S0-ARN-890

MAGAZINES
FOR
LIBRARIES

This edition of
Magazines For Libraries 2003
was prepared by R.R. Bowker's Database Publishing Group
and R.R. Bowker's Serials Bibliography Department

Michael Cairns, President
Gary Aiello, Senior Vice President, Operations
Belinda Tseo, Senior Vice President, Finance
Angela D'Agostino, Vice President, Product Development and Marketing
Boe Horton, Vice President, Worldwide Sales
Roy Crego, Senior Managing Director, Editorial
Andrew Grabois, Senior Director, Publisher Relations and Content Development
Doreen Gravesande, Senior Director, ISBN/SAN/PAD and Data Acquisition
Constance Harbison, Senior Director, BIP Editorial, Quality Assurance, and Subject Guide
Yvette Diven, Director of Product Management, Serials
Galen Strazza, Director, Creative Services

Editorial
Nancy Bucenec, Managing Editor
Valerie Mahon, Ewa Kowalska, Senior Editors
Martha David, Quality Control/Technical Manager
Christopher King, Vanessa Mitchell, Senior Associate Editors
Shawn Chen, Pappaparvathi Sankaranarayanan, Associate Editors
Halyna Testerman, Filippo Valli, and Michael Weingardner, Assistant Editors
Jeff Kosokoff (Head of Reference Services, Lamont Library of Harvard College Library),
Assistant Editor, Content and Development

Data Acquisition
Joseph Kalina, Director
O'Sheila Delgado, Editorial Coordinator
Jennifer Williams, Assistant Editor

Production
Gordon MacPherson, Director, Electronic and Print Production
Myriam Nunez, Project Manager, Content Integrity
Megan Roxberry, Managing Editor
Kennard D. McGill, Senior Editor
Jocelyn Kwiatkowski, Associate Editor

Manufacturing
Delia Tedoff, Director

Editorial Systems Group
Mark Heinzelman, Director
Frank Morris, Project Manager
Christopher Voser, David Weuste, Youliang Zhou, Programmer Analysts

Sales
Charlie Friscia, Director, Inside Sales

MAGAZINES FOR LIBRARIES™

TWELTH EDITION

Edited by Cheryl LaGuardia
with
consulting editors
Bill Katz and Linda Sternberg Katz

For the general reader and
school, junior college, college, university
and public libraries

Reviewing the best publications
for all serials collections
since 1969

New Providence, New Jersey

Published by R.R. Bowker LLC,

Printed and bound in the United States of America

International Standard Book Number 0-8352-4541-1
International Standard Serial Number 0000-0914
Library of Congress Catalog Card Number 86-640971

ISBN 0-8352-4541-1

9 780835 245418

CONTENTS

CONTENTS

CONTENTS

PREFACE

This 12th edition of *Magazines for Libraries*™ enters a very different publishing world than that of the first, 1969 edition. Serials librarianship has never been for the squeamish (title changes alone have always required mental fortitude and infinite flexibility) but the head-spinning rate of change in serials now is sure to give the hardiest librarian motion sickness. You cannot depend that a fact or statistic quoted today will hold true—or even in the same ballpark—tomorrow. Given the grim serials' statistics we've been hearing lately, that's daunting. Despite predications that electronic access could reduce production costs and bring down subscription rates, prices have not only climbed since the last edition was published, they are soaring. According to the EBSCO web site (http://www.ebsco.com/home/printsubs/priceproj.asp), at the time *MFL* was going to press, the 2004 price projections for printed serials being purchased by U.S. dollars will rise 8-10% for U.S. journals, 10-12% for U.K. journals, and 12-14% for European journals. In one year.

A number of factors and issues continue to transform serial acquisitions in the post-Tasini era. These include: the emergence of SPARC and other organizations like it (whose goals are to offer high-quality research publications at lower costs); the increasing formations of consortia among libraries (in an effort to increase buying power and influence with vendors); bundling subscriptions a.k.a. The Big Deal (whereby publishers offer packages to libraries at a discounted cost, giving access to both highly sought after and unwanted titles in the process); exclusivity deals between aggregators and publishers (in which a publisher contracts with a single aggregator to offer their title); embargoes (a refinement within an aggregator/publisher contract whereby the aggregator is "prevented" from offering content for a specified period of time, thereby encouraging libraries to continue print subscriptions); burgeoning open source access, and the on-going archiving issues that have dogged—and will continue to dog—e-content since its invention (given the rapidity with which aggregators gain and lose titles within their files, what library on earth can count on that access for archival access to journal material?).

Since aggregated vendors have assumed an even more important place in serial publishing since the last edition of *MFL*, we are adding a new section, Aggregators, to the front matter of this 12th edition. In it you will find more discussion on the issues noted above, as well as descriptions of various aggregated products. We hope this new material will offer additional guidance to readers on navigating the stormy waters of online access.

We're also analyzing the contents of *MFL* in greater explicit detail this time around. In addition to the content of the individual chapters and entries that *MFL* has always offered, we think our new analysis of what's included in *MFL*— as well as of what gets deleted by the contributors in subsequent editions—will be very useful information for librarians both in the short term and the long term. In this time of massive serials cuts in libraries we believe librarians will find *MFL* even more essential than ever before. Serials cancellation projects are necessarily based on local needs, but *MFL* listings serve as a guide for what's essential to keep, while at the same time the volume is a powerful tool for backing up an individual librarian's difficult decisions in making tough cuts.

Electronic Journals

The novelty of electronic journals has worn off, and they are now considered to be simply essential to study and research in many disciplines, particularly in the sciences. Aggregators are bringing to the Internet thousands of both new and standard titles, and as publishers become more comfortable with web-based business and pricing structures we may see costs stabilize. University-based publishing of scholarly journals is expanding gradually, and it continues to be interesting to watch this phenomenon and its influence on the broader publishing world. Thematic resources, such as Gale's Resource Centers, are expanding researchers' access to a variety of materials across disciplines. The increasingly interdisciplinary nature of research will challenge content producers to offer broader arrays of electronic content as demand for cross-disciplinary materials increases. As always, the realities of publishing will influence further developments: increased revenue potential versus costs will drive the trend.

Basic Lists

At the head of the chapters are listings, by type of audience, of those periodicals that the editors and contributors think absolutely essential for a basic collection. Also included is a list of the basic abstracts and indexes for that subject area. The lists may be used by the librarians or by a layperson as a guide through the scores of titles in a particular subject section. The lists should be carefully checked and modified for the needs of a library's particular users.

PREFACE

Selection Policy

Selection was made by the 179 subject-expert authors of the *MFL* chapters. Authors were asked to choose titles they believe basic. They were asked to consider the primary audience for the title, indicate how well the editors meet the needs of that audience, and the value of the title in relation to others covering much the same subject material. Primarily, it was left to the experience, education, and common sense of the consultants to select, sometimes from hundreds of titles, those best suited for a core collection in a library.

Annotations are intended to show purpose, scope, and audience for the periodicals, and most of them reflect some value judgment. On occasion, a title that is considered of limited value to the library is included—the reason being that the magazine is popular, widely read, and, even if not purchased by the librarian, should be known to the librarian.

The basic bibliographic data is current as of 2003, but subject to change. This is particularly true of subscription prices, which can be considered only relative; anyone will recognize that the prices quoted here are likely to be higher before the next edition of *Magazines for Libraries* is published.

An effort is made to show what titles are indexed in several basic indexes, but space limitations prevent a complete listing. Almost all of today's abstracting and indexing services are available online. This is so indicated, primarily in the Abstracts and Indexes section, which leads off the book. The only caveat that bears repeating is that coverage of titles in the abstracting and indexing services should be thoroughly checked and redundancies carefully compared.

Scope of Sections

As in previous editions, titles in *Magazines for Libraries* have been selected to include (1) some general, nonspecialist periodicals of interest to the layperson; (2) the main English-language research journals sponsored by distinguished societies in the United States, Canada, and Great Britain; and (3) a few high-quality commercial publications commonly found in academic/special libraries. Although titles cannot represent the full scope of research publications available for specialized collections, there has been an attempt to provide a balance, by discipline, between specialist versus general interest, student versus faculty use, and general versus research concerns. Consultants were asked to consider points set out in each of the previous editions. Given tight library budgets, a strong effort is made to indicate "best" and "better." In the deselection program, which is forced upon most librarians handling serials, it is essential to know the essential. It is the goal of the consultants to help the librarian make these difficult choices. Ultimate selections depend on the specific needs of the individual library: this must be stressed. The editor and consultants offer here a guide, a point of departure.

Some selection criteria include:

1. What is indexed, particularly in the basic print and electronic services found in most medium- to larger-sized libraries. (This argument of exclusion based on indexing rather than selection, is less valid than in times past, since nowadays just about everything is indexed. But it remains a consideration.)

2. What is found in citation studies and other efforts to quantitatively evaluate a collection.

3. What is being read and consulted by subject experts.

4. What is found in other lists, other choices recommended in books and magazines (*Library Journal*'s magazine review section, for example).

5. What is purchased by various types and sizes of libraries.

6. Price is a major consideration in what is listed as basic.

7. What was listed in the eleventh edition of this volume. Over the years, this work has become a basic selection aid in most libraries because initial and added choices seemed generally useful. The contributors and editors looked carefully at previously listed titles and annotations.

8. Refereeing is a consideration, particularly among scholarly journals and technical publications where rigorous evaluation of manuscripts is as much a tradition as, according to many, a necessity.

9. The publisher is an important factor. The better-known commercial and scholarly publishers have a well-earned reputation for accuracy and authority.

10. The intrinsic quality of the individual titles is considered. This ranges from how well it is edited to the format, illustrations, and degree and type of advertising. How well is the material presented? Do the authors write well? Do they have something to say that will hold the attention of the readers? Then there are the features: from the number and type of book reviews (if appropriate) to regular columns, summaries of events, calendars, letters to the editor, and so on.

11. Possibly most important: Who are the editors and do they appreciate the mission of their publication? Do they enlist the best possible authors? Do they depend entirely on staff for material, or do they go out in the field and seek out the experts? (Some titles may be legitimately written entirely by staff, but these are the exception.) Do they have the reputation and the credentials to sustain the quality of the periodical? Does the editor sense the importance of being honest, nonsensational, and informative—as well, often, as entertaining? Does the editor insist that the magazine challenges rather than caters to the tastes of the audience? Is the content superficial, or does it offer a new approach? And certainly one should ask for objectivity, or at least a forthright point of view that is clearly identified.

12. There are other considerations that may cause titles to be omitted here. A journal may be among the best in its field, but have an erratic publishing schedule. Another journal may be excellent, but often fail to consider proper layout. One must evaluate the title on its merits, not on the irregularities of the mails or a web connection. This is not to

downplay the importance of graphics, layout, and the total viewing experience of the exclusively web title. But the message is the most important aspect, at least for this reference work.

Additions, Deletions, and Omissions

Additions are made to chapters either because a chapter author decides that a newly published title merits inclusion or because the chapter author considers that a previously published title now merits inclusion. Deletions are made for a variety of reasons: (1) because a title has ceased publication; (2) because the chapter author decides it no longer merits inclusion in a core listing for libraries; (3) because another title now suits the chapter better; (4) because the cost of the title may have increased so much it was no longer considered a reasonable purchase for library collections; or (5) because, despite a chapter author's best attempts, the author was unable to examine issues of a particular title. Some publishers simply refuse to send chapter authors sample copies, or they charge for them. If that title was not readily available in libraries, it may therefore be impossible to consider it for inclusion. Our reasoning is that if a publisher is so dismissive about serving libraries that they will not provide review copies of the title, it is advisable to consider other titles for purchase instead. This is why a few titles that might otherwise be included are not listed in *Magazines for Libraries*.

Revision

This twelfth edition has been completely revised. Every title from the eleventh edition was reviewed and retained or deleted, and new titles were added as appropriate. Entries have been checked for currency and accuracy.

Designation of Consultants

The name of the consultant who compiled the particular section is given at the head of that section, along with title and address. In some cases, there is more than one contributor. Where the primary contributor is noted at the head of the section, that person's initials are not used within the section. However, sometimes initials are used within the section because: (1) in the Abstracts and Indexes section the initials identify who did one or more of the various annotations; (2) where more than one individual did a section, the initials indicate the division of labor; and (3) throughout the book, individuals contributed annotations to otherwise complete sections. The editor acted as overall evaluator of all the sections and individual titles. Here and there titles were added or dropped—usually after discussion with the consultants— and annotations revised as necessary. But the amount of revision of contributors' work is modest. An effort was made to retain individual contributor style and approach. Although contributors were asked to follow a basic pattern of selection and of writing annotations, they were urged to give a personal interpretation of editorial content. The editor takes full responsibility for the selection of the titles and for the annotations. As this is an ongoing effort, with new editions planned, readers are invited to write to the contributors and/or the editor when they have suggestions for new titles or for older titles that may have been missed, or comments on the evaluation of a particular periodical.

As always this book is the result of literally hundreds of peoples' work. My thanks especially to Nancy Bucenec at Bowker who is nothing short of an editing marvel and the one person you want on the other end of the phone line when you think it might be time to panic! and to Jeff Kosokoff for his very able assistance and insight. To the chapter authors I send heartfelt personal thanks and professional gratitude for thie invaluable contribution they make to the research world in creating this resource, which is truly unlike any other.

STATISTICS FROM THE TWELFTH EDITION

Statistical information on the content of the twelfth edition of *Magazines for Libraries* represents a new feature. The presentation of this information on titles and their publishers is provided as the basis for further analysis— not only of the titles included in or excluded from *Magazines for Libraries*, but of trends in the serials publishing industry. For this reason, future editions of *MFL* will include as a regular feature analysis and reports on the changing nature of serials publishing and the impact of serials trends on libraries. Regardless of library type or user community, an understanding of serials trends promotes a better understanding of the issues that impact collection decision-making and decision makers. The publishers and the editor of *Magazines for Libraries* welcome your suggestions for serials trend topics critical to you and your library's users.

This twelfth edition includes 6,856 titles published by large and small publishers alike. Overall, 3,893 publishers and imprints are represented. The following tables illustrate the range of publishers whose titles were selected for this edition—or whose titles have been dropped from *MFL* since the last edition.

Table 1 includes a report on the number of publishers in each *MFL* subject chapter. Further analysis of the 152 publishers with 5 or more entries is presented in Table 2, noting the characteristics of their titles— electronic format availability, refereed/peer-reviewed status, and inclusion in abstracting and indexing sources. Table 2 also includes aggregate information on the titles from publishers with 4 or fewer entries. All data in Table 2 should be evaluated by the individual reader within the context of his or her own collection decision-making.

As mentioned in the description of *Additions, Deletions, and Omissions* (see Preface), deletions since the previous edition were made for a variety of reasons: (1) because a title has ceased publication; (2) because the chapter author decides it no longer merits inclusion; (3) because another title now suits the chapter better; (4) because the cost of the title may have increased so much it was no longer considered a reasonable purchase for library collections; or (5) because, despite a chapter author's best attempts, the author was unable to examine issues of a particular title. Table 3 and Table 4 contain lists of each of the titles deleted since the last edition of *MFL*, sorted by publisher and by *MFL* subject. The prior edition's record sequence number is provided in both tables to allow the reader to reference the complete listing for a specific title in the older edition.

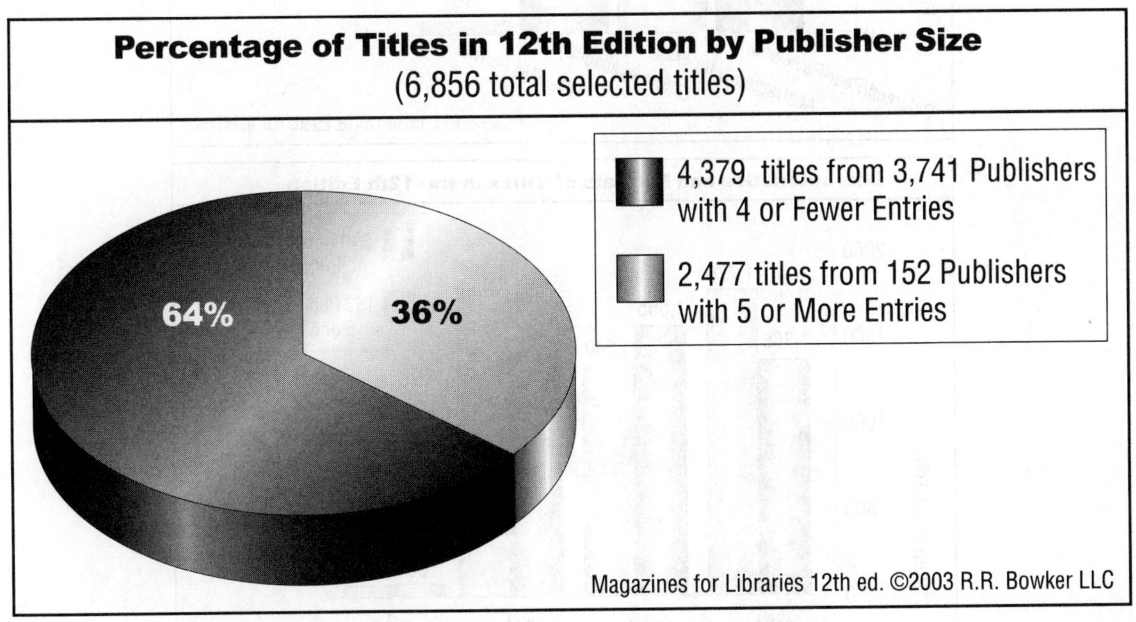

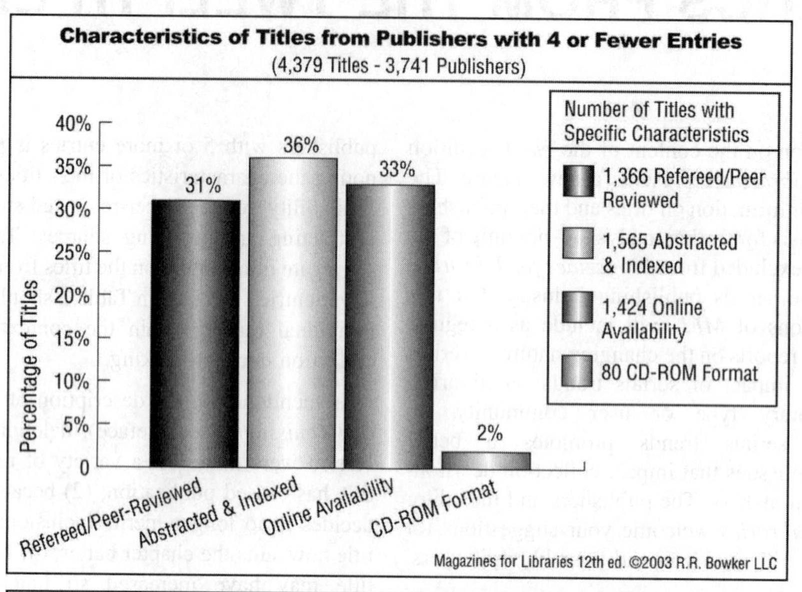
Characteristics of Titles from Publishers with 4 or Fewer Entries
(4,379 Titles - 3,741 Publishers)
Number of Titles with Specific Characteristics
1,366 Refereed/Peer Reviewed
1,565 Abstracted & Indexed
1,424 Online Availability
80 CD-ROM Format
Percentage of Titles
40%
35%
30%
25%
20%
15%
10%
5%
0
31%
36%
33%
2%
Refereed/Peer-Reviewed
Abstracted & Indexed
Online Availability
CD-ROM Format
Magazines for Libraries 12th ed. ©2003 R.R. Bowker LLC

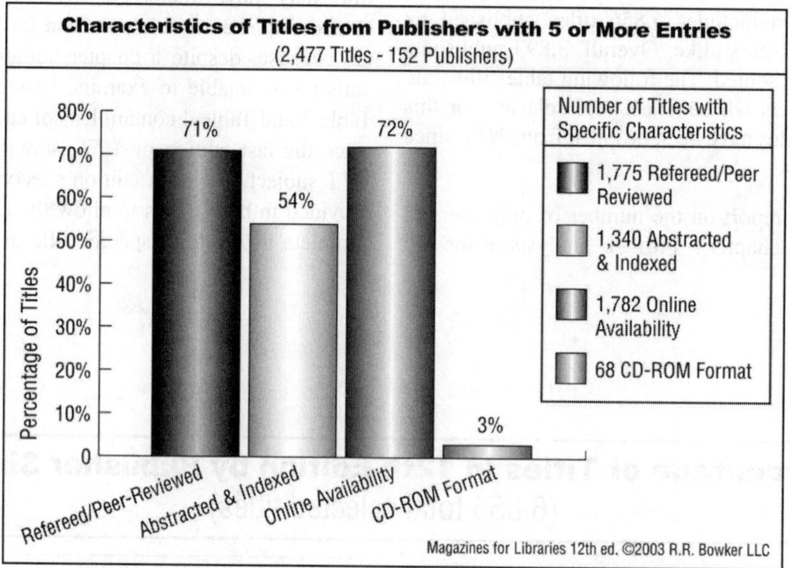
Characteristics of Titles from Publishers with 5 or More Entries
(2,477 Titles - 152 Publishers)
Number of Titles with Specific Characteristics
1,775 Refereed/Peer Reviewed
1,340 Abstracted & Indexed
1,782 Online Availability
68 CD-ROM Format
Percentage of Titles
80%
70%
60%
50%
40%
30%
20%
10%
0
71%
54%
72%
3%
Refereed/Peer-Reviewed
Abstracted & Indexed
Online Availability
CD-ROM Format
Magazines for Libraries 12th ed. ©2003 R.R. Bowker LLC

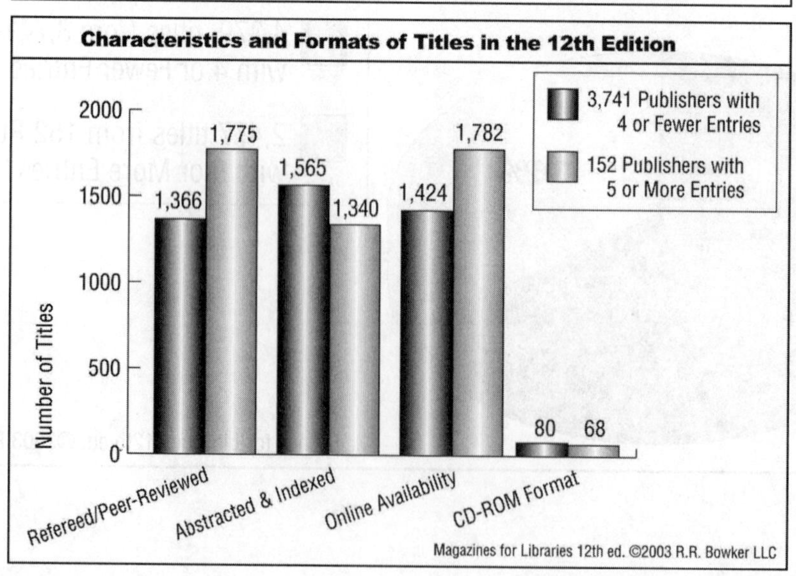
Characteristics and Formats of Titles in the 12th Edition
3,741 Publishers with 4 or Fewer Entries
152 Publishers with 5 or More Entries
Number of Titles
2000
1500
1000
500
0
1,366
1,775
1,565
1,340
1,424
1,782
80
68
Refereed/Peer-Reviewed
Abstracted & Indexed
Online Availability
CD-ROM Format
Magazines for Libraries 12th ed. ©2003 R.R. Bowker LLC

Table 1 / No. of Publishers by MFL Subject

Section	No. of Publishers
ABSTRACTS AND INDEXES	122
ACCOUNTING AND TAXATION	32
ADVERTISING, MARKETING, AND PUBLIC RELATIONS	25
AERONAUTICS AND SPACE SCIENCE	49
AFRICA	55
AFRICAN AMERICAN	47
AGING	30
AGRICULTURE	29
ALTERNATIVES	31
ANIMAL WELFARE	29
ANTHROPOLOGY	21
ANTIQUES AND COLLECTING	21
ARCHAEOLOGY	33
ARCHITECTURE	24
ARCHIVES AND MANUSCRIPTS	16
ART	49
ASIA AND THE PACIFIC	82
ASIAN AMERICAN	11
ASTROLOGY	7
ASTRONOMY	42
ATMOSPHERIC SCIENCES	24
AUTOMOBILES AND MOTORCYCLES	20
BIBLIOGRAPHY	20
BIOLOGICAL SCIENCES	56
BIRDS	21
BOATS AND BOATING	26
BOOKS AND BOOK REVIEWS	34
BUILDING AND CONSTRUCTION	12
BUSINESS	108
CANADA	38
CHEMISTRY	17
CHILDREN	27
CHINA	33
CIS AND EASTERN EUROPE	34
CITY, STATE, AND REGIONAL	39
CIVIL LIBERTIES	19
CLASSICAL STUDIES	30
CLASSROOM MAGAZINES	19
COLLEGE AND ALUMNI	11
COMIC BOOKS	17
COMMUNICATION	22
COMPUTER SCIENCE AND AUTOMATION	35
CONSUMER EDUCATION	8
CRAFT	41
CRIMINOLOGY AND LAW ENFORCEMENT	32
CULTURAL-SOCIAL STUDIES	36
DANCE	19
DEATH AND DYING	11
DISABILITIES	49
EARTH SCIENCES	46
ECONOMICS	48
EDUCATION	104
ELECTRONICS	18
ENERGY	30
ENGINEERING AND TECHNOLOGY	52
ENVIRONMENT AND CONSERVATION	46
ETHNIC STUDIES	8
EUROPE	96
FAMILY AND MARRIAGE	14
FICTION: GENERAL/MYSTERY AND DETECTIVE	28
FICTION: SCIENCE FICTION, FANTASY, AND HORROR	25

Table 1 / No. of Publishers by MFL Subject (cont.)

Section	No. of Publishers
FILMS	51
FINANCE	68
FIRE PROTECTION	9
FISH, FISHERIES, AND AQUACULTURE	21
FISHING	12
FOLKLORE	25
FOOD AND NUTRITION	14
FOOD AND WINE	22
FOOD INDUSTRY	13
FORESTRY	22
FRATERNAL, CLUB, AND SERVICE ORGANIZATIONS	19
FREE MAGAZINES AND HOUSE ORGANS	40
GAMES	32
GARDENING	27
GENEALOGY	77
GENERAL EDITORIAL	54
GENERAL EDITORIAL-INTERNET	24
GEOGRAPHY	30
GOVERNMENT PERIODICALS;b1FEDERAL	16
GOVERNMENT PERIODICALS;b1STATE AND LOCAL	36
HIKING, CLIMBING, AND OUTDOOR RECREATION	23
HISTORY	71
HOME	20
HORSES	22
HOSPITALITY/RESTAURANT	8
HUMOR	17
HUNTING AND GUNS	24
INTERDISCIPLINARY STUDIES	6
INTERIOR DESIGN AND DECORATION	12
INTERNET-WORLD WIDE WEB	21
JOURNALISM AND WRITING	32
LABOR AND INDUSTRIAL RELATIONS	36
LANDSCAPE ARCHITECTURE	14
LARGE PRINT	17
LATIN AMERICAN	52
LATINO STUDIES	21
LAW	86
LESBIAN, GAY, BISEXUAL, AND TRANSGENDER	45
LIBRARY AND INFORMATION SCIENCE	26
LINGUISTICS	23
LITERARY REVIEWS	56
LITERATURE	55
LITTLE MAGAZINES	41
MANAGEMENT, ADMINISTRATION, AND HUMAN RESOURCES	62
MARINE SCIENCE AND TECHNOLOGY	46
MATHEMATICS	22
MEDIA AND AV	14
MEDICINE AND HEALTH	100
MEN	35
MIDDLE EAST	26
MILITARY	25
MILITARY GAMES	27
MODEL MAKING AND COLLECTING	54
MUSIC	66
MUSIC REVIEWS	16
NATIVE AMERICANS	31
NEWS AND OPINION	33
NEWSPAPERS	20
NUMISMATICS	7
OCCUPATIONS AND CAREERS	20
OFFICE MANAGEMENT	4
PALEONTOLOGY	21

Table 1 / No. of Publishers by MFL Subject (cont.)

Section	No. of Publishers
PARAPSYCHOLOGY	9
PARENTING	19
PEACE	17
PETS	15
PHILATELY	14
PHILOSOPHY	49
PHOTOGRAPHY	22
PHYSICS	18
POLITICAL SCIENCE	46
POPULATION STUDIES	12
PRINTING AND GRAPHIC ARTS	25
PSYCHOLOGY	58
REAL ESTATE	13
RELIGION	58
ROBOTICS	17
SAFETY	15
SCIENCE AND TECHNOLOGY	31
SERIALS	6
SEXUALITY	31
SINGLES	16
SOCIOLOGY AND SOCIAL WORK	41
SPIRITUALITY AND WELL-BEING	9
SPORTS	65
STATISTICS	19
TEENAGERS	22
TELEVISION, VIDEO, AND RADIO	29
THEATER	40
TRANSPORTATION	75
TRAVEL AND TOURISM	24
URBAN STUDIES	24
VETERINARY SCIENCE	23
WEDDINGS	11
WOMEN	42
WOMEN: FEMINIST AND SPECIAL INTEREST	77
ZINES	77

Table 2 / Publishers with 5 or More Titles in This Edition (152 Selected Publishers)

Publisher	Total Titles	No. of Refereed Titles	Percentage (%) Refereed	No. of A&I Titles	Percentage (%) A & I	No. of Online Titles	Percentage (%) Online	No. of CD-ROM	Percentage (%) CD-ROM
Pergamon	119	115	97%	82	69%	116	97%	1	1%
Blackwell Publishing Ltd.	118	109	92	80	68	106	90	1	1
Sage Publications, Inc.	91	79	87	57	63	64	70	2	2
Kluwer Academic Publishers	81	79	98	47	58	79	98	0	0
Cambridge University Press	74	59	80	39	53	59	80	1	1
Blackwell Publishing, Inc.	73	70	96	54	74	66	90	3	4
Oxford University Press	71	71	100	46	65	60	85	0	0
Carfax Publishing Ltd.	64	53	83	35	55	57	89	0	0
Sage Publications Ltd.	55	48	87	27	49	29	53	0	0
Elsevier BV	54	52	96	39	72	51	94	0	0
Elsevier BV, North-Holland	52	51	98	42	81	50	96	0	0
Haworth Press, Inc.	44	40	91	4	9	16	36	0	0
Academic Press	43	43	100	28	65	42	98	0	0
Kluwer Academic / Plenum Publishers	43	44	102	23	53	43	100	0	0
Routledge	37	28	76	13	35	30	81	0	0
University of Chicago Press, Journals Division	36	36	100	31	86	34	94	0	0
Johns Hopkins University Press, Journals Publishing Division	32	34	106	19	59	33	103	0	0
Institute of Electrical and Electronics Engineers, Inc.	31	31	100	21	68	30	97	0	0
Springer-Verlag	31	30	97	17	55	26	84	0	0
Taylor & Francis Ltd	31	30	97	15	48	27	87	0	0
American Psychological Association	29	27	93	14	48	18	62	0	0
Heldref Publications	28	26	93	22	79	27	96	22	79
Reed Business Information	27	2	7	13	48	24	89	0	0
C S A	26	1	4	6	23	18	69	4	15
John Wiley & Sons Ltd.	26	25	96	11	42	16	62	0	0
Krause Publications, Inc.	24	0	0	4	17	3	13	0	0
M.E. Sharpe, Inc.	24	22	92	20	83	8	33	0	0
Duke University Press	23	16	70	11	48	20	87	0	0
Emerald	23	20	87	9	39	17	74	0	0
Frank Cass Publishers	22	22	100	12	55	12	55	0	0
Lippincott Williams & Wilkins	22	15	68	9	41	19	86	5	23

Primedia Enthusiast Group	21	0	0%	5	24%	2	10%	0	0%
University of California Press, Journals Division	21	21	100	16	76	19	90	0	0
American Chemical Society	19	17	89	16	84	17	89	0	0
John Wiley & Sons, Inc.	19	18	95	11	58	15	79	1	5
Scholastic Inc.	19	1	5	9	47	11	58	0	0
V N U Business Publications	19	0	0	7	37	17	89	0	0
Elsevier Inc.	18	17	94	9	50	17	94	0	0
Human Kinetics Publishers, Inc.	18	18	100	9	50	3	17	0	0
Lawrence Erlbaum Associates, Inc.	18	17	94	6	33	6	33	0	0
Conde Nast Publications Inc.	15	0	0	4	27	9	60	0	0
Hachette Filipacchi Media U.S., Inc.	15	0	0	5	33	13	87	0	0
M I T Press	15	13	87	7	47	11	73	0	0
Taylor & Francis Inc	15	14	93	10	67	15	100	0	0
American Institute of Physics	14	9	64	10	71	9	64	0	0
American Library Association	14	5	36	6	43	9	64	1	7
Association for Computing Machinery, Inc.	14	11	79	6	43	10	71	0	0
Institute of Physics Publishing	14	14	100	11	79	12	86	0	0
Transaction Publishers	14	11	79	8	57	10	71	1	7
Brill Academic Publishers, Inc.	13	11	85	6	46	6	46	0	0
Primedia Consumer Media & Magazine Group	13	0	0	4	31	9	69	1	8
University of Toronto Press, Journals Department	13	11	85	10	77	9	69	0	0
American Physical Society	12	10	83	8	67	7	58	0	0
CABI Publishing	12	2	17	5	42	11	92	0	0
Elsevier Ltd.	12	10	83	10	83	8	67	0	0
Primedia Business Magazines & Media, Inc.	12	0	0	2	17	9	75	0	0
American Geophysical Union	11	7	64	5	45	1	9	0	0
Baywood Publishing Co., Inc.	11	8	73	5	45	0	0	0	0
H.W. Wilson Co.	11	0	0	0	0	2	18	11	100
Indiana University Press	11	11	100	4	36	9	82	0	0
Kalmbach Publishing Co.	11	0	0	6	55	3	27	0	0
Time, Inc	11	0	0	2	18	4	36	2	18
Editorial Televisa	10	0	0	0	0	2	20	0	0
Penton Media, Inc.	10	0	0	5	50	9	90	0	0
Time4 Media, Inc.	10	0	0	1	10	8	80	2	20
University of Hawaii Press, Journals Department	10	9	90	4	40	10	100	0	0
American Anthropological Association	9	7	78	3	33	4	44	0	0
American Meteorological Society	9	9	100	8	89	9	100	0	0

Table 2 / Publishers with 5 or More Titles in This Edition (cont.)

Publisher	Total Titles	No. of Refereed Titles	Percentage (%) Refereed	No. of A&I Titles	Percentage (%) A & I	No. of Online Titles	Percentage (%) Online	No. of CD-ROM	Percentage (%) CD-ROM
Meredith Corp.	9	0	0%	1	11%	3	33%	0	0%
Mouton de Gruyter	9	9	100	3	33	2	22	0	0
N R C Research Press	9	9	100	9	100	9	100	0	0
Rodale	9	0	0	3	33	7	78	0	0
Royal Society of Chemistry	9	8	89	7	78	6	67	0	0
University of Illinois Press	9	8	89	7	78	8	89	0	0
W.B. Saunders Co.	9	9	100	9	100	3	33	0	0
Weekly Reader Corp.	9	0	0	3	33	7	78	0	0
American Institute of Aeronautics and Astronautics, Inc.	8	7	88	7	88	6	75	0	0
Crain Communications, Inc.	8	0	0	5	63	8	100	0	0
Fancy Publications, Inc.	8	0	0	6	75	1	13	0	0
Gale Group	8	0	0	2	25	1	13	0	0
Hearst Corporation	8	0	0	1	13	7	88	0	0
National Council of Teachers of English	8	5	63	5	63	6	75	0	0
Blackwell Publishing Asia	7	7	100	2	29	6	86	0	0
Cricket Magazine Group	7	0	0	0	0	3	43	0	0
D C Comics	7	0	0	0	0	0	0	0	0
Fairchild Publications, Inc.	7	0	0	1	14	4	57	0	0
Hanley-Wood, Llc.	7	0	0	2	29	3	43	0	0
PennWell Corp.	7	0	0	5	71	7	100	0	0
University of Wisconsin Press, Journal Division	7	6	86	6	86	4	57	0	0
A S M E International	6	5	83	5	83	4	67	0	0
Air Age Publishing	6	0	0	0	0	1	17	0	0
American Accounting Association	6	4	67	2	33	2	33	0	0
American Society of Civil Engineers	6	5	83	4	67	4	67	0	0
American Sociological Association	6	6	100	3	50	5	83	0	0
American Statistical Association	6	5	83	2	33	3	50	0	0
Blackwell Munksgaard	6	6	100	3	50	2	33	0	0
Business News Publishing Co.	6	0	0	5	83	6	100	0	0
Century Publishing Co.	6	0	0	0	0	0	0	0	0
Children's Better Health Institute	6	0	0	4	67	5	83	0	0

Cobblestone Publishing	6	0	0%	4	67%	0	0%	0	0%
EBSCO Publishing	6	0	0	2	33	1	17	1	17
Euromoney Institutional Investor plc.	6	0	0	3	50	4	67	0	0
Gruner + Jahr U.S.A. Publishing	6	0	0	0	0	1	17	1	17
I N F O R M S	6	6	100	4	67	6	100	0	0
Institute for Scientific Information	6	0	0	4	67	2	33	5	83
Institute of Mathematical Statistics	6	5	83	5	83	1	17	0	0
M A I K Nauka - Interperiodica	6	6	100	4	67	4	67	0	0
Maney Publishing	6	5	83	2	33	1	17	1	17
McGraw-Hill Companies, Inc.	6	2	33	3	50	5	83	0	0
National Communication Association	6	6	100	4	67	5	83	0	0
New York Times Company	6	0	0	1	17	2	33	1	17
Optical Society of America, Inc.	6	5	83	5	83	2	33	0	0
PRIMEDIA Special Interest Publications, History Group	6	0	0	2	33	2	33	0	0
Pro-Ed Inc.	6	6	100	3	50	5	83	0	0
Springer-Verlag, Journals	6	5	83	2	33	4	67	0	0
Taylor & Francis A S	6	4	67	3	50	5	83	0	0
University of Nebraska Press	6	6	100	3	50	4	67	0	0
University of Texas Press, Journals Division	6	5	83	4	67	5	83	0	0
World Publications LLC	6	0	0	1	17	2	33	0	0
Y-Visionary Publishing	6	0	0	0	0	0	0	0	0
American Economic Association	5	3	60	3	60	3	60	1	20
American Educational Research Association	5	5	100	3	60	5	100	0	0
American Fisheries Society	5	5	100	4	80	1	20	0	0
American Media, Inc.	5	0	0	0	0	0	0	0	0
American Society for Microbiology	5	5	100	5	100	5	100	0	0
C M P Media LLC	5	0	0	2	40	5	100	0	0
Caddo Gap Press	5	5	100	2	40	1	20	0	0
Christianity Today International	5	0	0	1	20	5	100	0	0
Cygnus Business Media, Inc.	5	0	0	1	20	2	40	0	0
Dell Magazines	5	0	0	2	40	1	20	0	0
Edinburgh University Press	5	2	40	2	40	3	60	0	0
F & W Publications, Inc.	5	0	0	1	20	2	40	0	0
Greenwood Publishing Group Inc.	5	1	20	3	60	0	0	0	0
John Benjamins Publishing Co.	5	5	100	1	20	2	40	0	0
K.G. Saur Verlag GmbH	5	0	0	2	40	0	0	0	0

Table 2 / Publishers with 5 or More Titles in This Edition (cont.)

Publisher	Total Titles	No. of Refereed Titles	Percentage (%) Refereed	No. of A&I Titles	Percentage (%) A & I	No. of Online Titles	Percentage (%) Online	No. of CD-ROM	Percentage (%) CD-ROM
Lifestyle Ventures, LLC	5	0	0%	1	20%	0	0%	0	0%
Marcel Dekker Inc.	5	4	80	5	100	3	60	0	0
Marvel Comics Group	5	0	0	0	0	0	0	0	0
National Geographic Society	5	0	0	3	60	3	60	0	0
Presses Universitaires de France, Departement des Revues	5	3	60	3	60	0	0	0	0
Primedia Business Magazines & Media, Inc. (Atlanta)	5	0	0	3	60	5	100	0	0
ProQuest Information & Learning	5	0	0	0	0	0	0	0	0
Reader's Digest Association, Inc	5	0	0	2	40	1	20	0	0
Society of American Foresters	5	4	80	4	80	5	100	0	0
Taunton Press, Inc.	5	0	0	4	80	0	0	0	0
Traplet Publications Ltd	5	0	0	2	40	0	0	0	0
U.S. National Climatic Data Center	5	0	0	1	20	0	0	0	0
University of North Carolina Press	5	5	100	4	80	5	100	0	0
V.H. Winston & Son, Inc.	5	4	80	5	100	0	0	0	0
Warren, Gorham and Lamont	5	0	0	2	40	2	40	0	0
Wiley - V C H Verlag GmbH	5	5	100	5	100	4	80	0	0
Count from 152 Publishers with 5 or more titles	**2,477**	**1,775**	**72**	**1,340**	**54**	**1,782**	**72**	**68**	**3**
Count from 3,741 Publishers with 4 or fewer titles	**4,379**	**1,366**	**31**	**1,565**	**36**	**1,424**	**33**	**80**	**2**
Total selected Publications in the 12th Edition	**6,856**	**3,141**	**46**	**2,905**	**42**	**3,206**	**47**	**148**	**2**

Table 3 / Titles Deleted Since the Last Edition, by Publisher

Publisher	Title	ISSN No.	11th Ed. Sequence No.
A S W G T Inc. Utopian Network	SandMUtopian Guardian	(1087-6316)	6132
Abbey Publications, Inc.	The Abbey Newsletter	(0276-8291)	4296
Aboriginal Science Fiction	Aboriginal Science Fiction	(0895-3198)	2950
Academic Partners, LLC	Lingua Franca	(1051-3310)	2507
Academic Press	Information and Computation	(0890-5401)	1915
	Journal of Computer and System Sciences	(0022-0000)	1920
Adams Business Media	Irrigation Journal	(0047-1518)	556
	Business Geographics	(1067-456X)	3577
Advanstar Communications Inc.	Geospatial Solutions	(1051-9858)	3596
Agra Europe (London) Ltd.	Environment Watch Europe		2894
Alba Publikation Alf Teloeken GmbH & Co. KG	Spielzeug Antik Revue	(1617-2582)	5120
Alliance for Community Media	Community Media Review	(1074-9004)	6422
Alpine Hansen Publishers	Specialty Travel Index	(0889-7085)	6598
Alternative Medicine	Alternative Medicine	(1081-4000)	5258
Amarillo Design Bureau	Star Fleet Times		5029
Amedia Inc.	A. Magazine	(1070-9401)	951
American Alliance for Health, Physical Education, Recreation, and Dance	Journal of Health Education	(1055-6699)	4902
American Association of Retired Persons	Modern Maturity	(0026-8046)	531
	My Generation	(1532-3935)	532
American Association of Teachers of Spanish and Portuguese, Inc.	Hispania	(0018-2133)	4356
American Bowling Congress	Bowling Magazine	(0162-0274)	6316
American City Business Journals, Inc. (Charlotte)	Hemmings Rods & Performance		1070
American Civil Liberties Union	ACLU Cyber-Liberties Update		1729
American Council on Consumer Interests	Advancing the Consumer Interest	(1044-7385)	1948
American Council on the Teaching of Foreign Languages, Inc.	Foreign Language Annals	(0015-718X)	4353
American Dental Association	Index to Dental Literature	(0019-3992)	127
American Educational Trust (A E T)	Washington Report on Middle East Affairs	(8755-4917)	4970
American Foundation for Preventive Medicine	Medical Update		4800
American Indian Library Association	American Indian Libraries Newsletter	(0193-8207)	5228
American Mathematical Society	Mathematics of Computation	(0025-5718)	4759
American Media, Inc.	AMI Auto World Magazine		1060
American Metal Market LLC	New Steel	(0897-4365)	1438
American Psychological Association	Psychological Abstracts	(0033-2887)	180
American Society for Horticultural Science	HortScience	(0018-5345)	3396
	HortTechnology	(1063-0198)	3397
	American Society for Horticultural Science. Journal	(0003-1062)	3381

Table 3 / Titles Deleted Since the Last Edition, by Publisher (cont.)

Publisher	Title	ISSN No.	11th Ed. Sequence No
Americans for Middle East Understanding, Inc.	The Link	(0024-4007)	4959
Amnews Corp.	New York Amsterdam News	(0028-7121)	5320
Amusing Yourself to Death	Amusing Yourself to Death		6863
Ancient History Bulletin	Ancient History Bulletin	(1700-3334)	3775
Andrews Publications	Breast Implant Litigation Reporter	(1062-1814)	6843
Annals of Improbable Research	The Mini-Annals of Improbable Research	(1076-500X)	3862
Archive Press	Art International	(0004-3230)	796
Arnold Publishers	Second Language Research	(0267-6583)	4396
Arnoldo Mondadori Editore SpA	Chi		2780
	Panorama	(0553-1098)	2841
Art Access	Art Access		841
Art Culinaire	Art Culinaire	(0892-1024)	3217
Art in the Public Interest	High Performance	(0160-9769)	815
Art of Eating	Art of Eating	(0895-6200)	3218
Arts Atlantic Inc.	ARTSatlantic	(0704-7916)	1460
Arts Communications	Arts Magazine	(0004-4059)	805
Asahi Shimbun Publishing Co.	Japan Quarterly	(0021-4590)	890
Ashdown Publishing Ltd.	Toy Soldier and Model Figure	(1359-7426)	5107
Asia Inc. Ltd.	Asia-Inc Magazine	(1019-2239)	944
Asian Arts	Asian Arts		945
Asiaweek Ltd.	AsiaWeek	(1012-6244)	863
Association des Historiens Africains	Afrika Zamani	(0257-5760)	396
Association for Computing Machinery	ACM Electronic Guide to Computing Literature	(1089-5310)	2
	Communications of the ACM	(0001-0782)	1891
Association for Management Education and Development	Organisations & People	(1350-6269)	4659
Association for the Advancement of Computing in Education	Web Net Journal	(1522-192X)	3934
Association of American Colleges and Universities	On Campus with Women	(0734-0141)	6850
Association of Arab-American University Graduates, Inc.	Arab Studies Quarterly	(0271-3519)	4951
Aster Publishing Corp.	Mercator's World	(1086-6728)	3605
August Home Publishing Co.	Cuisine	(1089-6546)	3225
Australian Mathematical Society	Australian Mathematical Society. Journal	(0263-6115)	4742
	The ANZIAM Journal	(1446-1811)	4736
Austrian Cultural Forum	Austria Kultur Online		2886
Axel Springer Verlag AG	Die Welt	(0173-8437)	2883
B V Dagblad de Telegraaf	De Telegraaf		2881
Bad Subjects Production Team	Bad Subjects		605
Baker Boulanger	Baker Boulanger		3241

Baybury Books	Baybury Review		4541
Becker Associates	Urban History Review/Revue d'Histoire Revue	(0703-0428)	1491
Belgian Film Music Society vzw	Soundtrack!	(0771-6303)	3014
Belvoir Publications, Inc.	American Gunsmith	(1060-0892)	3867
Berlin Online	Berlin Online		2888
Best Fares	Best Fares	(8750-2410)	6588
Big World Publishing, Inc.	Big World	(1079-5707)	6589
Bill Communications, Inc.	Supermarket Business	(0196-5700)	1449
Billian Publishing, Inc.	Textile Industries	(0890-9970)	1451
Birkhaeuser Verlag AG	Commentarii Mathematica Helvetici	(0010-2571)	4746
Black Flag Collective	Black Flag	(0045-2157)	5272
Black Plankton Press	The Rejected Quarterly	(1525-2671)	4571
Blackwell Publishing Ltd.	World Englishes	(0883-2919)	4404
	Politics	(0263-3957)	5708
Blackwell Publishing, Inc.	Middle East Policy	(1061-1924)	4963
Blades on Ice, Inc.	Blades on Ice	(1070-390X)	6314
Bloomberg L.P.	Bloomberg Personal Finance	(1523-0023)	3051
Bluffton News Printing and Publishing Co.	Boys' Quest	(1078-9006)	1541
Bonkers!	Bonkers	(1521-8139)	5479
BRAT Media	Brat		6868
Bummers and Gummers	Bummers and Gummers		6870
Burda Verlag GmbH	Bunte	(0172-2050)	2777
C M P Media LLC	Network Magazine	(1093-8001)	1936
	New Architect	(1537-9000)	3932
C X O Media Inc.	Darwin	(1536-2256)	1324
Cabinet Communications	Hobby Broadcasting		6426
Cambridge University Press	American Journal of Germanic Linguistics and Literature	(1040-8207)	4339
	English Today	(0266-0784)	4349
Canadian Institute of International Affairs	Behind the Headlines	(0005-7983)	1464
Canadian Nature Federation	Nature Canada	(0374-9894)	1478
Canadian PeaceKeeping Press Pearson Peacekeeping Centre	Peacekeeping & International Relations	(1187-3485)	5467
CAP Ventures	Printout	(0887-7556)	5803
Capco Marketing	Gourmet Connection		3245
Career Magazine	Career Magazine		5382
Carrier Aviation News	Carrier Aviation News		361
Center for Changes	Against the Current	(0739-4853)	5269
Central Newspapers, Inc.	High Technology Careers Magazine	(0749-2960)	5383
Centre National de la Recherche Scientifique Institut de l'Information Scientifique et Technique	PASCAL Folio 47	(1146-5247)	168
Charles Sturt University	Complexity International	(1320-0682)	2711

Table 3 / Titles Deleted Since the Last Edition, by Publisher (cont.)

Publisher	Title	ISSN No.	11th Ed. Sequence No
Cheever Publishing, Inc.	Accent on Living	(0001-4508)	2139
Chicago New Art Association	New Art Examiner	(0886-8115)	821
Children Now	Children Now		5446
Chinese Historical Society of America	Chinese America	(1051-7642)	954
Chip Rowe	Chip's Closet Cleaner	(1064-9719)	6873
Chitra Publications	Quilting Today	(1040-4457)	1999
Christian Singles International	Christian Singles		6145
Christianity and the Arts	Christianity and the Arts	(1080-7608)	5968
Coalition Web, Inc.	Berg's Review of Games		5011
Columbia College Leadership Institute	A Leadership Journal	(1088-5188)	6799
Commercial Law League of America	Commercial Law Journal	(0010-3055)	4157
Commitment	Commitment		6745
Community College of Southern Nevada Department of English	Red Rock Review	(1086-4342)	4570
Computer Publishing Group	Web Server OnLineMagazine	(1087-4232)	3942
Concord Press of Nigeria	Africa Economic Digest	(0144-8234)	375
Consumers Digest, Inc.	Consumers Digest	(0010-7182)	1951
Consumers Union of the United States, Inc.	Consumer Reports Travel Letter	(0887-8439)	6609
Contemporary Arts Press	Art Com	(0732-2852)	793
Contentious	Contentious		3975
Cork University Press	Irish Journal of Feminist Studies	(1393-306X)	6793
Corporate Watch	Corporate Watch		2757
Correctional Educational Association	The Journal of Correctional Education	(0740-2708)	2029
Council for Educational Diagnostic Services	Diagnostique	(0737-2477)	2149
Council for Exceptional Children	Exceptional Children	(0014-4029)	5433
Council on Christian Unity of the Christian Church	Mid-Stream	(0544-0653)	6008
Cradle Publishing, Inc.	Childbirth Instructor Magazine	(1075-9689)	4811
Crap Hound	Crap Hound		6877
Creative Classroom Publishing LLC	Creative Classroom	(0887-042X)	1795
Crone Corp.	Crone Chronicles	(1068-8684)	6853
D C Comics	Batman: Gotham Adventures		1822
	Superman Adventures		1839
DADAm@g	DADAm@g		2892
Dance Online	Dance Online		2126
Dance/U S A	Dance/USA journal	(1064-6515)	2120
Defense Language Institute Foreign Language Center	Applied Language Learning	(1041-679X)	4342
Democratic Socialists of America	Democratic Left	(0164-3207)	5276
Detroit Free Press, Inc.	The Freep (Detroit Free Press)		5343

Publisher	Title	ISSN	Entry
DieWoche Zeitungsverlag GmbH	Die Woche	(0945-2125)	2884
Documenter Journals Inc	Documenter	(1442-844X)	3020
Douglas Publications, Inc.	Robotics World	(0737-7908)	6054
Dow Jones & Co., Inc.	Asian Wall Street Journal Weekly	(0191-0132)	862
Downhome Publications, Inc.	Mississippi	(0747-1602)	1689
Drawing Society, Inc.	Drawing	(0191-6963)	811
Dropout	Dropout		6879
Duke University Press	Hopscotch	(1098-6995)	593
E E I Press	Editorial Eye	(0193-7383)	3949
E T P Ltd.	Blueprint	(0268-4926)	752
Earthwatch Expeditions, Inc.	EarthWatch Journal	(8750-0183)	2729
Eastern Publishing & Distributing, Inc.	Bowhunting News	(1066-7148)	3873
EBSCO Publishing	Academic Abstracts and Search titles	(1071-2720)	8
Economist Newspaper Ltd	Business Central Europe	(1350-1240)	1378
Eeeek Publishing Co.	Eeeek-Net		1578
Electric Power Research Institute	EPRI Journal	(0362-3416)	2597
Electronic Book Reviews	ebr		1286
Electronic Gourmet Guide	Global Gourmet		3244
Electronic Policy Network	Idea Central		2384
Elsevier Advanced Technology	Refocus	(1471-0846)	2627
Elsevier BV	Preventive Veterinary Medicine	(0167-5877)	6680
Elsevier BV North-Holland	Journal of Pragmatics	(0378-2166)	4370
Elsevier Inc.	Pharmacology and Therapeutics:	(0163-7258)	4826
Emap Active Ltd. (Angel House)	Car	(0008-5987)	1063
Emperor's Headquarters	Napoleon	(1093-2283)	5024
Empire Productions & Publishing	POV		3007
End-of-Life Choices	Timelines		2136
Enigma Communications	Fabulous Foods		3243
Environmental Business International Inc.	Environmental Business Journal	(1045-8611)	2734
Environmental Law Institute	Environmental Forum	(0731-5732)	2737
Equal Opportunity Publications, Inc.	Woman Engineer	(0887-2120)	6852
European Commission Office for Official Publications of the European Union	European Commission-Bulletin of the European Union		2895
European Commission The European Union's Publisher	Europe: the magazine of the European community	(0191-4545)	2790
Evenement	L'Evenement du Jeudi	(0765-412X)	2794
Fancy Publications, Inc.	Bird Breeder On-line	(1096-2115)	5491
	Pet Product News	(1076-5573)	5488
Fashion Dish	Fashion Dish		6746
Fashion Planet	Fashion Planet		6749
Fezziwig Publishing Co., L L C	Epicurean Traveler		3242
Film	Film International	(1021-6510)	2993

Table 3 / Titles Deleted Since the Last Edition, by Publisher (cont.)

Publisher	Title	ISSN No.	11th Ed. Sequence No
Fireweed Inc.	Fireweed	(0706-3857)	6832
First Intensity	First Intensity		4548
First Nations Development Institute	Business Alert		5230
Fish and Game Finder Magazines	Fish and Game Finder	(1081-910X)	3159
Flatland Books	Flatland	(1090-0683)	6888
Focus Magazin Verlag GmbH	Focus	(0943-7576)	2797
Focus on the Family, Inc.	Single-Parent Family	(1077-4092)	6151
Fondo de Cultura Economica	El Trimestre Economico	(0041-3011)	2376
Food and Agriculture Organization of the United Nations Sales and Marketing Group	Agrindex	(0254-8801)	16
Frank Schaffer Publications, Inc.	Challenge	(0745-6298)	1792
	Schooldays	(1529-160X)	1802
FrankAmato Publications, Inc	Salmon - Trout Steelheader	(0029-3431)	3170
Freedom Technology Media Group	Home Office Computing	(0899-7373)	1401
Fringe, Inc.	FringeGolf	(1534-9683)	6319
Fucktooth	Fucktooth		6890
Future Publishing Ltd.	.net	(1355-7602)	3930
Gale Group	Magazine Index Plus/ASAP		152
Gamers	Operations		5040
Gauntlet, Inc.	Gauntlet	(1047-4463)	588
Gay & Lesbian Alliance Against Defamation	Images (New York)		4256
General Learning Communications	Your Health & Fitness	(0279-9324)	4807
George Mason University Communication Department	Women and Language	(8755-4550)	4402
Girljock Magazine	Girljock		6892
Glas Publishers	Glas	(0869-3102)	1632
Globe and Mail Publishing	GlobeNet		5345
Glovebox Chronicles	The Glovebox Chronicles		6893
Gordon and Breach - Harwood Academic	Astrophysical Letters and Communications	(0888-6512)	983
	Fundamentals of Cosmic Physics	(0094-5846)	992
	Modern Geology	(0026-7775)	2270
Graham Powner	Theaterworld Internet Magazine		6502
Greenspun School of Communication	Journalism History	(0094-7679)	3958
Gruner + Jahr U.S.A. Publishing	Custom Builder	(0895-2493)	1301
	Rosie		6722
Gruner und Jahr AG & Co.	Brigitte	(0931-8763)	2776
	Stern Magazin	(0039-1239)	2858
Gulf Publishing Co.	Hydrocarbon Processing	(0018-8190)	2614
Hachette Filipacchi Media U.S., Inc.	Travel Holiday	(0199-025X)	6605

Table 3 / Titles Deleted Since the Last Edition, by Publisher (cont.)

Publisher	Title	ISSN No.	11th Ed. Sequence No
International Linguistic Association	Word	(0043-7956)	4403
International Press	Journal of Differential Geometry	(0022-040X)	4753
International Society for General Semantics	ETC	(0014-164X)	4351
International Union for Conservation of Nature and Natural Resources	Primate Conservation	(0898-6207)	640
Islands Publishing Company	Islands	(0745-7847)	6594
J. Paul Getty Museum	J. Paul Getty Museum Journal	(0362-1979)	836
Jane's Information Group	Islamic Affairs Analyst	(0969-4234)	4953
Japan P.E.N. Club	Japanese Literature Today	(0385-1044)	892
Jens Jurgen, Ed. & Pub.	Travel Companions	(1076-5719)	6156
Job Options	Job Options		5384
John Benjamins Publishing Co.	Functions of Language	(0929-998X)	4354
	Interpreting	(1384-6647)	4362
	Language International	(0923-182X)	4378
	Language Problems and Language Planning	(0272-2690)	4379
	Lingvisticae Investigationes	(0378-4169)	4389
	Pragmatics & Cognition	(0929-0907)	4394
	Terminology	(0929-9971)	4401
John Wiley & Sons, Inc.	Competitive Intelligence Review	(1058-0247)	4667
	Global Focus	(1525-0369)	1383
	Laboratory Robotics and Automation	(0895-7533)	6048
Johns Hopkins University Press Journals Publishing Division	Kennedy Institute of Ethics. Journal	(1054-6863)	1720
	Wide Angle	(0160-6840)	3016
Jones Publishing Inc.	Doll World	(1066-4726)	707
Journal for Vocational Special Needs Education	Journal for Vocational Special Needs Education	(0195-7597)	2162
Journal of Contemporary Art	Journal of Contemporary Art	(0897-2400)	818
Journal of Developing Areas	Journal of Developing Areas	(0022-037X)	2329
K C Publishing, Inc	Flower and Garden	(0162-3249)	3387
Kluwer Academic / Plenum Publishers	International Journal of Sexuality and Gender Studies	(1566-1768)	4257
Kluwer Academic / Plenum Publishers	Journal of Near-Death Studies	(0891-4494)	5422
Kluwer Academic / Plenum Publishers	Journal of Social Distress and the Homeless	(1053-0789)	6200
Kluwer Academic Publishers	Journal of Quantitative Anthropology	(0922-2995)	670
	Argumentation	(0920-427X)	1849
Knight Publishing Corporation	Adam Black Video Directory	(1533-5992)	6115
Korean Cultural Center	Korean Culture	(0270-1618)	897
Krause Publications, Inc.	Sports Cards	(1069-2282)	6260
Kurdish Library	Kurdish Life	(1061-8457)	4958
L A T N N, Inc.	Grafico		4108

L A Y A!	LAYA		6417
L F P, Inc.	Hustler Erotic Video Guide	(1059-9703)	6125
L R P Publications	Hospitality Law	(0889-5414)	3838
Larry Flynt Publications, Inc.	Code	(1522-0591)	4923
Larry Nocella	QECE	(1524-1114)	6922
Latin Girl Magazine	Latingirl	(1524-2218)	4123
LatinWorld	LatinWorld		4109
Lawrence Erlbaum Associates, Inc.	CBQ	(1094-8007)	1852
	Communication Law and Policy	(1081-1680)	1854
	Language Acquisition	(1048-9223)	4372
Left Curve Publications	Left Curve	(0160-1857)	4557
Legal Bytes	Legal Bytes		1944
Let It Rock, Inc.	Let It Rock		5202
Leukemia Society of America	Leukemia Society of America. Newsline		4863
Libra Publishers, Inc.	Adolescence	(0001-8449)	5429
LifeWay Press	ParentLife	(1074-326X)	5440
Los Alamos National Laboratory	Dateline Los Alamos		6103
Losers Magazine	Losers Magazine		609
Lotus Publishing Inc.	Personal Transformation	(1094-9917)	5265
M I T Press	Voo Doo Magazine		3866
M Magazine Ltd.	Northern Ohio Live	(0271-5147)	1696
Magnes Press	Israel Journal of Mathematics	(0021-2172)	4752
Male Media Inc.	Manshots		6126
Maney Publishing	Cartographic Journal	(0008-7041)	3578
Marcasite Press	The Amethyst Review	(1192-2478)	4538
Marvel Comics Group	The Defenders		1827
Mathematical Association of America	College Mathematics Journal	(0746-8342)	4745
	Mathematics Magazine	(0025-570X)	4758
Maxi	Maxi		6948
McMaster University Institute for Energy Studies	Energy Studies Review	(0843-4379)	2607
McMullen Argus Publishing, Inc.	Off Road	(0363-1745)	1075
	Today's SUV	(1528-0772)	1079
	Surfing	(0194-9314)	6341
Medical Economics Company	Business & Health	(0739-9413)	3039
Meme	Meme		610
Meredith Corp.	Better Homes and Gardens Hometown Cooking	(1524-7856)	3219
Merle Hoffman Enterprises, Ltd.	On the Issues	(0895-6014)	6809
Mester	Mester	(0026-0436)	4089
Miami University	The Old Northwest	(0360-5531)	3758
Micromedia ProQuest	Canadian Index	(1192-4160)	5327

Table 3 / Titles Deleted Since the Last Edition, by Publisher (cont.)

Publisher	Title	ISSN No.	11th Ed. Sequence No
Mid-American Review of Sociology Consortium	Social Thought and Research	(0732-913X)	6218
Middle East International (Publishers) Ltd.	Middle East International	(0047-7249)	4961
Moderna Tider Foerlags AB	Moderna Tider	(1101-6396)	2830
Mouton de Gruyter	IRAL	(0019-042X)	4357
MoXie Magazine	Moxie	(1521-5873)	6716
Multilingual Matters Ltd.	Language Awareness	(0965-8416)	4376
Murder Can Be Fun	Murder Can Be Fun		6911
Muuna Takeena	Muuna Takeena		6913
N D	ND	(0894-8585)	6916
Nando Media	The Nando Times		5347
National Academy of Sciences	National Research Council. NewsReport	(0027-8432)	6083
National Bureau of Asian Research	AccessAsia Review		942
National Conference of Editorial Writers	The Masthead (Rockville)	(0025-5122)	3959
National Council of Teachers of English	Primary Voices K-6	(1068-073X)	2439
National Council of Teachers of Mathematics	Mathematics Teaching in the Middle School	(1072-0839)	1799
	Teaching Children Mathematics	(1073-5836)	1805
National Federation of Business and Professional Women's Clubs, Inc.	Business Woman Magazine	(0027-8831)	6764
National Gardening Association	National Gardening	(1052-4096)	3400
National Interreligious Service Board for Conscientious Objectors	The Reporter for Conscience' Sake	(0034-4796)	5468
National Journal of Sexual Orientation Law	National Journal of Sexual Orientation Law		4293
National Research Center on the Gifted and Talented	The National Research Center on the Gifted and Talented Newsletter		5449
National Student Research Center	E-Journal of Student Research		2550
National Wildlife Federation	International Wildlife	(0020-9112)	2746
Near East Research, Inc.	Near East Report	(0028-176X)	4968
New Moon Publishing	New Moon Network	(1083-5970)	5436
New York Academy of Sciences	The Sciences	(0036-861X)	6097
New York Open Center	Lapis	(1529-0840)	5261
New York University School of Law	Annual Survey of American Law	(0066-4413)	4143
North American Media Group, Inc.	North American Hunter	(0194-4320)	3891
Northeast Sea Grant Programs	Nor'easter	(1066-8357)	4723
Nottingham Arabidopsis Stock Centre	Weeds World		576
Nouvel Observateur	Le Nouvel Observateur	(0029-4713)	2838
Nova Southeastern University	Online Chronicle of Distance Education and Communication		2560
O C L C Online Computer Library Center, Inc.	OCLC FirstSearch		163
Obzine	OBZINE!		6949

Odyssey Publications, Inc.	Pop Culture Collecting	(1527-4578)	696
Older Women's League	The OWL Observer		6848
Oryx Press	Consumer Health and Nutrition Index	(0883-1963)	70
Oxford University Press	Asian Art and Culture	(1352-2744)	807
	National Cancer Institute. Journal	(0027-8874)	3628
	Literary and Linguistic Computing	(0268-1145)	4390
Oxpecker Enterprises, Inc.	The Angling Report	(1045-3539)	3156
Pace Publications	Criminal Justice Newsletter	(0045-9038)	2020
Pakistan Institute of International Affairs	Pakistan Horizon	(0030-980X)	924
Panoff Publishing, Inc.	Porthole	(1070-9479)	6597
Parthenon Publishing Group	Climacteric	(1369-7137)	6844
Partisan Review, Inc.	Partisan Review	(0031-2525)	4437
Passages North	Passages North		4566
Pella Publishing Company	Journal of the Hellenic Diaspora	(0364-2976)	2820
Pergamon	Aircraft Design	(1369-8869)	317
	Journal of Second Language Writing	(1060-3743)	4371
Periodiques Reader's Digest Ltee.	Reader's Digest Canada	(0034-0413)	1485
Periph' Organisation	PeriphWeb Magazine		2898
Pestsearch International Pty. Ltd.	Online Journal of Veterinary Research	(1328-925X)	6693
Phoenix Newspapers, Inc.	Arizona Central		5339
Piemme	Il Mattino		2874
Pigulki	Pigulki	(1060-9288)	3863
Pira International	Printing Abstracts	(0031-109X)	178
Platts	Electrical World	(0013-4457)	1430
Poetry Atlanta, Inc.	Atlanta Review	(1073-9696)	4539
Poetry Today Online	Poetry Today Online		4584
Politico	Politico		4131
Population Reference Bureau, Inc.	Population Today	(0749-2448)	5782
Powerlifting U S A	Powerlifting USA	(0199-8536)	6330
Pressdram Ltd.	Private Eye	(0032-888X)	3858
Presses Universitaires de France Departement des Revues	Etudes Philosophiques	(0014-2166)	5524
Presson - North & Co.	The Woolly Times		601
Primary Source Microfilm	B N I	(1357-2598)	5326
Primedia Consumer Media & Magazine Group	Skin Diver	(0037-6345)	6337
Primedia Inc.	Ritmo Beat	(1534-4754)	4127
PRIMEDIA Special Interest Group	Cats Magazine	(0008-8544)	5481
Primedia Youth Entertainment Group	Bop	(8750-7242)	5172
Princeton University International Finance Section	Essays in International Economics	(0071-142X)	2315
Princeton University Office of Population Research	Population Index	(0032-4701)	177

Table 3 / Titles Deleted Since the Last Edition, by Publisher (cont.)

Publisher	Title	ISSN No.	11th Ed. Sequence No
Proud Parenting	Proud Parenting	(1534-5025)	4277
Psiren Publications	Siren		6136
PsychNews International	PsychNews International	(1366-9869)	5935
Psychology Press	Language and Cognitive Processes	(0169-0965)	4373
Public Citizen, Inc.	Public Citizen	(0738-5927)	595
Publish Media, LLC	Publish!	(0897-6007)	5805
Publishing Concepts Corp.	Marine Fish Monthly	(1045-3555)	5486
Purdue University	Down the Garden Path		3405
Putman Media	Food Processing	(0015-6523)	3261
Quale Press	edition key satch(el)	(1527-9579)	4545
Quest	Quest: philosophical discussions	(1011-226X)	430
R C S Editori SpA Periodici	Oggi	(0030-0705)	2840
R C S Editori SpA Quotidiani	Corriere della Sera	(1120-4982)	2865
R H C Media Inc.	Red Herring	(1080-076X)	1339
	Redherring.com		3561
R I A Group	Banking Law Journal	(0005-5506)	4144
Randall Publishing Company	Owner Operator	(0475-2112)	6550
RealPoetik	RealPoetik		4586
RedSun Institute	Native Monthly Reader	(1061-7884)	5245
Reformed Congregation of the Goddess - International	Of a Like Mind	(0892-5984)	6849
Regis Publishing, Inc.	Design Times	(1041-0422)	3908
Revue Noire	Revue Noire	(1157-4127)	433
Ripon Society	Ripon Forum	(0035-5526)	5297
River Oak Arts	River Oak Review	(1074-3693)	4573
Rocky Mountain Mathematics Consortium	Rocky Mountain Journal of Mathematics	(0035-7596)	4765
Rodale	Mountain Bike	(0897-5213)	6328
Routledge	European Romantic Review	(1050-9585)	2793
Royal Society of Chemistry	Royal Chemical Society. Journal. Perkin Transactions 1	(1472-7781)	1526
	Royal Chemical Society. Journal. Perkin Transactions 2	(1472-779X)	1527
Rump Parliament	Rump Parliament		6928
Russian Language Journal Consortium	Russian Language Journal	(0036-0252)	4395
S A M Publications	Scale Auto Modeller		5090
S B C Publishers	S B C		4280
S. Hirzel Verlag	Zeitschrift fuer deutsches Altertum und deutsche Literatur	(0044-2518)	2862
Safety Online	Safety Online		6071

Sage Publications India Pvt. Ltd.	Indian Journal of Gender Studies	(0971-5215)	6791
SalsaZine Publishing Group	SalsaZine		4132
SatireWire, LLC	SatireWire		3864
Scholars Press	Illinois Classical Studies	(0363-1923)	1753
Science and Environmental Health Network	The Networker		2762
Scientific American, Inc.	Scientific American Explorations	(1099-5005)	1782
Second Foundation	Birth Gazette	(0890-3255)	4810
Secretariat aux Affaires Autochtones	Rencontre	(0709-9495)	5249
Self Help for Her	Self Help for Her		6755
Sesame Workshop	Kid City	(0899-4293)	1558
Simon Fraser University	Critical Mass		1942
Simple Cooking	Simple Cooking	(0749-176X)	3234
Smithsonian Institution Office of Elementary and Secondary Education	Art to Zoo	(0882-6838)	3316
Socialist Party, U S A	Socialist	(0884-6154)	5298
Societa Italiana di Fisica	Journal of High Energy Physics	(1126-6708)	5683
Society of American Foresters	Forestry Source	(1084-5496)	3281
Society of Biblical Literature	Semeia	(0095-571X)	6020
Society of Financial Service Professionals	Journal of Financial Service Professionals	(1052-2875)	3043
Sojourner Feminist Institute	Sojourner	(0191-8699)	6815
Southern African Review of Books	Southern Africa Review of Books	(1606-2663)	442
Sovereign Media	Science Fiction Age	(1065-1829)	2965
SparrowHawk Press	Piano & Keyboard	(1067-3881)	5160
Special Libraries Association Geography and Map Division	Special Libraries Association Geography and Map Division. Bulletin	(0036-1607)	4330
Specialty Publishing Co.	Plastic Figure & Playset Collector	(1064-4350)	5112
St. Louis Journalism Review, Inc.	St. Louis Journalism Review	(0036-2972)	3964
Starlog Group, Inc.	Black Elegance/BE	(0885-9647)	6696
StartSpot Mediaworks, Inc.	GourmetSpot		3246
Stover Publishing Co., Inc.	Wing & Shot	(0892-1849)	3904
Student Affairs Journal Online	Student Affairs Journal Online		2561
Sunshine Farm & Gardens	Cyber-Plantsman		3404
Sunwest Publishing	Quick & Light	(1520-2879)	3232
Survival Foundation	Canadian Forum	(0008-3631)	1470
System Concepts Ltd	System Concepts Ltd.		6072
T A Media AG	Facts		2796
Tad Publishing Co.	Caregiving Online		540
Taylor & Francis A S	Norsk Geografisk Tidsskrift/Norwegian Journal of Geography	(0029-1951)	3606
Taylor & Francis Ltd	International Journal of Remote Sensing	(0143-1161)	3601
Teachers of English to Speakers of Other Languages	TESOL Journal	(1056-7941)	4399

Table 3 / Titles Deleted Since the Last Edition, by Publisher (cont.)

Publisher	Title	ISSN No.	11th Ed. Sequence No
10 Things Jesus Wants You to Know	Ten Things Jesus Wants You to Know	(1089-2869)	6861
Ten Thousand Things	Ten Thousand Things		6936
Tench	Kaspahraster		6947
Texas Cooking	Texas Cooking Online		3247
The Lesbian Review of Books	The Lesbian Review of Books	(1077-5684)	4270
The Textile Museum	Textile Museum Journal	(0083-7407)	1974
The Write Answer	Futures Past	(1068-3992)	2958
The Golf Digest Companies	Golf Digest Woman		6321
Tibetan Centre for Advanced Studies	High Asia		948
Tiempo S.A. de C.V.	Hispano Americano	(0018-2192)	4074
Time Inc. Sports Illustrated Group	Sports Illustrated Women	(1524-9409)	6725
Times Publishing Group	Asian Business	(0254-3729)	855
Titnotes	Titnotes		1224
Tocqueville Connection	Tocqueville Connection		2900
Today Media, Inc.	Delaware Today	(1086-8380)	1682
Totline Publications	Totline Newsletter	(0734-4473)	5444
Trader Publishing Co.	Walneck's Classic Cycle Trader	(1051-8088)	1082
Transportation Library	Current Literature in Traffic and Transportation	(0011-3654)	81
Triple International	Lumiere		6754
True West Publications	Old West Journal	(0030-2058)	3759
Trustworthy	Trustworthy		6937
Truth Consciousness at Desert Ashram	Light of Consciousness	(1040-7448)	5262
Turpion Ltd.	Russian Mathematical Surveys	(0036-0279)	4766
Two Queens, Inc	Empire Magazine		4243
U F O Magazine	UFO Magazine		5428
U S A Today	USA Today Baseball Weekly	(1057-9532)	6346
U S Global Change Research Information Office	Consequences	(1080-5702)	2755
U.S. Department of Agriculture * Economic Research Service	FoodReview	(1056-327X)	3633
U.S. Department of Agriculture Agricultural Research Service	U.S. Department of Agriculture. Agricultural Research Service Quarterly Report		575
U.S. Department of Agriculture Economic Research Service	Agricultural Outlook	(0099-1066)	567
U.S. National Aeronautics and Space Administration	Today@nasa.gov		368
Underground Experts United	uXu		612
Underground Informer	Underground Informer		613
UNESCO	Unesco Courier (Paris)	(0041-5278)	3527
Union Theological Seminary	Union Seminary Quarterly Review	(0362-1545)	6027
United Nations Population Fund	Populi	(0251-6861)	5784
Universite de Montreal Departement d'Etudes Anglaises	Tessera	(0840-4631)	6838

University of California, Berkeley School of Law	Berkeley Women's Law Journal	(0882-4312)	4146
University of California, Riverside Department of Spanish and Portuguese	Alaluz	(0044-7064)	4047
University of Chicago Press Journals Division	The Supreme Court Review	(0081-9557)	4216
University of Houston Department of Mathematics	Houston Journal of Mathematics	(0362-1588)	4748
University of Hull Department of History	Renaissance Forum	(1362-1149)	4536
University of Illinois at Urbana-Champaign College of Education	Ex Change		2553
University of Illinois at Urbana-Champaign Department of Mathematics	Illinois Journal of Mathematics	(0019-2082)	4750
University of Iowa College of Law	The Journal of Corporation Law	(0360-795X)	4179
University of Memphis Department of English	River City	(1048-129X)	4572
University of Michigan Department of Mathematics	Michigan Mathematical Journal	(0026-2285)	4760
University of Nevada at Reno Department of Curriculum Instruction	Electronic Journal of Science Education	(1087-3430)	2552
University of North Carolina at Chapel Hill Institute of African American Research	The Journal of African Travel-Writing	(1085-9527)	4555
University of Rhode Island Graduate School of Oceanography	Maritimes	(0025-3472)	4721
University of Toronto Press Journals Department	Cartographica	(0317-7173)	3579
	Canadian Modern Language Review/Revue Canadienne des Langues Vivantes	(0008-4506)	4346
University Press of Kentucky	Southern Folklore	(0899-594X)	3191
University Press of New England	International Environmental Affairs	(1041-4665)	2745
University Publishing Group, Inc.	AIDS and Public Policy Journal	(0887-3852)	1717
Up Here Publishing	Up Here	(0828-4253)	1490
Upside Publishing Company	Upside	(1052-0341)	1343
V N U Business Publications	Online Learning	(1092-5260)	3340
	ID Magazine	(1080-9015)	1435
V S P	Digital Printing:	(1566-1016)	5789
Vallecchi Editore	Il Ponte	(0032-423X)	2845
Vermont College of Norwich University	American Journal of Art Therapy	(0007-4764)	2513
Vienna Online	Vienna Online		2901
Vikas Publishing House Pvt. Ltd.	Indian Historical Review	(0376-9836)	919
Vogel Satellite TV Publishing	Satellite Entertainment Guide	(0843-8617)	6441
Voters Communications	Billwatch		1730
Warren, Gorham and Lamont	Estate Planning	(0094-1794)	4164
Webster University	Natural Bridge	(1525-9897)	4563
Weider Publications	Muscle & Fitness	(0744-5105)	6329
Western Association of Map Libraries	Western Association of Map Libraries. Information Bulletin	(0049-7282)	3617
Wichita State University Department of Criminal Justice	International Journal of Comparative and Applied Criminal Justice	(0192-4036)	2026
Woman and Earth	Woman and Earth Almanac		6821

Table 3 / Titles Deleted Since the Last Edition, by Publisher (cont.)

Publisher	Title	ISSN No.	11th Ed. Sequence No
Working Woman Network	Working Woman	(0145-5761)	6733
World Eagle	World Eagle	(0193-7871)	2100
World Media Live	Fashion Live		6757
Ziff Davis Media Inc.	Ziff Davis Smart Business	(1535-9891)	1344
	Computer Shopper	(0886-0556)	1929
	Yahoo! Internet Life	(1088-0070)	3937
	Family Internet Life	(1076-7754)	1931
Ziff-Davis Publishing Co.	Inter@ctive Week	(1078-7259)	3925

Table 4 / Titles Deleted Since the Last Edition, by MFL Subject

Section	Title	ISSN No.	Publisher	11th Ed. Sequence No.
ABSTRACTS AND INDEXES	Academic Abstracts and Search titles	(1071-2720)	EBSCO Publishing	8
	ACM Electronic Guide to Computing Literature	(1089-5310)	Association for Computing Machinery	2
	Agrindex	(0254-8801)	Food and Agriculture Organization of the United Nations Sales and Marketing Group	16
	Consumer Health and Nutrition Index	(0883-1963)	Oryx Press	70
	Current Literature in Traffic and Transportation	(0011-3654)	Transportation Library	81
	Index to Dental Literature	(0019-3992)	American Dental Association	127
	Magazine Index Plus/ASAP		Gale Group	152
	OCLC FirstSearch		O C L C Online Computer Library Center, Inc.	163
	PASCAL Folio 47	(1146-5247)	Centre National de la Recherche Scientifique Institut de l'Information Scientifique et Technique	168
	Population Index	(0032-4701)	Princeton University Office of Population Research	177
	Printing Abstracts	(0031-109X)	Pira International	178
	Psychological Abstracts	(0033-2887)	American Psychological Association	180
AERONAUTICS AND SPACE SCIENCE	Aircraft Design	(1369-8869)	Pergamon	317
	Carrier Aviation News		Carrier Aviation News	361
	Today@nasa.gov		U.S. National Aeronautics and Space Administration	368
AFRICA	Africa Economic Digest	(0144-8234)	Concord Press of Nigeria	375
	Afrika Zamani	(0257-5760)	Association des Historiens Africains	396
	Quest: philosophical discussions	(1011-226X)	Quest	430
	Revue Noire	(1157-4127)	Revue Noire	433
	Southern Africa Review of Books	(1606-2663)	Southern African Review of Books	442
AFRICAN AMERICAN	American Visions	(0884-9390)	Heritage Information Publishers	453
AGING	Caregiving Online		Tad Publishing Co.	540
	Modern Maturity	(0026-8046)	American Association of Retired Persons	531
	My Generation	(1532-3935)	American Association of Retired Persons	532
AGRICULTURE	Agricultural Outlook	(0099-1066)	U.S. Department of Agriculture Economic Research Service	567
	Irrigation Journal	(0047-1518)	Adams Business Media	556
	U.S. Department of Agriculture. Agricultural Research Service Quarterly Report		U.S. Department of Agriculture Agricultural Research Service	575
	Weeds World		Nottingham Arabidopsis Stock Centre	576
ALTERNATIVES	uXu		Underground Experts United	612
	Bad Subjects		Bad Subjects Production Team	605
	Gauntlet	(1047-4463)	Gauntlet, Inc.	588
	Hopscotch	(1098-6995)	Duke University Press	593
	Losers Magazine		Losers Magazine	609

Table 4 / Titles Deleted Since the Last Edition, by MFL Subject (cont.)

Section	Title	ISSN No.	Publisher	11th Ed. Sequence No.
	Meme		Meme	610
	Public Citizen	(0738-5927)	Public Citizen, Inc.	595
	The Woolly Times		Presson - North & Co.	601
	Underground Informer		Underground Informer	613
ANIMAL WELFARE	Primate Conservation	(0898-6207)	International Union for Conservation of Nature and Natural Resources	640
ANTHROPOLOGY	Journal of Quantitative Anthropology	(0922-2995)	Kluwer Academic Publishers	670
ANTIQUES AND COLLECTING	Doll World	(1066-4726)	Jones Publishing Inc.	707
	Pop Culture Collecting	(1527-4578)	Odyssey Publications, Inc.	696
ARCHITECTURE	Blueprint	(0268-4926)	E T P Ltd.	752
ARCHIVES AND MANUSCRIPTS	Library & Archival Security	(0196-0075)	Haworth Press, Inc.	780
ART	Art Access		Art Access	841
	Art Com	(0732-2852)	Contemporary Arts Press	793
	Art International	(0004-3230)	Archive Press	796
	Arts Magazine	(0004-4059)	Arts Communications	805
	Asian Art and Culture	(1352-2744)	Oxford University Press	807
	Drawing	(0191-6963)	Drawing Society, Inc.	811
	High Performance	(0160-9769)	Art in the Public Interest	815
	J. Paul Getty Museum Journal	(0362-1979)	J. Paul Getty Museum	836
	Journal of Contemporary Art	(0897-2400)	Journal of Contemporary Art	818
	New Art Examiner	(0886-8115)	Chicago New Art Association	821
ASIA AND THE PACIFIC	AccessAsia Review		National Bureau of Asian Research	942
	Asia-Inc Magazine	(1019-2239)	Asia Inc. Ltd.	944
	Asian Arts		Asian Arts	945
	Asian Business	(0254-3729)	Times Publishing Group	855
	Asian Wall Street Journal Weekly	(0191-0132)	Dow Jones & Co., Inc.	862
	AsiaWeek	(1012-6244)	Asiaweek Ltd.	863
	Central Asia Monitor	(1062-2314)	Institute for Democratic Development	905
	High Asia		Tibetan Centre for Advanced Studies	948
	Indian Historical Review	(0376-9836)	Vikas Publishing House Pvt. Ltd.	919
	Japan Quarterly	(0021-4590)	Asahi Shimbun Publishing Co.	890
	Japanese Literature Today	(0385-1044)	Japan P.E.N. Club	892
	Korean Culture	(0270-1618)	Korean Cultural Center	897
	Pakistan Horizon	(0030-980X)	Pakistan Institute of International Affairs	924
	A. Magazine	(1070-9401)	Amedia Inc.	951
	Chinese America	(1051-7642)	Chinese Historical Society of America	954
ASTRONOMY	Astrophysical Letters and Communications	(0888-6512)	Gordon and Breach - Harwood Academic	983
	Fundamentals of Cosmic Physics	(0094-5846)	Gordon and Breach - Harwood Academic	992

AUTOMOBILES AND MOTORCYCLES	AMI Auto World Magazine		American Media, Inc.	1060
	Car	(0008-5987)	Emap Active Ltd. (Angel House)	1063
	Hemmings Motor News		Hemmings Publishing	1069
	Hemmings Rods & Performance		American City Business Journals, Inc. (Charlotte)	1070
	Off Road	(0363-1745)	McMullen Argus Publishing, Inc.	1075
	Today's SUV	(1528-0772)	McMullen Argus Publishing, Inc.	1079
	Walneck's Classic Cycle Trader	(1051-8088)	Trader Publishing Co.	1082
BIRDS	Titnotes		Titnotes	1224
BOOKS AND BOOK REVIEWS	ebr		Electronic Book Reviews	1286
BUILDING AND CONSTRUCTION	Custom Builder	(0895-2493)	Gruner + Jahr U.S.A. Publishing	1301
BUSINESS	Business Central Europe	(1350-1240)	Economist Newspaper Ltd	1378
	Darwin	(1536-2256)	C X O Media Inc.	1324
	Electrical World	(0013-4457)	Platts	1430
	Global Focus	(1525-0369)	John Wiley & Sons, Inc.	1383
	Home Office Computing	(0899-7373)	Freedom Technology Media Group	1401
	ID Magazine	(1080-9015)	V N U Business Publications	1435
	New Steel	(0897-4365)	American Metal Market LLC	1438
	Red Herring	(1080-076X)	R H C Media Inc.	1339
	Supermarket Business	(0196-5700)	Bill Communications, Inc.	1449
	Textile Industries	(0890-9970)	Billian Publishing, Inc.	1451
	Upside	(1052-0341)	Upside Publishing Company	1343
	Ziff Davis Smart Business	(1535-9891)	Ziff Davis Media Inc.	1344
CANADA	ARTSatlantic	(0704-7916)	Arts Atlantic Inc.	1460
	Behind the Headlines	(0005-7983)	Canadian Institute of International Affairs	1464
	Canadian Forum	(0008-3631)	Survival Foundation	1470
	Nature Canada	(0374-9894)	Canadian Nature Federation	1478
	Reader's Digest Canada	(0034-0413)	Periodiques Reader's Digest Ltee.	1485
	Up Here	(0828-4253)	Up Here Publishing	1490
	Urban History Review/Revue d'Histoire Revue	(0703-0428)	Becker Associates	1491
CHEMISTRY	Royal Chemical Society. Journal. Perkin Transactions 1	(1472-7781)	Royal Society of Chemistry	1526
	Royal Chemical Society. Journal. Perkin Transactions 2	(1472-779X)	Royal Society of Chemistry	1527
CHILDREN	Boys' Quest	(1078-9006)	Bluffton News Printing and Publishing Co.	1541
	Eeeek-Net		Eeeek Publishing Co.	1578
	Kid City	(0899-4293)	Sesame Workshop	1558
CIS AND EASTERN EUROPE	Glas	(0869-3102)	Glas Publishers	1632
CITY, STATE, AND REGIONAL	Delaware Today	(1086-8380)	Today Media, Inc.	1682
	Mississippi	(0747-1602)	Downhome Publications, Inc.	1689
	Northern Ohio Live	(0271-5147)	M Magazine Ltd.	1696

Table 4 / Titles Deleted Since the Last Edition, by MFL Subject (cont.)

Section	Title	ISSN No.	Publisher	11th Ed. Sequence No.
CIVIL LIBERTIES	ACLU Cyber-Liberties Update		American Civil Liberties Union	1729
	AIDS and Public Policy Journal	(0887-3852)	University Publishing Group, Inc.	1717
	Billwatch		Voters Communications	1730
	Freedom Writer	(1059-6372)	Institute for First Amendment Studies, Inc.	1731
	Kennedy Institute of Ethics. Journal	(1054-6863)	Johns Hopkins University Press Journals Publishing Division	1720
CLASSICAL STUDIES	Illinois Classical Studies	(0363-1923)	Scholars Press	1753
CLASSROOM MAGAZINES	Challenge	(0745-6298)	Frank Schaffer Publications, Inc.	1792
	Creative Classroom	(0887-042X)	Creative Classroom Publishing LLC	1795
	Mathematics Teaching in the Middle School	(1072-0839)	National Council of Teachers of Mathematics	1799
	Schooldays	(1529-160X)	Frank Schaffer Publications, Inc.	1802
	Scientific American Explorations	(1099-5005)	Scientific American, Inc.	1782
	Teaching Children Mathematics	(1073-5836)	National Council of Teachers of Mathematics	1805
COMIC BOOKS	Batman: Gotham Adventures		D C Comics	1822
	Superman Adventures		D C Comics	1839
	The Defenders		Marvel Comics Group	1827
COMMUNICATION	Argumentation	(0920-427X)	Kluwer Academic Publishers	1849
	CBQ	(1094-8007)	Lawrence Erlbaum Associates, Inc.	1852
	Communication Law and Policy	(1081-1680)	Lawrence Erlbaum Associates, Inc.	1854
COMPUTER SCIENCE AND AUTOMATION	Communications of the ACM	(0001-0782)	Association for Computing Machinery, Inc.	1891
	Computer Shopper	(0886-0556)	Ziff Davis Media Inc.	1929
	Critical Mass		Simon Fraser University	1942
	Family Internet Life	(1076-7754)	Ziff Davis Media Inc.	1931
	Information and Computation	(0890-5401)	Academic Press	1915
	Journal of Computer and System Sciences	(0022-0000)	Academic Press	1920
	Legal Bytes		Legal Bytes	1944
	Maximum PC	(1073-1784)	Imagine Media, Inc.	1935
	Network Magazine	(1093-8001)	C M P Media LLC	1936
	NII Scan		Infocomm Development Authority of Singapore	1945
CONSUMER EDUCATION	Advancing the Consumer Interest	(1044-7385)	American Council on Consumer Interests	1948
	Consumers Digest	(0010-7182)	Consumers Digest, Inc.	1951
CRAFT	Quilting Today	(1040-4457)	Chitra Publications	1999
	Textile Museum Journal	(0083-7407)	The Textile Museum	1974
CRIMINOLOGY AND LAW ENFORCEMENT	Criminal Justice Newsletter	(0045-9038)	Pace Publications	2020
	International Journal of Comparative and Applied Criminal Justice	(0192-4036)	Wichita State University Department of Criminal Justice	2026
	The Journal of Correctional Education	(0740-2708)	Correctional Educational Association	2029

	Women Police		International Association of Women Police	2052
CULTURAL-SOCIAL STUDIES	World Eagle	(0193-7871)	World Eagle	2100
DANCE	Dance Online		Dance Online	2126
	Dance/USA journal	(1064-6515)	Dance/U S A	2120
DEATH AND DYING	Timelines		End-of-Life Choices	2136
DISABILITIES	Accent on Living	(0001-4508)	Cheever Publishing, Inc.	2139
	Diagnostique	(0737-2477)	Council for Educational Diagnostic Services	2149
	Hip Magazine	(1090-5707)	Hip Magazine	2158
	Journal for Vocational Special Needs Education	(0195-7597)	Journal for Vocational Special Needs Education	2162
EARTH SCIENCES	Modern Geology	(0026-7775)	Gordon and Breach - Harwood Academic	2270
ECONOMICS	El Trimestre Economico	(0041-3011)	Fondo de Cultura Economica	2376
	Essays in International Economics	(0071-142X)	Princeton University International Finance Section	2315
	Idea Central		Electronic Policy Network	2384
	Journal of Developing Areas	(0022-037X)	Journal of Developing Areas	2329
EDUCATION	American Journal of Art Therapy	(0007-4764)	Vermont College of Norwich University	2513
	Contemporary Education	(0010-7476)	Indiana State University School of Education	2398
	E-Journal of Student Research		National Student Research Center	2550
	Electronic Journal of Science Education	(1087-3430)	University of Nevada at Reno Department of Curriculum Instruction	2552
	Ex Change		University of Illinois at Urbana-Champaign College of Education	2553
	Growing Without Schooling	(0745-5305)	Holt Associates	2417
	International Education Daily		International Educators' Network Association	2555
	Lingua Franca	(1051-3310)	Academic Partners, LLC	2507
	Online Chronicle of Distance Education and Communication		Nova Southeastern University	2560
	Primary Voices K-6	(1068-073X)	National Council of Teachers of English	2439
	Student Affairs Journal Online		Student Affairs Journal Online	2561
ELECTRONICS	Electronics & Communication Engineering Journal	(0954-0695)	Institution of Electrical Engineers	2569
ENERGY	Energy Studies Review	(0843-4379)	McMaster University Institute for Energy Studies	2607
	EPRI Journal	(0362-3416)	Electric Power Research Institute	2597
	Hydrocarbon Processing	(0018-8190)	Gulf Publishing Co.	2614
	Refocus	(1471-0846)	Elsevier Advanced Technology	2627
ENGINEERING AND TECHNOLOGY	Complexity International	(1320-0682)	Charles Sturt University	2711
	Journal of Fluids Engineering	(0098-2202)	A S M E International	2704
ENVIRONMENT AND CONSERVATION	Consequences	(1080-5702)	U S Global Change Research Information Office	2755
	Corporate Watch		Corporate Watch	2757
	Earth Negotiations Bulletin		International Institute for Sustainable Development	2758

Table 4 / Titles Deleted Since the Last Edition, by MFL Subject (cont.)

Section	Title	ISSN No.	Publisher	11th Ed. Sequence No.
	EarthWatch Journal	(8750-0183)	Earthwatch Expeditions, Inc.	2729
	Environmental Business Journal	(1045-8611)	Environmental Business International Inc.	2734
	Environmental Forum	(0731-5732)	Environmental Law Institute	2737
	International Environmental Affairs	(1041-4665)	University Press of New England	2745
	International Wildlife	(0020-9112)	National Wildlife Federation	2746
	The Networker		Science and Environmental Health Network	2762
EUROPE	Austria Kultur Online		Austrian Cultural Forum	2886
	Berlin Online		Berlin Online	2888
	Brigitte	(0931-8763)	Gruner und Jahr AG & Co.	2776
	Bunte	(0172-2050)	Burda Verlag GmbH	2777
	Chi		Arnoldo Mondadori Editore SpA	2780
	Corriere della Sera	(1120-4982)	R C S Editori SpA Quotidiani	2865
	DADAm@g		DADAm@g	2892
	De Telegraaf		B V Dagblad de Telegraaf	2881
	Die Welt	(0173-8437)	Axel Springer Verlag AG	2883
	Die Woche	(0945-2125)	DieWoche Zeitungsverlag GmbH	2884
	Environment Watch Europe		Agra Europe (London) Ltd.	2894
	Europe: the magazine of the European community	(0191-4545)	European Commission The European Union's Publisher	2790
	European Commission-Bulletin of the European Union		European Commission Office for Official Publications of the European Union	2895
	European Romantic Review	(1050-9585)	Routledge	2793
	Facts		T A Media AG	2796
	Focus	(0943-7576)	Focus Magazin Verlag GmbH	2797
	Il Mattino		Piemme	2874
	Il Ponte	(0032-423X)	Vallecchi Editore	2845
	Journal of the Hellenic Diaspora	(0364-2976)	Pella Publishing Company	2820
	L'Evenement du Jeudi	(0765-412X)	Evenement	2794
	Le Nouvel Observateur	(0029-4713)	Nouvel Observateur	2838
	Moderna Tider	(1101-6396)	Moderna Tider Foerlags AB	2830
	Oggi	(0030-0705)	R C S Editori SpA Periodici	2840
	Panorama	(0553-1098)	Arnoldo Mondadori Editore SpA	2841
	Paris Match	(0397-1635)	Hachette Filipacchi Medias S.A.	2842
	PeriphWeb Magazine		Periph' Organisation	2898
	Stern Magazin	(0039-1239)	Gruner und Jahr AG & Co.	2858
	Tocqueville Connection		Tocqueville Connection	2900
	Vienna Online		Vienna Online	2901

Subject	Title	ISSN	Publisher	Entry
	Zeitschrift fuer deutsches Altertum und deutsche Literatur	(0044-2518)	S. Hirzel Verlag	2862
FICTION: SCIENCE FICTION, FANTASY, AND HORROR	Aboriginal Science Fiction	(0895-3198)	Aboriginal Science Fiction	2950
	Futures Past	(1068-3992)	The Write Answer	2958
	Science Fiction Age	(1065-1829)	Sovereign Media	2965
FILMS	Documenter	(1442-844X)	Documenter Journals Inc	3020
	Film International	(1021-6510)	Film	2993
	POV		Empire Productions & Publishing	3007
	Soundtrack!	(0771-6303)	Belgian Film Music Society vzw	3014
	Wide Angle	(0160-6840)	Johns Hopkins University Press Journals Publishing Division	3016
FINANCE	Bloomberg Personal Finance	(1523-0023)	Bloomberg L.P.	3051
	Business & Health	(0739-9413)	Medical Economics Company	3039
	Individual Investor	(1049-4596)	Individual Investor Group	3057
	Journal of Financial Service Professionals	(1052-2875)	Society of Financial Service Professionals	3043
	Mutual Funds Magazine	(8755-9889)	Institute for Econometric Research	3066
FISHING	Fish and Game Finder	(1081-910X)	Fish and Game Finder Magazines	3159
	International Angler	(0257-1420)	International Game Fish Association	3167
	Salmon - Trout Steelheader	(0029-3431)	Frank Amato Publications, Inc	3170
	The Angling Report	(1045-3539)	Oxpecker Enterprises, Inc.	3156
FOLKLORE	Southern Folklore	(0899-594X)	University Press of Kentucky	3191
FOOD AND WINE	Art Culinaire	(0892-1024)	Art Culinaire	3217
	Art of Eating	(0895-6200)	Art of Eating	3218
	Baker Boulanger		Baker Boulanger	3241
	Better Homes and Gardens Hometown Cooking	(1524-7856)	Meredith Corp.	3219
	Cuisine	(1089-6546)	August Home Publishing Co.	3225
	Epicurean Traveler		Fezziwig Publishing Co., L L C	3242
	Fabulous Foods		Enigma Communications	3243
	Global Gourmet		Electronic Gourmet Guide	3244
	Gourmet Connection		Capco Marketing	3245
	GourmetSpot		StartSpot Mediaworks, Inc.	3246
	Quick & Light	(1520-2879)	Sunwest Publishing	3232
	Simple Cooking	(0749-176X)	Simple Cooking	3234
	Texas Cooking Online		Texas Cooking	3247
FOOD INDUSTRY	Food Processing	(0015-6523)	Putman Media	3261
FORESTRY	Forestry Source	(1084-5496)	Society of American Foresters	3281
FREE MAGAZINES AND HOUSE ORGANS	Art to Zoo	(0882-6838)	Smithsonian Institution Office of Elementary and Secondary Education	3316
	Grassroots Development	(0733-6608)	Inter-American Foundation	3330
	Online Learning	(1092-5260)	V N U Business Publications	3340
GARDENING	Cyber-Plantsman		Sunshine Farm & Gardens	3404

Table 4 / Titles Deleted Since the Last Edition, by MFL Subject (cont.)

Section	Title	ISSN No.	Publisher	11th Ed. Sequence No.
	Down the Garden Path		Purdue University	3405
	Flower and Garden	(0162-3249)	K C Publishing, Inc	3387
	HortScience	(0018-5345)	American Society for Horticultural Science	3396
	HortTechnology	(1063-0198)	American Society for Horticultural Science	3397
	Journal of Herbs, Spices & Medicinal Plants	(1049-6475)	Haworth Press, Inc.	3399
	American Society for Horticultural Science. Journal	(0003-1062)	American Society for Horticultural Science	3381
	National Gardening	(1052-4096)	National Gardening Association	3400
GENERAL EDITORIAL	Unesco Courier (Paris)	(0041-5278)	UNESCO	3527
GENERAL EDITORIAL-INTERNET	Redherring.com		R H C Media Inc.	3561
GEOGRAPHY	Business Geographics	(1067-456X)	Adams Business Media	3577
	Cartographic Journal	(0008-7041)	Maney Publishing	3578
	Cartographica	(0317-7173)	University of Toronto Press, Journals Department	3579
	Geospatial Solutions	(1051-9858)	Advanstar Communications Inc.	3596
	International Journal of Remote Sensing	(0143-1161)	Taylor & Francis Ltd	3601
	Mercator's World	(1086-6728)	Aster Publishing Corp.	3605
	Norsk Geografisk Tidsskrift/Norwegian Journal of Geography	(0029-1951)	Taylor & Francis A S	3606
	Western Association of Map Libraries. Information Bulletin	(0049-7282)	Western Association of Map Libraries	3617
GOVERNMENT PERIODICALS–FEDERAL	FoodReview	(1056-327X)	U.S. Department of Agriculture, Economic Research Service	3633
	National Cancer Institute. Journal	(0027-8874)	Oxford University Press	3628
GOVERNMENT PERIODICALS–STATE AND LOCAL	Ideas in Action	(1082-9547)	International City/County Management Association	3639
	The Regionalist	(1083-6063)	Institute of Community and Area Development	3648
HISTORY	Ancient History Bulletin	(1700-3334)	Ancient History Bulletin	3775
	Old West Journal	(0030-2058)	True West Publications	3759
	The Journal of the Illinois State Historical Society	(1522-1067)	Illinois State Historical Society	3740
	The Old Northwest	(0360-5531)	Miami University	3758
HOME	Classic American Home	(1528-2864)	Hearst Corporation	3780
HOSPITALITY/RESTAURANT	Hospitality Law	(0889-5414)	L R P Publications	3838
HUMOR	Pigulki	(1060-9288)	Pigulki	3863
	Private Eye	(0032-888X)	Pressdram Ltd.	3858
	SatireWire		SatireWire, LLC	3864
	The Mini-Annals of Improbable Research	(1076-500X)	Annals of Improbable Research	3862
	Voo Doo Magazine		M I T Press	3866
HUNTING AND GUNS	American Gunsmith	(1060-0892)	Belvoir Publications, Inc.	3867

	Bowhunting News	(1066-7148)	Eastern Publishing & Distributing, Inc.	3873
	North American Hunter	(0194-4320)	North American Media Group, Inc.	3891
	Wing & Shot	(0892-1849)	Stover Publishing Co., Inc.	3904
INTERIOR DESIGN AND DECORATION	Design Times	(1041-0422)	Regis Publishing, Inc.	3908
INTERNET-WORLD WIDE WEB	.net	(1355-7602)	Future Publishing Ltd.	3930
	Inter@ctive Week	(1078-7259)	Ziff-Davis Publishing Co.	3925
	Web Net Journal	(1522-192X)	Association for the Advancement of Computing in Education	3934
	Web Server OnLineMagazine	(1087-4232)	Computer Publishing Group	3942
	New Architect	(1537-9000)	C M P Media LLC	3932
	Yahoo! Internet Life	(1088-0070)	Ziff Davis Media Inc.	3937
JOURNALISM AND WRITING	Contentious		Contentious	3975
	Editorial Eye	(0193-7383)	E E I Press	3949
	Journalism History	(0094-7679)	Greenspun School of Communication	3958
	The Masthead (Rockville)	(0025-5122)	National Conference of Editorial Writers	3959
	St. Louis Journalism Review	(0036-2972)	St. Louis Journalism Review, Inc.	3964
LATIN AMERICAN	Alaluz	(0044-7064)	University of California, Riverside Department of Spanish and Portuguese	4047
	Grafico		L A T N N, Inc.	4108
	Hispano Americano	(0018-2192)	Tiempo S.A. de C.V.	4074
	LatinWorld		LatinWorld	4109
	Mester	(0026-0436)	Mester	4089
	Latingirl	(1524-2218)	Latin Girl Magazine	4123
	Politico		Politico	4131
	Ritmo Beat	(1534-4754)	Primedia Inc.	4127
	SalsaZine		SalsaZine Publishing Group	4132
	Super Onda		Hispanic Business Inc.	4128
LAW	Annual Survey of American Law	(0066-4413)	New York University School of Law	4143
	Banking Law Journal	(0005-5506)	R I A Group	4144
	Berkeley Women's Law Journal	(0882-4312)	University of California, Berkeley School of Law	4146
	Commercial Law Journal	(0010-3055)	Commercial Law League of America	4157
	Estate Planning	(0094-1794)	Warren, Gorham and Lamont	4164
	The Journal of Corporation Law	(0360-795X)	University of Iowa College of Law	4179
	The Supreme Court Review	(0081-9557)	University of Chicago Press Journals Division	4216
LESBIAN, GAY, BISEXUAL, AND TRANSGENDER	Empire Magazine		Two Queens, Inc	4243
	Images (New York)		Gay & Lesbian Alliance Against Defamation	4256
	Hero	(1521-9658)	Hero	4254
	International Journal of Sexuality and Gender Studies	(1566-1768)	Kluwer Academic / Plenum Publishers	4257

Table 4 / Titles Deleted Since the Last Edition, by MFL Subject (cont.)

Section	Title	ISSN No.	Publisher	11th Ed. Sequence No.
	National Journal of Sexual Orientation Law		National Journal of Sexual Orientation Law	4293
	Proud Parenting	(1534-5025)	Proud Parenting	4277
	S B C		S B C Publishers	4280
	The Lesbian Review of Books	(1077-5684)	The Lesbian Review of Books	4270
	Special Libraries Association Geography and Map Division. Bulletin	(0036-1607)	Special Libraries Association Geography and Map Division	4330
	The Abbey Newsletter	(0276-8291)	Abbey Publications, Inc.	4296
LINGUISTICS	American Journal of Germanic Linguistics and Literature	(1040-8207)	Cambridge University Press	4339
	Applied Language Learning	(1041-679X)	Defense Language Institute Foreign Language Center	4342
	Canadian Modern Language Review/Revue Canadienne des Langues Vivantes	(0008-4506)	University of Toronto Press Journals Department	4346
	English Today	(0266-0784)	Cambridge University Press	4349
	ETC	(0014-164X)	International Society for General Semantics	4351
	Foreign Language Annals	(0015-718X)	American Council on the Teaching of Foreign Languages, Inc.	4353
	Functions of Language	(0929-998X)	John Benjamins Publishing Co.	4354
	Hispania	(0018-2133)	American Association of Teachers of Spanish and Portuguese, Inc.	4356
	Interpreting	(1384-6647)	John Benjamins Publishing Co.	4362
	IRAL	(0019-042X)	Mouton de Gruyter	4357
	Journal of Pragmatics	(0378-2166)	Elsevier BV North-Holland	4370
	Journal of Second Language Writing	(1060-3743)	Pergamon	4371
	Language Acquisition	(1048-9223)	Lawrence Erlbaum Associates, Inc.	4372
	Language and Cognitive Processes	(0169-0965)	Psychology Press	4373
	Language Awareness	(0965-8416)	Multilingual Matters Ltd.	4376
	Language International	(0923-182X)	John Benjamins Publishing Co.	4378
	Language Problems and Language Planning	(0272-2690)	John Benjamins Publishing Co.	4379
	Lingvisticae Investigationes	(0378-4169)	John Benjamins Publishing Co.	4389
	Literary and Linguistic Computing	(0268-1145)	Oxford University Press	4390
	Pragmatics & Cognition	(0929-0907)	John Benjamins Publishing Co.	4394
	Russian Language Journal	(0036-0252)	Russian Language Journal Consortium	4395
	Second Language Research	(0267-6583)	Arnold Publishers	4396
	Terminology	(0929-9971)	John Benjamins Publishing Co.	4401
	TESOL Journal	(1056-7941)	Teachers of English to Speakers of Other Languages	4399
	Women and Language	(8755-4550)	George Mason University Communication Department	4402
	Word	(0043-7956)	International Linguistic Association	4403

	World Englishes	(0883-2919)	Blackwell Publishing Ltd.	4404
LITERARY REVIEWS	Partisan Review	(0031-2525)	Partisan Review, Inc.	4437
LITERATURE	Renaissance Forum	(1362-1149)	University of Hull Department of History	4536
LITTLE MAGAZINES	Atlanta Review	(1073-9696)	Poetry Atlanta, Inc.	4539
	Baybury Review		Baybury Books	4541
	edition key satch(el)	(1527-9579)	Quale Press	4545
	First Intensity		First Intensity	4548
	Koja		Hive Press	4556
	Left Curve	(0160-1857)	Left Curve Publications	4557
	Natural Bridge	(1525-9897)	Webster University	4563
	Passages North		Passages North	4566
	Poetry Today Online		Poetry Today Online	4584
	RealPoetik		RealPoetik	4586
	Red Rock Review	(1086-4342)	Community College of Southern Nevada Department of English	4570
	River City	(1048-129X)	University of Memphis Department of English	4572
	River Oak Review	(1074-3693)	River Oak Arts	4573
	The Amethyst Review	(1192-2478)	Marcasite Press	4538
	The Journal of African Travel-Writing	(1085-9527)	University of North Carolina at Chapel Hill Institute of African American Research	4555
	The Rejected Quarterly	(1525-2671)	Black Plankton Press	4571
MANAGEMENT, ADMINISTRATION, AND HUMAN RESOURCES	Competitive Intelligence Review	(1058-0247)	John Wiley & Sons, Inc.	4667
	Organisations & People	(1350-6269)	Association for Management Education and Development	4659
MARINE SCIENCE AND TECHNOLOGY	Maritimes	(0025-3472)	University of Rhode Island Graduate School of Oceanography	4721
	Nor'easter	(1066-8357)	Northeast Sea Grant Programs	4723
MATHEMATICS	College Mathematics Journal	(0746-8342)	Mathematical Association of America	4745
	Commentarii Mathematica Helvetici	(0010-2571)	Birkhaeuser Verlag AG	4746
	Houston Journal of Mathematics	(0362-1588)	University of Houston Department of Mathematics	4748
	Illinois Journal of Mathematics	(0019-2082)	University of Illinois at Urbana-Champaign Department of Mathematics	4750
	Israel Journal of Mathematics	(0021-2172)	Magnes Press	4752
	Journal of Differential Geometry	(0022-040X)	International Press	4753
	Australian Mathematical Society. Journal	(0263-6115)	Australian Mathematical Society	4742
	Mathematics Magazine	(0025-570X)	Mathematical Association of America	4758
	Mathematics of Computation	(0025-5718)	American Mathematical Society	4759
	Michigan Mathematical Journal	(0026-2285)	University of Michigan Department of Mathematics	4760
	Rocky Mountain Journal of Mathematics	(0035-7596)	Rocky Mountain Mathematics Consortium	4765
	Russian Mathematical Surveys	(0036-0279)	Turpion Ltd.	4766

Table 4 / Titles Deleted Since the Last Edition, by MFL Subject (cont.)

Section	Title	ISSN No.	Publisher	11th Ed. Sequence No.
	The ANZIAM Journal	(1446-1811)	Australian Mathematical Society	4736
MEDICINE AND HEALTH	Birth Gazette	(0890-3255)	Second Foundation	4810
	Childbirth Instructor Magazine	(1075-9689)	Cradle Publishing, Inc.	4811
	Health Watch		Health Care Financing Administration	4912
	Journal of Health Education	(1055-6699)	American Alliance for Health, Physical Education, Recreation, and Dance	4902
	Medical Update		American Foundation for Preventive Medicine	4800
	Leukemia Society of America. Newsline		Leukemia Society of America	4863
	Pharmacology and Therapeutics:	(0163-7258)	Elsevier Inc.	4826
	Your Health & Fitness	(0279-9324)	General Learning Communications	4807
MEN	Code	(1522-0591)	Larry Flynt Publications, Inc.	4923
MIDDLE EAST	Arab Studies Quarterly	(0271-3519)	Association of Arab-American University Graduates, Inc.	4951
	Islamic Affairs Analyst	(0969-4234)	Jane's Information Group	4953
	Kurdish Life	(1061-8457)	Kurdish Library	4958
	Middle East International	(0047-7249)	Middle East International (Publishers) Ltd.	4961
	Middle East Policy	(1061-1924)	Blackwell Publishing, Inc.	4963
	Near East Report	(0028-176X)	Near East Research, Inc.	4968
	The Link	(0024-4007)	Americans for Middle East Understanding, Inc.	4959
	Washington Report on Middle East Affairs	(8755-4917)	American Educational Trust (A E T)	4970
MILITARY GAMES	Berg's Review of Games		Coalition Web, Inc.	5011
	Napoleon	(1093-2283)	Emperor's Headquarters	5024
	Operations		Gamers	5040
	Star Fleet Times		Amarillo Design Bureau	5029
MODEL MAKING AND COLLECTING	Plastic Figure & Playset Collector	(1064-4350)	Specialty Publishing Co.	5112
	Scale Auto Modeller		S A M Publications	5090
	Spielzeug Antik Revue	(1617-2582)	Alba Publikation Alf Teloeken GmbH & Co. KG	5120
	Toy Soldier and Model Figure	(1359-7426)	Ashdown Publishing Ltd.	5107
MUSIC	Bop	(8750-7242)	Primedia Youth Entertainment Group	5172
	Let It Rock		Let It Rock, Inc.	5202
	Piano & Keyboard	(1067-3881)	SparrowHawk Press	5160
NATIVE AMERICANS	American Indian Libraries Newsletter	(0193-8207)	American Indian Library Association	5228
	Business Alert		First Nations Development Institute	5230
	Native Monthly Reader	(1061-7884)	RedSun Institute	5245
	Rencontre	(0709-9495)	Secretariat aux Affaires Autochtones	5249
NEWS AND OPINION	Against the Current	(0739-4853)	Center for Changes	5269
	Black Flag	(0045-2157)	Black Flag Collective	5272

	Democratic Left	(0164-3207)	Democratic Socialists of America	5276
	Ripon Forum	(0035-5526)	Ripon Society	5297
	Socialist	(0884-6154)	Socialist Party, U S A	5298
	The Harris Poll	(0895-7983)	Harris Interactive	5279
NEWSPAPERS	Arizona Central		Phoenix Newspapers, Inc.	5339
	B N I	(1357-2598)	Primary Source Microfilm	5326
	Canadian Index	(1192-4160)	Micromedia ProQuest	5327
	GlobeNet		Globe and Mail Publishing	5345
	New York Amsterdam News	(0028-7121)	Amnews Corp.	5320
	The Freep (Detroit Free Press)		Detroit Free Press, Inc.	5343
	The Nando Times		Nando Media	5347
OCCUPATIONS AND CAREERS	Career Magazine		Career Magazine	5382
	High Technology Careers Magazine	(0749-2960)	Central Newspapers, Inc.	5383
	Job Options		Job Options	5384
PARAPSYCHOLOGY	Journal of Near-Death Studies	(0891-4494)	Kluwer Academic / Plenum Publishers	5422
	UFO Magazine		U F O Magazine	5428
PARENTING	Adolescence	(0001-8449)	Libra Publishers, Inc.	5429
	Children Now		Children Now	5446
	Exceptional Children	(0014-4029)	Council for Exceptional Children	5433
	New Moon Network	(1083-5970)	New Moon Publishing	5436
	ParentLife	(1074-326X)	LifeWay Press	5440
	The National Research Center on the Gifted and Talented Newsletter		National Research Center on the Gifted and Talented	5449
	Totline Newsletter	(0734-4473)	Totline Publications	5444
PEACE	Peacekeeping & International Relations	(1187-3485)	Canadian PeaceKeeping Press Pearson Peacekeeping Centre	5467
	The Reporter for Conscience' Sake	(0034-4796)	National Interreligious Service Board for Conscientious Objectors	5468
PETS	Bird Breeder On-line	(1096-2115)	Fancy Publications, Inc.	5491
	Bonkers	(1521-8139)	Bonkers!	5479
	Cats Magazine	(0008-8544)	PRIMEDIA Special Interest Group	5481
	Marine Fish Monthly	(1045-3555)	Publishing Concepts Corp.	5486
	Pet Product News	(1076-5573)	Fancy Publications, Inc.	5488
PHILOSOPHY	Etudes Philosophiques	(0014-2166)	Presses Universitaires de France Departement des Revues	5524
PHYSICS	Journal of High Energy Physics	(1126-6708)	Societa Italiana di Fisica	5683
POLITICAL SCIENCE	Policy Review	(0146-5945)	Heritage Foundation	5703
	Politics	(0263-3957)	Blackwell Publishing Ltd.	5708
POPULATION STUDIES	Population Today	(0749-2448)	Population Reference Bureau, Inc.	5782
	Populi	(0251-6861)	United Nations Population Fund	5784
PRINTING AND GRAPHIC ARTS	Digital Printing:	(1566-1016)	V S P	5789
	Printout	(0887-7556)	CAP Ventures	5803

Table 4 / Titles Deleted Since the Last Edition, by MFL Subject (cont.)

Section	Title	ISSN No.	Publisher	11th Ed. Sequence No.
	Publish!	(0897-6007)	Publish Media, LLC	5805
PSYCHOLOGY	PsychNews International	(1366-9869)	PsychNews International	5935
RELIGION	Christianity and the Arts	(1080-7608)	Christianity and the Arts	5968
	Greek Orthodox Theological Review	(0017-3894)	Holy Cross Orthodox Press	5978
	Mid-Stream	(0544-0653)	Council on Christian Unity of the Christian Church	6008
	Semeia	(0095-571X)	Society of Biblical Literature	6020
	Union Seminary Quarterly Review	(0362-1545)	Union Theological Seminary	6027
ROBOTICS	Laboratory Robotics and Automation	(0895-7533)	John Wiley & Sons, Inc.	6048
	Robotics World	(0737-7908)	Douglas Publications, Inc.	6054
SAFETY	Safety Online		Safety Online	6071
	System Concepts Ltd.		System Concepts Ltd	6072
SCIENCE AND TECHNOLOGY	Dateline Los Alamos		Los Alamos National Laboratory	6103
	National Research Council. NewsReport	(0027-8432)	National Academy of Sciences	6083
	The Sciences	(0036-861X)	New York Academy of Sciences	6097
SEXUALITY	Adam Black Video Directory	(1533-5992)	Knight Publishing Corporation	6115
	Hustler Erotic Video Guide	(1059-9703)	L F P, Inc.	6125
	Manshots		Male Media Inc.	6126
	SandMUtopian Guardian	(1087-6316)	A S W G T Inc. Utopian Network	6132
	Siren		Psiren Publications	6136
SINGLES	Christian Singles		Christian Singles International	6145
	Single-Parent Family	(1077-4092)	Focus on the Family, Inc.	6151
	Travel Companions	(1076-5719)	Jens Jurgen, Ed. & Pub.	6156
SOCIOLOGY AND SOCIAL WORK	Humboldt Journal of Social Relations	(0160-4341)	Humboldt State University Department of Sociology	6187
	Journal of Social Distress and the Homeless	(1053-0789)	Kluwer Academic / Plenum Publishers	6200
	Social Thought and Research	(0732-913X)	Mid-American Review of Sociology Consortium	6218
SPIRITUALITY AND WELL-BEING	Alternative Medicine	(1081-4000)	Alternative Medicine	5258
	Lapis	(1529-0840)	New York Open Center	5261
	Light of Consciousness	(1040-7448)	Truth Consciousness at Desert Ashram	5262
	Personal Transformation	(1094-9917)	Lotus Publishing Inc.	5265
	Yoga International	(1055-7911)	Himalayan International Institute (HII)	5268
SPORTS	Blades on Ice	(1070-390X)	Blades on Ice, Inc.	6314
	Bowling Magazine	(0162-0274)	American Bowling Congress	6316
	FringeGolf	(1534-9683)	Fringe, Inc.	6319
	Golf Digest Woman		The Golf Digest Companies	6321
	International Journal of Sport Nutrition & Exercise Metabolism	(1050-1606)	Human Kinetics Publishers, Inc.	6271

	Muscle & Fitness	(0744-5105)	Weider Publications	6329
	Mountain Bike	(0897-5213)	Rodale	6328
	Powerlifting USA	(0199-8536)	Powerlifting U S A	6330
	Skin Diver	(0037-6345)	Primedia Consumer Media & Magazine Group	6337
	Sports Cards	(1069-2282)	Krause Publications, Inc.	6260
	Surfing	(0194-9314)	McMullen Argus Publishing, Inc.	6341
	USA Today Baseball Weekly	(1057-9532)	U S A Today	6346
	VeloNews		Inside Communications	6355
TEENAGERS	LAYA		L A Y A!	6417
TELEVISION, VIDEO, AND RADIO	Community Media Review	(1074-9004)	Alliance for Community Media	6422
	Hobby Broadcasting		Cabinet Communications	6426
	Satellite Entertainment Guide	(0843-8617)	Vogel Satellite TV Publishing	6441
THEATER	Theaterworld Internet Magazine		Graham Powner	6502
TRANSPORTATION	Owner Operator	(0475-2112)	Randall Publishing Company	6550
TRAVEL AND TOURISM	Best Fares	(8750-2410)	Best Fares	6588
	Big World	(1079-5707)	Big World Publishing, Inc.	6589
	Consumer Reports Travel Letter	(0887-8439)	Consumers Union of the United States, Inc.	6609
	Islands	(0745-7847)	Islands Publishing Company	6594
	Journal of Travel & Tourism Marketing	(1054-8408)	Haworth Hospitality Press	6621
	Porthole	(1070-9479)	Panoff Publishing, Inc.	6597
	Specialty Travel Index	(0889-7085)	Alpine Hansen Publishers	6598
	The Shoestring Traveler	(1082-5304)	International Association of Air Travel Couriers (IAATC)	6612
	Travel Holiday	(0199-025X)	Hachette Filipacchi Media U.S., Inc.	6605
VETERINARY SCIENCE	Online Journal of Veterinary Research	(1328-925X)	Pestsearch International Pty. Ltd.	6693
	Preventive Veterinary Medicine	(0167-5877)	Elsevier BV	6680
WOMEN	Black Elegance/BE	(0885-9647)	Starlog Group, Inc.	6696
	Commitment		Commitment	6745
	Fashion Dish		Fashion Dish	6746
	Fashion Live		World Media Live	6757
	Fashion Planet		Fashion Planet	6749
	Lumiere		Triple International	6754
	Moxie	(1521-5873)	MoXie Magazine	6716
	Rosie		Gruner + Jahr U.S.A. Publishing	6722
	Self Help for Her		Self Help for Her	6755
	Sports Illustrated Women	(1524-9409)	Time Inc. Sports Illustrated Group	6725
	Woman's Journal	(0043-7344)	I P C SouthBank	6730
	Working Woman	(0145-5761)	Working Woman Network	6733
WOMEN: FEMINIST AND SPECIAL INTEREST	A Leadership Journal	(1088-5188)	Columbia College Leadership Institute	6799
	Breast Implant Litigation Reporter	(1062-1814)	Andrews Publications	6843

Table 4 / Titles Deleted Since the Last Edition, by MFL Subject (cont.)

Section	Title	ISSN No.	Publisher	11th Ed. Sequence No.
	Climacteric	(1369-7137)	Parthenon Publishing Group	6844
	Crone Chronicles	(1068-8684)	Crone Corp.	6853
	Equal Opportunities Review	(0268-7143)	I R S	6769
	Fireweed	(0706-3857)	Fireweed Inc.	6832
	Indian Journal of Gender Studies	(0971-5215)	Sage Publications India Pvt. Ltd.	6791
	Irish Journal of Feminist Studies	(1393-306X)	Cork University Press	6793
	Business Woman Magazine	(0027-8831)	National Federation of Business and Professional Women's Clubs, Inc.	6764
	Of a Like Mind	(0892-5984)	Reformed Congregation of the Goddess - International	6849
	On Campus with Women	(0734-0141)	Association of American Colleges and Universities	6850
	On the Issues	(0895-6014)	Merle Hoffman Enterprises, Ltd.	6809
	Sojourner	(0191-8699)	Sojourner Feminist Institute	6815
	Tessera	(0840-4631)	Universite de Montreal Departement d'Etudes Anglaises	6838
	The OWL Observer		Older Women's League	6848
	Woman and Earth Almanac		Woman and Earth	6821
	Woman Engineer	(0887-2120)	Equal Opportunity Publications, Inc.	6852
ZINES	Amusing Yourself to Death		Amusing Yourself to Death	6863
	Brat		BRAT Media	6868
	Bummers and Gummers		Bummers and Gummers	6870
	Chip's Closet Cleaner	(1064-9719)	Chip Rowe	6873
	Crap Hound		Crap Hound	6877
	Dropout		Dropout	6879
	Flatland	(1090-0683)	Flatland Books	6888
	Fucktooth		Fucktooth	6890
	Girljock		Girljock Magazine	6892
	Hodgepodge		Hodgepodge	6900
	Kaspahraster		Tench	6947
	Maxi		Maxi	6948
	Murder Can Be Fun		Murder Can Be Fun	6911
	Muuna Takeena		Muuna Takeena	6913
	ND	(0894-8585)	N D	6916
	OBZINE!		Obzine	6949
	QECE	(1524-1114)	Larry Nocella	6922
	Rump Parliament		Rump Parliament	6928
	Ten Things Jesus Wants You to Know	(1089-2869)	10 Things Jesus Wants You to Know	6861
	Ten Thousand Things		Ten Thousand Things	6936
	The Glovebox Chronicles		Glovebox Chronicles	6893
	Trustworthy		Trustworthy	6937

HOW TO USE THIS BOOK

*Title. *ISSN. Date Founded. *Frequency. *Price.
Editor. Publisher and Address, *Internet-WWW.
Illustrations, Index, Advertising. *Sample. *Refereed.
Circulation. *Date Volume Ends. *CD-ROM.
Microform. Reprint. *Online. *Indexed.
*Book Reviews. *Audience. * Annotation.

The bibliographic data in the entries contain the items shown in the box above. Items preceded by an asterisk are fully explained in the paragraphs that follow. For an explanation of how consultants', or contributors', names are handled, see Designation of Consultants in the Preface. The Abbreviations section lists the general abbreviations found in the bibliographic information and the acronyms used for the micropublishers, and abstracts and indexes.

The detailed Subject Index enables the user to access the enormous amount of information that may not be readily retrievable from the alphabetically arranged Title Index. All subject classifications used, as well as variations in wording of subject headings, and as many additional subject cross-references as the editors expected would be useful, are listed in the Subject Index. The numbers that appear in the indexes refer to the magazine entry numbers, not page numbers.

Title

The periodicals in this book are listed alphabetically, by title, under the subjects given in the Contents. They are numbered sequentially, beginning with 1 on page 1 and ending with 6856, the last magazine entry in the book, on page 1033.

ISSN Numbers

This international standard, which is used all over the world by serial publishers to distinguish similar titles from each other, directly follows the title. *Ulrich's Periodicals Directory* was used to verify this information.

Frequency and Price

The frequency is given immediately after the founding date, and the symbols used are explained in the General Abbreviations section. The price quoted is the annual subscription rate given by the publisher, usually as of 2003. Prices are relative and, of course, subject to change—probably upward. Furthermore, the fluctuation of the dollar makes the prices of foreign magazines even more relative. The phrase "Controlled Circ." is found after some titles. This means the magazine has a controlled circulation and is sent free to certain individuals whom the advertisers are trying to reach. Such a magazine is financed solely by advertisements, and the controlled circulation indicates the publisher has targeted a certain audience or audiences for the advertisers. For a listing of controlled circulation serials, with full addresses, see the index volume of *Ulrich's Periodicals Directory*. "Others" means those who are outside that select audience and must pay for the title. Often the publisher is willing to send the magazine free to libraries, but in any case an inquiry should be made.

Internet-World Wide Web

The web address (URL) represents the address at the time of the compilation. As anyone knows who uses the Internet, the address may change frequently. In a case where the address does not prove correct, try shortening the address back to the "root" or entering the name of the magazine in the search engine box. Normally this works.

Sample

Publishers were asked whether or not they would send a free copy of the magazine to a library if requested. Those who replied favorably are indicated by the single word "sample" The request should be made by the head of the library, or by the head of the serials department, and written on official stationery. The indication that publishers are willing to send samples to institutions does not mean they are necessarily interested in sending them to individual subscribers.

Refereed

This term is used to indicate that manuscripts submitted to a magazine are examined both by the editor and one or more specialists in the individual field before approval is given to publish. The readers (sometimes called an editorial board) apparently ensure a better chance that the final product will be a contribution to knowledge. Microform and Reprint Companies providing microform runs of magazines are indicated, and information concerning the publisher of some reprints is noted. Librarians should consult *Guide to Microforms in Print* (Munich: K.G. Saur Verlag) and *Ulrich's Periodicals Directory* for additional information.

Date Volume Ends

Librarians find it helpful to know when a publisher ends a volume—obviously for purposes of binding. The information provided is from the publisher.

CD-ROM

Like the online designation, this includes the basic sources of CD-ROM access to a particular title. Again, this is in reference to an index where the periodical is accessed, or the name of the CD-ROM publisher, not the periodical itself. *Ulrich's* listings include information on indexes in CD-ROM format for some titles. For additional information, see the *Gale Directory of Databases* (Detroit: Gale Research) and the annual *CD-ROMs in Print* (Detroit: Gale Research).

Online

This includes, where available, the basic source(s) of online access to a particular title. Normally, of course, the online notation is in reference to an index (not a periodical) that may be employed to access the journal or magazine. Therefore, one will find the online designation most often in the Abstracts and Indexes section.

Indexed

Information on where titles are indexed or abstracted is given—in abbreviated format—on the first line under the bibliographic data. Also indicated are major subject indexes in which the periodicals are indexed. Major must be emphasized. Not all indexing for each title is included. Indexes and abstracts that are employed are annotated in the Abstracts and Indexes section, which leads off this book. Here one finds, too, whether that index is available online and/or on CD-ROM. Note that all but the most esoteric titles are found in one of the three citation indexes: *Science Citation Index*, *Social Sciences Citation Index*, and *Arts and Humanities Citation Index*. The term index in the bibliographic description indicates that the publisher has an index to the periodical.

Book Reviews

Information given refers to the approximate number of reviews that appear in a typical issue of the periodical and the average length.

Audience

Ems (elementary and middle school students); Hs (high school students); Ga (General Adult); Ac (Academic audience); Sa (Special Adult). Each magazine has an indication of audience or type of library for which it is suited. The scale is specific, but as most magazines are for more than one audience, several audience levels are usually given for each title. Periodicals for elementary and middle school students (Ems) are not separated because it is often difficult to draw the line between these two age groups. The titles and descriptive annotations leave little doubt as to the level of maturity for which the magazine is intended. Generally, elementary and middle school means the age group from 4 to 14 years and/or those in elementary or middle school. The high school level (Hs) overlaps and may include middle school, but for the most part, these are titles suitable for those from 14 years up to 18 years and/or in high school. Magazines suitable for public libraries and college and university library reading rooms are rated General Adult (Ga). Publications designated Academic audience (Ac) should be considered for junior colleges, colleges, and universities. Magazines rated Special Adult (Sa) are for specialized audiences and will be read by few people other than professionals or students of a particular subject. It is assumed that the audience symbols are only guides, not designations for type of library—which is to say that the symbol Ga does not mean the magazine is only limited to public libraries any more than Ac means a magazine is only for academic libraries. Obviously the choice should be made by the librarian, and this will depend on his or her assessment of the audience to be served. Public libraries will often include many of the same magazines found in all other libraries.

Annotation

The annotations are generally short summaries describing the scope, purpose, and intent of each magazine, bias (if any), and target audience as described above. In making their recommendations chapter authors are assessing the usefulness and readability of articles in each journal for various audiences. The fact that a journal is listed in *Magazines for Libraries* indicates that it is considered to be a core title for the listed audience and recommended to the libraries serving them.

ABBREVIATIONS

■ GENERAL ABBREVIATIONS

a.	Annual
Ac	Academic (Junior Colleges, Colleges, Universities)
adv.	advertising
Aud.	Audience
bi-m.	Every two months
bi-w.	Every two weeks
Bk. rev	Book reviews
Circ.	circulation
CND	Canadian Dollar
d.	Daily
DEM	Deutsche Mark
Ed., Eds.	Editor(s)
Ems	Elementary and Middle School
fortn.	Fortnightly
FRF	French Franc
Ga	General Adult
GPB	British Pound
Hs	High School
illus.	illustrations
Irreg.	Irregular
ISSN	International Standard Serial Number
ITL	Italian Lira
m.	Monthly
N.S.	New Series
NLG	Dutch Guilder
no., #, nos.	number(s)
q.	Quarterly
rev.	reviews
Sa	Special Adult
s-a.	Twice annually
s-m.	Twice monthly
s-w.	Twice weekly
3/m.	Three times a month
3/w	Three times a week
3/yr.	Three times per year
USD	U.S. Dollars
vol., vols.	volume(s)
w.	Weekly
XEU	Euro
yr., yrs.	year(s)

Controlled Circ. Controlled circulation (free to certain groups)

■ ABSTRACTS AND INDEXES

A&AAb	Astronomy and Astrophysics Abstracts
ABCPolSci	C S A Political Science & Government (Cambridge Scientific Abstracts)
ABCT	ARTbibliographies Current Titles
ABIn	A B I - INFORM (American Business Information)
ABM	ARTbibliographies Modern
ABS&EES	American Bibliography of Slavic and East European Studies
API	Architectural Publications Index
AS&TI	Applied Science & Technology Index
ASD	African Studies Abstracts
ASFA	Aquatic Sciences & Fisheries Abstracts
ASG	Abstracts in Social Gerontology
ASIP	Access: The Supplementary Index to Periodicals
ASSIA	A S S I A Net (Applied Social Sciences Index & Abstracts)
AUNI	Air University Library Index to Military Periodicals
AbAn	Abstracts in Anthropology
AgeL	AgeLine
Agr	Agricola C R I S
AltPI	Alternative Press Index
AmH&L	America: History and Life.
AmHI	American Humanities Index
AmStI	American Statistics Index
AnBeAb	C S A Animal Behavior Abstracts
AnthLit	Anthropological Literature
ApMecR	Applied Mechanics Reviews

ABBREVIATIONS

Abbreviation	Meaning
ArtHuCI	Arts & Humanities Citation Index
ArtInd	Art Index
B&AI	Biological & Agricultural Index
B&I	Business and Industry (Beachwood)
BAS	Bibliography of Asian Studies (Online Edition)
BEL&L	Annual Bibliography of English Language and Literature
BHA	Bibliography of the History of Art
BIM	Bibliography and Index of Micropaleontology
BRD	Book Review Digest
BRI	Book Review Index
BioEngAb	BioEngineering Abstracts (Online Edition)
BiolAb	Biological Abstracts
BiolDig	Biology Digest
BrHumI	British Humanities Index
BrTechI	Abstracts in New Technologies and Engineering
BusEdI	Business Education Index
C&ISA	Computer and Information Systems Abstracts Journal
CABC	Current Advances in Protein Biochemistry
CACR	Current Advances in Cancer Research
CAPS	Current Advances in Plant Science
CBA	Conservation Biology Abstracts
CBCABus	Canadian Business and Current Affairs Business
CBCARef	Canadian Business and Current Affairs Reference
CBRI	Children's Book Review Index
CEI	Canadian Business and Current Affairs Education
CIJE	Current Index to Journals in Education
CINAHL	Cumulative Index to Nursing & Allied Health Literature
CJA	Criminal Justice Abstracts
CJPI	Criminal Justice Periodical Index
CLI	Current Law Index
CLPI	Canadian Literary Periodicals Index
CMPI	Canadian Music Periodical Index
CPI	Current Physics Index
CPL	The Catholic Periodical and Literature Index
CPerI	Canadian Periodical Index
CWI	Contemporary Women's Issues
CerAb	Ceramic Abstracts
ChLitAb	Children's Literature Abstracts
ChPerI	Chicano Index
ChemAb	Chemical Abstracts
ChrPI	Christian Periodical Index
CommAb	Communication Abstracts
CompLI	Computer Literature Index
CompR	Computing Reviews
CurCont	Current Contents
DAAI	Design and Applied Arts Index
DSA	Dairy Science Abstracts
DSR&OA	Oceanographic Literature Review
DYW	†Diversity Your World
EA	Ecology Abstracts
ECER	Exceptional Child Education Resources
EIP	Ekistic Index of Periodicals
EduInd	Education Index
EngInd	Engineering Index Monthly
EnvAb	Environment Abstracts
ErgAb	Ergonomics Abstracts
ExcerpMed	Excerpta Medica.
FPA	Forest Products Abstracts
FS&TA	Food Science and Technology Abstracts
FemPer	Feminist Periodicals
FoVS&M	Focus On: Veterinary Science and Medicine
ForAb	Forestry Abstracts
FutSurv	Future Survey
GLA	Gay & Lesbian Abstracts
GPAI	Genealogical Periodical Annual Index
GSI	General Science Index
GardL	Garden Literature
GendWatch	Gender Watch
GeogAbHG	Geographical Abstracts: Human Geography

GeoRef	Bibliography and Index of Geology
H&SSA	Health and Safety Science Abstracts (Online Edition)
HAPI	Hispanic American Periodicals Index
HRA	Human Resources Abstracts
HRIS	T R I S Electronic Bibliographic Data Base
HistAb	Historical Abstracts
HortAb	Horticultural Abstracts
HumInd	Humanities Index
IAA	International Aerospace Abstracts
IAPV	Index of American Periodical Verse
IBZ	I B Z - Internationale Bibliographie der Geistes- und Sozialwissenschaftlichen Zeitschriftenliteratur
IBibSS	International Bibliography of the Social Sciences: Anthropology, Political Science, Economics, Sociology
ICM	Children's Magazine Guide
IDP	Index to Dance Periodicals
IIBP	International Index to Black Periodicals Full Text
IIMP	International Index to Music Periodicals
IIPA	International Index to the Performing Arts
IJCS	Index to Journals in Communication Studies
IJP	Index to Jewish Periodicals
ILP	Index to Legal Periodicals & Books
IMFL	Family & Society Studies Worldwide
INI	International Nursing Index
IPB	Repertoire Bibliographique de la Philosophie
IUSGP	U.S. Government Periodicals Index
IndIslam	Index Islamicus
IndMed	Index Medicus
IndVet	Index Veterinarius
L&LBA	Linguistics and Language Behavior Abstracts
LISA	L I S A: Library & Information Science Abstracts
LR&TI	Lodging, Restaurant and Tourism Index
LRI	LegalTrac (Online)
LT&LA	Language Teaching
LibLit	Library Literature & Information Science
LingAb	Linguistics Abstracts
M&GPA	Meteorological and Geoastrophysical Abstracts
MEA&I	Middle East: Abstracts and Index
MLA-IB	M L A International Bibliography of Books and Articles on the Modern Languages and Literatures
MRD	Media Review Digest
MathSciNet	MathSciNet
MinerAb	Mineralogical Abstracts
MusicInd	Music Index
NTA	New Testament Abstracts
NumL	Numismatic Literature
NutrAb	Nutrition Abstracts and Reviews
OTA	Old Testament Abstracts
OceAb	Oceanic Abstracts
PAIS	P A I S International in Print
PLESA	Quarterly Index to Africana Periodical Literature
PRA	Peace Research Abstracts Journal
PetrolAb	Petroleum Abstracts
PhilInd	Philosopher's Index
PollutAb	Pollution Abstracts
PsycInfo	PsycINFO
R&TA	Religious & Theological Abstracts
RGPR	Readers' Guide to Periodical Literature
RI-1	Religion Index One: Periodicals
RILM	R I L M Abstracts of Music Literature Litterature Musicale)
RRTA	Leisure, Recreation and Tourism Abstracts
RiskAb	Risk Abstracts (Online Edition)
S&F	Soils and Fertilizers
SCI	Science Citation Index
SFSA	Sage Family Studies Abstracts
SSA	Social Services Abstracts
SSCI	Social Sciences Citation Index

ABBREVIATIONS

SSI	Social Sciences Index
ST&MA	Statistical Theory and Method Abstracts (CD-ROM Edition)
SUSA	Sage Urban Studies Abstracts
SWA	Studies on Women and Gender Abstracts
SWR&A	Social Work Abstracts
SWRA	Water Resources Abstracts (Bethesda, Online Edition)
SociolAb	Sociological Abstracts
V&AA	Violence & Abuse Abstracts
VetBull	Veterinary Bulletin
WAE&RSA	World Agricultural Economics and Rural Sociology Abstracts
WRCInf	Aqualine Abstracts
WSA	Women Studies Abstracts
WSI	Women's Studies Index (Year)
ZooRec	Zoological Record

CONSULTANTS

Full names and addresses are given for the consultants at the head of each section.

Adams, Roger C. (Comic Books)
Alexander, Harriet (Sports)
Altschiller, Donald (Ethnic Studies; Middle East)
Angelini, Mary Frances (Craft)
Ashmun, Julia D. (Boats and Boating)
Avery, Bonnie D. (Forestry)
Baird, Susan G. (General Editorial)
Barnett, Judith B. (Marine Science and Technology)
Bartley, Drew (Genealogy)
Baughman, Pauline (Hiking, Climbing, and Outdoor Recreation)
Becker, Nancy J. (Political Science)
Berard, G. Lynn (Engineering and Technology)
Blake, Laura Farwell (Literary Reviews)
Bliss, Laurel (Fiction: General/Mystery and Detective)
Bourneuf, Joe (Philately)
Boyd, C. Trenton (Veterinary Science)
Boyer, Clifton W. (Hunting and Guns)
Bradford, Jane (Consumer Education)
Bryce, Betty K. (Fraternal, Club, and Service Organizations)
Bunyan, Linda E. (Medicine and Health)
Burchsted, Fred (Geography)
Burg, Barbara A. (African American)
Burton, Donna L. (College and Alumni)
Burton, Jean Piper (Folklore)
Buxton, David (Architecture)
Campbell, Nancy F. (Communication)
Casper, Christianne L. (Astrology; Parapsychology)
Clack, Mary Beth (Literary Reviews)
Clark, George E. (Environment and Conservation)
Cochran, Myrtis (Aging)
Coe, Erica L. (Music Reviews)
Collins, Linda (Horses)
Conley, Kathleen M. (Free Magazines and House Organs)
Cramer, Jane (Labor and Industrial Relations)
Crane, Rachel (Fishing)
Creelan, Marilee M. (Medicine and Health)
Crohan, Catherine (Journalism and Writing)
Crowley, Gwyneth H. (Economics)
Culbertson, Michael (Atmospheric Sciences)
Dalrymple, Connie (Biological Sciences)
Dankert, Holly Stec (Art; Interior Design and Decoration)
Dawson, Patrick Jose (Games)
DeDecker, Sherry (Sociology and Social Work)
DeHart, Brian (Business)
Dekker, Harrison (Real Estate)
Desai, Christine M. (Asia and the Pacific)
Diaz, Joseph (Bob) (Latin American; Latino Studies)
Dolan, Meghan (Population Studies)
Donovan, Carrie (Fiction: Science Fiction, Fantasy, and Horror)
Dratch, Gladys I. (Education)
Dunn, Donald J. (Law)
Ellis, Allen (Comic Books)
Elsen, Carol J. (Finance)
Esty, Barbara (Finance)
Fehrmann, Paul (Psychology)
Firpo, Andy (Computer Science and Automation)
Fladger, Ellen (History)
Fusich, Monica (Women: Fashion)
Garson, Deborah S. (Education)
Gates, Thomas P. (Landscape Architecture)
Gauder, Heidi (Weddings)
Geary, Mary Kathleen (Transportation)
Gessesse, Kebede (Paleontology)
Giambi, M. Dina (Serials)
Gillie, Esther (Music: General)
Gilroy, Susan M. (Literature)
Goetsch, Lori A. (Women)
Golderman, Gail (Zines)
Hallman, Clark N. (Criminology and Law Enforcement)
Halporn, Barbara (Gardening)
Hamill, Sarah J. (Singles)
Hansen, Mary Ann (Electronics)

CONSULTANTS

Harnsberger, R. Scott (Philosophy)
Hedden, Holly (Pets)
Hemment, Michael J. (Humor; Photography)
Hess, Wendy (Medicine and Health)
Hicks, Emily A. (Television, Video, and Radio)
Hierl, Sebastian (Europe)
Hoeppner, Christopher (Accounting and Taxation)
Howarth, Rachel (Bibliography)
Howze, Philip C. (Animal Welfare; Ethnic Studies; Teenagers)
Jacoby, JoAnn (Urban Studies)
Jagodzinski, Cecile M. (Books and Book Reviews)
Jenkins, Fred W. (Classical Studies)
Jerabek, Alexander (Canada)
Jones, Marie F. (Civil Liberties)
Joubert, Douglas (Medicine and Health)
Kautzman, Amy M. (Lesbian, Gay, Bisexual, and Transgender)
Kent, Caroline M. (Journalism and Writing; Parenting; Theater)
Kilcullen, Maureen (Antiques and Collecting)
Kilpatrick, Thomas L. (Men)
Kooistra, Judith Ohles (Hospitality/Restaurant)
Kosokoff, Jeff (Aggregators; Travel and Tourism)
Kumar, Suhasini L. (Peace)
Kunkel, Lilith R. (Women: Feminist and Special Interest)
Ladwig, J. Parker (Mathematics)
Lagana, Gretchen (Alternatives)
Lener, Edward F. (Earth Sciences)
Lenkowski, Patricia A. (Anthropology)
Maas, Jan A. (Occupations and Careers)
Macfarlane, Carrie M. (Literature)
Maker, Ray (Computer Science and Automation)
Marshall, Jerilyn (Spirituality and Well-Being)
Matthews, Priscilla J. (Chemistry)
Matz, Pamela (Home)
Mayer, Constance A. (Music: Popular)
McCaffery, Erin K. (Family and Marriage)
McClusky, Duncan (Agriculture)
McCutcheon, Camille (Large Print)
McDaniel, Sarah (Little Magazines)
McKeigue, Elizabeth (Theater)
McMinn, Howard Stephen (Aeronautics and Space Science)
Meszaros, Rosemary (Government Periodicals—Federal; Government Periodicals—State and Local
Moberly, Heather K. (Food and Nutrition; Food and Wine)
Montilio, Ralph (Music: General)
Moore, Susan M. (Office Management)
Naylor, Sharon (Disabilities)
Neuhaus, Chris F. (General Editorial-Internet)
Neuhaus, Ellen (General Editorial-Internet)
Oftedahl, Lenora A. (Fish, Fisheries, and Aquaculture)
Oka, Christine K. (Asian American)
Oka, Susan (Films)
Olivares, Olivia (Latin American; Latino Studies)
Olsgaard, Jane K. (Medicine and Health)
Palmer, Pamela (Food Industry)
Park, Betsy (Sports)
Paster, Amy L. (Science and Technology)
Peterson, Elaine (Birds)
Plaid, Andrea (Sexuality; Sex Positive)
Poorbaugh, Susan R. (Medicine and Health)
Power, Margaret (Africa)
Prest, Loring A. (Religion)
Rankin, Sharon (Canada)
Reyes, Veronica (Latin American; Latino Studies)
Robinson, Chip (Gardening)
Robinson, Kara L. (News and Opinion)
Rogan, Michael J. (Lesbian, Gay, Bisexual, and Transgender)
Ronningen, Jim (Newspapers)
Rosati, Karen (Medicine and Health)
Rose, Michael J. (Communication)
Ruan, Lian (Fire Protection)
Ruppel, Margie (City, State, and Regional; Linguistics)
Salzmann, Katharine A. (Archaeology)
Sanudo, Manuel (CIS and Eastern Europe)
Saxton, Elna L. (Safety)
Schlipf, Frederick A. (Model Making and Collecting)
Schwartz, Vanette M. (Cultural-Social Studies)
Shrode, Flora G. (Earth Sciences)
Siegler, Sharon L. (Energy; Robotics)
Skewis, Charles A. (Men)
Smith, Donna B. (Printing and Graphic Arts)
Stam, Julian (Building and Construction)
Straw, Joseph (Military Games)
Sugrue, Edward Creighton, Jr. (Astronomy)
Sullivan, Laura A. (Communication)
Sutton, Allison (Death and Dying)
Swetland, Karen L. (Hunting and Guns)
Taylor, Terry (Classroom Magazines)
Thomas, Mary Augusta (Dance)
Thompson, Gary B. (Journalism and Writing)
Tsang, Daniel C. (Sexuality)
Tuliao, Miriam (Library and Information Science)

Tyckoson, David A. (Physics)

Tyler, Peggy (Management, Administration, and Human Resources)

Vallely, John R. (Military)

Van de Streek, David (Numismatics)

Weir, Katherine M. (Statistics)

Wies, Lorraine (History)

Williams, Clay (Advertising and Public Relations)

Williams, Helene (Computer Science and Automation; Literature)

Wisner, Melanie (Archives and Manuscripts)

Wones, Suzanne L. (Native Americans)

Wood, Wendy (Printing and Graphic Arts)

Wylie, Roslyn E. (Children)

Xue, Susan (China)

Young, Courtney L. (Interdisciplinary Studies)

Yu, Xiaochang (Internet-Worldwide Web; Media and AV)

CD-ROM PRODUCERS

R.R. Bowker LLC
(Subsidiary of: Cambridge Information Group)
630 Central Ave., New Providence, NJ 07974
TEL 908-219-1090, 800-521-8110, FAX 908-219-0182
E-mail info@bowker.com
URL http://www.bowker.com

C S A
(Subsidiary of: Cambridge Information Group)
7200 Wisconsin Ave, Ste 601, Bethesda, MD 20814
TEL 301-961-6700, FAX 301-961-6720
URL http://www.csa.com

Chadwyck-Healey Incorporated
(Subsidiary of: ProQuest Information & Learning)
300 N. Zeeb Rd., Ann Arbor, MI 48106-1346
TEL 734-761-4700, 800-521-0600
E-mail info@il.proquest.com, info@chadwyck.com
URL http://www.chadwyck.com

Context Ltd.
Grand Union Hse., 20 Kentish Town Rd., London NW1 9NR, United Kingdom
TEL 44-20-7267-8989, FAX 44-20-7267-1133
URL http://www.justis.com, http://www.context.co.uk

The Dialog Corporation
11000 Regency Parkway, Ste. 10, Cary, NC 27511
TEL 919-462-8600, 800-210-9768, FAX 919-468-9890
URL http://www.dialog.com

Galaxie Press
6302 Galaxie Rd, Garland, TX 75044
TEL 972-414-5322
URL http://www.galaxie.com

Institute for Scientific Information
3501 Market St., Philadelphia, PA 19104
TEL 215-386-0100, 800-336-4474, FAX 215-386-2911
E-mail sales@isinet.com
URL http://www.isinet.com

National Information Services Corp.
3100 St Paul St, Ste 6, Wyman Towers, Baltimore, MD 21218
TEL 410-243-0797, FAX 410-243-0982
E-mail sales@nisc.com
URL http://www.nisc.com

O C L C Forest Press
6565 Frantz Rd., Dublin, OH 43017-3395
TEL 614-764-6000, 800-848-5878, FAX 614-718-7434, 888-339-3921
E-mail orders@oclc.org
URL http://www.oclc.org/fp

Ovid Technologies, Inc.
333 Seventh Ave., New York, NY 10001
TEL 212-563-3006, 800-950-2035, FAX 212-563-3784
URL http://www.ovid.com

ProQuest Information & Learning
300 N Zeeb Rd., PO Box 1346, Ann Arbor, MI 48106-1346
TEL 734-761-4700, 800-521-0600, FAX 734-997-4040, 800-864-0019
E-mail info@proquest.com, library_sales@umi.com, info@umi.com
URL http://www.umi.com

R M I T Publishing
A'Beckett St, PO Box 12058, Melbourne, VIC 8006, Australia
TEL 61-3-9349-4994, 61-3-9341-8251, 61-3-9341-8210, FAX 61-3-9349-4583, 61-3-9349-3508
E-mail info@rmitpublishing.com.au, subscriptions@rmitpublishing.com.au
URL http://www.rmitpublishing.com.au, http://www.informit.com.au

K. G. Saur Verlag GmbH & Company
(Subsidiary of: Gale/Thomson Learning)
Ortlerstrasse 8, Munich 70 D-81373, Germany
TEL 49-89-769 02 230, FAX 49-89-769 02 277, TELEX 089-76902AUR-D
URL http://www.saur.de/

SilverPlatter Information, Incorporated
(Subsidiary of: Ovid Technologies, Incorporated)
100 River Ridge Dr., Norwood, MA 02062
TEL 781-769-2599, 800-343-0064, FAX 781-769-8763
E-mail info@silverplatter.com
URL http://www.silverplatter.com

Tsinghua Tongfang Optical Disc Co., Ltd.
Room 1300, Huaye Building, Tsing Hua University, PO Box 84-48, Beijing 100084, China
TEL 86-1-62791819, FAX 86-1-62791944
E-mail Beijing@cnki.net
URL http://www.cnki.net

H. W. Wilson
950 University Ave., Bronx, NY 10452-4224
TEL 718-588-8400, 800-367-6770, FAX 718-681-1511
FAX 800-590-1617
E-mail intlsales@hwwilson.com
URL http://www.hwwilson.com

DOCUMENT SUPPLIERS

AskIEEE
AskIEEE
10850 Wilshire Blvd, 8th Fl,
Los Angeles, CA 90024
TEL 734-459-8944, 800-949-4333
FAX 734-459-8990
E-mail askieee@ieee.org
URL http://ieee.org/services/askieee

BLDSC
British Library Document Supply Centre
Boston Spa, Wetherby LS23 7BQ,
United Kingdom
TEL 44-1937-546060
FAX 44-1937-546333
E-mail dsc-customerservice@bl.uk
URL
http://www.bl.uk/services/document/dsc.html

CASDDS
Chemical Abstracts Service Document Detective Service
2540 Olentangy River Rd, PO Box 3012,
Columbus, OH 43210-0012
TEL 614-447-3670, 800-678-4337
FAX 614-447-3648
TELEX 684086 via WUI
E-mail dds@cas.org
URL http://www.cas.org/Support/dds.html

CINDOC
CINDOC Suministro de Documentos Service
Joaquin Costa, 22, Madrid 28002, Spain
TEL 34-91-5635482
FAX 34-91-5642644
URL http://www.cindoc.csic.es
E-mail sdi@cindoc.scis.es

CIS
LexisNexis Academic & Library Solutions
(Subsidiary of: LexisNexis)
4520 East-West Hwy.,
Bethesda, MD 20814-3389
TEL 301-654-1550, 800-638-8380
FAX 301-657-3203,
E-mail academicinfo@lexisnexis.com
URL
http://www.nexis.com/academic/3cis/cismnu.asp

CISTI
CISTI
(Canada Institute for Scientific and Technical Information)
(Subsidiary of: National Research Council of Canada)
1200 Montreal Rd., Bldg, M-55,
Ottawa, ON K1A 0S2, Canada
TEL 613-993-9251, 800-668-1222
FAX 613-993-7619
E-mail info.sisti@nrc-cnrc.gc.ca
URL
http://cisti-icist.nrc-cnrc.gc.ca/docdel/docdel_e.shtml

East View
East View Publications, Inc.
3020 Harbor Ln. N., Minneapolis, MN 55447
TEL 612-550-0961, 800-477-1005
FAX 612-559-2931, 800-800-3839
E-mail eastview@eastview.com
URL http://www.eastview.com

Ei
Engineering Information, Incorporated
See Linda Hall Library Document Services

GNLM
German National Library of Medicine
Joseph-Stelzman-Str. 9, D-50924, Koeln,
Germany
TEL 49-221-4785600
FAX 49-221-4785697
E-mail zbmed.zbmed@uni-koeln.de
URL http://www.zbmed.de

Haworth
Haworth Press, Incorporated, The
10 Alice St., Binghamton, NY 13904-1580
TEL 607-722-5857, 800-429-6784
FAX 607-722-6362, 607-722-1424,
800-895-0582,
E-mail getinfo@haworthpressinc.com
URL http://www.haworthpressinc.com

IDS
ISI Document Solution (Institute for Scientific Information)
3501 Market St., Philadelphia, PA 19104
TEL 800-630-4367
FAX 856-787-1679
E-mail service@isidoc.com
URL http://www.isidoc.com

Infotrieve — Infotrieve
10850 Wilshire Blvd 8th Fl,
Los Angeles, CA 90024
TEL 310-208-1903, 800-422-4633
FAX 310-208-5971
E-mail orders@infotrieve.com, info@infotrieve.com
URL http://www.infotrieve.com/docdelivery.asp

ingenta — ingenta.com (Subsidiary of: Ingenta Inc.)
44 Brattle St., 4th Fl., Cambridge, MA 02138
TEL 617-395-4046, 800-296-2221
FAX 617-395-4099
E-mail ushelp@ingenta.com
URL http://www.ingenta.com

KNAW — NIWI (Netherlands Institute of Scientific Information Services)
Customer Service, 95180,
Amsterdam 1090 HD, Netherlands
TEL 31-20-462-8628
FAX 31-20-663-9257
E-mail info@niwi.knaw.nl
URL http://www.niwi.knaw.nl

Linda Hall — Linda Hall Library Document Services
5109 Cherry St, Kansas City, MO 64110-2498
TEL 816-363-4600, 800-662-1545
FAX 816-926-8785
E-mail requests@lindahall.org
URL http://www.lindahall.org/docserv

PADDS — Petroleum Abstracts Document Delivery System
University of Tulsa - McFarlin Library,
2933 E 6th St, Tulsa, OK 74104-3123
TEL 918-631-2231, 800-247-8678
FAX 918-613-3823
URL http://www.pa.utulsa.edu/

MICROPUBLISHERS AND DISTRIBUTORS

AGU American Geophysical Union
2000 Florida Ave, N W,
Washington, DC 20009-1277
TEL 202-462-6900, 800-966-2481
FAX 202-328-0566
E-mail service@agu.org
URL http://www.agu.org

AIP American Institute of Physics
1 Physics Ellipse, College Park, MD 20740-3843
TEL 301-209-3100
FAX 301-209-0843
E-mail aipinfo@aip.org
URL http://www.aip.org

AJP American Jewish Periodical Center
3101 Clifton Ave., Cincinnati, OH 45220
TEL 513-221-1875
FAX 513-221-0519

ALP Alpha Com
Sportallee 6, Hamburg 22335, Germany
TEL 49-40-51302-123, FAX 49-40-51302-111
URL http://www.alpha-com.de

AMP Adam Matthew Publications Ltd.
Pelham House, London Rd, Marlborough, Wiltshire
SN8 2AA, United Kingdom
TEL 44-1672-511921
FAX 44-1672-511663
E-mail info@ampltd.co.uk
URL http://www.ampltd.co.uk

BHP Brookhaven Press
(Subsidiary of: N M T Corporation)
E-mail brookhaven@nmt.com
URL http://www.brookhavenpress.com

BIO BIOSIS
(BioSciences Information Service of Biological Abstracts)
2 Commerce Sq., 2001 Market St, Ste 700,
Philadelphia, PA 19103-7095
TEL 215- 231-7500, 800-523-4806 (US & Canada)
FAX 215-578-2016
E-mail info@biosis.org
URL http://www.biosis.org

BNB British Library National Bibliographic Service
Boston Spa, Wetherby, W. Yorkshire LS23 7BQ,
United Kingdom
TEL 44-1937-546585
FAX 44-1937-546586
E-mail nbs-info@bl.uk
URL http://www.bl.uk

BNQ Bibliotheque Nationale du Quebec (B N Q)
2275 Rue Holt, Montreal, PQ H2G 3H1, Canada
TEL 514-873-1100 ext.158, 800-363-9028
FAX 514-873-7510
E-mail info@bnquebec.ca
URL http://www.bnquebec.ca

CDS Current Digest of the Soviet Press
E-mail subscriptions@currentdigest.org
URL http://www.currentdigest.org

CHL Chadwyck-Healey Limited
see ProQuest Information & Learning

CIS LexisNexis Academic & Library Solutions
(Subsidiary of: LexisNexis)
4520 East-West Hwy., Bethesda, MD 20814-3389
TEL 301-654-1550, 800-638-8380
FAX 301-657-3203
E-mail academicinfo@lexisnexis.com
URL http://www.nexis.com/academic/3cis/cismnu.asp

CML Commonwealth Imaging
P.O. Box 215, Ste 618, 555 Richmond St W.,
Toronto, ON M5V 3B1, Canada
TEL 416-703-3755 ext 224
FAX 416-703-6426
E-mail nvehrs@westcanadian.com
URL http://www.commonwealthimaging.com

EVP East View Publications, Inc.
3020 Harbor Ln. N., Minneapolis, MN 55447
TEL 763-550-0961, 800-477-1005
FAX 763-559-2931
E-mail eastview@eastview.com
URL http://www.eastview.com

FCM Fairchild Books
7 W. 34th St., New York, NY 10001
TEL 800-932-4724
FAX 212-286-3122
URL http://www.fairchildbooks.com

GCS Preston Publications, Inc. (Division of: Preston Industries, Inc.)
6600 W. Touhy Ave., Niles, IL 60714-4588
TEL 847-647-2900
FAX 847-647-1155
URL http://www.prestonpub.com

IAM SIAM Publications
3600 University City Science Center, Philadelphia, PA 19104-2688
TEL 215-382-9800
FAX 215-386-7999
E-mail service@siam.org
URL http://www.siam.org

IDC I D C Publishers
Microform Production Department, PO Box 11205, Leiden 2301 EE, Netherlands
E-mail info@idc.nl
URL http://www.idc.nl
In North America, IDC Publishers Inc., 350 Fifth Ave, Ste 1801, Empire State Bldg, New York, NY 10118
TEL 212-271-5945, 800-757-7441
FAX 212-271-5930
E-mail info@idcpublishers.com

IFA International Federation of Film Archives
1 rue Defacqz, Bruxels 1000, Belgium
TEL 32-2-534-3065
FAX 32-2-534-4774
E-mail info@fiafnet.org
URL http://www.fiafnet.org

ILO ILO Publications Center
PO Box 753, Waldorf, MD 20604-0753
TEL 301-638-3152
FAX 301-843-0159
E-mail ilopubs@tasco1.com
URL http://www.ilo.org

IMI Irish Microforms Limited
Unit 18, Southern Cross, Business Park, Bray, Wicklow, Ireland
TEL 353-1-286705
FAX 353-1-2867095

IPC Institute of Paper Science and Technology
500 Tenth St., NW, Rm. 258, Atlanta, GA 30318-5794
TEL 404-894-5726
FAX 404-894-9596
E-mail sharon.kirkes@ipst.edu
URL http://www.ipst.edu

LCP The Library of Congress Photoduplication Service
101 Independence Ave SE, Washington, DC 20540-5230
TEL 202-707-5640
FAX 202-707-1771
E-mail photoduplication@loc.gov
URL http://www.loc.gov/preserve-pds

LIB BMI Imaging Systems
1115 E. Arques Ave., Sunnyvale, CA 94086
TEL 408-736-7444, 800-359-3456
FAX 408-736-4397
E-mail info@bmiimaging.com
URL http://www.bmiimaging.com

MIM Elsevier Science, Limited
Lacon Hse., 84 Theobalds Rd., London WC1X 8RW, United Kingdom
TEL 44 20 7611 4000
FAX 44 20 7611 4001
URL http://www.elsevierscience.com

MIS Moody's Investors Service
Sales Department, 99 Church St., New York, NY 10007
TEL 212-553-0300
FAX 212-553-4700
URL http://www.moodys.com

MML Micromedia, ProQuest
(Subsidiary of: ProQuest Information & Learning)
20 Victoria St., Toronto, ON M5C 2N8, Canada
TEL 416-362-5211, 800-387-2689
FAX 416-362-6161
E-mail info@micromedia.ca, order@micromedia.ca
URL http://www.micromedia.ca

MMP McLaren Micropublishing Limited
PO Box 972, Sta. F, Toronto, ON M4Y 2N9, Canada
TEL 416-960-4801
FAX 416-964-3745
E-mail mmicro@interlog.com
URL http://www.interlog.com/~mmicro

MUE University Music Editions
PO Box 192, Ft. George Station, New York, NY 10040
TEL 212-569-5340, 800-448-2805
FAX 212-569-1269
E-mail ume@universitymusicedition.com
URL http://www.universitymusicedition.com

NBI Newsbank, Incorporated
5020 Tamiami Trail N, Ste 110, Naples, FL 34103
TEL 239-263-6004
FAX 203-966-6254
E-mail sales@newsbank.com
URL http://www.newsbank.com

NRP Norman Ross Publishing, Incorporated
See ProQuest Information & Learning

NTI National Technical Information Service, U. S. Department of Commerce
5285 Port Royal Rd., Springfield, VA 22161
TEL 703-605-6000, 800-553-6847
FAX 703-605-6900
E-mail info@ntis.gov
URL http://www.ntis.gov

NYL American Lawyer Media, Incorporated
345 Park Ave, S., New York, NY 10010
TEL 212-779-9200, 800-888-8300
FAX 212-481-8161, 212-481-8110
E-mail catalog@amlaw.com
URL http://www.americanlawyermedia.com

OEC Organization for Economic Cooperation and Development
No longer a micropublisher.

PMC Princeton Microfilm Corp.
PO Box 2073, Princeton, NJ 08543
TEL 609-452-2066, 800-257-9502
FAX 609-275-6201
E-mail info@princetonmicro.com
URL http://www.princetonmicro.com

PQC ProQuest Information & Learning (Divison of: ProQuest Company)
300 N Zeeb Rd., PO Box 1346,
Ann Arbor, MI 48106-1346
TEL 734-761-4700, 800-521-0600
FAX 734-997-4040
E-mail info@proquest.com,
URL http://www.umi.com

PSL The Pretoria State Library
PO Box 397, Pretoria 0001, South Africa
TEL 27-12-3218931
FAX 27-12-3255984
E-mail statelib@statelib.pwv.gov.za

RPI Primary Source Microfilm
(Subsidiary of: Gale Group)
12 Lunar Dr, Woodbridge, CT 06525
TEL 203-397-2600, 800-444-079
FAX 203-397-3893
E-mail psmcs@gale.com
URL http://www.galegroup.com/psm

SAL South African Library
Queen Victoria St, PO Box 496, Cape Town, South Africa
TEL 27-21-246320
FAX 27-21-244848

SAS Society for Applied Spectroscopy
201-B Broadway St., Frederick, MD 21701-6501
TEL 301-694-8122
FAX 301-694-6860
E-mail orders@press.com, sasoffice@aol.com
URL http://www.s-a-s.org

SOC Societe Canadienne du Microfilm Inc. /Canadian Microfilming Company Limited
464, rue Saint-Jean, Ste 110, Montreal, PQ H2Y 2S1, Canada
TEL 514-288-5404
FAX 514-843-4690
E-mail info@socami.qc.ca
URL http://www.socami.qc.ca

SWZ Swets & Zeitlinger Publishers
PO Box 800, Lisse 2160 SZ, Netherlands
TEL 31-252-435111
FAX 31-252-415888
E-mail info@swetsinc.com
URL http://www.swets.nl

TMI Tennessee Microfilms Inc.
PO Box 23075, Nashville, TN 37202
TEL 615-242-3632, 615-895-0535

VCI VCH Publishers, Incorporated
605 3rd Ave, New York, NY 10158
TEL 212-629-6200
E-mail vchsouth@vistana.com

VFN Voltaire Foundation Limited
99 Banbury Rd., Oxford 0X2 6JX, United Kingdom
TEL 44-1865-284600
FAX 44-1865-284610
E-mail vfweb.mail@www.server.volt.ox.ac.uk
URL http://www.voltaire.ox.ac.uk

WMP World Microfilm Publications Ltd.
Microworld House, 4 Foscote Mews,
London W9 2HH, United Kingdom
TEL 44-20-7266-2202
FAX 44-20-7266-2314
E-mail microworld@ndirect.co.uk
URL http://www.microworld.ndirect.co.uk

WSH William S. Hein & Company, Incorporated
1285 Main St, Buffalo, NY 14209-1987
TEL 800-828-7571
FAX 716-883-8100
E-mail mail@wshein.com
URL http://www.wshein.com

WWS Lippincott Williams & Wilkins
(Subsidiary of: Wolters Kluwer N.V.)
351 W Camden St, Baltimore, MD 21201
TEL 410-528-4000, 410-528-8517
FAX 410-528-4312
E-mail custserv@lww.com,
URL http://www.lww.com

ONLINE SERVICES

America Online, Inc.
(Subsidiary of: A O L Time Warner Inc.)
22000 AOL Way, Dulles, VA 20166
TEL 703-448-8700, FAX 703-265-2206
URL http://www.aoltimewarner.com/

Association for Computing Machinery, Inc.
One Astor Plaza, 1515 Broadway, New York, NY 10036-5701
TEL 212-869-1318, 212-869-7440, FAX 212-869-0481
E-mail SIGS@acm.org
URL http://www.acm.org

bigchalk
(Subsidiary of: ProQuest Information & Learning)
300 N. Zeeb Rd., Ann Arbor, MI 48103
TEL 800-521-0600 ext 7112
URL http://www.bigchalk.com

BioOne
c/o Susie Thompson, BioOne Sales Support Specialist, Amigos Library Services, 14400 Midway Rd, Dallas, TX 75244
TEL 972-851-8000 ext 180, 800-843-8482 ext 180, FAX 972/991-6061
E-mail thompson@amigos.org
URL http://www.bioone.org

The Bureau of National Affairs, Inc.
1231 25th St NW, Washington, DC 20037
TEL 202-452-4323, 800-372-1033, FAX 202-452-4226
E-mail customercare@bna.com
URL http://www.bna.com/

C S A
(Subsidiary of: Cambridge Information Group)
7200 Wisconsin Ave, Ste 601, Bethesda, MD 20814
TEL 301-961-6700, FAX 301-961-6720
URL http://www.csa.com

CEDOCAR
/Centre de Documentation de l'Armement
9 boulevard Liedot, 1602 Angouleme Cedex, France
TEL 33(5) 45 37 19 63, FAX 33(5) 45 37 19 98

Chadwyck-Healey Incorporated
(Subsidiary of: ProQuest Information & Learning)
300 N. Zeeb Rd., Ann Arbor, MI 48106-1346
TEL 734-761-4700, 800-521-0600
Po Box 1346, Ann Arbor, MI 48106-1346
E-mail info@chadwyck.com
URL http://www.chadwyck.com

CISTI
(Subsidiary of: National Research Council of Canada)
1200 Montreal Rd., Bldg, M-55, Ottawa, ON K1A 0S2, Canada
TEL 613-993-9251, 800-668-1222, FAX 613-993-7619
E-mail cisti.producthelp@nrc.ca
URL http://www.nrc.ca/cisti,

CompuServe Inc.
5000 Arlington Centre Blvd, Columbus, OH 43220
TEL 614-457-0802, 800-848-8199, FAX 614-538-4023
URL http://www.compuserve.com

Context Ltd.
Grand Union Hse., 20 Kentish Town Rd., London NW1 9NR, United Kingdom
TEL 44-20-7267-8989, FAX 44-20-7267-1133
URL http://www.context.co.uk

Data-Star
(Subsidiary of: The Dialog Corporation)
114 Jermyn St, Plaza Ste, London SW1Y 6HJ, United Kingdom
Radio Suisse AG, Laupenstr. 18A, Berne 38008, Switzerland
TEL 41-31-5609500, FAX 43-31-509675

The Dialog Corporation
11000 Regency Parkway, Ste. 10, Cary, NC 27511
TEL 919-462-8600, 800-210-9768, FAX 919-468-9890
URL http://www.dialog.com)

DIMDI
Weisshausstrasse 36-38a, Cologne D-50676, Germany
TEL 49-221-47240, FAX 49-221-411429
URL http://www.dimdi.de

Dow Jones Interactive
PO Box 300, Princeton, NJ 08543-0300
TEL 609-452-1511, 800-369-7466, FAX 609-520-4775
URL http://www.djinteractive.com

East View Publications, Inc.
3020 Harbor Ln. N., Minneapolis, MN 55447
TEL 612-550-0961, 800-477-1005, FAX 612-559-2931, 800-800-3839
E-mail eastview@eastview.com
URL http://www.eastview.com

EBSCO Publishing
(Subsidiary of: EBSCO Industries, Inc.)
10 Estes St, PO Box 682, Ipswich, MA 01938-0682
TEL 978-356-6500, 800-653-2726, FAX 978-356-6565

E-mail ep@epnet.com
URL http://www.epnet.com

Emerald
60-62 Toller Ln, Bradford, W Yorks BD8 9BY, United Kingdom
TEL 44-1274-777700, FAX 44-1274-785200
E-mail info@emeraldinsight.com,
URL http://www.emeraldinsight.com

European Space Agency
Via Galileo Galilei, Casella Postale 64, Frascati, RM 00044, Italy
TEL 39-6-9418-0951
URL http://www.esa.int

F I Z Technik
Ostbahnhofstrasse 13-15, Frankfurt a.M. 60314, Germany
TEL 49-69-4308-0, FAX 49-69-4308200
URL http://www.fiz-technik.de

Factiva
PO Box 300, Princeton, NJ 08543-0300
TEL 609-452-1511, 800-369-7466, FAX 609-520-4775
E-mail solutions@factiva.com
URL http://www.factiva.com

Florida Center for Library Automation
5830 NW 39th Ave, Gainesville, FL 32606
TEL 352-392-9020, FAX 352-392-9185
URL http://www.fcla.edu/index.html

G B I
Freischutzstrasse 96e, Munich 81927, Germany
TEL 49-89-9570064, FAX 49-89-954229
URL http://www.gbi.de

Gale Group
(Subsidiary of: The Thomson Corp.)
27500 Drake Rd, Farmington Hills, MI 48331-3535
TEL 248-699-4253, 800-347-4253, FAX 248-699-8035, 800-414-5043
E-mail galeord@galegroup.com
URL http://www.gale.com

HighWire Press
(Subsidiary of: Stanford University Libraries)
102 Green Library, Stanford University, Stanford, CA 94305-6004
TEL 650-723-2019, FAX 650-723-9325
E-mail contact@highwire.stanford.edu
URL http://www.highwire.org,
http://www.highwire.stanford.edu,
http://www.intl.highwire.org

Human Resources Information Network
(Subsidiary of: Executive Telecom System International)
9585 Valparaiso Ct., College Park N., Indianapolis, IN 46268
TEL 317-872-2045, FAX 317-872-2059

I E E E
3 Park Ave, 17th Fl, New York, NY 10016-5997
TEL 212-419-7900, FAX 212-752-4929
445 Hoes Ln, Box 1331, Piscataway, NJ 08855-1331
TEL 732-981-0600, FAX 732-981-1721
URL http://www.ieee.org

Infomart Ltd.
333 King St East, Toronto, ON M5A 4R7, Canada
TEL 416-350-6001, FAX 416-350-6066
URL http://www.infomart.ca

Ingenta Select
(Subsidiary of: Ingenta Inc.)
23-28 Hythe Bridge St., Ground Fl., Oxford OX1 2ET, United Kingdom
TEL 44-1865-799000, FAX 44-1865-799111
E-mail sales@catchword.com
URL http://www.catchword.com

ingenta.com
(Subsidiary of: Ingenta Inc.)
3-4 Riverside Ct., Lower Bristol Rd., Bath BA2 3D2, United Kingdom
TEL 44-1225-361000, FAX 44-1225-361155
E-mail info@ingenta.com
44 Brattle St., 4th Fl., Cambridge, MA 02138
TEL 617-395-4000, 800-296-2221, FAX 617-395-4099
23-28 Hythe Bridge St., Ground Fl., Oxford OX1 2ET, United Kingdom
TEL 44-1865-799000, FAX 44-1865-799111
E-mail sales@ingenta.com
URL http://www.ingenta.comg (CHE)

J-Stage
(Subsidiary of: Japan Science and Technology Corp.)
5-3, 4-Bancho, Chiyoda-ku, Tokyo 102-0081, Japan
TEL 81-3-5214-8455
E-mail contact@jstage.jst.go.jp
URL http://www.jstage.jst.go.jp/ja/index.html

JICST
5-3, Yonbancho, Chiyoda-Ku, Tokyo 102-0081, Japan
TEL 81-3-5214-8413, FAX 81-3-5214-8410
E-mail overseas@mr.jst.go.jp
URL http://www.jst.go.jp

JSTOR (Web-based Journal Archive)
120 Fifth Ave., 5th Fl., New York, NY 10011
TEL 212-229-3700, FAX 212-229-6841
E-mail clm@jstor.org
URL http://www.jstor.org

Kluwer Online
Kluwer Academic Publishers, Sales Dept., Spuiboulevard 50, PO Box 17, Dordrecht 3300 AA, Netherlands
TEL 31-78-6392179, FAX 31-78-6392300
E-mail Sales@wkap.nl
Kluwer Academic Publishers, Subscription Dept., 101 Philip Dr., Assinippi Park, Norwell, MA 02061
TEL 781-871-6600, FAX 781-871-6528
E-mail Kluwer@wkap.com
URL http://www.kluweronline.com

LexisNexis
(Subsidiary of: Reed Elsevier plc)
9443 Springboro Pike, Miamisburg, OH 45342
TEL 937-865-6800, 800-227-4908,
FAX 937-865-1666, 800-227-9597
URL http://www.lexisnexis.com

MD Consult
11830 Westline Industrial Dr, St. Louis, MO 63146
TEL 314-997-1176, 800-401-9962, FAX 314-997-5080
E-mail mdc.customerservice@elsevier.com

URL http://www.mdconsult.com

MediaStream, Inc.
(Subsidiary of: Newsbank, Inc.)
One Commerce Sq., Ste 1020, 2005 Market St., Philadelphia, PA 19103-7042
TEL 215-239-4100, FAX 215-239-4150
URL http://www.krmediastream.com

Micromedia ProQuest
(Subsidiary of: ProQuest Information & Learning)
20 Victoria St., Toronto, ON M5C 2N8, Canada
TEL 416-362-5211, 800-387-2689, FAX 416-362-6161
TELEX 065-24668
E-mail info@micromedia.ca
URL http://www.micromedia.ca, http://www.mmltd.com

Munksgaard & Blackwell Science's Synergy
35 Noerre Soegade, Box 2148, Copenhagen K, Denmark
TEL 45-77-333333, FAX 45-77-333377
URL http://www.munksgaard-synergy.com

National Data Corporation
2 National Data Plaza, Corporate Sq., Atlanta, GA 30329
TEL 404-728-2000, FAX 404-728-3635
URL http://www.ndcorp.com

National Library of Medicine
8600 Rockville Pike, Bethesda, MD 20209
TEL 301-594-5983, 888-346-3656, FAX 301-496-4000
URL http://www.nlm.nih.gov

Newsbank, Inc.
5020 Tamiami Trai N, Ste 110, Naples, FL 34103
TEL 239-263-6004, FAX 239-263-3004
URL http://www.newsbank.com

NewsNet
(Subsidiary of: Independent Publications)
945 Haverford Rd., Bryn Mawr, PA 19010
TEL 610-527-8030, 800-345-1301, FAX 610-527-0338
E-mail info@newsnet.com
URL http://www.newsnet.com

NISC
601 Wyman Towers, Ste 806, 3100 St Paul St, Baltimore, MD 21218
TEL 410-243-0797, FAX 410-243-0892
E-mail sales@nisc.com
URL http://www.nisc.com

Northern Light Technology, Inc.
One Broadway, 14th Fl., Cambridge, MA 02142
TEL 617-621-5960, FAX 621-242-6105
E-mail adsales@northernlight.com
URL http://www.northernlight.com

O C L C Online Computer Library Center, Inc.
6565 Frantz Rd, Dublin, OH 43017
TEL 800-848-5878, 614-764-6000, FAX 614-764-6096
E-mail oclc@oclc.org
URL http://www.oclc.org

OhioLINK
2455 North Star Rd, Columbus, OH 43221
TEL 614-728-3600, FAX 614-728-3610
E-mail charly@ohiolink.edu

Ovid Technologies, Inc.
333 Seventh Ave., New York, NY 10001
TEL 212-563-3006, 800-950-2035, FAX 212-563-3784
URL http://www.ovid.com

Oxford University Press Online Journals
(Subsidiary of: Oxford University Press)
Great Clarendon St, Oxford OX2 6DP, United Kingdom
TEL 44-1865 267907, FAX 44-1865-267485
E-mail jnl.info@oup.co.uk
URL http://www3.oup.co.uk/jnls/online/

Project MUSE
(Subsidiary of: Johns Hopkins University Press)
2715 N. Charles St., Baltimore, MD 21218-4319
TEL 410-516-6989, FAX 410-516-6968
URL http://muse.jhu.edu

ProQuest Information & Learning
300 N Zeeb Rd., PO Box 1346, Ann Arbor, MI 48106-1346
TEL 734-761-4700, 800-521-0600, FAX 734-997-4040, 800-864-0019
E-mail info@proquest.com, library_sales@umi.com, info@umi.com
URL http://www.umi.com

Questel Orbit Inc.
(Subsidiary of: France Telecom, Inc.)
8000 Westpark Dr., McLean, VA 22102
TEL 703-442-0900, FAX 703-893-4632
URL http://www.questel.orbit.com

QuickLaw Inc.
275 Sparks St., Ste. 901, St. Andrews Tower, Ottawa, ON K1R 7X9, Canada
TEL 613-238-3499

R M I T Publishing
A'Beckett St, PO Box 12058, Melbourne, VIC 8006, Australia
TEL 61-3-9349-4994, FAX 61-3-9349-4583
E-mail info@rmitpublishing.com.au,
URL http://www.rmitpublishing.com.au

Reed Information Services Limited
Windsor Ct., East Grinstead Hse., East Grinstead, West Sussex RH19 1XA, United Kingdom
TEL 44-1342-326972, FAX 44-1342-335665, TELEX 0342-326972R G

Research Libraries Group
1200 Villa St., Mountain View, CA 94041-1100
TEL 650-691-2333, 800-537-7546, FAX 650-964-0943
E-mail bl.ric@rlg.org
URL http://www.rlg.org

Reuters Business Briefing
85 Fleet St., London EC4P 4AJ, United Kingdom
TEL 44-170-250-1122, FAX 44-170-542-8006
URL http://www.reuters.com

RoweCom Information Quest
(Subsidiary of: RoweCom, Inc.)
5838 Edison Place, Carlsbad, CA 92008-6596
TEL 760-431-7474, 800-422-3223, FAX 760-431-8860
E-mail iqsales@eiq.com, iqcontent@eiq.com
URL http://www.informationquest.com

S T N International
c/o Chemical Abstracts Service, 2540 Olentengy River Rd.,
PO Box 3012, Columbus, OH 43210-0012
TEL 614-447-3600, 800-753-4227, FAX 614-447-3751,
TELEX 6842086 CHMAB
E-mail help@cas.org
URL http://www.cas.orgsical

Sage Publications, Inc.
2455 Teller Rd, Thousand Oaks, CA 91320
TEL 805-499-0721 800-818-7243, FAX 805-499-0871,
800-583-2665
E-mail info@sagepub.com
URL http://www.sagepub.com

SciELO
FAPESP - BIREME, Rue Botucatu 862, Sao Paulo SP
04023-901, Brazil
TEL 55-11-576-9863
CONICYT, Canada 308 Providencia, Santiago de Chile,
Chile
TEL 562-365-4400
E-mail scielo@conicyt.cl
INFOMED, Calle 27 No 110 M y N, Vedado, Havana, Cuba
TEL 537-55-3375, FAX 537-33-3063
E-mail webmaster@infomed.sld.cu
E-mail scielo@bireme.br
URL http://www.scielo.cl/, http://www.scielo.sld.cu/,
http://www.scielo.org, http://www.scielo.br

ScienceDirect
(Subsidiary of: Elsevier Science & Technology)
PO Box 945, New York, NY 10159-0945
TEL 212-462-1980, FAX 212-462-1985
E-mail usinfo@sciencedirect.com
URL http://www.sciencedirect.com

SilverPlatter Information, Incorporated
(Subsidiary of: Ovid Technologies, Incorporated)
100 River Ridge Dr., Norwood, MA 02062
TEL 781-769-2599, 800-343-0064, FAX 781-769-8763
E-mail info@silverplatter.com
URL http://www.silverplatter.com

SoftLine Information
20 Summer St, Stamford, CT 06901
TEL 203-975-8292, 800-524-7922, FAX 203-975-8347
E-mail cadavid@slinfo.com
URL http://enw.softlineweb.com/ethnic.htm

Springer LINK
Springer-Verlag, Tiergartenstr. 17, Heidelberg 69121,
Germany
FAX 49-6221-487-120
Springer-Verlag, 175 Fifth Ave., New York, NY 10010
FAX 212-539-1719
URL http://link.springer.de

Swets Blackwell
Heereweg 347 B, PO Box 830, Lisse 2160 SZ, Netherlands
TEL 31-252-435-111, FAX 31-252-415-888
E-mail swetsnetnavigator@nl.swetsblackwell.com
URL http://www.swetsblackwell.com

Telesystemes-Questel
83-85 blvd. Vincent-Auriol, Paris 75013, France
TEL 33-144236464, FAX 33-144236465

WanFang Data Corp.
Rm 432, 15 Fu Xing lu, Beijing 100038, China
TEL 86-1-68515544 ext 2432, 86-1-68515544 ext 2430,
86-1-68511818, FAX 86-1-68514021
E-mail chinainfo@chinainfo.gov.cn
URL http://www.periodicals.net.cn

West Group
(Subsidiary of: Thomson Corporation, The)
610 Opperman Dr., Eagan, MN 55123-1396
TEL 651-687-7000
E-mail customer.service@westgroup.com
URL http://west.thomson.com/

Wiley InterScience
(Subsidiary of: John Wiley & Sons, Inc.)
111 River St, Hoboken, NJ 07030
TEL 201-748-6000, FAX 201-748-6088
URL http://www.interscience.wiley.com

H. W. Wilson
950 University Ave., Bronx, NY 10452-4224
TEL 718-588-8400, 800-367-6770, FAX 718-681-1511
FAX 800-590-1617
E-mail intlsales@hwwilson.com
URL http://www.hwwilson.com

REPRINT SERVICES

CIS LexisNexis Academic & Library Solutions
(Subsidiary of: LexisNexis)
4520 East-West Hwy., Bethesda, MD 20814-3389
TEL 301-654-1550, 800-638-8380
FAX 301-654-4033
E-mail academicinfo@lexisnexis.com
URL http://www.nexis.com/academic/3cis/cismnu.asp

HAW Haworth Press, Incorporated, The
10 Alice St., Binghamton, NY 13904-1580
TEL 607-722-5857, 800-429-6784
FAX 800-895-0582
TELEX 49 325 99 HAWORTH
E-mail getinfo@haworthpress.com
URL http://www.haworthpressinc.com

IRC International Reprint Corporation
287 East H St, Benicia, CA 94510
TEL 707-746-8740
FAX 707-746-1643
E-mail irc@intlreprints.com
URL http://www.intlreprints.com

ISI Institute for Scientific Information
No longer provide reprint service

NRP Ross Publishing, Incorporated
330 W. 58th St., Ste 306, New York, NY 10019
TEL 212-765-8200, 800-648-8850
FAX 212-765-2393
E-mail info@rosspubl.com
URL http://www.rosspub.com

NTI National Technical Information Service, U. S. Department of Commerce
5285 Port Royal Rd., Springfield, VA 22161
TEL 703-605-6000, 800-553-6847
FAX 703-605-6900
TELEX 89-9405
E-mail info@ntis.gov
URL http://www.ntis.gov

PQC ProQuest Information & Learning
300 N Zeeb Rd., PO Box 1346, Ann Arbor, MI 48106-1346
TEL 734-761-4700, 800-521-0600
FAX 734-997-4040
E-mail info@proquest.com
URL http://www.umi.com

PSC Periodicals Service Company
11 Main St., Germantown, NY 12526
TEL 518-537-4700
FAX 518-537-5899
E-mail psc@backsets.com
URL http://www.backsets.com

RPI Primary Source Microfilm
(Subsidiary of: Gale Group)
12 Lunar Dr, Woodbridge, CT 06525
TEL 203-397-2600, 800-444-0799
FAX 203-397-3893
E-mail sales@gale.com
URL http://www.gale.com/psm

SCH Schmidt Periodicals GmbH
Ortsteil Dettendorf, Bad Feilnbach D 83075, Germany
TEL 49-8064221
FAX 49-8064557
E-mail schmidt@backsets.com
URL http://www.backsets.com

SWZ Swets & Zeitlinger Publishers
PO Box 825, Lisse 2160 SZ, Netherlands
TEL 31-252-435111
FAX 31-252-415888
E-mail pub@swets.nl
URL http://www.szp.swets.nl

WSH William S. Hein & Company, Incorporated
1285 Main St, Buffalo, NY 14209-1987
TEL 800-828-7571
FAX 716-883-8100
E-mail mail@wshein.com
URL http://www.wshein.com

AGGREGATORS

Publishers/E-Platform Providers/A&I-Based

Jeff Kosokoff, Head of Reference Services, Lamont Library of the Harvard College Library, Harvard University, Harvard Yard, Cambridge, MA 02138; kosokoff@fas.harvard.edu

Introduction

With the continued growth in the market for and availability of electronic full-text resources, there has been an explosion of products designed to deliver that text to libraries via the web. The major ways that most libraries will gain access to full text online will be through one of three major kinds of providers. In this new section, our goal is to give a broad overview of the services that these providers (whom we call, for want of a better, more precise term, aggregators) make available, and to discuss the advantages and pitfalls inherent in each type of service. The three types of aggregators we are considering here are:

Publishers: There is a considerable online presence of large publishers who provide their own online serials online themselves. The aggregators included are all large publishers with around 50 or more online titles, whether free-with-print, at a fee over print, or as discrete subscription services with little or no connection to print subscriptions.

Platform providers: These are services that act as online agents for journal titles, many or all of which they do not themselves publish. These aggregators frequently see publishers as their primary customers. Also included in this section are some of the emerging efforts to create new open-access models for publishing and accessing scholarly information. This section is something of a catch-all for a wide variety of publishing efforts that don't fit into the other categories. However, all these services provide browsable access to individual periodical titles, often with little or no value-added indexing and abstracting.

A&I-based aggregators: These providers lease content from a variety of sources and add a common search interface that allows users to search and retrieve content. Aggregations of this type began with the simple idea of taking traditional abstracting and indexing and enhancing it with full text. The most prevalent early example of this sort of service was *InfoTrac*, when it moved from giving references to its microtext set to offering the electronic full text directly. For public and school libraries, these may be the primary form of aggregations offered to users.

In all these services, an important feature has been gained through aggregation. Beyond the convenience of having many titles "grouped" together online for ease of access and searching, by pulling together a large group of diverse titles a searchable body of knowledge is created. Thus, in many aggregations, a new sort of "serendipity" is born, whereby searchers can find perspectives on a given topic coming from a more diverse set of disciplines than might be found via typical single subject indexes. Many of the larger publisher aggregations, and nearly all those that are A&I-based, have the potential to offer this advantage. Another nice by-product of many publisher and platform provider aggregations is that the abstracting and indexing is often freely available, whether or not a user has a subscription. Of course, for users with partial subscriptions, or without any subscriptions at all, the potential exists that users will be asked to pay for content themselves.

Sometimes it seems as though there are as many business and licensing models as there are aggregators, and buying into aggregations can be an expensive proposition. Many aggregators only make their content available as an all-or-nothing proposition, while others allow subscribers to pick and choose among modules (or even down to individual titles). Publishers and platform provider packages are the most likely to have high levels of such granularity. Whereas a library may only want access to a few titles within a service, some aggregators make libraries buy their whole package or offer steep pricing disincentives to selective licensing of part of the entire package. Under a model that many have labeled the "Big Deal," online access to a publisher's content is offered in exchange for a commitment to freeze the level of print or total expenditure, often with bonus access to some unsubscribed content for the duration of the agreement. Whether this kind of deal makes sense for a given library or consortium must be a local decision. Since large publisher aggregations are usually quite multidisciplinary, and many of the publishers have many very prominent titles, larger academic institutions can find the Big Deal quite tempting. Organizations with a more narrow or less scholarly focus may find the deal too big, too expensive, or too restrictive, especially in tough economic times. Some critics have also argued that when they agree contractually to link print and online subscriptions, whatever the deal, libraries are supporting an undesirable licensing model, i.e., enabling the publishers to work under a business model that we should not support.

As the availability of online full text has grown, there have been many attempts to make easier connections between citations, whether in abstracts and indexes or online full text, and the referred-to full text. References that library users find are destined to come from a variety of providers and interfaces—not to mention print, word of mouth, etc. Many of the services describe below provide links from citations to full text within the same service or out to another service from another vendor. Enabling readers to follow citation linkages to full text is a powerful capability that continues to grow in availability. And when services can extend beyond the text they provide (if any) to the wider world of online full text that the user has access to, an important connection has been achieved. However, given the complexities of authentication, creating seamless linking can be problematic. Two issues here are what the link should point to (publication title vs. article), and how to mediate so that users can gain the access that they are due as a consequence of their local/institutional affiliations.

In order to fill the need for linking at the *publication* level, libraries have been experimenting with a variety of Publication Access Management services (PAM). Initially, many institutions built their own database of titles to which their users are entitled online access. Local solutions seemed obvious, since users must be presented with local links in order to use local authentication services. However, the fluidity of content within A&I-based aggregations is a huge issue for linking. That is, for most large and many smaller institutions, a major portion of the serial titles to which they have electronic access is not on a title-by-title basis, but through purchasing an A&I-based aggregation, and such aggregations are especially likely to add and subtract titles over time. It has quickly become clear to those who have tried this at the local or consortial level that maintaining such a database is a huge effort and that the duplication of effort seems wasteful within the library community. Imagine if Library A and Library B both have a subscription to a given full-text aggregation; why would they both need to maintain a list of links to the contents in that aggregation? Commercial PAM from companies such as SerialsSolutions, JournalWebCite, and TD/Net have tried to move to fill this market need by maintaining a database of online content from all significant publishers (i.e., any publisher that any customer wanted to have included). They then allow customers to customize the database to reflect their actual aggregator and individual title online subscriptions. Add in the local authentication information, and this is a workable solution for linking to a periodical at the title level.

Linking at the *article* level is a bit more challenging; not every publisher maintains static URLs for individual articles, and if a publisher changes their web site structure, literally thousands of URLs need to be changed. Again, if everyone tried to maintain their own database of all the URLs of all the online articles to which they have access, the duplication of effort would be enormous, and the cost would be prohibitive. A promising early attempt to centralize maintenance was SilverPlatter's *SilverLinker. SilverLinker* was a database that acted as a service layer, allowing a citation that was sent to it in the proper format to be resolved into a link to the cited article. SilverPlatter maintains the *SilverLinker* database centrally, and offers subscriptions to it to libraries who subscribe to traditional databases through SilverPlatter. This solution is workable if a library has many SilverPlatter databases. However, as a proprietary solution, wider acceptance seems unlikely. The emergence of the DOI (central naming and URL repository), CrossRef (central database connecting DOI to metadata, i.e., citation information) and the OpenURL (standard way to pass metadata) looks promising as parts of a new model to use more open and voluntary standards to achieve the desired results. The key here is to allow users to turn citations—whether those come as links from within aggregations or databases, or from more conventional sources—into links to full text when and if the user is authorized to access the referenced article. The model here is to create a service layer that stands between the database (or user with a citation in hand) and do a lookup from the citation, resulting in a link to point the user at online full text, if available.

As more databases become more savvy at interoperating, the challenge is to maintain authorized access for users as they move from service to service. Complex proxy environments, which by definition are local in nature, are developing to cope with these problems. Perhaps more challenging for library users and the librarians who serve them is the possibility that a database will offer a link to a service to which the user is not entitled access, even though the particular article they are trying to access is available via another service or within the library itself, a nearby institution, or via interlibrary loan. This can also be true for users of any large aggregation that allows subscribers to purchase only a portion of the total content. Some publishers make it fairly obvious which content is "subscribed" and which is not, but this varies greatly between products, providers, and interfaces. While a more centralized solution seems desirable, for now, many of these links are being made more directly. For librarians, inappropriate direct links can also be a source of pressure to add new titles to an institutional subscription. The downside of the local service layer approach is that maintaining the local service, even when the lists of titles and link resolution is handled by external products and services, has significant overhead.

The author wishes to thank Cheryl LaGuardia, Ivy Anderson, and Kristin Stoklosa for taking the time to provide the benefit of their knowledge and experience during the creation of this new section.

Below are some terms that you will see used in the listings in this section.

Text-only: The full text provided is plain text, the format does not look or feel like it would in a printed publication. If images are available, they are placed as they would be on a web page.

PDF or page image: The full text provided is available as Adobe Acrobat files. Typically, this means that the online version is pretty much equivalent in look and feel to the printed version.

OpenURL: An emerging standard that allows services with references to articles and other objects to create a standard URL that refers to the article or other object. The result is that a citation within a database can be used to query another database to help locate the actual object referred to in the citation. See http://library.caltech.edu/openurl/.

DOI–Digital Object Identifier: A service/database in which publishers establish a permanent name for a digital object. Within the confines of this section, these objects would generally be journal articles, every article having its own, unique DOI. Content publishers maintain the precise association between the permanent DOI for a given object and the (possibly transitory) URL for that object within the DOI database. Services such as CrossRef and local services can then use the DOI to query the database and get the true URL for a particular object. See http://www.doi.org/.

CrossRef: A service that can resolve metadata—in this context, citation information for an article—into the DOI for the object the metadata describes. This linking registry service is frequently used by local link servers to get a DOI or metadata, for use in creating a link that a user would use to access the object in question that allows DOIs to be used to access journal content. See http://www.crossref.org.

Addressable: The individual articles within the service have URLs or can be retrieved via URLs. This functionality is especially important in the context of electronic reserves and emerging services such as ExLibris' SFX, which allows linking from citations directly to article content when possible. This relates closely to emerging standards and organizations such as OpenURL, CrossRef, and DOI.

TOC alerting: An alerting service whereby users can have tables of contents of newly posted online content e-mailed to them.

Embargo: The practice within some aggregations (usually from A&I-based aggregators) under which new content is not available for some period of time after publication. For example, titles in JSTOR are all behind what is called a "moving wall." If the moving wall is five years for a given title, then new content is not available until five years after publication.

Pay-per-view: Content is available to nonsubscribed titles (or to nonsubscribers to the service) by making a payment at the point of use. When a service has this sort of arrangement, it can be useful for librarians as a form of document delivery. On the other hand, it can be a frustration for users who may not see the rationale behind having what looks like free access to some content, and being asked to pay for other content.

References:

Dorn, Knut and Katharina Klemperer (2002), "E-journal aggregation systems: only part of the big picture," *Library Collections, Acquisitions, & Technical Services*, 26, 307-310.

Frazier, Kenneth (2001), "The Librarians' Dilemma: Contemplating the Costs of the "Big Deal," *D-Lib Magazine*, 7(3) March 2001. http://www.dlib.org/dlib/march01/frazier/03frazier.html

Huber, Charles (2000), "Electronic journal publishers: a reference librarian's guide," *Issues in Science and Technology Librarianship*, Summer 2000. http://www.library.ucsb.edu/istl/00-summer/article2.html, viewed 2/4/2003.

Peters, Thomas (2001), "What's the Big Deal?" *The Journal of Academic Librarianship,* 27(4), 302-304.

Watson, Paula D. (2003), "E-journal management: acquisition and control," *Library Technology Reports,* 39(2), March-April issue.

Publishers

While not traditionally considered to be aggregators, these companies are academic or specialist publishers who have brought together their own content in electronic form to provide their own online service. The body of knowledge thus created is an aggregation of a variety of journals, often in widely different disciplines, that creates new possibilities for users and offers unique challenges to libraries. To be included in this section, a publisher must put around fifty titles online in a browsable manner.

These publishers have made a business decision that it makes good sense to mount their own service. Some publishers provide their own service and also make their text available through other platforms, others have exclusive access to their content via their own service. Whether a given publisher's content is available widely or through only one service is a decision that each publisher makes based on their perceived role and mission. Publishing is a business, and we cannot really fault publishers who have tried to maximize their profits. On the other hand, many would argue that the business models employed by some large and small commercial and institutional publishers are impeding the dissemination of knowledge. Out of this conflict, a variety of new models are emerging, and it remains unclear if the future of publishing, especially scholarly publishing, will resemble its past.

Typically, these services allow the user to search, browse issues and tables of contents, as well as view individual articles in a variety of formats. The production stream for journals has been changed from a "print-then scan" model to a "digital to online+print" model. In this context, the online version is often a co-product, not a by-product of print publication, and there is thus a greater likelihood that the publisher will make high quality PDFs available.

In these services, content direct from publishers is available under a variety of models from free-with-print to online-only subscriptions, although availability of non-subscribed journals varies by publisher and their individual license terms. Some of the larger commercial publishers have complex and expensive licensing arrangements. Some publishers include access to large backfiles for free, others charge for access to part or all of their backfile. Archival rights associated with publisher aggregations vary widely.

When licensing a publisher aggregation at an additional cost above print, beware of long term commitments to maintain print subscription levels. Under some arrangements, the deal offered requires an institution to freeze their expenditures with the publisher at or above a certain level, with little regard for which format or formats those dollars go towards. Archival rights within publisher aggregations also deserves special consideration when looking at licensing. Many publishers will give libraries access to a backfile for the duration of the subscription, but will only guarantee archival rights for the years of publication that coincide with the online subscription period. That is, while the entire backfile is available to subscribers, only the years of subscription remain to those who later cancel.

ACM Digital Library. Association for Computing Machinery, 1515 Broadway, New York, NY 10036; acmhelp@acm.org; http://www.acm.org/.
Aud.: Ac, Sa.
An important resource for scholars and specialists in computing, the *ACM Digital Library* brings together disparate content, mostly published by the Association for Computing Machinery (ACM), into a cohesive and powerful collection. Content comes from journals, magazines, transactions, and proceedings; and from books, theses, and other ACM publications. It includes the *ACM Guide to Computing Literature,* a comprehensive finding aid for much of the computing literature published in a given year. The resulting collection is an indispensable resource for scholars, with a very sophisticated search interface.

Content dates from 1985 to the present, and is fully and usefully searchable. Bibliographic records are enhanced with abstracts, an Amazon.com-like feature that indicates which other ACM objects readers of the present citation looked at, and article bibliographies (with links to other *Digital Library* content). PDFs for all articles are very high quality. An important resource for academic and special libraries with a need for high-quality computing literature. All content is addressable. ACM is a participant in CrossRef and maintains DOIs to each article.

ACS Journal Archives. American Chemical Society, Member & Subscriber Services, PO Box 3337, Columbus, OH 43210; liblink@acs.org; http://pubs.acs.org/.
Aud.: Ac, Sa.
A massive collection comprised of the collective output of the American Chemical Society (ACS) journals from 1979 to the present. This is a high-powered resource for chemists and historians.

DOI and CrossRef enabled, PDF for all articles. Newer articles are also in enhanced-HTML, which delivers the text, thumbnails of images, and voluminous links to other ACS full-text, Medline searches, and other outside resources. Nonsubscribers can also have pay-per-view access to all the content. Enhanced searching for some levels of subscription includes the ability to search over all journal content ever published by the ACS. This resource is to chemistry what JSTOR is to many other fields.

Blackwell Synergy. Blackwell Publishing, 350 Main St., Malden, MA 02148; subscrip@blackwellpub.com; http://www.blackwell-synergy.com/ or http://www.blackwellpublishing.com/.
Aud.: Ac, Sa.
This is the online home for the journal output of Blackwell Publishing, covering 668 journal titles. The site is open to the public, but only subscribers have access to the actual articles. It allows browsing by title or subject, a fairly sophisticated search interface, and links from within HTML versions of articles (both from within the text and from selected items in the bibliography) to other indexing sources. There are also links to other online articles that cite the article being viewed. Most journals extend their coverage back to 1997. For certain levels of subscribers, articles are available online in advance of their appearance in print.

Articles are available in PDF and/or HTML. The HTML is quite embellished with links. Individual articles are addressable. Blackwell also participates in CrossRef, and most articles have their DOI given along with the HTML version of the article in a handy pre-built text that can be used to cite the article. Free sample issues of all currently published titles are available. Nonsubscribed content is available pay-per-view, although the *Synergy* interface makes it fairly easy to limit a search to subscribed content.

Cambridge Journals Online. Cambridge University Press, 40 West 20th St., New York, NY 10011-4211; sales@cup.org; http://www.cambridge.org/.
Aud.: Ac.
This is the gateway to over 100 journals from Cambridge University Press. Searching is free for all journals, although full-text access beyond online sample copies is restricted to subscribers. Searching can be limited to subscribed titles, and subject divisions provide another convenient way to focus searches. Online coverage of journals begins as early as 1990. This is solid content from a major publisher. Articles are addressable, and are typically available in PDF and HTML. Cambridge University Press uses DOI and participates in CrossRef.

Emerald FullText. Emerald, 44 Brattle St., 4th Fl., Cambridge, MA 02138; america@emeraldinsight.com; http://www.emeraldinsight.com/.
Aud.: Ac, Sa.
Formerly MCB University Press, Emerald is primarily a publisher of a wide range of management and library and information management journals. *FullText* is their online platform, offering access to Emerald's over 100 titles back to 1989.

A variety of search methods are available, and it is easy to limit a search to subscribed titles. Articles are in PDF and/or HTML, and the HTML versions are enhanced with links to other Emerald journals. Individual articles are addressable. Emerald is a CrossRef participant, and assigns a DOI to each article.

IEEE Xplore. The Institute of Electrical and Electronics Engineers, 1828 L St., N.W., Suite 1202, Washington, DC 20036-5104; ieeeusa@ieee.org; http://www.ieee.org/.
Aud.: Ac, Sa.
Xplore is a platform for accessing content produced by IEEE, a premier organization for electronics, electrical, manufacturing and IT professionals. Their *All-Society Periodicals Package* provides access to IEEE's journals, magazines and transactions from 1998 forward, the *Electronic Library* goes further by including proceedings and standards, as well as extending all the way back to 1988.

As one would expect from an engineering publisher, the aggregation is highly organized and efficient to use. Each abstracts is enhanced with a referenced article bibliography, and there are links from within that bibliography to other IEEE *Xplore* content. Another useful feature is citation index–style linking to later IEEE content that cites the article whose abstract one is viewing.

Articles are provided as PDF. They are addressable, and IEEE maintains DOIs and participates in CrossRef. Unfortunately, is not possible to limit searches to subscribed content.

Kluwer Online Journals. Kluwer Academic Publishers, 101 Philip Dr., Assinippi Park, Norwell, MA 02061; kluweronline@wkap.com.
Aud.: Ac, Sa.
Over 650 titles from Kluwer aggregated into a powerful body of knowledge. Coverage varies by title but extends as far back as 1997. Articles are available in HTML and/or PDF. Subscribing libraries can choose to buy any number of titles, either as online-with-print or online-only. There is a good search interface, although there seems to be no way to limit the search only to subscribed titles.

CrossRef and DOI compliant; TOC alerting is free to subscribers and nonsubscribers. The advanced search allows the user to highlight hits within search results in a variety of styles and colors. In the spring of 2003, the owners of Kluwer purchased BertelsmannSpringer, and they plan to merge the companies under the Springer name (see "SpringerLink," below) and presumably under the SpringerLink interface as well.

Oxford Journals. Oxford University Press, Journals Customer Services, 2001 Evans Rd., Cary, NC 27513; jnl.cust.serv@oup.co.uk; http://www.oup.co.uk/.
Aud.: Ac.
Most of the roughly 200 titles in Oxford Journals begin online with 1998. This represents nearly all of the journals from this respected academic publisher.

PDF is available for most all, and HTML for many of the articles. Unfortunately the search interface does not allow the user to limit a search to those journals to which they are registered for online access. However, it is possible to limit to a subset of the journals, either by title or subject. Individual articles are addressable, and Oxford University Press uses DOI and participates in CrossRef.

PsycARTICLES. American Psychological Association, 750 First St., N.E., Washington, DC 20002-4242; psycinfo@apa.org; http://www.apa.org. *Aud.:* Ac, Sa.

A hybrid database of articles from psychology publishers, mostly the American Psychological Association (APA), that could be in any of the three categories in this section. APA uses *PsycARTICLES* as a platform for 40 of its own journals. As a platform provider, this service makes three journals from the Canadian Psychological Association and eight from Hogrefe & Huber available electronically. As an A&I service, all this text comes with access to APA's PsycInfo database, which contains full-text links for *PsycARTICLES* coverage beginning in 1988 for most publications. Each article's bibliography has been enhanced with links to the *PsycInfo* record, where available; and to the full text within *PsycARTICLES*, where available. Full text is generally provided in both PDF and enhanced HTML (with links, as described above). Subscription fees are reduced for institutions that already subscribe to *PsycInfo*. Articles within *PsycARTICLES* are addressable and have DOIs, and the APA participates in CrossRef.

Sage Full-Text Collections. Sage Publications Ltd, 6 Bonhill St., London EC2A 4PU, UK; info@sagepub.com; http://www.sagepub.co.uk/. *Aud.:* Ac, Sa.

Sage has recently pulled much of its journal content out of abstracting and indexing aggregations in favor of providing access through the Cambridge Scientific Abstracts (CSA) Internet Database Service. As such, *Sage Full-Text Collections* is a journal aggregation within an interface that was designed to accommodate abstracting and indexing services. However, the result is a very usable tool for getting at Sage journal content from the early 1980s forward. The collection can be accessed though its own portal, branded as Sage, or along with other databases an institution subscribes to through CSA. Either way, the functionality is basically identical. The content is divided into four individually licensable subject collections: Communications, Criminology, Politics and International Relations, and Sociology.

Articles are provided in PDF, detailed abstracts allow basic searches to be fairly useful, and the tables of contents for each title are browsable. Sage is a DOI and CrossRef participant, and CSA's implementation should allow articles to be addressable, although it is too early to judge as of this writing.

ScienceDirect. Elsevier Science, PO Box 945, New York, NY 10159-0945; usinfo@sciencedirect.com; http://www.info.sciencedirect.com. *Aud.:* Ac, Sa.

ScienceDirect is a platform for the over 1,700 journals published by Elsevier. Begun through a variety of experiments in providing e-versions of print journals, the web-based product emerged more generally in 1999. The content has grown as Elsevier has continued to acquire additional journal titles and publishers. Notable among recent integrations is the content from Academic Press (formerly provided to libraries through Academic Press's *IDEAL*).

TOC altering service is available to all, regardless of subscription. Access to TOC and abstracts for all journals is freely available, with indications to users as to availability provided at point of access.

Elsevier is a CrossRef participant, and articles in *ScienceDirect* are in PDF (some also plain text), have DOIs and are addressable, and are generally posted simultaneously with print publication.

SpringerLink. BertelsmannSpringer, Springer-Verlag Heidelberg, Tiergartenstrasse 17, 69121 Heidelberg, Germany; subscriptions@springer.de; http://www.bertelsmannspringer.de/index_en.php. *Aud.:* Ac.

This service is a gateway to online journals published by BertelsmannSpringer, historically a major STN information provider. Through mergers and acquisitions, Springer has branched out to other areas. The content of all the journals is freely searchable, but only subscribers get access to the entire range of full text, which dates from the mid-1990s forward. The titles are sorted into 11 "Online Libraries" that also incorporate related book content alongside the approximately 500 serial titles. The areas are: chemical sciences, computer science, economics, engineering, environmental sciences, geosciences, law, life sciences, mathematics, medicine, and physics and astronomy. As of this writing, BertelsmannSpringer has been purchased by the firms Candover and Cinven, which also owns Kluwer (see above). Candover and Cinven plan to merge Kluwer and BertelsmannSpringer under a new company called Springer. This will create the second largest academic publisher (behind Elsevier).

The service includes free TOC alerting and some journals have online content available ahead of print. *SpringerLINK* has DOI and CrossRef functionality, and all content is addressable. PDF and HTML available, with enhanced linking to cited articles within the service.

Taylor & Francis Online Journals. Taylor & Francis Group, 325 Chestnut St., Suite 800, Philadelphia, PA 19106; journals.orders@tandf.co.uk; http://www.taylorandfrancis.com. *Aud.:* Ac, Sa.

While much of their content is available online through Ingenta (see entry in Platform Providers, subsection), Taylor & Francis also has their own service. *Taylor & Francis Online Journals* is a very basic platform that supports simple searching and retrieval of full articles from many Taylor & Francis journals, which includes the Taylor & Francis, Carfax, Routledge, and Spon Press imprints.

Individual journal titles are addressable, and Taylor & Francis uses DOI and participates in CrossRef. Article bibliographies are included with some abstracts, and the entire collection is searchable for subscribers. A handy TOC alerting service is available to authorized users who register.

Wiley InterScience. John Wiley & Sons, Inc, Attn: Wiley InterScience Coordinator, Subscription Dept., 111 River St., Hoboken, NJ 07030; uscs-wis@wiley.com; http://www.interscience.wiley.com/. *Aud.:* Ac.

The online presence for journals produced by Wiley, *InterScience* contains full text for over 300 titles, with coverage from the mid-1990s forward. The periodical content is enhanced with access to a variety of monographic titles. The archive is searchable, and provides PDFs for all journals and HTML for some. Articles in many journals appear online ahead of their print publication.

InterScience articles are assigned DOIs and Wiley is a CrossRef participant. Individual articles are addressable. Includes a TOC alerting service that is free to subscribers and nonsubscribers.

E-Platform Providers

Generally, platform providers enable smaller or less financially able publishers to make their publications available over the Internet. To users, these services often look and feel much the same as those provided by publishers. For librarians who license and provide access to the content, there are other issues and complexities, including the reality of dealing with the print publisher and/or one's subscription agent to secure access, and the platform provider for technical support. Some of these aggregators started as online publishers of their own content and have seen their service grow to include providing significant content from other publishers as well. Other e-platform providers publish nothing of their own, and are purely online platform providers for the true publishers or for other kinds of projects, such as the archival access provided by JSTOR.

Archival rights and licensing for this form of aggregation run the gamut from full purchase arrangements with permanent archival rights to lease agreements that hold only for the term of subscription. Again, since many of these organizations are acting as only providers on the behalf of publishers, licensing is frequently a matter between the library and the publisher, and does not involve the platform provider. Beyond technical issues, libraries can expect to have dealings with each individual publisher when gaining access to the varied content within many of these services. Also notable here are the efforts of two providers, BioOne and BioMed. These providers aim to lower the barriers/costs for providing and freely accessing research content. Further, some are trying to lower the hard and soft costs to libraries. The emerging open access models are evolving quickly as you read this, and the landscape of journal publishing will likely look very different in the near future.

BioMed Central. BioMed Central Ltd, Current Science Group, Middlesex House, 34-42 Cleveland St., London W1T 4LB, UK; info@biomedcentral.com; http://www.biomedcentral.com.

Aud.: Ac, Sa.

BioMed Central is an ongoing endeavor in association with SPARC (see http://www.arl.org/sparc) to promote an alternative to commercial publication of research articles in the biomedical sciences. The Institutional Membership Program provides the financial support for *BioMed Central* and fosters the growth of the online journals. Institutions join for an individual fee, and researchers at member institutions can publish articles in the service free of the normal article-processing charges. Authors of articles in the service retain copyright. Their "Open Access" model means that every peer-reviewed research article appearing in any *BioMed Central* journal is immediately and permanently available to anyone, free of charge. In addition, a community of researchers can create and maintain a journal within the service if they agree to certain copyright and archiving terms under the model.

Provisional PDFs of new articles are the first thing to appear in the database. Soon after, full articles are available in PDF and HTML. Individual users, subscribers or not, must register in order to use the handy search functionality. All articles are addressable, as the service is a CrossRef participant, and many articles have DOIs. The HTML versions of articles are enhanced with links to PubMed, author e-mail addresses, and links to other *BioMed Central* content referenced in article bibliographies.

BioOne. BioOne, 21 Dupont Circle, Ste. 800, Washington, DC 20036; geer@amigos.org; http://www.bioone.org/.
Aud.: Ac, Sa.

A growing aggregation of bioscience research journals. A majority of the publishers involved are small and noncommercial members of the American Institute of Biological Sciences (AIBS). Participating societies publish online in *BioOne* at no upfront cost to the societies. The aim of *BioOne* is to develop their service into a core collection for academic and research organizations that support investigation in the biological, geological and environmental sciences.

The over 200 titles are available in both PDF and HTML. Coverage begins for most titles in 2000, although the backfile in being enhanced by some of the participating publishers. All articles have DOIs and are addressable.

EBSCO Electronic Journals Service (EJS). EBSCO Information Services, EBSCO Subscription Services, PO Box 1943, Birmingham, AL 35201-1943; http://www.ebsco.com.
Aud.: Ems, Hs, Ga, Ac, Sa.

EBSCO has been able to leverage its access to periodical content in creating both online abstracting and indexing with full text and this stand-alone e-journal platform. The "Basic" service allows libraries to access e-journals purchased directly from EBSCO. Libraries that want to add access to titles purchased elsewhere will want the "Enhanced" service, which offers full-text access to over 8,000 titles. Additionally, the service indexes content that is available through other services, with direct links to *Ingenta* and others.

Like OCLC's *Electronic Collections Online*, *Ingenta*, this service provides basic access to a wide range and large number of electronic periodicals through a single interface. The *Electronic Journals* service offers basic search functionality plus a browsable list of available titles.

Articles are addressable, and any full text purchased through this service is available through any EBSCO database that indexes that title. TOC alerting is available, and artcles are generally available in PDF, although some are text-only. Like the other services mentioned above, this is the kind of service that can be extremely useful in the context of open linking through local resolvers.

Electronic Collections Online. Online Computer Library Center, Inc., 6565 Frantz Rd., Dublin, OH 43017-3395; oclc@oclc.org; http://www.oclc.org.
Aud.: Ga, Ac, Sa.

OCLC uses the FirstSearch platform to deliver over 4,100 individual journals online. Participating publishers agree to a very hearty archiving policy, and are able to offer their subscribers online access to their content, which is hosted by OCLC. A very wide range of publishers are represented, including many whose content is available online from other aggregators and/or from the publisher's own service. For nonsubscribers, articles are also available as pay-per-view.

Electronic Collections Online is a searchable collection whose interface allows searches to be easily limited by a single subject (i.e., by broad LC class), to content from a particular publisher, and/or to content owned by the user's home library. Individual journal titles, although not articles, are addressable. Like other aggregators that use an interface that was designed primarily for traditional abstracting and indexing database access, this service can seem a little clunky for accessing journal titles.

HighWire. HighWire Press, 1454 Page Mill Rd., Palo Alto, CA 94304-1124; http://www.highwire.org/.
Aud.: Ac, Sa.

HighWire began as the provider of an online presence for journals published by Stanford University Press, and is based at Stanford. The service now provides a platform for many other publishers, and contains full text for over 350 titles largely focused on the sciences and medicine.

HighWire does not manage subscription issues for non-Stanford titles, they simply host and provide an online presence so that publishers can offer online access for subscribers through the HighWire interface. Articles are provided as HTML, PDF, or special versions meant for PDAs (e.g., Palm OS or other handheld devices).

The entire service is searchable, and TOC alerting is available for all titles. Many titles are available for free after a set time that varies by title (usually between 6 and 24 months). Rights and access issues are covered by individual agreements between publishers and subscribers. Articles are addressable.

Ingenta. Ingenta, 44 Brattle St., 4th Fl., Cambridge, MA 02138; libraryinfo@ingenta.com; http://www.ingenta.com.
Aud.: Ga, Ac, Sa.

Through merger, acquisitions, and refocusing, a small spinoff of an academic abstracting and indexing platform (BIDS) has grown into a multidimensional electronic platform for a wide variety of users. Part (formerly) UnCover's table of contents and document delivery service, part (formerly) Catchword's publisher platform, *Ingenta* comprises one of the largest collections of full-text articles available anywhere. Hundreds of publishers work with Ingenta, and over 5,000 titles are included in some version of full text. *Ingenta Select* (formerly CatchWord) is a platform for publishers to provide online text for little or no cost to libraries over their print subscriptions. The rest of *Ingenta* is available to libraries that are subscribers or to individuals on a pay-per-view model. Much of this content can also be licensed as a "with print" option. As time passes, the two models seem to be growing together into a more seamless service. Individual articles are addressable, and are provided in PDF and/or HTML. This service is a particularly good fit for institutions who have a link resolution service of their own, as the search functionality is quite limited.

Journals @ Ovid. Ovid Technologies, 100 River Ridge Dr., Norwood, MA 02062; sales@ovid.com; http://ww.ovid.com.
Aud.: Ac, Sa.

Ovid has entered the full-text world with their journals platform. While there is some integration with the many indexes that OVID resells, the journals platform continues as a separate product. It is also possible to gain access to the full list of Kluwer journal titles (see Kluwer entry in the Publishers subsection) and titles from Lippincott, Williams, and Wilkins. Like the Sage content described above, this service provided journal content through an interface that was designed primarily for making abstracting and indexing available. However, the search interface is a good one, and content is readily accessible. Content is grouped into collections, and subscribers can choose to subscribe to one or more grouping of titles.

Ovid's focus is on providing full-text content in support of medicine and the allied health fields with a distinctly clinical focus, as well as science and technology. Subscribers to the Journals @ Ovid service gain linking between articles within the service, and from within bibliographic databases that the same subscriber has through Ovid. That is, Journals @ Ovid adds full text to databases such as CINAHL and PsycInfo if one has them through Ovid.

Most titles begin their full text in the mid-1990s. Searches can be limited to subscribed content. Articles are available as HTML plus images or as PDF, and do not appear to be addressable.

JSTOR. JSTOR, 301 E. Liberty, Suite 310, Ann Arbor, MI 48104-2262; jstor-info@umich.edu; http://www.jstor.org/.
Aud.: Ac.

Begun under the support of a Mellon Foundation grant, JSTOR provides archival access to page images of core academic journals in a variety of disciplines.

Coverage usually begins with the inception of the journal and continues up to a cutoff date that can vary from a few months to a few years before the present. Initially, the product aimed to cover titles in the social sciences and humanities, but has recently expanded to include titles in the sciences.

JSTOR is explicitly an archival resource, and the embargoes on the most current content are intended to mitigate competition with the sales of current issues. Most JSTOR content has been scanned from print, with OCR kept invisibly behind the scenes to enable the full-text searchability. All content is addressable.

Online Journal Publishing Service (OJPS). American Institute of Physics, One Physics Ellipse, College Park, MD 20740-3843; corr@aip.org; http://www.aip.org/.
Aud.: Ac, Sa.

Besides publishing some of the leading journals in physics, the American Institute of Physics (AIP) acts as provider of a wide range of services to enable AIP member societies to bring their physics journals to the scholarly community. Online, this means hosting journal content through their *Online Journal Publishing Service* (*OJPS*), which includes content from Russian publishers and scholarly societies. The content is browsable, and searchable through an *OJPS*-only search or through AIP's broader SPIN database, which dates back to the mid-1970s for many titles.

OJPS access includes enhanced abstracts, which often include full article bibliographies with links to other *OJPS* content as well as INSPEC records. Full text is available as PDF or GZipped Postscript. The set of journals is browsable to nonsubscribers, but searching is limited to subscribers. Nonsubscribed content is available on a pay-per-article basis. Recent content is in CrossRef, has DOIs, and is therefore addressable.

POESIS. InteLex, PO Box 859, Charlottesville, VA 22902-0859; order@pdcnet.org; http://www.nlx.com/.
Aud.: Ac.

POESIS is a platform for over 50 philosophy journals, most from small associations and societies. Full access to online content of any given title is dependent on having a print subscription to that title. All subscribers can search the database.

The InteLex interface is quite different from any other aggregator treated in this section in that it is more of a text browsing tool than a journal. In fact, this is the same interface InteLex has deployed for their philosophy texts collection called *Past Masters*. The result is a text browsing environment that is nowhere near the sophistication of tools that make close approximations of the feel of browsing a print journal. Individual journals, but not issues or articles, are addressable. Articles are text-only.

Project MUSE. The Johns Hopkins University Press, 2715 N. Charles St., Baltimore, MD 21218-4319; muse@muse.jhu.edu; http://muse.jhu.edu.
Aud.: Ac.

Project MUSE began as a platform for many journals from The Johns Hopkins University Press. Over time, other not-for-profit and association publishers came to MUSE to offer their text online as well. Now numbering nearly 200 titles from around 30 publishers, Project MUSE offers searchable full text for all the journals, some dating back to the mid-1990s. For titles in MUSE that are also covered in JSTOR, JSTOR coverage usually stops where MUSE coverage begins. Article URLs are stable, and all articles are thus addressable.

A&I-Based

Moving beyond the traditional index, these aggregations emerged as an obvious first step when digital technology was applied to enhance indexing and abstracting services. Many of these services are "partial full-text" in that their indexing and abstracting is more comprehensive than the full-text content they provide electronically (or the actual published content of a given publication). Since the content is leased by the aggregator, and such arrangements can change or cease over time, these aggregations are the most subject to gaps and content loss. However, the wide range of publications that many aggregators are able to acquire also means that these can be rich collections of content for researchers at all levels.

Within this section, there are a mixture of companies that provide multiple products and services that represent a single aggregated product and indexing. License agreements with this form of aggregator rarely include archival access. Further, rarely is any particular bit of content guaranteed to remain over time. While it is a problem within all three types of aggregation described here, especially within many large aggregations of this type there can be significant noise in the presence of potentially irrelevant or somewhat lower quality content. Potential purchasers would be wise to pay as much attention to the content that they would rather not have as they do to assuring that certain important publications are present.

Full-text coverage within A&I-based aggregations is not always cover-to-cover and is not always as granular as one might hope. Front matter, editorials, sidebars, or book reviews might not be included. For some publications in some aggregations, coverage may be even more selective, only including one or two articles per issue or only some issues from a given volume. Such gaps in coverage may be an important consideration when considering licensing such services. For many publications, the agreements that these aggregators have with publishers also results in an embargo of current issues that may be as long as one year. The granularity issue can be a little trickier. For example, if the book reviews section of a publication is a series of reviews run together in a single section, the aggregator may treat the section as an article. This can be frustrating when a user is looking to get at a single review, especially in the context of linking services, since addressing a single review as cited in a third-party index may fail.

EBSCO Publishing. EBSCO Information Services, 10 Estes St., PO Box 682, Ipswich, MA 01938-0682; ep@epnet.com; http://www.epnet.com.
Aud.: Ems, Hs, Ga, Ac, Sa.

Driven by one of the largest collections of full-text content, EBSCO repackages that content aiming to meet the needs of all types of libraries. Gaining leverage from its position as a serials vendor, EBSCO has turned their contacts toward providing full-text aggregations.

Major Products. Many come in two versions; full versions are called "Premier" and reduced versions are called "Elite":

Academic Search, a general database containing journal, newspaper, and magazine content.

Business Source, a comprehensive business aggregation, aims to be a competitor to Proquest's *ABI/InForm*.

Computer Source, over 300 full-text titles for IT professionals and scholars.

Health Source, a pair of products for allied health professionals, scholars, and consumers; comes in a "Consumer Edition" and a "Nursing/Academic Edition."

EBSCO's strengths lie in their comprehensive content, especially strong with academic publications. Articles are usually addressable. Full text is in HTML and/or PDF.

Factiva. Dow Jones Reuters Business Interactive, PO Box 300, Princeton, NJ 08543-0300; solutions@factiva.com; http://www.factiva.com/.
Aud.: Ac, Sa, Ga.

A powerful aggregation of business news and intelligence. The product most affluent libraries will purchase is *Factiva.com*, a collection of full text from over 7,000 publications (text-only), mostly magazines, but it includes over 1,000 newspapers. Content is international and is available in 22 languages.

This is one of the premier news information sources, and its focus on business does not preclude its usefulness to all who seek news content. This is one of the few aggregations that includes access to the *Wall Street Journal*, which is published by Factiva's parent company, Dow Jones.

Individual articles are not addressable, content is text-only, and licensing of selected content is possible, although it is not possible to block searching of nonsubscribed content. Since this service is aimed at individual and corporate subscribers, some features of the interface are less appropriate in library settings.

Gale. Thomson Gale, 27500 Drake Rd., Farmington Hills, MI 48331-3535; galeord@gale.com; http://www.gale.com.
Aud.: Ems, Hs, Ga, Ac.

In some ways, the idea of an abstracting and indexing–based aggregation begins with *InfoTrac*, a product that is now just one among many full-text offerings from Gale. With aggressive development for many years, accelerated when Gale was purchased by The Thomson Corporation, Gale's databases continue as major players, along with those from EBSCO and Proquest, in the

A&I-plus-full-text market. In recent years, one major strategy from Gale has been to create subject- or audience-based "Resource Center" products, which incorporate content from a variety of sources (including nonserial full text from Primary Source Media, which Gale purchased in the late 1990s) under specialized interfaces with the subject and/or audience in mind. Examples of this include *History Resource Center*, *Business & Company Resource Center*, *Student Resource Center*, and *Literature Resource Center*. This approach has allowed Gale to repackage content for different audiences. In general, Gale's market for these products has been in smaller academic, public, and school libraries, as larger academic institutions find that more general full-text resources are a better fit with their other abstracting services.

Selected Major Products. Gale has a wide diversity of aggregations, many repackaging content found in their other products:

Academic ASAP, Gale's general database of journal, magazine, and newspaper content; over 700 titles in full text back as far as the late 1980s.

InfoTrac, a customizable collection of periodical content; comes prepackaged in a complete file (OneFile) or for K-12 (Kids, Junior or Student versions). OneFile contains over 4,000 publications in full text back as far as the mid-1980s, though it is much more rich from the late 1990s forward.

Resource Centers, as mentioned above, these are specialized aggregations focused on pulling together content in support of audiences or topics. Biography, literature, and history have their own *Resource Centers*, as do audiences from K-12 to college students (various *Student Resource Centers*).

Individual articles are addressable within many of Gale's products, and full text is generally provided only in PDF.

LexisNexis. LexisNexis Group, PO Box 933, Dayton, OH 45401-0933; academicinfo@lexisnexis.com; http://www.lexis-nexis.com.
Aud.: Hs, Ga, Ac, Sa.

Born in 1973 as a legal research product, LexisNexis has grown into a major player in providing indexing and access to full-text content for a wide variety of users. While "traditional" LexisNexis is still the database of choice for many legal and research professionals, the penetration of LexisNexis into more general niches has come as they have portioned out their content in web-based products for broader use within schools, colleges, and universities.

Because LexisNexis licenses nearly all of their content from other publishers, their products have historically been subject to some depletion of content as those publishers have ended their agreements with LexisNexis. However, *LexisNexis Academic* remains a key resource at colleges and universities. *Scholastic Edition* has also had success, and is now available to millions of high school students. Most purchasers of LexisNexis subscribe through local or regional consortia, or gain access through statewide agreements.

Major Products:

- *LexisNexis Academic*, based on the commercial LexisNexis product used by professional researchers in journalism and law. The Nexis piece provides major newspaper and magazine content, and Lexis is the legal section, which is a huge collection of legal materials, including law reviews and other legal serials. The service also contains a fair amount of medical and business content, although most libraries that have the product have more significant resources from other providers to cover these subject areas.

- *Government Periodicals Index*, an index to 170 U.S. government publications, with links to full text.

- *Scholastic Edition*, a subset of the content in *LexisNexis Academic*, designed to meet the needs of secondary school students.

Individual articles and documents within LexisNexis products are not addressable, and content from periodicals is text-only. Much of the full-text content within LexisNexis is extremely current, some publications appearing online before most users would be able to access the same content in the print analog.

NewsBank. NewsBank, Inc, 5020 Tamiami Trail N., Suite 110, Naples, FL 34103; sales@newsbank.com; http://www.newsbank.com.
Aud.: Ems, Hs, Ga, Ac.

A provider of indexing and full text for newspapers, predominantly American. Coverage of many titles is not cover-to-cover. A good resource for basic news in text-only format. It does not match the coverage or scope of LexisNexis or Factiva, although NewsBank does have content from newspapers not found in either.

NewsBank repackages their content in various forms to target specific audiences with specialized products, i.e., "School Library Collection," "Middle School Edition." Business NewsBank targets business researchers. Content is plain text-only, and is not addressable.

Proquest. Proquest Information and Learning, 300 N. Zeeb Rd., PO Box 1346, Ann Arbor, MI 48106-1346; info@il.proquest.com; www.proquest.com.
Aud.: Ems, Hs, Ga, Ac.

Proquest is one of the largest players in the world of A&I-based full text. Born out of University Microfilms as an online provider, Proquest broadened its offerings with the purchase of Chadwyck-Healey in the mid-1990s. Recently, the acquisition of *bigchalk* marked a concerted effort to make inroads in the K-12 market. Proquest has been able to leverage their massive full-text archive by repackaging content to meet a wide variety of market needs. Besides reselling many A&I services that are available from other vendors, Proquest's flagship products include:

1. *Research Library*, a searchable index to thousands of magazines, newspapers, trade and academic journals, and other serial publications. It contains full text from over 1,500 publications. *Research Library* is made up of a core database of periodical indexing and full text, augmented by various subject-focused modules that are themselves available as stand-alone products.

2. *ABI/INFORM*, the premier business literature index. *ABI/INFORM* contains a very liberal amount of full text from regional, national, and international business, finance, and trade publications.

3. *bigchalk*, a wide-ranging, largely full-text resource aimed at the K-12 and public library markets. Users find full text here as well as graphical materials such as maps and diagrams.

4. *Proquest Historical Newspapers*, an online platform for a growing inventory of newspaper backfiles. Titles currently available from their inception include *The Wall Street Journal*, *The New York Times* and *The Washington Post*. PDF-only viewing.

5. *Ethnic Newswatch*, *Gender Watch* and *Alt-Press Watch*, three important databases that Proquest acquired when it absorbed Softline Information. *Ethnic NewsWatch* provides indexing for the regional ethnic press of the United States, *Alt-Press Watch* covers local alternative newspapers, and *Gender Watch* covers publications that focus on issues of gender. All contain text that is hard to find anywhere else. Text and publication/masthead information is provided for all publications.

Generally, full text is available in a variety of formats, including plain text and PDF. Individual articles in many databases are somewhat addressable (usually an additional single-click is required).

WilsonWeb. H. W. Wilson, 950 University Ave., Bronx, NY 10452; http://www.hwwilson.com/.
Aud.: Ems, Hs, Ga, Ac.

From the original indexing company, WilsonWeb is the online presence of all your favorite Wilson indexes. In the full-text era, Wilson created new indexes and enhanced others. The heart of the system is Wilson's *OmninFile*, which contains full text from 1982 forward, selectively pulling content together from over 1,600 publications. Wilson uses this content to enhance the classic Wilson indexes (e.g., *Readers' Guide*, *General Science*, and *Social Sciences*) and more subject-specific ones such as their education, art, and library science products.

Articles are addressable and are available as plain text or PDF. This is a selective service, so beyond the normal gaps and embargoes, one will not find cover-to-cover full text here.

MAGAZINES FOR LIBRARIES

■ ABSTRACTS AND INDEXES

See also Newspapers/Newspaper Indexes; and Newspapers/Commercial Web News Systems subsections.

Cheryl LaGuardia, Head of Instructional Services for the Harvard College Library, Widener Library, Research Services, Harvard University, Cambridge, MA 02138; claguard@fas.harvard.edu

Jeff Kosokoff, Head of Reference Services, Lamont Library of the Harvard College Library, Harvard University, Harvard Yard, Cambridge, MA 02138; kosokoff@fas.harvard.edu

Introduction

The major development affecting abstracts and indexes since the last edition of *MFL* is the proliferation of files offering full-text, including products with the ability to link to the full-text of material not created by that vendor; in other words: interoperability. The new Aggregators section details this growing phenomenon in research publishing at greater length, but it's important to emphasize here because both users' and librarians' expectations have been raised considerably in this area. We have much higher standards for online files now, and newly formed technological, consortial, and partnership arrangements make these higher standards very achievable.

Along with the increase in expectations for full-text accompanying developments with A&I, researchers are also expecting online availability of backfiles to be added to online databases, and companies have discovered a healthy market for archival content added to current files. H.W. Wilson's databases illustrate this clearly: Readers' Guide Retrospective will soon make the entire Readers' Guide Indexing file available via the web, and ISI has provided retrospective files for many years, as have other vendors. Given current trends, it seems that print publishers will be making most, if not all, retrospective files available on the web—and that's a very good thing for librarians, researchers, and the publishing industry. Now if only the wildly variant pricing structures for full-text indexing would come in line with reality. . .

Please note that each subject section in *MFL* begins with a Basic Abstract and Index list of the essential subject indexes in the field. (CML, JK)

1. *A B I - INFORM.* [ISSN: 1062-5127] 1971. m. U M I, 300 N Zeeb Rd, Ann Arbor, MI 48106; http://www.umi.com.
Illus. CD-ROM: ProQuest Information & Learning. Online: Data-Star; European Space Agency; Questel Orbit Inc.; STN International; SilverPlatter Information, Incorporated. *Aud.:* Ga, Ac, Sa.

Available through several vendors employing a variety of interfaces, this is the premier abstracting and indexing service that covers 1,800-plus academic business journals and trade magazines. The strengths of this database include a deep history dating back to 1971, a well-developed controlled vocabulary of subject terms, several searchable fields, and concise, informative abstracts. Full-text availability of articles is extensive, but certainly not complete across all publications indexed; it can be frustrating to discover that full-text coverage of some titles is only available for limited date ranges. Some vendors are now offering full image and graphics capabilities. This excellent product is a must for all libraries that support a large business collection; even general collections will find that it has a broad appeal to patrons researching social and political questions. (BD)

2. *A S S I A Net.* Supersedes (in 1999): *A S S I A: Applied Social Sciences Index & Abstracts (Print).* 1987. m. GBP 2060; USD 3900. CSA, 7200 Wisconsin Ave, Ste 715, Bethesda, MD 20814; journals@csa.com; http://www.csa.com. Illus. Sample. *Aud.:* Ac.

ASSIA indexes and abstracts articles from 650 English-language journals from the United Kingdom, United States, and other countries. It is available on CD-ROM (ASSIA PLUS) and online (ASSIAnet), with coverage from 1987. Coverage is of core social sciences journals, primarily from Great Britain, Canada, Australia, and the United States, with an emphasis on sociology, psychology, and medicine. Other subjects include anthropology, communication, criminology, education, ethnic studies, legal issues, political science, urban planning, and women's studies. The online version from Cambridge Scientific Abstracts is very user-friendly, with a thesaurus and multiple refining and limiting options. If your library subscribes to other Cambridge databases, there is the ability to search them simultaneously. Recommended for academic libraries. (SKD)

3. *Abstracts in Anthropology.* [ISSN: 0001-3455] 1970. 8x/yr. USD 483. Ed(s): Roger W Moeller, Jay F Custer. Baywood Publishing Co., Inc., 26 Austin Ave, Amityville, NY 11701; info@baywood.com; http://www.baywood.com. Illus., adv. Sample. *Aud.:* Ac, Sa.

Provides comprehensive abstracting coverage of international anthropological literature. Entries are fully indexed by author and subject, in the areas of cultural anthropology, physical anthropology, archaeology, and linguistics. Twice annual cumulative indexing for the volume.

4. *Abstracts in New Technologies and Engineering.* Former titles (until 1997): *Current Technology Index; British Technology Index.* [ISSN: 1367-9899] 1962. bi-m. 7 issues plus a. cumulation. USD 1865 combined subscription print & online eds. CSA, 7200 Wisconsin Ave, Ste 715, Bethesda, MD 20814; journals@csa.com; http://www.csa.com. Illus. Online: Data-Star. *Aud.:* Ac, Sa.

Covers over 350 periodicals in all branches of engineering, chemical technology, instrumentation, building, transport, and computerization technology. Noted for its abundance of cross-references and for an index that permits a high degree of specialty in searching. For large research collections. (LTB)

5. *Abstracts in Social Gerontology: current literature on aging.* Formerly (until 1990): *Current Literature on Aging.* [ISSN: 1047-4862] 1957. q. USD 542. Sage Publications, Inc., 2455 Teller Rd, Thousand Oaks, CA 91320; info@sagepub.com; http://www.sagepub.com. Illus. Circ: 8300. Vol. ends: Dec. *Aud.:* Ac, Sa.

Published in association with the National Council on the Aging, *ASG*'s coverage ranges widely across the multidisciplinary study of aging. Titles analyzed range from *Health Care Financing Review,* to *Educational Gerontology, Journal of Housing for the Elderly,* and *Journal of Cross-Cultural Gerontology.* Entries are by subject and cover medical, social, financial, and public policy material as well as additions to theory and method. A basic source for information in the study of aging, geriatrics, and gerontology.

6. ***Abstracts of Working Papers in Economics: the official journal of the AWPE database.*** [ISSN: 0951-0079] 1986. bi-m. USD 445 (Individuals, USD 150). Ed(s): Halbert White. Cambridge University Press, The Edinburgh Bldg, Shaftesbury Rd, Cambridge, CB2 2RU, United Kingdom; information@cambridge.org; http://uk.cambridge.org/journals. Illus., adv. Reprint: SWZ. *Aud.:* Ac.

Abstracts of Working Papers in Economics gathers information from over 70 research centers worldwide from more than 100 series of working papers. The database is a great "point of access for thousands of working papers in all areas of economics, finance and econometrics." This is a very useful tool for researchers, students, and economists alike. Each issue contains about 400 current abstracts, which include full bibliographic information and author addresses, JEL classification number, price, and availability. For easy accessibility, there is a series index, a keyword index, and a permuted title index. Abstracts are also included in the American Economic Association's online and CD-ROM databases, *Economic Literature Index*, and *EconLit,* respectively. Highly recommended for large college and university libraries. (GC)

7. ***Access: The Supplementary Index to Periodicals.*** Incorporates: *Monthly Periodical Index.* [ISSN: 0095-5698] 1975. s-a. USD 277.50. John Gordon Burke Publisher, Inc., PO Box 1492, Evanston, IL 60204-1492; info@jgburkepub.com; http://jgburkepub.com. Illus., index. *Aud.:* Hs, Ga, Ac.

Although this began as a supplement to the *Readers' Guide to Periodical Literature,* it now stands by itself as an excellent general index. It covers titles not included in the *Readers' Guide. Access* focuses primarily on popular music, travel, science fiction, arts and crafts, and regional and city magazines. About 140–150 periodicals are indexed in each issue. The index is published in two parts: author and subject. The third issue is the annual hardbound cumulation published in December.

8. ***Accounting and Tax Index.*** Formerly (until 1992): *Accountants' Index.* [ISSN: 1063-0287] 1920. q. plus a. cumulation. Ed(s): Paula McCoy. U M I, 300 N Zeeb Rd, Ann Arbor, MI 48106; http://www.umi.com. Illus. Microform: PQC. *Aud.:* Ac, Sa.

This index is the successor of the well-regarded *Accountants' Index,* published by the American Institute of Certified Public Accountants from 1921 to 1991. *Accounting and Tax Index* covers a wide range of accounting, finance, and business sources, including both periodicals and monographs. Coverage of international sources is also good. More than 1,000 sources are scanned for citations relating to accounting and taxation. A particularly helpful feature is the use of specific accounting standards, court decisions, and sections of the Internal Revenue Code and tax regulations as indexing terms, enabling the user to locate articles that discuss these authoritative documents. The online edition, *Accounting and Tax Database,* is among the databases offered through the publisher's web-based *ProQuest Direct. Accounting and Tax Database* covers a significantly larger number (approximately 1,900) of sources than the print index and also provides the full text of articles from approximately 200 sources. *Accounting and Tax Index,* either in print or online, is recommended for libraries that serve accountants or academic accounting programs.

ACM Electronic Guide to Computing Literature. See *ACM Digital Library* in the Aggregators/Publishers section in the front matter.

9. ***African Index Medicus.*** 1993. q. USD 100. Ed(s): Lucilda Hunter. W H O Regional Office for Africa, The Library & Documentation Centre, The African Index Medicus Coordinating Center, Belvedere, BO Box BE 773, Harare, Zimbabwe. Illus., adv. *Aud.:* Ac, Sa.

The *African Index Medicus* (*AIM*) was created "to give access to information published in or related to Africa and to encourage local publishing." It is produced by the Association for Health Information and Libraries in Africa (AHILA) with support from the World Health Organization. The index is available at no charge at http://www.who.int/hlt/countrysup/aim/English/aime.htm.

Authors and others can participate in the creation of *AIM* by writing to The African Index Medicus Coordinating Center, The Library & Documentation Centre, WHO Regional Office for Africa, B.O. Box BE 773, Belvedere, Harare, Zimbabwe.

According to information found at the web site, "[the] need for improved access to what has been published on health issues in African countries has long been felt by researchers, development agencies, health administrators and planners both inside and outside the continent. Very few African health and biomedical information sources are included in the world's leading bibliographic databases and there is a wealth of untapped information reports and studies from international development agencies, nongovernmental organizations and local institutions."

10. ***African Studies.*** q. ZAR 8270; USD 1116.06. National Inquiry Services Centre (Pty) Ltd, 22 Somerset St, Grahamstown, 6139, South Africa; info@nisc.co.za; http://www.nisc.co.za. *Aud.:* Ac, Sa.

NISC's *African Studies* database is an anthology, a compilation of 16 large databases from three continents with records of books, periodical articles, pamphlets, maps, and music recordings with publication years from the nineteenth century forward. Both versions, the compact disc and the online service, include the following major files (some of which are closed and other continuously updated): *African Studies Abstracts* (1994–) and its predecessor, *Documentatieblad* (1988–1993); ASC Leiden Library catalogue of books and periodicals on North and sub-Saharan Africa (1988–present); Africa Institute files of books and articles (1981–present); Southern African Database (Sardius) (1961–1997), indexing political and economic literature of the SADC region; School of Oriental & African Studies (SOAS) Library Catalogue: Africa (1989–present), including a broad range of African book and journal material; and Business & Industry: Africa (1994–present). The database includes other more specialized collections from the region. The pricing structure for this substantial archive and current index varies with choice of format and the number of users and work stations. Recommended for academic and specialist institutions. For related indexes and abstracts, see also the print *African Studies Abstracts, Black Studies on Disc*, and *Current Bibliography on African Affairs* (all in this section).

11. ***African Studies Abstracts.*** Former titles (until 1994): *Documentatieblad: The Abstracts Journal of the African Studies Centre Leiden;* (until 1980): *Afrika Studiecentrum. Documentatieblad.* [ISSN: 1352-2175] 1968. q. DEM 358; DEM 98 newsstand/cover per issue. Ed(s): Hans Zell. K.G. Saur Verlag GmbH, Ortlerstr. 8, Munchen, 81373, Germany; info@saur.de; http://www.saur.de. Illus. Circ: 500. *Aud.:* Ac, Sa.

From the African Studies Centre, University of Leiden, this abstracting journal is a source for keeping abreast of articles and edited works on Africa in the field of the social sciences and the humanities. Close to 250 scholarly journals in the field of African Studies are systematically scanned, as are edited works and some periodicals dealing with Third World and development studies. Some 40 percent of these are published in Africa. The arrangement of the some 450 abstracts per issue is geographical by subregion and then by individual country. About half of the journals covered are in English, with the remaining in French and German and a few in other languages. There are author and subject indexes and a list of journals and edited works abstracted in the issue. This is an extremely important and useful reference resource for the current study of Africa. Highly recommended for collections supporting African Studies at various levels. This abstracting service can be purchased in print, but is also available electronically as part of the NISC *African Studies* database (see above).

12. ***AgeLine.*** 1978. bi-m. American Association of Retired Persons, 601 E St, N W, Washington, DC 20049; ageline@aarp.org; http://research.aarp.org/ageline/about.html. CD-ROM: SilverPlatter Information, Incorporated. *Aud.:* Ac, Sa.

Produced by AARP (American Association of Retired Persons), AGELINE is a searchable online database with detailed summaries of books, articles from over 300 periodicals, videos, and research reports on the subject of aging and older persons. It is updated "regularly" (meaning irregularly) and selectively covers material back as far as 1966, with broader coverage commencing in 1978. The entire file continues to be searchable for free at http://research.aarp.org/ageline/access.html, or it can be accessed through commercial vendors via the web, online service, or CD-ROM (these vendors include Cambridge Scientific Abstracts, DIALOG, OVID, and SilverPlatter). Content is the same irrespective of where you search it, but the commercial vendors' products offer much more powerful and sophisticated search options than the free AARP site. A very important source for the study of aging. (CML)

13. ***Agricola C R I S.*** [ISSN: 0897-3237] 1970. q. U.S. National Agricultural Library, 10301 Baltimore Ave, Rm 204, Beltsville, MD 20705-2351; ag98help@nal.usda.gov; http://www.nal.usda.gov/ag98/. Online: NISC. *Aud.:* Ac, Sa.

AGRICOLA (AGRICultural OnLine Access) started in 1970 and is produced by the National Agricultural Library. Records of items back to the fifteenth century have been included in the database. This database is available for free on the web or can be accessed through a number of providers in a number of different formats. Journals indexed in this database are listed at http://www.nal.usda.gov.indexing.jia.html. The *NAL Agricultural Thesaurus* can be found at http://agclass.nal.usda.gov/agl/agl.htm. This is a valuable resource for agricultural research.

14. ***Agris.*** [ISSN: 1020-0320] Food and Agriculture Organization of the United Nations, Sales and Marketing Group, Viale delle Terme di Caracalla, Rome, 00100, Italy; http://www.fao.org. *Aud.:* Ga, Ac.

"AGRIS is a cooperative system in which participating countries input references to the literature produced within their boundaries and, in return, draw on the information provided by the other participants. To date, 240 national, international and intergovernmental centres participate from all over the world." A list of the journals indexed can be found at ftp://ext-ftp.fao.org/agris/Manuals/FAO-AGRIS-9/EN-ES-FR/. The database is searchable back to 1975. This index is a valuable tool for finding citations from developing countries.

15. ***Air University Library Index to Military Periodicals.*** [ISSN: 0002-2586] 1949. q. Free to qualified personnel. Ed(s): Evita M Siebert. U.S. Air Force, Air University Library, 600 Chennault Circle, Building 1405, Maxwell Afb, AL 36112-6424; evita.siebert@maxwell.af.mil; http://www.au.af.mil/au/aul/aul.htm. Illus. Circ: 1100 Controlled. Vol. ends: No. 4. *Aud.:* Ac.

An indexing service published to support the faculty and students of the U.S. Air Force's senior war college. The *Index to Military Periodicals* provides author and subject access to news articles, book reviews, and editorials published in 78 English-language military and aeronautical periodicals. The coverage includes a good mix of U.S. Department of Defense periodicals, as well as those produced by other publishers (e.g., military associations). Since the demise of the *Index to U.S. Government Periodicals* in 1987, this index offers researchers convenient access to the contents of military publications available through the U.S. depository program. The staff members of the Air University Library index all but five periodicals; the others are indexed by the other service libraries. An online version of the index (1990–present) is available at the above URL. For the list of titles indexed go to http://www.au.af.mil/au/aul/muir1/aulimp.htm.

16. ***Alternative Press Index: access to movements, news, policy, theory.*** [ISSN: 0002-662X] 1969. q. USD 300 (Individuals, USD 75). Ed(s): Charles D'Adamo, Les Wade. Alternative Press Center, Inc, PO Box 33109, Baltimore, MD 21218; http://www.altpress.org/api.html. Illus. Circ: 650 Paid. CD-ROM: National Information Services Corp. Online: NISC. *Aud.:* Hs, Ga, Ac, Sa.

The *Alternative Press Index* is a quarterly subject index to some 250 alternative, radical, and leftist periodicals, newspapers, and magazines. Some 90 percent of its coverage is not indexed in either *Readers' Guide to Periodical Literature* or the *Social Science Index*. Major topics include African American studies, alternative organizations, anarchism, community organizing, ecology, ethnic and racial studies, feminism, gay and lesbian studies, internationalism, labor studies, prisons, and social theory. It indexes all articles of five or more paragraphs, among them editorial, regular columns, essays, fiction, speeches, interviews, statistics, reprints, bibliographies, directories, resource lists, autobiographies, biographies, obituaries, memoirs, and reviews of books, films, CDs, TV, drama, arts, and multimedia. A web site offers information on the index (coverage, use, order), an online directory, sample citations, current features, and links to over 425 alternative online resources. *Alternative Press Index* serves multiple purposes. It indexes publications that many libraries subscribe to but, at the same time, lack the indexes for; serves as a collection development tool; and offers information about the alternative press world through its web presence and ties with groups such as the Independent Press Association. With the recent loss of the *Left Index,* its access to leftist and radical materials becomes even more important. The *Alternative Press Index* is a powerful tool that can only enrich library collections.

17. ***America: History and Life. Article Abstracts and Citations of Reviews and Dissertations Covering the United States and Canada.*** Formed by the merger of: *America: History and Life. Part A: Article Abstracts and Citation; America: History and Life. Part B: Index to Book Reviews; America: History and Life. Part C: American History Bibliography; America: History and Life. Part D: Annual Index.* [ISSN: 0002-7065] 1964. 5x/yr. Ed(s): Mary Bagne. A B C-Clio, 130 Cremona Dr, Santa Barbara, CA 93117; sales@abc-clio.com; http://www.abc-clio.com. Adv. *Bk. rev.:* Various number and length. *Aud.:* Ac, Sa.

America: History and Life is the authoritative abstracting and indexing reference for United States and Canadian history from prehistory to the present. It covers over 2,100 journals published worldwide. In addition to English-language journals, *AH&L* covers selected historical journals from major countries, state and local history journals, and other journals in the social sciences and humanities. More than 90 percent of the articles indexed are in English. The file also includes book and media reviews and dissertation citations and abstracts. Approximately 16,000 new entries are added to the database each year, and the file presently goes back to 1964. Updated monthly. Recent additions to the file include the CLIO Notes research guide, CLIO Alert SDI service, and a new Simple Search screen.

18. ***American Bibliography of Slavic and East European Studies.*** Formerly: *American Bibliography of Russian and East European Studies.* [ISSN: 0094-3770] 1956. m. American Association for the Advancement of Slavic Studies, Harvard University, 8 Story St, 3d Fl, Cambridge, MA 02138; aaass@fas.harvard.edu; http://www.fas.harvard.edu. Illus., adv. Circ: 250 Paid. *Aud.:* Ac, Sa.

Available in online format, this bibliography of English-language publications and selected foreign language materials published in the United States and Canada lists citations through author and subject indexes for books, journal articles, and book reviews on material relating to Eastern and Central Europe, the Balkans, the Baltics, and the former Soviet Union. The subjects covered are many and varied, including anthropology, ethnology, archaeology, culture and the arts, economics and foreign trade, education and scholarship, geography and demography, government, law, politics, history, international relations, language and linguistics, literature, military affairs, philosophy, psychology, religion, science and technology, and sociology.

19. ***American Humanities Index.*** [ISSN: 0361-0144] 1975. a. USD 499 print ed. Ed(s): Michael Laddin. Whitston Publishing Co. Inc., 1717 Central Ave, Ste 201, Albany, NY 12205-4759; whitston@capital.net; http://www.whitston.com. Illus. Circ: 300. *Aud.:* Ac, Sa.

This index is most useful for finding new creative writing and book reviews. Its scope includes many English-language literary journals and magazines, with an emphasis on American and Canadian works. At present it covers over 700 titles, and some of the little magazines and author newsletters that are included are not indexed elsewhere. In the printed version, citations to articles appear both under relevant subject headings and under the author's name. When an author's name is used as a subject heading, it appears in all uppercase letters. Subject headings are often subdivided by geographical location and historical period. Review articles are listed under subject, reviewer, and author of the work reviewed. An online version is available via EBSCOhost. Recommended for libraries that support the advanced study of literature. (CM)

20. ***American Statistics Index: a comprehensive guide and index to the statistical publications of the U.S. Government.*** [ISSN: 0091-1658] 1974. m. plus q. & a. cumulations. Ed(s): Paul Kesaris. Congressional Information Service, Inc., 4520 East West Hwy, Bethesda, MD 20814; cisinfo@lexis-nexis.com; http://www.cispubs.com. Illus. *Aud.:* Hs, Ga, Ac, Sa.

ASI is divided into two parts—an index section corresponding to a separately bound abstracts section. There are multiple access points: subject, issuing agency, name, type of data breakdown (e.g., by city, by occupation, or by educational attainment), publication title, and agency report number. Each index entry cites an accession number that corresponds to a specific publication description in the abstracts section. Available in print or on the web through LexisNexis Statistical database, *ASI* has won awards from *Library Journal* and *Database Magazine*. It is comprehensive and an effective resource for locating government statistics.

21. *L'Annee Philologique: bibliographie critique et analytique de l'antiquite greco-latine.* [ISSN: 0184-6949] 1924. a. FRF 850. Societe International de Bibliographie Classique, c/o Pierre-Paul Corsetti Ed., Tour Chephren, 7 square Dunois, Paris, Cedex 13 75646, France. Illus. Circ: 2000. Microform: BHP. Reprint: PSC. *Aud.:* Ac, Sa.

The primary source for bibliographical information in classical studies, *L'Annee Philologique* covers virtually all books and periodicals published in the field. It indexes about 1,500 journal titles. Each entry offers a one- or two-sentence summary of the content. These are written variously in French, English, or German, depending upon which editorial office prepares them. *L'Annee Philologique* also analyzes the contents of Festschriften and conference proceedings. Book reviews are noted under the entry for the work reviewed; listings are repeated as new reviews appear for up to five years. The first half of each volume covers authors and texts. The remainder is devoted to such special topics as literary history, grammar, archaeology, ancient law, and history. Indexes provide access by collective titles for anonymous works and corpora, ancient names, modern names, place names, and authors. An excessive lag time in production is the major flaw of this otherwise excellent tool; volumes generally appear about two years after the year covered. A web version covering the years 1969-2000 is now available. Highly recommended for all academic libraries. (FWJ)

22. *Annual Bibliography of English Language and Literature.* Formerly (until 1924): *Bibliography of English Language and Literature.* [ISSN: 0066-3786] 1921. a. GBP 150. Maney Publishing, Hudson Rd, Leeds, LS9 7DL, United Kingdom; maney@maney.co.uk; http://www.maney.co.uk. Illus. CD-ROM: Chadwyck-Healey Incorporated. Microform: BHP. *Aud.:* Ac, Sa.

This significant international bibliography covers scholarship about the English language and literatures in English. In the printed version the contents are divided into the following topical sections: "Festschriften and Other Collections"; "Bibliography"; "Scholarly Method"; "Language, Literature, and the Computer"; "Newspapers and Other Periodicals"; "The English Language"; "Traditional Culture, Folklore, and Folklife"; and "English Literature." The literature section includes works from Britain, the United States, Canada, Australia, Africa, and Asia, and is subdivided by time period, then by genre and author. Searching in the literature section of the printed version can be cumbersome due to the size and scope of the section. There can be up to two years of lag time in the publication of the printed version. An online version is available via Chadwyck-Healey and is relatively easy to use. Recommended for libraries that support the study of English and American literature. (CM)

23. *Annual Bibliography of the History of the Printed Book and Library.* [ISSN: 0303-5964] 1973. a. EUR 280 per vol.; GBP 174 per vol.; USD 260 per vol. Ed(s): H D L Vervliet. Kluwer Academic Publishers, van Godewijckstraat 30, PO Box 17, Dordrecht, 3300 AA, Netherlands; services@wkap.nl; http://www.wkap.nl. Illus. *Aud.:* Ac, Sa.

This major international index contains information on the history of printing and publishing, papermaking, bookbinding, book illustration, type design and typefounding, bibliophily and book collecting, libraries, and scholars. It is produced under the auspices of the Committee on Rare Books and Manuscripts of the International Federation of Library Associations and Institutions (IFLA) but does not cover the medieval manuscript book. Arrangement is classified by broad subject areas with subsections by country and century. There is an author index and subject index by proper names. Published in the Netherlands, but subject terms and prefatory material are in English. Recommended for larger academic libraries and important where there is serious interest in book or library history.

24. *Anthropological Index Online.* 1995. every 6 wks. Ed(s): Clare Warrior, Max Carocci. Royal Anthropological Institute, 50 Fitzroy St., London, W1P 5HS, United Kingdom; rai@cix.compulink.co.uk; http://rai.anthropology.org.uk. *Aud.:* Ac.

This free online index dates back to 1957 and is the comprehensive index of several thousand publications produced over almost 50 years. In addition, data was modified to include a searchable language field. The search engine is flexible and sophisticated enough to do nearly anything one might want.

25. *Anthropological Literature: an index to periodical articles and essays.* [ISSN: 0190-3373] 1979. q. USD 225. Ed(s): Emily Moss. Harvard University, Tozzer Library, 21 Divinity Ave, Cambridge, MA 02138; http://www.harvard.edu/. Illus. Circ: 600. Online: Research Libraries Group. *Aud.:* Ac.

This author and subject index covers articles in serials and over 1,300 edited works from the nineteenth century to the present. Coverage is international in scope. Articles indexed are in the fields of archaeology, biological and physical anthropology, linguistics, cultural and social anthropology, and folklore. It indexes materials received at Harvard's Tozzer Library, Peabody Museum of Archaeology and Anthropology. It continues the published catalogs of the Peabody Museum of Archaeology and Ethnology. The current editor is Emily M. Moss.

26. *Applied Mechanics Reviews: an assessment of world literature in engineering sciences.* [ISSN: 0003-6900] 1948. m. Members, USD 138 print & online eds.; Non-members, USD 741 print & online eds. Ed(s): A W Kenneth Metzner. A S M E International, Three Park Ave, New York, NY 10016-5990; infocentral@asme.org; http://www.asme.org. Illus. Circ: 5000. Microform: PQC. *Bk. rev.:* 20-25, 200-600 words. *Aud.:* Ac, Sa.

Mechanical engineering and related topics are the primary topics, but all areas of engineering are covered. Abstracts are organized through a classification scheme that is presented on the back of each issue. Each issue includes reviews of books, software, and databases, as well as several state-of-the-art review articles on a special topic.

27. *Applied Science & Technology Index.* Supersedes in part: *Industrial Arts Index.* [ISSN: 0003-6986] 1958. m. except Jul., plus q. & a. cumulations. Ed(s): Joyce Howard. H.W. Wilson Co., 950 University Ave, Bronx, NY 10452-4224; custserv@hwwilson.com; http://www.hwwilson.com. CD-ROM: SilverPlatter Information, Incorporated; H.W. Wilson. *Aud.:* Ga, Ac, Sa.

Indexes close to 500 English-language periodicals in the fields of science and technology, intended for the general reader. Subject fields indexed include acoustics, space science, ceramics and glass chemistry, data processing, energy resources, food industry, meterology, physics, robotics, telecommunication, and transportation. This index also covers a number of engineering disciplines including aeronautic, chemical, civil, electrical, environmental, mechanical, and nuclear. The index is arranged by subject in an alphabetical format. Following the subject index are two additional indexes, one for book reviews and another for product reviews. The online version is available three different ways. *Applied Science & Technology Abstracts Full-Text* offers full-text from articles as far back as 1997, library holdings indicator, graphical content and frequent updates. *Applied Science & Technology Abstracts* presents the same indexing and abstracts offered in *Applied Science & Technology Full-Text* but without links to full-text articles. The same journals are covered. *Applied Science & Technology Abstracts* is updated weekly on WilsonWeb, monthly on WilsonDisc. *Applied Science & Technology Index* is available in print as well as online. The online version is updated monthly. See, too, the same publisher's *General Science Index.*

28. *Aqualine Abstracts.* Formerly (until 1985): *W R C Information;* Supersedes: *Water Pollution Abstracts.* [ISSN: 0263-5534] 1927. bi-m. USD 1265 combined subscription print & online eds. CSA, 7200 Wisconsin Ave, Ste 715, Bethesda, MD 20814; journals@csa.com; http://www.csa.com. Index, adv. Online: Questel Orbit Inc.; Telesystemes-Questel. Reprint: PSC. *Aud.:* Hs, Ga, Ac, Sa.

Aqualine Abstracts' focus is on the scientific, technical, and trade literature covering all aspects of water resources, and thus it is a major resource for environmental studies. Subjects covered include water resources and supplies management, water legislation, water quality, potable water distribution, wastewater collection, water treatment technologies, wastewater and sewage treatment, and ecological and environmental effects of water pollution. Articles indexed by the file come from more than 300 journals plus conference proceedings, scientific reports, books, and theses, and entries include a bibliographic citation, abstract, geographic index terms, and subject index terms (from the Aqualine Thesaurus, which is available for online searching). Produced by the joint cooperation of the British WRC (Water Research Centre) and Cambridge Scientific Abstracts, the file covers as far back as the late 1950s up to the present, and is updated monthly, with approximately 700 records added each month. (CML)

29. ***Aquatic Biology, Aquaculture & Fisheries Resources.*** [ISSN: 1083-883X] 1995. q. ZAR 27420. National Inquiry Services Centre (Pty) Ltd, 22 Somerset St, Grahamstown, 6139, South Africa; info@nisc.co.za; http://www.nisc.co.za. CD-ROM: National Information Services Corp. *Aud.:* Ac, Sa.

Available as two CDs or online via Biblioline, this index is a compilation of several sources. Included are the CAB Aquaculture subset, Fish Database from the Fish and Wildlife Reference Service, FishLit, and the Fish subset from MEDLINE. The records officially go back to 1971, but several of the sources are listed as far back as 1960.

30. ***Aquatic Sciences & Fisheries Abstracts. Part 1: Biological Sciences and Living Resources.*** Supersedes in part: *Aquatic Sciences and Fisheries Abstracts;* Which was formed by the merger of: *Aquatic Biology Abstracts; Current Bibliography for Aquatic Sciences and Fisheries.* [ISSN: 0140-5373] 1971. m. USD 1665 combined subscription print & online eds.; USD 2625 combined subscription print, online & CD-ROM eds. of part.1, 2 & 3. Ed(s): Richard Pepe. CSA, 7200 Wisconsin Ave, Ste 715, Bethesda, MD 20814; journals@csa.com; http://www.csa.com. Online: Pub.; CISTI. *Aud.:* Ac, Sa.

Aquatic Sciences and Fisheries Abstracts (ASFA) is a bibliographic database in the field of aquatic resources. Its comprehensive coverage includes subfiles users can subscribe to and search individually. These are: ASFA 1: Biological Sciences and Living Resources (1978-); ASFA 2: Ocean Technology, Policy and Non-Living Resources (1978-); ASFA 3: Aquatic Pollution and Environmental (1990-); ASFA Aquaculture Abstracts (1984-); and ASFA Marine Biotechnology Abstracts (1989-). Content is provided by an international network of information centers monitoring more than 5,000 serial publications, books, reports, conference proceedings, translations, and limited distribution literature. This abstract is a component of the Aquatic Sciences and Fisheries Information System (ASFIS), formed by four United Nations agency sponsors of ASFA and two international partners. Coverage includes aquaculture, aquatic organisms, aquatic pollution, conservation, environmental quality, fisheries, brackish and freshwater environments, limnology, marine biotechnology and environments, meteorology, oceanography, policy and legislation, and wildlife management.

31. ***Architectural Publications Index.*** Formerly (until 1995): *Architectural Periodicals Index;* Supersedes: *R I B A Library Bulletin.* [ISSN: 1359-740X] 1973. q. GBP 180; GBP 190 foreign. Ed(s): C Dembsky. R I B A Publications, Finsbury Mission, 39 Moreland St, London, EC1V 8BB, United Kingdom; http://www.ribac.co.uk/. Illus., adv. Circ: 800. Vol. ends: Dec. *Aud.:* Ac, Sa.

The *Architectural Publications Index* is the published version of the British Architectural Library's own periodical subject index. It is designed as a general, though selective, index to more than 400 of the world's architectural periodicals. Periodicals from 45 countries are currently indexed. The *API* also offers details of recently published books on architecture and related topics including architecture and allied arts (current and historical), constructional technology, interior design, environmental studies, landscape, planning, conservation, and urban history. Each quarterly issue includes a name index and the list of subject headings used in each issue. The annual cumulation also includes a topical and building name index. *API* is also available on CD-ROM as *Architectural Publications Index* on disc.

32. ***ARTbibliographies Current Titles (Email Edition).*** Formerly (until 2003): *ARTbibliographies Current Titles (Print Edition).* [ISSN: 0307-9961] 1972. bi-m. USD 190. CSA, 7200 Wisconsin Ave, Ste 715, Bethesda, MD 20814; journals@csa.com; http://www.csa.com. Illus. Sample. Online: Pub. *Aud.:* Ac, Sa.

International in coverage, this publication reproduces the tables of contents of approximately 250 journals in art and design. It also includes annuals, museum bulletins, and some irregular publications.

33. ***ARTbibliographies Modern: abstracts of the current literature of modern art, photography and design.*** Supersedes (in 1971): *L O M A Literature on Modern Art.* [ISSN: 0300-466X] 1969. s-a. USD 1180 combined subscription print & online eds. for N. America & European Countries; USD 590 elsewhere. CSA, 7200 Wisconsin Ave, Ste 715, Bethesda, MD 20814; journals@csa.com; http://www.csa.com. Sample. Online: Pub. *Aud.:* Ac, Sa.

An essential title for libraries serving art researchers and historians, *ARTbibliographies Modern (ABM)* provides abstracts of journal articles from more than 500 periodicals, books, essays, exhibition catalogs, dissertations, and exhibition reviews on all forms of modern and contemporary art, with approximately 12,000 to 13,000 new entries added each year. Entries date back to the late 1960s. Major areas of coverage include art history and theory, cartoons, computer art, conservation and restoration, costume, folk art, illustration, interior decoration, photography, sculpture, woodwork, and more. The file covers the years 1974 to the present, and as of May 2003 there were over 289,200 records in the database. The printed equivalent is *ARTbibliographies Modern*; a companion and supplementary product is *ARTbibliographies Current Titles.* (CML)

34. ***Arts & Humanities Citation Index.*** [ISSN: 0162-8445] 1976. 3x/yr. USD 6490. Institute for Scientific Information, 3501 Market St., Philadelphia, PA 19104; http://www.isinet.com. Illus., index. CD-ROM: Pub. *Aud.:* Ac, Sa.

This is an international multidisciplinary index that covers journals in the arts and humanities. It provides references to over 1,000 arts and humanities journals as well as individually selected items from major science and social science journals. It has a broad scope that includes the fields of archaeology, architecture, art, classics, dance, film, folklore, history, language, linguistics, literature, music, philosophy, radio, religion, television, and theater. The printed version of the index is divided into four parts (Source Index, Permuterm Subject Index, Citation Index, and Corporate Index), with the main entry listed in the Source Index. Searching in the print version, and to some extent in the online and CD-ROM versions as well, can be difficult, as it is easy to lose one's bearings when viewing lists of cited works. However, the coverage of the index is relatively thorough, and it will sometimes point the user to important articles that are difficult to find elsewhere. Recommended for large libraries that support the study of the humanities. (CM)

35. ***Astronomy and Astrophysics Abstracts.*** Supersedes: *Astronomischer Jahresbericht.* [ISSN: 0067-0022] 1969. irreg. Springer-Verlag, Journals, 175 Fifth Ave., New York, NY 10010-7703; http://www.springer-ny.com. Illus. Reprint: ISI. *Aud.:* Ac.

Astronomy and Astrophysics Abstracts is prepared under the auspices of the International Astronomical Union, and provides comprehensive documentation of the literature of the world in all aspects of astronomy, astrophysics, and related fields. More than 100 subject headings provide a quick method of surveying the world of literature on a particular topic. Effort is made to use author-provided abstracts where applicable and to use English as much as possible for titles and abstracts. Although popular articles are not abstracted, some popular publications, such as *Astronomy,* are indexed.

36. ***Aviation Tradescan: monthly index and abstracts.*** [ISSN: 0899-1928] 1984. m. USD 175. Ed(s): Catherine Heinzer. Aerospace Research Group, Inc., 11 Atlantic Ave, Nanuet, NY 10954-3302. Sample. Circ: 500 Paid. Vol. ends: No. 12. *Aud.:* Ac, Sa.

The Aerospace Research Group publishes this handy index to aviation periodicals and offers a reprint service for many of its titles. The monthly issues are cumulated every year and provide manageable access to its contents. The subscription price is very reasonable for an index of its size. A simple and workable subject index is provided in each issue, and because the size is not overwhelming, finding things is not a problem. This is a general-interest, consumer-oriented index for aviation, and it provides coverage that *International Aerospace Abstracts* does not have. It is intended, however, to be more practical than scholarly. Indexed magazines include *Aviation Week & Space Technology, Aerospace America* and *Business and Commercial Aviation.* (HSM)

37. *Bibliography and Index of Geology.* Formed by the merger of (1907-1969): *Bibliography of North American Geology;* (1933-1969): *Bibliography and Index of Geology Exclusive of North America.* [ISSN: 0098-2784] 1969. 13x/yr. USD 1295 domestic; USD 1370 foreign. Ed(s): Sharon Tahirkheli. American Geological Institute, 4220 King St, Alexandria, VA 22302-1502; kyost@agiweb.org; http://www.agiweb.org/pubs. Sample. Circ: 170. Vol. ends: Dec. CD-ROM: SilverPlatter Information, Incorporated. *Aud.:* Ga, Ac, Sa.

Produced by the American Geological Institute, this bibliography and its electronic counterpart, *GeoRef*, provide access to literature in the earth sciences from around the world. Coverage of materials about North America begins in 1785, while materials for the rest of the world are indexed beginning with 1933. Over two million records enable researchers to locate journal articles, books, maps, conference proceedings, North American theses and dissertations, and government and technical reports. *GeoRef* is available via the web, online, or on CD-ROM and is supported by several database vendors. In addition to earth science materials, publications in the fields of paleontology and paleobotany are indexed. A basic index for college and university libraries with collections in geological sciences and related fields. (FS)

38. *Bibliography and Index of Micropaleontology.* [ISSN: 0300-7227] 1971. m. Corporations, USD 600; Non-profit organizations, USD 125. Ed(s): Susan Carroll. American Museum of Natural History, Central Park West at 79th St, New York, NY 10024-5192; http://www.micropress.org. Illus., index. Circ: 150. Reprint: PQC. *Aud.:* Ac, Sa.

The *Bibliography and Index of Micropaleontology* is published monthly by Micropaleontology Press of the American Museum of Natural History. Effective January 2003, *BIM* is produced only online. This source lists the literature of micropaleontology since 1972. It is arranged by microfossil group and contains an annual author index. About 2,500 references are provided each year and organized into 12 classes, such as Algae, Foraminifera, Palynomorphs, and Radiolarea, plus Miscellaneous (which includes papers that cover more than one microfossil group). Entries record illustrations, sheet maps, tables, and number of references. This specialized bibliography and index is produced in cooperation with the American Geological Institute. Highly relevant to petroleum exploration. (KG)

39. *Bibliography of Asian Studies (Online Edition).* 1992. 4x/yr. Individuals, USD 75 members. Ed(s): Auna Shulman. Association for Asian Studies, Inc., 1021 E Huron St, Ann Arbor, MI 48104; bassub@aasianst.org; http://www.aasianst.org/bassub.htm. Circ: 3000. Microform: PQC. Reprint: PQC. *Aud.:* Ac, Sa.

This index, produced by the Association for Asian Studies at the University of Michigan, is the primary source for locating articles, edited book chapters, proceedings papers, and the like, published in Western languages about East, Southeast, and South Asia. Other indexes also cover this ground, but *BAS* is the only one dedicated specifically to Asian Studies. It no longer covers individual monographs, and does not cover Inner or Central Asia, Australasia, or the Pacific area. It does include articles about Asia from sources not primarily concerned with Asia, such as *The American Political Science Review*. Emphasis is on the humanities and social sciences. *BAS* is now available online only. Currency is problematic with this source. Much of its content is also available in other more widely held databases (such as *PAIS*) and disciplinary indexes, such as *EconLit, Historical Abstracts, Sociological Abstracts,* and, surprisingly, *America: History and Life*. These other databases are often more current, even for journals *BAS* has identified for priority, "fast-track" indexing.

40. *Bibliography of the History of Art.* Formed by the merger of (1975-1996): *International Repertory of the Literature of Art / Repertoire International de la Litterature de l'Art (RILA);* (19??-1996): *Repertoire d'Art et d'Archeologie (CD-ROM).* [ISSN: 1085-5092] 1996. q. USD 1500. Getty Trust Publications, PO Box 49659, Los Angeles, CA 90049-0659; http://www.getty.edu/publications. Online: Research Libraries Group; Telesystemes-Questel. *Aud.:* Ac, Sa.

This major indexing tool emerged as the successor of two important print indexes that ceased publication in 1989 and 1990 respectively, *Repertoire international de la litterature de l'art* (*RILA*) and *Repertoire d'art et d'archeologie* (*RAA*). Co-sponsored by a number of international art history institutes, *BHA* is now overseen by the Research Institute of the J. Paul Getty Trust. It covers European art from the classical periods of Rome and Greece and American art post its European "discovery." *BHA* indexes and abstracts over 4,300 periodicals, including books, conference proceedings, dissertations, exhibition and dealers catalogs, and museum bulletins related to the history of European art. It includes Asian art only in its relation to the impact on Western art. The print edition of *BHA* ceased in 1999 and is now available only on the Internet. Dates of coverage are 1973 through the present. Although its scope is limited to Western art, it is highly recommended for academic libraries that support programs and degrees in the history of art.

41. *BioEngineering Abstracts (Online Edition).* m. USD 765. Ed(s): Evelyn Beck. CSA, 7200 Wisconsin Ave, Ste 715, Bethesda, MD 20814; journals@csa.com; http://www.csa.com. Online: Pub. *Aud.:* Ac, Sa.

Given the tremendously increased interest in this field (predicted to be one of the greatest areas of growth in the world economy for the twenty-first century), *Bioengineering Abstracts* is a tool most academic and many public libraries will want to add to their collections. It provides access to the international research literature on biochemical and microbial technology as applied to bioengineering. The file's material comes from journals, conference proceeding, directories, and sources that include Engineering Information's engineering database. The file runs from 1993 to the present and is updated monthly (about 1,000 new records are added each month). (CML)

42. *Biological Abstracts: references, abstracts, and indexes to the world's life sciences research literature.* Formed by the 1926 merger of: *Abstracts of Bacteriology; Botanical Abstracts.* [ISSN: 0006-3169] 1926. s-m. USD 9850; USD 16985 combined subscription print & electronic media; USD 18185 combined subscription includes print, cumulative indexes & electronic media. BIOSIS, 2 Commerce Sq., 2001 Market St, Ste 700, Philadelphia, PA 19103-7095; http://www.biosis.org/. Illus., index. Vol. ends: Dec. CD-ROM: SilverPlatter Information, Incorporated. Online: Data-Star; DIMDI; STN International. *Aud.:* Ac, Sa.

Biological Abstracts, indexing over 4,000 serials annually, is the most comprehensive indexing and abstracting source in the biological sciences. Approximately 370,000 new records are added annually, encompassing biology, botany, biochemistry, biotechology, pre-clinical and experimental medicine, zoology, veterinary science, agriculture, and pharmacology. Major changes were made to this source in 1998. The numbering of records, which had previously started over every six months, was changed to starting over annually. This makes it possible to search the print source one year at a time rather than six months at a time and lessens confusion on the part of users. Another change was moving away from the generic and biosystematic indexes to the organism index. In earlier years, one looked up one's taxonomic name alphabetically in the generic or biosystematic index. Now, the user looks up the organism within the hierarchically arranged organism index in order to access information by taxonomic name. This has advantages and disadvantages. The disadvantage is that many users need assistance in figuring out where the organism fits into the hierarchy. The advantage is that, once the organism is found, similar organisms are near it in the index. New to the electronic version are CAS registry numbers, MeSH, and relational indexing. The print version is published every two weeks with a cumulative index for the first six months appearing mid-year and an annual index covering the whole year. The database is also available on Dialog and STN as *Biosis Previews*. *Biological Abstracts/RRM (Reports, Reviews, Meetings)* expands coverage beyond the journals indexed in *Biological Abstracts,* covering meetings, symposia, and conference proceedings, patents, reviews, reports, books, CD-ROMs, and other media. While expensive, this is an important source for academic institutions with biology programs, especially those with graduate students and an emphasis on research.

Biological Abstracts/RRM (Reports, Reviews, Meetings). See under *Biological Abstracts.*

43. *Biological & Agricultural Index.* Formerly: *Agricultural Index.* [ISSN: 0006-3177] 1964. m. except Aug., plus q. & a. cumulations. Ed(s): Syed Shah. H.W. Wilson Co., 950 University Ave, Bronx, NY 10452-4224; custserv@hwwilson.com; http://www.hwwilson.com. Vol. ends: Jul. CD-ROM: SilverPlatter Information, Incorporated; H.W. Wilson. *Aud.:* Hs, Ga, Ac.

Biological and Agricultural Index indexes 291 periodicals in the core literature of biology and agriculture. Subject areas covered include agricultural chemicals, agricultural economics, agricultural engineering, agriculture and agricultural research, animal sciences, biochemistry, biology, biotechnology, botany, cytology, ecology, entomology, environmental science, fishery sciences, food science, forestry, genetics, horticulture, immunology, marine biology, limnology, microbiology, nutrition, paleontology, physiology, plant pathology, soil science, veterinary medicine, weed sciences, wildlife management, and zoology. Periodicals indexed are selected by subscriber vote and are listed on the index web site. A controlled list of subject headings is used, with numerous cross-references provided. An index to book reviews is included as a separate section in each issue. Monthly issues cumulate quarterly, and an annual hardbound cumulation is issued. Like other indexes from H.W. Wilson, *Biological and Agricultural Index* is sold with subscription price based on the number of indexed titles received by the library, as determined by a checklist filled out by the subscribing library. Available in print and electronically. This source is easy to use, and since it shares the same format with the other H.W. Wilson products, is a favored source of many library patrons seeking biology information.

44. *Biology Digest.* Incorporates: *Environmental Quality Abstracts.* [ISSN: 0095-2958] 1974. m. Sep.-May. USD 149 in US & Canada; USD 159 elsewhere. Ed(s): Thomas H Hogan. Plexus Publishing, Inc., 143 Old Marlton Pike, Medford, NJ 08055; info@plexuspublishing.com; http://www.plexuspublishing.com. Illus., index, adv. Sample. Circ: 2000 Paid. Vol. ends: May. Microform: PQC. *Aud.:* Hs, Ga, Ac.

Available on paper and electronically via NewsBank, OCLC FirstSearch, and Cambridge Scientific Abstracts, *Biology Digest* is a biology abstracting and indexing source aimed primarily at high school and undergraduate students. The source is arranged into the following categories: Diversity of Life; Ecology and Environmental Science; Cellular Biology, Genetics and Evolution; The Human Body; Health and Wellness; and General Topics. Approximately 300 articles are indexed in each monthly issue. Each volume has a cumulative index that is included with the subscription. This source will be useful in academic and large high school and public libraries.

45. *Book Review Digest: an index to reviews of current books.* [ISSN: 0006-7326] 1905. m. except Feb. and July plus q. & a. cumulations. Ed(s): Barbara Jo Riviello. H.W. Wilson Co., 950 University Ave, Bronx, NY 10452-4224; custserv@hwwilson.com; http://www.hwwilson.com. CD-ROM: SilverPlatter Information, Incorporated; H.W. Wilson. Online: The Dialog Corporation; SilverPlatter Information, Incorporated. *Aud.:* Ems, Hs, Ga, Ac, Sa.

This standard reference tool indexes and provides excerpts of book reviews in nearly 100 general-interest magazines and core journals in the social sciences, humanities, and general sciences. Juvenile and adult fiction and nonfiction titles are covered, but government publications, textbooks, and technical books in the sciences and law are excluded. Each issue, arranged by author, is indexed by subject; the annual cumulation also includes a directory of publishers. While the online versions of this title provide easier access, the paper version of *BRD* is still a nearly indispensable source for most libraries. (CMJ)

46. *Book Review Index: indexes all reviews in over 600 periodicals.* [ISSN: 0524-0581] 1965. 3x/yr. USD 299. Ed(s): Beverly Baer. Gale Group, 27500 Drake Rd, Farmington Hills, MI 48331-3535; galeord@galegroup.com; http://www.galegroup.com. Illus., index. Circ: 3000. Vol. ends: Dec. *Aud.:* Ems, Hs, Ga, Ac, Sa.

Book Review Index (*BRI*) includes reviews of books, periodicals, reference works, audiobooks, e-books, and electronic editions of printed books. Covering over 500 publications, *BRI* provides access, via author and title, to juvenile and adult popular and academic titles. Index entries are coded by age level (children and young adult); reviews of periodicals are labeled as well. An absolute necessity in all but the smallest libraries. (CMJ)

47. *British Humanities Index.* [ISSN: 0007-0815] 1915. q. plus a. cumulation. USD 1220. CSA, 7200 Wisconsin Ave, Ste 715, Bethesda, MD 20814. Illus. *Aud.:* Ac, Sa.

British Humanities Index is an international resource for English-language research in such fields as literature, history, folklore, art, film, and music. It also provides broad coverage of many fields more typically associated with the social sciences: politics, economics, women's studies, and the environment, for example. Like its American counterpart, the *Readers' Guide to Periodical Literature*, *BHI* draws its content from daily newspapers, general-interest weekly magazines, and academic journals. Most of the 300-plus titles indexed or abstracted in *BHI* are U.K. publications. The print version of *BHI* is released in quarterly numbers and information is arranged by subject; the annual cumulation includes an author index. *BHI* is also available online. (SG)

48. *Business A S A P.* d. Gale Group, 27500 Drake Rd, Farmington Hills, MI 48331-3535; galeord@galegroup.com; http://www.galegroup.com. *Aud.:* Ga, Ac.

This popular InfoTrac product, now owned by Gale, remains a strong competitor to *ABI/Inform.* Title coverage is not quite as extensive or as deep in years, but patrons find the subject headings/subheadings and cross-references easy to use. There is a rich mix of popular business magazines, scholarly management journals, trade magazines, and newspapers. Approximately 60 percent of titles are available full-text. Highly recommended for public libraries. Academic libraries might find the *Business and Company ASAP* version more attractive because it integrates corporate directory listings with direct links to relevant articles. (BD)

Business Abstracts. See *Wilson Business Abstracts.*

Business and Company ASAP. See *Business ASAP.*

49. *Business and Industry (Beachwood).* 1994. d. Responsive Database Services, 23611 Chagrin Blvd Ste 320, Beachwood, OH 44122. *Aud.:* Ga, Ac, Sa.

This product is one in a suite of indexes produced by Responsive Database Services, which is now part of the Gale Group. Its strength is twofold. First, it covers 1,000-plus business journals and trade titles, industry newsletters, and regional, national, and international newspapers. Approximately 65 percent of the articles are available full-text. Second, the unique interface design and multiple index terms allow for precise searching. The addition of more descriptive wording to ambiguous article titles enhances the search results. More sophisticated search strategies can incorporate concept terms, SIC codes, document types, and geographic limitations. Ideal for marketing and industry analysis.

A related product, *TableBase,* specializes exclusively in tabular data on company, industry, and product/brand market share and rankings, production and consumption statistics, demographics, and import/export statistics. Figures embedded in articles that otherwise might be missed by researchers are pulled out and indexed independently.

The third product in the suite, *Business & Management Practices,* focuses more on management methods and strategies. It is not, however, as comprehensive as *ABI/Inform.* Searching the trio simultaneously across a common interface is one advantage to subscribing to all three. *Business & Industry* can stand alone, but is complemented by the presence of *TableBase.* Both are strongly recommended for large public, academic, and special libraries with a need for business intelligence. (BD)

Business & Management Practices. See *Business and Industry (Beachwood).*

50. *Business Education Index.* [ISSN: 0068-4414] 1940. a. USD 25 domestic; USD 28 foreign. Ed(s): Cheryl Noll. Delta Pi Epsilon Graduate Business Education Society, National Office, PO Box 4340, Little Rock, AR 72214. Illus. Circ: 11000. Microform: PQC. Reprint: PQC. *Aud.:* Ac.

Delta Pi Epsilon, the national honorary professional graduate society in business education, publishes this annual print index. The format is a compact, soft-bound 225 pages. Citations of articles (there are no abstracts) are noted from approximately 40 business education journals and related publications that appear during the calendar year. The index can take as long as eight months after year-end to appear. Access is provided by subject and author entries. Citations can be listed multiple times under as many as four subject headings. Of interest primarily to specialists in the field. Most researchers will gravitate toward electronic indexes, such as *ABI/Inform*, that cover most of the same journals. (BD)

Business Periodicals Index. See *Wilson Business Abstracts.*

51. *C A B Abstracts.* unknown. CABI Publishing North America, 44 Brattle St, 4th Fl, Cambridge, MA 02138; cabi-nao@cabi.org; http://www.cabi-publishing.org/. *Aud.:* Ac, Sa.

Records from about 9,000 journals, conference proceedings, books, technical reports, and selective patents are added each year to this index of agricultural literature. Approximately 21 percent of the citations are on plant science, 18 percent on animal science, and 9 percent on "pathogen, pests and parasite and weed management." Publications in more than 50 languages are included, and English original-text articles make up approximately 76 percent of the index. Almost half of the indexed publications are published in the United Kingdom and Western Europe, and 26 percent of the entries are from publications produced in the United States. This index covers back to 1973, and there are about "45 electronic and printed abstract and index titles" produced from this index. It is a valuable resource for agricultural and forestry information.

52. *CSA Animal Behavior Abstracts.* Formerly: *Behavioural Biology Abstracts, Section A: Animal Behaviour.* [ISSN: 0301-8695] 1972. q. 5 issues. USD 935 combined subscription print & online eds. Ed(s): R Hilton. CSA, 7200 Wisconsin Ave, Ste 715, Bethesda, MD 20814; journals@csa.com; http://www.csa.com. Online: Pub.; STN International. *Aud.:* Ga, Ac, Sa.

Animal Behavior Abstracts is an essential tool for behavioral scientists and those in related disciplines. Major areas of coverage include aggression, behavioral ecology, biological correlates, communication, dominance, evolution, genetics of behavior, motivation, parental-filial behavior, sexual and reproductive behavior, and theoretical models and overviews. The file covers the literature from 1982 to the present, and is updated monthly. (CML)

53. *CSA Political Science & Government: a guide to periodical literature.* Formerly (until vol. 32, no. 6, 2000): *A B C Pol Sci.* [ISSN: 1542-9040] 1969. bi-m. USD 1150 combined subscription print & annual index in print & on CD-ROM with annual book fund amount greater than $200,000; USD 900 combined subscription print & annual index in print & on CD-ROM with annual book fund amount greater than $50,000-200,000; USD 750 combined subscription print & annual index in print & on CD-ROM with annual book fund amount less than $50,000. Ed(s): Jill Blaemers. CSA, 7200 Wisconsin Ave, Ste 715, Bethesda, MD 20814; journals@csa.com; http://www.csa.com. Adv. Online: Pub. *Aud.:* Ac.

An international index to journal literature, newspapers, books, and web sites in political science and related fields, this file indexes about 1,000 journals with more than 250,000 records from 1975 to the present, with some links to full-text. Indexed titles include *Asian Outlook, Contemporary Poland, India Today*, and *Italian Communists.* Records are derived from IFI/Plenum's former *Political Science Abstracts* and ABC-CLIO's ABC POLY SCI Database. One of the premier databases for political science and government research. (CML)

54. *Canadian Business and Current Affairs Education.* Formerly (until 1998): *Canadian Education Index (CD-ROM Edition).* [ISSN: 1481-7586] 1996. bi-m. CND 2100. Ed(s): Gail Randall. Micromedia ProQuest, 20 Victoria St., Toronto, ON M5C 2N8, Canada; http://www.micromedia.ca. Illus. Sample. Vol. ends: No. 3. *Aud.:* Ac.

This online resource covers Canadian educational materials from a variety of sources, books, journals, reports, Canadian federal and provincial publications, curriculum guides, and graduate education theses, including both French and English sources. There are over 150 education journals indexed and over 30 are online full-text. The resource also incorporates the ONTERIS database, which is an index of research reports and curriculum documents from the province of Ontario from May 1997, and the *Canadian Education Directory,* a directory for educational institutions and organizations in Canada, including public and private schools, school boards, educational associations, and government departments related to education in Canada. Entries are arranged by author, corporate name, title, and subject, and cover most education-related fields, such as computers, language, mathematics, psychology, sports, and schools. This is a useful resource for teachers, school administrators, researchers, parents and community leaders involved in education, legislators and civil servants. The *CBCA Education* online index is appropriate for libraries with education collections.

55. *Canadian Business and Current Affairs Reference.* Supersedes in part (in 1997): *C B C A Fulltext;* Which was formerly (until 1997): *Canadian Business and Current Affairs - Fulltext (CD-ROM).* [ISSN: 1484-6489] 1992. s-m. CND 3100. Ed(s): Susan Baumann. Micromedia ProQuest, 20 Victoria St., Toronto, ON M5C 2N8, Canada; http://www.micromedia.ca. *Aud.:* Ga, Ac.

This online resource combines the indexing of over 700 Canadian newspapers, magazines, and journals in the fields of business and current affairs, with direct access to the full-text content of approximately 180 Canadian periodicals and other sources of current affairs information. *CBCA Reference* is the online equivalent of the *Canadian News Index, Canadian Business Index,* and *Canadian Magazine Index.* The database contains more than two million records and is updated monthly. The publisher states that 30,000 full-text and 200,000 bibliographic records are added every year. The full-text coverage varies per title. The earliest date that full-text online appears is 1993. Several French-language periodicals are included. Searchable fields include author, title, corporate identifier, publication year, magazine/newspaper title, full-text available, file subsets, subject descriptor, ISBN/ISSN, publication type, and others. *CBCA Reference* is ideal for libraries that require indexing coverage of Canadian public affairs, multidisciplinary scholarly journals, and popular magazines.

Canadian Index. See *Canadian Business and Current Affairs Education.*

56. *Canadian Literary Periodicals Index.* [ISSN: 1188-2646] 1992. a. CND 185. Reference Press, PO Box, Teeswater, ON N0G 2S0, Canada. *Aud.:* Hs, Ga, Ac.

The *Canadian Literary Periodicals Index* is a unique online index to a large collection of Canadian primary materials (poems, short stories, novels, plays, and literary essays) and to a wealth of secondary materials (critical articles, book reviews, interviews, and bibliographies) in the field of Canadian literature. More than 80 Canadian literary journals, selected general-interest magazines, and scholarly publications are reviewed for entries. The current database consists of some 55,000 citations with current materials added as received. Retrospective indexing continues for the years 1994 through 2001. Indexing is complete for 1992, 1993, 1997, and 1998. Case-bound volumes were published in 1992 and 1997, but these are now out of print. The *CLPI* is no longer published in print form. This online index is suitable for large public and academic libraries with Canadian literature collections.

57. *Canadian Music Periodical Index.* m. National Library of Canada, Marketing and Publishing Services, 395 Wellington St, Ottawa, ON K1A 0N4, Canada; mus@nlc-bnc.ca; http://www.nlc-bnc.ca/cmpi/. *Aud.:* Ga, Ac.

The *CMPI* is an index of Canadian music periodicals (journals, newsletters, magazines) from the late nineteenth century to the present day. It focuses on articles and news items covering all aspects of musical activity in Canada. It contains nearly 30,000 entries from 500 Canadian music publications, almost 200 of which are active and continue to be indexed. In 1999, the index expanded its focus to include articles about non-Canadian subjects published in Canadian music journals, newsletters, and magazines. Searches in *CMPI* can be made by name (individuals, associations, institutions, ensembles), author, title, periodical, geographic area, type of article, date, or subject heading. The index is a free online service provided by the National Library of Canada and will be of interest to all libraries with music collections.

58. *Canadian Newsstand: the nation's news source.* d. Micromedia ProQuest, 20 Victoria St., Toronto, ON M5C 2N8, Canada. *Aud.:* Ga, Ac, Sa.

This web resource contains the full texts of selected English-language Canadian newspapers and CBC/CTV broadcast transcripts. The coverage of titles varies and can be verified online before searching. The resource is a subset of the *CBCA Reference* resource (above in this section), specifically focusing on news sources. The database contains the full text of every article, column, and feature published in daily newspapers from all major Canadian cites. The following newspapers are indexed: *Charlottetown Guardian, Calgary Herald, Edmonton Journal, Financial Post, Halifax Daily News, Hamilton Spectator, Montreal Gazette, Ottawa Citizen, Saint-John's Evening Telegram, St. John's Telegram, Toronto Sun, Vancouver Province, Vancouver Sun,* and the *Victoria Times Colonist.* This online index will be of interest to public, academic, and special libraries requiring Canadian current affairs resources.

59. *Canadian Periodical Index.* Formerly: *Canadian Index to Periodicals and Documentary Films.* [ISSN: 0008-4719] 1938. m. USD 595. Gale Group, 27500 Drake Rd, Farmington Hills, MI 48331-3535; galeord@galegroup.com; http://www.galegroup.com. *Aud.:* Hs, Ga, Ac.

This is a bilingual index to more than 400 popular and academic Canadian periodicals. Coverage in the print and CD-ROM formats is from 1947 to the present. *CPI.Q* is the online full-text version of the index; coverage in the online version is from 1988 to the present and includes full-text for over 160 periodicals, including selected sections of *The Globe and Mail*, Canada?s national newspaper. Information from Gale reference books on Canadian science, biography, and geography are also included, as well as over 30 American titles focused on international issues and over 80 business journals. The resource provides Canadian and worldwide coverage of Canadian companies, history, biographies, and society. The search interface has a browsable subject guide, advanced search, keyword search, and relevancy search. This index is a basic requirement for any public, academic, or school library with an interest in Canadian information.

60. *Canadian Research Index, Microlog.* Former titles (until 1992): *Microlog: Canadian Research Index; Microlog Index; Publicat Index to Canadian Federal Publications; Urban Canada; Canadian Urban Sources; Profile Index to Canadian and Municipal Government Publications.* [ISSN: 1196-099X] 1979. m. CND 10. Ed(s): Brian Terry. Micromedia ProQuest, 20 Victoria St., Toronto, ON M5C 2N8, Canada; http://www.micromedia.ca. *Aud.:* Ac, Sa.

This publication is a unique index to Canadian government publications from the federal, provincial, and municipal levels, as well as from selected research centers, nonprofit organizations, and educational institutions. All depository publications of research value are included; nondepository publications issued by Canadian government agencies and departments and Statistic Canada monographs and serials are indexed. This 200,000-record index is available in both print and electronic formats. Full-text of the government publications is available as a separate microfiche publication called *Microlog* from the same publisher. This index will be of interest to academic libraries, government agencies, and corporate and special libraries that are fulfilling research needs in Canadian governmental affairs and economics.

61. *The Catholic Periodical and Literature Index.* Former titles: *Catholic Periodical Index; Guide to Catholic Literature.* [ISSN: 0008-8285] 1930. q. plus a. cumulation. USD 400 per vol. Ed(s): Kathleen Spaltro, Ph.D. Catholic Library Association, 100 North St, Ste 224, Pittsfield, MA 01201-5109; http://www.cathla.org. Illus. Sample. Circ: 1500. Vol. ends: Dec. Microform: PQC. *Aud.:* Ga, Ac, Sa.

In addition to covering nearly 150 Roman Catholic periodicals, this index also provides access to papal documents, ecclesiastical statements, essays, and books about the Catholic faith authored by Catholics or produced by Catholic publishers. Subject headings are based on Library of Congress subject headings, supplemented by the *ATLA Thesaurus* for Bible subject headings and by *CathI*-specific subject headings. This will enable users to move easily between this index and the American Theological Library Association's *Religious Index One: Periodicals* (*RIO*, below in this section). By focusing on the Catholic tradition, *CathI* provides unique access to titles overlooked in more general indexes. Public and academic libraries that have extensive Catholic collections will find this depth of indexing useful. Libraries with smaller Catholic holdings, however, may find this index redundant, since the major Catholic periodicals are covered in the general religious indexes and abstracts (e.g., *RIO* and *RelAb*). A CD-ROM version of *CathI* is produced by the American Theological Library Association. This version contains indexing from 1981 to the fall of the year prior to the May release of the CD-ROM. Information about this index—in both its print and CD-ROM versions—can be found online at www.cathla.org/publications.html. (LAP)

CBCA. *See Canadian Business and Current Affairs Education.*

62. *Ceramic Abstracts.* Supersedes in part: *Journal of the American Ceramic Society;* Which was formerly (until 1917): *Transactions of the American Ceramic Society.* [ISSN: 0095-9960] 1922. q. 5 issues. USD 450 print & online eds. (Individuals, USD 225 print & online eds.). Ed(s): Kathleen Hickman. CSA, 7200 Wisconsin Ave, Ste 715, Bethesda, MD 20814; journals@csa.com; http://www.csa.com. Adv. Circ: 1500. *Aud.:* Ga, Ac, Sa.

A subfile of CSA's *Engineered Materials Abstracts, Ceramics Abstracts* covers the worldwide literature on ceramics. It is the central source of information on structural ceramics, and is designed for libraries serving materials sciences researchers, engineers, and scientists. The database runs from 1986 to the present and is updated monthly. Variant titles include *CSA Ceramic Abstracts Online* and *World Ceramic Abstracts.* (CML)

63. *Chemical Abstracts.* [ISSN: 0009-2258] 1907. w. USD 26000 includes CA Index Guide. Chemical Abstracts Service (C A S), 2540 Olentangy River Rd., Columbus, OH 43210-0012; help@cas.com; http://www.cas.org. Illus., index. Vol. ends: Jun/Dec. Microform: IDC. Online: STN International. *Aud.:* Ac, Sa.

One of the largest abstracting services in the world and the most comprehensive one for chemists, this index abstracts about 755,000 documents per year. *CA* tracks approximately 9,000 titles every year and includes the chemical research reported in journal articles, patents, symposia, conference proceedings, dissertations, technical reports, and new books in chemistry. Although this information comes from over 150 countries in any of 50 languages and includes patents from 26 different countries, abstracts are always in English and augmented where necessary to include appropriate chemical indexing, including structure and sequence information. Two volumes are published each year. Abstracts are assigned numbers sequentially from the beginning of the six-month volume period and are preceded by the volume number. The abstracts are organized according to the primary subject of the document and placed into categories to allow easy subject browsing in the print version. There are 80 sections divided into five broad categories: (1) Biochemistry, Sections 1–20; (2) Organic Chemistry, Sections 21–34; (3) Macromolecular Chemistry, Sections 35–46; (4) Applied Chemistry and Chemical Engineering, Sections 47–64; and (5) Physical, Inorganic and Analytical Chemistry, Sections 65–80. Sections 1–34 are published in the odd-numbered issues and sections 35–80 are published the following week (even-numbered issues). Individual sections may also be purchased separately. Each issue contains abstracts and author, patent number, and keyword indexes. Volume indexes, published every six months, include a General Subject Index, Chemical Substance Index, Formula Index, Ring System Index, Patent Index, and Author Index. An Index Guide is also provided, which links the names for chemical substances and general subject terms to the controlled terminology of the volume indexes. Collective indexes covering five years of the abstracts are also available for purchase. In addition, the *CAS Source Index* (*CASSI*), which provides information on the titles covered and includes abbreviations, title changes, history, and translation information, is also available for an additional fee.

Chemical Abstracts is available in print, in microform, on CD-ROM, and as an online database in varying forms. Online client-server versions include SciFinder (for commercial firms) and SciFinder Scholar (for academic institutions), both of which include coverage from 1967 to the present and the ability to search by chemistry-specific terms and by chemical structure. *CA* is available via DIALOG and STN as well; STN has proprietary software for searching this database and an easy-to-use web version. STN is pay-as-you-go; SciFinder is usually purchased as an annual subscription. Some form of *CA* should be available to all advanced researchers and academics.

64. ***Chicano Database on CD-ROM.*** [ISSN: 1056-2516] 1991. s-a. USD 495. Ed(s): Lillian Castillo Speed. University of California at Berkeley, Ethnic Studies Library Publications Unit, 30 Stephens Hall, 2360, Berkeley, CA 94702-2360; http://www.eslibrary.berkeley.edu. Adv. Online: Research Libraries Group. *Aud.:* Hs, Ga, Ac.

This excellent electronic index offers extensive coverage of all types of materials about Mexican Americans (Chicanos). Topics covered include art, bilingual education, economics, folklore, history, health, religion, women's studies, politics, literature, and music. Since 1992, coverage has broadened to include Puerto Ricans, Cuban Americans, and Central American immigrants. The database, produced by the University of California–Berkeley's Ethnic Studies Library, includes more than 45,000 citations to books, journal articles, book chapters, anthologies, and book reviews. Sources listed may be written in English, Spanish, Portuguese, or Calo. Publications can be searched by author, title, subject, journal title, language, and global keyword. Online access is provided by RLG's Eureka platform. A CD-ROM version is also available from the UC Berkeley Ethnic Studies Library. (JRD)

65. ***Children's Book Review Index.*** [ISSN: 0147-5681] 1976. a. USD 160. Ed(s): Neil E Walker, Beverly Baer. Gale Group, 27500 Drake Rd, Farmington Hills, MI 48331-3535; galeord@gale.com; http://www.gale.com. Illus., index. *Aud.:* Ems, Hs, Ga, Ac, Sa.

This index boasts of being "a master key providing access to reviews of thousands of children's books and periodicals." It includes citations to all books, periodicals, audiobooks, and book-related electronic media that appeared in *Book Review Index* during the previous year and that were recommended by at least one reviewer. Although this is a handy tool for those libraries that can afford it, its derivation from the parent *Book Review Index* means that only large public libraries or those with specializations in children's literature need to regard this title as a necessity. (CMJ)

66. ***Children's Literature Abstracts.*** [ISSN: 0306-2015] 1973. q. USD 32; USD 33 in Canada & Mexico; USD 35 elsewhere. Ed(s): Gillian Adams. International Federation of Library Associations, Children's Libraries Section, 5906 Fairlane Dr, Austin, TX 78757-4417; clabs@bga.com; http://www.nlc-bnc.ca/ifla/. Illus. Circ: 500. *Aud.:* Ac, Sa.

Children's Literature Abstracts, published by the Children's Libraries Section of the International Federation of Library Associations, is an excellent source of abstracts from a wealth of journals, books, and pamphlets. This is a quarterly publication with two supplements plus a yearly index. The quarterly issues give citations, abstracts, and annotations for approximately 400 articles from Australian, British, Canadian, U.S., and other international journals. The two supplements, summer and winter, abstract books and pamphlets. The yearly index issue contains an alphabetical list of authors, illustrators, subjects, and titles. Entries for articles, books, and pamphlets are arranged under 18 subject headings, e.g., authors and illustrators; awards, prizes and organizations; censorship, stereotyping and canon; critics and analytical approaches, and so on. A must for academic libraries supporting children's literature programs.

67. ***Children's Magazine Guide: subject index to children's magazines and web sites.*** Formerly: *Subject Index to Children's Magazines.* [ISSN: 0743-9873] 1948. 9x/yr. USD 69.95 domestic; USD 75 foreign. Greenwood Publishing Group Inc., 88 Post Rd W, PO Box 5007, Westport, CT 06881; http://www.greenwood.com. Illus. Sample. Circ: 13000. Vol. ends: Apr/May. *Aud.:* Ems, Sa.

Children's Magazine Guide indexes 53 children's magazines and 20 web sites per issue by subject. The entries are arranged alphabetically by subject heading. Bibliographic information is given for each magazine and web site. Appropriate cross-references that may include magazine titles and related web sites, URLs, and annotations are included with the bibliographic information. New and ceased magazine titles are included in the "Announcements" section, plus information on upcoming workshops and conferences. *CMG* is a valuable and necessary tool for curricular support in elementary and junior high school libraries as well as public library children's rooms.

68. ***Christian Periodical Index: an index to subjects, authors and book reviews.*** [ISSN: 0069-3871] 1959. 3x/yr. USD 105. Ed(s): Douglas J Butler. Association of Christian Librarians Inc., PO Box 4, Cedarville, OH 45314; http://www.acl.org. Illus. Circ: 450. *Aud.:* Ac, Sa.

There is a heavy emphasis on evangelical Christian periodicals in this index of more than 130 titles. Titles are chosen for their value to students training for the Protestant Christian ministry. Arrangement is an author-subject index with a separate section for book reviews. The electronic web version covers most titles from 1982 to the present and is updated quarterly. The CD-ROM version is updated annually and covers most titles from 1979 to the present. The index is extremely limited in both scope and content, but some libraries will find it useful because some titles are covered here that are not covered elsewhere.

CIP.Q. See under *Canadian Periodical Index.*

CLPI. See *Canadian Literary Periodicals Index.*

69. ***Communication Abstracts: an international information service.*** [ISSN: 0162-2811] 1978. bi-m. GBP 712 in Europe, Middle East, Africa & Australasia. Ed(s): Thomas F Gordon. Sage Publications, Inc., 2455 Teller Rd, Thousand Oaks, CA 91320; info@sagepub.com; http://www.sagepub.com. Illus., adv. Circ: 1200. *Aud.:* Ac, Sa.

An important file covering the recent literature in communications-related publications from around the world. It provides substantive abstracts to journal articles, reports, and books. Contents include an author index, subject index, and a "Briefly Noted" section. Coverage spans all areas of communication, excluding general film-related topics, from advertising and marketing to radio, speech, and television. A source list is contained in the October issue of each volume. (NFC)

70. ***Computer & Control Abstracts.*** [ISSN: 0036-8113] 1966. m. GBP 1410; USD 2400. INSPEC, I.E.E., Michael Faraday House, Six Hills Way, Stevenage, SG1 2AY, United Kingdom; inspec@iee.org.uk; http://www.iee.org.uk. Illus., adv. Online: CEDOCAR; CISTI; Data-Star; The Dialog Corporation; F I Z Technik; Questel Orbit Inc.; STN International; SilverPlatter Information, Incorporated. *Aud.:* Ac, Sa.

Contains short summaries of papers published in the computer and control arena, including all aspects of computer installations, applications, hardware, peripherals, software, robotics, control engineering, systems theory, and artificial intelligence. It provides about 72,000 items in 12 monthly issues. Each issue has subject, author, conference, and book indexes. This index is the most comprehensive one published today in the area of computer science and robotics. Available in many electronic versions.

71. ***Computer and Information Systems Abstracts Journal.*** Former titles: *Computer and Information Systems; Information Processing Journal.* [ISSN: 0191-9776] 1962. m. except Dec. USD 1750 combined subscription print & online eds. Ed(s): Evelyn Beck. CSA, 7200 Wisconsin Ave, Ste 715, Bethesda, MD 20814; journals@csa.com; http://www.csa.com. Illus., adv. Online: Pub.; STN International. *Aud.:* Ac.

An abstracting service with citations and annotations arranged in broad categories. Sections are broken down into the topics of civil, mining, mechanical, electrical, and general engineering. Each issue includes an author and subject index, and an Internet edition is also available to subscribers.

72. *Computer Literature Index.* Formerly (until 1979): *Quarterly Bibliography of Computers and Data Processing.* [ISSN: 0270-4846] 1971. q. plus a. cumulation. USD 245. EBSCO Publishing, 10 Estes St, PO Box 682, Ipswich, MA 01938-0682; ep@epnet.com; http://www.epnet.com. Illus. Vol. ends: No. 4. *Aud.:* Ga, Ac, Sa.

This is an annotated bibliography of books, articles, reports, and reference services concerning computers and computer science. Cumulated annually, the bibliography indexes over 300 publications and is arranged by author, subject, and publisher. Citations are classified under 300 subject headings, such as software development, expert systems, job markets, database systems, object-oriented programming, and computer operations management.

73. *Computing Reviews.* [ISSN: 0010-4884] 1960. m. USD 40 student members (Members, USD 45; Non-members, USD 190). Ed(s): Neal S. Coulter. Association for Computing Machinery, Inc., One Astor Plaza, 1515 Broadway, 17th Fl, New York, NY 10036-5701; sigs@acm.org; http://www.acm.org. Illus., adv. Sample. Refereed. Circ: 8500. Vol. ends: Dec. Microform: WWS; NRP. Online: Pub.; The Dialog Corporation; EBSCO Publishing. *Aud.:* Ac, Sa.

The "review journal of the Association for Computing Machinery," this title reviews computer-related resources "for persons in mathematics, engineering, the natural and social sciences, the humanities, and other fields with critical information about current publications in any area of the computing sciences." Citations are generally arranged according to the ACM Computing Classification System, and each issue also includes an "Author Index," "Books and Proceedings," and "Nonbook Literature." Particularly useful for busy professionals and scholars, providing valuable reviews across the computing science field.

74. *Contemporary Women's Issues.* 1997. w. Gale Group, 27500 Drake Rd, Farmington Hills, MI 48331-3535; http://www.galegroup.com. *Aud.:* Hs, Ga, Ac.

CWI, now published by Gale, provides indexing, abstracts, and very substantial full-text coverage of the wide range of issues and events shaping the lives of women. Coverage begins with 1992 and is multidisciplinary and international. The database contains more than 2,000 unique sources, and over 10,000 new records are added each year. *CWI* is valuable for access to "gray literature?? and the alternative press as well as to mainstream popular and scholarly periodicals. The web version is updated weekly; the CD-ROM version quarterly. Recommended for academic and public library patrons investigating family, reproductive or general health, sexuality, domestic violence, and social, political, and economic issues relating to gender.

75. *Criminal Justice Abstracts.* Former titles: *Abstracts on Crime and Juvenile Delinquency; Crime and Delinquency Literature;* Formed by the merger of: *Information Review on Crime and Delinquency; Selected Highlights of Crime and Delinquency.* [ISSN: 0146-9177] 1968. q. GBP 461 in Europe, Middle East, Africa & Australasia. Ed(s): Judith Anne Ryder. Sage Publications, Inc., 2455 Teller Rd, Thousand Oaks, CA 91320; info@sagepub.com; http://www.sagepub.com. Illus., index, adv. Sample. Circ: 1000. Vol. ends: Dec. CD-ROM: SilverPlatter Information, Incorporated. Microform: WSH; PMC; PQC. Online: SilverPlatter Information, Incorporated. Reprint: WSH. *Aud.:* Ga, Ac, Sa.

Sage Publications began publishing *Criminal Justice Abstracts* with the December 2000 issue. Willow Tree Press published *CJA* from 1983 through September 2000 and the National Council on Crime and Delinquency published it from 1968 to 1983. The publication continues to be produced in cooperation with the Criminal Justice Collection of Rutgers University Libraries. Sage has maintained the NCCD basic format and quality of this unique source of in-depth abstracts of current criminal justice literature. The often-lengthy abstracts describe each document's major findings and theoretical and practical implications. Entries are arranged in broad subject groupings, including "Crime, the Offender, and the Victim," "Juvenile Justice and Delinquency," "Police," "Courts and the Legal Process," "Adult Corrections," and "Crime Prevention and Control Strategies." A two-page "Quarterly Highlights" section at the beginning of each issue calls attention to abstracts of special interest within each subject section. A detailed subject and geographic index, and an author index are provided at the back of each issue, with annual cumulative indexes and a list of journals abstracted in the fourth issue. This publication provides comprehensive coverage of all major journals in criminology and selective coverage of journals in related disciplines, as well as extensive coverage of books, dissertations, and reports from worldwide sources. More than 1,500 records are added each year. Although comprehensive coverage of all topics related to criminal justice may require the use of additional resources, this selective abstracting publication is excellent as a single source that covers a variety of types of publications.

76. *Criminal Justice Periodical Index.* [ISSN: 0145-5818] 1975. 3x/yr. U M I, 300 N Zeeb Rd, Ann Arbor, MI 48106; http://www.umi.com. Illus., index. Sample. *Aud.:* Ga, Ac, Sa.

The *Criminal Justice Periodical Index,* formerly published by UMI, is no longer published in paper format. Beginning in June 1999, Bell & Howell Information and Learning began producing only the electronic database. Their ProQuest interface provides indexing from 1981 with abstracts from 1999. Full text and/or images for many titles from 1988 make this basic index for criminal justice periodicals a very useful resource. *CJPI* should be considered by any library where there is an interest in criminology, criminal law, corrections, law enforcement, juvenile justice, drug abuse, victimization studies, and related areas, if needs are not satisfied by less specialized indexes or databases. *CJPI* provides convenient bibliographic access to a good assortment of 190 journals and newsletters (mostly American, with a few British and Canadian titles) covering the broad spectrum of criminal justice. The database provides full-text and full-image access to the articles in approximately 50 of those publications that are frequently consulted by criminal justice researchers. Although *Criminal Justice Abstracts* provides better single-source bibliographic coverage of the literature with abstracts, *CJPI*'s coverage of the basic journals will be appreciated by the unsophisticated user, and the full-text articles provided by ProQuest will be appreciated by all users. Therefore, *CJPI* may be desirable even where other criminal justice bibliographic resources are available. Libraries that lack an extensive criminal justice periodicals collection will find the electronic full text for many of the publications to be very useful. The database is available via the publisher's ProQuest interface.

77. *Cumulative Index to Nursing & Allied Health Literature.* Incorporates: *Nursing and Allied Health Index;* Which was formerly (1956-1976): *Nursing Literature Index;* (until 1977): *Cumulative Index to Nursing Literature;* Incorporates: *C I N A H L'S List of Subject Headings;* Which was formerly (until 1977): *Cumulative Index to Nursing Literature, Nursing Subject Headings.* [ISSN: 0146-5554] 1961. q. USD 365. Ed(s): Sarah Marcarian. C I N A H L Information Systems, 1509 Wilson Terr, Glendale, CA 91209-0871; cinahl@cinahl.com; http://www.cinahl.com/. Illus., adv. Sample. Circ: 2500. CD-ROM: SilverPlatter Information, Incorporated. Microform: PQC. Online: Data-Star; EBSCO Publishing. Reprint: PQC. *Aud.:* Ga, Ac, Sa.

Cumulative Index to Nursing and Allied Health Literature indexes more than 800 English-language nursing and allied health-profession serial titles, as well as selected medical, hospital administration, and behavioral sciences titles. It also includes selected foreign-language titles. The online database retrospective to 1982 contains more than 250,000 citations. In addition to traditional nursing and allied health sources, *CINAHL* includes such topics as alternative therapies, health informatics, biomedical library resources, case management, medical equipment/supplies, consumer health, mental health, evidence-based practice, and pharmacology. (MMC)

78. *Current Advances in Plant Science.* [ISSN: 0306-4484] 1972. m. EUR 2200 (Qualified personnel, EUR 131). Elsevier BV, Sara Burgerhartstraat 25, Amsterdam, 1055 KV, Netherlands; nlinfo-f@elsevier.nl; http://www.elsevier.nl. Illus., adv. Circ: 1200. Vol. ends: No. 33. Microform: PQC. *Aud.:* Ac, Sa.

Current Advances in Plant Science is a current-awareness source covering approximately 1,800 journals, which provides a "subject categorized listing of titles, authors, bibliographic details and authors' addresses." Categories include: Molecular biology; Photosynthesis; Enzymes; Metabolism; Secondary products; Cell biology; Tissue culture; Water and nutrients; Stress physiology; Anatomy and morphology; Vegetative development; Reproductive development; Growth regulators; Photomorphogenesis and photoperiodism; Biotechnology; Crop physiology; Agronomy and horticulture; Tree growth and forest management; Crop protection; Plant pathology and symbioses; Breeding; Ecology; Taxonomy, systematics and evolutionary studies; Flora reports and plant geography; and Plant and medicine. An excellent source of current-awareness materials, although of limited usefulness as an index. A sample issue in pdf format is available online at the index web site. This source will prove useful to botanists, agricultural and environmental scientists, and ecologists.

79. ***Current Bibliography on African Affairs.*** [ISSN: 0011-3255] 1968. q. USD 257. Ed(s): Roger W Moeller, Roger Moeller. Baywood Publishing Co., Inc., 26 Austin Ave, Amityville, NY 11701; info@baywood.com; http://www.baywood.com. Illus., adv. Sample. Vol. ends: No. 4. *Bk. rev.:* 1, 1,000-1,500 words. *Aud.:* Ga, Ac, Sa.

This is an excellent general index to African periodicals, covering all major African titles as well as selected titles with African coverage from other countries. Abstracts cover not only periodicals, but also related matter, from books and dissertations to official documents and reports. Since volume 30 the format and content has changed; abstracts appear under broad subject headings, with topical, geographical, and author indexes in each issue as well as a cumulative index at the end of a volume. The previous strong focus on political issues and development of emerging economies has been expanded to include more coverage of archaeology, anthropology, natural history, and medical and environmental issues. Bibliographic essays as well as commentary and other features round out the issues. Suitable for all types of libraries with an interest in Africa.

80. ***Current Contents: Agriculture, Biology & Environmental Sciences.*** Formerly: *C C A F V (Current Contents, Agricultural, Food and Veterinary Sciences).* [ISSN: 0090-0508] 1970. w. USD 730. Institute for Scientific Information, 3501 Market St., Philadelphia, PA 19104; http://www.isinet.com. Index. CD-ROM: Pub. *Aud.:* Ac, Sa.

Current Contents: Agriculture, Biology and Environmental Sciences and *Current Contents: Life Sciences* [ISSN: 0011-3409] provide access to the tables of contents of journals and books in the biological sciences. *Agriculture, Biology and Environmental Sciences* includes about 1,040 journals and books in such fields as general biology, biotechnology, entomology, ecology, and plant sciences. *Life Sciences* includes about 1,370 titles in the fields of biochemistry, biophysics, immunology, cellular and developmental biology, neuroscience, microbiology, and physiology. Indexes include author and title keyword as well as journal name and are cumulated three times annually. Publisher and author address directories are also provided. Both titles are available in several different formats in addition to print, all of which are updated at least weekly. *Current Contents Desktop* is available on diskette or via ftp. *Current Contents Connect* is available via the Internet or Intranet. The Internet version is updated daily, while the Intranet version is updated weekly. *Current Contents on CD-ROM* is a rolling one-year file. These are excellent sources for researchers and students who want to keep current with publications in their areas of interest.

Current Contents/Life Sciences. See under *Current Contents: Agriculture, Biology & Environmental Sciences.*

81. ***Current Contents: Physical, Chemical & Earth Sciences.*** Formerly: *Current Contents, Physical and Chemical Sciences;* Which was formed by the merger of: *Current Contents, Physical Sciences; Current Contents, Chemical Sciences.* [ISSN: 0163-2574] 1961. w. USD 730. Institute for Scientific Information, 3501 Market St., Philadelphia, PA 19104; http://www.isinet.com. Illus., index. Sample. Vol. ends: Dec. CD-ROM: Pub. *Aud.:* Ac, Sa.

Provides access to the tables of contents from over 1,050 journals and books in the physical, chemical, and earth sciences. Disciplines covered include mathematics, applied physics, condensed matter, organic chemistry, polymer science, physics, space science, and analytical sciences. Weekly features include complete bibliographic data, title word index, author index and addresses, and current book contents. A publishers' address directory is included.

82. ***Current Law Index: multiple access to legal periodicals in print.*** [ISSN: 0196-1780] 1980. m. USD 725. Ed(s): Cheryl Ann Toliver. Gale Group, 27500 Drake Rd, Farmington Hills, MI 48331-3535; galeord@gale.com; http://www.gale.com. Illus. Online: The Dialog Corporation; West Group. *Aud.:* Ac, Sa.

This American Association of Law Libraries–sponsored index is substantially more extensive than its principal competitor, the *Index to Legal Periodicals & Books* (see below in this section). However, *ILP* indexing began in 1908, whereas *CLI* coverage is from 1980 on. Most periodicals indexed are in English, the exception being those in French from Canada, and coverage is from the United States, Canada, the United Kingdom, Ireland, Australia, and New Zealand. Inclusion is based on the material's "value" and not on length. *CLI* can be accessed by subject, author/title, by a Table of Cases, and by a Table of Statutes. (DD)

Current Mathematical Publications. See *MathSciNet.*

83. ***Current Physics Index.*** [ISSN: 0098-9819] 1975. q. USD 1780 domestic; USD 1815 in Canada, Mexico, Central and South America & Caribbean; USD 1865 in Europe, Asia, Middle East, Africa & Oceania. American Institute of Physics, 2 Huntington Quadrangle, Ste 1NO1, Melville, NY 11747-4502; http://www.aip.org/journal_catalog/. Illus., index. Microform: Pub. *Aud.:* Ac, Sa.

Primarily a current-awareness service for physics researchers, each quarterly issue of this title contains approximately 9,000 abstracts of recent research papers in all branches of the field of physics. Entries are organized by the Physics and Astronomy Classification Scheme, a physicists' version of the Dewey Decimal System. Effective use of the index requires the reader to become familiar with this classification scheme. *Current Physics Index* uses the author abstracts published with each journal article—no new abstracts are written for this publication. This index covers only the journals affiliated with the American Institute of Physics. While these journals are the most significant in the field and include approximately 90 percent of American research and 50 percent of Russian research, it does not cover any articles published in commercial physics journals. Although there are annual cumulative indexes, this index is best used for current-awareness purposes. *Physics Abstracts* (see below in this section) is the index to use for a comprehensive search because it indexes all journals relating to physics. (DAT)

Current Technology Index. See *Abstracts in New Technologies and Engineering.*

84. ***Dairy Science Abstracts.*** [ISSN: 0011-5681] 1939. m. GBP 745. Ed(s): E J Mann. CABI Publishing,Wallingford, OC10 8DE, United Kingdom; orders@cabi.org; http://www.cabi.org. Illus., index, adv. Circ: 1500. Online: The Dialog Corporation; DIMDI; STN International. *Aud.:* Ac, Sa.

This CAB (Commonwealth Agricultural Bureau) abstracting journal adds approximately 8,000 entries each year on the subject of "milk production, secretion, processing, and milk products." The major subject divisions are: Husbandry and Milk Production, Milk and Milk Products, Economics and Statistics, Legislation and Standards, Lactogenic Hormones, Mammary Glands and Lactation, Human Nutrition, Human Milk, Breast Feeding, Breast Cancer, Immunology and Immunoglobulins, Dairy Microorganisms, and Dairy Research and Education.

85. ***Design and Applied Arts Index.*** [ISSN: 1353-1298] q. Ed(s): Chris Mees. CSA, 7200 Wisconsin Ave, Ste 715, Bethesda, MD 20814; journals@csa.com; http://www.csa.com. Illus., adv. *Bk. rev.:* Various number and length. *Aud.:* Ac, Sa.

Design and Applied Arts Index is arranged in one alphabetical sequence by subject, author, and illustration. Some citations are briefly annotated; between 10,000 and 15,000 citations are added annually. *Design and Applied Arts Index* is a useful contribution to the increasing amount of material on craft and design.

86. ***Dissertation Abstracts International. Section C: Worldwide.*** Formerly: *Dissertation Abstracts International. Section C: European Abstracts.* [ISSN: 1042-7279] 1966. q. U M I, 300 N Zeeb Rd, Ann Arbor, MI 48106; http://www.umi.com. Illus. CD-ROM: ProQuest Information & Learning. Online: Data-Star; STN International. *Aud.:* Ac.

This is an index to dissertations and master's theses in the humanities, sciences, and social sciences (over 90 percent of the dissertations accepted in the U.S. each year). The file is available on the web, in CD-ROM, and in print, and coverage is from 1861 to the present. Dissertations published since July 1980 have author-written abstracts, master's theses published since 1988 have 150-word abstracts. Citations are available for dissertations from 1861 to the present, with over 55,000 citations added to the file each year. *ProQuest Digital Dissertations* on the web lets researchers "preview" the first 24 pages of thousands of documents online, and also gives researchers free access to digital copies of dissertations from their own institutions. (CML)

87. *Diversity Your World.* 2000. m. SoftLine Information, 20 Summer St, Stamford, CT 06901. *Aud.:* Hs, Ga, Ac, Sa.

Diversity Your World is a "full-text, general reference database of 120+ publications that reflect a wide variety of diversity issues, including ethnicity, religion, gender, physical and mental disabilities and more." Designed specifically for secondary schools and small libraries, this database has an excellent representation of ethnic periodicals from prominent newsletters, journals, newspapers, and magazines. Highly recommended for high school, public, and small academic libraries.

88. *E R I C on CD-ROM.* [ISSN: 1069-9279] q. USD 125 includes online. National Information Services Corp., Ste 6, Wyman Towers, 3100 St Paul St, Baltimore, MD 21218; sales@nisc.com; http://www.nisc.com. *Aud.:* Ems, Hs, Ga, Ac, Sa.

Established in 1966, the Educational Resources Information Center (*ERIC*) is a national information system from the U.S. Department of Education's Office of Educational Research and Improvement and is administered by the National Library of Education. It is designed to supply ready access to an extensive body of education-related literature. It provides access to information from journals and educational documents (formerly the contents of *Current Index of Journals in Education* (*CIJE*) and *Resources in Education Index*). *ERIC* provides full text of more than 2,200 digests along with references for additional information and citations and abstracts from over 1,000 educational and education-related journals, to research reports, curriculum and teaching guides, conference papers, and books.

The *ERIC* database is offered by several vendors including EBSCOhost and FirstSearch, and citations can also be searched for free at: http://askeric.org/Eric/adv_search.shtml.

EBSCO Publishing. See Aggregators/A&I-Based section in the front matter.

89. *EBSCOhost.* 1984. m. EBSCO Publishing, 10 Estes St, PO Box 682, Ipswich, MA 01938-0682; ep@epnet.com. *Aud.:* Ems, Hs, Ga, Ac, Sa.

EBSCO publishes and makes available a very large number of online resources across the disciplines, including: Academic Search products (Elite and Premier), Business Source products (Elite and Premier), Newspaper Source, MasterFILE titles (Elite, Premier, and Select), and much more. For a full listing of titles and their descriptions, please see their web site at http://www.epnet.com.

90. *Ecology Abstracts (Bethesda).* Formerly (until 1980): *Applied Ecology Abstracts.* [ISSN: 0143-3296] 1975. m. USD 1550 combined subscription print & online eds. Ed(s): Robert Hilton. CSA, 7200 Wisconsin Ave, Ste 715, Bethesda, MD 20814; journals@csa.com; http://www.csa.com. Adv. *Aud.:* Hs, Ga, Ac, Sa.

A core resource for environmental science research, *Ecology Abstracts* "focuses on how organisms of all kinds—microbes, plants, and animals—interact with their environments and with other organisms." The file indexes material on evolutionary biology, economics, and systems analysis related to ecosystems and the environment. A notable feature of the file is the information it contains on resource and ecosystems management, as well as information on the impact of climate, water resources, soil, and man. Environmental issues including depletion, erosion, and pollution are addressed. The file covers from 1982 to the present, and is updated monthly with approximately 1,300 new records. (CML)

91. *EconLit.* w. American Economic Association, 2014 Broadway, Ste 305, Nashville, TN 37203. *Aud.:* Ac.

This database from the American Economic Associations indexes over 600 international economics journals from 1969 to the present. Coverage includes every major topic, and most minor topics, in economics research. Citations for collective works, dissertations, and annotations of new books are also included. It corresponds to the *Index of Economics Articles,* and in part corresponds historically to the *Journal of Economic Literature* (articles are excluded) as well as the online version, *Economic Literature Index* . The premier index to economic literature. (GHC)

92. *Education Index.* [ISSN: 0013-1385] 1929. m. Sep.-Jun., plus q. & a. cumulation. Ed(s): Barbara Berry. H.W. Wilson Co., 950 University Ave, Bronx, NY 10452-4224; custserv@hwwilson.com; http://www.hwwilson.com. *Aud.:* Ac, Sa.

Education Index, available in print, online, and on CD-ROM, provides thorough indexing of about 527 education periodicals, using the subject-and-author approach that many users will know from other Wilson Company indexes. Although *EI* indexes less than half as many journals as *Current Index to Journals in Education,* it does index about 87 periodicals that *CIJE* does not. This, along with its ease of use and the fact that it is relatively inexpensive, makes it a basic choice for academic libraries. *Education Abstracts* is updated monthly on WilsonDisc. It covers the same material as the straight index, but it adds superior abstracts. Full-text is available for more than 500 journals. The service is updated weekly on WilsonWeb and updated monthly on WilsonDisc.

93. *Ekistic Index of Periodicals.* [ISSN: 0013-2934] 1968. s-a. USD 150. Ed(s): Panayotis C Psomopoulos. Athens Center of Ekistics, 24 Strategos Syndesmou, Athens, 106 73, Greece. Illus. Sample. *Aud.:* Ac, Sa.

Ekistics is a science dealing with human settlements and drawing on the research and experience of professionals in various fields (such as architecture, engineering, city planning, and sociology), and this index is a fine source of architectural materials. It selectively reviews 700 worldwide journals annually and regularly indexes 100 journals. The indexing is based on what will be of interest to readers—that is, architecture, city planning, urban renewal, and so forth. The computer-produced index lists articles by keyword, subject, and author and, much of the time, by country or region. This would be of primary value to large research libraries because the majority of indexed journals are foreign.

94. *Electrical & Electronics Abstracts.* [ISSN: 0036-8105] 1898. m. GBP 2120; USD 3605. INSPEC, I.E.E., Michael Faraday House, Six Hills Way, Stevenage, SG1 2AY, United Kingdom; inspec@iee.org.uk; http://www.iee.org.uk. Illus., index. Online: CEDOCAR; CISTI; Data-Star; The Dialog Corporation; F I Z Technik; Questel Orbit Inc.; STN International; SilverPlatter Information, Incorporated. *Aud.:* Ac, Sa.

Recent technical developments worldwide in all areas of electronics, radio, telecommunications, optoelectronics, and electrical power are represented here. It provides about 81,000 abstracts each year. Subject, author, conference, and book indexes are included. Cumulated indexes are published twice a year for convenient searching. *Section B* should always be purchased with *Section C: Computers & Control Abstracts,* because the subject areas will overlap tremendously. Can be accessed by a variety of online vendors.

95. *Engineering Index Monthly: abstracting and indexing services covering sources of the world's engineering literature.* Former titles: *Engineering Index Monthly and Author Index; Engineering Index.* [ISSN: 0742-1974] 1884. m. EUR 4862. Elsevier Engineering Information, Incorporated, One Castle Point Terr., Hoboken, NJ 07030-5996; eicustomersupport@elsevier.com; http://www.ei.org. Illus. CD-ROM: The Dialog Corporation. Microform: PMC. Online: CEDOCAR; CISTI; Data-Star; European Space Agency; Questel Orbit Inc.; STN International. *Aud.:* Ga, Ac, Sa.

Engineering Index is the major indexing and abstracting source for all areas of engineering, applied sciences, and related technical literature. The index covers over 5,000 international journals, conferences papers, and technical reports each year. Every aspect of engineering is covered, including aeronautics and astronautics, chemical, civil and construction, electrical and computer, industrial, mechanical, and nuclear engineering, and related disciplines. Most records include a concise abstract, produced by the author whenever available. The listing of publications included in the index is also published separately as *PIE—Publications Indexed for Engineering.* Likewise, the controlled vocabulary utilized in the electronic versions of the index is published separately, titled *EI Thesaurus.* It should be noted that the abstract numbers for entries in the monthly printed index differ from those in the annual volume. Cumulative multiyear indexes are also available. The electronic version of *Engineering Index,* containing data back to 1970, is titled *COMPENDEX (COMPuterized ENgineering InDEX)* and is available electronically from numerous sources. All engineering collections should be receiving this important and comprehensive title. (HSM)

96. *Environment Abstracts.* Incorporates (1985-1991): *Acid Rain Abstracts;* Formerly: *Environment Information Access.* [ISSN: 0093-3287] 1975. m. Ed(s): Larry Sheridan. Congressional Information Service, Inc., 4520 East West Hwy, Bethesda, MD 20814; cisinfo@lexis-nexis.com; http://www.cispubs.com. Illus., index. Vol. ends: Dec. Online: Data-Star; The Dialog Corporation; F I Z Technik; Questel Orbit Inc. *Aud.:* Ga, Ac, Sa.

Building on the abstracting and indexing of *Environment Abstracts, LexisNexis Environmental* is a comprehensive index to the environmental literature, including over 6,000 journals published worldwide, conference papers, news, codes and regulations, case law, agency activity, proceedings, and other significant environmental materials. The file covers air, noise, and water pollution; solid and toxic wastes; radiological contamination; toxicological effects; control technologies; resource management; population; endangered species; and climatic change. (JK)

97. *Ergonomics Abstracts.* [ISSN: 0046-2446] 1968. 2x/yr. GBP 1302. Ed(s): Christine Stapleton. Taylor & Francis Ltd, 11 New Fetter Ln, London, EC4P 4EE, United Kingdom; info@tandf.co.uk; http://www.tandf.co.uk/journals. Illus., index, adv. Sample. Online: Ingenta Select; JSTOR (Web-based Journal Archive); OCLC Online Computer Library Center, Inc.; RoweCom Information Quest. Reprint: PSC. *Bk. rev.:* 8, signed, length varies. *Aud.:* Ac, Sa.

The Ergonomics Information Analysis Centre at the University of Birmingham (U.K.) provides this international abstracting service for all areas of ergonomics and human factors. Nearly 6,000 abstracts per year are compiled using journals, books, reports, and conference proceedings from their collection. Full bibliographic details and a summary of the abstracted article are organized by a classification scheme and presented in a concise format. Each issue contains a book review section and an index arranged by application. A subscription to the print edition includes free access to the online edition. The online equivalent contains abstracts dating back to 1985, and is updated four times per year. Recommended for collections serving ergonomists, health and safety specialists, human factors engineers, systems designers, and industrial engineers. (ELS)

98. *Ethnic NewsWatch (Online): news, culture and history.* Formerly: *Ethnic NewsWatch (Print).* 1991. bi-m. ProQuest Information & Learning, 300 N Zeeb Rd., PO Box 1346, Ann Arbor, MI 48106-1346; info@proquest.com; http://www.umi.com. Illus. Vol. ends: Sep. *Aud.:* Hs, Ga, Ac, Sa.

Now published as a web-only product available exclusively through ProQuest, this full-text database includes articles from American ethnic publications. Ethnicities represented here are African American/Caribbean/African, Arab/Middle Eastern, Asian/Pacific Islander, European/Eastern European, Hispanic, Jewish, Multi-Ethnic, and Native People. This versatile file is useful for researchers in a wide variety of areas, including history, arts, business, and political science. Contains articles, editorials, interviews, and masthead information for all included publications. This is an excellent product for the serious researcher and the general reader interested in diversity and multiculturalism.

99. *Exceptional Child Education Resources.* Formerly (until May 1977): *Exceptional Child Education Abstracts.* [ISSN: 0160-4309] 1969. q. Members, USD 69; Non-members, USD 89; USD 26 newsstand/cover per issue. Ed(s): Kathleen McLane. Council for Exceptional Children, 1110 N. Glebe Rd., Arlington, VA 22201-5704; http://www.cec.sped.org/. Illus., adv. Circ: 1000 Paid. CD-ROM: SilverPlatter Information, Incorporated. *Aud.:* Ac, Sa.

ECER selectively indexes and abstracts material dealing with English-language references in the study of the exceptionalities in children (disabilities, giftedness, special education and related services, child abuse and neglect, special health problems, and current policies and issues). More than 200 journals are scanned regularly, and abstracts of books, dissertations, conference papers, government documents, and commercially available nonprint media resources (films, video, software) are included along with those of periodical articles. Each issue is indexed by author, title, and subject. Available online and on CD-ROM from SilverPlatter. This service is a must for academic libraries serving programs in special education.

100. *Exceptional Human Experience: studies of the psychic - spontaneous - imaginal.* Formerly (until 1990): *Parapsychology Abstracts International.* [ISSN: 1053-4768] 1983. s-a. USD 60 (Individuals, USD 30). Ed(s): Rhea A White. Exceptional Human Experience Network, 414 Rockledge Rd, New Bern, NC 28562; ehenwhite@coastalnet.com; http://www.ehe.org. Illus., index. Refereed. Circ: 350. Vol. ends: Dec. *Bk. rev.:* Book and film reviews. *Aud.:* Ga, Ac, Sa.

Exceptional Human Experience consists of case reports, articles, and abstracts of books, dissertations, and essays. The articles and abstracts focus on educating the public about exceptional human experiences (EHEs). These EHEs can be brought on through mystical or psychical experiences. This publication is in two parts. The first part contains articles on the study of EHEs and accounts of various types of EHEs. The second part has 300+ abstracts, including subject, title, and author indexes. Each issue averages 150 pages. An excellent resource for public, academic, and scholarly parapsychology collections. (CLC)

101. *Excerpta Medica. Abstract Journals.* [ISSN: 0921-822X] 1947. 12x/yr. EUR 53032 in Europe for the full set series; JPY, 7147500 Japan for the full set series; USD 59324 elsewhere for the full set series. Excerpta Medica Medical Communications BV, Rooseveltweg 15, Almere, 1314 SJ, Netherlands; http://www.excerptamedica.com. Illus. *Aud.:* Ac, Sa.

Excerpta Medica abstracts articles from more than 4,000 biomedical, pharmaceutical, and chemical journals, covering the most significant published papers in the field of biomedicine from 70 countries around the world. Every journal contains bibliographic references and abstracts summarizing original articles from primary research and clinical journals. There are 41 individual specialty abstract journals (sections) and two drug-related literature indexes.

Articles are indexed by subject and author and are summarized in an abstract journal. Consult the publisher's website for further details.

102. *F R A N C I S.* [ISSN: 1161-0395] 1991. s-a. FRF 5000. Institut de L'Information Scientifique et Technique, 2, Allee du Parc de Brabois, Vandoeuveles-Nancy, 54514, Spain; webmaster@inist.fr. *Aud.:* Ac.

FRANCIS is produced by the French Institut de l'Information Scientifique et Technique du Centre National de la Recherche Scientifique (INIST-CNRS) and the Getty Research Institute (GRI). *FRANCIS* indexes over 4,000 multilingual and multidisciplinary journals and includes citations from the humanities (67 percent), social sciences (30 percent), and economics (3 percent) from 1984 to the present. According to the publisher, *FRANCIS* is particularly strong in religion, the history of art, psychology, and literature. Coverage includes serials, journal articles, books, book chapters, conference papers, French dissertations, exhibition catalogs, legislation, teaching materials, and reports. Available through RLG, *FRANCIS* is updated monthly.

103. *Family & Society Studies Worldwide.* Former titles: *Family Studies Database; Family Resources;* Supersedes: *Inventory of Marriage and Family Literature;* Which was formerly: *International Bibliography of Research in Marriage and the Family.* q. USD 695. Ed(s): H Robert Cohen. National Information Services Corp., Ste 6, Wyman Towers, 3100 St Paul St, Baltimore, MD 21218. Adv. CD-ROM: Pub. Online: NISC. *Aud.:* Ga, Ac, Sa.

Family & Society Studies Worldwide is a comprehensive indexing and abstracting system for family and marriage literature. Indexing current literature from books, book chapters, journals, conference papers, government reports, web sites, and other sources relating to marriage and the family, it includes both popular and scholarly literature. Covering 1970 to the present, it has over 500,000 records. Abstracts have been added for new and older articles when available. Although many other indexes (for instance, *Psychological Abstracts* and *Sociological Abstracts*) include family literature, this database should also be considered for family studies programs, since it includes some unique citations. Most indexes exclude articles outside their focus, and because family studies are multidisciplinary, several indexes might otherwise need to be consulted. *Family & Society Studies Worldwide* is a convenient and relatively low-cost electronic database that covers all types of literature and would be useful in academic, clinic, and hospital libraries, as well as in offices of family therapists, psychologists, and social workers. It is available on CD-ROM and online but not in print. (KK)

Family Studies Database See *Family & Society Studies Worldwide.*

104. *Feminist Periodicals: a current listing of contents.* [ISSN: 0742-7433] 1981. q. USD 15 Univ. of Wisc. affiliated, Libraries, USD 22.50 Non-Univ. of Wisc. affiliated (Individuals, USD 8.50 Univ. of Wisc. affiliated). Ed(s): Phyllis Holman Weisbard, Ingrid Markhardt. University of Wisconsin System, Women's Studies Librarian, 430 Memorial Library, 728 State St, Madison, WI 53706; wisws1@library.wisc.edu. Illus. Circ: 1000. Vol. ends: Winter. *Aud.:* Ac.

Feminist Periodicals is a current-awareness service from the office of the University of Wisconsin System's Women's Studies Librarian. It reproduces the tables of contents of more than 130 women's studies journals and magazines, many of which are not indexed elsewhere. It focuses on scholarly or small-press English-language publications with a substantial national or regional readership. It also includes publishing and subscription information for each periodical. A subscription also includes *Feminist Collections* and *New Books on Women & Feminism.* An excellent resource for early identification of new serial titles.

105. *Film Literature Index.* [ISSN: 0093-6758] 1973. q. USD 475 in US & Canada includes bound a. cum.; USD 500 foreign includes bound a. cum.; USD 220 in US & Canada bound a. cum. only. Ed(s): Linda Provinzano, Deborah Sternklar. Film Literature Index, Film and Documentation Center, State University of New York at Albany, Richardson 390C, 1400 Washington Ave, Albany, NY 12222; fatdoc@albany.edu; http://www.albany.edu/sisp/fatdoc/fli.htm. Illus. Circ: 500 Paid. *Aud.:* Hs, Ga, Ac.

Still the first choice in film periodical research, *FLI* indexes 150 film and television journals from 30 countries cover-to-cover and another 200 periodicals selectively. The index is arranged alphabetically by author and subject (with over 2,000 subject headings continuously updated to reflect changes in the field), and includes cross-references by film title and director. Researchers will also find easy access to reviews, verified film production data, industry name lists, conferences, and award and festival information. Bibliographic entries indicate whether articles contain obituaries, filmographies, portraits, stills, discographies, and bibliographies.

106. *Focus On: Veterinary Science and Medicine.* [ISSN: 1067-8964] 1993. m. USD 375. Institute for Scientific Information, 3501 Market St., Philadelphia, PA 19104; sales@isinet.com; http://www.isinet.com. Sample. Vol. ends: Dec. *Aud.:* Ac, Sa.

There has long been a problem in the timeliness of the indexing of veterinary literature. Usually there is a delay of three to seven months from the time an article is published to when it appears in a printed index or an online database. ISI's *Current Contents/Agriculture, Biology and Environmental Sciences* resolved some of this problem as it provided the tables of contents of journals as soon as they were published, but the coverage of veterinary journals was limited. After surveying veterinary librarians and other interested parties, ISI created a highly targeted current-awareness database called *Focus On: Veterinary Science & Medicine* to provide immediate indexing and expanded coverage with the addition of abstracts. ISI has enhanced coverage of the veterinary literature by doing cover-to-cover indexing of 166 core titles. In addition, ISI scans its total database (8,000 journals, 8,000 conference proceedings and books) for other articles that have been added during the month regarding the study, care, and treatment of animals. From all these sources, a monthly diskette of all veterinary articles (including abstracts) is prepared and sent to the subscriber. This product has definitely found its niche and has proved to be popular with the end user. A yearly subscription includes 12 monthly diskettes (not available in paper format), documentation, and software. The cumulated backfiles from 1993 are available on CD-ROM for $230 plus postage. Technical support is available at no additional charge. All articles indexed can be obtained through ISI's full-text document delivery service, The Genuine Article. The latest information regarding this product, with a list of journals indexed, and other ISI products can be found at ISI's web site. *Focus On* has been designed so that search results can be exported to word processing or file management packages such as *Pro-Cite, Reference Manager,* etc. It is the most comprehensive veterinary database available at an affordable price for the veterinary practitioner. Researchers in veterinary medicine will also find this current-awareness tool useful. (CTB)

107. *Food Science and Technology Abstracts.* [ISSN: 0015-6574] 1969. m. GBP 1395; USD 2466. Ed(s): Sue Hill. International Food Information Service (I F I S Publishing), Lane End House, Shinfield Rd, Shinfield, Reading, RG2 9BB, United Kingdom; IFIS@ifis.org; http://www.foodsciencecentral.com/. Index. Circ: 1250. CD-ROM: SilverPlatter Information, Incorporated. Online: Data-Star; DIMDI; F I Z Technik; Questel Orbit Inc.; STN International. *Aud.:* Ac, Sa.

Food Science and Technology Abstracts(FSTA) provides comprehensive coverage of the international literature in the field of food sciences and technology, including all human food commodities and aspects of food processing, hygiene, toxicology, standards, laws, and regulations, as well as basic food sciences. Sources include about 1,800 journals, books, patents, theses, laws, and regulations. Bibliographic information, author's address, commercial names, patents, and abstracts (nearly 100 percent) are searchable in the electronic editions. *FSTA* is the essential source of published information for food industry collections. (JJA)

108. *Forest Products Abstracts.* [ISSN: 0140-4784] 1978. bi-m. USD 770. CABI Publishing, Wallingford, OC10 8DE, United Kingdom; orders@cabi.org; http://www.cabi.org. Illus. Vol. ends: Nov. Online: The Dialog Corporation; DIMDI; STN International. *Aud.:* Ac, Sa.

Forest Products Abstracts, a companion to *Forestry Abstracts,* is the foremost index covering the international forest products scholarly literature. With about 2,600 records added each year, it covers journal articles, reports, conference proceedings, and book chapters. Topics include wood properties; timber extraction, conversion, and measurement; damage to timber and timber protection; veneers, composite boards, laminated beams, panels, improved wood, and adhesives; pulp industries and other utilization; and marketing, trade, and economics. Occasional review articles are published. Subject and author indexes are included in each issue and cumulated annually. Electronic coverage is through the comprehensive *CAB* database online from a number of vendors and on *CABCD* and *TreeCD.* Subscription information, prices, and a list of serials scanned are available at http://tree.cabweb.org. *TreeCabweb* offers subscribers free online access to current issues. (CCG)

109. *Forestry Abstracts: compiled from world literature.* [ISSN: 0015-7538] 1939. m. GBP 820. Ed(s): S Harris. CABI Publishing, Wallingford, OC10 8DE, United Kingdom; http://www.cabi.org. Illus. Vol. ends: Dec. Online: The Dialog Corporation; DIMDI; STN International. *Aud.:* Ac, Sa.

Forestry Abstracts is the only indexing and abstracting service specializing in the international scholarly forestry literature. This index is a must for all forestry research collections. The 10,000 records included each year cover all aspects of forestry: silviculture; forest mensuration and management; the physical environment, fire, plant biology, genetics, mycology, and pathology; insects, game, wildlife, and fish; watersheds and soil conservation; nature conservation; arboriculture; dendrochronology; and dendroclimatology. Each issue contains author and subject indexes that cumulate annually. A list of serials scanned is available on the web site. The companion index *Forest Products Abstracts* once appeared in *Forestry Abstracts,* but it has been published separately since 1978. Online access is through the comprehensive *CAB* database or as *TreeCD* from

SilverPlatter. Subscribers can get free online access to current issues through TreeCabweb. Subscription information and prices are at the web site. *TreeCD* covers *Forest Products Abstracts, Forestry Abstracts,* and *Agroforestry Abstracts.* (CCG)

110. *Future Survey: a monthly abstract of books, articles, and reports concerning trends, forecasts, and ideas about the future.* Formerly: *Public Policy Book Forecast.* [ISSN: 0190-3241] 1979. m. USD 145 (Individuals, USD 98). Ed(s): Michael Marien. World Future Society, 7910 Woodmont Ave, Ste 450, Bethesda, MD 20814; info@wfs.org; http://www.wfs.org/. Illus., index. Circ: 1900. Vol. ends: Dec. Reprint: PQC. *Aud.:* Ga, Ac.

This publication lists, in over 70 subject divisions, book reviews, article abstracts, bibliographies, and overviews. It is a monthly guide "to the literature of social change, new technologies, futures studies, policy-making, environmental studies, organizational renewal, and related cross-disciplinary fields." Political science, educational philosophy and planning, energy production and control, and economic forecasting are some of the wide range of subjects discussed. Abstracts are detailed and well composed and run to about 500 words. Author and subject indexes are keyed to main articles in each issue. Sample before subscribing.

111. *Garden Literature: an index to periodical articles and book reviews.* [ISSN: 1061-3722] 1992. a. USD 29.95 domestic. Ed(s): Sally Williams. Garden Literature Press, 398 Columbus Ave, Ste 181, Boston, MA 02116; http://www.gardennet/gardenliterature. *Bk. rev.:* Number and length varies. *Aud.:* Hs, Ga, Ac.

Garden Literature's subject coverage is broad in order to reflect the wide-ranging interests of gardeners, horticulturists, designers, landscape architects, growers, conservationists, and individuals who appreciate plants in any setting, cultivated or natural, and who are curious and wish to learn more. *Garden Literature* aims to make the information found in the 12 periodicals covered as accessible as that found in books. (CR)

112. *Gay & Lesbian Abstracts.* 1999. q. National Information Services Corp., Ste 6, Wyman Towers, 3100 St Paul St, Baltimore, MD 21218. CD-ROM: Pub. Online: NISC. *Aud.:* Hs, Ga, Ac.

Gay and Lesbian Abstracts is the only reference tool that exists for the sole purpose of indexing and abstracting gay, lesbian, bisexual, and transgender materials. According to its web page, *Gay and Lesbian Abstracts* "primarily indexes publications addressing the social, legal, economic, political, cultural, historical, literary, and health concerns of the GLBT community." Note that *GLA* does not cover medical research associated with HIV/AIDS. In tune with its multidisciplinary nature, *Gay and Lesbian Abstracts* indexes a spectrum of titles. From academic journals and dissertations to newspapers, newsletters, and web sites, over 1,800 sources are indexed. There is a wonderful expansiveness to the titles indexed. Small presses have always been important to the GLBT community. This index appropriately includes hundreds of small titles that report big news. Recommended for all academic and major public research institutes. (AMK)

113. *Gender Watch.* Formerly: *Women 'R'.* 1996. q. ProQuest Information & Learning, 300 N Zeeb Rd., PO Box 1346, Ann Arbor, MI 48106-1346; info@proquest.com. *Aud.:* Ga, Ac.

This full-text database provides access to a mix of popular and scholarly items covering women's and gender issues in a broad spectrum of subject areas. It currently indexes 175 journals, magazines, newspapers, regional publications, and newsletters. It also includes alternative-press materials, some "gray literature," and archival materials from 1974 forward. *GenderWatch* now includes more than 80,000 articles and is updated quarterly. Coverage is international, with a primary emphasis on English-language materials. A key resource for public libraries and for academic women's studies collections. (LRK)

114. *Genealogical Periodical Annual Index: key to the genealogical literature.* 1962. a. Ed(s): Leslie K Towle. Heritage Books, Inc., 1540 E Pointer Ridge Pl, Ste 190, Bowie, MD 20716; http://www.heritagebooks.com. Circ: 300. *Aud.:* Ga, Ac.

GPAI indexes over 300 periodicals with nearly 14,000 citations indexed by such fields as surname, locality, topic, and book reviews. To be included in *GPAI,* a publisher must send a copy of its journal to Heritage Books. Although the publisher states in the introduction that this journal is the "only comprehensive" index available, *GPAI* covers only the major genealogical English-language periodicals. *GPAI* is a sleek and easy-to-use resource, and it is more compact than *Periodical Source Index* for bookshelves. However, there is no cumulative index, so every year must be consulted separately and it is also a few years behind, with the latest volume (35) covering the year 1996. It is the only alternative to *PERSI,* but *PERSI* should be librarians' first choice.

115. *General Science Index.* [ISSN: 0162-1963] 1978. m. except Jun. & Dec., plus q. and a. cumulations. Ed(s): Jim Shine. H.W. Wilson Co., 950 University Ave, Bronx, NY 10452-4224; custserv@hwwilson.com; http://www.hwwilson.com. CD-ROM: SilverPlatter Information, Incorporated; H.W. Wilson. *Aud.:* Hs, Ga, Ac.

Indexes over 400 journals and magazines from the United States and Great Britain. The index is arranged alphabetically by subject area. Subjects included are anthropology, pollution biology, earth science, and medicine and health. The first choice for all libraries serving all levels of undergraduates as well as public libraries. Following the subject index is a very useful index to book reviews. The index is available in print and online and is updated monthly *General Science Abstracts* online covers the same 400 periodicals, but includes abstracts. This dates from 1984 with abstracts for records from 1993 to the present. The *General Science Full-Text* database features full-text of articles as far back as 1995 plus graphs, charts, diagrams, photos, and illustrations. The database is updated four times a week online and monthly on disc.

116. *Geographical Abstracts: Human Geography.* Formed by the 1989 merger of: *Geographical Abstracts: Economic Geography; Geographical Abstracts: Social and Historical Geography; Geographical Abstracts: Regional and Community Planning; Geographical Abstracts: Economic Geography;* Which was formerly: *Geographical Abstracts C (Economic Geography); Geo Abstracts C (Economic Geography); Geographical Abstracts: Social and Historical Geography;* Which was formerly: *Geographical Abstracts D (Social and Historical Geography; Geo Abstracts D (Social and Historical Geography); Geographical Abstracts: Regional and Community Planning;* Which was formerly: *Geographical Abstracts F (Regional and Community Planning); Geo Abstracts F (Regional and Community Planning).* [ISSN: 0953-9611] 1966. m. EUR 1630. Elsevier - Geo Abstracts, Duke St., 34, Norwich, NR3 3AP, United Kingdom. Online: SilverPlatter Information, Incorporated; Swets Blackwell. *Aud.:* Ac, Sa.

The English-language abstracting journal for geography and related subjects. Each issue indexes over 1,100 journals. There are two sections. *Human Geography* includes environment; environmental resources; cultural and political geography; historical geography; demographic studies; rural and urban studies; national, regional, and community planning; environmental planning, economic development, and trade; agriculture and industry; transport and communications; recreational geography; gender studies; environmental economics; the service sector; and GIS applications. *Physical Geography* includes synoptic geography; applied geomorphology; landforms; the Quaternary; sedimentology; soils; hydrology; meteorology and climatology; and remote sensing, mapping, and GIS. The citations for the articles indexed include a brief signed annotation or abstract. Each issue also includes regional and subject indexes. A cumulative index—with subject, author, and regional sections—is also published. Information on the GeoBase online version and on this print version is available on the publisher's web site. Essential for collections supporting active geography programs; others should preview a sample issue prior to subscribing.

GeoRef. See *Bibliography and Index of Geology.*

117. *Health and Safety Science Abstracts (Online Edition).* m. USD 850. Ed(s): Evelyn Beck. CSA, 7200 Wisconsin Ave, Ste 715, Bethesda, MD 20814; journals@csa.com; http://www.csa.com. Index. Sample. Vol. ends: No. 4. Online: Pub. *Aud.:* Ac, Sa.

Cambridge offers this database in print or via the web. Major areas of coverage include occupational safety and health, transportation, environment and ecology, food and drugs, pesticides, natural disasters, civil defense and emergency management, fire safety, radiation safety, electrical safety, consumer and recreation safety, ergonomics and human factors, diseases, injuries and trauma, and public health. Government reports are included as well as journal articles, conference proceedings, books, and other publications. *Health and Safety Science Abstracts* monitors 1,140 titles, with cover-to-cover indexing of 12 core journals (including *Safety Science* and *Accident Analysis and Prevention*), and "priority coverage" providing 50 percent or greater coverage for 42 other titles. Coverage dates from 1981 to the present, with monthly updates adding approximately 445 new records. This is an essential database for libraries collecting in the broad, cross-disciplinary field of safety, public health, and industrial hygiene. (ELS)

118. ***Hispanic American Periodicals Index.*** [ISSN: 0270-8558] 1974. a. USD 400. Ed(s): Colleen Trujillo. Latin American Studies Center Publications, University of California, Los Angeles, Box 951447, Los Angeles, CA 90095-1447; bvalk@ucla.edu; http://hapi.gseis.ucla.edu. CD-ROM: National Information Services Corp. Online: Research Libraries Group. *Aud.:* Ga, Ac, Sa.

HAPI indexes more than 350 international journals in the social sciences and humanities whose coverage includes Latin American topics. The hard sciences and technology are excluded. It also indexes some of the leading journals covering the U.S. Latino experience. Book, film, and theatre reviews are cited in a separate section. Because the journals indexed are worldwide, many of the bibliographic references are in Spanish or in other Western European languages. The index has been made possible by an international panel of indexers who also assist in identifying new titles. A unique and essential tool for any library that collects material on Latin America. (JRD)

119. ***Historical Abstracts. Part A: Modern History Abstracts, 1450-1914.*** Supersedes in part: *Historical Abstracts.* [ISSN: 0363-2717] 1955. q. including a. index. Ed(s): Denves Compton. A B C-Clio, 130 Cremona Dr, Santa Barbara, CA 93117; http://www.abc-clio.com. Adv. *Aud.:* Ac.

Along with the companion product, *America: History and Life* (see above in this section), this is the major index for research in world history (i.e., everywhere but the United States and Canada), and includes abstracts of journal articles, books, book chapters, and dissertations. The time frame is 1450 to the present. More than 2,000 journals are abstracted. In the printed version, Part A, "Modern History Abstracts," covers 1450–1914 and Part B, "Twentieth History Abstracts," covers 1914 to the present. The online version includes both parts. (WFY)

120. ***Horticultural Abstracts: compiled from world literature on temperate and tropical fruits, vegetables, ornaments, plantation crops.*** [ISSN: 0018-5280] 1931. m. GBP 1150. Ed(s): K K S Bhat, S Harris. CABI Publishing, Wallingford, OC10 8DE, United Kingdom; orders@cabi.org; http://www.cabi.org. Illus., adv. Vol. ends: Dec. Online: The Dialog Corporation; DIMDI; European Space Agency; STN International. *Aud.:* Ac, Sa.

This major horticultural abstracting tool is one of several services produced by the Commonwealth Agricultural Bureaux and is derived from the CAB Abstracts database. Arrangement of entries is by eight main topics: general aspects of research and its applications; temperate tree fruits and nuts; small fruits; viticulture; vegetables—temperate, tropical, and greenhouse; ornamental plants; minor temperate and tropical industrial crops; subtropical fruit and plantation crops; and tropical fruit and plantation crops. Each main topic is then divided into the specific plant families covered in that particular issue. The abstracts can be used by scanning a topical grouping of interest or by using the detailed author and subject indexes. Citations to over 11,000 scholarly journal articles, reports, conferences, and books published worldwide in various languages are added to the abstract each year. Abstracts are in English, and cross-references to related entries are provided.

121. ***Human Resources Abstracts: an international information service.*** Formerly: *Poverty and Human Resources Abstracts.* [ISSN: 0099-2453] 1966. q. GBP 668 in Europe, Middle East, Africa & Australasia. Sage Publications, Inc., 2455 Teller Rd, Thousand Oaks, CA 91320; info@sagepub.com; http://www.sagepub.com. Illus., index, adv. Circ: 750. Vol. ends: Dec. Microform: PQC. Online: EBSCO Publishing; RoweCom Information Quest; Swets Blackwell. Reprint: PQC. *Aud.:* Ac, Sa.

As the title suggests, this indexing/abstracting service is international in scope, encompassing sociological issues in journals and books worldwide. Its major subdivisions cover the labor force, employment, labor markets, income and benefits, the EEO, working conditions and life, labor relations, and worker education and training. Social issues related to labor are also covered. Indexing is by subject and author.

122. ***Humanities Index.*** Supersedes in part: *Social Sciences and Humanities Index.* [ISSN: 0095-5981] 1974. q. plus a. cumulation. Ed(s): Joanna Greenspon. H.W. Wilson Co., 950 University Ave, Bronx, NY 10452-4224; custserv@hwwilson.com; http://www.hwwilson.com. Illus. CD-ROM: H.W. Wilson. *Aud.:* Hs, Ga, Ac.

This essential publication (and *Humanities Abstracts* [1082-3573]) is available in print and online. The print product is a cumulative index to 500 English-language periodicals in the subject areas of archaeology, classical studies, gender studies, folklore, history, language and literature, performing arts, philosophy, religion, and theology. It is published quarterly, with a bound annual cumulation. Author and subject entries are followed by a separate section for book reviews. SilverPlatter distributes Wilson Humanities Abstracts Full Text, providing for coverage of the periodicals in the index as well as full text of over 160 periodicals. This product is available with Internet, CD, and hard-disk access options, providing access to some 480,000 records (36,000-plus added annually).

123. ***I B Z - Internationale Bibliographie der Geistes- und Sozialwissenschaftlichen Zeitschriftenliteratur.*** Former titles (until 2000): *I B Z - Internationale Bibliographie der Zeitschriftenliteratur aus Allen Gebieten des Wissens;* (until 1984): *Internationale Bibliographie der Zeitschriftenliteratur aus Allen Gebieten des Wissens.* [ISSN: 1618-923X] 1965. 2x/yr. EUR 3066. K.G. Saur Verlag GmbH, Hirschberger Str. 17b, Osnabrueck, 49086, Germany; g.hochgeladen@saur.de; http://www.saur.de. Illus. *Aud.:* Ac.

IBZ is international in coverage and includes journal articles from over 12,000 English and European periodicals, books, and dissertations. Coverage begins with 1983, and the online database is updated monthly. The search interface from GBV (www.gbv.de), the online distributor of the *IBZ*, is rudimentary but functional, and the database may be searched by a combination of keywords or browsed by index entry. The interface is available in both English and German and includes an exhaustive help section. *IBZ* is also available on CD-ROM.

124. ***I C O N D A: International Construction Database.*** 1976. q. plus a. cumulation. SilverPlatter Information, Incorporated, 100 River Ridge Dr., Norwood, MA 02062; info@silverplatter.com; http://www.silverplatter.com. *Aud.:* Ac, Sa.

ICONDA, International Construction Database, is produced by the International Council for Building Research Studies and Documentation (CIB). The producing agency for the database is the Information Center for Regional Planning and Building Construction (IRB) of the Fraunhofer Society of Germany. The publisher of the quarterly CD-ROM is SilverPlatter Information. The *ICONDA* CD-ROM is accessed using WebSPIRS, a web interface for searching.

This powerful and user-friendly database contains over 450,000 international references of a specialized nature, concentrating on books, research reports, conference proceedings, and business reports; it also indexes over 540 periodicals, with the citations in English. The contents of *ICONDA* cover all aspects of architecture, design, construction, structures, materials, planning, finance and management, restoration and conservation, and computer-aided design. Approximately 25,000 citations are added annually and these are cumulative. The specialized nature of *ICONDA* makes it a sound candidate for a specialized academic architecture library audience. (TG)

125. ***Index Islamicus: a bibliography of publications on Islam and the Muslim world since 1906.*** Former titles (until 1995): *Quarterly Index Islamicus;* (until 1976): *Index Islamicus.* [ISSN: 1360-0982] 1958. 3x/yr.

EUR 825; USD 1025. Ed(s): G.J. Roper, C.H. Bleaney. Brill Academic Publishers, Inc., PO Box 9000, Leiden, 2300 PA, Netherlands; cs@brill.nl; http://www.brill.nl. Illus. Sample. *Aud.:* Ac, Sa.

Index Islamicus is the most widely respected and authoritative index to the serial literature on the Islamic world. Periodical articles, Festschriften, congresses, and other collective works are compiled by the Royal Academy for Islamic Civilization (Amman, Jordan) and University Library (Cambridge, England). Material is arranged geographically and thematically. Within the last few years the general subject indexing in the print index has gotten much more detailed, thus bringing out more of the literature on "new" topics such as gender and interdisciplinary cultural studies. The index covers literature by and about the entire geographic scope of Islam, including Africa and South Asia as well as the Middle East. The CD-ROM should make extremely detailed searching possible. *Index Islamicus* is the essential index for any Middle Eastern Studies program, as well as for libraries and institutions that do research in Africa, South Asia, and other parts of the Islamic world. See also *African Studies, Current Bibliography on African Affairs,* and *Black Studies on Disc* for related material.

126. *Index Medicus.* [ISSN: 0019-3879] 1960. m. USD 505; USD 65 for Medical Subject Headings Section; USD 38 for List of Journals Indexed Section. U.S. National Library of Medicine, Bldg 38, 8600 Rockville Pike, Bethesda, MD 20894; http://www.nlm.nih.gov. Illus. Circ: 6000. CD-ROM: CSA; The Dialog Corporation; SilverPlatter Information, Incorporated. Microform: PMC; PQC. Online: National Library of Medicine; STN International. *Aud.:* Ac, Sa.

Index Medicus is the premier medical indexing tool in the world, indexing more than 3,000 journals published worldwide. It has been described by enthusiastic physicians as "a national treasure." It includes the List of Journals Indexed in Index Medicus and the Medical Subject Headings. The automated *MEDLARS* is available through the National Library of Medicine's *MEDLINE.* It is available on the web at virtually all academic medical centers and colleges and many public libraries. In addition to various commercial electronic publishers, NLM's *Pubmed* format is now available free of charge to the public, and continues to include/add full-text titles to the product. For this reason, and due to the very large size of the paper version, only those libraries without Internet access must continue to purchase the paper *IM.* (MMC)

127. *Index of American Periodical Verse.* [ISSN: 0090-9130] 1971. a. Ed(s): Rafael Catata, James D Anderson. Scarecrow Press, Inc., 4720 Boston Way, Ste A, Lanham, MD 20706-4310; http://www.scarecrowpress.com. Illus. Circ: 3000. *Aud.:* Ga, Ac, Sa.

The *Index of American Periodical Verse* is an annual that identifies the poetry published in nearly 300 literary, scholarly, popular, general, and "little" magazines, journals, and reviews. The index restricts its scope to U.S., Canadian, and Caribbean publications, but the works of writers around the globe, from many cultures and lands, are represented. A recent volume, for example, included more than 7,100 individual poets and referenced more than 21,000 poems (including those in translation). Poems are indexed by author, translator (when applicable), and title; poems lacking titles are indexed by first line. Each volume also includes an alphabetical list of all journals indexed, plus information on periodical titles that have been added or deleted from previous volumes. An essential resource for most libraries. (SG)

128. *Index of Economic Articles in Journals and Collective Volumes.* [ISSN: 0536-647X] 1961. irreg. USD 160. American Economic Association, 2014 Broadway, Ste 305, Nashville, TN 37203. Illus. *Aud.:* Ac, Sa.

The 1996 print volume is to be the last in the series and was scheduled to be published before the end of 2001. Over the years, the journals indexed in the *Index of Economics Articles in Journals and Collective Volumes* have matched with *EconLit.* The Collective Volume information will be (and has been) included in all electronic versions of *EconLit.* By the end of 2001, all of the 1999 Collective Volume will be added. 1996, 1997, and 1998 are already included. This extensive and thorough index lists articles, by subject and author, from the major economics journals and collective volumes. Articles are written in English or have English summaries. The collective volumes contain conference proceedings and publications, collected essays, research papers, collections of papers by a single author, and Festschriften. It is classified by the *JEL* system, and geographic descriptors are used. Note: In past years, I have found a few citations included in the print volumes that were not in *EconLit.*

129. *Index to Black Periodicals.* Former titles (until 1974): *Index to Periodical Articles by and About Blacks;* (until 1973): *Index to Periodical Articles by and About Negroes; Index to Selected Periodicals.* [ISSN: 0899-6253] 1960. a. USD 195. G.K. Hall & Co., 12 Lunar Dr, Woodbridge, CT 06525; http://www.galegroup.com/gkhall. *Aud.:* Ga, Ac, Sa.

The *International Index to Black Periodicals Full Text* is a web-based multidisciplinary index, with some full text, to journal literature in Black Studies. Overall the *IIBP* includes current and retrospective coverage of 150 scholarly and popular journals, newspapers, and newsletters from the United States, Africa, and the Caribbean. The Current Title List contains 120 journals indexed from 1998 forward. Most of these records contain abstracts. Out of these 120 titles, full-text coverage is provided for 23 core periodicals, such as *The A.M.E. Church Review, Afro-Hispanic Review, Black Issues in Higher Education, The Griot, Howard Law Journal, The International Review of African American Art, The Langston Hughes Review,* and *The Western Journal of Black Studies.* Pre-1990 access is available for 45 titles, including *The Crisis* back to 1910, *Phylon* back to 1940, and *Colored American Magazine* back to 1900. In addition to offering a variety of keyword and subject searches from 11 combinable fields, the *IIBP* includes an option for searching for peer-reviewed articles only. The *IIBP* is a valuable resource for scholars, faculty, bibliographers, and students doing both undergraduate and graduate research in Black Studies, International Studies, Ethnic Studies, and American and World History.

130. *Index to Current Urban Documents.* [ISSN: 0046-8908] 1972. q. plus a. cumulation. USD 500. Ed(s): Gerry Lynch Katz. Greenwood Publishing Group Inc., 88 Post Rd W, PO Box 5007, Westport, CT 06881; webmaster@greenwood.com; http://www.greenwood.com/. Illus., index. Circ: 200 Paid. Vol. ends: May. *Aud.:* Ac, Sa.

A unique index to the local-government documents (from local governments, civic organizations, research organizations, public libraries, and regional planning agencies) of 500 selected American and Canadian cities, their counties, and regions. Over 2,400 documents are indexed yearly, using terms specifically developed for this publication (the subject index refers the user to the geographical list, which contains complete bibliographic data). The listing may also include a summary of the document and an indication of any appendix, bibliography, organizational charts, minutes of proceedings, and texts of ordinances or annual reports that are indexed. A yearly subscription to *ICUD* online includes a fully searchable online index with full-text documents available as pdf files.

131. *Index to Dance Periodicals.* [ISSN: 1058-6350] 1991. a. USD 295. G.K. Hall & Co., 12 Lunar Dr, Woodbridge, CT 06525; remmel.nunn@gale.com. Illus. *Aud.:* Hs, Ga, Ac, Sa.

Developed by the New York Public Library–Performing Arts Research Center, *Index to Dance Periodicals* indexes approximately 30 dance periodicals that are the most often referenced around the world. This remains the most useful guide to the major dance periodicals in print, and includes almost 4,000 indexed articles yearly.

132. *Index to Jewish Periodicals.* [ISSN: 0019-4050] 1963. a. USD 110. Ed(s): Lenore P Koppel. Index to Jewish Periodicals, PO Box 22780, Beachwood, OH 44122; index@jewishperiodicals.com; http://www.jewishperiodicals.com. Illus., adv. Circ: 400. *Aud.:* Ac, Sa.

An index to approximately 50 English-language magazines and journals, both general and scholarly, published within the Jewish community and with Jewish interests. Nearly all titles are published in the United States. The index is alphabetically arranged by author and subject, and book reviews are included—arranged by subject rather than separately. Good for general periodicals from the Jewish community, but limited in scope because much material on Jewish Studies will be found in periodicals not indexed here.

133. *Index to Journals in Communication Studies.* [ISSN: 1072-5733] 1974. irreg. approx. every 5 yrs. Members, USD 60; Non-members, USD 80. Ed(s): Ronald J Matlon, Sylvia Ortiz. Speech Communication Association, 5105 Backlick Rd, Bldg E, Annandale, VA 22003; http://www.natcom.org/publications/. Illus. *Aud.:* Ac, Sa.

In a somewhat unconventional arrangement, this indexing service offers access to primary articles in 24 communication studies journals. Organization is by table of contents, from the first issue of each title to the most recent one being indexed; contributor; subject (using a coded classification hierarchy—such as 05.11 Speech Communication, 05.11 02 Intercultural Communication, and 05.11 03 Interpersonal Communication); and keyword. Although its publication schedule is approximately every five years, creating a sizable gap before the next issue, this index is one of the most comprehensive for the discipline. *IJCS* is also available on CD-ROM as *CommSearch.* (NFC)

134. *Index to Legal Periodicals & Books.* Formerly (until 1994): *Index to Legal Periodicals.* [ISSN: 1079-4719] 1908. m. plus q. & a. cumulations. USD 490 in US & Canada; USD 540 elsewhere. Ed(s): Richard Dorfman. H.W. Wilson Co., 950 University Ave, Bronx, NY 10452-4224; custserv@hwwilson.com; http://www.hwwilson.com. CD-ROM: SilverPlatter Information, Incorporated; H.W. Wilson. Online: West Group. Reprint: WSH. *Aud.:* Ac, Sa.

This index includes coverage of about 800 legal periodicals published in the United States, Canada, Great Britain, Ireland, Australia, and New Zealand. *ILP* indexes periodicals that "regularly publish high quality legal articles which are of permanent reference value," as well as yearbooks, annual institutes, and annual reviews of the work in a given field or given topic. Articles must be at least two pages in length to qualify for inclusion. Biographies, bibliographies, book reviews, case notes, and notes on legislation must be two pages in length to be indexed. All entries are in proper legal citation form. A list of all titles indexed is in the front of each issue; subject headings and cross-references used in indexing are in the annual volume. *ILP* has four access points: 1. Author/Subject Index, in one alphabet, with complete bibliographic information; articles are indexed under subject and author; student pieces are indexed only under subject; 2. Table of Cases, for which student comments have been written; 3. Table of Statutes, for which students have provided analyses; arrangement is by jurisdiction, with federal laws first; and 4. Book Review Index. In 1994, *ILP* began to index the legal books listed in this publisher's *Cumulative Book Index.* Although *ILP* is more selective in journal coverage than the *Current Law Index* (see above in this section), it still gets at the heart of the legal materials. Because *ILP* has been around since 1908 and *CLI* only since 1980, *ILP* is the only indexing source for pre-1980 legal periodical materials. It is included in the publisher's *Wilsonline* database. (DD)

135. *Index Veterinarius: comprehensive monthly subject and author index to the world's veterinary literature available in print and on the internet.* [ISSN: 0019-4123] 1933. m. plus a. cumulation. GBP 1170. Ed(s): Rachel Duffy. CABI Publishing, Wallingford, OC10 8DE, United Kingdom; orders@cabi.org; http://www.cabi.org. Illus., adv. Sample. Circ: 750. Vol. ends: Dec. Online: The Dialog Corporation; DIMDI; STN International. *Aud.:* Ac, Sa.

Index Veterinarius is one of several indexes related to veterinary medicine that CAB International publishes. This is the premier index to the veterinary literature, and it attempts to be all-inclusive and worldwide in coverage. Titles are selected from approximately 3,500 serial publicatons and from books, annual reports, theses, and other nonserial publications. The 21,000 citations added yearly provide bibliographic information, the author's address, language of the article, and the language of any summaries. All *major* items of veterinary interest are abstracted in the index's companion volume, *Veterinary Bulletin* (see below in this section). A numbering system provides easy access between the two volumes. A hardbound cumulation is published annually. CAB International also provides a document delivery service for the articles it indexes. Both a print and online version are available. The online version includes access to a ten-year backfile. A must purchase for any veterinary collection. (CTB)

136. *International Aerospace Abstracts.* [ISSN: 0020-5842] 1961. m. except Dec. USD 2260 combined subscription print & online eds. CSA, 7200 Wisconsin Ave, Ste 715, Bethesda, MD 20814; journals@csa.com; http://www.csa.com. Illus. Refereed. CD-ROM: The Dialog Corporation. Microform: PMC. Online: Pub. *Aud.:* Ac, Sa.

This aerospace-focused index and abstract journal is devoted to the indexing and abstracting of worldwide technical literature related to the many subdisciplines of aeronautics, astronautics, space science, and related disciplines. The index emphasizes the technical and scientific information in the areas of aeronautics and astronautics rather than the theoretical aspects of space sciences. The index includes records taken from books, journals, conference proceedings, individual conference papers, translations of journals, government technical reports, and journal articles. Overall, there are 76 subjects divided into 11 broad classifications that cover aeronautics, astronautics, chemistry and materials, engineering, geosciences, life sciences, mathematics and computer science, physics, social sciences, space sciences, and general topics. There are four major indexes: subject, author, meeting paper and report number, and accession number. The cumulative index contains these same four indexes along with a list of sources indexed. The electronic version of this index is included in the *Aerospace Database,* which is available online from Cambridge Scientific Abstracts (CSA). This index remains an important tool for those working in the fields of aeronautics, astronautics, and space sciences. (HSM)

137. *International African Bibliography: current books, articles and papers in African studies.* [ISSN: 0020-5877] 1971. q. EUR 298; EUR 84 newsstand/cover. K.G. Saur Verlag GmbH, Ortlerstr. 8, Munchen, 81373, Germany; info@saur.de; http://www.saur.de. Illus., index, adv. Vol. ends: Nov. *Aud.:* Ac, Sa.

This index began as a supplement to the journal *Africa* (see also *Africa Bibliography* in the Africa section). No longer connected to the International African Institute, it is, since 1971, a separate publication, now compiled in association with the Centre of African Studies at the Library, School of Oriental and African Studies, University of London. *IAB* is an important African Studies index (see also *Current Bibliography on African Affairs*) listing books, articles, and papers in all fields of African Studies. The publisher claims to index 4,000 publications including contents of some 1,150 periodicals. Coverage includes both materials published in Africa and abroad. About one-third of the periodicals and other information sources are from Africa. The quarterly issues of bibliography are divided into two sections: articles and monographs, both arranged by region and country. The monographs section is particularly useful in that it lists full analytics for contents of the items. Each issue has a subject list for articles, but the last issue of the year includes indexes arranged by subject, author/personality, ethnic group, language, and special terms. There are ample cross-references to cope with the complexity of African names.

138. *International Bibliography of the Social Sciences.* 1951. a. British Library of Political and Economic Science, 10 Portugal St, London, WC2A 2HD, United Kingdom; http://www.lse.ac.uk/. *Aud.:* Ac, Sa.

An international interdisciplinary index for social scientists, this database has over two million references to journal articles, book reviews, books, and book chapters. Two thousand journals are currently reviewed, and approximately 500 of these are in the fields of anthropology, economics, political science, sociology, and general social science journals. Another strength of *IBSS* is the broad range of international data. Coverage is from 1952, and the index has been produced at the London School of Economics since 1989. Available online, on CD-ROM, or in print, this is a valuable tool for researchers and should not be overlooked.

139. *International Index to Black Periodicals Full Text.* [ISSN: 1528-3143] m. ProQuest Information & Learning, 300 N Zeeb Rd., PO Box 1346, Ann Arbor, MI 48106-1346; info@proquest.com; http://www.umi.com. Illus. *Aud.:* Ga, Ac.

Index to Black Periodicals is the only print index exclusively devoted to analyzing the contents of periodicals and selected newspapers about African Americans. While it does cover all the major African American periodicals and selected material about African Americans from other publications, its utility is limited by the fact that it comes out only once a year. While ideal for historical research, it has limited value for current events. Libraries will have better access to this same material in *Black Studies on Disc,* which also contains the catalog of the Schomburg Library; *Ethnic Newswatch,* an electronic resource that indexes and provides full-text of articles in 200 U.S. ethnic and minority news sources; and the H W Wilson Company's *Social Sciences Index,* available in print, CD-ROM, and online versions, which indexes major African American Studies journals.

140. ***International Index to Music Periodicals.*** [ISSN: 1087-6871] 1996. m. ProQuest Information & Learning, 300 N Zeeb Rd., PO Box 1346, Ann Arbor, MI 48106-1346; info@proquest.com; http://www.umi.com. *Aud.:* Ga, Ac, Sa.

The *International Index to Music Periodicals* contains over 340,000 records from over 370 current international music periodicals, and includes 185 retrospective titles that date back to 1874. *IIMP* also indexes feature music articles and obituaries from *The New York Times* and *The Washington Post.* Coverage includes both scholarly and popular periodical literature. Most entries after 1995 contain an abstract. Searches can be made from 12 combinable fields. Results of searches are displayed in reverse chronological order. *IIMP* is available online and on CD-ROM. The online database is updated monthly. Recommended for academic and large high school libraries.

141. ***International Index to the Performing Arts.*** 1998. m. Ed(s): Tarshel Beards. Chadwyck-Healey Inc., 300 N Zeeb Rd, PO Box 1346, Ann Arbor, MI 48103-1553; info@il.proquest.com; http://www.chadwyck.com. *Aud.:* Ga, Ac, Sa.

More than 200 scholarly and popular performing-arts works are indexed online monthly, with a 100-word abstract. Retrospective abstracts are included for 83 journals, some going as far back as 1864. *IIPA* also indexes performing arts–related articles and obituaries appearing in *The New York Times* and *The Washington Post,* and a variety of documents such as biographical profiles, conference papers, interviews, discographies, reviews, and events. The initial release of *IIPA Full Text* contains all of *IIPA* plus the full text of current articles from more than 30 important performing-arts journals.

142. ***International Nursing Index.*** [ISSN: 0020-8124] 1966. 3x/yr. USD 382 USD 138 newsstand/cover per issue. Lippincott Williams & Wilkins, 530 Walnut St, Philadelphia, PA 19106-3621; custserv@lww.com; http://www.lww.com. Illus. Circ: 1400. Vol. ends: No. 3. Reprint: PQC. *Aud.:* Ac, Sa.

The *International Nursing Index* is nursing's counterpart to medicine's *Index Medicus* (above in this section). *INI* is published in cooperation with the National Library of Medicine (NLM), utilizng MeSH headings, by Lippincott, Williams & Wilkins (http:www.lww.com). It covers over 270 international nursing journals, nursing material from MEDLINE, health planning, and health administration resources. It definitely covers the premier journals in all languages and complements the English-only *CINAHL,* which has broader topic coverage. This index should be available in some format in all nursing libraries and most academic libraries with health care programs. (MMC)

International Philosophical Bibliography. See *Repertoire Bibliographique de la Philosophie.*

143. ***Internet & Personal Computing Abstracts (Print Edition).*** Former titles (until Mar 2000): *Microcomputer Abstracts;* (until 1994): *Microcomputer Index.* [ISSN: 1529-7705] 1980. q. USD 269 domestic; USD 281 in Canada & Mexico; USD 297 elsewhere. Ed(s): Kevin George, Sean Layman. EBSCO Publishing, 10 Estes St, PO Box 682, Ipswich, MA 01938-0682; ep@epnet.com; http://www.epnet.com. Illus., index. *Aud.:* Ga, Ac.

Internet & Personal Computing Abstracts indexes and abstracts over 120 magazines concerned with the Internet and personal computers in general. The publication is divided into six sections: feature articles, news, and columns; book reviews; buyer and vendor guides; hardware reviews; product announcements; and software reviews. The focus is more on mass-market computer magazines that cover microcomputer operating systems such as Windows, Macintosh, and UNIX, with information on desktop publishing, Internet applications, client-server computing, multimedia, database management, etc. The web site provides more information on this title. (RK)

144. ***Kew Record of Taxonomic Literature (Year).*** a. GBP 40. H.S.M.O., Royal Botanical Gardens, Kew, PO Box 276, London, SW8 5DT, United Kingdom; http://www.itsofficial.co.uk. Circ: 200. *Aud.:* Ga, Ac.

This British free-access database will allow limited downloading of citations on the "taxonomy of flowering plants, gymnosperms, and ferns" that can be found with a simple search. There is a registration process that will allow the searcher to use more searching capabilities and to retrieve more citations.

145. ***L I S A: Library & Information Science Abstracts.*** Supersedes (in 1969): *Library Science Abstracts.* [ISSN: 0024-2179] 1950. 13x/yr. USD 1055 combined subscription print & online eds. CSA, 7200 Wisconsin Ave, Ste 715, Bethesda, MD 20814; journals@csa.com; http://www.csa.com. Illus., index. Circ: 2500. *Aud.:* Ac, Sa.

LISA: Library and Information Science Abstracts is an international abstracting and indexing resource for librarians and other information professionals. The file currently abstracts more than 440 periodicals from over 68 countries, in more than 20 different languages. Subjects covered range from artificial intelligence to information management, information technology, knowledge management, library use and users, publishing and bookselling, records management, technical services, and the web. Coverage runs from 1969 to the present, and the file is updated every two weeks (over 500 records are added each update). There are more than 230,000 records in the database. (CML)

146. ***Language Teaching: the international abstracting journal for language teachers and applied linguistics.*** Former titles (until 1982): *Language Teaching and Linguistics Abstracts;* (until 1975): *Language-Teaching Abstracts; English Teaching Abstracts.* [ISSN: 0261-4448] 1968. q. USD 150 (Individuals, USD 57). Ed(s): Janet Hooper. Cambridge University Press, The Edinburgh Bldg, Shaftesbury Rd, Cambridge, CB2 2RU, United Kingdom; information@cambridge.org; http://uk.cambridge.org/journals. Illus., index, adv. Vol. ends: Oct. Microform: PQC. Reprint: SWZ. *Aud.:* Ga, Ac.

Published with the support of the Centre for Information on Language Teaching & Research (UK), *LT* is complementary to the two other major abstracting sources in linguistics, with a focus on second-language and foreign-language education. *LT* "provides easy access to current international research in language learning and teaching, by bringing together in one journal English summaries of research findings in language education from around the world." A range of approximately 200 international periodicals is "scanned," from which a small percentage of the total content of any single issue is included in *LT.* Though "current work of significance and interest is selected and summarised," it is not clear what precise criteria are applied for inclusion. The abstracts are grouped into several subject areas: language teaching, language learning, reading, writing, language testing, teacher education, bilingualism and bilingual education, and sociolinguistics. In addition, each issue includes a lengthy "state-of-the-art survey article . . . specially commissioned from experts in the field and [each issue] features a comprehensive and up-to-date bibliography." Short book notices along with a list of books recently published are also included. If you keep in mind the emphasis is on European language research, this publication will be useful in large public libraries and wherever ESL/EFL programs are offered. (JM)

147. ***LegalTrac (Online).*** Former titles: *LegalTrac (Print); Legal Resource Index.* 1980. m. Gale Group, 27500 Drake Rd, Farmington Hills, MI 48331-3535; galeord@gale.com; http://www.gale.com. Illus. *Aud.:* Ac, Sa.

The *Legal Resource Index,* sponsored by the American Association of Law Libraries, provides access to legal periodical literature from 1980 in three versions—online, CD-ROM, and print. The *LRI* database—containing indexing for over 900 legal periodicals plus more than 70 legal newspapers and law-related articles from more than 1,000 additional business and general-interest periodicals—is also used in producing *Current Law Index* and *LegalTrac,* its paper and CD-ROM counterparts, respectively (see above and below in this section). The online *LRI* is updated daily in The Gale Group's *Newsearch,* the vendor's database holding tank of newly indexed materials awaiting monthly inclusion in the vendor's various online periodical indexes. The *LRI* database contains in excess of one million records, adds more than 5,000 new records each month, and is also available through the larger InfoTrac. The *Legal Resource Index* database is one of the most significant enhancements for legal research in recent years. (DD)

148. *Leisure, Recreation and Tourism Abstracts.* Formerly: *Rural Recreation and Tourism Abstracts.* [ISSN: 0261-1392] 1976. q. USD 610. Ed(s): P Trayhurn. CABI Publishing, Wallingford, OC10 8DE, United Kingdom; orders@cabi.org; http://www.cabi.org. Illus., index, adv. Sample. Circ: 350. Online: The Dialog Corporation; DIMDI; STN International. *Aud.:* Ac, Sa.

This subset of the *CAB Abstracts* and *CAB Health* databases provides 600 150-word abstracts of articles, conference papers, reports, and books. The publication covers the areas of leisure, tourism, recreation, and sports. Subject, author, and a serials-cited index are provided. Available online, with complete backfile access, at http://www.leisuretourism.com.

LexisNexis. See Aggregators/A&I-Based section in the front matter.

149. *Library Literature & Information Science.* Formerly (until 1999): *Library Literature.* [ISSN: 1528-0659] 1921. bi-m. Ed(s): Mary Brereton. H.W. Wilson Co., 950 University Ave, Bronx, NY 10452-4224; custserv@hwwilson.com; http://www.hwwilson.com. CD-ROM: SilverPlatter Information, Incorporated; H.W. Wilson. *Bk. rev.:* Number and length vary. *Aud.:* Ems, Hs, Ga, Ac, Sa.

This author and subject index to books, periodicals, and library school theses on library and information science covers the gamut of librarianship—from the philosophical to the practical, from church libraries to research libraries, from selecting children's books to systems analysis. Each issue contains a helpful checklist of monographs indexed and a separate book review section, two handy ways to keep up with the literature of librarianship. (CMJ)

150. *Linguistics Abstracts.* [ISSN: 0267-5498] 1985. q. GBP 702. Ed(s): Terence Langendoen. Blackwell Publishing Ltd., 9600 Garsington Rd, PO Box 805, Oxford, OX4 2DQ, United Kingdom; customerservices@oxon.blackwellpublishing.com; http://www.blackwellpublishing.com/. Illus., index, adv. Circ: 700. Online: EBSCO Publishing; RoweCom Information Quest; Swets Blackwell. Reprint: SWZ. *Aud.:* Ac, Sa.

This resource abstracts scholarly articles from journals in linguistics and related fields, as well as from selected university working papers. Among the areas abstracted are linguistic theory, semantics, syntax and morphology, phonology, pragmatics, sociolinguistics, psycholinguistics, computational linguistics, discourse analysis, reading and writing, and more. Short abstracts describe scholarly articles from approximately 100 publications. There is both an annual cumulative author index and an annual cumulative journal index. Some publications have as few as one of their articles included while others have as many as 20. There is some overlap in journal coverage with another index, *LLBA*. Appropriate for complete collections. (JM)

151. *Linguistics and Language Behavior Abstracts.* Incorporates (in 1989, vol.12): *Reading Abstracts;* Formerly (until 1985): *Language and Language Behavior Abstracts.* [ISSN: 0888-8027] 1967. 5x/yr. USD 460 combined subscription print & online eds. without a. cumulative index; USD 595 combined subscription print & online eds. with a. cumulative index; USD 230 combined subscription print & CD-ROM a. cumulative index. Ed(s): Stanley Novak. CSA, 7200 Wisconsin Ave, Ste 715, Bethesda, MD 20814; journals@csa.com; http://www.csa.com. Illus., index, adv. Circ: 900. Vol. ends: Dec. CD-ROM: National Information Services Corp.; SilverPlatter Information, Incorporated. Online: Pub.; SilverPlatter Information, Incorporated. *Aud.:* Ga, Ac, Sa.

Long the standard in the field, *LLBA* offers both evaluative and nonevaluative abstracts selected from the international and interdisciplinary literature in language, language behavior, linguistics, and related disciplines. Several hundred journals are "screened," and abstracts for selected titles are provided in the broad core areas of syntax, linguistic theory, diachronic linguistics, and second-language learning. Each issue organizes the paragraph-length abstracts in more than 20 classifications, including psycholinguistics, applied linguistics, phonology, semantics, morphology, descriptive linguistics, sociolinguistics, semiotics, learning disabilities, and more. There are four types of abstracts: evaluative and nonevaluative abstracts of articles in scholarly journals, and evaluative and nonevaluative abstracts of new books. Each issue includes a subject index, author index, source publication index, and books abstracted indexes. An annual cumulative index is published and sold separately. Though not comprehensive, *LLBA* is an indispensable abstracting source for linguistics. Electronic versions available from several vendors. (JM)

152. *Lodging, Restaurant and Tourism Index.* Formerly: *Lodging and Restaurant Index.* 1985. q. USD 265. Ed(s): Priscilla C Geahigan. CFS Library, Purdue University, 1002 Stone Hall, W, Lafayette, IN 47907-1002; http://www.cea.purdue.edu/rhimi/tour-idx/tour-idx.htm. Sample. Circ: 200. *Aud.:* Ga, Ac.

A quarterly index to over 70 of the most prominent international scholarly and trade publications in the travel and hospitality industries. The indexing is performed by a librarian at Purdue University. Available in print or on CD-ROM. The CD-ROM is especially useful as it contains every year's entries.

153. *M L A International Bibliography of Books and Articles on the Modern Languages and Literatures.* [ISSN: 0024-8215] 1922. a. USD 950. Ed(s): Barbara Chen. Modern Language Association of America, 26 Broadway, 3rd Fl, New York, NY 10004-1789; kathleen.hansen@mla.org; http://www.mla.org. Index. Circ: 3000. CD-ROM: SilverPlatter Information, Incorporated. Online: OCLC Online Computer Library Center, Inc.; SilverPlatter Information, Incorporated. *Aud.:* Ac, Sa.

The *MLA International Bibliography* is one of the most important and comprehensive indexes to the critical literature in the humanities. It indexes 3,500 journals that cover language, linguistics and literature, criticism, drama, and folklore. Other document types covered include series, monographs, dissertations, bibliographies, and proceedings. Over 50,000 new entries are added each year. The print edition began in 1921–25, as *MLA American Bibliography* until 1965, when it expanded its coverage to include books and articles written in English, French, German, Spanish, Italian, Portuguese, a Scandinavian language, and Dutch and became the *MLA International Bibliography*. Online editions cover 1963 to the present, with ten updates per year.

154. *MAS Ultra - School Edition.* d. EBSCO Publishing, 10 Estes St, PO Box 682, Ipswich, MA 01938-0682; http://www.epnet.com. *Aud.:* Hs, Ga, Ac.

MAS Ultra - School Edition, designed specifically for high school libraries, provides full text from over 515 popular general interest and current events publications covering general reference, health, science, and other areas. In addition to the full text, this database offers indexing and abstracts for all publications in the collection. Every full-text article is assigned a reading level indicator (Lexiles). This database also includes more than 3,000 charts, tables, and graphs; 5,000 full-text Magill book reviews; nearly 550 health- and science-related full-text pamphlets; coverage of more than 250 reference books (including the *Columbia Encyclopedia*, the *CIA World Fact Book*, and *World Almanac & Book of Facts*) and an image collection of 91,000 photos, maps, and flags.

Mathematical Reviews. See *MathSciNet*.

155. *MathSciNet: mathematical reviews on the Web.* d. USD 1921. American Mathematical Society, 201 Charles St, Providence, RI 02904-2294; ams@ams.org; http://www.ams.org. Online: SilverPlatter Information, Incorporated. Online: SilverPlatter Information, Incorporated. *Bk. rev.:* 200-500 words, signed. *Aud.:* Ac, Sa.

Produced by the American Mathematical Society (http://www.ams.org), MathSciNet is the web interface to the *Mathematical Reviews* database. It is the basic index for the academic literature of mathematics and is recommended for research libraries and special adults. It also includes reviews specifically written for the database. Entries cover articles and books that provide new contributions to mathematical research. Textbooks, expository papers, and videocassettes are also included. Each year, over 10,000 journal issues and books are acquired, over 100,000 are scanned, and over 70,000 items are added. The database is updated daily. MathSciNet may be searched by Mathematics Subject Classification (which unfortunately is not easily related to either Dewey or Library of Congress classifications). Searching for authors is its real strength because there are authority records for each author. A subscription includes a content fee and a format fee, and because it is costly, consortia and developing countries may be eligible for reduced fees. The *Mathematical Reviews* database, while most convenient with a web interface, is also available in other formats: *Mathemati-*

cal Reviews and *Current Mathematical Publications* are the print versions; MathSci on SilverPlatter R provides a CD-ROM and web interface. Though research libraries should subscribe to MathSciNet, other libraries may still get access to the database through DIALOG R File 239. For more detailed information about MathSciNet and the *Mathematical Reviews* database, download an overview booklet at www.ams.org/msnhtml/guidebook.pdf.

156. *Media Review Digest: the only complete guide to reviews of non-book media.* Formerly: *Multi Media Reviews Index.* [ISSN: 0363-7778] 1970. a. USD 255. Ed(s): Mary K Hashman. Pierian Press, PO Box 1808, Ann Arbor, MI 48106; http://www.pierianpress.com. Illus. *Aud.:* Ac, Sa.

MRD can be used primarily as an index to reviews on films, cassettes, CD-ROMs, DVDs, and other non-book media. With an emphasis on educational, instructional, and informational media, it collects reviews from some 115 periodicals and other sources worldwide. The reviews are classified under four major media types: film and video, audio, CD-ROM, and miscellaneous. The word "review" is used here in a broad sense: It includes not only critical evaluations or examinations, but also brief descriptions or comments. Also, this annual publication is more than an index service; it contains abstracts, citations, and other information on media. Unique features include "feature film ratings," "audience level indications," and "review ratings." It has four major indexes: general subject index, alphabetical subject index, geographical index, and reviewer index. Its web supplements are free of charge to print subscribers. *MRD* provides an excellent access point for media reviews.

157. *Metals Abstracts.* Formed by the merger of: *Review of Metal Literature; Metallurgical Abstracts.* [ISSN: 0026-0924] 1968. m. plus a. cumulation. USD 3790 combined subscription print & online eds.; USD 4730 combined subscription includes Metal Abstracts Index with print & online eds.; USD 5235 combined subscription includes Metal Abstracts Index & Metals Abstracts Annual Index with print & online eds. CSA, 7200 Wisconsin Ave, Ste 715, Bethesda, MD 20814; journals@csa.com; http://www.csa.com. Circ: 1500. Online: Pub.; CEDOCAR; CISTI; Data-Star; European Space Agency; F I Z Technik; Questel Orbit Inc.; STN International. Online: Pub. *Aud.:* Ac, Sa.

The comprehensive abstracting service for locating information in the metals field, *Metals Abstracts* covers international scholarly and trade journal articles, conference proceedings, books, patents, government reports, and selected dissertations. The main organization is by subject class. Cross-references point to abstracts in other relevant sections of the publicatin. Its companion index, *Metals Abstracts Index* (ISSN: 0026-0932), is published monthly and has complete subject, author, and company name listings. (GLB)

158. *Meteorological and Geoastrophysical Abstracts.* [ISSN: 0026-1130] 1950. bi-m. USD 1685. CSA, 7200 Wisconsin Ave, Ste 715, Bethesda, MD 20814; journals@csa.com; http://www.csa.com. Illus., adv. Circ: 334. Vol. ends: Dec. Microform: PMC. Online: EBSCO Publishing. *Aud.:* Ac, Sa.

This is the major abstracting source in the atmospheric sciences, covering over 600 journals; plus annuals, proceedings, and selected monographic series. Coverage includes important publications that appear in languages other than English, and is international in scope. Disciplines covered include meteorology, climatology, physical oceanography, hydrology, glaciology, and environmental science. Beyond the search functionality one would expect from most databases, it is possible to search on a classification scheme developed by the American Meteorological Society. Most abstracts in this index do come from the authors. This index is a fundamental resource for libraries supporting research and postsecondary instruction in the atmospheric sciences. (MiC)

159. *Middle East: Abstracts and Index.* [ISSN: 0162-766X] 1978. a. USD 300. Ed(s): James Joseph Sanchez. Aristarchus Publications, PO Box 45610, Seattle, WA 98145-0610. Illus., adv. *Aud.:* Ac, Sa.

Published annually in five volumes, the first four of which are arranged by geographical region, embracing the fields of anthropology, archaeology, art, business, current affairs, economic development, education, history, langugage, literature, politics and government, and sociology, and addressing religion and philosophy in related issues. The fifth volume provides a bibliography for particular topics. There are author, corporate, named person, and subject indexes, and subjects are cross-referenced. Entries cover journal articles from nearly 1,500 journals, editorials, government documents, research reports, press releases, annual reports, speeches, interviews, and news conferences.

160. *Mineralogical Abstracts: a quarterly journal of abstracts in English, covering the world literature of mineralogy and related subjects.* [ISSN: 0026-4601] 1959. q. issue numbers 1-4 and index. GBP 253.35; USD 393. Ed(s): R A Howie. Mineralogical Society, 41 Queens Gate, London, SW7 5HR, United Kingdom; http://www.minersoc.org. Illus. Circ: 1800. Vol. ends: Dec (No. 4). *Aud.:* Ac, Sa.

This abstracting service is a joint effort of the Mineralogical Societies of Great Britain and America along with the International Mineralogical Association and with several smaller professional societies. In all, over 30 societies contribute material for inclusion in the index. Entries are arranged under several broad subject categories related to different aspects of mineralogy, crystallography, geochemistry, and petrology. An annual cumulative index is a useful supplement and simplifies extensive searching. There is some overlap in coverage with the *Bibliography and Index of Geology,* but this is an important, useful and respected bibliographic tool. (EFL)

161. *Music Index: a subject-author guide to music periodical literature.* [ISSN: 0027-4348] 1949. q. USD 2195 domestic; USD 2225 foreign. Ed(s): Sonja Hempseed. Harmonie Park Press, 23630 Pinewood, Warren, MI 48091-4759; info@harmonieparkpress.com; http://www.harmonieparkpress.com. Circ: 900. *Aud.:* Ga, Ac, Sa.

The Music Index provides indexing of over 670 international music periodicals. Areas covered include music history, musicology, and ethnomusicology; subjects covered include performers, instruments past and present, musical genres, and computer generated music. Indexing includes book reviews, concert reviews, and recording reviews. First performances and obituaries are noted. Both quarterly and yearly issues include a Subject Heading List containing cross-references. *The Music Index* is available in both print and online formats; the CD-ROM format is being discontinued. The online index complements the print index and covers 1979 to the present, with quarterly updates. Searches can be made from five combinable fields. Recommended for all libraries.

162. *National Criminal Justice Reference Service Abstracts Database.* 1972. d. Free. National Criminal Justice Reference Service, PO Box 6000, Rockville, MD 20849-6000; askncjrs@ncjrs.org; http://www.ncjrs.org. *Aud.:* Ga, Ac, Sa.

The *NCJRS Abstracts Database* is a computer-searchable bibliographic file of more than 170,000 annotated citations. The database is produced by the National Criminal Justice Reference Service, which is a national clearinghouse of information about criminal justice and law enforcement sponsored by the National Institute of Justice, the research and development agency of the U.S. Department of Justice. All aspects of criminal justice are included: corrections, crime prevention, criminology, forensics, facility design, police, probation, prosecution, and so on. Information that is both practical and theoretical is included from federal, state, and local government reports, books, research reports, journal articles, unpublished research, and other sources. A large portion of the database (perhaps half) lists government reports/documents; journal articles make up the second-largest portion (perhaps 30 percent). Many of the publications (7,000+) listed in this database are available from *NCJRS Virtual Library* online through web links from the database records, and many others are available via mail. The *NCJRS Abstracts Database* is available free via the web from NCJRS at http://abstractsdb.ncjrs.org. In addition, it is available Cambridge Scientific Abstracts and DIALOG. In the past NCJRS produced a CD-ROM version of the database, but it is doubtful that the CD-ROM edition will be updated. More information about the National Criminal Justice Reference Service and its publications and services is available at its web site.

163. *New Testament Abstracts: a record of current literature.* [ISSN: 0028-6877] 1956. 3x/yr. USD 35 domestic; USD 38 foreign. Ed(s): D J Harrington. Weston Jesuit School of Theology, 3 Phillips Place, Cambridge, MA 02138; NTAweston@aol.com; http://members.aol.com/ntaweston/nta.html. Illus., index, adv. Sample. Circ: 2250. Vol. ends: No. 3. *Bk. rev.:* Various number and length. *Aud.:* Ac, Sa.

This is the standard source for abstracted information on the New Testament (NT). *NTAb* covers over 500 periodicals and 800-900 books per year from around the world. Sources come from a variety of languages, but all of the abstracts are in English. Two-thirds of each issue is devoted to periodical articles, while the remaining third reviews books (and occasionally, computer software). Both sections are arranged according to the same topical outline: "The New Testament: General," "Gospels—Acts," "Epistles—Revelation," "Biblical Theology," and "The World of the New Testament," plus subdivisions. This conceptual arrangement is better suited for searching broad subject areas or a particular NT book or passage than for locating items on a specific term. Included in the last issue of each volume are cumulative indexes for "Principle Scriptural Texts," "Authors of Articles and Book Reviews," "Book Reviews," and "Book Notices." This is an essential resource for researching the NT (for the Old Testament/Hebrew Bible, see *Old Testament Abstracts*, below in this section). A CD-ROM version, containing all abstracts and book notices from 1983 through 2000 (and perhaps 2003), should be available by the time this review is published. More information about this index can be found online at members.aol.com/ntaweston/nta.html. (LAP)

164. *Numismatic Literature.* [ISSN: 0029-6031] 1947. s-a. USD 44. Ed(s): Heath Sebastian, Oliver Hoover. American Numismatic Society, Broadway & 155th St, New York, NY 10032-7598; http://www.amnumsoc.org/. Illus., index, adv. Reprint: PQC. *Aud.:* Ac.

This annotated bibliography is the only comprehensive indexing source available for numismatics, referencing material on coins, medals, tokens, and paper money. This is not an exhaustive listing of numismatic resources, but represents material that is generally scholarly. Citations are predominantly for periodical articles, but include books and conference proceedings; these are overwhelmingly international and include many non-English items. Almost all citations are recent publications, and the majority of entries include an abstract of 50-200 words. This also indexes some book reviews plus obituaries of numismatic notables. The web site has both a current version and a retrospective version of this bibliography, both of which can be searched by keyword. The current version covers from 2002 to the present, and is essentially a web format of each printed index. The retrospective index spans from 1947 to 2000, but is lacking many years that have yet to be input. *Numismatic Literature* is clearly a source for scholarly rather than popular use, making it strictly for academic libraries and research-oriented institutions. (DV)

165. *Nutrition Abstracts and Reviews. Series A: Human and Experimental.* Incorporates: *Reviews in Clinical Nutrition;* Supersedes in part: *Nutrition Abstracts and Reviews.* [ISSN: 0309-1295] 1977. m. GBP 1050. CABI Publishing, Wallingford, OC10 8DE, United Kingdom; orders@cabi.org; http://www.cabi.org. Illus., index, adv. Sample. Vol. ends: Dec. Online: The Dialog Corporation; DIMDI; STN International. *Bk. rev.:* Various number and length. *Aud.:* Ac, Sa.

CAB International, an international, intergovernmental agency established in 1928, provides "information, scientific and development services for agriculture and allied disciplines throughout the world." *Nutrition Abstracts and Reviews,* published monthly, is compiled from CAB International's database of more than 12,000 serials and additional sources of information. The journal, designed for a scholarly/research audience, has a decidedly international flair. This publication uses the *CAB Thesaurus* as controlled vocabulary and presents abstracts in a classed arrangement—e.g., technique, foods, physiology, and biochemistry—followed by reports, conference proceedings, and nonevaluative book reviews. Each issue contains a subject and an author index. Issues are cumulated in the annual index volume, which also contains a list of the source journals for the abstracts from that year. Note: With the cessation of *CHNI* (*Consumer Health and Nutrition Index*) this is now the major index in the field and, as such, should be found in libraries that formerly subscribed to *CHNI.* Also note: With the availability of *CAB Abstracts,* a comprehensive electronic product, the information included in *Nutrition Abstracts and Reviews* is necessarily included in *CAB Abstracts,* comprising the *Nutrition (Human and Experimental)* subset. Depending upon the specific vendor of *CAB Abstracts,* it may be possible to search subsets separately. (HKM)

166. *OCLC First Search.* 1990. d. OCLC Online Computer Library Center, Inc., 6565 Frantz Rd, Dublin, OH 43017; http://www.oclc.org. *Aud.:* Ems, Hs, Ga, Ac, Sa.

FirstSearch provides access to over 72 online databases and is searchable in five languages. It offers access to the full text from 9,000 journals and to the full images of more than 4,000 journals online. Databases offered through the service range from ABI Inform to General Science Abstracts to PapersFirst to Worldscope. For a full listing of content, please see their web site at http://www.oclc.org/firstsearch/content.

167. *Oceanic Abstracts.* Supersedes: *Oceanic Index; Oceanic Citation Index.* [ISSN: 0748-1489] 1964. m. except Dec. USD 1645 combined subscription print & online eds. Ed(s): Catherine Deckard. CSA, 7200 Wisconsin Ave, Ste 715, Bethesda, MD 20814; journals@csa.com; http://www.csa.com. Illus., index, adv. CD-ROM: National Information Services Corp. Online: Pub.; European Space Agency; STN International. *Aud.:* Ac, Sa.

This publication indexes and abstracts worldwide technical literature on the marine and brackish-water environments, but excludes literature on freshwater environments. It is thus narrower in scope than *Aquatic Sciences and Fisheries Abstracts.* It includes fisheries, aquaculture, nonliving resources and technology, ships and shipping, navigation, and communications. It covers 3,000 journals, conference proceedings, books, government reports, documents, and trade publications. Abstracts are arranged by subject; author, subject, geographic, and taxonomic indexes appear in each issue, with an annual cumulative index on CD-ROM. (JBB)

168. *Oceanographic Literature Review.* Former titles (until 1993): *Deep-Sea Research. Part B: Oceanographic Literature Review;* (until 1979): *Oceanographic Abstracts and Bibliography;* (until 1977): *Deep-Sea Research. Oceanographic Abstracts and Oceanographic Bibliography Section.* [ISSN: 0967-0653] 1967. m. EUR 2117 (Qualified personnel, EUR 115). Ed(s): F K Cooper, N T Davey. Pergamon, The Boulevard, Langford Ln, East Park, Kidlington, OX5 1GB, United Kingdom. Illus., index, adv. Refereed. Vol. ends: No. 12. CD-ROM: National Information Services Corp. Microform: PQC. Online: The Dialog Corporation. *Aud.:* Ac, Sa.

This publication is an annotated bibliography to "the international research literature in all fields of oceanography including science, mathematics and methods as well as policy, laws, economics and resource management." About 2,500 journals, books, and conference proceedings are scanned; these include non-oceanographic material in the basic sciences useful to oceanographers. Each issue includes geographic, subject, author, and organism indexes; an annual cumulative index includes a listing of all journals cited. Essential for academic and specialized collections, it provides complementary coverage on *Oceanic Abstracts.* (JBB)

169. *Old Testament Abstracts.* [ISSN: 0364-8591] 1978. 3x/yr. USD 26. Ed(s): Christopher T Begg. Catholic Biblical Association of America, Catholic University of America, Washington, DC 20064. Illus., index, adv. Circ: 2050. Vol. ends: No. 3. *Aud.:* Ac, Sa.

OTAb is the standard source for abstracted information on the Old Testament (OT, as it is known by Christians) or Hebrew Bible. (See *New Testament Abstracts*, above in this section, for the similar New Testament standard.) Over 500 titles, covering antiquities, biblical archaeology, biblical theology, and philology are covered. This includes foreign-language publications, although all abstracts are in English. Issues are divided into two sections: periodical articles and book notices. Periodical abstracts are grouped under the headings "General"; "Ancient Near East: History, Texts, etc."; "Texts, Manuscripts, Versions, Canon"; "Archaeology, Epigraphy, Philology"; "History and Geography"; "Pentateuch;" "Historical Books;" "Writings;" "Major Prophets"; "Minor Prophets"; "Biblical Theology"; and "Intertestamental and Apocrypha." The book notices section uses the same categories from "Pentateuch" on, but replaces the previous headings with "Festschriften and Collected Essays" and "Introduction and General." Included in the last issue of each volume are cumulative indexes for "Author," "Scripture Text," and "Words in Hebrew and Other Ancient Languages." Although the use of a topical arrangement does not allow for precise term searching, *OTAb* works well for a great deal of OT research. This is an indispensable research tool for OT studies. The entire run of *OTAb,* from 1978 to 2001, is available on CD-ROM from the American Theological Library Association. More information about this index can be found online at cba.cua.edu/OTA.cfm. (LAP)

170. *P A I S International in Print.* Former titles (until 1990): *P A I S Bulletin;* (until 1985): *Public Affairs Information Service. Bulletin;* (until 1967): *Bulletin of the Public Affairs Information Service.* [ISSN: 1076-2094] 1915. a. plus 3/yr cumulation. USD 850. Ed(s): Catherine Korvin. OCLC Public Affairs Information Service, Inc., 521 W 43rd St, New York, NY 10036-4396; PAISInquiries@oclc.org; http://www.pais.org. Illus. CD-ROM: SilverPlatter Information, Incorporated. Online: OCLC Online Computer Library Center, Inc.; SilverPlatter Information, Incorporated. Reprint: PSC. *Aud.:* Hs, Ga, Ac.

PAIS provides indexing on public policy and social issues from around the world. Bibliographic information on books, periodical articles, hearings, reports, gray literature, goverment publications, and Internet resources are covered for 120 countries. Materials in English, French, German, Italian, Portugese, and Spanish are included with English-language abstracts and subject headings. Established in 1914, the online version covers from 1972 to the present.

171. *Peace Research Abstracts Journal.* [ISSN: 0031-3599] 1964. bi-m. GBP 698 print & online eds. in Europe, Middle East, Africa & Australasia. Ed(s): Dr. Hanna Newcombe. Sage Publications, Inc., 2455 Teller Rd, Thousand Oaks, CA 91320; info@sagepub.com; http://www.sagepub.com. Illus., adv. Circ: 400. Vol. ends: Dec. Online: ProQuest Information & Learning; RoweCom Information Quest; Swets Blackwell. *Aud.:* Ga, Ac.

Peace Research Abstracts Journal is considered the primary international abstracting journal in the field of peace and conflict studies. Sponsored and compiled by the Peace Research Institute, Dundas, this is a valuable source of literature concerning peace studies and international relations. Each issue has over 600 abstracts of articles from recent literature that deals with every aspect of peace, nonviolence, war, conflict resolution, and international relations. More than 3,000 documents are abstracted by volunteers each year. Monographs, articles, government documents, scholarly papers, international research studies, significant speeches, and fugitive materials are covered. The journal is arranged according to 20 subject areas. Access to abstracts is by a subject and an author index, and it is cross-indexed for easy reference. There is a source list and a cumulated subject and author index in the December issue. Although the journal covers a large number of Canadian periodicals, it also does justice to a fairly large number of American and British publications. An excellent resource for academic libraries, peace research centers, and institutions that specialize in peace studies and international relations. (SK)

172. *Periodical Abstracts.* Formerly: *Periodical Abstracts Ondisc.* 1988. m. Bell & Howell Information and Learning Co., 300 N Zeeb Rd, Ann Arbor, MI 48106. Online: The Dialog Corporation. *Aud.:* Hs, Ga, Ac.

This title provides excellent coverage of both popular and selected scholarly titles. Entries include full bibliographic citations and brief (typically 25 words or less) abstracts. Price is negotiated on a case-by-case basis. Coverage is from 1971 to the present. Updates are provided monthly or weekly (depending on version and pricing). *Periodical Abstracts* is only available as a CD-ROM, an online resource, or a magnetic tape that can be loaded and made available from a local server. One of the best of the general indexes, it includes over 2,000 periodicals that include academic publications, business periodicals, and popular magazines. It includes limited indexing of *The New York Times* and *The Wall Street Journal.*

There are additions to (or versions of) *Periodical Abstracts* that offer full text of some of the indexed publications. The full-text coverage does not go as far back as the indexing. What is available full-text changes frequently as new publishers agree to allow this option and other publishers decide no longer to permit it. Most of the full-text articles will offer two versions: a text-only (ASCII) version; and a pdf format version. Cost will vary depending on the number of titles available full-text. Consult the Bell & Howell web site for further information. (KLR)

173. *Periodical Source Index.* [ISSN: 1065-9056] 1987. a. USD 50. Ed(s): Michael B Clegg. Allen County Public Library Foundation, PERSI Project, PO Box 2270, Ft. Wayne, IN 46801; mclegg@everest.acpl.lib.in.us; http://www.acpl.lib.in.us/departments/genealogy.html. Illus. *Aud.:* Ga, Ac.

PERSI is the most comprehensive index to articles in genealogical journals available, with nearly 6,000 journals indexed annually. A 16-volume retrospective set for the years 1847–1985 is also available. Volumes are indexed by family name, subject, and place name. Because new titles are added annually, the entire run of new journals is indexed in that year, so volume dates are deceptive. The annual volumes contain all the articles that were indexed during the year. *PERSI* also acts as a document delivery service, and articles that cannot be found locally can be purchased for a fee from the Allen County Public Library, which owns all the titles indexed. The CD-ROM from Ancestry.com covers all 30 large volumes, with more than 1.1 million searchable citations. *PERSI* on the web can be searched at the Ancestry.com web site.

174. *Petroleum Abstracts.* [ISSN: 0031-6423] 1961. w. 50/yr. University of Tulsa, Information Services Division, 600 S College Ave, Tulsa, OK 74104-3189; question@tured.pa.utulsa.edu; http://www.pa.utulsa.edu/. Illus. Vol. ends: No. 50. CD-ROM: The Dialog Corporation. Online: Questel Orbit Inc.; STN International. *Aud.:* Ac, Sa.

This abstract bulletin and its electronic counterpart, the *TULSA* online database, are issued by a division of the University of Tulsa. In addition to indexing the scientific journal literature, relevant books, conference proceedings, dissertations, patents, and government reports are also included. Abstracts are arranged into several broad subject categories, such as drilling, well logging, and reservoir engineering. CD-ROMs with a rolling file with either the latest ten or twenty years of entries are also available. *Petroleum Abstracts* is a useful tool for academic and special libraries that serve a clientele interested in in-depth coverage of petroleum exploration and production. (EFL)

175. *Philosopher's Index: an international index to philosophical periodicals and books.* [ISSN: 0031-7993] 1967. q. plus a. cumulation. USD 238. Ed(s): Richard H Lineback. Philosopher's Information Center, 1616 E Wooster St, Box P, Bowling Green, OH 43402. Adv. Sample. Circ: 1150 Paid. Vol. ends: No. 4. *Aud.:* Ac.

Philosopher's Index treats approximately 350 serial publications, including those in all major philosophy journals in English, French, German, Spanish, and Italian, plus selected titles in other languages and related interdisciplinary journals. In print, the listings are divided into subject and author indexes, the latter including the complete citation and abstract. Author abstracts are usually used, and if a *PI* staff member provides the abstract, it is so noted. Subject descriptors include proper names, nationalities, historical periods, the major fields of philosophy, subdivisions of these major fields, specific topics and technical terms, and bibliographies. *PI* also indexes and abstracts books and monographic series; analytics for most anthologies are provided. An index to book reviews concludes each print issue. For print subscribers, a cumulative bound volume is issued annually and must be purchased separately. This is the basic indexing source for philosophy and philosophers. (RSH)

176. *Physics Abstracts.* [ISSN: 0036-8091] 1898. s-m. GBP 2705; USD 4600. INSPEC, I.E.E., Michael Faraday House, Six Hills Way, Stevenage, SG1 2AY, United Kingdom; inspec@iee.org.uk; http://www.iee.org.uk. Illus., index, adv. Online: CEDOCAR; CISTI; Data-Star; The Dialog Corporation; F I Z Technik; Questel Orbit Inc.; STN International; SilverPlatter Information, Incorporated. *Aud.:* Ac, Sa.

Physics Abstracts is the world's oldest and most comprehensive index to physics literature. It covers the entire range of subdisciplines within the field of physics, ranging from mathematics to history to applications to instrumentation. Nearly 200,000 abstracts are published each year, covering journals in every language and published in every nation. In addition to articles, *Physics Abstracts* also indexes books, conference papers, technical reports, patents, and dissertations. The biweekly issues are arranged by the Physics and Astronomy Classification Scheme, which organizes the literature of physics into a system similar to the Dewey Decimal classification. This system attempts to organize the different branches of physics into a hierarchical classification. Semi-annual author and subject indexes provide additional access. Separate indexes are included for books, conferences, and corporate authors. *Physics Abstracts* is one part of the INSPEC database, which is widely available through a number of vendors. *Physics Abstracts* remains the single most important indexing and abstracting service in the field of physics. (DAT)

177. *Pollution Abstracts.* [ISSN: 0032-3624] 1970. m. except Dec. USD 1390 combined subscription print & online eds.; USD 1515 combined subscription includes annual index for print & online eds. Ed(s): Craig Emerson. CSA, 7200 Wisconsin Ave, Ste 715, Bethesda, MD 20814; journals@csa.com; http://www.csa.com. Illus., adv. CD-ROM: The Dialog Corporation; National Information Services Corp.; SilverPlatter Information, Incorporated. Online: Pub.; Data-Star; European Space Agency; STN International. *Aud.:* Ac, Sa.

Pollution Abstracts offers access to information on the environment, from scientific research to public policy to government and regulatory issues. Conference proceedings and articles from primary journals in the field are abstracted, as well as hard-to-find documents. Major areas covered include air and water pollution, waste management, toxicology and health, emissions, pollution effects on people and animals, noise, radiation, and environmental action in response to global pollution issues. Dates covered by the file are 1981 to the present, and the database is updated monthly (except in December), with nearly 1,200 new records added each month. There are currently over 200,000 records in the file.

178. *Press.* Formed by the merger of (1946-2001): *Printing Abstracts;* (1983-2001): *World Publishing Monitor;* Which was formerly (until 1991): *Electronic Publishing Abstracts.* [ISSN: 1475-0910] 2001. m. GBP 850; USD 1275. Ed(s): Gillian Micklewright. Pira International, Randalls Rd, Leatherhead, KT22 7RU, United Kingdom; publications@pira.co.uk; http://www.piranet.com. Illus. Sample. *Aud.:* Ac, Sa.

Over 1,000 international printing trade magazines, journals, and conference proceedings are examined for this index. Each issue contains over 500 abstracts with each abstract being approximately 200 words in length. Also included are summaries of the pick of the month's longer features, technical articles, and conference papers. Subjects include company information, graphic reproduction, printing processes, inks, finishing processes, market trends, and management issues. The selective coverage of this index for the printing industry makes it an important addition to any printing collection.

179. *Primary Search.* d. EBSCO Publishing, 10 Estes St, PO Box 682, Ipswich, MA 01938-0682; http://www.epnet.com. *Aud.:* Ems, Hs, Ga.

Primary Search, designed specifically for elementary school libraries and public library children's rooms, contains full text for more than 50 popular elementary school magazines. All full-text articles are assigned a reading level indicator (Lexiles). In addition to the full text, this database offers indexing and abstracts for over 80 magazines. Full text is also available for over 100 student pamphlets. Examples of publications covered in *Primary Search* include *Appleseeds, Boys' Life, Cobblestone, Cricket, Highlights for Children, Hopscotch, Jack & Jill, Ladybug, Ranger Rick, Science World, Spider, SuperScience, Time for Kids, Turtle,* and various *Scholastic* magazines. This database also provides an image collection of 116,000 photos, maps, and flags.

Psychological Abstracts See *PsycINFO.*

180. *PsycINFO.* m. Non-members, USD 499. American Psychological Association, 750 First St, NE, Washington, DC 20002-4242; http://www.apa.org/. *Aud.:* Hs, Ga, Ac, Sa.

The best tool for accessing the psychology literature is *PsycINFO* (all records published in *Psychological Abstracts* are now in *PsycINFO.*). *PsycINFO* covers literature from 1887 to the present, and contains more than 1.9 million references to journal articles, books, book chapters, technical reports, and dissertations published in more than 50 countries. All abstracts in *PsycINFO* are written in English, but the covered literature includes material in more than 24 languages. An integrated thesaurus and "search limiting" offer powerful search options, and recently APA added to the research value of database records by including cited references appearing in journal articles, books, and book chapters. The "historical records" in *PsycINFO* cover psychological literature published from 1887 to 1966 with citations and abstracts from six sources: *Psychological Abstracts* (1927–1966), *Psychological Bulletin* (1921–1926), all APA journals, the *American Journal of Psychology,* from the first issue through 1966, the *Psychological Index* (1894–1935) (citations to English-language journals only), and *Harvard Book Lists* (1938–1971).

Interdisciplinary issues in psychology can call for additional indexes. However, *PsycINFO* also selectively covers such related fields as medicine, education, law, sociology, business, anthropology, physiology, speech pathology, and linguistics. Therefore, *PsycINFO* does serve as the central information search tool for students, researchers, and professionals in psychology. There are numerous considerations and options involved in pricing; those interested should contact APA for current information. (PF)

181. *Quarterly Index to Africana Periodical Literature.* Formerly: *Quarterly Index to Periodical Literature, Eastern and Southern Africa.* [ISSN: 1527-5388] 1991. q. Free. U.S. Library of Congress Office, Embassy of the United States of America, PO Box 30598, Nairobi, Kenya; nairobi@libcon-kenya.org; http://www.icipe.org/locnairobi. Illus. *Aud.:* Ac, Sa.

This invaluable index produced by the U.S. Library of Congress, Nairobi, Kenya Office, provides a continuing index to now 300 periodicals from 29 African countries. Beginning in 2000, the index's new title reflects the widening of the scope to include West Africa. The *Quarterly Index* consists of a register of citations and five indexes: author, geographical, subject term, article title, and journal title. Broad subject categories are used for the register of article citations. The journal index includes each periodical's publication address. This source is an extremely important addition to identify articles published in African magazines and journals.

182. *RILM Abstracts of Music Literature.* [ISSN: 0033-6955] 1967. q. USD 1395 (Individuals, USD 350). Ed(s): Barbara Dobbs Mackenzie. RILM Abstracts, City University of New York, 365 Fifth Ave, New York, NY 10016; LJackson@gc.cuny.edu; http://www.rilm.org. Illus. Circ: 1500 Controlled. CD-ROM: National Information Services Corp. Online: NISC. *Aud.:* Ac, Sa.

RILM Abstracts provides an international bibliography of scholarly music literature found in books, periodicals, bibliographies, catalogues, conference proceedings, discographies, dissertations, ethnographic recordings, Festschriften, films, iconographies, and videos from 1967 to the present. Most citations contain abstracts. *RILM* also contains indexes to author, subject, and journal titles.

RILM contains records in over 200 languages. Foreign-language entries contain English translations of titles, abstracts in English, and full bibliographic information. Over 20,000 new records are added each year. Areas of coverage include historical musicology, ethnomusicology, instruments and voice, performance practice and notation, theory and analysis, and interdisciplinary studies. Concert reviews, recording notes, and pedagogical manuals of scholarly interest are also indexed. *RILM* is available in print, online, and CD-ROM formats. Highly recommended for academic libraries.

183. *Readers' Guide to Periodical Literature.* [ISSN: 0034-0464] 1900. m. plus a. cumulation. USD 345 in US & Canada; USD 380 elsewhere. Ed(s): Donald Cannon. H.W. Wilson Co., 950 University Ave, Bronx, NY 10452-4224; custserv@hwwilson.com; http://www.hwwilson.com. CD-ROM: SilverPlatter Information, Incorporated; H.W. Wilson. *Aud.:* Hs, Ga, Ac.

Readers' Guide to Periodical Literature is one of the standard tools in the librarian's arsenal. This index to general-interest periodicals is found in most English-language libraries throughout the world. In addition to the familiar green-covered print version, Wilson also offers electronic versions. The electronic versions, available as CD-ROM, Wilson Web, or magnetic tape for local loading, include *Readers' Guide Abstracts,* with coverage back to September 1984, and *Readers' Guide Full-text,* with coverage back to January 1994. A new *Retrospective* version, covering 1890 to 1982 has been added to the product line. Any one of these versions is an excellent tool, so cost may be the deciding factor. (KLR)

184. *Religion Index One: Periodicals.* Formerly: *Index to Religious Periodical Literature.* [ISSN: 0149-8428] 1949. s-a. plus a. cumulation. Non-members, USD 530. Ed(s): Carolyn Coates. American Theological Library Association, 250 South Wacker Dr, Ste 1600, Chicago, IL 60606-5834; sales@atla.com; http://www.atla.com. Illus. Circ: 1200. Online: EBSCO Publishing. *Aud.:* Ga, Ac, Sa.

For broad, general coverage of religious periodicals, *RIO* has no equal. Over 520 periodicals are comprehensively indexed, along with about 100 more that are covered selectively. Although almost exclusively Christian in orientation when it began, over the years *RIO* has broadened its coverage to include other religions. In addition to using Library of Congress subject headings, the American Theological Library Association (ATLA) has developed its own religious subject headings (available separately as *ATLA Thesaurus*). The arrangement of these subject headings can be confusing at first, and should be clarified to users. The book of Genesis, for example, is not listed alphabetically, but is found under "Bible (OT)—Genesis," which comes *after* "Bible (OT)—Theology." This occurs because all of the "Bible (OT)" *subjects* (like "Theology") are listed first, followed by the books of the Old Testament arranged in *alphabetical*—rather than canonical—order (the NT uses the same pattern). Once users become accustomed to this scheme, however, they can easily negotiate the hierarchy. Searching for specific terms is facilitated by indexing that is much more specific and detailed than that found in *New Testament Abstracts, Old Testament Abstracts,* or *Religious and Theological Abstracts.* Helpful *see* and *see also* references are also included. There are separate indexes for "Subject," "Author and Editor," and "Scripture" (arranged in canonical, rather than alphabetical, order). This is a premier index that is essential for religious studies, and very highly recommended for academic and large public libraries.

In recent years, indexing products have moved to electronic versions, reflecting the preference of many libraries for these formats. ATLA has responded with CD-ROM, MARC, and online versions of *RIO.* These electronic products, known as *ATLA Religion Database,* provide full retrospective coverage and include several other ATLA indexes. The CD-ROM version includes *Religion Index One: Periodicals, Religion Index Two: Multi-Author Works* (providing detailed coverage of Festschriften and conference proceedings), *Index to Book Reviews in Religion,* and citations from *Methodist Reviews Index, 1818-1985.* The MARC version includes only three of the CD-ROM databases (*RIO, RIT, IBRR*), but provides the records in MARC format so they can be loaded into a library's online catalog system. This allows the user to search the *Religion Database* through the catalog's interface, retrieving both indexing and catalog records simultaneously. The online version of *Religion Database* is available through several vendors (Cambridge Scientific Abstracts, EBSCO, OCLC, Ovid, SilverPlatter).

In order to provide full-text journal access, ATLA offers another product, *ATLAS: ATLA Serials,* that builds on the online *Religion Database.* ATLA has already digitized 50 years of about 60 top journals in religion. Retrospective coverage ultimately will extend back to volume one—regardless of how many years are involved. The ongoing digitization process currently includes page images (GIF), but eventually will include fully searchable XML versions as well. *ATLAS* links results from *Religion Database* to this digital collection, providing the user with the full text (when available). Given the continued usefulness of older articles for religious research, this digital collection is a welcome resource. Due to the changing nature of electronic resources and the variables involved in pricing, those interested in these electronic options should contact ATLA (www.atla.com) for current pricing and information. Libraries supporting religious studies are strongly advised to consider the advantages provided by online access to *Religion Database* and *ATLAS.* These products represent the standard for electronic religious research and are very highly recommended. (LAP)

185. *Religious & Theological Abstracts.* [ISSN: 0034-4044] 1958. q. USD 165 (Individuals, USD 50). Ed(s): William S Sailer. Religious & Theological Abstracts, Inc., PO Box 215, Myerstown, PA 17067; rtabst@sunlink.net; http://www.rtabst.org/. Refereed. Circ: 800. Vol. ends: Dec. *Aud.:* Ac, Sa.

Reviewing over 400 periodicals, *RelAb* provides coverage of religion and theology that is similar to *Religion Index One* (above in this section). The difference between them is that *RIO* is a detailed index, while *RelAb* is a topically categorized list of abstracts. Abstracts are classified under the major headings: "Biblical," "Theological," "Historical," and "Practical," with further subdivisions under each heading. A "Subject Index" and "Author Index" are also included, which are cumulative throughout the yearly volume. The final issue of each volume also contains a cumulated "Scripture Index." Christianity, Judaism, and other world religions are included. English-language abstracts cover research in French, German, Dutch, Swedish, Norwegian, Afrikaans, Hebrew, Italian, and Spanish. A cumulative version of *RelAb* is available on CD-ROM. Information about this resource can be found online at rtabst.org. Highly recommended for academic libraries. (LAP)

186. *Repertoire Bibliographique de la Philosophie.* Former titles (until 1949): *Revue Philosophique de Louvain. Supplement. Repertoire Bibliographique;* (until 1946): *Revue Neoscolastique de Philosophie. Repertoire Bibliographique.* [ISSN: 0034-4567] 1934. q. EUR 120. Ed(s): A Van De Pute, G Gerard. Peeters, Bondgenotenlaan 153, Leuven, 3000, Belgium. Illus., index. Refereed. Circ: 1800. Vol. ends: No. 4. *Aud.:* Ac.

This index is published under the auspices of the International Institute of Philosophy, with the patronage of UNESCO and the support of the Communaute Francaise. The first three issues of each volume index both books and articles appearing in approximately 600 periodicals in the English, French, German, Italian, Dutch, Latin, Portugese, Spanish, and Catalan languages. The entries are listed in two sections: "History of Philosophy," which is arranged both geographically and chronologically; and "Philosophy," which is arranged according to the standard subdivisions of the subject. The fourth issue of each volume indexes book reviews, authors, and anonymous publications. Despite the fact that there are no abstracts such as one finds in *The Philosopher's Index,* this is an essential reference resource because of its broad coverage. (RSH)

187. *Risk Abstracts (Online Edition).* m. USD 350. Ed(s): Craig Emerson. CSA, 7200 Wisconsin Ave, Ste 715, Bethesda, MD 20814; journals@csa.com; http://www.csa.com. Illus., index. Vol. ends: Oct. Online: Pub. *Aud.:* Ac, Sa.

A complement to *Health and Safety Science Abstracts* (above in this section), *Risk Abstracts* offers a different focus. This abstracting and indexing publication is also an inexpensive alternative. This file is published in association with the Institute for Risk Research at the University of Waterloo, and covers areas such as natural hazards, technological risks, environmental risks, biological risks, medical and environmental health, industry and labor, and policy and planning. Dates of coverage are from 1990 to the present. Cambridge Scientific Abstracts offers this database in various formats: print, CD-ROM, or via the web. An important component of collections focused on the identification, evaluation, and elimination of risk across a wide range of occupational and environmental situations. (ELS)

188. *S T A R.* [ISSN: 0036-8741] 1963. m. U.S. National Aeronautics and Space Administration, Scientific and Technical Information Office, 7121 Standard Dr, Hanover, MD 21076-1320. Illus. Refereed. Microform: NTI; PMC; PQC. Online: European Space Agency. Reprint: PQC. *Aud.:* Ga, Ac, Sa.

Scientific and Technical Aerospace Reports (*STAR*), produced by the National Aeronautics and Space Administration (NASA) Scientific and Technical Information (STI) Office, provides informative abstracts as well as bibliographic citations to reports and literature on aerospace-related topics. This international index covers all aspects of aeronautics and space research as well as aerospace aspects of earth resources, energy development, conservation, environmental protection, and other areas related to aeronautics, astronautics, and space sciences. The index primarily includes NASA and NASA-contractor literature and reports issued from other U.S. government agencies, domestic and foreign institutions, universities, and private firms. This abstract index migrated from a printed resource to a web-accessible resource in 1995. There are two main access points, either by accessing an Adobe Acrobat version of the individual volumes or by searching the RECONselect database. The Adobe Acrobat version of the index is divided into 11 broad subject categories, along with a subject and a personal-author index. These broad subject categories are further divided into a total of 76 subject categories. The subject organization mirrors that of *International Aerospace Abstracts,* which focuses on the published journal and conference literature. This index fills an important role in the locating, organizing, and distributing of technical reports and related information, and is important for most general engineering collections. (HSM)

189. ***Sage Family Studies Abstracts.*** [ISSN: 0164-0283] 1979. q. GBP 584 in Europe, Middle East, Africa & Australasia. Sage Publications, Inc., 2455 Teller Rd, Thousand Oaks, CA 91320; info@sagepub.com; http://www.sagepub.com. Illus., adv. Sample. Circ: 500 Paid. Vol. ends: Nov. *Aud.:* Ac, Sa.

Sage Family Studies Abstracts is a print index to articles, books, and reports in most areas of family studies. Specific areas of coverage include adolescent development and parenthood; aging, child abuse and neglect; cross-cultural relations; death and dying; marriage and divorce; domestic abuse; family counseling and therapy; gender relations and gender roles; and sexuality. Coverage is selective and inclusion indicates quality. Broader and more comprehensive coverage is available in *Family & Society Studies Worldwide* (above in this section). Approximately 1,000 new entries are found in each year's indexing. Electronic service is available from several vendors. Some vendors of full-text services have implemented this as if it were an online journal instead of an abstracting and indexing service, making it somewhat confusing to users. (KK)

190. ***Sage Urban Studies Abstracts.*** [ISSN: 0090-5747] 1973. q. GBP 550 in Europe, Middle East, Africa & Australasia. Sage Publications, Inc., 2455 Teller Rd, Thousand Oaks, CA 91320; info@sagepub.com; http://www.sagepub.com. Illus., index, adv. Circ: 750. Vol. ends: Nov. *Aud.:* Ac, Sa.

Sage Urban Studies Abstracts indexes the core urban studies literature, including journal articles, books, research papers, and government documents published by scholars, practitioners, legislative groups, research institutes, and public agencies. All aspects of the field are covered, including urban development and planning, environment and land use, architecture and design, urban history and sociology, housing and real estate, transportation, economics, criminology, public services, social policy, and politics and government. Each quarterly update includes abstracts and citations to approximately 250 articles and other publications. The online version covers 1998 to the present, and the print indexes cover 1973 to the present. The November issue of the print index includes annual cumulative author and subject indexes, as well as a list of periodicals abstracted. Appropriate for large academic libraries supporting strong urban studies programs.

Science Abstracts. Section B. See *Electrical & Electronics Abstracts.*

Science Abstracts. Section C. See *Computer & Control Abstracts.*

191. ***Science Citation Index.*** [ISSN: 0036-827X] 1961. 6x/yr. USD 15020. Institute for Scientific Information, 3501 Market St., Philadelphia, PA 19104; http://www.isinet.com. Illus., index. Vol. ends: Dec. CD-ROM: Pub. Online: Data-Star; DIMDI; Questel Orbit Inc. *Aud.:* Ac, Sa.

A multidisciplinary index covering more than 3,600 of the leading scientific and technical journals, as well as some symposium proceedings and monographs. As part of the online service called *Web of Science* or *Web of Knowledge*, it covers more than 5,600 journals. Every major discipline in the physical and life sciences is treated. *SCI* provides the bibliographic information for the articles published during a specified time period. Like all of ISI's citation indexes, this product offers researchers the powerful ability to search by citation and therefore find references published after a citation-in-hand. The online version, despite its cost, is much more widely used now than the print version, both for general ease of use and for the multi-year search capability. A fundamental resource for academic researchers. (JK)

192. ***Social Sciences Citation Index.*** [ISSN: 0091-3707] 1969. 3x/yr. USD 6900. Institute for Scientific Information, 3501 Market St., Philadelphia, PA 19104; http://www.isinet.com. Illus. Sample. CD-ROM: Pub. Online: Data-Star; DIMDI. *Aud.:* Ac, Sa.

This index provides access to the core journal literature of the social, behavioral, and related sciences. The print version has three sections: Permuterm Subject Index, Source Index, and Citation Index. Permuterm Subject Index provides access to authors of works relating to a topic. Source Index includes the full description of the article, including the bibliographic references. Citation Index lists cited authors and works that cite them. There is also a CD-ROM version. Much easier to use is the *Web of Science*, the online version, with coverage from 1956 to the present; references for sources available through ISI are hotlinked. Access is also available for the Arts and Humanities and Sciences databases. Highly recommended for academic libraries. (SKD)

193. ***Social Sciences Index.*** Supersedes in part: *Social Sciences and Humanities Index.* [ISSN: 0094-4920] 1974. q. Ed(s): Cheryl Ehrens. H.W. Wilson Co., 950 University Ave, Bronx, NY 10452-4224; custserv@hwwilson.com; http://www.hwwilson.com. CD-ROM: SilverPlatter Information, Incorporated; H.W. Wilson. *Aud.:* Hs, Ga, Ac.

An index to over 500 English-language periodicals, with expanded coverage in 2003, covering a broad spectrum of social sciences. Index coverage begins with 1983, abstracts from 1994, and full text online for selected journals beginning with 1995. Although a print index and a CD-Rom version with abstracts are published, the online version would be much more useful. This greatly improved, user-friendly database has several useful options: a "no-results" search provides the user with a list of relevant results; the ability to limit search results to peer-reviewed journals; an online thesaurus; and the ability to connect to other catalogs and databases using SFX-powered technology. Book reviews are listed separately at the end of each print index, and are available in the online and CD-ROM versions as well. An online retrospective social sciences and humanities index covering 1907-1984 will be released in Fall 2003. Highly recommended. (SKD)

194. ***Social Services Abstracts.*** m. USD 1650 current & archive. CSA, 7200 Wisconsin Ave, Ste 715, Bethesda, MD 20814; journals@csa.com; http://www.csa.com. *Aud.:* Ac, Sa.

Social Services Abstracts provides indexes and abstracts to over 1,600 social services journals from 1980 to the present. Social service issues cover topics such as community development; crisis intervention; family issues such as domestic violence, poverty, and homelessness; social welfare services and support networks; gerontology; policy, planning, and forecasting; evaluation research; and professional issues in social work. The database is part of the Cambridge Social Services InfoNet; other portions link to topics relevant to social services professionals, such as organizations, pending legislation, newsletter lists, and book reviews. Recommended for academic and special libraries supporting social services programs or curricula. (SKD)

195. ***Social Work Abstracts.*** Supersedes in part (in 1994): *Social Work Research and Abstracts;* Which was formerly (until 1977): *Abstracts for Social Workers.* [ISSN: 1070-5317] 1965. q. USD 115 (Individuals, USD 80; Members, USD 50). N A S W Press, 750 First St, N E, Ste 700, Washington, DC 20002-4241; press@naswdc.org; http://www.naswpress.org. Illus., adv. Refereed. Circ: 2500. CD-ROM: SilverPlatter Information, Incorporated. Microform: PQC. Reprint: PQC. *Aud.:* Ac, Sa.

Produced by the National Association of Social Workers. Coverage is provided for over 400 journals, including international sources, in social work and social welfare. Abstracts in the print version are arranged under four major subject areas: Social Work Profession, Theory and Practice, Areas of Service, and Social Issues/Social Problems. There are CD-ROM and online versions, covering the entire *Social Works Abstracts* database from 1977 to the present, plus the *NASW Register of Clinical Social Workers.* Recommended, especially the online version, for libraries serving social services clientele. (SKD)

196. ***Sociological Abstracts.*** [ISSN: 0038-0202] 1953. bi-m. USD 720 combined subscription print & online eds.; USD 860 combined subscription includes a. cumulative index for print & online eds.; USD 262 combined subscription annual cumulative index in print & on CD-ROM. Ed(s): Jill Blaemers. CSA, 7200 Wisconsin Ave, Ste 715, Bethesda, MD 20814; journals@csa.com; http://www.csa.com. Illus., adv. Circ: 1900. *Aud.:* Ac, Sa.

Sociological Abstracts, online through Cambridge, indexes more than 1,700 journals, conference papers, books, and dissertations in all areas of sociology and related disciplines from 1963 to the present, with abstracts available from 1974. The database provides useful features such as an online thesaurus, several refining and limiting options, SFX-powered technology that links to library catalogs, and the ability to search simultaneously other Cambridge subscription databases. Highly recommended for academic libraries. (SKD)

197. ***Soils and Fertilizers.*** [ISSN: 0038-0792] 1937. m. USD 2170. CABI Publishing, Wallingford, OC10 8DE, United Kingdom; orders@cabi.org; http://www.cabi.org. Illus., adv. Online: The Dialog Corporation; DIMDI; STN International. *Aud.:* Ac, Sa.

This is a Commonwealth Agricultural Bureau (CAB)abstract journal that provides a comprehensive index to soil science literature. Entries are arranged in broad subject classifications that can be found in the beginning of the publication. Each issue has an author and subject index in the back for more specific searching. About 15,000 entries are added to this journal each year. The publisher now makes the journal available on the web, with weekly updates and a ten-year backfile, to individual or institutional subscribers.

198. ***SPORTDiscus.*** 1975. q. Sport Information Resource Centre (SIRC), 116 Albert St Ste 400, Ottawa, ON K1P 5G3, Canada. *Aud.:* Ac, Sa.

Published since 1975 by the Sport Information Resource Centre of Canada (SIRC), *SPORTDiscus* is a bibliographic database providing extensive international coverage of the sport, fitness, recreation, sports medicine, and related literature. Subjects include sports medicine, physical education, sport law, physical fitness, training, kinesiology, physical therapy, sport science, administration, coaching, and recreation. This international multidisciplinary database contains references from journal and magazine articles, books, book chapters, conference proceedings, theses, dissertations, and web sites. Coverage of theses and monographs extends back to 1949, while journal coverage ranges from 1975 to the present. In 1996 the database added citations from the previous Sport & Leisure bibliographic database of SIRLS, covering the research literature for the social and psychological aspects of sport and leisure, including play, games, and dance. The database is available on CD or online through SilverPlatter, OVID, EBSCO, Dialog, or DataStar. An appropriate acquisition for medical and academic libraries with physical education and sports science programs. (BP)

199. ***Statistical Theory and Method Abstracts (CD-ROM Edition).*** Former titles (until vol.42, 2002): *Statistical Theory and Method Abstracts (Print Edition);* (until 1964): *International Journal of Abstracts.* [ISSN: 1569-0636] 1959. 2x/yr. Non-members, EUR 120. Ed(s): Constance van Eeden, Fred Steutel. International Statistical Institute, Princes Beatrixlaan 428, PO Box 950, Voorburg, 2270 AZ, Netherlands; isi@cbs.nl; http://www.cbs.nl/isi. Illus., index, adv. Circ: 750 Paid. Vol. ends: No. 4. Reprint: PSC. *Aud.:* Ac, Sa.

Statistical Theory and Method Abstracts is produced by the International Statistical Institute, and is the primary abstracting and indexing service for mathematical statistics and probability. The publications provides comprehensive international coverage, with abstracts of articles from statistics and probability journals, journals largely devoted to other fields that regularly contain papers of interest, conference proceedings, Festschriften, commemorative volumes, research reports, and monographs in series. There are 97 journals receiving complete coverage. Entries are arranged according to a classification scheme composed of 15 broad categories, with as many as 39 subtopics in each category. Each listing includes just a single subject heading. Each issue contains an author index. A cumulative author index and a list of publications indexed are published as a supplement to the last issue each year. The file is also available online and on CD-ROM. (KW)

200. ***Studies on Women and Gender Abstracts.*** Formerly (until 2000): *Studies on Women Abstracts.* [ISSN: 1467-596X] 1983. bi-m. GBP 560 (Individuals, GBP 172). Ed(s): June Purvis. Carfax Publishing Ltd., 4 Park Sq, Milton Park, Abingdon, OX14 4RN, United Kingdom; enquiry@tandf.co.uk; http://www.tandf.co.uk/. Illus., index, adv. Online: Ingenta Select; ProQuest Information & Learning. Reprint: PSC. *Aud.:* Ac.

This international abstracting service, formerly *Studies on Women Abstracts*, covers the major international academic journals and books in women's studies from 1995 forward. It is available in print and online versions. The online version is free to institutions with print subscriptions and provides links to full text where possible. The publisher's web site offers a free online trial and a list of journals covered. Appropriate for academic and research libraries. (LRK)

201. ***T O C S - I N.*** 1992. irreg. Free. Ed(s): Jacques Poucet, Philippa M W Matheson. T O C S - I N, http://www.chass.utoronto.ca.amphoras/tocs/html. *Aud.:* Ac.

This free online service, maintained entirely by volunteers, provides table of contents information for around 160 journals in classical studies and related fields. Only print publicatinos are included; *TOCS-IN* does not cover electronic publications, but *TOCS-IN* has coverage of collections of articles, such as Festschriften. While coverage for most publications begins in 1992, *TOCS-IN* also has earlier coverage for a number of significant titles. Journals are arranged in groups by broad topics, including classics, archaeology, religion, and Near Eastern Studies. *TOCS-IN* provides direct links to full text, preprints, and abstracts when these are available on the web. While *L'Annee Philologique* is much more comprehensive, *TOCS-IN* is far more timely and is readily available to anyone with access to the Internet. (FWJ)

202. ***T R I S Electronic Bibliographic Data Base.*** Incorporates (in 1996): *Highway Research Abstracts;* Which was formerly (1968-1990): *H R I S Abstracts.* m. U.S. National Research Council, Transportation Research Board, 2101 Constitution Ave, N W, Washington, DC 20418; jmaccock@nas.edu; http://www.nas.edu/trb/index.html. CD-ROM: SilverPlatter Information, Incorporated. *Aud.:* Ac, Sa.

TRIS Online is the free, web-based bibliographic index published and maintained by the Transportation Research Board, in collaboration with other private, state, and federal transportation agencies. It is the largest transportation bibliographic utility, offering over 470,000 citations, including journal articles, books, conference proceedings, technical reports, and other media. It covers all transportation modalities, and absorbs several other transportation indexes, including *TRANweb, PATH, ITRD,* and the *Canadian Surface Transportation Research Database.* Many citations are annotated.

TableBase. See *Business and Industry.*

203. ***TRANweb: transportation article file.*** 1985. unknown. Transportation Library, 1935 Sheridan Rd, Evanston, IL 60208-2300; library@northwestern.edu; http://www.library.nwu.edu/transportation/. *Aud.:* Ac, Sa.

TRANweb is a free bibliographic index published and maintained on the web by the Transportation Library at Northwestern University. The database is comprised of references to articles on transportation, traffic, and law enforcement, providing full citations and subject headings for over 235,000 entries. Coverage includes journal articles, conference proceedings, technical reports, annual reports, environmental impact statements, and selected documents important to the disciplines. Generally, citations extend back to 1979, with a few of particular importance extending back to 1976, or even further for those of current interest. This is a core database for transportation researchers.

204. ***U.S. Government Periodicals Index.*** Supersedes (1970-1987): *Index to U.S. Government Periodicals.* [ISSN: 1076-3163] 1970. q. plus a. cumulation. USD 995; USD 1295 print & online eds. Ed(s): John Heffernan. Congressional Information Service, Inc., 4520 East West Hwy, Bethesda, MD 20814; cisinfo@lexis-nexis.com; http://www.cispubs.com. *Aud.:* Ac, Sa.

Covering articles in approximately 170 current federal periodicals, plus retrospective coverage from 1988 of over 60 additional federal publications that have major research, reference, or general-interest value, this resource appeals to a broad cross-section of researchers. Available in print and online through *LexisNexis Government Periodicals Index.* While the articles cited in the web-based index are not full-text, a list of full-text online periodicals is maintained on the web site for easy access to the online magazines.

205. ***Veterinary Bulletin: a monthly abstract journal on veterinary science.*** [ISSN: 0042-4854] 1931. m. USD 1660. Ed(s): Robert Taylor. CABI Publishing, Wallingford, OC10 8DE, United Kingdom; orders@cabi.org; http://www.cabi.org. Illus., index, adv. Sample. Vol. ends: Dec. Online: The Dialog Corporation; DIMDI; STN International. *Bk. rev.:* 10-30, 50-350 words. *Aud.:* Ac, Sa.

This journal contains abstracts for articles of major interest that are found during the process of creating *Index Veterinarius* (above in this section). Frequently, the authors' own abstracts are used, but if the indexer feels that an abstract is not adequate, it is enhanced for inclusion. Around 8,500 abstracts are added every year. A numbering system provides cross-referencing between this publication and *Index Veterinarius.* An average of 20 book reviews are included in each issue. An annual author and subject index is produced. Available in both a print and an online version that includes access to a ten-year backfile. (CTB)

206. *Violence & Abuse Abstracts: current literature in interpersonal violence.* [ISSN: 1077-2197] 1995. q. GBP 731 in Europe, Middle East, Africa & Australasia. Sage Publications, Inc., 2455 Teller Rd, Thousand Oaks, CA 91320; info@sagepub.com; http://www.sagepub.com. Adv. *Aud.:* Ac, Sa.

VAA provides abstracts and extended bibliographic citations of "recent literature on all types of interpersonal violence, including sexual, physical and psychological child abuse, domestic violence, rape, sexual assault and harassment, hate crimes, workplace violence, gang violence, elder abuse and neglect." Coverage begins with 1995 and includes about 1,200 abstracts of journal articles, books, conference proceedings, and reports annually. A free contents alert service is available from the publisher's U.S. web site. A useful resource for researchers, social workers, mental health practitioners, legal professionals, and others concerned with the problems of violence and abuse. (LRK)

207. *Water Resources Abstracts (Bethesda, Online Edition).* Formerly (until 1993): *Selected Water Resources Abstracts.* m. USD 3200 current & archive. CSA, 7200 Wisconsin Ave, Ste 715, Bethesda, MD 20814; journals@csa.com; http://www.csa.com. Illus. Microform: BHP. Online: Pub.; NISC. *Aud.:* Ac, Sa.

Continuing the fine work of *Selected Water Resources Abstracts*, produced by the U.S. Geological Survey from 1967 to 1993, this is a resource for bibliographic information and abstracts representing publications from around the world on all aspects of water resources. The majority of entries are for English-language publications and cover scientific journal articles, conference proceedings, U.S. government documents, patents, and court cases. Material indexed is drawn from sources in life, physical, and social sciences and includes relevant items on engineering, policy, and law. (FS)

208. *Wilson Business Abstracts.* [ISSN: 1057-6533] 1991. w. H.W. Wilson Co., 950 University Ave, Bronx, NY 10452-4224; custserv@hwwilson.com; http://www.hwwilson.com. CD-ROM: SilverPlatter Information, Incorporated; H.W. Wilson. *Aud.:* Ga, Ac.

Indexing over 600 international English-language business periodicals, this product covers all aspects of contemporary business. In addition to feature articles, there are citations to book reviews, interviews, biographical sketches, new-product reviews, corporate profiles, and obituaries. Letters to the editor, advertisements, and articles of less than one column are not included. *Wilson Business Full Text* includes full-text coverage of more than 350 periodicals back to January 1995. Wilson continues to publish the print counterpart, *Business Periodicals Index*, that contains only bibliographic citations under a subject heading hierarchy. At one time these were standard sources, but most researchers prefer *ABI/Inform* or *Business ASAP*, if available. (BD)

Wilson Business Full Text. See *Wilson Business Abstracts.*

209. *Women Studies Abstracts.* [ISSN: 0049-7835] 1971. q. USD 240 (Individuals, USD 102). Ed(s): Sara Stauffer Whaley. Transaction Publishers, 35 Berrue Circle, Rutgers University, Piscataway, NJ 08854-8042; trans@transactionpub.com; http://www.transactionpub.com. Illus., index, adv. Circ: 800. Vol. ends: Winter. CD-ROM: National Information Services Corp. Microform: PQC. Online: NISC. Reprint: PQC; PSC. *Aud.:* Ac.

This publication abstracts significant research in women's studies appearing since 1971 in some 60 journals. Entries are arranged by subject and cover key areas such as "education and socialization, psychology of women, sex roles, and characteristics; politics and government; employment; family; violence against women; mental and physical health; pregnancy, fertility, childbirth and neonatal care; finances; history; literature; art and music; interpersonal relations; and biography and criticism." Each volume includes a cumulative author and subject index. Also available in a CD-ROM version, updated semi-annually. Its broad scope, length of coverage, and affordable price make this a useful for publication for academic and public libraries.

210. *Women's Studies Index (Year).* [ISSN: 1058-6369] 1990. a. USD 295. G.K. Hall & Co., 12 Lunar Dr, Woodbridge, CT 06525; http://www.galegroup.com/gkhall. Illus. *Aud.:* Ga, Ac.

This annual index from G.K. Hall covers 100 popular and scholarly journals focusing on the diverse issues of concern to women's studies. Coverage is "predominantly but not exclusively American." Some lesbian, women of color, and international titles are included. Scholarly journals are fully indexed (book reviews, etc.) while popular magazines are indexed selectively. Entries are arranged by LC subject headings as modified by terms from M.E. Capek's *A Women's Thesaurus. WSI* offers solid coverage of core titles in women?s studies without the power and flexibility of computer searching. *Women's Studies on Disc* is based on this title. (LRK)

211. *Women's Studies International (Baltimore).* Formerly: *Women's Resources International.* 1996. s-a. National Information Services Corp., Ste 6, Wyman Towers, 3100 St Paul St, Baltimore, MD 21218; http://www.nisc.com. *Aud.:* Ac.

Formerly *Women's Resources International*, this broadly inclusive database provides access to "journals, newspapers, newsletters, bulletins, books, book chapters, proceedings, reports, theses, dissertations, NGO studies, important websites & web documents, and grey literature." It is made up of ten files including *Women's Studies Abstracts, Women's Studies Database, Women's Studies Bibliography Database*, four files from the University of Wisconsin System's Women's Studies Librarian, and a *MEDLINE Subset on Women.* The content and period of coverage varies from file to file, and some duplication of entries occurs. This product is available in web and CD-ROM versions, and offers a variety options for searching, printing, and downloading. (LRK)

212. *Women's Studies on Disc.* G.K. Hall & Co., 12 Lunar Dr, Woodbridge, CT 06525; remmel.nunn@gale.com. *Aud.:* Ga, Ac.

This cumulative version of *Women's Studies Index* provides access to popular and scholarly articles and book reviews in women's studies published since 1988. Scholarly journals are fully indexed (book reviews, etc.) while popular magazines are indexed selectively. Abstracts are included from 1997 forward. Entries are arranged by LC subject headings as modified by terms from M.E. Capek's *A Women's Thesaurus.* The current edition also includes *An Index to Women's Studies Anthologies, Research Across the Disciplines*, compiled by Sara Brownmiller and Ruth Dickstein, *Women's Periodicals and Newspapers From the 18th Century to 1981*, edited by James P. Danky, and *The Women's Movement: References and Resources*, by Barbara Ryan. This product is updated annually and is fully networkable at no extra charge. (LRK)

213. *World Agricultural Economics and Rural Sociology Abstracts: abstracts of world literature.* Supersedes: *Digest of Agricultural Economics and Marketing.* [ISSN: 0043-8219] 1959. m. USD 1425. CABI Publishing, Wallingford, OC10 8DE, United Kingdom. Illus., adv. Vol. ends: Dec. Online: The Dialog Corporation; DIMDI; STN International. *Aud.:* Ga, Ac, Sa.

This CAB abstract journal covers agriculture, including a wide variety of subtopics such as agricultural policy and development; agricultural economics, employment, and income; agrarian reform; environment and natural resources; supply, demand, and prices; input industries; food policies; international trade, finance, and credit; farm economics, marketing, and distribution; cooperatives; and rural sociology. Approximately 8,000 entries are added each year.

214. *Zentralblatt fuer Geologie und Palaeontologie. Teil II: Palaeontologie.* [ISSN: 0044-4189] 1807. 7x/yr. USD 87 per issue domestic; USD 88.10 per issue foreign. Ed(s): Adolf Seilacher, E Seilacher. E. Schweizerbart'sche Verlagsbuchhandlung, Johannesstr 3A, Stuttgart, 70176, Germany; mail@schweizerbart.de; http://www.schweizerbart.de. Illus., index, adv. *Bk. rev.:* Various number and length. *Aud.:* Ac, Sa.

This service covers all aspects of geology and paleontontology with over 900 abstracts each year. *Zentralblatt fuer Geologie und Palaeontologie. Teil 2* is a leading index for geological and paleontological journals, books, conference proceedings, reports, and theses. It consists of three sections: Allgemeine Palaeontologie, Palaeozoologie, and Palaeobotanik. Each bimonthly issue carries one or more review articles and a subject index. (KG)

215. ***Zoological Record.*** [ISSN: 0144-3607] 1864. a. USD 4825 print; USD 5830 electronic; USD 6430 combined subscription print & electronic. Ed(s): Marcia Edwards. BIOSIS, 2 Commerce Sq., 2001 Market St, Ste 700, Philadelphia, PA 19103-7095; info@biosis.org; http://www.biosis.org/. Illus., index. CD-ROM: SilverPlatter Information, Incorporated. Microform: BHP; PQC. *Aud.:* Ga, Ac, Sa.

The *Zoological Record* is an annual index to the world's zoological literature. It is the oldest continuously published and the most respected information service for life sciences in the world. The publication of this title dates back to 1865, and it is now published annually in separate sections, the first of which is "Comprehensive Zoology," followed by sections recording literature relating to the class of the animal kingdom. Each section contains five indexes: Author, Subject, Geographical, Paleontological, and Systematic. Approximately 6,000 serials published worldwide are reviewed for inclusion. *ZR* may be accessed in print, on the web, on CD-ROM, and online. (KG)

■ ACCOUNTING AND TAXATION

Christopher Hoeppner, Associate Director of Libraries, DePaul University, 2350 North Kenmore Avenue, Chicago, IL 60614; choeppne@depaul.edu

Introduction

Since the last edition of *Magazines for Libraries* appeared, events have made it clear that accounting is too important to be left to accountants. In a matter of months, the United States saw the failure of Enron, one of the nation's largest corporations, amid a variety of dubious accounting practices, and the consequent failure of its auditor, one of the world's largest and, previously, most highly regarded public accounting firms. News of the Enron debacle was soon followed by reports of accounting malfeasance at a number of other large and prominent publicly traded corporations. Discussions of accounting treatments and auditing activities that for so long were relegated to business and financial publications suddenly burst onto the front pages of daily newspapers and the covers of popular magazines. What will result from the legislative and regulatory reforms occasioned by these events remains uncertain. One effect has been to highlight the fact that—unlike in many disciplines where notions of truth are rooted in empirical observation and rational analysis—in accounting these ways of knowing influence and are influenced by received wisdom in the form of authority. This authority can take various forms: the Internal Revenue Service and other revenue agencies in the area of taxation; the Securities and Exchange Commission and other countries' regulators, where accounting information pertains to publicly traded stocks and other securities; and the Financial Accounting Standards Board and other standards-setting bodies for the principles that underlie the preparation of financial statements. Thus, the interpretation and application of authoritative pronouncements is a topic of much ongoing discussion for both accounting academics and practitioners. Periodicals in the field can fall into several categories: news sources used by readers to keep up with current developments; professional journals where practitioners elucidate principles and discuss how these are to be applied; and scholarly titles where academicians examine the impact of existing principles and structures and evaluate how these might be altered.

Basic Periodicals

Ac: *Accounting Review, The CPA Journal, Journal of Accountancy, Journal of Accounting Research.*

Basic Abstracts and Indexes

ABI/INFORM, Accounting and Tax Index, Business & Company ASAP, Business Periodicals Index, EBSCO Business Source Elite.

216. ***Abacus: a journal of accounting, finance and business studies.*** [ISSN: 0001-3072] 1964. 3x/yr. GBP 132 print & online eds. Ed(s): G W Dean. Blackwell Publishing Asia, 550 Swanston St, Carlton South, VIC 3053, Australia; subs@blackwellpublishingasia.com; http://www.blackwellpublishing.com/. Illus., adv. Refereed. Circ: 1200. Online: EBSCO Publishing; Gale Group; ingenta.com; OCLC Online Computer Library Center, Inc.; RoweCom Information Quest; Swets Blackwell. Reprint: PQC; SWZ. *Indexed:* ABIn, ATI, IBSS, PAIS, SSCI. *Aud.:* Ac.

Published on behalf of the Accounting Foundation, University of Sydney, this scholarly journal is international in scope, with an emphasis on the development of, and alternatives to, accounting standards and practices.

217. ***Accountancy International.*** Formerly (until 1998): *Accountancy.* 1889. m. USD 100 United States; GBP 5.10 newsstand/cover per issue domestic; USD 10 newsstand/cover per issue foreign. Ed(s): Brian Singleton Green. Institute of Chartered Accountants in England and Wales, Moorgate Pl, PO Box 433, London, EC2P 2BJ, United Kingdom; postmaster@theabg.demon.co.uk; http://www.accountancymag.co.uk. Illus., index, adv. Circ: 70000. Vol. ends: Jun/Dec. Microform: PQC. Online: Gale Group; Northern Light Technology, Inc. Reprint: PSC. *Indexed:* ABIn, ATI, BPI, ExcerpMed. *Bk. rev.:* 0-2, 500-750 words, signed. *Aud.:* Sa.

Published on behalf of the Institute of Chartered Accountants in England and Wales, the British professional association for public accountants, this magazine offers a mix of news, opinion pieces, and feature articles. The focus is on the practical, with articles on taxation, management issues in accounting practice, and implications of new standards. Frequently, summaries or the full texts of official releases, such as exposure drafts or new pronouncements, are included.

218. ***The Accountant.*** [ISSN: 0001-4710] 1874. m. IEP 349; USD 599; IEP 525 Print & Online eds. Ed(s): Paul Rogernon. Lafferty Publications Ltd., The Tower, IDA Enterprise Centre, Pearse St, Dublin, 2, Ireland; cuserv@lafferty.ie; http://www.lafferty.co.uk/newsletter/iaccount.html. Illus., index, adv. Online: Factiva; Florida Center for Library Automation; Gale Group; LexisNexis; Northern Light Technology, Inc.; OCLC Online Computer Library Center, Inc. Reprint: PSC. *Indexed:* ATI, B&I, LRI. *Aud.:* Ac, Sa.

This monthly newsletter, typically 20 pages in length, contains news articles describing trends and developments in accounting practice worldwide. Articles announce new standards, report news from accounting firms and associations, or survey the accounting profession within a particular country.

219. ***Accounting & Business.*** Former titles (until 1998): *Certified Accountant;* (until 1972): *Certified Accountants Journal.* [ISSN: 1460-406X] 1905. m. GBP 85 (Individuals, GBP 42; Students, GBP 25). Ed(s): John Prosser. Association of Chartered Certified Accountants, 29 Lincoln's Inn Fields, London, WC2A 3EE, United Kingdom; http://www.accaglobal.com/publications/accountingandbusiness/. Illus., index, adv. Circ: 59450. Vol. ends: Dec. *Indexed:* ATI. *Bk. rev.:* 3, 150-400 words, signed. *Aud.:* Sa.

This professional journal for British accountants, a publication of the Association of Chartered Certified Accountants, offers news of accounting and auditing trends and developments, information about association activities, and feature articles that frequently focus on business topics outside of accounting. It also presents information on official pronouncements of the association. An archive (1998-) of the full text of many articles is available at the journal's web site.

220. ***Accounting and Business Research.*** Formerly (until 1970): *Accounting Research.* [ISSN: 0001-4788] 1970. q. GBP 120 (Individuals, GBP 40). Ed(s): J A Darnill. Institute of Chartered Accountants in England and Wales, Moorgate Pl, PO Box 433, London, EC2P 2BJ, United

Kingdom; postmaster@theabg.demon.co.uk; http://www.icaew.co.uk/. Illus., index, adv. Refereed. Circ: 1500. Vol. ends: Autumn. Microform: PQC; WMP. Online: Gale Group. Reprint: SCH; SWZ. *Indexed:* ABIn, ATI, BPI, ExcerpMed, IBSS, PAIS. *Bk. rev.:* 0-4, 750-1,250 words, signed. *Aud.:* Ac.

This is the research journal of the Institute of Chartered Accountants in England and Wales, as opposed to the monthly news and practice-oriented magazine *Accountancy.* It presents empirical or analytical research in the fields of accounting and finance. Articles tend to be technical and may be international in scope. Sample topics include the effect of accounting information on investor and market behavior, international transfer pricing, and the market for audit services.

221. ***Accounting Auditing and Accountability Journal.*** Formerly (until 1989): *Accounting Auditing and Accountability.* [ISSN: 1368-0668] 1987. 5x/yr. EUR 3826.91 in Europe; USD 3069 in North America; AUD 3069 in Australasia. Ed(s): James E Guthrie, Lee D Parker. Emerald, 60-62 Toller Ln, Bradford, BD8 9BY, United Kingdom; info@emeraldinsight.com; http://www.emeraldinsight.com. Illus., index. Refereed. Vol. ends: No. 5. Reprint: PSC; SWZ. *Indexed:* ABIn, ATI, IBSS. *Bk. rev.:* 1-2, 500-1,500 words, signed. *Aud.:* Ac, Sa.

This is a scholarly journal that focuses on the interaction between accounting and auditing and their socioeconomic and political environments. Articles emphasize critical and historical perspectives on current issues. Topics are often international in scope, covering accounting practices in particular countries or doing cross-country comparisons.

222. ***Accounting Education.*** [ISSN: 0963-9284] 1992. q. GBP 369 (Individuals, GBP 50). Ed(s): Richard M S Wilson. Routledge, 11 New Fetter Ln, London, EC4P 4EE, United Kingdom; info@routledge.co.uk; http://www.routledge.com. Illus., index. Refereed. Vol. ends: Dec. Online: EBSCO Publishing; Ingenta Select; OCLC Online Computer Library Center, Inc.; RoweCom Information Quest; Swets Blackwell. Reprint: PSC. *Indexed:* ATI, BrEdI. *Bk. rev.:* 0-2, 500-750 words, signed. *Aud.:* Ac.

This journal addresses all aspects of accounting education. The scope is international, and topics addressed include curriculum issues, computing matters, teaching methods, and research pertinent to accounting education.

223. ***Accounting Historians Journal.*** Formerly (until 1977): *Accounting Historian.* [ISSN: 0148-4184] 1974. s-a. USD 55 (Individuals, USD 45). Ed(s): Stephen P Walker. Academy of Accounting Historians, c/o Culverhouse School of Accountancy, University of Alabama, Tuscaloosa, AL 35487; http://accounting.rutgers.edu/raw/aah/. Illus. Refereed. Circ: 900. Vol. ends: Dec. Online: Florida Center for Library Automation; Gale Group; Northern Light Technology, Inc.; ProQuest Information & Learning. *Indexed:* ATI, AmH&L. *Bk. rev.:* 4-5, 750-1,500 words, signed. *Aud.:* Ac, Sa.

Published by the Academy of Accounting Historians, this journal is unique in that it focuses on intellectual history and business history from the perspective of accountants and their profession. The journal presents scholarly articles on the history and development of accounting thought and practice. Citations and remarks from the annual inductions to the Accounting Hall of Fame are also reported here.

224. ***Accounting Horizons.*** [ISSN: 0888-7993] 1987. q. Non-members, USD 75. Ed(s): Eugene Imhoff. American Accounting Association, 5717 Bessie Dr, Sarasota, FL 34233; http://aaahq.org. Illus., index, adv. Refereed. Vol. ends: Dec. Reprint: PSC. *Indexed:* ABIn, ATI, BPI. *Aud.:* Ac, Sa.

A product of the American Accounting Association, this publication features articles with a broader intended audience than accounting academics, including practicing accountants, educators, regulators, and students. Material is presented in a less technical and quantitative manner than in most scholarly journals, including the association's own *Accounting Review.* Commentaries on current issues and reviews of authoritative pronouncements are also offered. The result is a journal that ties accounting theory to practice. Abstracts of articles from recent issues are presented on the publication's web site.

225. ***Accounting, Organizations and Society.*** [ISSN: 0361-3682] 1976. 8x/yr. EUR 1460 (Qualified personnel, EUR 266; Students, EUR 59). Ed(s): Anthony G. Hopwood. Pergamon, The Boulevard, Langford Ln, East Park, Kidlington, OX5 1GB, United Kingdom. Illus., adv. Refereed. Vol. ends: Nov. Microform: PQC. Online: Gale Group; ingenta.com; ScienceDirect; Swets Blackwell. *Indexed:* ABIn, ATI, AgeL, ArtHuCI, IBSS, RI-1, SSCI. *Aud.:* Ac, Sa.

This international scholarly journal focuses on the behavioral, organizational, and social aspects of accounting. Articles have addressed such topics as the social dimensions of international accounting standards, organizational behavior as it impacts management accounting, and historical studies of the accountant's role in business and society at a particular time and place.

226. ***Accounting Review.*** [ISSN: 0001-4826] 1926. q. Members, USD 85; Non-members, USD 110. Ed(s): Linda Smith Bamber. American Accounting Association, 5717 Bessie Dr, Sarasota, FL 34233. Illus., index, adv. Refereed. Circ: 18000 Paid. Vol. ends: Oct. Microform: PQC. Online: Chadwyck-Healey Incorporated; EBSCO Publishing; Gale Group; JSTOR (Web-based Journal Archive); OCLC Online Computer Library Center, Inc.; ProQuest Information & Learning; H.W. Wilson. Reprint: PSC. *Indexed:* ABIn, ATI, BPI, BRI, CBRI, CompLI, IBSS, IBZ, JEL, SSCI. *Bk. rev.:* 2-3, 350-1,500 words, signed. *Aud.:* Ac.

The American Accounting Association is the principal professional association in the United States for faculty in all areas of accounting. The association's Publications Committee has stated that the *Accounting Review* should be "the premier journal for publishing articles reporting the results of accounting research and explaining and illustrating related research methodology" and that the journal's primary audience is academicians, graduate students, and others interested in accounting research. Scholarly articles are accompanied by book reviews and placement ads for college and university accounting educators. This is among the most important core titles for academic libraries supporting accounting programs.

227. ***Accounting Today: the business newspaper for the tax and accounting community.*** [ISSN: 1044-5714] 1987. bi-w. except Apr., Aug. USD 84. Ed(s): Rick Telberg. Thomson Financial / I M G Media, 11 Penn Plaza, 17th Fl, New York, NY 10001-2006; http://www.faulknergray.com/account/today.htm. Illus., adv. Circ: 32000. Online: bigchalk; Florida Center for Library Automation; Gale Group; LexisNexis; Northern Light Technology, Inc.; OCLC Online Computer Library Center, Inc.; ProQuest Information & Learning. *Indexed:* ATI, LRI. *Aud.:* Ac, Sa.

This tabloid-size newspaper for accountants makes effective use of color, layout, and graphics. It reports on the activities of firms, individuals, and agencies in the tax and accounting community. Its annual surveys of regional accounting firms, of the top 100 firms nationally, and of the top 100 accounting software products are of particular interest. A web site produced by the publisher (Accountants Media Group, a unit of Thomson), *WebCPA,* offers some of the print publication's content free.

228. ***American Taxation Association. Journal.*** [ISSN: 0198-9073] 1979. s-a. USD 30. Ed(s): Terrence J Shevlin. American Accounting Association, 5717 Bessie Dr, Sarasota, FL 34233; http://aaahq.org. Illus., adv. Reprint: PSC. *Indexed:* ATI. *Bk. rev.:* 5-10, 500-1,000 words, signed. *Aud.:* Ac, Sa.

Published by the American Taxation Association (the Tax Section of the American Accounting Association), this journal presents several types of articles on tax topics. Articles and research notes may be quantitative, theoretical, or primarily legal research. Research on the teaching of taxation is also presented. In addition, abstracts of recent dissertations on taxation are included. The third issue of the volume is a Conference Supplement containing papers presented at the conference held by the journal in conjunction with the American Taxation Association's mid-year meeting.

229. ***Asia - Pacific Journal of Accounting & Economics.*** Formerly (until 2000): *Asia - Pacific Journal of Accounting.* [ISSN: 1608-1625] 1993. s-a. USD 50 (Individuals, USD 35). Ed(s): Dan A Simunic, Ferdinand A

Gul. City University of Hong Kong, Dept. of Accountancy, c/o Kate Walsh, 83 Tat Chee Ave, Kowloon, , Hong Kong; http://fbweb.cityu.edu.hk/ac/. *Aud.:* Ac.

This journal features empirical research with an emphasis on the application of legal and economic theory to accounting issues. Although there is a focus on issues important to the Asia-Pacific region, papers are also published on global topics in such areas as corporate governance, capital markets, and financial institutions.

230. ***Auditing: a journal of practice and theory.*** [ISSN: 0278-0380] 1981. s-a. Non-members, USD 25. Ed(s): William L Felix, Jr. American Accounting Association, 5717 Bessie Dr, Sarasota, FL 34233; http://aaahq.org. Illus., adv. Circ: 2000. Vol. ends: Fall. Reprint: PSC. *Indexed:* ABIn, ATI, SSCI. *Aud.:* Ac, Sa.

Published by the Auditing Section of the American Accounting Association, this journal's stated purpose is to contribute to the improvement of both the practice and theory of auditing. Several substantive research articles on auditing topics are featured in each issue. Abstracts of articles are available at the journal's web site, and lengthier executive summaries ("practice summaries") of the articles are presented at the front of each issue.

231. ***The C P A Journal.*** Former titles (until 1975): *The C P A;* (until 1975): *C P A Journal;* (until 1972): *Certified Public Accountant; New York Certified Public Accountant: C P A.* [ISSN: 0732-8435] 1930. m. USD 42 (Students, USD 18). New York State Society of Certified Public Accountants, 530 Fifth Ave. 5th fl., New York, NY 10036-5101; http://www.cpaj.com. Illus., adv. Circ: 46079. Vol. ends: Dec. Reprint: PQC. *Indexed:* ABIn, ATI, BPI. *Bk. rev.:* 0-1, 250-350 words, signed. *Aud.:* Sa.

Although published by a state accounting society, this magazine's scope is national, and it has long been among the most important publications directed at accounting practitioners in the United States. Pronouncements of the American Institute of Certified Public Accountants, Financial Accounting Standards Board, and other regulatory bodies are covered, as are developments in tax law, technology, and other topics of interest to the practicing professional. The full text of each issue since 1989 is available at the journal's web site.

232. ***Contemporary Accounting Research.*** [ISSN: 0823-9150] 1984. q. USD 140 (Individuals, USD 100). Ed(s): Gordon Richardson. Canadian Academic Accounting Association, 12 Donwoods Dr., Toronto, ON M4N 2G1, Canada; admin@caaa.ca; http://www.caaa.ca. Illus., adv. Refereed. Circ: 1400 Paid. Vol. ends: Winter. Online: Northern Light Technology, Inc.; ProQuest Information & Learning. Reprint: SWZ. *Indexed:* ABIn, ATI, IBSS. *Aud.:* Ac, Sa.

This journal presents scholarly and practical research in the field of accounting. Articles from other disciplines (such as economics or psychology) that have implications for accounting are also accepted. Despite the journal's Canadian origin, many articles are authored by academics from the United States or other countries. Articles may be in French or English, although most are in English, and abstracts are provided in both languages. The abstract in the language of the article is a standard 250-word synopsis, while the abstract in the other language is much more extensive, typically two to three pages long.

233. ***Corporate Taxation.*** Formerly (until Jan. 2001): *Journal of Corporate Taxation.* [ISSN: 1534-715X] 1973. bi-m. USD 400. Ed(s): Eugene Krader, Gersham Goldstein. Warren, Gorham and Lamont, 395 Hudson St, 4th Fl, New York, NY 10014; http://www.wgl.com/tax/jct.html. Illus., adv. Vol. ends: Winter. Microform: MIM; PQC. Online: Gale Group; ProQuest Information & Learning. Reprint: WSH. *Indexed:* ABIn, ATI, BLI, BPI, CLI, ILP, LRI, PAIS, SSCI. *Aud.:* Sa.

This is a more specialized title from the publisher of the *Journal of Taxation.* Compared to those in its sister publication, articles in this journal are fewer in number and treat their subjects in greater depth. In addition to the feature articles, there are regular departments discussing recent rulings and new developments.

234. ***Critical Perspectives on Accounting: an international journal for social and organizational accountability.*** [ISSN: 1045-2354] 1990. 8x/yr. EUR 593 (Individuals, EUR 135). Ed(s): David Cooper, Tony Tinker. Academic Press, Harcourt Pl, 32 Jamestown Rd, London, NW1 7BY, United Kingdom; apsubs@acad.com; http://www.elsevier-international.com/serials/. Illus., adv. Refereed. Vol. ends: Dec. Online: EBSCO Publishing; ingenta.com; OCLC Online Computer Library Center, Inc.; RoweCom Information Quest; ScienceDirect; Swets Blackwell. Reprint: SWZ. *Indexed:* ATI, IBSS. *Aud.:* Ac.

This journal provides a forum for scholarly articles that attempt to go beyond "conventional theory and practice" in examining accounting practices and corporate behavior in relation to the "many allocative, distributive, social, and ecological problems of our era." An aptly titled journal, *Critical Perspectives* publishes papers that very often take a contrarian view of established practices and institutions in the world of accounting and business.

235. ***Financial Management.*** Former titles: *Management Accounting;* (until 1965): *Cost Accountant.* [ISSN: 1471-9185] 1921. m. GBP 40; GBP 3 newsstand/cover per issue. Ed(s): Gemma Townley. Chartered Institute of Management Accountants, 63 Portland Pl, London, W1N 4AB, United Kingdom; journal@cima.org.uk; http://www.cima.org.uk. Illus., index, adv. Circ: 55000. Vol. ends: Dec. Online: EBSCO Publishing; Florida Center for Library Automation; Gale Group; OCLC Online Computer Library Center, Inc.; ProQuest Information & Learning. Reprint: SCH. *Indexed:* ABIn, ATI, JEL. *Aud.:* Sa.

This magazine is an official publication of the Chartered Institute of Management Accountants. It contains practical articles and columns on management accounting, as well as reports on activities of the association. Although most articles are primarily concerned with practical aspects of management accounting in the United Kingdom, many may also be of value to readers elsewhere.

236. ***Internal Auditing & Business Risk.*** Formerly: *Internal Auditing.* 1978. m. EUR 120. Ed(s): Neil Baker. Institute of Internal Auditors (UK and Ireland), 13 Abbeville Mews, 88 Clapham Park Rd, London, SW4 7BX, United Kingdom; info@iia.org.uk; http://www.iia.org.uk/. Illus., adv. Circ: 6000 Paid. *Bk. rev.:* 1-2, 500-1,000 words, signed. *Aud.:* Sa.

This is the official journal of the Institute of Internal Auditors–United Kingdom and Ireland. It includes articles that focus on the internal auditing function, written for practitioners. In addition to auditing techniques, articles discuss such areas as recruitment and retention of staff, e-commerce, and professional ethics. Association news and events are also covered. A free archive of full-image articles is available at the association's web site.

237. ***Internal Auditor.*** Formerly: *I I A Research Reports.* [ISSN: 0020-5745] 1944. bi-m. USD 60 in North America; USD 84 elsewhere. Ed(s): Joanne Hodges. Institute of Internal Auditors, Inc., 249 Maitland Ave, Altamonte Springs, FL 32701-4201; custserv@theiia.org; http://www.theiia.org/period/ia.htm. Illus., index, adv. Circ: 49500. Vol. ends: Dec. Microform: PQC. Online: EBSCO Publishing; Florida Center for Library Automation; Gale Group; Northern Light Technology, Inc.; OCLC Online Computer Library Center, Inc.; ProQuest Information & Learning; H.W. Wilson. Reprint: SCH. *Indexed:* ABIn, ATI, BPI, CompLI, ExcerpMed. *Bk. rev.:* 1-2, 500-1,000 words, signed. *Aud.:* Sa.

The magazine of the Institute of Internal Auditors offers articles of interest to the institute's membership of internal auditors and professionals in related fields. Topics include current auditing techniques and applications, information systems auditing, internal controls and quality assurance, corporate governance, and professional standards. Use of color graphics and sidebars makes the magazine appealing and easy to read.

238. ***The International Journal of Accounting.*** Formerly: *The International Journal of Accounting Education and Research.* [ISSN: 1094-4060] 1965. q. EUR 304 (Qualified personnel, EUR 118). Ed(s): A. R. Abdel-Khalik. Pergamon, The Boulevard, Langford Ln, East Park, Kidlington, OX5 1GB, United Kingdom. Illus., index. Refereed. Online: ingenta.com; ScienceDirect; Swets Blackwell. Reprint: SWZ. *Indexed:* ABIn, ATI, IBSS, PAIS. *Bk. rev.:* 5-6, 1,000-1,500 words, signed. *Aud.:* Ac.

A publication of the Vernon K. Zimmerman Center for International Education and Research in Accounting at the University of Illinois at Urbana-Champaign, this journal publishes scholarly articles that explore international aspects of accounting theory and practice. This may include the examination of accounting practices in a particular country or comparisons across countries. Articles that focus on the impact of cultural, political, and economic factors on accounting are encouraged, and the not-for-profit as well as the for-profit context is considered. The research tends to be empirical, with an emphasis on practical application.

239. ***International Journal of Auditing.*** [ISSN: 1090-6738] 1997. 3x/yr. USD 434 print & online. Ed(s): Anthony Chambers. Blackwell Publishing Ltd., 9600 Garsington Rd, PO Box 805, Oxford, OX4 2DQ, United Kingdom; customerservices@oxon.blackwellpublishing.com; http://www.blackwellpublishers.co.uk/Scripts/. Sample. Refereed. Online: ingenta.com; ScienceDirect; Swets Blackwell; Wiley InterScience. *Aud.:* Ac.

This journal provides an international forum for academics, professionals, and policy makers with research interests in new ideas, techniques, and approaches within all aspects of auditing. About once a year, it publishes an issue organized around a central theme; recent examples are audit pricing and research methods in auditing.

240. ***International Tax Journal.*** [ISSN: 0097-7314] 1974. q. USD 297. Ed(s): Tom Whitehill. Panel Publishers, Inc., 1185 Ave of the Americas, 37th Fl, New York, NY 10036; customer.service@aspenpubl.com; http://www.aspenpublishers.com. Illus., adv. Vol. ends: Fall. Microform: WSH; PQC. Online: EBSCO Publishing; Gale Group; OCLC Online Computer Library Center, Inc.; ProQuest Information & Learning. Reprint: WSH. *Indexed:* ABIn, ATI, BPI, CLI, ILP, LRI, PAIS. *Aud.:* Ac, Sa.

This journal publishes articles, often lengthy, that address a broad range of international tax topics. Foreign tax credit planning, business restructurings, and transfer pricing are examples of topics treated. Some issues focus on a particular country or region. This title will be of interest to both academics and practitioners.

241. ***Issues in Accounting Education.*** [ISSN: 0739-3172] 1983. s-a. USD 75. Ed(s): David E Stout. American Accounting Association, 5717 Bessie Dr, Sarasota, FL 34233; http://aaahq.org. Illus., adv. Refereed. Vol. ends: No. 4. Reprint: PSC. *Indexed:* ATI. *Bk. rev.:* 2-20, 500-1,500 words, signed. *Aud.:* Ac.

A publication of the American Accounting Association, this journal contains empirical research, commentaries, and cross-cultural comparisons pertaining to accounting education. Instructional materials and reviews of texts and other books are also included.

242. ***Journal of Accountancy.*** [ISSN: 0021-8448] 1905. m. Non-members, USD 61. Ed(s): Colleen Katz. American Institute of Certified Public Accountants, Harborside Financial Ctr., 201 Plaza Three, Jersey City, NJ 07311-9801; journal@aicpa.org; http://www.aicpa.org/pubs/joa/index.htm. Illus., index, adv. Circ: 363042. Vol. ends: Jun/Dec. Microform: MIM; PQC. Online: EBSCO Publishing; Florida Center for Library Automation; Gale Group; LexisNexis; Northern Light Technology, Inc.; OCLC Online Computer Library Center, Inc.; ProQuest Information & Learning; H.W. Wilson. Reprint: PQC. *Indexed:* ABIn, ATI, AgeL, BPI, BRI, BusEdI, CBRI, CLI, CompLI, LRI, PAIS, SSCI. *Aud.:* Ac, Sa.

The official magazine of the American Institute of Certified Public Accountants (AICPA) contains feature articles on such topics as financial reporting, auditing, taxation, and electronic commerce; news reports of the AICPA's activities, regulatory matters, and business trends; and columns on taxation, practice management, and technology. A list of outstanding exposure drafts from various accounting organizations, such as the Financial Accounting Standards Board, is presented in each issue. The full texts of new official releases are presented, as space permits. If a library subscribes to only one accounting magazine, it should be this one. Selected articles from recent issues, as well as an index and an archive of several years' length, are available on the AICPA's web site.

243. ***Journal of Accounting and Economics.*** [ISSN: 0165-4101] 1979. bi-m. EUR 825 (Individuals, EUR 67; Students, EUR 40). Ed(s): Ross L Watts, Jerold L Zimmerman. Elsevier BV, North-Holland, Sara Burgerhartstraat 25, Amsterdam, 1055 KV, Netherlands; nlinfo-f@elsevier.nl; http://www.elsevier.nl. Illus., index, adv. Refereed. Vol. ends: Jun/Dec. Microform: PQC. Online: EBSCO Publishing; Gale Group; ingenta.com; ScienceDirect; Swets Blackwell. Reprint: SWZ. *Indexed:* ABIn, ATI, IBSS, JEL, RiskAb, SSCI. *Aud.:* Ac.

Scholarly papers published here apply economic analysis to such accounting issues as the determination of accounting standards, government regulation of corporate disclosure and of the accounting profession, and the role of accounting in contracts and agency relationships.

244. ***Journal of Accounting and Public Policy.*** [ISSN: 0278-4254] 1982. 6x/yr. EUR 522 (Individuals, EUR 89). Ed(s): Lawrence A Gordon, Stephen E Loeb. Elsevier Inc., 360 Park Ave. S, New York, NY 10010-1710; usinfo-f@elsevier.com; http://www.elsevier.com. Illus., index, adv. Refereed. Vol. ends: Winter. Microform: PQC. Online: Gale Group; ingenta.com; ScienceDirect; Swets Blackwell. Reprint: SWZ. *Indexed:* ABIn, ATI, AgeL, IBSS, PAIS, RiskAb, SSCI. *Aud.:* Ac, Sa.

This journal publishes scholarly articles on the relationship between accounting and public policy, including public administration, political science, sociology, law, and economics. Interdisciplinary review papers are also encouraged. Also included are short papers linking current topics in accounting and auditing to public policy and corporate governance.

245. ***Journal of Accounting, Auditing & Finance.*** [ISSN: 0148-558X] 1977. q. USD 165 (Individuals, USD 70). Ed(s): K. R. Balachandran. Greenwood Publishing Group Inc., 88 Post Rd W, PO Box 5007, Westport, CT 06881; webmaster@greenwood.com; http://www.greenwood.com/jaaf.htm. Illus. Refereed. Circ: 1000. Vol. ends: Fall. Microform: PQC. Reprint: WSH. *Indexed:* ABIn, ATI, BLI, BPI, CLI, ILP, JEL. *Aud.:* Ac.

This journal is sponsored by the Vincent C. Ross Institute of Accounting Research at the Leonard N. Stern School of Business, New York University. The journal seeks to serve as a forum bringing together academics and practitioners. Each issue contains three to six articles, which frequently are highly quantitative in their methodology.

246. ***Journal of Accounting Education.*** [ISSN: 0748-5751] 1982. q. EUR 422 (Individuals, EUR 101). Ed(s): James E Rebele. Pergamon, The Boulevard, Langford Ln, East Park, Kidlington, OX5 1GB, United Kingdom. Illus., index, adv. Refereed. Circ: 1500. Vol. ends: Fall. Microform: PQC. Online: ingenta.com; ScienceDirect; Swets Blackwell. *Indexed:* ATI. *Aud.:* Ac.

Articles published here are typically empirical in nature and often deal with issues of instructional design. Each issue includes separate sections presenting cases for use in accounting classes as well as shorter papers on topics of interest to educators.

247. ***Journal of Accounting Literature.*** [ISSN: 0737-4607] 1982. a. USD 32 (Individuals, USD 22; Students, USD 12). Ed(s): Bipin B Ajinkya, Stephen K Asare. University of Florida, Accounting Research Center, Fisher School of Accounting-267 BUS, College of Business Administration, Gainesville, FL 32611. Illus. Refereed. Online: Northern Light Technology, Inc.; ProQuest Information & Learning. Reprint: PSC. *Indexed:* ATI. *Aud.:* Ac.

Publishes in-depth articles reviewing the scholarly literature on various topics in accounting. Papers presented at conferences held at the University of Florida also appear here. Articles typically conclude with a brief annotated bibliography and a comprehensive list of references.

248. ***Journal of Accounting Research.*** [ISSN: 0021-8456] 1963. s-a. USD 425 print & online eds. Blackwell Publishing, Inc., Commerce Place, 350 Main St, Malden, MA 02148; subscrip@blackwellpub.com; http://www.blackwellpublishing.com. Illus. Refereed. Circ: 2800.

Microform: MIM; PQC. Online: EBSCO Publishing; ingenta.com; JSTOR (Web-based Journal Archive); Northern Light Technology, Inc.; ProQuest Information & Learning; Swets Blackwell. Reprint: PQC. *Indexed:* ABIn, ATI, BPI, IBSS, IBZ, JEL, SSCI. *Aud.:* Ac.

Among the most important scholarly journals in accounting, this journal publishes academic research on a broad range of topics. Papers generally are highly quantitative and often address the impact of accounting standards on investors and the capital markets. Subscribers also receive an annual compilation of papers presented at an annual conference held at the University of Chicago.

Journal of Business Finance & Accounting. See Finance/Trade Journals section.

249. *Journal of Cost Management.* Formerly: *Journal of Cost Management for the Manufacturing Industry.* [ISSN: 1092-8057] 1987. bi-m. USD 123.98; USD 197.35 foreign. Ed(s): Tom Pryor. Warren, Gorham and Lamont, 395 Hudson St, 4th Fl, New York, NY 10014; tony.powell@riag.com. Circ: 2649. Microform: PQC. Reprint: PSC. *Indexed:* ATI, IBSS. *Aud.:* Sa.

This professional journal publishes articles written by academics and accounting professionals. Articles are practical in their orientation, and each includes a brief executive summary. Topics include performance measurement, costing systems, activity-based management, and the implications of e-business.

250. *The Journal of Government Financial Management.* Former titles: *Government Accountants Journal;* (until vol.25, 1976): *Federal Accountant.* [ISSN: 1533-1385] 1952. q. USD 90 domestic; USD 115 foreign. Ed(s): Marie S Force. Association of Government Accountants, 2208 Mount Vernon Ave, Alexandria, VA 22301-1314; jmccumber@agacgfm.org; http://www.agacgfm.org. Illus., adv. Refereed. Circ: 18000 Paid. Vol. ends: Winter. Microform: PQC. Online: Gale Group; Northern Light Technology, Inc.; OCLC Online Computer Library Center, Inc.; ProQuest Information & Learning. Reprint: PQC. *Indexed:* ABIn, ATI, PAIS. *Aud.:* Ac, Sa.

This publication of the Association of Government Accountants publishes peer-reviewed articles addressing all areas of government accounting and financial management at all levels of government: federal, state, and local. The emphasis is on articles that provide practical insights. News and activities of the association are reported as well.

251. *Journal of International Accounting, Auditing and Taxation.* [ISSN: 1061-9518] 1992. s-a. EUR 281 (Individuals, EUR 95). Ed(s): H. J. Dykxhoorn, Kathleen E. Sinning. Pergamon, The Boulevard, Langford Ln, East Park, Kidlington, OX5 1GB, United Kingdom. Illus., index. Refereed. Vol. ends: No. 2. Microform: PQC. Online: EBSCO Publishing; ingenta.com; ScienceDirect; Swets Blackwell. *Indexed:* ATI, IBSS. *Aud.:* Ac, Sa.

This journal's goal is to "bridge the gap between academic researchers and practitioners," addressing all areas of international accounting. Applied research findings and critiques of current practices and their impact on management decisions are among the areas covered. Many articles are internationally comparative.

Journal of International Financial Management and Accounting. See Finance/Scholarly section.

252. *Journal of Management Accounting Research.* [ISSN: 1049-2127] 1989. a. USD 15. Ed(s): Anthony A Atkinson. American Accounting Association, 5717 Bessie Dr, Sarasota, FL 34233; http://aaahq.org. Illus. Refereed. Online: EBSCO Publishing; Florida Center for Library Automation; Gale Group; Northern Light Technology, Inc.; ProQuest Information & Learning. Reprint: PSC. *Indexed:* ATI, JEL. *Aud.:* Ac, Sa.

This journal is an official publication of the Management Accounting Section of the American Accounting Association. Articles cover a variety of topics within the broad area of management accounting, such as budgeting, costing systems, internal reporting and the relationship between internal and external reporting, performance measurement, and behavioral aspects of accounting.

253. *Journal of Taxation: a national journal of current developments, analysis, and commentary for tax professionals.* [ISSN: 0022-4863] 1954. m. USD 250 in US & Canada; USD 325 elsewhere. Ed(s): Joseph I Graf. R I A Group, 395 Hudson St, New York, NY 10014; RIAhome@riag.com; http://www.riahome.com/. Illus., index, adv. Circ: 14000. Vol. ends: Jun/Dec. Microform: PQC. Online: EBSCO Publishing; Gale Group; ProQuest Information & Learning; West Group. Reprint: PQC; WSH. *Indexed:* ABIn, ATI, AgeL, BLI, BPI, CLI, ILP, LRI, PAIS, SSCI. *Aud.:* Sa.

Articles written by tax attorneys and CPAs seek to help practitioners reduce their time spent on research by summarizing, analyzing, and applying the law in specific areas. Issues are discussed in a practical but technical manner. Includes, in addition to feature articles, regular items updating readers on the latest tax law changes, court decisions, revenue rulings, and administrative actions.

Management Accounting. See *Financial Management.*

254. *National Public Accountant.* [ISSN: 0027-9978] 1949. 10x/yr. Non-members, USD 20. Ed(s): Jody Felski. National Society of Public Accountants, 1010 N Fairfax St, Alexandria, VA 22314. Illus., index, adv. Circ: 18000 Paid. Vol. ends: Dec. Microform: PQC. Online: EBSCO Publishing; Florida Center for Library Automation; Gale Group; OCLC Online Computer Library Center, Inc.; ProQuest Information & Learning; H.W. Wilson. Reprint: PQC. *Indexed:* ABIn, ATI, BPI, PAIS. *Aud.:* Sa.

Although some public accounting services can as a matter of law be provided only by Certified Public Accountants, this is not the case for many services. The National Society of Accountants is a professional association for public accountants who may or may not be CPAs, and this is the society's official publication. Articles focus on topics of interest to sole practitioners and those in smaller firms. Topics include issues in managing and marketing one's practice as well as tax, financial reporting, and other substantive practice areas. Information about the events and activities of the society is also included.

255. *National Tax Journal.* Formerly (until 1947): *National Tax Association. Bulletin.* [ISSN: 0028-0283] 1916. q. USD 150 (Individuals, USD 85). Ed(s): Douglas Hotz Eakin. National Tax Association, 725 15th St, N W, Ste 600, Washington, DC 20005-2109; natltax@aol.com; http://www.ntanet.org. Illus., index. Refereed. Circ: 3300. Vol. ends: Dec. Microform: WSH; PQC. Online: EBSCO Publishing; Florida Center for Library Automation; Gale Group; Northern Light Technology, Inc.; OCLC Online Computer Library Center, Inc.; ProQuest Information & Learning; H.W. Wilson. Reprint: PSC; WSH. *Indexed:* ABIn, ATI, AgeL, BLI, BPI, CJA, CLI, IBSS, IBZ, ILP, IPSA, JEL, LRI, PAIS, SSCI. *Aud.:* Ac, Sa.

Published by the National Tax Association, this journal presents refereed papers representing original research in government finance, evaluating particular policies, or reporting administrative developments. Papers from selected symposia are also included. The editors encourage authors to present their material in a manner that can be understood by all members of the association, including accountants, lawyers, tax administrators, and academicians, with technical and methodological discussions kept to a minimum or placed in an appendix.

256. *The Practical Accountant: providing the competitive edge.* Formerly: *Practical Accounting.* [ISSN: 0032-6321] 1967. m. USD 65. Ed(s): Howard Wolosky. Thomson Financial / I M G Media, 11 Penn Plaza, 17th Fl, New York, NY 10001-2006; howard.wolosky@ten.com; http://www.faulknergray.com/account/prac.htm. Illus., adv. Circ: 40000 Paid and controlled. Vol. ends: Dec. Microform: PQC. Online: Factiva; Florida Center for Library Automation; Gale Group; LexisNexis; Northern Light Technology, Inc.; OCLC Online Computer Library Center, Inc.; ProQuest Information & Learning. Reprint: PQC. *Indexed:* ABIn, ATI, AgeL, BPI. *Aud.:* Sa.

This magazine appears to be targeted to the public accounting practitioner in a small to medium-sized firm. A broad range of topics in accounting, auditing, financial planning, taxation, and accounting practice management are discussed. As the name suggests, the focus is on providing readily useful advice presented in a very accessible way, and the level of technical complexity is not as sophisticated as in many of the more specialized journals.

257. ***Practical Tax Strategies.*** Formed by the merger of (1966-1998): *Taxation for Accountants;* (1972-1998): *Taxation for Lawyers.* [ISSN: 1523-6250] 1998. m. USD 125. Ed(s): Sandra K Lewis. Warren, Gorham and Lamont, 90 Fifth Ave, New York, NY 10011; http://www.wgl.com/tax/txac.html. Illus., index, adv. Circ: 8544. Vol. ends: Jun/Dec. Microform: PQC. Online: Gale Group; ProQuest Information & Learning. Reprint: WSH. *Indexed:* ABIn, ATI, BPI, CLI, PAIS. *Aud.:* Sa.
Although its articles and columns, written by tax professionals, regularly cover technical tax topics, this journal seeks to be accessible to practitioners who are not tax specialists. Accordingly, many articles stress the broader business perspective relevant to tax planning. In each issue, about five feature articles are accompanied by regular departments that provide updates on recent developments.

258. ***Review of Accounting Studies.*** [ISSN: 1380-6653] 1996. q. USD 382 print or online ed. Ed(s): John S Hughes. Kluwer Academic Publishers, 101 Philip Dr, Assinippi Park, Norwell, MA 02061. Illus. Sample. Refereed. Vol. ends: No. 4. Online: EBSCO Publishing; ingenta.com; Kluwer Online; OCLC Online Computer Library Center, Inc.; Ovid Technologies, Inc.; RoweCom Information Quest; Swets Blackwell. *Indexed:* RiskAb. *Aud.:* Ac.
This journal presents academic research in accounting. Articles may be theoretical models or empirical studies. Contributors are welcome to draw from related disciplines, such as economics or finance, but all articles must contribute to the discipline of accounting.

259. ***S E C Accounting Report.*** [ISSN: 0146-485X] 1974. m. USD 285; USD 399 overseas. Ed(s): Paul J Wendell. Warren, Gorham and Lamont, 395 Hudson St, 4th Fl, New York, NY 10014. Illus., index. Vol. ends: Nov. *Indexed:* ATI. *Aud.:* Sa.
This newsletter reports on rulings and official releases of the Securities and Exchange Commission. Articles are brief, summarizing key provisions and offering commentary directed at practitioners, including interpretations and suggestions for planning and compliance. Reports on relevant court decisions and on pronouncements of other accounting standards-setting bodies, such as the Financial Accounting Standards Board, are also included.

260. ***Strategic Finance.*** Former titles (until 1999): *Management Accounting; N A A Bulletin - Management Accounting.* [ISSN: 1524-833X] 1919. m. USD 140 USD 70 United States Nonprofit Libraries. Ed(s): Kathy Williams. Institute of Management Accountants, 10 Paragon Dr, Montvale, NJ 07645-1760; info@strategicfinancemag.com; http://www.strategicfinancemag.com. Illus., index, adv. Circ: 85000. Vol. ends: Jun. Microform: PQC; NRP. Online: EBSCO Publishing; Florida Center for Library Automation; Gale Group; OCLC Online Computer Library Center, Inc.; ProQuest Information & Learning; H.W. Wilson. Reprint: PQC; SCH. *Indexed:* ABIn, ATI, AgeL, BPI, CompLI, EngInd, PAIS. *Aud.:* Sa.
This magazine was formerly known as *Management Accounting.* It is a publication of the Institute of Management Accountants, a professional association for U.S. accountants and financial managers who practice in industry as oppposed to public accounting. Thus, the range of topics discussed is broad and encompasses not only accounting standards and practices but also information technology, e-business, and methods of reporting business performance beyond the financial statements. Information on association activities and a useful annual career and salary guide are also provided.

261. ***The Tax Adviser: a magazine of tax planning, trends and techniques.*** [ISSN: 0039-9957] 1970. m. Members, USD 71; Non-members, USD 98. Ed(s): Nick Fiore. American Institute of Certified Public Accountants, Harborside Financial Ctr., 201 Plaza Three, Jersey City, NJ 07311-9801; nfiore@aicpa.org; http://www.aicpa.org. Illus., index, adv. Circ: 30000. Microform: WSH; PQC. Online: EBSCO Publishing; Florida Center for Library Automation; Gale Group; OCLC Online Computer Library Center, Inc.; ProQuest Information & Learning; H.W. Wilson. Reprint: PQC; WSH. *Indexed:* ABIn, ATI, BPI, CLI, ILP, LRI. *Aud.:* Sa.
This journal of the American Institute of Certified Public Accountants covers a broad range of tax information. Its focus is on the technical aspects of federal (and some state) taxation, providing practical commentary through feature articles and regular departments.

262. ***The Tax Executive.*** [ISSN: 0040-0025] 1944. bi-m. USD 120; USD 145 foreign. Ed(s): Fred F Murray. Tax Executives Institute, Inc., 1200 G St N W, 300, Washington, DC 20005-3814. Illus., adv. Circ: 5500. Vol. ends: Nov/Dec. Microform: PQC. Online: bigchalk; EBSCO Publishing; Florida Center for Library Automation; Gale Group; Northern Light Technology, Inc.; OCLC Online Computer Library Center, Inc.; ProQuest Information & Learning. Reprint: PQC; WSH. *Indexed:* ABIn, ATI, CLI, IBZ, ILP, LRI, PAIS. *Aud.:* Sa.
Each issue of this journal of the Tax Executives Institute includes articles on current issues of tax policy, administration, and management. The institute's position papers and testimony appear here, as do the minutes of official liaison meetings with federal, state, and provincial government officials.

263. ***Taxes - The Tax Magazine.*** Former titles: *Taxes (Riverwoods);* (until 1939): *Tax Magazine;* (until 1931): *National Tax Magazine;* (until 1930): *National Income Tax Magazine.* 1923. m. USD 235. C C H Inc., 2700 Lake Cook Rd., Riverwoods, IL 60015; cust_serv@cch.com; http://www.cch.com. Illus. Vol. ends: Dec. Microform: PQC. Online: Gale Group. Reprint: PSC; WSH. *Indexed:* ATI, AgeL, BPI, CLI, ILP, LRI, PAIS, SSCI. *Aud.:* Ac, Sa.
This magazine is aimed primarily at practitioners working with all areas of the tax law—state, federal, and international, though academics also find it of interest. Written by experts, articles are technical in nature and focus on current issues and trends as well as legislative developments. Regular columns provide information on tax trends, international issues, and other topics.

■ ADVERTISING, MARKETING, AND PUBLIC RELATIONS

See also Business; Communications; Journalism and Writing; and Serials sections.

Clay Williams, Coordinator for Bibliographic Instruction, Hunter College Library, Hunter College, New York, NY 10021

Introduction

In choosing the journals for inclusion here, one must recognize the profound influence that the online environment has upon scholarship and business. As predicted, the Internet as the medium of the journals themselves has become the issue. The web as a topic of intellectual discussion is now ubiquitous, but the polemics naturally change their focus as the directions the online world takes become more apparent. This was made manifest by the dot-com phenomenon at the turn of the millennium, whose demise has had a profound effect upon both advertising and librarianship. The journals directed at practitioners describe uses of the web in the various manifestations of advertising, while the academic journals explore the effects the Internet is having on advertising, marketing, and public relations and what effects the authors think it could or should have.

Practitioners already make proper use of all media to succeed, and the Internet is certainly the current one to understand and use. However, comprehending the online world in its many manifestations and hidden adendas, if you will, make things difficult to pin down for more than a moment. Many articles appear on this topic in journals focusing ostensibly on business and marketing. No one questions the importance of advertising, and certainly no one can avoid the role spin doctors or public relations practitioners are playing in the world today in business.

The inherent pitfalls of the Internet become problematic for a work such as *Magazines for Libraries* because some electronic journals (not to mention companies) do not stay around long enough for their importance to register, particularly in the academic world. Where are these journals archived and for how long and in what format? Consider, as well, that the full-text versions of some journals are best reached via such databases as Lexis-Nexis Academic Universe and EBSCO's various indexes, now ubiquitious in colleges and public libraries and available at home to subscribers. However, occasional lags in the promptness of recent articles in the promised full-text format speak of other forces at work. The inconsistency only frustrates users, as they see excellent articles abstracted and unavailable because of costs. The variety of formats we see are representative of the transitional period we are now in, and the scholarship reflects that as well.

Basic Periodicals

Ga: *Advertising Age, Adweek, B to B, Brandweek, Public Relations Quarterly;* Ac: *Advertising Age, B to B, Journal of Advertising, Journal of Advertising Research, The Journal of Consmer Marketing, Journal of Consumer Research, Journal of Macromarketing, Journal of Marketing, Journal of Marketing Research, Marketing News, Marketing Research, O'Dwyer's P R Services Report, Public Relations Review, Sales & Marketing Management.*

Basic Abstracts and Indexes

ABI/INFORM, Academic Index ASAP, Business Index, Business Periodicals Index, Lexis-Nexis. Business Elite, EBSCO.

264. ***Academy of Marketing Science. Journal.*** [ISSN: 0092-0703] 1973. q. USD 381 print & online eds. Ed(s): P. Rajan Varadarajan. Sage Publications, Inc., 2455 Teller Rd, Thousand Oaks, CA 91320; info@sagepub.com; http://www.sagepub.com. Illus., adv. Refereed. Circ: 3000. Vol. ends: Oct (No. 4). Online: The Dialog Corporation; Gale Group; ingenta.com; OCLC Online Computer Library Center, Inc.; ProQuest Information & Learning. Reprint: PQC; PSC. *Indexed:* ABIn, ATI, CommAb, HRA, PAIS, PsycholAb, SSCI. *Bk. rev.:* 2-6, 300-1,000 words. *Aud.:* Ac.

This is the official journal of the Academy of Marketing Science. Articles intended for theoreticians disseminate research results related to the international impact of economics, ethics, and social forces. A regular section concerns marketing and the law. Recent issues contain articles including a study that examines the effects of downsizing on organizational buying behavior, the concept of culture, the definition of organizational memory, and the dimensions of decision-making context. A reasonable price for an important journal dealing largely with theory.

265. ***Advertising Age: the international newspaper of marketing.*** Incorporates: *Advertising Age's Focus.* [ISSN: 0001-8899] 1930. w. USD 178.50 domestic; USD 198 Canada; USD 349 in Europe & Mexico. Ed(s): Rance Crain, Scott Donaton. Crain Communications, Inc., 360 N Michigan Ave, Chicago, IL 60601-3806; http://www.crain.com. Illus., index, adv. Sample. Circ: 80000. Vol. ends: Dec. Microform: CIS; PQC. Online: EBSCO Publishing; Factiva; Florida Center for Library Automation; Gale Group; LexisNexis; Northern Light Technology, Inc.; OCLC Online Computer Library Center, Inc.; ProQuest Information & Learning; H.W. Wilson. *Indexed:* ABIn, B&I, BPI, LRI, MagInd. *Aud.:* Ga, Ac, Sa.

For the student and the practitioner, this tabloid contains enormous amounts of fascinating and useful data. The coverage is thorough yet succinct and touches all aspects of advertising. Because it is a weekly, the information is current and topical. It covers important campaigns with text and graphics. The "Annual Agency Report" is a statistical issue covering the top agencies worldwide. The publication has feature articles on people, issues such as tobacco and alcohol advertising, and tells the reader of forthcoming campaigns and spots to watch for, such as those during the Super Bowl. Advertising on the web is not ignored. The title is one of the best for the price in this field. Highly recommended for college, public, and special collections.

266. ***Adweek: Eastern Edition.*** Formerly: *A N N Y (Advertising News of New York).* [ISSN: 0199-2864] 1960. w. 51/yr. USD 149 domestic (Students, USD 85.20). Ed(s): Sidney Holt, Alison Fahey. V N U Business Publications, 770 Broadway, 7th Fl, New York, NY 10003; bmcomm@vnuinc.com; http://www.vnubusinessmedia.com/. Illus., adv. Circ: 35940. Vol. ends: Dec. *Indexed:* ABIn, B&I, BPI, LRI, PAIS. *Bk. rev.:* short. *Aud.:* Ga, Ac, Sa.

This title is published in seven regional editions including Asia, with the Western edition being actually now larger than the Eastern, and the others having far less circulation than these two. They all have national and international articles, nonetheless. This is a trade publication, and the substance of the articles reflects that; the personalities and news within the industry are closely followed. Campaigns are covered graphically and in depth, and the regional aspects of the title allow in-depth reporting on topics and aspects of the field that would not otherwise be covered. An excellent choice for agency and public libraries though often carried by academic libraries because of the availability in popular databases.

267. ***Art Direction: the magazine of visual communication.*** [ISSN: 0004-3109] 1949. m. USD 29.97. Advertising Trade Publications, Inc., c/o Dan Barron, Ed, 456 Glenbrook Rd, Stamford, CT 06906-1800. Illus., adv. Sample. Circ: 7854. *Indexed:* ABS&EES, ArtInd, BRI, CBRI, DAAI. *Bk. rev.:* 3, 125-200 words. *Aud.:* Ga, Ac, Sa.

This title's circulation has fallen off a bit, but it still retains its attractions—namely, the coverage of graphic design, television, and print advertising. It is hoped that the smaller circulation does not reflect a lack of these skills in the computer industry. This work is written for the art design professional, but its glossy presentation is attractive to any reader. The regular features are news of people, a calendar, letters to the editor, and columns. The reasonable price allows many different kinds of libraries to subscribe, although it is directed at commercial artists and those in training to be such.

268. ***B to B: the magazine for marketing and e-commerce strategists.*** Former titles (until 1999): *Advertising Age's Business Marketing;* (until 1993): *Business Marketing;* (until 1983): *Industrial Marketing.* [ISSN: 1530-2369] 1935. 26x/yr. USD 59 domestic; USD 69 Canada; USD 89 elsewhere. Ed(s): Steve Yahn. Crain Communications, Inc., 360 N Michigan Ave, Chicago, IL 60601-3806; http://www.crain.com. Illus., index, adv. Circ: 47853 Controlled. Vol. ends: Dec. Microform: MIM; PQC. Online: EBSCO Publishing; Factiva; Florida Center for Library Automation; Gale Group; OCLC Online Computer Library Center, Inc.; ProQuest Information & Learning; H.W. Wilson. Reprint: PQC. *Indexed:* ABIn, ATI, B&I, BPI, CompLI, LRI, LogistBibl, PAIS. *Aud.:* Ga, Ac, Sa.

Also known as *Advertising Age's B to B*, this Crain publication's articles discuss e-commerce, publishing, business-to-business marketing, and a variety of face-to-face encounters including trade shows. Case studies provide the foundation for suggestions on creating and expanding a presence in existing and emerging international markets. News, statistics, software reviews, technology reports, analysis of research aids, and company market share information are regularly included. There is a web presence not as commonly asserted since the dot-com meltdown. There is certainly an effort to consider that the best customers will want their data quickly, and the web site provides e-mail updates to subscribers. Topics reflect changes in the information industry of interest to many librarians, and this should be available in public, academic, and special libraries.

269. ***Brandweek: the newsweekly of marketing communications.*** Former titles (until 1992): *Adweek's Marketing Week;* (until 1986): *Adweek (National Marketing Edition);* Which superseded (in 1985): *Ad Forum.* [ISSN: 1064-4318] 1980. w. 46/yr. USD 149 domestic; USD 342 Canada; USD 319 foreign. Ed(s): Karen Benezra. V N U Business Publications, 770 Broadway, New York, NY 10003; bmcomm@vnuinc.com; http://www.vnubusinessmedia.com/. Illus., adv. Circ: 24103. Vol. ends: Dec. Microform: PQC. Online: EBSCO Publishing; Factiva; Florida Center for Library Automation; Gale Group; LexisNexis; Northern Light Technology, Inc.; OCLC Online Computer Library Center, Inc.; ProQuest Information & Learning; H.W. Wilson. *Indexed:* ABIn, B&I, BPI, LRI. *Aud.:* Ga, Ac, Sa.

This title has a surprising amount of text, and it features major industries such as automobile companies. It does reflect the types of media as well: A major section, "From the Box," features various aspects of television advertising. This column reports on the actions of a product or the actions of players in Hollywood. There is extensive statistical information available, sometimes presented according to the product and sometimes the company. It is particularly good at keeping up with the various personalities in the field. There is a news update column as well, which can include the effect of politics and current events on advertising. An important element in all marketing collections.

270. *Campaign: the national weekly of the communications business, embracing advertising, marketing, newspapers and magazines, television, radios and posters.* [ISSN: 0008-2309] 1968. w. GBP 80; GBP 2.10 newsstand/cover per issue. Ed(s): Stefano Hatfield. Haymarket Magazines Ltd., 174 Hammersmith Rd, London, W6 7JP, United Kingdom; campaign@haynet.com. Illus., adv. Circ: 16452 Paid. Vol. ends: Dec. Online: EBSCO Publishing; Florida Center for Library Automation; Gale Group; MediaStream, Inc.; Northern Light Technology, Inc.; OCLC Online Computer Library Center, Inc. *Indexed:* ABIn, B&I, DAAI, PhotoAb. *Aud.:* Sa.

This title is included because of its prominence in Britain and the European Union. Political articles affecting American companies are available in the online version, *Campaignlive,* which also provides regular international news feeds. It is now full-text in mainstream databases as well, which certainly raises the profile. The articles are generally short, 150–500 words.

271. *Chemical Market Reporter.* Former titles (until 1996): *Chemical Marketing Reporter;* (until 1972): *Oil, Paint and Drug Reporter.* [ISSN: 1092-0110] 1871. w. USD 169 domestic; USD 290 Canada; USD 365 United Kingdom. Ed(s): Helga Tilton. Schnell Publishing Co., Inc., Two Rector St, 26th Fl, New York, NY 10006; http://www.chemexpo.com. Illus., adv. Circ: 10000. Vol. ends: Dec. Microform: PMC; PQC. Online: The Dialog Corporation; Factiva; Florida Center for Library Automation; Gale Group; Northern Light Technology, Inc.; OCLC Online Computer Library Center, Inc.; ProQuest Information & Learning. *Indexed:* ABIn, B&I, BPI, ChemAb, EngInd, EnvAb. *Aud.:* Sa.

Marketing professionals involved in the chemical industry can obtain company information, reports of industry and market activities and conditions, government regulations, and international and U.S. news and trends by reading this reasonably priced title. Each issue contains information on chemical imports, a chemical profile, and special reports on chemical manufacturing, as well as current reports of significant news such as fines related to price fixing of vitamins or chemical spills. Information is grouped by categories such as detergents, fats and waxes, and personal care products. Issues also provide information on jobs and a meeting calendar. There are industry statistics in each issue, including a long list of the latest chemical prices.

272. *Direct Marketing: using direct response advertising to enhance marketing database.* Former titles (until 1968): *Reporter of Direct Mail Advertising.* [ISSN: 0012-3188] 1938. m. USD 65. Ed(s): Debra Ray. Hoke Communications, 224 Seventh St, Garden City, NY 11530; 71410.2423@compuserve.com. Illus., index, adv. Circ: 11000. Vol. ends: Apr. Microform: PQC. Online: bigchalk; EBSCO Publishing; Florida Center for Library Automation; Gale Group; Northern Light Technology, Inc.; OCLC Online Computer Library Center, Inc.; ProQuest Information & Learning. Reprint: PQC. *Indexed:* ABIn, B&I, BPI. *Aud.:* Ga, Sa.

This title is an up-to-date, easy-to-read magazine dealing with all the major media and their needs regarding direct marketing. A recent article investigates the problems with rising postal costs; another discusses web-based marketing research, but the magazine certainly does not ignore catalog marketing. It has inclusive columns and a calendar of events. Essential for large public libraries, special libraries, and academic libraries.

273. *Industrial Marketing Management: the international journal of marketing for industrial and high-tech firms.* [ISSN: 0019-8501] 1971. 8x/yr. EUR 730 (Qualified personnel, EUR 112). Ed(s): Peter J. LaPlaca. Elsevier Inc., 360 Park Ave. S, New York, NY 10010-1710; usinfo-f@elsevier.com; http://www.elsevier.com. Illus. Refereed. Vol. ends: Nov. Microform: PQC. Online: ingenta.com; LexisNexis; ScienceDirect; Swets Blackwell. Reprint: SWZ. *Indexed:* ABIn, BPI, PAIS, SSCI. *Aud.:* Ac.

This very important scholarly journal provides eight to ten clear, well-written articles on topics such as product development, production presentation, advertising, sales, and pricing. Articles often focus on statistical analysis techniques, such as the recent one titled "A Conceptual Model for Building and Maintaining Relationships between Manufacturers' Representatives and their Principals." There is diversity however; for example, other recent topics include modeling of business-to-business partnerships and the impact of antitrust guidelines on competition.

274. *International Journal of Advertising: the quarterly review of marketing communications.* Formerly: *Journal of Advertising;* Which superseded (1978-1980): *Advertising Magazine;* Which was formerly: *Advertising;* (1964-1978): *Advertising Quarterly.* [ISSN: 0265-0487] 1982. q. N T C Publications Ltd., Farm Rd, Henley-on-Thames, RG9 1EJ, United Kingdom; ijoa@ntc.co.uk; http://www.warc.com. Illus., index, adv. Sample. Refereed. Circ: 800. Reprint: SWZ. *Indexed:* ABIn, BAS, BPI, LRI, PAIS, SSCI. *Aud.:* Ac.

This refereed academic journal is devoted to publishing authoritative studies for practitioners and academics in the fields of marketing, advertising, and public relations. The articles average about ten pages each. Recent articles include such topics as beer brand advertising and market share in the United States between 1977 and 1998 and a study of the response to banner ads on the web. This title is imperative for research libraries that have programs in advertising and marketing.

275. *International Journal of Research in Marketing.* [ISSN: 0167-8116] 1984. 4x/yr. EUR 539 (Individuals, EUR 75). Ed(s): H Gatignon. Elsevier BV, North-Holland, Sara Burgerhartstraat 25, Amsterdam, 1055 KV, Netherlands; nlinfo-f@elsevier.nl; http://www.elsevier.nl. Illus., index, adv. Refereed. Circ: 800. Vol. ends: Nov. Microform: PQC. Online: Gale Group; ingenta.com; ScienceDirect; Swets Blackwell. Reprint: SWZ. *Indexed:* ABIn, SSCI. *Bk. rev.:* 0-1. *Aud.:* Ac, Sa.

This title is intended to communicate developments in marketing theory and results of empirical research from all countries and a variety of disciplinary approaches. Coverage includes for-profit as well as nonprofit marketing, consumer behavior, products, pricing, marketing communication, marketing channels, strategic marketing planning, industrial marketing, and international marketing. Recent issues include five or six articles on such topics as consumer choice behavior in online and traditional supermarkets and the effects of brand name, price, and other search attributes; and homeostasis and consumer behavior across cultures. While expensive for a quarterly, it does cover areas that other journals don't.

276. *International Marketing Review.* Incorporates: *Industrial Marketing and Purchasing.* [ISSN: 0265-1335] 1983. bi-m. EUR 9177.41 in Europe; USD 8386 in North America; AUD 10189 in Australasia. Ed(s): Jeryl Whitelock. Emerald, 60-62 Toller Ln, Bradford, BD8 9BY, United Kingdom; info@emeraldinsight.com; http://www.emeraldinsight.com/journals/. Illus., index, adv. Refereed. Circ: 900. Vol. ends: No. 5. Online: Pub.; EBSCO Publishing; Gale Group; OCLC Online Computer Library Center, Inc.; ProQuest Information & Learning; RoweCom Information Quest; Swets Blackwell. Reprint: PSC; SWZ. *Indexed:* ABIn, SSCI. *Bk. rev.:* 2, 1,000 words. *Aud.:* Ac.

International marketing management is a complex and interesting area of marketing research. This expensive journal is part of an expensive group of marketing journals from MCB. Despite its small subscriber base and the high cost of subscription, it does have an international readership among academicians because of its research reports, literature reviews, and occasional book reviews. The articles are excellent, and single issues are often devoted to a topic, recently, for example, retailing. Despite its being indexed prominently, the price makes this journal impossible for many libraries. Naturally, this makes document delivery problematic.

277. ***Journal of Advertising.*** [ISSN: 0091-3367] 1972. q. USD 90 (Individuals, USD 69). Ed(s): Russell N Laczniak. M.E. Sharpe, Inc., 80 Business Park Dr, Armonk, NY 10504; custserv@mesharpe.com; http://www.mesharpe.com. Illus., index, adv. Refereed. Circ: 1850 Paid. Vol. ends: Dec. Microform: PQC. Online: Ingenta Select; Northern Light Technology, Inc. Reprint: PQC; PSC. *Indexed:* ABIn, AgeL, ArtHuCI, BPI, CommAb, PAIS, PsycholAb, SFSA, SSCI. *Bk. rev.:* 0-1, 1,000-2,000 words. *Aud.:* Ac.

This journal cleaves closely to the classic academic model: The articles are all well footnoted and abstracted. They are very theoretical with extensive use of statistics and well-defined methodologies. A recent issue includes an article titled "The Role of Myth in Creative Advertising Design," and another article explores managers' perceptions of the impact of sponsorship on brand equity. The review process is a blind one, but unfortunately, a call for papers does not come through when reached only through the indexes.

278. ***Journal of Advertising Research.*** [ISSN: 0021-8499] 1960. q. USD 275 print & online eds. (Individuals, USD 155 print & online eds.). Ed(s): Arthur J Kover. Cambridge University Press, The Edinburgh Bldg, Shaftesbury Rd, Cambridge, CB2 2RU, United Kingdom; information@cambridge.org; http://uk.cambridge.org. Illus., index, adv. Sample. Circ: 4977. Microform: PQC. Online: bigchalk; EBSCO Publishing; Florida Center for Library Automation; Gale Group; Northern Light Technology, Inc.; OCLC Online Computer Library Center, Inc.; ProQuest Information & Learning. Reprint: ISI; PQC. *Indexed:* ABIn, AgeL, BPI, CommAb, PsycholAb, SSCI, SUSA. *Aud.:* Ac, Sa.

This trade publication consists of well-researched and footnoted articles that are easier to read than those found in most academic journals. The charts and illustrations will not intimidate undergraduates with complicated explanations of methodology. A recent issue presents an article titled "Brain-Imaging Detection of Visual Scene Encoding in Long-Term Memory for TV Commercials." The editorial board is a blend of academics and professionals in the field. There is a calendar of foundation events in each issue.

279. ***The Journal of Business and Industrial Marketing.*** [ISSN: 0885-8624] 1985. 7x/yr. EUR 6262.91 in Europe; USD 1899 in North America; AUD 6959 in Australasia. Ed(s): W J Johnston. Emerald, 60-62 Toller Ln, Bradford, BD8 9BY, United Kingdom; info@emeraldinsight.com; http://www.emeraldinsight.com/journals/. Illus., index, adv. Refereed. Circ: 3000. Vol. ends: No. 4. Online: Pub.; EBSCO Publishing; Florida Center for Library Automation; Gale Group; OCLC Online Computer Library Center, Inc.; ProQuest Information & Learning; RoweCom Information Quest; Swets Blackwell. Reprint: PSC; SWZ. *Indexed:* ABIn, BPI, DSA, FS&TA. *Bk. rev.:* 1-4, 750-1,000 words. *Aud.:* Sa.

Academicians provide practical applications and new ideas based on marketing research to demonstrate the relationship of research to practice in each issue. This is another of MCB University Press's (Emerald Group) products. Recent articles explore sales force automation usage, effectiveness, and cost-benefit in Germany, England, and the United Kingdom; and studying distance learning for Malaysian sales forces. Marketing educators and practitioners are the intended audience.

280. ***The Journal of Consumer Marketing.*** [ISSN: 0736-3761] 1983. 7x/yr. EUR 6262.91 in Europe; USD 1999 in North America; AUD 7199 in Australasia. Ed(s): Richard Leventhal. Emerald, 60-62 Toller Ln, Bradford, BD8 9BY, United Kingdom; info@emeraldinsight.com; http://www.emeraldinsight.com/journals/. Illus., index, adv. Refereed. Circ: 4000. Vol. ends: Nov. Microform: PQC. Online: Pub.; EBSCO Publishing; Florida Center for Library Automation; Gale Group; OCLC Online Computer Library Center, Inc.; ProQuest Information & Learning; RoweCom Information Quest; Swets Blackwell. Reprint: PSC; SWZ. *Indexed:* ABIn, BPI, CommAb. *Bk. rev.:* 2, 500-1,000 words. *Aud.:* Ac, Sa.

Articles in this expensive title report on a wide range of research related to all aspects of consumer marketing. Book reviews are extensive and well written. It is indexed in mainstream databases, and students will appreciate that the articles are on current topics of interest. For example, a recent article reports on "Baby Boomers and Busters: an Exploratory Investigation of Attitudes toward Marketing, Advertising and Consumerism." A regular feature on franchising adds to the mix.

281. ***Journal of Consumer Psychology.*** [ISSN: 1057-7408] 1992. q. USD 430. Ed(s): Robert Wyer. Lawrence Erlbaum Associates, Inc., 10 Industrial Ave, Mahwah, NJ 07430-2262; journals@erlbaum.com; http://www.erlbaum.com/. Adv. Refereed. Reprint: PSC. *Indexed:* PsycholAb, SSCI. *Aud.:* Ac, Sa.

This title is very much directed toward academics in the field. Articles can include collaborations between faculty in management and psychology. There are peer-reviewed articles in the field of consumer psychology that include topics such as the role of advertising, consumer attitudes, decision making processes, and direct brand experience. Other topics covered include the development and change of consumer attitudes; judgment, choice, and decision processes; and social cognition research. A recent article is titled "Consumers' Responses to Negative Word-of-Mouth Communication: an Attribution Theory Perspective."

282. ***Journal of Consumer Research.*** [ISSN: 0093-5301] 1973. q. USD 152 (Individuals, USD 145; Members, USD 55). Ed(s): Dawn Iacobucci. University of Chicago Press, Journals Division, PO Box 37005, Chicago, IL 60637; subscriptions@press.uchicago.edu; http://www.journals.uchicago.edu. Illus., index, adv. Refereed. Circ: 3200. Vol. ends: Dec. Microform: PQC. Online: The Dialog Corporation; EBSCO Publishing; Florida Center for Library Automation; Gale Group; JSTOR (Web-based Journal Archive); ProQuest Information & Learning. Reprint: PQC; PSC. *Indexed:* ABIn, AgeL, ArtHuCI, BPI, CommAb, ErgAb, FS&TA, JEL, L&LBA, PsycholAb, SFSA, SSCI, SWA. *Aud.:* Ac, Sa.

A dozen associations cosponsor this journal, which reports on the research results from numerous disciplines in a dozen articles each issue. Culture swapping, price perception, consumer choice deferral, and the role of gifts in the reformulation of interpersonal relationships serve to represent the diversity of the contents. This title covers the latest hot topics in consumer research, and it is a good choice for both large public libraries and academic libraries.

283. ***Journal of Global Marketing.*** [ISSN: 0891-1762] 1987. q. USD 460 domestic print & online eds.; USD 621 Canada print & online eds.; USD 667 elsewhere print & online eds. Ed(s): Erdener Kaynak. Haworth Press, Inc., 10 Alice St, Binghamton, NY 13904-1580; getinfo@haworthpressinc.com; http://www.haworthpressinc.com. Illus., adv. Sample. Refereed. Circ: 425 Paid. Vol. ends: Winter (No. 4). Microform: PQC. Online: OCLC Online Computer Library Center, Inc. Reprint: HAW. *Indexed:* ABIn, BPI, BusEdI, CommAb, HRA, IBZ, IPSA, PAIS, RiskAb. *Bk. rev.:* 3-4, 500-1,000 words. *Aud.:* Ac, Sa.

Under the auspices of the International Business Press, this journal provides relatively inexpensive access to practical, and sometimes comparative, information on specific aspects of marketing in various countries and geographic regions. Topics address transborder information flow, intellectual property issues, counterfeit goods, market penetration strategies, and personal communication. Recent articles include "The Relationship Between Consumer Ethnocentrism and Human Values, On the Marketing of Nations: A Gap Analysis of Managers' Perceptions, Linking Product Evaluations and Purchase Intention for Country-of-Origin Effects" and "Increasing the Effectiveness of Export Assistance Programs: The Case of the California Environmental Technology Industry." A highly selective journal with about half international subscribers. Only information of interest to nonspecialists is considered for inclusion in this title.

284. ***Journal of Hospitality & Leisure Marketing: the international forum for research, theory & practice.*** [ISSN: 1050-7051] 1992. q. USD 315 domestic; USD 425.25 Canada; USD 456.75 elsewhere. Ed(s): Bonnie Knutson. Haworth Hospitality Press, 10 Alice St, Binghamton, NY 13904-1580; getinfo@haworthpressinc.com; http://www.haworthpressinc.com. Illus., index, adv. Sample. Refereed. Circ: 269 Paid. Vol. ends: Winter. Microform: PQC. Reprint: HAW. *Indexed:* HRA, LR&TI, PEI, RRTA, S&F, WAE&RSA. *Bk. rev.:* 1, 1,200-3,000 words. *Aud.:* Ac, Sa.

Edited by Michigan State's outstanding School of Hotel, Restaurant, and Institutional Management, this journal cannot be ignored by schools with hospitality programs. The articles are applicable beyond hospitality marketing. Several in-depth articles are included in each issue, along with selected abstracts and a lengthy signed book review. Issues are often thematic; for example, recently a volume dealt with the mature market, an important issue as baby-boomers age. The focus of the contents is understanding how consumer demographics, psychographics, and geographic location can be used to develop and enhance marketing strategies. This work is reasonably priced and invaluable for students in this area.

285. ***Journal of Macromarketing.*** [ISSN: 0276-1467] 1981. s-a. GBP 190 print & online eds. in Europe, Middle East, Africa & Australasia. Ed(s): Sanford Grossbart, Luis V Dominguez. Sage Publications, Inc., 2455 Teller Rd, Thousand Oaks, CA 91320; info@sagepub.com; http://www.sagepub.com. Illus. Refereed. Vol. ends: Fall (No. 2). Online: ingenta.com; Northern Light Technology, Inc.; OCLC Online Computer Library Center, Inc.; ProQuest Information & Learning; RoweCom Information Quest; Swets Blackwell. Reprint: PSC. *Indexed:* ABIn, CommAb, HRA, PRA. *Bk. rev.:* 2-6, 1,000-3,000 words. *Aud.:* Ac.

The scholarly articles in this semi-annual journal address a wide range of social issues, international and domestic, and the impact of marketing upon them. The authors approach topics from many perspectives: historical, analytical, theoretical, and general. Articles in recent issues discuss marketing and the natural environment and the role for morality, and a study that examines the marketing literature within the publications of the American Economic Association. Each issue has several extensive book reviews that are signed. This work is worth the price for a program concerned with business ethics.

286. ***Journal of Marketing.*** [ISSN: 0022-2429] 1934. q. USD 200 (Individuals, USD 80; Members, USD 45). Ed(s): Robert Lusch. American Marketing Association, 311 S Wacker Dr, Ste 5800, Chicago, IL 60606; info@ama.org; http://www.ama.org/pubs/jminfo/index.html; http://www.allenpress.com. Illus., index, adv. Refereed. Circ: 10000. Vol. ends: No. 4. Microform: PQC. Online: bigchalk; Chadwyck-Healey Incorporated; EBSCO Publishing; Gale Group; LexisNexis; Northern Light Technology, Inc.; OCLC Online Computer Library Center, Inc.; ProQuest Information & Learning. Reprint: PQC; PSC. *Indexed:* ABIn, ATI, BAS, BLI, BPI, BRI, CBRI, CommAb, IBZ, LogistBibl, PAIS, PsycholAb, SSCI. *Bk. rev.:* 3, 1,000-4,000 words. *Aud.:* Ac.

This official publication of the American Marketing Association includes research articles that must provide a practical link to an application. Articles must be theoretically sound, provide new information or a fresh insight into an unsolved problem, and benefit both practitioners and academicians. Articles tend to be thoughtful, well researched, and interesting. This is a core title for any academic library that supports business programs, especially marketing education programs. There are regular lengthy book reviews. Recent articles discuss the acquisition and utilization of information in new product alliances and two aspects of brand loyalty: purchase loyalty and attitudinal loyalty. Online subscriptions are now available directly from the publisher.

287. ***Journal of Marketing Education.*** [ISSN: 0273-4753] 1979. 3x/yr. GBP 243 print & online eds. in Europe, Middle East, Africa & Australasia. Ed(s): Craig A Kelly. Sage Publications, Inc., 2455 Teller Rd, Thousand Oaks, CA 91320; info@sagepub.com; http://www.sagepub.com. Illus., index. Sample. Refereed. Circ: 400. Vol. ends: Fall (No. 3). *Indexed:* ABIn, BusEdI. *Aud.:* Ac.

This journal is cosponsored by the Western Marketing Educators Association and the publisher. Each issue includes several papers of about ten pages in length on various aspects of marketing education. Recent articles discuss analyzing the perceptions and preferences of master of business administration (MBA) students regarding face-to-face versus distance-education methods for delivering a course in marketing management, and familiarizing marketing educators with the process of creative problem-solving. A wise investment as the makeup of marketing departments evolves.

288. ***Journal of Marketing Research.*** [ISSN: 0022-2437] 1964. q. USD 200 (Members, USD 45; Non-members, USD 80). Ed(s): Russ Winer. American Marketing Association, 311 S Wacker Dr, Ste 5800, Chicago, IL 60606; info@ama.org; http://www.ama.org/pubs/jmr/index.html. Illus., index, adv. Refereed. Circ: 9000. Vol. ends: Nov. Microform: PQC. Online: Chadwyck-Healey Incorporated; EBSCO Publishing; Gale Group; LexisNexis; Northern Light Technology, Inc.; OCLC Online Computer Library Center, Inc.; ProQuest Information & Learning. Reprint: PQC; PSC. *Indexed:* ABIn, ATI, AgeL, BPI, CommAb, FS&TA, IBZ, PAIS, PsycholAb, SSCI, ST&MA. *Bk. rev.:* Number and length vary. *Aud.:* Ac.

This core journal presents the results of scholarly and empirical research without the restriction (which accompanies the *Journal of Marketing*) of linking it to practical applications. Mathematical marketing research included in this journal requires readers to possess a strong background in quantitative methods. Papers in recent issues examine negative customer feedback and consumer reactions to corporate social responsibility. Each issue includes a section of research notes on topics such as an empirical analysis of the growth stage of the product life cycle or the design of research studies for maximum impact, and a section of book reviews.

289. ***The Journal of Services Marketing.*** [ISSN: 0887-6045] 1986. 7x/yr. EUR 6262.91 in Europe; USD 1999 in North America; AUD 7199 in Australasia. Ed(s): Charles Martin. Emerald, 60-62 Toller Ln, Bradford, BD8 9BY, United Kingdom; info@emeraldinsight.com; http://www.emeraldinsight.com/journals/. Illus., adv. Circ: 1000. Vol. ends: Nov (No. 4). Online: Pub.; EBSCO Publishing; Gale Group; OCLC Online Computer Library Center, Inc.; ProQuest Information & Learning; RoweCom Information Quest; Swets Blackwell. Reprint: PSC; SWZ. *Indexed:* ABIn. *Bk. rev.:* Number and length vary. *Aud.:* Ac, Sa.

This international marketing journal for practitioners provides research reports on a variety of topics related to all aspects of the service economy, including benchmarking, customer perception, customer satisfaction, quality and performance, marketing operations, and marketing management. A recent article concerns the influence of the musicscape within service environments. Each issue contains five to seven articles of 10 to 15 pages in length, abstracts of current research literature, and book reviews. This important journal is overpriced for many academic programs that could benefit from a subscription.

290. ***Marketing.*** [ISSN: 0025-3650] 1980. w. GBP 80; GBP 2.10 newsstand/cover per issue; GBP 115 in Europe. Ed(s): Conor Dignam. Haymarket Magazines Ltd., 174 Hammersmith Rd, London, W6 7JP, United Kingdom. Illus., adv. Circ: 40291. Vol. ends: Dec. Microform: PQC. Online: Gale Group; MediaStream, Inc.; Northern Light Technology, Inc. *Indexed:* ABIn, BPI, LRI. *Aud.:* Ga, Sa.

This publication is the newspaper of marketing. Functioning much like a trade magazine, it focuses on international marketing news regarding companies, individuals, brands, legal wrangles, technology, and general areas of market research, advertising, use of emerging technologies, image, and market positioning through dozens of short articles. Survey results and awards are reported, such as a recent report on awards for the best direct marketing campaigns.

291. ***Marketing News: reporting on marketing and its association.*** [ISSN: 0025-3790] 1967. bi-w. USD 130 (Non-members, USD 100). Ed(s): Lisa Keefe. American Marketing Association, 311 S Wacker Dr, Ste 5800, Chicago, IL 60606; info@ama.org; http://www.ama.org/pubs/mn/pub2.html. Illus., adv. Circ: 25871. Vol. ends: No. 26. Microform: MIM; PQC. Online: bigchalk; EBSCO Publishing; Gale Group; LexisNexis; Northern Light Technology, Inc.; OCLC Online Computer Library Center, Inc.; ProQuest Information & Learning; H.W. Wilson. *Indexed:* ABIn, B&I, BPI. *Aud.:* Ac, Sa.

The American Marketing Association produces this core trade and industry newspaper to provide timely information to practitioners about the most recent innovations and practices of today's leading companies. A calendar of events, association activities, and a variety of methods and techniques for achieving marketing goals in a company, for a product, or within the industry as a whole are presented in short articles. An annual directory of consultants is published each June. Sample articles include one on digital yellow-pages and another on the actual profile of baby boomers in marketing terms and marketing to them since the dot-com crash.

292. *Marketing Research: a magazine of management and applications.* [ISSN: 1040-8460] 1989. q. USD 120 (Members, USD 45; Non-members, USD 70). Ed(s): Chris Brennan. American Marketing Association, 311 S Wacker Dr, Ste 5800, Chicago, IL 60606; info@ama.org; http://www.ama.org/pubs/mr/index.html. Illus., index, adv. Sample. Refereed. Vol. ends: No. 4. Online: EBSCO Publishing; Gale Group; OCLC Online Computer Library Center, Inc.; ProQuest Information & Learning; H.W. Wilson. Reprint: PSC. *Indexed:* ABIn, BPI. *Aud.:* Ac, Sa.

In this core title, the American Marketing Association seeks to emphasize the advancement of the theoretical base of marketing science. Aimed at market research academicians and practitioners, each issue contains several well-written articles on the practical aspects of marketing research. Feature articles often examine cyber-research including techniques, software, methods, and models for data collecting. Regular departments focus on software reviews, legislative and regulatory issues, secondary research, research methods, and data collections. A recent article is titled "Safe Harbor Principles for the European Privacy Directive Are Finalized." The editorial board includes representatives of research firms and academicians.

293. *Marketing Science: the marketing journal of INFORMS.* [ISSN: 0732-2399] 1982. q. USD 248 (Individuals, USD 153). Ed(s): Steven M. Shugan. I N F O R M S, 901 Elkridge Landing Rd., Ste. 400, Linthicum, MD 21090-2909; informs@informs.org; http://www.informs.org. Illus., index, adv. Refereed. Circ: 1800. Online: ProQuest Information & Learning. *Indexed:* ABIn, BPI, JEL, SSCI. *Aud.:* Ac, Sa.

The Operational Research Society of America and the Institute of Marketing Science produce this journal in which authors use mathematics and statistics to evaluate marketing science. It presents papers offering significant new marketing insights and implications for academics and quantitatively oriented practitioners. One example is a paper on the "Direct Competitive Pricing Behavior in the Auto Market: A Structural Analysis." The wide variety of methodologies provides researchers with ideas for approaching research as well as reports on current concerns. Recent topics include "Patterns in Parameters of Buyer Behavior Models: Generalizing from Sparse Replication. A Model for the Analysis of Asymmetric Data in Marketing Research"; "Application, Predictive Test, and Strategy Implications for a Dynamic Model of Consumer Response"; and "Modelling Retail Customer Behavior at Merrill Lynch."

294. *Media Industry Newsletter.* Incorporates in part (in 2002): *m i n's New Media Report;* Which incorporated (1994-1997): *Interactive Video News;* Which was formed by the merger of (1993-1994): *Video Services News;* (1990-1994): *Video Marketing Newsletter;* Formerly: *Magazine Industry Newsletter.* [ISSN: 0024-9793] 1948. w. USD 795. Ed(s): Steven Cohn. P B I Media, LLC, 1201 Seven Locks Rd, Ste 300, Potomac, MD 20859-1130; clientservices@pbimedia.com; http://www.pbimedia.com. Illus., index. Circ: 2143. Vol. ends: Dec. Online: Gale Group; NewsNet; ProQuest Information & Learning. *Aud.:* Sa.

This loose-leaf title is devoted to the media industry, especially magazine and newspaper publications. Its eight to ten pages are filled with statistics regarding advertising in the consumer-magazine publishing industry. There is an opinion article in each issue and many short pieces on the various industries. This title describes itself as "the first source for magazine advertising data (boxscores)," and it does keep its readers up-to-date on what is happening in the field. Despite the importance of the data, it is a bit pricey for what it might bring to an academic library, but fortunately it is indexed in Lexis-Nexis Academic Universe.

295. *MediaWeek: the news magazine of the media.* Former titles (until 1990): *Marketing and Media Decisions;* (until 1979): *Media Decisions.* [ISSN: 1055-176X] 1966. w. 47/yr. USD 149 domestic; USD 342 Canada; USD 319 elsewhere. V N U Business Publications, PO Box 16569, North Hollywood, CA 91615-9465; bmcomm@vnuinc.com; http://www.vnubusinessmedia.com/. Illus., index, adv. Circ: 20982. Vol. ends: Dec. Microform: CIS; PQC. Online: The Dialog Corporation; EBSCO Publishing; Factiva; Florida Center for Library Automation; Gale Group; Northern Light Technology, Inc.; OCLC Online Computer Library Center, Inc.; ProQuest Information & Learning; H.W. Wilson. *Indexed:* ABIn, BPI, LRI. *Aud.:* Ga, Ac, Sa.

A core newsmagazine designed for the practitioner, this relatively short title presents pieces monitoring the several media it considers important. It naturally spends much effort on the world of television. It regularly reports on such matters as the ratings of the cable networks. The format is divided according to cable, magazines, new media, and media elite. The talk show competition is a good example of the kind of topics covered. The editors devote a lot of space to "Services and Resources," which includes listings of available jobs in the field. A good, breezy journal for practitioners that must be acknowledged by students of the field.

296. *O'Dwyer's P R Newsletter.* Former titles: *Jack O'Dwyer's Newsletter; Jack O'Dwyer's P R Newsletter.* 1968. w. USD 275. J.R. O'Dwyer Co., Inc., 271 Madison Ave, New York, NY 10016; http://www.odwyerpr.com. *Aud.:* Sa.

This indispensable weekly provides the latest news and information on public relations firms and professionals. It subdivides the news rather casually in the "PR Opinion/Items" and "Media News" sections. Under each are several stories that the editors have deemed important for professionals to know. The former gives editorial opinions on politics as they affect this field. In the latter recently, CCNY Communications Hall of Fame inductees are found next to the announcement of the winner of the McDonald's account. Recommended for all professionals and large public libraries.

297. *O'Dwyer's P R Services Report.* [ISSN: 1043-2957] 1987. m. USD 40. J.R. O'Dwyer Co., Inc., 271 Madison Ave, New York, NY 10016; http://www.odwyerpr.com. Adv. Circ: 4000. Online: Gale Group; LexisNexis. *Aud.:* Sa.

This newsletter publishes articles on current topics and trends of interest to PR professionals, including profiles of firms and discussions of legal and financial issues. It includes such columns as "Web Sitings," which reports on recent developments in the field on the web. This work differs from *Jack O'Dwyer's Newsletter* in that it is more news and less opinion. The columns are informational in intent without any particular political slant. Issues include a PR job market section.

298. *Potentials: ideas and products that motivate.* Formerly (until 1998): *Potentials in Marketing;* Which incorporated (1976-1989): *Marketing Communications.* [ISSN: 1522-9564] 1968. m. USD 59 domestic (Free to qualified personnel). V N U Business Publications, 770 Broadway, New York, NY 10003; bmcomm@vnuinc.com; http://www.vnubusinessmedia.com/. Illus., adv. Sample. Circ: 50450 Controlled. Vol. ends: Dec. Online: EBSCO Publishing; Florida Center for Library Automation; Gale Group; OCLC Online Computer Library Center, Inc.; ProQuest Information & Learning. *Indexed:* ABIn, AgeL, BPI. *Aud.:* Sa.

This title reports case studies, methods and trends in marketing, and sales promotions that are intended to help practitioners boost a company's competitive advantage. The primary function is to provide advertising and notice of available premiums and promotional items to potential buyers. Libraries will find this interesting for their own uses, as would some corporate special libraries. The title is available full-text via EBSCO.

299. *Psychology & Marketing.* [ISSN: 0742-6046] 1984. m. USD 1095 domestic; USD 1215 in Canada & Mexico; USD 1317 elsewhere. Ed(s): Dr. Ronald J Cohen. John Wiley & Sons, Inc., 111 River St, Hoboken, NJ 07030; uscs-wis@wiley.com; http://www.wiley.com. Illus., index, adv. Refereed. Circ: 800. Vol. ends: No. 6. Microform: PQC. Online: EBSCO Publishing; ScienceDirect; Wiley InterScience. Reprint: PSC. *Indexed:* ABIn, ASG, AgeL, BPI, CJA, CommAb, PsycholAb, SSCI. *Aud.:* Ac, Sa.

This title presents research that bridges academic and practice interests in marketing and advertising through the application of psychological principles to marketing strategy. Research reports are based on "fundamental factors that affect buying, social and cultural trends, psychological profiles of potential customers, and changes in customer behavior." Recent papers discuss the dangers of using deceptive practices in the mail-order business, using deception to measure service performance, and "Romancing the Past: Heritage Visiting and the Nostalgic Consumer." The journal is widely indexed, and the in-depth articles are well written. An important, although expensive, addition for academic and special libraries.

300. ***Public Relations Quarterly.*** Incorporates: *International Public Relations Review.* [ISSN: 0033-3700] 1955. q. USD 65 domestic; USD 70 in Canada & Mexico; USD 77 elsewhere. Ed(s): Howard Penn Hudson. Hudson Associates, 44 W Market St, Box 311, Rhinebeck, NY 12572-0311; hphudson@aol.com; http://www.newsletter-clearinghse.com. Illus., index. Circ: 5000 Paid. Vol. ends: Dec. Microform: PQC. Online: bigchalk; EBSCO Publishing; Florida Center for Library Automation; Gale Group; Northern Light Technology, Inc.; OCLC Online Computer Library Center, Inc.; ProQuest Information & Learning; H.W. Wilson. Reprint: PQC. *Indexed:* ABIn, ATI, BPI, CommAb. *Bk. rev.:* 4, 300-600 words. *Aud.:* Ga, Ac, Sa.

This title is primarily directed at the practitioner, but its articles would be of interest to students as well. A recent article claims that *The Wizard of Oz* by L. Frank Baum was part of the movement that officially established the field of public relations in the twentieth century. Another featured article describes the vital role that public relations can play in attracting investors and licensing partners. The assumptions characterizing litigation public relations is the subject of another article. For the professor, there is a piece describing how poetry can help people improve their prose. Recommended for large public libraries and academic libraries.

301. ***Public Relations Review: journal of research and comment.*** [ISSN: 0363-8111] 1975. 5x/yr. EUR 344 (Individuals, EUR 123). Ed(s): Ray E Hiebert. Elsevier Ltd., The Boulevard, Langford Ln, Oxford, OX5 1GB, United Kingdom. Illus., adv. Sample. Circ: 2500. Vol. ends: Dec. Microform: PQC. Online: Florida Center for Library Automation; Gale Group; ingenta.com; Northern Light Technology, Inc.; OCLC Online Computer Library Center, Inc.; ScienceDirect; Swets Blackwell; H.W. Wilson. Reprint: ISI; PQC. *Indexed:* ABIn, AgeL, ArtHuCI, BPI, CIJE, CommAb, HRA, PAIS, PRA, PSA, SSCI. *Bk. rev.:* 5-6, 500-1,000 words. *Aud.:* Ga, Ac, Sa.

This journal considers its title an important guide to its content: There are pieces that could be called research, although some might question the format of the methodology section in the articles. There are pieces that comment on how government policy directly affects aspects of a public relations officer's life. The book reviews alone are worth the cover price. They are extensive and could be considered articles in themselves, perhaps thus fulfilling the "review" promise in the title. A fifth issue published midyear is an extensive bibliography that will interest librarians.

302. ***Public Relations Strategist: issue and trends that affect management.*** [ISSN: 1082-9113] 1995. q. USD 48 domestic; USD 58 Canada; USD 68 elsewhere. Public Relations Society of America, Inc., 33 Irving Pl, New York, NY 10003-2376; john.elsasser@prsa.org; http://www.prsa.org. Adv. *Aud.:* Sa.

This journal is included in the price of Public Relations Society membership dues. It contains about ten articles of interest to the trade. The editors wish to emphasize the regular interviews with CEOs of the leading firms in the field. Recent articles include one on the "Ethical Challenge of Global Public Relations."

303. ***Public Relations Tactics.*** [ISSN: 1080-6792] 1994. q. USD 44 domestic (Students, USD 24). Ed(s): John Elasser. Public Relations Society of America, Inc., 33 Irving Pl, New York, NY 10003-2376; john.elsasser@prsa.org; http://www.prsa.org. Adv. Circ: 25000. *Aud.:* Sa.

This tabloid directs its articles toward professionals, and they are written by their peers. The articles can concern independent practitioners or employees of big firms. Each issue has a listing of upcoming events such as trade shows. Polls are included that are of interest and importance to the audience, but with little analysis. The articles also keep the readers abreast of recent court rulings that have an impact upon the field. This paper is an important mouthpiece for the profession.

304. ***Sales & Marketing Management.*** Formerly (until 1975): *Sales Management.* [ISSN: 0163-7517] 1918. m. USD 48 domestic; USD 67 Canada; USD 146 elsewhere. Ed(s): Melinda Ligos. V N U Business Publications, 770 Broadway, 7th Fl, New York, NY 10003; bmcomm@vnuinc.com; http://www.vnubusinessmedia.com/. Illus., adv. Circ: 60000. Microform: CIS; PQC. Online: EBSCO Publishing; Factiva; Florida Center for Library Automation; Gale Group; OCLC Online Computer Library Center, Inc.; ProQuest Information & Learning; H.W. Wilson. Reprint: PQC. *Indexed:* ABIn, BPI, LRI, MagInd, PAIS. *Aud.:* Sa.

This valuable trade magazine is aimed at executives who manage sales and marketing functions. Its annual surveys provide readers with "retail sales, effective buying income, and population data for both metro markets and media markets (DMAs), making comparisons between market types simpler." Regional and state-by-state tables are presented for market totals, five-year market summaries and projections, and merchandising line sales. A glossary and an alphabetical listing of hundreds of metro markets and their component communities are also included in this issue. Most issues contain numerous articles on all aspects of marketing. A core title for both public and academic libraries.

■ AERONAUTICS AND SPACE SCIENCE

Howard Stephen McMinn, Coordinator of Collection Development for Science, Technology and Medicine, Resource Services Department, Room 135 - Science and Engineering Library, Wayne State University, Detroit, MI 48202; hsmcminn@wayne.edu

Introduction

The terms *aeronautics, astronautics,* and *space science* do not conjure up the romantic images of early aviators and aviation pioneers or the excitement of space exploration, but they are the basic elements of these inspiring endeavors. This romanticism of flying, aircraft, and space exploration is displayed by many of the popular journals that capitalize on the adventure, excitement, and sport of all types of aviation and flight, from ballooning to spaceflight. This is especially true given that the 100th anniversary of flight was celebrated in 2003 (http://www.flight100.org), and almost every publication in this section paid homage to those pioneers and adventurers who participated in its history and development. However, the practical reality is that the areas of aeronautics, astronautics, and space science are highly technical fields that require very specific and technical information created by experts in their fields. There is still another side to these fields that revolves around the business and industry of aviation and spaceflight, from airlines to airports to manufacturing to military and government, to private, commercial, and corporate flying. Not only do these fields of study have many areas of application, but also the fields themselves are composed of numerous specialties. The journals included in this section comprise both the important technical journals required by researchers, scientists, and engineers and the leading general-interest publications in the numerous areas of aviation and flight.

From a library perspective, the field of aeronautics, astronautics, and space science has not seen the explosive growth in new technical journals that some disciplines have experienced in the past few years. The majority of the new research-level journals are focused on very specific research areas such as human factors or space debris, and these new titles seem to be struggling to find an audience, especially given the economic pressures faced by scientific and technical libraries directly related to journal price inflation. In terms of the general-interest publications, there has been some growth in titles both in terms of general publications and those targeted at specialized markets such as *Northern Pilot.* Most of these general-interest publications have some sort of Internet presence, but the amount of information available electronically varies vastly from title to title. Most provide some information about the journal and its sponsoring organization or publisher along with information that would be of interest to the subscriber such as tables of contents and articles. Most of the electronic journals included with this section are either trade publications or sites of interest to the general aviation population. The content of the electronic journals in the space sciences tends to overlap with the field of astronomy much more than the print journals. The list of journals that follows should provide enough information to develop a core collection for the researcher or for those interested in general aviation from the fields of aeronautics and space sciences.

Basic Periodicals

Hs: *Ad Astra, Air & Space - Smithsonian, Aviation Week & Space Technology, Flying, Spaceflight;* Ga: *Air & Space - Smithsonian, A O P A Pilot, Aviation Week & Space Technology, Flying, Plane and Pilot, Private Pilot, Soaring;* Ac (Nontechnical): *Aerospace America, Aviation Week & Space Technology, Flight International, Interavia, Space Policy, Vertiflite;* Ac (Technical): *Acta Astronautica, The Aeronautical Journal, A I A A Journal, Journal of Aircraft, Journal of Astronautical Sciences, Journal of Spacecraft and Rockets, Progress in Aerospace Sciences.*

Basic Abstracts and Indexes

Engineering Index, International Aerospace Abstracts, Scientific and Technical Aerospace Reports.

305. ***A A H S Journal.*** Formerly (until 1980): *American Aviation Historical Society Journal.* [ISSN: 0882-9365] 1956. q. USD 49; USD 64 foreign. Ed(s): Albert Hansen. American Aviation Historical Society, 2333 Otis St, Santa Ana, CA 92704; http://cwalton.jovanet.com/aahs/. Illus., adv. Vol. ends: No. 4. *Indexed:* AUNI, AmH&L. *Aud.:* Ac, Sa.

Produced by the American Aviation Historical Society (AAHS), this journal consists of well-researched scholarly articles on all areas of aviation history. The emphasis is on general aviation, but there are articles on military aircraft and history. The primary emphasis is on the history of aviation and commercial flight technology, not on military or space history and events, as is the case with most general-interest aviation history magazines. All areas of aviation history are included, from famous aviators and engineers to aircraft design and manufacture to the history of aerospace advancements and technical achievements. The journal contains primarily black-and-white photographs (appropriate for the time periods covered) and illustrations. The articles are well researched and are usually written by historians, military personnel, and scholars. The articles are produced by members of the organization and most have an American flavor. There are two ongoing departments—"Forum of Flight" (consisting of interesting or unusual black-and-white photographs of aircraft submitted by members) and "News and Comments from Members" (including items of interest, news, and conference activities). This scholarly and informative journal is appropriate for academic and public libraries.

306. ***A I A A Journal: devoted to aerospace research and development.*** Formed by the merger of (1934-1963): *Journal of the Aerospace Sciences;* Which was formerly (until 1958): *Journal of the Aeronautical Sciences;* (1945-1963): *A R S Journal;* Which was formerly (until 1959): *Jet Propulsion;* (until 1954): *American Rocket Society. Journal.* [ISSN: 0001-1452] 1963. m. Members, USD 68 Print & online eds.; Non-members, USD 890. Ed(s): Gerard M Faeth, Luke McCabe. American Institute of Aeronautics and Astronautics, Inc., 1801 Alexander Bell Dr, Ste 500, Reston, VA 20191; custserv@aiaa.org; http://www.aiaa.org/publications/journal/aiaa.html. Illus., index. Refereed. Circ: 3400 Paid. Vol. ends: No. 12. Microform: PMC; PQC. Online: EBSCO Publishing; Gale Group; Ingenta Select. Reprint: PQC. *Indexed:* AS&TI, ApMecR, C&ISA, ChemAb, EngInd, ExcerpMed, H&SSA, IAA, SCI. *Bk. rev.:* 1-2, 300-500 words. *Aud.:* Ac.

This journal is designed to disseminate original research papers discussing new theoretical developments or experimental results for the advancement of astronautics and aeronautics. The areas covered include aerodynamics, aeroacoustics, fluid mechanics, reacting flows, hydrodynamics, research instrumentation and facilities, structural mechanics and materials, propulsion, aircraft technology, STOL/VTOL, fluid dynamics, thermophysics and thermochemistry, and interdisciplinary topics. The journal is arranged into sections by broad subject classification: "Aircraft Technology, Conventional, STOL/VTOL," "Fluid Dynamics," "Interdisciplinary Topics," and "Structural Mechanics and Materials." Additional sections are added when appropriate, such as "Propulsion" and "Energy." The AIAA Dryden Lecture is also published in this journal. This is the leading journal of the American Institute of Aeronautics and Astronautics and covers all topics of broad interest to the membership as opposed to the more narrowly focused scope of the organization's other journals. A recently added feature is the table-of-contents information from non–U.S. aerospace journals. Appropriate for all academic, technical, and larger public libraries.

307. ***A O P A Pilot.*** [ISSN: 0001-2084] 1958. m. USD 21 to qualified organizations (Members, USD 39). Ed(s): Thomas B Haines, Mike Collins. Aircraft Owners and Pilots Association, 421 Aviation Way, Frederick, MD 21701; http://www.aopa.org/pilot/pwelcome.html. Illus., index, adv. Circ: 340000 Paid and controlled. Vol. ends: Dec. *Bk. rev.:* 1-2, 300-500 words. *Aud.:* Ga, Sa.

The journal is the primary vehicle of the Aircraft Owners and Pilots Association, which is the world's largest aviation organization that meets the needs of all pilots—from student pilots to space shuttle pilots. It is geared specifically toward meeting the needs of the private pilot and aircraft owner. The journal contains information pertinent to the members of this organization such as regulatory news, information on new aircraft and equipment, a calendar of events, and meeting and organizational notes. The articles include information on safety; flying; tips and techniques; airports and nearby accommodations and attractions; newly certified aircraft, along with specifications; and, of course, general-interest pieces on aircraft and flying. The journal provides many photographs, both color and black-and-white, and illustrations for aviation buffs that add to its appearance and highlight the text. A companion publication, *AOPA Flight Training,* provides in-depth information for pilots and pilots-in-training. One of the better general-interest aviation publications and a good addition to most general-aviation collections.

308. ***Acta Astronautica: journal of the International Academy of Astronautics.*** Supersedes (in 1974): *Astronautica Acta.* [ISSN: 0094-5765] 1955. s-m. EUR 3177. Ed(s): Jean-Pierre Marec. Pergamon, The Boulevard, Langford Ln, East Park, Kidlington, OX5 1GB, United Kingdom. Illus., index, adv. Sample. Refereed. Vol. ends: Dec. Microform: PQC. Online: ingenta.com; ScienceDirect; Swets Blackwell. *Indexed:* ApMecR, BiolAb, C&ISA, ChemAb, EngInd, GeoRef, H&SSA, IAA, M&GPA, RiskAb, SCI, SSCI. *Aud.:* Ac.

This research-level publication covering the field of astronautics, with contributions and readership on a global scale, is the journal of the International Academy of Astronautics. It presents original reviewed papers in the areas of life sciences, astronautics, space sciences, and space technology to promote the peaceful scientific exploration of space to aid humanity. In addition, the journal covers the design, development, research, and technological advances necessary to accomplish this goal. Articles cover microgravity, space station technology, power and propulsion, satellite technology, and space economics, along with traditional areas of research such as materials science, guidance and control, etc. The journal periodically publishes special issues either devoted to a specific topic or comprised of selected conference papers from the International Academy of Astronautics and the International Astronautical Federation, along with "Academy Transaction Notes" and other items of interest to members of the organization. Overall, a broad-coverage publication with an international scope. It is appropriate for academic and other research libraries.

Ad Astra. See Astronomy section.

309. ***Advances in Space Research.*** Incorporates (1960-1998): *C O S P A R Information Bulletin;* Formed by the merger of (1978-1980): *Advances in Space Exploration;* (1963-1980): *Life Sciences and Space Research;* (1960-1980): *Space Research.* [ISSN: 0273-1177] 1981. 27x/yr. EUR 3131. Ed(s): M A Shea, G Haerendel. Pergamon, The Boulevard, Langford Ln, East Park, Kidlington, OX5 1GB, United Kingdom; http://www.elsevier.nl. Illus., index. Refereed. Vol. ends: No. 24. Microform: PQC. Online: ingenta.com; ScienceDirect; Swets Blackwell. *Indexed:* BiolAb, ChemAb, DSR&OA, EngInd, GeoRef, GeogAbPG, IAA, M&GPA, SCI. *Aud.:* Ac, Sa.

As the official journal of the Committee on Space Research (COSPAR), a scientific committee of the International Council of Scientific Unions, *Advances in Space Research* covers all areas of fundamental research obtained with the use of balloons, rockets, rocket-propelled vehicles, or other aerospace vehicles regardless of political considerations. A sampling of the topics covered includes planets and small bodies of the solar system, space studies of the upper atmosphere, research in astrophysics from space, materials sciences in space, life sciences as related to space, and space studies of Earth's surface. Much of the information contained in the journal has been taken from various meetings and symposia sponsored by COSPAR. Therefore, most issues contain papers on a similar theme in a single area of interest. Even though papers are taken from various conferences, they are thoroughly reviewed before inclusion in the journal. Readers who cannot justify the expense of a subscription to this specialized international journal can purchase the issues individually. This journal presents information on fundamental research obtained by utilizing aerospace vehicles and is primarily of interest to physicists, astronomers, and the general field of space science.

310. ***The Aeronautical Journal.*** Incorporates: *Aeronautical Quarterly.* [ISSN: 0001-9240] 1897. 12x/yr. GBP 299. Ed(s): Mr. C S Male, J L Stollery. Royal Aeronautical Society, 4 Hamilton Pl, London, W1J 7BQ, United Kingdom; raes@raes.org.uk; http://www.aerosociety.com. Illus., index. Refereed. Circ: 1500. Vol. ends: Dec. Microform: PMC; PQC. *Indexed:* AS&TI, ApMecR, ChemAb, EngInd, ExcerpMed, H&SSA, IAA, SCI. *Bk. rev.:* 2-3, 300-500 words. *Aud.:* Ac.

The purpose of this longstanding aeronautical engineering research journal, produced by the Royal Aeronautical Society, is to foster the advancement of all aspects of aeronautical and space sciences. It includes papers on the research, design, development, construction, and operation of aircraft and space vehicles. Topics of the papers include fluid mechanics and aerodynamics, propulsion, structures and materials, rotocraft, astronautics, dynamics and control, noise and vibration, guided flight, air transport, test flying and flight simulation, and the history of aviation and flight. The journal also includes the sections "Technical Notes" and "Engineering Notes," to encourage rapid dissemination of information and to foster discussion on current research. The journal is presenting a series of survey articles covering the contribution that the United Kingdom has made toward the development of aeronautics. The journal has moved away from information that is geared solely to members, and now includes strictly technical articles on aeronautics and astronautics. Occasional special issues are comprised of technical papers presented at aeronautical conferences.

311. ***Aerospace America.*** Formerly (1963-1983): *Astronautics and Aeronautics;* Incorporating: *A I A A Bulletin.* [ISSN: 0740-722X] 1932. m. Non-members, USD 140. Ed(s): Elaine J Camhi. American Institute of Aeronautics and Astronautics, Inc., 1801 Alexander Bell Dr, Ste 500, Reston, VA 20191; custserv@aiaa.org. Illus., index, adv. Refereed. Circ: 41000 Controlled. Vol. ends: No. 12. Microform: PQC. Online: Gale Group; LexisNexis. Reprint: PQC. *Indexed:* ABS&EES, AS&TI, ApMecR, C&ISA, ChemAb, EngInd, ExcerpMed, IAA, SCI, SSCI. *Aud.:* Hs, Ga, Ac.

This general-interest journal is produced by the American Institute of Aeronautics and Astronautics (AIAA). It contains informative articles of interest to those within the field of aeronautics and space science rather than the more technical articles and papers presented in the other AIAA publications. Although these articles are broader and less technical than those presented in the other AIAA publications, they are still quite sophisticated and comprehensive. Like most journals produced by professional organizations devoted to keeping their membership up-to-date on major events and issues in their field, this journal contains many color photographs and illustrations. It is also the prime vehicle for relaying information to its membership on the association's activities, and it contains much valuable information on upcoming conferences and events. The journal also includes various information sections or departments, such as "International Beat" and "Washington Watch," with recent industry news, and "Conversations," interviews with important people in the industry or impacting the industry (such as lawmakers). Other sections providing items of interest to those within the field include information on new systems, software, materials, or products of note; an almanac of past aerospace items of interest; and career-related information. The two or three feature articles cover all aspects of the industry—economic issues, aircraft, materials, space transportation, spacecraft, and defense. The articles primarily interpret or review new research, engineering issues, program developments, and future trends in aeronautics or space sciences. The journal produces a special issue in December that reviews the year in aerospace. There are over 40 short articles in this special issue, each devoted to reviewing the progress made in these areas during the past year. Overall, a valuable addition to all types of libraries, from high school to academic.

312. ***Aerospace Engineering Magazine.*** Formerly: *S A E in Aerospace Engineering.* [ISSN: 0736-2536] 1981. m. USD 66; USD 118 foreign. Ed(s): Daniel J Holt. Society of Automotive Engineers, 400 Commonwealth Dr, Warrendale, PA 15096-0001; advertising@sae.org; http://www.sae.org/aeromag. Illus., index, adv. Circ: 33216. Vol. ends: Dec. Online: Questel Orbit Inc. *Indexed:* C&ISA, EngInd, IAA. *Bk. rev.:* 1-2. *Aud.:* Ac, Sa.

This journal, produced by the Society of Automotive Engineers (SAE), is designed to provide technical assistance and state-of-the-art technology information of interest to designers, manufacturers, and project managers of aerospace systems and components. Unlike most trade-oriented magazines, this journal's emphasis is more on applications, testing, and reliability of aerospace components than on theoretical or experimental results. There is very little information on people and events or on the business side of the industry. The journal covers all areas of interest to aerospace engineers, including propulsion systems, system and component design and maintainability, avionics, structural design, and related engineering topics. The journal is also important as a vehicle for new-product information, product literature, computer products, and related technical information. The journal is mainly utilized as a forum to convey practical technological information to those working in the field. The more theoretical and technical research information and papers presented at the various SAE conferences and symposia are included in *SAE Transactions. Aerospace Engineering* is an important publication for technical and academic libraries.

313. ***Aerospace Science and Technology.*** Formed by the merger of (1977-1997): *Recherche Aerospaciale;* (1963-1997): *Zeitschrift fuer Flugwissenschaften und Weltraumforschung;* Which was formerly: *Raumfahrtforschung.* [ISSN: 1270-9638] 1997. 8x/yr. EUR 277. Ed(s): Jean Carpentier, Fred Thomas. Elsevier France, Editions Scientifiques et Medicales, 23 Rue Linois, Paris, 75724, France; academic@elsevier-fr.com. Illus., index. Sample. Refereed. Vol. ends: No. 8. *Indexed:* ApMecR, C&ISA, ChemAb, EngInd, ExcerpMed, IAA, SCI. *Aud.:* Ac, Sa.

This journal originated by combining two of the leading aerospace journals from France and Germany. *Aerospace Science and Technology* boasts a binational editorial team consisting of important members of the European aerospace community. The recent addition of research organizations from Italy, Spain, the Netherlands, and Sweden has solidified its position as one of the leading European journals in the discipline. It is international in scope, presenting original research, review articles, and condensed versions of recently completed doctoral theses. Topics covered include all issues related to aerospace research from fundamental research to industrial applications for the design and manufacture of aircraft, helicopters, missiles, launch vehicles, and satellites. Included are articles on fluid dynamics, materials and structures, flight mechanics, guidance and control, automatic systems, and propulsion systems. Recommended for a research-level collection.

314. ***Air & Space Law.*** Formerly (until 1992): *Air Law.* [ISSN: 0927-3379] 1975. bi-m. USD 329 for print or online ed. Ed(s): Berend J H Crans. Kluwer Law International, Laan van Meerdervoort 70, PO Box 85889, The Hague, 2508 CN, Netherlands; sales@kluwerlaw.com; http://www.kluwerlaw.com. Illus., index. Refereed. Vol. ends: No. 6. Online: EBSCO Publishing; Gale Group; ingenta.com; Kluwer Online; OCLC Online Computer Library Center, Inc.; Ovid Technologies, Inc.; RoweCom Information Quest; Swets Blackwell. Reprint: SWZ; WSH. *Indexed:* CLI, IAA, ILP, LRI, PAIS. *Bk. rev.:* 1-5, 100-300 words. *Aud.:* Ac, Sa.

This journal provides current topical articles and research-level scholarly publications primarily covering the civil, commercial, administrative, and penal aspects of air and space law from an international perspective. The journal also covers related societal, technical, and business topics, such as civil and military aviation issues and policies, space transportation, trends in air transportation, regulatory and territorial issues, accident investigations and airworthiness, market access, environmental issues, regulation and deregulation matters, and self-service ticketing. The journal also includes such sections as "Case Law and Comment"; "Case Law Digest"; "Book Reviews"; and "EC Aviation Scene," which includes news from the International Aviation Organization and other international organizations. There is a wealth of information for those in the profession and for policy makers, scientists, and engineers. An additional feature is the annual bibliography of air law. Appropriate for specialized collections in law, aeronautics, and space sciences.

315. ***Air & Space - Smithsonian.*** Formerly: *Air & Space.* [ISSN: 0886-2257] 1986. bi-m. USD 24 domestic; USD 30 foreign; USD 3.99 newsstand/cover per issue. Ed(s): George C Larson. Smithsonian Institution, Air & Space Magazine, Victor Bldg 7100 MRC 951, P.O. Box 37012, Washington, DC 20013-7012; http://www.airspacemag.com. Illus., adv. Circ: 222305 Paid. Vol. ends: No. 6. *Indexed:* ASIP, AmH&L, BRI, CBRI, GeoRef, IAA. *Bk. rev.:* 4-5, 800-1,000 words. *Aud.:* Ems, Hs, Ga, Ac.

This magazine is the best overall journal for general-aviation and space enthusiasts, as every area of aerospace and aviation is covered in a comprehensive and entertaining fashion. It provides current topical information, historical information, future trends, and scientific advancements in all areas of aviation including military, general, and commercial, as well as space flight and exploration. It profiles people—both aviation pioneers and present-day decision-makers and innovators—as well as technological and scientific research advancements from both the pure and applied research areas of aerospace, aeronautics, and space sciences. The articles provide a great deal of scientific and technical information in an informative, educational, and entertaining format. The range of topics or articles is so broad that it is almost a disservice to mention only a few of the topics covered. This magazine is the closest thing to actually visiting the Air and Space Museum in Washington, D.C., and marveling at the history of aviation while imagining its future possibilities. The numerous departments are informative for both members and nonmembers. Two interesting departments are "Sightings" (which provides photographs of various aircraft) and "Reviews and Previews" (which includes reviews of books, videos, CD-ROMs, and software). This is one of those rare magazines that should be mandatory for any type of library.

Air International. See Military section.

316. ***Air Power History: the journal of air and space history.*** Former titles (until 1989): *Aerospace Historian; Airpower History.* [ISSN: 1044-016X] 1954. q. USD 45 (Individuals, USD 35; Students, USD 25). Ed(s): Jacob Neufeld. Air Force Historical Foundation, 1535 Command Drive, Ste A122, Andrews Afb, MD 20762-7002; bingem@andrews.af.mil; bausumh@vmi.edu; http://www.aon.af.mil/historic.html#power. Illus., adv. Refereed. Circ: 7000 Paid. Vol. ends: Dec. Microform: PQC. Online: bigchalk; EBSCO Publishing; Florida Center for Library Automation; Gale Group; Northern Light Technology, Inc.; OCLC Online Computer Library Center, Inc.; ProQuest Information & Learning. Reprint: ISI; PQC. *Indexed:* AUNI, AmH&L, BAS, BRI, CBRI. *Bk. rev.:* 5-10, 500-750 words. *Aud.:* Ac, Sa.

This periodical is the premier scholarly journal for aerospace, aviation, and space science history. The journal chronicles historic events in all of the various fields of aviation, including general aviation, space missions, and military aviation. The emphasis is primarily on military and general aviation. All time periods are covered, from the earliest use of aviation to current events/topics such as the Stealth bomber. All articles are solid history, with extensive bibliographies, and are written by historians, military personnel, museum curators, and others who possess both a strong academic foundation in history and a background in aviation. The articles are good reading and include many quotes. Numerous photographs and illustrations bring the text alive, but most of them are in black and white due to the time periods covered by most articles. The magazine also includes Air Force Historical Foundation symposium notices, book reviews, letters, news, notices, and reunions. This journal is highly recommended for aviation buffs, military history enthusiasts, and a general readership. It would be appropriate for all types of libraries based on its content, but its limited focus will not appeal to some general libraries.

317. ***Air Transport World.*** [ISSN: 0002-2543] 1964. m. USD 55 domestic; USD 80 Canada; USD 95 elsewhere. Ed(s): J A Donoghue. A T W Media Group, 1350 Connecticut Ave, NW, Ste 902, Washington, DC 20036. Illus., index, adv. Circ: 3742 Paid. Vol. ends: No. 12. Microform: PQC. Online: The Dialog Corporation; EBSCO Publishing; Factiva; Florida Center for Library Automation; Gale Group; Northern Light Technology, Inc.; OCLC Online Computer Library Center, Inc.; ProQuest Information & Learning; H.W. Wilson. Reprint: PQC. *Indexed:* ABIn, ABS&EES, B&I, BPI, C&ISA, EnvAb, PAIS. *Aud.:* Sa.

This magazine of world airline management covers all aspects of commercial aviation and the surrounding industries, primarily airport management and related issues. It is a business-oriented journal that covers an important segment of the aeronautics field. The industry aspects of commercial aviation also compose a major segment of the journal, with several informative segments that include data and statistics on such topics as commuter traffic, airport usage, fuel prices, and foreign exchange rates. Broad article categories include technology, airways, airlines, safety, marketing, maintenance, cargo, and passenger service. Articles on the people involved with this side of the aviation spectrum are informative and enlightening. Periodically, the journal includes directory information on specific topics that provides practical, factual information for industry insiders. The journal recently started to publish supplements that provide valuable information on recent trends, such as security, to those within the industry. Although the journal is primarily a trade publication for the commercial aviation segment of the industry, it can provide valuable information on all aspects of aviation.

318. ***Aircraft Engineering and Aerospace Technology: an international journal.*** Formerly: *Aircraft Engineering.* 1929. 6x/yr. EUR 2271.79 in Europe; USD 2069 in North America; AUD 2339 in Australasia. Ed(s): Terry Savage. Emerald, 60-62 Toller Ln, Bradford, BD8 9BY, United Kingdom; info@emeraldinsight.com; http://www.emeraldinsight.com/journals/. Illus., index, adv. Vol. ends: No. 6. Online: EBSCO Publishing; RoweCom Information Quest; Swets Blackwell. Reprint: PSC. *Indexed:* AS&TI, BrTechI, C&ISA, ChemAb, EngInd, ExcerpMed, H&SSA. *Bk. rev.:* 1-3, 100-250 words. *Aud.:* Ac, Sa.

This is primarily a trade publication for the European aerospace industry, with feature articles on all aspects of aircraft and aerospace technology. There is a unique blend of scholarly articles on practical topics combined with industry-related information. There are various departments that provide information on the business side of the industry. These items include news of recent and current activities, blurbs, industry highlights, profiles of equipment and tools, items on people in the industry, and a calendar of events. Also included is a page containing abstracts and keywords of the articles as an aid to readers. The main articles section contains the research-level papers. All subject areas of the aerospace industry are covered. The journal's strength is in getting leading practitioners in the field to contribute articles of interest to both researchers and fellow practitioners. It is geared primarily to the British and European aerospace industry and is appropriate for academic and major public libraries.

Airpower. See Military section.

319. ***American Helicopter Society. Journal.*** [ISSN: 0002-8711] 1956. q. USD 60; USD 75 foreign. Ed(s): David Jenney. American Helicopter Society, Inc., 217 N Washington St, Alexandria, VA 22314; http://www.vtol.org/journal/journal/html. Illus. Sample. Circ: 7400. Vol. ends: No. 4. *Indexed:* ApMecR, C&ISA, EngInd, IAA, SCI. *Aud.:* Ac.

Original technical papers dealing with all aspects of the design, theory, and practice of vertical flight make up this journal. Papers cover three main areas: research and engineering, design and manufacturing, and operations. They are designed to foster the exchange of significant new ideas, information, and research about helicopters and V/STOL aircraft. The emphasis is on dynamics, structures, aerodynamics (both basic and applied), handling qualities, and acoustics. Additional areas include vehicle and component design, manufacture, and testing; the operational aspects including support, noise and vibration, control and control failure, safety and reliability, materials, design criteria; and historical information. In addition to full articles, the "Technical Notes" section provides a forum for brief, timely updates on current research topics. This journal focuses on the more technical aspects of vertical flight, with the general-interest and membership information included in the organization's companion publication *Vertiflight* (below in this section). Valuable to any academic collection supporting aeronautics and engineering.

320. ***Aviation, Space, and Environmental Medicine.*** Formerly (until 1975): *Aerospace Medicine.* [ISSN: 0095-6562] 1930. m. USD 175 (Individuals, USD 160). Ed(s): Pamela Day. Aerospace Medical Association, 320 S Henry St, Alexandria, VA 22314-3579; pday@asma.org; http://www.asma.org. Illus., index, adv. Refereed. Circ: 4000 Paid. Vol. ends: No. 12. Microform: PQC. Online: Ingenta Select. *Indexed:* AUNI, BiolAb, C&ISA, CINAHL, ChemAb, ErgAb, ExcerpMed, H&SSA, IAA, IndMed, PEI, PsycholAb, SCI, SSCI. *Bk. rev.:* 1-2, 500 words. *Aud.:* Ac, Sa.

This scholarly journal is concerned with the medical aspects of humans in spaceflight, aviation, and other environmentally and physically hostile environments. The publication is produced by the Aerospace Medical Association and contains original articles, clinical investigations, and applied medicine as related to humans as a result of aerospace travel, flight, and the factors that impact on humans in these environments. Original articles in these subject areas compose the core of the journal. Additional features include technical notes, news items, and other information of interest to members. The journal occasionally publishes review articles and papers drawn from major conferences in these areas. Most articles deal with the effects of physical exertions on human bodies during flight and their reaction to the extreme environments and environmental changes during spaceflight. The wide variety of articles and research topics combined with information on conferences and symposia makes this a valuable information source for both medical specialists and engineers concerned with aircraft, space vehicles, or human factors.

321. ***Aviation Week & Space Technology.*** [ISSN: 0005-2175] 1916. w. USD 92 domestic; USD 109 in Canada & Mexico; USD 80 in Western Europe. McGraw-Hill Companies, Inc., 1221 Ave of the Americas, New York, NY 10020; http://www.mcgraw-hill.com/. Illus., adv. Circ: 107000 Paid. Vol. ends: No. 26. Microform: PQC. Online: Dow Jones Interactive; EBSCO Publishing; Factiva; LexisNexis; NewsNet; OCLC Online Computer Library Center, Inc.; ProQuest Information & Learning. *Indexed:* ABIn, ABS&EES, AS&TI, ApMecR, B&I, BPI, BrTechI, C&ISA, ChemAb, EngInd, EnvAb, ExcerpMed, IAA, LRI, MagInd, RGPR. *Aud.:* Ga, Ac.

This is the premier trade magazine covering aviation, aerospace, and aeronautics. All segments of the aerospace industry are featured and detailed, along with many short but insightful articles. The regular sections include "World News & Analysis" and "Headline News," which contain news items of note and other industry happenings; "Air Transport," covering commercial and general aviation; and "Business Aviation," which profiles commercial- and business-focused information. The magazine then segments the rest of its articles into topical sections: "Space Technology," "Aerospace Business," "Aeronautical Engineering," "Manufacturing Technology," and "Information Technology." Also provided is valuable, up-to-date information on the respective subject area. Special reports, such as information on the recent shuttle tragedy or the 100 years of aerospace, are included when appropriate. In addition, the magazine contains industry outlooks and profiles, features on people within the industry, a calendar of events, and news and information from government and other regulatory agencies. The special issue "Aerospace Source Book" provides outlook/specification tables for all areas of the aerospace industry. Major sections include a world military aircraft inventory, prime contractor and major manufacturer profiles, major airline profiles, leading regional airline profiles, and leading all-cargo airlines. This special issue is usually published the second week of the year. Other special issues are produced for the major air shows, Farnborough and Paris, each year. The combination of trade publication and general-interest articles makes this a valuable resource for all types of libraries, from high school to academic.

322. ***Ballooning.*** [ISSN: 0194-6854] 1977. bi-m. USD 45; USD 50 in Canada & Mexico; USD 85 elsewhere. Ballooning Magazine, PO Box 400, Indianola, IA 50125; ballon-fed@bfa.ycg.org; http://www.bfa.net/publications.htm. Illus., adv. Sample. Circ: 5100. Vol. ends: No. 6. *Bk. rev.:* 1-4, 300-500 words. *Aud.:* Ga, Sa.

This is the best general-interest magazine for the ballooning enthusiast. Major articles cover a wide range of topics including safety issues, equipment, profiles of members, descriptions of balloon trips, noteworthy events in ballooning, and other general-interest items. The magazine includes excellent color and black-and-white photographs, results from rallies, information on new products, reviews of products and literature, and a directory of the federation's officers. Although the journal is produced by the Ballooning Federation of America, it covers the sport from an international perspective. It provides quality content enhanced by a good layout and organization scheme. This general-interest magazine is suitable for all ages.

323. ***British Interplanetary Society Journal.*** [ISSN: 0007-084X] 1934. bi-m. GBP 290; USD 536. Ed(s): A R Martin. British Interplanetary Society, 27-29 S Lambeth Rd, London, SW8 1SZ, United Kingdom; mail@bis-spaceflight.com; http://bis-spaceflight.com. Illus., index. Refereed. Circ: 1500. Vol. ends: No. 12. Microform: PQC. Reprint: PQC; PSC. *Indexed:* EngInd, ExcerpMed, GeoRef, IAA. *Aud.:* Ac, Sa.

This publication of the British Interplanetary Society contains original papers covering all aspects of space exploration, with each issue dedicated to one or two particular subjects, topics, or themes. Emphasis is solely on space and space-based applications. Sample topics include the history of rocket development, the Earth-space environment, space missions and astrodynamics, new space concepts, and related areas of aeronautics, astronautics, and space sciences. Most issues contain five to ten articles in these and related areas of space exploration. Additionally, the journal contains brief information on the society's activities and announcements. It incorporates photographs and illustrations to supplement the text. Appropriate for major research libraries, whether in academe or the public sector.

324. ***Canadian Aeronautics and Space Journal.*** [ISSN: 0008-2821] 1955. q. CND 90 domestic; USD 80 foreign. Ed(s): D Simpson. Canadian Aeronautics and Space Institute, 1685 Russell Rd, Unit 1R, Ottawa, ON K1G 0N1, Canada; casi@casi.ca; http://www.casi.ca. Illus., index. Circ: 2000. Vol. ends: No. 4. Microform: MML; PQC. Reprint: PQC. *Indexed:* ApMecR, C&ISA, CBCARef, EngInd, ForAb, H&SSA, IAA. *Bk. rev.:* 2-3, 300-400 words. *Aud.:* Ac.

This official publication of the Canadian Aeronautics and Space Institute disseminates technical and research information in the areas of aeronautical and aerospace sciences to the international community. The journal includes articles on recent research and technical discoveries in all areas of aeronautics, including aerospace materials, spacecraft thermal design, de-icing studies, aerodynamics, aircraft design and analysis, aircraft component design, and wind tunnel investigations. Original articles cover such topics as flight testing, astronautics, structures and materials, simulation and training, aerospace operations, and aircraft design and development. The journal recently began to publish occasional special issues in which all articles are focused on a single topic, such as aerospace human factors or material problems in aging aircraft. The journal also periodically includes the section "CASI Bulletin," which provides information of interest to members, and book reviews. This research-oriented magazine belongs primarily in academic, technical, and major public libraries.

325. ***Flight International.*** [ISSN: 0015-3710] 1909. w. EUR 140 in Europe; GBP 89 elsewhere; USD 140 elsewhere. Ed(s): Murdo Morrison. Reed Business Information Ltd., Quadrant House, The Quadrant, Brighton Rd, Sutton, SM2 5AS, United Kingdom; http://www.reedbusiness.co.uk/. Illus., index, adv. Circ: 50500. Vol. ends: Dec. Microform: PQC. Online: Data-Star; EBSCO Publishing; Florida Center for Library Automation; Gale Group; LexisNexis; OCLC Online Computer Library Center, Inc.; H.W. Wilson. Reprint: PQC. *Indexed:* AUNI, B&I, BrTechI, C&ISA, ChemAb, EngInd, IAA. *Aud.:* Ga, Ac.

This trade publication provides a global perspective on the aerospace industry and covers every aspect—airframe systems and components, support equipment, air transport, general aviation, defense, spaceflight, and regulatory agencies and authorities worldwide. Sections include "Headlines," "Air Transport," "Business," "Defence," "General Aviation," "Spaceflight," "Features," and "Regulars." The "Features" section profiles important and interesting items, from industry predictions for the upcoming year to implementation of new safety ideas or methods. Periodically, the journal also provides classifieds, letters, aerospace awards, newsmakers, and similar topical sections. Occasionally, there are directories of maintenance facilities, military simulators, turbine engine manufacturers, and world airlines, as well as informative ranking information such as the top 100 aerospace companies, airline safety statistics, and space launch calendars. There are also occasional supplements on "hot" topics or industry trends. The magazine is similar to *Aviation Week & Space Technology,* with a greater international flavor. Recommended for both academic libraries and public libraries.

326. *Flying.* [ISSN: 0015-4806] 1927. m. USD 14.97 domestic; USD 22.97 foreign. Ed(s): J Mac McClellan. Hachette Filipacchi Media U.S., Inc., 1633 Broadway, New York, NY 10019; http://www.hfmus.com. Illus., index, adv. Circ: 310455 Paid. Vol. ends: No. 12. Microform: MIM; PQC. Online: America Online, Inc.; The Dialog Corporation; EBSCO Publishing; Gale Group. Reprint: PQC. *Indexed:* BRI, CBRI, ConsI, MagInd, RGPR, SportS. *Aud.:* Hs, Ga, Ac, Sa.

Flying has the broadest scope of the numerous magazines geared toward the private pilot and flying enthusiast. Most of the feature articles concern the various aspects of flying, from safety issues, historical articles, and airports to aircraft and instruments. Every aspect of general aviation is covered, with an emphasis on flying and contemporary aircraft. The feature articles are written primarily to enthuse the reader and instill or convey the love of flying. Other articles are designed to impart practical advice and cover items of interest to the flying public. The magazine includes the sections "Flying News and Notes," news for pilots and new product information; "Training," providing information ranging from FAA examinations to job and student statistics; "Flying Opinion," which informs and aids readers with information imparted in a personal manner through anecdotes and stories; "Flying Safely"; and letters to the editor, a calendar of flying rallies and events, and other aviation news. The major articles fall into the "Pilot Reports" section. There are occasional special issues, such as one devoted to learning how to fly. Overall, the magazine is informative and interesting, with excellent photography. It deserves a place in most libraries, from high school to academic.

327. *FlyPast: the UK's top selling aviation monthly.* [ISSN: 0262-6950] 1980. m. GBP 42 domestic; GBP 49.65 in Europe; USD 80.50 per issue United States. Ed(s): Ken Ellis. Key Publishing Ltd., PO Box 100, Stamford, PE9 1XQ, United Kingdom; ann.saundry@keypublishing.com; http://www.keypublishing.com. Illus., index, adv. Circ: 44081. Vol. ends: No. 12. *Aud.:* Ga, Sa.

This structured publication is essentially a general-interest, history-focused aviation journal. It is advertised as Britain's top-selling aviation monthly. Although the primary focus is historical, with a particular emphasis on military history, there is an additional focus on restoration and preservation of aircraft. All areas of history are covered, although articles tend to lean toward military conflicts throughout time. Unlike other historical aviation magazines, this journal is geared toward a general readership. The magazine includes many photographs and illustrations to highlight the text, but most of them are in black and white due to the historical nature of the journal. The articles are informative and interesting and cover many of the same topics as the general-interest aviation magazines, including events and news. The product review sections include memorabilia, books, videos, and art prints. Numerous advertisements for memorabilia and related items are found throughout. This magazine should appeal to military-history or general-history enthusiasts, and to those interested in military aviation, aviation history, and aircraft restoration and preservation.

328. *I C A O Journal.* Former titles (until 1990): *I C A O Bulletin;* (until 1952): *I C A O Monthly Bulletin;* (until 1948): *P I C A O Monthly Bulletin.* [ISSN: 1014-8876] 1946. m. 10/yr. USD 25 domestic; GBP 25 foreign; USD 3 newsstand/cover per issue. Ed(s): Eric MacBurnie. International Civil Aviation Organization, External Relations and Public Information Office, 999 University St, Montreal, PQ H3C 5H7, Canada; icaohq@icao.int; http://www.icao.int. Illus., adv. Vol. ends: Dec. Microform: CIS. *Indexed:* EnvAb, IAA. *Aud.:* Ac, Sa.

The primary mission of this journal is the dissemination of the accounts, activities, and progress of the International Civil Aviation Organization (ICAO) to the ICAO membership and the global aerospace community, primarily the international civil aviation community. It is published in English, French, and Spanish, with a quarterly digest in Russian. Although the stated mission of the magazine is to relate the organization's activities to its members, the journal provides articles that would be of interest to anyone involved with civil aviation and air transport, such as airports and airport management; regulations; air traffic control and air traffic management; environmental issues; airport and aircraft safety issues and methodologies; new guidance, control, and monitoring equipment; aerodynamics and vehicle control; and related civil aviation issues. The "ICAO Update" contains news of interest to members. The July/August issue is the annual report on the state of international civilian aviation. This journal provides valuable insight into and information on the civil and commercial aviation industry and is appropriate for most research libraries.

329. *I E E E Aerospace and Electronic Systems Magazine.* Supersedes (in 1986): *I E E E Aerospace and Electronic Systems Society Newsletter.* [ISSN: 0885-8985] 1961. m. USD 335 in North America; USD 370 elsewhere. Ed(s): Harry Oman. Institute of Electrical and Electronics Engineers, Inc., 445 Hoes Ln, Piscataway, NJ 08854-1331; subscription-service@ieee.org; http://www.ieee.org. Illus., index. Refereed. Vol. ends: No. 12. Online: EBSCO Publishing; I E E E. *Indexed:* C&ISA, EngInd, IAA. *Bk. rev.:* 1, 500-1,500 words. *Aud.:* Ac, Sa.

This publication is the main avenue for the dissemination of information to the members of the Aerospace and Electronics Systems Society of the Institute of Electrical and Electronics Engineers (IEEE). The society consists of those members of the IEEE interested in the fields of navigation, avionics, spacecraft, aerospace power, radar, sonar, telemetry, defense, transportation, automated testing, and command and control. The three to five short articles in each issue cover those areas in which the fields of computer and electrical engineering overlap the area of aeronautical and astronautical engineering, and they deal primarily with the organization, design, development, integration, and operation of complex systems for air, space, and ground environments in the above areas. The journal's objective is to provide timely, useful, and readable systems information for engineers. The journal also includes notices of upcoming meetings and conferences, book reviews, and other membership-related information. Primarily of importance to academic libraries, technical libraries, and some major public libraries.

330. *I E E E Transactions on Aerospace and Electronic Systems.* Formerly: *I E E E Transaction. Aerospace.* [ISSN: 0018-9251] 1965. q. USD 685 in North America; USD 720 elsewhere. Ed(s): Cary R Spitzer. Institute of Electrical and Electronics Engineers, Inc., 445 Hoes Ln, Piscataway, NJ 08854-1331; subscription-service@ieee.org; http://www.ieee.org. Illus., index. Refereed. Vol. ends: No. 4. Online: Gale Group; I E E E; Swets Blackwell. *Indexed:* AS&TI, ApMecR, C&ISA, ChemAb, DSR&OA, EngInd, ExcerpMed, IAA, SCI. *Aud.:* Ac.

This journal is primarily geared toward those individuals working or studying in the areas of aerospace electronic systems, which includes command, control, and communications systems; avionics; aircraft control; aircraft navigation; missile guidance; multisensor systems; electronic warfare systems; energy conversion systems; intelligent systems; radar systems; robotics systems; space systems; and support systems. The 20 to 30 articles per issue vary from specific papers on individual systems to those that cover general research, design, and testing of various systems and subsystems. Little or no membership-related information is included. The journal prides itself on being the most often cited scholarly journal in the areas of systems engineering, avionics, and related fields. Included with the full papers is a correspondence section for brief discussions of new research. This research publication contains numerous reviewed technical articles in the same areas of coverage as the *IEEE Aerospace and Electronic Systems Magazine* (above in this section). Recommended for all types of academic and technical libraries.

331. *Institution of Mechanical Engineers. Proceedings. Part G: Journal of Aerospace Engineering.* Supersedes in part (in 1989): *Institution of Mechanical Engineers. Proceedings. Part D: Transport Engineering;* Which superseded in part (1847-1982): *Institution of Mechanical Engineers. Proceedings.* [ISSN: 0954-4100] 1989. bi-m. USD 824 in the Americas; GBP 514 elsewhere. Ed(s): J Hodgkinson. Professional Engineering Publishing, Northgate Ave, Bury St Edmunds, IP32 6BW, United Kingdom; orders@pepublishing.com; http://www.pepublishing.com. Illus. Sample. Refereed. Circ: 800. Vol. ends: No. 6. Online: EBSCO Publishing; Ingenta Select; OCLC Online Computer Library Center, Inc.; ProQuest Information & Learning; RoweCom Information Quest; Swets Blackwell. *Indexed:* AS&TI, ApMecR, BrTechI, C&ISA, H&SSA, IAA. *Bk. rev.:* 1-2, 500-750 words. *Aud.:* Ac.

The *Journal of Aerospace Engineering* publishes papers primarily in the field of aeronautical engineering that will interest mechanical engineers. The publication provides both practical and theoretical articles designed to further the advancement of the field of aeronautical engineering, especially the areas of civil and military aircraft, along with space systems and their components. Topics cover research, design, development, testing, operation, and service and repair of vehicles and their components. Fields covered include aerodynamics, fluid mechanics, propulsion and fuel systems, avionics and flight control systems, structural and mechanical design, materials science, testing and performance, and airports and spaceports. The journal publishes five to ten articles per issue to accommodate the growth in submitted papers. This increase is due to the academic community's discovering this international aerospace engineering journal produced by the United Kingdom's mechanical engineering society. Appropriate for academic and technical libraries.

332. ***Interavia: business & technology.*** Formerly (until 1994): *Interavia, Aerospace World;* Which was formed by the merger of (1946-1992): *Interavia;* (1987-1992): *Aerospace World.* [ISSN: 1423-3215] 1992. m. USD 150 in Europe; USD 175 rest of world. Ed(s): Oliver Sutton. Aerospace Media Publishing SA, 33 Route de l'Aeroport, PO Box 56, Geneva, 1215, Switzerland; interavia@swissonline.ch; http://www.aerospacemedia.com. Illus., index, adv. Sample. Circ: 21000 Paid. Vol. ends: Dec. *Indexed:* AUNI, BPI, C&ISA. *Aud.:* Ga, Ac.

This trade journal covers the aerospace industry from a global perspective. It covers all aspects of the aerospace industry in such sections as "Finance, Markets, and Industry," "Air Transport and General Aviation," "Defence," "Space," and "Datelines" (news events from several regional offices, including London, Paris, Bonn, Moscow, and Washington, D.C.). The journal also contains one or two "Special Reports," covering important topics concerning the aerospace industry, such as analysis of regional markets, airline pilot training, or airline maintenance strategies. Each section details relevant news items and profiles people within the industry. Important dates are found in a calendar section. The journal covers the entire range of issues facing the commercial aviation and aerospace industries, including regulations, safety issues, defense issues, civil aviation issues and news, and new products and developments. The strength of this publication is its depth of analysis and thoroughness in reporting the news and events affecting the aerospace industry. Although the coverage is global in scope and not as timely as other trade publications covering the aerospace industry, this journal is appropriate for most academic and major public libraries.

333. ***Journal of Aerospace Engineering.*** [ISSN: 0893-1321] 1988. q. Members, USD 58; Non-members, USD 87. Ed(s): Manohar P Kamat. American Society of Civil Engineers, 1801 Alexander Graham Bell Dr, Reston, VA 20191-4400; http://www.pubs.asce.org. Illus., index. Refereed. Circ: 1300. Vol. ends: No. 4. Microform: PQC. Online: EBSCO Publishing; Gale Group; Swets Blackwell. *Indexed:* AS&TI, ApMecR, C&ISA, EngInd, EnvAb, GeoRef, H&SSA, M&GPA. *Aud.:* Ac.

The main emphasis of this journal, produced by the American Society of Civil Engineers, is toward the practical application and development of civil engineering concepts, designs, and methodologies for space and on Earth. This international journal provides information related to the civil engineering aspects of aerospace engineering, primarily structural aspects of space engineering, applied mechanics, aeronautics, and astronautics. Sample topics include MEMS, composite materials, lunar soil mechanics, environmental factors in inhabited space facilities, aerodynamics of structures, extraterrestrial construction, aerospace materials, advanced energy systems, remote sensing, and robotics as related to aeronautics and aerospace engineering. Both full papers (five to ten per issue) and technical notes are included, with the emphasis being on fully refereed papers designed to share information developed through space applications and concepts between civil engineers and related engineering disciplines. A valuable addition to academic and technical libraries.

334. ***Journal of Aircraft: devoted to aeronautical science and technology.*** [ISSN: 0021-8669] 1963. bi-m. USD 520 print only (Members, USD 55 print & online). Ed(s): Thomas M Weeks. American Institute of Aeronautics and Astronautics, Inc., 1801 Alexander Bell Dr, Ste 500, Reston, VA 20191; custserv@aiaa.org; http://www.aiaa.org/publications/journals/aircraft-scope.html. Illus., index. Refereed. Circ: 3500. Vol. ends: No. 6. Microform: PQC. Online: Gale Group; Ingenta Select. Reprint: PQC. *Indexed:* AS&TI, ApMecR, C&ISA, EngInd, H&SSA, IAA, M&GPA, SCI. *Aud.:* Ac.

This journal is devoted primarily to the dissemination of original papers for the advancement of airborne flight. The focus is on the promotion of applied science and technology related to airborne flight, including articles on significant advances in the operation of aircraft, advances in aircraft themselves, and the application of aircraft technologies to other disciplines. All types of vehicles related to airborne flight are covered, including commercial and military aircraft, STOL and V/STOL aircraft, and subsonic, supersonic, transonic, and hypersonic aircraft. Areas covered include aircraft and aircraft systems design and operation, flight mechanics, flight and ground testing, computational fluid dynamics, aerodynamics, and structural dynamics. Related areas—such as application of computer technology to aircraft and aircraft systems, artificial intelligence, production methods, engineering economic analysis, and logistics support—are also covered. Accompanying the full-length papers (20 to 25 per issue) are "Technical Comments" and "Engineering Notes," the latter designed to further communication within the field. The journal occasionally produces special issues related to a single topic. This highly technical journal is recommended for academic, technical, and other research libraries.

335. ***Journal of Astronautical Sciences.*** [ISSN: 0021-9142] 1954. q. USD 155 domestic; USD 175 foreign. Ed(s): Kathleen Howell. American Astronautical Society (Springfield), 6352 Rolling Mill Place, Ste 102, Springfield, VA 22152-2354; aas@astronautical.org; http://www.astronautical.org. Illus., index. Refereed. Circ: 1800. Vol. ends: No. 4. *Indexed:* AS&TI, C&ISA, CCMJ, EngInd, H&SSA, IAA, M&GPA, MathSciNet, SCI. *Aud.:* Ac.

This journal provides topical information, research, and reviews on state-of-the-art technologies in all areas of astronautics, including astrodynamics, celestial mechanics, flight mechanics, navigation and guidance, and space sciences. Topics of articles include such areas as altitude dynamics, orbit determination, altitude stability, orbital mechanics/dynamics, propulsion systems (both conventional and electric), trajectory optimization, space mission analysis, numerical methods, maneuvering of flight vehicles, dynamics and control, and new astronautical systems and their applications. The journal occasionally includes technical notes to speed up communication of new technological and scientific advances. Likewise, the journal occasionally consists of papers taken from important conferences or symposia. Most appropriate for academic and technical libraries.

336. ***Journal of Guidance, Control, and Dynamics: devoted to the technology of dynamics and control.*** Formerly: *Journal of Guidance and Control.* [ISSN: 0731-5090] 1978. bi-m. Members, USD 58 Print & online eds.; Non-members, USD 500. Ed(s): George T Schmidt, Aimee Munyan. American Institute of Aeronautics and Astronautics, Inc., 1801 Alexander Bell Dr, Ste 500, Reston, VA 20191; custserv@aiaa.org. Illus., index. Sample. Refereed. Circ: 2200 Paid. Vol. ends: No. 6. *Indexed:* AS&TI, ApMecR, C&ISA, EngInd, H&SSA, IAA, SCI. *Bk. rev.:* 1, 750-1,000 words. *Aud.:* Ac.

This journal's primary focus is the advancement of guidance, control, and dynamics through the publishing of original peer-reviewed papers highlighting development, design, and application of new technology in aeronautics, astronautics, celestial mechanics, and related fields. Topics of articles include dynamics, stability, guidance, control, navigation, systems optimization, avionics, and information processing. There are also articles highlighting advances in the guidance and control of new aircraft, spacecraft, and related systems. In addition to the 20 to 25 full-length papers, the journal includes engineering notes, survey papers, technical comments, and book reviews. For 2003, the journal includes a section titled "History of Key Technologies," highlighting historical achievements as a celebration of the history of flight. The various topics covered by the fields of guidance, control, and dynamics are important to other engineering fields besides aeronautics, making this journal a valuable addition for research collections in engineering.

337. ***Journal of Propulsion and Power: devoted to aerospace propulsion and power.*** [ISSN: 0748-4658] 1985. bi-m. Members, USD 47 Print & online eds.; Non-members, USD 615 Print & online eds. Ed(s): Vigor Yang, Aimee Munyan. American Institute of Aeronautics and Astronautics, Inc., 1801 Alexander Bell Dr, Ste 500, Reston, VA 20191; custserv@aiaa.org; http://www.aiaa.org. Illus., index. Refereed. Circ: 1600 Paid. Vol. ends: No. 6. Online: Ingenta Select. *Indexed:* ApMecR, C&ISA, ChemAb, EngInd, H&SSA, IAA, SCI. *Aud.:* Ac.

This journal focuses on the segment of aerospace dealing specifically with an engineer's interest in working on aerospace propulsion and power systems. This is the primary journal covering combustion, power generation and use, and overall propulsion systems and components as they relate to the fields of aeronautics, astronautics, and space sciences. Topics include air-breathing propulsion systems (from turbine engines to scramjets), electric propulsion systems, solid and liquid rocket systems, hybrid propulsion systems, and other advanced propulsion systems and components. Original papers are presented to highlight recent advances in the areas of research, development, design, and applications. Subjects include fuel and propellants, power generation and transmission in aerospace systems, combustion of fuels, fluid mechanics, and solid mechanics. Accompanying the full-length technical papers (20 to 25 per issue) are "Technical Notes" and "Technical Comments." These sections are designed for rapid dissemination of research results. The journal recently started publishing occasional issues devoted to a single topic or subject. An excellent addition to any research-oriented library.

338. ***Journal of Spacecraft and Rockets: devoted to astronautical science and technology.*** [ISSN: 0022-4650] 1964. bi-m. USD 330 (Members, USD 45; Non-members, USD 165). Ed(s): E Vincent Zoby. American Institute of Aeronautics and Astronautics, Inc., 1801 Alexander Bell Dr, Ste 500, Reston, VA 20191; custserv@aiaa.org; http://www.aiaa.org/publications/jornals/spacecraft-scope.html. Illus., index. Refereed. Circ: 3500. Vol. ends: No. 6. Microform: PQC. Online: Ingenta Select. Reprint: PQC. *Indexed:* AS&TI, ApMecR, C&ISA, ChemAb, EngInd, H&SSA, IAA, SCI. *Aud.:* Ac.

This journal covers recent research, design, and current developments in the broad area of spacecraft and rockets and their accompanying systems, subsystems, and components. Articles focus on space sciences, including spacecraft, space vehicles, tactical and strategic missile systems and subsystems, applications, missions, and environmental interactions. Information is given on spacecraft and missile systems configurations, launch and reentry vehicles, transatmospheric vehicles, system and subsystem design, application and testing, mission design and analysis, applied and computational fluid dynamics, applied aerothermodynamics, and structures and materials as related to vehicle design and analysis. In addition, the journal covers such topics as space processing and manufacturing, operations in space, interactions between space vehicles, design of sensors, ground support systems design, and the transfer of space technologies to other fields. All areas of aeronautics are covered, including propulsion, guidance and control, aircraft technology (both conventional and STOL/VTOL), structural systems of spacecraft and missiles, missile design, and performance of space vehicles. Occasionally, issues include engineering notes, technical notes, and special sections on specific topics. Recommended for all types of research libraries or collections.

339. ***Journal of Thermophysics and Heat Transfer: devoted to thermophysics and heat transfer.*** [ISSN: 0887-8722] 1987. q. Members, USD 40; Non-members, USD 165. Ed(s): Alfred L Crosbie. American Institute of Aeronautics and Astronautics, Inc., 1801 Alexander Bell Dr, Ste 500, Reston, VA 20191; custserv@aiaa.org; http://www.aiaa.org/publications/jornals/thermophysics-scope.html. Illus., index. Sample. Refereed. Circ: 1000. Vol. ends: No. 4. Online: Ingenta Select. Reprint: PQC. *Indexed:* ApMecR, C&ISA, ChemAb, EngInd, IAA, SCI. *Aud.:* Ac.

This publication provides a forum for technical papers in areas utilized by designers of aerospace systems and components, including all methods of heat transfer—radiative, conductive, convective, and combinations of these methods. In addition, the effects of these heat transfer methods are also included. Topics of interest in the corresponding area of thermophysics include mechanisms and properties involved with thermal energy transfer and storage in liquids, gases, solids, and systems composing one or more of the physical states. Articles cover such topics as radiative heat transfer, conductivity, vibrational kinetics, thermal control systems, convective flow, and other areas of thermophysics, thermodynamics, and heat transfer. These issues are of primary importance to many aerospace-related areas of study, from the obvious propulsion and space vehicle areas to computational fluid dynamics, which could be affected by extreme temperatures and energy transfer. The journal also includes survey papers and technical notes. The use of color illustrations and photographs aid in conveying technical information. Recommended for major research collections, whether academic, technical, or a large public library.

340. ***Kitplanes: the world's number one homebuilt aircraft magazine.*** [ISSN: 0891-1851] 1984. m. USD 29.95 domestic; USD 41.95 Canada; USD 57.95 elsewhere. Primedia Enthusiast Group, 6405 Flank Dr, Harrisburg, PA 17112; http://www.primedia.com. Illus., adv. Circ: 74000. Vol. ends: No. 12. *Indexed:* IHTDI. *Aud.:* Ga, Sa.

This magazine covers the specialized areas of hobbyists and enthusiasts who wish to design, build, and fly their own aircraft. Articles cover all aspects of flying, training, safety, and maintenance as well as theory and other technical issues related to aircraft design, construction, and flying. Along with feature articles, the magazine includes departments such as "Builder Spotlight," "Shop Talk," and "Designers Notebook," and provides news, a calendar of events, editorial and readers' comments, classifieds, and information on competitions and events. There are many color and black-and-white photographs and illustrations, plus information on products and services, in-flight reports, and information on new aircraft. Emphasis is placed on providing useful how-to tips and other practical information. Geared to the flying public, hobbyists, and enthusiasts.

341. ***Plane and Pilot.*** Incorporates (in 1987): *Homebuilt Aircraft; Airways.* [ISSN: 0032-0617] 1965. m. USD 9.97 domestic; USD 19.97 newsstand/cover per issue foreign; USD 3.99 newsstand/cover per issue. Ed(s): Steve Werner. Werner Publishing Corporation, 12121 Wilshire Blvd 1200, Los Angeles, CA 90025-1176; editors@planeandpilotmag.com. Illus., adv. Circ: 134000. Vol. ends: No. 12. Microform: PQC. Online: ProQuest Information & Learning. Reprint: PQC. *Indexed:* IHTDI, SportS. *Aud.:* Hs, Ga, Sa.

This "magazine for active piston-engine pilots" is an official membership publication of the Pilots International Association and is devoted primarily to the interests of recreational flyers or pilots. It includes articles on flying, aircraft, new products and aircraft, pilot aids, safety information, flying events, information on rules and regulations, and other general-interest items for pilots and aviation buffs. There are classifieds, editorials, and letters to the editor. Regular departments include a section on training; "NTSB Debriefer," covering safety issues; and "In Training," providing practical advice and tips. One of the distinctive features of this journal that makes it more attractive for public libraries is a special issue devoted to the various careers available in the aviation industry, with a review of the present situation of the industry and a discussion of future trends, needs, and opportunities. There are usually features on topics of interest, from purchasing aircraft to tips on better piloting.

342. ***Private Pilot.*** [ISSN: 0032-8901] 1965. m. USD 23.97; USD 31.97 Canada; USD 39.97 elsewhere. Ed(s): Steve Whitson. Y-Visionary Publishing, 265 S Anita Dr, Ste 120, Orange, CA 92868. Illus., adv. Circ: 85000. Vol. ends: No. 12. *Aud.:* Ga, Sa.

The focus of this journal is the pilot of private business and pleasure aircraft. The journal's feature articles are a blend of those related to pleasure and business flying. The magazine bills itself as the world's leading general aviation magazine, and there are sufficient articles of interest on all types of aircraft and general-aviation topics, such as training, safety, and maintenance, to interest any aviation enthusiast or pilot. The numerous articles and corresponding photographs and illustrations cover such topics as safety, maintenance, new products, descriptions and reviews of pilot aids and equipment, pilot training and services, and government regulations and information. Regular features include news of interest to aviators, editorials, mail, classifieds, web sites of interest, and a calendar of events. The journal also provides information on new and used aircraft to aid pilots in selecting the best aircraft based on their particular needs or purpose. Although geared toward commercial piloting, the magazine contains numerous practical-information articles on aircraft, safety, and events that will interest all general-aviation buffs.

343. ***Progress in Aerospace Sciences: an international journal.*** Formerly: *Progress in Aeronautical Sciences.* [ISSN: 0376-0421] 1961. 8x/yr. EUR 1371. Ed(s): A B Haines. Pergamon, The Boulevard, Langford Ln, East Park, Kidlington, OX5 1GB, United Kingdom. Illus., index. Sample. Refereed. Vol. ends: No. 12. Microform: PQC. Online: Gale Group; ingenta.com; ScienceDirect; Swets Blackwell. *Indexed:* ApMecR, C&ISA, EngInd, IAA, SCI. *Aud.:* Ac.

This review journal is designed to bring together current advances in the field of aerospace sciences for those involved with research and development and for other researchers who have a need for technical information. The review articles, which contain extensive bibliographies, provide a concise and orderly summary of topics with sufficient detail that even nonspecialists can gain insight into the most recent and advanced research available. All aspects of aeronautical engineering are covered, including aerodynamics and fluid dynamics, aircraft design and performance, avionics, vehicle dynamics, guidance and control, fracture mechanics, combustion and propulsion systems, composite materials, wind tunnel design and testing, wind shear, and flight safety. The journal usually contains two or three articles per issue. Color illustrations add to the clarity and understanding of the research presented. Highly recommended for any research collection, whether in academe or the research sector.

344. ***Soaring.*** [ISSN: 0037-7503] 1937. m. Members, USD 55; USD 5 newsstand/cover per issue. Ed(s): Mark Kennedy. Soaring Society of America, Inc, PO Box 2100, Hobbs, NM 88241-2100. Illus., adv. Circ: 14881. Vol. ends: No. 12. *Indexed:* BAS, MagInd, SportS. *Aud.:* Ga, Sa.

This journal is analogous to *Ballooning,* except its primary emphasis is on propulsionless-aircraft flight or glided flight. The publication is the main communication vehicle for the Soaring Society of America, and it includes articles, photographs, news, and other items of interest for enthusiasts of gliding or soaring. The journal's feature articles include contest reports, information on safety issues, and product reviews of aircraft and systems. Topics of general-interest articles include historical perspectives on gliding, pioneers, and aerial photography. There are additional regular features on soaring and gliding events, conferences and competitions, general news of the society, tips on safety, reader mail, and classified ads. A good general-interest magazine for hobbyists and other interested readers, and appropriate for all types of libraries.

345. ***Space Communications: an international journal.*** Formerly (until 1990): *Space Communication and Broadcasting.* [ISSN: 0924-8625] 1983. q. EUR 388. Ed(s): Geoffrey Hyde. I O S Press, Nieuwe Hemweg 6B, Amsterdam, 1013 BG, Netherlands; order@iospress.nl; http://www.iospress.nl. Illus., index, adv. Refereed. Circ: 300. Vol. ends: No. 4. *Indexed:* ABIn, C&ISA, CommAb, CompLI, EngInd, IAA. *Aud.:* Ac.

This refereed international journal is the primary publication vehicle for new and original papers and related research covering all aspects of satellite communication, satellite navigation, and satellite broadcast fields. The journal covers such topics as the design of communication systems, all aspects of satellite technology, and the design and operation of satellite systems, as well as system and user requirements for satellite and delivery systems. Recent subjects include alternative uses of satellite navigation technology, key trends in global satellite technology, satellite network technology, launch systems, artificial and mobile satellites, aerospace control, space vehicles and manned spacecraft, and military satellite constellations. The journal includes both the technical aspects of this field and the commercial side of space communications, covering such topics as financing, regulatory matters, legal aspects, and management of space programs. Appropriate for this specialized segment of the aerospace industry and for research libraries.

346. ***Space Policy.*** [ISSN: 0265-9646] 1985. q. EUR 1133 (Individuals, EUR 197). Ed(s): Frances Brown. Pergamon, The Boulevard, Langford Ln, East Park, Kidlington, OX5 1GB, United Kingdom. Illus., index, adv. Sample. Refereed. Vol. ends: No. 4. Microform: PQC. Online: Gale Group; ingenta.com; ScienceDirect; Swets Blackwell. *Indexed:* CommAb, PAIS, PSA, SSCI. *Bk. rev.:* 4-5, 500-1,000 words. *Aud.:* Ac, Sa.

This journal is one of the few interdisciplinary journals in the field of aeronautics and space science and is designed to provide a forum for the discussion of how space policies will shape the future of space exploration, utilization, and related issues. The issues discussed include the impact of scientific discoveries obtained through space applications and research, space activities and discoveries that impact industry and society, and the resulting economic, political, social, legal, and moral issues raised. The exchange of ideas and opinions is as much a part of this journal as the exchange of scientific and technical information on space activities and developments. Many of the articles center on the use of space and the implications of this use. Topics range from space law and space commercialization to the history and current status of space programs, to space exploration and lunar development, to satellite systems and global positioning systems. The journal also provides information on new international developments in space, book reviews, and news of upcoming conferences and meetings. This unique approach of blending political, philosophical, business, and societal issues with scientific and engineering issues makes this journal an attractive addition to most academic and technical libraries.

347. ***Space Science Reviews.*** [ISSN: 0038-6308] 1962. 16x/yr. EUR 2085 print or online ed. Kluwer Academic Publishers, van Godewijckstraat 30, PO Box 17, Dordrecht, 3300 AA, Netherlands; services@wkap.nl; http://www.wkap.nl. Illus., adv. Sample. Refereed. Vol. ends: No. 4. Microform: PMC; PQC. Online: EBSCO Publishing; ingenta.com; Kluwer Online; OCLC Online Computer Library Center, Inc.; Ovid Technologies, Inc.; RoweCom Information Quest; Swets Blackwell. Reprint: SWZ. *Indexed:* ChemAb, GeoRef, IAA, IBZ, M&GPA, SCI. *Bk. rev.:* 10-12, 100-300 words. *Aud.:* Ac.

This international journal is composed of review papers on various topics related directly to space sciences. The magazine defines space science as scientific research carried out by means of rockets, rocket-propelled vehicles, stratospheric balloons, and observatories on the Earth and the Moon. The journal is primarily oriented toward the advancement of pure science, with limited coverage of the technical aspects of space science. The papers, some of which are very lengthy and compose an entire volume, provide a synthesis of the current research and developments in the numerous branches of space science. The journal covers all areas of space science, including, but not limited to, the Big Bang theory, supernovae, cosmic rays, solar variability and climate, infrared space observation, airborne observatories, solar-wind phenomena, and characteristics of interstellar matter. In addition, the journal includes book reviews and a listing of books received. Appropriate primarily for academic libraries.

348. ***Sport Aviation.*** [ISSN: 0038-7835] 1953. m. Membership, USD 40. Ed(s): Scott M Spangler, Mike DiFrisce. Experimental Aircraft Association, Inc., PO Box 3086, Oshkosh, WI 54903-3086; editoral@eaa.org; http://www.eaa.org/. Illus., adv. Circ: 170000 Paid. Vol. ends: Dec. *Indexed:* IHTDI, SportS. *Aud.:* Ga, Sa.

Sport Aviation is a cross between magazines geared for pilots and aviation enthusiasts and those aimed at specific areas of aviation, such as ultralights and ballooning. The magazine promotes general aviation and highlights all types of aircraft, from military and private aircraft, helicopters, and rotocraft to purely sport aircraft. The primary emphasis is on the sport of aviation and sport planes. There are numerous feature articles and other information on all types of aircraft, plus many articles on air shows, air competitions, restoring aircraft, and classic aircraft from military and commercial aircraft to seaplanes. Besides the feature articles, the magazine contains the following major sections, "Commentary," "EAA in Action," "Nuts & Bolts," "Stick & Rudder," and "Departments." These sections provide the bulk of the information of interest to the members of the journal's parent organization, the Experimental Aircraft Association (EAA). "Commentary" consists of columns and editorials. "EAA in Action" provides information and news of interest to EAA members, such as a calendar of events, association news, a memorial section, and member services. The other sections provide practical information for those restoring aircraft along with training- and safety-related information. A worthwhile addition to general-interest collections and public libraries.

349. ***Technical Soaring.*** [ISSN: 0744-8996] 1976. q. Membership, USD 24; Non-members, USD 30. Ed(s): Mark Kennedy. Technical Soaring Society of America, Inc., P.O. Box 2100, Hobbs, NM 88241-2100; 74521.116@compuserve.com; http://ssa.org. Illus. Refereed. Circ: 750. Vol. ends: No. 4. *Indexed:* SportS. *Aud.:* Ac.

This journal is a joint publication of the Soaring Society of America (SSA) and OSTIVA (Organization Scientifique et Technique Internationale du Vol a Voile). The journal is primarily technical in nature, including scientific and technical information on propulsionless flight and aircraft. Its focus is on the technical and scientific aspects of soaring flight, which includes design, testing, development, aerodynamics, structures, materials, and instrumentation. Safety and technical improvements toward greater safety comprise a major part of the journal. Unlike most of the journals on flight and flying, *Technical Soaring* is devoted strictly to scientific and technical information. Promotional information and general-interest articles are published in the SSA's other, less technical journal, *Soaring* (above in this section). The specialized nature of the journal limits its appeal to academic and technical libraries.

350. *Ultralight Flying!: international magazine of ultralight aviation.* Formerly: *Glider Rider.* [ISSN: 0883-7937] 1976. m. USD 34.95 domestic; USD 36.95 foreign; USD 3.50 newsstand/cover per issue. Ed(s): Scott Wilcox, Sharon Hill. Glider Rider, Inc., Dept N, PO Box 6009, Chattanooga, TN 37401; http://www.ultralightflying.com. Illus., adv. Circ: 15500 Paid. Vol. ends: Dec. *Aud.:* Ga, Sa.

The journal is the magazine of the U.S. Ultralight Association (USUA) and contains feature articles, columns, and departments. The feature articles cover the various issues related to owning and flying ultralight aircraft. There are articles on aircraft, flying, safety, and training, as well as reports from rallies and contests. There are also numerous advertisements and photographs. The standard departments and columns contain news from members, reports from USUA headquarters, information on competitions, new-product announcements and reviews, safety items, and a calendar of events. The journal provides an abundance of information on products, equipment, and safety. The articles are well written, and the magazine provides much practical information for ultralight enthusiasts. Appropriate for most general libraries.

351. *Vertiflite.* [ISSN: 0042-4455] 1955. q. USD 55; USD 75 foreign. Ed(s): Kim Smith. American Helicopter Society, Inc., 217 N Washington St, Alexandria, VA 22314; http://www.vtol.org/journal/. Illus., index, adv. Circ: 6000 Paid and controlled. Vol. ends: No. 5. *Indexed:* EngInd, IAA. *Bk. rev.:* 1-2, 700-1,000 words. *Aud.:* Ga, Ac.

The basic membership publication of the American Helicopter Society (AHS), *Vertiflite* is aimed at providing information on the advances being made in the areas of vertical flight and promoting the wider use of helicopters and vertical-flight aircraft. Research articles on rotocraft technology can be found in the *Journal of the American Helicopter Society* (above in this section). *Vertiflite* provides feature articles on helicopters and rotocraft technology and other issues relevant to the membership, such as new aircraft, new technologies, safety issues, and military technology. Along with these feature articles are various departments, which include the table of contents of the *AHS Journal,* book reviews, a calendar of events, conference activities, industry briefs, a member update section, and related news items. Articles range from the value of helicopters as demonstrated by cruise ship rescues to reviews of civilian helicopters, addressing community concerns about vertical flight, and the problems of the dependency of the helicopter industry on defense spending. The "AHS Annual International Directory," a special issue, contains a wealth of practical information on members, sponsors, awards, the annual index, and surveys of engines and aircraft. Recommended for academic and technical libraries.

Electronic Journals

352. *A I A A Bulletin.* 1996. m. American Institute of Aeronautics and Astronautics, Inc., 1801 Alexander Bell Dr, Ste 500, Reston, VA 20191; http://www.aiaa.org. *Aud.:* Ga, Ac, Sa.

The *AIAA Bulletin* is an online service produced by the American Institute of Aeronautics and Astronautics. The site is more limited in the availability of information than AIAA journals such as *Aerospace America.* The online journal is designed to serve as a vehicle to keep the association's membership up-to-date with the latest news on association activities and events, including information on officers and candidates, calls for nominations, listings of new members, obituaries, and announcements of fellows and other awards. There are also general news items on future activities such as meeting schedules, calls for papers, and related items of interest to the membership.

353. *Aero - News Network.* [ISSN: 1530-9339] 1999. d. Free. Ed(s): Jim Campbell. Aero - News Network, PO Box 9132, Winter Haven, FL 33883-9132; editor@aero-news.net; http://www.aero-news.net/. *Aud.:* Hs, Ga.

This site caters to the sport and general aviation community with articles and news from the now-defunct *US Aviator* print magazine. The web site has the advantage of being fresh and timely in its reporting of the aviation industry. The site is committed to being accurate and entertaining, with a commitment to making flying safer through reporting consumer activism and education. Lots of columns, lots of color photographs, news, and editorials make this a worthwhile stop in the search for aviation information. This is similar to commercial newsstand publications, but in an electronic form, and it is a good place to get a fresh view of the aviation industry. The majority of the information is on general and sport aviation, but commercial aviation, space news, and political news are included. One of the refreshing things about the site is it doesn't seem to be bought and sold by its advertisers; you can actually distinguish the content from the ads. A good site that will keep you up-to-date and informed, especially if sport aviation is your primary interest.

354. *Aerotech News and Review.* 1997. w. Ed(s): Stuart Ibberson. Aerotech News and Review, 456 East Ave, K-4, Ste 8, Lancaster, CA 93535; http://www.aerotechnews.com. Adv. *Aud.:* Ga.

This web site is primarily a weekly news bulletin for the aerospace and defense industries. The news is divided into sections, including business news, defense news, space news, science and technology news, and international news. In addition to the news articles are sections on mergers and acquisitions, other financial news, people, and places, as well as an area titled "Viewpoints." These are editorials, speeches, or other commentary related to the aerospace industry from politicians, the military, NASA, or others within the industry. Some of the supplemental information available includes notices on upcoming air shows, events, a listing of other relevant aviation web sites organized by category, and a photo section of various aircraft. The strength of the site is the in-depth news on the business aspects of the aviation and defense industries.

355. *Air Letter On-Line.* d. GBP 935 domestic; GBP 935 in Europe; USD 1980 United States. The Air Letter, 50-52 Upper Village Rd, Sunninghill, SL5 7AQ, United Kingdom; info@airletter.com; http://www.airletter.com. *Aud.:* Sa.

This web site advertises itself as a daily newsletter reporting on international news, business, politics, technology, and economics in the aerospace industry for those working in the industry. The site provides daily updates, Monday through Friday, on the aerospace industry from a worldwide perspective. Sections include "Headlines," "Air Transport," "Military Affairs," and "Industry." The newsletter also archives previous editions and the latest week's articles. These archives are available in several formats, including ASCII text and Adobe Acrobat pdf format. There is also a search engine that supports case-sensitive Boolean searching as another way of locating previously published information. The newsletter also contains a searchable calendar of aerospace events and a searchable index of more than 600 web sites, with hyperlinks to these sites. It is available by subscription only, by airmail, fax, and the Internet.

356. *Avion Online Newspaper.* w. Embry-Riddle Aeronautical University, 600 S. Clyde Morris Blvd., Daytona Beach, FL 32114-3900; http://www.db.erau.edu/campus/student/sga/avion.html. *Aud.:* Ga, Ac.

This newspaper, published by the Embry-Riddle Aeronautical University, is produced by a volunteer student staff weekly throughout the academic year and biweekly throughout the summer. *Avion Online* is the electronic version of the *Avion Newspaper* and contains the same information as the printed version. The journal at the time of press is undergoing a major revision under new management. Hopefully, it will retain its historic role of providing information to both the academic and the general aerospace community. The journal is supported by advertising and includes articles of interest to those concerned with general aviation, space science, and technology. Articles are grouped into sections covering such topics as space technology, aeronautics, and data technology.

Other regular features are geared toward the university's students. The newsletter also provides a search engine for information within the site. A good site covering the broad areas of aeronautics, astronautics, and space science.

357. ***AvStop Magazine Online.*** d. AvStop Magazine Online, avstop@avstop.com; http://avstop.com/. Adv. *Aud.:* Ga, Sa.

This site provides general aviation information including news, history, articles, and legal guidance. It is different from most online trade journals covering aviation that include news, links, and ads. This journal provides these items as well as pieces on aviation history, full-text books, medical stories, legal stories and research tools, and employment listings. The site is organized by these categories and provides sections for various aircraft types such as seaplanes, helicopters, hot-air balloons, home-built aircraft, and general aviation. Typical aviation web site information is also included, such as weather, editorials, chat areas, aviation databases, and links. Another excellent general-aviation web site that should interest most pilots and aviation buffs.

358. ***AVWeb.*** 1995. w. Ed(s): Mike Busch. AVWeb, 5455 N Federal Hwy, Boca Raton, FL 33487; http://www.avweb.com/. *Aud.:* Ga.

This premier aeronautics web site offers a broad view of current aviation. The articles, usually by professionals (including the editor), highlight what is going on in every area from legislation to technology. The site provides valuable articles and columns as opposed to other aviation and aeronautics sites that are strictly news reporting services. Probably of most value to many are the numerous links to related web sites and to experts and others interested in various aspects of aviation. It covers general-aviation topics as opposed to the commercial aviation industry, space industry, or the defense industry. A good deal of the cost of this seems to be borne by advertisements for products and by classified ads.

359. ***F A A Aviation News.*** Former titles: *F A A General Aviation News; F A A Aviation News.* [ISSN: 1057-9648] 1962. 8x/yr. USD 28. Ed(s): Phyllis-Anne Duncan. U.S. Federal Aviation Administration, 800 Independence Ave S W, Washington, DC 20591; http://www.faa.gov/avr/news/newshome.htm. Illus. Circ: 35000. Microform: MIM; PQC. Reprint: PQC. *Indexed:* IUSGP. *Aud.:* Ga.

This is the electronic version of *FAA Aviation News*, and it includes all the information found in the printed magazine. The journal promotes aviation safety from cover to cover, with safety-related news from the Federal Aviation Administration (FAA) and much information on safety issues faced by pilots. Articles cover regulations, people within the aviation safety arena, FAA facilities, weather, night flying, and any aspect of aircraft, pilots, or equipment relating to safety. Major departments include "FlightFORUM," a feedback section with responses from the FAA; "AvNEWS," which provides aviation facts and figures, news, and safety tips; and "MEDICALStuff," the latest information on aviation medicine. Other departments include editorials, runway safety issues, reprints, and past issues.

360. ***Jonathan's Space Report.*** 1989. w. Free. Ed(s): Jonathan McDowell. Harvard-Smithsonian Center for Astrophysics, 60 Garden St, MS 6, Cambridge, MA 02138; http://hea-www.harvard.edu/QEDT/jcm/space/jsr/jsr.html. *Aud.:* Ac.

This electronic newsletter is designed to provide information on all space launches, including manned missions and automated satellites. The newsletter is fully archived and available via ftp (file transfer protocol) back to its original issue in January 1989. The newsletter can also be received via e-mail. A recent issue contains information about the space shuttle and the Mir space station, several tables about recent launches, and current shuttle processing status. A recent addition is a link to Jonathan's Space Home Page, which provides links to image files, historical articles, and other information and sites related to space exploration. Not very fancy, but if you are looking for space vehicle launch information and need it from a reliable source, this is the place.

361. ***Landings.com.*** 1994. d. Landings.com, 6280 S. Valley View Blvd., Ste. 314, Las Vegas, NV 89118; landings-ops@landings.com; http://www.landings.com/. Adv. *Aud.:* Ga, Sa.

Landings is one site that everyone associated with aviation should visit as a central meeting place as well as a jump-off to other specialized sites. The site is primarily devoted to general aviation, but covers military aspects. The news is timely and on focus, and the feature articles are brief but comparable to commercial aviation publications. There are numerous other resources such as flight planning guides, links to weather sources, pilot and aircraft supplies, regulations, and reports. There are also links to information on airports and airlines as well as specific types of general aviation and military aircraft. The strength of the site is its ability to locate any type of information along with current news and feature articles.

362. ***SatNews OnLine Magazine.*** 1998. w. Free. SatNews Publishers, 800 Siesta Way, Sonoma, CA 95476; http://www.satnews.com/. *Aud.:* Ga.

A weekly web magazine containing up-to-date information on the commercial satellite industry. A daily news update from the site requires a paid subscription. The primary focus of the site is on providing breaking news and feature stories related to the commercial side of the satellite industry. Other features include a glossary of satellite terms, a history of the satellite industry, links to other satellite web sites, and a calendar of industry events. Some of the business and financial news includes information on satellite companies, information on particular satellites and operators, financial and technical analysis, and telecommunications facts and figures. This is an online trade journal covering the satellite and space industry and highlighting business news, information on companies and industry executives, and government regulations. Appropriate for specialized collections.

363. ***Science at N A S A.*** d. Free. N A S A Headquarters, Code FEO-2, 300 E. St. SW., Washington, DC 20546; phillips@spacesciences.com. *Aud.:* Hs, Ga, Ac.

This web site is a source for informative scientific and research-level articles based on the activities of the National Aeronautics and Space Administration (NASA). It is produced by the Science Directorate at NASA's Marshall Space Flight Center but covers all areas of NASA research. The main page lists a number of articles and their publication date. Along the left hand side is a listing of further articles by subject—space sciences, astronomy, living in space, earth science, biological and physical sciences, and beyond rocketry. This is a good starting point for scientific information (for all levels) from NASA. There is additional information for teachers on the Science@NASA site; however, for students and teachers the Liftoff and NASA for Kids (http://www.nasa.gov/audience/forkids/home/index.html) and the Educator Astronaut Program (http://edspace.nasa.gov) sites are better sources of information. For an alternate look at NASA's activities, check out the NASA Watch site (http://www.nasawatch.com). Suitable for almost any age and certainly delightful for anyone interested in the space program.

364. ***Space Science News.*** 1996. irreg. Ed(s): Gregory Wilson. N A S A Marshall Space Flight Center, Space Sciences Laboratory, Huntsville, AL 12345. *Aud.:* Hs, Ga.

Space Science is a subset of the Science@NASA web site. Both this section and the entire web site serve as a gathering place for scientific and technical information and news releases on space events and phenomena. Some of the topics covered include space weather, planetary science, microgravity, science highlights, and technology transfer. Other sections of the Science@NASA site include "Scientific Inquiry," "Astronomy," "Living in Space," "Earth Sciences," "Biological & Physical Sciences," and "Beyond Rocketry." All of these sections provide a half-dozen or so stories highlighting NASA activities and discoveries. Additional information includes links to other sites and recent stories. The ability to search the site for items of interest is also available. The site provides a wealth of information that covers all areas of science and presents it in a readable, concise format highlighted with illustrations and color photographs. A worthwhile site for anyone interested in NASA activities.

365. ***SPACE.com.*** Incorporates (1989-200?): *SpaceViews.* 1999. d. SPACE.com, 120 W 45th St, New York, NY 10036; info@space.com; http://www.space.com. Adv. *Aud.:* Hs, Ga, Sa.

This is one of the premier web sites for space information. *Space.com* has incorporated several features that make it attractive to those interested in spaceflight and space science, including in-depth articles and special reports along with basic headline and business news. The main site is divided into major sections, which include "News," "SpaceFlight," "Science/Astronomy," "Technology," "SpaceViews," and "SETI" (Search for Extraterrestrial Intelligence Institute). Each section contains an area for top stories as well as related information including links, special reports, polls, and recent news. The exception is the "SpaceViews" section that provides access to stunning illustrations and art related to space. The site has a link to the online version of the *Space News* weekly newspaper that provides much of the current news content. However, in-depth information from this area of the site requires a subscription to the print publication. Free access is provided to news briefs from the United States, Europe, and Asia as well as information on upcoming events, company profiles, satellite operators, and a directory of space-related web sites. The heavily illustrated content and broad focus make this site worthwhile for anyone interested in space. Subscription options are attractive for those within the aerospace industry, but space enthusiasts will also find plenty of interesting and informative information.

SpaceViews. See *Space.com.*

■ AFRICA

Margaret Power, Head of Reference, John T. Richardson Library, DePaul University Libraries, 2350 N. Kenmore, Chicago IL 60614 773-325-7835 email: mpower@depaul.edu

Introduction

Africa is a very interdisciplinary area of study, a consideration which determines the arrangement of this section. Because many of the titles selected cannot be classified by a specific discipline or topic, and most do not focus on a single country or region, presentation is in a straightforward alphabetical list. Subject areas such as literature, philosophy, ecology, basic science, and art are represented as well as issue areas such as development, gender studies, and democratization. A selection of consumer magazines and newsmagazines is also included. The section aims to provide representation in both subjects and geography at the regional level. Most publications are in English. However, some titles in French are important for covering former francophone African regions as well as providing significant contributions to African Studies. The selections represent a mix of titles published in the United States, England, and Europe as well as a healthy representation of magazines and journals from Africa.

The publishing industry in Africa is not strong outside of South Africa and perhaps Nigeria. Publishing has also been greatly affected by the economic crises of the past decades and weak technological infrastructures. It is important to note also that the industrialized countries have dominated the production of knowledge about Africa. Despite delays in production or receipt of materials published on the continent, the selections reflect the importance of including the African point of view. This includes access to publications that communicate the African heritage and culture, provide commentary on current events, and present African scholarship. Scholarly journals in Africa have been particularly affected by socioeconomic issues as well as the "brain drain" to the North. In this edition daily newspapers have not been included. With over 50 nations on the continent, it has not been possible to include a truly representative sampling of the most prominent newspapers. However, an entry has been provided in the Electronic Journals subsection to a major news service, *allAfrica* (allAfrica-.com), whose stories come from newspapers, news agencies, and publications from all over the African continent. Links to major African newspapers' web sites are provided on that site as well. Except for large research collections and specialized African collections, access to electronic news and newspapers is probably a more realistic strategy than subscription to printed newspapers.

A significant development for all serials concerning Africa is the greater presence on the Internet of African Studies journals and African publications. Electronic access to contents information and full text has mushroomed along with the appearance of many new all-electronic journals. Following the trends in publishing, many journals from the United States and Europe are now available in part or in full on the web or through aggregator vendors. Even if the full text is not available except to subscribers, many offer tables of contents and current-awareness services. *African Journals Online* (www.inasp.org.uk/ajol/index.html), a project of International Network for the Availability of Scientific Publications, brings awareness of African published journals to a world audience, offering current contents and abstracts on the web, along with a document delivery service. To assess the totally expanded electronic presence, one can examine the web site of electronic journal links at Stanford University Library compiled by Karen Fung for the Electronic Technology Group, U S. African Studies Association (www-sul.stanford.edu/depts/ssrg/africa/journal.html) or the journals list at Columbia University's African Studies pages (http://www.columbia.edu/cu/lweb/indiv/africa/ejournals.html).

Basic Periodicals

Hs: *Focus on Africa;* Ga: *Africa Research Bulletin. Economic, Financial and Technical Series; Africa Research Bulletin. Political, Social and Cultural Series, African Business, Journal of Modern African Studies, New African, Transition, West Africa;* Ac: *Africa, Africa Confidential, Africa Today, African Affairs, African Studies Review, History in Africa, L'Intelligent, Presence Africaine, Research in African Literatures.*

Basic Abstracts and Indexes

African Studies, African Studies Abstracts, Current Bibliography on African Affairs, International African Bibliography, PAIS, Quarterly Index to Africana Periodical Literature.

366. *A S A News: a quarterly newsletter for African Studies Association members.* Former titles (until vol.13): *African Studies Newsletter; African Studies Association. Newsletter.* [ISSN: 0278-2219] 1968. 4x/yr. USD 99; USD 109 foreign. Ed(s): Christopher P Koch. African Studies Association, Rutgers, The State University of New Jersey, 132 George St, New Brunswick, NJ 08901-1400; ckoch@emory.edu. Illus. Circ: 3600. Vol. ends: Oct/Dec (No. 4). *Aud.:* Ac, Sa.

African Studies Association (ASA) members receive *ASA News* and two other publications, *African Studies Review* and *African Issues* (both in this section) with their membership. *ASA News* is the association's communication organ for news and information. The newsletter provides listings of grants and fellowships; news of awards, papers presented, and employment openings; ASA calls for papers; meeting schedules and minutes; other meeting calendars; letters; information on new members and donors; and a list of recent Africa-related dissertations. ASA publications are highly recommended for academic libraries and any libraries supporting interest in African Studies.

367. *Africa: journal of the International African Institute/revue de l'Institute Africain International.* [ISSN: 0001-9720] 1928. q. plus a. bibliography. Individuals, GBP 205. Ed(s): Murray Last. Edinburgh University Press, 22 George Sq, Edinburgh, EH8 9LF, United Kingdom; http://www.eup.ed.ac.uk. Illus., index, adv. Sample. Refereed. Circ: 1250. Vol. ends: No. 4. *Indexed:* AmH&L, AnthLit, ForAb, IBSS, IBZ, IIBP, MLA-IB, PAIS, RI-1, RRTA, S&F, SSCI, SSI, SWA, WAE&RSA. *Bk. rev.:* 10-15, 750-2,500 words. *Aud.:* Ac, Sa.

Africa is the venerable journal of the International African Institute in London, which has played a seminal role in the development of African Studies. The journal has an interdisciplinary approach, presenting topics in social sciences, history, the environment, and life sciences with strong emphasis on issues of development, links between local and national levels of society, and cultural studies. Each issue contains usually six major thematically grouped articles, well footnoted with extensive bibliographies. Articles are accompanied by abstracts in English and French. Book reviews and review essays are substantial. *Africa Bibliography* (see below in this section), a comprehensive, categorized, and indexed annual listing of published work in African Studies from the previous year, is included with the full subscription in every fourth issue or can be purchased separately. *Africa* is a basic African Studies periodical, highly recommended for all academic collections and large general collections.

368. *Africa Analysis: fortnightly bulletin on financial and political trends.* Incorporates: *Southern Africa Business Intelligence.* [ISSN: 0950-902X] 1986. fortn. GBP 250 (Individuals, GBP 350). Ed(s): Ahmed Rajab. Africa Analysis Ltd., Africa Analysis, Ludgate House 107-111, Fleet St, London, EC4A 2AB, United Kingdom; aa@africaanalysis.com;

http://www.africaanalysis.com. Illus., adv. Sample. Circ: 1000. Online: EBSCO Publishing; Florida Center for Library Automation; Gale Group; LexisNexis; OCLC Online Computer Library Center, Inc.; SoftLine Information. *Indexed:* IIBP. *Bk. rev.:* 3-4. *Aud.:* Ac, Sa.

Africa Analysis offers timely information on the African business and financial climate and political trends. Published biweekly, subscribers may access the stories on the web site (www.africaanalysis.com) or by e-mail the day of publication or by first-class or airmail post. Back issues are archived on the web site, available to subscribers via password. Billing itself as "information for decision makers," it offers analysis of current business conditions and also practical advice for doing business in various African countries. Regular features include diplomatic briefings, corporate updates, guest columns, African currency checklists, and market/industry sector reviews. Columns featuring "names in the news" with political and business gossip provide information similar to *Africa Confidential* (below). Now incorporated is *Gulf Analysis*, which reports on the dynamics of the Gulf States' economies and news of that region. Timely, informative, and expensive, this bulletin is recommended for business, economics, graduate schools of management, research, and corporate libraries. Other libraries may want to choose one or two other business and political news sources (see also *Africa Economic Digest, African Business,* and *Southern Africa Political & Economic Monthly*, all below in this section).

369. *Africa Bibliography.* [ISSN: 0266-6731] 1985. a. Ed(s): Christopher Allen. Edinburgh University Press, 22 George Sq, Edinburgh, EH8 9LF, United Kingdom; http://www.eup.ed.ac.uk. Illus. *Indexed:* IBZ. *Aud.:* Ga, Ac, Sa.

Begun anew in 1984 in conjunction with the International African Institute's journal *Africa*, this annual review reports on African publications (books, periodical articles, pamphlets, book chapters) primarily in the social sciences, humanities, and arts, with selected coverage of the medical, biological, and physical sciences as they are relevant to readers from a social sciences/arts background. The entire African continent and its associated islands are included. It is arranged by region and country and preceded by a section for the continent as a whole. The sections are divided by subject classes with author and subject indexes. It is an easy-to-use resource for locating current, popular, and scholarly African materials. This recommended reference is useful both for those developing comprehensive collections and libraries that can afford to select a few items for geographic coverage of current literature. Some libraries may opt to acquire the *Bibliography* with a subscription to *Africa* (see above in this section).

370. *Africa Confidential.* [ISSN: 0044-6483] 1960. fortn. 25/yr. GBP 422 print & online eds. GBP 517 combined subscription in Europe commercial companies; print & online eds. Ed(s): Patrick Smith. Blackwell Publishing Ltd., 9600 Garsington Rd, PO Box 805, Oxford, OX4 2DQ, United Kingdom; jnlinfo@blackwellpublishers.co.uk; info@africa-confidential.com; http://www.blackwellpublishers.co.uk; http://www.africa-confidential.com. Illus., index. Sample. Circ: 3500. Vol. ends: Dec. Online: EBSCO Publishing; Factiva; ingenta.com; OCLC Online Computer Library Center, Inc.; RoweCom Information Quest; Swets Blackwell. *Aud.:* Ga, Ac, Sa.

For over forty years, this newsletter has been a source of current political, military, and economic intelligence reporting and analysis. Biweekly issues provide "inside track" information on African leaders and analysis of general trends and specific events in Africa written by a network of correspondents in every country. *Africa Confidential* is now available in an online version from Blackwell Publishers for corporate subscribers. Access to back files from 1998 to the present is available on the web. OCLC's Electronic Collections Online also provides access to issues of *Africa Confidential*. Pricey, provocative, and current, this newsletter remains in heavy demand and is highly recommended for both general and academic collections.

371. *Africa Development.* [ISSN: 0850-3907] 1976. q. USD 32 (Individuals, USD 30; USD 7 newsstand/cover). Ed(s): Felicia Oyekanmi. Council for the Development of Social Science Research in Africa, BP 3304, Dakar, , Senegal; codesria@sentoo.sn; http://www.codesria.org. Illus., adv. Refereed. Circ: 600. *Indexed:* AbAn, IBSS, IBZ, PSA, RRTA, WAE&RSA. *Bk. rev.:* 2-5, 1,000-1,500 words. *Aud.:* Ac, Sa.

This quarterly bilingual journal of the Council for the Development of Social Science Research in Africa (CODESRIA), supports CODESRIA's principal objectives of "exchange of ideas among African scholars from a variety of intellectual persuasions and various disciplines." African authors contribute articles on cultural, social, political, and economic issues of society in Africa. The focus may be on an issue in a specific country, such as agricultural labor in Ethiopia or education for democracy in Kenya, or on continent-wide issues. Abstracts in French and English precede the articles, which may be in either language. The two-page book reviews are in French or English. *Africa Development* is the oldest regularly published social science journal in Africa. It is currently lagging in publication but still highly recommended for academic and special audiences and institutions interested in including social science analysis from African scholars. Tables of contents are available through African Journals Online (http://www.inasp.info/ajol/journals.html).

372. *Africa Insight.* Formerly: *South African Journal of African Affairs.* [ISSN: 0256-2804] 1971. 4x/yr. ZAR 160; USD 40. Ed(s): Elizabeth Le Roux. Africa Institute of South Africa, PO Box 630, Pretoria, 0001, South Africa; beth@ai.org.za. Illus., index, adv. Sample. Refereed. Circ: 5000. Microform: PQC. Reprint: PQC. *Indexed:* AbAn, IBSS, PAIS, RRTA, S&F, WAE&RSA. *Bk. rev.:* 3-5, 500-700 words. *Aud.:* Ga, Ac, Sa.

Africa Insight is a publication of the Africa Institute of South Africa, a think tank devoted to production of knowledge on Africa. The journal is a forum for diverse topics focusing on the process of change in Africa. Topics are wide ranging: political trends and events, democratization, economic issues, regional cooperation, international relations, conflict resolution, aspects of education and training, health, community development, food security, institutional capacity building. While many articles focus on southern Africa, the whole continent is within the scope. The articles are scholarly, well researched, and frequently illustrated. Of interest to educators, institutions, and decision makers in business and the public sector, but also to a wider audience interested in Africa, this publication is well recommended and suitable for academic and large public libraries as well as special audiences.

373. *Africa Quarterly: a journal of African affairs.* [ISSN: 0001-9828] 1961. q. INR 100; USD 40; INR 25 newsstand/cover per issue. Ed(s): K Matthews. Indian Council for Cultural Relations, Azad Bhavan, Indraprastha Estate, New Delhi, 110 002, India. Illus., index, adv. Circ: 1900. Vol. ends: Oct. Microform: PQC. Reprint: PQC. *Indexed:* ABCPolSci, IBSS, IBZ, IPSA, PAIS. *Aud.:* Ac, Sa.

This publication of the Indian Council for Cultural Relations promotes understanding between India and Africa with articles that examine important themes affecting both areas, e.g., justice and human rights, Asian–African relations, globalization, etc. Issues may have a country focus. Scholars from around the word contribute the six to eight well-researched and accessible articles in each issue. There are also three or four substantive book reviews. Africa-related activities in India and conference notes may also be included. Significant in the context of the growing importance of non-Western interregional cooperation, *Africa Quarterly* is a good addition to both large and modest Africana collections.

374. *Africa Research Bulletin. Economic, Financial and Technical Series.* [ISSN: 0001-9852] 1964. m. GBP 583 print & online eds. Ed(s): Pita Adams. Blackwell Publishing Ltd., 9600 Garsington Rd, PO Box 805, Oxford, OX4 2DQ, United Kingdom; jnlinfo@blackwellpublishers.co.uk; http://www.blackwellpublishing.com/. Illus., index, adv. Sample. Online: EBSCO Publishing; ingenta.com; RoweCom Information Quest; Swets Blackwell. *Aud.:* Ac, Sa.

Comment and analysis drawn from Africa and around the world add value to this monthly economic news digest from *Africa Research Bulletin*. In both print and web formats, the *Bulletin* extracts text and summaries from media sources, including African newspapers, news agencies, radio broadcasts, and United Nations agency publications, as well as information from government gazettes, international organizations, and selected European newspapers and journals. After a lead article, six sections cover, for specific countries and entities, issues related to cooperation, trade, economic policies, infrastructure, commodities, industry, and economic aid. Charts, graphs, and maps accompany articles. The web format (http://africa-research-bulletin.com) is available to subscribers.

This publisher issues a companion series, *Africa Research Bulletin: political, social, and cultural series.* Both are highly recommended for specialized and large public and academic libraries for the extensive (but expensive) coverage.

375. *Africa Research Bulletin. Political, Social and Cultural Series.* [ISSN: 0001-9844] 1964. m. GBP 583 print & online eds. Ed(s): Pita Adams. Blackwell Publishing Ltd., 9600 Garsington Rd, PO Box 805, Oxford, OX4 2DQ, United Kingdom; jnlinfo@blackwellpublishers.co.uk; http://www.blackwellpublishing.com/. Illus., index. Sample. Online: EBSCO Publishing; ingenta.com; OCLC Online Computer Library Center, Inc.; RoweCom Information Quest; Swets Blackwell. *Aud.:* Ga, Ac, Sa.

A companion to the *African Research Bulletin: economic series* (see above), this analysis service draws from more than 100 acknowledged sources to provide news and commentary on politics and society. Sources from Africa are complemented with information from government gazettes, international agencies, and the European and American press. Coverage includes major conference reports; government changes, with lists of new officials; internal security; the military; international relations; and cultural and social information. Principal content sections are geographically arranged by country with a geographic/subject index. Major political/military events often appear in chronological, tabular outlines, and charts, graphs, and maps illustrate the articles. The online format follows that of the print. In addition to providing a detailed index, the web allows full-text searching. Like the economic series, this is expensive but essential for specialized and academic libraries, especially large research institutions.

376. *Africa Today.* [ISSN: 0001-9887] 1954. q. USD 92.50 (Individuals, USD 41). Ed(s): Gracia Clark, John Hanson. Indiana University Press, 601 N Morton St, Bloomington, IN 47404. Illus., index, adv. Sample. Refereed. Circ: 1300 Paid. Vol. ends: Fall. Microform: PQC. Online: bigchalk; Chadwyck-Healey Incorporated; EBSCO Publishing; Florida Center for Library Automation; Gale Group; LexisNexis; OCLC Online Computer Library Center, Inc.; Project MUSE; ProQuest Information & Learning; RoweCom Information Quest; Swets Blackwell; H.W. Wilson. Reprint: PSC. *Indexed:* ABCPolSci, AbAn, ArtHuCI, BRI, CBRI, ForAb, IBSS, IIBP, IPSA, PAIS, PRA, PSA, PollutAb, RiskAb, S&F, SSCI, SSI, WAE&RSA. *Bk. rev.:* 5-15, 750 words. *Aud.:* Ga, Ac, Sa.

Africa Today presents solidly scholarly yet readable articles examining a wide variety of current (and historical) social, political, cultural, and media issues. A publication that had its origins as the bulletin of the antiapartheid American Committee on Africa, *Africa Today* is now an academic journal. Since the journal's move to Indiana University, the focus has broadened to become more interdisciplinary, including occasional articles in the arts and humanities and reform-minded research in the social sciences. Many issues are on specific themes. A recent two-part special issue presents topics on "Women, Language and Law in Africa." A small number of well-written and incisive book reviews are included in each issue. A list of books ends the issue. This is an affordable, well-recommended publication for both general audiences and academic collections. Available through Project Muse (muse.jhu.edu/journals/at). Document delivery of articles and single issues at the Indiana University Press site (iupjournals.org/africatoday).

377. *African Affairs.* [ISSN: 0001-9909] 1901. q. GBP 155; USD 255; GBP 163 combined subscription print & online. Ed(s): David Killingray, Stephen Ellis. Oxford University Press, Great Clarendon St, Oxford, OX2 6DP, United Kingdom; jnl.orders@oup.co.uk; http://www3.oup.co.uk/jnls. Illus., adv. Refereed. Circ: 2000. Vol. ends: Sep. Online: EBSCO Publishing; Florida Center for Library Automation; Gale Group; HighWire Press; ingenta.com; JSTOR (Web-based Journal Archive); Northern Light Technology, Inc.; OCLC Online Computer Library Center, Inc.; ProQuest Information & Learning; RoweCom Information Quest; Swets Blackwell. Reprint: PSC. *Indexed:* ABCPolSci, AICP, AbAn, AmH&L, ArtHuCI, BrHumI, HumInd, IBSS, IBZ, IIBP, IPSA, PAIS, PRA, PSA, RRTA, SSCI, SociolAb, WAE&RSA. *Bk. rev.:* 5-15, 500-1,500 words. *Aud.:* Ac, Sa.

This scholarly journal has a long tradition of covering Africa from a broad range of social science and cultural perspectives. Each issue includes several scholarly articles that focus on recent political, social, and economic developments in sub-Saharan countries. Also included are historical studies that illuminate the current events in the continent. The journal regularly posts news of meetings of the Royal African Society (United Kingdom) and includes the society's annual meeting minutes, announcements, and annual report. Very useful to scholars, students, and librarians is the large bibliographic section with review articles, book reviews, a bibliography of current publications by region, and a bibliography of Africa-related articles appearing in non-African periodicals. Beginning in 2000, the full text of each issue is available online to subscribers to the print copies, at no additional cost (http://afraf.oupjournals.org). Oxford University Press provides abstracts of major articles online and a search facility to search the online tables of contents and abstracts. A table of contents mailing list is also provided for current awareness. A valuable resource for researchers, students, scholars, librarians, and anyone interested in recent and historical literature on sub-Saharan Africa, *African Affairs* is a basic journal for all collections.

378. *African Archaeological Review.* [ISSN: 0263-0338] 1983. q. USD 260 print or online ed. Ed(s): Fekri A Hassan. Kluwer Academic / Plenum Publishers, 233 Spring St Fl 7, New York, NY 10013-1522; http://www.wkap.nl/. Illus., adv. Sample. Refereed. Microform: PQC. Online: EBSCO Publishing; ingenta.com; Kluwer Online; OCLC Online Computer Library Center, Inc.; Ovid Technologies, Inc.; RoweCom Information Quest; Swets Blackwell. *Indexed:* AICP, AbAn, AnthLit, GeoRef, HumInd, IBZ. *Bk. rev.:* 1-2, 1,000-1,500 words. *Aud.:* Ac, Sa.

An international scholarly journal published quarterly in collaboration with the Society of Africanist Archaeologists. Each issue features one or two authoritative and detailed articles on an aspect of African archaeology. Archaeological research and activities in all parts of Africa are treated, with emphasis on issues dealing with cultural continuities or discontinuities, interregional processes, key cultural changes and transitions, and the application of ethno-historical techniques. Field data from key sites or localities are reported. "On Microlithic Quartz Industries at the End of the Pleistocene in Central Africa: The Evidence from Shum Laka (NW Cameroon)" and "Stone Age Prehistory of the Songwe River Valley, Lake Rukwa Basin, Southwestern Tanzania" are two recent examples of the research and analysis published here. There is generally one long book review in each issue. This publication is an important one in the field and is recommended for institutions with anthropology and archaeology interests. It is available in print and electronically from Kluwer Academic–Plenum Publishers (www.wkap.nl).

379. *African Arts.* [ISSN: 0001-9933] 1967. q. USD 64 (Individuals, USD 42). Ed(s): Amy Futa. University of California at Los Angeles, James S. Coleman African Studies Center, 10244 Bunche Hall, 405 Hilgard Ave, Los Angeles, CA 90095-1310; afriarts@ucla.edu; http://www.isop.ucla.edu/jscass/afrart/afrart1.htm. Illus., index, adv. Sample. Refereed. Circ: 5000. Vol. ends: Autumn. Microform: PQC. Online: bigchalk; Chadwyck-Healey Incorporated; EBSCO Publishing; Florida Center for Library Automation; Gale Group; Northern Light Technology, Inc.; OCLC Online Computer Library Center, Inc.; ProQuest Information & Learning; H.W. Wilson. Reprint: PQC. *Indexed:* ABCT, ABM, AIAP, AICP, AnthLit, ArtHuCI, ArtInd, HumInd, IBSS, IIBP, MLA-IB, SSCI. *Bk. rev.:* 3-4, 200-700 words. *Aud.:* Hs, Ga, Ac, Sa.

African Arts is an attractive, glossy journal devoted to the plastic and graphic arts of Africa and its diaspora. Architecture, arts of personal adornment, and contemporary and popular arts are a focus, as well as music, film, theater, and other forms of expressive culture. Each issue usually includes four to eight articles with beautiful black-and-white and color illustrations and photos. Topical reviews and discussions are often featured. Recent issues feature articles on Makonde sculpture and on community murals in South Africa, with an exhibition preview on "Genesis: Ideas of Origin in African Sculpture." Exhibit announcements, descriptive reviews of major exhibits, and book, video, and/or theater reviews appear in each issue. The presentation, subject matter, and accessible writing make this a good choice for all audiences. Published out of the African Studies program at UCLA, the full text is available through several aggregators such as EBSCOHost and *International Index to Black Periodicals.*

380. ***The African Book Publishing Record.*** [ISSN: 0306-0322] 1975. q. EUR 328; EUR 88 newsstand/cover. Ed(s): Hans Zell. K.G. Saur Verlag GmbH, Ortlerstr. 8, Munchen, 81373, Germany; info@saur.de; http://www.saur.de. Illus., adv. Circ: 500 Controlled. Vol. ends: No. 4. *Indexed:* IIBP, MLA-IB. *Bk. rev.:* 35-55, 200-400 words. *Aud.:* Ac, Sa.

ABPR provides comprehensive bibliographic and acquisitions data on new and forthcoming publications from the African continent. It includes books published in English or French and also lists significant titles in African languages. Bibliographic lists arranged by subject, author, and country supplement large book review sections. Features include reviews of new periodicals, an annual annotated review of African reference books, articles, news relating to the African book trade or African publishing, and listings of book awards and prizes. The Hans Zell web site at www.hanszell.co.uk is highly recommended as a resource for Africana collection development. This publisher also produces *African Books in Print*. *ABPR* is recommended for academic, large public, and special libraries.

381. ***African Business.*** [ISSN: 0141-3929] 1966. 11x/yr. GBP 36 United Kingdom; USD 90 United States; GBP 50 elsewhere. Ed(s): Anver Versi. I.C. Publications Ltd., 7 Coldbath Sq, London, EC1R 4LQ, United Kingdom; http://www.icpublications.com. Illus., index, adv. Sample. Circ: 18961. Microform: PQC. Online: EBSCO Publishing; Florida Center for Library Automation; Gale Group; LexisNexis; Northern Light Technology, Inc.; OCLC Online Computer Library Center, Inc.; ProQuest Information & Learning; H.W. Wilson. *Indexed:* ABIn, BPI, PAIS, RRTA. *Bk. rev.:* 1-5, 100-500 words. *Aud.:* Hs, Ga, Ac, Sa.

In a familiar newsmagazine format, *African Business* provides information on business trends, risks, and opportunities in Africa. The focus is Pan-African. Each issue usually has three or four "cover stories," longer articles on timely, compelling, current business and economic issues. Surveys of major market sectors—energy, commodities, freight and transport, construction, technology—are included each month. The "Countryfile" section features several specific-country analyses of economic developments and trends. Shorter stories on "products and processes," an editorial page, and regular columnists with opinions and advice round out this newsy, upbeat review of Africa's business climate. The magazine also includes news of conferences, trade exhibition dates, African currency tables, and book reviews. With colorful production and a lively, readable style, *African Business* is recommended for general, academic, and special collections. For in-depth country analysis, see *Country Report* (below in this section).

382. ***African Communist.*** [ISSN: 0001-9976] 1959. q. ZAR 35; USD 30. Inkululeko Publications, PO Box 1027, Johannesburg, 2000, South Africa; sacp@wn.apc.org; http://www.arc.org.za/sacp/ac.html. Illus., adv. Circ: 10000. Microform: PQC. *Indexed:* IBZ. *Bk. rev.:* 1, 1,000-2,000 words. *Aud.:* Ac, Sa.

This is the journal of the South African Communist Party. It is a quarterly forum for Marxist-Leninist thought. Published furtively in Johannesburg at first and then produced abroad and smuggled into the country with false covers (as gardening magazines or antiques guides) throughout the 1970s and 1980s, this journal finally came home in 1990. The South African Communist Party (SACP) played a significant role in ending apartheid and shaping South African politics and, perhaps, the political future of the country. The major focus of the journal is the South African transition. Issues may be devoted to a specific theme, such as HIV/AIDS and development or socialism and gender equality. Included are articles of opinion and debate, SACP documents and addresses, international political reports on socialism and communism in other countries, interviews, letters to the editor, and editorial notes. Useful for watching South Africa's development as a multiparty state from the leftist perspective, the *African Communist* provides an insight into African opinion and debates. An appropriate selection for libraries and institutions with a graduate political science program or an African Studies program, for research centers, and for general academic collections.

383. ***African Development Review.*** [ISSN: 1017-6772] 1989. s-a. USD 188 print & online eds. Ed(s): Mohammed N Hussain. Blackwell Publishing Ltd., 9600 Garsington Rd, PO Box 805, Oxford, OX4 2DQ, United Kingdom; jnlinfo@blackwellpublishers.co.uk; http://www.blackwellpublishing.com/. Illus. Sample. Refereed. Online: EBSCO Publishing; ingenta.com; OCLC Online Computer Library Center, Inc.; RoweCom Information Quest; Swets Blackwell. *Indexed:* ASSIA, IBSS, JEL, PAIS, PSA, S&F, WAE&RSA. *Bk. rev.:* Irreg. *Aud.:* Ac, Sa.

Published for the African Development Bank, a regional, multilateral development-finance institution, the *Review* is a "professional journal devoted to the study and analysis of development policy in Africa." Emphasis is on the relevance of research findings to policy rather than purely theoretical or quantitative contributions. Published generally twice a year, each issue includes about six scholarly, technical articles on developmental economics, policy, and planning issues such as macroeconomic policies, private sector development, and income distribution and poverty alleviation. The focus may be on recent critical issues or empirical analyses and case studies, either comparative or of single countries. Articles are generally in English, very occasionally in French. All articles have both English and French abstracts. There are book reviews, conference reports, and comments on review articles. Online access is provided for subscribers via the Blackwell web site from Vol. 11, no.1, 1999. Full text is available to subscribers through third-party service providers such as OCLC ECO Firstsearch and Ebsco Online. More technical and more focused on economics than *Africa Development* (see above), this journal is recommended for academic and special audiences.

384. ***African Economic History.*** Formerly (until 1976): *African Economic History Review.* [ISSN: 0145-2258] 1974. a. USD 36 (Individuals, USD 18). Ed(s): Paul Lovejoy, Donna Maier. University of Wisconsin at Madison, African Studies Program, 205 Ingraham Hall, 1155 Observatory Dr, Madison, WI 53706. Illus., adv. Sample. Refereed. Circ: 250. Reprint: ISI; PSC. *Indexed:* AbAn, AmH&L, ArtHuCI, IBSS, JEL, PAIS, SSCI. *Bk. rev.:* 8-10, 600-1,000 words. *Aud.:* GA, Ac, Sa.

Articles in this annual dealing with African economic history from the precolonial era to the twentieth century contribute to historical knowledge and provide insights into contemporary economic and political issues on the continent. Scholarly, well-researched articles documenting historical topics such as marriage and bride wealth in Zambia or the history of timber trade in Ghana make this an important addition to collections with an interest in both African history and economics. The book review section is substantial. Although the publication schedule is slow, it is recommended for specialized collections, academic libraries, and large public libraries.

385. ***African Issues.*** Formerly: *Issue (New Brunswick).* 1972. 2x/yr. African Studies Association, Rutgers, The State University of New Jersey, 132 George St, New Brunswick, NJ 08901-1400; http://www.sas.upenn.edu/African_Studies/ASA/ASA_Journ.html. Illus., adv. Circ: 3600. *Indexed:* AICP, IBSS, MLA-IB, PAIS. *Aud.:* Ga, Ac., Sa.

Formerly *Issue: A Journal of Opinion*, this title is received by African Studies Association (www.africanstudies.org) members along with *African Studies Review* and *ASA News* (both below in this section). A venue for Africanist scholars and experts to present empirical research, theoretical analyses, and personal reflections on a wide variety of issues and topics relating to Africa, the publication aims to be a useful resource for teaching. Each number has several essays on a theme.

386. ***African Journal of Ecology.*** Formerly: *East African Wildlife Journal.* [ISSN: 0141-6707] 1962. q. GBP 469 for print & online eds. Ed(s): F I B Kayanja. Blackwell Publishing Ltd., 9600 Garsington Rd, Oxford, OX4 2ZG, United Kingdom; jnl.orders@blacksci.co.uk; http://www.blackwellpublishing.com. Illus., index, adv. Sample. Refereed. Circ: 380. Vol. ends: Dec. Microform: PQC. Online: EBSCO Publishing; ingenta.com; Munksgaard & Blackwell Science's Synergy; OCLC Online Computer Library Center, Inc.; RoweCom Information Quest; Swets Blackwell. Reprint: ISI. *Indexed:* AbAn, ApEcolAb, BiolAb, CAPS, DSA, FPA, ForAb, GeogAbPG, HortAb, IndVet, RRTA, S&F, SCI, SWRA, VetBull, WAE&RSA, ZooRec. *Bk. rev.:* 1-3, 250-800 words. *Aud.:* Ga, Ac, Sa.

This important journal publishes original research material on the plant and animal ecology of Africa. Six to eight scholarly scientific articles are included in each issue. Recent articles include a paper on the preservation of the Mkomazi Game Reserve in Tanzania and an examination of elephant refuges in

Zimbabwe. Graphs, tables, and high-quality illustrations accompany the articles on wildlife and plant ecology, with all of Africa as the geographic scope. Although articles are in English, a brief summary in French is included for each. Regularly featured book reviews and brief communications round out each issue. The editors see the readership as wildlife biologists, academics in biological sciences, undergraduates, and schoolteachers. It is published for the East African Wildlife Society. Tables of contents and reprint services are available at www.blackwell-science.com. The journal itself is also online through Blackwell's Synergy journals service for subscribers. Highly recommended for general science, biology, and botany collections and for research and academic libraries with an environment or ecology program.

387. ***African Research and Documentation.*** Supersedes: *African Studies Association of the United Kingdom. Bulletin; Library Materials on Africa.* [ISSN: 0305-862X] 1973. 3x/yr. GBP 20 domestic; USD 48 domestic; GBP 27 foreign. Ed(s): J McIlwaine. Standing Conference on Library Materials on Africa, University College London, School of Library, Archive and Information Studies, London, WC1E 6BT, United Kingdom; n.matthews@bradford.ac.uk; http://www.soas.ac.uk/scolma/. Illus., index, adv. Circ: 300. *Indexed:* AICP, AmH&L, BAS, IBZ. *Bk. rev.:* 2-3, 250-1,000 words. *Aud.:* Ac, Sa.

Publishing articles on all aspects of library, archives, and bibliographical matters relating to Africa and African Studies, this journal is a good tool for building Africana collections and for keeping up with current African publishing trends, African bibliographic research projects, reference sources, book reviews, major scholarly writings, and announcements relating to African research sources. Issues also include information on Africa-related conferences and meetings, especially in Great Britain. Periodically, the journal provides an updated listing of African Studies resources on the Internet. In "Notes and News" one can find a summary of activities in various institutions with Africana collections. Book reviews by librarians cover a wide variety of scholarly works including some very specialized items. Table of contents is available on the association web site (www.lse.ac.uk/library/scolma/ard.htm). Recommended as a very useful tool for Africana librarians and scholars.

388. ***African Rural and Urban Studies.*** Formed by the 1994 merger of: *Rural Africana; African Urban Studies;* Which was formerly (until 1978): *African Urban Notes.* [ISSN: 1073-4600] 1966. 3x/yr. USD 40 (Individuals, USD 30). Ed(s): David Wiley. Michigan State University Press, Manly Miles Bldg, Ste 25, 1405 S Harrison Rd, East Lansing, MI 48823-5202; africa@msu.edu. Illus. Circ: 200. *Indexed:* AICP, AmH&L, AnthLit, IBSS, IBZ, PAIS, WAE&RSA. *Aud.:* Ac, Sa.

Formed by the joining of two journals, *African Urban Studies* and *Rural Africana* (previously published by the African Studies Center), this scholarly publication focuses on urban society, urban and regional planning, and the institutions of a rapidly urbanizing continent as well as dealing with the rural society and economy of what at the same time remains also the world's most rural continent. A good addition to collections with a focus on social sciences in Africa or the less-developed countries. A recent issue is devoted to articles on mass media in Africa. The journal is being reinitiated in fall 2003 with the same name but beginning a new series under the co-editorship of professors Ellen Bassett and David Wiley of Michigan State University.

389. ***African Sociological Review.*** Incorporates (in 1995): *South African Sociological Review;* Which was formerly (until 1988): *A S S A Proceedings (Association for Sociology in South Africa).* [ISSN: 1027-4332] 1973. s-a. ZAR 70 (Individuals, ZAR 40). Ed(s): Fred Hendricks. Council for the Development of Social Science Research in Africa, BP 3304, Dakar, , Senegal; codesria@sonatel.senet.net; seth@warthog.ru.ac.za; http://www.codesria.org. Illus., adv. Refereed. Circ: 600. *Indexed:* IBSS, PSA, SociolAb. *Bk. rev.:* 1,200-1,500 words. *Aud.:* Ac.Sa.

Like other publications sponsored by CODESRIA (Council for Development of Social Science Research in Africa), *African Sociological Review* is a venue for research-based publishing by African scholars, in this case in sociology and anthropology. Each issue generally contains four or five articles, usually in English but with occasional French-language essays. Recent articles include one on the interface between religious and political discourses in Zimbabwe and a report on productivity among nurses and midwives in Botswana. Research reports, important addresses or speeches, review essays, or argument pieces ("Debates") are selectively included. A few critical book reviews appear in each issue. Important for academic institutions with advanced degrees in sociology as well as Africana collections. Table of contents is available through African Journals OnLine (www.inasp.info/ajol/journals.html).

390. ***African Studies: a biannual journal devoted to the study of African anthropology, history, sociology, literature and languages.*** Formerly (until 1938): *Bantu Studies.* [ISSN: 0002-0184] 1923. s-a. GBP 116 (Individuals, GBP 31). Ed(s): Deborah A James. Carfax Publishing Ltd., 4 Park Sq, Milton Park, Abingdon, OX14 4RN, United Kingdom; enquiry@tandf.co.uk; http://www.tandf.co.uk/. Illus., adv. Refereed. Circ: 600. Reprint: PSC. *Indexed:* AICP, ASSIA, AbAn, AnthLit, IBSS, IBZ, IIBP, IPSA, MLA-IB, PSA, S&F, SSCI, SSI, SociolAb, WAE&RSA. *Aud.:* Ac, Sa.

This scholarly South African journal is based at the University of the Witwatersrand, an English-speaking institution with a progressive climate. The journal encourages dialogue between scholars writing in and about various countries in the South, drawing on South African academics and those in other parts of Africa and abroad. Each issue includes six to nine articles with an equal complement of book reviews. Originally focused on anthropology and linguistics, the scope is now much broader—including history, sociology, politics, geography, and literary and cultural studies, primarily in southern Africa, but also treating other countries and regions. A recent thematic issue has as its focus "Ethnicity, Nationalism and Democracy in Kenya." Regular reports on conferences and workshops are included. At the publisher's web site (www.tandf.co.uk/journals) one can browse the contents pages of the issues. Users from institutions subscribing to this journal can access the full text free of charge. Recommended for larger collections.

391. ***African Studies Review.*** Formerly (until 1970): *African Studies Bulletin;* Incorporates (1975-1980): *A S A Review of Books.* [ISSN: 0002-0206] 1958. 3x/yr. Ed(s): Mitzi Goheen, Ralph Faulkingham. African Studies Association, Rutgers, The State University of New Jersey, 132 George St, New Brunswick, NJ 08901-1400. Illus., adv. Refereed. Circ: 3600. Vol. ends: Dec (No. 3). *Indexed:* ABCPolSci, AICP, AbAn, AmH&L, IBSS, IIBP, IPSA, MLA-IB, PAIS, RRTA, SSI, WAE&RSA. *Bk. rev.:* 10-15, one page each. *Aud.:* Ga, Ac, Sa.

This scholarly publication is the principal journal of the U.S. African Studies Association (ASA), received as part of a paid membership to the association. International scholars in African Studies publish original research and analyses, primarily in the humanities and social sciences. Each issue contains three to ten scholarly articles, sometimes around a particular theme. Review articles discussing three or four new titles are frequent. In addition, each issue contains at least 10 to 15 one-page book reviews, arranged by discipline. At the ASA web site (www.umass.edu/anthro/asr) one can find an index (a couple of years out of date) of the book reviews and a subject list of *ASR* articles. The journal is an excellent source for collection development and current awareness. Recommended for general collections, and a basic choice for academic and specialist collections.

392. ***Africana Libraries Newsletter.*** Former titles: *Boston University Africana Libraries. Newsletter; Africana Libraries Newsletter.* 1975. q. Free. Ed(s): Marion Frank Wilson. Africana Libraries Newsletter, c/o Marion Frank Wilson, Ed, Librarian for African Studies, Main Library E660, Indiana University, Bloomington, IN 47405-3907; mfrankwi@indiana@edu; http://www.indiana.edu/~libsalc/african/aln. Illus. Sample. Circ: 480 Controlled. *Bk. rev.:* 400-500 words. *Aud.:* Ac, Sa.

A forum for the exchange of ideas and opinions about issues in Africana librarianship, this eight- to twelve-page newsletter supports the work and activities of the Africana Librarians Council (ALC) of the African Studies Association. Issues contain news of the council's activities, including meeting minutes and information about the ALC, Cooperative Africana Microform Project (CAMP), meeting schedules, agendas, and news from relevant groups. The content is of particular benefit to Africana librarians and collection developers as it routinely includes items dealing with information resources in and about Africa, as well as vendor news, acquisitions, trip reports, book awards, serial title changes, new and ceased serials, and electronic resources for Africana. Published by the Office of the Librarian for African Studies at Indiana University, it is also available free online at http://www.indiana.edu/~libsalc/african/aln.

393. ***Afrique Contemporaine: documents d'Afrique noire et de Madagascar.*** [ISSN: 0002-0478] 1962. q. EUR 51.50 domestic; EUR 54.50 in the European Union; EUR 55.50 DOM-TOM. Ed(s): Michel Gavd. Documentation Francaise, 29-31 quai Voltaire, Paris, Cedex 7 75344, France. Illus., index, adv. Circ: 2000. *Indexed:* IBSS, IBZ, IPSA, PAIS. *Bk. rev.:* 95, 50-100 words. *Aud.:* Ac, Sa.

This French-language journal focuses on trends and issues in politics, development, economics, and country-to-country and international relations in contemporary Africa. Each issue provides a chronology of major political events listed by country and brief biographies of principal personages. Articles are usually footnoted. *Afrique Contemporaine* includes numerous brief book annotations classed by country and topic. Recommended for larger collections.

394. ***Afrique Magazine.*** Former titles (until 1989): *Jeune Afrique Magazine;* (until 1986): *J A Magazine;* (until 1985): *Jeune Afrique Magazine.* [ISSN: 0998-9307] 1981. m. Ed(s): Zyad Liman. A M International, 57 bis, rue d'Auteil, Paris, 75016, France. *Bk. rev.:* Occasional. *Aud.:* Hs, Ga, Ac.

One of several glossy publications from Le Groupe Jeune Afrique, this is a mass-consumption magazine, in French, aimed at a youthful, upwardly mobile African or African diasporic audience. It is editorially self-identified as "infotainment." Monthly issues contain lifestyle articles and features on international figures, food, health, sports, fashion, travel, and music. Lively and upbeat, it is a good purchase for French and African Studies undergraduate collections.

395. ***Arts d'Afrique Noire.*** [ISSN: 0337-1603] 1972. q. FRF 310; USD 62. Ed(s): Eric Lehuard. Arts d'Afrique Noire, B.P. 24, Arnouville-les-Gonesse, 95400, France. Illus., index, adv. Sample. *Indexed:* AICP, AnthLit, ArtInd. *Bk. rev.:* 6-10, 200-1,000 words. *Aud.:* Ac, Sa.

This French journal of African art includes well-illustrated articles on aspects of the arts of black Africa and reviews of exhibitions. It also includes information on museums, exhibitions, private collections, public auctions, and recent art prices. For larger art collections and Africana libraries.

396. ***Azania.*** [ISSN: 0067-270X] 1966. a. GBP 12.50 membership. Ed(s): P J Lane. British Institute in Eastern Africa, PO Box 30710, Nairobi, Kenya; oxbow@oxbowbooks.com; http://britac3.britac.ac.uk/institutes/eafrica. Illus., index. Refereed. *Indexed:* AICP, AnthLit, GeoRef, IBSS, PLESA. *Aud.:* Ac, Sa.

Azania is the ancient name for East Africa. This journal of the British Institute in Nairobi (sponsored by the British Academy) is devoted to eastern African precolonial history and archaeology. It reports on diverse research undertaken by staff, students, associated scholars, and grant recipients of the institute, but it also publishes relevant research on East Africa's precolonial past from other scholars, both local and international. Articles are technical and accompanied by photos, graphs, and data. More geographically focused than *African Archeological Review* (see above), but East Africa is broadly defined, with coverage from the Horn of Africa to Zimbabwe. Suitable for larger archaeology and Africana collections

397. ***Cahiers d'Etudes Africaines.*** [ISSN: 0008-0055] 1960. q. EUR 72 (Individuals, EUR 46). Ed(s): J L Amselle. Editions de l' Ecole des Hautes Etudes en Sciences Sociales, 131 bd. Saint-Michel, Paris, 75005, France; editions@ehess.fr; http://www.ehess.fr/editions/publications.html. Illus., adv. Sample. Circ: 760. Microform: IDC. *Indexed:* ABCPolSci, AICP, AmH&L, AnthLit, ArtHuCI, IBSS, IPSA, L&LBA, MLA-IB, PAIS, PSA, SSCI, SociolAb, WAE&RSA. *Bk. rev.:* 9-14, 100-1,400 words. *Aud.:* Sa.

International and interdisciplinary, this important French bilingual journal publishes scholarly articles on Africa and the diaspora—the Caribbean, the Americas, and Europe. Focus is primarily in the social sciences, but it also features scholarship in history, popular culture, archaeology, communication, and literature. One or two articles of the five or six in each issue are in English. Each article has an abstract in either French or English. There are frequent thematic numbers with essays on a region or a problem or issue. A recent issue is devoted to African world music. Issues include review essays, critical book reviews, and a list of publications received. For specialized audiences, larger academic collections, and those with interest in Francophone Africa.

398. ***Canadian Journal of African Studies.*** Supersedes: *Bulletin of African Studies in Canada.* [ISSN: 0008-3968] 1967. 3x/yr. Individuals, CND 70; Students, CND 35. Canadian Association of African Studies, Centre for Urban and Community Studies, University of Toronto, Toronto, ON M5S 2G8, Canada. Illus., adv. Sample. Refereed. Circ: 1000. *Indexed:* ABCPolSci, AICP, AbAn, AmH&L, ArtHuCI, HortAb, IBSS, IIBP, IPSA, MLA-IB, PAIS, RI-1, RRTA, SSCI, WAE&RSA. *Bk. rev.:* 30-40, 500-1,000 words. *Aud.:* Ac, Sa.

Each issue of this bilingual journal of the Canadian Association of African Studies includes articles, research notes, book review essays, and book reviews in English or French. Most articles are in English unless the theme of an issue is a Francophone country. Articles carry an abstract in French if the article is in English and vice versa. There is broad coverage of the social sciences and humanities with a focus on anthropology, political economy, history, geography, and development, especially assessment of development strategies. A section of "Debates and Commentaries" presents divergent viewpoints on current issues. Review essays and book reviews (in either language) are quite substantial. The extensive reviews and essays make this a bibliographic resource for librarians and researchers to keep up with research, debates, and publications in the field of African Studies.

399. ***Country Reports.*** Formerly: Quarterly Economic Reviews. 1952. q. USD 455; USD 215 newsstand/cover per issue. Economist Intelligence Unit, 111 W 57th St, New York, NY 10019; http://www.eiu.com. Circ: 40000. *Aud.:* Ga, Ac, Sa.

This series of analyst reports, published by the Economic Intelligence Unit, aims to assist executive business decisions by providing timely and impartial analysis on worldwide market trends and business strategies for close to 200 countries. The quarterly reports (with free monthly updates on the Internet) monitor and analyze developments and trends in politics, policy, and economy. Putting recent events in context, the reports provide a two-year outlook for each country. Graphs and charts illustrate the economic trends and data. Subscriptions for print or web access are $470 for each report, which also includes an annual country profile (the profile alone is $225/year), with essential background information on political and economic developments and long-term trends. From the same group that publishes *The Economist* and *EIU ViewsWire* (a daily intelligence service covering the same countries), the *Country Reports* are a long-standing source of data and country intelligence; formats are accessible and information is timely, especially with the Internet access and updates. At $470 per country, this is an expensive publication; however, specialized collections may want to consider reports on countries of interest.

400. ***Current Writing: text and reception in southern Africa.*** [ISSN: 1013-929X] 1989. s-a. USD 20 (Individuals, USD 15). Ed(s): J U Jacobs. University of Natal, Department of English, King George V Ave, Durban, 4001, South Africa; http://www.und.ac.za/und/english/curwrit/. Illus., index. Refereed. Vol. ends: Oct. *Bk. rev.:* 15-20, 300-1,200 words. *Aud.:* Ac, Sa.

Current Writing carries essays on contemporary and republished texts in southern Africa and on the reading of world texts from a southern African perspective. Scholars from southern Africa are the primary contributors. The review section, an important part of the journal, evaluates new publications that relate to the region. The journal is of interest to those studying developments in writing and literature in southern Africa, a region where tremendous political and social changes have had an effect on writing style and content. While there is sometimes a delay in printing and distribution of the annual issues, this specialized journal appears to be still in publication. Recommended for large academic and special collections.

401. ***Discovery and Innovation.*** [ISSN: 1015-079X] 1989. q. KES 1500 (Individuals, KES 1000). Academy Science Publishers, PO Box 14798, Nairobi, Kenya; asp@arcc.or.ke; http://www.aasciences.org/. Illus., adv. Refereed. *Indexed:* AbAn, BiolAb, ChemAb, DSA, FPA, ForAb, HortAb, IndVet, PAIS, PLESA, RRTA, S&F, SSCI, VetBull, WAE&RSA, ZooRec. *Aud.:* Ac, Sa.

For academic and specialized audiences, this international journal features peer-reviewed articles on science and technology in Africa. A wide range of subject areas is represented: the basic sciences, applied sciences, environment, traditional African sciences, and social and human sciences. Emphasis is on scientific research and development and policy, especially as the sciences, technology, and social sciences relate to concerns in Africa. Third World research is considered as it applies to the African situation. Each issue also includes review articles with extensive bibliographies, research reports, and conference announcements. A recent issue contains articles on information and communication technology in Africa and on rainfall erosion and poultry disease in Nigeria. Tables of contents and the means to order photocopies are available from African Journals Online, a project of the International Network for the Availability of Scientific Publications that offers the tables of content and abstracts from journals published in Africa in agricultural sciences, science and technology, and health and social sciences. The URL is http://www.inasp.org.uk/ajol/journals/dai/about.html.

402. ***Drum: Africa's leading magazine beating to the pulse of the times.*** [ISSN: 0419-7674] 1951. m. ZAR 27.16; ZAR 32.76 foreign. Ed(s): Barney Cohen. Drum Publications, National Magazines, PO Box 1802, Cape Town, 8000, South Africa. Illus., adv. Circ: 150000. Microform: SAL. *Bk. rev.:* Irreg. *Aud.:* Hs, Ga, Ac.

Since the early 1950s *Drum* (South Africa) has been a very popular, consumer-oriented magazine. Sports heroes, models, political figures, and entertainment personalities are featured on the covers of each weekly issue, along with headers of the stories on music, fashion, food, health, and features on popular figures, as well as some sensational stories. Sections for children and women appear in most issues in addition to regular columns offering advice, horoscopes, puzzles, etc. It has a bit of the flavor of both *People* and *The National Enquirer*. *Drum* reflects the multicultural, middle-class, youth-oriented new South Africa. A short history of *Drum* and its unique place as a vehicle for black expression in South Africa can be found on the *Afribeat* web site at www.afribeat.com/archiveafrica_drum.html. Highly recommended as a colorful and appealing popular source that offers insight on the values and aspirations of South Africans.

403. ***East African Journal of Peace and Human Rights.*** [ISSN: 1021-8858] 1993. s-a. USD 35 (Individuals, UGX 32000). Ed(s): James Katlikawe. Human Rights and Peace Centre, Makerere University, Faculty of Law, PO Box 7062, Kampala, Uganda; dasiimwe@huripec.ac.ug; http://www.huripec.ac.ug. Illus. Refereed. *Aud.:* Ac, Sa.

Makerere University's Human Rights and Peace Centre (HURIPEC) was established 1993 with a mandate of teaching, researching, and compiling of local/regional materials relating to human rights. This journal of the political center continues to be an important venue for the critical discussion of peace and human rights development for Africa. The primary focus of this publication "is the manner in which legal and policy intervention can effectively promote and enhance the struggle against underdevelopment, human rights and peace." Five or six articles per issue appear from scholars from all parts of Africa, plus shorter commentaries, book reviews, selected correspondence, and editorials. An appropriate acquisition for academic and specialized libraries with interest in human rights or Africa

404. ***The East African Medical Journal.*** [ISSN: 0012-835X] 1923. m. KES 60001; USD 375. Ed(s): W Lore. Kenya Medical Association, Chyulu Rd., PO Box 41632, Nairobi, Kenya; eamj@healthnet.or.ke. Illus., adv. Refereed. Circ: 4500 Paid. Reprint: IRC. *Indexed:* BiolAb, ChemAb, DSA, ExcerpMed, FS&TA, H&SSA, HortAb, IndMed, IndVet, RRTA, RiskAb, S&F, SCI, SSCI, VetBull, WAE&RSA. *Aud.:* Ac, Sa.

Since 1923, the Kenya Medical Society has published original research and clinical data in this well-produced monthly journal. While about half of the authors are Kenyan, medical researchers from all over Africa and elsewhere are contributors. All aspects of medicine including nursing and health topics are included, especially clinical and basic research on problems relevant to East Africa and other African countries. Conference announcements and job postings are included. Table of contents and purchase of reprints is available through African Journals OnLine (www.inasp.info/ajol/journals.html). To be considered in medical collections and research or specialized libraries with a focus on Africa or tropical medicine.

405. ***Eastern Africa Social Science Research Review.*** [ISSN: 1027-1775] 1985. 2x/yr. USD 28 in Africa; USD 35 elsewhere. Ed(s): Bahru Zewde, Mohamed Salih. Organization for Social Science Research in Eastern Africa, PO Box 31971, Addis Ababa, Ethiopia; pub.ossrea@telecom.net.et; http://www.ossrea.net. Refereed. Circ: 500. *Indexed:* IBSS, PLESA, WAE&RSA. *Bk. rev.:* Number and length vary. *Aud.:* Ac, Sa.

The Organization for Social Science Research in Eastern Africa (OSSREA) based in Ethiopia publishes this twice-yearly forum for articles on economic, political, and social and development issues of the countries and sub-regions within the Eastern and Southern Africa. The social sciences are broadly represented, and treatment of policies and issues in scholarly articles, book reviews and shorter communications are presumed to be of interest to development planners and policy makers as well as academics. Recent issues contain substantial essays on "The Historical Origin of African Debt Crisis," "Democracy and Multiparty Politics in Africa," and "Women and Land in Zambia." A solid and consistent venue for African scholars, it is a good addition to libraries supporting African Studies. The is online access to tables of contents through the African Journals OnLine program at www.inasp.info/ajol/journals/eassrr. Also, since 2002, full text is available via Project Muse at http://muse.jhu.edu/journals/eas.

406. ***English in Africa.*** [ISSN: 0376-8902] 1974. 2x/yr. ZAR 70 (Individuals, ZAR 60). Ed(s): Craig Mackenzie. Rhodes University, Institute for the Study of English in Africa, PO Box 94, Grahamstown, 6140, South Africa; http://www.ru.ac.za/affiliates/isea/. Illus., index, adv. Refereed. Circ: 500. Vol. ends: May/Oct (No. 2). Online: Florida Center for Library Automation; Gale Group. *Indexed:* ArtHuCI, BEL&L, IBSS, IBZ, MLA-IB. *Bk. rev.:* Irreg. *Aud.:* Ac, Sa.

English in Africa is a scholarly journal devoted to the study of African literature and English as a language of Africa. Published by the Institute for the Study of English in Africa, a research institute within Rhodes University, contributors are generally established writers or academics from South Africa, England, and the United States. *English in Africa* specializes in publishing previously unpublished or out-of-print primary material, including articles and letters by writers of Africa as well as scholarly articles on African writing in English, especially African literature. Most articles are historical or cultural studies rather than theoretical enquiries. Reviews, review articles, or discussions between writers regularly conclude each issue. More literary and broader in scope than *Current Writing* (see above), *English in Africa* is suitable for academic institutions with a strong English, cultural studies, or African Studies emphasis.

407. ***Focus on Africa.*** [ISSN: 0959-9576] 1990. q. GBP 14 in Europe; USD 32 United States; GBP 16 rest of world. Ed(s): Damian Zane. B B C African Service, Bush House, PO Box 76, London, WC2B 4PH, United Kingdom; focus.magazine@bbc.co.uk; http://www.bbc.co.uk/worldservice/focus. Illus., adv. Circ: 32000 Paid. *Bk. rev.:* Occasional. *Aud.:* Hs, Ga, Ac, Sa.

This colorful, well-produced news magazine from the BBC World Service is published in London with content from journalists in the BBC's African Service programs. Each issue features news reports, feature articles, and color pictures covering the political, social, cultural, and sporting developments in the countries of Africa. Besides the feature stories and regular columns each quarterly issue has an update on the previous three months of developments, sections on business, sports, and an entire section devoted to reader contributions showcasing short stories, poetry, letters, and articles. BBC programming schedules are also included. The BBC World Service has a web site on Africa with a link to the page containing the current issue of the *BBC Focus on Africa* with an archive of selections of current affairs and business articles from back issues of *Focus on Africa* magazine (http://www.bbc.co.uk/worldservice/africa/features/focus_magazine/index.shtml). Highly recommended for all collections.

408. ***History in Africa: an annual journal of method.*** [ISSN: 0361-5413] 1974. a. USD 35. Ed(s): David Henige. African Studies Association, Rutgers, The State University of New Jersey, 132 George St, New Brunswick, NJ 08901-1400; callasa@rci.rutgers.edu; http://www.africanstudies.org. Illus., adv. Refereed. Circ: 550. *Indexed:* AICP, AmH&L, ArtHuCI, IBSS. *Aud.:* Ac, Sa.

This annual publication of the African Studies Association contains 20 to 30 articles on aspects of African history and culture. Essays on historiography, historical methodology, and archival research within Africa make this a valuable resource for historians, researchers, and advanced graduate students. History teaching programs will find it an important resource as the essays often reflect new research trends in African historical research. An essential journal for institutions supporting African history programs and highly recommended as a basic journal for academic libraries.

409. ***L'Intelligent.*** Formerly (until 2000): *Jeune Afrique.* [ISSN: 1621-6032] 1960. w. FRF 710 domestic; FRF 1300 foreign. Ed(s): Bechir Ben Yahmed. J A Press, 57 bis rue d'Auteuil, BP 399, Paris, Cedex 16 75768, France; redaction@jeuneafrique.com; http://www.jeuneafrique.com. Illus., adv. Circ: 100000. Microform: NRP. *Indexed:* MLA-IB, PAIS. *Aud.:* Ga, Ac, Sa.

Formerly *Jeune Afrique*, *L'Intelligent* is the principal French-language newsweekly on Africa. Published in Paris with a format similar to U.S. weekly newsmagazines, it has very good coverage of North Africa and formerly Francophone sub-Saharan African countries. Each issue has news and interpretative and editorial commentary on Africa and includes feature articles on political, cultural, and economic developments. The corresponding web site is www.jeuneafrique.com. Recommended for collections with Francophone-area interest and for general academic collections. See also *BBC Focus on Africa* (above in this section) and *West Africa* (below in this section).

410. ***International Journal of African Historical Studies.*** Formerly: *African Historical Studies.* [ISSN: 0361-7882] 1968. 3x/yr. USD 116 (Individuals, USD 50). Ed(s): Jean Hay. Boston University, African Studies Center, 270 Bay State Rd, Boston, MA 02215; http://www.bu.edu/africa/publications/index.html. Illus., index, adv. Circ: 700. Vol. ends: No. 3. *Indexed:* ABS&EES, AICP, AbAn, AmH&L, ArtHuCI, HumInd, IBSS, IBZ, IIBP, LRI, SSCI. *Bk. rev.:* 65-80, 500-800 words. *Aud.:* Ac, Sa.

Published at the African Studies Center at Boston University, this scholarly periodical and reviewing source covers all aspects of African history from "prehistoric archaeology to the present problems of the continent, including the interaction between Africa and Afro-American people of the New World." The extensive book review section and the review essays in most issues make this journal a significant tool for collection development. For a similar journal, see *Journal of African History* (below in this section). Recommended for academic collections and large public libraries.

Jeune Afrique. See *L'Intelligent.*

411. ***Journal of African Cultural Studies.*** Formerly: *African Languages and Cultures.* [ISSN: 1369-6815] 1988. s-a. GBP 119 (Individuals, GBP 29). Ed(s): E D Elderkin. Carfax Publishing Ltd., 4 Park Sq, Milton Park, Abingdon, OX14 4RN, United Kingdom; enquiries@carfax.co.uk/; http://www.tandf.co.uk/. Illus., index, adv. Sample. Circ: 300. Vol. ends: Dec. Online: EBSCO Publishing; Ingenta Select; RoweCom Information Quest; Swets Blackwell. Reprint: PSC. *Indexed:* AICP, IIBP, MLA-IB, PSA, SociolAb. *Aud.:* Ac, Sa.

Journal of African Cultural Studies has a much broader scope than in its previous incarnation as *African Languages and Cultures. JACS* no longer carries articles dealing with technical linguistic descriptions of African languages, but rather focuses on languages of Africa as channels for the expression of culture. Articles address "literature (particularly African-language literatures), performance, art, music, the role of the media, the relationship between culture and power, etc., as well as issues within fields such as popular culture in Africa, sociolinguistic topics of cultural interest, and culture and gender." Many articles have a historical focus. The content remains very scholarly, providing a venue for essays on African culture from inside and outside Africa. E-mail table of contents alerts are free through the Carfax web site, as well as full text of articles to subscribers (www.tandf.co.uk/journals). Recommended for academic and general libraries with a large audience in Africana, cultural studies, literature, and linguistics interests.

412. ***Journal of African Economies.*** [ISSN: 0963-8024] 1992. q. GBP 185. Ed(s): Marcel Fafchamps, Marcel Fafchamps. Oxford University Press, Great Clarendon St, Oxford, OX2 6DP, United Kingdom; jnl.orders@oup.co.uk; http://www3.oup.co.uk/jnls. Illus., adv. Sample. Refereed. Circ: 650. Online: EBSCO Publishing; HighWire Press; ingenta.com; OCLC Online Computer Library Center, Inc.; RoweCom Information Quest; Swets Blackwell. Reprint: PSC. *Indexed:* GeogAbPG, IBSS, JEL, RRTA, S&F, SSCI, WAE&RSA. *Bk. rev.:* 4-6, 800-1,200 words. *Aud.:* Ac, Sa.

This journal's stated aim is to offer "rigorous economic analysis, focused entirely on Africa, for Africans and anyone interested in the continent—be they consultants, policymakers, academics, traders, financiers, development agents or aid workers." The scholarly articles are accompanied by tabular data and graphs to illustrate trends and theories on African fiscal and monetary policies, trade, agricultural labor, and production issues. Book reviews and annotated listings of recent working papers in developmental economics are featured in some issues. An annual supplement provides text of ongoing research presented at the plenary sessions of the African Economic Research Consortium (AERC). The full text of each issue and archives back to 1996 are available online in pdf format to users with a print subscription (http://jae.oupjournals.org). Highly recommended for large libraries and economics collections.

413. ***Journal of African History.*** [ISSN: 0021-8537] 1960. 3x/yr. USD 193 (Individuals, USD 40). Ed(s): Iris Berger, Gareth Austin. Cambridge University Press, The Edinburgh Bldg, Shaftesbury Rd, Cambridge, CB2 2RU, United Kingdom; information@cambridge.org; http://uk.cambridge.org/journals. Illus., index, adv. Sample. Refereed. Microform: PQC. Online: EBSCO Publishing; Florida Center for Library Automation; Gale Group; JSTOR (Web-based Journal Archive); OCLC Online Computer Library Center, Inc.; RoweCom Information Quest; Swets Blackwell. Reprint: SWZ. *Indexed:* AICP, AbAn, AmH&L, AnthLit, ArtHuCI, BrHumI, GeogAbPG, HumInd, IBSS, IBZ, IIBP, NumL, PSA, RI-1, SSCI, SociolAb. *Bk. rev.:* 20-35, 500-1,400 words. *Aud.:* Ac, Sa.

Each issue of this excellent journal includes five or six long scholarly articles dealing with all aspects and periods of African history from the "late Stone Age to the 1970s" including archaeology, political, economic, and social history; and Africa's relationship with the world. Major essay topics have included slavery, African population history, medical and labor history, gender roles, the construction of ethnicity, Islam in Africa, and environmental history. A recent issue, for example, provides several perspectives on colonial Zimbabwe. Extensive and substantial book reviews assist in selection. For a similar journal in quality and scope, see *International Journal of African Historical Studies* (above in this section). Tables of contents and abstracts are available free on the journal's web site along with some selected free articles, but full texts of journal articles are available only to subscribers. Also part of OCLC's Electronic Journals Collection.

Journal of African Languages and Linguistics. See Linguistics section.

414. ***Journal of African Law.*** [ISSN: 0021-8553] 1956. s-a. USD 125 (Individuals, USD 50). Ed(s): Fareda Banda, Nelson Enonchong. Cambridge University Press, The Edinburgh Bldg, Shaftesbury Rd, Cambridge, CB2 2RU, United Kingdom; information@cambridge.org; http://uk.cambridge.org/journals. Adv. Circ: 550. Microform: WSH; PMC. Online: EBSCO Publishing; OCLC Online Computer Library Center, Inc.; RoweCom Information Quest; Swets Blackwell. Reprint: WSH. *Indexed:* AICP, CLI, IBSS, IBZ, IIBP, ILP, IPSA, LRI, PAIS. *Bk. rev.:* Number and length varies. *Aud.:* Ga, Ac, Sa.

Published by Cambridge University Press for the School of Oriental and African Studies University of London, *The African Journal of Law* is a scholarly publication covering laws of the entire sub-Saharan continent. Comparative legal issues and those of international significance are highlighted. A separate section covers recent legislation, case law, law reform proposals, and international developments affecting Africa. The scope includes crime, family law, human rights, and nationality and constitutional law. With articles on such topics as South African land reform, forest management in Ghana, capital markets regulation in Nigeria, the aim of the journal to reach development workers and policy makers as well as academics and professional lawyers is well founded. Available in print and electronically.

415. *Journal of Contemporary African Studies.* [ISSN: 0258-9001] 1981. 3x/yr. GBP 282 (Individuals, GBP 60). Ed(s): Patrick McAllister. Carfax Publishing Ltd., 4 Park Sq, Milton Park, Abingdon, OX14 4RN, United Kingdom; enquiry@tandf.co.uk; http://www.tandf.co.uk/. Illus., adv. Sample. Refereed. Circ: 2000. Vol. ends: No. 2. Online: EBSCO Publishing; Ingenta Select; OCLC Online Computer Library Center, Inc.; RoweCom Information Quest; Swets Blackwell. Reprint: PQC; PSC. *Indexed:* ASSIA, AmH&L, FPA, ForAb, IBSS, IPSA, PSA, SociolAb, WAE&RSA. *Bk. rev.:* 5-15, 500-1,000 words. *Aud.:* Ac, Sa.

This interdisciplinary journal aims to provide a scholarly understanding of developments and change in Africa through publication of research and writing in the social sciences and humanities with the social sciences predominating. Sociology, urban studies, modern history, education, literature, development studies—the wide scope of research makes this an important journal for contemporary African Studies. While the editorial group is based in South Africa, the scope is the whole sub-Saharan continent and the contributors are wide ranging. Recent issues include articles on Ghanaian elections, entrepreneurial manufacturing in Nigeria, and parliamentary reform in Zambia. Book reviews appear in each semi-annual issue. Articles are available online to print subscribers at www.tandf.co.uk/journals. Recommended for academic collections and those with strong interest in contemporary Africa.

416. *Journal of Modern African Studies.* [ISSN: 0022-278X] 1963. q. USD 220 (Individuals, USD 76). Ed(s): Christopher Clapham. Cambridge University Press, The Edinburgh Bldg, Shaftesbury Rd, Cambridge, CB2 2RU, United Kingdom; information@cambridge.org; http://uk.cambridge.org/journals. Illus., index, adv. Sample. Refereed. Circ: 1700. Vol. ends: Dec. Microform: PQC. Online: EBSCO Publishing; Gale Group; JSTOR (Web-based Journal Archive); OCLC Online Computer Library Center, Inc.; RoweCom Information Quest; Swets Blackwell. Reprint: SWZ. *Indexed:* ABCPolSci, AbAn, AmH&L, ArtHuCI, BAS, BrHumI, FPA, ForAb, GeogAbPG, HortAb, IBSS, IIBP, IPSA, L&LBA, MLA-IB, NumL, PAIS, PRA, PSA, RRTA, S&F, SFSA, SSCI, SSI, SociolAb, WAE&RSA. *Bk. rev.:* 0-25, 500-2,000 words. *Aud.:* Ac, Sa.

The aim of this scholarly but accessible journal is to present fair and balanced views of "controversial issues," focusing on contemporary Africa, with emphasis on current issues in African politics, economies, societies, and international relations. Specialists and scholars in the field contribute articles on political, economic, and social policies that affect people and progress on the continent. Recent articles treat such topics as women and politics in Ghana and the role of business associations on the continent. Shorter pieces on literature, culture, and aspects of social history also appear. Issues also include critical book reviews. Available electronically to institutions via Cambridge Journals Online (uk.cambridge.org/journals). Guests can view abstracts of articles. Suitable for students, academics, and general readers, it is highly recommended for academic libraries and general collections.

417. *The Journal of North African Studies.* [ISSN: 1362-9387] 1996. q. GBP 203 print & online eds. Ed(s): John P Entelis, George Joffe. Frank Cass Publishers, Crown House, 47 Chase Side, Southgate, London, N14 5BP, United Kingdom; jnlsubs@frankcass.com; http://www.frankcass.com/jnls/. Adv. Sample. Refereed. Vol. ends: Winter. *Indexed:* BrHumI, IBSS, IPSA, PSA, SociolAb. *Bk. rev.:* Number and length vary. *Aud.:* Ac, Sa.

This relatively new journal is one of a few that treat this region with links to both sub-Saharan Africa and the Middle East. It provides a forum for scholars of and from North Africa. The peer-reviewed articles cover country-based and regional themes in historical topics and in the social sciences. There are five to eight articles per issue and book reviews. A recent issue features both contemporary analysis (economic liberalization in Algeria, privatization of the Internet in Morocco) and a historical article on the trans-Saharan slave trade in Morocco. Special issues also available as books appear regularly, such as a recent one devoted to the "Walled Arab City in Literature, Architecture and History." A positive addition covering a region rarely treated as coherent. Book reviews provide current awareness for this area of study. Recommended for academic and special libraries.

418. *Journal of Religion in Africa.* [ISSN: 0022-4200] 1967. q. EUR 179 print & online eds. (Individuals, EUR 100 print & online eds.). Ed(s): David Maxwell. Brill Academic Publishers, Inc., PO Box 9000, Leiden, 2300 PA, Netherlands; cs@brill.nl; http://www.brill.nl. Illus., adv. Refereed. Vol. ends: No. 4. *Indexed:* ArtHuCI, IBSS, IBZ, IIBP, R&TA, RI-1, SociolAb. *Bk. rev.:* 4-6, 750+ words. *Aud.:* Ac, Sa.

As the only English-language journal to be focused on the forms and history of religion within the African continent, particularly in sub-Saharan Africa, this is an important publication. Scholars from a variety of disciplines and countries contribute to each issue, which is normally on a particular topic introduced by editorial comment. The journal occasionally publishes religious texts in their original African language. There are book reviews and longer review articles. A leading international journal in religious studies but also of interest to a humanities and social science readership. Online access is through Ingenta Select (http://matilde.ingentaselect.com). For academic and larger collections.

419. *Journal of Southern African Studies.* [ISSN: 0305-7070] 1975. q. GBP 222 (Individuals, GBP 60). Ed(s): Jocelyn Alexander. Carfax Publishing Ltd., 4 Park Sq, Milton Park, Abingdon, OX14 4RN, United Kingdom; enquiry@tandf.co.uk; http://www.tandf.co.uk/. Illus., adv. Sample. Refereed. Circ: 900. Microform: PQC. Online: bigchalk; EBSCO Publishing; Ingenta Select; JSTOR (Web-based Journal Archive); Northern Light Technology, Inc.; OCLC Online Computer Library Center, Inc.; ProQuest Information & Learning; RoweCom Information Quest; Swets Blackwell. Reprint: PSC. *Indexed:* ABCPolSci, AICP, AmH&L, ArtHuCI, BrHumI, CJA, FPA, ForAb, GeogAbPG, IBSS, IIBP, IPSA, L&LBA, PSA, RRTA, S&F, SSCI, SWA, SociolAb, WAE&RSA. *Bk. rev.:* 4-6, 200-1,000 words. *Aud.:* Ac, Sa.

Academic scholarship presenting new perspectives from various disciplines in social sciences and allied fields are featured in this international journal. New theoretical approaches and scholarly inquiry are applied to issues and social problems in the region of southern Africa. Issues include six to ten extensive articles, excellent review essays, and signed book reviews. A recent issue has articles on water use in Zimbabwe and a historical study of the Amandiki of Zululand. One or two of each year's four issues are devoted to broad themes; another recent issue focuses on Botswana. Contents pages and full texts to institutional subscribers are available at www.tandf.co.uk/journals. Highly recommended for academic and specialized collections.

420. *The Maghreb Review: a quarterly journal on all aspects of North Africa, the Middle East, Sub-Saharan Africa and Islamic studies from earliest times to the present day.* [ISSN: 0309-457X] 1976. q. GBP 235. Ed(s): Mohamed Ben Madani. Maghreb Review, 45 Burton St, London, WC1H 9AL, United Kingdom. Illus., adv. Refereed. Circ: 10000. *Indexed:* AmH&L, IPSA, IndIslam. *Bk. rev.:* 4-6, 2,000-4,000 words. *Aud.:* Ac, Sa.

Independent, interdisciplinary, and bilingual, this journal is one of the oldest English/French publications devoted to the study of North Africa. The specific focus is the region of the Maghreb: Algeria, Tunisia, Libya, Morocco, and Mauritania. International scholars contribute studies in archaeology, anthropology, politics, history, religion, literature—the spectrum of the social sciences and humanities as they relate to the Berber, Arab, and Islamic heritage of this crossroads region and its interaction with sub-Saharan Africa, the Mediterranean, and the Middle East. Six to eight articles appear in each issue, some in both languages and some with translated abstracts. Special issues on topics are frequent, and conference papers are featured. Recommended for larger collections.

421. *Matatu: journal for African culture and society.* [ISSN: 0932-9714] 1987. s-a. Ed(s): Holger G Ehling. Rodopi, Tijnmuiden 7, Amsterdam, 1046 AK, Netherlands; orders-queries@rodopi.nl; http://www.rodopi.nl. Illus., adv. Refereed. Circ: 500. *Indexed:* IBZ, L&LBA, MLA-IB, PSA, SociolAb. *Aud.:* Ga, Ac, Sa.

Matatu is a semi-annual refereed journal devoted to African literatures and societies "promoting interdisciplinary dialogue between literary and cultural studies, historiography, the social sciences and cultural anthropology." The focus is on African (including Afro-Caribbean) culture and literature, providing a forum for critical debates and exploration of African modernities. While *Matatu* is a journal, each volume is on a specific theme and is priced to be purchased separately. Recent issues treat the relation of the museum to African cultures and visual arts, and Nigerian writing and the struggle for democracy. Considering Africa in the global context, this journal makes nice addition for arts and cultural studies for academic libraries.

422. ***N K A: journal of contemporary African art.*** [ISSN: 1075-7163] 1994. s-a. USD 43 (Individuals, USD 27). Ed(s): Salah Hassan, Okwui Enwezor. Mario Einaudi Center for International Studies, 170 Uris Hall, Africana Studies and Research Center, Ithaca, NY 14853-7601. Illus. Refereed. *Indexed:* ABM. *Bk. rev.:* Number and length vary. *Aud.:* Ga, Ac, Sa.

Published in conjunction with the Africana Studies and Research Center at Cornell, this beautifully produced magazine is focused not primarily on the ethnographic and traditional art forms, but on contemporary art from Africa and the diaspora. Arts from film to poetry to sculpture are treated. A recent issue has articles on hip-hop and contemporary art, filmmaker Ousmane Sembene, and the fashion scene in Senegal. The editors are art critics and curators who aim to make "significant contributions to the intellectual dialogue on world art and the discourse on internationalism and multiculturalism in the arts" and to bring an awareness of contemporary African art and culture to the world. A good choice for public and academic libraries.

423. ***New African.*** Former titles (until 1978): *New African Development;* (until 1977): *African Development.* [ISSN: 0142-9345] 1966. 11x/yr. GBP 36 United Kingdom; USD 90 United States; GBP 50 elsewhere. Ed(s): Baffour Ankomah. I.C. Publications Ltd., 7 Coldbath Sq, London, EC1R 4LQ, United Kingdom; http://www.icpublications.com. Illus., adv. Sample. Microform: PQC. Online: EBSCO Publishing; Florida Center for Library Automation; Gale Group; Northern Light Technology, Inc.; ProQuest Information & Learning. Reprint: PQC. *Indexed:* IIBP, PAIS, RRTA, WAE&RSA. *Aud.:* Hs, Ga, Ac.

From the same publishers as *African Business* (see above), this glossy consumer newsmagazine covers the entire spectrum of contemporary African life: political reporting, economic and financial analysis, and articles on culture and social affairs including art, music, fashion, and sport. Each issue includes more than one cover story dealing with a major social or political issue or personality. Many of the articles take a muckraking stance. The scope is Pan-African and the diaspora, although most features focus on sub-Saharan Africa. Each issue has a section called "Around Africa" that reports news of specific countries and presents longer special reports on a featured country. The online version (www.africasia.com/newafrican) offers summaries of the cover stories and the table of contents of issues, as well as text of some special reports. The same publisher releases the *New African Yearbook* with facts and figures on each of the 53 countries. As one of the oldest monthly magazines, *New African* is recommended for all collections with an interest in Africa.

424. ***Newswatch: Nigeria's weekly newsmagazine.*** [ISSN: 0189-8892] 1985. w. NGN 70 per issue. Ed(s): Dan Ochima Agbese. Newswatch Communications Ltd., Oregun, 3 Billingsway, PMB 21499, Ikeja, Nigeria. Illus., index, adv. Circ: 150084. *Aud.:* Hs, Ga, Ac.

This Nigerian newsmagazine (Africa's largest-selling weekly outside of South Africa) includes politically oriented news, primarily about Nigeria, but also African and international news, as well as news on business and the economy. Regular articles cover news in science, technology, politics, business and finance, the stock market, arts and society, and environment reports. Cheeky and muckraking and critical of the government, it has sometimes been banned in Nigeria. This important, critical, and risk-taking newsmagazine is recommended for all audiences. A new web site offers online subscriptions, and there are also some feature stories available for free (www.newswatchngr.com).

425. ***Philosophia Africana: analysis of philosophy and issues in Africa and the Black Diaspora.*** Former titles: *African Philosophy;* (until 1998): *SAPINA Newsletter.* [ISSN: 1539-8250] s-a. USD 180 (Individuals, USD 50). Ed(s): Emmanuel Chukwudi Eze. DePaul University, Department of Philosophy, 2219 N Kenmore Ave, Chicago, IL 60614; editors@philosophia-africana.org; http://condor.depaul.edu/~africana/index.html. Index. Refereed. Reprint: PSC. *Indexed:* IBZ, IPB, L&LBA. *Aud.:* Ac, Sa.

With African philosophy emerging as a distinct movement, this journal publishes "philosophical and interdisciplinary scholarly writings on the pluralistic experiences of Africa and the Black Diaspora from both universal and comparative points of view." Recent issues include essays on Kenyan philosopher Henry Odera Oruka and a piece by Julian Bond on 9/11. In tandem with the journal, a list-serv has been developed as a forum for the exchange of views, experiences, and techniques pertaining to the teaching and study of the philosophical thought of African and African-diaspora cultures (www.augustana.ab.ca/~janzb/AFRI-PHIL1.htm).

426. ***Politique Africaine.*** [ISSN: 0244-7827] 1981. q. FRF 370 domestic; FRF 440 in Europe; FRF 540 elsewhere. Ed(s): Richard Banegas. Editions Karthala, 22-24 bd. Arago, Paris, 75013, France; karthala@wanadoo.fr; http://www.karthala.com. Illus., adv. Refereed. Circ: 3500. *Indexed:* IBSS, IPSA, PAIS, WAE&RSA. *Bk. rev.:* 20-25, 50-200 words. *Aud.:* Ac, Sa.

Published in France, this quarterly political science journal includes contributed articles usually relating to a thematic topic, recently, for example, religion on the continent, and refugees in Africa. While some focus is on Francophone countries, the scope is really the entire continent. The remainder of each issue includes briefer articles, speeches, and recent political developments in sub-Saharan Africa. It also includes major meeting and conference announcements, book reviews, and lists of books received. Tables of contents and abstracts in English are available at www.politique-africaine.com and also at www.cean.u-bordeaux.fr/pubcean/polaf.html. Older issues, generally 2000 and earlier, have the full texts of the articles available for free in pdf format, while newer issues have abstracts only. For larger collections and those with Francophonic interests.

427. ***Presence Africaine: revue culturelle du monde noir.*** [ISSN: 0032-7638] 1947. s-a. FRF 300; FRF 150 newsstand/cover per issue. Societe Africaine de Culture, 25 bis rue des Ecoles, Paris, 75005, France. Illus. Refereed. Circ: 3000 Controlled. *Indexed:* IBSS, MLA-IB, PAIS, RRTA, WAE&RSA. *Aud.:* Ga, Ac, Sa.

Presence Africaine has a long, illustrious history and remains the most influential French-language journal on Africa. It was founded in 1947 by Alioune Diop, a Senegalese intellectual and seminal figure in the discourse on Africa. Its early years coincided with the struggles against colonialism as well as the development of the "Negritude" movement. *PA* was the leading journal of anticolonial intellectuals in France and Africa and a major publisher of African writers. Now bilingual (in French and English), *PA* remains a leading cultural journal of the African diaspora and is indispensable for academic collections, especially those supporting African Studies and literature. Issues feature critical and historical articles, book reviews and discussions, and creative writing.

428. ***Research in African Literatures.*** [ISSN: 0034-5210] 1970. q. USD 92.50 (Individuals, USD 41). Ed(s): Abiola Irele. Indiana University Press, 601 N Morton St, Bloomington, IN 47404. Illus., index, adv. Sample. Refereed. Circ: 900. Vol. ends: Winter. Microform: PQC; NRP. Online: bigchalk; RoweCom Information Quest; Swets Blackwell. Reprint: PQC; PSC. *Indexed:* AbAn, AnthLit, ArtHuCI, BEL&L, FLI, HumInd, IBSS, IBZ, IIBP, L&LBA, MLA-IB, SSCI. *Bk. rev.:* 5-21, 1,000-2,000 words. *Aud.:* Ac, Sa.

RAL is an official journal of both the African Literature Association and the African Literatures Division of the Modern Language Association. An important source for research on the literatures of Africa, it includes scholarly essays; extensive, useful bibliographies; and long reviews of all aspects of oral and written literatures, music, film, and theater of Africa. Articles are in English, but literature written in English, French, or African languages is treated. The scope also extends to literature of the black diaspora and other arts as well. A recent issue contains an essay on Caribbean writer Derek Walcott and a discussion of Yoruba wood carving among the eight articles. Contributions include discussions of short and long fiction, poetry, drama, important new writers, music, film, and theater, as well as literary developments. Issues include information on

African publishing and announcements of importance to Africanists. A standard and highly recommended source for academic and large public libraries and anyone interested in African literatures and literary criticism. Available electronically through Project Muse (muse.jhu.edu). Tables of contents for issues are available on the Indiana University Press web site (http://iupjournals.org).

429. *Review of African Political Economy.* [ISSN: 0305-6244] 1973. q. GBP 241 (Individuals, GBP 50). Ed(s): Jan Burgess, David Seddon. Carfax Publishing Ltd., 4 Park Sq, Milton Park, Abingdon, OX14 4RN, United Kingdom; enquiry@tandf.co.uk; http://www.tandf.co.uk/. Illus., adv. Sample. Refereed. Circ: 1500. Online: Chadwyck-Healey Incorporated; EBSCO Publishing; Northern Light Technology, Inc.; OCLC Online Computer Library Center, Inc.; ProQuest Information & Learning. Reprint: PSC. *Indexed:* ABIn, AltPI, DSA, ForAb, GeogAbPG, HortAb, IBSS, IBZ, IIBP, IPSA, JEL, PAIS, PSA, S&F, SWA, SociolAb, WAE&RSA. *Bk. rev.:* 4-7, 900-3,000 words. *Aud.:* Ac, Sa.

Articles in this journal focus on Africa's underdevelopment with a leftist analysis that examines imperialism, capitalism, and the social and political forces in the new global economy. Editorial policy proudly takes a definite political stance. Each themed issue begins with an editorial and contains five to nine articles dealing with such issues as transnational corporations, class struggle, peasant struggle and social welfare, structural adjustment programs (SAPs) and international financial institutions, and corruption. Recent issues are devoted to such topics as state failure in the Congo, African diaspora, and democracy in Zimbabwe. Shorter news articles and book reviews and announcements are also featured. Contributions by African scholars and activists are encouraged and published. The web site (www.roape.org/index.html) provides abstracts of articles from current and past issues. Highly recommended for academic and special audience categories.

430. *Southern Africa Political and Economic Monthly.* [ISSN: 1017-9208] 1987. m. USD 160 foreign. S A P E S Trust, Belgravia, Mt. Pleasant, Deary Ave 4, PO Box MP 111, Harare, Zimbabwe; sapes@mango.org; http://csf.colorado.edu/ipe/sapem/sapem.html. Illus., adv. Sample. *Indexed:* IIBP. *Bk. rev.:* 3-5, 200-500 words. *Aud.:* Ga, Ac, Sa.

This significant monthly is a publication of SAPES (Southern Africa Political and Economic Series) Trust, a nonprofit organization that promotes social science research, teaching, debate, and publications in the region. Published in Harare, Zimbabwe, the journal has a focus on the region of southern Africa but also presents news and analysis on Pan-African issues and other nations, interpreting the current political, economic, and social climate. Since 1998, it has incorporated another publication, *Southern African Economist.* The longer, signed articles assess political developments, individual country economies in the region, and regional issues. African policy makers and intellectuals are regular contributors. Gender issues, politics, environmental issues, ecology, entertainment, arts, culture, sports, and literary developments all receive attention. Book reviews, guest columns, and news from other African regions make this a highly recommended selection.

431. *Transition: an international review.* Former titles (until 1977): *Ch'indaba;* (until no.50, 1975): *Transition.* [ISSN: 0041-1191] 1961. q. USD 80 (Individuals, USD 27; Students, USD 19). Ed(s): Kwame Anthony Appiah, Henry Louis Gates, Jr. Duke University Press, 905 W Main St, Ste 18 B, Durham, NC 27701; subscriptions@dukeupress.edu; http://www.dukeupress.edu. Illus., adv. Sample. Circ: 1100. Vol. ends: Aug. Microform: PQC. Reprint: PSC. *Indexed:* ABS&EES, AltPI, IIBP, MLA-IB, PAIS, PSA, SociolAb. *Bk. rev.:* 2-3. *Aud.:* Ga, Ac, Sa.

Originally published in Uganda, and harkening to its earlier reputation as a forum for intellectual debate, this new series of *Transition* takes a critical look at culture, cultural icons, literature, visual imagery, and the arts. The scope of *Transition* is not just on Africa, but the entire postcolonial world with a multicultural perspective, billing itself as "an international review of politics, culture, and ethnicity from Beijing to Bujumbura." An official publication of the W. E. B. Du Bois Institute at Harvard University, and edited by Kwame Appiah and Henry Louis Gates, the editorial board is equally star-studded, headed by Wole Soyinka and featuring Carlos Fuentes, Jamaica Kincaid, and other leading intellectuals and literati as members of the board. The essays are clearly written, provocative, and engaging. Issues are well illustrated with high production values. While text is available via Project Muse (muse.jhu.edu) and other aggregators, the striking illustrations and photographs are not available electronically, so there is no substitute for the print journal. A three-time winner of the Alternative Press Award, this venue for cultural criticism is very highly recommended for both general and academic institutions.

432. *Ufahamu.* [ISSN: 0041-5715] 1970. 3x/yr. USD 28 (Individuals, USD 20). Ed(s): Shobana Shankar. University of California at Los Angeles, James S. Coleman African Studies Center, 10244 Bunche Hall, 405 Hilgard Ave, Los Angeles, CA 90095-1310. Illus., adv. Sample. Circ: 350. *Indexed:* IBSS, IBZ, MLA-IB. *Bk. rev.:* 1-2, 1,000-2,500 words. *Aud.:* Ga, Ac.

Ufahamu, from the Swahili word meaning "understanding, comprehension or being and remaining aware," is published by the African Activist Association, a graduate student organization at the University of California at Los Angeles. *Ufahamu* presents articles from established writers and academics as well as graduate students and nonacademic researchers. Founded as a journal of opinion on social issues, it continues to provide an interdisciplinary forum for those whose approach is both scholarly and activist. It includes articles on history, politics, economics, sociology, anthropology, law, planning and development, and literature and the arts about the African continent and diaspora. Creative writing is occasionally included. Addressing an audience of both scholars and general readers, it is recommended for academic institutions and larger general libraries.

433. *West Africa: the pan-African weekly.* [ISSN: 0043-2962] 1917. w. GBP 77 domestic; GBP 79 in Europe; USD 139 in US & Canada. Ed(s): Desmond Davies. Afrimedia International Ltd., 321 City Rd, London, EC1V 1LJ, United Kingdom; wa@westafricamagazine.co.uk; http://www.westafricamagazine.com/. Illus., adv. Circ: 30000. *Indexed:* IIBP, MLA-IB, RRTA, WAE&RSA. *Bk. rev.:* 1-2, 400-800 words. *Aud.:* Hs,Ga, Ac, Sa.

Weekly since 1917, this international newsmagazine has provided informative essays on various general-interest topics, including politics, economics, business and finance, art, culture, and sports. Publication faltered in 1999, but the magazine was relaunched with a new publisher, Afrimedia Ltd., a subsidiary of Graphic Communication of Ghana. Issues are produced in London. While the emphasis is on West African countries, there is good coverage of the continent as a whole, both for internal affairs and international issues. Four or five cover stories are followed by shorter reports on specific countries or topics such as food security, health issues, and the African Union. Business and finance is a regular feature, as well as news of the arts, religion, and sports. Stories and photos from past issues are an interesting regular inclusion. The attractive new web site (www.westafricamagazine.com) has full texts of a selection of stories from the "current" issue, but not cover-to-cover access. The web site indicates that an archives section is being constructed. *West Africa* is deservedly a popular newsweekly, recommended for most collections.

Electronic Journals

434. *Africa Update (New Britain).* [ISSN: 1526-7822] 1993. q. USD 25 (Individuals, USD 5). Ed(s): Gloria T Emeagwali. Central Connecticut State University, African Studies Program, PO Box 4010, New Britain, CT 06050-4010; emeagwali@ccsu.edu; http://www.ccsu.edu/afstudy/archive.html. Adv. *Bk. rev.:* Irreg. *Aud.:* Ga, Ac.

Students and scholars contribute to this electronic newsletter of the Central Connecticut State University African Studies program. It presents a wide variety of interdisciplinary research and reports on social, political, and cultural issues in African Studies. Each issue has a very broad thematic and/or geographic focus, e.g., "Politics and Culture in West Africa" and "Human Rights, Apartheid and Reparations." Available by subscription in print, the archive of issues is free on the web. Some pieces are summaries or even reprints of articles published elsewhere. Some are footnoted, others are not. The brief, unfootnoted style of many of the articles allows for opinion pieces, conference reports, and other more topical reports. Not a typical academic journal, but all in all a fine magazine for students and others interested in Africa and African Studies. Recommended for both general and undergraduate collections.

435. ***African Philosophy.*** [ISSN: 1533-1067] 2002. s-a. Ed(s): Nkiru Nzegwu. Africa Resource Center, Inc., Binghamton University, Dept of Africana Studies, Binghamton, NY 13902-6000. *Aud.:* Ac.

A brand new electronic-only journal sponsored by the International Society for African Philosophy and Studies (ISAPS). According to the lengthy editorial statement on the web site, the journal reflects the aims and objectives of the society: to promote the study of African philosophy; to provide a forum for discussion of philosophical issues related to politics, aesthetic sensibilities, values, metaphysics, and cultural traditions of Africa and the Diaspora; and to create a space for practical ideas on teaching philosophy. The inaugural issue features five essays on such topics as race and racism in the works of David Hume, and on monarchy and democracy. The web site is www.africaresource-.com. The publishers also present the electronic journals *Jenda* and *West Africa Review* (below in this section).

436. ***African Studies Quarterly: the online journal of African studies.*** [ISSN: 1093-2658] 1997. q. Free. Ed(s): Leonardo Villalon. University of Florida, Center for African Studies, 427 Grinter Hall, PO Box 115560, Gainesville, FL 32611-5560; asq@africa.ufl.edu; http://www.africa.ufl.edu/asq/index.htm. Illus., adv. Refereed. *Bk. rev.:* 3-4, 500-1,000 words. *Aud.:* Ac.

The Center for African Studies at the University of Florida publishes this interdisciplinary, refereed, online academic journal. Research and opinion in all disciplines are represented with a focus on contemporary Africa. Articles are in English and occasionally French. The journal is available free on the web, making available current research on Africa to a worldwide audience inside and outside academia. Each issue includes several book reviews.

437. ***allAfrica.com.*** 2000. d. Free. AllAfrica Global Media, 920 M St SE, Washington, DC 20003. *Aud.:* Hs, Ga , Ac, Sa.

allAfrica.com is the successor to *Africa News Online*. Like its predecessor the Africa News Service, the publisher AllAfrica Global Media is a content provider through partnership with media organizations in Africa. The news web site *allAfrica.com* provides news stories, analysis, and comment on a wide range of topics, drawing from newspapers, news agencies, and publications from all over the continent. Selected documents—key speeches, reports, and announcements—from governments, nongovernmental organizations, and other newsmakers are also posted. More than 500 new stories appear daily from over 80 African media organizations, as well as reporting and analysis from AllAfrica's own news staff. Links are also provided to the newspapers and other media organizations such as *The Mail & Guardian* of Johannesburg and Nairobi's *The Nation*. The web site is keyword searchable, and stories can be viewed by region, topic, or country. The archives of *African News Online* are housed and searchable. The design and graphics are outstanding. The organization claims to be the "largest electronic distributor of African news and information worldwide." This is an invaluable source for news of Africa at all levels.

438. ***Electronic Journal of Africana Bibliography.*** [ISSN: 1092-9576] 1996. irreg. Free. Ed(s): Edward A Miner, Afeworki Paulos. University of Iowa, University Libraries, 100 Main Library, Iowa City, IA 52242-1420; webmaster@www.lib.uiowa.edu. *Aud.:* Ga, Ac, Sa.

The late John Howell and the Africana Librarians Council of the African Studies Association established this refereed electronic journal as a means for scholars and librarians in the field to publish bibliographies on all aspects of Africa and its peoples. Topics may include the society, economy, sustainable development, politics, literature, creative arts, and the diaspora. A recent list centers on the environment and development in Western Sahel. Irregularly published (one to three issues per year), the bibliographies containing from 75 to close to 900 items can serve as research guides and collection development tools. No fee or registration is required to use the site.

439. ***Jenda: a journal of culture and African women studies.*** [ISSN: 1530-5686] 2001. 3x/yr. Africa Resource Center, Inc., Binghamton University, Dept of Africana Studies, Binghamton, NY 13902-6000; http://www.jendajournal.com/jenda/. *Aud.:* Ac, Sa.

Published on the web three times a year, free of charge, this e-journal promotes the research and scholarship of African women to the global African community and friends of Africa. Articles are centered on women's history and studies in African social, cultural, political, and economic systems. It creates a forum for African women scholars, analysts, and activists to participate with their contemporaries worldwide in debates, exchanges of ideas, and the creation and documentation of knowledge. Issues feature lengthy articles (in html and pdf files) on topics related to gender. A review essay and shorter pieces on current debates such as female circumcision are also offered, as well as links to relevant articles in other online sources.

440. ***Journal of Sustainable Development in Africa.*** [ISSN: 1520-5509] 1999. m. Nelson Mandela School of Public Policy and Urban Affairs, PO Box 9656, Baton Rouge, LA 70813. *Bk. rev.:* 1 per issue. *Aud.:* Ac, Sa.

The sustainability issues in African development are the focus of this electronic-only refereed journal. Four to five articles and generally a book review in each issue bring a multidisciplinary perspective to the economic, socio-political, cultural and environmental issues surrounding development and planning on the continent. Urban shelter, foreign direct investment, and hazardous waste shipment are some recent topics treated in this journal that seeks contributions of both theoretical and applied discussions of the debates on sustainable development in Africa.

441. ***West Africa Review.*** [ISSN: 1525-4488] 1999. s-a. Ed(s): Nkiru Nzegwu. Africa Resource Center, Inc., Binghamton University, Dept of Africana Studies, Binghamton, NY 13902-6000; http://www.westafricareview.com/war/right.htm. Refereed. *Aud.:* Ga, Ac, Sa.

A newcomer in the African Studies field, this e-journal is one of several published by the Africa Resource Center (see *Jenda* and *African Philosophy* above). According to editorial statements, *West Africa Review* is devoted to the promotion of research and scholarship of importance to the global African community, also accepting technical and scientific papers that further the understanding of the geography and life in the region, research findings, analyses, and interpretations of scholars in West African Studies. While the publication schedule is supposed to be twice a year, publication times vary, as does the volume of material included. Issues contain generally four to six articles not solely on West Africa, book reviews, and research reports. It makes available works that have been published elsewhere but deemed to deserve wider circulation. For example, a recent issue provides a link to the text of the U.N. Economic Commission for Africa's *Economic Report on Africa 2000.*

■ AFRICAN AMERICAN

Barbara A. Burg, Research Librarian, Widener Library, Harvard University, Cambridge, MA 02138; bburg@fas.harvard.edu

Introduction

The interesting variety of topics covered in the African American section will appeal to a diverse audience. While the journals in this section embody a rich and dynamic content, the titles in this section have remained fairly stable since the last edition of *Magazines for Libraries.* At the present time, only the arts and culture journal *American Visions* has suspended publication.

The range of topics covered in this section includes automobiles, book reviews, business and finance, communications, cultural studies, drama, economics, education, women?s studies, general interest, history, literary studies, gender studies, music, psychology, public policy, religion and theology, and youth culture. Notable are the title changes of two "classic" journals. The *Journal of Negro History* is now the *Journal of African American History,* and the *Negro History Bulletin* is now the *Black History Bulletin.* The newest title, *Blackgirl Magazine,* was founded by a 13-year-old and will especially appeal to teenage girls.

Freely available electronic journals and hybrid web portal sites still remain somewhat unstable. As previously mentioned, it is always worth scanning the web sites of black organizations, research centers, and the historically black colleges and universities in search of additional online publications.

Basic Periodicals

Ems: *American Legacy, Black History Bulletin, Blackgirl Magazine, Ebony, Right On!* Hs: *American Legacy, Black Collegian, Black Enterprise, Ebony, Essence, Jet, Journal of African American History, Savoy, Vibe, Vital Issues;* Ga: *African American Review, American Legacy, Black Enterprise, Black Issues Book Review, Black Scholar, Ebony, Essence (New York), Heart & Soul, Honey, Jet, The Messenger Magazine, Q B R: The Black Book Review, Savoy, Vibe, Vital Issues;* Ac: *African American Review, Black Collegian, Black Enterprise, Black History Bulletin, Black Issues Book Review, Black Issues in Higher Education, Black Music Research Journal, Black Scholar, Callaloo, Ebony, Essence, Harvard Journal of African American Public Policy, International Review of African American Art, Jet, Journal of African American History, Journal of Black Psychology, Journal of Black Studies, Journal of Blacks in Higher Education, Journal of Negro Education, National Black Law Journal, Q B R: The Black Book Review, The Review of Black Political Economy, Transition, Trotter Review, Vibe, Vital Issues, The Western Journal of Black Studies.*

Basic Abstracts and Indexes

America: History and Life, Arts & Humanities Citation Index, Bell-Howell Proquest, Black Studies on Disc, Current Index to Journals in Education, Ethnic NewsWatch, Humanities Abstracts, Humanities Index, Index to Black Periodicals, International Index to Black Periodicals Full Text, Modern Language Association International Bibliography, Social Sciences Citation Index, Social Sciences Index and Abstracts.

Abafazi. See Women: Feminist and Special Interest/Feminist and Women's Studies section.

442. *About Time.* [ISSN: 1060-3905] 1972. m. USD 14; USD 2.50 newsstand/cover per issue. Ed(s): Carolyne S Blount. About...Time Magazine Inc., 283 Genesee St, Rochester, NY 14611. Illus., adv. Sample. Circ: 28000. Vol. ends: Dec. *Indexed:* ENW, IIBP. *Bk. rev.:* 1-2, 500-1,500 words. *Aud.:* Hs, Ga.

Continuously published since 1972, this eclectic monthly seeks to stimulate ideas on issues of international, national, and regional importance to the African American community. *About Time* entertains as well as informs through in-depth interviews, commentaries, special reports, news briefs, and feature stories ranging from family life and education to business and culture. Although its articles and ads are often oriented toward readers in the Rochester, New York, area, the magazine remains relevant to the African American community at large. This worthwhile independent publication belongs in most public libraries.

443. *African American Pulpit.* [ISSN: 1094-0111] 1997. q. USD 48 USD 32.95 domestic. Ed(s): Frank Thomas, Martha Simmons. Judson Press, PO Box 851, Valley Forge, PA 19482-0851; http://www.judsonpress.com. Adv. Circ: 2450 Paid. *Indexed:* IIBP. *Bk. rev.:* 1, 500 words. *Aud.:* Ac, Sa.

Published by Judson Press, the publishing arm of American Baptist Churches in the U.S.A., *African American Pulpit* offers a dynamic compendium of sermons, narratives, essays, interviews, stories, book reviews, and articles relevant to preaching and issues related to the black church. Some examples of recent articles include "Sometimes It Causes Me to Tremble: Black Social Activism Now," "The Prophet Amos as a Model for Preaching on Issues of Social Justice," and "The Post-Soul Generation and the Black Church." This quality publication would be welcome in public and academic libraries, as well as in theological, seminary, and church collections.

444. *African American Review.* Former titles: *Black American Literature Forum;* (until 1976): *Negro American Literature Forum.* [ISSN: 1062-4783] 1967. q. USD 78 (Individuals, USD 38; USD 12 per issue). Ed(s): Joe Weixlmann. African American Review, Shannon Hall 199, 220 N Grand Blvd, St Louis, MO 63103-2007; keenanam@slu.edu; http://aar.slu.edu/. Illus., index, adv. Sample. Refereed. Circ: 3770 Paid. Microform: PQC. Online: bigchalk; Chadwyck-Healey Incorporated; EBSCO Publishing; Florida Center for Library Automation; Gale Group; JSTOR (Web-based Journal Archive); Northern Light Technology, Inc.; OCLC Online Computer Library Center, Inc.; ProQuest Information & Learning. Reprint: ISI; PQC. *Indexed:* ABS&EES, AmH&L, AmHI, ArtHuCI, BEL&L, BRI, CBRI, FLI, HumInd, IAPV, IBZ, IIBP, MLA-IB, MagInd. *Bk. rev.:* 5-20, 500-1,000 words. *Aud.:* Ga, Ac.

The *African American Review* (*AAR*), the official publication of the Division on Black American Literature and Culture of the Modern Language Association, "promotes a lively exchange among writers and scholars in the arts, humanities, and social sciences who hold diverse perspectives on African American literature and culture." Between 1967 and 1976, the journal appeared under the title *Negro American Literature Forum* and for the next 15 years was known as *Black American Literature Forum.* In 1992, *African American Review* changed its name for a third time and expanded its mission to include a broader range of cultural studies.

Leading scholars and writers contribute essays on African American literature, theater, film, the visual arts, and cultural studies in general; also included are interviews, poetry, fiction, and book reviews. *AAR* has received three American Literary Magazine Awards for editorial content. This is a required title for academic library collections and public libraries alike.

African Americans on Wheels. See Automobiles and Motorcycles section.

445. *Afro-Americans in New York Life and History.* [ISSN: 0364-2437] 1977. s-a. USD 8. Ed(s): Monroe Fordham. Afro-American Historical Association of the Niagara Frontier, PO Box 63, Buffalo, NY 14207. Illus. Refereed. Circ: 700 Paid. Vol. ends: Jul. Reprint: PQC. *Indexed:* AmH&L, IIBP. *Bk. rev.:* 1-2, 500-1,000 words. *Aud.:* Ac.

Introduced in 1977, this interdisciplinary journal publishes analytical, historical, and descriptive articles pertaining to the life and history of African Americans in New York State. Research and scholarship about local and and regional African American communities is particularly encouraged and viewed as "building blocks in establishing a continuous and connected body of scholarship aimed at enhancing our understanding of the larger African American experience."

The journal often includes articles on race relations and racial attitudes, as well on identifying the location of archival sources and materials relative to African Americans in New York. Examples of recent articles are "Adapting Cotton Comes to Harlem: From Inter- to Intra-racial Conflict" and "Buffalo's Prophet of Protest: The Political Leadership and Activism of the Rev. Dr. Bennett W. Smith, Sr." This is an important title for academic and special collections.

446. *Afro-Hispanic Review.* [ISSN: 0278-8969] 1982. s-a. USD 20 (Individuals, GBP 30). Ed(s): Edward J Mullen. University of Missouri at Columbia, Romance Languages Department, c/o Dr Edward Mullen, 143 Arts & Sciences, Columbia, MO 65211. Illus., adv. Sample. Refereed. Circ: 500. Online: bigchalk; Chadwyck-Healey Incorporated; EBSCO Publishing; Northern Light Technology, Inc.; ProQuest Information & Learning. *Indexed:* HAPI, IIBP, MLA-IB. *Bk. rev.:* 3-4, 1,000-2,500 words. *Aud.:* Ac.

The semi-annual *Afro-Hispanic Review,* a bilingual journal of Afro-Hispanic literature and culture, is published by the Department of Romance Languages and Literatures of the University of Missouri–Columbia. While seeking to reflect the richness of Afro-Hispanic culture, the *Afro-Hispanic Review* publishes literary criticism, translations, creative writing, and book reviews, in addition to introducing neglected works and authors. Examples of some recent articles include "Can(n)on Fodder: Afro-Hispanic Literature, Heretical Texts, and the Polemics of Canon-Formation," "Afro-Cuban Literature: Critical Junctures, Black Writers and the Hispanic Canon," and "Afro-Hispanic Literature: The Poetics of Refutation." An important title for academic collections.

447. *American Legacy: celebrating African-American history and culture.* Formerly (until 1996): *Legacy (New York).* [ISSN: 1086-7201] 1995. q. USD 9.95 domestic; USD 15.95 foreign; USD 2.95 newsstand/cover per issue. Ed(s): Audrey Peterson. American Heritage, 90 Fifth Ave, New York, NY 10011; http://www.americanheritage.com/amlegacy. Illus., adv. Sample. Circ: 86184 Paid. Vol. ends: Winter. Online: EBSCO Publishing. *Indexed:* AmH&L. *Aud.:* Ems, Hs, Ga, Ac.

American Legacy is a very appealing quarterly featuring African American history and culture. Published by the popular history magazine *American Heritage* and owned by Forbes, Inc., *American Legacy* offers stories, facts, and legends about people and events significant to American history. Characterized by *USA Today* as including "Fine writing and powerful tales!" this lavishly illustrated magazine is a required title for school and public libraries and is recommended for virtually all collections.

Black Collegian. See College and Alumni section.

448. *Black Enterprise.* [ISSN: 0006-4165] 1970. m. USD 17.95 domestic; USD 30.95 foreign; USD 3.95 newsstand/cover per issue domestic. Ed(s): Alfred Edmond. Earl G. Graves Publishing Co., Inc., 130 Fifth Ave, New York, NY 10011; beeditor@aol.com; http://www.blackenterprise.com. Illus., adv. Sample. Circ: 421103 Paid. Vol. ends: Jul. Microform: PQC. Online: bigchalk; EBSCO Publishing; Florida Center for Library Automation; Gale Group; LexisNexis; Northern Light Technology, Inc.; OCLC Online Computer Library Center, Inc.; ProQuest Information & Learning; SoftLine Information; H.W. Wilson. Reprint: PQC. *Indexed:* ABIn, ATI, B&I, BPI, BRI, CBRI, ENW, IIBP, LRI, MagInd, PAIS, RGPR. *Bk. rev.:* 2-3, 250-500 words. *Aud.:* Hs, Ga, Ac.

Black Enterprise (*BE*) is the flagship publication of Earl G. Graves, Inc., a business information company with wide-ranging interests. For more than 30 years, business owners, entrepreneurs, corporate executives, and professionals have looked to the magazine for its authoritative and inspirational articles about African Americans in business and industry. Overall, coverage includes money management, technology, business news and trends, small-business management, personal finance, career opportunities and development, and consumer affairs. Readers are treated annually to a number of special issues that feature in-depth information on specific topics such as "Careers and Opportunities"; the BE 100s—the nation's largest black-owned industrial/service companies and auto dealerships; and "Money Management." Monthly editorial features cover health care, franchising, start-up opportunities, and the best cities for African Americans to live and work in. The magazine's Board of Economists provides critical analysis and forecasts of the economic challenges facing the black community. *Black Enterprise* provides some of the most authoritative coverage of African American economic life and is highly recommended for public, academic, and business-oriented libraries.

449. *Black History Bulletin: a publication of the Association for the Study of African-American Life and History.* Formerly (until Jun. 2001): *Negro History Bulletin.* 1937. q. USD 35 (Individuals, USD 16.50). Ed(s): Ida Jones, Tamara Brown. Association for the Study of African-American Life and History, Inc., 7961 Eastern Ave, Ste 301, Silver Spring, MD 20910; asalh@earthlink.net; http://www.asalh.org. Illus., index, adv. Sample. Refereed. Circ: 22000. Microform: PMC; PQC. Online: Gale Group; Northern Light Technology, Inc. Reprint: PQC. *Indexed:* ArtHuCI, BRI, BiogInd, CBRI, CIJE, HumInd, IIBP, LRI, MagInd, NumL, RGPR, SSI. *Bk. rev.:* 2-3, 250-500 words. *Aud.:* Ems, Hs, Ga.

Historian Carter G. Woodson began publishing the *Black History Bulletin* (formerly the *Negro History Bulletin*) in 1937. Intended for schools and general readers, it continues to offer a fascinating mix of history, biography, current events, and book reviews, with features on writers, artists, and musicians. Some recent articles include "Carter G. Woodson as a Scholar" and "Historical Significance of Black History Month." Although the *Bulletin* is faced with competition from some of the newer, glossy titles, such as *American Legacy*, academic collections and public libraries should continue their support of this august title.

Black Issues Book Review. See Books and Book Reviews section.

450. *Black Issues in Higher Education.* [ISSN: 0742-0277] 1984. fortn. USD 40 domestic; USD 50 Canada; USD 60 elsewhere. Ed(s): Hilary Hurd. Cox, Matthews & Associates, Inc., 10520 Warwick Ave, Ste B 8, Fairfax, VA 22030; cmabiccw.com; http://www.ccw.com. Illus., index, adv. Sample. Circ: 200000. Vol. ends: Feb. *Indexed:* CIJE, ENW, EduInd, HEA, IIBP. *Aud.:* Ac.

This publication is the only national publication covering news and major issues in higher education affecting minorities in the United States and its territories. In addition to including feature stories, reports, and statistics analyzing critical trends and developments in academe, *BIHE* features articles about major issues concerning African Americans and other minorities, such as the top 100 institutions that graduate the most students of color. Each issue also contains an events calendar and academic position announcements. *BIHE* is mandatory for most colleges and universities and highly recommended for public and secondary school libraries serving minority communities.

451. *Black Masks: spotlight on Black art.* [ISSN: 0887-7580] 1984. bi-m. USD 20 domestic; USD 23 Canada; USD 30 elsewhere. Ed(s): Beth Turner. Black Masks, PO Box 2, Bronx, NY 10471; beth.turner@nyu.edu. Illus., adv. Sample. Circ: 1500 Paid. Vol. ends: May/Jun. *Indexed:* ENW. *Bk. rev.:* Various number and length. *Aud.:* Ga, Ac.

This small but excellent journal says that it contains "articles and papers on performing, literary or visual arts and artists of African descent." It does all of that exceedingly well, although it should be stated that its coverage of the performing arts, such as theater, is particularly good. It contains occasional book reviews, reviews of performances and showings, and a very good "Events" section. Its coverage is international, although like many American theater journals, it has a distinctly New York slant. It should be included in any library that contains substantive theater and/or African American Studies collections.

452. *Black Music Research Journal.* [ISSN: 0276-3605] 1980. s-a. USD 35 domestic; USD 40 foreign. Ed(s): Samuel A Floyd, Jr. Center for Black Music Research, Columbia College Chicago, 600 S Michigan Ave, Chicago, IL 60605; cbmr@cbmr.colum.ed; http://www.cbmr.org. Illus., index, adv. Sample. Refereed. Circ: 808. *Indexed:* ArtHuCI, HumInd, IBZ, IIBP, IIMP, MusicInd, RILM. *Aud.:* Ac.

Since 1980, the *BMRJ* has provided a forum for scholarship about the philosophy, esthetics, history, and criticism of black music. The journal is published by The Center for Black Music Research (CBMR) at Columbia College in Chicago, a research center devoted to the documentation, collection preservation, and dissemination of information about black music in all parts of the world. The center's stated mission is "to promote understanding of the common roots of the music, musicians, and composers of the global African diaspora." The range of topics examined is best illustrated by examples of articles from a recent issue: "Religion in Rhythm: William Grant Still's Orchestrations for Willard Robison's Deep River Hour," "Fletcher Henderson, Composer: A Counter-Entry to the International Dictionary of Black Composers," and "The Prairie View Co-Eds: Black College Women Musicians in Class and on the Road during World War II." Most issues are thematic, with recent special issues focusing on black music education and Thelonious Monk. The *BMRJ* is required for music libraries, black studies collections, and libraries serving African American communities.

453. *Black Renaissance.* [ISSN: 1089-3148] 1996. 3x/yr. USD 70 (Individuals, USD 35). Ed(s): Manthia Diawara. New York University, African Studies Program, 269 Mercer St., Ste 601, New York, NY 10003-6687; http://www.nyu.edu. Illus., adv. Vol. ends: Spring. Online: EBSCO Publishing; Factiva; Florida Center for Library Automation; Gale Group; LexisNexis; OCLC Online Computer Library Center, Inc.; ProQuest Information & Learning; RoweCom Information Quest; SoftLine Information. Reprint: PSC. *Indexed:* AmHI, IIBP. *Aud.:* Ga, Ac.

Named by *Library Journal* as one of the ten best magazines of 1996, this handsome multilingual publication includes essays, poetry, fiction, photography, reviews, and artwork "addressing the full range of contemporary black concerns." This journal is published under the auspices of the Africana Studies Program at New York University, and its editorial board includes such prominent intellectuals as Houston A. Baker, Jr., Kamau Brathwaite, Maryse Conde, Angela Y. Davis, Michel Fabre, Robin D. G. Kelley, Paule Marshall, and Ngugi wa Thiong'o. A recent issue features "The Ideology of Racial Hierarchy and the Construction of the European Slave Trade" by Molefi Kete Asante and "Myth Today: The Color of Ken Burns' Jazz." Recommended for academic collections.

454. *Black Scholar: journal of Black studies and research.* [ISSN: 0006-4246] 1969. q. USD 60 (Individuals, USD 30). Ed(s): Robert Chrisman. Black World Foundation, PO Box 2869, Oakland, CA 94609. Illus., index, adv. Sample. Refereed. Circ: 10000 Paid. Microform: MIM; PQC. Online: Chadwyck-Healey Incorporated; EBSCO Publishing; LexisNexis; Northern Light Technology, Inc.; OCLC Online Computer Library Center, Inc.; ProQuest Information & Learning. Reprint: PQC. *Indexed:* AgeL, AltPI, AmH&L, ArtHuCI, BRI, CBRI, CIJE, IIBP, PAIS, PSA, RI-1, SSCI, SSI, SWA, SWR&A, SociolAb. *Bk. rev.:* 2-3, 500-1,000 words. *Aud.:* Ga, Ac.

For over 30 years, *Black Scholar* has been a leading vehicle for the finest expressions of black cultural and political thought. *Black Scholar* provides a diversity of views in dealing with issues affecting African America and Africa as it draws from academics, public intellectuals, community activists, and national and international political leaders. Among its contributors have been Amiri Baraka, Angela Davis, Julian Bond, Shirley Chisholm, Kwame Ture (Stokely Carmichael), Nathan Hare, June Jordan, Haki Madhubuti (Don L. Lee), and Nelson Mandela. Each issue is theme-based and features book reviews, current books received, announcements, and employment listings from colleges and universities. The following examples of the wide range of topics covered illustrate the breadth of the *Black Scholar*: wonders of the African world, black women writers, black social issues, Ebonics, the crisis of the black male, the Nation of Islam, and black detective fiction. An important title for both academic and public library collections.

455. *Blackgirl Magazine.* 2002. bi-m. USD 24. Blackgirl Magazine, PO Box 90729, Atlanta, GA 30364; editor@blackgirlmagazine.com; http://www.blackgirlmagazine.com/. *Aud.:* Ems, Hs, Ga.

Blackgirl Magazine was founded in 2001 by 13-year-old Atlanta resident Kenya Jordana James. Committed to the empowerment of young African American women, as well as providing entertainment, *Blackgirl Magazine* "focuses on promoting positive messages and imagery among African American teens, while offering insightful coverage of history, culture, lifestyle, and entertainment news from a unique perspective."

Bimonthly issues feature articles about music, culture, and history, short stories, poetry, and interviews with people such as Lauryn Hill, Jill Scott, and Venus and Serena Williams, in addition to commentary from "elders" like Attorney Alton Maddox and Dr. Asa Hilliard. A welcome title for both school (K–12) and public library collections.

456. *C L A Journal.* [ISSN: 0007-8549] 1957. q. USD 40 domestic; USD 41.50 Canada; USD 45.50 elsewhere. Ed(s): Cason L Hill. College Language Association, Morehouse College, Atlanta, GA 30314. Illus., index, adv. Sample. Refereed. Circ: 2500 Paid. *Indexed:* ABS&EES, ArtHuCI, HumInd, IIBP, MLA-IB. *Bk. rev.:* 3-6, 500-1,500 words. *Aud.:* Ac.

The College Language Association, founded in 1937 by a group of African American scholars and educators, is an organization of college teachers of English and foreign languages. Since 1957, the association has published the *CLA Journal,* featuring scholarly research and reviews of books in the areas of language, literature, literary criticism, linguistics, and pedagogy. Only articles by members and subscribers are considered for publication. Additionally, the journal includes listings of available positions via the CLA Placement Service. Recommended for academic libraries.

457. *Callaloo: a journal of African-American and African arts and letters.* [ISSN: 0161-2492] 1976. q. USD 115 (Individuals, USD 39). Ed(s): Ginger Thornton, Charles H Rowell. Johns Hopkins University Press, Journals Publishing Division, 2715 N Charles St, Baltimore, MD 21218-4363; http://www.press.jhu.edu/. Illus., index, adv. Refereed. Circ: 1471. Vol. ends: Fall. Online: EBSCO Publishing; Florida Center for Library Automation; Gale Group; JSTOR (Web-based Journal Archive); OCLC Online Computer Library Center, Inc.; Project MUSE; ProQuest Information & Learning; RoweCom Information Quest; Swets Blackwell. *Indexed:* AmHI, ArtHuCI, BRI, CBRI, HumInd, IAPV, IBZ, IIBP, MLA-IB. *Aud.:* Ga, Ac.

First published in 1976 to highlight the creative and scholarly work of the Southern black writing community in the 1960s and 1970s, *Callaloo* (a Caribbean soup or stew) has become today's premier African American and African literary journal. It offers fiction, poetry, plays, critical essays, cultural studies, interviews, annotated bibliographies, original art, and photography. Special issues often feature individual authors, geographic areas, and/or genres. With an international scope and readership, articles are published in French and Spanish in addition to English. Readers can look to *Callaloo* for the writings of new and young writers from marginalized communities, as it is committed to their nurturance and publication. A required title for academic libraries and recommended for public libraries.

458. *Challenge (Atlanta): a journal of research on African American men.* [ISSN: 1077-193X] 1990. s-a. USD 25 (Individuals, USD 10). Ed(s): Obie Clayton. Morehouse Research Institute, 830 Westview Dr, S W, Atlanta, GA 30314; http://www.morehouse.edu/. Illus. Sample. Refereed. Vol. ends: Dec. Online: Chadwyck-Healey Incorporated. *Indexed:* CIJE, IIBP, SociolAb. *Aud.:* Ac.

Challenge is the official publication of the Morehouse Research Institute (MRI), an interdisciplinary research institute based at Morehouse College. The principal objectives of the MRI are to encourage relevant scholarship and to develop an information exchange network so that policies and programs, particularly those germane to the status of African American men and boys, will be grounded in research. Typically, issues of *Challenge* contain proceedings of the symposia, conferences, and focus groups sponsored by MRI, in addition to invited occasional papers and reports on concerns such as priorities for future research, policy analysis, and the identification and development of programs and agendas for change. *Challenge* welcomes scholarly papers that analyze any aspect of issues associated with African American men. Recommended for academic and public policy collections.

459. *The Crisis.* [ISSN: 0011-1422] 1910. bi-m. USD 12. Ed(s): Victoria L. Valentine. Crisis Publishing Co., 4805 Mt Hope Dr, Baltimore, MD 21215; http://www.thecrisismagazine.com. Illus., adv. Sample. Circ: 250000. Vol. ends: Nov/Dec. Microform: BHP; PQC; NRP. Online: Gale Group. *Indexed:* AmH&L, CIJE, IIBP, SSI. *Bk. rev.:* 2-3, 200-500 words. *Aud.:* Hs, Ga, Ac.

In 1910, W. E. B. Du Bois founded *The Crisis* magazine as the premier crusading voice for civil rights. It is the intent of the new bimonthly *New Crisis* to continue this mission. A respected journal of thought, opinion, and analysis, the magazine remains the official publication of the National Association for the Advancement of Colored People (NAACP). In essays, interviews, in-depth reporting, and feature stories, writers explore past and present issues concerning race and its impact on educational, economic, political, social, moral, and ethical issues. Each issue reports the news and events of the NAACP on a local and national level. Except for the stories featured about the NAACP, the opinions expressed in this journal may not represent the official position of the NAACP. A recent issue features a story titled "The Agenda—Can the Congressional Black Caucus Prevail with a GOP-Controlled White House and Congress?" In addition, it covers issues related to "Census 2000" and "Race and the Death Penalty." Committed to an integrated, nonviolent society that rejects all forms of racism, anti-Semitism, sexism, and homophobia, *The New Crisis* is a valuable title for school, public, and academic libraries.

460. *Drumvoices Revue: a confluence of literary, cultural and vision arts.* [ISSN: 1080-0522] 1992. s-a. USD 10. Ed(s): Eugene B Redmond. Southern Illinois University at Edwardsville, English Department, PO Box 1431, Edwardsville, IL 62026; http://www.siue.edu/ENGLISH/about.html#drumvoice. Illus., adv. Sample. *Indexed:* IAPV. *Aud.:* Ga, Ac.

Drumvoices Revue, a distinctive multicultural literary review, is produced and published by the poet/playwright Eugene Redmond. It showcases photographs, poetry, prose, interviews, and fiction, providing a welcome forum for young artists and scholars. While sustaining the flavor of the 1960s Black Arts Movement, *Drumvoices Revue* is in touch with both academia and "the street." A unique title recommended for both academic collections and urban public libraries.

461. *Ebony.* Incorporates (1985-Feb. 1998): *E M: Ebony Man;* Incorporates (in 1976): *Black World;* Which superseded (1950-1970): *Negro Digest.* [ISSN: 0012-9011] 1945. m. USD 16.97 domestic; USD 31.97 foreign. Ed(s): Kevin Chappell, Joy Bennet Kinnon. Johnson Publishing Co., Inc., 820 S Michigan Ave, Chicago, IL 60605; http://www.ebony.com. Illus., adv. Sample. Circ: 1700000 Paid. Vol. ends: Oct. CD-ROM: ProQuest Information & Learning. Microform: NBI; PQC. Online: bigchalk; Chadwyck-Healey Incorporated; EBSCO Publishing; Florida Center for Library Automation; Gale Group; LexisNexis; Northern Light Technology, Inc.; OCLC Online Computer Library Center, Inc.; ProQuest Information & Learning; H.W. Wilson. Reprint: PQC. *Indexed:* CPerI, FLI, IIBP, MLA-IB, MRD, MagInd, RGPR. *Bk. rev.:* 9-12, 25-50 words. *Aud.:* Ems, Hs, Ga, Ac.

After 60 years, one of the most engaging publications centered around African American life, *Ebony* continues to be the most widely read African American publication. Monthly features include articles about relationships, parenting, awards, entertainment, religion, and sports. Readers also look forward to regularly appearing departments about noteworthy people, recorded music, personal finance, travel, books, medical advice, memorable photographs, recipes, fashion, beauty, and style. *Ebony* is a very popular title and is highly recommended for all libraries.

Essence. See Women section.

Ethnic and Racial Studies. See Ethnic Studies section.

462. *Griot.* [ISSN: 0737-0873] 1981. s-a. USD 50 (Individuals, USD 35; USD 60 foreign). Ed(s): Andrew Baskin. Southern Conference on African-American Studies, Inc., Box 1715, Berea College, Berea, KY 40404. Illus., adv. Circ: 250. *Indexed:* IIBP, MLA-IB. *Bk. rev.:* 1-4, 500-1,000 words. *Aud.:* Ga, Ac.

The Griot is the official journal of the Southern Conference on African American Studies, Inc. (SCAASI). Founded in 1979, the SCAASI brought together all those interested in the interpretation and preservation of African American culture and history, especially that which originated in and/or affected the South. As stated in the journal, "*The Griot* solicits articles relative to any disciplinary perspective in the humanities that further enhances knowledge of the African's (including African American and Caribbean) experience." Recently published articles include "Anticipating the Fall: African American Theatre at the End of the 1970s," "A Potential Solution to the Digital Divide Dilemma for Africans," and "Men Who Make a Difference in *The Autobiography of Miss Jane Pittman.*" Recommended primarily for academic collections.

463. *Harvard Journal of African American Public Policy.* [ISSN: 1081-0463] 1989. 2x/yr. USD 80 (Individuals, USD 40). Harvard University, John F. Kennedy School of Government, 79 John F. Kennedy St., Cambridge, MA 02138; http://www.ksg.harvard.edu. Adv. Refereed. *Indexed:* PAIS. *Aud.:* Ac, Sa.

Founded in 1989, the *Harvard Journal of African American Public Policy* is published by graduate students at Harvard University's John F. Kennedy School of Government and is committed to a comprehensive and interdisciplinary examination of the interaction between public policy and the African American experience. Specifically, the journal seeks to provide an arena for sound, innovative, and solution-oriented discourse on issues affecting the African American community; encourage scholarship and communication among academics, policy makers, and practitioners with an interest in African American issues; and improve the public policy process by integrating the experience of African Americans into the formulation, implementation, and evaluation of public policy. A recent issue was a tribute to the Honorable A. Leon Higginbotham, Jr. and included articles titled "No Equal Justice: How the Criminal Justice System Uses Inequality," "The Relationship between Race and Mental Health Treatment," and "When a Stumble Is Not a Fall: Recovering from Employment Setbacks in the Welfare to Work Transition." Forthcoming issues will include articles about the digital divide, prison labor, and welfare reform. Highly recommended for academic and public policy collections.

464. *HealthQuest: total wellness for body, mind and spirit.* [ISSN: 1077-5668] 1993. bi-m. USD 12. Ed(s): Hilary Beard. Levas, Inc., 200 Highpoint Dr, Ste 215, Chalfont, PA 18914. Illus., adv. Sample. Circ: 500000. *Indexed:* ENW, IIBP. *Aud.:* Ga.

Founded in 1993, *HealthQuest* has become a respected consumer health information resource, offering health care news and information, feature articles, recipes and cooking tips, biographical profiles, and travel and exercise suggestions. Designed to enable people to make better-informed health care decisions, *HealthQuest* has received the Congressional Black Caucus's "Beacon of Light Award" for outstanding health coverage as well as the National Health Information Award for best consumer decision-making material. With a large national circulation, *HealthQuest* is made available free to the community at large and distributed through a network of retail outlets, churches, doctors' offices, and public health centers and as an insert within African American newspapers. Available to libraries by subscription and recommended for public libraries.

Heart & Soul. See Women section.

465. *Honey.* [ISSN: 1522-0478] 1999. m. USD 20. Ed(s): Amy Dubois Barnett, Angela Burt-Murray. Vanguarde Media, Inc, 315 Park Ave S, 11th fl, New York, NY 10010; http://www.vanguarde.com. Adv. Circ: 200000 Paid and controlled. *Aud.:* Hs, Ga, Sa.

Honey magazine is a glossy, visually appealing women's magazine that features the latest trends in fashion, beauty, style, and entertainment. All is not glitz, though, as monthly columns thoughtfully deal with issues of relationships, employment, and racism. While mostly recommended for public libraries, *Honey* would be welcome in academic libraries as well.

466. *Howard Journal of Communications.* [ISSN: 1064-6175] 1988. q. USD 208 (Individuals, USD 59). Ed(s): Carolyn A. Stroman. Taylor & Francis Inc, 325 Chestnut St, Suite 800, Philadelphia, PA 19016; info@taylorandfrancis.com; http://www.taylorandfrancis.com/. Illus., index, adv. Refereed. Vol. ends: Dec. Online: EBSCO Publishing; Ingenta Select; OCLC Online Computer Library Center, Inc.; RoweCom Information Quest; Swets Blackwell. Reprint: PSC. *Indexed:* ABS&EES, BAS, CINAHL, CommAb, FLI, HRA, IIBP, IJCS, IPSA, L&LBA, PRA, PSA, SFSA, SWA, SociolAb. *Aud.:* Ac.

The quarterly *Howard Journal of Communications* is the only scholarly journal that exclusively examines domestic and international communication issues with respect to ethnicity, gender, and culture. Recent articles include "An African American Perspective on Conversational Improvement Strategies," "Black, White, Hispanic, and Asian American Adolescents' Responses to Culturally Embedded Ads," and "Advertising of Alcoholic Beverages in African-American and Women's Magazines: Implications for Health Communication." This journal is a must for academic libraries and, in particular, for programs in speech, communications, theater, journalism, gender, and racial studies.

International Review of African American Art. See Art/Museum Publications section.

467. *Jet.* [ISSN: 0021-5996] 1951. w. USD 22 domestic; USD 37 foreign; USD 1.25 newsstand/cover per issue domestic. Johnson Publishing Co., Inc., 820 S Michigan Ave, Chicago, IL 60605; http://www.jetmag.com. Illus., adv. Sample. Circ: 952342 Paid. CD-ROM: ProQuest Information & Learning. Microform: NBI; PQC. Online: bigchalk; Chadwyck-Healey Incorporated; EBSCO Publishing; Florida Center for Library Automation; Gale Group; LexisNexis; Northern Light Technology, Inc.; OCLC Online Computer Library Center, Inc.; ProQuest Information & Learning; H.W. Wilson. Reprint: PQC. *Indexed:* IIBP, LRI, MagInd, RGPR. *Aud.:* Ems, Hs, Ga, Ac.

For over 50 years, *Jet* has been the leading weekly African American newsmagazine. Balancing news and entertainment, each issue carries the latest national and international news; a topical cover story; events in Africa; a report from Washington, D.C.; news on health, education, and labor; obituaries and wedding announcements; sports coverage; a historic calendar of events; the "Week's Best Photos"; entertainment news, celebrity profiles, and interviews; film reviews; top music sales; and a television schedule. *Jet* is a must for every library with African American constituents.

468. *Journal of African American History.* Formerly (until Jun. 2001): *Journal of Negro History.* 1916. q. USD 50 (Individuals, USD 27; USD 7 newsstand/cover per issue). Ed(s): V. P. Franklin. Association for the Study of African-American Life and History, Inc., 7961 Eastern Ave, Ste 301, Silver Spring, MD 20910; asalh@earthlink.net; http://www.asalh.org. Illus., adv. Refereed. Microform: PQC. Online: Gale Group. Reprint: PQC. *Indexed:* AmH&L, ArtHuCI, BRD, BRI, BiogInd, CBRI, CIJE, HumInd, IIBP, MLA-IB, MagInd, NumL, RGPR, SSI. *Bk. rev.:* 4-6; 500-1,500 words. *Aud.:* Ga, Ac.

Founded in 1916 by Carter G. Woodson, the "Father of Black History," the *Journal of African American History* (formerly the *Journal of Negro History*) was the prototype for all subsequent scholarly black studies journals. Even now, some 85 years later, it still retains its reputation as a vehicle for publishing influential articles of lasting interest. Recently published articles include "The Extracurricular Activities of Black College Students, 1868–1940," "The Response of the African American Press to the United States Occupation of Haiti, 1915–1934," and "Diamonds in Iowa: Blacks, Buxton, and Baseball." Each issue contains "Book Notes" and "Multi-Media Notes," sections that serve to highlight new print and nonprint African American history–oriented publications. A highly recommended title for public and academic libraries.

469. *Journal of African American Men: a publication of the National Council of African American Men.* Formerly (until 1995): *Journal of African American Male Studies.* [ISSN: 1081-1753] 1993. q. USD 192 (Individuals, USD 60). Ed(s): Gary Sailes, George Rowan. Transaction Publishers, 35 Berrue Circle, Rutgers University, Piscataway, NJ 08854-8042; trans@transactionpub.com; http://www.transactionpub.com. Illus., adv. Sample. Refereed. Circ: 400. Vol. ends: Aug. Online: Chadwyck-Healey Incorporated; EBSCO Publishing; Florida Center for Library Automation; Gale Group. Reprint: PSC. *Indexed:* HEA, IIBP, SociolAb. *Aud.:* Ac.

JAAM is the first refereed journal concerned with African American male issues in the United States. Published by the National Council of African American Men in collaboration with the David Walker Research Institute of Michigan State University, this interdisciplinary journal publishes theoretical and empirical articles that challenge current stereotypes and identify strategies and policies that can counter the unique problems African American men face. Recent articles include "Violence and the Politics of Black Males' Identity in Post-Modern America," "An Afrocentric Rites of Passage Program for Adolescent Males," and "African American Men in Nursing: A Career Opportunity that Challenges Structural Racism." An important title for academic libraries and public policy collections.

470. *Journal of Black Psychology.* [ISSN: 0095-7984] 1974. q. USD 411 print & online eds. Ed(s): Dr. Ann Kathleen Burlew. Sage Publications, Inc., 2455 Teller Rd, Thousand Oaks, CA 91320; info@sagepub.com; http://www.sagepub.com. Illus., adv. Refereed. Circ: 2600. Microform: PQC. Online: Chadwyck-Healey Incorporated; ingenta.com; OCLC Online Computer Library Center, Inc.; ProQuest Information & Learning; Swets Blackwell. Reprint: PQC. *Indexed:* ASSIA, AbAn, CIJE, CJA, HEA, HRA, IBSS, IIBP, IMFL, L&LBA, PRA, PsycholAb, RiskAb, SSI, SociolAb. *Bk. rev.:* 1, 1,000 words. *Aud.:* Ac.

The *Journal of Black Psychology* (*JBP*) has been the leading publication on the psychological study of black populations for over 25 years. Founded and sponsored by the Association of Black Psychologists, the *JBP* continues to provide innovative scholarly research and theory on the behavior of black and other populations from a black or Afrocentric perspective.

An international array of authors covers a variety of subjects, such as cognition, clinical psychology, personality, social behavior, child development, cross-cultural psychology, education, and physiological functioning. The journal provides coverage of the field's latest developments through original articles, research briefs, essays, commentaries, and book reviews. An important resource for students, scholars, and practitioners concerned with African American behavioral sciences, and it belongs in academic and health care collections.

471. *Journal of Black Studies.* [ISSN: 0021-9347] 1970. bi-m. GBP 401 print & online eds. in Europe, Middle East, Africa & Australasia. Ed(s): Molefi Kete Asante, Terry Kershaw. Sage Publications, Inc., 2455 Teller Rd, Thousand Oaks, CA 91320; info@sagepub.com; http://www.sagepub.com. Illus., index, adv. Refereed. Circ: 1750. Vol. ends: Jul. Microform: PQC. Online: Chadwyck-Healey Incorporated; EBSCO Publishing; Florida Center for Library Automation; Gale Group; ingenta.com; JSTOR (Web-based Journal Archive); OCLC Online Computer Library Center, Inc.; ProQuest Information & Learning; RoweCom Information Quest; Swets Blackwell. Reprint: PQC. *Indexed:* ASSIA, AgeL, AmH&L, ArtHuCI, BHA, BRI, BrArAb, CBRI, CIJE, CJA, HEA, HRA, IBSS, IIBP, IMFL, IPSA, L&LBA, PAIS, PRA, PSA, PsycholAb, RiskAb, SFSA, SSCI, SSI, SWR&A, SociolAb. *Aud.:* Ac.

Since 1970, the *Journal of Black Studies* has been a dynamic source for creative scholarship, covering a broad range of economic, political, sociological, historical, literary, and philosophical issues related to persons of African descent. A sampling of articles from a recent issue best illustrates its range of intellectually provocative content: "A Critical Inquiry of Enslaved African Females and the Antebellum Hospital Experience," "The Rehabilitation of Violence and the Violence of Rehabilitation: Fanon and Colonialism," and "W. E. B. Du Bois: Pioneering American Criminologist." The editorial board has an impressive international roster, and the journal contents reflect the diversity of thought within the African diaspora. The *JBS* is heavily cited by scholarly authors and is highly recommended for academic libraries, black studies collections, and urban public libraries.

472. *Journal of Blacks in Higher Education.* [ISSN: 1077-3711] 1993. q. USD 36. Ed(s): Robert Slater, Theodore Cross. The CH II Foundation, Inc., 200 W 57th St, New York, NY 10019. Illus., adv. Sample. Circ: 2500 Paid. Online: Northern Light Technology, Inc.; ProQuest Information & Learning. *Indexed:* ArtHuCI, CIJE, ENW, HEA, IIBP, SSCI. *Aud.:* Ac.

The scholarly *Journal of Blacks in Higher Education* is dedicated to the "conscientious investigation of the status and prospects for African Americans in higher education." Readers will find information about racial practices, policies, and governance in American colleges and universities. The journal often features the writings of college presidents, affirmative-action officers, deans, black studies scholars, and civil rights activists. Regular departments include scholarly research, race relations on campus, appointments, tenure decisions and promotions, minority-related grants, notable honors and awards, and "Vital Signs": statistics that measure the state of racial inequality. A requisite publication for academic libraries, colleges, and universities.

Journal of Health Care for the Poor and Underserved. See Medicine and Health/Health Care Delivery section.

473. *Journal of Multicultural Counseling and Development.* Formerly (until 1985): *Journal of Non-White Concerns in Personnel and Guidance.* [ISSN: 0883-8534] 1972. q. USD 60. Ed(s): Donald B Pope Davis. American Counseling Association, 5999 Stevenson Ave, Alexandria, VA 22304-3300; http://www.counseling.org. Illus., adv. Refereed. Circ: 2900. Vol. ends: Oct. Microform: PQC. Online: EBSCO Publishing; Florida Center for Library Automation; Gale Group; OCLC Online Computer Library Center, Inc.; ProQuest Information & Learning; H.W. Wilson. Reprint: PQC; PSC. *Indexed:* CIJE, EduInd, HEA, IIBP, PsycholAb, SSCI, SWR&A. *Aud.:* Ac.

The *Journal of Multicultural Counseling and Development,* published by the Association for Multicultural Counseling and Development, is dedicated to the publication of articles pertinent to multicultural and ethnic minority interests in all areas of counseling and human development. Coverage includes state-of-the-art multicultural research and reports on the application of the latest theoretical ideas and concepts, as the journal seeks to provide mental health practitioners with information and interventions from the latest clinical developments. Individuals and organizations involved with diverse communities will find the research within the journal's pages practical as well as scholarly.

474. ***Journal of Negro Education: a Howard University quarterly review of issues incident to the education of black people.*** [ISSN: 0022-2984] 1932. q. USD 20 (Individuals, USD 16). Ed(s): R C Saravanabhavan. Howard University Press, Marketing Department, 2600 Sixth St, N W, Washington, DC 20059; http://jne.law.howard.edu/. Illus., index, adv. Sample. Refereed. Circ: 2300 Paid. Vol. ends: Fall. Microform: MIM; PMC; PQC. Online: Gale Group; JSTOR (Web-based Journal Archive); Northern Light Technology, Inc.; OCLC Online Computer Library Center, Inc.; ProQuest Information & Learning. Reprint: PQC; PSC. *Indexed:* AgeL, AmH&L, BRI, CBRI, CIJE, ECER, EduInd, HEA, IIBP, IMFL, L&LBA, MagInd, PAIS, PsycholAb, SFSA, SSCI, SWR&A, SociolAb. *Bk. rev.:* 4-6, 1,000-2,500 words. *Aud.:* Ac.

For 70 years, the *Journal of Negro Education* has been a major resource for the investigation of issues related to the education of African Americans in the United States and developing countries. As one of the oldest continuously published periodicals by and about blacks, it continues to be the primary repository of scholarly information about every aspect of black education. Special features include regular reports on black college enrollments, listings of doctoral research, book and media reviews, and news and announcements in education. Required for academic libraries and education programs, in particular.

475. ***Journal of Religious Thought.*** [ISSN: 0022-4235] 1943. s-a. USD 20 (Individuals, USD 18; Students, USD 15). Howard University, School of Divinity, 1400 Shepherd St, NE, Washington, DC 20017; cjnewsome@howard.edu; http://www.howard.edu/schooldivinity/default.htm. Illus., adv. Refereed. Circ: 1500. Microform: PQC. Online: Chadwyck-Healey Incorporated; EBSCO Publishing; Gale Group; Northern Light Technology, Inc.; OCLC Online Computer Library Center, Inc.; ProQuest Information & Learning. Reprint: PQC. *Indexed:* AbAn, AmH&L, BAS, HumInd, IBZ, IIBP, NTA, R&TA, RI-1. *Bk. rev.:* 2-3, 250-1,500 words. *Aud.:* Ac.

The *Journal of Religious Thought* was established in 1943 by the faculty of the Howard University School of Divinity. For close to 60 years, the journal has sought to advance knowledge and share the results of scholarship in the field of religion generally, with special attention to the issues that variously pertain to ministry of the black church and related aspects of the black religious experience. The journal accepts articles from persons of varied theological and ethnic backgrounds. A regular feature, "Pastor's Corner," offers speeches and sermons, and its listing of books received provides a helpful bibliography. Theological collections, black church libraries, and African American studies collections will find its legacy welcome and its scholarship insightful.

476. ***Literary Griot: international journal of Black expressive culture studies.*** [ISSN: 1053-9344] 1988. s-a. USD 20 (Individuals, USD 15). Ed(s): Ousseynou B. Traore. Literary Griot, 300 Pompton Rd., Wayne, NJ 07470. Illus. Refereed. *Bk. rev.:* 2-3, 500-1,000 words. *Aud.:* Ac.

Committed to the critical and theoretical study of black expressive cultures in Africa, the Americas, the Caribbean, and other areas of the world, *Literary Griot* publishes essays, scholarly articles, and reviews of books on literature, film, music, theater, sculpture, painting, music, and oral traditions. The journal is particularly interested in the historical, theoretical, and critical perspectives of the native culture in which black expressive arts are produced, but it remains open to other modes of scholarly inquiry derived from non-black cultural and ideological traditions. Manuscripts are accepted in French, English, or any African language. Previous special issues have focused on Afrocentricity and music; signifying race and identity; and black womanhood. Academic and Africana/black studies collections should consider this title.

Living Blues. See Music/Popular section.

477. ***The Messenger Magazine.*** Formerly: *African American Magazine.* [ISSN: 1536-3600] 1998. bi-m. USD 20. Ed(s): Pat Mathis. Topaz Marketing & Distributing, 1014 Franklin S E, Grand Rapids, MI 49507-1327; http://www.africanamericanmag.com. Circ: 5000. *Bk. rev.:* 1-5. *Aud.:* Ems, Hs, Ga.

Although the *The Messenger Magazine* is oriented toward readers in Michigan and other Midwestern states, there is much here to recommend to a national audience. The magazine's stated mission articulates well its inspirational tone, i.e., to "strengthen our readers in the areas of economic and educational empowerment, such that the whole community is improved and unified in its economic goals." Each issue includes business briefs, home improvement tips, economic advice, and profiles of successful businesses and people, with many of the articles geared toward family and community. Recommended for secondary school and public libraries.

National Black Law Journal. See Law section.

National Medical Association. Journal. See Medicine and Health/Health Care Delivery section.

478. ***Negro Educational Review: a forum for discussion of Afro-American issues.*** [ISSN: 0548-1457] 1950. q. USD 30. Ed(s): William Jimmerson Holloway. Negro Educational Review, Inc., Box 70425, Florida A & M University, Tallahassee, FL 32307; ner@famu.edu. Illus., index, adv. Sample. Refereed. Circ: 1000. Vol. ends: Oct. *Indexed:* CIJE, EduInd, HEA, IIBP. *Bk. rev.:* 1-2, 500-1,500 words. *Aud.:* Ac.

For over 50 years, this international quarterly has been publishing scholarly articles and research reports on a wide range of issues regarding blacks in education. In addition to articles and book reviews, the journal covers the problems of the education profession and news about black educators. Recent issues have included articles such as "The Emergence of Multicultural Education: The Control and Dissemination of Information," "Issues Affecting the Recruitment and Retention of Black Students in Teacher Education," and "The Idea of a Historically Black University." Recommended for academic libraries and public libraries serving African American communities.

479. ***The Network Journal: Black professional and small business magazine.*** [ISSN: 1094-1908] 1993. m. USD 15; USD 2.50 newsstand/cover per issue. Ed(s): Akinshiju C Ola. Network Journal, 139 Fulton St, Ste 407, New York, NY 10038; http://www.tnj.com. Illus. Circ: 35000. Online: EBSCO Publishing; OCLC Online Computer Library Center, Inc.; SoftLine Information. *Indexed:* ENW. *Bk. rev.:* Various number and length. *Aud.:* Ga.

Founded in 1993 in order to assist African American small-business owners and professionals, *The Network Journal* provides readers with timely, thought-provoking cover articles and inspiring success stories. Monthly features cover personal finance, tax tips, travel, book reviews, and upcoming seminars and events. Unique is its annual "40-Under-Forty" Awards, where 40 people are highlighted for their excellence in careers and entrepreneurship. A worthwhile title for most public libraries.

480. ***Obsidian 3: Literature in the African Diaspora.*** Former titles (until 1999): *Obsidian 2: Black Literature in Review;* (until 1982): *Obsidian: Black Literature in Review.* [ISSN: 1542-1619] 1975. s-a. USD 15. Ed(s): Afaa M Weaver. North Carolina State University, English Department, PO Box 8105, Raleigh, NC 27695-8105; krsassan@unity.ncsu.edu; http://www2.ncsu.edu/ncsu/chass/obsidian.html. Illus., adv. Refereed. Circ: 500 Paid. Microform: PQC. Online: Gale Group. Reprint: PQC. *Indexed:* AmHI, ArtHuCI, IAPV, IIBP, MLA-IB. *Bk. rev.:* Various number and length. *Aud.:* Hs, Ga, Ac.

Signaling the arrival of its new editor, Afaa Michael Weaver, the former *Obsidian II* is now *Obsidian III: Literature in the African Diaspora.* A semi-annual literary review, *Obsidian III* provides an important venue for the cultivation and study of contemporary poetry, fiction, drama, and nonfiction prose by black writers worldwide, in addition to critical scholarly writing about these artists and their works. Book reviews are also included. As one of today's finest collections of creative writing and scholarship, *Obsidian III* is recommended for academic collections and for all black studies collections.

QBR: The Black Book Review. See Books and Book Reviews section.

481. ***The Review of Black Political Economy.*** [ISSN: 0034-6446] 1970. q. USD 192 (Individuals, USD 60). Ed(s): Thomas D Boston. Transaction Publishers, 35 Berrue Circle, Rutgers University, Piscataway, NJ 08854-8042; trans@transactionpub.com; http://www.transactionpub.com. Illus., adv. Refereed. Circ: 700. Microform: PQC. Online: Chadwyck-Healey Incorporated; EBSCO Publishing; Florida Center for Library Automation; Gale Group; Ingenta Select; OCLC Online Computer Library Center, Inc.; ProQuest Information & Learning. Reprint: PQC; PSC. *Indexed:* AgeL, AmH&L, IBSS, IIBP, JEL, LRI, PAIS, PSA, SSCI, SSI, SUSA, SociolAb. *Bk. rev.:* 1-3, 500-1,500 words. *Aud.:* Ac.

The Review of Black Political Economy, a publication of the National Economic Association and the Southern Center for Studies in Public Policy of Clark Atlanta University, examines issues related to the economic status of African American and Third World peoples. For over 30 years, it has been the leading scholarly journal devoted to identifying and analyzing policy prescriptions designed to reduce racial economic inequality. The journal is devoted to appraising public and private policies for their ability to advance economic opportunities without regard to their theoretical or ideological origins. Recent articles include "Racial and Gender Differences in an Urban Labor Market: The Case of Detroit," "Black Infant Health: Where to in the 21st Century?," and "Is There Discrimination in Mortgage Lending? What Does the Research Tell Us?" A highly recommended journal for academic and public policy collections.

482. ***Right On!*** [ISSN: 0048-8305] 1971. m. USD 21.95 domestic; USD 27.95 Canada; USD 29.95 elsewhere. Ed(s): Cynthia Horner. Sterling - Macfadden Partnership, 233 Park Ave S, 6th Fl, New York, NY 10003; http://www.sterlingmacfadden.com. Illus., adv. Sample. Circ: 100000 Paid. Vol. ends: Oct. *Bk. rev.:* 2-3, 250-500 words. *Aud.:* Ems, Hs.

Right On! has kept pace with the growth and changing interests of the youth-based African American popular culture in the United States for over 30 years, as it covers every personality, fad, and fashion of interest to African American adolescents. It has a more wholesome appeal than many of the hard-driving titles it competes with on the newsstand. Originally classified as a fan magazine, *Right On!* covers the leading screen, television, and recording stars and has become more of a lifestyle/entertainment magazine. *Right On!* is used in many schools for reading-enrichment programs and will appeal to school library users.

483. ***Savoy: power. substance. style.*** [ISSN: 1532-3692] 2001. 10x/yr. USD 10 domestic; USD 20 Canada; USD 25 elsewhere. Ed(s): Roy Johnson. Vanguarde Media, Inc, 315 Park Ave S, 11th fl, New York, NY 10010; http://www.vanguarde.com. Adv. *Indexed:* IIBP. *Aud.:* Hs, Ga, Ac.

Named after New York City's stylish ballroom, *Savoy* debuted in January 2001, replacing the popular issues-oriented newsmagazine *Emerge*, which discontinued publication in June 2000. Intended to reach a broader audience, this stylish lifestyle magazine covers entertainment, travel, politics, business, and fashion. *Savoy's* well-respected editor, Roy S. Johnson, likens it to "a dinner party where the topics are wide-ranging." *Savoy* has proven to be a popular title for public library collections.

484. ***Sister 2 Sister: giving it to ya' straight, no chaser!*** [ISSN: 1071-5053] 1988. m. USD 18; USD 2.99 newsstand/cover per issue; GBP 1.95 newsstand/cover per issue United Kingdom. Ed(s): Lorenzo Brown. Sister 2 Sister, Inc., PO Box 41148, Washington, DC 20018-0548. Illus., adv. Sample. Circ: 85000 Paid. Vol. ends: Dec. *Bk. rev.:* 1, 250 words. *Aud.:* Ga.

In 1988, Jamie Foster Brown launched *Sister 2 Sister* (*S2S*) as a monthly trade newsletter targeted at newly emerging black female executives in the music industry. Since then, the magazine has developed into one of the most powerful and respected voices in entertainment, focusing on black celebrity news. Each issue begins with a monthly diary of publisher Jamie Brown's latest adventures in the entertainment and media worlds, revealing the lives of African American movie, music, sports, and entertainment stars. The magazine also includes music, television, and film reviews, offers beauty and fashion tips, profiles successful women in the entertainment industry, and has lengthy transcripts of interviews with two famous people in each issue. Highly recommended for public libraries serving predominantly African American communities or popular-culture collections.

485. ***Slavery and Abolition: a journal of slave and post-slave studies.*** [ISSN: 0144-039X] 1980. 3x/yr. GBP 197 print & online eds. Ed(s): Gad Heuman, James Walvin. Frank Cass Publishers, Crown House, 47 Chase Side, Southgate, London, N14 5BP, United Kingdom; jnlsubs@frankcass.com; http://www.frankcass.com/jnls/. Illus., index, adv. Sample. Refereed. Vol. ends: Dec. Microform: PQC. Online: Ingenta Select. *Indexed:* AmH&L, BrHumI, IBZ, IIBP, PSA, SociolAb. *Bk. rev.:* 9-15+, 500-1,000 words. *Aud.:* Ac.

Slavery and Abolition is the only journal devoted in its entirety to a discussion of the demographic, socioeconomic, historical, and psychological aspects of human bondage from the ancient period to the present. Frequently, special thematic issues are published in addition to an important annual bibliographical supplement on slavery, providing the only comprehensive listing of books and articles in the field.

As its major focus is on the slave experience in Africa and the Americas, the publication has looked at slavery in Cuba, slave sugar boycotts, slave resistance, African response to abolition, and free blacks in slave societies. Recent articles have included "~Black Frenchman' and ~White Settlers': Race, Slavery, and the Creation of African-American Identities Along the Northwest Frontier, 1790–1840," "From Chattel to Citizen: The Transition from Slavery to Freedom in Richmond, Virginia," and "African-American Aspirations and the Settlement of Liberia." *Slavery and Abolition* is highly recommended for academic libraries.

486. ***Souls: a critical journal of Black politics, culture, and society.*** [ISSN: 1099-9949] 1999. q. USD 135 (Individuals, USD 49). Ed(s): Dr. Manning Marable. Taylor & Francis Inc, 325 Chestnut St, Suite 800, Philadelphia, PA 19016; http://www.taylorandfrancis.com/. Online: Ingenta Select. Reprint: PSC. *Bk. rev.:* 1, 1,000-2,000 words. *Aud.:* Ga, Ac.

Inspired by W. E. B. Du Bois's classic work *The Souls of Black Folk, Souls* is a relatively new quarterly journal edited by the notable activist scholar Manning Marable and sponsored by the Institute for Research in African-American Studies at Columbia University. Along the lines of the *Black Scholar, Souls* brings together intellectuals from both traditional academe and the black community to engage in a critical dialogue about contemporary problems and challenges facing black America today. Each quarterly issue includes feature articles, interviews, book reviews, and an extended "symposium" section drafted by prominent scholars, writers, and leaders on the central theme of each issue. Recommended for academic and black studies collections.

The Source. See Music/Popular section.

Transition: an international review. See Africa section.

487. ***Trotter Review.*** Formerly (until 1992): *Trotter Institute Review.* [ISSN: 1070-695X] 1987. a. USD 30 (Individuals, USD 15). Ed(s): James Jennings. William Monroe Trotter Institute, 10th Fl, Healey Library, University of Massachusetts Boston, Boston, MA 02125-3393; http://www.trotterinst.org. Adv. Circ: 2500. *Aud.:* Ac, Sa.

The William Monroe Trotter Institute of the University of Massachusetts–Boston was founded in 1984 to address the needs and concerns of the black community of Boston and Massachusetts through research, technical assistance, and public service. Since 1987, the *Trotter Review* has published scholarly, informative, and provocative articles addressing current issues in black studies, race, and race relations in the United States and abroad. The annual issues are theme-based, and recent issues have looked at "Women of Color and Economic Development," "Diversity, Pedagogy and Higher Education," and "The Black Church: Facing and Responding to Social, Economic and Political Challenges." Future issues will focus on the experiences of black children and the black community with public schools, the historical and contemporary relationships between the black and Native American communities in the United States, and the role of black educators in community service learning. An important title for academic libraries and public policy collections.

488. ***Upscale: the magazine for the success-oriented.*** [ISSN: 1047-2592] 1989. 9x/yr. USD 14.95; USD 3.50. Upscale Communications, Inc., 2141 Powers Ferry Rd, Marietta, GA 30067. Illus., adv. Sample. Circ: 237720. *Aud.:* Ga, Ac.

An early example of the lifestyle genre of magazines, the pages of *Upscale* feature the latest in business, style, entertainment, current events, fashion, beauty, health care, travel articles, and celebrity profiles. Targeting the African American middle class, *Upscale* reflects and promotes "the image of success; the flowing abundance of wealth, spirituality, intellect and style...." Reflecting its Southern orientation, the magazine covers news and personalities not often seen in a national publication. Particularly recommended for urban public libraries.

489. ***Vibe.*** [ISSN: 1070-4701] 1993. 12x/yr. USD 9.95 domestic; USD 24 Canada; USD 50 elsewhere. Ed(s): Emil Wilbekin. Vibe - Spin Ventures, 215 Lexington Ave, 6th Fl, New York, NY 10016; webmaster@vibe.com; http://www.vibe.com. Illus. Sample. Circ: 825000. *Indexed:* ASIP, IIBP, IIMP, IIPA, MusicInd, RGPR. *Aud.:* Hs, Ga.

Vibe is a lifestyle magazine aimed at young urban males, featuring rap, hip-hop, and related music; fashion; and celebrity interviews. Although *Vibe* has not been without controversy for its provocative covers, choice of features, opinions of writers, and behaviors of staff members, libraries that serve young people, particularly urban youth, should consider including *Vibe* when expanding their selection of titles for this audience.

490. ***Vital Issues: the journal of African American speeches.*** [ISSN: 1056-6368] 1950. q. USD 49. Ed(s): Teta V Banks. Bethune - Dubois Publications, 600 New Hampshire Ave, N W, Ste 1125, Washington, DC 20037. Illus., index, adv. Sample. Circ: 5000. Reprint: PQC. *Indexed:* IIBP, PAIS. *Aud.:* Hs, Ga, Ac.

The objective of this journal is to "present major speeches of African American professional leaders and to preserve their spirit and voices for all generations to come." Here are a sampling of some of these voices published in a recent issue: Colin L. Powell, remarks on mentoring: "Mentoring: The First Thing"; C. DeLores Tucker, remarks at the National Political Congress of Black Women's 16th Annual Awards Brunch: "Mandate for the Millennium"; and Hugh B. Price, keynote address at the 89th Annual National Urban League Conference. As stated by the Hon. William H. Gray, III, in vol. 137, no. 34 of the *Congressional Record,* "This publication will be a valuable resource for research and history of the issues that were confronted and perspectives taken by our leaders at the forefront of social change." This is an important resource for leaders, policy makers, students, and researchers, as well as a general audience. Special collections serving legislative entities might also find its inclusion useful.

491. ***The Western Journal of Black Studies.*** [ISSN: 0197-4327] 1977. q. USD 90 (Individuals, USD 30). Ed(s): Lincoln James. Washington State University Press, PO Box 645910, Pullman, WA 99164-5910; grunewan@wsu.edu; http://www.wsu.edu/~wjbs/. Illus., index. Refereed. Circ: 600. Vol. ends: Winter. Online: bigchalk; Chadwyck-Healey Incorporated; EBSCO Publishing; Florida Center for Library Automation; Gale Group; Northern Light Technology, Inc.; ProQuest Information & Learning. Reprint: PQC. *Indexed:* AmH&L, AmHI, CIJE, IIBP, L&LBA, PSA, PsycholAb, SWR&A, SociolAb. *Bk. rev.:* 1, 1,000-2,500 words. *Aud.:* Ac.

Devoted to the study of blacks and people of African descent, *The Western Journal of Black Studies* (*WJBS*) has been a leading scholarly interdisciplinary journal since 1977. Devoted to research, social and political analyses, literary criticism, and the arts, all articles are selected by blind peer review and exemplify rigorous scholarship. The following articles are from a recent issue: "Black Mothers/Black Sons: A Critical Examination of the Social Science Literature," "Feminism and the Subtext of Whiteness: Black Women's Experiences as a Site of Identity Formation and Contestation of Whiteness," and "Does Economic Culture and Social Capital Matter? An Analysis of African-American Entrepreneurs in Cleveland, Ohio."

WJBS was recently honored with the C. L. R. James award for promoting outstanding African American issue-oriented scholarship. Highly recommended for academic libraries and public libraries serving African American populations.

Electronic Journals

492. ***Africana: gateway to the black world.*** 1999. d. Free. Ed(s): Gary Dauphin. A O L Time Warner Inc., AOL Time Warner Bldg, 75 Rockefeller Plaza, New York, NY 10019; http://www.aoltimewarner.com/. *Aud.:* Ems, Hs, Ga, Ac, Sa.

Africana is both an online publication and an Internet portal committed to "providing provocative coverage of the whole world of Africa and her diaspora." *Africana* was first developed in 1999 by Henry Louis Gates, Jr. and Kwame Anthony Appiah in order to feature content from the *Encarta Africana* encyclopedia, a CD-ROM compendium of African and African American history edited by Gates and Appiah. Time-Warner acquired *Africana* in 2000, and now the guiding vision for the site, according to Africana.com CEO Kenn Turner, is more along the lines of a "black *Vanity Fair* on the World Wide Web." The content ranges from daily news, feature articles, and in-depth sections ("Channels") devoted to articles about movies and TV, music, books, people, arts, and health and beauty. Of special note is the section "The Research Center." Currently, it features topical sections about the Harlem Renaissance, slavery, Rosa Parks, and black soldiers. Within each of these topical sections are links to in-depth articles taken from the "Encarta Africana." Additional sections include sample lesson plans for students in grades 3–12 and an archive of recordings from a public radio show hosted by Prof. Henry Louis Gates, Jr., that features the stories of prominent African Americans throughout U.S. history. This type of special content places the web site a cut above most other similar sites.

493. ***Electronic Urban Report.*** 1995. 3x/w. Free. Ed(s): Kim Cohn. Electronic Urban Report, PO Box 412081, Los Angeles, CA 90041; info1@eurweb.com. *Aud.:* Hs, Ga.

The *Electronic Urban Report* provides daily coverage of African American celebrities in films, music, and writing, though most of the focus is on popular music and musicians. Includes interviews, comments, news notes, and occasional critical comments from readers.

494. ***The North Star (Poughkeepsie): a journal of African American religious history.*** [ISSN: 1094-902X] 1997. s-a. Free. Ed(s): Judith Weisenfeld. North Star (Poughkeepsie), c/o Vassar College, Dept. of Religion, 124 Raymond Ave, Poughkeepsie, NY 12604; jweisenfeld@vassar.edu. Illus. Refereed. *Indexed:* AmH&L. *Bk. rev.:* Various number and length. *Aud.:* Ga, Ac.

The North Star is supported by Vassar College and by a grant from the American Academy of Religion. It is published exclusively on the World Wide Web with two primary goals. First, in association with the Afro-American Religious History group of the American Academy of Religion, it provides information on events, new publications, research collections, and other resources in the field of African American religious history. Second, it presents peer-reviewed articles based on historical research that explore the religious cultures of people of African descent in the United States. Although primarily oriented to North America, the journal will occasionally publish work from other disciplines and/or work that deals in a comparative way with other areas of the African diaspora, as well as with regions in Africa. Graduate students working in this area are encouraged to submit articles and book reviews. In addition to featured articles, each issue includes "News and Announcements," recommended Internet resources, and book reviews.

■ AGING

Myrtis Cochran, Reference Librarian for the Humanities, Social Sciences, Area Studies, and Government Information, University of California at Berkeley, Berkeley, CA 94720-6000; mcochran@library.berkeley.edu

Introduction

"If the demographic focus of the twentieth century was on education and employment for the young, then the theme for the twenty-first century will be the elderly," stated Nitin Desai, United Nations Under-Secretary-General for Economic and Social Affairs, during the Second World Assembly on Aging (April, 2002). The assembly's goal was to raise public awareness of the issue of aging. To this end, a 44-page plan of action was adopted outlining numerous objectives to support the elderly in education, employment, housing and health care, guaranteed pensions, and women's rights. Other areas of focus include human rights and elder abuse, with special attention to medical and nutritional needs, promoting literacy and technology skills, and the aging work force. According to U.N. statistics, the world's population is expected to triple to two billion by 2050, at which time it is estimated that one in five people will be 60 or older and more than two million people will be 100 or older.

As a logical consequence of this shift in demographics, one would expect that more attention would be given to the elderly and that there would be an increase in the production of goods and services with the mature consumer in mind. Baby boomers (those born in the years following World War II), said to be the largest growing group, would be a primary target. The 50-plus crowd is considered to be the fastest-growing market, having money for discretionary spending and leading the way as the fastest-growing group of Internet users. Baby boomers are not expected to age quietly like their parents did. They will make demands for services and invest in products that will provide the quality of life they knew in their youth, according to Phil Goodman of the consulting firm Generation Transitional Marketing.

Given the predicted shift in demographics and the resulting need for information about the lifestyles and the care of the elderly, more researchers can be expected to monitor and conduct studies of the aging population. Current research regarding the elderly appears in the journal literature of gerontology (the study of aging) and the related area of geriatrics (a branch of medicine that focuses on the aged). The journal titles listed below cover all aspects of aging. Several scholarly publications presenting original research and a smaller number of general-interest journals have been selected for this section. Titles were selected primarily because of their accessibility to gerontology professionals and the general reader. In addition, their suitability for academic, special, and public libraries was considered. The majority of the titles are directed toward the scholar, practitioner, and student of the discipline. There are fewer general-interest magazines, but this will probably change in time in response to changing demographics. Available, but to a lesser degree, are government, state, and regional magazines and newsletters appearing in print, and as web sites.

Abstracts in Social Gerontology and *AGELINE* are the core abstracting service and index for the field of gerontology. These sources monitor publications in gerontology and related disciplines. Since the field of gerontology is interdisciplinary, indexes and abstracts in other subject areas such as women's studies, psychology, public policy, and religion may be consulted to locate information on aging.

Basic Periodicals

Ga: *A A R P The Magazine, Ageing and Society;* Ac: *American Geriatrics Society. Journal, Generations (San Francisco).*

Basic Abstracts and Indexes

Abstracts in Social Gerontology, AGELINE.

495. *A A R P: The Magazine.* Formed by the merger of (2001-2003): *My Generation;* (2002-2003): *A A R P Modern Maturity;* Which was formerly (until Mar. 2002): *Modern Maturity;* (until 1960): *We; Journal of Lifetime Living;* Modern Maturity incorporated (in 1986): *Dynamic Years;* Which was formerly (1965-1977): *Dynamic Maturity.* [ISSN: 1541-9894] 2003. bi-m. American Association of Retired Persons, 601 E St, N W, Washington, DC 20049; http://www.aarp.org. Circ: 2150000. *Aud.:* Ga.

The magazine for the 50-plus generation and "America's largest circulation magazine (21.5 million) and the best guide to the rest of your life" has a new name and design that combines the best features of *My Generation* and *Modern Maturity.* A publication of the American Association of Retired Persons, *AARP The Magazine* comes in three editions. Each edition has the same content, plus one or two articles targeted to one of three age groups: 50-59, 60-69, and over 70. The magazine includes feature articles and general interest articles on various topics including money, love, nutrition, and travel bargains. More information is available at the web site (www.aarpmagazine.org), such as enhanced versions of articles, an archive of stories from *My Generation* and *AARP Modern Maturity,* and the latest news on prescription drugs, Social Security updates, and more (surveys, crossword puzzles, recipes). Articles are timely and interesting. A benefit of an AARP membership, this publication is also suitable for public libraries and institutions serving seniors.

496. *Activities, Adaptation & Aging: the journal of activities management.* [ISSN: 0192-4788] 1980. q. USD 500 domestic; USD 675 Canada; USD 725 elsewhere. Ed(s): Linnea Couture. Haworth Press, Inc., 10 Alice St, Binghamton, NY 13904-1580; getinfo@haworthpressinc.com; http://www.haworthpress.com. Illus., adv. Sample. Refereed. Circ: 340 Paid. Vol. ends: Summer. Microform: PQC. Reprint: HAW. *Indexed:* ASG, AbAn, AgeL, BiolAb, CINAHL, ExcerpMed, IBZ, IMFL, MCR, PEI, PsycholAb, RRTA, SWA, SWR&A, SociolAb, WAE&RSA. *Bk. rev.:* 2-3, 600-800 words, signed. *Aud.:* Ac, Sa.

Longevity has been attributed to staying active. This journal promotes activity among the elderly by presenting research studies of interest to practitioners, healthcare professionals concerned with enhancing the lives of the elderly. A wide range of programs is covered, including physical, recreational, spiritual, and creative activities in various settings such as nursing homes, individual residences, or outpatient care. The journal includes a special section, "Announcements/What's New," which lists manufacturers of daily living aids and facts and information on particular health issues such as Alzheimer's disease. Occasionally, thematic issues are published; some recent titles are "Exercise Programming for Older Adults" and "The Abusive Elder: Service Considerations." Suitable for academic libraries.

497. *Advances (Chicago): progress in Alzheimer research and care.* Former titles (until Aug. 1997): *Alzheimer's Association Newsletter; A D R D A Newsletter.* 1981. q. Free. Ed(s): Barbara Harfmann. Alzheimer's Association, Inc., 225 N Michigan Ave, 17th Fl., Chicago, IL 60601; info@alz.org; http://www.alz.org. Circ: 160000. *Aud.:* Ga.

Advances is an important resource for caregivers of those with Alzheimer's disease. Published by the Alzheimer's Association, this short publication is rich in content. Available both electronically and in print, *Advances* provides practical information regarding Alzheimer's in the form of clinical studies, current reports, medical treatments and therapies, prescription drugs, and news. Personal questions about real-life situations are answered in a question-and-answer column. Suitable for practitioners and individual caregivers.

498. *Age and Ageing.* [ISSN: 0002-0729] 1972. bi-m. GBP 210. Ed(s): Gordon Wilcock. Oxford University Press, Great Clarendon St, Oxford, OX2 6DP, United Kingdom; jnl.orders@oup.co.uk; http://www3.oup.co.uk/jnls. Illus., index, adv. Sample. Refereed. Circ: 3700. Vol. ends: Nov. Online: bigchalk; EBSCO Publishing; Florida Center for Library Automation; Gale Group; HighWire Press; ingenta.com; OCLC Online Computer Library Center, Inc.; ProQuest Information & Learning; RoweCom Information Quest; Swets Blackwell. Reprint: PSC. *Indexed:* ASSIA, AbAn, AgeL, BiolAb, CINAHL, ChemAb, DSA, ErgAb, ExcerpMed, H&SSA, IndMed, SCI, SSCI, SSI. *Aud.:* Ac, Sa.

Age and Ageing is a joint publication of the British Geriatrics Society and the British Society for Research on Aging. The focus of this journal is on the medical aspects of aging and is very similar to the *Journal of the American Geriatrics Society* (see below) in intended audience and content. Original research and commissioned review articles are published along with editorials, letters, case studies, and news items. While the editorial board is mainly British, articles on research outside the United Kingdom are published. Occasionally, articles dealing with mental health are published, although the main focus is on medical research. The contributing authors are generally research physicians. Suitable for academic libraries with a geriatric medicine collection and medical libraries.

499. ***Ageing and Society: the journal of the centre for policy on ageing and the British society of gerontology.*** [ISSN: 0144-686X] 1981. bi-m. USD 227 (Individuals, USD 80). Ed(s): Tony Warnes. Cambridge University Press, The Edinburgh Bldg, Shaftesbury Rd, Cambridge, CB2 2RU, United Kingdom; information@cambridge.org; http://uk.cambridge.org/journals. Illus., index, adv. Sample. Refereed. Circ: 1050. Vol. ends: Nov. Microform: PQC. Online: EBSCO Publishing; Gale Group; RoweCom Information Quest; Swets Blackwell. *Indexed:* ASG, ASSIA, AgeL, ArtHuCI, IBSS, IPSA, PAIS, PSA, RI-1, SSCI, SSI, SWA, SociolAb. *Bk. rev.:* Number and length vary. *Aud.:* Ac.

An "international journal devoted to publishing contributions to the understanding of human ageing, particularly from the social and behavioural sciences and humanities." This journal takes a broadly based approach to aging and the human condition. Numerous topics related to aging are explored. Research articles are presented on aging as it relates to individuals, groups, institutions, or societies. In addition to original research, occasionally a review section is included that may feature review articles, symposia, progress reports on current research, book reviews, or abstracts of relevant articles in other journals. Recent articles cover nursing home vouchers, poverty and social assistance, growing old, and men's organizational affiliations. The intended audience is professionals in gerontology, sociology, and social work. Suitable for academic libraries, especially ones desiring a British perspective.

500. ***Ageing International: information bulletin of the International Federation on Ageing.*** [ISSN: 0163-5158] 1973. q. USD 192 (Individuals, USD 60). Ed(s): Prem Fry. Transaction Publishers, 35 Berrue Circle, Rutgers University, Piscataway, NJ 08854-8042; trans@transactionpub.com; http://www.transactionpub.com. Illus., index, adv. Sample. Circ: 500. Vol. ends: Winter. Reprint: PSC. *Indexed:* ASG, AgeL, CIJE, SociolAb. *Aud.:* Ga, Ac.

The International Federation on Ageing is a nonprofit organization whose membership is comprised of approximately 100 organizations that represent or serve the elderly in over 50 countries worldwide. *Ageing International* is its official publication. In addition to news briefs, each issue covers a theme. Recent topics include pensions and income security and global perspectives on lifelong learning. Articles describe programs, policies, and activities dealing with the elderly, and they are generally written by the person(s) responsible for the programs. The information is practical and presents a global view. This title is considered a core source in a general gerontology collection.

501. ***American Geriatrics Society. Journal.*** Supersedes (in 1952): *American Therapeutic Society. Transactions.* [ISSN: 0002-8614] 1953. m. USD 510 print & online eds. Ed(s): Thomas T Yoshikawa. Blackwell Publishing, Inc., Commerce Place, 350 Main St, Malden, MA 02148; subscrip@blackwellpub.com; http://www.blackwellpublishing.com. Illus., index, adv. Sample. Refereed. Circ: 9018. Vol. ends: Dec. Microform: WWS; PQC. Online: Gale Group; ingenta.com; MD Consult; OCLC Online Computer Library Center, Inc.; Ovid Technologies, Inc.; RoweCom Information Quest; Swets Blackwell; H.W. Wilson. Reprint: PQC. *Indexed:* ASG, ASSIA, AgeL, BiolAb, CINAHL, ChemAb, ExcerpMed, H&SSA, HortAb, IndMed, PsycholAb, RiskAb, SCI, SFSA, SSCI, SSI, SWR&A. *Bk. rev.:* 2, 500 words. *Aud.:* Ac, Sa.

The official journal of the American Geriatrics Society (AGS) was fifty years old in 2003. The goal of this well-established journal is "to publish articles that are relevant in the broadest terms to the clinical care of older persons" spanning a variety of disciplines with potential benefits to clinicians. The journal organizes original research articles into eleven sections: Progress in Geriatrics; Models and Systems of Geriatric Care; Geriatric Bioscience; International Health Affairs; Old Lives Tales, Geriatric Literature; Nursing; Ethnogeriatrics and Special Populations; Ethics; Public Policy and Medical Economics; Education and Training; and Drugs and Pharmacology. Each section has its own expert editor. Article content is presented in the form of research papers, brief reports, methodological reports, personal stories, assessments of models and systems, and research and product reviews dedicated to a specific topic. Abstracts of papers are included in the table of contents. Benefits to members of the AGS include reports of AGS news, announcements of upcoming conferences, courses, grants/awards, and job opportunities. It is intended for medical practitioners, researchers, gerontology and geriatrics scholars, and health care professionals in related fields. Considered a core journal for academic libraries with collections in geriatrics.

502. ***American Journal of Geriatric Psychiatry: official journal of the American Association for Geriatric Psychiatry.*** [ISSN: 1064-7481] 1993. bi-m. USD 289 print & online eds. (Individuals, USD 136 print & online eds.; Students, USD 60 print & online eds.). Ed(s): Dr. Dilip Jeste. American Psychiatric Publishing, Inc., 1000 Wilson Blvd, Ste 1825, Arlington, VA 22209; appi@psych.org; http://www.appi.org. Illus., index, adv. Sample. Refereed. Microform: PQC. Online: EBSCO Publishing; HighWire Press; Northern Light Technology, Inc.; ProQuest Information & Learning; RoweCom Information Quest. *Indexed:* ASG, AgeL, ExcerpMed, IndMed, PsycholAb, SSCI. *Bk. rev.:* 0-2. *Aud.:* Ac.

As an official organ of the American Association for Geriatric Psychiatry, this journal publishes "regular research articles" on various aspects of geriatric psychiatry and "special articles" that focus on scholarly and critical reviews of the literature. Also included are clinical reviews providing current information on a specific topic and directed toward clinicians, brief reports, and invited commentary. Mainly written by medical practitioners, a typical issue is generally composed of theme-based articles presided over by a guest editor and unsolicited papers, related or unrelated to the particular theme, with abstracts provided for the research articles. Recent coverage includes articles on brain imaging and on interventions for Alzheimer's disease. The intended audience is scholars in the field. Suitable for medical and large academic libraries.

503. ***Assisted Living Today.*** [ISSN: 1076-5743] 1993. 9x/yr. USD 30 domestic; USD 60 foreign. Ed(s): Angela Hickman Brady. Assisted Living Federation of America, 11200 Waples Mill Rd., Ste. 150, Fairfax, VA 22030-7407; altoday@strattonpub.com; http://www.alfa.org. Adv. Circ: 15000 Paid and controlled. *Indexed:* AgeL. *Aud.:* Sa.

Independent living is a quality of life not often afforded the elderly. Directed towards the assisted-living housing industry, this monthly magazine includes feature articles and regular sections devoted to conference and member news, educational and legal information, guest editorials, product advertisements, and services. Recent articles cover redefining the assisted-living business and discuss the economic environment. Practical advice and information is offered regarding financial services and assisted-living properties. Marketing information abounds, not only for promoting properties, but also for medical equipment and devices such as "eldercare interiors" (furniture), healthcare services and institutions, and insurance. Suitable for anyone with a personal or business interest in the senior housing industry.

504. ***Canadian Journal on Aging.*** [ISSN: 0714-9808] 1982. q. CND 65 (Individuals, CND 46; Students, CND 25). Ed(s): Francois Beland. The Canadian Association on Gerontology, 100-824 Meath St, Ottawa, ON K1Z 6E8, Canada; info@cagacg.ca; http://www.cagacg.ca/index.htm. Illus., adv. Sample. Refereed. Circ: 1600 Paid. Vol. ends: Winter. *Indexed:* ASG, AgeL, CBCARef, CIJE, CPerI, CommAb, ExcerpMed, PAIS, PsycholAb, SFSA, SSCI, SWR&A, SociolAb. *Bk. rev.:* 1-3, 500-700 words. *Aud.:* Ac, Sa.

A refereed journal published by the Canadian Association on Gerontology. Articles are original research with a Canadian perspective focusing on aging in the areas of biology, educational gerontology, health sciences, psychology, social sciences, and social policy and practice. Most of the authors are Canadian, and articles are written in English or French with abstracts in both languages. Recent articles include "Beauty in Later Life," "Higher Thresholds for Elder Abuse with Age and Rural Residence," and "Aging, Attention, and Bimanual Coordination." Intended for scholars in the field.

Caregiving Online. See *Spotlight on Caregiving* in Electronic Journals, this section.

505. *Clinical Gerontologist: the journal of aging and mental health.* Former titles: *Journal of Aged Care;* (until 1981): *Aged Care and Services Review.* [ISSN: 0731-7115] 1977. q. USD 535 domestic; USD 722.25 Canada; USD 775.75 elsewhere. Ed(s): Terry L Brink. Haworth Press, Inc., 10 Alice St, Binghamton, NY 13904-1580; getinfo@haworthpressinc.com; http://www.haworthpress.com. Illus., index, adv. Sample. Refereed. Circ: 350 Paid. Vol. ends: Summer. Microform: PQC. Reprint: HAW. *Indexed:* ASG, ASSIA, AbAn, AgeL, BiolAb, CINAHL, ExcerpMed, H&SSA, IMFL, MCR, PsycholAb, RiskAb, SFSA, SWR&A, SociolAb. *Aud.:* Ac, Sa.

Research articles written by "geriatric practitioners in settings where empirical observations are recorded and published to advance the work of scholars in geropsychology." Practitioners share their case studies on subjects related to aging such as long-term care and mental health. Periodically, special monographic issues are co-published simultaneously with the journal. Theme issues may extend into two issues; one such title is "Emerging Trends in Psychological Practice in Long-Term Care," Part I & II. Recent special issues cover "Holocaust Survivors' Mental Health" and "The Forgotten Aged: Ethnic, Psychiatric, and Societal Minorities." Abstracts precede articles and are included in the table of contents, making it easy to browse topics. This journal has a clinical focus as compared to the academic title *Journal of Mental Health and Aging.* Recommended for gerontology and mental health practitioners, and academic libraries with gerontology and psychology departments.

The Duplex Planet. See Zines section.

506. *Generations (San Francisco).* [ISSN: 0738-7806] 1976. q. USD 55 (Individuals, USD 38). Ed(s): Mary Johnson. American Society on Aging, 833 Market St, Ste 511, San Francisco, CA 94103-1824; pubsinfo@asaging.org; http://www.asaging.org. Illus., adv. Sample. Refereed. Circ: 10000. Microform: PQC. Online: bigchalk; EBSCO Publishing; Florida Center for Library Automation; Gale Group; OCLC Online Computer Library Center, Inc.; ProQuest Information & Learning; H.W. Wilson. Reprint: PSC. *Indexed:* ASG, AbAn, AgeL, BRI, CBRI, CIJE, CINAHL, HRA, PAIS, PsycholAb, RI-1, SFSA, SSCI, SSI, SociolAb. *Aud.:* Ac, Ga.

Presents in-depth current information about specific topics on aging, giving preference to practice, research, and policy. Recent issues focus on retirement—changing demographics, Social Security reforms, pension changes; and on mental health and mental illness—research in aging and mental health, progress in training specialists. A different type of research journal, *Generations* includes brief, easy-to-read articles (about 4-10 pages) on current issues instead of research studies. Guest editors oversee each issue, providing an introduction and an overview of the topic, including historical and current trends. Appearing irregularly is a useful section highlighting additional resources on the topic. A core resource for academic collections and suitable for large public libraries.

507. *Geriatric Nursing.* [ISSN: 0197-4572] 1980. bi-m. USD 112 (Individuals, USD 56; Students, USD 28). Ed(s): Leslie J. Flatt, Dr. Priscilla R. Ebersole. Mosby, Inc., 11830 Westline Industrial Dr, St Louis, MO 63146-3318; http://www.us.elsevierhealth.com. Illus., index, adv. Sample. Refereed. Circ: 11622. Vol. ends: Nov/Dec. Microform: PQC. Online: EBSCO Publishing; Ovid Technologies, Inc.; RoweCom Information Quest; ScienceDirect. Reprint: PQC. *Indexed:* ASG, AgeL, CINAHL, IndMed, PsycholAb, SSCI. *Bk. rev.:* 1-3, 300 words, signed. *Aud.:* Sa.

Nurses are important caregivers for the elderly, and with the predicted increase in this segment of the population, will become even more so, whether within or outside of the traditional hospital or nursing home setting. *Geriatric Nursing* is the official publication of the National Gerontological Nursing Association and the National Conference of Gerontological Nurse Practitioners. The journal is similar in content to *Journal of Gerontological Nursing.* Recent articles cover Alzheimer's disease, nursing intervention for patients with dementia, and dependency assessment. Although primarily focused on the elderly in the United States, perspectives from other countries are also presented. In addition to subject-based articles written by and directed to practicing nurses and nursing students, there is practical information on grants and awards, announcements of continuing-education opportunities (each issue contains an article and exam that can be submitted for CE credit), and association news. Primarily for practitioners and also suitable for medical and academic libraries with nursing programs.

508. *Geriatrics: medicine for midlife and beyond.* [ISSN: 0016-867X] 1946. m. USD 60 US & Possessions; USD 85 in Canada & Mexico; USD 120 elsewhere. Ed(s): Alice V Luddington. Advanstar Communications Inc., 201 Sandpointe Ave, Ste 600, Santa Ana, CA 92707-8700; info@advanstar.com; http://www.advanstar.com. Illus., index, adv. Sample. Refereed. Circ: 55571. Vol. ends: Dec. Online: bigchalk; EBSCO Publishing; Florida Center for Library Automation; Gale Group; Northern Light Technology, Inc.; OCLC Online Computer Library Center, Inc.; ProQuest Information & Learning; H.W. Wilson. *Indexed:* ASG, AbAn, AgeL, BiolAb, CINAHL, ChemAb, ExcerpMed, GSI, H&SSA, IndMed, PsycholAb, RiskAb, SCI, SSCI. *Aud.:* Sa.

While this title has the look of a doctor's waiting room magazine, it is actually a peer-reviwed monthly geared toward primary-care physicians. One must ignore the heavy advertising (which does manage to keep the subscription price reasonable). Issues include three or so refereed clinical reviews providing the latest research on topics common to general practice (drug interactions, diabetes, heart and prostate health). In addition, the "News Pulse" section contains news updates on matters concerning geriatric medicine; "Abstracts" presents detailed, page-long summaries of recent research in geriatric care; and "Medicare Matters" provides authoritative answers to Medicare-related questions. Although published for physicians, this title is also useful to geriatric nurse practitioners and clinical social workers. It is recommended for the libraries that support these types of programs or clientele.

509. *The Gerontologist.* [ISSN: 0016-9013] 1961. bi-m. USD 198. Ed(s): Laurence Branch. Gerontological Society of America, 1030 15th, NW, Ste 250, Washington, DC 20005-1503; hworley@geron.org; http://www.geron.org. Illus., index, adv. Sample. Refereed. Circ: 7200 Paid. Microform: PQC. Online: bigchalk; Gale Group; HighWire Press; Northern Light Technology, Inc.; OCLC Online Computer Library Center, Inc.; ProQuest Information & Learning. Reprint: PQC. *Indexed:* ASG, AgeL, ArtHuCI, BiolAb, CIJE, CINAHL, ChemAb, ErgAb, ExcerpMed, GSI, IBSS, IndMed, PsycholAb, SFSA, SSCI, SSI, SUSA, SWR&A, SociolAb. *Bk. rev.:* 4-6, 500-700 words. *Aud.:* Ga, Ac.

Published by the Gerontological Society of America, *The Gerontologist* is the most general of their publications (see *Journals of Gerontology, Series A* and *Series B*). The editorial board consists mainly of academics in the social sciences and public health. Research articles are accessible to undergraduates but still useful to scholars and practitioners. Most of the articles deal with social policy and mental health. Recent topics include the economic consequences of widowhood, Medicaid, retirement patterns, physician-assisted suicide, and ethnic and cultural differences in dementia. Each issue contains a "Practice Concepts" section that critically reviews innovations in education or practice. This title is recommended as part of a core collection for academic and special libraries that support a gerontology program.

510. *Gerontology & Geriatrics Education.* [ISSN: 0270-1960] 1980. q. USD 465 domestic; USD 627.75 Canada; USD 674.25 elsewhere. Ed(s): Pearl M. Mosher-Ashley. Haworth Press, Inc., 10 Alice St, Binghamton, NY 13904-1580; getinfo@haworthpressinc.com; http://www.haworthpressinc.com. Illus., index, adv. Sample. Refereed. Circ: 300 Paid. Reprint: HAW. *Indexed:* ASG, AbAn, AgeL, CINAHL, ExcerpMed, IBZ, IMFL, IndMed, PsycholAb, SFSA, SWA, SociolAb. *Aud.:* Ac, Sa.

Articles provide readers with information and ideas to rethink their approaches to teaching in the fields of gerontology and geriatrics. The primary focus is on issues faced in teaching such as program assessments and curriculum changes. Also included are current social and cultural issues, diversity, gender, aging, and technology. Recent articles include "Gender Bias in Gerontological Education," "Gerontology Telecourses," "Assessment of an Online Course on Adult Development, Aging, and Diversity," and "Geriatrics Curriculum for First Year Medical Students." Occasionally, the journal is co-published simultaneously as a monograph, such as the recent "Death Education and Research: Critical Perspectives." Medical students, instructors, physicians, social workers, and others interested in educational preparation of caregivers for the aging will benefit from the research presented in this journal. Recommended for academic libraries and scholars in the medical profession, social work, and gerontological education.

511. ***International Journal of Aging & Human Development: a journal of psychosocial gerontology.*** Formerly (until 1973): *Aging and Human Development.* [ISSN: 0091-4150] 1970. 8x/yr. USD 323 (Individuals, USD 82). Ed(s): Robert G Kunzendorf, Bert Hayslip, Jr. Baywood Publishing Co., Inc., 26 Austin Ave, Amityville, NY 11701; info@baywood.com; http://www.baywood.com. Illus., index, adv. Sample. Refereed. *Indexed:* ASG, ASSIA, AbAn, AgeL, BAS, BRI, BiolAb, CIJE, CommAb, ExcerpMed, HRA, IMFL, IndMed, PsycholAb, SFSA, SSCI, SSI, SWR&A, SociolAb. *Aud.:* Ac, Sa.

A journal presenting original research focusing on "psychological and social studies of aging and the aged." Research articles present observations from other fields to highlight the "human" side of gerontology, or conversely, gerontological observations are used to point out problems in other fields. About five articles are published per issue. Recent issues include such topics as coping with illnesses and grandparents as caregivers. Articles are in English, international in scope, and targeted to a scholarly audience. Recommended for special libraries and academic libraries with gerontology departments or programs.

512. ***Journal of Aging and Ethnicity.*** [ISSN: 1076-1624] 1996. 3x/yr. USD 78 (Individuals, USD 39). Ed(s): Donald E Gelfand. Springer Publishing Company, 536 Broadway, New York, NY 10012; springer@springerpub.com; http://www.springerpub.com. Illus., adv. Sample. Refereed. *Indexed:* AgeL, SWR&A, SociolAb. *Aud.:* Ac, Sa.

The *Journal of Aging and Ethnicity* is a multidisciplinary, peer-reviewed journal of use to individuals interested in research and current issues dealing with the relationship between aging and ethnicity. Original research, review, and historical analysis articles are published. Articles will be of primary use and interest to academics, but some are of interest to practitioners. Recent topics include caregiver burden among Mexican Americans and preventative health behaviors among older Asian and African Americans. This title is similar to the *Journal of Cross-Cultural Gerontology* (see below) but limits itself to groups in North America.

513. ***Journal of Aging and Health: an interdisciplinary research forum.*** [ISSN: 0898-2643] 1989. 5x/yr. GBP 293 print & online eds. in Europe, Middle East, Africa & Australasia. Ed(s): Kyriakos S Markides. Sage Publications, Inc., 2455 Teller Rd, Thousand Oaks, CA 91320; info@sagepub.com; http://www.sagepub.com. Illus., index, adv. Refereed. Circ: 1250. Vol. ends: Nov. *Indexed:* ASG, AgeL, CINAHL, ExcerpMed, H&SSA, IMFL, PsycholAb, SSCI, SociolAb. *Aud.:* Ac, Sa.

An interdisciplinary journal that serves as a "forum for the presentation of research findings and scholarly exchange in the area of aging and health." A broad view of social and behavioral factors related to aging and health is presented. Original research is the primary focus, but review and methodological articles are accepted. It covers disciplines such as public health, social work, medicine, and other related subject areas. A recent special issue is devoted to "From Philosophy to Practice: Selected Issues in Financing and Coordinating Long-Term Care." The intended audience is scholars and researchers since the contributors are primarily made up of these two groups. Health care professionals would also find this journal beneficial.

514. ***Journal of Aging and Physical Activity.*** [ISSN: 1063-8652] 1993. q. USD 184 (Individuals, USD 49). Ed(s): Jessie C. Jones, Debra J. Rose. Human Kinetics Publishers, Inc., PO Box 5076, Champaign, IL 61825-5076; orders@hkusa.com; http://www.humankinetics.com. Illus., adv. Sample. Refereed. Circ: 745 Paid. Vol. ends: Oct. Reprint: PSC. *Indexed:* ASG, AbAn, AgeL, CINAHL, ErgAb, ExcerpMed, IBZ, PEI, SSCI. *Aud.:* Ac, Sa.

This official journal of the International Society for Aging and Physical Activity provides original research articles focused on physical activity for the elderly, and reviews of articles on the subject of aging from related journals. Thematic issues are published occasionally. Recent articles include "Responses of Heart Rate and Vagus Tone to Treadmill Walking on Land and in Water in Healthy Older Adults" and "Effects of a Six-Week Resistance-Training Program on Functional Fitness of Older Adults." Suitable for academic and special libraries.

515. ***Journal of Aging & Social Policy: a journal devoted to aging & social policy.*** [ISSN: 0895-9420] 1989. q. USD 415 domestic; USD 560.25 Canada; USD 601.75 elsewhere. Ed(s): Francis G Caro, Robert Morris. Haworth Press, Inc., 10 Alice St, Binghamton, NY 13904-1580; getinfo@haworthpressinc.com; http://www.haworthpressinc.com. Illus., adv. Sample. Refereed. Circ: 402 Paid. Microform: PQC. Online: Gale Group. Reprint: HAW. *Indexed:* ASG, AbAn, AgeL, BiolDig, CINAHL, GeogAbPG, H&SSA, IBZ, IMFL, PAIS, PSA, RiskAb, SFSA, SSI, SWR&A, SociolAb. *Bk. rev.:* 3, 300-500 words. *Aud.:* Ac, Sa.

This journal publishes research papers on social policy and the aged. Journal issues are divided into two sections, "General Articles," covering social or public policy issues, and "International View," covering policy issues in countries other than the United States. Recent articles focus on such topics as health care, Social Security, crime, long-term care in prison, and consumer satisfaction. Article abstracts are conveniently located in the table of contents. Occasionally, thematic issues are published. A guest editor presides over the issue, usually consisting of 8 to 10 research papers and sometimes published as a hardcover book. Papers from conferences covering a current social or public policy issue are accepted, and authors may be solicited. A recent theme was "Social Security Reform: A Worldwide Phenomenon," which included articles on Social Security reform in the United States, Latin America, western Europe, Asia, and Africa. Suitable for policy makers and academic libraries with programs in gerontology and public policy.

516. ***Journal of Applied Gerontology.*** [ISSN: 0733-4648] 1982. q. USD 468 print & online eds. Ed(s): Larry C Mullins. Sage Publications, Inc., 2455 Teller Rd, Thousand Oaks, CA 91320; info@sagepub.com; http://www.sagepub.com. Illus., index, adv. Refereed. Circ: 1600. Vol. ends: Dec. *Indexed:* ASG, AgeL, ExcerpMed, H&SSA, HRA, IMFL, PsycholAb, RiskAb, SFSA, SSCI, SSI, SociolAb. *Bk. rev.:* 3, 900-1,000 words. *Aud.:* Ac.

Serving as the official journal of the Southern Gerontological Society, the *Journal of Applied Gerontology* includes articles that focus "explicitly on the application of knowledge and insights from research and practice to improvement of the quality of life of older persons." It functions as a forum for dialogue among practitioners, policy makers, and researchers. Some recent articles include "Correlates of Social Function: A Comparison of a Black and a White Sample of Older Persons in Los Angeles," "Driver License Renewal for the Elderly: A Case Study," and "Anatomy of a Choice: Deciding on Assisted Living or Nursing Home Care in Oregon." The journal is a good source of information offering solutions and answers to current issues and questions facing those working with the elderly. Intended for practitioners and also useful to other professionals in gerontology and related fields.

517. ***Journal of Cross-Cultural Gerontology.*** [ISSN: 0169-3816] 1986. q. EUR 362 print or online ed. Ed(s): John W Traphagan. Kluwer Academic Publishers, van Godewijckstraat 30, PO Box 17, Dordrecht, 3300 AA, Netherlands. Illus., index, adv. Sample. Refereed. Vol. ends: No. 4. Microform: PQC. Online: EBSCO Publishing; ingenta.com; Kluwer Online; OCLC Online Computer Library Center, Inc.; Ovid Technologies, Inc.; RoweCom Information Quest; Swets Blackwell. Reprint: SWZ. *Indexed:* ASG, AgeL, AnthLit, BiolAb, IBSS, IBZ, IndMed, PsycholAb, RiskAb, SFSA, SociolAb. *Aud.:* Ac, Sa.

International and interdisciplinary in scope, this journal is intended to serve as "a forum for scholarly discussion of the aging process and the problems of the aged throughout the world." It presents a broad range of articles, about four or five per issue, focusing on research, theory, and applications regarding non-Western societies. Secondarily, articles are included that focus on the aged in Western societies and present comparative studies of topics relevant to the social, economic, historical, and biological aspects of the aging process. Subjects covered are history, anthropology, sociology, political science, psychology, population studies, health, and biology. Special issues are published with assistance from guest editors. Gerontology scholars and faculty in sociology and anthropology would find this journal intellectually informative. Academic libraries would want to consider it for their gerontology collections.

518. ***Journal of Elder Abuse & Neglect.*** [ISSN: 0894-6566] 1988. q. USD 485 domestic; USD 654.75 Canada; USD 703.25 elsewhere. Ed(s): Pamela B. Teaster, Terry Fulmer. Haworth Press, Inc., 10 Alice St, Binghamton, NY 13904-1580; getinfo@haworthpressinc.com; http://www.haworthpressinc.com. Illus., adv. Sample. Refereed. Circ: 800 Paid. Microform: PQC. Online: Gale Group; ProQuest Information & Learning. Reprint: HAW. *Indexed:* ASG, AgeL, CINAHL, CJA, CJPI, H&SSA, IBZ, IMFL, RiskAb, SFSA, SSCI, SSI, SUSA, SWR&A, SociolAb. *Bk. rev.:* 1-3, 300-500 words, signed. *Aud.:* Ac, Sa.

The purpose of this journal is to "study the causes, effects, treatment, and prevention of the mistreatment of older people and disabled adults." Articles alert readers to problem of elder abuse, its causes, and strategies for prevention. Each issue is designed to address a single topic; recent thematic issues focus on "Self Neglect" and "Elder Mistreatment: Ethical Issues, Dilemmas and Decisions." Other topics available for authors to address are conflict resolution, financial exploitation, sexual abuse, and domestic violence. The journal also provides personal commentary and a place for scholars to discuss program development, policy initiatives, and scientific investigation. The scope is primarily abuse and neglect in the United States. It is suitable for researchers, educators, practitioners, and policymakers. A membership benefit of the National Committee for the Prevention of Elder Abuse.

519. ***Journal of Geriatric Psychiatry: a multidiciplinary journal of mental health and aging.*** [ISSN: 0022-1414] 1967. s-a. USD 125 (Individuals, USD 72). International Universities Press, Inc., 59 Boston Post Rd, Box 1524, Madison, CT 06443-1524; office@iup.com; http://www.iup.com. Illus., adv. Sample. Refereed. *Indexed:* ASG, ASSIA, AgeL, BiolAb, CINAHL, ExcerpMed, IMFL, IndMed, PsycholAb, SCI, SFSA, SSCI. *Bk. rev.:* Number varies, lengthy. *Aud.:* Ac, Sa.

A multidisciplinary journal of mental health and aging providing review articles, case histories, and recent treatment interventions for the psychiatric assessment and treatment of the elderly. Although the focus of this journal is mental health, "all relevant and timely subjects will be considered." The focus is on current issues and policies; therefore, the information presented is of immediate, practical use. Articles are written by and for mental health practitioners. Thematic issues are published occasionally focusing on theory, research and clinical application of a particular topic related to mental health and aging. Special issues have included "Recent Developments in Clinical Gerontology: Maximizing Lifespan Potential" and "Reminiscence and Life Review." Readership focus is geriatric psychiatrists, psychologists, social workers, and nurses.

520. ***Journal of Geriatric Psychiatry and Neurology.*** [ISSN: 0891-9887] 1988. q. USD 376 print & online eds. Ed(s): Alan M Mellow. Sage Publications, Inc., 2455 Teller Rd, Thousand Oaks, CA 91320; info@sagepub.com; http://www.sagepub.com. Illus., adv. Sample. Refereed. Circ: 450. Online: bigchalk; EBSCO Publishing; ingenta.com; ProQuest Information & Learning. *Indexed:* ExcerpMed, IndMed, PsycholAb, SCI, SSCI. *Aud.:* Ac, Sa.

The *Journal of Geriatric Psychiatry and Neurology* is the official publication of the Alzheimer's Foundation. It serves as a research publication devoted primarily to providing articles on various clinical and scientific aspects of the psychiatry and neurology of Alzheimer's disease. The majority of editorial board members and article authors have medical degrees and appointments associated with academic institutions. Issues reviewed contained articles on age-related impairments and health service utilization. Recent article titles include "Dementia with Lewy Bodies: Neuropathology" and "Association of Depression with Agitation in Elderly Nursing Home Residents." As described by the title, this publication is directed to clinicians and scientists. In addition, medical libraries and academic libraries with medical collections would want to consider subscribing.

521. ***Journal of Gerontological Nursing: for nursing care of older adults.*** [ISSN: 0098-9134] 1974. m. USD 89 (Individuals, USD 59; USD 19 newsstand/cover). Ed(s): Melissa Long Daddona, Dr. Kathleen C. Buckwalter. Slack, Inc., 6900 Grove Rd, Thorofare, NJ 08086-9447; http://www.slackinc.com. Illus., index, adv. Sample. Refereed. Circ: 9300 Paid. Vol. ends: Dec. Microform: PQC. Online: Northern Light Technology, Inc.; ProQuest Information & Learning. Reprint: PQC. *Indexed:* ASG, AgeL, CINAHL, PsycholAb, SUSA. *Bk. rev.:* 2, 100-300 words, signed. *Aud.:* Ac, Sa.

Similar in content, style, and format to *Geriatric Nursing,* this journal serves as a forum for nurses and nursing students (who are eligible for reduced rate subscriptions) to discuss nursing care of older adults. Most of the articles, written by fellow practitioners, present current information of immediate practical use. Each issue includes feature articles, for example, "Health and Safety Risk at a Skilled Nursing Facility" and "Family Caregiver Assessment." Special sections make up a large part of this journal, such as job announcements, a quiz that can be submitted for continuing-education credit, and "Your Turn," which is designed to support an open dialogue among peers. Other regular items of interest are guest editorials, personal essays, legal issues, and award citations. Written primarily for nurses and nursing students, it is suitable for medical libraries, health care institutions, and programs serving nurse practitioners.

522. ***Journal of Gerontological Social Work.*** [ISSN: 0163-4372] 1978. q. in 2 vols. USD 450 domestic; USD 607.50 Canada; USD 652.50 elsewhere. Ed(s): Rose Dobrof. Haworth Press, Inc., 10 Alice St, Binghamton, NY 13904-1580; getinfo@haworthpressinc.com; http://www.haworthpressinc.com. Illus., adv. Sample. Refereed. Circ: 639 Paid. Microform: PQC. Online: Gale Group. Reprint: HAW. *Indexed:* ASG, ASSIA, AgeL, CINAHL, CommAb, ExcerpMed, HRA, IBZ, IMFL, PSA, PsycholAb, SSCI, SSI, SWR&A, SociolAb. *Bk. rev.:* 0-2, 300-500 words, signed. *Aud.:* Ac, Sa.

Refereed journal publishing original research articles and reports on the elderly from a social work perspective. Articles are written mainly by social work professionals. Recent titles include "The Relationship Between Pre-Retirement Earnings and Health Status in Old Age: Black-White Differences" and "Predictors of Life Satisfaction in Frail Elderly." Occasionally, thematic issues are published, such as "Geriatric Social Work Education," and "Gerontological Social Work: Issues, Challenges, and Potential." Article abstracts are conveniently located in the table of contents and make it easy to browse topics. Recommended for gerontology and social work professionals and academic libraries supporting social work programs.

523. ***Journal of Housing for the Elderly.*** [ISSN: 0276-3893] 1983. s-a. USD 400 domestic; USD 540 Canada; USD 580 elsewhere. Ed(s): Benyamin Schwarz. Haworth Press, Inc., 10 Alice St, Binghamton, NY 13904-1580; getinfo@haworthpressinc.com; http://www.haworthpressinc.com. Illus., adv. Sample. Refereed. Circ: 179 Paid. Microform: PQC. Reprint: HAW. *Indexed:* API, ASG, ASSIA, AgeL, CINAHL, IBZ, IMFL, PAIS, PRA, PsycholAb, SFSA, SUSA, SociolAb. *Aud.:* Ac.

All volumes are published as special issues concentrating on particular topics regarding housing for the elderly. The journal includes special issues, but will soon "contain articles that vary in content, presentation and form without a common denominator." Recent articles focus on housing design, type, and affordability. Although the scope of most articles is the United States and Canada, occasionally an international perspective is presented, for example, "Housing Policy for Frail Elders in Norway: A Study of the Implementation of Housing Reforms in Norwegian Municipalities." Suitable for gerontology and social work professionals and academic libraries supporting architecture and city planning as well as gerontology programs.

524. ***Journal of Mental Health and Aging.*** [ISSN: 1078-4470] 1995. 4x/yr. USD 128 (Individuals, USD 58). Ed(s): Donna Cohen. Springer Publishing Company, 536 Broadway, New York, NY 10012; springer@springerpub.com; http://www.springerpub.com. Illus., adv. Sample. Refereed. Vol. ends: Winter. *Indexed:* ASG, AgeL, CINAHL, ExcerpMed, PAIS, SWR&A, SociolAb. *Bk. rev.:* 1-2, 500+ words. *Aud.:* Ac, Sa.

National and international in scope, this scholarly journal is "dedicated to the dissemination of current research findings, aging studies, policy analysis, and innovations in mental health care." Each issue features an editorial on a current issue and four to five articles on a particular aspect of mental health. Recent article titles inlcude "Social Support and Social Networks in the Last Year of

Life" and "Implications for Grandparents When They Lose Contact With Their Grandchildren." Suitable for a broad range of mental health professionals including clinical care, social services, law, and public policy.

525. *Journal of Nutrition for the Elderly.* [ISSN: 0163-9366] 1980. q. USD 540. Ed(s): Annette B Natow. Haworth Press, Inc., 10 Alice St, Binghamton, NY 13904-1580; getinfo@haworthpressinc.com; http://www.haworthpressinc.com. Illus., adv. Sample. Refereed. Circ: 354 Paid. Vol. ends: Summer. Microform: PQC. Reprint: HAW. *Indexed:* ASG, AbAn, AgeL, Agr, BiolAb, CINAHL, ChemAb, DSA, ExcerpMed, FS&TA, H&SSA, IMFL, MCR, PEI, PsycholAb, RiskAb, SWR&A, WAE&RSA. *Bk. rev.:* 4-5, 300-500 words. *Aud.:* Ac, Sa.

The goal of this journal is to "increase awareness in professionals and lay public of benefits to older adults from nutrition education that promotes... healthful eating habits." Articles present research and current practices in nutrition and aging. Special features include "From the Journals," reviews of journals in the field; and "Noteworthy," current news and reviews. Recent article topics cover nutrition management of hospitalized elderly, home-delivered meal participants, and nutrition programs and education. Nutrition issues of the elderly in other countries are also included, providing an international perspective. To promote browsing, article abstracts are located in the table of contents. Intended for professionals and researchers with an interest in nutrition education and aging. Suitable for medical libraries and academic libraries with medical programs.

526. *Journal of Religious Gerontology: the interdisiplinary journal of practice, theory & applied research.* Formerly (until vol.7, 1990): *Journal of Religion and Aging.* [ISSN: 1050-2289] 1985. q. USD 285. Ed(s): Rev. James W Ellor. Haworth Press, Inc., 10 Alice St, Binghamton, NY 13904-1580; getinfo@haworthpressinc.com; http://www.haworthpressinc.com. Illus., adv. Sample. Refereed. Circ: 380 Paid. Vol. ends: Fall. Reprint: HAW. *Indexed:* ASG, ASSIA, AgeL, ChrPI, IBZ, IMFL, PsycholAb, R&TA, RI-1. *Bk. rev.:* 3-8, 400-500 words. *Aud.:* Ac, Sa.

This interdisciplinary, interfaith professional journal, combining "practical innovation and scholarly insight," offers timely information regarding topics related to the religious and spiritual lives of the elderly. The only journal devoted to religion and aging, it provides original research that "aims to inform religious professionals about developments in new fields of gerontology." Other professionals, administrators, and practitioners who work with elderly people and their families within religious institutions also will benefit from the articles. Practice-based authors are encouraged to contribute work in theology, program development, and other direct service applications. Articles from past issues include "Intergenerational Relationships within the Local Congregation" and "Future of the Church as a Primary Health Place." The journal is also published as a separate thematic issue, with titles such as "Gerontology in Theological Education" and "New Directions in Religion and Aging." The intended audience is pastors, chaplains, educators, administrators, social workers, nurses, physicians, and graduate-school teachers. Suitable for libraries supporting theological seminaries and academic libraries with gerontology and religion collections.

527. *Journal of Women and Aging: the multidiciplinary quarterly of psychosocial practice, theory & research.* [ISSN: 0895-2841] 1989. q. USD 335. Ed(s): J Dianne Garner. Haworth Press, Inc., 10 Alice St, Binghamton, NY 13904-1580; getinfo@haworthpressinc.com; http://www.haworthpressinc.com. Illus., adv. Sample. Refereed. Circ: 366 Paid. Microform: PQC. Online: Gale Group; LexisNexis; ProQuest Information & Learning. Reprint: HAW. *Indexed:* ASG, AbAn, AgeL, CINAHL, CWI, FemPer, GendWatch, H&SSA, IBZ, IMFL, IndMed, SSCI, SWA, SWR&A, SociolAb, WSA, WSI. *Bk. rev.:* 1-3, 300-500 words. *Aud.:* Ga, Ac.

A journal of research studies focusing on various issues such as gender, race, ethnicity, elder care, retirement, sexuality and feminism, health and physical fitness, and nutrition as they relate to older women. Articles are more sociological than medical, unlike most research journals regarding the elderly; for example, "Women's Perceived Body Image: Relations with Personal Happiness" and "Midlife Myths and Realities: Women Reflect on Their Experiences." In addition to journal articles, thematic monographs are published, the most recent two being "Health Expectations for Older Women: International Perspectives" and "Fundamentals of Feminist Gerontology." It is the only title to focus solely on women and aging. Intended for scholars in gerontology, it would also be of interest to academic libraries supporting a women's studies program.

528. *Journals of Gerontology. Series A: Biological Sciences & Medical Sciences.* Supersedes in part (in 1995): *Journal of Gerontology.* [ISSN: 1079-5006] 1946. m. USD 485 (Individuals, USD 222). Ed(s): Dr. John A Faulkner, John Morley. Gerontological Society of America, 1030 15th, NW, Ste 250, Washington, DC 20005-1503; http://www.geron.org. Illus., index, adv. Sample. Refereed. Circ: 4373 Paid and controlled. Vol. ends: Dec. Microform: PQC. Online: Factiva; Gale Group; HighWire Press; OCLC Online Computer Library Center, Inc.; ProQuest Information & Learning. Reprint: PQC. *Indexed:* ASG, AbAn, AgeL, ArtHuCI, BRI, BiolAb, CBRI, CIJE, CINAHL, ChemAb, DSA, ErgAb, ExcerpMed, HortAb, IndMed, IndVet, PAIS, PsycholAb, RRTA, S&F, SCI, SFSA, SSCI, SSI, SUSA, SWR&A, VetBull. *Aud.:* Ac, Sa.

Published by the Gerontological Society of America, this journal is actually two journals issued as one. *Biological Sciences* publishes original research articles on the biological aspects of aging (including research using nonhuman subjects). Recent topics include cellular resistance to oxidative damage and the effect of aging and obesity on insulin responsiveness. *Medical Sciences* publishes original research articles that focus on all aspects of medical services related to aging. Articles published here are more practical in nature and include such subjects as protein requirements in elderly women and nutritional factors in Alzheimer's disease. Both sections have their own editor and editorial board and separate policies and pagination. This journal is heavily indexed and is considered a seminal journal in the field of gerontology; as such, it is core component of an academic collection.

529. *Journals of Gerontology. Series B: Psychological Sciences & Social Sciences.* Supersedes in part (in 1995): *Journal of Gerontology.* [ISSN: 1079-5014] 1946. bi-m. USD 210 (Individuals, USD 101). Ed(s): Margie Lachman, Fredric D Wolinsky. Gerontological Society of America, 1030 15th, NW, Ste 250, Washington, DC 20005-1503; http://www.geron.org. Illus., index, adv. Sample. Refereed. Circ: 6459 Paid and controlled. Vol. ends: Nov. Microform: PQC. Online: Factiva; HighWire Press; OCLC Online Computer Library Center, Inc.; ProQuest Information & Learning. Reprint: PQC. *Indexed:* ASG, AbAn, AgeL, ArtHuCI, BRI, BiolAb, CBRI, CINAHL, CJA, ChemAb, DSA, ErgAb, ExcerpMed, HRA, IndMed, PAIS, PsycholAb, SCI, SFSA, SSCI, SSI, SUSA, SWR&A. *Aud.:* Ac, Sa.

Similar to the title above, *Journals of Gerontology, Series B* is also published by the Gerontological Society of America and is two journals in one. *Psychological Sciences* publishes research and review articles on the clinical, developmental, and social psychology of aging. *Social Sciences* publishes research and review articles dealing with the issues of aging from a variety of disciplines, including anthropology, social work, economics, demographics, and political science. Both sections have their own editor and editorial board and separate policies and pagination. Like *Series A*, this journal is heavily indexed and considered a seminal journal in the field of gerontology; as such, it is a core component of an academic collection.

Modern Maturity. See *AARP: The Magazine.*

My Generation. See *AARP: The Magazine.*

530. *New Choices: the magazine for your health, money & travel.* Former titles (until 1995): *New Choices for Retirement Living;* (until 1992): *New Choices for the Best Years;* (until 1989): *50 Plus;* (1972-1978): *Retirement Living; Harvest Years.* [ISSN: 1085-1003] 1960. 10x/yr. USD 15; USD 2.95 newsstand/cover per issue. Ed(s): Greg Daugherty. Reader's Digest Association, Inc, Reader's Digest Rd, Pleasantville, NY 10570-7000; newchoices@readersdigest.com. Illus., adv. Sample. Circ: 619352 Paid. Vol. ends: Dec. Reprint: PQC. *Indexed:* AgeL, CINAHL, MagInd, RGPR. *Aud.:* Ga.

This general-interest publication from Reader's Digest is a lifestyle magazine primarily for those between 50 and retirement. The editor notes that readers "already enjoying retirement will also find useful and inspiring information in its pages." Each issue contains several feature-length articles covering a standard range of topics—travel, finances, careers, health, and medicine. There are also regular columns on these topics and others, such as cooking, taxes, retirement planning, bargains, and online, which provide short news briefs and information. Another regular section, "New Choices in Retirement," contains news and information for those who are already retired. While this publication is similar to *Modern Maturity* (see above), it is glossier and slightly more upscale.

531. *Physical & Occupational Therapy in Geriatrics: current trends in geriatric rehabilitation.* [ISSN: 0270-3181] 1980. q. USD 475. Ed(s): Ellen Dunleavey Taira. Haworth Press, Inc., 10 Alice St, Binghamton, NY 13904-1580; getinfo@haworthpressinc.com; http://www.haworthpressinc.com. Illus., adv. Sample. Refereed. Circ: 511 Paid. Microform: PQC. Reprint: HAW. *Indexed:* ASG, AgeL, BiolAb, CINAHL, ExcerpMed, IMFL, MCR, PAIS, PEI, PsycholAb, RiskAb, SWR&A. *Bk. rev.:* 1-4, 250-400 words, signed. *Aud.:* Ac, Sa.

A journal presenting articles devoted to practical application of the latest information regarding physical and mental rehabilitation therapies for the elderly. Topics have ranged from post-illness therapy to the use of computer technology. Issues reviewed contained articles on memory and motor learning, mobility devices, motor control, and assessing home modifications. Occasionally, separate issues are published as monographs with such titles as "The Mentally Impaired Elderly: Strategies and Interventions to Maintain Function" and "Therapeutic Interventions for the Person with Dementia." The primary intended audience is practitioners, academics, and students of occupational therapy.

532. *Psychology and Aging.* [ISSN: 0882-7974] 1986. q. USD 279 (Members, USD 56; Non-members, USD 114). Ed(s): Dr. Leah L Light. American Psychological Association, 750 First St, NE, Washington, DC 20002-4242; journals@apa.org; http://www.apa.org/. Illus., index, adv. Sample. Refereed. Circ: 2800. Vol. ends: Feb. Microform: PQC. Online: EBSCO Publishing; Gale Group; OCLC Online Computer Library Center, Inc.; Ovid Technologies, Inc.; ProQuest Information & Learning; ScienceDirect. Reprint: PSC. *Indexed:* ASG, ASSIA, AgeL, ExcerpMed, IMFL, IndMed, PsycholAb, SSCI, SSI, SWR&A. *Aud.:* Ac, Sa.

Psychology and Aging publishes "original research articles on adult development and aging, including reports of research that may be applied." Article titles include "Aging and Autobiographical Memory" and "Age and Ethnicity Differences in Storytelling to Young Children." Articles reporting theoretical analyses, clinical problems, or policy issues may appear even though the focus is on original research. A "Brief Reports" section consisting of short articles (and short seems to be the only distinguishing factor), as compared to research articles, is included in some issues. Written by academic psychologists for other professionals in psychology and related fields.

533. *Research on Aging: a quarterly of social gerontology and adult development.* [ISSN: 0164-0275] 1979. bi-m. GBP 382 print & online eds. in Europe, Middle East, Africa & Australasia. Ed(s): Angela O'Rand. Sage Publications, Inc., 2455 Teller Rd, Thousand Oaks, CA 91320; info@sagepub.com; http://www.sagepub.com. Illus., index, adv. Sample. Refereed. Circ: 1400. Vol. ends: Dec. *Indexed:* ASG, AbAn, AgeL, CJA, ExcerpMed, HRA, IMFL, PsycholAb, SFSA, SSCI, SSI, SWR&A, SociolAb. *Aud.:* Ac.

International and interdisciplinary in scope, *Research on Aging* publishes original research and review articles in the field of social gerontology. Editorial board members and contributing authors are professors and researchers in the fields of sociology, psychology, anthropology, public health, political science, and economics, as well as gerontology. Recent topics include attitudes toward governmental policies, caregiver and patient relationships, elder care programs, and older Americans and financial satisfaction. Thematic issues are occasionally published. This title is heavily indexed and is considered a core journal for an academic collection.

534. *Secure Retirement: the newsmagazine for mature Americans.* Formerly (until 1992): *Saving Social Security.* [ISSN: 1069-6911] 1983. bi-m. Members, USD 10. Ed(s): Angela Angerosa. National Committee to Preserve Social Security and Medicare, 10 G St, N E, Ste 600, Washington, DC 20002-4213; secure_retirement@ncpssm.org. Illus., adv. Sample. Circ: 1254000. Vol. ends: Dec. *Indexed:* AgeL. *Aud.:* Ga, Sa.

The future of Social Security in the United States is a topic currently under much debate. This magazine is the official publication of the National Committee to Preserve Social Security and Medicare (NCPSSM). NCPSSM claims to be the second largest senior lobbying group in the United States. Among other things, the NCPSSM aims to remove Social Security from the federal budget calculations and to protect the cost-of-living provisions of Social Security. *Secure Retirement* focuses on Social Security and Medicare programs in the United States. Each issue contains feature-length articles on how the current programs are administered and on pending and new legislation that would effect Social Security and Medicare. In addition, there are articles on travel and regular columns such as "Ask Mary Jane," which answers questions about benefits and rules of Social Security and Medicare, and "We Salute," which profiles members of NCPSSM. The political and policy goals of NCPSSM are evident in these articles; nonetheless, this title will be of interest to anyone already receiving these benefits and those who will in the future.

535. *Social Security Bulletin.* [ISSN: 0037-7910] 1937. q. USD 23. Ed(s): Marilyn R Thomas. U.S. Social Security Administration, Office of Research, Evaluation and Statistics (ORES), I T C Building, 8th Fl, 500 E St, S W, Washington, DC 20254; ores.publications@ssa.gov; http://www.ssa.gov. Illus., index. Sample. Vol. ends: Dec. Microform: MIM; CIS; PMC; PQC. Online: Chadwyck-Healey Incorporated; EBSCO Publishing; Florida Center for Library Automation; Gale Group; Northern Light Technology, Inc.; OCLC Online Computer Library Center, Inc.; ProQuest Information & Learning; H.W. Wilson. Reprint: CIS; PQC; WSH. *Indexed:* ABIn, ASG, AgeL, AmStI, BPI, CLI, ExcerpMed, ILP, IUSGP, IndMed, JEL, LRI, MCR, PAIS, SSCI, SSI, SWR&A. *Aud.:* Ac, Sa.

Published by the Social Security Administration (SSA), the *Social Security Bulletin* addresses all aspects of the Social Security system in the United States (i.e., income supplements for the aged, disabled, or orphaned). Each issue contains three of four research articles written by SSA staff members. These articles are laden with statistics and statistical analysis. A typical article contains five or more charts or tables. While some articles present a historical analysis, most articles reflect current issues or projections. New to the journal is a section called "Perspectives." It includes one or two articles authored by non-SSA researchers on topics that are related to social security and benefits. Recent titles include "What Stock Market Returns to Expect for the Future" and "Attrition in the New Beneficiary Survey and Follow-up." All of the research articles are also avaliable at www.ssa.gov/policy/pubs/SSB. In addition to the articles, each issue also presents current news in the field of Social Security, "Social Security at a Glance" (current information about payments), and "Current Operating Statistics." As a government document, this title can be selected by libraries in the federal depository program or purchased directly from the Government Printing Office. The *Annual Statistical Supplement* is also included with an annual subscription.

536. *Topics in Geriatric Rehabilitation.* [ISSN: 0882-7524] 1985. q. USD 199 (Individuals, USD 89). Lippincott Williams & Wilkins, 16522 Hunters Green Pkwy., Hagerstown, MD 21740; http://www.lww.com. Illus. Sample. Refereed. Circ: 2581 Paid. Online: EBSCO Publishing; Florida Center for Library Automation; Gale Group; Ovid Technologies, Inc.; ProQuest Information & Learning. *Indexed:* ASG, AgeL, CINAHL, ExcerpMed, IMFL, SSCI. *Aud.:* Sa.

This journal is aimed at the "health care professional practicing in the area of geriatric rehabilitation." As the title suggests, each issue has a topical theme. Recent topics include "Facilitating Communication in the Older Person" and "Home Care." Research articles are authored by academics and practitioners and are well written and accessible. This is a useful title because of the broad coverage it gives each topic and its focus on delivering useful information for the practitioner. See also *Physical and Occupational Therapy in Geriatrics* (above in this section).

Travel 50 & Beyond. See Travel and Tourism section.

Electronic Journals

537. ***A O A eNews.*** 2003. m. U.S. Department of Health and Human Services, Administration on Aging, 200 Independence Ave, SW, Washington, DC 20201; http://www.aoa.dhhs.gov. *Aud.:* Ga.

This monthly e-newletter is produced by the Administration on Aging (AoA). It is designed to provide "information of importance to the State and Area Agencies on Aging, members of the Leadership Council of Aging Organizations, grantees, tribal organizations, and service providers." The newsletter intends to be brief, and the format is conducive to providing up-to-date information to readers. There is also information about the AoA, its mission, organizational structure, budget, and more. The newsletter can be viewed in Microsoft Word and Adobe Acrobat pdf formats or downloaded. Although targeted to federal agencies serving the aged, the newsletter contains a wealth of information that would interest seniors and others working with the elderly. Suitable for policy makers and anyone interested in AoA news and government information concerning the aged.

538. ***N A I C Online Newsletter.*** 1996. q. National Aging Information Center, 7830 Old Georgetown Rd Ste 100, Bethesda, MD 20814; http://www.aoa.dhhs.gov/naic. *Aud.:* Sa.

A government publication of the National Aging Information Center, this is primarily for the professional who works with the elderly and/or is doing research in the area. Particularly useful for statistical data and reports on the latest laws and research in the field. (BK)

539. ***Senior World Online.*** 2000. w. Harlan Iowa Newspapers, 1114 7th St, Harlan, IA 51537; http://www.seniorworld.com. *Aud.:* Ga.

"For active seniors in the digital age," this attractive, colorful e-publication is directed toward active seniors interested in health, home, leisure and travel, the arts, and general news items. Each section includes a host of articles that are easy to access. A menu on each screen points the reader to an array of topics. Recent articles cover a personal account of a trip to Panama, a menopause diet and cookbook, and parent/child relationships. Photographs accompany many of the articles. *Senior World* also serves as a gateway to additional information on the Internet such as medical supplement insurance, weight loss programs, and senior housing. New sections are planned: directory, calendar, classifieds, shopping, forums, and more. When you enter the web site you are automatically subscribed. Suitable for active seniors of all ages and recommended for public libraries and institutions serving seniors.

540. ***Spotlight on Caregiving: caregiving newsletter online.*** Formerly: *Caregiving Online.* 1997. m. Free. Ed(s): Denise Brown. Tad Publishing Co., PO Box 224, Park Ridge, IL 60068; http://www.caregiving.com/. *Aud.:* Ga.

Written by the editor with assistance from readers and experts, this online newsletter provides tools and advice on how to handle most situations faced by caregivers. Although aimed at the caregiver, there is useful information for the elderly. The newsletter has three major content sections: "Our Care," timeout techniques and information for the caregiver, "Support Center," personal stories and more, and "E-mail Denise," described by the editor as "a Dear Abby for caregivers." Also presented are strategies for coping, including the six stages of caregiving, a tip of the week, and the latest how-to information related to elder care. For sources of additional information, the newsletter references the web site Caregiver.com, provides the reader with an opportunity to join a support group and makes available access to professional advice via "Ask an Expert." *Spotlight on Caregiving* is a survivor's manual for anyone caring for an aging relative or friend. Recommended to public libraries, institutions supporting elder care, and anyone currently or soon to be caring for an elderly person.

■ AGRICULTURE

Duncan McClusky, Branch Librarian, College of Agricultural and Environmental Sciences Tifton Campus, University of Georgia, Tifton, GA 31793

Introduction

It is difficult for farming families to keep their farms. Farmers in the United States continue to face difficult meteorological conditions and competition from crops produced in other countries. Urban sprawl is also encroaching on some agricultural land. Concerns over genetically modified foods have limited the selling of some crops in the marketplace. Research on agricultural water usage is being conducted due to the high demand for water by municipalities and other industries. Researchers continue investigating technological advances in precision agriculture, new cultivars, value-added agriculture, and variable-rate irrigation to assist the farmer. *Agricola* (http://www.nal.usda.gov/ag98/ag98.html), produced by the National Agricultural Library, and *Agris* (http://www.fao.org/agris), produced by the United Nations Food and Agriculture Organization, continue to be available for free on the web.

Basic Periodicals

Hs, Ga: *Amber Waves, Farm Journal, Progressive Farmer, Successful Farming;* Ac: *American Journal of Alternative Agriculture, Crop Science, Journal of Animal Science, Journal of Dairy Science, Poultry Science.*

Basic Abstracts and Indexes

Agricola, Biological and Agricultural Index, CAB Abstract Journals

541. ***The Agricultural Education Magazine.*** Formerly (until 1980): *Agricultural Education.* [ISSN: 0732-4677] 1929. m. USD 10; USD 20 foreign. Ed(s): Glenn Anderson. Agricultural Education Magazine, Inc., 10171 Suzanne Dr, Mechanicsville, VA 23116-4028. Illus., index. Sample. Circ: 4500. Vol. ends: No. 6. Microform: PQC. Online: OCLC Online Computer Library Center, Inc.; ProQuest Information & Learning; H.W. Wilson. Reprint: PQC. *Indexed:* Agr, CIJE, EduInd. *Aud.:* Hs, Ac.

Each year this professional journal from the National Council for Agricultural Education establishes a theme, and theme editors are chosen for each issue to concentrate on a subject within the theme. The intent of the journal is to be a resource for all those involved in agricultural education. Articles "based on research or debating current issues in agricultural education will be particularly welcome." A section of general articles is included in each issue as well.

542. ***Agricultural History.*** [ISSN: 0002-1482] 1927. q. USD 145 print & online eds. USD 35 newsstand/cover. Ed(s): R Douglas Hurt. University of California Press, Journals Division, 2000 Center St, Ste 303, Berkeley, CA 94704-1223; journals@ucop.edu; http://www.ucpress.edu/journals. Illus., index, adv. Sample. Refereed. Circ: 1200 Paid. Vol. ends: Fall. Microform: PQC. Online: EBSCO Publishing; Florida Center for Library Automation; Gale Group; Ingenta Select; Northern Light Technology, Inc.; OCLC Online Computer Library Center, Inc. *Indexed:* ABS&EES, Agr, AmH&L, ArtHuCI, B&AI, BAS, BiolAb, BrArAb, CJA, DSA, EnvAb, ForAb, HortAb, HumInd, IBSS, IBZ, NumL, RRTA, S&F, SSCI, VetBull, WAE&RSA. *Bk. rev.:* 15-30, 150-600 words. *Aud.:* Ac, Sa.

This journal focuses on all aspects of agricultural history and rural life from any country. There are approximately four articles in each issue as well as announcements and book reviews. One recent issue provides an index to 25 volumes (26-50) covering the period from 1952 to 1976. This publication would be of interest to academic agricultural researchers and agricultural history enthusiasts.

543. ***Agricultural Research.*** [ISSN: 0002-161X] 1953. m. USD 45 domestic. Ed(s): Robert Sowers. U.S. Department of Agriculture, Agricultural Research Service, 5601 Sunnyside Ave, Beltsville, MD 20705-5130; armag@asrr.arsusda.gov; http://www.ars.usda.gov/is/AR. Illus. Circ: 39000. Vol. ends: Dec. Microform: PQC. Online: bigchalk; EBSCO Publishing; Florida Center for Library Automation; Gale Group;

Northern Light Technology, Inc.; OCLC Online Computer Library Center, Inc.; ProQuest Information & Learning. *Indexed:* Agr, BiogInd, BiolAb, BiolDig, C&ISA, ChemAb, DSA, EnvAb, ExcerpMed, ForAb, GardL, GeoRef, HortAb, IndVet, PollutAb, S&F, VetBull. *Aud.:* Hs, Ga, Ac.

Research by U. S. Department of Agriculture (USDA) scientists that benefits farmers or prevents the outbreak of disease are reported in this publication. Most articles are less than two pages long and written so that a nonscientist can understand them. This journal is available online back to 1996, and there is an online index by title and keyword back to 1978. This publication is useful for those wanting to check on current USDA research. "Complimentary 1-year subscriptions are available directly from ARS to public libraries, schools, USDA employees, and the news media. Call 301-504-1660, or e-mail armag@ars.usda.gov."

544. ***Agriculture, Ecosystems and Environment.*** Incorporates (1979-1985): *Protection Ecology;* Formed by the merger of (1974-1982): *Agriculture and Environment;* (1974-1982): *Agro-Ecosystems.* [ISSN: 0167-8809] 1982. 18x/yr. EUR 1766. Ed(s): M R Carter. Elsevier BV, Sara Burgerhartstraat 25, Amsterdam, 1055 KV, Netherlands; nlinfo-f@elsevier.nl; http://www.elsevier.nl. Illus., adv. Sample. Refereed. Vol. ends: Dec. Microform: PQC. Online: ingenta.com; ScienceDirect; Swets Blackwell. Reprint: SWZ. *Indexed:* Agr, ApEcolAb, B&AI, BiolAb, ChemAb, DSA, EngInd, EnvAb, ExcerpMed, FPA, FS&TA, ForAb, GeoRef, GeogAbPG, HortAb, IndVet, PollutAb, RRTA, S&F, SCI, SSCI, SWRA, VetBull, WAE&RSA, ZooRec. *Bk. rev.:* 7, 500-1,000 words. *Aud.:* Ac, Sa.

Approximately eight articles are included in each issue covering the "interface between agriculture and the environment." Full-text pre-publication articles are available electronically on the publisher's web site for the journal. Selected articles on a particular theme or from a conference may be compiled in a special issue. A selection of articles from the journal is now being published as *Applied Soil Ecology.* This publication would be valuable to researchers interested in environmental issues.

545. ***Agronomy Journal: an international journal.*** Incorporates (1988-1999): *Journal of Production Agriculture;* Formerly: *American Society of Agronomy. Journal.* [ISSN: 0002-1962] 1907. bi-m. Non-members, USD 216. Ed(s): Calvin H Pearson. American Society of Agronomy, Inc., 677 S Segoe Rd, Madison, WI 53711; http://www.agronomy.org/. Illus., index, adv. Sample. Refereed. Circ: 7650 Paid. Vol. ends: Nov/Dec. Microform: PMC. Online: EBSCO Publishing; HighWire Press; OCLC Online Computer Library Center, Inc.; ProQuest Information & Learning; Swets Blackwell; H.W. Wilson. *Indexed:* Agr, B&AI, BiolAb, CAPS, ChemAb, DSA, EngInd, EnvAb, ExcerpMed, FS&TA, ForAb, HortAb, IndVet, M&GPA, RRTA, S&F, SCI, SWRA, VetBull, WAE&RSA. *Aud.:* Ac, Sa.

This society publication covers all aspects of agronomy and separates the papers into subjects such as corn, cotton, fertilizer management, instrumentation, modeling, mycorrhizal, nitrogen management, remote sensing, rice, seed, sorghum, tillage, and wheat. Selected conference symposium papers may be published together in one issue as well. This journal would be useful to an academic or research facility working in agronomy.

546. ***Amber Waves: the economics of food, farming, natural resources and rural America.*** Formed by the 2003 merger of: *Agricultural Outlook; Food Review; Rural America.* [ISSN: 1545-8741] 2003. 5x/yr. USD 49.95 domestic; USD 99.90 foreign. U.S. Economic Research Service, Department of Agriculture, 1800 M St, N W, Ste 3, Washington, DC 20036-5828; ersinfo@ers.usda.gov; http://www.ers.usda.gov. *Aud.:* Hs, Ga.

Three former Economic Research Service journals were merged into this one journal to report on the research and activities of the USDA. The electronic version will have additional articles that are not included in the print copy and will also be updated more frequently. This journal will be valuable to people interested in the economics of agriculture.

American Journal of Agricultural Economics. See Economics section.

547. ***American Journal of Alternative Agriculture.*** [ISSN: 0889-1893] 1986. q. USD 132 (Individuals, USD 45). CABI Publishing, Wallingford, OC10 8DE, United Kingdom; orders@cabi.org; http://www.cabi.org. Illus. Sample. Refereed. Circ: 1000. *Indexed:* Agr, B&AI, DSA, EngInd, EnvAb, FPA, FS&TA, ForAb, GeogAbPG, HortAb, PollutAb, RRTA, S&F, SSCI, VetBull, WAE&RSA. *Bk. rev.:* 2-4, 400-600 words. *Aud.:* Ga, Ac.

In 2002, CABI Publishing started this journal in print and electronically. It is "devoted to publishing original research and review articles on the biological, physical, social science, and policy aspects of alternative agriculture." Five to eight articles appear in each issue. Anyone interested in organic farming or other alternative farming activities would enjoy this journal.

548. ***American Society of Agricultural Engineers. Transactions.*** [ISSN: 0001-2351] 1958. bi-m. Members, USD 106; Non-members, USD 315. Ed(s): Glenn Laing. American Society of Agricultural Engineers, 2950 Niles Rd., St. Joseph, MI 49085-9659; hq@asae.org; http://www.asae.org. Illus., index. Sample. Circ: 1000. Vol. ends: Nov/Dec. *Indexed:* Agr, B&AI, BiolAb, C&ISA, CAPS, ChemAb, DSA, EngInd, EnvAb, ExcerpMed, FPA, FS&TA, ForAb, GeoRef, GeogAbPG, HortAb, IndVet, M&GPA, PollutAb, S&F, SCI, SWRA, VetBull, WAE&RSA. *Aud.:* Ac, Sa.

Articles are published for engineers working in agriculture, food, and other bioresource industries. Sections include Power and Machinery, Soil and Water, and Food and Process Engineering. In the Emerging Areas section are Information and Electrical Technologies and Biological Engineering. Issues are available online from 2000 forward, and as funds permit earlier years may be added. Approximately 20,000 pages are added electronically each year. Abstracts of papers in each issue are printed in the last few pages. This journal should be in any academic library providing support for agricultural or engineering programs.

549. ***Computers and Electronics in Agriculture: an international journal.*** Incorporates (in 1998): *A I Applications;* Which superseded (1987-1990): *A I Applications in Natural Resource Management.* [ISSN: 0168-1699] 1984. 12x/yr. EUR 1117. Ed(s): D L Schmoldt, Sidney W R Cox. Elsevier BV, Sara Burgerhartstraat 25, Amsterdam, 1055 KV, Netherlands; nlinfo-f@elsevier.nl; http://www.elsevier.nl. Illus. Sample. Refereed. Vol. ends: Dec. Microform: PQC. Online: ingenta.com; ScienceDirect; Swets Blackwell. *Indexed:* Agr, BiolAb, C&ISA, CAPS, DSA, EngInd, FPA, FS&TA, ForAb, GeogAbPG, HortAb, IndVet, RRTA, S&F, SWRA, VetBull, WAE&RSA. *Aud.:* Ac, Sa.

This international journal contains four to six articles per issue covering the use of computers, software, and electronic instrumentation in the fields of agriculture, forestry, horticulture, aquaculture, veterinary medicine, and food processing. Special issues have covered topics such as artificial intelligence in agriculture and advances in field instrumentation. Color images may be included in the online version whether they appear in the print edition or not. This journal is valuable in any agricultural collection, especially where researchers are working on precision agriculture.

Country Woman. See Women section.

550. ***Crop Science: a journal serving the international community of crop scientists.*** [ISSN: 0011-183X] 1961. bi-m. Non-members, USD 241. Ed(s): Nicholas Rhodehamed, Keith Karnok. Crop Science Society of America, 677 S Segoe Rd, Madison, WI 53711; http://www.crops.org. Illus., index, adv. Refereed. Circ: 7300. Vol. ends: Nov/Dec. Online: EBSCO Publishing; Florida Center for Library Automation; Gale Group; HighWire Press; Northern Light Technology, Inc.; ProQuest Information & Learning; ScienceDirect; Swets Blackwell. *Indexed:* Agr, B&AI, BioEngAb, BiolAb, BiolDig, CAPS, ChemAb, DSA, ExcerpMed, FS&TA, ForAb, HortAb, IndVet, RRTA, S&F, SCI, SWRA, WAE&RSA. *Aud.:* Ac.

This association journal covers research in crop breeding, genetics and cytology, crop physiology and metabolism, crop ecology, production and management, turfgrass science, crop quality and utilization, cell biology and molecular genetics, and plant genetic resources. New cultivars, germplasms, parental lines, and genetic stocks are registered in this publication. Short abstracts for selected articles are included near the beginning of the issue. This journal is valuable to any agriculture collection.

551. ***Experimental Agriculture.*** [ISSN: 0014-4797] 1965. q. USD 298. Ed(s): M K Carr. Cambridge University Press, The Edinburgh Bldg, Shaftesbury Rd, Cambridge, CB2 2RU, United Kingdom; information@cambridge.org; http://uk.cambridge.org/journals. Illus., adv. Refereed. Vol. ends: Nov/Dec. Microform: PQC. Online: EBSCO Publishing; OCLC Online Computer Library Center, Inc.; RoweCom Information Quest; Swets Blackwell. *Indexed:* Agr, B&AI, BiolAb, CAPS, ChemAb, DSA, EngInd, FS&TA, ForAb, HortAb, IndVet, PollutAb, RRTA, S&F, SCI, SWRA, VetBull, WAE&RSA. *Bk. rev.:* 5-10, 200 words. *Aud.:* Ac, Sa.

This scientific publication concentrates on agronomy as well as agricultural production systems in the tropical or warmer regions of the world. Authors may report on original research, survey methodology, discuss issues related to developing agricultural areas, review a book, or present an occasional invited review paper. Recent papers have reported on root characteristics of cowpeas, effects of fertilizer on maize and wheat yields, and responses of cassava to water stress. Full text is available electronically back to 1997. This journal would be useful in a research or specialized library serving patrons who are working in tropical agriculture.

552. ***Farm Journal: the magazine of American agriculture.*** [ISSN: 0014-8008] 1877. 12x/yr. USD 19.50 domestic. Ed(s): Karen Freiberg, Sonja Hillgren. Farm Journal, Corp., 1818 Market St 31st Fl, Philadelphia, PA 19103-3654; http://www.agweb.com. Illus., adv. Circ: 600000 Paid and controlled. Vol. ends: Dec. Microform: PQC. Online: Gale Group; ProQuest Information & Learning. Reprint: PQC. *Indexed:* MagInd, RGPR. *Aud.:* Hs, Ga.

This journal, which celebrated its 125th anniversary in 2001, covers business information for people who own farms or ranches. There are six to ten articles in each issue. Regular department features include Machinery Today, Technology Alert, $100 Ideas, and Kitchen Table. Regular columns include Washington, Outlook, John's World, Helpline, and Viewpoint. This journal is available free on the web and has links to other publications such as *Dairy Today, Beef Today, Top Producer,* and *Ag Day.*

553. ***Feedstuffs: the weekly newspaper for agribusiness.*** [ISSN: 0014-9624] 1929. w. USD 135. Ed(s): Sarah Muirhead. Farm Progress Companies, 191 S Gary Ave, Carol Stream, IL 60188; info@farmprogress.com; http://www.farmprogress.com/. Illus., adv. Sample. Circ: 15650. Vol. ends: Dec. Microform: PQC. Online: Florida Center for Library Automation; Gale Group; OCLC Online Computer Library Center, Inc. Reprint: PQC. *Indexed:* Agr, B&I, BiolAb, ChemAb, DSA, IndVet, LRI, RRTA, S&F, VetBull, WAE&RSA. *Aud.:* Ga, Ac, Sa.

This tabloid-format publication rotates a section among areas such as dairy, beef, and swine. USDA reports on cold storage, livestock slaughter, agricultural prices, chicken and eggs, hogs and pigs, and egg products rotate as well. Regular features include business report, bottom line, mill market, ingredient market, grains and ingredients, and livestock and poultry. The annual reference issue provides statistics on animal production, current information on animal nutrition, and information for feed manufacturers. Issues back to 1996 can be accessed online. Electronically, the publication has an events calendar and a feed market directory. Many articles are short, and this publication would be useful to someone trying to keep current on feeds.

554. ***Hoard's Dairyman: the national dairy farm magazine.*** [ISSN: 0018-2885] 1885. s-m. 20/yr. USD 16 domestic; USD 40 foreign. Ed(s): W D Knox. W.D. Hoard and Sons Co., PO Box 801, Fort Atkinson, WI 53538; hoards@hoards.com; http://www.hoards.com/. Illus., index, adv. Circ: 88160 Paid. Vol. ends: Dec. Microform: PQC. Reprint: PQC. *Indexed:* B&AI, DSA, FS&TA, RRTA, WAE&RSA. *Aud.:* Ga, Ac, Sa.

This folio-sized publication provides brief articles on subjects of interest to dairy farmers. Coverage includes articles on people in the field, information on feeds and feeding, business aspects, veterinary news, FFA and 4H, and government relations. The electronic version includes a youth corner, a youth quiz, and a farm survey. This journal would be valuable for a library near dairy cattle farms.

555. ***Journal of Agricultural and Food Chemistry.*** [ISSN: 0021-8561] 1953. bi-w. USD 991 (Individual members, USD 108; Students, USD 81). Ed(s): James N Seiber. American Chemical Society, 1155 16th St, N W, Washington, DC 20036; service@acs.org; http://pubs.acs.org. Illus., adv. Refereed. Circ: 2850. Vol. ends: Dec. Online: EBSCO Publishing; Swets Blackwell. *Indexed:* AS&TI, B&AI, BioEngAb, BiolAb, ChemAb, DSA, EnvAb, ExcerpMed, FPA, FS&TA, ForAb, H&SSA, HortAb, IndMed, IndVet, OceAb, PollutAb, S&F, SCI, VetBull. *Aud.:* Ac, Sa.

This journal publishes approximately 45 articles per issue on food biochemistry, food composition, analytical methods, nutrition, toxicology, flavors and aromas, chemical changes during processing or storage, environmental chemistry, and biotechnology. This journal will quickly fill your shelves, but it is important for any food science or agricultural research library.

556. ***Journal of Agricultural Safety and Health.*** [ISSN: 1074-7583] 1995. q. Members, USD 53; Non-members, USD 102. Ed(s): Glenn Laing. American Society of Agricultural Engineers, 2950 Niles Rd., St. Joseph, MI 49085-9659; hq@asae.org; http://www.asae.org. Illus. Refereed. Circ: 400. Vol. ends: Nov. *Indexed:* Agr, DSA, EngInd, ErgAb, FPA, ForAb, H&SSA, HortAb, IndMed, IndVet, RiskAb, WAE&RSA. *Aud.:* Ga, Ac.

This journal focuses on "areas such as engineering, occupational safety, public policy, education and public health." There are five to eight articles in each issue along with regular features such as an "editorial" a "guest editorial," and a "foreword." There is a concern for safety on the farm and preventing accidents. This journal would be valuable to any rural library.

557. ***Journal of Animal Science.*** [ISSN: 0021-8812] 1942. m. 1 vol./yr. USD 450 in North America; USD 500 elsewhere. Ed(s): John Edwards. American Society of Animal Science, 1111 N Dunlap Ave, Savoy, IL 61874; johne@assochq.org; http://www.asas.org. Illus., index. Refereed. Circ: 5000. Vol. ends: Dec. Microform: PMC; PQC. Online: EBSCO Publishing; Gale Group; Northern Light Technology, Inc.; OCLC Online Computer Library Center, Inc.; ProQuest Information & Learning. *Indexed:* B&AI, BiolAb, ChemAb, DSA, ExcerpMed, FPA, FS&TA, FoVS&M, ForAb, HortAb, IndMed, IndVet, RRTA, S&F, SCI, SSCI, VetBull, WAE&RSA, ZooRec. *Bk. rev.:* 1-5, 35-100 words. *Aud.:* Ac, Sa.

This journal of the American Society of Animal Science covers all aspects of the subject including applied animal science; breeding and genetics; contemporary issues; environment and behavior; growth and developmental biology; meat science; nonruminant nutrition; pharmacology and toxicology; physiology and endocrinology; rangeland, pasture, and forage utilization; ruminant nutrition; teaching; and a rapid-communications section for molecular genetics articles. Some news about society publishing is also included. This journal should be in any collection providing support to animal researchers.

558. ***Journal of Dairy Science.*** [ISSN: 0022-0302] 1917. m. USD 450 in North America; USD 500 elsewhere. Ed(s): Jean Rice. American Dairy Science Association, 1111 N Dunlap Ave, Savoy, IL 61874; jeanr@assochq.org; http://www.adsa.org. Illus., index, adv. Refereed. Circ: 5400. Vol. ends: Dec. Microform: PMC; PQC. *Indexed:* Agr, B&AI, BiolAb, ChemAb, DSA, EnvAb, ExcerpMed, FPA, FS&TA, FoVS&M, IndMed, IndVet, RRTA, S&F, SCI, SSCI, VetBull, WAE&RSA. *Aud.:* Ac, Sa.

The American Dairy Association publishes approximately 3,600 pages per year in this journal covering all aspects of dairy cattle research including dairy foods; physiology and management; nutrition, feeding and calves; genetics and breeding; and the dairy industry today. The announcements section can contain employment information. Some proceedings may be published jointly with the Journal of Animal Science. This journal is a must for any library supporting a cattle research program.

559. ***N A S S Ag. Newsletter.*** m. U S D A - N A S S, PO Box 1699, Boise, ID 83701; nass.id@nass.usda.gov; http://www.nass.usda.gov/id/homepage.htm. *Aud.:* Hs, Ga, Ac.

This is one example of the USDA National Agricultural Statistics Service's many serial reports that are available through its web site. This monthly publication provides "estimates, forecasts and projections mainly taken from recent publications of the National Agricultural Statistics Service, Economic Research Service, and the World Agricultural Outlook Board of the USDA." Anyone interested in tracking agricultural production, trade, prices, and the effects of weather on crops will enjoy these two-page newsletters.

560. ***National Hog Farmer.*** [ISSN: 0027-9447] 1956. m. USD 115 domestic; USD 127 Canada; USD 139 elsewhere. Ed(s): Dale Miller. Primedia Business Magazines & Media, Inc., 7900 International Dr, Ste 300, Minneapolis, MN 55425; inquiries@primediabusiness.com; http://www.primediabusiness.com. Illus., adv. Sample. Circ: 33000 Controlled. Vol. ends: Dec. *Aud.:* Ga, Sa.

Each issue contains four to six articles related to the "production technology, management practices in production and marketing" for pork producers. Current news on the field is also covered. This journal has been published for 45 years, and the online version can search issues back to November 1997. This publication is available at no cost to qualified readers. It would be valuable for libraries serving communities where hogs are raised.

561. ***Poultry Science.*** [ISSN: 0032-5791] 1908. m. USD 425 print & online eds. Ed(s): P. B. Siegel. Poultry Science Association Inc., 1111 N Dunlap Ave, Savoy, IL 61874; psa@assochq.org; http://www.poultryscience.org. Illus., index, adv. Refereed. Circ: 3500 Paid. Vol. ends: Dec. Microform: PQC. Reprint: PQC. *Indexed:* Agr, B&AI, BiolAb, ChemAb, DSA, ExcerpMed, FS&TA, FoVS&M, HortAb, IndMed, IndVet, RRTA, S&F, SCI, VetBull, WAE&RSA, ZooRec. *Bk. rev.:* 2-4, 200-500 words. *Aud.:* Ac, Sa.

This professional association journal covers all aspects of poultry science including genetics, production, health, metabolism and nutrition, molecular biology, physiology, reproduction, and processing. Employment opportunities and book reviews are included in the "Association Notes" section. The *Journal of Applied Poultry Research* is available at no charge when subscribing to *Poultry Science.* This journal would be valuable in any collection providing support to poultry farmers or researchers.

562. ***Progressive Farmer.*** [ISSN: 0033-0760] 1886. s-m. in Jan-June; m. in July-Dec. USD 18 domestic; USD 26 foreign; USD 3.95 newsstand/cover per issue. Ed(s): Jack Odle. Progressive Farmer, Inc., 2100 Lakeshore Drive, Birmingham, AL 35209; jodle@progressivefarmer.com; ads@progressivefarmer.com; http://www.pathfinder.com/PF. Illus., adv. Circ: 630000. Vol. ends: Dec. Microform: PQC. Online: ProQuest Information & Learning. *Aud.:* Hs, Ga, Ac.

This journal is written for people living on farms or involved in agriculture. There are numerous regular sections such as Farm Safety, Cotton, Rural Sportsman, and Countryplace. The Handy Devices department provides useful ideas from farmers. A library in a farming area would find this journal valuable.

Ram's Horn. See Zines section.

563. ***Resource (Niles): engineering & technology for a sustainable world.*** Formed by the merger of (1920-1994): *Agricultural Engineering;* (1983-1994): *Within A S A E.* [ISSN: 1076-3333] 1994. m. Members, USD 24; Non-members, USD 75. Ed(s): Jackie Elowsky. American Society of Agricultural Engineers, 2950 Niles Rd., St. Joseph, MI 49085-9659; hq@asae.org; http://www.asae.org. Illus., adv. Circ: 8000. Vol. ends: Dec. Microform: PQC. Online: Florida Center for Library Automation; Gale Group; OCLC Online Computer Library Center, Inc.; ProQuest Information & Learning. *Indexed:* B&AI, BiolAb, ChemAb, DSA, EngInd, EnvAb, ExcerpMed, FPA, ForAb, HortAb, S&F, SSCI, WAE&RSA. *Aud.:* Ac.

This association magazine is much smaller than the research publication *Transactions of the Society of Agricultural Engineers* (see below in this section) and contains news about the society, member news, an events calendar, and typically four short articles. Employment opportunities are also listed. One issue contains a special section of outstanding innovations and a listing of consultants. Most appropriate for academic libraries.

564. ***Soil Science Society of America Journal.*** Formerly (until 1976): *Soil Science Society of America. Proceedings.* [ISSN: 0361-5995] 1936. bi-m. USD 247 domestic; USD 277 foreign. Ed(s): Richard L Mulvaney. Soil Science Society of America, 677 S Segoe Rd, Madison, WI 53711; http://www.soils.org/. Illus., index, adv. Refereed. Circ: 6000. Vol. ends: Nov/Dec. Microform: PMC. Online: EBSCO Publishing; Gale Group; HighWire Press; ProQuest Information & Learning; ScienceDirect. *Indexed:* Agr, B&AI, BiolAb, C&ISA, CAPS, ChemAb, DSA, DSR&OA, EngInd, EnvAb, ExcerpMed, FPA, ForAb, GSI, GeoRef, GeogAbPG, HortAb, PetrolAb, PollutAb, S&F, SCI, SWRA, WAE&RSA, WRCInf. *Aud.:* Ac, Sa.

Articles are grouped by the various sections within the Soil Science Society of America, including soil physics, soil chemistry, soil biology and biochemistry, soil fertility and plant nutrition, pathology, soil and water management and conservation, forest and range soils, nutrient management and soil and plant analysis, soil mineralogy, and wetland soils. This would be a popular title in an academic library serving researchers in soil sciences.

565. ***Successful Farming: for families that make farming their business.*** [ISSN: 0039-4432] 1902. m. USD 15.95 for 2 yrs. domestic. Ed(s): Loren Kruse. Meredith Corp., 1716 Locust St, Des Moines, IA 50309-3023; http://www.meredith.com. Illus., adv. Circ: 465000 Paid. Vol. ends: Dec. Microform: NBI. Online: Factiva; Florida Center for Library Automation; Gale Group; Northern Light Technology, Inc.; ProQuest Information & Learning. *Indexed:* MagInd, RGPR. *Aud.:* Hs, Ga.

This journal contains articles about farms and farm life. It is a trade publication and contains many advertisements. An article in a recent issue discusses controlling spray and droplet size. In the electronic version, called *@g online,* articles are separated into sections called Top Talk, Top Stories, @gpoll, Markets, @g Worldwide, and Smart Farmer. In the Smart Farmer section, people can test their knowledge of crops, machinery, and livestock. The print version divides articles into Business, Production, Family, Personal, Humor, and Features. This journal would be valuable for any library in an agricultural area.

Electronic Journals

566. ***Farm Bureau News.*** Formerly: *American Farm Bureau Federations Official News Letter.* [ISSN: 0197-5617] 1921. 22x/yr. USD 10. Ed(s): Barbara E Knisely. American Farm Bureau Federation, 600 Maryland Ave, S W, Ste 800, Washington, DC 20024; fbnews@fb.com; http://www.fb.com/. Circ: 47000 Paid. *Aud.:* Ga.

This electronic publication from the American Farm Bureau Federation covers political and economic issues related to farming in 22 issues per year. The usual sections include: "Top Stories," "Viewpoint," "Capital Update," "Grassroots," "State FB Links," and "Trade Update." The "Corner Post" provides various statistical references. There is a link to a "Farm Facts" publication with various statistics on farming, and a few examples can be retrieved electronically. This publication is easy to read and would be useful to anyone wanting to stay up-to-date on farming issues.

567. ***Farmer's Market Online.*** 1995. w. Ed(s): Michael Hofferber. Hofferber, P.O. Box 441, Baker City, OR 97814-0441; http://www.farmersmarketonline.com/. *Aud.:* Ga.

This electronic shopping page is set up to "resemble an open air market" where producers can sell directly to the consumer. There are also helpful "booths" set up to provide helpful advice for web surfers. Subscribers can sign up to receive either or both weekly updates called "Food Edition" and "Farm and Garden Edition." It is an interesting site for those wanting to explore available products.

568. ***Food Outlook.*** 1995. bi-m. Food & Agriculture Association of the United Nations, Viale delle Terme di Caracalla, Rome, Italy. *Aud.:* Ga, Ac.

This publication tracks international financial information on "cereals and other basic food commodities." There are special reports on critical food shortages around the world and food supplies that are available. Statistical information is presented in tables and graphs. This publication would be useful to those interested in agricultural economics.

569. ***Horticulture & Home Pest News.*** 1996. m. Iowa State University Entomology Extension Service, Iowa State University, Ames, IA 50011. *Aud.:* Ga, Ac, Sa.

This publication is directed to the professional but has some material of interest and value to the amateur horticulturist. For example, the features and articles on plant care and how to handle disease and pests will be of value to almost anyone. On the other hand, some of the solutions and suggestions assume that the reader is a professional in the field. An unusual newsletter, but one that should have a wider readership than the title suggests. (BK)

570. ***Rural Development Perspectives.*** 1997. 3x/yr. Department of Agriculture, Economic Research Service, 1800 M St, N W, Rm 3100, Washington, DC 20036; http://www.ers.usda.gov/publications/rdp/rdp.htm. *Indexed:* Agr, CIJE, PAIS. *Aud.:* Ga, Ac.

The online version of the print edition is from the U.S. Department of Agriculture, Economic Research Service. Its purpose is to analyze and discuss economic, social, political, and related matters in terms of what they mean for rural agricultural development. The six or seven feature articles discuss such things as rural labor markets, commuting and the economic functions of small towns, industrial uses of agricultural products, and rural areas in the new telecommunications era. Most of this is supported by statistical data and will be of equal interest to working farmers, researchers, and laypersons. Anyone who wishes to take a new look at what it means to live and work in a rural area should put this on their regular reading list. (BK)

571. ***Sciences of Soils.*** [ISSN: 1432-9492] 1996. irreg. DEM 698 includes print & CD-ROM eds. (Individuals, DEM 198 includes CD-ROM). Ed(s): Dr. Thomas Hintze. Springer-Verlag, Tiergartenstr 17, Heidelberg, 69121, Germany; subscriptions@springer.de. Refereed. *Indexed:* GeoRef. *Aud.:* Ac.

This journal started in 1996, and in 1998 Springer Verlag started publishing the articles for the journal while the original web site still maintains many of the features for free. The journal covers all aspects of soil science, and the "XChange" portion allows readers and authors to communicate with each other via either a discussion group or a discussion list. Anyone is welcome to set up a group to discuss soil science issues, and the discussion lists are used to discuss articles published in the journals. This is an interesting site for people interested in soil science.

572. ***Weekly Weather and Crop Bulletin.*** Formerly (until 1924): *Weekly Weather Chronicle.* [ISSN: 0043-1974] 1872. w. USD 45 domestic; USD 55 foreign. Ed(s): David Miskus. U.S. National Oceanic and Atmospheric Administration, Climate Prediction Center, W/NP52, World Weather Bldg, Room 605, Camp Springs, MD 20746-4304; http://www.usda.gov/oce/waob/jawf/wwcb.html. Illus., index. Vol. ends: Dec. Reprint: CIS. *Indexed:* AmStI, GeoRef, IUSGP. *Aud.:* Ga, Ac.

This publication provides meteorological information for farmers as well as information on how various crops are doing. Tables of temperature and precipitation data are given, with written descriptions for each state, satellite photography, and figures showing general trends across the United States. International weather and crop information is also provided. The online version provides links to a current Crop Moisture Index and a current Palmer Drought Index, both of which cover the United States. This is a valuable resource for libraries that support patrons involved in agriculture.

■ ALTERNATIVES

General/Alternative Newspapers/Reviews and Bibliographies

Gretchen Lagana, Special Collections Librarian (Head) University of Illinois at Chicago, University Library, M/C 234, P.O. Box 8198, Chicago, IL 60680; glagana@uic.edu

Introduction

Resilience is the word that best describes the current alternative magazine scene. In the face of climbing postal rates and unstable newsstand sales, erosion of independent bookstores, and decline of ancillary issue-oriented foundations and organizations, alternatives continue to survive, even thrive. New titles replace ceased or suspended titles while troubled titles shift their focus or morph from print to electronic format.

In addition to their resilience, alternative magazines are accessible at all levels. They can be found in independent bookstores, super bookstores (particularly in urban areas), and thanks to the Independent Press Association (IPA), even in the local Wal-Mart. They have developed a distinct electronic presence. Nearly every title now has a web site with extensive links to alternative publications and organizations. Many provide full-text access, and exclusively electronic titles continue to increase in number.

Bibliographic access is anchored by groups such as the Alternatives in Publication Task Force (http://www.libr.org/AIP), a subgroup of the American Library Association's Social Responsibilities Round Table; the Independent Press Association, with an independent press membership of over 400 (http://www.indypress.org); and the Alternative Press Center (http://www.altpress.org), which publishes *Alternative Press Index.* These groups offer an excellent starting point for anyone interested in alternative magazines. Certainly, the economic, social, environmental, and political issues that currently roil the country offer alternatives a rich seedbed, and in this issue-oriented period there is no better time to explore alternative magazines.

Basic Periodicals

Hs: *Adbusters, Car Busters, Hope Magazine, Orion Afield, Utne* Ga: *Adbusters, Home Education Magazine, Orion Afield, San Francisco Bay Guardian, The Sun (Chapel Hill), Utne* Ac: *Alternatives Journal, The Baffler, City Limits, Orion Afield;* Sa: *Alternatives Journal.*

Basic Abstracts and Indexes

Alternative Press Index.

General

573. ***Adbusters: journal of the mental environment.*** [ISSN: 0847-9097] 1989. 6x/yr. CND 120 (Individuals, CND 40; CND 5.95 newsstand/cover per issue). Ed(s): Kalle Lasn. Adbusters Media Foundation, 1243 W Seventh Ave, Vancouver, BC V6H 1B7, Canada; adbusters@adbusters.org; http://www.adbusters.org. Illus., adv. Circ: 30000. Online: Gale Group. *Indexed:* AltPI, CBCARef, CPerI. *Bk. rev.:* Various number and length. *Aud.:* Ga.

Based in Vancouver, British Columbia, *Adbusters* is reader-supported and published by the Adbusters Media Foundation, a nonprofit organization. Its activism centers on problems and issues raised by consumerism, mass media, advertising, and marketing. Each issue reflects the magazine's aim to "forge a major rethinking of the way we will live in the 21st century." Articles tend to be brief, are well written, and cover a wide range of topics. Recent articles have centered on Internet taxes, pharmaceutical marketing, classroom advertising, antiglobilization, global warming, and Third World sweatshops. *Adbusters* is associated with Buy Nothing Day, TV Turn-off Week, Culture Jamming, and Creative Resistance. It is also one of the best designed of the alternatives and often features the work of designers of the caliber of the late Tibor Kalman. The Adbuster's Media Foundation web site offers additional information on the magazine as well as activities asociated with the foundation. *Adbusters* will appeal to activists, evironmentalists, corporate watchdogs, students, parents, and those interested in media issues.

Alternative Press Index. See Abstracts and Indexes section.

574. *Alternative Press Review: your guide beyond the mainstream.* [ISSN: 1072-7299] 1993. q. USD 16 domestic; USD 24 foreign. Ed(s): Jason McQuinn. A A L Press, PO Box 4710, Arlington, VA 22204-4710; jmcquinn@coin.org; http://www.altpr.org. Illus., adv. Sample. Circ: 6500 Paid. *Indexed:* ASIP, AltPI, BRI, CBRI. *Bk. rev.:* Various number and length. *Aud.:* Ga.

The *Alternative Press Review* bills itself as "your window on the world of independent media." Each issue is packed with commentary, essays, and excerpts from zines, tabloids, books, and magazines, along with columns devoted to the alternative press and alternative media. Additionally, there are about 100 reviews of current issues of alternative magazines and zines (50–60 titles, 80–100 words each), books, CDs, records, tapes, and videos. Titles are wide ranging and include political activism, literature, music, humor, and the environment. *Alternative Press Review* has a strong web presence, with a "review of the week," abstracts of featured essays, selected reviews, and subscription information. This title is a must for anyone interested in alternatives. However, the wait between issues can be lengthy.

575. *Alternatives Journal.* Formerly (until 1996): *Alternatives.* [ISSN: 1205-7398] 1971. q. CND 50 (Individuals, CND 25; Students, CND 19.95). Ed(s): Robert Gibson, Ray Tomalty. University of Waterloo, Faculty of Environmental Studies, 200 University Ave, W, Waterloo, ON N2L 3G1, Canada; editor@alternativesjournal.ca; http://www.alternativesjournal.ca. Illus., adv. Sample. Refereed. Circ: 2000. Microform: MML; PQC. Online: Florida Center for Library Automation; Gale Group; Northern Light Technology, Inc.; ProQuest Information & Learning; SoftLine Information. *Indexed:* AltPI, CIJE, CPerI, EnvAb, LRI, MagInd, PRA. *Bk. rev.:* 11, 700 words. *Aud.:* Ga, Ac.

An independent, nonprofit, 40-page Canadian environmental journal with theme-based issues, *Alternatives Journal* is published by the Faculty of Environmental Studies, University of Waterloo (Ontario). Its aim is to promote understanding and dialog among students, scholars, professionals, and activists concerned with the environment, including its social and political dimensions, while reflecting the Canadian perspective, which is informed by an understanding of global issues. Since 1995 it has been the official journal of the Environmental Studies Association of Canada. Solid, in-depth, well-documented, and very readable, it provides access to a wide range of information. Each issue contains refereed feature articles, news reports, commentaries, and reviews. This is an important, recognized source for environmental issues, especially valuable in those educational settings with interdisiciplinary studies. Its informative, attractive, and easy-to-navigate web site offers an impressive number of links to environmental sites, including what must be a nearly comprehensive compilation of links to Canadian environmental web sites. Highly recommended.

576. *The Baffler.* [ISSN: 1059-9789] 1988. irreg. USD 24 domestic; USD 25 in Canada & Mexico; USD 29 elsewhere. Ed(s): Thomas Frank. Baffler, PO Box 378293, Chicago, IL 60637; info@thebaffler.com; http://www.thebaffler.com. Illus., adv. Refereed. Circ: 20000. *Indexed:* AltPI. *Aud.:* Ga, Ac.

The Baffler, "the journal that blunts the cultural edge," is a Chicago-based, independent, 128-page journal of cultural criticism. Intellectual, defiant, and anticommerce, the consistent superiority of its investigative essays, articles, interviews, excerpts, cartoons, and coverage of pop music and the arts makes this an excellent choice for general and college collections.

577. *Briarpatch.* [ISSN: 0703-8968] 1973. 10x/yr. CND 35.31 (Individuals, CND 24.61; CND 3 newsstand/cover per issue). Ed(s): George Manz. Briarpatch Society, 2138 McIntyre St, Regina, SK S4P 2R7, Canada; http://www.cmpa.ca/no6.html. Illus., adv. Sample. Circ: 2300 Paid. Microform: MML. Online: Gale Group; LexisNexis; Micromedia ProQuest. *Indexed:* AltPI, CBCARef, CPerI. *Bk. rev.:* Various number and length. *Aud.:* Ga.

Briarpatch is Saskatchewan's award-winning independent, nonprofit alternative news magazine. Committed to building a socialist democratic society, it covers a wide range of topics both nationally and internationally. Themes and special issues offer in-depth treatment of politics, economic justice, the environment, labor, agriculture, human rights, and international solidarity. In the past few years, *Briarpatch* has strengthened its links with Canada's labor movement. The result is increased coverage of the peace and antiwar movement, solidarity with Third World revolutions and social justice movements, and the fight against free trade. Photos and cartoons have also increased in quality, and *Briarpatch* has added a web site with excerpts from and information about the magazine. Recommended for libraries with ties to Canadian readers and those seeking a leftist perspective on international issues.

578. *Car Busters.* 1998. q. CZK 230; EUR 15; USD 15. Car Busters, Kratka 26, Praha 10, 100 00 , Czech Republic. Illus., adv. Circ: 3000. *Bk. rev.:* 1, 450 words. *Aud.:* Hs, Ga.

Car Busters, a nonprofit, 32-page quarterly published by an international activist group in Prague, Czech Republic, aims both to serve as a source of information and a call to action. Inspired by the Canadian magazine *Adbusters*, it is international in scope, with summaries of articles provided in several languages. Content ranges from direct action skills to current research developments, with feature articles including such topics as driving as addiction, eco-city visions, sustainable transportation, and consumerism. This is an energetic, information-packed publication with much of interest to advocates of the autofree movement in North America that took root in the 1990s. Those concerned about consumerism, transportation, and urban issues will find *Car Busters* enjoyable and informative.

Centerfold. See *Fuse Magazine.*

579. *City Limits: New York's urban affairs news magazine.* [ISSN: 0199-0330] 1976. m. USD 35 (Individuals, USD 25). Ed(s): Robin Epstein, Glenn Thrush. City Limits Community Information Service, Inc., 120 Wall St, 20th Fl, New York, NY 10005-4001; citlim@aol .com. Illus., adv. Circ: 3000 Paid. Microform: PQC. Online: Gale Group; LexisNexis; Northern Light Technology, Inc.; OCLC Online Computer Library Center, Inc.; ProQuest Information & Learning; SoftLine Information. *Indexed:* AIAP, AltPI, CWI. *Bk. rev.:* Various number and length. *Aud.:* Ga, Ac.

Published by the City Limits Community Information Service, a nonprofit organization devoted to the dissemination of information on neighborhood revitalization, *City Limits* offers 42 pages of news, investigative reports, articles, reviews, resource information, and analysis of current urban issues. Its focus is the "other New York," but it will interest anyone concerned with urban housing issues.

580. *Communities: journal of cooperative living.* Supersedes: *Modern Utopian; Alternatives Newsmagazine; Communitarian; Communitas.* [ISSN: 0199-9346] 1972. q. USD 20; USD 6 newsstand/cover per issue. Ed(s): Diana Christian. Fellowship for Intentional Community, Rte 1, Box 156, Rutledge, MO 63563; http://www.ic.org/. Illus., adv. Circ: 5000. Microform: PQC. Online: Northern Light Technology, Inc.; ProQuest Information & Learning. *Indexed:* AltPI. *Bk. rev.:* 1-2, 200 words. *Aud.:* Hs, Ga.

Communities, published quarterly by the Fellowship for Intentional Community, is one of the best and most comprehensive sources on intentional communities and cooperative living. Theme-based issues have guest editors covering such topics as appropriate technology, student co-ops, communication, and the group process. In addition to articles that tend to be anecdotal, the magazine contains reviews, commentary, information updates, a community calendar, and a large classified section. A web site offers a vast array of resources and additional information, including excerpts from current and past issues.

Food & Water Journal. See *Wild Matters.*

581. ***Fourth Door Review.*** [ISSN: 1364-5110] 1996. a. USD 60 (Individuals, USD 50). Fouth Door Research, PO Box 2632, Lewes, BN7 2XZ, United Kingdom; fouthdoor@pavilion.co.uk; http://www.fouthdoor.co.uk. Illus. *Bk. rev.:* Various number and length. *Aud.:* Ga, Ac.

Fourth Door is a beautifully illustrated, annual review magazine published in Sussex, Great Britain. It aims to explore the new edges of the green world—to remove the differences between ecology and technology, land art and digital crafts, music and media. Running close to 100 pages in an oversized format, it features leading-edge sections on music, new media, and architecture, with in-depth articles, interviews, essays, and book reviews. This is a handsome and well-written alternative title, suitable for general and academic collections.

582. ***Fuse Magazine: a magazine about issues of art and culture.*** Former titles: *Fuse; Centerfold.* [ISSN: 0838-603X] 1976. 4x/yr. CND 32 (Individuals, CND 15; CND 5.50 newsstand/cover per issue). Arton's Publishing, 401 Richmond St W, Ste 454, Toronto, ON M5V 3A8, Canada; fuse@interlog.com; http://www.fusemagazine.org. Illus., adv. Sample. Refereed. Circ: 2500 Paid. Microform: MML. *Indexed:* AltPI, CBCARef, CPerl. *Aud.:* Ga, Ac.

Fuse, a 48-page Canadian magazine, is published by Arton's Cultural Affairs Society and Publishing, a nonprofit artists' organization. It is an arts and culture magazine that specializes in in-depth coverage of art that is politically engaged and relevant to understanding the contemporary world. Although it contains information on the Canadian, English-speaking, alternative-arts community, with a special emphasis on the Toronto area, many of its feature articles will also appeal to non-Canadians. The United States is frequently covered, particularly in the areas of film, television, and photography. Now over 20 years old, *Fuse* features articles, artists' projects, and critical analysis on issues in the arts concerning criticism and curation, the visual arts, independent film and video, new media and cultural diversity, visible minorities, First Nations, and community-based and gay- and lesbian-positive art. A web site provides additional information and resources, including an online directory with a comprehensive listing, city by city, of cultural organization happenings from coast to coast. This is one of the best of the alternative art publications.

583. ***Gray Areas.*** [ISSN: 1062-5712] 1991. irreg. USD 40 (Individuals, USD 23; USD 6.95 newsstand/cover). Ed(s): Netta Gilboa. Gray Areas, Inc., PO Box 808, Broomall, PA 19008-0808; http://www.grayarea.com/gray2.htm. Illus., adv. Circ: 10000 Paid. *Bk. rev.:* 75-80, 50-75 words. *Aud.:* Hs, Ga.

"In life there is no black and white, only . . . gray areas." It's the gray areas this magazine examines: "where lawbreakers can speak freely (we guarantee anonymity) and law abiders and enforcers can safely interact with them." Magazine issues are from 80 to 148 pages long, with a focus on music and musicians, computer privacy, computer hacking, plagiarism, video and audio tapes, and the adult film industry. Each issue has at least one interview. Librarians will welcome the many reviews of zines, concerts, books, computer software, CDs, films, comics, video games, and tapes. Software reviews are particularly detailed. In all, *Gray Areas* contains some 50 pages of reviews. A web site offers information on back issues, contents, and suscriptions. *Library Journal* has named *Gray Areas* as one of the top magazines.

584. ***Home Education Magazine.*** [ISSN: 0888-4633] 1984. bi-m. USD 32. Ed(s): Helen E Hegener. Home Education Magazine, PO Box 1083, Tonasket, WA 98855; hem-editor@home-ed-magazine.com. Illus., adv. Sample. Circ: 28000. Vol. ends: Dec. *Bk. rev.:* Various number and length. *Aud.:* Ga.

Home Education Magazine was founded during the early years of the home schooling movement, when American children being taught at home numbered only about 20,000. Today, with more parents choosing every day to teach their children at home, it serves a constituency of nearly a million. This magazine is one of the oldest and best of the home schooling magazines. Each 68-page issue includes articles, interviews, columns with practical advice written by experienced home schoolers, resource pages, reviews, networking, and a pen-pals feature. Its web site includes ordering and descriptive information, access to online newsletters, discussion boards, networking lists, and full-text selections from the magazine. *Home Education Magazine* is an excellent source of printed and electronic information on all aspects of home schooling.

585. ***Hope Magazine: finding the courage to change what we can.*** [ISSN: 1085-228X] 1996. bi-m. USD 15.95. Ed(s): Kimberly Ridley. Hope Publishing, Inc., Naskeag Rd, PO Box 160, Brooklin, ME 04616; info@hopemag.com; http://www.hopemag.com. Illus., adv. Circ: 85000 Paid. *Bk. rev.:* 1, 200-250 words. *Aud.:* Hs, Ga, Ac.

This award-winning quarterly magazine explores the ways individuals and organizations can work singly and together to make the world a better place. *Hope* searches out "fearless thinkers, passionate social innovators and giant local heros" to bring to its pages. There is no formal religious, political, or spiritual affiliation, and the writing is free of sentimentality. If there is a message, it is, as E. M. Forster urged, "connect, just connect." Recent issues have dealt with caring for aging parents, educating boys to be compassionate, healing, schooling, achieving balance in our lives, and getting off the consumption treadmill. A web site offers additional magazine information and resources.

586. ***HopeDance Magazine: radical solutions inspiring hope.*** [ISSN: 1533-8401] 1996. bi-m. Membership, USD 20. Ed(s): Bob Banner. HopeDance, PO Box 15609, San Luis Obispo, CA 93406; info@hopedance.org; http://www.hopedance.org. Adv. Sample. *Bk. rev.:* Various number and length. *Aud.:* Hs, Ga.

HopeDance Magazine is a grassroots, independent magazine published in San Luis Obispo, California, with a focus on the state's central coastal area. However, its concerns will appeal beyond the state to those interested in solutions to a wide range of environmental problems. *HopeDance* reports on the work of individuals and organizations trying to build ecologically sustainable, holistic communities, and it offers stories of people and organizations with creative solutions to housing needs. Issues are theme-based (for example, energy, media, water, natural building, sprawl and sustainable communities, globalization), and articles contain annotated source lists. A review section covers books and magazines, and the web site offers summaries of featured articles, with selected full-text access, links, and current issue information. Librarians serving smaller communities will find this title of interest.

587. ***Impact Press: covering issues the way the media should.*** 1996. bi-m. USD 10 domestic; USD 16 in Canada & Mexico; USD 28 elsewhere. Ed(s): Craig Mazer. Loudmouth Productions, Inc, 10151 University Blvd, Ste 151, Orlando, FL 32817; impact-press@mindspring.com; http://www.impactpress.com. *Aud.:* Hs, Ga.

Impact Press bills itself as a socio-political magazine that features aggressive journalism, pungent commentary, and a dose of satire. It aims to "cover issues the way the media should." Each 60-page issue, with its striking graphics, conveys a sense of currency and urgency. Sample topics covered range from terrorism, public school privatization, and the chemical industry to globilization, censorship, and ritalin. The last quarter of the magazine includes more than 200 succinct music reviews that are informed and fun to read. The online edition contains an equally interesting and unusual annotated list of music and politics/activism links.

MotherJones.com. See General Editorial-Internet section.

588. ***OnEarth.*** Former titles: *The Amicus Journal; Amicus;* Which incorporated (in 1992): *N R D C Newsline.* [ISSN: 1537-4246] 1979. q. USD 8 (Individuals, USD 10). Ed(s): Kathrin Day Lassila. Natural Resources Defense Council, Inc., 40 W 20th St, 11th Fl, New York, NY 10011; amicus@nrdc.igc.apc.org; http://www.igc.apc.org/nrdc/. Illus. Sample. Circ: 175000. Vol. ends: Winter. Microform: PQC. Online: bigchalk; Florida Center for Library Automation; Gale Group; Northern Light Technology, Inc.; OCLC Online Computer Library Center, Inc.; ProQuest Information & Learning. Reprint: WSH. *Indexed:* AltPI, B&AI, BiolDig, CLI, EnvAb, IAPV, ILP, PAIS, SSI. *Aud.:* Hs, Ga.

OnEarth is the quarterly magazine of the National Resources Defense Council, a nonprofit organization with the mission of safeguarding the earth: its people, plants, and animals, and the natural systems on which life depends. Formerly published under the title *Amicus Journal,* this well-known alternative took on a new title in 2001 in search of a more general audience. Issues run about 50 pages, are well written, with broad coverage and up-to-date information that includes news on environmental legislation, essays, and a poetry section. This is an excellent selection for high school and general collections.

589. *Orion Afield.* Formerly (until 1997): *Orion Society Notebook.* [ISSN: 1096-9144] 1997. bi-m. Individual members, USD 30; USD 8 newsstand/cover per issue. Ed(s): Jennifer Sahn. Orion Society, 187 Main St., Gt Barrington, MA 01230-1602; orion@orionsociety.org; http://www.orionsociety.org. *Indexed:* BiolDig. *Bk. rev.:* Various number and length. *Aud.:* Hs, Ga, Ac.

Orion Afield, published by the Orion Society, a group that aims "to heal the fractured relationship between people and nature," is a 37-page environmental education quarterly. Its goal is to inform and educate people of all ages and help individuals and grassroots organizations stay informed, motivated, and connected. Each issue contains a special section covering a given topic from multiple points of view. Recent sections examine hunting, economic globilization, myths, fiction that portrays the relationship between people and nature, wonder, and consumer waste. A "Features" section includes selections from the best nature writing currently being published, while other departments and columns explore spirituality and the arts, interviews, profiles, poetry, and reviews of books and magazines. Each issue includes portfolios from a variety of artists. There are no advertisements. This is a handsome and appealing magazine in its content, design, look, and feel (the recycled paper has a vellum-like texture). *Orion Afield* is an excellent choice for readers of all ages.

590. *Rain Taxi: review of books.* q. USD 12 domestic; USD 24 foreign. Ed(s): Eric Lorberer. Rain Taxi, Inc., PO Box 3840, Minneapolis, MN 55403. *Bk. rev.:* Various number and length. *Aud.:* Hs, Ga, Ac.

Rain Taxi is a nonprofit quarterly of 55 pages offering reviews, interviews, essays, fiction, nonfiction, poetry, audio, and graphic novels. Coverage includes alternative and independent press, university press, and some mainstream press selections. This is a good place to read informed interviews of hard-to-find figures important to the independent press. Each interview is proceeded by a biography, a summary of the subject's writing, and their photograph. The online edition offers fiction, nonfiction, poetry, and various resource features. *Rain Taxi* won the *Utne Reader* 2000 Alternative Press Award citation for best arts and literature coverage. Librarians will want to consider this title for their literature collections, especially poetry holdings. They will also find it a handy collection development tool.

591. *Ruminator Review: the independent book magazine.* Formerly (until 2000): *Hungry Mind Review.* [ISSN: 1529-0654] 1986. q. USD 14. Ed(s): Margaret Todd Maitland. Ruminator Review, 1648 Grand Ave., St. Paul, MN 55105; http://www.bookwire.com/HMR. Illus., adv. Circ: 45000. *Indexed:* BRI, CBRI. *Bk. rev.:* Various number and length. *Aud.:* Hs,Ga,Ac.

Ruminator Review is a theme-based, quarterly book magazine in tabloid format published at Macalester College, St. Paul, Minnesota. Issues cover independent and other press materials not covered by the mainstream review press and include original essays, interviews, in-depth and shorter reviews of new fiction, nonfiction, poetry, and children's books. Unusual graphics and photographs in color and black and white make this an especially interesting and handsome publication. Readers interested in non-mainstream titles and librarians seeking to identify new independent-press titles will find this a valuable guide.

592. *Sojourners.* Formerly: *Post American.* [ISSN: 0364-2097] 1971. bi-m. USD 39.95 domestic (Students, USD 15). Ed(s): Jim Wallis. Sojourners, 2401 15th St, N W, Washington, DC 20009; sojourners@sojo.net; http://www.sojourners.com. Illus., adv. Circ: 23000. Online: Florida Center for Library Automation; Gale Group; Northern Light Technology, Inc.; OCLC Online Computer Library Center, Inc.; H.W. Wilson. *Indexed:* AltPI, ChrPI, HumInd, MRD, PRA, RI-1. *Bk. rev.:* Various number and length. *Aud.:* Ga.

Sojourners is a grassroots and progressive Christian voice that refuses to "separate personal faith from social justice, prayer from peacemaking, contemplation from action, or spirituality from politics." Issues run about 60 to 70 pages, with five or six articles on current political, cultural, social, and theological topics. Each issue includes poetry, resources for group or individual study and action, and posted events and programs. Reviews cover books, the performing arts, and popular culture. Its accompanying web site is extensive and includes access to articles from current and back issues, information on internship programs and job openings, news briefs, book reviews, forums, and an online store. *Sojourners* is a well-respected publication that effectively balances a sense of humor with a quiet, yet determined, tone of activism. Librarians will find it a welome alternative to mainstream press coverage of topical events.

593. *The Sun (Chapel Hill): a magazine of ideas.* [ISSN: 0744-9666] 1974. m. USD 34 domestic; USD 49 in Canada & Mexico; USD 54 elsewhere. Ed(s): Sy Safransky. Sun Publishing Company, 107 N Roberson St, Chapel Hill, NC 27516; http://www.thesunmagazine.org. Illus., adv. Circ: 50000 Paid. Microform: PQC. *Indexed:* AltPI, IAPV. *Aud.:* Hs, Ga.

In its first issue, *The Sun* described itself as non-elitist (the sunlight shines on everybody), with the aim of bringing light where there was darkness, while serving as an alternative forum for those who didn't think like everyone else. That still holds true. Issues include fiction, essays, interviews, poetry, and photographs. The longest piece is 7000 words. Personal writing is favored, and reader submissions, which accompany those of professionl writers, are welcome. A readers' section on pre-announced subjects (recently on whirlwind romances, locked doors, begging, hair) and a page of juxtaposed quotations called "Sunbeams" are two of many excellent features. A web site offers summaries of articles, excerpts, and additional magazine information. Both *The Sun*'s circulation and the quality of its writing has improved over the years. As a result, it has received many awards, including *Utne Reader*'s Alternative Press Award for General Excellence. Librarians will find this an especially appropriate title for high school and general collections.

594. *Utne: a different read on life.* Formerly (until Nov. 2002): *Utne Reader.* [ISSN: 1544-2225] 1984. bi-m. USD 19.97 domestic; USD 30 Canada. Ed(s): Jay Walljasper. Lens Publishing Co., Inc., 1624 Harmon Pl, Ste 330, Minneapolis, MN 55403; editor@utne.com; http://www.utne.com. Illus., adv. Circ: 282433. Microform: PQC. Online: Gale Group. *Indexed:* ABS&EES, AltPI, BRI, CBRI, IIMP, IIPA, MagInd, RGPR, RI-1. *Bk. rev.:* Various number and length. *Aud.:* Hs, Ga.

Founded in 1984, *Utne Reader* is now simply *Utne.* Renamed, redesigned, with a new editorial approach, *Utne* offers much more original writing and far less reliance on reprinted material (reflective of the access role now played by the Internet). Other changes include expanded cultural coverage and a new focus on political advocacy. *Utne* remains an important source of information on alternatives. *Utne* librarian Chris Dodge, who has played a key role with alternatives for many years, offers reviews along with news and notes on the alternative press, and the magazine's annual roster of the best of the alternative press is always informative. This is an excellent title for high school and general collections.

Utne Reader. See *Utne.*

595. *Wild Matters.* Former titles (until 2003): *Food & Water Journal; Safe Food News.* 1992. 10x/yr. USD 25 domestic; USD 40 Canada; USD 45 elsewhere. Ed(s): Michael Colby. Food and Water, Inc., P.O. Box 543, Montpelier, VT 05601; fwi@together.net; http://www.foodandwater.org. Illus. Circ: 15000. *Indexed:* AltPI. *Aud.:* Ga.

Wild Matters was formerly *Food and Water Journal,* which targeted corporations poisoning the food supply through the use of pesticides, genetic engineering, and food irradiation. Its new focus expands to include politics, ecology, news, and views, with a self-proclaimed hard edge that calls for social and environmental justice. Published by Food & Water, Inc., a nonprofit education and advocacy organization, *Wild Matters* still maintains a literary voice along with its political and environmental information.

Alternative Newspapers

596. *Fifth Estate.* [ISSN: 0015-0800] 1965. q. USD 20 & libraries (Individuals, USD 10; Corporations, USD 50). Fifth Estate Newspaper, PO Box 6, Liberty, TN 37095; fifthestate@pumpkinhollow.net. Illus. Sample. Circ: 5000 Controlled. Microform: PQC. Reprint: PQC. *Indexed:* AltPI. *Bk. rev.:* Various number and length. *Aud.:* Ga, Ac.

The oldest survivor of the hundreds of underground newspapers that came out of the 1960s, the *Fifth Estate* is an anarchist paper devoted to far-left ideas and graphics. Each 32-page issue includes 1,000- to 2,000-word articles on local, national, and international topics, along with reviews of books, periodicals, and other radical information. Its graphics are excellent. Feature articles are signed and generally accompanied by resources information. In late 2002, *Fifth Estate* moved from Detroit and Detroit's rich counterculture to Pumpkin Hollow, a rural commune on the outskirts of Nashville, Tennessee. The paper is being run by a new editorial team that, so far, is carrying on the in-your-face tone and content of *Fifth Estate.*

In These Times. See News and Opinion section.

597. ***San Francisco Bay Guardian.*** [ISSN: 0036-4096] 1966. w. USD 32. Ed(s): Bruce B Brugmann. Bay Guardian Co., 520 Hampshire St, San Francisco, CA 94110; http://www.sfbg.com. Illus., adv. Circ: 153000. Microform: PQC. Reprint: PQC. *Bk. rev.:* Various number and length. *Aud.:* Ga, Ac.

"It is a newspaper's duty to print the news and raise hell." So says the weekly *San Francisco Bay Gaurdian.* Founded in 1966, it has established itself as an important newspaper, in part by following this philosophy. Although many of the investigative articles deal with local and state issues, topics are also wide ranging. Special features include reviews (books, theater, film, music, restaurants) and a "Books and Writers" section. Those interested in Northern California politics and lifestyle, energy, urban, AIDS, gay, and lesbian issues will find this title of interest.

Reviews and Bibliographies

598. ***Counterpoise: for social responsibilites, liberty and dissent.*** [ISSN: 1092-0714] 1997. q. USD 45 (Individuals, USD 35). Ed(s): Charles Willett. Civic Media Center and Library, Inc., 1716 S W Williston Rd, Gainesville, FL 32608-4049. Illus., adv. Sample. Refereed. *Indexed:* AltPI, BRI, CBRI. *Bk. rev.:* Various number and length. *Aud.:* Ga, Ac, Sa.

Published by the "conscience" of ALA, the American Library Association's Social Responsibilities Roundtable's Alternatives in Print Task Force, *Counterpoise* bills itself as the only review journal to make alternative points of view widely accessible to librarians, scholars, and activists. It appears quarterly, and each 65-page issue contains a wide range of contents: reviews, original essays, comparative review articles, letters to the editor, editor's notes, an annotated directory of bibliographic tools for the alternative press, a publisher/distributor directory and index, an author/title index, and a subject index. The reviews include books, periodicals, and nonprint materials not usually found in other review journals. Reviews tend toward the humanities and social sciences and include reprints from other alternative titles such as *Alternative Press Review, Women in Libraries, Workbook, Anarchy,* and *Librarians at Liberty.* Its web site contains information on and from *Counterpoise* as well as a selection of full-text articles. Librarians interested in alternative literature will want to use this title for selection purposes as well as add it to their collection.

Factsheet 5: the definitive guide to the zine revolution. See Zines section.

Electronic Journals

599. ***Freezerbox: culture technology and politics.*** 1998. bi-m. Freezerbox, Speridakis Terrace, Cambridge, MA 02139; submissions@freezerbox.com; http://www.freezerbox.com. *Aud.:* Hs, Ga.

Freezerbox, in operation since 1998, is an activist-oriented electronic magazine on culture, technology, and politics. Offering nonmainstream views on current events, links to further information sources, reviews, and nonpolitical essays, it is well written by professional and nonprofessional authors. Informative, with broad coverage, this is an excellent forum for the exchange of ideas.

600. ***The Hungry Soul.*** 1997. irreg. Ed(s): Patricia Burke. Hungry Soul, 997 Pequawket Trail, West Baldwin, ME 04091; bmhc@ime.net; http://w3.ime.net/~bmhc/soul.htm. *Aud.:* Ga, Ac.

The title of this alternative literary magazine comes from a Sufi (Muslim) mystic. What is the soul? What is the soul's hunger? These and other questions are explored through healing stories: food for the imagination; poetry: songs for the spirit; short fiction: food for the heart; articles: food for thought; viewpoint: grist for the mill; and woman to woman. Well edited, easy to read, and always informative, *Hungry Soul* will appeal both to feminists and men.

601. ***In Motion Magazine: a multicultural US publication about democracy.*** 1996. d. Ed(s): Nic Paget-Clarke. N P C Productions, PO Box 927482, San Diego, CA 92192; publish@cts.com; http://www.inmotionmagazine.com. Adv. *Aud.:* Ga, Ac.

In Motion Magazine is one of the better social-welfare magazines. It has great art, writing, design, and topic selection. It bills itself as a multicultural online publication about democracy, and it promotes grassroots organizing and art for social change among communities of color and working people. There are over 20 sections and columns, with some containing 50 or more articles and interviews. They include "Art Changes" (interviews, articles, poems, original works of fiction, and photo essays), "Rural America" (articles and interviews), "In Defense of Affirmative Action" (articles and interviews about various aspects of the history and effectivenes of affirmative action, with interviews and speeches by Rev. Jesse Jackson and a series on Dr. Martin Luther King, Jr.), "Education Rights," "Healthcare," "Humor and Civil Rights," "Global Eyes," "Reprints from Chiapas," "Essays from Ireland," and "En Espanol," which indexes both original articles in Spanish and translations of others.

602. ***Library Juice.*** 1998. w. USD 10 donation. Ed(s): Rory Litwin. Library Juice Research and Communication, PO Box 720511, San Jose, CA 95172; juice@libr.org; http://libr.org/Juice. Circ: 1600. *Aud.:* Ga,Ac.

Library Juice is a weekly news publication for librarians, library and information science students, and other interested persons. Edited and published by a single individual who has recently relocated to Sacramento, California, it is the outgrowth of his communication with students in the MLIS program at San Jose State University in San Jose, California. Topics include announcements, web resources, calls for papers, and news concerning the library world, with a focus on social responsibility and intellectual freedom. This is not a discussion list but a digest of materials from multiple sources. Full of information and easy to use, librarians, library students, and those interested in library issues will find it useful and interesting.

603. ***WebActive.*** 1996. w. Ed(s): Sam Tucker. RealNetworks, Inc., 2601 Elliot Ave., Seattle, WA 98121; webactive@prognet.com; http://www.webactive.com/. *Aud.:* Ga.

WebActive is designed to keep readers up to date on the latest in activism and progressive politics on the Internet. It serves as an electronic guide to progressive resources online. It contains a wide variety of material including commentary, news, short articles, interviews, audio-based multimedia content, and a searchable directory of over 2,100 web sites. Each issue also presents a site of the week in addition to other featured sites. Librarians will appreciate this site's ease of use and its access to a wide variety of activist materials.

■ ANIMAL WELFARE

See also Birds; Horses; Pets; and Veterinary Science sections.

Philip C. Howze, Social Sciences Librarian, Library Affairs, Morris Library 6632, Southern Illinois University–Carbondale, Carbondale, IL 62901-6632; phowze@lib.siu.edu; FAX: 618-453-3440

Introduction

Concern for the welfare of animals has grown over the years to the point where the community of the caring is an international one. Prominent animal welfare groups exist in many countries to promote the importance of social and legal issues relating to the humane treatment and conservation of animals. Ever since it became evident that certain animals could be tamed, or could at least earn their food by not biting the hand that tossed it to them, human beings have been kindly disposed toward keeping such animals as pets. Of particular value was the animal that could demonstrate domestication through affection, loyalty, or skill (herding, for example). Unfortunately, while dogs, cats, birds, monkeys, pigs, horses, and other animals have evolved into fine pets for loving owners with time and patience, not all humans have behaved in ways that make them suitable pet owners. Not all humans agree that an animal's sole utility is that of pet, either. The use of animals as biomedical models for human health research has proven lucrative for breeders with sufficient supply. Then there is the use of animals as food source; humans consume millions of pounds of meat per year.

As the pet care industry exploded and small-animal care grew as a veterinary medicine specialty during the 1960s, society began to witness the "humanization" of domesticated animals as creatures worthy of human-like care. It is not uncommon for pets to be described as "one of the family." Along with this family member status (promoted by television) grew sensitivity to how the animal feels, or more accurately, behaves—particularly when in pain.

Animal rights activists work to promote the notion that they who share the planet (and ecological balance) with us should have certain fundamental rights, whether they are domesticated or entirely in the wild, and that those rights should transcend property. Animal rights activists will need to convince the courts that the human concept of cruelty is applicable where the maltreatment of nonhuman animals exists. The following periodicals introduce the reader to the issues and organizations dedicated to animals "faring well."

Publications in the area of animal rights, as a general area, are attractive and fascinating to read and can be found for readers of all age groups.

Basic Periodicals

Ems: *A S P C A Animaland, Grrr!;* Hs: *The A V Magazine, P E T A's Animal Times;* Ga: *Act'ionLine, The A V Magazine, P E T A's Animal Times;* Ac: *Journal of Applied Animal Welfare Science, P E T A's Animal Times, Society & Animals;* Sa: *Alternatives to Laboratory Animals, Animal Welfare.*

Basic Abstracts and Indexes

Agricola, Humans & Other Species, UnCover.

604. *A S P C A Animal Watch.* Formerly (until 1992): *A S P C A Report;* Supersedes (in 1981): *A S P C A Bulletin;* Which superseded (in 1977): *Animal Protection.* [ISSN: 1521-6381] 1947. q. Members, USD 20. Ed(s): Marion S Lane. American Society for the Prevention of Cruelty to Animals, 345 Park Ave South 9th Fl, New York, NY 10010-1707; http://www.aspca.org/calendar/watch.htm. Illus. Sample. Circ: 330000. *Aud.:* Hs, Ga.

This magazine is the voice of the American Society for the Prevention of Cruelty to Animals (ASPCA) and is the organization's primary means of communicating with and educating its national membership. It features timely coverage and original reporting on such issues as companion-pet overpopulation and responsible care, horse and farm animal welfare, and zoo and circus animal welfare. This quarterly magazine is nicely laid out, with quality color photography throughout. The overall presentation is biased to the cause. Recommended for public libraries.

605. *A S P C A Animaland.* [ISSN: 1526-9779] bi-m. USD 16. American Society for the Prevention of Cruelty to Animals (A S P C A), 424 E 92nd St, New York, NY 10128-6804; publications@aspca.org; http://www.aspca.org. *Aud.:* Ems.

This magazine for children is sponsored by the American Society for the Prevention of Cruelty to Animals (ASPCA) to introduce them to pet care and basic knowledge of animals. There is a "Parents" section, as well as games and contests to introduce and sensitize young people to animal care and welfare. Appropriate for public and elementary school libraries.

606. *The A V Magazine.* Formerly: *A-V.* [ISSN: 0274-7774] 1892. q. Members, USD 20. Ed(s): Tina Nelson. American Anti-Vivisection Society, Noble Plaza, Ste 204, 801 Old York Rd, Jenkintown, PA 19046; aavsonline@aol.com; http://www.aavs.org/. Illus. Sample. Circ: 11000. Vol. ends: Winter. *Aud.:* Hs, Ga.

This magazine is a publication of the American Anti-Vivisection Society (AAVS), an animal advocacy and educational organization dedicated to ending (yes, ending) experimentation on animals in research, testing, and education, as well as other forms of cruelty to animals. Articles and campaigns are often presented with militant zeal, and at times the publication claims that the "real story" concerning the treatment of laboratory animals can only be found within its covers. Issues are thematically arranged.

607. *A W I Quarterly.* Former titles (until 1992): *Animal Welfare Institute Quarterly;* (until 1981): *Animal Welfare Institute Information Report.* [ISSN: 1071-1384] 1951. q. USD 25. Ed(s): Christine Stevens. Animal Welfare Institute, PO Box 3650, Washington, DC 20007; awi@awionline.org; http://www.awionline.org/. Illus. Sample. Circ: 4000 Paid. Vol. ends: Winter. *Indexed:* Agr. *Bk. rev.:* 2, 500-700. *Aud.:* Hs, Ga.

The Animal Welfare Institute (AWI) publishes this magazine for its members as an awareness tool, reinforcing the notion that as humans we have a long way to go in improving our relationships with and treatment of nonhuman animals. Regular departments are dedicated to farm animals, wildlife and forests, laboratory animals, and marine animals. Conservation issues are also treated regularly, such as cruel trapping and wildlife under threat. Book reviews are also provided. AWI has developed quite a web presence, with recent issues available online. Highly recommended for public libraries.

608. *Act'ionLine.* Former titles: *Friends of Animals Reports; Animals (New York); Actionline.* [ISSN: 1072-2068] 1977. q. USD 25. Ed(s): Priscilla Feral. Friends of Animals, Inc., 777 Post Rd, Ste 205, Darien, CT 06820-4721; http://www.friendsofanimals.org. Illus., index, adv. Sample. Circ: 200000. Vol. ends: Winter. *Bk. rev.:* Occasional. *Aud.:* Hs, Ga.

A magazine published by Friends of Animals (FoA), an international organization dedicated to protecting animals from cruelty, abuse, and institutionalized exploitation. Published quarterly, this magazine is largely a watch forum for FoA members. There are attractive color photographs, a legislative tally (how they voted) on animal rights bills before the U.S. Congress, and URLs and telephone numbers provided for additional information on animal-related topics.

609. *Advocate (Englewood).* Former titles (until 1983): *National Animal Protection Newsletter; Animal Protection News;* Which was formed by the merger of: *National Humane Review; Animal Shelter Shoptalk; National Humane Newsletter; National Humane Shoptalk; American Humane Association Annual Report; American Humane Association. National Humane Report.* [ISSN: 1040-2225] 1952. q. USD 15. Ed(s): Roxanne Hawn. American Humane Association, Animal Protection Division, 63 Inverness Dr E, Englewood, CO 80112-5117; http://www.amerhumane.org. Illus., adv. Sample. Circ: 35000. Vol. ends: No. 3 - No. 4. *Indexed:* Agr. *Aud.:* Hs, Ga.

This magazine is a watch publication of the American Humane Association, which is concerned not only with child protection but animal protection as well. Articles cover a number of areas, including legislative watch, campaigns, and education pieces on humane work in general. Philosophical pieces on why concern for animal welfare is good for society are also included from time to time.

610. *AllAnimals.* Former titles (until 1999): *H S U S News; Humane Society News; Humane Society of the United States. News.* 1954. q. 0 membership. Time, Inc, Time & Life Bldg, Rockefeller Center, 1271 Ave of the Americas, New York, NY 10020-1393. Illus. Circ: 450000. *Aud.:* Hs, Ga.

This magazine of the Humane Society of the United States, attractively laid out, contains numerous photographs and short articles related to the inhumane treatment of animals. Certain topics are regularly discussed, such as not wearing fur and cruel trapping practices. Material is presented in an interesting and readable manner, and animal rights victories are also chronicled. Recommended for large public libraries.

611. ***Alternatives to Laboratory Animals.*** Formerly (until 1983): *A T L A Abstracts.* [ISSN: 0261-1929] 1973. bi-m. Individuals, USD 220. Ed(s): Michael Balls. Fund for the Replacement of Animals in Medical Experiments, Russell & Burch House, 96-98 N Sherwood St, Nottingham, NG1 4EE, United Kingdom; http://www.frame.org.uk. Illus., index, adv. Sample. Refereed. Circ: 850. Vol. ends: Dec. *Indexed:* Agr, BiolAb, ChemAb, DSA, ExcerpMed, FoVS&M, HortAb, IndMed, IndVet, S&F, SCI, SSCI, VetBull. *Bk. rev.:* 4, 575 words. *Aud.:* Ac, Sa.

This journal publishes—according to the web site of Fund for the Replacement of Animals in Medical Experiments (FRAME)—articles on the latest research in any aspect of the development, validation, introduction, and use of alternatives to laboratory animals. International and scientific in its presentation, it regularly includes conference proceedings from major toxicology societies. In addition to scholarly articles, there are extended abstracts, comment, and book reviews. Highly recommended for academic and medical libraries.

612. ***Animal Action.*** Former titles (until 1994): *Animal World;* (until 1981): *Animal Ways.* [ISSN: 1354-7437] 1975. bi-m. GBP 5.40; GBP 6.90 foreign; GBP 1.30 newsstand/cover per issue. Ed(s): Michaela Miller. Royal Society for the Prevention of Cruelty to Animals, Wilberforce Way, Oakhurst Business Park, Southwater, Horsham, RH13 7WN, United Kingdom. Illus., adv. Sample. Circ: 75000. Vol. ends: Dec. *Aud.:* Ems, Hs.

When young persons up to the age of 13 are introduced to the Animal Action Club, the youth membership organization of the RSPCA, they receive the club's 32-page, full-color magazine *Animal Action.* Filled with activities, including games and drawings, this magazine draws on a number of things young people can do while learning about wild and domestic animals. Feature topics of interest include animal rescue and retrieval by the RSPCA and taking care of family pets during the summer. Nicely put together. Recommended for elementary school classes where every student can have a copy; otherwise, be prepared for a very short shelf life.

613. ***Animal Issues.*** Formerly: *Mainstream (Sacramento).* 1969. q. USD 35. Ed(s): Gil Lamont. Animal Protection Institute, PO Box 22505, Sacramento, CA 95822; info@api4animals.org; http://www.api4animals.org. Illus., adv. Sample. Refereed. Circ: 50000 Controlled. Vol. ends: Dec. *Indexed:* GeoRef. *Bk. rev.:* 1, 1,200 words. *Aud.:* Ac.

This quarterly full-color magazine is published to inform and educate the reader about animal protection issues. Published by the Animal Protection Institute, it reflects the organizational goals of investigation, campaign, and education. Feature articles range from the applied (living egg-free; how to treat common dog misbehavior) to the explanatory (a dairy cow's miserable life; grim animal shelters) to remedy (eating to save animal lives; saving the bighorn sheep). Reports and book reviews are also included. Recommended for public and academic libraries.

614. ***Animal Law.*** [ISSN: 1088-8802] 1995. a. USD 8. Ed(s): Kathleen Heimerl. Lewis and Clark College, Northwestern School of Law, 10015 S W Terwilliger Blvd, Portland, OR 97219. Illus. *Indexed:* CLI. *Bk. rev.:* 2, 3,000 words. *Aud.:* Ac, Sa.

This annual student-run law review is the first (and only) review devoted solely to animal issues in the nation. It is scholarly in presentation and legalistic in milieu. Many of the articles argue for the application of human rights to nonhuman animals. Topics include animals as property, correlating the propensity for pet abuse with child abuse, and free-speech protection when speaking out against animal welfare violations. It also contains essays, legislative reviews, and commentary on animal-related issues. The strength of this journal is its dedication to presenting balance in what is a relatively new, evolving law specialty. Highly recommended for academic libraries.

615. ***Animal Sheltering: the community animal care, control, and protection resource.*** Formerly (until 1996): *Shelter Sense.* 1978. bi-m. USD 8. Ed(s): Geoffrey L Handy. Humane Society of the United States, 2100 L St, N W, Washington, DC 20037; asm@ix.netcom.com; http://www.hsus.org/. Illus., adv. Sample. Circ: 3000. Vol. ends: Nov/Dec. *Bk. rev.:* Various number and length. *Aud.:* Sa.

Published by the Humane Society of the United States (HSUS) for animal care and control professionals and others who care about community animal protection, sheltering, and control. In addition to shelter and humane society management and companion animal protection issues, each issue includes a calendar for training and job listings. Feature articles complement regular departments such as "The Frontlines," "Shelterspeak," "How To," "Resources," and "Perspective." It could be of tremendous value to those contemplating a career in animal care and control and is therefore recommended for college libraries.

616. ***Animal Welfare.*** [ISSN: 0962-7286] 1992. q. GBP 70 non-members (Individuals, GBP 50 non-members; Institutional members, GBP 50). Ed(s): James Kirkwood. Universities Federation for Animal Welfare, The Old School, Brewhouse Hill, Wheathampstead, St Albans, AL4 8AN, United Kingdom; ufaw@ufaw.org.uk; http://www.ufaw.org.uk/. Illus., index. Sample. Refereed. *Indexed:* Agr, AnBeAb, BiolAb, ChemAb, DSA, EngInd, ExcerpMed, FS&TA, FoVS&M, IndVet, SCI, SSCI, VetBull, WAE&RSA, ZooRec. *Bk. rev.:* 9, 750 words. *Aud.:* Ac, Sa.

This journal is published by the Universities Federation for Animal Welfare (UFAW), a charitable organization that uses scientific and established expertise to improve the welfare of animals as pets, in zoos, in laboratories, on farms, and in the wild. Since 1926, UFAW has been involved in improving animal welfare. In 1992, it established this quarterly scientific and technical journal, which is distributed worldwide. Sample research titles include "Behavioral and Hormonal Indicators of Enduring Environmental Stress in Dogs" and "Zoo Animals and Their Human Audiences: What Is the Visitor Effect." Highly recommended for academic libraries.

Animals. See Pets section.

617. ***Animals' Agenda: helping people help animals.*** Formerly (until 1985): *Agenda (Westport).* [ISSN: 0892-8819] 1979. bi-m. USD 24; USD 30 in Canada & Mexico; USD 37 elsewhere. Ed(s): Kim W Stallwood. Animal Rights Network, Inc., PO Box 25881, Baltimore, MD 21224; office@animalsagenda.org; http://www.animalsagenda.org. Illus., index, adv. Sample. Refereed. Circ: 30000. Vol. ends: Nov. *Indexed:* AltPI. *Bk. rev.:* 5, 60 words. *Aud.:* Hs, Ga.

This magazine is published by the Animal Rights Network (ARN), which seems to have adopted a less harsh mission for its publication than the previous one—a dedication to the liberation of animals, to informing people about animal rights and cruelty-free living for the purpose of inspiring action for animals. It appears that ARN has both broadened its mission and its publication to become a true network, not just another animal rights organization. There are the usual departments in this bimonthly news magazine. What is new is the expanded reporting on stories and the inclusion of photographs found in other animal rights magazines. By doing this, the magazine seeks to bring together, as one-stop-shopping, all the animal welfare news of the day. The writing is succinct, and the call to activism is clear. The format is a bit crowded, which could mean that ARN members are definitely getting their money's worth. Highly recommended for public and academic libraries.

618. ***Animals Defender.*** Supersedes in part (in 1990): *Campaigner and Animal's Defender;* Which incorporated (in 1986): *Campaigner;* Which was formerly: *Animals: Defender and Anti-Vivisection News.* 1879. s-a. GBP 17; GBP 30 foreign. Ed(s): Jan Creamer. Animal Defenders, 261 Goldhawk Rd, London, W12 8EU, United Kingdom. Adv. *Aud.:* Ga.

Animal Defenders (AD) is a U.K.-based organization whose purpose is to educate, create awareness, and promote the interest of humanity in the cause of justice and the suppression of all forms of cruelty to animals; wherever possible, to alleviate suffering, and to conserve and protect animals and their environment. To this end, the organization investigates and exposes incidents of animal suffering, rescues animals, and supports practical projects to help animals. *Animals Defender* contains regular departments, much the same as any of this sort. What is different is the inclusion of a section, "Young Defenders," for kids, instead of a separate children's publication as many animal welfare organizations produce. It is available to AD members and by subscription.

619. *Animals International.* Formerly: *Animalia;* Which supersedes: *W F P A News.* [ISSN: 0254-3923] 1974. 2x/yr. GBP 12.50; USD 20. Ed(s): Jonathan Pearce. World Society for the Protection of Animals, 2 Langley Ln, London, SW8 1TJ, United Kingdom; wspa@wspa.org.uk; http://www.way.net.wspa/. Illus. Sample. Circ: 35000. Vol. ends: Summer/Fall. *Indexed:* Agr. *Bk. rev.:* 8, 50 words. *Aud.:* Hs, Ga.

This magazine provides information on campaigns, legislative watch, and animal rescues during natural disasters and wars. An "Action" section is also included. This publication is sponsored by the World Society for the Protection of Animals (WPSA), the world's largest network of animal protection specialists, having a membership of over 300 animal protection societies in 71 countries. This magazine provides a dramatic chronicle of abuse toward animals all over the world. Highly recommended for public libraries.

620. *Animals Today.* [ISSN: 1320-2464] 1993. 3x/yr. AUD 25 domestic; AUD 40 foreign. Ed(s): Lisa Curtin, Glenys Oogjes. Australian and New Zealand Federation of Animal Societies Inc., PO Box 1023, Collingwood, VIC 3066, Australia; enquiries@animalsaustralia.org; http://www.animalsaustralia.org. Illus., adv. Sample. Circ: 3000. Vol. ends: Nov. *Aud.:* Hs, Ga.

This magazine is published by Animals Australia, the Australian arm of the Australian and New Zealand Federation of Animal Societies (ANZFAS). The federation deals with most animal welfare and animal rights issues. The magazine includes interviews, news, reviews, and feature articles. It offers a view of the animal rights movement in action outside the United States, and it exposes the reader to the rescue of animals indigenous to other countries. Some examples of content include "Feedlots—A Time Bomb for Cattle" and "Tail Docking of Pups Gets the Chop." Recommended for public libraries.

Anthrozoos. See Pets section.

621. *Farm Animal Voice: better lives for animals and us.* Formerly (until 2001): *Agscene.* [ISSN: 1473-1800] 1967. q. Membership, GBP 21. Ed(s): Joyce D'Silva. Compassion in World Farming Ltd., Charles House, 5a Charles St, Petersfield, GU32 3EH, United Kingdom; http://www.ciwf.co.uk. Illus., adv. Sample. Circ: 20000. *Indexed:* IndVet. *Bk. rev.:* 1,150 words. *Aud.:* Ga.

This publication provides a watch forum for news items related to farming practices that are considered cruel to animals bred for consumption. The organization Compassion in World Farming, whose headquarters is in the United Kingdom, is particularly vigilant in reporting on European causes, such as foot-and-mouth disease, mass slaughter of farm animals, abuses associated with live transport of farm animals, and painful animal-rearing devices. Illustrated, with book reviews.

622. *Grrr!: kids bite back.* [ISSN: 1078-6244] 1994. 2x/yr. Free. Ed(s): Ingrid Newkirk. People for the Ethical Treatment of Animals, Inc., 501 Front St, Norfolk, VA 23510; peta@peta.org; http://www.peta.org. Illus. Sample. Circ: 60000 Free. *Aud.:* Ems.

This is PETA's zine for kids. Filled with simple and fun ways to help animals, it has photos of "regular" kids as well as young celebrities who spread the gospel of animal welfare. Sample content includes feature articles, role models, "Chow Time" (vegan recipes for kids), contests and quizzes, "Hot Times" (summertime dos and don'ts, such as leaving dogs in locked cars), and "Down on the Farm," to name some of the sections. A summer reading list for kids is also available, with titles appropriate to the cause. Recommended for elementary school libraries.

623. *I P P L News.* Formerly (Until 1992): *International Primate Protection League Newsletter.* 1973. 3x/yr. USD 20. Ed(s): Shirley McGreal. International Primate Protection League, PO Box 766, Summerville, SC 29484; info@ippl.org; http://www.ippl.org. Illus. Sample. Circ: 20000. Vol. ends: Nov. *Aud.:* Ga.

This is a publication of the International Primate Protection League (IPPL), an organization working to protect gibbons and all living primates. While the primary focus is on nonhuman primates (monkeys, gibbons, gorillas, chimpanzees, and others) and their well-being throughout the world, it also reports on the good works of human primates to save many animals from mutilation or certain death. There are regular departments and book reviews. It is also a watch magazine: Illegal smuggling activities are exposed, and legislative actions are highlighted. In addition, internationally famous people associated with the movement are occasionally mentioned.

624. *In Defense of Animals Magazine.* q. Ed(s): Laura Moretti. In Defense of Animals, 131 Camino Alto, Ste E, Mill Valley, CA 94941; ida@idausa.org; http://www.petropolitan.com/petpages/pet961025guestbyline.html. Circ: 70000. *Aud.:* Ga.

This magazine is the publishing venue of In Defense of Animals (IDA), an organization that works to end the institutionalized exploitation of animals worldwide. IDA got started in the early 1980s, when a group of activist researchers filed suit against the USDA for failing to order UC–Berkeley to "cease and desist" from running animal-testing laboratories in which animals were sick and dying from deplorable conditions, hygiene failure leading the list. They won their suit, and since then IDA has taken on a number of high-profile animal rescues. The magazine chronicles their activities, including the section "Highlights and Victories." Recommended for public and high school libraries.

625. *International Wolf: the quarterly publication of the International Wolf Center.* [ISSN: 1089-683X] 1990. q. USD 30; USD 6 newsstand/cover per issue. Ed(s): Mary Ortiz. International Wolf Center, 3300 Bass Lake Rd, 202, Minneapolis, MN 55429; mplspack@wolf.org; http://www.wolf.org. Illus., adv. Circ: 10000. *Aud.:* Ga.

This very attractive quarterly from the International Wolf Center is designed to educate its members and the public about wolves. Their social behaviors and migratory patterns, as well as why they need to be reintroduced into the wilderness areas around the world, are but a few of the topics discussed in easy-to-read language. The photography and layout are superb. There is even a section in each issue dedicated to children's education about wolves. Highly recommended for public libraries.

626. *Journal of Applied Animal Welfare Science.* Supersedes (in 1995): *Humane Innovations and Alternatives;* Which was formerly (until 1991): *Humane Innovations and Alternatives in Animal Experimentation.* [ISSN: 1088-8705] 1989. q. USD 270. Ed(s): Stephen Zawistowski, Kenneth Shapiro. Lawrence Erlbaum Associates, Inc., 10 Industrial Ave, Mahwah, NJ 07430-2262; journals@erlbaum.com; http://www.erlbaum.com/. Illus., index, adv. Sample. Refereed. Reprint: PSC. *Indexed:* Agr, ChemAb, DSA, ExcerpMed, IndVet, VetBull, WAE&RSA, ZooRec. *Aud.:* Ac, Sa.

This journal presents scholarly articles, commentary, and book reviews on aspects of the ethical use and treatment of animals used in laboratory and other controlled studies. In other words, ethical treatment itself is the subject of scientific study. When aspects of ethical treatment are translated into variables, these variables are measured for adverse impact on the animals. Examples include the degree of harm to the lab animals, if any, when subjected to deprivation of sleep, food, or social interaction and the degree of harm to the lab animals, if any, when subjected to procedural aspects of experimentation, such as repeated drawing of blood. Strong editing and careful writing make this journal noteworthy. Highly recommended for academic and large public libraries with research collections.

627. *K I N D News.* 1983. m. USD 30 domestic; USD 50 foreign. Ed(s): Jessica Vanase, Cathy Vicenti. National Association for Humane and Environmental Education, PO Box 362, E Haddam, CT 06423-0362; http://www.nahee.org. Circ: 1126400 Paid. *Aud.:* Ems.

KIND [Kids In Nature's Defense] News, published by the National Association for Humane and Environmental Education, has been available since 1983 to help elementary school students develop values of kindness toward people, animals, and the earth. Featured are contributions from readers, celebrity profiles, articles, puzzles, projects, and questions that test reading comprehension. Students learn critical-thinking skills as well as important humane and environmental issues. Subscriptions are available in three reading levels: grades K–2, 3–4, and 5–6. Suitable for elementary school use in the classroom.

628. ***N A V S Bulletin and N A V S Animal Action Report.*** Formerly (until 199?): *N A V S Bulletin.* 1930. q. Members, USD 25. Ed(s): Marcia Kramer. National Anti-Vivisection Society, 53 W Jackson Blvd, Ste 1552, Chicago, IL 60604-3795; navs@navs.org; http://www.navs.org. Illus., adv. Sample. Circ: 30000. Vol. ends: Winter. *Indexed:* CIJE. *Aud.:* Hs, Ga.

Vivisection is "the practice of cutting into or using invasive techniques on live animals or dissecting the bodies of animals." The National Anti-Vivisection Society (NAVS) has opposed the practice since 1929. The fundamental belief of NAVS is that confined laboratory animals may be subjected to extreme pain, deprivation, and distress, and their lives of agony often end in a premature and horrible death. Of equal importance is that, as a scientific methodology, animal experimentation is often invalid and misleading. The magazine, then, is largely a watch publication, with regular columns on animals in education, scientific research, and the law. The bulletin's features are crisp, well-written summaries of daily events related to animal research. Recommended for public and academic libraries.

Our Animals. See Pets section.

629. ***P E T A's Animal Times (English Edition).*** Formerly (until 1994): *P E T A News.* 1980. 5x/yr. Members, USD 16. Ed(s): Ingrid Newkirk. People for the Ethical Treatment of Animals, Inc., 501 Front St, Norfolk, VA 23510; peta@peta.org; http://www.peta.org. Illus. Sample. Circ: 700000. Vol. ends: Winter. *Aud.:* Hs, Ga.

This magazine is published by the famous animal rights organization PETA. It is a glossy magazine with regular departments, articles, and "watch" columns. The magazine has become trendy and includes vegan recipes and profiles of celebrities who support the cause. It has a nice layout and an easy-to-read format. This magazine is not for the reader who insists on bias-free journalism. It is highly recommended, however, for those who want to quickly tap into the information pulse of animal activism. Suggested for public libraries.

630. ***Satya: magazine of vegetarianism, environmentalism, and animal advocacy.*** 1993. m. USD 15. Ed(s): Martin Rowe. Stealth Technologies, Inc., 539 1st St., Brooklyn, NY 11215-2305; stealth@interport.net; http://www.montelis.com/satya/. Illus., adv. Circ: 20000. *Bk. rev.:* 3, 700 words. *Aud.:* Ga.

This magazine contains a rich mix of interviews and feature articles, all held together by a common mission: the promotion of nonviolent social change through vegetarianism, environmentalism, and animal advocacy. Sample topics include fitness, nutrition, animal activism, and avoiding activism burnout. This is also a watch magazine, exposing cruelty and opportunism in settings ranging from industry to processing plants to vivisection laboratories. An interesting, eclectic forum for animal activists.

631. ***Society & Animals: social scientific studies of the human experience of other animals.*** Former titles (until 1993): *P S Y E T A Bulletin;* (until 1986): *P S Y E T A Newsletter.* [ISSN: 1063-1119] 1983. q. EUR 119 print & online eds. (Individuals, EUR 42 print & online eds.). Ed(s): Kenneth Shapiro. Brill Academic Publishers, Inc., PO Box 9000, Leiden, 2300 PA, Netherlands; cs@brill.nl; http://www.brill.nl. Illus., index, adv. Sample. Refereed. Circ: 400. Online: EBSCO Publishing; Ingenta Select; OCLC Online Computer Library Center, Inc.; RoweCom Information Quest; Swets Blackwell. *Indexed:* Agr, CJA, FoVS&M, IBSS, SSCI, SociolAb, ZooRec. *Bk. rev.:* 4, 1,050 words. *Aud.:* Ac.

This journal is published by Psychologists for the Ethical Treatment of Animals (PSYETA), "comprised of psychologists working with other professional and animal rights organizations to change the way individuals and society as a whole treat non-human animals." While the journal purports to investigate the many ways that non-human animals figure in our lives, it is readily admitted that "findings regarding non-human animal experience and behavior are included only secondarily to that end." Sample topics include childhood socialization and companion animals, animals in children's lives, and functions of repetitive talk to dogs during play. Book reviews are also published. Recommended for academic libraries.

632. ***The Vegan.*** [ISSN: 0307-4811] 1946. q. GBP 7.80 domestic; GBP 9.80 overseas; GBP 1.95 newsstand/cover per issue. Ed(s): Richard Farhall. Vegan Society, 7 Battle Rd, St Leonards-on-Sea, TN37 7AA, United Kingdom; info@vegansociety.com; http://www.vegansociety.com/. Illus., adv. Sample. Circ: 7000. Vol. ends: Winter. *Aud.:* Ga.

Veganism is spreading! The desire to make a personal statement about compassion toward animals and their rights as beings, as well as a concern for one's own health, has prompted many to adopt the vegan lifestyle. Vegans avoid all animal products and their derivatives. According to the Vegan Society, people decide to adopt the vegan lifestyle for five reasons: animal rights/welfare, health, environment, resource use, and spiritual growth. This magazine, then, is devoted to nutrition, health concerns, and how to eat vegan. Recipes are provided in each issue, as well as ads for products endorsed by the society.

Electronic Journals

633. ***Ark Online: the online magazine for people who care about animals.*** irreg. Ed(s): Bob Schlesinger. Ark Online, bob@arkonline.com; http://www.arkonline.com/. *Aud.:* Ga.

Ark Online is an independent publication "staffed by a small group of people who care about animals and want to use the web to broadcast information about animal welfare to a wide array of readers." The editors acknowledge a wonderful group of contributors who help to make the e-zine a success (and it is). There are articles, news stories, action alerts, and activities for the reader, many to be found in regularly updated sections. The "Featured Links" section is very good, and the "Shelters and Adoptions" section is outstanding. Recommended for academic and public libraries.

■ ANTHROPOLOGY

Patricia A. Lenkowski, Instructional Media Librarian, F.H. Green Library, West Chester University of Pennsylvania, West Chester, PA 19383; plenkowski@wcupa.edu; FAX: 610-436-2251

Introduction

The study of humankind and the description and interpretation of the peoples of the world, past and present, defines anthropology. It studies all aspects of culture and society. It looks at group relationships, traditions, social structures, tools, language, economics, music, and art. The four major branches of anthropology are archaeology, physical anthropology, cultural or social anthropology, and linguistics. Each branch is further split into many subdivisions. Though archaeology and linguistics fall under the broad discipline of anthropology, they each have separate sections. The professional organization for anthropology is the American Anthropological Association (AAA). The AAA is a major publisher of anthropology serials, and several of its titles are listed in this section. A library's core journal collection should contain some of the association's titles.

Because there are several major branches as well as many subdivisions of the branches of anthropology, there are many journals published to cover the wide range of the discipline. Titles that represent the four branches were selected for inclusion and were chosen for breadth rather than depth in both subject material and geographic coverage. This selection of anthropological journals provides information for building a core periodical collection and enhancing weak collections.

Basic Periodicals

Ga: *American Anthropologist, Annual Review of Anthropology, Current Anthropology, Reviews in Anthropology;* Ac: *American Anthropologist, American Ethnologist, American Journal of Physical Anthropology, Current Anthropology, Royal Anthropological Institute. Journal.*

Basic Abstracts and Indexes

Abstracts in Anthropology, Anthropological Index, Anthropological Literature.

634. ***American Anthropologist.*** [ISSN: 0002-7294] 1899. q. USD 105 (Individuals, USD 50). Ed(s): Robert Sussman. American Anthropological Association, 4350 N Fairfax Dr, Ste 640, Arlington, VA 22203-1620; http://www.ameranthassn.org/ameranth.htm. Illus., index, adv. Refereed. Circ: 12000. Vol. ends: Dec. Microform: PQC. Online: bigchalk; Gale Group; JSTOR (Web-based Journal Archive); OCLC Online Computer Library Center, Inc.; ProQuest Information & Learning; H.W. Wilson. Reprint: PSC. *Indexed:* ABS&EES, AICP, AbAn, AgeL, AmH&L, AnthLit, ArtHuCI, B&AI, BAS, BEL&L, BRD, BRI, BiolAb, BrArAb, CBRI, CJA, CommAb, ExcerpMed, FLI, GSI, GeoRef, IBSS, IBZ, IPSA, L&LBA, MLA-IB, MRD, NumL, PRA, PSA, PsycholAb, RI-1, SSCI, SSI, SWA, SociolAb, WAE&RSA, ZooRec. *Bk. rev.:* 50-60, 250-300 words. *Aud.:* Ga, Ac.

More than 100 years in publication, this is the flagship journal of the American Anthropological Association. It is the most general and most comprehensive of all the association's publications. Articles, essays, commentaries, and research reports on the four major areas of the field—archaeology, biology, ethnology, and linguistics—are published, as well as many reviews of books, audiovisual materials, and exhibits. Issues average six or more major articles of 10–15 pages in length. A core title in anthropology.

635. ***American Ethnologist.*** [ISSN: 0094-0496] 1974. q. USD 70 (Individuals, USD 50). Ed(s): Carol Greenhouse. American Anthropological Association, 4350 N Fairfax Dr, Ste 640, Arlington, VA 22203-1620; http://www.ameranthassn.org/aespubs.htm. Illus., index, adv. Refereed. Circ: 3000. Vol. ends: Nov. Microform: PQC. Online: Gale Group; JSTOR (Web-based Journal Archive); OCLC Online Computer Library Center, Inc.; ProQuest Information & Learning; H.W. Wilson. *Indexed:* AICP, AbAn, AnthLit, ArtHuCI, BAS, BRI, CBRI, CommAb, IBSS, LRI, PRA, PsycholAb, RI-1, RILM, SSCI, SSI, SociolAb. *Bk. rev.:* 40, length varies. *Aud.:* Ac.

Articles concerning any human group or society are the focus of this journal. Major areas addressed include social organization, ecology, politics, ethnicity, ritual, and economy. This title would be a good basic journal in most academic collections. The book review section is substantial, averaging 40 reviews per issue, although a recent issue had only a few reviews and a lengthy review article. Most issues contain six to eight articles of 20 or more pages each.

American Indian Quarterly. See Native Americans section.

636. ***American Journal of Physical Anthropology.*** [ISSN: 0002-9483] 1918. 14x/yr. USD 1715 United States; USD 1855 in Canada & Mexico; USD 1974 elsewhere. Ed(s): Emoke J E Szathmary. John Wiley & Sons, Inc., 111 River St, Hoboken, NJ 07030; uscs-wis@wiley.com; http://www.wiley.com. Illus., index, adv. Refereed. Circ: 2550. Vol. ends: Dec. Microform: PQC. Online: EBSCO Publishing; Gale Group; ScienceDirect; Wiley InterScience. Reprint: PSC; SWZ. *Indexed:* AICP, AbAn, AnthLit, ArtHuCI, BAS, BiolAb, DSA, ExcerpMed, ForAb, GeoRef, IBSS, IndMed, IndVet, RRTA, SCI, SSCI, SSI, SWA, VetBull, WAE&RSA, ZooRec. *Bk. rev.:* 5-10, 1,200 words. *Aud.:* Ac.

This is a major scholarly journal in the area of physical anthropology. It is issued 14 times per year and publishes articles on human evolution, behavior, genetics, and primate physiology, among other topics. "Brief Communication" articles, technical reports, letters, book reviews, and a list of books received are in many issues. The proceedings of the American Association of Physical Anthropologists annual meeting is published as a supplement. Articles are 7–15 pages long, and there are about eight per issue. This is one of the most expensive journals in anthropology, and that alone may factor into subscription decisions. It is also available in an online version.

637. ***Annual Review of Anthropology.*** Formerly (until 1971): *Biennial Review of Anthropology.* [ISSN: 0084-6570] 1959. a. USD 150 (Individuals, USD 65). Ed(s): Samuel Gubins, William Durham. Annual Reviews, 4139 El Camino Way, Palo Alto, CA 94303-0139; service@annualreviews.org; http://www.annualreviews.org. Illus., index, adv. Refereed. Microform: PQC. Online: Gale Group; HighWire Press; Swets Blackwell. Reprint: PSC. *Indexed:* AICP, AnthLit, BAS, BiolAb, BrArAb, ChemAb, GeoRef, IBSS, IBZ, IPSA, L&LBA, MRD, NumL, PSA, PsycholAb, SSCI, SSI, SociolAb. *Aud.:* Ga, Ac.

Like most annual reviews, the *Annual Review of Anthropology* is used to keep current with recent trends and research in the discipline. The articles are written for general readership and for anthropologists, to make them aware of significant literature and current developments. Each article includes an abstract and keywords. A current subscription to an "Annual Reviews" series includes both print and online products.

Anthropological Linguistics. See Linguistics section.

638. ***Anthropological Quarterly.*** Formerly (until 1953): *Primitive Man.* [ISSN: 0003-5491] 1928. q. USD 59 (Individuals, USD 46). Ed(s): Roy Richard Grinker. Institute for Ethnographic Research, George Washington University, 2110 G St, NW, Washington, DC 20052. Illus., index, adv. Refereed. Circ: 913. Vol. ends: Oct. Microform: MIM; PQC. Online: bigchalk; Chadwyck-Healey Incorporated; EBSCO Publishing; Gale Group; Northern Light Technology, Inc.; OCLC Online Computer Library Center, Inc.; Project MUSE; ProQuest Information & Learning; RoweCom Information Quest; Swets Blackwell; H.W. Wilson. Reprint: PQC. *Indexed:* ABS&EES, AICP, AbAn, AgeL, AnthLit, ArtHuCI, BAS, CPL, CommAb, EIP, IBSS, IBZ, IMFL, L&LBA, MLA-IB, PSA, RI-1, SSCI, SSI, SWA, SociolAb, WAE&RSA. *Bk. rev.:* Various number and length. *Aud.:* Ga, Ac.

Focusing on social and cultural anthropology, this journal is cross-disciplinary and therefore of interest to many other disciplines in the social sciences. Both scholarly and review articles are featured. The journal averages three articles (15 pages) per issue, a section on thought and commentary, and five book reviews, as well as a lengthy list of books received.

639. ***Anthropology & Education Quarterly.*** Former titles: *Council on Anthropology and Education Quarterly; C A E Newsletter.* [ISSN: 0161-7761] 1970. q. USD 60 (Individuals, USD 40). Ed(s): Kathryn Anderson Levitt. American Anthropological Association, 4350 N Fairfax Dr, Ste 640, Arlington, VA 22203-1620; http://www.ameranthassn.org/caepubs.htm. Illus., index, adv. Refereed. Circ: 1000. Vol. ends: Dec. Microform: PQC. Online: OCLC Online Computer Library Center, Inc.; ProQuest Information & Learning; H.W. Wilson. Reprint: PQC. *Indexed:* ABS&EES, AICP, AnthLit, ArtHuCI, CIJE, EduInd, L&LBA, PsycholAb, RI-1, SSCI, SSI, SWA. *Aud.:* Ga, Ac.

This journal, the official publication of the Council on Anthropology and Education, publishes four or five articles per issue on human learning inside and outside of formal schools, on schooling in cultural or social context, and on the teaching of anthropology. Articles are about 20 pages in length and would interest educators, sociologists, and social workers in addition to anthropologists. Beginning in April 2001, book reviews are available only online. The list is cumulative from 1996 and arranged alphabetically by author.

640. ***Anthropology and Humanism.*** Formerly (until 1992): *Anthropology and Humanism Quarterly.* 1974. s-a. Members, USD 20; Non-members, USD 35. Ed(s): Edith Turner. American Anthropological Association, 4350 N Fairfax Dr, Ste 640, Arlington, VA 22203-1620; http://www.ameranthass.org/shapubs.htm. Illus. Circ: 455. Vol. ends: Dec. *Indexed:* AICP, AbAn, AnthLit, IBSS. *Bk. rev.:* 3-5, 1,200 words. *Aud.:* Ga, Ac.

A publication of the Society for Humanistic Anthropology, this title celebrates human reality and promotes multicultural understanding. Recent issues contain about seven scholarly articles as well as poetry and fiction. There are also a few book reviews in some issues.

641. ***Anthropos: revue internationale d'ethnologie et de linguistique.*** [ISSN: 0257-9774] 1906. 2x/yr. CHF 180. Editions Saint-Paul, Perolles 42, Fribourg, 1700, Switzerland. Illus., index. Refereed. Circ: 1000. *Indexed:* AICP, AbAn, AnthLit, BAS, IBSS, IBZ, L&LBA, MLA-IB, PSA, PsycholAb, RI-1, RILM, SSCI, SSI, SociolAb. *Bk. rev.:* 30, length varies. *Aud.:* Ac.

Its international character and its pluralistic approach are distinguishing marks of this journal. Articles on the anthropology of religion, economic and social anthropology, culture history, and linguistics are included in this publication. Every issue has about 700 pages, to which roughly 125 authors typically contribute. Each issue contains over ten articles of 15–20 pages, as well as reports and comments. Article abstracts are available on the web. Half of each issue is devoted to about 30 book reviews of a page or two in length.

642. ***Arctic Anthropology.*** [ISSN: 0066-6939] 1962. s-a. USD 150 (Individuals, USD 48). Ed(s): Susan Kaplan. University of Wisconsin Press, Journal Division, 1930 Monroe St., 3rd Fl, Madison, WI 53711; journals@uwpress.wisc.edu; http://www.wisc.edu/wisconsinpress/journals. Illus., index, adv. Refereed. Circ: 800. Microform: PQC. Online: EBSCO Publishing. Reprint: PQC; PSC. *Indexed:* ABS&EES, AICP, AbAn, AmH&L, AnthLit, ArtHuCI, BAS, BiolAb, GeoRef, GeogAbPG, SSCI, SWA. *Bk. rev.:* Various number and length. *Aud.:* Ga, Ac.

Scholarly, yet engaging and accessible, this journal focuses on arctic and subarctic cultures and peoples. Recent issues contain articles from international contributors writing on interdisciplinary Northern research and cultures of the circumpolar zone. Recent issues average eight articles, 15 pages in length, most with illustrations, photos, maps, or charts.

643. ***The Australian Journal of Anthropology.*** Formerly (until 1990): *Mankind.* [ISSN: 1035-8811] 1931. 3x/yr. AUD 100 (Individuals, AUD 60; Members, AUD 50). Ed(s): Michael Allen. Australian Anthropological Society, c/o Dept. of Anthropology, Univ. of Sydney, Sydney, NSW 2006, Australia; aas.taja@anthropology.usyd.edu.au. Illus., index, adv. Refereed. Circ: 450 Paid. Online: Chadwyck-Healey Incorporated; EBSCO Publishing; Florida Center for Library Automation; Gale Group; Northern Light Technology, Inc.; OCLC Online Computer Library Center, Inc.; ProQuest Information & Learning; RMIT Publishing. *Indexed:* AICP, AbAn, AnthLit, BAS, BrArAb, IBSS, MLA-IB, PSA, SSCI, SSI, SociolAb. *Bk. rev.:* Number varies, 800-1,000 words. *Aud.:* Ga, Ac.

This refereed scholarly journal of anthropology and related disciplines continues the journal *Mankind.* It publishes "theoretically focused analyses and fieldwork-based reports on research carried out in Australia and neighboring countries in the Pacific and Asian regions." One of the three annual issues is devoted to a special topic. One such issue examined the "politics of dance," summarizing and challenging current anthropological thinking on the subject. Recent articles have analyzed a fire-walking ritual as an act of aesthetic discovery, changing trends and methods in anthropology, and the relevance of the senses of taste and smell versus hearing and sight in Western metaphysics. Though intended for a scholarly audience, this journal, relatively jargon-free, may be of interest to a wider audience, including undergraduates and educated public. (ChD)

644. ***Cultural Anthropology.*** [ISSN: 0886-7356] 1986. q. USD 50 (Individuals, USD 40). Ed(s): Daniel Segal. American Anthropological Association, 4350 N Fairfax Dr, Ste 640, Arlington, VA 22203-1620; cultanth@email.pitzer.edu; http://www.pitzer.edu/~cultanth/. Illus., adv. Refereed. Circ: 1000. Vol. ends: Nov. Reprint: PQC; SWZ. *Indexed:* ABS&EES, AICP, ASSIA, AbAn, AmH&L, AnthLit, ArtHuCI, BAS, ForAb, IBSS, L&LBA, RI-1, RRTA, SSCI, SSI, SociolAb, WAE&RSA. *Aud.:* Ac.

This journal publishes articles on a broad array of cultural issues in many cultures. Each issue contains about four lengthy, 25-page articles. In about half the issues, there are one or two review essays under the feature title "In the News." The web version provides audio and video clips as companion pieces to the print journal; however, the web site does not contain the full text of the articles.

645. ***Current Anthropology.*** Formerly (until 1956): *Yearbook of Anthropology.* [ISSN: 0011-3204] 1955. 5x/yr. USD 200 and in Australia, Hong Kong, Japan, New Zealand, & W. Europe for print & online eds. (Individuals, USD 50 and in Australia, Hong Kong, Japan, New Zealand, & W. Europe for print & online eds.). Ed(s): Benjamin S Orlove. University of Chicago Press, Journals Division, PO Box 37005, Chicago, IL 60637; subscriptions@press.uchicago.edu; http://www.journals.uchicago.edu. Illus., index, adv. Refereed. Circ: 4000. Vol. ends: Dec. Microform: PQC. Online: bigchalk; EBSCO Publishing; Florida Center for Library Automation; Gale Group; JSTOR (Web-based Journal Archive); ProQuest Information & Learning. Reprint: ISI; PQC; PSC. *Indexed:* ABS&EES, AICP, AbAn, AgeL, AnthLit, ArtHuCI, BAS, BiolAb, BrArAb, CommAb, GeoRef, IBSS, IBZ, IPSA, L&LBA, MLA-IB, NumL, PSA, PsycholAb, RI-1, RILM, SCI, SSCI, SSI, SWA, SociolAb, ZooRec. *Bk. rev.:* 3-5, 2,000 words. *Aud.:* Ga, Ac.

A transnational journal devoted to research in a wide variety of areas, including social, cultural, and physical anthropology, as well as ethnology, archaeology, folklore, and linguistics. Each issue is comprised of two to four major articles with several comments and the authors' replies to the comments. Issues also include reports on research, professional news, a few book reviews, and a list of books received. Beginning in 2003 a new section, "Anthropological Currents," will summarize empirical research in other publications. For a professional and general readership.

646. ***Dialectical Anthropology: an independent international journal in the critical tradition committed to the transformation of our society and the humane union of theory and practice.*** [ISSN: 0304-4092] 1975. q. EUR 345 print or online ed. (Individuals, EUR 154 print or online ed.). Ed(s): Marie Josephine Diamond. Kluwer Academic Publishers, van Godewijckstraat 30, PO Box 17, Dordrecht, 3300 AA, Netherlands. Illus., index, adv. Vol. ends: Dec. Microform: PQC. Online: EBSCO Publishing; ingenta.com; Kluwer Online; OCLC Online Computer Library Center, Inc.; Ovid Technologies, Inc.; RoweCom Information Quest; Swets Blackwell. Reprint: SWZ. *Indexed:* AICP, AbAn, AltPI, AnthLit, ArtHuCI, BAS, IBSS, PRA, PSA, PhilInd, SSCI, SociolAb. *Aud.:* Ac.

"An independent international journal in the critical tradition committed to the transformation of our society and the humane union of theory and practice." This journal publishes social critiques of every aspect of contemporary civilization, comparative and historical essays, case studies of crisis and transition, and professional or personal memoirs. The journal is a contributor to the radical literature of our time. Issues average four or five essays of 20–30 pages in length. Available in print or electronic format.

Ethnohistory. See Ethnic Studies section.

647. ***Ethnology: an international journal of cultural and social anthropology.*** [ISSN: 0014-1828] 1962. q. USD 40 (Individuals, USD 21). Ed(s): Leonard Plotnicov. University of Pittsburgh, Department of Anthropology, 3H01 WWPH, Pittsburgh, PA 15260; ethnolog@pitt.edu; http://www.pitt.edu/~ethnolog. Illus., index, adv. Refereed. Circ: 2000 Paid. Vol. ends: Oct. Microform: PQC. Online: bigchalk; Chadwyck-Healey Incorporated; EBSCO Publishing; Florida Center for Library Automation; Gale Group; Northern Light Technology, Inc.; OCLC Online Computer Library Center, Inc.; ProQuest Information & Learning. Reprint: PQC; PSC. *Indexed:* ABS&EES, AICP, AbAn, AmH&L, AnthLit, ArtHuCI, BAS, BiolAb, BrArAb, IBSS, IBZ, IPSA, MLA-IB, PSA, RI-1, SSCI, SSI, SUSA, SWR&A, SociolAb, WAE&RSA. *Aud.:* Ga, Ac.

This journal offers a broad range of articles on cultural and social anthropology. It is highly readable and reflects a cross-section of specializations, making it useful for teaching, reference, and general readership. There are on average five articles per issue, each about 15 pages long.

648. ***Ethnos.*** [ISSN: 0014-1844] 1936. 3x/yr. GBP 174 (Individuals, GBP 57). Ed(s): Don Kulick, Wilhelm Oestberg. Routledge, 11 New Fetter Ln, London, EC4P 4EE, United Kingdom; info@routledge.co.uk; http://www.routledge.co.uk. Illus., index, adv. Refereed. Circ: 1000. Online: EBSCO Publishing; Ingenta Select; OCLC Online Computer Library Center, Inc.; RoweCom Information Quest; Swets Blackwell. Reprint: PSC; SWZ. *Indexed:* AIAP, AICP, ASSIA, AbAn, AnthLit, BAS, BiolAb, BiolDig, HAPI, IBSS, IBZ, L&LBA, PSA, RI-1, SSCI, SociolAb. *Bk. rev.:* Number varies, 1,000 words. *Aud.:* Ac.

Original papers on theoretical, methodological, and empirical developments in the discipline of sociocultural anthropology are featured in this publication. Contributors are international, and the scope is global. Each issue averages five articles of 25 pages, with book reviews and correspondence. Available in print or electronic format.

649. ***Ethos (Washington).*** [ISSN: 0091-2131] 1973. q. USD 60 (Individuals, USD 44). Ed(s): Thomas J Csordas, Janis H Jenkins. American Anthropological Association, 4350 N Fairfax Dr, Ste 640, Arlington, VA 22203-1620; ethos@po.cwru.edu; http://www.cwru.edu/orgs/spa/ethos.html. Illus., adv. Refereed. Circ: 1100. Vol. ends: Dec. Microform: PQC. Online: JSTOR (Web-based Journal Archive); ProQuest Information & Learning. Reprint: PQC. *Indexed:* AbAn, AnthLit, IBSS, L&LBA, PsycholAb, SSCI. *Aud.:* Ac.

This journal is the publication of the Society for Psychological Anthropology. It features the relationship between the individual and society. The editors "intend the journal to be instrumental in fostering the growth of an international, interdisciplinary community of scholars in psychocultural research and theory." Topics include psychodynamics, psychoanalysis, child development and socialization, interpersonal interaction, emotion, perception, motivation, self and identity, and religion. Most issues contain four to six articles approximately 30 pages in length, with occasional commentary. There are often theme issues.

650. ***Evolutionary Anthropology: issues, news, and reviews.*** [ISSN: 1060-1538] 1992. bi-m. USD 365 domestic; USD 425 in Canada & Mexico; USD 476 elsewhere. Ed(s): John Fleagle. John Wiley & Sons, Inc., 111 River St, Hoboken, NJ 07030; uscs-wis@wiley.com; http://www.wiley.com. Illus., adv. Refereed. Microform: PQC. Online: EBSCO Publishing; ScienceDirect; Wiley InterScience. *Indexed:* AICP, AbAn, AnthLit, IBSS, SSCI, ZooRec. *Aud.:* Ac.

This is a review journal that publishes four or five scholarly articles on contemporary research in paloeoanthropology and biological anthropology. In addition, the journal has articles on social biology, bone biology, and human biology. Book reviews, professional news, letters to the editor, and a calendar are included. Available in print or electronic format.

Human Ecology. See Environment and Conservation section.

651. ***Human Evolution: international journal.*** [ISSN: 0393-9375] 1986. q. ITL 200000 (Individuals, ITL 150000). Ed(s): A B Chiarelli. Angelo Pontecorboli Editore, Via Trieste 16, Florence, 50139, Italy; pontecorboli@fol.it; http://www.pontecorboli.com. Illus., index, adv. Circ: 700. Vol. ends: Dec. *Indexed:* AICP, AnthLit, BAS, ExcerpMed, GeoRef, ZooRec. *Aud.:* Ac.

Published in Italy with text in English and summaries in French, this journal is international in coverage and is devoted to the arena of primates and human evolution. Average issues contain five articles of varying length. Of interest to scholars and professionals.

652. ***Human Organization.*** Formerly: *Applied Anthropology.* [ISSN: 0018-7259] 1941. q. USD 75. Ed(s): Donald D Stull. Society for Applied Anthropology, PO Box 2436, Oklahoma City, OK 73101; info@sfaa.net; http://www.sfaa.net. Illus., index, adv. Refereed. Circ: 4700. Vol. ends: Winter. Online: bigchalk; Gale Group; Northern Light Technology, Inc.; OCLC Online Computer Library Center, Inc.; ProQuest Information & Learning. *Indexed:* ABIn, AICP, ASG, AbAn, AgeL, AnthLit, BAS, CIJE, CJA, CommAb, DSA, FPA, ForAb, HRA, IBSS, IBZ, IPSA, IndVet, MCR, PRA, PSA, PsycholAb, RRTA, S&F, SFSA, SSCI, SSI, SUSA, SWA, SWR&A, SociolAb, VetBull, WAE&RSA. *Aud.:* Ac.

This journal, a publication of the Society for Applied Anthropology, covers all areas of applied social science. Each issue contains eight to ten articles of ten pages focusing on case studies, comparative studies, and fieldwork with an international approach. Meeting and conference notes, comments on previously published pieces, and commentaries are also included.

653. ***International Journal of Anthropology.*** [ISSN: 0393-9383] 1986. q. ITL 150000 (Individuals, ITL 120000). Ed(s): Brunetto Chiarelli. Angelo Pontecorboli Editore, Via Trieste 16, Florence, 50139, Italy; pontecorboli@fol.it; http://www.pontecorboli.com. Illus., index, adv. Circ: 500. Vol. ends: Dec. *Indexed:* AICP, AnthLit, ExcerpMed. *Aud.:* Ac.

As the official organ of the European Anthropological Association, this journal is a good source for current research in the international anthropological community. Issues cover biological anthropology. Subjects include studies on paleoanthropology, primate ethology, paleopathology, and biosocial anthropology. The articles vary in number and length from issue to issue.

654. ***Journal of Anthropological Archaeology.*** [ISSN: 0278-4165] 1982. q. EUR 364 (Individuals, EUR 88). Ed(s): John M O'Shea. Academic Press, 525 B St, Ste 1900, San Diego, CA 92101-4495; apsubs@acad.com; http://www.academicpress.com. Illus. Refereed. Vol. ends: Dec. Online: EBSCO Publishing; Gale Group; ingenta.com; OCLC Online Computer Library Center, Inc.; RoweCom Information Quest; ScienceDirect; Swets Blackwell. *Indexed:* AICP, AbAn, AnthLit, ArtHuCI, BAS, BrArAb, GeoRef, HumInd, IBSS, NumL, SSCI. *Aud.:* Ac.

This journal publishes articles on the theory and methodology of archaeology as it relates to human societies, covering the broadest scope of time. Issues typically carry three or four scholarly articles ranging in length from 15 to 40 pages, with most being 30 pages long. An occasional special-topics issue will have shorter contributions. Available in print and electronic format, the online version posts the articles as they are finally accepted.

655. ***Journal of Anthropological Research.*** Formerly: *Southwestern Journal of Anthropology.* [ISSN: 0091-7710] 1945. q. USD 50 (Individuals, USD 30). Ed(s): Lawrence G Straus. University of New Mexico, Department of Anthropology, Anthropology Building, Room 240, Albuquerque, NM 87131; lstraus@unm.edu; jar45@unm.edu; http://www.unm.edu/~jar. Illus., index. Refereed. Circ: 1200 Paid. Vol. ends: Winter. Microform: PQC. Online: Gale Group. Reprint: PQC; PSC. *Indexed:* ABS&EES, AICP, AbAn, AmH&L, AnthLit, ArtHuCI, BAS, BiolAb, BrArAb, CommAb, IBSS, L&LBA, LRI, MLA-IB, NumL, PRA, RI-1, SSCI, SSI, SociolAb, WAE&RSA. *Aud.:* Ga, Ac.

Publishes recent research from all areas of anthropology, primarily on the Americas but with an occasional international piece. Most issues have four articles 20 pages in length and approximately 15 current, critical book reviews.

656. ***Journal of Human Evolution.*** [ISSN: 0047-2484] 1972. m. EUR 1258 (Individuals, EUR 474). Ed(s): T. Harrison, F. Spoor. Academic Press, Harcourt Pl, 32 Jamestown Rd, London, NW1 7BY, United Kingdom; apsubs@acad.com; http://www.elsevier-international.com/serials/. Illus., adv. Refereed. Vol. ends: Dec. Online: EBSCO Publishing; ingenta.com; OCLC Online Computer Library Center, Inc.; RoweCom Information Quest; ScienceDirect; Swets Blackwell. Reprint: SWZ. *Indexed:* AICP, AbAn, AnthLit, ArtHuCI, BiolAb, BrArAb, ExcerpMed, GeoRef, GeogAbPG, IBSS, IndMed, SCI, SSCI, ZooRec. *Bk. rev.:* Various number and length. *Aud.:* Ac.

This journal is devoted to publishing research papers on all aspects of human evolution, especially palaeoanthropological work on human and primate fossils. Three to six articles per issues are typical, most are 15–20 pages long. Additional features that may be included are communications on new discoveries, reports of meetings, and review papers. Also included are abstracts for the Paleoanthropology Society meeting. Available in print and electronic format.

657. ***Journal of Latin American Anthropology.*** [ISSN: 1085-7052] 1995. s-a. USD 40 (Individuals, USD 25). Ed(s): Wendy A Weiss. American Anthropological Association, 4350 N Fairfax Dr, Ste 640, Arlington, VA 22203-1620. *Indexed:* AbAn, AnthLit, SSI, SociolAb. *Aud.:* Ac.

The official publication of the Latin American Anthropology Section of the American Anthropological Association, this journal is devoted to publishing articles on anthropological research in Mexico, Central and South America, and the Caribbean. Articles may be published in Spanish or English. Each issue has five to seven articles, and theme issues are common.

658. ***Journal of Linguistic Anthropology.*** [ISSN: 1055-1360] 1991. s-a. USD 40 (Individuals, USD 38). Ed(s): Judith T Irvine. American Anthropological Association, 4350 N Fairfax Dr, Ste 640, Arlington, VA

22203-1620; http://www.ameranthassn.org/slapnbs.html. Illus. Refereed. Vol. ends: Dec. *Indexed:* AICP, AbAn, AnthLit, L&LBA, MLA-IB, SociolAb. *Bk. rev.:* Various number and length. *Aud.:* Ac.

This journal commonly publishes research results, critical essays, and book reviews on linguistic anthropology and closely related topics. Each issue typically has four articles and ten book reviews. Book reviews are available online as of December 2002. Some issues also contain commentaries and discussions, interviews, and brief translations. This is a specialist journal.

659. ***Man in India.*** [ISSN: 0025-1569] 1921. q. USD 32. Ed(s): Surajit Sinha. Man in India, 18 Church Rd., Ranchi, 834 001, India. Illus., index. Refereed. Circ: 800. Vol. ends: Dec. Reprint: SWZ. *Indexed:* AICP, AbAn, AgeL, AnthLit, ArtHuCI, BAS, BiolAb, FPA, ForAb, IBSS, RI-1, RRTA, SSCI, WAE&RSA. *Aud.:* Ga, Ac.

The "man" in this anthropology title refers to humankind. This scholarly journal publishes articles, notes, communications, and review articles on "biological and socio-cultural anthropology, archaeology, linguistics and folk-culture." Occasionally, special thematic issues are published, as one recent issue on tribal society that included articles on health-seeking behavior, crop rotation, and child-rearing practices among various tribal cultures. Other recent topics have included studies of economic development and its effects on sustainability, and genetic consequences of various mating systems, including inbreeding. The text is illustrated with sketches, tables, and graphs. A useful journal on Indian society for academic libraries serving anthropology or Asian Studies departments. (CMD)

660. ***Mankind Quarterly: an international quarterly journal dealing with both physical and cultural anthropology including related subjects such as psychology, demography, genetics, linguistics and mythology.*** [ISSN: 0025-2344] 1960. q. USD 89 (Individuals, USD 39.50). Ed(s): Richard Lynn. Scott - Townsend Publishers, PO Box 34070, N W, Washington, DC 20043; socecon@aol.com. Illus., index, adv. Refereed. Circ: 1025. Vol. ends: Winter. *Indexed:* AICP, ASSIA, AbAn, AnthLit, ArtHuCI, BAS, BiolAb, IBSS, IBZ, L&LBA, MLA-IB, PAIS, PsycholAb, RI-1, SSCI, SociolAb. *Bk. rev.:* Various number and length. *Aud.:* Ac.

The journal subtitle says it all: "an international quarterly journal dealing with both physical and cultural anthropology including related subjects such as psychology, demography, genetics, linguistics and mythology." It is international in both scope and authorship and takes a general approach to anthropology, but it is written for scholars and professionals. Book reviews vary in number and length.

661. ***Medical Anthropology Quarterly: international journal for the cultural and social analysis of health.*** Former titles: *Medical Anthropology Newsletter; Medical Anthropology.* [ISSN: 0745-5194] 1970. q. USD 80 (Individuals, USD 75). Ed(s): Mac Marshall. American Anthropological Association, 4350 N Fairfax Dr, Ste 640, Arlington, VA 22203-1620; http://www.ameranthassn.org/smapubs.htm. Illus., adv. Refereed. Circ: 2000. Vol. ends: Dec. Reprint: ISI; PQC. *Indexed:* AICP, AbAn, AgeL, AnthLit, ArtHuCI, IBSS, IndMed, SSCI, SSI, SociolAb. *Bk. rev.:* Various number and length. *Aud.:* Ac.

The range of subjects in this journal includes illness, disease, and health of individuals and groups, using an anthropological focus, including the cultural, linguistic, and biological aspects of health issues. This scholarly journal is cross-cultural and multidisciplinary and addresses topics of interest in public health, health policy, nutrition, and maternal-child health. Each issue includes articles, research reports, and book reviews of varying length. There are occasionally theme issues.

662. ***Oceania: devoted to the study of the indigenous peoples of Australia, Melanesia, Micronesia, Indonesia, Polynesia and Insular Southeast Asia.*** [ISSN: 0029-8077] 1930. q. AUD 84 (Individuals, AUD 72). Oceania Publications, University of Sydney (H42), 116 Darlington Rd, Sydney, NSW 2006, Australia; d.koller@oceania.usyd.edu.au. Illus., index, adv. Refereed. Circ: 900. Vol. ends: Jun. Microform: PQC. Online: bigchalk; Chadwyck-Healey Incorporated; EBSCO Publishing; Florida Center for Library Automation; Gale Group; Northern Light Technology, Inc.; OCLC Online Computer Library Center, Inc.; ProQuest Information & Learning; RMIT Publishing; H.W. Wilson. Reprint: PQC; PSC. *Indexed:* AICP, ASSIA, AbAn, AnthLit, ArtHuCI, BAS, IBSS, IBZ, MLA-IB, PAIS, RI-1, SSCI, SSI, ZooRec. *Bk. rev.:* 7, length varies. *Aud.:* Ac.

This refereed scholarly journal publishes research in social and cultural anthropology on the "indigenous peoples of Australia, Melanesia, Polynesia, Micronesia, and Southeast Asia." It is an important source for Australia and Pacific studies. It covers past and present customs, ceremonies, folklore, and belief systems of the region. Recent articles discuss Aborigine use of cars in initiation rites, the transformation of a tribal people in Papua New Guinea into a wage-earning workforce, and cave art in Vanuatu. Guest-edited thematic issues also appear, e.g., "Race Relations and Australian Ethnography." It includes maps and graphs, some illustrations, and an abstract for each article. This journal is recommended for academic libraries that serve anthropology or Asian, Pacific, or Australian Studies faculty. (ChD)

663. ***Practicing Anthropology.*** [ISSN: 0888-4552] q. USD 35; USD 40 foreign. Ed(s): Alexander Ervin. Society for Applied Anthropology, PO Box 24083, Oklahoma City, OK 73124-0083; sfaa@telepath.com; http://www.zoom1.telepath.com/sfaa/sfaapubs.html. Illus., index, adv. Vol. ends: Fall. Reprint: PSC. *Indexed:* AICP, AbAn, AnthLit. *Bk. rev.:* Various number and length. *Aud.:* Ac.

This journal publishes short, readable articles focused on a single topic. Applied or practicing anthropology is the focus. Some of the stated goals of the publication are to provide career information for anthropologists who work outside academia; to explore the use of anthropology in policy research and implementation; and to serve as a forum for inquiry into the present state and future of anthropology in general. In a typical issue, there are six to ten articles of three to five pages, several book reviews, letters, commentaries, "FYI Notes," and the column "Washington Watch."

664. ***Reviews in Anthropology.*** [ISSN: 0093-8157] 1974. q. GBP 311 (Individuals, GBP 62). Taylor & Francis Ltd, 11 New Fetter Ln, London, EC4P 4EE, United Kingdom; http://www.tandf.co.uk/journals. Illus., adv. Refereed. Vol. ends: Fall. Microform: PQC. Reprint: PQC; PSC. *Indexed:* ABS&EES, AbAn, AnthLit, BRI, CBRI, IBSS. *Aud.:* Ga, Ac.

A quarterly publication devoted to review commentary on recently published books in anthropology, including the subdisciplines of cultural anthropology, human biology, comparative linguistics, and archaeology. The papers, which are submitted by invitation only, are few (three or four) but lengthy (over 20 pages) and appeal to both generalists and specialists. A useful collection-development resource.

665. ***Royal Anthropological Institute. Journal.*** Formerly (until 1995): *Man;* Incorporates (1871-1965): *Royal Anthropological Institute of Great Britain and Ireland. Journal;* Which was formerly (until 1906): *Anthropological Institute of Great Britain and Ireland. Journal;* Which was formed by the merger of (1848-1871): *Ethnological Society of London. Journal;* Which was formerly (until 1869): *Ethnological Society of London.Transactions;* (until 1861): *Ethnological Society of London. Journal;* (1863-1871): *Journal of Anthropology;* Which was formerly (until 1870): *Anthropological Review.* [ISSN: 1359-0987] 1901. q. USD 368 print & online eds. Blackwell Publishing Ltd., 9600 Garsington Rd, PO Box 805, Oxford, OX4 2DQ, United Kingdom; customerservices@oxon.blackwellpublishing.com; http://www.blackwellpublishing.com/. Illus., index, adv. Refereed. Circ: 3200. Vol. ends: Dec. Microform: BHP; PQC. Online: EBSCO Publishing; Florida Center for Library Automation; Gale Group; ingenta.com; JSTOR (Web-based Journal Archive); OCLC Online Computer Library Center, Inc.; RoweCom Information Quest; Swets Blackwell; H.W. Wilson. Reprint: PQC. *Indexed:* AICP, AbAn, AgeL, AnthLit, BAS, BiolAb, BrArAb, ExcerpMed, GeoRef, GeogAbPG, IBSS, MLA-IB, PSA, RI-1, SSCI, SSI, SWA, SociolAb. *Bk. rev.:* 40, 350 words. *Aud.:* Ac.

This publication is international in both contributors and content. It covers all the subfields of anthropology. Abstracts are in English and French, and text is in English. Half of each recent issue is comprised of eight or so articles, and the other half contains more than 40 book reviews divided into subfields in anthropology.

666. ***Urban Anthropology and Studies of Cultural Systems and World Economic Development.*** Formerly (until 1984): *Urban Anthropology.* [ISSN: 0894-6019] 1972. q. USD 75. Ed(s): Jack R Rollwagen. The Institute, Inc., 56 Centennial Ave, Brockport, NY 14420; jrollwag@brockport.edu. Illus. Refereed. Circ: 500. *Indexed:* ABS&EES, AICP, AbAn, AnthLit, BAS, CIJE, DSA, IBSS, PRA, SSCI, SSI, SUSA, SWA, SociolAb, WAE&RSA. *Aud.:* Ac.

As the title suggests, this journal is devoted to urban anthropology and global economics development in the world's cultural systems. Articles focus on urbanization, development and underdevelopment, and colonialism and neocolonialism. A typical issue has two or three lengthy articles of 30 to 50 pages each. There are often theme issues.

667. ***Visual Anthropology.*** [ISSN: 0894-9468] 1987. q. GBP 437 (Individuals, GBP 95). Ed(s): Paul Hockings. Taylor & Francis Ltd, 11 New Fetter Ln, London, EC4P 4EE, United Kingdom; http://www.tandf.co.uk/journals. Illus. Refereed. Reprint: PSC. *Indexed:* AICP, AbAn, AnthLit, IBSS, IBZ. *Aud.:* Ac.

Published in cooperation with the Commission on Visual Anthropology, this journal aims to publish articles, comments, discussions, and film and book reviews that contribute to the study, use, and production of anthropological and ethnographic films, videos, and photographs for research and teaching. The journal also is concerned with the analysis of visual symbolic forms and the study of human behavior through visual means. This is an international journal in subject and contribution.

■ ANTIQUES AND COLLECTING

General/Doll Collecting

Maureen Kilcullen, Reference Librarian, Kent State University Stark Campus Library, 6000 Frank Ave., Canton, OH 44720; mkilcullen@stark.kent.edu; FAX: 330-494-6212

Introduction

America's fascination with antiques and collecting continues. The popularity of antiques and collectibles can be seen in the addition of another television program about collecting, *Flea Market Finds with the Kovels.* America can now view this show along with *Appraisal Fair, Collectible Treasures, At the Auction,* and *Antiques Roadshow.* Above and beyond these shows, the Internet is still making a huge impact on the antiques and collectibles field. Not only do most of the magazines reviewed here have their own web sites, more and more of them are offering feature articles (and more) from their print versions online. In addition, one of the strongest trends in the antiques and collectibles field is buying, selling, and collecting online through auction web sites such as eBay and Sothebys.com.

Trends also indicate that the interest in popular collectibles continues to rise. Unquestionably, interest in antique furniture has remained high, and auction prices still indicate that the most popular pieces are American, especially from the Arts and Crafts movement. Many standard titles remain, but the trends increasingly indicate that while interest in fine antiques will remain high, interest in collectible memorabilia continues to grow. Once again, the Jacqueline Kennedy Onassis estate "Sale of the Century" in 1996 can help define the differences between collecting antiques and collecting memorabilia. If one defines an antique as an object from the past that has artistic or historical value and is over 100 years old, then the small Louis XV gilt tooled red Morocco leather casket (trunk) once owned by Marie Antoinette and then by Mrs. Onassis is definitely an antique. At the auction, this trunk sold for $105,000. The walnut humidor that Milton Berle presented to John F. Kennedy in 1961 is not considered an antique, but because it was in the possession of both Kennedy and Berle, it is considered a collectible. At the auction, it sold for $574,000.

The field has lost another specialty magazine with the cessation of the publication *Pop Culture Collecting.* Despite this loss, the trend in collecting memorabilia can still be seen in other popular collecting magazines. Twentieth-century collectibles, rock-and-roll memorabilia, and television memorabilia are still gaining in popularity and market value. Traditional collectibles—such as depression glass, limited-edition plates, figurines, and ornaments—are still desirable, and this is also reflected in publishing trends.

Basic Periodicals

FINE ANTIQUES/OBJETS D'ART. Ga: *Antique Collecting, Antique Dealer and Collector's Guide, The Magazine Antiques.*

POPULAR ANTIQUES/COLLECTIBLES. Ga: *Antique Trader Weekly, Collector Editions, Collector Magazine & Price Guide, Maine Antique Digest.*

DOLL COLLECTING. Ga: *Contemporary Doll Collector, Doll Reader, Dolls: the collector's magazine.*

Basic Abstracts and Indexes

Readers' Guide to Periodical Literature.

General

668. ***Antique Collecting.*** Incorporates: *Antique Finder.* [ISSN: 0003-584X] 1965. m. except Aug. & Jan. GBP 25 United Kingdom; GBP 30 overseas. Ed(s): Susan Wilson. Antique Collectors Club, 5 Church St, Woodbridge, IP12 1DS, United Kingdom; http://www.antiquecc.com/. Illus., adv. Sample. Circ: 20000. Vol. ends: Apr. *Indexed:* BHA, DAAI. *Bk. rev.:* 2-6, 100-500 words. *Aud.:* Ga, Sa.

This fine British magazine is tastefully done and does not include the annoying "every-other-page" advertising found in other magazines. The signed articles range from antique clothing to furniture and are interesting and informative. The articles are written by dealers or collectors with first-hand knowledge of their subject. Photographs are mostly in color and large enough to see details. The information found in this magazine, written "for collectors, by collectors about collecting," focuses on sixteenth- through eighteenth-century European and British antiques and collectibles. Most of the articles offer advice on evaluating a piece and provide a list of recommended books. Regular features include an auction calendar, entertaining editorials, auction news, and a fairs preview calendar. Several full-text articles from past issues can be found at the magazine's web site. Highly recommended for public libraries with an interest in British and European antiques.

669. ***Antique Dealer and Collector's Guide: the international magazine for dealers and collectors.*** Incorporating: *Art and Antiques.* [ISSN: 0003-5866] 1946. m. GBP 33; GBP 44 overseas; GBP 2.75 newsstand/cover per issue. Ed(s): Philip Bartlam. Statuscourt Ltd., PO Box 805, London, SE10 8TD, United Kingdom. Illus., adv. Sample. Circ: 12000 Paid. Vol. ends: Jul. *Indexed:* AIAP, BHA, IBZ. *Bk. rev.:* 2-6, 50-200 words. *Aud.:* Ga, Sa.

Another British publication, *Antique Dealer and Collector's Guide* covers the international antiques scene and sees its role as "the international magazine for dealers and collectors." Not only does it contain complete information on the antique trade, auctions, antiques fairs, and dealer news, but the information is presented in an attractive, glossy format. The photographs are in color and in black and white. Its fine art correspondent regularly announces details of art exhibitions, and there are regular reviews of and recommendations for attending the best antiques fairs. Each issue usually contains a feature article on an artist as well as articles on antiques detailing the background and history of the pieces exhibited. Informative surveys of events, such as "Coming Up for Auction" and "In the Salesrooms," are regularly included. *Antique Dealer* is more reserved than *Antique Collecting,* and there is no doubt that it is popular in libraries—check the holdings! The web site offers a few older articles. Recommended for libraries with an interest in fine art and antiques.

670. ***Antique Review: serving the dealers & collectors of midAmerica.*** Formerly: *Ohio Antique Review.* [ISSN: 0883-833X] 1976. m. USD 23; USD 3.95 newsstand/cover per issue. Ed(s): Linda Kunkel. Krause Publications, Inc., 700 E State St, Iola, WI 54990-0001; info@krause.com; http://www.krause.com. Illus., index, adv. Sample. Circ: 5492 Paid and controlled. Vol. ends: Dec. *Bk. rev.:* 5, length varies. *Aud.:* Ga.

This publication offers informative articles on American antiques and auctions throughout mid-America. Expanded to four sections, *Antique Review* also examines trends in collecting and answers readers' questions. The articles about the auctions are interesting to read, and they offer both black-and-white photographs and prices for the pieces pictured. "Antique Review Preview" features upcoming events in the field of American antiques. *Antique Review* should be considered by all public libraries in the geographic area.

671. ***Antique Showcase.*** Formerly (until vol.17, Nov. 1981): *Ontario Showcase.* [ISSN: 0713-6315] 1963. 8x/yr. CND 23.53 domestic; USD 21.99 United States; CND 38.95 elsewhere. Ed(s): Barbara Sutton Smith. Trajan Publishing Corp., 103 Lakeshore Rd, Ste 202, St Catharines, ON L2N 2T6, Canada; office@trajan.com; http://www.trajan.com. Illus., adv. Sample. Circ: 9200. Vol. ends: Jun. *Bk. rev.:* 5, length varies. *Aud.:* Ga.

Antique Showcase advertises itself as being for antique lovers and collectors, and its extensive coverage is laid out in an attractive format. The factual and informative articles offer valuable information to the novice as well as the experienced collector. Departments such as "Around the Shows," "Antique Detective," and "Common Sense" keep the reader up to date. Regular features include museum exhibitions, book reviews, and an antique show calendar. Newer columns such as "Heirlooms" and "Q & A" appear periodically. Many antiques publications concentrate on antiques and collectibles in a specific market, whether it be fine art or collectible Americana. *Antique Showcase*'s focus is on the generalist and has much improved. There is a web site for this magazine, but it only features a brief description and access to one or two articles in the current issue. Recommended for those libraries searching for a general title about antiques and collectibles.

672. ***The Antique Trader Weekly: America's weekly antiques and collectibles marketplace.*** Formerly: *Antique Trader.* [ISSN: 0161-8342] 1957. w. USD 38; USD 21 for 6 mos.; USD 2.99 newsstand/cover per issue. Ed(s): Sharon Korbeck. Krause Publications, Inc., 700 E State St, Iola, WI 54990-0001; info@krause.com; http://www.krause.com. Illus., adv. Sample. Circ: 34666 Paid and free. Vol. ends: Dec. *Bk. rev.:* 30, length varies. *Aud.:* Ga.

Antique Trader Weekly is one of the most comprehensive newspapers available on the antique trade. It is popular in libraries if holdings are a consideration. The publication features thousands of classified ads in 75 categories, a question-and-answer section, articles and columns, a national shopping directory, book reviews, industry news, an Internet shopping directory, and show and auction calendars. This is combined with expert advice and in-depth articles on anything to do with antiques. The "Show and Auction AntiqCalendar" is arranged both chronologically and geographically and covers the United States. *Antique Trader Online* does not provide the complete print publication online, but it offers feature articles from past issues and weekly news stories.

Antiques. See *The Magazine Antiques.*

673. ***Antiques and Auction News: the most widely read collector's newspaper in the East.*** Formerly: *Joel Sater's Antiques and Auction News.* 1969. w. USD 18. Ed(s): Denise M Sater. Engle Publishing Company, PO Box 500, Mount Joy, PA 17552-0500. Illus., adv. Circ: 38000. *Aud.:* Ga.

This weekly newspaper focuses on the geographic area east of and including Pennsylvania and is written "for antiquers, collectors, auctioneers and show promoters." A few articles are included with tips for taking care of antiques as well as news from the field, but the real value lies in its extensive coverage of auctions, exhibitions, and shows. Regular columns such as the "Auction Calendar," "Auction Sales Bills," and " Shops & Centers" provide detailed information for collectors in the eastern United States. If your library does not carry *Antique Trader Weekly* (above in this section), this title should be considered for public libraries in the geographic region with patrons interested in antique shows and auctions.

674. ***Antiques & Collecting Magazine.*** Former titles (until Oct. 1993): *Antiques and Collecting Hobbies;* (until 1985): *Hobbies, the Magazine for Collectors.* [ISSN: 1084-0818] 1931. m. USD 32 domestic; USD 44 foreign; USD 3.50 newsstand/cover per issue. Ed(s): Theresa Nolan. Lightner Publishing Corporation, 1006 S Michigan Ave, Chicago, IL 60605; lightnerpb@aol.com. Illus., adv. Sample. Circ: 20000 Paid. Vol. ends: Feb. Microform: PQC. Online: bigchalk; EBSCO Publishing; Gale Group; Northern Light Technology, Inc.; OCLC Online Computer Library Center, Inc.; ProQuest Information & Learning; H.W. Wilson. Reprint: PQC. *Indexed:* BRI, CBRI, MagInd, MusicInd, RGPR. *Bk. rev.:* 4-6, 30-100 words. *Aud.:* Ga.

Antiques and Collecting Magazine averages five feature articles per issue. The focus of this magazine is eclectic, ranging from Americana to international antiques and collectibles. Articles are brief, and the photographs are in color and black and white. The magazine features regular columns such as "The Antique Detective," and "Rinker on Collectibles," where experts answer questions about antiques and collectibles and provide restoration tips. Recent issues feature "Celebrity Collectors," in which television and film stars share their collections with subscribers.

675. ***AntiqueWeek: weekly antique, auction and collectors' newspaper.*** Former titles (until 1986): *Antique Week - Tri-State Trader;* (until 1983): *Tri-State Trader.* [ISSN: 0888-5451] 1968. w. USD 32.95. Ed(s): Tom G Hoepf, Connie Swaim. D M G World Media, Inc., 27 N. Jefferson St., P.O. Box 90, Knightstown, IN 46148-0120; connie@antiqueweek.com; http://www.antiqueweek.com. Illus., adv. Sample. Vol. ends: Mar. *Bk. rev.:* 16, length varies. *Aud.:* Ga.

The Central and Eastern U.S. editions of this newspaper cover antique auctions, shows, and flea markets in their geographic areas. The articles are interesting and informative, and there is a lot of Internet coverage. Regular columns include "The World of Ceramics" and advice from the experts. Coverage, focusing on the United States, ranges from sporting collectibles to collectible cupids. *AntiqueWeek* includes helpful articles about identifying antiques. *AntiqueWeek*'s web site not only includes a discussion group, classified ads, and auction and flea market calendars, it also offers links to online auctions. Recommended for public libraries in the geographic region (depending on the edition) with an interest in popular collectibles.

676. ***Art & Antiques.*** Incorporates (1967-Jan. 1994): *Antique Monthly;* Formerly (until 1980): *American Art and Antiques.* [ISSN: 0195-8208] 1978. m. 11/yr. USD 24.95 domestic; USD 54.95 foreign; USD 4.99 newsstand/cover per issue. Ed(s): Barbara Tapp. Trans World Publishing, Inc., 2100 Powers Ferry Rd, Ste 300, Atlanta, GA 30339; service@www.billian.com. Illus., adv. Sample. Circ: 168999 Paid. Vol. ends: Dec. *Indexed:* ABM, ABS&EES, AIAP, ASIP, ArtInd, BHA. *Bk. rev.:* 6, length varies. *Aud.:* Ga.

This magazine presents beautiful photography and finely written articles on antique furniture and interesting but brief sketches of emerging artists. Regular departments include "Art Crimes" (art thefts), "Gallery Watch," and "Museum Scene." The publication focuses on antiques and regularly showcases a wide variety of art exhibitions. The web site (www.artantiquesmag.com) offers many feature articles as well as access to online auctions. Recommended for libraries wanting a title covering both art and antiques.

Blade. See Hunting and Guns section.

677. ***Collectibles, Flea Market Finds.*** Formerly: *Collectibles, Country and Americana.* [ISSN: 1086-1602] 1993. q. USD 18.97; USD 23.97 foreign; USD 3.99 newsstand/cover per issue. Ed(s): Stacy Durr Albert. Goodman Media Group, Inc., 250 W 57th St, Ste 710, New York, NY 10107-0799; http://www.goodmanmediagroup.com. Illus., adv. Circ: 200000. Vol. ends: Winter. *Bk. rev.:* 4-7, 50-75 words. *Aud.:* Ga.

Collectibles, Flea Market Finds reflects current trends in collecting by offering very informative articles that concentrate on such popular twentieth-century American collectibles as television memorabilia, rock-and-roll toys, and costume jewelry. Articles feature photographs of the various collectibles and also list the most recent prices realized for each collectible. The magazine offers practical tips on displaying collectibles and joining various collectors' clubs, and it gives advice on where to sell collections. A few libraries have already discovered this magazine. The web site at www.goodmanmediagroup.com/collectibles offers subscription information. Because of the rising popularity of twentieth-century collectibles, it would make an inexpensive addition to any public library's popular magazine section.

678. ***Collector Editions.*** Former titles (until 1981): *Collector Editions Quarterly;* (until 1977): *Acquire.* [ISSN: 0733-2130] 1973. q. USD 14.95; USD 4.99 newsstand/cover per issue. Ed(s): Linda Kruger. Pioneer Communications, Inc., 506 Second St, Grundy Center, IA 50638. Illus., adv. Circ: 100000 Paid. Microform: PQC. *Bk. rev.:* 4, 75-200 words. *Aud.:* Ga.

Now under new ownership, *Collector Editions* still features fascinating articles on such "traditional" collectibles as plates, figurines, prints, ornaments, and other limited-edition collectors' pieces. The magazine offers numerous columns: "Currents in Collecting" showcases the newest collectibles; "Artist Update" gives up-to-date information on artists and their most recent projects; "Ask the Expert" answers questions about readers' collectibles; "Auction Report" covers recent international sales of collectibles; "CIB Market Report" offers valuable information on the collectibles, with the current most dramatic market gains. This magazine is popular in many libraries. Public libraries with a clientele interested in limited-edition collectibles would be safe in adding this title to their holdings.

679. ***Collector Magazine & Price Guide.*** Formerly (until 1994): *Antique Trader Price Guide to Antiques and Collectors' Items.* [ISSN: 1077-2774] 1970. m. USD 21.95; USD 2.95 newsstand/cover per issue. Ed(s): Claire Fliess. Krause Publications, Inc., 2728 Asbury Rd, Cove Bldg, Ste 600, Dubuque, IA 52003; info@krause.com; http://www.krause.com. Illus., adv. Circ: 23173 Paid and free. Vol. ends: Dec. *Aud.:* Ga.

This publication has replaced the well-known *Antique Trader Price Guide to Antiques and Collectors' Items.* It is similar to the former title, covering recent market trends and auction analyses, and it also includes expert advice and practical collecting tips. Feature articles are usually about popular collectibles. Probably of the most value to libraries is the monthly price guide that lists the most current market price on hundreds of antiques and collectibles. The web site offers an online price guide, classified ads and a dealer directory. It also offers a service called "Collection Trader" where collectors can list items they want to sell or buy. For libraries whose patrons need current pricing information and descriptions of antiques and collectibles.

680. ***Collector's Mart.*** Former titles (until 2000): *Collector's Mart Magazine;* (until 199?): *Collectors Mart;* (until 198?): *Antique and Collectors Mart.* [ISSN: 1533-3000] 1976. q. USD 10 domestic; USD 38 foreign. Ed(s): Mary Sieber. Krause Publications, Inc., 700 E State St, Iola, WI 54990-0001; info@krause.com; http://www.krause.com. Illus., adv. Circ: 101429 Paid and free. Vol. ends: Dec. *Indexed:* ABCT. *Bk. rev.:* 5, 50-150 words. *Aud.:* Ga.

Similar to *Collector Editions* (above in this section), this magazine features articles on limited-edition collectibles such as figurines and ornaments. Regular columns are written by experts: "Bear World," "Figurine Finesse," "Ornaments," and "Doll Collecting Today." The magazine offers a calendar of events, guides to prices and trends, and previews of shows. The difference between the two magazines is that more information about the secondary market is provided in *Collector's Mart Magazine.* If your library does not subscribe to *Collector Editions,* you may want to consider *Collector's Mart Magazine,* since it is gaining in popularity in many libraries.

681. ***Kovels on Antiques and Collectibles: the newsletter for dealers, collectors and investors.*** [ISSN: 0741-6091] 1974. m. USD 46 in US & Canada; USD 56 elsewhere. Ed(s): Nancy Saada. Antiques, Inc., 49 Richmondville Ave, Westport, CT 06880; http://www.kovel.com. Illus. *Aud.:* Hs, Ga.

What distinguishes this newsletter from many of the others is not only the Kovels' 40 years of experience but also the lack of advertising. This simple, full color, 12-page monthly newsletter is filled with the most recent news affecting prices of antiques and collectibles. It includes information about fakes, sale reports, prices, and book reviews. Advice is given on what's hot, which items are rising in value, and where to find the best prices. The Kovels teach you how to distinguish originals from reproductions and how restoration affects value. The newsletter provides information on what's selling in flea markets and at auctions, and the Kovels answer questions about readers' antiques and collectibles. An annual index is provided with a subscription. The web site features excerpts from articles, a database of information from five of the Kovels' price books, and answers to collectors' questions.

682. ***The Magazine Antiques.*** Formerly: *Antiques.* [ISSN: 0161-9284] 1922. m. USD 34.95 USD 39.95. Ed(s): Allison Ledes. Brant Publications, Inc., 575 Broadway, 5th Fl, New York, NY 10012. Illus., index, adv. Circ: 66703. Vol. ends: Dec. Microform: PQC. Online: bigchalk; EBSCO Publishing; Gale Group; Northern Light Technology, Inc.; OCLC Online Computer Library Center, Inc.; ProQuest Information & Learning. *Indexed:* ABM, AIAP, ArtHuCI, ArtInd, BAS, BHA, BRI, CBRI, MagInd, RGPR. *Bk. rev.:* 1-9, length varies. *Aud.:* Ga, Ac, Sa.

There is no doubt that this American periodical is one of the finest offered on the topic of antiques. The articles are well written by experts. Although the focus is on antique furnishings, topics also include folk art, paintings, architecture, and art shows. Beautifully illustrated feature articles focus not only on the antique or historical piece but also on the person who created it. International in coverage, this journal should be in all libraries.

683. ***Maine Antique Digest: the worldwide marketplace for Americana.*** [ISSN: 0147-0639] 1973. m. USD 43 domestic; USD 55 foreign. Ed(s): Samuel C Pennington. Maine Antique Digest, Inc., PO Box 1429, Waldoboro, ME 04572; mad@maine.com; http://www.maineantiquedigest.com. Illus., adv. Sample. Circ: 30000. Vol. ends: Dec. Microform: PQC. *Bk. rev.:* 2-3, 500-2,000 words. *Aud.:* Ga, Sa.

This 300-page tabloid newspaper covers most of the information you need to know if you collect antiques or art either in Maine or across America. Regular features include auctions and shows and a few articles on all kinds of collectibles. Featured are articles covering everything from consignment to understanding furniture finishes. Intended for dealers and collectors on the East Coast, the focus is on fine antiques and Americana. Although this digest has traditionally concentrated on the East, it has always covered the United States in general, and it continues to be a basic title that all libraries should consider. After visiting the web site you will understand both the online and print popularity of this title. It is the best web site in this category previewed. Market concentration has been expanded to include the world. Included in the searchable, full-text database are hundreds of book reviews, a selection of recent articles, hot news items, a searchable price database (with descriptions), shareware and demo programs for antiquers, and online auction catalogs.

684. ***Teddy Bear Review.*** [ISSN: 0890-4162] 1986. bi-m. USD 24.95 domestic; USD 39.95 foreign. Ed(s): Tina Laube. Jones Publishing Inc., N 7450 Aanstad Rd, PO Box 5000, Iola, WI 54945; jonespub@jonespublishing.com; http://www.jonespublishing.com. Illus., adv. Circ: 60000 Paid. *Bk. rev.:* 2, 250-300 words. *Aud.:* Ga.

Collecting teddy bears has gained even more popularity in the past few years. This publication covers antique, contemporary, and miniature teddy bears. Teddy bear experts contribute well-written articles profiling bear manufacturers, interviewing bear artists, and showcasing the latest bear creations. An auction report is included. Recommended for public libraries whose clientele is interested in the subject.

685. ***Yesteryear: your monthly guide to antiques and collectibles.*** [ISSN: 0194-9349] 1975. m. USD 19. Ed(s): Michael Jacobi. Yesteryear Publications, Inc., PO Box 2, Princeton, WI 54968. Illus., adv. Circ: 6500 Paid. *Bk. rev.:* 2-10, 200-300 words. *Aud.:* Ga.

Yesteryear focuses on Wisconsin and neighboring Midwestern states. It offers valuable information in a variety of question-and-answer columns. There are hundreds of listings for upcoming antique shows, flea markets, auctions, and arts-and-crafts shows. Although the focus is Midwestern, the information is priceless. Recommended wherever there is a gap in information about antiques and collectibles.

Doll Collecting

It seems that much of doll collecting stems from nostalgia. What you played with when you were a child becomes a collectible when you become an adult. Doll collecting has become one of the largest hobbies in the United States today. This is evidenced in the enormous array of doll clubs and associations ranging from the Doll Artisan Guild, the Madame Alexander Doll Club, the Chatty Cathy Club to the National Organization of Miniaturists and Dollers. The hottest trend in doll collecting today appears to be in collecting fashion dolls. These are part of the group of contemporary or modern dolls but define themselves by their higher prices ($50 or more), and their extensive wardrobes. An example of the fashion doll is Ashton-Drake's Gene. Despite the popularity of the fashion doll, interest in collectible and antique dolls remains high. Trends indicate that despite the often high prices, fashion dolls are being collected due to their quality alternative to mass production of other dolls.

There are three distinct categories of dolls: antique dolls (those produced 75 years ago or earlier), collectible dolls (those produced between 25 and 75 years ago), and modern or contemporary dolls (those produced within the last 25 years). Although the field has lost *Doll World*, which was purchased recently by *Dolls*, the magazines included here range from coverage on how to make dolls and dollhouses to collecting and accessorizing antique and contemporary dolls.

686. ***Antique Doll Collector.*** Formerly (until 1997): *Antique Doll World.* [ISSN: 1096-8474] 1993. m. USD 39.95. Ed(s): Donna C. Kaonis. Puffin Co., LLC, 6 Woodside Ave., Ste. 300, Northport, NY 11768. Adv. Circ: 7000 Paid. *Aud.:* Ga.

If you are interested in antique dolls (of every kind) and their accessories, this magazine is for you. *Antique Doll Collector* truthfully advertises itself as "the ONLY magazine for collectors of antique and vintage dolls." Color photographs are extraordinarily detailed, and contributors to the articles are experts in the field. The magazine regularly features columns (such as "Doll News" and "Auction Gallery") and a calendar of shows, conventions, and auctions. Recently, descriptive articles have analyzed mysterious mold numbers, miniature dolls, and black folk-art dolls. There is a web site for this magazine; unfortunately, it only features brief snippets of information (with pictures) from the current issue and subscription information. *Antique Doll Collector* would be of value to museums and public libraries with an interest in this area.

687. ***Barbie Bazaar: the official Barbie doll collector's magazine.*** [ISSN: 1040-094X] bi-m. USD 23.95 domestic; USD 38.95 Canada; USD 58.95 elsewhere. Murat Caviale Inc, 5711 8th Ave, Kenosha, WI 53140. Adv. *Aud.:* Ems, Hs, Ga, Sa.

The interest in Barbie doll collecting originated with the baby boomers who played with Barbies as children and continues with today's children who are bombarded with Barbie ads and images morning, noon, and night. As indicated by the title, *Barbie Bazaar* is devoted to vintage and modern Barbie dolls, and although this remains the focus, new features cover a wide range of interests from 1960s to 1990s vintage dolls to today's designer dolls. In this publication, Barbie doll collectors will find well-written articles on collecting Barbie clothing and dolls, hair styling, making Barbie clothes and accessories, and news from Barbie collectors' clubs. Also featured are Barbie doll artists who discuss how they design and refurbish Barbies. Recommended for public libraries and museums where there is an interest.

688. ***Contemporary Doll Collector.*** Formerly (until 1994): *Contemporary Doll Magazine.* [ISSN: 1075-8674] 1990. bi-m. USD 19.90 domestic; USD 25.90 foreign. Ed(s): Barbara Campbell. Scott Publications, 30595 Eight Mile, Livonia, MI 48152-1798; contactus@scottpublications.com; http://www.scottpublications.com. Illus., adv. Sample. Circ: 40000 Paid. Vol. ends: Oct/Nov. *Aud.:* Ga, Sa.

The focus of this magazine is on contemporary and modern dolls, but it also offers advice on collecting, identifying, and preserving antique dolls. The importance of *Contemporary Doll Collector* lies in its clear advice and tips on how to collect dolls and its coverage of the doll industry's newest attractions such as fabric, felt, vinyl, plastic, and compositon dolls. As in other doll magazines, this one also offers a show calendar and auction report. Recommended for public libraries where patrons have an interest in collecting the newer modern dolls.

689. ***Doll Artisan.*** [ISSN: 1040-6336] 2003. bi-m. USD 25.95 domestic; USD 42.95 in Canada & Mexico; USD 47.95 elsewhere. Ed(s): Jenny Meachen. Jones Publishing Inc., N 7450 Aanstad Rd, PO Box 5000, Iola, WI 54945. Illus., adv. Sample. *Aud.:* Ga, Sa.

Doll Artisan features articles offering extremely detailed, step-by-step instructions not only on casting and firing the porcelain heads and bodies of dolls but also on painting and costuming them. Clothing and wig patterns are provided as well as a list of references and materials. Regular departments include "Studio Guide," "Show Calendar," and "On the Bookshelf." The web site provides a few feature articles from the current issue and classified ads. This magazine is highly recommended where there is interest in the subject.

690. ***Doll Castle News: the doll collector's magazine.*** 1961. 6x/yr. USD 19.95 domestic; USD 24 Canada; USD 39 elsewhere. Ed(s): Dorita M Mortenson. Castle Press Publications, Inc., PO Box 247, Washington, NJ 07882. Illus., adv. Sample. Circ: 4000. Vol. ends: Jan/Feb. *Bk. rev.:* 3-4, 100-150 words. *Aud.:* Ga, Sa.

Here you will find many projects and patterns for dolls. The instructions are very clear and well written. Feature articles are signed, well researched, and written in a familiar style, but the illustrations and photographs are strictly black and white. Recommended for public libraries whose clientele has an interest in the subject. The web site offers an online archive of previous articles.

691. ***Doll Crafter: published for creators and collectors.*** Incorporates (in 2003): *Doll Artisan;* (1994-2003): *Dollmaking;* Which was formerly (until 1996): *Dollmaking Crafts & Designs;* Which was formed by the merger of (1985-1994): *Dollmaking Projects & Plans;* (198?-1994): *Doll Designs.* [ISSN: 0746-9624] 1983. m. USD 39.95 domestic; USD 54.95 foreign; USD 4.95 newsstand/cover per issue domestic. Ed(s): Joyce Murch. Jones Publishing Inc., N 7450 Aanstad Rd, PO Box 5000, Iola, WI 54945; http://www.jonespublishing.com. Illus., adv. Circ: 60000. Vol. ends: Apr. *Indexed:* IHTDI. *Aud.:* Ga, Sa.

Doll Crafter is an invaluable publication for the doll creator and collector. Each of the feature articles provides very clear instructions and illustrations not only for creating or sculpting dolls but also for doll costuming and accessorizing. The brief articles include specific materials and color guides that are extremely useful to the doll crafter plus beautifully photographed examples of the finished doll or accessory. In this magazine, doll crafters re-create dolls from French bebes to modern original dolls. Regular departments include "Doll Dates," "Ask the Expert," "Doll Directory," and a "Pullout Pattern." Highly recommended wherever there is interest.

692. ***Doll Magazine.*** [ISSN: 1358-3506] 1992. bi-m. GBP 21 domestic; GBP 38.50 in Europe; USD 69.50 United States. Ed(s): Alison Sibley. Ashdown Publishing Ltd., Avalon Ct, Star Rd, Partridge Green, RH13 8RY, United Kingdom; esther.forder@btinternet.com; http://www.ashdown.co.uk. Adv. *Bk. rev.:* 1, 300-400 words. *Aud.:* Ga, Sa.

Doll Magazine offers more feature articles than any of the other doll magazines in this section. The articles offer in-depth research, are well written, and cover doll artists, dolls, and even company histories. The regular departments feature "Doll Talk," "Off the Bookshelf," and "Dollmaker's Diary." Instructions for making dolls and their accessories are clear and easy to follow. The web site offers an archive of articles, subscription information, a bookshop, and access to doll clubs online. Another fine British publication, this should be in every public library that has a clientele interested in the subject.

693. *Doll Reader: the ultimate doll authority.* [ISSN: 0744-0901] 1972. 9x/yr. USD 29.95; USD 4.99 newsstand/cover per issue domestic; USD 5.99 newsstand/cover per issue Canada. Ed(s): Marianne Clay. Ashton International Media, Inc., 44 Front St, Ste 280, Worcester, MA 01608; http://www.wbmagazine.com. Illus., adv. Circ: 95972. Vol. ends: Nov. *Aud.:* Ga, Sa.

One of the top doll-collecting magazines, *Doll Reader* deals with every facet of doll collecting. Eight to ten signed feature articles are offered in each issue, covering everything from antique, modern, artist, and play dolls to profiles of doll designers and artists. Regular departments include "Doll Scene," "Out & About," "Antique Q & A," and "Curious Collector." The articles are well written, beautifully photographed, and informative. The web site includes current and archived articles as well as tips on insuring doll collections, on the various types of dolls, and a glossary of doll terms. This magazine is essential for any library with patrons interested in the subject.

Dollhouse Miniatures. See Model Making and Collecting/Dollhouse Miniatures section.

694. *Dolls: the collector's magazine.* Incorporates (in 2003): *Doll World.* [ISSN: 0733-2238] 1982. 10x/yr. USD 24.95. Jones Publishing Inc., N 7450 Aanstad Rd, PO Box 5000, Iola, WI 54945; jonespub@jonespublishing.com; http://www.jonespublishing.com. Illus., adv. Circ: 95000 Paid. Vol. ends: Dec. *Bk. rev.:* 2-4,100-150 words. *Aud.:* Ga, Sa.

Dolls has recently purchased *Doll World.* With the merger, *Dolls* has added additional columns, articles, and writers. Most of the feature articles in this magazine are about doll artisans, their dolls, and fashion accessories. The photographs are beautiful, and the articles are often first-person accounts in which the artists discuss how and when the inspiration to create dolls struck them. Regular departments cover auction reports, the identification and valuation of dolls, antique dolls, and a calendar of doll events. The web site is an advertisement. *Dolls* is recommended for public libraries where there is an interest in doll artisans and fashion dolls.

695. *Dolls House World.* [ISSN: 0961-0928] 1990. m. GBP 42 domestic; GBP 73 in Europe; USD 74.50 United States. Ed(s): Joyce Dean. Ashdown Publishing Ltd., Avalon Ct, Star Rd, Partridge Green, RH13 8RY, United Kingdom; esther.forder@btinternet.com; http://www.ashdown.co.uk. Illus., index, adv. Circ: 30000. *Aud.:* Ga, Sa.

This British publication has beautiful photographs and will hold your interest. The several monthly articles are well written, humorous, and feature favorite doll houses as well as doll-house craftspeople and miniaturists. Very practical projects from decorating to furniture making are offered and have clear, easy-to-follow instructions. Regular departments include "Smalltalk," "My Favorite House," "Miniature Mail," and "Club News." Although you are required to create a login to enter the web site, the service is free, and you can access archived feature articles and projects as well as links to products you can buy. *Dolls House World* is a nice complement to the other doll magazines and should be considered by public libraries where there is an interest in the subject.

■ ARCHAEOLOGY

Katharine A. Salzmann, Curator of Manuscripts, Special Collections Research Center, Morris Library, Southern Illinois University Carbondale, Carbondale, IL 62901

Introduction

Archaeology can be defined as the scientific study of human behavior and culture through the examination of material remains dating anywhere from prehistoric times to the modern era. The broad field of archaeology, however, is as varied and complex as the cultures examined, the geographic areas and time periods explored, the scholars and professional organizations involved, and the methods used in research. In addition, it is nearly impossible to study archaeology without crossing over into closely related interdisciplinary fields such as anthropology, art and architecture, classical studies, history, and physical and earth sciences.

When considering reader needs, it is imperative that all of the above factors be considered. Each of the magazines and journals reviewed in this section are published or sponsored by organizations (usually archaeological societies) or institutions (primarily universities or academic departments) that address the scholarly interests of their targeted audiences. There are two basic types of journals: those that are defined by the cultures, time period, and geographic areas explored, and those that are defined by the methodology used in conducting the research. This methodology is often aligned to a cross-discipline such as history, geology, or anthropology. A final factor in considering reader needs should be the audience's level of subject knowledge. There are a number of general-interest archaeology magazines that cater to a wide range of amateur archaeologists, high school and college students, and other nonspecialists. The journals and magazines reviewed in this section represent the range of titles available in many significant areas of archaeology, but the list is in no way exhaustive. For literature on a specialized field, one should explore additional titles and organizations. Limitations in space and scope have made it necessary to exclude non-English journals with the exception of ones that publish an occasional paper in another language. Because virtually every state, province, and local archaeological society publishes its own newsletter or journal, the list is too long to include in these pages. Libraries should identify local or regional associations and include titles that relate to the focus of their researchers.

Basic Periodicals

Hs: *American Archaeology, Archaeology, Expedition;* Ga: *American Archaeology, Archaeology, Biblical Archaeology Review, Egyptian Archaeology, Expedition;* Ac: *American Antiquity, American Journal of Archaeology, Antiquity, Archaeology, Archaeometry, Expedition, Journal of Roman Archaeology, Near Eastern Archaeology, North American Archaeologist, World Archaeology.*

Basic Abstracts and Indexes

Abstracts in Anthropology, Anthropological Index Online, Art and Archaeology Technical Abstracts, British and Irish Archaeological Bibliography. (Some general indexes also cover a good number of archaeological publications.)

696. *Acta Archaeologica.* [ISSN: 0065-101X] 1930. a. USD 113 print & online. Ed(s): Klavs Randsborg. Blackwell Munksgaard, Rosenoerns Alle 1, PO Box 227, Copenhagen V, 1502, Denmark; customerservice@munksgaard.dk; http://www.blackwellmunksgaard.com. Illus., adv. Refereed. Circ: 650. Reprint: ISI. *Indexed:* AIAP, AICP, AbAn, AnthLit, ArtHuCI, BHA, BrArAb, NumL, SSCI. *Aud.:* Ac.

Published annually by the Institute of Archaeology in Copenhagen, this scholarly journal focuses primarily on Nordic and North Eastern studies. The institute describes its publishing aim and scope as, "full presentations of important new discoveries, archaeological analysis, and general and interdisciplinary studies with archaeological basis." Each issue includes a variety of 12 to 15 lengthy articles that are engaging and well illustrated. Contents are occasionally influenced by regional conferences, and one recent issue focuses entirely on Vikings in the West. While most articles are in English, publishers also consider those in French, German, or Italian.

African Archaeological Review. See Africa section.

697. *American Antiquity.* [ISSN: 0002-7316] 1935. q. USD 175. Ed(s): Timothy Kohler. Society for American Archaeology, 900 Second St, N W, 12, Washington, DC 20002-3557; publications@saa.org; http://www.saa.org/Publications/AmAntiq/amantiq.html. Illus., index, adv. Refereed. Circ: 6400. Vol. ends: Oct. Online: Florida Center for Library Automation; Gale Group; JSTOR (Web-based Journal Archive); Northern Light Technology, Inc. Reprint: PSC. *Indexed:* AICP, AbAn, AmH&L, AnthLit, ArtHuCI, ArtInd, BHA, BRI, BrArAb, CBRI, ChemAb, GeoRef, HAPI, HumInd, NumL, SSCI, SportS. *Bk. rev.:* 25, 500-700 words, signed. *Aud.:* Ac, Sa.

Published quarterly by the Society of American Archaeologists, American Antiquity presents articles on the archaeology of the Americas and on worldwide archaeological method, theory, and practice. Articles by scholars in archaeology and anthropology address current trends and research, and numerous shorter reports give an overview of specific projects in the Americas. The lengthy comment section provides an opportunity for members and readers to respond to articles previously published and to other topics of interest to the society. Occasionally, the editors publish a special issue with several papers on a specific topic. Recently, one such issue highlights work on Chaco Canyon, New Mexico. Articles on Latin American topics are accepted, but they are also published in the sister journal *Latin American Archaeology* (below in this section). Both journals have recently begun printing each other's tables of contents at the back of their issues.

698. *American Archaeology: a quarterly publication of the Archaeological Conservancy.* Formerly (until 1997): *Archaeological Conservancy Newsletter.* [ISSN: 1093-8400] 1980. q. USD 25; USD 3.95 newsstand/cover per issue. Ed(s): Michael Bawaya. Archaeological Conservancy, 5301 Central Ave, N E, Ste 402, Albuquerque, NM 87108-1517; archcons@nm.net; http://www.americanarchaeology.org. Illus., adv. Sample. Refereed. Circ: 28000 Paid. *Indexed:* AbAn, AnthLit, BHA. *Bk. rev.:* 2-4, 200-300 words, signed. *Aud.:* Ga.

As the primary publication of the Archaeological Conservancy, *American Archaeology* is "devoted to presenting the rich diversity of archaeology in the Americas." The magazine is tailored for a layperson audience and presents "the research breakthroughs, persistent puzzles, and unique personalities making news in this fascinating field." In addition to four or five full-length feature articles per issue, the magazine highlights upcoming events in the American archaeological community, provides book reviews, and keeps the reader informed of upcoming expeditions and the activities of the conservancy. *American Archaeology* replaced the conservancy's newsletter, and subscription is a benefit of membership.

699. *American Journal of Archaeology.* [ISSN: 0002-9114] 1885. q. USD 250 (Individuals, USD 75). Ed(s): R Bruce Hitchner. Archaeological Institute of America (Boston), c/o Mark Kurtz, 656 Beacon St, Boston, MA 02215-2006; aia@aia.bu.edu; http://www.archaeological.org. Illus., index, adv. Refereed. Circ: 3600. Vol. ends: Oct. Microform: PMC; PQC. Online: Gale Group; JSTOR (Web-based Journal Archive). *Indexed:* ABS&EES, AIAP, AICP, AbAn, AnthLit, ArtHuCI, ArtInd, BAS, BHA, BRD, BRI, BrArAb, CBRI, ChemAb, GeoRef, HumInd, IBZ, NTA, NumL, OTA, RI-1, SSCI. *Bk. rev.:* Number varies, 1-2 columns, signed. *Aud.:* Ac, Sa.

The Archaeology Institute of America, located at Boston University, publishes this critical scholarly journal four times a year to promote the research and interests of members of the society as well as the broader archaeological community. The editorial policy defines the scope of the journal as devoted to "art and archaeology of ancient Europe and the Mediterranean world, including the Near East and Egypt, from prehistoric to late antique times." Three to five peer-reviewed field reports and articles highlight current research in the field; "Necrology Notes" provides tributes to prominent archaeologists; and numerous short reviews keep the reader abreast of current literature. The fourth issue of each volume provides a cumulative contents listing for the year.

700. *Ancient Mesoamerica.* [ISSN: 0956-5361] 1990. s-a. USD 209 (Individuals, USD 90). Ed(s): William R Fowler, Jr. Cambridge University Press, The Edinburgh Bldg, Shaftesbury Rd, Cambridge, CB2 2RU, United Kingdom; information@cambridge.org; http://uk.cambridge.org/journals. Adv. Refereed. Reprint: SWZ. *Indexed:* AIAP, AICP, AbAn, AnthLit, HAPI. *Aud.:* Ac, Sa.

Defined by its editors as "the international forum for the method, theory, substance and interpretation of Mesoamerican archaeology, art history, ethnohistory, historical linguistics and related fields," this academic journal publishes articles primarily exploring pre-Columbian archaeology of the region. The credentials of the contributors reflect the interdisciplinary scope of the journal. Contributors are encouraged in the submission instructions to avoid technical language in order to appeal to nonspecialist readers as well as scholars in the field. Recent issues include articles on Maya women rulers, the Canek manuscript, and Mesoamerican evidence of pre-Columbian transoceanic contacts.

701. *Antiquaries Journal.* Formerly: *Society of Antiquaries. Proceedings.* [ISSN: 0003-5815] 1921. a. GBP 60; USD 100. Ed(s): David Morgan Evans. Society of Antiquaries of London, Burlington House, Piccadilly, London, W1V 0BE, United Kingdom; admin@sal.org.uk; http://www.sal.org.uk. Illus., index. Refereed. Microform: IDC; PQC. *Indexed:* A&ATA, AIAP, AICP, API, AbAn, AnthLit, BHA, BRI, BrArAb, BrHumI, NumL, SSCI. *Bk. rev.:* 25-26, 1-2 columns, signed. *Aud.:* Ac, Sa.

This annual publication of the Society of Antiquaries of London is an impressive work of scholarship, with each issue containing 10 to 12 illustrated articles, a number of shorter notes, and reviews. The journal also provides a full index to the issue's contents. The variety of topics covered, from the transcription of a London pewterer's 1551 manuscript fragment, to the exploration of Richard III and the knave of cards, to the description of architectural recording at the University of Cambridge's Old Schools, reveal the breadth of the society's interests.

702. *Antiquity: a periodical review of archaeology.* [ISSN: 0003-598X] 1927. q. GBP 35 (Individuals, GBP 35; Students, GBP 23). Ed(s): Caroline Malone, Simon Stoddart. Antiquity Publications Ltd., Bidder Bldg, 140 Cowley Rd, Cambridge, CB4 4DL, United Kingdom; sales@thecob.demon.co.uk; http://www.biologists.com. Illus., index, adv. Refereed. Vol. ends: Dec. Microform: MIM; IDC; PQC. Online: bigchalk; EBSCO Publishing; Florida Center for Library Automation; Gale Group; Northern Light Technology, Inc.; OCLC Online Computer Library Center, Inc.; ProQuest Information & Learning; H.W. Wilson. *Indexed:* A&ATA, AIAP, AICP, AbAn, AnthLit, ArtHuCI, ArtInd, BAS, BHA, BrArAb, BrHumI, GeoRef, GeogAbPG, HumInd, IBSS, MLA-IB, NumL, RI-1, SSCI. *Aud.:* Ac, Sa.

This British journal publishes 10 to 12 peer-reviewed articles per issue and a comprehensive notes and news section focusing on current research in areas ranging in scope from the Paleolithic to the present day. Recent issues include articles on diet and ethnicity during the Viking colonization of northern Scotland, stone tool technology in South India, and ostrich distribution and exploitation in the Arabian Peninsula. Notes to the contributor advise potential authors to "write in an accessible, scholarly style that can be understood by a wide range of readers, including amateurs, students, academics, and professionals." News and articles are lavishly illustrated with both color and black-and-white photographs and diagrams.

703. *Archaeology.* [ISSN: 0003-8113] 1948. bi-m. USD 21.95; USD 4.95 newsstand/cover per issue. Ed(s): Peter Young. Archaeological Institute of America, 36-36 33d St, Long Island City, NY 11106; peter@archaeology.org; http://www.he.net/~archaeol/. Illus., index, adv. Refereed. Circ: 200000 Paid. Vol. ends: Nov/Dec. Microform: PQC. Online: EBSCO Publishing; Gale Group. *Indexed:* A&ATA, ABS&EES, AIAP, AICP, AbAn, ArtHuCI, ArtInd, BAS, BHA, BRD, BRI, BiolDig, BrArAb, CBRI, GeoRef, HumInd, MagInd, NumL, RGPR, RI-1, SSCI. *Bk. rev.:* 3-4, 700 words, signed. *Aud.:* Hs, Ga, Ac, Sa.

Published by the Archaeological Institute of America, *Archaeology* is an excellent general-interest magazine that is a must for high school and college libraries. Cover stories and feature articles are well written and illustrated with glossy, engaging photographs and drawings. Further readings are suggested for each, encouraging readers to continue exploration of topics presented. Additional departments include letters to the editor and news notes highlighting activities and events in the field. The review section is versatile and covers not only books but also museum exhibits and multimedia productions.

704. *Archaeology in Oceania.* Formerly: *Archaeology and Physical Anthropology in Oceania.* [ISSN: 0003-8121] 1966. 3x/yr. AUD 60.50 domestic (Students, AUD 48.40). Ed(s): Dr. J P White. Oceania Publications, University of Sydney (H42), 116 Darlington Rd, Sydney, NSW

2006, Australia; d.koller@oceania.usyd.edu.au. Illus., adv. Refereed. Circ: 600. Vol. ends: Oct. Reprint: PQC; PSC. *Indexed:* AICP, AbAn, AnthLit, BAS, BiolAb, GeoRef, IBSS. *Bk. rev.:* 3-4, 2 columns, signed. *Aud.:* Ac, Sa.

This scholarly journal published through the University of Sydney includes peer-reviewed articles in the fields of archaeology and physical anthropology. Its geographic focus is the area between the western Pacific rim and all the islands of the Pacific Ocean including Australia. Three or four technical and sparsely illustrated articles per issue present current research in the field.

705. *Archaeology Ireland.* [ISSN: 0790-892X] 1987. q. USD 35. Archaeology Ireland, PO Box 69, Bray, Ireland.
Illus., adv. *Indexed:* BHA, BrArAb, NumL. *Bk. rev.:* 3-4, 400-500 words, signed. *Aud.:* Ga.

First published in 1987 by a small assemblage of individuals interested in the general field of archaeology, the magazine has evolved to cover many related disciplines including architecture, art, history, religion, science, and sociology. As the title suggests, the focus of the feature articles is on events and trends in archaeology in Ireland, however the magazine serves a broader audience with "the latest news, reviews and debates that are influencing archaeology and history in Ireland, Britain and the rest of the world." Contributors include academics and field professionals as well as members of the editorial team. The concise, well-written articles are accompanied by illuminating photographs and diagrams.

706. *Archaeology Odyssey.* [ISSN: 1096-9640] 1998. bi-m. USD 24 domestic; USD 33 foreign; USD 4.50 newsstand/cover per issue. Ed(s): Jack Meinhardt, Hershel Shanks. Biblical Archaeology Society, 4710 41st St, N W, Washington, DC 20016; bas@bib-arch.org; http://www.bib-arch.org/. Illus., adv. Sample. Circ: 70000 Paid. *Bk. rev.:* 3-4, 4 columns, signed. *Aud.:* Ga.

The newest publication by the Biblical Archaeological Society and editor Herschel Shanks, *Archaeology Odyssey* offers three or four feature articles per issue and provides an "exciting and informative journey to the ancient roots of the Western World." The scholarly content of the articles is made attainable for laypersons with engaging photographs and sidebars. "Keep reading" notices peppered throughout the magazine cite related articles and links available at the society's web site. In addition to the feature articles, contents include letters to the editor, field notes, reviews, and contributor credits.

707. *Archaeology of Eastern North America.* [ISSN: 0360-1021] 1973. a. USD 40. Ed(s): Arthur Spiess. Eastern States Archeological Federation, PO Box 386, Bethlehem, CT 06751. Illus. Circ: 500. *Indexed:* AICP, AbAn, AnthLit. *Aud.:* Ac.

Published by the Eastern States Archaeological Federation (ESAF), this scholarly journal provides seven to ten articles per issue on a variety of topics relating to the archaeological exploration of Eastern North America. Issues include articles on such diverse topics as Native American grave gods in Pennsylvania, petroglyphs in Maine, and farmsteads in Ohio. Papers presented at ESAF conferences are frequently published, as in a recent issue that includes four papers from the session "From the Prehistoric to the Historic Period in the Ohio River Valley."

708. *Archaeometry.* [ISSN: 0003-813X] 1958. biennial. USD 227 print & online eds. Ed(s): M S Tite. Blackwell Publishing Ltd., 9600 Garsington Rd, PO Box 805, Oxford, OX4 2DQ, United Kingdom. Illus., adv. Refereed. Circ: 1500. Vol. ends: Aug. Reprint: ISI. *Indexed:* A&ATA, AIAP, AICP, AbAn, AnthLit, ArtHuCI, BAS, BHA, BrArAb, ChemAb, NumL, SSCI. *Aud.:* Ac, Sa.

This scholarly journal published for Oxford University covers "the interaction between the sciences and archaeology, conservation, and art history" with methodology and application being the focal points. Eight to twelve articles per issue present the results of research in the field, involving either the development of new or the use of existing methods. The journal also publishes review articles and short notes, including comments on previously published articles.

709. *Australasian Historical Archaeology.* Formerly: *Australian Journal of Historical Archaeology;* Supersedes (in 1983): *Australian Society for Historical Archeology. (Annual Publication);* Which was formerly (until 1973): *Studies in Historical Archeology.* [ISSN: 1322-9214] a. AUD 50 for membership to individuals; AUD 60 for membership to institutions. Australasian Society for Historical Archaeology, University of Sydney, Holme Bldg, PO Box 220, Sydney, NSW 2006, Australia; asha_secretary@yahoo.co.uk. Refereed. Circ: 400. *Indexed:* AbAn, AmH&L, AnthLit. *Bk. rev.:* 3-5. *Aud.:* Ac.

The Australasian Society for Historical Archaeology represents the merger of Australian and New Zealand archaeologists dedicated to the promotion and "exchange of information, research, and reference materials relating to historical archaeology within Australia, New Zealand, and overseas." The society's scholarly organ, *Australasian Historical Archaeology*, serves as the vehicle for this exchange and publishes eight to ten research articles annually documenting historical sites, buildings, and relics reflecting all aspects of life in these areas. The journal also publishes book reviews and short reports on these topics.

The Biblical Archaeologist. See *Near Eastern Archaeology.*

710. *Biblical Archaeology Review.* [ISSN: 0098-9444] 1975. bi-m. USD 27 domestic; GBP 27 United Kingdom; GBP 29.70 elsewhere. Ed(s): Hershel Shanks, Steven Feldman. Biblical Archaeology Society, 4710 41st St, N W, Washington, DC 20016; http://www.tradepub.com/paid/TITLES/paid.Biblical_Archae_Revi.html. Illus., adv. Circ: 180000. Vol. ends: Nov/Dec. *Indexed:* AIAP, AbAn, ArtInd, ChrPI, GeoRef, HumInd, IJP, NTA, OTA, R&TA, RI-1. *Bk. rev.:* 3-4, length 2-3 columns, signed. *Aud.:* Ga, Ac, Sa.

Biblical Archaeology Review is an organ of the Biblical Archaeology Society, a nondenominational educational organization founded in 1974 to promote the research and study of archaeology in the biblical lands of the Old and New Testaments. Similar in both format and style to the broader publication by the same society, *Archaeology Odyssey* (above in this section), four or five feature articles "connect the academic study of archaeology to a general audience eager to understand the world of the Bible." Editor Herschel Shanks and his staff embrace the controversial nature of biblical archaeology and do an admirable job of printing all sides of the contemporary debates, whether in feature articles, letters to the editor, or book reviews.

711. *Cambridge Archaeological Journal.* [ISSN: 0959-7743] 1991. s-a. USD 130 print & online eds. (Individuals, USD 40). Ed(s): Chris Scarre. Cambridge University Press, The Edinburgh Bldg, Shaftesbury Rd, Cambridge, CB2 2RU, United Kingdom; information@cambridge.org; http://uk.cambridge.org/journals. Illus., index, adv. Refereed. Vol. ends: Oct. Reprint: SWZ. *Indexed:* AIAP, AICP, AnthLit, ArtHuCI, BrArAb, BrHumI, NumL. *Bk. rev.:* 5-6, 3-7 pages, signed. *Aud.:* Ac, Sa.

Published by Cambridge University Press on behalf of the McDonald Institute for Archaeological Research, this scholarly journal broadly covers all areas and periods of archaeology, with a notable focus on "the role of human intellectual abilities as reflected for example in art, religion, and symbolism of early societies." About five full-length articles comprise the bulk of each issue with additional shorter viewpoint and review pieces. Recent issues include such topics as demography and cultural innovation, tool standardization in the middle and upper Palaeolithic, and perception and expression in ancient Mesoamerica.

712. *Canadian Journal of Archaeology.* Formerly: *Canadian Archaeological Association. Bulletin.* [ISSN: 0705-2006] 1977. a. CND 100 (Individuals, CND 75; Students, CND 35). Ed(s): George Nicholas. Canadian Archaeological Association, c/o Butch Amundson, Sec -Treas, Dept of Anthropology and Archeology, Saskatoon, SK S7N 5B1, Canada; nicholas@sfu.ca; http://www.canadianarchaeology.com. Illus., adv. Refereed. Circ: 500. *Indexed:* AICP, AmH&L, AnthLit, BHA, BrArAb, CBCARef. *Bk. rev.:* 5-6, 3 pages, signed. *Aud.:* Ac, Sa.

Published annually by the Canadian Archaeological Association (CAA), this journal "serves as a means of communicating the interests and concerns of the Canadian archaeological community." Contributors are almost exclusively from Canadian universities and their scholarly articles are illustrated with black-

and-white maps, graphs, photographs, and drawings. Recent issues include articles on research and sites in the boreal forest of Vancouver Island and Baker Island in southeast Alaska. Occasionally, the journal also publishes statements and proceedings from the CAA's meetings.

713. *Egyptian Archaeology.* [ISSN: 0962-2837] 1991. s-a. GBP 4.95 per issue. Ed(s): Patricia Spencer. Egypt Exploration Society, 3 Doughty Mews, London, WC1N 2PG, United Kingdom; http://www.ees.ac.uk. Illus., index, adv. Circ: 5000. Vol. ends: Spring. *Bk. rev.:* Number and length vary. *Aud.:* Ac.

Relatively new to archaeological literature, *Egyptian Archaeology* provides readers with a colorful look at archaeological activities and research of interest to the Egyptian Exploration Society. Eight to ten short articles are lavishly illustrated with color photographs and charts. Regular features include "Notes and News," covering archaeological sites, online displays, and news stories and concerns; "Notice Board," highlighting forthcoming lectures, exhibits, and other events; "Bookshelf," featuring reviews of books on archaeology in Egypt; and "Membership Matters," showcasing activities and projects of the society.

714. *Expedition.* [ISSN: 0014-4738] 1958. 3x/yr. USD 27 domestic; USD 31 foreign; USD 9.95 newsstand/cover per issue. Ed(s): Beebe Bahrami. University of Pennsylvania Museum, 33rd & Spruce Sts, Philadelphia, PA 19104-6324; expedition@sas.upenn.edu; http://www.upenn.edu/museum. Illus., index. Refereed. Circ: 4250. Vol. ends: Winter. Microform: PQC. Online: EBSCO Publishing; Gale Group. Reprint: PQC. *Indexed:* A&ATA, AIAP, AICP, AbAn, AnthLit, ArtInd, BAS, BHA, NumL. *Aud.:* Hs, Ga, Ac.

In a popular, glossy format, *Expedition* provides articles and updates on current research on ancient civilizations, with an emphasis on how they relate to contemporary cultures for general readers, students, and scholars. Contributors tend to have a University of Pennsylvania affiliation, but the topics of the refereed feature articles appeal to a broad audience and are frequently assembled around a particular topic. Departments such as "From the Archives," "Museum Mosaic," and "What in the World" supplement the themes, with emphasis on the resources and activities of the museum. In addition, the magazine includes an insert, "Laying the Groundwork," a publication of the Office of Museum Development that highlights the people and events of the friends of the museum.

715. *Geoarchaeology: an international journal.* [ISSN: 0883-6353] 1986. 8x/yr. USD 1300 domestic; USD 1380 in Canada & Mexico; USD 1448 elsewhere. Ed(s): Jack Donahue. John Wiley & Sons, Inc., 111 River St, Hoboken, NJ 07030; uscs-wis@wiley.com; http://www.wiley.com. Refereed. Microform: PQC. *Indexed:* AbAn, AnthLit, BrArAb, GeoRef, NumL. *Aud.:* Ac, Sa.

This scholarly journal presents international research on the methodological and theoretical intersection of archaeology and the earth sciences. It includes within its scope interdisciplinary work focusing on understanding archaeological sites, their natural context, and particularly aspects of site formation processes. Submissions are encouraged that cover the interrelationship between archaeology and such fields as climatology, geochemistry, geography, geology, geophysics, oceanography, and pedology. Five to seven peer-reviewed articles explore these disciplines, and occasionally an entire issue may be dedicated to a specific topic, such as the recent special issue on rockshelter sediment records and environmental change in the Mediterranean region.

716. *Hesperia.* [ISSN: 0018-098X] 1932. q. USD 110 (Individuals, USD 60). Ed(s): Dr. Tracey Cullen. American School of Classical Studies at Athens, 6 - 8 Charlton St, Princeton, NJ 08540-5232; tc@ascsa.org; http://www.ascsa.edu.gr. Illus. Refereed. Circ: 1100. Reprint: SWZ. *Indexed:* AIAP, AbAn, ArtHuCI, ArtInd, IBZ, MLA-IB, NumL, SSCI. *Aud.:* Ac, Sa.

The American School of Classical Studies at Athens is a research and teaching institution dedicated to advanced study of the archaeology, art, history, philosophy, language, and literature of Greece and the Greek world. *Hesperia* serves as the scholarly organ of the school, dedicated to the "timely publication of reports on School-sponsored and School-directed projects." The editors welcome submissions from all scholars working in the fields of Greek archaeology, art, epigraphy, history, and literature, from prehistoric times onward. The refereed articles in the journal are thorough and lengthy (at times only three per issue) with abstracts and substantial notes, but the charts, photographs, and other illustrative material make the information accessible for audiences at any academic level.

717. *Historical Archaeology.* [ISSN: 0440-9213] 1967. q. USD 105 (Individuals, USD 75; Students, USD 40 includes S H A Newsletter). Ed(s): Ronald L Michael. Society for Historical Archaeology, PO Box 30446, Tucson, AZ 85751; the_sha@mindspring.com; http://www.sha.org. Illus., index, adv. Sample. Refereed. Circ: 2500 Paid. Vol. ends: Dec. *Indexed:* A&ATA, AbAn, AmH&L, AnthLit, ArtHuCI, BHA, BrArAb, HumInd, IBSS, IBZ, NumL. *Bk. rev.:* 15-20, 2 pages, signed. *Aud.:* Ac, Sa.

As the scholarly journal of the Society for Historical Archaeology, this publication presents articles and reports on historic-period archaeological research, method, and theory. Contributors are generally members of the society, and five or six articles per issue focus primarily on their North American subjects and research, with forages into international themes. Occasionally, a thematic, monograph-length work is published, for example, "Feeding Colonial Boston: A Zooarchaeological Study." A lengthy and comprehensive review section provides a look at relevant books and research publications in the field, and society news is frequently featured. Subscription is a benefit of membership.

718. *International Journal of Osteoarchaeology.* [ISSN: 1047-482X] 1991. bi-m. USD 820. John Wiley & Sons Ltd., The Atrium, Southern Gate, Chichester, PO19 8SQ, United Kingdom; customer@wiley.co.uk; http://www.wiley.co.uk. Adv. Refereed. Circ: 500. Microform: PQC. Online: EBSCO Publishing; ScienceDirect; Swets Blackwell; Wiley InterScience. Reprint: SWZ. *Indexed:* AnthLit, ArtHuCI, BrArAb, NumL, SSCI, ZooRec. *Aud.:* Ac, Sa.

This scientific journal publishes articles exploring all aspects of the study of human and animal bones in an archaeological context. Relatively new, it has evolved from a vehicle for publishing the work of its founding editors into an established scholarly journal with international contributors. Five to seven articles per issue covering bone research from any area of the world are accepted, and papers from the following disciplines are encouraged: palaeoanthropology, physical anthropology, epidemiology, chemical analysis, exploitation of animal resources, and taphonoly. The editors occasionally compile articles on a specific topic, such as a recent special issue on the zooarchaeology of oceanic coasts and islands.

719. *Journal of Archaeological Method and Theory.* [ISSN: 1072-5369] 1994. q. USD 345 print or online ed. Ed(s): James M Skibo, Catherine M Cameron. Kluwer Academic / Plenum Publishers, 233 Spring St Fl 7, New York, NY 10013-1522; http://www.wkap.nl/. Adv. Refereed. Online: EBSCO Publishing; ingenta.com; Kluwer Online; OCLC Online Computer Library Center, Inc.; Ovid Technologies, Inc.; RoweCom Information Quest. *Indexed:* AICP, AnthLit, ArtHuCI, BrArAb, NumL. *Aud.:* Ac, Sa.

As the title suggests, this journal's primary focus is on the examination of methods and theories used in conducting archaeological research. The editorial description indicates that each article "establishes a framework for synthesizing findings, provides incisive commentary on previous work, and identifies research priorities." Four to six articles cross the fields of archaeology, art history, cultural studies, ethnohistory, and related disciplines. Recent topics include exploration of the archaeology of childhood, experimental approaches to the process of information transmittal, and conceptual alternatives for consideration of stone tool production.

720. *Journal of Archaeological Science.* [ISSN: 0305-4403] 1974. m. EUR 1058 (Qualified personnel, EUR 124). Ed(s): K. W. Butzer, J. Grattan. Academic Press, Harcourt Pl, 32 Jamestown Rd, London, NW1 7BY, United Kingdom; apsubs@acad.com; http://www.elsevier-international.com/serials/. Illus., index, adv. Refereed. Vol. ends: Nov. Online: EBSCO Publishing; ingenta.com; OCLC Online Computer

Library Center, Inc.; RoweCom Information Quest; ScienceDirect; Swets Blackwell. Reprint: SWZ. *Indexed:* A&ATA, AIAP, AICP, AbAn, AnthLit, ArtHuCI, BHA, BiolAb, BrArAb, FS&TA, GeoRef, GeogAbPG, NumL, SSCI, ZooRec. *Bk. rev.:* Various number and length, signed. *Aud.:* Ac, Sa.

Published by Academic Press in association with the Society for Archaeological Science, this journal "aims to publish papers, reviews, focus articles, and short notes covering the interaction between the sciences and archaeology, with particular emphasis on methodological innovation." Any one issue may include articles relating archaeological research to the fields of botany, geology, chemistry, and anatomy. With the contents of the journal comprised almost solely of feature articles averaging ten pages in length, this journal is able to include many more titles than the average source.

721. ***Journal of Field Archaeology.*** [ISSN: 0093-4690] 1974. q. USD 60 (Individuals, USD 48). Ed(s): Curtis Runnels. Boston University, Journal of Field Archaeology, 675 Commonwealth Ave, Boston, MA 02215; jfa@bu.edu; http://jfa-www.bu.edu. Illus., adv. Sample. Refereed. Circ: 1200 Paid. Vol. ends: Winter. Microform: PQC. Online: Gale Group; JSTOR (Web-based Journal Archive). *Indexed:* A&ATA, ABS&EES, AIAP, AICP, AbAn, AnthLit, ArtHuCI, ArtInd, BAS, BHA, BrArAb, GeoRef, HumInd, IBZ, NumL, OTA, SSCI. *Bk. rev.:* 5, 2-4 pages, signed. *Aud.:* Ac, Sa.

Published quarterly by Boston University, this journal offers refereed articles "serving the interests of archaeologists, anthropologists, historians, scientists, and others concerned with the recovery and interpretation of archeological data." The scope is international, and types of articles include field reports, technical and methodological studies, review articles, articles on the history of archaeology, and preliminary reports describing field work or research. Contributors represent a wide range of academic institutions and field projects, and articles are accompanied by charts, diagrams, and photographs.

722. ***Journal of Mediterranean Archaeology.*** [ISSN: 0952-7648] 1988. 2x/yr. GBP 80 (Individuals, GBP 35; Students, GBP 26.50). Ed(s): A Bernard Knapp, John F Cherry. Sheffield Academic Press Ltd, Mansion House, 19 Kingfield Rd, Sheffield, S11 9AS, United Kingdom; jjoyce@continuumbooks.com; http://www.continuumjournals.com/. Adv. Online: EBSCO Publishing. *Indexed:* AnthLit, GeogAbPG, RI-1. *Aud.:* Ac.

Documenting the islands in the Mediterranean Sea and and the lands and regions that border it, the *Journal of Mediterranean Archaeology* examines all aspects of Mediterranean prehistory and history. Four to six sparsely illustrated articles per issue explore the "theoretical implications and methodological assumptions that can be extrapolated from the relevant archaeological data." Of particular note in this publication is the frequent inclusion of an engaging "Discussion and Debate" section devoted to colleague responses to articles published in the journal.

723. ***Journal of Roman Archaeology.*** [ISSN: 1047-7594] 1988. a. USD 100 (Individuals, USD 59.75). Ed(s): John H Humphrey. Journal of Roman Archaeology L.L.C., The Editor, JRA, 95 Peleg Rd, Portsmouth, RI 02871; jra@journalofromanarch.com; http://JournalofRomanArch.com. Illus. Refereed. Circ: 1050. *Indexed:* ArtInd, BrArAb, IBZ, NTA, NumL. *Bk. rev.:* 50, 4 pages, signed. *Aud.:* Ac, Sa.

This substantial annual publication serves as a vehicle for articles, archaeological reports, and notes of interest to classical scholars, archaeologists, art and architecture historians, and others interested in Roman archaeology. Eight to ten scholarly articles cover a wide spectrum of topics and interdisciplinary studies, with recent articles on Greek portraits, Herculean women statue types, wooden arena flooring, and aqueducts. Articles are primarily illustrated with black-and-white photographs and drawings, but there is an occasional color plate. One recent issue includes an impressive, glossy pullout photo-mosaic in color.

724. ***Kiva: the journal of Southwestern anthropology and history.*** [ISSN: 0023-1940] 1935. q. USD 40. Ed(s): Tobi Taylor. Arizona Archaeological and Historical Society, Arizona State Museum, University of Arizona, Tucson, AZ 85721. Illus., adv. Sample. Refereed. Circ: 1100. Vol. ends: Jun. *Indexed:* AICP, AbAn, AmH&L, AnthLit. *Bk. rev.:* 2-3, 2-3 pages, signed. *Aud.:* Ac, Sa.

The scholarly organ of the Arizona Archaeological and Historical Society, *Kiva* supports the society's mission to further research in and preservation of southwestern United States and Mexican archaeological and historical sites. Four to six sparsely illustrated articles per issue relate to the prehistoric and historic archaeology, ethnology, history, anthropology, linguistics, and ethnohistory of the region. Recent issues include articles on late archaic dog burial from the Tucson Basin, Hispano identity through the Santa Fe Fiesta, and migrations in late Anasazi prehistory. The society's other publication, *Glyphs*, serves as their newsletter. It is published monthly and announces lectures, field trips, classes, and news.

725. ***Latin American Antiquity.*** [ISSN: 1045-6635] 1990. q. USD 120 domestic; USD 33 in Latin America. Ed(s): Katharina Schreiber. Society for American Archaeology, 900 Second St, N W, 12, Washington, DC 20002-3557; publications@saa.org; http://www.saa.org/Publications/LatAmAnt/latamant.html. Illus., index, adv. Refereed. Circ: 1500. Vol. ends: Dec. *Indexed:* AICP, AbAn, AnthLit, ArtHuCI, BRI, CBRI, HAPI. *Bk. rev.:* 4-5, 300-700 words, signed. *Aud.:* Ac, Sa.

Published quarterly by the Society for American Archaeology, this journal is similar in format and editorial style to its sister journal, *American Antiquity* (above in this section), but its geographical scope is narrower. It publishes original papers on the archaeology, prehistory, and ethnohistory of Mesoamerica, Central America, South America, and adjacent culturally affiliated regions. Three to five feature articles, shorter reports, comments, and book reviews comprise the contents of a typical issue. As one might expect from the journal's geographical focus, the editors often publish Spanish-language articles.

MCJA. See *Midcontinental Journal of Archaeology.*

726. ***Medieval Archaeology.*** [ISSN: 0076-6097] 1957. a. USD 109 (Individuals, USD 36). Ed(s): J Hines. Maney Publishing, Hudson Rd, Leeds, LS9 7DL, United Kingdom; maney@maney.co.uk; http://www.maney.co.uk. Illus. Refereed. Circ: 1500. *Indexed:* A&ATA, AIAP, AbAn, BEL&L, BHA, BrArAb, HumInd, NumL. *Bk. rev.:* 40, 500-1,000 words, signed. *Aud.:* Ac, Sa.

Published by the Society for Medieval Archaeology, this journal supports the society's mission to further the study of the fifth to sixteenth centuries A.D. in Britain, Ireland, and, to a lesser extent, continental Europe. The editor's note comments that contributions "may be artifact or site based, but papers with a theoretical or methodological content related to medieval archaeology are also welcomed." Six to eight lengthy and sparsely illustrated feature articles are accepted by the editorial committee for this annual publication and are "subject to peer review." Each issue includes notes, news, and book reviews. The society also publishes a separate annual directory of fieldwork in the British Isles, *Medieval Britain and Ireland in xxxx*."

727. ***Midcontinental Journal of Archaeology.*** [ISSN: 0146-1109] 1976. s-a. USD 28 (Individuals, USD 19). Ed(s): William Green, David S Brose. University of Iowa, Office of State Archaeologist, 700 Clinton St Bldg, Iowa City, IA 52242-1030; http://www.uiowa.edu/~osa/publica/mcja/mcja.htm. Illus., index, adv. Refereed. Circ: 600. Vol. ends: Oct. Reprint: PQC. *Indexed:* AICP, AbAn, AmH&L, AnthLit, BrArAb. *Aud.:* Ac, Sa.

The editors of this American archaeological journal define the region it covers as "between the Appalachian Mountains and the Great Plains, from the Boreal Forests to the Gulf of Mexico." Published biannually by the Office of the State Archaeologist, University of Iowa, it contains four or five articles per issue highlighting research in the region with charts, diagrams, and black-and-white photographs as illustration. Each issue includes articles on a variety of topics, but one recent theme-based issue presents papers in honor of the retirement of a prominent North American archaeologist.

728. *Near Eastern Archaeology.* Formerly (until 1998): *Biblical Archaeologist.* [ISSN: 1094-2076] 1938. q. USD 75 (Individuals, USD 35). Ed(s): Theodore Lewis. American Schools of Oriental Research, 825 Houston Mill Rd, Atlanta, GA 30329; asorpubs@asor.org; http://www.asor.org. Illus., index, adv. Refereed. Circ: 4500 Paid. Vol. ends: Dec. Microform: PQC. Online: EBSCO Publishing; Gale Group; OCLC Online Computer Library Center, Inc.; ProQuest Information & Learning; H.W. Wilson. Reprint: PQC. *Indexed:* A&ATA, AICP, AbAn, AnthLit, ArtHuCI, ArtInd, BHA, CPL, ChrPI, HumInd, IBSS, IBZ, IJP, MLA-IB, NTA, NumL, OTA, R&TA, RI-1, SSCI. *Bk. rev.:* 3-4, 500-1,000 words, signed. *Aud.:* Ac, Sa.

Formerly *Biblical Archaeologist*, this magazine publishes articles exploring the cultural, historical, and literary heritage of the Middle East (i.e., Anatolia, Cyprus, Egypt, Mesopotamia, and Syro-Palestine) through all time periods. Four to six feature articles per issue present current research and trends in the field with numerous photographs and illustrations. Abstracts to the articles are published in the table of contents, and biographical sketches and photographs of authors are placed at the end of each article. The "Arti-facts" section serves as a vehicle for short notes on new finds or discoveries, rebuttals to articles previously published, and announcements of upcoming conferences.

729. *North American Archaeologist.* [ISSN: 0197-6931] 1979. q. USD 237 (Individuals, USD 60). Ed(s): Roger W Moeller. Baywood Publishing Co., Inc., 26 Austin Ave, Amityville, NY 11701; info@baywood.com; http://www.baywood.com. Illus., adv. Sample. Refereed. Vol. ends: No. 4. *Indexed:* AICP, AbAn, AmH&L, AnthLit, ArtHuCI, BHA, BrArAb, IBZ. *Bk. rev.:* 2-6, 2 pages, signed. *Aud.:* Ac, Sa.

Concerned with all aspects of American archaeology, this journal covers the United States and Mexico with topics that span the range of cultural evolution in America from paleo-Indian studies to modern industrial archaeology. Three to five theoretical and methodological articles per issue highlight state, provincial, and local archaeological research, and the editors encourage articles that cut across geographic and cultural boundaries. Lengthy book reviews provide insight into current trends and research in the field.

730. *Oxford Journal of Archaeology.* [ISSN: 0262-5253] 1982. q. GBP 287 print & online eds. Ed(s): Sir John Boardman, Barry Cunliffe. Blackwell Publishing Ltd., 9600 Garsington Rd, PO Box 805, Oxford, OX4 2DQ, United Kingdom; jnlinfo@blackwellpublishers.co.uk; http://www.blackwellpublishers.co.uk/scripts/webjrn1.idc. Illus., adv. Sample. Refereed. Circ: 550. Online: EBSCO Publishing; ingenta.com; OCLC Online Computer Library Center, Inc.; RoweCom Information Quest; Swets Blackwell. Reprint: SWZ. *Indexed:* A&ATA, AIAP, AnthLit, BHA, BrArAb, GeoRef, GeogAbPG, IBSS, L&LBA, NumL. *Aud.:* Ac, Sa.

Published for the Institute of Archaeology, Oxford University, this journal covers current research in prehistoric, classical, and later European archaeology within the geographic scope of Europe and Mediterranean areas. Five to seven quality articles per issue combine to present a highly respected, scholarly journal covering archaeology as it relates to "art, art history, architecture, numismatics, the applications of scientific analysis, and theoretical approaches." Occasionally, notes sections are included to inform readers about and spark discussion on relevant issues in archaeology.

731. *Prehistoric American.* Former titles (until 1990): *Prehistoric Artifacts of North America;* (until 1985): *Prehistoric Art Archaeology;* (until 1980): *The Resskin.* [ISSN: 1060-0965] 1966. q. Membership, USD 20. G.I.R.S. Inc., c/o Anthony Stein, 4739 Belleview, Ste 304, Kansas City, MO 64112; tony@mississippian-artifacts.com; http://www.thegirs.com/. *Aud.:* Hs, Ga, Ac, Sa.

This is the official publication of the Genuine Indian Relic Society, Inc., a nonprofit organization founded in 1964 to promote "friendship and trust among persons interested in the collection and preservation of genuine prehistoric North American artifacts by providing a medium of information and educational exchange." The magazine is lavishly illustrated with full-page color photographs. In fact, it has more visual content than text and appeals to younger readers as well as scholars in the field. Focusing primarily on artifacts, the articles are concise and lucidly written. Recent topics include ancient Texas art, a comparison of often confused point types, and Cahokie gempoints.

732. *World Archaeology.* [ISSN: 0043-8243] 1969. 3x/yr. GBP 172 (Individuals, GBP 51). Ed(s): Richard Bradley. Routledge, 11 New Fetter Ln, London, EC4P 4EE, United Kingdom; info@routledge.co.uk; http://www.routledge.co.uk. Illus., index, adv. Refereed. Vol. ends: Feb. Microform: NRP. Online: EBSCO Publishing; Gale Group; Ingenta Select; JSTOR (Web-based Journal Archive); OCLC Online Computer Library Center, Inc.; RoweCom Information Quest; Swets Blackwell. Reprint: PSC. *Indexed:* A&ATA, AIAP, AICP, AbAn, AnthLit, ArtHuCI, ArtInd, BAS, BHA, BrArAb, BrHumI, HumInd, IBSS, NumL, RI-1, SSCI. *Aud.:* Ac, Sa.

This scholarly journal, published by the respected Routledge Press, presents an entire issue dedicated to a particular theme. Each issue has a different editor, and seven to ten articles provide a worldwide, multi-period perspective on the topic. Articles are peer reviewed, and the editors provide a keyword listing and an abstract for each. Recent issues have covered archaeology in Southeast Asia, "queer" archaeology, and the cultural biography of objects. Future publications will include archaeology and aesthetics, ancient eco-disasters, and evolutionary ecology and archaeology.

■ ARCHITECTURE

David Buxton, Campus Librarian, Washington State University, Spokane, WA 99202-1495; buxton@wsu.edu

Introduction

Architecture is many things, and it is not surprising that the architectural periodical literature reflects this diversity. Architecture is a profession. As such it supports professional associations that promote the profession and accredit academic programs. Associations like the American Institute of Architects and the Society of Architectural Historians either publish or support journals, some of them scholarly, and the students and faculty in the accredited academic programs write articles for these publications. Architecture is also a trade, so there are trade publications that promote the business of architecture. More than any other profession or trade, however, there is an important aesthetic element to architecture; ideally, a building design should be a work of art. There are regional styles of building design, so there are magazines that take a geographic perspective on the architecture of different parts of the world. Finally, architecture and building and interior design are popular arts that anyone can enjoy, so there is a wealth of popular magazines that appeal to ordinary people, not just to professional designers and architects.

Architectural magazines tend to be different from other magazines in that they themselves are often "designed," and consequently they look different from other magazines. There are big, heavy "coffee table" magazines like *El Croquis* that make special demands on libraries since they don't fit well on standard library shelves. By virtue of the fact that they contain so many color illustrations and photographs, architecture magazines are often very heavy, even if they are normal size. They are also often very expensive, since color photographic artwork is costly to print.

Publishing architectural journals electronically on the web could address the cost issues, and attempts have been made to do this. *Architronic* and *Grey Room* are examples of architecture magazines published electronically on the web. Unfortunately, however, *Architronic* is no longer published. *Grey Room*, published by MIT Press and distributed by Ingenta, continues, although irregularly.

Basic Periodicals

Ga: *Architectural Record, Architecture, Inland Architect, Metropolis, Preservation, Taunton's Fine Homebuilding, World Architecture;* Ac: *A & U, L'Architecture d'Aujourd'hui, Architectural Design, Architectural Review, Architecture, Built Environment, El Croquis, Domus, Journal of the Society of Architectural Historians, Places, RIBA Journal.*

Basic Abstracts and Indexes

Architectural Index, Architectural Publications Index, Art Index, Avery Index to Architectural Periodicals.

733. ***A A Files: annals of the Architectural Association School of Architecture.*** Formerly: *A A Quarterly.* [ISSN: 0261-6823] 1981. 3x/yr. GBP 42 (Students, GBP 33). Ed(s): Mark Rappolt. Architectural Association, 36 Bedford Sq, London, WC1B 3ES, United Kingdom; publications@aaschool.ac.uk; http://www.aaschool.ac.uk. Illus., index. Circ: 2500. *Indexed:* AIAP, API, ArtInd, BHA. *Bk. rev.:* 6-8, 1,500 words. *Aud.:* Ac.

This heavy, oversized quarterly published by the Architectural Association School of Architecture in the United Kingdom carries no advertising. It deals with architecture from an aesthetic perspective and includes beautifully illustrated articles not only on architecture but also photography, poetry, short fiction, and painting. Contributors include architects, academics, and artists. Recommended for large public and academic libraries.

734. ***A & U.*** [ISSN: 0389-9160] 1971. m. JPY 30000 domestic; USD 232.55 domestic; JPY 35000 foreign. Ed(s): Nobuyuki Yoshida. A + U Publishing Co. Ltd., 30-8 Yushima 2-chome, Bunkyo-ku, Tokyo, 113-0034, Japan; aandu@nisiq.net; http://www.nisuiq.net/~aandu. Illus., index, adv. Circ: 25000. Vol. ends: Dec. *Indexed:* AIAP, API, ArtHuCI, ArtInd, BHA. *Bk. rev.:* Various number and length. *Aud.:* Ac, Sa.

This highly regarded Japanese periodical deals primarily with architecture as an art form. The feature articles usually include English translations. The only advertising appears on the inside front and back covers. A new regular section on schools of architecture began in January 2003 with a profile of Yale University's architecture program. The target audience appears to be architects and academics. Recommended for academic libraries.

735. ***Abitare: home, town and environmental living.*** Formerly (until 1962): *Casa Novita.* [ISSN: 0001-3218] 1961. 11x/yr. ITL 174000 in Europe; USD 115 United States; USD 12 newsstand/cover per issue United States. Ed(s): Italo Lupi. Editrice Abitare Segesta SpA, Corso Monforte, 15, Milan, 20122, Italy; abitaremag@abitare.it; http://www.abitare.it. Illus., adv. Circ: 42848. *Indexed:* AIAP, ArtInd, DAAI. *Bk. rev.:* Various number and length. *Aud.:* Ga, Sa.

This Italian quarterly sandwiches short news items and feature articles between display advertising in the front and classified advertising in the back. The articles deal with contemporary architecture worldwide and are richly illustrated with color photos. Regular departments include a section called "Nautilus" that features book reviews. The feature articles are grouped into categories: "Interiors," "Architecture," "Design," and "Production." Recent articles include one on the "Naked House" designed by Shigeru Ban and one on gypsy architecture in Romania. Articles are in Italian with English translations. Recommended for large public and academic libraries.

736. ***Architects' Journal.*** [ISSN: 0003-8466] 1895. w. GBP 119 foreign (Individuals, GBP 75; Students, GBP 49). Ed(s): Paul Finch. Emap Construct Ltd., 151 Rosebery Ave, London, EC1R 4GB, United Kingdom; tina@construct.emap.co.uk; http://www.emap.com/construct/. Illus., adv. Circ: 17180. *Indexed:* A&ATA, AIAP, API, ArtInd, BrHumI, BrTechI, C&ISA, CerAb. *Aud.:* Ga, Ac.

This weekly British trade publication covers current news and events in architecture, primarily from a British perspective, but with some attention to international architectural news. In addition to the typical departments and feature articles, the magazine includes display ads and classified ads for goods and services of interest to British architects and contractors. Recommended for architecture libraries.

737. ***Architectural Design.*** [ISSN: 0003-8504] 1930. bi-m. USD 270. John Wiley & Sons Ltd., The Atrium, Southern Gate, Chichester, PO19 8SQ, United Kingdom; customer@wiley.co.uk; http://www.wiley.co.uk. Illus., index, adv. Circ: 6500 Paid. Vol. ends: Nov/Dec. *Indexed:* AIAP, API, ArtHuCI, ArtInd, EIP, SSCI. *Bk. rev.:* 8, 250 words. *Aud.:* Ac, Sa.

This slick magazine covers a different theme in each issue, which is guest edited by an individual or design firm. Recent examples include "Food & Architecture" edited by Karen A. Franck and "Versioning: Evolutionary Techniques in Architecture" by the firm of SHoP/Sharples Holden Pasquarelli. Each issue is lavishly illustrated with color photographs and renderings. Profiles of the contributors and the projects discussed in the issue follow the feature articles, along with the regular departments "Practice Profile," "Building Profile," and "Engineering Exegesis." International in coverage, the magazine does not carry advertising. Recommended for academic libraries.

Architectural Digest. See Interior Design and Decoration section.

738. ***Architectural Record.*** [ISSN: 0003-858X] 1891. m. USD 59 domestic. Ed(s): Robert A Ivy. Architectural Record, 2 Penn Plaza, 9th Fl, New York, NY 10121; dialogue@mcgraw-hill.com; http://www.archrecord.com/. Illus., index, adv. Circ: 10115. Vol. ends: Dec. Microform: IDC; PQC. Online: Dow Jones Interactive; EBSCO Publishing; Factiva; Gale Group; LexisNexis; NewsNet; Northern Light Technology, Inc.; ProQuest Information & Learning. *Indexed:* ABS&EES, AIAP, API, AS&TI, ArchI, ArtHuCI, ArtInd, EngInd, LRI, MagInd, RGPR, RI-1, SSCI. *Bk. rev.:* 6, 50-250 words. *Aud.:* Ga, Ac, Sa.

This trade publication includes news and departments such as editorials, book reviews, and profiles. Features include the "Business Week/Architectural Record Awards." Regular sections include "Projects," showcasing recently completed building projects, "Building Types Study," on specific building types such as a recent study of restaurants, "Building Science & Technology," and "Lighting Products." "Continuing Education Opportunities" is another regular department, often sponsored by manufacturers and trade associations wishing to promote certain products. The target audience is U.S. architects and builders. Recommended for public and academic libraries as well as larger architectural firms.

739. ***Architectural Review.*** [ISSN: 0003-861X] 1897. m. Individuals, GBP 54; Students, GBP 40.50; GBP 5.95 newsstand/cover per issue. Emap Construct Ltd., 151 Rosebery Ave, London, EC1R 4GB, United Kingdom; lynnej@construct.emap.co.uk; http://www.emap.com/construct/arhome.htm. Illus., adv. Circ: 18500. Vol. ends: Jun/Dec. Microform: IDC. Online: bigchalk; Florida Center for Library Automation; Gale Group; Northern Light Technology, Inc.; OCLC Online Computer Library Center, Inc.; ProQuest Information & Learning. *Indexed:* A&ATA, AIAP, API, ArchI, ArtHuCI, ArtInd, BAS, BHA, BrHumI, BrTechI, DAAI, GardL. *Bk. rev.:* 4-6, 500 words. *Aud.:* Ac,Sa.

Each issue of this British publication has a theme, such as "Water," "Light," and "AR+D Emerging Architecture Awards." Departments include "Products Review," "Books," and "Delight," an essay celebrating a notable work of architecture. The articles are often unsigned; some are by the editorial staff, others are signed by authors who are otherwise unidentified (presumably well-known enough by regular readers that they need no further identification). The audience appears to be European architects and builders. The publication's web site is available for free. Recommended for large academic libraries and larger architectural firms.

740. ***Architecture.*** Incorporates (1992-1995): *Building Renovation;* (1920-1995): *Progressive Architecture;* Incorporates (1983-1986): *Architectural Technology;* Former titles (1957-1983): *A I A Journal; American Institute of Architects. Journal.* [ISSN: 0746-0554] 1913. m. USD 49 domestic; USD 69 Canada; USD 199 elsewhere. Ed(s): Emilie W Sommerhoff. V N U Business Publications, 770 Broadway, New York, NY 10003; http://www.vnubusinessmedia.com/. Illus., index, adv. Circ: 70516 Paid. Microform: PQC. Online: EBSCO Publishing; Florida Center for Library Automation; Gale Group; OCLC Online Computer Library Center, Inc.; ProQuest Information & Learning; H.W. Wilson. *Indexed:* ABS&EES, AIAP, API, AgeL, ArchI, ArtHuCI, ArtInd, BHA, EngInd, GardL, LRI, RGPR, SSCI. *Bk. rev.:* 4, 200 words. *Aud.:* Ga, Ac, Sa.

This monthly trade magazine is targeted toward the architecture and building industries. Its regular features include "Agenda," "On The Boards," "Protest," and "Specifications." Its features are divided into "Practice," which focuses on issues such as standards and sustainability, and "Design," which includes articles profiling firms and recent projects. Recommended for architecture libraries.

741. *L'Architecture d'Aujourd'hui.* Formerly: *Architecture Francaise.* [ISSN: 0003-8695] 1930. bi-m. FRF 710. Ed(s): Jean Michel Place. Editions Jean - Michel Place, 3 rue Lhomond, Paris, 75005, France; sowa@implace.com; http://www.jmplace.com. Illus., adv. Circ: 19275. *Indexed:* AIAP, API, ArtHuCI, ArtInd, BAS, IBZ, SSCI. *Bk. rev.:* Number and length vary. *Aud.:* Ac, Sa.

Very similar in format to *Techniques & Architecture*, this highly regarded French publication includes feature articles in French with English translations that deal with a common topic ("Getting Old," for example) written by contributors selected for each issue by the editorial staff. This magazine does a good job of balancing the commercial and aesthetic aspects of architecture by, for example, including a poem accompanying a photo-essay. The geographic focus is worldwide. Regular departments, which include book reviews and a calendar of events, are in French only. Recommended for academic architecture libraries.

742. *Architektur Aktuell.* [ISSN: 0570-6602] 1967. 12x/yr. EUR 82 domestic; EUR 91.50 foreign; EUR 10 newsstand/cover per issue. Ed(s): Liesbeth Waechter Boehm. Springer-Verlag Wien, Sachsenplatz 4-6, Vienna, 1201, Austria; journals@springer.at. Adv. Sample. Circ: 7500. *Aud.:* Ac, Sa.

This elegant Austrian monthly sandwiches feature articles that have a common theme ("Spirit & Space" and "Understanding" are recent examples) between recurring departments (book and product reviews, a calendar of events, thumbnail biographies of the architects whose works are discussed in the issue) and advertising. The text of the departments is in German only, but the feature articles, which are international in coverage, include English translations. The magazine is beautifully laid out, with lots of color photographs and drawings. Advertising is restricted to the front and back of the issues, away from the feature articles, each of which is laid out on contiguous, consecutive pages without jumps. Recommended for architecture libraries.

743. *Built Environment.* Formerly (until 1978): *Built Environment Quarterly.* [ISSN: 0263-7960] 1975. q. GBP 85 domestic; GBP 90 foreign. Ed(s): Sir Peter Hall, David Banister. Alexandrine Press, 1 The Farthings, Marcham, OX13 6QD, United Kingdom. Illus., adv. Sample. Circ: 645. *Indexed:* AIAP, API, ErgAb, SUSA, SWA. *Bk. rev.:* 2-4, 500 words. *Aud.:* Ac.

Each issue of this British scholarly quarterly has a guest editor or editors who present a theme that ties together a collection of approximately half a dozen articles by noted academics. Recently, for example, Noha Nasser guest-edited an issue on "Islam and Built Form: Studies in Regional Diversity." Each issue includes one or two book reviews. Recommended for academic architecture libraries.

744. *Casabella: rivista internazionale di architettura.* [ISSN: 0008-7181] 1928. m. 10/yr. ITL 159000. Ed(s): Francesco Dalco. Elemond SpA, Via Domenico Trentacoste, 7, Milan, 20134, Italy. Illus., index, adv. Circ: 46000. *Indexed:* AIAP, API, ArtHuCI, ArtInd, BHA. *Bk. rev.:* 8, 150 words. *Aud.:* Ac, Sa.

Along with *Domus* (below in this section), *Casabella* is a superb example of Italian design in the publication field. The focus here is on international architects and architecture. Recent issues included features on a beach house in Peru, several homes in Australia, an Italian church, a Dutch museum, and architects Sigurd Lewerentz, Mies, and Le Corbusier. The format and quality of color illustrations is exceptional. Unfortunately, only a few selected features have English translations. Recommended for architecture libraries.

745. *El Croquis: de arquitectura y diseno.* [ISSN: 0212-5633] 1982. 5x/yr. EUR 173 domestic; EUR 215 in Europe; EUR 250 in North America. Ed(s): Paloma Poveda. Croquis Editorial, Av. Reyes Catolicos, 9, El Escorial (Madrid), 28280, Spain; elcroquis@infornet.es; http://www.elcroquis.es/. Adv. Circ: 30000. *Indexed:* AIAP, API. *Aud.:* Ac, Sa.

This magazine has become one of the most respected international architectural publications. It is oversized and substantial, lavishly illustrated, and it has limited advertising located only at the front of the issue. Each issue is devoted entirely to an individual architect or firm, with a thematic approach to recent work. Examples published recently include "Annette Gigon/Mike Guyer; 1989-2000; The Variegated Minimal," "Zaha Hadid; 1996-2002; Landscape as a Plan," and "Dominique Perrault; 1990-2001; The Violence of Neutral." All text is in Spanish and English. Recommended for architecture libraries.

746. *Domus: architettura arredamento arte.* [ISSN: 0012-5377] 1928. m. 11/yr. USD 175. Ed(s): Maria Bordone. Editoriale Domus, Via Achille Grandi, 5/7, Rozzano, 20089, Italy. Illus., adv. Circ: 60000. *Indexed:* AIAP, API, ArtHuCI, ArtInd, BHA, DAAI. *Bk. rev.:* 7, 750 words. *Aud.:* Ac, Sa.

This is a beautiful, large-format magazine, one of several well-established Italian design publications (see also *Abitare* and *Casabella*). All of the text is in both Italian and English, including book reviews, editorials, exhibition calendars, and short news and events pieces. There are many advertisements, most located at the front of the magazine. Each issue has about ten feature articles that provide balanced coverage of trendy architecture and interior design worldwide. Recommended for architecture libraries and large academic libraries.

747. *Grey Room.* [ISSN: 1526-3819] 2000. q. USD 180 (Individuals, USD 65; Students, USD 40). Ed(s): Reinhold Martin, Felicity D Scott. MIT Press, 5 Cambridge Center, Cambridge, MA 02142-1493; journals-orders@mit.edu; http://mitpress.mit.edu. Refereed. *Aud.:* Ac.

The high expectations of the web as a medium for publishing architectural periodicals have not been realized, unfortunately. The cost of printing full-color, lavishly illustrated architectural periodicals on paper meant that few libraries, let alone individual readers, were able to afford them. Using the web, it was hoped that the high costs associated with color printing could be avoided. *Grey Room* is one of the few remaining electronic architectural periodicals, although the publication schedule for this quarterly has become irregular. It is also ironic that the illustrations in this periodical are in black and white. The half dozen or so articles in each issue focus on the intersection of architecture and a variety of other topics, such as psychology, sociology, politics, and the media. Recommended for academic libraries.

748. *Inland Architect.* [ISSN: 0020-1472] 1888. q. USD 50. Ed(s): Margaret Guzek. Real Estate News Corp, 3525 W Peterson Ave, Ste 401, Chicago, IL 60659; rencpublishing@earthlink.net. Illus., adv. Circ: 75000. Online: OCLC Online Computer Library Center, Inc.; H.W. Wilson. Reprint: PQC. *Indexed:* AIAP, API, AgeL, ArtInd. *Bk. rev.:* 1-2, 1,000 words. *Aud.:* Ga, Ac, Sa.

This attractive magazine is published in Chicago, and the advertising and many of the feature articles emphasize the Midwest. Recently, however, coverage includes architecture and design throughout the United States and occasionally abroad. The publication now bills iteself as "the international magazine for the building arts since 1883," harkening back to a magazine of the same name that flourished between 1883 and 1908. Regular departments focus on landscape architecture, travel, and architectural photography; book reviews and news briefs are also included. This magazine appeals to a broad audience. Recommended for public libraries and academic libraries.

749. *Journal of Architectural and Planning Research.* Supersedes: *Journal of Architectural Research.* [ISSN: 0738-0895] 1984. q. USD 180 (Individuals, USD 82). Ed(s): Andrew D Seidel. Locke Science Publishing Company, Inc., 28 E Jackson Bldg., 10th Floor L221, Chicago, IL 60604; lockescience@juno.com. Illus., adv. Sample. Refereed. Vol. ends: Winter. *Indexed:* ABS&EES, AIAP, API, AbAn, AgeL, ArtHuCI, ArtInd, C&ISA, EngInd, GeogAbPG, IBSS, PAIS, PRA, PsycholAb, SSCI, SUSA. *Aud.:* Ac.

This refereed quarterly "links research and practice in architecture, planning, and design from four broad areas: architectural research; urban planning research; architectural design; and urban design;" according to the editorial statement at the beginning of each issue. The authors tend to be affiliated with North American universities, not only from architecture departments, but from urban planning, psychology, and other disciplines. Recommended for academic libraries.

750. *Journal of Architectural Education.* Former titles (until 1983): *J A E;* (until 1974): *Journal of Architectural Education.* [ISSN: 1046-4883] 1947. q. USD 185 (Non-members, USD 50). Ed(s): Barbara Allen. MIT

Press, 5 Cambridge Center, Cambridge, MA 02142-1493; journals-orders@mit.edu; http://mitpress.mit.edu. Illus., index, adv. Refereed. Vol. ends: Aug. Microform: PQC. Online: EBSCO Publishing; Ingenta Select; RoweCom Information Quest; Swets Blackwell. Reprint: PQC. *Indexed:* AIAP, API, AgeL, ArchI, ArtHuCI, ArtInd, CIJE. *Bk. rev.:* 4, 1,500 words. *Aud.:* Ac.

Each issue of this quarterly published by the MIT Press and sponsored by the Association of the Collegiate Schools of Architecture contains several scholarly articles on a common topic. Recent examples include "Digital Technology and Architecture" and "Marking Domain." The articles are accompanied by black-and-white illustrations, and each issue usually contains several book reviews. Recommended for academic architectural libraries.

751. *The Journal of Architecture.* [ISSN: 1360-2365] 1996. q. GBP 270 (Individuals, GBP 95). Routledge, 11 New Fetter Ln, London, EC4P 4EE, United Kingdom; info@routledge.co.uk; http://www.routledge.co.uk. Illus., adv. Sample. Refereed. Online: EBSCO Publishing; Ingenta Select; OCLC Online Computer Library Center, Inc.; RoweCom Information Quest; Swets Blackwell. Reprint: PSC. *Indexed:* AIAP, API, C&ISA, IBZ, SUSA. *Aud.:* Ac.

The Royal Institute of British Architects sponsors three important titles in this section, and this is its refereed scholarly journal. (See also *Riba Journal* and *World Architecture.*) Each issue of *The Journal of Architecture* includes four to eight papers and several book reviews. Some issues are thematic, e.g., "Post-War Images . . . The Return of the Avant-Garde." Articles are often international in scope, and the editorial policy is "to encourage critical debate, outspokenness, and independence of entrenched interests and fashion." Topics covered include the interplay between cities, building, history and economic forces; problems of gender and ethnicity in architectural production and understanding; and professionalism, rhetoric, theory, and practice. Recommended for architecture libraries.

Landscape Architecture. See Landscape Architecture section.

Landscape Journal. See Landscape Architecture section.

752. *Metropolis: architecture <culture> design.* [ISSN: 0279-4977] 1981. 10x/yr. USD 32.95 domestic; USD 52.95 Canada; USD 72.95 elsewhere. Ed(s): Susan S Szenasy. Bellerophon Publications, Inc., 61 W 23rd St, 4th fl, New York, NY 10010; http://www.metropolismag.com. Illus., adv. Circ: 47000 Paid. Vol. ends: Jun. *Indexed:* AIAP, ASIP, DAAI. *Bk. rev.:* 2. *Aud.:* Ga, Ac, Sa.

This large-format monthly magazine (actually 11 issues a year) is characterized by regular departments and display advertising printed on glossy paper surrounding an advertising-free features section printed on heavy, matte paper in the middle. The features include interviews with and profiles of architects and designers, photo-essays, and architectural criticism that will appeal not only to design professionals but to sophisticated amateurs. Recent features include a brief article and photo-essay about the restoration of Edith Wharton's estate in the Berkshire mountains, which was done according to the design principles she and co-author architect Ogden Codman published in *Decoration of Houses* (1897). In addition to such typical departments as letters and product reviews, there are reviews of everything from CDs and books to videos, conferences, and web sites. Recommended for public and academic libraries.

753. *Places: a forum of environmental design.* [ISSN: 0731-0455] 1983. 3x/yr. USD 55. Ed(s): Donlyn Lyndon. Design History Foundation, 201B Higgins Hall, Pratt Institute, Brooklyn, NY 11205; places@allenpress.com; http://www.places-journal.org. Illus., adv. Refereed. Circ: 4200. Reprint: PQC. *Indexed:* AIAP, API, ArtHuCI, ArtInd, DAAI, GardL, PRA, SUSA. *Bk. rev.:* Various number and length. *Aud.:* Ac, Sa.

This superbly illustrated journal is published by the Design History Foundation. Its mission is "to establish forums in which designers, public officials, scholars, and citizens can discuss issues vital to environmental design, with particular emphasis on public spaces." Coverage is international, ranging from Havana to Philadelphia to London. Recent articles focus on golf courses, desert cities, civic squares, and waterfronts. Each issue has a few short pieces by the U.S. General Services Administration's Center for Urban Development. This title is important for its broad view, encompassing landscape architecture, urban planning, environment, engineering, and architecture. Recommended for academic libraries that support programs in architecture and urban planning.

754. *Preservation.* Formerly (until vol.48, no.4, 1996): *Historic Preservation;* Incorporates (in 1995): *Historic Preservation News;* Which was formerly (1961-1990): *Preservation News;* Historic Preservation was formerly (until 1951): *National Council for Historic Sites and Buildings Quarterly Report.* [ISSN: 1090-9931] 1949. bi-m. USD 20 membership. National Trust for Historic Preservation, 1785 Massachusetts Ave N W, Washington, DC 20036; http://www.nthp.org/. Illus., adv. Circ: 204149 Paid. Vol. ends: Nov. Microform: PQC. *Indexed:* A&ATA, ABS&EES, AIAP, API, AbAn, AmH&L, ArtHuCI, ArtInd, BHA, GardL, SSCI. *Bk. rev.:* 4, 300-500 words. *Aud.:* Ga, Ac, Sa.

Members of the National Trust for Historic Preservation receive a subscription to the bimonthly *Preservation* as a benefit of membership. Feature articles focus on notable historic building preservation and renovation projects. A recent article, for example, describes the conversion of a Cold War–era federal bunker in Culpepper, Virginia, to use as a media storage facility for the Library of Congress. Standard departments are supplemented with information of interest to National Trust members regarding the trust's activities. The advertising, mostly for travel and upscale real estate, appears to be aimed at a well-to-do, retired readership. Recommended for public libraries.

755. *R I B A Journal.* Incorporates (1986-2003): *R I B A Interiors;* Former titles (until 1993): *Royal Institute of British Architects. Journal;* (until 1987): *Architect; R I B A Journal.* [ISSN: 1463-9505] 1893. m. GBP 70 domestic; EUR 196 in Europe; USD 201 elsewhere. Ed(s): Amanda Baillieu. Builder Group plc., Exchange Tower, 2 Harbour Exchange Sq, London, E14 9GE, United Kingdom; http://www.riba.org/riba/advice2.htm. Illus., index, adv. Sample. Circ: 24180. Vol. ends: Dec. Microform: PQC. Online: Ingenta Select. Reprint: PQC. *Indexed:* AIAP, API, ArtHuCI, ArtInd, BAS, BHA, BrHumI, BrTechI, EIP. *Bk. rev.:* 3, 200 words. *Aud.:* Sa.

The Royal Institute of British Architects and the Builder Group publish this trade monthly, which deals primarily with news of interest to professional architects and builders in the United Kingdom. In addition to feature articles, each issue includes book reviews, interviews, editorials, letters, and both display and classified advertising. Recommended for architectural libraries.

756. *Society of Architectural Historians. Journal.* [ISSN: 0037-9808] 1940. q. USD 150 (Individuals, USD 80; Students, USD 30). Ed(s): Zeynep Celik. Society of Architectural Historians, 1365 North Astor St, Chicago, IL 60610-2144; http://www.sah.org. Illus., index, adv. Refereed. Circ: 4000. Vol. ends: Dec. Microform: PQC. Online: OCLC Online Computer Library Center, Inc.; H.W. Wilson. Reprint: ISI; PQC. *Indexed:* ABS&EES, AIAP, API, AmH&L, ArtHuCI, ArtInd, BAS, BHA, BrArAb, GardL, NumL. *Bk. rev.:* 20, 1,500 words. *Aud.:* Ac.

About a third of this publication from the Society of Architectural Historians is devoted to book reviews. The remainder of each issue is taken up primarily with scholarly articles, many or all of which may focus on a common topic, such as "Teaching the History of Architecture." The articles are illustrated with black-and-white photographs and drawings. The fourth quarterly issue of each volume includes an index to the full volume. Recommended for academic architecture and urban planning libraries.

757. *Taunton's Fine Homebuilding.* Formerly (until 1991): *Fine Homebuilding.* [ISSN: 1096-360X] 1980. bi-m. USD 37.95 in US & Canada; USD 45.95 elsewhere. Ed(s): Kevin Ireton. Taunton Press, Inc., 63, South Main St, PO Box 5506, Newtown, CT 06470-5506; http://www.taunton.com. Illus., adv. Circ: 278524 Paid. *Indexed:* AIAP, API, AS&TI, ASIP, BRI, CBRI, IHTDI. *Bk. rev.:* 3, 500 words. *Aud.:* Ga, Ac, Sa.

This popular bimonthly trade magazine is for the professional homebuilder, renovator, or enthusiastic do-it-yourselfer. Judging from the advertisements, of which there are many, confined primarily to the front and back quarters of the book, the primary target audience is the professional homebuilder/designer/

remodeler. Regular departments include a "Great Ideas" section with brief descriptions of innovative design and remodeling ideas contributed by architects, designers, and renovation contractors. One recent "Great Idea" is a "toe drawer," built into the toe space below most kitchen cabinets. Most issues treat a general topic, such as kitchens and baths, and the feature articles deal with various aspects of this topic. Recommended for public and architecture libraries.

758. *Techniques et Architecture.* [ISSN: 0373-0719] 1942. bi-m. FRF 880; FRF 1010 foreign. Ed(s): Marie Christine Loriers, Jean-Francois Pousse. Editions Jean - Michel Place, 3 rue Lhomond, Paris, 75005, France. Adv. Circ: 16800. *Indexed:* AIAP, BHA. *Bk. rev.:* Number and length vary. *Aud.:* Ac, Sa.

This is a French publication that features primarily commercial and public building projects in Europe, but occasionally also in the Americas. The feature articles, all related to a common topic (the "Alchemy of Concrete," for example), are written in French by the editorial staff and include English translations. The regular departments, which include brief news items, new product reviews, book reviews, and a calendar of events, are all in French only and are also written by the editorial staff. The advertising appears targeted to readers whose business is commercial architecture and construction in Europe. Recommended for academic architecture libraries and libraries in large architectural and contracting firms specializing in commercial buildings.

759. *World Architecture.* Formerly: *Interarchitecture (London).* [ISSN: 0956-9758] 1989. bi-m. GBP 110; USD 176. Ed(s): Nicola Jackson. Cheerman Ltd., Cheerman Ltd, 3 Kenrick Pl, London, W1H 3FF, United Kingdom; warch@atlas.co.uk; http://www.world-architecture.co.uk/. Illus., adv. Circ: 10000 Paid. *Indexed:* AIAP, API, ArtInd, DAAI. *Bk. rev.:* 3, 500 words. *Aud.:* Ac, Sa.

This title incorporates *RIBA International* and is sent as part of Royal Institute of British Architects membership to overseas members. It's a lavishly illustrated magazine that covers international news and events and includes opinion pieces and book reviews. Each issue includes several articles that focus on a country or region, analyzing particular subjects such as houses or transportation and discussing products such as door access systems or lighting. Recommended for large public libraries and academic libraries.

■ ARCHIVES AND MANUSCRIPTS

General/National, Regional, and State Newsletters/National, Regional, and State Newsletters—Canada/National, Regional, and State Newsletters—United States/Special-Interest Newsletters

See also Bibliography; History; and Library and Information Science sections.

Melanie Wisner, Manuscript Department, Houghton Library, Harvard University, Cambridge, MA 02138; mmwisner@fas.harvard.edu; FAX: 617-495-1376

Introduction

To quote from the Society of American Archivists' web site, "The primary task of the archivist is to establish and maintain control, both physical and intellectual, over records of enduring value." The literature of archives and manuscripts treats the fundamental archival activities of acquiring, appraising, accessioning, arranging, describing, preserving, and providing access to material of myriad types and formats, and managing archival institutions. It also examines the vast array of uses to which cultural resources are put. Librarians, records managers, and museum curators share this range of responsibilities with archivists to varying degrees and in various settings. Researchers and potential collectors can find direction and inspiration by reading in this field.

National and global crises these last few years have affected cultural heritage materials shockingly; the suddenness and connection to human upheaval have highlighted the fragility of material history. Document and artifact destruction and theft have altered future memory; in the political wake of these events, security, privacy, and public access have been pitted against each other internationally in an impossible gridlock. If there can be silver linings to tragedy and hardship, citizens of the world and of nations are ever more aware of the importance of responsible custodianship of existing records. The documentation of tragedy as it is happening and the memorializing of such events are in the public eye continually. The meaning of *archivist* may remain foggy, but the archivist's actions, as simple as gathering photographs and letters in a coherent story, are increasingly familiar activities in an increasingly wired world.

For some years the attention of archivists has been on adapting traditional practices to accommodate the electronic and the digital. Questions of defining, then collecting, describing, and keeping electronic records continue to populate archival journals and conferences. Internet-based practices and standards that have emerged now might be said to be maturing. Encoded Archival Description (EAD), now in its second version, is known to most practitioners; if not EAD, then another web-based system has been chosen by more and more archives to represent their holdings. Earlier national and local standards for archival content and communication are being "harmonized" at national and international levels, representing millions of person-hours in committees around the globe. Librarians, archivists, and records managers work more and more with the same information technology platforms; their records migrate toward each other's systems, mingling with sound, images, movies, and commerce. Reference archivists have their hands full dealing with the infinite expectations and/or confusion of researchers, but they have much more to work with.

The literature is debating copyright and its legal ramifications, from several sides of the fence: archivists champion access and they are anxious not to see their holdings used in unauthorized ways. Issues of secrecy and tightening governmental controls over records have brought leaders in the field to speak out in warning over the loss of freedom of information. Scandals in the corporate world have demonstrated the fluid nature of "records of enduring value," and the profession is struggling to reinforce its ethical foundations. Researchers and keepers of collections alike are seeking to document the previously undocumented, mining collections for evidence of people, movements, places, and ideas left behind, hoping that materials have survived enough to tell a story. And as ever, archives in most settings must continually justify their existence while watching for new funding opportunites; grant-funded projects pick up some of the slack left by institutional cuts in slim times, but the volume of work to be processed gallops ever faster beyond available staff time.

The literature of archives and manuscripts is predominantly scholarly in the larger journals, often quite theoretical, and practical in the newsletters. It aims to discover and illuminate best practices and to build community, among and between the custodians and the users of original cultural materials.

Basic Periodicals

Ga: *Archivist, Prologue;* Ac: *American Archivist, Archival Issues, Archivaria, Comma, The Information Management Journal.*

Basic Abstracts and Indexes

America: History and Life, Historical Abstracts, Library and Information Science Abstracts, Library Literature.

General

760. *American Archivist.* [ISSN: 0360-9081] 1938. s-a. USD 85; USD 100 overseas. Ed(s): Philip B Eppard. Society of American Archivists, 527 S Wells St, 5th Fl, Chicago, IL 60607; info@archivists.org; http://www.archivists.org/publications.html. Illus., index, adv. Refereed. Circ: 4600. Vol. ends: Fall. Microform: PMC. *Indexed:* A&ATA, ABS&EES, AgeL, AmH&L, ArtHuCI, BRI, CBRI, ConsI, IBZ, InfoSAb, LISA, LibLit, PAIS, SSCI. *Bk. rev.:* 9-11, 400-1,500 words. *Aud.:* Ac, Sa.

American Archivist is the premier journal of archival history, theory, and practice in the United States as well as the official forum for the national professional association, the Society of American Archivists. The nearly book-length semi-annual volumes often examine an issue, organization, or practice in depth in a special section or, occasionally, in a special issue. The journal composes an archival curriculum by itself (supplemented, perhaps, by the society's publications of basic archival texts), offering the literature that most often supports coursework in archival training programs across the nation. Regular content includes research articles, case studies, commentary and opinion, coverage of international issues, practical bibliographies and other professional tools, reviews of archival literature and end products, and letters to the editor. *American Archivist* is a vital part of the American archival profession and consistently representative of the trends in the field.

761. *Archival Issues.* Formerly (until 1992): *Midwestern Archivist.* [ISSN: 1067-4993] 1976. s-a. USD 60 (Individuals, USD 30). Ed(s): Mark Greene. Midwest Archives Conference, Menzi Behrnd-Klodt, 7422 Longmeadow Rd, Madison, WI 53717; http://www.midwestarchives.org. Illus., index, adv. Refereed. Circ: 1100. Vol. ends: No. 2. Reprint: PQC. *Indexed:* InfoSAb, LibLit. *Bk. rev.:* 6-8, 400-1,200 words. *Aud.:* Ac, Sa.

Archival Issues is not a journal of solely regional interests as its subtitle suggests. Its articles are interesting geographically and topically, providing wide-ranging current awareness, often from refreshing viewpoints. Recent topics include a surprising episode relating to the Richard Nixon archives; the universal concern about copyright; and "Listening to Users," a valuable survey and commentary on basic communication between archivists and users of archives. *Archival Issues* reviews publications in basic archival areas. This journal extends the range of *The American Archivist* and is equally well edited; it particularly invites archivists who have never published to submit work and awards an annual prize to a first-time author.

762. *Archival Science: international journal on recorded information.* Incorporates (in 2000): *Archives & Museum Informatics;* Which was formerly (1987-1989): *Archival Informatics Newsletter.* [ISSN: 1389-0166] 2000. q. USD 230 print or online ed. Kluwer Academic Publishers, van Godewijckstraat 30, PO Box 17, Dordrecht, 3300 AA, Netherlands; services@wkap.nl; http://www.wkap.nl. Refereed. Online: ingenta.com; Kluwer Online; OCLC Online Computer Library Center, Inc.; Ovid Technologies, Inc.; RoweCom Information Quest; Swets Blackwell. Reprint: SWZ. *Aud.:* Ac, Sa.

Archival Science is an "integrated, interdisciplinary, and intercultural" journal on "the whole field of recorded process-related information, analysed in terms of form, structure and context." The jargon of deconstruction and the postmodern can be an obstacle to the uninitiated, but this is cutting-edge territory where cultural-heritage theory joins with technology, and, after all, its target audience is researchers and educators in archival science. The ivory tower created here of "archival science as an autonomous scientific discipline" provides a home to seriously theoretical articles, some by practitioners who also frequent more traditional archival journals. Recent article titles include "Colonial Archives and the Arts of Governance," "Archival Temples, Archival Prisons: Modes of Power and Protection," and "The End of Collecting: Towards a New Purpose for Archival Appraisal." Attention is given to work in the non–English-speaking world. Online tables of contents and abstracts, as well as an online version, are available.

763. *Archivaria.* Supersedes: *Canadian Archivist.* [ISSN: 0318-6954] 1975. s-a. CND 276.08 (Individuals, CND 115.56). Ed(s): Barbara L Craig. Association of Canadian Archivists, PO Box 2596, Ottawa, ON K1P 5W6, Canada. Illus., index. Refereed. Circ: 1300. Vol. ends: Autumn. *Indexed:* A&ATA, BRI, CBCARef, CBRI, CPerI, LISA, LibLit. *Bk. rev.:* 10-20, 750-2,500 words. *Aud.:* Ac, Sa.

Archivaria is the journal of the Association of Canadian Archivists, focusing on Canadian activities and policies chiefly of interest to the professional but of value to the entire archival community. The journal aspires "to be a bridge of communication among archivists, and between archivists and users of archives." National archival policy, practice, and fundamental current issues in the field are present to some degree in every issue (recently, for instance, the impact of the Canadian Personal Information Act on archives and the definition of electronic series). Article abstracts are given in both French and English; a few book reviews are in French. The journal reviews books and exhibits and, lately, exchanges tables of contents with the journal *Archives* (published by the Association des archivistes du Quebec). The range of regular features, including "Counterpoint" and "Notes and Communications," offers a lively whole. *Archivaria* should be considered required reading alongside *The American Archivist.*

764. *Archives.* [ISSN: 0003-9535] 1949. s-a. Institutional members, GBP 45; Individual members, GBP 25; Non-members, GBP 50. British Records Association, 40 Northampton Rd, London, EC1R 0HB, United Kingdom; http://www.hmc.gov.uk/bra. Illus., index. Circ: 1300. Vol. ends: Oct. *Indexed:* AmH&L, ArtHuCI, BrArAb, BrHumI, LISA, LibLit, NumL. *Bk. rev.:* 25-30, 300-800 words. *Aud.:* Ac, Sa.

The British Records Association, parent of *Archives,* "co-ordinates and encourages the work of owners, individual scholars, archivists and librarians, institutions and societies interested in the preservation and use of archives." The journal is elegant and scholarly, sometimes densely so, perhaps austere, but it demonstrates fervent devotion to British heritage and its preservation. Its six or so articles and numerous book reviews are generally slanted toward the British user, rather than administrator, of collections, often publishing historical scholarship derived from hours spent in archives. It has lately covered issues of greater currency, including a collaborative database of clergyman, the difficulty of documenting infanticide, and "Hearing Slave Voices." The "Report and Comment" section offers a detailed picture of the health and activities of British archival agencies.

765. *Archives and Manuscripts.* [ISSN: 0157-6895] 1955. s-a. AUD 150. Ed(s): Maggie Shapley. Australian Society of Archivists Inc., PO Box 83, O'Connor, ACT 2602, Australia; asa@asap.unimelb.edu.au; http://www.archivists.org.au. Illus., adv. Refereed. Circ: 850. Vol. ends: Nov. Online: RMIT Publishing. *Indexed:* AmH&L, LISA. *Bk. rev.:* 15-20, 500-2,000 words. *Aud.:* Ac, Sa.

Archives and Manuscripts, the journal of the Australian Society of Archivists, covers issues of the South Pacific and Pacific Islands region, but it offers the rest of the English-speaking world a refreshing viewpoint from a diverse and culturally aware part of the archival world as well. As of the November 2002 issue, the journal is fully refereed, describing itself anew as a "professional and scholarly journal...about the theory and practice of archives and recordkeeping." Recent articles have examined the application of Encoded Archival Description, document destruction, web site appraisal, retention of national census data, and other issues sometimes painfully current all over the world. The "International Notes" section, organized geographically, describes regional activities in detail; extensive reviews and a review article are of interest to archivists beyond the region.

Archives and Museum Informatics. See *Archival Science.*

766. *Archivist: magazine of the National Archives of Canada.* [ISSN: 0705-2855] 1973. 2x/yr. Free. Ed(s): Rebecca Grace. National Archives of Canada, 395 Wellington St, Ottawa, ON K1A 0N3, Canada; publications@archives.ca; http://www.archives.ca/. Illus. Circ: 14000. *Indexed:* ABS&EES, AmH&L, BHA, CBCARef, CPerI. *Aud.:* Ga, Ac, Sa.

Archivist is the Canadian counterpart to *Prologue* (below in this section), the magazine of the National Archives of Canada. As of this writing, legislation to merge into one institution the National Archives and the National Library of Canada has been tabled; if the new entity is created, a period of uncertain retooling may follow. After a lengthy period between issues, the new editor has rolled out a glossy back-to-back bilingual format, previously in side-by-side translation, making an easier, continuous read for readers in both languages. Black-and-white photographs accompany feature articles that are often written by archives division heads highlighting particular collections. Digitization is the focus of the first redesigned issue; accessibility and relevance to the Canadian citizen are paramount. Regular features include "Acquisitions," an informative view of collecting activities, and "Virtual Exhibitions." *Archivist* is an excellent guide to the issues and collections native to the Canadian archival and records management environment.

Archivum. See *Comma.*

767. *Comma: international journal on archives.* Formed by the merger of (1951-2000): *Archivum;* (1983-2000): *Janus;* (1958-2000): *Conseil International des Archives. Table Ronde Internationale des Archives.*

Actes. [ISSN: 1680-1865] 2000. q. EUR 158; EUR 44 newsstand/cover. Ed(s): Nancy Bartlett. K.G. Saur Verlag GmbH, Ortlerstr. 8, Munchen, 81373, Germany; customerservice_saur@csi.com; http://www.saur.de. Index. *Aud.:* Ac, Sa.

Comma is the International Council on Archives' new journal, taking up the cut threads of both *Archivum* and *Janus*; the title is to suggest "reflective pause," the "pause in the continuum." The renewed focus of the only internationally-focused and -produced journal is "the research, administration, and development of archives and the archival profession worldwide." The new journal now includes abstracts in Arabic, Chinese, and Russian, as well as English, French, German, and Spanish (articles appear in English, French, and Spanish), and it encourages translation and dissemination in other languages. Rather than four separate issues per year, three double issues have appeared as of this writing: one featuring articles from underrepresented Latin America, Spain, and Portugal; one printing two major documents on preservation, in the tropics and when moving an archives; and the third one devoted to the 2001 Proceedings of the International Conference of the Round Table on Archives (CITRA). The multilingual format requires extra effort to navigate, and the journal cannot reflect quickly shifting events, but *Comma*'s work is impressive, and crucial to understanding the directions of the field globally.

History News. See History section.

768. *The Information Management Journal: the journal for the information management professionals.* Former titles: *Records Management Quarterly;* (until Jan. 1999): *A R M A Records Management Quarterly.* [ISSN: 1535-2897] 1967. bi-m. USD 53 (Non-members, USD 95). Ed(s): Cynthia Launchbaugh, Mike Pemberton. A R M A International, 13725 W 109th St, Ste101, Lenexa, KS 66215; http://www.arma.org/publications/journal/journal_about.cfm. Illus., index, adv. Circ: 10500 Paid. Vol. ends: Dec. Microform: PQC. Online: EBSCO Publishing; Gale Group; OCLC Online Computer Library Center, Inc.; ProQuest Information & Learning; H.W. Wilson. *Indexed:* ABIn, BPI, BusEdI, CompLI, ConsI, InfoSAb, LRI. *Bk. rev.:* 1-4, 1,000-2,500 words. *Aud.:* Ac, Sa.

As the professional journal of ARMA International (the Association for Information Management Professionals, previously known as the Association of Records Managers and Administrators), *IMJ* is an important forum for professionals involved in any of the allied fields within information and records management and for archivists of all types. From its origins in the New Deal era as the set of practices created to process mountains of newly generated governmental records, the field now encompasses "the management of records, information, and knowledge as corporate assets and as contributors to organizational success" in any setting. Its issues are largely indistinguishable from those of archivists, but late developments that pit security against liberty and corporate recordkeeping against individual investors point out the current bleeding-edge quality of life for records managers. The journal is glossy and highly professional, with regular columns on legislation and the international scene. The current table of contents is available online.

769. *Journal of Archival Organization.* [ISSN: 1533-2748] 2002. q. USD 200 domestic print & online eds.; USD 270 Canada print & online eds.; USD 290 elsewhere print & online eds. Ed(s): Ruth C. Carter, Thomas J. Frusciano. Haworth Press, Inc., 10 Alice St, Binghamton, NY 13904-1580; getinfo@haworthpressinc.com; http://www.haworthpressinc.com. Adv. Circ: 42 Paid. *Aud.:* Ac, Sa.

This is the newcomer in the lineup of basic archival periodicals, offered in 2002 by Haworth Press, publishers of scores of academic journals, some in library and information science. It is too early to tell if the journal will hold its own; its stated territory focuses on primary archival functions, arrangement, description, and the provision of access, emphasizing emerging standards and technologies. So far it has not achieved the international coverage or representation its publisher early mentioned, sticking close to American concerns and practices. The first issue ranged widely, setting the parameters for future work; the second examined, thematically, documentation of the experience of women in higher education. The journal looks drawn to practice over theory, and particularly changing practices, about which there is plenty to talk about. Haworth Press has a number of offerings already in library science and therefore has an established presence in library training curricula; this journal certainly will be worth tracking beyond its first heady issues as it determines its turf.

770. *Manuscripts.* [ISSN: 0025-262X] 1948. q. Membership, USD 45. Ed(s): David R Chesnutt. Manuscript Society, 1960 E Fairmont Dr, Tempe, AZ 85282-2844; manuscrip@home.com; http://www.manuscript.org. Illus., index, adv. Circ: 1500. Vol. ends: No. 4. Microform: NRP. *Indexed:* AmH&L, AmHI, MLA-IB. *Aud.:* Ga.

Manuscripts is the quarterly journal of the Manuscript Society, founded in 1948 as the National Society of Autograph Collectors. The journal provides community to its somewhat independent constituency of private historians, amateur antiquarians, and private and institutional collectors of literary and historical materials. "Excellent scholarly and collector articles" educate readers in the sometimes arcane, sometimes culturally hot culture of the document, from Sotheby's to flea markets, promoting ethical practices and preservation along the way. The issue current as of this writing is devoted to "Celebrating Ralph Waldo Emerson" at his bicentennial; fraudulent Internet trading was covered recently. Regular features include "Auction Trends," a very detailed survey of prices paid for specific items at auction, and a hefty section of advertising directing member-collectors to member-sellers. While harking back to a private-society tradition, the journal is well worth pointing out to users of archives, and archivists should take note of this community's viewpoints.

771. *Prologue (College Park): quarterly of the National Archives and Records Administration.* Formerly (until 1967): *National Archives Accessions.* [ISSN: 0033-1031] 1969. q. USD 16 domestic; USD 21 foreign. Ed(s): Mary C Ryan. National Archives and Records Administration, 8601 Adelphi Rd, Rm 4100, College Park, MD 20740-6001; mary.ryan@arch2.nara.gov; http://www.archives.gov. Illus., index. Circ: 3000 Paid. Vol. ends: Winter. Reprint: PSC. *Indexed:* AmH&L, ArtHuCI, HumInd, IUSGP, SSCI. *Aud.:* Ga.

Prologue celebrates the remarkable holdings and programs of the National Archives and Records Administration (NARA), the regional archives, and the presidential libraries. This handsomely produced pictorial quarterly in the Smithsonian style offers essays in American history based on original documents, black-and-white photographs and illustrations from the collections, and news of numerous outreach and education programs of interest to historians, students, and other archivists. Recent issues have reported on the new AAD (Access to Archival Databases) project, bringing the data within a large number of government databases direct to the citizenry; Harry Truman's poker game; the Cuban Missile Crisis; and the centennial of the Louisiana Purchase. Articles are particularly suited to middle and high school teachers and students (for whom NARA also created the suite of resources called the Digital Classroom). Notice is given of NARA's valuable publications, many of which will aid genealogical researchers.

772. *Provenance.* Formerly: *Georgia Archive.* [ISSN: 0739-4241] 1972. a. Members, USD 40. Ed(s): Susan Dick. Society of Georgia Archivists, PO Box 133085, Atlanta, GA 30333-3085; http://www.soga.org. Illus., index, adv. Refereed. Circ: 400 Paid. Vol. ends: No. 2. *Bk. rev.:* 3-4, 750-1,250 words. *Aud.:* Ac, Sa.

The first (1972) professional archival journal published by a state or regional organization, *Provenance* naturally covers regional issues for its parent, the Society of Georgia Archivists, but it also prints articles from archivists around the country in somewhat thematic issues. Its stated primary focus is the archival profession in the theory and practice of archival management. Recent issues have covered appraisal of university records; military archives; documentary editing; appraising congressional papers; ethics; and descriptive standards. *Provenance* samples American archival concerns in a format especially appealing to archival students, new professionals, and archivists in local and subject-oriented collections.

773. *The Public Historian: a journal of public history.* [ISSN: 0272-3433] 1978. q. USD 123 print & online USD 32 newsstand/cover. Ed(s): Anne Plane. University of California Press, Journals Division, 2000 Center St, Ste 303, Berkeley, CA 94704-1223; journals@ucop.edu; http://www.ucpress.edu/journals. Illus., index, adv. Refereed. Circ: 1600 Paid. Vol. ends: Fall. Microform: PQC. Online: EBSCO Publishing; Florida Center for Library Automation; Gale Group; Ingenta Select; OCLC Online Computer Library Center, Inc. *Indexed:* AmH&L, ArtHuCI, BRI, CBRI, GeoRef, PAIS, SSCI, SSI. *Bk. rev.:* 30-60, 1,000-2,800 words. *Aud.:* Ac, Sa.

The Public Historian is a multidisciplinary journal, the "voice of the public history movement." Its territory includes but is not limited to oral history, corporate information services, grassroots efforts in local history at all levels, historic preservation, museum and archives administration, cultural resources management, litigation support and expert witnessing, editing, publishing, and media. The journal pays particular attention to public land and cultural artifact issues. Archivists working in museum settings will find many issues covered in *The Public Historian* familiar. The diversity of approaches to defining public history makes for a provocative mix of articles on all aspects of the practice of collecting and presenting history but with an academic underpinning. Reviews cover books, museum exhibits, film, video, and electronic media. A recent issue is devoted to past and current documentation of World War II following that recent burst of commemorative "public history" events and artifacts. The journal may offer particular inspiration to the student fan of history who is facing school and career choices, especially if he or she has never heard of public history.

774. *R B M: A Journal of Rare Books, Manuscripts and Cultural Heritage.* Formerly (until 2000): *Rare Books and Manuscripts Librarianship.* [ISSN: 1529-6407] 1986. s-a. USD 35 domestic; USD 40 in Canada & Mexico; USD 50 elsewhere. Ed(s): Lisa Brower, Marvin Je Taylor. Association of College and Research Libraries, 50 East Huron St, Chicago, IL 60611; acrl@ala.org; http://www.ala.org/acrl. Illus., index, adv. Refereed. Circ: 450. Vol. ends: No. 2. Reprint: PQC. *Indexed:* LISA, LibLit, MLA-IB. *Aud.:* Ac, Sa.

RBM: A Journal of Rare Books, Manuscripts, and Cultural Heritage is the Association of College and Research Libraries' independent journal "covering issues pertaining to the world inhabited by special collections libraries and cultural heritage institutions." Noting that "rare book and manuscript libraries have metamorphosed into special collections libraries," the journal has flung open its doors, embracing the broader range of institutions that care for cultural heritage materials as well as the broader range of media being cared for. Content appeals chiefly to the rare book librarian who may carry responsibility for manuscripts and archives, but articles are also relevant to purely book or manuscript professionals, dealers, private collectors, auction houses, museums, practitioners of copyright and intellectual property law, and students. Articles appearing since the journal's makeover have been philosophical, delving into the compounding complexities of our digital world and the flood tide of material available to cultural heritage professionals working in these interesting times.

Rare Books & Manuscripts Librarianship. See *RBM*.

775. *Society of Archivists. Journal.* [ISSN: 0037-9816] 1955. s-a. GBP 143 (Individuals, GBP 57). Ed(s): Christopher Webb. Carfax Publishing Ltd., 4 Park Sq, Milton Park, Abingdon, OX14 4RN, United Kingdom; enquiry@tandf.co.uk; http://www.tandf.co.uk/. Illus., index, adv. Refereed. Circ: 1600. Microform: PQC. Online: EBSCO Publishing; Ingenta Select; OCLC Online Computer Library Center, Inc.; ProQuest Information & Learning; RoweCom Information Quest. Reprint: PQC; PSC. *Indexed:* AmH&L, ArtHuCI, BrArAb, BrHumI, LISA, NumL, SSCI. *Bk. rev.:* 15-25, 600-1,400 words. *Aud.:* Ac, Sa.

The *Journal of the Society of Archivists* offers a balanced picture of the well-developed archival profession in the United Kingdom and Ireland. It is oriented to British and Irish archivists, records managers, and conservation professionals, but articles report occasionally from other English-speaking territories. The tone is professional but can range from reflective and personal to fairly technically scientific; conservation issues, in particular, are covered in some depth. Issues often suggest, by clusters of articles, a focus. A recent issue very usefully surveys and compares archival training in the United Kingdom, Europe, Australia, Canada, and the United States, along with a look at archival employment and the marketing of archives. Numerous book reviews, notices of publications by the Society and the Royal Commission on Historical Manuscripts, and obituaries primarily serve the British archival community, but reviews of reference works and guides to collections will interest American researchers traveling to the United Kingdom.

National, Regional, and State Newsletters

State, provincial, and regional associations provide archivists in the field with current awareness of challenges and opportunities, a sense of community, and a forum for professional development. Newsletters issued at the local level track state and provincial legal trends, list professional and public workshops, announce and report on local meetings, describe funding opportunites, and publish job announcements, as well as gather news from member repositories. The larger or most active associations may publish articles on a par with the national journals, but they generally focus on shorter-range issues and resources to support the daily work of their members.

Publication can be irregular due to changes in activity levels and editorship within local associations. Quite a few newsletters have created online versions to supplement or replace paper copies distributed to members; organizational web sites can also function as de facto newsletters. As newsletters are usually a dividend of membership in a given organization, prices shown can be assumed to represent annual membership dues.

The following publications of national, regional, state, and provincial archival associations are arranged geographically.

National, Regional, and State Newsletters—Canada

ACA Bulletin. [ISSN: 0709-4604] 6/yr. John Macleod. Assn. of Canadian Archivists, Public Archives of Nova Scotia Site, Nova Scotia Archives and Records Management, 6016 University Ave., Halifax NS B3H 1W4.

ALBERTA

ASA Newsletter. q. $20. Archives Soc. of Alberta, P.O. Box 4067, South Edmonton Post Office Edmonton, Alberta T6E 4S8 (www.archivesalberta.org/newsl.htm).

BRITISH COLUMBIA

AABC Newsletter. [ISSN: 1183-3165] q. Robert Edwards. Archives Assn. of British Columbia, P.O. Box 78530, Univ. Post Office, Vancouver, BC V6T 1Z4 (aabc.bc.ca/aabc/newsletter).

MANITOBA

Communique [ISSN: 0827-0074] q. $25. Assn. for Manitoba Archives, P.O. Box 26005, Westminster Post Office, Winnipeg, MB R3C 4K9 (www.mbarchives.mb.ca/communique.htm).

NEWFOUNDLAND AND LABRADOR

ANLA Bulletin. [ISSN: 0821-7157] q. $25. Assn. of Newfoundland & Labrador Archivists, Colonial Bldg., Military Rd., St. John, NF A1C 2C9 (www.anla.nf.ca/).

NOVA SCOTIA

The Council of Nova Scotia Archives Newsletter. [ISSN: 0829-7142] s-a. $35. Anjali Vohra, John Macleod. Council of Nova Scotia Archives, 6016 University Ave., Halifax, NS B3H 1W4 (www.councilofnsarchives.ca/).

ONTARIO

Off the Record. q. $66.13. Patrick Cummins, Manda Vranic. Ontario Assn. of Archivists, and Ontario Council of Archives, P.O. Box 46009, College Park Post Office, 444 Yonge St., Toronto, ON M5B 2L8 (aao.fis.utoronto.ca/).

QUEBEC

La Chronique. Assn. des Archivistes du Quebec, Archives nationales du Quebec a Montreal, 535 ave Viger Est, local 5.27.1, Montreal H2L 2P3.

SASKATCHEWAN

SCAA Newsletter. Saskatchewan Council for Archives and Archivists, 301 Main Library, 3 Campus Drive, Saskatoon, SK S7N 5A4 (scaa.usask.ca/).

National, Regional, and State Newsletters—United States

Archival Outlook (Formerly: *SAA Newsletter*). [ISSN: 1520-3379] 6/yr. Teresa M. Brinati. Soc. of Amer. Archivists, 527 S. Wells, 5th Floor, Chicago, IL 60607 (www.archivists.org).

ALABAMA

The Alabama Archivist. s-a. $10. Jessica Lacher-Feldman. Soc. of Alabama Archivists, W.S. Hoole Special Collections Library, Univ. of Alabama Libraries, Box 870266, Tuscaloosa, AL 35487-0266 (www.auburn.edu/sala/).

CALIFORNIA

SCA Newsletter. q. $35. Terry Boom. Soc. of California Archivists, The Bancroft Library, Univ. of California Berkeley, Berkeley, CA 94720-6000 (www.calarchivists.org/).

DELAWARE VALLEY

Archival Arranger. $7.50. Joseph-James Ahern. Delaware Valley Archivists Group, American Philosophical Society Library, 105 S. Fifth St., Philadelphia, PA 19106.

FLORIDA

The Florida Archivist. q. $15. Kim Bateman. Soc. of Florida Archivists, P.O. Box 7694, Lakeland, FL 33807-7694.

GEORGIA

SGA Newsletter. q. Lamonica Jenkins Sanford. Soc. of Georgia Archivists, P.O. Box 133085, Atlanta, GA 30333 (www.soga.org).

INDIANA

SIA Newsletter. 3/yr. $10. Brenda Burk. Soc. of Indiana Archivists, IUPUI Univ. Library, 755 W. Michigan St., Indianapolis, IN 46202 (archives1.archives.nd.edu/sia/).

INTERMOUNTAIN

CIMA Newsletter. q. $10. Jeff Kintop. Conference of Inter-Mountain Archivists, P.O. Box 2048, Salt Lake City, Utah 84110-2048 (www.lib.utah.edu/cima/).

KENTUCKY

The Kentucky Archivist. s-a. $10. Jim Cundy. Kentucky Council on Archives, Eastern Kentucky Univ., Richmond, KY 40475.

LOUISIANA

LAMA Newsletter. [ISSN: 1073-1008] $15. Ann Wakefield. Louisiana Archives and Manuscripts Assn., P.O. Box 51213, New Orleans, LA 70151-1213 (nutrias.org/lama/lama.htm).

LOUISIANA, NEW ORLEANS

Greater New Orleans Archivists Newsletter. 3/yr. $10. Barbara Vaughn. Greater New Orleans Archivists, Nunez Community College Archives, 3710 Paris Rd., Chalmette, LA 70043 (nutrias.org/gnoa/gnoa.htm).

MICHIGAN

Open Entry. s-a. $15. Bonnie Walworth. Michigan Archival Assn., Ford Motor Co., 1338 Hollywood St., Dearborn, MI 48124 (www2.h-net.msu.edu/~maa/).

MID-ATLANTIC

Mid-Atlantic Archivist. [ISSN: 0738-9396] q. $35. Katy Rawdon-Faucett. Mid-Atlantic Regional Archives Conference, 8233 Old Courthouse Rd., Suite 210, Vienna, VA 22182 (lib.umd.edu/MARAC/).

MIDWEST

MAC Newsletter. [ISSN: 0741-0379] q. $30. Mark Shelstad. Midwest Archives Conference, Univ. of Wyoming, P.O. Box 3924, Laramie, WY 82071 (midwestarchives.org).

MINNESOTA, TWIN CITIES

TCART Newsletter. $5. Kathy M. L. Evavold. Twin Cities Archives Roundtable, c/o Augsburg Fortress Publishers, P.O. Box 1209, Minneapolis, MN 55440-1209.

MISSISSIPPI

The Primary Source. [ISSN: 0741-6563] q. $10. Irmgard Wolfe. Soc. of Mississippi Archivists, Univ. of Southern Mississippi, Box 5053, Hattiesburg, MS 39406-5053.

MISSOURI, KANSAS CITY

The Dusty Shelf. 3/yr. $15. Stan Ingersol. Kansas City Area Archivists, c/o Western Historical Manuscripts Collection, Univ. of Missouri-Kansas City, 320 Newcomb Hall, 5100 Rockhill Rd., Kansas City, MO 64110-2499 (www.umkc.edu/KCAA/).

MISSOURI, ST. LOUIS

The Acid Free Press. $5. Mike Everman. Assn. of St. Louis Area Archivists, Missouri Historical Soc., P.O. Box 11940, St. Louis, MO 63112 (library.wustl.edu/units/spec/archives/aslaa/).

NEW ENGLAND

NEA Newsletter. q. $20. Ellen Doon. New England Archivists, Massachusetts Archives, 220 Morrissey Blvd., Boston, MA 02125 (www.newenglandarchivists.org).

NEW YORK, CAPITAL DISTRICT

CAA Newsletter. $5. Vicki Weiss. Capital Area Archivists of New York, New York State Archives and Records Admin., Rm. 9C71-CEC, Albany, NY 12230 (www.albany.edu/sisp/people/students/saa/CAA/index.htm).

NEW YORK, LONG ISLAND

LIAC Newsletter. 3/yr. $10. Richard Harmond. Long Island Archives Conference, St. John's Univ., History Dept., Jamaica, NY 11439.

NEW YORK, NEW YORK

Metropolitan Archivist. $20. Joe Ciccone. Archivists Round Table of Metropolitan New York, Inc., Merck & Co., Inc., P.O. Box 100, Whitehouse Station, NJ 08889 (www.nyarchivists.org).

NORTH CAROLINA

North Carolina Archivist. q. $15. Laura Clark Brown. Soc. of North Carolina Archivists, Manuscripts Dept., CB#3926, Wilson Library, Chapel Hill, NC 27514 (ncarchivists.org).

NORTHWEST

Easy Access. q. $15. John Bolcer. Northwest Archivists, Inc., Univ. Washington, UW Libraries, Box 352900, Seattle, WA 98195-2900 (osulibrary.oregonstate.edu/archives/misc/nwa.html).

OHIO

The Ohio Archivist. [ISSN: 1047-5400] s-a, electronic only. $15. Judy Cobb. Soc. of Ohio Archivists, Wright State Univ., Special Collections and Archives, Dunbar Library, 3640 Colonel Glenn Highway, Dayton, OH 45435-0001 (www.ohiojunction.net/soa/).

ROCKY MOUNTAINS

The Rocky Mountain Archivist. q. $10. Ginny Kilander. Soc. of Rocky Mountain Archivists, American Heritage Center, Univ. of Wyoming, P.O. Box 3924, Laramie, WY 82071 (www.uwyo.edu/ahc/srma/).

SOUTHWEST

The Southwestern Archivist. [ISSN: 1056-1021] q. $10. Tara Zachary. Soc. of Southwest Archivists, Special Collections, LSU Libraries, Baton Rouge, LA 70803 (info.lib.uh.edu/ssa/ssa.htm).

TENNESSEE

Tennessee Archivist. q. $20. Steven P. Cox. Tennessee Archivists, Lupton Library, Rm. 103, Univ. of Tennessee at Chattanooga, 615 McCallie Ave., Chattanooga, TN 37403-2598 (www.geocities.com/tennarchivists).

Special-Interest Newsletters

Archivists who train formally are introduced to the whole spectrum of archival functions and settings, but there is a great need for cooperation among archivists caring for the same types of records, performing the same specialized functions, working with the same user groups, or collecting in the same areas. Numerous special-interest newsletters answer this need. Many are published by the sections and roundtables of the Society of American Archivists; most of these sub-groups meet at the SAA annual conference and consequently print meeting notes as well as news, reviews, and sometimes fuller articles.

The list below offers a selection, not a comprehensive list, of special interest publications. Many newsletters are available online. The allied profession of conservation publishes newsletters that include specialized topics of relevance to archivists, and several of these are included. Not listed are the newsletters and journals published by individual repositories. Newsletters published by subsections of the Society of American Archivists are listed under the section's name unless it forms part of the title; web addresses are given where known. These groups change editorship frequently, so readers are advised to contact the society directly for current information: Society of American Archivists, 527 S. Wells St., 5th Floor, Chicago, IL 60607 (archivists.org).

ACADEMIC

The Academic Archivist. College and Univ. Archives Section, Soc. of Amer. Archivists (www.archivists.org/saagroups/cnu/index.asp)

ACQUISITIONS

Acquisition & Appraisal News. Acquisition & Appraisal Section, Soc. of Amer. Archivists (www.archivists.org/saagroups/acq-app/acq-app.html).

AFRICAN AMERICAN AND THIRD WORLD

Archivists and Archives of Color Newsletter. Archivists and Archives of Color Roundtable. Soc. of Amer. Archivists (www.archivists.org/saagroups/aac/index.htm).

ARCHIVAL HISTORY

Archival History Newsletter. Archival History Roundtable, Soc. of Amer. Archivists

BUSINESS

Business Archives Newsletter. Business Archives Section, Soc. of Amer. Archivists (www.archivists.org/saagroups/bas/Welcome.asp).

CONGRESSIONAL PAPERS

Congressional Papers Roundtable Newsletter. Soc. of Amer. Archivists (www.lib.udel.edu/ud/spec/cpr/index.htm).

DESCRIPTION

Descriptive Notes. John Rees. Description Section, Soc. of Amer. Archivists (www.archivists.org/saagroups/descr/index.htm).

ELECTRONIC RECORDS

Err Not's. Electronic Records Section, Soc. of Amer. Archivists (www.archivists.org/saagroups/ers/index.asp).

FILM

AMIA Newsletter. [ISSN: 1075-6477] q. $50. Assn. of Moving Image Archivists, 8949 Wilshire Blvd., Beverly Hills, CA 90211 (www.amianet.org/).

Film Technology News. Irreg. Free. Alan Stark. Film Technology Co., 726 N. Cole Ave., Los Angeles, CA 90038.

GOVERNMENT RECORDS

Government Records News. Government Records Section, Soc. of Amer. Archivists (www.archivists.org/saagroups/gov/index.asp).

NAGARA Clearinghouse: news and reports on government records. 3/yr. $75. Stacie Byas. Natl. Assn. of Government Archives and Records Administrators, 48 Howard St., Albany, NY 12207 (nagara.org/clearinghouse/clearinghousehome.html).

MANUSCRIPTS

The Manuscript Society News. 4/yr. Evelyn Cooper. The Manuscript Society, 1960 East Fairmont Drive, Tempe, AZ 85282-2844 (manuscript.org/publications.html).

RBMS Newsletter. 2/yr. $4. Assn. of College and Research Libs., Amer. Library Assn., 50 E. Huron St., Chicago, IL 60611 (www.rbms.nd.edu/).

Manuscript Repositories Section Newsletter. 3/yr. Soc. of Amer. Archivists (www.library.yale.edu/%7Ekspicher/mssrepos/).

MUSEUMS

Museum Archivist. s-a. Museum Archives Section, Soc. of Amer. Archivists (www.chin.gc.ca/English/News/index.html), scroll down to "newsletters."

PERFORMING ARTS AND RECORDED SOUND

Performing Arts and Recorded Sound Newsletter. Performing Arts and Recorded Sound Roundtable, Soc. of Amer. Archivists.

PRESERVATION/CONSERVATION

The Abbey Newsletter: preservation of library and archival materials. [ISSN: 0276-8291] 8/yr. $47. Ellen McCrady, 7105 Geneva Dr., Austin, TX 78723-1510 (palimpsest.stanford.edu/byorg/abbey/an/index.html).

AIC News. [ISSN: 0887-705X] 6/yr. $120. Nora A. Armbruster. The Amer. Inst. for Conservation of Historic and Artistic Works, 1717 K St. N.W., Suite 200, Washington, DC 20006 (aic.stanford.edu/pubs/).

Conservation: The Getty Conservation Institute Newsletter. [ISSN: 0898-4808] 3/yr. Free. Jeffrey Levin. Getty Conservation Inst., 1200 Getty Center Dr., Suite 700, Los Angeles, CA 90049-1684 (www.getty.edu/conservation/resources/newsletter.html).

Guild of Book Workers Newsletter. [ISSN: 0730-3203] 6/yr. $60. Jody Beenk. Guild of Book Workers, 521 Fifth Ave., New York, NY 10175 (palimpsest.stanford.edu/byorg/gbw/news.shtml).

Infinity. (Formerly: *Consect News*). Preservation Section, Soc. of Amer. Archivists (is.gseis.ucla.edu/saapreserv/prindex.htm).

International Preservation News: a newsletter of the IFLA Core Activity for Preservation and Conservation. 3/yr. Preservation Program Office, Library of Congress, Washington, DC 20540 (www.ifla.org/VI/4/pac.htm).

WAAC Newsletter. [ISSN: 1052-0066] 3/yr. $30. Carolyn Tallent. Western Assn. for Art Conservation, 5905 Wilshire Blvd., Los Angeles, CA 90036 (palimpsest.stanford.edu/waac/wn/).

RECORDS MANAGEMENT

GRIST; newsletter of the Archives Industry Specific Group of ARMA International and the Records Management Round Table of the Soc. of Amer. Archivists (archives.syr.edu/saarmrt/).

Records & Information Management Report: issues in information technology. [ISSN: 1096-9624] 10/yr. $165. Ann Balough. Greenwood Press, 88 Post Rd. W., P.O. Box 5007, Westport, CT 06881-5007.

REFERENCE

RAO News. 3/yr. Reference, Access, and Outreach Section, Soc. of Amer. Archivists (www.archivists.org/saagroups/rao/RAOmain.asp).

RELIGIOUS

ACDA Bulletin. q. $15. Christine Taylor. Assn. of Catholic Diocesan Archivists, Archdiocese of Seattle, 910 Marion St., Seattle, WA 98104.

ACWR News. s-a. $25. Dolores Liptak. Archivists for Congregations of Women Religious, ACWR National Office, Trinity College, 125 Michigan Ave. N.E., Washington, DC 20017.

The Archival Spirit. Archivists of Religious Collections Section, Soc. of Amer. Archivists.

Catholic Archives Newsletter. s-a. Bro. David Richardson, Catholic Univ. of America Archives, Washington, DC 20006.

The Historiographer. Margaret Landis. Natl. Episcopal Historians and Archivists, Philadelphia Office of the Episcopal Church, 1201 Chestnut St., Philadelphia, PA 19107.

NEARI Newsletter. $10. New England Archivists of Religious Institutions, Boston CSJ Archives, 637 Cambridge St., Brighton, MA 02135-2801.

SCIENCE, TECHNOLOGY, AND HEALTH CARE

Archival Elements. Science, Technology, and Health Care Roundtable, Soc. of Amer. Archivists (www.archivists.org/saagroups/sthc/index.html).

VISUAL MATERIALS

Views. Visual Materials Section, Soc. of Amer. Archivists (www.lib.lsu.edu/SAA/VMhome.html).

■ ART

General/Museum Publications/Electronic Journals

See also Craft section.

Holly Stec Dankert, Reference Instruction Librarian, DePaul University Libraries, 2350 N. Kenmore, Chicago, IL 60614; hdankert@depaul.edu; FAX: 773-325-7870

Introduction

The audience for art publications remains primarily artists, dealers, museum curators, art historians, and scholars. Important also are art collectors, students, and the general reader. The term "art" as used in this section can be defined as two- or three-dimensional visual arts of all media including, but not limited to, paint, pencil, ink, found objects, clay, bronze, other metals, video, film, photography, decorative arts, and performance art. Sadly, the economic woes of the last year have affected the arts in the publishing arena, which saw the demise of eight journals previously covered in *Magazines for Libraries*, including important titles like *New Art Examiner* and *Gazette des Beaux Arts*; the latter's contribution to international art history will be missed.

The general section features core titles for art collections in a variety of libraries, including general-interest magazines, scholarly and professional journals, and instructional magazines for artists. Bulletins from major museums focusing on their own collections are divided into a separate category in this section.

Most titles include an online version; however, many of these provide only subscriber information. Core titles with additional web content are indicated in the description. The nature of full-color imagery is still dependent on print media for best quality reproduction, but faster Internet connections and more robust computers now available are encouraging more publishers to increase their web presence.

Basic Periodicals

GENERAL. Ems: *The Artist's Magazine;* Hs: *American Artist, Art in America, The Artist's Magazine;* Ga: *American Artist, Art & Antiques, Art in America, Artforum International, The Artist's Magazine;* Ac: *Art Bulletin, Art History, Art in America, Art Journal, Artforum International, Artnews.*

MUSEUM PUBLICATIONS. The *Metropolitan Museum of Art Bulletin* is the best multipurpose museum publication for all ages. A local museum publication should also be chosen for regional representation.

Basic Abstracts and Indexes

Art Index, Artbibliographies Modern, Bibliography of the History of Art (BHA) succeeded RILA.

African Arts. See Africa section.

General

776. *American Art.* Formerly (until 1991): *Smithsonian Studies in American Art.* [ISSN: 1073-9300] 1987. 3x/yr. USD 140 (Individuals, USD 45). Ed(s): Cynthia Mills. University of Chicago Press, Journals Division, PO Box 37005, Chicago, IL 60637; subscriptions@journals.uchicago.edu; http://www.journals.uchicago.edu. Illus., adv. Refereed. Vol. ends: Fall. Online: EBSCO Publishing; Gale Group. *Indexed:* ABM, AIAP, AmH&L, ArtInd, BHA. *Aud.:* Ga, Ac.

Produced by the Smithsonian American Art Museum, *American Art*'s scope encompasses the visual heritage of the United States from its beginning in the colonial era to the present. Interdisciplinary articles range from art and art history through archaeology, anthropology, and cultural studies, all with a focus on visual arts. While the editorial statement indicates that the scope is primarily fine arts, *American Art* includes works of popular culture, public art, film, photography, electronic multimedia, and decorative arts and crafts. Each issue offers a mix of scholarly feature articles and a commentary that focuses on an issue or artist of importance to the Smithsonian or to the American art world at large. Articles are written in accessible language, and the mix of color and black-and-white photographs makes this well suited to public libraries and to colleges and universities, especially if studio or history of art courses are taught.

777. *American Art Journal.* [ISSN: 0002-7359] 1969. a. USD 35 domestic; USD 40 foreign. Ed(s): Jayne A Kuchna. Kennedy Galleries, Inc., 730 Fifth Ave, New York, NY 10019; inquiry@kgny.com; http://www.kgny.com. Illus., index, adv. Refereed. Circ: 2000. Vol. ends: Fall. Microform: PQC. Online: Gale Group. *Indexed:* ABCT, AIAP, AmH&L, ArtHuCI, ArtInd, BHA, HumInd, IBZ. *Aud.:* Ac, Sa.

American Art Journal is published by the Kennedy Art Gallery in New York and has provided a venue for scholarly articles on American art during the eighteenth, nineteenth, and early twentieth centuries since the late 1970s. The journal is slightly behind in its production schedule and now publishes nos. 1 and 2 in a combined issue once yearly. A handful of articles in each issue feature painting, sculpture, prints, photography, and the decorative arts in America and are well documented with numerous black-and-white illustrations. Occasional coverage of cultural history of the United States may be of interest to scholars of other disciplines. *American Art Journal* will be most useful in research collections of academic libraries.

778. *American Artist.* [ISSN: 0002-7375] 1937. m. USD 29.95 domestic; USD 39.95 foreign; USD 42.98 combined subscription domestic print & online edis. Ed(s): Stephen Doherty. V N U Business Publications, 770 Broadway, New York, NY 10003; bmcomm@vnuinc.com; http://www.vnubusinessmedia.com/. Illus., index, adv. Circ: 123300 Paid. Vol. ends: Dec. Microform: NBI. Online: bigchalk; EBSCO Publishing;

Florida Center for Library Automation; Gale Group; OCLC Online Computer Library Center, Inc.; ProQuest Information & Learning. *Indexed:* A&ATA, ABCT, ABM, ABS&EES, AIAP, AS&TI, ArtInd, BEL&L, BHA, BRI, BiogInd, CBRI, IBZ, MagInd, RGPR. *Bk. rev.:* 2-3, 500 words. *Aud.:* Hs, Ga.

Geared to aspiring as well as professional artists, this consumer publication covers how-to information on oil painting, watercolor, acrylics, drawing, sculpture, and printmaking. The subject matter tends to be traditional representational art, with landscapes, still lifes, and portraiture predominating. Interviews with notable contemporary artists provide insights into the technical aspects of their work. Current news on societies and organizations of special interest to painters, notices on business and commercial opportunities, and advertising for supplies and materials will be useful to all artists. A subscription to *American Artist* includes the *Annual Directory of Art Schools & Workshops,* which is particularly useful for studio artists. Not to be missed is the web site at www.myamericanartist.com, with full-text articles and many other resources for artists. This periodical is suited for public libraries and institutions with fine arts programs.

Antiques. See *The Magazine Antiques* in the Antiques and Collecting section.

779. *Apollo: the international magazine of the arts.* [ISSN: 0003-6536] 1925. m. GBP 84; USD 148 in the Americas except Canada; GBP 93 Canada. Ed(s): Dr. David Euserdjian. Apollo Magazine Ltd., 1 Castle Ln, London, SW1E 6DR, United Kingdom. Illus., index, adv. Sample. Vol. ends: Dec. Microform: PQC. Reprint: PSC. *Indexed:* ABM, AIAP, API, ArtHuCI, ArtInd, BAS, BHA, BRI, CBRI, DAAI, IBZ. *Bk. rev.:* 6-7, 800-1,000 words. *Aud.:* Ga, Ac.

Tastefully illustrated and international in scope, *Apollo*'s themed issues revolve around broad categories (decorative arts, Asian arts, etc.), with six or seven articles aimed at an educated audience and written by curators, professors, and other art experts. The December issue reviews the year with feature articles on acquisitions, exhibitions, and a personality of the year. Each issue includes a diary of museum shows, book reviews, and loads of Paris, London, and New York gallery ads. It is geared toward collectors and curators but is also relevant to academicians. Appropriate for large public libraries and college and university libraries with art programs.

780. *Archives of Asian Art.* Formerly (until 1966): *Chinese Art Society of America. Archives.* [ISSN: 0066-6637] 1945. a. EUR 62.54 in the European Union; EUR 62 elsewhere. Ed(s): Kathryn Parker. Brepols Publishers, Begijnhof 67, Turnhout, 2300, Belgium; info.brepols@brepols.net; http://www.brepols.net. Illus., index. Refereed. Circ: 600. *Indexed:* AIAP, ArtHuCI, ArtInd, BAS. *Aud.:* Ac, Sa.

Published biennially by the Asia Society, a nonprofit, nonpolitical educational organization, *Archives of Asian Art* provides a forum for research by scholars on numerous topics concerning Asian art. Four to six lengthy articles are generously illustrated and feature Buddhist sculpture and imagery in China, India, and elsewhere, Chinese watercolors, Japanese textiles, and the art of a Han shrine, among others. The journal also documents significant acquisitions of Asian art by North American museums and other institutions covering a two-year period. This publication serves as one the few English-language resources for serious students and scholars. It is highly recommended for research collections in academic libraries.

Art & Antiques. See Antiques and Collecting section.

781. *The Art Book.* Formerly: *International Publishing Review (Fine Arts Edition).* [ISSN: 1368-6267] 1993. q. GBP 72 print & online eds. Ed(s): Sue Ward. Blackwell Publishing Ltd., 9600 Garsington Rd, PO Box 805, Oxford, OX4 2DQ, United Kingdom; jnlinfo@blackwellpublishers.co.uk; http://www.blackwellpublishing.com/. Illus., adv. Online: EBSCO Publishing; ingenta.com; OCLC Online Computer Library Center, Inc.; RoweCom Information Quest; Swets Blackwell. *Indexed:* ABM. *Bk. rev.:* 45-60. *Aud.:* Ga, Ac, Sa.

Different from the other art titles listed in this section, *The Art Book* is devoted exclusively to reviews of art books and articles related to the art book publishing industry. The Association of Art Historians in the United Kingdom provides authoritative and independent critical oversight of the contents, in conjunction with Blackwell staff. Three feature-length reviews, frequently thematic, are included in each issue; plus interviews; exhibition, museum, and gallery publications reviews; and commentary segments. Book reviews in general art, photography, and architecture genres and a bestseller list round out each issue. Librarians will find this a useful collection development tool. Highly recommended for all libraries.

782. *Art Bulletin.* [ISSN: 0004-3079] 1913. q. 0 membership. Ed(s): H. Perry Chapman. College Art Association, 275 Seventh Ave, New York, NY 10001. Illus., index, adv. Refereed. Circ: 9500. Vol. ends: No. 4. Microform: IDC; PQC. Online: bigchalk; Chadwyck-Healey Incorporated; EBSCO Publishing; Florida Center for Library Automation; Gale Group; Northern Light Technology, Inc.; OCLC Online Computer Library Center, Inc.; ProQuest Information & Learning; H.W. Wilson. Reprint: PSC. *Indexed:* ABCT, ABM, ABS&EES, AIAP, API, ArtHuCI, ArtInd, BAS, BHA, BRD, BRI, BrArAb, CBRI, HumInd, IBZ, NumL, RI-1. *Bk. rev.:* Numerous, essay length. *Aud.:* Ac.

Published quarterly by the College Art Association, *Art Bulletin* serves as a scholarly forum for dialogue among art history academicians. Research articles cover art from all historical periods but predominantly Western art, and they are usually accompanied by black-and-white photos in this slightly oversized, glossy journal. Abstracts of each article are provided in the table of contents. Book reviews, a list of books received, and an exhibition review are also included. *Art Bulletin* is considered essential for all research collections and academic libraries.

Art Education. See Education/Specific Subjects and Teaching Methods/The Arts section.

783. *Art History.* [ISSN: 0141-6790] 1978. 5x/yr. GBP 323 print & online eds. Ed(s): Deborah Cherry. Blackwell Publishing Ltd., 9600 Garsington Rd, PO Box 805, Oxford, OX4 2DQ, United Kingdom; jnlinfo@blackwellpublishers.co.uk; http://www.blackwellpublishing.com/. Illus., index, adv. Refereed. Circ: 2500. Vol. ends: Dec. Microform: PQC. Online: EBSCO Publishing; Gale Group; ingenta.com; OCLC Online Computer Library Center, Inc.; RoweCom Information Quest; Swets Blackwell. Reprint: PQC; SWZ. *Indexed:* ABCT, ABM, AIAP, API, AmH&L, ArtHuCI, ArtInd, BAS, BHA, BrHumI, DAAI, HumInd. *Bk. rev.:* 9-11, essay length. *Aud.:* Ac.

Published by the Association of Art Historians, a British-based group of international scholars, *Art History* provides a vehicle for research in the historical and theoretical aspects of traditional visual arts—primarily two-dimensional works on paper and canvas with occasional forays into three-dimensional art—from both Western and Eastern hemispheres. Articles that explore the arts in their interdisciplinary context are encouraged. Targeted to art and design professionals and others concerned with the advancement of the history of art, *Art History* seeks to consider related cultural, economic, and social issues as well. Illustrations are minimal and appropriate to the theses posited in the four papers that are presented in each issue. Librarians will especially appreciate the extensive scholarly book reviews written by experts in the field. Recommended for all academic libraries.

784. *Art in America.* [ISSN: 0004-3214] 1913. m. USD 34.95 USD 39.95 domestic. Ed(s): Richard Vine. Brant Publications, Inc., 575 Broadway, 5th Fl, New York, NY 10012. Illus., adv. Circ: 65000. Microform: PQC. Online: bigchalk; EBSCO Publishing; Florida Center for Library Automation; Gale Group; Northern Light Technology, Inc.; OCLC Online Computer Library Center, Inc.; ProQuest Information & Learning. *Indexed:* ABM, ABS&EES, AIAP, ArtHuCI, ArtInd, BHA, BRD, BRI, CBRI, DAAI, FLI, HumInd, IBZ, MagInd, RGPR, RI-1, SSCI. *Bk. rev.:* 2-3, 1,000 words. *Aud.:* Ga, Ac.

A standard in the field, *Art in America* strives to bring big-name artists, exhibitions, and performance pieces to the American art world. Brief articles cover both U.S. and international news items, issues, commentary, exhibitions, and occasional regional pieces, e.g., "Report from Milwaukee." A handful of feature articles focuses primarily on contemporary artists while including one on past masters of the nineteenth and twentieth centuries. Written for an educated audience of art collectors, dealers, and curators, *Art in America* nevertheless is suitable for large public and academic libraries whose users will find the many gallery and exhibition advertisements and show listings useful.

785. *Art Journal.* Former titles: *College Art Journal; Art Journal.* 1941. q. Ed(s): Patricia C. Phillips. College Art Association, 275 Seventh Ave, New York, NY 10001. Illus., adv. Refereed. Circ: 11000. Microform: PQC. Online: Gale Group. Reprint: PSC. *Indexed:* A&ATA, ABM, ABS&EES, AIAP, API, ArtHuCI, ArtInd, BAS, BHA, BRI, CBRI, DAAI, HumInd, IBZ, SSCI. *Bk. rev.:* 6, length varies. *Aud.:* Ac.

Art Journal is an academic periodical published by the College Art Association. It is a visionary work; the editorial board seeks to create a dialogue among educators teaching art, design, criticism and theory, art history, and visual culture. Articles are of a scholarly nature and focus on cultural change reflected in the visual arts selecting "vital, intellectually compelling, and visually engaging" subjects of the twentieth and twenty-first centuries. Contemporary works and artists are featured, with black-and-white and color illustrations. This journal is highly recommended for all academic libraries.

786. *The Art Newspaper (International Edition).* Incorporated (1988-1989): *Journal of Art.* [ISSN: 0960-6556] 1990. 11x/yr. GBP 47 United Kingdom; GBP 59 in Europe; GBP 77 rest of world. Ed(s): Anna Somers Cocks. The Art Newspaper, 70 South Lambeth Rd, London, SW8 1RL, United Kingdom; contact@theartnewspaper.com; http://www.artnewspaper.com. Adv. Sample. Circ: 14000 Paid. *Indexed:* ABM, ArtInd. *Aud.:* Ga, Ac, Sa.

The Art Newspaper is a true newspaper in its format and content. Its focus is commentary and news of the international art world. It is divided into two sections. The first is devoted to what's going on in private, national, and international museums, legislation/regulation in the arts, financial crises and funding issues, effects of world events on art collections, and scandals from all areas. Columnists and op/ed writers turn a critical eye on governments around the world and the effects their policies have on the arts, plus other regular commentaries. The second section lists "What's On," exhibitions around the globe, divided into New York, the rest of the United States, London, the rest of the United Kingdom, France, Germany, and the rest of the world. There is also an auction listing. The web site offers some free content and is worth bookmarking. An excellent source for keeping up with world art news and people. Highly recommended for all libraries.

787. *Art Now Gallery Guide: Collector's Edition.* Former titles: *Art Now Gallery Guide: International Edition; Art Now Gallery Guide: National Edition; Art Now: U S A - National Art Museum and Gallery Guide.* 1982. 10x/yr. USD 45 domestic; USD 52 foreign. Ed(s): Mary Lynn Rinker. Art Now, Inc., 97 Grayrock Rd, PO Box 5541, Clinton, NJ 08809; gil@galleryguideonline.com; http://www.gallery-guide.com. Illus., adv. Circ: 6000. *Aud.:* Ga, Ac, Sa.

Art Now Gallery Guide informs readers about exhibitions at art galleries and museums across the United States, serving as a current-awareness resource in the contemporary art world. Divided into regional publications—New York, Boston/New England, Philadelphia, Southeast, Chicago/Midwest, Southwest, and West Coast editions—this pocket-size monthly reference book offers events, highlights, and listings of private art dealers and services in each region. Area maps provide a special feature in these regional editions. A great value for the price, this title is useful for all types of libraries.

788. *Art Papers Magazine.* Formerly (until 1999): *Art Papers;* Formed by the 1980 merger of: *Contemporary Art - Southeast; Atlanta Art Papers;* Formerly (until 1978): *Atlanta Art Workers Coalition Newspaper.* [ISSN: 1524-9581] 1976. bi-m. USD 55 in Canada & Mexico (Individuals, USD 35; Members, USD 30). Ed(s): Michael Pittari. Atlanta Art Papers, Inc., PO Box 5748, Atlanta, GA 31107; info@artpapers.org; http://www.artpapers.org. Illus., adv. Circ: 155000. Vol. ends: Nov/Dec. Microform: PQC. *Indexed:* ABM, ABS&EES, ArtInd, BHA. *Bk. rev.:* 1, 1,000 words. *Aud.:* Ga, Ac, Sa.

Art Papers is the publication for the eponymous nonprofit organization dedicated to providing advocacy and a forum for the examination and exchange of diverse and independent perspectives on the role of art. The organization is located in and serves the southeastern United States, but it does not limit its scope geographically. Controversial topics and criticism cover cultural, social, and philosophical issues related to the arts including photography, mixed media, film, and all visual arts. The excellent web site, www.artpapers.org, plus departments featuring studio visits, interviews, collecting and art resources, regional artists' gallery shows, and reviews make this resource valuable for the professional artist and student as well as interested laymen. Appropriate for public, college, and university libraries.

789. *Artforum International.* Formerly (until 1982): *Artforum.* [ISSN: 1086-7058] 1962. m. 10/yr. Individuals, USD 46. Ed(s): Jack Bankowsky. Artforum International Magazine, Inc., 350 Seventh Ave, New York, NY 10001. Illus., adv. Circ: 30000. Vol. ends: Sep/Jun. Microform: PQC. Online: Florida Center for Library Automation; Gale Group; Northern Light Technology, Inc. *Indexed:* ABCT, ABM, ABS&EES, AIAP, ArtHuCI, ArtInd, BAS, BHA, DAAI, FLI, HumInd, RILM. *Bk. rev.:* 1, length varies. *Aud.:* Ga, Ac.

Published in an appealing coffee-table, art-book format, this international contemporary art magazine is accessible to a wide audience. Vying for attention amid the glossy advertisements, primarily from New York galleries but including others from around the world, are articles on sculpture, painting, mixed media, installation pieces, architecture, music, and popular culture, frequently including artist interviews. Regular departments cover film, music, and book reviews, top-ten lists, and individual artist and/or gallery reviews. Included three times a year are previews of upcoming exhibitions. A calendar of international art events is provided in every issue. Collectors and curators of contemporary art will find this magazine essential. Recommended for all libraries.

Artibus Asiae. See Asia and the Pacific/General section.

790. *The Artist: inspiration, instruction & practical udeas for all artists.* Incorporates: *Art and Artists.* [ISSN: 0004-3877] 1931. m. GBP 24 United Kingdom; USD 58 United States; CND 72 Canada. Ed(s): Sally Bulgin. The Artists' Publishing Company Limited, Caxton House, 62-65 High St, Tenterden, TN30 6BD, United Kingdom. Illus., index, adv. Sample. Circ: 19000. *Indexed:* AIAP, ArtInd. *Bk. rev.:* Notes. *Aud.:* Ga, Ac.

The British equivalent to *American Artist, The Artist* provides many instructional articles for the professional and amateur artist. A dozen articles offer practical advice on technique, materials to use, and other helpful technical information, and they are illustrated with lots of easy-to-follow color illustrations. The focus is generally representational art, landscapes, and figurative and still-life portrayals. Exhibition reviews, profiles of contemporary artists, interviews, and other current news in the United Kingdom make up the rest of the contents. This periodical is recommended for public libraries and institutions with fine arts programs.

791. *The Artist's Magazine.* [ISSN: 0741-3351] 1984. m. USD 27 domestic; USD 37 foreign; USD 3.99 newsstand/cover per issue. Ed(s): Sandra Carpenter. F & W Publications, Inc., 1507 Dana Ave, Cincinnati, OH 45207; http://www.artistsmagazine.com. Illus., adv. Circ: 200000 Paid. Vol. ends: Dec. *Indexed:* IHTDI. *Bk. rev.:* 50, 200 words. *Aud.:* Hs, Ga.

Artist's Magazine is a monthly publication designed for artists of all levels of accomplishment from beginner to professional. Most of the articles instruct and present various working methods, materials, tools, and techniques. Marketing information is provided, plus announcements of study opportunities and art competitions. The accompanying web site, www.artistsmagazine.com, is most useful to artists, providing business tips, technical questions and answers, clinics, and much more. This is an educational and instructive publication that would be most useful in school libraries with serious studio art programs.

792. *Artnews.* [ISSN: 0004-3273] 1902. 11x/yr. USD 39.95 domestic; USD 59.95 Canada; USD 99.95 elsewhere. Ed(s): Milton Esterow. Artnews LLC, 48 W 38th St, New York, NY 10018; http://www.artnewsonline.com. Illus., adv. Circ: 80000. Vol. ends: Dec.

Microform: MIM; PQC. Online: bigchalk. Reprint: PQC. *Indexed:* A&ATA, ABM, ABS&EES, AIAP, ArtHuCI, ArtInd, BHA, BRI, CBRI, DAAI, IIPA, MagInd, RGPR. *Bk. rev.:* 3-4, 300-500 words. *Aud.:* Hs, Ga, Ac.

Functioning much like a *Newsweek* for the art world, *ARTnews*, albeit a monthly, serves as the principle source for current information on both contemporary art in America and international art both contemporary and historical, and on collectors and collections. Five feature-length articles cover new genres, contemporary artists, and old masters, along with regular departments exploring personalities, national and international art news, new talent, the art market, book reviews, exhibition and competition listings, and a smattering of regional, national, and international exhibition reviews. The web site, www.artnewsonline.com, mirrors the print edition and offers some content for free along with table of contents to back issues since 1996. This standard art magazine is highly recommended for all libraries.

Arts of Asia. See Asia and the Pacific/General section.

793. ***Arts Review (London).*** Formerly: *Art News & Review.* [ISSN: 0004-4091] 1949. m. GBP 38 domestic; EUR 65 in Europe; USD 59.99 United States. Ed(s): David Lee. Art Review Ltd., Hereford House, 23-24 Smithfield St, London, EC1A 9LF, United Kingdom. Illus., index, adv. Circ: 15000. Microform: BNB; PQC. *Indexed:* ABCT, ABM, AIAP, ArtInd, BHA. *Bk. rev.:* Various number and length. *Aud.:* Ga, Ac.

A consumer publication reporting on the current international art scene, *Art Review* features five articles on contemporary visual arts, photography, design, or the artists themselves. The United Kingdom is primarily covered, but there are also segments devoted to international art, style, objects, collectors, and critics. Regional reviews and exhibition guides attempt a more inclusive overview of contemporary art. The magazine's glitzy, insider presentation of art news will appeal to all audiences. Useful for research collections that are trying to provide comprehensive coverage of the art world.

794. ***Artweek: West Coast art news criticism.*** [ISSN: 0004-4121] 1970. m. USD 36 (Individuals, USD 32). Ed(s): Meredith Tromble. Spaulding - Devlin, Inc., 2149 Paragon Dr, Ste 100, San Jose, CA 95131. Illus., index, adv. Circ: 14500. Vol. ends: Dec. Microform: MIM; PQC. Online: OCLC Online Computer Library Center, Inc.; H.W. Wilson. *Indexed:* ABCT, ArtInd, BHA, MagInd, RGPR. *Bk. rev.:* 2, 500 words. *Aud.:* Ga, Ac, Sa.

A monthly tabloid-style publication, *Artweek* is a standard source of information for contemporary fine arts, photography, and crafts on the West Coast. Arranged by state and region, it includes exhibition listings and reviews of artists in California, the Pacific Northwest, and Hawaii, and gives by far the most comprehensive descriptive overview of galleries and artists in the western United States. Additional content includes commentary, gallery guides, film and book reviews, regional and international competitions, and calendars of events that are geared toward art lovers as well as art professionals. It is well suited for public, academic, and museum collections on the West Coast, and large public and academic libraries with comprehensive art holdings.

795. ***Beaux Arts Magazine: actualite des arts.*** [ISSN: 0757-2271] 1983. m. 11/yr. FRF 398. Ed(s): Nicolas Chaudin. Editions Flammarion, Tour Maine Montparnasse, 33 av. du Maine, Paris, Cedex 15 75755, France. Illus., index, adv. Sample. Circ: 49000. *Indexed:* ABM, ArtInd, BHA. *Bk. rev.:* Number and length vary. *Aud.:* Ga.

Published in France, *Beaux Arts Magazine* is a beautifully illustrated periodical aimed at the art collector. Articles are written for a general audience, and the scope covers all of Europe. Included are auction news and sales, exhibition announcements, museum events, interviews, a calendar of events, book reviews, and occasional performance and movie reviews. Written in French, the American edition includes abstracts of the articles in English, which increases the utility of this attractive publication. Recommended for libraries with extensive art holdings.

796. ***Burlington Magazine.*** [ISSN: 0007-6287] 1903. m. USD 415. Ed(s): Caroline ELam. Burlington Magazine Publications Ltd., 14 Dukes Rd, London, WC1H 9AD, United Kingdom; editorial@burlington.org.uk. Illus., index, adv. Refereed. Vol. ends: Dec. Microform: IDC. Reprint: PSC. *Indexed:* A&ATA, ABCT, ABM, AIAP, API, ArtHuCI, ArtInd, BAS, BEL&L, BHA, BRI, BrArAb, CBRI, DAAI, IBZ, SSCI. *Bk. rev.:* 10-15, 1,000 words. *Aud.:* Ac.

Begun in 1903 to lavishly illustrate, attribute, discover, and document western European art for connoisseurs, *Burlington Magazine* has long maintained a well-respected reputation among art historians and other scholars. Its aim and scope today cover all historical periods from prehistoric art to modern Western art including works and artists outside of Europe. Its design is elegant and gracious, with lots of full-color images. Articles by experts in the field focus on new developments, historical documents, conservation practices, and the history of collecting art. Book reviews, shorter notices, obituaries, exhibition information, and a calendar of events round out this important journal. It is recommended for all research collections in academic and special libraries.

Calyx. See Women: Feminist and Special Interest/Literary and Artistic section.

797. ***Canadian Art.*** [ISSN: 0825-3854] 1984. q. CND 24 domestic; USD 32 United States; USD 40 elsewhere. Ed(s): Richard Rhodes. Canadian Art Foundation, 51 Front St E, Ste 210, Toronto, ON M5E 1B3, Canada. Illus., adv. Circ: 20000 Paid. Vol. ends: Winter. Microform: MML. Online: LexisNexis; Micromedia ProQuest. *Indexed:* ABM, ArtInd, BHA, CBCARef, CPerI. *Bk. rev.:* 1-3, 500 words. *Aud.:* Ga, Ac, Sa.

Published in part by the Canadian government, Canada Council, and the Ontario Arts Council, *Canadian Art* is a quarterly that is devoted to the visual arts of that country. It is beautifully designed with lots of full-color images, and the subject matter covers painting, sculpture, illustration, design, architecture, photography, and film. Articles are not limited to any particular time period; however, profiles of individual contemporary artists with reproductions of their works or group shows predominate, making this an invaluable resource for contemporary Canadian art. Also worth bookmarking is the web site, www.canadianart.ca. This magazine is aimed toward a general audience including art collectors and regular guests of art galleries.

Critical Inquiry. See Cultural-Social Studies section.

798. ***F M R.*** [ISSN: 0394-0462] 1982. bi-m. ITL 160000 domestic; ITL 200000 in Europe; ITL 260000 elsewhere. Ed(s): Carole Aghion. Franco Maria Ricci SpA, c/o Alfea, Via Marconi, 2, Lugano, 6900, Italy; ricci@fmrmagazine.it. Illus., adv. Circ: 43000. Vol. ends: Nov/Dec. *Indexed:* AIAP, ArtInd, BHA, DAAI. *Aud.:* Ga, Ac.

FMR, published by Italian fine arts book publisher Franco Maria Ricci, strives to create a magazine covering the arts that is itself a work of art. Lavishly illustrated in vibrant color images that regularly play across both pages, *FMR* highlights traditional, representational European paintings, places of architectural significance and objects elevated to the status of art. Its international coverage provides exhibition information arranged by country, indicating the museum, exhibition title, dates, and a short description, plus an international calendar of events. Recommended for general audiences in either public or academic libraries.

799. ***Flash Art International.*** [ISSN: 0394-1493] 1980. bi-m. EUR 50 in Europe; EUR 90 Oceania; EUR 70 elsewhere. Ed(s): Giancarlo Politi, Helena Kontova. Giancarlo Politi Editore, PO Box 95, Borgo Trevi, 06032, Italy; subscription@flashartonline.com; http://www.flashartonline.com. Illus., adv. Circ: 55000. *Indexed:* ABM, AIAP, ArtInd, BHA, DAAI. *Bk. rev.:* 2-3, 600-900 words. *Aud.:* Ga, Ac.

This self-proclaimed world's leading art magazine is filled with glossy ads from galleries as widely disparate as McLean, Virginia, and Milan to the Netherlands and New York. *Flash Art* has long used its journalistic tone to bring the North American and European contemporary art world into its readership, and it continues as a strong voice in current news and criticism in the visual arts. Each issue contains news updates, gallery reviews, interviews, and feature articles on two- and three-dimensional and performance art, video, and mixed media works and their creators. Recommended as an important basic international source for all libraries with an interest in art and art criticism.

800. ***Gazette des Beaux Arts.*** [ISSN: 0016-5530] 1859. 10x/yr. FRF 1500. Ed(s): Francois Souchal. Societe Les Beaux Arts, 140 rue du Faubourg Saint- Honore, Paris, 75008, France; gazette.des.beaux.arts@wanadoo.fr. Illus., index, adv. Refereed. Circ: 1650. Vol. ends: Dec. Microform: PMC. Online: OCLC Online Computer Library Center, Inc.; H.W. Wilson. *Indexed:* AIAP, ArtHuCI, ArtInd, BHA, IBZ. *Bk. rev.:* Number varies, lengthy. *Aud.:* Ac.

Gazette des Beaux-Arts was one of the earliest European journals devoted to the scholarship of art. With the last issue in December, 2002, it has ceased publication.

801. ***I F A R Journal.*** Formerly (until 1998): *I F A R Reports;* Which was formed by the merger of (1981-1984): *Art Research News;* (1979-1984): *Stolen Art Alert;* Which was formerly (until 1980): *Art Theft Archive Newsletter.* [ISSN: 1098-1195] 1984. q. USD 65 domestic; USD 85 foreign; USD 100 domestic associate (active subscriber)). Ed(s): Sharon Flescher. International Foundation for Art Research, Inc., 500 Fifth Ave, New York, NY 10110; http://www.ifar.org. Illus., index, adv. Circ: 1500. *Indexed:* ABM. *Aud.:* Sa.

IFAR Reports, the mouthpiece of the International Foundation for Art Research (IFAR), informs the art community about recent art theft, authentication, fraud, and art laws through feature articles. From its founding, IFAR has been a resource for scholarship in authentication research, maintaining a list of stolen art plus authenticating problematic works of art and providing a clearinghouse for legal issues. With its recent shift away from maintaining a stolen art database (now the purview of the Art Loss Register), IFAR is able to publish new depths of scholarship in authentication research. Featured in each issue are four or five well-researched articles, plus brief discussions of art and the law, updates, and news items. Selections from the Art Loss Register, consisting of art theft reports and recent items stolen, plus a recovery list, are printed in each issue. As an advocate for the entire art community, *IFAR Reports* provides important research about provenance and attribution not found in other art journals. Appropriate for research and municipal libraries.

Journal of Aesthetic Education. See Cultural-Social Studies section.

Journal of Aesthetics and Art Criticism. See Cultural-Social Studies section.

802. ***The Journal of Canadian Art History.*** [ISSN: 0315-4297] 1974. s-a. CND 25; CND 30 foreign. Ed(s): Sandra Paikowsky. Journal of Canadian Art History, 9 Campus Dr, Saskatoon, SK S7N 5A5, Canada. Illus., index, adv. Refereed. Circ: 700. Vol. ends: No. 2. Microform: MML. Online: OCLC Online Computer Library Center, Inc.; H.W. Wilson. *Indexed:* AIAP, AmH&L, ArtHuCI, ArtInd, BHA, CBCARef, CPerI. *Bk. rev.:* 4-5, lengthy. *Aud.:* Ac, Sa.

The national art history journal in Canada, *JCAH* is a scholarly periodical devoted to the research of Canadian art, architecture, decorative arts, and photography. It includes all historical and contemporary periods with articles that are sparingly illustrated in black and white. Both English- and French-language submissions are accepted, and three- or four-page summaries are translated into the other appropriate language. Also included on a regular basis are bibliographies, such as individual artists and architects; theses and dissertations in Canadian art and architecture; and book reviews and reviews of exhibition catalogs specific to Canadian art. Appropriate for research collections in academic libraries.

803. ***Journal of Pre-Raphaelite Studies.*** Former titles (until 1992): *Journal of Pre-Raphaelite and Aesthetic Studies;* (until 1987): *Journal of Pre-Raphaelite Studies;* (until 1980): *Pre-Raphaelite Review.* [ISSN: 1060-149X] 1977. 2x/yr. CND 40 (Individuals, CND 24). Ed(s): David Latham. Journal of Pre-Raphaelite Studies, 208 Stong College, York University, Toronto, ON M3J 1P3, Canada; dlatham@yorku.ca. Illus. Sample. Refereed. Circ: 450 Paid. *Indexed:* AmHI, ArtHuCI, BHA, HumInd, MLA-IB, SSCI. *Aud.:* Ac.

Founded to create a forum for the study of Pre-Raphaelite, Aesthetic, and Decadent art, culture, and literature of the nineteenth century, *JPRS* publishes research on such renowned artists as Dante Gabriel Rosetti, Christina Rosetti, Edward Burne-Jones, William Morris, and the cult of Pre-Raphaelites worldwide and its interaction with Victorian literary figures (Edith Wharton, Oscar Wilde) and Victorian culture and mores. A dozen papers, sparsely illustrated with black-and-white images, are printed in this small-scale semi-annual journal. Topics covered include historical examinations and interdisciplinary studies on the creation of sexual knowledge, Victorian masculinities, and consumerism and industrial art. Although targeting a fairly narrow topic, *JPRS* is important for academic libraries with studies in nineteenth-century literary and art history programs.

804. ***Koreana: Korean art and culture.*** [ISSN: 1016-0744] 1987. q. KRW 18000 domestic; USD 30 foreign. Ed(s): Jeong Yeop Park. Korea Foundation, Publication & Reference Materials Team, 1376-1 Seocho 2 dong, Seocho-gu, Seoul, 137072, Korea, Republic of; publication@kf.or.kr; http://www.kofo.or.kr/kdata.htm. Adv. Circ: 9000. Online: OCLC Online Computer Library Center, Inc.; H.W. Wilson. *Indexed:* ABM, ArtInd, BAS, MLA-IB. *Aud.:* Ga, Ac, Sa.

This beautifully illustrated quarterly magazine in English is devoted to traditional and contemporary Korean art and culture. Four to six feature articles typically revolve around a theme like weddings, traditional and contemporary; Korean perceptions of life and death; or national treasures such as the Gyujanggak archives. Regular departments include interviews with architects and artists, cuisine and arts of living, discovering Korea, a featured masterpiece, an art review, and a small section devoted to Korean literature. Much full-text content from current and archived issues can be found for free at www.koreana.or.kr. Recommended for academic libraries and large public libraries.

805. ***Master Drawings: devoted exclusively to the study and illustration of drawings.*** [ISSN: 0025-5025] 1963. q. USD 85 domestic; USD 95 foreign. Ed(s): Anne Marie Logan. Master Drawings Association, Inc., 29 E 36th St, New York, NY 10016. Illus., index, adv. Refereed. Circ: 1250 Paid and free. Vol. ends: No. 4. *Indexed:* AIAP, ArtHuCI, ArtInd, BHA, IBZ. *Bk. rev.:* Number varies, essay length. *Aud.:* Ac, Sa.

This journal is published by the Master Drawings Association of New York, and its audience is primarily art historians, collectors, and dealers. The academic quarterly provides a venue for the exclusive study of drawings and occasionally other works on paper, e.g., engraving and watercolor since the Renaissance. Thematic issues concentrate mainly on the old masters up to 1900 and are written for scholars. Authors tend to be art history fellows, professors, and museum curators, and focus on new developments and reattributions of specific drawings. Appropriate for academic libraries that support art history programs.

806. ***Mediamatic.*** [ISSN: 0920-7864] 1986. 4x/yr. NLG 150 (Individuals, NLG 90; NLG 170 foreign). Ed(s): Willem Velthouen. Mediamatic Foundation, Postbus 17490, Amsterdam, 1001 JL, Netherlands; subscriptions@mediamatic.nl; http://www.mediamatic.nl. Illus., adv. Circ: 4000. Vol. ends: No. 4. *Bk. rev.:* 6, 200 words. *Aud.:* Ac, Sa.

Mediamatic provides international coverage of new media, art, culture, and theory, and is published in Dutch and English. The journal specializes in electronic media and hardware design with a particular emphasis on video. Each issue is filled with a variety of material including theoretical and historical articles, interviews with artists, technical pieces, and announcements about upcoming events. The web site is www.mediamatic.net.

807. ***New Criterion.*** [ISSN: 0734-0222] 1982. m. 10/yr. USD 36. Ed(s): Hilton Kramer. Foundation for Cultural Review, 850 Seventh Ave, New York, NY 10019. Illus., adv. Circ: 8000. Microform: PQC. Online: EBSCO Publishing; Florida Center for Library Automation; Gale Group; OCLC Online Computer Library Center, Inc.; H.W. Wilson. *Indexed:* ABM, AmHI, ArtInd, BHA, IBZ, MLA-IB. *Bk. rev.:* 3, lengthy. *Aud.:* Ga, Ac.

New Criterion is published by the Foundation for Cultural Review, which gives the magazine a much wider scope than strictly visual arts. Poets, authors, public policy scholars, humanities lecturers, and critics all contribute to create a vehicle for poetry, arts criticism, and commentary on cultural life in America. Departments in theater, art, music, and the media provide substantial reviews, and exhibition listings and book reviews make regular appearances in this periodical. Engaging and interesting to the informed reader, *New Criterion* is recommended for both public and academic libraries.

n.paradoxa. See Women: Feminist and Special Interest/Literary and Artistic section.

808. *Oriental Art: devoted to the study of all forms of Oriental art.* [ISSN: 0030-5278] 1948. q. USD 64; GBP 46. Oriental Art Magazine Ltd., 12 Ennerdale Rd, Richmond, TW9 3PG , United Kingdom. Illus., index, adv. Vol. ends: Winter. Reprint: PSC. *Indexed:* A&ATA, ABCT, AIAP, ArtHuCI, ArtInd, BHA, RI-1. *Bk. rev.:* 4-5, length varies. *Aud.:* Ac, Sa.

Lavishly illustrated with full-color glossy reproductions, *Oriental Art* is an inclusive publication that extends coverage to art in India, the Islamic world, and all of Southeast Asia, beyond the traditional China and Japan focus. Five or six scholarly in-depth articles written by international experts in the field are featured. Similarly, book reviews are quite lengthy and written for scholars. Departments include the sales and auction reports from London and New York, and exhibition reviews and reports. It is one of the best publications on Oriental art and should be included in all research collections in academic and special libraries.

809. *Oxford Art Journal.* [ISSN: 0142-6540] 1978. s-a. GBP 105. Ed(s): Tamar Garb. Oxford University Press, Great Clarendon St, Oxford, OX2 6DP, United Kingdom; jnl.orders@oup.co.uk; http://www3.oup.co.uk/jnls. Illus., adv. Sample. Refereed. Circ: 1200. Vol. ends: No. 2. Online: Chadwyck-Healey Incorporated. Reprint: PSC. *Indexed:* ABM, AIAP, AltPI, ArtHuCI, ArtInd, BHA, DAAI. *Bk. rev.:* 8, essay length. *Aud.:* Ac.

The *Oxford Art Journal*'s content presents critical works in art history through the interpretation of artists' works within a social context. Seven to ten scholarly, peer-reviewed papers represent research in the visual arts and related historical and philosophical issues including studies in modern languages, history, and cultural studies. It is a high-quality publication well illustrated with black-and-white photos. Six or seven signed book reviews and the focus on the historical, social commentary of art make this appropriate for college and university libraries.

810. *Print Quarterly.* [ISSN: 0265-8305] 1984. q. GBP 42 domestic; USD 77 in US & Canada; GBP 50 elsewhere. Ed(s): David Landau. Print Quarterly Publications, 52 Kelso Pl, London, W8 5QQ, United Kingdom. Illus., adv. Refereed. Circ: 1300. Vol. ends: Dec. *Indexed:* ABM, AIAP, AmH&L, ArtHuCI, ArtInd, BHA. *Bk. rev.:* Number and length vary. *Aud.:* Ac, Sa.

Print Quarterly is the leading publication in its field. Devoted to the art of the printed image, whether engraving, intaglio, woodprint, lithograph, drypoint, or zincograph, it covers the history of printmaking from the fifteenth century to the present. Features include three to four peer-reviewed and in-depth book reviews. The publication is well illustrated, and the articles are written for such academicians as art historians, although collectors would also find this a very useful source of information. It includes unique sections devoted to news items in the print and graphic arts world (new attributions, the latest serial publications, brief articles on societies) that go beyond the ordinary current events news. This journal is recommended for academic art libraries, museums, and other special collections.

811. *R A C A R.* [ISSN: 0315-9906] 1974. s-a. CND 20; CND 30 foreign. Societe pour Promouvoir la Publication en Histoire de l'Art au Canada, Quebec, PQ , Canada. Illus. Circ: 900. Vol. ends: No. 2. *Indexed:* ABM, AIAP, AmH&L, ArtHuCI, ArtInd, BHA, CBCARef, CPerI. *Bk. rev.:* 6, essay length. *Aud.:* Ac.

RACAR is published by the Universities Art Association of Canada with the assistance of the Social Sciences and Humanities Research Council of Canada, and it is the leading Canadian art journal. A major drawback is the delay in the publication cycle, which has led to issues published in 2002 to be dated as 1999, volume 26. That said, the nine peer-reviewed articles feature lengthy treatments of Western art history illustrated with black-and-white photos, written in either French or English. The latest issues focus on art of nineteenth- and twentieth-century Europe. Appropriate for academic research collections.

812. *Revue de l'Art.* [ISSN: 0035-1326] 1968. q. EUR 69 domestic; FRF 81 foreign. Ed(s): Michel Laclotteh. Presses Universitaires de France, Departement des Revues, 6 av. Reille, Paris, 75685 Cedex 14, France; revues@puf.com. Illus. *Indexed:* A&ATA, AIAP, ArtHuCI, ArtInd, BHA, IBZ. *Bk. rev.:* 4-5, essay length. *Aud.:* Ac.

Emphasizing French art of the Neoclassic through Impressionist eras, this journal provides international scholarship. Abstracts occasionally summarize the contents of the French-language articles in English and German. Each issue includes book reviews, biographical essays, a calendar of museum exhibitions, and critical bibliographies. Appropriate for research collections in academic libraries with art history programs.

813. *Sculpture.* Former titles (until Jan. 1987): *International Sculpture;* (until Apr. 1985): *Sculptors International;* (until 1981): *International Sculpture Center Bulletin; National Sculpture Center Bulletin.* [ISSN: 0889-728X] 1982. 10x/yr. USD 50 in North America; USD 70 elsewhere. Ed(s): Glenn Harper. International Sculpture Center, 1529 18th St NW, Washington, DC 20036; jeff@sculpture.org; http://www.sculpture.org/. Illus., adv. Circ: 22000. Vol. ends: Dec. *Indexed:* ABM, AIAP, ArtInd, BHA. *Bk. rev.:* 10-12, 150 words. *Aud.:* Ga, Ac, Sa.

Published by the International Sculpture Center, this is the only international publication of its kind devoted exclusively to all forms of contemporary sculpture. Richly illustrated with full-color photography, the feature articles fill a gap by covering three-dimensional artwork exclusively. Filled with gallery ads, news briefs, exhibitions, interviews with sculptors, a column devoted to commissions (a major source of revenue), and reviews of installations, this a useful title to artists, collectors, and scholars. It is recommended to all academic libraries with significant art programs, and to larger public libraries for those interested in contemporary sculpture.

814. *Studies in the Decorative Arts.* [ISSN: 1069-8825] 1993. s-a. USD 30 domestic; USD 35 in Canada & Mexico; USD 37 elsewhere. Ed(s): Sarah B Sherrill. Bard Graduate Center for Studies in the Decorative Arts, 18 W 86th St, New York, NY 10024. Illus. Refereed. Circ: 1000 Paid. *Indexed:* ABM, AIAP, AmH&L, ArtInd, BHA, BRI, CBRI, DAAI. *Bk. rev.:* Number varies, essay length. *Aud.:* Ga, Ac.

According to its mission, *Studies in the Decorative Arts* emphasizes analytical and interpretative scholarly research of the decorative arts regardless of media, culture, era, or geographic location; however, recent issues have a decided preference for western European and American objects from the nineteenth and twentieth centuries. Focusing on the decorative arts as documents of material culture and placing them within their social and political contexts, the four to six peer-reviewed articles are sparsely illustrated with black-and-white photographs and focus on such diverse topics as Alvar Aalto's Paris Pavilion, Soviet Metro stations of the Stalin era, Art Nouveau lace, and Henry VIII's tapestries. Each issue includes signed reviews of important new books, exhibitions, and discussions of developments in conservation and restoration. It is recommended for larger public libraries and college and university libraries.

Umbrella. See Zines section.

815. *WittyWorld: international cartoon bulletin.* [ISSN: 0892-9807] 1987. 11x/yr. USD 56; USD 64 foreign. Ed(s): Joseph George Szabo. WittyWorld Publications, 214 School St, North Wales, PA 19454. Illus., adv. Circ: 5000. *Bk. rev.:* 5, 200 words. *Aud.:* Ga, Ac, Sa.

WittyWorld presents the creative wit and talent of international cartoonists and publishes political cartoons, comic strips, animation, and caricatures as well as articles about this art form. Regular features important to the practitioner include competitions announcements; reviews of comics, cartoons, animation, and journals; and interviews with famous cartoonists. The web site, www.wittyworld.com, is loaded with editorial/political cartoons, comics, caricatures, satire, animation, gag cartoons, humorous illustrations, and photo illustrations. Very useful for professional cartoonists, academicians, students, and collectors, as well as those in the fields of graphics, advertising, illustration, animation, and commercial arts, *WittyWorld* and especially the web site are highly recommended. Appropriate for public, academic, and special libraries.

Woman's Art Journal. See Women: Feminist and Special Interest/ Literary and Artistic section.

816. ***Word & Image: a journal of verbal/visual enquiry.*** [ISSN: 0266-6286] 1985. q. GBP 293 (Individuals, GBP 145). Ed(s): John Dixon Hunt. Taylor & Francis Ltd, 11 New Fetter Ln, London, EC4P 4EE, United Kingdom; info@tandf.co.uk; http://www.tandf.co.uk/journals. Illus., adv. Refereed. Circ: 750. Vol. ends: Dec. Online: EBSCO Publishing. Reprint: PSC. *Indexed:* ABM, ArtHuCI, ArtInd, BEL&L, BHA, L&LBA, MLA-IB. *Bk. rev.:* Number varies, 1 page. *Aud.:* Ac, Sa.
Word and Image is an interdisciplinary journal featuring the intersection of the printed word and visual imagery regardless of media and important to literary critics, art historians, linguisticians, social historians, philosophers, and psychologists alike. Scholarly articles examine the many complicated relationships between words and images, representing scholarship that is frequently developed from symposia. Infrequently, issues revolve around a central theme with guest editors invited to participate, but the majority cover a variety of subject matter. Articles are primarily in English, but French and German occasionally appear. Strictly a scholar's resource, it is recommended for all academic libraries, and universities that support programs in literature, art history, and communications will find this journal indispensable.

817. ***Zeitschrift fuer Kunstgeschichte.*** [ISSN: 0044-2992] 1932. 4x/yr. EUR 92. Ed(s): Andreas Beyer, Andreas Toennesmann. Deutscher Kunstverlag GmbH, Nymphenburger Str 84, Munich, 80636, Germany. Illus., index. Circ: 900. Vol. ends: No. 4. Reprint: PSC. *Indexed:* AIAP, AmH&L, ArtHuCI, ArtInd, BHA, IBZ, NTA. *Bk. rev.:* 3-4, lengthy. *Aud.:* Ac.
This German publication has been a standard in the field of art history since the 1930s. Black-and-white and some color photography illustrate the five or six peer-reviewed articles representing international research in the history of Western art. Published in German, English, French, or Italian, the research focuses on traditional painting and sculpture in Western art from the ancient Greeks through twentieth-century European artists. Lengthy book reviews provide extensive treatment of three or four books in each issue. Appropriate for all academic libraries, but especially for those with art history programs of study.

Museum Publications

818. ***Archives of American Art Journal.*** Formerly: *Archives Quarterly Bulletin.* [ISSN: 0003-9853] 1960. q. USD 35; USD 10 newsstand/cover per issue. Ed(s): Darcy Tell. Smithsonian Institution, Archives of American Art, Washington, DC 20560-0937; telld@aaa.si.edu; http://www.si.edu/autoarchives. Illus. Circ: 1700. *Indexed:* ABM, AIAP, AmH&L, ArtHuCI, ArtInd, BHA, IBZ. *Bk. rev.:* Number and length vary. *Aud.:* Ac, Sa.
This journal publishes research about the permanent collections of the Archives of American Art. Housed in the Smithsonian Institution, the Archives of American Art provide researchers with access to the largest collection of documents on the history of the visual arts in the United States. Three or four articles in each issue feature papers of artists, collectors, art historians, and other art world figures, and records of dealers, museums, and other institutions. Book reviews and regional reports covering new acquisitions to the archives round out this important resource of historical documentation. Highly recommended for research collections.

819. ***Art Institute of Chicago. Museum Studies.*** [ISSN: 0069-3235] 1966. s-a. USD 40 (Individuals, USD 25; Members, USD 20). Ed(s): Susan F Rossen, Gregory Nosan. Art Institute of Chicago, 111 S Michigan Ave, Chicago, IL 60603; pubsmus@artic.edu; http://www.artic.edu/aic/books. Illus., index. Circ: 1500 Paid. Vol. ends: No. 2. *Indexed:* AIAP, AmH&L, ArtHuCI, ArtInd, BHA. *Aud.:* Ac, Sa.
Museum Studies is published semi-annually, and more often that not is monothematic, covering such diverse subjects as European decorative arts, German art in the nineteenth and twentieth centuries, and American art during the Civil War. Anywhere from three to six articles, lavishly illustrated in color and black and white, feature the permanent collection and history of the Art Institute of Chicago. Contributors, who present recent scholarship, include museum curators, art historians, and lecturers from around the world, in addition to museum personnel. Recommended for all museum collections and academic libraries.

Clarion. See *Folk Art.*

820. ***Folk Art: magazine of the American Folk Art Museum.*** Formerly (until 1992): *Clarion.* [ISSN: 1067-3067] 1971. q. USD 6 newsstand/cover. Ed(s): Rosemary Gabriel. American Folk Art Museum, 1414 Ave. of the Americas, New York, NY 10019-2514; info@folkartmuseum.org; http://www.folkartmuseum.org. Illus., index, adv. Circ: 10000. Vol. ends: No. 4. *Indexed:* ABCT, ArtInd, BHA. *Bk. rev.:* 1-2, 300-500 words. *Aud.:* Hs, Ga, Ac, Sa.
Folk Art is the magazine of the American Folk Art Museum in New York, which is devoted to traditional and contemporary American folk art and self-taught art. Articles, essays, and reviews treat subjects such as ceramics, pottery, textiles, quilts, furniture, sculpture, painting, and prints. Regular departments briefly treat traveling exhibitions, museum shows, American antique shows, outsider art, seasonal programs, books, and museum news. There are a variety of contributors including scholars, curators, freelance writers, and collectors. It is recommended for academic, museum, and public libraries.

821. ***International Review of African American Art: an international publication.*** Formerly: *Black Art.* [ISSN: 1045-0920] 1976. q. USD 36. Ed(s): Juliette Bowles. International Review of African American Art, University Museum, Hampton University, Hampton, VA 23668-0101; jbowles@hamptona.edu. Illus., adv. Refereed. Circ: 5000. Vol. ends: No. 4. *Indexed:* ABM, AIAP, AmHI, ArtHuCI, ArtInd, BHA, IIBP. *Bk. rev.:* Number and length vary. *Aud.:* Hs, Ga, Ac, Sa.
This monthly magazine published by the Hampton University Museum features interviews, biographical essays, and articles about visual and performing artists of African American heritage. While stating that it is "international," *IRAAA* primarily covers African American artists in the United States and occasionally Caribbean and South American artists as well. This full-color, well-illustrated journal frequently chooses one aspect of African American art for the subject of an issue. It includes a handful of book or exhibition reviews and noteworthy news on rising artists or new acquisitions. Cultural history and social themes related to the experience of the African American artist make this of interest to anyone conducting research in African American culture or American Studies. It is recommended for all academic and large public libraries.

822. ***Metropolitan Museum Journal.*** [ISSN: 0077-8958] 1968. a. USD 70. Ed(s): Barbara Burn. Metropolitan Museum of Art, 1000 Fifth Ave, New York, NY 10028; http://www.press.uchicago.edu/. Illus. Refereed. *Indexed:* AIAP, ArtHuCI, ArtInd, BAS, BHA. *Aud.:* Ac, Sa.
This journal publishes new scholarly research that examines works of art in the permanent collection of the Metropolitan Museum of Art and related matters. Articles investigate the cultural context of these art objects and cover archival research and technical analyses. Contributors are usually specialists, researchers, or museum staff. Because the Metropolitan Museum is one of the premier museums in the United States, this publication is highly recommended for all research collections in academic, museum, and special libraries.

823. ***Metropolitan Museum of Art Bulletin.*** [ISSN: 0026-1521] 1905. q. USD 25. Ed(s): Joan Holt. Metropolitan Museum of Art, 1000 Fifth Ave, New York, NY 10028. Illus., index. Sample. Circ: 112000. Vol. ends: No. 4. *Indexed:* A&ATA, ABM, AIAP, ArtHuCI, ArtInd, BAS, BHA, NumL, RILM. *Aud.:* Ga, Ac, Sa.
One of the two Metropolitan Museum of Art publications, the *Bulletin* focuses on one artist, theme, historical period, or item from the permanent collection in one lengthy article. Most contributions are written by museum personnel, but occasionally outside scholars may compose an article. Recent acquisitions are noted in the fall issue. The primary audience for this publication is museum members and art historians, but it is highly recommended for all academic libraries.

824. ***La Revue du Louvre et des Musees de France.*** [ISSN: 0035-2608] 1951. bi-m. FRF 450; FRF 550 foreign. Ed(s): Jean Pierre Cuzin, Danielle Gaborit Chopin. Editions de la Reunion des Musees Nationaux, Centre de Distribution des Musees Nationaux, 1-31 allee du 12-Fevrier-1934, Noisei, 77186, France. Illus., adv. Refereed. Circ: 5500. *Indexed:* A&ATA, AIAP, ArtHuCI, ArtInd, BAS, BHA, IBZ. *Aud.:* Ac, Sa.

This beautiful publication with lavish illustrations provides coverage of the special collections and works of art in the Louvre. It also includes scholarly articles on the collections of other national art museums in France. Information on new acquisitions, temporary exhibitions, and restoration work is regularly featured. Exhibition reviews, subject bibliographies, and calendars of events are also included. Recommended for all academic and museum libraries.

825. ***Studies in Modern Art.*** [ISSN: 1058-997X] 1991. a. USD 25. Ed(s): John Elderfield. Museum of Modern Art, 11 W 53rd St, New York, NY 10019. Illus. *Indexed:* ArtInd, BHA. *Aud.:* Ga, Ac, Sa.

Issued by the Museum of Modern Art in New York, *Studies in Modern Art* might be more appropriately catagorized as a monograph published serially. It showcases important collections, important works of art, and special programs at the museum. The journal maintains high standards of scholarship and makes a significant contribution to the serious study of contemporary art. Issues are frequently monothematic. Appropriate for academic, museum, and large public libraries.

826. ***Studies in the History of Art.*** Formerly: *Report and Studies in the History of Art.* [ISSN: 0091-7338] 1971. irreg. National Gallery of Art, Constitution Ave, N W, between Third & Ninth Sts, Washington, DC 20565. Illus. Circ: 6000. *Indexed:* AIAP, ArtHuCI, ArtInd, BHA. *Aud.:* Ga, Ac, Sa.

Designed to document scholarly symposia, this series-as-book is sponsored in part by the National Gallery of Art's Center for Advanced Study of the Visual Arts. Each monothematic volume presents a dozen or so research papers from a single symposium that foster study of the history, theory, and criticism of art, architecture, and urbanism. Recent topics cover Renaissance bronzes, paintings of Hans Holbein, and Olmec art and archaeology. An important resource for research art collections in all institutions.

827. ***Winterthur Portfolio: a journal of American material culture.*** Incorporates: *Winterthur Conference Report.* [ISSN: 0084-0416] 1964. 3x/yr. USD 147 print & online eds. (Individuals, USD 36 print & online eds.; Students, USD 28 print & online eds.). Ed(s): Lisa L Lock. University of Chicago Press, Journals Division, PO Box 37005, Chicago, IL 60637; subscriptions@press.uchicago.edu; http://www.journals.uchicago.edu. Illus., adv. Refereed. Circ: 1000 Paid. Reprint: ISI; PQC; PSC. *Indexed:* ABCT, ABM, AIAP, API, AmH&L, ArtHuCI, ArtInd, BHA, IBZ, MLA-IB, RI-1, SSCI. *Aud.:* Ac.

Winterthur Portfolio provides an outlet for scholarship at the confluence of the visual arts and material culture. Interdisciplinary in nature, *WP*'s scope is presenting American art within the historical culture in which it was created. Unfortunately, this journal is currently published at a one-year lag. The articles are sparsely illustrated with black-and-white photos and give in-depth treatment to subjects as diverse as titillating Rococo paintings collected in Victorian New York to the domestic architecture of slavery. Appropriate for academic research libraries.

Electronic Journals

828. ***ArtNet Magazine.*** 1996. d. Free. Ed(s): Walter Robinson. ArtNet Worldwide Inc., 61 Broadway 23 Fl, New York, NY 10006-2701; artnet@artnet.com. Illus. *Bk. rev.:* Number and length vary. *Aud.:* Ga, Ac, Sa.

This web zine, which is part of artnet.com, an online resource for researching, buying, and selling fine art, can be viewed as a selling tool aimed at buyers and dealers. That said, it is useful to the artist and layperson because it includes a wide variety of information about the visual arts: color images of artworks, book reviews, exhibition reviews, and other news of the art world. Artists, art dealers, critics, and curators plus a handful of staff writers post frequent articles, dated accordingly. Heavily geared toward New York City, *ArtNet* coverage also focuses on the U.S. art world and mentions international artists and shows.

■ ASIA AND THE PACIFIC

General/Australia and the Pacific/East Asia/Inner Asia/South Asia/Southeast Asia/Online Newspapers

See also China; and CIS and Eastern Europe sections.

Christina M. Desai, Science Librarian, Morris Library, Southern Illinois University, Carbondale IL 62901-6632; cdesai@lib.siu.edu; FAX: 618-453-2704.

Introduction

Globalization both promises and threatens to lessen the economic and cultural differences among peoples of the world. Technology, increased travel, and migration bring us into closer contact, while divisive political forces magnify our differences. Given all these forces for change, the need to know more about Asia is more urgent than ever. The periodical selections below, because of their distant origins and often highly specialized content, are not likely to be found outside of libraries. It is therefore all the more critical that libraries continue to offer a range of periodicals representing the continent that is home to three-fifths of the world's population.

The types and varieties of periodicals available in and about Asia are almost as varied as the continent itself. This chapter of necessity focuses on those available in the United States and written in English, although some also include content in other European languages. The selections range from magazines about arts and culture to newsletters of displaced groups to scholarly journals on abstruse academic fields. Many resemble American popular magazines and academic journals. Most can be classed in one of four types. The first would be newspapers and news weeklies, including business news publications, very similar to *Newsweek* or *Business Week* both in content and format. Newspapers from almost every country are available online, offering much free content and color. A second type is the cultural magazine, often lavishly illustrated, presenting the artistic and cultural side of the country or continent, for connoisseurs or outsiders interested in an introduction. Thirdly, scholarly journals on the languages, histories, and antiquities of Asia also abound, many produced by scholarly societies in the United States or Europe, many others indigenously. Finally are the academic journals devoted to the contemporary scene. These include journals on the politics, international relations, environment, economy, and development of Asian and Pacific nations. They also analyze social and cultural trends, gender, artistic expression, and such matters as identity formation and the legacies of colonialism. Like their popular counterparts, these academic publications are increasingly available online. All four types offer information and perspectives not commonly found in American publications.

A good source for further investigation is the Asian Studies WWW Virtual Library, http://coombs.anu.edu.au/WWWVL-AsianStudies.html, the Association for Asian Studies, http://www.aasianst.org/, and the web sites of Asian Studies departments at major universities.

China is considered in a separate chapter, and Asian science journals are included with their appropriate disciplines.

Basic Periodicals

GENERAL. Hs: *Education about Asia.* Ga: *Arts of Asia, Education about Asia, Far Eastern Economic Review.* Ac: *Journal of Asian Studies, Modern Asian Studies.*

AUSTRALIA AND THE PACIFIC. Ga: *AQ, Nature Australia.* Ac: *Contemporary Pacific, Journal of Pacific History.*

EAST ASIA. Hs: *East.* Ga: *East, Japan Echo.* Ac: *Journal of Japanese Studies, Korean Studies.*

INNER ASIA. Ga: *Mongol Survey.* Ac: *Central Asian Survey.*

SOUTH ASIA. Hs: *India Perspectives.* Ga: *Economic and Political Weekly, Pakistan and Gulf Economist.* Ac: *Contributions to Indian Sociology, Indian Economic and Social History Review.*

SOUTHEAST ASIA. Ga: *Inside Indonesia.* Ac: *Journal of Southeast Asian Studies, Southeast Asian Affairs, Bulletin of Indonesian Economic Studies.*

Basic Abstracts and Indexes

Bibliography of Asian Studies, PAIS, Ingenta.

General

829. ***Acta Asiatica.*** [ISSN: 0567-7254] 1961. s-a. JPY 8400. Toho Gakkai, 4-1 Nishi-Kanda 2-chome, Chiyoda-ku, Tokyo, 101-0065, Japan; tohogakkai@mc.nextlink.ne.jp. Circ: 1000. *Indexed:* AnthLit, BAS, IBSS, MLA-IB. *Aud.:* Ac.

The Institute of Eastern Culture was founded to advance the study of China in Japan, but has since expanded its focus to include all of Asia, and all topics, including history, law, economics, ethnology, folklore, philosophy, thought, religion, literature, linguistics, art, archaeology, etc. This Japanese academic journal publishes research in English about any Asian country, but most frequently about Japan, by Japanese scholars. Each issue has a single theme, with an introduction and four or five articles. Some articles assess research trends in various area studies. The latest issue, for example, surveys the current state of research on traditional Japanese narrative tales. Other recent themes are "New Approaches to the History of Chinese Fiction" and "New Directions in the Study of Sung History." An earlier issue covers trends in the study of Mongolia, Tibet, and Vietnam. Illustrations, photographs, and original script amplify the text. Recommended for academic libraries serving Asian Studies departments.

830. ***African and Asian Studies.*** Supersedes in part: *Journal of Asian and African Studies.* [ISSN: 1569-2094] 2002. q. EUR 179 print & online subscription (Individuals, EUR 88 print & online subscription). Ed(s): Tukumbi Lumumba-Kasongo. Brill Academic Publishers, Inc., PO Box 9000, Leiden, 2300 PA, Netherlands; cs@brill.nl; http://www.brill.nl. Refereed. Microform: SWZ. Online: EBSCO Publishing; Gale Group; Ingenta Select; OCLC Online Computer Library Center, Inc. Reprint: SWZ. *Indexed:* ABCPolSci, AICP, AbAn, AmH&L, AnthLit, BAS, GeogAbPG, IBSS, IBZ, IIBP, IPSA, PRA, PSA, RI-1, SSCI, SSI, SociolAb, WAE&RSA. *Bk. rev.:* Various number and length. *Aud.:* Ac.

This new, refereed academic journal continues, in part, the well-established *Journal of Asian and African studies* and is similar to it. It publishes original research in anthropology, sociology, history, culture, and political science. The emphasis so far has been on contemporary affairs. The first special issue explores "Media, Identity, and the Public Sphere in Post-Apartheid South Africa." Other issues address topics such as obstacles to democracy in Cameroon, reasons for Asian success in business in East Africa, the roots of dowry harassment and deaths in India, and the applicability of various models of political mobilization to ethnic protest in the Middle East and Central Asia. Abstracts and author notes are included for each article. Book reviews are also included. Recommended for academic libraries.

831. ***American Oriental Society. Journal.*** [ISSN: 0003-0279] 1842. q. USD 90 domestic; USD 100 foreign. Ed(s): Edwin Gerow. American Oriental Society, Harlan Hatcher Graduate Library, University of Michigan, Ann Arbor, MI 48109-1205; http://www.umich.edu/vaos/. Illus., index, adv. Sample. Refereed. Circ: 2300. Vol. ends: Dec. Microform: IDC; PMC; PQC. Online: bigchalk; EBSCO Publishing; Florida Center for Library Automation; Gale Group; JSTOR (Web-based Journal Archive); OCLC Online Computer Library Center, Inc.; ProQuest Information & Learning; H.W. Wilson. Reprint: PQC. *Indexed:* ABS&EES, AIAP, AbAn, ArtHuCI, BAS, HumInd, IBSS, IBZ, IPB, L&LBA, LRI, MLA-IB, NTA, NumL, OTA, R&TA, RI-1, SSCI. *Bk. rev.:* 50-75, 250-3,000 words. *Aud.:* Ac, Sa.

This refereed scholarly journal, published since 1843, covers the language, literature, culture, and history of the Near East, North Africa, South and Southeast Asia, Inner Asia, the Far East, and the Islamic world. A listing of the scripts used in the journal reveals something of its slant: Greek and Hebrew scripts are reproduced as well as Chinese, Japanese, Cyrillic, and Arabic; Indian scripts are not. Articles may be about any time period, but most deal with ancient times. Originally devoted to the study of Asian languages and literatures, the society has broadened to include "intellectual and imaginative aspects of Oriental civilizations, especially of philosophy, religion, folklore and art." The emphasis is on close textual analysis of manuscripts to clarify linguistic, literary, or historical issues. A recent issue is devoted to Indic and Iranian Studies and recent articles include one on the date when Jesus died and a review article on Mandarin phonological structure. Maps and other illustrations enhance the text. Short abstracts precede the articles, which form only about a third of each issue. The remainder is given to review articles and book reviews, roughly 25 per issue. Recommended for academic libraries in universities with programs in Asian or Middle Eastern literature, history, or civilizations. Tables of contents from 1996 are available online at http://www.umich.edu/~aos/.

Archives of Asian Art. See Art/General section.

832. ***Ars Orientalis: the arts of Asia, Southeast Asia and Islam.*** Supersedes: *Ars Islamica.* [ISSN: 0571-1371] 1954. a. USD 40. Ed(s): Margaret A Lourie. Department of History of Art, Tappan Hall, University of Michigan, Ann Arbor, MI 48109-1357; http://www-personal.umich.edu/~plourie. Illus. Refereed. Circ: 500. Online: OCLC Online Computer Library Center, Inc.; H.W. Wilson. *Indexed:* AIAP, ArtInd, BAS. *Bk. rev.:* Various number and length. *Aud.:* Ac.

Though similar in appearance to *Archives of Asian Art*, this annual scholarly journal is broader in geographic and intellectual scope. It encompasses the "art and archaeology of Asia, including the ancient Near East and the Islamic world." The journal also encompasses architecture, and research in literature, philosophy, religion, and social sciences as they relate to the arts. For example, a recent article explores tomb architecture in the Punjab, tracing regional influences. Another analyzes creativity and talent vs. training in the management of a seventeenth-century Japanese painters' workshop, and another disputes the Buddhist origins of Chinese Daoist art. Articles include abstracts and are illustrated with excellent black-and-white photographs. Thematic issues occasionally appear. The journal also publishes book reviews and review articles. Table of contents and abstracts for the current issue are available on the journal's web site at http://www-personal.umich.edu/~plourie. Highly recommended for research libraries with an interest in art, archeology, history, Asian or Middle Eastern Studies.

833. ***Artibus Asiae: journal of Asian art and archaeology for scholars and connoisseurs.*** [ISSN: 0004-3648] 1925. s-a. CHF 160; USD 105. Ed(s): Francoise Louis, Anne McGannon. Museum Rietberg Zurich, Gablerstr 15, Zuerich, 8002, Switzerland; artibus.asiae@rietb.stzh.ch; http://www.rietberg.ch. Illus., index. Sample. Refereed. Reprint: SCH. *Indexed:* ABCT, AIAP, ArtHuCI, ArtInd, BAS, IBSS, IBZ. *Bk. rev.:* 2-5, up to 1,500 words. *Aud.:* Ac, Sa.

This refereed academic art journal presents studies of "previously unpublished art objects and documents, recent discoveries, new studies of other materials, book reviews" and is meant for art connoisseurs, libraries, museums, Asian Studies centers. Published by the Museum Rietberg Zurich and the Arthur M. Sackler Gallery of the Smithsonian and edited by a distinguished international board, each hefty volume combines fine scholarly articles with lovely presentation and high-quality drawings and black-and-white photographs. The authors expansively discuss newly unearthed art works and reinterpret well-known works. Emphasis is on art of ancient times. There are no abstracts, but most findings are summarized in a conclusion. Articles may contain original script and/or a glossary. Some articles are also published separately as supplements. The journal also contains book reviews and minimal advertising. An essential publication, especially for scholars of Chinese, Japanese, and Indian art. Also of interest to anthropologists, archaeologists, and historians specializing in Asia.

834. *Arts of Asia.* [ISSN: 0004-4083] 1970. bi-m. HKD 520 domestic; HKD 650 foreign; USD 85 foreign. Ed(s): Robin Markbreiter, Stephen Markbreiter. Arts of Asia Publications Ltd., 1309 Kowloon Centre, 29-39 Ashley Rd, Tsimshatsui, Hong Kong; info@artsofasianet.com; http://www.artsofasianet.com. Illus., index, adv. Sample. Circ: 18000. *Indexed:* A&ATA, ABCT, ABM, AIAP, ArtHuCI, ArtInd, BAS. *Bk. rev.:* 2-3, 750-1,000 words. *Aud.:* Ga, Ac, Sa.

This lavishly illustrated art magazine is an excellent source of information and illustration on every aspect of Asian art. The fine quality of the illustrations does justice to the artworks in the articles and even the ads. Well-researched, often commissioned articles delve into the history, techniques, and value of art objects and artistic periods, discuss archeological findings, and evaluate art at exhibitions and auctions. Authors are academic experts and curators of major museums. Special issues are sometimes devoted to a particular topic, museum, or region. Two recent thematic issues explore the new Asian Art Museum in San Francisco and Asian textiles in the Victoria and Albert Museum. A typical recent article addresses the history and value of Burmese kalagas, embroidered or appliqued textile pieces. Though published in Hong Kong, American and British collections are well represented. The magazine's web site, at http://www.artsofasianet.com/frameset.htm, is also a fine resource, including full-text editorials, a search feature for back issues, and links to major exhibitions, auctions, art book stores, galleries, and other Internet sources on Asian art searchable by country. A valuable reference source for scholars, students, collectors, dealers, and the general public, and highly recommended for all types of libraries.

835. *Asia Pacific Viewpoint: specialises in the study of development, change and underdevelopment.* Formerly (until 1996): *Pacific Viewpoint.* [ISSN: 1360-7456] 1960. 3x/yr. GBP 60 print & online eds. Blackwell Publishing Asia, 550 Swanston St, Carlton South, VIC 3053, Australia; subs@blackwellpublishingasia.com; http://www.blackwellpublishing.com/. Illus., adv. Refereed. Circ: 850. Microform: PQC. Online: EBSCO Publishing; ingenta.com; OCLC Online Computer Library Center, Inc.; RoweCom Information Quest; Swets Blackwell. Reprint: PSC. *Indexed:* AmH&L, AnthLit, BAS, GeogAbPG, IBSS, IBZ, IPSA, PAIS, PSA, SWA, SociolAb. *Bk. rev.:* 1-2 pages. *Aud.:* Ac.

This refereed multidisciplinary journal covers the Pacific region as well as East and Southeast Asia. The focus is on geography and related fields, especially economic and social growth and development and its effects on migration, demographics, gender issues, the environment, politics, and policy. It also considers such issues as globalization, urbanization, and the economic and political relationships among countries of the region. The emphasis is on contemporary affairs. Articles are of high quality and may be theoretical or research based. They include abstracts. Examples of recent topics are poverty and social adjustment problems of black refugees in New Zealand, adjustment of Filipina immigrants to rural Ohio, strategies for increasing sustainability of NGOs in the Pacific, and factors affecting upward mobility in Tonga. Special issues appear regularly, including an issue on environmental conflict and management and one on postcolonial transformations in Oceania. The journal includes maps, charts, illustrations, book reviews, and a year-end index. It is recommended for academic libraries with an interest in geography, Asian or Pacific Studies, economic development, or international affairs.

836. *AsiaMoney.* Former titles: *Asia Money and Finance;* (until Nov. 1991): *Asiamoney;* Which incorporated: *Billion and Asian Finance.* 1989. 10x/yr. HKD 3250 combined subscription domestic print & online eds.; USD 415 combined subscription foreign print & online eds. Asia Law & Practice Ltd., 5/F Printing House, 6 Duddell St, Central Hong Kong, Hong Kong. Illus., adv. Sample. Circ: 25000. Vol. ends: Dec/Jan. *Indexed:* ABIn, BPI. *Aud.:* Ga, Sa.

This aptly named financial monthly focuses exclusively on investment, management, and economic news and analysis. Read by "companies, bankers, brokers, investors, regulators and policy-makers," it covers the fast-developing Asian countries of Australia, China and Hong Kong, India, Indonesia, Japan, Korea, Malaysia, Philippines, Singapore, Taiwan, Thailand, and Vietnam. Articles are packed with facts and figures, offering detailed information on industries and specific companies as well as articles on regional trends. It is well designed and illustrated, with numerous tables, charts, and graphs, often in color. It also contains interviews, company and people profiles, an annual listing of the Asian "Big 500," and regular features such as "Deal Digest." Based in Hong Kong, the publication employs a network of correspondents throughout the region. It conducts surveys regularly, for example, of which countries offer the best return on assets, or which hotels, airlines, and airports are preferred by business travelers. A recent cover story described the financing for the Three Gorges project. Other recent topics include speculation on Hong Kong's new regulatory structure, second thoughts about privatization in Australia, and analysis of the link between democracy and economic progress. Many articles discuss changes in public policies and their effects on economic development. Supplements explore a specific topic or industry. The web site at http://www.asiamoney.com offers free access to its archives, including graphics, for all but the two most recent issues, as well as helpful features such as the "events diary" with links to relevant conferences. An excellent publication for any business library, academic or public.

837. *Asian Affairs.* Formerly: *Royal Central Asian Society. Journal.* [ISSN: 0306-8374] 1903. 3x/yr. GBP 44; USD 73. Ed(s): Michael Sheringham. Routledge, 11 New Fetter Ln, London, EC4P 4EE, United Kingdom; info@routledge.co.uk; http://www.routledge.com. Illus., index, adv. Sample. Circ: 1600 Paid. Vol. ends: Oct. Reprint: PSC. *Indexed:* AmH&L, BAS, CJA, IBZ, IPSA, PAIS, RI-1, SSI. *Bk. rev.:* 40-50, 250-1,000 words. *Aud.:* Ac, Ga.

Published under several titles since 1903, this journal records the activities of the Royal Society for Asian Affairs and publishes society lectures. It accepts other papers, often by academic experts, but is not peer reviewed. Articles cover a broader range of public-affairs topics than its American counterpart (above in this section), including broad analytical as well as narrowly focused descriptive and biographical pieces. They are frequently written from a British perspective: for example, a recent history of the first English school in Tibet and its headmaster, and an account of the experience of a British army intelligence officer in Persia at the turn of the century. More theoretical pieces include an article on Manchuria's importance to China's dynastic history; overview articles are also common, such as a "score card" on India's current state of economic development. Articles include brief biographical sketches of the authors. The journal is enlivened with photographs and maps. Book reviews form a substantial part of each issue. A valuable source of historical or overview material for the scholar or interested layperson.

838. *Asian Affairs: An American Review.* Formerly: *Southeast Asian Perspectives.* [ISSN: 0092-7678] 1973. q. USD 104 (Individuals, USD 52; USD 26 per issue). Ed(s): Jannette Whippy. Heldref Publications, 1319 18th St, NW, Washington, DC 20036-1802; subscribe@heldref.org; http://www.heldref.org. Illus., index, adv. Sample. Refereed. Circ: 337 Paid. Vol. ends: Spring. CD-ROM: ProQuest Information & Learning. Online: bigchalk; Chadwyck-Healey Incorporated; EBSCO Publishing; Florida Center for Library Automation; Gale Group; Northern Light Technology, Inc.; OCLC Online Computer Library Center, Inc.; ProQuest Information & Learning; H.W. Wilson. Reprint: PSC. *Indexed:* ABCPolSci, ABS&EES, BAS, IBZ, IPSA, PAIS, PSA, SociolAb. *Bk. rev.:* 3-10, 250-2,500 words. *Aud.:* Ga, Ac.

Published by the Helen Dwight Reid Education Foundation, this journal (not to be confused with the older *Asian Affairs: Journal of the Royal Society for Asian Affairs*) addresses "developments in politics, economics, security, and international relations, especially between Asian nations and the United States." Its intended audience is scholars, educators, policymakers, government officials, and business executives. It is peer reviewed and includes thought-provoking articles with a focus on public policy, political culture and economy, and international affairs, and book reviews. Recent issues feature articles on China's membership in the WTO and its impact on the region; an evaluation of current consensus on sustainability issues; and analysis of Japan's recent structural reforms. A volume-end index is organized by country and by author, and includes the book reviews. The web site at http://www.heldref.org/html/body_aa.html offers a searchable archive with access to abstracts from all issues. Purchase of individual electronic articles is very inexpensive; a monthly pass buys ten articles. Recommended for all academic libraries and larger public libraries.

839. ***Asian Cinema.*** [ISSN: 1059-440X] 1984. s-a. USD 30 (Individuals, USD 20). Asian Cinema Studies Society, c/o John A. Lent, Ed & Pub, 669 Ferne Blvd, Drexel Hill, PA 19026. Adv. Circ: 375. *Indexed:* BAS, FLI, IIFP, MLA-IB. *Bk. rev.:* yes. *Aud.:* Ga, Ac.

This journal is devoted to the scholarly study of all aspects of Asian cinema, including technique, national style, and genre, but the emphasis is on cinema as it reflects societal issues and identity. It also considers cultural and global influences on contemporary film and reactions outside the country of origin. A recent article analyzes women and relationships in Bengali film. Another explores the depiction of South Indians in independent and Hollywood films, especially with regard to race, class, religion, and sexual orientation. Another article discusses South Korea's emerging expressions of feeling on its participation in the Vietnam war by comparing a novel on the subject with its film adaptation. A recent thematic issue focuses on the impact of globalization. The journal also features illustrations, interviews, and book reviews. Each issue includes an impressive bibliography of "Recent Publications on Asian Cinema" grouped by region, country, and topics, such as criticism, history, personnel, and sometimes individual film titles. This journal's high quality and broad geographic scope make it a valuable source for any film studies or Asian Studies program.

Asian Folklore Studies. See Folklore section.

840. ***Asian Journal of Communication.*** [ISSN: 0129-2986] s-a. USD 40. Ed(s): Vijay Menon. Asian Media Information and Communication Centre, Publications Unit, PO Box 360, Jurong Point, 916412, Singapore; amicline@singnet.com.sg; http://www.amic.org.sg. Index. *Indexed:* BAS, CommAb, HRA, PSA, SociolAb. *Bk. rev.:* 3, 3-5 pages. *Aud.:* Ac.

This refereed scholarly journal "aims to facilitate the understanding of the process of communication in the Asia-Pacific region by publishing articles that develop communication theory, report empirical research, and describe advances made in research methodology." It is broader in scope than *Media Asia* (below in this section). A recent thematic issue on communication in Korea includes an article analyzing how use of the media affects cynicism among Korean voters, one on cultural values and Westernization as reflected in Korean magazine ads, and another on how U.S. network coverage of Japan and Korea differs. Other topics include advertising, TV, and the Internet. It also includes abstracts, tables, graphs, research notes, and three- to five-page book reviews. Recommended for academic libraries serving communications or mass-media studies or Asian Studies programs.

841. ***Asian Journal of Public Administration.*** [ISSN: 0259-8272] 1979. s-a. HKD 165 domestic; USD 42 in Asia; USD 47 elsewhere. Hong Kong University, Department of Politics and Public Administration, Pokfulam Rd, Hong Kong; psdhku@hkucc.hku.hk; http://www.hku.hk/ppaweb/index.htm. Circ: 500. *Indexed:* BAS, HRA, IBSS, IPSA, PAIS, PRA, SUSA. *Bk. rev.:* 9-10, 1-2 paragraphs. *Aud.:* Ac.

This peer-reviewed scholarly journal covers "public policy and administration in Asia, as well as in other regions and on more general themes." Recent issues cover the gamut of public-policy issues facing developed and developing countries, including articles such as "Banking on gender: uncovering masculinism in the World Bank's environmental policies," "Evolving strategies for environmental management in Asia: from command-and-control to voluntary compliance," and "Adverting the old age crisis: problems of the privately managed Mandatory Provident Fund Scheme." Comparative articles also appear, such as "Europe's Rhine River Delta and China's Pearl River Delta: Issues and Lessons for Integrated Water Resources Management." The journal also publishes symposia, for example, on the public-private-enterprise mix, and book notes of one or two paragraphs. Each article includes an abstract. The web site includes tables of contents for all issues. Highly recommended for academic libraries serving public affairs, international relations, economics, development, or Asian Studies departments.

842. ***Asian Music: journal of the Society for Asian Music.*** [ISSN: 0044-9202] 1968. s-a. USD 40. Ed(s): Sean Williams, Martin Hatch. Society for Asian Music, Department of Music, Cornell University, Ithaca, NY 14853; mfh2@cornell.edu; http://asianmusic.skidmore.edu. Illus., adv. Refereed. Circ: 600. Vol. ends: Spring/Summer. *Indexed:* AICP, ArtHuCI, BAS, IBSS, IIMP, MLA-IB, MusicInd, RILM. *Bk. rev.:* Various number and length. *Aud.:* Ac.

This refereed scholarly journal publishes in the area of music and the performing arts of Asia and Asians wherever they may be. All types of music are considered, though recent focus has been on contemporary music, including scholarly study of classical, experimental, and popular forms. It analyzes music as an expression of culture, and often treats the ways in which scattered Asian communities transform traditional and classical forms as they negotiate new identities, either in new host countries, or in new urban environments of their home countries. Examples of recent topics include the "hybridization" of Japanese pop in Singapore, Indonesian experimental composition, Nepali folk-pop as a blend of mountain-culture nostalgia and urban Western influences, development of the Balinese modal system, and the Indian-American pop music scene in Chicago. Contributors are musicologists and performers from around the world. Most articles are not highly technical and would be of interest to students of Asian culture as well as music. The journal also contains book reviews, audio and video reviews, and musical notation and illustrations as needed. Highly recommended for academic libraries serving music programs and others serving Asian or Asian American populations.

Asian Perspective. See Political Science/International Relations section.

843. ***Asian Perspectives: the journal of archaeology for Asia and the Pacific.*** [ISSN: 0066-8435] 1957. s-a. USD 50 (Individuals, USD 30). Ed(s): Miriam T. Stark. University of Hawaii Press, Journals Department, 2840 Kolowalu St, Honolulu, HI 96822-1888; uhpjourn@hawaii.edu; http://www.uhpress.hawaii.edu/. Illus., index, adv. Sample. Refereed. Circ: 450. Microform: PQC. Online: bigchalk; EBSCO Publishing; Florida Center for Library Automation; Gale Group; Northern Light Technology, Inc.; OCLC Online Computer Library Center, Inc.; Project MUSE; ProQuest Information & Learning; RoweCom Information Quest; Swets Blackwell; H.W. Wilson. Reprint: ISI; PQC; PSC. *Indexed:* AICP, AbAn, AnthLit, BAS, HumInd, IBSS, IBZ, SSCI. *Bk. rev.:* 0-5, 500-1,500 words. *Aud.:* Ac, Sa.

This scholarly journal presents in-depth articles on topics in prehistory throughout Asia and the Pacific. "In addition to archaeology, it features articles and book reviews on ethnoarchaeology, palaeoanthropology, physical anthropology, and ethnography." Occasional special issues are published on a particular topic or region. Excellent maps, drawings, photographs, charts, tables, and illustrations accompany the text. Although the articles are quite specialized, the writing style is free of jargon. Articles draw on the related fields of ethnology, historical linguistics, and anthropology, and include both Asia and the Pacific. Coverage of the vast region is balanced. Recent articles discuss adaptations of hunter-gatherers in Tamil Nadu, India, and the earlier settlers of Rapa Nui (Easter Island). Book reviews are substantial and balanced. Abstracts are not included in the print edition but are available with full content through Project MUSE. The journal's web site at http://www.uhpress.hawaii.edu/journals/ap/index.html offers tables of contents. An excellent choice for a university library.

844. ***Asian Philosophy: an international journal of Indian, Chinese, Japanese, Buddhist, Persian and Islamic philosophical traditions.*** [ISSN: 0955-2367] 1991. 3x/yr. GBP 342 (Individuals, GBP 96). Ed(s): Indira Mahalingam, Brian Carr. Carfax Publishing Ltd., 4 Park Sq, Milton Park, Abingdon, OX14 4RN, United Kingdom; enquiry@tandf.co.uk; http://www.tandf.co.uk/. Illus., index, adv. Sample. Refereed. Vol. ends: Nov. Online: EBSCO Publishing; Florida Center for Library Automation; Gale Group; Ingenta Select; Northern Light Technology, Inc.; OCLC Online Computer Library Center, Inc.; ProQuest Information & Learning; RoweCom Information Quest; Swets Blackwell. Reprint: PSC. *Indexed:* ArtHuCI, BAS, BrHumI, HumInd, IBZ, PhilInd. *Bk. rev.:* 3-5, 750-2,000 words. *Aud.:* Ac.

This fine scholarly publication discusses the ancient philosophical and religious traditions of India, China, Japan, Korea, and Persia. Articles are readable by educated nonscholars and often relate ancient traditions to modern philosophical or ethical dilemmas. Some compare Eastern and Western philosophical approaches. Recent articles, for example, compare Kant's concepts of self and the world with those of the Kyoto school of Buddhist philosophy and discuss the East Asian cultural-identity crisis stemming from globalization as it relates to Confucian ethics. Some articles apply concepts to practical applications, such as a recent article on how best to understand "Indian culture" and apply it in courses on multiculturalism. Abstracts and book reviews are also included. This title belongs in any academic library serving students of the liberal arts.

845. ***Asian Recorder: weekly record of Asian events with index.*** [ISSN: 0004-4644] 1955. w. USD 185. Ed(s): A K B Menon. Asian Recorder & Publications (Private) Ltd., A-126 Niti Bagh, New Delhi, 110 049, India. Illus. Sample. Circ: 3000. *Aud.:* Ga, Ac.

This publication continues *Asian Recorder* and follows its format. It is a weekly digest providing very brief summaries of the important stories of the week from leading Indian newspapers. It covers Middle Eastern and all Asian countries, excluding Australia and the Pacific. It is arranged alphabetically by country. Each story is followed by its news source and date, thus allowing readers to follow up on the stories in the original publication. A new and very useful feature that is sometimes included following a news item is "Background info," a page reference to an earlier *Digest* story on the same topic. Emphasis is on factual reporting rather than analysis, though the publication also includes selected regional news, world events, science and technology developments, essays, and documents. It can be received as a loose-leaf weekly or paper-bound monthly. The quarterly and yearly indexes make this an excellent reference source for anyone seeking factual information on recent Asian events, from the high school student in a public library to the Asian scholar in an academic institution. Like the news digest, the index is arranged by country, subdivided by topic, and may be further subdivided. The index also has sections on international news, international organizations, regional issues, and documents. The lag time in delivery of each issue is a hindrance, making this publication a prime candidate for an electronic version. Recommended for academic and public libraries serving Asian scholars or patrons.

846. ***Asian Studies Newsletter.*** Formerly (until 1971): *Association for Asian Studies. Newsletter.* [ISSN: 0362-4811] 1955. 5x/yr. USD 25; USD 35 foreign. Association for Asian Studies, Inc., 1021 E Huron St, Ann Arbor, MI 48104; http://www.assianst.org. Illus., adv. Sample. Circ: 8500. Reprint: PQC. *Indexed:* AICP. *Aud.:* Ga, Ac, Sa.

This well-produced newsletter of the Asian Studies Association serves students and faculty interested in Asian Studies. It provides news about upcoming conferences and other association business, conference reports, grants, fellowships, study and academic employment opportunities, and publication and other resource announcements. One issue per year is devoted to the annual conference. Much of this material is also available at the association's web site, http://www.aasianst.org, including the "Viewpoints" section, short essays on the study and teaching of Asian Studies, and public policy regarding Asia. A recent article touted the varied skills and talents of Asian Studies librarians. The print edition also publishes essays on the state of the profession. An essential publication for academic libraries serving Asian Studies departments.

847. ***Asian Survey: a monthly review of contemporary Asian affairs.*** Formerly (until 1961): *Far Eastern Survey; Institute of Pacific Relations. American Council. Memorandum.* [ISSN: 0004-4687] 1961. bi-m. Jan., Mar., May., Jul., Sep. USD 215 print & online eds. USD 36 newsstand/cover. Ed(s): David Frasen, Lowell Dittmer. University of California Press, Journals Division, 2000 Center St, Ste 303, Berkeley, CA 94704-1223; journals@ucop.edu; http://www.ucpress.edu/journals. Illus., index, adv. Sample. Refereed. Circ: 2700 Paid. Vol. ends: Dec. Microform: PQC. Online: EBSCO Publishing; Florida Center for Library Automation; Gale Group; Ingenta Select; JSTOR (Web-based Journal Archive); Northern Light Technology, Inc.; OCLC Online Computer Library Center, Inc. Reprint: PSC. *Indexed:* ABCPolSci, ABS&EES, AbAn, AgeL, BAS, FPA, ForAb, IBSS, IBZ, IPSA, PAIS, PSA, RI-1, RRTA, S&F, SSCI, SSI, SUSA, SociolAb, WAE&RSA. *Aud.:* Ga, Ac, Sa.

This well-established refereed scholarly journal focuses on contemporary issues in the "politics, economics, and foreign relations of Asian countries from the Philippines west to Afghanistan and from China to the South Pacific," often comparatively. Historical background is included when needed to elucidate current situations. It explores such topics as bureaucratic and political mechanisms used in China to suppress the Falungong, ethnic fragmentation in New Guinea and its consequences for building social capital and sustaining democracy, and comparison of economic liberalization in China and India. Occasional issues are devoted to a single topic, for example, violence in Indonesia. Tables and graphs enhance the text. The web site at http://ucpress.edu/journals/as offers tables of contents and full-text pdfs on a well-designed site. This journal is an excellent source of information on the current state of political and economic developments in Asian countries, accessible to the layman as well as the scholar. Highly recommended for any academic or large public library.

848. ***B C Asian Review (Online Edition).*** Formerly (until 1998): *B C Asian Review (Print Edition).* 1987. a. Ed(s): Allen Haaheim. University of British Columbia, Department of Asian Studies, Asian Centre, 403 - 1871 West Mall, Vancouver, BC V6T 1Z2, Canada; astudies@interchange.ubc.ca; http://www.asia.ubc.ca. Refereed. *Bk. rev.:* 6-8, 2-4 pp. *Aud.:* Ac.

This is a unique refereed academic journal in that it is written and published by graduate students. Produced annually since 1987 at the University of British Columbia's Asian Studies department, it has been in electronic format since 1998. Articles are generally well written and range from the narrowly focused to the broadly theoretical. It covers China, India, Japan, Korea, and Southeast Asia. Topics may address any aspect of Asian Studies, including historical and artistic studies, but articles on language and literature, philosophy, and religion predominate. Contributors may be past or present graduate students of UBC or elsewhere. The journal web site is attractive and user friendly. The archived issues show how the journal has matured. Tables of contents are available online from the second issue. From 1997 on, full text is available free online, and recent issues include abstracts as well as full text. In-depth book reviews have also been added. This is an excellent source for sampling the research of new Asian Studies scholars and a good way to introduce them to the peer-review process.

849. ***Business Asia: fortnightly report to managers of Asia operations index.*** [ISSN: 0572-7545] 1970. bi-w. USD 985; USD 75 newsstand/cover per issue. Economist Intelligence Unit, 111 W 57th St, New York, NY 10019; http://www.eiu.com. Illus. Sample. Vol. ends: Dec. Microform: PQC. *Indexed:* ABIn. *Bk. rev.:* Various number and length. *Aud.:* Ga, Sa.

This fortnightly newsletter, published by the Economist Intelligence Unit, which also publishes *The Economist*, is designed as a resource for business and industry managers with dealings in Asia. It provides the latest business news, assesses the outlook on up-and-coming industries and commercial opportunities, reports changes in laws and regulations that may affect business interests, analyzes trends, provides detailed company case studies, and analyzes economic and political risks in various countries. The impact of politics and international forces on business is a constant thread. A recent issue, for example, assesses the "political and operational risks in Asia" from the U.S. war in Iraq. Each issue includes an "Economic Outlook" for one Asian country, while the "Country Watchlist" gives a one-paragraph summary of business, economic, and political news for each Asian country. Articles are short (two or three pages) but focused. Occasional special issues are devoted to one topic. Recent articles have analyzed South Korean President Kim Dae-jung's record of achievements, problems with Japan's broadband market, and issues of corporate governance such as personal networks and shareholder rights. Helpful charts and graphs provide additional information. It is available in paper or online. Recommended for academic and public libraries serving business faculty or managers with Asian business interests.

850. ***Critical Asian Studies.*** Former titles (until 2000): *Bulletin of Concerned Asian Scholars; C C A S Newsletter.* [ISSN: 1467-2715] 1968. q. USD 166 (Individuals, USD 52). Ed(s): Tom Fenton. Taylor & Francis Inc, 325 Chestnut St, Suite 800, Philadelphia, PA 19016; info@taylorandfrancis.com; http://www.taylorandfrancis.com/. Illus., index, adv. Sample. Refereed. Circ: 1000 Paid. Vol. ends: Dec. Microform: PQC. Online: Ingenta Select. Reprint: ISI; PQC; PSC. *Indexed:* AltPI, AmH&L, BAS, IBSS, IBZ, PSA, SSCI, WAE&RSA. *Bk. rev.:* Number varies; essay length. *Aud.:* Ac.

This refereed scholarly journal focuses attention on injustice and inequalities facing Asian and Pacific countries and on their international relations. The emphasis is on political history and cultural identity. The journal seeks to challenge conventional, parochial thinking about Asia and examine the roots of poverty, cultural integrity, and the effects of imperialism and oppression. It is indexed, among other places, in the *Alternative Press Index*. Recent articles include a discussion of government denial of genocide to further a political agenda, using as cases genocides of natives of Australia and East Timor, and a historical review of smuggling in Southeast Asia, especially the trade in narcotics and human beings. Occasional special issues focus on one topic or region; for example, a recent issue examines Cambodian conflict from 1945 to the present, including articles on the fall of Pol Pot; the behavior of elites in the democratization process; forest exploitation strategies; and efforts to bring Khmer Rouge leaders to trial for genocide. The publication includes articles and documents, as well as "essays, reviews, translations, interviews, photo essays, and letters about Asia and the Pacific, particularly those that challenge the accepted formulas." A recent issue includes a selection of photographs of the Vietnam war taken in the North, and an excerpt from Arundhati Roy's *Power Politics*. It is sparingly but effectively illustrated. The journal includes abstracts and frequently, review essays. It awards yearly prizes for its best articles, particularly those "at the intersection of scholarship and activism." Highly recommended for academic libraries, particularly those with an interest in international or Asian affairs, history, and economic or political development.

851. *Education about Asia.* [ISSN: 1090-6851] 1996. 3x/yr. USD 20 (Individuals, USD 14). Ed(s): Anand A Yang. Association for Asian Studies, Inc., 1021 E Huron St, Ann Arbor, MI 48104; http://www.aasianst.org. Adv. Circ: 9000. *Indexed:* BAS. *Bk. rev.:* Various number and length. *Aud.:* Hs, Ga, Ac.

This refereed journal is intended to encourage and support teaching about Asia at all educational levels from elementary to university. Its primary focus is on support for high school classrooms in Asian history, culture, politics, current events, and the arts. The articles provide content as well as pedagogical ideas, so they could also be used as a resource outside the classroom. Articles are well illustrated with maps, graphs, photographs, and other graphics. Recent article topics include "Using Chinese Folktales in the Classroom" and "Reflections on Stereotypes in South Asian History." Numerous book reviews and review articles not only evaluate print titles, electronic media, and other materials, but also show how they might be used in the classroom. This journal excels at making Asian topics accessible and relevant. Thematic issues address such topics as "Teaching About Asia Through Film" and "Teaching the Korean War and Beyond." Its web site, at http://www.aasianst.org/eaa-toc.htm, provides tables of contents, sample articles, Asian "factoids" (interesting facts and statistics), and links to other resources. Highly recommended for school and public libraries and for academic libraries serving education students.

Europe-Asia Studies. See CIS and Eastern Europe section.

852. *Far Eastern Economic Review.* [ISSN: 0014-7591] 1946. w. HKD 950; HKD 40 newsstand/cover per issue. Ed(s): Michael Vatikiotis. Review Publishing Co. Ltd., GPO Box 160, Hong Kong; subscription@feer.com; http://www.feer.com. Illus., index, adv. Sample. Circ: 95622 Paid. Microform: RPI; PQC. Online: Dow Jones Interactive; Factiva; Gale Group; OCLC Online Computer Library Center, Inc.; ProQuest Information & Learning. Reprint: SCH. *Indexed:* ABIn, BAS, BPI, PAIS, RRTA, SSI, WAE&RSA. *Bk. rev.:* 3-4, 500-1,000 words. *Aud.:* Ga.

This is one of the most widely read news magazines on Asia and includes global news as it affects Asia. Though billed as a far-eastern business newsweekly, its coverage is much more broad both in subject matter and in regions covered. For example, a recent article reports on human rights abuses by Thai officials in the war on drugs. The magazine is similar to *Time* or *Newsweek* in format but more serious, with more emphasis on economic and business news. Issues include editorials; a regional news section with brief updates by country; and longer articles on major stories; a section on Innovation covering e-commerce, technology, and management; a Money section including country reports, with key economic data such as stock market and foreign exchange rates; and a Currents section, for art and entertainment news and trends. Special reports highlight a specific industry or corporation in one Asian country and report the results of reader surveys on the top ten multinational corporations. Recently a China section has been added. The Innovations section reported recently on Korea's efforts to compete with China's shoe industry and on the web browser *Opera*'s latest features, while the Currents section featured an article on India's new trend toward making films in English, or the hybrid "Hinglish." The Money section contains a half-page summary of the economic outlook of the major Asian countries. The publication is illustrated generously with photographs, maps, and tables of financial data. It also includes profiles of business leaders and book reviews. Highly recommended for academic and public libraries with an interest in Asian affairs or international business.

853. *Harvard Journal of Asiatic Studies.* [ISSN: 0073-0548] 1936. s-a. USD 45 (Individuals, USD 30). Ed(s): Wilt Idema, Joanna Handlin Smith. Harvard-Yenching Institute, 2 Divinity Ave, Cambridge, MA 02138; http://www-hcl.harvard.edu/hyl/hylhome.html. Illus., index. Sample. Refereed. Circ: 1200. Vol. ends: Dec. Microform: MIM; PQC. Online: Gale Group; JSTOR (Web-based Journal Archive). Reprint: PQC; SCH. *Indexed:* AmH&L, AnthLit, ArtHuCI, BAS, BRI, CBRI, HumInd, IBSS, MLA-IB, SSI. *Bk. rev.:* 8-12 pages. *Aud.:* Ac, Sa.

This important scholarly publication contributes substantial but very readable articles on the humanities (literature, history, thought/philosophy, religion, and art history, but not musicology or linguistics) of China, Korea, Japan, and Inner Asia. Contributors are academics from prestigious universities. A recent article examines the historical evidence for the Kija legend of eastward migration to form the first Korean state and discusses Japanese imperialistic as well as postcolonial nationalistic biases in past use of the evidence. Another article discusses differences between two versions of a sixteenth-century novel, *Jinpingmei*. Translations and textual points are amplified by original script in Chinese, Japanese, Korean, Manchu, Mongolian, Russian, Sanskrit, and Tibetan. Book reviews, 8 to 12 pages in length, provide in-depth analysis. Highly recommended for academic libraries.

854. *Journal of Asian Business.* Former titles: *Journal of Southeast Asia Business; Southeast Asia Business.* [ISSN: 1068-0055] 1983. q. USD 40 (Individuals, USD 25). Ed(s): Linda E Lim, Jason Eyster. Southeast Asia Business Program, University of Michigan, 914 Hill St, Ann Arbor, MI 48109-1234; jab@umich.edu. Illus. Sample. Refereed. Circ: 1000. Vol. ends: Fall. *Indexed:* ABIn, BAS, BPI, IBSS. *Bk. rev.:* 0-15, 500-1,000 words. *Aud.:* Ac, Sa.

This refereed academic journal seeks to facilitate communication among scholars of many disciplines and business professionals. Its scope is broad, including "business, management, economics, political economy, economic and business history, development studies, and comparative and cross-cultural studies" as relevant to Asian business. Formerly titled *Journal of Southeast Asia Business*, the journal still focuses almost exclusively on Southeast and East Asia. The journal contains research articles (with abstracts), case studies, comparative and empirical studies, review articles, and numerous book reviews (one or two pages each). Recent articles discuss such topics as profitability of less diversified companies in Korea, and managerial autonomy in China following privatization of rural firms. Broader-based issues are also studied; for example, a research report analyzes the data to dispute a correlation between increased foreign direct investment in China and declining foreign direct investment in Southeast Asian nations. An article on the reasons for the prevalence of counterfeit software in Thailand illustrates the emphasis in this publication on uncovering the cultural and historical underpinnings of economic phenomena in the region. The web site, at http://www.umich.edu/~cibe/JAB, is easy to navigate and provides tables of contents for current and back issues, with links to abstracts. Suitable for academic libraries, this lucid publication may be read by scholars and educated readers interested in Asian or international business and Asian affairs generally.

855. *Journal of Asian History.* [ISSN: 0021-910X] 1967. 2x/yr. EUR 84; CHF 142 Switzerland. Ed(s): Denis Sinor. Harrassowitz Verlag, Taunusstr 14, Wiesbaden, 65183, Germany; verlag@harrassowitz.de; http://www.harrassowitz.de. Illus., index, adv. Sample. Refereed. Circ: 600. Microform: PQC. Online: Gale Group. *Indexed:* AmH&L, ArtHuCI, BAS, HumInd, IBSS, IBZ, NumL, SSCI. *Aud.:* Ac, Sa.

This refereed academic journal publishes research on "any period and all regions of Asia with the exception of the Ancient Near East. It welcomes manuscripts that make use of primary sources on any aspect of East Asian, South Asian, Southeast Asian, Inner Asian, and Middle Eastern history." The word history is broadly defined to include any social science or humanities discipline as it relates to history. Recent issues place the emphasis on China, Japan, and South Asia. While the scope of the journal is broad, articles themselves tend to be narrowly focused on a particular incident, institution, or time period. For example, recent articles include "Military Poetry of Six Dynasties" of China, "Musical Instruments of the Huqin Family in the Late Nineteenth-Century Illustrated Periodical Dianshizai, and "The Learning of Pashto in North India and Pakistan." It typically publishes two to three articles and 10 to 15 book reviews per issue. The journal web site, at http://www.indiana.edu/~jahist/index.html, is not particularly helpful; it provides a list of articles from all past issues in one alphabetical list by author. The list is searchable by keyword. Suitable for a university library.

Journal of Asian Martial Arts. See Sports/Specific Sports section.

856. *Journal of Asian Studies.* Formerly (until 1956): *The Far Eastern Quarterly.* [ISSN: 0021-9118] 1941. q. USD 60; USD 70 foreign. Ed(s): Anand A Yang. Association for Asian Studies, Inc., 1021 E Huron St, Ann Arbor, MI 48104; http://www.aasianst.org. Illus., index, adv. Sample. Refereed. Circ: 10000. Vol. ends: Dec. Microform: PQC. Online: Chadwyck-Healey Incorporated; Gale Group; JSTOR (Web-based Journal Archive); Northern Light Technology, Inc.; OCLC Online Computer Library Center, Inc.; ProQuest Information & Learning. Reprint: PQC. *Indexed:* ABCPolSci, ABS&EES, AmH&L, AnthLit, ArtHuCI, BAS, BRI, CBRI, ForAb, HumInd, IBSS, IPSA, MLA-IB, RI-1, SSCI, SWA, WAE&RSA. *Aud.:* Ac.

The scope of this refereed journal includes "history, arts, social sciences, philosophy, and contemporary issues of East, South, and Southeast Asia." This is the most widely respected and widely indexed scholarly journal for Asian Studies. Though it does not include Pacific Island nations, it is otherwise very broad in scope, covering the past and present over a wide geographic area. Many of the articles break new theoretical grounds or challenge prevailing paradigms. Whether by narrow case study or by broad-brush historical or cultural survey, many of these weighty articles address the concept of identity formation and its implications for society. Recent issues include seemingly unrelated articles, but authors are asked to comment on and find common themes in each others' works. Their commentaries are included in the front matter to encourage readers to read and find connections "across disciplines and regions." One recent issue discussed the circulation of poetic texts in seventeenth-century China, while another analyzed intersection between colonial British rule in India, a princely state, and attempts to form a modern university based on an Indian rather than Western model. Another issue treats issues such as attempts to "scientifically" identify ethnic groups in China, Thailand, and Vietnam, and the barriers to democratic vision as expressed in Indian postcolonial monumental architecture. Special issues cover a single topic. The journal is illustrated with maps, charts, and photographs of artworks and manuscripts. Approximately half of each issue is devoted to short book reviews, one or two pages in length, grouped by the following regions: Asia—Comparative and Transnational, China, Inner Asia, Japan, Korea, South Asia, and Southeast Asia. An essential publication for the academic library. The web site, at http://www.aasianst.org/catalog/jas.htm, offers the introductory essay, table of contents, and one full-text article per issue. An essential publication for the academic library.

857. *Journal of Contemporary Asia.* [ISSN: 0047-2336] 1970. q. USD 71. Ed(s): Peter Limqueco. Journal of Contemporary Asia, P.O. Box 592, Manila, 1099, Philippines. Illus., adv. Sample. Refereed. Circ: 3500 Paid. Microform: PQC. Online: bigchalk; Chadwyck-Healey Incorporated; EBSCO Publishing; Florida Center for Library Automation; Gale Group; Northern Light Technology, Inc.; OCLC Online Computer Library Center, Inc.; ProQuest Information & Learning; H.W. Wilson. Reprint: SCH. *Indexed:* ASSIA, AmH&L, BAS, FPA, ForAb, IBSS, IPSA, PSA, RRTA, S&F, SSCI, SSI, WAE&RSA. *Bk. rev.:* 10-15, 750-1,500 words. *Aud.:* Ga, Ac, Sa.

This refereed scholarly journal addresses "broad problems of the economic, political and social development of Asia" with emphasis on "agriculture, planning and the working class." Also welcomed are articles of a theoretical nature on global issues. It includes research articles, review articles, and book reviews. The distinguished international editorial board includes Noam Chomsky of MIT. Well-researched, well-written articles draw attention to economic anomalies, oppressive colonial legacies, and undemocratic policies of the region in stark contrast to the coverage on contemporary Asia found in the glossy business weeklies. For example, a recent article analyzes the language of racial and ethnic division in Malaysia and shows how recognition of transethnic solidarities are obscured by the focus on race. Other articles analyze Japan's shift in economic policy away from dependence on the United States and decentralization and corruption in Vietnam. Tables and charts accompany the text. Book reviews (two to four pages in length) and review articles are also included. The journal is widely indexed in sources as diverse as *Historical Abstracts*, *Bibliography of Asian Studies*, and *Forestry Abstracts*. An important source of analysis of Asian affairs, and highly recommended for any academic or large public library.

858. *Media Asia: an Asian mass communication quarterly operations index.* [ISSN: 0129-6612] 1974. q. USD 44. Ed(s): Vijay Menon. Asian Media Information and Communication Centre, Publications Unit, PO Box 360, Jurong Point, 916412, Singapore; amicline@singnet.com.sg; http://www.amic.org.sg. Illus., index. Sample. Circ: 1500. *Indexed:* BAS, CommAb, HRA, IIFP, PAIS. *Bk. rev.:* 2-5, 500-1,500 words. *Aud.:* Ga, Ac, Sa.

This journal, published in Singapore, is dedicated to the exchange of information on mass communication in Asia and the Pacific for media professionals, scholars and laymen; it should not be confused with the Hong Kong magazine of the same name. It is narrower in scope than *Asian Journal of Communication* (above in this section), by the same publisher, in that it focuses on news media rather than all mass media. The authors are professors, journalists, or media experts and the tone is predominantly scholarly. Articles cover a wide range of media topics, from a survey of outdoor advertising in Vietnam as an expression of emerging capitalism, to an analysis of media coverage of ethnic conflict, to an overview of trends in international television. Most issues are thematic; for example, a recent issue covers media portrayal of terrorism including articles on how to define it, how to recognize and avoid bias, the role of media regulation in reducing conflict, use of cyber media to further terrorist aims, and media practitioners' need for education and greater sensitivity to the history of the conflicts. Cultural, social, and political aspects of mass communications are often addressed in research articles and commentary. Articles include abstracts. The scope is far reaching both in subject matter and geographic area. Highly recommended for any academic library, particularly those serving mass communications, Asian Studies, or public affairs departments.

859. *Modern Asian Studies.* [ISSN: 0026-749X] 1967. q. USD 268 (Individuals, USD 99). Ed(s): Gordon Johnson. Cambridge University Press, The Edinburgh Bldg, Shaftesbury Rd, Cambridge, CB2 2RU, United Kingdom; information@cambridge.org; http://uk.cambridge.org/journals. Illus., index, adv. Sample. Refereed. Vol. ends: Oct. Microform: PQC. Online: EBSCO Publishing; Gale Group; JSTOR (Web-based Journal Archive); OCLC Online Computer Library Center, Inc.; RoweCom Information Quest; Swets Blackwell. Reprint: SWZ. *Indexed:* ABCPolSci, AmH&L, ArtHuCI, BAS, ForAb, GeogAbPG, HumInd, IBSS, IBZ, IPSA, L&LBA, PSA, RI-1, RRTA, S&F, SSCI, SSI, SociolAb, WAE&RSA. *Bk. rev.:* 0-12, 1,500-3,500 words. *Aud.:* Ac, Sa.

This respected, widely indexed British scholarly journal, with a distinguished editorial board, "promotes an understanding of contemporary Asia and its rich inheritance," specifically in South and Southeast Asia, China, and Japan. Well-researched articles concern the "history, geography, politics, sociology, literature, economics, and social anthropology and culture," and the journal specializes in "the longer monographic essay based on archival materials and new field work." Articles on more recent history and its influence on the current political and cultural landscape predominate. For example, a recent article examines labor relations in precolonial India while critiquing the indigenist approach that assumes a clash of cultures between colonists and colonizers. Another looks at guru organizations in India, finding a trend toward secularization rather than toward Hindu nationalism. Another considers how cultural biases dictate attitudes toward taboo drugs of other countries while minimizing drug taboos in one's own. Occasionally special issues are devoted to one topic. Abstracts are available in the electronic version but not in the print. The books reviews average two to six pages but are limited in number. Highly recommended for the research library, of interest to scholars of Asian politics, culture, literature, or history.

860. *Orientations: the monthly magazine for collectors and connoisseurs of Oriental art.* [ISSN: 0030-5448] 1970. m. 10/yr., Jan-Jun, Sep-Dec. USD 105. Ed(s): Elizabeth Knight. Orientations Magazine Ltd., 17th Fl,

200 Lockhart Rd, Hong Kong; http://www.orientations.com.hk/. Illus., index, adv. Circ: 5000. Vol. ends: Dec. *Indexed:* A&ATA, AIAP, ArtInd, BAS, BHA. *Bk. rev.:* 2-6 pages. *Aud.:* Ga, Ac, Sa.

Though the subtitle addresses art collectors and connoisseurs, the journal is scholarly, and the articles on the art, archaeology, and architecture of Asia are aimed at academics as well. Most of the articles focus on art from museum collections and exhibitions. All forms of art objects are included. Stunningly illustrated, the articles discuss artistic influences and merit, technique, use and social or ritual significance, and historical environment, and include bibliographies for further reading. The authors are academics and museum experts and researchers. Recent representative articles include "A True Picture of Korean Buddhist Art and its Status in the Asian Art World" and "Demystifying Artifacts from Eastern Eurasia: Archaeology and the Study of Art History." The journal also includes commentary, interviews, and exhibition, art fair, and auction announcements for London, New York, and Hong Kong. The table of contents is preceded by about 30-50 pages of beautiful ads for art galleries and exhibitions. The journal's web site, at http://www.orientations.com.hk, provides tables of contents with a synopsis of articles and representative illustrations of the artwork discussed. It also contains links to dealers and galleries, exhibitions, bookstores, other art and academic sites, art foundations, and publications. Highly recommended for academic libraries serving art, archeology, or Asian Studies departments and for larger public libraries.

861. ***Pacific Affairs: an international review of Asia and the Pacific.*** Formerly (until 1928): *News Bulletin - Institute of Pacific Relations.* [ISSN: 0030-851X] 1926. q. CND 70 (Individuals, CND 45). Ed(s): Jacqueline Garnett. Pacific Affairs, University of British Columbia, 1855 West Mall, Ste 164, Vancouver, BC V6T 1Z2, Canada; pacifaff@interchange.ubc.ca; http://www.pacificaffairs.com. Illus., index, adv. Sample. Refereed. Circ: 2700 Paid. Vol. ends: Winter. Microform: MML; PQC. Online: bigchalk; Chadwyck-Healey Incorporated; EBSCO Publishing; Florida Center for Library Automation; Gale Group; JSTOR (Web-based Journal Archive); Micromedia ProQuest; Northern Light Technology, Inc.; OCLC Online Computer Library Center, Inc.; ProQuest Information & Learning. Reprint: PQC. *Indexed:* ABCPolSci, ABS&EES, AbAn, AgeL, AmH&L, ArtHuCI, BAS, BRD, BRI, CBCARef, CBRI, CPerI, ForAb, GeogAbPG, HumInd, IBSS, IPSA, PAIS, PRA, PSA, RRTA, SSCI, SSI, WAE&RSA. *Bk. rev.:* 50-75, 1,000-1,500 words. *Aud.:* Ac, Sa.

This highly regarded refereed journal includes in scope all of Asia and the Pacific. The book review section, which comprises about a third of each issue, is divided into the following regions, demonstrating its breadth: General Asia, China and Inner Asia, Northeast Asia, South Asia, Southeast Asia, and Australasia and the South Pacific. The focus is on contemporary political, economic, and social issues, but historical topics may be included if relevant to the present day. Recent issues include an article comparing post-independence nation-building in two neighboring Muslim majority states, refuting the common belief that Islam hinders secular nation-building. Another article examines the effect of the influx of Hollywood movies in China and its effects on the interests and tensions between independent and Party filmmakers. Another article examines the role of social structures in New Zealand's experience with returning land to the Maori. This journal is an excellent source of thoughtful, in-depth coverage of contemporary development, conflicts, and trends in the region. Biographical notes on article authors are lacking. Highly recommended for academic libraries and larger public libraries.

862. ***The Pacific Review.*** [ISSN: 0951-2748] 1988. q. GBP 213 (Individuals, GBP 53). Ed(s): Richard Higgott, Neil Renwick. Routledge, 11 New Fetter Ln, London, EC4P 4EE, United Kingdom; info@routledge.co.uk; http://www.routledge.co.uk. Adv. Refereed. Online: EBSCO Publishing; Ingenta Select; OCLC Online Computer Library Center, Inc.; RoweCom Information Quest; Swets Blackwell. Reprint: PSC. *Indexed:* AmH&L, BAS, BrHumI, GeogAbPG, IBSS, IBZ, IPSA, PAIS, PSA, SSCI. *Aud.:* Ac, Sa.

This is a peer-reviewed academic journal aimed at "more than just an academic audience,?? including government, media, and business professionals. It is widely indexed and interdisciplinary, covering "domestic politics, economics and international relations of the countries of the Asia-Pacific region,?? but also venturing into subjects as diverse as military strategy and cultural issues. The emphasis is on current policy and its historical roots. Frequent themes are nationalism, nation building, and ethnic conflict, as in recent articles on the idealized past in Philippine Muslim separatism and on Karen ethno-nationalism in Burma. Other recent articles analyze economic and international issues such as Russian-Japanese relations, globalization and trade friction between Japan and China, and the concept of "environmental security?? as a basis for regional cooperation. The web site offers tables of contents and abstracts for most articles. Highly recommended for larger public libraries and academic libraries serving economics, international business, public affairs, political science, or Asian Studies programs.

Philosophy East and West. See Philosophy section.

863. ***University of London. School of Oriental and African Studies. Bulletin.*** Formerly (until 1940): *University of London. School of Oriental Studies. Bulletin.* [ISSN: 0041-977X] 1917. 3x/yr. USD 178 (Individuals, USD 79). Ed(s): T H Barrett. Cambridge University Press, The Edinburgh Bldg, Shaftesbury Rd, Cambridge, CB2 2RU, United Kingdom; information@cambridge.org; http://uk.cambridge.org/journals. Adv. Refereed. Circ: 1000. Microform: IDC. Online: JSTOR (Web-based Journal Archive); OCLC Online Computer Library Center, Inc.; RoweCom Information Quest; Swets Blackwell. Reprint: PSC. *Indexed:* AICP, AmH&L, AnthLit, ArtHuCI, BAS, IBSS, L&LBA, MLA-IB, NumL, RI-1, SSCI. *Bk. rev.:* Various number and length. *Aud.:* Ac.

This well-established scholarly journal publishes articles and "shorter communications" on a broad range of Asian and African topics. It covers the "languages, cultures, and civilizations" of Asia, Africa, and the Middle East. Articles and book reviews on Asian topics predominate; there are fewer on Africa. The journal spans all time periods from antiquity to the present. Article topics range from the highly specialized to the more general. A recent issue includes articles on a Kothi gateway in Gujarat, India, disputing its British origin. Another article explores the significance of ancient coins found in Harran, Turkey. Many articles trace the development of or comparative influences on historical, artistic, or linguistic phenomena. For example, a recent article traces the influence of Sufi manuscripts in Egypt on Islamic mysticism and another analyzes ancient Indian works on poetics written in Pali, arguing that they do not draw from certain Sanscrit sources as supposed, but from earlier sources from which the Sanscrit sources also derive. About half of each issue is devoted to book reviews, about 1,000 words, grouped by geographic area. Full-text pdfs are available online by electronic subscription. Highly recommended for academic libraries serving graduate programs in Asian or Middle Eastern Studies, archeology, or world history.

Australia and the Pacific

864. ***A Q - Journal of Contemporary Analysis.*** Formerly: *Australian Quarterly.* [ISSN: 1443-3605] 1929. bi-m. AUD 95 (Individuals, AUD 55). Ed(s): Jim Morris. Australian Institute of Political Science, PO Box 145, Balmain, NSW 2041, Australia; aq@aips.net.au; http://www.aips.net.au. Illus., index, adv. Sample. Refereed. Circ: 900. Vol. ends: Summer. Reprint: PSC. *Indexed:* ABCPolSci, BAS, IBSS, IPSA, MLA-IB, SSCI. *Bk. rev.:* Various number and length. *Aud.:* Ga, Ac.

This refereed journal is published by the Australian Institute of Political Science, which promotes "understanding of the important political, economic and social issues facing Australia." Contributors are academics and researchers or media correspondents. The journal also contains occasional book excerpts, public documents, and transcripts of public addresses. Though written largely by academic specialists, the journal is aimed at the educated layman interested in understanding current events and trends in Australia, and world events as they affect Australia and the Pacific region. Recent issues analyze media coverage of specific events such as 9/11 and its effect on Australian election results, examples of deliberate government misinformation, and the inroads of green-party politics on support for labor. The journal also addresses issues of wider relevance, such as a comparison between presidential and parliamentary systems, democratization efforts in East Timor, and the issue of privacy vs. cost in health care. Recurring topics include ethics in political life, issues concerning the indigenous population, international affairs, mass media, and development and trade issues. It is well illustrated, with no advertising. An excellent source of information and commentary on present day Australia. Recommended for public and academic libraries.

865. *Australian Historical Studies.* Former titles (until Jan. 1988): *Historical Studies; Historical Studies: Australia and New Zealand.* [ISSN: 1031-461X] 1940. s-a. AUD 90 (Individuals, AUD 60; Students, AUD 30). Ed(s): Joy Damousi. University of Melbourne, Department of History, Melbourne, VIC 3010, Australia; ahs-history@unimelb.edu.au; http://www.unimelb.edu.au/infoserv81/anz/ahs/ahs.html. Illus., index, adv. Sample. Refereed. Circ: 1200 Controlled. Vol. ends: Oct. *Indexed:* AmH&L, ArtHuCI, BrHumI, IBSS, IBZ, IPSA. *Bk. rev.:* 20-30, 1,000-1,500 words. *Aud.:* Ga, Ac, Sa.

This refereed scholarly journal concerns Australian history and other histories as they relate to Australian history. Though restricted to one discipline and one country, this excellent journal is valuable for its inquiry into the uniqueness of this country and its insights into cultural identity in general. Under its new editor, Joy Damousi, each issue will focus on a group of related themes and include a forum section and a historical overview article, which will "develop one theme or debate across several decades." Recent articles examine such issues as the legacy of eugenics and racial aspects of migration policies. Abstracts accompany each article. In addition to the articles, review articles, and reviews of books and exhibitions, this publication contains a spirited and frank debate section. This well-written and well-illustrated journal belongs in academic and larger public libraries.

The Australian Journal of Anthropology. See Anthropology section.

866. *Australian Journal of Politics and History.* [ISSN: 0004-9522] 1955. q. GBP 75 print & online eds. Ed(s): Ian Ward, Andrew Bonnell. Blackwell Publishing Asia, 550 Swanston St, Carlton South, VIC 3053, Australia; subs@blackwellpublishingasia.com; http://www.blackwellpublishing.com/. Illus., adv. Sample. Refereed. Circ: 750. Microform: PQC. Online: EBSCO Publishing; Florida Center for Library Automation; Gale Group; ingenta.com; OCLC Online Computer Library Center, Inc.; RoweCom Information Quest; Swets Blackwell. Reprint: SCH. *Indexed:* ABCPolSci, AmH&L, ArtHuCI, BAS, IBSS, IBZ, IPSA, PAIS, PRA, PSA, SSCI, SociolAb. *Bk. rev.:* 20-30, 500-1,200 words. *Aud.:* Ga, Ac.

This refereed scholarly journal is not exclusively about Australia, but publishes serious research on "significant problems" in history, political science, and international affairs. Preference is given to the "politics and history of Australia and modern Europe, intellectual history, political theory, and the history of political thought," but also "international politics, Australian foreign policy, and Australia's relations with countries of the Asia-Pacific region." Recent issues focus more on the present and the history and politics of the last 200 years and include discussion of Tocqueville's influence on thinking about Australian democracy, and of the spread of right-wing political parties in Europe and Australia that appeal to xenophobia and populism. Economic change is also addressed in articles such as "Globalization and the End of Social Democracy" and "One Nation's Electoral Support: Economic Insecurity versus Attitudes to Immigration." Abstracts are included. Book reviews may account for up to half of an issue, though sometimes there are few or none. Review articles on several books are common. Thematic issues with guest editors are also published. The "Political Chronicles" feature provides summaries (6-8 pages each) of national and state events of note semi-annually. Well-researched and easy to read, this journal is highly recommended for libraries serving scholars or lay readers interested in recent history or politics.

867. *The Contemporary Pacific: a journal of island affairs.* [ISSN: 1043-898X] 1989. s-a. USD 30 Pacific Islands (Individuals, USD 23 Pacific Islands). Ed(s): Vilsoni Hereniko. University of Hawaii Press, Journals Department, 2840 Kolowalu St, Honolulu, HI 96822-1888; uhpjourn@hawaii.edu; http://www.uhpress.hawaii.edu/. Illus., index, adv. Sample. Refereed. Circ: 550. Vol. ends: Fall. Online: EBSCO Publishing; Florida Center for Library Automation; Gale Group; Northern Light Technology, Inc.; OCLC Online Computer Library Center, Inc.; Project MUSE; RoweCom Information Quest; Swets Blackwell. Reprint: PQC; PSC. *Indexed:* AICP, ArtHuCI, BAS, BRI, CBRI, FPA, ForAb, IBSS, L&LBA, PSA, RRTA, SSCI, SociolAb, WAE&RSA. *Bk. rev.:* 8-15, 1,200-2,000 words. *Aud.:* Ac, Sa.

This excellent scholarly journal is one of few devoted exclusively to the Pacific Islands, including Melanesia, Micronesia, and Polynesia. The journal covers contemporary public affairs through a wide range of disciplines. Using a minimum of jargon, it discusses contemporary "social, economic, political, ecological, and cultural topics, along with political reviews, book reviews, resource reviews, and a dialogue section of letters and short items." A recent issue is devoted to rethinking approaches to Pacific Studies and considering effects of colonization and decolonization on personal and national identity on the one hand and efforts to modernize and advance economically without suppressing indigenous values and knowledge on the other. It also includes discussions of the benefits and dangers of interdisciplinary approaches to Pacific Studies. Other features include book and media reviews, political review essays, and resource lists and dialogues. The political reviews provide very useful summaries of major political events in each nation for a one-year period. Tables of contents with abstracts and a ten-year index are available online through Project MUSE. Recommended highly for academic libraries.

868. *Journal of Pacific History.* [ISSN: 0022-3344] 1966. 3x/yr. GBP 154 (Individuals, GBP 48). Ed(s): Chris Ballard, Hank Nelson. Carfax Publishing Ltd., 4 Park Sq, Milton Park, Abingdon, OX14 4RN, United Kingdom; enquiry@tandf.co.uk; http://www.tandf.co.uk/. Illus., adv. Sample. Refereed. Circ: 800 Paid. Vol. ends: Oct. Online: EBSCO Publishing; Florida Center for Library Automation; Gale Group; Ingenta Select; OCLC Online Computer Library Center, Inc.; RMIT Publishing; RoweCom Information Quest; Swets Blackwell. Reprint: PSC. *Indexed:* AICP, AbAn, AmH&L, ArtHuCI, HumInd, IBSS, IBZ, PSA, RI-1, SSCI, SociolAb. *Bk. rev.:* 0-10, 750-1,500 words. *Aud.:* Ac, Sa.

This refereed scholarly journal published by Australian National University "serves historians, prehistorians, anthropologists and others interested in the study of mankind in the Pacific Islands (including Hawaii and New Guinea), and is concerned generally with political, economic, religious and cultural factors affecting human presence there. It publishes articles, annotated previously unpublished manuscripts, notes on source material and comment on current affairs." Articles on other regions as they relate to Pacific affairs are also published. Abstracts are available at the end of the articles and online. Most articles focus on historical events or phenomena, but some encompass current affairs. Recent articles include an examination of factors other than the obvious ethnic conflicts causing the current crisis in the governance of the Solomon Islands and an analysis of recent elections in Tonga and implications for democracy there. Another article speculates on the study of memory and the significance of forgetting and urges collaboration with medical researchers to enrich understanding of the significance of both. The notes on source materials and annotated manuscripts section are unique features of the journal. A year-end bibliography of sources is not limited to this journal and is searchable by subject or country. Book reviews average one to two pages. Highly recommended for academic libraries with interest in the Pacific Islands, including Australasia.

869. *Nature Australia.* Former titles (until 1995): *A N H;* (until 1992): *Australian Natural History;* (until 1962): *Australian Museum Magazine.* [ISSN: 1324-2598] 1921. q. AUD 33 domestic; AUD 45 foreign; AUD 8.95 newsstand/cover per issue. Ed(s): Jennifer Saunders. Australian Museum, 6 College St, Sydney, NSW 2010, Australia; http://www.austmus.gov.au. Illus., adv. Sample. Circ: 20000. Online: EBSCO Publishing. *Indexed:* BiolAb, GeoRef. *Bk. rev.:* 4-8, 500-750 words. *Aud.:* Hs, Ga.

This glossy nature magazine "specializes in bringing current scientific research to the general public." It is a nonprofit publication of the Australian Museum. Though written in nontechnical language, all articles are peer reviewed and most contain references to the scientific literature for further reading. Its contributors are academic experts, museum curators, and research institute scientists, mostly in zoology, entomology, ecology, and botany. Lavishly illustrated articles describe wildlife behavior, distribution, and ecological conditions for all sorts of species in the region. Topics range from the broad to the specific; for example, recent issues discuss the origins of art, purple wallabies, and the dearth of succulent plants in Australian deserts. Regular features include a full color poster, a Q&A column, "Wild Things," "Rare and Endangered," "Backyard Naturalist," a photo-art section, and a "Last Word" essay. The breathtaking photographs alone are worth the price. While highly recommended for undergraduates in academic libraries, it is also an excellent teaching tool and recommended especially for school and public libraries.

Oceania. See Anthropology section.

Pacific Historical Review. See History section.

Pacific Philosophical Quarterly. See Philosophy section.

870. ***Pacific Studies: an interdisciplinary journal devoted to the study of the Pacific - its islands and adjacent countries.*** [ISSN: 0275-3596] 1977. q. USD 40. Ed(s): Dale B. Robertson. Brigham Young University - Hawaii, The Pacific Institute, 55-220 Kulanui St, Laie, HI 96762; robertsd@byuh.edu; http://w3.byuh.edu/academics/thepacificinstitute. Adv. Refereed. Circ: 500. *Indexed:* AICP, AbAn, AmH&L, AnthLit, BRI, CBRI, IBSS, IBZ, IPSA, L&LBA, PAIS, PSA, RI-1, SociolAb. *Bk. rev.:* Various number and length. *Aud.:* Ac.

This is a refereed "multidisciplinary journal devoted to the study of the peoples of the Pacific Islands." Disciplines include anthropology, archaeology, art history, economics, ethnomusicology, folklore, geography, history, sociolinguistics, political science, and sociology. Using perspectives from all these disciplines, this journal analyzes culture and culture clashes and blending in the Pacific region. Economic and environmental change is a frequent theme, as are gender issues and belief. A recent article, for example, uses book cover photographs to analyze "an exotic eroticism" that has characterized popular and anthropological images of Pacific island women. A recent thematic issue explores strategies of migrants and dispersed groups for building "moral communities" in new environments. This is an excellent source for analysis of this vast region. The editorial board members are from prestigious academic institutions around the world. The journal is illustrated with maps, charts, and photographs. There are also abstracts for each article, book reviews, and visual media reviews. Recommended for academic libraries with an interest in the Pacific region.

East Asia

871. ***East.*** [ISSN: 0012-8295] 1964. 6x/yr. JPY 4800; USD 38. Ed(s): Burritt Sabin. East Publications Inc., Mamiana Arc Bldg, 1F, 2-1 Higashi-Azabu, 3 Minato-ku, Tokyo, 106-0044, Japan; east @japan.email.ne.jp. Illus., index, adv. Sample. Circ: 65000. Microform: PQC. Reprint: PQC. *Indexed:* ArtHuCI, BAS, SSCI. *Bk. rev.:* 1-3, 750-1,000 words. *Aud.:* Hs, Ga, Ac.

Begun in 1964, this magazine was started "to introduce overseas the quintessence of Japanese culture," foster understanding, and examine "how the inheritance of Japanese culture influences the values and thinking of present-day Japan in various fields." Tastefully illustrated, this lovely magazine contains a smorgasbord of features and topics, including history, travel, selections of essays and short stories, feature articles on art, popular culture, and technology, biographies of business leaders and historical figures, and film and book reviews. Recent issues include articles on Hojo Masako, "the nun general," powerful wife of ruler Yoritomo; a biographical sketch of the founder of the Japanese postal system; and a travel article on a colossal Buddha in Fukuoka. The web site previews new issues with imaginative animated use of images from the articles. Highly recommended as a source on Japanese arts, culture, economic culture, travel, and public affairs, especially for public and school libraries.

872. ***East Asian History.*** Formerly (until 1991): *Papers on Far Eastern History.* [ISSN: 1036-6008] 1970. s-a. USD 45 domestic; USD 50 foreign. Ed(s): Geremie Barme. Australian National University, Division of Pacific and Asian History, RSPAS, Canberra, ACT 0200, Australia; marion@coombs.anu.edu.au; http://rspas.anu.edu/au/eah. Illus., adv. Refereed. Circ: 400. Reprint: ISI. *Indexed:* AmH&L, ArtHuCI, BAS, IBZ. *Aud.:* Ac.

This refereed academic journal focuses primarily on China, but also on other East Asian countries, including recently Taiwan, Japan, and Korea. It spans history from ancient times to the recent past. For example, recent issues treat a case of environmental degradation in nineteenth-century China, cross-cultural influences on the religion of Chinese mariners, and Japanese colonization efforts by outcast groups and the process of becoming Japanese. But they also discuss more recent phenomena such as the Falon Gong movement. The journal is scholarly but very readable. Articles may be quite lengthy, treating subjects in detail but always relating them to larger issues or theoretical concepts. It is beautifully illustrated with art reproductions, photographs, lne drawings, cartoons, and original script. A recent issue contains an impressive photographic journal by a German traveler to Japanese-occupied Jehol in China in the 1930s. Highly recommended for large public and academic libraries serving Asian Studies or history scholars.

873. ***Japan and the World Economy: international journal of theory and policy.*** [ISSN: 0922-1425] 1988. q. EUR 413 (Individuals, EUR 48). Ed(s): Jeroen Loos. Elsevier BV, North-Holland, Sara Burgerhartstraat 25, Amsterdam, 1055 KV, Netherlands; nlinfo-f@elsevier.nl; http://www.elsevier.nl. Illus., adv. Sample. Refereed. Microform: PQC. Online: ingenta.com; ScienceDirect; Swets Blackwell. *Indexed:* BAS, IBSS, JEL, PAIS, SSCI. *Aud.:* Ac, Sa.

This scholarly economics journal "will publish original research in economics, finance, managerial sciences, and marketing" relating to the Japanese economy and its influence on U.S. and world affairs. It publishes empirically based scholarly articles, policy studies and theoretical analyses on "trade imbalance and friction, technological competition, internationalization of financial markets, exchange rate variation and macroeconomic coordination, comparative managerial and marketing practices and other related topics." The editors are from prestigious academic institutions. Examples of recent articles include "Can the rest of East Asia catch up with Japan," "The relative impact of the US and Japanese business cycles on the Australian Economy," and "Exchange-rate volatility, trade and ~fixing for life' in Thailand." Comparative studies of the United States and Japan are frequent. Thematic issues appear about once a year. Abstracts accompany each article. The journal's web site, at http://www.elsevier.com/homepage/sae/econworld/econbase/japwor/frame.htm, is logically arranged and searchable. Highly recommended for academic libraries serving economics or international business faculty and graduate programs.

874. ***Japan Echo: insight and analysis from the Japanese media.*** [ISSN: 0388-0435] 1974. bi-m. JPY 8400 domestic; USD 75 foreign. Ed(s): Sumiko Iwao. Japan Echo Inc, 1-3-13 Hirakawa-cho, Chiyoda-ku, Tokyo, 102-0093, Japan. Illus., adv. Sample. Microform: PQC. Online: bigchalk; Gale Group; Northern Light Technology, Inc.; OCLC Online Computer Library Center, Inc.; ProQuest Information & Learning. *Indexed:* BAS, IBSS. *Aud.:* Ga, Ac.

This excellent current-affairs journal publishes full or abridged translations of articles and opinion pieces from the Japanese media, written originally for a Japanese audience. Articles are accompanied by information on the authors' credentials; most are scholars or prominent journalists. Some articles are commissioned. Some issues include a series of articles grouped under three or four themes, providing alternative viewpoints on or different aspects of the issues. Recent issues include articles on refugee policy, environmental government in Asia, and opposing viewpoints on the declining scholastic achievement and the new curriculum guidelines recently implemented in the Japanese school system. Another set of articles assessed the Koizumi structural reforms. Emphasis is on political, economic, and international affairs, but there are also occasional cultural and historical pieces, such as a recent interview with architect Ando Tadao, articles on Japanese *manga*, and on parenting in the royal family and the possibility of female succession. Each issue also includes a two-month chronology of events, mostly political and economic. Though not a scholarly journal, it is well written and informed enough to be of interest to academics as well as to the general reader. The web site offers tables of contents and selected full text for current and back issues. Highly recommended for the academic, public, and high school library.

875. ***Japan Economic Review.*** [ISSN: 0449-4636] 1969. m. USD 7. Japan Economic Review, c/o Kyodo Tsushinsha, 9-20, Asaka 1-chome, Tokyo, 107, Japan. Illus. Sample. Vol. ends: Dec. *Aud.:* Ga, Ac, Sa.

This monthly newsletter, "created with the cooperation of the Ministry of Foreign Affairs and the business world," was designed to disseminate information about the Japanese economy and to promote "Japan's economic diplomacy and normalization of trade." Though only 12 pages long and in tabloid format, it is a good source of succinct economic news and commentary. It is well illustrated with graphs and photographs, some in color. It covers government trade agreements, industry and corporate developments, market trends, and forecasts. A fair amount of each issue reports technology news, especially automotive and telecommunications. Other features include broader issues such as trade relations with the United States and other countries, a few general interest items, interviews, and at least one non-economic topic per issue, such as recent features on Hirosaki Castle or international haiku competitions. This is not a flashy commercial business magazine but a more measured, attractive summary of economic news and trends. Recommended for public and academic libraries.

Japanese Journal of Religious Studies. See Religion section.

876. *Journal of Japanese Studies.* [ISSN: 0095-6848] 1974. s-a. USD 42 domestic; USD 47 foreign. Ed(s): Susan B Hanley, John Whitter Treat. Society for Japanese Studies, University of Washington, Box 353650, Seattle, WA 98195-3650; jjs@u.washington.edu; http://depts.washington.edu/jjs. Illus., adv. Refereed. Circ: 1900. Vol. ends: Summer. Reprint: PSC. *Indexed:* AmH&L, ArtHuCI, BAS, HumInd, IBSS, IPSA, MLA-IB, SSCI, SSI. *Bk. rev.:* 10-40, 1,500-3,000 words. *Aud.:* Ac, Sa.

This prestigious scholarly journal publishes "new information, new interpretations, and recent research results concerning Japan" including "broad, exploratory articles suggesting new analyses and interpretations, substantial book reviews, translations of Japanese articles of particular interest, and occasional symposia." The emphasis is on history and literary interpretation and on contemporary cultural, economic, and public affairs. It is multidisciplinary, providing fresh perspectives on Japan for an English audience. For example, a recent article discusses the effect of leadership in a case study of political change, while another compares the concept of "a good death" in America and Japan, exploring its cultural roots. Over half of each issue is devoted to substantial book reviews and review articles by academic experts. Abstracts and notes on contributors accompany the articles. An index and tables of contents for the last three years are available online. Highly recommended for academic and research libraries.

877. *Korea & World Affairs.* [ISSN: 0259-9686] 1977. q. USD 66 foreign. Research Center for Peace and Unification, Rm.1014, Daewoo Center Bldg, 5-541, Namdaemoon-ro, Choong-Ku, C.P.O. Box 6545, Seoul, 100-714, Korea, Republic of; rcpu@chollian.net. Illus., index. Sample. *Indexed:* IBSS, IPSA, PAIS, PRA. *Aud.:* Ac, Ga.

This scholarly journal, published by the Research Center for Peace and Unification of Korea, concerns public and international affairs in contemporary Korea. Its editorial board and authors are academic experts in Korea or abroad, and high-ranking government or agency officials. The focus is on relations between North and South Korea and the United States, and on events and factors affecting peace and security in the region and possibilities for unification of the divided nation. It also addresses wider topics such as culture and development, trade issues, and comparative policy studies. Recent topics include "Beijing, Moscow, and Pyongyang: Same Old Bed, Three Different Dreams," "The Impact of U.S.-North Korean Relations on Inter-Korean Relations," and "Orders to Attack," an analysis of secret orders in the Korean People's Army at the start of the Korean War. This very readable journal provides valuable historical background and analysis of the current situation in the two Koreas. Author notes provide credentials, current position, and major publications. The journal also provides "source materials" (texts of presidential addresses, press briefings, and other documents) and a chronology of events in North and South Korea for the quarter, presented side by side in two columns. There are no abstracts or web site. Recommended for academic and larger public libraries.

878. *Korea Journal.* [ISSN: 0023-3900] 1961. q. KRW 40000 domestic; USD 50 foreign. Ed(s): Yi Jeong Hyeon. Korean National Commission for UNESCO, CPO Box 64, Seoul, Korea, Republic of; kj@mail.unesco.or.kr; http://www.unesco.or.kr/. Illus. Sample. Refereed. Circ: 2100. Vol. ends: Winter. *Indexed:* AmH&L, BAS, IBSS, IPSA, MLA-IB, RILM. *Bk. rev.:* 2-4, 1,000-2,000 words. *Aud.:* Ga, Ac.

This scholarly UNESCO publication was founded to encourage Korean Studies, originally focusing on "traditional culture and the humanities," but now more concerned with the social sciences, especially but not exclusively as related to Korea. The emphasis is on society, politics, democratic processes, and economic development in contemporary Korea and the recent past, but the journal also includes broad topics such as an essay on "Asian values." Recent articles discuss government policies on gender equality, corporate restructuring, labor reform, and Korean wartime collaboration with the Japanese. Another focuses on the prospects for reunification of North and South, with comparisons to Vietnam and Germany. Articles are often grouped under common themes, such as human rights in Korea and the Korean economy. Short book reviews are also included in each issue. Recommended for academic libraries serving Asian Studies or international relations programs.

879. *Korea Observer.* [ISSN: 0023-3919] 1968. q. USD 40. Ed(s): Myong Whai Kim. Institute of Korean Studies, PO Box 3410, Seoul, 100634, Korea, Republic of. Illus., adv. Refereed. Circ: 3500. Vol. ends: Winter. *Indexed:* BAS, IBSS, IPSA, PAIS. *Aud.:* Ga, Ac, Sa.

This scholarly journal publishes articles on modern Korean Studies, "especially in the fields of the humanities and the social sciences," and includes articles on politics, economics, societies, and culture as they relate to Korea. The emphasis is on contemporary affairs and recent history (twentieth century) as it affects present-day Korea. The focus is mostly on North and South Korean politics, economic development, and international relations, from a South Korean perspective. This publication fills a niche for scholarly articles on public-affairs topics affecting modern Korea. Recent issues examine the future of the U.S. Forces in Korea, trace the history and possible future of civil society in South Korea, compare development of the IT industry in Korea and Australia, and analyze the influence of ideology on perceptions of Korea before the Korean War by the Soviet Union and the United States. A special issue published selected papers from the 2002 Seoul Ocean Seminar. Tables and charts and occasional photographs supplement the text and abstracts are provided. A limited number of book reviews are included. The journal also prints topical documents such as presidential speeches, including one by George Bush during a visit to South Korea. Recommended for academic libraries with an interest in Asian Studies or international relations.

880. *Korean Studies.* [ISSN: 0145-840X] 1977. s-a. a. pre-vol.25. USD 30 (Individuals, USD 20; Students, USD 15). University of Hawaii Press, Journals Department, 2840 Kolowalu St, Honolulu, HI 96822-1888; uhpjourn@hawaii.edu; http://www.uhpress.hawaii.edu/. Adv. Refereed. Circ: 180. Online: EBSCO Publishing; Florida Center for Library Automation; Gale Group; OCLC Online Computer Library Center, Inc.; Project MUSE; ProQuest Information & Learning; RoweCom Information Quest; Swets Blackwell. Reprint: ISI; PQC; PSC. *Indexed:* AmH&L, BAS, GeogAbPG, IBSS, L&LBA, MLA-IB, PAIS, PSA, SociolAb. *Bk. rev.:* Various number and length. *Aud.:* Ac.

This scholarly journal publishes articles in all academic disciplines about Korea and Koreans abroad. It welcomes interdisciplinary and multicultural studies, however, the most of articles are concerned with the history, public affairs, and international relations of South Korea, its relations with the North, or with Korean literature and language. The journal includes essays and a fair number of in-depth book reviews in the humanities and social sciences, both for specialists on Korea and nonspecialists. Recent issues include an article on an early Korean feminist painter and writer and an analysis of the impact of the 1997 IMF economic crisis on families and gender roles. A recent thematic issue explores Korean historiography, with articles on popular influences on the making of history, an overview of Korean literature of the diaspora, and views on Korean collaboration with occupying Japan. Abstracts accompany each article. Some are illustrated. The web site, at http://www.uhpress.hawaii.edu/journals/ks/index.html, offers tables of contents and abstracts from 1994 to the present, as well as indexes of articles and book reviews from 1977 to 2000, and a link to the Copyright Clearance Center for permissions. Full content is also available through Project MUSE. This very readable journal is highly recommended for academic libraries concerned with Asian Studies or international relations.

881. ***Monumenta Nipponica: studies in Japanese culture.*** [ISSN: 0027-0741] 1938. q. JPY 4280; USD 36. Ed(s): Lynne E. Riggs, Kate Wildman Nakai. Sophia University, 7-1 Kioi-cho, Chiyoda-ku, Tokyo, 102-8554 , Japan; http://monumenta.cc.sophia.ac.jp/. Illus., index, adv. Refereed. Circ: 1150. Vol. ends: Winter. Microform: PQC. Online: JSTOR (Web-based Journal Archive). *Indexed:* AmH&L, ArtHuCI, BAS, IBSS, MLA-IB, RI-1, SSCI. *Bk. rev.:* 8-15, 750-1,500 words. *Aud.:* Ac, Sa.

An excellent and well-established peer-reviewed journal about all things Japanese, publishing "original scholarship and translations in the fields of history, literature, art history, religion, thought, and anthropology." Many recent articles are historical studies of art and literature, but others cover music, education, and social issues such as prostitution. Some are illustrated. There are also translations of literary works, numerous books reviews, and review essays. Examples of recent articles include "The Ambiguous Legacy of Modern Japanese Philosophy," "Digitalizing Japanese Art," and "Apocryphal Texts and Literary Identity." It also addresses more contemporary social topics such as "Regendering Domestic Space: Modern Housing in Prewar Tokyo." It is addressed to an academic audience but is easily readable by anyone with an interest in Japanese culture. The journal web site, at http://monumenta.cc.sophia.ac.jp, contains tables of contents of recent issues and indexes of its articles, translations, and book reviews. There is also a link to *JSTOR* for full texts of back issues. Highly recommended for academic and larger public libraries.

882. ***Nichibunken Japan Review.*** [ISSN: 0915-0986] 1990. a. International Research Center for Japanese Studies (Nichibunken), 3-2 Oeyama-cho, Goryo, Nishikyo-ku, Kyoto-shi, 610-1192, Japan. *Indexed:* BAS. *Bk. rev.:* Various number and length. *Aud.:* Ac.

This scholarly journal serves as the bulletin of the International Research Center for Japanese Studies in Kyoto, Japan, which seeks to advance the "comparative and interdisciplinary studies of Japan." Contributors are members of the center, but articles are also invited or accepted on occasion. It is published once a year and distributed free to institutions where Japanese Studies programs exist. The journal includes articles, book reviews and review articles, research notes, technical reports, and occasional translations of articles on Japanese culture, art, language, literature, history, and society. Abstracts are included for each article. Topics range from a new interpretation of mythological deities to an analysis of attitude toward the lower class in an eleventh-century literary work to images of the family in early modern Japanese theater. Abstracts accompany the articles. A recent special issue reports on a team project analyzing the "Birth of Tardiness: The Formation of Time Consciousness in Modern Japan." The journal is illustrated with graphs, tables, and photographs; translation in Japanese script is liberally supplied. Useful for academic libraries serving Asian or Japanese Studies scholars.

883. ***Nipponia.*** [ISSN: 1343-1196] 1997. q. JPY 238 per issue. Ed(s): Tsuchiya Komei, Sanada Kuniko. Heibonsha Ltd., 2-29-4 Kakusan, Bunkyo-ku, Tokyo, 112-0001, Japan. *Aud.:* Hs, Ga.

This glossy magazine, published in 14 languages, "introduces modern Japan to people all over the world." Articles are short (one or two pages) and lavishly illustrated. Each issue contains a series of articles on one theme, usually concerning trends and changing lifestyles in Japan and focusing on the young. Regular features include a cover interview with a prominent personality, a mystery photograph, Trends Today, Living in Japan, Bon Appetit, and a Travelogue highlighting a Japanese tourist destination. Recent issues have featured articles on Japan underground (transportation, streets, and shops), Japanese seafood, and traditional Japanese footwear. The web site, at http://jin.jcic.or.jp/nipponia, is well designed, offering full texts and images from current and back issues, in Japanese, Chinese, English, Spanish, French, and Korean. Recommended for public and school libraries.

884. ***Pacific Friend: a window on Japan.*** 1973. m. JPY 8100; USD 60 per issue; JPY 60 newsstand/cover per issue. Ed(s): Hisashi Kondo. Jiji Gaho Sha Inc., Fonte Akasaka Bldg, 7-10-17 Akasaka, Tokyo, 107-0052, Japan; pf-info@jijigaho.or.jp; http://www.jijigaho.or.jp/index_e.html. Illus., adv. *Aud.:* Ga.

Similar to *Nipponia* in purpose, but more meaty, this "monthly pictorial" is designed "for anyone who wants to know more about Japan." It is published in English and in Japanese. Articles cover both serious and playful topics, from "The Spread of Universal Design," and "Preparing for Disaster" to "Tokyo Through Souvenirs." The photographs are excellent and the feature articles imaginative. The magazine frequently features articles on environmental, political, arts, and media topics, as well as nature, and social or cultural phenomena. A recent "Around the Pacific" feature compares photographically the contents of refrigerators in ten countries! This tasteful magazine is a good choice for libraries looking for nonacademic treatment of Japan.

885. ***Positions: East Asia cultures critique.*** [ISSN: 1067-9847] 1993. 3x/yr. USD 125 includes online access (Individuals, USD 33 includes online access). Ed(s): Tani Barlow. Duke University Press, 905 W Main St, Ste 18 B, Durham, NC 27701; subscriptions@dukeupress.edu; http://www.dukeupress.edu. Adv. Circ: 800. Online: EBSCO Publishing; Ingenta Select; OCLC Online Computer Library Center, Inc.; Project MUSE; RoweCom Information Quest; Swets Blackwell. Reprint: PSC. *Indexed:* AmH&L, ArtHuCI, BAS, MLA-IB, PSA, SociolAb. *Bk. rev.:* Various number and length. *Aud.:* Ac.

This journal offers scholarly articles of varying length, often multidisciplinary in approach, as well as works of poetry, lengthy book and film reviews, visuals, and commentary on East Asian cultures. The scope is broad, including social, artistic, historical, political, and other perspectives on East Asian culture and East Asians abroad. It critically examines the legacies of colonialism, recent profound economic and political changes, and Third World status of countries in the region as well as the creation of modern identities. Article topics are extremely varied. For example, recent articles explore writing about food and cooking as it relates to regional, class, and gender identities of Indians abroad; sexuality in Tibet; identity formation of Taiwanese doctors and med students under Japanese occupation; and representations of dogs in Japanese culture. A recent thematic issue explores ethnicity and culture. Recommended for academic libraries serving Asian Studies programs.

886. ***Social Science Japan Journal.*** [ISSN: 1369-1465] 1998. s-a. GBP 102. Ed(s): Akira Suehiro. Oxford University Press, Great Clarendon St, Oxford, OX2 6DP, United Kingdom; jnl.orders@oup.co.uk; http://www3.oup.co.uk/jnls. Adv. Refereed. Circ: 1050. Reprint: PSC. *Indexed:* AmH&L, BAS, IBSS, JEL, PAIS, PSA, SociolAb. *Bk. rev.:* Various number and length. *Aud.:* Ac.

This excellent refereed scholarly journal is a product of the Institute of Social Science at the University of Tokyo. It continues *Annals of the Institute of Social Science*, which suspended publication in 1995; the new title begins with volume 1 in 1998. It publishes comparative studies on contemporary Japan and international issues as they affect Japan. Disciplines include economics, law, political science, history, sociology, and anthropology. For example, recent articles study the effect of the economic crisis on Japanese crime syndicates, compare police-corruption data in Japan and the United States, and analyze perceptions of World War II as seen in *manga* in the postwar period. The journal also publishes commentaries, survey articles, review articles, and numerous book reviews. It is recommended for academic libraries with interests in Japanese or East Asian affairs. The institute also publishes a newsletter, *Social Science Japan* [ISSN: 1340-7155], accessible from the institute's web site at http://www.iss.u-tokyo.ac.jp. Newsletter issues address a single theme, such as Japanese education or China in transition, in a series of articles available in pdf format at no charge.

887. ***Vantage Point: developments in North Korea.*** [ISSN: 0251-2971] 1978. m. Free. Ed(s): Li Ik Sang. Naewoe Press, 42-2 Chuja dong, Chung-gu, PO Box 9708, Seoul, 100240, Korea, Republic of. Illus. Circ: 3000. *Indexed:* BAS, BRI, IPSA. *Aud.:* Ga, Ac, Sa.

This news and public affairs magazine is published in South Korea but reports on political and economic developments in North Korea and on the North's relations with South Korea and the United States. It provides a distinctly South Korean, highly critical view of the Northern regime. Each issue provides short articles on major developments, news summaries and excerpts from other sources, and a chronology of events and people. The editors monitor North Korean broadcast and print media; analysis is necessarily based largely on official North Korean sources. Each issue also includes one longer, more scholarly study. A recent feature article analyzes North Korea's declaration of policy priorities for the new year, finding a continuation of its "military first" policy and emphasis on "ideological indoctrination" rather than new economic initiatives. Other articles assess the nuclear policy crisis, stormy relations with the United States, and prospects for change under the new president-elect. The web site, at http://www.yonhapnews.co.kr/services/2220030000.html, is in Korean but offers tables of contents for the current issue and past year in English. The web site also links to Yonhapnews, a free full-text news service on Korea. Recommended for academic libraries with an interest in East Asian or international affairs.

Inner Asia

888. *Central Asian Survey.* [ISSN: 0263-4937] 1982. q. Individuals, GBP 83. Ed(s): Marie Broxup. Carfax Publishing Ltd., 4 Park Sq, Milton Park, Abingdon, OX14 4RN, United Kingdom; enquiry@tandf.co.uk; http://www.tandf.co.uk/. Illus., index, adv. Sample. Refereed. Online: EBSCO Publishing; Ingenta Select; Northern Light Technology, Inc.; OCLC Online Computer Library Center, Inc.; ProQuest Information & Learning; RoweCom Information Quest; Swets Blackwell. Reprint: PSC. *Indexed:* AICP, AmH&L, IBSS, IBZ, IPSA, PSA, RRTA, SWA, SociolAb, WAE&RSA. *Bk. rev.:* 4-7, 750-1,500 words. *Aud.:* Ac, Sa.

This refereed journal covers the "history, politics, cultures, religions and economics of the Central Asian and Caucasian regions," including nations from Anatolia to Mongolia. The articles often focus on contemporary public affairs and their historical roots in light of recent political, demographic, economic, and military changes in the region. Frequent themes include political culture and Islam, shifts of power between Russia and newly independent states, national identity formation, ethnic vs. political boundaries, and the effects of change on identity, gender issues, and society. Some articles engage in the rewriting of history given new access to Russian archival documents. Examples include a special issue on resistance to Russian expansion in the Caucasus region in the nineteenth century, and articles on "Broadcasting to Tibet," and "Modernity, Nationalism, Resistance: Identity Politics in Post-Soviet Kazakhstan." Countries discussed in one recent issue include Azerbaijan, Kazakhstan, Tajikistan, Russia, Chechnya, Tibet, and Turkey. Recent tables of contents are available online. Expensive but recommended for academic libraries for its quality and broad scope.

889. *Central Asiatic Journal: international periodical for the languages, literatures, history and archaeology of Central Asia.* [ISSN: 0008-9192] 1955. s-a. EUR 84; CHF 142 Switzerland. Ed(s): Giovanni Stary. Harrassowitz Verlag, Taunusstr 14, Wiesbaden, 65183, Germany; verlag@harrassowitz.de; http://www.harrassowitz.de. Illus., index, adv. Sample. Refereed. Circ: 550. *Indexed:* ArtHuCI, BAS, IBSS, IBZ, MLA-IB, NumL. *Bk. rev.:* 8-15, 750-2,500 words. *Aud.:* Ac, Sa.

This high-quality but highly specialized academic journal covers all the disciplines in the subtitle and more, for example, religion and music. One recent article, for instance, offers evidence for Tibetan Buddhist pilgrimage sites in Mongolia, while another uses chemical analysis of pottery to explore contacts between the Xiong-nu, a dominant Inner Asian ethnic group in the second and third centuries B.C., and the wider region. Textual analyses and translations of historic documents are also published. An example is a recent transcription and translation of a land-dispute document from nineteenth-century Mongolia showing friction between social classes and between Mongols and Chinese. Articles on history from the nineteenth century onward are not normally included. Emphasis is on the languages and literature of the region. For example, another recent article focuses on the translation of one word in a cache of Manichean documents found in China a century ago, written in Persian and Partian. The journal is well illustrated with sketches, photographs, tables, and maps; it includes original script where appropriate. It also includes book reviews, but not abstracts. Articles are in English, German, or French. Recommended for specialized research collections.

890. *Mongol Survey: a publication of the Mongolia Society.* Former titles: *Mongolia Survey;* (until 1995): *Mongolia Society Newsletter. New Series.* [ISSN: 1081-5082] 1962. irreg. Ed(s): Peter K Marsh. Mongolia Society, Inc., 322 Goodbody Hall, Indiana University, Bloomington, IN 47405-2401; http://www.bluemarket.net/~mitch/monsoc/monsocnews.html. Illus., adv. Sample. *Indexed:* BAS, IBSS. *Bk. rev.:* Various number and length. *Aud.:* Ga, Ac, Sa.

This is the newsletter of the Mongolia Society, which seeks to promote the study of Mongolia and its people, language, and culture. Members of the society receive this and *Mongolian Studies* (below) as part of membership. Members contribute news items, announcements, and articles. The articles range from nonscholarly travel accounts to research reports by academics on contemporary public affairs or historical eras, or research projects. For example, recent issues report on a project to survey the well-being of the Dukha community and the reindeer they herd, and on an archeological project that is surveying the ecology of ancient cultures in the Altay mountain region. General-interest articles include one that speculates on the reasons for the predominance of women in Mongolian universities, and one that promotes revival of interest in Mongolian Buddhist art. It also contains announcements of conferences and calls for papers, society news and reports, book reviews, and notices of festivals, jobs, grants, scholarships, and exhibitions. The events announced are for the most part in the United States. Other features are "Internet News," with links to web sites on Mongolia and "Recently Published" books on Mongolia. Recommended for specialized research collections and public libraries serving people of Mongolian origin.

891. *Mongolian Studies.* Supersedes (in 1974): *Mongolian Society Bulletin;* Which superseded: *Mongolia Society Newsletter.* [ISSN: 0190-3667] 1962. a. USD 20. Ed(s): Christopher Atwood. Mongolia Society, Inc., 322 Goodbody Hall, Indiana University, Bloomington, IN 47405-2401; monsoc@indiana.edu; http://www.bluemarket.net/~mitch/monsoc/monsocj.html. Illus., adv. Sample. Refereed. Circ: 475. *Indexed:* ABS&EES, AmH&L, BAS, IBSS, MLA-IB. *Bk. rev.:* 4-12, 750-3,000 words. *Aud.:* Ac, Sa.

This refereed journal "contains scholarly research articles, book reviews, and embraces cross-Asian and multi-disciplinary approaches to Mongolia, past and present." It is the scholarly journal of the Mongolia Society, whereas *Mongolian Survey* (above in this section) is its newsletter. The society also publishes scholarly *Occasional Papers.* This journal includes scholarly studies of Mongolian history, culture, and language as well as translations, book reviews, and review articles on any Mongolian topic. Most but not all of the articles are in English. Recent articles discuss the lack of written indigenous histories of the Golden Horde, "Mongolian Representations of the Body," and a translation of a Buddhist hymn. Charts, maps, and other scripts augment the text. The publication has been appearing approximately a year late. Nevertheless, this is an important source of scholarly work on this little-known region of the world.

892. *The Tibet Journal: a publication of Tibetian studies.* [ISSN: 0970-5368] 1975. q. INR 260; USD 30. Ed(s): Thupten K Rikey. Library of Tibetan Works and Archives, Dharmsala, 176 215, India; ltwa@ndf.vsnl.net.in; http://www.lib.virginia.edu/area-studies/Tibet/Tserials/Tibet.Jour/tibJour.html. Illus., index, adv. Sample. Refereed. Circ: 1000. Vol. ends: Winter. *Indexed:* BAS, IBSS. *Bk. rev.:* 0-4, 750-2,500 words. *Aud.:* Ga, Ac, Sa.

This journal, published in India by the Library of Tibetan Works and Archives of the Government of Tibet in Exile, provides "scholarly and general interest articles on Tibetan culture and civilization" in English or Romanized Tibetan. Most are scholarly; contributors are scholars and students of Tibetan Studies. Articles span a wide range of fields, from art to history to linguistics to public affairs. The journal also includes book reviews and review articles. The latest issue available for review contains articles on textual transmission and lineage of ancient manuscripts, cultural history of one Tibetan district before Chinese occupation, and East India Company's failed attempts to open trade with Tibet. The quality is generally high and the information not readily available elsewhere. The "unofficial" web site, at http://lib.virginia.edu/area-studies/Tibet/Tserials/TibetJour/tibJour.html, provides tables of contents from 1995 forward, but shows 2000 as the latest volume. Recommended for libraries serving Asian Studies programs or Tibetan populations.

893. *Tibetan Review: a monthly magazine on all aspects of Tibet.* Formerly: *Voice of Tibet.* [ISSN: 0040-6708] 1968. m. INR 90 domestic; USD 25 foreign. Ed(s): Pema Thinley. Tibetan Review, c/o Tibetan SOS

Youth Hostel, Sector 14 Ext. Rohini, New Delhi, 110 085, India; tibrev@vsnl.com; http://tibetan.review.to. Illus., index, adv. Sample. Circ: 4500. Vol. ends: Dec. *Indexed:* BAS, IBZ. *Aud.:* Ga.

This is a general news and public affairs magazine about modern Tibet and its people wherever they may reside, and about the problems of Tibet and activities related to it around the world. It invites articles from researchers and journalists interested in all aspects of Tibetan Studies. Most articles, however, are short and carry no byline. A few longer articles on Tibetan life and culture by journalists, academics, and others also appear. It is published from Delhi, and edited by Mr. Thinley, former Executive Editor of *Tibetan Bulletin*, the official journal of the Central Tibet Administration of the Dalai Lama. The magazine summarizes or reprints news stories found in world media sources, particularly about the latest suppressive measures and atrocities of the Chinese in Tibet, and about the activities of the Dalai Lama. The web site provides sample articles from the past, but has not been updated recently; it also contains links to Tibetan activist organizations such as the International Tibet Independence Movement. Recommended for any library with an interest in news on this underreported part of the world.

South Asia

894. ***Business India: the magazine of the corporate world.*** [ISSN: 0254-5268] 1978. fortn. INR 245; USD 110. Business India Group of Publications, Nirmal, Nariman Point, Mumbai, 400 021, India; http://www.indiaworld.co.in/biz/yp/bi-index.html. Illus., adv. Circ: 17508. Vol. ends: Dec. Online: bigchalk; Factiva; Florida Center for Library Automation; Gale Group; ProQuest Information & Learning. *Indexed:* B&I. *Bk. rev.:* 0-3, 500-1,000 words. *Aud.:* Ga, Ac.

This hefty biweekly magazine is aimed at Indian business and corporate executives. In addition to business news, it includes irreverent editorials on the political and economic climate, international and Internet news, interviews with prominent business figures, articles on technology, energy, resources, development, government policy and court decisions, and on marketing, advertising, manufacturing, and banking. There are brief news reports on companies and occasional articles on social issues. The Marketwatch section contains the usual economic indicators, currency, and stock exchange figures found in most business weeklies. A recent editorial comments on the Indian government's lack of commitment to the environment and sustainable development despite industry's environmental advances; another article describes the innovative business strategy of a retail chain. A good source of coverage of Indian business news.

895. ***Contributions to Indian Sociology.*** [ISSN: 0069-9667] 1957. 3x/yr. GBP 130 in Europe, Middle East, Africa & Australasia. Ed(s): Veena Das, Dipankar Gupta. Sage Publications India Pvt. Ltd., M-32 Market, Greater Kailash-I, PO Box 4215, New Delhi, 110 048, India; http://www.indiasage.com/. Adv. Refereed. Circ: 900. Microform: PQC. *Indexed:* AICP, AnthLit, ArtHuCI, BAS, IBSS, IBZ, IMFL, IPSA, PSA, RRTA, SSCI, SociolAb, WAE&RSA. *Bk. rev.:* Various number and length. *Aud.:* Ac.

This is an excellent, widely indexed academic journal comprising research articles, book reviews, review articles, and a discussion section. It provides a "forum for divergent views on Indian society." It also publishes articles on "themes of cross-civilisational significance, bringing in data from non-South Asian societies." It devotes some issues to a single significant topic, such as a recent one titled "Beyond Appearances? Visual Practices and Ideologies in Modern India," and occasionally the journal publishes comparative studies. The articles are well written and avoid jargon. The scope is all of South Asian society and culture, including such concerns as traditional culture and power as shown in the marketing of traditional Ayurvedic medicine in response to the modern market, and the shaping of women's citizenship rights during the independence movement and repercussions today. Another recent article discusses the relationship between democracy and communitarianism. Abstracts precede each article; however, the web site provides only tables of contents. The numerous book reviews are brief but well written. Highly recommended for academic libraries.

896. ***Economic and Political Weekly: a journal of current economic and political affairs.*** Formerly: *Economic Weekly.* [ISSN: 0012-9976] 1966. w. INR 800 (Individuals, INR 650; Students, INR 300). Ed(s): Krishna Raj. Sameeksha Trust, Hitkari House, 284 Shahid Bhagatsingh Rd., Mumbai, 400 038, India; epw@vsnl.com; http://www.south-asian-initiative.org/EPW. Illus., adv. Sample. Refereed. Circ: 14000 Paid. Vol. ends: Dec. Microform: IDC. *Indexed:* AgeL, ArtHuCI, BAS, DSA, FPA, ForAb, IPSA, PAIS, RI-1, RRTA, S&F, SSCI, WAE&RSA. *Bk. rev.:* 2-4, 1,500-3,000 words. *Aud.:* Ga, Ac.

Not a refereed academic journal, but more scholarly than the usual business or news weekly, this periodical is a widely read and respected source of political and economic analysis on contemporary India. Each issue contains thoughtful essays on large political, economic, and social issues, such as a theoretical discussion on sustainable development in the context of a concept of "human well-being," as well as more narrowly focused articles on more-local issues such as hybrid rice research and rural credit. Each issue includes political commentary and editorials, feature research articles, economic statistics, money market reports, book reviews, and letters. Highly recommended for academic and medium or large public libraries.

897. ***India Perspectives.*** [ISSN: 0970-5074] 1988. m. Free. Ed(s): Bharat Bhushan. Ministry of External Affairs, 149, 'A' Wing, Shastri Bhavan, New Delhi, 110 001, India; subeditor_ip@meadev.gov.in; http://www.indiagov.org/perspec/intro.html. Illus. Sample. Circ: 50000. *Aud.:* Hs, Ga.

This free monthly magazine is published by the Ministry for External Affairs of the Government of India. It is distributed abroad in ten languages through the Indian Embassy. Generously illustrated, it offers brief articles on travel, art, nature spots, literature, and culture in India, promoting its image abroad. It also includes book reviews and some current-affairs articles. A recent issue includes articles on Kaziranga National Park's rare wildlife; Jamia Masjid, Srinagar's noted mosque; and Kaifi Azmi, Urdu poet. Another recent issue is devoted to the Indian diaspora, with well-illustrated articles on Indian immigrants' impact on food, fashion, culture, etc., Indian success stories, and the experience of Indians in various parts of the world, from Fiji to Dubai to the United States. Recommended for school or public libraries.

898. ***India Quarterly: a journal of international affairs.*** [ISSN: 0251-3048] 1945. q. USD 100. Indian Council of World Affairs, Sapru House, Barakhamba Rd., New Delhi, 110 001, India; dgicwa@bol.net.in. Illus., index, adv. Sample. Circ: 2000. Vol. ends: Oct/Dec. *Indexed:* ABCPolSci, BAS, IBSS, IBZ, IPSA, PAIS. *Aud.:* Ac.

This is a scholarly journal but not refereed; its authors are academics, but the journal contains essays rather than empirical research. The focus is on contemporary political and economic issues, especially concerning India and its neighbors, but also events in the international arena. The essays also provide historical background on the issues. Some issues have a unifying theme. One recent issue is devoted for the most part to global terrorism. Many of the articles showed a decided nationalist (anti-Pakistan) perspective. Recent articles have discussed chances for peace between Israelis and Palestinians, and between India and Pakistan, and outlined the religious basis for terrorism in fundamentalist Islam. Useful for providing a non-Western perspective on international relations, for an academic library.

899. ***India Today.*** [ISSN: 0254-8399] 1975. w. INR 399; INR 10 newsstand/cover per issue; GBP 1.80 newsstand/cover per issue United Kingdom. Ed(s): Aroon Purie. Living Media India Pvt. Ltd., F-14-15, Connaught Place, New Delhi, India; http://www.india-today.com/itoday/index.html. Illus., adv. Sample. Circ: 414293. Vol. ends: Dec. *Indexed:* B&I, PAIS. *Bk. rev.:* 2-4, 500-1,000 words. *Aud.:* Hs, Ga.

This *Time* look-alike is an important source of news and commentary on what's going on in modern India. This newsweekly reports on government action and South Asian and international affairs and covers trends in business, technology, the arts, sports, entertainment and prominent personalities, and publishes interviews, editorials, and book, art, and film reviews. Recent feature articles describe the recent wave of Bharatiya Janata Party success at the polls, and legal obstacles faced by Indians returning from abroad. It is copiously illustrated with photographs and irreverent graphics. The international edition, published in the United States and widely read by Indians in America, also covers such events as the London stage production of Salmon Rushdie's *Midnight's Children* and discusses the Indian animated film *Alibaba*'s chances at the Oscars. There are also other Indian-language editions published in India. The web site is available in English and Hindi, but it limits all content to subscribers. Highly recommended for public, school, and academic libraries with an interest in contemporary India.

900. ***Indian Economic and Social History Review.*** [ISSN: 0019-4646] 1963. q. GBP 156 in Europe, Middle East, Africa & Australasia. Ed(s): Dr. Dharma Kumar. Sage Publications India Pvt. Ltd., M-32 Market, Greater Kailash-I, PO Box 4215, New Delhi, 110 048, India; http://www.indiasage.com/. Index, adv. Refereed. Circ: 900. Microform: PQC. Reprint: PQC. *Indexed:* AmH&L, ArtHuCI, BAS, IBSS, IBZ, JEL, NumL, PSA, SSCI, SociolAb. *Bk. rev.:* Various number and length. *Aud.:* Ac.

This refereed scholarly journal addresses the "history, economy and society of India and South Asia." It also includes comparative studies, especially as they relate to Indian history. Maps, photographs, and tables supplement the text. Contributors are from academic institutions worldwide. Articles focus on all aspects of Indian and South Asian history, but of late have focused on the colonial and postcolonial periods. Recent articles, for example, critique the British colonial jails for Indian women; explore eighteenth-century Italian missionaries' perceptions of Indian culture and religions and how they differed from British and French perceptions; and discuss political support for large-scale public works projects in postcolonial India. Abstracts are included beginning with the 2003 issue. Issues typically include about ten book reviews of two or three pages each. Thematic issues appear occasionally. A year-end index includes a separate listing of books reviewed. The web site, at http://www.sagepub.co.uk/journals/details/j0032.html, offers tables of contents for the last several volumes but little else. An excellent source on Indian and South Asian history, this journal is highly recommended for academic libraries serving history or Asian Studies departments.

901. ***Indian Economic Review.*** [ISSN: 0019-4670] 1952. s-a. INR 300; USD 50. Ed(s): Partha Sen. University of Delhi, Delhi School of Economics, New Delhi, 110 007, India; ier@cdedse.ernet.in. Adv. Refereed. Circ: 600. *Indexed:* BAS, IBSS, JEL, PAIS, RRTA, RiskAb, WAE&RSA. *Bk. rev.:* Various number and length. *Aud.:* Ac.

This refereed academic journal publishes research on economics in India and South Asia. The emphasis is on measuring the effects of public policies on the economy, and the effects of economic policies on development issues such as poverty reduction, gender equality, energy management, and globalization issues. Comparative studies are also included, such as "Characteristics of India's formal and informal trading with Nepal: A Comparative Analysis." Special issues, such as a recent issue on business cycles, sometimes appear. Articles include lucid abstracts as well as numerous tables, formulas, and graphs. Recommended for academic libraries serving economics, public affairs, and development studies programs.

902. ***Indian Literature: Sahitya Akademi's bi-monthly journal.*** [ISSN: 0019-5804] 1957. bi-m. INR 20; USD 12. Ed(s): D S Rao. National Academy of Letters, 35 Ferozeshah Rd., Rabindra Bhavan, New Delhi, 110 001, India. Illus., adv. Sample. Circ: 2500. *Indexed:* ArtHuCI, BAS, MLA-IB. *Bk. rev.:* 3-5, 1,500-2,000 words. *Aud.:* Ac, Sa.

This well-established literary journal presents Indian literature in English. It publishes poetry, short stories, and short plays, written in English, and translations of literary works from all the Indian languages, as well as some literary criticism, tributes, and interviews. The selections on this smorgasbord provide enough examples to give an idea of each writer's themes and style. Special issues focus on a particular genre, theme, or literary movement. The emphasis is on contemporary writing, but some space is now being given to classical and folk literature, even to oral, folk, and tribal literature. The scope has expanded to include nonofficial languages, including tribal and minority languages. Contributors are recognized authors, academics, journalists, and translators. Recommended for academic libraries serving world literature or Asian Studies faculties.

903. ***Indo-Iranian Journal.*** [ISSN: 0019-7246] 1957. q. EUR 416 print or online ed. Ed(s): J W De Jong, H W Bodewitz. Kluwer Academic Publishers, van Godewijckstraat 30, PO Box 17, Dordrecht, 3300 AA, Netherlands. Adv. Refereed. Microform: PQC. Online: EBSCO Publishing; ingenta.com; Kluwer Online; OCLC Online Computer Library Center, Inc.; Ovid Technologies, Inc.; RoweCom Information Quest; Swets Blackwell. Reprint: SWZ. *Indexed:* ArtHuCI, BAS, IBSS, IBZ, L&LBA, MLA-IB, PhilInd, RI-1. *Bk. rev.:* Various number and length. *Aud.:* Ac, Sa.

This refereed academic journal publishes scholarly work on three countries and the following subjects: "ancient and medieval Indian languages, literature, philosophy, and religion; ancient and medieval Iran, and papers on Tibet," but excludes "archaeological or specific historical studies." The major emphasis is on ancient and medieval Indian languages, but there is some attention to modern Dravidian languages and religion. An example of the former is a discussion on recent scholarship about the death of Sanskrit. Most contain detailed textual analysis, but articles relating linguistic considerations to philosophical or religious scholarship also appear, as in articles on the power of religion in the political and economic organization of Persian ruler Darius. The number of articles per issue is few; some are in German or French, with English abstracts. The articles are of high quality, but the journal's main value to scholars and librarians may be the many book reviews covering the three countries, including many non-English titles. The web site offers a free sample issue and tables of contents from the last five years. This very specialized journal is highly recommended for libraries serving language scholars in this area.

904. ***Journal of South Asian and Middle Eastern Studies.*** [ISSN: 0149-1784] 1977. q. USD 30 (Individuals, USD 25; USD 40 foreign). Ed(s): Dr. Hafeez Malik. Pakistan American Foundation, c/o Dr Hafeez Malik, Ed, 421 SAC, Villanova, PA 19085; http://www.vill.edu/academic/artsci/arts/pak/pak.htm. Illus., adv. Circ: 7500. Reprint: SCH. *Indexed:* ABS&EES, AmH&L, BAS, IPSA, PAIS. *Bk. rev.:* 0-25, 50-150 words. *Aud.:* Ac, Sa.

This scholarly journal, published by the Pakistan American Foundation of Villanova University, deals with "Islamic and non-Islamic societies in South Asia, the Middle East, and North Africa." Although it invites contributions from scholars as well as "leaders in public affairs," most of the articles are written by academics. And though the journal welcomes articles in all fields, including the sciences, most articles concern international relations, regional cooperation or conflict, economic trends, and to some extent, history of the region. Islam, as manifest in different political systems, is another significant theme. This aspect, and the journal's geographic scope, make this journal particularly relevant in today's context. Recent articles have dealt with the minimum nuclear deterrence policies of South Asian nations, foreign relations of India and Iran, and of Turkmenistan, and policies required for a stable Palestinian state. Other representative topics include Turkish foreign policy in the aftermath of the breakup of the Soviet Union, a comparative study of Israeli and Indian intelligence gathering, and Pakistan's effect on Indo-U.S. relations. The book review section categorizes new books and sometimes videos by subject and provides a one-line description. Recommended for research libraries.

Man in India. See Anthropology section.

905. ***Pakistan and Gulf Economist.*** Incorporating: *Pakistan Economist;* Which was formerly: *Finance and Industry.* [ISSN: 0253-1941] 1962. w. PKR 1170; PKR 30 newsstand/cover per issue; USD 160 in Asia. Ed(s): Suhail Abbas. Economist Publications (Pvt.) Limited, 3 A, Falcon Arcade, BC - 3, Block - 7, Karachi, Pakistan; information@pak-economist.com; http://www.pak-economist.com/. Illus., adv. Sample. Circ: 35000. Vol. ends: Dec. *Indexed:* BAS, RRTA, WAE&RSA. *Bk. rev.:* 0-2, 750-1,000 words. *Aud.:* Ac, Sa.

This weekly magazine is a good source of economic information on Pakistan and its neighbors, although most coverage is of Pakistan. It also features news highlights from around the world, especially as they impact Pakistan's economic situation. Recent articles, for example, assess the effects of the U.S. war in Iraq on its own economy, on World Bank resources, and on Pakistan's access to oil. Another reports the results of the latest Corruption Perception Index. Each issue contains brief news summaries on Pakistan's industry, trade, finance, and policy, as well as international economic news. Major sections include Weekly News, Industry & Economy, Finance & Markets, Market Watch, and "Etc.," which may contain articles on society, politics, company or executive profiles, science and technology or IT trends, and new-product news. The Market Watch and PAGE Data Base sections provide commodity reports, stock market prices, foreign exchange rates, and other investment data in paragraph, graph, and tabular form. Some full-text articles are available online through the journal's attractive web site, at http://www.pakistaneconomist.com, which also provides links to back issues and to other news sources such as CNN and regional sources. A useful source of current economic information on Pakistan for any academic or public library serving business or economics faculty or those doing business in the region.

906. ***Quarterly Review of Historical Studies.*** [ISSN: 0033-5800] 1961. q. INR 100 domestic; USD 10 foreign. Ed(s): Sukumar Bhattacharyya. Institute of Historical Studies, Shakespeare Sarani, 35 Theatre Rd., Kolkata, 700 017, India. Illus., adv. Circ: 900. *Indexed:* ArtHuCI, BAS. *Bk. rev.:* Various number and length. *Aud.:* Ac.

This academic journal on Indian history is produced by the Institute of Historical Studies, Calcutta. Publication has been consistently delayed (the 2000 issue was received in and refers to events in 2002); print and binding quality is poor. However, these faults aside, the journal is a good source of descriptive scholarship on Indian history from ancient to modern times. It publishes brief articles, book reviews, institute lectures, and an editorial that is actually a report by the editor/director on the institute's finances, programs, and publications. The journal deals with intellectual as well as social, political, and economic history in articles on such topics as progress in deciphering ancient Harappan script; the development of women's education in ancient India; Hindu-Muslim riots and Gandhi's leadership; and early agrarian reforms and the rights of peasants in Bengal. Contributors are academics of Indian universities. Recommended for academic libraries serving Indologists.

907. ***South Asia: Journal of South Asian Studies.*** [ISSN: 0085-6401] 1971. 3x/yr. AUD 130 (Individuals, AUD 92). Ed(s): H.V. Brasted. South Asian Studies Association, c/o Department of Classics, History & Religion, University Of New England, Armidale, NSW 2351, Australia; hbrasted@metz.une.edu.au; http://www.southasiaonline.net. Adv. Refereed. Circ: 450. Reprint: PSC. *Indexed:* AmH&L, ArtHuCI, BAS, IBSS, IBZ. *Bk. rev.:* Various number and length. *Aud.:* Ac.

This very readable refereed academic journal explores the history, public affairs, culture, and development of the Indian subcontinent. While articles about India predominate, it is more inclusive of other South Asian countries and of the subcontinent as a whole than *South Asia Research* (below in this section). Authors are from academic institutions throughout the world. The journal deals with the present as well as past history of the subcontinent. Recent articles, for example, show how contemporary political currents have resulted in more militaristic representations of Hindu deities and how elites in nineteenth-century Gujarat worked to standardize the language so as to establish its standing, help create a regional identity, and establish their own power and cultural dominance. Colonial politics and the dislocations and nation building that followed independence are frequent themes. Guest editors are invited to prepare special thematic issues. Each issue contains a sizeable number of book reviews, one or two pages in length. The journal's web site provides tables of contents for several past volumes, text of book reviews, and a sample full-text article, but the site has not been kept up to date. Recommended for academic libraries seeking wider perspective on the region.

908. ***South Asia Research.*** [ISSN: 0262-7280] 1980. s-a. GBP 150 print & online eds. in Europe, Middle East, Africa & Australasia. Ed(s): Werner F Menski. Sage Publications Ltd., 6 Bonhill St, London, EC2A 4PU, United Kingdom; info@sagepub.co.uk; http://www.sagepub.co.uk/. Refereed. Circ: 500. Online: ingenta.com. *Indexed:* AmH&L, BAS, GeogAbPG, IBSS, MLA-IB, PSA, SociolAb. *Bk. rev.:* Various number and length. *Aud.:* Ac.

This respected interdisciplinary academic journal covers the "history, politics, law, economics, sociology, visual culture, languages and literature of South Asian countries," including "works of theory, review and synthesis as well as detailed empirical studies" by scholars from around the world. Emphasis is on the social sciences and literature, almost exclusively on India. One recent article explores possibilities for a framework for analyzing Muslim traditions in India, their history, origins, variety, and evolution. Another analyzes nonarranged marriages in India and scholars' failure to recognize and study the growing phenomenon. Guest editors sometimes publish special issues. There are no abstracts or author notes. Contents for the most recent issues are available online. Recommended for academic libraries.

Southeast Asia

909. ***A S E A N Economic Bulletin.*** [ISSN: 0217-4472] 1984. 3x/yr. SGD 97 in Singapore, Malaysia & Brunei (Individuals, SGD 61 in Singapore, Malaysia & Brunei). Ed(s): Mrs. Triena Ong. Institute of Southeast Asian Studies, 30 Heng Mui Keng Terrace, Pasir Panjang, Singapore, 119614, Singapore; pubsunit@iseas.edu.sg; http://www.iseas.edu.sg/. Illus., index, adv. Refereed. Vol. ends: Dec. Microform: PQC. Online: Chadwyck-Healey Incorporated; EBSCO Publishing; Florida Center for Library Automation; Gale Group; OCLC Online Computer Library Center, Inc.; ProQuest Information & Learning. Reprint: SCH. *Indexed:* BAS, FPA, HRA, IBSS, IBZ, JEL, PAIS, PRA, WAE&RSA. *Bk. rev.:* 5-10, 500-1,000 words. *Aud.:* Ac, Sa.

Published by Singapore's Institute of Southeast Asian Studies, this refereed scholarly journal deals with contemporary economic issues affecting the countries of the Association of Southeast Asian Nations (ASEAN). Emphasis is on "economic issues affecting ASEAN as a whole; the region's links with its major trading partners; and it interfaces and relationships with the world political economy in general." The journal uses empirical data and economic models to analyze economic crises, income trends, foreign investment behavior, poverty, growth, development, international trade, and the effects of political and economic policies of member nations and of their international trading partners on the economies of the region. Recent topics include analysis of the relationship between strength in market and non-market services and economic growth, and between foreign direct investment and reduction of poverty. "Special focus" issues address such topics as globalization. Abstracts accompany each article. Also included are book reviews (2-4 pages in length), ASEAN chronology, and a documentation section, which presents full text of ASEAN addresses and presentations. The journal's web site offers tables of contents of recent issues with abstracts only for the current issue. This is a rather technical but very well-written journal, recommended for any academic library serving economics, international relations, business, or public affairs faculty.

910. ***American Historical Collection. Bulletin.*** [ISSN: 0115-3226] 1972. q. Ed(s): Lewis E Gleeck, Jr. American Historical Collection Foundation, c/o Rizal Library, Ateneo de Manila University, PO Box 154, Quezon City, , Philippines; http://www.rizal.lib.admu.edu.ph. Adv. *Indexed:* AmH&L, BAS. *Bk. rev.:* Various number and length. *Aud.:* Ac.

This journal focuses on American involvement in the Philippines, especially from the beginning of the twentieth century to the end of World War II. It is the journal of the American Historical Collection Foundation, and was started to publicize this large collection of sources on Philippine-American history located at Ateneo de Manila University. It traces the history of American involvement in the Philippines, often based on memoirs, reminiscences, and primary sources. Recent issues feature a reconstruction of Pearl Harbor Day based on a contemporary diary and other sources, an investigation of rumors of a massacre by Americans in the Philippine-American War, and an account of "London and the Philippine Commonwealth 1935-1946" based on documents in the British Public Records Office. While the articles are definitely written from the American point of view, the journal does provide firsthand accounts of Philippine life and American influence there, useful to the historian. It includes book reviews. Recommended for research libraries.

911. ***Bulletin of Indonesian Economic Studies.*** [ISSN: 0007-4918] 1965. 3x/yr. GBP 117 (Individuals, GBP 27). Ed(s): Ross H McLeod. Carfax Publishing Ltd., 4 Park Sq, Milton Park, Abingdon, OX14 4RN, United Kingdom; enquiry@tandf.co.uk; http://www.tandf.co.uk/. Illus., adv. Refereed. Circ: 1200. Reprint: PSC; SCH. *Indexed:* BAS, DSA, ForAb, IBSS, JEL, PAIS, S&F, SSCI, WAE&RSA. *Bk. rev.:* Various number and length. *Aud.:* Ac, Sa.

This refereed academic journal, published by the Indonesia Project, Australian National University, is an excellent source of information on the economic condition of Indonesia, its development history, and the impact of government policy of social conditions. Each issue features "articles, shorter notes and reviews of books reporting empirical research and policy analysis," as well as a very readable Survey of Recent Developments, which provides a detailed summary of economic activity and trends, government policy changes, political developments and other events. The journal defines economics broadly to include articles on economic and development aspects of education, law, the environment, and health. For example, a recent issue publishes a study evaluating Indonesia's antipoverty efforts, finding most success in health and education programs, where most money was spent, while another study finds the minimum-wage policy to have disproportionate negative effects on women, the young, and less-educated workers. There are also numerous articles on traditional economics topics, such as the effects of the new competition regulations and analysis of the recent banking crisis. The articles are accompanied by abstracts and numerous graphs, charts and tables. The web site, at http://rspas.anu.edu.au/economics/bies/, is logically arranged and provides tables of contents and abstracts for recent issues. Highly recommended for academic libraries with an interest in Asian Studies, economics, economic development, or policy studies.

912. ***Contemporary Southeast Asia: a journal of international and strategic affairs.*** [ISSN: 0129-797X] 1979. 3x/yr. SGD 102 in Singapore, Malaysia & Brunei (Individuals, SGD 66 in Singapore, Malaysia & Brunei). Ed(s): Mrs. Triena Ong. Institute of Southeast Asian Studies, 30 Heng Mui Keng Terrace, Pasir Panjang, Singapore, 119614, Singapore; pubsunit@iseas.edu.sg; http://www.iseas.edu.sg/. Illus., index, adv. Refereed. Vol. ends: Dec. Microform: PQC. Online: bigchalk; EBSCO Publishing; Florida Center for Library Automation; Gale Group; Northern Light Technology, Inc.; OCLC Online Computer Library Center, Inc.; ProQuest Information & Learning. Reprint: SCH. *Indexed:* AmH&L, BAS, IBSS, IBZ, IPSA, PAIS, PRA, PSA, RRTA, SociolAb, WAE&RSA. *Bk. rev.:* 5-10, 500-1,500 words. *Aud.:* Ac.

This refereed journal addresses "politics and strategic and international affairs as they impinge on the Southeast Asian and Asia-Pacific geographical region." The emphasis is on stability and security issues as they relate to Southeast Asia and the "wider geostrategic environment." Articles are addressed to an academic audience while providing enough historical background to make them readable by nonspecialists. Article authors are academics or institute fellows. The journal also addresses domestic politics and socio-economic change. Examples of recent topics include articles on the sharing of sovereignty with international organizations such as the United Nations and consequent effects on security, and an analysis of the Islamic state or state of Islam in Malaysia. The focus is on Southeast Asian concerns, but the journal also addresses superpower and nearby regional influences and regional security; for example, a recent article discusses the destabilizing and unproven benefits of Bush's plans to develop a ballistic missile defense system. The book reviews are balanced and thought provoking. Special issues appear on "particular national situations or on major strategic trends in both Southeast Asia and the wider Asia-Pacific region." The journal's web site offers tables of contents of recent issues with abstracts; free pdfs are available to subscribers. Highly recommended for academic and larger public libraries.

913. ***Crossroads: An Interdisciplinary Journal of Southeast Asian Studies.*** [ISSN: 0741-2037] 1983. s-a. USD 25; USD 14.95 newsstand/cover per issue. Ed(s): Peter Ross. Southeast Asia Publications, Center for Southeast Asian Studies, Adams 412, DeKalb, IL 60115; seap@niu.edu; http://www.niu.edu/cseas/seap. Illus., adv. Refereed. Circ: 300. *Indexed:* AmH&L, IBSS, L&LBA, MLA-IB, PAIS, PSA, SociolAb. *Bk. rev.:* 10-12, 1-4 pgs. *Aud.:* Ac.

This refereed academic journal publishes Southeast Asian research in a wide variety of disciplines and also addresses theoretical concerns in Southeast Asian Studies. The journal publishes three to four scholarly articles, with abstracts, and ten or more book reviews grouped by country. It covers such areas as culture, literature and the arts, public affairs, and history. Topics range from a discussion of the role of historical memory in Thai Buddhist ritual to analysis of recent threats to government legitimacy in Malaysia and its exploitation of divisive ethnic politics to reestablish it; to consideration of Chinese and indigenous influences on Vietnamese poetry; to analysis of the social meaning of Khmer Rouge songs. The journal is valuable for its historical and geographical breadth (especially the seldom-covered countries of Myanmar, Vietnam, and Cambodia) and for its multidisciplinary and theoretical approach. Recommended for academic libraries with an interest in Southeast Asian Studies.

914. ***Indonesia.*** [ISSN: 0019-7289] 1966. s-a. USD 32; USD 34 foreign. Ed(s): Deborah Homsher. Cornell University, Southeast Asia Program, 640 Stewart Ave, Ithaca, NY 14850; SEAP-Pubs@cornell.edu. Illus., index, adv. Sample. Refereed. Circ: 900. Vol. ends: Oct. Microform: PQC. Online: Northern Light Technology, Inc.; ProQuest Information & Learning. Reprint: PQC. *Indexed:* AmH&L, BAS, IBSS, IPSA, MLA-IB. *Bk. rev.:* 0-4, 1,000-2,500 words. *Aud.:* Ac.

This refereed journal publishes scholarly articles, interviews, book reviews, and review essays on historical and contemporary Indonesian affairs, art, and culture. Comparative studies are also published. Most but not all articles are in English. While the articles deal with a wide range of topics, from literary studies to gender issues to economic and religious concerns, the emphasis in most of them is on the broadly political aspects of these topics. For example, a study of Western influences on Indonesian popular music explores the "xenocentrism" in the attitudes of young people toward various genres; and a study of the women's labor focuses on their role in industry rather than agriculture and home production. The book reviews and review essays contain thorough discussion of contents as well as evaluation. There is also a yearly update on the Indonesian military elite, and translations of literary and journalistic pieces. Recommended for academic libraries.

915. ***Inside Indonesia.*** [ISSN: 0814-1185] 1983. q. AUD 45 (Individuals, AUD 30). Ed(s): Gerry Van Klinken. Indonesia Resources & Information Programme, PO Box 1326, Collingwood, VIC 3066, Australia; editor@insideindonesia.org; http://www.insideindonesia.org. Illus., adv. Sample. Circ: 2000. *Indexed:* AltPI. *Bk. rev.:* 4-8, 1,500-2,000 words. *Aud.:* Hs, Ga, Ac.

This Australian magazine about Indonesia is primarily concerned with contemporary public and international affairs. Its publisher, the Indonesian Resources and Information Program (IRIP), seeks to promote understanding and cooperation between Australia and Indonesia and to "increase international awareness of issues facing Indonesian people today." The magazine focuses attention on human rights abuses, economic and environmental exploitation, democratic political movements, social and women's issues, and artistic responses. It also publishes news briefs, articles on cultural and artistic trends, and short book reviews. Though many of the authors are academic experts on Indonesia, articles are quite short and the magazine is intended for the nonspecialist. Other authors are action group, trade union, or international aid agency members of IRIP. Examples of recent articles are "Law, globalization, and military terror," about civil suits against U.S. corporations operating with the support of military regimes; "Power to the people," about public radio; and "Consuming passions," about Indonesia's addictive soap operas. Most issues devote a cluster of articles to a single topic, such as the terrorist bombing in Bali; "Outside Indonesia: East Timor," about conditions there; and "Militarized society," about security forces, police, and militia. The publication's excellent web site, at http://www.insideindonesia.org, provides tables of contents and selected full-text articles for the current edition as well as complete full texts of earlier editions (minus the graphics). It also features a subject index, search engine, links to related sites, an educational resources page, and a news digest. A fine source of information on present day Indonesian affairs, this publication is recommended for any academic, public, or school library with an interest in Indonesia.

916. ***Journal of Burma Studies.*** [ISSN: 1094-799X] 1997. a. USD 16. Ed(s): Catherine Raymond. Southeast Asia Publications, Center for Southeast Asian Studies, Adams 412, DeKalb, IL 60115; seap@niu.edu; http://www.niu.edu/cseas/seap. Illus., adv. Refereed. Circ: 350. *Indexed:* AmH&L, PAIS. *Aud.:* Ac, Sa.

This annual academic journal is of recent origin and not widely held. It is, however, the only academic journal to focus exclusively on Burma (Myanmar) Studies, and it is fully refereed. Topics range from the historical to present day issues and include many disciplines. Examples are an article, based on Dutch archival documents, on the importance of Burma to the fortunes of the Dutch East India Company, and articles on the practice of Burmese martial arts and worship of Buddhist relics. It is appropriately illustrated with maps, sketches, tables, and original script. Burmese terms are translated and explained. The web site, at http://www.niu.edu/cseas/seap/jbs.html, provides tables of contents and abstracts for all issues. Recommended for academic libraries serving Asian or Southeast Asia Studies programs.

917. ***Journal of Southeast Asian Studies.*** Supersedes (in 1970): *Journal of Southeast Asian History.* [ISSN: 0022-4634] 1970. 3x/yr. USD 90 (Individuals, USD 42). Ed(s): Bruce Lockhart, Paul H. Kratoska. Cambridge University Press, The Edinburgh Bldg, Shaftesbury Rd, Cambridge, CB2 2RU, United Kingdom; information@cambridge.org; http://uk.cambridge.org/journals. Illus., index, adv. Sample. Refereed. Vol. ends: Sep. Online: Florida Center for Library Automation; Gale Group; Northern Light Technology, Inc.; OCLC Online Computer Library Center, Inc.; Swets Blackwell; H.W. Wilson. *Indexed:* ABCPolSci, AbAn, AmH&L, ArtHuCI, CJA, ForAb, GeogAbPG, HumInd, IBSS, IPSA, PRA, PSA, RRTA, S&F, SSCI, SociolAb, WAE&RSA. *Bk. rev.:* 12-18, 1,000-2,000 words. *Aud.:* Ac.

Though published by Cambridge University Press for the Department of History of the National University of Singapore, this refereed academic journal encompasses not only history but also the humanities and social sciences generally. Articles address issues of significance to the region or to the individual countries of Brunei, Indonesia, Laos, Malaysia, Myanmar, Philippines, Singapore, Thailand, and Vietnam. They deal with major historical and cultural events, often using primary historical and literary documents and artifacts, to explore themes such as the development of a national identity, modernity, nationalism, colonial legacies, and occasionally economic matters as they affect the social fabric. A recent issue deals with Japanese use of Islam in aid of war propaganda during its occupation of Malaya, and with Buddhism's appeal to women as a factor in its spread throughout Southeast Asia. The journal also publishes symposia periodically, including one recently on eroticism in Southeast Asian literature and another on Chinese business networks. Brief abstracts are included for each article. It is occasionally illustrated with color photographs, graphs, and maps. Review essays and book reviews take up about a third of each issue and are categorized by country. Most of the contributors are historians, but there are also anthropologists, economists, linguists, and Asian Studies specialists. Highly recommended for any academic library with an interest in this region or any of its individual countries.

918. ***Philippine Studies.*** [ISSN: 0031-7837] 1953. q. PHP 600; USD 40. Ed(s): Antonette P Angeles. Ateneo de Manila University Press, PO Box 154, Manila, 1099, Philippines; unipress@admu.edu.ph; http://www.ateneopress.com. Illus., adv. Refereed. Circ: 650. *Indexed:* AmH&L, BAS, BHA, CPL, IBSS, IBZ, IPSA, MLA-IB, RI-1. *Bk. rev.:* Various number and length. *Aud.:* Ac.

This scholarly journal focuses on the study of Philippine public affairs, history, social sciences, culture, communications, and Filipinos abroad. Many of its articles address American colonial involvement and its aftermath. Others treat a range of topics from the timber trade to U.S.-Philippine relations to ethnic heritage to rapid urbanization. A recent article analyzes the film *Apocalypse Now*, filmed in the Philippines, and its role in creating U.S. popular history of the Vietnam conflict and implication for the Philippines. Another article addresses the Philippine struggle for economic development in pre-war years. An article on more recent times looks for household characteristics affecting a family's ability to cope with disaster. The journal also publishes book reviews and review articles, and brief articles as "Notes and Comments." Recommended for academic libraries interested in Asian affairs.

919. ***Sojourn: journal of social issues in Southeast Asia.*** [ISSN: 0217-9520] 1986. s-a. Apr. & Oct. SGD 65 in Spingapore, Malaysia & Brunei (Individuals, SGD 36 in Spingapore, Malaysia & Brunei). Ed(s): Mrs. Triena Ong. Institute of Southeast Asian Studies, 30 Heng Mui Keng Terrace, Pasir Panjang, Singapore, 119614, Singapore; pubsunit@iseas.edu.sg; http://www.iseas.edu.sg/. Adv. Refereed. Microform: PQC. Online: EBSCO Publishing; Florida Center for Library Automation; Gale Group. Reprint: SCH. *Indexed:* AmH&L, BAS, IBSS, PAIS, PRA, PSA, RRTA, SociolAb, WAE&RSA. *Bk. rev.:* 4-5, 3-4 pgs. *Aud.:* Ac.

This refereed academic journal treats social issues of the past and present in Southeast Asian countries. Political, social, historical, and economic aspects of society are examined in these research- or theory-based articles. Gender, ethnicity, national identity, urbanization, development, migration, and literature are representative themes. A recent issue includes analysis of the Indonesian Muhammadiyah movement, an Islamic social organization and its potential contribution to civil society; two articles explore use and interpretation of Islamic doctrine with regard to women. Other topics include changing expectations of Vietnamese graduates seeking employment and opium reduction programs in Laos. Topics and approaches are often quite original, as in a recent discussion of batik and pewter as national symbols of Malaysia. Articles include abstracts, tables, graphs, and illustrations where appropriate, research notes, and thorough book reviews. The web site, at http://bookshop.iseas.edu.sg, offers tables of contents and abstracts from 1996 to the present. Recommended for academic libraries with an interest in Asian, intercultural, or international affairs.

920. ***South East Asia Research.*** [ISSN: 0967-828X] 1993. 3x/yr. USD 164 print & online eds. (Individuals, USD 64 print & online eds.). Ed(s): Ian Brown. I P Publishing Ltd., Coleridge House, 4-5 Coleridge Gardens, London, NW6 3HQ, United Kingdom; JEdmondIP@aol.com; http://www.ippublishing.com. Sample. Refereed. *Indexed:* AmH&L, BAS, IBSS, IPSA, PSA. *Bk. rev.:* Occasional. *Aud.:* Ac.

This fairly new refereed academic journal publishes research on "archaeology, art, history, economics, geography, language, and literature, law, music, political science, social anthropology and religious studies." It is published by the University of London's School of Oriental and African Studies. Recent issues include articles on the roots of Muslim vigilante groups in Indonesia, the effect of economic liberalization policy in Thailand, the spread of a Burmese origin myth, ethnic mix in the Dutch colonial army, and election funding by the United States in Singapore in the 1950s. Recent volumes focus predominantly on recent history and the roots of current situations, especially on colonial legacies and local response. Abstracts accompany each article. Occasional book reviews are also published. Recommended for academic libraries serving Asian Studies interests.

921. ***South East Asian Studies.*** [ISSN: 0563-8682] 1963. q. Kyoto University, Centre for Southeast Asian Studies, 46 Shimoadachi-cho, Yoshida, Sakyo-ku, Kyoto, 606-8501, Japan; hp@cseas.kyoto-u.ac.jp; http://www.cseas.kyoto-u.ac.jp/. Refereed. *Indexed:* AmH&L. *Bk. rev.:* 1-5 (in Japanese). *Aud.:* Ac.

This academic journal, peer-reviewed starting with volume 7, publishes articles, book reviews, special issues, and field reports on the ecology, society, culture, politics, and economy of Southeast Asian countries. It is also known by its Japanese title, *Tonan Ajia Kenkyu.* About half the articles and reviews are in English, the rest in Japanese. Abstracts or more extensive summaries in English accompany each article. Economic development, social change and policy, agriculture and natural resource management, institution building, power dynamics, and colonial legacies are frequent topics. For example, a recent thematic issue offers comparative perspectives on state formation in former African and Asian colonies. Other recent articles analyze mechanisms for consolidation of authoritarian power in post-independence Burma, Indonesia, and the Philippines, the dynamics of insurgencies without ideology, and language and culture policy in Indonesia. One recent article is titled "Some Things Poetry Can Tell Us about the Process of Social Change in Vietnam." Authors are Southeast Asian scholars from academic institutions worldwide. Tables of contents and full-text articles are available online, at http://www.cseas.kyoto-u.ac.jp/documents/index_en.htm, from 1988 to the present, except for most recent issues. Highly recommended for academic libraries serving Asian Studies, economics, development studies, and public or international affairs departments.

922. ***Southeast Asian Affairs.*** Formerly: *Institute of Southeast Asian Studies. Annual Review.* [ISSN: 0377-5437] 1974. a. Ed(s): Daljit Singh. Institute of Southeast Asian Studies, 30 Heng Mui Keng Terrace, Pasir Panjang, Singapore, 119614, Singapore; pubsunit@iseas.edu.sg; http://www.iseas.edu.sg/. Online: East View Publications, Inc.; EBSCO Publishing. Reprint: SCH. *Indexed:* BAS, IBSS, IPSA, PSA. *Aud.:* Ac.

Published by the Institute of Southeast Asian Studies in Singapore, this publication offers an annual review of economic and political trends in the countries of this region, individually and collectively. Each issue begins with an introduction and several articles addressing regional developments, followed by one or more articles on each of the following ten countries: Brunei Darussalam, Cambodia, Indonesia, Laos, Malaysia, Myanmar, Philippines, Singapore, Thailand, and Vietnam. The articles discuss major news stories of the year and political, economic, and social situations and trends. Many articles offer a longer historical perspective; for example, one article analyzes the paradox of the promising beginnings and current disappointing economic progress in the Philippines. Authors are experts from universities and research centers around the world. This annual publication can be considered a reference work rather than a periodical. It is valuable for its quality and balanced coverage, especially since some of the countries, Laos and Myanmar, for example, receive little attention in either the popular or academic press. Statistics and tabular data are included. Recommended for all academic and public libraries.

Online Newspapers

Many Asian newspapers are now available online. Web access provides a quick and cheap (usually free) alternative to print subscriptions. Those listed below are free or provide at least some free content. Most are dailies and have at least a limited archive. All those listed provide content in English and many are also available in the local language. For more links to online newspapers, see the directories at http://www.newsdirectory.com/news/press/as/ or http://www.samachar.com/newsasia/.

ASIA

Wall Street Journal: Asia. http://online.wsj.com/public/asia

AFGHANISTAN

AfghanNews. http://www.afghannews.net/

AUSTRALIA

The Australian. http://www.theaustralian.news.com.au/
The Herald Sun. http://heraldsun.news.com.au/
The Sydney Morning Herald. http://www.smh.com.au/

BANGLADESH

The Daily Star. http://www.dailystarnews.com/
The Independent. http://independent-bangladesh.com/

BRUNEI DARUSSALAM

Borneo Bulletin. http://www.brunei-online.com/bb/

CAMBODIA

The Phnom Penh Post. http://www.vais.net/~tapang/ppp/

HONG KONG

The Standard. http://www.thestandard.com.hk/

INDIA

Deccan Chronicle. http://www.deccan.com/
The Hindu. http://www.hinduonnet.com
The Indian Express. http://www.indian-express.com/
The Statesman. http://www.thestatesman.org/
The Times of India. http://www.timesofindia.com/today/pagehome.htm

INDONESIA

The Jakarta Post. http://www.thejakartapost.com/
Tempo Interaktif. http://www.tempo.co.id/index.uk.asp

JAPAN

The Japan Times. http://www.japantimes.co.jp/news.htm
Asahi.com. http://www.asahi.com/english/english.html

MALAYSIA

Daily Express. http://www.dailyexpress.com.my/
Sarawak Tribune. http://www.jaring.my/tribune/
The Star. http://thestar.com.my/news/
Bernama. http://www3.bernama.com/web/index.html

MONGOLIA

Montsame. http://www.montsame.mn/

MYANMAR

The New Light of Myanmar. http://www.myanmar.com/nlm/

NEPAL

Nepal News. http://www.nepalnews.com/
Kathmandu Post. http://www.nepalnews.com.np/ktmpost.htm
The Rising Nepal. http://www.nepalnews.com.np/trn.htm

NEW ZEALAND

The New Zealand Herald. http://www.nzherald.co.nz/nznews/

NORTH KOREA

Korean News. http://www.kcna.co.jp/index-e.htm
The People's Korea. (weekly) http://www.korea-np.co.jp/pk/

PAKISTAN

Dawn. http://www.dawn.com/
The News. http://www.jang-group.com/thenews/
Business Recorder. http://www.brecorder.com/

PHILIPPINES

The Manila Bulletin. http://www.mb.com.ph/
Manila Times. http://www.manilatimes.net/
Sun Star Daily. http://www.sunstar.com.ph/
Business World. http://www.bworld.com.ph/current/today.html

SINGAPORE

The Straits Times. http://straitstimes.asia1.com.sg/singapore/

SOUTH KOREA

Korea Herald. http://www.koreaherald.co.kr/national/
Chosun. http://english.chosun.com/

SRI LANKA

The Daily News. http://www.dailynews.lk/
The Island http://www.island.lk/index.html

TAIWAN

Taipei Times. http://www.taipeitimes.com/News/
The China Post. http://www.chinapost.com.tw/taiwan/

THAILAND

Bangkok Post. http://www.bangkokpost.net/
Business Day. http://www.bday.net/
The Nation. http://www.nationmultimedia.com/new/national.shtml

VIETNAM

Nhan Dan. http://www.nhandan.org.vn/ english/today/

Electronic Journals

923. *A S E A N Review of Biodiversity and Environmental Conservation.* m. USD 215. Association of South East Asian Nations (ASEAN), ASEAN Secretariat, Jalan Sisingamangaraja 70 A, Jakarta, 12110, Indonesia; public@aseansec.org. *Aud.:* Hs, Ga, Ac.

This journal reports on the state of biodiversity and conservation issues for the South East Asian region, particularly in Malaysia. It provides updates on conservation initiatives by ARBEC and other world organizations. It also publishes well-illustrated articles and special reports on the state of the environment and links to related articles in other electronic journals. This is an excellent site for tracking conditions of specific species as well as the progress of national and regional efforts to protect the environment and inform the public. Examples of recent features are articles on forest conservation in Borneo, the near-extinction of leatherback turtles in Malaysia, and successful attempts to protect raptors. There are also links to abstracts of conference papers on turtle conservation and to Malaysia's Biodiversity Policy. The journal is free, but there is no archive. This is not a site intended primarily for children, but it could be very useful in educational settings.

924. *Asia Environmental Review: the business report for environmental decision-makers with operations in Asia.* [ISSN: 1360-1644] 1995. 10x/yr. GBP 300; GBP 250 email edition. Ed(s): Dylan Tanner. Asia Environmental Trading Ltd., 55 Exhibition Rd, London, SW7 2PG, United Kingdom; AET@asianenviro.com; http://www.asianenviro.com. Illus. *Aud.:* Ga, Ac, Sa.

This newsletter is designed to provide "environment, health and safety business news" by monitoring government regulatory activity and policy, nongovernmental organization activity, and corporate responses to environmental health and safety risks. While the publication is designed to benefit business rather than environmental interests, the philosophy of the editors is that "to attain long-term profitability, business should operate within a sustainable framework, optimising resource utilisation across the supply chain and being accountable for their external impacts." This practical publication provides brief digests (one to four paragraphs each) of environmental news affecting business, such as new governmental regulations, policies, or programs, announcements of conferences and workshops, and reviews of new web sites. News items are grouped by country for easy scanning. The focus is on South and Southeast Asia and China. It is available online only, delivered by e-mail or the web twice per month, with improved search access to the archive. Related titles also available are: *Japan Environmental Review* and *China Environmental Review.* A very useful but expensive resource for libraries serving business interests in Asia, business students or scholars, and environmentalists.

925. *Asian Development Review: studies of Asian and Pacific economic issues.* [ISSN: 0116-1105] 1983. s-a. USD 8. Ed(s): Satish C Jha. Asian Development Bank, Publications Unit, P.O. Box 789, Manila, 0980, Philippines; adbpub@adb.org; http://www.adb.org. Illus., adv. Sample. Refereed. *Indexed:* BAS, DSA, IBZ, JEL, PAIS, SWA, WAE&RSA. *Aud.:* Ac, Sa.

This refereed journal is an excellent source of data and analysis on development issues in Asia. Published by the Asian Development Bank, it presents "the results of economic and development research carried out by staff and resource persons" of the bank. The journal looks at the human and environmental as well as the economic costs and effects of poverty and development, stressing "policy and operational relevance" rather than "technical aspects." The journal is intended not only for academics but also for professional economists and social scientists in government, nongovernmental organizations, and the private sector. Recent articles assess the optimal balance between pro-growth and pro-poor policies in reducing poverty, show the relevance of early-twentieth-century European social policies as opposed to those of the postwar period, and suggest institutional changes necessary for Asia to capitalize on globalization. Special issues are sometimes devoted to one topic, for example, the relationship between economic growth and inequality. Online issues are available free in pdf format beginning with 1997; print copies are available individually for $5.00. Highly recommended for libraries serving academics or policy makers with interests in public or international affairs, economics, development, social reform, or environmental policy.

926. *Asian Studies W W W Monitor.* Formerly: *What's New in W W W Asian Studies.* [ISSN: 1329-9778] 1994. every 10 days. Free. Ed(s): T Matthew Ciolek. Australian National University, G.P.O. Box 4, Canberra, ACT 2601, Australia; tmciolek@ciolek.com; http://coombs.anu.edu.au/asia-www-monitor.html. Illus. *Aud.:* Ga, Ac.

This review journal is a major part of the Asian Studies WWW Virtual Library. It is designed to monitor the Internet for new web sites of interest to Asian Studies scholars and to evaluate the web sites. Evaluations are based on the accuracy, quality, currency, and scholarly usefulness of the resource, using a five-star system. Not included are resources that have no scholarly value or contain inaccurate information. A distinguished editorial board oversees the evaluation process; but the reviews do not elaborate on the ratings and do not consider aesthetics or usability issues such as navigability or layout. Each entry contains a link to the site and quotes its "self description." It also gives a brief summary of contents and features. This resource split in 2000 to create a similar resource for Pacific Studies (below in this section). A search engine for all Asian Studies WWW Virtual Library resources has been added, making this a very useful tool for locating web resources on a variety of Asian and Pacific Studies topics. The journal has grown from a quarterly in 1994 to a roughly fortnightly publication, updated daily. The entire archive is available online, though understandably the links and even the web sites reviewed in older issues may no longer be valid. E-mail notification of new issues is also available. This is an essential resource in Asian Studies.

927. *Business Times.* 1976. d. except Sun. SGD 288 domestic; SGD 1607 in Brunei, China, Hong Kong, India, Indonesia, Korea, Philippines, Pakistan, Sri Lanka, Thailand, Taiwan, Vietnam & Asia Pacific countries (excluding Hawaii).; USD 1925 in Australia, Japan & New Zealand). Ed(s): Patrick Daniel. Singapore Press Holdings Ltd., 1000 Tea Payoh North, News Centre, Singapore, 318994, Singapore; http://www.sph.com.sg/. Illus., adv. Circ: 31205 Paid. Microform: NRP. *Indexed:* B&I. *Aud.:* Ga, Sa.

This online daily newspaper is an excellent source of business and financial news for Singapore and the region (South and Southeast Asia). It also covers major world economic news. The site is extensive and well organized. The "front page" contains leading news stories from Singapore, with links to regional and world news. There are reports on specific industries and companies, U.S. and regional stock indexes, international market news, shipping news, feature articles, polls, statistics, and editorials. There are also weekly sections on such topics as "Executive Lifestyle" and "Executive Money." The site also provides a searchable seven-day archive. "Premium content," labeled with a red star, is restricted to subscribers between 4:00 a.m. and 2:00 p.m. Singapore time. Articles can be e-mailed or printed easily using the link to a "printer friendly version." Links to parent company AsiaOne include such services as a "My Stocks" page and a currency converter. Recommended for any library with business or academic interests in the Asian economy.

928. *Journal of South Asia Women Studies.* [ISSN: 1085-7478] 1995. s-a. USD 50. Ed(s): Enrica Garzilli. Journal of South Asia Women Studies, 1306 Massachusetts Ave, Apt 511, Cambridge, MA 02138; jsaws@asiatica.org; http://www.asiatica.org. Adv. Refereed. *Indexed:* PAIS. *Bk. rev.:* Various number and length. *Aud.:* Ac.

This journal covers all aspects of Asian women's experience, including "law, civil rights, gender issues, religion, philosophy, politics, feminism and ecofeminism, classical and modern literature, poetry, dance, music, drama, language, translations, history, folklore, customs, medicine, architecture, discoveries and cultural or social products by women, etc." Countries included for consideration are India, Nepal, Tibet, Afghanistan, Pakistan, Sri Lanka, Bangladesh, Bhutan, Burma, Thailand, Laos, Vietnam, Cambodia, Taiwan, Maldives, Malaysia, Indonesia, and the Philippines. The journal includes articles, book reviews, and news items. Tables of contents for all issues are available online along with article preview pages; full-text requires a subscription. There is free access to the book reviews and to a moderated distribution list. Publication is irregular and the number of articles per issue is limited. A recent issue contains one article on ethics and ecological awareness in women's storytelling in Maharastra, India. From time to time a compilation of past volumes is issued in print. Recommended for academic libraries serving women's studies or Asian Studies programs.

929. ***The Pacific Studies W W W Monitor.*** [ISSN: 1443-8976] 2000. m. Ed(s): Matthew Ciolek. Australian National University, Research School of Pacific & Asian Studies, Pacific Manuscripts Bureau, Canberra, ACT 0200, Australia; http://coombs.anu.edu.au/pacific-www-monitor.html. *Aud.:* Ga, Ac.

This review journal is part of the Asian Studies WWW Virtual Library. It is "modelled on its sister publication *Asian Studies WWW Monitor"* (above in this section), and shares its search engine of Asian Studies WWW Virtual Library resources. The format and quality of the two monitors are the same, except that there are fewer resources on Pacific Studies reviewed. The issues are dated bimonthly but are updated more often. The complete archive is available online, although older issues may contain links to no-longer-existing web sites. Anyone may submit suggestions for new entries, using an online form. Entries may include a "self description" taken from the web site itself and/or a "supplied note" from the person who suggested the site. The journal includes links to related sites such as the Melanesia, Micronesia, and Polynesia Virtual Library pages. E-mail notification of new issues is also available. Recommended for academic or public libraries serving Pacific Studies interests.

■ ASIAN AMERICAN

Christine K. Oka, Bibliographic Instruction Coordinator, 270 Snell Library, Northeastern University, Boston, MA 02115; c.oka@neu.edu; FAX: 617-373-5409

Introduction

Asian Americans are an incredibly diverse ethnic, religious, and socioeconomic group that defies (and sometimes denies) the single descriptor. The official U.S. Census description identifies "Asian and Pacific Islanders" as people having origins in the Far East, Southeast Asia, or the Indian subcontinent, with Pacific Islanders having origins from Hawaii, Guam, Samoa, or other Pacific Islands. On the other side of the categorization coin, standard periodical directories do not use "Asian American" as a subject. For example, *The Standard Periodical Directory* uses the entry "Ethnic" with a note to check under the specific ethnic group subheading, which includes Asian, Chinese, Filipino, Indian, Japanese, Korean, and Vietnamese. *Ulrich's Periodicals Directory* has "Ethnic Interests" with an alphabetical listing of all titles in that category. The lack of a specific Asian American descriptor in most serials directories is a challenge to academic librarians developing collections to support new research at their institutions, and to collection managers at public libraries searching for periodicals for their changing user population. I did find "Asian American" in the subject index of the *International Directory of Little Magazines and Small Presses*, but occasionally some titles in this directory appeared more "Asian" than "Asian American." This dilemma places *Amerasia Journal*, the oldest scholarly journal in the field of Asian American Studies, under the classification of "History" in *The Standard Periodical Directory* and under "Sociology" in *Ulrich's International Periodical Directory.* To be fair, when *Amerasia Journal* began publication in 1971, the field of Asian American Studies was new.

Today, college students of Asian descent question Asian American Studies scholars about the choice of the label "Asian American," derived from the social activism of the 1960s. In a survey about Asian American Studies, some participants (these students would fall into the U.S. Census description of the group) specifically asked NOT to be identified as "Asian American." These varying perspectives on Asian Americans are challenging bibliographically.

Many promising titles have come in and out of existence since the last edition, while other titles are published infrequently or irregularly or are of inherent interest only to geographically focused groups (e.g., student publications). Therefore, covered here are those titles likely to be longer-term, continuing publications that libraries can reasonably expect to obtain, and that are of interest to a broad spectrum of library readers throughout the country. Of course, the difficult economic environment can change this status quo; since the last edition, *A.Magazine: Inside Asian America*, with a reported circulation of 125,000 subscribers, has folded. In the interests of "truth in advertising," I have concentrated on those magazines in English that I have had the opportunity to examine.

Note well, the full texts of a number of Asian American publications are available on the web by subscription. Most notably, in the Diversity Studies Databases published by ProQuest Information and Learning (http://www.il.proquest.com): *Ethnic NewsWatch, Ethnic NewsWatch: A History*, and *Diversity Your World.*

Basic Periodicals

Hs: *Filipinas, India Currents, KoreAm Journal, Yolk;* Ga: *Amerasia Journal, Filipinas, KoreAm Journal, Monolid Magazine, PoliticalCircus, Yolk* Ac: *Amerasia Journal, Asian American and Pacific Islander Journal of Health, Asian American Movement Ezine, Asian American Policy Review, Journal of Asian American Studies, KoreAm Journal, PoliticalCircus.*

Basic Abstracts and Indexes

America: History and Life, Sage Race Relations Abstracts, Ethnic NewsWatch.

930. ***Amerasia Journal: the national interdisciplinary journal of scholarship, criticism, and literature on Asian and Pacific American.*** [ISSN: 0044-7471] 1971. 3x/yr. USD 55 (Individuals, USD 35). Ed(s): Ku Charles. University of California at Los Angeles, Asian American Studies Center, 3230 Campbell Hall, Box 951546, Los Angeles, CA 90095-1546; rleong@ucla.edu; http://www.sscnet.ucla.edu/aasc/. Illus., index, adv. Sample. Refereed. Circ: 1500 Paid. Vol. ends: No. 3. Microform: PQC. Online: Gale Group. *Indexed:* AmH&L, ArtHuCI, BAS, BRI, CBRI, CIJE, FLI, HumInd, IBZ, MLA-IB, MagInd, PSA, RI-1, SSCI, SociolAb. *Bk. rev.:* Number varies, 3-4 pages. *Aud.:* Ga, Ac.

The leading scholarly periodical dedicated to Asian American Studies, *Amerasia Journal* is the oldest academic journal in the field. In addition to being indexed in a number of sources, the journal published a 30th Anniversary Cumulative Index documenting 1971 to 2001. During that period, "over 900 scholarly articles, more than 450 book and film reviews, and 27 bibliographies" appeared in the journal. *Amerasia Journal* publishes articles by writers of all ethnicities and disciplines, as well as interviews with noted Asian American scholars and authors. It also includes in-depth book reviews. Each issue is arranged around a theme. A recent issue, "Asians in the Americas: Transculturations and Power," looks beyond the United States and Canada with articles about Asians in Latin America and the Caribbean. In 2001–2002, two issues were consolidated into one, "After Words: Who Speaks on War, Peace, and Justice?," with interviews and articles about the 9/11 attack and its subsequent effect on immigrant communities. Essential for academic libraries and highly recommended for public libraries serving an Asian American community.

931. ***Asian American and Pacific Islander Journal of Health.*** [ISSN: 1072-0367] 1993. s-a. USD 64. Ed(s): Moon S Chen, Jr. Asian American and Pacific Islander Health Promotion, 5525 Corey Swirl Dr, Dublin, OH 43017-3057. Illus. *Aud.:* Ac, Sa.

I had heard about *Asian American and Pacific Islander Journal of Health* but had difficulty finding it in libraries or contacting the publishers for review copies. I took advantage of a visit to one of the 27 libraries in the world that owns the title (according to OCLC) and reviewed issues in-library. One reason this publication slips below the research radar is the lack of indexing; another reason may be a delay in publishing. Despite that, I was impressed by its focus on health and medical issues regarding Asian American and Pacific Islander populations. Articles included "Patterns and Factors Associated with Healthcare Utilization Among Korean American Elderly" and "Depathologizing Asian-American Perspectives of Health and Healing," which examines services that did not always address Asian American medical and "psychological concerns in a culturally meaningful way." Highly recommended for special and academic libraries serving medical and public health researchers and practitioners.

932. ***Asian American Policy Review.*** [ISSN: 1062-1830] 1990. a. USD 40 (Individuals, USD 15; Students, USD 10). Ed(s): Anne Im, Omar Brownson. Harvard University, John F. Kennedy School of Government, 79 John F. Kennedy St., Cambridge, MA 02138; http://www.ksg.harvard.edu. Illus., adv. Refereed. Circ: 500 Paid and controlled. *Indexed:* BAS, CIJE, PSA. *Bk. rev.:* Various number and length. *Aud.:* Ga, Ac.

This independent, student-run journal is published annually by graduate students at the John F. Kennedy School of Government at Harvard University. It has a respected academic advisory board for every issue and publishes in-depth scholarly articles by researchers in Asian American Studies. Predictably, it concentrates on the political science/public policy issues facing the Asian Pacific American community. In addition to interviews with prominent Asian American politicians at the local and national levels, it contains sections for book reviews, a forum, and commentary, and a section highlighting the works of emerging and established scholars. Recent articles range from "Acculturation and Quality of Life: A Comparative Study of Asian Indians, Japanese Americans, and Korean American in Los Angeles, California" to "An Analysis of Public Funding Provided to Social Service Organizations Serving the Asian American Community in New York City." Before you think the *AAPR* publishes only articles about the bicoastal enclaves of Asian America, read "Hate Crimes in the Aftermath of September 11" or "Transforming Patterns of Contemporary Asian American Community Politics." Recommended for special libraries and academic libraries serving Asian American Studies, ethnic studies, or public policy programs.

Bamboo Girl. See Zines section.

933. ***Filipinas: a magazine for all Filipinos.*** [ISSN: 1063-4630] 1992. m. USD 18; USD 2.95 newsstand/cover per issue. Ed(s): Mona Lisa Yuchengco. Filipinas Publishing, Inc., 1486 Huntington Ave, Ste 300, South San Francisco, CA 94080. Illus., adv. Sample. Circ: 30000 Paid. Vol. ends: Dec. *Indexed:* BAS, ENW. *Aud.:* Hs, Ga, Ac.

The only nationally circulated Filipino American monthly, *Filipinas* is a glossy current-events compendium that features historical articles, travel notes, recipes, and stories about achievers, role models, and politics in the United States and the Philippines. It covers all facets of Filipino life and culture, topics of interest to both immigrant and U.S.–born Filipinos as well as those interested in Filipino culture. A recent cover story features Rodney Salines, political consultant and "the brain behind the popular political website www.politicalcircus.com." An essential title for public and academic libraries serving a substantial Filipino clientele or supporting Asian American Studies and ethnic studies programs.

Giant Robot. See Zines section.

934. ***India Currents: North America's magazine of Indian arts, entertainment & dining.*** [ISSN: 0896-095X] 1987. m. USD 19.95. Ed(s): Arvind Kumar. India Currents, PO Box 21285, San Jose, CA 95151; publisher@indiacur.com; http://www.indiacur.com/indiacur/. Illus., adv. Sample. Circ: 26000 Paid and free. *Indexed:* ENW. *Bk. rev.:* Number varies, 300 words. *Aud.:* Ems, Hs, Ga, Ac.

India Currents describes itself as "the nation's leading Indian-American monthly with features, reviews, opinion, analysis, and a detailed calendar of Indian events nationwide." The newsprint-quality paper is surprising, but on the plus side it is printed using soy ink and is fully indexed by *Ethnic NewsWatch.* The magazine is "devoted to the exploration of the heritage and culture of India as it exists in the United States," and it covers a wide range of topics for readers of all backgrounds: Indian American news, lifestyles, recipes, business, politics, dance, film, art, and literature. A recent issue features an interview with film director Amol Palekar and an article called "Feel the Beat" about the world-music ensemble Global Rhythms, which performs with "instruments from Asia, Africa, South America and Europe." Recommended for libraries serving Indian American communities and readers of all ages with an interest in India and Indian American culture.

935. ***Journal of Asian American Studies.*** [ISSN: 1097-2129] 1998. 3x/yr. USD 85 domestic; USD 91 in Canada & Mexico; USD 92.35 elsewhere. Ed(s): Traise Yamamoto, John M Liu. Johns Hopkins University Press, Journals Publishing Division, 2715 N Charles St, Baltimore, MD 21218-4363; http://www.press.jhu.edu/. Illus., adv. Sample. Refereed. Circ: 860. Vol. ends: Oct. Online: EBSCO Publishing; OCLC Online Computer Library Center, Inc.; Project MUSE; RoweCom Information Quest; Swets Blackwell. Reprint: PSC. *Indexed:* AmH&L, BAS, SociolAb. *Bk. rev.:* Number varies, 2-3 pages. *Aud.:* Ga, Ac.

The Association for Asian American Studies was founded in 1979 with the mission of advancing excellence in teaching and research in the field and promoting closer ties and understanding among the various groups within it—Chinese, Japanese, Korean, Filipino, Hawaiian, Southeast Asian, South Asian, and Pacific Islander, among others. This official association journal publishes articles that explore the historical, social, and cultural aspects of the Asian American experience along with book, media, and exhibition reviews. Article topics in recent issues range from popular culture, as in "He Wanted to Be Just Like Bruce Lee: African Americans, Kung Fu Theater and Cultural Exchange at the Margins"; to regional politics, as in "Public Resistance to Electing Asian Americans in Southern California"; and history, as in "The Chinese Creoles of Nicaragua: Identity, Economy, and Revolution in a Caribbean Port City." The online version of the journal is available at Project Muse. Essential for academic libraries supporting Asian American Studies and other ethnic studies programs.

936. ***KoreAm Journal: Korean American Experience.*** 1990. m. USD 28 domestic; USD 48 Canada; USD 3.95 newsstand/cover domestic. Ed(s): James Ryu. Korean American Publications, 17813 S Main St, Ste 112, Gardena, CA 90248; info@koreamjournal.com. Illus., adv. Circ: 33723 Paid. *Bk. rev.:* Various number and length. *Aud.:* Hs, Ga, Ac, Sa.

Originally a tabloid-format publication, *KoreAm Journal* has burst into the glossy magazine market. Established "to provide a forum nationwide for English-speaking Korean Americans," it includes a cover story, features, and departments, with columns titled "Street Talk," "Miscellaneous Mutterings," "Sports," and reaction pieces by "Banana Man." Two recent issues explore and celebrate the centennial of Korean immigration and the subsequent Korean American experience. Other articles highlight the economic, political, and cultural life in Korea. Many achieve a balance between informing and entertaining. Other fun educational features include "The KoreAm Kitchen" and "Artists' Trax," ranging from book and performance reviews to an interview with a transgender entertainer in Korea. There is a unique section titled "Community Network," which is reserved for providing information about local and national Korean American nonprofit organizations. Recommended for public libraries serving Korean American populations as well as academic libraries supporting Asian American and ethnic studies programs.

937. ***Monolid Magazine.*** 2000. q. USD 12. Ed(s): Carrie Chang. Monolid Magazine, 368 Broadway, Ste 516, New York, NY 10013; admin@monolid.com; http://www.monolid.com/. Adv. *Aud.:* Hs, Ga, Ac.

Self-described on their web site as "a back-atcha 'zine with verve and chutzpah that dares to say no to a bleached-out culture," *Monolid* is an edgy new publication targeting college students and young professionals. Be warned, they don't pull any punches! In "A Word About Our Name," Editor in Chief and founder Carrie Chang explains that she "cooked up this magazine with the hopes that Asians would stop annihilating their God-given features and, instead, put up a yellow fist." The table-of-contents format looks different with each issue, and a recent issue demonstrates the range of topics covered, with sections titled "Reviews and Lifestyle," "Religion and Philosophy," "Photography," "Don't Blink: Poetry and Fiction from the Yellow Underground," and "Departments." Sample articles range from "Honda's Crusade: Why Congressman Mike Honda Won't Let Japan Forget," to "David Henry Hwang's *Flower Drum* is a Song for a New Generation," to writings by prominent Asian American authors like Janice Mirikitani, Amy Uyematsu, and Arthur Sze. If it continues to explore diverse topics, *Monolid*, which published an expose on the demise of *aMagazine*, could make the leap to reaching that wider audience. Special note: The magazine's covers have the best graphics and photography in this genre. Instead of showing scantily clad women in provocative poses, *Monolid*'s covers have featured civil rights activists like Ling-chi Wang and Yuri Kochiyama. Recommended for public libraries serving Asian American communities, or for readers wanting to know more about Asian Americans. Also appropriate for academic libraries supporting Asian American Studies and ethnic diversity programs.

938. ***Yolk: generasian next.*** [ISSN: 1077-6907] 1994. bi-m. USD 18 domestic; USD 30 Canada; USD 60 elsewhere. Informasia Media Group, Inc., PO Box 3607, Alhambra, CA 91803. Adv. *Bk. rev.:* Various number and length. *Aud.:* Hs, Ga.

According to the 2000 U.S. Census, the number of Asians and Pacific Americans living in the United States had doubled since 1990. *Yolk* is a slick publication aimed at the growing portion of this population between the ages of 18 and 34 ("Generasian Next") with articles on entertainers, films, supermodels, and fashion. In addition to the usual articles about Asian American/Asian celebrities, *Yolk* has explored some unusual subjects. A recent issue contains an interview with Masuimi Max, a fire-eating performance artist who performs in the nude, and in the same issue, an investigative article titled "Play But No Pay: the Fleecing of Asian American Actors." Regular departments include "Editor's Slant"; "Yakkity Yolk," reader letters and e-mails; "Yin & Yolk," pointed perspectives on the tag line "you all look alike"; and "EmbrYolk," reviews of films, music, books, and web sites. Recommended for libraries serving young adult Asians and Asian Americans and for readers interested in the Asian American cultural scene.

Electronic Journals

939. ***Asian American Movement Ezine.*** 1999. m. Asian American Movement Ezine, yellowpower@aamovement.net; http://www.aamovement.net/. *Bk. rev.:* Occasional. *Aud.:* Hs, Ga, Ac, Sa.

Started in 1999 by a group of Asian Americans in the Boston area, the stated goals of this online publication were to provide a noncommercial, "alternative medium for political, cultural and social exchange on Asian American issues" as well as "a vehicle in which to organize for mass social change, and a place for social and artistic expression." This is a tall order for an e-zine run by volunteers with only donated funds (no advertising dollars accepted). It more than meets the challenge, with pages produced by members of the collective on history, news, community, narratives, art/culture, hate crimes, immigration/labor, and race/identity. While looking at the present and future with frequent updates and new articles, *Asian American Movement Ezine* also honors the Asian American movement of the past with article reprints. A recent issue has a speical section: The "War on Terrorism" (quote marks theirs), with links to "IQ Test on the War on Iraq" and "List of Countries the U.S. Has Bombed since WWII." A disclaimer states, "This website documents the Movement for historical and educational use and makes NO claim as being the authoritative source for the Asian Left of the Movement." An informative and accessible resource, recommended for students, researchers, and activists.

940. ***PoliticalCircus.*** 2001. irreg. USD 15. Rainmaker Political Group LLC, mail@rainmakerpolitical.com; http://www.politicalcircus.com/. *Aud.:* Hs, Ga, Ac, Sa.

PoliticalCircus.com is a weekly e-zine for political information and news about the Asian Pacific American community. Owned and operated by the Rainmaker Political Group based in Alexandria, Virginia, it relies on editors from all across the country to monitor and review local, state, and national publications, press releases, action alerts, and other sources for the weekly report, published every Monday. Supported by donations and banner advertisements, the site is well organized, and it reportedly receives over 30,000 viewings per week. Perhaps "the pen is mightier with a click." In May, Asian Pacific American Heritage Month, the site publishes daily profiles ("31 Days, 31 Profiles") of Asian Pacific American advocacy leaders, elected officials, appointed officials, political insiders, and political intellectuals. There is a links page inviting anyone to add their link to the relevant directory: Academic, Campaigns and Elections, Forums and Communities, Federal Government, Humor and Parody, Issues and Activism, Local Government, Merchandise, News and Commentary, Nonprofits and Community Groups, Political Parties, Publications and Magazines, Research and Dirt, and State Government, in order to "build a bigger and better online political resource for the Asian Pacific American community." Recommended for anyone interested in the latest information about Asian Americans and politics or public policy.

■ ASTROLOGY

Christianne Casper, Faculty Librarian, Broward Community College, South Campus, 7200 Pines Blvd., Pembroke Pines, FL 33024; a012724t@bc.seflin.org

Introduction

Astrology involves observations, measurements, and calculations about the stars and planets to produce a framework for symbolic patterns according to their positions and aspects. Analyzing these patterns, astrologists attempt to explain and predict social, political, emotional, and other important aspects of life on Earth. Some popular astrology journals include *American Astrology, Dell Horoscope, Mountain Astrologer*, and *Welcome to Planet Earth*. These journals provide information on personal horoscopes and guides to world events. Other journals, *Considerations, Mercury Hour,* and *Today's Astrologer*, focus on a more scholarly, research-oriented approach. The following list includes publications for all levels of interest.

Basic Periodicals

Hs: *American Astrology, Dell Horoscope;* Ga: *American Astrology, Dell Horoscope, The Mountain Astrologer, Welcome to Planet Earth;* Sa: *Considerations, Mercury Hour, The Mountain Astrologer, Today's Astrologer;* Ac: *American Astrology, Considerations, The Mountain Astrologer, Today's Astrologer.*

941. ***American Astrology.*** [ISSN: 0002-7529] 1933. m. USD 18.98. Ed(s): Ken Irving, Lee Chapman. Starlog Group, Inc., 475 Park Ave S, 8th Fl, New York, NY 10016; http://www.starlog.com. Illus., index, adv. Circ: 185000. Vol. ends: Feb. Microform: PQC. *Bk. rev.:* 2. *Aud.:* Hs, Ga, Ac.

American Astrology is one of the oldest and most popular astrology magazines. Its focus is on the practical application of astrology to everyday life. Each issue is divided into three sections. "Features" contains articles that cover topics from astrology for a new age to astrology of famous personalities. "Popular Astrology" includes book reviews, astrology for ages 50-plus, birthday forecasts, and astro-crosswords. The final section, "Forecasts," includes monthly, weekly, and daily horoscopes.

942. ***Considerations.*** [ISSN: 1066-4920] 1983. q. USD 35 domestic; USD 40 foreign. Ed(s): Kennet Gillman. Considerations, PO Box 655, Mount Kisco, NY 10549. Illus. Sample. Circ: 1500 Paid. *Bk. rev.:* 3-6, signed. *Aud.:* Ac, Sa.

As an international, scholarly journal, *Considerations* provides a forum for scholars, professionals, students, and astrology buffs to discuss, question, and develop thought-provoking ideas. The majority of the articles focus on the astrology of an individual. However, other topics may include business or financial matters as well as historical aspects of astrology. "Let's Consider" is a section of letters to and responses from the editor. Toward the end of the issue there is an excellent list of Internet-based astrological resources. The online version includes the table of contents of the current issue, an index of articles searchable by subject or author, some full-text sample articles, and links to recommended web sites.

943. ***Dell Horoscope.*** Formerly (until 199?): *Horoscope.* [ISSN: 1080-1421] 1935. 13x/yr. USD 27.97 domestic; USD 37.97 foreign. Ed(s): Ronnie Grishman. Dell Magazines, 475 Park Ave S, 11 Fl, New York, NY 10016-6901; juliamcevoy@dellmagazines.com. Illus., adv. Circ: 111684 Paid. Vol. ends: Dec. Reprint: PQC. *Indexed:* BRI, CBRI. *Bk. rev.:* 3 signed. *Aud.:* Hs, Ga.

Dell Horoscope is one of the most popular astrology magazines. The articles cover general-interest topics ranging from world and national affairs to personal problems. Also included are yearly, monthly, and daily guides. The regular features include letters to the editor, lucky numbers, celebrity snapshots, and book and product reviews. *Dell* is written with both professional astrologers and amateurs in mind. The online version includes daily horoscopes, a readers' forum, and links to other astrology web sites. Also of interest is "Cosmic Connections," which lists astrological activities in the United States.

944. ***Mercury Hour: the astrologer's astrology magazine.*** 1974. q. Ed(s): Jewel Cook Fahey. Mercury Hour, 283 Gardenpark Ave., Lynchburg, VA 24502-2397. Illus., adv. *Bk. rev.:* 3. *Aud.:* Sa.

Mercury Hour is a unique publication, providing an international forum for discussing anything and everything astrological. The letters, opinions, and articles are all contributed by astrologers for astrologers. Research is presented, and questions are posed seeking answers from other readers. All branches of astrology are discussed. The online version includes previously published articles, a bulletin board, chat rooms, conference listings, and links to other web sites.

945. ***The Mountain Astrologer.*** [ISSN: 1079-1345] 1987. 6x/yr. USD 36 in US & Canada; USD 54 elsewhere in the Americas; USD 64 in Europe. Ed(s): Nan Geary. Mountain Astrologer, PO Box 970, Cedar Ridge, CA 95924-0970; subs@mountainastrologer.com; http://www.mountainastrologer.com. Illus., adv. Sample. Circ: 20000 Paid. Vol. ends: Nov/Dec. *Bk. rev.:* 4-7. *Aud.:* Ga, Ac, Sa.

The Mountain Astrologer provides a wealth of information for professional and amateur astrologers alike. Standard features include a "Forecast Calendar," "New and Full Moon Reports," "Where's that Moon?," "Astrology News," letters to the editor, a professional directory, and signed book and astrological web site reviews. The web site reviews and the abundance of charts are extremely helpful. The web site lists the table of contents of the current issue, provides an index of articles from 1992 to 2000, and offers an article archive. Web site recommendations are also available. In addition there is a "Beginner Information" section, which provides an overview of basic concepts of astrology.

946. ***Today's Astrologer.*** Formerly: *American Federation of Astrologers Bulletin.* [ISSN: 1067-1439] 1938. m. USD 35. Ed(s): Kris Brandt Riske. American Federation of Astrologers, Inc., 6535 S Rural Rd, Box 22040, Tempe, AZ 85283-9760. Illus., index. Sample. Circ: 2700 Controlled. *Aud.:* Ac, Sa.

Today's Astrologer, the bulletin of the American Federation of Astrologers, was established as a forum to promote astrology through research and education. There is an average of five articles per issue. Regular departments include "Data Exchange," "The Question Box," and "The Communication Center." This last department is a calendar of activities of member organizations and other astrology affiliates. Finally, a "Lunation / Full Moon" chart is provided.

947. ***Welcome to Planet Earth: journal of new astrology in the contemporary world.*** Former titles: *Pass the Word; Great Bear.* [ISSN: 0747-8968] 1979. m. USD 25. Ed(s): Mark Lerner. Great Bear Press, PO Box 5164, Eugene, OR 97405. Illus., adv. Sample. Circ: 2100. *Aud.:* Ga.

Welcome to Planet Earth includes astrology articles on individuals as well as information on current and historical events. The articles are written for a general audience in order to provide a deeper understanding of contemporary astrology. The monthly features include letters to the editor, "Your Cosmic Kalendar," and "Astro-Shamanic Perspectives." The online journal includes current articles covering world events, astro-software, computer reports, back articles, celebrity profiles, and educational materials.

■ ASTRONOMY

See also Aeronautics and Space Science; and Atmospheric Sciences sections.

Edward Creighton Sugrue Jr., Wolbach Library, Harvard-Smithsonian Center for Astrophysics, 60 Garden St., Cambridge, MA 02138; edsugrue@hotmail.com

Introduction

In these days of unprecedented technological advances, our understanding of the universe is growing, expanding, and accelerating as quickly as the universe itself. But even so—why study astronomy? What is the draw of the pursuit? The lure and the lore of astronomy spring from the ancient, essential human sense of wonder at the immensity of our universe. Although there was a time, long ago, when mankind sought to explain the heavens through recourse to mythological explanations, today's astronomers (at least the successful ones!) prefer to employ the methodology of science. Today's science of astronomy begins with the universal language of mathematics. Using this language, it attempts to express and therefore define the fundamental science of physics. In turn, astronomy employs the fundamental science of physics in order to elucidate the underlying form and shape, the warp and woof, of the basic principles behind the true nature and origins of the universe.

This ongoing process involves a perpetual balancing act between the essential human desire for mathematical certainty, or "that which is known or knowable," and the equally essential human love of Mystery in the largest sense possible, or "that which is unknowable, and beyond the ken of humanity." The draw of astronomy can be best understood in terms of this balancing act, this pair of inherently opposite human drives, locked together in the pursuit we call astronomy. But as for the actual daily work involved in this pursuit, modern astronomers' jobs are made vastly easier by being kept well informed about recent developments in their fields, and one of the best ways to keep themselves informed is by means of the journals discussed in this section.

In an interesting way, astronomy has a lot in common with the mission of libraries, especially public libraries. Both are inherently very democratic, and by their nature they are open to anyone. Anyone can experience wonder about the origin and nature of our universe, and anyone can walk into a library to read a book or periodical.

There is a wide range of astronomical periodicals available, many of which are indeed quite democratic in spirit, and aim at a wider audience. However, librarians need to take extra care concerning which periodicals they select for their institutions, in this area of study. While many of the following periodicals are aimed at the general public, other periodicals are so esoteric that even undergraduate astronomy students have trouble wading through them. Please take care, also, not to assume that the periodicals listed in the Basic Periodicals part of this section are "basic" in the sense of being "simple." Many of them are overflowing with high-level equations, and are only "basic" in the sense that they are invaluable components of any serious academic astronomy library. Please also note that "basic" periodicals are distinct from "core" periodicals. Core periodicals are chosen and agreed upon by specialized science libraries. They can be identified by consulting PAMNET and/or ASTROWEB, which are each described, three paragraphs down, in this introduction. In determining a periodical's prospective value to your library, pay attention to the audience codes that periodicals have been assigned, and take time to examine their annotations and their web sites.

That said, a lot of these periodicals do provide terrific information to committed amateur astronomers, of whom there are many. Amateur astronomers make major contributions to the field on a regular basis. The Hale-Bopp comet was discovered by amateurs, and Albert Einstein himself, whose discoveries eventually led to the search for black holes, among so many other things, was just a clerk when he made his discoveries. The general audience periodicals serve a role that is at least as valuable as the specialized journals, as many thoughtful people, children, etc., harbor a great love of astronomy, yet simply don't have the time to study it in any great depth. Many periodicals listed here are somewhere between the abstruse journals and the nontechnical ones. Quite a few of these tend to specialize in a particular area of astronomical research, such as meteors, cosmology, or the planets of our solar system.

The selections put forward here include titles of interest to a diverse range of readers, ranging from Spanish-speaking children, to the average intelligent adult, to hobbyists with a specific astronomical interest, to professional astronomers. Most of the publications, although not all, can be found on the Internet. Several excellent periodicals are available free of charge in this way. This section includes a couple of journals that are designed entirely to translate research being done in the former Soviet Union. For journals with a similar function, seek out *Ulrich's International Periodicals Directory*. A word to the wise—if you are new to this field, do not confuse *Astronomy and Astrophysics Abstracts* with *Astronomy and Astrophysics*. They sound like they should be connected somehow, but they are completely unrelated publications, and the similarity in their titles is merely an annoying coincidence. Special mention in this category goes to a publication that is technically not a serial, but that needs to be mentioned in this context. A valuable, beautifully illustrated, eye-catching resource, *Astronomical Calendar* by Guy Ottewell, published by Furman University in Greenville, South Carolina, is generally considered to be the most beautiful, and one of the most treasured, of all the annual sky atlases.

Academic librarians who are new to the field also need to be aware of *PAMNET* and *ASTROWEB*. *PAMNET* is a valuable, professional online forum, useful for discussing astronomy periodicals and other information sources with fellow information professionals and librarians. *PAMNET* can easily be found online at http://pantheon.yale.edu/~dstern/astro.html. *ASTROWEB* is maintained by an international group of astronomers, and provides easy access to a host of astronomical databases and other resources that are just outside the scope of the section you are reading right now. *ASTROWEB* can be located at http://www.stsci.edu/science/net-resources.html. *Astronomy and Astrophysics Abstracts,* NASA's *ADS*, which is at http://adswww.harvard.edu, and *INSPEC* are excellent indexing services.

Basic Periodicals

Ems: *Abrams Planetarium Sky Calendar, Odyssey, SkyWatch;* Hs, Ga: *Astronomy, Griffith Observer, Mercury, Sky & Telescope, SkyWatch;* Ac: *Astronomical Journal, Astronomy, Astronomy & Astrophysics, The Astrophysical Journal, Royal Astronomical Society. Monthly Notices.*

Basic Abstracts and Indexes

ADS, Astronomy and Astrophysics Abstracts, INSPEC, NASA Astrophysics Data System (ADS). Note: The highly respected *Astronomy and Astrophysics Abstracts* ceased print publication in 2000. It still exists in its online form, as a repository for information up to that point, but the German government, which administers it, is attempting to phase it out.

948. ***A A V S O Journal.*** [ISSN: 0271-9053] 1972. s-a. USD 40 (Individuals, USD 25). Ed(s): Charles A Whitney. American Association of Variable Star Observers, 25 Birch St, Cambridge, MA 02138; aavso@aavso.org; http://www.aavso.org/journal.html. Illus., index. Refereed. Circ: 1500. Vol. ends: No. 2. *Bk. rev.:* 1-2, 400-600 words. *Aud.:* Ac, Sa.

The American Association of Variable Star Observers (AAVSO) has members in more than 40 countries. These members include both amateur and professional astronomers. AAVSO is the largest organization of variable-star observers in the world. Members watch and track variable stars (those whose luminosity changes over time), and then submit their observations to the AAVSO. Amateur astronomers play a very important role in the tracking of variable stars, as there are far too many for only professionals to follow. The AAVSO web site has such features as a search engine designed to locate variable stars in the AAVSO charts; a variety of online tools to assist observers in processing their information; and even a "variable star of the month." The journal publishes scientific papers on variable-star research, activities of the AAVSO, letters to the editor, and the Annual Report of the Director. Both are valued, valuable sources of information within the astronomical community.

949. ***Abrams Planetarium Sky Calendar: an aid to enjoying the changing sky.*** [ISSN: 0733-6314] 1969. q. USD 10; USD 14. Ed(s): Robert C Victor. Michigan State University, Talbert & Leota Abrams Planetarium, 113 Angell Bldg, East Lansing, MI 48824-1234; ladiski@pilot.msu.edu; http://www.pa.msu.edu/abrams/SkyCalendar. Illus. Circ: 15000. *Aud.:* Ems, Hs, Ga, Ac.

Sky Calendar, as the name suggests, presents a page for each month that is laid out like a calendar. The reverse side of each page presents a simplified sky map for that month, printed for use at mid-evening and approximately 43 degrees north latitude. Diagrams in the boxes invite the reader to track the moon's rapid motion past the planets and bright stars of the zodiac, as well as to follow the more leisurely pace of the planets in their conjunctions with bright stars and other planets. This is a very specialized publication that serves only the purpose described here. You will not find articles, book reviews, or evaluations of software, for example—just the charts. The highly illustrated format and easy-to-follow guide make the loose-leaf calendar popular. Information presented in the calendar can be used (with permission) as a teaching tool by members of astronomical societies, teachers, and park interpreters.

950. ***Ad Astra: to the stars: the magazine of the National Space Society.*** [ISSN: 1041-102X] 1989. 6x/yr. USD 40 (Individuals, USD 35). Ed(s): Pat Dasch. National Space Society, 600 Pennsylvania Ave, S E, Ste 201, Washington, DC 20003-4316; adastraed@aol.com; http://www.nss.org/adastra/home.html. Illus., adv. Circ: 30000. Vol. ends: No. 6. *Indexed:* ABS&EES, IAA, MagInd, RGPR. *Aud.:* Hs, Ga, Ac, Sa.

Ad Astra contains articles and news stories concerning U.S. and international space programs, federal space policy formation, commercial space endeavors, new technologies, and recent scientific achievements pertaining to astronomy. It is the membership publication of the National Space Society, and its articles can be read by space and astronomy enthusiasts, as well as those with extensive education in the field. Regular departments in the publication include "Launch Pad," "Mission Control," "Countdown," "Space Community," and "Lifting Off." Obviously, the primary focus is on the space program, but often there are articles dealing with broader astronomical issues such as cosmology, or wholly speculative articles about possible future space-related ventures. This popular journal has numerous beautiful illustrations and photographs, and has helped spark an early interest in space in many people. A valuable addition to any library, whether it specializes in astronomy or not.

951. ***American Astronomical Society. Bulletin.*** [ISSN: 0002-7537] 1969. q. USD 55 domestic; USD 70 in Canada, Mexico, Central and South America & Caribbean; USD 80 in Europe, Asia, Middle East, Africa & Oceania. Ed(s): P B Boyce. American Astronomical Society, c/o Dawn Marie Craig, 2000 Florida Ave, N W, Ste 400, Washington, DC 20009; http://www.aas.org. Illus. Vol. ends: No. 4. Microform: AIP. *Indexed:* GeoRef. *Aud.:* Ac, Sa.

The function of the *Bulletin* is to give the American Astronomical Society (AAS) a forum to present the abstracts of papers from conferences and meetings, and to present notices of the society that are likely to be of interest to the astronomical community. Annual observatory reports and reports of the society itself are also published here. The observatory reports are particularly useful to people wanting to determine the observational capabilities and major research programs of various observatories. The *Bulletin* sometimes includes such interesting papers as "The Most Frequently-Cited Astronomical Papers Published during the Past Decade," Alvin Toffler-esque discussions of likely cultural changes in the twenty-first century and their impact on astronomy, and the real value of a Ph.D. The AAS reserves its *Astronomical Journal* and *Astrophysical Journal* (both below in this section) for original research papers.

952. ***Annual Review of Astronomy and Astrophysics.*** [ISSN: 0066-4146] 1963. a. USD 180 (Individuals, USD 80). Ed(s): Samuel Gubins, Geoffrey Burbidge. Annual Reviews, 4139 El Camino Way, Palo Alto, CA 94303-0139; service@annualreviews.org; http://www.annualreviews.org. Adv. Refereed. Microform: PQC. Online: EBSCO Publishing; Gale Group; HighWire Press; ProQuest Information & Learning; Swets Blackwell. Reprint: PSC. *Indexed:* ChemAb, GSI, IAA, M&GPA, MRD, SCI. *Aud.:* Ac, Sa.

This is a valuable synthesis of the current state of research in a wide range of astronomical fields. Each volume contains about 15–20 articles, each dealing with a currently "hot" topic in astronomy. The article gives the reader a detailed overview of what kind of research is being done, and upon what specific problems and issues researchers are striving to focus more energy. Each article is followed up by a select bibliography of several dozen of the most important published articles in the particular area of inquiry for the year, chosen by some of the top people in the world in that specific field. Be aware that the articles assume a certain scientific sophistication and awareness on the part the reader. *ARAA* is a tremendously useful volume for librarians and astronomers, and is often kept behind the circulation desk in science libraries to keep it safe.

953. ***Association of Lunar and Planetary Observers. Journal.*** [ISSN: 0039-2502] 1947. q. USD 23 in US & Canada; USD 33 elsewhere. Ed(s): John E Westfall. Association of Lunar and Planetary Observers, PO Box 13456, Springfield, IL 62791-3456; poshedly@bellsouth.nt; http://www.LPL.Arizona.edu/~rhill/alpo/member.html. Illus., adv. Sample. Refereed. Circ: 410 Paid. Vol. ends: No. 4. *Bk. rev.:* 1-2, 300-500 words. *Aud.:* Ac, Sa.

Sometimes known by its alternate title, *The Strolling Astronomer*, this journal is a publication of the Association of Lunar and Planetary Observers (ALPO), and is regularly mailed to members of this international organization of amateur and professional astronomers. Not an easy magazine to leaf through, it is definitely designed for the reader who really knows physics and astronomy.

ALPO has many subdivisions, each with its own publication, and subscriptions to these other publications need to be handled directly with each division. The ALPO web site can help settle questions concerning which publications might be best for you. This specific journal is considered to be the means of coordinating all the various areas of ALPO research under a single cover. Reports and observations from readers and staff are always welcome for all publications, provided they have not been published elsewhere.

954. ***The Astronomical Almanac.*** Supersedes: *Astronomical Ephemeris; American Ephemeris and Nautical Almanac; Nautical Almanac and Astronomical Ephemeris.* [ISSN: 0737-6421] 1855. a. USD 47. U.S. Naval Observatory, c/o Dr D D McCarthy, Department of the Navy, Washington, DC 20392-5100. *Aud.:* Hs, Ga, Ac, Sa.

The *Astronomical Almanac* contains precise ephemerides of the Sun, Moon, planets, and satellites, data for eclipses, and information on other astronomical phenomena for a given year. Most data are tabulated at one-day intervals. It includes geocentric positions of the Sun, Moon, planets, and bright stars; heliocentric positions of the planets and their orbital elements; universal and sidereal times; daily polynomials for the Moon's position; physical ephemerides of the Sun, Moon, and planets; elongation times and differential coordinates of selected satellites of the planets; rise, set, and transit times of the Sun and Moon; eclipse data and maps; tables of reference data for various celestial objects; useful formulas; and other information. Don't miss the "Explanatory Supplement" to this publication. The supplement is an authoritative source on astronomical phenomena and calendars, and offers detailed directions for performing practical astronomy. All in all, this is a very valuable, esteemed resource—generally given pride of place in any serious astronomy collection.

955. ***The Astronomical Journal.*** [ISSN: 0004-6256] 1849. m. USD 505 combined subscription domestic print and online eds.; USD 545 combined subscription Mexico print and online eds.; USD 580.35 combined subscription Canada print and online eds. Ed(s): Paul Hodge. American Astronomical Society, c/o Dawn Marie Craig, 2000 Florida Ave, N W, Ste 400, Washington, DC 20009; http://www.aas.org. Illus., index. Refereed. Vol. ends: No. 6. Microform: AIP. Online: EBSCO Publishing. *Indexed:* ApMecR, CPI, ChemAb, CompR, GeoRef, SCI. *Aud.:* Ac, Sa.

A vehicle for publishing original observations and research with a fairly short publication time, the *Journal* publishes many seminal papers. Coverage includes the traditional areas of astronomy and expanded topics, including such topical areas as detection of new planets; large-scale structure of the universe; asteroids that are likely to strike the Earth; and every imaginable other topic pertaining to astronomy. This journal and *Astrophysical Journal* (below in this section) comprise the main U.S. publications of new research in the fields of astronomy and astrophysics, similar to the European *Astronomy and Astrophysics* (below in this section). Considered to be one of the five or six "core" journals in any serious astronomy collection, *AJ* is essential for any academic institute with an astronomy program and indispensable to serious astronomers.

956. ***Astronomy.*** [ISSN: 0091-6358] 1973. m. USD 39.95 domestic; USD 50 foreign; USD 4.95 newsstand/cover per issue domestic. Ed(s): David Eicher. Kalmbach Publishing Co., PO Box 1612, Waukesha, WI 53187-1612; http://www.kalmbach.com. Illus., index, adv. Sample. Circ: 160745 Paid. Vol. ends: Dec. Online: bigchalk; EBSCO Publishing; Florida Center for Library Automation; Gale Group; Northern Light Technology, Inc.; OCLC Online Computer Library Center, Inc.; ProQuest Information & Learning; H.W. Wilson. Reprint: PQC. *Indexed:* BRI, CBRI, CPerI, GSI, GeoRef, IHTDI, MagInd, RGPR. *Bk. rev.:* 5-6, 50-500 words. *Aud.:* Hs, Ga, Ac.

As indicated by its circulation, this is one of the most popular astronomy publications among casual sky watchers. Insightful, well-written articles, aimed at a popular audience, are brought together here with some truly spectacular photographs of some of the most "stellar" sights in the heavens. *Astronomy* provides readers with news reports, hobby information, copious reviews of astronomy equipment, and the latest news on space exploration. A very helpful sky chart, as well as observing tips for locating specific objects in the sky, are to be found here in a visually appealing format that is both pleasant and stimulating to read. This would surely be a welcome addition to virtually any library.

957. ***Astronomy & Astrophysics: a European journal.*** Superseded in part (in 1968): *Zeitschrift fuer Astrophysik;* Incorporated (1947-1992): *Astronomical Institutes of Czechoslovakia. Bulletin;* (1966-2000): *Astronomy & Astrophysics. Supplement Series;* Which was formerly (until 1970): *Astronomical Institutes of the Netherlands. Bulletin. Supplement Series;* Which incorporated (1900-1960): *Kapteyn Astronomical Laboratory at Groningen. Publications;* Which was formerly (until 1924): *Astronomical Laboratory at Groningen. Publications.* [ISSN: 0004-6361] 1930. 48x/yr. EUR 3301. E D P Sciences, 17 Ave du Hoggar, B P 112, Les Ulis, 91944 Cedex A, France; subscribers@edpsciences.org; http://www.edpsciences.org. Illus., index, adv. Sample. Refereed. Vol. ends: No. 3. Microform: PQC. Online: EBSCO Publishing; RoweCom Information Quest; ScienceDirect; Springer LINK; Swets Blackwell. Reprint: ISI. *Indexed:* ApMecR, ChemAb, EngInd, SCI. *Aud.:* Ac, Sa.

Sponsored by the European Southern Observatory, this publication represents scientific organizations in 17 European countries. The journal is a cooperative effort that grew out of the merger of the publications of several of the represented organizations. It once had a supplement, published separately, but today the main journal and the supplement are published under a single cover. Papers present all aspects of astronomy and astrophysics, regardless of the techniques used to obtain the results. Some items that will *not* be found in this journal include observatory reports, review papers, and conference proceedings. Especially since the merging of this title with its supplement, coverage includes all areas of astronomy and astrophysics, including connected fields. Therefore, for example, this journal might include articles on such subjects as computational techniques that might have applications in astronomy, atomic or molecular physics, or even statistical mathematics. It is intended that all important fields relevant to the study of astronomy and astrophysics be reviewed from time to time, where frequency of review is dictated by the amount of activity in an area. This research publication is comparable to *Astronomical Journal* and *Astrophysical Journal.*

958. ***Astronomy & Geophysics: journal of the Royal Astronomical Society.*** Formerly (until 1997): *Royal Astronomical Society. Quarterly Journal.* [ISSN: 1366-8781] 1960. bi-m. GBP 166 print & online eds. Ed(s): Sue Bowler. Blackwell Publishing Ltd., 9600 Garsington Rd, PO Box 805, Oxford, OX4 2DQ, United Kingdom; customerservices@oxon.blackwellpublishing.com; http://www.blackwellpublishing.com/. Illus., index, adv. Sample. Refereed. Circ: 3700. Vol. ends: No. 6. Microform: PQC. Online: EBSCO Publishing; ingenta.com; Munksgaard & Blackwell Science's Synergy; OCLC Online Computer Library Center, Inc.; RoweCom Information Quest; Swets Blackwell. Reprint: ISI. *Indexed:* ChemAb, DSR&OA, GeoRef, SCI. *Bk. rev.:* Variable number and length. *Aud.:* Ac, Sa.

After a redesign in 1996, *Astronomy and Geophysics* replaced the *Quarterly Journal* of the Royal Astronomical Society as its topical publication. One objective of the journal is to promote communication among general astronomers and planetary scientists. Therefore, it often has exceptionally strong coverage of planetary sciences, yet it also has excellent coverage of cosmology, black holes, astrophotography, etc. Articles are written in accessible language, without many equations or formulae, and include related topics such as interdisciplinary research, information about upcoming international conferences, science policy, social issues within the astronomical community, news, and book and software reviews. Many of the traditions from the *Quarterly Journal* remain, such as the journal being a forum for discussion of fundamental and controversial scientific issues.

959. ***Astronomy Reports.*** Former titles: *Soviet Astronomy; Soviet Astronomy A.J.* [ISSN: 1063-7729] 1924. m. USD 2432 combined subscription domestic; USD 2457 combined subscription in Canada, Mexico, Central and South America & Caribbean; USD 2462 combined subscription in Europe, Asia, Middle East, Africa & Oceania. Ed(s): Alexander A Boyarchuk. M A I K Nauka - Interperiodica, Profsoyuznaya ul 90, Moscow, 117997, Russian Federation; compmg@maik.ru; http://www.maik.rssi.ru. Illus., index. Sample. Refereed. Vol. ends: No. 6. Microform: AIP. Online: EBSCO Publishing; RoweCom Information Quest; Swets Blackwell. *Indexed:* CPI, IAA, SCI. *Aud.:* Ac, Sa.

Astronomy Reports is a cover-to-cover translation of the principal Russian astronomy journal, *Astronomicheskii Zhurnal,* and is available simultaneously with the Russian edition from Maik Nauka/Interperiodica Publishing. Russia has a long and proud tradition of producing great astrophysicists, and a lot of cutting-edge science is first reported in the Russian journals. This journal is displayed prominently at any serious astronomy library. Issues consist of about 10–20 articles in many areas of astronomy, including radio astronomy, physics of the sun, planetary science, and issues having to do with cosmological large-scale structure. Proceedings of international conferences and book reviews are also included.

960. *The Astrophysical Journal: an international review of astronomy and astronomical physics.* [ISSN: 0004-637X] 1895. 36x/yr. USD 1470 domestic; USD 1680 combined subscription domestic print & online eds.; USD 1712.90 Canada. American Astronomical Society, c/o Dawn Marie Craig, 2000 Florida Ave, N W, Ste 400, Washington, DC 20009; http://www.aas.org. Illus., index. Refereed. Circ: 2900 Paid. Microform: PMC; PQC. Online: EBSCO Publishing. Reprint: ISI; PQC. *Indexed:* ChemAb, EngInd, GeoRef, SCI. *Aud.:* Ac, Sa.

Many astronomy and astrophysics discoveries of the twentieth century have first been reported in this peer-reviewed official publication of the American Astronomical Society. Any major astronomy library considers this to be part of its "core" collection. The astrophysics presented here is as esoteric as it ever gets, with many equations and graphs in every article. A supplement series accompanies it, with its main purpose being to present substantial and extensive support for material found in the main journal. Access to a full-text electronic version is free with a paid print subscription.

961. *Astrophysics.* [ISSN: 0571-7256] 1965. q. USD 2053 print or online ed. Ed(s): D M Sedrakyan. Kluwer Academic / Plenum Publishers, 233 Spring St Fl 7, New York, NY 10013-1522; http://www.wkap.nl/. Illus., index. Sample. Refereed. Vol. ends: No. 4. Microform: PQC. Online: ingenta.com; Kluwer Online; OCLC Online Computer Library Center, Inc.; Ovid Technologies, Inc.; RoweCom Information Quest; Swets Blackwell. *Indexed:* ApMecR, ChemAb. *Aud.:* Ac, Sa.

Data obtained at all principal observatories in Russia, along with recent theoretical and experimental advances in astrophysics, are published in this journal. Fortunately for those of us who do not read Russian, much of the scientific literature from this part of the world is translated into English in a timely fashion. Like *Astronomy Reports,* this is full of cutting-edge Russian science and is geared toward a higher-level audience. It contains data obtained at the Sternberg Astronomical Institute and all principal Russian observatories, which data deals with the entire range of astronomical and astrophysical phenomena. The Consultants Bureau, a subsidiary of Plenum Publishing, is responsible for publishing dozens of English translations of Russian journals, including *Astrophysics,* which is a cover-to-cover translation of *Astrofizika.* Topics of papers include planetary atmospheres, interstellar matter, solar physics, and space astrophysics, among a broad range of related topics.

962. *Astrophysics and Space Science: an international journal of astronomy, astrophysics and space science.* Incorporates (1970-1972): *Cosmic Electrodynamics;* (1975-1981): *Space Science Instrumentation.* [ISSN: 0004-640X] 1968. s-m. EUR 3063 print or online ed. Ed(s): John E Dyson, Susan A Lamb. Kluwer Academic Publishers, van Godewijckstraat 30, PO Box 17, Dordrecht, 3300 AA, Netherlands; services@wkap.nl; http://www.wkap.nl. Illus., index, adv. Sample. Refereed. Vol. ends: No. 2. Microform: PQC. Online: EBSCO Publishing; ingenta.com; Kluwer Online; OCLC Online Computer Library Center, Inc.; Ovid Technologies, Inc.; RoweCom Information Quest. *Indexed:* CCMJ, ChemAb, EngInd, GeoRef, M&GPA, SCI. *Aud.:* Ac, Sa.

This journal publishes original contributions, invited reviews, and conference proceedings over the entire range of astronomy and astrophysics. It includes observational and theoretical papers as well as those concerned with the techniques of instrumentation. Observational papers can include data from ground-based, space, and atmospheric facilities. *Astrophysics and Space Science* has published, and continues to publish, landmark papers in its field. It is widely considered to be an indispensable source of information for professional astronomers, astrophysicists, and space scientists. The supplemental publication *Experimental Astronomy* (below in this section) is included with the subscription at no extra cost.

963. *Astrum.* [ISSN: 0210-4105] 1960. bi-m. Membership, ESP 10700. Agrupacio Astronomica de Sabadell, Apdo de Correos 50, Sabadell, 08200, Spain; secretaria@astrosabadell.org; http://www.astrosabadell.org. Illus., adv. Circ: 2000. *Aud.:* Hs, Ga.

Astrum is a colorful astronomy magazine in Spanish, aimed at a popular audience. Bowker chose this year to survey some astronomy periodicals in Spanish, so that librarians serving constituencies with a growing Spanish-speaking population can accommodate the needs of those patrons. *Astrum* serves this role quite well. It is not a commercial magazine—it is mailed free to members of the Agrupacio Astronomica de Sabadell, and to astronomical centers and libraries. However, if your library seeks to foster an interest in science in Hispanic children, you might consider e-mailing the publishing part of the Agrupacio. *Astrum* includes articles, sky charts, ephemerides, and even surveys of Spanish-language Internet resources having to do with astronomy. Furthermore, it is full of very colorful, high-resolution photographs of many of the more beautiful areas in the sky.

964. *British Astronomical Association. Journal.* [ISSN: 0007-0297] 1890. bi-m. GBP 35.10. Ed(s): H McGee. British Astronomical Association, Burlington House, Picadilly, London, W1J 0DU, United Kingdom; 100257.735@compuserve.com; http://www.britastro.org. Illus., index, adv. Sample. Refereed. Circ: 3500. Vol. ends: No. 6. *Bk. rev.:* 6-20, 500-1,000 words. *Aud.:* Ac, Sa.

Since its founding in 1890, this journal has published the observations and work of British Astronomical Association (BAA) members, and members receive the journal free. However, nonmembers are eligible to receive the journal if they contact the publisher at the above e-mail address. Many articles and items of interest to all amateur astronomers are published, along with the observations and work of BAA members. The letters to the editor are often lively, with discussions on any subject having to do with astronomy, especially at the amateur level. Subscribers are offered special deals on astronomy-related products from time to time, such as CD-ROMs or software. Although this publication is geared to amateur astronomers and professionals who focus on observational techniques, it does not include the star charts and viewing guides that are published by equivalent American publications, such as *Astronomy* and *Sky & Telescope.*

965. *Earth in Space.* [ISSN: 1040-3124] 1988. 9x/yr. USD 12 domestic; USD 16 foreign. American Geophysical Union, 2000 Florida Ave, N W, Washington, DC 20009-1277; http://www.agu.org. Illus. Vol. ends: No. 9. *Indexed:* GeoRef. *Aud.:* Hs, Ga, Sa.

A concise, colorful 16-page magazine that is designed to stimulate educators and provoke top high school students to become interested in pursuing science. Articles and news in *Earth in Space* are written by real scientists, cover research and applications in geophysics, and discuss the social context of science. Issues are published monthly during the school year, September–May, and provide a window on current earth and space science.

966. *Earth, Moon, and Planets: an international journal of comparative planetology.* Former titles: *Moon and the Planets; Moon.* [ISSN: 0167-9295] 1969. m. EUR 938 print or online ed. Ed(s): Mark E Bailey. Kluwer Academic Publishers, van Godewijckstraat 30, PO Box 17, Dordrecht, 3300 AA, Netherlands. Illus., index, adv. Sample. Refereed. Vol. ends: Dec. Microform: PQC. Online: EBSCO Publishing; ingenta.com; Kluwer Online; OCLC Online Computer Library Center, Inc.; RoweCom Information Quest; Swets Blackwell. Reprint: SWZ. *Indexed:* ChemAb, DSR&OA, GeoRef, GeogAbPG, IAA, M&GPA, SCI. *Bk. rev.:* Variable number and length. *Aud.:* Ac, Sa.

Earth, Moon, and Planets, an international journal of solar system science, publishes original contributions on subjects ranging from star and planet formation and the origin and evolution of the solar and extra-solar planetary systems, to asteroids, comets, meteoroids, and near-Earth objects. The research done in this journal on near-Earth objects (NEOs) includes studies on asteroids that are considered likely candidates to one day strike the Earth. The journal also publishes relevant special issues and topical conference proceedings, review articles on problems of current interest, and book reviews. The editor welcomes proposals from guest editors for special thematic issues.

967. ***Experimental Astronomy: an international journal on astronomical instrumentation and data analysis.*** [ISSN: 0922-6435] 1989. bi-m. EUR 557 print or online ed. Ed(s): A Boksenberg. Kluwer Academic Publishers, van Godewijckstraat 30, PO Box 17, Dordrecht, 3300 AA, Netherlands. Illus. Sample. Refereed. Vol. ends: No. 4. Microform: PQC. Online: EBSCO Publishing; ingenta.com; Kluwer Online; OCLC Online Computer Library Center, Inc.; Ovid Technologies, Inc.; RoweCom Information Quest. *Aud.:* Ac, Sa.

Experimental Astronomy acts as a medium for the publication of papers on the instrumentation and data handling necessary for the conduct of astronomy at all wavelength fields. *Experimental Astronomy* publishes full-length articles, research letters, and reviews on developments in detection techniques, instruments, and data analysis and image-processing techniques. Occasionally, special issues are published to provide in-depth coverage on the instrumentation or analysis connected with a particular project, such as satellite experiments. Subscribers to *Astrophysics and Space Science* (above in this section) receive this publication as a supplement, but it can also be purchased alone.

968. ***Griffith Observer.*** [ISSN: 0195-3982] 1937. m. USD 18 domestic; USD 25 Canada; USD 26 Mexico. Ed(s): E C Krupp. Griffith Observatory, 2800 E Observatory Rd, Los Angeles, CA 90027; info@GriffithObs.org; http://www.griffithobs.org/Observer.html. Illus., index. Sample. Circ: 2000 Paid. Vol. ends: Dec. *Aud.:* Hs, Ga.

Published monthly by the observatory, this journal provides information about the activities at the Griffith Observatory as well as popular articles about astronomy. This journal is comparable in aims and scope to the Spanish-language journal *Astrum.* Sky charts, illustrations, guides to useful Internet links, and photographs enhance this publication, which strives to create a lifelong interest in science in its readers. For its efforts at popularizing astronomy, the *Griffith Observer* has been characterized as "the Carl Sagan of astronomy periodicals."

969. ***Icarus (San Diego): international journal of solar system studies.*** [ISSN: 0019-1035] 1962. m. EUR 3887 (Individuals, EUR 1890; Students, EUR 210). Ed(s): P. D. Nicholson. Academic Press, 525 B St, Ste 1900, San Diego, CA 92101-4495; apsubs@acad.com; http://www.academicpress.com. Illus., index, adv. Refereed. Vol. ends: No. 2. Online: EBSCO Publishing; Gale Group; ingenta.com; OCLC Online Computer Library Center, Inc.; RoweCom Information Quest; ScienceDirect; Swets Blackwell. *Indexed:* ChemAb, DSR&OA, GeoRef, M&GPA, SCI. *Bk. rev.:* 2-3, 150-2,000 words. *Aud.:* Ac, Sa.

Devoted to publishing original contributions in planetary science and the science of solar systems, this is another very prominent journal for academic libraries. Librarians should note that these fields are focused primarily on relatively local astronomy. Articles are generally about planets, moons, the Sun, or asteroids within our solar system. Coverage of cosmology, black holes, quasars, or theoretical physics is very rarely included. The main exception to this general rule is the appearance of articles concerning extrasolar planets, that is, planets revolving around stars other than the sun. This field is quite new, but it is increasingly important. All aspects of planetary system research are included, such as results of new research and observations. Special sections or issues are also a feature. All articles appear in English, but occasional abstracts are in German, French, or Russian.

970. ***International Astronomical Union. Minor Planet Center. Minor Planet Circulars - Minor Planets and Comets.*** Former titles (until 1978): *Cincinnati Observatory. Minor Planet Circulars; Smithsonian Institution. Astrophysical Observatory. Minor Planet Circulars - Minor Planets and Comets.* [ISSN: 0736-6884] 1947. irreg. approx. m. Ed(s): Brian G Marsden. Smithsonian Institution Astrophysical Observatory, 60 Garden St, Cambridge, MA 02138; iausubs@cfa.harvard.edu; http://cfa-www.harvard.edu/cfa/ps/services/MPC.html. Illus. Circ: 250. *Aud.:* Ac, Sa.

Generally published on the date of the full moon (hence, the approximately monthly frequency), *Minor Planets Circulars* are available in both print and electronically as the *Minor Planets Electronic Circulars.* Astrometric observations on comets and minor planets are included, although some information is summarized in observatory code. For those who may not be aware of this, "minor planets" is another accepted term for "asteroids." These circulars are published by the agency in charge of keeping an eye out for asteroids that may one day strike the Earth. The circulars were once sent out as telegrams, and retain the pithiness of the telegram. No space is wasted, and there is seldom anything resembling actual articles. New numberings and namings of asteroids/minor planets are also announced in the *Circulars.*

971. ***International Comet Quarterly.*** [ISSN: 0736-6922] 1979. q. plus a. handbook. USD 31; USD 46 foreign. Ed(s): Daniel W.E. Green. International Comet Quarterly, Smithsonian Astrophysical Observatory, M S 18, 60 Garden St, Cambridge, MA 02138; icq@cfa.harvard.edu; http://cfa-www.harvard.edu/cfa/ps/icq.html. Illus., index, adv. Refereed. Circ: 500. Vol. ends: No. 4. *Aud.:* Ac, Sa.

The *International Comet Quarterly (ICQ)* is the primary location for information about comets and observing comets, and it serves as a link between professional and serious amateur astronomers. Observations, discoveries, and research relating to comets can be found in this publication. Also published are announcements concerning international conferences that have to do with the extremely important work of detecting comets and asteroids that are likely to someday strike the Earth. The annual subscription cost includes a copy of the annual *Comet Handbook,* which contains ephemerides and orbital elements for comets observable in the coming year. This journal is not geared to general readership; only professionals and serious amateurs who focus on comets will need this publication for their research.

972. ***International Journal of Astrobiology.*** [ISSN: 1473-5504] 2002. q. USD 192 (Individuals, USD 82). Cambridge University Press, The Edinburgh Bldg, Shaftesbury Rd, Cambridge, CB2 2RU, United Kingdom; information@cambridge.org; http://uk.cambridge.org. *Aud.:* Ga, Ac, Sa.

A new publication, this fascinating journal provides an introduction to the burgeoning world of "astrobiology." This topic includes not only the search for extraterrestrial life, but also related inquiries into such issues as adaptations made by lifeforms to extreme environments on Earth. The journal includes peer-reviewed research papers, book reviews, and overviews of this fast-evolving discipline. Intended primarily as a forum for biochemists, astronomers, and other professionals in allied fields, the inherently fascinating nature of the topic could make some readers choose to put in the extra effort required to wade through an issue.

973. ***Journal for the History of Astronomy.*** Incorporates (1979-2002): *Archaeoastronomy.* [ISSN: 0021-8286] 1970. 4x/yr. USD 180 in the Americas & Japan; GBP 90 elsewhere; USD 56 per issue. Ed(s): M A Hoskin. Science History Publications Ltd., 16 Rutherford Rd, Cambridge, CB2 2HH, United Kingdom; http://www.shpltd.co.uk. Illus., index. Sample. Refereed. Circ: 650. Vol. ends: No. 4. *Indexed:* AbAn, AmH&L, BrArAb, CCMJ, IBZ, NumL. *Bk. rev.:* 6-16, 300-1,000 words. *Aud.:* Ac, Sa.

The only journal of its type, this covers the history of astronomy from its earliest times. The research presented is a pleasant, fascinating change of pace from the heavily math- and science-oriented publications so common (and so important) in astronomy. Few journals capture more successfully the spirit of astronomy, in the sense of the important role it has played throughout the historical struggle between reason and superstition. Subject matter is not rigidly restricted to the history of astronomy per se. For example, sometimes intellectual forays are made into relevant topics in the study of the history of mathematics or physics. A supplemental publication, *Archaeoastronomy,* is included with a subscription. The supplement is dedicated to investigating astronomical practice and celestial lore in ancient societies from all over the world. Sample articles might include, for example, discussion of ancient Mayan, Inca, Greek, or Egyptian astronomical traditions and edifices, by experts who are learned in the field.

974. ***Mercury (San Francisco).*** [ISSN: 0047-6773] 1972. bi-m. USD 48 domestic; USD 57 foreign. Ed(s): Robert Naeye. Astronomical Society of the Pacific, 390 Ashton Ave, San Francisco, CA 94112; editor@astrosociety.org; http://www.astrosociety.org. Illus., index, adv. Sample. Circ: 7000. Vol. ends: No. 6. Online: EBSCO Publishing; Florida Center for Library Automation; Gale Group; OCLC Online Computer Library Center, Inc.; H.W. Wilson. Reprint: PQC. *Indexed:* CIJE, GSI. *Bk. rev.:* 2-6, 50-200 words. *Aud.:* Hs, Ga, Sa.

The purpose of *Mercury* is to provide the necessary perspective for understanding astronomy. This nonspecialist magazine features articles on topics ranging from astronomy research, education, archaeoastronomy, history, and public policy. It is the most widely read publication of the Astronomical Society of the Pacific (ASP), a nonprofit organization whose goal is to promote public interest and awareness of astronomy through education and outreach programs. As the membership magazine of the ASP, it has made a name for itself as *the* location for teachers to follow innovations in astronomy education. There are frequently articles dealing with the role of education in science, and the role of science in society. The magazine includes sky calendars and sky maps for use in the Northern Hemisphere. Book reviews are included, as are regular sections on current observing prospects, "armchair astrophysics," and news highlights from the world of astronomy.

975. ***The Messenger.*** [ISSN: 0722-6691] 1974. q. Free. Ed(s): M H Ulrich. European Southern Observatory, Karl Schwarzschild Str 2, Garching, 85748, Germany; ips@eso.org; http://www.eso.org. Illus., index. Sample. Vol. ends: Dec. *Aud.:* Ac, Sa.

Published by the European Southern Observatory (ESO) in La Silla, Chile, this magazine presents the activities of the ESO to the public. It is roughly comparable to the *Griffith Observer,* in that it acts as a window into the activities of a major observatory, but it adds an international flavor. As the audience codes indicate, many of the articles are quite high-level, full of equations, graphs, etc. However, the photographs of the ESO staff happily toiling away at their astro-projects make the reader feel like a guest in the home of an interesting extended family. The ESO observatory is supported by eight countries—Belgium, Denmark, France, Germany, Italy, Sweden, Switzerland, and the Netherlands—and it receives 800 proposals a year for research that would require use of the facility.

976. ***Meteorite!*** [ISSN: 1173-2245] 1995. q. USD 27. Ed(s): Joel Schiff. Pallasite Press, Takapuna, PO Box 33-1218, Auckland, New Zealand; j.schiff@auckland.ac.nz; http://www.meteor.co.nz. *Aud.:* Ga, Ac, Sa.

Some past articles from this publication are available at the publisher's web site, but the only way to get the full articles and the photos is to subscribe. It is a forum for publishing information and research on collecting, new falls and finds, asteroids, craters, and historical meteorite events. Of the several journals described in this section that focus on meteors, this is perhaps the best suited for the amateur enthusiast.

977. ***Meteoritics and Planetary Science.*** Formerly (until 1996): *Meteoritics.* [ISSN: 1086-9379] 1953. bi-m. USD 830 in North America; USD 880 elsewhere. Ed(s): Derek W Sears. Meteoritical Society, c/o Hazel Sears, Managing Editor, Department of Chemistry and Biochemistry, Fayetteville, AR 72701; http://www.uark.edu/meteor. Illus., index, adv. Sample. Refereed. Circ: 1200 Paid. Vol. ends: No. 6. Microform: PQC. Online: Ingenta Select. *Indexed:* ChemAb, DSR&OA, GeoRef, IAA, MinerAb, SCI. *Aud.:* Ac, Sa.

This scholarly journal is published by the Meteoritical Society, an international organization that studies the smallest bodies in the solar system. It is free to society members. It provides a forum for discussing the study of extraterrestrial matter and history, including asteroids, impact craters, and interplanetary dust—uniting professionals from a variety of backgrounds including geology, physics, astronomy, and chemistry. Of the several journals dealing with meteors and asteroids, this is the one that deals most directly with what we can *learn* from meteors, especially about the origins of our solar system. This journal is different from, for example, the *Minor Planet Circulars,* in that it includes articles as well as raw data.

Minor Planets Circulars. See *International Astronomical Union. Minor Planets Center. Minor Planets Circulars—Minor Planets and Comets.*

978. ***New Astronomy Reviews: an international review journal.*** Formerly: *Vistas in Astronomy;* Incorporates (1977-1991): *Astronomy Quarterly.* [ISSN: 1387-6473] 1958. m. EUR 768. Ed(s): J. Audouze. Elsevier BV, North-Holland, Sara Burgerhartstraat 25, Amsterdam, 1055 KV, Netherlands; nlinfo-f@elsevier.nl; http://www.elsevier.nl. Illus., index, adv. Sample. Refereed. Vol. ends: No. 45. Microform: PQC. Online: ingenta.com; ScienceDirect; Swets Blackwell. *Indexed:* BAS, ChemAb, GeoRef, IAA. *Aud.:* Ac, Sa.

Although the name of this journal has changed, there has been no significant content change. The journal still includes historical perspectives and in-depth reports, review articles, and surveys of findings on major activities in astronomical research. Contributions include reprints in specific areas and in-depth review articles surveying major areas of astronomy. The journal covers solar, planetary, stellar, galactic, and extragalactic astronomy and astrophysics. It reports on original research in all wavelength bands, ranging from radio to gamma-ray. This journal might be seen as taking the broad-based coverage of *Mercury* to a higher level, for reading by professional scientists. Written for astronomers, astrophysicists, and space scientists.

979. ***The Observatory: a review of astronomy.*** [ISSN: 0029-7704] 1877. bi-m. GBP 48 GBP 10 newsstand/cover per issue. Observatory, c/o Dr. D.J. Stickland, Ed, Space and Astrophysics Div., Rutherford Appleton Laboratory, Didcot, OX11 0QX, United Kingdom. Illus., index, adv. Refereed. Circ: 1000 Paid. Vol. ends: No. 6. *Indexed:* ChemAb, SCI. *Aud.:* Ga.

This journal is sent free to members of the Royal Astronomical Society (RAS), and it is owned and managed by the editors. Meetings of the RAS are reported, but information does not generally overlap with what appears in the official RAS publications *Monthly Notices* and *Astronomy and Geophysics.* Those are considered the most important publications of this society—*The Observatory* is more of a supplement. Papers and correspondence tend to be short but scholarly, with few illustrations.

Odyssey. See Children section.

980. ***Planetarian.*** [ISSN: 0090-3213] 1972. q. USD 50. Ed(s): John E Mosley. International Planetarium Society, Griffith Observatory, 2800 E Observatory Rd, Los Angeles, CA 90027; jmosley@griffithObs.org; http://www.griffithobs.org/IPSPlanetarian.html. Illus., index, adv. Circ: 750. Vol. ends: No. 4. Microform: PQC. Reprint: PQC. *Aud.:* Hs, Ac, Sa.

Planetarian is free with membership in the International Planetarium Society, but there is also the option for libraries to purchase the journal separately. The majority of the publication is devoted to astronomy education, with special emphasis on the role planetariums can play. For example, articles discuss the value of planetariums as teaching aids to help students develop a three-dimensional vision of the structure of our galaxy, or planetariums acting aids in helping students visualize actual or potential space voyages. This is a fairly specialized journal, but certainly a very interesting and very readable one. It includes much information of interest to astronomers, academic libraries, school libraries, and science teachers.

981. ***Planetary and Space Science.*** [ISSN: 0032-0633] 1959. 15x/yr. EUR 2718 (Qualified personnel, EUR 306). Ed(s): T. Encrenaz. Pergamon, The Boulevard, Langford Ln, East Park, Kidlington, OX5 1GB, United Kingdom. Illus., index, adv. Sample. Refereed. Circ: 1250. Vol. ends: No. 12. Microform: PQC. Online: EBSCO Publishing; ingenta.com; ScienceDirect; Swets Blackwell. *Indexed:* ApMecR, ChemAb, EngInd, ExcerpMed, GeoRef, IAA, M&GPA, SCI, SSCI. *Aud.:* Ac, Sa.

Significant reorganization during 1998 changed some aspects of this official journal of the European Geophysical Society, Planetary and Solar Systems Sciences Section. While still focusing primarily upon coverage of planetary and solar system research, the scope has broadened to include extra-solar systems and astrobiology, comprehensive review articles, and meetings papers. Articles still tend to be focused upon planetary systems—but with recent advances in astronomy, some of the planets studied lie outside of our solar system. Ground-based and space-borne instrumentation and laboratory simulation of solar system processes are included. This journal has a fairly similar mission and audience to *Icarus,* and libraries may want to compare these two excellent journals to consider which best meets their needs. The intended audience includes professional astronomers, astrophysicists, atmospheric physicists, geologists, and planetologists.

982. ***Popular Astronomy.*** Formerly: *Hermes.* [ISSN: 0261-0892] 1953. q. GBP 12; GBP 16 in Europe; GBP 20 elsewhere. Society for Popular Astronomy, c/o Tom Hosking, Ed, 6 Queensberry Pl, Richmond, TW9 1NW, United Kingdom. Illus., adv. Circ: Controlled. *Aud.:* Hs, Ga, Ac.

This highly readable publication covers all aspects of astronomy. Each issue is packed with articles and photographs, many in color. Regular features include a review of developments in astronomy and space science; methods, advice, and ideas for the practical amateur astronomer; and a sky diary of what's upcoming in the next week. There is an unusual section called "Amateur Scene," which provides interviews and surveys dealing with the very active amateur astronomy scene—astronomy clubs, "open sky nights" at college observatories, and the like. The clear, readable style will appeal to beginners and more experienced amateurs alike. This journal is roughly comparable in scope and approach to *Astronomy* and *Sky and Telescope.*

983. ***Publications of the Astronomical Society of the Pacific.*** [ISSN: 0004-6280] 1889. m. USD 350 print & online eds. USD 34.20 per issue. University of Chicago Press, Journals Division, PO Box 37005, Chicago, IL 60637; subscriptions@press.uchicago.edu; http://www.journals.uchicago.edu. Illus., index. Refereed. Circ: 3000. Microform: AIP. Online: EBSCO Publishing. Reprint: PQC. *Indexed:* ChemAb, EngInd, SCI. *Aud.:* Ac, Sa.

The Astronomical Society of the Pacific (ASP) publishes several titles, among them *Mercury* (below in this section), *Publications of the ASP,* and *Selectory,* a catalog of equipment for astronomy. The ASP's mission is "to advance the science of astronomy and disseminate astronomical information," and it uses some of its publications to this end. Be aware that *Publications* is an actual title—it does not simply refer to a group of publications, but rather constitutes an actual periodical in and of itself. *Publications* is the ASP's technical journal, which includes refereed reports on current research, Ph.D. thesis abstracts, and review articles on astronomy and astrophysics. It prides itself on giving equal coverage to "all wavelengths and distance scales" of astronometric data.

984. ***Royal Astronomical Society. Monthly Notices.*** [ISSN: 0035-8711] 1827. 36x/yr. GBP 2660 print & online eds. Ed(s): A C Fabian. Blackwell Publishing Ltd., 9600 Garsington Rd, Oxford, OX4 2ZG, United Kingdom; customerservices@oxon.blackwellpublishing.com; http://www.blackwellpublishing.com. Illus., adv. Refereed. Circ: 1130. Microform: PQC. Online: EBSCO Publishing; ingenta.com; Munksgaard & Blackwell Science's Synergy; OCLC Online Computer Library Center, Inc.; RoweCom Information Quest; Swets Blackwell. Reprint: ISI. *Indexed:* ChemAb, GeoRef, IAA, SCI. *Aud.:* Ac, Sa.

This journal is considered to be a "core" publication for any high-level astronomy library. Since 1827, it has published timely articles on all areas of astronomy, including positional and dynamical astronomy, astrophysics, radio astronomy, cosmology, space research, instrument design, and more. Replete with equations, this periodical is indispensable for the serious astronomer, but rather slow going for anyone but the most committed amateur. Note that *The Observatory: A Review of Astronomy* (above in this section) is an optional companion to this journal.

985. ***Royal Astronomical Society of Canada. Observer's Handbook.*** [ISSN: 0080-4193] 1908. a. CND 23.56; USD 22.95. Ed(s): Dr. Rajiv Gupta. Royal Astronomical Society of Canada, 136 Dupont St, Toronto, ON M5R 1V2, Canada; nationaloffice@rasc.ca; http://www.rasc.ca. Illus., index. Circ: 12000. Microform: PQC. *Indexed:* GeoRef. *Aud.:* Ems, Hs, Ga, Ac, Sa.

The *Observer's Handbook* is a guide published annually since 1907 by The Royal Astronomical Society of Canada. Through its long tradition and the highly respected expertise of its contributors, it has come to be regarded as the standard North American reference for data concerning the sky. The material in it is of interest to professional and amateur astronomers, scientists, teachers at all levels, students, science writers, campers, scout and guide leaders, and others. The guide is an integral part of many astronomy courses at the secondary and university levels, and it is on the reference shelf of many libraries of various kinds. This useful annual volume is comparable in aims and scope to the *Annual Review of Astronomy and Astrophysics.*

Royal Astronomical Society. Quarterly Journal. See *Astronomy & Geophysics.*

Science. See Science and Technology section.

986. ***The Science Teacher.*** [ISSN: 0036-8555] 1934. 9x/yr. USD 77. Ed(s): Janet Gerking. National Science Teachers Association, 1840 Wilson Blvd, Arlington, VA 22201; thescienceteacher@nsta.org; http://www.nsta.org/pubs/tst. Illus., index, adv. Circ: 26000. Vol. ends: May. Microform: PQC. Online: Gale Group; ProQuest Information & Learning. Reprint: PQC. *Indexed:* BiolDig, CIJE, EduInd, GeoRef, MRD. *Aud.:* Ems, Hs.

Science Teacher is not exclusively an astronomy periodical, but it frequently devotes a lot of coverage to astronomy. This is one of the publications of the National Science Teachers Association (NSTA), and is aimed at secondary school teachers. *Science and Children* is a parallel journal published by the same association, directed at teachers of a younger age bracket. Both of these are highly respected journals that take a hands-on approach to education. They are each constantly brimming over with specific ideas for age-appropriate activities, as opposed to the jargon of educational theory. If your library includes teachers among its patrons, you should be aware of these journals for their utility in the communication of the wonder of astronomy to young minds. NSTA journals are a member benefit and are not available by subscription.

987. ***Sky & Telescope: the essential magazine of astronomy.*** Former titles: *Telescope: Drama of the Skies; Sky.* [ISSN: 0037-6604] 1941. m. USD 39.95 United States; USD 47.95 Canada; USD 59.95 elsewhere. Ed(s): Richard T Fienberg, Bud Sadler. Sky Publishing Corp., 49 Bay State Rd, Cambridge, MA 02138; postmaster@skypub.com; skytel@skypub.com. Illus., index, adv. Circ: 132727 Paid. Vol. ends: Jun/Dec. Microform: PQC. Online: bigchalk; Gale Group; Northern Light Technology, Inc.; OCLC Online Computer Library Center, Inc.; ProQuest Information & Learning. *Indexed:* BRI, BiogInd, CBRI, GSI, GeoRef, IAA, IHTDI, LRI, MagInd, RGPR. *Bk. rev.:* 4-5, 350-1,000 words. *Aud.:* Hs, Ga, Ac.

Since it began publication in 1941, *Sky and Telescope* has been a leader in providing accurate and up-to-date information on astronomy and space science. The magazine chose its subtitle of "the essential magazine of astronomy" itself, but it is able to get away with it. It is written so that it appeals to all astronomy enthusiasts, from the youngest novice to the most seasoned professional; its articles are painstakingly edited to be easily understood by both technically savvy readers and those who benefit from clear descriptive language and graphics. Regular features include book reviews, a sky calendar, news notes, and tips on imaging the sky. Annually, the journal prints a directory of organizations, institutions, and businesses related to astronomy.

988. ***SkyNews: the Canadian magazine of astronomy and stargazing.*** [ISSN: 0840-8939] bi-m. CND 24 domestic; CND 30 United States; CND 40 elsewhere. Ed(s): Terence Dickinson. Canada Science and Technology Museum, PO Box 9724, Ottawa, ON K1G 5A3, Canada; cmgroup@interlog.com. Illus. Vol. ends: No. 6. *Indexed:* CBCARef, CPerI. *Aud.:* Hs, Ga, Ac.

A useful, very popular publication for novice stargazers. Each colorful issue contains news, columns, features, an excellent sky chart, and equipment reviews. Articles are directed primarily, but not exclusively, at a Canadian audience. What this may mean to an American library is simply that some of the tables presented will have been calibrated with more northerly latitudes in mind. This may have a certain impact on the utility of *some* of the information provided, but the articles and equipment reviews, of course, will still be quite useful, enjoyable, and engrossing.

989. ***SkyWatch: tour guide for stargazing and space exploration.*** 1996. a. USD 4.99 newsstand/cover per issue domestic; USD 5.99 newsstand/ cover per issue foreign. Sky Publishing Corp., 49 Bay State Rd, Cambridge, MA 02138; orders@skypub.com; http://www.skypub.com. Adv. Circ: 85000 Paid and controlled. *Aud.:* Ems, Hs, Ga.

Published by the people who bring us *Sky and Telescope,* this annual listing of sky events is meant for beginners or serious amateurs. A portable, uncomplicated guide to the night sky, *SkyWatch* is a useful observing tool. Included are star charts from September of one year through December of the following year; a map of the lunar surface; a gallery of state-of-the-art astrophotography; and articles on choosing telescopes, binoculars, and other astronomy gear. Also helpful is the featured how-to article on finding 16 of the most popular objects for viewing in the night sky. This publication can be compared to the *Observer's Handbook* (see *Royal Astronomical Society of Canada. Observer's Handbook* above in this section).

990. ***Solar Physics: a journal for solar and solar-stellar research and the study of solar terrestrial physics.*** [ISSN: 0038-0938] 1967. 14x/yr. EUR 3315 print or online ed. Kluwer Academic Publishers, van Godewijckstraat 30, PO Box 17, Dordrecht, 3300 AA, Netherlands; services@wkap.nl; http://www.wkap.nl. Illus., index, adv. Sample. Refereed. Vol. ends: No. 14. Microform: PQC. Online: EBSCO Publishing; ingenta.com; Kluwer Online; OCLC Online Computer Library Center, Inc.; Ovid Technologies, Inc.; RoweCom Information Quest; Swets Blackwell. Reprint: SWZ. *Indexed:* ChemAb, EngInd, GeoRef, IAA, IBZ, M&GPA, SCI. *Aud.:* Ac, Sa.

Solar Physics was founded in 1967 and is the principal journal for the publication of the results of fundamental research on the Sun. The journal treats all aspects of solar physics, ranging from the internal structure of the Sun and its evolution, to the outer corona and solar wind in interplanetary space. Papers on solar-terrestrial physics and on stellar research are also published when their results have a direct bearing on our understanding of the Sun.

991. ***Solar System Research.*** [ISSN: 0038-0946] 1967. bi-m. EUR 2477 print or online ed. Ed(s): M Ya Marov. M A I K Nauka - Interperiodica, Profsoyuznaya ul 90, Moscow, 117997, Russian Federation; compmg@maik.ru; http://www.maik.rssi.ru. Illus. Sample. Refereed. Vol. ends: No. 6. Microform: PQC. Online: ingenta.com; Kluwer Online; OCLC Online Computer Library Center, Inc.; Ovid Technologies, Inc.; RoweCom Information Quest; Swets Blackwell. *Indexed:* EngInd, GeoRef. *Aud.:* Ac, Sa.

This journal is translated into English by MAIK Nauka/Interperiodica Publishing and is published simultaneously with the Russian edition. Review papers appear regularly, along with notes on observational results and communications on scientific meetings and colloquiums. *Solar System Research* is the only journal from Russia dealing with the topics of planetary exploration, including the results of original study obtained through ground-based and/or space-borne observations and theoretical/computer modeling. In recent years the journal has significantly expanded the scope of its interest through the involvement of new research fields, such as planetary geology and cosmophysics, planetary plasma physics and heliosphere, atmospheric sciences, and general problems in comparative planetology.

Soviet Astronomy. See *Astronomy Reports.*

992. ***Spaceflight: the magazine of astronautics and outer space.*** Incorporates: *Space Education.* [ISSN: 0038-6340] 1956. m. GBP 48; USD 90; GBP 2.50 newsstand/cover per issue. Ed(s): Clive Simpson. British Interplanetary Society, 27-29 S Lambeth Rd, London, SW8 1SZ, United Kingdom; mail@bis-spaceflight.com; http://bis-spaceflight.com. Illus., index, adv. Circ: 8000. Vol. ends: No. 12. Microform: PQC. Online: OCLC Online Computer Library Center, Inc.; H.W. Wilson. Reprint: PQC. *Indexed:* AS&TI, ApMecR, BrArAb, BrTechI, C&ISA, ChemAb, EngInd, IAA. *Aud.:* Hs, Ga, Ac, Sa.

Published since 1956, this is considered to be a core journal by most astronomy libraries. Considered an authoritative periodical, *Spaceflight* focuses primarily upon national, international, and commercial efforts to explore space. Articles cover such topics as ongoing space shuttle missions, details of space station life, and educational efforts aimed at popularizing these initiatives. In general, articles are aimed at a presumably intelligent audience that may or may not be professionally involved in space exploration.

993. ***StarDate.*** Formerly: *McDonald Observatory News.* [ISSN: 0889-3098] 1972. bi-m. USD 21 domestic; USD 25 in Canada & Mexico; USD 36 elsewhere. Ed(s): Damond Beeningfield, Gary Harrison. University of Texas, Austin, McDonald Observatory, PO Box 1337, Fort Davis, TX 79734-1337; http://stardate.org. Illus. Sample. Circ: 11000 Paid. *Aud.:* Ems, Hs, Ga.

StarDate is known to many as a radio show, but you can find the same information and more in the online edition, *StarDate Online*, at http:// stardate.utexas.edu, or by purchasing a paper copy. The magazine is perfect for amateur astronomers and anyone interested in celestial events and space exploration. It is updated daily, and includes such helpful features as an astronomical "Tip of the Day," which concerns interesting things to observe in the sky; a section called "Today on Stardate," which presents articles on all kinds of topics from astronomy and the history of astronomy, including archaeo-astronomy; and daily astronomical questions to ponder, Internet links about astronomy, and an astronomical search engine for online research.

Vistas in Astronomy. See *New Astronomy Reviews.*

Electronic Journals

994. ***Celestial Mechanics and Dynamical Astronomy: an international journal of space dynamics.*** Formerly: *Celestial Mechanics.* [ISSN: 0923-2958] 1969. m. EUR 1620 print or online ed. Ed(s): Jacques Henrard. Kluwer Academic Publishers, van Godewijckstraat 30, PO Box 17, Dordrecht, 3300 AA, Netherlands. Illus., index, adv. Sample. Refereed. Vol. ends: No. 4. Microform: PQC. Online: EBSCO Publishing; ingenta.com; Kluwer Online; OCLC Online Computer Library Center, Inc.; Ovid Technologies, Inc.; RoweCom Information Quest; Swets Blackwell. Reprint: SWZ. *Indexed:* ApMecR, CCMJ, GeoRef, IAA, MathSciNet, SCI. *Aud.:* Ac, Sa.

This international publication is concerned with the broadest range of dynamical astronomy and its applications, as well as with peripheral fields. It is heavily math- and physics-oriented, which can make reading difficult for those not well versed in these fields. Articles cover all aspects of celestial mechanics: mathematical, physics-related, and computational, including computer languages for analytical developments. The majority of the articles are in English. This noteworthy publication is considered in the astronomical community to be the journal of record in its area, and belongs in any complete astronomical library.

995. ***Journal of Cosmology and Astroparticle Physics.*** [ISSN: 1475-7516] 2003. irreg. Free. Scuola Internazionale Superiore di Studi Avanzati, Via Beirut 4, Trieste, 34014, Italy; http://www.sissa.it. Refereed. *Aud.:* Ac, Sa.

A new journal, *JCAP* is an ambitious, selective online periodical focusing on the interrelationships beween the smallest subatomic particles and the nature of the universe "in the large." Common topics include string theory, gravitational waves, black holes, large-scale structure of the universe, and other cosmological issues. Criteria for article acceptance are "scientific quality, originality and relevance." It is probably too advanced for most amateur hobbyists, but this publication has been placed on many "core" reading lists for academic science libraries, even in these financially strapped times.

996. ***Lunar and Planetary Information Bulletin.*** [ISSN: 0891-4664] 1970. q. Free. Ed(s): D Brian Anderson. Lunar and Planetary Institute, 3600 Bay Area Blvd, Houston, TX 77058-1113; lpibed@lpi.usra.edu; http://www.lpi.usra.edu. Illus. Circ: 5500. *Indexed:* GeoRef, IAA. *Aud.:* Ac, Ga.

Here is a real treat for the layperson who has the background and command of vocabulary. The subject of the *Bulletin* is astronomical topics that are likely to be of interest to the average, involved reader, such as potential fossils on Mars, or the adaptation of hydroponic plant cultures to possible long-term space missions for life-support purposes. There is a "New in Print" section that takes the reader on a tour of recently published books in the field. Often, one of these titles is singled out for an in-depth review, which sometimes includes an interview with the author. Also, the "News from Space" section is excellent, containing six or seven short articles about exciting goings-on in astronomy. Intelligent, well-written discussions can be found dealing with such questions as the origin of the solar system or of the asteroid belt. An objective and scientific approach, written in an delightfully accessible style.

997. ***New Astronomy: an international journal in astronomy and astrophysics.*** [ISSN: 1384-1076] 1996. 8x/yr. EUR 570 (Individuals, EUR 149). Ed(s): W. D. Cochran. Elsevier BV, North-Holland, Sara Burgerhartstraat 25, Amsterdam, 1055 KV, Netherlands; nlinfo-f@elsevier.nl; http://www.elsevier.nl. Illus. Sample. Refereed. Vol. ends: No. 8. Online: EBSCO Publishing; ingenta.com; ScienceDirect; Swets Blackwell. *Indexed:* EngInd. *Aud.:* Ac, Sa.

An institutional subscription provides web access for everyone at a subscribing institute, an archival paper edition, and an electronic copy for LAN distribution. Slightly lower prices for smaller institutions and for individuals are available upon request, and a two-month free trial is available for individuals. This journal includes full-length research articles and letter articles. It aims to have a very short publication time, which keeps it very close to the cutting edge of astronomy. It prides itself on sending personal e-mails to astronomers about upcoming articles in their specialties. It covers solar, planetary, stellar, galactic, and extragalactic astronomy and astrophysics, and reports on original research in all wavelength bands, ranging from radio to gamma-ray. Topics include all fields of astronomy and astrophysics: theoretical, observational, and instrumental.

998. ***North American Skies.*** 1996. m. Ed(s): Larry Sessions. Final Copy, 6874 E Harvard Ave., Denver, CO 80224; starman@usa.net; http://webcom.com/safezone/NAS/. *Aud.:* Ems, Hs, Ga.

This is a layperson's guide to the stars and planets, suitable for both young people and adults. *North American Skies* provides information on stars, planets, eclipses, meteor showers, and other events visible in the sky. Times are given for the Mountain Time Zone, and some information, such as the Sun and Moon rise and set tables, is specific to Denver. However, most information is applicable throughout North America, given the appropriate time-zone change. Each issue provides a feature article (with past articles also available online) and a sky chart and instructions for its use. Another regular feature is a monthly sky calendar that lists only events that can be seen in North America with the unaided eye. Other helpful features include links about sighting satellites or shuttlecraft, telescope-related questions, and forms to facilitate reporting meteor sightings.

999. ***SpaceDaily.com.*** d. Free. SpaceDaily.com, free-subscribe@spacer.com. *Aud.:* Hs, Ga, Ac.

This web site, updated on a daily basis, is a highly useful resource to be aware of. Consisting of a broad range of articles on topics both astronomical and aeronautical in nature, it serves to keep the public informed about technological and administrative issues in the areas of astronomical and aerospace progress. Sections of the journal are devoted to such matters as the exploration of the asteroid Eros; advances in our understanding of comets; satellites that can be expected to increase our understanding of the cosmos; and general issues germane to our understanding of the universe.

1000. ***Universo Online.*** 1997. m. Ed(s): Gary Harrison. University of Texas, Austin, McDonald Observatory, PO Box 1337, Fort Davis, TX 79734-1337; http://universo.utexas.edu/. *Aud.:* Ems, Hs, Ga.

A valuable online Spanish-language resource for astronomy. There is much variety in the coverage, which is updated daily. Interesting features include an observer's tip of the day, or "Aviso del dia para mirar las estrellas"; a daily interesting fact in the "Hoy en Universo" section; and a daily question of cosmic import, such as "Will we ever visit the stars?" The site is searchable by keyword in Spanish.

ATMOSPHERIC SCIENCES

See also Marine Science and Technology section.

Michael Culbertson, Engineering and Atmospheric Science Librarian, The Libraries, Colorado State University, Fort Collins, CO 80523-1019; michael.culbertson@colostate.edu

Introduction

Atmospheric science includes meteorology, climatology, atmospheric chemistry, weather forecasting, and other disciplines concerned with weather and the study of the atmosphere. This is an exciting time for research into the atmosphere. Data available from earth-orbiting satellites and other technologies, combined with computer modeling techniques, have, within the last generation, begun to give atmospheric scientists a coherent picture of how the earth's atmosphere operates as a system. It is even possible now to make predictions concerning the cycles of weather phenomena such as hurricanes. Data obtained from interplanetary spacecraft is also beginning to make serious research into the atmospheres of the other planets in the solar system possible. This section provides a list of important journals and general-interest periodicals devoted to the study of weather and the atmosphere. The list provides information concerning important titles for libraries in North America that collect materials in meteorology, climatology, atmospheric chemistry, atmospheric physics, weather forecasting, and related areas. Foreign-language journals have not been included, however, some journals published outside of the United States and Canada that appear in English have been included because of their interest to researchers. Selected publications from the U.S. government and the World Meteorological Organization, which provide data about weather and atmospheric phenomena, are also included.

Basic Periodicals

Hs: *Weatherwise;* Ga: *Bulletin of the American Meteorological Society, Local Climatological Data, Weather, Weatherwise, WMO Bulletin*; Ac: *Bulletin of the American Meteorological Society, Journal of Applied Meteorology, Journal of Climate, JGR: Journal of Geophysical Research: Section D: Atmosphere, Journal of the Atmospheric Sciences, Monthly Weather Review, Royal Meteorological Society. Quarterly Journal, Weather, Weather and Forecasting, Weatherwise, WMO Bulletin.*

Basic Abstracts and Indexes

Meteorological and Geoastrophysical Abstracts. Chemical Abstracts, INSPEC, and *Science Citation Index* are also useful tools in this area.

1001. ***Acta Meteorologica Sinica.*** [ISSN: 0894-0525] 1987. 4x/yr. USD 300. Ed(s): Zhou Xiuji. China Meteorological Press, 46 Zhongguancun Nandajie, Haidian District, Beijing, 100081, China; ams@rays.cma.gov.cn. Illus., index, adv. Refereed. Circ: 300 Paid. Microform: PQC. *Indexed:* ChemAb, GeogAbPG, IAA, M&GPA. *Aud.:* Ac, Sa.

Intended as a forum for the exchange of ideas between Chinese atmospheric scientists and those from outside China. It accomplishes this by publishing papers translated from the Chinese edition of this journal, along with papers submitted in English from other countries. It focuses on the following areas: pure and applied meteorology, climatology, marine meteorology, atmospheric physics and chemistry, cloud physics, remote sensing, and air pollution meteorology. Publishing original research and review articles, this is an excellent source for keeping up with meteorological research in China. Recommended for research collections.

Agricultural and Forest Meteorology. See Forestry section.

1002. ***American Meteorological Society. Bulletin.*** [ISSN: 0003-0007] 1920. m. USD 100 (Members, USD 70). Ed(s): Ronald McPherson. American Meteorological Society, 45 Beacon St, Boston, MA 02108; amsinfo@ametsoc.org; http://www.ametsoc.org/ams. Illus., index, adv. Refereed. Circ: 11528. Vol. ends: Dec. Microform: PMC. Online: Gale Group.

Indexed: ABS&EES, AS&TI, ApMecR, BiolAb, ChemAb, DSR&OA, EngInd, EnvAb, ExcerpMed, GSI, GeoRef, GeogAbPG, IAA, M&GPA, OceAb, PollutAb, RRTA, S&F, SCI, SSCI, SWRA, WAE&RSA. *Bk. rev.:* Occasional, 200-500 words. *Aud.:* Ga, Ac.

This publication, the official organ of the American Meteorological Society, includes research articles, editorials, book reviews, notices from the society, and meeting reviews. Particularly helpful is the "Announcements/Call for Papers" section, which lists upcoming conferences in atmospheric science and related areas. There is also a calendar of professional meetings. Of note for librarians is the regular supplement listing current publications available from the society. This title is essential for professionals and students in the field and should be part of the collection in any library supporting teaching and research in atmospheric science, meteorology, climatology, and related fields. Because it reports current news in atmospheric science, the online version of this title is particularly helpful.

1003. ***Atmosfera.*** [ISSN: 0187-6236] 1988. q. MXP 70. Ed(s): Julian Adem. Universidad Nacional Autonoma de Mexico, Centro de Ciencias de la Atmosfera, Circuito Exterior, Ciudad Universitaria, Mexico, D.F., 04510 , Mexico. Illus., index. Refereed. Vol. ends: Dec. *Indexed:* GeogAbPG, M&GPA. *Aud.:* Ac.

Publishes "a theoretical, empirical and applied research on all aspects of the atmospheric sciences." Articles appear in either Spanish or English, with abstracts in both languages. This journal is particularly strong in reporting meteorological and climatological research on Latin America and surrounding ocean areas. Articles are of high quality and are suitable for serious researchers. Recommended for research collections.

1004. ***Atmosphere - Ocean.*** Supersedes (with vol.16, 1978): *Atmosphere.* [ISSN: 0705-5900] 1963. q. CND 125 (Individuals, CND 45). Ed(s): Steven Lambert, Patrick Cummins. Canadian Meteorological and Oceanographic Society, Station D, PO Box 3211, Ottawa, ON K1P 6H7, Canada; Pubs@meds-sdmm.dfo-mpo.gc.ca; http://www.cmos.ca. Illus., index. Refereed. Circ: 600 Paid. Online: EBSCO Publishing. *Indexed:* ApMecR, DSR&OA, EngInd, GeogAbPG, M&GPA, OceAb, PollutAb, SCI, SWRA. *Bk. rev.:* Occasional, 750-1,000 words. *Aud.:* Ac, Sa.

Publishes original research and survey articles, along with editorial notes and comments. Covering atmospheric sciences, oceanography, hydrology, and related fields, the journal is particularly good in reporting research studies of Canada and surrounding ocean areas, including the Canadian Arctic. Because this is the major research publication of the Canadian Meteorological and Oceanographic Society, many of the authors are Canadian, although contributions from outside Canada are encouraged. The articles are technical, adhere to high standards of scholarship, and are oriented toward professionals and graduate students. The journal publishes occasional special issues on topics of interest in meteorology and related fields. All articles are in English, while abstracts are in English and French.

1005. ***Atmospheric Environment.*** Formed by the 1993 merger of: *Atmospheric Environment. Part A, General Topics; Atmospheric Environment. Part B, Urban Atmosphere;* Each of which superseded in part (in 1990): *Atmospheric Environment.* [ISSN: 1352-2310] 1967. 40x/yr. EUR 4798 (Qualified personnel, EUR 385). Ed(s): P Brimblecombe, H. B. Singh. Pergamon, The Boulevard, Langford Ln, East Park, Kidlington, OX5 1GB, United Kingdom. Illus., adv. Refereed. Circ: 2600. Microform: MIM; PQC. Online: ingenta.com; ScienceDirect; Swets Blackwell. *Indexed:* AS&TI, ApMecR, B&AI, BiolAb, C&ISA, CEA, ChemAb, DSA, DSR&OA, EngInd, EnvAb, ExcerpMed, FPA, ForAb, GeogAbPG, H&SSA, HortAb, IndMed, M&GPA, OceAb, PollutAb, RRTA, S&F, SCI, SSCI, SWRA, WAE&RSA, WRCInf. *Aud.:* Ac.

Atmospheric Environment focuses on natural and human induced effects on the earth's atmosphere. Atmospheric pollution and air quality are major themes of the papers in this journal but its scope is by no means limited to these areas. The articles are intended for scientists and advanced students in atmospheric science, engineering, chemistry, and environmental studies.

1006. ***Atmospheric Research: clouds - precipitation - aerosols - radiation - weather modification.*** Formerly (until 1986): *Journal de Recherches Atmospheriques.* [ISSN: 0169-8095] 1963. 16x/yr. EUR 1517. Ed(s): Dr. Clive P.R. Saunders, Dr. J T Snow. Elsevier BV, Sara Burgerhartstraat 25, Amsterdam, 1055 KV, Netherlands; nlinfo-f@elsevier.nl; http://www.elsevier.nl. Illus., index. Refereed. Circ: 350. Online: ingenta.com; ScienceDirect; Swets Blackwell. *Indexed:* ChemAb, EngInd, EnvAb, GeoRef, GeogAbPG, M&GPA, OceAb, SCI, SWRA. *Aud.:* Ac.

This journal focuses on meteorological processes occurring in the troposphere. Special attention is given to the physics of clouds and precipitation. Specifically, this includes atmospheric aerosols, microphysical processes, cloud dynamics and thermodynamics, numerical simulation of cloud processes, clouds and radiation, meso- and macrostructure of clouds and cloud systems, and weather modification. Abstracts are in English and French; articles (with rare exceptions) are in English. Recommended for research collections in meteorology and related areas.

1007. ***Australian Meteorological Magazine.*** [ISSN: 0004-9743] 1952. q. AUD 43 domestic; AUD 50 in Asia; AUD 55 elsewhere. Ed(s): Clara Walton. Bureau of Meteorology, 150 Lonsdale St, Melbourne, VIC 3000, Australia; http://www.bom.gov.au. Illus. Refereed. *Indexed:* ChemAb, DSR&OA, GeogAbPG, M&GPA, OceAb, SCI, SWRA. *Bk. rev.:* 300-400 words, signed. *Aud.:* Ac.

This title covers the meteorology of Australia and the Southern Hemisphere. The articles are intended for scientists and advanced students in atmospheric science, meteorology, and related fields. Most of the contributors are Australian. This journal fills a valuable role by publishing research articles dealing with the meteorology of not only Australia but also the South Pacific and Indian Oceans.

1008. ***Boundary-Layer Meteorology: an international journal of physical and biological processes in the atmospheric boundary layer.*** [ISSN: 0006-8314] 1970. m. EUR 2222 print or online ed. Ed(s): John R Garratt, P A Taylor. Kluwer Academic Publishers, van Godewijckstraat 30, PO Box 17, Dordrecht, 3300 AA, Netherlands. Illus., index, adv. Refereed. Vol. ends: Dec. Microform: PQC. Online: EBSCO Publishing; ingenta.com; Kluwer Online; OCLC Online Computer Library Center, Inc.; Ovid Technologies, Inc.; RoweCom Information Quest; Swets Blackwell. Reprint: SWZ. *Indexed:* ApMecR, BiolAb, DSR&OA, EngInd, ExcerpMed, ForAb, GeoRef, GeogAbPG, HortAb, IAA, M&GPA, OceAb, S&F, SCI, SWRA. *Bk. rev.:* Occasional, 350-500 words. *Aud.:* Ac.

Boundary-Layer Meteorology focuses on physical and biological processes in the lowest kilometers of the atmosphere. It concentrates on interactions that take place between the earth's surface and the atmosphere in what is called the "boundary layer." Articles are highly technical and are intended for professionals in atmospheric science. Specific subject areas covered are forest meteorology, air pollution, hydrology, micrometeorological instruments, planetary boundary layer, surface boundary layer, mesometeorology, numerical modeling of boundary layers, remote sensing, and urban meteorology. Recommended for all atmospheric science collections, particularly those supporting research.

1009. ***Climatic Change: an interdisciplinary, international journal devoted to the description, causes and implications of climatic change.*** [ISSN: 0165-0009] 1977. 16x/yr. USD 1977 for print or online ed. Ed(s): Stephen H Schneider. Kluwer Academic Publishers, van Godewijckstraat 30, PO Box 17, Dordrecht, 3300 AA, Netherlands. Illus., index, adv. Refereed. Microform: PQC. Online: EBSCO Publishing; Gale Group; ingenta.com; Kluwer Online; OCLC Online Computer Library Center, Inc.; Ovid Technologies, Inc.; RoweCom Information Quest; Swets Blackwell. Reprint: SWZ. *Indexed:* ArtHuCI, BiolAb, ChemAb, DSR&OA, EngInd, EnvAb, ExcerpMed, FPA, ForAb, GeoRef, GeogAbPG, HortAb, IBZ, M&GPA, OceAb, PollutAb, RRTA, S&F, SCI, SSCI, SWRA, WAE&RSA. *Aud.:* Ac.

As the title indicates, this journal publishes papers on climatic variability from authors in a number of different disciplines: meteorology, anthropology, agriculture, astronomy, biology, chemistry, engineering, geology, ecology, and history. The editor, in fact, intends the journal to be a vehicle for cross-disciplinary communication on climatic change. The papers tend to be descriptive in nature;

some are review papers. Most of the papers are standard scientific articles, but some are essays. Editorials can also be found in most issues. Some numbers are special issues devoted to discussion of a specific topic. This journal should be of interest to academic libraries, particularly those that support programs in the earth sciences.

1010. ***Climatological Data.*** [ISSN: 0009-8949] 1897. m. plus a. update. USD 45 per region. U.S. National Climatic Data Center, Federal Bldg., 151 Patton Ave, Asheville, NC 28801-5001; orders@ncdc.noaa.gov; http://www.ncdc.noaa.gov/pdfs/samplepubs/cdsep42.pdf. Illus. Circ: 23000. *Aud.:* Hs, Ga, Ac, Sa.

Provides monthly temperature and precipitation data for each state. The New England states are combined in a regional edition, as are Maryland and Delaware. Average maximum and minimum temperatures are given for each station, along with temperature extremes; total precipitation and deviation from normal are also provided. Maps showing current weather patterns and charts based on historic data are included. This is an invaluable reference tool, and all libraries should at least have the part that covers their state.

Contributions to Atmospheric Physics. See *Meteorologische Zeitschrift.*

1011. ***Daily Weather Maps (Weekly Series): weekly series.*** [ISSN: 0898-6592] 1967. w. USD 60. Ed(s): Paul Kocin. U.S. Department of Commerce, U.S. Climatic Prediction Center, W NP 53, Rm 811, 4700 Silver Hill Rd Stop 9910, Washington, DC 20233-9910; http://www.ncdc.noaa.gov/. Illus. Circ: 3400. *Aud.:* Ga, Ac.

Maps for each day of a given week are included, one page per day. Most prominent is a surface weather map that codes data for specific stations throughout the continental United States. Contours of barometric pressure are also included in four-millibar increments. Other maps give temperature extremes, precipitation areas and amounts, and wind speed and direction. Explanations of the maps and a specimen station model showing the codes used on the surface weather map are given on the first page of each issue.

1012. ***Dynamics of Atmospheres and Oceans: planetary fluids, climatic and biogeochemical systems.*** [ISSN: 0377-0265] 1977. 8x/yr. EUR 1036. Ed(s): Dr. Allan R Robinson, Dr. D. B. Haidvogel. Elsevier BV, Sara Burgerhartstraat 25, Amsterdam, 1055 KV, Netherlands; nlinfo-f@elsevier.nl; http://www.elsevier.nl. Illus., index, adv. Sample. Refereed. Vol. ends: Jan. Microform: PQC. Online: ingenta.com; ScienceDirect; Swets Blackwell. Reprint: SWZ. *Indexed:* ApMecR, DSR&OA, EnvAb, GeogAbPG, M&GPA, OceAb, SCI, SWRA. *Aud.:* Ac, Sa.

The scope of this journal is research of atmospheres and oceans as fluid dynamic systems. A particular area of concentration is the interaction of atmospheres and oceans. The articles are technical and assume a high degree of mathematical literacy. Authors are usually oceanographers, atmospheric scientists, or, occasionally, engineers. Some numbers are special issues that include papers presented at particular conference sessions. Recommended for research collections in both atmospheric science and oceanography.

1013. ***Hourly Precipitation Data.*** m. USD 65; USD 7 per month per state. U.S. National Climatic Data Center, Federal Bldg., 151 Patton Ave, Asheville, NC 28801-5001; http://lwf.ncdc.noaa.gov/oa/ncdc.html. *Aud.:* Sa.

Gives precipitation data, arranged by state, for the United States. The data are obtained from rain gauges at "National Weather Service, Federal Aviation Administration or cooperative observer stations." Included are hourly precipitation, daily precipitation totals, and monthly maximums. Annual precipitation summaries for each state and territory are also provided. An online version is at http://www5.ncdc.noaa.gov/pubs/publications.html.

1014. ***International Journal of Biometeorology: the description, causes, and implications of climatic change.*** [ISSN: 0020-7128] 1957. q. EUR 498 domestic; EUR 507.90 foreign; EUR 150 newsstand/cover per issue. Ed(s): M Iriki. Springer-Verlag, Tiergartenstr 17, Heidelberg, 69121, Germany. Illus., index, adv. Refereed. Circ: 1300. Vol. ends: Mar. Online: EBSCO Publishing; RoweCom Information Quest; ScienceDirect; Springer LINK; Swets Blackwell. *Indexed:* Agr, BiolAb, ChemAb, DSA, ExcerpMed, ForAb, GeoRef, HortAb, IndMed, IndVet, M&GPA, PollutAb, S&F, SCI, SSCI, SWRA, VetBull, ZooRec. *Aud.:* Ac.

Focuses on the interactions of climate and weather with living organisms. In particular, this journal addresses the relationships of weather and air pollution with health and disease, indoor air pollution, and health effects of electric, magnetic, and electromagnetic fields. Reports of field, laboratory, and theoretical studies are included. Review articles occasionally appear, and editorials and book reviews are included in most issues. Abstracts of papers presented at conferences dealing with biometeorology appear from time to time. Recommended for libraries supporting programs in atmospheric science, health science, and medicine.

1015. ***International Journal of Climatology.*** Formerly: *Journal of Climatology.* [ISSN: 0899-8418] 1981. 15x/yr. USD 2265. John Wiley & Sons Ltd., The Atrium, Southern Gate, Chichester, PO19 8SQ, United Kingdom; customer@wiley.co.uk; http://www.wiley.co.uk. Illus., index, adv. Refereed. Circ: 578. Vol. ends: Dec. Microform: PQC. Online: EBSCO Publishing; ScienceDirect; Wiley InterScience. Reprint: PQC; SWZ. *Indexed:* DSR&OA, EngInd, ForAb, GeoRef, GeogAbPG, HortAb, M&GPA, OceAb, PollutAb, RRTA, S&F, SCI, SSCI, SWRA, WAE&RSA. *Bk. rev.:* 300-500 words. *Aud.:* Ac, Sa.

Publishes research and review papers on climate at the global, regional, local, and microclimatological levels. The journal is also concerned with long-range forecasting and climatic change. Articles often reflect the interdisciplinary nature of interest in climate and touch on such fields as geology, agriculture, geology, forestry, and geography. Recent climatic maps of the Northern and Southern Hemispheres (using polar projections) are also included in some issues. Recommended for libraries that support research and both undergraduate and graduate course work in the atmospheric sciences.

1016. ***J G R: Journal of Geophysical Research: Atmosphere.*** Supersedes in part (in 1991): *J G R: Journal of Geophysical Research;* Which was formerly (until 1948): *Terrestrial Magnetism and Atmospheric Electricity;* (until 1898): *Terrestrial Magnetism.* 1896. s-m. USD 3700. Ed(s): A F Spilhaus. American Geophysical Union, 2000 Florida Ave, N W, Washington, DC 20009-1277; http://www.agu.org. Illus. Microform: Pub.; AIP. *Indexed:* EngInd, EnvAb, GeoRef, GeogAbPG, SCI. *Aud.:* Ac, Sa.

The scope of this title is the physics and chemistry of the atmosphere of the earth and other planets. Papers tend to be highly technical and require a thorough grounding in atmospheric chemistry. Much of the work reported is interdisciplinary with other earth sciences, especially hydrology, oceanography, and planetary studies. This is a high-quality research journal, which professionals and graduate students will expect to find on the shelves of any library supporting a serious program in atmospheric science or related subjects, such as meteorology.

1017. ***Journal of Applied Meteorology.*** Supersedes in part (in 1988): *Journal of Climate and Applied Meteorology;* Formerly (until 1983): *Journal of Applied Meteorology.* [ISSN: 0894-8763] 1962. m. USD 410 (Individuals, USD 365; Members, USD 55). Ed(s): Michael Garstang. American Meteorological Society, 45 Beacon St, Boston, MA 02108; amsinfo@ametsoc.org; http://ams.allenpress.com. Illus., index, adv. Refereed. Circ: 1978. Vol. ends: Dec. Online: EBSCO Publishing; Gale Group; Northern Light Technology, Inc. *Indexed:* AS&TI, ApMecR, B&AI, BiolAb, ChemAb, DSR&OA, EngInd, ExcerpMed, ForAb, GeoRef, GeogAbPG, HortAb, IAA, M&GPA, OceAb, PollutAb, S&F, SCI, SWRA, WAE&RSA. *Aud.:* Ac, Sa.

Published by the American Meteorological Society, this journal reports on applied research in physical meteorology, hydrology, weather modification, cloud physics, satellite meteorology, air pollution meteorology, agricultural meteorology, and forest meteorology. Articles are scholarly and technical. Each volume includes an author and subject index. The online version provides the research articles and an author index only. Highly recommended for libraries supporting research and graduate course work in not only atmospheric science but also earth resources, agriculture, forestry, or engineering.

1018. ***Journal of Atmospheric and Oceanic Technology.*** [ISSN: 0739-0572] 1984. m. USD 335 (Members, USD 50). Ed(s): Kevin Leaman, Edward V Browell. American Meteorological Society, 45 Beacon St, Boston, MA 02108. Illus., index, adv. Refereed. Circ: 798. Vol. ends: Dec. Online: EBSCO Publishing. *Indexed:* AS&TI, ChemAb, DSR&OA, EngInd, GeogAbPG, M&GPA, OceAb, SCI, SWRA. *Aud.:* Ac.

Focuses on the methodology and instrumentation pertinent to atmospheric science and oceanography. A specific area of emphasis is the instruments and techniques used for data acquisition and interpretation. Articles tend to be detailed and quite technical. A "Notes and Correspondence" section reports both preliminary results and works in progress. The online version provides the research articles and an author index only. Recommended for research collections that support programs in atmospheric sciences and oceanography.

1019. ***Journal of Atmospheric Chemistry.*** [ISSN: 0167-7764] 1983. 9x/yr. EUR 996 print or online ed. Ed(s): Dieter H Ehhalt, Brian A Ridley. Kluwer Academic Publishers, van Godewijckstraat 30, PO Box 17, Dordrecht, 3300 AA, Netherlands. Illus., adv. Refereed. Microform: PQC. Online: EBSCO Publishing; ingenta.com; Kluwer Online; OCLC Online Computer Library Center, Inc.; Ovid Technologies, Inc.; RoweCom Information Quest; Swets Blackwell. Reprint: SWZ. *Indexed:* ChemAb, DSR&OA, EngInd, EnvAb, ExcerpMed, FPA, ForAb, GeoRef, GeogAbPG, HortAb, IAA, M&GPA, OceAb, PollutAb, S&F, SCI, SWRA. *Aud.:* Ac.

Publishes research on the chemical interactions in the earth's atmosphere. The emphasis is on the region below 100 Km. The research reported in the journal focuses increasingly on how human activities affect the chemistry of the atmosphere. Other areas of emphasis are composition of air and precipitation, physiochemical processes in the atmosphere, and chemical interaction of oceans and land surfaces with the atmosphere.

1020. ***Journal of Climate.*** Supersedes in part (in 1988): *Journal of Climate and Applied Meteorology;* Formerly (until 1983): *Journal of Applied Meteorology.* [ISSN: 0894-8755] 1986. s-m. USD 565 (Members, USD 80). Ed(s): Dave Randall. American Meteorological Society, 45 Beacon St, Boston, MA 02108; amsinfo@ametsoc.org; http://ams.allenpress.com. Illus., index, adv. Refereed. Circ: 1689. Vol. ends: Dec. Online: EBSCO Publishing; Northern Light Technology, Inc. *Indexed:* Agr, EngInd, ForAb, GeoRef, GeogAbPG, M&GPA, OceAb, PollutAb, S&F, SCI, SSCI, SWRA, WAE&RSA. *Aud.:* Ac, Sa.

Publishes technical research papers dealing with climate and its impacts. Specific areas of focus are large-scale atmospheric variability, changes in the climate system, climate modeling, forecasting of climate, and impacts of climate change on society. Each issue also contains a list of forthcoming papers. The online version provides the research articles and an author index only. Highly recommended for collections supporting programs in atmospheric science and recommended for those supporting programs in earth sciences and geography.

1021. ***Journal of Hydrometeorology.*** [ISSN: 1525-755X] 1999. bi-m. USD 160 (Members, USD 40). Ed(s): Dennis P Lettenmaier, Dara Entekhabi. American Meteorological Society, 45 Beacon St, Boston, MA 02108; amsinfo@ametsoc.org. Refereed. Online: EBSCO Publishing; OCLC Online Computer Library Center, Inc. *Indexed:* M&GPA, SWRA. *Aud.:* Ac, Sa.

Focuses on interactions of water with the boundary layer and lower atmosphere. Including processes of hydrology related to precipitation, radiation, and other atmospheric impacts, this journal publishes contributions from atmospheric scientists, earth scientists, civil engineers, and others. In addition to research articles, it also publishes "Notes and Correspondence." This section provides a forum for discussion of research topics in hydrometeorology and related areas. The online version provides the research articles and an author index only.

1022. ***Journal of the Atmospheric Sciences.*** [ISSN: 0022-4928] 1944. s-m. USD 545 (Members, USD 80). Ed(s): Theodore G Shepherd. American Meteorological Society, 45 Beacon St, Boston, MA 02108; amsinfo@ametsoc.org; http://ams.allenpress.com. Illus., index, adv. Refereed. Circ: 2136. Online: EBSCO Publishing; Gale Group; Northern Light Technology, Inc. *Indexed:* AS&TI, ApMecR, CCMJ, ChemAb, EngInd, ExcerpMed, GSI, GeoRef, GeogAbPG, IAA, M&GPA, MathSciNet, OceAb, PollutAb, SCI, SWRA. *Aud.:* Ac, Sa.

This is the American Meteorological Society journal that is devoted to basic research. Its specific orientation is the "physics, dynamics and chemistry of the earth and other planets." Articles rely heavily on quantitative methods, and much of the work reported is theoretical. A "Notes and Correspondence" section presents brief reports, often of research in progress. There is also an extensive list of papers slated to appear in future issues. The online version of this journal includes the research articles and an author index only. This is a prestigious journal and should be on the shelves of every library that supports research in atmospheric science and planetary studies.

1023. ***Local Climatological Data.*** m. USD 32; USD 5 per station, month, or year. U.S. National Climatic Data Center, Federal Bldg., 151 Patton Ave, Asheville, NC 28801-5001; http://lwf.ncdc.noaa.gov/oa/ncdc.html. *Aud.:* Hs, Ga, Ac, Sa.

This is a source for monthly meteorological data on nearly 300 cities throughout the United States. The data, given for each day of the month reported, include temperature, degree days, weather types, snow cover, precipitation, barometric pressure, wind speed, sunshine, and sky cover (cloudiness). Observations of temperature, wind, sky cover, and visibility taken at three-hour intervals are also provided, as is a table of hourly precipitation. Most libraries will want to have the summary for their immediate area. Public and school libraries should find this source especially valuable for ready reference. An online version of this publication is at www5.ncdc.noaa.gov/pubs/publications.html.

1024. ***Mariners Weather Log: a climatic review of North Atlantic and North Pacific Ocean and Great Lake areas.*** [ISSN: 0025-3367] 1957. 3x/yr. USD 16 domestic; USD 20 foreign. Ed(s): Robert A Luke. U.S. National Oceanographic Data Center, NOAA NESDIS, E OC2, Universal Bldg 1, Rm 415, Washington, DC 20235; http://www.nws.noaa.gov/om/mwl.mwl.htm. Illus., index, adv. Circ: 8100. Vol. ends: Dec. Reprint: CIS. *Indexed:* AmStI, DSR&OA, IUSGP, M&GPA, OceAb. *Aud.:* Hs, Ga, Ac.

This is a general-information publication for sailors and others interested in marine weather. Each issue contains a summary of buoy data and of weather reports from ships. Charts also give tracks of recent cyclones in the Northern Hemisphere. In addition, narrative accounts of tropical cyclones are provided. These include how the storm developed, its track, reports of damage, and accounts of any unique features exhibited by the storm. Feature articles summarize weather in particular ocean areas. News of NOAA is also included.

1025. ***Meteorological Applications.*** [ISSN: 1350-4827] 1994. q. USD 309. Ed(s): John Thornes. Cambridge University Press, The Edinburgh Bldg, Shaftesbury Rd, Cambridge, CB2 2RU, United Kingdom; information@cambridge.org; http://uk.cambridge.org/journals. Adv. Online: EBSCO Publishing; OCLC Online Computer Library Center, Inc.; RoweCom Information Quest; Swets Blackwell. Reprint: ISI. *Indexed:* M&GPA, PollutAb, SCI, SWRA. *Aud.:* Ac.

Meteorological Applications is oriented toward applied meteorology. It focuses on "applications of meterological information; analysis and prediction of weather hazards; performance, verification and value of numerical models and forecasting aids; and practical applications of ocean and climate models." This title also concentrates on the education and training of meteorologists.

1026. ***Meteorological Society of Japan. Journal.*** [ISSN: 0026-1165] 1882. bi-m. JPY 10200 (Individuals, JPY 6600). Ed(s): M Murakami. Meteorological Society of Japan, c/o Japan Meteorological Agency, 3-4 Ote-Machi 1-chome, Tokyo, 100-0004, Japan; http://www-cmpo.mit.edu/met_links/full/imsjap.full.html. Illus. Refereed. Circ: 2000. Vol. ends: Dec. *Indexed:* ChemAb, DSR&OA, GeogAbPG, M&GPA, SCI. *Aud.:* Ac.

Reports primary research in all areas of atmospheric science, particularly in analysis of weather patterns over East Asia and the Western Pacific. Most authors are Japanese, but the journal also includes contributions from throughout the world. Articles are in English. Summaries in Japanese are published in a separate publication titled *Tenki.* Recommended for libraries supporting research-level collections in the atmospheric sciences.

1027. ***Meteorologische Zeitschrift.*** Incorporates (1957-2000): *Contributions to Atmospheric Physics;* Formerly: *Meteorologische Rundschau.* [ISSN: 0941-2948] 1948. 6x/yr. EUR 276; USD 315. Ed(s): Michael J Kerschgens. Gebrueder Borntraeger Verlagsbuchhandlung, Johannesstr. 3A, Stuttgart, 70176, Germany; mail@borntraeger-cramer.de; http://www.schweizerbart.de. Illus., adv. Refereed. *Indexed:* ApMecR, ChemAb, DSR&OA, ExcerpMed, GeoRef, IAA, M&GPA. *Bk. rev.:* Occasional, 200-500 words. *Aud.:* Ac.

Sponsored by the German Meteorological Society, the Austrian Society for Meteorology, and the Swiss Society for Meteorology, this is a major journal for reporting research in the atmospheric sciences from German-speaking countries. Most articles are in English (occasionally they are in German); abstracts are in German and English. It publishes original research papers on meteorology and atmospheric physics. Papers on atmospheric circulation and air pollution are also included. Recommended for libraries supporting research-level collections in the atmospheric sciences.

1028. ***Meteorology and Atmospheric Physics.*** Formerly (until 1986): *Archives for Meteorology, Geophysics, and Bioclimatology. Series A: Meteorology and Geophysics - Archiv fuer Meteorologie, Geophysik und Bioklimatologie. Series A.* [ISSN: 0177-7971] 1948. 12x/yr. EUR 1232 domestic; EUR 1255.10 foreign; EUR 124 newsstand/cover per issue. Ed(s): E R Reiter, L Bengtsson. Springer-Verlag Wien, Sachsenplatz 4-6, Vienna, 1201, Austria; journals@springer.at. Illus., adv. Sample. Refereed. Vol. ends: Dec. Microform: PQC. Online: EBSCO Publishing; RoweCom Information Quest; Springer LINK; Swets Blackwell. *Indexed:* DSR&OA, EngInd, GeoRef, M&GPA, SCI. *Bk. rev.:* 200-500 words. *Aud.:* Ac, Sa.

Concentrates on physical and chemical processes in the atmosphere, including radiation, optical effects, electricity, atmospheric turbulence, and transport processes. Also covers atmospheric dynamics, general circulation in the atmosphere, and analyses of weather systems in specific regions. Articles report original research and tend to be highly technical. This is a true international journal: authors and reviewers are located throughout the world. Recommended for research collections in the atmospheric sciences.

1029. ***Monthly Climatic Data for the World.*** [ISSN: 0027-0296] 1948. m. USD 55 domestic; USD 75 foreign. U.S. National Climatic Data Center, Federal Bldg., 151 Patton Ave, Asheville, NC 28801-5001; orders@ncdc.noaa.gov; http://www.ncdc.noaa.gov/pdfs/samplepnbs/mcdw.pdf. Illus. Circ: 500. Vol. ends: Dec. Microform: CIS. Reprint: CIS. *Indexed:* AmStI, GeoRef. *Aud.:* Ga, Ac.

Publishes updates of climatic data in cooperation with the World Meteorological Organization. Includes surface data, which is arranged by continent and country. Each station reports mean air pressure at altitude and at sea level, mean temperature and departure for the month, mean vapor pressure and departure, and precipitation. Most stations also report hours of sunshine. Data are also given for the upper air, including height of air pressure contours, mean temperatures at various altitudes, and wind vectors at various altitudes. An annual summary is also included. Limited access to this title online is free to some agencies and individuals. For others, subscriptions are $7 a month or $55 annually. Information can be found at http://www5.ncdc.noaa.gov/pubs/publications.html. This title provides important information for atmospheric scientists.

1030. ***Monthly Weather Review.*** [ISSN: 0027-0644] 1872. m. USD 500 (Members, USD 65). Ed(s): Ying Hwa Kuo, David Jorgensen. American Meteorological Society, 45 Beacon St, Boston, MA 02108; amsinfo@ametsoc.org; http://www.ametsoc.org/ams. Illus., index, adv. Refereed. Circ: 2327. Vol. ends: Dec. Microform: PMC. Online: EBSCO Publishing; Northern Light Technology, Inc. *Indexed:* AS&TI, ApMecR, ChemAb, EngInd, ExcerpMed, ForAb, GeoRef, GeogAbPG, IAA, M&GPA, PollutAb, S&F, SCI, SSCI, SWRA. *Aud.:* Ga, Ac, Sa.

This research journal publishes papers on the analysis and forecasting of weather, including papers on observed and modeled atmospheric circulation. Much of the research reported is based on models of weather patterns. Articles are technical in nature and intended for professionals and graduate students. Brief reports, usually of research in progress, are given in a "Notes and Correspondence" section. The online version provides the research articles and an author index only. Recommended for all atmospheric science collections.

1031. ***National Weather Digest.*** [ISSN: 0271-1052] 1976. q. USD 29. Ed(s): Kenneth Mielke, Peter Roohr. National Weather Association, 6704 Wolke Ct, Montgomery, AL 36116-2134; natweaasoc@aol.com; http://www.nwas.org. Illus., index, adv. Circ: 3100. Vol. ends: Nov. *Indexed:* M&GPA. *Bk. rev.:* 1-2, 500-700 words. *Aud.:* Ga, Ac.

This title, the official publication of the National Weather Association, focuses on applied research of specific meteorological incidents that have occurred in the United States. It also includes technical notes, correspondence, and news pertinent to the association.

1032. ***Royal Meteorological Society. Quarterly Journal: a journal of the atmospheric sciences, applied meteorology, and physical oceanography.*** [ISSN: 0035-9009] 1871. 8x/yr. GBP 305; USD 520. Ed(s): K P Shine, J D Haigh. Royal Meteorological Society, 104 Oxford Rd, Reading, RG1 7LL, United Kingdom; qj@royal-met-soc.org.uk; http://www.royal-met-soc.org.uk. Illus., index, adv. Refereed. Circ: 1100. Vol. ends: Oct. *Indexed:* BiolAb, DSR&OA, EngInd, ExcerpMed, GeoRef, GeogAbPG, HortAb, IAA, M&GPA, OceAb, S&F, SCI. *Aud.:* Ac, Sa.

This is one of the major research journals in the atmospheric sciences. It publishes articles on all aspects of meteorology, climatology, atmospheric chemistry, and physical oceanography. The journal attracts contributions from throughout the world, though the editorial board, naturally, is primarily British. The papers are scholarly and technical. Each issue is divided into two separately bound parts. Book reviews appear in selected issues. Particularly recommended for academic libraries that support programs in the atmospheric sciences.

1033. ***Russian Meteorology and Hydrology.*** Formerly (until 1993): *Soviet Meteorology and Hydrology.* [ISSN: 1068-3739] 1976. m. USD 1915 in US & Canada; USD 2190 elsewhere. Ed(s): Yu A Izrael. Allerton Press, Inc., 18 W 27th St, New York, NY 10001; journals@allertonpress.com; http://www.allertonpress.com/. Illus. Sample. Refereed. *Indexed:* DSR&OA, ExcerpMed, ForAb, GeogAbPG, S&F. *Aud.:* Ac.

This journal publishes high-quality scholarly articles reporting research done by atmospheric scientists in Russia, much of which would otherwise remain unknown to scientists in the West. The articles cover meteorology, climatology, atmospheric physics and chemistry, and related areas. Recommended for research-level collections.

1034. ***Storm Data.*** [ISSN: 0039-1972] 1922. m. USD 70. U.S. National Climatic Data Center, 14th St and Constitution Ave, N W, Washington, DC 20230; webmaster@ncdc.noaa.gov; http://www5.ncdc.noaa.gov/pubs/publications.html. Illus., index. Circ: 1500. Vol. ends: Dec. Microform: CIS. Reprint: CIS. *Indexed:* AmStI. *Aud.:* Ga, Ac.

Data on storms and other unusual weather are summarized in this volume. Incidents are listed by state, then chronologically. For each incident, the date is given, then the local time, number of persons killed or injured, estimated damage, and character of the storm. For tornadoes, the path length and width are also given. Characteristics of significant or unusual storms are summarized, and maps of cyclone tracks and confirmed tornadoes for the month are included.

1035. ***Tellus. Series A: Dynamic Meteorology and Oceanography.*** Supersedes in part: *Tellus.* [ISSN: 0280-6495] 1949. 5x/yr. USD 243 print & online eds. Ed(s): H Sundquist. Blackwell Munksgaard, Rosenoerns Alle 1, PO Box 227, Copenhagen V, 1502, Denmark; info@mks.blackwellpublishing.com; http://www.munksgaard.dk/chemica/toc.html. Illus., index. Refereed. Circ: 1470. Vol. ends: Oct. Reprint: ISI. *Indexed:* ApMecR, BiolAb, ChemAb, DSR&OA, EnvAb, ExcerpMed, GeoRef, GeogAbPG, IAA, M&GPA, OceAb, S&F, SCI, SWRA. *Aud.:* Ac, Sa.

One of two parts of the original *Tellus, Series A* concentrates on dynamic meteorology and oceanography, which includes synoptic meteorology, weather forecasting, dynamic climatology, and theoretical and experimental fluid dynamics. The journal contains original research and review articles. Interaction of the atmosphere and the oceans is a recurring theme in many of the articles. A significant number of other articles deal with numerical analysis in atmospheric science and oceanography. This is an important title for atmospheric scientists and oceanographers.

1036. ***Tellus. Series B: Chemical and Physical Meteorology.*** Supersedes in part: *Tellus.* [ISSN: 0280-6509] 1949. 5x/yr. USD 243 print & online eds. Ed(s): H Rodhe. Blackwell Munksgaard, Rosenoerns Alle 1, PO Box 227, Copenhagen V, 1502, Denmark; info@mks.blackwellpublishing.com; http://www.munksgaard.dk/. Illus., index. Refereed. Circ: 1000. Vol. ends: Nov. Reprint: ISI. *Indexed:* ApMecR, BiolAb, ChemAb, DSR&OA, EngInd, EnvAb, ExcerpMed, GeoRef, GeogAbPG, IAA, M&GPA, OceAb, PollutAb, S&F, SCI, SWRA. *Aud.:* Ac, Sa.

The second part of the original *Tellus*, this journal concentrates on chemistry of the atmosphere, long-range and global transport, aerosol science, cloud physics, and biogeochemical cycles. The articles are scholarly and technical, with an emphasis on chemical interactions in the atmosphere. This, in fact, is one of the most important research titles in atmospheric chemistry. Authorship from many countries gives a scope to the journal that is truly international. As an important forum for researchers in atmospheric science, this journal would also be of interest to scholars and students in hydrology, oceanography, environmental studies, and geography.

1037. ***W M O Bulletin.*** [ISSN: 0042-9767] 1952. q. CHF 85. Ed(s): Hong Yan. World Meteorological Organization, 7 bis Avenue de la Paix, Case postale 2300, Geneva, 1211, Switzerland; pubsales@gateway.wmo.ch; http://www.wmo.ch. Illus., index, adv. Circ: 6500. Vol. ends: Oct. *Indexed:* GeoRef, M&GPA, OceAb, SWRA. *Bk. rev.:* 2-5, 300-500 words. *Aud.:* Ga, Ac.

This is both a serious meteorological journal and a medium for communication of news and information concerning the World Meteorological Organization (WMO). The aim of this publication is to further worldwide cooperation in the observation and measurement of meteorological phenomena and to further the study of weather and climate in general. Along with scholarly articles, it includes descriptions of recent weather events. Each issue also features an interview with a prominent person in meteorology. Extensive coverage is given to conferences, projects, and programs sponsored by the WMO. Libraries with research collections in the atmospheric sciences will need this title.

1038. ***Weather.*** [ISSN: 0043-1656] 1946. m. GBP 33; USD 62; GBP 3.80 per issue. Ed(s): G Bigg. Royal Meteorological Society, 104 Oxford Rd, Reading, RG1 7LL, United Kingdom; weather@royal-met-soc.org.uk; http://www.royal-met-soc.org.uk. Illus., index, adv. Refereed. Circ: 5300. Vol. ends: Dec. *Indexed:* ChemAb, DSR&OA, EngInd, ForAb, GeoRef, HortAb, IAA, M&GPA, PollutAb, S&F, SWRA. *Aud.:* Hs, Ga, Ac.

This is the more popular publication issued by the Royal Meteorological Society. The articles are scholarly but intended more for the educated layperson than the meteorological professional. The articles tend to be oriented toward the British Isles. Most issues also include book reviews and short summaries of meetings sponsored by the society. There's even a crossword puzzle of meteorological terms. Recommended for both academic and public libraries.

1039. ***Weather and Forecasting.*** [ISSN: 0882-8156] 1986. bi-m. USD 180 (Members, USD 40). Ed(s): Robert Maddox. American Meteorological Society, 45 Beacon St, Boston, MA 02108; amsinfo@ametsoc.org. Illus., index, adv. Refereed. Circ: 1640. Online: bigchalk; EBSCO Publishing; OCLC Online Computer Library Center, Inc.; ProQuest Information & Learning. *Indexed:* EngInd, GeogAbPG, M&GPA, SCI. *Aud.:* Ac.

Reports experimental testing of models of weather forecasting. Many papers concentrate on the accuracy of models in predicting specific weather events. The journal also publishes analyses of forecasting techniques. Short summaries of research are given in a "Notes and Correspondence" section. The online version provides the research articles and an author index only. Intended for professionals in the area of weather forecasting, it would also be of interest to atmospheric scientists in general.

1040. ***Weatherwise.*** [ISSN: 0043-1672] 1948. bi-m. USD 80 (Individuals, USD 38; USD 13.50 per issue). Ed(s): Doyle S Rice. Heldref Publications, 1319 18th St, NW, Washington, DC 20036-1802; subscribe@heldref.org; http://www.heldref.org. Illus., index, adv. Circ: 34000. CD-ROM: ProQuest Information & Learning. Microform: PQC. Online: bigchalk; EBSCO Publishing; Florida Center for Library Automation; Gale Group; Northern Light Technology, Inc.; OCLC Online Computer Library Center, Inc.; ProQuest Information & Learning; H.W. Wilson. *Indexed:* ChemAb, DSR&OA, EnvAb, GSI, GeoRef, IAA, M&GPA, MagInd, RGPR. *Aud.:* Ga, Ac, Sa.

This popular magazine publishes articles on weather, particularly on weather anomalies. The articles are written for the intelligent layperson; indeed, the primary audience seems to be amateur weather observers. It regularly publishes a review of weather over North America during the preceding two months. Areas such as influence of weather in history, weather in the arts, and photography of weather are recurring themes. The February issue includes weather records from the previous year. Recommended for all libraries that serve users with an interest in weather.

Weekly Weather and Crop Bulletin. See Agriculture/Electronic Journals section.

Electronic Journals

In addition to the journal listed below, here are three government sites that link to publications that provide important meteorological information:

National Weather Service, Internet Weather Source. http://weather.noaa.gov/index.html. This is a very useful web site of weather and forecasting data from the National Weather Service. The links included are: *United States Weather, Marine Weather, Radar Graphics, Weather Maps, International Weather Conditions,* and *Aviation Weather*. The United States Weather link gives current conditions for each National Weather Service observing station throughout the country. The specific conditions provided are: Wind, Visibility, Sky Conditions, Temperature, Dew Point, Relative Humidity, and Barometric pressure. Summaries of the previous 24 hours for each station are also included.

NCDC Online Document Library, Publications. http://www.ncdc.noaa.gov/pubs/publications.html. This web site serves as a gateway to the publications of the National Climatic Data Center. Among the publications available are: *Monthly Climatic Data for the World, Local Climatological Data, Storm Data, Hourly Precipitation Data, Heating and Cooling Degree Day Data, Climate Maps of U.S., Climates of the World, Wind Climatology,* and *Freeze/Frost Data for the U.S.*. Together, these publications constitute a cornucopia of climatological information.

U.S. Joint Agricultural Weather Facility, Publications. http://www.usda.gov/oce/waob/jawf. This web site provides access to publications that provide important meteorological information to those engaged in agriculture. The publications linked are: *U.S. Agricultural Weather Highlights, Weekly Weather and Crop Bulletin, Major World Crop Areas and Climatic Profiles,* and *Monthly World Agricultural Weather Highlights.* These publications include specific information for farmers, such as drought monitors and crop calendars. The agency that hosts this site, the Joint Agricultural Weather Facility, is sponsored by both the U.S. Department of Agriculture and National Oceanic and Atmospheric Administration. It utilizes data and services from both agencies.

1041. ***Earth Interactions.*** [ISSN: 1087-3562] 1996. d. Ed(s): A F Spilhaus. American Geophysical Union, 2000 Florida Ave, N W, Washington, DC 20009-1277; http://earthinteractions.org/; http://www.agu.org. Illus. Refereed. *Indexed:* M&GPA, SWRA. *Aud.:* Ac.

According to its editors, this interdisciplinary journal deals "with the interactions between the lithosphere, hydrosphere, atmosphere, and biosphere in the context of global issues or global change. It exploits the capabilities of electronic communications technology and provides its authors the opportunity to use animations and other visualization techniques that traditional publications cannot accommodate." *Earth Interactions* adheres to the same rigorous scholarly standards as the print journals issued by the copublishers. A conscious decision has also been made by the editors to go beyond the limits of the printed page to take full advantage of the capabilities of the web. In particular, the journal seeks to provide access to extensive datasets and to computer-generated graphics to expand upon the information reported in research articles. Authors are, in fact, encouraged to take "maximum advantage of the capabilities of the electronic medium." Articles can be viewed in html abstract and full-text files, and pdf full-text files.

■ AUTOMOBILES AND MOTORCYCLES

Amy Kautzman, Head, Research, Reference, and Collections, Doe/Moffitt Libraries, 212 Doe Library, #6000; University of California, Berkeley, CA 94720-6000; akautzma@library.berkeley.edu

Introduction

Considering that an automobile is a gas-powered proxy for our inner selves, it shouldn't surprise anyone that there is a wide range of periodicals to represent the multitudes of cars and motorcycles in the world today. While an automobile can signify financial security (if it is the only way we can get to work and earn a paycheck), specific makes and models also embody part of who we are, such as our wild sides, practical selves, or class standing. Similarly, motorcycles have personified a range of identities for their owners, from the untrustworthy hoodlum to the 45-year-old man in a midlife crisis who has just purchased his first Harley Davidson. (My apologies to the steady riders who have always been the core of biking.)

How did Henry Ford's "you can paint it any color, so long as it's black" sensibility become a candy-apple-red lifestyle? Madison Avenue is partly to blame for this shift in automotive meaning, but as consumers, we are responsible for taking our Ids on Wheels to an extreme. The convergence of expendable incomes and a growing sense of entitlement to endless consumer choice has resulted in a personalized and diverse market in which SUVs share the sales lot with the retro-classic car, and automobile advertising is used to sell pop music. In addition, cars are extremely important to us not only because they provide mobility in a country that worships freedom, but also because they are the second most expensive purchase (the first being a house) that most of us will ever make.

A quick perusal through the titles below (despite the fact that hundreds of magazines have not been included in the following list) show that Christians, African Americans, Latinos, truck drivers, and those boisterous motorcycle aficionados all have print materials that represent their clans and their passions. When choosing titles for your library, it is important to understand the demographics of your local audience. NASCAR is popular in the South in a way it will never be in the West. And while moto-cross isn't huge in large urban centers, there are regions where it is extremely important. And almost everybody wants to read the general automobile titles that show and critique the newest offerings.

We all have some interest in our vehicles; the array of print matter on the subject testifies to this. In full disclosure, I have a practical, boring car, but the motorcycles I've been driving since age 14 more than make up for any four-cylinder faux pas!

Basic Periodicals

Automobile, Car and Driver, Cycle World, Motor Trend, Motorcyclist, Roadbike.

1042. *African Americans on Wheels.* 1995. 6x/yr. USD 13.97. Ed(s): Jacqueline Mitchell. On Wheels, Inc., 585 E. Larned St., Ste. 100, Detroit, MI 48226; aaow@aol.com; http://www.automag.com. Illus., adv. Circ: 750000 Controlled. *Aud.:* Hs, Ga, Ac.

African Americans On Wheels is an interesting amalgam of an industry/minority voice magazine, written and published by and for an African American audience. The strength of this title is its reportage in the "Around Town" section. Here is where you'll find celebratory vignettes (in the tradition of *Jet* magazine) of African Americans in the automotive world. Topics include Detroit partnerships with minority charities and foundations. One month's cover story reports on Henry Ford and how his employment policies helped to create the black middle class. Another article highlights the Chrysler Group as being supportive of minority businesses. The car reviews are not in-depth or very critical. The same publisher also puts out the partially bilingual *Latinos On Wheels*, one of the nation's 35 leading Latino publications. Sample articles focus on Latino auto dealers, diversity in car ads, and the growing Latino NASCAR fan base. Text is available on the web site. These two titles represent important ethnic groups and should be considered for public libraries supporting a diverse audience.

1043. *American Iron Magazine: for people who love Harley-Davidsons.* [ISSN: 1059-7891] 1989. m. USD 19.95; USD 3.99 newsstand/cover per issue. Ed(s): Chris Maida. T A M Communications Inc., 1010 Summer St, Stamford, CT 06905-5503. Adv. Circ: 80000 Paid. *Aud.:* Hs, Ga.

This year, the 100th anniversary of Harley-Davidson, represents nothing less than a 365-day celebration of America's most iconic vehicle. *American Iron* is the standard for reading about and looking at this fabulous line of motorcycles. Dream inducing and instructional, this title features glossy photographs of bikes throughout each issue. Harley fans can read about new and historical models, from the featured hog on the cover to hundreds of bikes within (including Buell, H-D's sport bike). This is a participatory magazine, and most of the letters to the editor include photos of readers' bikes. Travel information, reviews (detailed if not highly critical), and wrenching advice abound. Chock-full of text and photos, this magazine is a true joy to read and drool over. Suggested for all public libraries with a large cruising population.

1044. *American Motorcyclist: journal of the American Motorcyclist Association.* Former titles (until Sep. 1977): *A M A News; American Motorcycling.* [ISSN: 0277-9358] 1947. m. USD 12.50; USD 15 foreign. Ed(s): Greg Harrison. American Motorcyclist Association, 13515 Yarmouth Dr, Pickerington, OK 43147-8214; http://www.ama-cycle.org/magazine/index.html. Illus., adv. Circ: 186598. Vol. ends: Dec. *Bk. rev.:* 1-5, 500-2,000 words. *Aud.:* Ga, Sa.

Available to the more than 250,000 members of the American Motorcyclist Association (AMA), this magazine covers every facet of motorcycling. Each monthly issue details the people, places, and events—from road rallies to road races—that make up the American motorcycling experience. The AMA is the world's largest motorsports sanctioning body, and this title is where you'll find the official, AMA-sanctioned rules and events. The AMA also acts as a political lobby for motorcyclists, and there is excellent reporting on legislation and activities, state-by-state and nationally. The social lives of bikers are also covered with Daytona, Sturgis, and other rallies covered in a family friendly format (i.e., no naked babes). For responsible riders who consider their bikes an extension of their personality, this title is absolutely necessary. Recommended for large public libraries.

1045. *Automobile.* Formerly (until 1987): *Automobile Magazine.* [ISSN: 0897-8360] 1986. m. USD 12 domestic; USD 25 Canada; USD 27 elsewhere. Ed(s): Jean Jennings, Mark Gillies. Primedia Broad Reach Group, 120 E. Liberty St., Ann Arbor, MI 48104-2186; rconnery@automobilemag.com; http://www.primedia.com. Illus., adv. Sample. Circ: 609000 Paid. Vol. ends: Dec. Online: Gale Group. Reprint: PQC. *Indexed:* ASIP. *Aud.:* Hs, Ga, Ac.

Automobile is your average generic car title. Highlighting the most recent models from Detroit, Germany, Japan, and the rest of the world, it is a fanzine with shiny metal objects in lieu of Hollywood superstars. That said, it can be a useful tool when doing research for a new car purchase. Part of the huge Primedia publishing empire, it has a professional design on glossy paper with lots of photos, and text that is never too critical of the automotive industry. The writing is interesting but not in-depth. Reviews appreciate size and speed while rarely commenting on gasoline mileage. If you can only buy one general automobile title for a public library collection, either *Car and Driver* or *Road and Track* would be a better choice.

1046. *Automotive Engineering International.* Former titles (until Dec. 1997): *Automotive Engineering;* (until 1972): *S A E Journal of Automotive Engineering.* 1905. m. USD 96 in North America; USD 150 elsewhere. Ed(s): Kevin Jost. Society of Automotive Engineers, 400

Commonwealth Dr, Warrendale, PA 15096-0001; advertising@sae.org; http://www.sae.org/automag. Illus., adv. Circ: 128520. Vol. ends: Dec. Microform: PMC. Online: Gale Group; Questel Orbit Inc. *Indexed:* AS&TI, C&ISA, EngInd, ErgAb, ExcerpMed, H&SSA, RRTA. *Aud.:* Ac, Sa.

Published by The Society of Automotive Engineers, *Automotive Engineering International* is "your one-stop resource for technical information and expertise used in designing, building, maintaining, and operating self-propelled vehicles for use on land or sea, in air or space." A combination of trade journal and academic resource, *AEI* features an editorial, technical briefs, and many articles on computers, material innovations, product briefs, and more. This is very much a technical title, and the casual reader may not find it accessible. A necessary purchase for academic and special engineering and design libraries.

1047. *Automotive Industries.* Former titles (until 1994): *Chilton's Automotive Industries;* (until 1976): *Automotive Industries.* [ISSN: 1099-4130] 1895. m. Free. Randall Publishing Company, 24901 Northwestern Hwy Ste 505, Southfield, MI 48075; http://www.randallpub.com. Illus., adv. Circ: 100834. Microform: CIS; PMC; PQC. Online: The Dialog Corporation; Florida Center for Library Automation; Gale Group; ProQuest Information & Learning. Reprint: PQC. *Indexed:* AS&TI, B&I, BPI, C&ISA, EduInd, EngInd, EnvAb, ExcerpMed. *Aud.:* Ga, Ac, Sa.

According to its web site, "*Automotive Industries* is a monthly publication devoted to providing global coverage of all aspects of the automobile marketplace, with an emphasis on the people, products and processes that shape the industry." Founded in 1895 as *The Horseless Age*, this title puts a strong emphasis on news that affects automotive manufacturing. If you truly care about production scheduling, inventory control, materials development, personnel management techniques, robotics and automation applications, and European manufacturing, you will find a little bit of nirvana in this read. Highly recommended for public libraries with constituents in the automotive industry, and for academic libraries supporting programs in automotive design, engineering, business, and other affiliated studies.

1048. *Car and Driver.* [ISSN: 0008-6002] 1956. m. USD 11.97 domestic; USD 19.97 foreign. Ed(s): Daniel Pund. Hachette Filipacchi Media U.S., Inc., 1633 Broadway, New York, NY 10019; http://www.hfmus.com. Illus., adv. Sample. Circ: 1381909 Paid. Vol. ends: Jun. Microform: NBI; PQC. Online: America Online, Inc.; The Dialog Corporation; EBSCO Publishing; Gale Group. Reprint: ISI. *Indexed:* ConsI, LRI, MagInd, RGPR. *Aud.:* Hs, Ga.

In publication since 1956, *Car and Driver* reviews and tests domestic and foreign automobiles, yet it is more like a print representation of cars in our lives. It is slick and full of photographs, well-written reviews, and interesting articles; one can get caught up in a good read even when not looking for a new car. The cover story is generally a comparative review of a vehicle genre, such as middleweight sedans or four-seater sports cars. Featured articles cover the gamut from car racing history to travel tips and carjacking in South Africa. Also covered are previews of specific models, at times a dream car that the average buyer can't afford, such as the 2004 Rolls-Royce Phantom. That aside, most of the magazine is devoted to educating buyers and enthralling enthusiasts. *Car and Driver* does this competently and with a bit of elan. Recommended for high school and public libraries.

1049. *Car Craft: do-it-yourself street performance.* [ISSN: 0008-6010] 1953. m. USD 10 domestic. Ed(s): Matt King. Primedia Consumer Media & Magazine Group, 200 Madison Ave, New York, NY 10016; http://www.primedia.com. Illus., adv. Circ: 375186 Paid. Microform: PQC. Online: Gale Group. *Aud.:* Hs, Ga.

Car Craft is the entry-level title for every weekend "rebuilt" warrior. Supporting all aspects of owning, maintaining, and customizing high-performance street cars, this title is a must have for any wrenching fool who likes to do it her/himself. It is uncannily like a magazine for teenage girls, except—instead of working on one's thighs or getting a facial—a Musclecar Makeover is the road to popularity. Technical articles give the basics on nitrous fuel and diagnosing used engines. The featured articles show amazing cars (at least five to seven of them). The columns are funny, irreverent, and actually pretty enjoyable. With 375,186 paid subscribers, this magazine obviously fulfills some basic American need. Suggested for high school and public libraries.

1050. *Christian Motorsports Illustrated.* Incorporates (in 1999): *Chrysler Power.* [ISSN: 1099-9396] 1996. q. USD 19.96; USD 3.99 newsstand/cover per issue. Ed(s): Tom Winfield. C PO, PO Box 129, Mansfield, PA 16933-0129; cpo@epix.net; http://www.christianmotorsports.com. Illus., adv. Circ: 10000. *Aud.:* Hs, Ga.

This title is representative of Christianity?s influence in racing. According to the blurb, it is "a colorful, exciting motorsports magazine reporting on God?s invasion of the world of motorsports." Muscular Christianity indeed! With a mix of color and black-and-white print, this magazine is an interesting combination of technical information, NASCAR worship, and proselytizing. Although the audience for this title is limited, it is a strong and vocal one. The publication should be considered for libraries with conservative Christian patrons.

1051. *Collectible Automobile.* Formerly: *Consumer Guide Elite Cars.* [ISSN: 0742-812X] 1984. bi-m. USD 37.95; USD 6.65 newsstand/cover per issue. Ed(s): John Biel. Publications International Ltd., 7373 N Cicero Ave, Lincolnwood, IL 60646. Illus., adv. Circ: 100000. *Bk. rev.:* 1-5, 500-2,000. *Aud.:* Ga, Sa.

Imagine, if you will, the automotive equivalent of *National Geographic*, a magazine on high-gloss paper with amazing photography and text; the writing incorporates automobile history with mechanical talk and places it in its proper place in the historical/sociological continuum. That magazine exists, and it is *Collectible Automobile.* This is the premier title on automotive restoration—not muscle-car wrenching but the careful reconstitution of older vehicles. Four cars are featured in each issue, with magnificent photos and great supporting text. Sections include a calendar of events, lots of letters, future collectibles (cars and more), and other interesting tidbits. If a public library can purchase only one auto-restoration/old-car-buff title, *Collectible Automobile* should be it. Also of interest to academic libraries that collect in automotive history.

Consumer Reports New Car Issue. See *Consumer Reports* in the Consumer Education section.

1052. *Consumer Reports New Car Preview.* Formerly (until 1999): *Consumer Reports New Car Yearbook.* [ISSN: 1528-3267] 1994. a. USD 5.95. Consumers Union of the United States, Inc., 101 Truman Ave, Yonkers, NY 10703-1057; http://www.consumerreports.org. *Aud.:* Ga, Ac, Sa.

Most of the titles included in this section have reviews of the newest car models rolling off of the factory floor. And while many reviewers present a fair and nuanced opinion, nobody has the respect, the history, and the firewall separating them from the industry like *Consumer Reports.* Consumers Union was founded in 1936 as an independent, nonprofit testing and information organization, with the motto "Test, Inform, Protect." The annual *New Car Preview*, a great value for the price, has two sections. The first includes articles on how to shop for a new car, overviews on new models and trends, and hints for haggling on price. The second is filled with 150 car reviews. Lacking the lyrical content of most auto appraisals, there is a short chapter of text and then information on safety, specs, reliability history, forecasts, and "From the Test Track." These nit-picky facts are more useful than the perceptions and specifications that fill most automotive reviews and can be implicitly trusted as unbiased. Highly recommended for public and academic libraries.

1053. *Cycle World.* Incorporated (in Oct. 1991): *Cycle (New York, 1952).* [ISSN: 0011-4286] 1961. m. USD 12.97 domestic; USD 20.97 foreign. Hachette Filipacchi Media U.S., Inc., 1633 Broadway, New York, NY 10019; http://www.hfmus.com. Illus., adv. Sample. Circ: 310000 Paid. Vol. ends: Dec. Microform: NBI; PQC. Online: America Online, Inc.; Gale Group. Reprint: PQC. *Indexed:* ConsI, LRI, MagInd, RGPR, SportS. *Bk. rev.:* Various number and length. *Aud.:* Hs, Ga.

Cycle World goes toe-to-toe with *Motorcyclist* for the best generalist bike title. Although *Motorcyclist* is older, *Cycle World* has a healthy 100,000+ lead on subscribers. *Cycle World* has the same combination of reviews, comparisons, and worshipful praise that are staples of all motorcycling publications. In addition, there are lifestyle articles, reporting on races and rallies, video game reviews, book reviews, and more. If it came to a tie-breaker I'd chose *Motorcyclist*, if only for its informative, text-rich web site. Otherwise, it's up to you to decide which of these two should be added to your public library collection.

1054. *Drag Racer Magazine.* [ISSN: 1094-5547] 1997. bi-m. USD 16.95; USD 3.99 newsstand/cover per issue. Ed(s): Scott Cochran. Y-Visionary Publishing, 265 S Anita Dr, Ste 120, Orange, CA 92868; yvis03@cogent.net; http://www.dragracermag.com. Illus., adv. *Bk. rev.:* Various number and length. *Aud.:* Hs, Ga.

Motorsports is a growing industry with an audience that expands each year. This title is a starting place for technical information, interviews, an industry news. According to its web site, "*Drag Racer* magazine is where you will find entertaining, action-packed, in-depth features on the cars, personalities, and events that make up the entire sport of drag racing. Also featured are comprehensive how-to articles for both the enthusiast and the professional, as well as coverage on nostalgia racing, new product information and the latest news in the drag racing industry." If automobile racing is popular in your neck of the woods, this is a title you should strongly consider for your library.

1055. *Hot Rod.* [ISSN: 0018-6031] 1948. m. USD 10 domestic. Ed(s): David Freiburger. Primedia Consumer Media & Magazine Group, 200 Madison Ave, New York, NY 10016; http://www.primedia.com. Illus., adv. Sample. Circ: 805035 Paid. Vol. ends: Dec. Microform: PQC. Online: The Dialog Corporation; Gale Group; OCLC Online Computer Library Center, Inc.; ProQuest Information & Learning. Reprint: PQC. *Indexed:* ASIP, CPerI, ConsI, MagInd, RGPR. *Bk. rev.:* 1-3, 200-500 words. *Aud.:* Hs, Ga.

Hot Rod is a prime example of car porn. Directed towards men and visually oriented, with hundreds of photographs of cars, this hugely popular title takes most of its readers into a fantasyland. Focusing on high-performance vehicles, the technical (chassis, drive train, engine) and how-to (painting, oiling, installing, etc.) articles take up much of the magazine's real estate. The rest of the pages (featured cars and project cars) highlight beautiful examples of owners' personalities incorporated into metal and gas sculptures. With over 800,000 subscribers (double that of *The Atlantic Monthly* and equivalent to *The New Yorker*), public libraries should seriously consider this title for their popular periodicals collection.

1056. *Hybrid & Electric Vehicle Progress.* Formerly: *Electric Vehicle Progress.* 1979. bi-m. USD 477 in North America; USD 507 elsewhere. Ed(s): Layne Holley. Alexander Communications Group, Inc., 28 W. 25th St., Flr. 8, New York, NY 10010-2705; info@alexcommgrp.com; http://www.alexcommgrp.com. Illus. Sample. *Aud.:* Ga, Ac, Sa.

For more than two decades, *Hybrid & Electric Vehicle Progress* has provided worldwide news concerning research, development, and commercialization of battery-electric, hybrid, and fuel cell vehicles. From this long-range perspective, it distills important information and market intelligence to bring you a clear, concise picture of the industry. It is published twice each month, and short articles focus on research and development, alternative power sources, real world applications, marketing strategies, and more. With today's focus on alternative fuels, *EVP* is a necessary purchase for large public, academic, and special engineering and design libraries.

Lowrider. See Latino Studies section.

1057. *Moto Kids.* 2002. bi-m. USD 9.95 domestic; USD 21.95 foreign; USD 3 newsstand/cover per issue. Ed(s): Paul Carruthers. Cycle News, Inc., 3503-M Cadillac Ave, Costa Mesa, CA 92626; advertising@moto-kids.com; http://www.moto-kids.com. Adv. Circ: 70000. *Aud.:* Hs, Ga, Sa.

It is assumed that children are drawn to shiny things. Perhaps this is why *Moto Kids* uses high-gloss paper and full-color, full-page photos. This "WOW" publication is like MTV for the kinder-racer. Busily designed pages, product evaluations, personality profiles, riding tips, and motorcycle maintenance help make this a must-read for any young rider. The text is written to be accessible and youthful in style, which is not to say that it is dumbed down. The focus is on the "future of our sport," and lest we forget, the parents are paying for an inexpensive magazine but a very expensive hobby. Ya gotta love their web site quote: "*Moto Kids*—Not Your Daddy's Motorcycle Magazine!" Recommended for public libraries where there is a strong motocross community.

1058. *Motor Trend.* Incorporates: *Car Life; Sports Car Graphic; Wheels Afield.* [ISSN: 0027-2094] 1949. m. USD 18 domestic; USD 31 in Canada & Mexico; USD 33 elsewhere. Ed(s): Kevin Smith. Primedia Consumer Media & Magazine Group, 200 Madison Ave, New York, NY 10016; information@primedia.com; http://www.primedia.com. Illus., index, adv. Circ: 1263725. Vol. ends: Dec. CD-ROM: ProQuest Information & Learning. Microform: PQC. Online: The Dialog Corporation; Gale Group; OCLC Online Computer Library Center, Inc.; ProQuest Information & Learning. *Indexed:* BPI, ConsI, MagInd, RGPR. *Aud.:* Hs, Ga, Ac.

Even if you've never picked up a copy of *Motor Trend*, you've more than likely heard of the "Motor Trend Car of the Year Award." Around since 1949, *Motor Trend* is a stellar title that will compete with *Car and Driver* and *Road and Track* for your subscription money. It covers news and trends in the worldwide auto market along with excellent road tests and reviews. The writing is breezy, funny, and critical when it needs to be. Unlike some car reviews, those in *Motor Trend* tend to take into account what sort of driver is drawn to a car and why. This mix of the sociological with the automotive makes for a fuller read. Features on car care, auto shows, and race results round out a fun and sometimes useful title. Recommended for public libraries and specialized academic collections.

1059. *Motorcyclist.* Incorporates (1970-1988): *Motorcycle Buyer's Guide.* [ISSN: 0027-2205] 1912. m. USD 10 domestic. Ed(s): Mitch Boehm. Primedia Consumer Media & Magazine Group, 200 Madison Ave, New York, NY 10016; http://www.primedia.com. Illus., adv. Circ: 255456 Paid. Microform: PQC. Online: Gale Group. *Indexed:* ConsI, IHTDI, SportS. *Aud.:* Hs, Ga.

If you can only afford one motorcycle magazine for your library, *Motorcyclist* should be it. Published since 1912, it covers a little bit of everything: racing bikes, cruisers, American bikes vs. others, reviews, and more. The cover story is generally some new bike that simply screams for attention, or so it would seem when the tilted bike is pictured being driven at full speed and surrounded by text in a huge yellow font ending with exclamation points. There are really enjoyable non-feature articles, columns, and departments written by experienced writers/bikers. The "Up to Speed" section focuses on what is "hot, hot, hot," and the "Real World" articles consist of "tips, tweaks, fixes, and facts." Safety is given a priority throughout the magazine. Unlike most Harley magazines, there are no riders without helmets on these pages. *Motorcyclist* is akin to the older sister or brother biker that every youth should learn from. Highly recommended for public libraries.

1060. *Racer X Illustrated.* [ISSN: 1099-6729] 1998. bi-m. USD 24; USD 4.95 newsstand/cover per issue. Ed(s): Davey Coombs. Racer X Illustrated, 166 Harner Run, Morgantown, WV 26508; davey@racerxill.com; http://www.racerxill.com. Illus., adv. *Bk. rev.:* Various number and length. *Aud.:* Hs, Ga.

If *Moto Kids* is the entry-level title for motocross racing, *Racer X Illustrated* is the next logical step up as the motocross racer reaches young adulthood. Covering all aspects of motocross racing and recreation, this kinetically designed magazine seeps testosterone through its text, ads, and photographs. Columnists include X-Games gold-medal-winner Travis Pastrana, former champion and ESPN color analyst David Bailey, and off-road star Shane Watts. This monthly extravaganza of over 200 pages constantly features words like "broken clavicle" and "mild concussion." For libraries that support motocross enthusiasts and their parents.

1061. *Road & Track.* [ISSN: 0035-7189] 1947. m. USD 11.97 domestic; USD 19.97 foreign. Hachette Filipacchi Media U.S., Inc., 1633 Broadway, New York, NY 10019; http://www.hfmus.com. Illus., index, adv. Sample. Circ: 737362 Paid. Vol. ends: Dec. Microform: NBI; PQC. Online: America Online, Inc.; EBSCO Publishing; Gale Group. Reprint: PQC. *Indexed:* ASIP, ConsI, MagInd, RGPR. *Bk. rev.:* 1-2, 2000 words. *Aud.:* Hs, GA.

Started in 1947, *Road & Track* is the original automotive enthusiast magazine. It is not that different from *Car and Driver* or *Motor Trend* in that it focuses on automotive subjects such as design, engineering, driving reports, road tests, racing coverage, and in-depth technical discussions. The magazine's road tests are detailed and fun to read, the technical articles truly interesting (for example, on intercultural differences and automotive global positioning systems), and the photographs ensure car lust. The news features cover industry insiders, automotive shows, and trends. A strong contender for collections in public and academic libraries, especially those supporting an automotive industry audience.

1062. *RoadBike.* Former titles (until 2002): *Motorcycle Tour & Cruiser; Motorcycle Tour and Travel.* [ISSN: 1538-4748] 1993. m. USD 19.94 domestic; USD 31.94 foreign; USD 3.99 newsstand/cover per issue domestic. Ed(s): Buzz Kanter, Laura Brengalman. T A M Communications Inc., 1010 Summer St, Stamford, CT 06905-5503; mtcmagazine@earthlink.net. Illus., adv. Sample. Circ: 35000 Paid. Vol. ends: Nov. *Aud.:* Hs, Ga.

There are two reasons why libraries should consider getting *Roadbike* (formerly *Motorcycle Tour & Cruiser*). The first, and most important to this reviewer, is that it is edited by a man and a woman, features a good number of female authors, and even has the audacity to put a woman on the cover (on her bike, not in her bikini)! The second reason is specialization. If your library can afford to buy more than one motorcycle magazine, it should consider a touring/travel title, and this is a superior example. There are bike reviews, articles on paint jobs and customizations, up to seven mechanical/tech articles, and a bunch of gear write-ups. What makes this title different, other than its respect for women riders, are the three roadtrip articles included each month. From Bike Week in Daytona to riding the roads of Norway to exploring War Eagle Mill in Arkansas, these articles include history, maps, events, and contact information. With roadbike cruising growing in popularity, this would be a superb addition to any public library travel or motorcycle collection.

1063. *Stock Car Racing.* [ISSN: 0734-7340] 1964. m. USD 12 domestic; USD 25 Canada; USD 27 elsewhere. Ed(s): David Bourne. Primedia Consumer Media & Magazine Group, 200 Madison Ave, New York, NY 10016; http://www.primedia.com. Illus., adv. Circ: 257296 Paid. *Aud.:* Hs, Ga.

Published since 1964, *Stock Car Racing* has been along for the ride as NASCAR has risen in popularity. Interestingly, a recent editorial questions how much growth is too much before the sport "turns its back on the folks who were behind it all." Recognizing its core audience, it continues to cover all aspects of the racing lifestyle, profiling drivers, reporting on events, and reviewing equipment. A recent issue features a NASCAR driver's humble beginnings, NASCAR's focus on safety (not far behind a full-color, several-page spread of an extreme Daytona crash-and-burn), lots of tech talk, and new products. Do I respect this title? Not really. But it accurately reflects a sport that is all about noise, hero worship, safety (barely), and the quick reflexes of men willing to risk their lives for riches. Recommended for public libraries whose audience loves racing.

1064. *Truckin': world's leading sport truck publication.* [ISSN: 0277-5743] 1975. m. USD 24.95. Ed(s): Steve Warner. McMullen Argus Publishing, Inc., 2400 E Katella Ave, Ste 1100, Anaheim, CA 92806; http://www.mcmullenargus.com. Illus., adv. Circ: 202255 Paid. Vol. ends: Dec. *Aud.:* Hs, Ga.

Truckin' is an example of the genre specialization that exists in the automotive publishing world. Tilted toward the enthusiast, this title emphasizes all things truck. Customization, new model reviews (domestic and imported), tech tips, and lots of interaction between readers and the publisher fill the pages for those who can't get enough from more generalist magazines. Recommended only for specialized collections.

1065. *Vintage Motorsport: the journal of motor racing history.* [ISSN: 1052-8067] 1982. bi-m. USD 35 domestic; USD 45 in Canada & Mexico; USD 65 in Europe. Ed(s): Randy Riggs. Vintage Motorsport Inc., PO Box 7200, Lakeland, FL 33807. Adv. Circ: 9350. *Bk. rev.:* Various number and length. *Aud.:* Hs, Ga, Ac.

According to its web site, "*Vintage Motorsport*, the Journal of Motor Racing History, celebrates the heroes of motorsport, the people, cars, and venues that have given the sport its rich heritage. In addition, the magazine covers current vintage racing, which continues to reach new levels in participation and attendance." While NASCAR and drag racing are huge, the magazines that support them seldom look deeply into the past. This one views racing history through an international lens. Sample articles include one on a world champion Argentinean racer, on the French Deutsch-Bonnet, and on historic racing events. For the public library that supports the full racing enthusiast.

1066. *Woman Rider.* 2000. q. USD 11.95 domestic; USD 15.95 Canada; USD 19.95 elsewhere. Ed(s): Genevieve Schmitt. Ehlert Publishing Group, Inc., 6420 Sycamore Ln. N. Ste 100, Maple Grove, MN 55369-6003; editor@ridermagazine.com; http://ww.ehlertpowersports.com. Illus., adv. Circ: 43852 Paid. *Bk. rev.:* 150-200 words. *Aud.:* Hs, Ga, Sa.

Introduced in 2000, *Woman Rider* fills an important void in motorcycle publications. While many of the mainstream publishers are becoming more inclusive of women riders, this title sole focus is on supporting them. With many features that encourage first-time riders, it introduces new products from a female point of view and includes readers in the cycling lifestyle. The magazine pays admirably close attention to handling and size issues inherent when shorter people ride large bikes. Its articles on safe touring, maintenance, and reviews are fun to read and well written. At times the editorial and advertising departments don't seem far enough apart, but the bonus of seeing smaller-sized gear spotlighted almost makes up for the inclusion of product in the stories. Strongly suggested for public libraries as a counterpoint to the dominant male titles and for academic libraries that focus on gender issues.

Electronic Journals

1067. *Woman Motorist: Internet magazine.* [ISSN: 1523-5742] 1996. d. Ed(s): Sandra Kinsler. CyberAd, 2674 E Main St, Ste D 240, Ventura, CA 93003-2899; editor@womanmotorist.com; http://www.womanmotorist.com. Adv. *Aud.:* Ga.

A very active web site, *Woman Motorist* is updated daily and is chock-full of interesting bits of news, articles, and links to other automotive sites. There is nothing specifically female about this site other than that the text is written in gender-neutral tones, the design is a bit lavender, and there are quite a few articles that mention safety for children. I can't imagine, however, that this topic matters only to mothers and not to fathers as well. The writers are of all genders and the focus on reviews, automobile law, new products, safety, etc., transcends any sexing of engines. RVs, motorcycles, and racing are also featured. A rich, enjoyable resource.

1068. *Women with Wheels (Online).* 2000. irreg. update as needed. Free. Ed(s): Susan Frissell. Women with Wheels, 1885 Willowview Terrace, Northfield, IL 60093-2934. *Bk. rev.:* 1: 200-1000. *Aud.:* Hs, Ga, Ac, Sa.

Women With Wheels began in 1989 as the first automotive publication written expressly for women. In 2001, it ceased its print version and became a web resource. Publisher Susan Frissell is a syndicated columnist in over 120 newspapers, and her writing is found in a number of big-name automotive publications. As the web site claims, "Because today?s women are savvy, *WWW* became an important publication for those who wanted to become informed about such things as basic automotive maintenance and automotive recalls. *Women With Wheels* compiled all the automotive news and synthesized it into an easily readable format." This site is actually fairly gender neutral, and both men and women will appreciate the lack of too many pronouns while enjoying the good reviews, interesting articles, and rich resources and links.

■ BIBLIOGRAPHY

See also Books and Book Reviews; Library and Information Science; and Printing and Graphic Arts sections.

Rachel Howarth, Head of Public Services, Houghton Library of the Harvard College Libraries, Harvard University, Cambridge, MA 02138; rhowarth@fas.harvard.edu

Introduction

Bibliography is the study of books. While the word is most commonly associated with a simple listing of publications, the field is much richer and more complex. Traditionally bibliography has been divided into three parts: enumerative bibliography (book lists); analytical (or critical) bibliography; and descriptive (in a detailed and meaningful way) bibliography. Bibliography includes the study of the physical aspects of books such as bindings, papers, typography, and methods of illustration; it includes textual criticism, manuscript studies, and the study of the transmission of texts; it extends from the study of paleography and codicology to the history of editing, printing, and publishing. The gathering and examination of physical bibliographical evidence, along with the careful study of context, enables new insights into of all aspects of books. It connects the study of book production, authorship, and reception, and the book's role in social, cultural, and economic history.

There are a few different types of bibliographical periodicals. The most fundamental to the field are produced by bibliographical societies. These interdisciplinary groups exist in many countries including Canada, Australia, New Zealand, and most Western European countries, each with its own (or more than one) publication. American librarians, depending on their focus, may wish to explore beyond the examples from the United States and England that are listed here. Another large portion of periodicals are the publications of libraries themselves, and they focus on research coming out of their rare books and manuscript special collections. The most well-known of these publications have been included here. While each of these library journals has a certain local flavor, the real distinction between them lies in the different holdings at each particular institution. Certain very important international journals have also been included. Even though the majority of their contents is not in English, their inclusion gives a clearer sense of the field's deeply international character.

The field of bibliography, although long and well established, continues to expand. It has most recently been intimately associated with the relatively new field known as "history of the book," an area that has spawned new conferences, new academic departments, new national and international projects, and even a new journal, *Book History.* While the majority of contributors to the field continue to be academics, important contributions also come from outside the academy, from collectors, book dealers, and other bibliophiles.

Basic Periodicals

Ga: *Bulletin of Bibliography;* Ac: *Bibliographical Society of America. Papers, The Library, Studies in Bibliography.*

Basic Abstracts and Indexes

America: History and Life, Annual Bibliography of the History of the Printed Book and Library, Historical Abstracts, Library Literature, MLA International Bibliography.

1069. ***American Antiquarian Society. Proceedings: journal of American history and culture through 1876.*** [ISSN: 0044-751X] 1812. s-a. USD 45 domestic; USD 53 foreign. Ed(s): Jonathan Lane. American Antiquarian Society, 185 Salisbury St, Worcester, MA 01609; jkeenum@mwa.org; http://www.americanantiquarian.org. Illus., index, adv. Refereed. Circ: 1000. Microform: PQC. Reprint: PSC. *Indexed:* A&ATA, AmH&L, ArtHuCI, BHA, MLA-IB, RILM. *Aud.:* Ac.

Self-described as "one of the country's oldest learned journals," *Proceedings* "publishes articles within the general field of American history and culture through 1876, with a particular emphasis on the publication of bibliographies, primary sources, and other basic tools for scholarship." Each hefty issue (approximately 250 pages) contains three to five well-researched articles with helpful abstracts in the table of contents. Occasionally, articles appear exploring new acquisitions and/or innovations at the American Antiquarian Society (AAS) Library, and contributors are often drawn from the list of library fellows or former fellows. Regular features include obituaries of members and of those otherwise connected to the society; actual proceedings of the AAS meetings including lists of current fellows and their projects; the report of the council, giving news of the society and the library; and the report of the treasurer. An important journal for collections focusing on early American history and literature.

Antiquarian Book Monthly. See Books and Book Reviews section.

1070. ***La Bibliofilia: rivista di storia del libro e di bibliografia.*** [ISSN: 0006-0941] 1899. 3x/yr. EUR 64 domestic; EUR 79 foreign. Ed(s): Luigi Balsamo. Casa Editrice Leo S. Olschki, Casella Postale 66, Florence, 50100, Italy; celso@olschki.it; http://www.olschki.it. Illus., adv. Circ: 1000. Vol. ends: Sep/Dec. *Indexed:* AmH&L, BHA, IBZ, LibLit, LingAb, MLA-IB. *Bk. rev.:* 7-9, 500-2,000 words. *Aud.:* Ac.

La Bibliofilia is devoted to the publication of scholarly articles about Italian books, their history, publishers, and artistic production. Though mostly in Italian, the editor often includes English-language and French-language articles. Each volume includes three or four well-researched main articles, two or three shorter articles, and several substantial book reviews. All issues are oversize and printed on fine paper with many illustrations. A gray paper section at the back of each volume consists of international publication announcements and advertisements. The particularly rich history of Italian printing and publishing makes this elegant journal an important contribution to the field.

1071. ***Bibliographical Society of America. Papers.*** [ISSN: 0006-128X] 1904. q. USD 50. Ed(s): Trevor Howard Hill. Bibliographical Society of America, PO Box 1537, New York, NY 10021; bsa@bibsocamer.org; http://www.bibsocamer.org. Illus., index, adv. Circ: 1300. Vol. ends: Dec. Reprint: PSC. *Indexed:* AmH&L, ArtHuCI, BEL&L, BHA, BRI, CBRI, HumInd, LibLit, MLA-IB, SSCI. *Bk. rev.:* 7-10 of 1,000-1,500 words; plus 4-6 more of 200-500 words. *Aud.:* Ac.

Perhaps the most influential journal in the field of American bibliography, *Papers of the Bibliographical Society of America* features four or five meticulously researched scholarly articles by academics and librarians. Specifics about subject matter are outlined in the editor's instructions to contributors: "Contributions to the *Papers* may deal with books and manuscripts in any field, but should involve consideration of the book or manuscript (the physical object) as historical evidence, whether for establishing a text or illuminating the history of book production, publication, distribution, or collecting, or for other purposes. Studies of the printing, publishing, and allied trades are also welcome." A substantial and high quality review section follows the articles. An occasional "Notes and News" section is included, as well as the annual report of the society. This is an important work for collections dealing with the serious study of bibliography, textual studies, and the history of the book.

1072. ***Bodleian Library Record.*** Formerly (until 1938): *Bodleian Quarterly Record.* [ISSN: 0067-9488] 1917. s-a. GBP 18 in the European Union; GBP 20 elsewhere. Ed(s): Martin Kauffmann. Bodleian Library, Bodleian Library, Broad St, Oxford, OX1 3BG, United Kingdom; mrk@bodley.ox.ac.uk. Illus., index. Refereed. Circ: 1500 Paid. Vol. ends: Apr. Microform: PQC. Reprint: PQC; PSC. *Indexed:* AmH&L, BHA, BrHumI, IBZ, MLA-IB. *Aud.:* Ac.

This slim journal published by Oxford University's Bodleian Library manages to be both local and international at the same time. It has three regular features: "Notes and News," a section devoted to happenings in the library, staff departures and arrivals, changes in administrative structure, new programs, exhibition summaries, and announcements of interest to Bodleian friends groups all over the world; "Notable Accessions," which provides narrative description of recent acquisitons; and "Notes and Documents," where brief pieces about important research discoveries in the collection are printed. Two to four longer articles based on the collections but with broad scholarly relevance fill out each volume. A notable journal for those particularly interested in the Bodleian's exceptional collections.

1073. *Book Collector.* [ISSN: 0006-7237] 1952. q. EUR 42; USD 68. Ed(s): Nicolas Barker. Collector Ltd., PO Box 12426, London, W11 3GW, United Kingdom; http://www./thebookcollector.co.uk. Illus., index, adv. Vol. ends: Winter. Microform: NRP. Reprint: PSC. *Indexed:* ArtHuCI, BEL&L, BHA, BRI, BrHumI, CBRI, IBZ, LibLit, LingAb, MLA-IB, RI-1. *Bk. rev.:* 3-6, 500-3,000 words. *Aud.:* Ac, Sa.

The Book Collector is self-described as "the most interesting and lively current journal for collectors, bibliographers, antiquarian book sellers and custodians of rare books. Leading authorities contribute regularly on all aspects of bibliophily, from medieval manuscript to modern first editions, and each issue offers new and original insight into the world of books." Less strictly academic than other journals in this field, each issue includes three to five articles on such topics as the history of books, binding styles, printing types, paper, illustrators, specific book collections or libraries, book sales, the wonders revealed through detailed book description, and the pleasures of collecting. Regular sections include "English and Foreign Bookbindings," "News and Comment," "Exhibitions and Exhibition Catalogues," "Obituaries" of prominent collectors or bibliographers, "Books Received," and "Book Reviews," as well as an annual "Christmas Catalog" of "bibliographical nonsense" (i.e., humorous errors in printed catalogs). Advertisements for rare book auctions and sales are also included, making this journal useful as well as readable.

1074. *Book History.* [ISSN: 1098-7371] 1998. a. USD 56 domestic (Students, USD 25). Ed(s): Ezra Greenspan, Jonathan Rose. Pennsylvania State University Press, 820 N. University Dr., USB-1, Ste C, University Park, PA 16802-1003; pspjournals@psu.edu; http://www.psupress.org. Illus. Circ: 1000. Online: EBSCO Publishing; OCLC Online Computer Library Center, Inc.; Project MUSE; RoweCom Information Quest. *Indexed:* AmH&L, MLA-IB. *Aud.:* Ac.

Growing out of the activities of SHARP (the Society for the History of Authorship, Reading, and Publishing), *Book History* is a recent addition to the field and already receiving high acclaim. The editors describe the journal as "devoted to the history of the book, broadly defined as the creating, dissemination, reception, and use of script, print, and mediacy." Interdisciplinary in its mission, *Book History* welcomes articles on "the social, economic and cultural history of authorship, editing, printing, publishing, media, the book arts, the book trade, periodicals, newspapers, ephemera, copyright, censorship, literary agents, libraries, literary criticism, canon formation, literacy, literary education, reading habits, and reader response." Each cloth-bound volume includes a dozen articles, both readable and scholarly, by experts in various academic disciplines, book collectors, dealers, and unaffiliated specialists. An excellent selection for those interested in the latest developments in this exciting area of scholarship.

1075. *Bulletin of Bibliography.* Formerly: *Bulletin of Bibliography and Magazine Notes.* [ISSN: 0190-745X] 1897. q. USD 125 domestic; USD 145 foreign. Ed(s): Bernard McTigue. Greenwood Publishing Group Inc., 88 Post Rd W, PO Box 5007, Westport, CT 06881; webmaster@greenwood.com; http://www.greenwood.com/bob.html. Illus., index, adv. Circ: 1000. Vol. ends: Dec. *Indexed:* ABS&EES, AmH&L, BEL&L, BiogInd, MLA-IB, RI-1. *Bk. rev.:* 2-10, 200-1,000 words. *Aud.:* Ga, Ac.

Bulletin of Bibliography "publishes articles on a wide range of topics in the humanities, social sciences, and fine arts." Issues include "topics of scholarly and general interest that contain bibliographical material not accessible through other published sources." Articles demonstrate subject and enumerative bibliography more than descriptive or analytical, and the titles reveal an enormously broad range. Recent entries include "Carson McCullers since 1980: A Bibliography," "Ancient Roman Concrete Construction: An Annotated Bibliography," and "Blondie and Deborah Harry: A Comprehensive Bibliography, 1975-2000," which even lists current Deborah Harry web sites. Each issue includes one to ten book reviews of just-published bibliographies from Greenwood among others. A useful item for more general, or general academic, collections.

1076. *Cambridge Bibliographical Society. Transactions.* [ISSN: 0068-6611] 1949. a. GBP 12; USD 25. Ed(s): Elisabeth Leedham Green. Cambridge Bibliographical Society, c/o Cambridge University Library, West Rd, Cambridge, CB3 9DR, United Kingdom. Illus. Circ: 500. *Indexed:* BHA, IBZ, MLA-IB. *Aud.:* Ac.

Editors of this locally focused publication prefer to publish articles with "some Cambridge connections; those, for example, which deal with manuscripts or printed books in Cambridge libraries, books printed at Cambridge or written by Cambridge authors." The *Transactions* typically includes four to seven well-researched articles along with a brief "Summary of the Society's Activities." Occasional illustrations accompany such articles as John Morehen's "Thomas Snodham, and the Printing of William Byrd's *Psalmes, songs, and sonnets* (1611)" or Nicholas Rogers's "Two Fifteenth-Century *Polychronicions* in Cambridge Collections." For libraries with a strong connection to English book history and libraries, this would be a good selection.

1077. *Gutenberg - Jahrbuch.* [ISSN: 0072-9094] 1926. a. Membership, EUR 60; Non-members, EUR 75. Ed(s): Stephan Fuessel. Gutenberg-Gesellschaft e.V., Liebfrauenplatz 5, Mainz, 55116, Germany; gutenberg-gesellschaft@freenet.de; http://www.gutenberg-gesellschaft.uni-mainz.de. Illus., adv. Circ: 2200. Reprint: PSC. *Indexed:* BHA, IBZ, MLA-IB. *Aud.:* Ac.

The *Yearbook* is published by the International Gutenberg Society, which has more than 2,000 members in nearly 40 countries. This important international journal goes beyond Gutenberg research, encouraging articles on "the early history of printing, the history of printing from the beginning to the present, the history of paper, the history of the library, the history of the book trade and publishing houses, the history of type design, modern typesetting and printing processes, developments in typography and in the new media, book illustration, book binding, newspapers and the press, literature reports on book printing and the art of book-binding." According to the editor, each issue "comes to approximately 400 pages each year, contains up to 30 contributions by authors of international standing from many different countries in English, French, German, Italian, and/or Spanish." All issues are handsomely bound and well illustrated.

1078. *Harvard Library Bulletin.* Former titles (until 1942): *Harvard University Library Notes;* (until 1940): *Harvard Library Notes.* [ISSN: 0017-8136] 1920. q. USD 35 domestic; USD 41 foreign. Ed(s): William P. Stoneman. Harvard University Library, Wadsworth House, Cambridge, MA 02138; libraries@harvard; http://www.harvard.edu/. Illus. Circ: 1500. Vol. ends: Winter. Microform: MIM; PQC. Reprint: PQC. *Indexed:* ABS&EES, AmH&L, ArtHuCI, BAS, BHA, IBZ, IDP, LISA, LibLit, MLA-IB, SSCI. *Aud.:* Ac.

The *Harvard Library Bulletin* is designed to showcase research based on the holdings of the Harvard University Libraries. In articles often written by Harvard faculty and staff, specific topics are as varied as the libraries' enormous collections and are certainly of interest to those beyond the Harvard community. Recent issues include such wide-ranging titles as "Thomas Hollis of London and his Gifts: 275 Years of Piety and Philanthropy at Harvard" by Peter J. Gomes, and "The Measure of Ruins: Dilettanti in the Levant, 1750-1770" by Bruce Redford. While many issues consist of three or four well-researched articles, often around a particular theme, some issues are entirely devoted to catalogs of exhibitions or definitive bibliographies of authors, collections, or areas of research. The journal is elegantly printed in an oversized format and generously illustrated.

1079. *Huntington Library Quarterly: studies in English and American history and literature.* [ISSN: 0018-7895] 1937. q. USD 120 print & online eds. USD 40 newsstand/cover. Ed(s): Susan Green. University of California Press, Journals Division, 2000 Center St, Ste 303, Berkeley, CA 94704-1223; journals@ucop.edu; http://www.ucpress.edu/journals. Illus., index, adv. Sample. Refereed. Circ: 800 Paid. Vol. ends: Fall. Microform: PQC. Online: Gale Group; Northern Light Technology, Inc.; OCLC Online Computer Library Center, Inc.; ProQuest Information & Learning. Reprint: PQC; PSC. *Indexed:* AmH&L, AmHI, BHA, HumInd, MLA-IB, RI-1, SSCI. *Bk. rev.:* 1-4, 1,000-2,500 words. *Aud.:* Ac.

The *Huntington Library Quarterly* invites "scholars working in the history, literature, or art history of the early modern period to submit." Contributors are generally academics, and content is inclusive of diverse theoretical approaches. Recent articles include "Berosus and the Protestants: Reconstructing Protestant Myth" by Glyn Parry, "Elizabethan Parliamentary Oratory" by Peter Mack, and "Spenser's Complaints and the New Poet" by Katharine A. Craik. Articles are followed by a "Notes and Documents" section that includes "short pieces on specific subjects or pieces of up to 15,000 words devoted to the content of archival material (including transcriptions of manuscripts)," reviews, and "Intramuralia." In 1999, a new section was introduced: "Intramuralia: Acquisitions of Rare Materials," which "will present an annual comprehensive list of current additions to the Library's research collections." This is in addition to the ongoing "Intramuralia Notes" section in which curators report on single significant acquisitions. This is a valuable journal from one of the most prominent private libraries in the United States.

1080. *John Rylands University Library of Manchester. Bulletin.* Formerly: *John Rylands Library. Bulletin.* [ISSN: 0301-102X] 1903. 3x/yr. GBP 60. Ed(s): Dorothy Clayton. John Rylands University Library, John Rylands University, Oxford Rd, Manchester, M13 9PP, United Kingdom; d.clayton@man.ac.uk; http://rylibweb.man.ac.uk. Illus., index, adv. Refereed. Circ: 700. Vol. ends: Autumn. Microform: IDC. *Indexed:* AmH&L, ArtHuCI, BAS, BEL&L, BHA, BrArAb, BrHumI, IBZ, MLA-IB, NTA, NumL, OTA, R&TA, RI-1. *Aud.:* Ac.

This bulletin "publishes methodological, interpretive or substantive articles in any subject from the arts and social sciences (understood in the broadest possible sense) and on the historical or philosophical aspects of the natural and physical sciences." The editor notes that "in selecting contributions, special interest will always be shown in those which are of an interdisciplinary nature and/or which incorporate the results of research in the extensive collections of the John Rylands University Library of Manchester." Each issue includes three or four scholarly articles by academic contributors and the occasional catalog or finding aid for materials at the Rylands Library. Recent contributions include David Adams's "Jean-Baptiste de Secondat's marginalia in Boulainvilliers's 'Etat de la France'" and Peter B. Nockles's "A disputed legacy: Anglican historiographies of the Reformation from the era of the Caroline divines to that of the Oxford Movement." A thoughtful journal that explicity recognizes interdisciplinary possibilities for bibliographic research.

1081. *The Library: the transactions of the Bibliographical Society.* [ISSN: 0024-2160] 1899. q. GBP 110. Ed(s): Dr. Oliver Pickering, Nicolas Bell. Oxford University Press, Great Clarendon St, Oxford, OX2 6DP, United Kingdom; jnl.orders@oup.co.uk; http://www3.oup.co.uk/jnls. Illus., index, adv. Refereed. Circ: 1200. Vol. ends: Dec. Microform: PQC. *Indexed:* AmH&L, ArtHuCI, BHA, BRI, BrArAb, CBRI, LibLit, LingAb, MLA-IB, NumL. *Bk. rev.:* 6-13, 1,000-2,000 words. *Aud.:* Ac.

Founded in England in 1892, the Bibliographical Society is the oldest learned society dealing with the study of the book and its history. *The Library* is published by Oxford University Press on behalf of the society. It covers "all aspects of descriptive and historical bibliography that come within its scope, including the general and economic history of the production and distribution of books, paper, printing types, illustration, and binding, as well as the transmission of texts and their authenticity." Issues generally include four or five scholarly articles such as Robert Costomiris's "Some new light on the early career of William Thynne, Chief Clerk of the Kitchen of Henry VIII and Editor of Chaucer" and David Stoker's "William Proctor, Nathaniel Ponder, and the financing of *Pilgrim's Progress*." Articles are followed by a substantial book review section followed by a listing of recent books and periodicals organized by country. A comprehensive index is issued annually. One of the most prominent journals in the field, it is a staple item in most American academic research libraries.

1082. *Matrix (Herefordshire): a review for printers and bibliophiles.* [ISSN: 0261-3093] 1981. a. GBP 90. Ed(s): John Randle. Whittington Press, Lower Marston Farm, Near Risbury, HR6 0NJ, United Kingdom; http://www.whittingtonpress.com. Illus. Circ: 1000. *Indexed:* ABM. *Bk. rev.:* 4-12, 1,000-2,500 words. *Aud.:* Ac, Sa.

Designed to appeal to printers and bibliophiles, each *Matrix* is limited to 850 copies and finely printed by the Whittington Press on laid paper with great attention the details of illustration and typography. One recent issue was advertised as containing "the usual kaleidoscope of ingredients: autolithographic posters, Vietnamese papers, Dard Hunter, private press proprietary types, *La Compagnie Typographiqe*, Warren Editions, 84- to 228-point Caslon, German typefounders specimens, Robert Gibbings, Parisian Printers, *The Architectural Review*, Compton Press, the engravings of Raymond Hawthorn, and much else besides, all profusely illustrated." This beautiful, book-length journal (approximately 240 pages each) might best be placed in a library's special collection or rare book room.

1083. *Princeton University Library Chronicle.* [ISSN: 0032-8456] 1939. 3x/yr. USD 30 (Membership, USD 50). Ed(s): Gretchen N Oberfrane. Friends of Princeton University Library, 1 Washington Rd, Princeton, NJ 08544; principi@princeton.edu; http://www.priceton.edu/~rbsc/Friends. Illus., index. Refereed. Circ: 1250 Paid. Vol. ends: Spring. Microform: PQC. *Indexed:* AmH&L, BAS, BHA, HumInd, LibLit, MLA-IB. *Aud.:* Ac.

The purpose of the *Princeton University Library Chronicle* is threefold: "to record noteworthy acquisitions of the Princeton University Library; to describe the Library's special collections; and to publish articles of general literary, bibliographical, and historical interest, particularly on subjects relating to materials in the Library." It generally contains three to five high quality articles on varied topics. Occasionally, an issue may consist of a catalog of an exhibition or the celebration of a gift to the library. Special thematic issues may include several articles and an introductory essay by the editor. For example, a recent special issue is entirely devoted the collection of literature and poetry pertaining to Jewish literature and literary culture with over 60 articles, poems, and extracts from works of fiction. The *Chronicle* closely resembles British models (especially the *Bodleian Library Record*) in its local flavor. Regular features include "Library Notes," news and information such as the latest winner of the Princeton book-collecting prize essay; "New and Notable," remarks on new acquisitions; and a "Friends of the Library" section. Each issue also contains a "Cover Note," a short essay on the significance of the illustration on the cover including its connection to the issue's contents.

1084. *The Private Library.* [ISSN: 0032-8898] 1957. q. GBP 25; USD 40. Ed(s): David Chambers, Paul Nash. Private Libraries Association, Ravelston, South View Rd, Pinner, HA5 3YD, United Kingdom. Illus., adv. Sample. Circ: 800. Vol. ends: Winter. *Indexed:* BHA, LISA, LibLit. *Bk. rev.:* 1-3, 500-3,000 words. *Aud.:* Sa.

Based in the United Kingdom, the Private Libraries Association is "an international society of book collectors—collectors of rare books, fine books, single authors, special subjects and, above all, collectors of books for the simple pleasures of reading and ownership." *The Private Library*, a journal for true bibliophiles and book collectors, contains signed articles, checklists, and book reviews. Volumes are slim, illustrated, and directed toward a more popular audience than other journals in the field. Often a list of "Recent Private Press Books" is included. Said to concentrate on "books that can be collected *today,*" *The Private Library* accurately boasts that its essays contain "any aspect of the mania likely to appeal to collectors."

1085. *Publishing History: the social, economic and literary history of book, newspaper, and magazine publishing.* [ISSN: 0309-2445] 1977. s-a. GBP 67 (Individuals, GBP 33). Ed(s): Peter Cockton. Chadwyck-Healey Inc., 300 N Zeeb Rd, PO Box 1346, Ann Arbor, MI 48103-1553; info@il.proquest.com; http://www.chadwyck.com. Illus., adv. Circ: 500. *Indexed:* AmH&L, ArtHuCI, BEL&L, BrHumI, MLA-IB. *Bk. rev.:* 1-2, 1,500-4,500 words. *Aud.:* Ac.

A significant journal in the emerging field of "history of the book," *Publishing History* "covers the whole spectrum of publishing from the author to the reader, and contains scholarly articles; memoirs by contemporary publishers; conference papers; archive listings; and reviews, annotations and facsimile reprints of important documents relating to the history of publishing." While most contributors are academics, independent scholars and book-history specialists also publish here. Each issue contains two to four well-documented articles firmly grounded in primary source research, such as John R. Turner's "Joint Publishing Agreements 1850-1919" and Warwick Gould's "Yeats in the States: Piracy, Copyright and the Shaping of the Canon," as well as the occasional checklist (e.g., Clare Hutton's "A Checklist of the Publications of Maunsel and Co., Irish Publishers, 1905-1925"). This important journal, like its cousin *Book History,* crosses disciplinary boundaries in important new ways.

Quaerendo: a quarterly journal from the Low Countries devoted to manuscripts and printed books. See Printing and Graphic Arts section.

1086. ***Scriptorium: international review of manuscript studies and bulletin codicologique (book reviews).*** [ISSN: 0036-9772] 1947. s-a. BEF 6050. Ed(s): P Cockshaw. Centre d'Etudes des Manuscrits, Bd de l'Empereur 4, Brussels, 1000, Belgium. Illus., adv. Circ: 900. Vol. ends: No. 2. *Indexed:* ArtHuCI, BEL&L, BHA, IPB, MLA-IB, NTA, RILM. *Bk. rev.:* 0-14, 1,000-3,000 words. *Aud.:* Ac.

An important journal in international bibliography and medieval studies, *Scriptorium* generally includes scholarly articles in French, English, German, Italian, and Spanish. A recent issue publishes several papers from the Ninth International Colloquium on International Paleography held at the Vatican Library. Most issues include three or four articles on medieval manuscripts followed by notes, book reviews, and a large section devoted to abstracts of publications in the field. Each *Scriptorium* concludes with a comprehensive index of all titles noted in the journal. Taken together, the run forms an indispensable ongoing index of information about medieval manuscripts.

1087. ***Studies in Bibliography.*** [ISSN: 0081-7600] 1948. a. USD 40. Ed(s): D Vander Meulen. University Press of Virginia, PO Box 400318, Charlottesville, VA 22904-4318; dlv8g@virginia.edu; webmaster@www.upress.virginia.edu; http://etext.lib.virginai.edu/bsuva.html; http://www.upress.virginia.edu. Illus. Circ: 2000. *Indexed:* ArtHuCI, IBZ, MLA-IB. *Aud.:* Ac.

A very highly respected journal, *Studies in Bibliography* has been stewarded by some of America's best known bibliographers including founding editor Fredson Bowers, current editor David L. Vander Meulen, and frequent contributor G. Thomas Tanselle. "The editors invite articles and notes on analytical bibliography, textual criticism, manuscript study, the history of printing and publishing, as well as related matters of method and evidence." Recent contributions include "Back at Chaucer's Tomb—Inscriptions in Two Early Copies of Chaucer's *Workes*" by Joseph A. Dane and Alexandra Gillespie, and "~A Sort of Bird's Eye View of the British Land of Letters': *The Monthly Magazine* and its Reviewers, 1796-1811" by David Chandler. Each annual volume contains up to fifteen scholarly articles and a list of society publications. Articles are generally unillustrated and thoroughly documented. The first 52 volumes are now available online at etext.lib.virginia.edu/bsuva/sb.

1088. ***Yale University Library Gazette.*** [ISSN: 0044-0175] 1926. s-a. USD 20. Ed(s): Stephen Parks. Yale University Library, PO Box 208240, New Haven, CT 06520-8240; stephen.parks@yale.edu; http://www.library.yale.edu/. Illus., index. Circ: 1500. Vol. ends: Apr. Online: EBSCO Publishing. *Indexed:* AmH&L, BEL&L, BHA, IBZ, LibLit, MLA-IB. *Aud.:* Ac.

The semiannual *Yale University Library Gazette* "contains articles based on the collections in the various divisions of the Yale Library, along with news of recent acquisitions and occasionally, catalogs of current exhibitions." Three to six scholarly articles, based on in-depth research with primary sources found at Yale, make up each issue. Recent examples include "The Odious, Canting, Worthless Author of this Book": Edmond Malone's Annotations to Sir John Hawkins' *Life of Samuel Johnson, LL.D.* (1787)" by Michael F. Suarez and "Edith Wharton and Ronald Simmons: Documenting a Pivotal Wartime Friendship" by Frederick Wegener. Regular features are "The Gazette," a recounting of newsworthy events at Yale libraries including lectures, conferences, tours, awards, readings, exhibitions, and celebrations; "Notable Bindings;" "Marginalia," brief narrative descriptions of the history and importance of specific items in the collections; obituaries of Yale Library notables; a list of "Beinecke Library Visiting Fellows" and their research topics; and "Recent Acquisitions Briefly Noted." Another valuable journal showcasing research done in an exceptional library collection.

■ BIOLOGICAL SCIENCES

Biochemistry and Biophysics/Botany/Cell Biology/Developmental Biology/Ecology/Genetics/Microbiology/Molecular Biology/ Multidisciplinary/Physiology/Specialty Titles/Vertebrate and Invertebrate Zoology

See also Agriculture; Birds; Environment, Conservation, and Outdoor Recreation; Marine Science and Technology; and Science and Technology sections.

Connie Dalrymple, Life and Health Sciences Librarian, Wichita State University Libraries, Wichita State University, Wichita, KS 67260-0068

Introduction

The biological sciences have an enormous publishing presence and consist of a wide array of disciplines, including biochemistry and biophysics, botany, cell biology, developmental biology, ecology, evolutionary biology, genetics, molecular biology, microbiology, physiology, and zoology. Many of these areas also have subdisciplines, each with researchers requiring their own bodies of literature. Genetics, biochemistry, and molecular biology are areas where there is much crossover into other biological disciplines.

The literature of the biological sciences, which is published by various societies and by commercial publishers, has proliferated along with the development of areas of research interest. New specialty titles and new competitors for established journals appear every year. This area also experiences the merging and splitting and changing of titles that occurs in other disciplines, reflecting the ever-changing nature of this branch of science.

Most of the journals in the biological sciences focus primarily on the publication of original research articles, but with a review or minireview, often commissioned, appearing regularly. Another category is the review journal, in which all of the articles consist of reviews of the existing literature on various topics. Other information found in many biology journals includes book reviews, news and announcements, and communications that often discuss work previously published in the journal. Journals publishing original research are preferred by most researchers; it may be necessary to carefully consider the importance of review journals to students and generalists during the inevitable serials review.

Time is of the essence in scientific publishing; many titles are moving toward some form of rapid publication. Some maintain an accelerated publication schedule and advertise the average number of weeks between manuscript acceptance and print publication. Others publish at least some of their contents electronically before the print publication appears. Sometimes this early online information is only a table of contents; in other cases, it is the full text. Many titles now have online supplemental material that is not published in the print version. Another variant is to publish some sections online with only a summary appearing in the print publication.

Online content is increasingly important. Every journal in this section has at least some online presence. Most of the web sites are updated regularly and are quite useful; a few leave something to be desired in terms of user-friendliness, content, and or timely updating. Information can range from subscription and contact information to full text, free online sample issues, and lists of frequently cited articles. Many sites also offer free alerting services, which can be great for current-awareness purposes. In a welcome move, many publishers make freely available their older issues, commonly older than one year, in an effort to share scientific information more freely.

In selecting the titles for inclusion in this section, an attempt was made to mention important titles and to cover as broad a range of subdisciplines as possible. For the most part, the subject-specific nature of these journals, the depth of scientific knowledge required to benefit from the papers, and the high subscription costs will restrict these journals to academic and research library collections. A select few are appropriate for a more general readership, which is indicated in the annotations.

Basic Periodicals

Hs: *American Biology Teacher;* Ga: *BioScience;* Ac: *American Journal of Botany, Biochemistry, Cell, Ecology, Genetics, Integrative and Comparative*

Biology, Microbiology and Molecular Biology Reviews, Physiological Reviews, National Academy of Sciences. Proceedings, Quarterly Review of Biology.

Basic Abstracts and Indexes

Biological Abstracts, Biological Abstracts/RRM, Biological and Agricultural Index, Biology Digest, Current Contents/Agriculture, Current Contents/Life Sciences.

Biochemistry and Biophysics

1089. *Analytical Biochemistry: methods in the biological sciences.* [ISSN: 0003-2697] 1960. 24x/yr. EUR 5393 (Individuals, EUR 2622). Ed(s): William B Jakoby, J.K. Baker. Academic Press, 525 B St, Ste 1900, San Diego, CA 92101-4495; apsubs@acad.com; http://www.academicpress.com. Illus., index, adv. Refereed. Online: EBSCO Publishing; ingenta.com; OCLC Online Computer Library Center, Inc.; RoweCom Information Quest; ScienceDirect; Swets Blackwell. *Indexed:* BiolAb, ChemAb, DSA, DSR&OA, ExcerpMed, FS&TA, HortAb, IndMed, IndVet, S&F, SCI, VetBull. *Bk. rev.:* 0-2, 240-500 words. *Aud.:* Ac, Sa.

This journal publishes methods and methodology of interest to the biological sciences and biochemistry. The scope includes cell biology; cell, tissue, and organ culture; membranes and membrane proteins; recombinant technology; molecular genetics; novel and generally applicable purification of enzymes and other proteins; immunological techniques; and pharmacological and toxicological research. Article types include full-length research articles; short "Notes and Tips"; and reviews of current interest. Online content is available through Elsevier's ScienceDirect. An online sample issue is available. This journal is expensive but well-regarded and widely used in academic and research libraries. Document delivery is available from BLDSC, CASDDS, CISTI, EMDOCS, The Genuine Article, LHLDS, UMI, and UnCover.

1090. *B B A - Biochimica et Biophysica Acta: international journal of biochemistry and biophysics.* [ISSN: 0006-3002] 1947. 133x/yr. EUR 13218 in Europe subscription to all 9 sections; JPY, 1757500 Japan subscription to all 9 sections; USD 14786 elsewhere subscription to all 9 sections. Ed(s): Dr. G. Evan. Elsevier BV, Sara Burgerhartstraat 25, Amsterdam, 1055 KV, Netherlands; nlinfo-f@elsevier.nl; http://www.elsevier.nl. Illus., index, adv. Refereed. Circ: 4500. Microform: PQC. Online: EBSCO Publishing. *Indexed:* Agr, BiolAb, ChemAb, ExcerpMed, FS&TA, GeoRef, IndMed, VetBull. *Aud.:* Ac, Sa.

This important collection of journals publishes papers in biochemistry, biophysics, and molecular biology. There are currently nine individual sections, and subscribers may order the full set or individual titles. The individual sections are *BBA-Bioenergetics, BBA-Biomembranes, BBA-Gene Structure and Expression, BBA-General Subjects, BBA-Molecular and Cell Biology of Lipids, BBA-Molecular Basis of Disease, BBA-Molecular Cell Research, BBA-Proteins and Proteomics*, and *BBA-Reviews on Cancer.* The focus is primarily on original research but all of the sections also publish review articles, most of which are invited. A helpful cumulative author/title index is published annually. Online content, including full text and a free sample issue, are available on Elsevier's ScienceDirect. This journal, while expensive, is considered a core title for researchers. Libraries supporting biology programs should consider purchasing individual titles that would support their patron base. Further information about the individual sections, including a publication schedule, pricing, and tables of contents, may be viewed at Elsevier's web site. Document delivery is available from ADONIS, CASDDS, CISTI, The Genuine Article, LHLDS, and UnCover.

1091. *Biochemical and Biophysical Research Communications.* [ISSN: 0006-291X] 1959. w. EUR 6095 (Individuals, EUR 3850; Students, EUR 1927). Ed(s): W. Baumeister. Academic Press, 525 B St, Ste 1900, San Diego, CA 92101-4495; apsubs@acad.com; http://www.academicpress.com. Illus., index, adv. Refereed. Online: EBSCO Publishing; ingenta.com; OCLC Online Computer Library Center, Inc.; RoweCom Information Quest; ScienceDirect; Swets Blackwell. *Indexed:* Agr, BiolAb, ChemAb, DSA, ExcerpMed, FPA, FS&TA, ForAb, HortAb, IndMed, IndVet, S&F, SCI, VetBull, ZooRec. *Aud.:* Ac, Sa.

This journal is "very rapid dissemination (six weeks) of timely and significant experimental results in the diverse fields of biological research." The range of coverage of the journal is broad, including Biochemistry, Biophysics, Cell Biology, Developmental Biology, Immunology, Molecular Biology, Neurobiology, Plant Biology, and Proteomics. Online full text is available from 1993 forward via Elsevier's ScienceDirect. An online sample issue is also available. Useful for researchers and graduate students in academic and special libraries. Document delivery is available from BLDSC, CASDDS, CISTI, EMDOCS, The Genuine Article, LHLDS, and UnCover.

1092. *Biochemical Journal.* Formed by the merger of: *Biochemical Journal. Part 1: Cellular Aspects; Biochemical Journal. Part 2: Molecular Aspects.* [ISSN: 0264-6021] 1906. s-m. USD 2414 combined subscription in US & Canada for print & online eds.; GBP 1373 combined subscription elsewhere for print & online eds. Ed(s): P J Parker. Portland Press Ltd., 59 Portland Pl, London, W1B 1QW, United Kingdom; editorial@portlandpress.com; http://www.portlandpress.com. Illus., index, adv. Sample. Refereed. Circ: 2300. Microform: PMC; PQC. Online: EBSCO Publishing; RoweCom Information Quest; Swets Blackwell. *Indexed:* Agr, BiolAb, ChemAb, DSA, EngInd, ExcerpMed, FS&TA, ForAb, HortAb, IndMed, IndVet, S&F, SCI, VetBull. *Aud.:* Ac, Sa.

Biochemical Journal, published for the Biochemical Society, presents papers in "all fields of biochemistry and cellular and molecular biology." Reports of theoretical and experimental work are both accepted. Article types include research papers, research communications, and reviews. The online edition is available one week earlier than the paper edition, and online issues from past years are available free to all Internet users. Full text is available from 1996 with abstracts being available from 1975 on at the Biochemical Society's Portland Press web site. An online sample issue and a current awareness service are available. The current year's issues are available online only to subscribers, while previous issues are freely available. This is a valuable and highly cited title. Document delivery is available from BLDSC, CASDDS, CISTI, EMDOCS, The Genuine Article, LHLDS, NIWI, UnCover, and UMI.

1093. *Biochemistry.* [ISSN: 0006-2960] 1962. 51x/yr. USD 2906 (Individual members, USD 380; Students, USD 285). Ed(s): Dr. Gordon G Hammes. American Chemical Society, 1155 16th St, N W, Washington, DC 20036; service@acs.org; http://pubs.acs.org. Illus., index, adv. Refereed. Circ: 6200. Vol. ends: Dec. Online: EBSCO Publishing; Gale Group; Swets Blackwell. *Indexed:* Agr, B&AI, BiolAb, ChemAb, DSA, DSR&OA, EngInd, EnvAb, ExcerpMed, FS&TA, ForAb, GSI, HortAb, IndMed, IndVet, S&F, SCI, VetBull, ZooRec. *Aud.:* Ac, Sa.

This weekly journal, publishing approximately 17,000 pages annually, covers such topics as the structure, function, and regulation of biologically active molecules, gene structure and expression, protein biosynthesis and folding, membrane structure-function relationships, bioenergetics, and immunochemistry. A subscription to ACS Web Editions allows online access to the current year's subscription plus the four previous years. Older issues, back to 1962, may be accessed online via a separate subscription to the ACS Journal Archives. *Biochemistry* is an important journal for academic or special libraries with biology or chemistry collections. Document delivery is available from BLDSC, CASDDS, CISTI, EMDOCS, The Genuine Article, LHLDS, NIWI, UMI, and UnCover.

1094. *Biochemistry and Cell Biology.* Former titles (until 1986): *Canadian Journal of Biochemistry and Cell Biology - Revue Canadien de Biochimie et Biologie Cellulaire;* (until 1983): *Canadian Journal of Biochemistry;* Which supersedes in part (in 1963): *Canadian Journal of Biochemistry and Physiology;* Which was formerly (until 1954): *Canadian Journal of Medical Sciences;* (until 1950): *Canadian Journal of Research. Section E: Medical Sciences.* [ISSN: 0829-8211] 1929. bi-m. CND 350 (Individuals, CND 116). Ed(s): Dr. David L Brown, Martin Tenniswood. N R C Research Press, Building M 55, Ottawa, ON

K1A 0R6, Canada; http://www.nrc.ca/cisti/journals/. Illus., index, adv. Sample. Refereed. Circ: 913. Vol. ends: Nov/Dec. Microform: MML; PMC; PQC. Online: CISTI; EBSCO Publishing; ingenta.com; RoweCom Information Quest; Swets Blackwell. Reprint: PQC. *Indexed:* Agr, B&AI, BiolAb, CBCARef, ChemAb, DSA, EngInd, ExcerpMed, FS&TA, HortAb, IndMed, IndVet, S&F, SCI, VetBull, ZooRec. *Aud.:* Ac, Sa.

First published in 1929, this journal explores every aspect of general biochemistry, and includes up-to-date coverage of experimental research into cellular and molecular biology, review articles on topics of current interest, and notes contributed by recognized international experts. Special issues are dedicated to expanding new areas of research in biochemistry and cell biology. Papers are published electronically within 6 weeks of acceptance. While both English and French papers are published, the majority seem to be in English. Print and electronic access are separate subscriptions. An online sample issue is available. Published by the respected National Research Council of Canada, this journal is appropriate for most biology collections. Document delivery is available from ADONIS, BLDSC, CASDDS, CISTI, The Genuine Article, LHLDS, NIWI, UMI, and UnCover.

1095. *Biophysical Journal.* [ISSN: 0006-3495] 1960. m. USD 865 domestic; USD 980 Canada; USD 915 elsewhere. Ed(s): Robert Callender. Biophysical Society, 9650 Rockville Pike, Bethesda, MD 20814; ckenney@biophysics.org; http://www.biophysics.org/. Illus., index, adv. Refereed. Microform: PQC. Online: EBSCO Publishing; HighWire Press; Northern Light Technology, Inc.; ProQuest Information & Learning; RoweCom Information Quest. *Indexed:* Agr, ApMecR, BiolAb, ChemAb, DSA, DSR&OA, EngInd, ExcerpMed, FS&TA, HortAb, IndMed, IndVet, SCI, VetBull. *Aud.:* Ac, Sa.

Biophysical Journal publishes "original articles, letters and reviews on biophysical topics, emphasizing the molecular and cellular aspects of biology." Article categories vary slightly from issue to issue but include bioenergetics; biophysical theory and modeling; cell biophysics; channels, receptors, and transporters; membranes; muscle and contractility; nucleic acids; photobiophysics; supramolecular assemblies; electrophysiology; proteins; and spectroscopy, imaging, and other techniques. The program and abstracts for the annual meeting of the Biophysical Society are included as part of the subscription. The online edition of the journal, available on Stanford's HighWire Press, is a separate subscription and contains content from 1976 to the present, with coverage varying from tables of contents through full text. Also included on the site is a useful "Biophysics on the Internet" listing maintained by the Biophysical Society. A leading journal in the area of biophysics, this title is suitable for academic and special libraries. Document delivery is available from BLDSC, CASDDS, CISTI, EMDOCS, The Genuine Article, LHLDS, UnCover, and UMI.

1096. *European Journal of Biochemistry: the FEBS journal.* Formerly (Until 1967): *Biochemische Zeitschrift.* [ISSN: 0014-2956] 1906. fortn. GBP 1800 print & online eds. Ed(s): Richard Perham. Blackwell Publishing Ltd., 9600 Garsington Rd, Oxford, OX4 2ZG, United Kingdom; customerservices@oxon.blackwellpublishing.com; http://www.blackwellpublishing.com. Illus., index, adv. Refereed. Circ: 1950. Microform: PQC. Online: EBSCO Publishing; HighWire Press; ingenta.com; Munksgaard & Blackwell Science's Synergy; OCLC Online Computer Library Center, Inc.; Ovid Technologies, Inc.; RoweCom Information Quest; Swets Blackwell. Reprint: ISI. *Indexed:* Agr, B&AI, BiolAb, ChemAb, DSA, EngInd, ExcerpMed, FPA, FS&TA, ForAb, HortAb, IndMed, IndVet, S&F, SCI, VetBull, ZooRec. *Aud.:* Ac, Sa.

Published by the respected Federation of European Biochemical Societies (FEBS), the *European Journal of Biochemistry* prints "original research in the areas of biochemistry, molecular and cell biology, and molecular biophysics." Reviews and minireviews are also published. Online content is made available through Blackwell's Synergy and Stanford's HighWire Press. A free sample issue, an alerting service, and full text from 1998 forward are available. As a service to the scientific community, review articles in all issues are freely available, as are all articles one year after publication. This journal will be useful in libraries supporting biology and chemistry researchers. Document delivery is available from ADONIS, BLDSC, CASDDS, CISTI, EI, EMDOCS, The Genuine Article, LHLDS, NIWI, UMI, and UnCover

1097. *F E B S Letters.* [ISSN: 0014-5793] 1968. 69x/yr. EUR 3856 (Individuals, EUR 574). Ed(s): F. Wieland. Elsevier BV, Sara Burgerhartstraat 25, Amsterdam, 1055 KV, Netherlands; nlinfo-f@elsevier.nl; http://www.elsevier.nl. Illus., index, adv. Refereed. Circ: Controlled. Microform: PQC. Online: ingenta.com; ScienceDirect. Reprint: ISI. *Indexed:* BiolAb, ChemAb, DSA, EnvAb, ExcerpMed, FPA, FS&TA, ForAb, GeoRef, HortAb, IndMed, IndVet, S&F, SCI, VetBull. *Aud.:* Ac, Sa.

Published by the Federation of European Biochemical Societies (FEBS), *FEBS Letters* purpose is the "most rapid possible publication of essentially final short papers in the field of biochemistry, biophysics and molecular cell biology."' Some of the subjects treated include protein chemistry, enzymology, nucleic acid chemistry, metabolism, immunochemistry, and structural biology. Papers fall into "Research Letters," "Minireviews," and "Hypotheses" categories. Online access to the full text of current issues is restricted to print subscribers via Elsevier's ScienceDirect. After 12 months, access becomes free to all. Several special issues are published annually and may consist of conference papers or papers on a specific topic. Special issues and minireviews are available free to all online. Statistics on impact factor and citations to the journal are included on the journal's web site. An expensive but important journal for researchers in academic or special libraries. Document delivery is available from ADONIS, BLDSC, CASDDS, CISTI, EMDOCS, The Genuine Article, LHLDS, UMI, and UnCover.

1098. *Journal of Biochemistry.* [ISSN: 0021-924X] 1922. m. USD 240. Japanese Biochemical Society, 26-16 Hongo 5-chome, Bunkyo-ku, Tokyo, 113-0033, Japan; jbs-ho@bcasj.or.jp; http://jb.bcasj.or.jp/. Illus., index, adv. Refereed. Circ: 2650. Microform: PMC. *Indexed:* Agr, BiolAb, ChemAb, DSA, DSR&OA, EngInd, ExcerpMed, FS&TA, ForAb, HortAb, IndMed, IndVet, S&F, SCI, VetBull. *Aud.:* Ac, Sa.

Journal of Biochemistry, published by the Japanese Biochemical Society, features articles on biochemistry, biotechnology, molecular biology, and cell biology. Articles consist of regular research papers, shorter rapid communications, and short reviews, all published in English. More details about specific areas of interest are available on the journal's web site in the information section. Tables of contents and full text since 1996 are available for free to all on the web site. This journal, with its broad scope and inexpensive subscription price, is appropriate for academic and special libraries supporting biologists, chemists, physiologists, and physicians. Document delivery is available from BLDSC, CASDDS, CISTI, EI, The Genuine Article, LHLDS, UMI, and UnCover.

1099. *Journal of Biological Chemistry.* [ISSN: 0021-9258] 1905. w. USD 1600; USD 1962 Canada; USD 1850 elsewhere. Ed(s): Herbert Tabor. American Society for Biochemistry and Molecular Biology, Inc., 9650 Rockville Pike, Bethesda, MD 20814-3996; asbmb@asbmb.faseb.org; http://www.asbmb.org. Illus., index, adv. Refereed. Circ: 6000. Vol. ends: Dec. Microform: PMC; PQC. Online: EBSCO Publishing; HighWire Press; RoweCom Information Quest. Reprint: PQC. *Indexed:* Agr, B&AI, BiolAb, ChemAb, DSA, DSR&OA, EngInd, ExcerpMed, FPA, FS&TA, ForAb, HortAb, IndMed, IndVet, S&F, SCI, VetBull, ZooRec. *Aud.:* Ac, Sa.

Journal of Biological Chemistry is an authoritative journal published by the American Society for Biochemistry and Molecular Biology. Issues consist of around 1,000 pages and contain a wide range of topics including developmental biology, computational biology, metabolism, protein chemistry, and nucleic acids. Research articles are complemented by minireviews and "Accelerated Publications," which present new or novel information of special interest to readers. Relevant announcements are also published. Subscription options include print only, online only, and print and online combined. Online full text is available from 1965 to the present via Stanford's HighWire Press and is available for free to issues published before the current year. Essential for academic and special libraries supporting biology programs. Document delivery is available from BLDSC, CASDDS, CISTI, The Genuine Article, LHLDS, NIWI, UMI, and UnCover.

Botany

1100. *American Journal of Botany: devoted to all branches of plant sciences.* [ISSN: 0002-9122] 1914. m. USD 295 domestic; USD 305 in Canada & Mexico; USD 320 elsewhere. Ed(s): Karl V Niklas. Botanical Society of America, Inc. (Columbus), Business Office, 1735 Neil Ave, Columbus, OH 43210-1293; orders@allenpress.com; http://www.botany.org/bsa/ajb/index.html; http://www.allenpress.com. Illus., adv. Refereed. Circ: 5000. Microform: IDC; PMC. Online: EBSCO Publishing; Gale Group; HighWire Press; JSTOR (Web-based Journal Archive); OCLC Online Computer Library Center, Inc.; H.W. Wilson. *Indexed:* Agr, ApEcolAb, B&AI, BiolAb, BiolDig, CAPS, ChemAb, DSR&OA, ExcerpMed, FPA, ForAb, GSI, GeoRef, HortAb, OceAb, PollutAb, RRTA, S&F, SCI, SWRA, ZooRec. *Aud.:* Ac, Sa.

The official publication of the Botanical Society of America (BSA), *American Journal of Botany* covers all areas of plant science. Papers (18 to 22 per issue) appear in the following subject areas: genetics and molecular biology, anatomy and morphology, development and morphogenesis, ecology, evolution, paleobotany, population biology, reproductive biology, structure and development, and systematics. "Brief Communications" occasionally appear. BSA membership includes *American Journal of Botany, Plant Science Bulletin* (irregular), and a directory of members. Future issues' tables of contents are available four to six weeks in advance on the journal's web site. Online access to the journal is through HighWire Press. For general biology collections. Document delivery is available from BLDSC, CASDDS, CISTI, EMDOCS, The Genuine Article, LHLDS, and UnCover.

1101. *Annals of Botany.* [ISSN: 0305-7364] 1887. 13x/yr. GBP 483. Ed(s): Michael Jackson. Oxford University Press, Great Clarendon St, Oxford, OX2 6DP, United Kingdom; jnl.orders@oup.co.uk; http://www3.oup.co.uk/jnls. Illus., index, adv. Refereed. Microform: IDC; PMC. Online: EBSCO Publishing; HighWire Press; ingenta.com; OCLC Online Computer Library Center, Inc.; Ovid Technologies, Inc.; RoweCom Information Quest; ScienceDirect; Swets Blackwell. Reprint: SWZ. *Indexed:* Agr, ApEcolAb, B&AI, BiolAb, CAPS, ChemAb, ExcerpMed, FPA, FS&TA, ForAb, GeoRef, GeogAbPG, HortAb, OceAb, S&F, SCI, SWRA. *Bk. rev.:* 0-7, 400-900 words. *Aud.:* Ac, Sa.

Annals of Botany serves "to publish on all aspects of the plant sciences, whether observational, experimental, theoretical or applied." Editors cite technical advances in molecular biology, molecular genetics, biochemistry, and computing, as well as increasing concerns for the environment and the ability to support the growing population of the earth, as issues of special importance to the journal. At least once annually a special issue focusing on specific theme is published. Papers fall into one of several categories: research papers, short communications, and invited and submitted review articles and book reviews. Online abstracts and text are available from 1993 forward via Oxford Journals Online. An online sample issue is available. This journal is appropriate for academic institutions with programs in botany. Document delivery is available from BLDSC, CASDDS, CISTI, EMDOCS, The Genuine Article, and UnCover.

1102. *The Botanical Review: interpreting botanical progress.* [ISSN: 0006-8101] 1935. q. USD 96 (Individuals, USD 82). Ed(s): Dennis W Stevenson. New York Botanical Garden Press, The New York Botanical Garden, Bronx, NY 10458-5126; http://www.nybg.org. Illus., adv. Sample. Refereed. Circ: 2000. Vol. ends: Oct/Dec. Microform: IDC; PMC; PQC. Online: Florida Center for Library Automation; Gale Group; Northern Light Technology, Inc.; OCLC Online Computer Library Center, Inc.; H.W. Wilson. *Indexed:* Agr, B&AI, BiolAb, ChemAb, DSR&OA, EnvAb, FPA, ForAb, GSI, GeoRef, HortAb, S&F, SCI, SSCI. *Aud.:* Ac, Sa.

Botanical Review publishes "syntheses of the state of knowledge and understanding of individual segments of botany." Articles are primarily obtained via invitation, but unsolicited manuscripts are also considered. Between one and four reviews are published in most issues, generally with extensive bibliographies that can be very helpful in giving researchers an overview of the literature in an area. The publication schedule appears to be slightly irregular. The most recent online content, featuring abstracts, available through the New York Botanical Garden web site is from 2000 and was more than two years out of date at this writing. This journal will be useful in academic and special libraries in institutions with biology programs. Document delivery is available from BLDSC, CASDDS, CISTI, The Genuine Article, LHLDS, UMI, and UnCover.

1103. *Canadian Journal of Botany.* Formerly (until 1950): *Canadian Journal of Research. Section B: Botanical Sciences;* Which superseded in part (in 1935): *Canadian Journal of Research.* [ISSN: 0008-4026] 1929. m. CND 627 (Individuals, CND 207). Ed(s): I E P Taylor. N R C Research Press, Building M 55, Ottawa, ON K1A 0R6, Canada; http://www.nrc.ca/cisti/journals/. Illus., index, adv. Refereed. Circ: 1506. Vol. ends: Dec. Microform: MML; PMC; PQC. Online: CISTI; EBSCO Publishing; ingenta.com; RoweCom Information Quest; Swets Blackwell. Reprint: PQC. *Indexed:* ABS&EES, Agr, ApEcolAb, B&AI, BiolAb, CBCARef, ChemAb, DSR&OA, EngInd, EnvAb, ExcerpMed, FPA, FS&TA, ForAb, GeoRef, GeogAbPG, HortAb, IndVet, PollutAb, RRTA, S&F, SCI, SWRA, WAE&RSA, ZooRec. *Aud.:* Ac, Sa.

The *Canadian Journal of Botany* publishes "comprehensive research in all segments of plant science including cell and molecular biology, ecology, mycology, physiology and biochemistry, structure and development, systematics, phytogeography, and paleobotany." Articles, notes, commentaries, and reviews are the categories into which the papers fall, though conference papers may also be published. Papers in both English and French are published, though English predominates. Published by the well-regarded National Research Council of Canada, this journal is appropriate for most collections serving biology programs. Tables of contents and a sample issue are freely available on the NRC web site. Online full-text access and print are separate subscriptions, though a discount is available to libraries wishing to purchase both. Document delivery is available from BLDSC, CASDDS, CISTI, EMDOCS, The Genuine Article, LHLDS, UMI, and UnCover.

1104. *Economic Botany: devoted to applied botany and plant utilization.* [ISSN: 0013-0001] 1947. q. USD 102 (Individuals, USD 88). Ed(s): Lawrence Kaplan. New York Botanical Garden Press, The New York Botanical Garden, Bronx, NY 10458-5126; nybgpress@nybg.org; http://www.nybg.org. Illus., index, adv. Sample. Refereed. Circ: 2000. Vol. ends: Oct/Dec. Microform: PMC; PQC. Online: BioOne; OCLC Online Computer Library Center, Inc.; H.W. Wilson. *Indexed:* A&ATA, Agr, ArtHuCI, B&AI, BAS, BiolAb, BiolDig, CAPS, ChemAb, DSA, EnvAb, ExcerpMed, FPA, FS&TA, ForAb, HortAb, IndVet, PollutAb, RRTA, S&F, SCI, SSCI, SWRA, VetBull, WAE&RSA. *Bk. rev.:* 2-18, 200-1,200 words. *Aud.:* Ac, Sa.

This quarterly publication of the Society for Economic Botany focuses on "the botany, history, and evolution of useful plants and their modes of use," including the effects of plants on humans and civilization and human impacts on plants. Accompanying the research articles are special reports, news, letters, descriptions of plant collections, and book reviews. Online content through the society's web site included freely available tables of contents and pdf full text at the time of this writing. Due to the broad focus of this journal, it will be of interest to researchers in many disciplines, including anthropologists and agronomists, in addition to botanists. Document delivery is available from BLDSC, CASDDS, CISTI, EMDOCS, The Genuine Article, UMI, and UnCover.

1105. *International Journal of Plant Sciences.* Former titles (until Mar. 1992): *Botanical Gazette;* (until 1876): *Botanical Bulletin.* [ISSN: 1058-5893] 1875. bi-m. USD 588 print & online eds. (Individuals, USD 50 print & online eds.; Students, USD 33 print & online eds.). Ed(s): Manfred Ruddat, Peter R Crane. University of Chicago Press, Journals Division, PO Box 37005, Chicago, IL 60637; subscriptions@journals.uchicago.edu; http://www.journals.uchicago.edu. Illus., index, adv. Sample. Refereed. Circ: 1500. Vol. ends: Nov. Microform: IDC; PMC; PQC. Online: EBSCO Publishing; Florida Center for Library Automation; Gale Group; JSTOR (Web-based Journal Archive); ProQuest Information & Learning. Reprint: ISI; PQC; PSC. *Indexed:* Agr, ApEcolAb, B&AI, BiolAb, BiolDig, CAPS, ChemAb, DSR&OA, ExcerpMed, FPA, FS&TA, ForAb, GSI, GeoRef, HortAb, S&F, SCI, SWRA. *Aud.:* Ac, Sa.

International Journal of Plant Sciences publishes original research papers on such topics as "plant-microbe interactions, development, structure and systematics, molecular biology, genetics and evolution, ecology, paleobotany, and physiology and ecophysiology." Occasionally, a special issue devoted to in-depth analysis of a specific topic or group is published. Online materials are available through the University of Chicago Press from November 1998 forward. JSTOR makes available online full text of issues from 1992 through 1998. A five-year moving wall of coverage in JSTOR will be restored in 2005. Precursors *Botanical Gazette* and *Botanical Bulletin* are also available in JSTOR. This title will be useful in academic and special libraries supporting botany and general biology programs. Document delivery is available from BLDSC, CASDDS, CISTI, EMDOCS, The Genuine Article, LHLDS, UMI, and UnCover.

1106. *Journal of Experimental Botany.* [ISSN: 0022-0957] 1950. 14x/yr. GBP 733. Ed(s): W J Davies. Oxford University Press, Great Clarendon St, Oxford, OX2 6DP, United Kingdom; jnl.orders@oup.co.uk; http://www3.oup.co.uk/jnls. Illus., index, adv. Sample. Refereed. Circ: 1400. Vol. ends: Dec. Microform: PQC. Online: EBSCO Publishing; HighWire Press; ingenta.com; RoweCom Information Quest; Swets Blackwell. Reprint: PSC. *Indexed:* Agr, B&AI, BiolAb, CAPS, ChemAb, DSA, DSR&OA, EngInd, ExcerpMed, FPA, FS&TA, ForAb, HortAb, IndMed, PollutAb, RRTA, S&F, SCI, SWRA. *Aud.:* Ac, Sa.

Journal of Experimental Botany is a forum for plant research covering a "range of disciplines from molecular and cellular physiology and biochemistry through whole plant physiology to community physiology." Research articles, methods papers, short communications, novel gene sequences, opinion papers, and reviews of research areas that are "particularly exciting and important, topical or controversial" are accepted. At least one additional special issue is published annually, containing articles from specialized meetings or conference sessions. Online full text, through Stanford's HighWire Press, is available for the years 1997 onward. This journal is appropriate for academic and research institutions with botany or agriculture programs. Document delivery is available from BLDSC, CASDDS, CISTI, EMDOCS, The Genuine Article, LHLDS, UMI, and UnCover.

1107. *Journal of Phycology.* [ISSN: 0022-3646] 1965. bi-m. USD 520 except Canada & Mexico, print & online eds. Ed(s): Susan Brawley. Blackwell Publishing, Inc., Commerce Place, 350 Main St, Malden, MA 02148; subscrip@blackwellpub.com; http://www.blackwellpublishing.com. Illus., index, adv. Sample. Refereed. Circ: 2000. *Indexed:* BiolAb, CAPS, ChemAb, DSR&OA, ForAb, GeoRef, HortAb, IndVet, OceAb, SCI, VetBull, ZooRec. *Aud.:* Ac, Sa.

Published by the Phycological Society of America, this journal presents papers on "all aspects of basic and applied research on algae to provide a common medium for the ecologist, physiologist, cell biologist, molecular biologist, morphologist, taxonomist, geneticist, and biochemist." The editors are especially interested in receiving papers emphasizing "algal interactions with other organisms and the roles of algae as components of natural ecosystems." Research papers, researcher notes, reviews, minireviews, meeting announcements, and comments are published. Subscription options include print, online, and print plus online combined. Stanford's HighWire Press makes available the online content for this title, including full text from 1998 forward. This journal will be useful to a wide range of researchers. Document delivery is available from BLDSC, CASDDS, CISTI, EMDOCS, The Genuine Article, LHLDS, UMI, and UnCover.

1108. *Mycologia.* Formed by the merger of: *Mycological Bulletin; Journal of Mycology.* [ISSN: 0027-5514] 1909. bi-m. USD 160 in US & Canada; USD 172 elsewhere. Ed(s): James Ginns. Mycological Society of America, c/o Joan W. Bennett, Dept. of Cell & Molecular Biology, Tulane University, New Orleans, LA 70118; http://msafungi.org/. Illus., index, adv. Sample. Refereed. Circ: 2000. Vol. ends: Nov/Dec. Microform: PMC; PQC. *Indexed:* Agr, B&AI, BiolAb, CAPS, ChemAb, DSA, DSR&OA, EnvAb, FPA, FS&TA, ForAb, GeoRef, HortAb, IndVet, S&F, SCI, VetBull, ZooRec. *Aud.:* Ac, Sa.

Mycologia is the official publication of the Mycological Society of America, covering all aspects of research on fungi, including lichens. Topics appropriate for publication in the journal include "physiology and biochemistry, ecology, pathology, development and morphology, systematics, cell biology and ultrastructure, genetics, molecular biology, evolution, applied aspects, and new techniques." Article categories include regular research articles, notes or brief articles reporting research or new techniques, invited papers, and reviews. Subscription options include online only and print plus online. Stanford's HighWire Press makes available the electronic content for this journal, including full text from 2002 forward. Reasonably priced and appropriate for general botany collections as well as institutions supporting more-specialized research in mycology. Document delivery is available from BLDSC, CASDDS, CISTI, EMDOCS, The Genuine Article, LHLDS, UMI, and UnCover.

1109. *Phytochemistry: international journal of plant biochemistry.* [ISSN: 0031-9422] 1962. s-m. EUR 3729 (Qualified personnel, EUR 583). Ed(s): G. P. Bolwell, N G Lewis. Pergamon, The Boulevard, Langford Ln, East Park, Kidlington, OX5 1GB, United Kingdom. Illus., index, adv. Sample. Refereed. Circ: 2500. Microform: MIM; PQC. Online: ingenta.com; ScienceDirect; Swets Blackwell. *Indexed:* Agr, B&AI, BiolAb, ChemAb, DSA, DSR&OA, EnvAb, ExcerpMed, FPA, FS&TA, ForAb, GeoRef, HortAb, IndMed, IndVet, S&F, SCI, VetBull, WAE&RSA. *Bk. rev.:* 0-2, 200-350 words. *Aud.:* Ac, Sa.

Phytochemistry publishes "research on all aspects of plant chemistry, plant biochemistry, plant molecular biology and chemical ecology." Full-length articles, review articles, and accelerated publications are published. The journal is divided into seven general areas: protein biochemistry, molecular genetics and genomics, metabolism, ecological biochemistry, chemotaxonomy, bioactive products, and chemistry. Online content is available through Elsevier's ScienceDirect and includes full text from 1961 forward. This title will be useful in academic or special libraries supporting botanists. Document delivery is available from BLDSC, CASDDS, CISTI, EMDOCS, The Genuine Article, UMI, and UnCover.

1110. *The Plant Cell.* [ISSN: 1040-4651] 1989. m. USD 1970 for print & online eds. Plant Physiology & The Plant Cell incl. (Individual members, USD 150 includes online access; Non-members, USD 300 Print & online eds.). Ed(s): Dr. Ralph S Quatrano, Beth Straehle. American Society of Plant Biologists, 15501 Monona Dr, Rockville, MD 20855; beths@aspp.org; http://www.plantcell.org. Illus., index, adv. Sample. Refereed. Circ: 3600 Paid. Online: HighWire Press; ProQuest Information & Learning. *Indexed:* Agr, B&AI, BioEngAb, BiolAb, CAPS, ChemAb, EngInd, FPA, FS&TA, ForAb, HortAb, IndMed, S&F, SCI. *Aud.:* Ac, Sa.

The editors of *Plant Cell* say that one of the main goals of the journal is to publish "novel research of special significance in plant biology, especially in the areas of cellular biology, molecular biology, genetics, development, and evolution." The journal features research papers, review articles, and meeting reports. Stanford's HighWire Press provides access to the online content which includes full text from 1989 forward. Online access is free with a print subscription but institutions can also purchase an online only subscription. A subscription includes a print and online subscription to the sister title, "Plant Physiology". Excellent journals for libraries supporting botanists. Document delivery is available from BLDSC, CASDDS, CISTI, EMDOCS, The Genuine Article, LHLDS, UMI, and UnCover.

1111. *Plant Molecular Biology: an international journal on molecular biology, biochemistry and genetic engineering.* [ISSN: 0167-4412] 1981. 18x/yr. EUR 2712 print or online ed. Ed(s): Stephen H Howell. Kluwer Academic Publishers, van Godewijckstraat 30, PO Box 17, Dordrecht, 3300 AA, Netherlands; services@wkap.nl; http://www.wkap.nl. Illus., index, adv. Sample. Refereed. Microform: PQC. Online: EBSCO Publishing; ingenta.com; Kluwer Online; OCLC Online Computer Library Center, Inc.; Ovid Technologies, Inc.; RoweCom Information Quest; Swets Blackwell. Reprint: SWZ. *Indexed:* Agr, BioEngAb, BiolAb, CAPS, ChemAb, DSA, EngInd, FS&TA, ForAb, HortAb, IndMed, S&F, SCI. *Aud.:* Ac, Sa.

Plant Molecular Biology concentrates on providing publications of interest to researchers working on the molecular biology, biochemistry, and molecular genetics of higher and lower plants, though work on higher plants seems to predominate. Full-length research papers and minireviews are published. Online content is available through Kluwer Online. Subscribers may receive either the paper or the electronic version of the journal for the subscription price, but if both are required, a 20 percent surcharge is applied. This journal is appropriate for academic and special libraries supporting botanists. Document delivery is available from BLDSC, CASDDS, CISTI, EMDOCS, The Genuine Article, LHLDS, UMI, and UnCover.

1112. ***Plant Physiology.*** [ISSN: 0032-0889] 1926. m. USD 1690 print & online eds. Plant Physiology & The Plant Cell incl. (Individual members, USD 165; USD 125 student member). Ed(s): Melissa Junior, Natasha V Raikhel. American Society of Plant Biologists, 15501 Monona Dr, Rockville, MD 20855; mjunior@aspp.org; http://www.plantphysiol.org. Illus., index, adv. Sample. Refereed. Circ: 3700 Paid. Microform: MIM; PMC; PQC. Online: HighWire Press; ProQuest Information & Learning. Reprint: PQC. *Indexed:* Agr, B&AI, BioEngAb, BiolAb, CAPS, ChemAb, DSA, DSR&OA, EngInd, EnvAb, ExcerpMed, FPA, FS&TA, ForAb, HortAb, IndMed, S&F, SCI, WAE&RSA. *Aud.:* Ac, Sa.

Plant Physiology is "devoted to physiology, biochemistry, cellular and molecular biology, genetics, biophysics, and environmental biology of plants." Some more specific areas of interest include development, bioenergetics, understanding the plant as an organism, and interactions with the environment, symbionts, pathogens, and pests. Research articles, editorials, new technology, correspondence, meeting reports, updates, and articles on genome analysis are published. Online content is available through Stanford's HighWire Press and includes full text from 1993 forward. A subscription includes online access to this and also a print and online subscription to the sister title, *The Plant Cell.* This journal will be necessary for collections supporting botanists. Document delivery is available from BLDSC, CASDDS, CISTI, EMDOCS, The Genuine Article, LHLDS, UMI, and UnCover.

1113. ***Planta: an international journal of plant biology.*** [ISSN: 0032-0935] 1925. m. EUR 3190 domestic; EUR 3238.20 foreign; EUR 319 newsstand/cover per issue. Ed(s): R L Jones, A Sievers. Springer-Verlag, Tiergartenstr 17, Heidelberg, 69121, Germany. Illus., index, adv. Sample. Refereed. Microform: PMC; PQC. Online: EBSCO Publishing; RoweCom Information Quest; ScienceDirect; Springer LINK; Swets Blackwell. Reprint: ISI. *Indexed:* Agr, B&AI, BiolAb, CAPS, ChemAb, DSA, DSR&OA, EngInd, FPA, FS&TA, ForAb, GeoRef, HortAb, IAA, IndMed, S&F, SCI. *Aud.:* Ac, Sa.

Planta presents papers on "all aspects of plant biology, particularly in molecular and cell biology, ultrastructure, biochemistry, metabolism, growth, development and morphogenesis, ecological and environmental physiology, biotechnology, and plant-microorganism interactions." Research papers, invited reviews, and rapid communications are published. Basic electronic access to full text from 1997 forward is available via SpringerLink and is included with a print subscription. Appropriate for collections supporting botanists. Document delivery is available from BLDSC, CASDDS, CISTI, EMDOCS, The Genuine Article, LHLDS, UMI, and UnCover.

1114. ***Torrey Botanical Society. Journal.*** Formerly (until 1997): *Torrey Botanical Club. Bulletin;* Which incorporated (1901-1945): *Torreya.* [ISSN: 1095-5674] 1870. q. USD 55 domestic; USD 60 foreign. Torrey Botanical Society, Box 1897, Lawrence, KS 66044-8897; orders@allenpress.com; http://www.torreybotanical.org. Illus., index, adv. Refereed. Circ: 1304. Vol. ends: Oct/Dec. Microform: PQC. Online: JSTOR (Web-based Journal Archive); ProQuest Information & Learning. Reprint: ISI; PQC. *Indexed:* Agr, ApEcolAb, BiolAb, CAPS, ChemAb, DSR&OA, EnvAb, ExcerpMed, FPA, ForAb, GeoRef, GeogAbPG, HortAb, RRTA, S&F, SCI, SWRA. *Bk. rev.:* 0-2, 350-1,000 words. *Aud.:* Ac, Sa.

The objective of the Torrey Botanical Society, whose membership includes professional and amateur biologists, students, and naturalists, is "to promote interest in botany, and to collect and disseminate information on all phases of plant science." This journal, published in two parts, presents original research; review papers; papers on distribution, floristics, conservation, and environmental concerns; field trip reports; obituaries; book reviews; and other articles of interest to botanists. Online full text for this journal and its predecessor is available through JSTOR from 1870 up to a three-year moving wall. Allen Press' APT Online provides online abstracts for the more recent years. Written for generalists as well as specialists in the field, this journal would be appropriate for academic and special-library collections and for some larger public libraries depending on the patron base. Document delivery is available from CASDDS, CISTI, EMDOCS, The Genuine Article, LHLDS, UMI, and UnCover.

Cell Biology

1115. ***Cell.*** [ISSN: 0092-8674] 1974. bi-w. USD 949 (Individuals, USD 159 print & online eds.). Cell Press, 1100 Massachusetts Ave, Cambridge, MA 02138; http://www.cellpress.com/. Illus., index, adv. Refereed. Circ: 15500. Online: Gale Group; ingenta.com; ScienceDirect. Reprint: ISI; PQC. *Indexed:* B&AI, BiolAb, ChemAb, DSA, EngInd, ExcerpMed, FS&TA, GSI, HortAb, IndMed, IndVet, S&F, SCI, SSCI, VetBull, ZooRec. *Aud.:* Ac, Sa.

Cell focuses on publishing novel results in all areas of experimental biology. Papers are expected to be as concise as possible (55,000 words or under) and to report work that is not only "of unusual significance within its field but also of interest to researchers outside the immediate area." Issues contain papers of 10 to 15 pages representing full-length research articles, as well as several minireviews. Longer review articles may also appear. Papers are published in a timely manner, within 12 weeks of acceptance. Issues also feature conference announcements and job advertisements. Print and online full text require a separate subscription and site license. Freely accessible tables of contents can be reviewed at the Cell Press web site. An alerting service is also freely available. Relatively inexpensive, this important journal will be useful in any library supporting biology programs. Document delivery is available from BLDSC, CASDDS, CISTI, EMDOCS, KNAW, NIWI, LHLDS, and UnCover.

1116. ***Experimental Cell Research.*** [ISSN: 0014-4827] 1950. 20x/yr. EUR 5170 (Individuals, EUR 606). Ed(s): U. Lendahl. Academic Press, 525 B St, Ste 1900, San Diego, CA 92101-4495; apsubs@acad.com; http://www.academicpress.com. Illus., index, adv. Refereed. Online: EBSCO Publishing; ingenta.com; OCLC Online Computer Library Center, Inc.; RoweCom Information Quest; ScienceDirect; Swets Blackwell. *Indexed:* Agr, B&AI, BiolAb, ChemAb, DSA, ExcerpMed, IndMed, IndVet, SCI, VetBull. *Aud.:* Ac, Sa.

Experimental Cell Research presents papers on the general organization and activity of cells, including all aspects of cell biology, from the molecular level to the level of cell interaction and differentiation. Online content is provided by Elsevier's ScienceDirect and includes materials from 1993 to the present. This title is appropriate for academic or special libraries supporting researchers in cell or molecular biology or cancer. Document delivery is available from BLDSC, CASDDS, CISTI, The Genuine Article, LHLDS, and UnCover.

1117. ***Journal of Cell Biology.*** [ISSN: 0021-9525] 1955. bi-w. USD 1025 print ed. Ed(s): Ira Mellman. Rockefeller University Press, 1114 First Ave, New York, NY 10021-8325; rupcd@rockefeller.edu; http://www.jcb.org; http://www.rockefeller.edu/rupress. Illus., index, adv. Sample. Refereed. Circ: 3931. Microform: PQC. Online: HighWire Press; RoweCom Information Quest. Reprint: ISI; PQC. *Indexed:* Agr, B&AI, BiolAb, ChemAb, DSA, ExcerpMed, ForAb, GSI, HortAb, IndMed, IndVet, S&F, SCI, VetBull, ZooRec. *Aud.:* Ac, Sa.

The *Journal of Cell Biology* publishes new research on cellular structure and function, including "nuclear organization and structure, protein and membrane trafficking, signal transduction, cytoskeleton and molecular motors, cell cycle and division, cell growth, survival and death, cellular adhesion and motility, and intercellular communication." Article sections include comments, minireviews, research papers, and research reports. Subscription options include print only, online only, and print and online combined. Online full text begins in 1975 and is made available via Stanford's HighWire Press. This is a well-regarded journal, appropriate for academic and special libraries. Document delivery is available from BLDSC, CASDDS, CISTI, The Genuine Article, LHLDS, UMI, and UnCover.

1118. ***Journal of Cell Science.*** Formerly (until 1966): *Quarterly Journal of Microscopical Science.* [ISSN: 0021-9533] 1852. s-m. USD 1995 (Individuals, USD 380; Members, USD 256). Ed(s): Dr. Fiona M Watt. The Company of Biologists Ltd., Bidder Building, 140 Cowley Rd, Cambridge, CB4 4DL, United Kingdom; sales@thecob.demon.co.uk;

http://www.biologists.com. Illus., index, adv. Sample. Refereed. Circ: 1550. Vol. ends: Dec. Microform: BHP. Online: EBSCO Publishing; HighWire Press; RoweCom Information Quest. *Indexed:* Agr, B&AI, BiolAb, ChemAb, DSA, ExcerpMed, ForAb, GeoRef, HortAb, IndMed, IndVet, S&F, SCI, VetBull, ZooRec. *Aud.:* Ac, Sa.

The *Journal of Cell Science* publishes articles on the "complete range of topics in cell biology." Issues include research articles, review articles commissioned from experts in their fields, brief syntheses, and topical comments. Subscription options include print only, online only, and print plus online. Online full text from 1992 forward is available through Stanford's HighWire Press. Articles published prior to the current subscription year are available for free on the journal's web site. This title will be of interest to a broad range of researchers, including cell biologists, developmental biologists, molecular biologists, and geneticists. Document delivery is available from BLDSC, CASDDS, CISTI, LHLDS, NIWI, UMI, and UnCover.

Developmental Biology

1119. ***Development (Cambridge).*** Formerly: *Journal of Embryology and Experimental Morphology.* [ISSN: 0950-1991] 1953. s-m. USD 2435 (Individuals, USD 482; Members, USD 289). Ed(s): Dr. Jim Smith. The Company of Biologists Ltd., Bidder Building, 140 Cowley Rd, Cambridge, CB4 4DL, United Kingdom; sales@biologists.com; http://www.biologists.com/development. Illus., index, adv. Refereed. Circ: 2700. Vol. ends: Dec. Online: EBSCO Publishing; HighWire Press; RoweCom Information Quest. *Indexed:* B&AI, BiolAb, ChemAb, DSA, ExcerpMed, ForAb, IndMed, IndVet, S&F, SCI, VetBull, ZooRec. *Aud.:* Ac, Sa.

Development, one of the most respected journals in the field of developmental biology, is a "forum for research that offers a genuine insight into mechanisms of development" covering the topic on the molecular, cellular, and tissue levels. While plant and animal studies are included, most papers focus on animals. Experimental studies are given top priority, though review articles and high-quality descriptive studies are considered. The new Development and Disease section highlights research on developmental disease processes. A Company of Biologists journal, a separate print subscription and online site license are required. At year's end, however, all online content becomes freely accessible. Appropriate for supporting researchers in academic and special libraries with biology programs. Document delivery is available from BLDSC, CASDDS, CISTI, EMDOCS, LHLDS, UMI, and UnCover.

1120. ***Developmental Biology: an international journal.*** [ISSN: 0012-1606] 1959. 24x/yr. EUR 7073 (Individuals, EUR 493; Students, EUR 405). Ed(s): Dr. Eric N Olson. Academic Press, 525 B St, Ste 1900, San Diego, CA 92101-4495; apsubs@acad.com; http://www.academicpress.com. Illus., index, adv. Refereed. Online: EBSCO Publishing; Gale Group; ingenta.com; OCLC Online Computer Library Center, Inc.; RoweCom Information Quest; ScienceDirect; Swets Blackwell. *Indexed:* Agr, B&AI, BiolAb, ChemAb, DSA, ExcerpMed, GSI, HortAb, IndMed, IndVet, S&F, SCI, VetBull, ZooRec. *Aud.:* Ac, Sa.

Developmental Biology publishes papers on the molecular genetics of development, the control of gene expression, cell and cell matrix interactions, mechanisms of differentiation, growth factors and oncogenes, the regulation of stem cell populations, gametogenesis and fertilization, developmental endocrinology, and plant development. Most papers describe research done on animal species. Conference announcements, advertisements for publications, and position announcements are also useful features. Online content is available via Elsevier's ScienceDirect. *Developmental Biology* while very expensive, is considered one of the top journals in the field and will be useful to researchers in academic and special libraries. Document delivery is available from BLDSC, CASDDS, The Genuine Article, LHLDS, UMI, and UnCover.

1121. ***Genes & Development.*** [ISSN: 0890-9369] 1987. s-m. USD 980 (Individuals, USD 140). Ed(s): T Grodzicker. Cold Spring Harbor Laboratory Press, Publications Department, 500 Sunnyside Blvd., Woodbury, NY 11797-2924; cshpress@cshl.edu; http://www.cshl.org. Illus., index, adv. Sample. Refereed. Vol. ends: Dec. Online: EBSCO Publishing; Gale Group; HighWire Press. Reprint: PSC. *Indexed:* AbAn, B&AI, BiolAb, BiolDig, ChemAb, DSA, ExcerpMed, GSI, HortAb, IndMed, IndVet, S&F, SCI, SSCI, VetBull. *Aud.:* Ac, Sa.

This well-regarded journal, published by Cold Spring Harbor Laboratory Press in association with the Genetical Society of Great Britain, features papers of general interest and biological significance in molecular biology and molecular genetics. Research papers, research communications, review articles, and perspectives are paper categories. Conference announcements and advertisements for products and publications are also included. Online content, which is made available through Stanford's HighWire Press, is included with a print subscription. The 2001 ISI impact factor for this journal places it among the top ten primary research journals in the sciences. Document delivery is available from BLDSC, CASDDS, CISTI, EMDOCS, The Genuine Article, LHLDS, NIWI, UMI, and UnCover.

Ecology

1122. ***American Midland Naturalist.*** Formerly (until 1909): *Midland Naturalist.* [ISSN: 0003-0031] 1909. q. USD 85 N. & S. America & the Caribbean (Individuals, USD 45; Students, USD 25). Ed(s): William Evan. University of Notre Dame, Department of Biological Sciences, Rm 285 GLSC Box 369, Notre Dame, IN 46556; ammidnat./@nd.edu; http://www.nd..edu/~ammidnat. Illus., index. Refereed. Circ: 1400. Microform: IDC; PQC. Online: BioOne; EBSCO Publishing; Florida Center for Library Automation; Gale Group; JSTOR (Web-based Journal Archive); Northern Light Technology, Inc.; OCLC Online Computer Library Center, Inc.; ProQuest Information & Learning; H.W. Wilson. *Indexed:* Agr, AnBeAb, ApEcolAb, B&AI, BiolAb, CAPS, ChemAb, DSA, DSR&OA, FPA, ForAb, GSI, GeoRef, GeogAbPG, HortAb, IndVet, RRTA, S&F, SCI, SSCI, SWRA, VetBull, WAE&RSA, ZooRec. *Aud.:* Ac, Sa.

Published since 1909, *American Midland Naturalist* "welcomes articles reporting original research in any field of biological science and review articles on topics of current interest in biology." Each issue includes 17 to 22 full-length papers and a few shorter "Notes and Discussions." Despite its title, the geographical coverage of this journal includes all of North America and occasionally areas outside North America. Issues prior to the latest three years are available on JSTOR. BioOne provides online coverage for the years 1998 through the present. A frequently cited and well-respected core journal for academic as well as specialized natural-history collections. Document delivery is available from BLDSC, CASDDS, CISTI, EMDOCS, The Genuine Article, JSTOR, LHLDS, UMI, and UnCover.

1123. ***The American Naturalist.*** [ISSN: 0003-0147] 1867. m. USD 433 print & online eds. (Individuals, USD 75 print & online eds.; Students, USD 49 print & online eds.). Ed(s): Jonathan Losos. University of Chicago Press, Journals Division, PO Box 37005, Chicago, IL 60637; orders@press.uchicago.edu; http://www.journals.uchicago.edu. Illus., index, adv. Refereed. Circ: 2600 Paid. Microform: IDC; PMC; PQC. Online: EBSCO Publishing; Florida Center for Library Automation; Gale Group; JSTOR (Web-based Journal Archive); ProQuest Information & Learning. Reprint: PSC. *Indexed:* AnBeAb, ApEcolAb, B&AI, BiolAb, CAPS, ChemAb, DSA, DSR&OA, EngInd, ForAb, GSI, GeoRef, HortAb, IndVet, OceAb, S&F, SCI, SSCI, VetBull, ZooRec. *Aud.:* Ac, Sa.

The official journal of the American Society of Naturalists, *American Naturalist* is "one of the world's most renowned peer-reviewed publications in ecology, evolution, and population and integrative biology research." The six to eight full-length papers emphasize population, behavioral, and genetic aspects of ecology and evolution in both animal and plant communities. Typical papers include such subjects as mate selection, ecosystem models, food webs, reproductive fitness, and larval dispersal strategies. "Notes and Comments" includes brief articles, criticism, and comments on other publications. Tables of contents alert users when articles have online "enhancements." Subscriptions include electronic access, made available through the University of Chicago. The journal's web site includes a search engine, tables of contents, abstracts, and forthcoming papers. Subscribers and nonsubscribers alike can have tables of contents e-mailed to them. Appropriate for professionals and all levels of academic libraries. Document delivery is available from BLDSC, CASDDS, CISTI, EI, EMDOCS, The Genuine Article, LHLDS, UMI, and UnCover.

Ecological Monographs. See under *Ecology.*

1124. *Ecology.* [ISSN: 0012-9658] 1920. m. USD 470 in North America; USD 548 elsewhere. Ed(s): Robert K Peet. Ecological Society of America, 1707 H St, N W, Ste 400, Washington, DC 20006; esahq@esa.org. Illus., index, adv. Refereed. Circ: 6400. Vol. ends: Dec. Microform: IDC; PMC; PQC. *Indexed:* AbAn, Agr, AnBeAb, ApEcolAb, B&AI, BRI, BiolAb, CBRI, ChemAb, DSR&OA, ExcerpMed, FPA, FS&TA, ForAb, GSI, GeoRef, GeogAbPG, HortAb, IndVet, M&GPA, OceAb, RI-1, S&F, SCI, SSCI, SWRA, ZooRec. *Bk. rev.:* 5-7, 500-1,000 words. *Aud.:* Ac, Sa.

Published in *Ecology* are papers on "physiological responses of individual organisms to their biotic and abiotic environments, ecological genetics and evolution, the structure and dynamics of populations, interactions among individuals of the same or different species, the behavior of individuals and groups of organisms, the organization of biological communities, landscape ecology, and ecosystems processes." Articles are divided into several categories, which are described on the journal's web site. Full text of this title is available via JSTOR from 1920 up to the current four years. The Ecological Society of America's web site makes available online tables of contents from 1920 forward, some with abstracts. The Ecological Society of America (ESA) maintains the Ecological Archives, with the purpose of making supplemental material to all ESA journals available on the Internet. This is a core title for academic and special libraries supporting biology programs. Document delivery is available from BLDSC, CASDDS, CISTI, LHLDS, UMI, and UnCover.

1125. *Freshwater Biology.* [ISSN: 0046-5070] 1971. 12x/yr. GBP 1820 print & online eds. Ed(s): Dr. Colin R. Townsend, Dr. Alan G. Hildrew. Blackwell Publishing Ltd., 9600 Garsington Rd, Oxford, OX4 2ZG, United Kingdom; customerservices@oxon.blackwellpublishing.com; http://www.blackwellpublishing.com. Illus., index. Sample. Refereed. Circ: 840. Microform: PQC. Online: EBSCO Publishing; ingenta.com; Munksgaard & Blackwell Science's Synergy; OCLC Online Computer Library Center, Inc.; RoweCom Information Quest; Swets Blackwell. Reprint: ISI. *Indexed:* ApEcolAb, B&AI, BiolAb, CAPS, ChemAb, DSR&OA, EnvAb, ExcerpMed, FPA, ForAb, GeoRef, GeogAbPG, IndVet, PollutAb, RRTA, S&F, SCI, SWRA, VetBull, WAE&RSA, WRCInf, ZooRec. *Bk. rev.:* 0-3, 500-2,000 words. *Aud.:* Ac, Sa.

Freshwater Biology, a limnology journal, publishes papers on "all aspects of the ecology of inland surface waters, including rivers and lakes, connected ground waters, flood plains and other wetlands." Included are research papers, applied-research papers, and opinion pieces. Online content, available through Blackwell's Synergy and several intermediaries, includes a free sample issue, full text from 1998 forward, and an alerting service. There are three subscription choices available to institutions: premium online plus print, standard online plus print, and premium online alone. Standard online includes only the current and one previous volume while premium allows access to all online content. This title will be useful in libraries supporting limnologists, ecologists, and environmental scientists. Document delivery is available from BLDSC, CASDDS, CISTI, EMDOCS, The Genuine Article, LHLDS, UMI, and UnCover.

1126. *Journal of Animal Ecology.* [ISSN: 0021-8790] 1932. bi-m. GBP 412 print & online eds. Ed(s): D Raffaelli, S Albon. Blackwell Publishing Ltd., 9600 Garsington Rd, Oxford, OX4 2ZG, United Kingdom; customerservices@oxon.blackwellpublishing.com; http://www.blackwellpublishing.com. Illus., index, adv. Refereed. Circ: 2715. Vol. ends: Nov. Microform: PQC. Online: EBSCO Publishing; ingenta.com; JSTOR (Web-based Journal Archive); Munksgaard & Blackwell Science's Synergy; OCLC Online Computer Library Center, Inc.; RoweCom Information Quest; Swets Blackwell. Reprint: ISI. *Indexed:* AbAn, AnBeAb, ApEcolAb, B&AI, BiolAb, ChemAb, DSR&OA, FS&TA, ForAb, GeoRef, GeogAbPG, HortAb, IndVet, S&F, SCI, SWRA, VetBull, ZooRec. *Bk. rev.:* 0-8, 300-1,200 words. *Aud.:* Ac, Sa.

Published by the British Ecological Society, the papers in *Journal of Animal Ecology* represent all aspects of animal ecology. Recently, articles on population ecology, behavioral ecology, community ecology, physiological ecology, and evolutionary ecology have appeared. The editors express an interest in supporting traditional research as well as research in emerging fields like molecular ecology. Research articles are the main focus, but reviews on topics central to animal ecology are also considered. JSTOR covers online full text of this title from its inception in 1932 up to a three year moving wall. Online full text from 1998 forward is available on Blackwell Synergy. ISI ranks this among the top ecology and zoology journals. Accessible to everyone from upper-division undergraduates through researchers. Document delivery is available from BLDSC, CISTI, EMDOCS, The Genuine Article, LHLDS, UMI, and UnCover.

1127. *Journal of Ecology.* [ISSN: 0022-0477] 1913. bi-m. GBP 412 print & online eds. Ed(s): A Davy, M Hutchings. Blackwell Publishing Ltd., 9600 Garsington Rd, Oxford, OX4 2ZG, United Kingdom; customerservices@oxon.blackwellpublishing.com; http://www.blackwellpublishing.com. Illus., index, adv. Refereed. Circ: 3190. Vol. ends: Dec. Microform: PQC. Online: EBSCO Publishing; Gale Group; ingenta.com; JSTOR (Web-based Journal Archive); Munksgaard & Blackwell Science's Synergy; OCLC Online Computer Library Center, Inc.; RoweCom Information Quest; Swets Blackwell. Reprint: ISI. *Indexed:* Agr, AnBeAb, ApEcolAb, B&AI, BiolAb, BrArAb, CAPS, ChemAb, DSR&OA, EnvAb, ExcerpMed, FPA, ForAb, GSI, GeoRef, GeogAbPG, HortAb, OceAb, RRTA, S&F, SCI, SWRA, WRCInf, ZooRec. *Aud.:* Ac, Sa.

The British Ecological Society publishes *Journal of Ecology* to present papers on all aspects of ecology of plants in aquatic and terrestrial ecosystems. Articles focusing primarily on agriculture and cultivated plants are not included. Subscription options include print plus premium online, print plus standard online, and premium online alone. The difference between premium and standard online subscriptions is that a standard online subscription includes only the current volume plus the previous volume, while a premium subscription includes all online issues, currently 1998 to the present. JSTOR covers this title from its inception in 1913 to a moving wall of the current three years. *Journal of Ecology* is appropriate for undergraduates through specialists and would be useful in any academic library with a biology program. Document delivery is available from BLDSC, CASDDS, CISTI, EMDOCS, The Genuine Article, LHLDS, UMI, and UnCover.

1128. *Oecologia.* Formerly: *Zeitschrift fuer Morphologie und Oekologie der Tiere.* [ISSN: 0029-8549] 1924. 16x/yr. EUR 3300 domestic; EUR 3364.20 foreign; EUR 248 newsstand/cover per issue. Ed(s): J R Ehleringer, M Schaefer. Springer-Verlag, Tiergartenstr 17, Heidelberg, 69121, Germany. Illus., adv. Sample. Refereed. Microform: PQC. Online: EBSCO Publishing; RoweCom Information Quest; ScienceDirect; Springer LINK; Swets Blackwell. Reprint: ISI. *Indexed:* Agr, AnBeAb, ApEcolAb, B&AI, BiolAb, CAPS, DSA, DSR&OA, ExcerpMed, FPA, ForAb, GeoRef, GeogAbPG, HortAb, IndVet, OceAb, S&F, SCI, SWRA, VetBull, WAE&RSA, ZooRec. *Aud.:* Ac, Sa.

Oecologia publishes rapid publications, reviews, advances in methodology, and original contributions in ecology, with an emphasis on the following areas: ecophysiology, population ecology, plant-animal interactions, ecosystems ecology, global change, and conservation ecology. Coverage seems to be fairly balanced between plant and animal studies. SpringerLink makes available the online content for this title, including full text from 1997 to the present. A print subscription includes basic online access. Appropriate for academic and special libraries supporting ecology programs.

1129. *Oikos: a journal of ecology.* [ISSN: 0030-1299] 1948. 12x/yr. USD 778 print & online eds. Ed(s): Nils Malmer. Blackwell Munksgaard, Rosenoerns Alle 1, PO Box 227, Copenhagen V, 1502, Denmark; customerservice@munksgaard.dk; http://www.blackwellmunksgaard.com. Illus., adv. Refereed. Circ: 1550. Online: ingenta.com; Munksgaard & Blackwell Science's Synergy; OCLC Online Computer Library Center, Inc.; Ovid Technologies, Inc.; Swets Blackwell. Reprint: ISI. *Indexed:* AnBeAb, ApEcolAb, BiolAb, CAPS, ChemAb, DSR&OA, FPA, ForAb, GSI, GeoRef, GeogAbPG, HortAb, IndVet, OceAb, S&F, SCI, SWRA, VetBull, WAE&RSA, ZooRec. *Aud.:* Ac, Sa.

Oikos focuses on ecology without regard to "taxon, biome or geographical region." Research papers, minireviews, and opinion pieces are published, as well as new hypotheses and challenges to current thinking on ecological issues. Approximately 2,500 pages are published annually. Online content is made available via Blackwell Synergy and includes full text from 2000 forward. Subscription options include print plus either premium or standard online access, and premium online access only. Premium and standard access differ in that standard allows for access to the current and the previous volume while premium allows access to all online content. This journal is very accessible and will be useful in any library supporting a biology program. Document delivery is available from BLDSC, CASDDS, CISTI, EMDOCS, The Genuine Article, LHLDS, UMI, and UnCover.

Genetics

1130. *American Journal of Human Genetics.* [ISSN: 0002-9297] 1948. m. USD 895 USD 79.60 per issue. Ed(s): Stephen T. Warren. University of Chicago Press, Journals Division, PO Box 37005, Chicago, IL 60637; subscriptions@press.uchicago.edu. Illus., index, adv. Refereed. Circ: 7500 Paid. Vol. ends: Dec. Microform: MIM; PQC. Online: EBSCO Publishing; Florida Center for Library Automation; Gale Group; OCLC Online Computer Library Center, Inc. Reprint: PSC. *Indexed:* AICP, AbAn, B&AI, BAS, BiolAb, ChemAb, DSA, ExcerpMed, GSI, IndMed, SCI. *Bk. rev.:* 0-3, 200-1,200 words. *Aud.:* Ac, Sa.

Published since 1948 for the American Society of Human Genetics, the *American Journal of Human Genetics* is "record of research and review relating to heredity in man and to the application of genetic principles in medicine, psychology, anthropology, and social services, as well as in related areas of molecular and cell biology." Papers appear on such topics as behavioral, biochemical, or clinical genetics; immunogenetics; genetic counseling; and epidemiology. Many papers discuss genetic aspects of medical conditions or diseases. Issues include review articles, full-length research articles, reports (rapid publication of original research), letters to the editor, and announcements. Professionals will find the employment notices, conference announcements, and calls for papers very helpful. Subscriptions include access to the online edition of the journal, which is published earlier than the paper edition. The online edition is published for the society by the University of Chicago. Online access to issues older than 6 months is free on the Internet. Document delivery is available from BLDSC, CASDDS, CISTI, EMDOCS, The Genuine Article, LHLDS, NIWI, UMI, and UnCover.

Genes & Development. See Developmental Biology subsection.

1131. *Genetics: a periodical record of investigations bearing on heredity and variation.* [ISSN: 0016-6731] 1916. m. USD 735 print & online eds. Ed(s): Elizabeth W Jones. Genetics Society of America, 9650 Rockville Pike, Bethesda, MD 20814; staff@dues.faseb.org; http://www.genetics.org. Illus., index, adv. Refereed. Circ: 5000. Microform: MIM; PMC; PQC. Online: EBSCO Publishing; Gale Group; HighWire Press; RoweCom Information Quest. Reprint: PQC. *Indexed:* AbAn, Agr, B&AI, BiolAb, BiolDig, ChemAb, DSA, ExcerpMed, FS&TA, ForAb, GSI, HortAb, IndMed, IndVet, OceAb, S&F, SCI, VetBull, ZooRec. *Aud.:* Ac, Sa.

Genetics publishes papers that represent original research in the field of genetics and related disciplines. "Perspectives" consists of essays that may outline the history of an event or present a tribute to an important figure in the field. "Investigations" are original, full-length research articles, while "Notes" consist of shorter research papers. Letters to the editor are usually comments on earlier publications in the journal and responses to those comments. Special issues occasionally appear. Online content for this title is available via Stanford's HighWire Press and is provided along with a print subscription. Full text is available from 1988 forward with abstracts only available from 1980 through 1987. The articles vary greatly in experimental organisms used and in the types of research conducted, making this journal appealing to a wide audience. This title will useful for upper-division undergraduates through specialists. Document delivery is available from BLDSC, CASDDS, CISTI, The Genuine Article, LHLDS, UMI, and UnCover.

1132. *Genome Research.* Formerly (until Aug 1995): *P C R Methods and Applications (Polymerase Chain Reaction).* [ISSN: 1088-9051] 1991. m. USD 930 (Individuals, USD 117). Ed(s): L Goodman. Cold Spring Harbor Laboratory Press, Publications Department, 500 Sunnyside Blvd., Woodbury, NY 11797-2924; cshpress@cshl.edu; http://www.cshl.org. Illus., adv. Refereed. Online: EBSCO Publishing; HighWire Press. Reprint: PSC. *Indexed:* BiolAb, ChemAb, DSA, ExcerpMed, FS&TA, HortAb, IndMed, IndVet, S&F, SCI, VetBull. *Aud.:* Ac, Sa.

Genome Research seeks to provide a "nexus point where genomic information, applications, and technology come together with biological information to create a more global understanding of all biological systems." Topics treated include gene discovery, comparative genome analyses, molecular and human evolution, informatics, genome structure and function, proteomics, technological innovations and applications, statistical and mathematical methods, cutting-edge genetic and physical mapping and DNA sequencing, systems biology and other reports that present data where sequence information is used to address biological concerns. Electronic access is free with a paid print subscription. Online content, including full text from 1997 forward, is provided through Stanford's HighWire Press. The broad scope of this journal will appeal to upper-level undergraduates through specialists in the biological sciences.

1133. *Heredity.* [ISSN: 0018-067X] 1947. m. USD 611 print & online eds. (Individuals, USD 207 print & online eds.). Ed(s): Dr. J F Brookfield. Nature Publishing Group, The MacMillan Building, 4 Crinan St, London, N1 9XW, United Kingdom; subscriptions@nature.com; http://www.nature.com/. Illus., index, adv. Sample. Refereed. Circ: 1075. Microform: PQC. Online: EBSCO Publishing; Gale Group; ingenta.com; Munksgaard & Blackwell Science's Synergy; OCLC Online Computer Library Center, Inc.; Ovid Technologies, Inc.; RoweCom Information Quest; Swets Blackwell. *Indexed:* AbAn, Agr, ApEcolAb, B&AI, BiolAb, ChemAb, ExcerpMed, FPA, FS&TA, ForAb, GSI, HortAb, IndMed, IndVet, S&F, SCI, VetBull, ZooRec. *Bk. rev.:* 4-5, 400-2,000 words. *Aud.:* Ac, Sa.

Published by the Nature Publishing Group for The Genetics Society, *Heredity* presents articles covering "original research and theoretical insights in all areas of genetics." Research papers, news and commentary, and book reviews are published. There is a good mix of plant and animal genetics. Subscription options include print only, online only, and print and online combined. Online full text is available from 1996 forward. Appropriate for academic and special libraries catering to researchers interested in genetics. Document delivery is available from BLDSC, CASDDS, CISTI, EMDOCS, The Genuine Article, LHLDS, UMI, and UnCover.

1134. *Human Biology (Detroit): the international journal of population biology and genetics.* [ISSN: 0018-7143] 1929. bi-m. USD 190; USD 266 combined subscription. Ed(s): Dennis O'Rourke. Wayne State University Press, The Leonard N Simons Bldg, 4809 Woodward Ave, Detroit, MI 48201-1309; http://wsupress.wayne.edu/. Illus., index, adv. Refereed. Circ: 1654. Vol. ends: Dec. Microform: PQC. Online: bigchalk; Chadwyck-Healey Incorporated; Florida Center for Library Automation; Gale Group; OCLC Online Computer Library Center, Inc.; Project MUSE; ProQuest Information & Learning; Swets Blackwell; H.W. Wilson. Reprint: PQC. *Indexed:* A&ATA, ABS&EES, AICP, AbAn, AgeL, AnthLit, B&AI, BAS, BiolAb, BiolDig, ChemAb, DSA, ExcerpMed, GSI, IndMed, PsycholAb, SCI, SSCI, SociolAb. *Bk. rev.:* 1-3, 500-1,400 words. *Aud.:* Ac, Sa.

Human Biology, published by Wayne State University Press for the American Association of Anthropological Genetics (AAAG), publishes papers in human population biology and genetics. Topics of interest include population genetics, evolutionary and genetic demography, quantitative genetics, genetic epidemiology, behavioral genetics, molecular genetics, growth, and physiological parameters focusing on genetic/environmental interactions. Online content is available for the years 2001 forward via a subscription to Project Muse. This title is appropriate for anthropology, biology, and medical collections. Document delivery is available from BLDSC, CASDDS, CISTI, EMDOCS, The Genuine Article, LHLDS, NIWI, UMI, and UnCover.

1135. ***Journal of Heredity.*** [ISSN: 0022-1503] 1910. bi-m. GBP 176. Ed(s): Stephen O'Brien. Oxford University Press, Great Clarendon St, Oxford, OX2 6DP, United Kingdom; jnl.orders@oup.co.uk; http://www3.oup.co.uk/jnls. Illus., index, adv. Refereed. Circ: 2300. Vol. ends: Nov/Dec. Microform: IDC; PMC; PQC. Online: EBSCO Publishing; Gale Group; HighWire Press; ingenta.com; OCLC Online Computer Library Center, Inc.; Oxford University Press Online Journals; RoweCom Information Quest; Swets Blackwell. Reprint: PQC; PSC. *Indexed:* AbAn, Agr, B&AI, BiolAb, ChemAb, DSA, ExcerpMed, FPA, FS&TA, ForAb, GSI, GeoRef, HortAb, IndMed, IndVet, PsycholAb, SCI, VetBull, ZooRec. *Bk. rev.:* 0-5, 300-900 words. *Aud.:* Ac, Sa.

Journal of Heredity publishes articles focusing on gene action, regulation, and transmission in both plant and animal species, including the genetic aspects of botany, cytogenetics and evolution, zoology, and molecular and developmental biology. Research papers, short communications, computer notes, and review articles are accepted. The reasonably priced print subscription includes online access. Online content, available on Stanford's HighWire Press, includes full text from 1998 to the present. This journal will be of interest to a wide range of biologists, including geneticists, zoologists, botanists, and ecologists. Document delivery is available from BLDSC, CASDDS, CISTI, The Genuine Article, LHLDS, UMI, and UnCover.

1136. ***Molecular Genetics and Genomics: an international journal.*** Former titles (until 2001): *Molecular and General Genetics;* (until 1966): *Zeitschrift fuer Vererbungslehre;* (until 1957): *Zeitschrift fuer Induktive Abstammungs- und Vererbungslehre.* [ISSN: 1617-4615] 1908. m. EUR 2998 domestic; EUR 3046.20 foreign; EUR 300 newsstand/cover per issue. Ed(s): C P Hollenberg, W Arber. Springer-Verlag, Tiergartenstr 17, Heidelberg, 69121, Germany. Illus., index, adv. Refereed. Microform: PQC. Online: EBSCO Publishing; RoweCom Information Quest; Springer LINK; Swets Blackwell. Reprint: ISI. *Indexed:* Agr, B&AI, BiolAb, ChemAb, DSA, ExcerpMed, FPA, FS&TA, ForAb, HortAb, IndMed, IndVet, S&F, SCI, VetBull, ZooRec. *Aud.:* Ac, Sa.

Molecular Genetics and Genomics publishes "original research and reviews in all areas of general and molecular genetics, developmental genetics, somatic cell genetics, and genetic engineering, irrespective of the organism involved." SpringerLink makes available the electronic content for the title, including full text from 1996 forward. A basic site license is included in the price of a print subscription. An important, though expensive, journal for molecular geneticists. Document delivery is available from ADONIS, BLDSC, CASDDS, CISTI, The Genuine Article, UMI, and UnCover.

1137. ***Nature Genetics.*** [ISSN: 1061-4036] 1992. m. USD 825 (Individuals, USD 199). Ed(s): Bette Phimister. Nature America, Inc., 345 Park Ave S, 10th Fl, New York, NY 10010. Illus., index, adv. Refereed. Circ: 3000. Online: EBSCO Publishing; Swets Blackwell. *Indexed:* ArtHuCI, B&AI, BiolAb, BiolDig, ChemAb, DSA, ExcerpMed, IndMed, IndVet, S&F, SCI, SSCI, VetBull. *Bk. rev.:* 1, 700-1,000 words. *Aud.:* Ac, Sa.

Nature Genetics was founded in 1992 as a companion journal to *Nature.* The emphasis of the journal is on genomics and mammalian genetics but all fields of genetic research are treated. Original research articles, editorials, news, commentary, progress articles, and articles about new technology are published. Print and online subscriptions are separate and accessed through Nature Publishing Group. Online content for this title includes full text from mid-1997 forward. This journal is frequently cited and well-respected and is appropriate for any library supporting a biology program. Document delivery is available from BLDSC, CASDDS, CISTI, EMDOCS, The Genuine Article, and UMI.

1138. ***R N A.*** [ISSN: 1355-8382] 1995. m. USD 710 (Individuals, USD 260). Ed(s): Dr. Timothy W Nilsen. Cold Spring Harbor Laboratory Press, Publications Department, 500 Sunnyside Blvd., Woodbury, NY 11797-2924; cshpress@cshl.edu; http://www.cshl.org. Adv. Refereed. Online: EBSCO Publishing; HighWire Press; RoweCom Information Quest; Swets Blackwell. *Indexed:* IndMed, SCI. *Aud.:* Ac, Sa.

RNA "provides rapid publication of significant original research in all areas of RNA structure and function in eukaryotic, prokaryotic, and viral systems." Papers may cover a broad range of topics including structural analysis; rRNA, mRNA and tRNA structure, function and biogenesis; alternative processing; ribosome structure and function; translational control; RNA catalysis; RNA editing; RNA transport and localization; regulatory RNAs; large and small RNP structure, function and biogenesis; viral RNA metabolism; RNA stability and turnover; in vitro evolution; and RNA chemistry. Institutions may choose from a two subscription options: print plus online, and online only. Online content is provided through Stanford's HighWire Press and includes full text from the inception of the journal in 1995 to the present. While this is a specialty title, it will appeal to upper-level undergraduates through researchers in a broad range of biological and medical disciplines.

Microbiology

1139. ***Applied and Environmental Microbiology.*** Formerly (until 1976): *Applied Microbiology.* [ISSN: 0099-2240] 1953. m. Members, USD 64; Non-members, USD 421. Ed(s): Judy D Wall. American Society for Microbiology, 1752 N St N W, Washington, DC 20036-2904; subscriptions@amsusa.org; http://www.asmusa.org. Illus., index, adv. Refereed. Circ: 7100 Paid. Vol. ends: Dec. Microform: PQC. Online: EBSCO Publishing; Gale Group; HighWire Press. Reprint: PQC. *Indexed:* Agr, ApEcolAb, B&AI, BioEngAb, BiolAb, ChemAb, DSA, EngInd, EnvAb, ExcerpMed, FPA, FS&TA, ForAb, GSI, GeoRef, GeogAbPG, HortAb, IndMed, IndVet, OceAb, PetrolAb, PollutAb, RRTA, S&F, SCI, SWRA, VetBull, WRCInf, ZooRec. *Aud.:* Ac, Sa.

This journal publishes current research in the areas of biotechnology, microbial ecology, food microbiology, and industrial microbiology. Articles cover a very broad range of topics and are divided into several sections, including genetics and molecular biology, enzymology and protein engineering, physiology and biotechnology, mycology, public-health microbiology, environmental microbiology and biodegradation, microbial ecology, geomicrobiology, food microbiology, plant microbiology, invertebrate microbiology, and methods. Online full text is available from 1995 forward and abstracts only from 1992 to 1994 on the ASM web site. Free access is granted to issues more than 12 months old. One of many valuable sources from the well-respected American Society for Microbiology, this source is an inexpensive and important source for academic libraries and for special libraries with an interest in microbiology. Document delivery is available from BLDSC, CASDDS, CISTI, EI, EMDOCS, The Genuine Article, LHLDS, NIWI, UMI, and UnCover.

1140. ***Canadian Journal of Microbiology.*** [ISSN: 0008-4166] 1954. m. CND 422 (Individuals, CND 151). Ed(s): Dr. Jim J Germida, H G Deneer. N R C Research Press, Building M 55, Ottawa, ON K1A 0R6, Canada; http://www.nrc.ca/cisti/journals/. Illus., index, adv. Sample. Refereed. Circ: 1341. Vol. ends: Dec. Microform: MML; PMC; PQC. Online: CISTI; EBSCO Publishing; ingenta.com; RoweCom Information Quest; Swets Blackwell. Reprint: PQC. *Indexed:* Agr, B&AI, BiolAb, CBCARef, ChemAb, DSA, DSR&OA, EngInd, EnvAb, ExcerpMed, FPA, FS&TA, ForAb, HortAb, IAA, IndMed, IndVet, PollutAb, S&F, SCI, SWRA, VetBull. *Aud.:* Ac, Sa.

Published by the National Research Council of Canada, *Canadian Journal of Microbiology* covers a wide range of microbiological topics, including "applied microbiology and biotechnology; microbial structure and function; fungi and other eucaryotic protists; infection and immunity; microbial ecology; physiology, metabolism, and enzymology; and virology, genetics, and molecular biology." The majority of the journal's papers are in English, although French is also accepted. Tables of contents and a sample issue are freely available on the NRC web site. Online full text access and print are separate subscriptions, though a discount is available to libraries wishing to purchase both. This journal will be useful for researchers in academic or special-library settings. Document delivery is available from ADONIS, BLDSC, CASDDS, CISTI, EMDOCS, The Genuine Article, LHLDS, UMI, and UnCover.

1141. ***International Journal of Systematic and Evolutionary Microbiology.*** Former titles (until 1999): *International Journal of Systematic Bacteriology;* (until 1966): *International Bulletin of Bacteriological Nomenclature and Toxonomy.* [ISSN: 1466-5026] 1951. bi-m. GBP 420. Ed(s): Dr. Peter Kaempfer. Society for General Microbiology, Marlborough House, Basingstoke Rd, Spencers Wood, Reading, RG7 1AG, United Kingdom; http://www.sgm.ac.uk. Illus., index, adv. Refereed. Circ: 1100. Vol. ends:

Oct/Dec. Microform: PQC. Online: EBSCO Publishing; HighWire Press. Reprint: PQC. *Indexed:* Agr, BiolAb, ChemAb, DSA, DSR&OA, ExcerpMed, FPA, FS&TA, ForAb, HortAb, IndMed, IndVet, S&F, SCI, VetBull, ZooRec. *Bk. rev.:* 1, 1,000-1,200 words. *Aud.:* Ac, Sa.

Sponsored by the Society for General Microbiology, this journal, formerly entitled *International Journal of Systematic Bacteriology* publishes "papers dealing with all phases of the systematics of all micro-organisms, including taxonomy, nomenclature, identification, characterization and culture preservation." Articles make up the vast majority of the contents, but reviews may occasionally appear. Stanford's HighWire Press makes available the online content, which is included with a print subscription. A section of the web site makes available articles' online supplementary material. This journal will be of use in libraries providing services to bacteriologists and evolutionary biologists.

1142. ***Journal of Bacteriology.*** [ISSN: 0021-9193] 1916. fortn. Non-members, USD 688. Ed(s): Graham C Walker. American Society for Microbiology, 1752 N St N W, Washington, DC 20036-2904; subscriptions@asmusa.org; http://www.asmusa.org. Illus., index, adv. Refereed. Circ: 5400 Paid. Vol. ends: Dec. Microform: PQC. Online: EBSCO Publishing; Gale Group; HighWire Press. Reprint: PQC. *Indexed:* Agr, B&AI, BiolAb, BiolDig, ChemAb, DSA, DSR&OA, ExcerpMed, FPA, FS&TA, GSI, HortAb, IAA, IndMed, IndVet, S&F, SCI, VetBull, WRCInf. *Aud.:* Ac, Sa.

Papers in *Journal of Bacteriology* cover all aspects of microorganisms and fall into the following categories: general microbiology, structure and function, models and cell growth, plant microbiology, genetics and molecular biology, plasmids and transposons, eukaryotic cells, cell surfaces, physiology and metabolism, enzymes and proteins, bacteriophages, population genetics, and evolution. Papers on genetics and molecular biology make up most of the contents, while some categories may not contain any papers in a given month. Minireviews also appear. Print and online subscriptions are separate. Online full text is available from 1995 to the present. Free online access is available to all for issues more than six months old. Published by the well-regarded American Society for Microbiology, this is a prominent microbiology journal and core biology title. Document delivery is available from BLDSC, CASDDS, CISTI, The Genuine Article, LHLDS, NIWI, UMI, and UnCover.

1143. ***The Journal of Eukaryotic Microbiology.*** Formerly (until 1993): *Journal of Protozoology.* [ISSN: 1066-5234] 1954. bi-m. Members, USD 87; Non-members, USD 180. Ed(s): Dennis Lynn. Allen Press Inc., PO Box 1897, Lawrence, KS 66044; orders@allenpress.com; http://www.allenpress.com/. Illus., index, adv. Refereed. Circ: 1800. Vol. ends: Nov/Dec. *Indexed:* Agr, B&AI, BiolAb, BiolDig, ChemAb, DSA, DSR&OA, ExcerpMed, ForAb, GeoRef, IndMed, IndVet, S&F, SCI, VetBull, ZooRec. *Aud.:* Ac, Sa.

Published by the Society of Protozoologists, the *Journal of Eukaryotic Microbiology* is a forum for "original research on protists, including lower algae and fungi." It covers all aspects of these organisms, including their behavior, biochemistry, cell biology, chemotherapy, development, ecology, evolution, genetics, molecular biology, morphogenetics, parasitology, systematics, and ultrastructure. Papers fall into the following categories: research articles, communications, and invited reviews. Special reports generated from workshops are published as supplements. Online content is provided by Allen Press' APT Online and includes tables of contents and abstracts from 1998 to the present. Appropriate for academic, medical, and special library biology collections. Document delivery is available from BLDSC, CASDDS, CISTI, EMDOCS, The Genuine Article, LHLDS, NIWI, UMI, and UnCover.

1144. ***Journal of Virology.*** [ISSN: 0022-538X] 1967. fortn. Non-members, USD 772. Ed(s): Thomas E Shenk. American Society for Microbiology, 1752 N St N W, Washington, DC 20036-2904; subscriptions@asmusa.org; http://www.asmusa.org. Illus., index, adv. Refereed. Circ: 4300 Paid. Vol. ends: Dec. Microform: PQC. Online: EBSCO Publishing; HighWire Press. Reprint: PQC. *Indexed:* Agr, B&AI, BiolAb, ChemAb, DSA, ExcerpMed, FS&TA, ForAb, HortAb, IndMed, IndVet, SCI, VetBull. *Aud.:* Ac, Sa.

Producing approximately 13,400 pages in 2003, the *Journal of Virology* publishes original research concerning viruses, regardless of vector. Sections include "Structure and Assembly," "Replication," "Recombination and Evolution," "Virus-Cell Interactions," "Transformation and Oncogenesis," "Pathogenesis and Immunity," "Vaccines and Antiviral Agents," "Gene Therapy," and "Minireviews." As one might expect, much of the journal is devoted to viruses impacting humans, especially HIV. Online content is provided through Stanford's HighWire Press and includes full text from 1995 forward. This title is one of the most highly respected in the field and will be useful in academic libraries or special libraries supporting biology or medical programs. Document delivery is available from BLDSC, CASDDS, CISTI, EMDOCS, The Genuine Article, LHLDS, NIWI, UMI, and UnCover.

1145. ***Microbiology.*** Formerly (until 1993): *Journal of General Microbiology.* [ISSN: 1350-0872] 1947. m. GBP 695. Ed(s): C M Thomas. Society for General Microbiology, Marlborough House, Basingstoke Rd, Spencers Wood, Reading, RG7 1AG, United Kingdom; http://www.sgm.ac.uk Illus., index, adv. Refereed. Circ: 2440. Vol. ends: Dec. Microform: PMC. Online: EBSCO Publishing; Gale Group; HighWire Press; Kluwer Online. *Indexed:* Agr, B&AI, BiolAb, BiolDig, ChemAb, DSA, DSR&OA, ExcerpMed, FPA, FS&TA, ForAb, GSI, GeoRef, HortAb, IndMed, IndVet, S&F, SCI, VetBull. *Aud.:* Ac, Sa.

Published by the Society for General Microbiology in approximately 3,000 pages annually, this journal presents research papers, reviews and minireviews, and informal communications on all areas of microbiology. Sections vary from issue to issue and may include "Biochemistry and Molecular Biology," "Biodiversity and Evolution," "Cell and Developmental Biology," "Environmental Microbiology," "Genes and Genomes," "Pathogens and Pathogenicity," "Physiology," "Plant-Microbe Interactions," and "Theoretical Microbiology." Online access is free with a print subscription. Full text online from 1997 forward is provided through Stanford's HighWire Press. Useful for institutions with researchers in biology and medical disciplines. Document delivery is available from BLDSC, CASDDS, CISTI, EMDOCS, The Genuine Article, LHLDS, NIWI, and UnCover.

1146. ***Microbiology and Molecular Biology Reviews.*** Former titles (until 1997): *Microbiological Reviews;* (until 1978): *Bacteriological Reviews.* [ISSN: 1092-2172] 1937. q. Members, USD 48; Non-members, USD 320. Ed(s): Catherine L Squires. American Society for Microbiology, 1752 N St N W, Washington, DC 20036-2904; subscriptions@asmusa.org; http://www.asmusa.org. Illus., index, adv. Refereed. Circ: 8200 Paid. Vol. ends: Dec. Microform: PQC. Online: EBSCO Publishing; Gale Group; HighWire Press. Reprint: PQC. *Indexed:* B&AI, BiolAb, BiolDig, ChemAb, DSA, DSR&OA, ExcerpMed, FS&TA, GSI, HortAb, IndMed, IndVet, S&F, SCI, VetBull, WRCInf, ZooRec. *Aud.:* Ac, Sa.

Microbiology and Molecular Biology Reviews (*MMBR*) is the review journal of the American Society for Microbiology, focusing on critical, evaluative reviews of the current state of research in microbiology, immunology, and molecular and cellular biology. Topics covered include cellular biology, ecology, genetics, host-parasite relationships leading to disease, molecular biology, physiology and enzymology, and virology. Subscription options include print only and online only, with multiple online subscription levels depending on the institution's FTE in the life sciences. Online content for this title is provided through Stanford's HighWire Press and includes full text from 1995 forward. Access to articles more than one year old is freely available to all. The accessibility of the articles, the wonderful bibliographies, and the low cost of this journal make it an excellent choice for academic or special libraries supporting biology programs. Document delivery is available from BLDSC, CASDDS, CISTI, The Genuine Article, LHLDS, and UnCover.

1147. ***Virology.*** [ISSN: 0042-6822] 1955. 26x/yr. EUR 5884 (Individuals, EUR 801; Students, EUR 134). Ed(s): Robert Lamb. Academic Press, 525 B St, Ste 1900, San Diego, CA 92101-4495; http://www.academicpress.com. Illus., index, adv. Refereed. Online: EBSCO Publishing; ingenta.com; OCLC Online Computer Library Center, Inc.; RoweCom Information Quest; ScienceDirect; Swets Blackwell. *Indexed:* Agr, B&AI, BiolAb, ChemAb, DSA, ExcerpMed, FS&TA, HortAb, IndMed, IndVet, SCI, VetBull. *Aud.:* Ac, Sa.

Virology is a forum for research on viruses regardless of vector. The editors cite the following as areas of interest: virus replication and gene expression, virus structure and assembly, virus-cell interaction, viral pathogenesis and immunity, viral vectors/gene therapy, and molecular aspects of prevention of viral infection. Of particular interest is information on emerging viruses and unconventional agents. Minireviews are also published. Elsevier's ScienceDirect makes available the online content for this title, including full text from 1993 forward. Appropriate for upper-division undergraduates through specialists and a useful title for medical and biology collections. Document delivery is available from BLDSC, CASDDS, CISTI, The Genuine Article, LHLDS, UMI, and UnCover.

Molecular Biology

1148. ***BioEssays: advances in molecular, cellular and developmental biology.*** [ISSN: 0265-9247] 1984. m. USD 895.25 in North America; USD 955 elsewhere; USD 935.75 combined subscription in North America for print and online eds. Ed(s): Adam S Wilkins. John Wiley & Sons Ltd., The Atrium, Southern Gate, Chichester, PO19 8SQ, United Kingdom; customer@wiley.co.uk; http://www.wiley.co.uk. Adv. Refereed. Reprint: SWZ. *Indexed:* ChemAb, DSA, ExcerpMed, HortAb, IndMed, IndVet, S&F, SCI, VetBull, ZooRec. *Bk. rev.:* 0-3, 500-600 words. *Aud.:* Ac, Sa.

BioEssays publishes "short news-and-views articles plus broad reviews plus insightful discussion articles about the latest findings and ideas in molecular cell biology, developmental biology, plant science and neurobiology - all within a broad context." Reviews, discussions, meeting overviews, book reviews, editorials, and hypotheses appear. Special issues focusing on particular themes are published occasionally. Online full text is provided via Wiley InterScience with a full rate subscription. An online sample issue is available, as are tables of contents and alerts, with registration. The broad coverage and style of this journal will appeal to upper-division undergraduates through specialists.

1149. ***The E M B O Journal.*** [ISSN: 0261-4189] 1982. s-m. GBP 875 (Individuals, GBP 150; Members, GBP 130). Ed(s): Herbert Jaeckle, John Tooze. Oxford University Press, Great Clarendon St, Oxford, OX2 6DP, United Kingdom; jnl.orders@oup.co.uk; http://www3.oup.co.uk/jnls. Illus., index, adv. Sample. Refereed. Circ: 4200. Vol. ends: Dec. Online: EBSCO Publishing; HighWire Press; ingenta.com; OCLC Online Computer Library Center, Inc.; Ovid Technologies, Inc.; RoweCom Information Quest; Swets Blackwell. Reprint: SWZ. *Indexed:* Agr, B&AI, BiolAb, ChemAb, DSA, ExcerpMed, FS&TA, ForAb, HortAb, IndMed, IndVet, S&F, SCI, VetBull, ZooRec. *Aud.:* Ac, Sa.

The EMBO Journal, published by Oxford for the European Molecular Biology Organization, is dedicated to making available "novel results of significant general interest that provide new functional insight into molecular or cellular processes." Authors are instructed to write for as wide an audience as possible. The journal is restricted to publishing not more than 6,500 pages annually and even receiving a majority of favorable reviews from the journal's reviewers does not guarantee that a paper will be published. Online content is available through Stanford's HighWire Press and includes full text and abstracts from 1997 to the present, while abstracts only are available from 1984 to 1996. The online content is free with a print subscription. A table of contents alerting service is available. Highly respected and heavily cited, this title is appropriate for academic or special libraries with biology programs. Document delivery is available from BLDSC, CASDDS, CISTI, EMDOCS, The Genuine Article, LHLDS, UMI, and UnCover.

1150. ***Journal of Molecular Biology.*** [ISSN: 0022-2836] 1959. 50x/yr. EUR 6321 (Individuals, EUR 851). Ed(s): P Wright. Academic Press, Harcourt Pl, 32 Jamestown Rd, London, NW1 7BY, United Kingdom; apsubs@acad.com; http://www.elsevier-international.com/serials/. Illus., index, adv. Sample. Refereed. Online: EBSCO Publishing; ingenta.com; OCLC Online Computer Library Center, Inc.; RoweCom Information Quest; ScienceDirect; Swets Blackwell. Reprint: SWZ. *Indexed:* Agr, B&AI, BiolAb, ChemAb, DSA, ExcerpMed, FPA, FS&TA, ForAb, HortAb, IndMed, IndVet, S&F, SCI, VetBull, ZooRec. *Aud.:* Ac, Sa.

Among the topics covered by the weekly *Journal of Molecular Biology* are molecular structure, physical chemistry, molecular engineering of proteins, organelle structure and function, nucleic acids and other macromolecules, and the structure, expression, replication, and sequencing of genes. Article types include research papers, editorials, reviews, innovative techniques, controversial topics, and historical perspectives. Elsevier's ScienceDirect provides the online presence for this journal, including full text from 1993 to the present. While expensive, this is a well-regarded title, appropriate for any research institution supporting biologists. Document delivery is available from BLDSC, CASDDS, CISTI, The Genuine Article, LHLDS, UMI, and UnCover.

1151. ***Molecular and Cellular Biology.*** [ISSN: 0270-7306] 1981. fortn. Members, USD 99; Non-members, USD 644. Ed(s): James N Ihle. American Society for Microbiology, 1752 N St N W, Washington, DC 20036-2904; subscriptions@asmusa.org; http://www.asmusa.org. Illus., index, adv. Sample. Refereed. Circ: 4700 Paid. Vol. ends: Dec. Microform: PQC. Online: EBSCO Publishing. Reprint: PQC. *Indexed:* B&AI, BiolAb, ChemAb, DSA, ExcerpMed, HortAb, IndMed, IndVet, S&F, SCI, VetBull, ZooRec. *Aud.:* Ac, Sa.

Published in approximately 8,600 pages in 2003 by the well-regarded American Society for Microbiology, *Molecular and Cellular Biology* accepts papers presenting "fundamental knowledge and new developments in all aspects of the molecular biology of eukaryotic cells." The scope of the journal includes gene expression, transcriptional regulation, cell growth and development, nucleocytoplasmic communication, and cell and organelle structure and assembly, among other subjects. Minireviews appear in some issues. Print and online subscriptions are available, with varying fees for online depending on the institution's FTE in the life sciences. Stanford's HighWire Press makes available the full text of this journal from 1995 forward. Accessible to upper-division undergraduates through specialists. Document delivery is available from BLDSC, CASDDS, CISTI, EMDOCS, The Genuine Article, LHLDS, NIWI, UMI, and UnCover.

1152. ***Molecular Biology and Evolution.*** [ISSN: 0737-4038] 1983. m. GBP 341. Ed(s): Simon Easteal. Oxford University Press, Great Clarendon St, Oxford, OX2 6DP, United Kingdom; jnl.orders@oup.co.uk; http://www3.oup.co.uk/jnls. Illus., index, adv. Refereed. Circ: 1000. Vol. ends: Nov. Microform: PMC; PQC. Online: EBSCO Publishing; HighWire Press; ingenta.com. Reprint: ISI; PQC; PSC. *Indexed:* AbAn, BiolAb, ChemAb, DSA, ExcerpMed, ForAb, GeoRef, HortAb, IndMed, IndVet, S&F, SCI, VetBull, ZooRec. *Aud.:* Ac, Sa.

Molecular Biology and Evolution publishes research at the interface of molecular biology and evolution, including "investigations of molecular evolutionary patterns and processes; tests of evolutionary hypotheses that use molecular data; and studies that use molecular evolutionary information to address issues in fields such as anthropology, biochemistry, developmental biology, ecology, genetics, genomics, and molecular medicine." Articles fall into two categories: full-length research papers and short research communications, published under "Letters to the Editor." Subscription options to this reasonably priced journal include online-only and print plus online. Substantial online content is made available through Stanford's HighWire Press and includes full text from 1983 to the present. This title is accessible to upper-division undergraduates through specialists. Document delivery is available from BLDSC, CASDDS, CISTI, EMDOCS, The Genuine Article, LHLDS, UMI, and UnCover.

1153. ***Molecular Cell.*** [ISSN: 1097-2765] 1997. 24x/yr. EUR 1227 (Individuals, EUR 275). Ed(s): Vivian Siegel. Cell Press, 1100 Massachusetts Ave, Cambridge, MA 02138; editor@cell.com; http://www.cellpress.com/. Adv. Refereed. Online: ingenta.com. *Indexed:* BiolAb, ChemAb, EngInd, ExcerpMed, IndMed, IndVet, SCI, VetBull. *Aud.:* Ac, Sa.

Molecular Cell "focuses on analyses at the molecular level in any area of biology, particularly that of molecular biology (including replication, recombination, repair, gene expression, RNA processing, translation, and protein folding, modification and degradation)." Research articles make up most of the journal with shorter papers making up the balance. Position announcements are also included. Print and online subscriptions are available. Cell Press makes available the online content for the title, including full text from 1997 forward. Useful to researchers in this area in academic or special library settings.

1154. ***Nucleic Acids Research.*** [ISSN: 0305-1048] 1974. s-m. GBP 1502. Ed(s): Michael Gait, Richard J Roberts. Oxford University Press, Great Clarendon St, Oxford, OX2 6DP, United Kingdom; jnl.orders@oup.co.uk; http://www3.oup.co.uk/jnls. Illus., index, adv. Sample.

Refereed. Circ: 2800. Vol. ends: Dec. Online: EBSCO Publishing; HighWire Press; ingenta.com; RoweCom Information Quest; Swets Blackwell. Reprint: PSC; SWZ. *Indexed:* Agr, BioEngAb, BiolAb, ChemAb, DSA, ExcerpMed, FS&TA, ForAb, HortAb, IndMed, IndVet, S&F, SCI, VetBull. *Aud.:* Ac, Sa.

Nucleic Acids Research publishes the results of "leading edge research into physical, chemical, biochemical and biological aspects of nucleic acids and proteins involved in nucleic acid metabolism and/or interactions." "Nucleic Acids Research Methods" provides a forum for online access to methods papers, listed in the journal's table of contents. Online content for this title is available via Stanford's HighWire Press and includes full text from 1996 forward. A print subscription includes online access. Expensive, but appropriate for biology, chemistry, and medical collections. Document delivery is available from BLDSC, CASDDS, CISTI, EMDOCS, The Genuine Article, LHLDS, UMI, and UnCover.

Multidisciplinary

1155. ***The American Biology Teacher.*** [ISSN: 0002-7685] 1938. m. during school year. USD 75 domestic; USD 90 foreign. Ed(s): Randy Moore. National Association of Biology Teachers, Inc., 12030 Sunrise Valley Dr, 110, Reston, VA 20191; NABTer@aol.com; http://www.nabt.org. Illus., index, adv. Refereed. Circ: 12000. Vol. ends: Nov/Dec. Microform: PQC. Online: BioOne; Gale Group; OCLC Online Computer Library Center, Inc.; ProQuest Information & Learning. *Indexed:* ABS&EES, BiolAb, BiolDig, CIJE, DSA, EduInd, EnvAb, ForAb, GSI, HortAb, IndVet, MRD, S&F, SSCI, VetBull. *Bk. rev.:* 4-8, 300-800 words. *Aud.:* Ems, Hs, Ac.

This is the official journal of the National Association of Biology Teachers, and it is aimed at teachers of high school and undergraduate biology students. Most authors are biology educators (mainly at the college level, though some are high school teachers) or professional biologists. The journal publishes three to five articles monthly. These may include reviews of biology research or topics of current interest, discussion of social and ethical issues in biology education, results of studies on teaching techniques, or approaches for use in the classroom. The "How-to-Do-It" section includes four to six articles focusing on specific projects for the laboratory or field. Most issues have reviews of audiovisual materials or computer resources in "Classroom Technology Reviews." "Biology Today" presents essays by the section editor on interesting topics of current interest. Announcements and society news are also featured. Given the concern about science education in this country, this title should be of interest to anyone teaching undergraduate introductory biology courses, junior and senior high teachers, and even parents home-schooling older children. Excerpts from the journal can be viewed at the association's web site. Document delivery is available from BLDSC, CASDDS, CISTI, The Genuine Article, LHLDS, UMI, and UnCover.

1156. ***Biological Reviews.*** Former titles (until 1997): *Cambridge Philosophical Society. Biological Reviews;* (until 1937): *Cambridge Philosophical Society. Biological Reviews and Biological Proceedings;* (until 1926): *Cambridge Philosophical Society. Proceedings. Biological Sciences.* [ISSN: 1464-7931] 1923. q. USD 210. Ed(s): W A Foster. Cambridge University Press, The Edinburgh Bldg, Shaftesbury Rd, Cambridge, CB2 2RU, United Kingdom; information@cambridge.org; http://uk.cambridge.org/journals. Illus., index. Refereed. Vol. ends: Nov. Microform: IDC; PQC. Online: EBSCO Publishing; Gale Group; RoweCom Information Quest; Swets Blackwell. *Indexed:* AnBeAb, ApEcolAb, B&AI, BiolAb, ChemAb, ExcerpMed, FPA, ForAb, GSI, GeoRef, HortAb, IndMed, IndVet, S&F, SCI, SSCI, VetBull, ZooRec. *Aud.:* Ac, Sa.

Covering the entire range of the biological sciences, *Biological Reviews* presents review articles aimed at general biologists as well as specialists in the field. Each issue contains about five articles, each containing a detailed table of contents, an introduction, a summary, and a substantial bibliography. Online access is available through Cambridge Journals Online. The basic subscription is for the online journal. With a small additional fee one can have the print subscription as well. This is an excellent source for general academic as well as research collections supporting biology programs. Individuals interested in biology are likely to find at least one article of interest in every issue. Document delivery is available from BLDSC, CASDDS, EMDOCS, The Genuine Article, UMI, and UnCover.

1157. ***BioScience.*** [ISSN: 0006-3568] 1951. m. USD 267 print & online eds. (Individuals, USD 70). Ed(s): Rebecca Chasan. American Institute of Biological Sciences, 1313 Dolley Madison Blvd, Ste 402, McLean, VA 22101; http://www.aibs.org. Illus., index, adv. Refereed. Circ: 9000. Vol. ends: Dec. Microform: PQC. Online: bigchalk; BioOne; EBSCO Publishing; Florida Center for Library Automation; Gale Group; Ingenta Select; Northern Light Technology, Inc.; OCLC Online Computer Library Center, Inc.; ProQuest Information & Learning; H.W. Wilson. Reprint: PQC. *Indexed:* Agr, AnBeAb, ApEcolAb, B&AI, BRI, BiolAb, BiolDig, CAPS, CBRI, CIJE, ChemAb, DSA, DSR&OA, EnvAb, FPA, ForAb, FutSurv, GSI, GardL, GeoRef, HortAb, IndVet, MagInd, PollutAb, RGPR, RRTA, S&F, SCI, SSCI, SWRA, VetBull, WAE&RSA, ZooRec. *Bk. rev.:* 2-7, 600-2,000 words. *Aud.:* Ga, Ac, Sa.

BioScience is published for "a broad audience of professional biologists, biology teachers, and advanced students." The journal features recent advances in the field, opinion pieces, essays on the teaching of biology, news, legislative developments, and calendars of meetings. Online access from 1999 forward is included with a print subscription and is hosted by Ingenta Select. Table of contents alerting is available. This journal features interesting articles accessible to general readers as well as students, researchers, and professionals, and is appropriate for academic libraries, special libraries, and large public libraries. Document delivery is available from BLDSC, CIS, CISTI, EMDOCS, The Genuine Article, LHLDS, UMI, and UnCover.

Chickadee. See Children section.

1158. ***Current Biology.*** [ISSN: 0960-9822] 1991. s-m. EUR 1186 (Individuals, EUR 275). Ed(s): Geoffrey North. Cell Press, 1100 Massachusetts Ave, Cambridge, MA 02138; http://www.cellpress.com/. Illus., adv. Sample. Refereed. Circ: 9100. Vol. ends: Dec. Online: EBSCO Publishing; ingenta.com; ScienceDirect; Swets Blackwell. *Indexed:* AnBeAb, BiolAb, BiolDig, ChemAb, HortAb, IndMed, IndVet, S&F, SSCI, VetBull, ZooRec. *Aud.:* Ga, Ac, Sa.

Current Biology "publishes research papers in any area of biology, provided that the research clearly represents an important advance of especially broad interest to biologists." Contents include news and features, brief review articles, research papers, and shorter research papers called "Brief Communications." Review of papers takes place within three weeks of receipt of articles and publication of papers is targetted for the first issue after proofs are returned, making for a relatively quick publication schedule. Online content, available via the Cell Press web site, features full text and summaries for 1994 to the present. Online content and a print subscription require separate site license and subscription. The general coverage of the publication and the news and short reviews make this title one that would be useful in any academic or special library supporting a biology program. Document delivery is available from ADONIS, BLDSC, CASDDS, CISTI, EMDOCS, The Genuine Article, UMI, and UnCover.

1159. ***The F A S E B Journal.*** Supersedes: *Federation of American Societies for Experimental Biology. Federation Proceedings.* [ISSN: 0892-6638] 1987. 14x/yr. USD 693 print & online eds. (Individuals, USD 170 print & online eds.; Members, USD 99 print & online eds.). Ed(s): Vincent T Marchesi. Federation of American Societies for Experimental Biology, 9650 Rockville Pike, Bethesda, MD 20814-3998; http://www.faseb.org. Illus., index, adv. Refereed. Circ: 6000 Paid. Vol. ends: Dec. Online: EBSCO Publishing; HighWire Press; RoweCom Information Quest. Reprint: PQC. *Indexed:* Agr, B&AI, BiolAb, ChemAb, DSA, ExcerpMed, FS&TA, ForAb, HortAb, IndMed, IndVet, S&F, SCI, SSCI, VetBull, ZooRec. *Aud.:* Ac, Sa.

The Federation of American Societies for Experimental Biology (FASEB) is made up of the following member organizations: American Physiological Society, American Society for Biochemistry and Molecular Biology, American Society for Pharmacology and Experimental Therapeutics, American Society for Investigative Pathology, American Society for Nutritional Sciences, American Association of Immunologists, Biophysical Society, American Association of Anatomists, Protein Society, American Society for Bone and Mineral Research, American Society for Clinical Investigation, Endocrine Society, American Society of Human Genetics, Society for Developmental Biology, American Peptide Society, Association of Biomolecular Resource Facilities, Society for the Study of Reproduction, Teratology Society, Radiation Research Society, Society for Gynecologic Investigation, and Environmental Mutagen Society. *The FASEB Journal* focuses on manuscripts that integrate one or more of the disciplines of the represented societies. The section "FJ Express" provides a mechanism for rapid dissemination of information, consisting of brief outlines of online articles. These summaries appear two months after the online versions. Also published are review articles, research communications, and hypotheses. Online content is via Stanford's HighWire Press and is included with the cost of a print subscription. Full text online is available from 1998 forward while abstracts are available from 1987 through 1997. The broad coverage of this journal make this a good choice for most biology collections. Document delivery is available from BLDSC, CASDDS, CISTI, EMDOCS, The Genuine Article, LHLDS, NIWI, UMI, and UnCover.

1160. ***National Academy of Sciences of the United States of America. Proceedings.*** Former titles (until 1985): *National Academy of Sciences of the United States of America. Proceedings. Physical Sciences; National Academy of Sciences of the United States of America. Proceedings. Biological Sciences;* Which superseded in part: *National Academy of Sciences. Proceedings.* [ISSN: 0027-8424] 1914. bi-w. USD 1320 Print & Online eds. (Individuals, USD 125 print ed.). Ed(s): Nicholas R Cozzarelli. National Academy of Sciences, 2101 Constitution Ave., NW, Washington, DC 20418; subspnas@nas.edu; http://www.pnas.org. Illus., index, adv. Sample. Refereed. Circ: 10132. Vol. ends: Dec. Microform: PQC. Online: EBSCO Publishing; Gale Group; HighWire Press; JSTOR (Web-based Journal Archive); RoweCom Information Quest. *Indexed:* Agr, AnBeAb, ApEcolAb, ArtHuCI, B&AI, BiolAb, ChemAb, DSA, DSR&OA, EngInd, ExcerpMed, FPA, FS&TA, ForAb, GSI, GeoRef, HortAb, IndMed, IndVet, OceAb, S&F, SCI, SSCI, VetBull, WAE&RSA, ZooRec. *Aud.:* Ac, Sa.

Proceedings of the National Academy of Sciences (NAS) covers the biological, social, and physical sciences, but a large proportion of the material is biological in nature. The papers fall into the following categories: research reports, commentaries, reviews, perspectives, colloquium papers, and actions of the NAS. All areas of the biological sciences may be represented, but the most heavily published areas are cell biology and biochemistry. This is a heavily cited and important journal. The price of the journal is relatively low considering its prestigious nature. Online access is currently included with a print subscription, but individuals can subscribe to the online version alone. Stanford's HighWire Press provides access to full text from 1990 forward. JSTOR makes available the full text of items published prior to 1990. An essential title for science collections. Document delivery is available from BLDSC, CASDDS, CISTI, EI, EMDOCS, The Genuine Article, LHLDS, NIWI, UMI, and UnCover.

Natural History. See Science and Technology section.

Nature. See Science and Technology section.

Owl. See Children section.

1161. ***Perspectives in Biology and Medicine.*** [ISSN: 0031-5982] 1957. q. USD 110 (Individuals, USD 40). Ed(s): Richard L Landau, Robert L Perlman. Johns Hopkins University Press, Journals Publishing Division, 2715 N Charles St, Baltimore, MD 21218-4363; http://www.press.jhu.edu/. Illus., index, adv. Sample. Refereed. Circ: 1620. Vol. ends: Summer. Microform: PQC. Online: EBSCO Publishing; Florida Center for Library Automation; Gale Group; OCLC Online Computer Library Center, Inc.; Project MUSE; ProQuest Information & Learning; RoweCom Information Quest; Swets Blackwell. Reprint: ISI; PQC; PSC. *Indexed:* AmH&L, B&AI, BiolAb, BiolDig, ChemAb, DSR&OA, ExcerpMed, GSI, IndMed, IndVet, PsycholAb, SCI, SSCI, VetBull, ZooRec. *Bk. rev.:* 2-9, 300-1,200 words. *Aud.:* Ac, Sa.

Perspectives in Biology and Medicine publishes "essays that place biological and medical topics in broader contexts, including scientific, ethical, historical, and cultural perspectives." Conference proceedings may also be published. Subscription options include print only, online only, and print plus online combined. Online full text from 2000 forward is provided through Johns Hopkins' Project Muse. This journal can provide historical perspective and a thought-provoking read for biologists and medical professionals. Appropriate for academic, medical, and special-library collections. Document delivery is available from BLDSC, CASDDS, CISTI, The Genuine Article, LHLDS, NIWI, UMI, and UnCover.

1162. ***The Quarterly Review of Biology.*** [ISSN: 0033-5770] 1926. q. USD 233 print & online eds. (Individuals, USD 42 print & online eds.; Students, USD 28 print & online eds.). Ed(s): Albert D Carlson, James D Thomson. University of Chicago Press, Journals Division, PO Box 37005, Chicago, IL 60637; subscriptions@press.uchicago.edu; http://www.journals.uchicago.edu. Illus., index, adv. Refereed. Circ: 3200 Paid and controlled. Vol. ends: Dec. Microform: PQC; NRP. Online: EBSCO Publishing; Florida Center for Library Automation; Gale Group; JSTOR (Web-based Journal Archive). Reprint: PSC. *Indexed:* AbAn, AnBeAb, ApEcolAb, B&AI, BRI, BiolAb, BiolDig, CBRI, ChemAb, DSR&OA, ExcerpMed, GSI, GeoRef, HortAb, IndMed, IndVet, SCI, SWRA, VetBull, ZooRec. *Bk. rev.:* 100 or more, 200-1,500 words. *Aud.:* Ac, Sa.

The goal of *Quarterly Review of Biology* is to present "insightful historical, philosophical, and technical treatments of important biological topics." At least half of each issue is made up of book reviews, arranged by subject, which provides a good source for biologists to regularly scan for information on new publications in areas of interest. JSTOR provides access to full text from 1926 through 1996. The University of Chicago Press makes available full text from March 2002 forward. This very readable, broadly based journal is appropriate for even very basic biology collections. Document delivery is available from BLDSC, CASDDS, CISTI, The Genuine Article, LHLDS, UMI, and UnCover.

Ranger Rick. See Children section.

Science. See Science and Technology section.

1163. ***Systematic Biology.*** Formerly (until 1991): *Systematic Zoology.* [ISSN: 1063-5157] 1952. bi-m. USD 157. Ed(s): Richard Olmstead, Chris Simon. Taylor & Francis Inc, 325 Chestnut St, Suite 800, Philadelphia, PA 19016; info@taylorandfrancis.com; http://www.taylorandfrancis.com/. Illus., index. Refereed. Circ: 2800. Vol. ends: Dec. Microform: PQC. Online: EBSCO Publishing; Ingenta Select; RoweCom Information Quest; Swets Blackwell. Reprint: PQC. *Indexed:* B&AI, BiolAb, ChemAb, DSR&OA, ForAb, GeoRef, HortAb, IndMed, IndVet, OceAb, S&F, SCI, SSCI, VetBull, ZooRec. *Bk. rev.:* 0-2, 800-2,000 words. *Aud.:* Ac, Sa.

Systematic Biology is concerned with the "advancement of the science of systematic biology in all its aspects of theory, principles, methodology, and practice, for both living and fossil organisms, with emphasis on areas of common interest to all systematic biologists regardless of individual specialization." The journal includes research papers, discussion pieces, and software and book reviews. Online full text from 1998 forward is available through the Taylor & Francis web site and is free with a print subscription. Appropriate for academic and special-library collections. Document delivery is available from BLDSC, CISTI, The Genuine Article, LHLDS, UMI, and UnCover.

Physiology

1164. ***American Journal of Physiology (Consolidated).*** [ISSN: 0002-9513] 1898. m. USD 3175 (Members, USD 820 print & online eds.; Non-members, USD 2110). Ed(s): Brenda B Rauner. American Physiological Society, 9650 Rockville Pike, Bethesda, MD 20814-3991;

info@the-aps.org; http://www.the-aps.org. Illus., index, adv. Refereed. Circ: 2500. Microform: PMC; PQC. Online: Gale Group. Reprint: ISI; PQC. *Indexed:* Agr, B&AI, BiolAb, ChemAb, DSA, FPA, ForAb, GSI, HortAb, IndMed, IndVet, RRTA, S&F, SCI, SSCI, VetBull, ZooRec. *Aud.:* Ac, Sa.

The *American Journal of Physiology* (*AJP*) is made up of seven individual titles, each preceded by *AJP*: *Cell Physiology, Endocrinology and Metabolism, Gastrointestinal and Liver Physiology, Heart and Circulatory Physiology, Lung Cellular and Molecular Physiology, Regulatory, Integrative and Comparative Physiology*, and *Renal Physiology*. Each of the titles is available separately, as well as part of the total *AJP* package. The majority of the journal is made up of research articles, though reviews and special communications also appear. The online content, made available through HighWire Press, includes tables of contents, abstracts, full texts, advance information on future issues, and search capability. CiteTrack is a free alerting service. This important title is appropriate for medical and biology collections. Document delivery is available from BLDSC, CASDDS, CISTI, The Genuine Article, LHLDS, NIWI, UMI, and UnCover.

1165. *Journal of Applied Physiology.* Former titles: *Journal of Applied Physiology: Respiratory, Environmental and Exercise Physiology;* (until 1977): *Journal of Applied Physiology.* [ISSN: 8750-7587] 1948. m. USD 1010 (Members, USD 300 print & online eds.; Non-members, USD 670). Ed(s): Margaret Reich, Gary C Sieck. American Physiological Society, 9650 Rockville Pike, Bethesda, MD 20814-3991; info@the-aps.org; http://www.the-aps.org. Illus., adv. Refereed. Circ: 3286 Paid and free. Microform: PQC. Online: HighWire Press; RoweCom Information Quest. Reprint: PQC. *Indexed:* AbAn, AgeL, B&AI, BiolAb, ChemAb, DSA, ErgAb, ExcerpMed, H&SSA, IAA, IndMed, IndVet, PEI, RRTA, SCI, SSCI, SportS, VetBull, ZooRec. *Aud.:* Ac, Sa.

Journal of Applied Physiology publishes papers dealing with "diverse areas of research in applied physiology." Articles are mostly research papers, but some communications, historical papers, and reviews are also published. Subscription options include print-only, print plus online, and online-only. Online content from is provided through Stanford's HighWire Press and includes full text from 1996 to the present. The American Physical Society is in the process of putting all of its publications online from the first issue to the present, calling this product the *APS Journal Legacy Content*. This package is currently available for free to APS members and to institutions for a one time charge of $1,500. This journal will be useful to physiologists as well as researchers and practitioners in various medical specialties. Document delivery is available from BLDSC, CASDDS, CISTI, EMDOCS, The Genuine Article, LHLDS, NIWI, UMI, and UnCover.

1166. *Journal of General Physiology.* [ISSN: 0022-1295] 1918. m. USD 575. Ed(s): Dr. Olaf S Andersen. Rockefeller University Press, 1114 First Ave, New York, NY 10021-8325; rupcd@rockefeller.edu; http://www.jgp.org; http://www.rockefeller.edu/rupress. Illus., index, adv. Sample. Refereed. Circ: 1790 Paid. Microform: PQC. Online: EBSCO Publishing; Gale Group; HighWire Press; RoweCom Information Quest. Reprint: ISI; PQC. *Indexed:* B&AI, BiolAb, ChemAb, ExcerpMed, GSI, IndMed, IndVet, PEI, SCI, VetBull, ZooRec. *Aud.:* Ac, Sa.

The *Journal of General Physiology* publishes research on "basic biological, chemical, or physical mechanisms of broad physiological significance." The articles fall into three categories: invited papers, research papers, and comments. Subscription options include print, online, and print plus online. Substantial online content, available on Stanford's HighWire Press, includes full text from 1975 to the present. This journal is appropriate for academic and special libraries supporting biologists, physiologists, and physicians. Document delivery is available from BLDSC, CASDDS, CISTI, The Genuine Article, LHLDS, UMI, and UnCover.

1167. *Journal of Physiology.* [ISSN: 0022-3751] 1878. s-m. plus proceedings 5/yr. GBP 1900 print & online. Ed(s): George Augustine, Stewart Sage. Blackwell Publishing Ltd., 9600 Garsington Rd, PO Box 805, Oxford, OX4 2DQ, United Kingdom; customerservices@oxon.blackwellpublishing.com; http://www.blackwellpublishing.com/. Illus., index, adv. Sample. Refereed. Circ: 3100. Microform: PMC; PQC. Online: EBSCO Publishing; HighWire Press; RoweCom Information Quest. *Indexed:* B&AI, BiolAb, ChemAb, DSA, DSR&OA, ErgAb, ExcerpMed, IndMed, IndVet, PEI, SCI, SSCI, VetBull, ZooRec. *Aud.:* Ac, Sa.

The *Journal of Physiology* presents physiology research papers at levels of organization ranging from the cell membrane up through systems. While the main emphasis of the journal is on human and mammalian physiology, papers that present work on other organisms may be accepted provided that the work furthers the understanding of other organisms, including mammals. Issues contain research papers, "Rapid Reports," "Topical Reviews," and "Perspectives." Stanford's HighWire Press makes available the online content for this journal, including full text from 1997 forward. A print subscription also entitles the institution to online access. Online access to papers older than one year is freely available. This well-regarded journal is useful for upper-division undergraduates through specialists. Document delivery is available from BLDSC, CASDDS, CISTI, The Genuine Article, LHLDS, UMI, and UnCover.

1168. *Physiological Reviews.* [ISSN: 0031-9333] 1921. q. USD 380 (Members, USD 115 print & online eds.; Non-members, USD 250). Ed(s): S L Hamilton. American Physiological Society, 9650 Rockville Pike, Bethesda, MD 20814-3991; info@the-aps.org; http://www.the-aps.org. Illus., index, adv. Refereed. Circ: 3352. Vol. ends: Oct. Microform: PMC; PQC. Online: EBSCO Publishing; Gale Group; HighWire Press; Northern Light Technology, Inc.; RoweCom Information Quest. Reprint: PQC. *Indexed:* B&AI, BiolAb, ChemAb, DSA, ExcerpMed, GSI, IndMed, PEI, SCI, SSCI, ZooRec. *Aud.:* Ac, Sa.

Published quarterly by the American Physiological Society, *Physiological Reviews* presents review articles on topics of interest to physiologists. Articles have detailed tables of contents and extensive bibliographies. Subscription options include print only, online online, and print plus online combined. Stanford's HighWire Press makes available the online content for this title, including full text from 1998 to the present. By the end of 2004, the APS plans to make all back issues of its journals accessible online through APS Legacy Content. This package is currently available for a one-time charge of $1,500. Articles provide a great starting point, overview, and bibliography builder for researchers and students. Document delivery is available from BLDSC, CASDDS, CISTI, The Genuine Article, LHLDS, and UnCover.

Specialty Titles

1169. *Biology of Reproduction.* [ISSN: 0006-3363] 1969. m. in 2 vols. USD 550 domestic print & online eds.; USD 600 foreign print & online eds. Ed(s): Virendra B Mahesh. Society for the Study of Reproduction, 1619 Monroe St., Madison, WI 53711-2063; ssr@ssr.org; http://www.ssr.org. Illus., adv. Sample. Refereed. Circ: 3750 Paid. Microform: PQC. Online: BioOne; EBSCO Publishing; HighWire Press. *Indexed:* AbAn, Agr, BiolAb, ChemAb, DSA, ExcerpMed, FoVS&M, IndMed, IndVet, SCI, VetBull, ZooRec. *Aud.:* Ac, Sa.

Biology of Reproduction publishes "original research on a broad range of topics in the field of reproductive biology, as well as minireviews on topics of current importance or controversy." Journal sections vary somewhat from issue to issue but include "Embryo," "Female Reproductive Tract," "Gamete Biology," "Male Reproductive Tract," "Ovary," "Neuroendocrinology," "Pregnancy," "Testis," "Reproductive Technology," "and "Special Papers." " Myriad animal species are represented among the experimental animals used in the research in this title. The journal's policy is to allow free Internet access 18 months after publication. The journal's web site includes a table of contents service, sample issue, and online information from 1969 to the present with varying levels of access from tables of contents through full text, with search capabilities. Online content is provided by Stanford's HighWire Press. Useful for academic collections supporting research in reproductive biology, as well as medical and veterinary libraries.

1170. *Endocrinology.* [ISSN: 0013-7227] 1917. m. USD 768 (Individuals, USD 369; Members, USD 135). Ed(s): Kenneth Korach. Endocrine Society, 8410, Connecticut Ave., Ste 900, Chevy Chase, MD 20815-5817; endocrinology@endo-society.org; http://www.endo-society.org. Illus., index, adv. Refereed. Circ: 5800. Vol. ends: Dec. Microform: PMC. Online: EBSCO Publishing; HighWire Press; Ovid Technologies, Inc. *Indexed:* BiolAb, ChemAb, DSA, ExcerpMed, HortAb, IndMed, IndVet, S&F, SCI, VetBull, ZooRec. *Aud.:* Ac, Sa.

Endocrinology , published by the Endocrine Society, is considered one of the foremost biomedical research journals in the world and focuses on "nonprimate subcellular biochemical and physiological studies, although work on material of primate origin is not necessarily excluded." Published in approximately 6,000 pages annually, journal sections cover receptors, neuroendocrinology, intracellular signal systems, and others. Also useful are the employment opportunities, conference announcements, and other advertisements that appear. Online content is made available via Stanford's HighWire Press and includes full text from 1992 onward and a mix of tables of contents and tables of contents plus abstracts from 1965 to 1992. Subscription options include online access only or print plus online access. *Endocrinology* is a core journal in this discipline and is appropriate for both medical and biology collections. Document delivery is available from ADONIS, BLDSC, CASDDS, CISTI, The Genuine Article, LHLDS, NIWI, UMI, and UnCover.

1171. ***Evolution: international journal of organic evolution.*** [ISSN: 0014-3820] 1947. m. USD 190 (Individuals, USD 65). Ed(s): Donald M Waller. Society for the Study of Evolution, c/o Allen Press, Inc, Box 1897, Lawrence, KS 66044-8897; ssoe@allenpress.com; http://www.lsvl.la.asu.edu/evolution. Illus., index, adv. Refereed. Circ: 4500. Vol. ends: Dec. Microform: PQC. Online: BioOne; Northern Light Technology, Inc. *Indexed:* AbAn, Agr, AnBeAb, ApEcolAb, B&AI, BiolAb, CAPS, ChemAb, DSR&OA, ExcerpMed, FPA, FS&TA, ForAb, GSI, GeoRef, HortAb, IAA, IndMed, IndVet, OceAb, S&F, SCI, SSCI, VetBull, ZooRec. *Bk. rev.:* 0-2, 1,000-3,000 words. *Aud.:* Ac, Sa.

Evolution is devoted to the understanding of evolutionary biology phenomena and processes. Perspectives, brief communications, comments, and book reviews are published. JSTOR provides full text of this title from 1943 up to a moving wall of the most recent three years. Allen Press provides online access to the more recent years. *Evolution* is highly respected, reasonably priced, and a core title for libraries supporting biology programs. Document delivery is available from BLDSC, CASDDS, CISTI, EMDOCS, LHLDS, and UMI.

1172. ***Journal of Immunology.*** [ISSN: 0022-1767] 1916. 2x/m. USD 470 (Individuals, USD 270; USD 20 newsstand/cover per issue). Ed(s): Dr. Robert Rich. American Association of Immunologists, 9650 Rockville Pike, Bethesda, MD 20814; infoji@faseb.org; http://www.jimmunol.org. Illus., index, adv. Refereed. Circ: 8600 Paid. Microform: PQC. Online: EBSCO Publishing; HighWire Press. *Indexed:* B&AI, BiolAb, ChemAb, DSA, ExcerpMed, ForAb, HortAb, IAA, IndMed, IndVet, SCI, VetBull. *Aud.:* Ac, Sa.

The official journal of the American Association of Immunologists, *Journal of Immunology* publishes research papers on all areas of experimental immunology. Articles cover cellular immunology and immune regulation, molecular and structural immunology, host defense, inflammation, and clinical immunology. The section "Cutting Edge" consists of brief research articles of significance or discussions of controversial subjects of broad interest to immunologists. Stanford's HighWire Press provides access to the journal's online content, which includes full text from 1980 forward. The journal is useful for programs in microbiology, virology, and medicine, as well as immunology. Document delivery is available from BLDSC, CASDDS, CISTI, The Genuine Article, LHLDS, UMI, and UnCover.

1173. ***Journal of Neuroscience.*** [ISSN: 0270-6474] 1981. w. Institutional members, USD 1924; Individual members, USD 336. Ed(s): David C Van Essen. Society for Neuroscience, 11 Dupont Circle, N W, Ste 500, Washington, DC 20036; http://www.sfn.org/. Illus., index, adv. Refereed. Circ: 4100. Vol. ends: Dec. Microform: PQC. Online: EBSCO Publishing; HighWire Press. *Indexed:* AnBeAb, B&AI, BiolAb, ChemAb, ExcerpMed, IndMed, IndVet, PsycholAb, S&F, SCI, SSCI, VetBull, ZooRec. *Aud.:* Ac, Sa.

Journal of Neuroscience publishes on a "broad range of topics of general interest to those working on the nervous system." Rapid communications and research articles are published. Articles can range from cellular and molecular research to developmental and behavioral studies. Site-wide online access is included with a print subscription. Stanford's HighWire Press makes available the online content for this title, including full text from 1996 onward. This journal will be useful in biology and medical collections. Document delivery is available from BLDSC, CASDDS, CISTI, EMDOCS, The Genuine Article, LHLDS, UMI, and UnCover.

1174. ***Reproduction.*** Formed by the merger of (1996-2000): *Reviews of Reproduction;* (1960-2000): *Journal of Reproduction and Fertility;* Which was formerly (1949-1958): *Society for the Study of Fertility. Proceedings.* [ISSN: 1470-1626] 2001. m. GBP 595 combined subscription; USD 1040 combined subscription. Ed(s): Dr. C A Doberska. Society for Reproduction and Fertility, 22 Newmarket Rd, Cambridge, CB5 8DT, United Kingdom; http://www.srf-reproduction.org/. Adv. Sample. Refereed. *Indexed:* B&AI, BiolAb, ChemAb, DSA, ExcerpMed, FoVS&M, IndMed, IndVet, VetBull. *Aud.:* Ac, Sa.

Reproduction, formed by the union of *Reviews of Reproduction* and *Journal of Reproduction and Fertility* in 2001, publishes "papers covering the whole range of reproductive biology and species, including humans." Editors express an interest in receiving papers on genomics, proteomics, and the study of the metabolome and on cloning, nuclear reprogramming, stem cell biology and developmental biology, while still maintaining their interests in whole-animal physiology. Research and review articles are published. Full text online is available for 1996 forward through the Society for Reproduction and Fertiligy web site. Useful for academic, medical, and veterinary collections.

Vertebrate and Invertebrate Zoology

1175. ***Animal Behaviour.*** [ISSN: 0003-3472] 1953. m. EUR 960. Ed(s): Jeffrey R. Lucas, Leigh W. Simmons. Academic Press, 24-28 Oval Rd, London, NW1 7DX, United Kingdom; apsubs@acad.com; http://www.elsevier-international.com/serials/. Illus., index, adv. Refereed. Microform: PMC; PQC. Online: EBSCO Publishing; Gale Group; ingenta.com; OCLC Online Computer Library Center, Inc.; RoweCom Information Quest; ScienceDirect; Swets Blackwell. Reprint: SWZ. *Indexed:* Agr, AnBeAb, ApEcolAb, B&AI, BiolAb, ChemAb, DSA, DSR&OA, ExcerpMed, FS&TA, ForAb, GSI, HortAb, IndMed, IndVet, MLA-IB, OceAb, PsycholAb, SCI, SSCI, VetBull, WAE&RSA, ZooRec. *Bk. rev.:* 2-8, 400-1,200 words. *Aud.:* Ac, Sa.

This journal, published by the Association for the Study of Animal Behaviour, presents original papers, reviews, and commentaries related to all aspects of animal behavior, including human behavior. Papers testing explicit hypotheses are preferred, with less emphasis given to papers presenting descriptive studies. An online forum section allows for commentaries. Online materials include tables of contents, abstracts, full text, and free sample issues via Elsevier's ScienceDirect. This is an important title for academic libraries. Document delivery is available from BLDSC, CASDDS, CISTI, EMDOCS, The Genuine Article, LHLDS, UMI, and UnCover.

Auk. See Birds section.

1176. ***Biological Bulletin.*** [ISSN: 0006-3185] 1897. bi-m. 2 vols./yr. USD 280 (Individuals, USD 105). Ed(s): Michael J Greenberg. Marine Biological Laboratory, 7 MBL St, Woods Hole, MA 02543-1015; wchild@mbl.edu; http://www.mbl.edu/. Illus., index, adv. Refereed. Circ: 1850. Microform: PMC; PQC. Online: Florida Center for Library Automation; Gale Group; HighWire Press; Northern Light Technology, Inc.; OCLC Online Computer Library Center, Inc.; ProQuest Information & Learning. *Indexed:* AnBeAb, ApEcolAb, B&AI, BiolAb, ChemAb, DSR&OA, ForAb, GSI, GeoRef, IAA, IndMed, IndVet, OceAb, PsycholAb, S&F, SCI, VetBull, ZooRec. *Aud.:* Ac, Sa.

The *Biological Bulletin* presents research papers and occasional solicited review articles focusing on the saltwater and freshwater environments. Article topics range from behavior to development to physiology to evolution. Stanford's HighWire Press makes available the online version of the journal, including a free sample issue and full text from 1990 to the present. This is a quality title, published by the Marine Biological Laboratory, which will be useful in academic and special libraries supporting research on freshwater or saltwater organisms and ecosystems. Online access is included with a subscription to the paper copy. Document delivery is available from BLDSC, CASDDS, CISTI, The Genuine Article, LHLDS, UMI, and UnCover.

1177. ***Canadian Journal of Zoology.*** Formerly (until 1950): *Canadian Journal of Research. Section D: Zoological Sciences;* Which superseded in part (in 1935): *Canadian Journal of Research.* [ISSN: 0008-4301] 1929. m. CND 680 (Individuals, CND 227). Ed(s): Dr. K. G. Davey, Dr. A. S.M. Saleuddin. N R C Research Press, Building M 55, Ottawa, ON K1A 0R6, Canada; http://www.nrc.ca/cisti/journals/. Illus., index, adv. Refereed. Circ: 1125. Vol. ends: Dec. Microform: MML; PMC; PQC. Online: CISTI; EBSCO Publishing; ingenta.com; RoweCom Information Quest; Swets Blackwell. Reprint: PQC. *Indexed:* Agr, AnBeAb, ApEcolAb, B&AI, BiolAb, CBCARef, ChemAb, DSA, DSR&OA, EngInd, EnvAb, ExcerpMed, FPA, ForAb, GeoRef, HortAb, IndVet, MLA-IB, OceAb, S&F, SCI, SWRA, VetBull, ZooRec. *Aud.:* Ac, Sa.

The *Canadian Journal of Zoology* publishes "in the areas of behaviour, biochemistry and physiology, developmental biology, ecology, genetics, morphology and ultrastructure, parasitology and pathology, and systematics and evolution" relating to zoology. Papers are published only if they contain "significant new findings of fundamental and general zoological interest." Tables of contents and a sample issue are freely available on the NRC web site. Online full text access and print are separate subscriptions, though a discount is available to libraries wishing to purchase both. Published by the well-regarded National Research Council of Canada, the broad coverage in this journal is appropriate for undergraduate students through specialists. Document delivery is available from BLDSC, CASDDS, CISTI, EMDOCS, The Genuine Article, LHLDS, UMI, and UnCover.

1178. ***Copeia.*** [ISSN: 0045-8511] 1913. q. USD 90 (Individuals, USD 50). Ed(s): Robert Kenley. American Society of Ichthyologists and Herpetologists, c/o Karen Hickey, Allen Press Inc, Lawrence, KS 66044-8897; orders@allenpress.com; http://www.utexas.edu.depts/asih/; http://www.allenpress.com. Illus., index, adv. Refereed. Circ: 3600 Controlled. Vol. ends: Dec. Microform: PQC. Online: BioOne; OCLC Online Computer Library Center, Inc. *Indexed:* AnBeAb, ApEcolAb, B&AI, BiolAb, ChemAb, DSR&OA, ForAb, GeoRef, IndVet, OceAb, SCI, SWRA, VetBull, ZooRec. *Bk. rev.:* 5-7, 800-1,800 words. *Aud.:* Ac, Sa.

The papers focus on research where "fish, amphibians, or reptiles are used as study organisms" in *Copeia*, the official publication of the American Society of Ichthyologists and Herpetologists. Articles fall into one of four categories: full-length articles of 15 to 50 manuscript pages, shorter contributions of 15 pages or less, comments on previous publications, and announcements and news. Meeting minutes may also appear. Online content, available on Allen Press' APT Online, features citations and abstracts from 1998 to the present, including author indexes. This journal is very reasonably priced and will be found useful in academic and special libraries supporting biology programs. Document delivery is available from BLDSC, EMDOCS, The Genuine Article, LHLDS, UMI, and UnCover.

1179. ***Herpetologica.*** [ISSN: 0018-0831] 1936. q. USD 95. Ed(s): Robert G Jaeger. Herpetologists League, c/o East Tennessee State University, Dept of Biology, Johnson City, TN 37614; sievert@esumail.emporia.edu; http://www.herplit.com. Illus., index. Refereed. Circ: 2000 Paid. Vol. ends: Dec. Microform: PQC. Online: BioOne. Reprint: PQC. *Indexed:* BiolAb, ChemAb, DSR&OA, GeoRef, SCI, SSCI, ZooRec. *Aud.:* Ac, Sa.

Published by the Herpetologists League, *Herpetologica* publishes original-research papers, essays, and book reviews about amphibians and reptiles. Longer research articles, syntheses, and symposia papers are published in the annual supplement, *Herpetological Monographs.* The society's web site allows access to some online tables of contents but is outdated, with the most recent table of contents being four years old at the time of this review. This title is useful for general biology, ecology, and herpetology collections. Document delivery is available from BLDSC, CISTI, EMDOCS, LHLDS, UMI, and UnCover.

1180. ***Integrative and Comparative Biology.*** Formerly (until 2002): *American Zoologist.* [ISSN: 1540-7063] 1961. 6x/yr. USD 460 (Individuals, USD 230). Ed(s): John S. Edwards. Society for Integrative and Comparative Biology, 1313 Dolley Madison Blvd, #402, McLean, VA 22101-3926; sicb@burkinc.com; http://www.sicb.org. Illus., index, adv. Refereed. Circ: 6300. Vol. ends: Dec. Microform: PQC. Online: BioOne; Gale Group; Northern Light Technology, Inc.; OCLC Online Computer Library Center, Inc.; ProQuest Information & Learning; H.W. Wilson. Reprint: PQC. *Indexed:* AnBeAb, ApEcolAb, B&AI, BiolAb, BiolDig, ChemAb, DSA, DSR&OA, GSI, GeoRef, IndVet, SCI, VetBull, ZooRec. *Aud.:* Ac, Sa.

This journal, formerly *American Zoologist*, published by the Society for Integrative and Comparative Biology, includes invited papers, most of them derived from symposia sponsored by the society, its divisions, or its affiliates. Each issue focuses on one or two symposia, publishing papers up to ten pages long that generally are reviews or synthetic in nature, but that may report original research. Programs and abstracts of papers for the society's annual meeting are published in the issue just prior to the meeting. Also included are book reviews, reports, and special bulletins. Tables of contents and abstracts of recent issues can be found on the web site, accessible via Allen Press APT Online. The concentration on review articles, the range of topics, and the generally nonmolecular approach of the journal make this a useful resource for undergraduate biology students through professionals. Document delivery is available from BLDSC, CASDDS, CISTI, The Genuine Article, LHLDS, UMI, and UnCover.

1181. ***Journal of Economic Entomology.*** [ISSN: 0022-0493] 1908. bi-m. USD 250 (Individuals, USD 117). Ed(s): John T Trumble. Entomological Society of America, 9301 Annapolis Rd, Lanham, MD 20706; esa@entsoc.org; http://www.entsoc.org. Illus., index, adv. Refereed. Circ: 4300. Vol. ends: Dec. Microform: PMC; PQC. Online: BioOne; OCLC Online Computer Library Center, Inc. *Indexed:* Agr, AnBeAb, B&AI, BiolAb, BiolDig, CAPS, ChemAb, DSA, ExcerpMed, FPA, FS&TA, ForAb, HortAb, IndMed, IndVet, PsycholAb, RRTA, S&F, SCI, SSCI, VetBull, WAE&RSA, ZooRec. *Bk. rev.:* 0-3, 200-1,200 words. *Aud.:* Ac, Sa.

The *Journal of Economic Entomology* reports research on the economic significance of insects. The following subjects are covered: apiculture and social insects, arthropods in relation to plant disease, insecticide resistance and resistance management, ecotoxicology, biological and microbial control, ecology and behavior, sampling and biostatistics, household and structural insects, and medical and veterinary entomology, among others. Articles include research articles, letters to the editor, interpretive or evaluative articles, and book reviews. Print and online subscriptions are available at the same rate. If both are purchased, a discount of 25 percent applies. Tables of contents, abstracts, and full text are available on the journal's web site. For agriculture and horticulture collections as well as biology collections supporting entomologists. Document delivery is available from BLDSC, CASDDS, CISTI, EMDOCS, The Genuine Article, LHLDS, UMI, and UnCover.

1182. ***The Journal of Experimental Biology.*** Formerly (until 1925): *British Journal of Experimental Biology.* [ISSN: 0022-0949] 1923. bi-m. USD 1995 (Individuals, USD 354; Members, USD 233). Ed(s): Dr. R G Boutilier. The Company of Biologists Ltd., Bidder Building, 140 Cowley Rd, Cambridge, CB4 4DL, United Kingdom; sales@thecob.demon.co.uk; http://www.biologists.com. Illus., index, adv. Sample. Refereed. Circ: 1250. Online: EBSCO Publishing; Gale Group; HighWire Press; RoweCom Information Quest. *Indexed:* AnBeAb, B&AI, BiolAb, ChemAb, DSA, DSR&OA, ExcerpMed, ForAb, GSI, HortAb, IndMed, IndVet, PsycholAb, S&F, SCI, SSCI, VetBull, ZooRec. *Aud.:* Ac, Sa.

The *Journal of Experimental Biology* is a forum for papers on comparative animal physiology from the molecular level to the whole animal. Research papers, reviews, and commentary are published. Subscription options include print, online, and print plus online. Stanford's HighWire Press provides the substantial online content, including tables of contents from 1965 through 1974, abstracts from 1975 through 1992, and full text from late 1992 to date. Full text of each year's articles is made freely available at the end of the calendar year. The broad subject matter of this title will appeal to academic and special-library patrons in a wide range of biological specialities. Document delivery is available from BLDSC, CASDDS, CISTI, EMDOCS, LHLDS, NIWI, UMI, and UnCover.

1183. *Journal of Mammalogy.* [ISSN: 0022-2372] 1919. q. USD 170. Ed(s): David M Leslie. American Society of Mammalogists, c/o Dr H Duane Smith, Sec -Treas, Monte L Bean Life Science Museum, Provo, UT 84602-0200; asm@allenpress.com; http://www.mammalogy.org. Illus., index, adv. Refereed. Vol. ends: Nov. Microform: PMC; PQC. Online: BioOne; Gale Group; Northern Light Technology, Inc.; OCLC Online Computer Library Center, Inc.; ProQuest Information & Learning. Reprint: PQC. *Indexed:* AbAn, Agr, AnBeAb, ApEcolAb, B&AI, BiolAb, DSA, DSR&OA, FPA, ForAb, GSI, GeoRef, IndMed, IndVet, OceAb, S&F, SCI, SSCI, VetBull, ZooRec. *Bk. rev.:* 1-3, 800-2,100 words. *Aud.:* Ac, Sa.

Journal of Mammology covers research in the broad field of mammal biology, including both marine and terrestrial mammals and paleontology. Approximately 1,200 pages are published annually including original research, society news, meeting announcements, research and award proposals, and committee reports. Online content is available through Allen Press' APT Online, including abstracts from 2000 to the present. The journal is reasonably priced and written to be accessible to readers from undergraduates through specialists. A good title for academic and special libraries supporting biology programs. Document delivery is available from BLDSC, CISTI, EMDOCS, LHLDS, UMI, and UnCover.

1184. *The Journal of Wildlife Management.* [ISSN: 0022-541X] 1937. q. USD 140. Ed(s): R Scott Lutz. The Wildlife Society, 5410 Grosvenor Ln, Ste 200, Bethesda, MD 20814; tws@wildlife.org; http://www.wildlife.org. Illus., index. Refereed. Circ: 7000. Vol. ends: Oct. Microform: PQC. Online: Gale Group. Reprint: PQC. *Indexed:* Agr, AnBeAb, ApEcolAb, B&AI, BiolAb, ChemAb, DSA, DSR&OA, ExcerpMed, FPA, FoVS&M, ForAb, GSI, GeoRef, HortAb, IAA, IndVet, RRTA, S&F, SCI, SWRA, VetBull, WAE&RSA, ZooRec. *Bk. rev.:* 4-5, 600-2,500 words. *Aud.:* Ac, Sa.

Journal of Wildlife Management publishes papers on the science of wildlife management. Population dynamics, natural history, ecology, physiology, habitat use, nutrition, systematics, modeling, and research techniques are all topics of interest. Papers are very accessible to everyone from undergraduates on up, making this journal useful to support general programs in ecology and biology as well as those in wildlife management. Document delivery is available from BLDSC, CASDDS, CISTI, EMDOCS, LHLDS, UMI, and UnCover.

1185. *Physiological and Biochemical Zoology.* Formerly (until 1999): *Physiological Zoology.* [ISSN: 1522-2152] 1928. bi-m. USD 515 print & online eds. (Individuals, USD 78 print & online eds.; Students, USD 47 print & online eds.). Ed(s): James W Hicks. University of Chicago Press, Journals Division, PO Box 37005, Chicago, IL 60637; subscriptions@press.uchicago.edu; http://www.journals.uchicago.edu. Illus., index, adv. Refereed. Circ: 3300 Paid. Microform: PMC; PQC. Online: EBSCO Publishing; Florida Center for Library Automation; Gale Group. Reprint: ISI; PQC; PSC. *Indexed:* B&AI, BiolAb, ChemAb, DSA, DSR&OA, ExcerpMed, ForAb, IndMed, IndVet, OceAb, PollutAb, S&F, SCI, SSCI, VetBull, ZooRec. *Aud.:* Ac, Sa.

Physiological and Biochemical Zoology presents "current research in environmental, adaptational, and comparative physiology and biochemistry." Some of the important research areas represented include circulation, environmental acclimation, evolutionary physiology, metabolic physiology and biochemistry, osmotic and ionic regulation, respiration, and thermoregulation. Most of the contents consist of research papers, though occasionally an "Invited Perspectives" paper will appear. Also published are symposium proceedings. Online access to full text from mid-1997 forward is available through the University of Chicago press and is included with a print subscription. Accessible to upper-division undergraduates through specialists, this journal would be an excellent choice for all academic biology collections. Document delivery is available from BLDSC, CASDDS, CISTI, EMDOCS, The Genuine Article, LHLDS, UMI, and UnCover.

1186. *Systematic Entomology.* Formerly: *Journal of Entomology (B).* [ISSN: 0307-6970] 1976. q. GBP 447 print & online eds. Ed(s): P Eggleton, R E Harbach. Blackwell Publishing Ltd., 9600 Garsington Rd, Oxford, OX4 2ZG, United Kingdom; customerservices@oxon.blackwellpublishing.com; http://www.blackwellpublishing.com. Illus., index, adv. Refereed. Circ: 635. Vol. ends: Oct/Dec. Microform: PQC. Online: EBSCO Publishing; ingenta.com; Munksgaard & Blackwell Science's Synergy; OCLC Online Computer Library Center, Inc.; RoweCom Information Quest; Swets Blackwell. Reprint: ISI. *Indexed:* BiolAb, ForAb, GeoRef, IndVet, S&F, SCI, VetBull, ZooRec. *Bk. rev.:* 1-3, 500-800 words. *Aud.:* Ac, Sa.

Dealing with the systematics of insects, *Systematic Entomology* presents "original contributions to insect taxonomy and systematics, although descriptive morphology and other subjects bearing on taxonomy may be considered." Blackwell Synergy provides access to the electronic content for this title, including full text from 1998 forward. This publication will be of interest to evolutionary biologists and zoologists in addition to the primary audience of entomologists.

1187. *Systematic Parasitology.* [ISSN: 0165-5752] 1979. 9x/yr. EUR 1083 print or online ed. Ed(s): D I Gibson. Kluwer Academic Publishers, van Godewijckstraat 30, PO Box 17, Dordrecht, 3300 AA, Netherlands; services@wkap.nl; http://www.wkap.nl. Illus., index, adv. Refereed. Vol. ends: Oct/Dec. Microform: PQC. Online: EBSCO Publishing; ingenta.com; Kluwer Online; OCLC Online Computer Library Center, Inc.; Ovid Technologies, Inc.; RoweCom Information Quest; Swets Blackwell. Reprint: SWZ. *Indexed:* Agr, BiolAb, ForAb, IndMed, IndVet, S&F, SCI, VetBull, ZooRec. *Aud.:* Ac, Sa.

Systematic Parasitology publishes papers on the systematics, taxonomy, and nomenclature of parasites, including the following groups: Nematoda, Monogenea, Digenea, Cestoda, Acanthocephala, Aspidogastrea, Cestodaria, Arthropoda, and Protozoa, and parasitic genera in other groups, such as the Mollusca and Turbelleria. Research papers, brief communications, and major revisions are published. Institutions can subscribe to paper or electronic versions for the same price, but a 20 percent surcharge is applied when both are required. Full text online through Kluwer is available from 1997 forward. Useful in supporting academic biology, medical, and veterinary programs.

■ BIRDS

See also Environment and Conservation; and Pets sections.

Elaine Peterson, Special Collections Librarian, The Libraries, Montana State University, Bozeman, MT 59717-3320; elainep@montana.edu

Introduction

Poets have relied on birds for such inspirational phrases as "the green freedom of a cockatoo" or "casual flocks of pigeons make ambiguous undulations as they sink." And yet, while poets like Wallace Stevens penned lyrical words about birds, scientists were already studying the creatures using modern scientific methods. To examine the literature about birds is to experience this dichotomy between the aesthetic and the scientific. One journal might try to capture the poetic beauty of birds with glossy color photographs, while another quantifies an ornithological experience through modern technology, such as a spreadsheet or sonogram. The abundance and variety of journals devoted to ornithology demonstrates that there is room for all types of queries, expressions, and research. Selected here are the best titles, ranging from those for amateur birders to professional ornithologists. Those marked as recommended for High School/General Adult audience are devoted to casual birding, list activities, photography, field trips, and group activities, while those identified as Academic contain original, documented research in the scientific study of bird biology.

Basic Periodicals

Hs: *Bird Watcher's Digest, Living Bird, Wildbird;* Ga: *Birder's World, Living Bird, North American Birds, Wildbird;* Ac: *The Auk, Condor, Ibis, Journal of Field Ornithology, North American Birds.*

Basic Abstracts and Indexes

Biological Abstracts.

Audubon. See Environment and Conservation section.

1188. *The Auk: a quarterly journal of ornithology.* Supersedes (1876-1883): *Nuttall Ornithological Club. Bulletin.* [ISSN: 0004-8038] 1884. q. USD 70 in North America; USD 85 elsewhere. Ed(s): Kimberly G Smith. American Ornithologists' Union, c/o Frederick Sheldon, Museum of Natural History, Louisiana State University, Baton Rouge, LA 70803; order@allenpress.com; http://www.aou.org/aou/auk.html. Illus., index, adv. Refereed. Circ: 4500. Vol. ends: Oct (No. 4). Microform: IDC; PQC. Online: bigchalk; BioOne; Gale Group; Northern Light Technology, Inc.; OCLC Online Computer Library Center, Inc.; ProQuest Information & Learning. Reprint: PSC. *Indexed:* AnBeAb, ApEcolAb, B&AI, BiolAb, ChemAb, DSR&OA, ForAb, GeoRef, HortAb, IndVet, OceAb, PsycholAb, S&F, SCI, VetBull, ZooRec. *Bk. rev.:* 10, 500 words. *Aud.:* Ac, Sa.

The Auk, a well-regarded journal, publishes original reports on the biology of birds. Topics include documentation, analysis, and interpretation of laboratory and field studies, theoretical or methodological developments, and reviews of information or ideas. Tables of contents of upcoming issues and tables of contents and full texts of articles from 2000 to the present are available on the journal's web site. Appropriate for academic or special libraries with collections supporting ornithology, zoology, and ecology. (CD)

1189. *Bird Study: the science of pure and applied orinthology.* [ISSN: 0006-3657] 1954. 3x/yr. GBP 76 in Europe; EUR 115 in Europe; USD 140 in US & Canada. Ed(s): Mary Fox, John O'Halloran. British Trust for Ornithology, The Nunnery, Nunnery Pl, Thetford, IP24 2PU, United Kingdom; general@bto.org; http://www.bto.org/. Illus., index, adv. Refereed. Circ: 2400. Vol. ends: No. 3. Microform: PQC. Online: ingenta.com. *Indexed:* AnBeAb, ApEcolAb, BiolAb, EnvAb, FPA, ForAb, IndVet, S&F, SCI, VetBull, ZooRec. *Bk. rev.:* 1, 50 words. *Aud.:* Ac, Sa.

This is the official journal of the British Trust for Ornithology, an organization that has been a prime contributor to ornithological research in Great Britain for many years. It is noted for its original papers on all aspects of field ornithology, especially distribution, census information, migration, habitat, and breeding ecology. Although it concentrates on the birds of Western Europe, significant papers from elsewhere are also welcomed. Recommended for the professional and serious students of bird life.

Bird Talk. See Pets section.

1190. *Bird Watcher's Digest.* [ISSN: 0164-3037] 1978. bi-m. USD 18.95 domestic; USD 23.95 in Canada & Mexico; USD 28.95 elsewhere. Ed(s): W.H. Thompson, III. Pardson, Inc., 149 Acme St, PO Box 110, Marietta, OH 45750; editor@birdwatchersdigest.com. Illus., adv. Circ: 90000. Vol. ends: Jul/Aug. Microform: PQC. *Indexed:* BiolDig. *Bk. rev.:* 8, 50 words. *Aud.:* Hs, Ga.

This popular magazine publishes articles as well as such regular columns as "The Backyard" on backyard birdwatching and "My Way," with reader tips and helpful hints. Although its target audience is the amateur bird observer, many of the articles are written by professional ornithologists. Other regular features include letters from readers, humor, and cartoons. Color photographs appear in all issues. Recommended for the general public.

1191. *Birder's World: exploring birds in the field and backyard.* [ISSN: 0895-495X] 1987. bi-m. USD 22.50; USD 4.95 newsstand/cover per issue. Ed(s): Diane Jolie, Chuck Hagner. Kalmbach Publishing Co., PO Box 1612, Waukesha, WI 53187-1612; http://www.kalmbach.com. Adv. Circ: 60689 Paid. *Indexed:* BiolDig, MagInd. *Bk. rev.:* Various number and length. *Aud.:* Hs, Ga.

Birder's World offers readers a print and online version, both with superb color photography. Articles are geared to enthusiasts ranging from casual birdwatchers to more serious birders. Includes helpful hints for backyard feeding and landscaping, identification tips, photography pointers, and advice for traveling birders. An excellent magazine for the beginning birder.

1192. *Birding.* [ISSN: 0161-1836] 1969. bi-m. Individuals, USD 45 includes Winging It. Ed(s): Paul Baicich. American Birding Association, PO Box 6599, Colorado Springs, CO 80934. Illus., index, adv. Refereed. Circ: 19000. Vol. ends: Dec (No. 6). *Indexed:* ZooRec. *Bk. rev.:* 3, 200 words. *Aud.:* Ga, Ac.

The stated mission of the American Birding Association is to educate the general public in the appreciation of birds and their relationship to the environment, to study birds in their natural habitats, and to contribute to the development of improved methods of population studies of birds. *Birding* contains excellent information to assist the birder in the field, including identification methods, locations to find birds, and observations of behavior. Articles are well written and illustrated. Recommended for the field ornithologist. Association membership includes the monthly newsletter *Winging It*.

1193. *British Birds.* [ISSN: 0007-0335] 1907. m. GBP 72. Ed(s): Dr. R Riddington. British Birds, The Banks, Mountfield, Roberts Bridge, TN32 5JY, United Kingdom. Illus., index, adv. Sample. Refereed. Circ: 9000. Vol. ends: Dec. Microform: IDC; PQC. Reprint: PQC. *Indexed:* BiolAb, SCI, ZooRec. *Bk. rev.:* 2, 200 words. *Aud.:* Ga, Ac.

Publishes original research dealing with observations of birds of Europe, North Africa, and the Middle East. Bird identification, status, and behavior are emphasized. Other regular features include letters, official reports on rare birds in Great Britain, announcements, and surveys of equipment. Much useful birding-trip information is also included.

1194. *Condor (Tempe): an international journal of avian biology.* [ISSN: 0010-5422] 1899. q. Membership, USD 40. Cooper Ornithological Society, Inc., c/o Glenn E Walsberg, Ed, Zoology Department, Tempe, AZ 85287-1501; http://www.cooper.org. Illus., index, adv. Refereed. Circ: 3300. Vol. ends: Nov. Microform: PQC. Online: bigchalk; BioOne; Gale Group; OCLC Online Computer Library Center, Inc.; ProQuest Information & Learning. *Indexed:* AnBeAb, ApEcolAb, B&AI, BiolAb, ChemAb, ForAb, GeoRef, IndVet, OceAb, S&F, SCI, VetBull, ZooRec. *Bk. rev.:* 1, 2,000 words. *Aud.:* Ac, Sa.

Condor publishes original research on the biology of wild species of birds anywhere in the world. Studies based on extensive field observations as well as modeling are presented. Each article, including those in the section "Short Communications," is supported by substantial references. Occasional news and notes for the society also appear. Recommended for institutions that support advanced ornithological research.

1195. *Emu: Austral Ornithology.* [ISSN: 0158-4197] 1901. q. AUD 250 print & online eds. Ed(s): David W Morton. C S I R O Publishing, 150 Oxford St, Collingwood, VIC 3066, Australia; publishing@csiro.au; http://www.publish.csiro.au/. Illus., index, adv. Refereed. Circ: 1500. Vol. ends: Dec. Microform: IDC; PQC. Online: Ingenta Select; OCLC Online Computer Library Center, Inc.; Swets Blackwell. Reprint: PQC. *Indexed:* AnBeAb, ApEcolAb, BiolAb, ForAb, GeoRef, SCI, ZooRec. *Bk. rev.:* 2, 1,000 words. *Aud.:* Ac, Sa.

Emu prints original papers and short communications on the ornithology of the Australasian region (Australia, New Zealand, New Guinea, Pacific Islands, and Antarctica). Articles are accompanied by extensive references and charts. The variety of species covered by this geographic area make it a recommended title for research libraries serving ornithologists.

1196. *Ibis: the international journal of avian science.* [ISSN: 0019-1019] 1859. q. GBP 240 print & online eds. Ed(s): Andrew G Gosler. Blackwell Publishing Ltd., 9600 Garsington Rd, PO Box 805, Oxford, OX4 2DQ, United Kingdom; customerservices@

oxon.blackwellpublishing.com; http://www.blackwellpublishing.com/. Illus., index, adv. Refereed. Circ: 2650. Vol. ends: Oct. *Indexed:* AnBeAb, ApEcolAb, B&AI, BiolAb, EnvAb, ForAb, GeoRef, IndVet, OceAb, S&F, SCI, VetBull, ZooRec. *Bk. rev.:* 25, 300 words. *Aud.:* Ac, Sa.

The British Ornithologists' Union was founded for the advancement of the science of ornithology. Its activities include the encouragement of active research and the publication of that research in this journal. Long, well-documented articles and short communications are published on all aspects of bird behavior and biology throughout the world. Includes abstracts of papers appearing in the online version. Recommended for academic and research collections.

1197. ***Journal of Field Ornithology.*** Formerly: *Bird-Banding.* [ISSN: 0273-8570] 1930. q. USD 45 in North America; USD 51 elsewhere. Ed(s): Charles R Brown. Association of Field Ornithologists, Inc., Dept of Biology, Georgia Southern University, Statesboro, GA 30460; osna@allenpress.com; http://www.afonet.org. Illus., index. Refereed. Circ: 2200. Vol. ends: No. 4. Microform: PQC. Online: BioOne; OCLC Online Computer Library Center, Inc. Reprint: PQC. *Indexed:* AnBeAb, ApEcolAb, BiolAb, DSR&OA, ForAb, HortAb, IndVet, S&F, SCI, VetBull, ZooRec. *Bk. rev.:* 4, 200 words. *Aud.:* Ac, Sa.

Includes original articles that emphasize the descriptive or experimental study of birds in their natural habitats. Bird-banding information is a key component. Most articles report techniques, emphasize conservation, or comment on published studies of existing theories. A subscription includes the supplement "Resident Bird Counts," including a breeding-bird census and a winter-bird population study. All articles are written in English but have a Spanish translation of the title and abstract. A standard title for professional ornithologists.

1198. ***Journal of Raptor Research.*** Formerly (until vol.20, 1987): *Raptor Research.* [ISSN: 0892-1016] 1967. q. USD 50 (Individuals, USD 33). Ed(s): James C Bednarz. Raptor Research Foundation, Inc., Allen Press Box 1897, Lawrence, KS 66044-8897; osna@allenpress.com; http://www.biology.boisestate.edu/raptor/. Illus., index, adv. Sample. Refereed. Circ: 1200 Paid. Vol. ends: No. 4. *Indexed:* BiolAb, EnvAb, ForAb, IndVet, S&F, SCI, VetBull, WAE&RSA, ZooRec. *Bk. rev.:* 3, 800 words. *Aud.:* Ac, Sa.

A quarterly journal of the Raptor Research Foundation (RRF) devoted to all aspects of predatory birds. The journal consists of research articles, short communications, letters, and book reviews. RRF members also receive the newsletter *Wingspan,* which contains current news, job postings, and meeting information. More information about RRF and its publications can be found on the Internet.

1199. ***Living Bird.*** Former titles (until 1991): *Living Bird Quarterly;* (until 1982): *Living Bird.* [ISSN: 1059-521X] 1962. q. Members, USD 35. Ed(s): Tim Gallagher. Cornell University, Laboratory of Ornithology, 159 Sapsucker Woods Rd, Ithaca, NY 14850; http://www.omith.cornell.edu/PUBS/LB/main.html. Illus., index, adv. Circ: 22000. Microform: PQC. *Indexed:* BiolAb, ZooRec. *Aud.:* Hs, Ga, Ac.

This handsome magazine, produced by the Cornell Laboratory of Ornithology, presents readable articles on all aspects of bird life, from biology, behavior, and environmental concerns to art, humor, and equipment for birds. It reviews current research and activities related to ornithology and includes regular columns. Many travel opportunities for birding are listed. It contains color photographs and paintings. The online version includes bird sounds and a virtual birding excursion.

1200. ***Loon.*** Formerly (until 1964): *Flicker.* [ISSN: 0024-645X] 1929. q. USD 35 (Individual members, USD 25; Students, USD 15). Ed(s): Anthony Hertzel. Minnesota Ornithologists' Union, James Ford Bell Museum of Natural History, University of Minnesota, Minneapolis, MN 55455-0104; mou@biosci.cbs.umn.edu; http://biosci.cbs.um.edu/mou/. Illus., index. Circ: 1400. Vol. ends: Winter. Reprint: ISI; PQC. *Indexed:* BiolAb, ZooRec. *Bk. rev.:* 1, 200 words. *Aud.:* Ga, Ac.

The purpose of the Minnesota Ornithologists' Union is to foster the study of birds, increase public interest in birds, and promote the preservation of bird life and bird habitats. These aims are carried out through *Loon,* which includes articles and shorter "Notes of Interest" accompanied by black-and-white photos. The journal concentrates on birds in the Minnesota area, but it's one of the best regional bird journals available.

1201. ***North American Bird Bander.*** Incorporates (in 1986): *Inland Bird Banding Newsletter;* Formed by the 1976 merger of: *Western Bird Bander;* (until vol.39): *E B B A News.* [ISSN: 0363-8979] 1976. q. Membership, USD 15. Ed(s): Robert Pantle. North American Bird Bander, 35 Logan Hill Rd, Candor, NY 13743; rjpl@cornell.edu. Illus., index, adv. Sample. Circ: 2000. Vol. ends: Oct/Dec. Microform: PQC. *Indexed:* BiolAb, ZooRec. *Bk. rev.:* 1,250 words. *Aud.:* Ac, Sa.

This essential journal for the serious bird bander contains information on techniques and equipment for bird banding. Recent books on banding are listed with brief annotations. Also contains the findings about bird migration following bird banding.

1202. ***North American Birds: a quarterly journal of ornithological record.*** Former titles (until 1999): *National Audubon Society Field Notes;* (until 1994): *American Birds;* (until 1971): *Audubon Field Notes.* [ISSN: 1525-3708] 1947. q. USD 33 (Individuals, USD 30). Ed(s): Edward S Brinkley. American Birding Association, PO Box 6599, Colorado Springs, CO 80934. Illus., index, adv. Circ: 6000. Vol. ends: Winter. Microform: PQC. *Indexed:* B&AI, BiolAb, BiolDig, DSR&OA, ZooRec. *Aud.:* Ga, Ac.

The ornithological field journal of the National Audubon Society is now published by the American Birding Association. The format is the same, detailing the distribution and abundance, range, ecology, behavior, and natural history of bird life of the entire North American continent and Hawaii. Reports from 27 regions highlight key articles in ornithology, as well as color photos and artwork. The Annual Christmas Bird Count issue, which contains the complete results of the world's largest survey of winter bird life, is no longer included with the subscription but can be purchased separately.

Owl. See Children section.

1203. ***Pacific Seabirds: a publication of the Pacific Seabird Group.*** Formerly: *Pacific Seabird Group Bulletin.* [ISSN: 1089-6317] 1974. 2x/yr. USD 25. Ed(s): Steven Speich. Pacific Seabird Group, 4505 University Way, N E, Box 179, Seattle, WA 98105; sspeich@azstarnet.com. Illus., adv. Sample. Circ: 400. Vol. ends: Fall (No. 2). *Indexed:* ZooRec. *Bk. rev.:* 2,500 words. *Aud.:* Ac, Sa.

The Pacific Seabird Group (PSG) was formed to create better communication among Pacific seabird researchers. Its official publication informs its members and the general public of conservation issues relating to seabirds and marine environment. Although the PSG's primary area of interest is the west coast of North America and adjacent areas of the Pacific Ocean, other seabird enthusiasts also contribute to PSG. Contains forums, articles, news, abstracts, reports, and book reviews.

1204. ***Western Birds: quarterly journal of Western Field Ornithologists.*** Formerly (until 1973): *California Birds.* [ISSN: 0160-1121] 1973. q. USD 25 domestic; USD 35 foreign. Ed(s): Philip Unitt. Western Field Ornithologists, c/o Robbie Fischer, Treasurer, 1359 Solano Dr, Pacifica, CA 94044-4258; robbie22@pacbell.net; http://www.wfo-cbrc.org/. Illus., index, adv. Sample. Refereed. Circ: 1000 Paid. *Indexed:* BiolAb, ZooRec. *Bk. rev.:* 1, 1,000 words. *Aud.:* Ga, Ac.

This journal contains articles that are useful to amateur field ornithologists, but also contribute to scientific research. Topics include distribution, migration, status, identification, geographic variation, behavior, techniques for censusing, sound recording, and photographing birds in the field. The focus is on birds found in the Rocky Mountain and Pacific states, including Alaska and Hawaii, western Texas, northwestern Mexico, and the northeastern Pacific Ocean. Excellent photographs, sketches, and maps.

1205. ***Wildbird.*** [ISSN: 0892-5534] 1987. bi-m. USD 19.97 domestic; USD 25.22 Canada; USD 27.97 elsewhere. Ed(s): June Kikuchi. Fancy Publications, Inc., 3 Burroughs, Irvine, CA 92618-2804; j.cain@fancypubs.com; http://www.animalnetwork.com. Illus., index, adv. Circ: 114000 Paid. Vol. ends: Dec. *Aud.:* Hs, Ga.

A monthly magazine devoted to watching and identifying birds, as well as attracting and feeding them. Species profiles and birding "hotspots" are included. Excellent color photographs are featured. It provides product directories and information on equipment for birding. Highly recommended for a general audience.

1206. ***Wilson Bulletin: a quarterly journal of ornithology.*** [ISSN: 0043-5643] 1889. q. USD 40 in North America; USD 45 elsewhere. Ed(s): Robert Beason. Wilson Ornithological Society, c/o Robert C Beason, Ed, Biology Dept, State University of New York, Geneseo, NY 14454; http://www.ummz.lsa.umich.edu/birds/wos.html. Illus., index. Refereed. Circ: 3500 Paid. Vol. ends: Dec. Microform: PQC. Online: BioOne; Florida Center for Library Automation; Gale Group; Northern Light Technology, Inc.; OCLC Online Computer Library Center, Inc.; ProQuest Information & Learning. *Indexed:* AnBeAb, ApEcolAb, BiolAb, FPA, ForAb, GSI, GeoRef, IndVet, OceAb, S&F, SCI, VetBull, ZooRec. *Bk. rev.:* 3, lengthy. *Aud.:* Ac, Sa.

The *Wilson Bulletin* contains articles based on worldwide research conducted on all aspects of ornithology. Articles are well documented, with extensive footnotes and charts. "Short Communications" cover field observations of bird behavior, and "Ornithological Literature" contains extensive book reviews. A key journal for ornithological research.

1207. ***Winging It: the monthly newsletter of the American Birding Association.*** [ISSN: 1042-511X] 1989. m. USD 41 (Individuals, USD 36; Students, USD 18). Ed(s): Matthew L Pelikan. American Birding Association, PO Box 6599, Colorado Springs, CO 80934; member@aba.org; http://www.americanbirding.org. Illus., adv. Sample. Vol. ends: Dec. *Aud.:* Ga.

Once a thin newsletter, *Winging It* has expanded. It publishes many special issues, including a monthly summary of the previous month's rare-bird reports from throughout the American Birding Association area. Members supply much of the information in the newsletter, including bird-finding articles, letters, site guides, and field notes.

Electronic Journals

1208. ***BirdSource: birding with a purpose.*** unknown. Free. National Audubon Society, 700 Broadway, New York, NY 10003; editor@audubon.org; http://www.audubon.org. *Aud.:* Ga.

BirdSource is an electronic journal formed by a partnership between scientists and citizens. It is an interactive web site where the enthusiasm of birders is combined with state-of-the-art technology to promote conservation and environmental learning. Readers are invited to record and share their counts of birds online. *BirdSource*'s interactive information system hopes to become the long-term record of North American bird populations.

1209. ***InterBirdNet Online.*** 1997. m. InterBirdNet Online, PO Box 1, Studley, B80 7JG, United Kingdom; http://www.birder.co.uk/indexmain.htm. *Aud.:* Ga., Sa.

Originating in England and updated monthly, this web site offers book reviews, featured birds of the month, a diary section of events, an "Ask Us" feature for posing birding queries, and a "Links" section to bird-related sites worldwide. The focus is very much on birding in the United Kingdom, but the links will be of interest to a North American audience. A useful site for the enthusiast. (BK/CML)

1210. ***The Virtual Birder: the internet magazine for birders.*** 1996. m. Ed(s): Don Crockett. Great Blue Publications, TVB@greatblue.com; http://www.virtualbirder.com. *Aud.:* Ga.

A magazine available only on the Internet, with a goal of bringing content to birders via the web. In addition to standard articles about birds, the site is able to incorporate the type of interactivity available through a CD-ROM. The photo and sound galleries are particularly exciting to use, as are the virtual birding tours of various locations, primarily in the northeastern United States. The site maintains links to other bird web sites and discussion groups.

■ BOATS AND BOATING

See also Fishing; Hunting and Guns; and Sports sections.

Julia D. Ashmun, Systems Analyst/Programmer, Information Technology Services, Widener Library, Harvard University, Cambridge, MA 02138; ashmun@fas.harvard.edu

Introduction

The boating community in the United States is large and diverse, with enthusiasts having widely different tastes in boat styles, boating activities, and boating lifestyles. Boats range from portable to large, oceangoing craft and may be powered by sail, motor, or paddle. Boating environments include oceans, lakes, or navigable rivers, and boating activities can be day outings or extended cruises. Many boat for leisure, others competitively.

Boating periodicals are similarly diverse. Few attempt to represent the whole boating world. Although some are general in their approach, most focus on particular kinds of boats, e.g., sailboats or powerboats, or deal with particular aspects of boating, e.g., navigation or competition. Others confine coverage to a specific geographic area, such as the Great Lakes region or the Pacific Ocean.

Publications included here were selected for their general coverage, or to represent specific regional areas, or to address the many specialized boating interests. Only periodicals published in the United States have been included because boating interests of most U.S. boaters tend to be national and because most of the magazines listed contain international news events and frequent articles on worldwide cruises or racing events.

Numerous boating magazines exist on the web, but almost all of these also have an established print version. Without exception, wherever there is both a print and a web version, the web version provides only a sampling of what is available in the print edition. Almost all of the remaining sites that call themselves online magazines are not magazines in the traditional sense, but rather are newsletters or a collection of links to directories of products or services; these are almost always lacking feature material. One of these, however, *By-the-Sea* (www.by-the-sea.com), does have some articles and stories and is the best of this style.

Basic Periodicals

Hs: *Boating World, Personal Watercraft Illustrated;* Ga: *Boating* or *Boating World, Canoe & Kayak, Personal Watercraft Illustrated, Sail, The Woodenboat;* Ac: *Boating World, Canoe & Kayak, Sail, The Woodenboat.*

1211. ***Blue Water Sailing: the magazine of cruising and offshore sailing.*** [ISSN: 1091-1979] 1996. m. USD 29.95 domestic; USD 39.95 Canada; USD 44.95 elsewhere. Ed(s): Quentin Warren. Blue Water Sailing, 747 Aquidneck Ave, Ste 201, Middletown, RI 02842. Adv. *Aud.:* Ga, Sa.

The magazine is focused on various aspects of offshore sailing. Article subjects are balanced between sailing passages, ports of interest, offshore seamanship, safety, design, boat reviews, events (including racing), news, live-on-board suggestions, a readers' forum, dispatches, and special sections (i.e., a section on various aspects of offshore navigation that includes articles on electronic navigation, electronic charts, raster versus vector charts, radar, GPS, etc.).

1212. ***Boating.*** Incorporates (1973-1980): *Motorboat;* Which incorporated (in 1975): *Family Houseboating;* Formerly: *Popular Boating.* [ISSN: 0006-5374] 1956. m. USD 17.97 domestic; USD 27.97 foreign; USD 4.99 newsstand/cover per issue domestic. Ed(s): Randy Steele. Hachette

Filipacchi Media U.S., Inc., 1633 Broadway, 41st Fl, New York, NY 10019; http://www.hfmus.com. Illus., adv. Sample. Circ: 202265 Paid. Vol. ends: Dec. Microform: MIM; PQC. Online: America Online, Inc.; The Dialog Corporation; Gale Group. *Indexed:* ASIP, ConsI, MagInd. *Aud.:* Ga.

This has long been the highest-circulation boating magazine, and it is one that offers a wide range of material for power boaters. Much of its material is written to increase boaters' knowledge, with regular instructive features on seamanship, navigation, equipment, maintenance, and safety. A major part of its coverage is new-boat testing and evaluation, which usually accounts for a considerable part of each issue. Other material ranges over many aspects of boating and can include articles on trips, recreational activities, and news of the boating industry. Visually, the magazine is highly polished, with extensive color and graphics. It also contains a substantial amount of advertising, although it is generally integrated well with the text. The magazine emphasizes midsize to large boats, but it does offer a broad perspective for power boaters and can be useful as part of a basic collection.

1213. ***Boating World.*** Former titles: *Boat Journal; Small Boat Journal.* [ISSN: 1059-5155] 1979. 10x/yr. USD 18 domestic; USD 38 foreign; USD 3.95 newsstand/cover per issue. Trans World Publishing, Inc., 2100 Powers Ferry Rd, Ste 300, Atlanta, GA 30339. Illus., adv. Sample. *Indexed:* IHTDI, RGPR. *Aud.:* Hs, Ga.

This title focuses on powered boats of 35 feet or less, a widely owned size used for short trips, water-sport activities, and fishing. The magazine offers a very wide range of material on boats and equipment, activities on and off the water, and the general environment of boating. Each issue has a lengthy feature article on a special topic and an article focusing on a boat of the month. Articles offer practical advice either for hands-on upkeep and maintenance or for consumer benefit, such as buying a used boat or insuring boats. A nicely done production, with colorful graphics. Because of its breadth of coverage and its focus on the boat size that makes up a substantial part of the boating community, this useful publication should merit strong consideration as part of a library's core collection.

1214. ***Canoe & Kayak: the #1 paddlesports resource.*** Formerly: *Canoe;* Supersedes (in 1978): *American Canoeist.* [ISSN: 1077-3258] 1973. bi-m. USD 17.95 domestic; USD 26 Canada; USD 38 elsewhere. Ed(s): Ross Prather. Primedia Enthusiast Group, 260 Madison Ave, 8th Fl, New York, NY 10016; http://www.primedia.com. Illus., adv. Sample. Circ: 86690. Vol. ends: Dec. *Indexed:* PEI, SportS. *Aud.:* Ga, Ac.

An excellent magazine offering a good balance of information for canoe and kayak enthusiasts in all kinds of paddling environments. The primary emphasis is on descriptions of paddling trips, ranging from casual day outings to rigorous white-water excursions. There is also considerable coverage of paddling techniques, skills, safety, and health. This is rounded out by material on boat design and construction and new products and accessories. Articles often voice environmental concerns and are usually very thorough and well written. Tastefully done, the magazine is informative, instructional, and enjoyable to read. The web site has selected articles and the contents listings from the two most recently printed issues, with a limited archive of selected feature articles from prior issues. *Canoe & Kayak* offers thorough and well-balanced paddle sports coverage, and it should be appreciated by a wide audience.

1215. ***Cruising World.*** [ISSN: 0098-3519] 1974. m. USD 28 domestic; USD 40 Canada; USD 64 elsewhere. World Publications LLC, 460 N Orlando Ave, Ste 200, Winter Park, FL 32789; info@worldpub.net; http://www.worldpub.net. Illus., adv. Sample. Circ: 160020 Paid. Vol. ends: Dec. Microform: PQC. Online: EBSCO Publishing; Gale Group. Reprint: PQC. *Indexed:* MagInd. *Bk. rev.:* 3, 50 words. *Aud.:* Ga.

A very popular magazine dedicated to open-water sailing and enjoyment of the sailing life. Most of its content centers either on descriptive narratives of cruising trips and situations or on practical solutions and techniques useful or necessary for long-term cruising. Trip narratives usually convey a good sense of the open-water experience and provide interesting glimpses of the character, history, and culture of various international areas visited. The practical material covers many different topics, which can include navigational techniques, fishing, and boat maintenance. Supporting material includes news items and reviews of new equipment and new boats. The writing is sound, the graphics are pleasing, and the overall quality of the magazine is good. Although this has a considerable amount of advertising and classifieds, these are relegated to the last third of the magazine, where they do not interfere with the magazine's content. Its web version includes selected articles from the current print issue and an archive of boat reviews and cruises from many past issues; it also has tables of contents from each issue since 1991. The magazine is useful and informative, and with its emphasis on living on the water, it offers a different approach than most other boating magazines.

1216. ***D I Y Boat Owner: the marine maintenance magazine.*** [ISSN: 1201-5598] 1995. q. USD 18; CND 16.60; CND 39 foreign. Ed(s): Jan Mundy. D I Y Boat Owner, PO Box 167000, Dallas, TX 75261-9652. Adv. *Aud.:* Ga, Sa.

A technical how-to magazine for powerboat and sailboat owners aimed at increasing their knowledge of boat maintenance, upgrade, and repair. It offers articles on engine maintenance, building projects, electrical problems, installing accessories, troubleshooting engines and electronics, rigging, hull and deck maintenance, and more. Also included are reviews and articles on equipment, tools, parts, and products.

1217. ***Good Old Boat.*** 1998. bi-m. USD 39.95. Partnership for Excellence, Inc., 7340 Niagara Lane N, Maple Grove, MN 55311-2655. *Bk. rev.:* Number and length vary. *Aud.:* Ga, Sa.

Aimed at average, do-it-yourself sailors who are not sailing the latest and greatest new yachts but are instead "celebrating older-model sailboats." Like WoodenBoat, the magazine has in-depth reviews about models of boats (including trailerable boats) that include the history, design, biography of the designer(s), and articles about the owner(s) of that model, along with photos of the boat—inside and out—in an attractive, glossy format. Most material is focused on increasing a sailor?s knowledge of boat maintenance, seamanship, safety, and do-it-yourself improvement projects. Issues include design lessons, book reviews, equipment reviews, and features about fellow sailors relating their experiences and favorite weekend or extended cruise spots.

1218. ***Houseboat Magazine: the family magazine for American houseboaters.*** 1990. 10x/yr. USD 29.95 United States; USD 44.95 elsewhere; USD 3.95 newsstand/cover per issue. Ed(s): Steve Smede. Harris Publishing, Inc. (Idaho Falls), 360 B St, Idaho Falls, ID 83402; hbsubscriptions@houseboatmagazine.com; http://www.harrispublishing.com. Illus., adv. Circ: 25000. *Aud.:* Ga.

The sole publication focusing exclusively, and extensively, on houseboats, this title covers all facets of boat ownership and maintenance, interesting boating locales, and activities and lifestyles of houseboaters. One of the defining features of the magazine is its focus on a different destination in each issue, including some of the history, scenic qualities, and services found at that body of water. This is a thin but attractively packaged publication that fills a need for a unique group of boaters. The web site has only one or two articles found in each print issue, but it is a very comprehensive site, with links to much useful information for houseboaters. Houseboats are seen most frequently on large lakes and rivers, especially in the Western and Midwestern regions, so libraries in those areas would be the most likely to consider this magazine.

1219. ***Lakeland Boating: the Great Lakes boating magazine.*** Former titles (until 1983): *Lakeland Boating Incorporating Sea;* (until 1980): *Lakeland Boating; Lakeland Yachting.* [ISSN: 0744-9194] 1946. m. USD 21.95 domestic; USD 27.95 Canada; USD 55.90 elsewhere. Ed(s): Randall Hess. O'Meara - Brown Publications, Inc., 500 Davis St, Ste 1000, Evanston, IL 60201-4643. Illus., adv. Sample. Circ: 36133. Vol. ends: Nov/Dec. Microform: PQC. *Indexed:* ConsI, SportS. *Aud.:* Ga.

For boaters in the Great Lakes region this is a well-established and good general-purpose magazine. Its focus is almost exclusively on powerboats, save for an occasional article on sailing, and it has a good balance of material about boats, boating equipment, and boating-related activities. One of its best features is coverage of boating destinations throughout the region. These are usually thorough treatments of a specific location or waterway, including historical information, points of interest, put-in sites, marina services, and hospitality services. Frequently, articles address either safety equipment or safety procedures and know-how. The web site consists largely of consumer information and links, but it does have all the feature columns of the currently published issue plus a listing of the tables of contents for all print issues since 1984. A solid and tastefully done magazine that should be considered strongly by libraries in the Great Lakes region.

1220. *Maritime Life and Traditions.* [ISSN: 1467-1611] 1998. q. USD 35 United States; USD 41 Canada; USD 51 elsewhere. Ed(s): Bernard Cadoret. WoodenBoat Publications, Inc., Naskeag Rd, PO Box 78, Brooklin, ME 04616-0078; subscriptions@woodenboat.com. Illus., adv. *Aud.:* Ga, Sa.

Jointly published by the publishers of *Le Chasse-Maree* and *WoodenBoat* and produced in France, this magazine elegantly describes international maritime culture in superb detail combined with glossy photos. Each issue covers naval history, nautical archaeology, boat building and restoration, naval architecture, yachting history, maritime art, merchant maritime history, maritime trades and crafts, social and cultural issues, model making, exploration, and/or contemporary maritime industries.

1221. *Motor Boating.* Former titles (until 2000): *Motor Boating & Sailing;* (until 1970): *Motor Boating.* [ISSN: 1531-2623] 1907. m. USD 17.97 domestic; USD 33.97 foreign; USD 3.99 newsstand/cover per issue. Ed(s): Louisa Rudeen, John Wooldridge. Time4 Media, Inc., 2 Park Ave, New York, NY 10016. Illus., adv. Sample. Circ: 125473 Paid. Vol. ends: Jun/Dec. Microform: NBI; PQC. Online: EBSCO Publishing; Gale Group; Northern Light Technology, Inc. *Indexed:* ConsI, MagInd, RGPR, SportS. *Aud.:* Ga.

One of the oldest boating magazines available, this high-circulation title is for powerboaters only. Its scope includes powerboats of all sizes, with feature material covering a variety of boating topics. The emphasis is on reviews of new boats, with supporting material covering both the pleasure and the practical aspects of boating. A particularly useful feature is the "Boatkeeper" section, designed as a cut-out section for hands-on boaters and containing a number of practical ideas and applications for boat maintenance, upkeep, and problem solving. Like several other high-circulation magazines, this has abundant advertising plus a classified and brokerage section that take up close to half of each issue. This effectively obscures some of the informational content that has been relegated to the latter part of the magazine. Its web site has the table of contents for the current issue, but no material is available in full-text; prior issues are not archived, but material from the "Boatkeeper" section is, along with keyword search capability. *Motor Boating* could serve as a general-interest boating magazine for a core collection.

1222. *Multihulls.* [ISSN: 0749-4122] 1975. bi-m. USD 21; USD 27 foreign. Ed(s): Ava M Burgess. Chiodi Advertising & Publishing, Inc., 421 Hancock St, N, Quincy, MA 02171; multimag@aol.com. Illus., adv. Sample. Circ: 49000. Vol. ends: Nov/Dec. *Bk. rev.:* 1-3, 100-600 words. *Aud.:* Ga.

Devoted to sailing craft with two hulls (catamarans) or three (trimarans), this title offers insightful knowledge about the "buying, building, racing, cruising, and safety of multihulls." Most articles cover either cruising or racing activities, but these are supplemented nicely by articles on boat design and construction, navigation, seamanship, and safety. Most articles are written by multihull sailors rather than magazine staff, and they are lengthy and detailed, almost always relating sailing experiences. Some material is geared toward boaters who do their own maintenance and repair work. The magazine is not as flashy as most in this field, but it is tastefully done. And because it has considerably less advertising than others, its contents remain free from distraction. Its web site has the contents listed for articles in the current print version, but none are available in full-text. An archive does have text for selected past articles, and there is also a search engine that searches contents from the prior three years. This magazine is the only one that specifically represents the interests of multihull sailors and should be considered as a complement for a basic sailing collection.

1223. *Ocean Navigator: marine navigation and ocean voyaging.* Formerly (until Dec. 1985): *Navigator.* [ISSN: 0886-0149] 1985. bi-m. USD 26 domestic; USD 30 Canada; USD 32 elsewhere. Ed(s): Tim Queeney. Navigator Publishing LLC., 58 Fore St., Portland, ME 04101-4842; subscriptions@oceannavigator.com. Illus., adv. Sample. Circ: 43000 Paid. *Indexed:* RiskAb. *Bk. rev.:* 2-4, 75-200 words. *Aud.:* Ga.

Ocean boating requires skills and knowledge about navigation, and this is the only magazine whose major focus is on that topic. While primary content is about the art, tools, and techniques of navigation and seamanship, there is also a good sampling of articles on other aspects of ocean voyaging, such as boat maintenance or inviting cruise destinations. Some articles give accounts of voyages in which navigational skills or equipment have been a significant or crucial factor in the trip's outcome. Most topics offer detailed, in-depth coverage and are interesting, informative, and sometimes instructional. Although most of the material applies to sailing craft, the navigational features can be valuable for all boaters. A very good supplement to basic collections for libraries near oceans or large lakes.

1224. *Offshore (Needham).* Formerly: *New England Offshore.* 1976. m. USD 19.95; USD 3.50 newsstand/cover per issue. Offshore Communications, 220 Reservoir St, 9, Needham, MA 02494-3133. Illus., adv. Sample. Circ: 36000 Paid. Vol. ends: Dec. *Bk. rev.:* 2, 200-300 words. *Aud.:* Ga.

The general-purpose magazine for boaters in coastal areas of the Northeast from New Jersey to Maine. Material is well balanced between articles on boats and those about cruising destinations and lifestyle aspects of boating. Articles cover evaluation and design of new boats and equipment and related areas such as maintenance, navigation, and safety. Material about cruising offers very descriptive pieces on interesting destinations, including some of their history and color, local activities, and area marinas and services. Other articles touch on any number of things related to boating, like sport fishing and water recreation. Nicely done, with conversational writing and a good sense of design.

1225. *Paddler.* Formerly: *River Runner.* [ISSN: 1058-5710] 1981. 6x/yr. USD 18 domestic; USD 23 Canada; USD 30 elsewhere. Ed(s): Eugene Buchanan, Tom Bie. Paddlesport Publishing, Inc., PO Box 775450, Steamboat Springs, CO 80477; bieline@paddlermagazine.com. Illus., adv. Sample. Circ: 100000. Vol. ends: Nov/Dec. *Indexed:* SportS. *Bk. rev.:* 1-2, 400 words. *Aud.:* Ga, Sa.

The membership magazine of the American Canoe Association, this is intended for canoe, kayak, and raft enthusiasts on both white water and flat water. Much of its material, however, is about white-water kayaking, which gives the magazine its allure and probably much of its readership. Featured articles are predominantly about paddling destinations or narratives of paddling experiences, balanced by news items and material on boat and gear evaluations and paddling skills and techniques. Throughout, there is an emphasis on a paddler's health and safety and on environmental concerns. The quality of the publication is good, and it is enhanced by many action photos. Its web site has many articles from each current issue plus all back issues beginning with 1998. A good choice for libraries needing a title focused on white-water paddle sports.

1226. *Personal Watercraft Illustrated: the personal watercraft recreation magazine.* [ISSN: 1041-567X] 1987. m. USD 18.95 domestic; USD 65 foreign. Ed(s): Paul Carruthers. C N Publishing Group, 3505-M Cadillac Ave, Costa Mesa, CA 92626; http://www.watercraft.com. Illus., adv. Sample. Circ: 68115. Vol. ends: Dec. *Aud.:* Hs, Ga.

Personal watercraft are fast, maneuverable boatlike machines—the water-going equivalent of motorcycles and snowmobiles. They can seat up to four people and are seen on virtually any body of water. This magazine provides comprehensive coverage of the sport, mixing articles about equipment and accessories with competition news and information about boating spots. The major focus is on various watercraft and accessories, which are tested and reviewed usually with an emphasis on technical aspects or performance qualities. Some material is directed toward do-it-yourself maintenance and repair. Articles are usually well written and often have a technical slant. The web version has some but not all of the material found in the print edition.

1227. ***Powerboat: the world's leading performance boating magazine.*** [ISSN: 0032-6089] 1968. m. 11/yr. USD 27; USD 38 foreign; USD 3.95 newsstand/cover per issue. Ed(s): Doug Thompson. Nordskog Publishing, Inc., 1691 Spinnaker Dr, Ste 206, Ventura, CA 93001-4378; edit-dept@powerboatmag.com. Illus., adv. Sample. Circ: 62575 Paid. Vol. ends: Dec. *Indexed:* SportS. *Aud.:* Ga.

This artfully done magazine is targeted at high-performance powerboat enthusiasts. Its main focus is on evaluations of new boats, with an emphasis on performance features. These reviews are thorough and detailed, testing a boat's speed and handling characteristics, its construction and workmanship, and its interior design and overall impact. Many of these boats are also tested for their qualities as water-skiing boats. The magazine also features powerboat racing coverage, with commentary and results of racing events plus articles about significant figures in powerboat racing. Additional material includes information on products, accessories, and various water sport activities. The magazine has excellent photography and graphics, complemented by intelligent and informative writing. The web site has a few of the articles from the print version and an archive of those dating from April 1998. *Powerboat* is a very complete magazine for performance-minded boaters and would be a good complement to a basic collection.

1228. ***Practical Sailor.*** [ISSN: 0161-8059] 1974. bi-w. USD 96. Ed(s): Dan Spurr, Doug Logan. Belvoir Publications, Inc., 10 Bluff Ave., # 111, Clinton, CT 06413. Circ: 50000 Paid. *Indexed:* SportS. *Aud.:* Ga, Sa.

Practical Sailor is the *Consumer Reports* of sailing. The focus is on reviewing equipment and supplies with also a review of one sailboat (new and old). The magazine is in plain black-and-white format and accepts no commercial advertising. The sailboat reviews contain quotes from previous or existing customers about items they like or don't like; value/price graphs over the years starting with original cost; interior, exterior, hull, and manufacturing quality information; and how the boat handles under sail. The most of the magazine is dedicated to reviewing equipment and supplies, such as the best bottom paint by region, testing of hand-held radios, ladders, radar, autopilots, etc.

1229. ***Sail.*** [ISSN: 0036-2700] 1970. m. USD 23.94 domestic; USD 30.97 Canada; USD 33.94 elsewhere. Ed(s): Peter Nielsen. Primedia Enthusiast Group, 98 N Washington St, Boston, MA 02114; http://www.primedia.com. Illus., adv. Sample. Circ: 172740 Paid. Vol. ends: Dec. Microform: PQC. Online: Gale Group. Reprint: PQC. *Indexed:* ConsI, MagInd, RGPR, SportS. *Bk. rev.:* 1-2, 200 words. *Aud.:* Ga, Ac.

This very popular magazine provides a balanced selection of material on a variety of sailing topics. The emphasis is on boating knowledge and skills as applied to equipment, maintenance, navigation, and seamanship. Articles address these issues in very practical terms. Another area of focus is cruising and racing activities. These are usually narratives describing interesting cruise destinations or situations that demonstrate sailing skills and experiences. The magazine's content applies to both small and large boats and to both novice and expert sailors. The consistent focus on the enhancement of sailing skills. This is one of the highest-circulating boating periodicals, and, as is common with these, it contains a lot of advertising that sometimes seems to overwhelm the text. Still, the magazine is informative and well done and should probably be a core holding for most boating collections.

1230. ***Sailing: the beauty of sail.*** Formerly: *Lake Michigan Sailing.* [ISSN: 0036-2719] 1966. m. USD 28 domestic; USD 30 Canada; USD 40 elsewhere. Ed(s): Gregory O Jones. Port Publications, Inc., 125 E Main St, Port Washington, WI 53074. Illus., adv. Sample. Circ: 38860 Paid. Vol. ends: Aug. Microform: PQC. *Bk. rev.:* 2-4, 200-400 words. *Aud.:* Ga.

An oversized magazine that combines lengthy, sound feature articles, often as first-person narratives, with pictorial beauty. Its primary content is balanced between cruising locales and thorough reviews of boats and equipment. Additional material covers maintenance skills, sailing techniques, and racing news. What separates this magazine from others is its sense of artistry. Not only is it tastefully done, but the photography is often stunning. The large format allows full-page photos to convey the panorama of certain places or the sensation of skimming through the water. The web site has contents listings and a few articles in full-text from the current printed issue plus an archive of past issues from 1995 onward. An interesting, enjoyable, and often instructive magazine that does a very good job of portraying the sailing experience.

1231. ***Sailing World: the authority on performance sailing.*** Former titles: *Yacht Racing and Cruising; Yacht Racing; One-Design and Offshore Yachtsman.* [ISSN: 0889-4094] 1962. 10x/yr. USD 28 domestic; USD 38 Canada; USD 48 elsewhere. World Publications LLC, 460 N Orlando Ave, Ste 200, Winter Park, FL 32789; info@worldpub.net; http://www.worldpub.net. Illus., adv. Sample. Circ: 51376 Paid. Vol. ends: Dec/Jan. Microform: PQC. Online: EBSCO Publishing; Gale Group. Reprint: PQC. *Indexed:* SportS. *Aud.:* Ga.

The definitive periodical for performance- and competition-oriented sailors. Its coverage includes narratives about competitive events and articles focusing on sailing techniques, boat technology, and racing tactics and strategies. The material is primarily oriented toward larger boats, but it is also applicable to smaller ones. Most articles are thorough and informative, with the intent of enhancing sailing skills and performance. The magazine also includes boat reviews and evaluations of high-performance equipment and gear. Racing news and results are included for many levels of competition. This is a visually appealing publication, with good photography, graphics, and layout design. The web site largely links to racing news and events, but it does provide an index for all magazine issues since 1991 and an archive of selected published articles. Intended for serious sailors involved in competitions, this is an excellent choice for libraries near sailing centers.

1232. ***Sea: America's western boating magazine.*** Incorporates (1993-1997): *Waterfront Northwest News;* (1993-1997): *Waterfront Southern California News;* Formerly (until 1984): *Sea and Pacific Skipper;* Incorporates (in 1977): *Rudder;* Which superseded: *Sea, Eastern Edition; Sea and Pacific Motor Boat.* [ISSN: 0746-8601] 1908. m. USD 16.97 domestic; USD 26.97 foreign; USD 3.50 newsstand/cover per issue. Ed(s): Eston Ellis. Duncan McIntosh Co. Inc., 17782 Cowan., Ste. A, Irvine, CA 92614-6041. Illus., adv. Sample. Vol. ends: Dec. *Indexed:* SportS. *Aud.:* Ga.

The only boating periodical that represents boating interests and activities for the entire Pacific Coast region, with coverage extending from Alaska to Mexico. It is intended for oceangoing boaters only, and it focuses almost exclusively on mid- to large-sized powerboats. Its articles broadly cover a variety of topics on boating and the boating environment. A large portion of these highlight pleasure cruising throughout the region, quite often providing extensive detail about the area's recreational activities, sport-fishing opportunities, marina facilities, and general services. Other material includes boat and equipment evaluations and a number of articles about practical, hands-on aspects of boat ownership and maintenance. One of the magazine's strengths is frequent material with a consumer focus, written in a way that allows boaters to make informed decisions about product choices. The web site includes most of the feature material from each issue, with an archive beginning in mid-1998. This is a good general-interest publication that should be popular in coastal areas of the West.

1233. ***Sea Kayaker.*** [ISSN: 0829-3279] 1984. bi-m. USD 20.95 domestic; USD 24 Canada; USD 27 elsewhere. Ed(s): Chris Cunningham. Sea Kayaker Inc., PO Box 17029, Seattle, WA 98117; mail@seakayakermag.com; http://www.seakayakermag.com. Illus., adv. Sample. Circ: 25000. Vol. ends: Dec. *Indexed:* SportS. *Bk. rev.:* 1-2, 500 words. *Aud.:* Ga, Sa.

The only publication dedicated specifically to the sport of sea kayaking. Interesting and informative, its primary content is lengthy first-person narratives of paddling adventures and related aspects, such as conditioning and health, food, safety, and camping. Additional feature material is usually instructional, dealing with techniques such as navigation or paddling. Coverage is rounded out with reviews of new kayaks, equipment, and products. There are occasional articles on environmental issues or wildlife. The feature material is generally well written, and the magazine is visually pleasing despite having a somewhat small type font. Advertising is less obtrusive than in most other boating magazines, allowing readers to focus more on the content. The web site has selected articles from each month's print counterpart and a three-year back file of articles; there is also an index of every feature article ever printed in the published magazine, arranged by topic. This publication will likely find an audience in libraries located in coastal regions or near large, open bodies of water.

1234. ***Southern Boating: the South's largest boating magazine.*** [ISSN: 0192-3579] 1972. m. USD 15 domestic; USD 35 foreign; USD 2.95 newsstand/cover per issue. Ed(s): Timothy Banse. Southern Boating and Yachting, Inc., 330 North Andrews Ave, Fort Lauderdale, FL 33301; sboating@southernboating.com; http://www.southernboating.com. Illus., adv. Sample. Circ: 40000. Vol. ends: Aug. *Aud.:* Ga.

A title aimed at covering recreational and pleasure aspects of boating in the Southern and Gulf region, emphasizing Florida and the Caribbean, with very good features on cruises throughout the area. These are well-written treatments filled with historical information and usually paired with inviting photographs. Additional material profiles new boats, sometimes extensively, and new products and technology. Practical and technical issues are regularly addressed, usually on a knowledge basis rather than as a hands-on approach. Coverage of area racing is also a standard feature. The web site offers selected abridged articles from the printed magazine, but it has no archive of previous issues. *Southern Boating* is well written, has good graphic style, and would be a good selection for libraries in Florida.

1235. ***Trailer Boats: America's only trailer boating magazine.*** [ISSN: 0300-6557] 1971. m. USD 16.97 domestic; USD 32 Canada; USD 57 elsewhere. Ed(s): Jim Hendricks. Poole Publications, Inc., 20700 Belshaw Ave, Carson, CA 90746. Illus., adv. Sample. Circ: 85000. Vol. ends: Nov/Dec. Microform: PQC. Online: Gale Group; Northern Light Technology, Inc.; OCLC Online Computer Library Center, Inc.; ProQuest Information & Learning. *Indexed:* ConsI, MagInd. *Aud.:* Ga.

A magazine dedicated exclusively to boats small enough to be towed on a trailer (generally powerboats less than 30 feet long). Most content consists of thorough, detailed evaluations of new boats and engines and towing equipment and vehicles. It is the only boating resource that regularly features articles on towing vehicles and techniques and regulatory issues involved with towing. Additional material covers gear and accessories, seamanship, and boating activities. Much of the material has enough detail and technical description to make it very useful for boaters who do their own maintenance. The magazine is well written, has pleasing graphics, and is enjoyable to read. With its emphasis on those smaller, portable boats that are owned by a sizable segment of the boating community, this publication will appeal to a wide readership.

1236. ***The Woodenboat: the magazine for wooden boat owners, builders and designers.*** [ISSN: 0095-067X] 1974. bi-m. USD 29 domestic; USD 34 in Canada & Mexico; USD 42 elsewhere. Ed(s): Matthew P Murphy. WoodenBoat Publications, Inc., Naskeag Rd, PO Box 78, Brooklin, ME 04616-0078; subscriptions@woodenboat.com; http://www.woodenboat.com. Illus., adv. Sample. Circ: 106000 Paid. Vol. ends: Nov/Dec. *Indexed:* IHTDI. *Bk. rev.:* 2, 500-1,000 words. *Aud.:* Ga, Ac.

Most modern boats are made of synthetic materials, but the tradition of building boats of wood still has a devoted following. This magazine is dedicated to preserving that tradition, and it is one of the finest and most informative of all boating periodicals. It covers the history, design, building, and preservation of wooden boats of any size or style. Feature articles range from highly detailed descriptions and plans for building or restoring a boat to historical pieces on a style of boat or a boat-building operation. Articles often include substantive biographical profiles of individuals prominent in some area of the wooden-boat industry. There is also material on wood technology and tools and techniques for working with wood. The detailed feature articles provide more depth than is usually found in boating periodicals. The color photography, illustrations, and design all lend a sense of artistry to the magazine. The web site has the contents page for the current issue, but no articles are available in full-text. There is also a keyword index to all the material published in the magazine since its inception. This stylish magazine is a pleasure to read and should be in a core collection.

1237. ***Yachting: power and sail.*** [ISSN: 0043-9940] 1907. m. USD 15.97 domestic; USD 45.98 foreign; USD 3.99 newsstand/cover per issue. Ed(s): Kenny Wooton. Time4 Media, Inc. (Greenwich), 20 E Elm St, Greenwich, CT 06830; editor@yachtingnet.com; http://www.yachtingnet.com. Illus., adv. Sample. Circ: 133016 Paid. Vol. ends: Jun/Dec. Microform: PQC. Online: EBSCO Publishing; Gale Group; Northern Light Technology, Inc. *Indexed:* ASIP, BRI, CBRI, ConsI, MagInd, RGPR. *Aud.:* Ga.

This long-lived title's coverage emphasizes large, upscale yachts plus activities and lifestyles associated with those boats. It is intended for experienced, knowledgeable yachtsmen of both powerboats and sailboats and contains lengthy, well-written articles on a variety of boating topics. Evaluations of new boats are numerous, as are cruise narratives describing interesting, exotic, or out-of-the-way places to visit. Additionally, there are a number of informational articles on boating know-how, especially relating to equipment. The magazine has high production values and a very good sense of style. There is also much advertising, with the latter half of each issue given over to ads for boat brokerages and chartering services. The web site connects to the Yachting Net, which is not an electronic journal but which does have some material from both current and recently printed issues. This is a sound, stylish, and useful magazine, and it represents the high end of boating very well.

Electronic Journals

1238. ***BoatSafe and BoatSafeKids: boating courses, boating tips, boating safety, boating contests.*** m. Nautical Know How, Inc., 5102 S E Nassau Terrace, Stuart, FL 34997; http://Boatsafe.com. *Aud.:* Ems, Hs, Ga.

This comprehensive web magazine, sponsored by International Marine Educators, Inc., is dedicated to promoting boating knowledge and safety. The archive is filled with articles dealing with safety issues for both boats and people plus instructional material and narratives about navigation, equipment, boat maintenance, and boat handling. A number of other articles dealing with the same topics are written specifically for children. In addition, the magazine has a state-by-state listing of boating regulations and online boating courses that are designed to satisfy most boating-education requirements. A very useful site for most boaters, one that may also help libraries' reference services.

1239. ***By-the-Sea: the online boating magazine.*** 1998. d. By-the-Sea, 1315 Samoset Rd, Eastham, MA 02642; http://www.by-the-sea.com. *Aud.:* Ga.

Here is a web-based smorgasbord for boaters: *By-the-Sea* includes feature articles and stories, posts message boards, and lists boats for sale as well as boat builders and boat dealers. There's a huge amount of information readily available, and this is a title all those interested in boating will want to know.

■ BOOKS AND BOOK REVIEWS

See also Archives and Manuscripts; Bibliography; Library and Information Science; and Printing and Graphic Arts sections. Book reviews in subject areas are located within their specific subject areas (e.g., *Science Books and Films* in the Science and Technology section).

Cecile M. Jagodzinski, Assistant Director for Collection Development, Indiana University Libraries, 1320 E. 10th St., Bloomington, IN 47405; cjagodzi@indiana.edu

Introduction

"Of making many books there is no end." This is as true today in the twenty-first century as it was in biblical times, and the dire predictions about the death of the book seem in no danger of coming to fulfillment. Instead, book publishing is at an all-time high, and computers and the digital age, rather than obliterating the written word, appear to be fueling interest in books and reading. The birth of megastores and the proliferation of large bookstore chains have been accompanied by new scholarly work on the history of books and reading, by a fascination with what television celebrities read, and burgeoning numbers of reading groups for people of all ages and interests. The magazines and journals listed below review, study, and revel in the printed word in its most tangible form, the codex. Their audiences are children and scholars, booksellers and librarians, hoi polloi and academicians. Surprisingly, reading and talking about books has blossomed on the Internet as traditional reviewing sources extend their reach into both the electronic marketplace and the marketplace of ideas. The selections below are just a starting place for the librarian seeking news about books, authors, and the world of publishing. What is gratifying is that the focus of our professional lives and the information, knowledge, and delights contained in books are still so alive and well, sure to keep us in business for decades to come.

Basic Periodicals

Ems: *Booklist, Center for Children's Books. Bulletin, The Horn Book Magazine;* Hs: *Booklist, Kirkus Reviews;* Ga: *Booklist, Kirkus Reviews, New York Review of Books, New York Times Book Review, Publishers Weekly;* Ac: *Choice, London Review of Books, New York Review of Books, New York Times Book Review, Publishers Weekly, T L S.*

Basic Abstracts and Indexes

Book Review Digest, Book Review Index, Children's Book Review Index, Library Literature.

1240. *American Book Review.* [ISSN: 0149-9408] 1977. bi-m. USD 30 (Individuals, USD 24; USD 35 foreign). Ed(s): Rebecca Kaiser. Writers Review, Inc., c/o Unit for Contemporary Literature, Campus Box 4241, Normal, IL 61790-4241; rakaise@ilstu.edu; http://www.litline.org/abr. Illus., adv. Sample. Circ: 5000. Vol. ends: Sep/Oct. Online: H.W. Wilson. *Indexed:* AmHI, ArtHuCI, BRD, BRI, CBRI, SSCI. *Bk. rev.:* 25-30, 500-2,500 words. *Aud.:* Ac, Sa.

The *ABR* is a guide to current books of literary interest, with a focus on the products of small, university, regional, Third World, and women's presses. Graphic novels and university press poetry are the themes of two recent issues. Its reviews are more critical than those of the *Small Press Review* (below in this section), which covers much of the same ground; *ABR*'s reviewers, primarily literary critics and university professors, do not take for granted that "small press" means fine writing. Contributing and advisory editors include such literary stars as Andrei Codrescu, Joyce Carol Oates, John Ashbery, and Robert Creeley. The electronic edition makes available the table of contents and selected reviews from each issue. Academic libraries that aggressively select modern literature will want to add this review source to their collections.

1241. *Antiquarian Book Review: opening up the world of rare books.* Formerly (until 2002): *Antiquarian Book Monthly.* [ISSN: 1477-4755] 1974. 10x/yr. GBP 4.50 newsstand/cover per issue; USD 5.95 newsstand/cover per issue. Ed(s): Emma Lewis. Countrywide Editions Ltd., Countrywide Editions Ltd, PO Box 97, High Wycombe, HP14 4GH, United Kingdom; subs@abmr.demon.co.uk. Illus., index, adv. Sample. Refereed. Circ: 5000. Vol. ends: Dec. *Indexed:* DAAI. *Bk. rev.:* 2-5, 300-500 words. *Aud.:* Ac, Sa.

Newsier than the more scholarly *The Library* (see Bibliography section) but less business-oriented than *The Bookseller,* (below in this section), *Antiquarian Book Review* covers the peculiar amalgam of commerce and scholarship that is the antiquarian book trade. Feature articles focus on fine presses, eminent bibliographers, authors, and illustrators and on topics of current and historical interest, e.g., old libraries and societies devoted to the book. A calendar of book fairs and auctions, columns of commentary on auctions and new catalogs (the stock-in-trade of the book collector), and notices on exhibitions and lectures round out the magazine. The book review section caters to the interests of the bibliophile; reviewers comment incisively on new catalogs, bibliographical studies, and ventures into the history of printing. This attractive periodical is recommended for large academic and public libraries with rare book collections and for the individual with an interest in book-related matters.

1242. *Black Issues Book Review.* [ISSN: 1522-0524] 1999. bi-m. USD 14.95 domestic; USD 21.95 Canada; USD 28 elsewhere. Ed(s): Mondella Jones, Evette Porter. Cox, Matthews & Associates, Inc., Empire State Bldg, 350 Fifth Ave, Ste 1215, New York, NY 10118; cmabiccw.com; http://www.ccw.com. Illus., adv. Sample. Vol. ends: Nov/Dec. *Indexed:* AmHI, BRI, CBRI, IIBP, RGPR. *Bk. rev.:* 15-20 (100-250 words). *Aud.:* Ga.

This glossy consumer-oriented magazine is devoted to books by and about "the people of the great African diaspora." It focuses on issues that shape black culture, ranging from music and the visual arts to sports, politics, and history. The feature articles by and about black authors are supplemented by short reviews of new titles, including a "Children's Bookshelf." A column entitled "Tribute" highlights the life of blacks who have made a significant contribution to society and culture, while "Between the Lines" provides news about the publishing industry. The online version of the periodical complements the print with tables of contents and the full text of some articles and reviews. This title should be essential reading for public librarians and selectors who are intent on serving the reading interests of all their users.

1243. *Book: magazine for the reading life.* [ISSN: 1520-3204] 1998. bi-m. USD 20 domestic; USD 24 Canada; USD 38 elsewhere. Ed(s): Jerome Kramer. West Egg Communications LLC, 252 W 37th St, 5th Fl, New York, NY 10018; feedback@bookmagazine.com; http://www.bookmagazine.com. Illus., adv. Circ: 150000. *Indexed:* BRI, CBRI, RGPR. *Bk. rev.:* 50 (100-150 words). *Aud.:* Ga.

A sort of *People* magazine for the serious reader, this delightful magazine is an invitation to reading and an introduction to the famous and not-so-famous people who write and read books. There are feature articles on best-selling authors ranging from Hunter Thompson to Louise Erdrich, stories about the genesis of important new nonfiction writing, and the inevitable lists of best books. Regular columns on crime fiction, children's books, poetry, and books for teens are supplemented by engaging stories on great local bookstores and geographical locations with literary associations. The "Group Dynamics" column capitalizes on the current book-group phenomenon by talking about people reading together, either virtually or in person. Information on book fairs and festivals and author appearances are available both in print and online. The web version of the periodical adds recent book- and publishing-related news, along with a complete archive of earlier issues. Already widely available in chain bookstores, this *Book* is a must purchase for most libraries.

1244. *Book Links: connecting books, libraries, and classrooms.* [ISSN: 1055-4742] 1991. bi-m. USD 28.95 domestic; USD 35 foreign. Ed(s): Laura Tillotson. American Library Association, 50 E Huron St, Chicago, IL 60611-2795; http://www.ala.org. Illus., index, adv. Circ: 30000. Vol. ends: Aug. *Bk. rev.:* 50-75, 50-150 words. *Aud.:* Ems, Ga.

This attractive periodical targets the adult lover of children's books with bright colors, beautiful reproductions of book illustrations, and articles that discuss books meant for both pleasure reading and classroom use. Aimed at librarians, teachers, parents, and booksellers, *Book Links* offers feature articles on children's books (e.g., best books of the year, a Newbery/Caldecott retrospective) and regular columns that suggest ways to incorporate fine children's literature into the curriculum and into day-care and nursery school programming. Background information on special topics (e.g., the environment, polar regions, Native Americans) is accompanied by an annotated bibliography, complete with appropriate grade level. Columns devoted to specific children's books and interviews with authors and illustrators are a plus for the adult who wants to read to, or select books for, children.

1245. *Booklist.* Formerly: *Booklist and Subscription Books Bulletin.* [ISSN: 0006-7385] 1905. s-m. 22/yr. USD 79.95 domestic; USD 95 foreign. Ed(s): Bill Ott. American Library Association, 50 E Huron St, Chicago, IL 60611-2795; http://www.ala.org. Illus., index, adv. Circ: 25696. Vol. ends: Sep. CD-ROM: SilverPlatter Information, Incorporated. Microform: PQC. Online: bigchalk; EBSCO Publishing; Florida Center for Library Automation; Gale Group; Northern Light Technology, Inc.; OCLC Online Computer Library Center, Inc.; ProQuest Information & Learning. Reprint: PQC. *Indexed:* ABS&EES, BRD, BRI, CBRI, ConsI, GardL, InfoSAb, LibLit, MRD, MagInd, MicrocompInd. *Bk. rev.:* 200-250, 75-150 words. *Aud.:* Ems, Hs, Ga, Ac.

"A review in *Booklist* constitutes a recommendation for library purchase." Intended chiefly as a guide for librarians in public and school libraries, each issue covers titles in five major areas: advance reviews, adult books, books for youth, media, and reference books. Outstanding titles are starred; adult books suitable for young adults or curriculum use are labeled, and bibliographic citations include Dewey class number. Most issues spotlight a special topic (e.g., poetry, foreign language titles, black history)—a useful way for librarians to assess their collection in popular and/or important subject areas. The longer reviews of reference materials—a separate section edited by a separate editorial board—also include notices of new editions, continuations, and paperback reprints. An online version of the magazine offers additional services and a cumulative index not available in print. Because of its selectivity, its early reviews, and its broad coverage of popular nonprint media, *Booklist* is essential reading for public, school, and many academic librarians.

1246. *Bookmarks: your guide to the best in books.* [ISSN: 1546-0657] 2002. bi-m. USD 24.95 domestic; USD 30.95 Canada; USD 36.95 elsewhere. Ed(s): Jon Phillips. Phillips & Nelson Media, Inc., 63 Bovet Rd, no.108, San Mateo, CA 94402; subs@bookmarksmagazine.com. Illus. *Bk. rev.:* 55-65, 500 words. *Aud.:* Ga, Ac.

To call this the "reader's digest" version of book reviews would do a disservice to this attractive new periodical. It's an interesting take on book reviewing, targeted at avid readers who haven't read everything and know they won't ever have the time to read everything they'd like. The unique feature of *Bookmarks* is its rating system: the editors read hundreds of reviews in publications such as the *New York Times Book Review* and the *Chicago Tribune*, provide brief excerpts, and apply a one- to five-star rating of the book based on the original review itself. Along with the collected reviews, we get a summary of the plot or thesis of the book, critical themes, and a critical summary. Discussions of new books are complemented by feature stories on well-known contemporary and classic authors (recently, Mark Twain and Gabriel Garcia Marquez), a news section, and a column with advice from readers on what to read next. An excellent title that most public libraries ought to consider for their collections.

1247. *Books.* Formerly: *Books and Bookmen;* Which superseded (in 1987): *Book Choice.* [ISSN: 0952-987X] 1987. q. GBP 1.50 newsstand/cover per issue. Publishing News Ltd., 39 Store St, London, WC1E 7DB, United Kingdom. Illus., adv. Circ: 100000. Vol. ends: Nov/Dec. *Indexed:* BRI, CBRI. *Bk. rev.:* 70-80, 25-50 words. *Aud.:* Ga.

Intended for the avid reader, not the librarian-selector, *Books* talks about what's new in the world of books. News, gossip, contests, and lots of color ads compete with features on specific genres (e.g., travel books, biography) and articles on the histories of specific titles. Interviews with famous and not-yet-famous authors reveal interesting facts, not only about the person behind the book, but the genesis of the book itself. The regular column "Books Choice" presents the editors' pick of the best hardcover, paperback, fiction, nonfiction, and children's books. Although this magazine has a distinctively British flavor and focuses on British imprints, even U.S. public libraries will want to have *Books* on their shelves.

1248. *Books in Canada: the Canadian review of books.* [ISSN: 0045-2564] 1971. m. 9/yr. CND 39.97 (Individuals, CND 27.98; CND 4.50 newsstand/cover per issue). Ed(s): Paul Stuewe. Canadian Review of Books Ltd., 427 Mount Pleasant Rd, Toronto, ON M4S 2L8, Canada. Illus., index, adv. Circ: 10000. Vol. ends: Dec. Microform: MMP; MML. *Indexed:* BRD, BRI, CBCARef, CBRI, CPerI. *Bk. rev.:* 20-30, 500-2,000 words. *Aud.:* Ga, Ac, Sa.

Librarians sometimes forget that books are not just for selecting, buying, cataloging, and reviewing. This refreshing tabloid helps remind us, the book professionals, of the pleasures of reading. The articles feature Canadian authors and publishers who write and publish in the English language; French Canadian works translated into English are covered as well. Contributors to the magazine share two things: their love of reading and their concern for the promotion of Canadian culture. In addition to columns on first novels and children's books, there are substantive reviews, regular interviews with Canadian authors, and the occasional poem. A *Books in Canada* best-seller list, derived from Amazon.ca sales figures, is also included in each issue. This publication is not just for Canadians, but for anyone with an interest in fine writing and the culture of the book.

1249. *The Bookseller.* [ISSN: 0006-7539] 1858. w. GBP 170 domestic; EUR 311 in Europe; GBP 184 in Europe. Ed(s): Nicholas Clee. V N U Entertainment Media UK Ltd, 5th Fl, Endeavour House, 189 Shaffedary Ave, London, WC2H 8TJ, United Kingdom. Illus., adv. Circ: 11250. Vol. ends: Dec. Online: EBSCO Publishing; Factiva; Gale Group. *Indexed:* BrHumI, LISA. *Bk. rev.:* 30-40, 100-150 words. *Aud.:* Ga, Ac, Sa.

This magazine is to the British book trade what *Publishers Weekly* is to the publishing industry in the United States. The news and trade notes sections and numerous publishers' ads are complemented by feature articles on book men and women, both authors and those behind the scenes. "Publications of the Week" lists, by subject, newly published English-language titles. The bulky spring and autumn special issues—available as a separate subscription—list forthcoming books by subject and publisher. The magazine's electronic counterpart offers "Digital Dialogues," a "Books in the Media," column, job listings in the trade, and a five-year archive of articles. For those interested in the publishing industry across the pond, and for collection-development librarians in academic or large public libraries, *The Bookseller* is essential reading.

1250. *Boston Review: a political and literary forum.* Formerly (until 1982): *New Boston Review.* [ISSN: 0734-2306] 1975. bi-m. USD 20 (Individuals, USD 17). Ed(s): Joshua Cohen. Boston Critic, Inc., c/o MIT, E53 407, Cambridge, MA 02139-4307; bostonreview@mit.edu; http://www.bostonreview.org. Illus., index, adv. Sample. Circ: 170000 Paid and controlled. Vol. ends: Dec/Jan. Microform: LIB; PQC. Reprint: PQC. *Indexed:* AltPI, AmHI, BRI, CBRI, IAPV, IBZ, MLA-IB. *Bk. rev.:* 20-25, 250-2,000 words. *Aud.:* Ga, Ac, Sa.

The *Boston Review* is a highly acclaimed and award-winning publication dealing with politics, culture, and the arts. Poetry, short fiction, essays on current events, literature, the role of the fine arts in American society, and a few book reviews constitute most of each issue. "The New Democracy Forum" presents significant social and political issues (e.g., "Democracy and Defense," "Crime and Punishment") from multiple viewpoints, and is typical of the magazine's breadth of vision and its provocative and intelligent writing. A free electronic version offers the full text of articles, "Rave Reviews," awards lists, contests, and "Literary Links" to other web sites. Highly recommended for both public and academic libraries.

1251. *Center for Children's Books. Bulletin.* [ISSN: 0008-9036] 1947. m. except Aug. USD 70 (Individuals, USD 50). Ed(s): Deborah Stevenson. University of Illinois Press, 1325 S Oak St, Champaign, IL 61820-6903; uipress@uillinois.edu; http://www.press.uillinois.edu. Illus., index, adv. Circ: 5000. Vol. ends: Jul/Aug. Microform: PQC. Online: bigchalk; ProQuest Information & Learning; H.W. Wilson. Reprint: ISI; PQC. *Indexed:* BRD, BRI, CBRI. *Bk. rev.:* 70, 50-100 words. *Aud.:* Ems, Hs, Ga, Ac.

This highly regarded reviewing source covers selected titles from the thousands of children's books published each year. In addition to complete bibliographic information, the critical annotations are supplemented by an indication of suitable age and/or grade level and a shorthand code noting a range of quality, from "books of special distinction" to "NR" (for not recommended). A signed column, "The Big Picture," provides a longer review by the editor of a particular title, while "Professional Connections: Resources for Teachers and Librarians" covers curricular and professional bibliography. The "Subject and Use Index" points to genres and subject areas of the curriculum covered by the books reviewed in each issue. The electronic edition contains highlights from the current issue, lists of starred reviews, and a "Blue Ribbon Archive" of the previous year's best. Unique to the online edition is the "Bulletin Dozen," an annotated listing of books based on a particular theme. Librarians in schools, public libraries, and academic libraries with children's literature collections will find this journal an indispensable guide to the field.

1252. *Choice Magazine: current reviews for academic libraries.* [ISSN: 0009-4978] 1963. m. 11/yr. USD 237 in North America; USD 287 elsewhere. Ed(s): Irving E Rockwood. Association of College and Research Libraries, 50 East Huron St, Chicago, IL 60611; acrl@ala.org; http://www.ala.org/acrl. Illus., index, adv. Refereed. Circ: 35000 Paid. Vol. ends: Jul/Aug. CD-ROM: SilverPlatter Information, Incorporated. Microform: PQC. Online: EBSCO Publishing; Gale Group. *Indexed:* BAS, BRD, BRI, CBRI, IBZ, InfoSAb, LibLit. *Bk. rev.:* 600, 100-250 words. *Aud.:* Ga, Ac.

Published under the auspices of the Association of College and Research Libraries "to support undergraduate library collections," *Choice* is a basic selection tool for academic librarians. Each issue includes a lengthy bibliographic essay that, in addition to listing key sources on the topic, provides a fine introduction to the subject under discussion. The remainder of the issue (besides numerous publishers' announcements) is devoted to reviews. Within the constraints of a 100- to 250-word annotation, reviewers (college and university faculty and librarians with subject specialties) offer a summary of each title's thesis, a comparison with similar titles and audience, and a recommendation for purchase. Reviews of web sites and other electronic media supplement the reviews on general reference materials, and an occasional author interview looks at the people behind the books. ChoiceReviews.online, available for an additional cost, provides a mechanism for searching the periodical online, along with the ability to create individual profiles, manage lists of titles, and receive e-mail bulletins of new materials.

1253. ***Criticas: an English speaker's guide to the latest Spanish language titles.*** [ISSN: 1535-6132] 2001. quadrennial. USD 39.95 domestic; USD 49.95 Canada; USD 59.95 elsewhere. Ed(s): Adriana Lopez, Joe Tessitore. Reed Business Information, 360 Park Ave South, New York, NY 10010; http://www.reedbusiness.com. Adv. *Bk. rev.:* 100, 75-200 words. *Aud.:* Ga, Sa.

This new review source aims to "gather, critique, translate, and report on" the Spanish-language titles being published in Latin America, Spain, and the United States. The look and feel of this magazine will be familiar to readers of *Library Journal* and *School Library Journal.* A recent issue features best book published last year, industry news, interviews with Hispanic authors, and a substantial number of reviews of both adult and juvenile titles. Even the ads can be helpful to acquisitions staffs who have trouble acquiring Spanish materials. Recommended for both public libraries that serve the fastest-growing segment of the population and all others who want to expose their traditional audiences to other cultures and languages.

1254. ***Firsts: the book collector's magazine.*** [ISSN: 1066-5471] 1991. m. USD 40 domestic; USD 60 in Canada & Mexico; USD 95 elsewhere. Ed(s): Kathryn Smiley. Firsts Magazine, Inc., PO Box 65166, Tucson, AZ 85728-5168. Illus., index, adv. Sample. Circ: 6000 Paid. Vol. ends: Dec. *Bk. rev.:* 1-5, 100-500 words. *Aud.:* Ac, Sa.

There seems to have been an explosion of periodicals in recent years directed at the amateur book collector. This one has found its niche with a focus on first editions of specific authors (mostly contemporary). Both book dealers and *amateurs du livre* offer articles on individual authors' publishing histories, checklists and bibliographies, and discussions of special bindings and illustrations. Amid the expected columns on auctions, catalogs, and upcoming book-related events, the "Ten Years Ago" column updates checklists published in earlier issues and "Books into Film" provides the connection between two very different formats. Especially suited to libraries with special collections on contemporary authors.

1255. ***Horn Book Guide to Children's and Young Adult Books.*** [ISSN: 1044-405X] 1989. s-a. USD 48 domestic; USD 58 in Canada & Mexico; USD 68 elsewhere. Ed(s): Jennifer Brabander, Kitty Flynn. Horn Book, Inc., 56 Roland St, Ste 200, Boston, MA 02129-1235; info@hbook.com; http://www.hbook.com. Illus., index, adv. Sample. Circ: 4000 Paid. Vol. ends: Jan/Jun. Online: ProQuest Information & Learning. *Indexed:* BRD, BRI, CBRI. *Bk. rev.:* 2,000, 40-50 words. *Aud.:* Ems, Hs, Ga.

This offshoot of *The Horn Book Magazine* provides critical annotations on all hardcover trade children's and young adult books published in the United States during the previous six months. Fiction is arranged by grade level and genre (e.g., picture books, readers), while nonfiction is arranged by the ten broad Dewey classes and then narrower topics. Each review (by a specialist in children's literature) bears a number from 1 to 6, with 1 denoting books of the highest quality and 6 marking those not recommended; a small triangle marking books rated 1 or 2 makes for easier reading and selection. Numerous indexes (author, illustrator, title, series, subject, and new editions and reissues) help the librarian track down particular titles. The reliability of the publisher, the useful arrangement by subject and level of quality, and the critical annotations make this a valuable source for selectors of children's books.

1256. ***The Horn Book Magazine: recommending books for children and young adults.*** [ISSN: 0018-5078] 1924. bi-m. USD 47 domestic; USD 67 per issue in Canada & Mexico; USD 77 per issue elsewhere. Ed(s): Roger Sutton. Horn Book, Inc., 56 Roland St, Ste 200, Boston, MA 02129-1235. Illus., index, adv. Sample. Circ: 18000 Paid and free. Vol. ends: Nov/Dec. Microform: NBI; PQC. Reprint: PQC. *Indexed:* ASIP, BRD, BRI, CBRI, CIJE, ICM, LISA, LibLit, MRD, MagInd, RGPR. *Bk. rev.:* 70-120, 100-300 words. *Aud.:* Ems, Hs, Ga, Ac.

One of the first magazines to treat children's literature as serious material for discussion and review, *The Horn Book* nevertheless avoids the temptation of burying children's books under a mountain of footnotes. Interviews, personal essays, and historical essays on great children's authors and illustrators, and reflections on topics such as book reviewing or multiculturalism in children's literature anchor each issue. The book reviews, most of which are for recommended titles, are grouped by age level and/or format (picture books, folklore, etc.). Other sections of the magazine include lists of new paperbacks and reissues, books in Spanish, and audiobooks, while "The Hunt Breakfast" is an invaluable guide to conference events and awards in the field of children's literature. Online, *The Horn Book*'s "Parents' Page" provides lists of recommended books, tips for reading with your child, and a library of "Children's Classics."

1257. ***Journal of Scholarly Publishing.*** Formerly: *Scholarly Publishing.* [ISSN: 1198-9742] 1969. q. CND 70. Ed(s): Bill Harnum. University of Toronto Press, Journals Department, 5201 Dufferin St, Toronto, ON M3H 5T8, Canada; journals@utpress.utoronto.ca; http://www.utpjournals.com. Illus., index, adv. Sample. Refereed. Circ: 1200. Vol. ends: Jul. Microform: MML; PQC. Online: EBSCO Publishing; LexisNexis; Micromedia ProQuest. *Indexed:* AmH&L, ArtHuCI, BAS, CBCARef, CLI, HEA, IBZ, ILP, InfoSAb, LISA, LibLit, MLA-IB, SSCI. *Bk. rev.:* 1-2, 400-500 words. *Aud.:* Ac, Sa.

This journal, as its title suggests, focuses on the academic side of publishing, from publishing or perishing to essays on the future of scholarly communication, the changing nature of authorship, and the effects of the electronic revolution on the printed scholarly monograph. Articles provide philosophical analysis and practical advice on topics such as the peer-review process, electronic publishing, copyright and permissions, and the business and management end of scholarly publishing. This title is a necessary acquisition for any college or university library with an interest in publishing, the history of the book, and the scholarly transmission of ideas.

1258. ***Kirkus Reviews: adult, young adult and children's book reviews.*** [ISSN: 0042-6598] 1933. s-m. USD 450 combined subscription print & online eds. Ed(s): Anne Larsen. V N U Business Publications, 770 Broadway, New York, NY 10003; bmcomm@vnuinc.com; http://www.vnubusinessmedia.com/. Illus., index. Circ: 5000 Paid and controlled. Microform: PQC. Online: EBSCO Publishing; Florida Center for Library Automation; Gale Group; LexisNexis. *Indexed:* BRI, CBRI. *Bk. rev.:* 150, 200-250 words. *Aud.:* Ems, Hs, Ga, Ac.

Divided into two main sections (adult and children's books), this handy preview of new books is a valued collection development tool for public librarians. Adult books are categorized by genre (i.e., fiction, mystery, science fiction, nonfiction). Along with bibliographic information, expected date of publication and the names of literary agents for individual titles are provided. Starred reviews serve several functions: In the adult section, they mark potential best-sellers, major promotions, book club selections, and just very good books; in the children's section, they denote books "of unusually high quality." The reviews manage to be discerning and critical without being too serious or self-righteous. Even when the editors review potboilers, they recognize that they might "sell millions" and will therefore be in demand in most public libraries. Online, the previews of forthcoming reviews and "Book-2-Film" makes a great complement to the print resource.

1259. ***Kliatt: reviews of selected current paperbacks, hardcover fiction, audiobooks, and educational software.*** Former titles: *Kliatt Young Adult Paperback Book Guide; Kliatt Paperback Book Guide.* [ISSN: 1065-8602] 1967. 6x/yr. USD 39 domestic; USD 41 foreign. Ed(s): Claire Rosser. Kliatt, 33 Bay State Rd, Wellesley, MA 02481-3244; kliatt@aol.com. Illus., index, adv. Sample. Circ: 2300. Vol. ends: Nov. Microform: PQC. Reprint: PQC. *Indexed:* BRI, CBRI, MRD. *Bk. rev.:* 150-200, 150-200 words. *Aud.:* Hs, Ga.

This title, with its focus on the reading of young adults, is "valuable . . . for supplementing the curriculum, for encouraging students' leisure reading, for promoting learning with computers." This review service is devoted chiefly to paperback books, hardcover YA fiction, audiobooks, educational software, and reference books suitable for high school libraries. Each review is coded for reading level and difficulty (junior high, senior high, advanced/adult). The reviews, by high school and college teachers and librarians, are arranged by broad subject area and seem to be universally positive; especially good books are asterisked. Additionally, a feature article covers an educational issue, a longer review, or a critical essay on a theme in young adult fiction. A recommended selection tool for junior high, high school, and YA librarians.

Literary Review. See Literary Reviews section.

1260. ***Logos: the professional journal of the book world.*** [ISSN: 0957-9656] 1990. q. USD 170 (Individuals, USD 78). Ed(s): Gordon Graham. Whurr Publishers Ltd., 19b Compton Terr, London, N1 2UN, United Kingdom; http://www.whurr.co.uk. Illus., adv. Sample. Circ: 309 Paid. *Indexed:* IBZ, LISA, LibLit. *Bk. rev.:* 5-10, 500-1,000 words. *Aud.:* Ac, Sa.

As the electronic age continues its incursions into our lives and reading matter, this scholarly journal studies "the word" within the context of the printed book. Attending to the interests of librarians, publishers, commercial book people, and scholars, and eschewing news and advertising, *Logos* is international in scope; its key characteristic is bridging: "between nations; between disciplines and professions; between specialists and generalists; between private and public enterprise." Typical articles focus on the textbook of the future, reading in the electronic era, translation, media mergers, and publishing in developing countries. The book review section is small but interesting, and it provides a useful overview of new work in the fields of bibliography, publishing, and book history. A recommended title for college and university libraries with programs in publishing, information studies, or the history of the book.

1261. ***London Review of Books.*** [ISSN: 0260-9592] 1979. s-m. GBP 70.80 domestic; GBP 85 in Europe; USD 42 United States. Ed(s): Mary-Kay Wilmers. L R B Ltd., 28-30 Little Russell St, London, WC1A 2HN, United Kingdom; subs@lrb.co.uk. Illus., index, adv. Circ: 42525. Vol. ends: Dec. Microform: PQC. Reprint: PQC. *Indexed:* BEL&L, BHA, BRD, BRI, BrHumI, CBRI, IDP, MLA-IB, RI-1. *Bk. rev.:* 15-20, 1,500-2,500 words. *Aud.:* Ga, Ac.

Similar in format and coverage to the *Times Literary Supplement* and *The New York Review of Books* (both below in this section), this periodical has an equally elite readership in mind. With an editorial board including distinguished literary critic Frank Kermode, the *London Review of Books* (*LRB*) examines, at essay length, new titles by major British and American university presses and quality trade publishers. Frequent groupings of new books by theme offer readers and buyers the chance to comparison-shop and the reviewers the opportunity to display their learning and their opinions. There is a frequently contentious letters-to-the-editor column, some new poetry, and a regular "Diary" column—a personal essay on people and places that helps balance the ivory-tower tone of the rest of the publication. Online, the *LRB* web site offers letters from the current issue, a full-text archive of past reviews and letters, and contributors' and subject indexes. Recommended for large public libraries and most academic libraries.

The Medieval Review. See History/Electronic Journals section.

MultiCultural Review. See Ethnic Studies section.

1262. ***New York Review of Books.*** [ISSN: 0028-7504] 1963. 20x/yr. USD 64; USD 4.50 newsstand/cover per issue. Ed(s): Robert Silvers, Barbara Epstein. N Y R E V, Inc., 1755 Broadway, 5th Fl, New York, NY 10019-3780; mail@nybooks.com; http://www.nybooks.com/nyrev. Illus., adv. Circ: 120000 Paid. Vol. ends: Jan. Microform: PQC. Online: bigchalk; Gale Group; Northern Light Technology, Inc. Reprint: PQC. *Indexed:* A&ATA, ABS&EES, AltPI, AnthLit, ArtHuCI, BHA, BRD, BRI, CBRI, FLI, FutSurv, IAPV, IDP, LRI, MLA-IB, MagInd, MusicInd, RGPR, RI-1, RILM, SSCI. *Bk. rev.:* 15-20, 2,000-3,500 words. *Aud.:* Ga, Ac, Sa.

The letters to the editor in this publication (complete with footnotes) provide more interesting and challenging reading than the lead articles in most other magazines. The major essays and lengthy book reviews that form the more substantial part of *The New York Review of Books* are contributed by some of the best and best-known contemporary writers. One can read Garry Wills on nativity scenes, Doris Lessing on Zimbabwe, or a poem by John Ashbery. The thoughtful and often acerbic comments of reviewers on important new books and the larger issues they raise are frequently accompanied by the clever caricatures of artist David Levine. The *Review*'s web presence offers, in addition to a table of contents and selected editorial material, a Levine Gallery in which Count Basie and Margaret Thatcher are neighbors, and the text of its first issue in 1963. Although it certainly does not cater to mass-market tastes, the *NYRB* is a basic title for all academic and most public libraries.

1263. ***New York Times Book Review.*** [ISSN: 0028-7806] 1896. w. USD 54.60 domestic; USD 74.36 foreign. Ed(s): Charles McGrath. New York Times Company, 229 W 43rd St, New York, NY 10036; http://www.nytimes.com/books/home/. Illus., index, adv. Circ: 1638908. Vol. ends: Dec. Microform: PQC. Online: bigchalk; Gale Group; ProQuest Information & Learning. *Indexed:* ABS&EES, ArtHuCI, BEL&L, BHA, BRD, BRI, CBRI, GardL, IDP, LRI, MLA-IB, MagInd, MusicInd, NewsAb, RGPR, RI-1. *Bk. rev.:* 45-50, 250-2,500 words. *Aud.:* Ga, Ac, Sa.

A supplement to the hefty Sunday edition of *The New York Times,* the *Book Review* (*NYTBR*) reviews not only the best books but the books that make the best news. Scholarly works, literary fiction, bad books by famous authors, good ones by first-time novelists, children's books, and pop culture—all are surveyed by the *NYTBR.* The featured article-length reviews are accompanied by shorter notices and regular columns on children's books, mysteries, and paperback reissues. Particularly scathing or sloppy reviews can generate numerous letters to the editor, often from well-known persons; these, as well as the brief authors' queries, give some sense of the level of the *NYTBR*'s readership. Librarians in most types of libraries will find both the best-seller lists and the editors' lists of best books useful. The *NYTBR* is not just a book selection tool, however; as the reviewing arm of one of the country's most widely circulated newspapers, it is a source with which any librarian worth her or his salt must be familiar.

1264. ***Publishers Weekly: the international news magazine of book publishing.*** [ISSN: 0000-0019] 1872. 51x/yr. USD 214 domestic; USD 264 Canada; USD 350 elsewhere. Ed(s): Nora Rawlinson, Joe Tessitore. Reed Business Information, 360 Park Ave South, New York, NY 10010; http://www.reedbusiness.com. Illus., index, adv. Circ: 38500. Vol. ends: Dec. Microform: CIS; PQC. Online: EBSCO Publishing; Florida Center for Library Automation; Gale Group; LexisNexis; OCLC Online Computer Library Center, Inc.; ProQuest Information & Learning; H.W. Wilson. Reprint: PQC. *Indexed:* ABIn, ABS&EES, BAS, BPI, BRI, CBRI, ConsI, GardL, LISA, LRI, LibLit, MagInd, PAIS, RGPR, RI-1. *Bk. rev.:* 70, 50-150 words. *Aud.:* Ga, Ac, Sa.

Books are still the meat and potatoes of libraries, and only the library that no longer needs to keep abreast of trends in the book business can afford to do without *Publishers Weekly* (*PW*). Chock-full of news on publishers and publishing, with an emphasis on the American scene, *PW* talks with and about the authors, editors, designers, and marketers of books. For the public librarian who needs to fill requests for popular materials, *PW*'s most useful feature is the "Forecasts" section, which reviews new titles, with notes on special promotions or ad campaigns. The regular issues in specific subject areas (e.g., children's books, religion) are useful checklists for academic libraries and libraries with particular subject concentrations, and the columns on audiobooks, multimedia, and movie tie-ins reflect the increasingly symbiotic relations between the traditional print and new media industries. The *PW* web site supplements the print version, with lists of best-sellers, job openings in the field, and an opportunity to sign up for e-mail newsletters on the latest books and book news.

1265. *Publishing Research Quarterly.* Formerly (until 1991): *Book Research Quarterly.* [ISSN: 1053-8801] 1986. q. USD 192 (Individuals, USD 68). Ed(s): Robert Baensch. Transaction Publishers, 35 Berrue Circle, Rutgers University, Piscataway, NJ 08854-8042; trans@transactionpub.com; http://www.transactionpub.com. Illus., index, adv. Refereed. Circ: 500. Vol. ends: Winter. Online: bigchalk; EBSCO Publishing; Florida Center for Library Automation; Gale Group; Ingenta Select; Northern Light Technology, Inc.; ProQuest Information & Learning. Reprint: PSC. *Indexed:* AbAn, AgeL, IBZ, InfoSAb, LISA, MLA-IB, PAIS, SSCI. *Bk. rev.:* 2-3, 1,000 words. *Aud.:* Ac, Sa.

Publishing Research Quarterly is a journal that "aims to clarify the process that enables writers to connect with their readers." Although this journal has always viewed "the book" in its broadest possible sense, its contents now reflect even more the interdisciplinary nature of the study of the book: the journal now encompasses the fields of journalism, communications, library science, and printing as they relate to publishing. Articles explore the commercial aspects of publishing, copyright, and computerization, as well as historical studies of books, printing, and reading, while the book review section provides a good overview of scholarly work in these fields. A useful title for most academic library collections.

1266. *Q B R: The Black Book Review: our lives, our words, our stories.* Formerly (until 1995): *Quarterly Black Review of Books.* [ISSN: 1087-7088] 1993. bi-m. USD 16 domestic; USD 27 foreign. Ed(s): Max Rodriguez. Quarterly Black Review of Books, 9 West 126 St, 2nd Fl, New York, NY 10027. Illus., adv. Sample. Vol. ends: Aug. *Indexed:* IIBP. *Bk. rev.:* 15-20, 500-1000 words. *Aud.:* Ga, Ac.

Quarterly Black Review reviews the latest fiction, nonfiction, poetry, children's books, health-related titles, and other publications of interest to the black community, including works by African and Caribbean writers. Frequently *QBR* includes book excerpts and interviews with authors of note. Essays on topics such as reviewing black literature and articles on black publishers and authors round out the periodical. This is a required title for academic libraries, black studies collections, and libraries serving African American readers.

1267. *Reference and Research Book News: annotations and reviews of new books for libraries.* Incorporates (1989-1992): *University Press Book News.* [ISSN: 0887-3763] 1986. q. USD 175 (Individuals, USD 130). Ed(s): Jane Erskine. Book News, Inc. (Portland), 5739 N E Sumner St, Portland, OR 97218; BookNews@BookNews.com. Illus., adv. Circ: 1700. Vol. ends: Nov. *Indexed:* BRI, CBRI. *Bk. rev.:* 2,500, 25-75 words. *Aud.:* Ga, Ac.

Similar to *Choice* (above in this section) in its presentation and function, *Reference and Research Book News* is targeted at acquisitions librarians in academic, special, and public libraries. It has some unique features, some of marginal value (e.g., book size, cataloging main entry). Each entry in the LC-classed arrangement includes standard bibliographic information, pagination, and cost. Titles listed in "Guide to Reference Books" and "Books for College Libraries" are flagged. The reviews—which cover scholarly monographs, continuations, reference books, and reprints—are, for the most part, summary rather than evaluative. Due to space constraints, some annotations are available only in electronic form; these asterisked titles (and the complete database) are searchable in various online sources, including Amazon.com, Barnes & Noble, and Powell's. Collection development librarians should find this title a useful current-awareness tool.

Science Books & Films. See Science and Technology section.

1268. *Small Press Review - Small Magazine Review.* Formerly (until Feb. 1994): *Small Press Review;* Incorporates (1993-1994): *Small Magazine Review.* 1967. bi-m. USD 35 (Individuals, USD 25). Ed(s): Len Fulton. Dustbooks, PO Box 100, Paradise, CA 95967; publisher@dustbooks.com; http://www.dustbooks.com. Illus., adv. Circ: 3500. *Indexed:* ASIP, BRI, CBRI. *Bk. rev.:* 10-15, 200-500 words. *Aud.:* Ac, Sa.

Small-press aficionados, readers of modern poetry, and special collections librarians will find this magazine in newsprint a good place to learn about the world of little presses. The *Small Press Review* covers titles that the better-known reviewing sources neglect; selectors should note, however, that many of the reviewers, in their zeal to promote the small-press gospel, frequently comment favorably. There is a regular "picks" column, practical advice to writers and editors, and news of writing contests and writers' conferences. With the absorption of *Small Magazine Review* comes the bonus of reviews of new periodical titles and specific issues of little magazines. The publication also updates the *International Directory of Little Magazines and Small Presses* (brought out by the same publisher) with its listings of new magazines and new publisher start-ups.

T L S: the Times literary supplement. See Newspapers/General section.

1269. *The Women's Review of Books.* [ISSN: 0738-1433] 1983. m. except Aug. USD 40 (Individuals, USD 25; USD 4 newsstand/cover per issue). Ed(s): Linda Gardiner. Wellesley College, Center for Research on Women, 106 Central St, Wellesley, MA 02481; http://www.wcwonline.org/. Illus., index, adv. Circ: 16000 Paid. Vol. ends: Sep. Microform: PQC. Online: EBSCO Publishing; Gale Group; LexisNexis; Northern Light Technology, Inc.; OCLC Online Computer Library Center, Inc.; H.W. Wilson. *Indexed:* ABS&EES, AltPI, AmHI, BRD, BRI, CBRI, CWI, FemPer, IBZ, RI-1, RILM, SWA, WSA, WSI. *Bk. rev.:* 15-20, 1,000-1,500 words. *Aud.:* Ac, Sa.

The Women's Review of Books announces itself as "feminist" without restricting itself to any one conception of feminism. In its reviews of books by and about women, it attempts to represent the "widest possible range of feminist perspectives." The tabloid's bent, however, is clearly scholarly and academic; most of the reviewers are college and university professors, and the books reviewed are more likely to be found in academic than in public libraries. The reviews themselves, and an occasional article or group of articles on women's issues, are literate, incisive, and personal, revealing as much about the reviewer's viewpoints as the author's. A monthly listing of books received is useful, if not as informative as the full-length reviews. Online, *The Women's Review* presents the table of contents, letters to the editor, and job postings from the most recent issue, along with links to feminist bookstores and feminist literary magazines and journals. On the whole, an important source for academic and large public libraries with women's literature collections.

1270. *The Yale Review of Books.* 1998. q. USD 20. Ed(s): Joshua Foer. Yale Review of Books, Box 206560, New Haven, CT 06520-6560; Cesar.Garza@yale.edu. Adv. *Bk. rev.:* 15-20, 1,000 words. *Aud.:* Ac.

This quarterly, which claims to be the oldest undergraduate book review source in the nation, contains reviews of fiction and nonfiction titles, author interviews, and personal essays, most written by Yale University undergraduates. An occasional piece by a Yale faculty member rounds out each issue, and the faculty's influence is evidenced in the periodical's advisory board, a veritable who's who of literary scholars and writers. A "Profs' Picks" column tells the reader what faculty at Yale are reading and why; "Can't Judge a Cover by Its Book" is a clever student-authored essay on books that happen to be in the news. Available both in print and online, the editors' target audiences are the local Yale and New Haven community, "influential opinion-makers," and university libraries. Scanning this appealing review would be an excellent way for academic librarians to keep up with not only new and important books, but with what some of our brightest college students think about literature, politics, and the written word.

Electronic Journals

1271. *BookEnds: the book pl@ce magazine.* 1997. m. Free. Ed(s): Chris Martin. Book Data, Globe House, 1 Chertsey Rd, Twickenham, TW1 1LR, United Kingdom; editor@thebookplace.com; http://www.bookends.co.uk/. *Aud.:* Ems, Hs, Ga.

This British cousin to Amazon.com is at once more readable, less cluttered, and more literate than its relative across the pond. Along with author interviews and extracts from new books, one can find publishing industry news, a calendar of events, and books offered for purchase. The reviews include a reader's advisor (i.e., other titles you might like), and there is a summary of the Sunday newspaper rankings of the latest in print. Avid readers can browse by subject (science fiction, crime, travel, etc.), and children can link to "The Book Monster" to read about authors and books they might enjoy. And *BookEnds*' "Bookmarks" section is a great monthly guide to the best web sites for book lovers. A recommended site to accompany the human reader's advisor in your own library.

1272. *BookWire.* 1999. irreg. approx. m. Free. R.R. Bowker LLC, 630 Central Ave., New Providence, NJ 07974; info@bowker.com; http://www.bookwire.com/bookwire/. Adv. *Aud.:* Ga, Ac, Sa.

Strictly speaking, *BookWire* is not a periodical; it's not regular, and it's not numbered. But this online portal into the book industry is a great starting place for everything you might want to know about books, bookselling, and the people who write, create, and lend them. Although Bowker publications comprise a large portion of the table of contents, there are also useful links to indispensable resources such as professional associations, bestseller lists, author biographies, literary events, and statistical data. In addition to book industry news, the site also provides links to review sources, directories of publishers, and book dealers. A good reference source for all sorts of book-related queries.

1273. *C M Magazine: Canadian review of materials.* Former titles (until Dec. 1994): *C M: Canadian Materials for Schools and Libraries;* (until 1979): *Canadian Materials.* [ISSN: 1201-9364] 1995. bi-w. Ed(s): Peter Tittenberger. Manitoba Library Association, 606 100 Arthur St, Winnipeg, MB R3B 1H3, Canada; cm@mts.net; http://www.umanitoba.ca/cm. Illus., adv. Online: Micromedia ProQuest. *Indexed:* BRD, BRI, CBCARef, CBRI, CEI, CPerI, MRD. *Bk. rev.:* 30-35, 200 words. *Aud.:* Ems, Hs, Ga, Ac.

With its reviews of books, videos, audio recordings, and CD-ROMs, this online magazine courts a broad audience, from children and teenagers to parents and librarians. Along with a focus on Canadian subject matter (and the option of reading some of the text in French), *CM* publishes profiles of authors and illustrators and feature articles on important issues such as censorship and the freedom to read. The entire archive of *CM*'s print predecessor is also available online. Public libraries and academic libraries with teaching materials centers will want to point their browsers to this award-winning title.

1274. *E-Streams (Contoocook): electronic reviews of science and technology references covering engineering, agriculture, medicine and science.* [ISSN: 1098-4399] 1998. m. Free. Ed(s): H Robert Malinowsky. Yankee Book Peddler, Inc., 999 Maple St, Contoocook, NH 03229; estreams@ybp.com; http://www.e-streams.com. *Indexed:* BRI, CBRI. *Bk. rev.:* 30-50, 100-250 words. *Aud.:* Ga, Ac.

This collaborative venture between a practicing librarian and well-known book jobber Yankee Book Peddler yokes together the perspectives of both consumers and purveyors of books. Each issue has short reviews of basic books in engineering, agriculture, medicine, and science that will appeal to the academic and public library reader. The reviews, written by and for librarians, can be read in either html or pdf format, and include bibliographic information, tables of contents, and, if relevant, a list of contributors. Each review also provides a link to YBP's online ordering system. A reliable, welcome addition to the rather specialized world of science and scientific publishing.

1275. *January Magazine.* 1997. d. Free. Ed(s): Linda Richards. January Publishing Inc., 101-1001 W Broadway, Ste 192, Vancouver, BC V6H 4E4, Canada; scribe@mindlink.bc.ca; http://www.januarymagazine.com. *Aud.:* Ga.

With a relaxed, bookstore approach to readers and reading, this online magazine calls itself *January* because it offers "something different . . . Renewal. New beginnings. New ideas." Along with book reviews, excerpts from books, and lists of bestsellers (based on sales among international online booksellers), *January*'s editors profile contemporary authors ranging from Margaret Atwood to Anne Rice, from Judy Blume to Thomas Keneally. Sections on children's books, crime fiction, sci-fi, and cookbooks cater to the fans of these genres, while the musically inclined reader can link to "Blue Coupe," a record-review site "where words and music collide." Libraries can help their patrons collide with the written word more easily by placing a link from their own home pages to *January*.

1276. *The Journal of Electronic Publishing.* [ISSN: 1080-2711] 1995. q. Ed(s): Eve Trager, Judith Axler Turner. University of Michigan Press, 839 Greene St, Box 1104, Ann Arbor, MI 48106-1104; um.press@umich.edu; http://www.press.umich.edu. Refereed. *Indexed:* LISA, PAIS. *Aud.:* Ac, Sa.

This e-journal is intended for "the thoughtful forward-thinking publisher, librarian, scholar, or author." Dedicated to examining the issues that shape publishing policy in an electronic environment, it includes short invited contributions from experts working in the field and longer pieces by scholars. A recent issue includes papers on alternatives to peer review, the effect of computers on writing, and lessons learned from editing an online refereed journal. Academic libraries and all those interested in what electronic publishing implies for scholarship and libraries should provide a link from their catalog to this university press publication.

■ BUILDING AND CONSTRUCTION

See also Architecture; Home; and Interior Design and Decoration sections.

Julian Stam, Preservation Manager, Thomas P. O'Neill Library, Boston College, 140 Commonwealth Ave., Chestnut Hill, MA 02460

Introduction

Professional contractors, builders, designers, engineers, and developers are the primary users of magazines in the Building and Construction section. The journals are most often highly technical and specific. Most readers with a general interest in design, carpentry, restoration, or architecture will find other sections, including Architecture, Home, and Interior Design and Decoration, to be of more interest.

Special libraries with a construction clientele should consider a number of these titles but must also be aware of the many online resources currently available. One excellent resource is an international list of "Refereed Journals" (http://cwis.livjm.ac.uk/lea/misc/ARCref.htm) provided and updated by ARCLIB, the Architecture Librarians Group. Many others of them are provided by the publishers of building and construction magazines, which often put content from their print publications online, and some of this information is free. Related web sites are noted in title descriptions. It should also be noted that many titles in this section are associated with a particular trade organization and may not be available through general circulation or may be free for trade members only. Because of the technical nature of this field, the following is not a complete list of related publications, but rather a compilation of major titles that will support construction businesses and educational programs.

Basic Periodicals

Sa: *Builder, Building Design & Construction, Constructor, Old House Journal, Professional Builder.*

Basic Abstracts and Indexes

Applied Science and Technology Index, Engineering Index.

1277. *A C I Materials Journal.* Supersedes in part (Mar. 1987): *American Concrete Institute. Journal.* [ISSN: 0889-325X] 1929. bi-m. USD 135 domestic; USD 143 foreign. Ed(s): Rebecca A Hartford. American Concrete Institute, PO Box 9094, Farmington, MI 48333; webmaster@aci-int.org; http://www.aci-int.org. Illus., index, adv. Refereed. Circ: 11700. Reprint: PQC. *Indexed:* AS&TI, ChemAb, EngInd, GeoRef, H&SSA, SCI. *Aud.:* Ac, Sa.

ACI Materials Journal provides technical information and research on the properties and use of concrete. American Concrete Institute (ACI) standards and committee reports are also included. The ACI web site is searchable and includes abstracts, with full-text articles available via traditional mail for a fee.

1278. ***A C I Structural Journal.*** Supersedes in part (Mar. 1987): *American Concrete Institute. Journal.* [ISSN: 0889-3241] 1929. bi-m. USD 135 domestic; USD 143 foreign. Ed(s): Rebecca A Hartford. American Concrete Institute, PO Box 9094, Farmington, MI 48333; webmaster@aci-int.org; http://www.aci-int.org. Illus., index, adv. Refereed. Circ: 17400. Microform: PQC. Reprint: PQC. *Indexed:* AS&TI, ApMecR, C&ISA, ChemAb, EngInd, ExcerpMed, GeoRef, H&SSA, SCI. *Aud.:* Ac, Sa.

ACI Structural Journal provides technical information and research on structural design, analysis and analysis theory, and the elements and structures of concrete. ACI standards and committee reports are also included. The ACI web site is searchable and includes abstracts, with full-text articles available via traditional mail for a fee.

1279. ***Aberdeen's Magazine of Masonry Construction.*** Formerly (until 1990): *Magazine of Masonry Construction.* [ISSN: 1055-4408] 1988. m. USD 30 domestic; USD 39 in Canada & Mexico; USD 93 elsewhere. Ed(s): William D Palmer. Aberdeen Group, 426 S Westgate St, Addison, IL 60101; cschierhorn@wocnet.com; httpp://www.worldofmasonry.com. Illus., adv. Circ: 40000 Paid. Online: Florida Center for Library Automation; Gale Group; H.W. Wilson. *Indexed:* C&ISA, CerAb, EngInd. *Aud.:* Sa.

A wide variety of uses for masonry in building and construction are included in this primary source. Paving and architectural designs are examples that demonstrate an emphasis on engineering and technical processes, but new products and the economics of the industry are also included. An annual buyers' guide is also published.

Air Conditioning, Heating & Refrigeration News. See Business/Trade and Industry section.

1280. ***Builder (Washington): NAHB, the voice of America's housing industry.*** Former titles: *N A H B Builder; Builder (Washington); N A H B Journal-Scope;* Which was formed by the merger of: *N A H B Journal; N A H B Washington Scope.* [ISSN: 0744-1193] 1942. m. USD 29.95 domestic; USD 35.95 Canada; USD 67 elsewhere. Ed(s): Boyce Thompson. Hanley-Wood, Llc., One Thomas Circle, N W, Ste 600, Washington, DC 20005-5701; tjackson@hanley-wood.com; http://www.hanley-wood.com. Illus., adv. Circ: 160696. Microform: PQC. Online: Florida Center for Library Automation; Gale Group; OCLC Online Computer Library Center, Inc.; ProQuest Information & Learning; H.W. Wilson. *Indexed:* ABIn, AIAP, API, BPI, LRI. *Aud.:* Ac, Sa.

This National Association of Home Builders (NAHB) publication provides information for builders of residential units. Design and new products are featured. Sections also include plans; economic, real estate, and political news and trends; marketing ideas; and industry news. A buyers' guide, the nation's 100 biggest builders, and award-winning homes are also published annually. The attractive format and coverage of design ideas make this a technical publication that may also be of interest to current homeowners. *Builder Online* includes business, design, and architecture news, discussion groups, links, house plans, and an online interactive products guide to more than 10,000 products from 3,000 manufacturers. Full-text articles are available.

1281. ***Building Design & Construction: the magazine for the building team.*** Formerly (until 1958): *Building Construction.* [ISSN: 0007-3407] 1950. m. USD 119 domestic; USD 164 Canada; USD 159 Mexico. Ed(s): Robert Cassidy. Reed Business Information, 8878 S Barrons Blvd, Highlands Ranch, CO 80129-2345; http://www.reedbusiness.com. Illus., index, adv. Circ: 76743. Microform: CIS. Online: EBSCO Publishing; Florida Center for Library Automation; Gale Group; LexisNexis; Northern Light Technology, Inc.; OCLC Online Computer Library Center, Inc.; ProQuest Information & Learning; H.W. Wilson. Reprint: PQC. *Indexed:* ABIn, AIAP, ArchI, BPI, LRI. *Aud.:* Ac, Sa.

The subtitle says it best. Topics will be of primary interest to design and building teams that include engineers, contractors, owners, and facilities managers. Emphasis is, logically, on large, commercial building projects. Topics focus on projects and project development, economic trends, industry news, and building technologies. Construction outlook, reconstruction, the 300 largest owners, and the 300 largest design/construction firms are also regularly featured. The online magazine provides news, products, suppliers, and associations links, literature, and data, as well as article archives that include abstracts. There is also a fee-based article delivery service.

1282. ***Buildings: the source for facilities decision-makers.*** [ISSN: 0007-3725] 1906. m. USD 70 domestic; USD 85 Canada; USD 150 elsewhere. Ed(s): Linda K Monroe. Stamats Buildings Media, Inc., PO Box 1888, Cedar Rapids, IA 52406-1888; http://www.buildings.com. Illus., index, adv. Circ: 57000 Controlled. Vol. ends: Dec. Microform: PQC. Online: The Dialog Corporation; EBSCO Publishing; Florida Center for Library Automation; Gale Group; Northern Light Technology, Inc.; OCLC Online Computer Library Center, Inc.; ProQuest Information & Learning; H.W. Wilson. *Indexed:* ABIn, AIAP, AgeL, BPI, C&ISA, EngInd. *Aud.:* Ac, Sa.

The design and construction of large commercial and industrial buildings is the major focus of this magazine. Contents also include forecasts for trends and products in commercial/institutional buildings. Most articles are brief and written by journal staff. This publication contains an abundance of colorful advertisements for services and products. Some of the regular monthly sections of this magazine are "Smarter Buildings," "Industry411," and "Tools of the Trade." Many issues have a theme. There is a feature article and all others relate to it. The table of contents contains a brief summary for each article in the issue. Select articles are available for browsing at the publisher's web site.

1283. ***C E E News.*** Former titles (until 1990): *Electrical Construction Technology;* (until 1989): *C E E; Contractors' Electrical Equipment.* [ISSN: 1045-2710] 1949. m. USD 30. Ed(s): Jim Lucy. Primedia Business Magazines & Media, Inc., 9800 Metcalf Ave., Overland Park, KS 66212; http://www.primediabusiness.com. Illus., adv. Circ: 105700. *Aud.:* Sa.

Electrical contractors will find this tabloid-format publication to be a primary source. New products, installation methods, and personnel and office management are featured. Editorial content will also be of interest. An annual product issue is also published. *CEE News Online* includes a searchable buyer's guide, calendar, full-text articles, and industry links.

Another title of similar scope but available only with National Electrical Contractors Association membership is

Electrical Contractor. [ISSN: 0033-5118] 1939. m. Membership. Natl. Electric Contractors Assn., 3 Bethesda Metro Center, Suite 1100, Bethesda, MD 20814. Circ: 68,000.

1284. ***Concrete Construction.*** Former titles (until Nov.1999): *Aberdeen's Concrete Construction;* (until 1990): *Concrete Construction.* [ISSN: 1533-7316] 1956. m. USD 30 domestic; USD 39 in Canada & Mexico; USD 93 elsewhere. Ed(s): William D. Palmer. Hanley-Wood, Llc., One Thomas Circle, N W, Ste 600, Washington, DC 20005-5701; tjackson@hanley-wood.com; http://www.hanley-wood.com. Illus., index, adv. Circ: 73580 Paid. Microform: PQC. Online: Florida Center for Library Automation; Gale Group; OCLC Online Computer Library Center, Inc.; ProQuest Information & Learning; H.W. Wilson. *Indexed:* AS&TI, EngInd. *Aud.:* Ac, Sa.

A wide variety of uses for concrete in building and construction are included in this primary source. Paving and architectural designs are typical subjects that demonstrate the emphasis on engineering and technical processes, but new products and the economics of the industry are also included. There is an annual reference guide published. Articles and a "problem clinic" can be found at www2.worldofconcrete.com.

1285. ***Construction Equipment.*** Former titles: *Construction Equipment Magazine; Construction Equipment and Materials Magazine.* [ISSN: 0192-3978] 1949. 13x/yr. USD 99.90 domestic (Free to qualified personnel). Ed(s): Rod Sutton. Reed Business Information, 2000 Clearwater Dr, Oak Brook, IL 60523; http://www.reedbusiness.com. Illus., index, adv. Circ: 80000 Controlled. Online: EBSCO Publishing;

Florida Center for Library Automation; Gale Group; Northern Light Technology, Inc.; OCLC Online Computer Library Center, Inc.; ProQuest Information & Learning. Reprint: PQC. *Indexed:* ABIn, EngInd. *Aud.:* Sa.

What could be better than knowing, really knowing, you've got the best truck? Well, this publication will help you figure out if you do. Content focuses on the purchase, maintenance, and use of all types of construction equipment. Safety issues, legislative updates, and economics are discussed. Advertisements are prominent, and do-it-yourself tips are often included. *Construction Equipment On-Line* (www.coneq.com) includes a buyers' guide, a specification guide, a market watch, links to other sites, and product and industry updates.

1286. *Construction Specifier: for commercial and industrial construction.* [ISSN: 0010-6925] 1950. m. USD 30 (Non-members, USD 36). Ed(s): Jack Reeder. Construction Specifications Institute, 99 Canal Center Plz, Ste 300, Alexandria, VA 22314-1588; http://www.csinet.org. Illus., index, adv. Circ: 19000. *Indexed:* AIAP, ArchI, C&ISA, EngInd. *Aud.:* Sa.

This is the official publication of the Construction Specifications Institute (CSI) and is appropriate for specifying architects, engineers, and writers, or others responsible for the selection and specification of construction products, materials, equipment, and methods. It features news, commentary, and editorial viewpoints regarding specification writing, CSI and education, technical commentary, and the CSI specification series. The CSI web site gives members full-text access to articles published since 1995, while the latest three issues are available free of charge to all.

1287. *Constructor: the management magazine of the construction industry.* [ISSN: 0162-6191] 1919. m. Members, USD 15; Non-members, USD 250. Ed(s): Ben Herring. A G C, 333 John Carlyle St, Ste 200, Alexandria, VA 22314-5745; http://www.agc.org. Illus., index, adv. Circ: 40000 Paid and controlled. *Aud.:* Sa.

The official publication of the Associated General Contractors of America (AGCA), this magazine focuses on the economics, marketing, and management of the construction industry. It will be of particular interest to managers and business executives. Economic and political news, and coverage of legal, tax, and labor issues affecting the construction industry are included. A complete AGCA directory of members is included annually, while member activities are reported throughout the regular issues. The searchable AGCA web site includes a construction marketplace, news, legislative information, and safety and risk management information.

1288. *Contractor: the newsmagazine of mechanical contracting.* [ISSN: 0897-7135] 1954. m. USD 60 domestic; USD 85 Canada; USD 100 elsewhere. Penton Media, Inc., 1300 E 9th St, Cleveland, OH 44114-1503; http://www.penton.com. Illus., adv. Circ: 50377 Controlled. Online: EBSCO Publishing; Florida Center for Library Automation; Gale Group; Northern Light Technology, Inc.; OCLC Online Computer Library Center, Inc.; ProQuest Information & Learning. Reprint: PQC. *Indexed:* ABIn. *Aud.:* Sa.

This is a tabloid-format publication for heating, plumbing, and air-conditioning contractors. New products and materials, legislative updates, and labor issues are discussed. *Contractormag.com* includes news, product updates, columnists, a data bank, and links to related associations, regulatory groups, and unions.

1289. *Custom Home.* Incorporates (1976-1999): *Custom Builder.* [ISSN: 1055-3479] 1991. 7x/yr. Ed(s): Leslie Ensor. Hanley-Wood, Llc., One Thomas Circle, N W, Ste 600, Washington, DC 20005-5701; tjackson@hanley-wood.com; http://www.hanley-wood.com. Illus., adv. Circ: 45000. *Aud.:* Sa.

This trade publication discusses building techniques, practices, and products for custom homes. Architects and builders of top-of-the-line custom residences will be particularly interested.

1290. *E C & M.* Incorporates (in 2002): *Power Quality Assurance;* Formerly (until 199?): *Electrical Construction & Maintenance.* [ISSN: 1082-295X] 1901. m. Free to qualified personnel. Ed(s): Mike Eby. Primedia Business Magazines & Media, Inc., 9800 Metcalf Ave., Overland Park, KS 66212; inquiries@primediabusiness.com; http://www.primediabusiness.com. Illus., adv. Circ: 106618 Controlled. Online: Gale Group; ProQuest Information & Learning. *Indexed:* AS&TI, EngInd, RiskAb. *Aud.:* Ac, Sa.

This highly technical journal provides professionals with data for the design, installation, maintenance, and national codes for electrical systems. Some management issues are also discussed. Each issue usually focuses on a specific topic such as testing, the National Electrical Codes, safety issues, or remote monitoring. The *EC&M* web site includes news, National Electrical Code issues, a contractors' corner, product updates, commentary, full-text articles from 1995 to the present, and a searchable supplier directory.

Electrical Contractor. See under *CEE News.*

The Family Handyman. See Home section.

1291. *Heating-Piping-Air Conditioning Engineering.* Formerly (until 1999): *Heating, Piping and Air Conditioning.* [ISSN: 1527-4055] 1929. m. USD 65 domestic; USD 80 Canada; USD 100 elsewhere. Ed(s): Michael Ivanovich. Penton Media, Inc., 1300 E 9th St, Cleveland, OH 44114-1503; information@penton.com; http://www.penton.com. Illus., adv. Circ: 52000 Controlled. Microform: PQC. Online: Gale Group; OCLC Online Computer Library Center, Inc.; ProQuest Information & Learning; H.W. Wilson. Reprint: PQC. *Indexed:* AS&TI, ApMecR, C&ISA, ChemAb, EngInd, ExcerpMed, H&SSA. *Aud.:* Ac, Sa.

Technical aspects of heating, air conditioning, and refrigeration systems are covered in this technical publication. Engineers will find the title of particular interest. Topics have included industrial processes, power piping systems, mold, efficiency issues, and codes and standards. *HPAC Engineering Interactive* provides full-text articles; news; product, equipment, and data information; event listings; design and IT tips; a learning center; and editorial content.

1292. *Journal of Light Construction.* Formerly: *New England Builder.* [ISSN: 1040-5224] 1982. m. USD 39.95; USD 4.95 newsstand/cover per issue. Ed(s): Dan Jackson. Hanley-Wood, Llc., 186 Allen Brook Ln, Williston, VT 05495; tjackson@hanley-wood.com; http://www.hanley-wood.com. Illus., index, adv. Sample. Circ: 62500 Paid. *Aud.:* Sa.

This title isn't quite for the shed-building "weekend warrior," but it's the closest you'll find in this category, being of use for residential and light-commercial building contractors and remodelers. Topics range from practical information on building technology, management, and products to technical aspects of materials and design. *JLC Online* provides selected articles, builder forums, a bookstore, information on links and events, and a searchable product directory.

1293. *Old House Journal.* [ISSN: 0094-0178] 1973. 6x/yr. USD 21.97 domestic; USD 31.97 Canada; USD 51.97 elsewhere. Ed(s): Gordon Bock. Hanley-Wood, Llc., One Thomas Circle, N W, Ste 600, Washington, DC 20005-5701; tjackson@hanley-wood.com; http://www.hanley-wood.com. Illus., adv. *Indexed:* A&ATA, AIAP, API, GardL, IHTDI, RGPR. *Aud.:* Sa.

This magazine is designed specifically to address restoration and maintenance of homes built before 1939 while targeting a general audience through a very attractive format. It can be very technical but is of general appeal to the layperson, with articles covering preservation, renovation, restoration, and repair techniques; product evaluation; and histories. There are many advertisements of interest to the old-house owner or renovation/restoration do-it-yourselfer. Highlights of *Old House Journal Online* (www.oldhousejournal.com) are full-text articles, a new-products list, the "Restoration Directory," and chat areas.

1294. *Plumbing Engineer.* [ISSN: 0192-1711] 1973. 12x/yr. USD 50. Ed(s): Tom Klemens. T M B Publishing, 1838 Techny Ct, Northbrook, IL 60062. Illus., adv. Circ: 23000 Controlled. Microform: PQC. Reprint: PQC. *Indexed:* EngInd. *Aud.:* Ac, Sa.

A technical journal for engineers, this title deals with all levels of fluid-handling systems. "Nuts and Bolts of Sprinkler Installations" is a good example. New materials and products are highlighted along with discussions of engineering solutions. Professional organizations are also featured regularly. The associated web site also features a "Manufacturer, Distributor and Product Directory."

1295. ***Professional Builder.*** Former titles (until 1993): *Professional Builder and Remodeler;* (until 1990): *Professional Builder;* (until 1985): *Professional Builder and Apartment Business;* (until 1972): *Professional Builder;* (until 1967): *Practical Builder.* [ISSN: 1072-0561] 1936. m. USD 109.90 domestic; USD 179.90 Canada; USD 164.90 Mexico. Ed(s): Heather McCune. Reed Business Information, 2000 Clearwater Dr, Oak Brook, IL 60523; http://www.reedbusiness.com. Illus., adv. Circ: 127260. Microform: CIS. Online: EBSCO Publishing; Florida Center for Library Automation; Gale Group; Northern Light Technology, Inc.; OCLC Online Computer Library Center, Inc.; ProQuest Information & Learning; H.W. Wilson. *Indexed:* ABIn, BPI, C&ISA, EnvAb. *Aud.:* Sa.

Builders of single-family houses and small multifamily units will find this attractive magazine to be of interest. Departments cover economics, real estate trends, and political news; industry news; new products; and architectural plans. Current design concepts and products are highlighted. This is a colorful magazine full of design ideas, and homeowners, prospective homeowners, and remodelers will be interested or entertained. The *Professional Builder* web site (http://www.housingzone.com/pb/) provides full-text articles, real estate news, product links, and house plans.

1296. ***Qualified Remodeler.*** Incorporates (1985-1991): *Kitchen and Bath Concepts.* [ISSN: 0098-9207] 1975. a. Ed(s): Roger Stanley. Cygnus Business Media, Inc., 1233 Janeville Ave, Fort Atkinson, WI 53538-0803; paul.bowers@cygnuspub.com. Illus., adv. Circ: 83510 Paid and controlled. *Aud.:* Sa.

Don't be misled by the general term "remodeler." This magazine is not for those looking for remodeling ideas, it is designed for the professional builder who specializes in remodeling work. Articles often focus on business, with additional material on design principles for interior and exterior remodeling projects. The layperson may, however, benefit from product information and some construction tips. The *Qualified Remodeler* web site (http://www.qualifiedremodeler.com) provides full-text articles and product information.

1297. ***Remodeling.*** Formerly: *Remodeling World;* Incorporates (1948-1987): *Remodeling Contractor (Washington);* Which was formerly (until 1983): *Home Improvement Contractor;* (until 1976): *Home Improvements;* (until 1969): *Building Specialties and Home Improvements.* [ISSN: 0885-8039] 1985. m. USD 24.95 domestic; USD 39.95 Canada; USD 192 elsewhere. Ed(s): Paul Deffenbaugh, Christine Fishburn. Hanley-Wood, Llc., One Thomas Circle, N W, Ste 600, Washington, DC 20005-5701; tjackson@hanley-wood.com; http://www.hanley-wood.com. Illus., adv. Circ: 80000 Controlled. Microform: PQC. Online: Florida Center for Library Automation; Gale Group. Reprint: PQC. *Aud.:* Sa.

This colorful magazine is designed for the residential remodeling market. Articles focus on design, management and marketing techniques, and construction tips. Homeowners and remodelers will find the design concepts and product information to be of great usefulness. *Remodeling Online* includes sections devoted to business, design/architecture, product information, and how-to tips. Full-text articles are also included.

Taunton's Fine Homebuilding. See Architecture section.

1298. ***Welding Journal.*** [ISSN: 0043-2296] 1922. m. 0 membership. Ed(s): Jeff Weber. American Welding Society, 550 N W LeJeune Rd, Miami, FL 33126; info@awsparc.amweld.org; http://www.amweld.org/wj/wj.htm. Illus., adv. Circ: 40000. Microform: PMC; PQC. Online: OCLC Online Computer Library Center, Inc.; H.W. Wilson. *Indexed:* AS&TI, ApMecR, C&ISA, ChemAb, EngInd, ErgAb, ExcerpMed, IAA, SCI, SSCI. *Aud.:* Sa.

This is an official publication of the American Welding Society. It focuses on equipment, processes, techniques, quality control, and industry news. The web site includes full-text articles from the latest issue, news, a buyers' guide, links, classifieds, and an article index covering 1922 to the present.

■ BUSINESS

General/Computers and Systems/Ethics/International/Small Business/State and Regional/Trade and Industry

See also Accounting and Taxation; Advertising and Public Relations; Economics; Finance; Management, Administration, and Personnel; Office Management; and Real Estate sections.

Brian DeHart, Reference/Instruction Librarian, DePaul University Libraries, 1 E. Jackson Blvd., Chicago, IL 60604; bdehart@depaul.edu with Holly Stec Dankert, Reference/Instruction Librarian, DePaul University Libraries

Introduction

Magazines monitor trends and innovations that businesses—both big and small—cannot afford to ignore. The titles included in this section provide timely news and insight impacting not just corporations and industries, but also individuals, organizations, and governments. The information and analysis they provide are invaluable to institutional as well as personal investors. For their part, scholarly journals report best practices, research findings, and theories that advance the understanding of how business dynamics interact with each other and the world at large.

Publishers nowadays frequently offer additional web-based content, such as exclusive features, access to archives, buyers' guides, and industry statistics, that complements their print products. Online versions of magazines rarely function as replacements for their print counterparts because they usually lack charts, graphs, advertisements, and a full complement of article sidebars and news items. Furthermore, such web sites can require users to register or pay additional subscription fees in order to gain full access.

The global economic slowdown has taken its toll on business press publishers. Several titles launched during the 1990s that sought to cover the networked global economy have ceased publication. Many venerable trade titles included here in the past have also folded operations or merged with competitors—casualties of a jittery worldwide economy.

Basic Periodicals

GENERAL. Ga: *Barron's, Business 2.0, Business Week, The Economist, eWEEK, Fast Company, Forbes, Fortune, IndustryWeek, Survey of Current Business, Wall Street Journal.* Ac: *Business History Review, Business Horizons, Harvard Business Review, Journal of Business, The Journal of Business Research, Journal of Education for Business, Journal of Retailing.*

COMPUTERS AND SYSTEMS. Ga: *CIO.* Ac: *Industrial Engineer, International Journal of Forecasting, International Journal of Production Research, Operational Research Society. Journal.*

ETHICS. Ac: *Business and Society Review, Journal of Business Ethics.*

INTERNATIONAL. Ga: *The Economist, Export America, Financial Times, Journal of Commerce.* Ac: *Journal of International Business Studies, Journal of World Business.*

SMALL BUSINESS. Ga: *Franchising World, Entrepreneur, Inc.* Ac: *Entrepreneurship: Theory and Practice, The Journal of Business Venturing, Journal of Small Business Management, Success.*

STATE AND REGIONAL. Will vary.

TRADE AND INDUSTRY. Will vary.

Basic Abstracts and Indexes

ABI/Inform, Business ASAP, Business Source, Business and Industry, Wilson Business Abstracts.

General

1299. *Across the Board: reporting to management on business affairs.* Formerly (until 1976): *Conference Board Record;* Supersedes: *Conference Board Business-Management Record.* [ISSN: 0147-1554] 1939. 6x/yr. Members, USD 39; Non-members, USD 59. Ed(s): A J Vogl. Conference Board, Inc., 845 Third Ave, New York, NY 10022; atb@conference-board.com; http://www.conference-board.org. Illus., index, adv. Circ: 35000. Vol. ends: Dec. Online: EBSCO Publishing; Northern Light Technology, Inc.; OCLC Online Computer Library Center, Inc.; ProQuest Information & Learning; H.W. Wilson. *Indexed:* ABIn, ABS&EES, ATI, AgeL, BAS, BLI, BPI, FutSurv, PAIS, SSCI. *Bk. rev.:* 1-2, 1,500 words. *Aud.:* Ga, Ac.

The Conference Board's stated goals are to help "executives build strong professional relationships, expand their business knowledge, and find solutions to a wide range of business problems." Whereas the primary audience is intended to be senior executives of the Fortune 500, this publication also appeals to a general audience because of its wide range of topics and interviews. Articles are written in an irreverent and accessible style. Selected features and departments from current and previous issues are available full-text through www.conference-board.com.

1300. *American Business Review.* [ISSN: 0743-2348] 1983. s-a. USD 14. Ed(s): Thomas Katsaros. University of New Haven, School of Business, 300 Orange Ave, West Haven, CT 06516. Illus. Refereed. Vol. ends: No. 2. *Indexed:* ABIn. *Aud.:* Ga,Ac.

This journal covers a wide array of topics intended to stimulate the exchange of ideas. Each issue includes approximately a dozen articles five to ten pages in length. Although written mainly for business and economic scholars, the variety and quality of articles would be of interest to a general readership as well.

1301. *Barron's: the Dow Jones business and financial weekly.* Former titles (until vol.74, no.13, 1994): *Barron's National Business and Financial Weekly;* (until 1942): *Barron's.* [ISSN: 1077-8039] 1921. w. USD 145; USD 3.50 newsstand/cover per issue. Ed(s): Finn Edwin. Dow Jones & Co., Inc., 200 Liberty St, New York, NY 10281; http://www.barrons.com. Illus., adv. Circ: 310000 Paid. Vol. ends: Dec. Microform: BHP; PQC; NRP. Online: bigchalk; Dow Jones Interactive; Factiva; Gale Group; ProQuest Information & Learning. Reprint: PQC. *Indexed:* ABIn, ATI, BPI, BRI, CBRI, EnvAb, LRI, MagInd, NewsAb. *Bk. rev.:* Various number and length. *Aud.:* Ga, Ac, Sa.

Published each Monday, this newspaper-format publication provides general business information that serves the needs of investors. Stories about current business, economic, and political trends are accompanied by reports on companies and people in the news. Financial and economic statistics for commodities, all major stock exchanges, and money markets make up the bulk of the paper. This is a core business and investment title for public and academic libraries.

1302. *Business 2.0.* Formed by the merger of (2000-2001): *eCompany Now;* (1995-2001): *Business 2.0 (Brisbane);* Which was formerly (until 1998): *The Net - Your Cyberspace Companion.* [ISSN: 1538-1730] 2001. m. USD 19.99 domestic; CND 32.50 Canada; USD 59 elsewhere. Ed(s): James Aley, Ned Desmond. Time Inc., Fortune Group, 1 California St., San Francisco, CA 94111; http://www.business2.com. Illus., adv. Sample. Circ: 550000. Vol. ends: Dec. Online: EBSCO Publishing. *Indexed:* CompLI. *Aud.:* Ga.

Strives to discover and report on innovative business practices and the people behind them in an ever changing marketplace driven by the Internet and other technologies. Editorial control changed in the summer of 2001 when AOL Time Warner purchased this title and merged it with their own publication of a similar scope, *eCompany Now.* More inclusion by major indexes would improve visibility; there is, however, ready access to a complete web-based archive at www.business2.com.

Business 2.0 Online. See General Editorial-Internet section.

1303. *Business Communication Quarterly.* Former titles (until 1994): *Association for Business Communication. Bulletin;* (until 1985): *A B C A Bulletin (American Business Communication Association); A B W A Bulletin (American Business Writing Association).* [ISSN: 1080-5699] 1935. q. USD 160 (Members, USD 65). Ed(s): Deborah C Andrews. Association for Business Communication, c/o Dr Robert J Myers, Dept of Speech Communication, Baruch College, 17 Lexington Ave, New York, NY 10010; http://www.theabc.org. Illus., index, adv. Sample. Refereed. Circ: 2475. Microform: PQC. Online: EBSCO Publishing; Florida Center for Library Automation; Gale Group; Northern Light Technology, Inc.; OCLC Online Computer Library Center, Inc.; ProQuest Information & Learning. Reprint: PQC. *Indexed:* ABIn, BPI, BusEdI, CIJE, PAIS. *Bk. rev.:* 2-3, 750-1000 words. *Aud.:* Ac, Sa.

This interdisciplinary journal is aimed primarily at an international readership directly involved in the teaching of business communication. Like its sister publication, *Journal of Business Communication*, submissions are invited from educators in a wide variety of fields including management, rhetoric, organizational behavior, composition, speech, mass communication, pyschology, linguistics, advertising, sociology, information technology, education, and history. Topics cover teaching methods in a variety of settings: two?year college, technical institute, four-year college, university, corporate or agency training program, and the like; case studies of specific classroom techniques; reports on strategies for program development; research on classroom teaching or assessment; summary reviews of literature on teaching business communication; and book reviews of both textbooks and other items of interest to faculty.

Business Economics. See Economics section.

1304. *Business Education Forum.* [ISSN: 0007-6678] 1947. 4x/yr. USD 70. National Business Education Association, 1914 Association Dr, Reston, VA 20191-1596; http://www.nbea.org. Illus., index, adv. Circ: 15000. Vol. ends: Apr. Microform: PQC. Reprint: PQC. *Indexed:* BusEdI, CIJE, EduInd. *Aud.:* Ac.

Articles range from 1,500 to 2,500 words and cover business education issues in high schools, technical schools, colleges, and universities. The Curriculum Forum section includes articles on accounting, basic business, communication, international business, marketing, methods, and technology. Special sections appear quarterly: research (October), student organizations (December), entrepreneurship (February), and administration and supervision (April). Association news, a professional leadership directory, and award announcements are also included.

1305. *Business Facilities: the location advisor.* Formerly: *A I P R (American Industrial Properties Report).* [ISSN: 0746-0023] 1968. m. USD 30. Ed(s): Donna Clapp. Group C Communications, 121 Monmouth St, Box 2060, Red Bank, NJ 07701; jcarzon@group.com. Illus., adv. Circ: 43500 Controlled and free. *Aud.:* Ga, Ac, Sa.

Written in practical language, short features analyze local, state, and regional communities in areas of real estate; utilities, infrastructure, and workforce issues; economic development at both national and international levels; and facility design, construction, and management topics. The journal's companion web site, www.FacilityCity.com, offers online access to selected articles from the current issue along with exclusive news and special reports. Follow links to the sister publication *Today's Facility Manager* and the *TFM Show* (formerly *Facility Forum*), the premier conference event for this industry. An important magazine for the corporate expansion field, this is a bargain for all public, academic, and corporate libraries.

1306. *Business Forum (Los Angeles).* Formerly (until 1982): *Los Angeles Business and Economics.* [ISSN: 0733-2408] 1975. q. USD 35 domestic; USD 45 foreign. Ed(s): Tom H Woods. California State University, Los Angeles, School of Business & Economics, 5151 State University Dr, Los Angeles, CA 90032-8120; http://cbe.calstatela.edu/publication/index.htm. Illus., index, adv. Refereed. Circ: 3000 Paid. Microform: PQC. Online: EBSCO Publishing; Florida Center for Library Automation; Gale Group; OCLC Online Computer Library Center, Inc.; ProQuest Information & Learning. Reprint: PQC. *Indexed:* ABIn, PAIS. *Bk. rev.:* irregular. *Aud.:* Ga, Ac.

Typical readers are business people, academic faculty, and students. Articles are intended to add to their awareness of developments in specific fields of business without being overly technical. The editorial review board and advisors include faculty, corporate executives, and military leaders. Each issue contains five to seven short articles written at a general level. Some issues are thematic.

1307. *Business History.* [ISSN: 0007-6791] 1959. q. GBP 246 print & online eds. Ed(s): Charles Harvey, Geoffrey Jones. Frank Cass Publishers, Crown House, 47 Chase Side, Southgate, London, N14 5BP, United Kingdom; jnlsubs@frankcass.com; http://www.frankcass.com/jnls/. Illus., index, adv. Refereed. Microform: PQC. Online: EBSCO Publishing; Florida Center for Library Automation; Gale Group; Ingenta Select; Northern Light Technology, Inc. Reprint: PSC. *Indexed:* AmH&L, ArtHuCI, BAS, BPI, BrHumI, IBSS, IBZ, JEL, PAIS, SSCI, SociolAb. *Bk. rev.:* approx. 40 per issue, each one page long. *Aud.:* Ac.

Each issue contains five feature articles 20–40 pages in length, with an emphasis on U.K. and European history. Subject coverage includes profiles of global enterprises, analysis of specific industries, and the evolution of economic integration. Because of the pervasive nature of business in society, this title is of potential interest to all social scientists and historians.

1308. *Business History Review.* Formerly: *Business Historical Society. Bulletin.* [ISSN: 0007-6805] 1926. q. USD 75 (Individuals, USD 35; Students, USD 20). Ed(s): Thomas K McCraw. Harvard Business School Publishing, 60 Harvard Way, Boston, MA 02163; kdonahue@hbsp.harvard.edu. Illus., index, adv. Refereed. Circ: 2000. Vol. ends: No. 4. Microform: PQC. Online: Chadwyck-Healey Incorporated; The Dialog Corporation; Florida Center for Library Automation; Gale Group; Northern Light Technology, Inc.; OCLC Online Computer Library Center, Inc.; ProQuest Information & Learning; H.W. Wilson. Reprint: PSC. *Indexed:* ABIn, ABS&EES, ATI, AmH&L, ArtHuCI, BAS, BPI, BRD, BRI, CBRI, IBSS, JEL, LRI, PAIS, SSCI, SSI. *Bk. rev.:* 25-30, 750-1,000 words. *Aud.:* Ga, Ac.

Each issue is comprised of three feature articles 40–50 pages in length along with numerous book reviews. Subjects cover biographical profiles, corporate culture, and studies of specific industries with emphasis on North American history. Photographs and illustrations appear on the cover and accompany articles. Of interest to all social scientists, historians, and fans of Americana.

1309. *Business Horizons.* [ISSN: 0007-6813] 1957. bi-m. EUR 275 (Individuals, EUR 93). Ed(s): Dennis Organ. Elsevier Ltd., The Boulevard, Langford Ln, Oxford, OX5 1GB, United Kingdom. Illus., index, adv. Circ: 3000. Vol. ends: No. 6. Microform: PQC. Online: EBSCO Publishing; Florida Center for Library Automation; Gale Group; ingenta.com; Northern Light Technology, Inc.; OCLC Online Computer Library Center, Inc.; ScienceDirect; Swets Blackwell; H.W. Wilson. Reprint: PQC. *Indexed:* ABIn, ABS&EES, ATI, AgeL, BAS, BLI, BPI, BRD, BRI, CBRI, CompLI, ExcerpMed, FutSurv, LRI, LogistBibl, MagInd, PAIS, PMA, RI-1, SSCI. *Bk. rev.:* 0-3, 1,500 words. *Aud.:* Ga, Ac.

Now published by Elsevier, this publication remains edited by the Indiana University Kelley School of Business. Each issue contains ten scholarly articles of seven to ten pages in length. Subject matter is wide ranging and covers all business disciplines, ethics, and the impact of business on society. Contributors are encouraged to avoid nontechnical language. Each issue contains a cumulative index for the current volume year. Of interest to all libraries.

1310. *Business Today (Princeton).* [ISSN: 0007-7100] 1968. q. Ed(s): John Taylor. Foundation for Student Communication, Inc., 305 Aaron Burr Hall, Princeton University, Princeton, NJ 08540; FSCINT@phoenix.princeton.edu. Illus., adv. Circ: 200000. Microform: MIM; PQC. Reprint: PQC. *Bk. rev.:* Various number and length. *Aud.:* Ac.

This student-run magazine serves as a forum for diverse topics and is designed to give students a broader understanding of business leadership, industry innovation, government policies, international perspectives, and career track advice. The content will appeal to the undergraduate population at large, not just business majors; ideal for browsing collections in academic libraries.

1311. *Business Week.* [ISSN: 0007-7135] 1929. w. last of volume is a double issue. USD 45.97 domestic; CND 69 Canada; USD 90 in Asia. Ed(s): Stephen B Shepard. McGraw-Hill Companies, Inc., 1221 Ave of the Americas, New York, NY 10020; http://www.mcgraw-hill.com/. Illus., index, adv. Circ: 923786 Paid. Microform: PQC. Online: bigchalk; Dow Jones Interactive; EBSCO Publishing; Factiva; Florida Center for Library Automation; Gale Group; LexisNexis; NewsNet; Northern Light Technology, Inc. Reprint: PQC. *Indexed:* ABIn, ATI, AgeL, B&I, BLI, BPI, BRI, BrTechI, CBRI, CPerI, ChemAb, CompLI, EnvAb, FutSurv, GeoRef, InfoSAb, LRI, MagInd, MicrocompInd, PAIS, RGPR, RI-1. *Bk. rev.:* Various number and length. *Aud.:* Ga.

This title profiles industries, companies, and individuals, tracks political and legal issues, analyzes the impact of information technology, and reports on major developments in international business. Other sections cover commentary on social issues and lifestyle topics such as travel and consumer product reviews. Editorials generally take a moderate position. The table of contents also highlights offerings available at www.businessweek.com. It is written at a level appreciated by a general readership. If a library could purchase only one business magazine, this would be it.

The Economist. See Economics section.

1312. *eWEEK: the enterprise newsweekly.* Incorporates (1994-2001): *Inter@ctive Week;* Formerly (until 2000): *P C Week.* [ISSN: 1530-6283] 1984. w. Free. Ed(s): Eric Lundquist. Ziff Davis Media Inc., 28 E 28th St, New York, NY 10016-7930; info@ziffdavis.com; http://www.ziffdavis.com. Illus., adv. Circ: 400000 Controlled. Microform: PQC. Online: America Online, Inc.; CompuServe Inc.; EBSCO Publishing; Factiva; Florida Center for Library Automation; Gale Group; ProQuest Information & Learning. *Indexed:* BPI, C&ISA, CompLI, ConsI, InfoSAb, LRI, MagInd, MicrocompInd. *Aud.:* Ga.

Focusing on companies and individuals that provide hardware, software, and application hosting to businesses, this title gives an insider's picture of the twists and turns involved in an online economy. Brief news and analysis articles make up the bulk of the weekly, with management and infrastructure tips, reviews, and opinions rounding out the content. The web site at www.eweek.com offers daily updates, resources in IT services, and a careers center—worth bookmarking even if you do not subscribe. Best for all libraries that wish to have the latest information on the e-business industry.

1313. *Fast Company.* [ISSN: 1085-9241] 1995. m. USD 12 domestic; USD 29 Canada. Ed(s): John Byrne. Fast Company, Inc., 375 Lexington Ave, New York, NY 10017; subscriptions@fastcompany.com. Illus., adv. Circ: 500000. Online: bigchalk; EBSCO Publishing; Factiva; Florida Center for Library Automation; Gale Group; LexisNexis; OCLC Online Computer Library Center, Inc.; ProQuest Information & Learning; H.W. Wilson. *Indexed:* BPI. *Aud.:* Ga.

Chronicles how companies create and compete by showcasing the people who are inventing the future and the companies that are reinventing business. Broad themes include the Internet in business, information technology, marketing, best practices, personal growth and development, teamwork and philanthropy. Full text of the current and back issues is available through the web site. Content unique to its complementary web site is highlighted. This newer title has established itself as a leader in reporting on the digital economy and its impact on companies, employees, and customers.

1314. *Forbes.* [ISSN: 0015-6914] 1917. bi-w. USD 59.95 domestic; CND 89.95 Canada; USD 137.95 elsewhere. Ed(s): William Baldwin. Forbes, Inc., 60 Fifth Ave, New York, NY 10011; http://www.forbes.com/forbes. Illus., index, adv. Circ: 819884. Vol. ends: Dec. Microform: PQC. Online: The Dialog Corporation; Dow Jones Interactive; EBSCO Publishing; Factiva; Florida Center for Library Automation; Gale Group; OCLC Online Computer Library Center, Inc.; ProQuest Information & Learning. *Indexed:* ABIn, ATI, AgeL, B&I, BLI, BPI, ChemAb, CompLI, EnvAb, InfoSAb, LRI, MagInd, MicrocompInd, RGPR, RI-1, SSCI. *Aud.:* Ga, Ac.

The focus of this title is on news and analysis impacting executives, managers, and investors. In addition to the cover story, each issue contains numerous short articles analyzing economic trends and profiling industries, corporations, and key individuals. Recurring sections include Marketing, Entrepreneurs, Technology, Money & Investing, and Health. The table of contents highlights exclusive web content available at www.forbes.com. This is a core title for both public and academic libraries. The subscription is complemented by the occasional supplements *Forbes ASAP*, which covers information technology topics, and *Forbes FYI*, which contains lifestyle features.

1315. *Fortune.* [ISSN: 0015-8259] 1930. bi-w. USD 59.95 domestic; USD 79 Canada; USD 106.60 elsewhere. Time Inc., Business Information Group, 1271 Ave of the Americas, New York, NY 10020; http://www.fortune.com. Illus., index, adv. Circ: 818791 Paid. Vol. ends: Dec. Microform: PQC. Online: bigchalk; EBSCO Publishing; Factiva; Florida Center for Library Automation; Gale Group; LexisNexis; OCLC Online Computer Library Center, Inc.; ProQuest Information & Learning; H.W. Wilson. *Indexed:* ABIn, ABS&EES, AIAP, ATI, AgeL, BPI, BRI, CBRI, CPerI, CompLI, EnvAb, ExcerpMed, GeoRef, InfoSAb, LRI, MagInd, MicrocompInd, PAIS, RGPR, RI-1, SSCI. *Bk. rev.:* Various number and length. *Aud.:* Ga, Ac, Sa.

Less news driven than *Business Week*, this title offers lengthier features analyzing major corporate and industry developments. It tends to cover smaller companies and more industry sectors than *Forbes*. Emphasis is on investing and personal finance. Thus, articles inform the reader about general concepts and issues related to industry and the economy, management, and information technology. Articles are frequently accompanied by explanatory sidebars and related commentary. The April issue containing the *Fortune500* ranking is much anticipated; other thematic rankings appear regularly throughout the year. This is a core title for all business collections.

1316. *Harvard Business Review.* [ISSN: 0017-8012] 1922. m. USD 118 domestic; USD 128 in Canada & Mexico; USD 165 elsewhere. Ed(s): Suzi Wetlawfer. Harvard Business School Publishing, 60 Harvard Way, Boston, MA 02163; hbr_editorial@hbsp.harvard.edu; http://www.hbsp.harvard.edu/groups/hbr/index.html. Illus., index, adv. Refereed. Circ: 245000. Vol. ends: Dec. Microform: PQC. Online: bigchalk; Data-Star; EBSCO Publishing; Florida Center for Library Automation; Gale Group; Human Resources Information Network. Reprint: PSC. *Indexed:* ABIn, ABS&EES, ASIP, ATI, AgeL, BAS, BLI, BPI, BRI, CBRI, CIJE, CommAb, CompLI, CompR, EngInd, EnvAb, ExcerpMed, FutSurv, IBZ, LogistBibl, MagInd, PAIS, PMA, PsycholAb, RGPR, SSCI. *Bk. rev.:* Various number and length. *Aud.:* Ga, Ac.

Each issue contains about a dozen articles ten pages in length along with a short case study. *HBR* provides readers with the current thinking of scholars and industry leaders on the topics of human resources management, manufacturing, strategic planning, globalization of markets, competitiveness, and related general business interests. Articles, although rarely containing footnotes, are highly regarded if not considered scholarly. This is a core business title for academic libraries and larger public libraries.

Inc. See under Small Business, this section.

1317. *Industrial and Corporate Change.* [ISSN: 0960-6491] 1991. bi-m. GBP 280. Ed(s): J. Chytry. Oxford University Press, Great Clarendon St, Oxford, OX2 6DP, United Kingdom; jnl.orders@oup.co.uk; http://www3.oup.co.uk/jnls. Illus., index, adv. Refereed. Circ: 950. Online: EBSCO Publishing; HighWire Press; ingenta.com; OCLC Online Computer Library Center, Inc.; RoweCom Information Quest; Swets Blackwell. Reprint: PSC. *Indexed:* BPI, HRA, IBSS, JEL. *Bk. rev.:* Various number and length. *Aud.:* Ac, Sa.

The scope of this interdisciplinary journal draws on sociology, political science, social psychology, and organizational and economic theories. Aimed at industrial historians, the eight to ten lengthy articles (25–40 pages) focus on the history and evolution of technologies and industries; the nature of competition and relationships between individual firms and the environment, organizations, and markets; and the performance of industries over time. Recommended for academic libraries offering advanced degrees in the social sciences.

1318. *IndustryWeek: the management resource.* Incorporates (1985-1995): *Electronics;* Which was formerly (1984-1985): *Electronics Week;* (1930-1984): *Electronics.* [ISSN: 0039-0895] 1882. 22x/yr. USD 65 domestic (Free to qualified personnel). Ed(s): John R Russell. Penton Media, Inc., 1300 E 9th St, Cleveland, OH 44114-1503; information@penton.com; http://www.penton.com. Illus., index, adv. Circ: 233000 Controlled. Vol. ends: Dec. Microform: PQC. Online: bigchalk; The Dialog Corporation; EBSCO Publishing; Factiva; Florida Center for Library Automation; Gale Group; LexisNexis; Northern Light Technology, Inc.; OCLC Online Computer Library Center, Inc.; ProQuest Information & Learning; H.W. Wilson. Reprint: PQC. *Indexed:* ABIn, AS&TI, AgeL, B&I, BPI, CompLI, EngInd, EnvAb, LRI, MagInd. *Aud.:* Ga, Ac, Sa.

This trade magazine profiles individuals and companies active in manufacturing industries. Widely read among executives and managers, it reports on emerging technologies, e-business, globalization, best practices in management and marketing, and regulatory pressures. Back pages are devoted to financial and economic trends. The table of contents highlights the web site's complementary offerings. Most content from the current issue and a selective archive are available online. Of interest to all business collections.

1319. *Journal of Applied Business Research.* [ISSN: 0892-7626] 1985. q. USD 300. Ed(s): Ronald C Clute. Western Academic Press, PO Box 620760, Littleton, CO 80162; cluter@wapress.com; http://www.wapress.com. Adv. Sample. Refereed. Circ: 600. *Indexed:* ABIn, ATI, AgeL, BAS, BPI, JEL. *Aud.:* Ac.

Each issue of this refereed journal contains approximately ten articles, 10–15 pages in length. Both theoretical and applied research manuscripts are considered for publication. Topics cover all areas of business and economics and can include ethical, pedagogical, and technological analysis. Recommended for all academic business collections.

1320. *Journal of Business and Economic Statistics.* [ISSN: 0735-0015] 1983. q. USD 90. American Statistical Association, 1429 Duke St, Alexandria, VA 22314-3415; asainfo@amstat.org; http://www.amstat.org/publications/index.html. Illus. Refereed. Vol. ends: Oct. *Indexed:* ABIn, BPI, CCMJ, IBSS, JEL, MathSciNet, SSCI, ST&MA, WAE&RSA. *Aud.:* Ac.

The professional journal of the American Statistical Association, this scholarly title focuses on a broad range of topics in applied economic and business statistical problems. Using empirical methods, these highly technical articles presume knowledge of mathematical theory. Topics include demand and cost analysis, forecasting, economic modeling, stochastic theory control, and impact of societal issues on wages and productivity. Recommended for academic libraries.

1321. *The Journal of Business (Chicago).* Former titles (until 1954): *University of Chicago. Journal of Business;* (until 1927): *The University Journal of Business.* [ISSN: 0021-9398] 1922. q. USD 125 (Individuals, USD 31; Students, USD 25). Ed(s): Albert Madansky. University of Chicago Press, Journals Division, PO Box 37005, Chicago, IL 60637; subscriptions@press.uchicago.edu; http://www.press.uchicago.edu/. Illus., index, adv. Refereed. Circ: 3100 Paid. Vol. ends: Oct. Microform: MIM; PMC; PQC. Reprint: ISI; PQC; PSC; SCH. *Indexed:* ABIn, ATI, AgeL, BAS, BLI, BPI, CommAb, CompLI, IBSS, IBZ, JEL, MCR, PAIS, SSCI, WAE&RSA. *Aud.:* Ac.

There are approximately six research articles per issue. Subject coverage is comprehensive: money and banking, marketing, security markets, business economics, accounting practices, social issues and public policy, management organization, statistics and econometrics, administration and management, international trade and finance, and personnel, industrial relations, and labor. Some mathematical or statistical background is required to fully appreciate the use of equations and models.

Journal of Business Communication. See Communication section.

1322. *Journal of Business Research.* Formerly (until 1978): *Southern Journal of Business.* [ISSN: 0148-2963] 1973. m. EUR 1315 (Qualified personnel, EUR 162). Ed(s): Arch G Woodside, M Laroche. Elsevier Inc., 360 Park Ave. S, New York, NY 10010-1710; usinfo-f@elsevier.com; http://www.elsevier.com. Illus., index, adv. Refereed. Vol. ends: Nov. Microform: PQC. Online: ingenta.com; LexisNexis; ScienceDirect; Swets Blackwell. Reprint: PQC; SWZ. *Indexed:* ABIn, AgeL, BPI, CommAb, PAIS, PMA, PsycholAb, SSCI. *Aud.:* Ac, Sa.

The editorial review board of this pricey journal includes scholars in many disciplines related to economics, organizational theory, and buyer behavior. Each issue presents a dozen articles 8–20 pages in length that apply theory to actual business situations. Occasionally, issues are devoted to a theme, e.g., doing business in China or case studies in Latin American business. Intended for executives, researchers, and scholars alike.

Journal of Business Strategy. See Management, Administration, and Human Resources/Strategic Analysis section.

Journal of Commerce. See under International, this section.

Journal of Consumer Research. See Advertising, Marketing, and Public Relations section.

1323. *Journal of Education for Business.* Formerly: *Journal of Business Education.* [ISSN: 0883-2323] 1924. bi-m. USD 87 (Individuals, USD 51; USD 14.50 per issue). Ed(s): Isabella Owen. Heldref Publications, 1319 18th St, NW, Washington, DC 20036-1802; subscribe@heldref.org; http://www.heldref.org. Illus., adv. Refereed. Circ: 1200. CD-ROM: ProQuest Information & Learning. Online: bigchalk; EBSCO Publishing; Florida Center for Library Automation; Gale Group; LexisNexis; Northern Light Technology, Inc.; OCLC Online Computer Library Center, Inc.; ProQuest Information & Learning; H.W. Wilson. Reprint: PSC. *Indexed:* BPI, BRI, BusEdI, CBRI, CIJE, EduInd, IBZ, MRD, PAIS, SWA. *Bk. rev.:* irregular; 500-750 words. *Aud.:* Ac.

Each issue contains approximately eight articles that address trends and issues surrounding curriculum development and evaluation. Because the process of instruction—particularly successful innovations and best practices—in the various business disciplines is emphasized, this publication is of most interest to business faculty and higher education administrators.

1324. *Journal of Retailing.* [ISSN: 0022-4359] 1925. q. EUR 313 (Individuals, EUR 118). Ed(s): Michael Levy, Dhruv Grewal. Pergamon, The Boulevard, Langford Ln, East Park, Kidlington, OX5 1GB, United Kingdom. Illus., index, adv. Refereed. Circ: 3200. Vol. ends: Winter. Microform: PQC. Online: The Dialog Corporation; EBSCO Publishing; Florida Center for Library Automation; Gale Group; ingenta.com; Northern Light Technology, Inc.; OCLC Online Computer Library Center, Inc.; ScienceDirect; Swets Blackwell; H.W. Wilson. Reprint: ISI; PQC; PSC. *Indexed:* ABIn, ATI, AgeL, BPI, CompLI, IBZ, PAIS, PsycholAb, SSCI, WAE&RSA. *Aud.:* Ac, Sa.

Each issue offers five or six articles 20–25 pages in length. Topics examined include all activities supporting the sale of services and products, consumer behavior and satisfaction, and the supply chains and distribution channels that serve retailers. There is liberal use of mathematical models for the benefit of other academicians; a general readership will appreciate the nontechnical executive summaries.

Long Range Planning. See Management, Administration, and Human Resources/Strategic Analysis section.

1325. *Mid-American Journal of Business.* Formed by the merger of (1971-1985): *Ball State Business Review;* (1929-1982): *Ball State Journal for Business Educators;* Which was formerly (until 1965): *Ball State Commerce Journal.* [ISSN: 0895-1772] 1985. s-a. USD 12 domestic; USD 17 foreign. Ed(s): Ashok Gupta, Judy Lane. Ball State University, Bureau of Business Research, Muncie, IN 47306. Illus., index, adv. Refereed. Circ: 2000 Paid and controlled. Microform: PQC. Online: Gale Group; OCLC Online Computer Library Center, Inc.; ProQuest Information & Learning; H.W. Wilson. *Indexed:* ABIn, BusEdI, PAIS. *Bk. rev.:* 1, length varies. *Aud.:* Ac.

Aimed at researchers, practicing managers, and teachers, this journal gets its title from the Midwestern affiliations of its editorial board and not its content, which is general business administration practices and education in the United States. Shorter papers 8–10 pages in length are the norm, along with editorials, "Dean's Forum," "Executive Viewpoint," and one book review rounding out each issue. Occasional special issues present specific management themes, and many articles focus on teaching business administration in higher education. Academic libraries and faculty will benefit most from this title.

1326. *The Service Industries Journal.* [ISSN: 0264-2069] 1981. bi-m. GBP 348 print & online eds. Ed(s): Gary Akehurst, Ronald Goldsmith. Frank Cass Publishers, Crown House, 47 Chase Side, Southgate, London, N14 5BP, United Kingdom; jnlsubs@frankcass.com; http://www.frankcass.com/jnls/. Adv. Sample. Refereed. Microform: PQC. Online: EBSCO Publishing; Gale Group; Ingenta Select; Northern Light Technology, Inc.; OCLC Online Computer Library Center, Inc.; ProQuest Information & Learning. *Indexed:* ABIn, BrHumI, CommAb, FS&TA, GeogAbPG, HRA, IBZ, PRA, RRTA, SSCI, SWA, WAE&RSA. *Bk. rev.:* 5-6, 750-1000 words. *Aud.:* Ac.

The publisher's web site claims that "service industries generate over two-thirds of GNP and employment in developed countries, and their importance is growing in developing countries. Service industries include retailing and distribution; financial services, including banking and insurance; hotels and tourism; leisure, recreation, and entertainment; professional and business services, including accountancy, marketing, and law." Each issue contains 10 to 12 articles 20–30 pages in length. Geographic emphasis seems split between Europe and the United States. Of interest primarily to academic collections supporting business programs.

1327. *Site Selection.* Former titles (until 1994): *Site Selection and Industrial Development;* (until 1984): *Site Selection Handbook;* (until 1977): *Industrial Development's Site Selection Handbook;* (until 1976): *Site Selection Handbook;* (until 1970): *Industrial Development's Site Selection Handbook;* Incorporated (in 1984): *Industrial Development;* Which was formerly (until 1967): *Industrial Development and Manufacturers Record;* Which was formed by the 1958 merger of: *Manufacturers Record;* (1954-1958): *Industrial Development.* [ISSN: 1080-7799] 1956. bi-m. USD 85 per issue domestic; USD 125 per issue foreign; USD 22 per vol. Ed(s): Ron Starner. Conway Data, Inc., 35 Technology Pkwy, Ste 150, Norcross, GA 30092; http://www.sitenet.com. Illus., adv. Circ: 45000. Microform: PQC. Online: Gale Group; OCLC Online Computer Library Center, Inc.; H.W. Wilson. Reprint: ISI; PQC. *Indexed:* ABIn, BPI, GeoRef, LRI, PAIS. *Aud.:* Ac, Sa.

This offical publication of the International Development Research Council Foundation offers original research and analysis, interviews, and case studies for those involved in commercial real estate. Industry reviews provide forecasting and address key topics such as new plant construction, utilities and other infrastructure concerns, political and business climates, and labor demographics. Detailed economic development reports on specific cities, states, regions, and foreign countries fill out each issue.

1328. *Survey of Current Business.* [ISSN: 0039-6222] 1921. m. USD 49. U.S. Department of Commerce, Bureau of Economic Analysis, 1441 L St NW, Washington, DC 20230; http://www.bea.doc.gov/bea/. Illus., index. Circ: 7600 Paid. Vol. ends: Dec. Microform: CIS. Online: bigchalk; The Dialog Corporation; EBSCO Publishing; Florida Center for Library Automation; Gale Group; Northern Light Technology, Inc.; OCLC Online Computer Library Center, Inc.; ProQuest Information & Learning; H.W. Wilson. Reprint: CIS. *Indexed:* ABIn, AmStI, BPI, IUSGP, JEL, PAIS. *Aud.:* Ga, Ac.

Each month's issue provides trends in industry, business, and the general economy. It is primarily comprised of charts and tables displaying National Income and Product Accounts (NIPA) data. These statistics include current and historical figures on U.S. international trade in goods and services, gross domestic product, personal income and outlays, foreign direct investment, and similar statistics. Two or three feature articles analyze specific industries or sectors. Available in print through the Federal Depository Libraries program. Most patrons will find the online version more timely and appreciate the ability to download tables as spreadsheets.

Wall Street Journal. See Newspapers section.

Computers and Systems

1329. ***Business Communications Review.*** [ISSN: 0162-3885] 1971. m. USD 45 in US & Canada; USD 70 elsewhere. Key3Media Group, Inc., 5700 Wilshire Blvd., Ste 325, Los Angeles, CA 90036; http://www.key3media.com/. Illus., adv. Circ: 14713. Microform: PQC. Online: bigchalk; EBSCO Publishing; Florida Center for Library Automation; Gale Group; Northern Light Technology, Inc.; OCLC Online Computer Library Center, Inc.; ProQuest Information & Learning; H.W. Wilson. Reprint: PQC. *Indexed:* ABIn, BPI, CompLI. *Aud.:* Ac, Sa.

Aimed at professionals working in the enterprise network and telecommunications fields. *BCR* offers analysis of the technologies, trends, management issues, pricing, and regulation that helps managers break down the complex combination of factors for easier decision making. Limited content is available online through the web site at www.bcr.com/bcr.

1330. ***C I O: the magazine for information executives.*** Incorporates (1995-1997): *WebMaster.* [ISSN: 0894-9301] 1987. s-m. 23/yr. USD 150 in US & Canada (Free to qualified personnel). Ed(s): Tom Field, Abbie Lundberg. C X O Media Inc., 492 Old Connecticut Path, Box 9208, Framingham, MA 01701-9208; lundberg@cio.com; http://www.cio.com. Illus., adv. Circ: 125000. Online: Factiva; Gale Group; ProQuest Information & Learning. *Indexed:* ABIn, CompLI, LogistBibl, MicrocompInd. *Aud.:* Ga, Ac, Sa.

This major trade title provides semi-monthly industry updates, news and events, tips, trends, and opinions by and for managing executives in the information technology and computer systems departments of medium to large public and private organizations. Feature articles cover management skills, outsourcing, recruiting and other human resource management topics, emerging technologies, e-commerce, and IT strategies. Offering content from current and past issues plus daily columns, news updates, and a host of career related materials, www.cio.com is a terrific resource for chief information officers. Aimed at working professionals, *CIO* is well suited for public libraries that serve the business community and academic libraries with advanced business degrees.

1331. ***Computers in Industry: a new international journal of experience and practice on computer applications in industrial and technological processes.*** [ISSN: 0166-3615] 1980. 9x/yr. EUR 946 (Qualified personnel, EUR 165). Ed(s): J. C. Wortmann. Elsevier BV, Sara Burgerhartstraat 25, Amsterdam, 1055 KV, Netherlands; nlinfo-f@elsevier.nl; http://www.elsevier.nl. Illus., index, adv. Refereed. Vol. ends: No. 44 - No. 46. Microform: PQC. Online: Gale Group; ingenta.com; ScienceDirect. *Indexed:* ABIn, AS&TI, C&ISA, CEA, CompLI, EngInd, EnvAb, SSCI. *Aud.:* Ac, Sa.

Focusing on information and communication technology (ICT) in industry where there is substantial contribution in architecture, modeling, and technology, this international scholarly journal reports on trends in ICT with an applied scientific focus. Articles are technical and generally require a strong background in information systems and computer science, making this strictly a scholar's journal.

Decision Sciences. See Management, Administration, and Human Resources/Operations Research and Management Science section.

1332. ***Decision Support Systems: an international journal.*** [ISSN: 0167-9236] 1985. 8x/yr. EUR 780. Ed(s): A B Whinston. Elsevier BV, North-Holland, Sara Burgerhartstraat 25, Amsterdam, 1055 KV, Netherlands; nlinfo-f@elsevier.nl; http://www.elsevier.nl. Illus., index, adv. Refereed. Reprint: SWZ. *Indexed:* ABIn, AS&TI, C&ISA, CompLI, ErgAb, PollutAb, SSCI. *Aud.:* Ac.

Highly technical and scholarly journal covering the concept of using computers for supporting the decision process in managerial settings. Articles discuss operations research, management science, cognitive psychology, and organizational behavior. The high cost and theoretical focus make it appropriate for academic libraries offering programs in advanced business administration and information systems.

1333. ***European Journal of Operational Research.*** [ISSN: 0377-2217] 1977. 24x/yr. EUR 4063. Ed(s): R. Slowinski, Canon J. Teghem. Elsevier BV, North-Holland, Sara Burgerhartstraat 25, Amsterdam, 1055 KV, Netherlands; nlinfo-f@elsevier.nl; http://www.elsevier.nl. Illus. Refereed. Microform: PQC. Online: Gale Group; ingenta.com; ScienceDirect; Swets Blackwell. Reprint: SWZ. *Indexed:* ABIn, C&ISA, CJA, EngInd, ExcerpMed, GeoRef, MathSciNet, RiskAb, SSCI, ST&MA. *Bk. rev.:* 6, 100 words. *Aud.:* Ac, Sa.

Case studies and invited papers by the Association of European Operational Research Societies focus on theoretical developments and the role computers play in operations research and the practice of decision making. Theory and methodology papers, society communications, and software and book reviews fill out each issue. Targeted to scientists and researchers at a postgraduate level, this title will find a limited audience due to its high cost. Strictly for large academic institutions.

eWEEK. See Computer Science and Automation/Popular Computer Titles section.

1334. ***Government Technology: solutions for state and local government in the information age.*** [ISSN: 1043-9668] 1987. m. Free to qualified personnel. Ed(s): Dennis McKenna. E. Republic Inc., 100 Blue Ravine Rd, Folsom, CA 95630-4703; donpears@govtech.net; http://www.govtech.net/. Illus., adv. Circ: 72201 Controlled. *Indexed:* CompLI. *Aud.:* Sa.

Aimed at executives and managers, this magazine offers a network of integrated products and services for technology providers in the government IT sector. Content of both print and web site (www.govtech.net) are free, providing news, case studies, publications, conferences and events, a solution center, and product sources. Features include interviews with key personnel in local and national government departments and agencies who apply technology to improve service to citizens. Areas covered include justice, welfare, transportation, human services, and homeland security. Appropriate for municipal and government libraries or public and academic libraries with a large government administration audience.

1335. ***I N F O R Journal: information systems and operations research/ systemes d'information et recherche operationnelle.*** Formed by the merger of: *Canadian Information Processing Society. Quarterly Bulletin; Canadian Journal of Operational Research and Information Processing.* [ISSN: 0315-5986] 1963. q. CND 80. Ed(s): Michel Gendreau. University of Toronto Press, Journals Department, 5201 Dufferin St, Toronto, ON M3H 5T8, Canada; journals@utpress.utoronto.ca; http://www.utpjournals.com. Illus., index, adv. Sample. Refereed. Circ: 400. Online: EBSCO Publishing; OCLC Online Computer Library Center, Inc.; ProQuest Information & Learning. *Indexed:* ABIn, CBCARef, CompLI, CompR, EngInd. *Aud.:* Ac, Sa.

This purely academic journal is published by the Canadian Operational Research Society, whose aim is to integrate the concepts of both operations research and information systems to allow for communication between both theoreticians and practitioners. Highly technical in nature, each issue includes a few contributed papers by international scholars and five or six invited articles on the practical application of and situations in managerial decision analysis, distributed and cellular systems, and information technology management, among others. The majority of articles are in English, occasionally in French, and abstracts in both English and French. Recommended for academic collections supporting advanced degree programs.

1336. ***Industrial Engineer: engineering & management solutions at work.*** Former titles (until 2002): *I I E Solutions;* (until 1995): *Industrial Engineering;* Which superseded: *Journal of Industrial Engineering.*

[ISSN: 1542-894X] 1969. m. USD 73 domestic; USD 94 foreign; USD 7 newsstand/cover. Ed(s): Jane Gaboury. Institute of Industrial Engineers, 3577 Parkway Ln., Ste. 200, Norcross, GA 30092; cs@iienet.org; http://www.iienet.org. Illus., index, adv. Circ: 17000. Microform: PQC. Online: The Dialog Corporation; Gale Group. Reprint: PQC. *Indexed:* ABIn, AS&TI, ApMecR, BiolAb, CompLI, EngInd, ErgAb, ExcerpMed. *Aud.:* Ac, Sa.

Formerly *IIE Solutions, Industrial Engineer* is the official magazine of the Institute of Industrial Engineers. Designed specifically for managers and engineers in business, industry, and government, this monthly contains practical articles for improving commercial productivity and increasing efficiency. Standard columns include news, trends, profiles, and marketplace; buyers' guides, software reviews, a calendar, association happenings, and job listings lend value to practitioners. Feature articles cover industry topics: quality, production, and inventory control; ergonomics; worker safety; material handling; and management strategies. The web site offers access only to subscribers for the magazine contents; however, useful trade information on careers and other advice is available to all. Suitable for both academic and public libraries.

1337. ***Industrial Relations Journal.*** Incorporates: *European Annual Review.* [ISSN: 0019-8692] 1970. bi-m. GBP 422 print & online eds. Ed(s): Brian Towers. Blackwell Publishing Ltd., 9600 Garsington Rd, PO Box 805, Oxford, OX4 2DQ, United Kingdom; customerservices@oxon.blackwellpublishing.com; http://www.blackwellpublishing.com/. Illus., index, adv. Refereed. Circ: 1100. Vol. ends: Sep. Microform: PQC. Online: EBSCO Publishing; Gale Group; ingenta.com; OCLC Online Computer Library Center, Inc.; RoweCom Information Quest; Swets Blackwell. Reprint: PQC; SWZ. *Indexed:* ABIn, BPI, IBSS, PAIS, PSA, SWA, SociolAb. *Bk. rev.:* 4-8, signed, 1,500 w. *Aud.:* AC.

The aim of this scholarly journal is international coverage of broadly defined research in the manufacturing and service sectors of the economy. Four or five articles are featured, reflecting practical applications and new developments primarily in information, communication, and telecommunication systems and their impact on workers in terms of productivity, management, and quality of work life. Of interest to human resources scholars, consultants, and practitioners, this title is recommended for academic libraries with advanced degrees in management.

1338. ***Information and Management: international journal of information systems applications.*** Incorporates (1981-1985): *Systems, Objectives, Solutions;* Former titles (until 1977): *Management Datamatics;* (until 1975): *Management Informatics; I A G Journal.* [ISSN: 0378-7206] 1968. 8x/yr. EUR 578. Ed(s): E H Sibley. Elsevier BV, North-Holland, Sara Burgerhartstraat 25, Amsterdam, 1055 KV, Netherlands; nlinfo-f@elsevier.nl; http://www.elsevier.nl. Illus., index, adv. Refereed. Circ: 2500. Microform: PQC. Online: Gale Group; ingenta.com; ScienceDirect; Swets Blackwell. Reprint: SWZ. *Indexed:* ABIn, AS&TI, CompLI, EngInd, InfoSAb, SSCI. *Bk. rev.:* Various number and length. *Aud.:* Ac, Sa.

This scholarly journal aimed at managers, database administrators, and senior executives covers a wide range of developments in applied information systems and their use with strategies and policies in business, public administration, and international organizations. Papers focus on trends in methodology and applications of information systems and training and educational materials in administrative data systems. The technical language in the four to six papers presented in each issue makes this title appropriate for researchers and practitioners involved in the management of information systems.

Interfaces. See Management, Administration, and Human Resources/ Operations Research and Management Science section.

1339. ***International Journal of Forecasting.*** [ISSN: 0169-2070] 1985. q. EUR 508. Ed(s): Jan G de Gooijer, Michael Lawrence. Elsevier BV, North-Holland, Sara Burgerhartstraat 25, Amsterdam, 1055 KV, Netherlands. Adv. Refereed. Microform: PQC. Online: EBSCO Publishing; ingenta.com; ScienceDirect; Swets Blackwell. Reprint: SWZ. *Indexed:* ABIn, BAS, FPA, IBSS, JEL, PAIS, PSA, RiskAb, SSCI, ST&MA. *Bk. rev.:* Various number and length. *Aud.:* Ac, Sa.

This official publication of the International Institute of Forecasters is the leading journal of forecasting for all aspects of business. It aims at bridging the gap between theory and practice for those policy and decision makers who utilize forecasting methods. Articles by international scholars are featured each quarter along with notes, book and software reviews, and reviews of current research in forecasting, which also makes this title a better buy for half the cost than the *Journal of Forecasting.* Recommended for academic libraries.

1340. ***International Journal of Operations and Production Management.*** [ISSN: 0144-3577] 1980. m. EUR 10003.91 in Europe; USD 9229 in North America; AUD 10784 in Australasia. Ed(s): Bernard Burns, Dr. Robert Hollier. Emerald, 60-62 Toller Ln, Bradford, BD8 9BY, United Kingdom; info@emeraldinsight.com; http://www.emeraldinsight.com/journals/. Illus., index. Refereed. Online: Pub.; EBSCO Publishing; Florida Center for Library Automation; Gale Group; OCLC Online Computer Library Center, Inc.; ProQuest Information & Learning; RoweCom Information Quest; Swets Blackwell. Reprint: PSC; SWZ. *Indexed:* ABIn, C&ISA, EngInd, ErgAb, SSCI. *Aud.:* Ac, Sa.

Associated with the European Operations Management Association, this scholarly title is aimed at academicians, managers, and consultants. Lengthy articles focus on management versus technical content and blend theory and application in developing and implementing operation systems. Topics include operational strategy, industrial engineering, performance measurement, and computer applications in both service and manufacturing sectors. Prohibitively expensive for most libraries, this title is appropriate for large research institutions.

1341. ***International Journal of Physical Distribution & Logistics Management.*** Former titles (until 1990): *International Journal of Physical Distribution and Materials Management;* (until 1977): *International Journal of Physical Distribution;* Which incorporated (in 1975): *International Journal of Physical Distribution Monograph;* Which was formerly (1970-1974): *P D M. Physical Distribution Monograph.* [ISSN: 0960-0035] 1970. 10x/yr. EUR 12929.29 in Europe; USD 11868 in North America; AUD 14549 in Australasia. Ed(s): James Stock. Emerald, 60-62 Toller Ln, Bradford, BD8 9BY, United Kingdom; info@emeraldinsight.com; http://www.emeraldinsight.com/journals/. Illus., index. Refereed. Online: Pub.; EBSCO Publishing; Florida Center for Library Automation; Gale Group; OCLC Online Computer Library Center, Inc.; ProQuest Information & Learning; RoweCom Information Quest; Swets Blackwell. Reprint: PSC; SWZ. *Indexed:* ABIn, ExcerpMed, LogistBibl, PAIS, SSCI. *Aud.:* Ac, Sa.

This is the self-proclaimed leader in the field of logistics, but the high cost this scholarly journal makes it out of reach of most libraries. Combining the practical and scholarly in the latest developments of distribution and logistics management, *IJPDLM* offers four articles in each issue, which are sometimes thematic, e.g., logistics and supply chain risk and uncertainty. Targeted to both business planners and researchers, it is appropriate for large research institutions only.

1342. ***International Journal of Production Research.*** [ISSN: 0020-7543] 1961. 18x/yr. GBP 2110. Ed(s): J E Middle. Taylor & Francis Ltd, 11 New Fetter Ln, London, EC4P 4EE, United Kingdom; info@tandf.co.uk; http://www.tandf.co.uk/journals. Illus., index, adv. Refereed. Microform: MIM; NRP. Online: EBSCO Publishing; Ingenta Select; OCLC Online Computer Library Center, Inc.; RoweCom Information Quest; Swets Blackwell. Reprint: PSC. *Indexed:* C&ISA, EngInd, ErgAb, PsycholAb, SCI, SSCI. *Aud.:* Ac, Sa.

Associated with a number of trade associations, Institution of Production Engineers (U.K.), Society of Manufacturing Engineers, and the Institute of Industrial Engineers, *IJPR* is one of the top-ranked journals in the field of operations management. Papers each month feature cross-disciplinary problems in manufacturing technology and the design of production systems with an emphasis on empirical and theoretical studies. Aimed at research engineers and industrial practitioners, academic libraries will find this title important to support advanced business administration degree programs.

1343. ***International Journal of Technology Management.*** [ISSN: 0267-5730] 1986. 16x/yr. USD 1200; USD 1550 combined subscription for print & online eds. Ed(s): Dr. M A Dorgham. Inderscience

Enterprises Ltd., IEL Editorial Office, PO Box 735, Olney, MK46 5WB, United Kingdom; editor@inderscience.com; http://www.inderscience.com. Illus., index, adv. Refereed. Circ: 20000. *Indexed:* ABIn, Agr, BPI, BrTechI, C&ISA, EngInd, SSCI. *Bk. rev.:* Various number and length. *Aud.:* Ac, Sa.

Supported in part by UNESCO, this refereed journal disseminates advances in the science and practice of technology management, with the goal of fostering communication between government officials, technology executives, and academic experts worldwide. Each issue contains research reports and case studies on technology transfers, supply chain management, sourcing, R&D systems, and information technology. Geared to academics, researchers, professionals, and policy makers, *IJTM* is best suited to academic libraries with advanced degree programs in the management sciences.

1344. ***Journal of Business Forecasting Methods and Systems.*** [ISSN: 0278-6087] 1981. q. USD 85 domestic; USD 110 foreign. Ed(s): Chaman L Jain. Graceway Publishing Co., PO Box 670159, Flushing, NY 11367-0159; ibf@ibf.org; http://www.ibf.org. Illus., index, adv. Circ: 3500. Vol. ends: No. 4. Microform: PQC. Online: EBSCO Publishing; Gale Group; OCLC Online Computer Library Center, Inc.; ProQuest Information & Learning. *Indexed:* ABIn, ATI, RiskAb. *Bk. rev.:* 1, 750 words. *Aud.:* Ac, Sa.

Managers who must compile data to be used in forecasting business and economic trends, as well as forecasters themselves, are the target market of this highly specialized resource. Clearly written and jargon-free articles provide practical information that help managers with inventory control, supply chain management, production scheduling, budgeting, marketing strategies, and financial planning. Also featured are international and domestic economic outlooks and corporate earnings analysis by industry. Primarily of interest to academic and corporate libraries.

1345. ***Journal of Forecasting.*** [ISSN: 0277-6693] 1981. 8x/yr. USD 1115. John Wiley & Sons Ltd., The Atrium, Southern Gate, Chichester, PO19 8SQ, United Kingdom; customer@wiley.co.uk; http://www.wiley.co.uk. Illus., adv. Refereed. Vol. ends: Nov. Reprint: PQC; PSC; SWZ. *Indexed:* ABIn, EngInd, IBSS, IndVet, PAIS, RiskAb, SSCI, ST&MA, VetBull. *Aud.:* Ac.

Edited by an international board of scholars, this title offers a forum for forecasting practical, methodological, theoretical, and computational methods. As in the many journals dealing with forecasting, this title is concerned with the relationship of decision-making processes to forecasting systems. Feature articles in each issue cover a variety of theoretical and empirical applications in the fields of technology, government, business, and the environment. Presupposes a knowledge of mathematical theory; appropriate for academic and corporate libraries.

1346. ***Journal of Intelligent Information Systems: integrating artificial intelligence and database technologies.*** [ISSN: 0925-9902] 1992. bi-m. USD 667 print or online ed. Ed(s): Larry Kerschberg, Zbigniew Ras. Kluwer Academic Publishers, 101 Philip Dr, Assinippi Park, Norwell, MA 02061. Illus., adv. Refereed. Microform: PQC. Online: EBSCO Publishing; ingenta.com; Kluwer Online; OCLC Online Computer Library Center, Inc.; Ovid Technologies, Inc.; RoweCom Information Quest; Swets Blackwell. Reprint: SWZ. *Indexed:* CompLI, CompR, EngInd, ErgAb, InfoSAb. *Aud.:* Ac, Sa.

Focused on the design, implementation, and applications of intelligent information systems. Articles are related to the following topics: foundations and principles including models; methodologies for analysis and design; data representation; expert systems; logic and databases; storage and retrieval; distributed systems; data mining and knowledge management; user models and visual representation. Strictly a scholar's journal.

Journal of Management Information Systems. See Computer Science and Automation/Computer Science section.

Journal of Operations Management. See Management, Administration, and Human Resources/Operations Research and Management Science section.

1347. ***Journal of Productivity Analysis.*** [ISSN: 0895-562X] 1989. bi-m. USD 563 print or online ed. Ed(s): C A Knox Lovell. Kluwer Academic Publishers, 101 Philip Dr, Assinippi Park, Norwell, MA 02061. Illus., index, adv. Sample. Refereed. Vol. ends: No. 4. Online: EBSCO Publishing; ingenta.com; Kluwer Online; OCLC Online Computer Library Center, Inc.; Ovid Technologies, Inc.; RoweCom Information Quest; Swets Blackwell. Reprint: PQC; SWZ. *Indexed:* JEL, SSCI. *Aud.:* Ac, Sa.

This international title is included in highly specialized operations research indexes. Each issue contains four to six lengthy empirical studies on "theoretical and applied research that addresses issues involved with the management, explanation and improvement of productivity" in industry and public administration. Titles frequently tout the use of decision-making models and data envelopment analysis (DEA). Appropriate for scholars and practitioners in the fields of productivity and quality management.

1348. ***M S I.*** Former titles (until 2001): *Manufacturing Systems;* (until 198?): *Manufacturing Operations.* [ISSN: 1533-7758] 1983. m. USD 84.99 domestic (Free to qualified personnel). Ed(s): Roberto Michel. Reed Business Information, 2000 Clearwater Dr, Oak Brook, IL 60523; http://www.reedbusiness.com. Illus., adv. Circ: 103500 Controlled. Microform: PQC. Online: Gale Group; OCLC Online Computer Library Center, Inc.; ProQuest Information & Learning; H.W. Wilson. *Indexed:* ABIn, AS&TI, B&I, C&ISA, CompLI, EngInd, H&SSA. *Aud.:* Ac, Sa.

Much of this magazine's content is available at www.manufacturingsystems.com, plus additional industry links. *MSI*, a monthly trade magazine, focuses on IT approaches to enhancing manufacturing management applications, including articles that feature "improving productivity, eliminating bottlenecks, decreasing inventory and scrap, implementing automation in its many forms, and/or motivating a workforce to meet current challenges." Regular departments each month include manufacturing issue analyses, an industry focus, editorials, and association information. Aimed at managers who develop or oversee systems in manufacturing sectors, this title is recommended for public and academic collections and corporate libraries.

MIS Quarterly. See Management, Administration, and Human Resources/Functional Management section.

Organization Studies. See Management, Administration, and Human Resources/Organizational Behavior and Studies section.

Organizational Dynamics. See Management, Administration, and Human Resources/Organizational Behavior and Studies section.

1349. ***Technological Forecasting and Social Change: an international journal of the Dargon Project.*** Formerly (until 1970): *Technological Forecasting.* [ISSN: 0040-1625] 1969. 9x/yr. EUR 751 (Individuals, EUR 118). Ed(s): Harold A Linstone, J P Martino. Elsevier Inc., 360 Park Ave. S, New York, NY 10010-1710; usinfo-f@elsevier.com; http://www.elsevier.com. Illus., adv. Refereed. Vol. ends: No. 66 - No. 68. Microform: PQC. Online: Gale Group; ingenta.com; ScienceDirect; Swets Blackwell. Reprint: SWZ. *Indexed:* ABS&EES, Agr, ArtHuCI, BAS, BPI, C&ISA, EngInd, ExcerpMed, FutSurv, GeogAbPG, IPSA, JEL, PSA, SSCI, SUSA, SociolAb. *Bk. rev.:* 0-2, 1,000-2,500 words. *Aud.:* Ac, Sa.

Deals primarily with technological forecasting (TF) and social impact analysis (technology assessment) in a wide range of fields. Five to six papers provide research and case studies in "methodology and practice of TF as a planning tool, or the analysis of the interaction of technology with the social behavior and environmental aspects of integrative planning." Of interest to policy makers and scholars in advanced economics and social sciences.

Technology Review. See Science and Technology section.

1350. ***Technovation: an international journal of technical innovation and entrepreneurship.*** [ISSN: 0166-4972] 1981. m. EUR 1111. Ed(s): G Hayward, G Rosegger. Pergamon, The Boulevard, Langford Ln, East Park, Kidlington, OX5 1GB, United Kingdom. Illus., adv. Refereed. Vol. ends: No. 166 - No. 4972. Online: Gale Group; ingenta.com; ScienceDirect; Swets Blackwell. Reprint: SWZ. *Indexed:* ABIn, EngInd, RiskAb, SSCI. *Bk. rev.:* 1-3, 500-1,000 words. *Aud.:* Ac, Sa.

Published in the United Kingdom, this interdisciplinary journal reports on scholarly research related to moving a new product or process from development to the point of commercialization. Trends, innovations, and entrepreneurial strategies are hallmarks of this refereed journal where papers are presented through case studies, reviews, and analyses. Book reviews, a conference calendar, and news of the International Society for Professional Innovation Management (ISPIM) are included as well.

Ethics

Asia Environmental Review. See Asia and the Pacific/Electronic Journals section.

1351. ***Business & Professional Ethics Journal.*** [ISSN: 0277-2027] 1981. q. USD 95 (Individuals, USD 30). Ed(s): Robert J Baum. University of Florida, Center for Applied Philosophy and Ethics in the Professions, PO Box 15017, Gainesville, FL 32604; http://web.phil.ufl.edu. Illus., index, adv. Refereed. Circ: 800 Paid. *Indexed:* BPI, EngInd, LRI, PAIS, PhilInd, RI-1, SSI. *Bk. rev.:* Various number and length. *Aud.:* Ac.

Broadly interdisciplinary in aim, lengthy articles explore "the similarities and differences between the ethical situations that arise in two or more professions," including marketing, health care, human resource management, global labor, and business ethics. Half of the issues are devoted to reprinting selected papers from professional ethics conferences around the globe. Announcements are frequently included each quarter. Because of the pervasive awareness of applied ethics in society, this journal will be useful in all academic libraries.

1352. ***Business and Society: a journal of interdisciplinary exploration.*** [ISSN: 0007-6503] 1960. q. GBP 277 in Europe, Middle East, Africa & Australasia. Ed(s): Jeanne Logsdon. Sage Publications, Inc., 2455 Teller Rd, Thousand Oaks, CA 91320; info@sagepub.com; http://www.sagepub.com. Illus., index, adv. Refereed. Circ: 3500. Microform: PQC. Online: EBSCO Publishing; Florida Center for Library Automation; Gale Group; ingenta.com; OCLC Online Computer Library Center, Inc.; ProQuest Information & Learning; RoweCom Information Quest; Swets Blackwell. Reprint: PQC; SCH. *Indexed:* ABIn, BPI, CommAb, CompR, HRA, PAIS, PMA, RiskAb, SociolAb. *Bk. rev.:* 1-3, 750-1,000 words. *Aud.:* Ac.

This is the official publication of the International Association for Business and Society, which publishes "original research, book reviews and dissertation abstracts relating to business ethics, business-government relations, corporate governance, corporate social performance, and environmental management issues." Topical issues generally include several feature articles, one to three lengthy signed book reviews, and related dissertation abstracts.

1353. ***Business and Society Review: journal of the Center for Business Ethics at Bentley College.*** Formerly (until 1974): *Business and Society Review/Innovation;* Which was formed by the merger of (1962-1972): *Innovation; Business and Society Review.* [ISSN: 0045-3609] 1972. q. USD 179 print & online eds. Blackwell Publishing, Inc., Commerce Place, 350 Main St, Malden, MA 02148; subscrip@blackwellpub.com; http://www.blackwellpublishing.com. Illus., adv. Circ: 2000 Paid. Microform: PQC. Online: EBSCO Publishing; Gale Group; ingenta.com; OCLC Online Computer Library Center, Inc.; RoweCom Information Quest; Swets Blackwell; H.W. Wilson. Reprint: WSH. *Indexed:* ABIn, ATI, AgeL, BPI, CLI, CompR, FutSurv, ILP, LRI, PAIS, PMA, PRA, RI-1, SSI. *Bk. rev.:* irregular, 500-2,500 words. *Aud.:* Ga, Ac.

This scholarly publication includes a dozen articles 8–20 pages each covering a wide range of ethical issues concerning corporate citizenship and responsibility. Some issues are thematic. Articles are of interest to business people, academics, and others involved in the contemporary debate about the proper role of business in society. Expect to find this title in academic collections supporting business programs and larger public libraries.

1354. ***Business Ethics: a European review.*** [ISSN: 0962-8770] 1992. q. USD 846 print & online eds. Ed(s): June Collier. Blackwell Publishing Ltd., 9600 Garsington Rd, PO Box 805, Oxford, OX4 2DQ, United Kingdom; customerservices@oxon.blackwellpublishing.com; http://www.blackwellpublishing.com/. Illus. Refereed. Online: EBSCO Publishing; Gale Group; ingenta.com; OCLC Online Computer Library Center, Inc.; RoweCom Information Quest; Swets Blackwell. Reprint: SWZ. *Indexed:* IBSS, PhilInd, SSI. *Bk. rev.:* Brief. Number varies. *Aud.:* Ac.

This primarily European-focused journal provides a forum for dialogue at "every level on all issues related to ethics in business." Original theoretical research covers ethical challenges and their solutions, analysis of the ethics of business policies and practices, and the concept of good ethical thinking. Each issue contains several major articles, an occasional special focus with thematic articles, interviews, brief book reviews, comments, and responses to previously published articles.

1355. ***Business Ethics: corporate social responsibility report.*** [ISSN: 0894-6582] 1987. 6x/yr. USD 49 domestic; USD 59 foreign. Ed(s): Marjorie Kelly. Business Ethics, PO Box 8439, Minneapolis, MN 55408-0439; bizethics@aol.com; http://www.business-ethics.com. Adv. Sample. Circ: 10000 Paid and free. *Indexed:* AltPI. *Aud.:* Ga, Ac, Sa.

The format is modest and newsletter-like in appearance, but the editor packs much information into 25 pages. Each issue contains case studies presenting ethical dilemmas, news reports on corporate citizenship and environmental transgressions, articles advocating social justice, and analysis of socially responsible investing (SRI). Selected articles from the current issue and the annual ranking "100 Best Corporate Citizens" are available at the web site.

1356. ***Business Ethics Quarterly.*** [ISSN: 1052-150X] 1991. q. USD 155 (Individuals, USD 60; Students, USD 30). Ed(s): George Brenkert. Philosophy Documentation Center, PO Box 7147, Charlottesville, VA 22906-7147. Adv. Refereed. Circ: 900. Microform: PQC. Online: Gale Group; OCLC Online Computer Library Center, Inc.; H.W. Wilson. Reprint: PSC. *Indexed:* ABIn, ABS&EES, BPI, IBSS, IBZ, LRI, PhilInd, RI-1, SSI. *Bk. rev.:* 2-3, 1,000-2,000 words. *Aud.:* Ac.

This official journal of the Society for Business Ethics looks at how business ethics in particular are influenced by gender, race, ethnicity, and nationality. Article submissions addressing global business and economic concerns are encouraged. There are approximately six to twelve feature articles in each issue, accompanied by one or more review articles. Of most interest to academic business collections.

1357. ***Ethikos: examining ethical and compliance issues in business.*** Incorporates (1991-1999): *Corporate Conduct Quarterly.* [ISSN: 0895-5026] 1987. s-m. Corporations, USD 145; Non-profit organizations, USD 95. Ed(s): Andrew W Singer. Ethikos, Inc., 154 E Boston Post Rd, Mamaroneck, NY 10543. Adv. Online: Northern Light Technology, Inc. *Bk. rev.:* 1, 1,000-1,500 words. *Aud.:* Ac, Sa.

Analysis of federal regulatory compliance, reports on corporate policies/practices, and case studies are written primarily by the editors; outside contribution is limited. Each issue also contains an extensive review article. Of interest to academic and special libraries supporting corporate law programs.

1358. ***International Journal of Value-Based Management.*** [ISSN: 0895-8815] 1988. 3x/yr. EUR 211 for print or online ed. Ed(s): Anthony F Libertella, Samuel M Natale. Kluwer Academic Publishers, van Godewijckstraat 30, PO Box 17, Dordrecht, 3300 AA, Netherlands; services@wkap.nl; http://www.wkap.nl. Refereed. Circ: 500. *Indexed:* PAIS, RiskAb. *Aud.:* Ac.

"A forum for clarifying the role of values in organizational behavior and in the process of decision making." Each issue contains approximately six case studies and empirical research articles 10–20 pages in length. Comparative cultural points of view are encouraged from contributors worldwide. Of interest to academic collections supporting international business programs.

1359. ***Journal of Business Ethics.*** Incorporates (1997-2004): *Teaching Business Ethics;* (1988-2004): *International Journal of Value-Based Management.* [ISSN: 0167-4544] 1982. 28x/yr. EUR 1453 print or online ed. Ed(s): Alex C Michalos, Deborah C Poff. Kluwer Academic Publishers, van Godewijckstraat 30, PO Box 17, Dordrecht, 3300 AA, Netherlands. Illus., adv. Refereed. Vol. ends: Dec. Microform: PQC. Online: Chadwyck-Healey Incorporated; EBSCO Publishing; Gale Group; ingenta.com; Kluwer Online; OCLC Online Computer Library Center, Inc.; Ovid Technologies, Inc.; ProQuest Information & Learning; RoweCom Information Quest; Swets Blackwell. Reprint: SWZ. *Indexed:* ABIn, ATI, AgeL, ArtHuCI, BPI, CJA, CommAb, IBSS, IBZ, PAIS, PRA, PhilInd, RI-1, RiskAb, SSCI, SSI. *Aud.:* Ac.

This journal of international research analyzes systems of production, consumption, marketing, advertising, social and economic accounting, labor relations, public relations, and organizational behavior. Ethics is defined broadly by the publisher as "all human action aimed at securing a good life." Articles on speculative philosophy and empirical research are included. Since 1997, submissions of specific interest to instructors are referred to the sister publication, *Teaching Business Ethics.* Both titles are recommended for academic business collections.

1360. ***Multinational Monitor.*** Supersedes: *Elements.* [ISSN: 0197-4637] 1980. m. Individuals, USD 25; Corporations, USD 40; Non-profit organizations, USD 30. Ed(s): John Richard, Robert Weissman. Essential Information, PO Box 19405, Washington, DC 20036. Illus., index, adv. Refereed. Circ: 10000. Microform: PQC. Online: EBSCO Publishing; Florida Center for Library Automation; Gale Group; Northern Light Technology, Inc.; ProQuest Information & Learning. *Indexed:* AltPI, PAIS. *Bk. rev.:* 0-1, 750-1,500 words. *Aud.:* Ga, Sa.

This title provides coverage, often in a highly critical fashion, of multinational corporations' impact on society and the environment. Articles and interviews address topics involving labor, pollution, corporate crime, regulatory laws and government policy, multilateral banks, and development. Of interest to general and academic collections with a focus on business ethics. Corporate libraries will find it useful to monitor themselves and competitors in the court of public opinion.

Teaching Business Ethics. See *Journal of Business Ethics.*

International

African Business. See Africa section.

Business India. See Asia and the Pacific/South Asia section.

1361. ***Business Latin America: weekly report to managers of Latin American operations.*** [ISSN: 0007-6880] 1966. w. USD 1250; USD 75 newsstand/cover per issue. Ed(s): Anna Szterenfeld, Steven Murphy. Economist Intelligence Unit, 111 W 57th St, New York, NY 10019; newyork@eiu.com; http://www.eiu.com. Illus. Microform: PQC. *Indexed:* ABIn. *Aud.:* Ac, Sa.

This weekly report provides news briefs that feature political and economic analysis of Central and South American countries, giving important insights for companies that wish to operate in those markets. Segments include Investment Environment, Industry Monitor, Infrastructure, and Business Outlook, which forecasts the business climate of individual countries. The editorial board consists of individuals from large multinational corporations, making it a vital source of international business intelligence, although cost-prohibitive to all but the largest academic and corporate libraries. Similar titles exist from this publisher for other regions/countries, e.g., Africa, Asia, China, Europe, and Eastern Europe.

1362. ***Business Mexico.*** Formed by the merger of (1981): *American Chamber of Commerce of Mexico. Quarterly Economic Report;* (1939-1981): *Mexican-American Review.* [ISSN: 0187-1455] 1981. m. USD 134. Ed(s): Matthew Brayman, Armando Saliba. American Chamber of Commerce of Mexico A.C., Lucerna 78, Col. Juarez, Mexico City, 06600, Mexico; amchamm@amcham.com.mx; http://www.amcham.com.mx/. Illus., adv. Circ: 11000. CD-ROM: ProQuest Information & Learning. Microform: PQC. Online: Florida Center for Library Automation; Gale Group; LexisNexis; Northern Light Technology, Inc.; OCLC Online Computer Library Center, Inc.; ProQuest Information & Learning; H.W. Wilson. *Indexed:* ABIn, B&I, BPI, HAPI, PAIS. *Aud.:* Ga, Ac, Sa.

Regular columns cover politics, management, banking and finance, technology, and living conditions in Mexico. Also included are interviews with newsmakers and profiles of companies and industries. This title provides English-language insights into how Mexican businesses are positioning themselves for growth and globalization. Of interest to academic programs supporting international business studies and to public libraries serving local import/export businesses.

1363. ***Business Review Weekly.*** Incorporates (1935-1987): *Rydge's;* (1985-1987): *Rydge's Management and Marketing Update;* (1984-1986): *Today's Computers.* [ISSN: 0727-758X] 1980. w. AUD 175; AUD 160 renewals. Ed(s): Neil Shoebridge. Fairfax Business Media, c/o Elda Rebechi, Marketing Manager, GPO Box 55A, Melbourne, VIC 3000, Australia; http://www.fxj.com.au/. Illus., adv. Circ: 63578. *Indexed:* ABIn, PAIS. *Aud.:* Ga.

Australia's leading business magazine, covering economic, financial, management, marketing, and e-business topics each week. Company and individual profiles spotlight successes—and failures. An index of names on the back inside cover indicates whether the report was negative, positive, or neutral. Articles that have additional information in their online version are flagged with a "web extra" image.

Business Strategy Review. See Management, Administration, and Human Resources/Strategic Analysis section.

Business Times [Singapore]. See Asia and the Pacific/Electronic Journals section.

1364. ***Business Today.*** 1992. fortn. INR 215 domestic; USD 19.50 foreign. Ed(s): Aroon Purie. Living Media India Pvt. Ltd., F-14-15, Connaught Place, New Delhi, India; http://www.india-today.com. Adv. Circ: 127378. *Aud.:* Ga, Ac.

India's leading fortnightly that covers all aspects of Indian business with emphasis on information systems and technologies. Articles are written clearly, for a general audience, and are accompanied by colorful, detailed graphics. Each issue also includes news and trends, profiles of people, case studies, policy analysis, and discussions on career development. Of interest to larger public libraries and academic collections supporting international business programs or South Asian Studies.

Canadian Business. See Canada section.

China Business Review. See China section.

Emerging Markets Finance and Trade. See CIS and Eastern Europe section.

1365. ***EuroBusiness.*** [ISSN: 0953-0711] 1988. m. GBP 35 in Europe; EUR 57 elsewhere; FRF 26 newsstand/cover per issue France. Ed(s): Tom Rubython. European Business Press Ltd., Flat 8-16, Newspaper House, 8-16 Great New St, London, EC4A 3BN, United Kingdom; mail@eurobusiness.uk.com; http://www.eurobusiness.net. Adv. *Aud.:* Ga.

Written by Europeans for Europeans, this glossy title exudes new energy since the adoption of the euro. In the past, the cover story usually offered a lengthy profile on a prominent business leader whereas nowadays it is more likely to be topical in nature. Still personality driven, executive and corporate profiles along with news reports are covered in a section called "Insight." Features can address all aspects of business, economic, social, and regulatory trends affecting commerce within the European Union as well as trade with external markets. Special reports are devoted to a single country, region, or industry. Highly recommended for any academic collection supporting international business or European Studies. Of interest to larger public libraries, too.

Euromoney. See Finance/Investment section.

Export America. See under Small Business, this section.

Far Eastern Economic Review. See Asia and the Pacific section.

Financial Times. See Newspapers section.

International Small Business Journal. See under Small Business, this section.

1366. *International Trade Forum.* [ISSN: 0020-8957] 1964. q. USD 20 in developing nations; USD 65 elsewhere. Ed(s): Natalie Domeisen. International Trade Centre, Plais des Nations, Geneva, 1211, Switzerland; itcreg@intracen.org; http://www.intracen.org. Illus. Circ: 30000. Microform: PQC. Online: EBSCO Publishing; Florida Center for Library Automation; Gale Group; Northern Light Technology, Inc.; OCLC Online Computer Library Center, Inc.; ProQuest Information & Learning; H.W. Wilson. Reprint: PQC. *Indexed:* ABIn, BPI, FS&TA, LRI, PAIS, RRTA, WAE&RSA. *Aud.:* Ga, Ac.

The International Trade Centre (ITC) is the cooperative agency of the United Nations Conference on Trade and Development (UNCTAD) and the World Trade Organization (WTO). The *Forum* "focuses on trade promotion, export development and import methods, as part of [the ITC's] technical cooperation programme with developing countries and economies in transition." Issues contain short, practical articles; the trade statistics, import/export news, cross-cultural tips, and market profiles should appeal to a wide audience interested in the opportunities offered by a global economy. The web site is available at www.tradeforum.org.

Japan Economic Review. See Asia and the Pacific/East Asia section.

1367. *The Journal of Commerce.* Former titles (until 2002, vol.3, issue 42: *J o C Week;* (until 2000): *Journal of Commerce;* (until 1996): *Journal of Commerce and Commercial;* (until 1927): *Journal of Commerce.* 1827. w. USD 146. Ed(s): Peter M Tirschwell. Journal of Commerce, Inc., 33 Washington St, 13th Fl, Newark, NJ 07102; customersvs@joc.com; http://www.joc.com. Adv. Circ: 22000 Paid. Microform: NRP. Online: The Dialog Corporation; Gale Group; MediaStream, Inc. *Indexed:* ChemAb, LRI, LogistBibl, PAIS. *Aud.:* Ga, Ac, Sa.

This weekly provides authoritative editorial content for international business executives to help them plan their global supply chain and better manage their day-to-day international logistics and shipping needs. This information is delivered through news, analysis of the political landscape surrounding the latest regulatory issues, case studies, and perspective pieces. Recommended for all international business and transportation collections.

1368. *Journal of International Business Studies.* [ISSN: 0047-2506] 1970. bi-m. GBP 107 print & online. Ed(s): Arie Y Lewin. Palgrave Macmillan Ltd., Houndmills, Basingstoke, RG21 6XS, United Kingdom; journal-info@palgrave.com; http://www.palgrave-journals.com/. Adv. Refereed. Circ: 4100. Microform: PQC. Online: bigchalk; EBSCO Publishing; Florida Center for Library Automation; Gale Group; JSTOR (Web-based Journal Archive); Northern Light Technology, Inc.; OCLC Online Computer Library Center, Inc.; ProQuest Information & Learning; H.W. Wilson. Reprint: PQC; SCH. *Indexed:* ABIn, ABS&EES, BAS, BPI, CPerI, IBSS, JEL, PAIS, RiskAb, SSCI. *Aud.:* Ac.

This journal publishes empirical and hypothetical research articles that are frequently interdisciplinary in nature. Also included are case studies of corporate activities, strategies, and managerial processes that cross national boundaries; submissions that focus on the interactions of such firms with their economic, political, and cultural environments is encouraged. Recommended for all academic business collections.

1369. *Journal of Japanese Trade and Industry.* [ISSN: 0285-9556] 1982. 6x/yr. JPY 45. Ed(s): Yoshimichi Hori T Iwasaki. Maruzen Co., Ltd., 3-10 Nihonbashi 2-chome, Chuo-ku, Tokyo, 103-0027, Japan. Illus., adv. Circ: 35000. *Indexed:* BAS, BPI, EnvAb, PAIS. *Aud.:* Ac, Sa.

The purpose of the Japan Economic Foundation is to foster communication between Japan and its trading partners. Although emphasis is placed on manufacturing industries, the overall perception of Japan, Inc., and Japanese culture in general are addressed. The cover story sets the theme of the business-oriented features inside. The balance of the publication is devoted to an eclectic mix of articles on business history, ethics, finance, travel, and the arts. Current issue contents and archive are available through the foundation's web site at www.jef.or.jp/en. Recommended for academic collections supporting programs in international business or Japanese Studies; a must for corporations doing business with Japan.

1370. *Journal of Teaching in International Business.* [ISSN: 0897-5930] 1989. q. USD 315. Ed(s): Erdener Kaynak. Haworth Press, Inc., 10 Alice St, Binghamton, NY 13904-1580; getinfo@haworthpressinc.com; http://www.haworthpressinc.com. Adv. Sample. Refereed. Circ: 242 Paid. Reprint: HAW. *Indexed:* BusEdI, CIJE, IBZ. *Aud.:* Ac.

"Examines issues, problems, opportunities, and solutions related to teaching and learning in international business in diverse cultures and educational environments." Some issues are thematic and are simultaneously published as monographs. Of interest to business curriculum developers in higher education worldwide.

1371. *Journal of World Business.* Formerly (until 1997): *Columbia Journal of World Business.* [ISSN: 1090-9516] 1965. q. EUR 281 (Individuals, EUR 118). Ed(s): F. Luthans, J W Slocum, Jr. Pergamon, The Boulevard, Langford Ln, East Park, Kidlington, OX5 1GB, United Kingdom. Illus., index, adv. Refereed. Circ: 3500. Vol. ends: No. 4. Microform: PQC. Online: EBSCO Publishing; Florida Center for Library Automation; Gale Group; ingenta.com; OCLC Online Computer Library Center, Inc.; ScienceDirect; Swets Blackwell; H.W. Wilson. Reprint: ISI; PQC. *Indexed:* ABIn, ABS&EES, ATI, BLI, BPI, CommAb, IBSS, JEL, PAIS, PRA, RRTA, SSCI, WAE&RSA. *Aud.:* Ac.

Each issue includes a half-dozen articles written by leading academic researchers, top government officials, and prominent business leaders on issues related to financial markets, free trade, transition economies, emerging markets, privatization, joint ventures, mergers and acquisitions, human resource management, and marketing. Separate editorial boards are designated for contributors in the United States, Europe, Latin America, and the Pacific Rim. Recommended for all academic collections supporting international business studies.

1372. *Latin Trade: your business source for Latin America.* Formerly (until 1996): *U S - Latin Trade.* [ISSN: 1087-0857] 1993. m. USD 36 domestic; USD 48 foreign; USD 3.95 newsstand/cover per issue. Ed(s): Sabrina R Crow. Freedom Publications, Inc. (Miami), 200 S Biscayne Blvd, Ste 1150, Miami, FL 33131; lattrade@aol.com; http://www.latintrade.com. Illus., adv. Circ: 74000. Online: EBSCO Publishing; Florida Center for Library Automation; Gale Group; LexisNexis; Northern Light Technology, Inc.; OCLC Online Computer Library Center, Inc.; ProQuest Information & Learning. *Indexed:* B&I. *Bk. rev.:* Various number and length. *Aud.:* Ac, Sa.

This newsmagazine covers all aspects of corporate business in Central and South America. Feature articles tend to be few and short. Four departments fill out the remainder of each issue, providing timely information, statistics, and opinion pieces on people, companies, regulations, technology, import/export, and various trade and industry topics of the region. Special issues include the Annual Bravo Awards to recognize outstanding leadership in Latin America, and the annual ranking of Latin America's 100 largest publicly traded companies. The web site, www.latintrade.com, contains regional trade information and access to articles from the print version.

Law and Policy in International Business. See Law section.

1373. *Look Japan.* [ISSN: 0456-5339] 1953. m. USD 83 Southeast Asia; USD 83 East Asia (execpt Japan); USD 88 Oceania). Ed(s): Kunio Nishimura. Look Japan Ltd., Asahi Seimei Hibiya Bldg., 1-5-1, Yurakucho, Tokyo, 100-0006, Japan; mail@lookjapan.com; http://www.lookjapan.com. Illus., index, adv. Circ: 75000. Vol. ends: Dec. Online: Factiva; Gale Group. *Indexed:* BAS, PAIS. *Bk. rev.:* Various number and length. *Aud.:* Ac, Sa.

Each issue contains a cover story and several features in each of the main sections: Economy & Business, Society & Culture, and Science & Technology. Opinion pieces address such topics as the Japanese economy and politics, U.S.-Japan relations, globalization, small business development, and the impact of technology. There are news reports, interviews, company profiles, and new product announcements. Of interest to high school and public libraries because of the general coverage on the society. Academic collections supporting international studies or business programs will find value in having access to a Japanese perspective written in English. Chinese- and Spanish-language editions are also available.

1374. *Multinational Business Review.* [ISSN: 1525-383X] 1993. s-a. USD 60 (Individuals, USD 30; Students, USD 15). Ed(s): Suk H Kim. University of Detroit Mercy, College of Business Administration, PO Box 19900, Detroit, MI 48219-0900; kimsuk@udmercy.edu; http://www.mich.lom/~kimsuk/. Refereed. Circ: 375 Paid. CD-ROM: ProQuest Information & Learning. Microform: PQC. Online: EBSCO Publishing; OCLC Online Computer Library Center, Inc.; ProQuest Information & Learning; H.W. Wilson. *Indexed:* ABIn, BPI, PAIS. *Aud.:* Ac.

Published by an academic institution whose stated goal is application-oriented issues, *MBR* contains feature-length and short articles as well as case studies exploring contemporary international issues in finance, accounting, management, marketing, and economics. Focusing on practical applications such as operations management, investing and debt management, and import/export practices, this journal provides a bridge between international business theory and practice. Best suited for academic libraries with international business programs.

1375. *The Nikkei Weekly.* Formerly (until June 1991): *Japan Economic Journal.* [ISSN: 0918-5348] 1962. w. JPY 21600 domestic; USD 129 United States; CND 195 Canada. Ed(s): Nobuo Oneda. Nihon Keizai Shimbun Inc., 1-9-5 Ote-Machi, Chiyoda-ku, Tokyo, 100-0004, Japan; http://www.nni.nikkei.co.jp/. Illus., index, adv. Circ: 36500. Online: LexisNexis. *Indexed:* B&I, ChemAb, EnvAb. *Aud.:* Ga, Ac, Sa.

This newspaper is the leading English-language source of information about business and trade from a Japanese perspective. Similar in format to the *Financial Times*, it provides coverage of the economy, politics, science and technology, industry trends, management, labor, and financial sectors. Regular reports profile people, corporations, and new products. Summaries of business conditions in other Asian and Pacific markets are provided as well.

Pakistan and Gulf Economist. See Asia and the Pacific/South Asia section.

1376. *Project Finance.* Formed by the merger of (1992-1997): *Infrastructure Finance;* (1990-1997): *Project and Trade Finance (London, 1989);* Which was formerly (until 1990): *Trade Finance and Banker International;* Which was formed by the 1989 merger of: *Trade Finance; Banker International;* Which was formerly (until 1987): *Euromoney Bank Report.* [ISSN: 1462-0014] 1997. 10x/yr. GBP 499 combined subscription domestic print & online eds.; EUR 787 combined subscription in Europe print & online eds.; USD 740 combined subscription elsewhere print & online eds. Ed(s): Sean Keating. Euromoney Institutional Investor plc., Nestor House, Playhouse Yard, London, EC4V 5EX, United Kingdom; information@euromoneyplc.com; http://www.euromoney.com. Illus., index, adv. Circ: 6000. Microform: PQC. Online: Gale Group; LexisNexis. *Indexed:* ABIn, B&I. *Aud.:* Ac, Sa.

Stating that it is "the global authority for the project finance industry," this trade title offers news and short features covering people, agencies, countries, deals analysis, and developments by large corporations and regional authorities worldwide related to infrastructure, trade, and project finance. The online version, www.projectfinancemagazine.com, offers all this and more for industry insiders. Aimed at corporate insiders, this title may appeal to academic libraries with programs in international strategic planning and risk management.

1377. *S T I Review.* [ISSN: 1010-5247] 1986. s-a. FRF 330; USD 63. Organization for Economic Cooperation and Development, 2 rue Andre Pascal, Paris, Cedex 16 75775, France; sales@oecd.org; http://www.oecd.org/PUBS/PRINTPUBS/period.html. Illus. *Indexed:* EnvAb, PAIS. *Aud.:* Ac, Sa.

Primarily a tool for policy makers and analysts of member countries of the Organization for Economic Co-operation and Development (OECD), this title presents summary findings of studies by the OECD in the fields of industry, science, and technology. Each issue presents about ten articles on a similar theme, such as technology and innovation policy, sustainable development, public/private partnerships, and the global research village. It is inconsistently issued, thus the delay in publication makes it useful more for academic instruction and public policy review and less for current industry analysis.

1378. *Thunderbird International Business Review.* Formerly (until 1998): *International Executive;* Incorporates (1988-2001): *Global Focus;* Which was formerly (until 1999): *Global Outlook;* (until 1998): *Business and the Contemporary World.* [ISSN: 1096-4762] 1959. bi-m. USD 489. Ed(s): Yahia H Zoubir. John Wiley & Sons, Inc., 111 River St, Hoboken, NJ 07030; uscs-wis@wiley.com; http://www.wiley.com. Adv. Refereed. Circ: 2500. Microform: PQC. Online: ScienceDirect; Wiley InterScience. Reprint: PQC; PSC. *Indexed:* ABIn, ABS&EES, BPI, PAIS, RiskAb. *Bk. rev.:* 0-8, 450-2,000 words. *Aud.:* Ac, Sa.

The target audience of this publication includes "international managers, academicians, and executives in business and government," with the goal of exchanging ideas and research between scholars and practitioners worldwide. Articles and case studies address a wide range of topics: analysis of multinational corporations, small business development, marketing ethics, market entry, doing business in a specific country, and trade among several countries. Issues are frequently thematic.

Small Business

Black Enterprise. See African American section.

1379. *Entrepreneur (Irvine).* Formerly (until 1977): *Insider's Report.* [ISSN: 0163-3341] 1973. m. USD 19.97 domestic; USD 39.97 foreign; USD 4.99 newsstand/cover per issue domestic. Ed(s): Rieva Lesonsky. Entrepreneur Media, Inc., 2445 McCabe Way, Ste 400, Irvine, CA 92614; http://www.entrepreneur.com. Illus., adv. Sample. Circ: 540000. Online: bigchalk; Factiva; Florida Center for Library Automation; Gale Group. *Indexed:* BPI, MagInd, PAIS. *Aud.:* Ga, Sa.

A leading magazine covering trends, issues, and problems of starting and running a business. Written in an engaging style, short features include individual and company profiles, success stories, strategies for improvement, and rankings of top companies and individuals. News coverage includes national, global, women-oriented, industry-specific, and hot topics. Each issue contains tips on technology, money, management and marketing, classified ads, and a products and services directory. The web site, www.entrepreneur.com, contains full-text features and columns from the current issue along with online exclusives. Archival content is available back to 1997. A core title for business collections in most public and academic libraries.

1380. ***Entrepreneurship & Regional Development: an international journal.*** [ISSN: 0898-5626] 1989. q. GBP 156 (Individuals, GBP 70). Ed(s): Bengt Johannisson. Routledge, 11 New Fetter Ln, London, EC4P 4EE, United Kingdom; info@routledge.co.uk; http://www.routledge.co.uk. Adv. Refereed. Online: EBSCO Publishing; Ingenta Select; RoweCom Information Quest. Reprint: PSC. *Indexed:* IBSS, SSCI. *Bk. rev.:* infrequent. *Aud.:* Ac.

Focuses on the diverse and complex characteristics of local and regional economies (primarily European) that lead to entrepreneurial vitality. Provides a multidisciplinary forum for researchers, students, and practitioners in the field of entrepreneurship and small firm development within the larger context of economic growth and development. Each issue contains four or five articles, each 15-25 pages in length. Of interest to academic collections catering to small business studies or economics.

1381. ***Entrepreneurship: Theory and Practice.*** Formerly (until vol.12): *American Journal of Small Business.* [ISSN: 1042-2587] 1976. q. USD 280 print & online. Ed(s): D Bagby. Blackwell Publishing, Inc., Commerce Place, 350 Main St, Malden, MA 02148; subscrip@blackwellpub.com; http://www.blackwellpub.com. Illus., index, adv. Circ: 1600 Paid. Vol. ends: No. 4. Microform: PQC. Online: bigchalk; ingenta.com. Reprint: PQC. *Indexed:* ABIn, ATI, BPI, IBSS, PAIS. *Aud.:* Ac.

Blending theoretical and applied methods, this official journal of the U.S. Association for Small Business and Entrepreneurship features a wide range of refereed articles on issues in entrepreneurship, including "creation of enterprises, management of small firms, and issues in family business." Case studies, research notes, announcements, and guest editors' commentary occur sporadically throughout the year. Most appropriate for academic libraries.

1382. ***Export America.*** [ISSN: 1534-3588] m. USD 65. U.S. Department of Commerce, International Trade Administation, 1401 Constitution Ave, N W, Room 3414, Washington, DC 20230; http://www.ita.doc.gov/. *Aud.:* Ga, Ac, Sa.

This publication from the Department of Commerce is full of practical advice for businesses both small and large seeking to export their products. Each issue alerts readers to new opportunities via trade fairs, government initiatives and services, changes in federal regulations, and basic export statistics. The section titled "Success Stories" spotlights one exemplary small business. The back cover lists export assistance centers and their telephone numbers; the web site offers even more contact information and links to partner sites including the portal www.export.gov. Of interest to academic collections supporting business programs and to public libraries serving business owners looking to sell their products overseas.

1383. ***Family Business Review.*** [ISSN: 0894-4865] 1988. q. USD 175 print & online. Ed(s): Joseph H Astrachan. Blackwell Publishing, Inc., Commerce Place, 350 Main St, Malden, MA 02148; subscrip@blackwellpub.com; http://www.blackwellpublishing.com. Illus., index. Sample. Refereed. Circ: 1300. Vol. ends: No. 4. *Indexed:* ABIn. *Bk. rev.:* Various number and length. *Aud.:* Ac, Sa.

An international editorial board oversees this scholarly publication from the Family Firm Institute dedicated to furthering knowledge and increasing interdisciplinary skills of educators, consultants, and researchers of family-owned businesses. Four features, comprised of method papers and case studies, are presented in each issue, with invited commentaries, interviews, and books reviews. Not surprisingly, topics specific to family-owned enterprises predominate, with occasional special issues devoted to family business practices in a particular region of the world. Recommended for academic libraries with programs in small business and entrepreneurship.

1384. ***Franchising World.*** Former titles: *Franchising Opportunities; International Franchise Association. Quarterly Legal Bulletin; International Franchise Association. Legal Bulletin.* [ISSN: 1041-7311] 1960. 8x/yr. USD 18. Ed(s): Terry Hill. International Franchise Association, 1350 New York Ave, N W, Ste 900, Washington, DC 20005. Adv. Circ: 12000. Microform: PQC. Online: EBSCO Publishing; Florida Center for Library Automation; Gale Group; Northern Light Technology, Inc.; OCLC Online Computer Library Center, Inc.; ProQuest Information & Learning; H.W. Wilson. *Indexed:* ABIn, BPI. *Aud.:* Ga.

Official publication of the International Franchise Association. Each issue contains eight articles offering practical advice for both franchisors and franchisees. Anybody interested in franchising as a small business opportunity will want to consult this publication. Regular columns address management and operations, industry trends, case studies, legal issues and regulations, minority ownership opportunities, international development, and coverage of association events and activities.

Hispanic Business Magazine. See Latino Studies section.

1385. ***Home Business Magazine: the home-based entrepreneur's magazine.*** Formerly: *National Home Business.* [ISSN: 1092-4779] 1993. bi-m. 6 issues per volume. USD 15 domestic; USD 50 Canada; USD 70 foreign. Ed(s): Stacy Ann Henderson. United Marketing & Research Company, Inc., 9582 Hamilton Ave, PMB 368, Huntington Beach, CA 92646. Illus., adv. Circ: 100000. *Aud.:* Ga.

Featuring five or six articles on strategy along with an individual success story, this magazine offers readers practical advice. There is a strong online presence at www.homebusinessmag.com that will be useful for all libraries to bookmark for their patrons even if they do not subscribe to this bimonthly publication. Helpful information is organized by channels: Expo, Start Up, Opportunities, Marketing & Sales, Home Office, Web Mastery, Tele-commuters, Management, and Money.

1386. ***In Business (Emmaus): the magazine for environmental entrepreneuring.*** [ISSN: 0190-2458] 1979. bi-m. USD 33; USD 37 foreign. Ed(s): Jerome Goldstein. J G Press, Inc., 419 State Ave, Emmaus, PA 18049. Illus., adv. Circ: 3000. Vol. ends: No. 6. Online: bigchalk; EBSCO Publishing; OCLC Online Computer Library Center, Inc.; ProQuest Information & Learning. *Indexed:* ABIn. *Bk. rev.:* Various number and length. *Aud.:* Ga, Sa.

Profiling individuals who have created "green" enterprises, this environmentally conscious newsprint publication presents practical advice for sustainable growth. A dozen articles describe practices and trends in the green business industry, renewable energy sources, recycling, financing options, environmental and conservation news, and new product announcements. An important source of alternative business practices and products for the owner of small- to medium-sized companies. See also the online version at www.inbusiness.org/inbusine.htm for selected articles, a deep archive, and links to other titles from this publisher.

1387. ***Inc: the magazine for growing companies.*** Incorporates (1995-2000): *Self-Employed Professional.* [ISSN: 0162-8968] 1979. 18x/yr. USD 14 domestic; USD 31 Canada; USD 50 elsewhere. Inc., 38 Commercial Wharf, Boston, MA 02110. Illus., index, adv. Sample. Circ: 650000 Paid. Vol. ends: Dec. Microform: CIS. Online: The Dialog Corporation; EBSCO Publishing; Florida Center for Library Automation; Gale Group; LexisNexis; OCLC Online Computer Library Center, Inc.; ProQuest Information & Learning; H.W. Wilson. Reprint: PQC. *Indexed:* ABIn, ATI, BPI, BRI, CBRI, EnvAb, LRI, LogistBibl, MagInd. *Bk. rev.:* 0-2, 200-1,000 words. *Aud.:* Ga, Ac, Sa.

The premier magazine aimed at owners and managers of small- to mid-sized businesses. Articles feature individuals and companies and their proven strategies for success in marketing, management, finance, and customer relations. Each issue includes a dozen columns and departments that provide timely information on small business trends, new Internet technology, tips from CEOs, best web sites, advice on managing people, and editorials. Varying only slightly from one another are a dozen regional issues of this title; the Northeast edition is the one indexed in most services. *Inc. Technology* is a supplemental issue appearing three or four times per year. The web site, www.inc.com, offers more information, products, services, and online tools for members, and it is free to all. This core business title is well suited for all public and academic libraries.

1388. *International Small Business Journal.* Incorporates: *European Small Business Journal.* [ISSN: 0266-2426] 1982. bi-m. GBP 497 print & online eds. in Europe, Middle East, Africa & Australasia. Ed(s): Dr. Robert Blackburn. Sage Publications Ltd., 6 Bonhill St, London, EC2A 4PU, United Kingdom; info@sagepub.co.uk; http://www.sagepub.co.uk/. Illus. Refereed. Online: bigchalk; EBSCO Publishing; Florida Center for Library Automation; Gale Group; ingenta.com; Northern Light Technology, Inc.; OCLC Online Computer Library Center, Inc.; ProQuest Information & Learning; Swets Blackwell; H.W. Wilson. *Indexed:* ABIn, BPI, IBSS, PAIS. *Bk. rev.:* 0-2, 500-1,500 words. *Aud.:* Ac, Sa.

Targeting academics, policy makers, business and trade associations, small business consultants, and managers, this scholarly journal provides a venue for research on the small business sector worldwide. Articles presume a knowledge of business processes and strategies, focusing on "theoretical and methodological developments, empirical studies, practical applications and reviews of relevant literature." Each issue includes content summaries in English, French, Spanish, and German; abstracts with commentaries of related articles in other journals; book reviews; and tables of contents from previous volumes. Recommended for academic and corporate libraries, especially those with an entrepreneurship focus.

1389. *The Journal of Business Venturing.* [ISSN: 0883-9026] 1985. bi-m. EUR 687 (Individuals, EUR 132). Ed(s): S Subramony, S Venkataraman. Elsevier Inc., 360 Park Ave. S, New York, NY 10010-1710; usinfo-f@elsevier.com; http://www.elsevier.com. Illus., index. Refereed. Microform: PQC. Online: ingenta.com; LexisNexis; ScienceDirect; Swets Blackwell. *Indexed:* ABIn, SSCI. *Aud.:* Ac, Sa.

Leading scholars and practitioners contribute rigorously developed theoretical and empirical studies to fulfill the editor's stated aims of knowledge advancement in "international entrepreneurship, new business development, technology and innovation." Four to five articles 20–30 pages in length make up each issue covering entrepreneurship theory and venture capital issues. Occasionally included are invited papers devoted to a particular topic. The last issue of each volume includes a cumulative index for the volume year. An important journal for academic libraries offering advanced degrees in business.

1390. *Journal of Developmental Entrepreneurship.* [ISSN: 1084-9467] 1996. 3x/yr. USD 135. Miami University, School of Business Administration, Oxford, OH 45056-9978. http://www.sba.muohio.edu/PageCenter/JDE. *Indexed:* ABIn. *Aud.:* Ac, Sa.

Publishes empirical, theoretical, and descriptive research that centers on international "issues concerning microenterprise and small business development." *JDE* editors also place a significant priority on increasing the opportunity for new enterprise among women and minorities. Aimed at scholars, each issue includes four refereed articles and one short article ranging from processes and strategies to legislation, education, and training issues. Recommended for academic libraries.

1391. *Journal of Small Business Management.* [ISSN: 0047-2778] 1963. q. USD 166 print & online eds. Blackwell Publishing, Inc., Commerce Place, 350 Main St, Malden, MA 02148; subscrip@blackwellpub.com; http://www.blackwellpublishing.com. Illus., index, adv. Sample. Refereed. Circ: 3500. Vol. ends: Nov. Online: Gale Group; ingenta.com; Northern Light Technology, Inc.; Swets Blackwell. Reprint: PQC; SWZ. *Indexed:* ABIn, AgeL, BPI, CJA, LRI, MagInd, PAIS, PMA, RiskAb, SSCI. *Aud.:* Ac, Sa.

Supporting the goals and objectives of the International Council for Small Business, this official journal broadly covers education and research in entrepreneurship and small business management, including financial, strategic, operational, and cultural issues. Divided into two sections, each issue contains five or six rigorously researched articles that include "pragmatic advice for practitioners." Three or four smaller articles follow that focus on small enterprise endeavors outside the United States. Aimed at the international academic community, this title is appropriate for academic collections, especially those offering advanced degrees in business administration.

1392. *Minority Business Entrepreneur.* [ISSN: 1048-0919] 1984. bi-m. USD 16. Ed(s): Jeanie Barnett. Minority Business Entrepreneur, 3528 Torrance Blvd, Ste 101, Torrance, CA 90503-4803; mbewbe@ix.netcom.com; http://www.mbemag.com. Illus., index, adv. Circ: 40000. Vol. ends: No. 6. *Indexed:* ENW. *Bk. rev.:* Various number and length. *Aud.:* Ga, Ac.

This title serves to inform, educate, and inspire ethnic-minority and women business owners. Articles profile entrepreneurs, report on success stories, analyze failures, and provide best-practice examples designed to enhance small business management. Typical articles describe corporate and government programs and the positive benefits of supplier diversity. Ideal for public libraries serving small businesses; of interest to academic collections supporting entrepreneurship programs.

1393. *Small Business Economics: an international journal.* [ISSN: 0921-898X] 1989. 10x/yr. EUR 875 print or online ed. Ed(s): Zoltan J Acs, David B Audertsch. Kluwer Academic Publishers, van Godewijckstraat 30, PO Box 17, Dordrecht, 3300 AA, Netherlands; services@wkap.nl; http://www.wkap.nl. Illus., index. Sample. Refereed. Microform: PQC. Online: EBSCO Publishing; ingenta.com; Kluwer Online; OCLC Online Computer Library Center, Inc.; Ovid Technologies, Inc.; RoweCom Information Quest. Reprint: SWZ. *Indexed:* ABIn, IBSS, JEL, SSCI. *Bk. rev.:* 0-1, 750-1,000 words. *Aud.:* Ac, Sa.

Aimed at scholars, this international title provides a forum for studies in the activity of small and mid-sized firms. Each issue features six to eight articles of economic analysis and the role of small businesses and entrepreneurs in developed and developing countries. The scope is interdisciplinary and cross-national; best for academic libraries.

Success. See General Editorial section.

State and Regional

Most states and many cities produce some form of business newsmagazine. The Association of Area Business Publications provides a directory of titles at their web site, www.bizpubs.org. Only a select few are included here. See also the City and Regional section.

1394. *Alaska Business Monthly.* [ISSN: 8756-4092] 1985. m. USD 21.95. Ed(s): Ron Dalby. Alaska Business Publishing Co., PO Box 241288, Anchorage, AK 99524-1288. Illus., index, adv. Circ: 10000. Online: The Dialog Corporation; Florida Center for Library Automation; Gale Group; Northern Light Technology, Inc.; OCLC Online Computer Library Center, Inc.; ProQuest Information & Learning. *Aud.:* Ga, Ac, Sa.

This title covers issues and trends affecting Alaska's business sector and features stories on the individuals, organizations, and companies that shape the Alaskan economy. Each issue carries current news, interviews, human interest stories, and reports on a major industry sector including tourism, commercial fishing, construction, technology, manufacturing, mining, oil, gas, and timber.

1395. *Business & Economic Review.* [ISSN: 0007-6465] 1954. q. Free. Ed(s): Jan K Collins. University of South Carolina, Darla Moore School of Business, 1705 College St, Columbia, SC 29208; janc@darla.badm.sc.edu; http://research.badm.sc.edu/research/bereview/contents.htm. Illus., index. Circ: 5419. Microform: PQC. Online: EBSCO Publishing; Northern Light Technology, Inc.; ProQuest Information & Learning. Reprint: PQC. *Indexed:* ABIn, AgeL, PAIS, PMA. *Aud.:* Ga, Ac.

This magazine's goal is to address general trends and management techniques while at the same time discussing "current business and economic topics of particular interest to South Carolina and the Southeast." Along with an economic outlook and facts on the state, features include personal finances, health care, technology, and environmental reports. Academic libraries that support business programs generally have this type of business school publication in their collections; also of interest to public libraries in the southeastern United States.

1396. ***ColoradoBiz.*** Former titles (until 1999): *Colorado Business Magazine;* (until 1986): *Colorado Business.* [ISSN: 1523-6366] 1973. m. USD 24. Ed(s): David Lewis. Wiesner Publishing, Inc., 7009 S Potomac St., Ste 200, Englewood, CO 80112; ttol@ttol.com; http://www.cobizmag.com. Illus., adv. Circ: 16810 Paid. Microform: PQC. Online: The Dialog Corporation; Florida Center for Library Automation; Gale Group; OCLC Online Computer Library Center, Inc.; ProQuest Information & Learning. *Indexed:* LRI, MagInd, PAIS. *Aud.:* Sa.

"Business insight as colorful as Colorado," claims the cover of this handsome monthly. The cover story is accompanied by five features emphasizing business and industry trends statewide; general topics are usually put into a Colorado context. Departments include Attitude/Altitude, shorter reports on statewide business activities; SmallBiz; Colorado Career, a "day in the life" type profile of an individual business person or government official; and ITech, reports on information technology trends. Of interest to libraries in the region.

1397. ***Crain's Chicago Business.*** Incorporates (1993-1997?): *Crain's Small Business (Chicago ed.).* [ISSN: 0149-6956] 1978. w. USD 94.95 in state; USD 109 out of state; USD 149 foreign. Ed(s): Rance Crain. Crain Communications, Inc., 360 N Michigan Ave, Chicago, IL 60601-3806; http://www.crain.com. Adv. Circ: 51000. Microform: PQC. Online: The Dialog Corporation; EBSCO Publishing; Factiva; Florida Center for Library Automation; Gale Group; LexisNexis; Northern Light Technology, Inc.; OCLC Online Computer Library Center, Inc.; ProQuest Information & Learning; H.W. Wilson. Reprint: PQC. *Indexed:* B&I, BPI, GeoRef, LRI. *Aud.:* Ga, Ac, Sa.

Premier business newsmagazine for the greater Chicago area. Clearly written articles profile companies and individuals, report on industry trends, and examine the general economic situation in the city and suburbs beyond. Each issue contains a Crain's List—a topical ranking of companies. A web portal is available at www.chicagobusiness.com. Of most interest to public, academic, and corporate libraries maintaining business collections within the metropolitan area. Larger libraries outside the area might consider subscribing in acknowledgement of Chicagoland's business acumen.

1398. ***Crain's New York Business.*** Former titles (until 1985): *Citybusiness;* (until 1984): *New York CityBusiness.* [ISSN: 8756-789X] 1984. w. USD 69.95 domestic; USD 124.95 foreign; USD 2.50 newsstand/cover. Ed(s): Rance Crain. Crain Communications, Inc., 711 Third Ave, New York, NY 10017-4036; http://www.crain.com. Adv. Circ: 65000. Online: The Dialog Corporation; Gale Group; Northern Light Technology, Inc. *Indexed:* B&I, BPI, LRI. *Aud.:* Ga, Sa.

Similar in format to *Crain's Chicago Business.* In addition to news items, editorials, and recurring columns, departments include IT, real estate, executive moves, small business, restaurant reviews, and the week in review. Of interest to libraries in the Northeast and others that support large business collections.

1399. ***Florida Trend: magazine of Florida business.*** [ISSN: 0015-4326] 1958. m. USD 29.95; USD 39.95 out of state; USD 3.95 newsstand/ cover per issue. Ed(s): Mark R Howard. Trend Magazine, Inc., PO Box 611, St. Petersburg, FL 33731; http://www.floridatrend.com. Illus., adv. Circ: 50000. Microform: PQC. Online: bigchalk; The Dialog Corporation; Florida Center for Library Automation; Gale Group; Northern Light Technology, Inc.; OCLC Online Computer Library Center, Inc.; ProQuest Information & Learning. Reprint: PQC. *Indexed:* AgeL, PAIS. *Aud.:* Ga.

Created in the 1950s when agriculture and tourism dominated the Florida economy (and they still do, but are now joined by high tech), this title chronicles business in what has become one of the most populous states in the country. The publisher's aim is to "create a sense of community in Florida, tying together Florida's diverse, competitive and often difficult-to-understand regions in a statewide context." A cover story is accompanied by two to three features; the "Talk of Florida" section spotlights news, companies, and individuals. Each issue also contains a topical ranking of businesses.

1400. ***Indiana Business Review.*** [ISSN: 0019-6541] 1926. q. Free. Ed(s): Morton J Marcus. Indiana University, School of Business, 107 S Indiana Ave, Bloomington, IN 47405. Illus. Circ: 4000. Microform: CIS. Online: bigchalk; EBSCO Publishing; Florida Center for Library Automation; Gale Group; Northern Light Technology, Inc.; OCLC Online Computer Library Center, Inc.; ProQuest Information & Learning. *Indexed:* ABIn, PAIS, PMA. *Aud.:* Ga, Ac.

Published by the Indiana Business Research Center, this title provides analysis and insight on economic and demographic issues in the state. It is, however, of interest to a wider audience than just Hoosiers. Articles can spotlight trends and draw conclusions applicable to the country at large. Of interest to all libraries in the Midwest and to larger business collections nationwide.

1401. ***Los Angeles Business Journal.*** [ISSN: 0194-2603] 1979. w. USD 99.95 combined subscription print & online eds. Ed(s): Mark Lacter. California Business Journals, 5700 Wilshire Blvd, Ste 170, Los Angeles, CA 90036. Adv. Circ: 40000. Microform: PQC. Online: Florida Center for Library Automation; Gale Group; Northern Light Technology, Inc.; OCLC Online Computer Library Center, Inc.; ProQuest Information & Learning. *Aud.:* Ga.

This weekly newspaper covers local business activity in the second largest metropolitan area in the United States. Regular columns feature articles on media and technology, small business, investment and finance, and real estate. Each issue has a special report containing several brief articles on a specific industry or topic. There is also a topical ranking of companies. "The Lists," along with selected articles from the current newsstand issue, are now available online after free registration through the web site: www.labusinessjournal.com. Links are provided to sister publications covering Orange County, San Diego, and San Fernando Valley.

1402. ***New Jersey Business: the magazine of industry and business.*** [ISSN: 0028-5560] 1954. m. USD 21 domestic; USD 22 foreign; USD 2.50 newsstand/cover per issue. Ed(s): James T Prior. New Jersey Business Magazine, 310 Passaic Ave, Fairfield, NJ 07004. Illus., adv. Circ: 20000 Paid. Online: bigchalk; Northern Light Technology, Inc.; OCLC Online Computer Library Center, Inc.; ProQuest Information & Learning. *Indexed:* PAIS. *Aud.:* Ga, Sa.

This glossy title offers coverage of New Jersey legislation impacting business—summary information, opposing viewpoints, and current status. A dozen articles provide economic information on counties, selected industries, small businesses, technologies, and other related news and information. Monthly departments include people, advertising, construction, health care, and financial services.

1403. ***Oregon Business Magazine.*** [ISSN: 0279-8190] 1978. m. USD 19.95. Ed(s): Kathy Dimond. Oregon Business Media, 610 S W Broadway, 200, Portland, OR 97205-3431; http://www.oregonbusiness.com. Illus., adv. Circ: 20487. Microform: PQC. Online: Florida Center for Library Automation; Gale Group; OCLC Online Computer Library Center, Inc.; ProQuest Information & Learning. *Bk. rev.:* Various number and length. *Aud.:* Ga, Sa.

Oregon is home to an increasing number of small and medium-sized businesses; this title is dedicated to helping them grow. Each issue includes a cover story and features that emphasize a specific topic, interviews, company and industry profiles, advice, and savvy marketing strategies. Regular departments include insights, comments, feedback, and advice.

Trade and Industry

1404. ***Air Conditioning, Heating & Refrigeration News: the HVACR contractor's weekly newsmagazine.*** [ISSN: 0002-2276] 1926. w. USD 87 domestic; USD 117 Canada; USD 169 elsewhere. Ed(s): Mark Skaer. Business News Publishing Co., 755 W Big Beaver Rd, Ste 1000, Troy, MI 48084-4903; http://www.bnp.com. Illus., index, adv. Sample. Circ: 34608 Paid. Microform: CIS; PQC. Online: Dow Jones Interactive; Gale Group. Reprint: PQC. *Indexed:* ABIn, BPI. *Aud.:* Ac, Sa.

This tabloid-style magazine reports HVAC (heating, ventilating, and air conditioning) industry news with a half dozen articles on training and education, contracting and manufacturing, and management and association items, in addition to featuring a particular HVAC system, e.g., rooftop cooling and ductless split systems. Regular departments include updates on energy matters, historical practices, views and opinions, industry newsmakers, and classified ads. Appropriate for public libraries serving patrons in regions with active construction and renovation industries, as well as academic libraries supporting programs in engineering, architecture, and related fields.

1405. ***American Machinist: strategies & innovations for competitive manufacturing.*** Former titles (until 1988): *American Machinist and Automated Manufacturing;* (until 1986): *American Machinist;* (until 1968): *American Machinist - Metalworking Manufacturing;* (until 1960): *American Machinist.* [ISSN: 1041-7958] 1877. m. USD 75 domestic (Free to qualified personnel). Ed(s): Thomas Grasson. Penton Media, Inc., 1300 E 9th St, Cleveland, OH 44114-1503; ameditor@penton.com; http://www.penton.com. Illus., index, adv. Circ: 82079 Controlled. Microform: PMC; PQC. Online: bigchalk; EBSCO Publishing; Florida Center for Library Automation; Gale Group; Northern Light Technology, Inc.; OCLC Online Computer Library Center, Inc.; ProQuest Information & Learning; H.W. Wilson. *Indexed:* AS&TI, C&ISA, ChemAb, EngInd, LRI. *Bk. rev.:* Various number and length. *Aud.:* Sa.

Feature articles provide overviews on new tools, manufacturing equipment, materials, production management and quality control issues, and an assessment of one industry outside the United States. Extensive coverage of products and services, plus numerous departments relating to business and technology trends, software and hardware developments, testing and measurement advancements, practical ideas, casebooks, and liability and regulatory updates, as well as reader service and advertising information make this a valuable trade magazine to the cutting and tooling manufacturing industry. Current issue content and archives are available on the web site: www.americanmachinist-.com.

1406. ***Amusement Business: international live entertainment and amusement industry newsletter.*** [ISSN: 0003-2344] 1894. w. USD 149 domestic; USD 175 Canada; USD 185 elsewhere. V N U Business Publications, 770 Broadway, New York, NY 10003; bmcomm@vnuinc.com; http://www.vnubusinessmedia.com/. Illus. Circ: 12000 Paid. Microform: PQC. Online: The Dialog Corporation; EBSCO Publishing; Factiva; Florida Center for Library Automation; Gale Group; Northern Light Technology, Inc.; OCLC Online Computer Library Center, Inc.; ProQuest Information & Learning. *Indexed:* ABIn, B&I. *Aud.:* Sa.

This weekly reports news of interest to the live indoor and outdoor entertainment industry. Coverage includes people, company news, industry events, venue and facilities management, food concessions, advertising and marketing campaigns, special promotions, touring theater and musical acts, parks and attractions, fairs, carnivals, and expositions across North America. New product announcements, event grosses, and extensive classified advertising are in each issue.

Beverage Industry. See Food Industry section.

1407. ***Beverage World.*** Former titles (until 199?): *Soft Drinks;* (until 1996): *National Bottler's Gazette.* [ISSN: 0098-2318] 1882. m. USD 79 domestic; USD 84 Canada; USD 148 elsewhere. V N U Business Publications, 770 Broadway, New York, NY 10003; bmcomm@vnuinc.com; http://www.vnubusinessmedia.com/. Illus., index, adv. Circ: 34000. Vol. ends: Dec. Microform: PQC. Online: The Dialog Corporation; EBSCO Publishing; Factiva; Florida Center for Library Automation; Gale Group; LexisNexis; OCLC Online Computer Library Center, Inc.; ProQuest Information & Learning; H.W. Wilson. Reprint: PQC. *Indexed:* ABIn, BPI, ExcerpMed, PAIS. *Aud.:* Ac, Sa.

This publication tracks all aspects of the U.S. beverage industry providing market share and industry statistics to manufacturers, bottlers, distributors, and retailers of soft drinks, fruit juices, iced teas and coffees, wines and spirits, and bottled waters. Articles and interviews cover diverse topics including advances in packaging and vending, quality control, consumer preferences, marketing efforts, and fleet management. Sister publications are *Beverage World International* and *Beverage World en Espanol.* The web site, www.beverageworld.com, offers exclusive features, a deep archive of the print magazine, a buyer's guide (called Databank Directory) and assorted industry statistics.

Boxoffice. See Films section.

Broadcasting & Cable. See Television, Video, and Radio section.

Builder. See Building and Construction section.

1408. ***Chain Store Age: the news magazine for retail executives.*** Former titles (until Aug. 1995): *Chain Store Age Executive with Shopping Center Age;* (until 1975): *Chain Store Age Executives Edition Including Shopping Center Age.* [ISSN: 1087-0601] 1925. m. USD 105 domestic; USD 125 Canada; USD 165 foreign. Ed(s): Murray Forseter. Lebhar-Friedman, Inc., 425 Park Ave, New York, NY 10022; mforseter@lf.com; http://www.chainstoreage.com. Illus., adv. Circ: 35000. Vol. ends: Dec. Microform: CIS. Online: EBSCO Publishing; Gale Group; LexisNexis; OCLC Online Computer Library Center, Inc.; ProQuest Information & Learning. *Indexed:* ABIn, B&I, BPI, LogistBibl. *Aud.:* Ac, Sa.

This title, from the same publishers as *DSN Retailing Today,* serves the decision makers who manage chain stores and shopping centers. Nearly two dozen short articles in each issue discuss current news, events, and issues related to real estate, store planning and operations, electronic retailing, payment systems, and related products and technologies. Appropriate for larger public libraries and for academic libraries that support business programs.

Chemical Market Reporter. See Advertising, Marketing, and Public Relations section.

1409. ***Chemical Week.*** Former titles (until 1952): *Chemical Industries Week;* (until 1951): *Chemical Industries;* (until 1933): *Chemical Markets.* [ISSN: 0009-272X] 1914. w. 49/yr. USD 139 domestic; USD 169 Canada; USD 299 in Latin America. Ed(s): David Hunter. Chemical Week Associates, 110 William St 11th Fl, New York, NY 10038; webmaster@chemweek.com; http://www.chemweek.com. Illus., index, adv. Circ: 33000. Vol. ends: Dec. Microform: PQC. Online: bigchalk; EBSCO Publishing; Factiva; Florida Center for Library Automation; Gale Group; LexisNexis; Northern Light Technology, Inc.; OCLC Online Computer Library Center, Inc.; ProQuest Information & Learning; H.W. Wilson. *Indexed:* A&ATA, ABIn, B&I, BPI, C&ISA, CEA, ChemAb, EngInd, EnvAb, ExcerpMed. *Aud.:* Sa.

Weekly news source for chemical manufacturers and related industries including pharmaceuticals and plastics. A cover story running 2—3 pages accompanies brief business and finance news articles organized by region–United States/Americas, Europe/Mideast, Asia/Pacific. Other sections cover construction projects, mergers and acquisitions, information technology, speciality chemical production, environmental issues, laws and regulations, company and market profiles, management trends, and newsmakers in the industry. Most online content at www.chemweek.com is restricted to current subscribers only.

1410. ***Coal Age.*** Formerly (until 1996): *Coal;* Which was formed by the merger of (1911-1988): *Coal Age;* (1984-1988): *Coal Mining;* Which was formerly (1964-1984): *Coal Mining and Processing.* [ISSN: 1091-0646] 1988. m. Free to qualified personnel. Ed(s): Steve Fiscor. Primedia Business Magazines & Media, Inc., 29 N Wacker Dr, Chicago, IL 60606; inquiries@primediabusiness.com; http://www.primediabusiness.com. Illus., index, adv. Circ: 19038 Paid and free. *Indexed:* AS&TI, BPI, ChemAb, EngInd, EnvAb, ExcerpMed, GeoRef, LRI. *Aud.:* Sa.

Reports on technology and development of mining and processing in the coal industry. Two or three brief articles each week feature production operations, maintenance, and transportation issues of U.S. companies. Other departments include people, worldwide company news, marketwatch, regulatory matters, new media, classified ads, and association and conference news. Of interest to libraries that are located in mining regions or that collect in areas of energy production and industrial trends.

Constructor. See Building and Construction section.

1411. ***Customer Interaction Solutions.*** Incorporates (199?-2002): *Communications Solutions;* Which was formerly (until 2000): *C T I;* Former titles (until 2000): *C@ll Center C R M Solutions;* (until 1999): *Call Center Solutions;* (until 1996): *Telemarketing.* [ISSN: 1533-3078] 1982. m. USD 49 domestic; USD 69 Canada; USD 85 elsewhere. Ed(s): Linda Driscoll. Technology Marketing Corporation, One Technology Plaza, Norwalk, CT 06854; tmc@tmcnet.com. Adv. Online: Florida Center for Library Automation; Gale Group; OCLC Online Computer Library Center, Inc.; ProQuest Information & Learning. *Indexed:* ABIn, BPI. *Aud.:* Ac, Sa.

This is the primary trade title for call center (also known as contact center) management. With the advent of e-commerce, customer relationship management (CRM) has evolved into a sophisticated industry and is changing the face of direct marketing. Articles cover topics including call center design, products and technologies, best practices, and outsourcing. An annual buyers' guide is published in December. Deep archives and some exclusive web content are available at www.tmcnet.com/cis.

1412. ***D S N Retailing Today.*** Formerly: *Discount Store News.* [ISSN: 1530-6259] 1962. fortn. 23/yr. USD 119 domestic; USD 125 Canada; USD 195 elsewhere. Lebhar-Friedman, Inc., 425 Park Ave, New York, NY 10022; http://www.dsnretailingtoday.com. Illus., adv. Circ: 32805. Microform: CIS; PQC. Online: The Dialog Corporation; EBSCO Publishing; Florida Center for Library Automation; Gale Group; LexisNexis; Northern Light Technology, Inc.; OCLC Online Computer Library Center, Inc.; ProQuest Information & Learning. Reprint: PQC. *Indexed:* ABIn, B&I, PAIS. *Aud.:* Sa.

Targeted toward managers of all mass retail segments including full-line discount department stores, catalog showrooms, specialty chains, off-price retailers, mid-tier department stores, membership warehouse clubs, and super centers. Articles report on apparel, home products, soft and hard lines, hot ticket items, new product developments, licensing agreements, merchandising and store plans, operations, market share, and industry trends in general. Regular departments provide classified advertising, columns from the perspective of buyer and seller, reports on regulatory and market news and newsmakers. Special reports focus on the activities of specific companies and strategic business groups. The web site provides deep, full-text archives as well as complementary content.

1413. ***Dealerscope: product & strategy for consumer technology retailing.*** Former titles (until Mar. 2000): *Dealerscope Consumer Electronics Marketplace;* (until Oct. 1995): *Dealerscope Merchandising;* Which was formed by the merger of (1958-1986): *Dealerscope;* (1964-1986): *Merchandising;* Which was formerly (until 1976): *Merchandising Week; Electrical Merchandising Week.* [ISSN: 1534-4711] 1986. m. USD 79 domestic (Free to qualified personnel). Ed(s): Janet Pinkerton. North American Publishing Company, 401 N Broad St, 5th Fl, Philadelphia, PA 19108-1074; http://www.dealerscope.com. Illus., index, adv. Sample. Circ: 21161 Controlled. Vol. ends: Nov. Online: The Dialog Corporation; Gale Group. *Indexed:* ABIn, BPI. *Aud.:* Ga, Sa.

In the past, this title featured primarily new product announcements in the fields of consumer electronics, major appliances, and computing products; it was light on business solutions and management advice. A new mission is "to inform readers how to more profitably market and sell consumer electronics, as well as assist manufacturers and distributors in communicating best practice strategies to retail." It should continue to be of interest to general readers who like to keep up with the latest electronic gadgets and innovations. Retail professionals should find the enhanced content more relevant than ever. Current issue features, article archives, and web exclusives are available at www.dealerscope.com.

1414. ***Electronic Business: the management magazine for the electronics industry.*** Former titles (until 1997): *Electronic Business Today;* (until 1995): *Electronic Business Buyer;* (until Sep. 1993): *Electronic Business;* (until 1975): *Electronic Purchasing; Electro-Procurement.* [ISSN: 1097-4881] 1961. m. USD 100.99 domestic (Free to qualified personnel). Ed(s): Adrian Mello. Reed Business Information, 1101 S Winchester Blvd, Bldg N, San Jose, CA 95128-3901; http://www.reedbusiness.com. Illus., index, adv. Circ: 52000 Controlled. Microform: CIS. Online: The Dialog Corporation; EBSCO Publishing; Florida Center for Library Automation; Gale Group; OCLC Online Computer Library Center, Inc.; ProQuest Information & Learning; H.W. Wilson. *Indexed:* ABIn, BPI. *Bk. rev.:* Occasional. *Aud.:* Ac, Sa.

This magazine serves the information needs of senior managers employed in the multifaceted electronics industry, which spans components, computers, peripherals, and communications equipment. Each issue provides an in-depth cover story and four feature articles in addition to the regular departments. Topics covered include product development, trends, the Internet, the economy, regulation, distribution, human resources issues, and individual company profiles. Current issue content is available at the web site; access to archives requires free registration.

Electronic News. See Electronics section.

ENR. See Engineering and Technology/Civil Engineering section.

Farm Journal. See Agriculture section.

Fleet Owner. See Transportation section.

Food Processing. See Food Industry section.

1415. ***Footwear News.*** [ISSN: 0162-914X] 1945. w. USD 72 domestic; USD 59 domestic to retailers; USD 145 in Canada & Mexico. Ed(s): Stephen Dowdell. Fairchild Publications, Inc., 7 W 34th St, New York, NY 10001-8191; customerservice@fairchildpub.com; http://www.fairchildpub.com. Illus., adv. Circ: 14256. Microform: FCM. Online: The Dialog Corporation; Factiva; Florida Center for Library Automation; Gale Group; LexisNexis; Northern Light Technology, Inc.; OCLC Online Computer Library Center, Inc. *Indexed:* B&I. *Aud.:* Ga, Sa.

The readership of this weekly includes designers, retailers, manufacturers, importers, wholesalers, suppliers, tanners, finishers, and members of related fields. It offers extensive coverage of trends in women's, men's, and children's footwear across the dress, casual, and athletic categories. A typical issue is more visual than textual in content; articles tend to be brief profiles of designer lines and manufacturers. The web site at www.footwearnews.com does not provide much complementary information and lacks the graphic punch of its print counterpart. Of most interest to libraries collecting in fashion design.

1416. ***Global Cosmetic Industry.*** Former titles (until 1999): *D C I;* (until May 1997): *Drug and Cosmetic Industry;* Which incorporated (1931-1997): *Drug and Cosmetic Catalog.* [ISSN: 1523-9470] 1914. 13x/yr. USD 43 United States & Possessions; USD 59 in Canada & Mexico; USD 99 elsewhere. Allured Publishing, 362 S Schmale Rd, Carol Stream, IL 60188-2787; allured@allured.com; http://www.allured.com. Illus., index, adv. Circ: 14145. Vol. ends: Dec. Microform: PMC; PQC. Online: bigchalk; The Dialog Corporation; EBSCO Publishing; Factiva; Florida Center for Library Automation; Gale Group; Northern Light Technology, Inc.; OCLC Online Computer Library Center, Inc.; ProQuest Information & Learning; H.W. Wilson. *Indexed:* ABIn, B&I, BPI, BiolAb, ChemAb, H&SSA. *Aud.:* Ga, Ac, Sa.

This publication primarily intended for personal care products professionals is a showcase of R&D, market trends, and marketing efforts. Features are short in length and mix the practical (product application) with the technical (formulas and ingredient analysis). Of interest to academic collections supporting marketing programs and to special libraries supporting personal care product manufacturers, marketers, and retailers. Of interest somewhat to public libraries because of the practical information imparted to consumers, e.g., new product previews and general fashion forecasts. Web site available at www.globalcosmetic.com.

1417. ***H F N: the newsweekly of home products retailing.*** Former titles (until 1994): *H F D - Home Furnishing Daily; H F D - Retailing Home Furnishings;* (until 1976): *Home Furnishings Daily.* [ISSN: 1082-0310] 1929. w. USD 295 USD 99 domestic. Ed(s): Warren Schoulberg. Fairchild Publications, Inc., 7 W 34th St, New York, NY 10001-8191;

customerservice@fairchildpub.com; http://www.fairchildpub.com. Illus., index, adv. Sample. Circ: 30245 Controlled. Microform: FCM. Online: The Dialog Corporation; Florida Center for Library Automation; Gale Group; LexisNexis; OCLC Online Computer Library Center, Inc. *Indexed:* B&I. *Aud.:* Sa.

This is the industry news source for suppliers, manufacturers, wholesalers, and retailers of the interior design and retail market that specialize in home furnishing products, which includes furniture, major appliances, housewares, bedding, floor coverings, lighting and decorative accessories, giftware, and do-it-yourself decorating. Content covers new materials, products and processes, industry news and newsmakers, market conditions, and general industry trends. Online content at www.hfnmag.com is limited to article summaries from the current issue only, but daily news briefs, job postings, and a trade show calendar will nicely complement a paid print subscription.

Hotel and Motel Management. See Hospitality/Restaurant section.

1418. ***Household & Personal Products Industry: the magazine for the detergent, soap, cosmetic and toiletry, wax, polish and aerosol industries.*** Formerly: *Detergents and Specialties.* [ISSN: 0090-8878] 1964. m. USD 48; USD 52 in Canada & Mexico; USD 64 elsewhere. Ed(s): Hamilton Carson. Rodman Publications, Inc., 70 Hilltop Rd, Ramsey, NJ 07446. Illus., adv. Circ: 17000. *Indexed:* B&I, ChemAb, ExcerpMed. *Aud.:* Sa.

Covering soaps, detergents, cosmetics and toiletries, fragrances, waxes and polishes, insecticides, aerosols, and related chemical specialties, *HAPPI* is published monthly throughout the year for people involved in the personal care, household, industrial, and institutional fields. Four to six features join regular columns and departments including patent reviews, regulations, marketing, and packaging. Selected text from the current issue is available at www.happi.com along with web-only content.

Industry Week. See under General, this section.

Logistics Management. See Transportation section.

1419. ***Meetings and Conventions: the meeting & incentive planner's resource.*** Incorporates: *Incentive World.* [ISSN: 0025-8652] 1969. 12x/yr. USD 82.90 domestic; USD 113.25 Canada; USD 113.90 Mexico. Ed(s): Lori Cioffi. Northstar Travel Media LLC, 500 Plaza Dr, Secaucus, NJ 07094; http://www.ntmllc.com. Illus., adv. Sample. Circ: 76000. Vol. ends: Dec. Online: EBSCO Publishing; Florida Center for Library Automation; Gale Group; OCLC Online Computer Library Center, Inc. *Indexed:* ABIn, LR&TI. *Bk. rev.:* Various number and length. *Aud.:* Sp.

Meeting and convention planning has become an increasingly more visible and more competitive industry. Four or five feature articles cover a wide range of topics including economic outlook, best paractices in marketing and management, and career guidance for planners. Several departments report on industry events, newsmakers, travel advice, and legal issues. Every issue includes extensive destination guides.

1420. ***Modern Plastics.*** [ISSN: 0026-8275] 1925. m. USD 65 domestic; USD 110 in Canada & Mexico; USD 245 elsewhere. Canon Communications LLC, 11444 W Olympic Blvd, Ste 900, Los Angeles, CA 90064-1549; feedback@cancom.com; http://www.cancom.com. Illus., index, adv. Circ: 75782 Paid. Vol. ends: Dec. Microform: PQC. Online: Dow Jones Interactive; Factiva; Florida Center for Library Automation; Gale Group; NewsNet; Northern Light Technology, Inc.; OCLC Online Computer Library Center, Inc.; ProQuest Information & Learning. *Indexed:* A&ATA, ABIn, AS&TI, B&I, C&ISA, ChemAb, EngInd, SSCI. *Aud.:* Sa.

Covering all aspects of the plastics industry, each issue reports on international news, research and development, product innovations, manufacturing equipment and processes, marketing, distribution, industry trends, and conferences and trade shows. An annual buying guide is filled with company contacts, industry information, and specifications. A portal to industry information can be found at www.modplas.com along with magazine archives. For corporate libraries; also recommended for academic libraries supporting programs in chemistry and engineering.

1421. ***Packaging Digest.*** Incorporates (1983-1994): *Packaging;* Which was formerly: *Package Engineering Including Modern Packaging;* Which was formed by the merger of (1927-1979): *Modern Packaging;* (1956-1979): *Package Engineering;* Which incorporated (in 1974): *Package Engineering New Products;* Which superseded (1972-1973): *Package Engineering New Products News.* [ISSN: 0030-9117] 1963. 13x/yr. USD 119.90 domestic; USD 160.90 Canada; USD 148.50 Mexico. Ed(s): Mary Ann Falkman. Reed Business Information, 2000 Clearwater Dr, Oak Brook, IL 60523; http://www.reedbusiness.com. Illus., adv. Sample. Circ: 106600. Vol. ends: Dec. Microform: PQC. Online: Gale Group; Northern Light Technology, Inc. Reprint: PQC. *Indexed:* ABIn, AS&TI, B&I, BPI, EngInd, LRI. *Aud.:* Ga, Ac, Sa.

Aimed at managers, marketers, and manufacturers in the packaging industry, this monthly tabloid covers trends and news extensively. Ten to twelve articles feature company and product information, new technologies, environmental concerns, fusion of art and design with new materials and manufacturing methods, effective packaging ideas, retail display, and related information. Advertising, news, legislation and regulation, and new product announcements are well represented in regular departments, as well as specific examples and illustrations of packaging ideas. Articles, news updates, and industry links are available online at www.packagingdigest.com. An important source for marketing and advertising trends; recommended for all libraries.

1422. ***Platt's Energy Business and Technology.*** Formed by the merger of (1999-2002): *Global Energy Business;* (1995-2002): *Energy I T;* Which was formerly (until 2000): *Utilities I T;* (until 199?): *Information Technologies for Utilities.* [ISSN: 1540-367X] 2002. bi-m. Ed(s): Jon Arnold. Platts, 2 Penn Plaza, 25th Fl, New York, NY 10121-2298; http://www.platts.com/. Adv. Circ: 37000. *Aud.:* Ga, Ac, Sa.

This title's primary audience is executives in the energy production and delivery industries. Emphasis is placed on the role of information technology in worldwide energy markets. A wider audience will also appreciate its coverage of trends and developments in matters of regulation, mergers and acquisitions, finance and investment, and strategic management that affect energy companies. Selected articles are available through the online archives at www.platts.com/businesstech.

1423. ***Progressive Grocer (New York, 2002).*** Formed by the merger of (1946-2001): *Supermarket Business;* (1922-2001): *Progressive Grocer (New York, 1922).* 2002. 18x/yr. USD 129 domestic (Free to qualified personnel). V N U Business Publications, 770 Broadway, New York, NY 10003; bmcomm@vnuinc.com; http://www.vnubusinessmedia.com/. Illus., adv. Circ: 50365. *Indexed:* ABIn, B&I, BPI. *Aud.:* Ga,Ac, Sa.

Intended for the supermarket manager, this title covers such topics as personnel and labor issues, security, customer service, new products, store design, and market conditions in general. Retailers, both foreign and domestic, utilizing unique approaches to management are spotlighted in a "Store of the Month" feature. Articles are categorized as grocery, fresh food, or nonfoods business. Regular departments address consumer preferences, in-store promotions, technology, equipment, distribution, and issues unique to independent stores. Of interest to academic libraries supporting marketing and management programs and to public libraries because of the general appeal of food.

1424. ***Recycling Today.*** Formerly: *Recycling Today (Scrap Market Edition);* Which superseded in part (in May 1990): *Recycling Today;* Which was formerly: *Secondary Raw Materials.* [ISSN: 1096-6323] 1963. m. USD 30 domestic; USD 47 Canada; USD 105 elsewhere. Ed(s): Brian Taylor. G.I.E., Inc. Publishers, 4012 Bridge Ave, Cleveland, OH 44113-3320; http://www.recyclingtoday.com/. Illus., adv. Online: Florida Center for Library Automation; Gale Group; OCLC Online Computer Library Center, Inc. *Indexed:* AS&TI, C&ISA, EngInd, EnvAb, ExcerpMed. *Aud.:* Ga, Ac, Sa.

This title addresses social, political, and environmental issues impacting and impacted by recycling efforts from both a local and global perspective. Articles monitor trends in waste management technologies and processes, environmental regulations, and volatility of recycled commodity prices. Each issue provides updates on the status of the nonmetallic, ferrous, nonferrous, and construction/demolition debris sectors.

Restaurant Business. See Hospitality/Restaurant section.

1425. *Retail Merchandiser.* Formerly (until May 2000): *Discount Merchandiser.* [ISSN: 1530-8154] 1961. m. USD 99 domestic; USD 109 Canada; USD 171 elsewhere. V N U Business Publications, 770 Broadway, New York, NY 10003; bmcomm@vnuinc.com; http://www.vnubusinessmedia.com/. Illus., adv. Circ: 34188 Controlled. Vol. ends: Dec. Microform: PQC. Online: EBSCO Publishing; Factiva; Florida Center for Library Automation; Gale Group; Northern Light Technology, Inc.; OCLC Online Computer Library Center, Inc.; ProQuest Information & Learning; H.W. Wilson. Reprint: PQC. *Indexed:* ABIn, BPI, PAIS. *Aud.:* Sa.

All aspects of merchandising are covered in this publication, including manufacturing, distribution, marketing, advertising, and sales. Articles discuss products, famous brands and private labels, security, technology enhancements, staffing, and related issues. The news and newsmakers of the industry and its competition are spotlighted. The convention issue includes over 20 pages of editorial commentary on the current and future state of mass retailing. The web site is www.retail-merchandiser.com.

1426. *Retail Traffic.* Formerly (until May 2003): *Shopping Center World;* Incorporates (1975-1991): *Shopping Center World Product and Service Directory.* [ISSN: 1544-4236] 1972. m. USD 74 domestic; USD 134 foreign. Ed(s): Brannon Boswell. Primedia Business Magazines & Media, Inc. (Atlanta), 6151 Powers Ferry Rd, N W, Atlanta, GA 30339-2941; inquiries@primediabusiness.com; http://www.primediabusiness.com/. Illus., adv. Circ: 36553. Microform: PQC. Online: bigchalk; EBSCO Publishing; Factiva; Gale Group; LexisNexis; Northern Light Technology, Inc.; OCLC Online Computer Library Center, Inc.; ProQuest Information & Learning; H.W. Wilson. Reprint: PQC. *Indexed:* B&I, BPI. *Aud.:* Sa.

Formerly *Shopping Center World*, this trade title continues to cater to retail real estate executives, shopping center developers, owners and managers, retail chain store executives, construction personnel, marketing professionals, leasing agents, brokers, architects, and designers. Articles report on successful shopping center properties, projects proposed and underway, specific design elements and materials, financing, and retail store profiles. Regular departments include Shows and Events, Retail Design Trends, Lease Language, International News, and Sales Figures of Major Retailers. The web site is www.retailtrafficmag.com.

1427. *Rock Products: the aggregate industry's journal of applied technology.* [ISSN: 0747-3605] 1897. m. USD 56 in US & Canada; USD 77 foreign. Ed(s): Rick Markley. Primedia Business Magazines & Media, Inc., 9800 Metcalf Ave., Overland Park, KS 66212; inquiries@primediabusiness.com; http://www.primediabusiness.com. Illus., adv. Circ: 22860 Controlled. Vol. ends: Dec. Microform: PQC. Online: bigchalk; Northern Light Technology, Inc.; ProQuest Information & Learning. Reprint: PQC. *Indexed:* AS&TI, ChemAb, EngInd, ExcerpMed, GeoRef. *Aud.:* Sa.

This trade magazine is devoted to the quarried stone, sand, gypsum, lightweight aggregate, and earthmoving industries. Regular features include a handful of articles on manufacturing technologies, processes, business practices and labor, and regulatory and safety issues. Additional trade-specific departments include industry news, environmental issues, a Washington letter, new products, and a calendar of events. Occasional supplements focusing on niche industries, e.g., *Cement America*, and the annual buyers' guide and dealer directory, make this an important title for the aggregate industry. Libraries serving communities with these trades may wish to subscribe.

1428. *Rubber World.* [ISSN: 0035-9572] 1889. 16x/yr. USD 34 domestic; USD 39 Canada; USD 89 elsewhere. Ed(s): Don R Smith. Lippincott & Peto, Inc., 1867 W Market St, Akron, OH 44313; http://www.rubberworld.com/rwol/rwol.htm. Illus., adv. Circ: 11400 Controlled. Vol. ends: Dec. Microform: PMC; PQC. Online: bigchalk; EBSCO Publishing; Factiva; Florida Center for Library Automation; Gale Group; Northern Light Technology, Inc. Reprint: PQC. *Indexed:* C&ISA, ChemAb, EngInd, RRTA, WAE&RSA. *Aud.:* Sa.

This monthly trade publication offers timely updates aimed at rubber industry managers. Regular departments include Business Briefs, Patent News, Market Focus, Tech Service, Process Machinery, Supplies Showcase, Meetings, and Calendar of Events. A handful of feature articles present new technology to improve factory processes. The subscription includes additional quarterly issues devoted to special topics. Current news, industry links, and magazine archives can be found at www.rubberworld.com. Libraries that support industrial marketing research, chemistry, and engineering may find this useful.

Sea Technology. See Marine Science and Technology section.

Snack Food & Wholesale Bakery. See Food Industry section.

1429. *Special Events Magazine.* Formerly: *Special Events.* [ISSN: 1079-1264] 1982. m. USD 48 domestic; USD 59 Canada; USD 110 elsewhere. Ed(s): Lisa Hurley. Primedia Business Magazines & Media, Inc., 9800 Metcalf Ave., Overland Park, KS 66212; inquiries@primediabusiness.com; http://www.primediabusiness.com. Adv. Circ: 24109 Controlled. Online: EBSCO Publishing; Factiva; Florida Center for Library Automation; Gale Group; OCLC Online Computer Library Center, Inc.; H.W. Wilson. *Aud.:* Ga, Sa.

The mission of this trade title is to serve as a resource for event professionals who design and produce social, corporate, and public events in hotels, resorts, banquet facilities, and other venues. Coverage of galas is extensive; photos are a feast for the eyes. Departments provide practical advice on event management and tout new products and innovative ideas. The publication has a cooperative alliance with the International Special Events Society. In each issue, five pages are reserved for news and promotion of the society's web site. Exclusive features and contents of the current issue are available at www.specialevents.com.

1430. *Stores.* [ISSN: 0039-1867] 1912. m. USD 120 (Free to qualified personnel). Ed(s): Timothy P Henderson, Mary Alice Elmer. N R F Enterprises, Inc., 325 7th St, N W, Ste 1000, Washington, DC 20004-2802; http://www.stores.com/. Illus., adv. Circ: 33577. Vol. ends: Dec. Online: Gale Group. *Indexed:* ABIn, B&I, BPI, PAIS. *Aud.:* Ac, Sa.

This title features corporate and industry news for all kinds of retail chain stores and wholesale clubs, restaurants, drug stores, and direct mail and marketing firms engaged in specialty and general merchandising. The focus is on technology, management, and operations. Special issues include ranked lists of department stores in July and specialty chains in August, both including sales and earnings figures. Current issue contents, archives, and rankings are available at www.stores.org. Appropriate for larger public libraries and for academic libraries that support business programs.

1431. *Street & Smith's SportsBusiness Journal.* [ISSN: 1098-5972] 1998. w. USD 199. Ed(s): Barry Lovette. American City Business Journals, Street & Smith, 120 W Morehead St, Ste 310, Charlotte, NC 28202; info.sportsbiz@amcity.com; http://www.sportsbusinessjournal.com. Illus., adv. *Aud.:* Ac, Sa.

In addition to numerous small articles on events, individual athletes, advertising campaigns, and coast-to-coast news blurbs, each issue contains "Pro Sports Tracker" showing stadium attendance to date and a "Sports Profile" highlighting an individual city's sports-related demographics. Of interest to academic libraries supporting marketing programs; special libraries supporting advertising agencies, marketing firms, teams, and sport associations will want to subscribe, too.

1432. ***Telephony: intelligence for the broadband economy.*** Incorporates (in 2001): *Upstart.* [ISSN: 0040-2656] 1901. bi-w. Free. Primedia Business Magazines & Media, Inc., 9800 Metcalf Ave., Overland Park, KS 66212; inquiries@primediabusiness.com; http://www.primediabusiness.com. Illus., index, adv. Circ: 65000 Controlled. Microform: PQC. Online: bigchalk; EBSCO Publishing; Factiva; Florida Center for Library Automation; Gale Group; LexisNexis; OCLC Online Computer Library Center, Inc.; ProQuest Information & Learning; H.W. Wilson. *Indexed:* ABIn, BPI, LRI. *Bk. rev.:* Various number and length. *Aud.:* Ga, Ac, Sa.

This title covers all aspects of the rapidly evolving broadband industry that includes telecommunications, wireless and PCS technologies, cable, DSL, and optics. Each issue contains current news that impacts businesses, alliances, product development, policies, regulations, and perspectives. Given the importance of the digital economy and the technology behind it all, this magazine will be of interest to most libraries.

1433. ***Textile World.*** Former titles (until 1931): *Textile Advance News;* (until 1924): *Textiles;* (until 1923): *Posselt's Textile Journal;* (until 1915): *Textile World Journal.* [ISSN: 0040-5213] 1868. m. Billian Publishing, Inc., 2100 Powers Ferry Rd, Ste 300, Atlanta, GA 30339; http://www.billian.com/. Illus., adv. Circ: 32340 Paid and controlled. Vol. ends: Dec. Microform: PMC; PQC. Online: bigchalk; EBSCO Publishing; Factiva; Florida Center for Library Automation; Gale Group; LexisNexis; OCLC Online Computer Library Center, Inc.; ProQuest Information & Learning; H.W. Wilson. *Indexed:* ABIn, AS&TI, B&I, BPI, ChemAb, EngInd, ExcerpMed. *Aud.:* Sa.

Included in this title are reports on technologies such as yarn manufacturing, fabric forming, chemical treatment and finishing, industrial and specialty textiles, carpet manufacturing and marketing, manufacturing systems, and management issues on an international basis. Articles and advertisements introduce suppliers, new products and techniques, and industry trends. Departments provide industry news and statistics, legal and legislative news, profiles of companies and executives, and occasional special reports.

1434. ***Vending Times: vending - feeding - coffee service - music & games.*** Incorporates (in 1974): *Vend; V-T Music and Games.* [ISSN: 0042-3327] 1961. m. USD 35. Ed(s): Timothy Sanford. Vending Times, Inc., 1375 Broadway, 6th Fl, New York, NY 10018-7001; http://www.vendingtimes.com. Illus., adv. Circ: 16500. Microform: PQC. Online: Gale Group. *Indexed:* BPI. *Aud.:* Sa.

There are few areas of the public landscape where vending in some form is not evident: commercial and industrial establishments, hospitals, schools, airports and other transportation hubs, hotels and motels, restaurants and bars, and family entertainment centers. Readership is broad-based and can include independent and national-chain vending and manual foodservice operators, mobile caterers, office refreshment service operators, music and amusement operators, and bulk vending operators, as well as manufacturers, suppliers, distributors, and brokers of equipment, products, and support services to the industry. Each monthly issue includes sections presenting news, market trends, product innovations, interviews, and coverage of industry events. Selected content is also available online at the web site.

1435. ***W W D: the retailer's daily newspaper.*** Formerly (until 197?): *Women's Wear Daily.* [ISSN: 0149-5380] 1892. d.(Mon.-Fri.). USD 195 domestic; USD 99 domestic to retailers; USD 135 domestic to manufacturers. Fairchild Publications, Inc., 7 W 34th St, New York, NY 10001-8191; customerservice@fairchildpub.com; http://www.fairchildpub.com. Illus., adv. Circ: 55000. Microform: FCM; NRP. Online: The Dialog Corporation; Florida Center for Library Automation; Gale Group; OCLC Online Computer Library Center, Inc. *Indexed:* B&I, LRI. *Aud.:* Ac, Sa.

This newspaper format provides extensive coverage of the women's apparel and couture fashion industries. Each weekday issue focuses on a rotating theme of accessories, ready-to-wear, sportswear, or beauty, with commentary on the season's colors, styles, and fabrics. Designers are profiled, and their shows are lavishly photographed. There is extensive reporting on the social scene that is intrinsic to the concept of "image." Manufacturing and distribution problems, marketing and distribution channels, and retail issues are discussed in brief.

1436. ***Wines and Vines: the authoritative voice of the grape and wine industry.*** [ISSN: 0043-583X] 1919. m. s-m. Dec. USD 32.50 domestic; USD 39 in Canada & Mexico; USD 50 elsewhere. Ed(s): Philip E Hiaring. Hiaring Co., 1800 Lincoln Ave, San Rafael, CA 94901-1298. Illus., adv. Circ: 3500. *Indexed:* ChemAb. *Bk. rev.:* Various number and length. *Aud.:* Ga, Ac, Sa.

Although aimed at wine producers, this monthly publication will be enjoyed by anyone interested in the business aspects of the wine industry. Focusing on a different theme each month, *W&V* features valuable, scientific winemaking articles and covers marketing, management and import/export issues, and all aspects of wine production. It also covers trends and varietals produced outside the United States. Regular departments are devoted to practical advice for business owners—"Commonsense Winemaking," "Financial Health"—and include newsmakers, political, legal, and regulatory developments. See www.winesandvines.com for a table of contents and links to other important industry sources.

1437. ***Wood & Wood Products: furniture, cabinets, woodworking and allied products management and operations.*** [ISSN: 0043-7662] 1896. 13x/yr. USD 55. Ed(s): Richard Christianson. Vance Publishing Corporation (Lincolnshire), 400 Knightsbridge Pkwy, Lincolnshire, IL 60069. Illus., adv. Circ: 52500 Controlled. Microform: PQC. Online: EBSCO Publishing; Florida Center for Library Automation; Gale Group; Northern Light Technology, Inc.; OCLC Online Computer Library Center, Inc.; H.W. Wilson. *Indexed:* AS&TI, EngInd, ExcerpMed, FPA, ForAb. *Aud.:* Sa.

Focusing on the manufacture of wood products and woodworking companies, this trade title offers a half-dozen features on technology, tools, and processes in the manufacture of residential and commercial furniture. Regular departments provide timely information on trends, news, management matters, furniture design, digital woodworking, product news, new literature, and coming events, plus featuring a different professional association each month. Industry news, links, and selected articles can be found at www.iswonline.com/index-wwp.html.

■ CANADA

Alexander Jerabek and Sharon Rankin, McGill University Libraries, 3459 McTavish St., Montreal, PQ, Canada H3A 1Y1; alexander.jerabek@mcgill.ca, sharon.rankin@mcgill.ca

Introduction

The Canadian section is composed of a selection of magazines published in Canada containing articles about Canada and Canadians. The listing is a sample of the best, most representative magazines from all Canadian provinces. Magazines and journals were selected based on their overall quality and appearance, their availability in Canadian libraries, and countrywide circulation figures. Titles with general content describing the cultural, regional, and political diversity of the country were selected. The list also includes a selection of academic titles that contain the best research and scholarly articles about Canada and Canadian life. Canadian publications of a specialized consumer or academic nature are found in the subject listings elsewhere in this book. The editors have excluded split-run publications for the entries, e.g., foreign magazines containing some Canadian content and advertising, for example, *Time, Reader's Digest* and *Sports Illustrated.*

The Canadian magazine and journal publishing industry has historically received financial assistance from the Canadian federal government's Department of Canadian Heritage. The Canadian Magazine Fund provides editorial content support and the Publications Assistance Program provides mailing and distribution support. Many of the magazines selected also receive financial support from the Canada Council for the Arts and arts councils in their province of publication. Two associations represent magazine publishers, the Canadian Magazine Publishers Association (CMPA), a membership lobby group for the industry, and Magazine Canada, a nonprofit marketing board. The leaders of both these groups are committed to merging the associations to create a stronger, single voice for the industry. Readers who would like to follow the developments in the Canadian magazine industry are referred to *Masthead Online* (www.masthead.online), the news source for Canadian magazine publishing. There is a marketing campaign by the CMPA to promote Canadian magazines, to increase readership of lesser-known smaller magazines, and to identify Canadian titles at newsstands. A number of public relations events and reading series have been scheduled across the country to create awareness of the variety and quality of Canadian journalism.

The majority of the magazines and journals selected in this section also have web sites with complementary content summaries, interactive features, directories, and subscription and online renewal information. Hard copy is still the primary publishing medium for Canadian magazines.

Basic Periodicals

Hs, Ga, Ac: *Canadian Business, Maclean's, Saturday Night.*

Basic Abstracts and Indexes

CPI.Q, Canadian Business & Current Affairs - Fulltext Reference.

1438. ***Acadiensis: journal of the history of the Atlantic region.*** [ISSN: 0044-5851] 1971. s-a. CND 37.45 (Individuals, CND 26.75; CND 9.95 newsstand/cover per issue). Ed(s): Rusty Bitterman. University of New Brunswick, Department of History, PO Box 4400, Fredericton, NB E3B 5A3, Canada; acadnsis@unb.ca. Illus., index, adv. Sample. Refereed. Circ: 850. Vol. ends: Spring (No. 2). Microform: MML. *Indexed:* AmH&L, ArtHuCI, CBCARef, CPerI, IBSS, IBZ, SSCI. *Bk. rev.:* 2-4, 12-24 pages. *Aud.:* Ga, Ac.

Acadiensis is a bilingual, biannual journal devoted to Eastern Canadian history and regional studies. The journal publishes original research articles by scholars in the fields of history, geography, political science, folklore, literature, sociology, economics, and other areas. Each issue includes reviews and review essays of publications in Canadian Studies. Discussions by scholars are presented in an occasional Forum section. An authoritative bibliography compiled by librarians is also included. Articles range in scope from "Music, Song and Dance in Cape Breton" to "The British Military's Building of Wellington Barracks and Brick Construction in 19th-Century Halifax." *Acadiensis*'s focus on specialized and neglected areas of study makes it an appropriate choice for special and academic libraries.

1439. ***L'Actualite.*** [ISSN: 0383-8714] 1961. 20x/yr. CND 36.75 domestic; CND 49 United States; CND 112 overseas. Ed(s): Carole Beaulieu. Rogers Media Publishing Ltd, 1001 boul de Maisonneuve Ouest, Rm 1100, Montreal, PQ H3A 3E1, Canada; http://www.rogers.com. Illus., adv. Circ: 240000. Microform: MML. *Indexed:* CPerI. *Bk. rev.:* 1, 1-2 pages, signed. *Aud.:* Hs, Ga, Ac.

L?Actualite is the most popular French-language news magazine in Canada, with a subscription base of over 240,000. It focuses on events and issues in the province of Quebec and also includes stories of significant international interest. Each 100-page issue has regular columns, synopses of world events, opinion essays, health and personal finance items, and a calendar of events for the province. The magazine frequently uses a Q&A format for in-depth feature interviews with politicians and media personalities. A section titled "L?entretien" interviews an expert on an issue of international political concern. Every two months, the Royal Canadian Geographical Society publishes an insert called "Geographica," a colorful description with maps of a particular Canadian region or city. The January issue of *L?Actualite* spotlights Quebec personalities of the year and winners of an amateur geographical photography contest. Recommended for libraries wishing to offer information about French-Canadian culture, and suitable for French-language readers in high school and public libraries.

1440. ***Alberta History.*** Formerly (until 1975): *Alberta Historical Review.* [ISSN: 0316-1552] 1953. q. Non-members, CND 30. Ed(s): Hugh A Dempsey. Historical Society of Alberta, 95 Holmwood Ave, N W, Calgary, AB T2K 2G7, Canada. Illus., index. Sample. Refereed. Circ: 1200 Paid. Vol. ends: No. 4. Microform: PQC. *Indexed:* AmH&L, BHA, CBCARef, CPerI. *Bk. rev.:* 15-20, 1-2 pages. *Aud.:* Ga, Ac.

Alberta History, originally known as the *Alberta Historical Review*, is a quarterly magazine published by the Historical Society of Alberta with assistance from the Alberta Historical Resources Foundation. Primary source material by pioneers and settlers is presented along with scholarly articles about historical figures and events. Although the focus is on Albertan history, the occasionally paper will address current concerns and issues. Social aspects of early settlement, reflections on settlers' accounts and writings, and original research make this journal a valuable addition to large public libraries and to academic libraries with strong collections specializing in North American history.

1441. ***Arctic.*** [ISSN: 0004-0843] 1947. q. CND 120; USD 120. Ed(s): Karen M McCullough. Arctic Institute of North America, University of Calgary, MLT 11th Fl, 2500 University Dr N W, Calgary, AB T2N 1N4, Canada; kmccullo@acs.ucalgary.ca; http://www.ucalgary.ca/aina/. Illus., index. Sample. Refereed. Circ: 2000. Vol. ends: Dec (No. 4). Microform: PQC. Online: Florida Center for Library Automation; Gale Group; LexisNexis; Micromedia ProQuest. Reprint: PQC. *Indexed:* ABS&EES, AbAn, AnthLit, ApEcolAb, BHA, BiolAb, CBCARef, CPerI, ChemAb, DSA, DSR&OA, EnvAb, ExcerpMed, FPA, ForAb, GeoRef, GeogAbPG, IndVet, M&GPA, OceAb, PetrolAb, PollutAb, RRTA, S&F, SCI, SSCI, SWRA, VetBull, WAE&RSA, ZooRec. *Bk. rev.:* 7-10, 1-3 pages. *Aud.:* Ac.

Arctic is a cross-disciplinary journal of original scholarship dealing with issues affecting the circumpolar world. Each issue includes "peer reviewed articles, reviews of new books on the North, profiles of significant people, places and Northern events, and topical commentaries." The subject scope covers anthropology, astronomy, biology, ecology, education, engineering, fine arts, humanities, medicine, and paleoethnology, resulting in the journal being widely indexed. While the scope of articles is broad and covers all aspects of arctic research, the articles themselves can be highly specialized and technical. Although most articles are clearly intended for specialists, for example, "Levels of cadmium, lead, mercury and 137caesium in caribou (Rangifer tarandus) tissues from Northern Quebec," some articles may be of more popular interest, such as an account of the creation of an exhibition about Rockwell Kent, "painter, printmaker, illustrator, and architect; a designer of books, ceramics, and textiles, and a prolific writer." Also included in each issue is a general-interest section titled "Info North" containing an essay of Northern interest, Northern news, and institute news. *Arctic* is supported in part by a grant from the Social Sciences and Humanities Research Council of Canada. It is suitable for large academic libraries and specialized collections.

1442. ***B C Studies: the British Columbian quarterly.*** [ISSN: 0005-2949] 1969. q. CND 50 (Individuals, CND 35). Ed(s): Jean Barman, Cole Harris. University of British Columbia, Buchanan E158, 1866 Main Mall, Vancouver, BC V6T 1Z1, Canada; http://www.interchange.ubc.ca/bcstudie. Illus., index, adv. Sample. Refereed. Circ: 1000. Vol. ends: Summer. Microform: MML; PQC. Online: bigchalk; EBSCO Publishing; ProQuest Information & Learning. Reprint: PSC. *Indexed:* AbAn, AmH&L, BHA, CBCARef, CPerI, IBSS. *Bk. rev.:* 4-20, 2-6 pages, signed. *Aud.:* Ga, Ac.

Since 1969, *BC Studies* has published interdisciplinary research dealing with British Columbia's cultural, economic, and political life, past and present. Each issue includes articles, review essays, book reviews, interviews, poetry, and a bibliography of recent publications. Articles cover a broad range and are of interest to a wide audience. Issues are occasionally thematic, covering topics such as "Perspectives on Aboriginal Culture" or "Scientific Expedition into BC Interior." A section titled "Digital Domain" provides links to selected Internet resources on subjects covered. The web site also provides a cumulative subject index and book review index. The journal's authoritative and informative content make it a suitable resource for academic and large public libraries.

1443. ***The Beaver: Canada's history magazine.*** [ISSN: 0005-7517] 1920. bi-m. CND 27.50 domestic; CND 31.50 United States; CND 33.50 elsewhere. Ed(s): Annalee Greenberg. Canada's National History Society, 167 Lombard Ave, 478, Winnipeg, MB R3B 0T6, Canada; cnhs@historysociety.ca. Illus., index, adv. Sample. Refereed. Circ:

49300. Vol. ends: Dec/Jan (No. 6). Microform: MML. Online: EBSCO Publishing; Gale Group; LexisNexis; Micromedia ProQuest. *Indexed:* AICP, AbAn, AmH&L, AnthLit, BRI, CBRI, CPerI, GeoRef, ICM, MagInd. *Bk. rev.:* 3-6, 1-3 pages. *Aud.:* Hs, Ga, Ac.

The Beaver is one of Canada's oldest history magazines. It contains articles on Canadian history, famous Canadians, and literary, art, and political history, as well as interviews with prominent Canadians. Features include "Currents" and "Explorations," columns devoted to current events related to history and Canada. Splendid illustrations and photographs accompany articulate and well-written pieces. Reviews of books, films, exhibits, and events are included. This highly readable and handsome journal is well suited for a broad audience and is appropriate for most libraries and collections.

1444. *Border Crossings: a magazine of the arts.* Formerly: *Arts Manitoba.* [ISSN: 0831-2559] 1982. q. CND 23 domestic; USD 23 foreign; CND 6 newsstand/cover per issue. Ed(s): Meeka Walsh. Arts Manitoba Publications Inc., 500 70 Arthur St, Winnipeg, MB R3B 1G7, Canada; bordercr@escape.ca; http://www.cmpa.ca/va1.html. Illus., index, adv. Sample. Circ: 3300 Paid. Vol. ends: No. 4. Microform: MML. Online: LexisNexis; Micromedia ProQuest; OCLC Online Computer Library Center, Inc.; H.W. Wilson. *Indexed:* ABM, ArtInd, BHA, CBCARef, CPerI. *Bk. rev.:* 1-3, 2 pages, signed. *Aud.:* Ga, Ac.

This award-winning arts magazine has been profiling Canadian artists and their work for over 20 years. Art is defined broadly to include all visual, performing, and literary arts, painting, photography, architecture, film, drama, dance, music, poetry, and fiction. Each issue is centred on a particular national or international theme. Examples of themes from past issues include love, censorship, technology, First Nations art, and landscapes. There are regular columns describing current artists, exhibits, projects, and publications. Photographic portfolios with color reproductions of art works and extensive interviews with established artists are regular sections in each 100-page issue. *Border Crossings* continues to be one of the top grant recipients for funding from the Canada Council for the Arts. It has received 37 awards from national and western Canadian magazines. This magazine will be of interest to large public and academic libraries.

1445. *British Columbia Magazine.* Formerly (until 2002): *Beautiful British Columbia.* 1959. q. CND 19.95 domestic; CND 26.95 foreign. Ed(s): Bryan McGill. Tourism British Columbia, 802-865 Hornby St, Vancouver, BC V6Z 2G3, Canada; Yvette.Chamberlain@tourism.bc.ca; http://www.tourism.bc.ca. Illus., adv. Circ: 244000 Paid. Online: Northern Light Technology, Inc. *Indexed:* CBCARef, CPerI. *Aud.:* Hs, Ga.

This magazine is famous for its high-quality color photography and well-researched articles on beautiful places, remarkable people, and intriguing wildlife in Canada's most western province. Each issue contains photo essays, educational articles and useful travel information on the magnificent scenery, parks, wilderness, wildlife, geography, ecology, and heritage of the province. The editors pride themselves on seeking out "the exotic, unknown, rare and surprising." A supplement titled *Beautiful BC Traveller* is included with selected issues. The magazine has a worldwide subscriber base and is suitable for high school and public libraries.

Broken Pencil. See Zines section.

1446. *C A R P Fifty Plus.* Former titles (until 2001): *C A R P News Fifty Plus;* (until 1999): *C A R P News;* (until 1994): *C A R P;* (until 1992): *C A R P News;* (until 1986): *C A R P News Letter.* [ISSN: 1701-3674] 1985. m. CND 7.95; CND 2.50 newsstand/cover per issue. Ed(s): Bonnie Baker Cowan. Canadian Association of Retired Persons, 27 Queen St E, Ste 1304, Toronto, ON M5C 2M6, Canada; info@50plus.com; http://www.50plus.com/. Circ: 43000. *Aud.:* Ga, Ac, Sa.

The Canadian Association for Retired People (CARP) is a nonprofit organization that acts as a national voice for over 400,000 Canadians. The association and its magazine are autonomous and do not accept operating funds from any level of government. The magazine is a compendium of information on health, nutrition, money matters, travel, and community affairs. In each 100-page issue, CARP also provides members an update on their advocacy work and governmental legislation and financial changes effecting people over fifty. The magazine includes special reports on seniors? concerns such as safety of food, aging well, and fighting cancer. Three focused issues on retirement, finance, and travel are published throughout the year. CARP negotiates member discounts for accommodations, insurance, and other products, and the magazine highlights these services. Additional services, directories, community chat rooms, and discussion forums are available on the association?s web site. This magazine will be of interest to public libraries.

1447. *Canada. Statistics Canada. Canadian Social Trends.* [ISSN: 0831-5698] 1982. q. CND 36 domestic; USD 36 foreign. Ed(s): Susan Crompton. Statistics Canada, Operations and Integration Division, Circulation Management, Jean Talon Bldg, 2 C12, Ottawa, ON K1A 0T6, Canada; cstsc@statcan.ca; http://www.statcan.ca/english/IPS/data/11-008-XPE.htm. Illus., index, adv. Vol. ends: No. 4. Microform: MML. Online: EBSCO Publishing; Gale Group; LexisNexis; Micromedia ProQuest. *Indexed:* CBCARef, CPerI, PAIS. *Aud.:* Hs, Ga, Ac, Sa.

This bilingual journal is published and compiled by Statistics Canada's Housing, Family, and Social Statistics Division, and features articles on social, economic, and demographic conditions in Canada. The focus is on statistics and statistical analyses of major social, demographic, and economic indicators. Far from being dry statistical descriptions, the articles discuss relevant topics including culture, education, family, health, income, justice, labor, population, and trends. Charts, graphs, and other representations of data illustrate the articles. Examples of recent subjects include "Studying and working," "Motherhood and paycheques," and "Family violence against seniors." A section called "Educator's Notebook" provides resources and lesson plans for teachers. New publications by Statistics Canada are listed in the bulletin "Keeping Track." There is an online edition. A worthwhile addition to all libraries.

Canadian Art. See Art/General section.

1448. *Canadian Business.* Former titles (until 1977): *Canadian Business Magazine;* (until 1972): *Canadian Business;* (until 1932): *Commerce of the Nation;* Incorporates (1981-1982): *Energy.* [ISSN: 0008-3100] 1928. bi-w. CND 39.95 domestic; CND 64.95 United States; CND 129.95 overseas. Ed(s): Joe Chidley, Luba Krekhovetsky. Canadian Business Media, 1 Mount Pleasant Rd, 11th Fl, Toronto, ON M4Y 2Y5 , Canada; mcruz@cbmedia.ca; http://www.canbus.com. Illus., index, adv. Sample. Circ: 83000 Paid. Vol. ends: Dec (No. 12). Microform: MML. Online: bigchalk; EBSCO Publishing; Florida Center for Library Automation; Gale Group; LexisNexis; Micromedia ProQuest; Northern Light Technology, Inc.; OCLC Online Computer Library Center, Inc.; ProQuest Information & Learning; H.W. Wilson. *Indexed:* ABIn, BPI, CBCARef, CPerI, LRI, MagInd, PAIS, SportS. *Bk. rev.:* 2-3, 1-3 pages. *Aud.:* Ga, Ac.

Canadian Business covers all aspects of investing, industry analyses, and technology as they relate to Canadian business and the Canadian economy. It also provides timely topical management information on ideas and opportunities for senior executives. Each issue has a lengthy cover article. There are several feature articles, personal profiles, commentaries, and industry reports. The magazine is supported by full-page color advertising, and includes smaller business ads and job postings. There are a number of special issues throughout the year: "Investor 500," annual best investments; "Tech 100," annual top technology firms; and "Tech Education," a guide to technical schools. Libraries that require a general magazine documenting and predicting the future of Canadian business will find this magazine useful.

1449. *Canadian Dimension: for people who want to change the world.* [ISSN: 0008-3402] 1963. bi-m. CND 37 (Individuals, CND 26.50; Students, CND 19.50). Dimension Publishing Inc., 91 Albert St, Rm 2 B, Winnipeg, MB R3B 1G5, Canada. Illus., index, adv. Sample. Circ: 3200. Vol. ends: Nov/Dec (No. 6). Microform: MML; PQC. Online: EBSCO Publishing; Florida Center for Library Automation; Gale Group; LexisNexis; Micromedia ProQuest; Northern Light Technology, Inc.; ProQuest Information & Learning; SoftLine Information. *Indexed:* AltPI, BAS, CBCARef, CPerI, MagInd. *Bk. rev.:* 2-4, 1 page, signed. *Aud.:* Hs, Ga, Ac.

In 2003, *Canadian Dimension* celebrated 40 years of continuously publishing an "avowedly radical, anti-capitalist magazine," As the oldest alternative and independently published magazine in Canada, it consistently challenges mainstream public opinion. The magazine has an editorial collective dedicated to bringing about social change by encouraging open debate in Canadian society. The magazine's readership is broadly based. A recent survey revealed subscribers from four political generations who describe themselves as activists with concerns for globalization, environment, health care, labor, and human rights. Each issue contains 48 pages of ad-free articles written by Canadians about Canadian and international issues. Color advertisements are confined to the magazine's cover pages. Each black-and-white issue has political cartoons, illustrations, and photographs. This magazine is a valuable addition to high school, public, and academic library collections wanting to offer a well-written alternative political viewpoint.

1450. ***Canadian Ethnic Studies.*** [ISSN: 0008-3496] 1969. 3x/yr. CND 80 (Individuals, CND 60; Students, USD 25). Ed(s): James Frideres, A W Rasporich. Canadian Ethnic Studies Association, c/o Dept. of History, University of Calgary, 2500 University Dr, N W, Calgary, AB T2N 1N4, Canada; ces@ucalgary.ca; http://www.ss.ucalgary.ca/ces. Illus., index, adv. Sample. Refereed. Circ: 800 Paid. Vol. ends: No. 3. Microform: MML; PQC. Online: EBSCO Publishing; Florida Center for Library Automation; Gale Group; LexisNexis; Micromedia ProQuest; OCLC Online Computer Library Center, Inc.; ProQuest Information & Learning; SoftLine Information. Reprint: PSC. *Indexed:* ABS&EES, AICP, AgeL, AmH&L, CBCARef, CPerI, IBSS, L&LBA, MLA-IB, PAIS, RILM, SociolAb. *Bk. rev.:* 15-20, 1-4 pages, signed. *Aud.:* Ga, Ac.

Canadian Ethnic Studies is a bilingual refereed journal "devoted to the study of ethnicity, immigration, inter-group relations and the history and cultural life of ethnic groups in Canada." It publishes original research articles. Conference reports, evaluations, case studies, critical essays, practitioner reflections, and reviews are listed in separate sections such as "Ethnic Voice" or "Perspective/ Opinions." Book and occasional film reviews are included, and there is an annual bibliography. Each issue contains lists of contributors, books received, and an index. Issues may have a thematic focus such as diversity and identity, education for a pluralistic society, or Canadian immigration. This journal's interdisciplinary nature makes it a valuable addition to academic and public libraries.

1451. ***Canadian Gardening.*** [ISSN: 0847-3463] 7x/yr. CND 24.56 domestic; CND 37.95 United States; CND 57.95 overseas. Ed(s): Beckie Fox. Avid Media Inc., 340 Ferrier St, Ste 210, Markham, ON L3R 2Z5, Canada; howe@avidmediainc.com; http://www.canadiangardening.com. Adv. Circ: 135000 Paid. *Indexed:* CBCARef, GardL. *Bk. rev.:* 1-2, 1 pages, signed. *Aud.:* Hs, Ga.

This home gardening magazine will interest beginners and veterans alike. It has plant profiles, practical advice on gardening techniques, beautiful photographic tours of unique Canadian gardens, and descriptions of new trends in flower and vegetable gardening. Both the urban and country gardener will find articles of interest that provide information specific for growing in Canadian climatic conditions. A small recipe section is included in each issue. Gardening events, fairs, and society meetings from across Canada are included by region in the calendar of events. Sources for all products and plants featured in each issue are listed. The publisher?s web site is a useful complement to the magazine, providing seed catalogues, lists of Canadian garden clubs and societies, and a chat forum. This colorful magazine is recommended for public libraries.

1452. ***Canadian Geographic.*** Formerly (until 1978): *Canadian Geographical Journal.* [ISSN: 0706-2168] 1930. 6x/yr. CND 29.95 domestic; CND 37.95 United States; CND 49.95 overseas. Ed(s): Rick Boychuk. Canadian Geographical Enterprises, 39 McArthur Ave, Ottawa, ON K1L 8L7, Canada; editorial@canadiangeographic.ca. Illus., index, adv. Sample. Circ: 240000 Paid. Vol. ends: Nov/Dec (No. 6). Online: bigchalk; EBSCO Publishing; Florida Center for Library Automation; Gale Group; LexisNexis; Micromedia ProQuest; Northern Light Technology, Inc.; OCLC Online Computer Library Center, Inc.; ProQuest Information & Learning; H.W. Wilson. *Indexed:* ABS&EES, BAS, BRI, CBCARef, CBRI, CPerI, GeoRef, MagInd, PAIS, RGPR, SSI. *Bk. rev.:* 1-5, 1 page, signed. *Aud.:* Hs, Ga, Ac.

The Royal Canadian Geographical Society, a nonprofit educational organization founded in 1929, publishes this magazine. Last year, *Canadian Geographic* won two best-magazine awards, one from the National Magazine Publishers Association and one from the Canadian Association of Magazine Editors. Its editorial goal is "to make Canada better known to Canadians," and it does this superbly. The subject of this magazine is Canada, its people, resources, environment, heritage, and any major issue of concern, with a significant geographical dimension. Each 100-page issue has five features, often related to a similar theme, and is well illustrated with color photographs and maps. Biographies of the Canadian contributors and web sites for background reading for the feature stories are also included. *Canadian Geographic* sponsors an annual amateur photographic contest and publishes the winning photos. There is a small amount of advertising and adventure classified ads. A valuable geographic resource for high school, public, and academic collections.

1453. ***Canadian Historical Review.*** [ISSN: 0008-3755] 1920. q. CND 95. Ed(s): Peter Gossage, Wendy Mitchinson. University of Toronto Press, Journals Department, 5201 Dufferin St, Toronto, ON M3H 5T8, Canada; journals@utpress.utoronto.ca; http://www.utpjournals.com. Illus., index, adv. Sample. Refereed. Circ: 2580. Vol. ends: Dec (No. 4). Microform: MML; PMC; PQC. Online: EBSCO Publishing; LexisNexis; Micromedia ProQuest. Reprint: PQC. *Indexed:* ABS&EES, AbAn, AmH&L, ArtHuCI, BHA, BRD, BRI, CBCARef, CBRI, CPerI, HumInd, IBSS, IBZ, MagInd, PSA, SSCI, SociolAb. *Bk. rev.:* 20-30, 1-3 pages, signed. *Aud.:* Ga, Ac.

The Canadian Historical Review covers a broad range of subjects. Issues include five to eight scholarly articles, a listing of new publications in Canadian history, occasional film reviews, and forum debates. Bilingual abstracts are provided for main articles. Topics discussed vary, covering multiculturalism, politics, the environment, religion, gender studies, and people and events of note. A comprehensive bibliography lists new materials and dissertations from a range of authoritative sources. The bibliography includes a subject index. Book reviews are provided by experts in the field. This journal is suitable for both academic and public libraries.

1454. ***Canadian House & Home.*** Formerly: *House and Home.* [ISSN: 0826-7642] 1982. 8x/yr. CND 26.95 domestic; CND 28.96 in Nova Scotia, Newfoundland & New Brunswick; CND 46.95 United States. Ed(s): Cobi Ladner. Canadian Home Publishers, 511 King St W, Ste 120, Toronto, ON M5V 2Z4, Canada; mail@canhomepub.com; http://www.canadianhouseandhome.com. Adv. Circ: 110700. Online: Gale Group. *Indexed:* CBCARef, CPerI. *Bk. rev.:* 5-10, 100 words, unsigned. *Aud.:* Hs,Ga.

This magazine contains the latest trends in decorating and renovating with a Canadian focus. A popular consumer magazine for those who desire stylish living, each issue contains ideas and practical information for transforming living spaces and decorating homes. Each issue contains color photographs of interior rooms and exterior landscaping of model Canadian homes, as well as interviews with interior design experts, describing their favorite trends and showcasing samples of their work. A small recipe section, decorating advice for entertaining, and a cross-Canada listing of sources for new products and material featured in the articles is also included. A general-interest magazine suitable for public library collections.

1455. ***Canadian Issues.*** Incorporates: *A C S Bulletin.* [ISSN: 0318-8442] 1975. a. Non-members, CND 20. Ed(s): Gregory Slogar. Association for Canadian Studies, PO Box 8888, Montreal, PQ H3C 3P8, Canada; c1015@er.ugam.ca. Adv. Refereed. Circ: 1200. *Indexed:* AmH&L, CBCARef, CEI, CPerI, IPSA. *Bk. rev.:* 1-2, 1 page, signed. *Aud.:* Hs, Ga, Ac.

This journal is a bilingual publication of the Association for Canadian Studies, a nonprofit scholarly society dedicated to disseminating knowledge about Canada through research and publications. As a general magazine of public opinion, it is readable and informative. Each issue has a dozen opinion essays written by distinguished academics, politicians, or lawyers surrounding a theme. Examples of past themes include cities, sports and Canadian identity, Canada and the world after 9/11, and Canadian rights and freedoms. Not all essays are translated, however there is an English abstract for all French-language material. Color photographs add to the readability of each 50-page issue. Advertising is limited to forthcoming books from university presses, meeting announcements, and university recruitment. This journal will be of interest to high school, public, and academic libraries.

1456. ***Canadian Living.*** [ISSN: 0382-4624] 1975. m. CND 27.80 domestic; CND 38 United States. Transcontinental Media, Inc., 25 Sheppard Ave West, Ste 100, Toronto, ON M2N 6S7, Canada; info@transcontinental.ca; http://www.transcontinental-gtc.com. Adv. Circ: 555118 Paid. *Indexed:* CBCARef, CPerI. *Aud.:* Hs, Ga.

This is the most popular Canadian family magazine with a circulation of over half a million. Its colorful articles and advertising are primarily focused on three areas, food and nutrition, health and wellness, and family and community. By far the largest component is the recipe section prepared by the *Canadian Living* Test Kitchens, 50 to 75 recipes per issue, collected from across the country, including a nutritional analysis of each dish. Readers are invited to contribute stories about individuals in their community who deserve recognition for their accomplishments, and a regular "O Canada" column provides an opportunity for readers to share experiences about being Canadian. Each issue includes a read-out-loud family story. Practical parenting and relationship advice organized by children?s ages is included in every 100-page issue. Suitable for public library collections.

1457. ***Canadian Public Policy.*** [ISSN: 0317-0861] 1975. q. CND 115 (Individuals, CND 55; CND 16 per issue). Ed(s): Kenneth McKenzie. University of Toronto Press, Journals Department, 5201 Dufferin St, Toronto, ON M3H 5T8, Canada; journals@utpress.utoronto.ca; http://www.utpjournals.com. Illus., index, adv. Sample. Refereed. Circ: 1800 Paid. Vol. ends: Dec (No. 4). Microform: MML. *Indexed:* ABIn, ASG, AgeL, AmH&L, ArtHuCI, CBCARef, CPerI, DSA, FPA, ForAb, FutSurv, HRA, IBZ, IPSA, JEL, PAIS, PSA, RRTA, SSCI, SUSA, SWA, SociolAb, WAE&RSA. *Bk. rev.:* 15-25, 1-2 pages, signed. *Aud.:* Ga, Ac.

This refereed journal publishes works in economics, political science, law, sociology, anthropology, geography, social work, administrative and public sciences, and business. The scholarly yet accessible articles strive to "stimulate research and discussion of public policy problems in Canada." Featured articles discuss a broad range of topics from employment and income issues to gambling to technological change. Each issue includes reviews and editorials, notices of new and forthcoming publications in the field, and indexes. Recommended for academic and public libraries.

1458. ***Canadian Wildlife.*** Formerly: *International Wildlife (Canadian Edition);* Incorporates: *Wildlife Update;* Formerly: *Canadian Chronicle;* Supersedes: *Wildlife News.* [ISSN: 1201-673X] 1965. 5x/yr. Members, CND 26.75. Ed(s): Martin Silverstone. Malcolm Publishing Inc., 11 450 Albert Hudon Blvd, Montreal, PQ H1G 3J9, Canada. Circ: 77000. Online: EBSCO Publishing; Gale Group. *Indexed:* CBCARef, CPerI. *Aud.:* Hs, Ga, Ac.

This magazine is a colorful introduction to Canadian wildlife, published by the Canadian Wildlife Federation, an association dedicated to "fostering awareness and enjoyment of our natural world." The wide range of subjects covered include wildlife, wild areas, nature-related research, endangered species, wildlife management, land use issues, character profiles, and the politics of conservation. Of particular interest are the profiles and behind-the-scenes interviews with prominent scientists. Each 50-page issue has five feature articles and regular editorial columns. For children, the field guide trivia contest and backyard habitat sections encourage reading and interest in nature close to home. The color photographs and text layout are excellent. Advertising is very minimal. Recommended for all high school, public, and academic libraries.

Canadian Woman Studies. See Women: Feminist and Special Interest/ Feminist and Women's Studies section.

1459. ***Globe and Mail Report on Business.*** [ISSN: 0017-1212] 1962. d. Ed(s): Margaret Wente. Globe and Mail Publishing, 444 Front St W, Toronto, ON M5V 2S9, Canada. Adv. *Indexed:* CBCARef. *Bk. rev.:* 1-3, 500 words, signed. *Aud.:* Hs, Ga, Ac.

This business magazine is published monthly in Canada?s national newspaper, the *Globe and Mail.* The focus of each 100-page issue is Canadian business personalities, the individuals and the corporations they lead, and in-depth reporting on the successes, scandals, and failures in the Canadian economy. Some international stories are also included. The regular columnists also provide critical commentary of business practices and government policies. The magazine has many color photographs of the profiled individuals, and there is advertising throughout each issue. Regular columns track trends, review hotels and golf courses, and conduct city profiles for business travelers. The magazine is printed on recycled paper. Public and academic libraries will find this a readable source of background information about Canadians in business.

1460. ***Journal of Canadian Studies.*** [ISSN: 0021-9495] 1966. q. CND 55 (Individuals, CND 40). Ed(s): Robert M Campbell. Trent University, 1600 West Bank Dr, Peterborough, ON K9J 7B8, Canada; jcs_rec@trentu.ca; http://www.trentu.ca. Illus., index, adv. Refereed. Circ: 1400. Vol. ends: Winter (No. 4). Microform: MML. Online: bigchalk; EBSCO Publishing; Gale Group; LexisNexis; Micromedia ProQuest; Northern Light Technology, Inc.; OCLC Online Computer Library Center, Inc.; ProQuest Information & Learning; H.W. Wilson. *Indexed:* AbAn, AgeL, AmH&L, ArtHuCI, BEL&L, CBCARef, CPerI, HumInd, IBSS, IBZ, MLA-IB, SSCI. *Bk. rev.:* 1-2, 8-15 pages, signed. *Aud.:* Ga, Ac.

This journal is now published by the University of Toronto Press. Articles are of moderate length, bilingual, and of both scholarly and general interest, and deal with "some aspect of Canada or Canadian life." Issues include several main articles, bilingual abstracts, and book reviews. There is a useful listing of new books organized by subject. There is also a "Canadian Studies News and Notes" section that lists events of note. The Council of Editors of Learned Journals recently awarded this publication the runner-up prize for the Phoenix Award for Significant Editorial Achievement, and determined that the journal's special Millennium Series, a four-issue set commemorating the journal's 35th anniversary, was an outstanding example of scholarly work. The *Journal of Canadian Studies* is highly recommended for both public and academic libraries.

1461. ***Labour: journal of Canadian labour studies - revue d'etudes ouvrieres Canadiennes.*** [ISSN: 0700-3862] 1976. s-a. CND 35 (Individuals, CND 25; Students, CND 15). Ed(s): Bryan D Palmer. Canadian Committee on Labour History, Department of History, Memorial University of Newfoundland, St. John's, NF A1C 5S7, Canada; ccelh@mun.ca; http://www.mun.ca/cclh/. Illus., index, adv. Sample. Refereed. Circ: 1200. Vol. ends: No. 2. *Indexed:* AltPI, AmH&L, ArtHuCI, CPerI, HRA, IBSS, PAIS, PRA, SFSA, SSCI. *Aud.:* Ga, Ac.

This bilingual interdisciplinary journal has a goal of fostering "imaginative approaches to both teaching and research in labour studies." Articles cover a broad range of labor-related subjects. Issues also include obituaries, research reports, critiques, book and film reviews, announcements, minutes, abstracts, and a history section. A short feature called "Notebook/Carnet," provides room for op-ed pieces and brief essays and commentaries. The bibliography section is organized by publication format. Recommended for general and academic collections.

1462. ***Maclean's: Canada's weekly newsmagazine.*** [ISSN: 0024-9262] 1905. w. CND 55.64 domestic; USD 90 United States; USD 215 elsewhere. Rogers Media Publishing Ltd, One Mount Pleasant Rd, Toronto, ON M4Y 2Y5, Canada; http://www.rogers.com. Illus., index, adv. Sample. Circ: 503497. CD-ROM: ProQuest Information & Learning. Microform: MML; NBI; NRP. Online: bigchalk; EBSCO Publishing; Florida Center for Library Automation; Gale Group; Infomart Ltd.; LexisNexis; Micromedia ProQuest; Northern Light Technology, Inc.; OCLC Online Computer Library Center, Inc.; ProQuest Information & Learning; H.W. Wilson. *Indexed:* BRI, CBCARef, CBRI, CPerI, LRI, MagInd, PAIS, RGPR. *Bk. rev.:* 1-2, 2-4 pages. *Aud.:* Hs, Ga, Ac.

This is the most widely read news magazine in Canada. Each issue summarizes world events and highlights Canadian events in politics, health, sport, and science. It is designed in an easy-to-read three-column format and includes many color photographs and some advertising. Each issue has commentaries, essays, and opinion pieces written by politically informed Canadians. There are regular columns reviewing the best picks in Canadian books, movies, music, and art. Awards, medals, deaths, and nominations are included in the "Passages" column. The *Maclean's Guide to Universities* is an award-winning special issue published each year, ranking and evaluating Canadian universities based on resources and reputation. This guide is an essential selection tool for students and parents evaluating post-secondary educational choices. *Maclean's* is recommended for all high school, public, and academic libraries for its general coverage of Canadian current affairs and world events from a Canadian perspective.

1463. *Manitoba History.* [ISSN: 0226-5044] 1980. s-a. CND 19.50 domestic; CND 20.50 United States; CND 22.50 elsewhere. Ed(s): Morris Mott, Bob Coutts. Manitoba Historical Society, 470 167 Lombard Ave, Winnipeg, MB R3B 0T6, Canada. Illus. Sample. Refereed. Circ: 1000. Vol. ends: Fall (No. 2). *Indexed:* AmH&L, CBCARef, CPerI. *Bk. rev.:* 4-8, 1-3 pages. *Aud.:* Hs, Ga, Ac.

This journal is devoted primarily to Manitoban history. Longer main articles are accompanied by photographs and illustrations, shorter articles, and both substantial and brief reviews. The articles are scholarly and well-documented, and the subject scope is varied. Certain issues may have a focus or theme, such as "The North in Manitoba History" or the historical role of women in the province. The publication is attractively presented with care given to art reproductions and graphics. It combines articles of scholarly interest with articles and reviews of popular appeal in a well-designed format. An annual bibliography serves researchers in this area well. This journal is recommended for academic and larger public libraries and special collections.

1464. *Newfoundland Studies.* [ISSN: 0823-1737] 1985. s-a. CND 20 (Individuals, CND 15; CND 10 newsstand/cover per issue). Ed(s): Richard Buehler. Memorial University of Newfoundland, Department of English, Arts and Administration 3026, Elizabeth Ave, St. John's, NF A1C 5S7, Canada; irenew@plato.ucs.mun.can; http://www.ucs.mun.ca/~nflds/. Illus., index, adv. Sample. Refereed. Circ: 250. Vol. ends: Fall (No. 2). *Indexed:* AmH&L, CBCARef. *Bk. rev.:* 6-7, 2-5 pages, signed. *Aud.:* Ac.

This is a "biannual, interdisciplinary journal devoted to publishing essays about the society and culture of Newfoundland, past and present." Issues present refereed scholarly articles, original documents with introductions and annotations, and book reviews and review articles. A yearly comprehensive bibliography of Newfoundlandia is published. Occasional special theme issues are published, most recently "a 308-page volume containing eight specially commissioned articles written to commemorate and analyze the first fifty years of Newfoundland's presence in the Canadian confederation." Suitable for academic and large public libraries.

1465. *Ontario History.* [ISSN: 0030-2953] 1899. s-a. CND 42.80 domestic; USD 45 United States; USD 50 foreign. Ed(s): Gabriele Scardellato. Ontario Historical Society, 34 Parkview Ave, Willowdale, ON M2N 3Y2, Canada; oh5@ontariohistoricalsociety.ca; http://www.ontariohistoricalsociety.ca. Illus., index, adv. Refereed. Circ: 1200. Vol. ends: Dec (No. 4). Reprint: PSC. *Indexed:* AmH&L, CBCARef, CPerI. *Bk. rev.:* 5-12, 500-1,000 words. *Aud.:* Ga, Ac.

Ontario History is a publication of the Ontario Historical Society assisted by funding from the Ontario Ministry of Culture and the Social Sciences and Humanities Research Council of Canada. Articles cover political, military, and constitutional history as well as First Nations history, women's history, immigration and ethnic history, labor history, and "other recently developed areas of the discipline." Several research articles are presented in each issue, often with accompanying photographs and illustrations. There is a book review section and list of books received. Suitable for academic and public libraries.

1466. *Outdoor Canada: the total outdoor experience.* [ISSN: 0315-0542] 1972. 8x/yr. CND 25.98 domestic; CND 39 United States; CND 69 overseas. Ed(s): James Little. Avid Media Inc., 340 Ferrier St, Ste 210, Markham, ON L3R 2Z5, Canada; oceditorial@outdoorcanadamagazine.com; http://www.outdoorcanada.ca. Illus., adv. Sample. Circ: 93000 Paid. Vol. ends: Nov/Dec. Microform: MML. Online: LexisNexis; Micromedia ProQuest. *Indexed:* CBCARef, CPerI, SportS. *Aud.:* Hs,Ga.

Outdoor Canada is the country's most widely read publication for the traditional outdoor sportsman. The magazine describes hunting, fishing, canoeing, exploring, and winter sports in the top sporting destinations across Canada. Each issue is well illustrated with color photographs and has four feature articles on an outdoor sport, wildlife, or conservation topic. Regular columns highlight the latest in gear and transportation for outdoor recreation, and authoritative experts provide techniques and answer readers' questions concerning all aspects of hunting and fishing. The magazine has a lively opinion column that is reproduced on the magazine's web site. Suitable for high school and public libraries.

1467. *Parachute: contemporary art magazine.* [ISSN: 0318-7020] 1975. q. CND 110 (Individuals, CND 49; CND 16 newsstand/cover per issue). Ed(s): Chantal Pontbriand. Editions Parachute, 4060 bd St Laurent, Ste 501, Montreal, PQ H2W 1Y9, Canada; parachut@citenet.net; http://www.parachute.ca. Adv. Circ: 5000. *Indexed:* ABM, ArtInd, BHA, CBCARef, CPerI. *Bk. rev.:* 10 -12, 200 - 500 words, signed. *Aud.:* Ga, Ac.

Parachute is among the finest avant-garde visual-arts journals in the world. It is noted for its graphic design and color reproductions. Each issue is bilingual and presents contemporary Canadian and international art and critical essays of substance. Its contributors are both Canadian and international. Interviews with artists, exhibits, book reviews, and an opinionated debate section are regular components of the magazine. Once a year, a special issue is devoted to a city where artistic practices of particular interest are in the process of developing. The authors examine the art of the city by profiling leading artists and individuals. Back pages of each issue are devoted to gallery exhibition announcements. This journal of art "ideas" will be of interest to large public library and academic collections.

1468. *Policy Options.* [ISSN: 0226-5893] 1979. 10x/yr. CND 37.40 domestic; CND 40.20 in Quebec; CND 49.95 United States. Ed(s): William Watson. Institute for Research on Public Policy, 1470 Peel St, Ste 200, Montreal, PQ H3A 1T1, Canada; policy@irpp.org; http://www.irpp.org. Illus. Sample. Circ: 2500. Vol. ends: Dec (No. 10). *Indexed:* CBCARef, CPerI, PAIS. *Bk. rev.:* 0-1, 500 words. *Aud.:* Ga, Ac.

This bilingual journal publishes independent research on a broad range of public policy issues, ranging from bank mergers to social determinants of health. It is sponsored by the Institute for Research on Public Policy, an independent, national, nonprofit organization that funds original research. Short book reviews of relevant titles are included in each issue. This useful and informative publication is appropriate for academic and larger public libraries.

1469. *Prairie Forum.* [ISSN: 0317-6282] 1976. s-a. CND 29.96 (Individuals, CND 24.61; CND 14.50 newsstand/cover per issue). Ed(s): Patrick Douaud. Canadian Plains Research Center, University of Regina, Regina, SK S4S 0A2, Canada; canadian.plains@uregina.ca; http://www.cprc.ca. Illus., index, adv. Sample. Refereed. Circ: 350. Vol. ends: Fall (No. 2). Microform: MML. *Indexed:* ABS&EES, AmH&L, CBCARef, CPerI, GeogAbPG. *Bk. rev.:* 2-10, 2-4 pages. *Aud.:* Ga, Ac.

Prairie Forum publishes research devoted to the Northern Plains region. This interdisciplinary journal spans provincial boundaries and covers a range of subjects and disciplines dealing with the prairies. "The journal of the Canadian Plains Research Center is seen as an important step towards bridging both the geographic and disciplinary boundaries." Topics covered include art and culture, farming, history, economic development, and sociology. Occasional special issues have dealt with "Changing Prairie Landscapes" and "Prairie Theatre and Drama." Issues include research articles with abstracts, essays, review articles, book reviews, forums, and editorial notes and introductions. Appropriate for academic libraries, special collections, and public libraries.

1470. *Queen's Quarterly: a Canadian review.* [ISSN: 0033-6041] 1893. q. CND 40 (Individuals, CND 20; CND 6.50 newsstand/cover per issue). Ed(s): Boris Castel. Queen's Quarterly, Queen's University, Kingston, ON K7L 3N6, Canada; http://info.queensu.ca/quarterly. Illus., adv. Sample. Refereed. Circ: 3000. Vol. ends: No. 4. Microform: MML; PQC. Online: Florida Center for Library Automation; Gale Group; LexisNexis; Micromedia ProQuest. Reprint: PQC. *Indexed:* ABS&EES, AmH&L, ArtHuCI, BAS, BEL&L, BRI, CBCARef, CBRI, CPerI, IBZ, IPSA, MLA-IB, PAIS, SSCI. *Bk. rev.:* Various number and length. *Aud.:* Ga, Ac.

Since *Queen's Quarterly* was founded in 1893, "the journal's commitment has always been to offer both the academic and the general reader a lively collection of analysis and reflection, in fields as diverse as international relations, science policy, literary criticism, travel writing, economics, religion, short fiction, and poetry." Over the years it has published works by such eminent Canadians as Ed Broadbent, Gwynne Dyer, Michael Ignatieff, Margaret Laurence, and Joyce Carol Oates. Issues include an editorial, several main articles, and sections on photography, reviews, science, and short fiction. It is "always trying to satisfy the curiosity of the congenial reader, the general reader who wants to be both educated and entertained, a reader who appreciates an intellectual overview of the world." Suitable for academic and large public libraries.

1471. *Quill and Quire: Canada's magazine of book news and reviews.* Incorporates (in 1989): *Books for Young People.* [ISSN: 0033-6491] 1935. m. CND 59.95 domestic; CND 95 foreign; CND 4.95 newsstand/cover per issue. Ed(s): Scott Anderson. Key Publishers Co. Ltd., 70 The Esplanade, 4th Fl, Toronto, ON M5E 1R2, Canada; quill@idirect.com; http://www.quillandquire.com. Illus., adv. Circ: 6244. Microform: MMP; MML. *Indexed:* BRD, BRI, CBCARef, CBRI, CPerI. *Aud.:* Hs, Ga, Ac.

Established in 1935, *Quill and Quire* is a periodical whose aim is to be the "leading source of information about the Canadian book industry." Each issue includes news and feature articles, opinion columns, book reviews, and bestseller lists. *Q&Q* also provides a twice-weekly pdf newsletter with breaking news stories about Canadian publishing sent to subscribers via e-mail. This journal is of interest to "booksellers, librarians, publishers, writers, educators and anyone interested in books and the book industry." Feature articles cover such topics as marketing to the United States, the fate of nonfiction, and the state of book reviewing. Interviews with notable figures are often included. Highly readable and informative, *Q&Q* is well suited for academic and public libraries.

1472. *Saltscapes.* 2000. bi-m. Ed(s): Diane leBlanc. Saltscapes Publishing Limited, 40 Alderney Dr, Ste 303, Dartmouth, NS B2Y 2N5, Canada; subscriptions@saltscapes.com; http://www.saltscapes.com. *Aud.:* Hs, Ga.

This new family owned magazine profiles the people, places, and culture of Atlantic Canada's four eastern provinces, Nova Scotia, New Brunswick, Prince Edward Island, and Newfoundland. Subjects included in each 100-page issue are people, recreation, crafts, gardens, and traditions of the region. Writers and photographers are from across Atlantic Canada. Professional chefs' and favorite home-cooking recipes are included as well as projects and profiles of craftspeople. The magazine is adjusting to readers? opinions and appears to have the right recipe for a solid-general interest magazine for those who live in the region as well as those who don't. The letters-to-the-editor column and the back page, authored by well-known columnist Harry Bruce, are popular with readers. The magazine is suitable for high school and public libraries.

1473. *Saskatchewan History.* [ISSN: 0036-4908] 1948. 2x/yr. CND 15. Ed(s): Bruce Dawson. Saskatchewan Archives Board, Murray Building, University of Saskatchewan, Saskatoon, SK S7N 5A4, Canada. Illus., index, adv. Sample. Refereed. Circ: 700. Vol. ends: Fall (No. 2). *Indexed:* AmH&L, CBCARef, CPerI. *Bk. rev.:* 7-8, 1-2 pages. *Aud.:* Ga, Ac.

This journal is published by Saskatchewan Archives and dedicated to the province's history. "The magazine has established itself as a pre-eminent source of information and narration about Saskatchewan's unique heritage." Each issue contains scholarly research and general-interest articles, book reviews, heritage and archives news, and illustrations and photographs. Articles have dealt with such topics as "the fur trade era, ethnic groups and immigration, pioneer life, the history of medical care, business and trade unionism, religion on the prairies, women's history, First Nations and Metis history." Suitable for academic and public libraries.

1474. *Saturday Night: Canada's leading magazine of comment and opinion.* [ISSN: 0036-4975] 1887. 10x/yr. Multi-Vision Publishing, Inc., 111 Queen St E, Ste 450, Toronto, ON M5C 1S2, Canada. Illus., index, adv. Sample. Circ: 375000. Vol. ends: Dec/Jan (No. 10). *Indexed:* ABS&EES, BRI, CBCARef, CBRI, CPerI, MagInd, PAIS, RGPR. *Aud.:* Hs, Ga, Ac.

This general-interest magazine has a 116-year history of survival. It is well known for its in-depth articles uncovering the stories and personalities behind news events in Canada. Its most recent transformation occurred in 2002 under the leadership of a new editor, after a year-long publication suspension. It has refocused on Canadian current and historical events and has reduced the number of issues published to six per year. The magazine is now broadsheet in size and includes full-color advertisements for lifestyle products. There are four lengthy feature articles per issue and regular Canadian-authored columns and departments. The magazine has been described by a former contributor as "one of the most consistent observers of the evolution of Canadian culture." *Saturday Night* is an important weathervane of opinion for any library building a collection on Canadian current affairs. Suitable for high school, public, and academic libraries.

1475. *This Magazine: because everything is political.* Former titles (until 1998): *This Magazine - Education, Culture, Politics;* (until 1973): *This Magazine Is About Schools.* [ISSN: 1491-2678] 1966. 6x/yr. CND 37 (Individuals, CND 23.99; CND 4.95 newsstand/cover per issue). Ed(s): Ms. Julie Crysler. Red Maple Foundation, 401 Richmond St W. Ste 396, Toronto, ON M5V 3A8, Canada. Illus., index, adv. Sample. Microform: MML; PQC. Reprint: PQC. *Indexed:* AltPI, CBCARef, CEI, CPerI. *Bk. rev.:* 1-2 pages. *Aud.:* Hs, Ga, Ac.

The Red Maple Foundation, a registered charity with support from the Canadian Race Relations Foundation, publishes *This Magazine.* The magazine's independent roots allow the distinguished editorial board to publish critical and intelligent writing about culture, politics, and art in Canada. Its contributors come from all Canadian provinces and include well-known authors Margaret Atwood, Linda McQuaig, and Rick Salutin. Its feature articles provide an alternative interpretation to mainstream political analysis of cultural and political issues. Recent issues feature arctic poverty, recreation, gambling, shopping, the politics of science, and fund raising. The magazine won the 2001 National Magazine Award for investigative reporting. In its fall issue each year, it hosts the Great Canadian Literary Hunt, judging submissions from across Canada and publishing the winning new poetry. Each 50-page issue is printed on recycled paper. *This Magazine* will provide readers in high school, public, and academic libraries a fresh perspective on Canadian culture.

1476. *Toronto Life.* Incorporates (1969-1982): *Toronto Calendar Magazine;* (1962-1966): *Ontario Homes and Living.* [ISSN: 0049-4194] 1966. m. CND 25.68 domestic; CND 44 foreign; CND 3.95 newsstand/cover per issue. Ed(s): John Macfarlane. Toronto Life Publishing Co. Ltd., 59 Front St E, 3rd Fl, Toronto, ON M5E 1B3, Canada; http://www.torontolife.com. Illus., index, adv. Sample. Circ: 93872. Microform: MML. *Indexed:* ASIP, CBCARef, CPerI. *Aud.:* Hs, Ga.

This magazine highlights culture, politics, and personalities in Canada's largest city. There are five feature articles in each issue written by well-known Canadian journalists on such urban topics as municipal politics, transportation, health care, real estate, sports, and entertainment. The focus of each feature is on the individual personalities in the stories. The calendar of arts events lists theater openings, music, dance, and nightlife in Toronto. Advertisements are sprinkled throughout the magazine. There are classified ads on the back pages, and best shopping and restaurants are highlighted in regular columns. *Toronto Life* provides a trendy urban perspective for high school and public library collections.

University of Toronto Quarterly. See Literature/General section.

1477. *Windspeaker.* Formerly (until 1986): *A M M S A.* [ISSN: 0834-177X] 1983. m. CND 40 domestic; CND 52 United States; CND 60 elsewhere. Ed(s): Debora Lockyer. Aboriginal Multi-Media Society of Alberta, 15001 112 Ave, N W, Edmonton, AB T5M 2V6, Canada; http://www.ammsa.com/. Illus., adv. Circ: 12000 Paid. Microform: MML. Online: EBSCO Publishing; Gale Group; LexisNexis; Micromedia ProQuest; OCLC Online Computer Library Center, Inc.; ProQuest Information & Learning; SoftLine Information. *Indexed:* CBCARef, CPerI. *Bk. rev.:* 1-5, 1 page, signed. *Aud.:* Hs, Ga, Ac.

This is a news magazine published by the Aboriginal Multi-Media Society of Alberta, an independent association dedicated to reporting events in Canada?s aboriginal communities. Most articles are written by *Windspeaker* staff and contributors and are not reprints of newswire reports. The magazine is published in black and white in a large newssheet edition. The following regular sections are found in each issue: opinion, news, entertainment, sports, health, business, careers and training, a community events calendar list and government public notices, and extensive classified ads. Each summer, a "Guide to Indian Country," a special 25-page insert, has news of summer celebrations, events, and festival locations across the country. The publisher?s web site contains full-text articles from back issues and selected articles from the current issue. This magazine is an excellent general resource on aboriginal issues and culture and will be of interest to high school, public, and academic libraries.

1478. ***YES Mag: Canada's science magazine for kids.*** [ISSN: 1203-8016] 1996. bi-m. CND 19.95 domestic; CND 26 United States; CND 32 elsewhere. Ed(s): Shannon Hunt. Peter Piper Publishing Inc., 3968 Long Gun Pl, Victoria, BC V8N 6H1, Canada. Adv. Circ: 17000 Paid. *Bk. rev.:* 1-3, 300 words, signed. *Aud.:* Ems, Hs, Ga, Ac.

YES Mag is a very attractive and readable science magazine for children aged 8 to 14. The Canadian Children?s Book Centre has chosen *YES Mag* for its "Our Choice" list for six consecutive years. Published in partnership with Actua, a national nonprofit organization and registered charity that supports the development and delivery of hands-on science, technology, and engineering for youth. Each colorful 32-page issue presents an in-depth look at a scientific topic, such as the chemistry of candy making, magnetism, ocean life, marvelous math, and alternative energy. A try-this-at-home feature describes experiments and explains the science behind each project. Young Canadian readers write the book and software reviews. The magazine is advertisement free. It will be of interest to young readers in elementary, high school, and public libraries, and useful for academic libraries with teaching resource collections.

■ CHEMISTRY

General/Analytical/Inorganic/Organic/Physical

Priscilla J. Matthews, Illinois State University, 8900 Milner Library, Normal, IL 61790-8900; pjmatth@ilstu.edu

Introduction

Chemistry is a fundamental scientific discipline essential to the understanding of related sciences. It continues to rely on older as well as current literature. It is inextricably linked to the fields of medicine, biology, physics, and the science of materials. The journal literature of chemistry reflects its central position in modern scientific research exploring our world, its elements, their properties, and their interactions.

Publications in chemistry continue several trends noted in the previous editions of *Magazines for Libraries.* Prices continue to rise. Electronic publishing and web presence continue to increase, with journals published only in print now being exceptions rather than common. In the last edition, *Acta Chimica Scandinavica* being merged with the RSC's *Dalton Transactions, Perkin Transactions I,* and *Perkin Transactions II* was the most prominent example of journal mergers and title changes. New title changes have solidified the previous round of changes: the short title *Dalton* is now again the familiar *Dalton Transactions. Perkin I* and *Perkin II* have combined to form *Organic & Biomolecular Chemistry.* The trend of domination by professional society publications also continues. A good collection will have the basic journals from the American Chemical Society and the Royal Society of Chemistry in all major areas of chemistry (general, analytical, inorganic, organic, and physical). The remainder of each collection will depend on acquisitions funds allotted and the institution's research and curricular interests.

Basic Periodicals

Hs: *Journal of Chemical Education;* Ac: *Accounts of Chemical Research, Analytical Chemistry, Chemical Reviews, Inorganic Chemistry, The Journal of Organic Chemistry, The Journal of Physical Chemistry Part A, American Chemical Society. Journal.*

Basic Abstracts and Indexes

Chemical Abstracts; Current Contents/Physical; Chemical and Earth Sciences; Science Citation Index.

General

1479. ***Accounts of Chemical Research.*** [ISSN: 0001-4842] 1968. m. USD 446 (Individual members, USD 47; Students, USD 35). Ed(s): Joan Selverstone Valentine. American Chemical Society, 1155 16th St, N W, Washington, DC 20036; service@acs.org; http://pubs.acs.org. Illus., index. Sample. Refereed. Circ: 4780. Vol. ends: Dec. Online: EBSCO Publishing; Swets Blackwell. *Indexed:* ChemAb, DSA, EnvAb, ExcerpMed, GeoRef, IndMed, SCI. *Aud.:* Ac, Sa.

This essential ACS journal provides "an easy-to-read overview of basic research and applications in all areas of chemistry and biochemistry." Recommended for all chemistry libraries and libraries with strong chemistry collections. Full text available online to subscribers.

1480. ***American Chemical Society. Journal.*** [ISSN: 0002-7863] 1879. w. USD 2684 (Individual members, USD 180; Students, USD 135). Ed(s): Peter J Stang. American Chemical Society, 1155 16th St, N W, Washington, DC 20036; service@acs.org; http://pubs.acs.org. Illus., index, adv. Refereed. Circ: 9300. Vol. ends: Dec. Microform: PMC. Online: EBSCO Publishing; Gale Group; Swets Blackwell. *Indexed:* AS&TI, ApMecR, BiolAb, ChemAb, DSA, EngInd, ExcerpMed, FS&TA, GSI, GeoRef, HortAb, IndMed, PetrolAb, S&F, SCI. *Bk. rev.:* 5-15, 350-400 words. *Aud.:* Ac, Sa.

The web site information page of the *Journal of the American Chemical Society* proudly proclaims that it is the "most cited journal in chemistry." As such, it is an essential title for all chemical research collections. *JACS* includes research articles in all fields of chemistry, communications to the editor, book reviews, and computer software reviews. Full text is available online.

1481. ***Angewandte Chemie (International Edition, Print).*** Formerly (until 1998): *Angewandte Chemie: International Edition in English.* [ISSN: 1433-7851] 1961. 48x/yr. EUR 3118 in Europe; CHF 5774 in Switzerland & Liechtenstein; USD 4090 elsewhere. Ed(s): P Goelitz. Wiley - V C H Verlag GmbH, Boschstrasse 12, Weinheim, 69469, Germany; subservice@wiley-vch.de; http://www3.interscience.wiley.com/cgi-bin/home. Illus., index, adv. Sample. Refereed. Circ: 3390. Vol. ends: Dec. Microform: VCI. Online: ScienceDirect; Wiley InterScience. Reprint: PSC. *Indexed:* ChemAb, EngInd, FS&TA, GeoRef, HortAb, IndVet, SCI, VetBull. *Bk. rev.:* Various number and length. *Aud.:* Ac, Sa.

An English translation of the Gesellschaft Deutscher Chemiker's *Angewandte Chemie.* This unique journal is known for its mix of review articles that summarize current research, highlights evaluating trends in chemical research, and short communications reporting selected research results. Full text is available online. Highly recommended for academic libraries.

1482. ***Canadian Journal of Chemistry.*** [ISSN: 0008-4042] 1929. m. CND 876 (Individuals, CND 286). Ed(s): Dr. Dick Puddephatt. N R C Research Press, Building M 55, Ottawa, ON K1A 0R6, Canada; http://canjchem.nrc.ca. Illus., index, adv. Refereed. Circ: 1488. Vol. ends: Dec. Microform: MML; PMC; PQC. Online: CISTI; EBSCO Publishing; Gale Group; ingenta.com; RoweCom Information Quest; Swets Blackwell. Reprint: PQC. *Indexed:* BiolAb, CBCARef, ChemAb, DSA, DSR&OA, EngInd, ExcerpMed, FPA, ForAb, GSI, GeoRef, HortAb, IndVet, PetrolAb, S&F, SCI. *Aud.:* Ac, Sa.

This journal cites international contributors from all major areas of chemistry research, supplemented by periodic review articles. Previous editions of *Magazines for Libraries* have noted the primarily Canadian emphasis. Abstracts are available online in English and French. Recommended for research libraries and larger academic collections.

1483. ***Chemical & Engineering News: the newsmagazine of the chemical world.*** [ISSN: 0009-2347] 1923. w. USD 210. Ed(s): Madeleine Jacobs, Rudy M Baum. American Chemical Society, 1155 16th St, N W, Washington, DC 20036; service@acs.org; http://pubs.acs.org. Illus., index, adv. Refereed. Circ: 73500. Vol. ends: Dec. *Indexed:* A&ATA, ABIn, AS&TI, B&I, BPI, BiolAb, C&ISA, CEA, CIJE, ChemAb, EngInd, EnvAb, ExcerpMed, FS&TA, GeoRef, InfoSAb, M&GPA, PetrolAb, S&F, SCI, SSCI, WRCInf. *Aud.:* Ga, Ac, Sa.

Chemical & Engineering News is the chemists' equivalent of *Time* or *Newsweek,* published by the American Chemical Society. This journal covers breaking news that impacts chemistry and the chemical industry. Reports cover research, business, industrial, and regulatory trends. The journal contains significant classified job advertising. It is appropriate for collections serving patrons with diverse backgrounds interested in chemical technology. Full text is online, free to ACS members.

1484. ***Chemical Communications.*** Former titles (until 1996): *Journal of the Chemical Society - Chemical Communications;* (until 1972): *Chemical Communications.* [ISSN: 1359-7345] 1965. s-m. Individuals, GBP 878. Ed(s): Dr. Sarah Thomas. Royal Society of Chemistry, Thomas Graham House, Science Park, Milton Rd, Cambridge, CB4 0WF, United Kingdom; sales@rsc.org; http://www.rsc.org/. Illus., index, adv. Refereed. Vol. ends: Dec. Microform: PQC. Online: EBSCO Publishing; Ingenta Select; OCLC Online Computer Library Center, Inc.; STN International. Reprint: PQC. *Indexed:* BiolAb, ChemAb, DSR&OA, EngInd, ExcerpMed, GeoRef, PollutAb, SCI. *Aud.:* Ac, Sa.

This important journal focuses on rapid publication of short articles describing new chemical research in all major areas of chemistry. Most communications are supplemented by full articles in the relevant section of the *Journal of the Chemical Society.* Recommended for research libraries, especially those emphasizing organic research literature. Full text is available online.

1485. ***Chemical Reviews.*** [ISSN: 0009-2665] 1924. m. USD 823 (Individual members, USD 82; Students, USD 62). Ed(s): Josef Michl. American Chemical Society, 1155 16th St, N W, Washington, DC 20036; service@acs.org; http://pubs.acs.org. Illus., index, adv. Sample. Refereed. Circ: 4300. Vol. ends: Dec. Online: EBSCO Publishing; Gale Group; Swets Blackwell. Reprint: PSC. *Indexed:* AS&TI, ApMecR, BiolAb, ChemAb, DSA, EngInd, ExcerpMed, GSI, GeoRef, IndMed, S&F, SCI. *Aud.:* Ac, Sa.

Dr. Josef Michl, editor of *Chemical Reviews,* describes its mission as "to provide comprehensive, authoritative, critical, and readable reviews of important recent research in all areas of chemistry, from authors located all over the world." The journal is increasing its coverage of biological subjects. In addition, for the past 18 years, special thematic issues have collected review articles on special research areas and are available individually as well as part of the subscription. For example, thematic issues were published on protein design, protein phosphorylation and signaling, X-rays in chemistry, aromaticity, and mass spectroscopy. Essential for research chemists; recommended for academic collections.

1486. ***The Chemical Society of Japan. Bulletin.*** [ISSN: 0009-2673] 1926. m. USD 309 in North America. Ed(s): Renji Okazaki. Chemical Society of Japan, 1-5, Kanda-Surugadai 1-Chome, Chiyoda-ku, Tokyo, 101-0062, Japan; info@chemistry.or.jp; http://www.chemistry.or.jp/. Illus., index. Refereed. Circ: 3500. Vol. ends: Dec. Microform: PMC; PQC. Online: J-Stage. Reprint: PQC. *Indexed:* ApMecR, BiolAb, ChemAb, DSA, DSR&OA, EngInd, ExcerpMed, ForAb, GeoRef, HortAb, PetrolAb, S&F, SCI. *Aud.:* Ac, Sa.

This title is distributed in the United States through ACS. As "Japan's most cited international chemistry journal," this publication covers topics in all chemical research areas. An ideal source for current awareness of chemical research in Japan. Recommended for research libraries and larger academic collections.

1487. ***Chemical Society Reviews.*** Superseded: *Chemical Society, London. Quarterly Reviews; Royal Institute of Chemistry Reviews.* [ISSN: 0306-0012] 1972. bi-m. Individuals, GBP 180. Ed(s): Jeremy Sanders. Royal Society of Chemistry, Thomas Graham House, Science Park, Milton Rd, Cambridge, CB4 0WF, United Kingdom; sales@rsc.org; http://www.rsc.org/. Illus., index. Refereed. Vol. ends: Dec. Online: EBSCO Publishing; Ingenta Select; OCLC Online Computer Library Center, Inc.; RoweCom Information Quest; Swets Blackwell. *Indexed:* ApMecR, BiolAb, ChemAb, DSA, DSR&OA, EngInd, FS&TA, GeoRef, SCI. *Aud.:* Ac, Sa.

Targeted at advanced undergraduates, postgraduates, and experienced researchers, *Chemical Society Reviews* publishes reader-friendly articles that give a basic overview of topics of current chemical interest. Coverage is not restricted to a particular chemical specialty, but rather introduces chemists to other areas outside of their own individual specialization. Full text is available online. Ideal for academic libraries.

1488. ***Chemistry: a European journal.*** [ISSN: 0947-6539] 1995. s-m. EUR 2374. Ed(s): Neville Compton. Wiley - V C H Verlag GmbH, Boschstrasse 12, Weinheim, 69469, Germany; subservice@wiley-vch.de; http://www3.interscience.wiley.com/cgi-bin/home. Illus., index, adv. Sample. Refereed. Vol. ends: Dec. Online: EBSCO Publishing; ScienceDirect; Wiley InterScience. *Indexed:* BAS, ChemAb, IndMed, SCI. *Aud.:* Ac, Sa.

Quickly established as a leading publication despite its short publishing history, *Chemistry, a European journal* highlights both European and international chemical research across a broad range of topics. The "Concepts" section is targeted to the nonspecialist reader. Full text is available online.

1489. ***Chemistry & Industry.*** [ISSN: 0009-3068] 1881. s-m. USD 560 (Members, USD 160; USD 36 newsstand/cover per issue United States). Ed(s): Mr. Simon Robinson. Society of Chemical Industry, 14 Belgrave Sq, London, SW1X 8PS, United Kingdom; enquiries@chemind.org; http://www.soci.org. Illus., adv. Sample. Circ: 9161 Paid. Vol. ends: No. 24. Online: Florida Center for Library Automation; Gale Group; OCLC Online Computer Library Center, Inc.; H.W. Wilson. *Indexed:* AS&TI, BiolAb, BrTechI, CEA, ChemAb, DSA, EngInd, EnvAb, ExcerpMed, FPA, FS&TA, HortAb, IndVet, PetrolAb, S&F, SCI, SSCI, VetBull, WAE&RSA. *Bk. rev.:* 10-15. *Aud.:* Ac, Sa.

Published by the Society of Chemical Industry (SCI), the emphasis of this publication is on news and trends in the application of chemical sciences in the industrial world. Headquartered in London and somewhat focused on British and European news, SCI is including more reports to reflect the international chemical industrial network. Job advertisements are still primarily British and European; book reviews are included regularly. Recommended for academic and industrial libraries. Full text available online.

1490. ***Chemistry in Britain.*** [ISSN: 0009-3106] 1965. m. Individuals, GBP 379. Ed(s): Richard Stevenson. Royal Society of Chemistry, Thomas Graham House, Science Park, Milton Rd, Cambridge, CB4 0WF, United Kingdom; sales@rsc.org; http://www.rsc.org/. Illus., index, adv. Refereed. Circ: 45000. Vol. ends: Dec. *Indexed:* A&ATA, BiolAb, BrTechI, ChemAb, DSA, EngInd, EnvAb, ExcerpMed, FS&TA, GeoRef, S&F, SCI, SSCI, SWRA. *Bk. rev.:* 8-12. *Aud.:* Ga, Ac, Sa.

The monthly newsmagazine of the Royal Society of Chemistry, *Chemistry in Britain* fulfills the same functions for British chemists as *Chemical and Engineering News* does for the American chemical community. European coverage is expanding, as is the job advertising for European positions in addition to British positions. It provides a useful overview of current trends for diverse patrons of wide-ranging technical backgrounds. Full text available online.

1491. ***Chemistry of Materials.*** [ISSN: 0897-4756] 1989. m. USD 1182 (Individual members, USD 163; Students, USD 122). Ed(s): Leonard V Interrante. American Chemical Society, 1155 16th St, N W, Washington, DC 20036; service@acs.org; http://pubs.acs.org. Illus., index. Sample. Refereed. Circ: 1700. Vol. ends: Dec. Online: EBSCO Publishing; Swets Blackwell. *Indexed:* C&ISA, ChemAb, EngInd, SCI. *Aud.:* Ac, Sa.

Chemistry of Materials fills a unique niche in chemical literature by providing "a molecular-level perspective at the interface of chemistry, chemical engineering, and materials science." Highlighted research areas include solid-state and polymer chemistry, especially that directed to the development of materials with unusual or practical properties. It includes occasional review articles and special issues on focused topics. Full text is available online.

1492. ***Green Chemistry.*** [ISSN: 1463-9262] 1999. bi-m. Individuals, GBP 525. Ed(s): Harpal Minhas. Royal Society of Chemistry, Thomas Graham House, Science Park, Milton Rd, Cambridge, CB4 0WF, United Kingdom; sales@rsc.org; http://www.rsc.org/. Refereed. Online: EBSCO Publishing; OCLC Online Computer Library Center, Inc.; RoweCom Information Quest; Swets Blackwell. *Indexed:* ChemAb, DSA, EnvAb, FPA, ForAb, HortAb, S&F, SCI. *Aud.:* Ac, Sa.

Founded by the Royal Society of Chemistry in response to the pressure on the international chemistry community to utilize nonpolluting technology, *Green Chemistry* publishes primary research papers, communications, and reviews. The primary focus is reporting "chemical aspects of clean technology from academic, industrial and public sectors." Recommended for academic libraries. Full text available online.

1493. ***Journal of Chemical Education.*** [ISSN: 0021-9584] 1924. m. USD 105 (Individuals, USD 42). Ed(s): J W Moore. American Chemical Society, 1155 16th St, N W, Washington, DC 20036. Illus., index, adv. Sample. Refereed. Circ: 15000 Paid. Vol. ends: Dec. Microform: PMC; PQC. Online: East View Publications, Inc.; EBSCO Publishing; Gale Group; Northern Light Technology, Inc.; OCLC Online Computer Library Center, Inc.; ProQuest Information & Learning. Reprint: PQC. *Indexed:* A&ATA, BRI, BiolAb, CBRI, CIJE, ChemAb, DSA, DSR&OA, EduInd, ExcerpMed, GSI, GeoRef, SCI, SSCI. *Bk. rev.:* Various number and length. *Aud.:* Hs, Ac, Sa.

The essential journal for the chemical educator from high school teachers to research professors. Articles focus on laboratory examples and pedagogical techniques for communicating chemical concepts. Abstracts and full text of most articles are available online to subscribers. An important title for both high school and academic libraries.

1494. ***Journal of Chemical Research. Synopses (Print Edition).*** [ISSN: 0308-2342] 1977. m. GBP 312.50. Science Reviews Ltd., PO Box 314, St Albans, AL1 4ZG, United Kingdom; scilet@scilet.com; http://www.scilet.com. Illus., index. Refereed. *Indexed:* BiolAb, ChemAb, DSR&OA, GeoRef, SCI. *Aud.:* Ac, Sa.

This two-part journal is now published by Science Reviews instead of the three founding societies (Royal Society of Chemistry, Gesellschaft Deutscher Chemiker, and the Societe Francaise de Chimie). Part S (Synopses) provides English abstracts of research papers on a monthly basis. Part M (Miniprint) includes the full texts of the original papers abstracted in Synopses in a microfiche or miniprint version and may be in English, French, or German. All branches of chemistry are covered. Full text available online.

1495. ***Journal of Physical and Chemical Reference Data.*** [ISSN: 0047-2689] 1972. 6x/yr. USD 795 combined subscription domestic print and online eds.; USD 815 combined subscription in Canada, Mexico, Central and South America and Caribbean for print and online eds.; USD 825 combined subscription in Europe, Asia, Middle East, Africa and Oceania for print & online eds. . Ed(s): Malcolm Chase, Jr. National Institute of Standards and Technology, 100 Buvean Dr, Stop 8401, Gaithersburg, MD 20899-8401; http://www.nist.gov/. Illus., index. Refereed. Circ: 220. Vol. ends: Dec. Microform: AIP. Online: EBSCO Publishing; RoweCom Information Quest; Swets Blackwell. *Indexed:* AS&TI, ApMecR, CPI, ChemAb, GeoRef, S&F. *Aud.:* Ac, Sa.

The *Journal of Physical and Chemical Reference Data* "provides critically evaluated reference data in the physical sciences." Published jointly by the National Institute of Standards and Technology and the American Institute of Physics, the journal's mission is to provide physical and chemical property data supported by full documentation as to the original sources and the criteria used for evaluation. Critical reviews of measurement techniques are also included when the purpose is to evaluate data accuracy in a specific technical area. Most useful to researchers in the disciplines of chemistry and physics.

Journal of the American Chemical Society. See *American Chemical Society. Journal.*

1496. ***Pure and Applied Chemistry.*** Formerly: *International Congress of Pure and Applied Chemistry. Lectures.* [ISSN: 0033-4545] 1960. m. USD 1166 (Individuals, USD 99; USD 50 newsstand/cover per issue). Ed(s): J. W. Jost. International Union of Pure and Applied Chemistry, IUPAC Secretariat, PO Box 13757, Research Triangle Park, NC 27709-3757. Illus., index, adv. Sample. Refereed. Circ: 845. Vol. ends: Dec. Microform: PQC. Online: EBSCO Publishing; Munksgaard & Blackwell Science's Synergy; OCLC Online Computer Library Center, Inc.; RoweCom Information Quest. *Indexed:* A&ATA, BiolAb, ChemAb, DSA, DSR&OA, EngInd, ExcerpMed, FPA, FS&TA, ForAb, GeoRef, HortAb, IndMed, S&F, SCI. *Aud.:* Ac, Sa.

This is the official journal of the International Union of Pure and Applied Chemistry (IUPAC) and now published by the society, and it has long been a record of IUPAC's recommendation for nomenclature and symbols, a source of reports on standardization and recommended procedures, and a record of main invited lectures of symposia and conferences sponsored by IUPAC. Abstracts are available online.

Analytical

1497. ***Acta Crystallographica. Section A: Foundations of Crystallography.*** Formerly (Until 1982): *Acta Crystallographica. Section A: Crystal Physics, Diffraction, Theoretical and General Crystallography;* Which superseded in part (Until 1967): *Acta Crystallographica.* [ISSN: 0108-7673] 1948. bi-m. USD 496 print & online. Ed(s): C E Bugg. Blackwell Munksgaard, Rosenoerns Alle 1, PO Box 227, Copenhagen V, 1502, Denmark; customerservice@munksgaard.dk; http://www.munksgaard.dk/. Illus., index, adv. Refereed. Circ: 1500. Microform: PMC. Online: EBSCO Publishing; Swets Blackwell. Reprint: ISI. *Indexed:* BiolAb, C&ISA, CCMJ, ChemAb, EngInd, GeoRef, IndMed, MathSciNet, S&F, SCI. *Aud.:* Ac, Sa.

The International Union of Crystallography publishes four related titles under the collective title of *Acta Crystallographica.* Each title concentrates on one area of specialization within crystallography. *Section A: Foundations of Crystallography* focuses on papers covering advances in the underlying principles of crystallography. *Section B: Structural Science* focuses on structural topics. *Section C: Crystal Structure Communications* publishes short reports of crystal structures of inorganic, metallo-organic, and organic molecules. *Section D: Biological Crystallography* concentrates on biological macromolecular crystallography. Section E was added in 2001 to be a "rapid communication journal for the publication of concise reports on inorganic, metal-organic and organic structures." Section E continues the electronic papers section of *Acta Crystallographica, Section C, Crystal Structure Communications.*

1498. ***American Society for Mass Spectrometry. Journal.*** [ISSN: 1044-0305] 1990. m. EUR 375. Ed(s): Michael L Gross. Elsevier Inc., 360 Park Ave. S, New York, NY 10010-1710; usinfo-f@elsevier.com; http://www.elsevier.com. Illus., index, adv. Sample. Refereed. Circ: 5110 Paid. Vol. ends: Dec. Online: ingenta.com; ScienceDirect; Swets Blackwell. *Indexed:* C&ISA, ChemAb, EngInd, EnvAb, ExcerpMed, FS&TA, IndMed, SCI. *Aud.:* Ac, Sa.

This official society publication focuses on rapid publishing of research papers covering all facets of mass spectrometry. The journal publishes papers from all sciences in which mass spectrometry is utilized, including chemistry. Papers cover both applications and fundamentals of the discipline. Regular features include "Short Communications" and "Brief Accounts of Research." Full text available online.

1499. ***The Analyst.*** Incorporates (in 2000): *Analytical Communications;* Which was formerly (until 1996): *Analytical Proceedings;* Which superseded (in Jan. 1981): *Chemical Society. Analytical Division. Proceedings;* Which was formerly (1964-1975): *Society for Analytical Chemistry. Proceedings.* [ISSN: 0003-2654] 1876. m. GBP 813; USD 1341. Ed(s): Sarah J R Day, L A Colon. Royal Society of Chemistry,

Thomas Graham House, Science Park, Milton Rd, Cambridge, CB4 0WF, United Kingdom; sales@rsc.org; http://www.rsc.org/. Illus., index, adv. Refereed. Vol. ends: Dec. Microform: PQC. Online: EBSCO Publishing; Ingenta Select; OCLC Online Computer Library Center, Inc.; RoweCom Information Quest; Swets Blackwell. *Indexed:* A&ATA, BiolAb, C&ISA, ChemAb, DSA, DSR&OA, ExcerpMed, FPA, FS&TA, ForAb, GeoRef, HortAb, IndMed, IndVet, S&F, SCI, VetBull, WAE&RSA, WRCInf. *Bk. rev.:* 8-10, 300-500 words. *Aud.:* Ac, Sa.

The Analyst is an international journal focusing on "the development and application of analytical and bioanalytical techniques." It publishes full papers and brief communications on varied aspects of analytical science, in the following sections: "Bioanalytical," "Chemometrics/Statistics," "Electroanalytical," "Mass Spectrometry," "Microscale," "Sample Handling," "Sensors," "Separations," "Spectroscopy," and "Surface Analysis." Book and software reviews are also included.

1500. ***Analytica Chimica Acta: international journal devoted to all branches of analytical chemistry.*** Incorporates: *Analytica Chimica Acta - Computer Technique and Optimization.* [ISSN: 0003-2670] 1947. 52x/yr. EUR 7224. Ed(s): L Buydens, R P Baldwin. Elsevier BV, Sara Burgerhartstraat 25, Amsterdam, 1055 KV, Netherlands; nlinfo-f@elsevier.nl; http://www.elsevier.nl. Illus., index, adv. Sample. Refereed. Microform: PQC. Online: ingenta.com; STN International; ScienceDirect; Swets Blackwell. *Indexed:* BiolAb, C&ISA, ChemAb, DSA, DSR&OA, EngInd, ExcerpMed, FPA, FS&TA, ForAb, GeoRef, HortAb, IndMed, IndVet, M&GPA, PollutAb, S&F, SCI, SWRA, VetBull, WRCInf. *Bk. rev.:* 6-10, 200-300 words. *Aud.:* Ac, Sa.

This journal covers all branches of analytical chemistry, focusing on analytical development. Rapid publication letters and invitational review articles are also included. Recommended for large research libraries with a significant patron base of analytical chemists. Full text available online.

1501. ***Analytical Chemistry.*** Formerly (until 1946): *Industrial and Analytical Chemistry. Analytical Edition.* [ISSN: 0003-2700] 1929. s-m. plus Review Issue and Labguide. USD 1165 (Individual members, USD 100; Students, USD 75). Ed(s): Royce W Murray. American Chemical Society, 1155 16th St, N W, Washington, DC 20036; service@acs.org; http://pubs.acs.org. Illus., index, adv. Refereed. Circ: 11680. Vol. ends: Dec. Online: EBSCO Publishing; Gale Group; Swets Blackwell. *Indexed:* AS&TI, BioEngAb, BiolAb, CIJE, CJPI, ChemAb, DSA, DSR&OA, EngInd, EnvAb, ExcerpMed, FPA, FS&TA, ForAb, GSI, GeoRef, HortAb, IndMed, IndVet, MinerAb, OceAb, PetrolAb, S&F, SCI, SSCI, SWRA, VetBull, WRCInf. *Bk. rev.:* 2-3, 300 words. *Aud.:* Ac, Sa.

The "most cited journal in analytical chemistry" is published by the American Chemical Society. Editorials, news, and special A-page articles written for the discerning general adult population complement leading research articles in the exacting field of analytical measurement, both theorectical and applied. Recommended for both research and general science collections.

1502. ***The Journal of Chromatography A.*** Incorporates: *Chromatographic Reviews;* Supersedes (in 1958): *Chromatographic Methods.* [ISSN: 0021-9673] 1956. 78x/yr. EUR 11036. Ed(s): U. A.Th. Brinkman, J G Dorsey. Elsevier BV, Sara Burgerhartstraat 25, Amsterdam, 1055 KV, Netherlands; nlinfo-f@elsevier.nl; http://www.elsevier.nl. Illus., index, adv. Refereed. Circ: 1700. Microform: PQC. Online: ingenta.com; ScienceDirect; Swets Blackwell. *Indexed:* Agr, BiolAb, ChemAb, DSA, DSR&OA, EngInd, ExcerpMed, FPA, FS&TA, ForAb, GeoRef, HortAb, IndMed, IndVet, PollutAb, RRTA, S&F, SCI, SSCI, VetBull, WAE&RSA, WRCInf. *Aud.:* Ac, Sa.

The Journal of Chromatography A publishes research papers "dealing with chromatographic and electrophoretic theory, instrumental developments and their analytical and preparative applications" in all areas except biomedical sciences and applications. *The Journal of Chromatography B,* the companion journal, focuses on those areas. Full text available online.

Inorganic

1503. ***Dalton Transactions: an international journal of inorganic chemistry.*** Former titles (until 2003): *Journal of the Chemical Society. Dalton Transactions;* (until 2001): *Dalton (Cambridge);* Incorporates in part (in Jan. 2000): *Acta Chemica Scandinavica;* Which was formed by the 1989 merger of: *Acta Chemica Scandinavica. Series A: Physical and Organic Chemistry; Acta Chemica Scandinavica. Series B: Organic Chemistry and Biochemistry;* Which superseded in part (1947-1973): *Acta Chemica Scandinavica; Dalton Transactions;* Supersedes in part: *Chemical Society, London. Journal. Section A: Inorganic, Physical and Theoretical Chemistry.* [ISSN: 1477-9226] 1972. s-m. Individuals, GBP 1500. Ed(s): Graham McCann. Royal Society of Chemistry, Thomas Graham House, Science Park, Milton Rd, Cambridge, CB4 0WF, United Kingdom; sales@rsc.org; http://www.rsc.org/. Illus., index, adv. Refereed. Vol. ends: Dec. Microform: PQC. Online: EBSCO Publishing; Ingenta Select; RoweCom Information Quest; Swets Blackwell. *Indexed:* AS&TI, BiolAb, ChemAb, GeoRef, SCI. *Aud.:* Ac, Sa.

Dalton Transactions continues with a return to a former title as one of the most respected inorganic chemistry journals. Formerly *Dalton,* incorporating Nordic contributions previously published in *Acta Chemica Scandinavica,* which merged with *Dalton Transactions, Perkin Transactions 1,* and *Perkin Transaction 2* in 2000, *Dalton Transactions* focuses on rapid publication of "papers on all aspects of the chemistry of inorganic and organometallic compounds." The journal also includes the features "Dalton Communications," preliminary accounts of original research published within 2 to 3 months of receipt, and "Dalton Perspectives," invited, short, specialist personal accounts or critiques. Full text available online.

1504. ***European Journal of Inorganic Chemistry.*** Formed by the merger of (1947-1998): *Chemische Berichte;* Part of (1946-1998): *Societe Chimique de France. Bulletin;* Part of (1945-1998): *Societes Chimiques Belges. Bulletin;* Part of (1871-1998): *Gazzetta Chimica Italiana;* Part of (1990-1998): *Anales de Quimica;* Part of (1905-1998): *Revista Portuguesa de Quimica;* Part of (1969-1998): *Chimika Chronika;* Part of (1951-1998): *Acta Chimica Hungarica: Models in Chemistry;* Part of (1920-1998): *Recueil des Travaux Chimiques des Pays-Bas;* Which was formerly (until 1920): *Recueil des Travaux Chimiques des Pays-Bas et de la Belgique;* (1882-1897): *Recueil des Travaux Chimiques de Pays-Bas.* [ISSN: 1434-1948] 1998. s-m. EUR 2268. Ed(s): Karen J Hindson. Wiley - V C H Verlag GmbH, Boschstrasse 12, Weinheim, 69469, Germany; subservice@wiley-vch.de; http://www3.interscience.wiley.com/cgi-bin/home. Illus., index. Sample. Refereed. Vol. ends: Dec. Online: EBSCO Publishing; ScienceDirect; Wiley InterScience. *Indexed:* ChemAb, EngInd, GeoRef, SCI. *Aud.:* Ac, Sa.

European Journal of Inorganic Chemistry is the complement to the *European Journal of Organic Chemistry.* Both titles were formed by the consolidation of many European journals to form journals that were focused on a major chemical specialty. *European Journal of Inorganic Chemistry* continues the publication of "full papers, short communications, and microreviews from the entire spectrum of inorganic, organometallic, bioorganic, and solid-state chemistry" that were formerly published in *Chemische Berichte. Bulletin des Societe Chimique Belges; Bulletin de la Societe Chimique de France; Gazzetta Chimica Italiana; Recueil des Travaux Chimiques des Pays-Bas; Anales de Quimica; Chimika Chronika;* and *Revista Portuguesa Quimica.* Full text is available online.

1505. ***Inorganic Chemistry.*** [ISSN: 0020-1669] 1962. bi-w. USD 318 (Individual members, USD 154; Students, USD 116). Ed(s): Richard Eisenberg. American Chemical Society, 1155 16th St, N W, Washington, DC 20036; service@acs.org; http://pubs.acs.org. Illus., index, adv. Refereed. Circ: 3150. Vol. ends: Dec. Online: EBSCO Publishing; Gale Group; Swets Blackwell. *Indexed:* ChemAb, EngInd, ExcerpMed, GSI, IndMed, S&F, SCI. *Aud.:* Ac, Sa.

Indispensable for inorganic specialists, *Inorganic Chemistry* "publishes fundamental studies in all phases of inorganic chemistry." Publications are primarily experimental and theoretical reports of varying lengths. "Emphasis is placed on the synthesis, structure, thermodynamics, reactivity, spectroscopy, and bonding properties of significant new and known compounds." Full text is available online.

1506. *Inorganica Chimica Acta: the international inorganic chemistry journal.* Incorporates: *Chimica Acta Reviews.* [ISSN: 0020-1693] 1967. 15x/yr. EUR 7331 (Qualified personnel, EUR 398). Ed(s): U. Belluco. Elsevier BV, Sara Burgerhartstraat 25, Amsterdam, 1055 KV, Netherlands; nlinfo-f@elsevier.nl; http://www.elsevier.nl. Illus., index, adv. Sample. Refereed. Microform: PQC. Online: ingenta.com; ScienceDirect; Swets Blackwell. *Indexed:* ChemAb, ExcerpMed, GeoRef, S&F, SCI. *Aud.:* Ac, Sa.

This journal publishes original articles (full research reports) and notes (short research reports) from international contributors covering coordination and metallorganic compounds; catalytic reactions in inorganic systems; "structural, spectroscopic and bonding properties of inorganic molecules"; electron transfers in inorganic systems; and "basic studies of bioinorganic molecular models." This journal places more emphasis on organometallic and bioinorganic chemistry than the related title *Polyhedron.* Full text is available online.

1507. *Polyhedron: international journal for inorganic and organometallic chemistry.* Incorporated: *Journal of Inorganic and Nuclear Chemistry; Inorganic and Nuclear Chemistry Letters.* [ISSN: 0277-5387] 1982. 18x/yr. EUR 5986 (Qualified personnel, EUR 286). Ed(s): G. Christou, C. E. Housecroft. Pergamon, The Boulevard, Langford Ln, East Park, Kidlington, OX5 1GB, United Kingdom. Illus., index. Sample. Refereed. Microform: MIM; PQC. Online: ingenta.com; ScienceDirect; Swets Blackwell. Reprint: PQC. *Indexed:* BiolAb, ChemAb, EngInd, GeoRef, SCI. *Aud.:* Ac, Sa.

Polyhedron publishes fundamental, experimental, and theoretical work in all the major areas of inorganic chemistry. These include synthetic chemistry, coordination chemistry, organometallic chemistry, bioinorganic chemistry, and solid-state and materials chemistry. This journal is targeted more toward biochemists than the related title *Inorganica Chimica Acta.* Libraries formerly purchasing both titles may wish to choose based on their collection emphasis due to the significant price increases. Full text is available online.

Organic

1508. *Biomacromolecules.* [ISSN: 1525-7797] 2000. bi-m. USD 767 (Individual members, USD 93; Students, USD 70). Ed(s): Ann-Christine Albertsson. American Chemical Society, 1155 16th St, N W, Washington, DC 20036; service@acs.org; http://pubs.acs.org. *Indexed:* BiolAb, ChemAb, ExcerpMed. *Aud.:* Ac, Sa.

Biomacromolecules is a new journal from the respected publishing program of the American Chemical Society. It was founded to provide a single source for interdisciplinary research articles "at the interface of polymer science and the biological sciences." Full text available online.

1509. *European Journal of Organic Chemistry.* Formed by the merger of (1979-1998): *Liebigs Annalen;* Which was formerly (until 1995): *Liebigs Annalen der Chemie;* Part of (1946-1998): *Societe Chimique de France. Bulletin;* Part of (1945-1998): *Societes Chimiques Belges. Bulletin;* Part of (1871-1998): *Gazzetta Chimica Italiana;* Part of (1920-1998): *Recueil des Travaux Chimiques des Pays-Bas;* Part of (1990-1998): *Anales de Quimica;* Part of (1905-1998): *Revista Portuguesa de Quimica;* Part of (1969-1998): *Chimika Chronika;* Part of (1951-1998): *Acta Chimica Hungarica: Models in Chemistry.* [ISSN: 1434-193X] 1998. s-m. EUR 2784. Ed(s): Robert Temme. Wiley - V C H Verlag GmbH, Boschstrasse 12, Weinheim, 69469, Germany; adsales@wiley-vch.de; http://www3.interscience.wiley.com/cgi-bin/home. Illus., index. Sample. Refereed. Online: EBSCO Publishing; ScienceDirect; Wiley InterScience. *Indexed:* ChemAb, DSA, EngInd, ForAb, GeoRef, HortAb, IndVet, PollutAb, SCI, VetBull, ZooRec. *Aud.:* Ac, Sa.

European Journal of Organic Chemistry, like its counterpart *European Journal of Inorganic Chemistry,* was formed by the consolidation of all or part of several European journals to publish a journal focused on the major chemical specialty of synthetic organic, bioorganic, and physical-organic chemistry. The full papers, brief communications, and microreviews were formerly published in *Liebigs Annalen, Bulletin des Societe Chimiques Belges, Bulletin de la Societe Chimique de France, Gazzetta Chimica Italiana, Recueil des Travaux Chimiques des Pays-Bas, Anales de Quimica, Chimika Chronika,* and *Revista Portuguesa Quimica.* Full text is available online.

1510. *Journal of Heterocyclic Chemistry: international journal.* Incorporates: *Lectures in Heterocyclic Chemistry.* [ISSN: 0022-152X] 1964. 6x/yr. USD 650; USD 1110 combined subscription print & online eds. Ed(s): Lyle Castle. HeteroCorporation, PO Box 170, Provo, UT 84603-0170; jhetchem@yahoo.com; http://www.jhetchem.com/. Illus., index, adv. Refereed. Circ: 1600 Paid. *Indexed:* BiolAb, ChemAb, EngInd, ExcerpMed, IndVet, SCI. *Aud.:* Ac, Sa.

The *Journal of Heterocyclic Chemistry* publishes articles of varying lengths on any phase of heterocyclic chemistry research. Review articles are also included. The unique ring index included in each issue lists parent rings for each compound as well as the page number, with a collective ring index included in the last issue of each volume. Full text is available online, with a drawing program enabling web subscribers to search the structure index for all volumes. Recommended for academic libraries supporting an organic chemistry curriculum.

1511. *The Journal of Organic Chemistry (Washington).* [ISSN: 0022-3263] 1936. bi-w. USD 1814 (Individual members, USD 131; Students, USD 98). Ed(s): C Dale Poulter. American Chemical Society, 1155 16th St, N W, Washington, DC 20036; service@acs.org; http://pubs.acs.org. Illus., index, adv. Refereed. Circ: 8800. Vol. ends: Dec. Online: EBSCO Publishing; Gale Group; Swets Blackwell. *Indexed:* BiolAb, ChemAb, DSA, DSR&OA, EngInd, ExcerpMed, FS&TA, GSI, HortAb, IndMed, IndVet, S&F, SCI, VetBull. *Aud.:* Ac, Sa.

This leading organic chemistry journal accepts manuscripts via a secure web site to expedite processing and speed publication of current research. The *Journal of Organic Chemistry* publishes "full articles and notes, invited topical mini-reviews, as well as invited contributions from all the recipients of the annual national ACS awards in the field of organic chemistry." Full text is available online. Recommended for research collections.

1512. *Macromolecules.* [ISSN: 0024-9297] 1968. bi-w. USD 2214 (Individual members, USD 213; Students, USD 160). Ed(s): Timothy P Lodge. American Chemical Society, 1155 16th St, N W, Washington, DC 20036; service@acs.org; http://pubs.acs.org. Illus., index, adv. Refereed. Circ: 2800 Paid. Vol. ends: Dec. Online: EBSCO Publishing; Swets Blackwell. *Indexed:* C&ISA, ChemAb, EngInd, FS&TA, IAA, SCI. *Aud.:* Ac, Sa.

Macromolecules covers "significant advances in all fundamental aspects of polymer chemistry" concerning organic, inorganic, and naturally occurring polymers. The journal publishes original research in comprehensive reports and brief communications. Recommended for academic chemistry collections. Full text available online.

1513. *Organic & Biomolecular Chemistry.* Formed by the 2003 merger of: *Royal Chemical Society. Journal. Perkin Transactions 1;* Which was formerly (until 2001): *Perkin 1;* (until 1999): *Royal Society of Chemistry. Journal: Perkin Transactions 1;* (until 1971): *Chemical Society, London. Journal. Section C. Organic Chemistry;* and of: *Royal Chemical Society. Journal. Perkin Transactions 2;* Which was formerly (until 2001): *Perkin 2;* (until 1999): *Royal Society of Chemistry. Journal: Perkin Transactions 2;* (until 1971): *Chemistry Society, London. Journal. Section B. Physical Organic Chemistry;* Both of which superseded in part (1848-1877): *Chemical Society. Journal;* Perkin Transactions 1 incorporated (1994-1998): *Contemporary Organic Synthesis;* Perkin 1 & Perkin 2 incorporated in part (in Jan. 2000): *Acta Chemica Scandinavica;* Which was formed by the 1989 merger of: *Acta Chemica Scandinavica A: Physical and Inorganic Chemistry;* Which was formerly (until 1986): *Acta Chemica Scandivavica. Series A: Physical and Inorganic Chemistry;* and of: *Acta Chemical Scandinavica B: Organic Chemistry and Biochemistry;* Which was formerly (until 1986): *Acta Chemica Scandinavica. Series B: Organic and Biochemistry;* *Both of which superseded in part (1947-1973):*

Acta Chemica Scandinavica. [ISSN: 1477-0520] 2003. 24x/yr. GBP 1995; USD 3300. Ed(s): Caroline V Potter. Royal Society of Chemistry, Thomas Graham House, Science Park, Milton Rd, Cambridge, CB4 0WF, United Kingdom; rsc1@rsc.org; http://www.rsc.org/. Adv. *Indexed:* ChemAb. *Aud.:* Ac, Sa.

Organic & Biomolecular Chemistry is designed as a journal with "broad scope and high visibility" that follows the tradition of its predecessors by including rapid publication of new research in "Communications," traditional articles, and the "Perspectives" section for review of new developments in specific areas of organic chemistry. A new innovation is the "Emerging Areas" section, which includes short feature articles by "young and eminent chemists."The journal "brings together molecular design, synthesis, structure, function and reactivity in one journal. It publishes fundamental work on synthetic, physical and biomolecular organic chemistry as well as all organic aspects of: chemical biology, medicinal chemistry, natural product chemistry, supramolecular chemistry, macromolecular chemistry, theoretical chemistry, and catalysis." Highly recommended for academic and research collections. Full text available online.

1514. *Organometallics.* [ISSN: 0276-7333] 1982. bi-w. USD 2081 (Individual members, USD 163; Students, USD 122). Ed(s): Dr. Dietmar Seyferth. American Chemical Society, 1155 16th St, N W, Washington, DC 20036; service@acs.org; http://pubs.acs.org. Illus., index, adv. Refereed. Circ: 2800 Paid. Online: EBSCO Publishing; Swets Blackwell. *Indexed:* ChemAb, EngInd, SCI. *Aud.:* Ac, Sa.

Organometallics concentrates on the chemistry of specialized compounds bridging the fields of inorganic and organic chemistry and including the synthetic aspects of materials science and solid-state chemistry. The journal publishes articles, communications, mini-reviews, and notes regarding "the synthesis, structure, bonding, chemical reactivity and reaction mechanisms, and applications of organometallic and organometalloidal compounds." Full text is available online.

1515. *Synlett: accounts and rapid communications in synthetic chemistry.* [ISSN: 0936-5214] 1989. 15x/yr. EUR 822.80 (Individuals, EUR 169.80; EUR 64 newsstand/cover). Ed(s): K Vollhardt. Georg Thieme Verlag, Ruedigerstr 14, Stuttgart, 70469, Germany; kunden.service@thieme.de; http://www.thieme.de/chemistry/. Illus., index, adv. Sample. Refereed. Circ: 2800. Vol. ends: Dec. Online: EBSCO Publishing; Swets Blackwell. *Indexed:* ChemAb, EngInd, ExcerpMed, SCI. *Aud.:* Ac, Sa.

Synlett is designed for rapid publication and rapid reading: brief research articles of personalized research accounts and a flexible "Letters" format. The section "New Tools in Synthesis" provides practical current information for the laboratory chemist; the "Spotlight" section highlights reagent characteristics. Full text is available online.

1516. *Synthesis: journal of synthetic organic chemistry.* [ISSN: 0039-7881] 1969. 18x/yr. EUR 1190.80 (Individuals, EUR 293.80; EUR 77 newsstand/cover). Ed(s): D Enders. Georg Thieme Verlag, Ruedigerstr 14, Stuttgart, 70469, Germany; kunden.service@thieme.de; http://www.thieme.de. Illus., index, adv. Sample. Refereed. Circ: 3700. Vol. ends: Dec. Microform: PQC. Online: EBSCO Publishing; Swets Blackwell. Reprint: PQC. *Indexed:* ChemAb, ExcerpMed, HortAb, SCI. *Bk. rev.:* Various number and length. *Aud.:* Ac, Sa.

Synthesis publishes specialized research and review articles in the field of synthetic chemistry, emphasizing synthesis of organic molecules. Special issues cover special topics such as organometallic chemistry. Book reviews are also included in some issues. The feature "Synthesis Alerts" highlights new reagents, catalysts, and ligands, as well as innovative uses of established reagents. Recommended for academic libraries supporting an organic chemistry curriculum. Full text is available online.

1517. *Tetrahedron Letters: international journal for the rapid publication of preliminary communications in organic chemistry.* [ISSN: 0040-4039] 1959. 52x/yr. EUR 9850 (Qualified personnel, EUR 409; Students, EUR 206). Ed(s): Derek Barton, L Ghosez. Pergamon, The Boulevard, Langford Ln, East Park, Kidlington, OX5 1GB, United Kingdom. Illus., index, adv. Refereed. Circ: 3380. Vol. ends: Dec (No. 42). Microform: MIM; PQC. Online: EBSCO Publishing; ingenta.com; ScienceDirect; Swets Blackwell. *Indexed:* Agr, BiolAb, ChemAb, DSA, DSR&OA, EngInd, ExcerpMed, FPA, ForAb, GeoRef, HortAb, SCI. *Aud.:* Ac, Sa.

The purpose of *Tetrahedron Letters* is to publish rapidly the latest developments in "techniques, structures, methods and conclusions in experimental and theoretical organic chemistry." Full text is available online. Recommended for academic libraries supporting a significant research program.

Physical

1518. *Chemical Physics Letters.* [ISSN: 0009-2614] 1967. 102x/yr. EUR 10504 (Qualified personnel, EUR 518). Ed(s): D C Clary, V Sundstroem. Elsevier BV, North-Holland, Sara Burgerhartstraat 25, Amsterdam, 1055 KV, Netherlands; nlinfo-f@elsevier.nl; http://www.elsevier.nl/homepage/about/us/regional_sites.htt. Illus., index, adv. Refereed. Microform: PQC. Online: EBSCO Publishing; ingenta.com; ScienceDirect; Swets Blackwell. *Indexed:* ChemAb, EngInd, GeoRef, IAA, SCI. *Aud.:* Ac, Sa.

This journal publishes short reports of original research deemed appropriate for rapid publication. *Chemical Physics Letters* focuses on reports that emphasize theoretical interpretation or experimental reports of "direct importance to a theoretical analysis." Most suitable for academic libraries that support a large science research curriculum.

Journal of Chemical Physics. See Physics section.

1519. *The Journal of Physical Chemistry Part A: Molecules, Spectroscopy, Kinetics, Environment and General Theory.* Supersedes in part (in 1997): *Journal of Physical Chemistry;* Which was formerly (until 1952): *Journal of Physical and Colloid Chemistry.* [ISSN: 1089-5639] 1896. w. USD 3355 includes Part B (Individual members, USD 208 includes Part B; Students, USD 156 includes Part B). Ed(s): Dr. Mostafa A El-Sayed. American Chemical Society, 1155 16th St, N W, Washington, DC 20036; service@acs.org; http://pubs.acs.org. Adv. Refereed. Circ: 2939. Online: EBSCO Publishing; Gale Group. *Indexed:* AS&TI, CEA, ChemAb, DSA, EngInd, FS&TA, GSI, GeoRef, IAA, IndMed, M&GPA, OceAb, PetrolAb, S&F, SCI, SWRA, WRCInf. *Aud.:* Ac, Sa.

Both portions of this weekly ACS journal are available full-text online and contain letters, articles, feature articles, and comments. *JPC:A* focuses on molecular studies such as dynamics, spectroscopy, bonding, quantum chemistry, and general theory. *JPC:B* (ISSN: 1089-5647) concentrates on studies on materials such as nanostructures, macromolecules, condensed matter, and biophysical chemistry, as well as studies on surface structure and properties. Recommended for large academic libraries.

1520. *Langmuir: the A C S journal of surfaces and colloids.* [ISSN: 0743-7463] 1985. bi-w. USD 407 (Individual members, USD 251; Students, USD 188). Ed(s): David G Whitten. American Chemical Society, 1155 16th St, N W, Washington, DC 20036; service@acs.org; http://pubs.acs.org. Illus., index, adv. Refereed. Circ: 1750. Vol. ends: Dec. Online: EBSCO Publishing; Swets Blackwell. *Indexed:* C&ISA, ChemAb, EngInd, SCI. *Aud.:* Ac, Sa.

Langmuir reports experimental and theoretical research in the fields of surface and colloid chemistry. Topics covered include emulsions, gels, surfactants, colloids, crystal growth and liquid crystals, imaging spectroscopy, electrochemistry, biological colloids and interfaces, biopolymers, multicomponent systems, and materials. Recommended for research and academic libraries with significant collections in physical chemistry. Full text is available online.

PhysChemComm. See under Electronic Journals subsection.

1521. *Physical Chemistry Chemical Physics: Journal of European Chemical Societies.* Formed by the merger of (1990-1998): *Journal of the Chemical Society. Faraday Transactions;* Which was formed by the merger of (1972-1989): *Journal of the Chemical Society. Faraday Transactions I;* (1972-1989): *Journal of the Chemical Society. Faraday*

Transactions II; Incorporates (1968-1984): *Faraday Society. Symposia;* Which superseded (1905-1971): *Faraday Society Transactions;* and (1897-1998): *Berichte der Bunsen-Gesellschaft;* Which was formerly (until 1980): *Berichte der Bunsengesellschaft fur Physikalische Chemie;* (until 1962): *Zeitschrift fuer Elektrochemie;* (until 1951): *Zeitschrift fuer Elektrochemie und Angewandte Physikalische Chemie.* [ISSN: 1463-9076] 1999. 24x/yr. Individuals, GBP 1450. Ed(s): Susan Appleyard, J Troe. Royal Society of Chemistry, Thomas Graham House, Science Park, Milton Rd, Cambridge, CB4 0WF, United Kingdom; sales@rsc.org; http://www.rsc.org/. Illus., index, adv. Sample. Refereed. Vol. ends: Dec. Online: EBSCO Publishing; Ingenta Select; OCLC Online Computer Library Center, Inc.; RoweCom Information Quest; Swets Blackwell. *Indexed:* BiolAb, C&ISA, CEA, ChemAb, EngInd, GeoRef, S&F, SCI. *Aud.:* Ac, Sa.

Incorporating the former titles *Faraday Transactions* and *Berichte der Bunsen-Gesellschaft,* the Royal Society of Chemistry (RSC) and the Deutsche Bunsen-Gesellschaft fuer Physikalische Chemie (DBG) joined initially with the Societa Chimica Italiana (SCI) and the Koninklijke Nederlandse Chemische Vereniging (KNCV) and later with the Nordic Chemical Societies (Denmark, Finland, Norway, and Sweden), the Real Sociedad Espanola de Quimica, the Polskie Towarzystwo Chemiczne, and the Israel Chemical Society to publish a research journal covering physical chemistry, chemical physics, and biophysical chemistry. A new classic in academic and research libraries, as was its predecessors. Full text is available online.

Electronic Journals

1522. ***Internet Journal of Chemistry.*** [ISSN: 1099-8292] 1998. irreg. USD 489 (Individuals, USD 49). Ed(s): Steven M Bachrach. InfoTrust Ltd., 143 Old Marlton Pike, Medford, NJ 08055; steven.bachrach@trinity.edu; http://www.ijc.com. Refereed. *Aud.:* Ac, Sa.

This electronic-only journal states that its purpose is to "focus on the use of the Internet by chemists." Major areas of concentration include web site reviews and publications that "take advantage of the special attributes of the Internet," i.e., those that incorporate video, interactive programs, etc., that effectively utilize the resources of a distributed computing environment. The journal also includes original research on development and implementation of Internet resources for chemists.

1523. ***PhysChemComm.*** [ISSN: 1460-2733] 1998. irreg. Individuals, GBP 60. Ed(s): Jamie Humphrey. Royal Society of Chemistry, Thomas Graham House, Science Park, Milton Rd, Cambridge, CB4 0WF, United Kingdom; sales@rsc.org; http://www.rsc.org/. Illus., index. Refereed. *Aud.:* Ac, Sa.

An electronic-only journal supported by the Scholarly Publishing and Academic Resources Coalition (SPARC) initiative to "encourage new solutions to scientific journal publishing," *PhysChemComm* is published by the Royal Society of Chemistry and thus enjoys the benefit of the society's prestige. The journal concentrates on publishing brief articles describing "innovative research covering all aspects of physical chemistry and chemical physics." Also included are articles on surface science and condensed matter physics.

■ CHILDREN

See also Parenting; and Teenagers sections.

Roslyn E. Wylie, Teaching Materials Center Librarian, Milner Library, Illinois State University, Normal, IL 61790; rewylie@ilstu.edu

Introduction

The world of children's magazines includes titles covering a broad range of subjects appealing to a diverse population of child readers. The magazines covered in this section are most appropriate for children through age 14.

Magazines serve several purposes: they provide recreational reading on general-interest topics, informational reading for specific interests, reading for research and school assignments, and reading for the joy and love of reading.

A number of reviewed titles will be useful as additional sources of topical information for school use. Those topics include history, world history and geography, African American history, anthropology, and consumer information. Additional magazines can support the school subjects of science, nature, sports, creative writing, art, and health and fitness. Pre-reading skills and activities found in those magazines written specifically for beginning readers will be useful in preschool settings. Several magazines, both print and electronic, focus on literary or multicultural themes.

The large number of titles in the general-interest category can serve to create an interest in unexplored territories.

Specific-interest magazines appeal to readers interested in sports, scouting, collecting, crafts, and other specialities.

The electronic journals included in this section will appeal to both general-interest and specialized readers.

While the quality of individual titles may vary somewhat, the overall quality of children's magazines included in this section is very good.

Basic Periodicals

American Girl, AppleSeeds, Ask, Biography for Beginners, Boys' Life, Calliope, Chickadee, ChildArt, Click, Cobblestone, Consumer Reports for Kids Online, Cricket, Cyberkids, Faces, Footsteps, Girl Tech, Highlights for Children, Ladybug, MidLink Magazine, Muse, National Geographic Kids, New Moon, Odyssey, Owl, Ranger Rick, Skipping Stones, Spider, Sports Illustrated for Kids, Stone Soup.

Basic Abstracts and Indexes

Children's Magazine Guide.

1524. ***American Girl: celebrating girls, yesterday and today.*** [ISSN: 1062-7812] 1992. bi-m. USD 19.95 domestic; USD 24 foreign; USD 3.95 newsstand/cover per issue. Ed(s): Kristi Thom. Pleasant Company Publications, 8400 Fairway Pl, Middleton, WI 53562; readermail@ab.pleasantco.com; http://www.americangirl.com. Illus. Circ: 700000 Paid. Vol. ends: Nov/Dec. *Indexed:* ICM. *Aud.:* 6-12 yrs.

American Girl invites creative participation from readers in many of its sections. Special features include an advice column and opportunities to respond to monthly polls on many topics. The magazine features articles about girls, both of today and the past, with diverse backgrounds and interests. It is colorful, engaging, and filled with photographs and pictures. Each issue includes a historical story featuring one of the *American Girl* characters from the books and dolls. A punch-out paper doll with clothes of a real American girl is included in each issue. This magazine is highly recommended for school and public libraries.

1525. ***AppleSeeds.*** [ISSN: 1099-7725] 1998. m. except June, July, August. USD 29.95 domestic; USD 39.95 foreign. Ed(s): Susan Buckley. Cobblestone Publishing, 30 Grove St, Ste C, Peterborough, NH 03458; custsvc@cobblestone.mv.com; http://www.cobblestonepub.com. Illus., index. Sample. Circ: 5000 Paid. Vol. ends: May. *Bk. rev.:* 3-5, 20-40 words. *Aud.:* 7-9 yrs.

AppleSeeds, a wonderful publication from Cobblestone, is written for children ages 7–9. The purpose of *Appleseeds* is to aid in the development of vocabulary, geography, math, and science skills. Each issue is theme oriented, with articles and activities of interest to a diverse population of readers. Illustrations and pictures add interest to the text. *AppleSeeds* is recommended for school and public libraries.

1526. ***Ask!: arts and sciences for kids.*** [ISSN: 1535-4105] 2002. bi-m. USD 19.70. Ed(s): Marianne Carus. Cricket Magazine Group, 315 Fifth St, PO Box 300, Peru, IL 61354; http://www.cricketmag.com. *Aud.:* 7-10 yrs.

Ask! is a new magazine from the publishers of *Cricket* and *Smithsonian Magazine* with a focus on science, history, technology, and the arts. Each issue has a single theme with illustrated feature articles and activities related to that theme. Opportunities for reader participation include inventing/drawing contests, reader letters responding to features, and "Ask Jimmy the Bug."

Regular departments include "Harpo's World" and "Marvin and Friends." *Ask!* should be of interest to many children because of the multi-curricular approach within each theme. Recommended for school and public libraries and personal subscriptions.

1527. *Biography for Beginners: sketches for early readers.* [ISSN: 1081-4973] 1995. s-a. USD 40. Ed(s): Laurie Harris. Favorable Impressions, PO Box 69018, Pleasant Ridge, MI 48069. Illus., index. Sample. Circ: 4000. Vol. ends: May/Oct. *Aud.:* 6-9 yrs.

While *Biography for Beginners* is not a magazine, it is included in the children's magazine section. Each issue contains nine or ten biographical sketches arranged alphabetically and written on a mid-second- to third-grade reading level to acquaint young readers with the biography genre. The sketches include a mix of authors, world figures, sports stars, and television personalities. There are illustrations within the entries: action shots, photographs, book covers, and book illustrations. Within each ten-page biographical sketch, the reader will find information on the subject's early life and schooling, career preparation and work, and family. Addresses and web sites are included for classroom writing projects. Cumulative name and subject indexes and a birthday index are found in each issue. A list of subjects for upcoming issues will encourage young biography buffs to look for the next issue. Appropriate for school and public libraries.

1528. *Boys' Life: the magazine for all boys.* [ISSN: 0006-8608] 1911. m. USD 18 domestic; USD 27 foreign; USD 3 newsstand/cover per issue. Ed(s): J D Owen, William E Butterworth, IV. Boy Scouts of America, PO Box 152079, Irving, TX 75015-2079. Illus., adv. Circ: 1300000 Paid. Microform: NBI; PQC. Online: bigchalk; EBSCO Publishing; Gale Group; ProQuest Information & Learning; H.W. Wilson. *Indexed:* ASIP, CPerI, ICM, IHTDI, MagInd. *Aud.:* 8-18 yrs.

Boys' Life is the publication of the Boy Scouts of America and is designed for Cub Scouts and Boy Scouts. The magazine, which has been published for over 90 years, includes fiction, articles related to sports, science, hobbies, Scouting, and cartoons and jokes. Reader input is welcomed. A free braille edition is available to those who qualify. It is written for boys involved in Scouting, but girls will enjoy the magazine also.

1529. *Calliope (Peterborough): exploring world history.* Supersedes (in Sep. 1990): *Classical Calliope.* [ISSN: 1050-7086] 1981. 9x/yr. USD 29.95 domestic; USD 39.95 foreign. Ed(s): Rosalie F Baker, Charles Baker. Cobblestone Publishing, 30 Grove St, Ste C, Peterborough, NH 03458; custsvc@cobblestonepub.com; http://www.cobblestonepub.com. Illus., index. Circ: 12000 Paid. Vol. ends: May. *Indexed:* ICM. *Bk. rev.:* 5, 50-75 words. *Aud.:* 9-15 yrs.

Calliope provides readers with in-depth material on world history themes. Content includes age-appropriate research articles, often written by academics in the field. Readers will find photographs and drawings, maps, timelines, and activities in each issue. This is a quality magazine from Cobblestone Publishing. *Calliope* publishes original short poems, essays, and artwork submitted by readers. A helpful feature is the review section where books, reference materials, magazines, and videos are noted. Cross-references to previous issues with similar themes are given. A recommended useful magazine for school and public libraries.

1530. *Chickadee.* [ISSN: 0707-4611] 1979. 10x/yr. CND 29.95 domestic; CND 32.19 in Maritimes & Quebec; USD 22 United States. Ed(s): Hilary Bain. Bayard Canada, The Owl Group, 49 Front St E, 2nd Fl, Toronto, ON M5E 1B3, Canada; bayard@owl.on.ca; http://www.owlkids.com/. Illus., index, adv. Circ: 100000. Vol. ends: Dec. *Indexed:* CBCARef, CPerI, ICM. *Aud.:* 6-9 yrs.

Chickadee is a nature-oriented magazine for early elementary school age children. It is bright, colorful, and filled with interesting content. Each issue follows a single theme through several avenues of interest. A two-page poster is included in each issue. The web site has a sampling of word games, activities, games, and links to other web sites. Recommended for school, public libraries, and personal subscriptions.

1531. *Child Life: the children's own magazine.* Incorporates: *Young World;* Which was formerly: *Golden Magazine.* [ISSN: 0009-3971] 1921. bi-m. USD 15.95 domestic; USD 19.95 foreign. Ed(s): Jack Grambling. Children's Better Health Institute, 1100 Waterway Blvd, PO Box 567, Indianapolis, IN 46206; g.joray@cbhi.org; http://www.cbhi.org. Illus., index, adv. Sample. Circ: 54000. Vol. ends: Dec. Microform: PQC. Online: bigchalk; EBSCO Publishing; Florida Center for Library Automation; Gale Group; Northern Light Technology, Inc.; ProQuest Information & Learning. *Indexed:* ICM, MagInd. *Bk. rev.:* 2-4, 40-50 words. *Aud.:* 9-11 yrs.

Child Life is a health-related magazine for middle-grade elementary school readers published by the Children's Better Health Institute. Many of the stories and articles found in this magazine are classics that are reprinted from past *Child Life* issues. This magazine, which is best suited for personal subscriptions, presents wholesome features that include book reviews, web site reviews, word puzzles, and the creative work of readers.

1532. *ChildArt.* [ISSN: 1096-9020] 1998. q. USD 30 domestic to libraries, schools, museums & art organazations; USD 40 foreign to libraries, schools, museums & art organazations. International Child Art Foundation, 1350 Connecticut Ave, N W, Washington, DC 20036-1702. *Aud.:* 8-12 yrs.

ChildArt is a publication for visually creative children. Each issue is filled with interesting articles about children around the world creating art. The reader can find art projects and activities—for example, suggestions for making sand castles and for creating an abstract sculpture. Children's art is prominently featured in the magazine. This specialized magazine would be useful for personal subscriptions and for schools.

1533. *Children's Digest.* Former titles (Mar.-Nov. 1980): *Children's Digest and Children's Playcraft;* (Until 1980): *Children's Digest (1950).* [ISSN: 0272-7145] 1950. bi-m. USD 15.95 domestic; USD 19.95 foreign. Ed(s): Penny Radall. Children's Better Health Institute, 1100 Waterway Blvd, PO Box 567, Indianapolis, IN 46206; g.joray@cbhi.org; http://www.cbhi.org. Illus., index, adv. Circ: 120000. Vol. ends: Dec. Microform: PQC. Online: bigchalk; EBSCO Publishing; Gale Group; Northern Light Technology, Inc.; ProQuest Information & Learning; H.W. Wilson. *Indexed:* ICM, MagInd. *Bk. rev.:* 3-5, 80-100 words. *Aud.:* 10-12 yrs.

Children's Digest promotes good health and fitness for pre-teen readers of all races and cultures. Readers may submit original poetry, jokes, and riddles. "Ask Doctor Cory" offers an opportunity for reader-initiated health questions and answers. Regular features include stories, puzzles, and interesting articles. Most suitable for personal subscriptions.

1534. *Children's Playmate.* [ISSN: 0009-4161] 1929. bi-m. USD 15.95 domestic; USD 19.95 foreign. Ed(s): Terry Harshman. Children's Better Health Institute, 1100 Waterway Blvd, PO Box 567, Indianapolis, IN 46206; g.joray@cbhi.org; http://www.cbhi.org. Illus., index, adv. Circ: 115000 Paid. Vol. ends: Dec. Microform: PQC. Online: bigchalk; EBSCO Publishing; Gale Group; Northern Light Technology, Inc.; ProQuest Information & Learning; H.W. Wilson. *Indexed:* ICM, MagInd. *Aud.:* 6-8 yrs.

Children's Playmate is written to promote health, fitness, and well-being through stories, games, recipes, and activities. This magazine solicits the creative work of early elementary age children and publishes their pictures, poems, jokes, and riddles. The stories and illustrations in *Children's Playmate* do not reflect the racial and ethnic diversity that may be present among the readers.

1535. *Click: opening windows for young minds.* [ISSN: 1094-4273] 1998. 10x/yr. USD 32.97. Cricket Magazine Group, 315 Fifth St, PO Box 300, Peru, IL 61354; http://www.cricketmag.com. Illus. Vol. ends: Dec. Online: EBSCO Publishing. *Bk. rev.:* 12-16, length varies. *Aud.:* 3-7 yrs.

Click is a delightful magazine with a science orientation and a theme approach for each issue. A cartoon story featuring Click, the resident mouse, is featured each month, as well as colorfully illustrated and informational articles. *Click* includes takeout pages that become games for the reader. There is a helpful parent's companion section with suggestions of follow-up activities, plus additional related book titles. A useful title for home or library. This magazine is a joint publication of *Cricket* and *Smithsonian Magazine.*

1536. ***Cobblestone: discover American history.*** [ISSN: 0199-5197] 1980. 9x/yr. USD 29.95 domestic; USD 39.95 foreign. Ed(s): Meg Chorlian. Cobblestone Publishing, 30 Grove St, Ste C, Peterborough, NH 03458; custsvc@cobblestonepub.com; http://www.cobblestonepub.com. Illus., index. Circ: 31000. Vol. ends: Dec. *Indexed:* ICM. *Bk. rev.:* 10, length varies. *Aud.:* 9-14 yrs.

Cobblestone is a history magazine written for upper-elementary and junior-high age students. Each issue focuses in depth on a single topic. Unfamiliar words are highlighted in the text and defined in sidebars throughout the magazine. The illustrations are meaningful and interesting. Book, media, and web site reviews provide additional information for readers and teachers. *Cobblestone* is a quality magazine and is recommended for school and public library use.

1537. ***Cricket: the magazine for children.*** [ISSN: 0090-6034] 1973. m. USD 35.97 domestic; CND 45.97 Canada; CND 45.97 foreign. Ed(s): Marianne Carus, Deborah Vetter. Cricket Magazine Group, 315 Fifth St, PO Box 300, Peru, IL 61354. Illus. Circ: 65000 Paid. Vol. ends: Aug. Reprint: PQC. *Indexed:* CPerI, ICM. *Aud.:* 9-14 yrs.

Cricket is a quality magazine with general-interest stories and poetry about people and events throughout the world. Activities found include crossword puzzles and recipes. There are some opportunities for reader participation in a letters-to-the-editor section and monthly art contests. Words found within stories and articles that might be new to readers are italicized and defined. *Cricket* is also available on audiocassette. An excellent choice for school and public libraries as well as personal subscriptions.

1538. ***Faces: people, places, cultures.*** [ISSN: 0749-1387] 1984. 9x/yr. USD 29.95 domestic; USD 39.95 foreign. Ed(s): Elizabeth Crooker-Carpentiere. Cobblestone Publishing, 30 Grove St, Ste C, Peterborough, NH 03458; custsvc@cobblestonepub.com; http://www.cobblestonepub.com. Illus., index. Circ: 12000. *Indexed:* AIAP, ICM. *Bk. rev.:* 5, 35-50 words. *Aud.:* 9-14 yrs.

Faces is another quality publication from Cobblestone. The magazine's mission is to study the beliefs, lifestyles, and cultures of people. Each issue has a single focus, perhaps a country or a group of people. The issue explores the theme in depth through articles, maps, timelines, recipes, and folk tales. Color illustrations add interest to the text. Original letters, poems, and drawings are published monthly. Books, audio, video, and web sites are reviewed in the issues. This magazine is a valuable source of multicultural information, and it would be useful in school and public libraries.

1539. ***Footsteps: African-American history for kids.*** [ISSN: 1521-5865] 1999. 5x/yr. USD 23.95 domestic; USD 33.95 Canada; USD 29.95 rest of world. Ed(s): Charles Baker. Cobblestone Publishing, 30 Grove St, Ste C, Peterborough, NH 03458; custsvc@cobblestonepub.com; http://www.cobblestonepub.com. Illus., adv. Circ: 3500 Paid. Vol. ends: May/Jun. *Bk. rev.:* 8-12, length varies. *Aud.:* 9-14 yrs.

Footsteps is a wonderful magazine for middle- and upper-elementary readers that focuses on black history. Each issue is theme oriented with articles, activities, poetry, and artwork related to the theme. Book, museum, and film reviews provide additional resources for the reader or teacher. *Footsteps* encourages readers to submit their original poetry, essays, and artwork. This is a valuable resource for school and public libraries.

1540. ***Girls' Life.*** [ISSN: 1078-3326] 1994. bi-m. USD 14.95 domestic; USD 19.95 Canada; USD 45 elsewhere. Ed(s): Karen Bokram. Monarch Avalon, Inc., 4517 Harford Rd., Baltimore, MD 21214-3122; publisher@girlslife.com. Illus., adv. Online: EBSCO Publishing; Gale Group; OCLC Online Computer Library Center, Inc.; H.W. Wilson. *Indexed:* CPerI, ICM. *Bk. rev.:* Various number and length. *Aud.:* 10-14 yrs.

Girls' Life is a general-interest magazine for preteen girls. Readers will find articles and features on fashion and celebrities and discussions about school, family, and boys. Craft activities, horoscopes, and pen pal opportunities can be found in *Girls' Life.* Each issues includes some book, video, and CD-ROM reviews. Most appropriate for personal subscriptions.

1541. ***Highlights for Children: fun with a purpose.*** Incorporates: *Children's Activities.* [ISSN: 0018-165X] 1946. m. USD 29.64 domestic; USD 43.71 Canada; USD 3.95 newsstand/cover per issue. Ed(s): Kent L Brown, Jr. Highlights for Children, Inc., PO Box 269, Columbus, OH 43216-0269. Illus., index. Circ: 2800000 Paid. Vol. ends: Dec. Microform: PQC. Online: bigchalk; EBSCO Publishing; Gale Group; Northern Light Technology, Inc.; ProQuest Information & Learning; H.W. Wilson. *Indexed:* ICM. *Aud.:* 4-11 yrs.

Highlights for Children continues to be a magazine with consistently excellent stories, articles, activites, and crafts for children ages 4-11. This magazine can be used by nonreaders as well as readers because of the parent–child participation activities. It includes riddles, hidden pictures, and matching activities. Original pictures, poetry, and stories are solicited from readers. "Dear Highlights" gives readers an opportunity to express their concerns. Recommended for school and public libraries as well as personal subscriptions.

1542. ***Hopscotch (Bluffton): for girls.*** [ISSN: 1044-0488] 1989. bi-m. USD 24 domestic; USD 36 foreign. Ed(s): Marilyn Edwards. Bluffton News Printing and Publishing Co., PO Box 227, Bluffton, OH 45817-0164; http://www.hopscotchmagazine.com. Illus., adv. Sample. Circ: 15000 Paid. Vol. ends: Apr/May. Online: EBSCO Publishing; Gale Group. *Indexed:* ICM, MagInd. *Aud.:* 6-10 yrs.

Hopscotch publishes fiction and nonfiction, poetry, crafts, puzzles, and recipes on specific themes. The purpose of the magazine is to promote childhood by developing childhood interests and values through worthwhile reading and activities. It contains no advertising and may be most appealing to children ages 6-10. Appropriate for public libraries and personal subscriptions.

1543. ***Humpty Dumpty's Magazine.*** Formerly (until 1979): *Humpty Dumpty's Magazine for Little Children.* [ISSN: 0273-7590] 1952. bi-m. USD 15.95 domestic; USD 19.95 foreign. Ed(s): Nancy Axelrad. Children's Better Health Institute, 1100 Waterway Blvd, PO Box 567, Indianapolis, IN 46206; g.joray@cbhi.org; http://www.cbhi.org. Illus., index, adv. Circ: 200000. Vol. ends: Dec. Microform: PQC. Online: bigchalk; EBSCO Publishing; Gale Group; Northern Light Technology, Inc.; ProQuest Information & Learning. Reprint: PQC. *Indexed:* ICM, MagInd. *Aud.:* 4-6 yrs.

The aim of *Humpty Dumpty's Magazine,* another publication from the Children's Better Health Institute, is to promote good health among young children. The magazine includes fiction, poetry, science activities, and coloring pages on a monthly theme. Regular features include the "Ask Dr. Cory" column, where parent's questions are answered. This title is best suited to personal subscriptions.

1544. ***Jack and Jill (Inkprint Edition).*** [ISSN: 0021-3829] 1938. bi-m. USD 15.95 domestic; USD 19.95 foreign. Ed(s): Daniel Lee. Children's Better Health Institute, 1100 Waterway Blvd, PO Box 567, Indianapolis, IN 46206; g.joray@cbhi.org; http://www.cbhi.org. Illus., adv. Circ: 215000. Microform: PQC. Online: bigchalk; EBSCO Publishing; Gale Group; ProQuest Information & Learning; H.W. Wilson. Reprint: PQC. *Indexed:* ICM, MagInd. *Aud.:* 7-10 yrs.

Jack and Jill is a health and safe-living magazine for elementary grade readers from the Children's Better Health Institute. Each issue includes stories, recipes, puzzles, and activities relating to health issues. There are regular features including the "Ask Dr. Cory" column, where health-related questions are answered. *Jack and Jill* would be most useful for personal subscribers.

1545. ***Kids Discover.*** [ISSN: 1054-2868] 1991. 12x/yr. USD 26.95 domestic. Ed(s): Stella Sands. Kids Discover, 149 5th Ave, 12th Fl, New York, NY 10010. Illus. Circ: 450000 Paid. *Indexed:* ICM. *Aud.:* 8-12 yrs.

Kids Discover is a science magazine written for elementary school–age readers. There is a single theme for each issue with short articles, diagrams, and activities about this theme. Color photographs and illustrations add to the enjoyment of the theme approach. A table of contents would be helpful in finding the articles highlighted on the cover. *Kids Discover* is most suitable for individual subscribers.

1546. ***Ladybug: the magazine for young children.*** [ISSN: 1051-4961] 1990. m. USD 35.97 domestic; USD 45.97 Canada; USD 4.95 newsstand/cover per issue domestic. Ed(s): Marianne Carus, Paula Morrow. Cricket Magazine Group, 315 Fifth St, PO Box 300, Peru, IL 61354; http://www.cricketmag.com. Illus. Circ: 121000 Paid. Vol. ends: Aug. Online: EBSCO Publishing. *Indexed:* ICM. *Aud.:* 2-6 yrs.

Ladybug is a delightful beginning literary magazine for young children ages 2-6. The stories, poetry, and illustrations are engaging and new information is presented in delightful stories and articles. A parent section offers parent–child art activities. A "Meet the Author" page and a list of book titles by the featured author is also included. Recommended for libraries, preschools, and personal subscriptions.

1547. ***Muse (Chicago).*** [ISSN: 1090-0381] 1996. 10x/yr. USD 32.97; USD 4.95 newsstand/cover per issue. Cricket Magazine Group, 315 Fifth St, PO Box 300, Peru, IL 61354; http://www.cricketmag.com. Illus., adv. Vol. ends: Dec. *Indexed:* ICM. *Aud.:* 8-14 yrs.

Muse is a science-related magazine from the publishers of *Cricket* and *Smithsonian Magazine.* The in-depth articles include photographs, pictures, and diagrams plus suggested web sites and book titles. Article subjects are varied and will appeal to a wide range of readers. This is an interesting and valuable magazine for middle- and upper-elementary children as well as junior-high students. Recommended for school and public libraries and personal subscriptions.

1548. ***National Geographic Kids.*** Formerly (until Oct. 2002): *National Geographic World.* [ISSN: 1542-3042] 1975. 10x/yr. USD 17.95 domestic; USD 23.50 Canada; USD 27 elsewhere. Ed(s): Melina Gerosa Bellows. National Geographic Society, 17th & M Sts, N W, Washington, DC 20036; jagnone@ngs.org; http://www.nationalgeographic.com/world/. Illus., index, adv. Circ: 1000000. Microform: PQC. Online: Gale Group. Reprint: PQC. *Indexed:* CPerl, ICM, MagInd, RGPR. *Aud.:* 6-12 yrs.

National Geographic World is a high-interest children's geography magazine from the National Geographic Society. Topics covered include science, travel, wildlife, exploration, history, anthropology, careers, biography, and just-for-fun articles. A regular feature, "Kids Did It," relates accomplishments of children and includes a photo of the child. The magazine also has tear-out science cards in each issue. Recommended for public and school libraries and personal subscriptions.

1549. ***New Moon: the magazine for girls and their dreams.*** [ISSN: 1069-238X] 1993. bi-m. USD 29 domestic; USD 35 Canada; USD 41 elsewhere. Ed(s): Dawn Gorman. New Moon Publishing, 34 E. Superior St. #200, Duluth, MN 55802; newmoon@newmoon.org; http://www.newmoon.org. Illus., index. Circ: 22000 Paid. Vol. ends: Jul/Aug. *Indexed:* AltPI, CWI, GendWatch, ICM. *Bk. rev.:* Various number and length. *Aud.:* 8-14 yrs.

New Moon presents a strong positive image for girls ages 8-14. It is international in flavor and content with features and articles about customs, ceremonies, and life written by girls from many countries. *New Moon* provides opportunities for reader participation through submission of opinions, ideas, advice, and poetry. This publication promotes unity among girls worldwide and has an editorial board of girls ages 8-14. Valuable for school and public libraries and personal subscriptions.

1550. ***Nickelodeon Magazine.*** [ISSN: 1073-7510] 1993. 10x/yr. USD 15.95; USD 3.50 newsstand/cover per issue. Nickelodeon Magazine, Inc., 1515 Broadway, New York, NY 10036; NickEditor@aol.com; http://www.nick.com/. Illus., adv. Vol. ends: Dec. *Aud.:* 8-14 yrs.

Nickelodeon magazine is fun reading for children ages 8-14. It is the print companion to the cable television network. Each issue has a theme with features consistent with that theme. Advertisements, of which there are many, are labeled as such. Best suited for personal subscriptions.

1551. ***Odyssey (Peterborough): adventures in science.*** [ISSN: 0163-0946] 1979. 9x/yr. USD 29.95 domestic; USD 39.95 foreign. Ed(s): Elizabeth Lindstrom. Cobblestone Publishing, 30 Grove St, Ste C, Peterborough, NH 03458; custsvc@cobblestonepub.com; http://www.cobblestonepub.com. Illus., adv. Sample. Circ: 22000. *Indexed:* ICM. *Aud.:* 9-14 yrs.

Odyssey is a publication that focuses on science, especially earth science and space. It is written for upper-elementary and junior high school students. Each issue has a single theme that is explored in some depth. Color pictures and illustrations throughout each issue add interest. There are regular features as well as opportunities for reader input. Recommended for school and public libraries and personal subscriptions.

1552. ***Owl: the discovery magazine for kids.*** [ISSN: 0382-6627] 1976. 10x/yr. CND 29.95 domestic; CND 32.19 in Maritimes & Quebec; USD 22 United States. Ed(s): Hilary Bain. Bayard Canada, The Owl Group, 49 Front St E, 2nd Fl, Toronto, ON M5E 1B3, Canada; bayard@owl.on.ca; http://www.owlkids.com/. Illus., index. Circ: 100000. *Indexed:* CBCARef, CPerl, ICM. *Aud.:* 8-14 yrs.

Owl is a discovery magazine written for children ages eight and up and is a companion magazine to *Chickadee. Owl* contains entertaining and informative articles, projects, and lots of activities to interest readers. Each page is filled with things to make and do. There are pen pal opportunities, photography and art contests, an opinion page, and usually a removable poster. Recommended for school and public libraries and personal subscriptions.

1553. ***Pack-o-Fun.*** [ISSN: 0030-901X] 1951. 6x/yr. USD 16.97 domestic; USD 19.48 Canada; USD 20.97 elsewhere. Ed(s): Billie Ciancio. Clapper Communications Companies, 2400 E Devon Ave, Ste 375, Des Plaines, IL 60018-4618; imueller@clapper.com; http://www.pack-o-fun.com. Illus., adv. Circ: 102000. *Aud.:* 5-13 yrs.

Pack-o-Fun is a craft magazine designed for children who love to make things. It is filled with seasonal projects and crafts and includes the patterns for many of the activities. Materials needed for the projects and crafts are easily accessible. Some regular features include ideas useful for baby-sitters and family craft activities. A good title for personal subscriptions.

1554. ***Ranger Rick.*** Formerly (until 1983): *Ranger Rick's Nature Magazine.* [ISSN: 0738-6656] 1967. m. USD 17 domestic; USD 26 foreign. Ed(s): Gerry Bishop. National Wildlife Federation, 11100 Wildlife Center Dr., Reston, VA 20190-5362; rick@nwf.org; http://www.nwf.org. Illus., index, adv. Circ: 600000 Paid. Vol. ends: Dec. Microform: NBI; PQC. Online: bigchalk; EBSCO Publishing; Gale Group; Northern Light Technology, Inc.; ProQuest Information & Learning; H.W. Wilson. Reprint: PQC. *Indexed:* CBCARef, CPerl, ICM, MagInd. *Aud.:* 6-12 yrs.

Ranger Rick is a 48-page nature magazine for elementary school age readers published by the National Wildlife Federation. The magazine is filled with short stories and articles that are accompanied by colorful, often full-page pictures and illustrations. The web site has a number of departments and sample activities from the current month's print magazine. *Ranger Rick* is a high-interest magazine for girls and boys and is recommended for school and public libraries and individual subscriptions.

1555. ***Sesame Street.*** [ISSN: 0049-0253] 1971. 10x/yr. USD 19.90. Ed(s): Susan Lapinski, Rebecca Harman. Time Publishing Ventures, 1325 Ave of the Americas, 27th Fl, New York, NY 10019; http://www.ctw.org. Illus., adv. Circ: 1100000. Vol. ends: Dec. *Indexed:* ICM. *Aud.:* 2-6 yrs.

Sesame Street is a wonderfully engaging magazine for preschool children. Familiar characters from the television show are used throughout the magazine. *Sesame Street* includes several activity pages that allow readers to use such skills as cutting, tracing, and coloring. "Big Bird's Gallery" displays children's artwork and solicits questions and drawings from readers. *Sesame Street Parents* is included with each subscription. Most suitable for individual subscriptions but useful in preschools.

1556. ***Skipping Stones: a multicultural magazine.*** [ISSN: 0899-529X] 1988. 5x/yr. USD 35; USD 4.75 newsstand/cover per issue; USD 40 foreign. Ed(s): Arun N Toke. Skipping Stones, PO Box 3939, Eugene, OR 97403-0939; skipping@efn.org; http://www.efn.org/~skipping. Illus. Circ: 2500. *Indexed:* MagInd. *Bk. rev.:* 16, 30-50 words. *Aud.:* 8-14 yrs.
Skipping Stones emphasizes cultural and linguistic diversity within the United States and throughout the world. Much of the writing is contributed by children ages 8-15. Some interesting features are the international pen pals listings, book reviews, reader-contributed artwork, stories and articles, and a guide for parents and teachers. Recommended for school and public libraries and personal subscriptions.

1557. ***Soccer Jr: the soccer magazine for kids.*** [ISSN: 1060-9911] 1992. bi-m. USD 15.97 domestic; USD 28.97 Canada; USD 34.97 elsewhere. Ed(s): Joe Provey. Alyson Schenck Scholastic, 11 Commerce Blvd, P.O. Box 420235, Palm Coast, FL 32142-0235. Illus., adv. Circ: 130000 Paid and controlled. *Aud.:* 7-17 yrs.
Soccer Jr. is written for children and teen soccer enthusiasts. Included in the magazine are interviews with soccer stars, articles about soccer worldwide, playing tips, and short highlights from soccer teams and matches. The focus of *Soccer Jr.* is to promote good sportsmanship and positive attitudes. Advertisements include information on soccer camps. The subscription includes a "Soccer for Parents" pull-out issue twice a year.

1558. ***Spider: the magazine for children.*** [ISSN: 1070-2911] 1993. m. USD 35.97 domestic. Ed(s): Marianne Carus, Heather Delabre. Cricket Magazine Group, 315 Fifth St, PO Box 300, Peru, IL 61354; http://www.cricketmag.com. Illus. Circ: 73000 Paid. Vol. ends: Dec. Online: EBSCO Publishing. *Indexed:* ICM. *Aud.:* 6-9 yrs.
Spider, another quality magazine from the Cricket Magazine Group, is a general-interest magazine with fiction, fairy and folk tales, poetry, crafts, and puzzles to interest early-elementary-age boys and girls. The large, lovely illustrations enhance the writing. Opportunities are available for reader input and participation. *Spider* would be welcomed in school and public libraries and by individuals.

1559. ***Sports Illustrated for Kids.*** [ISSN: 1042-394X] 1989. m. USD 29.99 domestic; USD 39.95 Canada; USD 49 elsewhere. Ed(s): Neil Cohen. Sports Illustrated For Kids, 135 W 50th St, New York, NY 10020-1393. Illus., adv. Circ: 934000 Paid. *Indexed:* CPerI, ICM, MagInd, PEI. *Aud.:* 8-13 yrs.
Sports Illustrated for Kids is a consumer publication written for youngsters, both girls and boys, who are interested in all kinds of sports. It is colorful, with lots of photographs. The magazine features human-interest articles about professional athletes, short summaries and photos of kids who participate in sports, and several regular features. One regular feature, "Funny Photos," prints captions submitted by readers along with the photos. There is a large amount of advertising in this magazine, but school and public libraries will find this a popular title. The online counterpart to *Sports Illustrated for Kids* is *sikids.com.* The content changes at least daily and contains news, games, and interactive features.

1560. ***Stone Soup: the magazine by young writers and artists.*** [ISSN: 0094-579X] 1973. 6x/yr. USD 33 domestic; USD 39 Canada; USD 45 elsewhere. Ed(s): Gerry Mandel. Children's Art Foundation, PO Box 83, Santa Cruz, CA 95063. Illus., adv. Circ: 20000 Paid. Vol. ends: Summer. Online: EBSCO Publishing; Gale Group. *Indexed:* CPerI, MagInd. *Aud.:* 8-13 yrs.
Stone Soup provides young writers and artists with a wonderful opportunity to submit their creative work for publication. All of the stories, poetry, book reviews, and artwork found in the magazine are the original work of the young contributors. Contributors are encouraged to submit writing and artwork based on their experiences and observations. Photographs of the writers and artists are included with their creations. *Stone Soup* is also available in a braille edition. Useful for school creative writing classes and personal subscriptions.

1561. ***Turtle: magazine for preschool kids.*** [ISSN: 0191-3654] 1979. bi-m. USD 15.95 domestic; USD 19.95 foreign. Ed(s): Terry Harshman. Children's Better Health Institute, 1100 Waterway Blvd, PO Box 567, Indianapolis, IN 46206; g.joray@cbhi.org; http://www.cbhi.org. Illus., adv. Circ: 370000. Vol. ends: Dec. *Aud.:* 2-5 yrs.
Turtle is a magazine written with a focus on health and well-being for preschool children. The content includes stories, poems, dot-to-dot pictures, mazes, simple science experiments, recipes, and coloring pages. Two regular features display children's artwork. "Ask Doctor Cory" answers health-related questions for parents and teachers. *Turtle* includes little racial or ethnic diversity in the stories and illustrations. Best suited for personal subscriptions.

Electronic Journals

1562. ***Consumer Reports for Kids Online.*** Former titles: *Zillions (Online Edition);* (until 2000): *Zillions (Print Edition);* (until 1990): *Penny Power.* 1980. irreg. Ed(s): Charlotte Baecher. Consumers Union of the United States, Inc., 101 Truman Ave, Yonkers, NY 10703-1057; http://www.zillions.org. Illus. Circ: 200000. Microform: NBI; PQC. *Indexed:* CPerI, ConsI, ICM. *Aud.:* Age 8 and up.
Consumer Reports for Kids Online is the electronic version of the former print publication *Zillions.* The purpose is to help children make informed decisions concerning use and purchase of consumer products and to develop consumer literacy skills. Products reviewed, tested, and rated are high-interest items for the readers: toys, sports supplements, cameras, etc. Money management issues are discussed, with reader input included as possible solutions to the problems. *Consumer Reports for Kids Online* has good graphics and is easy to navigate. Appropriate for school use as well as public library and home use.

1563. ***Cyberkids.*** 1995. q. Mountain Lake Software, 298 Fourth Ave., San Francisco, CA 94118; http://www.cyberkids.com. *Aud.:* 7-12 yrs.
Cyberkids is a cool electronic magazine for 7- to 12-year-olds. It offers several opportunities for children's creative work to be shared. The art gallery displays original work by children throughout the world and the young-composers pages feature original music by young people. There are 55 family-oriented interactive games available to play. *Cyberkids* offers chat rooms and a message board for its readers to connect with their peers. Creative and educational contests are sponsored by this e-journal, for example, the National Young Game Inventor's Contest. Links to other sites are organized by subject. Most appropriate for personal use.

1564. ***Girl Tech.*** 1996. m. Radica Games, Ltd., http://www.girltech.com. *Aud.:* Ems, Hs.
Girl Tech is a great electronic magazine for girls and young teens. It publishes material on topical issues, health matters, women in sports and other professions, science and math games, and word games. Profiles of women in various professions offer readers a glimpse of possibilities for themselves. There are many interactive opportunities on *Girl Tech.* Some of the more interesting interactive areas include "Story Starter," "Girls Rule" (sign language), and "Invention." The "Invention" page solicits original inventions, offers quotes about inventions, gives information about female inventors, lists resources for kid inventors, and offers tips for teaching about inventions. *Girl Tech* is devoted to encouraging technology use by girls and to raising awareness and confidence in using technology by its readers.

1565. ***A Girl's World.*** 1996. m. A Girl's World Productions, Inc., 825 College Blvd. PMB 102-442, Oceanside, CA 92057; http://www.agirlsworld.com. *Aud.:* Ems, Hs.
The subtitle for this e-journal is "where girls and teens rule the web!" It encourages and empowers 7- to 17-year-old girls to become active contributors through a variety of opportunities. Writing contests, articles, quizzes, and problem-solving activities are examples of the varied interest areas found here. A "Book Club" offers an opportunity for readers to write book reviews. The "City Walk" section includes entertainment features with movie reviews and

articles about celebrities. *Girl's World* has an e-mail option to connect girls with similar experiences, problems, or challenges without publishing their e-mail addresses. Advice columns and opinion polls are included in the journal. Fun reading!

1566. ***MidLink Magazine.*** 1994. q. Ed(s): Caroline McCullen. Ligon Middle School, 706 E Lenoir St, Raleigh, NC 27601; http://longwood.cs.ucf.edu/~MidLink/. *Aud.:* Ems.

Subtitled "the digital magazine by students, for students from 8 to 18," *MidLink Magazine* is designed to highlight excellent work from creative classrooms around the world. There are several sections to the magazine. The Articles section showcases school/class web projects prepared for elementary, middle grades, or upper grades. The Honor Roll of Best Web Sites is organized by broad subjects and includes pages for Students, Teachers, ESL, Web Masters, Just for Fun, and Links to other web sites. Classrooms wishing to collaborate with others on online projects can find a list of possible schools. *MidLink Magazine* has a historical archive of articles back to 1994. Teachers are the editors of this great magazine. This will be valuable to both students and teachers in school classrooms and libraries, and helpful for public libraries and student homework assignments.

■ CHINA

See also Asia and the Pacific section.

Susan Xue, State and Foreign Documents Librarian, Norlin Library, University of Colorado at Boulder, Boulder, CO 80309; susan.xue@colorado.edu

Introduction

China, in addition to maintaining its strong development momentum, is experiencing even more changes in external relations and the domestic arena. Officially becoming a member of WTO in 2001 and winning both the bid to host the World Expo in 2010 and the Olympic Games in 2008, China has further improved its external position in foreign trade and investment, but it has also faced challenges from opening up more to the outside world. The social, economic, and cultural changes within the country have affected, and will continue to affect, its internal policies and practices. It also remains to be seen how the new generation of leaders will respond to both the external and domestic issues. Current hot issues in China include the WTO, environmental deterioration, an increasing gap between the poor and the rich, unemployment, political and economic reform, business and investment, and relations with leading countries in the world. Journals selected in this section touch upon all these issues but go beyond them to cover other topics. Because business is such an important issue in China, even general-interest publications provide at least brief business news. Some business titles in this section would be good choices for international business collections. General-interest journals, news and business magazines, newspapers, and annual publications from and about China, Hong Kong, and Taiwan are all considered for this section. Interestingly in scholarly publications, most of them show a gradual increase in contributors from mainland China, which furnishes an improved access to research done by scholars who live in this fourth-largest country. As the strong and frequently opposing viewpoints of the People's Republic of China and the Republic of China are reflected in their publications, care has been taken to balance the selection of journals to provide local, regional, and international perspectives; annotations about any political viewpoints are included when possible. There are increasingly more online newspapers and journals from and about China; however, quality and language limit the number of titles selected. For further information, readers may wish to consult the Internet Guide for Chinese Studies (part of WWW Virtual Library) at http://sun.sino.uni-heidelberg.de/igcs, which provides an excellent index to Chinese and China-related publications and links to some online journals. Harvard-Yenching Library Chinese Studies Online Resources (http://hcl.harvard.edu/harvard-yenching/chinadatabase.html) facilitates links to news, electronic newspapers and journals, databases in Chinese, and Chinese library and academic resources. The web directory http://chinasites.com provides links by subject category on China. The Digital Chinese Library of UC Berkeley (http://library.berkeley.edu/CCSL) focuses on electronic social sciences resources in China, while the Gateway Service Center of Chinese Academic Journal Publications (http://www.library.pitt.edu/gateway) at the University of Pittsburgh provides free delivery of full-text Chinese-language academic journal articles to any researcher in the United States.

Basic Periodicals

Ems: *China Pictorial;* Hs, Ga: *Beijing Review, China Business Review, China Today, Sinorama;* Ac: *Beijing Review, China Business Review, The China Journal, The China Quarterly, Modern China.*

Basic Abstracts and Indexes

America: History and Life, Historical Abstracts, PAIS, Social Sciences Index.

1567. ***American Journal of Chinese Studies.*** Former titles: *Journal of Chinese Studies; American Association for Chinese Studies. Bulletin; American Association for Chinese Studies Newsletter; American Association of Teachers of Chinese Language and Culture. Newsletter.* [ISSN: 0742-5929] 1984. s-a. USD 30. Ed(s): Dr. Thomas J Bellows. American Association for Chinese Studies, Dept od Political Science, University of Texas at San Antonio, San Antonio, TX 78249-0603. Illus., adv. Refereed. Circ: 550 Paid. Vol. ends: Oct. *Indexed:* AmH&L, BAS, MLA-IB, PAIS. *Bk. rev.:* 5-6, length varies. *Aud.:* Ac.

This journal is the official publication of the American Association for Chinese Studies. Contributed by international authors and referred, articles are in all disciplines of the social sciences and humanities. Although the content is relevant to both Taiwan and mainland China, the journal has a strong Taiwan focus or a major Taiwan component. Several book reviews appear in each issue. Articles in recent issues cover election in Taiwan and China after WTO. In general, business and politics topics dominate, but there are also articles about literature and history. This academic journal would be appropriate for both Asian Studies collections and most general academic collections because of its coverage of a wide range of disciplines. For balance of viewpoint, libraries that select this title may also want to consider *China Journal* and *Journal of Contemporary China* (below in this section).

1568. ***Beijing Review: a magazine of Chinese news and views.*** Formerly (until 1979): *Peking Review.* [ISSN: 1000-9140] 1958. w. USD 75.30 United States; CND 111 Canada; GBP 48.10 United Kingdom. Ed(s): Haibo Lii, Yu Zhaohui. Beijing Review Publishing Co., 24 Baiwanzhuang Rd, Beijing, 100037, China; http://www.bjreview.com.cn/. Illus., index, adv. Sample. Circ: 100000. Vol. ends: No. 52. Microform: LIB; MIM; PQC. Online: Factiva; Gale Group; LexisNexis; ProQuest Information & Learning. *Indexed:* BAS, ExcerpMed, LRI, SSI. *Bk. rev.:* 1-2, 500-1,000 words. *Aud.:* Hs, Ga, Ac.

The weekly *Beijing Review* (North American edition) contains short capsules describing events across China and the world. Originated in China, this journal has a strong government perspective and reflects China's position on domestic and international issues. Medium-length feature articles address major national and international events, while short articles brief the political, social, and economic developments within the country. Chinese Communist Party documents and commentary dominate the contents and provide excellent materials for students and scholars. Regular sections include Global Observer, Regional Feature, Business, Weekly Watch (with color photographs), and Travel Guide. The online version (www.bjreview.com.cn/bjreview/EN) is a free alternative. Recommended for public or academic libraries that support China Studies programs, or libraries with general interest in China.

1569. ***China Business Review.*** Formerly (until 1977): *U S China Business Review.* [ISSN: 0163-7169] 1974. bi-m. USD 99 domestic; USD 150 foreign. Ed(s): Catherine Gelb. United States - China Business Council, 1818 N St, N W, Ste 200, Washington, DC 20036-2406; info@uschina.org; http://www.chinabusinessreview.com/. Illus., index, adv. Sample. Circ: 3000 Paid. Vol. ends: Nov/Dec (No. 6). Microform: PQC. Online: bigchalk; The Dialog Corporation; Northern Light Technology, Inc. *Indexed:* ABIn, B&I, BAS, BPI, LRI, PAIS. *Bk. rev.:* 1-5, 500 words. *Aud.:* Ac, Sa.

This official magazine of the U.S.–China Business Council provides unique insight into the business and investment environment in China, legal developments, impending legislation, and industrial-sector issues. Each issue contains a few articles examining one particular topic. Two recent examples discuss China's WTO membership and intellectual property rights in China. Topics cover all sectors of the Chinese economy and all business issues, from human resources and management to operational issues and broader policy issues. Small business, securities markets, relations between economic reform and political reform, and China's e-commerce are examples in recent issues. Regular columns include www.china—Internet resources, a letter from the president of the U.S.–China Business Council, and the Council Bulletin. The China Business column provides lists organized by industry including recent contracts and negotiations underway. The first issue each year contains a cumulative index for the preceding year. Online access for subscribers is also available at a special price (http://www.chinabusinessreview.com). Recommended for both academic and public libraries serving communities with an interest in China or business.

1570. ***China Daily.*** [ISSN: 0748-6154] 1983. d. USD 140. Ed(s): Zhu Yinghuang. China Daily, 15 Huixin Dongjie, Beijing, 100029, China; cdweb@chinadaily.net; http://www.chinadaily.net/. Illus., adv. Microform: NRP. Online: The Dialog Corporation; Factiva; Florida Center for Library Automation; Gale Group; LexisNexis; Northern Light Technology, Inc.; ProQuest Information & Learning. *Indexed:* B&I, ChemAb. *Aud.:* Ga, Ac.

As the first English-language newspaper distributing news to overseas audiences after the Chinese Cultural Revolution, *China Daily* has grown in 12 years into a leading newspaper about China. Available in over 150 countries and regions around the world, it covers news in all areas, including national and international, government, industry, trade, information technology, research, and entertainment. The Monday issue contains a Business Weekly supplement. Like other publications originating from China, the articles and editorials are written from a government perspective. There is also a web edition (see Electronic Journals in this section). Recommended for both public and academic libraries.

1571. ***China Facts and Figures Annual.*** [ISSN: 0190-602X] 1978. a. USD 77. Academic International Press, PO Box 1111, Gulf Breeze, FL 32562-1111; info@ai-press.com; http://www.ai-press.com. Illus., index. *Aud.:* Ga, Ac, Sa.

This yearly publication accumulates all basic and statistical information about the People's Republic of China. Topics includes government, military affairs, population, cities, economy, natural resources, industry, agriculture, communications, trade, finance, science and technology, environment, health and medicine, education, law and criminal justice, and sports. Although current statistical information about China is now available on the Internet, this annual compilation has proven to be a valuable reference since it incorporates extensive and detailed data all in one place. Each volume also includes maps, China's constitution, current policies, government leaders, basic market prices, and regional information. Recommended for academic and public library collections.

1572. ***The China Journal.*** Formerly (until Jul. 1995): *Australian Journal of Chinese Affairs.* [ISSN: 1324-9347] 1979. s-a. Jan. & Jul. USD 40 (Individuals, USD 25; Students, USD 20). Ed(s): Anita Chan, Jonathan Unger. Contemporary China Centre, Australian National University, Research School of Pacific and Asian Studies, Canberra, ACT 0200, Australia; ccc@coombs.anu.edu.au; http://rspas.anu.edu.au/ccc/home.htm. Illus., index, adv. Sample. Refereed. Circ: 1300. Microform: PQC. Online: JSTOR (Web-based Journal Archive). *Indexed:* AmH&L, ArtHuCI, BAS, IBSS, IBZ, IPSA, PAIS, PSA, RRTA, SSCI, SUSA, WAE&RSA. *Bk. rev.:* Number varies, 25-1,000 words. *Aud.:* Ac.

China Journal is devoted to research on events and issues in China, Hong Kong, and Taiwan after 1949, with a focus on studies contributing to the understanding of Communist Party history and contemporary events. Refereed externally, articles cover a wide range of topics but have a strong focus on political, economic, and social matters. A notable feature of this journal is its well-written and extensive book reviews, covering new publications on China on all subjects. Recent issues address such subjects as China's economic system, China's rural periodic market, and housing issues in urban China. The web site includes tables of contents, author and topic index, abstracts of articles since 1997, and other information. Libraries with site licenses to *JSTOR* (www.jstor-.org) will have access to the full texts of earlier issues through 1995. Given its international authorship, excellent quality of book reviews, and extensive indexing, this journal is recommended for all Chinese and Asian Studies collections.

1573. ***China Mail.*** [ISSN: 0218-1517] 1988. q. SGD 26 domestic; SGD 40 Malaysia; SGD 57 in Asia. Ed(s): Tang Kin Eng. T W L Publishing (Singapore) Pte. Ltd., Soon Seng Bldg, 25 Genting Rd 07-01, Singapore, 349482, Singapore; cic@pacific.net.sg; http://www.nihao.com/cic. Adv. Circ: 51650. *Aud.:* Ga, Sa.

Published in Singapore, this journal is aimed at business people and others with a general interest in China. It informs readers of China's recent developments in economics, property, law, tourism, and arts and culture. The Travel column is a guide to the provinces and autonomous regions of China, featuring popular attractions and useful tips on local cuisine, entertainment, and accommodations. The Arts and Culture section introduces China through its artistic and cultural fabric. The Exhibitions and Conferences column reports on upcoming events in China. This journal is now available online by subscription. Given its low price and quick updates of events, this journal is worth consideration for both public and academic libraries.

1574. ***China Pictorial.*** [ISSN: 0009-4420] 1950. m. USD 24.60. Ed(s): Zhang Jiahua. China Pictorial Publishing House, Haich'an-qu, Cheong-zhuang, 33, Xi-lu, Beijing, 100044, China. Illus., index, adv. Circ: 500000. Microform: IDC; PQC. *Indexed:* BAS, GeoRef. *Aud.:* Ems, Hs, Ga.

This large-format monthly magazine features fine photographs and informative articles. Its purpose is to introduce life and culture in the People's Republic of China to foreign audiences. Subjects include arts and culture, environment, history, people, sports, daily life, tourism, and major political events. Although some articles and photos show arts, history, and tourist attractions, the focus is more on portraits of the social, economic, and political situation in mainland China. This publication is now available online without subscription in French, Japanese, German, Russian, Spanish, Arabic, Italian, and English, while the print version is published in 16 languages at a low price. *China Pictorial*'s high-quality photos and well-written articles will appeal to libraries with a general interest in China.

1575. ***The China Quarterly: an international journal for the study of China.*** [ISSN: 0305-7410] 1959. q. USD 142 (Individuals, USD 69). Ed(s): Julia Strauss. Cambridge University Press, The Edinburgh Bldg, Shaftesbury Rd, Cambridge, CB2 2RU, United Kingdom; information@cambridge.org; http://uk.cambridge.org. Illus., index, adv. Sample. Refereed. Circ: 4200. Microform: PQC. Online: EBSCO Publishing; JSTOR (Web-based Journal Archive); OCLC Online Computer Library Center, Inc.; ProQuest Information & Learning; RoweCom Information Quest. *Indexed:* ABCPolSci, AmH&L, ArtHuCI, BAS, CJA, IBSS, IPSA, JEL, MLA-IB, PAIS, PRA, RRTA, SSCI, SSI, WAE&RSA. *Bk. rev.:* 10-15, 500-750 words. *Aud.:* Ga, Ac.

This academic journal covers all aspects of contemporary China including the People's Republic of China, Taiwan, Hong Kong, and Macao. Its interdisciplinary approach allows a range of subjects including anthropology and sociology, literature and the arts, business and economics, geography, history, international affairs, law, and politics. International in scholarship, this journal provides readers with historical perspectives, in-depth analyses, and a deeper understanding of China and Chinese culture. In addition to major articles and research reports, each issue contains a comprehensive book review section, and also a Quarterly Chronicle, which keeps readers informed of events during the previous three-month period in and affecting China. There is a special issue annually, most recently on religions in China. A comprehensive index appears in the December issue. Highly recommended for academic libraries and for any library with an interest in Chinese or other Asian Studies.

1576. ***China Report: a journal of East Asian studies.*** [ISSN: 0009-4455] 1964. q. GBP 144 in Europe, Middle East, Africa & Australasia. Ed(s): Giri Deshinakar. Sage Publications India Pvt. Ltd., M-32 Market, Greater

Kailash-I, PO Box 4215, New Delhi, 110 048, India; http://www.indiasage.com/. Illus., index, adv. Sample. Refereed. Circ: 700. Vol. ends: Nov. Microform: PQC. *Indexed:* AmH&L, BAS, IBSS, IPSA, PSA, RRTA, SociolAb, WAE&RSA. *Bk. rev.:* 2-5, 750-1,000 words. *Aud.:* Ac, Sa.

This academic quarterly of the Centre for the Study of Developing Societies (India) "encourages the increased understanding of contemporary China and its East Asian neighbors, their cultures and ways of development and their impact on India and other South Asian countries." Articles address current issues in the areas of politics, economy, culture, and other disciplines. It also offers a unique focus on China's relationship with many nations and philosophies, while many journals in this section focus on China's relationship with the United States. Each issue consists of scholarly articles, a commentary, the text of documents and agreements between China and other nations, book reviews, and bibliographies of specific topics in the field. Recommended for academic libraries.

1577. *China Review International: a journal of reviews of scholarly literature in Chinese studies.* [ISSN: 1069-5834] 1994. s-a. USD 45 (Individuals, USD 30; Students, USD 18). Ed(s): Ronald C. Brown. University of Hawaii Press, Journals Department, 2840 Kolowalu St, Honolulu, HI 96822-1888; uhpjourn@hawaii.edu; http://www.uhpress.hawaii.edu/. Illus., adv. Sample. Circ: 550. Vol. ends: Sep. Microform: PQC. Online: EBSCO Publishing; Florida Center for Library Automation; Gale Group; OCLC Online Computer Library Center, Inc.; Project MUSE; RoweCom Information Quest; Swets Blackwell. Reprint: PQC; PSC; WSH. *Indexed:* AmH&L, BRI, CBRI, IBSS, L&LBA. *Bk. rev.:* 5-8, 2,000-3,000 words. *Aud.:* Ac.

This journal contains primarily substantive book reviews, responses to previously published reviews, and a list of books received. All reviews are in English, generally by invitation only, and each issue includes over 50 reviews. Feature reviews are usually in-depth examinations of new publications ranging from four to forty pages in length, while other reviews are from two to five pages. Contributors are leading scholars in the field. Reviews are of books and monographs on all disciplines, including translations and collections of papers from China, Hong Kong, Japan, Europe, the United States, and elsewhere. Its multidisciplinary scope and international coverage make it an indispensable tool for all those interested in Chinese culture and civilization, but particularly valuable for scholars. With its low price and high quality, it is a necessary selection for any academic library, and essential for libraries with an Asian Studies collection. The table of contents, as well as current and back issues, can be found on the journal's web site at http://muse.jhu.edu/journals/cri.

1578. *China Rights Forum: the journal of human rights in China.* Formerly (until 1993): *Human Rights Tribune.* [ISSN: 1068-4166] 1990. q. USD 50 (Individuals, USD 35; Students, USD 25). Ed(s): Stacy Mosher. Human Rights in China, 350 Fifth Ave, 3309-10, New York, NY 10118; hrichina@hrichina.org; http://www.hrichina.org. Illus. Sample. Refereed. Circ: 3500. *Indexed:* BAS, PAIS. *Bk. rev.:* 1-3, 800 words. *Aud.:* Ga, Ac.

Started as a bilingual journal in 1990 (in English only since 1997) by an independent organization, *China Rights Forum* is dedicated to documenting human rights developments in China and informing the Chinese people about international standards on human rights. Articles are on many human rights topics ranging from sexuality to elections. Recently, the revamped journal adopted a thematic focus for each issue while retaining existing features. Recent themes include China as partner to the world, corporate citizenship and human rights, and human rights and sports. Regular columns include editorials, a publisher bulletin, news updates, book reviews, a list of Internet resources, opportunities for activism, and prisoner profiles. Contributions are generally from activists in the human rights movement and exiles. The contents tend to be narrative and descriptive rather than scholarly research. Full-text articles since 2000 are accessible online at http://www.hrichina.org. Recommended for libraries serving patrons interested in Chinese government policy on human rights or human rights in general.

1579. *China Today (N. American Edition).* Formerly (until 1990): *China Reconstructs.* [ISSN: 1003-0905] 1952. m. USD 32.10 in US & Canada; USD 34.40 elsewhere. Ed(s): Meng Jiqing. Jinri Zhongguo Zazhishe, 24 Baiwanzhuang Lu, Beijing, 100037, China; http://www.chinatoday.com/. Illus., index, adv. Sample. Vol. ends: Dec. Microform: IDC; PQC; NRP. Online: The Dialog Corporation. *Indexed:* BAS, GeoRef, PRA. *Bk. rev.:* 2-3, 400-600 words. *Aud.:* Hs, Ga.

China Today (formerly *China Reconstructs*) was founded in 1952 by the late honorary chairwoman of China, Soong Ching Ling, wife of Sun Yat-sen. It is published in five languages by the China Welfare Institute. It gives "the latest information on China's economic construction, culture, arts, science, technology, sports, health, politics, social life, ethnic minorities, scenery, tourism, history, archaeology, international friendship and other aspects" of the People's Republic of China. Although similar in intent to *China Pictorial* (above in this section), *China Today* contains more long articles on social, environmental, scientific, cultural, and travel subjects. Special columns include the Language Corner, for students and teachers of the Chinese language, and Voice of Readers. As this journal has a strong government perspective, libraries who subscribe may also want to select *Sinorama* (below in this section) as the counterpart for Taiwan. Recommended for libraries with a general interest in China.

1580. *China's Foreign Trade.* [ISSN: 0009-4498] 1956. m. USD 99.40. Ed(s): Xinyi Li. China Chamber of International Commerce (CCOIC), China Council for the Promotion of International Trade (CCPIT), 1 Fuxingmenwai St, Beijing, 100860, China; http://www.ccpit.org/publisher/ccpit24.html. Illus., adv. Circ: 70000. Vol. ends: Dec. *Indexed:* BAS. *Aud.:* Ga, Ac, Sa.

This publication presents official Chinese government views of China's laws, regulations, and policies regarding foreign trade. Its primary purpose is to introduce the business and economic environment in the People's Republic of China to the outside world in a promotional way. Each issue contains news on major economic and trade events, market analyses, industry-specific reports, corporate profiles, foreign enterprise experiences in China, and tourism information. Given its position in interpreting Chinese government regulations and policies, this magazine is a necessity for both academic and public libraries with interest in international business or China's foreign trade. This title supplements the more academic *China Business Review* (above in this section).

1581. *Chinese Language Teachers Association. Journal.* [ISSN: 0009-4595] 1966. 3x/yr. USD 80. Ed(s): Shou Hsin Teng. Chinese Language Teachers Association, c/o Kalamazoo College, 1200 Academy St, Kalamazoo, MI 49006. Illus., adv. Sample. Circ: 525. Microform: PQC. Reprint: PQC. *Indexed:* BAS, BRI, CIJE, HumInd, L&LBA, MLA-IB. *Aud.:* Ac.

This is an official publication of the Chinese Language Teachers Association. Articles are in both Chinese and English and cover Chinese-language pedagogy, Chinese linguistics, Chinese literature, and curriculum ideas. Authors are primarily members of the association. Chinese language teachers will want to read this journal, and many students may be interested as well. Book reviews provide valuable comments on reference books, dictionaries, and general books on China, which may be useful to those responsible for collection development in language, education, and Asian Studies. Recommended for libraries that serve Chinese language and Asian Studies programs.

1582. *Chinese Literature: Essays, Articles, Reviews.* Formerly (until 1980): *Chinese Literature.* [ISSN: 0887-8099] 1979. a. USD 50 (Individuals, USD 25). Ed(s): Eugene Eoyang, William Nienhauser. Chinese Literature: Essays, Articles, Reviews, c/o Dept of Comparative Literature, Ballantine Hall Rm 914, Bloomington, IN 47405. Illus., index, adv. Refereed. Microform: PQC. *Indexed:* ArtHuCI, BAS, MLA-IB. *Bk. rev.:* 10-15, 1,000-1,500 words. *Aud.:* Ac.

This is an annual scholarly publication covering both modern and classical Chinese literature but with more focus on the latter. Each issue contains articles and book reviews on poetry, literary history, the arts, and philosophy. Book reviews written by experts cover a broad range of new publications, translations, and studies. The journal's in-depth treatment of topics and the extensive bibliographies make it particularly useful to scholars. A recent issue was devoted to the study of narratives written during the Ming and Qing periods. Recommended for academic libraries.

1583. ***Chinese Translation Series.*** 1984. irreg. M.E. Sharpe, Inc., 80 Business Park Dr, Armonk, NY 10504. *Aud.:* Ac, Sa.

Titles in this series include

Chinese Economy. (Formerly: *Chinese Economics Studies*) [ISSN: 1097-1475] 1967. bi-m. USD 979. Joseph Fewsmith. *Indexed:* CurrCont, JEL, PAIS, SOCI, WAERSA.

Chinese Education and Society (Formerly: *Chinese Education*). [ISSN: 1061-1932] 1968. bi-m. USD 1055. Stanley Rosen. *Indexed:* CIJE, CurrCont, EdI, SOCI.

Chinese Law and Government. [ISSN: 0009-4609] 1968. bi-m. USD 979. Michael Y. M. Kau. *Indexed:* CLI, CurrCont, ILegPer, PAIS, SOCI.

Chinese Sociology and Anthropology. [ISSN: 0009-4625] 1968. q. USD 670. Anita Chan. *Indexed:* CurrCont, LingAb, SOCI, StudWomAb.

Chinese Studies in History (Formerly: *Chinese Studies in History and Philosophy*). [ISSN: 0009-4633] 1967. q. USD 670. Li Yu-ning. *Indexed:* AmerH, CurrCont, HistAb.

Contemporary Chinese Thought (Formerly: *Chinese Studies in Philosophy* and *Chinese Studies in History and Philosophy*). [ISSN: 1097-1467] 1967. q. USD 670. Carine Defoort. *Indexed:* AHCI, CurrCont, PhilosI.

This series is devoted to locating and translating the most important Chinese studies in the disciplines covered and making them accessible to English-speaking scholars. Chinese sources are primarily scholarly journals, collections of articles published in book form, and newspapers. Original citations are listed for each translation, with a brief note about the source. Recent topics include cross-strait relations (Chinese Law and Government), eldercare issues in China (Chinese Sociology and Anthropology), history of American-educated Chinese (Chinese Studies in History), and Chinese-style urbanization (Chinese Economy). Special thematic issues bring together the best studies from a wide variety of sources, which is of high value to scholars in these fields. The prices for these titles are high, but they are of critical importance for research libraries that support Chinese Studies. Subscriptions are available for individual titles, and libraries may also want to consider other document delivery options as an alternative.

1584. ***Issues & Studies: an international quarterly on China, Taiwan, and East Asian affairs.*** [ISSN: 1013-2511] 1964. q. Mar., Jun., Sep & Dec. USD 48. Ed(s): Szu-Yin Ho. Institute of International Relations, 64 Wanshou Road, Wenshan District, Taipei, 116, Taiwan, Republic of China; iir@nccu.edu.tw; http://www.iir.nccu.edu.tw. Illus., index, adv. Sample. Refereed. Circ: 550 Paid. Microform: PQC. Reprint: ISI; PQC. *Indexed:* ABCPolSci, AgeL, AmH&L, ForAb, IBSS, IPSA, IndVet, PRA, PSA, SSCI, SociolAb, VetBull, WAE&RSA. *Aud.:* Ac, Sa.

Published by the Institute of International Relations (IIR) at the National Chengchi University in Taiwan, this is an "interdisciplinary journal devoted to the discussion and analysis of problems related to the domestic and international affairs of China, Taiwan, and East Asia." Particular focus is given to issues on China and Taiwan. Some of the articles have an anti-Communist perspective and a Taiwanese point of view, but most studies are objective. A newly added Policy Analysis section in 2002 offers insight into domestic and international policy in Taiwan and China. Recent topics include U.S.-China relations, state-owned enterprises in China, and China-Taiwan relations. Contributors are international, although the editorial board is almost solely drawn from the IIR. Recommended for academic libraries with an interest in Asian affairs. A balanced collection can be achieved by also selecting journals from mainland China.

1585. ***Journal of Chinese Linguistics.*** [ISSN: 0091-3723] 1973. s-a. USD 45 (Individuals, USD 30). Ed(s): William S Y Wang. Project on Linguistic Analysis, 2222 Piedmont Ave, Berkeley, CA 94720; jcl@socrates.berkeley.edu; http://socrates.berkeley.edu/~JCL. Illus., index, adv. Refereed. Circ: 450. Vol. ends: Jun. *Indexed:* ArtHuCI, BAS, CIJE, IBZ, L&LBA, LingAb, MLA-IB, SSCI. *Bk. rev.:* 3-5, 100-200 words. *Aud.:* Ac, Sa.

This journal contains studies of both classical and modern Chinese languages and dialects. Due to its in-depth discussion of linguistics and theory, it is more appropriate for scholars interested in linguistic analysis, not for beginning students and teachers of Chinese language. A recent issue sampled covers the multiple origins of old Chinese, animal metaphors in Chinese political disclosure, and grammaticalization of verbs. The web site provides indexes to all journal issues and monographic series, while the journal publishes a cumulative index every five years. Recommended for academic libraries that serve Chinese language programs, along with the *Journal of the Chinese Language Teachers Association* (below in this section).

1586. ***Journal of Chinese Philosophy.*** [ISSN: 0301-8121] 1973. q. USD 405 print & online eds. Blackwell Publishing, Inc., Commerce Place, 350 Main St, Malden, MA 02148; subscrip@blackwellpub.com; http://www.blackwellpublishing.com. Illus., index, adv. Sample. Refereed. Circ: 600. Vol. ends: Dec. *Indexed:* ArtHuCI, BAS, IBSS, IPB, MLA-IB, PhilInd, RI-1, SSCI. *Bk. rev.:* 2-3, 2,000-3,000 words. *Aud.:* Ac, Sa.

This journal is "devoted to the study of Chinese philosophy and Chinese thought in all their phases and stages of articulation and development." Scholarly articles focus on historical Chinese philosophical studies; interpretation and expositions of traditional Chinese texts; and comparative studies within a Chinese philosophical framework, or in relation to schools of thought in the Western tradition. Topics generally are on any of four major historic periods (pre-Ch'in and Han eras, neo-Taoism and Chinese Buddhism, neo-Confucianism, and Chinese philosophy since the nineteenth century), as well as five major disciplinary emphases (logic and scientific thinking, metaphysical theories, moral philosophy and the philosophy of religion, art theories and aesthetics, and social and political philosophies). A recent issue sampled focuses on "Ethics in Greek Philosophy and Chinese Philosophy." Book reviews are essay treatments of a few titles per issue. Recommended for academic libraries.

1587. ***Journal of Contemporary China.*** [ISSN: 1067-0564] 1992. q. GBP 251 (Individuals, GBP 67). Ed(s): Suisheng Zhao. Carfax Publishing Ltd., 4 Park Sq, Milton Park, Abingdon, OX14 4RN, United Kingdom; enquiry@tandf.co.uk; http://www.tandf.co.uk/. Illus. Sample. Refereed. Online: EBSCO Publishing; Ingenta Select; Northern Light Technology, Inc.; OCLC Online Computer Library Center, Inc.; ProQuest Information & Learning; RoweCom Information Quest; Swets Blackwell. Reprint: PSC. *Indexed:* AmH&L, BAS, BrHumI, IBZ, IPSA, MLA-IB, PSA, SociolAb. *Bk. rev.:* 5-8, 700-1,500 words. *Aud.:* Ac.

This journal provides excellent coverage of theoretical and policy research on contemporary Chinese affairs. Its "fields of interests include economics, political science, law, culture, history, international relations, and sociology, literature, business and other social sciences and humanities." Book reviews cover publications from mainland China, Taiwan, Hong Kong, and other countries when the topic is contemporary China. With authors from many countries, this journal has an international perspective. The web site provides many valuable added features, including tables of contents and announcements of forthcoming articles. The online version is free with institutional subscriptions. Recommended for academic libraries supporting Asian or Chinese Studies.

1588. ***Late Imperial China.*** Formerly (until 1984): *Ch'ing-shih Wen-t'i.* [ISSN: 0884-3236] 1975. 2x/yr. USD 90 (Individuals, USD 28). Ed(s): William T Rowe. Johns Hopkins University Press, Journals Publishing Division, 2715 N Charles St, Baltimore, MD 21218-4363; http://www.press.jhu.edu/. Illus., adv. Refereed. Circ: 553. Vol. ends: Dec. Online: EBSCO Publishing; OCLC Online Computer Library Center, Inc.; Project MUSE; RoweCom Information Quest; Swets Blackwell. Reprint: PSC. *Indexed:* AmH&L, ArtHuCI, BAS, PSA, SociolAb. *Aud.:* Ac.

This is the principal scholarly journal for historians of China specializing in the Ming (1368-1644) and Qing (1644-1912) dynasties. Articles cover political and historical subjects, business and economics, literature, religion, art, language, culture, gender history, and philosophy. Each issue contains three or four lengthy articles and occasionally one or two research notes. New work by historians in Europe, Japan, Taiwan, and the People's Republic of China is often featured. Although published almost entirely in English, each article has a glossary in Chinese. Subscriptions can be print, electronic, or both with a substantial discount. Recommended for academic libraries.

1589. ***Modern China: an international quarterly of history and social science.*** [ISSN: 0097-7004] 1975. q. GBP 343 print & online eds. in Europe, Middle East, Africa & Australasia. Ed(s): Philip C C Huang.

Sage Publications, Inc., 2455 Teller Rd, Thousand Oaks, CA 91320; info@sagepub.com; http://www.sagepub.com. Illus., index, adv. Sample. Refereed. Circ: 1250 Paid. Vol. ends: Oct. Reprint: PSC. *Indexed:* ABCPolSci, AgeL, AmH&L, ArtHuCI, BAS, GeogAbPG, IBSS, IBZ, IPSA, PAIS, PRA, PSA, SFSA, SSCI, SSI, SUSA, SociolAb. *Aud.:* Ac.

This journal provides new answers to old questions, or new understanding and interpretation of the contemporary history and social sciences of the People's Republic of China. While covering the entire modern period of China (i.e., from about 1500 to the present) it particularly focuses on the revolutionary experience. Originated in the United States, this journal is in English and authors are international. Each issue contains four or five substantial articles, and only substantial article-length book reviews are published. A recent issue examines the revolution in the Yangzi Delta area, prostitution taxes in the late Qing Dynasty, and women taxi drivers in China. Recommended for academic libraries that support Chinese history or Asian Studies programs.

1590. ***Renditions: a Chinese-English translation magazine.*** [ISSN: 0377-3515] 1973. s-a. USD 42 (Individuals, HKD 130). Ed(s): Dr. Eva Hung. Chinese University of Hong Kong, Research Centre for Translation, Sha Tin, Hong Kong; renditions@cuhk.edu.hk; http://www.renditions.org/renditions/magazines/m-menu.html. Illus., adv. Sample. Refereed. Circ: 1000 Paid. Vol. ends: Nov. *Indexed:* ArtHuCI, BAS, MLA-IB. *Aud.:* Ac.

This refereed journal contains English translations of a wide variety of Chinese literature including poetry, prose, articles, memoirs, editorials, chronologies, essays, reviews, and original fiction. Concentration is on the humanities and social sciences; content is drawn from both classical and contemporary Chinese literature. Short biographical entries are supplied on the contributors, an international group. Tables of contents, information on contributors and special issues, and sample issues are available on the web site at http://www.renditions.org/renditions. Every fourth issue includes an index, and a separately bound index for numbers 1-32 is also available. Recommended for academic libraries supporting Chinese Studies program.

1591. ***Sinorama.*** [ISSN: 0256-9043] 1976. m. USD 32; TWD 1500. Kwang Hwa Publishing Co., 6300 Wilshire Blvd, Ste 1510A, Los Angeles, CA 90048-5217. Illus., adv. Circ: 110000. Vol. ends: Dec. *Indexed:* IBZ. *Bk. rev.:* 2-3, length varies. *Aud.:* Hs, Ga, Ac.

This bilingual monthly is devoted to distributing information about Taiwan to an international audience. Articles focus on news and culture in the Republic of China. A recent issue includes a cover section on Taiwanese industry and nanotech, the overseas Chinese community, news across the strait, people and society, and science and technology. Articles are normally short but well written and translated. This magazine provides an alternative viewpoint of Taiwan and mainland China to *China Today* or *China Pictorial* (above in this section). The free and well-designed online version can be found at www.sinorama.com.tw/en. This title is a good choice for libraries serving patrons with a general interest in Taiwan and mainland China. Essential for a general collection.

1592. ***Social Sciences in China.*** [ISSN: 0252-9203] 1980. q. USD 65.20. Ed(s): Li Xinda. Shehui Kexue Zazhishe, 1-158 Gulou Xidajie, Beijing, 100720, China. Illus., index. Refereed. *Indexed:* BAS, IBSS, PAIS. *Bk. rev.:* 1-3, 1,000-2,000 words. *Aud.:* Ac, Sa.

Published by the Chinese Academy of Social Sciences (CASS), this academic journal covers the social sciences from a Marxist, socialist, and current Chinese leadership viewpoint. Topics covered include economics, politics, international relations, sociology, law, history, philosophy, and occasionally literature and traditional Chinese religions. Articles and book reviews are translated from CASS's and other Chinese-language journals. Each issue also contains a list of Selected Titles from Chinese Periodicals, a bibliography of articles grouped by subject category, including journals published outside of China. Academic libraries that select this title may want to consider other academic journals from Taiwan in order to have a balanced collection.

1593. ***South China Morning Post.*** [ISSN: 1021-6731] 1946. d. HKD 2028; HKD 7 newsstand/cover per issue. Ed(s): Robert Keatley. South China Morning Post Ltd., PO Box 47, Hong Kong; scmphkh@attmail.com; http://www.scmp.com. Adv. Circ: 114446 Paid. Microform: PQC; NRP. Online: Gale Group; Northern Light Technology, Inc. *Aud.:* Hs, Ga, Ac, Sa.

This English-language Hong Kong daily provides broad coverage of local and global news. Increasingly, it offers more political and business news on the People's Republic of China with a viewpoint different from the leading papers in China. It includes both a Business and a Markets section, which makes it an excellent place to keep up with international business. The Technology section provides fresh news on IT development and trends. The online version (www.scmp.com) offers PostPhoto, which has a collection of over 169,000 images, and a Companies section. It also includes several sections useful to locals or tourists only, such as city and hotel guides, online shopping, and local entertainment information. Recommended as the first-choice newspaper for libraries that want a Chinese daily. Libraries wanting a well-balanced collection may also wish to subscribe to the *People's Daily* (above in this section).

1594. ***Taipei Journal.*** Former titles: *Free China Journal;* (until 1983): *Free China Weekly.* [ISSN: 1605-6906] 1964. w. TWD 600; USD 24. Ed(s): Henry Hu. Kwang Hwa Publishing Co., 2 Tientsin St, Taipei, 10041, Taiwan, Republic of China; http://gio.gov.tw. Illus. Circ: 35000. Microform: PQC. Online: LexisNexis. Reprint: PQC. *Aud.:* Ga, Ac.

Taiwan Journal, formerly *Free China Journal*, is an official publication of the Republic of China. The weekly tabloid presents articles on political and social developments in both Taiwan and the People's Republic of China. Emphasis is on editorial content as well as texts of official documents and speeches. Regular columns include business, statistical summaries, political news, and arts and culture. Libraries that collect *Beijing Review* (above in this section) may want to consider this journal to get differing perspectives on issues in the People's Republic of China and the Republic of China. The online version of this journal and additional information are available from the Republic of China's web site at http://publish.gio.gov.tw/FCJ/fcj.html.

1595. ***Taipei Review.*** Formerly: *Free China Review.* [ISSN: 1608-702X] 1951. m. TWD 600 domestic; USD 22 United States; USD 28 elsewhere. Ed(s): Jiang Ping Lun. Kwang Hwa Publishing Co., 2 Tientsin St, Taipei, 10041, Taiwan, Republic of China; http://www.gio.gov.tw. Illus., index, adv. Sample. Circ: 53000. Vol. ends: Dec. Microform: PQC. *Indexed:* BAS, EngInd, MLA-IB, PAIS. *Bk. rev.:* 1, 1,500-3,000 words. *Aud.:* Ga, Ac, Sa.

Taipei Review, formerly *Free China Review*, is a major English-language monthly that has been published by the Republic of China Government Information Office since 1951. It provides in-depth features on political and business trends, society, the arts, cross-strait relations, key books, special reports, and interviews. Regular columns include politics, business, government, religion, health, society, and arts. This magazine is illustrated with color photos. Free online subscription is available from http://publish.gio.gov.tw/FCR/fcr.html. Recommended for libraries with a general interest in Taiwan as well as mainland China. It should be complemented by *Beijing Review* or *China Today* (above in this section) to balance the collection.

1596. ***T'oung Pao: revue internationale de sinologie.*** [ISSN: 0082-5433] 1890. s-a. EUR 198 print & online eds. (Individuals, EUR 184 print & online eds.). Ed(s): P E Will, B ter Haar. Brill Academic Publishers, Inc., PO Box 9000, Leiden, 2300 PA, Netherlands; cs@brill.nl; http://www.brill.nl. Illus., index. Refereed. Microform: BHP. Online: Chadwyck-Healey Incorporated; EBSCO Publishing; Ingenta Select; OCLC Online Computer Library Center, Inc.; Swets Blackwell. *Indexed:* AIAP, AmH&L, ArtHuCI, BAS, IBZ, MLA-IB. *Bk. rev.:* 8-10, 500-1,500 words. *Aud.:* Ac.

This distinguished international journal has been published for over a century. Articles are mainly in English but sometimes in French or German. The journal is devoted to traditional Chinese Studies, with an emphasis on history, classic literature, and the arts. The focus is on humanities, while articles on politics, anthropology, and sciences are also occasionally published. Recent article topics include social issues in Song and Ming Dynasty and religion. Its book review section and literature reviews are invaluable to scholars of Sinology. This journal is unique for its global perspective. Recommended for academic libraries.

1597. ***Zhongguo Jingji Xinwen.*** [ISSN: 1000-9094] w. USD 430. Zhongguo Jingji Xinwen, P.O. Box 8025, Beijing, China. *Aud.:* Ac, Sa.

This Chinese-English bilingual weekly is published in Hong Kong and provides up-to-date news and analysis on Hong Kong, China, and the worldwide economy. For more than 50 years, it has been known for its in-depth and broad coverage. In each issue, the Focus column contains news briefs reporting new developments in industries; feature articles provide in-depth analysis of particular topics; Industrial Profile outlines a few industrial sectors; and the Statistics/ Data column provides the most recent economic data. Some issues contain Regulations and Policies, Exhibitions and Fairs, and a Market Trends column. Due to its high price, libraries may want to consider choosing between *China Business Review* and *China Economic News*. However, those who support patrons with interests in international business may want to subscribe to this title.

Electronic Journals

1598. ***China Daily (Hong Kong Edition).*** d. HKD 5 newsstand/cover per issue. China Daily, 15 Huixin Dongjie, Beijing, 100029, China; cdweb@chinadaily.net; http://www.chinadaily.net/. *Aud.:* Ems, Hs, Ga, Ac, Sa.

Another subsidiary of *China Daily* (above in this section), this online English-language newspaper focuses on news and events in Hong Kong. While its sister publication *China Daily Web Edition* has national coverage of news, this site reports local Hong Kong news with from a lightly governmental viewpoint. Regular news sections include Nation, Business, and Campus Life. In-depth articles can be found in the Focus section. Government Information provides policy- and regulation-related news releases. Metropolitan, Shanghai Focus, Hong Kong/Taiwan, and Snapshot cover activities in major cities and provinces. Accompanied by *China Daily* and *Shanghai Star* (in this section), this newspaper is recommended for all libraries.

1599. ***China Daily Web Edition.*** China Daily, 15 Huixin Dongjie, Beijing, 100029, China; http://www.chinadaily.net/. *Aud.:* Ga, Ac, Sa.

This is a leading online English-language newspaper with a government perspective on China. It presents news and business news topics on China and the world. Free sections are General News, Business and Economics, Information Technology, Sports, and Entertainment, and Education, while BizChina requires a subscription. Business Weekly (http://www1.chinadaily.com.cn/bw/bw.html), a sub-section, provides in-depth business and economic coverage once a week. Business Daily Update, a section of BizChina, provides more detailed business reports at a subscription cost ranging from USD 300 to 1,900. Industry statistics, market reports, and other publications are also available online at a cost. Although most of the site is in English, there are two sections entirely in Chinese: the World Report and Newsphoto sections, which provide access to a large collection of color images. There is a Language Tip section to help English speakers with Chinese. Recommended as a good news source about the People's Republic for both public and academic libraries.

1600. ***People's Daily Online.*** Renmin Ribao Chubanshe, 2 Jintai Xilu, Chaoyangmenwai, Beijing, 100733, China; http://english.people.com.cn/. *Aud.:* Hs, Ga, Ac, Sa.

Launched in 1998, this online newspaper has become another major English publication like *China Daily Web Edition* (above in this section). It translates from the *People's Daily* print edition (Chinese-language only, with a subscription of three million) major news releases and new policies, resolutions, and statements of the Chinese government. An About China section provides access to the country?s constitution, government structure, white papers of the Chinese government, other official publications, and basic facts on China. This newspaper has a strong Chinese government perspective that is reflected in the columns China, Business, Opinion, World, and Sci-Edu. It is light on sports and lifestyle columns common to other newspapers. Recommended for all libraries, but should be supplemented by papers such as the *Shanghai Star* or *China Today* (both in this section).

1601. ***Perspectives (Sharon).*** [ISSN: 1533-1105] 1999. bi-m. Ed(s): Xujun Ying. Overseas Young Chinese Forum, 46 Longmeadow Ln, Sharon, MA 02067; oycf_editor@hotmail.com; http://www.oycf.org/. *Aud.:* Hs, Ga, Ac, Sa.

Published by the Overseas Young Chinese Forum, this new online journal is primarily designed to exchange ideas, facilitate cross-disciplinary dialogue, and popularize abstract ideas for purposes of education and development. Articles are in the form of commentaries and essays related to China and other current issues, and accessible to general readers as well as academics. The focus is on law, humanities, politics, economics, business, and sociology. One of the strengths of this journal is its coverage of up-to-date issues. A recent issue discusses Professor Ronald Dworkin's trip to China and the U.S. invasion of Iraq. Recommended for all libraries.

1602. ***Shanghai Star.*** 1992. w. Thu. Shanghai Daily, 395 Wanhangdu Rd, Shanghai, 200042, China; Shhstar@sh163a.sta.net.cn; http://chinadaily.chinadaily.com.cn/star/. Illus. *Aud.:* Hs, Ga, Ac, Sa.

This tabloid provides exclusive in-depth reports on people and issues in Shanghai, the leading industrial city in China, and neighboring regions. Well-known for its socially conscious, human-interest, informative, and entertaining approach, this online paper appeals to white-collar workers and English-speaking residents of Shanghai. Regular sections include World, Nation/City, Culture, People, Fashion, Technology, Health, Travel, Dining Out, Stage, Events, Sports, and Business. Although *Shanghai Star* is a local paper, it provides coverage on both local and international topics in each section. Originated in mainland China, it surprisingly does not have a particular government perspective on domestic and international political issues. Articles are entertaining and well written. Recommended for every library's news collection.

1603. ***World News Connection.*** 1996. d. U.S. Department of Commerce, National Technical Information Service, 5285 Port Royal Rd, Springfield, VA 22161; info@ntis.gov; http://www.ntis.gov/. *Aud.:* Ga, Ac, Sa.

This online news service covers news and events worldwide, not only China. However, it offers an extensive array of translated and English-language news and information from global media sources on the People's Republic of China, and it is particularly effective in its coverage of local media sources. The material in *WNC* is provided by the Foreign Broadcast Information Service, a U.S. government agency that has monitored and analyzed overseas news for over 60 years. The information is obtained from full texts and summaries of newspaper articles, conference proceedings, television and radio broadcasts, periodicals, and nonclassified technical reports. New information is entered every government business day. Generally, this information is available within 24-72 hours from the time of original publication or broadcast. Users can conduct unlimited interactive searches with a subscription, and have the ability to set up automated searches known as "profiles." Although many regions are covered by this service, China can be selected as a regional search criterion. Pricing information can be found at http://wnc.fedworld.gov/subscription.html. Recommended for academic and large public libraries.

■ CIS AND EASTERN EUROPE

See also Asia; China; Europe; and Middle East sections.

Manuel Sanudo, Assistant Professor, Reference Librarian, Queens College, Rosenthal Library, Flushing, NY 11367; msanudo@qc1.qc.edu; 718-997-3769; FAX: 718-997-3753

Introduction

The Russia of today was first created in 1985 when the glasnost and perestroika reforms of Mikhail Gorbachev began to alter the political, economic, and social institutions of the Soviet Union. These revolutionary processes changed an outmoded system into an open society, with December 1991 becoming a benchmark year in the transformation of Russia, the Commonwealth of Independent States, and Eastern Europe. The changes that took place affected all aspects of life, including the publishing world. Throughout the last dozen years, all serials have undergone a painful transition from the planned economies of the communist regimes to the current free-market economies. Many older serials and some newer ones could not withstand these changes and ceased to exist. Others have changed in one form or another, merged, or acquired a completely new outlook. In spite of the constant fluctuations of the ruble since 1991, the supply and distribution of publications has begun to settle. In addition, a continued growth of the middle class, a habitual interest in reading, which the people of this region have fostered through decades, and the liberalization of society, which has created an open atmosphere for reading, have all combined to produce a vital publishing atmosphere.

Most of the periodicals listed here are published in the United States and Western Europe and all are available through their publishers directly and/or through subscription agencies like EBSCO.

Basic Periodicals

Hs: *Moscow News, Russian Life;* Ga: *Current Digest of the Post-Soviet Press, Moscow News, Russian Life;* Ac: *The Russian Review, Studies in East European Thought.*

Basic Abstracts and Indexes

Historical Abstracts; MLA International Bibliography; PAIS International in Print.

1604. ***Anthropology and Archeology of Eurasia: a journal of translations.*** Formerly: *Soviet Anthropology and Archeology.* [ISSN: 1061-1959] 1962. q. USD 825 (Individuals, USD 140). Ed(s): Marjorie M Balzer. M.E. Sharpe, Inc., 80 Business Park Dr, Armonk, NY 10504; custserv@mesharpe.com; http://www.mesharpe.com. Illus., index, adv. Sample. Refereed. Vol. ends: Spring (No. 4). Reprint: PSC. *Indexed:* AICP, AbAn, AgeL, AnthLit, BAS, SSCI. *Aud.:* Ac, Sa.

"This journal contains unabridged translations of manuscripts, journal articles and parts of books. Materials are selected which best reflect developments in anthropology and archeology in the Newly Independent States and are of most interest to those professionally concerned with these fields." Among the Russian-language journals used in translation are *Ethnographic Review, Russian Archaeology, Works of the Institute of Ethnography, Collection of the Museum of Anthropology and Ethnography, Problems of Philosophy, Problems of History, New in Ethnography, Science and Religion, Social Sciences, The North Star, The East,* and *Friendship of the People.* Each issue begins with a five- to ten-page introduction by the editor. Articles vary in length, with the original source of each article cited in a footnote and the name of the translator. Recommended as an important purchase for academic and special libraries with an interest in anthropology, archaeology, and ethnology.

1605. ***Canadian - American Slavic Studies.*** Formerly (until 1972): *Canadian Slavic Studies - Revue Canadienne d'Etudes Slaves.* [ISSN: 0090-8290] 1967. q. USD 45 (Individuals, USD 20). Ed(s): Charles Schlacks, Jr. Charles Schlacks, Jr., Publisher, PO Box 1256, Idyllwild, CA 92549. Illus., index. Sample. Refereed. Circ: 700. Vol. ends: Winter (No. 4). Microform: BHP. *Indexed:* ABS&EES, AmH&L, ArtHuCI, BHA, MLA-IB, RI-1, SSCI. *Bk. rev.:* 20-30, 300-1,000 words, signed. *Aud.:* Ac, Sa.

This scholarly journal publishes articles in the fields of literature, linguistics, and history dealing with Russia and Eastern Europe. Each issue is about 125 pages in length and contains about four well-documented articles of which one might be in Russian or French, with the rest in English. Each issue includes an extensive book review section and a "Books Received" section covering publications dealing with all areas of the social sciences and humanities. These sections are a useful selection tool for librarians. Recent issues have articles on pictograms and ideograms in contemporary Russian visual poetry, Lev Rubinstein's conceptualism in theory and practice, a reinterpretation of Malevich, and religious dissent in seventeenth-century Russia. Recommended as an important journal for academic libraries with Slavic Studies programs and for public libraries with a clientele interested in Russia and Eastern Europe.

1606. ***Canadian Slavonic Papers: an interdisciplinary journal devoted to Central and Eastern Europe.*** [ISSN: 0008-5006] 1956. q. CND 50 domestic; CND 55 foreign. Ed(s): Oleh S Ilntyzkyj. Canadian Association of Slavists, c/o Gust Olson, University of Alberta, Edmonton, AB T6G 2E6, Canada; golson@gpu.srv.ualberta.ca; http://www.utoronto.ca/slavic/cas. Illus., index, adv. Refereed. Circ: 700. Reprint: PSC. *Indexed:* ABS&EES, AmH&L, ArtHuCI, BHA, CBCARef, L&LBA, MLA-IB, PAIS, PSA, SSCI, SociolAb. *Bk. rev.:* 35-40, 300-500 words, signed. *Aud.:* Ac, Sa.

This is a multidisciplinary journal publishing in English and French original research on topics relating to Russia and Central and Eastern Europe and covering the fields of language and linguistics, literature, history, political science, sociology, economics, anthropology, geography, and the arts. The editors have stated that "the collapse of the Soviet Union and the rise of new independent states has sharpened interest in the region, [and] presented scholars with unexpected problems and issues, while opening for them completely new opportunities for research by giving them access to totally unanticipated sources." The book review section in each issue provides scholars and collection-development librarians with an excellent source of books on Russia and Eastern Europe. An important journal for academic library collections at institutions with Slavic Studies programs and for research and larger public libraries with a clientele interested in Slavic Studies.

1607. ***Communist and Post-Communist Studies.*** Former titles (until 1992): *Studies in Comparative Communism;* (until 1968): *Communist Affairs.* [ISSN: 0967-067X] 1962. q. EUR 344 (Individuals, EUR 123). Ed(s): Andrzej Korbonski, Luba Fajfer. Pergamon, The Boulevard, Langford Ln, East Park, Kidlington, OX5 1GB, United Kingdom. Illus., index, adv. Sample. Refereed. Vol. ends: Dec (No. 4). Microform: PQC. Online: Gale Group; ingenta.com; ScienceDirect; Swets Blackwell. *Indexed:* ABCPolSci, ABS&EES, AmH&L, ArtHuCI, BAS, IBSS, IPSA, PAIS, PRA, SSCI, SSI, SWA. *Aud.:* Ac, Sa.

This international journal covers all communist and post-communist states and communist movements, including their international relations. It is focused on the analysis of historical as well as current developments in the communist and post-communist world, including ideology, economy, and society. The editors "aim to provide comparative foci on a given subject, e.g. education in China, by inviting comments of a comparative nature from scholars specializing in the same subject matter, but in different countries, like Poland or Romania." In addition to the traditional disciplines of history, political science, economics, and international relations, the editors encourage the submission of articles in less developed fields of social sciences and humanities, such as cultural anthropology, education, geography, religion, and sociology. Recent issues contain articles on topics like gender and the experience of poverty in Eastern Europe and Russia after 1989, the hidden dimension of poverty among Polish women, and fertility and childbearing practices among poor Gypsy women in Hungary. Recommended for both academic and public libraries with readers interested in communist and post-communist states throughout the world.

1608. ***Current Digest of the Post-Soviet Press.*** Formerly (until 1992): *Current Digest of the Soviet Press;* Incorporates: *Current Abstracts of the Soviet Press.* [ISSN: 1067-7542] 1949. w. USD 1175 domestic; USD 1215 foreign. Ed(s): Gordon Livermore. Current Digest of the Soviet Press, 3857 N. High St., Columbus, OH 43214; fowler.40@osu.edu; http://www.cohums.ohio-state.edu/. Illus., index. Circ: 1000. Vol. ends: No. 52. Microform: Pub. Online: Gale Group. *Indexed:* BAS, CDSP, PAIS. *Aud.:* Hs, Ga, Ac.

This weekly periodical presents a selection of Russian-language press materials carefully translated into English (or summarized in whole or in part). The translations are intended for use in teaching and research and are therefore presented as documentary materials without elaboration or comment and state the opinions of the original authors. Each issue in its about 24 pages contains around four feature articles and the "News of the Week" section, which is further divided into "The Russian Federation," "Other Post-Soviet States," and "International Affairs" subsections. Articles range from one paragraph to several pages in length and cover broad topics from economics, finance, and politics to education, religion, crime, and labor. This is an invaluable source of information on current events in Russia and the surrounding countries. A basic source for academic, public, and high school libraries with current interests in Russian affairs.

1609. ***Demokratizatsiya: the journal of post-soviet democratization.*** [ISSN: 1074-6846] 1992. q. USD 98 (Individuals, USD 47; USD 24.50 per issue). Heldref Publications, 1319 18th St, NW, Washington, DC 20036-1802; subscribe@heldref.org; http://www.heldref.org. Adv. Reprint: PSC. *Indexed:* IPSA, PSA, SociolAb. *Bk. rev.:* Varies, 500-600 words, signed. *Aud.:* Ac, Sa.

This international journal covers the historical and current transformations in the Soviet Union and its successor states. Scholars from around the world write on the politics, government, political economics, social issues, legal systems, international relations, human rights, and other topics as well as the history of Soviet totalitarianism and its transformation during the perestroika period. A recent issue contains articles on social capital and grassroots democracy in Russia, regional variations in the implementation of Russia's federal district reform, and human rights in post-Soviet Russia. Most issues contain a book review section of works published in the United States. Recommended for academic libraries with programs in Russian Studies and for larger academic libraries with patrons interested in this field.

1610. ***East European Constitutional Review.*** [ISSN: 1075-8402] 1992. q. Free. Ed(s): Stephen Holmes. University of Chicago, Law School, 1111 E 60th St, Chicago, IL 60637; http://www.law.uchicago.edu/Publications/CSCEE/EECR. Illus. Vol. ends: Fall (No. 4). *Indexed:* ABS&EES, ILP. *Aud.:* Ac, Sa.

This journal covers the challenges and obstacles of post-socialist law and politics in Eastern Europe. According to its editor, it gives an in-the-trenches understanding of the dilemmas of post-socialist legal reform, serves as a vital and lively forum for discussion and debate about pressing issues of the rule of law, and tracks the constitutional development of the region through academic articles, roundtables, and symposia given by regional and foreign scholars. It also offers country-by-country updates of regular, balanced, empirical information gathered and presented by local experts; these updates, which map the process of contitutional and legal change, currently cover 19 countries. Together with its Russian-language sister edition in Moscow, the journal reaches academics, policymakers, lawyers, judges, students, and activists in over 50 countries. Recent issues include articles on Putin's judicial reform, the future of jury trials in Russia, a Siberian criminal court, and Eurasia's nonstate states . Recommended for academic and research libraries with programs of study and a clientele interested in Eastern European Studies.

1611. ***East European Jewish Affairs.*** Formerly (until 1991): *Soviet Jewish Affairs.* [ISSN: 1350-1674] 1971. s-a. GBP 93 print & online eds. Ed(s): Howard Spier. Frank Cass Publishers, Crown House, 47 Chase Side, Southgate, London, N14 5BP, United Kingdom; jnlsubs@frankcass.com; http://www.frankcass.com/jnls/. Illus., index, adv. Sample. Refereed. Vol. ends: Winter (No. 2). Microform: PQC. Reprint: PQC. *Indexed:* AmH&L, IBSS, IJP, RI-1. *Bk. rev.:* 5-10, 300-500 words, signed. *Aud.:* Ac, Sa.

Published under the aegis of the Department of Hebrew and Jewish Studies, University College–London, and the Oxford Institute for Jewish Studies, this is a journal of interdisciplinary studies relevant to an understanding of the position and prospect of Jews in the former Soviet Union and East-Central Europe; the journal deals with these topics in historical depth and within the context of general, social, economic, political, and cultural developments. Each issue contains several book reviews, some long review articles, and the "Books Received" section with brief annotations of new books. These book sections are particularly useful to librarians. Recent issues contain articles on the ethnicity of Russian and Ukrainian Jews, Jewish immigrants from the former Soviet Union in Canada, Jewish identity in post-communist Poland, and Passover in the Soviet Union from 1917 to 1941. This is an important, highly recommended journal for academic or large public libraries collecting in these areas.

1612. ***East European Politics & Societies.*** [ISSN: 0888-3254] 1987. q. USD 243 & Caribbean. Ed(s): Vladimir Tismaneanu. Sage Publications, Inc., 2455 Teller Rd, Thousand Oaks, CA 91320; info@sagepub.com; http://www.sagepub.com. Illus., adv. Refereed. Circ: 1200. Vol. ends: No. 3. Microform: PQC. Online: Pub.; EBSCO Publishing; Florida Center for Library Automation; Gale Group; ingenta.com; Northern Light Technology, Inc.; OCLC Online Computer Library Center, Inc. *Indexed:* ABCPolSci, ABS&EES, AmH&L, ArtHuCI, IBSS, IPSA, PSA, SSCI, SSI, SociolAb. *Aud.:* Ac, Sa.

This international journal, published in association with the American Council of Learned Societies, examines the social, political, and economic issues in Eastern Europe. It offers holistic coverage of every country in the region, ranging from detailed case studies to comparative analysis and theoretical issues. The editor points out that the reason for the journal is to consider Eastern Europe's unique role in producing ideas and experimental solutions for solving the major problems of the modern world. Recent issues include articles on Greek communism from 1968 to 2001, the Second World War and the East European revolution, the federation of young democrats in post-communist Hungary, and Popovici's theory on the Austro-Hungarian monarchy. Recommended for special collections and academic libraries with departments in Russian and Eastern European Studies.

1613. ***East European Quarterly.*** [ISSN: 0012-8449] 1967. q. USD 20 (Individuals, USD 15). Ed(s): Stephen Fischer Galati. East European Quarterly, University of Colorado, Box 29, Regent Hall, Boulder, CO 80309; eestudies@mailstation.com. Illus., index, adv. Refereed. Circ: 950. Vol. ends: Winter (No. 4). Microform: PQC. Online: bigchalk; Chadwyck-Healey Incorporated; EBSCO Publishing; Florida Center for Library Automation; Gale Group; Northern Light Technology, Inc.; OCLC Online Computer Library Center, Inc.; ProQuest Information & Learning; H.W. Wilson. Reprint: PQC. *Indexed:* ABS&EES, AmH&L, ArtHuCI, BHA, HumInd, IBSS, IPSA, PAIS, SSCI, SSI. *Bk. rev.:* 1-5, 300-800 words, signed. *Aud.:* Ac, Sa.

The mission of this scholarly journal is "to be a channel for the publication of significant contributions in the fields of East European history, sociology, economics, politics, and civilization by scholars from the countries of East Central Europe, Western Europe, North America and, for that matter, throughout the world and to promote a better understanding of the place of Eastern Europe in world history, politics and civilization." Each issue contains five to eight articles that are all well documented. Book reviews cover publications from North America, Western Europe, and Eastern Europe. This journal is quite inexpensive and is highly recommended for academic libraries with research collections in Eastern European Studies and for large public libraries with patrons interested in countries of this area.

1614. ***Eastern European Economics: a journal of translations.*** [ISSN: 0012-8775] 1962. bi-m. USD 1190 includes online access (Individuals, USD 140). Ed(s): Josef Brada. M.E. Sharpe, Inc., 80 Business Park Dr, Armonk, NY 10504; custserv@mesharpe.com. Illus., index, adv. Sample. Refereed. Vol. ends: Nov/Dec (No. 6). Online: EBSCO Publishing; Ingenta Select; OCLC Online Computer Library Center, Inc.; Swets Blackwell. Reprint: PSC. *Indexed:* ABIn, JEL, PAIS, SSCI, WAE&RSA. *Aud.:* Ac, Sa.

This journal contains original articles and translations of both published and unpublished works on the economies of Central and Eastern Europe. According to the editor, "articles are selected which best reflect developments in Eastern European economic theory and practice and which are of most interest to those professionally concerned with this field." Each issue is almost 100 pages long, with three to five well-documented articles written by scholars from various Eastern European countries. A recent issue deals with privatization in Serbia, southeastern Europe and the Euroization debate, and the economic performance and structure of Albania, Bulgaria, Macedonia, and Greece. Highly recommended for acquisition by academic and special libraries with programs covering Eastern European economics and business.

1615. ***Emerging Markets Finance & Trade.*** Former titles (until 2002): *Russian and East European Finance and Trade;* (until 1992): *Soviet and Eastern European Foreign Trade; American Review of Soviet and Eastern European Foreign Trade.* [ISSN: 1540-496X] 1965. bi-m. USD 1150 (Individuals, USD 140). Ed(s): Ali M Kuton. M.E. Sharpe, Inc., 80

Business Park Dr, Armonk, NY 10504; custserv@mesharpe.com; http://www.mesharpe.com. Illus., index, adv. Sample. Refereed. Vol. ends: Nov/Dec (No. 6). Reprint: PSC. *Indexed:* ABIn, JEL, PAIS, SSCI. *Aud.:* Ac, Sa.

This journal publishes original research papers in the fields of economics, finance, international business and trade. It focuses on the economies of the former Soviet Union, including the Caucasus and Central Asia, and Central and Eastern Europe. Policy-oriented empirical and less technical papers are also included. One of the journal's primary purposes is to translate previously published papers on the region in order to make important research findings available in English. Each issue contains three or four well-documented and well-translated articles and covers areas such as the determinants of interest rates in Turkey, labor market developments in Hungary from a Central Bank perspective, and foreign trade and factor intensity in an open developing country. Recommended for academic and special libraries.

1616. ***Eurasian Geography and Economics.*** Former titles (until 2002): *Post-Soviet Geography and Economics;* (until 1995): *Post-Soviet Geography;* (until 1992): *Soviet Geography; Soviet Geography - Review and Translation.* [ISSN: 1538-7216] 1960. 8x/yr. USD 468 (Individuals, USD 80). Ed(s): C Cindy Fan, Stanley D Brunn. V.H. Winston & Son, Inc., c/o Bellwether Publishing, Ltd, 8640 Guilford Rd, Ste 200, Columbia, MD 21046; bellpub@bellpub.com; http://www.bellpub.com. Illus., index, adv. Refereed. Circ: 650. Vol. ends: No. 8. Reprint: PSC. *Indexed:* ABS&EES, BAS, ExcerpMed, GeoRef, GeogAbPG, JEL, PAIS, SSCI, SSI. *Aud.:* Ac, Sa.

This journal publishes original papers in geography and economics covering all states of the former Soviet Union and Eastern Europe as well as selected regions on their borders. The economic and geographical issues most emphasized include economic development, environmental protection, urban and rural settlement, nationalities, and related issues confronting the transition economies of Russia and Eastern and Central Europe. Related subjects like demography and ethnic studies that have a pronounced spatial element and/or significant economic content will also be considered for inclusion. Recent issues contain articles on Russian revenues from oil and gas exports, national territory and the reconstruction of history in Kazakhstan, and economic reform in Tajikistan. This journal is recommended for academic libraries with programs in these areas of study and for research and larger public libraries whose clientele also requires materials in these areas.

1617. ***Europe - Asia Studies.*** Formerly (until 1993): *Soviet Studies.* [ISSN: 0966-8136] 1949. 8x/yr. GBP 460 (Individuals, GBP 128). Ed(s): R A Clarke. Carfax Publishing Ltd., 4 Park Sq, Milton Park, Abingdon, OX14 4RN, United Kingdom; enquiry@tandf.co.uk; http://www.tandf.co.uk/. Illus., index, adv. Sample. Refereed. Vol. ends: Dec (No. 8). Online: EBSCO Publishing; Florida Center for Library Automation; Gale Group; Ingenta Select; JSTOR (Web-based Journal Archive); OCLC Online Computer Library Center, Inc.; ProQuest Information & Learning; RoweCom Information Quest; Swets Blackwell. Reprint: PSC; SCH. *Indexed:* ABCPolSci, ABS&EES, AmH&L, ArtHuCI, BAS, BrHumI, CJA, HumInd, IBSS, IBZ, IPSA, LRI, PAIS, PSA, RRTA, SSCI, SSI, SociolAb, WAE&RSA. *Bk. rev.:* 20-25, 500-1,000 words, signed. *Aud.:* Ac, Sa.

This journal is devoted to researching the political, historical, economic, and social affairs of what were once the Soviet bloc countries. The focus of the research is intended to reflect the way in which the transformation of these countries' political and economic systems is affecting their relationship with the rest of Europe and the growing links between what was Soviet Central Asia and other countries in both Europe and Asia. The comparison with similar transformations taking place in China is a further element in the scope of this journal. The "Reviews" and "Books Received" sections are especially useful as selection tools for acquisiton librarians. A recent issue includes articles such as tax evasion in Russia, popular support for nationalism in Russia's ethnic republics, and peasant support for the Socialist Revolutionary Party during 1917. Highly recommended for academic and research libraries with advanced-level scholars interested in the economics and politics of the region.

1618. ***Journal of Baltic Studies.*** Formerly (until 1972): *Bulletin of Baltic Studies.* [ISSN: 0162-9778] 1970. q. USD 95. Ed(s): Thomas Salumets. Association for the Advancement of Baltic Studies, 14743 Braemar Crescent Way, Darnestown, MD 20878-3911; aabs@starpower.net; http://www.balticstudies-aabs.lanet.lv. Illus., index, adv. Refereed. Circ: 1300. Vol. ends: Winter (No. 4). Microform: PQC. Reprint: PQC. *Indexed:* ABS&EES, AmH&L, ArtHuCI, BHA, MLA-IB, NumL, SSCI. *Bk. rev.:* 5-10, 300-500 words, signed. *Aud.:* Ac, Sa.

This journal seeks to promote research and education in all aspects of Baltic Studies, including history, language, literature, culture, the arts, and the people of the Baltic area. Each issue of about 100 pages contains around four well-documented and well-researched articles on topics such as Finland's eastern border after the Treaty of Noteborg, a study of the Baltic Sea area from nation-centric to multinational history, and the impact of homeland independence on the Latvian community in Great Britain. Most of the books reviewed are from American or English publishers; however, some titles in German or Baltic languages are also included. All the reviews are in English. A recently added new section, "Shorter Contributions," is designed to accommodate research notes and essays that are approximately five to fifteen manuscript pages in length. Recommended for academic and research libraries with programs in Russian and Eastern European Studies and for larger public libraries with a clientele interested in those fields.

1619. ***The Journal of Communist Studies and Transition Politics.*** Formerly (until 1994): *Journal of Communist Studies.* [ISSN: 1352-3279] 1985. q. GBP 235 print & online eds. Ed(s): Stephen White, Ronald J Hill. Frank Cass Publishers, Crown House, 47 Chase Side, Southgate, London, N14 5BP, United Kingdom; jnlsubs@frankcass.com; http://www.frankcass.com/jnls/. Illus., index, adv. Sample. Refereed. Vol. ends: No. 4. Microform: PQC. Online: EBSCO Publishing; Ingenta Select. *Indexed:* ABCPolSci, AmH&L, BrHumI, GeogAbPG, IBSS, IBZ, IPSA, PSA. *Bk. rev.:* Varies, 500-800 words, signed. *Aud.:* Ac, Sa.

As the face of Europe has been transformed by the demise of the Soviet Union and the collapse of communist party rule in Eastern Europe, a deep process of adjustment is under way. This journal devotes particular attention to this epochal process of regime change, including its material contributions from within the affected societies. It also follows the effects of this upheaval on communist parties, ruling and nonruling, in Europe and the rest of the world. Recent issues contain articles on sources of civic and ethnic nationalism in Ukraine; nation- and state-building in Estonia, Macedonia, and Moldova; democratization in Mongolia; and women's employment in Soviet and post-Soviet Russia. This journal is recommended for purchase by academic, special, and research libraries that have programs or clientele interested in this field.

1620. ***Journal of Russian and East European Psychology: a journal of translations.*** Formerly: *Soviet Psychology.* [ISSN: 1061-0405] 1962. bi-m. USD 1100 (Individuals, USD 140). Ed(s): Pentti Hakkarainen. M.E. Sharpe, Inc., 80 Business Park Dr, Armonk, NY 10504; custserv@mesharpe.com; http://www.mesharpe.com. Illus., index, adv. Sample. Refereed. Vol. ends: Nov/Dec (No. 6). Online: EBSCO Publishing. Reprint: PSC. *Indexed:* BiolAb, PAIS, PsycholAb. *Aud.:* Ac, Sa.

This scholarly research journal contains unabridged translations of original submissions as well as articles published in scholarly journals or in collections. Articles are selected that best reflect developments in psychology in this region and that are of most interest to those professionally concerned with this field. The editor introduces each issue with a thematic overview of the topics that will be presented, and each article lists in a footnote the original title, name of journal, date of original publication, and pages. One recent issue deals entirely with developmental psychology and the act of development and contains articles on psychological analysis of the crises in mental development and on transitional forms of sign mediation in teaching six-year-old children. This well-documented and well-translated journal is a valuable tool in the field of psychology and is recommended for academic and research libraries.

1621. ***Journal of Slavic Linguistics.*** [ISSN: 1068-2090] 1993. s-a. USD 40 (Individuals, USD 30). Ed(s): Steven Franks. Slavica Publishers, Inc., 2611 E 10th St, Bloomington, IN 47408-2603; slavica@indiana.edu; http://www.slavica.com. Illus., adv. Refereed. Circ: 250. Vol. ends: No. 2. *Indexed:* ABS&EES, L&LBA, MLA-IB. *Bk. rev.:* 1-3, 500-1,000 words, signed. *Aud.:* Ac, Sa.

This journal contains articles on major research in Slavic linguistics; it addresses issues of general interest to Slavic linguists regardless of theoretical orientation. The editors focus on material that "deals with any aspect of synchronic or diachronic Slavic phonetics, phonology, morphology, syntax, semantics, and pragmatics." The editors endeavor to include articles that raise substantive problems of broad theoretical concern or purpose, but significant descriptive generalizations are the mainstay of this publication. A typical issue has about 200 pages, including full-length articles and a book review section. Recent issues contain articles on Russian morphosyntax, Slavic semantics, expressing ingressity in Slavic, and American Russian. This journal is worthwhile to any academic or research library with a clientele using Slavic linguistics materials.

1622. ***Journal of Southeast European and Black Sea Studies.*** [ISSN: 1468-3857] 2001. 3x/yr. GBP 153 print & online eds. Ed(s): Theodore Couloumbis, Franz-Lothar Altmann. Frank Cass Publishers, Crown House, 47 Chase Side, Southgate, London, N14 5BP, United Kingdom; jnlsubs@frankcass.com; http://www.frankcass.com/jnls/. Adv. Sample. Refereed. *Indexed:* AmH&L, PSA. *Bk. rev.:* 3-4; 1000-1500 words; signed. *Aud.:* Ac, Sa.

The editors launched this journal to fill a void in the scholarly area studies of the post-Communist countries of Albania, Bulgaria, the successor states of the former Yugoslavia, Greece, Romania, and Turkey. The principal disciplines covered are politics, political economy, international relations and modern history. Each issue of about 200 pages contains full-length articles and a book review section. Some recent issues include articles on the decline of Ukrainian agriculture, Jewish socialism in Ottoman Salonica, fishery management in the Black Sea, and Greece's new policy toward Israel. It is recommended for academic libraries with courses of study in this area and for larger research libraries; it provides a new line of communication in an area of Europe that is in need of serious study.

1623. ***Lituanus: Baltic states quarterly journal of arts and sciences.*** [ISSN: 0024-5089] 1954. q. USD 30 (Individuals, USD 15). Ed(s): Antanas Klimas. Lituanus Foundation, Inc., 47 Polk St, Ste 100-300, Chicago, IL 60605. Illus., index. Circ: 4000. Vol. ends: Winter (No. 4). Microform: PQC. Reprint: PQC; SCH. *Indexed:* ABS&EES, AmH&L, BHA, IPSA, MLA-IB, PAIS, RILM. *Bk. rev.:* 3-4, 500-1,000 words, signed. *Aud.:* Ac, Sa.

This journal of arts and sciences is dedicated to the presentation and examination of all questions pertaining to the countries and peoples of the Baltic states, particularly Lithuania. Articles that include general problems related to all Eastern Europe are also considered for publication. Each issue of about 80 pages contains anywhere from three to six articles and a book review section. Recent issues deal with topics such as the evidence of language loss or linguistic innovation in American Lithuanian, Lithuanian in the twenty-first century, Lithuania's campaign for NATO membership, and new representations in the languages of contemporary Lithuanian theatre. Most of the well-documented articles are written by American scholars of Lithuanian heritage. Recommended as an excellent purchase for academic libraries with programs in this area and for public libraries with a Lithuanian clientele.

1624. ***Moscow News: international weekly.*** [ISSN: 0027-1306] 1930. 52x/yr. USD 90 United States. Ed(s): Sergei Roy. Moskovskie Novosti, Tverskaya ul 16-2, Moscow, 103829, Russian Federation; mosnews@sovam.com; periodicals@eastview.com; http://www.moscownews.ru. Illus., adv. Circ: 37000. Vol. ends: Jan (No. 52). Microform: NRP. Online: Gale Group; LexisNexis. *Aud.:* Hs, Ga, Ac.

This popular Russian-based newspaper is published in Russian while the United States edition is in English. It is based primarily on materials from *Moskovskiye Novosti* as well as articles by its own writers. The articles cover politics, the economy, business, cultural issues, society, sports, comments, city life, and all current events in Russia from the Russian point of view. Each issue is usually 12 pages in length with articles on the first page covering the most current political and economic issues. It often contains supplements translated from official speeches and documents along with reviews of films, theater, television, literature, and art exhibitions. An interesting section, especially for students who are learning Russian, is the "Linguist's Corner," which offers a side-by-side English and Russian version of an article. Commentaries are inserted in both languages to enable a student to better understand the translation. This is an excellent acquisition for all libraries; it offers a well-translated source of current news and views on Russia.

1625. ***Nationalities Papers.*** [ISSN: 0090-5992] 1972. q. GBP 296 (Individuals, GBP 81). Ed(s): Nancy Wingfield. Carfax Publishing Ltd., 4 Park Sq, Milton Park, Abingdon, OX14 4RN, United Kingdom; enquiry@tandf.co.uk; http://www.tandf.co.uk/. Illus., adv. Sample. Refereed. Circ: 1200. Vol. ends: Dec (No. 4). Online: EBSCO Publishing; Ingenta Select; Northern Light Technology, Inc.; OCLC Online Computer Library Center, Inc.; ProQuest Information & Learning; RoweCom Information Quest; Swets Blackwell. Reprint: ISI; PQC; PSC. *Indexed:* ABS&EES, AmH&L, GeogAbPG, IBSS, IBZ, IPSA, L&LBA, MLA-IB, PAIS, PSA, SWA, SociolAb. *Bk. rev.:* 15-25, 500-800 words, signed. *Aud.:* Ac, Sa.

This is "the only journal in the world which deals exclusively with all non-Russian nationalities of the former USSR and national minorities in Eastern and Central European countries. The problems and importance of over 160 million people are treated within the disciplinary and methodological contexts of post-Soviet and Europe-Asia studies. Of central concern is the fate of the Balts, Ukrainians, Jews, Gypsies, Croats, Muslims, etc. and the peoples of Central Asia and the Caucasus." Included in each issue of this international and multidisciplinary journal are in-depth articles focusing on the latest developments with some original documents and a "Book Reviews" section. This is an important journal that is highly recommended to those interested in current CIS and Eastern European developments among the national minorities.

1626. ***Polish Review.*** [ISSN: 0032-2970] 1956. q. USD 35 (Non-members, USD 30). Ed(s): Joseph W Wieczerzak. Polish Institute of Arts and Sciences of America, Inc., 208 E 30th St, New York, NY 10016; piasa@worldnet.att.net; http://home.att.net. Illus., index, adv. Refereed. Circ: 1500. Vol. ends: Dec (No. 4). Microform: PQC. Reprint: PQC. *Indexed:* ABS&EES, AmH&L, IPSA, MLA-IB, PAIS. *Bk. rev.:* 4-5, 300-1,000 words, signed. *Aud.:* Ac, Sa.

This journal aims to further interest in scientific and scholarly achievement in Polish affairs. The emphasis is on Polish history, politics, and literature from the point of view of the Polish emigre to the West. Scholarly articles written primarily by American and Canadian academics and journalists of Polish descent deal with such topics as the views of Polish peasants in Europe and the United States from the 1890s to the 1930s, trends in Polish audiovisual culture after 1989, Elsner and the flourishing of opera in Poland before 1830, and Polish messianism in regard to Polish-Russian relations. There is also a book review section that provides an overview of books dealing with all aspects of Polish Studies. This important publication should be included in academic and research library collections of Eastern European materials as well as public libraries with patrons interested in Poland.

1627. ***Post-Communist Economies.*** Former titles (until 1998): *Communist Economies and Economic Transformation; Communist Economies.* [ISSN: 1463-1377] 1989. q. GBP 373 (Individuals, GBP 109). Carfax Publishing Ltd., 4 Park Sq, Milton Park, Abingdon, OX14 4RN, United Kingdom; enquiry@tandf.co.uk; http://www.tandf.co.uk/. Illus., index, adv. Sample. Refereed. Online: EBSCO Publishing; Ingenta Select; OCLC Online Computer Library Center, Inc.; ProQuest Information & Learning; RoweCom Information Quest; Swets Blackwell. Reprint: PSC. *Indexed:* BAS, IBSS, IBZ, JEL, SSCI. *Aud.:* Ac, Sa.

Over the last ten years the focus of this journal has changed from the investigation of basic economic transformation processes of the former communist countries to a new focus on the establishment of market economies in the post-communist countries. These new economies still present distinctive problems that make them a particular focus of research, especially as they try to catch up with the long-established market economies of Western Europe and the European Union. Each issue contains about 150 pages, and recent articles have included such topics as inequalities in income distribution in Slovenia, the role of non-monetary trade in Russian transition, foreign investment and national interests in the Russian oil and gas industry, and tax policy and tax administration in Russia. This journal is recommended for academic libraries with programs in Russian Studies and for research libraries whose clientele requires materials in this area.

1628. ***Post-Soviet Affairs.*** Formerly (until 1992): *Soviet Economy.* [ISSN: 1060-586X] 1985. 4x/yr. USD 278 in North America; USD 249 elsewhere. Ed(s): George Breslauer. V.H. Winston & Son, Inc., c/o Bellwether Publishing, Ltd, 8640 Guilford Rd, Ste 200, Columbia, MD 21046; bellpub@bellpub.com; http://www.bellpub.com. Illus., index. Refereed. Circ: 500. Vol. ends: Dec (No. 4). *Indexed:* ABS&EES, IBSS, IPSA, JEL, PAIS, SSCI. *Aud.:* Ac, Sa.

This journal features the work of Western scholars on the republics of the former Soviet Union and provides up-to-the-minute analyses of the state of the economy and societal progress toward economic reform and linkages between political and social changes and economic developments. A typical issue contains about four articles in almost 100 pages. Each article begins with an abstract and ends with a well-documented list of references. Recent issues have articles on Russia's economic rebound, Putin's war on terrorism, and the Russian debt problem in the 1990s. Recommended for college and university libraries with programs in economics and Russian Studies. Large public libraries with a clientele interested in this field may also want to acquire it.

1629. ***Problems of Economic Transition: a journal of translations from Russian.*** Formerly: *Problems in Economics.* [ISSN: 1061-1991] 1958. m. USD 1290 includes online access (Individuals, USD 165). Ed(s): Ben Slay. M.E. Sharpe, Inc., 80 Business Park Dr, Armonk, NY 10504; custserv@mesharpe.com; http://www.mesharpe.com. Illus., index, adv. Sample. Refereed. Vol. ends: Apr (No. 12). Reprint: PSC. *Indexed:* ABIn, JEL, PAIS, RiskAb, SSCI, SSI. *Aud.:* Ac, Sa.

This journal contains unabridged translations of both original submissions and published articles from economic journals of the successor states to the former Soviet Union. The materials selected are intended to reflect developments in economic theory and practice in the Soviet successor states and to be of interest to those professionally concerned with this field. Each issue contains about five translations of scholarly, well-documented articles that identify the original source of publication by the name of the journal, title of article, original date of publication, pages, author, and the author's credentials. One of the most recent issues is devoted to social policy and tax reform in Russia and the CIS with articles on budgeting for federal health care institutions and investing the balance of the pension fund of the Russian Federation. This is a valuable source of information for scholars interested in Russian economics and is recommended for academic and special libraries.

1630. ***Problems of Post-Communism.*** Formerly (until Jan. 1995): *Problems of Communism.* [ISSN: 1075-8216] 1951. bi-m. USD 225 (Individuals, USD 49). Ed(s): James Millar. M.E. Sharpe, Inc., 80 Business Park Dr, Armonk, NY 10504; custserv@mesharpe.com; http://www.mesharpe.com. Illus., index, adv. Sample. Refereed. Circ: 34000. Vol. ends: Nov/Dec (No. 6). Microform: PQC. Online: EBSCO Publishing. Reprint: ISI; PQC; PSC. *Indexed:* ABCPolSci, ABS&EES, BAS, IBSS, IBZ, IUSGP, PAIS, PRA, SSCI, SSI. *Aud.:* Ac, Sa.

This journal features readable analysis, reliable information, and lively debate about the communist and post-communist world with an emphasis on thoughtful but timely coverage of current economic, political, and international issues. It seeks to serve as a place where scholars from various disciplines may converse with one another and with other serious students of communist and post-communist affairs. A typical issue offers about six articles and a "News and Notes" section. Recent issues contain articles on assessing international involvement in Bosnia, land reform and farm restructuring, German foreign policy toward the Yugoslav successor states from 1991 to 1999, and information sources on terrorism. Recommended for purchase by academic libraries and large public libraries.

1631. ***Religion, State and Society: The Keston Journal.*** Formerly (until 1992): *Religion in Communist Lands.* [ISSN: 0963-7494] 1973. q. GBP 327. Ed(s): Philip Walters. Carfax Publishing Ltd., 4 Park Sq, Milton Park, Abingdon, OX14 4RN, United Kingdom; enquiry@tandf.co.uk; http://www.tandf.co.uk/. Adv. Refereed. Circ: 2000. Microform: PQC. Online: bigchalk; EBSCO Publishing; Ingenta Select; OCLC Online Computer Library Center, Inc.; ProQuest Information & Learning; RoweCom Information Quest; Swets Blackwell. Reprint: PQC; PSC. *Indexed:* IBSS, IBZ, IPSA, PSA, RI-1, SociolAb. *Bk. rev.:* 1-2, 400-800, signed. *Aud.:* Ac, Sa.

According to the editor, this journal is the only English-language academic publication devoted to the issues of religion in communist and formerly communist countries. It reflects the conviction that the experiences of religious communities in their encounters with communism are central to the evolution of the new Europe and the Western world in general. A typical issue contains around 100 pages with articles on topics such as the Ukrainian Greek Catholic Church today, the role of the Russian Orthodox Church in nationalist tendencies in Russia, and the schism in the Bulgarian Orthodox Church. Also included is a book review section that reviews mostly English-language publications. Recommended for academic libraries with programs in this area and for larger public libraries.

1632. ***Revolutionary Russia: journal of the Study Group on the Russian Revolution.*** [ISSN: 0954-6545] 1988. s-a. GBP 148 print & online eds. Ed(s): Jonathan D Smele. Frank Cass Publishers, Crown House, 47 Chase Side, Southgate, London, N14 5BP, United Kingdom; jnlsubs@frankcass.com; http://www.frankcass.com/jnls/. Adv. Sample. Refereed. *Indexed:* AmH&L, IBZ, IPSA, PSA. *Bk. rev.:* 10-12, 800-1,000 words, signed. *Aud.:* Ac, Sa.

This interdisciplinary journal covers the history, politics, economics, sociology, literature, and intellectual history of Russia in the Revolutionary period. According to its editor, it is the first English-language journal to concentrate on this segment of Russian history and the Revolutions of 1905 and 1917. Scholars from all over the world, including from the former states of the Soviet Union, contribute to the approximately 150 pages per issue. Recent issues contain articles on the Lena Massacre of April 1912, the evolution of Communist Party control over trade unions around 1921, the Bolshevik seizure of power in Tver, and Russian military censorship during the First World War. Each issue also contains a book review section of English-language publications in this field. Recommended for research libraries and academic libraries that specialize in this area of historical studies.

1633. ***Romanian Panorama.*** Former titles (until 1991): *Romania; Romania Today.* [ISSN: 1220-5028] 1955. m. USD 58. Ed(s): Corneliu Rades. Foreign Languages Press Group "Romania", Piata Presei Libere 1, PO Box 33-28, Bucharest, 71341, Romania; rps@dial.kappa.ro; http://www.wsp.ro/rps. Illus., adv. Circ: 40000. Microform: BHP. *Aud.:* Ga, Ac.

This magazine, which frequently combines two months into one issue, publishes articles on Romania's history, economy, domestic and foreign policy, culture, literature, arts, sports, and other general areas. Besides this English edition, it is published in French, German, Spanish, and Russian. It very much resembles American newsmagazines in its size and layout. Most issues are about 35 pages long and all are well illustrated with clear, crisp photographs in color. A typical issue has articles on Romania's plan for military integration into NATO, the benefits of Romanian research and development, and Bucharest's plan against terrorism. Recommended for public libraries with patrons of Romanian nationality and descent or for academic libraries with programs dealing with Eastern Europe and its culture.

1634. ***Russian Education and Society: a journal of translations.*** Formerly (until 1992): *Soviet Education.* [ISSN: 1060-9393] 1958. m. USD 1245 (Individuals, USD 172). Ed(s): Anthony Jones. M.E. Sharpe, Inc., 80 Business Park Dr, Armonk, NY 10504; custserv@mesharpe.com; http://www.mesharpe.com. Illus., index, adv. Sample. Refereed. Vol. ends: Dec (No. 12). Reprint: PSC. *Indexed:* ArtHuCI, CIJE, CJA, EduInd, PAIS, SSCI. *Aud.:* Ac, Sa.

The editor of this journal selects material for translation from more than 35 Russian-language periodicals and newspapers, from empirical research reports, and from books. The materials cover preschool and primary, secondary, vocational, and higher education; curricula and methods of the subject fields taught in the schools; the pedagogy of art, music, and physical education; issues related to family life, employment, and youth culture; and special education programs. Journals and newspapers of ministries of education and higher education and the teachers' unions are also covered, as well as popular educational magazines for children, young people, and parents. Each issue is about 100 pages long. A recent issue includes such topics as school reform as seen by teachers, the present state and prospects of technological training, college students' dispositions toward property ownership, and teacher anxiety levels. Recommended for research and academic libraries, especially those with active departments of education.

1635. ***Russian History.*** [ISSN: 0094-288X] 1974. q. USD 45 (Individuals, USD 20). Ed(s): Richard Hellie. Charles Schlacks, Jr., Publisher, PO Box 1256, Idyllwild, CA 92549. Illus., index, adv. Sample. Refereed. Circ: 500. Vol. ends: Winter (No. 4). *Indexed:* ABS&EES, AmH&L, ArtHuCI, SSCI. *Bk. rev.:* 15-20, 500-1,000 words, signed. *Aud.:* Ac, Sa.

Each issue of this scholarly journal devoted to Russian history contains about four well-documented and well-written research articles. Almost all are in English with an appearance of an article in Russian and to a lesser extent one in French. Recent issues contain articles on observations regarding the early Russian collections belonging to the Library of Congress, the possilble death of 12,000 gulag prisoners on Dzhurma, and entertainers in the Mongolian Empire. All issues contain a book review section usually covering recent English-language books written and reviewed by American and Canadian scholars. This section is especially useful for collection development librarians in purchasing the newest English-language books on Russian history. This is an important tool for research and academic libraries that support programs in Russian Studies.

1636. ***Russian Life: a monthly magazine of culture, history and travel.*** Former titles (until 1991): *Soviet Life;* Which incorporated (in 1977): *Soviet Panorama;* And was formerly (until 1965): *U S S R.* [ISSN: 1066-999X] 1956. m. USD 33 domestic; USD 38 foreign; USD 5.25 newsstand/cover per issue. Ed(s): Mikhail V Ivanov. Russian Life, PO Box 567, Montpelier, VT 05601-0567; sales@rispubs.com; http://www.rispubs.com. Illus., adv. Sample. Circ: 15000 Paid. Vol. ends: Dec (No. 12). Microform: PQC. Online: bigchalk; EBSCO Publishing; Florida Center for Library Automation; Gale Group; Northern Light Technology, Inc.; OCLC Online Computer Library Center, Inc.; ProQuest Information & Learning; SoftLine Information. Reprint: PQC. *Indexed:* ABS&EES, ENW, MagInd, MusicInd, PAIS. *Aud.:* Ga, Ac.

This monthly magazine covers Russian culture, art, history, politics, and language. Since its inception, it has offered insights into the forces shaping life in Russia, but now it is independent of all government, agency, foundation, or organizational influence. According to the editor, it views Russia from the inside: free of illusions, but not blemishes, and full of hope, but not ideology. The magazine's regular sections include "Survival Russian," "Travel Journal," "Practical Traveler," "Russian Cuisine," and "Readers' Letters." The magazine always has excellent photographs and art reproductions in vivid color. Some recent issues contain articles on Marina Raskova and Soviet women aviators of World War II, the face of Russian political correctness, and an exhibition of photographs and etchings of St. Petersburg. Recommended for both public and academic libraries as a current events and news source of information about almost everything in Russia.

1637. ***Russian Linguistics: international journal for the study of the Russian language.*** [ISSN: 0304-3487] 1974. 3x/yr. EUR 434 print or online ed. Kluwer Academic Publishers, van Godewijckstraat 30, PO Box 17, Dordrecht, 3300 AA, Netherlands; services@wkap.nl; http://www.wkap.nl. Illus., index, adv. Sample. Refereed. Vol. ends: Nov (No. 3). Microform: PQC. Online: EBSCO Publishing; ingenta.com; Kluwer Online; OCLC Online Computer Library Center, Inc.; Ovid Technologies, Inc.; RoweCom Information Quest; Swets Blackwell. Reprint: SWZ. *Indexed:* ArtHuCI, IBZ, L&LBA, LT&LA, LingAb, MLA-IB. *Bk. rev.:* 6-9, 800-1,500 words, signed. *Aud.:* Ac, Sa.

According to the editor, this journal is an international forum for all scholars working in the field of Russian linguistics, including phonetics and phonology, syntax, linguistic analysis of texts (text grammar), and both diachronic and synchronic problems. Topics within the scope of this publication include Russian dialectology, history of Russian literary language, Russian grammar in relation to linguistic universals, philological problems of Russian and Old Russian texts, and Russian phonetics and phonology. Any library considering this item for acquisition must realize that about 70 percent of the articles are in Russian and only about 30 percent are in English; in addition, the book reviews are mostly in Russian. This journal is recommended for academic libraries with programs of study in Russian linguistics and for large research libraries with clientele requiring some English, but mostly Russian-language, material in this field.

1638. ***Russian Literature: Croatian and Serbian, Czech and Slovak, Polish.*** [ISSN: 0304-3479] 1973. 8x/yr. EUR 833. Ed(s): W G Weststeijn. Elsevier BV, North-Holland, Sara Burgerhartstraat 25, Amsterdam, 1055 KV, Netherlands; nlinfo-f@elsevier.nl; http://www.elsevier.nl/homepage/about/us/regional_sites.htt. Illus., index. Sample. Refereed. Vol. ends: No. 4 - No. 8. Microform: PQC. Reprint: ISI; SWZ. *Indexed:* ArtHuCI, MLA-IB. *Aud.:* Ac, Sa.

This journal publishes articles in Russian and English (only in exceptional cases will articles in French or German be published), which are devoted to topics in Russian literature with related subjects on Croatian, Serbian, Czech, Slovak, and Polish literatures. The editor states that all methods and viewpoints will be welcome, provided they contribute something new, original, or challenging to the understanding of Russian and other Slavic literatures. Recent issues contain English-language articles on Tolstoy's dialogue with Gercen in "Anna Karenina," postrealism in "Russland," and a typological study of Andres Platonov and Franz Kafka. Any library selecting this item must bear in mind that in a recent year a little over half the articles were in English and the rest in Russian. This journal is recommended for academic libraries and large research libraries whose programs of study and clientele need both English- and Russian-language material on Russian literature.

1639. ***Russian Politics and Law.*** Former titles: *Russian Politics;* (until 1992): *Soviet Law and Government.* [ISSN: 1061-1940] 1962. bi-m. USD 1150 (Individuals, USD 135). Ed(s): Nils H Wessell. M.E. Sharpe, Inc., 80 Business Park Dr, Armonk, NY 10504; custserv@mesharpe.com; http://www.mesharpe.com. Illus., index, adv. Sample. Refereed. Vol. ends: Nov/Dec (No. 6). Microform: WSH; PMC. Online: EBSCO Publishing; Gale Group; OCLC Online Computer Library Center, Inc.; H.W. Wilson. Reprint: PSC; WSH. *Indexed:* CJA, CLI, IBSS, ILP, IPSA, PAIS, PSA, SSCI, SSI. *Aud.:* Ac, Sa.

This scholarly journal contains unabridged translations of articles chiefly from Russian-language publications in the fields of politics, law, public affairs, public administration, and related fields. Articles cover topics such as domestic and foreign policy, legislative development, law enforcement, intra- and intergovernmental relations, and political party development. The editor introduces each issue, which consists of about 100 pages, and tries to select articles that afford new insights and information, reveal political undercurrents, represent departures from conventional thinking, or are emblematic of an emerging consensus on a particular question. Recent issues contain articles on the disappearance of totalitarianism in the twentieth century, the post-Soviet stage of study of totalitarianism, the war in Yugoslavia, and democratic and liberal reforms in Russia. This journal is recommended as an important purchase for special, academic, and research libraries.

1640. ***The Russian Review: an American quarterly devoted to Russia past and present.*** [ISSN: 0036-0341] 1941. q. USD 149 print & online eds. Blackwell Publishing, Inc., Commerce Place, 350 Main St, Malden, MA 02148; subscrip@blackwellpub.com; http://www.blackwellpublishing.com. Illus., index, adv. Sample. Refereed. Circ: 1700 Paid. Vol. ends: Oct (No. 4). Microform: PQC. Online: EBSCO Publishing; Gale Group; ingenta.com; JSTOR (Web-based Journal Archive); OCLC Online Computer Library Center, Inc.; RoweCom Information Quest; Swets Blackwell; H.W. Wilson. *Indexed:* ABS&EES, AmH&L, ArtHuCI, BHA, BRI, CBRI, CJA, HumInd, MLA-IB, PAIS, PSA, SSCI, SociolAb. *Bk. rev.:* 25-40, 300-1,000 words, signed. *Aud.:* Ac, Sa.

This scholarly journal covers all subject fields dealing with the culture, history, and civilization of Russia and Eastern Europe. According to the editor, the publication's mission is to keep abreast of the best in scholarship and to bring about fruitful communications among all the disciplines that concern themselves with Russia, past and present. Each issue contains several research articles on a variety of topics with an emphasis on history and literature, social sciences, art, and other humanistic studies. Recent issues contain articles such as Turkmen women under Soviet rule from 1924 to 1929, the Free Economic Society's battle against smallpox, and the purging of public intellectuals during the 1922 expulsions from Soviet Russia. There is a substantial book review section and a "Publications Received" section. This outstanding journal should constitute an integral part of any academic or public library with patrons interested in Russian or Slavic Studies.

1641. ***Russian Social Science Review: a journal of translations.*** Formerly (until 1992): *Soviet Review.* [ISSN: 1061-1428] 1960. bi-m. USD 284 (Individuals, USD 95). Ed(s): Patricia A Kolb. M.E. Sharpe, Inc., 80 Business Park Dr, Armonk, NY 10504; custserv@mesharpe.com; http://www.mesharpe.com. Illus., index, adv. Sample. Refereed. Vol. ends: Nov/Dec (No. 6). Microform: PQC. Online: EBSCO Publishing; Gale Group; Northern Light Technology, Inc.; OCLC Online Computer Library Center, Inc.; ProQuest Information & Learning; H.W. Wilson. Reprint: PSC. *Indexed:* MLA-IB, PAIS, SSI. *Aud.:* Ac, Sa.

This scholarly journal contains unabridged translations from a wide range of Russian-language periodicals, including the following journals in their translated titles: *Problems of Economics, Problems of History, Problems of Philosophy, Problems of Psychology, Problems of Literature, Sociological Research, Free Thought,* and *New World.* The articles selected for this publication by Western experts provide readers with a cross-section of significant articles published in Russian-language periodicals in the social sciences and related fields. Each issue is about 100 pages long with about five or six articles per issue. Recent issues cover topics such as the transformation of values in Russian society, theoretical sociology in Russia, a study of money or power as channels of mobility in Russian society, and sociology under totalitarianism. This important journal in the field of social sciences is recommended for academic libraries and large public libraries.

1642. ***Russian Studies in History: a journal of translations.*** Formerly (until 1992): *Soviet Studies in History.* [ISSN: 1061-1983] 1962. q. USD 825 (Individuals, USD 140). Ed(s): Joseph Bradley, Christine Ruane. M.E. Sharpe, Inc., 80 Business Park Dr, Armonk, NY 10504; custserv@mesharpe.com; http://www.mesharpe.com. Illus., index, adv. Sample. Refereed. Vol. ends: Spring (No. 4). Reprint: PSC. *Indexed:* AmH&L, BAS, IBZ, SSI. *Aud.:* Ac, Sa.

This scholarly research journal contains unabridged translations of articles from the following journals whose titles are translated into English: *Problems of History, Journal of Moscow University History Series, Modern and Contemporary History, The Past, Native Land, National History,* and *Centaur: a Political-Historical Journal.* The editors state that articles are selected that best reflect developments in Russian historiography and are of greatest interest to those professionally concerned with this field. Recent issues of this well-documented journal of about 100 pages per issue cover topics such as the nationality question, documents and commentary on the the second conquest of the Caucasus, the Bolsheviks and the national banner, and Russia's annexation of the Caucasus. Recommended for purchase by special and academic libraries with programs in Russian history.

1643. ***Russian Studies in Literature: a journal of translations.*** Formerly (until 1992): *Soviet Studies in Literature.* [ISSN: 1061-1975] 1964. q. USD 825 (Individuals, USD 140). Ed(s): John Givens. M.E. Sharpe, Inc., 80 Business Park Dr, Armonk, NY 10504; custserv@mesharpe.com; http://www.mesharpe.com. Illus., index, adv. Sample. Refereed. Vol. ends: Fall (No. 4). Reprint: PSC. *Indexed:* ArtHuCI, HumInd, MLA-IB, SSCI. *Aud.:* Ac, Sa.

This journal publishes translations from Russian in literary criticism and scholarship, including both contemporary and historical material. Selections are drawn primarily from the following Russian-language periodicals: *Friendship among Peoples, News, Continent, Foreign Literature, Literary Gazette, Literary Review, New Literary Review, New World, October, Russian Literature, Problems of Literature,* and *Banner.* Each issue of about 100 pages contains literary-analysis articles that provide insight into the current literary scene in Russia. Recent issues focus their articles on one theme, e.g., Dostoevsky, with articles on Dostoevsky and "Relations between the Sexes," Dostoevsky and Bakhtin, and "The Idiot" and "The Eccentric." This journal is highly recommended for research and academic libraries with programs and a clientele interested in Russian and comparative literatures.

1644. ***Russian Studies in Philosophy: a journal of translations.*** Formerly (until 1992): *Soviet Studies in Philosophy.* [ISSN: 1061-1967] 1962. q. USD 740 (Individuals, USD 130). Ed(s): Taras Zakydalsky. M.E. Sharpe, Inc., 80 Business Park Dr, Armonk, NY 10504; custserv@mesharpe.com; http://www.mesharpe.com. Illus., index, adv. Sample. Refereed. Vol. ends: Spring (No. 4). Reprint: PSC. *Indexed:* ArtHuCI, PhilInd, SSCI. *Aud.:* Ac, Sa.

This scholarly research journal contains unabridged translations of articles chiefly from the following Russian-language publications: *Problems of Philosophy; Philosophical Sciences; Moscow University Herald, Philosophy Series;* and *Leningrad University Herald, Economics, Philosophy, and Law Series.* The materials selected are intended to reflect developments in Russian philosophy, and to be of interest to those professionally concerned with this field. The editor begins each issue with a short introduction that gives an overview of the central topic that will be investigated. For example, a recent issue discusses ethical studies with articles on the subjunctive mood of morality, Talion and the Golden Rule, and the Roerich movement in Russia. This important journal is recommended for specialized academic and research library collections.

1645. ***Slavic & East European Information Resources.*** [ISSN: 1522-8886] 2000. q. USD 145. Ed(s): Karen Rondestvedt. Haworth Press, Inc., 10 Alice St, Binghamton, NY 13904-1580; getinfo@haworthpressinc.com; http://www.haworthpressinc.com. Illus., adv. Sample. Refereed. Circ: 111 Paid. *Indexed:* ABS&EES, IBZ, InfoSAb. *Bk. rev.:* 10-14; 300-1200 words; signed. *Aud.:* Ac, Sa.

The editor states that the central purpose of this journal is to serve as a focal point for the international exchange of information in the field of Slavic and East European librarianship. Information includes news of the profession, technical developments, reviews of literature, original research, and all related to Slavic librarianship in North America and the rest of the world. In addition to the articles, shorter pieces appear in such columns as "The Internet"; "In Our Libraries," which contains case studies and current news of the field; "Vendors' Column," which offers news from vendors of Slavic materials and focuses on acquisition practices; and "Reviews," which gives readers an assessment of books and other materials; all are important parts of this periodical. This newly created journal is highly recommended for librarians who have responsibility for Slavic and East European collections.

1646. ***Slavic and East European Journal.*** [ISSN: 0037-6752] 1957. 4x/yr. Members, USD 60. Ed(s): Gerald Janecek. American Association of Teachers of Slavic and East European Languages, c/o Kathleen E. Dillon, Executive Director, AATSEEL, PO Box 7039, Berkeley, CA 94707-2306; AATSEEL@Earthlink.net; http://clover.slavic.pitt.edu/~aatseel. Illus., index, adv. Refereed. Circ: 1600. Vol. ends: Winter (No. 4). Microform: PQC. Online: Gale Group. Reprint: PSC. *Indexed:* ABS&EES, ArtHuCI, BHA, CIJE, HumInd, L&LBA, LT&LA, MLA-IB, SociolAb. *Bk. rev.:* 25-30, 250-500 words, signed. *Aud.:* Ac, Sa.

This journal publishes research studies in all areas of Slavic languages, literatures, and pedagogy. It may also publish articles on non-Slavic East European subjects if they are of interest to Slavicists. Recent articles include such topics as Russian synonyms under a magnifying glass, orientalism in Adam Mickiewicz's Crimean sonnets, and the subjective turn in Polish literary biography in the 1860s. Of interest equal to that of the articles is the book review section, which provides many critical reviews of recently published works on Slavic languages and literatures. There is also the shorter "Publications Received" section. Both of these sections are very useful as an aid in identifying items for purchase by collection-development librarians. This journal is highly recommended for academic libraries with programs in Slavic languages and literatures.

1647. ***Slavic Review: American quarterly of Russian, Eurasian and East European studies.*** Formerly (until 1961): *American Slavic and East European Review;* (until 1944): *Slavonic and East European Review. American Series;* (until 1942): *Slavonic Year-Book. American Series.* [ISSN: 0037-6779] 1941. q. Non-members, USD 65. Ed(s): Diane

Koenker. American Association for the Advancement of Slavic Studies, Harvard University, 8 Story St, 3d Fl, Cambridge, MA 02138; aaass@fas.harvard.edu; http://www.fas.harvard.edu. Illus., index, adv. Refereed. Circ: 5000. Vol. ends: Winter (No. 4). Online: Gale Group. *Indexed:* ABCPolSci, ABS&EES, AmH&L, ArtHuCI, BRI, CBRI, HumInd, IBSS, MLA-IB, PAIS, RILM, SSI. *Bk. rev.:* 55-60, 300-1,000 words, signed. *Aud.:* Ac, Sa.

This is one of the major American scholarly research journals published in the field of Slavic and Eastern European Studies. Articles deal mainly with the areas of history, literature, economics, and political science. All issues have six to ten major articles contributed by American academics and a substantial number of book reviews, plus the shorter "Books Received" section. The book reviews are an outstanding tool for book selection by collection-development librarians. This journal is a highly recommended acquisition for academic and research libraries as well as for some larger public libraries with readers interested in Russia and Eastern Europe.

1648. ***Slavonic and East European Review.*** [ISSN: 0037-6795] 1922. q. GBP 106. Ed(s): M Rady. Maney Publishing, Hudson Rd, Leeds, LS9 7DL, United Kingdom; maney@maney.co.uk; http://www.lib.cam.ac.uk/MHRA/SEER/. Illus., index, adv. Refereed. Circ: 1000. Vol. ends: Oct (No. 4). Reprint: SCH. *Indexed:* AmH&L, ArtHuCI, BHA, BrHumI, HumInd, IBSS, L&LBA, LT&LA, MLA-IB, PSA, SSCI, SociolAb. *Bk. rev.:* 50-60, 300-750 words, signed. *Aud.:* Ac, Sa.

Produced by the Modern Humanities Research Association, this research journal publishes scholarly articles on all subjects related to the field of Slavic and East European Studies. Each issue of about 200 pages consists of articles on aspects of the languages, literatures, philosophies, and histories of the region. Also contained in each issue is a section of shorter review articles, a lengthy "Reviews" section of recent book reviews in all areas of Slavic Studies, and, in some issues, a "Publications Received" section. This journal is one of the oldest and most prestigious in the field of Slavic and East European Studies and is highly recommended for all academic libraries with a clientele in this field and for larger public libraries with a similar clientele.

1649. ***Social Sciences: a quarterly journal of the Russian Academy of Sciences.*** [ISSN: 0134-5486] 1970. q. USD 293 (Individuals, USD 58). Ed(s): L Mitrokhin. East View Publications, Inc., 3020 Harbor Ln. N., Minneapolis, MN 55447; periodicals@eastview.com. Illus., index. Refereed. Circ: 300 Paid. Vol. ends: No. 4. *Indexed:* EIP, IBSS, IBZ, PAIS, PSA, SociolAb. *Bk. rev.:* 3-5, 100-1,000 words, signed. *Aud.:* Ac, Sa.

This journal publishes translated articles in the disciplines of philosophy, history, economics, politics, sociology, law, philology, psychology, ethnography, and archaeology. The articles are taken from books and journals that are published by 30 institutes and 25 academic Russian-language journals in the humanities and social sciences. Each issue of about 200 pages begins with a one-page overview of the articles contained therein. A recent issue contains articles on monetary policy and structural reform in post-Soviet Russia's economy, the modern Russian revolution, Russia's strategic response to the challenges of the new century, and a nontraditional outlook of a market transformation in Russia. The editor tries to "select papers that do not skim the surface but delve deeply into problems and take a serious look at everything that happened in reality, that is, papers marked by respect for truth." The book reviews are generally written by Russian scholars. Highly recommended for academic and research libraries.

1650. ***Sociological Research: a journal of translations from Russian.*** Formerly (until 1992): *Soviet Sociology.* [ISSN: 1061-0154] 1962. bi-m. USD 1100 (Individuals, USD 140). Ed(s): Anthony Jones. M.E. Sharpe, Inc., 80 Business Park Dr, Armonk, NY 10504; custserv@mesharpe.com; http://www.mesharpe.com. Illus., index, adv. Sample. Refereed. Vol. ends: Nov/Dec (No. 6). Reprint: PSC. *Indexed:* ABS&EES, PAIS, PSA, SFSA, SSCI, SSI, SociolAb. *Aud.:* Ac, Sa.

This scholarly research journal contains unabridged translations of articles chiefly from the following publications, whose titles have been translated into English from Russian: *Sociological Journal, Economic and Social Changes: Monitoring Public Opinion, The Social Sciences and the Present, Sociological Research, Region: Economics and Sociology, Free Thought, Political Research,* and other relevant journals and books. The editor states that "the materials selected are intended to reflect developments in sociology in Russia and other successor states of the USSR, and to be of interest to those professionally concerned with this field." Each issue is about 100 pages long with about six well-translated articles per issue. Each article lists the original bibliographic information from the Russian article and includes the affiliation of the author. Recent articles include such topics as Moscow's working pensioners, the image of Russia in Russian public opinion, the formation of a middle class in Russia, and the birth rate in post-Soviet Georgia. This journal is highly recommended for academic and large public libraries with patrons interested in Russian sociological development.

1651. ***The Soviet and Post Soviet Review.*** Formerly (until 1992): *Soviet Union.* [ISSN: 1075-1262] 1974. 3x/yr. USD 30 (Individuals, USD 15). Ed(s): Vladimir P Buldakov. Charles Schlacks, Jr., Publisher, PO Box 1256, Idyllwild, CA 92549. Illus., index, adv. Refereed. Circ: 500. Vol. ends: No. 3. *Indexed:* ABS&EES, AmH&L. *Bk. rev.:* 1, 1,000 words, signed. *Aud.:* Ac, Sa.

This scholarly journal contains articles on the politics, international relations, history, and related areas of Russia past and present. The editor states that the publication will "offer readers subjective interpretive material on the former Soviet Union and the other post-Soviet successor states." A recent issue with well-documented articles written by mostly American scholars contains the following: the non-Science Fiction prose of Stanislaw Lem; Coca-Cola, MTV and the laboratory of culture in the new Russia; and the consciousness of scene in Elena Guro's work. Most issues have a book review section that deals with materials on Russia and the countries of Eastern Europe. This journal is highly recommended for academic libraries with Russian Studies programs and for larger public libraries with clientele interested in Russian Studies.

1652. ***Statutes and Decisions: The Laws of the U S S R & Its Successor States: a journal of translations.*** Formerly (until 1992): *Soviet Statutes and Decisions.* [ISSN: 1061-0014] 1964. bi-m. USD 1275 (Individuals, USD 170). Ed(s): Sarah Reynolds. M.E. Sharpe, Inc., 80 Business Park Dr, Armonk, NY 10504; custserv@mesharpe.com; http://www.mesharpe.com. Illus., index, adv. Sample. Refereed. Microform: WSH; PMC. Reprint: PSC; WSH. *Indexed:* CLI, ILP, PAIS. *Aud.:* Ac, Sa.

This journal contains translations from the following Russian-language sources: *Bulletin of Normative Acts; Information; Russian Newspaper; Russian Justice; Russian News; Collection of Acts of the President and the Government of the Russian Federation; Collection of Legislation of the RF; The State and the Law; Gazette of the Federal Assembly of the Russian Federation; RF Constitutional Court Herald; RSFSR Supreme Court Herald; RF Higher Arbitrazh Court Herald; Law, Legality, Legislation and the Economy;* and items from other publications as warranted. Each issue is about 100 pages long, with topics such as the evolution of constitutional jurisprudence in the Russian Federation and the development of Russian federalism. Recommended primarily for law libraries and large research libraries with collections in Russian Studies.

1653. ***Studies in East European Thought.*** Formerly (until 1992): *Studies in Soviet Thought.* [ISSN: 0925-9392] 1961. q. EUR 344 print or online ed. Ed(s): Edward M Swiderski. Kluwer Academic Publishers, van Godewijckstraat 30, PO Box 17, Dordrecht, 3300 AA, Netherlands; services@wkap.nl; http://www.wkap.nl. Illus., index, adv. Sample. Refereed. Vol. ends: Dec (No. 4). Microform: PQC. Online: EBSCO Publishing; ingenta.com; Kluwer Online; OCLC Online Computer Library Center, Inc.; Ovid Technologies, Inc.; RoweCom Information Quest; Swets Blackwell. Reprint: SWZ. *Indexed:* ABCPolSci, ABS&EES, AmH&L, ArtHuCI, BAS, IBZ, IPB, IPSA, PSA, PhilInd, SSCI, SociolAb. *Bk. rev.:* 1-10, 500-2,000 words, signed. *Aud.:* Ac, Sa.

This journal "is intended to provide a forum for Western-language (mostly English and German) writings on philosophy and philosophers who identify with the history and cultures of East and Central Europe, including Russia, Ukraine, and the Baltic States. The editors do not advocate a program or defend a position as to the nature and limits of philosophy in its manifold interactions with other disciplines and in its role in articulating cultural values and marking intellectual dissonances. They welcome descriptive, critical, comparative, and historical studies of individuals, schools, currents, and institutions whose works and influence are widely regarded in their own environments to be philosophical or provide insight into the socio-cultural conditions of philosophical life in Eastern Europe." Some recent issues contain articles on gender studies in post-Soviet society; Lithuanian philosophy in the twentieth century; and a dialogue on Russian Orthodox theologians and Augustine of Hippo. This journal is important for academic and research libraries with collections in philosophy and Russian-area Studies.

Electronic Journals

1654. ***Central Europe Review: the weekly journal of Central and Eastern European politics, society and culture.*** [ISSN: 1212-8732] 1999. fortn. USD 80 (Individuals, USD 20). Ed(s): Susan Abbott. Central Europe Review, Ltd., Holly Cottage, Ellerdine Heath, Telford, TF6 6RP, United Kingdom; http://www.ce-review.org/. Index, adv. Circ: 15000. *Aud.:* Ga, Ac.

This Internet journal provides current news and analysis from all the countries of Central Europe and archives of the publication with an index back to its first year in 1999. It includes a section on books, another on e-books, and interviews as well as its feature articles in a country news section. An innovative feature is CER Direct, which allows a user to sign up for a weekly summary of the journal via personal e-mail. Highly recommended as a useful source of current information on Central and Eastern Europe.

Folklore. See Folklore/Electronic Journals section.

1655. ***Intermarium: the first online journal of East Central European postwar history and politics.*** 1997. 3x/yr. Ed(s): Andrzej Paczkowski, John S Micgiel. Columbia University, Institute on East Central Europe, 420 W 118th St, New York, NY 10027; http://www.columbia.edu/cu/sipa/regional/ece/newintermar.html. *Indexed:* AmH&L. *Aud.:* Ac, Sa.

According to the editor, this publication provides an electronic medium for noteworthy scholarship and provocative thinking about the history and politics of Central and Eastern Europe after World War II. It will broaden the discourse on aspects of national histories that are undergoing change thanks to the availability of new documents from recently opened archives. By making research, essays, commentaries, documents, and reviews from the region available in English, this publication should be quite welcomed by the scholarly community.

1656. ***Military News Bulletin.*** 1991. m. USD 229.95. R.I.A. Novosti, Zubovskii bulv 4, Moscow, 119021, Russian Federation; marketing@rian.ru; http://en.rian.ru. *Aud.:* Ga, Ac.

The Russian Information Agency, Novosti (RIA Novosti), is the state news and analytical agency of the Russian Federation that publishes this online periodical. It contains articles and information about Russia's military policy and the reformation of its armed forces. Although it is specialized, it is of considerable interest to anyone following the activities in Russia's Defense Ministry, military treaties and agreements between Russia and other states, and documents from military archives. Published in Russian, English, and Spanish, it offers insight into the Russian armed forces.

1657. ***Russian Economic News.*** 1997. m. R I A Novosti, Zubovsky boulevard 4, Moscow, 119021, Russian Federation; marketing@rian.ru; http://old.rian.ru/e-main.htm. *Aud.:* Ga, Ac.

This publication of an official government agency and a commercial publisher contains official statistics, analyses, and forecasts concerning industries and industrial regions, agriculture, construction, transportation, and finance and banking. The online news feature offers up to 20 messages a day to supplement the monthly issues. Published both in Russian and in English, it offers a timely source of social and economic information on Russia.

1658. ***Sarmatian Review.*** Formerly: *Houston Sarmatian.* [ISSN: 1059-5872] 1981. 3x/yr. USD 21 (Individuals, USD 15). Ed(s): Ewa M Thompson. Polish Institute of Houston, PO Box 79119, Houston, TX 77279-9119; sarmatia@rice.edu; http://www.ruf.rice.edu/~sarmatia. Illus., adv. Refereed. Circ: 400 Paid. *Aud.:* Ac.

This scholarly online journal provides a forum for the issues affecting Central and Eastern Europe, especially Poland, and the impact of those issues on the United States. It looks at all aspects of the political, economic, social, and literary conditions of the area. In a "Books and Periodicals Received" section, reviews of both English-language and Polish-language materials are listed (all reviews are in English). A print version of this journal is also published. This publication presents a good overall picture of events in Eastern Europe.

1659. ***Transition Newsletter.*** World Bank Publications, 1818 H St, NW, Washington, DC 20433; http://www.worldbank.org/html/prddr/trans/WEB/trans.htm. *Aud.:* Ga, Ac.

This newsletter is a regular publication of the World Bank's Development Economic Research Group and reports on the latest economic, social, and business developments in the post-socialist and socialist transition countries of Eastern and Central Europe and Asia. During the past decade it has become an important tool in disseminating ideas on topics like privatization, banking reform, capital market development, and pension reform. A Russian-language version is also available.

1660. ***Transitions Online.*** 1999. m. updated daily. USD 75, Libraries, USD 160 (Individuals, USD 35). Ed(s): Jeremy Druker. Transitions, Chlumova 22, Prague, 130 00, Czech Republic; transitions@ijt.cz; http://www.ijt.cz/transitions. Adv. Online: OCLC Online Computer Library Center, Inc.; SoftLine Information. *Bk. rev.:* Various number and length. *Aud.:* Ga, Ac.

This Internet publication covers Central and Eastern Europe, the Balkans, and the former Soviet Union. It is the online successor to *Transitions* magazine. Using a network of local correspondents, it seeks to provide a cross-regional analysis of the developments in the region's 28 post-communist countries. It includes the following sections: "In Focus" (articles on a monthly theme), "Features," "Media" (media reviews), "Books" (reviews), "Opinion" (editorials), "In Their Own Words," and "Week in Review" (news update). It also maintains an archive of back issues, including articles from its print predecessor publication. This is a good source for up-to-date news of the CIS and all the former Soviet bloc countries.

■ CITY, STATE, AND REGIONAL

City Magazines/State and Regional

Margie Ruppel, Reference Librarian, Morris Library, Southern Illinois University–Carbondale, 605 Agriculture Drive, Mail Code 6632, Carbondale, IL 62901; mruppel@lib.siu.edu

Introduction

American places and thought are represented and chronicled in hundreds of city, state, and regional magazines throughout the United States. "For most of us, however long our lines of communication and cosmopolitan our knowledge and experience, we are more or less habitual inhabitants of a place. This connection indeed constitutes a rich and continuing theme of American thought" (Pierce, 1999). Acknowledging such an abundance of place magazines, I narrowed the selections in this section to the best magazines of the 50 states and capitals, Washington D.C., the 20 most populous cities, and regions of the United States (e.g., Midwest). In this section, a magazine about a place is "good" if it goes beyond advertising an area and becomes a learning resource for local personalities, traditions, and folklore; environmental concerns; and historical research and enlightenment; in addition to being a guide to community, cultural, and entertainment events.

Two main questions guided my selections: (1) Does the magazine include high-quality journalism that discusses the background of an event, person, or region, or is it merely filled with advertisements, dates, and times? and (2) Does the staff take time to research events, persons, and regions and turn this research into feature articles? The richness of the content is the main factor in determining which magazines to include here. *Albemarle, Arizona Highways, Hudson Valley Regional Review,* and *Yankee* are prime examples of place magazines with rich content. This marks the main difference between the magazines in this section and the magazines in the Travel and Tourism section.

A criterion I considered to a lesser degree is how much the magazine involves its readers. Asking readers to vote on their favorite restaurants or cultural institutions are two examples. A recent issue of *Mpls.St.Paul*, for example, features its readers' top ten favorite restaurants in approximately 50 categories.

In many cases, a magazine does not exist for a city, state, or region. In other cases, there is only one magazine for a place, but it doesn't meet the stated criteria, so these are also not included. Additionally, many good publications are omitted because publishers did not send sample copies to me.

City magazines have an inherent urban focus, while state and regional magazines must balance both urban and rural interests. City magazines generally have more articles about fashion, the social scene, and real estate, as well as decorating tips, detailed calendars of events, and articles on how to accomplish day-to-day activities. I focused on reviewing magazines for the 20 most populous U.S. cities and all 50 state capitals (which produced a slight overlap) plus Washington D.C. Of the 20 most populous cities, only four do not have magazines (San Antonio, El Paso, and Austin, Texas, and San Jose, California). Of the 50 state capitals, only 20 have magazines. *Honolulu, Salt Lake, Harrisburg Magazine,* and *Tallahassee Magazine* are state capital magazines new to the 12th edition. *Los Angeles Magazine, Baltimore Magazine, Columbus Monthly*, and *HOUR Detroit* are populous city magazines new to the 12th edition. *Phoenix Magazine* and *5280: Denver's Mile-High Magazine*, representing cities that are both state capitals and two of the 20 most populous cities, are new as well. The list also includes a few magazines for other well-known cities that are not capitals or among the most populous cities and some others for less well-known cities just because they are too good not to include (e.g., *Cincinnati, Evansville Living, Hampton Roads Monthly, New Orleans Magazine, Pittsburgh,* and *Tucson Lifestyles*).

State magazines typically examine the history, people, wildlife, folk tales, scenery, and current events in the state. My original goal was to include at least one quality magazine for each state, but some states do not have a magazine (Utah, Washington, and Wyoming) and other states have magazines that do not meet my criteria for inclusion. Some of the states that do not have a state magazine (California, Illinois, and New York) have large cities with substantial city magazines. Of the states lacking a state magazine, about 75 percent are represented by regional or city publications. Nevertheless, there are some state magazines new to the 12th edition: *Illinois Magazine, The Iowan, Louisiana Life, Ohio* and *Virginia Living*. Titles published by state historical societies are excluded, on the basis that their scope does not extend far beyond history.

Regional magazines represent geographical areas in the United States as large as the Route 66 corridor (*Route 66 Magazine*) or as small as southern Louisiana (*Acadiana Profile Magazine*); they may span several states (e.g., *Blue Ridge Country* and *Midwest Living*) or only one part of a state (*Adirondack Life*). Regional magazines sometimes cover a geographical area (*Big Sky Magazine*), while other times they cover a historical era (*Albemarle: Living in Jefferson's Virginia*) or a cultural region (*Yankee*). *Albemarle: Living in Jefferson's Virginia* appears to cover a small area, but because its scope includes all areas related to Virginia's early history, it actually covers almost the entire state. Among the regional magazines is the *Hudson Valley Regional Review*, the only scholarly journal in this section. It covers "regionalism" as an academic topic. According to the *Hudson Valley Regional Review*'s web site, the content of this magazine is taken directly from its environment: "The region's towns and countryside, libraries and museums, commerce and transportation, and natural environment provide an enormous cultural and scientific laboratory for analysis of its past and present." Regional magazines new to the 12th edition include *Acadiana Profile: The Magazine of the Cajun Country, Albemarle: Living in Jefferson's Virginia,* and *Route 66 Magazine*.

Which city, state, and regional magazines individual libraries should subscribe to will be based on geographical interest. Public libraries may want to consider subscribing to magazines related to the city, state, and region in which they are located, as well as nearby cities. Taking into consideration that about 95 percent of place magazines have web sites, public libraries could also bookmark URLs for the magazines representing their patrons' common travel destinations. Academic libraries may want to follow these guidelines and, if an academic program related to regionalism on their campus exists, subscribe to the *Hudson Valley Regional Review.*

If you wish to find out what other city, state, and regional magazines exist, check the following two web sites: International Regional Magazines Association (IRMA) (http://www.regionalmagazines.org/default.htm) and the City and Regional Magazines Association (CRMA) (http://www.citymag.org).

References: Pierce, David C., and Richard C. Wiles. 1999. "A Place for Regionalism?" *The Hudson Valley Regional Review.* <http://www.bard.edu/hvrr/essays/regional.shtml.

Basic Periodicals

No titles in this section have a general focus. Selection will depend on geographic interest.

Basic Abstracts and Indexes

Access; Magazine Index Plus; Reader's Guide to Periodical Literature.

City Magazines

5280: Denver's Mile-High Magazine. [ISSN: 1082-6815] 1993. 8/yr. $18.00. Daniel Brogan. 5280 Publishing, Inc., 1224 Speer Blvd., P.O. Box 40789, Denver, CO 80204; letters@5280.com; www.5280.com.

Akron Life & Leisure [ISSN: 1542-4456] 2003. m. $19.95. Kurt Kleidon. Baker Publishing, Inc., 168 E. Market St., Ste. 208, Akron, OH 44308; publisher@bakerpublishing.com; www.akronlifeandleisure.com. See also: *Cincinnati Magazine, Columbus Monthly.*

Atlanta. [ISSN: 0004-6701] 1961. 13/yr. $19.95. Rebecca Poyner Burns. Emmis Publishing, 1330 W. Peachtree St., Ste. 450, Atlanta, GA 30309; rburns@atlantamag.emmis.com; www.atlantamagazine.com. See also: *Blue Ridge Country; Augusta Magazine; Macon Magazine.*

Augusta Magazine. [ISSN: 0004-797X] 1973. bi-m. $15.95. Sherry Foster. Morris Communications Group, 127A Seventh St., Augusta, GA 30901; P.O. Box 1405, Augusta, GA 30903; foster@augustamagazine.com; www.augustamagazine.com. See also: *Blue Ridge Country; Atlanta; Macon Magazine.*

Baltimore Magazine. [ISSN: 0005-4453] 1907. m. $18. Richard M. Basoco. Rosebud Entertainment L.L.C., 1000 Lancaster St., Ste. 400, Baltimore, MD 21202; letters@baltimoremag.com; www.baltimoremagazine.net.

Birmingham. [ISSN: 0006-369X] 1961. m. $15. Joe O'Donnell. Birmingham Area Chamber of Commerce, 505 N. 20th St., Birmingham, AL 35203; jodonnell@bhammag.com; www.bhammag.com.

Boston Magazine. [ISSN: 0006-7989] 1962. m. $18. Jon Marcus. Boston Magazine, 300 Massachusetts Avenue, Boston, MA 02115; editor@bostonmagazine.com; www.bostonmagazine.com.

Buffalo Spree. [ISSN: 0300-7499] 1967. 7/yr. $12. Elizabeth Licata. David Laurence Publications, Inc., 5678 Main St., Williamsville, NY 14221; info@buffalospree.com; www.buffalospree.com. See also: *Adirondack Life, Hudson Valley Regional Review.*

Charleston Magazine. [ISSN: 0162-2722] 1987. bi-m. $15. Darcy Shankland. GulfStream Communications, P.O. Box 1794, Mt. Pleasant, SC 29465-1794; dshankland@charlestonmag.com; www.charlestonmag.com. See also: *Sandlapper: the Magazine of South Carolina; Blue Ridge Country.*

Charlotte. [ISSN: 1083-1444] 1988. m. Richard Thurmond. Abarta Media, 127 W. Worthington Ave., Ste. 208, Charlotte, NC 28203-4474; rthurmond@abartapub.com; www.charlottemagazine.com.

Chicago (Formerly: *Chicago Guide*). [ISSN: 0362-4595] 1952. m. $19.90. Richard Babcock. Chicago Tribune Company, 500 N. Dearborn St., Ste. 1200, Chicago, IL 60610; rbabcock@chicagomag.com; www.chicagomag.com. See also: *Illinois Magazine.*

Cincinnati Magazine (Formerly: *Cincinnati Monthly*). [ISSN: 0746-8210] 1967. 13/yr. $19.95. Kitty Morgan. 705 Central Ave., Ste. 175, Cincinnati, OH 45202. Emmis Communications, Inc., 40 Monument Circle, Ste. 100, Indianapolis, IN 46204; editors@cintimag.emmis.com; www.cincinnatimagazine.com. See also: *Ohio; Columbus Monthly; Akron Life & Leisure.*

Columbus Monthly. 1975. m. $18 (in OH). Lenore Egan Brown. CM Media Inc., 5255 Sinclair Rd., P.O. Box 29913, Columbus, OH 43229-7513; letters.monthly@cm-media.com; www.columbusmonthly.com. See also: *Cincinnati Magazine; Akron Life & Leisure.*

D Dallas/Fort Worth. [ISSN: 0164-8292] 1974. m. $18. Wick Allison. Magazine Limited Partners, 4311 Oak Lawn Ave., 1st Fl., Dallas, TX 75219; feedback@dmagazine.com; www.dmagazine.com. See also: *Texas Monthly; Texas Highways.*

Detroiter. [ISSN: 0011-9709] 1910. m. $18. Chris Mead. Detroit Regional Chamber, One Woodward Avenue, Suite 1700, P.O. Box 33840, Detroit, MI 48232-0840; cmead@detroitchamber.com; www.detroitchamber.com. See also: *Traverse: Northern Michigan's Magazine; HOUR Detroit; Midwest Living; Grand Rapids.*

Evansville Living. 2000. bi-m. $18. Kristen K.Tucker. Tucker Publishing Group, 100 NW Second St., Evansville, IN 47708; ktucker@evansvilleliving.com; www.evansvilleliving.com. See also: *Outdoor Indiana; Indianapolis Monthly; Midwest Living.*

Grand Rapids. [ISSN: 1055-5145] 1964. m. $19. Carole Valade-Copenhaver. Gemini Publications, 549 Ottawa Ave. NW, Ste. 201, Grand Rapids, MI 49503-1444; grminfo@grmag.com; www.grmag.com. See also: *Traverse: Northern Michigan's Magazine; HOUR Detroit; Midwest Living; Detroiter.*

Greenwich Magazine. [ISSN: 1072-2432] 1947. 11/yr. $27. Donna Moffly. Moffly Publications Inc., 39 Lewis St., Greenwich, CT 06830; mail@greenwichmagazine.com; www.greenwichmag.com. See also: *Westport Magazine, Connecticut.*

Hampton Roads Monthly (also called *H R Monthly*). [ISSN: 1533-8599] 2000. m. $19.95. Bonn L. Garrett III. VistaGraphics Inc., 1264 Perimeter Pkwy., Virginia Beach, VA 23454; editor@hrmonthly.com; www.hrmonthly.com. See also: *Virginia Living; Blue Ridge Country; The Roanoker; Albemarle: Living in Jefferson's Virginia; Richmond Magazine.*

Harrisburg Magazine. 1995. m. $19.95. Lisa Paige. 22 S. Third, Ste. 1, Harrisburg, PA 17101; editor@harrisburgmagazine.com; www.hbgmag.com. See also: *Pennsylvania Magazine; Philadelphia Magazine; Pittsburg.*

Honolulu. [ISSN:0441-2044] 1888. m. $15. John Heckathorn. PacificBasin Communications, 1000 Bishop St., Ste. 405, Honolulu, HA 96813-4204; johnh@pacificbasin.net; www.honolulumagazine.com.

HOUR Detroit. 1996. m. $17.95. Ric Bohy. Hour Media, L.L.C., 117 W. Third St., Royal Oak, MI 48067; editorial@hourdetroit.com; www.hourdetroit-.com. See also: *Traverse: Northern Michigan's Magazine; Midwest Living; Detroiter; Grand Rapids.*

Indianapolis Monthly. [ISSN: 0899-0328] 1977. 14/yr. $24. Deborah Way. Indianapolis Monthly, One Emmis Plaza, 40 Monument Circle, Ste. 100, Indianapolis, IN 46204; dway@indymonthly.emmis.com; www.indianapolismonthly.com. See also: *Outdoor Indiana; Midwest Living; Evansville Living.*

Jacksonville Magazine (Formerly: *Jacksonville Today; Jacksonville Magazine; Jacksonville*). [ISSN: 1070-5163] 1985. m. $19.90. Joseph White. White Publishing Co., 534 Lancaster St., Jacksonville, FL 32204; mail@jacksonvillemag.com; www.jacksonvillemag.com. See also: *Tallahassee Magazine; Sarasota Magazine.*

Las Vegas Life. [ISSN: 1533-4643] 1997. m. $19.95. Phil Hagen. Greenspun Media Group, 2290 Corporate Circle Dr., Ste. 250, Henderson, NV 89074; feedback@lvlife.com; www.lvlife.com.

Los Angeles Magazine (Formerly *Los Angeles*). [ISSN: 1522-9149] 1960. m. $19. Kit Rachlis. Emmis Publishing, L.P., 5900 Wilshire Blvd., 10th Fl., Los Angeles, CA 90036; letters@lamag.com; www.losangelesmagazine.com. See also: *Sacramento Magazine; San Francisco; San Diego Magazine; Palm Springs Life.*

Macon Magazine. [ISSN: 1090-3267] 1986. bi-m. $14.98. James and Jodi Palmer. Macon Magazine Inc., 227 Orange St., Macon, GA 31201-1627; feedback@maconmagazine.com; www.maconmagazine.com. See also: *Blue Ridge Country; Atlanta, Augusta Magazine.*

Madison Magazine (Formerly: *Madison Select*). [ISSN: 0192-7442] 1978. m. $17. Brian Howell. Madison Magazine Inc., 211 S. Paterson St., Ste. 100, Madison, WI 53703; bhowell@madisonmagazine.com; www.madisonmagazine.com. See also: *Wisconsin Trails: the Magazine of Life in Wisconsin; Milwaukee Magazine.*

Milwaukee Magazine (Formerly: *Milwaukee*). [ISSN: 0741-1243] 1979. m. $18. John Fennell. Quad Creative, L.L.C., 417 E. Chicago St., Milwaukee, WI 53202; milmag@qg.com; www.milwaukeemagazine.com. See also: *Wisconsin Trails: the Magazine of Life in Wisconsin; Madison Magazine.*

Mpls.St.Paul Magazine. [ISSN: 0162-6655] 1971. m. $19.95 (in MN and WI; other states, $23.95). Brian E. Anderson. MSP Communications, 220 S. 6th St., Ste. 500, Minneapolis, MN 55402-4507; edit@mspcommunications.com; www.mspmag.com. See also: *Minnesota Monthly.*

Nashville Lifestyles. 2000. bi-m. $15. Stacie Standifer. City Publications, 1602 W. Northfield Blvd., Ste. 510, Murfreesboro, TN 37129; info@nashvillelifestyles.com; www.nashvillelifestyles.com.

New Orleans Magazine (Formerly: *New Orleans; New Orleans Magazine; Metro New Orleans*). [ISSN: 0897-8174] 1966. m. $19.95. Errol Laborde. MCMedia, LLC., 111 Veterans Blvd., Ste. 1800, Metairie, LA 70005; elaborde@mcmediallc.com; www.neworleansmagazine.com. See also: *Louisiana Life.*

Palm Springs Life. [ISSN: 0331-0425] 1947. 13/yr. $38. Steven Biller. Desert Publications Inc., 303 N. Indian Canyon Dr., Palm Springs, CA 92262; desertpubs@aol.com; www.palmspringslife.com. See also: *Los Angeles Magazine; Sacramento Magazine; San Francisco; San Diego Magazine.*

Philadelphia Magazine (Formerly: *Greater Philadelphia*). [ISSN: 0031-7233] 1908. m. $12. Larry Platt. MetroCorp, 1818 Market St., Philadelphia, PA 19103; mail@phillymag.com; www.phillymag.com. See also: *Pennsylvania Magazine; Pittsburg; Harrisburg Magazine.*

Phoenix Magazine (Formerly: *Phoenix; Phoenix Metro; Phoenix Magazine*). [ISSN: 1074-1429] 1966. m. $18. Robert Stieve. Cities West Publishing, Inc., 8501 E. Princess Dr., Ste. 190, Scottsdale, AZ 85255; knoreen@citieswestpub.com. See also: *Arizona Highways; Tucson Lifestyles.*

Pittsburg(Formerly *Pittsburgh Renaissance; Q E D Renaissance*). [ISSN: 0194-8431] 1969. m. $17.95 for non-WQED supporters. Betsy Benson. WQED Multimedia, 4802 Fifth Ave., Pittsburg, PA 15213; editor@wqed.org; www.wqed.org. See also: *Pennsylvania Magazine; Harrisburg Magazine; Philadelphia Magazine.*

Richmond Magazine. 1980. m. $12. Susan Winiecki. Target Communications, 2201 W. Broad St., Ste. 105, Richmond, VA 23220; editor@richmag.com; www.richmondmagazine.com. See also: *Virginia Living; Blue Ridge Country; The Roanoker, Hampton Roads Monthly; Albemarle: Living in Jefferson's Virginia.*

Sacramento Magazine. [ISSN: 0747-8712] 1975. m. $18 (outside of CA $21). Krista Minard. Sacramento Magazines Corp., 706 56th St., Ste. 210, Sacramento, CA 95819; sacmag@sacmag.com; www.sacmag.com. See also: *Los Angeles Magazine; Palm Springs Life; San Francisco; San Diego Magazine.*

Salt Lake Magazine (Formerly *Salt Lake City*). [ISSN: 1062-8177] 1989. bi-m. $15. Andrea Malouf. Utah Partners Publishing, 240 E. Morris Ave. Ste. 200, Salt Lake City, UT 84115; magazine@saltlakemagazine; www.saltlakemagazine.com.

San Diego Magazine. [ISSN: 0036-4045] 1948. m. $16 in CA (other states $19). Tom Blair. San Diego Magazine Publishing Company, 1450 Front St./P.O. Box 85409, San Diego, CA 92101; tblair@sandiegomag.com; www.sandiegomag.com. See also: *Los Angeles Magazine; Sacramento Magazine; San Francisco; Palm Springs Life.*

San Francisco (Formerly *San Francisco Focus; San Francisco*). [ISSN: 1097-6345] 1953. m. $23.95. Bruce Kelley. San Francisco Focus, 243 Vallejo St., San Francisco, CA 94111; letters@sanfran.com; www.sanfran.com. See also: *Los Angeles Magazine; Sacramento Magazine; Palm Springs Life; San Diego Magazine.*

Sarasota Magazine (Formerly *Sarasota; Clubhouse*). [ISSN: 1048-2245] m. $19.95. Pam Daniel. Gulfshore Media Inc., 601 S. Osprey Ave., Sarasota, FL 34236; info@sarasotamagazine.com; www.sarasotamagazine.com. See also: *Tallahassee Magazine; Jacksonville Magazine.*

Seattle [ISSN: 1081-4469] 1989. 10/yr. $18.95. Rachel Hart. Tiger Oak Publications, 423 Third Ave. W., Seattle, WA 98119; editor@seattlemag.com; www.seattlemagazine.com.

Springfield! [ISSN: 0195-0894] 1979. m. $16.99. Robert C. Glazier. Springfield Communications Inc., 520 S. Union, P.O. Box 4749, Springfield, MO 65802; pub@sgfmag.com; www.sgfmag.com. See also: *Missouri Life; St. Louis Magazine.*

St. Louis Magazine. [ISSN: 1090-5723] 1963. m. $18. Elaine X. Grant. St. Louis Magazine LLC, 1034 S. Brentwood, Ste. 1220, St. Louis, MO 63117; feedback@stlmag.com; www.stlouismagazine.com. See also: *Missouri Life; Springfield!*

The Roanoker. [ISSN: 0274-9734] 1974. bi-m. $14.95. Kurt Rheinheimer. Leisure Publishing Co., 3424 Brambleton Ave. S.W./P.O. Box 21535, Roanoke,

VA 24018; info@theroanoker.com; www.theroanoker.com. See also: *Virginia Living; Albemarle: Living in Jefferson's Virginia; Hampton Roads Monthly; Richmond Magazine.*

Tallahassee Magazine. 1979. bi-m. $19.95. Julie Strauss Bettinger. Rowland Publishing Inc., 1932 Miccosukee Rd., Tallahassee, FL 32308; krolfs@rowlandinc.com; www.rowlandinc.com. See also: *Sarasota Magazine; Jacksonville Magazine.*

Tucson Lifestyles. [ISSN: 1062-2861] 1982. m. $18. Sue Giles. Conley Magazines, LLC., 7000 E. Tanque Verde Rd., Ste. 11, Tucson, AZ 85715-5318; tlm@tucsonlife.com; www.tucsonlife.com. See also: *Arizona Highways; Phoenix Magazine.*

Washingtonian. [ISSN: 0043-0897] 1965. m. $24 in DC, MD, and VA. John A. Limpert. Washington Magazine Inc., 1828 L St., NW, Ste. 200, Washington, DC 20036; editorial@washingtonian.com; www.washingtonian.com.

Westport Magazine. 11/yr. $24.95. Donna Moffly. 205 Main St., Westport, CT 06880. Moffly Publications Inc., 39 Lewis St., Greenwich, CT 06830; mail@westportmag.com; mail@mofflypub.com; www.westportmagazine.com. See also: *Connecticut; Greenwich Magazine.*

State and Regional

1661. *Acadiana Profile: magazine of the Cajun country.* [ISSN: 0001-4397] 1968. bi-m. USD 17; USD 2.50 newsstand/cover. Ed(s): Trent Angers. Acadian House Publishing, Inc., PO Box 52247, Lafayette, LA 70505; info@acadianhouse.com; http://www.acadianhouse.com. Illus., adv. Sample. Circ: 2000 Controlled. *Bk. rev.:* 2, 500 words. *Aud.:* Ga.

Acadiana Profile Magazine has recently published feature articles on Mardi Gras, Cajun artist Floyd Sonnier, and Hurricane Lili. Regular columns include biographies, interesting book reviews, Cajun recipes, artist profiles, genealogy research, book excerpts, and travel related to the Acadiana area of southern Louisiana. Feature articles are often published in series format, in three different issues. One issue per year is devoted to Cajun cooking. Emphasis is placed on content related to high-interest topics, making it an excellent regional magazine. See also: *Louisiana Life* and *New Orleans Magazine.*

1662. *Adirondack Life.* [ISSN: 0001-8252] 1970. 8x/yr. USD 21.95; USD 3.95 newsstand/cover per issue. Ed(s): Elizabeth Folwell. Adirondack Life, PO Box 410, Jay, NY 12941; aledit@primelinkl.net; http://www.adirondacklife.com. Illus., adv. Circ: 50000. *Bk. rev.:* 10, 100 words. *Aud.:* Ga.

Adirondack Life thoroughly covers the history, culture, recreation, and wildlife of New York's Adirondack Park. Regular columns include "Adirondack Made," "Yesteryear," and "Our Towns." "Inside and Out" provides a list of exhibitions, lectures, workshops, music, theater, festivals, and outdoor events. Many how-to articles are included, such as how to make syrup or mittens. An Annual Guide and an annual Collectors Issue are also published. See also: *Hudson Valley Regional Review.*

1663. *Albemarle: living in Jefferson's Virginia.* [ISSN: 1052-7974] 1987. bi-m. Ed(s): Ruth Hart. Carden Jennings Publishing, 375 Greenbrier Dr., # 100, Charlottesvle, VA 22901-1618. Circ: 10000. *Bk. rev.:* 10, 25 words. *Aud.:* Ga.

Award-winning *Albemarle* showcases the culture of areas related to Virginia's history, such as Monticello, Williamsburg, Jamestown, Richmond, Mount Vernon, the University of Virginia, and Washington, D.C. Regular columns include a food column, a biographical essay, and "Bookmark," a column covering books for adults, young adults, and children. Recent feature articles were "Lewis and Clark Expedition: A Brief Account" and "Service Dogs of Virginia." The events calendar covers entertainment, arts, gardening, lectures, exhibitions, symposia, seminars, and Monticello events. *Albemarle* is the only place magazine in this section based on a historical region. Hopefully, however, the magazine will improve its amount of journalistic content. See also *Blue Ridge Country, Hampton Roads Monthly, Richmond Magazine, The Roanoker,* and *Virginia Living.*

1664. *Arizona Highways.* [ISSN: 0004-1521] 1925. m. USD 24 domestic; USD 34 in Canada; USD 37 elsewhere. Ed(s): Robert J Early. Arizona Department of Transportation, 2039 West Lewis Ave, Phoenix, AZ 85009; http://www.dot.state.az.us. Illus. Circ: 315000 Paid. Vol. ends: Dec. *Indexed:* ASIP, GeoRef, MagInd, RGPR. *Aud.:* Ga.

High-quality journalism and deep regard for Arizona's heritage and people have given this magazine its excellent national reputation. Each issue keeps with this tradition by featuring, for example, local hikes, Native American legends, local humor, amusing yet thought-provoking columns, travel destinations, a photographic portfolio, historical events, backroad adventures, and local flora and fauna. Recent featured subjects are butterflies in Indian folklore, a Navajo policeman, and the Salt River Project. The magazine does not accept advertising. Highly recommended. See also *Phoenix Magazine,* and *Tucson Lifestyles.*

1665. *Big Sky Journal.* [ISSN: 1094-4680] 1994. 5x/yr. USD 30 domestic; USD 58 foreign; USD 5.95 newsstand/cover per issue. Ed(s): Michelle Stevens-Orton. Spring Creek Publishing, Inc., 101 E Main, 2nd Fl, PO Box 1069, Bozeman, MT 59771-9975. Adv. Circ: 20000 Paid. *Bk. rev.:* 3-10, 450 words. *Aud.:* Ga.

Big Sky Journal covers regional history, art, architecture, and photography of Montana and the Northern Rockies. Every issue features original work by local artists and writers, as well as outdoor activities in the area. Regular columns include "Local Knowledge," "Images of the West," and "Western Designs." Recent articles are about Lewis and Clark's interpretation of grizzly bears and the local history of drive-in theaters. Fly-fishing and arts issues are published annually. Highly recommended. See also *Montana Magazine.*

1666. *Blue Ridge Country.* [ISSN: 1041-3456] 1988. bi-m. USD 17.95; USD 3.95 newsstand/cover per issue. Ed(s): Kurt Rheinheimer. Leisure Publishing Co. (Roanoke), 3424 Brambleton Ave, S W, Roanoke, VA 24018; http://www.6.roanoke.infi.net/~leisure/brc.html. Illus., adv. Sample. Circ: 75000 Paid. Vol. ends: Nov/Dec. *Indexed:* GeoRef. *Bk. rev.:* 3, 100 words. *Aud.:* Ga.

Blue Ridge Country covers points of interest, history, and events in the Southern Appalachian Mountain region, encompassing Georgia, Kentucky, Maryland, North Carolina, South Carolina, Tennessee, Virginia, and West Virginia. Some regular departments are "Creature Feature" and "Mountain Delicacies." A recent feature article discusses Rugby, Tennesse, a former Utopian society. Both area natives and tourists will be particularly interested in its calendar of events and the breadth of coverage given to outdoor activities and sites in the Blue Ridge Mountains area. Includes a separate annual travel guide. See also *Albemarle: Living in Jefferson's Virginia, Our State: Down Home in North Carolina, Sandlapper: The Magazine of South Carolina, Virginia Living,* and *Wonderful West Virginia.*

1667. *Connecticut Magazine.* Formerly: *Connecticut.* [ISSN: 0889-7670] 1971. m. USD 18 domestic; USD 23 Canada; USD 28 elsewhere. Ed(s): Charles Monagan. Communications International, 35 Nutmeg Dr, Trumbull, CT 06611; http://www.connecticutmag.com. Illus., adv. Sample. Circ: 87174 Paid. Vol. ends: Dec. Microform: NRP. Reprint: PQC. *Indexed:* ASIP. *Aud.:* Ga.

Topics are geared toward affluent middle-aged citizens and cover people, restaurants, activities, and general news. Care is taken to involve readers, as illustrated by articles about reader survey results. Among several "Best of Connecticut" topics is a recent list of Reader's Choice Restaurant Award winners. Other recent articles feature a state health care guide, a compilation of the state's largest companies, and Connecticut college campus points of interest. A thorough calendar of events is presented by county. Each issue concludes with Connecticut Public Television news and a program guide. See also *Greenwich Magazine, Westport Magazine* and *Yankee.*

1668. *Down East Magazine: the magazine of Maine.* [ISSN: 0012-5776] 1954. m. USD 26 domestic; USD 38 foreign; USD 4.95 newsstand/cover domestic. Ed(s): Dale Kuhnert. Down East Enterprise, Inc., PO Box 679, Camden, ME 04843-0370. Illus., adv. Sample. Circ: 100000. Vol. ends: Jul. *Indexed:* ASIP. *Bk. rev.:* 1-5, 500 words. *Aud.:* Ga.

Down East covers the Pine Tree State's events, activities, people, locales, dining, and concerns. Two recent pieces discuss the state's future and reinventing its cities' downtowns. Each issue includes a collection of interesting articles from newspapers in Maine and at least one extensive book review. Recollections submitted by Mainers conclude every issue. See also *Yankee.*

1669. *Hudson Valley Regional Review: a journal of regional studies.* [ISSN: 0742-2075] 1984. s-a. USD 12 domestic; USD 16 foreign. Marist College, Hudson River Valley Institute, 3399 N Rd, Poughkeepsie, NY 12601-1387; hrvi@Marist.edu; http://www.hudsonrivervalley.net. Illus., index. Sample. Circ: 375. Vol. ends: Sep. *Indexed:* AmH&L. *Bk. rev.:* 6, 500-2,000 words. *Aud.:* Ac.

This journal covers all aspects of history in New York State's Hudson River Valley region (ten counties, from Westchester to the Capital District) and relates the information to the academic concept of regionalism. Articles are scholarly and discuss the region's architecture, literature, art, and music; intellectual, political, economic, and social history; and pre-history. Essays include local poetry and photographs. "Riding to the Rescue: How Theodore Roosevelt Saved the Erie Canal" is the title of a recent feature article. All research articles include an extensive list of notes. Highly recommended for all academic and public libraries in the region, as well as libraries outside of the region that collect in the area of regional studies. See also *Adirondack Life.*

1670. *Idaho Magazine.* 2001. m. USD 31.45. Ed(s): Kitty Delorey Fleischman. Idaho Magazine, Inc., 4301 W Franlin Rd, Boise, ID 83705. *Aud.:* Ga.

Idaho Magazine delivers on its promise to tell "the story of Idaho, one month at a time," by relating the state's history, arts, literature, geology, geography, people, humor, wildlife, made-in-Idaho products, and recreation. Its focus is on the "personal history of people who forged the state, and those who remember Idaho in its infancy." Monthly departments include "Free Range Verse," a biography; foliage, gardening, and "Buddy...His Trials and Treasures," about a boy growing up in Grace, Idaho, in the 1940s. Recent articles include one on the Craig Mountain Wildlife Management Area. Although advertising is accepted, it is minimal compared to the content. As a rather new publication, *Idaho Magazine* shows real promise as a state magazine.

1671. *Illinois Magazine.* Former titles: *Illinois; Outdoor Illinois.* [ISSN: 0747-9794] 1962. bi-m. USD 21.95. Ed(s): Lee J Schuster. Henrichs Publications, Inc., 1712 N. Van Buren St., Litchfield, IL 62056-1258. Illus., adv. Circ: 15800. *Aud.:* Ga.

Absorbing several small-city magazines in Illinois, *Illinois Magazine*'s mission is to "inform, educate, and entertain readers with stories that tell why Illinois is such a special place to work and play." A few recent features include Lisa Madigan, the new Attorney General; the history of the few remaining lighthouses in the state; and how to stop telemarketing phone calls. Regular columns include "Alphabetical Illinois" (e.g., N is for North Shore Shipwrecks), CD reviews, personal advice, health, home decorating, money, and travel. An opinion piece, written by the publisher, concludes each issue. As a new state publication, libraries in Illinois may consider subscribing to *Illinois Magazine.*

1672. *Kansas!* [ISSN: 0022-8435] 1945. q. USD 15. Ed(s): Nancy Nowick Romberg. Kansas. Department of Commerce and Housing, 1000 SW Jackson St., Ste 100, Topeka, KS 66612-1354. Illus. Sample. Circ: 53000. Vol. ends: Winter. Microform: PQC. *Indexed:* GeoRef. *Bk. rev.:* 5-10, 100 words. *Aud.:* Ga.

Kansas! is unique because a human-interest thread runs through almost every piece of writing. It covers people, history, cultural events, and places to visit. Recent topics include murals throughout Kansas and modern-day saddlemaking. It presents a positive, friendly view of the Sunflower State and includes interesting topics, but it is not content-heavy. *Kansas!* does not accept advertising.

1673. *Lake Superior Magazine.* Formerly: *Lake Superior Port Cities.* [ISSN: 0890-3050] 1979. bi-m. USD 21.95 domestic; USD 31.95 foreign. Ed(s): Konnie LeMay. Lake Superior Port Cities, Inc., 325 Lake Ave S, Duluth, MN 55802. Adv. Circ: 20000 Paid. *Bk. rev.:* 2-5, 100 words. *Aud.:* Ga.

Lake Superior Magazine covers the history, current events, lifestyles, environment, tourism, and business of the Lake Superior region, which includes Michigan, Minnesota, Wisconsin, and Ontario, Canada. While it is well known for its photography, the magazine also does a nice job of balancing coverage of the region's arts and business. Columns include "Lake Superior's Own," "Huck's Corner," and "Lake Pride." Recent articles feature several local lighthouses and the history of regional breweries. See also *Minnesota Monthly, Traverse: Northern Michigan's Magazine,* and *Wisconsin Trails.*

1674. *Louisiana Life.* Former titles (until 1989): *New Louisiana Life;* (until 1988): *Louisiana Life.* [ISSN: 1042-9980] 1981. q. USD 16 domestic; USD 2.95 newsstand/cover per issue. Ed(s): Faith Dawson. New Orleans Publishing Group, 111 Veterans Blvd, Ste 1810, Metairie, LA 70005. Illus., adv. Circ: 32324. Online: EBSCO Publishing. *Indexed:* ASIP. *Bk. rev.:* 6, 100 words. *Aud.:* Ga.

The most distinct feature of *Louisiana Life* is that it describes most events in the state for each month, rather than merely listing them. Equally pleasant are the two columns that work together to cover the state: "Louisianian at Large" features several pages of interesting newsworthy information from around the state, while "Around Louisiana" presents the people and places of north, central, and southwestern Louisiana; Baton Rouge; Plantation Country; and Greater New Orleans. Brief biographies, art, music, travel, excerpts from books pertaining to the state, and the "Great Louisiana Quiz" are also featured in each issue. Recent articles focus on "plantation hopping," museum exhibits, a book excerpt about the Louisiana Purchase's bicentennial, and perique tobacco, a native crop. A nice balance of content and advertising, of entertaining and serious topics. See also *Acadiana Profile Magazine* and *New Orleans Magazine.*

1675. *Midwest Living.* [ISSN: 0889-8138] 1986. bi-m. USD 19.97; USD 3.95 newsstand/cover. Ed(s): Dan Kaercher. Meredith Corp., 1716 Locust St, Des Moines, IA 50309-3023; http://www.meredith.com. Illus., adv. Circ: 850000. Vol. ends: Dec. *Indexed:* ASIP, MagInd. *Bk. rev.:* 2, 300 words. *Aud.:* Ga.

Midwest Living encompasses all aspects of life in the Midwest, including food, gardening, places to visit, and public events. Travel comprises a large portion of each issue, and an extensive listing of events in the region is included, as well as articles about some of the featured places. A regular department is devoted to specific Midwesterners. A recent article is about Iowa author Leigh Michaels. See also *Illinois Magazine, The Iowan, Minnesota Monthly, Outdoor Indiana, Traverse,* and *Wisconsin Trails.*

1676. *Minnesota Monthly.* [ISSN: 0739-8700] 1967. m. USD 17.95. Ed(s): Pamela Hill Nettleton. Minnesota Monthly Publications, Inc., 10 S Fifth St, Ste 1000, Minneapolis, MN 55402-1012. Illus., adv. Circ: 70000. Vol. ends: Dec. *Bk. rev.:* 1, 600 words. *Aud.:* Ga.

Published on behalf of Minnesota Public Radio (MPR), a considerable amount of space is given to MPR news and its listening guide. The calendar of events is divided into an arts guide and a dining guide. A monthly book club selection reviews one book. A distinctive feature of the magazine is its reports on research done within the state and results from polls and surveys it has conducted, allowing readers' voices to give the magazine a unique perspective. Recent features include St. Paul's Irish residents; and Minnesotans' favorite restaurants, places of employent, books, and entertainment venues. See also *Lake Superior Magazine, Midwest Living,* and *Mpls.St.Paul Magazine.*

1677. *Missouri Life.* Former titles: *Missouri Magazine;* (until 1988): *Missouri Life.* 1973. bi-m. USD 21.99 domestic; USD 29.99 Canada; USD 40.99 elsewhere. Ed(s): Danita Allen Wood. Missouri Life, Inc., PO Box 421, Fayette, MO 65248. Illus., adv. Circ: 50000 Paid and controlled. Vol. ends: Dec. *Indexed:* ASIP. *Bk. rev.:* 3-5, 50 words. *Aud.:* Ga.

This magazine of the Show-Me State shows residents and tourists what to do and where to go in Missouri, along with information about the state's history, culture, and way of life. A majority of the articles focus on cultural events and sites and cities to visit. Some recent articles feature Jesse James and the history of the Mastadon State Historic Site. Regular departments include "Best of Missouri," an almanac-style listing of cultural tidbits; and "Made in Missouri," a column featuring products native to the state. See also *Midwest Living, St. Louis Magazine,* and *Springfield!*

1678. *Montana Magazine.* [ISSN: 0274-9955] 1970. bi-m. USD 23 domestic; USD 28 foreign. Ed(s): Beverly R Magley. Lee Enterprises, PO Box 5630, Helena, MT 59604; http://www.montanamagazine.com. Illus., adv. Sample. Circ: 40000. Vol. ends: Nov. Microform: PQC. *Indexed:* ArtHuCI. *Bk. rev.:* 3, 500 words. *Aud.:* Ga.

Photography, history, and nature make up the bulk of this magazine, with photographs and text maintaining an almost equal proportion. Each issue has a portfolio of nature and Montana locales, as well as articles on historical events, a summary of current events across the state, and three or four reviews of Montana-based books. National Wildlife Refuges in Montana and the "great Montana history exam" are two recent article topics. See also *Big Sky Journal.*

1679. *Nebraska Life.* [ISSN: 1091-2886] 1997. bi-m. USD 17. Nebraska Life, 210 N Broadway, PO Box 577, Hartington, NE 68739; publisher@nebraskalife.com; http://www.nebraskalife.com. *Bk. rev.:* 4, 250 words. *Aud.:* Ga.

Nebraska Life features articles about people, locales, and the history of the Cornhusker State, as well as original writing and art by Nebraska artists. Recent pieces reveal Lewis and Clark's route through Nebraska and the state capital's new murals. "The Warbler" is an interesting column that brings together tidbits of news from around the state. Each issue also has four or five reviews about books with a Nebraska connection.

1680. *New Hampshire Magazine.* [ISSN: 1532-0219] m. USD 11.97; USD 2 newsstand/cover per issue. NewHampshire Magazine, 150 Dow St, Manchester, NH 03101; editor@nh.com; http://www.nhmagazine.com. Adv. *Aud.:* Ga.

Thin in appearance but thick with high-interest information, this magazine covers business, travel, home design, politics, events, dining, and products. Recent articles feature the history of vaudeville families in the Granite State, an annual list of top doctors, the best chocolates, and ratings of suburbs. Each issue also includes a short calendar of events (the complete list is on the web site), a brief dining guide, a fashion guide, and a product-sampling column. See also *Yankee.*

1681. *New Jersey Monthly.* Incorporates (1987-1991): *Garden State Home and Garden;* Which incorporated: *New Jersey Home and Garden.* [ISSN: 0273-270X] 1976. m. USD 19.95. Ed(s): Christopher Hahn. New Jersey Monthly L.L.C., 55 Park Pl, Box 920, Morristown, NJ 07963-0920; editor@njmonthly.com. Illus., adv. Sample. Circ: 93000 Paid. Vol. ends: Dec. Online: Florida Center for Library Automation; Gale Group. *Indexed:* ASIP, BHA. *Bk. rev.:* 1-2, 500 words. *Aud.:* Ga.

This slick, lively magazine balances serious topics with entertainment options, both geared slightly toward young professionals in the Garden State. "Out and About" lists events for both adults and children. Some recent articles cover "Myth and Mystery along New Jersey's Forgotten Border," Bruce Springsteen, and efforts to improve a public school system.

1682. *New Mexico Magazine.* Former titles (until 1974): *New Mexico;* (until 1970): *New Mexico Highway Journal.* [ISSN: 0028-6249] 1923. m. USD 23.95; USD 35.95 foreign. Ed(s): Emily Drabanski. Tourism Department, 495 Old Santa Fe Trail, Santa Fe, NM 87501. Illus., adv. Sample. Circ: 125000 Paid. Vol. ends: Dec. *Indexed:* ASIP, GeoRef. *Bk. rev.:* 5-10, 300 words. *Aud.:* Ga.

As the oldest state magazine in the United States, it is not surprising to see many articles on New Mexico's history in this publication. Equal space, however, is given to current events, environmental issues, places to visit, legends and folklore, architecture, nature, and residents. Classical architecture in New Mexico and El Malpais National Monument are the focus of two recent feature articles. The calendar of events is divided by region as well as by subject. Seventy percent of the total circulation is from out of state, which indicates a national readership.

1683. *Ohio.* Formerly (until 1980): *Ohio Magazine.* [ISSN: 0279-3504] 1978. m. USD 24. Ed(s): Alyson Borgerding. Ohio, 62 E Broad St, Columbus, OH 43215-3522; editorial@ohiomagazine.com; http://www.ohiomagazine.com. Illus., adv. Sample. Circ: 98000 Paid. Vol. ends: Mar. Microform: PQC. Online: OCLC Online Computer Library Center, Inc.; ProQuest Information & Learning. *Indexed:* ASIP. *Bk. rev.:* 1-5, 75-200 words. *Aud.:* Ga.

An Ohio State University Chimpanzee Center primatologist, Ohio-born President Rutherford B. Hayes, and Ohio's key historical events have all been recent topics in this magazine. Regular columns include Ohioan biographies, profiles of Ohio towns, travel within and outside of the state, Kent State University news, a "Living" section, a calendar of events, and "Ohio Digest," a compendium of local news. Although the magazine balances content and advertising, the travel section almost overwhelms the feature articles. See also *Akron Life & Leisure, Cincinnati Magazine,* and *Columbus Monthly* (none listed here).

1684. *Oklahoma Today: official magazine of the State of Oklahoma.* [ISSN: 0030-1892] 1956. bi-m. USD 17.95 domestic; USD 27.95 foreign; USD 4.95 newsstand/cover per issue. Ed(s): Louisa McCune. Tourism and Recreation Department, 15 N Robinson, Ste 100, Box 53384, Oklahoma City, OK 73152. Illus., adv. Circ: 43000 Paid. Vol. ends: Nov. *Aud.:* Ga.

Topics are covered from all angles, educating readers about Oklahoma's diverse culture. For example, an article on the revival of *Oklahoma!* includes thumbnail biographies of its stars, photographs of collectible items, a timeline of the musical's development and debut, and an accompanying article on its enduring popularity. Regular departments cover Sooner State locales, unique products, events, institutions, buildings, and restaurants. The calendar of events is divided by city. Recent articles report on the 30 highest-ranked public schools in Oklahoma, the 2002 Oklahoman of the Year, and 88 free activities across Oklahoma. Most issues, such as the Business Issue, are thematic.

1685. *Our State: down home in North Carolina.* Formerly (until 1996): *State.* [ISSN: 1092-0838] 1933. m. USD 21.95; USD 3.95 newsstand/cover per issue. Ed(s): Mary Best Ellis. Mann Media, Inc., 800 Green Valley Rd, 106, Greensboro, NC 27408; ourstate@ourstate.com; http://www.ourstate.com. Illus., adv. Sample. Circ: 77570 Paid. Vol. ends: May. *Bk. rev.:* 1-5, 500 words. *Aud.:* Ga.

Well-written and carefully designed articles cover the issues, people, arts, places, and events in North Carolina. Each issue includes columns on local quotes, towns, counties, Tar Heel history, unique people, food, and locally authored books. A 52-week guide to the best of North Carolina attractions and the people "who make extraordinary things happen" are the focus of two recent issues. See also *Blue Ridge Country.*

1686. *Outdoor Indiana.* [ISSN: 0030-7068] 1934. bi-m. USD 12 domestic; USD 20 foreign. Ed(s): Steve Sellers. Indiana Department of Natural Resources, 402 W Washington St, W 255B, Indianapolis, IN 46204-2748. Illus. Circ: 29000. *Bk. rev.:* 5, 250 words. *Aud.:* Ga.

This exceptional state magazine covers the culture of Indiana by featuring articles on traditions, trails, museums, people, state parks and forests, historical sites, plants, animals, and ideas for travel. Both native Hoosiers and tourists will enjoy the magazine, and well-written articles are as integral as the photography. Recent topics include Wyandotte Cave, the invention of fishing lures, and the Butler University Apothecary Garden. See also *Evansville Living, Indianapolis Monthly* , and *Midwest Living.*

1687. *Pennsylvania Magazine.* [ISSN: 0744-4230] 1981. bi-m. USD 19.97; USD 3.50 newsstand/cover per issue. Ed(s): Matthew K Holliday. Pennsylvania Magazine Co., PO Box 755, Camp Hill, PA 17001-0755. Illus., adv. Sample. Circ: 30000 Paid. Vol. ends: Dec. *Bk. rev.:* 20, 100 words. *Aud.:* Ga.

This magazine is mostly read by well-educated middle-aged residents. Each issue includes a photo essay and a section that lists several points of interest in Pennsylvania. Three recent articles discuss Pennsylvania Impressionist art, covered bridges in the state, and the Kutztown German festival. The calendar lists events by area: western, central, and eastern Pennsylvania. Advertising is not accepted. See also *Harrisburg Magazine, Philadelphia Magazine,* and *Pittsburgh.*

1688. *Rhode Island Monthly.* [ISSN: 1041-1380] 1988. m. USD 18. Ed(s): Paula Bodah. Rhode Island Monthly Communications, Inc., 280 Kinsley Ave., Providence, RI 02903. Illus., adv. Circ: 39192. Vol. ends: May. *Aud.:* Ga.

Rhode Island Monthly highlights events and discusses specific places, people, and issues pertinent to residents and tourists. Providence mayor David Cicilline's plans for the city and a special article on Rhode Island public radio are topics in recent issues. A viewer's guide to public television for southern New England and a travel column aptly named "Rhode Trip" conclude each issue. A December Holiday Issue is published. See also *Yankee.*

1689. *Route 66 Magazine.* [ISSN: 1069-1405] 1994. q. USD 16 domestic; USD 33 Canada; USD 44 elsewhere. Ed(s): Paul Taylor. Route 66 Magazine, 401 W. Railroad Ave., Williams, AZ 86046-2454; info@route66magazine.com; http://www.route66magazine.com. Adv. Circ: 13000. *Bk. rev.:* 4, 50 words. *Aud.:* Ga.

The topics in *Route 66 Magazine* are as diverse as the culture and attractions along "The Mother Road." Also called "America's Main Street" and "America's Highway," Route 66 was once the primary highway from Chicago to Santa Monica. The magazine is written for the Route 66 "roadie," which makes it sound like a travel magazine, but the articles are a blend of narratives and documentaries that more often relay the history and culture of the famous highway. Regular columns include "Highway Haunts" and "Route 66 Corridor Update." The Big Texan Steak House in Amarillo, TX (where eating a 72-ounce steak in an hour is desirable), Devil's Elbow, Missouri, and Navajo Code Talkers of World War II are recent topics of feature articles. Very interesting reading.

1690. *Sandlapper: the magazine of South Carolina.* [ISSN: 1046-3267] 1968. q. USD 25; USD 6 newsstand/cover per issue. Ed(s): Robert Pierce Wilkens. Sandlapper Society, Inc., PO Box 1108, Lexington, SC 29071. Adv. Circ: 8000 Paid and free. Vol. ends: Winter. *Bk. rev.:* 10, 50 words. *Aud.:* Ga.

Filled with a plethora of information and well-written articles, this first-rate magazine showcases all facets of life in South Carolina. Topics range from sports to well-known locals to cities and institutions of higher education. The "South Carolina Potpourri" section features brief articles on specific geographic regions. Photography is also an integral component of the magazine. The calendar of events is maintained on the web site, where it can be updated more frequently. See also *Blue Ridge Country* and *Charleston Magazine.*

1691. *South Dakota Magazine.* [ISSN: 0886-2680] 1985. bi-m. USD 17 domestic; USD 20 foreign. Ed(s): Bernie Hunhoff. South Dakota Magazine, 410 E Third St, Yankton, SD 57078-0175. Illus., adv. Circ: 35000 Paid. *Bk. rev.:* 6, 500 words. *Aud.:* Ga.

"Deadwood: The Town Built by Lady Luck" is the cover story of a recent issue. Drawing attention to what is unique about the Coyote State seems to be the goal of this publication, and its culture, history, and current points of interest are highlighted in every issue. A regular column, "Dakotiana," includes quotations, trivia, and stories related to the state. Wine-making in South Dakota is the topic of another recent feature article. Each issue also has a small-town profile, a brief calendar of events, and orginal art.

Southern Living. See General Editorial section.

Sunset: the magazine of Western living. See General Editorial section.

1692. *Texas Highways.* [ISSN: 0040-4349] 1974. m. USD 17.50 domestic; USD 25.50 foreign; USD 3.50 newsstand/cover per issue. Ed(s): Jack Lowry. Department of Transportation, Travel and Information Division, PO Box 141009, Austin, TX 78714-1009; editors@texashighways.com; http://www.texashighways.com. Illus., index. Sample. Circ: 300000 Paid. Vol. ends: Dec. *Bk. rev.:* 2, 100 words. *Aud.:* Ga.

Texas Highways offers varied views of the Lone Star State by writing about the many facets of its culture: people, history, public institutions, events, and travel. Readers' opinions are often solicited, as evidenced by reader's choice surveys. Recently, two articles focused on gargoyles on state buildings and the new Women's Museum in Dallas. The magazine is published by the Texas Department of Transportation and does not accept advertising. *Texas Highways* is targeted to a general readership, exhibiting a balance of urban and nonurban topics, while *Texas Monthly* is more of an urban publication. See also *D Dallas/Fort Worth.*

1693. *Texas Monthly.* [ISSN: 0148-7736] 1973. m. USD 18 domestic; USD 40 elsewhere; USD 3.95 newsstand/cover per issue. Ed(s): Evan Smith. Emmis Communications Corporations, One Emmis Plaza, 40 Monument Circle, Ste 100, Indianapolis, IN 46204; http://www.texasmonthly.com. Illus., adv. Circ: 30000 Paid. Vol. ends: Dec. Microform: PQC. Online: EBSCO Publishing; Gale Group; LexisNexis; Northern Light Technology, Inc.; OCLC Online Computer Library Center, Inc.; ProQuest Information & Learning; H.W. Wilson. *Indexed:* ASIP, LRI, MagInd, RGPR, RI-1. *Bk. rev.:* 3, 200 words. *Aud.:* Ga.

Intended for a younger professional audience, this publication contrasts with *Texas Highways* because of its emphasis on current events and popular culture in Texas. Entertainment and the arts command a lot of space, as do people, sports, and business. Articles may be more meaningful to Texans, although event and restaurant guides are useful to both residents and tourists. Topics cover both the humorous and the serious, such as the 2003 Bum Steer Awards (given to the lamest and most embarrassing happenings in Texas) and the withered Rio Grande river. Advertising is extensive but does not overshadow the emphasis on content. See also *D Dallas/Fort Worth* .

1694. *TRAVERSE: Northern Michigan's magazine.* Formerly: *Traverse, The Magazine.* [ISSN: 1071-3719] 1981. m. USD 27.95 domestic; USD 47.95 foreign; USD 3.95 newsstand/cover per issue. Ed(s): Deborah W Fellows. Prism Publications Inc., 148 E Front St, Traverse City, MI 49684; traverse@traversemagazine.com; traversemagazine.com. Illus., adv. Sample. Circ: 22000 Paid. Vol. ends: Dec. *Aud.:* Ga.

Traverse stays true to the Upper Peninsula's roots by including only events, people, places, and traditions unique to Northern Michigan's heritage and modern culture. The magazine's strengths lie in its ability to highlight general-interest topics, as well as environmental concerns and legends and folklore. It maintains a focus on families and young children. Haunted landmarks and how to make pickles are examples of two recent topics. See also *Lake Superior Magazine* and *Midwest Living.*

1695. *Vermont Life.* [ISSN: 0042-417X] 1946. q. USD 20; USD 4.95 newsstand/cover per issue. Ed(s): Tom K Slayton. Vermont Life Magazine, 6 Baldwin St., Montpelier, VT 05602; vtlife@life.state.vt.us; http://www.vtlife.com. Illus., adv. Sample. Circ: 90000. Vol. ends: No. 4. *Indexed:* ASIP. *Bk. rev.:* 5, 300 words. *Aud.:* Ga.

With a focus on culture and photography, this magazine includes articles and information about events, specific places, pastimes, work, food, and traditions. "Green Mountain Post Boy" and "Vermontiana" are regular departments. Special attention is given to the review of books of Vermont interest and to articles about residents. A recent issue contains a wonderful spread of 1936–1942 photographs of Vermont and a feature article on the state's many writers. Published by the State of Vermont. Advertising is not accepted. See also *Yankee.*

1696. *Virginia Living.* [ISSN: 1543-9984] 2002. bi-m. USD 18. Cape Fear Publishing, 109 E Cary St, 2nd Fl, Richmond, VA 23219. Adv. *Aud.:* Ga.

The recent debut of this glossy, large-scale publication fills the long-standing void of a state magazine for Virginia. In several monthly columns and two to three feature articles, each issue of *Virginia Living* covers the people and places of the state. Regular columns include "UpFront," a calendar of events; "Food"; "Virginia Living Interview," and "Fashion." Perhaps the most informative column is "UpFront," which is filled with many interesting tidbits of information, such as Alexandria's month-long George Washington birthday celebration and Marion, Virginia, the hometown of Mountain Dew. A creatively illustrated, annotated calendar of events is included. Two recent articles exhibit the balance of serious and entertaining topics: the North Atlantic Treaty Organization's U.S. headquarters in Norfolk and the return of oyster gardening in Virginia. See also *Albemarle: Living in Jefferson's Virginia* and *Blue Ridge Country.*

1697. *Wisconsin Trails: the magazine of life in Wisconsin.* Formerly: *Wisconsin Tales and Trails.* [ISSN: 0095-4314] 1960. bi-m. USD 24.95 domestic; USD 30.95 foreign. Ed(s): Kate Bast. Trails Media Group, Inc., 1131 Mills St., PO Box 317, Black Earth, WI 53515; info@wistrails.com; http://www.trailsmediagroup.com. Illus., adv. Circ: 55000 Paid. *Indexed:* ASIP, ICM, RGPR. *Bk. rev.:* 2, 100 words. *Aud.:* Ga.

Part travel magazine, part history magazine, this publication presents Wisconsin through articles about local history, events, conservation, and interesting places and the stories behind them. A calendar of events, a photographic portfolio, a restaurant review, sections on home decorating and gardening, and in-depth articles on various subjects comprise each issue. Illustrating the history side of the magazine are two recent examples of articles: Wisconsin WWII veterans' stories and the history behind Milwaukee's Basilica of St. Josaphat. See also *Lake Superior Magazine, Madison Magazine, Midwest Living,* and *Milwaukee Magazine.*

1698. *Wonderful West Virginia.* Formerly: *Outdoor West Virginia.* [ISSN: 0030-7157] 1936. m. USD 17 domestic; USD 30 foreign. Ed(s): Arnout Hyde, Jr. West Virginia Division of Natural Resources, Capitol Complex, Building 3, Rm 662, 1900 Kanawha Blvd E, Charleston, WV 25305; hpuce@dnr.state.wv.us; http://www.wonderfulwv.com. Illus. Sample. Circ: 49500. Vol. ends: Dec. Microform: PQC. *Bk. rev.:* 1-5, 100-500 words. *Aud.:* Ga.

Published by West Virginia's Division of Natural Resources, this magazine's articles are generally related to the outdoors. They tell the story of the state's culture as manifested in its people, history, places, and events. It concentrates on culture rather than on travel. Each issue has plenty of photography but a limited calendar of events. See also *Blue Ridge Country.*

1699. *Yankee.* [ISSN: 0044-0191] 1935. m. except Aug. & Feb. USD 15.97 domestic; USD 22 foreign; USD 2.99 newsstand/cover per issue domestic. Ed(s): Judson D Hale, Sr., Elizabeth Folwell. Yankee Publishing, Inc., PO Box 520, Dublin, NH 03444-0520; http://www.newengland.com. Illus., adv. Circ: 700625 Paid. Vol. ends: Dec. *Indexed:* ABS&EES, ASIP, MagInd, RGPR. *Bk. rev.:* 1, 500 words. *Aud.:* Ga.

Yankee is an almanac-sized magazine that publishes articles on topics unique to New England. Its excellent, engaging writing focuses on a variety of topics, including food, history, poetry, travel, and people. Columns include "Yarns, Snippets and Whatnots" and the "Original Swopper's Column." Recent issues feature articles on the new Eric Carle Museum (children's book's author and illustrator), Senator Ted Kennedy, and the inventor of the snowboard. "Traveler's Calendar" lists events in Massachusetts, Maine, Connecticut, Rhode Island, New Hampshire, and Vermont. Highly recommended; superior example of a regional magazine. See also *Connecticut, Down East: The Magazine of Maine, New Hampshire Magazine, Rhode Island Monthly,* and *Vermont Life.*

■ CIVIL LIBERTIES

General/Bioethics: Reproductive Rights, Right-to-Life, and Right-to-Die/ Freedom of Expression and Information/Freedom of Thought and Belief/ Groups and Minorities/Political-Economic Rights

See also Alternatives; News and Opinion; and Political Science sections.

Marie F. Jones, Extended Campus Services Librarian, East Tennessee State University, Johnson City, TN 37614; jonesmf@mail.etsu.edu

Introduction

As "homeland security" intrudes further into the freedoms of individual rights, library users will need an ever-increasing amount of information in the arena of civil liberties, civil rights, and human rights. Every person—regardless of age, race, gender, ability, or sexual orientation—has a right to freedom of thought, freedom of conscience, freedom of expression, freedom of movement, freedom to enjoy privacy and autonomy in one's personal affairs, and freedom to participate politically. Civil liberties are generally considered those freedoms that are restricted to the private sphere; civil rights are those that are more public and political; human rights are those universal rights that are guaranteed not by a single constitution, but by broader human principles. This section includes publications that address each of these forms of rights.

This chapter is divided into a number of subsections that, together, merely sample the range of materials available in this area. The "General" category contains only publications that are national or international in scope, but many states and regions have excellent civil liberties publications of interest to regional members. Librarians should seek out their regional political activist organizations and their state's ACLU chapter to identify appropriate titles. The "Electronic Journals" subsection has changed drastically since the last edition of *Magazines for Libraries*—partially due to a trend away from organizational web sites that merely re-create print publications. For example, the national ACLU web site, which used to house an online newsletter, has become a more fluid information resource, with constant news updates rather than a static biweekly publication. Finally, librarians should explore other *Magazines for Libraries* sections dedicated to individual groups: African American; Aging; Asian American; Disabilities; Ethnic Interests; Latino Studies; Lesbian, Gay, Bisexual and Transgender; Native Americans; and Women: Feminist and Special Interest to augment the titles listed in the "Groups and Minorities" subsection. It is important for the civil liberties interests of these groups that librarians support a broad range of voices in the library and the community and that they encourage use of library resources by diverse populations.

Basic Periodicals

Hs: *Liberty, New Perspectives Quarterly, Progressive;* Ga: *The Advocate, Amnesty Now, Cultural Survival Quarterly, Hastings Center Report, Human Rights, Index on Censorship, Newsletter on Intellectual Freedom, Reason, Ragged Edge, SIECUS Report, Voice of Reason;* Ac: *Cultural Survival Quarterly, Harvard Civil Rights—Civil Liberties Law Review, Human Rights Quarterly, Index on Censorship, Journal of Information Ethics;* Sa: *Bioethics, Harvard Civil Rights—Civil Liberties Law Review, Journal of Information Ethics, New York Law School Journal of Human Rights, Social Theory and Practice.*

Basic Abstracts and Indexes

Alternative Press Index, Current Law Index, Public Affairs Information Service.

General

1700. *Amnesty Now.* q. Members, USD 25. Ed(s): Terry J Allen. Amnesty International U S A, 322 Eighth Ave, New York, NY 10001; http://www.amnestyusa.org. *Aud.:* Ga, Ac, Sa.

This publication of Amnesty International USA features exposes, essays, and analysis on issues of human rights around the globe and reports on campaigns and actions of Amnesty International activists. Striking full-color photography throughout the glossy publication makes it visually attractive, while the content offers meaningful analysis of important issues. Recent articles include "Political Profiling: Police Spy on Peaceful Activists" and "False Confessions: Scaring Subjects to Death." A wide range of human rights violations are discussed, including genocide, institutionalized racism, sexism, misuse of police power, profiling, invasion of privacy, inhumane laws, and torture. Recommended for all libraries.

1701. *Constitutional Commentary.* [ISSN: 0742-7115] 1984. 3x/yr. USD 18. Ed(s): Daniel Farber. Constitutional Commentary Inc., 229 19th Ave S, Minneapolis, MN 55455; http://www.law.umn.edu/. Illus., adv. Circ: 600. Vol. ends: Winter. Microform: WSH. Online: EBSCO Publishing; Florida Center for Library Automation; Gale Group; LexisNexis; Northern Light Technology, Inc.; West Group. Reprint: WSH. *Indexed:* CLI, ILP, LRI. *Bk. rev.:* 1-4, 1,500-6,000 words. *Aud.:* Ac, Sa.

One of the few faculty-edited law school journals in the country, *Constitutional Commentary* carries short, "less ponderous" articles on constitutional law and history, written in a style that is more readable than other law reviews. Articles tend to be topical rather than focusing on case law. Recent articles include "What Does the Second Amendment Restrict?" and "The Supreme Court and the Brethren." Also includes review essays and book reviews.

Criminal Justice Ethics. See Criminology and Law Enforcement section.

1702. *Harvard Civil Rights - Civil Liberties Law Review.* [ISSN: 0017-8039] 1966. 2x/yr. USD 30 domestic; USD 38 Canada; USD 36 elsewhere. Ed(s): Elena Goldstein, Laura Weinrib. Harvard University, Law School, Publications Center, Hastings Hall, Cambridge, MA 02138; hlscrc@law.harvard.edu; http://www.law.harvard.edu/studorgs/crcl/lawreview/. Illus., adv. Circ: 1100. Vol. ends: Summer. Microform: WSH; PMC; PQC. Online: Gale Group; LexisNexis; OCLC Online Computer Library Center, Inc.; West Group; H.W. Wilson. Reprint: PQC; WSH. *Indexed:* ArtHuCI, CIJE, CJA, CLI, HRA, ILP, LRI, PAIS, RI-1, SSCI, SUSA. *Bk. rev.:* 1, 2,800-4,500 words. *Aud.:* Ac, Sa.

This readable law journal was founded in the mid-1960s, during the wave of constitutional reform produced by the Warren court, and it has tracked the erosion of civil rights and liberties through the years. Editorial viewpoints change with the editors, every two years, but the common themes of social justice and civil liberties continue throughout, covering "the struggle of victims against victimizers." Recent issues examine same-sex marriage, housing segregation, legal feminism, and "The New McCarthyism." Each issue contains lengthy essays, articles, notes, and some book reviews.

1703. *Human Rights (Chicago).* [ISSN: 0046-8185] 1970. q. Members, USD 5; Non-members, USD 17. Ed(s): Vicki Quade. American Bar Association, 750 N Lake Shore Dr, Chicago, IL 60611; quadev@attmail.com; http://www.abanet.org. Illus., index, adv. Circ: 7000. Microform: WSH. Online: bigchalk; EBSCO Publishing; Gale Group; OCLC Online Computer Library Center, Inc.; ProQuest Information & Learning; West Group. Reprint: WSH. *Indexed:* AgeL, ArtHuCI, CLI, IBZ, ILP, LRI, PAIS, SSCI, SSI. *Aud.:* Hs, Ga, Ac.

As the title indicates, this periodical covers issues of human rights and civil rights. Each thematic issue covers some aspect of human rights in a series of brief articles by practicing attorneys and prominant legal scholars. Recent issues have covered the right to healthcare, privacy in cyberspace, individual rights versus community rights, and disability rights. Although published by the American Bar Association Section of Individual Rights and Responsibilities for their section members, the format of this publication, more glossy trade magazine than heavy legal journal, makes it suitable for all types of libraries.

1704. *Human Rights Quarterly: a comparative and international journal of the social sciences, humanities and law.* Formerly (until 1981): *Universal Human Rights.* [ISSN: 0275-0392] 1979. q. USD 140 domestic; USD 146 in Canada & Mexico; USD 157.40 elsewhere. Ed(s): Bert B Lockwood, Jr. Johns Hopkins University Press, Journals Publishing Division, 2715 N Charles St, Baltimore, MD 21218-4363; http://www.press.jhu.edu/. Illus., index, adv. Sample. Refereed. Circ: 1770. Vol. ends: Nov. Microform: WSH; IDC; PQC. Online: EBSCO Publishing; Florida Center for Library Automation; Gale Group; OCLC Online Computer Library Center, Inc.; Project MUSE; RoweCom Information Quest; Swets Blackwell. Reprint: PQC; PSC; WSH. *Indexed:* ABCPolSci, ABS&EES, ArtHuCI, BAS, CLI, IBSS, ILP, IPSA, LRI, PAIS, PRA, PSA, PhilInd, RI-1, RiskAb, SSCI, SSI, SociolAb. *Bk. rev.:* 1-4, 1,100-3,000 words. *Aud.:* Ac, Sa.

This international journal addresses the complex issues of human rights from an interdisciplinary perspective. Basing its vision on the Universal Declaration of Human Rights, the journal provides a forum for noted international experts in the fields of law, philosophy, and the sciences to present comparative and international research on public policy. The quarterly provides up-to-date information on the United Nations and regional human rights organizations, both governmental and nongovernmental, and includes human rights research and policy analysis, book reviews, and philosophical essays on the nature of human rights.

Journal of Criminal Law & Criminology. See Law section.

1705. *Law & Inequality: a journal of theory and practice.* [ISSN: 0737-089X] 1983. 2x/yr. USD 15. Ed(s): John H Goolsby. University of Minnesota, Law School, 229 19th Ave S, Minneapolis, MN 55455; http://www.law.umn.edu/students/publicat.htm. Illus., adv. Refereed. Circ: 5600. Vol. ends: Jun. Microform: WSH. Online: Gale Group; LexisNexis. Reprint: WSH. *Indexed:* CLI, ILP, LRI, RI-1. *Bk. rev.:* 1, 2,000 words. *Aud.:* Ac, Sa.

This journal focuses on issues of inequality in law and society written by law school professors, students, and lawyers as well as those in other disciplines. Published by law students at the University of Minnesota, the journal examines such issues as gender, sexuality, age, ability, race, and socioeconomic status, always with a legal emphasis. Articles appear in standard law journal formats or in personal essays or creative writing. Recommended for academic libraries.

New Perspectives Quarterly. See News and Opinion section.

1706. *New York Law School Journal of Human Rights.* Formerly (until 1987): *New York Law School Human Rights Annual.* [ISSN: 1046-4328] 1982. 3x/yr. USD 22; USD 27 foreign. New York Law School, 57 Worth St, New York, NY 10013-2960; http://www.nyls.edu/. Illus., adv. Refereed. Circ: 1000. Vol. ends: Spring. Reprint: WSH. *Indexed:* CLI, ILP, LRI, PAIS. *Bk. rev.:* 1-2, 2,400 words. *Aud.:* Ac, Sa.

"Dedicated to the preservation and extension of human rights through the legal system," this journal solely addresses the human rights field. It covers legal issues and offers viable legal alternatives that "develop rather than discuss law." Interdisciplinary in scope, the journal contains articles designed to inform legal practitioners of new and changing areas of human rights law.

Social Philosophy and Policy. See Philosophy section.

Social Policy. See Sociology and Social Work/General section.

Social Theory and Practice. See Cultural-Social Studies section.

Bioethics: Reproductive Rights, Right-to-Life, and Right-to-Die

1707. *Bioethics.* [ISSN: 0269-9702] q. GBP 327 print & online eds. Ed(s): Ruth Chadwick, Udo Schuklenk. Blackwell Publishing Ltd., 9600 Garsington Rd, PO Box 805, Oxford, OX4 2DQ, United Kingdom; customerservices@oxon.blackwellpublishing.com; http://www.blackwellpublishing.com/. Illus. Refereed. Online: EBSCO Publishing; Gale Group; ingenta.com; OCLC Online Computer Library Center, Inc.; Ovid Technologies, Inc.; RoweCom Information Quest; Swets Blackwell. Reprint: SWZ. *Indexed:* ASSIA, ArtHuCI, ExcerpMed, GSI, IBSS, IBZ, PhilInd, RI-1, SSCI, SSI, SWA, SociolAb. *Bk. rev.:* 6-10, 400-1,300 words. *Aud.:* Ac, Sa.

The official journal of the International Association of Bioethics, this weighty publication discusses ethical issues raised in the biological and medical sciences. Each issue of the scholarly, refereed journal contains articles, discussion, and book reviews, from an international perspective. Articles are either theoretical or practical and are written by experts in the field. Topics such as human-subject research, research and informed consent, and justice and medical research appear. Recent articles include "Genes and Social Justice" and "Utilitarianism and the Disabled." Issues sometimes center around themes, such as biochemical warfare research or consensus in public bioethics commissions.

Hastings Center Report. See Medicine and Health/Medicine and Society section.

1708. *Issues in Law and Medicine.* [ISSN: 8756-8160] 1985. 3x/yr. USD 79 (Individuals, USD 59). Ed(s): James Bopp, Jr., Larry Ligget. National Legal Center for the Medically Dependent and Disabled, Inc., 3 S 6th St, Terre Haute, IN 47807-3510; http://www.elibrary.com. Illus., adv.

Refereed. Circ: 1000. Vol. ends: Spring. Microform: WSH. Online: bigchalk; EBSCO Publishing; Florida Center for Library Automation; Gale Group; LexisNexis; National Library of Medicine; OCLC Online Computer Library Center, Inc.; ProQuest Information & Learning; West Group; H.W. Wilson. Reprint: WSH. *Indexed:* AgeL, ArtHuCI, BiolAb, CJA, CLI, ECER, HRA, ILP, IndMed, LRI, PRA, PsycholAb, RI-1, SSCI, SUSA. *Bk. rev.:* 5, 200-400 words. *Aud.:* Ac, Sa.

Published by the National Center for the Medically Dependent and Disabled and foundation funds, this peer-reviewed professional journal discusses medical treatment rights of persons with disabilities and in need of life-sustaining treatment or care. Articles are sometimes technical in nature because the target audience includes attorneys, health care professionals, educators, and administrators concerned with people who have severe disabilities and therefore are discriminated against in the delivery of medical care. A wider audience will appreciate the juxtaposition of opposing views on controversial topics and the abstracts of relevant articles from other journals. The editorial policy states that the journal is opposed to euthanasia and assisted suicide. Recommended for academic and research collections.

1709. ***S I E C U S Report.*** Formerly: *S I E C U S Newsletter.* [ISSN: 0091-3995] 1972. bi-m. USD 75. Ed(s): Mac Edwards. Sexuality Information and Education Council of the U S, 130 W 42nd St, Ste 350, New York, NY 10036; siecus@siecus.org; http://www.siecus.org/pubs/srpt.html. Illus., index, adv. Circ: 3500. Vol. ends: Aug/Sep. Online: Florida Center for Library Automation; Gale Group; LexisNexis; OCLC Online Computer Library Center, Inc.; ProQuest Information & Learning. Reprint: ISI; PQC. *Indexed:* CWI, EduInd, IMFL, MRD. *Bk. rev.:* 2, 200-600 words. *Aud.:* Ga, Ac.

SIECUS (Sexuality Information and Education Council of the United States) publishes this respected journal in the field of sexuality and sexual health. The scholarly articles are written by practitioners in the field. Each report concentrates on a specific topic and includes a comprehensive bibliography. Recent reports focus on sexual health, HIV/AIDS, sexuality and people with disabilities, sexual abuse, and sexuality through midlife and aging. The SIECUS Report web site includes full text of back issues of the reports, from volume one to recent issues.

Freedom of Expression and Information

1710. ***CovertAction Quarterly.*** Formerly (until 1993): *Covert Action Information Bulletin.* [ISSN: 1067-7232] 1978. q. USD 57 (Individuals, USD 22). Ed(s): Karen Talbot. CovertAction Publications, Inc., 1500 Massachusetts Ave, N W, Ste 732, Washington, DC 20005. Circ: 11000 Paid. Microform: PQC. Reprint: PQC. *Indexed:* AltPI, PAIS. *Aud.:* Ga, Ac, Sa.

Through in-depth investigative journalism and analysis, this periodical reports on hidden activities of intelligence agencies and corporations, including those activities that infringe on civil rights and liberties. The editors say, "Covert action includes all the ways in which government and corporations act quietly to confuse the public." Speaking out on issues of free speech and governmental openness, the journal examines areas of national and international importance, exposing greed and malfeasance wherever it is found. The web site provides full tables of contents of archived issues, with some articles in full text.

1711. ***Index on Censorship: for free expression.*** [ISSN: 0306-4220] 1972. q. USD 80 (Individuals, USD 48; GBP 9.50 newsstand/cover per issue domestic). Ed(s): Ursula Owen. Writers & Scholars International Ltd., Lancaster House, 33 Islington High St, London, N1 9LH, United Kingdom; contact@indexoncenership.org; http://www.indexoncensorship.org/. Illus., index, adv. Circ: 10000. Vol. ends: Nov/Dec. Online: Gale Group. Reprint: ISI. *Indexed:* AltPI, ArtHuCI, BAS, BrHumI, IBZ, L&LBA, MLA-IB, PAIS, SSCI. *Bk. rev.:* 3, 800-1,800 words. *Aud.:* Ga, Ac.

Index on Censorship reports on freedom of speech, censorship, and censored topics worldwide and acts as a political forum on a broad range of topics. Each sizable issue contains articles surrounding a particular timely theme, such as the recent examination of Iran, Iraq, and the People's Republic of North Korea, "Inside the Axis of Evil." These essays take an approach to controversial issues not found in mainstream news and political commentary. Regular sections cover human rights, minorities, and the media. Most notably, the Index Index chronicles censorship and free-expression abuses in some 70 countries worldwide. The layout is attractive, including photo essays and outstanding graphics. Contributors to this periodical are internationally renowned. Highly recommended for all libraries.

Journal of Information Ethics. See Library and Information Science section.

1712. ***Newsletter on Intellectual Freedom.*** [ISSN: 0028-9485] 1952. bi-m. USD 40 in North America; USD 50 elsewhere; USD 8 newsstand/cover per issue. Ed(s): Judith F Krug. American Library Association, 50 E Huron St, Chicago, IL 60611-2795; http://www.ala.org. Illus., index. Circ: 3200. Vol. ends: Jan. Microform: PQC. Online: OCLC Online Computer Library Center, Inc.; H.W. Wilson. Reprint: PQC. *Indexed:* LibLit. *Bk. rev.:* 1-4, 500-700 words. *Aud.:* Hs, Ac, Ga.

This outstanding periodical published by the Office of Intellectual Freedom of the American Library Association covers intellectual-freedom infringements, especially in the United States, but also worldwide. Notable features include "Censorship Dateline," reporting on censorship activities in U.S. libraries, schools, and universities, on the Internet, and in other countries; "From the Bench," reporting on legal cases; and "Success Stories," reporting incidents where first-amendment rights have been upheld. Some longer articles related to intellectual freedom and censorship also appear. Recent topics of major concern have been CIPA, homeland security measures, and privacy issues. Recommended for all types of libraries.

Freedom of Thought and Belief

1713. ***Free Inquiry.*** [ISSN: 0272-0701] 1980. 11x/yr. USD 32.50 domestic; USD 39.50 foreign; USD 5.95 newsstand/cover domestic. Ed(s): Lewis Vaughn, Timothy Madigan. Council for Secular Humanism, PO Box 664, Amherst, NY 14226-0664; fivaughn@aol.com; http://www.secularhumanism.org. Illus., index, adv. Circ: 23000 Paid. Vol. ends: Fall. Microform: PQC. Online: Florida Center for Library Automation; Gale Group; Northern Light Technology, Inc.; OCLC Online Computer Library Center, Inc.; ProQuest Information & Learning. Reprint: PQC. *Indexed:* IBZ, PAIS, PhilInd. *Bk. rev.:* 3-5, 500-1,500 words. *Aud.:* Ga, Sa.

Published by the Journal for Secular Humanism, *Free Inquiry* "celebrates reason and humanity." Editor Paul Kurtz is an emeritus philosophy professor from SUNY–Buffalo and author of 22 books on humanism. *Free Inquiry* presents scholarly and popular articles relating to secular humanism, atheism, church–state separation, and issues affecting the rights of religious minorities. Recent issues include articles like "Citizens Resist War on the Bill of Rights" and "Thomas Jefferson's Famous ~Wall of Separation between Church and State' Letter."

The Humanist. See Religion section.

Journal of Church and State. See Religion section.

1714. ***Journal of Law and Religion.*** [ISSN: 0748-0814] 1983. s-a. USD 35 (Individuals, USD 25; Students, USD 10). Ed(s): Marre A Failinger. Hamline University School of Law, Journal of Law and Religion, 1536 Hewitt Ave., Saint Paul, MN 55104; lberglin@gw.hamline.edu; http://www.hamline.edu/law/jlr. Illus., index, adv. Refereed. Microform: WSH; PMC. Online: Gale Group. Reprint: WSH. *Indexed:* CLI, ILP, LRI, PRA, PSA, R&TA, RI-1, SociolAb. *Bk. rev.:* 1-2, 2,000 words. *Aud.:* Ac, Sa.

The *Journal of Law and Religion* is an international, interdisciplinary forum committed to studying law in its social context, including moral and religious views of law and life for policy makers, scholars, and educators. Examining the "intersection and interaction" of law and religion, the journal includes a broad range of topics, including historical studies, theoretical questions of jurisprudence and theology, essays on the meaning of justice and rights, power and authority, and law and religion in the social arena. Although issues of separation of church and state are included, they are by no means the main thrust of this publication.

1715. *Liberty (Hagerstown): a magazine of religious freedom.* [ISSN: 0024-2055] 1906. bi-m. USD 6.95. Ed(s): Lincoln Steed. Review and Herald Publishing Association, 55 W Oak Ridge Dr, Hagerstown, MD 21740; http://www.rhpa.org. Illus., adv. Circ: 200000. Vol. ends: Nov/Dec. Microform: PQC. Reprint: PQC. *Aud.:* Hs, Ga.

This inexpensive magazine speaks strongly on issues of separation of church and state. Its online edition (http://libertymagazine.org) includes full text of current articles and archives, with printer-friendly versions and e-mail options. Articles cover timely topics and sometimes present opposing viewpoints. Recent issues touch on everything from conscientious objection to whether "under God" should be in the Pledge of Allegiance. Published by the Seventh-Day Adventist church, this readable magazine is not proselytizing and treats the issues with "quiet diplomacy."

Mental and Physical Disability Law Reporter. See Law section.

1716. *Voice of Reason.* 1981. q. USD 20; USD 25 foreign. Ed(s): Edd Doerr. Americans for Religious Liberty, PO Box 6656, Silver Spring, MD 20916; arlinc@erols.com. Circ: 3500. *Aud.:* Ga.

This black-and-white newsletter is "dedicated to preserving the American tradition of religious, intellectual, and personal freedom in a secular democratic state." Every issue contains reports on Supreme Court and state court actions related to church and state issues, detailed political analysis and news summaries from national news services, and contributed items of importance concerning religious liberty and the freedom of conscience in the United States. Ongoing topics include the Istook Amendment, school vouchers and school funding, abortion rights, religious displays in public places, the activities of the "Religious Right," and actions of groups like People for the American Way, the ACLU, and the National Committee for Public Education and Religious liberty. Reports on political candidates? positions on church and state issues also appear, as do analyses of elections. Includes book and media reviews. While the publication distinctly favors the separation of church and state, its reporting style is relatively unbiased, using language that subsumes opinion to fact. Readers on both sides of these issues will find this publication informative. Full text available on the web site. Recommended for general audiences.

Groups and Minorities

The Advocate. See Lesbian, Gay, Bisexual, Trangender section.

American Indian Law Review. See Native Americans section.

Children's Legal Rights Journal. See Sociology and Social Work section.

Columbia Journal of Gender and the Law. See Women: Feminist and Special Interest section.

1717. *Cultural Survival Quarterly: world report on the rights of indigenous peoples and ethnic minorities.* Formerly (until 1982): *Cultural Survival Newsletter.* [ISSN: 0740-3291] 1976. q. USD 40 to individuals for membership; USD 60 to institutions for membership. Ed(s): Amy Stoll. Cultural Survival, Inc., 215 Prospect St, Cambridge, MA 02139; csinc@cs.org; http://www.culturalsurvival.org/. Illus., index, adv. Circ: 10000. Vol. ends: Winter. Reprint: PSC. *Indexed:* ABS&EES, AICP, AltPI, AnthLit, ForAb, GeogAbPG, WAE&RSA. *Bk. rev.:* 1-3, 350-500 words. *Aud.:* Ga, Ac.

Cultural Survival Quarterly began in 1981 as a newsletter for Cultural Survival, an organization that "has helped indigenous people and ethnic minorities deal as equals in their encounters with industrial society." Since then, the quarterly has expanded to report on the interconnected issues that affect indigenous and ethnic minority communities around the world, including environmental destruction, land rights, sustainable development, and cultural integrity. News, resources, book and media reviews, and notes from the field are also included in each issue. Issues center on a theme and are edited by guest editors. Articles are written for general readers.

Disability & Society. See Disabilities section.

Lesbian-Gay Law Notes. See Lesbian, Gay, Bisexual and Transgender section.

Mainstream. See Disabilities/Electronic Journals section.

Migration World. See Ethnic Studies section.

Mouth. See Zines.

National Black Law Journal. See Law section.

Off Our Backs. See Women: Feminist and Special Interest/Feminist and Women's Studies section.

Ragged Edge. See Disabilities/Electronic Journals section.

Southern California Review of Law and Women's Studies. See Women: Feminist and Special Interest/Feminist and Women's Studies section.

Political-Economic Rights

Clearinghouse Review. See Law section.

Eat the State! See Zines section.

Employee Relations Law Journal. See Labor and Industrial Relations section.

Progressive. See News and Opinion section.

1718. *Reason: free minds and free markets.* [ISSN: 0048-6906] 1968. m. USD 15 domestic; USD 25 foreign. Ed(s): Virginia I Postrel, Nick Gillespie. Reason Foundation, 3415 S Sepulveda Blvd, Ste 400, Los Angeles, CA 90034-6060; michaelo@reason.com; http://www.reason.org/pwatch.html. Illus., index, adv. Circ: 60000. Vol. ends: Apr. Microform: PQC. Online: bigchalk; EBSCO Publishing; Florida Center for Library Automation; Gale Group; Northern Light Technology, Inc.; OCLC Online Computer Library Center, Inc.; ProQuest Information & Learning; H.W. Wilson. *Indexed:* ABS&EES, BRI, CBRI, LRI, MRD, MagInd, PAIS, RGPR. *Bk. rev.:* 3-4, 1,500-2,300 words. *Aud.:* Hs, Ga, Ac.

This libertarian magazine reports on public policy and culture, including civil liberties issues. Interviews, satire and humor, columns, and media reviews make the attractive publication interesting to a popular audience. The online site includes both current and archived issues. Recent articles cover intellectual property and copyright law changes, OxyContin crackdowns and their negative effects on patients in pain, and a critique of NASA after the *Columbia* incident.

The Review of Black Political Economy. See African American section.

Electronic Journals

Asian American Movement Ezine. See Asian American/Electronic Journals section.

In Motion Magazine. See Alternatives/Electronic Journals section.

Library Juice. See Alternatives/Electronic Journals Section.

Webactive. See Alternatives/Electronic Journals section.

■ CLASSICAL STUDIES

See also Archaeology; Art; History; Linguistics; and Literature sections.

Fred W. Jenkins, Coordinator and Head of Collection Management, Roesch Library, University of Dayton, Dayton, OH 45469; fred.jenkins@udayton.edu

Introduction

Although displaced from the central role in education that it enjoyed in the past, classical scholarship has continued to flourish. University faculty and graduate students produce and consume a large volume of scholarly papers in a variety of journals. Latin and the study of classical civilization have also maintained a modest presence in schools and colleges, although relatively few periodicals are directed toward this audience.

The journal-publishing environment in classical studies is a stable one. Most journals are well-established titles that have existed for decades, although there are the inevitable shifts in quality and character among them. The few new classical journals introduced in recent years have been devoted largely to highly specialized subdisciplines. Associations and university presses issue the bulk of the titles; there are few commercial publishers in the field. As a result, nearly all the journals aim at an academic audience. Many are highly technical in content, contain extensive passages of untranslated Latin and Greek, and will interest only professional scholars. *Arethusa, Arion, Classics Ireland,* and *Greece and Rome* are among the few exceptions that might appeal to a broader audience.

Two particular groups of journals deserve comment. First, there are several good periodicals aimed at teachers of the classics at the high school and college levels. *Classical Journal, Classical Outlook,* and *Classical World* all offer articles and columns of pedagogical interest. Classical studies are also well served by journals devoted solely to book reviews and bibliographical essays. These include *Bryn Mawr Classical Review, Classical Review, Gnomon,* and *Lustrum.* Both librarians and scholars will find these to be valuable resources.

Classics was also one of the first disciplines to experiment with electronic publishing. *Bryn Mawr Classical Review*, a notable success in this arena, claims to be the second-oldest online scholarly journal in the humanities. While a majority of the print journals found below now have online avatars, new freestanding electronic journals have been slow to appear. Several efforts to create traditional peer-reviewed journals on the web have sputtered after one or two issues. One notable new venture is *Ancient Narrative*, which combines some elements of the traditional journal with features of an online discussion forum. It reviews and posts articles continuously and then allows authors an opportunity to revise them based on readers' comments before the final version is placed in the journal's archive.

Journals listed here include the most important English-language titles for students and scholars. Only a handful of European journals are noted—those that publish a substantial number of studies in English or provide exceptional bibliographical resources. Because classics has always been an international discipline, libraries supporting research programs in classics will need many additional foreign-language journals.

Basic Periodicals

Hs: *Classical Journal, Classical Outlook, Classical World, Greece and Rome.* Ac: *American Journal of Philology, Bryn Mawr Classical Review Online, Classical Journal, Classical Outlook, Classical Philology, Classical World, Greece and Rome, Transactions of the American Philological Association.*

Basic Abstracts and Indexes

L'Annee Philologique, Arts and Humanities Citation Index, Humanities Index, TOCS-IN.

1719. *American Journal of Philology.* [ISSN: 0002-9475] 1880. q. USD 130 (Individuals, USD 39). Ed(s): Barbara Gold. Johns Hopkins University Press, Journals Publishing Division, 2715 N Charles St, Baltimore, MD 21218-4363; http://www.press.jhu.edu/. Illus., index, adv. Sample. Refereed. Circ: 1205. Vol. ends: Winter. Microform: IDC; PMC; PQC. Online: EBSCO Publishing; Florida Center for Library Automation; Gale Group; JSTOR (Web-based Journal Archive); OCLC Online Computer Library Center, Inc.; Project MUSE; ProQuest Information & Learning; RoweCom Information Quest; Swets Blackwell. Reprint: PQC; PSC; SWZ. *Indexed:* ArtHuCI, BRI, CBRI, HumInd, IBZ, IPB, L&LBA, NTA, NumL, PhilInd, SSCI, SSI. *Bk. rev.:* 8-10, 2-5 pages. *Aud.:* Ac.

One of the oldest and most prestigious American journals in the field, the *American Journal of Philology* publishes scholarly contributions in all areas of classical studies, with special emphasis on languages and literature. Contents include both substantial articles and book reviews. These are aimed at professional scholars and generally require a good working knowledge of Latin and Greek. Tables of contents for recent issues and sample issues are available on the publisher's web site. Indispensable for any academic collection supporting a classics program.

1720. *American Philological Association. Transactions.* Supersedes in part (until 1972): *American Philological Association. Transactions and Proceedings;* Which was formerly (until 1986): *American Philological Association. Transactions.* [ISSN: 0360-5949] 1870. s-a. USD 85 (Individuals, USD 25). Ed(s): Cynthia Damon. Johns Hopkins University Press, Journals Publishing Division, 2715 N Charles St, Baltimore, MD 21218-4363; http://www.press.jhu.edu/. Illus., adv. Refereed. Circ: 3000 Paid. Microform: PMC. Online: JSTOR (Web-based Journal Archive); OCLC Online Computer Library Center, Inc.; Project MUSE; RoweCom Information Quest; Swets Blackwell. *Indexed:* ArtHuCI, L&LBA. *Aud.:* Ac.

As the official journal of the American Philological Association (APA), the major professional association for American classicists, this is one of the most widely read titles in the field. It covers all aspects of classical studies and usually offers a good mix of articles on classical literature and history. In its current manifestation, each volume begins with the annual address by the president of the association, followed by seven to ten articles. Some issues also include papers from a panel presentation at the previous APA conference. A brief final section, "Paragraphoi," consists of short editorial pieces on items of professional, pedagogical, or scholarly concern. The publications section of the association's web site (www.apaclassics.org) includes useful materials on the *Transactions,* including abstracts of articles and the full text of the presidential address from the recent volumes. A basic title for any academic library.

1721. *Ancient World: a scholarly journal for the study of antiquity.* [ISSN: 0160-9645] 1978. s-a. USD 40 (Individuals, USD 30). Ed(s): Martin C J Miller. Ares Publishers, Inc., PO Box 16970, Golden, CO 80402-6016; order.arespublisherscatt.net; http://www.arespublishers.com. Illus., adv. Refereed. Circ: 1200 Paid. *Indexed:* ArtHuCI, OTA. *Bk. rev.:* 2-5, 1-3 pages. *Aud.:* Ac.

This journal is "dedicated to original research in Classical Studies, especially in Archaeology, History, Epigraphy, Numismatics, Geography, and Topography." Although the content can be technical on occasion, many of the articles are accessible to a general audience. A typical issue includes about eight articles. Issues often focus on a particular theme.

1722. *Arethusa.* [ISSN: 0004-0975] 1968. 3x/yr. USD 85 (Individuals, USD 31). Ed(s): Martha Malamud. Johns Hopkins University Press, Journals Publishing Division, 2715 N Charles St, Baltimore, MD 21218-4363; http://www.press.jhu.edu/. Illus., adv. Sample. Refereed. Circ: 759 Paid. Vol. ends: Fall. Microform: PQC. Online: EBSCO Publishing; RoweCom Information Quest; Swets Blackwell. Reprint: PQC; PSC. *Indexed:* AmHI, ArtHuCI, IBZ, L&LBA, MLA-IB. *Aud.:* Ac.

Focusing on literary criticism, this journal includes both traditional and new approaches to classical literature. Although scholarly, the articles are often accessible to general readers and students. Thematic issues are not uncommon; among recent topics are "The Personal Voice in Classical Scholarship" and "The Reception of Ovid in Antiquity." A typical issue includes four to eight articles. Tables of contents for recent issues and sample issues are available electronically through the publisher's web site. Recommended for all academic collections.

CLASSICAL STUDIES

1723. ***Arion: a journal of humanities and the classics.*** [ISSN: 0095-5809] 1962. 3x/yr. USD 35 (Individuals, USD 19; Students, USD 12). Ed(s): Herbert Golder. Boston University, 10 Lenox St, Brookline, MA 02146; arion@acs.bu.edu; http://web.bu.edu/arion/. Illus., adv. Circ: 800 Controlled. Vol. ends: Fall. Microform: PQC. Online: LexisNexis. Reprint: PSC. *Indexed:* AmHI, ArtHuCI, HumInd, IAPV, MLA-IB, PhilInd. *Bk. rev.:* 2-5, 5-20 pages. *Aud.:* Ac.

One of the more lively and controversial journals in the field, *Arion* covers classical literature and its influence. It tends to avoid the technical baggage found in most classical journals and often features nontraditional and comparative approaches. Original poetry and translations from Greek and Latin literature also appear in most issues. Tables of contents for current and past issues are available on the journal's web site. *Arion* would be a good addition to any academic library supporting literature programs, as well as a worthwhile selection for larger public libraries.

1724. ***Classical and Modern Literature.*** [ISSN: 0197-2227] 1980. s-a. USD 26 (Individuals, USD 23). Ed(s): Daniel M. Hooley. C M L, c/o Daniel Hooley, Editor, Dept of Classical Studies, University of Missouri-Columbia, Columbia, MO 65211-4150. Illus., index, adv. Refereed. Circ: 500. Vol. ends: Fall. *Indexed:* BEL&L, BRI, CBRI, HumInd, IBZ, MLA-IB. *Aud.:* Ac.

This journal focuses on the relation of classical and modern literatures. The modern literatures involved are, for the most part, English and western European. Articles take a variety of approaches, from theoretical to the more traditional study of allusion and influence. Subjects include both high and pop culture; recent issues have featured articles on the Terminator movies and Eminem. Contents are usually accessible to students and general readers; most quotations from classical and European literature are accompanied by translations. A useful addition to any collection supporting literary studies.

1725. ***Classical Antiquity.*** Formerly (until 1982): *California Studies in Classical Antiquity.* [ISSN: 0278-6656] 1968. s-a. USD 120 print & online eds. USD 60 newsstand/cover. Ed(s): Leslie Kurke. University of California Press, Journals Division, 2000 Center St, Ste 303, Berkeley, CA 94704-1223; journals@ucop.edu; http://www.ucpress.edu/journals. Illus., adv. Sample. Refereed. Circ: 650 Paid. Vol. ends: Oct. Microform: PQC. Online: EBSCO Publishing; Florida Center for Library Automation; Gale Group; Ingenta Select; OCLC Online Computer Library Center, Inc. *Indexed:* ArtHuCI, HumInd, SSCI. *Aud.:* Ac.

This journal covers all aspects of ancient Greek and Roman civilization, although literature receives the most attention. An editorial preference for articles with a broad view of the subject over strictly technical pieces enhances its appeal. A typical issue includes five or six articles; there are no book reviews. A good general title, appropriate for most academic libraries.

1726. ***Classical Bulletin.*** [ISSN: 0009-8337] 1925. s-a. USD 50 (Individuals, USD 25; USD 20 newsstand/cover per issue). Ed(s): Ladislaus J Bolchazy. Bolchazy - Carducci Publishers, Inc, 1000 Brown St, Unit 101, Wauconda, IL 60084; info@bolchazy.com; http://www.bolchazy.com. Illus., index, adv. Refereed. Circ: 700. Microform: PQC. Online: Chadwyck-Healey Incorporated; Northern Light Technology, Inc.; ProQuest Information & Learning. Reprint: PQC. *Indexed:* ABS&EES, ArtHuCI, BEL&L, SSCI. *Bk. rev.:* 8-10, 1,000-2,000 words. *Aud.:* Ac.

For many years a general classics title of average quality suitable for high school and college students, *Classical Bulletin* has undergone extensive transformations in recent years since passing into the hands of commercial publishers (Ares in 1987, and then the present owner in 1992). Various changes in format, subtitles, and content have followed. The journal currently publishes articles on all aspects of classical studies, with the most recent issues focusing on Greek and Latin literature. A useful, but not essential, title.

1727. ***Classical Journal.*** [ISSN: 0009-8353] 1905. bi-m. USD 35. Ed(s): Peter E Knox. Classical Association of the Middle West and South, Inc., c/o John F Miller, Ed, Dept of Classics, University of Virginia, Charlottesville, VA 22903; http://www.rmc.edu/~gdaugher/cj.html. Illus., index, adv. Refereed. Circ: 3500. Vol. ends: May. Microform: PMC; PQC. Online: Gale Group; OCLC Online Computer Library Center, Inc.; H.W. Wilson. *Indexed:* ArtHuCI, BHA, BRI, CBRI, EduInd, HumInd, IIMP, MLA-IB, NTA, NumL. *Bk. rev.:* 3-5, 1-5 pages. *Aud.:* Hs, Ac.

As the official journal of the largest regional classical association in the United States, *Classical Journal* aims at a broad audience of scholars, teachers, and students. Its contents normally include three or four articles, "The Forum" (a regular column dealing with pedagogical matters), various association announcements, and a number of book reviews. The articles and reviews, which focus primarily on classical literature and history, are scholarly but usually well within the grasp of college students. The journal's web site offers tables of contents for recent issues. This title belongs in any library supporting a classics program.

1728. ***Classical Outlook.*** [ISSN: 0009-8361] 1923. q. USD 35. Ed(s): Richard La Fleur. American Classical League, Miami University, Oxford, OH 45056. Illus., adv. Circ: 4000. Vol. ends: Summer. *Indexed:* BRI, CBRI, CIJE. *Bk. rev.:* 6-8, 300-1,000 words. *Aud.:* Hs, Ac.

Intended for teachers of classical studies at all levels from elementary school through college, this journal mainly addresses pedagogical concerns. A typical issue contains three or four articles focusing on practical aspects of teaching Latin or classical civilization. Several regular columns discuss teaching materials and electronic resources for the study of the classics. A poetry section includes original verse on classical themes, translations from Greek and Latin, and original Latin verse. Also, *Classica Americana,* which appears on an occasional basis, offers biographical sketches of prominent American classicists. A necessary publication for high schools where Latin is taught and for colleges that train Latin teachers.

1729. ***Classical Philology.*** [ISSN: 0009-837X] 1906. q. USD 183 print & online eds. (Individuals, USD 50 print & online eds.; Students, USD 31 print & online eds.). Ed(s): Shadi Bartsch. University of Chicago Press, Journals Division, PO Box 37005, Chicago, IL 60637; subscriptions@journals.uchicago.edu; http://www.journals.uchicago.edu. Illus., adv. Sample. Refereed. Circ: 1100 Paid. Vol. ends: Oct. Microform: IDC; PMC; PQC. Online: EBSCO Publishing; Florida Center for Library Automation; Gale Group; JSTOR (Web-based Journal Archive); ProQuest Information & Learning. Reprint: ISI; PQC; PSC; SCH. *Indexed:* ArtHuCI, HumInd, IBZ, IPB, L&LBA, LRI, NTA, NumL, SSCI. *Bk. rev.:* 4-6, 3-5 pages. *Aud.:* Ac.

Long regarded as one of the premier journals in the field, *Classical Philology* is an important resource for advanced students and scholars. Each issue includes three to five full-length articles and as many brief notes. Several substantial book reviews and the occasional review essay round out the contents. Articles tend to focus on language and literature, although history and philosophy are not neglected. The sometimes technical nature of the contents and the large amount of untranslated Greek and Latin make the journal somewhat difficult for general readers and beginning students. The journal's web site offers a variety of information, including tables of contents for recent issues. Required for all academic libraries supporting classics programs.

1730. ***The Classical Quarterly.*** [ISSN: 0009-8388] 1906. s-a. GBP 66 combined subscription print & online; USD 122 combined subscription print & online. Ed(s): R. Maltby, Dr. M. Griffin. Oxford University Press, Great Clarendon St, Oxford, OX2 6DP, United Kingdom; jnl.orders@oup.co.uk; http://www3.oup.co.uk/jnls. Illus., index, adv. Refereed. Circ: 1600. Microform: PQC. Online: bigchalk; Florida Center for Library Automation; Gale Group; ingenta.com; JSTOR (Web-based Journal Archive); Northern Light Technology, Inc.; OCLC Online Computer Library Center, Inc.; ProQuest Information & Learning; Swets Blackwell. Reprint: PSC. *Indexed:* ArtHuCI, BrArAb, BrHumI, HumInd, IBZ, IPB, LRI, MLA-IB, MathSciNet, NTA, NumL, PhilInd, RI-1, SSCI. *Aud.:* Ac.

Sponsored by the Classical Association of Great Britain, this austere journal is one of the most highly regarded in the field. Although historical and philosophical topics make an occasional appearance, the primary focus of the journal is Greek and Latin philology. The level of scholarship is high and the content sometimes technical; those with "small Latin and less Greek" will find relatively little of benefit. A typical number includes about 20 articles and another dozen brief notes. There are no book reviews; these appear in a sister publication, *Classical Review.* Essential for libraries supporting strong programs in classics.

1731. ***The Classical Review.*** [ISSN: 0009-840X] 1886. s-a. GBP 74 combined subscription print & online; USD 129 combined subscription print & online. Ed(s): Jonathan Powell, David Scourfield. Oxford University Press, Great Clarendon St, Oxford, OX2 6DP, United Kingdom; jnl.orders@oup.co.uk; http://www3.oup.co.uk/jnls. Illus., index, adv. Refereed. Circ: 1600. Vol. ends: Winter. Microform: PMC; PQC. Online: EBSCO Publishing; Gale Group; ingenta.com; JSTOR (Web-based Journal Archive); OCLC Online Computer Library Center, Inc.; RoweCom Information Quest; Swets Blackwell. Reprint: PSC. *Indexed:* ArtHuCI, BRD, BRI, CBRI, HumInd, IBZ, IPB, MLA-IB, NumL, RI-1, SSCI. *Bk. rev.:* 150, 100-2,000 words. *Aud.:* Ac.

Devoted solely to book reviews, this journal covers works in all areas of classical studies and in a variety of languages. Reviews are normally in English, with occasional exceptions. They tend to be quite scholarly and are frequently critical. A typical issue includes approximately 90 full reviews and 60 brief notices. Tables of contents are available at the journal's web site. Although highly respected and extensive in its coverage, *Classical Review* is rarely timely: Reviews often appear several years after the initial appearance of a book. In spite of this, it remains an important collection development tool for libraries and belongs in any collection supporting a classics program.

1732. ***Classical World.*** [ISSN: 0009-8418] 1907. q. USD 30. Ed(s): Matthew S Santirocco. Classical Association of the Atlantic States, University of the Sciences, 600 S 43rd St, Philadelphia, PA 19104-4495. Illus., adv. Refereed. Circ: 3000. Vol. ends: Jun/Aug. Microform: MIM; PQC. Online: H.W. Wilson. *Indexed:* ArtHuCI, BRD, BRI, CBRI, IBZ, IPB, NTA, NumL, SSCI. *Bk. rev.:* 15-20, 300-500 words. *Aud.:* Hs, Ac.

Aimed at high school and college teachers of classics, this journal covers all aspects of classical civilization, with primary emphasis on literature and history. In addition to scholarly articles in these areas, *Classical World* includes several regular features dealing with pedagogical topics and an extensive "Notes and News" column that provides information about study programs, conferences, fellowships, and scholarships. The journal is also well known for the many valuable bibliographical surveys that it publishes. These include annual surveys of audiovisual materials and classical textbooks, as well as review essays on particular authors and topics. Accessible to a wide audience, including students and general readers, *Classical World* is suitable for high school, college, and larger public libraries.

1733. ***Classics Ireland.*** [ISSN: 0791-9417] 1994. a. IEP 5. Ed(s): Andrew Smith. Classical Association of Ireland, Department of Classics, University College, Dublin, 4, Ireland; andrewsmith@ucd.ie. Illus. Refereed. Circ: 400. *Bk. rev.:* 6-10, 500-800 words. *Aud.:* Ga, Ac.

The lively and well-written articles in *Classics Ireland* cover a variety of topics: classical literature and its influence, ancient history, classical archaeology, the study of classical antiquity in Ireland, and, occasionally, Byzantine Studies. While the contributors are mostly professional scholars, they tend to aim at a broad audience. *Classics Ireland* is one of the few titles in the field that can be warmly recommended to beginning students and general readers. The full text of the first seven volumes (1994-2000) is available at www.ucd.ie/~classics/ClassicsIreland.html.

1734. ***Glotta: Zeitschrift fuer griechische und lateinische Sprache.*** [ISSN: 0017-1298] 1909. 2x/yr. EUR 54. Vandenhoeck und Ruprecht, Robert-Bosch-Breite 6, Goettingen, 37079, Germany; info@vandenhoeck-ruprecht.de; http://www.vandenhoeck-ruprecht.de. Illus., index, adv. Refereed. Circ: 600 Paid and controlled. Reprint: SCH. *Indexed:* ArtHuCI, IBZ, MLA-IB. *Aud.:* Ac.

The only journal to focus solely on Greek and Latin linguistics, *Glotta* will interest students of Indo-European and Romance linguistics as well as classicists. Articles are generally written in German or English, and the contents tend to be rather technical. There are no book reviews. A keyword index, arranged by language, appears in the final issue of each volume. For academic libraries supporting strong programs in classics or linguistics.

1735. ***Gnomon: kritische Zeitschrift fuer die gesamte klassische Altertumswissenschaft.*** [ISSN: 0017-1417] 1924. 8x/yr. EUR 154. Ed(s): Ernst Vogt, H W Noerenberg. Verlag C.H. Beck oHG, Wilhelmstr 9, Munich, 80801, Germany; abo.service@beck.de; http://www.beck.de. Illus., index, adv. Circ: 1400. *Indexed:* ArtHuCI, BHA, IPB, MLA-IB, NumL, RI-1, RILM. *Bk. rev.:* 20-25. *Aud.:* Ac.

This review journal is an invaluable bibliographical resource. It covers books in all areas of classical studies. A typical issue includes a dozen substantial scholarly book reviews and as many more brief reviews. Most are in German. Odd-numbered issues include the *Bibliographische Beilage,* a detailed subject bibliography of recent publications that includes both books and articles. Its entries often provide table-of-contents information for conference proceedings, *Festschriften,* and collected papers. These listings are perhaps the most timely printed source of bibliography in the field. The publisher now produces an electronic bibliographical database based on the backfiles (without the reviews) on CD-ROM; a smaller version of the database (about 15 percent of the total content), covering 1997 forward, is available online at www.gnomon.ku-eichstaett.de/Gnomon/en/Gnomon.html. An indispensable journal for any library supporting serious research in the classics.

1736. ***Greece and Rome.*** [ISSN: 0017-3835] 1931. s-a. GBP 60 print & online. Ed(s): Dr. Katherine Clarke, Dr. Christopher Burnand. Oxford University Press, Great Clarendon St, Oxford, OX2 6DP, United Kingdom; jnl.orders@oup.co.uk; http://www3.oup.co.uk/jnls. Illus., adv. Sample. Refereed. Circ: 1600. Vol. ends: Oct. Microform: PQC. Online: Florida Center for Library Automation; Gale Group; ingenta.com; JSTOR (Web-based Journal Archive); OCLC Online Computer Library Center, Inc.; ProQuest Information & Learning; Swets Blackwell. Reprint: PSC. *Indexed:* ArtHuCI, BrArAb, BrHumI, HumInd, IBZ, IPB. *Bk. rev.:* 2-3, 500-1,000 words. *Aud.:* Hs, Ga, Ac.

One of the most readable classical journals, *Greece and Rome* aims "to publish scholarly but not technical articles that will be of use to all those who are interested in Classical Civilization, whether or not they are professionally engaged in its study, whether or not they can read Greek or Latin." It succeeds. A typical issue includes about six articles, evenly divided between literature and history, along with an occasional piece on archaeology and several book reviews. In addition to individual book reviews, each issue also includes a varying number of "subject reviews," covering such areas as Greek and Roman history and literature, archaeology and art, philosophy, and general works. These brief review essays cover important recent works in summary fashion. Subscribers to *Greece and Rome* also receive *New Surveys in the Classics,* a series of extended bibliographical essays on individual ancient authors and topics. An excellent journal that belongs in all libraries.

1737. ***Greek, Roman and Byzantine Studies.*** [ISSN: 0017-3916] 1958. q. USD 30 domestic; USD 36 foreign. Ed(s): E. L. Wheeler, Kent J Rigsby. Duke University, Department of Classical Studies, PO Box 90199, Durham, NC 27708-0199. Illus., adv. Refereed. Circ: 850. Vol. ends: Winter. Microform: PQC. Online: bigchalk; Gale Group; OCLC Online Computer Library Center, Inc.; ProQuest Information & Learning. Reprint: PSC. *Indexed:* ArtHuCI, BHA, HumInd, IBZ, NTA, NumL, RI-1. *Aud.:* Ac.

The use of "Roman" in this journal's title is somewhat misleading because "articles concerned primarily with Latin are excluded." Its focus is on the Greek world from the prehistoric period through Byzantine times. In practice, the majority of contributions deal with classical Greek literature and history, although a significant number of articles fall into the realm of later Greek Studies. Many of the articles require a working knowledge of Greek. A typical issue includes four to six articles. The journal does not publish book reviews. Recommended for academic libraries supporting a strong classics program.

1738. ***Harvard Studies in Classical Philology.*** [ISSN: 0073-0688] 1890. a. USD 45. Ed(s): Charles Segal. Harvard University, Department of the Classics, Boylston 320, Cambridge, MA 02138; http://www.fas.harvard.edu/~classics/hscp.html. Illus. Refereed. *Indexed:* ArtHuCI, RI-1. *Aud.:* Ac.

This somewhat irregularly issued annual has traditionally published articles by Harvard faculty and graduate students. In recent years, the cast of contributors has expanded, although the majority still have Harvard connections. Most articles concern Greek and Latin language and literature, although there are occasional excursions into ancient history and archaeology. *Harvard Studies* often includes lengthy articles; papers of 50 pages or more are not uncommon. Summaries of recent Harvard dissertations in classical philology appear at the end of most volumes.

1739. ***Helios: a journal devoted to critical and methodological studies of classical culture, literature, and society.*** [ISSN: 0160-0923] 1974. s-a. USD 40 (Individuals, USD 25). Ed(s): Steve M Oberhelman. Texas Tech University Press, 2903 4th St, PO Box 41037, Lubbock, TX 79409-1037. Illus., adv. Refereed. Circ: 536. Reprint: PSC. *Indexed:* ArtHuCI, BEL&L, IBZ. *Aud.:* Ac.

Once a nondescript classical periodical of middling quality, *Helios* has found a niche for itself as a venue for "innovative approaches to the study of classical culture." These approaches include "anthropological, deconstructive, feminist, reader response, social history, and text theory." Although contributors tend to overuse trendy jargon and occasionally have blatant political agendas, they do sometimes offer fresh and interesting perspectives on the classics. Greek and Latin are usually translated. *Helios* should be of interest to a wide range of cultural and literary scholars. Suitable for most academic libraries.

1740. ***International Journal of the Classical Tradition.*** [ISSN: 1073-0508] 1994. q. USD 208 (Individuals, USD 80). Ed(s): Meyer Reinhold, Wolfgang Haase. Transaction Publishers, 35 Berrue Circle, Rutgers University, Piscataway, NJ 08854-8042; trans@transactionpub.com; http://www.transactionpub.com. Illus., adv. Refereed. Circ: 300. Vol. ends: Spring. Online: EBSCO Publishing. Reprint: PSC. *Indexed:* IBZ. *Bk. rev.:* 5, 2-5 pages. *Aud.:* Ac.

As the official journal of the International Society for the Classical Tradition, this title focuses on the influence of classical antiquity on other cultures and on the reception of the classical heritage from ancient times to the present. Articles cover a wide range of topics, including art, literature, history, music, and philosophy. In addition, the journal offers review articles, book reviews, and news of professional interest (conference announcements, calls for papers, etc.) Students and scholars from all areas of the humanities are likely to find something of interest in its pages.

1741. ***Journal of Hellenic Studies.*** [ISSN: 0075-4269] 1880. a. GBP 55 per issue. Ed(s): Robert Fowler. Society for the Promotion of Hellenic Studies, Senate House, Malet St, London, WC1E 7HU, United Kingdom; http://www.sas.ac.uk/icls/hellenic/. Illus., adv. Refereed. Circ: 3000. Microform: PQC. Online: Gale Group; JSTOR (Web-based Journal Archive). Reprint: PQC; PSC. *Indexed:* AIAP, AICP, ArtHuCI, ArtInd, BHA, BrHumI, HumInd, IBZ, IPB, LRI, MLA-IB, NTA, NumL, PhilInd, RI-1, SSCI. *Bk. rev.:* 60-70, 1,000-2,000 words. *Aud.:* Ac.

This venerable and highly regarded journal publishes studies in Greek literature, history, archaeology, and philosophy. Contributors traditionally have been predominantly British, although more American and European scholars now appear among them. A typical issue includes about ten articles, many of substantial length. The extensive book review section is a particularly valuable feature; it covers most important books on classical Greek Studies in English and western European languages. Frequently, there are one or two review articles that discuss several books on related themes. Subscriptions also include the annual publication *Archaeological Reports,* which consists largely of reports on current British excavations of classical sites.

1742. ***Journal of Roman Studies.*** [ISSN: 0075-4358] 1911. a. GBP 45 (Individuals, GBP 36; Students, GBP 20). Ed(s): M D Goodman. Society for the Promotion of Roman Studies, The Roman Society, Senate House, Malet St, London, WC1E 7HU, United Kingdom; http://www.sas.ac.uk/icls/Roman/. Illus., adv. Refereed. Circ: 3200. Reprint: PSC. *Indexed:* ArtHuCI, BHA, BrArAb, BrHumI, HumInd, IBZ, NTA, NumL, SSCI. *Bk. rev.:* 60, 1,000-2,000 words. *Aud.:* Ac.

This companion publication to the *Journal of Hellenic Studies* covers all aspects of Roman civilization. The primary emphasis is on history, although important work on archaeology and Latin literature also appears. Its content is scholarly and sometimes technical. An issue usually offers about eight articles (often quite lengthy), one or more substantial surveys or review articles on a specific topic, and a large number of book reviews. The reviews continue to cover most important works in English on Roman Studies, but with fewer European-language titles than in the past. This is an important title for any library supporting a program in ancient history or the classics.

1743. ***Lustrum: Internationale Forschungsberichte aus dem Bereich des Klassischen Altertums.*** [ISSN: 0024-7421] 1956. irreg. Ed(s): Hans Gaertner, Hubert Petersmann. Vandenhoeck und Ruprecht, Robert-Bosch-Breite 6, Goettingen, 37079, Germany; info@vandenhoeck-ruprecht.de; http://www.vandenhoeck-ruprecht.de. Illus., index, adv. Refereed. Circ: 750 Paid and controlled. *Indexed:* IBZ. *Aud.:* Ac.

An important source of bibliographical information for researchers, *Lustrum* publishes extensive annotated bibliographies and review essays that focus on particular classical authors or topics. They are generally written by well-known specialists. Often the bibliographies attempt exhaustive coverage for a period of years. Most issues include two or three works, although a few contain only a single book-length bibliography. Recommended for libraries supporting a strong classics program.

1744. ***Mnemosyne: a journal of classical studies.*** [ISSN: 0026-7074] 1852. bi-m. EUR 280 print & online eds. (Individuals, EUR 147 print & online eds.). Ed(s): H Pinkster, S.R. Slings. Brill Academic Publishers, Inc., PO Box 9000, Leiden, 2300 PA, Netherlands; cs@brill.nl; http://www.brill.nl. Illus., index. Refereed. Vol. ends: Nov. Microform: SWZ. Online: Chadwyck-Healey Incorporated; EBSCO Publishing; Gale Group; Ingenta Select; OCLC Online Computer Library Center, Inc.; Swets Blackwell. Reprint: SWZ. *Indexed:* ArtHuCI, HumInd, IBZ, IPB, MLA-IB. *Bk. rev.:* 10-12, 500-1,500 words. *Aud.:* Ac.

As befits one of the oldest journals in the field, *Mnemosyne* continues to offer traditional studies of Greek and Latin literature. The articles tend to be philological and technical, although most are now written in English rather than the Dutch or Latin of years gone by. Most issues offer three to five articles, as many more short notes (Miscellanea), and a dozen substantial book reviews. A valuable journal, but primarily for collections catering to graduate students and scholars.

1745. ***Mouseion: journal of the Classical Association of Canada.*** Formerly (until 2000): *Classical Views/Echos du Monde Classique.* [ISSN: 1496-9343] 1956. 3x/yr. CND 40 (Individuals, CND 25). Ed(s): Mark Joyal, James Butrica. University of Calgary Press, University of Calgary, Faculty of Education ETD 722, 2500 University Dr N W, Calgary, AB T2N 1N4, Canada; wgee@ucalgary.ca; http://www.ucalgary.ca/ucpress. Adv. Refereed. Circ: 750. Reprint: PSC. *Indexed:* BHA, CBCARef, IBZ. *Bk. rev.:* 8-10, 2-5 pages. *Aud.:* Ac.

Mouseion, one of the two journals sponsored by the Classical Association of Canada, began life under the title *Echos du Monde Classique / Classical News and Views* as a source of news items and pedagogical articles for teachers of classics in Canada. In recent years it has evolved into a scholarly journal of good quality. A typical issue includes three to five articles and several substantial book reviews. These cover a wide range of topics, including Greek and Latin literature, ancient history, and classical archaeology. Most articles are in English with the remainder in French. This title is appropriate for academic libraies supporting strong classics programs.

1746. ***Phoenix (Toronto, 1946).*** [ISSN: 0031-8299] 1946. q. CND 100 (Individuals, CND 70). Ed(s): A M Keith. Classical Association of Canada, Trinity College, Toronto, ON M5S 1H8, Canada; phoenix@chass.utoronto.ca; http://www.chass.utoronto.ca. Illus., index, adv. Refereed. Circ: 1250 Paid and controlled. *Indexed:* ArtHuCI, IBZ, IPB, L&LBA, MLA-IB, NumL. *Bk. rev.:* 15-20, 500-1,000 words. *Aud.:* Ac.

This journal covers primarily Greek and Latin literature with sporadic ventures into history and philosophy. Articles are scholarly but generally accessible to a wider audience; Greek and Latin are usually translated. As one would expect of a journal published by the Classical Association of Canada, contributors are predominantly Canadian and write mostly in English, occasionally in French. A typical issue includes half a dozen articles and a selection of book reviews. Suitable for most academic libraries.

1747. ***Ramus: critical studies in Greek and Roman literature.*** [ISSN: 0048-671X] 1972. s-a. AUD 39.50 (Individuals, AUD 27.70; Students, AUD 20). Ed(s): A J Boyle, J L Penwill. Aureal Publications, PO Box 49, Bendigo North, VIC 3550, Australia; http://www.bendigo.latrobe.edu.au/publicat/ramus/index.html. Illus., adv. Refereed. Circ: 300 Paid. Online: RMIT Publishing. Reprint: ISI. *Indexed:* ArtHuCI, IBZ. *Aud.:* Ac.

Ramus covers Greek and Latin literature, with an emphasis on literary criticism rather than philology. The articles are both scholarly and readable. A typical issue includes four to six articles; there are no book reviews or other features. The journal occasionally publishes theme-oriented issues, most recently on "Ovid and Exile." Recommended for any academic library supporting programs in literature.

1748. ***University of London. Institute of Classical Studies. Bulletin.*** [ISSN: 0076-0730] 1954. a. GBP 28. University of London, Senate House, Malet St, London, WC1E 7HU, United Kingdom. Illus. *Indexed:* ArtHuCI, NumL. *Aud.:* Ac.

Although the substantial volumes of this annual cover all aspects of classical studies, emphasis tends to be on Greek literature and history, ancient philosophy, and Bronze Age archaeology. Roman Studies receive limited attention. Most contributors are connected to the University of London in some capacity. Each issue includes 8 to 10 substantial articles; there are no book reviews. This is an important title for collections that support large programs in classical studies.

1749. ***Vergilius.*** Former titles (until 1959): *Vergilian Digest;* (until 1940): *Vergilius.* [ISSN: 0506-7294] 1938. a. USD 25 in US & Canada; USD 30 elsewhere. Ed(s): Raymond J Clark. Vergilian Society, 22 Bluetop Rd., Setauket, NY 11733; VergSoc@aol.com; http://www.vergil.clarku.edu. Illus., adv. Refereed. Circ: 1400. Reprint: PSC. *Bk. rev.:* 6-8, 2-4 pages. *Aud.:* Ac.

Everything in this journal relates to the poet Vergil in one way or another. In addition to contributions directly concerned with his life and writings, there are studies of his later influence. Over time, the contents have ranged from general interest to scholarly; but in recent years, scholarly articles have predominated, most assuming some knowledge of Latin. An important feature is the annual bibliography of Vergilian studies. There are also notices about the society's programs and activities.

Electronic Journals

1750. ***Ancient Narrative.*** [ISSN: 1568-3532] 2001. 3x/yr. EUR 84 (Individuals, EUR 42). Ed(s): Maaike Zimmerman. Ancient Narrative, Zuurstukken 37, Eelde KP, 9761, Netherlands; info@narrative.com; http://www.ancientnarrative.com. *Aud.:* Ac.

Ancient Narrative is a new journal devoted to the novel in antiquity and its subsequent reception and influence. It covers Jewish, early Christian, and Byzantine narrative texts as well as classical Latin and Greek writings. Contributors take a wide range of approaches, ranging from traditional philological and historical studies to those applying critical theory and methods drawn from the social sciences. This primarily electronic journal represents something of a hybrid. Articles are posted continuously on the web, taken down periodically to allow the authors to revise them in light of comments received, and then appear in final form in the annual volume (both in print and in the electronic archive of *Ancient Narrative*).

1751. ***Bryn Mawr Classical Review Online.*** [ISSN: 1063-2948] 1990. Bryn Mawr Commentaries, Inc, Bryn Mawr College, Thomas Library, Bryn Mawr, PA 19010; http://www.ccat.sas.upenn.edu/bmcr. Illus. Refereed. *Bk. rev.:* 1,500-2,000 words. *Aud.:* Ac.

Claiming to be the "second oldest online scholarly journal in the humanities," this journal provides book reviews that are both timely and scholarly. It is the best single source for evaluations of recent books in classical studies; *BMCR* reviewed over 400 books in 2002. Reviewers, who are normally specialists in the relevant area, offer substantial, detailed, and critical treatments. Important or controversial books sometimes receive multiple reviews; authors' responses are also published. In addition to reviews, the journal includes occasional announcements concerning items of professional interest. Access to the *Review* is free. Subscribers receive new reviews irregularly by e-mail, as they become available. The backfiles are maintained on the publisher's web site and are searchable. An electronic subscription form is available at the *Review* web site. The journal's print version ceased publication in 1998.

1752. ***Didaskalia: ancient theater today.*** [ISSN: 1321-4853] 1994. bi-m. Free. Ed(s): C W Marshall, Hugh Denard. University of Warwick, United Kingdom; didaskalia@csv.warwick.ac.uk; http://www.warwick.ac.uk/didaskalia/. Illus. *Bk. rev.:* 2-3, 1,000-2,000 words. *Aud.:* Ac.

Didaskalia publishes articles about staging and performance aspects of Greek and Roman drama, dance, and music, both in antiquity and today. It also includes announcements and reviews of current productions and reviews of books about ancient drama. The character of contributions varies widely; some are scholarly, others are more popular in nature. Recent issues have featured papers from symposia linked to the performance of a paricular play, most recently the 2001 Cambridge Greek Play, Sophocles' *Electra*. *Didaskalia* is a very useful source of information, particularly for those interested in seeing or reading about contemporary productions of the ancient plays.

1753. ***Electronic Antiquity: communicating the classics.*** [ISSN: 1320-3606] 1993. irreg. Free. Ed(s): Terry Papillon. Digital Library and Archives at Virginia Polytechnic Institute and State University, Department of Classics, 331 Major Williams Hall, Blacksburg, VA 24061-0225; electronic.antiquity@vt.edu; http://scholar.lib.vt.edu/ejournals/ElAnt/. Illus., adv. Refereed. *Bk. rev.:* 2-4; 1,500-4,000 words. *Aud.:* Ac.

One of the first electronic classical journals to appear, *Electronic Antiquity* was intended to facilitate rapid communication in the field. It offered a selection of brief articles, book reviews, and news items in each issue. This is no longer the case. New issues have appeared sporadically in recent years and now average about one per year. A typical issue includes one or two articles followed by half a dozen book reviews. The book reviews tend to be substantial and are the most attractive feature of *EA*'s current manifestation. All back issues are available on the journal's web site.

■ CLASSROOM MAGAZINES

Art/Foreign Language/Language Arts/Life Skills/Mathematics/Science/Social Studies and Current Events/Teacher and Professional

See also Children; Education; and Teenagers sections.

Terry Taylor, Instruction Coordinator, DePaul University, 2350 N. Kenmore Ave., Chicago, IL 60614-3274; ttaylor@depaul.edu

Introduction

This section highlights magazines intended for use in K–12 classrooms. Most classroom magazines are written for students at appropriate reading levels and are available as classroom sets at a discounted per-issue or subscription price. Often these titles are accompanied by supplementary teacher resources, such as audiotapes for foreign language titles and teacher's guides containing activities, learning goals, and assessment techniques. Student titles are listed by subject in this section. Other classroom magazines are written for teachers and provide resources and ideas for classroom use. Examples of classroom activities that lend themselves to interactivity, collaborative learning, and interdisciplinary instruction in the classroom make these magazines ready-to-use practical tools for developing and enriching curriculum. These titles are listed in this section under the category "Teacher and Professional." Several publishers offer web sites with material to complement the content of the printed magazines.

Classroom magazines are geared to the practical application of current theory and standards to classroom activity. Periodicals that cover primarily educational issues or theory are described in the Education section of this volume or in the appropriate subject discipline, e.g., Mathematics. Magazines that may be used in the classroom but that are more likely to be personal subscriptions are described in the Children and Teenagers sections.

Basic Periodicals

Select by subject and audience level.

Basic Abstracts and Indexes

ProQuest, Children's Magazine Guide, Current Index to Journals in Education/ ERIC, MAS Ultra-School Edition, Primary Search, Education Index/Wilson Education Full Text, InfoTrac, Readers' Guide to Periodical Literature.

Art

Dramatics. See Theater section.

1754. *Scholastic Art.* Formerly (until 1992): *Art and Man;* Incorporates: *Artist Junior.* [ISSN: 1060-832X] 1970. 6x/yr. USD 8.95. Ed(s): Margaret Howlett. Scholastic Inc., 555 Broadway, New York, NY 10012-0399; http://www.scholastic.com. Illus., index. Sample. Circ: 245000. Vol. ends: Apr/May. Microform: PQC. Online: bigchalk; Gale Group; Northern Light Technology, Inc.; ProQuest Information & Learning; H.W. Wilson. Reprint: PQC. *Indexed:* ICM. *Aud.:* Ems, Hs.

Published in cooperation with the National Gallery of Art, this beautifully illustrated magazine introduces junior high and high school students to art and artists from around the world. The "Artist of the Month" column features an interview with a student artist from among the winners of the Scholastic Art and Writing Award. Each issue features a "Masterpiece of the Month" with a poster of the featured artist's work in the teacher's edition and mini-posters in each student issue. The teacher's guide also includes a lesson plan and discussion questions for the "Art Workshop," a hands-on activity related to the monthly theme, as well as a reproducible question sheet for the featured theme.

Stone Soup. see Children section.

Foreign Language

1755. *Ciao Italia: il mensile per il tuo italiano.* 8x/yr. USD 19.95. E L I s.r.l., Casella Postale 6, Recanati, 62019, Italy; http://www.mep-eli.com. Illus. *Aud.:* Hs.

One of many foreign-language magazines from this publisher, *Ciao Italia* is intended for students in their second year of Italian. Other magazines target various levels of language proficiency from elementary school through college. All include comic strips, puzzles, and games to teach vocabulary. Topical articles provide reading practice and enhance comprehension.

Elementary-level magazines include pullout pages with stickers for use in classroom activities, and many include a collectible poster with each issue. Intermediate levels place greater emphasis on civilization and culture and contain articles about music, sports, movies, and the Internet. More-advanced levels provide excerpts from contemporary literature, enhanced glossaries, and a wider variety of articles. Teachers' guides and audiocassettes can be purchased separately but are included, where available, with classroom orders of 20 or more subscriptions. A free teacher's desk copy accompanies classroom orders. *Resource*, published in English four times a year, provides practical ideas and tips for language teachers. English as a second language titles are also available.

Other magazines from this publisher include:

Italian: *Azzurro*—for students of different ages beginning to learn Italian, *Ragazzi*—two or more years, *Tutti Insieme*—three or more years, *Oggitalia*—for advanced students.

German: *Fertig...los*—for students beginning to study German, *Kinder*—second year, *Freunde*—two or more years, *Zusammen*—three or more years.

Spanish: *Vamos!*—for students beginning to study Spanish, *Chicos*—second year, *Muchachos*—two or more years, *Todos Amigos*—three or more years.

French: *Voila*—for beginning French in elementary school, *C'est Facile*—for students beginning to study French, *Mome*—second year, *Jeunes*—two or more years, *Ensemble*—three or more years, *Presse-Papiers*—for advanced students.

Latin: *Adulescens*—for students with one year's knowledge of Latin, *Iuvenis*—two or more years.

Russian: *Davai*—for students studying Russian at an intermediate level.

1756. *Que Tal.* Formerly: *Oye.* [ISSN: 0033-5940] 1963. 6x/yr. USD 7.95 Includes workbook. Mary Glasgow Magazines, Commonwealth House, 1-19 New Oxford St, London, WC1A 1NU, United Kingdom; http://www.link2english.com. Illus. Vol. ends: May/Jun. Microform: PQC. Reprint: PQC. *Aud.:* Hs.

Distributed through Scholastic, this colorful Mary Glasgow magazine (London) is aimed at first-year students of Spanish. Teen-interest content—such as interviews, activities, puzzles, and games—helps build language proficiency and cultural awareness. Some foreign-language magazines from this publisher include activity workbooks with orders of ten or more student copies. The teacher's guide, free with class subscriptions, provides additional assignments as well as a table that correlates content to teaching topics, activities, and national standards, where applicable.

Other Mary Glasgow magazines include:

Spanish: *Ahora*—2nd year, *El Sol*—3rd year, *Hoy Dia*—4th year

French: *Allons-y!*—1st year, *Bonjour*—2nd year, *Ca Va?*—3rd year, *Chez Nous*—4th year

German: *Das Rad*—1st year, *Schuss*—2nd year, *Actuell*—3rd year

Language Arts

Cricket. see Children section.

1757. *Literary Cavalcade.* [ISSN: 0024-4511] 1948. 8x/yr. USD 8.95. Ed(s): Cynthia Sosland. Scholastic Inc., 555 Broadway, New York, NY 10012-0399; http://www.scholastic.com. Illus., index, adv. Sample. Circ: 23000. Vol. ends: May. Microform: MIM; PQC. Online: bigchalk; EBSCO Publishing; Northern Light Technology, Inc.; ProQuest Information & Learning. Reprint: PQC. *Aud.:* Hs.

An excellent introduction to literary forms for high school students. *Literary Cavalcade* offers a variety of readings in prose, poetry, and drama, including selections from literary works and authors' insights into the writing process. As students read, they also build their vocabulary, develop language arts skills, and prepare for the SAT and ACT tests. The "Pop-up Literature" feature provides annotations to facilitate analysis of the text. Suggestions for a "20-Minute Essay" after each selection encourage students to think independently about what they've read. The "Writer's Craft" writing workshop helps students to hone their writing skills. The web site includes an editorial calendar that gives a preview of feature articles in upcoming issues.

1758. *Read Magazine.* [ISSN: 0034-0359] 1951. 18x/yr. USD 34.50 per academic year. Ed(s): D Nevins, N Neff. Weekly Reader Corp., 200 First Stamford Pl, PO Box 120023, Stamford, CT 06912-0023; http://www.weeklyreader.com. Illus. Sample. Circ: 345340 Paid. Vol. ends: May. Microform: PQC. Online: EBSCO Publishing; ProQuest Information & Learning. Reprint: PQC. *Indexed:* ICM. *Aud.:* Ems, Hs.

This language arts magazine for grades 6–10 includes plays, short stories, poetry, and nonfiction, both classical and contemporary. It introduces students to literature while developing vocabulary, comprehension, and critical-thinking skills. The "Current Scene" feature takes its theme from popular media, such as spy films, and connects it to literature by including an insert with facts from published works on the topic. Questions and quizzes help students to understand what they have read, and a teacher's guide contains more discussion questions and extension activities as well as recommendations for accommodating the needs of ESOL students. *Read*'s web site contains supplementary material for some of the readings as well as sample articles and stories from the magazine. An online planning guide (also in the teacher's guide) correlates specific topics, standards, and skills in upcoming issues.

1759. ***Scholastic Action.*** [ISSN: 0163-3570] 1977. 14x/yr. USD 7.95. Ed(s): Zoe Kashnerd. Scholastic Inc., 555 Broadway, New York, NY 10012-0399; http://www.scholastic.com. Illus. Sample. Circ: 230000. Microform: PQC. Online: bigchalk; EBSCO Publishing; Northern Light Technology, Inc.; ProQuest Information & Learning. Reprint: PQC. *Indexed:* ICM. *Aud.:* Hs.

A reading and language arts magazine covering teen topics for at-risk readers in grades 7–12 with an accessible 3–5 reading level. Celebrity profiles, debate topics, and real-life skill activities such as job hunting provide engaging reading material for teens. A series of read-aloud plays based upon current movie and TV screenplays is designed to be integrated into the curriculum. The "True Teen" feature uses controversial age-appropriate topics such as parents' divorce, shoplifting, and teen depression to challenge teens to think as they read. Skills features such as "Graphic Organizers," "Fluency Workout," and "Persuasive Writing" help students to improve their reading comprehension and suggest strategies for reading, writing, and vocabulary building. The teacher's edition includes "Issue at a Glance," which ties articles to skills, activities, and related standards. It contains lesson plans and reproducible worksheets as well as professional articles and book recommendations.

1760. ***Scholastic Scope.*** [ISSN: 0036-6412] 1964. 18x/yr. USD 8.50. Ed(s): Cate Baily. Scholastic Inc., 555 Broadway, New York, NY 10012-0399; http://www.scholastic.com. Illus., adv. Circ: 424843. Microform: PQC. Online: EBSCO Publishing; Northern Light Technology, Inc.; ProQuest Information & Learning. Reprint: PQC. *Indexed:* ICM. *Aud.:* Ems.

Scholastic Scope provides literature and writing activities for middle school students, including read-aloud plays, writing workshops, vocabulary builders, and reading strategies. The "Debate" feature in each issue encourages students to think critically by presenting two sides of a controversial issue and asking students to write in with their opinion on the subject. Each issue provides writing prompts, puzzles, a play, and regular features such as "Wordhunt," a text with accompanying word list and a fill-in-the-blank format, and "True Teen Stories," with inspiring real-life accounts. Skill-building features and test preparation lessons are tied to state and national standards. *Scholastic Scope* works on skills such as sequencing, listening, graph reading, and comprehension. The teacher's edition includes lesson plans with prereading activities and postreading discussion questions as well as reproducible pages.

1761. ***Storyworks.*** [ISSN: 1068-0292] 1993. 6x/yr. USD 6.75. Ed(s): Lauren Tarshis. Scholastic Inc., 555 Broadway, New York, NY 10012-0399; http://www.scholastic.com. Illus. Sample. Vol. ends: Apr/May. *Bk. rev.:* 4-5, 125 words. *Aud.:* Ems.

A literature magazine for grades 3–6, *Storyworks* features fiction, nonfiction, poetry, and plays by well-known children's authors. Activities that develop grammar, writing, vocabulary, and test-taking skills complement the readings. "Reviews by You" publishes students' reviews of books they've read. A new feature, "Sentence Chef," supplies writing skills exercises. Contests and author interviews offer students the opportunity to experience literature in more active and personal ways. The teacher's guide's "Issue at a Glance" feature lists articles with corresponding themes and teaching strategies, lesson plans, extension activities, and bibliographies of related readings. The web site has additional lessons, quizzes, activities, and contests.

1762. ***Writing (Stamford): the magazine of effective communication.*** Formerly (until 1981): *Current Media.* [ISSN: 0279-7208] 1974. 6x/yr. USD 33.95. Ed(s): Charles Piddock. Weekly Reader Corp., 200 First Stamford Pl, PO Box 120023, Stamford, CT 06912-0023; http://www.weeklyreader.com. Illus. Sample. Circ: 127343 Paid. Vol. ends: May. Microform: PQC. Online: Chadwyck-Healey Incorporated; EBSCO Publishing; Gale Group; ProQuest Information & Learning. Reprint: PQC. *Aud.:* Ems, Hs.

A magazine aimed at helping students in grades 6–10 build effective communication skills through learning the craft of writing. Each issue links reading and writing with high-interest articles focusing on aspects of one subject per issue, such as music or advertising. Most of the articles are categorized with one of three important aspects of writing: aims, language, process. The "Write Now" section at the end of each article suggests writing exercises to spark students' creativity and get them started on their own writing. The "Student Writing" segment features an article written by a student on that month's topic. The "Author's Craft" segment analyzes the work of well-known authors to illustrate such literary elements as plot, setting, perspective, and style.

The "Teacher's Guide" provides suggested discussion questions, pre-reading/pre-writing and extension activities, and link content to NCTE/IRA standards. The "Planning Calendar," included in the "Teacher's Guide," is also on the *Weekly Reader* web site.

Life Skills

Career World. See Occupations and Careers section.

1763. ***Current Health 1: the beginning guide to health education.*** [ISSN: 0199-820X] 1974. 8x/yr. USD 34.50. Ed(s): Carole Rubenstein. Weekly Reader Corp., 200 First Stamford Pl, PO Box 120023, Stamford, CT 06912-0023; http://www.weeklyreader.com/features/wrch.html. Illus. Sample. Circ: 165783 Paid. Vol. ends: May. Microform: PQC. Online: bigchalk; EBSCO Publishing; Northern Light Technology, Inc.; ProQuest Information & Learning; H.W. Wilson. Reprint: PQC. *Indexed:* ICM, MagInd, RGPR. *Aud.:* Ems, Hs.

This magazine is a wonderful resource for teachers looking for engaging material for health education. *Current Health 1* covers topics in personal health, fitness and exercise, diet and nutrition, and first aid and safety. Filled with full-color photographs, it focuses on health issues relevant to students and follows most state health curricula for grades 4–7. Each month, "Focus," the main article, provides an in-depth treatment of a current topic, such as how to avoid alcohol, dealing with stress, or how to maintain a healthy body image. The "Just Ask Us" column provides a forum for students to ask health-related question and have the answers published so that other readers can benefit from them. The "Getting Along" feature helps students explore issues of conflict resolution, communication, and interpersonal relations. The teacher's guide provides key objectives, links to standards and relevant subject areas as well as a planning calendar.

Current Health 2: the continuing guide to health education. [ISSN: 0163-156X] 1975. 8/yr. USD 34.50 (Students, USD 9.95 each/15+, USD 19.90 each/2–14 subscriptions). Carole Rubenstein. Weekly Reader Corporation, 200 First Stamford Pl., Box 120023, Stamford, CT 06912-0023; http://www.weeklyreader.com. Illus. Sample. Circ: 250000. Vol. ends: May. Microform: UMI.

Indexed: RG, InfTr, EBSCOHost, Bell & Howell ProQuest *Aud:* Hs.

Health information in a similar format for grades 7–12. The "Human Sexuality Supplement," available for an additional charge, covers such topics as HIV, sexual responsibility, and teen parenting. A separate teacher's guide is available.

1764. ***Imagine (Baltimore): opportunities and resources for academically talented youth.*** [ISSN: 1071-605X] 1993. 5x/yr. USD 30 (Individuals, USD 25). Johns Hopkins University, Center for Talented Youth, 3400 N Charles St, Baltimore, MD 21218. Adv. Sample. Refereed. *Bk. rev.:* Number and length vary. *Aud.:* Hs.

This exciting periodical for junior high and high school students won the Parents Choice Award in the spring of 2003. Each issue focuses on a general subject area, such as history, visual arts, biological sciences, mathematics, or language and linguistics. Emphasis is given to activities that students can do *now* to pursue that interest as well as career opportunities in that field. Each issue includes articles about summer programs and extracurricular activities written by student participants, student reviews of selective colleges, advice on planning for college, career profiles of accomplished professionals, book reviews written by students, puzzles, and web resources.

1765. ***Scholastic Choices: personal development & living skills.*** Incorporates (in 1999): *Health Choices;* Supersedes (in 1985): *Co-Ed;* Incorporates (in 1991): *Forecast for the Home Economist;* Which superseded (in 1986): *Forecast for Home Economics;* (1963-1966): *Practical Forecast for Home Economics.* [ISSN: 0883-475X] 1956. 6x/yr. USD 10.75 for 1-9 copies; USD 21.75 for Teacher's ed. Ed(s): Denise Rinaldo. Scholastic Inc., 555 Broadway, New York, NY 10012-0399; http://www.scholastic.com. Illus., index, adv. Sample. Circ: 185562. Vol. ends: May. Microform: PQC. Online: bigchalk; The Dialog Corporation; EBSCO Publishing; Gale Group; ProQuest Information & Learning; H.W. Wilson. Reprint: PQC. *Indexed:* EduInd, ICM, MRD, MagInd. *Aud.:* Ems, Hs.

This magazine for grades 7–12 features articles about health and nutrition, family, decision making, careers, and personal development, using examples of interest to this age group. Dating, sunburn and skin cancer, adoption, sexual harassment, travel abroad, and weight management are some of the topics covered. Each article includes an activity that encourages students to apply what they've learned. The teacher's edition summarizes the articles, ties them to applicable standards, and provides discussion questions and additional activities for the featured stories. The tone is upbeat and not condescending; difficult issues are presented honestly. Because of the high interest of the subject matter, this magazine could be used as discussion material in a variety of subjects or settings, for example, language arts, health, or social studies.

Mathematics

1766. ***Scholastic Dynamath.*** Formerly (until 1982): *Scholastic Math Power.* [ISSN: 0732-7773] 8x/yr. USD 6.75. Ed(s): Matt Friedman. Scholastic Inc., 555 Broadway, New York, NY 10012-0399; http://www.scholastic.com. Illus. Vol. ends: May. Reprint: PQC. *Aud.:* Ems.

A workbook/magazine for grades 3–6, *Dynamath* reinforces basic math skills with colorful pictures, problems, and puzzles. Telling time, measurements, map reading, and problem solving are among the skills taught. There is a statistics or graphing story in every issue. New features include "Testing 1-2-3," to prepare students for standardized tests, and a "Numbers in the News" column. The free web site presents a "Mindbender of the Month," skill review quizzes, web links related to the current issue, and bonus pages with timely online articles and resources. The teacher's edition includes an answer key, lesson plans, and a table that correlates math concepts covered with national math standards.

1767. ***Scholastic Math.*** [ISSN: 0198-8379] 1980. 12x/yr. USD 7.95. Ed(s): Jack Silbert. Scholastic Inc., 555 Broadway, New York, NY 10012-0399; http://www.scholastic.com. Illus. Circ: 190000. Microform: PQC. Online: bigchalk; EBSCO Publishing; ProQuest Information & Learning; H.W. Wilson. Reprint: PQC. *Aud.:* Ems, Hs.

Scholastic Math for grades 6–9 is designed to prepare junior high students for pre-algebra. Math problems are illustrated in articles on age-appropriate topics. Skills exercises, quizzes, and practice tests help prepare students for standardized tests. Movies, celebrities, comics, sports, and game show themes make complex math concepts accessible and entertaining. The teacher's edition contains teaching tips, extension activities, and a skills guide that correlates the articles to National Council for Teachers of Mathematics standards covered in each issue.

Science

1768. ***Current Science.*** [ISSN: 0011-3905] 1927. 16x/yr. USD 34.50 per academic year; USD 2 per issue. Ed(s): H Westrup. Weekly Reader Corp., 200 First Stamford Pl, PO Box 120023, Stamford, CT 06912-0023; pr@weeklyreader.com; http://www.weeklyreader.com. Illus., index. Sample. Circ: 289892 Paid. Vol. ends: May. Microform: PQC. Online: bigchalk; EBSCO Publishing; Gale Group; Northern Light Technology, Inc.; OCLC Online Computer Library Center, Inc.; ProQuest Information & Learning; H.W. Wilson. Reprint: PQC. *Indexed:* ChemAb, FS&TA, GeogAbPG, ICM, IndVet, SCI, SSCI, VetBull. *Aud.:* Ems, Hs.

Published biweekly, this heavily illustrated magazine uses current news to make science more accessible to students in grades 6–10. Each issue contains sections dealing with physical science, life science, and earth science as well as health and technology. Hands-on activities, related to the National Science Education standards, help students to apply what they?ve learned in the featured articles. Science trivia, puzzles, and mystery photos are regular features. A teacher's guide contains additional background information and answers to quizzes. A planning guide, which can also be found on the web site (www.weeklyreader-.com) includes curriculum topics to be covered in the coming school year.

1769. ***Scholastic Let's Find Out.*** Formerly (until 1995): *My First Magazine.* [ISSN: 0024-1261] 32x/yr. USD 4.95. Scholastic Inc., 555 Broadway, New York, NY 10012-0399; http://www.scholastic.com. Illus. Sample. Circ: 615000. Vol. ends: May/Jun. Reprint: PQC. *Aud.:* Ems.

Each month, *LFO* provides teaching ideas for the five critical areas of early reading: phonemic awareness, phonics, fluency, vocabulary, and comprehension. Pictures, stories, and activities help pre-K and kindergarten children discover the world around them. Each activity in the children's magazine has a teacher's note outlining points to emphasize in teaching. "Clifford Activity Pages" develop early reading and math skills. Mini-books contain emergent reader texts with lots of illustrations. Other regular sections are "Science"(nonfiction articles), and "People and Places" (social studies features). The teacher's guide, included with each subscription, contains cross-curricular activities and recommended supplementary materials. There is also a Spanish edition of *LFO* [ISSN: 1076-6766].

1770. ***Science News: the weekly newsmagazine of science.*** Former titles (until 1966): *Science News Letter; Science News Bulletin.* [ISSN: 0036-8423] 1921. w. USD 54.50 domestic; USD 72.50 foreign; USD 3 newsstand/cover per issue. Ed(s): Julie Ann Miller. Science Service, 1719 N St, N W, Washington, DC 20036; subnews@sciserv.org; http://www.sciencenews.org/. Illus., index, adv. Circ: 160000 Paid. Vol. ends: Dec. Microform: PQC. Online: bigchalk; EBSCO Publishing; Florida Center for Library Automation; Gale Group; Northern Light Technology, Inc.; OCLC Online Computer Library Center, Inc.; ProQuest Information & Learning; H.W. Wilson. Reprint: PQC. *Indexed:* AgeL, BiolDig, CBCARef, CIJE, CPerI, ChemAb, DSR&OA, EngInd, EnvAb, GSI, GardL, GeoRef, IAA, MagInd, RGPR. *Bk. rev.:* 6-8, 125 words. *Aud.:* Hs, Ga.

A slim magazine (16 pages), *Science News* contains approximately twenty news articles and is packed with information about what's happening in the science community. It has three main sections. "This Week" contains brief articles on current science news topics, and each issue features two longer articles. "Research Notes" addresses current research in specific disciplines, e.g., anthropology, biology, materials science. *Science News Online* (www.sciencenews.org) provides a searchable archive back to 1992 for subscribers. (Each week editors select three or four articles from the print edition for posting online in their entirety.) Also available on the web site are special features: "Math Trek," "Food for Thought," "Science Safari," and "Timeline." *Science News* stories are also available in digital audio format for playback on personal computers or mobile devices (www.audible.com/sciencenews). Although the magazine is not specifically aimed at K–12 students, it is very popular in middle and high schools and is highly recommended.

1771. ***Science World.*** Former titles (until 1987): *Scholastic Science World;* (until 1974): *Science World;* (until 1965): *Senior Science and Science World.* [ISSN: 1041-1410] 1959. 13x/yr. USD 9.25. Ed(s): Mark Bregman. Scholastic Inc., 555 Broadway, New York, NY 10012-0399; http://www.scholastic.com. Illus., index, adv. Sample. Circ: 390298. Vol. ends: May. Microform: PQC. Online: bigchalk; EBSCO Publishing; Gale Group; Northern Light Technology, Inc.; OCLC Online Computer Library Center, Inc.; ProQuest Information & Learning; H.W. Wilson. Reprint: PQC. *Indexed:* ICM, MagInd. *Aud.:* Ems.

A science magazine with articles and hands-on experiments for grades 7–10. Each issue features interesting articles on topics in the physical, earth, and life sciences. "You Can Do It" regularly features puzzles and brain teasers. The teacher's edition provides lesson plans that include cross-curricular connections, linking science to social studies, history, and English, with suggested activities. It also contains an answer key, reproducible skills pages, and additional quizzes to test vocabulary, reading comprehension, and understanding of graphs and maps.

1772. *SuperScience.* Formed by the merger of (1989-1997): *SuperScience Blue;* (1989-1997): *SuperScience Red.* 1997. 8x/yr. USD 6.75. Ed(s): Kathryn Kukula. Scholastic Inc., 555 Broadway, New York, NY 10012-0399; http://www.scholastic.com. Illus., index. Sample. Vol. ends: Apr/May. *Indexed:* ICM. *Aud.:* Ems.

A science news magazine for grades 3–6. Each issue is theme-based and includes many color photos. Hands-on activities, experiments, and quizzes on the news stories actively engage students in the content. The teacher's guide provides background information, teaching strategies, discussion prompts, additional activities, reproducible worksheets, and answer keys. Feature articles are tied to curriculum areas through process skills addressed in each activity (e.g., observe, compare, use numbers, hypothesize, etc.). *SuperScience* features help teachers meet local, state, and national science education standards. The web site provides extension activities and live web interviews.

Social Studies and Current Events

1773. *Biography Today: profiles of people of interest to young readers.* [ISSN: 1058-2347] 1992. 3x/yr. USD 57; USD 19 per issue. Ed(s): Cherie D. Abbey. Omnigraphics, Inc., 615 Griswold St, Detroit, MI 48226; info@omnigraphics.com; http://www.omnigraphics.com. Illus., index. Circ: 12000. Vol. ends: Sep (No. 3). *Indexed:* ICM. *Aud.:* Ems.

Written for the young reader, age nine and above, each issue includes profiles of 10–12 current, high-profile individuals, many from the arts, sports, or politics. Each entry provides at least one picture of the person. Biographical information traces the person's life from childhood, including education, first jobs, marriage and/or family, memorable experiences, hobbies, and accomplishments (e.g., honors and awards). Each profile includes a short bibliography for further reading as well as a current address and web site address, where available. Librarians and teachers submit suggestions for subjects to be included. An advisory board comprised of librarians, children's literature specialists, and reading instructors reviews each issue. A cumulative index in every issue contains the names of all individuals who have appeared in either the general series or the subject series as well as listings of occupations, nationalities, and ethnic origins. The edition of *Biography Today* reviewed here is the general series. Special subject series have been published in the following categories: artists, authors, scientists and inventors, sports figures, world leaders, and, new in 2003, performing artists. These series expand and complement the general series but do not duplicate any of the entries. The subject series are available as individual hardbound volumes, usually published annually. Highly recommended for elementary and middle school libraries as well as children's collections in public libraries. Beginning in 2003, a selection of current profiles will be published in Spanish as *Biografias Hoy!* Vol.1, ISBN 0-7808-0664-6, $39.00.

Cobblestone. see Children section.

1774. *Current Events.* [ISSN: 0011-3492] 1902. 25x/yr. USD 8.95 10 or more subscriptions; USD 34.50. Ed(s): C Colbert. Weekly Reader Corp., 200 First Stamford Pl, PO Box 120023, Stamford, CT 06912-0023; science@weeklyreader.com; http://www.weeklyreader.com. Illus., index. Sample. Circ: 205153 Paid. Vol. ends: May. Microform: PQC. Online: bigchalk; EBSCO Publishing; Gale Group; Northern Light Technology, Inc.; OCLC Online Computer Library Center, Inc.; ProQuest Information & Learning; H.W. Wilson. Reprint: PQC. *Indexed:* ICM, MagInd. *Aud.:* Ems, Hs.

This weekly publication highlights current issues in national and international news for students in grades 6–10. Photographs and maps aid in recognition of important places and people and illustrate the ideas presented. Articles present different perspectives and encourage debate about controversial issues. *Current Events* has teamed up with Accelerated Reader to provide students with quizzes based on *Current Events* content. Nine in-depth Special Reports provide comprehensive coverage of key news stories. The accompanying teacher's guide contains more background information, a quiz, a crossword puzzle, and a planning guide that targets specific social studies, geography, and language arts skills. The planning guide and updates of news articles are available on the *Weekly Reader* web site.

1775. *Junior Scholastic.* [ISSN: 0022-6688] 1937. 18x/yr. USD 8.25 for orders of 10 or more copies; USD 12.75 for orders of 1-9 copies; USD 21.75 for teacher's edition. Ed(s): Susanne McCabe, Lee Baier. Scholastic Inc., 555 Broadway, New York, NY 10012-0399; http://www.scholastic.com. Illus., index, adv. Sample. Circ: 570000 Paid. Vol. ends: May. Microform: PQC. Online: bigchalk; EBSCO Publishing; Gale Group; ProQuest Information & Learning; H.W. Wilson. Reprint: PQC. *Indexed:* ICM. *Aud.:* Ems.

A colorful current-events magazine for grades 5–8, *Junior Scholastic* features U.S. and world news, biographical profiles, first-person reports, and excellent maps. Articles focus on people in the news, and the many photos and illustrations help students understand complex issues. History and geography features are included in each issue. Additional features include activities at the end of each article to enhance comprehension and a crossword puzzle on a related topic. The teacher's edition contains lesson plans based on the stories in the issue with references to additional resources (print, video, web) and answer keys. *Junior Scholastic Online* (www.juniorscholastic.com) links to the *Scholastic News* site, which contains news updates, special reports, games and quizzes, links to web sites, and teacher tips.

1776. *Know Your World Extra.* Formerly (until 1977): *Know Your World.* [ISSN: 0163-4844] 1967. 12x/yr. USD 34.50; USD 10.50 10 or more subscriptions. Ed(s): M Letourneau. Weekly Reader Corp., 200 First Stamford Pl, PO Box 120023, Stamford, CT 06912-0023; http://www.weeklyreader.com. Illus. Sample. Circ: 129353 Paid. Vol. ends: May. Microform: PQC. Online: bigchalk; EBSCO Publishing; Gale Group; Northern Light Technology, Inc.; ProQuest Information & Learning. Reprint: PQC. *Indexed:* ICM. *Aud.:* Ems, Hs.

A high–low magazine for preteens and teenagers who read at a second- or third-grade level (2.0–3.9). *Extra* covers a wide range of high-interest topics and challenging activities that encourage students to read. Action photography, age-appropriate stories, and controlled vocabulary help students with special needs stay engaged and enjoy reading success. Features include news stories, science articles, true-life adventures, games, and a play to help students develop language and critical thinking skills while reading aloud. A teacher's guide links content to state and NCTE/IRA standards and included recommendations for accommodating ESOL students.

1777. *The New York Times Upfront: the news magazine for teens.* Supersedes (in Sep. 1999): *Scholastic Update;* Which was formed by the merger of (1972-1983): *Scholastic Search;* (1920-1983): *Senior Scholastic;* Which incorporated: *American Observer; World Week.* [ISSN: 1525-1292] 1983. 14x/yr. Individuals, USD 15.95; USD 2.25 newsstand/cover per issue. Ed(s): Peter S Young. Scholastic Inc., 555 Broadway, New York, NY 10012-0399; http://www.scholastic.com. Illus., index, adv. Sample. Refereed. Circ: 297029 Paid and free. Vol. ends: May. Microform: PQC. Online: The Dialog Corporation; EBSCO Publishing; Gale Group; OCLC Online Computer Library Center, Inc.; ProQuest Information & Learning; H.W. Wilson. Reprint: PQC. *Indexed:* ICM, LRI, MagInd, RGPR. *Aud.:* Hs.

Upfront is a newsmagazine for teens featuring in-depth coverage of current events, entertainment, and trends. Informative articles about national and international events, special reports, and interviews encourage high school students to consider different points of view. Recent articles examine alternative energy sources, school lunch programs and obesity, and reality TV. Each issue includes a "Key to Using This Issue" that lists key teaching points for each article and correlates the articles to curriculum standards of the National Council for the Social Studies. The teacher's edition includes lesson plans for the national, international, and history sections with teaching objectives, classroom strategies, and quizzes. The "Voices" column gives students a forum in which to share personal stories. "Drawing on the News" in each issue includes political cartoons from around the country. The web site, *Upfront Online*(http://

teacher.scholastic.com/upfront), supplements the print newsletter during the school year and provides a summer edition that features stories from *The New York Times* chosen especially for teens.

1778. ***Scholastic News (Senior Edition).*** Formed by the merger of (1952-1998): *Scholastic News (Edition 6);* Which was formerly (until 1993): *Scholastic Newstime;* (until 1989): *Scholastic News (Newstime Edition);* (until 1982): *Scholastic Newstime;* (1941-1998): *Scholastic News (Citizen Edition);* Which was formerly (until 1982): *Scholastic News Citizen;* (until 1973): *Young Citizen.* 1998. 24x/yr. USD 3.85. Ed(s): Lucille Renwick. Scholastic Inc., 555 Broadway, New York, NY 10012-0399; http://www.scholastic.com. Illus. Microform: PQC. Reprint: PQC. *Indexed:* ICM. *Aud.:* Ems.

A colorful current events weekly published in several editions to target different reading levels and interests. *Scholastic News,* 1st-grade edition (32 issues per year), helps students learn reading skills by introducing them to real-world events, seasons, and holidays. Grade 1 and 2 editions include posters, take-home activity pages, e-news tips for teachers, and big issues twice a month for guided reading. Editions 2 (32 issues per year), 3, and 4 (26 issues each per year) build on those skills and introduce history and geography topics. Grade 3 edition has a "Weekly Test-Taking Tip" and a "Standard of the Week" skill feature.

The senior edition, aimed at 4th-, 5th-, and 6th-grade students, adds read-aloud plays on American history and interactive thematic pages with graphs, puzzles, student book reviews, contests, and debates. The "GeoSkills Program" is a year-long geography feature with maps, map skill-builders, quizzes, games, and a free map skills book. Editions sometimes include two-sided posters, and all have teacher's guides with lesson plans, reproducible pages, and additional resources. All content can be extended with material from the *Scholastic News Online* web site (www.scholasticnews.com).

Scholastic News en espanol for grades 1–3 is directly translated from the English-language editions of *Scholastic News.* Every issue gives students an opportunity to maintain and develop literacy skills while learning English, to transition more easily to mainstream English classes, and to have a better time understanding and adjusting to U.S. culture.

1779. ***Teen Newsweek.*** [ISSN: 1527-6775] 1999. 26x/yr. USD 7.35 for 15 or more copies; USD 9.50 for 10-14 copies. Ed(s): Deborah Dolan Nevins. Weekly Reader Corp., 200 First Stamford Pl, PO Box 120023, Stamford, CT 06912-0023. Adv. Sample. Circ: 150000 Paid and controlled. *Aud.:* Ems, Hs.

Teen Newsweek covers hot topics in world and national news tailored for grades 6–9. It reinforces the social studies curriculum with articles that link history, geography, government, and cultures to the news. News-related activities also sharpen reading, writing, and critical thinking skills. Each issue contains a cover story; "Top of the Week," national and international news; "Focus," on a specific area such as music or movies; and "News Debate," coverage of a controversial news topic with an e-mail address for students to respond with their opinions. A teacher's guide and a planning guide accompany each issue. The *Teen Newsweek* web site links to news highlights, a question of the week, and games, activities, and contests.

1780. ***Time for Kids News Scoop (Grade 2-3).*** Supersedes in part (in 1997): *Time for Kids.* 1995. w. USD 3.50. Ed(s): Claudia Wallis. Time, Inc, Time & Life Bldg, Rockefeller Center, 1271 Ave of the Americas, New York, NY 10020-1393. Illus. Sample. Vol. ends: May. *Indexed:* ICM. *Aud.:* Ems.

This newsmagazine for elementary school students is published in multiple editions. The *Time for Kids News Scoop* edition is for grades 2–3 and features a cover story with glossy photos, two shorter articles, and a game page called "Time for Fun." *Big Picture* (ISSN 1528-6584), 30 issues, is for beginning readers with photos and easy-access text in two levels appropriate for emergent readers and readers moving into fluency. Connections to science, social studies, math, and the arts build vocabulary and prepare kids to read in the content areas. *World Report,* 26 issues, introduces current events across the curriculum, and improves nonfiction reading skills. Writing assignments develop critical thinking skills, and passages similar to those found on benchmark tests help to prepare students for taking standardized tests.

The web site (www.timeforkids.com) has a wealth of resources for subscribers: student activities, current events updates, a reproducibles library, early access to teachers' guides, and personalized weekly news quizzes. There is also a free sample of "Going Places with TFK," which explores countries and cultures around the world. The *Time for Kids Classroom* web site is loaded with teacher resources, including reproducibles, links to state and national standards, and an archive of past issues.

1781. ***Weekly Reader, Edition 4.*** Former titles: *Weekly Reader News Parade;* (until 1976): *My Weekly Reader News Parade Edition 4.* [ISSN: 0890-3190] 1934. 25x/yr. USD 24.95. Ed(s): Charles Piddock. Weekly Reader Corp., 200 First Stamford Pl, PO Box 120023, Stamford, CT 06912-0023; science@weeklyreader.com; http://www.weeklyreader.com. Illus. Sample. Circ: 850176 Paid. Vol. ends: May. Microform: PQC. Reprint: PQC. *Indexed:* ICM. *Aud.:* Ems.

Weekly Reader publishes seven editions of its newsmagazine covering pre-K through 5th/6th grade. *Weekly Reader* Pre-K and Kindergarten editions (28 issues) develop pre-reading, critical thinking, and social skills and are written to NAEYC guidelines. *Weekly Reader* Edition 1 (32 issues) offers high-interest theme-based content that support the curriculum. *Weekly Reader* Edition 2 continues to build reading and vocabulary skills through relevant, high-interest nonfiction, and engages students to increase class participation. *Weekly Reader* Edition 3 provides age-appropriate nonfiction content to develop reading, grammar, and vocabulary skills. *Weekly Reader* Edition 4 provides students with a greater awareness and understanding of the world while encouraging reading, discussions, and critical thinking.

Weekly Reader Senior Edition provides more sophisticated and engaging nonfiction and helps students build skills while gaining a greater understanding of the world. This edition also provides real-life practice for assessment testing. All editions include a free teacher's guide with curriculum correlations, and a planning calendar to facilitate incorporating the magazine into lesson plans. Editions 2, 3, 4, and Senior include periodic Reading Assessment Tests, and free access to WRToolkit, an online database with a searchable archive, extension activities, graphs, charts, and quizzes that reinforce curriculum, and access to special features drawing on *The World Almanac for Kids* and *Funk & Wagnall's New Encyclopedia.*

Weekly Reader Corporation publishes Skills Books with grade-specific editions, such as *Using Maps* (grades 1–6), *Geography Connections* (grades 2–6), *Great Moments in U.S. and World History* (grades 5–6), *Staying Healthy* (grades 1–6), *Science Matters* (grades 2–5), *Exploring the Environment* (grades 2–6), and *Infographics: Tables and Graphs for Today*(grades 2–6). Free access to the Weekly Reader web site provides story updates, extension activities, games, and more.

Teacher and Professional

Arts & Activities. see Education/Specific Subjects and Teaching Methods, The Arts section.

1782. ***Classroom Connect Newsletter.*** Formerly (until 1999): *Classroom Connect.* [ISSN: 1526-3673] 1994. 9x/yr. Ed(s): Christine Hofer Borror. Classroom Connect, Inc., 2221 Rosecrans Ave, Ste 237, El Segundo, CA 90245-4954. Illus., index. Sample. Vol. ends: Jun. *Aud.:* Sa.

Filled with prescreened web sites, lesson plans, and activities, this newsletter is designed to help K–12 educators integrate the Internet into their classrooms. Regular columns such as "Lesson Plan Goldmines" and "A+ Web Gallery" review web sites. The "Internet Activities" section provides detailed instructions that include learning goals, activities, and suggestions for assessment. "School Webmaster" and "Guest Expert" provide advice and problem-solving expertise. Feature articles focus on topics such as helping students evaluate online information and differentiated instruction. Technical articles offer helpful instruction in using web browsers and other Internet tools. Other columns present news about upcoming Internet projects in which classes may participate. The *Classroom Connect* web site offers additional web site reviews, online courses for professional development, and opportunities to connect with other teachers for interactive Internet projects. Free membership on the web site provides access to "Community" area services that include discussion groups, "Ask the Expert," and a browsable gallery of student projects and artwork. Classroom Connect, Inc. is a business unit within Harcourt, Inc.

Computing Teacher. See *Learning and Leading with Technology.*

1783. *Copycat Magazine: ideas and activities for K-3 teachers.* [ISSN: 0886-5612] 1985. bi-m. USD 18.95. Ed(s): Jo Anne Wood, Sharon Tuttle. Copycat Press, Inc., 2625 Lathrop Ave, Racine, WI 53405; subscriber_services@copycatpress.com; http://www.copycatpress.com. Illus., adv. Sample. Circ: 45000 Paid. *Bk. rev.:* 13, 100 words. *Aud.:* Sa.

A popular magazine for K–3 teachers, *Copycat* is full of activities, patterns, and reproducibles that cover reading, math, science, fine arts, social studies, and language. Emphasis is on hands-on learning with seasonal activities and patterns that make this a useful year-round teaching tool. Each issue contains two giant monthly calendars to display in the classroom or library. Articles include instructions for teachers and references to additional resources on the featured topic. The last issue each year includes a year-end index with general curriculum categories, such as "Arts and Crafts," "Holidays," "Games," "Language Arts," and "Special Fun." The web site (www.copycatpress.com) has descriptions of articles for a year's worth of issues and sample reproducibles that can be printed or downloaded.

1784. *Early Childhood Today.* Formerly (until 1993): *Scholastic Pre-K Today.* [ISSN: 1070-1214] 1986. 8x/yr. USD 19.95. Scholastic Inc., 555 Broadway, New York, NY 10012-0399; http://www.scholastic.com. Illus., adv. Circ: 220000. *Indexed:* CIJE, EduInd. *Aud.:* Ac, Sa.

A leading magazine for child care center owners and directors and early childhood educators, *Early Childhood Today* features research, teaching tips, activities, management strategies, and technology updates. "Teaching with Technology" highlights reviews of toys and software, "Staff Workshop" provides background information, goals, preparation, and process for workshops on topics such as "Why Read Aloud" or "Building Your Math Program." "Ages and Stages" discusses behavior and development issues in 3–6 year olds. The web site contains age-appropriate online activities for threes and fours, fives and sixes, and mixed grades, as well as a professional discussion group to share questions and advice about issues specific to early childhood.

Instructor. See Education/General, K-12 section.

1785. *Learning and Leading with Technology.* Formerly (until 1995): *Computing Teacher.* [ISSN: 1082-5754] 1979. 8x/yr. Members, USD 58; Non-members, USD 65; Students, USD 35. Ed(s): Kate Conley. International Society for Technology in Education, 1787 Agate St, Eugene, OR 97403-1923; http://www.iste.org/. Illus., index, adv. Sample. Refereed. Circ: 12000. Vol. ends: May. Microform: PQC. Online: Florida Center for Library Automation; Gale Group; OCLC Online Computer Library Center, Inc.; H.W. Wilson. *Indexed:* CIJE, EduInd, InfoSAb, MicrocompInd. *Aud.:* Sa.

This membership publication of the International Society for Technology in Education (ISTE) is for K–12 teachers and teacher educators with a broad range of experience integrating technology into the classroom. Articles emphasize practical applications of technology. "In the Curriculum" focuses on uses of technology for specific subjects (language arts, social studies, math, science) and project-based learning. "For Tech Leaders" offers teacher-to-teacher advice on technology issues. In "Student Voices," a student presents an activity or project. Each article includes a table that lists the applicable subject(s), teaching audience, grade level, and required technology for the ideas or activities presented. Each issue reviews several new software releases. The web site (www.iste.org) provides full texts of the articles to members.

1786. *The Mailbox: the idea magazine for teachers.* [ISSN: 0199-6045] 1972. bi-m. USD 24.95 domestic; USD 33.95 foreign. Ed(s): Angie Kutzer. Education Center Inc., 3515 W Market St, PO Box 9753, Greensboro, NC 27403; http://www.themailboxcompanion.com. Illus., index, adv. Sample. Vol. ends: Dec/Jan. *Aud.:* Sa.

A colorful and engaging resource for teachers, *The Mailbox* is published in four editions: Preschool, Kindergarten, Primary (1–3), and Intermediate (4–6). The Kindergarten edition, reviewed for this section, contains many reproducibles as well as a centerfold pullout for use with the regular "Calendar Connections" and "Seasonal Projects" segments. Feature articles cover teaching tips, book-related projects, and activities for subjects across the curriculum. *Mailbox Companion* is a free online service for subscribers that complements the print issue and contains skill-based reproducibles, forms for classroom management, student awards, clip art, and a daily calendar of tips and activity suggestions.

Teacher's Helper: skillbuilders for your classroom [ISSN 1078-6570] 6/yr. USD 19.95. Margaret Michel. Education Center, 3515 W. Market St., Suite 200, Greensboro, NC 27403; http://www.themailbox.com. Illus. Vol. ends: Dec./Jan. *Aud:* Sa.

Skill-based reproducible activity worksheets in four editions: kindergarten, grade 1, grades 2–3, and grades 4–5.

1787. *Mailbox Bookbag: the teachers' idea magazine for children's literature.* [ISSN: 1088-6397] 1996. bi-m. USD 29.95. Ed(s): Christine Thuman. Education Center Inc., 3515 W Market St, PO Box 9753, Greensboro, NC 27403. Illus. Sample. Vol. ends: Jun/Jul. *Aud.:* Sa.

An excellent resource for elementary and middle school teachers and librarians, The *Mailbox Bookbag* provides brief descriptions of books and suggests activities for each title. Teaching units for chapter books and novels lay out chapter-by-chapter questions and follow-up activities to integrate literature with skills instruction. Reproducible worksheets reinforce reading vocabulary and comprehension skills and make connections to writing and math skills where applicable. The "Bulletin Boards for Books" section illustrates classroom displays designed to attract students' attention while encouraging them to read.

A subscription includes free access to *The Bookbag Companion,* an online resource that contains a searchable archive of *Bookbag* issues, editors' monthly picks of author reviews, literature units and bulletin board ideas as well as publishers' special literature sections created just for *Bookbag* subscribers.

Mathematics Teacher. See Mathematics section.

Mathematics Teaching in the Middle School. See under *Mathematics Teacher* in the Mathematics section.

Media & Methods. see Media and AV.

1788. *Micromath.* [ISSN: 0267-5501] 1985. 3x/yr. Institutional members, GBP 67; Individual members, GBP 49. Ed(s): David Wright, Julie-Ann Edwards. Association of Teachers of Mathematics, 7 Shaftesbury St, Derby, DE23 8YB, United Kingdom; atm@atm.org.uk; http://www.atm.org.uk/journals/micromath.html. Illus., adv. Circ: 3800. Online: EBSCO Publishing; OCLC Online Computer Library Center, Inc.; H.W. Wilson. Reprint: SWZ. *Indexed:* BrEdI, EduInd. *Aud.:* Sa.

This British title carries articles ranging from research to purely anecdotal pieces. It emphasizes classroom strategies for teaching children mathematics and stresses the use of computers and technology. Each issue is devoted to a particular topic, such as using an interactive whiteboard in the classroom or dynamic geometry software to support teaching and learning. Regular features include software reviews and "WebWatch," a review of interactive mathematics resources on the web.

1789. *P C Teach It: integrating technology into the classroom.* 2001. 6x/yr. USD 29.99; USD 4.95 newsstand/cover per issue; USD 6.95 newsstand/cover per issue Canada. Ed(s): Linda Dennis. Rosewood Press, 802 A-B S Edisto Ave, Columbia, SC 29205. Illus., adv. Sample. *Aud.:* Sa.

This project-based magazine and online resource is geared to integrating technology into the classroom. It contains content relevant to students of all ages, with a concentration on the K-4-6 levels. *PC Teach-It*'s content follows the academic calendar, and the hands-on projects and cross-curricular lessons are correlated to the National Education Technology Standards (NETS). Each issue provides reproducible worksheets, columns by technology experts, and

Internet links and activities. The companion web site (www.pcteachit.com) contains projects, games, and tools not included in the print magazine, as well as a store from which to purchase project supplies. Access to the web site is included with a subscription.

School Arts. see Education/Specific Subjects and Teaching Methods, The Arts section.

1790. ***Science and Children: the journal for elementary school science teachers.*** [ISSN: 0036-8148] 1963. 8x/yr. USD 77 (Individuals, USD 67). Ed(s): Joan McShane. National Science Teachers Association, 1840 Wilson Blvd, Arlington, VA 22201; http://www.nsta.org/pubs/sc/. Illus., index, adv. Refereed. Circ: 22000. Vol. ends: May. *Indexed:* CIJE, ECER, EduInd, GeoRef, MRD, WSA. *Bk. rev.:* 7, 300 words. *Aud.:* Sa.

A magazine for kindergarten through middle-level science classroom teachers, science teacher administrators, and teacher educators. Feature articles discuss pedagogy and educational issues relevant to science teaching. "In the News" highlights discoveries and current research of interest to the science community. Regular features include "Finds & Sites," a list of free or inexpensive materials, publications, and events; "Teaching Through Trade Books," activities inspired by children's literature; and "Evening Skies," a monthly astronomical chart and calendar. A "Dragonfly TV" pullout in each issue can be duplicated for classroom use. It can also be used with videotapes of the particular episode of the pubic television program. "Home Zone" highlights science activities for families to share, and in "Science 101" experts answer teachers' questions about everyday science. "NSTA Recommends" reviews both student texts and professional literature for science teachers. These reviews and others are also available online at www.nsta.org/recommends.

1791. ***Science Scope: a journal for middle-junior high science teachers.*** [ISSN: 0887-2376] 1978. 8x/yr. USD 72. Ed(s): Inez Fugate Liftig. National Science Teachers Association, 1840 Wilson Blvd, Arlington, VA 22201; science.scope@nsta.org; http://www.nsta.org/pubs/scope. Illus., index, adv. Sample. Refereed. Circ: 15000. Vol. ends: May. Online: ProQuest Information & Learning. *Indexed:* CIJE, EduInd, GeoRef, MRD. *Bk. rev.:* 2-3, 300 words. *Aud.:* Sa.

A professional journal for middle and junior high school science teachers. Peer-reviewed articles provide ready-to-use activities and teaching strategies for life science, physical science, and earth science. Regular features include "Science Sampler," short activities and strategies; "Tried and True," classic demonstrations and experiments; "After the Bell," extracurricular science activities; "Tech Trek," incorporating technology in the classroom; and "Scope's Scoops," summaries of recent scientific research. "NSTA Recommends" highlights trade books. These reviews and others are available online at www.nsta.org/recommends.

Teaching Children Mathematics. See under *Mathematics Teacher* in the Mathematics section.

Teaching Exceptional Children. see Disabilities section.

Teaching Pre K–8. See Education/General, K–12 section.

The Science Teacher. See Astronomy section.

1792. ***Web Feet: the Internet traveler's desk reference.*** [ISSN: 1097-4210] 1998. m. USD 165. Ed(s): Terry Schneider. RockHill Communications, 14 Rock Hill Rd, Bala Cynwyd, PA 19004; info@rockhillcommunications.com; http://www.rockhillcommunications.com. *Aud.:* Ems, Hs, Ac, Sa.

Web Feet is a multidisciplinary guide to web sites that have been reviewed and annotated by librarians, educators, subject specialists, and editors. It is an excellent source of up-to-date curriculum resources. This valuable collection is available in several editions: K–8 (appropriate for elementary and middle schools and public libraries), K–12 (for K–12 schools and districts and public libraries), the Core Collection (for K–12 schools and districts, public and academic libraries), and a specialized Health Collection (for K–12 schools and districts, and public, academic, and medical libraries). All editions are available online and as downloadable MARC records that can be integrated into a library catalog. The K–8 and Core Collections are also available as print, looseleaf services, which are updated monthly. The Health Collection is also offered as a softcover book.

One of the new features in *Web Feet* is a selection of teaching tools and professional development and library management resources for teachers and librarians. A ready-reference section has been added to each collection. Subscribers to the online or MARC products now have access to monthly projects with activities that are aligned with curriculum standards. Subscribers to any *Web Feet* product may receive a monthly e-mail newsletter, "Web Feet WIRE," that not only highlights timely topics in *Web Feet* but also provides lesson plans, "WebQuests," and classroom activities on the featured topics. There is even a downloadable research guide that teachers can send home to help inform parents about *Web Feet.*

Web Feet Online provides browsing capability by LC subject, author/sponsor, site title, and LC or Dewey call number. The expanded search feature supports more complex keyword searching options. Search tips provide help with searches by grade level or curriculum area. An online training manual and guided tour help users to orient themselves to searching *Web Feet Online.* "Guide to Search Tools" is the equivalent, free supplement to the print products.

Highly recommended for school, public, and academic libraries.

Electronic Journals

1793. ***MultiMedia Schools: a practical journal of technology for education, including multimedia, CD-ROM, Online, Internet and hardware in K-12.*** [ISSN: 1075-0479] 1994. 6x/yr. USD 39.95 domestic; USD 54 in Canada & Mexico; USD 63 elsewhere. Ed(s): Ferdi Serim. Information Today, Inc., 143 Old Marlton Pike, Medford, NJ 08055-8750; custserv@infotoday.com; http://www.infotoday.com. Illus., adv. *Indexed:* CIJE, CPerI, CompLI, EduInd, InfoSAb, MicrocompInd. *Bk. rev.:* 4. *Aud.:* Ac, Sa.

A practical how-to magazine for librarians, teachers, and media specialists, *Multimedia Schools* reports on, reviews, and discusses a wide array of electronic media, including Internet resources, online databases, CD-ROMs and videodiscs, educational software, and the hardware needed to make those technologies work. Articles and columns address issues associated with using electronic information resources in K–12 schools. Other features include news items and reviews of books and software. All are contributed by practicing educators who use new technologies in the classroom or media center. *Multimedia Schools* is addressed primarily to K–12 librarians and media specialists, but also will be of interest to technology coordinators, principals, and other administrators. The web site (www.infotoday.com/MMSchools) provides full texts of selected articles from each issue as well as recent editorials.

1794. ***The Onestop Magazine: the magazine for English language teachers.*** d. Ed(s): Tim Bowen. Macmillan Education, Macmillan Oxford, Between Towns Rd, Oxford, OX4 3PP, United Kingdom; elt@mhelt.com; http://www.macmillaneducation.com. *Aud.:* Sa.

The Onestop Magazine is an e-journal published by Macmillan Education, "one of the world's leading publishers of English Language Teaching materials for teachers and students of English as a foreign or second language." The journal offers a range of free resources, including lesson plans and study skills extensions, teaching strategies in the "Methodology" section, ELT and ESL news from "The Guardian Weekly," and tips for teaching pre-K. Other free resources such as worksheets in American, British, and Business English (updated monthly); methodology texts; and interactive games are links on the web site. "Lesson Share" is a databank of lessons contributed by teachers for other teachers to share. The "Culture" page of music, art, and writing to use in the classroom has worksheets, "WebQuests," and a poetry competition. There is a "Professional Support" section for teachers to share anecdotes, find links to other relevant web sites, and even to ask grammar questions. A full-featured site for ESL instruction, this is a very useful resource for teachers and students.

1795. ***Scholastic.com.*** Formerly: *Scholastic Network.* w. Scholastic Inc., 555 Broadway, New York, NY 10012-0399. *Aud.:* Ems, Sa.

An excellent source of information and classroom resources for families, kids, and teachers. With separate areas for each of its target audiences, this web site emphasizes participation and interaction. The teacher's section (teacher.scholastic.com) includes lesson plans, reproducibles, thematic units, and activities for pre-K through 8th grade. Information about authors and books, teaching with technology, reading resources, and a class web site builder are some of the available resources. The "Teacher Toolkit" allows teachers to edit standards-based lessons to fit their needs, make resources to use in class, and post resources for students. Using "Classport," teachers can set up online communication for their classes with classrooms in 182 countries, and collaborate with teachers around the world. "Scholastic Wireless" can be used with AvantGo to download Scholastic.com's latest news, activities, and events to a Palm, Handspring, or Pocket PC device.

1796. ***WWW4Teachers.*** irreg. University of Kansas, High Plains Regional Technology in Education Consortium, http://hprtec.org/. *Aud.:* Sa.

Part of a web site filled with information and resources for teachers, *WWW4Teachers* is a free e-journal from the High Plains Regional Technology in Education Consortium, one of ten such consortia funded by the U.S. Department of Education. On the web site "you will find a combination of development and collaboration tools and resources, designed for online access, that address problems [teachers] face daily." The webzine features "Teacher Testimony," first-person accounts of teaching experiences, and "KidSpeak," students reporting on how they use technology. Other sections include ready-to-use web lessons, collections of classroom activities, puzzles and games, and "Tech-Along," a how-to technology guide with a glossary. The "Tools" section contains a variety of useful applications, including "Casa Notes," a set of templates teachers can use to make, and customize, typical notes that are sent home to parents or given to the students; "Assign-A-Day," an online teacher-managed calendar; a quiz maker; a rubric maker; a note-taking tool; and much more. This webzine is highly recommended and should be bookmarked and referred to frequently by elementary and middle school teachers.

■ COLLEGE AND ALUMNI

Donna L. Burton, Reference and Government Documents Librarian, Schaffer Library, Union College, Schenectady, NY 12308; burtond@union.edu; FAX: 518-388-6641

Introduction

Most colleges and universities are taking the time and money to produce some sort of compilation of campus and/or alumni news in the form of a magazine, bulletin, or newsletter that may also target prospective students and parents. Increasingly, these are available as well in electronic format on the Internet as promotional and public relations tools. They can also act as informational resources with archived full-text issues and search options for locating specific topics. Although the majority of them are not likely to be of widespread national interest, and they are rarely commercially indexed, there are some that routinely incorporate fare of universal appeal and may even be peer reviewed and indexed. The generally low subscription fees for paper copies and the free online versions broaden their appeal. Libraries within a reasonable geographic radius to a college or university should consider adding any such relevant publications to the periodical collection or bookmarking online versions of them for local interest.

Basic Periodicals

Hs: *Black Collegian, Circle K;* Ga: *Black Collegian;* Ac: *Black Collegian, Brown Alumni Magazine, Circle K, College Student Affairs Journal, Harvard Divinity Bulletin, Phi Kappa Phi Forum, University of New Hampshire Magazine.*

1797. ***Black Collegian.*** [ISSN: 0192-3757] 1970. s-a. Individuals, USD 8; Students, USD 4. Black Collegian, 909 Poydras St, 36th Fl, New Orleans, LA 70112; scott@black-collegian.com for on line version; http://www.black-collegian.com/. Illus. Sample. Microform: PQC. *Bk. rev.:* 50 words. *Aud.:* Hs, Ga, Ac.

Published twice annually in a glossy hardcopy format, this title focuses on such topics as career planning and job searching, top diversity employers, opportunities in the federal government, financial services, and the job outlook for the current graduating class. Most contributors are academics or professionals in relevant fields. The issues run about 120 pages, are in full color, and are fairly heavy on the advertising, not counting the top-employer articles that generate some incidental corporate promotion. There is a companion web site that features articles from the current issue as well as some online-only "specials." It includes channels for specially directed topics, such as a military opportunity job bank, and a full-text archive of back issues. In spite of infrequent paper issues, there is good value relative to cost for the well-presented information on job hunting and career development.

1798. ***Brown Alumni Magazine.*** Formerly: *Brown Alumni Monthly.* [ISSN: 1520-863X] 1900. bi-m. USD 35 (Free to qualified personnel). Ed(s): Norman Boucher. Brown University, PO Box 1854, Providence, RI 02912. Illus., adv. Sample. Circ: 77000 Controlled. *Bk. rev.:* 1, 650 words. *Aud.:* Ga, Ac.

This glossy, professionally produced magazine has an equally top-notch, free, full-text online counterpart, including archived issues going back to 1995. Articles and the "Under the Elms" news brief section feature numerous topics of general interest that retain a specific relevancy to the Brown University community. A majority of the articles are authored by Brown alumni, students, or faculty, and relate to views of the world, slices of life, points of view, and campus events. As is typical with alumni publications, nearly a quarter to a half the magazine is taken up by alumni class notes. Outside advertising is minimal.

1799. ***Circle K: a magazine for student leaders.*** Formerly: *Circle K Magazine.* [ISSN: 0745-1962] 1956. 5x/yr. USD 6. Ed(s): Casey Keller. Circle K International, 3636 Woodview Trace, Indianapolis, IN 46268-3196. Sample. Circ: 15000. Vol. ends: Apr. *Aud.:* Hs, Ac.

Subtitled "a magazine for student leaders," this publication states that "*Circle K Magazine* was established to promote the Objects of Circle K International." It "includes articles promoting the service initiative of CKI and articles of general interest to college students." CKI is affiliated with Kiwanis International and seeks to develop leadership and friendship principles in students during the course of volunteer service. Only 15 pages or so on average and ad-free, this is more a glossy newsletter than magazine, and it has numerous reports of CKI projects targeted to their 570 clubs and over 12,000 members. But the one or two short articles per issue would find a general audience. Sample topics include letting go of control, volunteerism, promoting reading, handling pressure, and honing your skills for job hunting. There is no online counterpart.

1800. ***College Student Affairs Journal.*** Formerly: *Southern College Personnel Association Journal.* [ISSN: 0888-210X] 1978. s-a. USD 25. Ed(s): Robert L Bowman. Northwestern State University of Louisiana, Southern Studies Institute, 203 Russell Hall, Natchitoches, LA 71497; bownmanr@nsula.edu. Sample. Refereed. Circ: 1200. Vol. ends: Spring. Microform: PQC. *Indexed:* CIJE, HEA. *Aud.:* Ac.

As described in the manuscript guidelines, this journal "...focuses on concepts, practices, and research that have implications and applicability for practitioners involved in college student affairs work." Although this title does not have any access online, the print publication is free of advertising, refereed, illustrated only with occasional graphs, charts, tables, or diagrams, and averages between 80 and 100 pages. It is indexed in two educationally related commercial indexing sources. Opinion pieces and book reviews supplement such recent research articles as sexual harassment preventive practices at colleges and universities, student press censorship, term paper mill cheating, student event policies and student affairs staffing practices and supervision.

1801. ***Columbia College Today.*** [ISSN: 0572-7820] 1954. 6x/yr. Free to alumni, students, faculty and friends of Columbia College. Ed(s): Alex Sachare. Columbia College, Office of Alumni Affairs and Development, 475 Riverside Dr, Rm 917, New York, NY 10115; http://www.college.columbia.edu/cct/index.html. Illus., adv. Sample. Circ: 46000 Controlled. *Bk. rev.:* Various number and length. *Aud.:* Ga, Ac, Sa.

This is a full-color, slickly produced magazine that carries minimal advertising and dedicates half its 60 or so pages to alumni class notes. The articles, written by students, faculty, and freelancers, are targeted to the institutional interests, but also to New York, both city and state, with most stories focusing on high-profile graduates, professorial specialties, and acadmic research projects. Few full-length book reviews are included, with the focus mainly on annotations of alumni output, which is considerable. This magazine also boasts a nicely presented web edition, including full-text access to archives of issues from winter 1999 to the present.

1802. *Harvard Divinity Bulletin.* Formerly (until 1958): *Harvard Divinity School Bulletin.* [ISSN: 0017-8047] 1908. q. Ed(s): Will Joyner. Cambridge U. Press, 45 Francis Ave, Cambridge, MA 02138; will_joyner@harvard.edu. Illus., index. Sample. Circ: 25000. *Indexed:* RI-1. *Bk. rev.:* 7, 750 words. *Aud.:* Ac, Sa.

This is printed in a no-advertising, black-and-white, tabloid-sized format, averaging 30 to 40 pages for the main content. As self-described, this publication is "composed of faculty and alumni/ae news; articles on current issues in theological education and the study of religion, especially pertaining to how religion affects contemporary culture and politics; book reviews; interviews; essays; and transcribed lectures, as well as news of school activities and events." These essays deal such contemporary topics as human rights, comparative religion, moral leadership and religion in public life, and faith afer tragedy. In-depth book reviews are a welcome feature, and the *Bulletin* is indexed in *Religion Index One: Periodicals* (in print or CD-ROM). Some key articles found in the current issue are accessible on the web site. An entire issue can be viewed in pdf, and a year's worth of past issues are full-text online, with others available on request.

1803. *Insider (Skokie): careers, issues and entertainment for the next generation.* Formerly: *Collegiate Insider.* [ISSN: 1070-6534] 1984. bi-m. USD 24.95. Ed(s): Rita Cook, Mark Jansen. College Marketing Bureau, Inc., 11168 Acama St., Ste. 3, North Hollywood, CA 91602; insideread@aol.com; http://www.incard.com/insider.htm. Adv. Circ: 1018350 Controlled. *Bk. rev.:* 4-8, 150-400 words. *Aud.:* Ga, Ac.

"INsider magazine is printed six times a year featuring a specific theme for each guide: Computer, Software & Football Guide; Skiing & Winter Sports Guide; Travel & Extreme Sports Guide; Automotive & Basketball Guide; Outdoor & Adventure Guide and Orientation Issue." Distributed by subscription and also directly to college newspapers and radio stations, it boasts over 15 individualized local editions for metropolitan markets. Averaging around 50 pages, it is mostly written by twentysomethings for the target 18- to 34-year-old market. Articles are rarely more than a page long, and there is much advertising. Some of the web site (www.incard.com) seems to need updating, but there are archived, full-text back issues. Fortunately, the print product, although still issued on newsprint, has toned down the busy backgrounds and fonts, corralled the ads, and vastly improved its legibility. Both web and print versions feature media and book reviews, career information, and features on hot topics. Given the newsprint and lack of indexing, the value of this title lies mostly in its currency.

1804. *Notre Dame Magazine.* Supersedes (in 1971): *Notre Dame Alumnus.* [ISSN: 0161-987X] 1923. q. USD 20 to non alumni. University of Notre Dame, Notre Dame, IN 46556. Illus. Sample. Circ: 135000 Controlled. *Indexed:* RI-1. *Aud.:* Ga, Sa.

Slightly larger than the typical format, this full-color magazine has intriguing covers that open into the introductory column, "Notre Dame News." Each issue includes the expected alumni briefs and "Classes" section in the back, comprising about a quarter of the 90 or so pages. Sandwiched between these sections are feature articles on such topics as church scandal with the priesthood in peril, power of the pope, international relations tied to religious beliefs, tracking money that funds global terrorism, and athletics versus academics, all delivered with a generally religious slant. Interestingly, in addition to replicating and archiving some of the print content, the nicely done web version is being used to expand on stories and other information that was too extensive to print or that arrived after deadline. This magazine and web site should appeal to general audiences and is indexed in *Religion Index One: Periodicals.*

1805. *Pennsylvania Gazette.* [ISSN: 1520-4650] 1902. bi-m. USD 28. Ed(s): John Prendergast. University of Pennsylvania, 3533 Locust Walk, Philadelphia, PA 19104-6226; gazette@ben.dev.upenn.edu; http://www.upenn.edu/gazette. Adv. Circ: 140000. *Bk. rev.:* 1, 1,500 words. *Aud.:* Ga, Ac, Sa.

Sporting an excellent full-text web site for the current issue as well as archived issues from 1997, this 90–100 page print publication has minimal advertising and well-written columns, book reviews, and feature articles. Not surprisingly, it is primarily tailored to campus events and information, and nearly half the issue is dedicated to alumni profiles, news, notes, and obituaries. The cited credentials of its feature and column contributors indicate a combination of students, alumni, faculty, and editorial staff, who write opinion pieces and articles, most often on prominent alumni or special faculty research interests or philosophies. Recent article topics include putting a Sumerian dictionary online, biological and environmental threads of nicotine addiction, hip-hop culture and social justice, Iraq and the Middle East, and minorities on campus.

1806. *Phi Kappa Phi Forum.* Former titles (until 2002): *National Forum (Auburn); Phi Kappa Phi National Forum.* [ISSN: 1538-5914] 1913. q. Non-members, USD 25. Ed(s): James Kaetz. Honor Society of Phi Kappa Phi (Auburn), Louisiana State University, PO Box 16000, Baton Rouge, LA 70893; kaetzjp@mail.auburn.edu. Illus., adv. Sample. Circ: 105000 Controlled. Vol. ends: Fall. Microform: PQC. Reprint: PQC. *Indexed:* AgeL, BRI, CBRI, CIJE, EnvAb, HEA, LRI, MagInd, PAIS, PhilInd. *Bk. rev.:* Various number and length. *Aud.:* Ga, Ac.

Polished-looking and professionally presented, this journal offers thematic issues that focus on a single "big topic" of current interest. Formerly ad-free, it now accepts advertising targeted to academics. Its stated mission is to "enhance the image of The Honor Society of Phi Kappa Phi and promote the pursuit of academic excellence in all fields through a quality, intellectually stimulating publication for its membership." Each issue has informative articles and columns on education and academics, business and economics, science and technology, and the arts, written by educators, editors, and published authors, with the added bonus of being indexed in multiple sources. Included are poetry and book review sections. There is no online access except to the table of contents of recent issues, however, its timely and interesting topics, such as food and culture, space exploration, and cancer research and treatment, make this is a good choice for high school, public, and academic collections.

1807. *University of New Hampshire Magazine.* Former titles (until 1998): *Alumni Companion;* (until 1991): *New Hampshire Alumnus;* (until 1984): *New Hampshire State Alumnus.* 1924. 3x/yr. USD 12 domestic; USD 15 foreign. Ed(s): Maggie Paine. University of New Hampshire, Alumni Association, Elliott Alumni Center, 9 Edgewood Rd, Durham, NH 03824; alumni@unh.edu; http://www.alumni.unh.edu/. Adv. Refereed. Circ: 100000 Controlled. *Bk. rev.:* Varous number and length. *Aud.:* Hs, Ga, Ac.

This is a nicely done, full-color college magazine, with minimal advertising. Columns include "Campus Currents; the ebb and flow of the UNH community," "Inquiring Minds; highlights from UNH research," "Colloquium; discourse across the disciplines" on academic projects or performances, and reviews in "Cover to Cover; books by UNH faculty and alumni." A sampling of article topics includes Sudanese refugee students adapting to American education, teaching mute children to communicate, mysteries of solar storms, mothering orphaned bear cubs, sailboat racing, and wrestling. "Class Notes" makes up about a third of each issue's approximately 60 pages. An excellent web site allows full-text access to the current issue and three years of archived issues.

■ COMIC BOOKS

General/Publications about Comics

Allen Ellis, Associate Professor of Library Services, W. Frank Steely Library, Northern Kentucky University, Highland Heights, KY 41099-6101; ellisa@nku.edu; FAX: 859-572-5390

Doug Highsmith, Reference Librarian, University Library, California State University-Hayward, Hayward, CA 94542; dhighsmi@bay.cshayward.edu

Roger C. Adams, Rare Books Librarian/Associate Professor, Special Collections, Hale Library, Kansas State University, Manhattan, KS 66506-1200; rcadams@ksu.edu; FAX: 785-532-7415

Introduction

Comics Books: Then and Now

Although the development of comics as an art form can be traced back over several centuries, the American comic book industry had its beginnings in 1933 with the publication of what is generally considered the first "modern" comic book, *Funnies on Parade.* Given away as a premium for Proctor & Gamble, *Funnies on Parade* featured reprints of several weeks' worth of various popular newspaper comic strips of the day. Such reprints provided nearly all the content for comic books until 1935, when the company that would eventually become known as DC Comics began publishing original material in *New Fun Comics.* Three years later, the appearance of Superman in the premiere issue of DC's *Action Comics* (June 1938) established the superhero as the pre-eminent genre in the medium and launched what is nostalgically regarded as the Golden Age of comics. This Golden Age is generally considered to have lasted until the end of World War II.

In the 1950s, comics' popularity—particularly that of the superhero genre—began to wane. One related problem was an alarming increase of antisocial behavior by juveniles. As video games and other violent media are today blamed for such phenomena, comic books were the scapegoat fifty years ago. Rising public outcry and threatened government intervention forced comics publishers to band together to self-police their products. The result was the Comics Code, which sanitized and sterilized the content of comic books for over two decades. Still, despite vocal critics demanding their banishment and the emerging competition from television, comic books managed to carry on.

In late 1956, the DC title *Showcase* debuted "The Flash," an updated version of a popular Golden Age hero, and his popularity led to resurgence not only of the superhero genre, but also of the medium of comic books itself. This resulted in what is considered the Silver Age of comics. Just when the Silver Age ended, and what "age" replaced it, is a matter of much debate.

Since the Silver Age, American comic books have experienced many ups and downs, both financially and creatively. Today, comic book publishing is an industry in crisis, suffering through a sales slump that has lasted the better part of a decade and continues to show little sign of going away. Industry sales, which into the early 1990s were estimated at $800 million to $1 billion per year, entered the new century at around $300 million per year. While comic books face increasingly stiff competition from video games, movies, television, the Internet, and various other types of mass entertainment, many of the problems encountered by the industry in recent years stem from the decision of publishers to cater to short-term investors and speculators. Spurred by news reports of true collectibles like that first issue of *Action Comics* being valued at $145,000, thousands of would-be investors with little interest in comic books as an art form or as an entertainment medium were led to believe (wrongly) that in buying current comics they were investing in surefire collectibles guaranteed to soar in value. To attract this segment of the market, many comics publishers focused their time and energies on such gimmicks as limited editions and specialty or variant covers, frequently at the expense of compelling, or even coherent, storytelling.

However, since the 1960s comic books have been systematically collected, and a well-developed resale market has been established for back issues. Comic books do indeed enjoy considerable popularity as collectibles (as witnessed by the success of auctions held by the likes of Sotheby's and Christie's, and by the number of comic books available for sale at any given time on eBay), but the likelihood of any particular modern comic book being as valuable as its Golden Age and early–Silver Age ancestors is not very great—particularly when one considers all of the Golden Age comics that were contributed to WWII paper drives by patriotic youngsters (who were spurred on by the comics themselves). Once this painful reality became apparent to them, short-term investors deserted the market, and those who remained were less than thrilled with the changes the speculators had helped bring to the industry.

With many old-time readers and collectors alienated by what was seen as pandering to speculators, comics sales went into a tailspin. Nevertheless, while it is possible that comic books, like pulp magazines and "big little books" before them, will fade from the scene, the comics industry has a history of bouncing back from periodic sales downturns. Prior to the current crisis, for instance, the industry suffered through a creative and economic nadir in the late 1970s and early 1980s, only to spring back to unprecedented growth and prosperity. That renaissance was fueled in large part by the emergence of the comic specialty shop as a stable, predictable venue for the sales of comic books. Over the years, comic books lost their once-common positions on newsstands and racks in drugstores, variety stores, supermarkets, and department stores, in favor of more profitable fare. Comics are now mostly sold through these comics specialty stores. About 3,000 comics stores are found throughout the United States. The existence of these specialty retail outlets, combined with improvements in distribution channels and in the printing and publishing facilities available to them, allowed many new publishers to enter the market, bringing with them an exciting new variety of approaches to what had become a creatively stagnant medium.

Comic Books Today: Publisher Overview

Today there are over 500 publishers of comics. While this may seem an impressive number, it is somewhat misleading. Both entries into and departures from the comic book marketplace are frequent. Many of the smallest publishers issue very few books per year—in fact, about a third put out only one comic book per year. Abstract Studios, which publishes *Strangers in Paradise*, and Exhibit A Press (*Supernatural Law*) are among the best of the one-title publishers. Both are discussed in entries below.

Unfortunately, space limitations, and the desire to focus on ongoing titles that interested libraries can acquire on a continuing basis, preclude providing entries below for the offerings from many other small publishers. Nevertheless, libraries interested in comic books should be aware that companies other than the industry's dominant players are publishing many interesting titles, particularly in genres other than superheroics.

Among the more interesting and noteworthy of the publishers not represented below are Antarctic Press, Cartoon Comics (home of Jeff Smith's wonderful *Bone* —left out of this edition only because the series concluded with issue 55), Claypool Comics, Fantagraphics Press (publisher of Chris Ware's award-winning *Acme Novelty Library* and an eclectic array of other mature reader-oriented non-superhero titles), NBM Publishing, and Oni Press. Much of this comics output is reprinted in trade paperback or hardcover collections that desire to find their way onto library shelves, such as the Jimmy Corrigan collection from Fantagraphics, which features stories that originally appeared in *Acme Novelty Library.*

So, who are the "dominant players" of the modern comic book industry? Currently, just five companies—Marvel, DC, Image, CrossGen Publications, and Dark Horse Comics. Dark Horse Comics, while by all indications on generally solid financial footing, has nevertheless curtailed its publication of standard comic books in order to give greater attention to the production of other comics-inspired items (statues of comics characters, motion pictures, books and graphic novels, tee-shirts, etc.)—although that trend currently shows some signs of reversing itself. CrossGen Comics—the most recent addition to the "Big Five"—is in many respects proving to be the most "library friendly" of all comic book publishers. Focusing more on fantasy and science fiction motifs than "pure" superheroics, CrossGen offers a line-up of titles produced by a number of top comics professionals (For more about CrossGen, see the entry below for *Ruse*). These five companies account for 80–90 percent of U.S. comics sales and occupy much of the available display space in most comics shops, bookstores, and other outlets.

But even as the smaller companies struggle to find room on the stands for their comics (or to find room in this book for coverage of their comics), those at the top have had their share of problems as well. Longtime industry leader Marvel Comics, which fell into hands of corporate owners little interested in comic book publishing as such, spent much of the 1990s making a series of questionable business decisions that alienated both comics fans and comics retailers. As a result, the self-styled "House of Ideas," home of such characters as Spider-Man, the X-Men, the Avengers, Captain America, Thor, the Fantastic Four, and the Incredible Hulk, stumbled into a bankruptcy from which it is still recovering. However, creatively speaking, Marvel is back on much firmer footing. Its recent renaissance, which includes publishing some books under the Marvel Knights or Max (read: "mature") imprints, allows it to once more match and, arguably surpass perennial second-banana DC Comics when it comes to producing quality mainstream comics (although neither company's current output is of a uniform quality). DC, benefiting from the stability afforded by being a (rather minor) part of the AOL Time-Warner corporate family, continues to offers a line of diverse, quality publications, including perennial favorites *Superman, Batman, Justice League of America,* and *Wonder Woman*), while edgier, more "adult"-oriented material appears primarily under the company's Vertigo imprint.

Comic Books Today: Still a Major Influence in American Popular Culture

Despite all the travails and instability experienced by the American comic book industry during the past decade, a strong case still can be made that, while this is economically one of the worst times for the industry, it is creatively among the best. As with any medium, there is a lot of junk, but there are also some precious jewels to be found. There is something to be said, after all, for any medium that not only develops such talents as Alan Moore, Frank Miller, Jeff Smith, Terry Moore, and Neil Gaiman (to name but a few), but also attracts such established creators as filmmaker Kevin Smith and writers Joss Whedon, J. Michael Straczynski, and Brad Meltzer to work in it. (Straczynski's recent work on *Amazing Spider-Man* is discussed below; Smith's most recent major contribution to the medium was as inaugural writer of the recently revived and highly successful *Green Arrow* title for DC Comics (for which, see below), to be followed by Metzer. Whedon's *Buffy the Vampire Slayer* and its spin-offs *Angel* and *Frey* (written by Whedon exclusively for the comics) are published by Dark Horse.)

Not only are a variety of creators from other popular media drawn into trying their hand at comics, comic books exert a strong influence on various other popular culture media. Michael Chabon's *Amazing Adventures of Kavalier and Clay*, set in world of comic book publishing during that industry's Golden Age, was awarded 2001's Pulitzer Prize for Fiction. Movies and television, for their part, have mined comic books for story ideas for decades, albeit with varying degrees of success.

Comics characters and series that have appeared in big screen movies and/or television adaptations include Spider-Man (star of 2002's biggest summer blockbuster), the X-Men (whose tremendously successful 2000 big-screen debut was followed by a 2003 sequel), Daredevil, and the Hulk (both of whom also headlined high-profile major motion pictures in 2003). In addition to these Marvel stalwarts, Batman, Superman, Wonder Woman, the Flash, Teenage Mutant Ninja Turtles, the Mask, Blade, Richie Rich, Casper the Friendly Ghost, Dennis the Menace, the Crow, Timecop, the Phantom, Dick Tracy, Barb Wire, Men in Black, Mystery Men, Static, The Tick, Witchblade, *From Hell, Road to Perdition, Ghost World, The League of Extraordinary Gentlemen,* and Howard the Duck have all appeared on the big and/or small screens during the past quarter century—with several others in the works.

The cross-pollination works in both directions, of course. Comics have offered adaptations of such Hollywood properties as *X-Files; Predator; Alien; Star Trek; Xena, Warrior Princess;* the aforementioned *Buffy the Vampire Slayer; Star Wars,* and *Powerpuff Girls*. And no discussion of the comics/movies connection would be complete without a mention of the movie M. Night Shyamalan made in between mega-hits *The Sixth Sense* and *Signs—Unbreakable,* a film that was nothing other than a variation on the classic superhero origin story.

While the superheroes that provided the inspiration for Shyamalan's film continue to be the dominant genre of the comics medium itself, there is, as indicated above, as wide a variety of types of material available as there is in any other entertainment medium. Westerns, war comics, science fiction, historical fiction, humor, horror, fantasy—they are all out there, though it may take some vigilance to find them.

Comic Books Today: Comic Books Are NOT Just for Kids (Update on the Comics Code)

The once-mighty Comics Code is today little more than a facade, not even acknowledged by most publications. What may ultimately prove be the final death knell of the Code as we know it was sounded in mid-2001 by Marvel Comics' new Editor in Chief Joe Quesada, who announced that the company would no longer be submitting its books to the Code for approval, but would instead be utilizing an in-house ratings systems, intended to indicate what Marvel deemed to be the appropriate reading age level for its various publications.

The declining influence of the Code, while to be applauded for the greater creative freedom it allows comics storytellers, nevertheless presents a potential problem, since the popular perception of comics continues to be that they are children's fare, even though most are actually targeted at teenage and young adult markets. Generally, publishers have resisted content ratings as seen with motion pictures, although Marvel's current system comes close to emulating the MPAA's approach. Indeed, comics may be considered as ranging from G-rated to XXX-rated.

The same conservative groups that have given libraries an increasingly hard time in recent years also target comic book establishments. Unfortunately, comics shops are typically small businesses and do not enjoy the same kind of defense by First Amendment supporters as do libraries. Increasingly, lives and livelihoods have been shattered by groups that feel they can dictate what people should and shouldn't read, necessitating the formation of a Comic Book Legal Defense Fund (P.O. Box 693, Northampton, MA 01601, 1-800-99-CBLDF, http://www.cbldf.org/index.shtml) to assist victims of such groups. Writer Peter David once wrote after visiting Spain: "In Spain, tax dollars go towards celebrating comics as an art form; in the United States, tax dollars go towards paying the salaries of DAs and cops so that they can shut down comic book stores and prosecute creators." How ironic that this innately American art form has yet to achieve in its native land the widespread respect and prestige it enjoys in Asia, Europe, and Latin America.

Bottom line: Don't expect comic books to be the "kids' stuff" they are popularly considered to be. Know your audience and choose carefully.

Comic Books Today: Who Reads Comics?

The audience for American comic books is estimated to be 90 percent male, with an average age in the mid-20s. Given the cost of the product, it makes sense that the age groups with the most disposable income are the major comics buyers. The complexity of the various publishers' "universes" and narratives crossing from one title to another do little to accommodate the casual reader, and the increasing average age of the comics buyer is partially a result of lack of product for and promotion to younger readers. Indeed, comics publishers rival major league baseball in their ability to alienate established fans and disinterest new ones. Female readers are particularly neglected, a situation being addressed by the Friends of Lulu (http://www.friends-lulu.org). Friends of Lulu, named after the classic comics character, Little Lulu, is "a national nonprofit organization whose purpose is to promote and encourage female readership and participation in the comic book industry" (see also *Sequential Tart* under Electronic Sources, below.

Comic Books and Librarians

Even while struggling to regain their appeal to the reading public, American comic books at their best remain an exciting, entertaining, relatively inexpensive communications medium. It is a medium that has long since earned a spot on library shelves, albeit not necessarily in its original cheaply produced magazine format.

Traditionally, librarians and comic books have had an oil/water relationship, and librarianship as a profession offers little to educate librarians about the medium (your humble contributors Ellis and Highsmith have offered a study of this relationship as "About Face: Comic Books in Library Literature," in *Serials Review* vol. 26, no. 2, 2000). Popular culture in general inhabits a vacuum in most professional training. Librarians wishing to know more about comic art as a medium should read Scott McCloud's 1993 *Understanding Comics.* This analysis of comics as an art is itself in comic art form, prompting some librarians to display their ignorance by cataloging it under such headings as "Periodicals, Publishing of, Juvenile Literature." A sequel, *Reinventing Comics,* published in 2000, is also recommended. A good introduction from a professional point of view is still Randall W. Scott's *Comic Book Librarianship* (McFarland, 1990). Also still of possible use are Steve Weiner's *The 101 Best Graphic Novels,* (NBM Publishing, 2001) and D. Aviva Rothschild's *Graphic Novels: A Bibliographic Guide to Book-Length Comics* (Libraries Unlimited, 1995). For intellectual freedom advocates, a fascinating history of the Comics Code is Amy Kiste Nyberg's *Seal of Approval: The History of the Comics Code* (University Press of Mississippi, 1998).These are just a few sources of possible interest. Information about the comics medium for librarians is available as never before, as a perusal of the Electronic Sources below will bear out. The days of librarians and comics as enemies are over!

Comics Acquisition for Libraries: Comic Books, Graphic Novels, Trade Paperbacks, and Hard Cover Collections

The average cost of a standard-format comic book is around $2.80 with prices being affected by rising paper costs and wide variations in paper quality and publishing formats. The standard comic book is still 32 pages, but instead of being on cheap newsprint, is published on high-quality paper designed to show off the modern, complex computerized coloring processes.

Comic books are usually available by subscription, particularly from the major publishers, and special subscription deals are often advertised within comics and at publishers' web sites. Subscription services are also available, and advertising for them can be found in most comic-related publications. However, the precariousness of today's market makes using them a calculated risk. Orders usually precede receipt by two months; if a subscription service goes under, that investment is lost. Notice too that some of the recommended titles below are not available by subscription—in fact, as was indicated in the discussion of the small comic book publishers, much of the best quality material appears in one-shot issues or mini-series rather than as open-ended serials. It is most recommended that customers establish a relationship with a local comics retailer (the closest can be found by calling 1-888-COMIC-BOOK). Another alternative is to work directly with Diamond Comics Distributors, whose web site, http://www.diamondcomics.com, has a "Librarians" tab. Custom orders may be placed from a monthly catalog (see *Previews,* below).

The real future of comics is believed by some to be electronic as Internet and CD-ROM comics tentatively make their way onto the scene. The dot-com implosion, however, took many pioneering comics-related sites down with it. The future of comics may indeed remain in "hard copy," but possibly in traditional book form rather than as periodicals.

For many years the only real choice for libraries wanting to add comic books to their collections has been to subscribe to selected titles, and then deal with the subsequent preservation and access headaches as best they could. Today, though, a strong case could be made that most libraries wishing to bring the best of contemporary (and classic) comic book stories into their collection would be best served by bypassing the stories in their original comic book format in favor of focusing on building a collection of hard cover and trade paperback volumes and original graphic novels. Such a collection, if chosen thoughtfully, could easily provide a library's clientele with a representative cross section of the very best the comic book medium has to offer, while allowing the library to avoid some of the access and preservation problems alluded to above.

[Note: For the purposes of this discussion, "graphic novels" should be considered books containing graphic narratives that are original to and conceived and designed for this format. Most graphic novels appear in trade paperback format, although some are also published in hardcover. "Trade paperbacks" and hardcover collections refer to books that reprint stories that originally appeared in the comic book (or comic strip) format. Such collections can be either devoted to a single comics series, or specific creator or team of creators, or can be anthologies built around a specific theme or time period, and featuring stories selected from a variety of different series.]

While the authors of this section are not endorsing this as the best single strategy for all libraries to adopt (especially not within the pages of *Magazines for Libraries*), we feel that it is important to make libraries aware of just how much of the best of the comic book medium can be acquired in long-lived, arguably more "library-friendly" traditional book formats. For that reason, we have added a paragraph to the end of many of the entries below discussing the availability of the cited comic book series in trade paperback or hardcover collections. Many of these books richly merit consideration for inclusion in library collections.

DC Comics in particular is to be commended for their Archives series of quality (and expensive) hardback reprint collections of classic material. Over eighty Archives volumes have been published thus far, covering such series as the original *Justice Society of America, Superman, Batman, Plastic Man, Wonder Woman, The Flash* (both Silver Age and Golden Age versions), *Green Lantern* (also both Silver and Golden Age versions), and the original *Captain Marvel.* Particularly noteworthy is the award-winning *Spirit Archives* series, which will eventually constitute a permanent library of the masterfully written and drawn early stories of Will Eisner's classic creation.

For their part, Marvel Comics has recently relaunched its Marvel Masterworks series of reprint collections, in both hardback and more affordable paperback editions, re-presenting classic early adventures of characters such as Spider-Man, X-Men, Fantastic Four, Daredevil, Hulk, Captain America, Thor, and the Avengers. Complementing these volumes is the less expensive "Essential" series, which offers much larger collections of stories, but in black-and-white trade paperbacks, printed on much cheaper paper.

And, as already mentioned, CrossGen has been particularly systematic in repacking and reprinting in trade paperback format the adventures of the company's various characters.

Librarians around the United States are discovering that there is a whole world of art and entertainment just waiting to be enjoyed by otherwise reluctant library users. Try comic books in your library. Respect them, promote them, then stand back and watch what happens!

(Statistics provided above were provided by John Jackson Miller, the editor of *Comics & Games Retailer,* the monthly trade magazine for the comics industry [available to all the retailers and publishers] and editorial director of the Comics & Games Division of Krause Publications, "The World's Largest Hobby Publisher.")

General

1808. ***Amazing Spider-Man.*** [ISSN: 0274-5232] 1963. m. Ed(s): Axel Alonso. Marvel Comics Group, 10 E. 40th St., New York, NY 10016; mail@marvel.com; http://www.marvel.com. *Aud.:* Ems, Hs, Ga.

Spidey's back! He never went away, you say? Well, Spider-Man made his comics debut nearly forty years ago, and any continuously published series that's been around for that long is bound to grow a bit stale over time. Certainly the Webspinner spent much of the 1990s in a creative doldrums (as did many other longtime Marvel characters). Happily, the dawn of a new century heralded a new beginning for the wondrous Wallcrawler. First came the launch of *Ultimate Spider-Man,* an ongoing series set outside of the mainstream Marvel Universe and its established continuity and internal history. The *Ultimate* books are designed to appeal to a wider, more broadly based audience than the readership attracted to comic books through their primary outlet of comics specialty shops. Not required to follow established "Marvel Universe" continuity, this new imprint allows creators such as Brian Michael Bendis (*Ultimate Spider-Man*) and Mark Millar (*Ultimate X-Men* and *The Ultimates*) to take a different approach with some of Marvel's premier characters and their histories. In the case of Bendis and his *Ultimate Spider-Man* collaborator, artist Mark Bagley, the result has been a fresh and entertaining look at a Spider-Man who (in the Ultimate universe) is once more a fifteen-year-old high-schooler just beginning to come to grips with his newfound powers. Readily accessible even to the newest reader, the expertly done *Ultimate Spider-Man* is highly recommended to libraries, and could easily stand as the Spider-Man book to purchase. But thanks to another top-notch writer, Peter Parker's original home, *Amazing Spider-Man,* has re-energized itself to the point where it deserves equal consideration. The writer who has brought the "buzz" back to Spider-Man's flagship title is J. Michael Straczynski (a.k.a. JMS), best known as the creative force behind the award-wining television series *Babylon 5.* In collaboration with penciller John Romita, Jr., JMS has brought a real sense of excitement the book, and made it once more a "must-read" for virtually all fans of superhero comics.

Other Spider-Man titles include *Peter Parker, Spider-Man* and *Tangled Webs,* both of which are set in the mainstream Marvel universe, and *Ultimate Marvel Team-Up,* which pairs Spider-Man with a succession of co-stars such as Wolverine, the Hulk, Iron Man, and Captain America. Each of these stalwarts gets both a different top-notch artist for his/her/their story, and an Ultimate universe "rethinking" along the same lines as the one given to Spidey himself. *Ultimate Marvel Team-Up* is recommended to libraries looking to add a third Spider-Man title to go with *Ultimate Spider-Man* and *Amazing Spider-Man.*

Early issues of *Ultimate Spider-Man* have already been gathered into a trade paperback, and more will be doubtless forthcoming. Similarly, one can expect that trade paperback collection of current issues of *Amazing Spider-Man* and *Ultimate Marvel Team-Up* will appear in due course. In the meantime, a veritable library of vintage Spider-Man adventures are available in numerous trade paperback collections, most notably the *Essential Spider-Man* volumes, which collect over 500 pages of stories within their covers (albeit in black and white rather than in full color) at a very affordable price (currently $14.95). (DH)

1809. ***Archie.*** 1942. m. USD 21.48. Ed(s): Victor Gorelick. Archie Comic Publications, Inc., 325 Fayette Ave, Mamaroneck, NY 10543-2318; talkback@archiecomics.com/; http://www.archiecomics.com. *Aud.:* Ems, Hs, Ga.

Comic books are replete with characters who are incredibly long-lived or even theoretically immortal. But if there were one comic book character who could truly be considered to be ageless, it would have to be Archie Andrews, the pride and joy of Riverdale High School, and Dick Clark's only rival to the title of "World's Oldest Teenager." Sixty-plus years after his debut in 1941, Archie maintains a publishing pace that even the estimable Mr. Clark would be hard-pressed to emulate. Probably the ultimate "franchise" character in the history of comics publishing, Archie has an entire comics company (i.e., Archie Comics) named after him. The energetic redhead appears in several comics every month—either as star or in support of such pals'n'gals as Betty, Veronica, Reggie, and the one-and-only Jughead. Archie and company seem destined to remain locked in a neverland of perpetual high school, and the appeal of Archie Comics for older readers remains almost exclusively nostalgic. Still, the publisher has made efforts to keep the characters relatively current by having them occasionally confront such pressing contemporary issues as hunger, illiteracy, and pollution. Also adding a bit of spice to the mix is *Archie's Mysteries,* which, as the title indicates, puts our hero and his gang in somewhat more perilous situations than they usually encounter (albeit always with happy results). *Archie's Mysteries* is also notable for superhero fans due to recent welcome guest appearances in its pages of the little-seen super-team, the Mighty Crusaders. (The Crusaders have shown up twice in the book as of this writing.) In addition to the Archie-related titles (which also include *Archie and Friends, Betty & Veronica, Jughead,* and others), Archie Comics is also home to *Sabrina the Teenage Witch, Sonic the Hedgehog,* and, occasionally, *Josie and the Pussycats.*

Libraries interested in acquiring trade paperback collections of Archie Comics' stories will be interested in the *Archie Americana* "Best of the Decade" series. (DH)

1810. ***The Avengers.*** [ISSN: 0274-5240] 1998. m. USD 27. Ed(s): Tom Breevort. Marvel Comics Group, 10 E. 40th St., New York, NY 10016; mail@marvel.com; http://www.marvel.com. *Aud.:* Ems, Hs, Ga.

Marvel's mightiest solo heroes unite monthly in what is, of late, a solid example of mainstream superheroic storytelling. Though the lineup may change, you may expect to see the likes of Captain America, Iron Man, the Norse god Thor, in league against whatever may threaten our planet.

Marvel publishes several other books that might be considered part of an unofficial family of Avenger-related titles. The three most popular members of the team—Thor, Captain America, and Iron Man—each stars in his own solo monthly book, as does fellow-Avenger the Black Panther. All four are, like *Avengers,* reasonable candidates for purchase by libraries.

Avengers issues are being regularly being collected in trade paperback form. Older issues of the original run of the book are available both as volumes of the Marvel Masterworks series, as well as in the Essentials series of mammoth (500+ pages), inexpensive, black-and-white trade paperbacks. The same is true for Thor, Captain America, and Iron Man. (DH)

1811. ***Batman Adventures.*** 2003. m. USD 27; USD 2.25 newsstand/cover. D C Comics, 1700 Broadway, New York, NY 10019; dcconline@aol.com; http://www.dccomics.com/. *Aud.:* Ems, Hs, Ga.

No one should approach the Batman family of comic books expecting the 1960s TV-show silliness or the bad storytelling of the popular motion picture series. It's all darkness, grit, and violence, as Bruce Wayne continues his obsessive war on crime in several Bat-titles. The main Batman continuity is chronicled in the monthly *Batman, Detective Comics,* and *Batman: Gotham Knights.* Several of Batman's partners against crime also have their own regular titles, including Robin, Nightwing, and Batgirl. Unfortunately, storylines may cross over between these and other titles, making subscriptions to one and not others a problem. Another title, *Batman: Legends of the Dark Knight,* usually takes place outside the ongoing continuity, and is a series of mini-series within a series as creators offer their takes on what makes Batman tick. Significant storylines from the comics, such as *Bruce Wayne: Fugitive* and *Batman: A Death in the Family,* are offered as trade paperbacks, while many other mini-series and graphic novels contribute to the overkill of the Batman franchise. Most highly recommended, however, is *Batman Adventures,* which promises to carry on the tradition of former Bat-titles that were based on the animated version of Batman that were proven so successful for the WB and Fox TV networks. Here, Batman and his colleagues are given a lighter, simpler approach, making it an excellent choice for younger readers, as well as for older readers who may not care for the *Sturm und Drang* of the "official" continuity. Perhaps best of all, the stories are told in single issues. What a concept! See also *Birds of Prey.*

1812. ***Birds of Prey.*** 1999. m. USD 30. D C Comics, 1700 Broadway, New York, NY 10019; dcconline@aol.com. *Aud.:* Ems, Ga, Hs.

Never mind that their TV series on the WB Network did not fly. *Birds of Prey* focuses on the crimebusting activities of Black Canary and Oracle, two of comics' most interesting female characters, who are remarkably well rounded in more than the comics' conventional physical sense. The Black Canary, daughter of the Golden Age character of the same name, is a resourceful martial artist who don't take no $#&% from nobody. Oracle is Barbara Gordon, former librarian and Batgirl, who uses her training in these roles as a mistress of information technology since a disability limits her physical effectiveness. As such, she is the DC universe's *deus ex machina,* able to manipulate computer technology to do her every whim. From her hidden lair, she directs Black Canary as they quite effectively bring down the bad guys. An excellent superhero title for (but not just for!) female readers. At least one trade collection has been published, *Birds of Prey: Old Friends, New Enemies.* The presence of Oracle makes *Birds of Prey* a peripheral Batman title, and the same goes for a "Bat-villain" (more like "Bat-anti-hero") with her own title, *Catwoman. Catwoman* also features a strong, independent female hero, and though its "urban jungle" setting makes it for more of a mature audience, it, too, is highly recommended. (AE)

1813. ***Buffy the Vampire Slayer.*** 1998. m. USD 2.95 newsstand/cover per issue. Ed(s): Scott Allie. Dark Horse Comics, 10956 SE Main St, Milwaukie, OR 97222; dhs@dhorse.com; http://www.darkhorse.com. *Aud.:* Ems, Hs, Ga.

From the literary landmarks that appeared in *Classics Illustrated* to Edgar Rice Burroughs's Tarzan of the Apes; from Disney's Mickey Mouse and Donald Duck to Lucas's Luke Skywalker and Darth Vader, any number of characters and concepts have made a successful transition from other storytelling media into comic books. Licensing costs and owner-imposed storytelling restrictions have helped to substantially reduce the number of comic book adaptations of other-media property in recent years. One company that has been successful in bucking the trend away from comics adaptations of licensed properties is Dark Horse Comics. Dark Horse's stable includes *Star Wars* (which appears in both one ongoing monthly series and a variety of limited series), and Joss Whedon's *Buffy the Vampire Slayer,* who also holds down her own ongoing monthly title. Buffy's vampire-with-a-soul, Angel, has been spun off into his own comic book series in parallel with his being granted his own television series. Angel's book, though, has now ceased ongoing monthly publication in favor of self-contained limited series. Other members of the Buffy supporting cast also appear from time to time in miniseries or one-shot specials of their own, attesting to the continuing popularity of Whedon's characters. While Buffy's own book is indeed an ongoing story, most Buffy adventures are multi-issue story arcs, in effect making the *Buffy* comic a succession of miniseries. Admittedly, the typical issue of the comic book does not fully capture the sharp dialogue and insightful characterization of the TV series. Nevertheless, the comic book adventures of Buffy and the Scooby Gang are consistently enjoyable in their own right, and they merit consideration by libraries wishing to add comic books to their holdings. Given the multi-issue story arc format that *Buffy* utilizes, it is to be expected that Buffy trade paperbacks appear regularly, as indeed is the case. These paperback collections offer an attractive alternative to libraries that want to appeal to Buffy's comics-reading fans without subscribing to the ongoing series. (DH)

1814. ***Comics Revue: 50 pages of your favorite comic strips.*** Formerly: *Comics Review.* 1983. m. USD 45 domestic; USD 60 foreign. Ed(s): Rick Norwood. Manuscript Press, Inc., PO Box 336, Mountain Home, TN 37684. Circ: 3000. *Aud.:* Ems, Hs, Ga.

There are a number of publications devoted to comic strips, and these help address the frustration of comic strip enthusiasts whose hometown newspapers may not carry particular strips. In *Comics Revue,* the emphasis is on adventure strips, which appear in fewer and fewer newspapers. Although the lineup is subject to change, each issue has more than 60 pages with several weeks' worth of such current and classic strips as *The Phantom, Buz Sawyer, Modesty Blaise,* Harold Gray's *Little Orphan Annie,* George Herriman's *Krazy Kat,* and *Tarzan of the Apes.* All strips are in black and white, except for what might appear on the cover. (AE)

1815. *Daredevil.* [ISSN: 0279-8271] 1964. m. USD 30. Ed(s): Nancy Dakesian. Marvel Comics Group, 10 E. 40th St., New York, NY 10016; mail@marvel.com; http://www.marvel.com. *Aud.:* Ems, Hs, Ga.

While certainly not the first blind superhero, Daredevil finds continually interesting ways around what would seem to be an insurmountable disability. The fact that his secret identity as attorney Matt Murdock has been revealed to the world does not help things, however. Following the groundbreaking run on the book by Frank Miller several years ago, *Daredevil* essentially languished, seemingly in danger of becoming permanently lost in the shuffle among Marvel's many long-running superhero titles. Sharing the credit for restoring *Daredevil* to past glories with was filmmaker Kevin Smith, who wrote the first multi-issue story arc of *Daredevil* under the "Marvel Knights" imprint. Since then, *Daredevil's* newfound popularity has remained undiminished—surviving even a yearlong stretch that saw the publication of only five issues of the supposedly monthly title. Reflecting this popularity was the release of the *Daredevil* motion picture in 2003, which, while not a blockbuster at the level of *Spider-Man,* still sat atop the box-office lists for a time and pulled in enough money to make the filming of one or more sequels a strong possibility.

Although not specifically targeted to "mature audiences," *Daredevil* is likely to be most in demand by and most suitable for older comics readers. *Daredevil* is the headliner title for the Marvel Knights imprint (although since the Avengers' Captain America's solo book is also now published under the same imprint, an argument could be made that he at least contests DD for that headliner status). Also published under the Marvel Knights imprint are the adventures of the Punisher—a once wildly popular character who fell on even harder times than Daredevil, but who has regained a substantial portion of his former popularity in his Marvel Knights incarnation.

Nearly everything that appears under the Marvel Knights banner makes its way quickly into trade paperback form, and may be more attractive to many libraries in that format. In addition to the collections of his recent story arcs, Daredevil has been around long enough that his earliest adventures are being included in both the Marvel Masterworks series and the Essentials line of cheap, massive, black-and-white collections. (DH)

1816. *Fantastic Four.* [ISSN: 0274-5291] 1961. m. USD 27. Ed(s): Bobbie Chase. Marvel Comics Group, 10 E. 40th St., New York, NY 10016; mail@marvel.com; http://www.marvel.com. *Aud.:* Ems, Ga, Hs.

Created by the legendary team of writer Stan Lee and artist Jack Kirby in 1961, *Fantastic Four* has been going strong for well over forty years now. During that time, the book has built a remarkably rich internal history (classic characters such as the Silver Surfer, the Black Panther, and the Inhumans made their debuts in its pages), and with the greatest super-villain of them all, Dr. Doom, frequently on hand as the team's primary antagonist. Thanks to such characters, and thanks most of all to the storytelling of Lee and Kirby, the book has for much of its storied run richly deserved the "World's Greatest Comic Magazine" sobriquet that graces its cover. Unfortunately, the 1990s was a decade in which fans of the team were hard-pressed to say that *Fantastic Four* lived up to that billing, but capable hands have helped Marvel's oldest title once more lay claim to being worthy of its impressive legacy. While every competent new creative team brings something fresh to the book, what makes it work, ultimately, is the relationship between its four main characters, established at the series' outset by Lee and Kirby. More than just a team, the FF—Reed (Mr. Fantastic) Richards; his wife, Susan (Invisible Woman) Storm Richards; her brother, Johnny (the Human Torch) Storm; and family friend Ben (the Thing) Grimm—is the First Family of superhero comic books. It is this family dynamic (also involving Reed and Sue's young son, Franklin, and their infant daughter Valeria) that has enabled the book to survive during lean times and to remain as vital in the twenty-first century as it was in the middle of the twentieth. It should be mentioned that the youngest member of the FF, the hot-tempered Human Torch, has been awarded his own ongoing monthly comic book. It is, however, too soon to tell how successful or how in-demand this new title will prove to be.

As with other Marvel titles, libraries interested in providing their users with adventures of the Fantastic Four in book rather than periodical form have various options. Early classic adventures can be found most readily in the Essentials black-and-white trade paperback series, and are also in the full-color Marvel Masterworks series. More contemporary adventures are available in a variety of stand-alone collections. (DH)

1817. *Green Arrow.* 2001. m. USD 30. D C Comics, 1700 Broadway, New York, NY 10019; dcconline@aol.com; http://www.dccomics.com/. *Aud.:* Hs, Ga.

Green Arrow first appeared in 1941 as not so much a Robin Hood ripoff as Batman ripoff. He was rich millionaire Oliver Queen, with a kid sidekick (Speedy), an Arrowcave, an Arrowcar, an Arrowplane (!), and a physics-defying quiver full of physics-defying arrows (most infamously, the "boxing-glove arrow"). In the 1960s he lost his fortune, gained a personality, and was portrayed as a loudmouthed liberal reactionary. In the 1980s he eschewed his trick arrows for real ones, becoming a murderous vigilante. In 1995 he died. In 2001 he got better, revived by filmmaker Kevin Smith. Now, he is portrayed as one of DC's more mature characters (physically if not emotionally—but he is working on that), who is adjusting to having been dead, having screwed up most of his relationships, and being a non-superpowered archer in a world of superheroes. Hot tempered, chauvinistic, stubborn, violent, and generally maddening, Oliver Queen has a complicated personal life in addition to fighting the occasional criminal. Besides Smith, *Green Arrow* has attracted other "celebrity" creators, such as *New York Times* bestselling author Brad Melzer and MTV's *Real World* alumnus Judd Winick, and this has made the book a fan favorite and certainly one to watch. Look for trade paperback collections, such as Kevin Smith's *Quiver,*and *Sounds of Violence.*(AE)

1818. *J L A.* 1997. m. USD 27. Ed(s): Mike Carlin, Dan Raspler. D C Comics, 1700 Broadway, New York, NY 10019; dcmarc@aol.com; http://www.dccomics.com/. *Aud.:* Ems, Hs, Ga.

DC Comics invented the concept of various superheroes uniting in a common cause with the Justice Society of America in the 1940s (see *JSA,* below). The tradition continues with the Justice League of America (JLA), which has been around since 1960 in one form or another. While the lineup may fluctuate, expect to see some combination of DC's classic "big three": Superman, Batman, and Wonder Woman, along with Flash, Green Lantern, Aquaman, the Martian Manhunter, or possibly others. The overall appeal, of course, is in seeing the interaction between favorite characters as they face menaces theoretically too tough for them to handle individually. Of late, this has been accomplished in a consistently entertaining manner. Also worthy of library consideration is *Justice League Adventures,* based on the hit Cartoon Network animated series. *Justice League Adventures* presents the Justice League in a less complex fashion (like *Batman Adventures,* above) making it an excellent choice for younger readers, as well as for older readers who may find the "official" continuity of *JLA* too grim or too convoluted. Story arcs are regularly collected into trade paperback form, e.g., *JLA: New World Order* and *JLA: American Dreams.* (AE)

1819. *J S A.* 1999. m. USD 30. Ed(s): Peter Tomasi. D C Comics, 1700 Broadway, New York, NY 10019; dccommail@aol.com; http://www.dccomics.com/. *Aud.:* Hs, Ga, Ems.

Granddaddy of all comic book superhero teams, the Justice Society of America made its debut in 1940 in the pages of *All-Star Comics #3.* The team's original series lasted until 1951, and, for many, its demise marks the official end of comics' Golden Age. Aside from a shortlived series in the mid-1970s, the JSA has spent the past half-century functioning primarily as guest stars in other DC comic books—most notably, *Justice League of America,* home of the JSA's direct successor as DC Comics' premier superteam (for more, see *JLA* above). Following the JLA's extremely successful relaunch in 1997, *JSA* proved to be one of the most successful title launches of the late 1990s, surviving and (relatively speaking) thriving despite the tough economic climate facing the contemporary comic book industry. While *JSA* adventures are often steeped in the sixty-plus year history of DC Comics, stories are nevertheless easily accessible to newer readers. Still, because of the inherent nostalgia appeal, *JSA* is likely to be of greatest interest to older teen and adult comic book readers.

At the moment, the only active JSA member who stars in his/her own title is *Hawkman*, co-starring with fellow JSAer Hawkgirl. *Hawkman* should appeal to many of the same readers who enjoy *JSA*. So far, all major story arcs in *JSA* are being collected in trade paperback format soon after publication, while at least one Hawkman trade paperback collection has appeared as well. These books are highly recommended for purchase by libraries wishing to own the best in contemporary superhero comics. Those wishing to own the best in classic Golden Age superheroics should be sure to pick up DC's *All-Star Comics Archives* editions. This series of hardcover books is reprinting in chronological order all the original 1940s adventures of the Justice Society of America as they appeared in the pages of *All-Star Comics*. (DH)

1820. *Kabuki.* 1997. irreg. USD 2.95 newsstand/cover per issue. Ed(s): David Mack. Image Comics, 1071 N Batavia St, Ste A, Orange, CA 92867; http://www.imagecomics.com/. *Aud.:* Hs, Ga.

Writer/artist David Mack's visionary *Kabuki* may be the most sophisticated comic book on the market today. His stories are intense psychological and emotional studies that set *Kabuki* well above other Asian-oriented comics. The themes are profound, the stories are evocative, and the prose is lyrical: intellectualism as rarely achieved in comic form. Mack's superb watercolor artwork pulls the reader into the dreamlike narrative unlike any other comic. In addition, his familiarity with Japanese culture and history is quite impressive and brings more depth to *Kabuki* than most Pacific-rim theme comics. Mack's work is often said to be "disturbing." Indeed, it is. The reader is forced to seriously contemplate the story at hand, the characters, and the setting. To many interested only in "brain candy" comics, this book is the equivalent of Kafka on mescaline. For that reason alone, *Kabuki* should be required reading in college psychology courses. It has a strong appeal to older adolescents and adults, and generally the themes would not be readily understood by younger readers. Further, *Kabuki*'s popularity and readership has grown significantly since becoming part of the Image family in 1997 (having been previously published by Caliber). Many of the earlier stories in the series have been collected into graphic novels (trade paperbacks and hardcovers) and published anew by Image, thus allowing a reader new to the series to follow the full story line. Titles in the series include *Circle of Blood, Dreams, Masks of the Noh, Metamorphosis, Agents: Scarab, Skin Deep, Reflections* (sketches, designs, etc.), and *Images* (poster art). (RA)

1821. *Liberty Meadows.* 1999. bi-w. USD 2.95 newsstand/cover per issue. Image Comics, 1071 N Batavia St, Ste A, Orange, CA 92867; http://www.imagecomics.com/. *Aud.:* Hs,Ga.

Well, this *is* an oddity: a "funny book" that is, by most standards, actually funny. *Liberty Meadows* revolves around the adventures of the personnel and patients at a veterinary hospital, including veterinarian Frank, who secretly longs for the stunningly beautiful "animal psychiatrist" Brandy, as they both deal with a host of anthropomorphic trouble makers, among others. *Liberty Meadows* was originally a syndicated newspaper comic strip until writer/artist Frank Cho had his fill of weak-kneed newspaper editors who did not always appreciate his sense of humor or his politically incorrect appreciation for the female form. The award-winning Cho is one of the comics medium's most gifted illustrators, and this title would be amazing to look at even were it not well written. Wildly inventive and—again— funny. (AE)

1822. *The Powerpuff Girls.* 2000. m. USD 27. Ed(s): Joan Hilty. D C Comics, 1700 Broadway, New York, NY 10019; dcocartoon@aol.com; http://www.dccomics.com/. *Aud.:* Ems, Hs, Ga.

Based on the hit Cartoon Network animated series, the Powerpuff Girls, Blossom, Bubbles, and Buttercup none-too-delicately use their superpowers to protect Townsville from whatever harm they themselves don't cause. Wonderfully wild, silly, cartoonish nonsense, but, importantly, one of those rare comic books that can be enjoyed by all ages, especially children, especially *young* children, for whom there are far too few comic books available. DC Comics is a leader in providing kids' comics, publishing such titles as *Cartoon Cartoons*, featuring other Cartoon Network favorites (Dexter's Laboratory, Johnny Bravo, and Cow & Chicken); and *Looney Tunes* starring the Warner Brothers stable of cartoon stars, such as Bugs Bunny, Daffy Duck, Elmer Fudd, and so forth, and which passed its 100th issue in 2003. (AE)

1823. *Powers.* 2000. m. USD 2.95 newsstand/cover per issue. Ed(s): K C McCrory. Image Comics, 1071 N Batavia St, Ste A, Orange, CA 92867; http://www.imagecomics.com/. *Aud.:* Ga, Hs.

Arriving on the scene in the early 1990s, Image Comics has been one of the industry's dominant players for the past decade—seemingly poised at one time to displace DC Comics as the second-largest comic book publishers. Those heady days are gone now, particularly after the departures of Image co-founders Jim Lee, who sold his Wildstorm Publications operation to DC, and Rob Leifeld, who struck out none too successfully on his own after coming to a parting of the ways with his partners at Image. Nevertheless, Image—home of Todd Macfarlene's *Spawn, Witchblade, Tomb Raider,* and the other titles published under Marc Silvestri's Top Cow imprint; and home of Eric Larsen's venerable *Savage Dragon*—remains a major force on the comics scene. As has always been the case, Image, which still functions more as a coalition of semi-independent imprints than the traditional monolithic comics publisher, offers a rather eclectic line. Some surviving Image titles still tend to emphasize artwork over storytelling, but happily, one can now find some of the best written contemporary comics at Image as well. Notable among these are the books being written for Top Cow by J. Michael Straczynski, *Rising Stars* and the recently completed *Midnight Nation.* As limited series, these titles have not been included in this chapter, but the trade paperback reprint collections of both are strongly recommended for purchase consideration. An equally strong recommendation can be given to another relatively new but ongoing series at Image—Brian Michael Bendis's *Powers,* which chronicles the adventures of homicide cop Christian Walker and his partner, Deena Pilgrim, who investigate murders involving the superpowered heroes and villains who populate their world. One of the most intriguing aspects of the series is that Walker himself is a former superhero, who operated under the codename of Diamond until his powers mysteriously disappeared and he was forced to look for another line of work. *Powers* succeeds on many levels. It functions effectively both as a classical whodunit, and as a character study of Detectives Walker and Pilgrim and their fellow inhabitants of a world in which superpowered beings operate both within and outside the law. In addition, *Powers* serves as one of the best examples of a trend that helped to successfully reinvigorate superhero comic book storytelling during the latter part of the 1990s. This approach, pioneered by Kurt Busiek and Alex Ross in the (highly recommended in reprint) *Marvels* limited series, provides a "street-level" point of view of a world populated by superpowered beings, chronicling how their presence and their actions impact the lives of ordinary citizens. Given its mature plots and storytelling, *Powers* is best suited for readers of high school age and older.

The book's first major story arc, "Powers: Who Killed Retro Girl?," has already been collected into a trade paperback that belongs on the shelves on many libraries. Subsequent story arcs have similarly been collected and released in trade paperback form. Another Bendis-written trade paperback worthy of library consideration is *Torso,* which depicts Elliot Ness's search for a serial killer in his post-Untouchables days as head of Public Safety in Cleveland. (DH)

1824. *The Red Star.* 2000. irreg. USD 2.95 newsstand/cover per issue. Archangel Studios, 11642 Camarillo St, No.9, North Hollywood, CA 91602. *Aud.:* Hs, Ga, Ac.

This fascinating series is told from the points of view of several characters from the United Republics of the Red Star (U.R.R.S.), which appears to encompass countries once belonging to the Soviet Union. The setting is in a future time unknown to the reader and we retrospectively learn about a war fought against the Nistaani people of Al'Istaan—an unknown Muslim country situated in what would be largely Afghanistan today. The war which ended nine years ago was a crushing defeat for the Red Star armies at the Battle of Kar Dathra's Gate. Although the plot is somewhat muddled (numerous story lines have been introduced recently), readers will enjoy the combination of history, politics, spiritualism, nationalism, and human drama in this book. Lay this upon the canvas of three-dimensional backgrounds created by Allen Coulter, and *The Red Star* is a interesting, complex comic book that is enjoyable to read over and over again. Each issue includes a lexicon with pronunciation help, definitions, and background information not directly mentioned in the story line. Overall, the stories are directed toward adolescents and adults, though some parents may object to the violent scenes for younger teens. Numerous publishing problems have plagued this title from its beginning. Team Red Star left Image Comics in 2002 and briefly partnered with CrossGen Entertainment. That partnership has since ended and *The Red Star* has resumed publication as an independent comic. Titles in the series include *Makita* and *The Red Star* (trade paperbacks and hardcovers). (RA)

1825. *Ruse.* 2001. m. USD 2.95 newsstand/cover. CrossGen Entertainment, Inc., 4023 Tampa Rd, Ste 2400, Oldsmar, FL 34677; info@crossgen.com; http://www.crossgen.com/. *Aud.:* Ems, Hs, Ga.

While controversial in some comics circles for some of their behind-the-scenes publishing and editorial policies and practices, CrossGen Publications has been a reliable source of smoothly put together and generally interesting comic books since arriving on the scene at the tail end of the last century. Setting its core titles on various worlds in a shared universe, and eschewing protagonists who don colorful costumes and adopt dramatic codenames in an ongoing fight against evil, CrossGen has rolled out a line-up of titles that meld elements of science fiction (e.g., *Sigil*), heroic fantasy (*Scion, Mystic*), horror (*Route 666*), and high adventure (*Sojourn*)—even while offering enough superpowered action in books such as *Crux* to appeal to the fan of traditional superheroic fare. Relying on veteran writers (Barbara Kesel, Ron Marz, Chuck Dixon, et al.) and a stable of excellent-to-above-average artists (George Perez, Greg Land, Butch Guice, and Bart Sears among them), CrossGen has been able to maintain a consistent level of quality, as well as a very reliable publishing schedule. Also notable is CrossGen?s frequent use of strong and appealing female protagonists in books such as the excellent *Meridian* and the aforementioned *Sojourn, Mystic,* and *Route 666,* making CrossGen one of the most "female friendly" of the major comic book companies. Another area in which CrossGen has been an industry leader is in the consistent, regular repacking and reprinting of their materials into library-friendly formats. Every CrossGen title that has been around long enough has had its issues collected and reprinted in handsome and relatively affordable trade paperbacks.

All of this makes choosing any one particular CrossGen title to spotlight rather arbitrary (although had the monthly compendium titles *Edge* and *Forge* not been cancelled the choice would have been very easy indeed). While both *Meridian* and *Scion* deserve serious consideration to be singled out, the award-nominated *Ruse* gets the nod. Stylishly drawn by Jackson "Butch" Guice, *Ruse* chronicles the adventures of master detective Simon Archard and his helper (or partner, depending upon who's describing the relationship) Emma Bishop. Although the setting is the city of Paddington on a planet that isn?t even Earth, the look and the feel is, quite intentionally, that of Victorian London—albeit a London replete with technological wonders (both good and bad) more reminiscent of Jules Verne than of Arthur Conan Doyle and Sherlock Holmes—with the adventures and interplay of Archard and Bishop echoing as much the relationship between TV's *Avengers* John Steed and Emma Peel as that of Holmes and Watson. Again, *Ruse* is only one of several CrossGen titles that libraries might want to consider—and all CrossGen series are probably best acquired in trade paperback format rather than by subscription to the monthly issues (which the publisher, to date, does not offer). (DH)

1826. *Simpsons Comics.* [ISSN: 1073-6395] 1993. bi-m. USD 2.50 newsstand/cover per issue. Ed(s): Bill Morrison. Bongo Comics, 1440 S Sepulveda Blvd, Third Fl, Los Angeles, CA 90025; bongo@primenet.com. *Aud.:* Ems, Hs, Ga.

Rather than license the characters to an established comics publisher, Simpsons creator Matt Groening joined with others to launch their own company—Bongo Comics—to bring his popular cartoon creations onto the comics page. And a decade later, the comic book is still going strong (as is the animated series that spawned it). While Mr. Groening's direct involvement in the actual writing and drawing of *Simpsons Comics* has been minimal, he nonetheless has managed to a surprisingly large degree to transfer the sensibilities of the TV series into the comic books. While the quality of the book arguably declined when the original team of writers left after a dozen issues, those who enjoy the antics of Homer, Marge, Bart, et al., on the Fox network are still likely to enjoy the nuclear family's similar misadventures in *Simpsons Comics.*

Given the current economic climate for comic books, Bongo Comics has been only sporadically successful in expanding its lineup beyond the monthly *Simpsons Comics.* Currently, however, Bongo does offer a second regularly published title: *Futurama Comics,* based on Groening & Company's now-cancelled other animated primetime series. Appearing more sporadically are occasional comics focusing on Bart Simpson or other members of his clan, as well as a book starring Bart's favorite comic book hero, Radioactive Man.

Although they do not appear as regularly as do other trade paperback collections, issues of *Simpsons Comics* and other Bongo Comics are occasionally reprinted in book format. (DH)

1827. *Spawn.* 1992. m. USD 2.50 newsstand/cover per issue. Image Comics, 1071 N Batavia St, Ste A, Orange, CA 92867; http://www.imagecomics.com/. *Aud.:* Ga, Hs.

Few comics of the 1990s achieved the level of success and rabid fandom as that of *Spawn.* To be certain, *Spawn* was *the* most successful comic enterprise of the last quarter of the twentieth century and may eventually surpass Superman and Batman in its marketability. Not only is the series well over 125 issues, but it has "spawned" (who could resist?) three animated series for Home Box Office, a live-action motion picture, trading cards, games (video and collectible cards), a full line of action figures, as well as numerous other collectible fandom products. The first issue sold an amazing 1.7 million copies; it is purported to be the best-selling independent comic book in printing history. *Spawn* has consistently been in the top five best-selling comics since its debut, with total sales of over 133 million issues in 120 countries and 16 languages.

The stories involve classic themes of love and hate, repentance and redemption, light and dark, and good versus evil. To distill the story lines to these levels is a great understatement and unfair, but they are powerful, pervasive themes in much of great Western literature. Al Simmons was an army-trained operative, doublecrossed and assassinated by a manipulative superior. He awakens one day as HellSpawn with flashes of past memories and no understanding of who or what he has become. Over time, Simmons learns that he has bargained with Malebolgia for a return trip to Earth to see his wife Wanda five years after his death. The bargain obligates Simmons to lead the forces of darkness against Heaven in the coming Armageddon. But, of course, things only get more complicated from there. Spawn is an introspective character haunted by feelings of love and betrayal. He develops a cadre of unlikely allies, including a renegade angel from Heaven, the enigmatic and beautiful Angela. Spawn is not your father's superhero. Numerous writers (namely, Neil Gaiman, Brian Holguin, Frank Miller, and Alan Moore) have contributed to the *Spawn* story arc, keeping it fresh over the last nine years. As well, several characters from the series have been given special one-shots, mini-series, and ongoing series of their own. Other titles in the *Spawn* universe include *Angela* (1994), *Curse of the Spawn* (1996), *Cy-Gor* (1999), *Hellspawn* (2000), *Sam and Twitch* (1999), *Spawn: The Dark Ages* (1999), and *Spawn: The Undead* (1999). *Sam and Twitch* is a notable continuing series named for two police officers introduced in the first *Spawn*, and is worthy of acquisition by libraries.

Spawn is a visual paradise for the comics lover. Beautiful artwork from Todd McFarlane and Greg Capullo have dominated the series providing layer upon layer of haunting textures and terrifying nightmares. The graphic violence, occasional nudity, and adult stories are not suitable for younger audiences. However, with parental approval, *Spawn* is an acceptable book for middle-school children. Librarians will find that *Spawn, Angela,* and *Curse of the Spawn* have all been collected and published as trade paperbacks, making them more friendly for circulation. (RA)

1828. *Strangers in Paradise.* 1996. 6 every x wks. USD 2.75 newsstand/cover per issue. Ed(s): Robyn Moore. Abstract Studios, PO Box 271487, Houston, TX 77277-1487; spinet@strangersinparadise,com; http://www.strangersinparadise.com. *Aud.:* Hs, Ga.

Aside from humor titles such as *Archie, Liberty Meadows,* and *The Simpsons, Strangers in Paradise* is about as far removed from a superhero comic book as can be found on this list. This does not mean the lives of Francine and her best friend Katchoo are devoid of adventure—far from it. Katchoo, after all, has lived one of the most colorful lives imaginable, most notably as the employee of a ruthless criminal mastermind. But the focus of Terry Moore's consistently excellent series has been resolutely on the personalities and personal lives of the resourceful and deadly Katchoo and her more mundane but equally fascinating longtime friend, the much-put-upon but ultimately resilient Francine. The result has been one of the most compellingly comic books of the past decade—one that should have a presence in any library with any holdings at all in graphic literature. Although being recommended for consideration by libraries in its original comic book format, *Strangers in Paradise* is one of the best examples of the comics series that might find its way into even more libraries in collected form. Issues of *SiP* are being systematically gathered up and reprinted in an excellent series of trade paperbacks. Even libraries that don't choose to purchase the ongoing series are encouraged to seek out these outstanding volumes. (DH)

1829. *Superman.* 1987. m. USD 19.95. D C Comics, 1700 Broadway, New York, NY 10019; dcconline@aol.com; http://www.dccomics.com/. *Aud.:* Ems, Hs, Ga.

Appropriately, some of the best comics in production today feature the guy who, for all intents and purposes, started it all. Aided by his wife, Lois Lane, and fighting such foes as U.S. President Lex Luthor, the Last Son of Krypton is in a never-ending battle for truth, justice, and the American way, and this struggle is chronicled in *Superman, Adventures of Superman,* and *Action Comics.* Surprisingly, although not nearly as grim as the *Batman* titles, the *Superman* titles are not always appropriate for younger readers. Unfortunately as well, subscribers may occasionally find storylines crossing from one title to another. Some librarians may decide that they are best served by collecting major story arcs in trade paperback form, as well as in many of the myriad mini-series and graphic novels devoted to the Man of Steel. (AE)

1830. *Supernatural Law.* Formerly (until 1999): *Wolff & Byrd, Counselors of the Macabre.* 1994. bi-m. USD 2.50 newsstand/cover per issue. Ed(s): Jackie Estrada. Exhibit A Press, 4657 Cajon Way, San Diego, CA 92115; mail@exhibitapress.com; http://www.exhibitapress.com. *Aud.:* Ems, Ga, Hs.

Aside from a title change inspired by the planned *Supernatural Law* movie adaptation, Batton Lash's creation remains what it has always been—one of the best-produced, most intelligent ongoing comic books around. Like Jeff Smith's *Bone* (omitted from this edition of *Magazines for Libraries* because its run is completed), Lash's *Supernatural Law* is a black-and-white comic that deftly blends fantasy/horror elements with marvelous humor. However, whereas *Bone* is set in a fantasy realm of undisclosed locale and uncertain time, *Supernatural Law* is clearly set in the here-and-now of contemporary America. Of course, this is a "here-and-now" in which various creatures of the night, such as those from classic horror literature and films, not only exist, but also are often brought into court to face the civil and criminal repercussions of their antisocial behavior. As the book's title suggests, Alanna Wolff and Jeff Byrd are lawyers specializing in representing such special clients before the law—which they do in a most effective and entertaining manner. In addition to the book's strong element of humor, the depiction of its characters is among the best in comics, and artist/writer Lash's familiarity with lawyers and the law is such that the legal aspects of the book benefit from a strong sense of verisimilitude. Although this entry indicates that its intended audience includes elementary school students, libraries should note that *Supernatural Law* might be both a bit too intense and a bit too sophisticated for the youngest readers.

Aside from the occasional special starring Wolff & Byrd's secretary Mavis, Batton Lash's Exhibit A Press is basically a one-book operation. Happily, collected issues of *Wolff & Byrd/Supernatural Law* occasionally find their way into book form in trade paperback collections. (DH)

1831. *Tom Strong.* 1999. bi-m. USD 2.95 newsstand/cover per issue. Ed(s): Scott Dunbier. America's Best Comics, LLC, 7910 Ivanhoe Ave, #438, La Jolla, CA 92037; http://www.wildstorm.com. *Aud.:* Ga, Hs, Ems.

Along with fellow Englishman Neil Gaiman, Alan Moore has established himself as one of the premier comic book writers of the past twenty years—indeed, of all time. Even more than Gaiman, Moore has been one of the industry's dominant trendsetters in terms of writing style and storytelling sensibilities. Along with Frank Miller's *Batman: the Dark Knight Returns,* Moore's seminal *Watchmen* has been credited (or blamed) with the trend toward "grim-and-gritty" comic book heroes/antiheroes that dominated so much of the industry from the late 1980s until deep into the 1990s. However, disturbed by the excesses and ineptitudes of all too many far less talented writers who followed unsuccessfully in his wake, by the late 1990s Moore was determined to do his part to help put the "fun" back into superhero comic books. This effort started most noticeably in the pages of the late, lamented *Supreme* from Awesome Comics, but has reached its full fruition in the titles being published under the America's Best Comics banner, all of which are fully written by Moore. America's Best Comics are being published under the auspices of Wildstorm Publications, which is in turn an imprint of DC Comics, which bought Wildstorm from founder Jim Lee in 1999. Happily, while the story behind America's Best Comics as a publishing imprint may be a bit convoluted, the stories that Moore tells are not. So far every book that Moore has put out as part of the ABC line has been a winner. These books include the brilliantly written if heavily metaphysical *Promethia* and the multi-series *Tomorrow Stories* (both ongoing titles), and limited series such as *Top Ten* (a superpowered street-cop book) and *The League of Extraordinary Gentlemen.* The latter (the inspiration for the similarly titled major motion picture) offers "new" adventures of an apocryphal team of Victorian stalwarts like Allan Quatemain, the Invisible Man, and Dr. Jekyll and Mr. Hyde. But, while a very good argument could be made that *Promethia* is the best written and most "substantial" of the books in the ABC line, if that line can be said to have a "flagship" title, it would have to be *Tom Strong.* A wonderful pastiche/updating of pulp heroes such as Doc Savage (whom the book's eponymous hero closely resembles in many respects), *Tom Strong* is a near-perfect melding of Moore's remarkable storytelling strengths with his desire to bring a sense of fun back into superhero comics. (Primary artist Chris Sprouse, who also worked with Moore on the aforementioned *Supreme,* presents Tom's adventures in a clean, "heroic" style very much in keeping with the upbeat tone of Moore's stories.) Much like the classic cartoon series *Rocky and Bullwinkle, Tom Strong* entertains on many levels (a trait it shares with *Tomorrow Stories, Promethia,* and the rest of the ABC line), with a surface story sure to entertain younger readers and plenty of subtextual content to keep older readers plenty interested.

Various ABC titles, including the ones mentioned above, have been collected into book form, and are highly recommended for purchase in that format by libraries with any sort of graphic story collection. (DH)

1832. *Ultimate X-Men.* 2001. m. USD 27. Ed(s): Mark Powers. Marvel Comics Group, 10 E. 40th St., New York, NY 10016; mail@marvel.com; http://www.marvel.com. *Aud.:* Ems, Ga, Hs.

Now with two honest-to-gosh successful big budget movies to their credit, Marvel's misunderstood mutants started the twenty-first century where they ended the twentieth—sitting on top of the comic book sales heap. But, since the overall market continues to decline even if the X-Men titles' collective market share remains steady, some major changes have been made in the X-Men family of titles by Marvel's new management. At the time of this writing, the entire line-up of "mainstream" X-Men titles is undergoing a substantial overhaul, with some new titles starting, others being cancelled, and the rest receiving "makeovers" of new creative staff, new characters, and/or new storyline directions. As a result, it is virtually impossible to recommend any one of these titles over any of the others in terms of either quality or future reader demand. Perhaps fortuitously, though, the X-Men, along with Spider-Man, have also been the first to get the "Ultimate" treatment from Marvel. This means that, in addition to all the other X-books, the team is now the star of a new ongoing series set outside of the mainstream Marvel Universe, with its massive established continuity and internal history. Like *Ultimate Spider-Man, Ultimate X-Men* is intended to appeal to a wider, more broadly based audience than simply fans who frequent comics specialty shops. Under the direction of writer Mark Millar and artist Adam Kubert, *Ultimate X-Men* has rocketed to the top of the comic industry?s monthly sales charts, where it joins the longer running "core" X-men titles—*Uncanny X-Men, Wolverine,* and *New X-Men.* (Somewhat further down the sales lists are the other "X-books"—among them *X-Force, Cable,* and the new *X-treme X-Men.*) What this means to libraries is that for the first time in more than twenty years, there is a "self-contained" X-Men title—one that does not directly tie into an entire "family" of related titles. This would argue that *Ultimate X-Men* is now the logical X-book of choice for libraries looking to subscribe to but a single X-Men–related title. The book will likely continue to be a top seller and in heavy demand in libraries with comic book holdings. (DH)

World War Three Illustrated. See Zines section.

Publications about Comics

1833. *Comic Book Marketplace.* 1991. m. USD 60. Ed(s): Russ Cochran. Gemstone Publishing, Inc., 1966 Greenspring Dr., Ste. 405, Timonium, MD 21093-4117; cbm@gemstonepub.com; http://www.gemstonepub.com. *Aud.:* Ems, Hs, Ga, Ac.

From the publisher of *The Overstreet Comic Book Price Guide,* this is "The Magazine for Golden Age, Silver Age, & Bronze Age Collectors." *Comic Book Marketplace* is a slick, professional magazine tailored for anyone interested in premodern comic books. The emphasis is on history, be it of a character, title, publisher, creator, genre, or theme. Art is handsomely reproduced, often in vivid color. Market values are traced, and collectors young and old share their experiences in the letters page. An excellent choice for those interested in collecting vintage comics or in comics history in general. (AE)

1834. ***Comics Buyer's Guide.*** Incorporates: *Comics Buyer's Guide Price Guide.* [ISSN: 0745-4570] 1971. w. USD 38.95; USD 20.95 for 6 mos.; USD 3.99 per issue. Ed(s): Maggie Thompson. Krause Publications, Inc., 700 E State St, Iola, WI 54990-0001; info@krause.com; http://www.krause.com. Illus., adv. Sample. Circ: 10046 Paid and free. Microform: PQC. *Bk. rev.:* Various number and length. *Aud.:* Ems, Hs, Ga.

The weekly *Comics Buyer's Guide (CBG),* the trade paper for the comics industry, is *the* source for news and information on the ever-changing comics scene and, to some extent, on such related interests as trading cards and animation. Along with advertisements from publishers, retailers, and collectors, each issue is packed with news, reviews, columns, Internet guides, convention schedules, monthly price guides, and a consistently fascinating letters column (a neutral forum wherein various viewpoints are shared on such wide-ranging topics as literacy, censorship, the moral responsibilities of publishers and retailers, perceptions of comics readers by non–comics readers, as well as discussions of comics in general). The annual *CBG* Fan Awards are a popular barometer of what fans are enjoying. Editor Maggie Thompson, with her late husband Don, was among the founders of comics fandom and is an articulate supporter of both comics and literacy in general. The voice and marketplace of comics fandom (and pros as well), *CBG* is often more interesting than the comics themselves. (AE)

1835. ***International Journal of Comic Art.*** [ISSN: 1531-6793] 1999. s-a. USD 40 (Individuals, USD 30). John A. Lent, Ed & Pub, 669 Ferne Blvd, Drexel Hill, PA 19026. Illus., adv. *Indexed:* MLA-IB. *Aud.:* Ac.

This is an excellent choice for college and university libraries, particularly when one considers the multidisciplinary nature of the growing academic interest in comic art. Scholarly articles on comics appear in such publications as the *Journal of Popular Culture,* but, since the demise of the wonderful *Inks: Cartoon and Comic Art Studies,* there had been no single scholarly journal to serve as outlet for the growing comics scholarship. Editor John A. Lent, professor of communications at Temple University and an authority on the international aspects of comic art, says "scholarly, but not stuffy" is his aim. Recent article titles include "Gary Groth and Kim Thompson: Interviews with the Heart of the Alternative Comics Industry," "Swedish Comics and Comics in Sweden," "Tezuka Osamu and the Star System," "William Faulkner and the Graphic Novel," and "Early Creative Responses to 9-11 by Comic Artists." (AE)

1836. ***The Overstreet Comic Book Price Guide.*** Former titles (until 1992): *Official Overstreet Comic Book Price Guide;* (until 1987): *Comic Book Price Guide.* [ISSN: 1073-2276] 1970. a. USD 32 newsstand/cover per issue. Ed(s): Arnold T Blumberg. Gemstone Publishing, Inc., 1966 Greenspring Dr., Ste. 405, Timonium, MD 21093-4117. Illus. Circ: 150000. *Aud.:* Ems, Hs, Ga, Ac.

This annual is commonly referred to simply as *Overstreet*—or perhaps as often, the bible of the comic book hobbyist, investor, collector, student, and fan. Most mainstream comic books from 1900 to the present are represented, with their current valuation based upon condition. There are other comics price guides available, but *Overstreet* is still the standard. Each issue—besides featuring articles on significant series, publishers, or characters—provides an omnibus of information ranging from invaluable historical and bibliographic data to guidelines for obtaining, grading, storing, and selling comic books. Highly recommended as a reference tool whether a library offers comics or not. (AE)

1837. ***Previews (Timonium).*** 1991. m. USD 3.95 newsstand/cover per issue. Ed(s): Marty Grosser. Diamond Comic Distributors, 1966 Greenspring Dr, Ste 300, Timonium, MD 21093; http://www.diamondcomics.com/previews/. *Aud.:* Ems, Hs, Ga.

Previews has described itself as the "*TV Guide* of the comics industry." It is a preview of comics scheduled for shipment to comics shops two months hence—not only comics, but also trading cards (including sports cards), games, toys, apparel, videos, posters, magazines, books, collectors supplies, and other products at least loosely related to the world of comics. It provides short descriptions of content and format, price, and expected delivery date, supplemented with articles and interviews promoting coming products. Available primarily through comics specialty shops and subscription services, it includes ordering forms for retailers. This system is a good way for libraries to customize a comics-ordering program. Even if not used as an ordering tool, *Previews* is still fun to browse through, but if you are making it available to your patrons, be aware that there are many images of human beings in various stages of what is commonly considered undress. (AE)

1838. ***Wizard: the comics magazine.*** [ISSN: 1065-6499] 1991. m. USD 29.95 domestic; CND 48 Canada; USD 70 elsewhere. Ed(s): Patricia McCallum. Wizard Entertainment, Wizard Editorial Dept, 151 Wells Ave, Congers, NY 10920; http://www.wizardworld.com. Illus., adv. Sample. Circ: 208000. *Bk. rev.:* Various number and length. *Aud.:* Ems, Hs, Ga.

Far more than just a monthly update of comic book collector prices (mostly superhero titles from the late 1950s to the present), *Wizard* is a slick, well-produced news/opinion fanzine loaded with information. The emphasis is on modern superhero comics, and features may provide in-depth examinations of particular creators, publishers, characters, and series, while regular departments spotlight reviews, art tips, reader art and letters, news of comics merchandising, and interpretations of comics characters in other media (a major concern of many fans). Similar fanzines come and go, but with its price and content, *Wizard* maintains its edge. (AE)

Electronic Sources

Hundreds of sites of comics-related information may be found on the Internet. Many publishers, creators, characters, and series have their own web sites, both official and fan-produced. The *Comics Buyer's Guide* is a good source for keeping up with comics web sites, and *The Incredible Internet Guide to Comic Books & Superheroes* (2000, Facts on Demand Press) by James R. Flowers, Jr., might still be useful, particularly for mainstream superhero comics. The following sites are particularly recommended:

BRIDGES: CrossGen Comics for Education. http://www.crossgen.com/education. ". . .where teachers, students and parents [and librarians?] can learn about using CrossGen's comics and our one-of-a-kind Teacher's Guides as a supplemental reading comprehension program. Using Meridian as the basis for intermediate elementary students (grades 4-8), and Ruse for high school students (9-12), CrossGen has engaged the help of five teachers with more than 100 combined years of classroom teaching experience to create a truly universal supplemental reading program."

Comic Art Collection Home Page. http://www.lib.msu.edu/comics. The web site for the world's largest research collection of comic art.

Comic Art in Scholarly Writing: A Citation Guide. http://www.sp.uconn.edu/~epk93002/CAC/cite.html. Guidelines for citing comic books in papers, articles, and so forth.

Comic Book Network Electronic Magazine. http://digitalwebbing.com/cbem. A weekly online magazine of comics news and opinion.

Comic Book Resources. (Formerly: *Jonah Weiland's Comic Book Resources*). http://www.comicbookresources.com. News, opinions, reviews, and many, many links; updated daily.

Comics Librarianship Resource Page. http://www.geocities.com/Athens/7875/comics.html. Notes on building a comic book research collection, and "links to online resources that may be of use to those interested in comics scholarship and related fields."

Comics Scholars' Discussion List. http://www.english.ufl.edu/comics/scholars. "An academic forum for those involved in research, criticism and teaching related to comics art. All aspects of comics and cartooning from around the world are open for discussion. Likewise, theoretical and critical perspectives from all academic fields are invited."

Comics.com: The Home of Comics on the Web. http://www.comics.com/. Provides access to popular newspaper comic strips and editorial cartoons, updated periodically.

ComicsOnCDRom, http://www.comicsoncdrom.com, is a wonderful source for vintage comics and other printed matter in CD-ROM format.

ComicsResearch.org. http://www.comicsresearch.org. Featuring "The Comics Scholarship Annotated Bibliographies" along with numerous links of interest to comics scholars.

FRESH. http://www.ORCAfresh.net. The site of "Organized Readers of Comics Associated, or ORCA, an international comic book association that is as aggressive and different as a 'killer whale' in its mission to promote the reading of comic books." Reviews, news, etc.

GNLIB: Graphic Novels in Libraries. http://www.angelfire.com/comics/gnlib. Home of the Graphic Novels in Libraries discussion list.

The Grand Comic-Book Database Project. http://www.comics.org. An impressive labor of love. From their charter: "We intend to catalog key story information, creator information, and other information which is useful to readers, fans, hobbyists, researchers. Our goal is to include all the comic books ever published."

MicroColour International Limited, http://www.microcolour.com/mci01.htm. A source for Golden Age comics on microfiche.

NACAE: National Association of Comics Art Educators, http://www.teachingcomics.org. "A resource for individuals and institutions involved in teaching visual storytelling."

The New York City Comic Book Museum. http://www.nyccomicbookmuseum.org. "Striving to be the most respected museum in the U.S. for interpreting comic book history and art." Also check out their "C.O.M.I.C.S. Curriculum Challenging Objective Minds: an Instructional Comicbook Series."

*The Periodic Table of Comic Books.*http://www.uky.edu/Projects/Chemcomics. A handsome, fun site, combining science and comics. "Click on an element to see a list of comic book pages involving that element."

Recommended Graphic Novels for Public Libraries. http://my.voyager.net/~sraiteri/graphicnovels.htm. Selected and annotated by Steve Raiteri, who reviews graphic novels for *Library Journal.*

The Secret Origin of Good Readers: A Resource Book. http://www.night-flight.com/secretorigin/index.html. A downloadable guide for educators who wish to utilize the comics medium.

Sequential Tart, http://www.sequentialtart.com/home.shtml, is "a Web Zine about the comics industry, published by an eclectic band of women."

Finally,

World Famous Comics. http://www.wfcomics.com. "Online since 1995, World Famous Comics brings the some of the very best of comics and entertainment to the Web by providing exclusive columns, contests and comics, interactive features, online resources and current news about the entertainment industry. World Famous Comics is a daily destination for a new era of comic book and entertainment fans." Particularly noteworthy is the outstanding daily opinion and review column by comics pro/fan Tony Isabella. (AE)

■ COMMUNICATION

See also Education; Journalism and Writing; Media and AV; and Television, Video, and Radio sections.

Laura A. Sullivan, Grants Coordinator, Northern Kentucky University, Steely Library, Highland Heights, KY 41099; sullivanl@nku.edu; FAX: 859-572-6181

Nancy F. Campbell, Assistant to the Associate Provost for Library Services, Northern Kentucky University, Steely Library, Highland Heights, KY 41099; campbelln@nku.edu; FAX: 859-572-6181

Michael J. Rose, Web Development Librarian, Steely Library, Highland Heights, KY 41099; rosemi@nku.edu; FAX: 859-572-6181

Introduction

This section features representative and significant titles in the field of communication. Titles chosen cover all types of communication: mass, speech, interpersonal, organizational, rhetoric, and applied communication, among others. Many well-known core periodicals within the discipline are provided, yet some specialized and interdisciplinary titles are included to bring balance. This basic list may include more specialized titles in the future to showcase the discipline's broad range and interdisciplinary characteristics. Four notable electronic titles are recommended here, one more since the last update. Particularly noticeable this review period is the increase in cost for many of the titles, almost a 50 percent increase. This, however, seems to be reflective of the rise in serials costs in general. Of the communication titles here, the average cost is $170, with costs ranging from a low of $30 to a high of $548.

Basic Periodicals

Ac: *Argumentation and Advocacy, Communication Education, Communication Monographs, Communication Quarterly, Communication Reports, Communication Research, Communication Research Reports, Critical Studies in Media Communication, Human Communication Research, Journal of Applied Communication Research, Journal of Communication, Quarterly Journal of Speech, Southern Communication Journal, Western Journal of Communication.*

Basic Abstracts and Indexes

Communication Abstracts, ERIC, Humanities Index, Index to Journals in Communication Studies through 1995, Psychological Abstracts, Social Sciences Citation Index, Sociological Abstracts.

1839. ***Argumentation & Advocacy: journal of the American Forensic Association.*** Formerly (until vol.25, 1989): *American Forensic Association. Journal.* [ISSN: 1051-1431] 1964. q. USD 70 (Individual members, USD 60; Students, USD 20). Ed(s): Dale Herbeck. American Forensic Association, PO Box 256, River Falls, WI 54022-0256; http://www.americanforensics.org. Illus., adv. Sample. Refereed. Circ: 1000. Vol. ends: Spring. Microform: PQC. Online: bigchalk; EBSCO Publishing; Florida Center for Library Automation; Gale Group; Northern Light Technology, Inc.; OCLC Online Computer Library Center, Inc.; ProQuest Information & Learning. Reprint: PQC. *Indexed:* CIJE, IJCS, LRI. *Bk. rev.:* 2-6, lengthy. *Aud.:* Ac.

This journal of the American Forensic Association advances the study of argumentation. Critical and theoretical articles are included in the areas of argumentation theory, public argument, critical and cultural perspectives, and forensics and pedagogy. Special issues occur occasionally (i.e., forensics, John Dewey), and a review essay and book reviews are provided as well. A title for academic collections.

1840. ***Association for Communication Administration. Journal.*** Former titles (until 1992): *A C A Bulletin; Association of Departments and Administrators in Communication. Bulletin.* 1972. 3x/yr. Membership, USD 75. Ed(s): Ronald Applbaum. Association for Communication Administration, 5105 F Backlick Rd, Annandale, VA 22003. Adv. Circ: 400. Reprint: PQC. *Indexed:* CIJE, IJCS. *Bk. rev.:* Occasional. *Aud.:* Ac, Sa.

This journal focuses on research related to communication in the academic setting (i.e., "Making Good Tenure Decisions," "Unique Characteristics of a Graduate Program in Applied Communication"). Manuscripts are considered in the fields of speech communication, mass communication, journalism, and theater. Types of articles published are diverse, ranging from special-topic papers to essays to research reports. Approaches to the material also vary—philosophical, theoretical, methodological, critical, applied, pedagogical, or empirical. Although not a regular feature, book reviews are published on topics of communication, administration, and/or organizational processes. This publication will obviously be of interest to communication administrators, as well as to communication faculty and scholars.

Broadcasting & Cable. See Television, Video, and Radio section.

Columbia Journalism Review. See Journalism and Writing section.

1841. ***Communication Education.*** Formerly (until 1976): *Speech Teacher.* [ISSN: 0363-4523] 1952. q. USD 110; USD 120 foreign. Ed(s): Joe Ayres. National Communication Association, 1765 N St., N W, Washington, DC 20036; weadie@natcom.org; http://www.natcom.org. Illus., index, adv. Sample. Refereed. Circ: 4200. Vol. ends: Oct. Microform: PQC. Online: Factiva; Northern Light Technology, Inc.; OCLC Online Computer Library Center, Inc.; ProQuest Information & Learning. Reprint: PQC; PSC. *Indexed:* BRI, CBRI, CIJE, CommAb, EduInd, IJCS, LISA, MLA-IB, MRD, PsycholAb, SSCI. *Bk. rev.:* 3-5, lengthy. *Aud.:* Ac, Sa.

This journal covers scholarship on discourse and instruction. Research and pedagogical articles may address teaching communication in traditional academic environments as well as in nontraditional settings, e.g., health and legal. Areas of focus include technology in mediated instruction, classroom discourse, life-span development of communication competence, and diverse backgrounds of learners and teachers in instructional settings. Some issues feature a special topic, such as "Racial, Cultural, and Gendered Identities in Educational Contexts: Communication Perspectives on Identity Negotiation." *CE* routinely publishes book reviews and nonprint learning resources; a recent addition to the journal is the Scholarship of Teaching and Learning in Communication section of articles. This is a critical publication for communication faculty and researchers. Valuable for its focus and a necessary resource for academic libraries.

1842. *Communication Monographs.* Formerly (until vol.42): *Speech Monographs.* [ISSN: 0363-7751] 1934. q. USD 110 domestic; USD 120 foreign. National Communication Association, 1765 N St., N W, Washington, DC 20036; weadie@natcom.org; http://www.natcom.org. Illus., index. Refereed. Circ: 3400. Vol. ends: Dec. Microform: PQC. Online: Factiva; Gale Group; Northern Light Technology, Inc.; OCLC Online Computer Library Center, Inc.; ProQuest Information & Learning. Reprint: PQC; PSC. *Indexed:* ArtHuCI, BAS, BiolAb, CIJE, CommAb, ECER, EduInd, IJCS, L&LBA, LT&LA, MLA-IB, PsycholAb, SFSA, SSCI, SociolAb. *Aud.:* Ac.

Communication Monographs publishes scientific and empirical research on communication processes, and is open to a variety of theoretical or methodological perspectives. The journal's editorial policy claims a "tradition of rigorous review and high intellectual standards," and manuscripts must show strong quantitative empirical research. Emphasis is also on the contributor's ability to explain clearly how the understanding of communication is advanced by the research submitted. Recommended for academic libraries.

1843. *Communication Quarterly.* Formerly: *Today's Speech.* [ISSN: 0146-3373] 1953. q. USD 50; USD 56 foreign. Ed(s): John Courtright. Eastern Communication Association, c/o Paul E Scovell, Exec Sec, Department of Communication Arts, Salisbury, MD 21801. Illus., index, adv. Circ: 3000. Vol. ends: Fall. Microform: PQC. Online: bigchalk; Factiva; Florida Center for Library Automation; Gale Group; Northern Light Technology, Inc.; OCLC Online Computer Library Center, Inc.; ProQuest Information & Learning; H.W. Wilson. *Indexed:* CIJE, CommAb, EduInd, HumInd, IJCS, L&LBA, LRI, PRA, RI-1, SSI, SWA, SociolAb. *Aud.:* Ac.

This journal publishes all types of manuscripts (topical interest papers, research reports, state-of-the-art reviews, supported opinion) that advance the understanding of human communication. Recent articles include "Theodore Roosevelt and the Rhetoric of Citizenship: On Tour in New England, 1902" and "Interpersonal Communication Motives in Everyday Interactions." An average of seven articles are published each issue. This publication also includes *Qualitative Research Reports in Communication* (with its own editorial board and independently volumed) following the *CQ* articles. *Communication Quarterly* is a regional communication association publication and a core title for academic libraries.

1844. *Communication Reports.* [ISSN: 0893-4215] 1988. s-a. USD 70; USD 80 foreign. Western States Communication Association, c/o Connie J Conlee, WSCA Executive Director, Department of Speech Communication, Fresno, CA 93740-0046; http://www.communication.ilstu.edu/. Illus., adv. Vol. ends: Summer. Online: EBSCO Publishing; Florida Center for Library Automation; Gale Group; Northern Light Technology, Inc.; ProQuest Information & Learning. *Indexed:* IJCS, L&LBA, SociolAb. *Aud.:* Ac.

This journal seeks short, original, data-based articles on broadly defined human communication topics. Theoretical or speculative reports are not accepted; rather, emphasis should be on research data analysis. Manuscripts are limited to 2,500 words, and one issue may have as many as ten reports. Recommended for academic collections.

1845. *Communication Research.* [ISSN: 0093-6502] 1974. bi-m. GBP 413 in Europe, Middle East, Africa & Australasia. Ed(s): Pamela Shoemaker, Michael E Roloff. Sage Publications, Inc., 2455 Teller Rd, Thousand Oaks, CA 91320; info@sagepub.com; http://www.sagepub.com. Illus., index, adv. Refereed. Circ: 1600. Vol. ends: Dec. Reprint: PSC. *Indexed:* AbAn, AgeL, ArtHuCI, CIJE, CommAb, FLI, HRA, HumInd, IBSS, IJCS, L&LBA, PRA, PSA, PsycholAb, SFSA, SSCI, SSI, SUSA, SWA, SociolAb. *Aud.:* Ac.

The editorial goal of *Communication Research* is "to offer a special opportunity for reflection and change in the new millennium." While requiring submissions of theoretically driven communication research, the journal is not limited to a specific methodology and is receptive to original research efforts, as long as that research is "directly linked to the most important problems and issues facing humankind." Although the title is expensive, it should be required for academic collections.

1846. *Communication Research Reports.* [ISSN: 0882-4096] 1984. q. USD 50. Ed(s): Jerry L Allen. Eastern Communication Association, c/o Paul E Scovell, Exec Sec, Department of Communication Arts, Salisbury, MD 21801. Illus., index, adv. Circ: 1500. Vol. ends: Fall. Microform: PQC. *Indexed:* CommAb, IJCS, L&LBA, PSA, PsycholAb, SociolAb. *Aud.:* Ac.

A publication of the Eastern Communication Association, *Communication Research Reports* publishes brief empirical articles (11 or more in each issue). Studies on human communication in a wide variety of areas are accepted, including intercultural, interpersonal, organizational, persuasive, political, nonverbal, instructional, relational, or mediated. Articles emphasize the reporting and interpretation of the results rather than theory. A title for academic collections.

1847. *Communication Studies.* Formerly: *Central States Speech Journal.* [ISSN: 1051-0974] 1949. q. USD 40. Ed(s): J Kevin Barge. Communication Studies, Baylor University, Waco, TX 76798; ADaniel@csca.ecok.edu; http://www.baylor.edu/. Illus., index, adv. Refereed. Circ: 2700. Vol. ends: Winter. Online: bigchalk; Factiva; Florida Center for Library Automation; Gale Group; Northern Light Technology, Inc.; OCLC Online Computer Library Center, Inc.; ProQuest Information & Learning. Reprint: PSC. *Indexed:* CIJE, CommAb, IJCS, MLA-IB, PRA, PsycholAb, SSCI, SociolAb. *Aud.:* Ac.

A publication of the Central States Communication Association, *Communication Studies* publishes excellent original research on human communication processes, with the expectation that the essays and studies advance human communication scholarship. Article topics are varied (i.e., "Cancer Communications Research and Health Outcomes: Review and Challenge," "Presidential Television Advertising and Public Policy Priorities, 1952-2000") and reflect communication studies in broad contexts. An easily affordable and very useful title for academic libraries.

1848. *Communication Theory.* [ISSN: 1050-3293] 1991. q. USD 172. Ed(s): Michael J. Cody. Oxford University Press, 2001 Evans Rd, Cary, NC 27513; http://www3.oup.co.uk/jnls/. Illus., adv. Refereed. Circ: 4100. Vol. ends: Nov. Reprint: PQC; PSC. *Indexed:* ArtHuCI, CJA, CommAb, IBSS, IJCS, L&LBA, PSA, SSCI, SociolAb. *Bk. rev.:* 1, lengthy. *Aud.:* Ac, Sa.

This journal publishes "high quality, original research into the theoretical development of communication." Many disciplines are represented, including communication studies, psychology, cultural/gender studies, sociology, political science, philosophy, linguistics, and literature. Articles are in-depth and lengthy. Recommended for larger research libraries.

1849. ***Communication World.*** Former titles (until 1982): *Journal of Communication Management;* (until 1981): *Journal of Organizational Communication;* (until 1974): *I A B C Journal.* [ISSN: 0744-7612] 1973. 7x/yr. USD 95 Free to members. Ed(s): Gloria Gordon. International Association of Business Communicators, One Hallidie Plaza, Ste 600, San Francisco, CA 94102; ggordon@iabc.com; http://www.abc.com. Illus., adv. Circ: 125000 Paid and free. Vol. ends: Dec. Online: bigchalk; The Dialog Corporation; EBSCO Publishing; Florida Center for Library Automation; Gale Group; Northern Light Technology, Inc.; OCLC Online Computer Library Center, Inc.; ProQuest Information & Learning. *Indexed:* ABIn. *Aud.:* Ga, Ac, Sa.

This official publication of the International Association of Business Communicators (IABC) combines practical articles with global communication issues in the area of communication management. *CW Bulletin* is IABC's online supplement to *Communication World* magazine. The monthly newsletter features critical communication issues and provides IABC information (membership, chapters) and programs, while the print version provides in-depth reports and features. Topics in a recent *CW* issue cover communicating in a crisis and merger success. For large public libraries and academic business and communication collections.

1850. ***Critical Studies in Media Communication.*** Formerly (unti 1999): *Critical Studies in Mass Communication.* [ISSN: 1529-5036] 1984. q. USD 110 domestic; USD 120 foreign. National Communication Association, 1765 N St., N W, Washington, DC 20036; weadie@natcom.org; http://www.natcom.org. Illus., index, adv. Sample. Refereed. Circ: 2800. Vol. ends: Dec. Online: Gale Group; OCLC Online Computer Library Center, Inc.; ProQuest Information & Learning. Reprint: PSC. *Indexed:* ABS&EES, ArtHuCI, CIJE, CommAb, HumInd, IJCS, PRA, PSA, RI-1, SSCI, SSI, SociolAb. *Aud.:* Ac.

Critical Studies publishes articles that reflect a concentration on mediated communication. Mediated communication includes "print and broadcast media, film, video, and new media forms such as the Internet and the World Wide Web." Submissions focus on analysis of mass media institutions, histories, technologies, and messages, as well as the relationship between culture and mass media. A publication of the National Communication Association, this is a valuable source for academic libraries.

1851. ***Discourse & Society: an international journal for the study of discourse and communication in their social, political and cultural contexts.*** [ISSN: 0957-9265] 1990. bi-m. GBP 401 in Europe, Middle East, Africa & Australasia. Ed(s): Teun A van Dijk. Sage Publications Ltd., 6 Bonhill St, London, EC2A 4PU, United Kingdom; info@sagepub.co.uk; http://www.sagepub.co.uk/. Adv. Refereed. *Indexed:* ASSIA, ArtHuCI, CommAb, FLI, HRA, IBSS, IBZ, IPSA, L&LBA, LingAb, MLA-IB, PRA, PSA, SFSA, SSCI, SUSA, SWA, SociolAb. *Bk. rev.:* 7 average, medium/lengthy. *Aud.:* Ac.

Discourse & Society is a multidisciplinary journal of discourse analysis. Editorial policy requires articles to "provide a detailed, systematic and theoretically based analysis of text and talk." Emphasis is on discourse in different societal contexts, the discursive dimensions of social structures, or any other relation between discourse and society (including politics and culture). Diversity is valued and may be reflected in authorship, theories, methods, data, and use of scholarly literature. The journal requires accessibilty as one criterion; that is, articles should be accessible to readers of various levels of expertise and specialization, including students, and to readers from varied disciplines. Articles from a recent issue include "Expressions of Gender: An Analysis of Pupils' Gendered Discourse Styles in Small Group Classroom Discussions" and "Racial insult in Brazil." Book reviews are included and issues are occasionally devoted to special topics (i.e., political correctness). Recommended for large academic collections.

Howard Journal of Communications. See African American section.

1852. ***Human Communication Research.*** [ISSN: 0360-3989] 1974. q. GBP 189. Ed(s): John O. Greene. Oxford University Press, 2001 Evans Rd, Cary, NC 27513; http://www3.oup.co.uk/jnls/. Illus., adv. Sample. Refereed. Circ: 4400. Vol. ends: Jun. Microform: PQC. Online: Florida Center for Library Automation; Gale Group; HighWire Press; ingenta.com; OCLC Online Computer Library Center, Inc.; ProQuest Information & Learning; Swets Blackwell. Reprint: PQC; PSC. *Indexed:* ASG, AbAn, AgeL, ArtHuCI, CIJE, CommAb, FLI, IJCS, IMFL, L&LBA, LRI, PRA, PsycholAb, SFSA, SSCI, SSI, SociolAb. *Aud.:* Ac, Sa.

This official journal of the International Communication Association has a strong social science approach to the study of communication. It is touted as one of the top two journals in human communication, and articles emphasize human symbolic processes in the areas of interpersonal, nonverbal, organizational, intercultural, and mass communication; language and social interaction; new technologies; and health communication. The journal will appeal not only to communication studies scholars but also to those in psychology, sociology, linguistics, and anthropology. For large public and academic libraries.

JACA. See *Association for Communication Administration. Journal.*

1853. ***Journal of Applied Communication Research.*** [ISSN: 0090-9882] 1973. q. USD 110 domestic; USD 120 foreign. Ed(s): H Dan O'Hair. National Communication Association, 1765 N St., N W, Washington, DC 20036; weadie@natcom.org; http://www.natcom.org. Illus., adv. Sample. Refereed. Circ: 2000. Vol. ends: Nov. Microform: PQC. Online: Gale Group; Ingenta Select; Northern Light Technology, Inc.; OCLC Online Computer Library Center, Inc.; ProQuest Information & Learning. Reprint: PSC. *Indexed:* ASG, AgeL, CIJE, CommAb, HRA, IJCS, L&LBA, PRA, SFSA, SSCI, SociolAb. *Aud.:* Ac, Sa.

This journal publishes articles that study actual communication situations or show results that can be applied to the solution of communication problems. Articles can be any of the following: original research applied to practical situations/problems; application articles that offer ways of improving or expanding upon a particular communication setting through specific research or theory; or commentaries on applied communication issues. Any methodological or theoretical approach is considered. Valuable for its pertinent topics and recommended for academic libraries.

1854. ***Journal of Business Communication.*** Former titles (until 1973): *The A B C A Journal of Business Communication;* (until 1969): *The Journal of Business Communication.* [ISSN: 0021-9436] 1963. q. USD 160 (Individuals, USD 65). Ed(s): Kitty O Hocker, Steve Ralston. Association for Business Communication, c/o Dr Robert J Myers, Dept of Speech Communication, Baruch College, 17 Lexington Ave, New York, NY 10010; abcrjm@compuserve.com; http://www.theabc.org. Illus., index, adv. Refereed. Circ: 1875. Vol. ends: Oct. Microform: PQC. Online: Florida Center for Library Automation; Gale Group; Northern Light Technology, Inc.; OCLC Online Computer Library Center, Inc.; ProQuest Information & Learning; H.W. Wilson. Reprint: PQC. *Indexed:* ABIn, AbAn, BPI, BusEdI, CIJE, CommAb, L&LBA. *Bk. rev.:* 1, lengthy. *Aud.:* Ac, Sa.

A publication of the Association for Business Communication, *JBC* is interested in all aspects of business communication. Manuscripts submitted may cover the role of communication in various areas as it pertains to organizations—international, information systems, managerial, organizational, corporate, and business composition/technical writing. Examples of recent article titles are "Could Communication Form Impact Organizations' Experience with Diversity?" and "Successful Sino-Western Business Negotiation: Participants' Accounts of National and Professional Cultures." The two issues examined each included one lengthy book review. A quality business communication title for academic libraries.

1855. ***Journal of Communication.*** [ISSN: 0021-9916] 1951. q. GBP 152. Ed(s): Dr. Jon Nussbaum. Oxford University Press, 2001 Evans Rd, Cary, NC 27513; http://www3.oup.co.uk/jnls/. Illus., index, adv. Refereed. Circ: 6150. Microform: PQC. Online: Gale Group; HighWire Press; ingenta.com; Northern Light Technology, Inc.; OCLC Online Computer Library Center, Inc.; ProQuest Information & Learning; Swets Blackwell. Reprint: PQC. *Indexed:* ABIn, ABS&EES, AgeL, AmH&L, ArtHuCI, BAS, BRI, CBRI, CIJE, CJA, CommAb, EduInd, ExcerpMed, FLI, FutSurv, HRA, HumInd, IBSS, IIFP, IJCS, IPSA, IndMed, InfoSAb, L&LBA, LISA, MLA-IB, PRA, PSA, PsycholAb, R&TA, SFSA, SSCI, SSI, SociolAb. *Bk. rev.:* 10+, length varies. *Aud.:* Ac.

Considered an official journal of the International Communication Association, this journal is interdisciplinary and concentrates broadly on communication theory, research, practice, and policy. Articles are written by scholars, professors from a variety of disciplines, and graduate and doctoral students. Recent issues include articles on public journalism; Jewish American identity; stereotypes of older adults; and TV and images of motherhood. The valuable "Review and Criticism" section includes review essays as well as shorter book reviews. A necessary publication for large public libraries and academic libraries.

1856. ***Journal of Communication Inquiry.*** [ISSN: 0196-8599] 1974. q. GBP 170 print & online eds. in Europe, Middle East, Africa & Australasia. Ed(s): Matthew Cecil. Sage Publications, Inc., 2455 Teller Rd, Thousand Oaks, CA 91320; info@sagepub.com; http://www.sagepub.com. Illus., adv. Sample. Refereed. Circ: 1000 Paid. Vol. ends: Oct. *Indexed:* AmH&L, CommAb, FLI, HumInd, IBZ, MLA-IB, PRA, PSA, SWA, SociolAb. *Aud.:* Ac.

This journal approaches the study of communication and mass communication from cultural and historical perspectives. The interdisciplinary aspects of communication are emphasized as articles reflect a variety of approaches, from philosophical to empirical to legal. The journal also publishes thematic special issues on any of the following critical topics: Deconstructing Popular Culture; Technology and Culture; Feminist Cultural Studies; and Race, Media, and Culture. For large research collections.

1857. ***Journal of Nonverbal Behavior.*** Formerly (until 1979): *Environmental Psychology and Nonverbal Behavior.* [ISSN: 0191-5886] 1976. q. USD 589 print or online ed. Ed(s): Ronald E Riggio. Kluwer Academic / Plenum Publishers, 233 Spring St Fl 7, New York, NY 10013-1522; http://www.wkap.nl/. Illus., adv. Sample. Refereed. Vol. ends: Winter. Microform: PQC. Online: EBSCO Publishing; Gale Group; ingenta.com; Kluwer Online; OCLC Online Computer Library Center, Inc.; Ovid Technologies, Inc.; ProQuest Information & Learning; RoweCom Information Quest; Swets Blackwell. Reprint: ISI; PQC. *Indexed:* AgeL, BiolAb, CIJE, CJA, CommAb, HRA, IMFL, L&LBA, MLA-IB, PRA, PsycholAb, SFSA, SSCI, SSI, SWA, SWR&A, SociolAb. *Aud.:* Ac, Sa.

This specialized journal publishes research on the varying components of nonverbal communication—interpersonal distance, gaze, facial expressiveness, kinesics, paralanguage, posture, gestures, and related behaviors. Research submitted can be empirical, theoretical, or methodological. Recognizing the interdisciplinary nature of nonverbal communication, manuscripts are welcomed from a variety of research fields. This publication also includes a "Notes in Brief" section, which publishes short/informal reports, reviews, and notes. Special issues are also published. An expensive but worthwhile title for comprehensive research collections.

Journalism and Mass Communication Educator. See Journalism and Writing/Journalism section.

1858. ***Management Communication Quarterly: an international journal.*** [ISSN: 0893-3189] 1987. q. GBP 281 print & online eds. in Europe, Middle East, Africa & Australasia. Ed(s): Ted Zorn. Sage Publications, Inc., 2455 Teller Rd, Thousand Oaks, CA 91320; info@sagepub.com; http://www.sagepub.com. Illus., adv. Refereed. Circ: 1100. Vol. ends: May. Online: EBSCO Publishing; ingenta.com; RoweCom Information Quest; Swets Blackwell. *Indexed:* CIJE, CommAb, HRA, PRA, RiskAb, SFSA. *Bk. rev.:* 1-4, lengthy. *Aud.:* Ac, Sa.

MCQ is devoted to theory and practice in the field of organizational communication. Open to varied methodologies and theories, the journal covers a variety of topics, i.e., intercultural communication, business writing, emotion in organizations, interpersonal communication/practices at work, group decision making, and communication technologies. Research must reflect originality and rigor. The journal also includes the Forum section where a reader will find book reviews, book review essays, research notes, commentaries, and case analyses. This title is a fine addition to academic business communication collections.

1859. ***Mass Communication and Society.*** Formerly (until 1998): *Mass Communications Review.* [ISSN: 1520-5436] 1973. q. USD 295. Ed(s): Carol J Pardun, George Gladney. Lawrence Erlbaum Associates, Inc., 10 Industrial Ave, Mahwah, NJ 07430-2262; journals@erlbaum.com; http://www.erlbaum.com/. Illus., adv. Sample. Refereed. Vol. ends: Summer/Fall. Reprint: PSC. *Indexed:* PSA, SociolAb. *Bk. rev.:* 2-5, lengthy. *Aud.:* Ac.

This is the official journal of the Mass Communication & Society Division of the Association for Education in Journalism and Mass Communication. Research and scholarship is published on mass communication theory from various perspectives, although the macrosocial perspective (i.e., societal, institutional, cross-cultural, global) is encouraged. This is a cross-disciplinary publication drawing from sociology, law, philosophy, history, psychology, and anthropology. Examples of article titles are "An Idea Whose Time Has Come: International Communication History" and "A Descriptive Analysis of NBC's Coverage of the 2000 Summer Olympics." A worthwhile title for academic collections.

Philosophy and Rhetoric. See Philosophy section.

1860. ***Quarterly Journal of Speech.*** [ISSN: 0033-5630] 1915. q. USD 110 domestic; USD 120 foreign. Ed(s): Andrew King. National Communication Association, 1765 N St., N W, Washington, DC 20036; weadie@natcom.org; http://www.natcom.org. Illus., index, adv. Refereed. Circ: 5400. Vol. ends: Nov. Microform: PMC; PQC. Online: bigchalk; Gale Group; Northern Light Technology, Inc.; OCLC Online Computer Library Center, Inc.; ProQuest Information & Learning. Reprint: PQC; PSC. *Indexed:* ABS&EES, AmH&L, ArtHuCI, BEL&L, BRI, CBRI, CIJE, CommAb, ECER, EduInd, HRA, HumInd, IJCS, L&LBA, LT&LA, MLA-IB, PRA, PSA, PsycholAb, RI-1, SSCI, SUSA, SociolAb. *Bk. rev.:* 5-10, lengthy. *Aud.:* Ac.

A respected and established journal in the field, *QJS* publishes articles that focus primarily on rhetorical theory and methods of analysis. The journal seeks essays that aid understanding of discourse practices and that investigate alternative approaches to discourse study. Each issue may include a book review essay or Forum section (responses to earlier *QJS* articles) and additional critical book reviews. A necessary title for academic libraries.

1861. ***Rhetoric Society Quarterly.*** Formerly: *Rhetoric Society Newsletter.* [ISSN: 0277-3945] 1968. q. USD 40 (Individuals, USD 30; Students, USD 15). Ed(s): Jeffrey Walker. Rhetoric Society of America, c/o Department of English, Pennsylvania State University, University Park, PA 16802-6200; rsq@psu.edu. Illus., index, adv. Refereed. Circ: 700 Paid. Vol. ends: Oct. *Indexed:* MLA-IB. *Bk. rev.:* 3-6, length varies. *Aud.:* Ac.

A publication of the Rhetoric Society of America, *RSQ* presents cross-disciplinary scholarship on all aspects of rhetoric. Approaches to rhetoric include historical, theoretical, pedagogical, and practical criticism. Editorial expectations are that the scholarship submitted will advance and/or contribute to the field of rhetoric. To serve its mission as a publication for the society, *RSQ* also publishes book reviews, announcements, and general information. A solid journal in its field and recommended for academic collections.

1862. ***Southern Communication Journal.*** Former titles (until 1988): *Southern Speech Communication Journal;* (until 1971): *Southern Speech Journal.* [ISSN: 1041-794X] 1935. q. USD 30. Ed(s): Craig Smith. Southern States Communication Association, c/o Dr Richard R Ranta, Exec Dir, College of Communication & Fine Arts, Memphis, TN 38152. Illus., index, adv. Refereed. Circ: 2500. Vol. ends: Summer. Microform: PQC; NRP. Online: Gale Group; Northern Light Technology, Inc.; OCLC Online Computer Library Center, Inc.; ProQuest Information & Learning. Reprint: PSC. *Indexed:* CIJE, CommAb, IJCS, L&LBA, MLA-IB, PRA, SociolAb. *Bk. rev.:* 20+, medium-length. *Aud.:* Ac.

Another publication of a regional communication association, *SCJ* publishes scholarly research on human communication. The journal is not limited to any topic, simply those topics of interest to scholars, researchers, teachers, and practitioners in the communication field. Any methodological and theoretical orientation is welcomed. There is a book review section with 32 reviews in the issue examined. An affordable, recommended title for academic libraries.

1863. ***Text and Performance Quarterly.*** Formerly (until 1989): *Literature and Performance.* [ISSN: 1046-2937] 1980. q. USD 110 domestic; USD 120 foreign. Ed(s): Judith Hamera. National Communication Association, 1765 N St., N W, Washington, DC 20036; weadie@natcom.org; http://www.natcom.org. Illus. Sample. Refereed. Vol. ends: Oct. Reprint: PSC. *Indexed:* IJCS, L&LBA, MLA-IB, SociolAb. *Bk. rev.:* 2-12, length varies. *Aud.:* Ac, Sa.

This journal publishes readable scholarship that examines and advances the study of performance as a "social, communicative practice; as a technology of representation and expression; and as a hermeneutics." Material is often presented in diverse styles such as narratives and photographic essays. A variety of perspectives to performance are considered—historical, ethnographic, feminist, rhetorical, political, aesthetic. A featured section is "Performance in Review," performance analyses from all types of venues. "Books in Review" includes one or more critical essays plus shorter book reviews. This unique source is recommended for rounding out communication collections in academic libraries.

1864. ***The Toastmaster: for better listening, thinking, speaking.*** [ISSN: 0040-8263] 1933. m. Members, USD 36. Ed(s): Suzanne Frey. Toastmasters International, 23182 Arroyo Vista, Rancho Santa Margarita, CA 92688; pubs@toastmasters.org; http://www.toastmasters.org/. Illus., index, adv. Sample. Circ: 170000. Vol. ends: Dec. *Aud.:* Ga, Sa.

This is a monthly magazine for members of Toastmasters International, although libraries may purchase a subscription. The publication provides helpful information to those interested in learning and improving public speaking and leadership skills. Newsy article topics include humor, speaking techniques, leadership, famous speakers, self-development, and language usage; notices and articles about the activities of the organization are included as well. An "Idea Corner" allows fellow Toastmasters to share ideas that have helped their clubs with membership growth and programming. Of benefit to business professionals and community people with these special interests, this is a title for public libraries.

1865. ***Vital Speeches of the Day.*** [ISSN: 0042-742X] 1934. bi-m. USD 45 domestic; USD 50 foreign; USD 3 newsstand/cover per issue. Ed(s): Thomas F Daly, IV. City News Publishing Co. Inc., PO Box 1247, Mt. Pleasant, SC 29465-1247; vitalspeeches@awod.com; http://www.votd.com/. Microform: PMC. Online: EBSCO Publishing; Florida Center for Library Automation; Gale Group; Northern Light Technology, Inc.; OCLC Online Computer Library Center, Inc.; ProQuest Information & Learning; H.W. Wilson. *Indexed:* ABIn, AgeL, BAS, FutSurv, LRI, MagInd, RGPR, RI-1. *Aud.:* Hs, Ga, Ac.

Vital Speeches prints the "best thought of the best minds on current national questions" twice a month. Speeches are printed in full, and editorial policy is committed to covering both sides of public questions in the areas of politics, education, sociology, government, criminology, finance, business, taxation, health, law, labor, economics, etc. Important addresses from a wide variety of national leaders are published; recent issues include speeches by George W. Bush; Jim Copeland, CEO of Deloitte & Touche ("Post-Enron Challenges for the Auditing Profession"); and James V. Schall, Professor, Georgetown University ("The Best Explanation for Our Existence"). Not only is this title important for the general public, it is also an excellent resource for the student of public speaking. Recommended for public and academic libraries.

1866. ***Western Journal of Communication.*** Former titles: *Western Journal of Speech Communication; Western Speech Communication; Western Speech.* [ISSN: 1057-0314] 1937. q. USD 121.50 domestic to agency (Individuals, USD 135). Ed(s): Sandra Petronio. Western States Communication Association, c/o Connie J Conlee, WSCA Executive Director, Department of Speech Communication, Fresno, CA 93740-0046; dennis.alexander@m.c.c.utah.edu. Illus., index, adv. Sample. Refereed. Circ: 2400. Vol. ends: Fall. Microform: PQC. Online: EBSCO Publishing; Florida Center for Library Automation; Gale Group; Northern Light Technology, Inc.; OCLC Online Computer Library Center, Inc.; ProQuest Information & Learning. Reprint: PQC. *Indexed:* BAS, CIJE, CommAb, IJCS, L&LBA, PsycholAb, SSCI, SociolAb. *Aud.:* Ac.

This journal publishes scholarly articles in all areas of human communication—rhetorical and communication theory, interpersonal communication, gender studies, small group communication, language behavior, cultural and critical theory, oral interpretation, freedom of speech, and applied communication (i.e., health, family, organizations). All methodological and theoretical perspectives are encouraged. Editorial policy encourages research that is accessible both to a scholarly audience and a learned public. A good title for academic libraries.

1867. ***Women's Studies in Communication.*** [ISSN: 0749-1409] 1977. s-a. USD 40 (Individuals, USD 25; Students, USD 15). Ed(s): Bonnie Dow, Celeste Condit. Organization for Research on Women and Communication, c/o Bonnie Dow, Celeste Condit, Eds, Department of Speech Comm, CSU, Long Beach, CA 90840-2407; sdowney@sculb.edu. Illus., adv. Refereed. Circ: 700. Vol. ends: Fall. *Indexed:* FLI, FemPer, HumInd, IJCS, MLA-IB, PsycholAb, WSA. *Bk. rev.:* Various number and length. *Aud.:* Ac, Sa.

The editorial policy of *WSC* states that it provides a "feminist forum for research, reviews and commentary that advance our understanding of the relationships between communication and women, gender, and feminisms." This journal seeks research from all communication scholars on the above topic in any area of communication (interpersonal, media, organizational, small group, rhetorical theory, etc.). Article examples are "Transmitters, Caregivers, and Flowerpots: Rhetorical Constructions of Women's Early Identities in the AIDS Pandemic" and "She Who Must be Obeyed: The Media and Political Spouses in Israel." The publication is open to any methodology, perspective, scope, and context, as long as there is a connection between communication and gender/women/the feminine. The editors also encourage submissions from novice scholars. Also included is a "Conversation and Commentary" section. As the journal of the Organization for Research on Women and Communication of the Western Speech Communication Association, this is a worthwhile title for academic collections.

Electronic Journals

1868. ***American Communication Journal.*** [ISSN: 1532-5865] 1996. 3x/yr. Free. Ed(s): Stephanie L Coopman. American Communication Association, c/o Stephanie Coopman, San Jose State University, San Jose, CA 95192-0112; acjournal@email.com; http://www.americancomm.org/. Refereed. *Bk. rev.:* Irreg. *Aud.:* Ac, Sa.

As described by the editor, this journal is "dedicated to the conscientious analysis and criticism of significant communication artifacts." In appreciation of the multiplicity of methodologies and research interests within the field of communication, essays on any relevant topic may be included. Themes from recent issues range from "Organizational Orienteering" to "Creativity and Scholarship." Each issue contains a special section that consists of essays addressing a single issue from various perspectives. A search engine makes it easy to find items throughout the journal's entire publication period. Articles are available in html or pdf format.

1869. ***Electronic Journal of Communication Online.*** Communication Institute for Online Scholarship, PO Box 57, Rotterdam Junction, NY 12150; http://www.cios.org/www/ejcmain.htm. *Bk. rev.:* Occasional. *Aud.:* Ac, Sa.

Presented in English with French abstracts, this journal addresses all areas of communication studies including theory, research, practice, and policy. Each issue is devoted to a theme and has its own editor. Themes from recent issues include "Communication Perspectives on Work and Family," "Computer Mediated Communication as a Teaching Method," and "The Future of the Internet." Nonsubscribers may access the editor's introduction to the issue and view abstracts for each article. A subscription is required to access the articles and the search engine that indexes every word in the issue. Occasionally an issue will include special features with book reviews.

1870. ***Journal of Computer-Mediated Communication.*** [ISSN: 1083-6101] q. Free. Ed(s): Margaret McLaughlin. Hebrew University of Jerusalem, School of Business Administration, Jerusalem, 91905, Israel; mmclaughlin@alnitak.usc.edu; http://jcmc.huji.ac.il; http://www.usc.edu/dept/annenberg/journal.html. Illus., index. Refereed. *Aud.:* Ac, Sa.

This journal provides a forum for research and essays based on any of the social sciences on the topic of computerized communication. Subscriptions are free, but those who choose to fill out a brief survey are notified of new issues and may receive the *JCMC Newsletter.* Each issue is devoted to a specific aspect of computer-mediated communication such as online journalism, electronic commerce, and Internet research. An integrated search engine is useful for the researcher searching for keywords or concepts across the full run of issues.

1871. ***Web Journal of Mass Communication Research.*** 1997. q. Free. Ed(s): Robert Stewart, Guido Stempel. Ohio University, E. W. Scripps School of Journalism, Athens, OH 45701. Refereed. *Aud.:* Ac, Sa.

This journal publishes scholarly investigations in mass communication research. It is designed in a very straightforward manner that, refreshingly, offers few frills and unnecessary graphics. Each issue contains one article, and topics from past issues range from a study of integrated marketing communication to the effects of television viewing on college students? use of alcohol. Frames are used to display endnotes as footnotes.

■ COMPUTER SCIENCE AND AUTOMATION

Computer Science/Popular Computer Titles

See also Business; Electronics; Engineering and Technology; Internet-World Wide Web; and Library and Information Science sections.

Andy Firpo, Manager, Acquisitions and Integrations, Technology Integration Group, Washington Mutual Inc., P.O. Box 194, Belmont, MA 02478; andy.firpo@wamu.net. FAX: 707-222-7507

Ray Maker, Acquisitons and Integrations Engineer, Technology Integration Group, Washington Mutual, Inc., 1111 3rd Ave, Seattle, WA 98101; ray.maker@wamu.net. FAX: 509-695-4879

Helene Williams, English Bibliographer for the Humanities, Widener Library of the the Harvard College Library, Harvard University, Cambridge, MA 02138; helene_williams@harvard.edu

Introduction

The entries herein represent publications to be considered for inclusion primarily in computer science collections, although titles may cross subject boundaries to some extent. This section is split into three subsections: Computer Science, Popular Computer Titles, and Electronic Journals. Journals in the Computer Science subsection tend toward the scholarly, intended largely for computer scientists and researchers. These titles also tend to focus on the more complicated, theoretical or conceptual aspects of computer use, large-scale or enterprise systems, or a perspective that treats an entire facet of the involved technologies as a single unit. Magazines in the Popular Computer Titles subsection are publications that will provide practical information to an "average" user of personal computers, whether at home or at work.

The title of the last subsection, Electronic Journals, is somewhat misleading in that every publication in the entire section has some corresponding electronic presence on the World Wide Web; one clear differentiation is that the listings in Electronic Journals are only available electronically. The move away from print editions to electronic formats continues; the speed of change in this field of study and its associated industries may be a large contributor to that trend.

Although this section contains more than 70 titles, please note that there are many more publications available in the Computer Science and Automation subject area. While not unique to this field, growing parochialism and fragmentation into ever-more-finely divided fields of study were evident in the range of serials available for consideration. Maturation from emerging technology to popular product can also drive a counter-trend, however: as an example, mobile technology is so popular that every title in the Popular Computer Titles subsection and several of those in the Computer Science subsection now deal with it directly.

Here are some things to consider when reviewing the titles presented in this section. While a goal of our selection process was to avoid including titles whose scope was narrowly defined, a decision was made to expand the definition of "personal computer" to include the most popular operating systems and associated software; thus, individual titles that focus on a single operating system are included. Also, although an effort was made to add titles specific to the "Automation" component of the "Computer Science and Automation" section, the titles available whose topics were not very narrow in scope were surprisingly few. And, in an attempt to avoid duplication, where two or more titles were sufficiently similar in scope, content, intent, and layout, only one (generally, the most well-known) was annotated, with mention at the end of that annotation of the other near-duplicate(s).

Basic Periodicals

Ems: *Smart Computing;* Hs: *Byte.com, PC World;* Ga: *Byte.com, MacWorld, PC Magazine, PC World, Smart Computing;* Ac: *Association for Computing Machinery. Journal; Byte.com, The Computer Journal, Computerworld.*

Basic Abstracts and Indexes

Computer and Control Abstracts (INSPEC), Computer Literature Index, Computing Reviews, Internet & Personal Computing Abstracts.

Computer Science

1872. ***A C M Computing Surveys: the survey and tutorial journal of the ACM.*** Formerly: *Computing Surveys.* [ISSN: 0360-0300] 1969. q. Members, USD 26; Non-members, USD 160; Students, USD 21. Ed(s): Peter Wegner. Association for Computing Machinery, Inc., One Astor Plaza, 1515 Broadway, 17th Fl, New York, NY 10036-5701; sigs@acm.org; http://www.acm.org. Illus., index. Refereed. Circ: 33000. Vol. ends: No. 4. Microform: WWS; NRP. Online: Pub.; EBSCO Publishing; Florida Center for Library Automation; Gale Group; OCLC Online Computer Library Center, Inc.; ProQuest Information & Learning. *Indexed:* ABIn, AS&TI, C&ISA, CompLI, CompR, EngInd, ErgAb, SCI. *Aud.:* Ac, Sa.

This publication of the Association for Computing Machinery (ACM) "publishes surveys, tutorials, and special reports on all areas of computing research." Articles focus primarily on the existing literature in the field, although articles do cover a variety of topics of interest in the study of computer science. While surveys tend to be conceptual and aimed at the more knowledgeable reader, tutorials are written for those with less experience, and have specific examples on a particular subject. Recent examples include "Information technology and economic performance: A critical review of the empirical evidence," "A survey of processors with explicit multithreading," and "Some facets of complexity theory and cryptography: A five-lecture tutorial." Short articles of about 1,000 words are sometimes included, on any topic deemed of interest to the ACM membership. Issues usually include up to six scholarly articles and an introductory "About This Issue" piece. Sometimes an entire issue is devoted to a particular symposium topic and may contain more articles. The web site includes the complete table of contents for present and past issues. Full-text content of the actual articles is available to members in pdf format. (AF)

1873. ***A C M Transactions on Computer Systems.*** [ISSN: 0734-2071] 1983. q. USD 32 student members (Members, USD 37; Non-members, USD 170). Ed(s): Larry Peterson. Association for Computing Machinery, Inc., One Astor Plaza, 1515 Broadway, 17th Fl, New York, NY 10036-5701; sigs@acm.org; http://www.acm.org. Illus. Refereed. Circ: 7100. Vol. ends: No. 4. Online: Pub.; EBSCO Publishing; Florida Center for Library Automation; Gale Group. *Indexed:* AS&TI, C&ISA, CompLI, EngInd, SCI. *Aud.:* Ac, Sa.

The charter of this publication of the Association for Computing Machinery is "to present research and development results on the design, specification, realization, behavior, and use of computer systems. The term ~computer systems' is interpreted broadly and includes systems architectures, operating systems, distributed systems, and computer networks." The presentations discuss the individual experiences of the researchers as well as recent developments for designers and users of computer systems. Issues usually contain three scholarly papers on various subjects. Recent topics include "A SMART scheduler for multimedia applications," "Size-based scheduling to improve web performance," and "Measuring thin-client performance using slow-motion benchmarking." Occasional special issues focus on a single topic, such as operating system design or system architecture. The web site includes tables of contents for recent issues, with full text of articles available to subscribers. (AF)

1874. ***A C M Transactions on Database Systems.*** [ISSN: 0362-5915] 1976. q. USD 34 student members (Members, USD 39; Non-members, USD 164). Ed(s): Richard T. Snodgrass. Association for Computing Machinery, Inc., One Astor Plaza, 1515 Broadway, 17th Fl, New York, NY 10036-5701; sigs@acm.org; http://www.acm.org. Illus., index. Refereed. Circ: 3300. Vol. ends: No. 4. Microform: WWS; NRP. Online: Pub.; EBSCO Publishing; Florida Center for Library Automation; Gale Group. *Indexed:* AS&TI, C&ISA, CompLI, CompR, EngInd, ErgAb, InfoSAb, SCI, SSCI. *Aud.:* Ac, Sa.

This journal of the Association for Computing Machinery "publishes original archival papers in the area of databases and closely related disciplines," presenting research on computerized data storage and processing. Articles may focus on database management theory, or design and implementation of database systems, or real-world experience with database systems administration. Most articles "address the logical and technical foundation of data management," with recent topics including "Description logics for semantic query optimization in object-oriented database systems," "Adaptive algorithms for set containment joins," and "Understanding the global semantics of referential actions using logic rules." Issues usually contain up to five scholarly articles that span a variety of approaches to database system research. The web site includes tables of contents for current and past issues as well as full-text content in pdf format available to members. (AF)

1875. ***A C M Transactions on Graphics.*** [ISSN: 0730-0301] 1982. q. USD 36 student members (Members, USD 41; Non-members, USD 170). Ed(s): John Hart. Association for Computing Machinery, Inc., One Astor Plaza, 1515 Broadway, 17th Fl, New York, NY 10036-5701; sigs@acm.org; http://www.acm.org. Illus., index. Refereed. Circ: 3100 Paid. Vol. ends: No. 4. Online: Pub.; EBSCO Publishing. *Indexed:* AS&TI, C&ISA, CompLI, CompR, EngInd, ErgAb, GeoRef, IAA, SCI. *Aud.:* Ac, Sa.

This journal of the Association for Computing Machinery "is the foremost peer-reviewed journal in the graphics field." Unlike other ACM publications, it is published in color, with articles on "breakthroughs in computer-aided design, synthetic image generation, rendering, solid modeling and other areas." Each issue contains up to six articles in three sections: original refereed papers in "Research"; articles on use and implementation in "Practice and Experience"; and shorter articles on how humans interact with graphics applications. Recent topics include "Constraint-based approach for automatic hinting of digital typefaces," "Planning biped locomotion using motion capture data and probabilistic roadmaps," "Anisotropic diffusion of surfaces and functions on surfaces," and "A search engine for 3D models." Some issues focus on a single topic of specific interest. Tables of contents can be found on the web site, and members can find full text in pdf format. (AF)

1876. ***A C M Transactions on Information Systems.*** Formerly (until 1988): *Transactions on Office Information Systems.* [ISSN: 1046-8188] 1983. q. USD 32 student members (Members, USD 37; Non-members, USD 170). Ed(s): Gary Marchionini. Association for Computing Machinery, Inc., One Astor Plaza, 1515 Broadway, 17th Fl, New York, NY 10036-5701; sigs@acm.org; http://www.acm.org. Illus., adv. Refereed. Circ: 5800. Vol. ends: No. 4. Online: Pub.; EBSCO Publishing; Florida Center for Library Automation; Gale Group. *Indexed:* AS&TI, ArtHuCI, C&ISA, CompLI, EngInd, ErgAb, InfoSAb, LISA, SCI, SSCI. *Aud.:* Ac, Sa.

The scope of this journal of the Association for Computing Machinery "encompasses all aspects of computerized information systems," with articles that cover "issues in information retrieval and filtering, information interfaces, and information systems design." Examples of recent topics include "Performance issues and error analysis in an open-domain question answering system," "A hierarchical access control model for video database systems," and "Exploiting hierarchical domain structure to compute similarity." Issues generally contain up to four articles, and occasionally are focused entirely on a specific topic. Both tables of contents and abstracts of articles for previous and current issues can be found on the web site. (AF)

1877. ***A C M Transactions on Modeling and Computer Simulation.*** [ISSN: 1049-3301] 1991. q. USD 36 student members (Members, USD 41; Non-members, USD 160). Association for Computing Machinery, Inc., One Astor Plaza, 1515 Broadway, 17th Fl, New York, NY 10036-5701; sigs@acm.org; http://www.acm.org. Illus. Refereed. Vol. ends: No. 4. Online: Pub.; EBSCO Publishing. *Indexed:* AS&TI, C&ISA, EngInd. *Aud.:* Ac, Sa.

This journal of the Association for Computing Machinery focuses on systems modeling and computer simulation concepts, two of the important tools for development and troubleshooting in computer science. "Emphasizing discrete event simulation, this journal publishes applications, reviews, and tutorials on such topics as combined, distributed, and hybrid simulation, simulation and computer graphics, process generators, and random number generation." Issues usually contain up to four articles, and recent topics include "On the processor scheduling problem in time warp synchronization," "Parallel simulation of chip-multiprocessor architectures," and "A two-stage modeling and simulation process for web-based modeling and simulation." Occasionally, issues are published with focus on a single topic, for example, "Computer automated multi-paradigm modeling." Correspondence is often included and provides a forum for criticism and defense of published concepts. Full text of articles is available to members in pdf format on the web site, which also includes tables of contents and abstracts for articles in current and recent issues. (AF)

1878. ***A C M Transactions on Programming Languages and Systems.*** Incorporates (1992-1993): *Letters on Programming Languages and Systems.* [ISSN: 0164-0925] 1979. bi-m. USD 44 student members (Members, USD 49; Non-members, USD 225). Ed(s): William Pugh. Association for Computing Machinery, Inc., One Astor Plaza, 1515 Broadway, 17th Fl, New York, NY 10036-5701; sigs@acm.org; http://www.acm.org. Illus., index. Refereed. Circ: 10500. Vol. ends: No. 6. Microform: WWS. Online: Pub.; EBSCO Publishing; Florida Center for Library Automation; Gale Group. *Indexed:* AS&TI, C&ISA, CompLI, EngInd, ErgAb, SCI. *Aud.:* Ac, Sa.

The focus of this journal of the Association for Computing Machinery is "to present research results on all aspects of the design, definition, implementation, and use of programming languages and programming systems." Recent topics include "A foundation for embedded languages," "Eliminating synchronization bottlenecks using adaptive replication," and "A transformational approach to binary translation of delayed branches." The web site contains tables of contents and abstracts for current and recent issues, and full text of articles is available for members in pdf format. (AF)

1879. ***A C M Transactions on Software Engineering and Methodology.*** [ISSN: 1049-331X] 1992. q. USD 28 student members (Members, USD 33; Non-members, USD 150). Ed(s): Axel Lamsweerde. Association for Computing Machinery, Inc., One Astor Plaza, 1515 Broadway, 17th Fl, New York, NY 10036-5701; sigs@acm.org; http://www.acm.org. Illus. Refereed. Vol. ends: No. 4. Online: Pub.; EBSCO Publishing. *Indexed:* AS&TI, C&ISA, EngInd, SCI. *Aud.:* Ac, Sa.

This journal of the Association for Computing Machinery publishes papers on all aspects of designing and building large, complex software systems, including specification, design, development and maintenance. "It covers tools and methodologies, languages, data structures, and algorithms...reports on successful efforts, noting practical lessons that can be scaled and transferred to other projects, and often looks at applications of innovative technologies." Issues usually contain up to four articles, with recent topics including "Architecting families of software systems with process algebras," "Temporal abstract classes and virtual temporal specifications for real-time systems," and "Equivalence analysis and its application in improving the efficiency of program slicing." The web site contains tables of contents and abstracts for current and recent issues, and full text of articles is available for members in pdf format. (AF)

1880. ***Acta Informatica.*** [ISSN: 0001-5903] 1971. 9x/yr. EUR 720 domestic; EUR 749.70 foreign; EUR 96 per issue. Ed(s): J Becvar, F L Bauer. Springer-Verlag, Tiergartenstr 17, Heidelberg, 69121, Germany. Illus., adv. Refereed. Microform: PQC. Online: EBSCO Publishing; RoweCom Information Quest; ScienceDirect; Springer LINK; Swets Blackwell. Reprint: ISI. *Indexed:* CCMJ, CompR, EngInd, MathSciNet, SCI. *Aud.:* Ac, Sa.

This long-published journal "provides international dissemination of contributions on the art, discipline and science of informatics. Its scope covers design, description, presentation and analysis of programs, information structures, computing systems and interaction between components thereof." Distinctions between informatics and computer science can be hard to discern. Recent articles include "Stepwise development of fair distributed systems," "Fundamentals of control flow in workflows," and "Preference rankings in the face of uncertainty." Tables of contents and abstracts of articles from past and current issues are available on the web site, as is full text (for subscribers) in pdf format. (AF)

1881. ***Algorithmica: an international journal in computer science.*** [ISSN: 0178-4617] 1986. m. USD 899; USD 89 per issue. Ed(s): C K Wong. Springer-Verlag, Journals, 175 Fifth Ave., New York, NY 10010-7703; journals@springer-ny.com; http://www.springer-ny.com. Illus., adv. Refereed. Vol. ends: No. 6. Microform: PQC. Online: EBSCO Publishing; RoweCom Information Quest; ScienceDirect; Springer LINK; Swets Blackwell. Reprint: SWZ. *Indexed:* C&ISA, CCMJ, EngInd, MathSciNet, SCI. *Aud.:* Ac, Sa.

An algorithm is a described approach to solve a problem or achieve a goal, with a defined endpoint. Problem: I'm hungry, but flour, raw eggs, butter, sugar, and baking chocolate are not very palatable individually. I apply an algorithm (Chocolate Cake Recipe) to achieve a goal: yummy chocolate cake. Similarly, almost all computer programs (except some artificial intelligence programs) can be viewed as algorithms, and as such are integral to the study of computer science. As noted in the Algorithmica Aims and Scope statement: "The increasing complexity and scope of computer applications makes the design of efficient algorithms essential...fields of interest include algorithms in applied areas such as: VLSI, distributed computing, parallel processing, automated design, robotics, graphics, data base design, software tools, as well as algorithms in fundamental areas such as sorting, searching, data structures, computational geometry, and linear programming." Recent topics include "Efficient External Memory Algorithms by Simulating Coarse-Grained Parallel Algorithms," "Time-Constrained Scheduling of Weighted Packets on Trees and Meshes," and "Multicast Pull Scheduling: When Fairness Is Fine." In addition, the publication sometimes includes the special sections "Application Experience," which documents the results of applying theory to practical situations, and "Problems," which are short papers that present problems on selected computer science topics. Tables of contents and abstracts of articles are available on the web site, and full text is available to subscribers in TeX and pdf formats. (AF)

1882. ***Circuit Cellar: the magazine for computer applications.*** Formerly (until 1999): *Circuit Cellar Ink.* [ISSN: 1528-0608] 1988. m. USD 21.95 domestic; USD 31.95 in Canada & Mexico; USD 49.95 elsewhere. Ed(s): Ken Davidson. Circuit Cellar, Inc., 4 Park St., Ste. 20, Vernon, CT 06066; edit@circellar.com. Illus., index, adv. Sample. Circ: 35000 Paid. Vol. ends: Dec. *Aud.:* Ac, Sa.

Circuit Cellar touts itself as "the magazine for computer applications...by engineers, for engineers." This very technical publication is intended primarily for readers who take a much more "hands-on" approach to computing hardware than the average personal computer user, with specific focus on use, circuit design for and programming of microcontrollers, embedded controllers, and associated hardware devices. Issues present four feature articles all on a single topic with circuit schematics, troubleshooting information, and program source code presented; the recent "Signal Processing" issue includes articles on a "2-D Optical Position Sensor," "Rotary Encoder Input Devices," "Home Automation Upgrade," and "Switching vs. Linear Supply." Other articles on related topics are also included. An index of tables of contents going back to 1988 is available on the web site, with access to full text of articles for subscribers. (AF)

1883. ***Computer Graphics World.*** Formerly: *Computer Graphics (Eugene).* [ISSN: 0271-4159] 1978. m. USD 55 domestic; USD 75 in Canada & Mexico; USD 115 elsewhere. Ed(s): Phil LoPiccolo. PennWell Corp., 1421 S Sheridan Rd, Tulsa, OK 74112; Headquarters@PennWell.com; http://www.pennwell.com. Illus., adv. Circ: 63915. Vol. ends: Dec. Microform: PQC. Online: The Dialog Corporation; EBSCO Publishing; Florida Center for Library Automation; Gale Group; Northern Light Technology, Inc.; OCLC Online Computer Library Center, Inc. *Indexed:* AS&TI, BrTechI, CompLI, EngInd, MicrocompInd. *Aud.:* Ga, Ac, Sa.

Billed as "The Magazine for Digital Content Professionals," *Computer Graphics World* provides content on computer graphics, 3D modeling, CAD, animation, and visual computing. Topics covered range across a broad spectrum, including the use of computer-generated imagery as an art medium, commercial application of image-processing hardware and software, process descriptions, product reviews, and editorial content on various facets of industries that use these media, processes, and products. Many detailed images are provided along with text content in both the print and web page versions. On computers with slower connections to the Internet this can cause somewhat long page-loading times, but the high quality and relevance to the topic being covered make the wait well worth it even on these systems, and a pure delight on computers with broadband or networked access. Most issues provide four feature articles; recent examples are "Character Driven," a detailed description of the creation of a new computer game, and "Pyramid Scheme," a technical look at the tools and techniques used in a 3D model reconstruction of the Great Pyramid of Giza. (AF)

1884. ***The Computer Journal.*** [ISSN: 0010-4620] 1958. bi-m. GBP 515. Ed(s): F. Murtagh. Oxford University Press, Great Clarendon St, Oxford, OX2 6DP, United Kingdom; jnl.orders@oup.co.uk; http://www3.oup.co.uk/jnls. Illus., index, adv. Refereed. Circ: 4500. Vol. ends: No. 8. Microform: PQC; NRP. Online: EBSCO Publishing; ingenta.com; OCLC Online Computer Library Center, Inc.; RoweCom Information Quest; Swets Blackwell. Reprint: PSC. *Indexed:* AS&TI, BRI, BrTechI, C&ISA, ChemAb, CompLI, CompR, EngInd, ErgAb, ExcerpMed, MLA-IB, SCI, SSCI. *Aud.:* Ac, Sa.

One of the oldest and most respected scholarly journals in the field, *The Computer Journal* is published by Oxford University Press for the British Computer Society, and "publishes research papers in a full range of subject areas, as well as regular feature articles and occasional themed issues...provides a complete overview of developments in the field of Computer Science." Issues generally include up to eight articles, and examples from the current issue are "Optimal Placement of Web Proxies for Replicated Web Servers in the Internet," "Balancing Traffic Load for Multi-Node Multicast in a Wormhole 2-D Torus/Mesh," "Probability-based Fault-tolerant Routing in Hypercubes," "A Logical Model for Information Retrieval Based on Propositional Logic and Belief Revision," "A Local Approach to the Testing of Real-time Systems," and "An Efficient and Secure Protocol for Multi-party Key Establishment." The themed issues have all papers focused on a specific topic. The web site offers the usual abstracts and tables of contents, with full text for subscribers, as well as the very unusual resource of links to issues going back to 1958! Older issues provide abstracts as well as full text presented via scans in tiff format, and there is a large group of issues from 1973 to 1992 not available. (AF)

1885. ***Computer Languages, Systems and Structures.*** Formerly (until 2003): *Computer Languages.* [ISSN: 1477-8424] 1976. 4x/yr. EUR 850 (Individuals, EUR 239). Ed(s): Dr. Robert S Ledley, Blaire V Mossman. Pergamon, The Boulevard, Langford Ln, East Park, Kidlington, OX5 1GB, United Kingdom. Illus., adv. Refereed. Circ: 1025. Vol. ends: No. 27. Microform: PQC. Online: EBSCO Publishing; Gale Group; ingenta.com; ScienceDirect; Swets Blackwell. *Indexed:* C&ISA, CompLI, CompR, EngInd, ErgAb. *Aud.:* Ac, Sa.

[Note: As of Volume 28 (2003), the journal will be known as *Computer Languages, Systems and Structures.*] This journal covers "both articles presenting original work and also review articles, on programming languages, systems, structures, and theories...topics to be included are syntax, parsing, compilers, complexities, computability, semantics, automatic programming languages, special purpose languages, programming theories, programming documentation, memory management, micro programming, process control programming, real-time programming, programming for interactive systems, streaming methods, Internet surfing technologies, composite hypermedia, server management, routing technique architecture, scalable Internet communication services, on-line economic systems for Internet resource allocation, bottleneck detection, adaptive network services, mobile computing techniques, network protocol development, distributed computer languages, cluster based network services, Web hosting services, and so forth." Surprisingly, even more descriptive information about the journal is available on the web site, as are abstracts and tables of contents, and full text for subscribers. (AF)

1886. ***Computer Networks.*** Former titles (until 1999): *Computer Networks and ISDN Systems;* (until 1985): *Computer Networks.* [ISSN: 1389-1286] 1976. 18x/yr. EUR 1545 print & online eds. Ed(s): I. F. Akyildiz, H. Rudin. Elsevier BV, North-Holland, Sara Burgerhartstraat 25, Amsterdam, 1055 KV, Netherlands; nlinfo-f@elsevier.nl; http://www.elsevier.nl. Illus., index. Refereed. Circ: 2500. Vol. ends: Nov (No. 35 - No. 37). Microform: PQC. Online: EBSCO Publishing; Gale Group; ingenta.com; ScienceDirect; Swets Blackwell. Reprint: SWZ. *Indexed:* ABIn, C&ISA, CommAb, CompLI, EngInd, ErgAb, LISA, SSCI. *Aud.:* Ac, Sa.

With a focus on innovation and the most current trends in the field, this journal of the International Council for Computer Communication "is an international, archival journal providing a publication vehicle for complete coverage of all topics of interest to those involved in the computer communications networking area...the audience includes researchers, managers and operators of networks as well as designers and implementers." Technical topics covered include communication network architectures, protocols, services and applications, security and privacy, operation and management, discrete algorithms and discrete modeling; nontechnical topics include business model studies, pricing strategies, social impacts and legal concerns. An entire issue is commonly devoted to a single topic; recent examples are "Small and Home Networks" and "Towards a New Internet." Also common are calls for papers for special issues and for other related journals, and announcements for upcoming conferences. The web site includes abstracts and tables of contents for current and archive issues, as well as full content for subscribers. (AF)

Computer Networks and ISDN Systems. See *Computer Networks.*

1887. ***Computer (New York).*** Former titles (until 1970): *I E E E Computer;* Supersedes: *I E E E Computer Group News.* [ISSN: 0018-9162] 1966. m. USD 1060 in North America; USD 1095 elsewhere. Ed(s): Edward A Parrish. Institute of Electrical and Electronics Engineers, Inc., 445 Hoes Ln, Piscataway, NJ 08854-1331; subscription-service@ieee.org; http://www.ieee.org. Illus., adv. Refereed. Circ: 96859. Vol. ends: Dec. Online: EBSCO Publishing; Gale Group; I E E E. *Indexed:* AS&TI, C&ISA, CompLI, CompR, DSR&OA, ErgAb, IAA, SCI, SSCI. *Bk. rev.:* 5, 500 words. *Aud.:* Ac, Sa.

The flagship publication of the IEEE Computer Society, *Computer* provides a forum where "practitioners, managers, and researchers can talk to each other in plain language about what works and what doesn't, what resources are available, and what might be next." Each issue has 15–20 brief (two to five pages each) articles on topics ranging from the popular to the technical, with writing and illustrations that are accessible to readers from all backgrounds. Recent topics have included business use of instant messaging, embedded system design challenges, server workloads in commercial settings, and an essay entitled "Me and My Theremin." Of all the IEEE publications, this has the most appeal to a general audience. Subscribers can access the full text of issues from 1988 to the present from the web site. (HW)

1888. ***Computer Standards and Interfaces: the international journal devoted to computer standards, their implementation and utilization.*** Formed by the merger of (1982-1986): *Computers and Standards;* (1983-1986): *Interfaces in Computing.* [ISSN: 0920-5489] 1986. 6x/yr. EUR 739. Ed(s): H. Schumny. Elsevier BV, North-Holland, Sara Burgerhartstraat 25, Amsterdam, 1055 KV, Netherlands; nlinfo-f@elsevier.nl; http://www.elsevier.nl. Illus. Refereed. Vol. ends: No. 23. Microform: PQC. Online: EBSCO Publishing; ingenta.com; ScienceDirect; Swets Blackwell. *Indexed:* C&ISA, CompLI, EngInd. *Aud.:* Ac, Sa.

Computer systems and components can't work together without adherence to defined standards in design and manufacture, making the subject matter of this journal vital to the basic usability of all commonly available computer hardware and software, and a required part of their evolution and development. Described as "the international journal devoted to computer standards, their implementation and utilization," specific topics covered include standards, information management, formal methods, design and implementation, software quality and process, distributed and open systems, e-commerce, data acquisition, process control, electromagnetic compatibility and standardization of digital instruments. More general topics include aspects of the standardization process itself, "such as technical, political and commercial aspects of standards, their impact on the marketplace, cost/benefit analyses, legislative issues, and relationships among national and international standards bodies." Some issues focus on a single standard, and usually contain more articles. Abstracts and tables of contents for current and archive issues are found on the web site. The last issue of each volume contains subject and author indexes. (AF)

1889. ***Computer Vision and Image Understanding.*** Formerly (until 1995): *C V G I P: Image Understanding;* Which superseded in part (in 1991): *Computer Vision, Graphics, and Image Processing;* Which was formerly (until 1983): *Computer Graphics and Image Processing.* [ISSN: 1077-3142] 1969. m. EUR 1399 (Individuals, EUR 680). Ed(s): Avinash C Kak. Academic Press, 525 B St, Ste 1900, San Diego, CA 92101-4495; apsubs@acad.com; http://www.academicpress.com. Illus. Refereed. Vol. ends: No. 3. Online: EBSCO Publishing; ingenta.com; OCLC Online Computer Library Center, Inc.; RoweCom Information Quest; ScienceDirect; Swets Blackwell. *Indexed:* AS&TI, C&ISA, EngInd, GeoRef, GeogAbPG, SCI, SSCI. *Aud.:* Ac, Sa.

Unlike other publications that focus on computer image generation, this scholarly journal covers computer analysis of pictorial information, with focus on "all aspects of image analysis from the low-level, iconic processes of early vision to the high-level, symbolic processes of recognition and interpretation." Theoretical topics include shape, range, motion, architecture and languages, data structures and representations, vision systems, and fundamental problems in image understanding by humans and machines; practical topics include medical image processing, face and object recognition in video monitoring, battle surveillance, and video-assisted operation of remote vehicles. Most issues have up to ten articles. Abstracts and tables of contents are available on the web site, with full text available for subscribers. (AF)

1890. ***Computers & Graphics: international journal of systems applications in computer graphics.*** [ISSN: 0097-8493] 1975. 6x/yr. EUR 1574 (Qualified personnel, EUR 162). Ed(s): Jose L. Encarnacao. Pergamon, The Boulevard, Langford Ln, East Park, Kidlington, OX5 1GB, United Kingdom. Illus., adv. Refereed. Circ: 1050. Vol. ends: No. 25. Microform: PQC. Online: ingenta.com; ScienceDirect; Swets Blackwell. *Indexed:* ApMecR, C&ISA, CompLI, CompR, EngInd, ErgAb, GeoRef, MathSciNet, SSCI. *Aud.:* Ac, Sa.

This scholarly journal provides "information concerning graphical man/machine interaction and the applications of computer graphics." The emphasis is on graphic processes as the means of interaction using "CRT-type consoles and manual input devices such as light-pens, tablets, and function keyboards. . .graphical models, data structures, attention-handling languages, picture manipulation algorithms and related software." Topics covered include computer-aided design, simulation, process control, computer-aided education, pattern recognition, graphic arts, medical research, architectural design, display techniques, and evaluation of hardware and software involved. Some issues explore a single specific topic; symposia announcements are common. The web site offers tables of contents, full text for subscribers, and a sample issue with full content. (AF)

1891. ***Computers & Operations Research: and their application to problems of world concern.*** Incorporates (1993-1998): *Location Science.* [ISSN: 0305-0548] 1974. 14x/yr. EUR 2289 (Individuals, EUR 284). Ed(s): Gilbert Laporte. Pergamon, The Boulevard, Langford Ln, East Park, Kidlington, OX5 1GB, United Kingdom. Illus., adv. Refereed.

Circ: 1000. Vol. ends: Dec. Microform: PQC. Online: Gale Group; ingenta.com; ScienceDirect; Swets Blackwell. *Indexed:* ABIn, BiolAb, C&ISA, CCMJ, CompLI, EngInd, ExcerpMed, GeoRef, GeogAbPG, MathSciNet, SSCI. *Aud.:* Ac, Sa.

"Operations research and computers meet in a large number of scientific fields, many of which are of vital current concern to our troubled society. These include, among others, ecology, transportation, safety, reliability, urban planning, economics, inventory control, investment strategy and military analysis." The focus of this international journal is the application of computers and operations research techniques to solving problems in these fields. Issues typically include six to ten scholarly articles and announcements for upcoming conferences. Frequent single-topic special issues are produced; recent examples are "Analytic Hierarchy Process," "Emerging Economics," and "Location Analysis." The web site offers tables of contents, full text for subscribers, and a sample issue with full content. (AF)

1892. *Computers & Society.* Formerly: *S I G C A S Newsletter.* [ISSN: 0095-2737] 1968. q. Membership, USD 99. Ed(s): Richard S Rosenberg. Association for Computing Machinery, Inc., One Astor Plaza, 1515 Broadway, 17th Fl, New York, NY 10036-5701; sigs@acm.org; http://www.acm.org. Illus. Circ: 1500. Vol. ends: Dec. *Indexed:* EngInd, ErgAb. *Bk. rev.:* 1-2, 500-750 words. *Aud.:* Ac, Sa.

This quarterly newsletter for members of the Special Interest Group on Computers and Society (SIGCAS) of the Association for Computing Machinery also serves "the public at large...to address concerns and raise awareness about the ethical and societal impact of computers...to gather and report information, thus stimulating the exchange and dissemination of ideas...." Issues may contain articles on a variety of topics or a single specific topic, as well as book excerpts or reviews, student papers and case studies, and may include proceedings from the various conferences sponsored by the special interest group. Recent articles include "All About the Blog," "Prostitution, Sex Tourism on the Internet: Whose Voice is Being Heard?" and "Open Source Software." The web site provides an index to articles and tables of contents with full text available for members; through the "Related Links" section, it also acts as a portal to a wealth of information on social and ethical concerns. (AF)

1893. *Computers and the Humanities.* [ISSN: 0010-4817] 1966. q. EUR 477 for print or online ed. Ed(s): Elli Mylonas, Nancy Ide. Kluwer Academic Publishers, van Godewijckstraat 30, PO Box 17, Dordrecht, 3300 AA, Netherlands. Illus., index, adv. Refereed. Vol. ends: No. 4. Microform: PQC. Online: EBSCO Publishing; Gale Group; ingenta.com; Kluwer Online; OCLC Online Computer Library Center, Inc.; RoweCom Information Quest; Swets Blackwell. *Indexed:* ABS&EES, AmHI, ArtHuCI, BAS, BHA, BRI, BrArAb, CBRI, CIJE, CompLI, CompR, HumInd, L&LBA, MLA-IB, MusicInd, NumL, RI-1, RILM, SCI, SSCI. *Aud.:* Ac, Sa.

This well-established journal began in the 1960s, to "report on significant new research concerning the application of computer methods to humanities scholarship." Those reports come from a broad range of humanities fields, which now incorporate media, hypertext theory, and digital text applications, among others. The journal also serves as a forum for discussion of standards, resource management, and the increasing legal concerns in the creation, use, and management of digital resources. Issues contain from three to nine scholarly articles as well as brief project reports. Topics of recent articles include tracking dialect changes over time and geographic distance, and creating a digital reconstruction of Rome's first theater. Special issues provide the proceedings of the Association for Computers and the Humanities conferences. The web site provides tables of contents and, for subscribers, full-text articles, back to 1997. (HW)

1894. *Control Engineering Practice.* [ISSN: 0967-0661] 1993. 12x/yr. EUR 1314 (Qualified personnel, EUR 67). Ed(s): A. H. Glattfelder. Pergamon, The Boulevard, Langford Ln, East Park, Kidlington, OX5 1GB, United Kingdom. Refereed. Vol. ends: No. 9. Microform: PQC. Online: ingenta.com; ScienceDirect; Swets Blackwell. *Indexed:* C&ISA, GeogAbPG. *Aud.:* Ac, Sa.

Similar in scope to its sister publication *Automatica,* this journal of the International Federation of Automatic Control is focused less on theoretical studies and experimental research and more on "direct application of control theory and its supporting tools in all possible areas of automation." Each monthly issue contains up to a dozen highly technical articles; recent examples include "A survey of industrial model predictive control technology," "Supervisory control for a telerobotic system: a hybrid control approach," and "Fuzzy logic based full-envelope autonomous flight control for an atmospheric re-entry spacecraft." Occasionally an entire issue is devoted to a single topic; there are also occasional papers on aspects of the application of automation including social and cultural effects, project planning, and economic and management issues. The web site offers abstracts and tables of contents for current and past issues, full content in pdf format for subscribers or for purchase, and a complete sample issue with free access. (AF)

1895. *Dr. Dobb's Journal: software tools for the professional programmer.* Former titles (until 1989): *Dr. Dobb's Journal of Software Tools;* (until 1986): *Dr. Dobb's Journal: Software Tools for Advanced Programmers;* (in 1984): *Dr. Dobb's Journal for the Experienced in Microcomputing;* (until 1984): *Dr. Dobb's Journal for Users of Small Computer Systems;* (until 1981): *Dr. Dobb's Journal of Computer Calisthenics and Orthodontia.* [ISSN: 1044-789X] 1977. m. USD 34.95 domestic (Qualified personnel, USD 9.95). Ed(s): Jonathan Erickson, Deirdre Blake. C M P Media LLC, 2800 Campus Dr, San Mateo, CA 94403; http://www.cmp.com. Illus., adv. Circ: 184050. Vol. ends: Dec. Microform: PQC. Online: EBSCO Publishing; Gale Group; OCLC Online Computer Library Center, Inc. *Indexed:* AS&TI, CompLI, EngInd, InfoSAb, MicrocompInd. *Bk. rev.:* 2-6, 100-200 words. *Aud.:* Ac, Sa.

With its focus on "Software Tools for the Professional Programmer," this magazine has been in print since 1976, covering all languages, platforms, and tools. The authors and the intended audience are "professional software developers who want to revise proposed standards, explore new technologies, argue over programming style, and share tricks of the trade." The web site provides some of the content of the print version, as well as tables of contents and a full-text search of articles from present issues back through 1988, and additional content not in the print version. (AF)

1896. *Evolutionary Computation.* [ISSN: 1063-6560] 1993. q. USD 250 print & online eds. (Individuals, USD 62 print & online eds.). Ed(s): Marc Schoenauer. MIT Press, 5 Cambridge Center, Cambridge, MA 02142-1493; journals-orders@mit.edu; http://mitpress.mit.edu. Adv. Refereed. Microform: PQC. Online: Ingenta Select; RoweCom Information Quest; Swets Blackwell. *Indexed:* BiolAb, CompLI, IndMed. *Aud.:* Ac, Sa.

The focus of this scholarly journal is "the exchange of information among researchers involved in both the theoretical and practical aspects of computational systems of an evolutionary nature." Topics include an emphasis on evolutionary models of computation such as genetic algorithms, evolutionary strategies, classifier systems, and evolutionary programming. Issues usually contain four to ten articles; a recurring section called "Electronic Calendar and Other EC-Related Activities" provides information and web addresses for electronic mailing lists specific to areas of evolutionary computational interest. The journal web site offers abstracts and tables of contents from current and past issues, as well as sample articles in pdf format. (AF)

1897. *Expert Systems: the international journal of knowledge engineering and neural networks.* Formerly: *Expert Systems User;* Which incorporated: *Artificial Intelligence Business.* [ISSN: 0266-4720] 1984. 5x/yr. USD 489 print & online eds. Ed(s): James L. Alty, Gordon Rugg. Blackwell Publishing Ltd., 9600 Garsington Rd, PO Box 805, Oxford, OX4 2DQ, United Kingdom; customerservices@oxon.blackwellpublishing.com; http://www.blackwellpublishing.com/. Illus., index. Refereed. Circ: 1000. Vol. ends: No. 4. Online: EBSCO Publishing; ingenta.com; OCLC Online Computer Library Center, Inc.; RoweCom Information Quest; Swets Blackwell. *Indexed:* AS&TI, CompLI, GeoRef, H&SSA, InfoSAb, LISA, MicrocompInd, RiskAb. *Bk. rev.:* 1, 500 words. *Aud.:* Ac, Sa.

[Note: The name of this journal was to change to *Expert Systems with Applications.*] An international refereed journal with a focus "on the exchange of information relating to expert systems applied in industry, government and universities worldwide...." Issues usually contain ten or more articles on design, development, testing, implementation, and management of such systems used in the areas of finance, accounting, engineering, marketing, audit, law, procurement and contracting, information retrieval, stock trading, network management, telecommunications, archaeology, economics, energy, and defense. Occasional special issues focus on a single topic; announcements of conferences, workshops, courses, and calls for paper are common. The web site includes tables of contents and abstracts, with full text available in pdf format for subscribers or for purchase. (AF)

1898. ***Graphical Models.*** Former titles (until 1998): *Graphical Models and Image Processing;* (until 1995): *C V G I P: Graphical Models and Image Processing;* Which supersedes in part (in 1991): *Computer Vision, Graphics, and Image Processing;* Which was formerly (until 1983): *Computer Graphics and Image Processing.* [ISSN: 1524-0703] 1969. bi-m. EUR 777 (Individuals, EUR 379). Ed(s): Dr. Norman I. Badler, Ingrid Carlbom. Academic Press, 525 B St, Ste 1900, San Diego, CA 92101-4495; apsubs@acad.com; http://www.academicpress.com. Illus., index. Refereed. Vol. ends: Nov. Online: EBSCO Publishing; ingenta.com; OCLC Online Computer Library Center, Inc.; RoweCom Information Quest; ScienceDirect; Swets Blackwell. Reprint: SWZ. *Indexed:* AS&TI, C&ISA, CompR, EngInd, ErgAb, GeoRef, GeogAbPG, IAA, SCI, SSCI. *Aud.:* Ac, Sa.

Formerly titled *Graphical Models and Image Processing,* this journal is focused on "the interaction between computer graphics, computer vision, and image processing" in areas that include algebraic surface models, animation, biomedical imaging, computer vision techniques, curves and surfaces, geometrical algorithms, motion capture and retargeting, physics-based modeling, scientific visualization, three-dimensional displays, and virtual environments. Issues usually present up to four scholarly papers, with occasional single-topic special issues. The web site provides tables of contents and abstracts, with full text in pdf format available for subscribers or for purchase. (AF)

1899. ***I E E E Computer Graphics and Applications.*** [ISSN: 0272-1716] 1981. bi-m. USD 695 in North America; USD 730 elsewhere. Ed(s): Jim Thomas, Robin Baldwin. Institute of Electrical and Electronics Engineers, Inc., 445 Hoes Ln, Piscataway, NJ 08854-1331; subscription-service@ieee.org; http://www.computer.org/. Illus., adv. Refereed. Circ: 8000 Paid. Vol. ends: Nov/Dec. Online: EBSCO Publishing; Gale Group; I E E E. *Indexed:* AS&TI, CompLI, DSR&OA, EngInd, ErgAb, IAA, MicrocompInd, SCI, SSCI. *Aud.:* Ac, Sa.

Aimed at specialized readers with some experience in computer graphics, *Computer Graphics and Applications* presents information on the applications for computer graphics. Each issue provides about a dozen articles ranging from two to ten pages, covering thematic topics, such as web graphics, graphics applications for grid computing, and 3D reconstruction. Some articles are quite technical, but the extensive illustrations help make them accessible. New application and product reviews, as well as conference announcements, keep readers updated, although this information is not all available in the web version of the journal. The online subscription version does include the full text of articles from 1988 to the present. (HW)

1900. ***I E E E Design & Test of Computers.*** [ISSN: 0740-7475] 1984. bi-m. USD 550. Ed(s): Yervent Zorian. Institute of Electrical and Electronics Engineers, Inc., 445 Hoes Ln, Piscataway, NJ 08854-1331; subscription-service@ieee.org; http://www.ieee.org. Illus., adv. Refereed. Circ: 6046. Vol. ends: No. 4. Online: EBSCO Publishing. *Indexed:* CompLI, EngInd, IAA. *Bk. rev.:* 1, 100 words. *Aud.:* Ac, Sa.

Co-published by the IEEE Computer Society and IEEE Circuits and Systems Society, this journal "offers original works describing the body of methods used in designing and testing the complete range of electronic product hardware and supportive software." The intended audience is users, developers, and researchers who design and test chips, assemblies, and integrated systems. Issues contain about ten articles of seven to ten pages each; guest editors introduce the issue and the three or four feature articles, which are linked by subject. Often these articles stem from conference presentations, with recent thematic contributions on board testing and application-specific microprocessors. Reviews and announcements do not appear in the online subscription version, but the full text of articles from 1988 to the present is available online. (HW)

I E E E Expert. See *IEEE Intelligent Systems.*

1901. ***I E E E Intelligent Systems: Putting A I into Practice.*** Former titles (until 2000): *I E E E Intelligent Systems and Their Applications;* (until 1997): *I E E E Expert.* [ISSN: 1541-1672] 1986. bi-m. USD 650 in North America; USD 685 elsewhere. Ed(s): Daniel O'Leary. Institute of Electrical and Electronics Engineers, Inc., 445 Hoes Ln, Piscataway, NJ 08854-1331; subscription-service@ieee.org; http://www.ieee.org. Illus., adv. Refereed. Circ: 6864. Vol. ends: Dec. Microform: Pub. Online: EBSCO Publishing; Gale Group. *Indexed:* AS&TI, C&ISA, CompLI, ErgAb, LISA, PollutAb, RiskAb, SCI, SSCI. *Bk. rev.:* 5-7, 750 words, signed. *Aud.:* Ac, Sa.

This journal of the IEEE Computer Society emphasizes current practice as well as promising ideas from across the spectrum of intelligent systems—from knowledge-based systems to data mining to robotics. Articles are aimed at professionals who deal with any part of intelligent systems, including designing and testing, maintaining, teaching, and managing. Several articles in each issue are oriented to a theme, such as natural-language processing in both web documents and in student essays, and information customization applications. Departments cover industry and research news, and issue-based editorials help connect the technological discussions with the larger world. Full text of articles from 1998 to the present is available with an online subscription. (HW)

1902. ***I E E E Micro.*** [ISSN: 0272-1732] 1981. bi-m. USD 650 in North America; USD 685 elsewhere. Ed(s): Stephen L Diamond. Institute of Electrical and Electronics Engineers, Inc., 445 Hoes Ln, Piscataway, NJ 08854-1331; subscription-service@ieee.org; http://www.ieee.org. Illus., index, adv. Refereed. Vol. ends: No. 6. Online: EBSCO Publishing; Gale Group; I E E E. *Indexed:* AS&TI, CompLI, EngInd, ErgAb, SCI, SSCI. *Aud.:* Ac, Sa.

IEEE Micro focuses on the design, performance, and application of microcomputer and microprocessor systems. Each issue generally has a cluster of articles on one theme, such as papers from an interconnectivity conference, or research on ubiquitous computers. Other regular features include news, reviews, legal aspects of microprocessing research and use, and standards. The articles are technical, and are aimed at practitioners and researchers rather than the general reader. Subscribers can access online the full text of articles back to 1988. (HW)

1903. ***I E E E MultiMedia Magazine.*** [ISSN: 1070-986X] 1994. q. USD 560 in North America; USD 595 elsewhere. Ed(s): William Grosky. Institute of Electrical and Electronics Engineers, Inc., 445 Hoes Ln, Piscataway, NJ 08854-1331; subscription-service@ieee.org; http://www.ieee.org. Illus., adv. Refereed. Vol. ends: Dec. Online: EBSCO Publishing; I E E E. *Indexed:* CompLI, EngInd, SCI. *Aud.:* Ac, Sa.

This IEEE publication provides technical information on a wide range of multimedia systems and applications issues, including hardware and software for media compression, storage, and transport, workstation support, and data modeling. One of the goals of this journal is to make even technical material easily understood by the reader, and it succeeds. Articles cover a variety of conceptual and practical topics; some recent pieces include "Fair User for Digital Imaging Technologies," "Interactive and Informative Art," and "Evaluating and Designing Web Site Quality." Issues also contain new product descriptions and reviews, and conference and workshop announcements. Subscribers to the online version can access the full text of articles from 1994 to the present. (HW)

1904. ***I E E E Network: the magazine of global information exchange.*** [ISSN: 0890-8044] 1987. bi-m. USD 250 in North America; USD 285 elsewhere. Ed(s): Jorg Leibeherr. Institute of Electrical and Electronics Engineers, Inc., 445 Hoes Ln, Piscataway, NJ 08854-1331; subscription-service@ieee.org; http://www.ieee.org. Illus., adv. Refereed. Vol. ends: No. 6. Online: EBSCO Publishing; Gale Group; I E E E. *Indexed:* C&ISA, EngInd, SCI. *Aud.:* Ac, Sa.

This IEEE journal calls itself "the magazine of global information exchange," and covers a range of issues surrounding the development, use, and management of computer networks. Topics include network protocols and architecture, protocol design and validation, communications software, distributed telecommunication systems, and network implementation. Special issues and guest editorials combine concepts with actual practice. New books and media are reviewed in a regular column. Overall coverage in *Network* is similar to that in *Computer Networks,* so libraries with limited budgets may want to select just one of these for their collection. Subscribers have online access to the full text of articles back to 1988. (HW)

1905. ***I E E E Software.*** [ISSN: 0740-7459] 1984. bi-m. USD 695 in North America; USD 730 elsewhere. Ed(s): Alan M Davis. Institute of Electrical and Electronics Engineers, Inc., 445 Hoes Ln, Piscataway, NJ 08854-1331; subscription-service@ieee.org; http://www.ieee.org. Illus., adv. Sample. Refereed. Vol. ends: No. 6. Microform: Pub. Online: EBSCO Publishing; Gale Group; I E E E. *Indexed:* AS&TI, CompLI, EngInd, ErgAb, SCI, SSCI. *Bk. rev.:* 4-5, 500 words. *Aud.:* Ac, Sa.

The mission of this IEEE Computer Society publication is to be the "authority on translating software theory into practice, [positioning] itself between pure research and pure practice, transferring ideas, methods, and experiences among researchers and engineers." IEEE views this as a magazine more than a scholarly journal, with an emphasis on shorter, readable articles. All aspects of the software industry are covered, including project management, process improvement, software maintenance, web applications, testing, and usability. Each issue presents several articles on a specific themes, such as security or knowledge management. Other regular features include interviews and book reviews. Full text of articles from 1988 to the present is available online. (HW)

1906. ***Information Sciences: an international journal.*** Incorporates (1994-1995): *Information Sciences - Applications.* [ISSN: 0020-0255] 1969. 36x/yr. EUR 3179 (Individuals, EUR 96). Ed(s): Paul P Wang. Elsevier Inc., 360 Park Ave. S, New York, NY 10010-1710; usinfo-f@elsevier.com; http://www.elsevier.com. Illus., adv. Refereed. Vol. ends: No. 4. Microform: PQC. Online: EBSCO Publishing; ingenta.com; ScienceDirect; Swets Blackwell. Reprint: SWZ. *Indexed:* C&ISA, CCMJ, ChemAb, CompR, EngInd, GeoRef, GeogAbPG, InfoSAb, L&LBA, MLA-IB, MathSciNet, SCI, SSCI. *Aud.:* Ac, Sa.

This scholarly journal is "designed to serve researchers, developers, managers, strategic planners, and others interested in state-of-the art research activities in information, knowledge engineering and intelligent systems." The broad scope of topics fall into three large categories: Foundations of Information Science (information theory, cognitive science, bioinformatics, etc.); Implementations and Information Technology (intelligent systems, artificial neural networks, data engineering, etc.); and Applications (manufacturing automation, virtual reality, search engine design, etc.). Most issues contain several papers for each category; occasional special issues focus on a single topic, for example "Photonics, Networking, and Computing." The web site provides tables of contents and abstracts, with full text in pdf format available for subscribers or for purchase. (AF)

1907. ***Information Systems: data base: their creation, management and utilization.*** Incorporates (1988-1992): *Database Technology.* [ISSN: 0306-4379] 1975. 8x/yr. EUR 1389. Ed(s): Mathias Jarke, Dr. Dennis Shasha. Pergamon, The Boulevard, Langford Ln, East Park, Kidlington, OX5 1GB, United Kingdom. Illus., adv. Refereed. Circ: 1200. Vol. ends: No. 8. Microform: PQC. Online: EBSCO Publishing; ingenta.com; ScienceDirect; Swets Blackwell. Reprint: PQC. *Indexed:* BiolAb, C&ISA, CIJE, CompLI, CompR, EngInd, ExcerpMed, InfoSAb, LISA, SCI. *Aud.:* Ac, Sa.

This journal defines "information systems" as "the software and hardware systems that support data-intensive applications" and has a focus on "data-related issues from the fields of data mining, information retrieval, natural language processing, internet data management, visual and audio information systems, scientific computing, and organisational behaviour." Issues usually contain four to eight scholarly papers on a variety of topics; recent single-topic special issues included "Data Management in Bioinformatics" and "Best Papers from EDBT 2002." The web site provides tables of contents and abstracts, with full text in pdf format available for subscribers or for purchase, as well as a sample issue with full content freely available for download. (AF)

1908. ***International Journal of Human-Computer Studies.*** Incorporates (1989-1995): *Knowledge Acquisition;* Formerly (1969-1993): *International Journal of Man-Machine Studies.* [ISSN: 1071-5819] 1969. m. EUR 2101 (Individuals, EUR 609). Ed(s): B R Gaines. Academic Press, Harcourt Pl, 32 Jamestown Rd, London, NW1 7BY, United Kingdom; apsubs@acad.com; http://www.elsevier-international.com/serials/. Illus., adv. Refereed. Online: EBSCO Publishing; ingenta.com; OCLC Online Computer Library Center, Inc.; RoweCom Information Quest; ScienceDirect; Swets Blackwell. Reprint: SWZ. *Indexed:* AS&TI, BiolAb, ChemAb, CommAb, CompR, EngInd, ErgAb, ExcerpMed, LISA, LingAb, PsycholAb, SCI, SSCI. *Aud.:* Ac, Sa.

Incorporating *Knowledge Acquisition* and formerly known as *International Journal of Man-Machine Studies,* this scholarly journal includes content on the "whole spectrum of work on both the theory and practice of human-computer interaction and the human-machine interface. The journal covers the boundaries between computing and artificial intelligence, psychology, linguistics, mathematics, engineering, and social organization." Issues generally contain four to seven articles, on subjects including user interfaces, natural language and speech interaction, expert systems, and innovative interaction techniques. Occasional special issues contain more articles; a recent example is "Notification User Interfaces." The web site provides tables of contents and abstracts, with full text in pdf format available for subscribers or for purchase. (AF)

1909. ***International Journal of Parallel Programming.*** Formerly (until 1987): *International Journal of Computer and Information Sciences.* [ISSN: 0885-7458] 1972. bi-m. USD 991 print or online ed. Kluwer Academic / Plenum Publishers, 233 Spring St Fl 7, New York, NY 10013-1522; http://www.wkap.nl/. Illus., adv. Refereed. Vol. ends: Dec. Microform: PQC. Online: EBSCO Publishing; Gale Group; ingenta.com; Kluwer Online; OCLC Online Computer Library Center, Inc.; Ovid Technologies, Inc.; RoweCom Information Quest; Swets Blackwell. *Indexed:* ABIn, C&ISA, ChemAb, CompLI, CompR, EngInd, ErgAb, InfoSAb, MLA-IB, SCI. *Aud.:* Ac, Sa.

This highly technical journal focuses "specifically on programming aspects of parallel computing systems. Such systems are characterized by the coexistence over time of multiple coordinated activities." What may not be obvious about this characterization is the large and growing number of computer systems and software to which it applies, from the laptop used to write this annotation to the largest mainframe and enterprise systems in existence. Issues usually contain only two to four articles; recent examples are "Non-Strict Execution in Parallel and Distributed Computing," "An Extended ANSI C for Processors with a Multimedia Extension," and "Alloyed Branch History: Combining Global and Local Branch History for Robust Performance." The web site provides tables of contents and abstracts, with full text in pdf format available for subscribers or for purchase, as well as a sample issue with full content freely available. (AF)

International Journal of Robotics and Automation. See Robotics section.

1910. ***Journal of Computer-Assisted Learning.*** [ISSN: 0266-4909] 1985. bi-m. GBP 433 print & online eds. Ed(s): R Lewis. Blackwell Publishing Ltd., 9600 Garsington Rd, Oxford, OX4 2ZG, United Kingdom; customerservices@oxon.blackwellpublishing.com; http://www.blackwellpublishing.com. Illus., adv. Refereed. Circ: 515. Microform: PQC. Online: EBSCO Publishing; ingenta.com; Munksgaard & Blackwell Science's Synergy; OCLC Online Computer Library Center, Inc.; RoweCom Information Quest. *Indexed:* BrEdI, CIJE, ErgAb, L&LBA, PsycholAb, SSCI. *Bk. rev.:* Occasional. *Aud.:* Ac.

This is a quarterly, peer-reviewed, international journal, "which covers the whole range of uses of information and communication technology to support learning and knowledge exchange. It aims to provide a medium for communication between researchers and the practitioners and to foster collaborative research." Topics covered include collaborative learning, knowledge engineering, open, distance and networked learning, developmental psychology, and evaluation. Issues often include a dozen or more articles; special issues covering a single topic occur (at least) annually, with a recent example being "Teaching Research Methods." The web site offers abstracts and tables of contents for current and past issues, plus the opportunity to purchase individual articles online. (AF)

1911. ***Journal of Computer Security.*** [ISSN: 0926-227X] 1992. 6x/yr. EUR 542. Ed(s): Sushil Jajodia, Jonathan Millen. I O S Press, Nieuwe Hemweg 6B, Amsterdam, 1013 BG, Netherlands; order@iospress.nl; http://www.iospress.nl. Refereed. Circ: 250. *Indexed:* C&ISA, CompLI, EngInd. *Aud.:* Ac.

This scholarly journal "presents research and development results of lasting significance in the theory, design, implementation, analysis, and application of secure computer systems and networks...the meaning and implications of security and privacy, particularly those with important consequences for the technical community." Issues usually contain three or four articles that can be very technical; recent examples include "A Comparative Experimental Evaluation Study of Intrusion Detection System Performance in a Gigabit Environment" and "Eliminating Counterevidence with Applications to Accountable Certificate Management." The web site includes tables of contents for current and past issues. (AF)

1912. ***Journal of Management Information Systems.*** [ISSN: 0742-1222] 1984. q. USD 569 includes online access (Individuals, USD 88). Ed(s): Vladimir Zwass. M.E. Sharpe, Inc., 80 Business Park Dr, Armonk, NY 10504; custserv@mesharpe.com; http://www.mesharpe.com. Illus., index, adv. Refereed. Reprint: PSC. *Indexed:* ABIn, BPI, CompLI, ConsI, EngInd, SSCI. *Aud.:* Ac, Sa.

This quarterly journal "serves those investigating new modes of information delivery and the changing landscape of information policy making, as well as practitioners and executives managing the information resource. A vital aim of the quarterly is to bridge the gap between theory and practice of management information systems." While there are occasional special issues that focus on a single topic, most issues have special sections with several articles on one topic along with other, more diverse articles; recent topics are "Management and Valuation of Advertisement-Supported Web Sites" and "A Model of Neutral B2B Intermediaries." The web site offers tables of contents and abstracts from issues going back to 1984. (AF)

1913. ***Journal of Systems and Software.*** [ISSN: 0164-1212] 1979. 15x/yr. EUR 1459. Ed(s): D. N. Card. Elsevier Inc., 360 Park Ave. S, New York, NY 10010-1710; usinfo-f@elsevier.com; http://www.elsevier.com. Illus. Refereed. Vol. ends: No. 3. Microform: PQC. Online: EBSCO Publishing; Gale Group; ingenta.com; ScienceDirect; Swets Blackwell. Reprint: SWZ. *Indexed:* ABIn, AS&TI, C&ISA, CompLI, CompR, EngInd. *Aud.:* Ac, Sa.

This journal covers "all aspects of programming methodology, software engineering and related hardware/software systems issues." Topics include software systems, prototyping issues, high-level specification techniques, procedural and functional programming techniques, data-flow concepts, multiprocessing, real-time, distributed, concurrent, and telecommunications systems, software metrics, reliability models for software, performance issues, and management concerns. Issues usually contain up to ten articles, with occasional special issues focused on a single topic. The web page provides tables of contents and abstracts, with full text in pdf format available for subscribers or for purchase, as well as a sample issue with full content freely available. (AF)

1914. ***New Generation Computing: computing paradigms and computational intelligence.*** [ISSN: 0288-3635] 1983. q. JPY 38000 domestic; EUR 330 combined subscription foreign print & online eds. Ed(s): Koichi Furukawa. Springer-Verlag Tokyo, 3-13 Hongo 3-chome, Bunkyo-ku, Tokyo, 113-0033, Japan; http://www.springer-tokyo.co.jp/. Illus. Refereed. Vol. ends: No. 4. Microform: PQC. Online: Springer LINK. Reprint: ISI. *Indexed:* CompLI, EngInd, SSCI. *Aud.:* Ac, Sa.

This journal is "specially intended to support the development of new computational paradigms stemming from the cross-fertilization of various research fields. These fields include, but are not limited to, programming (logic, constraint, functional, object-oriented), distributed/parallel computing, knowledge-based systems and agent-oriented systems." Some issues have articles on a variety of topics, others are single-topic issues; recent examples are "Decision Process Modeling across Internet and Real World by Double Helical Model of Chance Discover," "Discovering Validation Rules from Microbiological Data" and "An Approach to Discovering Risks in Development Process of Large and Complex Systems." The web site provides tables of contents, calls for papers, and a link to download a sample paper. (AF)

1915. ***Operating Systems Review.*** [ISSN: 0163-5980] 1970. 5x/yr. Members, USD 15; Non-members, USD 42. Ed(s): William Waite. Association for Computing Machinery, Inc., One Astor Plaza, 1515 Broadway, 17th Fl, New York, NY 10036-5701; sigs@acm.org; http://www.acm.org. Illus., index, adv. Circ: 8000. *Indexed:* C&ISA, EngInd. *Aud.:* Ac, Sa.

This publication of the Association for Computing Machinery is "an informal publication of the ACM Special Interest Group on Operating Systems (SIGOPS), whose scope of interest includes: computer operating systems and architecture for multiprogramming, multiprocessing, and time sharing; resource management; evaluation and simulation; reliability, integrity, and security of data; communications among computing processors; and computer system modeling and analysis." Issues include articles on a broad range of topics within the scope, and vary from scholarly to practical. The web site provides tables of contents and abstracts, with full text in pdf format available for subscribers. (AF)

1916. ***P C - A I Magazine: intelligent solutions for today's computers.*** [ISSN: 0894-0711] 1987. bi-m. USD 25 domestic; USD 41 in Canada & Mexico; USD 57 elsewhere. Ed(s): Terry Hengl. Knowledge Technology, PO BOX 30130, Phoenix, AZ 85046-0130; info@pcai.com; http://www.pcai.com. Illus., adv. Sample. Circ: 10000. Vol. ends: No. 6. *Indexed:* CompLI, InfoSAb, MicrocompInd. *Bk. rev.:* 1, 1,000 words, signed. *Aud.:* Ac, Sa.

While artificial intelligence (AI) may be more commonly found on larger systems, this journal focuses on AI computing using personal computers. Topics include business rules and business forecasting; data mining; decision support; expert systems; intelligent tools; natural language processing; modeling and simulation; neural networks; and object-oriented development languages. Issues generally include articles on several topics relating to building expert systems and the application of AI in a variety of business and industrial settings, as well as hardware and software reviews and regular columns. The web site provides tables of contents, abstracts, and an index of past articles, plus links to other AI resources. (AF)

1917. ***S I A M Journal on Computing.*** [ISSN: 0097-5397] 1972. bi-m. USD 480 (Individual members, USD 92). Ed(s): M Yannakakis. Society for Industrial and Applied Mathematics, 3600 University City Science Center, Philadelphia, PA 19104-2688; siam@siam.org; http://www.siam.org. Illus., adv. Refereed. Circ: 1711. Vol. ends: Dec. *Indexed:* AS&TI, ApMecR, C&ISA, CompR, EngInd, SCI, SSCI. *Aud.:* Ac, Sa.

This scholarly journal published by the Society for Industrial and Applied Mathematics "contains research articles on the mathematical and formal aspects of computer science and nonnumerical computing. Many of the foundations of computer science are mathematical and derive from a wide spectrum of mathematical disciplines. The purpose of this journal is to provide a medium for the cross-fertilization of mathematics and computer science that should benefit both the computing and mathematical communities...." Issues usually contain at least ten articles; recent examples include "Computing the Median with Uncertainty," "New Bounds for Variable-Sized Online Bin Packing," and "Backward Consistency and Sense of Direction in Advanced Distributed Systems." The web site provides abstracts and tables of contents, with full content in several formats available for subscribers. (AF)

1918. ***Software: Practice & Experience.*** [ISSN: 0038-0644] 1971. 15x/yr. USD 2830. Ed(s): A Wellings, Douglas E Comer. John Wiley & Sons Ltd., The Atrium, Southern Gate, Chichester, PO19 8SQ, United Kingdom; customer@wiley.co.uk; http://www.wiley.co.uk. Illus., index, adv. Refereed. Circ: 1800. Vol. ends: No. 15. Microform: PQC. Online: EBSCO Publishing; Wiley InterScience. Reprint: ISI; PQC; SWZ. *Indexed:* AS&TI, BrTechI, C&ISA, CompLI, EngInd, GeoRef, InfoSAb. *Aud.:* Ac, Sa.

The focus of this scholarly journal is "the dissemination and discussion of practical experience with new and established software for both systems and applications." This journal is intended for sophisticated programmers, and topics can include details on completed projects as templates for future work in the same field, short reports on techniques useful in a variety of areas, or explanation of methods for dealing with large-scale software projects. Issues usually contain about four articles, and can also include comments on articles as well as author responses to comments; occasional special issues focus on a single topic. The web site provides tables of contents and abstracts, with full text in pdf format available for subscribers or for purchase. (AF)

1919. *World Wide Web.* [ISSN: 1386-145X] q. EUR 392 print or online ed. Ed(s): Osman Balci. Baltzer Science Publishers B.V., Hooftlaan 51, Bussum, 1401 EC, Netherlands; subscribe@baltzer.nl; http://www.baltzer.nl. Sample. Refereed. Online: EBSCO Publishing; ingenta.com; Kluwer Online; OCLC Online Computer Library Center, Inc.; Ovid Technologies, Inc.; RoweCom Information Quest; Swets Blackwell. *Indexed:* CompLI. *Aud.:* Ac.

This scholarly journal is "an international, archival, peer-reviewed journal which covers all aspects of the World Wide Web, including issues related to architectures, applications, Internet and Web information systems, and communities." Topics include application program interfaces, authoring tools and environments, browsing and navigation techniques and tools, collaborative learning, data and link management, digital libraries, and innovative applications among many others. Issues usually include three to six articles; occasional special issues on a single topic usually have more. The web site offers abstracts and tables of contents for current and past issues, full content in pdf format for subscribers or for purchase, and a free sample issue. (AF)

Popular Computer Titles

1920. *Computerworld: newsweekly for information technology leaders.* [ISSN: 0010-4841] 1967. w. USD 190 domestic; USD 220 Canada; USD 250 in Central America. Ed(s): Mary Fran Johnson. Computerworld, Inc., 500 Old Connecticut Path, Box 9171, Framingham, MA 01701-9171; http://www.computerworld.com. Illus., adv. Circ: 250707. Vol. ends: Dec. Microform: PQC. Online: bigchalk; EBSCO Publishing; Factiva; Florida Center for Library Automation; Gale Group; LexisNexis; Northern Light Technology, Inc.; OCLC Online Computer Library Center, Inc.; ProQuest Information & Learning; H.W. Wilson. Reprint: PQC. *Indexed:* ABIn, BPI, CompLI, InfoSAb, LRI, MagInd, MicrocompInd. *Aud.:* Ga, Ac, Sa.

Describing itself as "America's #1 publication for IT Leaders" and available by paid subscription, free subscription (to professionals with almost any conceivable connection to computing), and web site, this weekly tabloid/magazine provides vast amounts of timely information on a wide range of topics of interest to "IT executives and professionals who are at the forefront of the move to e-business and adoption of new technologies." Foci include news, analysis, and "Knowledge Centers": integrated print and online information packages that consist of in-depth coverage of a specific topic in the weekly print issue as well as ongoing coverage of the same topic in a section of the web site. These include Careers, Data Management, Development, E-Business, Hardware, IT Management, Mobile & Wireless, Networking, Operating Systems and Storage, and others. Other content includes commentary, editorials, and letters to the editor. The web site content largely matches the print version, although the web site format allows for updates more frequently than weekly. This is a good source for anyone needing or wanting to stay current on hardware, software, and industry news and trends. (AF)

1921. *Information Today: the newspaper for users and producers of electronic information services.* [ISSN: 8755-6286] 1983. 11x/yr. USD 68.95 domestic; USD 92 in Canada & Mexico; USD 101 elsewhere. Ed(s): John Eichorn. Information Today, Inc., 143 Old Marlton Pike, Medford, NJ 08055-8750; custserv@infotoday.com; http://www.infotoday.com. Illus., adv. Circ: 10000 Paid. Vol. ends: No. 11. Microform: PQC. Online: bigchalk; EBSCO Publishing; Factiva; Florida Center for Library Automation; Gale Group; Northern Light Technology, Inc.; OCLC Online Computer Library Center, Inc.; ProQuest Information & Learning; H.W. Wilson. *Indexed:* ABIn, B&I, CompLI, InfoSAb, LISA, LRI, LibLit, MicrocompInd. *Bk. rev.:* 10, 100 words. *Aud.:* Ac, Sa.

While this monthly newspaper is similar in format and layout to *Computerworld,* the intended audience is different: subtitled "The Newspaper for Users and Producers of Electronic Information Services," the primary focus is on topics of interest to librarians and other information professionals. Issues include features, book reviews, product news and reviews, interviews, and regular columns titled "NewsBytes," "NewsBreak," "Legal Issues," "Internet Waves," "Focus on Publishing," and "Database Review." Also included are conference reports, previews, and registration announcements. Recent tables of contents are available on the web site, as are the full text of selected articles and additional web-only content. (AF)

1922. *InfoWorld: defining technology for business.* Formerly (until 1981): *Intelligent Machines Journal.* [ISSN: 0199-6649] 1979. w. USD 195 domestic (Free to qualified personnel). Ed(s): Michael Vizard. InfoWorld Media Group, 501 Second St, San Francisco, CA 94107; http://www.infoworld.com. Illus., index, adv. Circ: 370000. Vol. ends: Dec. Microform: PQC. Online: bigchalk; EBSCO Publishing; Factiva; Florida Center for Library Automation; Gale Group; LexisNexis; Northern Light Technology, Inc.; OCLC Online Computer Library Center, Inc.; ProQuest Information & Learning; H.W. Wilson. Reprint: PQC. *Indexed:* ABIn, C&ISA, CBCARef, ConsI, InfoSAb, MagInd, MicrocompInd. *Aud.:* Ac, Sa.

The web site for this journal is so similar to those of *Computerworld* and *Datamation* in terms of content and layout that differentiation can be difficult; the print version is also very close to that of *Computerworld* (*Datamation* is only available via web site). This is another good source for anyone needing or wanting to stay current on hardware, software, and industry news and trends. (AF)

Internet World. See Internet–World Wide Web section.

1923. *Linux Magazine: open source. open standards.* [ISSN: 1536-4674] 1999. m. USD 29.95 domestic; USD 59.95 Canada; USD 89.95 elsewhere. Ed(s): Adam M Goodman. Linux Magazine, 330 Townsend St, Ste 112, San Francisco, CA 94107. Adv. *Aud.:* Ga.

Linux is an "open source" and increasingly common operating system platform, particularly on servers. *Linux Magazine* provides information for all levels of Linux users from beginner to experienced. Recent examples of feature topics are "The Year of Desktop Linux," "Software Development," and "Linux on Wall Street: A Strong Buy." The largest of the regular sections are the "How To" and "Developer?s Den" areas, with a wealth of in-depth practical content and articles on Linux program code; product reviews are also prominent. The web site offers abstracts and selected content from current and recent issues, along with web-only content and a section for downloads. Other titles with very similar content (and equally worthy of consideration) are the nearly identically titled *Linux-Magazine* and *Linux Journal.* (AF)

1924. *MacWorld: the Macintosh magazine for the network professional.* Incorporates (1985-1997): *MacUser;* Which was formerly: *MacLetter.* [ISSN: 0741-8647] 1984. m. USD 19.97 domestic; USD 29.97 foreign. Ed(s): Andy Gore. Mac Publishing, L.L.C., 301 Howard St., 15th Fl, San Francisco, CA 94105; letters@macworld.com; http://www.macworld.com. Illus., adv. Circ: 532702. Vol. ends: Dec. Microform: NBI; PQC. Online: America Online, Inc.; bigchalk; EBSCO Publishing; Florida Center for Library Automation; Gale Group; Northern Light Technology, Inc.; OCLC Online Computer Library Center, Inc.; ProQuest Information & Learning. *Indexed:* ABIn, B&I, BPI, ConsI, InfoSAb, MRD, MagInd, MicrocompInd, RGPR. *Aud.:* Hs, Ga, Ac, Sa.

With a focus on a common non-Microsoft operating system platform, *Macworld* ("The Mac Product Experts") provides in-depth coverage of the Apple Macintosh line of personal computers. Issues contain feature articles on Mac-specific hardware, software, and other products; product reviews are prevalent and extensive. Departments include "Opinion," with editorial content and letters to the editor; "Mac Beat," with timely news items; and "Secrets," with how-to information largely in response to reader questions. The web site offers selected content from the current issue, a limited archive of past issues, and search engines for products and articles. Another Mac-focused magazine that is very similar in content, layout, and intent, *MacAddict,* is equally deserving of consideration. (AF)

1925. *P C Magazine: the independent guide to personal computing and the Internet.* Formerly (until 1986): *P C: The Independent Guide to I B M Personal Computers.* [ISSN: 0888-8507] 1982. bi-w. USD 34.97 domestic; USD 70.97 foreign. Ziff Davis Media Inc., 28 E 28th St, New York, NY 10016-7930; info@ziffdavis.com; http://www.ziffdavis.com. Illus., adv. Circ: 1225000. Online: EBSCO Publishing; Florida Center for Library Automation; Gale Group; ProQuest Information & Learning. *Indexed:* CompLI, ConsI, EngInd, InfoSAb, LRI, MRD, MagInd, MicrocompInd. *Aud.:* Hs, Ga, Ac, Sa.

This magazine caters to nearly all levels of computing users—from beginners to IT professionals. Offering "First Looks" at new products including reviews and product comparisons it then continues to provide "tips, tricks, tools, and techniques" to help a user enhance or ease their computing experience in its "Solutions" section. The publication also provides sections geared towards computing entertainment, including its "Gears and Gadgets" section as well as "After Hours" sections. In addition, the publication offers a wide variety of topics and reviews on the web site, as well as current and archived issues. (RM)

1926. *P C World: the no. 1 source for definitive how-to-buy, how-to-use advice on Personal Computing systems and software.* Incorporates (1985-1992): *Lotus;* (in 1991): *Windows (San Francisco);* (1987-1990): *P C Resource.* [ISSN: 0737-8939] 1982. m. USD 29.90 domestic; USD 45.90 in Canada & Mexico; USD 75.90 elsewhere. Ed(s): Kevin McKean. I D G Communications Inc., 501 Second St, Ste 600, San Francisco, CA 94107-4133. Illus., adv. Circ: 1000000 Paid. Vol. ends: Dec. Microform: PQC. Online: CompuServe Inc.; EBSCO Publishing; Factiva; Florida Center for Library Automation; Gale Group; LexisNexis; OCLC Online Computer Library Center, Inc.; ProQuest Information & Learning; H.W. Wilson. *Indexed:* BPI, CPerI, CompLI, ConsI, InfoSAb, LRI, MagInd, MicrocompInd, RGPR. *Aud.:* Hs, Ga, Ac, Sa.

Similar to *PC Magazine,* this publication caters to a wide spectrum of computing users, but is most appropriate for the consumer market. The magazine offers editorials and stories featuring the latest technology in the personal computer market, as well as covering a wide variety of peripherals and software. One of the most-used features is the comparison of the latest hardware and software in table format, including performance, vendor service, price, and overall customer satisfaction—most comparisons are offered in top-10 format. A regular section regarding helpful hints geared toward solving computer application problems, operating system issues, and hardware resolution is also included in the "Here's How" section. Both archived and current issues are available on the web site. (RM)

PC Novice. See *Smart Computing.*

1927. *PocketPC.* Formerly: *Handheld P C Magazine.* [ISSN: 1528-5456] 1997. bi-m. one bonus issue. USD 19.95 domestic; USD 25.95 in Canada & Mexico; USD 37.95 elsewhere. Ed(s): Hal Goldstein, Richard Hall. Thaddeus Computing, Inc., c/o Wayne Kneeskern, Controller, Box 869, Fairfield, IA 52556-0869; http://www.hpcmag.com/. Illus., adv. *Aud.:* Ga.

Pocket PCs are rapidly becoming more popular as users look to run more applications on mobile devices. This magazine focuses on a variety of concepts surrounding mobile computing devices, including news, editorials, and detailed reviews of products as well as how-to guides. In addition, it features regular columns such as letters to the editor, tips and tricks, and the news. In addition, the magazine offers a web site that provides a wealth of information and archived articles. (RM)

1928. *Smart Computing.* Formerly (until May 1997): *P C Novice.* [ISSN: 1093-4170] 1990. m. USD 29 domestic; USD 37 Canada; USD 59 elsewhere. Ed(s): Ronald D Kobler. Sand Hill Publishing, 120 W Harvest Dr, Lincoln, NE 68521; feedback@sandhills.com; http://www.sandhills.com. Illus., adv. Circ: 205837. Vol. ends: Dec. *Indexed:* CompLI, InfoSAb, MicrocompInd, RGPR. *Aud.:* Ems, Hs, Ga.

This magazine and its "Learning Series" and "Reference Series" titles represent information specifically tailored for the very beginning personal computer user, presented in a format that minimizes the jargon and potential intimidation of the technical aspects of computing. The dramatic rise in the number of U.S. households with computers will likely make this type of information more important to a growing number of users for some time to come. Topics include basic training on common operating system functions and usage, practical information on purchasing peripherals (printers, scanners, digital cameras, etc.) and software, and in-depth help using popular personal computer applications. The web site includes a search engine for product reviews, a computing dictionary and encyclopedia, and selected content from and tables of contents for current print issues. (AF)

Wired. See Internet–World Wide Web section.

Electronic Journals

1929. *Automatica.* [ISSN: 0005-1098] 1963. m. EUR 2085 (Qualified personnel, EUR 67). Ed(s): H Kwakernaak. Pergamon, The Boulevard, Langford Ln, East Park, Kidlington, OX5 1GB, United Kingdom. Illus., index, adv. Refereed. Circ: 2000. Microform: PQC. Online: ingenta.com; ScienceDirect; Swets Blackwell. *Indexed:* ApMecR, C&ISA, CCMJ, CompR, EngInd, ErgAb, ExcerpMed, MathSciNet, SCI, WRCInf. *Bk. rev.:* Occasional. *Aud.:* Ac, Sa.

This scholarly publication of the International Federation of Automatic Control is focused on "theoretical and experimental research and development in the control of systems, involving all facets of automatic control theory and its applications." Each monthly issue contains 20 to 25 articles on topics including theory and design of systems and components, adaptive control, robotics, neural networks, fuzzy and expert systems, and computers as used for control of industrial processes, space vehicles, ships, traffic, power systems, agriculture, and natural resources. Occasionally an entire issue is devoted to a single topic; there are also occasional book reviews and software reviews. The web site offers abstracts and tables of contents for current and past issues, full content in pdf format for subscribers or for purchase, and a complete sample issue with free access. (AF)

1930. *Byte.com.* Supersedes (1975-1999): *Byte (Print Edition);* And (1995-1999): *Byte on CD-ROM.* 1975. w. Free. Ed(s): Paul E Schindler, Jr. C M P Media LLC, 600 Community Dr, Manhasset, NY 11030; http://www.byte.com. Illus., index, adv. Circ: 500000. Microform: PQC. Online: Dow Jones Interactive; NewsNet. Reprint: PQC. *Indexed:* ABIn, ABS&EES, AS&TI, B&I, BPI, BRI, C&ISA, CBRI, CompLI, ConsI, ErgAb, GeoRef, IHTDI, LRI, MRD, MagInd, MicrocompInd, RGPR, SCI. *Aud.:* Hs, Ga, Ac, Sa.

Not available in print since 1998, *Byte* (or rather, Byte.com) is a fee-based web site that is usually updated weekly. The somewhat busy home page offers subscribers links to very current information on a variety of topics in categories of "In The News," features, and regular columns, as well as the entire content of past weekly editions since 1999. Columns include or have included "The Upgrade Advisor," "NT Technology," "Hot Toys," "Advanced Software and Technologies," "Mobile & Web," and "Media Lab," among others. An interesting aspect of this resource is that, unlike most of the other titles in the Popular Computer Titles subsection, *Byte* provides information on personal computer platforms other than Apple Macintosh and the various Windows releases, including AmigaOS, BeOS, DOS, FreeBSD, Linux, Solaris, and Unix. (AF)

1931. *I E E E - A C M Transactions on Networking.* [ISSN: 1063-6692] 1993. bi-m. USD 395 in North America; USD 430 elsewhere. Ed(s): Simon S Lam. Institute of Electrical and Electronics Engineers, Inc., 445 Hoes Ln, Piscataway, NJ 08854-1331; subscription-service@ieee.org; http://www.ieee.org. Illus., adv. Refereed. Vol. ends: No. 6. Online: Association for Computing Machinery, Inc.; EBSCO Publishing; I E E E. *Indexed:* AS&TI, C&ISA, CompLI, EngInd, SCI. *Aud.:* Ac, Sa.

A collaborative publication between IEEE and ACM, *Transactions on Networking* succeeds in combining the speed of online publishing with the solid scholarship of a peer-reviewed publication. Issues offer "broad coverage of research and experience in network architecture and design, communication protocols, network software and technologies, services and applications, and network operations and management." There are about ten articles per issue, and all are aimed at the practitioner or researcher. The writing is highly technical, and though some papers espouse new theories, nearly all of them have practical application to today's networking technologies. Abstracts and past tables of contents are available free at the web site, http://www.ton.cc.gatech.edu. (HW)

1932. ***Journal for Universal Computer Science (Online Edition).*** [ISSN: 0948-6968] 1995. m. EUR 220 (Individuals, EUR 110). Ed(s): H Maurer. Springer-Verlag, Tiergartenstr 17, Heidelberg, 69121, Germany. Online: EBSCO Publishing; RoweCom Information Quest. *Indexed:* CCMJ, MathSciNet. *Aud.:* Ac.

This monthly electronic journal "deals with all aspects of computer science." With uninterrupted publication since its foundation in 1995, it claims to be one of the oldest electronic journals online. A broad range of topics are covered, with submissions categorized by general literature, hardware, computer systems organization, software, data, theory of computation, mathematics of computing, information systems, computing methodologies, computer applications, and computing milieux. Special editions with a specific focus are common; recent examples are "Tools for System Design and Verification," "Spatial and Temporal Reasoning," and "Hypermedia—State of the Art 2002." Access is organized by volume, with tables of contents listings that link to abstracts and to full text in pdf or PostScript formats for subscribers. There is also a link to sample issues. (AF)

1933. ***Linux Gazette.*** m. Specialized Systems Consultants, Inc. (SSC), PO Box 85867, Seattle, WA 98145. *Bk. rev.:* Occasional. *Aud.:* Ga.

This electronic journal describes itself as "an on-line WWW publication dedicated to two simple ideas: Making Linux just a *little* more fun [and] sharing ideas and discoveries." With the growing number of personal computers (and particularly servers) using this "open source" operating system, the information provided by resources like this becomes important to a growing number of users. Each monthly issues contains articles on a variety of topics; recent examples are "Fonts for the Common Desktop Environment," "Security Administration with Debian GNU/Linux," and "Laurel and Hardy Try to Write a C Program." Regular sections include "2-Cent Tips," "News Bytes," and "The MailBag." Occasional book reviews are also included. (AF)

1934. ***PlugIn Datamation: profit and value from information technology.*** Formerly (until 1998): *Datamation.* 1957. m. Ed(s): Esther Shein. EarthWeb, 23 Old Kings Hwy, Darien, CT 06820; info@earthweb.com; http://www.datamation.com. Illus., index, adv. Circ: 200300. Microform: CIS. Online: The Dialog Corporation; Gale Group. Reprint: PQC. *Indexed:* ABIn, AS&TI, ATI, ApMecR, BPI, C&ISA, ChemAb, CompLI, ConsI, ErgAb, ExcerpMed, LRI, MagInd, MicrocompInd, PAIS, SCI, SSCI. *Aud.:* Ac, Sa.

Formerly available in print, this venerable and well respected journal has been found only on the Internet for some time. Very similar in scope and content to *Computerworld,* the two publications have largely duplicate web site elements. This is another good source for anyone needing or wanting to stay current on hardware, software, and industry news and trends. (AF)

1935. ***TechWeb.*** w. Ed(s): Jeff Pundyk. TechWeb, http://www.techweb.com. Illus. *Aud.:* Ga, Ac, Sa.

While very accessible to interested amateurs, this electronic resource is specifically geared toward enterprise IT professionals, with a focus on providing "a comprehensive, intelligent directory of the best IT information on the Web." The site acts not only as a direct portal to a variety of content providers collectively labeled the "TechWeb Network," it provides contextual linking between related items of news, reviews, analysis, opinion, research, and conference information, and it groups those into categories of interest: Mobile and Wireless, Software, Security, E-business and Management, Networking, and Hardware. Industry news is also a focus, updated daily and arranged by date and by topic. (AF)

■ CONSUMER EDUCATION

Jane T. Bradford, Reference/Instruction Librarian, duPont-Ball Library, Stetson University, DeLand, FL 32723, jbradfor@stetson.edu

Introduction

The importance of being an educated consumer, like an educated voter, cannot be overstated. As British author J. G. Ballard says, "The technological landscape of the present day has enfranchised its own electorates—the inhabitants of marketing zones in the consumer goods society, television audiences, and news magazine readerships . . . vote with money at the cash counter rather than with the ballot paper at the polling booth." ["The Consumer Consumer," *Ink,* (5 June, 1971)] One would definitely add web surfers to the list of electorates in today's technological landscape.

Being educated consumers not only benefits the pocketbooks of these economic electorates, but also their health and environment. Especially in times of an economic downturn, people look for ways to maximize what their money will purchase, to make their money work harder for them, and to conserve what they have. Educated consumers may also want to know which products are the most environmentally friendly or which companies have the best records in employee relations. In other words, consumers may want to consider factors in addition to the bottom line of cost.

Most consumer-oriented publications now recognize that consumers want to be able to compare not only products but also services. Consumers want to know not only what is the highest-rated garbage disposal but also how to choose a reputable plumber to install it. They still want to know how to evaluate products such as baby equipment, appliances, and cars, but they also want to know how to evaluate vacation packages and doctors and web site auctions.

The World Wide Web has become the first place many people look for information on products and services. The web contains much good information. Indeed, most of the magazines and journals listed in this section have a web site (the URLs are listed with each publication). In addition, the U.S. government Consumer Information Center in Pueblo, Colorado, at http://www.pueblo.gsa.gov, contains lists of dozens of government consumer publications available in print at little cost and available free on the web. The major web search engines also contain links to consumer information. For example, Yahoo's Directory of Society and Culture: Issues and Causes has a section of more than 600 links for Consumer Advocacy and Information: http://dir.yahoo.com/. Google's Directory section on consumers lists more than 30 categories with more than 6,000 links to subcategories: http://directory.google.com/Top/Home/Consumer_Information/. For a more controlled list, a search for the word *consumers* on *Librarians' Index to the Internet* (http://lii.org) turns up approximately 200 reviewed sites dealing with consumer issues.

For more information on a specific product, check the manufacturer's web site. For information on an industry (manufacturing or service), check with appropriate trade associations for that product or service from among the hundreds of trade associations. The standard list of trade associations can be found in the annual *National Trade and Professional Associations of America* (Washington, D.C.: Columbia Books, found in many libraries). Another alternative is the *Encyclopedia of Associations* (Detroit: Gale Research, also held by many libraries). Also available to help you determine reputable products and businesses or to file a complaint is the Better Business Bureau (http://www.bbb.org), 4200 Wilson Blvd., Suite 800, Arlington, VA 22203-1838; phone: (703)276-0100. On the bureau's web site is a locator to help consumers find their local Better Business Bureau.

In short, there are literally thousands of opportunities for consumers to become better educated. This section of *Magazines for Libraries* aims to provide a core list of consumer education magazines and journals. Some titles listed here are newsletters of consumer-oriented organizations; some are oriented toward consumer education in the very practical activities associated with day-to-day life; and some represent scholarly research being done on consumer behavior and its relationship to the marketplace. Consult other sections of *Magazines for Libraries* for more subject-specific entries. Also, check the cross-references to additional specific sources.

Basic Periodicals

Hs: *Consumer Information Catalog, Consumer Reports*; Ga: *Consumer Information Catalog, Consumer Reports, Consumers' Research Magazine*; Ac: *Consumer Reports, Journal of Consumer Affairs, Journal of Consumer Policy.*

Basic Abstracts and Indexes

Consumers Index to Product Evaluations and Information Sources.

Adbusters. See Alternatives/General section.

1936. ***Co-op America Quarterly.*** Formerly (until 1991): *Building Economic Alternatives.* 1985. q. USD 60 (Individuals, USD 20). Ed(s): Dennis Greenia. Co-op America Inc., 1612 K St, N W, Ste 600, Washington, DC 20006; info@coopamerica.org; http://www.coopamerica.org. Illus., adv. Sample. Circ: 60000 Paid. *Indexed:* AltPI. *Aud.:* Ga, Ac.

Co-op America Quarterly is a free publication to members of Co-op America, whose mission is "to harness economic power—the strength of consumers, investors, businesses, and the marketplace—to create a socially just and environmentally sustainable society." The magazine's issues suggest how consumers can use their spending and investing power to bring about social justice and environmental sustainability, highlight socially and environmentally responsible businesses, and expose irresponsible companies. Co-op America maintains several web sites focusing on its areas of interest. Their main site is at http://www.coopamerica.org. This is a solid choice for public and academic libraries.

Consumer Information Catalog. See Free Magazines and House Organs section.

1937. ***Consumer Reports.*** [ISSN: 0010-7174] 1936. m. except s-m. Dec. USD 24; USD 4.95 newsstand/cover. Ed(s): Julia Kagan. Consumers Union of the United States, Inc., 101 Truman Ave, Yonkers, NY 10703-1057; http://www.zillions.org. Illus., index. Sample. Circ: 4100000 Paid. Vol. ends: Dec. Microform: NBI. Online: America Online, Inc.; The Dialog Corporation; EBSCO Publishing; Gale Group; LexisNexis; ProQuest Information & Learning. *Indexed:* ABIn, AgeL, BLI, CBCARef, CINAHL, CPerI, ConsI, EnvAb, FLI, LRI, MagInd, PAIS, RGPR. *Aud.:* Hs, Ga, Ac.

Consumer Reports is probably THE most well known and frequently used magazine that evaluates consumer goods, services, health, and personal finance. It is published by Consumers Union, a nonprofit, independent consumer organization, established in 1936 to test products, inform the public, and protect consumers. Each issue contains feature articles evaluating all sorts of products and services such as kitchen equipment, exercise equipment, baby products, cars, theme parks, cruise lines, and electronics. Each article explains the importance of the features being evaluated, the criteria used to evaluate the products/services, how the tests were carried out, the results of the tests, and finally *Consumer Reports*' recommendations. Each issue also has a column on product updates and product recalls and a column called "Selling It" that highlights misleading advertising. The annual *Consumer Reports Buying Guide* refers to relevant *Consumer Reports* articles in its evaluation of products. The web site of *Consumer Reports* at http://www.consumerreports.org contains much free information, including the product recall notices, "e-Ratings," a guide to online shopping, and "Consumer WebWatch," a site whose mission is to investigate, inform, and improve consumer information on the web. If one can subscribe to only one consumer-oriented magazine, this would be the one.

Consumer Reports for Kids Online. See Children/Electronic Journals section.

1938. ***Consumers' Research Magazine: analyzing consumer issues.*** Formerly (1957-1973): *Consumer Bulletin.* [ISSN: 0095-2222] 1927. m. USD 24; USD 32 foreign. Ed(s): Peter Spencer. Consumers' Research, Inc., 800 Maryland Ave, N E, Washington, DC 20002. Illus., index, adv. Sample. Circ: 14000. Vol. ends: Dec. CD-ROM: ProQuest Information & Learning. Microform: NBI; PQC. Online: bigchalk; EBSCO Publishing; Florida Center for Library Automation; Gale Group; OCLC Online Computer Library Center, Inc.; ProQuest Information & Learning; H.W. Wilson. *Indexed:* AgeL, ConsI, FLI, LRI, MagInd, RGPR. *Aud.:* Ga, Ac.

Produced by the nonprofit organization, Consumers' Research, Inc., founded in 1928, *Consumers' Research Magazine* goes beyond product testing to report scientific, technical, and educational information on subjects of interest to consumers. Recent topics have included nutrition, automobiles, charities, college costs, energy, the environment, food safety, fraud, gardening, health care, investing, drugs, new technology, real estate, safety, taxes, telemarketing, managed care, social security, and many more. Recurring columns include Dateline Washington, Food for Thought (food topics), Automotive Consumer, The Green Thumb, What the Critics Say About Movies, and Computer Savvy, among others. All articles are signed, with brief credentials and contact information for the authors given. There are no ads, and the publication is not supported by any manufacturers, dealers, or government agencies. There is an annual cumulative index of topics covered. A solid choice for public and academic libraries.

Family Economics and Nutrition Review. See Home Economics section.

FDA Consumer. See Medicine and Health/Consumer Health section.

1939. ***Journal of Consumer Affairs.*** [ISSN: 0022-0078] 1967. s-a. USD 100 for membership to individuals; USD 240 for membership to institutions. Ed(s): Herbert Jack Rotfeld. American Council on Consumer Interests, 61 Stanley Hall, University of Missouri, Columbia, MO 65211-0001; acci@missouri.edu; http://www.consumerinterests.org/. Illus. Sample. Refereed. Circ: 1500. Vol. ends: Winter. Microform: MIM; PQC. Online: EBSCO Publishing; Florida Center for Library Automation; Gale Group; Northern Light Technology, Inc.; OCLC Online Computer Library Center, Inc.; ProQuest Information & Learning; H.W. Wilson. Reprint: PQC; PSC. *Indexed:* ABIn, AgeL, ArtHuCI, BPI, BRI, BusEdI, CBRI, CIJE, CommAb, ConsI, DSA, IBSS, IndVet, JEL, PAIS, SSCI, WAE&RSA. *Bk. rev.:* 12-13, 1,000-2,000 words. *Aud.:* Ac.

The *Journal of Consumer Affairs* is the scholarly journal of the American Council on Consumer Interests (ACCI). The *Journal of Consumer Affairs* is a refereed journal focusing on "the household, firms, and/or governmental agencies as they affect market and nonmarket perceptions, actions, interactions, and policies involving individuals and households as economic agents." The import of the articles has "implications for government, household and/or business policy, and decision making." Each issue also includes book reviews. A subscription to the *Journal of Consumer Affairs* is included in individual or institutional membership in ACCI. Because of its scholarly nature, this journal is a good choice for academic libraries.

1940. ***Journal of Consumer Policy: consumer issues in law, economics and behavioral sciences.*** Formerly (until 1983): *Zeitschrift fuer Verbraucherpolitik.* [ISSN: 0168-7034] 1977. q. USD 389 print or online ed. Kluwer Academic / Plenum Publishers, 233 Spring St Fl 7, New York, NY 10013-1522; http://www.wkap.nl/. Adv. Refereed. Microform: PQC. Online: EBSCO Publishing; Gale Group; ingenta.com; Kluwer Online; OCLC Online Computer Library Center, Inc.; Ovid Technologies, Inc.; ProQuest Information & Learning; RoweCom Information Quest; Swets Blackwell. Reprint: SWZ. *Indexed:* ABIn, H&SSA, IBSS, IBZ, JEL, LRI, PAIS, RiskAb, SSCI, WAE&RSA. *Bk. rev.:* Various number and length. *Aud.:* Ac.

A refereed journal that publishes theoretical and empirical studies of consumer and producer conduct. This journal reports research on a broad range of issues relating to consumer affairs, including discussion of social, legal, and economic structures influencing consumer interests. It also extensively and systematically covers issues in consumer law and legislation in transnational communities such as the EC and analyzes trends in the implementation of consumer legislation, including its impact on the producer. A very scholarly journal appropriate for academic libraries that support upper-division or graduate programs in business, economics, or law.

Kiplinger's Personal Finance. See Finance/Investment section.

1941. ***National Consumers League Bulletin.*** [ISSN: 1055-923X] 1937. bi-m. Individuals, USD 20; Corporations, USD 100. Ed(s): Holly Anderson. National Consumers League, Inc., 1701 K St, N W, Ste 1200, Washington, DC 20006. Illus. Sample. Circ: 5000. Vol. ends: Dec. *Aud.:* Hs, Ga.

First published in the early 1930s, the *NCL Bulletin* is the bimonthly publication of the National Consumers League, the United States's oldest nonprofit consumer group. Subscriptions to the *NCL Bulletin* are included in NCL membership. The mission of the National Consumers League is to "identify, protect, represent, and advance the economic and social interests of consumers and workers." The 12-page *NCL Bulletin* is billed as a newsletter, but it contains more than just information about the NCL. It contains articles about specific consumer products or services, such as over-the-counter pain medications, fake check fraud, and computer security. It also contains news about consumer-oriented action taken by other groups such as the Government Accounting Office and the Center for Disease Control as well as by individuals. The topics covered in the *NCL Bulletin* would be of interest to all consumers, but are most likely to be sought by those in high school and public libraries.

Priorities for Health. See Medicine and Health/Electronic Journals section.

1942. ***Refundle Bundle: your bi-monthly guide to refund and coupon offers.*** [ISSN: 0194-0139] 1973. bi-m. USD 19.87. Ed(s): Stephen M Samtur. Refundle Bundle, PO Box 140, Yonkers, NY 10710. Illus. Sample. Circ: 70000. *Aud.:* Ga.

Begun and still published by well-known "Coupon Queen" Susan Samtur, *Refundle Bundle* is a bimonthly guide to refund and coupon offers. Each issue contains dozens of announcements of coupon offers, tips for taking maximum advantage of coupon and refund offers, lists of refund groups, web sites devoted to couponing and refunding, an explanation of refunding terms, news on labels for education initiatives, and announcements of new products. Each subscription includes a Manual for Refunders that explains the various varieties of refunds and coupons, tips for changing shopping habits in order to maximize refund values, what parts of packaging to save for refunds, and tips on how to write companies regarding refund offers. A very practical, straightforward approach to this consumer subject. A good choice for public libraries.

1943. ***Robb Report: the magazine for the luxury lifestyle.*** [ISSN: 0279-1447] 1976. m. USD 65 domestic; USD 75 Canada; USD 1057.99 elsewhere. Ed(s): Larry Bean. CurtCo Robb Media LLC., One Acton Pl, Acton, MA 01720. Illus., adv. Sample. Circ: 115000 Paid. *Indexed:* NumL. *Aud.:* Ga, Sa.

For those looking at high-end products and services, the *Robb Report* lives up to its subtitle, "for the luxury lifestyle." While not comparative in its treatment of products, the magazine and its accompanying *Robb Report Collection* do explain the special features and materials of expensive products. For example, in one recent issue the meaning and import behind the French word *manufacture* as it relates to watchmaking is explained. In that same issue is an article on how to hire and keep household employees. Each issue of the *Robb Report Collection,* a supplement to the *Robb Report,* is centered around a single product, such as cars, homes, or antique furniture. The publication's web site, http://www.robbreport.com, allows one to see the table of contents of recent issues and the full texts of some articles in older issues. Since this magazine does not review products most people can afford, this magazine would be a serious choice only for those who want to fantasize about expensive purchases or have serious money to spend. However, libraries serving affluent patrons may find this title in demand.

Electronic Journals

1944. ***Consumer News and Reviews.*** Former titles (until 1989): *A C C I Newsletter;* (until 1969): *Council on Consumer Information. Newsletter.* [ISSN: 1086-9107] 1953. bi-m. USD 100 (Individuals, USD 25). Ed(s): Patricia Bonner. American Council on Consumer Interests, 61 Stanley Hall, University of Missouri, Columbia, MO 65211-0001; http://www.consumerinterests.org/. Illus. Sample. Circ: 1200. Vol. ends: Dec. *Aud.:* Ga, Ac.

One can either access this online-only publication as part of a membership in the American Council of Consumer Interests (ACCI) or subscribe to this publication separately, without membership in ACCI. Issues contain summaries of important articles and news concerning consumer and personal finance topics; news about educational materials available for kindergarten through adult educators—many are free or low-cost; links to Internet sites that can be used as reference tools and as part of the student learning experience; updates on court decisions, legislation, and regulation; and noteworthy statistics and research reports. As part of a subscription, members will be able to access past issues and use a search engine to find items by subject, target audience, resource type, and keyword. More information about this title and a subscription to it can be found at http://www.consumerinterests.org. The ACCI is well known in the area of consumer education, and this title is a standard of ACCI's publications.

■ CRAFT

General/Calligraphy/Clay/Fiber/Glass/Jewelry-Metal/Knitting and Crochet/Needlework/Quilting/Wood

Mary Frances Angelini, Electronic Resources Librarian, Godfrey Lowell Cabot Science Library, Harvard University, One Oxford St., Cambridge, MA 02138; angelini@fas.harvard.edu

Introduction

Fine craft is art, and many of the artists shown in fine craft magazines display their works in museums. Home crafting may be excellent technically but is essentially done in a crafter's spare time. Some crafts are skills that were formerly necessary to create useful items (quilting and embroidery, for example), while others, such as gold and silversmithing, require specialized tools and training. Useful crafts can certainly also be beautiful, as artisans of the guilds have shown. I have chosen to review magazines from all places along the continuum of home crafting and art craft, focusing on the more commonly practiced crafts—with an occasional exception.

Magazines are listed by subject. Not all the truly wonderful magazines are listed here, nor are all catagories—only those that have magazines that are necessary to a good, general crafts collection.

Basic Periodicals

GENERAL. *American Craft, Crafts, SAC Newsmonthly.*

CLAY. *Ceramic Review, Ceramics Monthly.*

FIBER. *Fiberarts, Threads.*

JEWELRY-METAL. *Ornament.*

KNITTING AND CROCHET. *Knitter's.*

NEEDLEWORK. *Piecework, Stitcher's World.*

QUILTING. *Quilter's Newsletter Magazine.*

WOOD. *Fine Woodworking, Woodsmith.*

Basic Abstracts and Indexes

Art Index, Artbibliographies Modern, Index to How to Do It Information, Magazine Article Summaries.

General

1945. *American Craft.* Former titles: *Craft Horizons with Craft World;* (until 1979, vol.39, no.3): *Craft Horizons;* Incorporates: *Craft World.* [ISSN: 0194-8008] 1941. bi-m. USD 40 domestic; USD 5 newsstand/cover per issue. Ed(s): Patricia Dandignac, Lois Moran. American Craft Council, 72 Spring St, New York, NY 10012; http://www.craftcouncil.org. Illus., adv. Circ: 42850 Paid and free. Vol. ends: Dec/Jan. CD-ROM: ProQuest Information & Learning. Microform: PQC. Online: bigchalk; Gale Group; Northern Light Technology, Inc.; OCLC Online Computer Library Center, Inc.; ProQuest Information & Learning. *Indexed:* ABM, AIAP, ArtInd, BAS, BRI, CBRI, DAAI, IBZ, MRD, MagInd, RGPR. *Bk. rev.:* 3-4, 500 words, critical, signed. *Aud.:* Ga, Ac, Sa.

It would be difficult to overstate the depth and breadth of this journal. It covers crafts from the contemporary to the historical to the prehistoric in any medium and analyzes the current state of craft in America. While it concentrates on American crafts and artisans, *American Craft* also looks at trends and artisans from all over the world. There are about six feature articles that focus on artists, collectors, technique, the history of a genre or technique, or trends and philosophies. The "Portfolio" section looks at the work of practicing artisans. The "Gallery" section shows photographs submitted by galleries, museums, and individuals to announce upcoming exhibits. The "Focus" section reviews two or three exhibits around the nation. Craft Council news has its own section. Galleries and museums list upcoming shows where other magazines would place ads. A beautiful, glossy publication full of articles and ideas, inspiration and information, for artists, craftspeople, students, and the interested public.

1946. *Crafts: the decorative & applied arts magazine.* [ISSN: 0306-610X] 1973. bi-m. GBP 33 (Individuals, GBP 27). Ed(s): Geraldine Rudge. Crafts Council, 44a Pentonville Rd, London, N1 9BY, United Kingdom. Illus., index, adv. Circ: 15500 Paid. Vol. ends: Nov/Dec. Microform: PQC. Online: OCLC Online Computer Library Center, Inc.; H.W. Wilson. Reprint: PQC. *Indexed:* ABM, ArtInd, DAAI. *Bk. rev.:* 1-4, critical, lengthy. *Aud.:* Ga, Ac, Sa.

Crafts is much more than a "decorative and applied arts magazine." It covers all media and does not limit itself to current practice. Every issue has a "Writers and Thinkers" article that studies the influence of a historic artist or craftsperson. Other articles are also in-depth studies of subjects ranging from the works and life of a practitioner to some facet of a particular medium. Exhibition reviews are more numerous than book reviews (as one might expect); both kinds of reviews are weighty and critical. Also interesting is the "Sources of Inspiration" where one artist/craftperson talks to another about their shared art/craft. There is also a "News, Reviews, and Previews" section with brief reviews in the front of the magazine. A serious, occasionally scholarly journal that beautifully conveys insight into craft in the United Kingdom, and a must purchase for any library that collects crafts periodicals.

1947. *Crafts News.* [ISSN: 0899-9724] 1986. q. USD 35. Crafts Center, 1001 Connecticut Ave, N W, Ste 525, Washington, DC 20036-5528; info@craftscenter.org; http://www.craftscenter.org. Adv. Circ: 6000 Paid and controlled. *Bk. rev.:* 3-7, descriptive. *Aud.:* Ga, Ac, Sa.

This unusual and wonderful publication "serves the interests and needs of low-income artisans and provides technical assistance and information to help artisans achieve greater quality, productions, and sales." While the focus of this newsletter is indigenous artisans and craftspeople all over the world, the articles are about craftways, trade laws, and environmental, economic, and sociocultural issues important to them. There are very few publications that cover these issues, and this newsletter covers them very competently, providing much-needed information to the interested consumer. The web site has more information about the organization and member organizations as well as some of the articles from the current issue of the newsletter. *Craft News* is not just for craft collections; this could also find a home in international and business collections.

1948. *Handcraft Illustrated.* [ISSN: 1072-0529] 1993. q. USD 24.95; USD 30.95 Canada; USD 36.95 elsewhere. Ed(s): Mary Ann Hall. Boston Common Press, 17 Station St, Box 470 589, Brookline, MA 02445. Illus. *Aud.:* Ga.

This is a project magazine, with 20 or so per issue. There are sewing, stenciling, beading, painting, cooking, candlemaking, paper, glass, wood, dried and fresh plant projects, and more. The instructions are clear and detailed, and the patterns are included. The only caveat is that some projects have some of the materials listed below the main list in smaller print under the heading "You'll Also Need" rather than with the rest of the materials where they ought to be. The "Notes from Readers" and "Quick Tips" columns are both well done. The layout and design of the magazine is excellent, and the lack of advertising is refreshing. An excellent choice.

1949. *Object.* Formerly (until 1995): *Crafts New South Wales.* [ISSN: 1038-1856] 1964. q. AUD 44 (Individuals, AUD 34). Ed(s): Ian Were. Centre for Contemporary Craft, 3rd Fl, Customs House, 31 Alfred St, Circular Quay, NSW 2000, Australia; object@object.com.au; http://www.object.com.au. Illus., adv. Refereed. Circ: 10000. *Indexed:* DAAI. *Aud.:* Ga, Ac, Sa.

Object was once more of a cultural critique/commentary journal, quite different from *Craft* and *American Craft.* In the past few years, it has become a peer-reviewed journal. It offers reviews of artists, exhibits, and the like, but the articles have become more scholarly. The focus is still Australia/Pacific Rim/Australasia, but occasional articles also cover other areas of the world. Although this journal's American and British counterparts are not peer reviewed, *Object* now seems more like them. The "tone" of this journal is just as refreshingly unique as always, even if the articles are more scholarly.

1950. *S A C Newsmonthly: national news and listings of art & craft shows.* Incorporates: *Art and Crafts Catalyst;* Former titles: *National Arts and Crafts Network; National Calendar of Open Competitive Exhibitions; Lisa's Report; Craft Show Bulletin.* 1986. m. USD 24 print edition only; USD 36 print and online editions. Ed(s): Wayne Smith. S A C, Inc, PO Box 159, Bogalusa, LA 70429-0159; http://www.SACNewsmonthly.com. Adv. Circ: 4000. *Aud.:* Ga, Sa.

This is a newsprint publication that lists art and craft show events for the current month and for the following 11 months. Within each month, listings are alphabetical by state, and then by date. Event information is concise, giving dates, times, the name of the event, location, contact phone numbers, and any other pertinent entry or display requirements. While there is not much information about each listing, the number of listings is remarkable; it is national in scope, updated each issue, and very affordable. There are some news articles on various events, but the focus, and the importance, of this publication is its events listings. An important resource for craftspeople and artisans looking to sell their works, and for those of us who like to go to these events.

Calligraphy

1951. *The Edge (London).* [ISSN: 1358-6688] 1995. bi-m. GBP 21 in Europe; GBP 27 elsewhere; GBP 3 newsstand/cover per issue. Ed(s): Susan Cavendish. Calligraphy and Lettering Arts Society, 54 Boileau Rd, London, SW13 9BL, United Kingdom; 101344.3245@compuserve.com. Illus., index, adv. Circ: 1800 Paid. Vol. ends: Mar/Apr (No. 6). *Bk. rev.:* 2, 250-500 words, critical. *Aud.:* Ga, Sa.

There are few journals on the subject of calligraphy or the art of lettering. *Letter Arts Review* is the better-known title, but this, *The Edge,* also deserves a place next to it on your shelves. This is a brief black-and-white magazine with no wasted space in the pages. Ads are few, and only in the back; content is king. The articles cover various topics such as the history of styles (an in-depth look at a particular style), library and museum collections, and examining a particular manuscript. Every issue includes the "Diary," a listing of events in date order; "Courses"; and similar informative sections. If *Letter Arts Review* is part of your collection, make *The Edge* part of it as well.

1952. *Letter Arts Review.* Former titles (until vol.11, no.2, 1994): *Calligraphy Review;* (until 1987): *Calligraphy Idea Exchange.* [ISSN: 1076-7339] 1982. q. USD 42 domestic; USD 45 in Canada & Mexico; USD 62 elsewhere. Ed(s): Karyn L Gilman. Letters Arts Review, vnc., 212 Hillsboro Dr, Silver Spring, MD 20902; http://www.letterarts.com. Illus., index, adv. Circ: 5500. *Indexed:* ArtInd, DAAI, IBZ. *Bk. rev.:* 2-3, critical. *Aud.:* Sa.

Letter Arts Review is "dedicated to the recognition and advancement of the lettering arts and to the artists throughout the world who labor in this cause." This is a beautiful magazine. There are five to eight articles in each issue ranging from opinion pieces to studies of a calligraphic artist's work, to graphic design education, to historical studies, to discussions on the state of this art form. *Letter Arts Review* belongs in any museum library, any library where there might be instructional or programmatic use for graphic design, bookbinding, or publishing, and libraries where there is a rare book collection.

Clay

1953. *Ceramic Review.* [ISSN: 0144-1825] 1970. bi-m. GBP 32; GBP 37 overseas. Ed(s): Emmanuel Cooper. Ceramic Review Publishing Ltd., 21 Carnaby St, London, W1V 1PH, United Kingdom; http://www.gold.net/users/dj94/creview.html. Illus., index, adv. Circ: 8300. *Indexed:* ABM, ArtInd, DAAI. *Bk. rev.:* 5-6, critical. *Aud.:* Ac, Sa.

Ceramic Review is a beautiful, thought-provoking, and practical British journal. It includes technical information about clay, glazes, and kilns; articles on practicing potters; reviews of exhibitions; and tips and techniques. There are also articles on historical influences and techniques and the craft as it is practiced in other parts of the world. The ads, which are numerous but confined to the front and back of the magazine, the classified section, and the gallery listings, are as critical to the magazine's functionality as the articles themselves—although not as useful for readers on this side of the Atlantic. *Ceramic Review* belongs in most crafts collections, and any ceramics collection.

1954. *Ceramics Monthly.* [ISSN: 0009-0328] 1953. 10x/yr. Members, USD 24; Non-members, USD 30; USD 6 newsstand/cover. Ed(s): Ruth C Butler. American Ceramic Society, 735 Ceramic Pl, Westerville, OH 43081-8720; customersrvc@acers.org; http://www.ceramics.org. Illus., index, adv. Circ: 40000 Paid. Microform: NBI; PQC. Online: EBSCO Publishing; Gale Group; OCLC Online Computer Library Center, Inc.; ProQuest Information & Learning; H.W. Wilson. Reprint: PQC. *Indexed:* A&ATA, ABM, ABS&EES, ASIP, ArtInd, BAS, BHA, BRI, BiogInd, CBRI, DAAI, IHTDI, MagInd. *Bk. rev.:* 5-6, descriptive, approx. 300 words. *Aud.:* Ga, Sa.

Ceramics Monthly is one of the most important journals in this field. Regular features include "Call for Entries," which lists application deadlines for exhibitions from the regional to the international; "Calendar," which lists conferences, exhibitions, fairs, and workshops; a "Classified" section that is, predictably, very large; the "Up Front" section, which shows reader-submitted photos and writing about potters or events; and the "Questions" column, which answers technical questions from readers. Feature articles look at individual potters and their work, sources of inspiration, software, exhibitions, competitions, potter-written thought pieces, materials and methods, and articles about historical and ethnic techniques. While not limited to ceramics in the United States, this is the main focus of the coverage. The numerous advertisements provide a great resource for equipment and suppliers. *Ceramics Monthly* is a necessity in any ceramics collection, and an important part of any basic crafts/decorative arts collection.

1955. *Pottery in Australia.* [ISSN: 0048-4954] 1962. q. Membership, AUD 88. Ed(s): Suzanne Buckle. Potters' Society of Australia, PO Box 105, Erskineville, NSW 2043 , Australia; society@potteryinaustralia.com; http://www.potteryinaustralia.com/PS/index_ab.html?about.html~main. Illus., index, adv. Circ: 5000. *Indexed:* ABM, DAAI. *Bk. rev.:* 1-2, critical. *Aud.:* Ga, Ac, Sa.

This is a publication of the Potters' Society of Australia, and it is the counterpart of *Ceramics Monthly* in the United States and *Ceramic Review* in the United Kingdom. Each issue has a "Focus" section, with 10–13 articles, all on the theme of the issue, and all on different potters. The "Reviews" section looks at four to six current exhibitions. As with all society publications, there is a section devoted to society news. There is also technical information, reviews of practicing potters' life's work, and articles about issues of practicing this craft today. A beautiful, substantive magazine, *Pottery in Australia* is equally valuable for inspiration and for a look at the practice of this craft in another nation.

Fiber

1956. *Fiberarts: the magazine of textiles.* Formerly (until 1977): *Fibercraft Newsletter.* [ISSN: 0164-324X] 1974. bi-m. 5/yr. USD 22 domestic; USD 27 foreign; USD 5.50 newsstand/cover per issue. Ed(s): Sunita Patterson. Altamont Press, 67 Broadway St., Asheville, NC 28801-2919; editor@fiberartsmagazine.com; http://www.fiberartsmagazine.com/. Illus., adv. Circ: 24500. Vol. ends: Mar/Apr. *Indexed:* A&ATA, ArtInd, DAAI, IHTDI. *Bk. rev.:* 5-9, length varies. *Aud.:* Ga, Ac, Sa.

Fiberarts covers fiber work of all description, from weaving to quilting, from textile manufacturing to knitting, from wearable art to fiber art that is not intended to be worn. Many items are short—one or two pages—covering ethnic fiber, wearable fiber art traditions, or artist profiles. The feature articles cover the same range of topics but in more depth, and look at artists, themes, trends, exhibits, and the future of fiber arts in general. All articles can be understood by nonspecialists. The "Reviews" section covers exhibits, events, and books, with the emphasis on exhibits. The "Fibermart" section and the advertising would prove useful for fiber artisans. In addition to this section, there are advertisments throughout the magazine. There are also columns for travel, education, competition opportunities, and exhibits (both current and upcoming) by state and in other countries. A beautiful magazine that covers a broad subject area very well.

1957. *Handwoven.* Incorporates (in 1981): *Interweave.* [ISSN: 0198-8212] 1979. 5x/yr. USD 22; USD 28 foreign. Ed(s): Jean Scorgie. Interweave Press, Inc., 201 E Fourth St, Loveland, CO 80537; http://www.interweave.com. Illus., adv. Circ: 36000. *Indexed:* IHTDI. *Bk. rev.:* 4-5, critical. *Aud.:* Ga, Ac, Sa.

Handwoven is for the serious weaver, for those who want to be, and for those who follow the craft. Issues are centered on three or four themes, and there are one to five articles on each theme. These themes may be about a weaving technique, or a nation's or a people's historic method of weaving or creating cloth or projects for a season. There are regular columns such as "Beginner's Corner" that give simple, clear explanations of techniques. There is also a calendar that lists exhibits, shows, and sales by state. There is an extensive advertising section, which is thankfully confined to the front and the back. There are many projects to try, and a "Project Guide" in each issue. If fiber arts are a focus, or even just an aspect of your collection, consider adding this title.

1958. *Journal for Weavers, Spinners & Dyers.* Former titles (until 1984): *Weavers Journal;* (until 1976): *Guilds of Weavers, Spinners and Dyers. Quarterly Journal.* [ISSN: 0267-7806] 1952. q. GBP 12.50 domestic; GBP 14.65 foreign. Ed(s): Jenny Aisbitt. Association of Guilds of Weavers Spinners & Dyers, Setters Glade Brewery Lane, Holcombe, Radstock, BA3 5EG, United Kingdom; journal@jonsmith.demon.co.uk. Illus., adv. Circ: 2500. *Indexed:* DAAI, IHTDI. *Bk. rev.:* 2-4, 150-300 words, critical. *Aud.:* Ga, Sa.

This interesting publication covers the world in its articles. It looks at textile fibers, methods, projects, and people. Articles are one to four pages; some pictures are in color. As this is a guild publication, there is plenty of guild news. There are also exhibition reviews and a listing of current exhibits in the United Kingdom. "News and Views" offers brief, descriptive, and critical reviews of these exhibits. The areas of focus are quite broad, and thus the content is wonderfully varied. A good addition to a crafts collection.

1959. *Rug Hooking.* [ISSN: 1045-4373] 1989. 5x/yr. USD 27.95 domestic; USD 35.26 Canada; USD 40.95 elsewhere. Ed(s): Patrice Crowley. Stackpole Magazines, 1300 Market St., Ste. 202, Lemoyne, PA 17043-1420; rughook@paonline.com. Illus., index, adv. Circ: 10869 Paid. *Bk. rev.:* 3-5. *Aud.:* Ga, Ac, Sa.

If you think rug hooking is limited to latch hook kits with their short pieces of yarn, this magazine will open your eyes to the past and present art of rug hooking. It is full of information for enthusiasts of all skill levels. It contains patterns, instructions on basic techniques, regular columns such as "Dear Beginning Rug Hooker," which includes a pattern; "Recipes from the Dye Kitchen"; and "Camps and Workshops." There are four or five feature articles per issue covering a variety of topics, including exhibiting your works, historical techniques, the state of the craft, copyright law, and tips and techniques. The ads do not overwhelm the content and may prove helpful to those searching for supplies. This excellent journal is worthy of a place in any craft collection, especially those libraries where there is an interest in rug hooking or where there is a strong crafting community.

1960. ***Spin-Off: the magazine for handspinners.*** [ISSN: 0198-8239] 1977. q. USD 21; USD 26 foreign. Ed(s): Linda C Ligon. Interweave Press, Inc., 201 E Fourth St, Loveland, CO 80537; http://www.interweave.com. Illus., adv. Circ: 18000. Vol. ends: Dec. *Indexed:* IHTDI. *Bk. rev.:* 5, 300-350 words, critical and descriptive. *Aud.:* Ga, Ac, Sa.

This magazine encompasses many aspects of fiber art. There are in-depth articles on various animal fibers (e.g., alpaca) and the animals; rare breeds, their wool, and its historical/cultural importance; carding and spinning techniques; caring for items made from natural fibers; museums and their collections; artist interviews; and projects (knitting, weaving, etc.). There is a calendar section that lists festivals, exhibits, conferences, instructional opportunities, and travel. The extensive classifieds section lists everything from carding supplies to animals. There are ads throughout, and they are occasionally distracting from the otherwise excellent content.

1961. ***Textile History.*** [ISSN: 0040-4969] 1968. s-a. USD 92 (Individuals, USD 38). Ed(s): Stanley Chapman. Maney Publishing, Hudson Rd, Leeds, LS9 7DL, United Kingdom; maney@maney.co.uk; http://www.maney.co.uk. Illus., index, adv. Refereed. Vol. ends: Nov. *Indexed:* A&ATA, AIAP, AmH&L, ArtInd, BAS, BHA, BrArAb, BrHumI, GeogAbPG, IBZ, NumL. *Bk. rev.:* 6-8, 300-500 words, critical. *Aud.:* Ac.

This journal was launched in 1968 by the Passold Research Fund to foster research and publication about the history of textiles; their technical development, design, conservation; the history of dress; and other uses of textiles. It is a substantial publication. While more than half of the five or so articles are about English textile history, other countries are covered as well. Because this is a scholarly journal, it will not suit a library that is searching only for popular material, but if yours is an academic, museum, or special library where textiles are a focus, then consider adding this title to your collection.

1962. ***Threads.*** [ISSN: 0882-7370] 1985. bi-m. USD 32.95 in US & Canada; USD 38.95 elsewhere. Ed(s): Renee Lewinter. Taunton Press, Inc., 63, South Main St, PO Box 5506, Newtown, CT 06470-5506; http://www.taunton.com. Illus., index, adv. Circ: 100000. Vol. ends: Dec. *Indexed:* ASIP, DAAI, IHTDI, MagInd. *Bk. rev.:* 1,350 words, critical. *Aud.:* Ga, Sa.

This is not a project magazine. *Threads* covers all aspects of sewing: clothing, non-clothing, measuring, software, tools and equipment, fabrics, decoration, machine embroidery, and so on. Projects seem designed to teach techniques, style, and design concepts, rather than being there for their own sake or to give the reader something to do. There are regular columns such as "Tools of the Trade" and "Basics." An excellent and important resource for sewers. *Threads* belongs in all general crafts collections.

Glass

1963. ***Glass Art Society Journal.*** [ISSN: 0278-9426] 1981. a. Non-members, USD 27. Ed(s): Susan Frantz. Glass Art Society, 1305 Fourth Ave, Ste 711, Seattle, WA 98101-2401; info@glassart.org; http://www.glassart.org. Illus., adv. Circ: 2500. *Indexed:* DAAI. *Aud.:* Ac, Sa.

This journal consists of the annual conference proceedings of the Glass Art Society, and the papers and presentations therefore cover a wide range of topics. These include history, art criticism, techniques, science and technology, education, current practice, the relationship of art glass to other forms of art, individual artists and their works, and even memorial notices. There is some advertising, but it is confined to the back pages. This is an important resource for academic libraies that cover art, art history, and related topics.

1964. ***Glass on Metal: the enamelist's magazine.*** [ISSN: 1083-6888] 1982. 5x/yr. USD 45 domestic; USD 52 in Canada & Mexico; USD 59.10 in Europe. Ed(s): Tom Ellis. Enamelist Society, PO Box 310, Newport, KY 41072; http://www.craftweb.com/org/enamel/enamel.htm. Illus., adv. Refereed. Circ: 1100 Paid. Vol. ends: Dec. *Indexed:* ABM. *Bk. rev.:* Occasional, descriptive and critical. *Aud.:* Sa.

Glass on Metal is a publication of the Enamelist Society. There are about eight feature articles in each issue. Most articles are short, about two pages, and guild news articles can run to three or four pages. The topics are varied, from works to gallery and museum reviews to techniques to news of the craft and artisans. As with any guild publication, guild news is plentiful. For collections where there is instructional or programmatic need, or interest.

1965. ***Journal of Glass Studies.*** [ISSN: 0075-4250] 1959. a. USD 43 per issue domestic; USD 43.75 per issue foreign. Ed(s): Richard Price. Corning Museum of Glass, One Museum Way, Corning, NY 14830-2253. Illus., index, adv. Refereed. Circ: 1500. Microform: PQC. Reprint: PQC. *Indexed:* A&ATA, AIAP, AICP, ArtHuCI, ArtInd, BHA, BrArAb, ChemAb, IBZ, NumL. *Aud.:* Ac.

Journal of Glass Studies is devoted to scholarly research in the history, art, and early technology of glass. It does not accept articles concerned with living artists or glassmakers. Articles can be in English, French, Spanish, Italian, or German, but non-English articles have a 100- to 150-word summary. There are usually many articles, but the editors may also choose to devote an issue to a single, extensive article. There is also a section called "Recent Important Acquisitions" covering both private and public collections in the United States and abroad. The "Notes" section has brief articles (two to six pages), letters, announcements, and obituaries. This is an important, scholarly publication that belongs in museums, art school libraries, and academic collections where there is interest.

1966. ***New Glass Review.*** Formerly (until 1979): *Contemporary Glass;* Supersedes (in 1978): *Contemporary Glass Microfiche Program.* [ISSN: 0275-469X] 1976. a. USD 11.50 per vol. domestic; USD 12 per vol. foreign. Ed(s): Richard Price. Corning Museum of Glass, One Museum Way, Corning, NY 14830-2253. Illus., adv. Reprint: PQC. *Indexed:* DAAI. *Aud.:* Ga, Sa.

New Glass Review has more in common with an exhibition than with other magazines. It displays 100 glass art pieces selected by a jury from submissions by artists from all over the world. It is looking for the best of the new—all artwork must have been done in the preceding calendar year. The magazine is divided into four sections. The first is statements from the four jury members. The second is the exhibition, with pictures of the works, their titles, and artist information. The third is called "Some of the Best in Recent Glass" and focuses on recent work that may or may not have been submitted or may not have made the date cutoff, and fuller descriptions of artists and their works. Finally, there is a bibliography of recent books, articles, films, and videotapes. This last section alone is a boon to collections librarians. *New Glass Review* is an important journal, not only for its look at practicing artists, but also for the bibliography.

1967. ***Stained Glass: devoted to the craft of architectural stained and decorative art glass.*** Former titles (until 1990): *Stained Glass Quarterly;* (until 1986): *Stained Glass.* [ISSN: 1067-8867] 1906. q. USD 36 domestic; USD 44 in Canada & Mexico; USD 50 elsewhere. Ed(s): Richard Gross. Stained Glass Association of America, 6 S W Second St, Ste 7, Lees Summit, MO 64063-2352; http://www.stainedglass.org. Illus., index, adv. Circ: 6000. Vol. ends: Spring/Winter. Online: OCLC Online Computer Library Center, Inc.; H.W. Wilson. *Indexed:* AIAP, ArtInd, BHA, DAAI, IBZ. *Bk. rev.:* 1-4, descriptive. *Aud.:* Ga, Ac, Sa.

Stained Glass is the official publication of the Stained Glass Association of America. Articles cover all aspects of the craft. There are features on older works and past artists, restoration and preservation techniques, technical issues, business issues, and photography. No article is so full of jargon as to exclude the interested layperson. As a society publication, it has information about the guild, conferences, workshops, scholarships, and society news. As one would expect from a magazine that endeavors to be useful as well as interesting, there is an extensive "Sources of Supply" section. *Stained Glass* should be part of any glass craft collection.

Jewelry-Metal

1968. ***The Anvil's Ring.*** [ISSN: 0889-177X] 1973. q. USD 35 (Individuals, USD 45; Senior citizens, USD 40). Ed(s): Rob Edwards. Artists-Blacksmith Association of North America, Inc., PO Box 816, Farmington, GA 30638-0816; abana@abana.org; http://www.abana.org. Illus., adv. Circ: 5000 Paid. *Bk. rev.:* 1-3, 100-300 words, critical. *Aud.:* Sa, Ga.

If you have thought at all about blacksmithing, you have probably thought that all it involved was shoeing horses and that it is a dying art. Both are partially correct, but both are a long way from the truth. The artistry of blacksmithing is alive in the world and on display in this magazine. There are four to five feature articles in each issue, covering various topics such as blacksmith artists, equipment, blacksmiths from other parts of the world, and examples of blacksmithing's art. Regular departments include "New Works" and "International Report." There are black-and-white and color photos throughout. The advertisements are plentiful and should prove useful for those in the craft. There is also a classified section and a "Calendar of Events" listing exhibitions, classes, and courses, organized by date.

1969. ***Bead & Button: creative ideas and profjects for the art of beads and jewelry.*** [ISSN: 1072-4931] 1994. bi-m. USD 24.95; USD 4.95 newsstand/cover per issue. Ed(s): Alice Korach. Kalmbach Publishing Co., PO Box 1612, Waukesha, WI 53187-1612; webmaster@kalmbach.com; http://www.kalmbach.com. Illus., adv. Circ: 130000 Paid. *Indexed:* IHTDI. *Aud.:* Ga.

Bead and Button is devoted to beading, and is not limited to jewelry. All but one or two of the articles are projects, the others are artists' profiles or information about materials. The projects are well designed and appealing. The instructions are clear and well written. The "department" columns are also quite good. They cover such topics as computers; ethnic, cultural, or historical beads and techniques; tool and equipment reviews; a calendar; and basic stitches. If your library is in need of a beading projects magazine, *Bead and Button* is an excellent choice.

1970. ***Beadwork.*** [ISSN: 1528-5634] 1998. q. USD 24.95 domestic; USD 31.95 foreign. Ed(s): Jean Campbell. Interweave Press, Inc., 201 E Fourth St, Loveland, CO 80537; http://www.interweave.com. Illus., adv. Vol. ends: Fall. *Aud.:* Ga.

This is predominantly a project magazine. There are ten to thirteen projects in each issue, four feature articles, and a variety of departments. The projects are not rated for difficulty, but most seem to be accessible to beginners. Each project has a materials and notions list and clear directions that include diagrams. The feature articles cover beads, artists, and beaded costumes and objects. The departments include a calendar of events, calls for entries, basic stitches, columns, letters to the magazine, and readers' works. A solid, single-focus magazine geared toward the beginner hobbyist rather than the professional.

1971. ***Lapidary Journal.*** [ISSN: 0023-8457] 1947. m. USD 29.95 domestic; USD 42.95 foreign. Ed(s): Merle White. Primedia Enthusiast Group, 60 Chestnut Ave, Ste 201, Devon, PA 19333-1312; http://www.primedia.com. Illus., index, adv. Circ: 60000. Vol. ends: Mar. *Indexed:* A&ATA, ChemAb, GeoRef, IHTDI, MagInd. *Bk. rev.:* 1-2, critical. *Aud.:* Ga, Sa.

Lapidary Journal is about more than gemstones and gem cutting, although these are the primary focus. Feature articles cover jewelry artists and their works, gemstones and gemstone carving, historical themes, beads, mining, shows, techniques, and tools. Regular features include a calendar, a classifieds section, and "Facets," which looks at a particular aspect of jewelry. The "Jewelry Journal" is a "step by step gem jewelry and bead workshop" that shows readers how to do a particular technique, set up a studio, facet a stone, or create an item of jewelry through projects. The articles are beautifully illustrated for those in search of inspiration, and the advertising is plentiful enough to please those who use the magazine for supply sources.

1972. ***Ornament: a quarterly of jewelry and personal adornment.*** Formerly (until 1979): *Bead Journal.* [ISSN: 0148-3897] 1974. q. USD 23 domestic; USD 27 foreign. Ed(s): Robert K Liu, Carolyn L E Benesh. Ornament Inc., PO Box 2349, San Marcos, CA 92079-2349. Illus., adv. Circ: 45000 Paid. Vol. ends: Summer. *Indexed:* ABM, AICP, ArtInd, BrArAb, DAAI, IBZ. *Aud.:* Ga, Ac, Sa.

This magazine is about "the art of personal adornment" in styles from the contemporary to the ancient and the art craft to the ethnic. It covers everything used to adorn the body: jewelry, beadwork, fiber/textiles, wood, and things that might be used but are considered works of art. There are six to eight feature articles in each issue covering artists, techniques, sociocultural issues, various peoples and their ornaments, and decoration. The regular columns cover exhibition reviews, shows, fairs, and exhibits. It is a beautiful magazine that treats an extremely broad topic with richness and depth. Well worth purchasing for a crafts section.

Knitting and Crochet

1973. ***Cast On.*** 1984. 5x/yr. Membership, USD 25. Ed(s): Jean Lampe. Knitting Guild of America, 1100H, Brandywine Blvd, Zanesville, OH 43701; tkga@tkga.com; http://www.tkga.com. Illus., adv. Circ: 10000. *Indexed:* IHTDI. *Bk. rev.:* 2-4, descriptive. *Aud.:* Ga.

Cast On is the official publication of the Knitting Guild of America. Its varied contents include six or seven patterns in each issue that are rated for difficulty, and it is indicated whether they are for hand or machine knitting or both. There are articles on designers, knitting with kids, master's tips, new product reviews, techniques, and a variety of other topics. There is an extensive "Guild" section covering news, conventions, and individuals. More than a pattern magazine, *Cast On* is about guild efforts to expand its craft and the quality of workmanship. A excellent choice for your collection if there is a lot of interest in this handicraft.

1974. ***Crochet Fantasy.*** [ISSN: 8750-8877] 1983. 9x/yr. USD 21.97 domestic; USD 30.97 Canada; USD 35.47 elsewhere. Ed(s): Karen Manthey, Marie Arnold. All American Crafts, Inc., 243 Newton Sparta Rd, Newton, NJ 07860-2748; editors@crochetfantasy.com. Illus., adv. Circ: 150000. *Aud.:* Hs, Ga.

This is a magazine of projects, and, with very few exceptions, that is all there is here. The exceptions are three pages of crochet stitch instructions that give good, clear explanations of the stitches; a "Sources of Supply" section; conversion charts; and "Coming Attractions." Patterns run the gamut from sweaters to afghans, from doilies to toys. Unlike many pattern magazines, this has all the pictures in the front and back, and the patterns on newsprint in the middle. All pattern pictures are numbered to correspond to the location of the pattern. Each pattern is given one of three ratings for level of difficulty. It is hard to say if any one crochet pattern magazine is "better" than any other; generally, it is a matter of taste and need. The mixture of types of projects is good in *Crochet Fantasy,* so it is worth reviewing if your collection needs more in this area.

1975. ***Interweave Knits.*** [ISSN: 1088-3622] 1996. q. USD 24 domestic; USD 31 foreign. Ed(s): Pam Allen. Interweave Knits, Dept A KA, 201 E Fourth St, Loveland, CO 80537-5655; nancy@interweave.com; http://www.interweave.com. Illus., adv. Circ: 51500. *Bk. rev.:* 7, 100-150 words, descriptive. *Aud.:* Ga.

This is a project magazine. For every article there are eight or more projects. The articles might be about wool or other materials, or artist profiles, or histories of knitting around the world. The projects range from sweaters to socks to toys to scarves to purses to pillows. All projects have detailed instructions and diagrams of new or difficult stitches and techniques. The "Departments" section has a glossary with explanations and diagrams of the stitches, as well as a "Beyond the Basics" column. The ads are numerous, and there is even an advertisers' index. If readers cannot find the product they are seeking, it will not be for lack of listings.

1976. ***Knitters's Magazine.*** [ISSN: 0747-9026] 1984. q. USD 18 domestic; USD 23 foreign; USD 5.50 newsstand/cover per issue domestic. Ed(s): Rick J Mondragon. X R X, Inc., 231 S. Phillips Ave., Ste 400, PO Box 1525, Sioux Falls, SD 57101; http://www.knittinguniverse.com. Illus., adv. Circ: 30000 Paid. *Bk. rev.:* 4-6, 200-300 words, critical. *Aud.:* Ga.

Knitter's is divided into three sections, but the bulk of the content is devoted to projects. The "Features" section has letters, an instructions and abbreviations section, classified section, book reviews, and the like. There is also an "Articles" section with four to six nonproject items on things like design issues, profiles, common problems, and reviews of classes. The "Projects," of which there are about 27, are mainly sweaters, but there are some home decor patterns—afghans, doilies, and other decorating or seasonal projects. Ads are plentiful and throughout the magazine. A solid magazine for your collection if there are knitters looking for something more.

1977. *Vogue Knitting International.* [ISSN: 0890-9237] 1982. 3x/yr. USD 11.95. Ed(s): Trisha Malcolm. Butterick Co., Inc., 161 Ave of the Americas, New York, NY 10013; knitting@vogueknitting.com; http://www.vogueknitting.com. Illus., adv. *Aud.:* Ga.

This is a knitting magazine with more than just patterns. It also includes techniques, designer profiles, information about types of yarn, handling difficult stitches in garments, and events and conferences. The majority of the patterns are for clothes. The instructions are all clear and easy to understand, are rated for difficulty, and have pictures of the yarns used in the project. At the beginning of the pattern instruction section is a guide and information section about the yarns used in the issue, techniques, and abbreviations. As one would expect from a publication with the name *Vogue,* the magazine is also an excellent resource for what is fashionable, in this case, both for clothing and for the home. An excellent resource for fashionable knitting patterns that are both trendy and timeless.

Needlework

1978. *Just Cross Stitch.* [ISSN: 0883-0797] 1983. bi-m. USD 19.98 domestic; USD 31.98 foreign; USD 3.95 newsstand/cover per issue. Ed(s): Lorna Reeves. Hoffman Media, Inc, 405 Riverhills Business Park, Birmingham, AL 35242. Illus., adv. *Aud.:* Ga.

Just Cross Stitch is a project magazine, and a fine one. There are 10 or 11 articles per issue, one of which comes with a needle-artist profile. There is a good variety of difficulty and the designs are attractive. The instructions are clear and all materials are listed. The explanation of basic stitches is also clear and well written. While there are some ads, they are limited and do not interrupt the flow of the designs. An excellent choice for a library looking to add to this area of their collection.

1979. *Lace.* [ISSN: 0308-3039] 1976. q. GBP 21 domestic; GBP 25 in Europe; GBP 29 elsewhere. Ed(s): D Robinson. Lace Guild, The Hollies, 53 Audnam, Stourbridge, DY8 4AE, United Kingdom; http://www.laceguild.org. Illus., adv. Sample. Circ: 6000. *Bk. rev.:* 3, 120-140 words, critical. *Aud.:* Ga.

This magazine is principally devoted to bobbin lace. The content is varied; there are articles on lacemakers, design issues, collections, and patterns to do. In addition, there is plentiful guild news and information about guild courses and workshops. The magazine is mostly in black and white to show the detail of the laces. The advertising is confined to the back so that it does not distract from the content—a good layout decision. If there are lace makers in your community or you are looking for an interesting or unusual inclusion in your crafts collection, try reviewing this journal.

1980. *Needle Arts.* [ISSN: 0047-925X] 1970. q. Membership, USD 24. Ed(s): Jody Jeroy. Embroiderers Guild of America, 335 W Broadway, Ste 100, Louisville, KY 40202; egahq@aol.com. Illus., adv. Circ: 21000. Vol. ends: Dec (No. 4). *Indexed:* A&ATA, BHA. *Bk. rev.:* 3-4, 150-300 words, some descriptive, some critical. *Aud.:* Ga.

This is the official publication of the Embroiderers' Guild of America (EGA) for its members. As such there is quite a lot of guild news including classes, correspondence courses, gatherings, competitions, a newsletter and the like. What this is not is a project magazine, and thus it might appeal to a different audience than the project magazines do. There are about eight feature articles in each issue ranging from two to four pages long and covering a variety of topics such as members' activities, projects, artist profiles, techniques, shows, a particular work, historical techniques, conservation of works, and the history of needlework. Columns that appear in every issue include "Letters," the "EGA Marketplace," "Chapter News," and the "EGA Master Calendar."

1981. *Piecework: all this by hand.* [ISSN: 1067-2249] 1993. bi-m. USD 24 domestic; USD 31 foreign. Ed(s): Jeane Hutchins. Interweave Press, Inc., 201 E Fourth St, Loveland, CO 80537; http://www.interweave.com. Illus., adv. Circ: 47000 Paid and controlled. *Indexed:* AICP, ArtInd. *Bk. rev.:* 6-9, critical. *Aud.:* Ga, Sa.

The purpose of this magazine seems to be to promote historical and ethnic handwork by offering articles on history, techniques, and individual items and people, and then offering projects based on the article using techniques such as needlework, knitting, quilting, crocheting, beading, drawn thread, and other crafts. Occasionally, issues are devoted to one theme. The projects all have clear instructions and are well designed. This is not a magazine that will teach a technique in simple terms; if the reader is at all shy about picking up new techniques, then some of the projects may be difficult. This is a beautiful magazine devoted to the history and the current state of common and ethnic handicraft arts. It is a wonderful addition to any craft collection.

1982. *Stitcher's World.* Formerly (until 1999): *Stitchery Magazine.* [ISSN: 1524-4466] 1995. bi-m. USD 22; USD 37 foreign; USD 4.95 newsstand/cover per issue. Ed(s): Michelle Howard. StitchWorld, Inc., 6350 Regency Pkwy, Ste 540, Norcross, GA 30071-2338. *Aud.:* Ga.

This is one of the best needlework project magazines available. The projects cover the spectrum of needlework, from cross stitch to needlepoint to beadwork to huck. The instructions are clear and the charts are in color. There are also designer profiles and some wonderful columns about technique. If there is room for only one needlework magazine in your collection, this could be it.

Quilting

1983. *For the Love of Quilting: as seen on PBS with Fons and Porter.* Formerly: *Sew Many Quilts.* [ISSN: 1525-1284] 1996. bi-m. USD 19.95; USD 4.95 newsstand/cover per issue. Ed(s): Nancy Fitzpatrick Wyatt, Rhonda Richards. Oxmoor House, 2100 Lakeshore Dr, Birmingham, AL 35209. Adv. Circ: 100000. *Aud.:* Ga.

This is a well-designed, high-quality publication focused on projects. There are eight to ten projects in each issue and about three feature articles. The articles are usually short, one to three pages, and are usually about designing or techniques. The project instructions are clear and easy to read, with good pictures and assembly instructions. There are several columns appearing in each issue that are about tips, techniques, and products. There are ads, but they are no more obtrusive or plentiful than in other craft project magazines. The quilting duo responsible for this magazine, Marianne Fons and Liz Porter, also record a show for public television. Well worth adding to your quilting collection, especially if the television show airs in your area.

1984. *Quilter's Newsletter Magazine: the magazine for quilt lovers.* [ISSN: 0274-712X] 1969. 10x/yr. USD 23.97; USD 33.97 foreign; GBP 2.50 newsstand/cover per issue. Ed(s): Mary Leman-Austin. PRIMEDIA Special Interest Publications, PO Box 4101, Golden, CO 80401-0101. Illus., adv. Vol. ends: Dec. *Indexed:* IHTDI. *Bk. rev.:* 4-5, descriptive. *Aud.:* Ga.

This magazine is for both the beginner and the experienced quilter. Regular features include a calendar of events that lists events by state, a section listing items for trade or sale, and "Quilting Bee," which displays reader-submitted works. The "Quilt Show" section is a spectacular inspiration. About half of the articles in each issue are projects that have easy-to-understand, clear instructions, and they are rated for difficulty. The remaining articles are on such topics as techniques, exemplary quilts on various themes, quilters, museums and other quilt collections, and technical aspects of quilting such as needles, thimbles, and sewing machines. The numerous ads seem to offer everything a quilter could need or want. Articles are accompanied by color photographs. The magazine belongs in every quilting collection and in more general collections as well, given the popularity of this craft.

1985. *Quiltmaker: tips, techniques & patterns for today's quilters.* [ISSN: 1047-1634] 1982. bi-m. USD 21.98 domestic; USD 29.95 foreign; USD 2.50 newsstand/cover foreign. Ed(s): Caroline Reordon. PRIMEDIA Special Interest Publications, PO Box 4101, Golden, CO 80401-0101; http://www.quiltmaker.com. Illus., index, adv. Sample. Circ: 150000. Vol. ends: Nov/Dec. *Indexed:* IHTDI. *Aud.:* Ga.

There are two general types of articles in this journal. First, there are patterns and projects, of which there are generally nine or ten. All are graded for difficulty and are of excellent quality and design. Interspersed with these, there are three or four articles, usually about technique, readers' completed projects, letters, product reviews, and basic lessons explaining how to read patterns and assemble quilts. An excellent addition to a quilting section, or a good place to begin one.

Wood

1986. *Chip Chats.* [ISSN: 0577-9294] 1953. bi-m. USD 14 domestic; USD 16 foreign. Edward F. Gallenstein, Ed. & Pub., 7424 Miami Ave, Cincinnati, OH 45243; http://www.terranet.ab.ca:80/~bjndt/ChipChats_Mag/ChipChats.html. Illus., adv. Circ: 40000 Paid. *Indexed:* IHTDI. *Aud.:* Ga, Sa.

Chip Chats, a publication of the National Woodcarvers Association, is "dedicated to the interests of amateur and professional carvers and whittlers." The main focus of the magazine is reporting on shows from all over the country and occasionally beyond the United States, including numerous black-and-white and color photos of prizewinners at the competitions. Other articles are about individual work, craftspeople, plans and projects, and tools, plus regular columns on techniques and opinion pieces. The ads in the "Sources of Supplies" section at the end are great for locating just about anything you might need. As with most guild publications, there is also a calendar of upcoming events.

1987. *Creative Woodworks and Crafts.* [ISSN: 1055-6729] 1988. 7x/yr. USD 41.65. Ed(s): Robert Becker. All American Crafts, Inc., 243 Newton Sparta Rd, Newton, NJ 07860-2748. Illus., adv. Circ: 95000. *Aud.:* Ga.

Creative Woodworks and Crafts is a project magazine intended for hobbyists. There are about ten projects in each issue, many of which focus on scroll saw work, with intarsia projects running a close second. There is a pullout pattern section (with patterns for all the projects in that issue that require them). There is also a separate "Carving Section" with about three projects of its own. Ads appear on every page, and while they do not cross the line into distracting, they come very close. If your readers are looking for woodworking projects that are primarily scroll saw or intarsia, then this magazine is worth reviewing.

1988. *Fine Woodworking.* Incorporates (in 1998): *Home Furniture;* Which superseded (in 1997): *Taunton's Home Furniture;* (1994-1996): *Fine Woodworking's Home Furniture.* [ISSN: 0361-3453] 1975. bi-m. USD 34.95 in US & Canada; USD 41.95 elsewhere. Ed(s): Timothy D Schreiner. Taunton Press, Inc., 63, South Main St, PO Box 5506, Newtown, CT 06470-5506; http://www.taunton.com. Illus., index, adv. Circ: 250000 Paid. Vol. ends: Nov/Dec. *Indexed:* ASIP, ArtInd, BHA, DAAI, IHTDI. *Bk. rev.:* 2-4, critical. *Aud.:* Ga, Sa.

Fine Woodworking is for the professional carpenter or cabinetmaker, those who would like to be, and those with an interest in these crafts. This magazine uses projects as examples of techniques, or as the basis of articles, rather than as projects for the reader to do—materials lists and measured drawings are not provided, but there are plenty of diagrams and pictures. Other articles review tools and equipment, discuss health and safety issues, look at designs of current or historic importance, and occasionally profile people or groups—past or present—of woodworkers that are important to the craft. There is an extensive Q&A section, and the "Methods of Work" and "Notes and Comment" sections are also substantial. Of special interest to the practicing woodworker are the supplier advertisements. Taunton Press provides excellent production quality; thus this magazine is not only a joy to read for content, but also for presentation. This belongs in every crafts collection.

1989. *ShopNotes.* [ISSN: 1062-9696] 1992. bi-m. USD 19.95. Ed(s): Tim Robertson. August Home Publishing Co., 2200 Grand Ave, Des Moines, IA 50312-5306; shopnotes@shopnotes.com; http://www.augusthome.com. Illus. Circ: 165000. Vol. ends: Nov. *Indexed:* IHTDI. *Aud.:* Ga.

This is not just a project magazine; it is a magazine about all the other aspects of woodworking. There are tool tests, articles about wood, organizing a workshop, and anything else pertaining to the craft of woodworking. While most woodworking magazines have more of a project focus (except the guild magazines, which focus on the guild), this is one of the few, like *Fine Woodworking,* where the craft is the subject of the magazine. The difference is that this is geared more to the hobbyist, while *Fine Woodworking* is more for the professional woodworker and cabinetmaker. If there is a good woodworking section in your library, consider adding this title to round it out.

The Woodenboat. See Boats and Boating section.

1990. *Woodshop News.* [ISSN: 0894-5403] 1986. m. USD 21.95; USD 3.95 newsstand/cover per issue; USD 5.95 newsstand/cover per issue Canada. Ed(s): A J Hamler. Soundings Publications, L L C, 35 Pratt St, Essex, CT 06426-1122. Illus., adv. Circ: 206375. Vol. ends: Jan. *Aud.:* Ga, Sa.

Woodshop News is a newsmagazine for the professional woodworker and the serious hobbyist. This is not a project magazine; the information it contains is as much a tool for the practicing woodworker as a saw. It tracks wood markets, job markets, reviews new tools and other products, tracks legislation, and discusses all aspects of wood and the wood industry. Feature articles cover individual rare wood species suppliers and dealers and individual woodworkers or communities. There are regular columns that cover health and ergonomic issues, and design issues. If there are serious woodworkers in your community, this magazine is worth adding to your collection.

1991. *Woodsmith.* [ISSN: 0164-4114] 1979. bi-m. USD 24.95 domestic; USD 34.95 foreign; USD 4.95 newsstand/cover per issue. Ed(s): Terry Strohman. August Home Publishing Co., 2200 Grand Ave, Des Moines, IA 50312-5306; woodsmith@woodsmith.com; http://www.augusthome.com. Illus., adv. Circ: 325000. Vol. ends: Dec. *Indexed:* IHTDI. *Aud.:* Ga.

This is a project magazine, and an excellent one at that. There are four or so projects in each issue with detailed instructions, cutting lists, and diagrams. Of these projects, one or two are designed to teach a technique or process. Every issue contains a "Tips and Techniques" section that has short explanations on general topics. In addition to having good, useful, well-designed projects, there is no advertising—a welcome change. A solid choice.

1992. *Woodturning.* [ISSN: 0958-9457] 1990. m. USD 82.80 United States; GBP 41.40 elsewhere. Ed(s): Mark Baker. G M C Publications Ltd., 166 High St, Lewes, BN7 1XU, United Kingdom; mags@thegmcgroup.com. Illus., adv. Circ: 31311. *Indexed:* IHTDI. *Bk. rev.:* 2-3. *Aud.:* Ga, Sa.

Woodturning is for the amateur, professional, or student of this craft. This very polished British magazine is a publication of the Guild of Master Craftsman. Articles are divided into five categories: projects, techniques, features, tool tests, and regulars. There are three or four projects in each issue, ranging from the practical to the decorative. While this is a guild publication, there is not as much emphasis on this aspect of the magazine as there is in many American guild publications. In addition to guild news, there are exhibit reviews in the regular columns. It might seem expensive, but if there are woodworkers or woodturners in your community, this is worth the asking price.

1993. *Woodwork.* [ISSN: 1045-3040] 1989. bi-m. USD 17.95 domestic; USD 24 foreign. Ed(s): John Lavine. Ross Periodicals, 42 Digital Dr, Ste 5, Novato, CA 94949. Illus., adv. Circ: 50000. Vol. ends: Nov. *Indexed:* IHTDI. *Aud.:* Ga, Sa.

Woodwork is more for the serious hobbyist than the professional carpenter, but the latter might find it useful as well. All aspects of woodworking are covered, from furniture, toys, and turned pieces, to species of wood, joining techniques, and profiles of current craftspeople. In each issue there are about nine articles, and two or three of these are projects complete with measured drawings and materials lists. There is also a "Gallery" where readers can submit finished works for display. The "Events" section lists classes, apprenticeship opportunities, shows, and juried shows by state. *Woodwork* is an excellent choice for a general crafts or woodworking collection.

Electronic Journals

There is a plethora of craft resources available online. The majority of these, however, are not crafts journals. *American Craft* has an online counterpart (available through Dialog) as does the *Professional Crafter's Market Guide* (available on the web at http://www.auntie.com/craftzine/main.asp). What is available on the web is a range of people and stores selling items, information about crafts in locations around the globe, museums and exhibitions, and various suppliers' catalogs, as well as the various Usenet chat groups and listservs. All of these resources are valuable, and while they do some of the same things as a magazine, they fill quite a different niche from the traditional magazines listed in this resource. What is on the Internet tends to be more personal, more surface than substance. This should not be construed as disapproval; the Internet does allow individuals to show their own works and talk about why they do what they do; and it may even help them sell their works. It also allows groups and consortia of individuals to do the same—all without having to break through the old barriers of galleries. What you may not find—and what I did not find—are substantive articles. I found displays, projects, and personal opinions in great profusion, but rarely did I see detailed technical discussions, historical perspectives, or studies of styles and trends. Given these differences—and the fact that there are few traditional magazines on the Internet—I will not give a list of online magazines that I have reviewed and given some kind of seal of approval. What I will do is give you places to explore or bookmark in your library. Remember that these are just guides; there is so much out there and it is changing all the time.

If you want to bookmark places to start, try search engines such as Yahoo (http://www.yahoo.com) in either the recreation: hobbies and crafts section or the arts: design arts section. Both of these sections list individual crafts as well as magazines. Excite (http://www.excite.com) also indexes sites, but the sites listed here are given ratings, and there are far fewer of them. The sections of potential interest are hobbies (http://www.excite.com/Reviews/Hobbies) and arts (http://www.excite.com/Reviews/Arts). Excite also offers the option of just searching the Internet for whatever is out there, which can also be done from many search sites. My advice is to start from the indexed sites and then use the big search engines to find all kinds of other stuff. Remember to bookmark what you like or you may never see it again! Happy searching, and I hope you find both what you want and what you did not know you wanted.

■ CRIMINOLOGY AND LAW ENFORCEMENT

See also Law; and Sociology and Social Work sections.

Clark N. Hallman, Head of Public Services, Briggs Library, South Dakota State University, Brookings, SD 57007-1098; E-mail: clark_hallman@sdstate.edu; FAX: 605-688-4688

Introduction

"Criminology is the body of knowledge regarding crime and delinquency as a social phenomenon. It includes within its scope the processes of making laws, breaking laws, and reacting to the breaking of laws" (Edwin H. Sutherland, Donald R. Cressey, & David F. Luckenbill, *Principles of Criminology,* Eleventh Edition. [Dix Hills, NY: General Hall, Inc., 1992], p. 3). This section describes many fine criminology journals that present scholarly material from many perspectives, including those of sociology, psychology, social work, and others. It also includes titles that deal with the agencies of social control, for example, police and corrections, which Zalman would categorize as criminal justice (Marvin Zalman, *A Heuristic Model of Criminology and Criminal Justice* [Chicago: Joint Commission on Criminology Education and Standards, Univ. of Illinois at Chicago Circle, 1981], p. 9). These include many titles focusing on the needs of practitioners, for example, police officers, corrections officers, probation officers, and social workers, and on the needs of law enforcement administrators and/or public administrators involved with criminal justice institutions. Also, a few titles cover news, legal decisions, and other recent developments, which may be useful to practitioners as well as to students and interested laypersons. The periodicals described here are representative samples of useful publications from subgroups covering most aspects of criminology. They were chosen as the most important, most useful, and/or best-quality periodicals from each subgroup; and a few were chosen because they are unique in their representation of specific practice areas, theoretical perspectives, or type of content. These journals cover law enforcement and corrections administration and practice; criminal behavior; characteristics, etiology, and prevention of crime; ethics; and other components of criminology and the criminal justice arena. Although jurisprudence, which can be broadly defined as the science of law, is certainly relevant to criminology and criminal justice, its periodicals are more appropriately covered in the Law section. Likewise, sociology produces much material of interest to criminology, but it is also given its own section. Therefore titles like *Deviant Behavior, Law and Society Review,* and *Social Problems* are not included here. As stated above, the titles listed here are not limited to those for a scholarly audience. Many are oriented to practitioners in the field, and many general readers could find any of the titles to be of interest.

Basic Periodicals

Ga: *American Jails, Corrections Compendium, Corrections Today, FBI Law Enforcement Bulletin, Law and Order Magazine, Law Enforcement News, National Institute of Justice Journal, Police Chief, Police Times, Sheriff Magazine;* Ac: *The British Journal of Criminology, Crime & Delinquency, Criminal Justice & Behavior, Criminology, The Howard Journal of Criminal Justice, Journal of Offender Rehabilitation, Journal of Research in Crime and Delinquency, Justice Quarterly, Policing and Society, The Prison Journal.*

Basic Abstracts and Indexes

Criminal Justice Abstracts, Criminal Justice Periodical Index.

1994. ***American Jails: the magazine of the American Jail Association.*** [ISSN: 1056-0319] 1987. bi-m. USD 30 domestic; USD 36 Canada; USD 42 elsewhere. Ed(s): Ken Kerle. American Jail Association, 2053 Day Rd, Ste 100, Hagerstown, MD 21740-9795; jails@worldnet.att.net; http://www.corrections.com/aja. Illus., index, adv. Sample. Circ: 6000. Vol. ends: Nov/Dec. *Indexed:* CJA, CJPI. *Aud.:* Ga, Ac, Sa.

The American Jail Association (membership: 5,000) works to enhance the standards of local detention facilities and the professionalism of jail personnel. Its attractively packaged bimonthly magazine contains news and informative articles that are useful to practitioners, faculty and students in criminal justice, and the interested public. It specifically focuses on jail issues with articles covering both the American and foreign scenes. However, it also provides broader information useful to corrections professionals. About 20 to 25 percent of the articles are contributed by academics. Criminal justice professionals write the remaining 75 to 80 percent. Each issue features a specific theme such as the private sector and contractual services; assessing the treatment of women staff and inmates; jail industry programs; holding illegal aliens, alleged terrorists, and inmates from other jurisdictions; keeping the best employees; and jail security in the twenty-first century. Although many articles focus on the narrower issues of techniques and practical proposals for improvement of local detention activities and facilities, many others deal with broader issues such as the image of the corrections field, corrections in the twenty-first century, correctional officer stress and suicide, alternatives to incarceration, bail bonds, gangs in jails, inmate classification, inmate communications, jail standards and inspections, legal issues in jails, privatization, suicides in jail, women in jails, medical care for inmates, jail programming, the National Institute of Corrections, and the training of correctional personnel. Regular departments present much useful information. More information and article reprints are available at AJA's web site.

1995. ***Australian and New Zealand Journal of Criminology.*** [ISSN: 0004-8658] 1968. triennial. AUD 203.25 domestic; AUD 184 New Zealand; AUD 205 elsewhere. Ed(s): Dr. John Pratt. Australian Academic Press Pty. Ltd., 32 Jeays St, Bowen Hills, QLD 4006, Australia; http://www.australianacademicpress.com.au. Illus., adv. Sample. Refereed. Vol. ends: No. 3. Reprint: WSH. *Indexed:* CBRI, CJA, CJPI, CLI, ILP, LRI, SSCI. *Bk. rev.:* 2-3, 1,000 words, signed. *Aud.:* Ac, Sa.

Australian Academic Press, an independent publisher for the behavioral sciences, now publishes the official journal of the Australian and New Zealand Society of Criminology. For over 30 years, this peer-reviewed journal has been promoting quality research and debate on crime and criminal justice by publishing theoretical and methodological articles, reviews of contemporary issues, special features that cover topics such as indigenous crime and justice, and shorter research notes. It focuses on crime, law enforcement, corrections, and courtroom practices in both countries. Most authors are Australian or New Zealand academics from disciplines including psychology, law, politics, history, sociology, and the forensic sciences. Many of the topics covered are area-specific—such as policing Aboriginal towns or punishment and welfare in Queensland—but the concepts and theories have wider appeal. The journal is aimed at university-affiliated readers and criminal justice professionals and policymakers. It would be useful in any international or comparative criminology collection and, of course, anywhere there is interest in Australia or New Zealand. More information about the journal is available on the publisher's web site. Online access to the journal is provided by Ingenta.

1996. ***The British Journal of Criminology: delinquency and deviant social behaviour.*** Supersedes (in 1960): *British Journal of Delinquency.* [ISSN: 0007-0955] 1950. q. GBP 225. Ed(s): Richard Sparks, G Pearson. Oxford University Press, Great Clarendon St, Oxford, OX2 6DP, United Kingdom; jnl.orders@oup.co.uk; http://www3.oup.co.uk/jnls. Illus., adv. Refereed. Circ: 1700. Vol. ends: Oct. Online: EBSCO Publishing; Florida Center for Library Automation; Gale Group; HighWire Press; ingenta.com; Northern Light Technology, Inc.; OCLC Online Computer Library Center, Inc.; ProQuest Information & Learning; RMIT Publishing; RoweCom Information Quest; Swets Blackwell. Reprint: PSC; SWZ; WSH. *Indexed:* ASSIA, AgeL, BrEdI, CJA, CJPI, CLI, IBSS, ILP, IMFL, LRI, PAIS, PSA, PsycholAb, RiskAb, SSCI, SSI, SWA, SociolAb. *Bk. rev.:* 8-10, signed. *Aud.:* Ac, Sa.

This is a quality journal published by Oxford University Press for the Centre for Crime and Justice Studies (formerly the Institute for the Study and Treatment of Delinquency). It aims to advance the education of the public, particularly criminal justice practitioners, in the causes and prevention of delinquency and crime, the treatment of offenders, and the principles of the criminal justice process both in the United Kingdom and abroad. Each issue of the journal presents 8 to 12 erudite, well-documented articles examining delinquency, deviant behavior, and social problems, usually from a theoretical or research perspective. A psychological or sociological approach is often used. Authors include both academics and practitioners from many fields. In addition, each issue contains a lengthy book review section (eight to ten reviews) that is very useful, especially for British publications. Often several articles present various viewpoints on a common theme such as "Crime and Criminology in China" or "Practice, Performance and Prospects for Restorative Justice"; and an occasional "Notes" section presents short, informative reports on research projects. Recent topics have included minority perspectives on racism, ethnicity, and criminology; the decline in non-lethal violence in England, Australia, and New Zealand, 1880–1920; co-offending as social exchange; elderly fear of crime; and the decline in support for penal welfarism. This journal's multidisciplinary approach makes it important for academic social science collections as well as crime and delinquency collections. It is very useful to academics and researchers in criminology, probation, and social work, and professionals concerned with law, criminal justice, and penology. Tables of contents and electronic full text, subscription information, indexing and abstracting information, and instructions to authors are available on the publisher's web site. An e-mail contents alerting service is also available.

1997. ***Campus Law Enforcement Journal: professional publication for campus law enforcement administrators, campus safety, security adm.*** [ISSN: 0739-0394] 1970. bi-m. USD 30; USD 35 foreign. Ed(s): Karen E Breseman, Peter J Berry. International Association of Campus Law Enforcement Administrators, 342 N Main St, West Hartford, CT 06117-2500; ljohnson@iaclea.org; http://www.iaclea.org. Illus., adv. Sample. Circ: 1700. Vol. ends: Nov/Dec. Microform: PQC. Reprint: PQC. *Indexed:* CJPI. *Aud.:* Ac, Sa.

It is increasingly important that college and university officials take a proactive and professional approach to crime prevention and public safety on campus. *CLEJ* is a publication of the International Association of Campus Law Enforcement Administrators (IACLEA). IACLEA works to advance public safety for educational institutions by providing educational resources, advocacy, and professional development opportunities. This organization's 1,600 members represent over 1,000 colleges and universities located in the United States, Canada, Australia, Europe, and elsewhere. The members include campus law enforcement staff members, criminal justice faculty members, municipal chiefs of police, and individuals from private companies or organizations offering campus law enforcement–related products and services. The journal acts as the voice of the campus law enforcement and security community and as a forum for the study of new ideas, trends in law enforcement, and relevant legislation. It attempts to promote professional ideals and standards of practice among law-enforcement personnel at institutions of higher education. The target audience consists of campus public safety administrators and personnel as well as those responsible for student affairs and residential life and housing. Practitioners write most articles with an emphasis on practical information and program reviews. It is an attractively packaged professional magazine with many photographs, much relevant advertising, and some organizational news. The IACLEA web site provides additional information about *CLEJ,* including article submission guidelines, subscription information, and advertising rates.

1998. ***Canadian Journal of Criminology and Criminal Justice.*** Former titles (until 2003, vol.45): *Canadian Journal of Criminology;* (until vol.19): *Canadian Journal of Criminology and Corrections;* (until vol.13): *Canadian Journal of Corrections.* 1958. q. CND 107 (Individuals, CND 53.50). Ed(s): Julian V Roberts. Canadian Criminal Justice Association, 383 Parkdale Ave, Ste 304, Ottawa, ON K1Y 4R4, Canada; http://home.istar.ca/~ccja/angl/. Illus., index, adv. Sample. Refereed. Circ: 1300. Vol. ends: Oct. Microform: PQC. Online: bigchalk; EBSCO Publishing; Florida Center for Library Automation; Gale Group; Micromedia ProQuest; Northern Light Technology, Inc.; OCLC Online Computer Library Center, Inc.; ProQuest Information & Learning. Reprint: PQC; PSC. *Indexed:* ASSIA, CBCARef, CJA, CJPI, CLI, CPerI, HRA, LRI, PRA, PsycholAb, RiskAb, SFSA, SSCI, SSI, SUSA, SWR&A. *Bk. rev.:* 5-8, 500-1,000 words, signed. *Aud.:* Ac, Sa.

The Canadian Criminal Justice Association is a voluntary national organization that represents all elements of the criminal justice system, as well as the public. It exists to promote informed debate in an effort to develop a more humane, equitable, and effective justice system. Until 1970 *The Canadian Journal of Criminology*'s focus was on corrections, but then it began to broaden its focus. Now it is an interdisciplinary journal that publishes articles on all aspects of criminology and criminal justice. It presents both theoretical treatments on the study of crime and methodological or program studies in law enforcement, administration of justice, and offender rehabilitation. Although most information is relevant to any geographical area, preference is given to articles with Canadian content or to those related in some way to a Canadian project, institution, or practice. Most articles are in English (with French abstracts), some are in French (with English abstracts); both types are well documented. In addition to featured articles, book reviews, research notes, commentaries, and lists of coming events frequently appear in *CJC.* The journal would be appealing to justice administrators, researchers and practitioners, academics, and anyone else wishing to stay informed on recent criminological findings and opinions. The Canadian Criminal Justice Association's web site contains tables of contents and article abstracts for *CJC* from 1997 to the present. Full-text articles form this journal are available via EBSCO Online and ProQuest.

1999. ***Corrections Compendium: the national journal for corrections.*** [ISSN: 0738-8144] 1976. m. USD 75. Ed(s): Susan Clayton. American Correctional Association, 4380 Forbes Blvd, Lanham, MD 20706-4322; gdaley@aca.org; http://www.corrections.com/aca/. Illus., adv. Sample. Circ: 1000 Paid and controlled. Vol. ends: Dec. *Indexed:* CJA, CJPI. *Aud.:* Ga, Ac, Sa.

This peer-reviewed monthly journal is published by the American Correctional Association, a multidisciplinary organization of more than 20,000 members from all facets of corrections and criminal justice, including federal, state, and military correctional facilities and prisons, county jails and detention centers, probation/parole agencies, and community corrections/halfway houses. Each monthly issue is packed with fascinating and useful information on all aspects of corrections. Feature articles and brief articles present research findings and trends and examine events in corrections and criminal justice. Often information derived from statistical data is presented. State and national corrections news, including legal case reports and commentary, is also included. A unique aspect of this publication is a monthly national survey of correctional systems that presents statistical data or other information related to specific corrections concerns. These surveys are especially useful to policymakers and analysts, corrections administrators, legislators at all levels, faculty and students of criminal justice, and business professionals involved with corrections. The surveys cover state, federal, and Canadian correctional systems (52 U.S. and 13 Canadian correctional systems). The 2003 surveys address staff wages and compensation, staff education and training, inmate transportation, drug testing and screening, juvenile offenders, inmate grievance procedures and lawsuits, DNA testing, religion, high-level security inmates, correctional health care—part 1 and part 2, and budgets. Other topics such as prison and jail construction, inmate populations and projections, probation and parole activities, community-based corrections, private corrections, and many others have been reported in the surveys during previous years. The data presented in these surveys make this publication desirable in almost any library where social problems are of interest. More information about *Corrections Compendium* is available on the American Correctional Association web site. Electronic versions of articles from this journal are available via InfoTrac.

2000. ***Corrections Today.*** Former titles (until 1979): *American Journal of Correction;* (until 1954): *Prison World;* (until 1941): *Jail Association Journal.* [ISSN: 0190-2563] 1939. 7x/yr. USD 25. Ed(s): Susan Clayton, Gabrielle Degoot. American Correctional Association, 4380 Forbes Blvd, Lanham, MD 20706-4322; http://www.corrections.com/aca/pubs.html. Illus., adv. Sample. Circ: 20000 Controlled. Vol. ends: Dec. Reprint: PSC. *Indexed:* ABS&EES, CJA, CJPI, PAIS, SSI. *Bk. rev.:* 1, 300-500 words, signed. *Aud.:* Ga, Ac, Sa.

This is the official publication of the American Correctional Association (ACA), which currently has over 20,000 members. It provides a forum for the presentation and discussion of issues related to the advancement of corrections. Its scope is extremely broad and includes topics from administration and management to community programs, minorities, history and philosophy, probation and parole, correctional industries, volunteer and service organizations, high-profile inmates, and others. Each issue contains several feature articles on a central theme (e.g., female offenders, correctional architecture and design, special-needs offenders, juvenile corrections, standards, etc.) and two to three articles related to a "Subtheme." In addition, other news, program descriptions, and columns are included. Most articles are short and not heavily documented; they focus on practical applications and programs; and they are written by corrections professionals or practitioners. An annual buyers' guide of correctional products and services is published in the July issue. *Corrections Today* is not for in-depth research, but the clearly written articles and the broad spectrum of its contents—along with its popular magazine format with glossy cover, numerous photographs, and much advertising—make it appealing to a large audience. A subscription also includes *On the Line,* a bimonthly newsletter from ACA. The ACA web site provides full-text access to five or so articles from the most recent issue issue of *Corrections Today.*

2001. ***Crime & Delinquency.*** Formerly (until 1960): *National Probation and Parole Association Journal.* [ISSN: 0011-1287] 1955. q. GBP 413 in Europe, Middle East, Africa & Australasia. Ed(s): Ron Vogel. Sage Publications, Inc., 2455 Teller Rd, Thousand Oaks, CA 91320; info@sagepub.com; http://www.sagepub.com. Illus., index, adv. Sample. Refereed. Circ: 2900. Vol. ends: Oct. Microform: WSH; PMC. Online: Pub.; EBSCO Publishing; Florida Center for Library Automation; Gale Group; ingenta.com; OCLC Online Computer Library Center, Inc.; ProQuest Information & Learning; RoweCom Information Quest; Swets Blackwell. Reprint: WSH. *Indexed:* ABS&EES, ASSIA, AgeL, CIJE, CJA, CJPI, CLI, ExcerpMed, IBSS, ILP, IMFL, LRI, PAIS, PRA, PsycholAb, RI-1, RiskAb, SFSA, SSCI, SSI, SUSA, SociolAb. *Aud.:* Ac, Sa.

Crime & Delinquency is published in cooperation with the National Council on Crime and Delinquency. The journal is policy-oriented and presents literate, well-documented articles on all aspects of crime and the administration of justice, including etiology, prevention, corrections, and rehabilitation. It is intended for the professional with direct involvement in the criminal justice field, and articles address policy or program implications; social, political, or economic implications; the victim and the offender; and the criminal justice response. Both quantitative and qualitative articles are published. However, statistical or quantitative articles must be presented in a manner that is understandable to practitioners. Both adult and juvenile offenses are discussed. A multidisciplinary view of crime is presented, with an emphasis on society's interrelationships with and responses to its crime problems. Most authors are academics, usually from the fields of criminal justice, sociology, public and policy studies, and social services. This scholarly publication should not be limited to criminal justice collections. It would be valuable to policymakers, administrators, and scholars in most social science disciplines. More information about this journal is available at the Sage web site, and the electronic version of the journal is available from Sage via OCLC FirstSearch Electronic Collections Online, EBSCO Online, Ingenta, and SwetsNet.

2002. ***Crime, Law and Social Change: an interdisciplinary journal.*** Formerly: *Contemporary Crises;* Incorporates (1986-1992): *Corruption and Reform.* [ISSN: 0925-4994] 1977. 8x/yr. EUR 899 print or online ed. Ed(s): Alan Block. Kluwer Academic Publishers, van Godewijckstraat 30, PO Box 17, Dordrecht, 3300 AA, Netherlands. Illus. Sample. Refereed. Microform: PQC. Online: EBSCO Publishing; Gale Group; ingenta.com; Kluwer Online; OCLC Online Computer Library Center, Inc.; RoweCom Information Quest; Swets Blackwell. Reprint: SWZ. *Indexed:* ABCPolSci, ArtHuCI, BAS, CJA, IBSS, IPSA, PAIS, PSA, SSCI, SSI, SociolAb. *Aud.:* Ac, Sa.

Crime, Law, and Social Change remains an international and interdisciplinary journal that publishes articles in the critical, leftist tradition. The journal addresses the "interplay between crime, development and legal change; between class structures and crime, policing and punishment" and comparative crime control. It places special emphasis on the relationships among social structure, criminal behavior, and the creation and enforcement of law. The journal's scope encompasses the traditional subject matter of crime, deviance, law, social problems, and social control. It publishes work on the smuggling of weapons, narcotics, people, and natural resources; money laundering; fraud; tax evasion; and economic crime. It also covers the issues of health, welfare, social policy, and other areas such as imperialism, gender, race and ethnic equality, rebellion, revolution, political corruption, environmental crime, and corporate crime, and human rights. Of particular interest is the political economy of organized crime, including international, national, regional, or local levels. The journal is a forum for scholars in such fields as criminology, sociology, anthropology, history, law, and political science. This scholarly journal's broad, and international, coverage of social problems makes it useful to a large social science audience. Unfortunately, its price is relatively high. More information about *Crime, Law, and Social Change,* including tables of contents from 1994 to the present, is available at the Kluwer web site. The online version of the journal is available from Kluwer Online.

Criminal Justice Abstracts. See Abstracts and Indexes section.

2003. ***Criminal Justice & Behavior.*** Supersedes: *Correctional Psychologist.* [ISSN: 0093-8548] 1973. bi-m. USD 551. Ed(s): Dr. Curt R Bartol. Sage Publications, Inc., 2455 Teller Rd, Thousand Oaks, CA 91320; info@sagepub.com; http://www.sagepub.com. Illus., index, adv. Refereed. Circ: 1950 Paid. Vol. ends: Dec. Microform: WSH; PMC; PQC. Online: Pub.; EBSCO Publishing; Florida Center for Library Automation; Gale Group; ingenta.com; OCLC Online Computer Library Center, Inc.; ProQuest Information & Learning; RoweCom Information Quest; Swets Blackwell. Reprint: PQC; WSH. *Indexed:* ASSIA, AgeL, BRI, CBRI, CIJE, CJA, CJPI, CLI, ExcerpMed, HRA, LRI, PAIS, PRA, PsycholAb, RiskAb, SFSA, SSCI, SSI, SUSA, SociolAb. *Aud.:* Ac, Sa.

Published in association with the American Association of Correctional Psychology, this publication is an excellent scholarly journal that examines the behavioral, psychological, and interactional factors of clientele and employees in the criminal justice system. Although the journal emphasizes correctional psychology, topics may include etiology of crime, the processes of law violation, victimology, offender classification and treatment, deterrence, and incapacitation. Indeed, any behavioral aspect of criminal justice could be included. Although original empirical research is emphasized, theoretical treatments, analyses of innovative programs and practices, and critical reviews of literature and theory on important topics of criminal justice are also included.

Occasional special issues focus on specific criminal justice concerns such as victimology and domestic violence, risk assessment, and coerced psychological treatment. Each issue contains five to seven well-documented articles written mostly by academicians. Recent article topics have included reporting of sexual victimization, neighborhood ecology and burglary victimization, the decision to end abusive relationships, stalking, psychopathy in female offenders, deception in eyewitness identification, and sex offender recidivism. More information about this journal is available at the Sage web site, and electronic versions of articles from this journal are available from several sources including OCLC FirstSearch Electronic Collections Online, EBSCO Online, Infotrac, and ProQuest. This is a fine addition to any criminal justice collection and is potentially useful for any behavioral scientist or criminal justice practitioner.

2004. ***Criminal Justice Ethics.*** [ISSN: 0731-129X] 1982. s-a. USD 12.50 student & senior citizen members (Institutional members, USD 40; Individual members, USD 15). Ed(s): John Kleinig, William Hefferman. Institute for Criminal Justice Ethics, John Jay College of Criminal Justice, City University of New York, New York, NY 10019-1029; cjejj@cunyvm.cuny.edu; http://www.lib.jjay.ainy.edu/cje. Illus. Sample. Refereed. Circ: 1200 Paid. Vol. ends: Summer/Fall. Microform: PQC. Online: bigchalk; Chadwyck-Healey Incorporated; EBSCO Publishing; Factiva; Florida Center for Library Automation; Gale Group; Northern Light Technology, Inc.; OCLC Online Computer Library Center, Inc.; ProQuest Information & Learning; H.W. Wilson. *Indexed:* CJA, CJPI, CLI, IBZ, LRI, Philnd, RI-1, SSI. *Bk. rev.:* 1-2, review essays. *Aud.:* Ac, Sa.

The Institute for Criminal Justice Ethics at John Jay College of Criminal Justice was established to foster greater concern for ethical issues among practitioners and scholars in the criminal justice field. It serves as a national clearinghouse for information and as a stimulus to research and publication. *Criminal Justice Ethics* is a scholarly publication addressing the ethical and moral issues concomitant with law enforcement, correctional, and court activities. Such issues as the use of deadly force, the decision to prosecute, plea bargaining, representation of the guilty, capital punishment, the right to privacy, and the influence of prior convictions are discussed in well-documented articles. The journal's audience includes lawyers, philosophers, judges, police officers and other practitioners, theoreticians, and students of criminal justice, law, philosophy, and sociology. The journal attempts to focus greater attention on ethical issues by members of these groups and by the general public. Each issue contains thought-provoking feature articles along with regular features such as "Commentary," "Exchange," and "Symposium," each presenting a few articles focusing on the same general topic such as gun control or the death penalty. It also contains review articles that cover recent literature of importance. This journal belongs in all academic collections and anywhere else that there is a serious interest in criminal justice. The journal's web site provides an article-title index, a subject index, an author index, and tables of contents. Electronic articles from the journal can be accessed via EBSCO Online and ProQuest.

Criminal Justice Periodical Index. See Abstracts and Indexes section.

2005. ***Criminal Justice Review.*** [ISSN: 0734-0168] 1976. s-a. USD 40 (Individuals, USD 25). Ed(s): Michael S. Vaughn. Georgia State University, PO Box 4018, Atlanta, GA 30302-4018. Adv. Refereed. Circ: 1200. Microform: PQC. Online: Gale Group. Reprint: PQC; WSH. *Indexed:* CJA, CJPI, CLI, ILP, PAIS, PSA, PsycholAb, RiskAb, SFSA, SSCI, SSI, SUSA, SociolAb. *Bk. rev.:* 2-3 essays. *Aud.:* Ac, Sa.

Criminal Justice Review is a peer-reviewed journal that addresses a broad spectrum of criminal justice topics. Potentially any aspect of crime or the justice system may be covered in three to six articles in each issue. Local, state, and national concerns may be addressed, using either quantitative or qualitative methods. Recent topics have included race and presentencing decisions in the United States, racial desegregation and violence in the Texas prison system, female sex offenders, conjugal visitations and prison violence in Mississippi, police drug testing and race bias, and sexual assault of college women. Occasional research notes and commentaries are also included. Most issues also contain two to three book review essays covering published material on issues such as critical criminology—then and now; coping with trauma; perspectives on domestic violence; and issues of substance abuse. In addition, each issue contains a lengthy book review section, which provides 20 to 25 signed reviews of recent books and a "Recent Legal Developments" section covering relevant case law. *Criminal Justice Review* is an inexpensive scholarly journal from the Department of Criminal Justice, College of Health and Human Sciences at Georgia State University, where the editor is an Associate Professor. The department also publishes the annual *International Criminal Justice Review,* which addresses worldwide criminal justice concerns.

2006. ***Criminal Justice Studies.*** Formerly: *The Justice Professional.* [ISSN: 1478-601X] 1986. q. GBP 144 (Individuals, USD 65; Corporations, GBP 233). Routledge, 29 W 35th St, New York, NY 10001; info@routledge-ny.com; http://www.routledge-ny.com. *Indexed:* CJA. *Aud.:* Ac, Sa.

After publishing 15 volumes under the title *The Justice Professional,* this journal changed its title to *Criminal Justice Studies* beginning with volume 16, number 1, 2003. It is still a quarterly peer-reviewed journal, and the editor remains Roslyn Muraskin at Long Island University. The journal focuses on all substantive criminal justice and criminological concerns. It provides interdisciplinary examinations of relevant issues, mostly written by academics and researchers in criminal justice and related fields such as sociology, political science, public administration, public affairs, and others. Occasional articles by criminal justice professionals are also published. Both quantitative and qualitative methodologies are presented, along with sporadic literature reviews and research notes that describe innovative research projects. In addition, approximately one issue per year has been devoted to a special topic such as capital punishment or minorities. The Taylor and Francis web site provides additional information about *Criminal Justice Studies,* including tables of contents and article abstracts from 2002 to the present, a free contents e-mail alert service, and electronic access to the journal.

2007. ***Criminology: an interdisciplinary journal.*** Formerly: *Criminologica.* [ISSN: 0011-1384] 1963. q. USD 140 (Individuals, USD 120). Ed(s): Robert J Bursik, Jr. American Society of Criminology, 1314 Kinnear Rd, Columbus, OH 43212. Illus., index. Sample. Refereed. Circ: 4000. Vol. ends: Nov. Microform: PQC. Online: bigchalk; EBSCO Publishing; Gale Group; Northern Light Technology, Inc.; OCLC Online Computer Library Center, Inc.; ProQuest Information & Learning. Reprint: PQC; WSH. *Indexed:* AgeL, CJA, CJPI, CLI, ExcerpMed, H&SSA, IBSS, ILP, LRI, PAIS, PsycholAb, RiskAb, SSCI, SSI, SWR&A, SociolAb. *Aud.:* Ac, Sa.

As "The Official Publication of the American Society of Criminology," this scholarly, multidisciplinary journal provides excellent, thoroughly documented articles that examine crime and deviant behavior as described in the disciplines of law, criminal justice, history, and the social and behavioral sciences. Each issue contains five to seven articles, which usually emphasize theoretical and empirical research. However, historical and current issues related to crime and justice may also be covered. In addition, one or two "Research Notes" present new viewpoints and new methods and/or findings in criminological research. Miscellaneous other inclusions may include commentary about previously published research along with responses from the authors of the examined studies or published addresses such as the ASC presidential address. Most authors are from criminal justice/criminology or sociology departments at academic institutions, but occasional contributions from professionals/practitioners in the criminal justice field are also included. Recent topics have included Chinese human smuggling organizations, the social ecology of police misconduct, unemployment and property crime, the reporting and nonreporting of domestic violence, and juvenile transfers to adult court. The ASC web site provides subject and author indexes and abstracts for all the articles published in this journal since 1980. Electronic versions of articles from the journal are available from several sources including EBSCO Online, InfoTrac, and ProQuest. This journal is highly recommended for any higher-education environment where there is an interest in criminology or criminal justice.

2008. ***Criminology and Public Policy.*** [ISSN: 1538-6473] 2001. 3x/yr. USD 120 domestic; USD 140 foreign. American Society of Criminology, 1314 Kinnear Rd, Columbus, OH 43212; http://www.bsos.umd.edu/asc/. *Aud.:* Ac, Sa.

As "An Official Publication of the American Society of Criminology," this new journal claims that it will match the outstanding scholarship of the ASC's longstanding research journal, *Criminology.* This interdisciplinary journal is devoted to policy discussions of criminology research findings, and the editorial policy states that the journal attempts to strengthen the role of research findings in the formulation of crime and justice policy through its empirically based articles. The journal seeks to foster and enhance public discussion of policy questions regarding criminology and criminal justice. Its unique format presents an editorial introduction preceding each article, which outlines the article's significant policy implications. In addition, some articles are followed by brief "Reaction Essays" by invited specialists, which comment on the policy issues of the articles. Recent topics have include federal legislation of the firearms licensing system, drug testing, stalking, federal prosecution of international terrorists, the consequences of "Three Strikes" sentencing policies, and private prisons. The ASC web site provides subject and author indexes and abstracts for all the articles published in this journal. A very interesting addition to the literature of criminology and criminal justice from ASC.

2009. ***F B I Law Enforcement Bulletin.*** [ISSN: 0014-5688] 1932. m. USD 36 domestic; USD 45 foreign. Ed(s): John E Ott. U.S. Federal Bureau of Investigation, F B I Academy, Madison Bldg, Rm 209, Quantico, VA 22135; leb@fbiacademy.edu; http://www.fbi.gov/leb/leb.htm. Illus., index. Sample. Circ: 43000. Vol. ends: Dec. Microform: MIM; PQC. Online: bigchalk; EBSCO Publishing; Florida Center for Library Automation; Gale Group; OCLC Online Computer Library Center, Inc.; ProQuest Information & Learning; H.W. Wilson. Reprint: PQC. *Indexed:* AgeL, CJA, CJPI, ExcerpMed, IUSGP, PAIS, SSI. *Bk. rev.:* Occasional, 400-500 words. *Aud.:* Ga, Ac, Sa.

This bulletin from the FBI is a real bargain. Each 34-page issue presents three or four feature articles on either operations or management issues, such as current police techniques, crime problems, personnel and management techniques and problems, equipment, and training. Law enforcement professionals write most of the articles, and criminal justice professionals are the primary audience for the bulletin. The articles are clearly written, and many are footnoted. The attractive format, use of photographs, and choice of topics make it similar to *Law and Order* (below in this section), but the *Bulletin*'s absence of advertising and its use of footnoting make it a slightly more scholarly publication. The *Bulletin* is very suitable for an academic environment, although most articles can be understood by laypersons. Recent articles have covered such topics as drug paraphernalia and drug gangs, Hmong gangs and rape, warrantless entry based on previous consent to undercover agents, stalkers, law enforcement ethics, and use of force. There are numerous recurring departments including "VICAP Alert," which allows the FBI's Violent Criminal Apprehension Program to ask other law enforcement agencies to review their case files for information that may be helpful on specific cases; "Bulletin Reports," which lists criminal justice studies, reports, and project findings; "Case Study," which reports on specific cases; "Police Practice," which presents noteworthy methods/techniques; "Perspective," which allows law enforcement professionals to address ethical, legal, or management issues or suggest improvement methods; "Crime Data," which presents statistical data; and "Focus on Communications/Management/Technology," which presents tips on better communication or better management techniques or descriptions of new technology. This title should be in any criminal justice or law enforcement collection. The price can't be beat. The full text of this journal from November 1989 to the present is also available free of charge from the FBI web site.

2010. ***Federal Probation: a journal of correctional philosophy and practice.*** Formerly: *U.S. Probation System. News Letter.* [ISSN: 0014-9128] 1937. 3x/yr. USD 16 domestic; USD 22.40 foreign. Ed(s): Ellen Wilson Fielding. Administrative Office of the United States Courts, Federal Corrections and Supervision Division, 1 Columbus Circle, NE, Washington, DC 20544. Illus., index. Sample. Refereed. Circ: 6500. Vol. ends: Dec. Microform: MIM; PQC. Online: bigchalk; EBSCO Publishing; Gale Group; Northern Light Technology, Inc.; OCLC Online Computer Library Center, Inc.; H.W. Wilson. Reprint: PQC; WSH. *Indexed:* AgeL, BRI, CBRI, CJA, CJPI, CLI, ExcerpMed, ILP, IUSGP, LRI, PAIS, PsycholAb, SSCI, SSI. *Bk. rev.:* 2-3, 900-1,500 words, signed. *Aud.:* Ga, Ac, Sa.

This scholarly publication from the U.S. government publishes articles on all aspects of preventive and correctional activities for both adults and juveniles. Now published three times per year, each issue contains eight to ten well-documented short articles written by either practitioners or academics. Many contributions are of a theoretical, philosophical, or research nature, although practical applications are emphasized. The publication's main audience consists of criminal justice and corrections professionals, students and academicians, and social service professionals. Occasional special issues may be edited by guest editors and may focus on specific aspects of corrections or criminal justice, such as one that focuses on "What Works In Corrections." Recent articles address the response of the federal courts to September 11th, sex offender supervision in Texas, a comparison of oral fluid and urinalysis drug testing, day reporting centers for adult offenders, gender-responsive programming for girls in Oregon, school-based substance abuse prevention, and treatment of antisocial and conduct-disordered offenders. Regular departments include the "Reviews of Professional Periodicals" section, which presents signed reviews of selected articles from various professional journals; an excellent "Your Bookshelf on Review" section; "Looking at the Law," which provides advice or practice guidelines to help probation-related practitioners adhere to legal requirements; and "The Cutting Edge," which alerts practitioners to technological innovations. The column "It Has Come to Our Attention" presents brief entries covering news of interest to practitioners. Although not refereed, this is a quality journal that takes a scholarly approach. It is useful to anyone with a serious interest in probation and corrections and, as with other U.S. government publications, the price is a real bargain.

2011. ***Homicide Studies: an interdisciplinary & international journal.*** [ISSN: 1088-7679] 1997. q. GBP 323 in Europe, Middle East, Africa & Australasia. Ed(s): Jay Corzine, Thomas Petee. Sage Publications, Inc., 2455 Teller Rd, Thousand Oaks, CA 91320; info@sagepub.com; http://www.sagepub.com. Illus. Refereed. *Indexed:* ASG, CJA, H&SSA, IBZ, PRA, PSA, RiskAb, SFSA, SUSA, SociolAb. *Aud.:* Ac, Sa.

Homicide Studies remains a scholarly, multidisciplinary journal that focuses on research, public policy, and applied knowledge related to homicide. The journal is published in association with the Homicide Research Working Group, which was formed at the 1991 American Society of Criminology (ASC) meeting by homicide experts from public health, criminology, geography, medicine, political science, sociology, criminal justice, and a variety of other disciplines. This international group now includes over 350 scholars and practitioners devoted to the study of homicide. *Homicide Studies* presents both qualitative and quantitative empirical studies, along with occasional theoretical papers, research summaries, and public policy reviews. All articles must focus on homicide, but other violent behaviors may be covered if the relationship between those behaviors and homicide is shown. Topics addressed include the effects of capital punishment in deterring homicides, feminist theories of homicide, trends in homicide offending and victimization, support groups for family members of homicide victims, and homicide investigative techniques, the effects of television on homicide, the effects of economic distress on homicide rates, and stress among homicide investigators. More information about this fine specialized journal is available at the Sage web site and the Homicide Research Working Group web site. The Working Group's web site provides complete tables of contents for all issues of the journal. The electronic version of the journal is available from Sage via OCLC FirstSearch Electronic Collections Online, EBSCO Online, Ingenta, and SwetsNet.

2012. ***The Howard Journal of Criminal Justice.*** Formerly (until Feb. 1984): *Howard Journal of Penology and Crime Prevention.* [ISSN: 0265-5527] 1941. q. GBP 285 print & online eds. Ed(s): Tony Fowles, David Wilson. Blackwell Publishing Ltd., 9600 Garsington Rd, PO Box 805, Oxford, OX4 2DQ, United Kingdom; customerservices@oxon.blackwellpublishing.com; http://www.blackwellpublishing.com/. Illus. Sample. Refereed. Circ: 1700. Vol. ends: Nov. Microform: PQC. Online: EBSCO Publishing; Gale Group; ingenta.com; OCLC Online Computer Library Center, Inc.; RoweCom Information Quest; Swets Blackwell. Reprint: PQC; PSC. *Indexed:* ASSIA, BrHumI, CJA, CJPI, CLI, IBSS, IBZ, LRI, PAIS, PSA, SociolAb. *Bk. rev.:* 5-7, 700-1,200 words. *Aud.:* Ac, Sa.

The Howard League for Penal Reform, founded in 1866, is the oldest penal reform organization in the United Kingdom. The League is funded by voluntary donations and works to establish a more humane and effective penal system through researching and publishing material on criminal justice policy and practice, organizing and hosting conferences and debates, and organizing programs in schools and prisons. This long-standing journal, sponsored by the Howard League for Penal Reform, has broadened its scope to include well-researched and -documented material on all aspects of the criminal justice process, including penal policy and crime prevention, and both theory and practice. Although it has some foreign contributions, the journal continues to emphasize research and analysis of the criminal justice system in the United Kingdom. Most authors are from academic institutions, and they seem to reflect the principal audience for the journal. However, policymakers and administrators in government departments and practitioners in the field also read the journal and often contribute material. The articles are of excellent academic quality, although specialist jargon and technical style are discouraged. The regular "Penal Policy File" column provides summaries of recent developments in penal policy in the United Kingdom. There are also review articles and an excellent book review section that emphasizes books published in the United Kingdom. Recent topics have included victimization of probationers, increasing imprisonment numbers in Germany, electronic monitoring of offenders in England and Wales, homicide and the media, stalking, the role of community service in reducing crime, feminist perspectives on self-help groups for prisoners' partners, magistrates' attitudes toward domestic violence, and death penalty resistance in the U.S. This has become a leading journal in the criminal justice field. The publisher's web site provides more information about this journal, including tables of contents and abstracts from 1997 to the present. The electronic version of the journal is available from Blackwell and Ingenta.

2013. *International Journal of Offender Therapy and Comparative Criminology.* Former titles (until 1972): *International Journal of Offender Therapy;* (until 1966): *Journal of Offender Therapy;* (until 1961): *Association for Psychiatric Treatment of Offenders. Journal.* [ISSN: 0306-624X] 1957. bi-m. GBP 348 print & online eds. in Europe, Middle East, Africa & Australasia. Ed(s): George Palermo. Sage Publications, Inc., 2455 Teller Rd, Thousand Oaks, CA 91320; info@sagepub.com; http://www.sagepub.com. Illus., index, adv. Sample. Refereed. Circ: 1000. Vol. ends: Winter. Microform: PQC. Online: EBSCO Publishing; Gale Group; ingenta.com; OCLC Online Computer Library Center, Inc.; ProQuest Information & Learning; RoweCom Information Quest; Swets Blackwell. Reprint: WSH. *Indexed:* ABS&EES, ASSIA, AgeL, CJA, CJPI, CLI, ExcerpMed, H&SSA, IBSS, IBZ, ILP, IMFL, LRI, PSA, PsycholAb, RiskAb, SFSA, SSCI, SSI, SUSA, SociolAb. *Bk. rev.:* 1, 500-600 words, signed. *Aud.:* Ac, Sa.

For more than 40 years, this scholarly journal has provided a forum for research and discussion of all variables associated with the treatment of offenders. It publishes both theoretical and clinical practice papers from the fields of criminology, law, psychiatry, psychology, social work, sociology, and related health sciences professions. The journal addresses psychological, biological, genetic, and environmental (life history) aspects of offender treatment. Each issue presents six to eight articles, an editorial, and occasional commentary. Recent topics have included youth homicide, empirical assessment in criminal psychological profiles, filicide in families with autistic children, inpatient evaluation and treatment of a self-professed serial killer, animal cruelty to serial murder, shame and guilt in child offenders, group-based intervention with incarcerated young offenders, psychological profiling of serial arson crimes, and the use of community service. This journal is similar to, and complements, both *Criminal Justice and Behavior* (above in this section) and *Journal of Offender Rehabilitation* (below in this section), but it is perhaps more international. If possible, all three titles should be included in any collection where there is a scholarly interest in criminal psychology, rehabilitation, or corrections. More information about this journal is available at the Sage web site, and the electronic version of the journal is available from Sage via OCLC FirstSearch Electronic Collections Online, EBSCO Online, Ingenta, and SwetsNet.

2014. *Journal of Contemporary Criminal Justice.* [ISSN: 1043-9862] 1978. q. GBP 267 print & online eds. in Europe, Middle East, Africa & Australasia. Ed(s): Chris Eskridge. Sage Publications, Inc., 2455 Teller Rd, Thousand Oaks, CA 91320; info@sagepub.com; http://www.sagepub.com. Illus., adv. Sample. Refereed. Vol. ends: Nov. Online: Pub.; EBSCO Publishing; ingenta.com; OCLC Online Computer Library Center, Inc.; ProQuest Information & Learning; RoweCom Information Quest; Swets Blackwell. Reprint: WSH. *Indexed:* CJA, CJPI, IBZ, PRA, PSA, RiskAb, SUSA, SociolAb. *Bk. rev.:* 3-5, 300-500 words. *Aud.:* Ac, Sa.

Sage took over publication of this unique scholarly journal in February 1997. Previously it was published by the Department of Criminal Justice at California State University, Long Beach, where the then editor-in-chief was a professor. Sage has maintained the unique format that enables each issue to present an in-depth exploration of topics by devoting all articles to a single theme. In each issue, authoritative guest editors assemble five to seven articles that provide interdisciplinary, thorough coverage of the specified theme. At least one issue in each volume is sponsored by the International Association for the Study of Organized Crime and is devoted to an examination of organized crime. Recent themes have included mental health needs and services of offenders, transnational organized crime, social capital and criminal justice, and post-conviction issues of the juvenile justice system. The journal's interdisciplinary nature and one-theme format make it very useful for a scholarly or research audience. More information about this journal, including a contents-alert service, is available at the Sage web site, and the electronic version of the journal is available from Sage via OCLC FirstSearch Electronic Collections Online, EBSCO Online, Ingenta, and SwetsNet.

2015. *Journal of Criminal Justice: an international journal.* [ISSN: 0047-2352] 1973. bi-m. EUR 816 (Qualified personnel, EUR 203). Ed(s): Kent B Joscelyn, Arnold Binder. Pergamon, The Boulevard, Langford Ln, East Park, Kidlington, OX5 1GB, United Kingdom. Illus., index, adv. Sample. Refereed. Circ: 3000. Vol. ends: No. 6. Microform: PQC. Online: Gale Group; ingenta.com; ScienceDirect; Swets Blackwell. Reprint: PQC; WSH. *Indexed:* ASSIA, AgeL, CJA, CJPI, CLI, ILP, LRI, PAIS, PsycholAb, SSCI, SSI. *Aud.:* Ac, Sa.

This is a fine, multidisciplinary journal that covers all aspects of the criminal justice system. It seeks to provide new ideas, new information, and new methods to both practitioners and academicians. Innovative thought is emphasized, along with relationships and interactions of individual elements within the criminal justice system. Its high-quality articles are scholarly. The journal strives to be international, and although most authors are from the United States, the topics are certainly not geographically limited. Most contributors to this journal are academicians. Recent topics have included administrative determinants of inmate violence, police liability for inappropriate response to domestic violence victims, the effect of cocaine price on cocaine use, conflict theory and racial profiling, offer acceptance of community policing, and urban crime in Ghana. This is an excellent journal for any criminal justice collection. Unfortunately, its relatively high price may cause many libraries to bypass it. The publisher's web site provides more information, and electronic access to articles from this journal is available from ScienceDirect and selected other sources including InfoTrac, ProQuest, and Wilson.

2016. *Journal of Criminal Justice Education.* [ISSN: 1051-1253] 1990. s-a. USD 125; USD 62.50 per issue. Ed(s): Craig Hemmens. Academy of Criminal Justice Sciences, 7319 Hanover Pkwy., Ste. C, Greenbelt, MD 20770-3615; info@acjs.org; http://www.acjs.org. Illus., index, adv. Sample. Refereed. Circ: 3000. Vol. ends: Fall. *Indexed:* CJA, CJPI. *Bk. rev.:* 1 article per issue. *Aud.:* Ac, Sa.

In addition to fostering excellence in education in criminal justice, the Academy of Criminal Justice Sciences encourages understanding and cooperation among those engaged in teaching and research and practitioners in criminal justice agencies. *JCJE* is a scholarly journal that seeks to provide a forum for the examination, discussion, and debate of issues concerning postsecondary education in criminal justice, criminology, and related areas. Its overall goal is to enhance the quality of higher education in these fields by encouraging new empirical research and debate. N. Prabha Unnithan, who recently finished a three-year term as editor, advised that *JCJE* focuses on the study of the nature of teaching, and examines various innovations in the teaching of criminal justice. Referring to the quality of the scholarship, he commented that the manuscripts are subjected to multiple readings and evaluations by internal and external reviewers. The journal includes articles dealing with best practices, i.e., teaching methods and innovations, as well as research. In addition to seven or eight theoretical or conceptual articles, each issue contains several "Practical Pedagogy" articles focusing on teaching methods. Most issues also include a "Resources" section with review articles covering materials useful to CJ education; and occasional commentary is also included. Recent topics have included distance learning for CJ professionals in the United Kingdom, student attitudes on juvenile justice policy, student attitudes toward internship experiences, student perceptions of policing as a profession, teaching criminological theory, CJ courses with university students and youthful offenders, and curricular resources for international CJ education. The popularity and proliferation of criminal justice programs in colleges and universities in recent years, along with the concerns about the quality of all educational programs, make this an important journal. The publisher's web site provides more information, and electronic access to articles from this journal is available through ProQuest.

Journal of Criminal Law & Criminology. See Law section.

2017. *Journal of Interpersonal Violence: concerned with the study and treatment of victims and perpetrators of physical and sexual violence.* [ISSN: 0886-2605] 1986. m. GBP 543 print & online eds. in Europe, Middle East, Africa & Australasia. Ed(s): Jon R Conte. Sage Publications, Inc., 2455 Teller Rd, Thousand Oaks, CA 91320; info@sagepub.com; http://www.sagepub.com. Illus., index, adv. Sample. Refereed. Circ: 3250 Paid. Vol. ends: Dec. *Indexed:* ASG, ASSIA, AgeL, CIJE, CJA, CJPI, IBZ, IMFL, PsycholAb, RiskAb, SFSA, SSCI, SSI, SWA, SWR&A, SociolAb. *Bk. rev.:* 1, 700-1,000 words, signed. *Aud.:* Ac, Sa.

This scholarly, interdisciplinary journal is devoted to the study and treatment of both victims and perpetrators of interpersonal violence. Contributors address the concerns and activities of professionals interested in domestic violence, child sexual abuse, rape and sexual assault, physical child abuse, and other violent crimes. The journal examines the causes, effects, characteristics, treatment, and prevention of all types of violence. It publishes both qualitative and quantitative research articles, but quantitative methods are emphasized. Theoretical links between all types of interpersonal violence are explored, using perspectives from a variety of disciplines including psychology, psychiatry, sociology, social work, and others. Each issue contains six articles and an occasional lengthy book review and/or very infrequent "Brief Notes" that describe ongoing research projects or specific innovations, methods, or practice experiences. The interdisciplinary nature of this publication makes it useful in any social science collection, as well as criminology collections. More information about this journal is available at the Sage web site, and the electronic version of the journal is available from Sage via OCLC FirstSearch Electronic Collections Online, EBSCO Online, Ingenta, and SwetsNet.

2018. *Journal of Offender Rehabilitation: a multidisciplinary journal of innovation in research, services, and programs in corrections and criminal justice.* Former titles (until 1990): *Journal of Offender Counseling, Services and Rehabilitation;* (until 1980): *Offender Rehabilitation.* [ISSN: 1050-9674] 1976. q. USD 390 domestic; USD 526.50 Canada; USD 565.50 elsewhere. Ed(s): Nathaniel J Pallone. Haworth Press, Inc., 10 Alice St, Binghamton, NY 13904-1580; getinfo@haworthpressinc.com; http://www.haworthpressinc.com. Illus., adv. Sample. Refereed. Circ: 328 Paid. Vol. ends: Spring/Summer. Microform: PQC. Online: Gale Group. Reprint: HAW. *Indexed:* AltPI, CIJE, CJA, CJPI, H&SSA, HRA, IBZ, IMFL, PRA, PsycholAb, RiskAb, SFSA, SSI, SUSA, SWA, SWR&A, SociolAb. *Aud.:* Ac, Sa.

This is an interdisciplinary journal that deals with all aspects of the treatment of offenders and the reentry of ex-offenders into society. It presents research and programs that demonstrate the importance of offender and ex-offender services to the criminal justice system. It also includes empirical research and conceptual analyses of issues relevant to offender rehabilitation. The content includes concise, well-documented articles that focus on measurement and appraisal in offender rehabilitation, clinical practices, professional roles, policy and program evaluation, special populations, special problems, and new approaches and conceptual paradigms. Many issues of the journal are edited by guest editors and focus articles on different aspects of the same broad topic, e.g., volume 35, numbers 3–4, focused on religion, the community, and the rehabilitation of criminal offenders. Other recent topics have covered social work in CJ and correctional settings, MCMI-III personality profiles of incarcerated female substance abusers, county jail nonpsychiatric mental health services, antisocial personality disorders of imprisoned adult males, and recidivism of boot camp graduates. This publication is highly recommended for any corrections or social service collection, and its interdisciplinary approach makes it desirable for all collections with an interest in social problems. It is similar to, but somewhat narrower in scope than, the *International Journal of Offender Therapy and Comparative Criminology* (above in this section). More information, including tables of contents back to 1991 and an e-mail alerting service, is available at the Haworth Press web site. An electronic version of this journal is also available from Haworth Press.

2019. *Journal of Quantitative Criminology.* [ISSN: 0748-4518] 1984. q. USD 594 print or online ed. Ed(s): David McDowall. Kluwer Academic / Plenum Publishers, 233 Spring St Fl 7, New York, NY 10013-1522; http://www.wkap.nl/. Illus., index, adv. Sample. Refereed. Vol. ends: Dec. Microform: PQC. Online: EBSCO Publishing; ingenta.com; Kluwer Online; OCLC Online Computer Library Center, Inc.; Ovid Technologies, Inc.; RoweCom Information Quest; Swets Blackwell. Reprint: WSH. *Indexed:* CJA, CJPI, PsycholAb, SSCI, SociolAb. *Aud.:* Ac, Sa.

JQC publishes quantitative research in crime and justice from many fields, including sociology, psychology, economics, statistics, geography, political science, and engineering, as well as criminology. Each issue presents four or five papers that may apply any type of quantitative techniques, present original research, or explore new methods for studying criminological topics. Occasional special issues focus on one topic. Book review essays that cover areas where significant quantitative research is ongoing are sometimes included. This journal seems most useful to an academic readership (especially above the undergraduate level). Virtually all authors are from academic institutions. In addition to its unique emphasis on quantitative methods, this journal is broader in scope than other scholarly research journals such as the *Journal of Research in Crime and Delinquency* or *Justice Quarterly* (both below in this section). Recent topics have included the epidemic of youth violence in Boston; strain theory among African Americans; Poisson latent class analyses of sex differences in age patterns of delinquent/criminal careers; the cross-national relationship between income inequality and homicide rates; routine activities and deviant behaviors among American, Dutch, Hungarian, and Swiss youth; and the impact of the 1994 federal assault weapons ban on gun markets. More information, including tables of contents from 1999 to the present, is available on the Kluwer web site. The electronic version of this journal is also available from Kluwer.

2020. *Journal of Research in Crime and Delinquency.* [ISSN: 0022-4278] 1964. q. GBP 304 print & online eds. in Europe, Middle East, Africa & Australasia. Ed(s): Clayton Hartjen. Sage Publications, Inc., 2455 Teller Rd, Thousand Oaks, CA 91320; info@sagepub.com; http://www.sagepub.com. Illus., index, adv. Sample. Refereed. Circ: 1650 Paid. Vol. ends: Nov. Microform: WSH; PMC. Online: Pub.; EBSCO Publishing; Florida Center for Library Automation; Gale Group; ingenta.com; OCLC Online Computer Library Center, Inc.; ProQuest Information & Learning; RoweCom Information Quest; Swets Blackwell. Reprint: WSH. *Indexed:* ASSIA, AgeL, CIJE, CJA, CJPI, CLI, ExcerpMed, IBSS, IBZ, ILP, IMFL, PRA, PsycholAb, RiskAb, SFSA, SSCI, SSI, SUSA, SWR&A, SociolAb. *Aud.:* Ac, Sa.

This long-standing scholarly journal is published in cooperation with the National Council on Crime and Delinquency, which emphasizes the relationship between postconviction sanctions (e.g., incarceration and community programs) and the prevention, treatment, and control of crime and delinquency. Each issue presents four or five lengthy reports on original research in crime and delinquency or critical analyses of either old or new theories or concepts. In addition to theory, methodological studies, experimental results, statistical analyses, evaluation research, and empirical research are included to enhance the knowledge of crime and society's relationship with it. The journal provides an excellent sampling of recent research that uses a variety of methods, both qualitative and quantitative, and it illustrates the application of sophisticated analytic techniques. It is interdisciplinary, with perspectives from economics, psychology, public administration, social work, and sociology, as well as criminology and criminal justice fields. The articles deal with both the etiology and characteristics of crime and criminals, and the criminal justice system itself. The new editor advises that he intends to expand the scope to cover "a wider range of readings more reflective of the field's diversity." Review essays, research notes, and commentaries are occasionally included. Recent topics have included the relationship between low-wage employment opportunities and violent adolescent delinquency, the relationship between punishment and offending, racial and ethnic typification of crime, fear of gang crime, and recidivism in juveniles. This journal is very useful in an academic setting for graduate/

advanced student and faculty research and in other research settings. Its presentation of a variety of research methods and theoretical models and concepts makes it appealing to a broader audience than the *Journal of Quantitative Criminology* (above in this section). More information about this journal is available at the Sage web site, and the electronic version of the journal is available from Sage via OCLC FirstSearch Electronic Collections Online, EBSCO Online, Ingenta, and SwetsNet.

2021. ***Justice Quarterly.*** [ISSN: 0741-8825] 1984. q. USD 250; USD 65 per issue. Ed(s): Donna Bishop. Academy of Criminal Justice Sciences, 7319 Hanover Pkwy., Ste. C, Greenbelt, MD 20770-3615; info@acjs.org; http://www.acjs.org. Illus., adv. Sample. Refereed. Circ: 3000. Vol. ends: Dec. Online: bigchalk; EBSCO Publishing; ProQuest Information & Learning. *Indexed:* CJA, CJPI, PRA, SFSA, SSCI, SUSA, SociolAb. *Bk. rev.:* 2, 1,000-2,000 words, signed. *Aud.:* Ac, Sa.

The Academy of Criminal Justice Sciences attempts to foster excellence in education and research in the field of criminal justice. Its other stated purposes are to encourage cooperation among criminal justice teaching and research personnel, to build cooperation between education programs and criminal justice agencies, and to serve as a clearinghouse for collection and dissemination of criminal justice information produced by educational or research programs. As an official journal of the academy, *Justice Quarterly* is a fine multidisciplinary journal that presents scholarly, well-documented articles addressing all aspects of criminal justice. Academic authors write virtually all articles, and research articles that represent a broad range of methodologies seem to have an edge in the selection process. Donna M. Bishop, Northeastern University, recently began a three-year term as editor. She advised that she will continue publishing articles from diverse perspectives and that she will favor articles that make significant contributions to CJ knowledge and stimulate theoretical research and/or policy advances. In addition, she will continue to welcome research notes and review essays. The journal also includes occasional "Exchange" articles that present lengthy and well-documented responses to articles previously published in *JQ*. This journal seems to focus more on the criminal justice system than does the *Journal of Research in Crime and Delinquency* (above in this section), which includes much about the etiology of crime and the characteristics of crime and criminals. However, the research articles in *JQ* compare favorably with the National Council on Crime and Delinquency title. Both journals should be part of academic library collections where graduate or advanced research is being conducted. The publisher's web site provides more information, and electronic access to articles from this journal is available ProQuest.

2022. ***Law and Order Magazine: the magazine for police management.*** [ISSN: 0023-9194] 1953. m. USD 24.95 domestic; USD 84.95 foreign. Ed(s): Ed Sanow. Hendon Publishing Company, 130 Waukegan Rd, Deerfield, IL 60015; info@hendonpub.com; http://www.lawandordermag.com. Illus., index, adv. Sample. Circ: 35000 Controlled. Vol. ends: Dec. Microform: PQC. Online: CompuServe Inc.; ProQuest Information & Learning. Reprint: PQC. *Indexed:* CJA, CJPI. *Bk. rev.:* 0-5, 75-150 words. *Aud.:* Ga, Ac, Sa.

Law and Order is a management-oriented publication that emphasizes practical solutions to problems encountered by law enforcement agencies. Concise, well-written articles focus on communications, training, fleet management, uniforms, weapons, community relations, patrol operations, administration, and personnel management. Articles are not footnoted, and practitioners write most of them, while magazine staff writes a few. Regular departments provide brief practical information that covers national and international news, law enforcement training, computer equipment and applications, other police equipment, and commentary. The magazine contains much useful advertising relevant to law enforcement products and services and some job ads. Each issue focuses a number of articles on a specific editorial focus. The 2003 issues focused on weapons technology/use/training, policing techniques from around the world, community relations, police technology, police training, law enforcement vehicles, police communications, uniforms and equipment, investigation techniques, and computing and Internet. In addition, one issue presents detailed information about the IACP conference and another presents the annual buyer's guide. Other recent topics have included special reports on hiring/recruiting and ethics, as well as articles on police wellness programs, first things to do at an accident scene, lessons from 30 years of policing, California Highway Patrol Safety and Farm Labor Vehicle Education Program, civil rights policy, ruggedized computers (strengthened to withstand rugged use), the use of digital video in law enforcement, the National Association of Women Law Enforcement Executives (NAWLEE), and bloodstain pattern analysis. This magazine's broad scope and its modest price make it appropriate wherever there is an interest in law enforcement. The publisher's web site provides many online articles, an online buyer's guide, an employment database, and other useful information. Electronic versions of articles from *Law and Order* are available via ProQuest.

2023. ***Law Enforcement News.*** Formerly: *John Jay College of Criminal Justice. Criminal Justice Center. Monographs.* [ISSN: 0364-1724] 1975. 22x/yr. USD 28. Ed(s): Peter Dodenhoff. John Jay College of Criminal Justice, 899 Tenth Ave, New York, NY 10019; http://www.jjay.cuny.edu/. Illus., adv. Sample. Circ: 7000. Microform: PQC. Reprint: PQC. *Indexed:* CJPI. *Aud.:* Ga, Ac, Sa.

Law Enforcement News is a long-standing, newspaper-format publication from John Jay College of Criminal Justice at the City University of New York. Each 15-page issue presents numerous feature articles, some lengthy, covering crime and law enforcement concerns around the nation. The publication is intended for law enforcement practitioners at all levels, but it is also of interest to academics and the general public. Police techniques, procedures, programs, equipment, education, and training; crime demographics and statistics; and social, political, and policy implications are among the topics included, with emphasis on what's being done and where. Many articles are written by publication staff, but many others are by outside contributors, mostly practitioners. Each issue contains several regular sections that cover short news items from around the country, present information on specific law enforcement professionals, and provide opinions or lengthy commentaries from practitioners. Recent topics have included LAPD gang enforcement, a Florida sheriff's hybrid (gas-electric) cars, federal dollars for local law enforcement, criticism of the Houston Police Department's DNA testing, NYPD surveillance guidelines, cyber-crime investigation, domestic violence in Milwaukee, a National Violent Death Reporting System, characteristics associated with the prevalence and severity of force used by the police, and whether Sioux Falls police are too aggressive. *Law Enforcement News* is an excellent and inexpensive way to keep track of law enforcement news from around the country. The journal's web site provides subscription information and many article excerpts from 1996 to the present.

2024. ***Law Officers' Bulletin.*** [ISSN: 0145-6571] 1976. bi-w. USD 169. Ed(s): Mary B Murphy. Pike & Fischer, Inc., 1010 Wayne Ave, Ste 1400, Silver Springs, MD 20910-5600; pike@pf.com; http://www.pf.com. Illus. Sample. Vol. ends: No. 26. *Indexed:* CJPI. *Aud.:* Ga, Ac, Sa.

A subsidiary of The Bureau of Nations Affairs, Inc., Pike & Fisher publishes authoritative legal and business reference services, conferences and seminars, newsletters, and special reports and directories; and it produces various software. They produce legal reference services in Internet law, communications law, administrative law, criminal law, and other areas. *Law Officers' Bulletin* is one of the legal digests from the attorney-editors at Pike & Fisher. This newsletter reporter provides brief information about recent interpretations of constitutional and statutory law relevant to law enforcement. Each issue presents summaries of recent court decisions from local, state, and federal jurisdictions, which affect law enforcement practice. Coverage could include any case that could impact law enforcement procedures, including arrest, search and seizure, interrogation, right to counsel, and others. Reports are grouped by broad topics and cases are also listed alphabetically. Regular sections cover U.S. Supreme Court decisions, trends of multiple decisions regarding especially important issues, and law officers' constitutional and legal problems. "You Be the Judge" tests the reader's knowledge by presenting federal or state court decisions in a "you are there" style. Special feature issues provide in-depth coverage of specific topics. The focus on case law makes this digest narrower in scope than other digests that address criminal justice topics. This legal digest is informative and readable and would be useful anywhere there is interest in legal ramifications of law enforcement. More information is available on the publisher's web site.

2025. ***N C J R S Catalog.*** bi-m. National Criminal Justice Reference Service, PO Box 6000, Rockville, MD 20849-6000; http://www.ncjrs.org. Circ: 80000. *Aud.:* Ga, Ac, Sa.

The *NCJRS Catalog,* while not a magazine or journal that publishes articles, is an important resource for criminal justice information. It contains information, including abstracts and ordering instructions, on criminal justice publications, videos, and related materials available from the National Criminal Justice Reference Service, which is a national clearinghouse of information sponsored by the National Institute of Justice. In fact NCJRS is one of the most extensive criminal justice information sources in the world. The *NCJRS Catalog* features publications produced by the bureaus of the Office of Justice Programs, including the Bureau of Justice Statistics, the National Institute of Justice, the Bureau of Justice Assistance, the Office of Juvenile Justice and Delinquency Prevention, and the Office for Victims of Crime. The *Catalog* also features the publications of the National Institute of Corrections, the Office of Community Oriented Policing Services, and the Office of National Drug Control Policy. These publications are listed under broad topic headings that include corrections, courts, juvenile justice, law enforcement, and victims. In addition, the *Catalog* describes a few key articles from professional journals, lists some relevant web sites, and describes recent grants awarded by the Office of Justice Programs agencies. Each issue also contains "Spotlight On," which lists publications and web sites that focus on a specific timely topic such as gangs, community safety, substance abuse prevention and education, and law enforcement and corrections technology. The *NCJRS Catalog* is a very useful, and free, current-awareness listing of mostly free government resources. The *Catalog* is available on the web at the NCJRS web site, and many of the resources noted in it are also available free via the web.

National Criminal Justice Reference Service Abstracts Database. See Abstracts and Indexes section.

2026. *National Institute of Justice Journal (Print Edition).* Superseded in part (in 1992): *National Institute of Justice Reports;* Which was formerly (until 1991): *N I J Reports;* (until 1983): *S N I: Selective Notification of Information.* [ISSN: 1067-7453] 1972. q. Free. Ed(s): Jolene Hernon. U.S. Department of Justice, National Institute of Justice, 810 Seventh St, NW, Rockville, MD 20531; http://www.ojp.usdoj.gov/nij/. Illus. Sample. Circ: 80000. Online: Gale Group; LexisNexis; OCLC Online Computer Library Center, Inc. *Indexed:* CJA, PAIS. *Aud.:* Ga, Ac, Sa.

The National Institute of Justice (NIJ) is the primary research and development agency of the U.S. Department of Justice within the Office of Justice Programs. It sponsors special projects, research, and programs designed to improve and strengthen the criminal justice system. NIJ also conducts evaluations to determine the effectiveness of programs, especially those funded by the Institute, and recommends programs for continuation or implementation at other locations. The *National Institute of Justice Journal* publishes information about NIJ research and programs in an attempt to ensure that research findings influence practice. Each issue presents four or five interesting, well-written articles that emphasize policy-relevant research and initiatives. In addition, regular columns include brief reports of recent research findings, announcements regarding grants and award winners, information about noteworthy publications and reports, and announcements of upcoming relevant conferences and meetings. This journal is useful anywhere that crime and criminal justice concerns are relevant, and it's free. The NIJ web site provides online full-text access to this journal and many other NIJ publications, and a free subscription to the paper version of the journal can also be ordered on the site.

2027. *Police: the law officer's magazine.* Formerly: *Police Product News.* [ISSN: 0893-8989] 1976. m. USD 25 domestic; USD 38.95 foreign. Ed(s): David Griffith. Bobit Publishing Company, 21061 S Western Ave, Torrance, CA 90501. Illus., adv. Sample. Circ: 52000. Vol. ends: Dec. *Indexed:* CJPI. *Aud.:* Ga, Ac, Sa.

Police remains an attractively packaged trade magazine for working law enforcement officers, who constitute 90 percent of its paid readership. The publication's primary target audience includes line officers through middle management, but also among its subscribers are several thousand chiefs of police. Each issue presents six or seven feature articles that may cover any topic of concern to law enforcement officers—for example, the latest crime prevention programs, the emotional and physical trauma police officers often face, profiles of exceptional individuals or departments, profiles of unusual cases or services, and weapons or technology. Regular columns include "Officer Survival," which focuses on skills and methods; "Arsenal," which discusses the safe and effective use of weapons; and "The Beat," in which officers share experiences on the job. Each issue also provides a "News Briefs" section that covers law enforcement news; the "Product Patrol," which presents information about law enforcement equipment and products; the "Briefing Room" section, which presents letters to the editor; and an editorial. Like *Law and Order, Police* is appropriate anywhere there is an interest in law enforcement. More information, including the selected full-text articles from 2001 to the present, some job listings, and product information, is available at the *Police* web site.

2028. *Police Chief: professional voice of law enforcement.* [ISSN: 0032-2571] 1934. m. USD 25. Ed(s): Charles E Higginbotham. International Association of Chiefs of Police, Inc., 515 N Washington St, Alexandria, VA 22314-2340; information@theiacp.org; http://www.theiacp.org/. Illus., index, adv. Circ: 22000. Vol. ends: Dec. Microform: PQC. Online: Gale Group. Reprint: PQC. *Indexed:* CJA, CJPI, PAIS, SSCI, SSI. *Aud.:* Ga, Ac, Sa.

The International Association of Chiefs of Police (IACP) is a leading organization of police executives that strives to advance the science and practice of police services. This official publication of the IACP provides a forum for law enforcement practitioners to share their collective expertise. The publication's mission is to enhance the reader's understanding of the latest trends and practices in law enforcement. Most issues focus on a specific theme of interest to police executives as determined by reader feedback. Recent themes have included law enforcement science and technology, proactive policing, highway safety, use of force, and defeating terrorism. The magazine is attractively packaged, with feature articles from a supervisory/command viewpoint, some membership news and job ads, and much advertising. Articles are contributed by practitioners in law enforcement and related fields, and are concise and not heavily footnoted. Regular columns/departments include "Legislative Alert"; "Chief's Counsel," which examines case law and liability issues; "Technology Talk"; "Product Update"; and "Survivors' Club," which documents the benefits of protective devices such as seatbelts and body armor. The April issue contains the annual "Buyers' Guide." This magazine is particularly useful for law enforcement executives or administrators. However, it is also very useful in academic collections where law enforcement administration is taught, and it is of interest to anyone involved in or studying law enforcement. More information about the IACP and *The Police Chief,* including annual subject and author indexes, is available at the IACP web site.

2029. *Police Review.* [ISSN: 0309-1414] 1893. w. GBP 70 domestic; GBP 90 in Europe; USD 215 in the Americas. Ed(s): Gary Mason. Jane's Information Group, Sentinel House, 163 Brighton Rd, Coulsdon, CR5 2YH, United Kingdom; info@janes.co.uk; http://www.janes.com. Illus., adv. Sample. Circ: 25000 Paid. *Indexed:* ASSIA, CLI, ILP, SSI. *Aud.:* Ga, Ac, Sa.

Police Review, now part of Jane's Information Group, is aimed at police officers primarily in the United Kingdom. It is a long-standing high-circulation trade magazine, which celebrated its 110th anniversary in 2003. It focuses on news and current affairs relevant to British police forces. Each weekly issue publishes five or so feature articles and numerous shorter pieces on the realities of law enforcement written by magazine staff or police practitioners. Included are editorials, news items, information on current and planned legislation, technological developments, case law, and promotion study guides relevant to British policing. More information about the magazine is available on the publisher's web site. The online version of *Police Review* is available from the publisher. *Police Review* provides a useful and interesting view of law enforcement in the United Kingdom.

2030. *Police Times.* Former titles: *Police Times and Police Command; Police Times.* 1964. q. Free to membership. Ed(s): Jim Gordon. American Federation of Police & Concerned Citizens, 6250 Horizon Dr, Titusville, FL 32780. Illus., adv. Circ: 50000. Vol. ends: Nov/Dec. *Bk. rev.:* 2, 350-450 words. *Aud.:* Ga, Sa.

Police Times is a low-cost, long-standing, organizational magazine that presents thought-provoking articles to a large readership. It is the official voice of the American Federation of Police and Concerned Citizens, an organization of more than 100,000 law enforcement and security personnel and concerned citizens. AFP&CC is dedicated to the prevention of crime and the apprehension of criminals. It also assists family members of officers killed in the line of duty, promotes the training of policy reserves, encourages citizens to volunteer in crime prevention programs, and educates the public about the contributions and sacrifices of law enforcement professionals. The magazine's tabloid-style format and content are similar to the more frequently published *Law Enforcement News* (above in this section), but *Police Times* includes more photographs and organizational news. The publication presents news, essays, and editorials on issues relevant to law enforcement, often focusing on what's being done and where. Police procedures, programs, equipment, and education and training; crime demographics; and political/policy implications are discussed. The editorial policy advises that stories involving smaller police departments or individuals who have made a significant contributions to law enforcement are emphasized. Regular sections cover legislative and judicial issues, equipment and technological innovations, recent facts, and off-the-wall items. *Police Times* has potential readership among academics and the general public in addition to its many law enforcement readers. More information about this publication and the American Federation of Police and Concerned Citizens is available on the organization's web site.

2031. *Policing: an international journal of police strategies and management.* Formerly (until 1997): *Police Studies;* Incorporates (1981-1997): *American Journal of Police.* [ISSN: 1363-951X] 1978. q. EUR 1477.91 in Europe; USD 1229 in North America; AUD 1979 in Australasia. Ed(s): Lawrence F Travis, III. Emerald, 60-62 Toller Ln, Bradford, BD8 9BY, United Kingdom; info@emeraldinsight.com; http://www.emeraldinsight.com/journals/. Illus. Sample. Refereed. Microform: PQC. Online: Pub.; EBSCO Publishing; OCLC Online Computer Library Center, Inc.; ProQuest Information & Learning; RoweCom Information Quest; Swets Blackwell. Reprint: PSC. *Indexed:* ABS&EES, CJA, CJPI, IBSS, PAIS, PRA, PSA, SSCI, SUSA, SociolAb. *Bk. rev.:* 1, 900-1,500 words, signed. *Aud.:* Ac, Sa.

In 1997, *Policing* was formed by the merger of *American Journal of Police,* which focused on policing in the United States, and *Police Studies,* which emphasized comparative and international law enforcement. Like its forerunners, *Policing* is an interdisciplinary scholarly journal that covers theory and research related to law enforcement. It aims to provide a global look at the latest developments on matters of police policy, practice, management, operations, education, training, and science and technology. Its scholarly examination of law enforcement issues is useful to senior law enforcement officers, policymakers, and especially to academics. *Policing* is very useful in libraries where there is an academic or research interest in law enforcement or the social sciences. The journal's sections include refereed articles, reviews of recent research, occasional book reviews, and debates. Recent topics have included effective policing in rural Australia, gender and police stress, community policing training and policy implications, a multivariate analysis of predictors of police shootings, the impact on women and minority candidates of raising the age and education requirements for police officers, policing in Northern Ireland, and justice and law enforcement in Afghanistan under the Taliban. More information about the journal is available on the publisher's web site, including tables of contents and article abstracts back to 1997. The publisher also provides a free table of contents e-mail alert service and an electronic version of the journal.

2032. *Policing and Society: an international journal of research & policy.* [ISSN: 1043-9463] 1991. q. GBP 325 (Individuals, GBP 95; Corporations, GBP 534). Ed(s): James Sheptycki. Taylor & Francis Ltd, 11 New Fetter Ln, London, EC4P 4EE, United Kingdom; http://www.tandf.co.uk/journals. Illus. Refereed. Online: EBSCO Publishing; OCLC Online Computer Library Center, Inc. Reprint: PSC. *Indexed:* CJA, IBSS, PSA, SociolAb. *Aud.:* Ac, Sa.

Policing and Society is a scholarly journal concerned with law enforcement. Any subject relevant to law enforcement may be covered, although the relationship between police and the overriding political and economic realities is stressed. Scientific investigations of police policies and procedures, legal analyses of police powers, and management-oriented studies of police organization are presented. Recent topics have covered policing in countries where police have historically been ineffective, video surveillance and related technologies, education of the Brazilian paramilitary police, the media influence on citizen attitudes toward police, and policing Dutch-Moroccan youth. Occasional special issues focus all articles on different aspects of the same broad theme, e.g., police accountability in Europe. The editor is in the Department of Sociology, University of Durham in the United Kingdom. The editorial/advisory board includes members from many countries where serious research and academic inquiry into policing take place, including Australia, Canada, Japan, the Netherlands, and the United States. Each issue presents five or six well-written and -documented articles, most written by college or university faculty. This international journal is of potential use to police and other criminal justice practitioners and academics from most social science disciplines. However, the price may be too high for many libraries. More information about *Policing and Society* is available at the publisher's web site, which also provides tables of contents and article abstracts for recent years and an e-mail alerting service.

2033. *The Prison Journal.* [ISSN: 0032-8855] 1845. q. GBP 261 print & online eds. in Europe, Middle East, Africa & Australasia. Ed(s): Rosemary L Gido. Sage Publications, Inc., 2455 Teller Rd, Thousand Oaks, CA 91320; info@sagepub.com; http://www.sagepub.com. Illus., index, adv. Sample. Refereed. Circ: 1000. Vol. ends: Dec. Microform: PQC. Online: Pub.; Florida Center for Library Automation; Gale Group; ingenta.com; OCLC Online Computer Library Center, Inc.; ProQuest Information & Learning; RoweCom Information Quest; Swets Blackwell. *Indexed:* ASG, AltPI, CJA, CJPI, PAIS, PRA, SSCI, SSI, SUSA, SociolAb. *Aud.:* Ac, Sa.

Although *The Prison Journal* is published by Sage, it is the official publication of the Pennsylvania Prison Society, founded in 1787 and the oldest prison reform organization in the United States. Members of the society believe that offenders should be held accountable for breaking laws and that punishments should be constructive. Among its other noble goals, the society works to convince policy makers to avoid politicizing criminal justice issues and to recognize the value of a restorative approach to corrections. This long-standing, well-respected, interdisciplinary journal presents learned articles on all aspects of corrections, including adult and juvenile confinement, treatment interventions, and alternative sanctions. Articles, research notes, and review essays present theoretical treatments, research, policy analyses, historical analyses, and practice descriptions and evaluations. Occasional special issues focus on specific aspects of corrections, such as American corrections and Native Americans or corrections, health care, and public health. Articles are well documented and are contributed by both academic authors and practitioners, including correctional employees, attorneys, and others. Recent articles have addressed the Indian prison reform movement, Native American identities among women prisoners, benchmarking juvenile justice facilities, the literature on older prisoners, the legal liability of inmate suicide, and inmate racial integration. This journal is of interest to the corrections community and anyone interested in current correctional practices, theories, or reforms. It should be part of any collection emphasizing corrections. More information about *The Prison Journal,* including a contents e-mail alerting service, is available at the Sage web site, and the electronic version is available from Sage via OCLC FirstSearch Electronic Collections Online, EBSCO Online, Ingenta, and SwetsNet.

Sexual Abuse. See Psychology section.

2034. *Sheriff Magazine.* Formerly (until 1991): *National Sheriff.* [ISSN: 1070-8170] 1948. bi-m. USD 25 domestic; USD 50 foreign. Ed(s): Mike Terault. National Sheriffs' Association, 1450 Duke St, Alexandria, VA 22314-3490; nsamail@sherrifs.org; http://www.sheriffs.org/. Illus., adv. Sample. Circ: 19000 Paid. Vol. ends: Nov/Dec. *Indexed:* CJA, CJPI. *Aud.:* Ga, Ac, Sa.

The National Sheriffs' Association (NSA) is a nonprofit organization that has worked for over 60 years to enhance the level of professionalism in the law enforcement field. *Sheriff Magazine* focuses on law enforcement concerns as they relate to the office of sheriff. It is the official publication of NSA and the primary magazine for sheriffs and deputies. Articles deal with best practices, procedures, and research in law enforcement, corrections, and court security. Each issue has a "Special Focus," presenting three or four feature articles addressing a chosen theme such as responding to critical incidents, use of force, direct supervision and classification of inmates, coping with law enforcement stress, high-speed pursuit, terrorism, traffic safety, jail privatization, or disaster preparedness. In addition, two to four additional articles address other relevant issues. Sheriffs and other law enforcement professionals write most articles from a practitioner's viewpoint. Regular departments present information on successful law enforcement programs, laws and legislation, news about appointments, retirements, and deaths, NSA activities, and a calendar of industry events. Although *Sheriff Magazine* focuses on the concerns of sheriffs and their personnel, it has broad appeal to anyone interested in law enforcement, including investigators, court officers, corrections officials, police chiefs, and police officers. More information is available at the National Sheriffs' Association web site.

2035. *Theoretical Criminology: an international journal.* [ISSN: 1362-4806] 1997. q. GBP 296 print & online eds. in Europe, Middle East, Africa & Australasia. Ed(s): Lynn Chancer, Tony Jefferson. Sage Publications Ltd., 6 Bonhill St, London, EC2A 4PU, United Kingdom; info@sagepub.co.uk; http://www.sagepub.co.uk/. Illus., adv. Refereed. Vol. ends: Nov. *Indexed:* CJA, IBZ, SFSA, SSCI, SUSA, SociolAb. *Aud.:* Ac, Sa.

Theoretical Criminology is a scholarly journal, now in its seventh year of publication, focusing on the theoretical aspects of criminology. It is concerned with concepts and theories, focusing on criminal behavior, social deviance, criminal law, morality, justice, social regulation, and related concerns. The journal aims to foster theoretical debate, explore the relationship between theory and data in empirical research, and advance the link between criminological analysis and general social and political theory. It is interdisciplinary, presenting perspectives from criminology, sociology, law, history, psychology, anthropology, philosophy, economics, and other disciplines. As would be expected, the journal's scope is broad, including information about the nature of crime and justice, penal policy, the history of crime and criminal justice, comparisons of local and international forms of crime and social control, and the relationships between crime and social development. Occasional theme issues focus on specific issues. One of the co-editors is at a university in the United States and the other is at a university in the United Kingdom. In addition, the editorial board consists of associate editors and international advisory editors from many countries, including Australia, Canada, Italy, Japan, the Netherlands, New Zealand, Norway, and Spain in addition to the United Kingdom and United States. Presumably, this international editorial board has contributed to this journal's ability to publish the scholarship of an international group of authors. Sixty-seven percent of the papers that were published in the last ten issues of this journal were written by authors from universities outside the United States. More information about *Theoretical Criminology,* including tables of contents and a contents e-mail alerting service, is available at the Sage web site. The electronic version of the journal is available from Sage via OCLC FirstSearch Electronic Collections Online, EBSCO Online, Ingenta, and SwetsNet.

Violence Against Women. See Women: Feminist and Special Interest/ Feminist and Women's Studies section.

2036. *Women & Criminal Justice.* [ISSN: 0897-4454] 1989. q. USD 325. Ed(s): Donna C Hale. Haworth Press, Inc., 10 Alice St, Binghamton, NY 13904-1580; getinfo@haworthpressinc.com; http://www.haworthpressinc.com. Illus., adv. Sample. Refereed. Circ: 397 Paid. Vol. ends: No. 2. Microform: PQC. Online: Gale Group; LexisNexis. Reprint: HAW; WSH. *Indexed:* AltPI, CJA, CJPI, CWI, FemPer, GendWatch, IBZ, IMFL, PAIS, SFSA, SSI, SUSA, SWA, SociolAb, WSA, WSI. *Bk. rev.:* 5-10, 500-1,500 words. *Aud.:* Ac, Sa.

Women & Criminal Justice (now semi-annual) is an interdisciplinary refereed journal for academicians and professionals. It is still the only scholarly journal devoted to interdisciplinary research on all issues specifically pertaining to women in criminal justice. It addresses both domestic and international topics and features original research, but also includes commentaries that allow authors to discuss methodological issues, present reports of ongoing research and findings, or comment on practice issues. In addition, the journal contains biographical essays on women who have made contributions to the criminal justice field as practitioners, criminologists, or theorists, and occasional special issues focus articles on themes such as women and domestic abuse. Topics range from women criminal justice practitioners or academicians, to women as victims or perpetrators, to incarcerated women, to women in crime and punishment literature, and more. *Women & Criminal Justice* is a quality journal that presents well-documented articles using many methodological approaches, including gender studies, historical studies, cross-cultural studies, and others. Its focus on women makes it unique and enhances its importance. The Haworth Press web site provides more information about the journal, including tables of contents with article abstracts and an e-mail contents alerting service.

■ CULTURAL-SOCIAL STUDIES

See also History; Literature; and Political Science sections.

Vanette M. Schwartz, Social Sciences Librarian, 8900 Milner Library, Illinois State University, Normal, IL 61790-8900; vmschwa@ilstu.edu

Introduction

The study of culture and its intersection with social issues is central to discourse in the humanities and social sciences. Especially in the last decades of the twentieth century, culture wars and their impact on society grew dramatically. Issues of race, ethnicity, class, and gender have become fundamental in academic dialogue and in popular culture. Cultural issues and conflicts have become an integral part of the political landscape of nations and of the global community. These conflicts have made for a rich and diverse body of literature in the field of cultural-social studies. Many cultural-social studies publications are both interdisciplinary and international. Every periodical in this area addresses issues of race, class, and gender. Many cultural studies journals blend philosophy, history, politics, and literature with social issues; others emphasize popular culture and future studies. Many journals cover history, theory, and research in social science disciplines, while other publications focus on modernism and postmodernism. More specialized journals examine the relationship of technology and human behavior, including the impact on culture. Aesthetics, the arts, and criticism are also an integral part of cultural-social studies. Variations in format, style, and modes of expression have become more predominant, especially in electronic journals. The literature of cultural-social studies offers diverse themes, wide-ranging controversy, and constant intellectual challenge for both writers and readers.

Basic Periodicals

Hs: *The Futurist;* Ga: *The Futurist, Humanities, Journal of Popular Culture;* Ac: *American Quarterly, Critical Inquiry, Humanities, Journal of Popular Culture, Postmodern Culture, Prospects.*

Basic Abstracts and Indexes

America: History and Life, Humanities Index, MLA International Bibliography, PAIS, Social Sciences Index, Sociological Abstracts.

2037. *American Quarterly.* [ISSN: 0003-0678] 1949. q. USD 115. Ed(s): Lucy Maddox, Teresa Murphy. Johns Hopkins University Press, Journals Publishing Division, 2715 N Charles St, Baltimore, MD 21218-4363; http://www.press.jhu.edu/. Illus., index, adv. Refereed. Circ: 6655. Vol. ends: Dec (No. 4). Microform: PQC. Online: EBSCO Publishing; Gale Group; JSTOR (Web-based Journal Archive); OCLC Online Computer Library Center, Inc.; Project MUSE; RoweCom Information Quest; Swets Blackwell. Reprint: PSC. *Indexed:* AIAP, AgeL, AmH&L, ArtHuCI, BAS, BEL&L, BRD, BRI, CBRI, FLI, HumInd, IBZ, MLA-IB, PSA, RI-1, SSCI, SociolAb. *Bk. rev.:* 5-8, essay length. *Aud.:* Ac.

As the major publication of the American Studies Association, this journal aims to "provide a sense of direction to studies of U.S. culture both past and present." *American Quarterly* publishes lengthy research articles, often on cross-disciplinary studies, and review essays on American culture. Recent articles cover such topics as jazz, mass consumption and gender, racial identity, and documentary films. In addition to book reviews, exhibition reviews appear in each issue. Each volume includes an annotated list of completed dissertations in American Studies. The full text of issues from 1996 to the present is available through Project Muse. Earlier full-text issues are available through JSTOR. Essential for academic libraries.

2038. ***American Studies.*** Former titles (until 1970): *Midcontinent American Studies Association. Journal;* (until 1961): *Central Mississippi Valley American Studies Association. Journal.* [ISSN: 0026-3079] 1960. 3x/yr. USD 35 (Individuals, USD 20; Students, USD 8). Ed(s): David Katzman, Norman Yetman. University of Kansas at Lawrence, American Studies Department, 213 Bailey Hall, Lawrence, KS 66045-2117; amerstud@ku.edu; http://www.urc.ukansas.edu/. Illus., index, adv. Refereed. Circ: 1300 Paid. Vol. ends: No. 3. Microform: PQC. Online: Gale Group. *Indexed:* AmH&L, AmHI, HumInd, IBZ, LRI, MLA-IB, PAIS, SSI. *Bk. rev.:* 10-45, 400-500 words, in some issues. *Aud.:* Ac, Ga.

This regional interdisciplinary journal is the publication of the Mid-America American Studies Association and the University of Kansas. The focus of *American Studies* is on broadly based research that provides insights into American society or culture. Research articles cover literature and the arts, along with politics, social issues, and popular culture. Recent articles explore such topics as school segregation and desegregation, the immigrant press, Native American assimilation, and race, gender, and global violence. One or more issues in each volume are devoted to a single theme such as a critical retrospective on American Studies or libraries and American culture. Review essays and book reviews appear in some issues, with at least one issue per year offering a substantial number of reviews. The web site for this journal provides basic editorial information and the contents of recent issues. This journal is a must for academic collections, and it will have broad appeal for many general collections.

2039. ***American Studies International.*** Former titles (until 1975): *American Studies; American Studies News.* [ISSN: 0883-105X] 1962. 3x/yr. USD 42.50 (Individuals, USD 30). Ed(s): Bernard Mergen, Brian Finnegan. George Washington University, American Studies Program, 2108 G St N W, Washington, DC 20052. Illus., index, adv. Refereed. Circ: 1100 Paid. Vol. ends: Oct (No. 3). Microform: PQC. Online: bigchalk; EBSCO Publishing; Florida Center for Library Automation; Gale Group; Northern Light Technology, Inc.; OCLC Online Computer Library Center, Inc.; ProQuest Information & Learning; H.W. Wilson. *Indexed:* ABS&EES, AmH&L, AmHI, ArtHuCI, BRI, CBRI, HumInd, IBZ, MLA-IB, SSCI. *Bk. rev.:* 25-30, length varies. *Aud.:* Ac.

"Promoting international scholarship in American studies" is the aim of this journal. Many contributors are international scholars, although writings by American academics are also included. Coverage is broadly based, ranging from history and literature to film, politics, crime, and social issues. Some issues focus on a theme, such as Post-Soviet American studies or Native American history and culture. Other topics covered in recent articles include global media, Latino ethnicity, Melville's dramatic poetry, and the decade of the 1950s. *American Studies International* also publishes review essays and individual reviews in "Book Notes." Each issue includes an announcements section with brief information on American Studies conferences, calls for papers, grants, fellowships, and publications. The full text of selected articles is available from EBSCO and OCLC databases. The journal's web site, based at George Washington University, includes complete contents and the full text of some articles from earlier issues. For academic collections.

2040. ***Behaviour and Information Technology: an international journal on the human aspects of computing.*** [ISSN: 0144-929X] 1982. bi-m. GBP 431 (Individuals, GBP 175). Ed(s): Krys Kaniasty, Reinhard Pekrun. Taylor & Francis Ltd, 11 New Fetter Ln, London, EC4P 4EE, United Kingdom; info@tandf.co.uk; http://www.tandf.co.uk/journals. Illus., index, adv. Sample. Refereed. Online: EBSCO Publishing; Ingenta Select; OCLC Online Computer Library Center, Inc.; RoweCom Information Quest; Swets Blackwell. Reprint: PSC. *Indexed:* ASG, AgeL, C&ISA, CommAb, CompLI, EngInd, ErgAb, HRA, L&LBA, PsycholAb, SSCI. *Bk. rev.:* in some issues, 500-1,000 words. *Aud.:* Ac.

The aim of this journal is to explore the design, use, and impact of telecommunications, office systems, industrial automation, robotics, and consumer products on human beings. Contributors are drawn from the academic world as well as business, industry, and research centers. Each issue includes six to eight articles, mostly empirical research, on topics such as ethics training for IT managers, software piracy, verbal protocol analysis, and the benefits of user involvement. Occasionally, technical notes and case studies are also published, along with book reviews. The articles are well researched and clearly written. This journal will appeal to an academic and research audience and to readers with background in areas of information technology. The full text of recent issues is available through OCLC Electronic Collections Online (ECO).

2041. ***Body & Society.*** [ISSN: 1357-034X] 1995. q. GBP 305 in Europe, Middle East, Africa & Australasia . Ed(s): Mike Featherstone, Bryan Turner. Sage Publications Ltd., 6 Bonhill St, London, EC2A 4PU, United Kingdom; info@sagepub.co.uk; http://www.sagepub.co.uk/. Adv. Refereed. Circ: 800. *Indexed:* ASSIA, AltPI, IBSS, PEI, SociolAb. *Bk. rev.:* Occasional, 1-4 reviews, 500-1000 words. *Aud.:* Ac.

A companion journal to *Theory, Culture and Society, Body & Society* focuses on the social and cultural analysis of the human body. The two journals share the same philosophy, namely a theoretical openness, an emphasis on the critical exploration of traditions, and a commitment to the analysis of a diverse range of themes. Articles in *Body & Society* center on themes related to feminism, postmoderism, medicine, ethics, and consumerism. The content of this journal ranges across many disciplines from anthropology to communications and from art history to leisure studies. The philosophical writings of theorists such as Bourdieu, Elias, and Foucault often form the basis for articles in this journal. Recent articles cover such topics as the embodiment of addiction, children in family relationships, and portrayals of suffering. The full text of articles is available through OCLC's Electronic Collections Online (ECO). This unique journal will interest social scientists and scholars in health and medicine.

2042. ***Cabinet.*** [ISSN: 1531-1430] 2000. q. USD 24; USD 34; USD 8 newsstand/cover per issue. Ed(s): Sina Najafi. Immaterial Incorporated, 181 Wyckoff St, Brooklyn, NY 11217; subscriptions@immaterial.net; http://www.immaterial.net. *Aud.:* Ga, Ac.

Cabinet is an international and interdisciplinary publication of art and culture. Each issue contains several articles, along with interviews, photography, works of art, postcards, poetry, recordings, and web sites. Some issues are supplemented with audio compact discs. Recent articles cover a wide range of topics, such as copyright law, pharmacopia, coffee houses, Israeli West Bank settlements, and a special issue on property. Contributors range from academics to freelance writers and artists to filmmakers, sound designers, and musicians. Special sections appear in some issues. The publisher's web site contains a table of contents and information on contributors, along with additional readings, artwork, sound tracks, and musical works. A fascinating publication that will appeal to the art community and academia, as well as many general readers.

Canada. Statistics Canada. Canadian Social Trends. See Canada section.

2043. ***Canadian Review of American Studies.*** Formerly (until 1970): *C A A S Bulletin.* [ISSN: 0007-7720] 1965. 3x/yr. CND 75 (Individuals, CND 55; Students, CND 35). Ed(s): Priscilla Walton. University of Toronto Press, Journals Department, 5201 Dufferin St, Toronto, ON M3H 5T8, Canada; journals@utpress.utoronto.ca; http://www.utpjournals.com. Illus., index, adv. Refereed. Circ: 400. Vol. ends: No. 3. *Indexed:* AmH&L, AmHI, ArtHuCI, CBCARef, MLA-IB, SSCI. *Bk. rev.:* 2-3, 1,000-1,500 words. *Aud.:* Ac.

Published by the Canadian Association for American Studies, this journal emphasizes cross-disciplinary studies of U.S. culture from both historical and contemporary perspectives. It also includes articles on the relationship between U.S. and Canadian cultures. Written mainly by Canadian scholars, each issue includes research articles and review essays. Many articles focus on literary works or themes, while others explore social and cultural issues. Recent articles cover such topics as baseball and masculinity, awards for spectacle type movies, nineteenth-century black Americans in Canada, and teaching American Studies abroad. The journal's web site gives basic information and contents for some issues. Full text of selected articles is available through EBSCO databases. For comprehensive collections on American Studies.

2044. ***Comparative American Studies.*** [ISSN: 1477-5700] 2003. q. GBP 270 in Europe, Middle East, Africa & Australasia. Ed(s): Richard Ellis. Sage Publications Ltd., 6 Bonhill St, London, EC2A 4PU, United Kingdom; info@sagepub.co.uk; http://www.sagepub.co.uk/. Adv. *Aud.:* Ac.

This journal aims to "extend scholarly debates about American Studies beyond the geographical boundaries of the United States, and to reposition discussions about American culture within an international, comparative framework." With the contemporary focus on globalization and on the relationship between the United States and other nations, *Comparative American Studies* seeks to draw out the conflicts and common themes especially in the areas of literature, film, popular culture, photography, and visual arts. Each issue contains five or six articles on topics such as South American perspectives on comparative American Studies, wealth in American culture and trans-Pacific globalization. Since literature is a focus of this publication, some articles cover comparative themes in the works of writers such as Edith Wharton, Robert Frank, and Charles W. Chesnutt. More scholarly than *American Studies International*, this journal is a welcome addition to the field of American Studies publications.

2045. *Configurations: a journal of literature, science and technology.* [ISSN: 1063-1801] 1993. 3x/yr. USD 88 (Individuals, USD 33). Ed(s): T Hugh Crawford, James J Bono. Johns Hopkins University Press, Journals Publishing Division, 2715 N Charles St, Baltimore, MD 21218-4363; http://www.press.jhu.edu/. Illus. Sample. Refereed. Circ: 781. Vol. ends: Fall. Online: EBSCO Publishing; OCLC Online Computer Library Center, Inc.; Project MUSE; RoweCom Information Quest; Swets Blackwell. Reprint: PSC. *Indexed:* ArtHuCI, BEL&L, HumInd, IBZ, L&LBA, RI-1, SSCI, SociolAb. *Bk. rev.:* 2-3, 500-1,000 words. *Aud.:* Ac.

As the official journal of the Society for Literature and Science, this publication's focus is cultural studies of scientific knowledge. Published in cooperation with the Georgia Institute of Technology, "the journal explores the relations of literature and the arts to the sciences and technology." Each issue includes research articles plus review essays and/or book reviews. Individual articles investigate topics ranging from philosophy to medical science to virtual reality. Recent special issues cover such themes as cultural history after Foucault and the writings of Michel Serres. Especially valuable are the bibliographies of recent works in literature, science, and technology. For academic collections with an emphasis on cross-disciplinary studies. Full text of issues from 1993 to the present is available through Project Muse.

2046. *Critical Inquiry.* [ISSN: 0093-1896] 1974. q. USD 165 print & online eds. (Individuals, USD 42 print & online eds.; Students, USD 28 print & online eds.). Ed(s): W J T Mitchell. University of Chicago Press, Journals Division, PO Box 37005, Chicago, IL 60637; subscriptions@press.uchicago.edu; http://www.journals.uchicago.edu. Illus., index, adv. Refereed. Circ: 2700. Vol. ends: Summer. Microform: PMC; PQC. Online: EBSCO Publishing; Florida Center for Library Automation; Gale Group; ProQuest Information & Learning. Reprint: ISI; PQC; PSC. *Indexed:* ABM, ABS&EES, AmHI, ArtHuCI, BEL&L, BHA, FLI, HumInd, IBZ, LRI, MLA-IB, MRD, PSA, PhilInd, RILM, SSCI, SociolAb. *Aud.:* Ac.

Critical Inquiry uses the art of criticism to explore a wide range of issues in the humanities and social sciences. Each issue includes six to eight articles on topics from the arts, philosophy, literature, film, history, politics, and social issues. Recent issues include articles on subjects ranging from Viking America to abstract art and from pragmatism and character to lesbian and gay taxonomies. Some issues include a "Critical Responses" section in which contributors react to earlier articles or continue the debate on previous topics. Some volumes include a special issue on a single topic or specific author. Contents and excerpts from the latest years of the journal are available on the University of Chicago web site. The full text of selected articles is available through EBSCO databases. The major interdisciplinary criticism journal for academic libraries.

2047. *Critical Review (Columbus): an interdisciplinary journal of politics and society.* [ISSN: 0891-3811] 1987. q. USD 64 (Individuals, USD 29; Students, USD 15). Ed(s): Jeffrey Friedman. Critical Review Foundation, Inc., PO Box 8306, Columbus, OH 43201; info@criticalreview.com; http://www.criticalreview.com. Illus., index, adv. Refereed. Circ: 2000 Paid. Vol. ends: Fall. Microform: PQC. Online: Northern Light Technology, Inc.; ProQuest Information & Learning. Reprint: PQC. *Indexed:* AmH&L, ArtHuCI, BRI, IBSS, IPSA, JEL, L&LBA, PAIS, PSA, PhilInd, SSCI, SociolAb. *Bk. rev.:* 1-3, review essays in some issues. *Aud.:* Ac.

Originally a libertarian journal, *Critical Review* has broadened its focus over the years, and now focuses on "understanding the nature, politics, and history of modern states and societies, and especially to evaluate their effects on human well-being." Contributors are primarily from U.S. academic circles, with a few authors from other countries. Articles are theoretical or historical but do not advocate or criticize policies. Most issues concentrate on a particular theme, such as globalization or state autonomy. Each issue contains four or five research articles or essays, well written and extensively documented. Articles explore topics such as free markets and the Asian crisis, Marxist state theory, and the manipulation of ethnic identity by the state. One or more review essays are included in most issues. The journal's web site includes tables of contents for all issues and summaries of articles from recent years. An important supplementary title for major collections, especially those supporting research in economics and political science.

2048. *Cross-Cultural Research: the journal of comparative social science.* Former titles (until 1993): *Behavior Science Research; Behavior Science Notes.* [ISSN: 1069-3971] 1966. q. GBP 284 in Europe, Middle East, Africa & Australasia. Ed(s): Melvin Ember. Sage Publications, Inc., 2455 Teller Rd, Thousand Oaks, CA 91320; info@sagepub.com; http://www.sagepub.com. Illus., index, adv. Refereed. Circ: 500. Vol. ends: Nov. Microform: PQC. Online: Gale Group; ingenta.com; OCLC Online Computer Library Center, Inc.; ProQuest Information & Learning; RoweCom Information Quest; Swets Blackwell. Reprint: PQC. *Indexed:* ABS&EES, AICP, AbAn, AgeL, AnthLit, BAS, CJA, HRA, IBSS, IBZ, IMFL, IPSA, L&LBA, PRA, PSA, PsycholAb, SSCI, SSI, SociolAb. *Aud.:* Ac.

This is the official journal of the Society for Cross-Cultural Research and is sponsored by Human Relations Area Files, Inc. The journal aims to publish comparative studies from all areas of the social and behavioral sciences. It stresses the methodology of the research and requires that studies include statistical measures linking dependent and independent variables. Recent articles have covered topics such as aggression among children, child care in India, Puerto Rican homelessness, and religion and intragroup cooperation. Occasional special issues are published on themes such as culture-bearing units and the units of culture. *Cross-Cultural Research* is available in full text through OCLC Electronic Collections Online (ECO). Full text of selected articles also is available in EBSCO databases. The technical writing style of this journal will appeal most to researchers and scholars.

2049. *Cultural Critique: an international journal of cultural studies.* [ISSN: 0882-4371] 1985. 3x/yr. USD 78 (Individuals, USD 30). Ed(s): Keya Ganguly, John Mowitt. University of Minnesota Press, 111 Third Ave S, Ste 290, Minneapolis, MN 55401-2520. Illus., index, adv. Sample. Refereed. Circ: 700. Vol. ends: Oct. Microform: PQC. Online: OCLC Online Computer Library Center, Inc.; Project MUSE; RoweCom Information Quest; Swets Blackwell. *Indexed:* AltPI, ArtHuCI, FLI, IPSA, MLA-IB, PSA, RI-1, SSCI, SociolAb. *Aud.:* Ac.

Cultural Critique offers an international and interdisciplinary forum to explore "intellectual controversies, trends, and issues in culture, theory and politics." Most issues are devoted to a single topic, such as the politics of impeachment, Eurocentrism, theories of modernity, or globalization. Other issues publish articles on two or three major subjects, such as the masses and media, psychoanalysis and cultural studies, and critical theory in Latin American cultural studies. Some articles involve literary criticism, while others focus on sociological, anthropological, and philosophical issues. Both historical topics and contemporary social and aesthetic studies are included. Recent articles cover such subjects as Latino poetic method, traumatic shame, and virtual empires. International in scope, this journal offers excellent coverage of race, class, and gender issues. Most contributors are scholars from U.S. institutions, although some international writers and researchers are included. Full text of this journal is available through Project Muse. An important title for major academic collections.

2050. *Cultural Studies.* [ISSN: 0950-2386] 1987. bi-m. GBP 288 (Individuals, GBP 50). Ed(s): Lawrence Grossberg, Della Pollock. Routledge, info@routledge.co.uk; http://www.routledge.com. Illus., adv. Refereed. Circ: 1650. Vol. ends: Oct. Online: EBSCO Publishing; Gale Group;

Ingenta Select; OCLC Online Computer Library Center, Inc.; RoweCom Information Quest; Swets Blackwell. Reprint: PSC. *Indexed:* ASSIA, AltPI, ArtHuCI, BrHumI, CommAb, HumInd, IBSS, PRA, PSA, RI-1, SSCI, SWA, SociolAb. *Bk. rev.:* 2-6; essay length. *Aud.:* Ac.

An international publication, *Cultural Studies* provides "a forum for response and strategic discussion of the historically and geographically diverse field of cultural studies." This journal emphasizes race, class, and gender, while addressing major questions of community, identity, agency, and change. Contributors are mainly from the United States, the United Kingdom, and Australia, with occasional articles by authors from other countries. Each issue is composed of six to eight articles; a review section is included in some issues. Frequently, special issues concentrate on single themes such as consumption in Eastern Europe, cultural intermediaries, and Austrian cultural studies. Articles have explored such topics as rap music and Trinidad carnival; and immigration, national identity, and transnationalism. The full-text electronic version of *Cultural Studies* is available via Catchword. Electronic Collections Online (ECO) from OCLC also offers full text of recent issues. For academic collections with extensive international coverage of cultural issues.

2051. ***Cultural Studies - Critical Methodologies.*** [ISSN: 1532-7086] 2001. q. GBP 253 in Europe, Middle East, Africa & Australasia. Ed(s): Norman K Denzin. Sage Publications, Inc., 2455 Teller Rd, Thousand Oaks, CA 91320; info@sagepub.com; http://www.sagepub.com. *Indexed:* PSA, SociolAb. *Aud.:* Ac.

This journal is devoted to the "interdisciplinary analysis of the relationship between cultural studies, cultural critique and interpretive, methodological inquiry." Although "methods talk" is frequently relegated to a lower level in cultural studies, this journal seeks to make methodological practice a major feature. Articles in this publication cover such issues as "local and global, text and context, voice, writing for the other, and the presence of the author in the text." Some issues of *Cultural Studies–Critical Methodologies* deal with a single theme such as 9-11 and its aftermath. Recent articles cover such topics as biography in the social sciences, cultural images of public schooling, and corporate capitalism and political agency. Alternative forms of writing make up much of this publication, including autoethnography, ethnodrama, ethnographic poetry, performance texts, creative nonfiction, and critical, reflexive essays. The full text of articles is available in OCLC's Electronic Collections Online (ECO). This journal fills a gap in cultural studies by providing a methodological focus and by encouraging experimentation with new writing forms.

2052. ***Futures: the journal of forecasting, planning and policy.*** [ISSN: 0016-3287] 1968. 10x/yr. EUR 833 (Qualified personnel, EUR 208). Ed(s): Zia Sardar. Pergamon, The Boulevard, Langford Ln, East Park, Kidlington, OX5 1GB, United Kingdom. Illus., index, adv. Sample. Refereed. Vol. ends: Dec. Microform: PQC. Online: Gale Group; ingenta.com; ScienceDirect; Swets Blackwell. *Indexed:* ABIn, AIAP, ArtHuCI, EngInd, FutSurv, HortAb, InfoSAb, PSA, RRTA, RiskAb, SSCI, SSI, SociolAb, WAE&RSA. *Bk. rev.:* 2-4, 500-1,500 words. *Aud.:* Ac, Sa.

Drawing upon a wide range of disciplines, this journal "seeks to examine possible and alternative futures of all human endeavors." *Futures* has a worldwide advisory board, but authors are mainly American and British scholars, with a sampling from other countries. The papers that begin each issue are international in scope and cover such subjects as Internet access for the rural poor, Caribbean medicinal plant research, robot futures, and the information society. Many volumes include special issues on such themes as learning at work, limits to growth, and sustainable futures. Shorter review articles, essays, and reports are included along with book reviews. The full text of articles is available through Elsevier Science-Direct. A specialized journal for the academic community, as well as business and public policy researchers.

2053. ***Futures Research Quarterly.*** Formerly (until 1985): *World Future Society Bulletin.* [ISSN: 8755-3317] 1967. q. Members, USD 77; Non-members, USD 99. Ed(s): Timothy Mack. World Future Society, 7910 Woodmont Ave, Ste 450, Bethesda, MD 20814; info@wfs.org; http://www.wfs.org/. Illus. Refereed. Circ: 1700. Microform: PQC. *Indexed:* CIJE, FutSurv. *Bk. rev.:* 3-8, 300-1,000 words. *Aud.:* Ga, Ac.

Futures Research Quarterly is a scholarly publication of the World Future Society. Published in cooperation with the Institute for Technology Assessment, the focus of this journal is on both applications of futures research and theory and methodology. The role of futures research in long-range planning and overall decision making is also a central aim of this publication. Each issue includes scholarly articles on such topics as corporate intranets, the future of racism, technology forecasting, and sustainable communities. Contributors are primarily from colleges and universities and research institutes. The writing is scholarly and engaging, appealing to academics as well as laypersons with an interest in future studies. The World Future Society web site includes basic information and contents of recent issues.

2054. ***Futurics: a quarterly journal of futures research.*** [ISSN: 0164-1220] 1976. q. USD 65 in North America; USD 82 elsewhere. Ed(s): Earl C Joseph. Minnesota Futurists, 365 Summit Ave., St. Paul, MN 55102; josep027@tc.umn.edu; ejoseph@waldenu.edu. Illus., adv. Refereed. Circ: 300. Vol. ends: Oct/Dec. Microform: PQC. Online: Northern Light Technology, Inc.; ProQuest Information & Learning. Reprint: PQC. *Indexed:* FutSurv. *Bk. rev.:* 2-6, 250-500 words. *Aud.:* Ga, Ac.

Futurics is published by the Minnesota chapter of the World Future Society. The aim of the journal is to "facilitate communication between researchers and writers who are interested in the exploration of alternative futures." It includes full-length articles, responses to articles, short notes, reviews of books and films, and information on recent developments in futures research. Articles cover such topics as wireless telecommunications, electronic marketing, management of privacy in electronic information systems, and the future of health care and computer technology. Most contributors are academics from selected institutions in the metropolitan Minneapolis area. Many of the articles are reviews of the literature on a specific topic rather than empirical research. This journal will be of greatest interest to libraries in the state of Minnesota and the upper Midwest. An optional title for libraries with heavy interest in futures studies.

2055. ***The Futurist: a journal of forecasts, trends, and ideas about the future.*** [ISSN: 0016-3317] 1967. bi-m. USD 55 & institutions Free to members. Ed(s): Cynthia G Wagner, Edward S Cornish. World Future Society, 7910 Woodmont Ave, Ste 450, Bethesda, MD 20814; info@wfs.org; http://www.wfs.org/. Illus., index, adv. Refereed. Circ: 30000 Paid and controlled. Vol. ends: Dec. Microform: PQC. Online: The Dialog Corporation; EBSCO Publishing; Florida Center for Library Automation; Gale Group; Northern Light Technology, Inc.; OCLC Online Computer Library Center, Inc.; ProQuest Information & Learning; H.W. Wilson. Reprint: PQC. *Indexed:* ABIn, AgeL, ArtHuCI, BRI, CBRI, CIJE, CPerI, EIP, EnvAb, FutSurv, MagInd, RGPR, RI-1, SSCI, SSI. *Bk. rev.:* 1-3, 400-1,000 words. *Aud.:* Hs, Ga, Ac.

A popular publication of the World Future Society, *The Futurist* will appeal to many levels of readers in public, academic, and high school libraries. Each issue includes half a dozen well-written, illustrated articles on such topics as human cloning, extraterrestrial intelligence, space tourism, and wearable computers. Articles are contributed by well-known researchers and writers on the future. The "World Trends and Forecasts" section offers brief reports on trends in government, economics, and demography, as well as technology, the environment, and society. "Tomorrow in Brief" presents notices, comments, and news items, some of which are gleaned from other publications. "Future View," a one-page opinion piece, concludes each issue. A special "Outlook" section of compiled forecasts is featured in each year's final issue. The World Future Society web site contains contents from recent issues of *The Futurist.* The full text of selected articles is available in EBSCO and OCLC databases. Highly recommended.

Gender & Society. See Women: Feminist and Special Interest/Feminist and Women's Studies section.

2056. ***History of the Human Sciences.*** [ISSN: 0952-6951] 1988. q. GBP 411 in Europe, Middle East, Africa & Australasia. Ed(s): Irving Velody, James Good. Sage Publications Ltd., 6 Bonhill St, London, EC2A 4PU, United Kingdom; info@sagepub.co.uk; http://www.sagepub.co.uk/. Illus., index, adv. Refereed. Circ: 750. Vol. ends: Nov. *Indexed:* ASSIA, AmH&L, ArtHuCI, BrHumI, IBSS, IBZ, IPB, IPSA, PSA, PhilInd, SCI, SSCI, SSI, SociolAb. *Bk. rev.:* 1-2, essay length. *Aud.:* Ac.

This journal "promotes research on a broad range of disciplines covered by the human sciences." It aims to link research from traditional social science disciplines, including sociology, psychology, anthropology, and political science, with the areas of philosophy, literary criticism, art history, linguistics, psychoanalysis, aesthetics, and law. Some issues focus on one theme, such as the historical imagination, rhetoric and science, or politics and modernity. Other issues cover a range of topics, such as authenticity and historic preservation, repression and recovered memory, and intellectual and cultural history. Review articles are often included. Most contributors are academics from British, European, and U.S. institutions. The full text of articles is available from OCLC Electronic Collections Online (ECO). For history and social science collections in larger academic libraries.

2057. *Humanities: the magazine of the national endowment for the humanities.* [ISSN: 0018-7526] 1980. bi-m. USD 24. Ed(s): Mary Lou Beatty. U.S. National Endowment for the Humanities, 1100 Pennsylvania Ave, N W, Washington, DC 20506; publications@neh.gov; http://www.neh.gov/publications/index.html. Illus., index. Sample. Circ: 12000. Vol. ends: Nov/Dec. Microform: PQC. Online: EBSCO Publishing; Northern Light Technology, Inc.; OCLC Online Computer Library Center, Inc.; ProQuest Information & Learning; H.W. Wilson. *Indexed:* CIJE, FLI, HumInd, IUSGP, RI-1, RRTA. *Aud.:* Hs, Ga, Ac.

The National Endowment for the Humanities (NEH) issues this publication featuring articles on history, literature, music, art, film, and material culture. Contributors are academics, freelance writers, and NEH staff and administrators. Many issues feature one or more sections on specific topics, such as the digital revolution, American music, the Civil War, and profiles of famous people. A section labeled "Around the Nation" describes exhibits, lectures, festivals, and programs sponsored by state humanities councils. The "Calendar" section describes and pictures current endowment-sponsored exhibitions. The "Deadlines" page lists NEH grants, fellowships, seminars, etc., with application dates. The NEH web site offers selected articles and contents from *Humanities.* The full text of selected articles also is available through EBSCO databases. This publication will appeal to a range of readers from high school students to the general public.

2058. *International Journal of Politics, Culture, and Society.* Formerly: *International Journal of Politics, Culture, and State.* [ISSN: 0891-4486] 1987. q. USD 568 print or online ed. Ed(s): Arthur J Vidich. Kluwer Academic / Plenum Publishers, 233 Spring St Fl 7, New York, NY 10013-1522; http://www.wkap.nl/. Illus., index, adv. Refereed. Circ: 500. Vol. ends: Summer. Microform: PQC. Online: EBSCO Publishing; ingenta.com; Kluwer Online; OCLC Online Computer Library Center, Inc.; RoweCom Information Quest; Swets Blackwell. *Indexed:* IBSS, IMFL, IPSA, PAIS, PSA, RiskAb, SSI, SWR&A, SociolAb. *Bk. rev.:* essay length, in some issues. *Aud.:* Ac.

This interdisciplinary and international journal explores issues "that arise at the intersections of nations, states, civil societies, global institutions and processes." Each issue includes essays and research articles on one or more themes. Recent articles have covered issues such as consumerism as a civilizing process, art in postmodernity, the cultural cold war, and Colombian politics and society. Some issues include essay-length book reviews or a review and commentary section. The journal has contributors from many countries and frequently discusses political and social issues in the context of a particular nation or region. The publisher's web site includes basic information and contents from recent issues. Full text is available through Kluwer Online. For comprehensive academic collections.

2059. *International Review of Social History.* Formerly (until 1956): *International Institute for Social History. Bulletin.* [ISSN: 0020-8590] 1937. 3x/yr. USD 148 (Individuals, USD 64). Ed(s): Marcel van der Linden. Cambridge University Press, The Edinburgh Bldg, Shaftesbury Rd, Cambridge, CB2 2RU, United Kingdom; information@cambridge.org; http://uk.cambridge.org/journals. Adv. Refereed. Microform: PQC. Online: EBSCO Publishing; Gale Group; OCLC Online Computer Library Center, Inc.; RoweCom Information Quest; Swets Blackwell. *Indexed:* AmH&L, ArtHuCI, IBSS, IBZ, IPSA, PSA, SSCI, SSI, SWA, SociolAb. *Bk. rev.:* 8-12, 1,000 words, some essay length. *Aud.:* Ac.

Issued by the International Institute for Social History, this journal's contributors are mainly from American and British institutions, with some from European countries. The research articles that begin each issue cover a range of countries, usually Britain, the United States, or European states, but also Latin America, India, Nigeria, and New Zealand. Many articles explore issues of workers' groups and labor history, but other topics such as migration, social mobility, and marriage and household formation also appear. Without doubt, a major section of this journal is its extensive annotated bibliography. Usually covering some 30 pages, the bibliography begins with a general section and is then subdivided by continent and country. Annual supplements have concentrated on such subjects as the categories of race, class, gender, and ethnicity, and household strategies for survival. Articles are in English, with some reviews in French or German. The full text of recent issues is available both through Cambridge Journals Online and OCLC Electronic Collections Online (ECO). Recommended for history collections.

2060. *International Social Science Journal.* [ISSN: 0020-8701] 1949. q. GBP 115 print & online eds. Ed(s): David Makinson, John Crowley. Blackwell Publishing Ltd., 9600 Garsington Rd, PO Box 805, Oxford, OX4 2DQ, United Kingdom; customerservices@oxon.blackwellpublishing.com; http://www.blackwellpublishing.com/. Illus., index, adv. Sample. Refereed. Circ: 4500. Vol. ends: Dec. Microform: MIM; PQC. Online: East View Publications, Inc.; EBSCO Publishing; Gale Group; ingenta.com; OCLC Online Computer Library Center, Inc.; RoweCom Information Quest; Swets Blackwell. Reprint: PQC; PSC. *Indexed:* ABCPolSci, AICP, ASSIA, AbAn, AgeL, AmH&L, ArtHuCI, BAS, CIJE, CJA, ExcerpMed, FutSurv, GeoRef, IBSS, IPSA, MLA-IB, PAIS, PRA, PSA, PsycholAb, RRTA, SFSA, SSCI, SSI, SWA, SociolAb, WAE&RSA. *Aud.:* Ga, Ac.

Issued for the United Nations Educational, Social and Cultural Organization (UNESCO), this is truly an international journal. It is published in six languages (French, Spanish, Chinese, Arabic, English, and Russian), and the contributors to the journal are drawn from many countries. Each issue is devoted to a single topic such as changing roles of the state, youth in transition, international migration, or federalism. Eight to ten articles explore regional and worldwide issues related to the overall theme. Occasionally, other sections are included. "Continuing Debate" follows up on previous articles or presents contrasting views on major questions. "Social Science Sphere" offers articles on the social sciences as a whole, concentrating on interdisciplinary aspects. "Open Forum" presents shorter articles on topics other than the theme of the issue. The journal's web site offers full text (in Spanish only) of issues from the past several years. Full text of articles also is available through OCLC Electronic Collections Online (ECO). A journal with wide appeal for those interested in global concerns.

2061. *Journal of Aesthetic Education.* [ISSN: 0021-8510] 1966. q. USD 65 (Individuals, USD 40; USD 14 newsstand/cover per issue). Ed(s): Pradeep A. Dhillon. University of Illinois Press, 1325 S Oak St, Champaign, IL 61820-6903; http://www.press.uillinois.edu. Illus., index, adv. Refereed. Circ: 1100 Paid. Vol. ends: Winter. Microform: MIM; PQC. Online: Northern Light Technology, Inc.; Project MUSE; ProQuest Information & Learning. Reprint: PQC. *Indexed:* ABM, ArtHuCI, ArtInd, BAS, BEL&L, BHA, BRI, CBRI, CIJE, EduInd, FLI, HumInd, IBZ, PhilInd, PsycholAb, RILM, SSCI. *Bk. rev.:* 3-5, 500-1,500 words. *Aud.:* Ac.

This journal provides a forum to explore issues in aesthetic education, both in instructional settings and in society at large. Contributors cover issues of aesthetics and public policy, cultural administration, arts and humanities instruction, aesthetics and new communications media, and the art of teaching and learning. Each issue includes articles on theory and philosophy and analyses of specific works in literature, art, or music. Recent issues feature articles on such topics as music and autism, critical thinking and artistic creation, instruction in visual art, and the dancer's role in the art of dance. Some issues contain commentary sections with brief essays or responses to earlier articles. The publisher's web site includes a brief description of the journal along with contents from recent issues. An important publication for educators, writers, and artists, and for those administering cultural programs and arts instruction.

2062. ***Journal of Aesthetics and Art Criticism.*** [ISSN: 0021-8529] 1941. q. USD 136 print & online eds. Blackwell Publishing, Inc., Commerce Place, 350 Main St, Malden, MA 02148; subscrip@blackwellpub.com; http://www.blackwellpublishing.com. Illus., index, adv. Refereed. Circ: 2500. Vol. ends: Fall. Microform: MIM; PQC. Online: Gale Group; ingenta.com; RoweCom Information Quest; Swets Blackwell. Reprint: PQC. *Indexed:* ABM, ABS&EES, AIAP, ArtHuCI, ArtInd, BAS, BHA, BRD, BRI, CBRI, FLI, HumInd, IBZ, IIMP, IIPA, IPB, MLA-IB, MusicInd, PhilInd, PsycholAb, RILM, SSCI. *Bk. rev.:* 7-15, 1,000-2,000 words. *Aud.:* Ac.

This is the official journal of the American Society for Aesthetics. Most issues include six to eight research articles along with a lengthy section of book reviews. Articles cover theoretical and philosophical research on aesthetics as well as critical analyses of specific works and artists, historical treatment of the arts, and social and political questions related to aesthetics. Most issues include a variety of topics, such as documentary photographs, art forgery, identifying with metaphor, and rock art aesthetics. Occasional special issues or symposia are published covering one theme, such as improvisation in the arts, or historicity of the eye. The journal's web site includes general information and table of contents listings. A very scholarly publication of interest to philosophers and artists, but with broader appeal to many scholars in the humanities. For large academic collections.

2063. ***Journal of American Ethnic History.*** [ISSN: 0278-5927] 1981. q. USD 100 (Individuals, USD 30). Ed(s): Ronald H Bayor. Transaction Publishers, 35 Berrue Circle, Rutgers University, Piscataway, NJ 08854-8042; trans@transactionpub.com; http://www.transactionpub.com. Illus., index, adv. Refereed. Circ: 900. Vol. ends: Summer (No. 4). Microform: PQC. Online: bigchalk; Chadwyck-Healey Incorporated; EBSCO Publishing; Florida Center for Library Automation; Gale Group; Ingenta Select; Northern Light Technology, Inc.; OCLC Online Computer Library Center, Inc.; ProQuest Information & Learning. Reprint: PQC; PSC. *Indexed:* ABS&EES, AbAn, AmH&L, ArtHuCI, BAS, HumInd, IBZ, IIBP, IMFL, PSA, RI-1, SSCI, SociolAb. *Bk. rev.:* 15-25; 300-500 words. *Aud.:* Ga, Ac.

As the official journal of the Immigration and Ethnic History Society, this publication is devoted to the history of North American immigration, ethnicity, and race. Each issue contains research articles, research comments, review essays, and book reviews. The journal covers many social and cultural aspects of immigration and ethnicity, including the migration process, adjustment and assimilation, group identity and group relations, mobility, politics, and culture. Articles cover such topics as integration of Brooklyn schools, black union members in Chicago's stockyards, loss of immigrant identity, marriage of Chinese immigrant women, and the rise of Tejano music. The web site for this journal includes general information along with contents of recent issues. Print subscribers receive free online access through Catchword. Selected full-text articles from this journal are available through EBSCO and OCLC databases. Although published primarily for the academic community, this journal may also appeal to genealogists and others interested in ethnic groups in the United States.

2064. ***Journal of American Studies.*** Formerly (until 1967): *British Association for American Studies. Bulletin.* [ISSN: 0021-8758] 1967. 3x/yr. USD 186 (Individuals, USD 72). Ed(s): Susan Castillo, S. Jay Kleinberg. Cambridge University Press, The Edinburgh Bldg, Shaftesbury Rd, Cambridge, CB2 2RU, United Kingdom; information@cambridge.org; http://uk.cambridge.org/journals. Illus., index, adv. Refereed. Vol. ends: Dec. Microform: PQC. Online: EBSCO Publishing; Gale Group; OCLC Online Computer Library Center, Inc.; RoweCom Information Quest; Swets Blackwell. Reprint: PQC; SWZ. *Indexed:* AmH&L, ArtHuCI, BHA, BRI, BrHumI, CBRI, FLI, HumInd, IBSS, IPSA, LRI, MLA-IB, PSA, SSCI, SociolAb. *Bk. rev.:* 30-40, 250-750 words. *Aud.:* Ac.

Sponsored by the British Association for American Studies, this journal covers American literary works, politics, history, and economics, as well as art, music, film, and popular culture. Most contributors are from British universities, although some articles are by U.S. authors. Many articles explore American literary classics or historical topics, but cross-disciplinary and comparative cultural studies are also included. Recent articles cover such topics as race and social control, U.S. currency in the early republic, Latina literature, and slavery in Washington's presidency. Review essays are also a regular feature. Biennially, the journal publishes a list of theses on American Studies in progress or completed at British universities. The full text of recent issues is available both through Cambridge Journals Online and OCLC Electronic Collections Online (ECO). For most academic collections.

2065. ***Journal of British Studies.*** [ISSN: 0021-9371] 1961. q. USD 134 (Individual members, USD 74.50; Non-members, USD 53.50). Ed(s): Nicholas Rogers, James Epstein. University of Chicago Press, Journals Division, PO Box 37005, Chicago, IL 60637; subscriptions@press.uchicago.edu; http://www.journals.uchicago.edu. Illus., index, adv. Refereed. Circ: 2000. Vol. ends: Oct. Microform: PQC. Online: EBSCO Publishing; Florida Center for Library Automation; Gale Group; JSTOR (Web-based Journal Archive); ProQuest Information & Learning. Reprint: PQC; PSC. *Indexed:* AmH&L, ArtHuCI, BrArAb, HumInd, IBSS, LRI, MLA-IB, RI-1, SSCI. *Bk. rev.:* 3-5, essay length. *Aud.:* Ac.

Sponsored by the North American Conference on British Studies, this journal includes research articles and review essays. Articles most often cover British history, politics, economics, religion, law, and demographics, along with gender and cultural studies. Most writing in this journal deals with Great Britain, although some articles focus on areas of the former British Empire. New editors are expanding the scope of the journal to include comparative history, colonial and postcolonial history, and cross-disciplinary studies. Recent articles cover such topics as the Labour Party culture, religion in the early Tudor court, the election of 1900, and marriage discourse in the early eighteenth century. Contents from the latest issues of the journal are available on the University of Chicago Press web site. An important journal for academic collections serving British history scholars.

2066. ***Journal of Popular Culture.*** [ISSN: 0022-3840] 1967. q. USD 132 print & online eds. Ed(s): Gary C Hoppenstand. Blackwell Publishing, Inc., Commerce Place, 350 Main St, Malden, MA 02148; subscrip@blackwellpub.com; http://www.blackwellpublishing.com. Illus., index, adv. Refereed. Circ: 3500. Vol. ends: Spring. Microform: PQC; NRP. Online: bigchalk; Chadwyck-Healey Incorporated; EBSCO Publishing; Florida Center for Library Automation; Gale Group; ingenta.com; Northern Light Technology, Inc.; OCLC Online Computer Library Center, Inc.; ProQuest Information & Learning; H.W. Wilson. Reprint: PQC. *Indexed:* ABS&EES, AmH&L, ArtHuCI, BAS, BEL&L, BHA, BRI, CBRI, CommAb, DAAI, FLI, HumInd, IBSS, IBZ, IIMP, IIPA, MLA-IB, MRD, MusicInd, PRA, RI-1, SFSA, SSCI, SSI. *Bk. rev.:* 15-20, 100-500 words. *Aud.:* Ga, Ac.

This journal is the official publication of the Popular Culture Association and the Popular Culture sections of the Modern Language Association (MLA) and the Midwest MLA. Each issue contains 12 to 15 articles on a wide variety of topics ranging from cowboy music to television shows to romance novels to roller coasters. In addition to its interdisciplinary coverage of U.S. culture, the *Journal of Popular Culture* also has an international focus. In-depth sections on popular culture in Australia and Africa have been published, along with articles on political cartoons in Singapore, Tokyo's Disneyland, and Mexican television programming. The publisher's web site provides a brief description of the journal. The full text of selected articles is available in EBSCO and OCLC databases. As the major U.S. publication on popular culture, this journal is aimed at academics, but it will appeal to many readers beyond the campus. Essential for most libraries.

2067. ***Journal of the History of Ideas: an international quarterly devoted to intellectual history.*** [ISSN: 0022-5037] 1940. q. USD 90 (Individuals, USD 30). Ed(s): Donald R Kelley, Robin Ladrach. Johns Hopkins University Press, Journals Publishing Division, 2715 N Charles St, Baltimore, MD 21218-4363; http://www.press.jhu.edu/. Illus., index, adv. Sample. Refereed. Circ: 2795 Paid. Vol. ends: Oct/Dec. Microform:

PMC; PQC; NRP. Online: EBSCO Publishing; Gale Group; JSTOR (Web-based Journal Archive); OCLC Online Computer Library Center, Inc.; Project MUSE; RoweCom Information Quest; Swets Blackwell. Reprint: PQC; PSC. *Indexed:* AmH&L, ArtHuCI, BAS, BHA, BRI, CBRI, CCMJ, ChemAb, DSR&OA, HumInd, IBSS, IBZ, IPB, IPSA, MLA-IB, MathSciNet, PRA, PSA, PhilInd, RI-1, SSCI. *Aud.:* Ga, Ac, Sa.

This journal aims to explore the "evolution of ideas and their influence on historical developments" in many fields including philosophy, literature, the social sciences, religion, and the arts. Each issue contains eight to ten scholarly articles covering such topics as liberty in nineteenth-century Japan, Schiller's theory of landscape depiction, and the rise of Nazi science. Most articles deal with philosophical writings, historiography, theology, scientific theories, or literary works. Contributors to the journal are academics, mostly historians with some from the fields of philosophy, classics, and literature. This journal is a very scholarly publication with excellent research and writing. The full text of current issues is available through Project Muse. Full text of all older issues is available through JSTOR. For most academic libraries.

Journal of Thought. See Education/General, K-12 section.

2068. ***Knowledge, Technology and Policy: the international journal of knowledge transfer and utilization.*** Former titles (until 1998): *Knowledge and Policy;* (until 1991): *Knowledge in Society.* 1988. q. USD 212 (Individuals, USD 76). Ed(s): David Clarke. Transaction Publishers, 35 Berrue Circle, Rutgers University, Piscataway, NJ 08854-8042; trans@transactionpub.com; http://www.transactionpub.com. Illus., index, adv. Refereed. Circ: 400. Vol. ends: Winter. Reprint: PSC. *Indexed:* IBSS, IBZ, IPSA, LISA. *Bk. rev.:* 2-6; 500-1000 words. *Aud.:* Ac, Sa.

Knowlege, Technology and Policy covers technological aspects of how people think, how they organize, access, and use information, and the policy implications of these processes. The journal is aimed at people working in the areas of policy analysis, program evaluation, and technology assessment. Each issue includes four or five articles, book notes, and "Techscope," which contains brief comments on technology issues from e-mail groups or online newsletters. Article topics include standardization/innovation trade-offs, knowledge-based development assistance, and technology and morality. Theme issues are published frequently on such topics as information technology standards, compatibility and infrastructure development, and science wars. Authors are largely academics, along with contributors from business, the government sector, and research institutes. Full text of articles is available through EBSCO. For academic collections, corporate or government libraries.

2069. ***Midwest Quarterly: a journal of contemporary thought.*** [ISSN: 0026-3451] 1961. q. USD 15 domestic; USD 20 foreign; USD 5 newsstand/cover per issue. Ed(s): James B M Schick. Pittsburg State University, Midwest Quarterly, Pittsburg, KS 66762. Index. Refereed. Circ: 570 Paid. Vol. ends: Summer. Microform: PQC. Online: EBSCO Publishing; Florida Center for Library Automation; Gale Group; Northern Light Technology, Inc.; OCLC Online Computer Library Center, Inc.; ProQuest Information & Learning; H.W. Wilson. *Indexed:* AmH&L, ArtHuCI, BAS, HumInd, IAPV, IBZ, LRI, MLA-IB, PAIS, RI-1, SSCI. *Bk. rev.:* 2-5, 500-750. *Aud.:* Ac.

This regional journal differs from other such publications in both focus and content. Reaching well beyond the Midwest, the quarterly focuses on "analytical and speculative treatment of its topics, rather than heavily documented research studies." Each issue includes articles analyzing specific literary works and themes and discussions of historical and political issues. Recent articles explore the writings of Herman Melville, Socrates, Virginia Woolf, and Raymond Carver. Other articles cover such subjects as assimilation of immigrants, race and genealogy, and Europe's neutral nations. A unique feature is the inclusion of several poems in each issue from both freelance writers and scholars. Full text of selected articles is available in EBSCO and OCLC databases. For comprehensive academic collections.

2070. ***Modernism/Modernity.*** [ISSN: 1071-6068] 1994. q. USD 115 (Individuals, USD 40). Ed(s): Robert von Hallberg, Lawrence Rainey. Johns Hopkins University Press, Journals Publishing Division, 2715 N Charles St, Baltimore, MD 21218-4363; http://www.press.jhu.edu/. Illus., index, adv. Refereed. Circ: 637. Vol. ends: Sep. Online: EBSCO Publishing; OCLC Online Computer Library Center, Inc.; Project MUSE; ProQuest Information & Learning; RoweCom Information Quest; Swets Blackwell. *Indexed:* ABM, AmH&L, AmHI, ArtHuCI, ArtInd, BEL&L, HumInd, MLA-IB, PSA, SociolAb. *Bk. rev.:* 10-20, 500-1,500 words. *Aud.:* Ac.

As the official journal of the Modernist Studies Association, the aim of *Modernism/Modernity* is to explore the arts in "their social, political, cultural and intellectual contexts from the late nineteenth through the mid-twentieth century." This journal combines the writings, theories, and methodology of modernist studies. Coverage is international and cross-disciplinary, encompassing the social sciences and humanities. Some articles are devoted to modernist writers, including Virginia Woolf, James Joyce, Marcel Proust, and T. S. Eliot. Other articles cover art, music, theater, philosophy, and politics. The writing is scholarly and well documented but also engaging and very appealing to a range of readers. The full text of issues from 1994 to the present is available through Project Muse. A good addition to most academic libraries.

2071. ***New Formations: a journal of culture/theory/politics.*** [ISSN: 0950-2378] 1987. 3x/yr. GBP 125 (Individuals, GBP 40). Ed(s): Scott McCracken. Lawrence & Wishart Ltd, 99a Wallis Rd, London, E9 5LN, United Kingdom; lw@l-w-bks.demon.co.uk; http://www.l-w-bks.co.uk/. Illus., adv. Refereed. Circ: 1500. Vol. ends: Winter. *Indexed:* IBSS, MLA-IB, RI-1. *Bk. rev.:* 2-3; 1,000-3,000 words, plus Book Notes, 2-3, c.500 words. *Aud.:* Ac.

To explore and critically investigate the culture, its ideology, its power structure, and its impact are the aims of this multidisciplinary journal. Each issue includes several articles and essays, many of which focus on one specific theme, such as the future of dialogue, the idea of childhood, or culture in China. Themes are explored from many points of view—political, sociological, literary, or philosophical. Articles range from modern applications of classical philosophy to popular culture essays. *New Formations* provides a fresh perspective on historical and contemporary international culture and politics. The publisher's web site includes basic information along with contents from the last several issues. Recommended for large academic collections.

2072. ***Prospects: an annual of American cultural studies.*** [ISSN: 0361-2333] 1975. a. USD 59. Ed(s): Jack Salzman. Cambridge University Press, The Edinburgh Bldg, Shaftesbury Rd, Cambridge, CB2 2RU, United Kingdom; information@cambridge.org; http://uk.cambridge.org/journals. Illus., index, adv. *Indexed:* AmH&L, BrEdI, MLA-IB, PSA, SociolAb. *Aud.:* Ac.

This annual volume of essays combines research and critical works from many disciplines to explore aspects of American society and the American character. Each volume includes some 15 to 20 lengthy essays, many on literary works or on such writers as Herman Melville, Nathaniel Hawthorne, Ralph Waldo Emerson, and Harriet Beecher Stowe. Other essays explore slave narratives, nineteenth-century novels, modern consumerism, and propaganda. Articles on art, music, and photography are included on such topics as African American music, vaudeville, and race in art. Still other articles relate to historical events and social issues, such as the Quaker legal system, Polish American identity, and Black Power and masculinity. *Prospects* is an excellent yearly volume of essays on American culture.

2073. ***Public Culture: society for transnational cultural studies.*** [ISSN: 0899-2363] 1988. 3x/yr. USD 136 includes online access (Individuals, USD 37 includes online access). Ed(s): Elizabeth A Povinelli. Duke University Press, 905 W Main St, Ste 18 B, Durham, NC 27701; subscriptions@dukeupress.edu; http://www.dukeupress.edu. Illus., index, adv. Refereed. Circ: 1000. Vol. ends: Spring. Online: EBSCO Publishing; Ingenta Select; OCLC Online Computer Library Center, Inc.; Project MUSE; RoweCom Information Quest; Swets Blackwell. Reprint: PSC. *Indexed:* ABS&EES, AICP, AltPI, AnthLit, ArtHuCI, CommAb, FLI, IBSS, IBZ, IPSA, MLA-IB, PSA, RRTA, S&F, SSCI, SociolAb. *Aud.:* Ac.

This publication "provides a forum for the internationalization of cultural studies." *Public Culture* includes research articles and essays on contemporary media and social and political issues. Articles cover such topics as weather and the media, medical care in a Nigerian village, technoculture, and same-sex marriages. Special issues are published frequently on specific themes, such as translation in a global market, reflections on disability, and new imaginaries. Photos, drawings, and paintings often accompany articles. The "artworks" section includes illustrations along with concise reports on film, theater, dance, music, art, or mass media. Full text of *Public Culture* from 1999 to the present is available through Project Muse. A unique publication for academic or large general collections with heavy interest in international media and culture studies.

2074. *Renaissance Quarterly.* Incorporated (1954-1974): *Studies in the Renaissance;* Formerly (until 1967): *Renaissance News.* [ISSN: 0034-4338] 1954. q. USD 80 (Individuals, USD 60). Renaissance Society of America, 365 5th Ave., # 5400, New York, NY 10016-4309; rsa@is.nyu.edu; http://www.r-s-a.org. Illus., index, adv. Refereed. Circ: 3500 Paid. Vol. ends: Winter. Microform: PQC; NRP. Online: bigchalk; Chadwyck-Healey Incorporated; Florida Center for Library Automation; Gale Group; JSTOR (Web-based Journal Archive); Northern Light Technology, Inc.; OCLC Online Computer Library Center, Inc.; ProQuest Information & Learning. Reprint: PSC. *Indexed:* AmH&L, AmHI, ArtHuCI, BEL&L, BHA, BRI, CBRI, HumInd, IBZ, MLA-IB, RI-1, SSCI. *Bk. rev.:* 40-50, 400-500 words. *Aud.:* Ac.

This journal is a must for Renaissance scholars and students. Each issue contains research studies, review essays, and many book reviews. Literary works and themes are the focus of many articles in addition to specialized studies in the arts, religion, or social aspects of the Renaissance. Recent articles cover such topics as geography and empire, social uses of theater, early modern print culture, and physicians in Renaissance culture. Review essays and reviews of individual works make up nearly half of each issue. English-language works predominate, but some titles in French, Italian, etc., are included. As the official publication of the Renaissance Society of America, the journal also includes reports of society meetings. Full text of selected articles is available through OCLC databases; full text of all issues prior to 1999 is available through JSTOR. For larger academic collections.

2075. *Representations.* [ISSN: 0734-6018] 1983. q. USD 168 print & online eds. USD 42 newsstand/cover. University of California Press, Journals Division, 2000 Center St, Ste 303, Berkeley, CA 94704-1223; journals@ucop.edu; http://www.ucpress.edu/journals. Illus., index, adv. Refereed. Circ: 1800. Vol. ends: Fall. Microform: PQC. Online: Gale Group; Ingenta Select. *Indexed:* ABM, AmH&L, AmHI, ArtHuCI, BEL&L, BHA, FLI, MLA-IB, SSCI, SociolAb. *Aud.:* Ac.

This publication is a multidisciplinary journal of interest to many scholars in the humanities and social sciences. Most issues include several articles on a variety of topics, with occasional issues focusing on one particular theme. Many articles analyze aspects of a particular literary or philosophical writing, while other essays examine historical, political, or social issues. Recent articles explore topics ranging from bibliomania in Britain to carnival during the French Revolution. The essays are written in a very engaging style and present a fresh perspective on literary, historical, or social subjects. Occasional special issues focus on such themes as "Philosophies in Time" and "Grounds for Remembering." Most contributors are scholars in English or other areas of the humanities. Full text of earlier issues is available through JSTOR. For comprehensive academic collections.

Sexualities. See Sexuality section.

Social Epistemology. See Philosophy section.

2076. *Social Identities: journal for the study of race, nation and culture.* [ISSN: 1350-4630] 1995. q. GBP 283 (Individuals, GBP 86). Ed(s): Abebe Zegeye, David Theo Goldberg. Carfax Publishing Ltd., 4 Park Sq, Milton Park, Abingdon, OX14 4RN, United Kingdom; enquiry@tandf.co.uk; http://www.tandf.co.uk/. Illus., index, adv. Sample. Refereed. Vol. ends: Dec. Online: EBSCO Publishing; Ingenta Select; OCLC Online Computer Library Center, Inc.; RoweCom Information Quest; Swets Blackwell. Reprint: PSC. *Indexed:* ASSIA, GeogAbPG, IBSS, IPSA, PSA, SWA, SociolAb. *Bk. rev.:* 1-3, essay length. *Aud.:* Ac.

Race, nationality, ethnicity, and cultural issues form the basis of this journal, published in conjunction with the African American Studies department at the University of California at Berkeley. The focus of *Social Identities* is on exploring the cross-disciplinary relationships of race, nationality, and ethnicity, both globally and in specific regions and countries of the world. Given the recent changes in economic and political conditions, this journal seeks to explore the postmodern and postcolonial context of racism and nationalism. Each issue begins with several research papers on topics ranging from race and imprisonment to the Truth and Reconciliation Commission. Special issues are published occasionally on such themes as African cinema and humor in the ancient world. Contributors are mainly from U.S. and South African universities, with some writers from the Middle East and Latin America. Full text of selected articles is available through EBSCO databases. An excellent addition to the journal literature on racial and ethnic cultural studies.

2077. *Social Justice Research.* [ISSN: 0885-7466] 1986. q. EUR 491 print or online ed. Ed(s): Leo Montada, Ronald C Dillehay. Kluwer Academic / Plenum Publishers, 233 Spring St Fl 7, New York, NY 10013-1522; http://www.wkap.nl/. Illus., index, adv. Refereed. Vol. ends: Dec. Microform: PQC. Online: EBSCO Publishing; ingenta.com; Kluwer Online; OCLC Online Computer Library Center, Inc.; Ovid Technologies, Inc.; Swets Blackwell. Reprint: WSH. *Indexed:* ASSIA, BAS, CJA, IBZ, PSA, SociolAb. *Bk. rev.:* 2-3, essay length. *Aud.:* Ac.

Social Justice Research aims to explore "the origins, structures and consequences of justice in human affairs." This publication takes a cross-disciplinary view of justice, covering social science and policy studies nationally and internationally. Each issue includes five or six research studies on the concept of justice as applied to such areas as the value of justice in the workplace, injustice and destructive employee behavior, drug testing and procedural fairness, and equality in the distribution of family inheritance. The articles are well written and thoroughly documented. Contributors are mainly from U.S., Canadian, and European universities. The publisher's web site offers contents and abstracts of recent articles. The full text of this journal is available through Kluwer Online. An important journal, especially for scholars in the fields of law and political science.

2078. *Social Science History.* [ISSN: 0145-5532] 1976. q. USD 95 includes online access (Individuals, USD 60 includes online access). Ed(s): Katherine A Lynch. Duke University Press, 905 W Main St, Ste 18 B, Durham, NC 27701; subscriptions@dukeupress.edu; http://www.dukeupress.edu. Illus., index, adv. Sample. Refereed. Circ: 1500. Vol. ends: Winter. Online: bigchalk; EBSCO Publishing; Ingenta Select; Northern Light Technology, Inc.; OCLC Online Computer Library Center, Inc.; Project MUSE; ProQuest Information & Learning; RoweCom Information Quest; Swets Blackwell. Reprint: PSC; SCH. *Indexed:* ABS&EES, AgeL, AmH&L, ArtHuCI, BAS, CJA, IBSS, IPSA, PSA, SSCI, SUSA, SWA, SociolAb. *Aud.:* Ac.

As the official journal of the Social Science History Association, this publication emphasizes "improving the quality of historical explanation, in teaching and research of relevant theories and methods from the social science disciplines." Research studies focus on the family, demography, economic issues, social classes, the labor force, crime, and poverty. Each issue includes five or six articles on such subjects as economic voting, religion in working-class history, Congress and the welfare state, and jury power in nineteenth-century Chicago. Frequently, an issue is devoted to a single theme, such as the working classes and urban public space or historical geographic information systems. Commentaries and responses on the works of specific authors are also included. Many articles focus on U.S. historical research, but British and European history are also covered. The Social Science History Association web site provides contents and abstracts from the latest issues of the journal. Full text of this journal is available through Project Muse from 1999 to the present. A specialized journal for historians and social scientists.

2079. *Social Science Information: information sur les sciences sociales.* Formerly: *Social Sciences Information - Information sur les Sciences Sociales.* [ISSN: 0539-0184] 1954. q. GBP 313 print & online eds. in Europe, Middle East, Africa & Australasia. Ed(s): Anna Rocha Perazzo, Veronique Campion-Vincent. Sage Publications Ltd., 6 Bonhill St,

London, EC2A 4PU, United Kingdom; info@sagepub.co.uk; http://www.sagepub.co.uk/. Illus., index, adv. Refereed. Vol. ends: Dec. Reprint: PSC. *Indexed:* ABCPolSci, AICP, ASSIA, BAS, HRA, IBSS, IBZ, IPSA, MLA-IB, PSA, PsycholAb, SFSA, SSCI, SociolAb, WAE&RSA. *Aud.:* Ac.

This publication of the International Social Sciences Council "aims to present new areas of research, with special focus on theoretical debates, methodology, and comparative and cross-cultural research." Most issues include eight to ten articles grouped into one of the following sections: anthropology of food, biology and social life, studies of science, theory and methods, or trends and developments. Articles on such subjects as gender inequality, theories of power, incest taboos, and cultural pluralism indicate the range of issues covered by *Social Science Information.* Frequently, special issues or symposia are published on such topics as the future of emotion, speed and social life, and qualitative methods in the study of culture and development. Text is in English or French. The publisher's web site provides an extensive description of the journal and contents from the latest issues. Full text of this journal is available through OCLC Electronic Collections Online (ECO). Strong global coverage of social science research issues.

2080. *The Social Science Journal.* Formerly (until 1976): *Rocky Mountain Social Science Journal.* [ISSN: 0362-3319] 1963. q. EUR 318 (Individuals, EUR 127). Ed(s): D A Freeman. Elsevier Inc., 360 Park Ave. S, New York, NY 10010-1710; usinfo-f@elsevier.com; http://www.elsevier.com. Illus., index, adv. Refereed. Circ: 2000. Vol. ends: Oct. Online: EBSCO Publishing; Florida Center for Library Automation; Gale Group; ingenta.com; Northern Light Technology, Inc.; OCLC Online Computer Library Center, Inc.; ScienceDirect; Swets Blackwell; H.W. Wilson. *Indexed:* ABCPolSci, ABS&EES, AbAn, AgeL, ArtHuCI, CJA, CommAb, IPSA, PAIS, PRA, PSA, PsycholAb, RiskAb, SSCI, SSI, SWA, SWR&A, SociolAb. *Aud.:* Ac.

This journal is the official publication of the Western Social Science Association. Although the organization primarily serves the western United States, the journal's coverage is much more broadly based. The journal publishes research articles, statistical analyses, and case studies covering topics from all social science disciplines. Articles on history, economics, politics, and gender are included, along with coverage of social theories, research methods, and curricular issues. Representative articles have covered such subjects as parental liability laws, women's suffrage in Iowa, tobacco policies in male prisons, and development strategy in Korea. Research notes are also included on such topics as religion and gambling in Las Vegas, tipping and service quality, and racism on college campuses. The full text of selected articles is available through EBSCO and OCLC databases. For comprehensive academic collections.

2081. *Social Science Quarterly.* Formerly: *Southwestern Social Science Quarterly.* [ISSN: 0038-4941] 1920. q. USD 195 print & online eds. Ed(s): Robert Lineberry. Blackwell Publishing, Inc., Commerce Place, 350 Main St, Malden, MA 02148; subscrip@blackwellpub.com; http://www.blackwellpublishing.com. Illus., index, adv. Refereed. Circ: 3000. Vol. ends: Dec. Microform: PQC; NRP. Online: Chadwyck-Healey Incorporated; EBSCO Publishing; Florida Center for Library Automation; Gale Group; ingenta.com; ProQuest Information & Learning; RoweCom Information Quest; Swets Blackwell. Reprint: PQC; PSC; SCH. *Indexed:* ABCPolSci, ABS&EES, ASSIA, AgeL, AmH&L, ArtHuCI, BAS, BRI, CBRI, CIJE, CJA, CommAb, HRA, IBSS, ILP, IMFL, IPSA, JEL, LRI, PAIS, PRA, PSA, PsycholAb, RI-1, SFSA, SSCI, SSI, SUSA, SWA, SociolAb, WAE&RSA. *Bk. rev.:* 10-15, 500 words. *Aud.:* Ga, Ac.

Although *Social Science Quarterly* is the official publication of the Southwestern Social Science Association, this journal stretches well beyond the organization's geographical boundaries. Both editors and contributors are drawn from the full spectrum of U.S. colleges and universities. The journal is aimed at multidisciplinary and public-policy issues, and it includes both theoretical approaches and quantitative research. Each issue contains general-interest articles on such topics as poverty among working families, antigay hate crime, and the Internet and opinion measurement. Another regular section, "Research Notes," includes shorter articles on such topics as term limits, charter schools, and political culture in the United States and Canada. The journal also includes a "Forum" section featuring a major article followed by responses from other scholars in the field. Recent "Forums" have focused on child-parent living arrangements, environmental justice, and the Phillips Curve. Full text of articles is available through EBSCO databases. There is good coverage of contemporary social questions from a research standpoint. For academic libraries, but this title will also appeal to general readers with an interest in social issues.

2082. *Social Science Research: a quarterly journal of social science methodology and quantitative research.* [ISSN: 0049-089X] 1972. q. EUR 596 (Individuals, EUR 129; Students, USD 464). Ed(s): James D Wright. Academic Press, 525 B St, Ste 1900, San Diego, CA 92101-4495; apsubs@acad.com; http://www.academicpress.com. Illus., index, adv. Refereed. Vol. ends: Dec. Online: East View Publications, Inc.; EBSCO Publishing; Gale Group; ingenta.com; OCLC Online Computer Library Center, Inc.; RoweCom Information Quest; ScienceDirect; Swets Blackwell. *Indexed:* ABCPolSci, AgeL, ArtHuCI, BAS, CJA, IBSS, PSA, PsycholAb, RiskAb, SSCI, SSI, SWA, SociolAb. *Aud.:* Ac.

This journal covers quantitative research studies as well as methodologies in all areas of the social sciences. Empirical research is the focus of this publication, especially research that emphasizes cross-disciplinary issues or methods. Each issue offers four to six lengthy articles on such topics as marital assimilation, the gender gap in suicide, race and wealth inequality, child care surveys, and public assistance for immigrants. Contributors are drawn from U.S. colleges and universities, with a good representation from universities abroad and from private research groups. This journal is more research-oriented than other comparable publications, such as *Social Science Journal* or *Social Science Quarterly.* A full-text version of this journal is available through Elsevier Science Direct. Recommended for university collections.

2083. *Social Text: theory, culture, ideology.* [ISSN: 0164-2472] 1979. q. USD 143 includes online access (Individuals, USD 33 includes online access). Ed(s): Michele Sharon-Glassford, Brent Edwards. Duke University Press, 905 W Main St, Ste 18 B, Durham, NC 27701; subscriptions@dukeupress.edu; http://www.dukeupress.edu. Illus., adv. Refereed. Circ: 700. Vol. ends: Winter. Online: EBSCO Publishing; Ingenta Select; JSTOR (Web-based Journal Archive); OCLC Online Computer Library Center, Inc.; Project MUSE; RoweCom Information Quest; Swets Blackwell. Reprint: PSC. *Indexed:* ABS&EES, AltPI, MLA-IB, PSA, RI-1, SociolAb. *Aud.:* Ac.

Cultural and political analysis with an emphasis on "questions of gender, sexuality, race and the environment" is the focus of *Social Text.* The journal is sponsored by the Center for the Critical Analysis of Contemporary Culture at Rutgers University. Contributors are largely U.S. scholars, critics, artists, and writers, although works of international writers are also included. Articles deal with such topics as nuclear weapons, knowledge workers, the African diaspora, and women's legal status in India. Special issues on one theme are common and have covered such subjects as globalization and world secularisms. *Social Text* offers engaging articles on current cultural phenomena and a unique perspective on political and social issues. The full text of recent issues is available through Project Muse.

2084. *Social Theory and Practice: an international and interdisciplinary journal of social philosophy.* [ISSN: 0037-802X] 1970. q. USD 52 (Individuals, USD 28; Students, USD 20). Ed(s): Margaret Dancy, Russell Dancy. Florida State University, Department of Philosophy, 151 Dodd Hall, Tallahassee, FL 32306-1500; journals@mailer.fsu.edu; http://www.fsu.edu/~philo/STP. Illus., index, adv. Sample. Refereed. Circ: 700. Microform: PQC. Online: Chadwyck-Healey Incorporated; EBSCO Publishing; Florida Center for Library Automation; Gale Group; OCLC Online Computer Library Center, Inc.; ProQuest Information & Learning; H.W. Wilson. Reprint: PQC. *Indexed:* ABCPolSci, ABS&EES, ASSIA, IBZ, IPB, IPSA, PRA, PSA, PhilInd, RI-1, SSCI, SSI, SociolAb. *Aud.:* Ac.

The major emphasis of this journal is philosophy, in "social, political, legal, economic, educational and moral" contexts. Articles cover the theories of historical figures in philosophy including Aristotle, Kant, Mill, and Locke, as well as more contemporary theorists such as Rawls, Habermas, and Foucault. Other writings address such controversies as genetic manipulation, liberal education, moral justification, and workplace democracy. Although its subtitle includes the word "international," most contributors are American and

Canadian. The writing is scholarly and encompasses a broad range of the humanities and social sciences as well as public policy issues. The journal's web site provides basic information and contents of recent issues. Full text of selected articles is available through EBSCO and OCLC databases. For college and university collections.

2085. ***Southern Quarterly: a journal of the arts in the South.*** [ISSN: 0038-4496] 1962. q. USD 35 (Individuals, USD 18). Ed(s): Neol Polk. University of Southern Mississippi, 2701 Hardy St, Hattiesburg, MS 39406; lol.norris@usm.edu; http://www.usm.edu. Illus., index, adv. Refereed. Circ: 950. Vol. ends: Summer. Microform: PQC. Online: OCLC Online Computer Library Center, Inc.; ProQuest Information & Learning; H.W. Wilson. Reprint: ISI; PQC. *Indexed:* AmH&L, AmHI, ArtHuCI, BEL&L, FLI, GeoRef, HumInd, MLA-IB, RI-1. *Bk. rev.:* 4-10, 400-1,000 words. *Aud.:* Ga, Ac.

Truly a regional journal, this publication focuses exclusively on the South, specifically on the arts and culture of the region. Each issue presents articles on Southern writers and artists, including interviews, critical analyses of particular works, or themes from Southern literature, music, visual arts, or popular culture. Frequently, special issues or features on one writer or subject are published. Recent special issues focus on Donald Harrington, Robert Hazel, and William Gilmore Simms. Some review essays and bibliographies are included, along with book reviews and occasional film and exhibition reviews. The fall issue of each volume includes a "Bibliography of the Visual Arts and Architecture in the South." The *Southern Quarterly* web site includes basic information about the journal, along with table of contents listings. For academic collections and public libraries with heavy patron interest in the South.

2086. ***Systems Research and Behavioral Science.*** Former titles (until 1997): *Systems Research; International Journal of Systems Research.* [ISSN: 1092-7026] 1984. bi-m. USD 510. Ed(s): Mike C Jackson. John Wiley & Sons Ltd., The Atrium, Southern Gate, Chichester, PO19 8SQ, United Kingdom; customer@wiley.co.uk; http://www.wiley.co.uk. Illus., adv. Sample. Refereed. Vol. ends: No. 4. Microform: PQC. Online: EBSCO Publishing; Florida Center for Library Automation; Gale Group; ScienceDirect; Wiley InterScience. *Indexed:* AgeL, BAS, CompLI, ExcerpMed, IBSS, IPSA, SSCI, SSI. *Bk. rev.:* 5-6, 700-1,000 words, in some issues. *Aud.:* Ac.

Systems Research and Behavioral Science aims to publish theoretical and empirical articles on "new theories, experimental research, and applications relating to all levels of living and non-living systems." The journal has a very broad, interdisciplinary scope, covering systems in society, organizations, and management, as well as systems related to quality of life and values. Each issue includes a half dozen research articles on such topics as competence development and learning organizations, systems hierarchies and management, simulation gaming in policy making, and conceptual tools for delivering systems. Some issues include shorter news items or "Notes and Insights," along with book reviews. The articles, uniformly well written and documented, vary greatly from highly technical studies to more theoretical approaches. Special issues appear frequently on such subjects as designing educational systems, systemic research on competence, or the development of systems thinking in southern Africa. One issue of each volume is devoted to the General Systems Yearbook of the International Society for the Systems Sciences. Contributors are academics or systems researchers from the private sector. The full text of this journal is available online from Wiley Interscience. For specialized libraries or those with extensive collections in systems research.

2087. ***Thesis Eleven: rethinking social and political theory.*** [ISSN: 0725-5136] 1980. q. GBP 317 print & online eds. in Europe, Middle East, Africa & Australasia. Ed(s): Johann P Arnason, Peter Beilha. Sage Publications Ltd., 6 Bonhill St, London, EC2A 4PU, United Kingdom; info@sagepub.co.uk; http://www.sagepub.co.uk/. Illus., index, adv. Sample. Refereed. Vol. ends: Nov. Microform: PQC. Online: ingenta.com; OCLC Online Computer Library Center, Inc.; ProQuest Information & Learning; RoweCom Information Quest; Sage Publications, Inc.; Swets Blackwell. Reprint: PQC. *Indexed:* AltPI, HRA, IBSS, IBZ, IPB, IPSA, PAIS, PSA, SUSA, SociolAb. *Bk. rev.:* 4-6, 1,000-3,000 words. *Aud.:* Ac.

The emphasis of *Thesis Eleven* is on social theory, incorporating both social sciences and liberal arts disciplines, from sociology and politics to philosophy, cultural studies, and literature. "The journal is international and interdisciplinary, with a central focus on theories of society, culture, politics and the understanding of modernity." Issues focus on such themes as civilizations, art and myth, post-Western Europe, and the new age of personality. A small number of research articles make up each issue, along with review essays and book reviews. A "Notes and Discussions" section features shorter essays or responses to previous articles. The publisher's web site provides general information and contents from the last three years. Full text of this journal is available through OCLC Electronic Collections Online (ECO). An optional title for comprehensive academic collections.

Electronic Journals

2088. ***Enculturation.*** [ISSN: 1525-3120] 1997. s-a. Ed(s): Byron Hawk. George Mason University, Department of English, 4400 University Dr, Fairfax, VA 22030-4444; http://www.gmu.edu. *Indexed:* MLA-IB. *Bk. rev.:* 1-2. *Aud.:* Ac.

A unique online publication, *Enculturation* is "devoted to contemporary theorizations of rhetoric, writing and culture." Each issue includes 10 to 12 feature articles, plus reviews of books, films, CDs, and web sites. Some issues cover a variety of topics while others focus on one theme, such as post-digital studies, visual rhetorics, or electronic publishing. Recent articles have centered on such topics as the dream of the mechanical brain, cyberpunk, and bioinformatics. Most contributors are faculty or graduate students in literature or the humanities, although some authors are independent artists and writers. The articles are scholarly yet engaging and will appeal to readers from many disciplines. The journal also includes a "Web-bin" with links to sites on rhetoric, composition, critical theory, postmodern theory, cultural studies, and computers, and to other journals. A substantial contribution to the online literature in cultural studies.

2089. ***Other Voices (Philadelphia): the (e)journal of cultural criticism.*** [ISSN: 1094-2254] 1997. irreg. Free. Ed(s): Vance Bell. Other Voices (Philadelphia), Box 31907, Philadelphia, PA 19104; http://www.othervoices.org/. *Indexed:* MLA-IB. *Bk. rev.:* 1-3, essay length. *Aud.:* Ac.

The focus of *Other Voices* is on cultural criticism in the arts and humanities, including literature, art, film, photography, and music, as well as philosophy and theory. The journal is "dedicated to fostering interdisciplinary dialogues while maintaining respect for the strengths of traditional academic disciplines." Each issue includes scholarly essays, interviews or lectures, reviews of books and exhibitions, and electronic-text projects. Current issues cover a variety of topics, including Holocaust denial, killing in Kosovo, the psychology of uncertainty, and psychosis in a cyberspace age. Occasionally, special issues are published on such themes as genocide, pseudography, literary hoaxes, and forgery. Founded by faculty and students from the University of Pennsylvania, this journal encourages submissions from students and seeks to be a part of the alternative publishing movement in academia. *Other Voices* offers engaging articles, well written and illustrated, along with unique electronic-text projects.

2090. ***Postmodern Culture: an electronic journal of interdisciplinary criticism.*** [ISSN: 1053-1920] 1990. 3x/yr. USD 80. Ed(s): Jim F English, Stuart Marlthrop. Johns Hopkins University Press, Journals Publishing Division, 2715 N Charles St, Baltimore, MD 21218-4363; http://www.press.jhu.edu/. Illus. Refereed. Online: EBSCO Publishing; OCLC Online Computer Library Center, Inc.; Project MUSE; RoweCom Information Quest. *Indexed:* ArtHuCI, BEL&L, HumInd, MLA-IB. *Bk. rev.:* 5-7, essay length. *Aud.:* Ga, Ac.

The focus of *Postmodern Culture* is on the literature, philosophy, art, film, and social issues of the last decades of the twentieth century. Each issue features essays or creative works on such topics as otherness, the prosody of space, and Hong Kong cinema. Essays usually include links between citations in the text and notes at the end of each article. Reviews of films, exhibitions, and performances are included along with book reviews. A "Related Readings" section provides links to other popular-culture sites, collections, journals, newsgroups, and readings. An interactive, annotated "Bibliography of Postmodernism and Critical Theory" is available with each issue. Readers who register with the database may add new items to the bibliography. From its beginnings as one of the first scholarly electronic journals, *Postmodern Culture* continues to combine engaging writing with popular media to explore contemporary literary, philosophical, and social themes. The full text of all issues is available through Project Muse.

2091. ***Standards: the international journal of multicultural studies.*** 1992. a. Standards, http://www.colorado.edu/journals/standards. Illus. *Bk. rev.:* 6-8, 500-1,000 words, in some issues. *Aud.:* Ac, Ga.

In 1995, when *Standards* appeared online, it became the first e-journal for international cultural studies. The editors of this journal interpret multiculturalism very broadly and look beyond race, class, ethnicity, and gender to include physical disability, sexual orientation, and recovery from addiction. "The aim of *Standards* is to engage visual artists, writers and thinkers around the world in an active dialogue on the appearance and effectiveness of cultural and postcultural studies." Each issue is an interesting mix of fiction, poetry, book reviews, essays, interviews, and mixed media. The latest issues have a central theme, such as "Complexities" or "Revolutions." This journal gives an annual "Best of the Small Press Award" to encourage and publicize the works of small publishers. Each issue also includes a series of links to web sites on cultural studies. A unique e-journal that encourages controversy.

■ DANCE

Mary Augusta Thomas, Associate Director, Readers Services and Strategic Planning, Smithsonian Institution Libraries, Washington, DC 20560-0154

Introduction

International dance, along with the growth in popularity for all styles of dance, has changed the content of many dance magazines in the past two years. On stage, more companies perform to bigger audiences than before. The number of dance schools and programs continues to increase while drill teams and dance companies flourish in many communities. Most journals continue to cover well-known companies, but each has its own perspective, and a true student will want to compare and contrast his or her reporting or research.

Journals in dance serve a diverse audience of students, researchers, and dance professionals, as well as the dance audience. To appeal to a wider readership, editors have broadened the types of dance they include by presenting reviews or research on social dancing, stage dancing, and rock and roll. All of us seek guidance to appreciate what we see at performances, whether as entertainment or as an indication of our cultural identity. Many journals have embraced the sense of the universality of dance, without boundaries of technique, venue, and nationality. Since scholars in other disciplines study how dance relates to fields as diverse as archaeology, psychology, sociology, and medicine, dance periodicals have increased their own scope.

The online journals, based on print titles, have grown in both number and quality. The sense of community is strong in most dance magazines and is most evident in the online environment. Dance magazine editors want to build on this connection by encouraging reader interaction and by providing customer services, a trend for online versions in particular.

Basic Periodicals

Ems: *Dance Magazine;* Hs: *Attitude, Dance and the Arts, Dance Magazine, Dance Spirit, Pointe;* Ga: *Dance Magazine, Dance Spirit, Dance Teacher, Dance Today!; The Hedgehog, Pointe;* Ac: *Ballet Review, Ballettanz Dance Chronicle, Dance Now, Dance Research Journal, Dance Theatre Journal, Dancing Times, Pointe;* Sa: *American Journal of Dance Therapy, Dance Research Journal, Dance Teacher, DanceView.*

Basic Abstracts and Indexes

American Bibliography of Slavic and Eastern European Studies, Arts and Humanities Citation Index, Current Contents, Humanities Index, Index to Dance Periodicals, International Index to the Performing Arts, Music Index.

2092. ***American Journal of Dance Therapy.*** Supersedes (in 1977): *American Dance Therapy Association. Monograph.* [ISSN: 0146-3721] 1968. s-a. EUR 309 print or online ed. Ed(s): Anne C Fisher, Joan L Lewins. Kluwer Academic / Plenum Publishers, 233 Spring St Fl 7, New York, NY 10013-1522; kluwer@wkap.com; http://www.wkap.nl/. Illus., index, adv. Sample. Refereed. Online: EBSCO Publishing; ingenta.com; Kluwer Online; OCLC Online Computer Library Center, Inc.; Ovid Technologies, Inc.; RoweCom Information Quest; Swets Blackwell. *Indexed:* AgeL, ArtHuCI, ExcerpMed, IDP, IIPA, PsycholAb, SSCI. *Bk. rev.:* 2-3, 1,000 words. *Aud.:* Ac.

Behavior and movement are closely linked. Essays and original research in this journal reflect the important role of dance and movement in therapeutic practice. Articles present original, scholarly research on the psychology of movement and dance, which is becoming more intertwined with other areas of dance research. As the relationship between movement and psychological health becomes better understood, use of dance in therapy has been steadily growing to deal with physical and mental illness, societal problems like homelessness, and individual personal development. In the past few years, research on dance therapy and its effects has developed, and recent issues deal with how to improve both research and practice. Clinicians and educators in dance therapy serve as journal contributors. This is a good source for administrators, psychiatrists, psychologists, social workers, and creative arts therapists in the disciplines of music, art, and drama.

2093. ***American SquareDance: square dance and round dance.*** Formerly: *Square Dance.* [ISSN: 0091-3383] 1945. m. USD 25 domestic; USD 27.50 Canada; USD 32.50 elsewhere. Ed(s): William Boyd. American Squaredance Magazine, 34 E Main St, Apopka, FL 32703. Illus., adv. Circ: 20000. Microform: PQC. *Bk. rev.:* Occasional, short. *Aud.:* Hs, Ga.

For 55 years, this magazine has covered square dance worldwide. Regular monthly features cover dances and conventions, clubs and venues, a "Callerlab," tips on steps and patterns, notes on travel, events, a calendar of dances, and "Sewing 101." As of May 2003, it was transferred to a new publisher.

2094. ***Attitude: the dancers' magazine.*** [ISSN: 0882-3472] 1982. q. USD 20 domestic; USD 25 in Canada & Mexico; USD 40 elsewhere. Ed(s): Arthur T Wilson. Dance Giant Steps, Inc., 1040 Park Pl, Ste C 5, Brooklyn, NY 11213-1946. Illus., adv. Circ: 2500. Vol. ends: Winter. Online: Chadwyck-Healey Incorporated. *Indexed:* IDP, IIPA. *Bk. rev.:* 5-10, 250-500 words. *Aud.:* Hs, Ga, Ac.

Attitude fills a major need by providing good documentation for contemporary dance and sharp, perceptive criticism of classical dance companies as well. Well-known dance writers, critics, educators, and choreographers contribute both reviews and features, enhanced by quality black-and-white illustrations. There are numerous reviews of video releases, recordings, and books. Recent issues include feature stories on contemporary dance companies and articles about choreographers. Reviews of international dance performances have featured Turkish folk dance and a Mongolian dance festival, along with the Bolshoi Ballet tour of the United States. In addition to contemporary dance, flamenco, tap, jazz, and classical ballet performances are reviewed.

2095. ***Attitudes and Arabesques.*** [ISSN: 0889-8847] 1980. m. USD 35 (Individuals, USD 25). Ed(s): Leslie Getz. Mid-Peninsula Dance Guild, Cultural Center, 1313 Newell Rd, Palo Alto, CA 94303; jogil415@aol.com. Illus., index. Sample. Circ: 248. Vol. ends: Aug. *Indexed:* SportS. *Aud.:* Ac, Sa.

Dance professionals, students of dance, dance historians, and bibliographers rely on editor Leslie Getz to analyze dance periodicals for articles on ballet and modern dance. Each issue provides brief but well-prepared annotations for articles in 30 or more dance periodicals and nonspecialized journals, including the *New Yorker, New Republic,* and *Cambridge Archeological Journal.* Recent listings also contain references to biographies of dancers that appear in *Current Biography* and other reference works. Its photocopy-newsletter appearance aside, this publication should be considered for academic libraries and any good-sized public library collection because it would be impossible to find a substitute. To ensure timeliness, the editor has limited content to periodical articles, brief publication notices for books, and brief conference reports. The books-received section includes mysteries and novels related to dance.

2096. ***Ballet Review.*** [ISSN: 0522-0653] 1965. q. USD 42 (Individuals, USD 23). Ed(s): Francis Mason. Dance Research Foundation, Inc., 37 W 12th St 7J, New York, NY 10011; info@balletreview.com; http://www.balletreview.com. Illus., adv. Circ: 2000 Paid. Microform: PQC. Online: Gale Group. *Indexed:* ABS&EES, ArtHuCI, HumInd, IDP, IIPA. *Bk. rev.:* Various number and length. *Aud.:* Ga, Ac, Sa.

Founded by Arlene Croce, the famed dance critic for the *New Yorker*, this periodical remains central to academic and specialized collections. Not limited to classical ballet alone, recent issues include modern dance and avant-garde companies in reviews written by both researchers and practitioners. Their blend of familiarity and scholarship makes the information accessible and entertaining. The clear, readable, well-researched text, often with unusual historic and contemporary black-and-white photographs and drawings, and the contributions of leading dance historians and critics combine to lend credibility to this journal as a major resource. Topics for the six or seven longer articles include dance history, choreography, trends in dance criticism, biographical features on important dancers, dance music, costume, and company performances. In a recent issue, a former dancer for George Balanchine provides insight into his teaching ideals and methods. This kind of in-depth focus is essential to any student of either the history or performance of dance.

2097. ***Ballettanz: Europe's leading dance magazine.*** Formerly (until 2002): *Ballett International - Tanz Aktuell;* Which was formed by the merger of (1986-1994): *Tanz Aktuell;* (1982-1994): *Ballett International;* Which incorporated (1990-1991): *Tanz International;* (1958-1989): *Tanz.* 1994. m. 11/yr. EUR 99 domestic; EUR 110 in Europe; EUR 115 elsewhere. Ed(s): Arnd Wesemann, Hartmut Regitz. Friedrich Berlin Verlagsgesellschaft mbH, Reinhardtstr 29, Berlin, 10117, Germany; verlag@friedrichberlin.de; http://www.friedrichberlin.de. Illus., adv. Sample. Circ: 15000 Paid. Vol. ends: Dec. *Indexed:* ArtHuCI, IBZ, IDP, IIPA, SSCI. *Bk. rev.:* 2-3 short reviews. *Aud.:* Ac.

Europe's leading dance magazine serves as "a forum for international discussion on the classical ballet and contemporary dance" and appears in German with some English translations. Online readers may choose an English or German web version. The journal's scope includes all of Europe, Eastern Europe, and the Middle East, making it especially valuable for the serious student of dance criticism or history. The editors present features that cross boundaries with themes of general interest, including politics, future planning, and finance, offering an interesting insight into the European arts community. Reviews of all companies performing in a region or country, contemporary as well as classical, are supported by excellent illustrations that serve as a source for researchers. Of all the dance magazines, this is the most visually exciting. Many of the companies featured here will not be profiled elsewhere. The European calendar of performances, auditions, and schools will help those seeking dance careers as well as performances while abroad. For researchers, the calendars will build chronologies for particular works in performance. For any sizable collection, this journal is important for its wide range and contemporary dance perspective.

2098. ***Contact Quarterly: a vehicle for moving ideas.*** [ISSN: 0198-9634] 1975. 2x/yr. USD 25 (Individuals, USD 14). Ed(s): Nancy Stark Smith, Lisa Nelson. Contact Collaborations, Inc., PO Box 603, Northampton, MA 01060. Illus., index, adv. Sample. Circ: 2400. Vol. ends: Fall. *Indexed:* IDP, IIPA. *Bk. rev.:* Number and length vary. *Aud.:* Ac, Sa.

Started over 25 years ago as a journal to cover the then basically unknown field of dance improvisation, *Contact Quarterly* is a sophisticated journal covering all forms of movement improvisation. Substantial and well designed, it may be the only dance performance magazine to deal with a broad range of social issues, including studies on the philosophical and psychological dimensions of movement for all people, including those with mental or physical disabilities. Fiction and poetry are included, along with health and alternative healing, to emphasize the all-encompassing nature of movement. *Contact Quarterly,* one of the few sources of analytical writing about movement as opposed to formal choreography, also provides information on small nontraditional companies, especially those in improvisation. The editors cover worldwide events, festivals, and schools, documenting what teachers of movement improvisation are doing internationally.

2099. ***Dance and the Arts.*** Former titles (until 1995): *Dance Pages Magazine;* (until 1989): *Dance Pages.* 1983. bi-m. USD 18 domestic; USD 30 Canada; USD 36 in Europe. Ed(s): Donna Gianell. Dance Pages, Inc., 1818 20 Amsterdam Ave, New York, NY 10031; http://www.arts-online.com/danceart.htm. Adv. *Indexed:* IDP. *Bk. rev.:* 3-5, short. *Aud.:* Hs, Ga, Ac.

Aimed at both professionals and the public, this journal contains numerous short articles and photographs covering many types of dance in performance. One of its strengths is the inclusion of Broadway musicals and show dancing, which are often overlooked in other dance periodicals. Teachers and students of tap dance, tango, salsa, and other popular dance styles will find regular features that include an events calendar, short news notes from teachers and dance companies, and book and video reviews.

2100. ***Dance Chronicle: studies in dance & the related arts.*** [ISSN: 0147-2526] 1978. 3x/yr. USD 675. Ed(s): George Dorris, Jack Anderson. Marcel Dekker Inc., 270 Madison Ave, New York, NY 10016-0602; journals@dekker.com; http://www.dekker.com. Illus., index, adv. Sample. Circ: 450. Vol. ends: Winter. Microform: RPI. Online: Chadwyck-Healey Incorporated; EBSCO Publishing; Gale Group; OCLC Online Computer Library Center, Inc.; RoweCom Information Quest; Swets Blackwell. *Indexed:* ABS&EES, ArtHuCI, HumInd, IDP, IIPA, MusicInd, PEI. *Bk. rev.:* 3-5 signed, 500-1,000 words. *Aud.:* Ac, Sa.

With topics ranging in time from classical antiquity to Broadway, this is the oldest journal devoted exclusively to the scholarly study of dance and its history. The research included here is essential for serious students of dance history, performance, and criticism. The contents represent the history of all periods and styles of dance and the interplay between dance and music. Detailed research on costuming and staging is also presented. The style is highly polished and readable, with extensive references to sources for further study. Both editors, among the most respected writers in the field, contribute regularly to all the major dance periodicals. Recent issues include a two-issue study of the career of eighteenth-century Italian choreographer Gaetano Grossatesta and a description of perhaps the earliest working version of Petipa's *Giselle.* The profiles of companies and dancers are an especially good source for tracing the development and work of renowned choreographers. Subject experts, established dance historians, and scholars review books in lengthy and carefully supported articles. Contents of several other scholarly dance journals are listed, along with books received. Although it's the highest-priced journal on dance, it must be included in any serious dance collection.

2101. ***Dance Europe.*** 1995. m. GBP 33.50 domestic; GBP 43 in Europe; GBP 55 elsewhere. Ed(s): Emma Manning. Dance Europe, PO Box 12661, London, E5 9TZ, United Kingdom. *Aud.:* Hs, Ga, Ac, Sa.

Dance Europe magazine, founded in 1995, is published monthly in London. The editorial policy aims to provide "unbiased platforms for dance throughout Europe and beyond," and many of the contributors are professional dancers or ex-dancers. Handsomely designed and well illustrated, it covers ballet and modern dance from many of the smaller companies across Europe. Well-written interviews with dancers and choreographers will open access to European trends to U.S. students. Recent issues included flamenco, a subject not well represented in the literature, and reviews of the new Irish dance companies. There are lists of auditions and a performance diary. *Dance Europe* may be the broadest source for European dance that is currently available. The online version at http://www.danceeurope.net includes numerous links to dancers, companies, and festivals.

2102. ***Dance Magazine.*** [ISSN: 0011-6009] 1926. m. USD 34.95; USD 3.95 newsstand/cover per issue. Ed(s): K C Patrick. Dance Magazine, Inc., 111 Myrtle St, Ste 203, Oakland, CA 94607. Illus., index, adv. Sample. Vol. ends: Dec. Microform: PQC. Online: bigchalk; EBSCO Publishing; Florida Center for Library Automation; Gale Group; Northern Light Technology, Inc.; OCLC Online Computer Library Center, Inc.; ProQuest Information & Learning. *Indexed:* ABS&EES, ArtHuCI, BRI, BiogInd, CBRI, FLI, HumInd, IDP, IIPA, MRD, MagInd, PEI, RGPR. *Bk. rev.:* 250-2,500 words. *Aud.:* Ems, Hs, Ga, Ac.

Dance Magazine remains the one journal that any collection, whether general or specific, must include to provide information on current dance performance and education in the United States. Recently given a crisp new look through an attractive redesign, it covers all regions and companies in depth, and its sections on people, events, an annual audition calendar, and even gossip make this a basic tool. As the oldest continuously published dance periodical (more than 75 years) in the country, it attracts leading dance writers from all over the world and is the first magazine consulted by professionals and dance-goers. Because of its painstaking coverage of ballet, modern, and theatrical styles throughout the country, it is required reading for the professional dancer and teacher. Richard Philp, the former editor, is now a regular columnist, as is Clive Barnes, the dean of dance critics, who has written a monthly column since 1958. Each issue contains listings of jobs and schools nationwide. An abbreviated, attractive online version is available.

2103. ***Dance Now.*** [ISSN: 0966-6346] 1992. q. GBP 17.50 domestic; GBP 20 foreign. Ed(s): David Leonard, Allen Robertson. Dance Books Ltd., The Old Bakery, 4 Lenten St, Alton, GU34 1HG, United Kingdom; dl@dancebooks.co.uk; http://www.dancebooks.co.uk. Illus., adv. Circ: 5000 Paid. Vol. ends: Winter. *Indexed:* IDP, IIPA. *Bk. rev.:* 2-3, short. *Aud.:* Ga, Ac.

Britain's liveliest dance magazine continues to present contributions by well-known writers and critics. Their long profiles of dancers and companies, reviews of the season, readable histories of dance in performance, and interviews with dancers, choreographers, and critics meet the needs of students, professional dancers, and the general reader. Recent issues feature an in-depth profile on French ballerina Sylvie Guillem and a retrospective on Merce Cunningham. It is a good source for information on dance in Russia, with regular reviews from the Kirov and other ballet companies.

2104. ***Dance Research Journal.*** Formerly: *C O R D News.* [ISSN: 0149-7677] 1969. s-a. USD 115 (Individuals, USD 65; Students, USD 30). Ed(s): Jill Green, Ann Dils. Congress on Research in Dance, Department of Dance, SUNY, College at Brockport, Brockport, NY 14420; gcarlson@brockport.edu; http://www.cordance.org. Illus., adv. Sample. Refereed. Circ: 850. Vol. ends: Winter. Reprint: ISI. *Indexed:* ABS&EES, ArtHuCI, BRI, CBRI, HumInd, IDP, IIPA, RILM. *Bk. rev.:* 15-20. *Aud.:* Ac.

Dance Research Journal, published by the Congress on Research in Dance for its members, remains one of the best academic journals for dance studies. Written mostly by the best dance historians and critics at major institutions, it presents current research that employs quantitative and qualitative analysis of international dance and related fields. Focused on dance education, articles may include dance studied through deconstruction, ethnography, linguistics, and semiotics. Papers are well documented and usually accompanied by bibliographies. One of the strongest attributes is the book review section, which contains many in-depth reviews that are signed and often accompanied by additional references, making this journal a major source for bibliographic information. A regular feature lists papers of major conferences and descriptions of research collections and archives.

2105. ***Dance Spirit.*** [ISSN: 1094-0588] 1997. 10x/yr. USD 16.95 domestic; USD 28 foreign; USD 3.95 newsstand/cover per issue domestic. Ed(s): Kimberly Gdula. Lifestyle Ventures, LLC, 250 W 57th St, Ste 420, New York, NY 10107; editors@dancespirit.com; http://www.dancespirit.com. Adv. Circ: 85000 Paid and controlled. *Aud.:* Hs, Ga, Ac, Sa.

A well-designed, glossy magazine that covers all forms of dance. Its features are aimed at students of dance, teachers, and professionals from the Broadway stage to the ballet and graduate dance programs. This is the one source to meet the needs of amateurs who are interested in tap dance, swing dance, and ballroom dancing, along with students who are on drill teams. Lifestyle Ventures, the publisher, also produces *American Cheerleader, Dance Spirit In Motion, Dance Teacher,* and *Pointe.*

2106. ***Dance Teacher: the magazine for dance professionals.*** Formerly (until 1999): *Dance Teacher Now.* [ISSN: 1524-4474] 1979. 10x/yr. USD 24.95 United States; USD 38 in Canada & Mexico; USD 48 elsewhere. Ed(s): Julie Davis. Lifestyle Ventures, LLC, 250 W 57th St, Ste 420, New York, NY 10107. Illus., index, adv. Circ: 18000 Paid. *Indexed:* IDP, IIPA. *Bk. rev.:* 5, 250 words. *Aud.:* Ga, Ac.

Dance Teacher, which has been published for more than 20 years, is the only nationwide magazine addressed to dance teachers of all disciplines. Articles on tap, ballroom, and aerobic dance appear along with those on ballet and modern performance. Recent issues include techniques for team competition, health and diet issues for students, and descriptions of competitions. Lifestyle Ventures, the new publisher, is responsible for a string of dance-related publications ranging from ballet to cheerleading and drill teams. Since it covers such a wide range, the content is useful for any student or teacher, grade school through college, not just for the professional. Profiles of dance teaching institutions and curricula development, classified advertising for training courses, and good articles on dance music make this a fine resource for all dance teachers. There is a nice online version at www.dance-teacher.com.

2107. ***Dance Theatre Journal: the voice of dance.*** Formerly (until 1983): *Labanews.* [ISSN: 0264-9160] 1982. q. GBP 17 (Individuals, GBP 15). Ed(s): Ian Bramley. Laban, Creekside, London, SE8 3DZ, United Kingdom; info@laban.org; http://www.laban.org. Illus., index, adv. Circ: 2000. Vol. ends: Dec. *Indexed:* ArtHuCI, IDP, IIPA. *Bk. rev.:* Number and length vary. *Aud.:* Ga, Ac, Sa.

Published by the Laban Centre in London, the preeminent school for dance notation and development, and focused on contemporary dance and dance theater in Europe, especially England, this is a sophisticated journal that aims to both cover dance and foster critical debate among a community of dance intellectuals. *Dance Theatre* incorporates dance, drama, music, and visual art. Interviews and in-depth articles cover the entire setting of dance performances, detailing not only choreography but costumes, sets, lighting, and music. The contents are wide ranging, incorporating long, reflective pieces on such topics as the role of the dramaturge in making art readable for audiences, the choreography of Martha Graham, and the current interest in dance being featured in movies. Extensive footnotes enhance the serious quality of the journal. The articles and reviews encompass ballet, modern dance, and contemporary hybrids, described in a lively fashion for performers, dance writers, and a general audience. Well-written text and visually stimulating black-and-white photographs support the lengthy signed reviews and interviews. A pullout guide provides the national listings for all performances of the season.

2108. ***Dance Today!*** Formerly (until 2001): *Ballroom Dancing Times.* [ISSN: 1475-2336] 1956. m. GBP 16 domestic; GBP 18 foreign; GBP 1.10 newsstand/cover per issue. Ed(s): Sylvia Boerner. Dancing Times Ltd., Clerkenwell House, 45-47 Clerkenwell Green, London, EC1R 0EB, United Kingdom; http://www.dt-ltd.dircon.co.uk. Illus., adv. Vol. ends: Sep. *Indexed:* IDP, IIPA. *Aud.:* Ga, Sa.

In 2001, *Dance Today!* succeeded the venerable *Ballroom Dancing Times.* The new publication is colorful and glossier, has a larger format, and covers a broader area that includes Flamenco, stage musicals, and salsa. For ballroom/social dancers in England, this is the main source for news on national competitions and steps of the winning dances. The most useful sections for general audiences, as well as teachers and judges, are the well-illustrated and -described scripts and sequences performed by competition winners. Tips on how to improve ballroom dancing may benefit any amateur or professional. Recent issues include lists of judges, demonstrators, and teachers, and reviews of compact discs, videos, and tapes.

2109. ***DanceView: a quarterly review of dance.*** Formerly (until 1992): *Washington Danceview.* [ISSN: 1077-0577] 1988. q. USD 20. Ed(s): Alexandra Tomalonis. DanceView, PO Box 34435, Washington, DC 20043. Illus. Vol. ends: Winter. Online: Chadwyck-Healey Incorporated. *Indexed:* IDP, IIPA. *Bk. rev.:* 10, length varies. *Aud.:* Ac, Sa.

DanceView covers companies and dance events worldwide. It includes thoughtful, in-depth interviews with dancers, often conducted by other dancers and dance writers, and reviews of exhibitions and other forms of research on dance and dance history. Its contributors, including Robert Greskovic and Mary Cargill, are professional dance critics who provide analysis of the major companies in the United States, England, and occasionally Russia. Features include regular "Reports" from New York, London, and the Bay Area. In addition, overviews of the season, video reviews, and book reviews make for a complete and satisfying read. A good addition to serious dance collections and to those that serve dance devotees.

2110. ***Dancing Times.*** [ISSN: 0011-605X] 1910. m. GBP 28; GBP 32 foreign; GBP 2.10 newsstand/cover per issue. Ed(s): Mary Clarke. Dancing Times Ltd., Clerkenwell House, 45-47 Clerkenwell Green, London, EC1R 0EB, United Kingdom; http://www.dt-ltd.dircon.co.uk. Illus., adv. Circ: 12000. *Indexed:* ArtHuCI, IDP, IIPA. *Bk. rev.:* 4-5. *Aud.:* Hs, Ga, Ac.

For all types of theatrical dance, and especially for British companies and the season, this remains a primary source. Now in its 92nd year of publication, it is the oldest continuing periodical on dance in existence. Britain continues as a major center for dance performance with a growing audience for contemporary dance, which is fully reflected in *Dancing Times.* Because dance students often study abroad, the coverage of dance schools is especially valuable. Regular sections are devoted to dance on video and television. "Into Dance!" is a regular section for children that makes dance themes more approachable by profiling young dancers and recent ballets like *Toad,* based on the *Wind in the Willows.* Although the emphasis is on education and training, frequent articles about the great companies, their history, and past reviews broaden its usefulness to research collections. In-depth reviews of principal dancers from the major companies continue, along with notes on all the schools, competitions, and awards. There is much to offer U.S. audiences, particularly regular reporting from Russia. Its online version, http://www.dancing-times.co.uk, includes archives and additional information on dance education.

2111. ***Folk Music Journal.*** Supersedes: *English Folk Dance and Song Society. Journal.* [ISSN: 0531-9684] 1965. a. GBP 7.50 per issue. Ed(s): Michael Heaney. English Folk Dance and Song Society, Cecil Sharp House, 2 Regents Park Rd, London, NW1 7AY, United Kingdom; efdss@efdss.org; http://www.efdss.org. Illus., index, adv. Refereed. Circ: 5000. Microform: PQC. Online: Gale Group. Reprint: PSC. *Indexed:* ArtHuCI, BrHumI, HumInd, IBZ, IDP, IIMP, IIPA, MLA-IB, MusicInd, SSCI. *Bk. rev.:* Number varies, 500 words, signed, shorter notices section. *Aud.:* Ac, Sa.

In 1911, Cecil Sharp formed the English Dance and Song Society, which serves to "collect, research and preserve our heritage of folk dances, songs, and music." While adopting a new, larger format, it continues a tradition of almost 90 years. Carefully researched articles present the history of English folk dance and music, with texts and musical scores. The consistent, well-written style makes this journal of interest to historians, as well as to the audience for folk music and dancing, and to the many people who are active in folk music and dance as a hobby. The emphasis on considering dance and music together reflects the interdisciplinary approach in most current dance scholarship and incorporates social and cultural history. Its value to serious students lies not only in the articles but also in the accompanying extensive references. A recent issue included an in-depth analysis of John Playford's *The English Dancing Master.* Lengthy scholarly reviews of new books and sound recordings are, in effect, research papers. Subscribers become members of the society and also receive the quarterly *English Dance and Song,* which contains shorter informational articles, events calendars, and news items.

2112. ***The Hedgehog (San Francisco): international arts review.*** [ISSN: 1091-9708] 1996. q. USD 20 domestic; USD 30 foreign. Ed(s): Jonathan Clark, Leslie Friedman. The Lively Foundation, 2565 Washington St., San Francisco, CA 94115; http://www.livelyfoundation.org. *Bk. rev.:* Various number and length. *Aud.:* Hs, Ga, Ac, Sa.

The Lively Foundation underwrites many types of art performances, including dance. Started by supporters of dancer/choreographer Leslie Friedman, the foundation presents works from African nations, the Middle East, Asia, and Western Europe. A good source for small company news and for dance-related subjects, recent issues feature the music director of the San Francisco Ballet and flamenco. The high quality of its design makes it visually stimulating and pleasurable reading.

2113. ***Pointe: ballet at its best.*** [ISSN: 1529-6741] 2000. bi-m. USD 12.95; USD 4.99 newsstand/cover domestic; USD 5.99 newsstand/cover Canada. Ed(s): Virginia Johnson. Lifestyle Ventures, LLC, 250 W 57th St, Ste 420, New York, NY 10107; vjohnson@lifestyleventures.com; http://www.pointemagazine.com. Illus., adv. Circ: 30000 Paid. *Aud.:* Hs, Ga, Ac, Sa.

Pointe, published six times a year, is intended as an international ballet periodical exclusively for the serious dancer. Regular features cover the business of ballet, and an online web site at http://www.pointemagazine.com includes a chat room and message board. Subjects range from contracts to clothes to technique, each handled by a practitioner/expert in the field. "BodyWatch" has the most recent developments in health care and the prevention of injuries. Since the focus is on working dancers and students, its style is crisp and clear, with very good photographs and drawings for illustrations. *Pointe* will also inform the ballet fan who wants to understand more about the dancer's craft and preparations for performance.

Electronic Journals

Most online journals in dance are based on a print title or focused on a single company, geographic area, or dance style. Online versions of print publications are noted in the appropriate print title annotation. There are some excellent regional dance web sites, including www.danceadvance.org for the Philadelphia area and www.nyfa.org/for New York state, with national resources included.

http://www.danceusa.org is the web site for Dance/USA, "an organization founded in 1982 following the release of a report by the Task Force for a National Dance Organization, which called for the establishment of a national service organization for professional dance. Dance/USA's members include over 400 ballet, modern, ethnic, jazz and tap companies, dance service and presenting organizations, individuals, and other organizations nationwide."

■ DEATH AND DYING

See also Medicine and Health section.

Allison Sutton, Psychology and Social Work Subject Specialist Assistant Social Science Librarian Assistant Professor of Library Administration University of Illinois at Urbana-Champaign Education and Social Science Library 1408 West Gregory Drive Urbana, IL 61801

Introduction

Issues of death and dying roam freely across the globe. Growing interest and concern in addressing these are evident in the increasing quantity of information available in both news headlines and research studies of this decade. We are no longer in denial—or at least no longer in complete denial. Research and information regarding terminal illness, bereavement, caregiver support, palliative care, medical staff and patient communication, suicide/patient-assisted suicide, preventative buffers, end-of-life choices, and many other pertinent topics have grown in the last decade. And, there is no shortage of commercials marketing pharmaceuticals and financial planning solicitations either. Perhaps all of this is a reflection of the aging baby-boom population and its zest for life. Most people, whether classified in this age group or not, have begun to live their lives with a forcefulness and vigor that was nonexistent decades earlier. There is a movement to incorporate plans for death and dying into life plans, which living wills and estate planning seminars can attest to. The About.com web site has Death and Dying listed under the Health and Fitness category, which seems to further validate death and dying as a life issue. As an aging population, we find the subject moving up on our list of high priorities.

We live comfortably. Expending energy, time, and money on comforts to enhance our daily lives and perhaps our longevity is prevalent among adults. It is common practice to converse with some regularity about our participation in activities like exercising, cooking, spiritual practices, family gatherings, and our latest "toys." These are the things that provide us with constructive reasons to step away from the duties and responsibilities of work life. We share our interests with others in an almost subliminal effort to persuade others to take stock of the value of life, especially their own lives. We choose to protect others through construction of living wills, provisions of bereavement counseling, and hospice and palliative care education. Luckily, there is a willingness by medical professionals, psychologists, religious leaders, and everyday caregivers to verbalize the painful parts of death and dying with very poignant anecdotal vignettes that soothe those in the midst of related experiences. Efforts in the research and education arenas are encouraging. Many medical schools and nursing programs have made changes to the curriculum to increase the knowledge level of professionals who will be (directly or indirectly) involved in palliative care issues. Service providers, social workers, and others are attentive to the results of research that documents and demonstrates the call for more communication to reveal the patient's psychosocial, spiritual, and environmental needs when facing death. Standard medicine has not, however, drowned in the sea of alternatives. Instead, it has found a willing companion. Research on therapeutic and complementary approaches to tackling pain and other less severe side effects continues to create a balance sought by patients and their team of health experts and supporters. Comparative analyses of varied groups have pointed to racial, ethnic, and cultural differences that are pertinent to the dialogue with the patients and their families. As consumers, we are learning to be aggressive about our health and in turn, about our death. Compassion and not complacency is key. Armed with reviews of research and other informative pieces, we are armed with greater understanding of the medical advancements, legislative initiatives, and psychosocial variables, enabling us to face death with greater inner strength, claiming dignity as a right and requirement.

Basic Periodicals

Ac, Sa: *American Journal of Hospice and Palliative Care; Death Studies; End-of-Life Choices; European Journal of Palliative Care; Journal of Pain & Palliative Care Pharmacotherapy; Journal of Palliative Care; Journal of Palliative Medicine; Loss, Grief & Care; Omega; Palliative Medicine; Suicide and Life-Threatening Behavior.*

2114. ***The American Journal of Hospice and Palliative Care.*** Formerly (until 1990): *American Journal of Hospice Care.* [ISSN: 1049-9091] 1983. bi-m. USD 193 (Individuals, USD 136). Ed(s): Dr. Robert E Enck. Prime National Publishing Corp., 470 Boston Post Rd, Weston, MA 02493; hospice@pnpco.com; http://www.pnpco.com. Illus., index, adv. Sample. Refereed. Circ: 3000. Vol. ends: Nov/Dec. *Indexed:* AgeL, CINAHL, SWR&A. *Bk. rev.:* Number and length vary. *Aud.:* Ac, Ga., Sa.

This journal covers a broad spectrum of topics, blending standard and complementary medicine. It serves as a good resource for applied research studies. The unique multi-professional approach to hospice and palliative care is evident in its content, which includes "Original Articles," "What's New in Therapeutics?," "Pain and Symptom Management," "Hospice News Briefs and Vignettes," and "Book Reviews." Recent articles include "Family Distress in Palliative Medicine," "Connecting the Medical and Spiritual Models in Patients Nearing Death," "Management of Hiccups in the Palliative Care Population," and "Complicated Bereavement: A National Survey of Potential Risks Factors." Hospice Abstracts (1994+) provides online contents and abstracts on the journal's web site. Will appeal to those in the medical profession and those counseling patients and families in transition due to terminal illness.

2115. ***Death Studies: education - counseling - care - law - ethics.*** Formerly (until 1985): *Death Education.* [ISSN: 0748-1187] 1977. 10x/yr. USD 483 (Individuals, USD 183). Ed(s): Robert A Neimeyer. Brunner - Routledge (US), 325 Chestnut St, Ste 800, Philadelphia, PA 19106; info@taylorandfrancis.com; http://www.brunner-routledge.com/. Illus., adv. Sample. Refereed. Circ: 800. Vol. ends: Dec. Microform: PQC. Online: bigchalk; EBSCO Publishing; Gale Group; Ingenta Select; OCLC Online Computer Library Center, Inc.; ProQuest Information & Learning; RoweCom Information Quest; Swets Blackwell. Reprint: PQC; PSC. *Indexed:* ASG, AgeL, CIJE, CINAHL, ExcerpMed, LRI, PsycholAb, RI-1, SFSA, SSCI, SSI, SWA, SWR&A, SociolAb. *Bk. rev.:* Number and length vary. *Aud.:* Ac., Sa.

This peer-reviewed journal targets five key areas: counseling, research, education, care, and ethics. Special emphasis is placed on legal and therapeutics issues and presentation of some alternative approaches to encourage improvement in professional practices. Editors are academics, primarily representing the disciplines of counseling, psychology, philosophy, and social work. Although the journal's primary aim is to provide information to those in the medical profession, a wider professional audience will find its articles engaging and useful, including educators, pastoral counselors, and lobbyists. Regular sections include "Research Articles," "Professional Practice," "Book Reviews," and "News and Notes." Recent articles include "Gun Control (Bill C-51) on Suicide in Canada," "A Quarter Century of End-of-Life Issues in U.S. Medical Schools," "Why Do We Fear Death? The Construction and Validation of the Reasons for the Death Fear Scale," and "Spiritual Issues and Quality of Life Assessment in Cancer Care."

2116. ***End-of-Life Choices.*** Former titles (until 2003): *Timelines;* (until 1994): *Hemlock Quarterly.* 1980. q. USD 35. Ed(s): James C Moore. End-of-Life Choices, PO Box 101810, Denver, CO 80250-1810; hemlock@hemlock.org; http://www.endoflifechoices.org/. Adv. Circ: 40000. *Aud.:* Ga.

Formerly *Timelines*, this is the official journal of the Hemlock Society. It contains current news and information regarding the movement to "curtail suffering of terminally ill people" by maximizing the options for death with dignity. Issues vary in coverage, but typically include a mix of legal news, consumer information, statistical data, and public advocacy updates. The society's political and legislative arm regularly reviews elected officials and applauds other advocates who are proponents of the society's agenda. Recent stories include "Disability Survey Results," "Estate Planning, a Supportive Voice from the Pulpit," "New Survey: Younger Docs OK Assisted Dying," and "Save Your Loved Ones Trouble After You've Moved On."

2117. ***European Journal of Palliative Care.*** [ISSN: 1352-2779] 1994. bi-m. GBP 48 in Europe; USD 75 United States; GBP 72 elsewhere. Ed(s): Dr. Andrew Hoy. Hayward Medical Communications Ltd., Covent Garden, Seven Dials Warehouse, London, WC2H 9LA, United Kingdom; admin@hayward.co.uk; http://www.hayward.co.uk. Circ: 2000. *Indexed:* CINAHL. *Aud.:* Ac, Sa.

This journal of review articles continues as the official voice of the European Association for Palliative Care and now shares a common bond with *Palliative Medicine*, which was recently selected as the association's official peer-reviewed journal. *EJPC* remains a multidisciplinary resource serving many, whether they are members of a medical staff or a part of other important affinity groups. *EJPC* is at the forefront of the movement to increase the knowledge level of professionals concerning palliative care, with detailed coverage of the attempt to advance the understanding of palliative care issues around the world. It is published simultaneously in English and French and provides opinions on published articles or material of general interest to the readership. Recent review articles include "Ethical Questions at the End of Life," "Putting the Plans for French Palliative Care into Action," "Infection Control in Hospices," and "Suffering—a Problem that Also Affects Nurses." The journal's web site provides article summaries from 1995 forward and an alphabetical listing of recent article titles.

2118. ***Journal of Pain & Palliative Care Pharmacotherapy: advances in acute, chronic and end of life symptom control.*** Formerly (until 2002): *Journal of Pharmaceutical Care in Pain & Symptom Control;* Incorporates (1985-2002): *The Hospice Journal.* [ISSN: 1536-0288] 1993. q. USD 435; USD 587.25; USD 630.75. Ed(s): Arthur Lipman. Haworth Press, Inc., 10 Alice St, Binghamton, NY 13904-1580; getinfo@haworthpressinc.com; http://www.haworthpressinc.com. Adv. Sample. Refereed. Circ: 529 Paid. Reprint: HAW. *Indexed:* CINAHL, ExcerpMed. *Aud.:* Ac.

This new journal title reflects an increased focus on symptom control in end-of-life care. It is the result of the merger of two journals, *Hospice Journal* and *Journal of Pharmaceutical Care in Pain and Symptom Control.* It supports research advances in acute, chronic, and end-of-life pain and symptom control. The articles, reports, and commentaries represent varied disciplines: medicine, nursing, pharmacy, psychology, bioethics, and health policy. Recent articles include "Clinical Pharmacokinetics of Morphine," "Newer Anticonvulsant Drugs in Neuropathic Pain and Bipolar Disorder," "Outcomes and Pharmacoeconomic Analyses," and "Complementary and Alternative Medicine: Information for Practitioners and Consumers," plus "An Annotated Guide to Pain and Palliative Care on the World Wide Web."

2119. ***Journal of Palliative Care.*** [ISSN: 0825-8597] 1985. q. CND 120 (Individuals, CND 80). Ed(s): Dr. David J Roy. Centre for Bioethics - Clinical Research Institute of Montreal, 110 Pine Ave W, Montreal, PQ H2W 1R7, Canada; marcotc@ircm.qc.ca; http://www.ircm.qc.ca/bioethique/english/publications/journal_of_palliative_care.html. Illus.

Sample. Refereed. Vol. ends: Winter. Microform: MML. Online: Micromedia ProQuest; Northern Light Technology, Inc.; ProQuest Information & Learning. *Indexed:* AgeL, CBCARef, CINAHL, CPerI, IndMed, PsycholAb, SCI, SSCI. *Bk. rev.:* Number and length vary. *Aud.:* Ac, Sa.

This is an international journal of refereed research articles that easily connects theory and practice. Coverage of topics is broad and representative of the needs of professionals seeking innovative ideas to apply with terminally ill patients and their families. Research articles are complemented by sections titled "Front Line Dispatch," "Global Exchange," "Forum," "Book Reviews," and "N.B. Notewell," which is a listing of announcements, awards, and continuing-education and conference information. Recent articles include "Symptomatic Uses of Caffeine in Patients with Cancer," "Using Patients with Cancer to Educate Residents about Giving Bad News," "The Cultural Differences in Perceived Value of Disclosure and Cognition: Spain and Canada," "Evidence-Based Palliative Care," and "The Impact on Families of a Children's Hospice Program." Thematic issues are biannual. A complete listing of contents from 1985 through 1998 and titles of the thematic issues are given on the journal's web site.

2120. ***Journal of Palliative Medicine.*** [ISSN: 1096-6218] 1998. bi-m. USD 436 (Individuals, USD 229). Ed(s): Dr. David E Weissman. Mary Ann Liebert, Inc. Publishers, 2 Madison Ave, Ste 210, Larchmont, NY 10538-9957; info@liebertpub.com; http://www.liebertpub.com. Illus., adv. Sample. Refereed. Vol. ends: Winter. Reprint: PSC. *Indexed:* ExcerpMed. *Aud.:* Ac, Sa.

This is the official journal of the American Academy of Hospice and Palliative Medicine. It is peer reviewed and inclusive in content and structure. Much of the content assists in improving practices by igniting interest in and providing recommendations for innovative approaches in palliative medicine through research studies, case discussion, and real-life anecdotal segments. Particularly notable are the myriad of subject groups and settings explored in the research studies and discussed in the informational pieces. Although there is a definite slant toward those currently enrolled in medical school, in training within the medical profession, or practicing, the journal will draw a wider audience. Content includes "Original Articles," "Case Discussion," "Fast Facts & Concepts," "Dilemmas in Palliative Care Education," and "Personal Reflection." Recent research articles are "The Medical Facility Debate," "Existential Concerns of Families of Late-Stage Dementia Patients: Questions of Freedom, Choices, Isolation, Death, and Meaning," "Olanzapine for Intractable Nausea in Palliative Care Patients," and "Long-Term Palliative Care Workers: More Than a Story of Endurance." Other informational pieces include "How to Write a Condolence Letter," "Tube Feed or Not Tube Feed?," "Integrating Palliative Care into Nursing Homes," and "Do We Really Care about Doctor-Patient Communication or Is It Just Talk?"

2121. ***Loss, Grief & Care: a journal of professional practice.*** [ISSN: 8756-4610] 1986. irreg. USD 250. Ed(s): Austin H Kutscher. Haworth Press, Inc., 10 Alice St, Binghamton, NY 13904-1580; getinfo@haworthpressinc.com; http://www.haworthpressinc.com. Illus., adv. Sample. Refereed. Circ: 232 Paid. Vol. ends: Winter. Microform: PQC. Reprint: HAW. *Indexed:* ASSIA, CINAHL, IBZ, IMFL, IPSA, PsycholAb, SWR&A, SociolAb. *Aud.:* Ac, Sa.

This journal's aim is to serve as a resource for professionals working with seriously ill or dying patients and their families. Critical, terminal, and long-term care issues are addressed in both a scholarly and practical manner. Each issue has a special focus that is harmonically presented: An initial introduction of the topic and articles that follow provide a thorough overview and understanding, tying the current subject matter to the journal's overarching theme—"quality of life." Research articles consider the physical and/or psychological aspects of treatment, review and evaluate surgical procedures, and discuss communication and rehabilitation practices. A recent thematic issue deals with "Multidisciplinary Care of the Stroke Patient." Articles include "Surgical Treatment to Prevent Stroke," "Rehabilitation of Strokes in Children," "Patient Education for Individuals with Communication and Sensory Impairment," and "Quality of Life after Stroke: Developing Meaningful Life Roles through Occupational Therapy." Past themes have included Parkinson's disease and dermatology. The journal is widely indexed. Contents and titles of thematic issues are available on the web site.

2122. ***Omega: Journal of Death and Dying.*** [ISSN: 0030-2228] 1969. 8x/yr. USD 323 (Individuals, USD 82). Ed(s): Michon Lartigue, Kenneth Doka. Baywood Publishing Co., Inc., 26 Austin Ave, Amityville, NY 11701; info@baywood.com; http://www.baywood.com. Illus., adv. Sample. Refereed. Vol. ends: No. 4. *Indexed:* ASG, ASSIA, AbAn, AgeL, ArtHuCI, BiolAb, CIJE, CINAHL, CJA, ExcerpMed, IBZ, PsycholAb, RI-1, SSCI, SSI, SociolAb. *Aud.:* Ac, Sa.

As the official publication of the Association for Death Education and Counseling, this refereed journal focuses on end-of-life issues. There is a heavy emphasis on research that centers around either the psychosocial challenge associated with death and bereavement or the examination of service structures and support networks. Uniquely and commendably, this journal includes research studies that promote greater understanding of cultural differences among people from varied countries, community groups uncommonly studied (i.e., funeral service providers), and studies that are internationally diverse. Recent research articles include "Sibling Support Systems in Childhood after a Parent Dies," "Death and the Discourse of the Body," "The State of Hospice Ethics Committees and the Social Workers Role," and "Death, Anxiety and Depression: A Comparison between Egyptian, Kuwaiti and Lebanese Undergraduates."

2123. ***Palliative Medicine: a multiprofessional journal.*** [ISSN: 0269-2163] 1987. bi-m. GBP 473 (Individuals, GBP 148; Members, GBP 118 qualified associations). Ed(s): Geoffrey Hanks. Arnold Publishers, 338 Euston Rd, London, NW1 3BH, United Kingdom; http://www.palliativemedjournal.com. Illus., adv. Sample. Refereed. Circ: 1400. Vol. ends: Nov. Online: EBSCO Publishing; OCLC Online Computer Library Center, Inc.; RoweCom Information Quest. *Indexed:* ASSIA, BiolAb, CINAHL, ExcerpMed, IMFL, IndMed, SCI. *Bk. rev.:* Number and length vary. *Aud.:* Ac, Sa.

In 2003, this was designated the the official peer-reviewed research journal of the European Association of Palliative Care. It continues to cover many strictly medical concerns related to palliative care issues, but includes articles that appeal to a wide audience of other palliative care professionals. Coverage is varied; topics include molecular biology of pain through symptom management, bereavement, ethics, and more. There have been a few changes to the journal's structure and its distribution. There are now eight issues per year instead of six, and monthly circulation is planned for the near future. Contents include original articles, research abstracts (e.g., from the Annual Palliative Care Congress), journal abstracts (from standard medical journals), book reviews, and a calendar of worldwide events. There are two new regular features. One emphasizes "evidence-based medicine" through reviews of protocol in pain management and offers recommendations to medical staff. The other is "Journal Club," which presents a critical review of new publications in the field of palliative medicine. Research articles that provide answers to questions about psychosocial (i.e., bereavement, spirituality) needs of the patients, support services, government, and policies remain prevalent. Recent titles include "Training in Pediatric Palliative Medicine," "The Experiences of Donor Families in the Hospice," "Intravenous Morphine for Rapid Control of Severe Cancer Pain," and "The Development of Palliative Care in National Government Policy." Contents from 1998 forward are available through a direct link on the journal's web site.

2124. ***Suicide and Life-Threatening Behavior: the official journal of the American Association of Suicidology.*** Former titles: *Suicide; Life Threatening Behavior.* [ISSN: 0363-0234] 1970. q. USD 305 (Individuals, USD 75). Ed(s): Morton Silverman. Guilford Publications, Inc., 72 Spring St, 4th Fl, New York, NY 10012; info@guilford.com; http://www.guilford.com. Illus., index, adv. Refereed. Circ: 2000. Vol. ends: Winter. Microform: PQC. Online: Gale Group; Ingenta Select; OCLC Online Computer Library Center, Inc.; ProQuest Information & Learning; RoweCom Information Quest; Swets Blackwell. Reprint: ISI; PQC. *Indexed:* ASG, AbAn, AgeL, BiolAb, CIJE, CJA, CommAb, ExcerpMed, HRA, IndMed, PRA, PsycholAb, SFSA, SSCI, SSI, SUSA, SociolAb. *Bk. rev.:* Number and length vary. *Aud.:* Ac, Sa.

This peer-reviewed journal addresses biological, sociological, psychological, and environmental factors that influence and/or are associated with suicide. It is particularly adept in applying theory to real-life scenarios. Important also is the regular inclusion of cutting-edge research that explores and validates multicultural and international differences related to suicidal behavior, original research articles, speeches and lectures, and case consultations. It also includes book reviews. Recent article titles are "Risk-Taking Behavior and Adolescent Suicide Attempts," "African-American College Women's Suicide Buffers," "Development of a Questionnaire on Attitudes Towards Suicide," "Ling's Death: An Ethnology of a Chinese Woman's Suicide," and "Why People Engage in Parasuicide: A Cross-Cultural Study of Intentions."

2125. *World Right-to-Die Newsletter.* [ISSN: 0742-535X] 1979. s-a. Free. Ed(s): Luis H Gallop. World Federation of Right-to-Die Societies, PO Box 570, Mill Valley, CA 94942; libbydrake@optushome.com.au.; http://www.worldrtd.org/nletter_list.html. Circ: 300. *Aud.:* Ga, Sa.

Now in its eighth year of publication, this newsletter provides a medium for proponents of the right to die, which is viewed as a basic human right. The newsletter's content clearly supports the idea that this right should be recognized worldwide. With an unquestionably logical approach to furthering its agenda, the newsletter is heavily laden with laws, views on "government control," and legislative initiatives in the United States and around the globe. Constant attention is given to increasing membership, and there are notifications and detailed coverage of conference events. Recent articles include "In Law and Actions, an Eventful Year," "Euthanasia Decriminalized under Tight Rules," "How It's Done in Switzerland," and "Birth and Growth of a World Group." All issues are also available online at www.worldrtd.org. It continues national distribution from the state of Oregon, where a right-to-die law was passed in 1995.

■ DISABILITIES

See also Education; and Medicine and Health sections.

Sharon Naylor, Education Librarian, Milner Library, Illinois State University, Campus Box 8900, Normal, IL 61790-8900; sknaylor@ilstu.edu

Introduction

Disability has always been a problematic term to define. Traditionally, the term *disability* covered a fairly narrow range of conditions. Now, the term may refer to a mild learning disability, a behavioral disorder, a severe orthopedic or mental disorder, a disease, or even a gender or age-related condition. Not surprisingly, periodicals related to disabilities cover a broad spectrum, including medical journals that publish highly scientific empirical research studies; inexpensive, limited-circulation publications that primarily convey self-help and consumer information; publications written for professionals in the field; and newsletters that are primarily legislative updates and action alerts. Many professional organizations publish one journal devoted to theory and empirical research and another devoted to practice-oriented articles.

The start of the "disability rights" movement is difficult to pinpoint, but the passage of the Americans with Disabilities Act (ADA) has undoubtedly generated an increased awareness of and interest in serving people with disabilities. There has probably been an even more marked change in the way that society now views persons with disabilities, and the periodical literature reflects this shift in attitude. Historically, people who had disabilities were primarily regarded as needing to either be cured or cared for. Now, many persons with a disability see themselves as members of a minority group that has been discriminated against, and they have demanded and received recognition. Magazines targeting this audience focus on political activity, advocacy issues, legal updates, and consumer news. In the past, much of the nonscholarly literature was generated by nonprofit organizations or charities and was frequently inspirational or devotional in tone. Many of the newer magazines are outspoken advocates for disability rights. *New Mobility* and *Mainstream* are two publications that represent an upbeat and "can do" point of view.

Although relatively few colleges and universities offer degrees in "disability studies," it is a growing field that draws primarily on theories and perspectives from sociology, social work, education, and cultural studies. Among the goals of those in this newly formed field is developing the research needed to shape disability policy. A premise of "disability studies" is that disability is a social construction. This perspective differs from the perspectives of the physician, the physical therapist, or the professional educator. Several scholarly publications reflect this emerging field, e.g., *Disability and Society* and *Journal of Disability Policy Studies.*

Another area that has emerged and is of increasing importance is the area of assistive technology. Publications about assistive technology include highly technical articles that relate to the design and engineering of assistive devices, practice-oriented publications directed to the professional educator, and consumer-oriented newsletters written specifically for persons with physical disabilities. Two examples of periodicals devoted to assistive technology issues are *Closing the Gap* and *Information Technology and Disabilities.*

Although "disabilities" has never been a distinct field of study, the current interest in educational inclusion, Universal Design, and compliance with ADA and the Individuals with Disabilities Education Act (IDEA) has resulted in far more being published in mainstream publications about disability concerns.

An attempt has been made to include a variety of types of publications in this list. However, because libraries usually purchase titles that are well established and well indexed, scholarly and professional journals are predominant.

Basic Periodicals

Ga: *Mainstream, New Mobility, Sports 'n Spokes*; Ac: *American Annals of the Deaf, American Journal of Mental Retardation, Education and Training in Developmental Disabilities, Focus on Exceptional Children, Journal of Speech, Language, and Hearing Research, Journal of Visual Impairment and Blindness, RE:View.*

Basic Abstracts and Indexes

Current Index to Journals in Education (CIJE), Exceptional Child Education Resources (ECER), Excerpta Medica, Linguistics and Language Behavior Abstracts, Psychological Abstracts.

2126. *Ability.* [ISSN: 1062-5321] 1992. bi-m. USD 29.70. C 2 Publishing, 1001 W 17th St, Costa Mesa, CA 92627; advertising@abilitymagazine.com. Illus., adv. Sample. Circ: 165000 Paid. *Aud.:* Hs, Ga, Sa.

Ability claims to be "the first publication focusing on disabilities to crossover into mainstream America." Most issues include an interview with a high-profile personality. Kirk Douglas and Danny Glover are among those recently interviewed. Also included are articles about new technologies, the Americans with Disabilities Act, travel, employment, and human-interest stories. One goal of the magazine is to help remove the misunderstandings and erase the stereotypes that surround disability issues. The web site includes the full text of the featured interviews and other selected articles, suggested links and resources, and information about the Americans with Disabilities Act. This inexpensive magazine is a good choice for libraries desiring to add a popular title, and it will appeal to persons with a broad variety of disabilities.

AccessWorld. See Large Print section.

2127. *Adapted Physical Activity Quarterly.* [ISSN: 0736-5829] 1984. q. USD 184 (Individuals, USD 49). Ed(s): David L. Porretta. Human Kinetics Publishers, Inc., PO Box 5076, Champaign, IL 61825-5076; orders@hkusa.com; http://www.humankinetics.com. Illus., index, adv. Sample. Refereed. Circ: 977 Paid and free. Vol. ends: Oct. Reprint: PSC. *Indexed:* CINAHL, ECER, ExcerpMed, IBZ, PEI, PsycholAb, SSCI, SportS. *Aud.:* Ac, Sa.

This scholarly, multidisciplinary journal is the official journal of the International Federation of Adapted Physical Activity and publishes "the latest scholarly inquiry related to physical activity for special populations." Populations that are considered range from the infant to the elderly. The focus of the articles may be on an adaptation of the equipment, activity, facility, methodology, or setting. Most issues include from five to seven research articles and one "Viewpoint" article that contains commentary on current opinions, legislation, and trends in the profession. Issues also include book and media reviews and abstracts. An author index is included in the October issue. Contents information and abstracts for issues from 1995 to the present are available on the magazine's web site.

2128. ***American Annals of the Deaf.*** Formerly: *American Annals of the Deaf and Dumb.* [ISSN: 0002-726X] 1847. 5x/yr. USD 60 (Individuals, USD 50). Ed(s): Mary E Carew, Dr. Donald Moores. Convention of American Instructors of the Deaf, FH, 409, 800 Florida Ave, NE, Washington, DC 20002. Illus., index, adv. Refereed. Circ: 4000 Paid and controlled. Vol. ends: Dec. Microform: PQC. Online: bigchalk; Gale Group; Northern Light Technology, Inc. Reprint: PQC. *Indexed:* AgeL, BiolAb, CIJE, CINAHL, ECER, EduInd, ExcerpMed, IndMed, PAIS, PsycholAb, SSCI. *Aud.:* Ac, Sa.

First published in 1847, the *Annals* is the official organ of the Convention of American Instructors of the Deaf (CAID) and of the Conference of Educational Administrators of Schools and Programs for the Deaf (CEASD). It is directed and administered by a committee made up of members of the executive committees of both of these organizations, and the intended audience is primarily professional educators. Topics covered include communication methods and strategies, language development, mainstreaming and residential schools, parent-child relationships, teacher training, and teaching skills. Topics also extend to covering the broad interests of educators in the general welfare of deaf children and adults. Each year the *Annals* publishes four literary issues (March, July, October, and December) and an annual reference issue that lists schools and programs in the United States and Canada for students who are deaf or hard of hearing (April). The reference issue also provides demographic, audiological, and educational data about students who are deaf and hard of hearing and the schools they attend. An annual author and subject index is included in the December issue. The web site includes abstracts of articles in the current issue and a subject index to previous issues. This key journal should be included in libraries that support a program for hearing-impaired.

2129. ***American Journal of Mental Retardation.*** Formerly (until 1987): *American Journal of Mental Deficiency.* [ISSN: 0895-8017] 1876. bi-m. USD 209 for print & online eds. (Individuals, USD 109 for print & online eds.; USD 30 per issue domestic). Ed(s): William Maclean. American Association on Mental Retardation, 444 N Capitol St, Ste 846, Washington, DC 20001-1512; orders@allenpress.com; http://www.aamr.allenpress.com. Illus., adv. Refereed. Circ: 8000. Vol. ends: Nov. Microform: PQC. Online: OCLC Online Computer Library Center, Inc.; H.W. Wilson. *Indexed:* AgeL, BRI, BiolAb, CBRI, CIJE, ChemAb, ECER, EduInd, ExcerpMed, IndMed, L&LBA, PsycholAb, SCI, SSCI, SWR&A. *Bk. rev.:* 2-3, 600-1,000 words. *Aud.:* Ac, Sa.

The *American Journal on Mental Retardation* is published by the American Association on Mental Retardation. Articles include reports of empirical research on characteristics of people with mental retardation, reviews and theoretical interpretations of relevant research literature, and reports of evaluative research on new treatment procedures. In general, the approach is scientific, experimental, and theory-oriented. Bibliographies, case studies, and descriptions of treatment procedures or programs are generally not included. Each issue includes abstracts of the articles in French. An author, subject, and book review index for the year appears in the November issue. Since researchers and professional educators are the target audience, this is primarily recommended for academic libraries.

2130. ***American Journal of Occupational Therapy.*** Former titles (until 1978): *A J O T: The American Journal of Occupational Therapy;* (until 1977): *American Journal of Occupational Therapy.* [ISSN: 0272-9490] 1947. 6x/yr. USD 120 (Individuals, USD 50; USD 130 foreign). Ed(s): Betty Hasselkus. American Occupational Therapy Association, Inc., 4720 Montgomery Lane, Bethesda, MD 20814-3425; http://www.aota.org. Illus., index, adv. Refereed. Circ: 58000. Vol. ends: Nov/Dec. Microform: PQC. *Indexed:* ASG, ASSIA, AgeL, BiolAb, CIJE, CINAHL, ECER, ExcerpMed, IMFL, IndMed, PsycholAb, SSCI. *Bk. rev.:* Various number and length. *Aud.:* Ac, Sa.

The *American Journal of Occupational Therapy* is an official publication of the American Occupational Therapy Association. Intended for practitioners, it focuses on research, practice, and health care issues in the field of occupational therapy. Issues include news and features about hands-on approaches, clinical technique and technology updates, careers and continuing education, legislative issues, and professional trends. Information about the association, edited speeches, and editorials representing differing viewpoints are also included. There are occasional issues centered around a theme; a recent issue is devoted to "Qualitative Research Issues." The November/December issue includes an author and subject index for the year and a listing of educational programs. This journal is recommended for academic, medical, and special libraries.

2131. ***American Journal of Physical Medicine and Rehabilitation.*** Formerly: *American Journal of Physical Medicine.* [ISSN: 0894-9115] 1921. m. USD 309 (Individuals, USD 182). Ed(s): Bradley R. Johns. Lippincott Williams & Wilkins, 351 W Camden St, Baltimore, MD 21201. Illus., adv. Refereed. Circ: 4828. Microform: Pub. Online: Ovid Technologies, Inc.; Swets Blackwell. *Indexed:* BioEngAb, BiolAb, CINAHL, ChemAb, EngInd, ErgAb, ExcerpMed, IndMed, PEI, PsycholAb, SCI, SSCI, SportS. *Aud.:* Ac, Sa.

The *American Journal of Physical Medicine & Rehabilitiation* is the official journal of the Association of Academic Physiatrists (AAP). Issues usually include seven research articles and one "CME Article" (a research article that is selected by the editors to be published as an educational activity). The journal focuses on the physical treatment of neuromuscular impairments and the use of electrodiagnostic studies. It is a good choice for academic and hospital libraries.

2132. ***American Rehabilitation.*** [ISSN: 0362-4048] 1975. q. USD 15. Ed(s): Frank Romano. U.S. Department of Education, Mary E Switzer Bldg, Rm 3030, 330 C St, S W, Washington, DC 20202; frank_romano@ed.gov; http://www.ed.gov/pubs/AmericanRehab. Illus., index. Sample. Circ: 8000. Microform: PQC. Online: bigchalk; EBSCO Publishing; Florida Center for Library Automation; Gale Group; Northern Light Technology, Inc.; OCLC Online Computer Library Center, Inc.; ProQuest Information & Learning. *Indexed:* AgeL, CINAHL, ECER, IUSGP, LRI, MCR. *Bk. rev.:* 7-10, 50 words. *Aud.:* Ga, Ac, Sa.

American Rehabilitation is the official publication of the Rehabilitation Services Administration. Each issue includes four or five fairly short articles, generally centered on a theme. Available government services are emphasized and articles are easy to read and frequently include statistical information. Each issue has a section that reviews new publications and films and a short "News" section. This publication will be automatically shipped to some government depository libraries, and the minimal cost will make it attractive to libraries with limited budgets. After a period in which no issues of *American Rehabilitation* were published, the journal was scheduled to resume publication with its Summer 2003 issue, sometime in June 2003.

2133. ***Annals of Dyslexia: an interdisciplinary journal of specific language disability.*** Formerly (until 1981): *Orton Society. Bulletin.* [ISSN: 0736-9387] 1951. a. Members, USD 55. Ed(s): Cindy Cressi. International Dyslexia Association, 8600 LaSalle Rd, Ste 382, Chester Bldg, Baltimore, MD 21286-2044. Refereed. Circ: 10000. Microform: PQC. Online: OCLC Online Computer Library Center, Inc.; ProQuest Information & Learning; H.W. Wilson. Reprint: PQC. *Indexed:* CIJE, ECER, EduInd, L&LBA, PsycholAb, SSCI. *Aud.:* Ac, Sa.

Published annually by the International Dyslexia Association, the *Annals* contains updates on current research and selected proceedings from the association's conferences. The focus of the journal is on "the understanding, prevention, and remediation of written language difficulties." Most articles discuss original research and are directed toward the scholar. A subject and name index is included at the end of each volume. Recommended for academic libraries.

2134. ***Archives of Physical Medicine and Rehabilitation.*** [ISSN: 0003-9993] 1920. m. USD 345 (Individuals, USD 236; Students, USD 99). Ed(s): Dr. Kenneth M Jaffe, Michael A. Vasko. W.B. Saunders Co., Independence Sq W, Ste 300, the Curtis Center, Philadelphia, PA 19106-3399; http://www.us.elsevierhealth.com/product.jsp?isbn=1055937x. Illus., index, adv. Refereed. Circ: 10050 Paid. Vol. ends: Dec. *Indexed:* AgeL, BiolAb, CINAHL, ChemAb, ExcerpMed, FPA, ForAb, IndMed, IndVet, RRTA, SCI, SSCI, SportS. *Bk. rev.:* Various number and length. *Aud.:* Ac, Sa.

This journal is published jointly by the American Congress of Rehabilitation Medicine and the American Academy of Physical Medicine and Rehabilitation. It disseminates organizational news and presents current research. The majority of the articles are research-based and intended for the professional clinician or researcher. Each issue also includes a section entitled "Clinical Notes," which includes shorter articles that report on an observation that is "interesting, new, or sufficient to warrant attention." The web site includes contents information, article abstracts, and a search engine that covers from 1996 to the present. Information about upcoming issues is also included. Journal subscriptions include print and online versions. This is an important title for medical and academic libraries.

2135. ***Assessment for Effective Intervention.*** Formerly: *Diagnostique.* [ISSN: 1534-5084] 1976. q. USD 28 domestic; USD 32 foreign. Ed(s): Linda K. Elksnin. Council for Educational Diagnostic Services, 1920 Association Dr., Reston, VA 22091; http://www.unr.edu/educ/ceds/. Illus., adv. Refereed. Circ: 1800. Vol. ends: Summer. Microform: PQC. *Indexed:* CIJE, ECER. *Aud.:* Ac, Sa.

Assessment for Effective Intervention is the official journal of the Council for the Educational Diagnostic Services, a division of the Council for Exceptional Children. The primary purpose of the journal is to publish empirical research that has implications for practitioners. Articles describe relationships between assessment and instruction, innovative assessment strategies, diagnostic procedures, relationships between existing instruments, and review articles of assessment techniques. Recent "theme" issues were "Issues in Postsecondary Assessment" and "Assessment of Children and Youth with Autism Spectrum Disorders." Recommended primarily for academic libraries.

Behavior Modification. See Psychology section.

2136. ***Behavioral Disorders.*** [ISSN: 0198-7429] 1976. q. USD 50 (Individuals, USD 20). Ed(s): Gary Sasso, Jo Hendrickson. Council for Exceptional Children, 1110 N. Glebe Rd., Ste. 300, Arlington, VA 22201-4795; http://www.unr.edu/educ/ceds/indexceds.html. Adv. Refereed. Circ: 9000. Microform: PQC. Online: bigchalk; ProQuest Information & Learning. Reprint: PQC. *Indexed:* CIJE, CJA, ECER, EduInd, PsycholAb, SSCI. *Aud.:* Ac, Sa.

Behavioral Disorders is published by the Council for Children with Behavioral Disorders, a Division of the Council for Exceptional Children. It publishes reports of research, program evaluations, and position papers related to children and youth with emotional and behavioral disorders. The emphasis is on publishing applied research, especially studies related to assessment and intervention. The articles are directed primarily to teacher educators, teachers, psychologists, administrators, and researchers. Most issues include from four to seven research articles and one shorter "Brief" article. Recent articles have included "The Effects of Social Skills Instruction on the Social Behaviors of Students at Risk for Emotional or Behavioral Disorders" and "Teaching Anger Management Skills to Students with Severe Emotional or Behavioral Disorders." Recommended for libraries that serve Special Education programs.

The Braille Forum. See Large Print section.

2137. ***Career Development for Exceptional Individuals.*** [ISSN: 0885-7288] 1978. s-a. USD 20; USD 24 foreign. Ed(s): Michael Bullis, Michael Benz. Council for Exceptional Children, 1110 N. Glebe Rd., Ste. 300, Arlington, VA 22201-4795; http://www.ed.uiuc.edu/sped/dcdt/. Illus. Circ: 2700. Microform: PQC. *Indexed:* CIJE, ECER. *Bk. rev.:* 10, 200 words. *Aud.:* Ac, Sa.

Career Development for Exceptional Individuals is the official journal of the Division on Career Development and Transition, a division of the Council for Exceptional Children. The journal specializes in the fields of secondary education, transition, and career development for persons with disabilities. Articles emphasize their roles as students, workers, consumers, family members, and citizens. The journal includes original quantitative and qualitative research, scholarly reviews, and program descriptions and evaluations. Recent issues have included five articles. There is considerable interest in transitioning, and this journal should be a welcome addition in libraries serving professional educators and researchers.

2138. ***Closing the Gap.*** [ISSN: 0886-1935] 1982. bi-m. USD 32 domestic; USD 47 Canada; USD 63 elsewhere. Ed(s): Budd Hagen. Closing the Gap, PO Box 68, Henderson, MN 56044; info@closingthegap.com; http://www.closingthegap.com. Adv. Circ: 10000. Online: Northern Light Technology, Inc. *Indexed:* CWI. *Aud.:* Ac, Sa.

Closing the Gap is a tabloid-style publication that explores the ways that technology is being used to enhance the lives of people with special needs. The articles are written in a style that is accessible to the general public and cover all aspects of assistive technology as it relates to special education, rehabilitation, and independent living. The primary focus is on hardware, software applications, and procedures that are currently available for immediate use. The web site contains the table of contents of the current issue and numerous "forums" where readers can ask questions and share information. The web site also includes a searchable database of over 2,000 products and features a "Product of the Week." The intended audience is parents and professionals as well as the disabled. A good choice for libraries that serve populations or programs related to assistive technology.

2139. ***Disability & Society.*** Formerly (until 1993): *Disability, Handicap and Society.* [ISSN: 0968-7599] 1986. 7x/yr. GBP 516 (Individuals, GBP 125). Ed(s): Len Barton. Carfax Publishing Ltd., 4 Park Sq, Milton Park, Abingdon, OX14 4RN, United Kingdom; enquiry@tandf.co.uk; http://www.tandf.co.uk/. Illus., index, adv. Sample. Refereed. Online: bigchalk; EBSCO Publishing; Ingenta Select; Northern Light Technology, Inc.; OCLC Online Computer Library Center, Inc.; ProQuest Information & Learning; RoweCom Information Quest; Swets Blackwell. Reprint: PSC. *Indexed:* ASSIA, AgeL, ArtHuCI, ECER, IBSS, L&LBA, PSA, PsycholAb, RI-1, SSCI, SWA, SociolAb. *Aud.:* Ac, Sa.

Disability & Society is "an international journal providing a focus for debate about such issues as human rights, discrimination, definitions, policy and practices." A custodial approach is viewed as unacceptable, and an emphasis is placed on community care and integration. Recent articles include "Development of Parenting Skills in Individuals with an Intellectual Impairment," "What Disability Civil Rights Cannot Do," "Curriculum Access for Pupils with Disabilities: an Irish Experience," and "Disability Discourses for Online Identities." Substantial book reviews are included in each issue. The publisher's web site includes a request form for a sample copy and table of contents information. This expensive title is primarily for comprehensive collections.

2140. ***Disability Resources Monthly: the newsletter that monitors, reviews and reports on resources for independent living.*** [ISSN: 1070-7220] 1993. m. USD 30 domestic; USD 40 foreign. Ed(s): Julie Klauber. Disability Resources, 4 Glatter Ln, Centereach, NY 11720-1032; info@disabilityresources.org; http://www.disabilityresources.org. *Aud.:* Sa.

The mission of *Disability Resources Monthly* is "to disseminate information about resources that can help people with disabilities live, learn, love, work, and play independently." The primary audience is libraries, disability organizations, health and social service providers, educators, consumers, individuals with disabilities, and their family members. The organization monitors audiovisual materials; online services; free, inexpensive, and hard-to-find books, pamphlets, and videotapes; and online sources; and includes reviews of worthwhile materials in the newsletter. Newsletters also include short articles. Recent newsletters have featured short articles such as "Jobs & Careers: Recent Resources," "Mind Over Matter: Coping with Neurological Disorders," and "Beginning Communication: New Resources for Parents of Children Who Are Deaf." The web site is appealing, easy to navigate, and probably one of the most comprehensive and well-organized sites available that deals with disability concerns. The extensive collection of links and other information makes it an extremely valuable resource. The web site is highly recommended, and the newsletter will be useful to libraries and other organizations or agencies that collect or purchase books and other materials for persons with disabilities.

2141. ***Education and Training in Developmental Disabilities.*** Former titles (until 2003): *Education and Training in Mental Retardation and Developmental Disabilities;* (until 1994): *Education and Training in Mental Retardation;* (until Dec. 1986): *Education and Training of the Mentally Retarded.* 1966. q. USD 75 (Individuals, USD 30; USD 20 newsstand/cover per issue). Ed(s): H Stanley Zucker. Council for

Exceptional Children, Division on Developmental Disabilities, 1110 N Glebe Rd., Ste 300, Arlington, VA 22201-5704; http://www.mrddcec.org. Illus., index, adv. Circ: 8000 Controlled. Vol. ends: Dec. Microform: PQC. Reprint: PQC. *Indexed:* AgeL, CIJE, ECER, EduInd, ExcerpMed, L&LBA, PsycholAb, SSCI, SWR&A. *Aud.:* Ac, Sa.

This journal is the publication of the newly named Division on Developmental Disabilities, a division of the Council for Exceptional Children. The journal's focus is on the education and welfare of persons who have developmental disabilities. Topics covered include identification and assessment, educational programming, training of instructional personnel, rehabilitation, community understanding and provisions, and legislation. Each issue includes six articles that may be either theory-based or practice-oriented. Recent articles have included "Using Self-Monitoring to Improve Performance in General Education High School Classes," "Friendships of Children with Disabilities in the Home Environment," and "Effects of Embedded Instruction on Students with Moderate Disabilities Enrolled in General Education Classes." The primary audience is professional educators.

Exceptional Parent. See Parenting section.

2142. *Exceptionality: a special education journal.* [ISSN: 0936-2835] 1990. q. USD 305. Ed(s): Edward J Sabornie. Lawrence Erlbaum Associates, Inc., 10 Industrial Ave, Mahwah, NJ 07430-2262; journals@erlbaum.com; http://www.erlbaum.com/. Illus., index, adv. Refereed. Reprint: PSC. *Indexed:* CIJE, ECER, EduInd, PsycholAb. *Aud.:* Ac, Sa.

Exceptionality publishes scholarly articles related to Special Education. Subjects include persons of all ages with mental retardation, learning disabilities, behavior disorders, speech and language disorders, hearing and/or visual impairment, physical limitations, and giftedness. Areas of scholarship published in the journal include quantitative, qualitative, and single-subject research designs, reviews of the literature, discussion pieces, invited works, and position papers. Articles in recent issues have included "Teaching Writing Strategies to Children with Disabilities" and "Parents' Expectations about Postschool Outcomes of Children with Hearing Disabilities." Occasionally, issues are oriented around a theme. Topics in recent theme issues have included "Academic Strategy Instruction" and "Gifted and Talented Behavior and Education." Recommended for academic libraries that support teacher education programs.

2143. *Focus on Autism and Other Developmental Disabilities.* Formerly (until vol.11, 1996): *Focus on Autistic Behavior.* [ISSN: 1088-3576] 1986. q. USD 114 (Individuals, USD 44). Ed(s): Richard Simpson, John Kregel. Pro-Ed Inc., 8700 Shoal Creek Blvd, Austin, TX 78757-6897; journals@proedinc.com; http://www.proedinc.com. Illus., adv. Sample. Refereed. Circ: 3000 Paid and free. Microform: PQC. Online: bigchalk; EBSCO Publishing; Florida Center for Library Automation; Gale Group; Ingenta Select; ProQuest Information & Learning. Reprint: PSC. *Indexed:* CIJE, ECER, IBZ, L&LBA, PsycholAb. *Aud.:* Ac, Sa.

Focus on Autism and Other Developmental Disabilities addresses issues concerning individuals with autism and other developmental disabilities and their families. Included are original research reports, position papers, effective intervention procedures, and descriptions of successful programs. Most issues include six to eight articles, and some issues include a book review. Articles cover topics throughout the life span in home, school, work, and community settings. Recent issues have included articles on respite care, development of communication skills, Supplemental Security Income, managed care, and workplace supports. Two recent issues devoted to a special theme include an issue devoted to multicultural aspects related to educating autistic children and a special issue on Asperger syndrome. Recommended primarily for academic libraries.

2144. *Focus on Exceptional Children.* [ISSN: 0015-511X] 1969. 9x/yr. USD 36. Ed(s): Stanley F Love. Love Publishing Co., PO Box 22353, Denver, CO 80222. Illus., adv. Circ: 3000. Vol. ends: May. Microform: PQC. Online: bigchalk; EBSCO Publishing; Florida Center for Library Automation; Gale Group; Northern Light Technology, Inc.; OCLC Online Computer Library Center, Inc.; ProQuest Information & Learning; H.W. Wilson. Reprint: PQC. *Indexed:* CIJE, ECER, EduInd, SSCI. *Aud.:* Ac, Sa.

Each newsletter features one scholarly, but not necessarily research-based, article on a topic of current interest to teachers, special educators, administrators, or others concerned with the education of exceptional children. The focus is on practice rather than theory. Recent articles include "Supporting Students with Health Needs in Schools: An Overview of Selected Health Conditions" and "Planning the IEP for Students with Emotional and Behavioral Disorders." This inexpensive title is a good choice for libraries that serve teachers and teacher educators.

The Future of Children. See Free Magazines and House Organs section.

2145. *Hearing Health: the voice on hearing issues.* Formerly (until 1992): *Voice.* 1984. q. USD 24 domestic; USD 43 foreign; USD 4.95 newsstand/cover per issue. Ed(s): Paula Bonillas. Voice International Publications, Inc., 2989 Main St, Box V, Ingleside, TX 78362-0500. Illus., adv. Circ: 20000. *Indexed:* L&LBA. *Aud.:* Sa.

After being published privately for 19 years, *Hearing Health* became a publication of the Deafness Research Foundation with the Spring 2003 issue. *Hearing Health's* mission is to increase awareness of real-world applications of research, technology, and trends, and to educate people about the effects of hearing loss on health and quality of life. The language is nontechnical and articles are written for persons with hearing impairments and their families. The full text of selected articles and "News Flashes" are available on the magazine's web site. Recent articles include "Why People Reject Hearing Aids" and "Anxiety and Hearing Loss." Recommended for libraries that serve populations with the deaf or hard-of-hearing.

2146. *Hearing Loss: the journal of self help for hard of hearing people.* Former titles: *S H H Journal; Shhh.* [ISSN: 1090-6215] 1980. bi-m. Individuals, USD 25. Ed(s): Barbara Kelley. Self Help for Hard of Hearing People, Inc., 7910 Woodmont Ave, Ste 1200, Bethesda, MD 20814; http://www.shhh.org. Adv. Circ: 30000. *Indexed:* AgeL, ECER. *Aud.:* Sa.

Hearing Loss is published by the organization SHHH (Self Help for Hard of Hearing People), which has 250 chapters throughout the United States and claims to represent over 26 million consumers. At the local level, *SHHH* chapters provide self-help programs, technical information, social activities, and referrals. At the national level, the organization sponsors conferences and an annual convention, and publishes *Hearing Loss,* a magazine that seeks "to make mainstream society more accessible to people who are hard of hearing" and "to improve the quality of life for hard-of-hearing people through education, advocacy, and self-help." It includes short, informative articles and updates on a variety of subjects related to hearing loss. Much of the information relates to technological and medical advances. Recommended for libraries serving deaf or hard-of-hearing populations.

2147. *International Journal of Disability, Development and Education.* Former titles (until 1990): *Exceptional Child; Slow Learning Child.* [ISSN: 1034-912X] 1954. q. GBP 221 (Individuals, GBP 81). Ed(s): Christa van Kraayenoord. Carfax Publishing Ltd., 4 Park Sq, Milton Park, Abingdon, OX14 4RN, United Kingdom; enquiry@tandf.co.uk; http://www.tandf.co.uk/. Illus., index, adv. Sample. Refereed. Circ: 1400. Microform: NRP. Online: EBSCO Publishing; Ingenta Select; OCLC Online Computer Library Center, Inc.; RMIT Publishing; RoweCom Information Quest; Swets Blackwell; H.W. Wilson. Reprint: PSC. *Indexed:* ASSIA, CIJE, ECER, EduInd, L&LBA, PsycholAb, SSCI. *Aud.:* Ac, Sa.

This scholarly journal is multidisciplinary, with an international focus. Research and review articles that concern "all aspects of education, human development, special education, and rehabilitation" are published. Recent articles have included "Self-Concept of Young People with Physical Disabilities: Does Integration Play a Role?" and "How German Teachers in Special Education Perceive and Describe Children with a Learning Disability." An online sample, an order form, and contents information are located on the journal's web site. Recommended for academic libraries.

2148. *International Journal of Rehabilitation Research.* [ISSN: 0342-5282] 1977. q. USD 373 for print & online eds. (Individuals, USD 144 for print & online eds.; Qualified personnel, USD 73 for print & online eds.). Ed(s): Juhani Wikstroem. Lippincott Williams & Wilkins, 530 Walnut St, Philadelphia, PA 19106-3621; http://www.lww.com. Illus., index, adv. Refereed. Circ: 1000. Vol. ends: Dec. Online: EBSCO Publishing; Swets Blackwell. *Indexed:* AgeL, BiolAb, CIJE, CINAHL, CJA, ECER, EngInd, ErgAb, ExcerpMed, IndMed, PsycholAb, SSCI. *Bk. rev.:* Various number and length. *Aud.:* Ac, Sa.

The *International Journal of Rehabilitation Research* is the official journal of the European Federation for Research in Rehabilitation. As such, it is international in scope and includes research information on both industrialized and Third World countries. Most issues include at least five "Original Articles" and several, shorter "Brief Research Reports." The journal is interdisciplinary and targets such fields as rehabilitation medicine, nursing, social and vocational rehabilitation, special education, social policy, social work and social welfare, sociology, psychology, psychiatry, and rehabilitation technology. Areas of interest include disability throughout the life cycle; rehabilitation programs for persons with physical, sensory, mental, and developmental disabilities; measurement of disability; special education and vocational rehabilitation; equipment, access, and transportation; independent living; and consumer, legal, economic, and sociopolitical aspects of disability. The December issue includes annual author and keyword indexes. For comprehensive collections.

2149. *Intervention in School and Clinic.* Former titles (until 1990): *Academic Therapy;* (until 1968): *Academic Therapy Quarterly.* [ISSN: 1053-4512] 1965. 5x/yr. USD 114 (Individuals, USD 39). Ed(s): Brenda Smith Myles. Pro-Ed Inc., 8700 Shoal Creek Blvd, Austin, TX 78757-6897; journals@proedinc.com; http://www.proedinc.com. Illus., index, adv. Sample. Refereed. Circ: 2800. Vol. ends: May. Microform: PQC. Online: EBSCO Publishing; Florida Center for Library Automation; Gale Group; Ingenta Select; OCLC Online Computer Library Center, Inc.; ProQuest Information & Learning; H.W. Wilson. Reprint: PSC. *Indexed:* ASSIA, ArtHuCI, CIJE, ECER, EduInd, IBZ, L&LBA, PsycholAb, SSCI. *Bk. rev.:* 4, 150 words. *Aud.:* Ac, Sa.

This practitioner-oriented publication is designed to provide practical, research-based ideas to those who work with students who have severe learning disabilities or emotional/behavioral problems and for whom typical classroom instruction is not effective. Issues usually include four main articles. Topics frequently deal with assessment, curriculum, instructional techniques, management, social interventions, and vocational issues. Recent articles were "Developing Person-Centered IEP's," "Science and Students With Mild Disabilities," and " Teaching Self-Advocating Strategies Through Drama." Regular columns are "20 Ways to...," a brief listing of 20 techniques related to a specific theme; "What Works for Me," suggestions from practitioners on effective instructional strategies; and "Conference Dateline," which lists a variety of upcoming conferences. Recent issues have included "20 Ways to Eliminate Bullying in Your Classroom" and "What Works for Me—Integrated Processing: A Strategy for Working Out Unknown Words." Highly recommended for libraries that serve teachers, administrators, and teacher educators.

2150. *Journal of Autism and Developmental Disorders.* Formerly (until 1979): *Journal of Autism and Childhood Schizophrenia.* [ISSN: 0162-3257] 1971. bi-m. EUR 801 print or online ed. Ed(s): Gary B Mesibov. Kluwer Academic / Plenum Publishers, 233 Spring St Fl 7, New York, NY 10013-1522; http://www.wkap.nl/. Illus., index, adv. Refereed. Vol. ends: Dec. Microform: PQC. Online: EBSCO Publishing; ingenta.com; Kluwer Online; Ovid Technologies, Inc.; RoweCom Information Quest. *Indexed:* ASSIA, BiolAb, CIJE, CINAHL, ChemAb, ECER, EduInd, ExcerpMed, IMFL, IndMed, PsycholAb, SSCI, SWR&A. *Aud.:* Ac, Sa.

This scholarly journal covers "all severe psychopathologies in childhood and is not necessarily limited to autism and childhood schizophrenia." Articles include experimental studies on the biochemical, neurological, and genetic aspects of the disorder; the implication of normal development for deviant processes; interaction between disordered behavior of individuals and social or group factors; research and case studies involving interventions, including behavioral, biological, education, and community aspects; and diagnosis and classification of disorders reflecting new knowledge. Original research, theoretical papers, critical reviews, and case studies are included. A recent issue includes the articles "Contextualized Behavioral Support in Early Intervention for Children with Autism and Their Families," "Lack of Benefit of Intravenous Synthetic Human Secretin in the Treatment of Autism," and a review of the Asperger Syndrome Diagnostic Scale. An online sample copy and contents information for recent issues are available on the web site. For medical and academic libraries.

Journal of Developmental Education. See Education/Higher Education section.

2151. *Journal of Disability Policy Studies.* [ISSN: 1044-2073] 1990. 4x/yr. USD 114 (Individuals, USD 44). Ed(s): Billie Jo Rylanie, Craig R Fiedler. Pro-Ed Inc., 8700 Shoal Creek Blvd, Austin, TX 78757-6897; journals@proedinc.com; http://www.proedinc.com. Illus., adv. Refereed. Circ: 500. Reprint: PSC. *Indexed:* ECER, PAIS, PSA, PsycholAb, SociolAb. *Aud.:* Ac, Sa.

Discusses disability policy topics and issues and addresses ethics, policy, and law related to individuals with disabilities. Regular features include "From My Perspective," which provides readers with discussions of the issues currently confronting a particular disability discipline or area, and "Disability Policy Newsbreak!," which offers a listing of the activities of specific disability organizations. Occasionally, special series discuss current problems or areas that need more in-depth research. Past topics have included rehabilitation for people with psychiatric impairments, political participation of people with disabilities, and the status of policy affecting women with disabilities. Recommended for comprehensive collections.

2152. *Journal of Early Intervention.* Formerly (until 1989): *Council of Exceptional Children. Division for Early Childhood. Journal.* [ISSN: 1053-8151] 1979. q. USD 70 (Individuals, USD 50). Ed(s): Patricia Snyder. Council for Exceptional Children, Division for Early Childhood, 634 Eddy Ave, Missoula, MT 59812; dec@selway.unit.org. Illus., index, adv. Refereed. Circ: 7000. Vol. ends: Fall. *Indexed:* CIJE, ECER, PsycholAb, SSCI. *Bk. rev.:* 2-3, 600-900 words. *Aud.:* Ac.

Publishes articles related to research and practice in early interventions for infants and young children with special needs and their families. The childhood years in which early intervention might occur begin at birth, or before birth for some prevention programs, and extend through the years that children traditionally begin elementary school. Articles are generally research reports, scholarly reviews, or policy analyses. Most articles relate directly to or have a clear relevance for practice. Recent issues include one feature article, three to five regular articles, and two shorter articles designated "Reactions from the Field," which allow readers to respond to current issues. Articles designated "Innovative Practices" are frequently included. These describe unique or innovative programs, curricula, techniques, or practices related to any aspect of early intervention. Tables of contents for current and past issues are included on the journal's web site. For academic and special libraries.

Journal of Learning Disabilities. See Education/Educational Psychology and Measurement, Special Education, Counseling section.

2153. *Journal of Rehabilitation.* [ISSN: 0022-4154] 1935. q. USD 65 United States; USD 75 Canada; USD 90 elsewhere. Ed(s): Paul Alston. National Rehabilitation Association, 633 S Washington St, Alexandria, VA 22314-4109; info@nationalrehab.org; http://www.nationalrehab.org. Illus., adv. Refereed. Circ: 11000 Controlled. Vol. ends: Oct/Dec. Microform: PQC. Online: EBSCO Publishing; Florida Center for Library Automation; Gale Group; Northern Light Technology, Inc.; OCLC Online Computer Library Center, Inc.; ProQuest Information & Learning; H.W. Wilson. *Indexed:* AgeL, CIJE, CINAHL, ECER, ExcerpMed, IndMed, PsycholAb, SSCI, SSI. *Aud.:* Ac, Sa.

This journal serves as the official publication of the National Rehabilitation Association. Most issues include six or seven articles that cover a broad range of disability-related issues. A recent issue included articles that dealt with mental retardation, Prader-Willi Syndrome, and AIDS. Articles are frequently international in scope, and are research-based and practice-oriented. Organization news; job advertisements; and book, audiovisual, and software reviews are included in some issues. Contents information and article abstracts from 1999 to the present are available on the journal's web site. This inexpensive and well-indexed title is primarily for academic and hospital libraries.

2154. *Journal of Speech, Language, and Hearing Research.* Formerly (until 1996): *Journal of Speech and Hearing Research;* Which incorporates (1948-1991): *Journal of Speech and Hearing Disorders;* Which was formerly (1936-1947): *Journal of Speech Disorders.* [ISSN: 1092-4388] 1958. bi-m. USD 300 (Individuals, USD 105). Ed(s): Claire Stathopoulos, Susan Ellis Weismer. American Speech - Language - Hearing Association, 10801 Rockville Pike, Rockville, MD 20852; sghoting@asha.org. Illus., index, adv. Refereed. Circ: 73000. Vol. ends: Dec. Microform: PQC. Online: bigchalk; EBSCO Publishing; Florida Center for Library Automation; Gale Group; OCLC Online Computer Library Center, Inc.; ProQuest Information & Learning; H.W. Wilson. Reprint: PQC. *Indexed:* ASSIA, AgeL, ArtHuCI, BiolAb, CIJE, CINAHL, ChemAb, ECER, EduInd, ExcerpMed, IndMed, L&LBA, LingAb, MLA-IB, PsycholAb, SSCI, SSI. *Bk. rev.:* Various number and length. *Aud.:* Ac, Sa.

The American Speech-Language-Hearing Association publishes the *Journal of Speech, Language, and Hearing Research.* Each issue is divided into three major categories: "Language," "Speech," and "Hearing." Each of these categories has a separate editor and most issues feature from three to nine significant articles in each area. Articles "pertain broadly to studies of the processes and disorders of speech, language, and hearing, and to the diagnosis and treatment of such disorders." Articles may be reports of original research; theoretical, tutorial, or review articles; or research notes. Topics that are covered include screening, assessment, treatment techniques, prevention, professional issues, supervision, and administration. Author, title, and subject indexes are included in each December issue. Contents information and abstracts back to February 1999 are available on the web site. This scholarly journal will primarily interest researchers and professional educators.

2155. *Journal of Visual Impairment & Blindness.* Formed by the merger of (1951-1977): *New Outlook for the Blind;* (1962-1977): *A F B Research Bulletin.* [ISSN: 0145-482X] 1977. m. USD 180 (Individuals, USD 130). Ed(s): Alan J Koenig. American Foundation for the Blind Press, 11 Penn Plaza, Suite 300, New York, NY 10001; afbinfo@afb.net; http://www.afb.org. Illus., adv. Refereed. Circ: 7000. Vol. ends: Nov/Dec. Online: EBSCO Publishing; OCLC Online Computer Library Center, Inc.; H.W. Wilson. Reprint: PQC. *Indexed:* AgeL, ArtHuCI, CIJE, CINAHL, ECER, EduInd, ExcerpMed, L&LBA, PsycholAb, SSCI, SWR&A. *Bk. rev.:* Various number, brief. *Aud.:* Ac, Sa.

The *Journal of Visual Impairment and Blindness* includes both research articles and shorter articles and is a key resource for practitioners. In addition to major research articles, the journal includes "Practice Reports" (descriptions of innovative techniques and summaries of best practices from the field) and "Research Reports" (brief reports on new research, new inventions and technology, unpublished studies, relevant work from other fields, ongoing research, and innovative methodology). Some issues also include "Perspectives"(invited discussion on a timely and important and perhaps controversial topic); "Employment Updates" (reports on innovative vocational rehabilitation programs and employment trends); "USABLE Data Reports" (demographic and other statistical information about blindness and low vision); "Reviews" (reviews of new scholarly as well as general interest titles, and videos related to blindness); "From the Field" (extensive news reports about the people, projects, and events in visual impairment); and "News" (announcements of new products and publications). Classified ads feature products, services, and situations available. December issues include a "Subjects and Names" annual index. A free sample can be requested, and a table of contents and article abstracts are available on the journal's web site. Also available in Braille and on cassette. Highly recommended for all libraries that serve the visually impaired or programs that train persons to work with the visually impaired.

Learning Disability Quarterly. See Education/Educational Psychology and Measurement, Special Education, Counseling section.

Mental and Physical Disability Law Reporter. See Law section.

2156. *Mental Retardation: a journal of practices, policy and perspectives.* [ISSN: 0047-6765] 1963. bi-m. USD 199 for print & online (Individuals, USD 99 for print & online; USD 30 per issue domestic). Ed(s): Steven Taylor. American Association on Mental Retardation, 444 N Capitol St, Ste 846, Washington, DC 20001-1512. Illus., index, adv. Refereed. Circ: 7500. Vol. ends: Dec. Online: OCLC Online Computer Library Center, Inc.; H.W. Wilson. *Indexed:* AgeL, BiolAb, CIJE, EduInd, ExcerpMed, IndMed, L&LBA, PsycholAb, SSCI, SociolAb. *Bk. rev.:* 3-4, 750-1,200 words. *Aud.:* Ac, Sa.

Mental Retardation is a peer-reviewed journal that includes "policy, practices, and perspectives in the field of mental retardation." It is the official publication of the American Association on Mental Retardation, and some organization business is published in the journal. Topics covered include new teaching approaches, program developments, administrative tools, program evaluation, service utilization studies, community surveys, public policy issues, training and case studies, and research. Although it is research-oriented, the focus is on applied research. The editors state that two main criteria for acceptance include "relevance to policy or practice" and "potential reader interest." The "Perspectives" section offers short, non-research-based articles. "Trends and Milestones" includes current demographic information. A subject index back to 1990 is also available on the web site. Researchers and practitioners are the intended audience. Recommended for academic and special libraries.

Mouth. See Zines section.

2157. *New Mobility: total resource magazine for the disability community.* Former titles (until 1994): *Spinal Network's New Mobility;* (until 1992): *Spinal Network EXTRA.* [ISSN: 1086-4741] 1989. m. USD 27.95 domestic; USD 35.95 Canada; USD 57.95 elsewhere. Ed(s): Jean Dobbs. No Limits, Inc., PO Box 220, Horsham, PA 19044. Illus., adv. Sample. *Aud.:* Ga, Ac, Sa.

This glossy, upbeat magazine helps fill the need for popular, general-interest publications for persons who have disabilities, especially persons with mobility impairments. *New Mobility* covers "people and issues that matter to people with disabilities: medical news and cure research; jobs; benefits; civil rights; sports, recreation and travel; fertility, pregnancy and child care." Feature articles from current issues can be read on *New Mobility*'s web site. The web site also features a search engine for the magazine and several interactive options, including a users' message center, an advertising board, an online chat option, and a "Classified" section. It also includes a well-developed list of links to other sites. Both the magazine and the web site represent a lifestyle. The editor writes, "Disability isn't all misery or triumph, pity or admiration. Disability is news, art, politics, humor, healing, recreation, travel, show-biz and rehab-biz, and that's what we do." They do it well. A good choice for both public and academic libraries.

2158. *O T J R: Occupation, Participation and Health.* Formerly (until 2002): *Occupational Therapy Journal of Research.* [ISSN: 1539-4492] 1981. q. USD 89 (Individuals, USD 59; Students, USD 29). Ed(s): Carolyn Baum. Slack, Inc., 6900 Grove Rd, Thorofare, NJ 08086-9447; http://www.slackinc.com. Illus., index, adv. Refereed. Circ: 900. Vol. ends: Fall. *Indexed:* AgeL, CIJE, CINAHL, ExcerpMed, PsycholAb, SSCI. *Aud.:* Ac, Sa.

This journal, published by the American Occupational Therapy Foundation, offers original research articles of professional interest to the occupational therapist. Issues generally include three or four feature articles. Recent articles have included "Occupational Embeddedness During a Reaching and Placing Task With Survivors of Cerebral Vascular Accident" and "Validation of School Function Assessment With Elementary School Children." The fall issue includes annual title and author indexes. The web site includes subscription information, requests for a trial subscription, and links to nursing and health professionals' resources. Recommended for academic and medical libraries.

2159. *Odyssey: New Directions in Deaf Education.* Former titles (until 2000): *Perspectives in Education and Deafness;* (until 1989): *Perspectives for Teachers of the Hearing Impaired.* 1982. q. Ed(s): Cathryn Carroll. Gallaudet University, Laurent Clerc National Deaf Education Center, 800 Florida Ave, NE, Washington, DC 20002-3695. Illus., index, adv. Refereed. Circ: 4000. Vol. ends: May/Jun. *Indexed:* CIJE, CompLI, ECER, SSI. *Aud.:* Hs, Ac, Sa.

Odyssey is published three times a year by the Laurent Clerc National Deaf Education Center at Gallaudet University and is distributed free of charge. The full text of issues back to Winter 2000 is also available on the magazine's web site. Articles are written in a practical, conversational style and cover a wide range of issues important to the families of deaf and hard-of-hearing children and to those involved in deaf education. Articles describe effective teaching techniques and strategies, learning activities, and innovative projects, research, information, and personal experiences that relate to current issues in education, deafness, and raising deaf children. Recommended primarily for academic libraries that serve teacher education programs, but appropriate for any library that serves a deaf or hard-of-hearing population.

2160. *P N - Paraplegia News.* Formerly (until 1992): *Paraplegia News.* 1946. m. USD 23 domestic; USD 32 foreign. Ed(s): Cliff Crase. P V A Publications, 2111 E Highland Ave. Ste 180, Phoenix, AZ 85016-4702; http://www.pvamagazines.com. Illus., index, adv. Circ: 30000. Vol. ends: Dec. Online: Gale Group; Northern Light Technology, Inc.; OCLC Online Computer Library Center, Inc. *Indexed:* SportS. *Aud.:* Ga, Ac, Sa.

This appealing magazine is published by the Paralyzed Veterans of America and is a vehicle for relaying organization news as well as for presenting all news concerning paraplegics (civilians and veterans) and wheelchair living. The format includes numerous color photographs, and topics target the latest on spinal-cord-injury research, new products, legislation, people with disabilities, accessible travel, and computers. The publisher's web site features an index of articles from previous issues, an extensive list of resources, and a calendar of upcoming events. This inexpensive title is a good choice for libraries that serve persons with spinal cord injuries.

2161. *Palaestra: forum of sport, physical education and recreation for those with disabilities.* [ISSN: 8756-5811] 1984. q. USD 25 (Individuals, USD 19). Ed(s): William Lorton, David P Beaver. Challenge Publications, Ltd., Circulation Department, PO Box 508, Macomb, IL 61455-0508. Illus., index, adv. Circ: 5500. Microform: PQC. Online: Gale Group; Northern Light Technology, Inc.; OCLC Online Computer Library Center, Inc.; ProQuest Information & Learning. *Indexed:* PEI, SportS. *Bk. rev.:* 5-7, 150-200 words. *Aud.:* Ac, Sa.

This colorful, upbeat magazine has a threefold mission: "to enlighten parents in all aspects of physical activity, making them the best advocates for their children during IEP discussions with school or community recreation staffs; to increase the knowledge base of professionals working with children or adults with disabilities, making them aware of the ~can do' possibilities of their students/clients; and to show the value physical activity holds for adult readers' increased wellness." The emphasis is on practical research and descriptions of successful programs or suggested techniques for use with a wide variety of disabilities. Sports nutrition, new product updates, legislative updates, and training tips are regular features. An author and title index is included in the fall issue. Recommended for public and academic libraries that serve programs in special education, physical education, or therapeutic recreation.

2162. *Physical Therapy.* Former titles (until 1962): *Physiotherapy Review;* (until 1926): *P.T.Review.* [ISSN: 0031-9023] 1921. m. USD 95 (Individuals, USD 70). Ed(s): Jan P Reynolds, Dr. Jules Rothstein. American Physical Therapy Association, 1111 N Fairfax St, Alexandria, VA 22314-1488; ptunderscorejournal@apta.org; http://www.apta.org. Illus., index, adv. Refereed. Circ: 77000 Controlled. Vol. ends: Dec. Microform: PQC. Online: Central Institute for Scientific & Technical Information; EBSCO Publishing; Florida Center for Library Automation; Gale Group; Northern Light Technology, Inc.; OCLC Online Computer Library Center, Inc.; ProQuest Information & Learning. Reprint: PQC. *Indexed:* AgeL, CINAHL, ECER, ExcerpMed, IndMed, PEI, SCI, SSCI, SportS. *Bk. rev.:* Various number and length. *Aud.:* Ac, Sa.

The official journal of the American Physical Therapy Association. Articles include case reports that describe an element of practice not previously documented in the literature; reports on original research; technical reports that describe and document the specifications or mechanical aspects of a device used by physical therapists; literature reviews; papers that present clinical perspectives on a specific clinical approach; and discussions of issues in physical therapy, health care, and related areas. Book, software, and video reviews; letters to the editor; product news; and association business are included. December issues include a list of education programs that lead to qualifications as a physical therapist. The journal's web site also includes a search engine, abstracts of articles published since January 1995, and free full-text access to many articles. Primarily for academic and special libraries.

2163. *Preventing School Failure.* Formerly: *Pointer (Washington).* [ISSN: 1045-988X] 1956. q. USD 101 (Individuals, USD 49; USD 25.25 per issue). Ed(s): Stephanie Fain. Heldref Publications, 1319 18th St, NW, Washington, DC 20036-1802; subscribe@heldref.org; http://www.heldref.org. Illus., index, adv. Refereed. Circ: 550. CD-ROM: ProQuest Information & Learning. Online: bigchalk; EBSCO Publishing; Florida Center for Library Automation; Gale Group; OCLC Online Computer Library Center, Inc.; ProQuest Information & Learning; SoftLine Information; H.W. Wilson. Reprint: PQC; PSC. *Indexed:* CIJE, ECER, EduInd, PsycholAb. *Aud.:* Ac, Sa.

Preventing School Failure is designed "for educators and other professionals seeking strategies to promote the success of students who have learning and behavior problems." It includes examples of programs and practices that help children and youth in schools, clinics, correctional institutions, and other settings. Each issue publishes six to eight articles that detail classroom applications and practical examples of successful teaching strategies. Recent articles have included "The Impact of Looping Classroom Environments on Parental Attitudes" and "What Teachers Can Do to Prevent Behavior Problems in Schools." There are occasional theme issues, such as a recent issue entitled "Teaching Reading: Strategies for Success with Challenging Learners." Teachers and teacher educators write the majority of articles, and the emphasis is on practice as opposed to theory. An annual author and title index is included in the summer issues. Highly recommended for libraries that serve teachers and teacher educators.

2164. *R E: view: rehabilitation and education for blindness and visual impairment.* Former titles: *Education of the Visually Handicapped; International Journal for the Education of the Blind.* [ISSN: 0899-1510] 1969. q. USD 94 (Individuals, USD 28; USD 23.50 per issue). Ed(s): Helen Strang. Heldref Publications, 1319 18th St, NW, Washington, DC 20036-1802; subscribe@heldref.org; http://www.heldref.org. Illus., index, adv. Refereed. Circ: 4300. CD-ROM: ProQuest Information & Learning. Online: bigchalk; EBSCO Publishing; Florida Center for Library Automation; Gale Group; OCLC Online Computer Library Center, Inc.; ProQuest Information & Learning; SoftLine Information; H.W. Wilson. Reprint: PSC. *Indexed:* CIJE, ECER, EduInd, IBZ, PsycholAb, SSCI. *Bk. rev.:* Various number and length, signed. *Aud.:* Ac, Sa.

RE:view is a peer-reviewed journal published in conjunction with the Association for Education and Rehabilitation of the Blind and Visually Impaired. The intended audience is "people concerned with services to individuals of all ages with visual disabilities, including those with multiple disabilities and deaf-blindness." Although written for professionals, the articles are accessible to the general public who have an interest in the topic. Articles include reports on useful practices and controversial issues, research findings, experiments, and professional experiences. Topics cover education and rehabilitation, administrative practices, counseling, technology, and other services to people with visual disabilities. The editors encourage contributions from people who have visual impairments. "Springboard" is a regular column designed for practitioners to use to get their ideas out in front of their peers. The winter issue includes a title and author index. Libraries that serve institutions that have programs for the visually impaired should own this key title.

2165. *Reading and Writing Quarterly: overcoming learning difficulties.* Former titles: *Journal of Reading, Writing, and Learning Disabilities International; Chicorel Abstracts to Reading and Learning Disabilities.* [ISSN: 1057-3569] 1984. q. USD 322 (Individuals, USD 122). Ed(s): Howard Margolis. Taylor & Francis Inc, 325 Chestnut St, Suite 800, Philadelphia, PA 19016; info@taylorandfrancis.com; http://www.taylorandfrancis.com/. Illus., index. Refereed. Vol. ends: Oct/Dec. Microform: PQC. Online: EBSCO Publishing; Ingenta Select; OCLC Online Computer Library Center, Inc.; RoweCom Information Quest. Reprint: PQC; PSC. *Indexed:* CIJE, ECER, L&LBA, PsycholAb. *Aud.:* Ac, Sa.

Reading and Writing Quarterly ". . . disseminates critical information to improve instruction for regular and special education students who have difficulty learning to read and write." Articles address such issues as adjustments for language-learning style, literature-based reading programs, teaching reading and writing in the mainstream, study strategies, language-centered computer curricula, oral language connections to literacy, cooperative learning approaches to reading and writing, direct instruction, curriculum-based assessment, the impact of environmental factors on instructional effectiveness, and improvement of self-esteem. The emphasis is practical rather than theoretical. Most issues will feature a theme; for example, recent themes have been "Motivation and Self-Efficacy Belief" and "Motivating Struggling Readers to Succeed." A recent special issue was devoted to "Closing the Gap: Providing Late Intervention for Struggling Learners in Grades 4-8." The web site includes the table of contents back to 1999 and an online sample copy. Recommended for libraries that serve professional educators.

2166. ***Research and Practice for Persons with Severe Disabilities.*** Former titles (until 2002): *The Association for Persons with Severe Handicaps. Journal;* (until 1983): *Association for the Severely Handicapped. Journal (JASH);* (until vol.5, no.1): *A A E S P H Review (American Association for the Education of the Severely-Profoundly Handicapped).* [ISSN: 1540-7969] 1975. q. USD 200 (Individuals, USD 88; Students, USD 45). Ed(s): Linda Bambara. T A S H, 29 W Susquehanna Ave, Ste 210, Baltimore, MD 21204-5201; http://www.tash.org. Illus., adv. Refereed. Circ: 3800. Vol. ends: Winter. Microform: PQC. Online: OCLC Online Computer Library Center, Inc.; H.W. Wilson. Reprint: PQC. *Indexed:* AgeL, CIJE, ECER, EduInd, L&LBA, SSCI. *Aud.:* Ac, Sa.

This scholarly journal (formerly *Journal of the Association for Persons with Severe Handicaps*) publishes original research, comprehensive reviews, conceptual and practical position papers that offer assessment and intervention methodologies, and program descriptions. Although the journal is research-based, putting theory into practice is emphasized. Some issues offer a "Special Topic," including a "Featured Article" and "Invited Commentaries." A recent Featured Article was "How Science Can Evaluate and Enhance Person-Centered Planning." A subject index for 1997–2000 is located on the journal's web site. An important title for libraries that support programs for persons with severe disabilities.

2167. ***Rural Special Education Quarterly.*** [ISSN: 8756-8705] 1984. q. USD 50; USD 56 foreign. Ed(s): Barbara Ludlow. American Council on Rural Special Education, Kansas State University, 2323 Anderson Ave., Ste. 226, Manhattan, KS 66502-2912. Illus., index. Circ: 650. Vol. ends: Fall. Online: EBSCO Publishing; ProQuest Information & Learning. *Indexed:* Agr, CIJE. *Aud.:* Ac, Sa.

Rural Special Education Quarterly is a scholarly journal produced by the American Council on Rural Special Education (ACRES). The aim is to provide rural educators and administrators with information about federal initiatives and other events relevant to rural individuals with disabilities. Most issues include three articles that generally "focus on identified service delivery systems, applied theory/research, or practical, field-tested solutions." Practical, problem-solving approaches and strategies used in successful programs are featured. Issues are occasionally written around a theme. An archive of article abstracts back to Winter 1992 is available on the journal's web site. This modestly priced periodical is recommended for libraries that serve teacher education programs or special educators in rural areas.

2168. ***Sexuality and Disability: a journal devoted to the psychological and medical aspects of sexuality in rehabilitation and community settings.*** [ISSN: 0146-1044] 1978. q. EUR 514 print or online ed. Ed(s): Stanley Ducharme. Kluwer Academic / Plenum Publishers, 233 Spring St Fl 7, New York, NY 10013-1522; http://www.wkap.nl/. Illus., index, adv. Sample. Refereed. Vol. ends: Winter. Microform: PQC. Online: EBSCO Publishing; ingenta.com; Kluwer Online; OCLC Online Computer Library Center, Inc.; RoweCom Information Quest; Swets Blackwell. Reprint: ISI; PQC. *Indexed:* AgeL, BiolAb, CINAHL, ExcerpMed, IMFL, PsycholAb, SFSA, SSCI, SWA. *Bk. rev.:* Various number and length. *Aud.:* Ac, Sa.

This international scholarly journal publishes articles "that address the psychological and medical aspects of sexuality in the field of rehabilitation." It covers developments in the areas of sexuality related to a wide range of disabilities. Articles include clinical practice reports, case studies, research and survey data, guidelines for clinical practice, developments in special programs in sex education, and counseling for disabled individuals. The editor particularly encourages contributions related to consumer issues, community programs, and independent living programs. Although scholarly in approach, most articles are accessible to the general public who have an interest in the subject. Issues will occasionally focus on a theme. Recent special issues have been devoted to parents with disabilities and to sexuality and cancer. Contents information and abstracts from fall 1998 are available on the web site. Subscribers can choose to receive either the paper version, the online version, or both for an additional 20 percent. Primarily for academic collections.

Sharing Solutions. See Large Print section.

2169. ***Sign Language Studies.*** [ISSN: 0302-1475] 1972. q. USD 90 (Individuals, USD 40). Ed(s): David F Armstrong. Gallaudet University, Department of English, 800 Florida Ave, NE, Washington, DC 20002. Illus., adv. Circ: 485. Online: OCLC Online Computer Library Center, Inc.; Project MUSE; ProQuest Information & Learning; RoweCom Information Quest; Swets Blackwell. *Indexed:* AICP, BAS, CIJE, ECER, L&LBA, LT&LA, MLA-IB, PsycholAb. *Bk. rev.:* 1-2. *Aud.:* Ac, Sa.

Published by Gallaudet University Press, this scholarly journal generally includes in each issue three or four research articles and one or two book reviews. Topics include linguistics, anthropology, semiotics, deaf culture, and deaf history and literature. Recent articles include "Indo-Pakistani Sign Language Grammar" and "Variable Subject Presence in ASL Narratives." Two recent issues were devoted to dictionaries and lexicography. The web site includes table of contents information and abstracts of articles back to the fall of 2000. Recommended primarily for academic libraries or libraries that serve the visually impaired.

2170. ***Silent News.*** [ISSN: 0049-0490] 1969. m. USD 30 domestic; USD 40 in Canada & Mexico; USD 50 in South America. Silent News, Inc., 133 Gaither Dr., Ste. E., Mt. Laurel, NJ 08054-1710; silentnews@aol.com. Adv. Circ: 11500 Paid. *Aud.:* Sa.

Silent News is written and published by and for deaf and hard-of-hearing people. This tabloid-style newspaper was established in 1969 and covers world, national, and community events; arts; sports; and health issues for the deaf and hard-of-hearing as well as the deaf/blind community. Personal profiles of deaf individuals and professionals are frequently featured. Employment ads, a calendar of events by state, and regular columnists are also included. Libraries that serve deaf or hard-of-hearing populations will want to subscribe to *Silent News.*

2171. ***SpeciaLiving Magazine.*** [ISSN: 1537-0747] 2002. q. USD 12. Ed(s): Betty Garee. SpeciaLiving, PO Box 1000, Bloomington, IL 61702-1000; garee@aol.com; http://www.SpeciaLiving.com. Illus., adv. Circ: 12000. *Aud.:* Sa.

This new publication is similar in style and content to *Accent on Living,* a magazine that ceased publication in 2001. The same editor as for that magazine started this new magazine, but one that maintains the previous one's tone and purpose. *SpeciaLiving Magazine* focuses on products, travel, accessible housing, people, inspiration, and humor. Short articles feature practical advice and consumer information, primarily for persons with mobility impairments. A regular column by Joni Eareckson Tada offers inspirational advice. Another regular columnist is Shelley Schwarz, who answers questions submitted by readers and offers tips about accessibility and quality-of-life issues. Cartoons, humor, and new product information are also included. This inexpensive and useful publication is recommended primarily for public libraries.

2172. ***Sports 'n Spokes: the magazine for wheelchair sports and recreation.*** [ISSN: 0161-6706] 1975. 6x/yr. USD 21 domestic; USD 27 foreign. Ed(s): Cliff Crase. P V A Publications, 2111 E Highland Ave. Ste 180, Phoenix, AZ 85016-4702; http://www.pvamagazines.com. Illus., index, adv. Sample. Circ: 14000. *Indexed:* PEI, SportS. *Aud.:* Hs, Ga, Sa.

This glossy, upbeat magazine will appeal to the wheelchair athlete and to any adults or teens who have a disabling condition and an interest in sports. There are numerous color photographs and short, informative articles on a variety of current topics. The focus is on coverage of wheelchair competitive sports, but other sports covered include bowling, fencing, handcycling, hockey, racing, sailing, shooting, skiing, rugby, fishing, and tennis. Some other topics covered include nutrition and assistive devices used in sports and recreation. Each issue includes a list of sports associations for the disabled. A calendar of sporting events and a well-developed list of resources are available on the web site. This is a good choice for school, public, and academic libraries.

2173. ***Teaching Exceptional Children.*** [ISSN: 0040-0599] 1968. bi-m. Non-members, USD 58. Ed(s): Dave Edyburn. Council for Exceptional Children, 1110 N. Glebe Rd., Ste. 300, Arlington, VA 22201-4795; http://www.cec.sped.org/bk/tec-jour.htm. Illus., index, adv. Refereed. Circ: 55000. Vol. ends: Jul/Aug. Microform: PQC. Online: EBSCO Publishing; Northern Light Technology, Inc.; OCLC Online Computer Library Center, Inc.; ProQuest Information & Learning; H.W. Wilson. Reprint: PQC. *Indexed:* CIJE, ECER, EduInd, IBZ. *Aud.:* Ac, Sa.

This colorful magazine is published specifically for teachers and administrators. It provides information on technology, assistive technology, and procedures and techniques for teaching students with exceptionalities. The focus of its practical content is on immediate application. Recent articles have included "What Every Special Educator Should Know about High-Stakes Testing" and "Instructional Tips for Teachers of Students with Autistic Spectrum Disorder (ASD)." Contents information, a keyword search, and some full-text articles are available on the journal's web site. Libraries that serve teacher education programs or special educators should own this popular title.

2174. ***Therapeutic Recreation Journal.*** [ISSN: 0040-5914] 1967. q. USD 66; USD 72 foreign. Ed(s): Michael Mabin, Mark Searle. National Recreation and Park Association, 22377 Belmont Ridge Rd, Ashburn, VA 20148-4501; http://www.nrpa.org/. Illus., index, adv. Refereed. Circ: 4000. Microform: PQC. Online: Northern Light Technology, Inc.; ProQuest Information & Learning. *Indexed:* ASSIA, AgeL, CIJE, PEI, RRTA, SportS. *Bk. rev.:* 2-3, 600-1,000 words. *Aud.:* Ac, Sa.

Therapeutic Recreation Journal (*TRJ*) is the official journal of the National Therapeutic Recreation Society, a branch of the National Recreation and Park Association. Some society business is included in the journal. Articles are "scholarly and substantive" and relevant to the field of therapeutic recreation. Each issue generally publishes four articles that are classified as either "Research," "Conceptual Paper," or "Practice Perspectives." Occasionally there will be a theme-related issue. For example, one issue deals with the role and function of therapeutic recreation with families. Most issues include one substantive book review. *TRJ* will be of interest primarily to practitioners and professional educators, but it is a key title in its field and should be owned by libraries that serve therapeutic recreation programs.

2175. ***Topics in Early Childhood Special Education.*** [ISSN: 0271-1214] 1981. q. USD 109 (Individuals, USD 43). Ed(s): Judith Carta. Pro-Ed Inc., 8700 Shoal Creek Blvd, Austin, TX 78757-6897; journals@proedinc.com; http://www.proedinc.com. Illus., index, adv. Refereed. Circ: 1800 Paid and free. Vol. ends: Winter. Microform: PQC. Online: bigchalk; EBSCO Publishing; Florida Center for Library Automation; Gale Group; Ingenta Select; OCLC Online Computer Library Center, Inc.; ProQuest Information & Learning; H.W. Wilson. Reprint: PQC; PSC. *Indexed:* ASSIA, CIJE, ECER, EduInd, IBZ, IMFL, L&LBA, PsycholAb, SSCI, SWA. *Aud.:* Ac, Sa.

The editor defines early intervention to include "services provided to (a) infants, toddlers, and preschoolers who are at risk for or display developmental delays and disabilities, and (b) the families of such youngsters." Articles discuss such issues as personnel preparation, policy issues, the operation of intervention programs, deciphering the complexities of IDEA, and strategies for engaging professionals and family members. Articles are scholarly and generally research-based. Each year, three of the four issues revolve around a topic or theme and one issue is nontopical. Recent topics have included "Innovations in Assessment" and "Evaluating Large-Scale Interventions for Low-Income Families." Practitioners and professional educators are the targeted audience. Recommended primarily for academic libraries.

2176. ***Topics in Language Disorders.*** [ISSN: 0271-8294] 1981. q. USD 199 (Individuals, USD 79). Ed(s): Beth Guthy. Lippincott Williams & Wilkins, 530 Walnut St, Philadelphia, PA 19106-3621; http://www.lww.com. Illus., adv. Refereed. Circ: 4550 Paid. Vol. ends: Aug. *Indexed:* AgeL, CIJE, CINAHL, ECER, EduInd, L&LBA, PsycholAb, SSCI. *Bk. rev.:* Various number and length. *Aud.:* Ac, Sa.

This journal publishes scholarly, but not always researched-based, articles. The emphasis is on "bridging the gap between theory, research, and everyday practice." Each issue publishes from three to six articles based on a central theme. Recent themes have been "The Child Language Specialist in a Digital Environment" and "Alternative Measures for Evaluating Treatment Outcomes." The journal also offers an ASHA-Sponsored Continuing Education program that provides four CEUs per volume. Professional educators and practitioners are the intended audience.

2177. ***The Volta Review.*** [ISSN: 0042-8639] 1898. q. USD 52. Alexander Graham Bell Association for the Deaf and Hard of Hearing, Inc., 3417 Volta Place, NW, Washington, DC 20007; http://www.agbell.org. Illus., adv. Sample. Refereed. Circ: 6000. Vol. ends: Fall. Microform: PQC. Online: EBSCO Publishing. Reprint: PQC. *Indexed:* CIJE, CINAHL, ECER, EduInd, L&LBA, PsycholAb, SSCI. *Bk. rev.:* 4-7, length varies. *Aud.:* Ac, Sa.

The Volta Review is the official journal of the Alexander Graham Bell Association. Each year, four regular issues are published. These issues usually include two research articles, association news, and book reviews. Recent articles have included "The Role of Early Language Experience in the Development of Speech Perception and Language Processing Abilities in Children with Hearing Loss," and "Acoustic Consequences of Evaluating Hearing Aids via Stethoscopes and Listening Tubes." The November issue, a longer "monograph," centers on a specific theme and has a special editor. A recent theme was "Cochlear Implantation: Speech and Language Benefits." Monographs include scholarly articles that present original research or describe successful programs. Contents information back to 1994 is located on the web site. Recommended for libraries that serve teachers and professionals who work with hearing-impaired children and adults.

2178. ***World Around You.*** [ISSN: 0199-8293] 1978. 5x/yr. USD 10 domestic; USD 15 foreign. Ed(s): Cathryn Carroll. Gallaudet University, National Deaf Educ Network & Clearinghouse, 800 Florida Ave, NE, KDES PAS 6, Washington, DC 20002-3695; cmcarrol@gallux.gallaudet.edu; http://clerccenter.gallaudet.edu/. Adv. Circ: 6500. *Aud.:* Hs.

Published at Gallaudet University since 1978, the intended audience of *World Around You* is deaf teens. Each issue has stories about deaf teens and adults who are succeeding in today's world. Other features include information about careers, role models, technology, laws, and deaf culture. The full text of the current issue and most of the back issues dating to November/December 1996 are available on the magazine's web site. Discounts are available for subscriptions of ten or more mailed to the same address. Teachers' guides are available. Although the magazine is designed to be used in the classroom, libraries that serve teacher education programs may want to consider purchasing this title.

Electronic Journals

2179. ***Breaking New Ground: cultivating independence for farmers and ranchers with disabilities.*** 1982. a. Free. Ed(s): Bill Field. Breaking New Ground Resource Center, Purdue University, 1146 Agricultural and Biological Engineering Bldg, West Lafayette, IN 47907-1146; bng@ecn.purdue.edu; http://www.agrability.org. Illus. Circ: 11000. *Aud.:* Ac, Sa.

Although publication of the newsletter ceased with the Winter 2000 edition, *Breaking New Ground Newsnotes* now appears quarterly on the web site. *Breaking New Ground* is part of the Indiana AgrAbility Project, which was started in 1991 to assist farmers and ranchers who have disabilities. Emphasis is on assistive technology and networking. Additional features on the web site are listings of resource materials and audiovisual resources. The "Barn Builders and Caregivers Directory" lists members of a voluntary peer support network of farmers and ranchers with disabilities from across the nation. The list includes people willing to become personally involved in the lives of others who might benefit from their prior experiences. Recommended for libraries serving farmers and/or ranchers and for libraries that serve agricultural engineering programs.

2180. ***DeafDigest.*** 1996. w. Ed(s): Barry M Strassler. Silent News, Inc., 133 Gaither Dr., Ste. E., Mt. Laurel, NJ 08054-1710; barry@deafdigest.com; http://www.deafdigest.org. *Aud.:* Sa.

This free weekly newsletter is available through e-mail subscription. Information on subscribing is available on the web site, which includes the text of the current issue. Brief articles include news items of interest to the deaf community and information about upcoming events. Job openings appropriate for the deaf and hard-of-hearing are included. *DeafDigest* subscribers can also subscribe to the *DeafSportZine* newsletter.

2181. ***I D E A News.*** m. Free. I D E A Practices, Office of Special Education Programs, US Dept of Education, Washington, DC 20202; ideapractices@cec.sped.org; http://idea-live.2rad.net/index.php. *Aud.:* Sa.

This free monthly e-mail newsletter publishes updates and news about the Individuals with Disabilities Education Act (IDEA). The focus is on what is happening nationally and how it affects the local level. It is a cooperative venture of four government-sponsored agencies. Text and HTML versions of archived newsletters are available back to January 2002 on the web site.

2182. ***Incitement.*** irreg. American Disabled for Attendant Programs Today, 1319 Lamar Sq Dr #101, Austin, TX 78704; http://www.adapt.org/incintro.htm. *Aud.:* Sa.

ADAPT is the acronym for American Disabled for Attendant Programs Today, and *Incitement* is their newsletter. ADAPT is an activist organization. Their focus is on promoting services in the community instead of "warehousing people with disabilities in institutions and nursing homes." The organization is very politically active and frequently demonstrates at conventions and national events. According to their web site, "ADAPT has a long history of organizing in the disability community and using civil disobedience and similar non-violent direct action tactics to achieve its goals." The organization's web site includes updates of actions and is usually published after a major ADAPT action. This site is included as an example of a publication of one of the more extreme disability organizations. The newsletter is also available on cassette tapes.

2183. ***Journal of Rehabilitation Research and Development.*** Former titles: *Journal of Rehabilitation R and D; Bulletin of Prosthetics Research.* [ISSN: 0748-7711] 1964. q. Free to qualified personnel. Department of Veterans Affairs, Veterans Health Administration, 103 S Gay St, Baltimore, MD 21202-3517; mail@rehab-balt.med.va.gov; http://www.va.gov. Illus., index. Refereed. Circ: 27000. Microform: PQC. Online: bigchalk; EBSCO Publishing; OCLC Online Computer Library Center, Inc.; ProQuest Information & Learning. Reprint: PQC. *Indexed:* AgeL, ApMecR, BRI, BioEngAb, BiolAb, C&ISA, CBRI, CINAHL, ECER, EngInd, ExcerpMed, H&SSA, IndMed, PEI, SSCI. *Aud.:* Ac, Sa.

The Journal of Rehabilitation Research and Development publishes research that enhances the quality and relevance of Department of Veterans Affairs (VA) rehabilitation research and disseminates information on biomedical and engineering advances. Priority areas are prosthetics, amputations, orthotics, and orthopedics; spinal cord injury and other neurological disorders (with particular focus on traumatic brain injury, multiple sclerosis, and restorative therapies); communication, sensory, and cognitive aids; geriatric rehabilitation; and functional outcome research. The December issues includes an author and title index. The full text of all issues back to October 1999 are available on the journal's web site. The primary audience is researchers, especially engineers.

2184. ***L D Online: the interactive guide to learning disabilities for parents, teachers, and children.*** w. L D Online, http://www.ldonline.org. *Aud.:* Ac, Sa.

Updated weekly, this colorful and well-designed web site features articles geared to families, teachers, and students dealing with learning disabilities. Each week, an "Artist of the Week" and a "Writer of the Week" are featured. Students between the ages of 5 and 18 with learning disabilities are encouraged to submit their work. The "Finding Help" section lists national organizations, federal agencies, state-by-state resource guides, Canadian resources, and resources by phone. The "LD in Depth" section features articles written by leading experts, research findings reported by top researchers, and the latest news in the field. "The ABC's of LD/ADD" answers frequently asked questions. "First Person" offers personal essays on firsthand experiences with the challenges of learning disabilities. Essays authored by teachers, parents, and students offer advice on and insight into living with learning disabilities. Readers can submit questions to a psychiatrist who specializes in the treatment of LD and ADHD, and selected responses are included on the web site. Numerous bulletin boards on such topics as "Parenting a Child With ADHD" and "Teaching an Inclusive Classroom" are also featured. The "LD OnLine Newsletter" is a free e-mail newsletter that keeps readers informed about new features, events, and information on *LD OnLine.* A wealth of information is available on this web site, which will appeal to parents, teachers, and children. Highly recommended.

2185. ***Mainstream (San Diego): magazine of the able-disabled.*** [ISSN: 0278-8225] 1975. 10x/yr. USD 24; USD 44.50 foreign. Ed(s): William G Stothers. Exploding Myths, Inc., 2980 Beech St., San Diego, CA 92102-1534; editor@mainstream-mag.com; http://www.mainstream-mag.com. Illus., index, adv. Sample. Circ: 19400. Vol. ends: Dec. *Indexed:* CompLI. *Aud.:* Ga.

Mainstream was a print magazine from 1975 until the final issue in December 1998/January 1999. Now, *Mainstream Online* is an outspoken zine that has emerged as a strong advocate for disability rights. The online archive includes selected features from the former print magazine as well as current commentaries. It covers "news and current affairs, new products and technology, profiles of movers and shakers, education, employment, sexuality and relationships, housing, transportation, travel and recreation." The tone is frequently strident.

2186. ***Ragged Edge.*** Former titles (until 1997): *Disability Rag and Resource; Disability Rag.* [ISSN: 1095-3949] 1980. bi-m. USD 35 (Individuals, USD 17.50; USD 42 foreign). Ed(s): Mary Johnson. Advocado Press, PO Box 145, Louisville, KY 40201. Adv. Circ: 3000 Paid. Online: ProQuest Information & Learning; SoftLine Information. *Indexed:* AltPI. *Bk. rev.:* Various number and length. *Aud.:* Sa.

Ragged Edge is the successor to *Disability Rag,* one of the first and most vocal vehicles to take a strong stance supporting disability rights. It claims that "you'll find the best in today's writing about society's ragged edge issues: medical rationing, genetic discrimination, assisted suicide, long-term care, attendant services." Each issue includes current news as well as short articles. Persons who have been mistreated or underserved by current systems write many of the stories. A wide variety of conditions are included. For example, a recent article was written by a person with "multiple chemical sensitivity" (MCS). The web site at www.ragged-edge-mag.com includes an archive of past issues back to September/October 1997 and features a section in which individuals can post their personal stories. Both print and e-mail subscriptions are available.

2187. ***The Special Ed Advocate Newsletter.*** [ISSN: 1538-3202] 1998. irreg. Free. Ed(s): Pamela Wright. Wrightslaw, webmaster@wrightslaw.com; http://www.wrightslaw.com/. *Aud.:* Sa.

The Special Ed Advocate is a free online newsletter. Each issue includes updates about special education law, new court cases, and information about effective advocacy. The newsletter and Wrightslaw web site are operated by a lawyer who represents children with special needs and his wife, who is a psychotherapist with training in psychology and clinical social work. Although the Wrights use the web site and newsletter as vehicles for advertising their books and seminars, the information they disseminate without cost provides an important service to professionals attempting to keep abreast of legal issues. Parents will find invaluable information about how to become effective advocates for their children with special needs. Back issues of the newsletter are available on the web site.

■ EARTH SCIENCES

See also Agriculture; Engineering and Technology; Geography; and Paleontology sections.

Edward F. Lener, College Librarian for the Sciences, University Libraries, Virginia Tech, P.O. Box 90001, Blacksburg, VA 24062; lener@vt.edu

Flora G. Shrode, Interim Head, Reference Services, University Libraries, Utah State University, Logan, UT 84322; fshrode@cc.usu.edu

Introduction

Due to heavy media coverage, geologic hazards and natural disasters are often the first thing that comes to mind when one mentions the earth sciences. This is only one small part, however, of the full picture. In fact, the earth sciences touch on many different aspects of our daily lives from the buildings we live in to the energy that powers our industries and our cars. Research spans the range from field reconnaissance, using a simple rock hammer, compass, and hand lens, to advanced three-dimensional computer modeling. The earth sciences are also highly interdisciplinary, drawing heavily on work in biology, chemistry, geography, physics, and mathematics.

As a general rule, publications in the earth sciences tend to have a long lifespan. The importance of older work is reflected in the fact that indexing coverage in the GeoRef database actually extends back to the 1700s. Of course, while much of the older research and descriptive material is still quite valid, new theories and analytical techniques often allow for a better understanding of the true nature of the underlying processes involved. Also, the increasing use of color illustrations in recent years helps readers to understand complex visual information more easily.

The number of good publications for general audiences continues to be limited but there are many excellent academic and specialist journals in the field. When selecting materials in the earth sciences, it is also necessary to consider the issues of geographic coverage and time frame. Work done at sites from around the world and examining different periods of geologic history are essential to developing a well-rounded collection. Obtaining a good mix of both theoretical and applied research is also important. There are not yet many electronic-only journals in the earth sciences, but increasing numbers now offer full texts online. Supplementary material is also available in some cases, as, for example, at the Geological Society of America web site.

The American Geological Institute has developed a list of "priority journals." These are titles recommended by the GeoRef Users Group Steering Committee to receive first priority for database indexing as new issues come out. These titles are indicated in the annotations where applicable. While this is a good general indication of the importance of these titles, one should always be cautious of relying too heavily on any single selection criterion. For the full list of all 99 priority journals, contact the American Geological Institute or access the information on their web site (http://www.agiweb.org/georef/priorjs.html).

Basic Periodicals

Hs, Ga: *Geology Today, Geotimes, Rocks and Minerals;* Ac, Sa: *Geological Society. Journal, Geological Society of America. Bulletin, Geology, Geophysics, Journal of Geology.*

Basic Abstracts and Indexes

Bibliography and Index of Geology.

2188. ***A A P G Bulletin.*** Formerly: *American Association of Petroleum Geologists. Bulletin.* [ISSN: 0149-1423] 1917. m. USD 280 domestic; USD 305 foreign; USD 330 domestic Print & online eds. Ed(s): Carol Christopher, John Lorenz. American Association of Petroleum Geologists, PO Box 979, Tulsa, OK 74101-0979; bulletin@aapg.org; http://www.aapg.org. Illus., index, adv. Refereed. Circ: 31000 Paid. Vol. ends: Dec (No. 12). Microform: PMC; PQC. *Indexed:* ABS&EES, AS&TI, BiolAb, C&ISA, ChemAb, DSR&OA, EngInd, EnvAb, GeoRef, GeogAbPG, MinerAb, OceAb, PetrolAb, PollutAb, SCI, SSCI, SWRA. *Bk. rev.:* 0-4, 300-700 words, signed. *Aud.:* Ac, Sa.

The official journal of the American Association of Petroleum Geologists, this monthly bulletin provides information of interest to the society's members and others in the field, including abstracts from section meetings, new book releases, and calendars of meetings and educational opportunities. More importantly, the many fine research articles cover such topics as reservoir characterization, depositional environments, and basin modeling. The web site offers free searching and previews of upcoming articles. Full-text access to recent issues is available for a fee, either by subscription or per article. Suitable for academic and specialized collections. A GeoRef priority journal.

2189. ***American Journal of Science: devoted to the geological sciences and to related fields.*** Former titles (until 1880): *American Journal of Science and Arts;* (until 1820): *American Journal of Science (1818).* [ISSN: 0002-9599] 1818. 10x/yr. USD 175 (Individuals, USD 75; Students, USD 35). Ed(s): Mary Casey. American Journal of Science, 217 Kline Geology Laboratory, Yale University, PO Box 208109, New Haven, CT 06520-8109; ajs@hess.geology.yale.edu; http://love.geology.yale.edu/. Illus., index. Refereed. Circ: 1727 Paid. Vol. ends: Dec (No. 10). Microform: PMC; PQC. Online: Gale Group. *Indexed:* AS&TI, BiolAb, ChemAb, DSR&OA, EngInd, EnvAb, ExcerpMed, ForAb, GSI, GeoRef, GeogAbPG, MinerAb, OceAb, PetrolAb, S&F, SCI, SSCI, SWRA. *Aud.:* Ac, Sa.

The oldest continuously published scientific journal in the United States, this title is devoted to geology and related sciences. It publishes articles from around the world presenting results of major research from all earth sciences. Readers are primarily earth scientists in academia and government institutions. Some topics of special volumes include functional morphology and evolution, Proterozoic evolution and environments, frontiers in petrology, and studies in metamorphism and metasomatism. The web site provides tables of contents and abstracts for recent issues. Appropriate for academic and research collections. A GeoRef priority journal.

2190. ***American Mineralogist: an international journal of earth and planetary materials.*** [ISSN: 0003-004X] 1916. 8x/yr. USD 580. Ed(s): Dr. Lee Groat, Dr. Robert Dymek. Mineralogical Society of America, 1015 Eighteenth St., N W, Ste 601, Washington, DC 20036-5212; http://www.minsocam.org. Illus., index, adv. Sample. Refereed. Circ: 3000 Paid and free. Vol. ends: Nov/Dec (No. 11 - No. 12). Reprint: PSC. *Indexed:* AS&TI, ChemAb, DSR&OA, EngInd, GeoRef, MinerAb, OceAb, PetrolAb, PhotoAb, S&F, SCI, SWRA. *Bk. rev.:* 0-3, 500-1,200 words, signed. *Aud.:* Ac, Sa.

One of the key titles in the field of mineralogy, this journal is the official publication of the Mineralogical Society of America. Research articles cover many topics including crystal structure, crystal chemistry, and mineral occurrences and deposits. Work in closely related areas such as crystallography, petrology, and geochemistry is also included. In addition, most issues include a section featuring newly named minerals with a brief description and citation to the literature for each of them. (Recent issues include such tongue-twisters as Oswaldpeetersite and Tischendorfite.) Long mineral names aside, this journal is invaluable for academic and special libraries alike. Tables of contents are available on the web site from 1916 to present along with article abstracts, full-text, and supplemental data for more recent issues. Articles published before 2002 are free to download while newer ones are available only to society members. A GeoRef priority journal.

2191. ***Annales Geophysicae: atmospheres, hydrospheres and space sciences.*** Formerly (until 1988): *Atmospheres, Hydrospheres, Space Sciences;* Formed by the 1985 merger of: *Annales de Geophysicae. Serie A: Upper Atmosphere and Space Sciences;* part of: *Annales Geophysicae. Serie B: Terrestrial and Planetary Physics.* [ISSN: 0992-7689] 1983. m. EUR 1100; EUR 120 newsstand/cover per issue. Ed(s): Denis Alcayde. European Geophysical Society, Max Planck Str 13, Katlenburg-Lindau, 37191, Germany; egs@copernicus.org; http://www.copernicus.org/egs/egs.html. Illus., index, adv. Sample. Refereed. Circ: 600. Vol. ends: Dec (No. 12). Online: EBSCO Publishing; RoweCom Information Quest; ScienceDirect; Springer LINK; Swets Blackwell. *Indexed:* ChemAb, DSR&OA, EngInd, GeoRef, M&GPA, SCI, WRCInf. *Aud.:* Ac, Sa.

This official journal of the European Geophysical Society features research articles and short communications pertaining to a broad range of geophysical topics. Some areas of emphasis include atmospheric physics and dynamics, the magnetosphere and ionosphere of the earth, solar and heliospheric physics, and the oceans and their physical interactions with the land and air. Special issues may feature conference papers or an in-depth report on selected geophysical studies. This monthly also makes extensive use of color illustrations where appropriate. Online access is available from the former publisher's web site (SpringerLink) where tables of contents and abstracts appear for articles published from 1994 forward, and subscribers may view full text from mid-1996 through 2001. A GeoRef priority journal.

2192. *Applied Geochemistry: journal of the International Association of Geochemistry and Cosmochemistry.* [ISSN: 0883-2927] 1986. m. EUR 969. Ed(s): Ron Fuge, H Armannsson. Pergamon, The Boulevard, Langford Ln, East Park, Kidlington, OX5 1GB, United Kingdom. Illus., index. Sample. Refereed. Vol. ends: Nov (No. 6). Microform: PQC. Online: ingenta.com; ScienceDirect; Swets Blackwell. *Indexed:* ChemAb, EngInd, EnvAb, ForAb, GeoRef, GeogAbPG, HortAb, MinerAb, PetrolAb, PollutAb, S&F, SCI, SWRA, WRCInf. *Bk. rev.:* 0-2, 400-2,000 words. *Aud.:* Ac, Sa.

This international journal emphasizes research in geochemistry and cosmochemistry that has practical applications to areas such as environmental monitoring and preservation, agriculture, health, waste disposal, and the search for resources. Reports of original research, rapid communications, and some reviews are published in the fields of inorganic, organic, and isotope geochemistry. As the official publication of the International Association of Geochemistry and Cosmochemistry, occasional issues include reports of association activities. This journal is appropriate for academic or corporate research collections. The web site provides free access to tables of contents and abstracts beginning with 1995 issues. Full-text articles from 1995 to present are also available to libraries that purchase access to ScienceDirect. A GeoRef priority journal.

2193. *Basin Research.* [ISSN: 0950-091X] 1988. q. GBP 499 for print & online eds. Ed(s): Hugh D Sinclair, Philip Allen. Blackwell Publishing Ltd., 9600 Garsington Rd, PO Box 805, Oxford, OX4 2DQ, United Kingdom; customerservices@oxon.blackwellpublishing.com; http://www.blackwellpublishing.com/. Illus., index, adv. Sample. Refereed. Circ: 700. Vol. ends: No. 4. Microform: PQC. Online: EBSCO Publishing; ingenta.com; Munksgaard & Blackwell Science's Synergy; OCLC Online Computer Library Center, Inc.; RoweCom Information Quest; Swets Blackwell. *Indexed.* EngInd, GeoRef, GeogAbPG, PetrolAb. *Bk. rev.:* 0-4, 500-1,500 words, signed. *Aud.:* Ac, Sa.

This journal is a joint publication effort of the European Association of Geoscientists and Engineers and the International Association of Sedimentologists. It features interdisciplinary work on sedimentary basins that addresses such important issues as sediment transport, fluid migration, and stratigraphic modeling. Special thematic issues are also published from time to time. Free tables of contents can be found on the web site beginning with 1997. Full-text articles beginning with 1998 are available for print subscribers or on a per-article basis. Recommended for comprehensive collections, but libraries on a tight budget may first want to consider its more general counterpart *Sedimentology,* also published by Blackwell Science Ltd., for the International Association of Sedimentologists.

Bibliography and Index of Geology. See Abstracts and Indexes section.

2194. *Boreas: an international journal of quaternary research.* [ISSN: 0300-9483] 1972. q. GBP 144 (Individuals, GBP 78). Ed(s): Jan A Piotrowski. Taylor & Francis A S, Cort Adelersgt. 17, Solli, PO Box 2562, Oslo, 0202, Norway. Illus., index, adv. Sample. Refereed. Circ: 700. Vol. ends: Dec (No. 4). Microform: PQC. Online: EBSCO Publishing; Ingenta Select; OCLC Online Computer Library Center, Inc.; RoweCom Information Quest; Swets Blackwell. Reprint: ISI; PSC. *Indexed:* AbAn, ApEcolAb, BiolAb, BrArAb, ChemAb, DSR&OA, GeoRef, GeogAbPG, M&GPA, NumL, S&F, SCI, SWRA, ZooRec. *Bk. rev.:* 0-3, 500-1,200 words, signed. *Aud.:* Ac, Sa.

Sponsored in partnership by the National Councils for Scientific Research in Denmark, Finland, Iceland, Norway, and Sweden, this journal deals exclusively with research on the Quaternary period. This time period extends from about two million years ago to the present, and many of the topics covered, such as climatic variations and sea-level changes, are of particular relevance. Other papers examine the stratigraphy, glacial dynamics and landforms, and the flora and fauna of the period. Full-text web access beginning with 1999 is available free to print subscribers. A GeoRef priority journal.

2195. *Bulletin of Volcanology.* Formerly (until 1984): *Bulletin Volcanologique.* [ISSN: 0258-8900] 1924. 8x/yr. EUR 768 domestic; EUR 789.80 foreign; EUR 116 newsstand/cover per issue. Ed(s): T H Druitt. Springer-Verlag, Tiergartenstr 17, Heidelberg, 69121, Germany. Illus., index, adv. Sample. Refereed. Vol. ends: Jul (No. 8). Online: EBSCO Publishing; RoweCom Information Quest; ScienceDirect; Springer LINK; Swets Blackwell. *Indexed:* ChemAb, DSR&OA, GeoRef, GeogAbPG, MinerAb, SCI. *Aud.:* Ac, Sa.

The official journal of the International Association of Volcanology and Chemistry of the Earth's Interior. As suggested by its title, the emphasis is on volcanoes, including their characteristics, their behavior, and their hazards. Coverage is international in scope and includes related material on magmatic systems and igneous petrology. All issues also contain a useful summary of recent volcanic activity based on data from the Smithsonian Institution's Global Volcanism Network. The web site offers tables of contents and abstracts from 1994 on and full-text access from mid-1996 forward for print subscribers. A GeoRef priority journal.

2196. *Canadian Journal of Earth Sciences.* [ISSN: 0008-4077] 1963. m. CND 701 print ed. (Individuals, CND 229 print ed.). Ed(s): Bruce P. Dancik. N R C Research Press, Building M 55, Ottawa, ON K1A 0R6, Canada; http://www.cisti.nrc.ca/cisti/journals/. Illus., index, adv. Refereed. Circ: 1572. Vol. ends: Dec (No. 12). Microform: MML; PMC; PQC. Online: CISTI; EBSCO Publishing; ingenta.com; RoweCom Information Quest; Swets Blackwell. Reprint: PQC. *Indexed:* BiolAb, C&ISA, CBCARef, ChemAb, DSR&OA, EngInd, EnvAb, GeoRef, GeogAbPG, M&GPA, MinerAb, PetrolAb, PollutAb, S&F, SCI, SWRA, ZooRec. *Aud.:* Ac, Sa.

Published monthly by the National Research Council of Canada, the majority of the articles are in English, and those in French include English abstracts. Articles are divided into sections covering geochronology, tectonics, geophysics, geochemistry, sedimentology, geomorphology, and petrology among others. All are more technical than those found in *Geoscience Canada.* As one might expect, for site-specific topics the focus is heavily on Canadian geology, but many of the underlying principles are transferable to other regions. The web site offers free tables of contents and abstracts from 1998 on, with full-text access for an added fee. A GeoRef priority journal.

2197. *Canadian Mineralogist: crystallography, geochemistry, mineralogy, petrology, mineral deposits.* [ISSN: 0008-4476] 1957. q. CND 295 (Individuals, CND 80). Ed(s): R F Martin. Mineralogical Association of Canada, Business Office, Cityview 78087, Nepean, ON K2G 5W2, Canada. Illus. Sample. Refereed. Circ: 2000. Vol. ends: Dec. *Indexed:* C&ISA, ChemAb, EngInd, GeoRef, GeogAbPG, MinerAb, PetrolAb, SCI. *Bk. rev.:* 0-2, 300-1,000 words. *Aud.:* Ac, Sa.

Publishes research papers on crystallography, geochemistry, mineralogy, mineral deposits, and petrology as well as discussions of and replies to previously published articles. On average, one thematic issue is published each year, usually reporting on symposia at the Geological Association of Canada/MAC. Similar in content to *American Mineralogist, European Journal of Mineralogy,* and *Mineralogical Magazine,* this journal places a slightly greater emphasis on ore minerals and deposits. Text is in English or French with summaries in both languages. Abstracts for papers from 2000 to present may be viewed on the web site, and full-text access is available to subscribers. A GeoRef priority journal.

2198. *Canadian Petroleum Geology. Bulletin.* [ISSN: 0007-4802] 1979. q. Members, CND 22.50; Non-members, CND 30. Ed(s): L V Hills. Canadian Society of Petroleum Geologists, No.160, 540 Fifth Ave SW,

Calgary, AB T2P 0M2 , Canada; http://www.cspg.org. Illus., index, adv. Circ: 3500. Vol. ends: Dec (No. 4). *Indexed:* BiolAb, ChemAb, EngInd, GeoRef, PetrolAb, SCI. *Bk. rev.:* 0-4, 500-1,200 words, signed. *Aud.:* Ac, Sa.

As the official publication of the Canadian Society of Petroleum Geologists, some space is devoted to society business such as awards and a report of activities. However, the journal also features high-quality research articles on different aspects of petroleum geology in a wide range of geologic environments. Articles are well illustrated and feature color where appropriate. Regional coverage emphasizes Canada and Alaska, but the title is still a valuable addition to larger academic or special libraries.

2199. ***Chemical Geology: an international journal.*** Incorporates (in 1993): *Chemical Geology. Isotope Geoscience Section;* Which was formerly (1983-1985): *Isotope Geoscience.* [ISSN: 0009-2541] 1966. 44x/yr. EUR 3237. Ed(s): Claude J Allegre, Dr. Peter Deines. Elsevier BV, Sara Burgerhartstraat 25, Amsterdam, 1055 KV, Netherlands; nlinfo-f@elsevier.nl; http://www.elsevier.nl. Illus., index, adv. Sample. Refereed. Vol. ends: No. 4. Microform: PQC. Online: ingenta.com; ScienceDirect; Swets Blackwell. Reprint: SWZ. *Indexed:* ChemAb, DSR&OA, GeoRef, GeogAbPG, MinerAb, OceAb, PetrolAb, PollutAb, S&F, SCI, SWRA. *Aud.:* Ac, Sa.

Incorporating *Isotope Geoscience: Journal of the European Association for Geochemistry,* this title serves as the official publication of the European Association for Geochemistry. It has an international scope and aims to provide broad coverage of the growing field of organic and inorganic geochemistry, including reports about Earth and other planets. Papers address topics such as low temperature geochemistry, organic/petroleum geochemistry, analytical techniques, isotope studies, environmental geochemistry, and experimental petrology and geochemistry. The web site provides free access to tables of contents and abstracts beginning with 1995 issues. Full-text articles from 1995 to present are also available to libraries that purchase access to ScienceDirect. A GeoRef priority journal.

2200. ***Clay Minerals: journal of the European Clay Groups.*** Formerly: *Clay Minerals Bulletin.* [ISSN: 0009-8558] 1947. q. issue numbers 1-4 last issue includes index. GBP 152.65; USD 234. Ed(s): D C Bain. Mineralogical Society, 41 Queens Gate, London, SW7 5HR, United Kingdom; http://www.minersoc.org. Illus., index, adv. Refereed. Circ: 1500. Vol. ends: Dec (No. 4). *Indexed:* C&ISA, CerAb, ChemAb, DSR&OA, EngInd, GeoRef, GeogAbPG, MinerAb, S&F, SCI. *Bk. rev.:* 0-2, 600-1,000 words, signed. *Aud.:* Ac, Sa.

Published by the Mineralogical Society, this journal represents the combined efforts of several clay research groups based primarily in Europe. Papers are occasionally printed in French, German, or Spanish but are predominantly in English. Many articles focus on research concerning hydrothermal interactions related to clay weathering and diagenesis. Analytical techniques and their use in the determination of structure and physical properties of clay minerals are also emphasized.

2201. ***Clays and Clay Minerals.*** Formerly: *Clay Minerals Society. Annual Proceedings.* [ISSN: 0009-8604] 1968. bi-m. USD 235 in North America includes online access; USD 250 elsewhere includes online access. Ed(s): Derek Bain. The Clay Minerals Society, PO Box 460130, Aurora, CO 80046; cms@clays.org; http://www.cms.lanl.gov. Illus., index, adv. Refereed. Circ: 1400. Vol. ends: Dec (No. 6). Online: Ingenta Select. Reprint: ISI. *Indexed:* C&ISA, CerAb, ChemAb, DSR&OA, EngInd, ExcerpMed, ForAb, GeoRef, GeogAbPG, IAA, MinerAb, PetrolAb, S&F, SCI, SWRA. *Aud.:* Ac, Sa.

This journal serves as the official publication of the Clay Minerals Society and was originally issued as an annual proceedings volume. The focus is on the "latest advances in research and technology concerning clays and other fine-grained minerals." Chemically, clays are important because the small size of the particles results in a high surface area, making them more reactive. They also often have some unique physical properties, such as the ability to absorb water into their crystal structure. Tables of contents are provided on the web site from 1980 to present, with abstracts available from 1998 forward. Coverage is similar to *Clay Minerals* but with a greater emphasis on interdisciplinary applications. Together, the two journals provide very thorough coverage of the field. A GeoRef priority journal.

2202. ***Compass (Norman): an honorary scientific society magazine devoted to the earth sciences.*** Formerly: *Compass of Sigma Gamma Epsilon.* [ISSN: 0894-802X] 1920. q. USD 24. Ed(s): R Nowell Donovan. Society of Sigma Gamma Epsilon, c/o Charles J Mankin, University of Oklahoma, Norman, OK 73019; cjmankin@ou.edu; bbellis-sge@ou.edu. Illus., index. Sample. Refereed. Circ: 1800. *Indexed:* GeoRef, GeogAbPG, PetrolAb. *Aud.:* Ac.

Sigma Gamma Epsilon is an honorary scientific society devoted to the earth sciences. Published since 1920, this quarterly includes a generous dose of society- and chapter-related news and historical information. Nevertheless, this small journal also features many quality research articles on a wide range of topics. A significant number of these come from students presenting the findings of their research, often in the form of a special issue from one of the society's chapters. In addition, these research papers are refereed and indexed in the major sources. Given the modest price, this title is one that most academic libraries should strongly consider, particularly if they have graduate programs in earth sciences.

2203. ***Computers & Geosciences.*** Incorporates: *Geocom Programs.* [ISSN: 0098-3004] 1975. 10x/yr. EUR 1818 (Qualified personnel, EUR 202). Ed(s): Graeme Bonham-Carter. Pergamon, The Boulevard, Langford Ln, East Park, Kidlington, OX5 1GB, United Kingdom. Illus., index, adv. Refereed. Circ: 1100. Vol. ends: Dec (No. 27). Microform: PQC. Online: EBSCO Publishing; ingenta.com; ScienceDirect; Swets Blackwell. *Indexed:* AS&TI, C&ISA, ChemAb, DSR&OA, EngInd, ForAb, GeoRef, GeogAbPG, InfoSAb, M&GPA, PetrolAb, PollutAb, S&F, SCI, SSCI, ST&MA, SWRA. *Bk. rev.:* 0-4, 500-2,500 words. *Aud.:* Ac, Sa.

This journal publishes papers on all aspects of computing applications in geosciences and often makes datasets and program codes available to readers via the Internet. Articles address all types of computational activities in the fields of geology, geochemistry, geophysics, oceanography, hydrology, geography, GIS, and remote sensing. Some example topics are algorithms, databases, data structures, numerical methods, computer graphics, simulation models, image analysis, and statistical and expert system methods. Thorough software reviews appear in most issues. The web site provides free access to tables of contents and abstracts beginning with 1995 issues. Full-text articles from 1995 to present are also available to libraries that purchase access to ScienceDirect. A GeoRef priority journal.

2204. ***Contributions to Mineralogy and Petrology.*** [ISSN: 0010-7999] 1947. 12x/yr. EUR 2850 domestic; EUR 2898.20 foreign; EUR 285 newsstand/cover per issue. Ed(s): T L Grove, J Hoefs. Springer-Verlag, Tiergartenstr 17, Heidelberg, 69121, Germany. Illus., index, adv. Refereed. Vol. ends: No. 6. Microform: PQC. Online: EBSCO Publishing; Gale Group; RoweCom Information Quest; ScienceDirect; Springer LINK; Swets Blackwell. Reprint: ISI. *Indexed:* ChemAb, DSR&OA, GeoRef, MinerAb, PetrolAb, SCI. *Aud.:* Ac, Sa.

This journal provides in-depth technical coverage of the mineralogy and petrology of all major rock types. Related areas such as isotope geology and element partitioning are also featured. There is a heavy emphasis on geochemistry and many of the articles consist of theoretical and experimental work such as determining mineral phase relations and chemical equilibria. For those papers that are site specific, each volume also features a handy location index. The web site offers tables of contents and abstracts from 1995 on and full-text access from mid-1995 forward for print subscribers. A GeoRef priority journal.

2205. ***Cretaceous Research: an international journal.*** [ISSN: 0195-6671] 1980. bi-m. EUR 988 (Individuals, EUR 317). Ed(s): D. J. Batten, Douglas J. Nichols. Academic Press, Harcourt Pl, 32 Jamestown Rd, London, NW1 7BY, United Kingdom; apsubs@acad.com; http://www.elsevier-international.com/serials/. Illus., index, adv. Sample. Refereed. Vol. ends: Dec (No. 6). Online: EBSCO Publishing;

ingenta.com; OCLC Online Computer Library Center, Inc.; RoweCom Information Quest; ScienceDirect; Swets Blackwell. Reprint: SWZ. *Indexed:* BiolAb, ChemAb, DSR&OA, GeoRef, GeogAbPG, PetrolAb, SCI, ZooRec. *Bk. rev.:* 0-2, 700-1,000 words, signed. *Aud.:* Ac, Sa.

Like *Quaternary Research* (below in this section), this journal is interdisciplinary and focuses on a single major geological period. The Cretaceous period ended about 65 million years ago, a time best known for the extinction of the dinosaurs. Several of the articles focus on this "K/T boundary," but this is by no means the only topic covered. Stratigraphy and paleontology in particular receive considerable attention. Special topical issues on significant sites or geologic events during the Cretaceous period are also featured. The web site provides free access to tables of contents and abstracts beginning with 1993 issues. Full-text articles from 1993 to present are also available to libraries that purchase access to ScienceDirect.

2206. *Earth and Planetary Science Letters.* [ISSN: 0012-821X] 1966. 48x/yr. EUR 3206 (Qualified personnel, EUR 187). Ed(s): E. Bard, Dr. E. Boyle. Elsevier BV, Sara Burgerhartstraat 25, Amsterdam, 1055 KV, Netherlands; nlinfo-f@elsevier.nl; http://www.elsevier.nl. Illus., index. Sample. Refereed. Vol. ends: No. 4. Microform: PQC. Online: EBSCO Publishing; ingenta.com; ScienceDirect; Swets Blackwell. Reprint: SWZ. *Indexed:* BrArAb, ChemAb, DSR&OA, EngInd, ExcerpMed, GeoRef, GeogAbPG, IAA, M&GPA, MinerAb, OceAb, PetrolAb, SCI, SWRA. *Aud.:* Ac, Sa.

Publishes basic research in physical, chemical, and mechanical properties of the earth's crust and mantle, atmosphere, and hydrosphere, as well as lunar studies, papers on plate tectonics, ocean floor spreading, and continental drift. Also included is "Express Letters," a forum for shorter communications with rapid turnaround. The web site offers article abstracts from 1996, author and subject searching, a keyword thesaurus, directories of authors and researchers with e-mail addresses, and background data sets not available in the print edition. The web site provides free access to tables of contents and abstracts beginning with 1966 issues. Full-text articles are also available to libraries that purchase access to ScienceDirect. A GeoRef priority journal.

2207. *Earth Surface Processes and Landforms.* Formerly (until Jan. 1981): *Earth Surface Processes.* [ISSN: 0197-9337] 1976. 13x/yr. USD 2510. John Wiley & Sons Ltd., The Atrium, Southern Gate, Chichester, PO19 8SQ, United Kingdom; customer@wiley.co.uk; http://www.wiley.co.uk. Illus., index, adv. Refereed. Circ: 1050. Vol. ends: Winter (No. 13). Microform: PQC. Online: EBSCO Publishing; Wiley InterScience. Reprint: ISI; PQC; SWZ. *Indexed:* ChemAb, EngInd, FPA, ForAb, GeoRef, GeogAbPG, PollutAb, S&F, SCI, SWRA, WAE&RSA. *Bk. rev.:* 0-2, 200-600 words, signed. *Aud.:* Ac, Sa.

This far-ranging journal publishes "research papers on all aspects of geomorphology interpreted in its widest sense." This encompasses the complex process of landform evolution by the processes of weathering, erosion, transport, and deposition. Landslides and other natural hazards are also considered. Much of the work is highly interdisciplinary in nature and shows how different chemical, mechanical, and hydrologic factors have interacted to shape the landscape both in the past and in the present. Free tables of contents and abstracts from 1996 to present are provided at the web site, with full-text access from 1997 on for subscribers. A GeoRef priority journal.

2208. *Economic Geology and the Bulletin of the Society of Economic Geologists.* Formerly (until 1930): *Economic Geology.* [ISSN: 0361-0128] 1905. irreg. USD 145 (Individuals, USD 75). Ed(s): Marco T Einaudi. Economic Geology Publishing Co., 7811 Shaffer Pkwy, Littleton, CO 80127; seg@segweb.org; http://www.segweb.org. Illus., index, adv. Sample. Refereed. Circ: 5000 Paid. Vol. ends: Dec (No. 8). Microform: PMC; PQC. *Indexed:* AS&TI, ChemAb, DSR&OA, EngInd, GeoRef, IBZ, PetrolAb, SCI, SWRA. *Bk. rev.:* 0-4, 600-1,000 words. *Aud.:* Ac, Sa.

Articles feature research on theoretical and experimental aspects of economic geology; these are balanced with field-based papers. This bulletin includes an international editorial board that reviews papers from around the world. A map series is planned to present sets of important maps that have not previously been publicly available. Each issue contains selected tables of contents from journals in related fields and a calendar of relevant events. A GeoRef priority journal.

2209. *Engineering Geology: an international journal.* Incorporates (in 1992): *Mining Science and Technology.* [ISSN: 0013-7952] 1965. 24x/yr. EUR 1535 (Qualified personnel, EUR 146). Ed(s): E L Krinitzsky, M. Arnould. Elsevier BV, Sara Burgerhartstraat 25, Amsterdam, 1055 KV, Netherlands; nlinfo-f@elsevier.nl; http://www.elsevier.nl. Illus., index, adv. Sample. Refereed. Vol. ends: No. 4. Microform: PQC. Online: ingenta.com; ScienceDirect; Swets Blackwell. Reprint: SWZ. *Indexed:* ApMecR, C&ISA, ChemAb, DSR&OA, EngInd, ExcerpMed, GeoRef, GeogAbPG, OceAb, PetrolAb, PollutAb, SCI, SWRA. *Bk. rev.:* 0-2, 500-1,000 words. *Aud.:* Ac, Sa.

This international journal publishes geological studies relevant to engineering, environmental concerns, and safety, including research papers, case histories, and reviews. Although English is the primary language, articles are accepted in French and German as well. The web site provides free access to tables of contents and abstracts beginning with 1995 issues. Full-text articles from 1995 to present are also available to libraries that purchase access to ScienceDirect. A GeoRef priority journal.

2210. *Environmental and Engineering Geoscience: serving professionals in engineering, environmental, and ground-water geology.* Formerly (until 1995): *Association of Engineering Geologists. Bulletin.* [ISSN: 1078-7275] 1963. q. Members, USD 42; Non-members, USD 125. Ed(s): Normetan R Tilford. Geological Society of America, 3300 Penrose Pl, Boulder, CO 80301-1806; http://www.geosociety.org. Illus., index, adv. Sample. Refereed. Circ: 3500. Vol. ends: Dec (No. 4). *Indexed:* C&ISA, ChemAb, ExcerpMed, GeoRef, GeogAbPG, OceAb, SWRA. *Bk. rev.:* 0-9, 800-3,000 words. *Aud.:* Ac, Sa.

Publishes research articles and technical papers and notes in areas of interest to geohydrologists and environmental and engineering geologists. The journal is cosponsored by the Association of Engineering Geologists and the Geological Society of America. Topics include site selection, feasibility studies, design or construction of civil engineering projects, waste management, and ground water. Appropriate for corporate and academic collections. Listed as a GeoRef priority journal under its former name, *Bulletin of the Association of Engineering Geologists* (ISSN 0004-5691).

2211. *Environmental Geology: international journal of geosciences.* Former titles (until 1993): *Environmental Geology and Water Sciences;* (until 1984): *Environmental Geology.* [ISSN: 0943-0105] 1975. m. EUR 1300 domestic; EUR 1364.20 foreign; EUR 98 newsstand/cover per issue. Ed(s): P E LaMoreaux, G Doerhoefer. Springer-Verlag, Tiergartenstr 17, Heidelberg, 69121, Germany. Illus., index, adv. Sample. Refereed. Microform: PQC. Online: EBSCO Publishing; RoweCom Information Quest; ScienceDirect; Springer LINK; Swets Blackwell. Reprint: ISI. *Indexed:* AS&TI, Agr, BiolAb, ChemAb, DSR&OA, EngInd, EnvAb, ExcerpMed, FPA, ForAb, GeoRef, GeogAbPG, HortAb, MinerAb, PetrolAb, PollutAb, RRTA, S&F, SCI, SSCI, SWRA, WAE&RSA, ZooRec. *Bk. rev.:* 2-7, 300-1,800 words, signed. *Aud.:* Ac, Sa.

The application of geological principles and data to environmental issues has become an increasingly important area of research in recent years. This monthly includes both research articles and applied technical reports on specific cases and solutions. Much of the work is multidisciplinary in nature and covers such areas as soil and water contamination, radioactive waste disposal, remediation techniques, and the effects of mining and industrial activities. Special topical issues often focus in greater detail on one of these specific subject areas. The web site offers tables of contents and abstracts from 1996 on and full-text access from mid-1996 forward for print subscribers. A GeoRef priority journal.

2212. *Eos: transactions, American Geophysical Union.* Formerly (until 1969): *American Geophysical Union. Transactions.* [ISSN: 0096-3941] 1919. w. USD 440. Ed(s): A F Spilhaus. American Geophysical Union, 2000 Florida Ave, N W, Washington, DC 20009-1277; http://www.agu.org/eos_elec; http://www.agu.org. Illus., index, adv. Sample. Refereed. Circ: 36500. Vol. ends: No. 52. Microform: Pub.; AIP. Reprint: ISI. *Indexed:* A&ATA, BiolAb, DSR&OA, EngInd, EnvAb, GeoRef, GeogAbPG, M&GPA, PetrolAb. *Bk. rev.:* 0-2, 100-400 words. *Aud.:* Ac, Sa.

This tabloid-format weekly publishes refereed articles on current geophysics research and on the relationship of geophysics to social and political issues. News, book reviews, announcements from the American Geophysical Union, a calendar of events, and ads for grants, fellowships, and employment make this appropriate for professional geophysicists and graduate students. A hardcover volume published annually contains the articles, news, and editorials from the weekly. An electronic supplement available at http://www.agu.org/pubs/eos.html provides deeper coverage of selected items than appears in print. Recommended for academic and corporate libraries. A GeoRef priority journal.

2213. ***Episodes: journal of international geoscience.*** Supersedes: *International Union of Geological Sciences. Geological Newsletter.* [ISSN: 0705-3797] 1978. q. USD 24. International Union of Geological Sciences, IUGS Secretariat, Geological Survey of Norway, Trondheim, 7491, Norway; http://www.iugs.org. Illus., index, adv. Sample. Refereed. Circ: 3000. Vol. ends: Dec (No. 4). *Indexed:* ChemAb, ExcerpMed, GeoRef, PetrolAb, SCI. *Bk. rev.:* 0-4, 500-1,500 words. *Aud.:* Ga, Ac, Sa.

Articles generally have more international orientation than those in *Geotimes,* and cover developments of regional and global importance in earth science research programs and techniques, organizations, and science policy. The International Union of Geological Sciences is a large, active, nongovernmental scientific organization that facilitates international and interdisciplinary cooperation in the earth sciences, promoting and supporting study of geological problems of worldwide significance. Each issue of *Episodes* includes a comprehensive calendar of future international geoscience events and training opportunities; issues regularly include reports from international conferences. Tables of contents and article abstracts for issues from 1997 to present and an events calendar are accessible at the web site.

2214. ***European Journal of Mineralogy.*** Formed by the merger of (1950-1988): *Fortschritte der Mineralogie;* (1968-1988): *Rendiconti della Societa Italiana di Mineralogia e Petrologia;* (1978-1988): *Bulletin de Mineralogia;* Which was formerly (1949-1977): *Societe Francaise de Mineralogie et de Cristallographie. Bulletin;* (1886-1948): *Societe Francaise de Mineralogie. Bulletin;* (1878-1885): *Societe Mineralogique de France. Bulletin.* [ISSN: 0935-1221] 1878. 6x/yr. USD 317.20 domestic; USD 323.60 foreign. E. Schweizerbart'sche Verlagsbuchhandlung, Johannesstr 3A, Stuttgart, 70176, Germany; mail@schweizerbart.de; http://www.schweizerbart.de. Illus., index, adv. Sample. Refereed. Vol. ends: Nov/Dec (No. 6). *Indexed:* C&ISA, ChemAb, ExcerpMed, GeoRef, GeogAbPG, MinerAb, SCI. *Aud.:* Ac, Sa.

The result of a cooperative publication effort among several European mineralogical societies, this journal replaced their individual journals when it came out in 1989. Contributions are primarily in English but articles in French, German, and Italian are also accepted. Papers are international in scope, with an emphasis on European localities. They cover a wide range of topics in mineralogy, petrology, and crystallography. Occasional thematic issues have included such topics as experimental mineralogy, fluid interactions, and phase transitions in minerals. The web site offers tables of contents from 1994 forward. More recent issues include abstracts and full-text for print subscribers. A GeoRef priority journal.

2215. ***Exploration & Mining Geology.*** [ISSN: 0964-1823] 1992. q. CND 325 (Members, CND 35 CIM; Non-members, CND 140). Canadian Institute of Metallurgy, 3400 de Maisonneuve Blvd, W, Ste 1210, Montreal, PQ H3Z 3B8, Canada; http://www.cim.org/. Illus., index. Refereed. Microform: PQC. *Indexed:* ChemAb, GeoRef, MinerAb. *Aud.:* Ac, Sa.

Published for the Geological Society of the Canadian Institute of Mining (CIM), Metallurgy, and Petroleum, this journal presents papers on mineral deposits, mining geology, and ore reserves from around the world. Although nearly all papers are published in English, some are in French. Abstracts of the annual CIM meeting are also included. Abstracts of articles from 1997 to present are available free at the web site. Appropriate for specialized academic and corporate research collections.

2216. ***Geo-Marine Letters: an international journal of marine geology.*** [ISSN: 0276-0460] 1980. q. EUR 498 domestic; EUR 508.90 foreign; EUR 150 newsstand/cover per issue. Ed(s): W F Burg, A H Bouma. Springer-Verlag, Tiergartenstr 17, Heidelberg, 69121, Germany. Illus., index, adv. Sample. Refereed. Vol. ends: No. 4. Microform: PQC. Online: EBSCO Publishing; RoweCom Information Quest; ScienceDirect; Springer LINK; Swets Blackwell. Reprint: ISI. *Indexed:* ChemAb, DSR&OA, EngInd, GeoRef, GeogAbPG, OceAb, PetrolAb, PollutAb, SCI, SWRA. *Bk. rev.:* 0-3, 700-1,200 words, signed. *Aud.:* Ac, Sa.

Newer techniques and equipment have opened up the vast areas of the earth under the oceans to intensive study. *Geo-Marine Letters* is an "international journal for the publication of short original studies and reviews dealing with all marine geological aspects." Major topics of coverage include depositional environments, sedimentary processes, stratigraphy, and post-depositional movement. Other areas of emphasis include marine geochemistry and geophysics. Recent topical issues highlight such subjects as continent-ocean margins and deep-sea sedimentation. The web site offers free tables of contents and abstracts as well as full-text access from 1997 on for print subscribers.

2217. ***Geochemistry International.*** Formerly: *Geochemistry.* [ISSN: 0016-7029] 1956. m. USD 3234 in North America; USD 3707 elsewhere. Ed(s): Evgenii B Kurdyukov, Olga P Fedorova. M A I K Nauka - Interperiodica, Profsoyuznaya ul 90, Moscow, 117997, Russian Federation; compmg@maik.ru; http://www.maik.rssi.ru. Illus., index, adv. Refereed. Circ: 675. Vol. ends: Dec (No. 12). Microform: PQC. Reprint: PSC. *Indexed:* DSR&OA, ExcerpMed, GeoRef, GeogAbPG, MinerAb, OceAb, PetrolAb, PollutAb, SCI, SWRA. *Aud.:* Ac, Sa.

The American Geophysical Union and the American Geological Institute together with the Russian Academy of Sciences sponsor publication of this journal. Articles are translated from the Russian journal *Geokhimiya.* Concentrating on the geology of the Eurasian continent, research papers in the journal address multidisciplinary aspects of theoretical and applied topics such as cosmochemistry; geochemistry of magmatic, metamorphic, hydrothermal and sedimentary processes; organic geochemistry; applied geochemistry; and chemistry of the environment. Occasional reports appear from symposia and international meetings. The web site provides tables of contents and article abstracts beginning with 1996 issues. Appropriate for comprehensive collections.

2218. ***Geochimica et Cosmochimica Acta.*** [ISSN: 0016-7037] 1950. 24x/yr. EUR 2210. Ed(s): F A Podosek, L Trower. Pergamon, The Boulevard, Langford Ln, East Park, Kidlington, OX5 1GB, United Kingdom. Illus., index, adv. Sample. Refereed. Circ: 3800. Vol. ends: No. 24. Microform: PQC. Online: ingenta.com; ScienceDirect; Swets Blackwell. Reprint: PQC. *Indexed:* BiolAb, ChemAb, DSR&OA, EngInd, ExcerpMed, ForAb, GeoRef, GeogAbPG, IAA, M&GPA, MinerAb, OceAb, PetrolAb, PollutAb, S&F, SCI, SWRA, WRCInf. *Aud.:* Ac, Sa.

Publishes research papers in the areas of terrestrial geochemistry, meteoritics and meteorite impacts, and planetary geochemistry aimed at an international audience. Topics include chemical processes in Earth's atmosphere, hydrosphere, biosphere, and lithosphere; organic and isotope geochemistry; and lunar science. The web site provides free access to tables of contents and abstracts beginning with 1995 issues. Full-text articles from 1995 to present are also available to libraries that purchase access to ScienceDirect. Text is in English, French, and German. Appropriate for academic and corporate research collections. A GeoRef priority journal.

2219. ***Geological Journal.*** Formerly (until 1964): *Liverpool and Manchester Geological Journal.* [ISSN: 0072-1050] 1966. q. USD 1050. John Wiley & Sons Ltd., The Atrium, Southern Gate, Chichester, PO19 8SQ, United Kingdom; customer@wiley.co.uk; http://www.wiley.co.uk. Illus., index, adv. Refereed. Circ: 700. Reprint: ISI; PQC. *Indexed:* ChemAb, DSR&OA, EngInd, GeoRef, GeogAbPG, MinerAb, PetrolAb, PollutAb, SCI, SWRA, ZooRec. *Bk. rev.:* 0-7, 500-2,000 words. *Aud.:* Ac, Sa.

This journal provides broad coverage of geology with an emphasis on interdisciplinary work and regional case studies. The United Kingdom and other areas of Europe receive the most attention, although studies from around the world are included. Free tables of contents and abstracts from 1996 to present are provided at the web site along with full-text access from 1997 on for subscribers who pay an added fee. This title is a good complement to others of a general nature such as *Geology* or *Geological Magazine* and is appropriate for comprehensive collections.

2220. *Geological Magazine.* [ISSN: 0016-7568] 1864. bi-m. USD 438. Ed(s): Graham E Budd, M J Bickle. Cambridge University Press, The Edinburgh Bldg, Shaftesbury Rd, Cambridge, CB2 2RU, United Kingdom; information@cambridge.org; http://uk.cambridge.org/journals. Illus., index, adv. Sample. Refereed. Vol. ends: Nov (No. 6). Microform: BHP. Online: EBSCO Publishing; Gale Group; OCLC Online Computer Library Center, Inc.; RoweCom Information Quest; Swets Blackwell. Reprint: PQC. *Indexed:* BiolAb, ChemAb, DSR&OA, EngInd, ForAb, GSI, GeoRef, GeogAbPG, MinerAb, PetrolAb, PollutAb, SCI, SWRA, ZooRec. *Bk. rev.:* 5-20, 50-500 words. *Aud.:* Ac, Sa.

Publishes research and review articles in all areas of earth sciences and emphasizes interdisciplinary papers of interest to geologists from several specialties. Discussion and reply pieces explore reader response to previous articles. This magazine is appropriate for comprehensive academic collections. Free tables of contents and abstracts from 1997 forward are available on the web site, and full-text access for subscribers. A GeoRef priority journal.

2221. *Geological Society. Journal.* Former titles (until 1971): *Geological Society of London. Quarterly Journal;* (until 1845): *Geological Society of London. Proceedings.* [ISSN: 0016-7649] 1826. bi-m. GBP 465 domestic; GBP 530 foreign; USD 885 foreign. Ed(s): Nick Rogers. Geological Society Publishing House, Unit 7, Brassmill Enterprise Centre, Brassmill Ln, Bath, BA1 3JN, United Kingdom; rebecca.toop@geolsoc.org.uk; http://www.geolsoc.org.uk. Illus., index, adv. Refereed. Circ: 5200. Vol. ends: Nov (No. 6). *Indexed:* BiolAb, BrArAb, ChemAb, EngInd, GeoRef, GeogAbPG, MinerAb, PetrolAb, SCI, ZooRec. *Aud.:* Ac, Sa.

This is the primary journal of the Geological Society of London, one of the oldest geological societies in the world. It is international in scope, with papers covering the full range of the earth sciences. These include both full-length research articles and shorter, rapid-publication "specials." The editors also often publish thematic sets of papers as all or part of an issue. Top-quality throughout and heavily cited, this journal is highly recommended for academic and special library collections. Full-text access is available through the Ingenta web site for issues starting in 1979 for subscribers or through a pay-per-view option. A GeoRef priority journal.

2222. *Geological Society of America. Bulletin.* [ISSN: 0016-7606] 1890. m. USD 475 domestic; USD 485 foreign; USD 600 domestic print & online ed. Geological Society of America, 3300 Penrose Pl, Boulder, CO 80301-1806; pubs@geosociety.org; http://www.geosociety.org. Illus., adv. Sample. Refereed. Circ: 7500. Vol. ends: Dec (No. 12). Microform: PMC; PQC. Online: Gale Group. Reprint: PQC. *Indexed:* AS&TI, BiolAb, C&ISA, ChemAb, DSR&OA, EngInd, EnvAb, GSI, GeoRef, GeogAbPG, IAA, M&GPA, MinerAb, OceAb, PetrolAb, S&F, SCI, SWRA, ZooRec. *Aud.:* Ac, Sa.

This journal is the more research-oriented periodical published by the Geological Society of America and contains longer articles than *Geology.* Although coverage of international projects is included, work in North America is emphasized. High quality, large-format inserts (usually maps) appear in occasional issues. The web site provides tables of contents and article abstracts beginning in 1988, full-text articles for subscribers, as well as a data repository of supplementary files for some articles. Strongly recommended for academic and corporate collections. A GeoRef priority journal.

2223. *Geology (Boulder).* [ISSN: 0091-7613] 1973. m. Members, USD 80; Non-members, USD 475. Geological Society of America, 3300 Penrose Pl, Boulder, CO 80301-1806; pubs@geosociety.org; http://www.geosociety.org. Illus., adv. Sample. Refereed. Circ: 9500. Vol. ends: Dec (No. 12). Microform: PQC. Online: Gale Group. Reprint: PQC. *Indexed:* A&ATA, AS&TI, BiolAb, ChemAb, DSR&OA, EngInd, ExcerpMed, GSI, GeoRef, GeogAbPG, IAA, M&GPA, OceAb, PetrolAb, PollutAb, SCI, SWRA, ZooRec. *Aud.:* Ac, Sa.

This title publishes short, provocative articles (about 20 per issue) on a wide range of geological topics of interest to a broad audience. *Geology* is oriented more toward new investigations and recent discoveries in the field than GSA's *Geological Society of America Bulletin.* The "Forum" section provides for comment and discussion in response to articles. Article abstracts are accessible on the web from 1988 to the present; full-text access to articles is available to subscribers. Strongly recommended for academic and corporate collections. A GeoRef priority journal.

2224. *Geology Today.* [ISSN: 0266-6979] 1985. bi-m. GBP 243 print & online eds. Ed(s): P Smith. Blackwell Publishing Ltd., 9600 Garsington Rd, Oxford, OX4 2ZG, United Kingdom; customerservices@oxon.blackwellpublishing.com; http://www.blackwellpublishing.com. Illus., index, adv. Sample. Refereed. Circ: 2550. Microform: PQC. Online: EBSCO Publishing; Gale Group; ingenta.com; Munksgaard & Blackwell Science's Synergy; OCLC Online Computer Library Center, Inc.; RoweCom Information Quest; Swets Blackwell. *Indexed:* GSI, GeoRef, GeogAbPG, ZooRec. *Bk. rev.:* 0-10, 200-500 words. *Aud.:* Ga, Ac.

Published in association with the Geological Society of London, this journal is similar in many respects to *Geotimes.* Lots of news and current awareness briefings are provided, supplemented by short feature articles. The latter often gravitate toward popular topics but are generally well written and illustrated. There are also two excellent series on the origin, classification, and identification of significant fossils and minerals aimed toward the novice. Given the nature of the publication, one might expect to see greater use of color. However, each issue still makes for interesting reading and is quite accessible to general audiences. Tables of contents can be found on the web site beginning with 1997. Full-text access is available for subscribers; articles are also available for individual purchase. A GeoRef priority journal.

2225. *Geomorphology: an international journal of pure and applied geomorphology.* [ISSN: 0169-555X] 1987. 32x/yr. EUR 1707. Ed(s): A. M. Harvey, R. A. Marston. Elsevier BV, Sara Burgerhartstraat 25, Amsterdam, 1055 KV, Netherlands; nlinfo-f@elsevier.nl; http://www.elsevier.nl. Illus., adv. Sample. Refereed. Microform: PQC. Online: ingenta.com; ScienceDirect; Swets Blackwell. *Indexed:* ForAb, GeoRef, GeogAbPG, OceAb, S&F, SCI, SWRA. *Bk. rev.:* 0-3, 500-1000 words. *Aud.:* Ac, Sa.

Publishes research papers, review articles, and book reviews on landform studies at all scales, including extraterrestrial landforms. Applied, tectonic, and climatological geomorphology are other topics included in this journal. Occasional issues include the newsletter of the International Association of Geomorphologists. Special issues present papers on such topics as "Biogeomorphology" and "Geomorphology in the Public Eye: Political Issues, Education, and the Public." The web site provides free access to tables of contents and abstracts beginning with 1995 issues. Full-text articles from 1995 to present are also available to libraries that purchase access to ScienceDirect. Appropriate for academic collections.

2226. *Geophysical Journal International.* Formerly (until 1989): *Geophysical Journal;* Which was formed by the 1987 merger of part of: *Annales Geophysicae. Series B: Terrestrial and Planetary Physics; Royal Astronomical Society Geophysical Journal;* Which was formerly: *Royal Astronomical Society. Monthly Notices. Geophysical Supplement.* [ISSN: 0956-540X] 1958. m. GBP 930 print & online eds. Ed(s): K Bahr, C Barton. Blackwell Publishing Ltd., 9600 Garsington Rd, Oxford, OX4 2ZG, United Kingdom; customerservices@oxon.blackwellpublishing.com; http://www.blackwellpublishing.com. Illus., adv. Refereed. Circ: 1585. Microform: PQC. Online: EBSCO Publishing; ingenta.com; Munksgaard & Blackwell Science's Synergy; OCLC Online Computer Library Center, Inc.; RoweCom Information Quest; Swets Blackwell. *Indexed:* ChemAb, GeoRef, GeogAbPG, IAA, MathSciNet, PetrolAb, SCI. *Bk. rev.:* 0-2, 700-1,500 words, signed. *Aud.:* Ac, Sa.

Formed by a merger of three journals, this title continues the numbering of the *Geophysical Journal of the Royal Astronomical Society.* It endeavors to provide international coverage of "all aspects of theoretical, computational, and observational geophysics." Some of the subject areas covered include seismology, crustal structure, geomagnetism, and rock rheology. A "fast-track" mechanism is provided for rapid publication of selected papers. Issues are bigger than most and include a large volume of top-quality research. Tables of contents can be found on the web site beginning with 1997. Full-text access is available for print subscribers; articles are available for individual purchase as well. A GeoRef priority journal.

2227. *Geophysical Prospecting.* [ISSN: 0016-8025] 1953. bi-m. GBP 504 print & online eds. Ed(s): R Silva. Blackwell Publishing Ltd., 9600 Garsington Rd, Oxford, OX4 2ZG, United Kingdom; customerservices@oxon.blackwellpublishing.com; http://www.blackwellpublishing.com. Illus., adv. Refereed. Circ: 4750. Microform: PQC. Online: EBSCO Publishing; ingenta.com; Munksgaard & Blackwell Science's Synergy; OCLC Online Computer Library Center, Inc.; RoweCom Information Quest; Swets Blackwell. Reprint: SWZ. *Indexed:* C&ISA, ChemAb, DSR&OA, EngInd, GeoRef, GeogAbPG, PetrolAb, SCI. *Aud.:* Ac, Sa.

Published on behalf of the European Association for Geoscientists and Engineers, *Geophysical Prospecting* emphasizes research on geophysics as applied to exploration. Many articles report on work in the oil and mineral exploration industries but are appropriate also for academic researchers in geophysics. Full-text access to articles from 1998 to present is available to subscribers at the web site.

2228. *Geophysical Research Letters.* [ISSN: 0094-8276] 1974. s-m. USD 1405. Ed(s): A F Spilhaus. American Geophysical Union, 2000 Florida Ave, N W, Washington, DC 20009-1277; http://www.agu.org. Illus., index. Sample. Refereed. Vol. ends: Dec. Microform: Pub.; AIP. Reprint: ISI. *Indexed:* ChemAb, DSR&OA, EngInd, ExcerpMed, ForAb, GeoRef, GeogAbPG, IAA, M&GPA, MinerAb, OceAb, PetrolAb, PollutAb, S&F, SCI, SWRA, WAE&RSA. *Aud.:* Ac, Sa.

Aimed at scientists in diverse disciplines within geophysics, *Geophysical Research Letters* may focus on broad or specific areas. As a letters journal, manuscripts are of limited length in order to expedite review and publication. Issues contain sections on topics such as atmospheric science, oceans, and climate; solid earth and planets; and hydrology and climate. Special sections address hot topics with a limited number of papers of broad interest to the geophysics research community. Full-text articles from 1994 to present are available for subscribers on the American Geological Union web site. A GeoRef priority journal.

2229. *Geophysics.* [ISSN: 0016-8033] 1936. m. USD 375 domestic; USD 410 in Canada, Mexico, Central and South America and Caribbean; USD 435 in Europe, Asia, Middle East, Africa and Oceania. Ed(s): Christopher L. Liner. Society of Exploration Geophysicists, PO Box 702740, Tulsa, OK 74170-2740; books@seg.org; http://www.seg.org. Illus., index, adv. Refereed. Circ: 16000. Vol. ends: Nov/Dec (No. 6). Microform: PQC. Online: EBSCO Publishing. Reprint: PQC. *Indexed:* AS&TI, ApMecR, BiolAb, C&ISA, ChemAb, DSR&OA, EngInd, GeoRef, GeogAbPG, PetrolAb, PollutAb, SCI, SWRA, WRCInf. *Aud.:* Ac, Sa.

Published by the Society of Exploration Geophysicists, this is one of the leading journals in the field and is available at a surprisingly reasonable price. A substantial percentage of the articles focus on seismic data acquisition, processing, and interpretation. Other areas such as mechanical properties of rock, borehole geophysics, and remote sensing are also covered. Extensive use is made of color figures and illustrations. Access to tables of contents and article abstracts from 1936 to present are available at the web site. Full-text articles are available to subscribers. Highly recommended. A GeoRef priority journal.

GeoRef. See *Bibliography and Index of Geology* in the Abstracts and Indexes section.

2230. *Geoscience Canada.* [ISSN: 0315-0941] 1974. q. CND 75. Ed(s): R Macqueen. Geological Association of Canada, Dept. of Earth Sciences, Memorial Univ. of Newfoundland, St. John's, NF A1B 3X5, Canada; http://www.esd.mun.ca/~gac/. Illus., adv. Sample. Refereed. Circ: 3300. Vol. ends: Dec (No. 4). Microform: PQC. Reprint: PQC. *Indexed:* DSR&OA, EngInd, GeoRef, PetrolAb, SCI, SWRA. *Bk. rev.:* 1-7, 400-1,200 words, signed. *Aud.:* Ac, Sa.

This engaging quarterly is published by the Geological Association of Canada and is geared toward the nonspecialist. Many of the papers deal with historical and policy issues related to the geology of Canada. Others, however, address topics of broader interest such as sedimentation processes, glacial geology, geothermal energy, and plate tectonics. For many years this journal has published an excellent series on mineral deposit models, and others, such as one on environmental marine geoscience, have recently been added. The web site offers tables of contents and article summaries in English and French from 1997 forward.

2231. *Geothermics: international journal of geothermal research and its applications.* [ISSN: 0375-6505] 1972. bi-m. EUR 1004. Ed(s): Enrico Barbier. Pergamon, The Boulevard, Langford Ln, East Park, Kidlington, OX5 1GB, United Kingdom. Illus., index, adv. Sample. Refereed. Circ: 1075. Vol. ends: Dec. Microform: PQC. Online: ingenta.com; ScienceDirect; Swets Blackwell. Reprint: PQC. *Indexed:* C&ISA, ChemAb, DSR&OA, EngInd, EnvAb, GeoRef, GeogAbPG, HortAb, PetrolAb, PollutAb, S&F, SWRA, WAE&RSA. *Bk. rev.:* 0-2, 400 words. *Aud.:* Ac, Sa.

Devoted to research and development of geothermal energy, this journal publishes articles on theory, exploration techniques, and all aspects of the use of geothermal resources. It serves as the official publication of the International Institute for Geothermal Research. Occasional special issues concentrate on one area of the world or a technique useful in a specific region. Sections of the journal are devoted to "recent literature" (citations to relevant journal articles and book announcements), recently issued patents, and a calendar of meetings in the discipline. The web site provides free access to tables of contents and abstracts beginning with 1972 issues. Full-text articles from 1972 to present are also available to libraries through ScienceDirect. Appropriate for academic and specialized collections.

2232. *Geotimes: newsmagazine of the earth sciences.* [ISSN: 0016-8556] 1956. m. USD 80 (Individuals, USD 39.95; Members, USD 24.95). American Geological Institute, 4220 King St, Alexandria, VA 22302-1502; agi@agiweb.org; http://www.agiweb.org/pubs. Illus., index, adv. Sample. Circ: 10000. Vol. ends: Dec (No. 12). Microform: PQC. Online: Gale Group. *Indexed:* BiolAb, CIJE, DSR&OA, GSI, GeoRef, OceAb, PetrolAb, SSCI, SWRA. *Bk. rev.:* 1-3, 500-1,000 words. *Aud.:* Ga, Ac, Sa.

This monthly newsmagazine by professional geoscientists reports on geoscience research and education, political activities, technological advances, and recent geological phenomena. Articles are aimed at both geologists and the general public. Books, maps, audiovisual material, and software are reviewed. This magazine tracks trends in industry relevant to engineering and environmental geology. Each issue includes classified ads and a calendar of events, and these along with news items and abstracts of feature articles are accessible at the web site (from 1996 to the present). Strongly recommended for academic and corporate collections.

2233. *Ground Water.* [ISSN: 0017-467X] 1963. bi-m. Members, USD 19; Non-members, USD 260. Ed(s): Mary P. Anderson. National Ground Water Association, 601 Dempsey Rd, Westerville, OH 43081-8978; ngwa@ngwa.org; http://www.ngwa.org. Illus., index, adv. Refereed. Circ: 11000. Vol. ends: Nov/Dec (No. 6). Microform: PQC. Online: bigchalk; Florida Center for Library Automation; Gale Group; Northern Light Technology, Inc.; OCLC Online Computer Library Center, Inc.; ProQuest Information & Learning. *Indexed:* AS&TI, Agr, BiolAb, C&ISA, ChemAb, EngInd, EnvAb, ExcerpMed, GeoRef, GeogAbPG, IndMed, PetrolAb, PollutAb, S&F, SCI, SWRA, WRCInf. *Bk. rev.:* 0-5, 300-800 words, signed. *Aud.:* Ac, Sa.

This is one of two major journals published for the Association of Ground Water Scientists and Engineers by Ground Water Publishing Company. It provides in-depth coverage of an area of research that has expanded as we have come to better appreciate the importance of this often overlooked natural resource in our daily lives. Emphasis is on modeling of ground water flow in aquifers and other geologic environments. Chemical interactions and solution transport are also heavily covered. Monitoring and remediation techniques, however, are largely dealt with in its sister publication, *Ground Water Monitoring and Remediation.* Tables of contents are available on the web site from 1997 forward. A GeoRef priority journal.

2234. ***Hydrogeology Journal.*** Formerly: *Applied Hydrogeology.* [ISSN: 1431-2174] 1992. 6x/yr. EUR 415 domestic (Free to members). Ed(s): Clifford Voss. Springer-Verlag, Tiergartenstr 17, Heidelberg, 69121, Germany. Illus., index, adv. Sample. Refereed. Vol. ends: No. 6. Online: EBSCO Publishing; RoweCom Information Quest; ScienceDirect; Springer LINK. *Indexed:* C&ISA, GeoRef, PollutAb, SWRA. *Aud.:* Ac, Sa.

This journal addresses a rapidly growing area of interest in the earth sciences. *Hydrogeology Journal* is the official journal of the International Association of Hydrogeologists and publishes theoretical and research-oriented papers as well as applied reports. The first issue of each year is a thematic one. Recent topics include groundwater recharge, microbial processes, and the role of groundwater as a geologic agent. The web site now offers full-text access from the start of publication for subscribers, along with free table of contents and abstracts.

2235. ***Hydrological Processes: an international journal.*** [ISSN: 0885-6087] 1987. 18x/yr. USD 2830. John Wiley & Sons Ltd., The Atrium, Southern Gate, Chichester, PO19 8SQ, United Kingdom; customer@wiley.co.uk; http://www.wiley.co.uk. Illus., adv. Refereed. Circ: 600. Microform: PQC. Online: EBSCO Publishing; ScienceDirect; Swets Blackwell; Wiley InterScience. Reprint: SWZ. *Indexed:* C&ISA, DSA, EngInd, EnvAb, FPA, ForAb, GeoRef, GeogAbPG, HortAb, M&GPA, PollutAb, RRTA, S&F, SCI, SWRA, WAE&RSA. *Bk. rev.:* 0-1, 500 - 1,000 words. *Aud.:* Ac, Sa.

This international journal publishes original scientific and technical papers in hydrology. The editors state that its primary objective is to improve understanding of hydrological processes. Articles present research on physical, biogeochemical, mathematical, and methodological aspects of hydrological processes as well as reports on instrumentation and techniques. Occasional special issues address such topics as "Application of Geographic Information Systems and Remote Sensing for Quantifying Patters of Erosion and Water Quality" and "Runoff Generation and Implications of River Basin Modeling." The journal includes a rapid-communications section called *HPToday* that provides invited commentaries, letters to the editor, refereed scientific briefings, current awareness, book reviews, lists and reviews of web sites and software, and conference listings. Full-text articles are available online to subscribers. Appropriate for corporate or academic collections.

2236. ***Hydrological Sciences Journal.*** Former titles (until 1981): *Hydrological Sciences Bulletin;* (until 1971): *International Association of Scientific Hydrology. Bulletin.* [ISSN: 0262-6667] 1956. bi-m. GBP 180 domestic; USD 300 foreign. Ed(s): Zbigniew Kundzewicz. I A H S Press, Centre for Ecology and Hydrology, Wallingford, OX10 8BB, United Kingdom; frances@iahs.demon.co.uk; http://www.cig.ensmp.fr/~iahs. Illus., index, adv. Sample. Refereed. Circ: 700. Vol. ends: Dec (No. 6). Reprint: ISI. *Indexed:* C&ISA, ChemAb, EngInd, ExcerpMed, ForAb, GeoRef, GeogAbPG, IBZ, M&GPA, PollutAb, RRTA, S&F, SWRA, WAE&RSA, WRCInf. *Aud.:* Ac, Sa.

Issued by the International Association of Hydrological Sciences, this journal publishes scientific papers that are primarily written in English but also include some in French. The range of topics covered is quite broad and includes modeling of hydrologic systems, use of water resources, runoff and erosion, and groundwater pollution and chemistry. The journal also features announcements, book reviews, and a handy "diary" of forthcoming hydrology-related events. The web site offers tables of contents and abstracts along with an author index from 1996 forward.

2237. ***Hydrology and Earth System Sciences.*** [ISSN: 1027-5606] 1997. q. EUR 300 (Individuals, EUR 100). Ed(s): J S G McCulloch. European Geophysical Society, Max Planck Str 13, Katlenburg-Lindau, 37191, Germany; egs@linaxi.mpae.gwdg.de. Refereed. *Indexed:* GeoRef, GeogAbPG, M&GPA, SWRA, WRCInf. *Aud.:* Ac, Sa.

A relative newcomer, this journal publishes interdisciplinary research in all areas of hydrology with an emphasis on physical, chemical, and biological processes. Some topics covered include the hydrological cycle, transport of dissolved and particulate matter, water budgets and fluxes, climate and atmospheric interactions, and the effects of human activity. Free tables of contents and abstracts are available on the web site from 1997 to present. Older, full-text articles are also available for free, with the most recent year's articles limited to subscribers only.

2238. ***International Geology Review.*** [ISSN: 0020-6814] 1958. m. USD 985 in North America; USD 997 elsewhere. Ed(s): W G Ernst, Brian J Skinner. V.H. Winston & Son, Inc., c/o Bellwether Publishing, Ltd, 8640 Guilford Rd, Ste 200, Columbia, MD 21046; bellpub@bellpub.com; http://www.bellpub.com. Illus., index, adv. Circ: 500. Vol. ends: Dec (No. 12). Reprint: PSC. *Indexed:* ChemAb, DSR&OA, EngInd, GeoRef, GeogAbPG, OceAb, PetrolAb, PollutAb, SWRA. *Aud.:* Ac, Sa.

This monthly is published in association with *Economic Geology* and the International Division of the Geological Society of America. It features in-depth review articles as well as original research. Specific areas of emphasis include petrology, tectonics, and mineral and energy resources. Coverage is global in scope, but the editors particularly encourage submission of papers about such less-frequently studied areas as Africa, Asia, and South America, making this an especially useful resource.

2239. ***International Journal of Coal Geology.*** [ISSN: 0166-5162] 1981. 16x/yr. EUR 1686 (Qualified personnel, EUR 116). Ed(s): J C Hower. Elsevier BV, Sara Burgerhartstraat 25, Amsterdam, 1055 KV, Netherlands; nlinfo-f@elsevier.nl; http://www.elsevier.nl. Illus., adv. Sample. Refereed. Vol. ends: No. 4. Microform: PQC. Online: ingenta.com; ScienceDirect; Swets Blackwell. *Indexed:* C&ISA, ChemAb, EngInd, EnvAb, GeoRef, GeogAbPG, MinerAb, PetrolAb, SCI. *Bk. rev.:* 0-2, 500-1000 words. *Aud.:* Ac, Sa.

Publishes both basic and applied research articles on the geology and petrology of coal from around the world. Some areas of special focus are the geology of coal measures, mechanisms of coal genesis, and studies of modern coal forming environments. Proceedings of symposia appear in some issues. The web site provides free access to tables of contents and abstracts beginning with 1995 issues. Full-text articles are also available online from 1995 forward through ScienceDirect. Appropriate for comprehensive research collections. A GeoRef priority journal.

2240. ***International Journal of Earth Sciences.*** Formerly (until 1998): *Geologische Rundschau.* [ISSN: 1437-3254] 1910. bi-m. EUR 730 domestic; EUR 769.70 foreign; EUR 146 newsstand/cover per issue. Ed(s): C W Dullo. Springer-Verlag, Tiergartenstr 17, Heidelberg, 69121, Germany. Illus., index, adv. Sample. Refereed. Vol. ends: Dec (No. 4). Microform: BHP. Online: EBSCO Publishing; RoweCom Information Quest; Springer LINK; Swets Blackwell. Reprint: IRC. *Indexed:* ChemAb, DSR&OA, EngInd, GeoRef, GeogAbPG, MinerAb, PetrolAb, PollutAb, SCI, SWRA, ZooRec. *Aud.:* Ac, Sa.

This bimonthly publishes "process-oriented original and review papers on the history of the earth." Some areas of particular focus include tectonics, volcanology, sedimentology, mineral deposits, and surface processes. Coverage is international in scope but with a European emphasis. Most papers are in English, but articles in German and French are also accepted. Recent thematic issue topics include island volcanic systems and the dynamics of alpine mountain belts. A special supplementary volume was issued in 2002 that featured milestone papers from the early history of the journal with English translations. The web site offers tables of contents and abstracts from 1995 forward and full-text access from mid-1996 forward for print subscribers. Listed as a GeoRef priority journal under its earlier title, *Geologische Rundschau.*

Isotope Geoscience. See *Chemical Geology.*

2241. ***J G R: Journal of Geophysical Research.*** [ISSN: 0148-0227] 1896. m. American Geophysical Union, 2000 Florida Ave, N W, Washington, DC 20009-1277; service@agu.org; http://www.agu.org. *Aud.:* Ac, Sa.

A comprehensive, interdisciplinary journal presenting research on the physics and chemistry of the earth, its environment, and the solar system, *JGR* is published in five parts: atmospheres, oceans, space physics, solid earth, and planets. A new sixth part, earth surface, is planned. Individual issues often contain special sections with multiple papers devoted to one topic. Full-text articles from 1994 to present are available for subscribers on the American Geological Union web site. Parts *B: Solid Earth, C: Oceans,* and *E: Planets* are GeoRef priority journals.

2242. *Journal of Applied Geophysics.* Formerly (until 1992): *Geoexploration.* [ISSN: 0926-9851] 1963. m. EUR 971. Ed(s): A. Hoerdt, J. W. Rector, III. Elsevier BV, Sara Burgerhartstraat 25, Amsterdam, 1055 KV, Netherlands; nlinfo-f@elsevier.nl; http://www.elsevier.nl. Illus., adv. Refereed. Microform: PQC. Online: ingenta.com; ScienceDirect; Swets Blackwell. Reprint: SWZ. *Indexed:* ChemAb, EngInd, ExcerpMed, GeoRef, GeogAbPG, OceAb, PetrolAb, PollutAb, SCI, SWRA. *Aud.:* Ac, Sa.

Originally published for mining geophysicists, this journal now emphasizes environmental, geotechnical, engineering, and hydrological aspects of geophysics and petrophysics including soil and rock mechanical properties. Special issues feature single topics and conference reports; examples are the report of a meeting on ground penetrating radar and a conference on electric, magnetic, and electromagnetic methods applied to cultural heritage. The web site provides free access to tables of contents and abstracts beginning with 1995 issues. Full-text articles from 1995 to present are also available online to libraries through ScienceDirect.

2243. *Journal of Geochemical Exploration.* [ISSN: 0375-6742] 1972. m. EUR 1220 (Individuals, EUR 189). Ed(s): R Swennen. Elsevier BV, Sara Burgerhartstraat 25, Amsterdam, 1055 KV, Netherlands; nlinfo-f@elsevier.nl; http://www.elsevier.nl. Illus., index. Sample. Refereed. Vol. ends: No. 3. Microform: PQC. Online: ingenta.com; ScienceDirect; Swets Blackwell. Reprint: ISI; SWZ. *Indexed:* ChemAb, DSR&OA, EngInd, EnvAb, ExcerpMed, GeoRef, GeogAbPG, MinerAb, PetrolAb, S&F, SCI, WRCInf. *Bk. rev.:* 0-2, 800-2,000 words. *Aud.:* Ac, Sa.

The major emphasis in this journal is the application of geochemistry to the exploration and study of mineral resources and related fields, including geochemistry of the environment. Papers present international research on geochemical exploration, sampling and analytical techniques, and geochemical distributions and dispersion in rocks, soils, and waters. Tables of contents and article abstracts from 1995 to present are available on the web site. Full-text articles are also available online beginning with 1995 issues through ScienceDirect. Appropriate for comprehensive and research collections. A GeoRef priority journal.

2244. *Journal of Geodynamics.* [ISSN: 0264-3707] 1984. 10x/yr. EUR 1358. Ed(s): G. Ranalli, Wolf R. Jacoby. Pergamon, The Boulevard, Langford Ln, East Park, Kidlington, OX5 1GB, United Kingdom. Adv. Refereed. Circ: 900. Microform: PQC. Online: ingenta.com; ScienceDirect; Swets Blackwell. *Indexed:* DSR&OA, GeoRef, GeogAbPG, IAA, SCI, SSCI. *Aud.:* Ac, Sa.

This journal provides an international forum for research in the solid earth sciences with an emphasis on large-scale processes. Papers address a wide range of topics such as physical properties of rocks and changes with pressure and temperature, mantle convection and heat flow, plate tectonics and kinematics, and magma generation, transport, and emplacement. Tables of contents and abstracts from 1995 forward are available free on the web site. Full-text is also available there through Elsevier Science Direct.

2245. *The Journal of Geology.* [ISSN: 0022-1376] 1893. bi-m. USD 149 print & online eds. (Individuals, USD 50 print & online eds.; Students, USD 22 print & online eds.). Ed(s): Alfred T Anderson, Jr. University of Chicago Press, Journals Division, PO Box 37005, Chicago, IL 60637; subscriptions@press.uchicago.edu; http://www.journals.uchicago.edu. Illus., index, adv. Sample. Refereed. Circ: 1800 Paid. Vol. ends: Nov. Microform: PMC; PQC. Online: EBSCO Publishing; Gale Group. Reprint: ISI; PQC; PSC. *Indexed:* AS&TI, BiolAb, ChemAb, DSR&OA, GSI, GeoRef, GeogAbPG, IAA, MinerAb, OceAb, PetrolAb, PollutAb, S&F, SCI, SSCI, SWRA. *Bk. rev.:* 0-4, 300-750 words. *Aud.:* Ac, Sa.

This prestigious journal, in print since 1893, is a true must-have for academic and special libraries. Contributions deal with all aspects of geology and are chosen in part for their broad applicability. Both the full-length articles and the shorter geological notes reflect high editorial standards, adding to the archival value of this outstanding publication. Full texts are available on the web site starting with 1997 for subscribers. A GeoRef priority journal.

Journal of Geophysical Research. See *JGR: Journal of Geophysical Research.*

2246. *Journal of Geoscience Education.* Formerly (until vol.44, 1996): *Journal of Geological Education.* [ISSN: 1089-9995] 1951. 5x/yr. USD 75 domestic; USD 87 foreign. Ed(s): Carl N Drummond. National Association of Geoscience Teachers, Inc., PO Box 5443, Bellingham, WA 98227-5443; xman@cc.wwu.edu; http://www.nagt.org. Illus., index, adv. Refereed. Circ: 2800 Paid. Vol. ends: Nov (No. 5). Microform: PQC. Reprint: PQC. *Indexed:* CIJE, ChemAb, EduInd, EngInd, ExcerpMed, GeoRef, GeogAbPG. *Bk. rev.:* 5-10, 200-800 words. *Aud.:* Ac, Sa.

Aimed at earth science teachers from elementary school through college, this journal reports on techniques, resources, and innovations useful for both formal and informal instruction. Regular features also include reviews of web resources, new books for geoscientists, museum and gallery information, as well as a column on errors in geoscience textbooks. Author and subject indexes beginning with 1980 are available on the web site of the National Association of Geoscience Teachers. Listed as a GeoRef priority journal under its earlier title, *Journal of Geological Education* (ISSN 0022-1368).

2247. *Journal of Glaciology.* [ISSN: 0022-1430] 1947. q. GBP 210. Ed(s): W D Harrison. International Glaciological Society, Lensfield Rd, Cambridge, CB2 1ER, United Kingdom; Int_Glaciol_Soc@compuserve.com. Illus., index. Refereed. Circ: 1300. *Indexed:* ChemAb, DSR&OA, GeoRef, GeogAbPG, M&GPA, SCI, SSCI, SWRA. *Bk. rev.:* 0-1, 600-1,200 words. *Aud.:* Ac, Sa.

Issued by the International Glaciological Society, this journal publishes findings and theories on all aspects of snow and ice with particular emphasis on studies of glaciers and their mechanics, meltwater, and energy. Some issues also include a section called "Instruments and Methods" describing new techniques and equipment for glacial investigation. Appropriate for comprehensive academic and specialized collections.

2248. *Journal of Hydrology.* [ISSN: 0022-1694] 1963. 60x/yr. EUR 4387. Ed(s): R Krzysztofowicz, M Sophocleous. Elsevier BV, Sara Burgerhartstraat 25, Amsterdam, 1055 KV, Netherlands; nlinfo-f@elsevier.nl; http://www.elsevier.nl. Illus., index, adv. Sample. Refereed. Vol. ends: No. 4. Microform: PQC. Online: EBSCO Publishing; ingenta.com; ScienceDirect; Swets Blackwell. Reprint: ISI; SWZ. *Indexed:* Agr, ApMecR, BiolAb, C&ISA, ChemAb, DSR&OA, EnvAb, ExcerpMed, FPA, ForAb, GeoRef, GeogAbPG, HortAb, M&GPA, OceAb, PollutAb, RRTA, S&F, SCI, SWRA, WAE&RSA, WRCInf. *Aud.:* Ac, Sa.

Publishes research papers and reviews on topics related to hydrology, such as physical, chemical, biogeochemical, stochastic, and systems aspects of surface and groundwater hydrology, hydrometeorology, and hydrogeology. Examples of titles of special issues are "Reactive Transport Modeling of Natural Systems" and "Biospheric Aspects of the Hydrological Cycle." Tables of contents and abstracts are available on the web site. Full-text articles from 1995 forward are also available online to libraries through ScienceDirect. Appropriate for comprehensive academic and research collections. A GeoRef priority journal.

2249. *Journal of Metamorphic Geology.* [ISSN: 0263-4929] 1982. 9x/yr. GBP 843 print & online eds. Blackwell Publishing Ltd., 9600 Garsington Rd, Oxford, OX4 2ZG, United Kingdom; customerservices@oxon.blackwellpublishing.com; http://www.blackwellpublishing.com. Illus., adv. Refereed. Circ: 364. Vol. ends: Nov (No. 6). Online: EBSCO Publishing; ingenta.com; Munksgaard & Blackwell Science's Synergy; RoweCom Information Quest; Swets Blackwell. *Indexed:* ChemAb, DSR&OA, EngInd, GeoRef, MinerAb, SCI. *Aud.:* Ac, Sa.

Publishes papers on a full range of metamorphic topics. International research is presented on properties of metamorphic minerals, theoretical and experimental studies of metamorphic reactions, structural deformation and geochemical changes associated with metamorphism, and regional analysis of metamorphic terranes. The web site provides full-text access beginning with 1999 for subscribers. A GeoRef priority journal.

Journal of Paleontology. See Paleontology section.

2250. *Journal of Petroleum Geology.* [ISSN: 0141-6421] 1978. q. GBP 180 (Individuals, GBP 50). Scientific Press Ltd., Scientific Press Ltd, PO Box 21, Beaconsfield, HP9 1NS, United Kingdom; ct@jpg.co.uk. Illus., index, adv. Sample. Refereed. Vol. ends: Oct (No. 4). Online: Ingenta Select. *Indexed:* ChemAb, DSR&OA, EngInd, GeoRef, GeogAbPG, MinerAb, PetrolAb, SCI. *Bk. rev.:* 0-3, 500-1,200 words, signed. *Aud.:* Ac, Sa.

This quarterly is from a smaller publisher, but it still compares quite favorably with its competitors. Articles deal with the geology of oil and gas with a particular focus on regions outside of North America. Some areas of emphasis include petroleum exploration and development, basin modeling, and reservoir evaluation. Each issue also includes a calendar of upcoming events. The web site provides tables of contents from the start of publication and abstracts for recent issues. A GeoRef priority journal.

2251. *Journal of Petrology.* [ISSN: 0022-3530] 1960. m. GBP 643. Ed(s): M Wilson. Oxford University Press, Great Clarendon St, Oxford, OX2 6DP, United Kingdom; jnl.orders@oup.co.uk; http://www3.oup.co.uk/jnls. Illus., index, adv. Sample. Refereed. Circ: 1200. Vol. ends: Dec (No. 12). Microform: PQC. Online: EBSCO Publishing; HighWire Press; ingenta.com; OCLC Online Computer Library Center, Inc.; RoweCom Information Quest; Swets Blackwell. Reprint: PSC. *Indexed:* BAS, ChemAb, DSR&OA, EngInd, GeoRef, MinerAb, SCI. *Bk. rev.:* 0-2, 600-1,000 words, signed. *Aud.:* Ac, Sa.

A top-notch journal from Oxford University Press that features research in igneous and metamorphic petrology, this title is recommended for academic and special libraries. Subjects covered include magmatic processes, petrogenesis, trace element and isotope geochemistry, and experimental studies and theoretical modeling. Special thematic issues or collections of selected papers from conferences are also published from time to time. Tables of contents with abstracts are available at the web site from 1996 forward. Full-text articles from 1997 on are available to subscribers. A GeoRef priority journal.

2252. *Journal of Quaternary Science.* [ISSN: 0267-8179] 1986. 8x/yr. USD 1295. John Wiley & Sons Ltd., The Atrium, Southern Gate, Chichester, PO19 8SQ, United Kingdom; customer@wiley.co.uk; http://www.wiley.co.uk. Illus., index, adv. Refereed. Circ: 700. Vol. ends: No. 8. Microform: PQC. Online: EBSCO Publishing; Florida Center for Library Automation; Gale Group; ScienceDirect; Wiley InterScience. Reprint: SWZ. *Indexed:* EngInd, GeoRef, GeogAbPG, M&GPA, S&F, SCI, SWRA, ZooRec. *Bk. rev.:* 2-10, 300-1,000 words, signed. *Aud.:* Ac, Sa.

Published for the Quaternary Research Association, this journal focuses on the earth's history during the last two million years. This time period is the same as that covered by the journal *Boreas*, and there are many similarities between the two. Papers span a wide range of topics and many are interdisciplinary in nature. In particular, there is an emphasis on the stratigraphy, glaciation, and paleoclimatology of the period. Occasional special issues may focus on a particular region or environment. Full-length research papers, short rapid communications, and invited reviews are all included. Free tables of contents and abstracts from 1996 to present are provided at the web site, along with full-text access from 1997 on for subscribers.

2253. *Journal of Sedimentary Research.* Formed by the merger of (1994-1996): *Journal of Sedimentary Research. Section A: Sedimentary Petrology and Processes;* (1994-1996): *Journal of Sedimentary Research. Section B: Stratigraphy and Global Studies;* Both superseded in part (1931-1994): *Journal of Sedimentary Petrology.* [ISSN: 1527-1404] 1996. bi-m. Members, USD 70; Non-members, USD 210; Students, USD 35. Ed(s): Mary J Kraus, David A Budd. S E P M, 1741 E. 71st St., Tulsa, OK 74136-5108; http://www.sepm.org. Illus., adv. Refereed. Circ: 5000. Microform: PMC; PQC. *Indexed:* BiolAb, ChemAb, DSR&OA, ExcerpMed, GeoRef, GeogAbPG, M&GPA, OceAb, PetrolAb, PollutAb, S&F, SCI, SWRA. *Bk. rev.:* 0-3, 200-600 words. *Aud.:* Ac, Sa.

This is the primary journal of the Society for Sedimentary Geology (SEPM). Topics from all branches of sedimentary geology are addressed, including inherent characteristics of sediments themselves, their impacts on other aspects of the sediment record, and sedimentary processes. These range from detailed papers concentrating on very specific, often small-scale topics to "big picture" papers describing research on larger spatial and temporal scales. Each issue includes research articles, research methods papers, and discussions. The SEPM web site provides tables of contents from 1995 forward, data files supplementing some papers, and full texts of recent book reviews. A GeoRef priority journal.

2254. *Journal of Seismology.* [ISSN: 1383-4649] 1997. q. EUR 385 print or online ed. Ed(s): A Udias. Kluwer Academic Publishers, van Godewijckstraat 30, PO Box 17, Dordrecht, 3300 AA, Netherlands. Adv. Refereed. Microform: PQC. Online: East View Publications, Inc.; EBSCO Publishing; ingenta.com; Kluwer Online; OCLC Online Computer Library Center, Inc.; Ovid Technologies, Inc.; RoweCom Information Quest; Swets Blackwell. *Indexed:* GeoRef, H&SSA, RiskAb, SWRA. *Aud.:* Ac, Sa.

This international journal specializes in the study of earthquakes and their occurrence. Areas of particular focus include seismicity and seismotectonics, earthquake prediction, seismic hazards, and earthquake engineering. Many papers are regional or historical studies. However, broader theoretical work can also be found along with short communications on new analytical techniques and instrumentation. The web site provides free table of contents and abstracts from 1997 to present. Full-text access is also available for subscribers.

2255. *Journal of Structural Geology.* [ISSN: 0191-8141] 1979. m. EUR 1296 (Qualified personnel, EUR 167). Ed(s): Thomas G. Blenkinsop, D. A. Ferrill. Pergamon, The Boulevard, Langford Ln, East Park, Kidlington, OX5 1GB, United Kingdom. Illus., adv. Sample. Refereed. Circ: 2000. Vol. ends: Dec (No. 12). Microform: PQC. Online: ingenta.com; ScienceDirect; Swets Blackwell. *Indexed:* ApMecR, C&ISA, ChemAb, DSR&OA, EngInd, GeoRef, MinerAb, PetrolAb, SCI, SWRA. *Bk. rev.:* 0-2, 500-1,000 words. *Aud.:* Ac, Sa.

This international journal publishes research and review articles on structural geology, tectonics, and the associated rock deformation processes on any scale. Some specific topics include faults, folds, fractures, strain analysis, rock mechanics, and theoretical and experimental modeling. Regional structural accounts are published when they are of broad interest. Occasional special issues are devoted to a theme or report on conference proceedings. Tables of contents and article abstracts from 1995 on are accessible free on the web site. Full-text articles from 1995 forward are also available online to libraries through ScienceDirect. A GeoRef priority journal.

2256. *Journal of Volcanology and Geothermal Research: an international journal on the geophysical, geochemical, petrological and economic aspects of geothermal and volcanological research.* [ISSN: 0377-0273] 1976. 40x/yr. EUR 2451 (Qualified personnel, EUR 179). Ed(s): B D Marsh, M. T. Mangan. Elsevier BV, Sara Burgerhartstraat 25, Amsterdam, 1055 KV, Netherlands; nlinfo-f@elsevier.nl; http://www.elsevier.nl. Illus., index, adv. Sample. Refereed. Vol. ends: No. 4. Microform: PQC. Online: ingenta.com; ScienceDirect; Swets Blackwell. Reprint: ISI; SWZ. *Indexed:* ChemAb, DSR&OA, EngInd, EnvAb, GeoRef, GeogAbPG, IAA, MinerAb, PetrolAb, PollutAb, SCI, SWRA. *Aud.:* Ac, Sa.

Presents recent research on geochemical, petrological, geophysical, economic, tectonic, and environmental aspects of volcanic activity. Occasional special issues address particular processes, environments, or locales, e.g., magmatic systems in the ocean crust or the geology and geophysics of the Canary Islands. Tables of contents and abstracts are available free from 1995 on at the web site. Full-text articles from 1995 to present are also available online to libraries through ScienceDirect. A GeoRef priority journal.

Lethaia. See Paleontology section.

2257. ***Lithos: an international journal of mineralogy, petrology, and geochemistry.*** [ISSN: 0024-4937] 1968. 28x/yr. EUR 1262 (Qualified personnel, EUR 264). Ed(s): S Foley. Elsevier BV, Sara Burgerhartstraat 25, Amsterdam, 1055 KV, Netherlands; nlinfo-f@elsevier.nl; http://www.elsevier.nl. Illus., index, adv. Sample. Refereed. Circ: 1000. Vol. ends: No. 4. Microform: PQC. Online: ingenta.com; ScienceDirect; Swets Blackwell. *Indexed:* ChemAb, DSR&OA, GeoRef, MinerAb, PollutAb, SCI, SSCI. *Bk. rev.:* 1-3, 800-1,000 words. *Aud.:* Ac, Sa.

Publishes research papers, reviews, discussions, and book reviews in the fields of mineralogy, petrology, and geochemistry with an emphasis on applications to petrogenetic problems. Occasional special issues are published. The web site provides free tables of contents and article abstracts from 1995 to present. Full-text articles are also available online from 1995 forward to libraries through ScienceDirect. A GeoRef priority journal.

2258. ***Marine and Petroleum Geology.*** [ISSN: 0264-8172] 1984. 10x/yr. EUR 1649 (Qualified personnel, EUR 216). Ed(s): D. G. Roberts, A. Tankard. Elsevier Ltd., The Boulevard, Langford Ln, Oxford, OX5 1GB, United Kingdom. Illus., index, adv. Sample. Refereed. Microform: PQC. Online: ingenta.com; ScienceDirect; Swets Blackwell. *Indexed:* ChemAb, EngInd, EnvAb, GeoRef, GeogAbPG, OceAb, PetrolAb, SCI. *Aud.:* Ac, Sa.

Marine and Petroleum Geology provides an international forum for the exchange of multidisciplinary concepts, interpretations, and techniques for all concerned with marine and petroleum geology. A selection of paper topics includes basin analysis and evaluation; organic geochemistry; geophysical interpretation; reserve/resource estimation; seismic stratigraphy; sedimentary geology; continental margins; and well logging. Full-color illustrations and occasional fold-out seismic sections and maps enhance many issues. Sets of thematic papers are occasionally published on selected basins or depositional environments. Tables of contents and abstracts from 1995 forward are available free at the web site; full-text articles are also available online from 1995 on to libraries through ScienceDirect.

Marine Geology. See Marine Science and Technology section.

2259. ***Mathematical Geology.*** Formerly (until 1986): *International Association for Mathematical Geology. Journal.* [ISSN: 0882-8121] 1969. 8x/yr. EUR 958 print or online ed. Ed(s): W E Sharp. Kluwer Academic / Plenum Publishers, 233 Spring St Fl 7, New York, NY 10013-1522; http://www.wkap.nl/. Illus., adv. Refereed. Vol. ends: Nov (No. 8). Microform: PQC. Online: EBSCO Publishing; ingenta.com; Kluwer Online; OCLC Online Computer Library Center, Inc.; Ovid Technologies, Inc.; RoweCom Information Quest; Swets Blackwell. *Indexed:* ApMecR, C&ISA, CCMJ, ChemAb, DSR&OA, EngInd, GeoRef, GeogAbPG, MathSciNet, PetrolAb, SCI, SWRA. *Bk. rev.:* 0-5, 400-700 words, signed. *Aud.:* Ac, Sa.

This is one of the main journals of the International Association for Mathematical Geology, which also publishes *Computers and Geosciences* and *Natural Resources Research.* The ability to work efficiently with large quantities of numerical data has become especially important in recent years. As suggested by the title, papers in *Mathematical Geology* are primarily concerned with the application and use of math, statistics, and computing in the earth sciences. Some specific areas of concentration include modeling and simulation, fluid mechanics, filtering techniques, fractals, and spatial analysis. Tables of contents and article abstracts from late 1997 forward are on the web site, with full-text access available for subscribers. A GeoRef priority journal.

Micropaleontology. See Paleontology section.

2260. ***Mineralium Deposita: international journal of geology, mineralogy, and geochemistry of mineral deposits.*** [ISSN: 0026-4598] 1966. 8x/yr. EUR 1140 domestic; EUR 1172.20 foreign; EUR 171 newsstand/cover per issue. Ed(s): R J Goldfarb, B Lehmann. Springer-Verlag, Tiergartenstr 17, Heidelberg, 69121, Germany. Illus., index, adv. Sample. Refereed. Vol. ends: No. 8. Microform: PQC. Online: EBSCO Publishing; RoweCom Information Quest; ScienceDirect; Springer LINK; Swets Blackwell. Reprint: ISI. *Indexed:* ChemAb, EngInd, GeoRef, MinerAb, PollutAb, SCI. *Bk. rev.:* 0-5, 400-700 words, signed. *Aud.:* Ac, Sa.

This journal is the official bulletin of the Society for Geology Applied to Mineral Deposits. It focuses on economic geology including field studies, experimental and applied geochemistry, and ore deposit exploration. Issues contain a mixture of full-length papers, rapid-communication letters, and notes, all dealing with economic geology and related topics in mineralogy and geochemistry. Many of the illustrations are in color, especially those of mineral thin sections. Coverage is truly international in scope and includes such often under-represented areas as Africa, Asia, Australia, and South America. There are also thematic issues on selected ore deposits or other topics of general interest. The web site offers free tables of contents and abstracts from mid-1996 on and full-text access from 1997 forward for print subscribers. A GeoRef priority journal.

2261. ***Mineralogical Magazine.*** [ISSN: 0026-461X] 1876. bi-m. issue numbers 428-433 - last issue includes index. GBP 238.65; USD 366. Ed(s): Dr. S A T Redfern. Mineralogical Society, 41 Queens Gate, London, SW7 5HR, United Kingdom; http://www.minersoc.org. Illus., index, adv. Sample. Refereed. Circ: 2000. Vol. ends: Dec (No. 6). Microform: BHP. Online: Ingenta Select; OCLC Online Computer Library Center, Inc.; Swets Blackwell. *Indexed:* ChemAb, DSR&OA, EngInd, GeoRef, MinerAb, SCI. *Bk. rev.:* 3-8, 500-900 words. *Aud.:* Ac, Sa.

Published by the Mineralogical Society, this well-respected journal has been in print for more than 125 years. Topics covered include not only mineralogy but also geochemistry and petrology. Both full-length original research papers and shorter letters for rapid communication are included. Along with *American Mineralogist,* this title is highly recommended for larger academic library collections. Full-text access is available from 1998 forward through Ingenta. A GeoRef priority journal.

2262. ***The Mineralogical Record.*** [ISSN: 0026-4628] 1970. bi-m. USD 120 (Individuals, USD 47). Ed(s): Wendell E Wilson. Mineralogical Record, Inc., 7413 N Mowry Place, Tucson, AZ 85741-2573; minrec@aol.com; http://www.minrec.org/. Illus., index, adv. Sample. Refereed. Circ: 7400. Vol. ends: Nov/Dec (No. 6). Microform: PQC. Online: Florida Center for Library Automation; Gale Group; Northern Light Technology, Inc.; OCLC Online Computer Library Center, Inc.; ProQuest Information & Learning; H.W. Wilson. Reprint: PQC. *Indexed:* ChemAb, GSI, GeoRef, MinerAb. *Bk. rev.:* 0-4, 100-800 words. *Aud.:* Ga, Ac, Sa.

This journal includes both nontechnical and technical articles written for mineral collectors, curators, and researchers. Each issue has numerous high-quality color photographs, and even many of the advertisements are visually stunning. Reports from mineral shows around the world appear in a column called "What's New in Minerals," and special issues focus on single topics such as minerals of a particular region, history of equipment used by mineraologists, and specific mines. The International Mineral Association's recommended guidelines for mineral nomenclature are published in *Mineralogical Record.* The web site provides searchable tables of contents back to the first issue, published in 1970. Recommended for public and academic libraries.

2263. ***Netherlands Journal of Geosciences.*** Formerly: *Geologie en Mijnbouw.* 1921. q. NLG 560. Ed(s): J Smit. Netherlands Journal of Geosciences Foundation, PO Box 80015, Utrecht, 3508, Netherlands. Illus., index, adv. Refereed. Circ: 2250. Vol. ends: No. 4. Microform: PQC; SWZ. Online: EBSCO Publishing; ingenta.com; RoweCom Information Quest; Swets Blackwell. *Indexed:* BiolAb, ChemAb, DSR&OA, EngInd, GeoRef, GeogAbPG, OceAb, PetrolAb, SWRA, ZooRec. *Aud.:* Ac, Sa.

The official journal of the Royal Geological and Mining Society of the Netherlands, this title represents a merger of two titles, *Geologie en Mijnbouw* and *Mededelingen Nederlands Instituut voor Geowetenschappen–TNO,* and the first issue appeared in March 2000. Articles feature research on geology and mining with emphasis on the Netherlands, the North Sea, and neighboring areas. A special strength is in geological aspects of coastal and deltaic lowlands, both ancient and modern. Tables of contents, abstracts, and supplementary material are available on the web site. Listed as a GeoRef priority journal under its earlier title, *Geologie en Mijnbouw*.

2264. *Organic Geochemistry.* [ISSN: 0146-6380] 1978. m. EUR 2571. Ed(s): J R Maxwell, L R Snowden. Pergamon, The Boulevard, Langford Ln, East Park, Kidlington, OX5 1GB, United Kingdom. Illus., index, adv. Sample. Refereed. Circ: 1100. Vol. ends: No. 32. Microform: PQC. Online: ingenta.com; ScienceDirect; Swets Blackwell. *Indexed:* C&ISA, ChemAb, DSR&OA, EngInd, ExcerpMed, FPA, ForAb, GeoRef, GeogAbPG, PetrolAb, PollutAb, S&F, SCI, SWRA, WRCInf. *Bk. rev.:* 0-2, 300-1,000 words. *Aud.:* Ac, Sa.

The official journal of the European Association of Organic Geochemists, this journal publishes papers on all phases of organic geochemistry including biogeochemistry, environmental geochemistry, and geochemical cycling. Types of articles include original research papers, comprehensive reviews, technical communications, and discussions and replies. The web site provides free tables of contents and article abstracts from 1995 forward. Full-text articles from 1995 on are also available online to libraries through ScienceDirect. A GeoRef priority journal.

Palaeogeography, Palaeoclimatology, Palaeoecology. See Paleontology section.

Palaeontology. See Paleontology section.

2265. *Petroleum Geoscience.* [ISSN: 1354-0793] 1995. q. USD 265 United States; GBP 160 in Europe; GBP 180 elsewhere. Ed(s): J R Parker. Geological Society Publishing House, Unit 7, Brassmill Enterprise Centre, Brassmill Ln, Bath, BA1 3JN, United Kingdom; http://www.geolsoc.org.uk. Illus., index, adv. Refereed. Circ: 3500. Vol. ends: Nov (No. 4). *Indexed:* C&ISA, GeoRef, GeogAbPG, PetrolAb, SCI. *Bk. rev.:* 0-6, 250-600 words, signed. *Aud.:* Ac, Sa.

This quarterly is published by the Geological Society of London and the Petroleum Division of the European Association of Geoscientists and Engineers. Although a relative newcomer, it has already established a strong reputation for quality and has been widely indexed. It covers a full range of geoscience aspects "involved in the exploration, appraisal, and development of hydrocarbon resources." Coverage is international in scope and includes both theoretical and applied articles. Color is used to good effect for many illustrations. Full-text access is available through the Ingenta web site for issues starting in 1999 for subscribers or through a pay-per-view option.

2266. *Physics and Chemistry of Minerals.* [ISSN: 0342-1791] 1977. 10x/yr. EUR 1550 domestic; EUR 1577.20 foreign; EUR 186 newsstand/cover per issue. Ed(s): M Akaogi, M Rieder. Springer-Verlag, Tiergartenstr 17, Heidelberg, 69121, Germany. Illus., index, adv. Sample. Refereed. Vol. ends: No. 10. Microform: PQC. Online: EBSCO Publishing; RoweCom Information Quest; ScienceDirect; Springer LINK; Swets Blackwell. Reprint: ISI. *Indexed:* ChemAb, EngInd, GeoRef, MinerAb, S&F, SCI. *Aud.:* Ac, Sa.

This journal is published in cooperation with the International Mineralogical Association. Papers focus on the chemistry and physics of minerals and related solids. Some areas of emphasis include atomic structure, spectroscopy, chemical reactions and bonding, and analysis of physical properties. Recommended for larger academic or special libraries. The web site offers full-text access to print subscribers for issues starting in 1997. A GeoRef priority journal.

2267. *Physics of the Earth and Planetary Interiors: a journal devoted to observational and experimental studies of the chemistry and physics of planetary interiors and their theoretical interpretation.* [ISSN: 0031-9201] 1967. 24x/yr. EUR 2232 (Qualified personnel, EUR 136). Ed(s): K. Creager, D Gubbins. Elsevier BV, Sara Burgerhartstraat 25, Amsterdam, 1055 KV, Netherlands; nlinfo-f@elsevier.nl; http://www.elsevier.nl. Illus., index. Sample. Refereed. Vol. ends: No. 124 - No. 129. Microform: PQC. Online: ingenta.com; ScienceDirect; Swets Blackwell. Reprint: SWZ. *Indexed:* ChemAb, DSR&OA, EngInd, GeoRef, GeogAbPG, IAA, M&GPA, PetrolAb, SCI. *Bk. rev.:* 0-1, 300-800 words. *Aud.:* Ac, Sa.

Devoted to studies of the planetary physical and chemical processes, this title publishes research in three main areas: geophysics and geodesy; hydrology, oceans, and atmospheres; and solar-terrestrial and planetary science. Papers present observational and experimental studies along with theoretical interpretation. Occasional issues present papers from symposia or are devoted to special topics. Some recent examples include magnetic fields of Earth's and planetary interiors, subduction zones, and accurate earthquake location. The web site offers free access to tables of contents and abstracts for issues from 1995 forward. Full-text articles are also available online to libraries through ScienceDirect. A GeoRef priority journal.

2268. *Precambrian Research.* [ISSN: 0301-9268] 1974. 32x/yr. EUR 2215 (Qualified personnel, EUR 298). Ed(s): K A Eriksson, A Kroener. Elsevier BV, Sara Burgerhartstraat 25, Amsterdam, 1055 KV, Netherlands; nlinfo-f@elsevier.nl; http://www.elsevier.nl. Illus., index, adv. Sample. Refereed. Vol. ends: No. 4. Microform: PQC. Online: ingenta.com; ScienceDirect; Swets Blackwell. *Indexed:* BiolAb, ChemAb, EngInd, GeoRef, GeogAbPG, MinerAb, PetrolAb, SCI, ZooRec. *Bk. rev.:* 0-2, 200-600 words. *Aud.:* Ac, Sa.

The Precambrian era extended for some four billion years of Earth's history, representing a substantial majority of the geological time scale. This journal publishes research on all aspects of the early history and evolution of Earth and its planetary neighbors, emphasizing interdisciplinary studies. Topics include the origin of life, evolution of the oceans and atmosphere, the early fossil record, paleobiology, geochronology, and Precambrian mineral deposits. Tables of contents and abstracts are available on the web site from 1995 forward. Full-text articles from 1995 to present are also available online to libraries through ScienceDirect. A GeoRef priority journal.

2269. *Pure and Applied Geophysics.* Formerly: *Geofisica.* [ISSN: 0033-4553] 1939. m. EUR 2288; EUR 228 newsstand/cover per issue. Ed(s): B J Mitchell. Birkhaeuser Verlag AG, Viaduktstr. 42, Postfach 133, Basel, 4051, Switzerland; info@birkhauser.ch; http://www.birkhauser.ch/journals. Illus. Refereed. Vol. ends: No. 4. Online: EBSCO Publishing; ScienceDirect; Springer LINK; Swets Blackwell. *Indexed:* ApMecR, BAS, ChemAb, DSR&OA, EngInd, ExcerpMed, GeoRef, GeogAbPG, IAA, M&GPA, PetrolAb, SCI, SWRA. *Bk. rev.:* 0-12, 400-1,200 words, signed. *Aud.:* Ac, Sa.

Often referred to as PAGEOPH, this journal features full-length papers on all aspects of geophysics. The vast majority of articles are in English although contributions in French and German are also accepted. Special issues, sometimes representing multiple numbers within a volume, are often featured on topics of interest. The web site offers full-text access from 1997 forward for print subscribers. Strongly recommended for academic and special libraries. A GeoRef priority journal.

2270. *Quarterly Journal of Engineering Geology and Hydrogeology.* Formerly (until 1999): *Quarterly Journal of Engineering Geology.* [ISSN: 1470-9236] 1967. q. GBP 235 domestic; GBP 265 foreign; USD 445 foreign. Ed(s): M Packman. Geological Society Publishing House, Unit 7, Brassmill Enterprise Centre, Brassmill Ln, Bath, BA1 3JN, United Kingdom; http://www.geolsoc.org.uk. Illus., index, adv. Refereed. Circ: 3300. Vol. ends: Nov (No. 4). *Indexed:* C&ISA, ChemAb, EngInd, ExcerpMed, GeoRef, GeogAbPG, MinerAb, SCI. *Bk. rev.:* 0-7, 300-800 words, signed. *Aud.:* Ac, Sa.

Another high-quality journal from the Geological Society of London, this title focuses specifically on geology as applied to civil engineering, mining, and water resources. This makes it of considerable value to both engineers and earth scientists. Coverage is international in scope. In addition to original research, it includes review articles, technical notes, and lectures. Supplements to the regular issues are also issued on an occasional basis. Full-text access is available through the Ingenta web site for issues starting in 1999. Listed as a GeoRef priority journal under its earlier title, *Quarterly Journal of Engineering Geology*.

2271. *Quaternary International.* [ISSN: 1040-6182] 1989. 14x/yr. EUR 864. Ed(s): N R Catto, Dirk van Husen. Pergamon, The Boulevard, Langford Ln, East Park, Kidlington, OX5 1GB, United Kingdom. Illus. Refereed. Vol. ends: Dec (No. 4). Microform: PQC. Online: ingenta.com; ScienceDirect; Swets Blackwell. *Indexed:* EngInd, GeoRef, GeogAbPG, ZooRec. *Aud.:* Ac, Sa.

Publishes international, interdisciplinary research on global climate changes and the succession of glacial and interglacial ages during the Quaternary period, approximately the last two million years of the earth's history. Complex environmental changes and interactions are studied, with appropriate connections to both present processes and future climatological implications. Each issue is thematic; collected papers from symposia and workshops sponsored by the International Union for Quaternary Research are often included. Full-text articles from 1995 to present are available online to libraries through ScienceDirect. Free access to tables of contents and abstracts is also available on the web site.

2272. *Quaternary Research: an interdisciplinary journal.* [ISSN: 0033-5894] 1970. bi-m. EUR 839 (Individuals, USD 407; Students, EUR 104). Ed(s): A. R. Gillespie. Academic Press, 525 B St, Ste 1900, San Diego, CA 92101-4495; apsubs@acad.com; http://www.academicpress.com. Illus., index. Sample. Refereed. Vol. ends: Nov (No. 3). Online: EBSCO Publishing; ingenta.com; OCLC Online Computer Library Center, Inc.; RoweCom Information Quest; ScienceDirect; Swets Blackwell. Reprint: SWZ. *Indexed:* AbAn, AnthLit, ApEcolAb, ArtHuCI, BiolAb, BrArAb, ChemAb, DSR&OA, FPA, ForAb, GeoRef, M&GPA, OceAb, S&F, SCI, SWRA, WAE&RSA, ZooRec. *Bk. rev.:* 0-2, 500-1,000 words. *Aud.:* Ac, Sa.

Papers in this journal present interdisciplinary studies in the earth and biological sciences. Articles cover areas of geoarcheology, geochemistry and geophysics, geochronology, geomorphology, glaciology, paleobotany and paleoecology, paleoclimatology, paleogeography, and volcanology. Geographic emphasis is on North and South America. Tables of contents and abstracts for articles from 1993 to present are available on the web site. Full-text access is also available from 1993 to present through ScienceDirect. Recommended for college and university libraries. A GeoRef priority journal.

2273. *Rocks and Minerals: mineralogy, geology, lapidary.* [ISSN: 0035-7529] 1926. bi-m. USD 91 (Individuals, USD 48; USD 15.25 per issue). Ed(s): Marie Huizing. Heldref Publications, 1319 18th St, NW, Washington, DC 20036-1802; subscribe@heldref.org; http://www.heldref.org. Illus., index, adv. Sample. Refereed. Circ: 3900. Vol. ends: No. 6. CD-ROM: ProQuest Information & Learning. Online: bigchalk; EBSCO Publishing; Florida Center for Library Automation; Gale Group; OCLC Online Computer Library Center, Inc.; ProQuest Information & Learning; H.W. Wilson. Reprint: PSC. *Indexed:* BRI, CBRI, ChemAb, GeoRef, MinerAb, PetrolAb. *Bk. rev.:* 0-7, 100-800 words, signed. *Aud.:* Ga, Hs, Ac, Sa.

Spectacular full-color photographs and a modest price make this an ideal choice for libraries of all sizes. The emphasis is on minerals more than on rocks, and the specimens featured in the articles are generally of "museum quality." There is also a considerable amount of other material to interest collectors, such as mineral localities, sample preparation, historical background, and so on. Museum notes, announcements, and a calendar of upcoming events are also included. The web site offers a searchable archive from mid-1998 forward with full-text access available for a fee.

2274. *Sedimentary Geology: international journal of pure and applied sedimentology.* [ISSN: 0037-0738] 1967. 40x/yr. EUR 2558 (Qualified personnel, EUR 163). Ed(s): K A W Crook. Elsevier BV, Sara Burgerhartstraat 25, Amsterdam, 1055 KV, Netherlands; nlinfo-f@elsevier.nl; http://www.elsevier.nl. Illus., index, adv. Sample. Refereed. Vol. ends: No. 4. Microform: PQC. Online: EBSCO Publishing; ingenta.com; ScienceDirect; Swets Blackwell. Reprint: SWZ. *Indexed:* BiolAb, ChemAb, DSR&OA, EngInd, GeoRef, GeogAbPG, OceAb, PetrolAb, PollutAb, SCI, SWRA, ZooRec. *Bk. rev.:* 0-4, 300-3,000 words. *Aud.:* Ac, Sa.

Publishes research papers on sediments and sedimentary rocks at all spatial and temporal scales. Examples of topics addressed include analytical techniques such as numerical modeling, regional studies of sedimentary systems, and chemical sedimentology. Some recent special issues focus on coastal depositional environments and on advanced techniques in provenance analysis of sedimentary rocks. It tends to emphasize the Eurasian region more than *Journal of Sedimentary Research.* Tables of contents and abstracts from 1995 are available at the web site. Full-text articles from 1995 to present are also available online to libraries through ScienceDirect. A GeoRef priority journal.

2275. *Sedimentology.* [ISSN: 0037-0746] 1952. bi-m. GBP 619 print & online eds. Ed(s): J Best, B Fielding. Blackwell Publishing Ltd., 9600 Garsington Rd, Oxford, OX4 2ZG, United Kingdom; customerservices@oxon.blackwellpublishing.com; http://www.blackwellpublishing.com. Illus., index, adv. Sample. Refereed. Circ: 2870. Vol. ends: Dec (No. 6). Microform: PQC. Online: EBSCO Publishing; ingenta.com; Munksgaard & Blackwell Science's Synergy; OCLC Online Computer Library Center, Inc.; RoweCom Information Quest. Reprint: ISI; SWZ. *Indexed:* BiolAb, ChemAb, DSR&OA, EngInd, GeoRef, GeogAbPG, OceAb, PetrolAb, PollutAb, SCI, SWRA, ZooRec. *Aud.:* Ac, Sa.

This bimonthly publication is the official journal of the International Association of Sedimentologists. Full-length papers deal with every aspect of sediments and sedimentary rocks. These are well illustrated and of consistently high quality. Virtually all are in English, but contributions in French and German are also accepted. This journal is recommended for academic and special library collections. Free tables of contents can be found on the web site beginning with 1997. Full-text access is available for print subscribers or on a per-article basis. A GeoRef priority journal.

2276. *Seismological Society of America. Bulletin.* [ISSN: 0037-1106] 1911. bi-m. USD 390 print & online eds. Ed(s): Michael Fehler. Seismological Society of America, 201 Plaza Professional Bldg, El Cerrito, CA 94530-4003; info@seismosoc.org; http://www.seismosoc.org/ssa/. Illus., index. Sample. Refereed. Circ: 2500 Paid. Vol. ends: Dec (No. 6). Online: OCLC Online Computer Library Center, Inc. *Indexed:* AS&TI, ApMecR, CCMJ, DSR&OA, EngInd, GeoRef, GeogAbPG, IAA, MathSciNet, PetrolAb, S&F, SCI. *Aud.:* Ac, Sa.

Publishes research papers, reviews, short notes, comments, and replies in the areas of seismology, earthquake geology, and earthquake engineering. Specific topics include investigation of specific earthquakes; theoretical and observational studies of seismic waves; seismometry; earthquake hazard and risk estimation; and seismotectonics. The web site provides tables of contents for the last three years, abstracts from 1996 to the current issue, links to supplemental data, and the *BSSA Web Index.* The index covers 1911 to the present. It is searchable by author and title for all years and, from 1996 to present, also by words in the abstracts. Society members may view the journal's electronic edition online. A GeoRef priority journal.

2277. *Tectonics.* [ISSN: 0278-7407] 1982. bi-m. USD 528. Ed(s): B Wernicke. American Geophysical Union, 2000 Florida Ave, N W, Washington, DC 20009-1277; http://www.agu.org. Illus., index. Sample. Refereed. Vol. ends: Dec (No. 6). Microform: Pub.; AIP. Online: Gale Group. *Indexed:* DSR&OA, EngInd, GeoRef, GeogAbPG, IAA, PetrolAb, SCI. *Aud.:* Ac, Sa.

Cosponsored by the American Geophysical Union (AGU) and the European Geophysical Society, this journal publishes reports of original analytical, synthetic, and integrative studies on the structure and evolution of the terrestrial lithosphere. Commentaries and replies address previously published papers. The AGU web site provides full-text articles from 1994 to the present for subscribers. Recommended for academic research collections. A GeoRef priority journal.

2278. *Tectonophysics: international journal of geotectonics and the geology and physics of the interior of the earth.* [ISSN: 0040-1951] 1964. 68x/yr. EUR 4188 (Qualified personnel, EUR 417). Ed(s): J P Burg, K P Furlong. Elsevier BV, Sara Burgerhartstraat 25, Amsterdam, 1055 KV, Netherlands; nlinfo-f@elsevier.nl; http://www.elsevier.nl. Illus., adv. Sample. Refereed. Vol. ends: No. 327 - No. 343. Microform: PQC.

Online: EBSCO Publishing; ingenta.com; ScienceDirect; Swets Blackwell. Reprint: SWZ. *Indexed:* ChemAb, DSR&OA, EngInd, GeoRef, GeogAbPG, IAA, M&GPA, MinerAb, OceAb, PetrolAb, PollutAb, SCI, SSCI, SWRA. *Bk. rev.:* 0-3, 400-1,500 words. *Aud.:* Ac, Sa.

Publishes research papers on geology and physics of the earth's crust and interior, addressing large-scale topics such as regional and plate tectonics, seismology, crustal movements, gravity, and structural features. The journal's international editorial board represents multiple disciplines, and special issues on single topics are edited by authorities in the field. Journal issues frequently include large-scale geological maps, seismic sections, and other diagrams. The web site provides searchable tables of contents and paper abstracts from 1995 forward. Full-text articles from 1995 to the present are also available online to libraries through ScienceDirect. A GeoRef priority journal.

2279. *Terra Nova: the european journal of geosciences.* [ISSN: 0954-4879] 1989. bi-m. GBP 432 print & online eds. Ed(s): Max Coleman, Alfred Kroener. Blackwell Publishing Ltd., 9600 Garsington Rd, Oxford, OX4 2ZG, United Kingdom; customerservices@oxon.blackwellpublishing.com; http://www.blackwellpublishing.com. Illus., index, adv. Sample. Refereed. Circ: 1765. Vol. ends: No. 6. Microform: PQC. Online: EBSCO Publishing; ingenta.com; Munksgaard & Blackwell Science's Synergy; OCLC Online Computer Library Center, Inc.; RoweCom Information Quest; Swets Blackwell. *Indexed:* ArtHuCI, GeoRef, PetrolAb, SCI. *Aud.:* Ac, Sa.

Terra Nova is the result of a collaboration between the European Union of Geosciences and 18 national geoscience societies throughout Europe. It includes a mix of original papers and review articles covering "the broadest spectrum of the solid earth and planetary sciences, including interfaces with the hydrosphere and atmosphere." Except for the review articles, all contributions are 2,500 words or less. Free tables of contents can be found on the web site beginning with 1997. Full-text access is available for print subscribers or on a per-article basis.

2280. *Water Resources Research.* [ISSN: 0043-1397] 1965. m. USD 980. Ed(s): A F Spilhaus. American Geophysical Union, 2000 Florida Ave, N W, Washington, DC 20009-1277; http://www.agu.org. Illus., index. Sample. Refereed. Circ: 4000. Vol. ends: No. 12. Microform: Pub.; AIP. Reprint: ISI. *Indexed:* AS&TI, Agr, ApMecR, BiolAb, ChemAb, DSR&OA, EngInd, EnvAb, ExcerpMed, FPA, ForAb, GeoRef, GeogAbPG, HortAb, IAA, JEL, M&GPA, OceAb, PetrolAb, PollutAb, RRTA, S&F, SCI, SSCI, SWRA, WAE&RSA, WRCInf. *Aud.:* Ac, Sa.

Research papers present water-related studies concentrating in hydrology; physical, chemical, and biological sciences; economics; systems analysis; and law. Each issue includes research articles, technical notes, commentaries, and replies. Tables of contents and abstracts of the latest three issues are available free on the web; full-text articles from 1990 are available to subscribers on the American Geophysical Union web site. A GeoRef priority journal.

Electronic Journals

Earth Interactions. See Atmospheric Sciences/Electronic Journals section.

2281. *G3: Geochemistry, Geophysics, Geosystems: an electronic journal of the earth sciences.* [ISSN: 1525-2027] bi-m. American Geophysical Union, 2000 Florida Ave, N W, Washington, DC 20009-1277; http://g-cubed.org/. *Indexed:* GeoRef. *Aud.:* Ac, Sa.

Sponsored by the American Geophysical Union and the Geochemical Society, this innovative electronic-only journal publishes original research, reviews, and technical briefs in geophysics and geochemistry. The focus is on interdisciplinary work pertaining to understanding the earth as a system and contributions span a wide range of topics. Many submissions include material such as large data sets, sound clips, or movies that could not be included in a print journal. Access to abstracts of recent articles is available free from the web site, but full-text articles only to subscribers.

■ ECONOMICS

Gwyneth H. Crowley, Head of Information Services, The Levy Economics Institute of Bard College, Annandale-on-Hudson, NY 12504-5000, crowley@levy.org

Introduction

What's new with economic journals? Subscription prices and the number of specialized journals are still rising, and the number of e-journals is slowly growing. For this edition, a number of new journals and cross-references have been added to reflect the interdisciplinary direction that economics is taking, which illustrates that economic behavior can be more than rational thought. 2002 Nobel Prize winners Daniel Kahneman and Vernon L. Smith were recognized for contributions that proved just that. To reflect the growing field of economics, *Journal of Economic Psychology, Journal of Human Development, Review of Income and Wealth, World Development* (despite its price), and two core type journals, *Journal of Economic Growth* and *The Scandinavian Journal of Economics*, have been added. *Applied Economics* has been put back into the section. Given developments and trends in journal publishing (with many associations "taking back" ownership of their publications from commercial vendors, for example) it will be very interesting to watch where journal prices go in the next two years.

Basic Periodicals

Ga: *The American Prospect, Challenge, Contemporary Economic Policy, The Economist, Journal of Economic History, Journal of Economic Literature, Journal of Economic Perspectives, OECD Observer, Review of Black Political Economy, Review of Political Economy, World Bank Research Observer;* Ac: *American Economic Review, Brookings Papers on Economic Activity, Cambridge Journal of Economics, Econometrica, Economic History Review, The Economic Journal, Economica, International Economic Review, Journal of Econometrics, Journal of Economic Literature, Journal of Economic Perspectives, Journal of Economic Theory, Journal of Monetary Economics, Journal of Political Economy, Journal of Public Economics, Manchester School, OECD Observer, Public Choice, Quarterly Journal of Economics, Rand Journal of Economics, The Review of Economic Studies, The Review of Economics and Statistics, The Review of Economics and Statistics, The World Bank Economic Review.*

Basic Abstracts and Indexes

ABI/Inform, EconLit, International Bibliography of the Social Sciences, Public Affairs Information Service International, Wilson Business Abstracts, World Agricultural Economic and Rural Sociology.

2282. *American Economic Review.* [ISSN: 0002-8282] 1911. 5x/yr. USD 195. Ed(s): Ben S Bernanke. American Economic Association, 2014 Broadway, Ste 305, Nashville, TN 37203; aeainfo@ctrvax.vanderbilt.edu; http://www.vanderbilt.edu/AEA/. Illus., index, adv. Refereed. Circ: 27000. Vol. ends: Dec. Microform: MIM; PMC; PQC. Online: Gale Group; Ingenta Select. Reprint: PQC. *Indexed:* ABIn, ABS&EES, ATI, AgeL, AmH&L, ArtHuCI, BAS, BLI, BPI, BRD, BRI, CBRI, DSR&OA, EnvAb, ExcerpMed, IBSS, IBZ, JEL, LRI, MagInd, PAIS, RI-1, RRTA, RiskAb, SSCI, SSI, SWA, WAE&RSA. *Aud.:* Ga, Ac, Sa.

Published by the American Economic Association (AEA), this highly cited journal in the field of economics is well respected. Each issue includes 12 to 14 technical articles on a wide range of timely and pertinent topics and four to seven shorter papers, all written by leading academic economists, usually at American universities. This journal is a must for academic institutions. Membership in the AEA includes free subscriptions to this journal, the *Journal of Economic Literature,* and the *Journal of Economic Perspectives.* Very highly recommended for colleges, universities, and large public libraries.

2283. *American Journal of Agricultural Economics.* Formerly (until 1968): *Journal of Farm Economics.* [ISSN: 0002-9092] 1919. 5x/yr. USD 183 print & online eds. Ed(s): Robert J Meyers, Ian M Sheldon. Blackwell Publishing, Inc., Commerce Place, 350 Main St, Malden, MA

02148; subscrip@blackwellpub.com; http://www.blackwellpublishing.com. Illus., index, adv. Refereed. Circ: 7000. Microform: PMC. Online: bigchalk; EBSCO Publishing; Factiva; Florida Center for Library Automation; Gale Group; ingenta.com; Northern Light Technology, Inc.; OCLC Online Computer Library Center, Inc.; RoweCom Information Quest; Swets Blackwell; H.W. Wilson. *Indexed:* ABIn, AgeL, Agr, B&AI, BAS, BPI, DSA, EngInd, EnvAb, ExcerpMed, FPA, FS&TA, ForAb, GeoRef, GeogAbPG, HortAb, IBSS, IndVet, JEL, PAIS, RRTA, RiskAb, S&F, SCI, SSCI, VetBull, WAE&RSA. *Bk. rev.:* 10, 600-700 words, signed. *Aud.:* Ac, Sa.

This well-respected journal contains 15 or so articles in each issue on "the economics of agriculture, natural resources and the environment, and rural and community development." The authors are usually American academics. Also included are invited papers, conference proceedings, book reviews, comments and replies, and biographies of recent fellows. The May issue carries the proceedings from the annual meeting of the American Agricultural Association. Recommended for all colleges and universities with agricultural economics and related programs.

2284. *American Journal of Economics and Sociology.* [ISSN: 0002-9246] 1941. 5x/yr. USD 168 print & online eds. Ed(s): Laurence S Moss. Blackwell Publishing, Inc., Commerce Place, 350 Main St, Malden, MA 02148; subscrip@blackwellpub.com; http://www.blackwellpublishing.com. Illus., index. Sample. Refereed. Circ: 2200. Vol. ends: Nov. Microform: PQC. Online: EBSCO Publishing; Florida Center for Library Automation; Gale Group; ingenta.com; OCLC Online Computer Library Center, Inc.; RoweCom Information Quest; Swets Blackwell; H.W. Wilson. Reprint: ISI; NTI; PQC. *Indexed:* ABCPolSci, ABIn, ABS&EES, AgeL, AmH&L, ArtHuCI, BAS, BRI, CBRI, CIJE, CJA, EIP, HRA, IBSS, IBZ, IMFL, IPSA, JEL, PAIS, PRA, PSA, RRTA, RiskAb, SSCI, SSI, SUSA, SWA, SWR&A, SociolAb, WAE&RSA. *Bk. rev.:* 1, 50-100 words. *Aud.:* Ga, Ac.

This esteemed journal is "published in the interest of constructive synthesis in the social sciences," and promotes "no ideological standards for contributors." It is problem-oriented and, as such, explores developments in economics, sociology, psychology, and philosophy, and also discusses social trends and problems. Each issue contains 8 to 11 articles by distinguished scholars. An annual index appears in the October issue. Recommended for large public and university libraries.

2285. *The American Prospect: a journal for the liberal imagination.* [ISSN: 1049-7285] 1990. 10x/yr. Individuals, USD 29.95. Ed(s): Robert Kuttner, Harold Meyerson. The American Prospect, Inc., 5 Broad St, Boston, MA 02109; editors@prospect.org; http://www.prospect.org. Adv. Circ: 55000 Paid and free. Microform: PQC. Online: Florida Center for Library Automation; Gale Group; LexisNexis; Northern Light Technology, Inc.; OCLC Online Computer Library Center, Inc.; ProQuest Information & Learning; H.W. Wilson. *Indexed:* ABS&EES, AgeL, AltPI, JEL, LRI, PAIS, PRA, RI-1, SSI. *Aud.:* Hs, Ga, Ac, Sa.

With a moderate left-wing slant, this magazine is for the general reader, and began publishing in 1990. Its aim is to present "a practical and convincing vision of liberal philosophy, politics and public life." It is now published every month except August, and in every other issue there is a 24-page special report that has been happily received. Tom Tomorrow's political cartoons are a must-see. There are daily updates on their web site at www.prospect.org. The Moving Ideas Network (formerly the Electronic Policy Network) is a project of this publication and "has news and resources from more than 120 research and advocacy organizations." A valuable resource and recommended for high schools, public, academic, and special libraries.

2286. *Brookings Papers on Economic Activity.* [ISSN: 0007-2303] 1970. s-a. USD 45 (Individuals, USD 28; Students, USD 19). Ed(s): George L Perry, William C Brainard. Brookings Institution Press, 1775 Massachusetts Ave, NW, Washington, DC 20036-2188. Illus., index. Refereed. Microform: PQC. Online: EBSCO Publishing; Florida Center for Library Automation; Gale Group; JSTOR (Web-based Journal Archive); Northern Light Technology, Inc.; OCLC Online Computer Library Center, Inc.; Project MUSE; ProQuest Information & Learning; RoweCom Information Quest; Swets Blackwell; H.W. Wilson. Reprint: PQC. *Indexed:* ABIn, ABS&EES, AgeL, BPI, HRA, IBSS, JEL, PAIS, SFSA, SSCI, SSI, WAE&RSA. *Aud.:* Ga, Ac.

This esteemed publication from the Brookings Institution, an independent organization, is a forum for "nonpartisan research, education, and publication in economics, government, foreign policy, and the social sciences generally" and works to help develop "sound public policies and to promote public understanding of issues of national importance." The journal is comprised exclusively of invited contributions and "articles, reports, and highlights of the discussions from conferences of the Brookings Panel on Economic Activity." Highly recommended for universities and colleges.

2287. *Bulletin of Economic Research.* Formerly: *Yorkshire Bulletin of Economic and Social Research.* [ISSN: 0307-3378] 1949. q. GBP 275 print & online eds. Ed(s): Gianni De Fraja, Indrajit Ray. Blackwell Publishing Ltd., 9600 Garsington Rd, PO Box 805, Oxford, OX4 2DQ, United Kingdom; customerservices@oxon.blackwellpublishing.com; http://www.blackwellpublishing.com/. Illus., index, adv. Refereed. Circ: 650. Vol. ends: Oct. Microform: PQC. Online: EBSCO Publishing; ingenta.com; OCLC Online Computer Library Center, Inc.; RoweCom Information Quest; Swets Blackwell. Reprint: SWZ. *Indexed:* ABIn, CCMJ, CJA, IBSS, JEL, MathSciNet, PAIS. *Bk. rev.:* 1, lengthy. *Aud.:* Ac, Sa.

This international, refereed technical journal from England includes papers across the entire spectrum of economics, both theoretical and applied. Each issue usually contains "an authoritative survey article, as well as other long articles, short-notes and memoranda," and a specially commissioned book review. Economists, postdoctoral candidates, and researchers should find this journal very useful.

2288. *Business Economics: designed to serve the needs of people who use economics in their work.* [ISSN: 0007-666X] 1965. q. USD 85 in North America; USD 100 elsewhere. Ed(s): Robert Thomas Crow. National Association for Business Economics, 1233 20th St, N W, Ste 505, Washington, DC 20036-2304; nabe@nabe.com; http://www.nabe.com. Illus., index, adv. Circ: 4700. Vol. ends: Oct. Microform: PQC. Online: bigchalk; EBSCO Publishing; Florida Center for Library Automation; Gale Group; Northern Light Technology, Inc.; OCLC Online Computer Library Center, Inc.; ProQuest Information & Learning; H.W. Wilson. Reprint: PQC; SCH. *Indexed:* ABIn, BLI, BPI, JEL, MagInd, PAIS. *Bk. rev.:* 1-4, 1,000-1,500 words. *Aud.:* Ga, Ac.

Created to provide a forum for economists in private business; to provide communications among the business community, educational institutions, and the government; and to stimulate discussion and research in public policy. Book reviews are included. Future issues will rely on contributed papers. Academic and large public libraries should consider this journal for their collections.

2289. *Cambridge Journal of Economics.* [ISSN: 0309-166X] 1950. bi-m. GBP 230. Ed(s): Ann Newton. Oxford University Press, Great Clarendon St, Oxford, OX2 6DP, United Kingdom; jnl.orders@oup.co.uk; http://www3.oup.co.uk/jnls. Illus., index, adv. Refereed. Circ: 1750. Vol. ends: Nov. Online: Chadwyck-Healey Incorporated; EBSCO Publishing; Gale Group; HighWire Press; ingenta.com; OCLC Online Computer Library Center, Inc.; RoweCom Information Quest; Swets Blackwell. Reprint: PSC; SWZ. *Indexed:* ABIn, ArtHuCI, BAS, IBSS, JEL, PAIS, PSA, RRTA, SSCI, SSI, SociolAb, WAE&RSA. *Bk. rev.:* Occasional, 6-8 pages. *Aud.:* Ac, Sa.

The Cambridge Political Economy Society founded this journal in 1977 "in the tradition of Marx, Keynes, Kalecki, Joan Robinson, and Kaldor." It focuses on "theoretical, applied, policy, and methodological research," with a strong emphasis on economic and social issues. Critical thinking is emphasized in the process of analyzing data, the development of theory, and the construction of policy. The journal's scope and editors are international. Five to eight articles per issue is typical. Material is solicited in the areas of "unemployment, inflation, the organisation of production, the distribution of social product, class conflict, economic underdevelopment, globalisation and international economic integration, changing forms and boundaries of markets and planning, and uneven development and instability in the world economy." This journal is an excellent addition for academic libraries.

2290. ***Canadian Journal of Economics.*** Supersedes in part (1928-1967): *Canadian Journal of Economics and Political Science;* Which was formerly (until 1934): *Contributions to Canada Economics.* [ISSN: 0008-4085] 1968. q. USD 155 except Canada, print & online eds. Ed(s): Michel Poitevin. Blackwell Publishing, Inc., Commerce Place, 350 Main St, Malden, MA 02148; subscrip@blackwellpub.com; http://www.blackwellpublishing.com. Illus., index, adv. Refereed. Circ: 2600. Microform: MML. Online: EBSCO Publishing; Gale Group; ingenta.com; JSTOR (Web-based Journal Archive); OCLC Online Computer Library Center, Inc.; Swets Blackwell. *Indexed:* ABIn, ABS&EES, AgeL, BAS, CBCARef, CLI, CPerI, DSA, IBSS, IBZ, ILP, JEL, PAIS, RRTA, RiskAb, SSCI, SSI, SWA, WAE&RSA. *Bk. rev.:* 2-4, 1,500-2,200 words. *Aud.:* Ac, Sa.

This is the "primary academic economics journal based in Canada," with material written in English and some in French by Canadian authors. It covers "original and significant research in all areas of economics and focuses on problems of the Canadian economy and policy issues." Methodology may be theoretical, applied, historical, or policy oriented. Some recent topics are poverty trends, income distribution dynamics, borders and trade, monetary exchange rates, and manufacturer performance. The November issue includes a presidential address delivered to the annual meeting of the Canadian Economics Association. This widely recognized journal—comparable to the *American Economic Review* (see above in this section)—would be an excellent addition to large academic libraries. Free to members of the Canadian Economics Association.

The Cato Journal. See Political Science/Comparative and American Politics section.

2291. ***Challenge (Armonk): the magazine of economic affairs.*** [ISSN: 0577-5132] 1952. bi-m. USD 220 print & online eds. (Individuals, USD 52). Ed(s): Jeffrey Madrick. M.E. Sharpe, Inc., 80 Business Park Dr, Armonk, NY 10504; custserv@mesharpe.com; http://www.mesharpe.com. Illus., index, adv. Sample. Refereed. Circ: 5000. Vol. ends: Nov/Dec. Microform: PQC. Online: EBSCO Publishing; Florida Center for Library Automation; Gale Group; Ingenta Select; OCLC Online Computer Library Center, Inc.; ProQuest Information & Learning; Swets Blackwell; H.W. Wilson. Reprint: PSC. *Indexed:* ABIn, ASIP, BAS, BPI, IBSS, IBZ, JEL, MagInd, PAIS, SSI. *Bk. rev.:* 1, 2-4 pages. *Aud.:* Hs, Ga, Ac.

The goal of *Challenge* is "to present a wide range of views on national and international economic affairs in the belief that an informed dialogue can result in more rational and effective public policy." Written in a clear, nontechnical manner, the articles are by prestigious economists and well-respected scholars, and the editorial board includes Nobel laureates Robert Solow and Kenneth Arrow. In-depth book reviews are also included. Recommended for high school, public, academic, and government libraries.

2292. ***Contemporary Economic Policy.*** Formerly (until 1994): *Contemporary Policy Issues.* [ISSN: 1074-3529] 1982. q. USD 272 USD 206 academics. Ed(s): Darwin C. Hall. Oxford University Press, 2001 Evans Rd, Cary, NC 27513; http://www3.oup.co.uk/jnls/. Illus., index, adv. Refereed. Circ: 3000. Vol. ends: Oct. Microform: PQC. Online: EBSCO Publishing; Florida Center for Library Automation; Gale Group; HighWire Press; ingenta.com; Northern Light Technology, Inc.; OCLC Online Computer Library Center, Inc.; ProQuest Information & Learning; RoweCom Information Quest; Swets Blackwell; H.W. Wilson. Reprint: PSC. *Indexed:* ABIn, ABS&EES, AgeL, CJA, HRA, IBSS, IBZ, JEL, PAIS, PRA, RI-1, SSCI, SSI, SUSA, WAE&RSA. *Aud.:* Ga, Ac.

This solid journal publishes scholarly research and analysis on current policy issues to business, government, and other decision makers, and is concerned with presenting high quality material in accessible language that will be widely read. Three Nobel laureates are among the authors. Membership in the Western Economic Association International includes subscriptions to this journal and *Economic Inquiry* (see below). Each issue contains about ten articles. A very solid recommendation for public, academic, and government libraries.

2293. ***Econometric Theory.*** [ISSN: 0266-4666] 1985. bi-m. USD 412 (Individuals, USD 153). Ed(s): Peter C B Phillips. Cambridge University Press, The Edinburgh Bldg, Shaftesbury Rd, Cambridge, CB2 2RU, United Kingdom; information@cambridge.org; http://uk.cambridge.org/journals. Illus., adv. Refereed. Microform: PQC. Online: EBSCO Publishing; OCLC Online Computer Library Center, Inc.; RoweCom Information Quest; Swets Blackwell. Reprint: SWZ. *Indexed:* CCMJ, IBSS, JEL, MathSciNet, SSCI, ST&MA. *Bk. rev.:* Various number and length. *Aud.:* Ac, Sa.

The aim of this leading international journal is to advance theoretical research in econometrics. It includes "original theoretical contributions in all major areas of econometrics and seeks to foster the multidisciplinary features of econometrics that extend beyond the subject of economics." Its scope includes, but is not limited to, "statistical theory of estimation, testing, prediction, and decision procedures in traditionally active areas of research, such as linear and nonlinear modeling, simultaneous equations theory, time series, studies of robustness, nonparametric methods, inference under misspecification, finite-sample econometrics," etc. Also included are "historical studies in the evolution of econometric thought," interviews with leading scholars, and periodic book reviews. Recommended for econometricians and large universities.

2294. ***Econometrica.*** [ISSN: 0012-9682] 1933. 6x/yr. GBP 301 print & online. Ed(s): Glenn Ellison. Blackwell Publishing Ltd., 9600 Garsington Rd, PO Box 805, Oxford, OX4 2DQ, United Kingdom; customerservices@oxon.blackwellpublishing.com; http://www.blackwellpublishing.com/. Illus., index, adv. Refereed. Circ: 6000. Vol. ends: Nov. Microform: PMC; PQC. Online: EBSCO Publishing; Gale Group; JSTOR (Web-based Journal Archive); OCLC Online Computer Library Center, Inc.; ProQuest Information & Learning; RoweCom Information Quest. Reprint: PQC; PSC; SWZ. *Indexed:* ABIn, AgeL, BAS, CCMJ, EngInd, IBSS, IBZ, IPSA, JEL, MathSciNet, RRTA, SCI, SSCI, SSI, ST&MA, WAE&RSA. *Aud.:* Ac, Sa.

This excellent journal "promotes the unification of the theoretical-quantitative and the empirical-quantitative approach to economic problems." It publishes original, refereed articles for the Econometric Society "in all branches of economics, theoretical, empirical, applied, and abstract." The journal also includes programs for regional society meetings, announcements and calls for papers, forthcoming articles, nominations for fellows, a list of the journal's referees, a directory of fellows, and news notes on "scholarly societies in economics, econometrics, mathematics, and statistics." Abstracts and contents are available on the publisher's web site. Highly recommended for universities and special libraries.

2295. ***Economic Development and Cultural Change.*** [ISSN: 0013-0079] 1952. q. USD 218 (Individuals, USD 50; Students, USD 38). Ed(s): Lia Green, D Gale Johnson. University of Chicago Press, Journals Division, PO Box 37005, Chicago, IL 60637; subscriptions@press.uchicago.edu; http://www.journals.uchicago.edu. Illus., index, adv. Refereed. Circ: 3100 Paid. Vol. ends: Jul. Microform: PMC; PQC. Online: EBSCO Publishing; Florida Center for Library Automation; Gale Group; ProQuest Information & Learning. Reprint: ISI; PQC; PSC; SCH. *Indexed:* ABCPolSci, ABIn, ABS&EES, AICP, ASSIA, AbAn, AgeL, AmH&L, BPI, DSA, DSR&OA, FPA, ForAb, GeogAbPG, HAPI, HortAb, IBSS, IMFL, IPSA, JEL, PAIS, PRA, PSA, RRTA, S&F, SFSA, SSCI, SSI, SUSA, SWA, SociolAb, WAE&RSA. *Bk. rev.:* 8-9, lengthy. *Aud.:* Ga, Ac, Sa.

A journal that examines "the study of noneconomic variables in the development process," this highly regarded periodical presents articles on developing nations in regard to the social and economic forces that affect culture. The journal includes book reviews. Scholars and researchers in economics, sociology, political science, and geography consider this journal important.

Economic Geography. See Geography section.

2296. ***Economic History Review: a journal of economic and social history.*** [ISSN: 0013-0117] 1927. q. GBP 136 print & online eds. Ed(s): Nicholas Crafts, J Hatcher. Blackwell Publishing Ltd., 9600 Garsington Rd, PO Box 805, Oxford, OX4 2DQ, United Kingdom; customerservices@oxon.blackwellpublishing.com; http://www.blackwellpublishing.com/. Illus., index, adv. Refereed. Circ:

5000. Vol. ends: Nov. Microform: IDC; NRP. Online: EBSCO Publishing; Gale Group; ingenta.com; JSTOR (Web-based Journal Archive); OCLC Online Computer Library Center, Inc.; RoweCom Information Quest; Swets Blackwell. Reprint: PSC; SWZ. *Indexed:* AgeL, AmH&L, ArtHuCI, BrArAb, BrHumI, IBSS, IBZ, JEL, NumL, PAIS, PSA, SSCI, SSI, SociolAb. *Bk. rev.:* 28-40, 600-1,200 words. *Aud.:* Ga, Ac, Sa.

This is the journal of the Economic History Society. A typical issue of *Economic History Review* contains a long essay in the "Surveys and Speculations" section that "discusses a particular problem in economic and social history in an adventurous way," five to six articles, "Notes and Comments," and book and software reviews. This well-written, easy-to-understand journal is recommended to historians, students, and researchers alike.

2297. *Economic Inquiry.* Formerly: *Western Economic Journal.* [ISSN: 0095-2583] 1962. q. USD 258. Ed(s): Dennis W. Jansen. Oxford University Press, 2001 Evans Rd, Cary, NC 27513; http://www3.oup.co.uk/jnls/. Illus., index, adv. Sample. Refereed. Circ: 3550. Vol. ends: Oct. Microform: PQC. Online: bigchalk; Chadwyck-Healey Incorporated; The Dialog Corporation; EBSCO Publishing; Florida Center for Library Automation; Gale Group; HighWire Press; ingenta.com; Northern Light Technology, Inc.; OCLC Online Computer Library Center, Inc.; ProQuest Information & Learning; RoweCom Information Quest; Swets Blackwell; H.W. Wilson. Reprint: PQC; PSC. *Indexed:* ABIn, AgeL, AmH&L, BAS, CJA, HRA, IBSS, IBZ, JEL, LRI, PAIS, PRA, RRTA, RiskAb, SSCI, SSI, SUSA, WAE&RSA. *Aud.:* Ac, Sa.

The goal of this scholarly journal is "to make each article understandable to economists who are not necessarily specialists in the article's topic area." It has research and analysis in all areas of economics. Larger academic libraries would benefit from a subscription, which also includes four issues of *Contemporary Economic Policy* (above in this section).

2298. *The Economic Journal.* [ISSN: 0013-0133] 1891. 8x/yr. GBP 273 print & online eds. Ed(s): M Wickens. Blackwell Publishing Ltd., 9600 Garsington Rd, PO Box 805, Oxford, OX4 2DQ, United Kingdom; customerservices@oxon.blackwellpublishing.com; http://www.blackwellpublishing.com/. Illus., index, adv. Sample. Refereed. Circ: 7000. Vol. ends: Nov. Microform: PMC; PQC. Online: EBSCO Publishing; Gale Group; ingenta.com; JSTOR (Web-based Journal Archive); OCLC Online Computer Library Center, Inc.; RoweCom Information Quest; Swets Blackwell. Reprint: PQC; PSC. *Indexed:* ABIn, AmH&L, BAS, BRI, CBRI, ExcerpMed, IBSS, IBZ, JEL, PAIS, RRTA, RiskAb, SSCI, SSI, WAE&RSA. *Bk. rev.:* 25, lengthy. *Aud.:* Ac, Sa.

This frequently cited periodical continues to be a preeminent source on economic issues, both theoretical and empirical. Each issue typically contains 9 to 11 papers. A discussion forum, datasets, and book notes can be found on its web site. Selected papers from the annual conference of the Royal Economic Society (the journal's sponsor) and the Association of University Teachers of Economics are an annual issue. Highly recommended for academic, government, business, and financial libraries.

2299. *Economic Policy: a European forum.* [ISSN: 0266-4658] 1985. 3x/yr. USD 331 print & online eds. Ed(s): Georges de Menil, Richard Portes. Blackwell Publishing Ltd., 9600 Garsington Rd, PO Box 805, Oxford, OX4 2DQ, United Kingdom; customerservices@oxon.blackwellpublishing.com; http://www.blackwellpublishing.com/. Illus., index, adv. Refereed. Microform: PQC. Online: EBSCO Publishing; ingenta.com; OCLC Online Computer Library Center, Inc.; RoweCom Information Quest; Swets Blackwell. Reprint: SWZ. *Indexed:* ABIn, BAS, IBSS, IPSA, JEL, PAIS, RRTA, RiskAb, SSCI, WAE&RSA. *Aud.:* Ga, Ac, Sa.

This reputable journal "acts as a forum for debate between analysts with a wide range of views" dealing with the timely and relevant policy issues in nontechnical language from experts. In other words, it will tell you what is really going on in Europe and with other key international issues. It "emphasizes the possibilities for cross-country comparisons; the balance between conflict and cooperation in national policy formation; and the constraints imposed on individual economies by their integration in the world economy." The web version has value-added features. Readership consists of economists, policy makers, researchers, government officials, business leaders, and students.

2300. *The Economic Record.* [ISSN: 0013-0249] 1925. q. GBP 96 print & online eds. Blackwell Publishing Asia, 550 Swanston St, Carlton South, VIC 3053, Australia; subs@blackwellpublishingasia.com; http://www.blackwellpublishing.com/. Illus., index, adv. Refereed. Circ: 3800. Vol. ends: Dec. Microform: PQC. Online: EBSCO Publishing; Florida Center for Library Automation; Gale Group; ingenta.com; OCLC Online Computer Library Center, Inc.; ProQuest Information & Learning; RMIT Publishing; RoweCom Information Quest; Swets Blackwell. Reprint: ISI; PQC. *Indexed:* ABIn, BAS, IBSS, IBZ, JEL, PAIS, RRTA, SSCI, SWA, WAE&RSA. *Bk. rev.:* 3-7, lengthy, signed. *Aud.:* Ac, Sa.

Published by the Economic Society of Australia, this is a general economics journal that provides a forum for research on the Australian economy. It publishes theoretical, applied, and policy papers in all fields of economics. Six articles are typical, and book reviews are included. Recommended for economists and university libraries with international interests.

2301. *Economic Theory.* [ISSN: 0938-2259] 1991. 8x/yr. EUR 930 domestic; EUR 982.90 foreign; EUR 140 newsstand/cover per issue. Ed(s): C D Aliprantis. Springer-Verlag, Tiergartenstr 17, Heidelberg, 69121, Germany. Illus., adv. Sample. Refereed. Online: EBSCO Publishing; RoweCom Information Quest; ScienceDirect; Springer LINK; Swets Blackwell. *Indexed:* AgeL, CCMJ, IBSS, JEL, MathSciNet, SSCI. *Aud.:* Ac, Sa.

The official journal of the Society for the Advancement of Economic Theory, this is "an outlet for research in all areas of economics based on rigorous theoretical reasoning and on specific topics in mathematics which is motivated by the analysis of economic problems." The range of subjects covered includes "classical and modern equilibrium theory, cooperative game theory, macroeconomics, social choice and welfare, uncertainty and information, intertemporal economics (including dynamical systems), public economics, international and developmental economics, financial economics, money and banking, and industrial organization." This journal also includes the section "Exposita," which encompasses "brief notes of substantial theoretical interest" that must contribute to the understanding of "substantial economic problems." For economists and graduate students.

2302. *Economica.* [ISSN: 0013-0427] 1921. q. USD 224 print & online eds. Ed(s): Frank Cowell, Alan Manning. Blackwell Publishing Ltd., 9600 Garsington Rd, PO Box 805, Oxford, OX4 2DQ, United Kingdom; customerservices@oxon.blackwellpublishing.com; http://www.blackwellpublishing.com/. Illus., index, adv. Sample. Refereed. Circ: 3800. Vol. ends: Nov. Online: EBSCO Publishing; Gale Group; ingenta.com; JSTOR (Web-based Journal Archive); OCLC Online Computer Library Center, Inc.; RoweCom Information Quest; Swets Blackwell. Reprint: PSC. *Indexed:* ABIn, ArtHuCI, BAS, EIP, ExcerpMed, IBSS, IBZ, IPSA, JEL, PAIS, RRTA, SSCI, SSI, ST&MA, WAE&RSA. *Bk. rev.:* 5-11, 275-1,800 words. *Aud.:* Ac, Sa.

One of the top economics journals, published on behalf of the London School of Economics and Political Science, this highly cited journal is international in scope and covers "all branches of economics." The authors are primarily British, Canadian, and American. Some recent topics are social mobility, international trade, the psychological impact of unemployment, and modelling business cycles. In addition to the articles, the journal contains numerous book reviews and an annual author/title index. Recommended for academic libraries, professional economists, and researchers.

2303. *Economics and Philosophy.* [ISSN: 0266-2671] 1985. s-a. USD 121 (Individuals, USD 46). Ed(s): Geoffrey Brennan, Luc Bovens. Cambridge University Press, The Edinburgh Bldg, Shaftesbury Rd, Cambridge, CB2 2RU, United Kingdom; information@cambridge.org; http://uk.cambridge.org/journals. Illus., index, adv. Refereed. Vol. ends: Oct. Microform: PQC. Online: EBSCO Publishing; OCLC Online Computer Library Center, Inc.; RoweCom Information Quest; Swets Blackwell. Reprint: SWZ. *Indexed:* IBSS, IPB, JEL, PhilInd, SSCI. *Bk. rev.:* 3-7, 4-8 pages. *Aud.:* Ac, Sa.

Created to be a forum for the interdisciplinary study of economics and philosophy, the core of this growing journal is substantial essays from esteemed scholars. The scope covers articles linking the disciplines of economics and philosophy. The current editors continue the tradition of publishing about "the epistemology and methodology of economics, the foundations of decision theory and game theory, the nature of rational choice in general, historical work on economics with a philosophical purpose, ethical issues in economics, the use of economic techniques in ethical theory, and many other subjects."

2304. *Economics & Politics.* [ISSN: 0954-1985] 1988. 3x/yr. GBP 264 print & online eds. Ed(s): Jagdish Bhagwati. Blackwell Publishing Ltd., 9600 Garsington Rd, PO Box 805, Oxford, OX4 2DQ, United Kingdom; customerservices@oxon.blackwellpublishing.com; http://www.blackwellpublishing.com/. Illus., index, adv. Sample. Circ: 300. Vol. ends: Oct. Online: EBSCO Publishing; ingenta.com; OCLC Online Computer Library Center, Inc.; RoweCom Information Quest; Swets Blackwell. Reprint: SWZ. *Indexed:* BAS, IBSS, IPSA, JEL, PRA, PSA, RiskAb, WAE&RSA. *Bk. rev.:* Number varies, 20 pages. *Aud.:* Ac, Sa.

Focusing on analytical political economy, "broadly defined as the study of economic phenomena and policy in models that include political processes," each issue of this solid journal contains six or seven technical articles and an extensive book review section. Readers are professionals and students in economics, political science, sociology, and psychology.

2305. *Economics Bulletin.* [ISSN: 1545-2921] 2001. irreg. Ed(s): John Conley. Economics Bulletin, c/o John Conley, Dept. of Economics, 414 Calhoun Hall, Nashville, TN 37235. *Aud.:* Ac, Sa.

Initiated to encourage free and extremely fast scientific communication within the field of research economics, *Economics Bulletin* publishes original notes, comments, and preliminary results. Submissions are refereed and a decision to publish is made within eight weeks. Accepted papers are published immediately. Also included are letters to the editor, announcements of conferences, and research announcements. There is a handy e-mail notification in your subject of interest. Hopefully, this publication will continue to grow and compete more effectively with the expensive *Economics Letters* (below).

2306. *Economics Letters.* [ISSN: 0165-1765] 1978. m. EUR 1736 (Individuals, EUR 287). Ed(s): Dr. Eric Maskin. Elsevier BV, North-Holland, Sara Burgerhartstraat 25, Amsterdam, 1055 KV, Netherlands; nlinfo-f@elsevier.nl; http://www.elsevier.nl. Illus., index, adv. Sample. Refereed. Vol. ends: Dec. Microform: PQC. Online: EBSCO Publishing; ingenta.com; ScienceDirect; Swets Blackwell. *Indexed:* AgeL, CCMJ, IBSS, JEL, MathSciNet, SSCI, WAE&RSA. *Aud.:* Ac, Sa.

As the only letters journal in the field of economics, it was conceived and designed to "provide a means of rapid and efficient dissemination of new results, models, and methods in all fields of economic research." Each contribution is limited to four pages, with a four-month turnover time for publication. An author/subject index is published in the last issue of every volume. This mathematical-oriented journal is intended for researchers and those wanting to know the latest trends. Recommended for university and special libraries.

2307. *The Economist.* [ISSN: 0013-0613] 1843. w. 51/yr. USD 125 United States (Individuals, GBP 86). Ed(s): Bill Emmott. Economist Newspaper Ltd, 25 St James's St, London, SW1A 1HG, United Kingdom; letters@economist.com; http://www.economist.com. Illus., index, adv. Sample. Circ: 722984 Paid. Vol. ends: Dec. Microform: PQC. CD-ROM: Chadwyck-Healey Incorporated. Online: bigchalk; EBSCO Publishing; Factiva; Florida Center for Library Automation; Gale Group; LexisNexis; MediaStream, Inc.; OCLC Online Computer Library Center, Inc.; ProQuest Information & Learning. *Indexed:* ABIn, AgeL, B&I, BAS, BPI, BRD, BRI, BrHumI, BrTechI, CBRI, DSA, EnvAb, FutSurv, IAA, IndVet, LogistBibl, MagInd, PAIS, RI-1, RRTA, SSI, WAE&RSA. *Bk. rev.:* 3-4, 450-500 words. *Aud.:* Ems, Hs, Ga, Ac, Sa.

Founded more than 150 years ago "to support the cause of free trade" and read in more than 180 countries, this easy-to-read weekly is well respected and authoritative for information on "world politics, global business, finance and economics, science and technology, and the arts." The magazine includes 16 news categories, including summaries on politics and business, short articles on world leaders, science, technology, finance and economics, surveys of countries and regions, obituaries, etc. The back of each issue includes handy economic, financial, and market indicators. Selected articles are available online, and political and business summaries are e-mailed free to subscribers. A must-have for all libraries.

Economy and Society. See Sociology and Social Work/General section.

Energy Economics. See Energy section.

Energy Journal. See Energy section.

2308. *European Economic Association. Journal.* [ISSN: 1542-4766] 2003. bi-m. USD 325 print & online eds. Ed(s): Roberto Perotti, Patrick Bolton. MIT Press, 5 Cambridge Center, Cambridge, MA 02142-1493; journals-orders@mit.edu; http://mitpress.mit.edu. *Aud.:* Ac, Sa.

This journal was created to be the new journal of the European Economic Association, and it will be fully owned and directed by them. It was defintely a good move to lower cost and help disseminate information, since the price is quite favorable compared to the association's previous journal, *European Economic Review.* Most of the editorial board will transfer to this new journal. The journal includes European and global articles, and each annual volume will include a double issue with the proceedings from the previous year. A hearty recommendation for this new, competing journal.

2309. *European Economic Review.* [ISSN: 0014-2921] 1969. bi-m. EUR 1093 (Individuals, EUR 50). Ed(s): Z. Eckstein, T. Gylfason. Elsevier BV, North-Holland, Sara Burgerhartstraat 25, Amsterdam, 1055 KV, Netherlands; nlinfo-f@elsevier.nl; http://www.elsevier.nl. Illus., index, adv. Sample. Refereed. Vol. ends: Dec. Microform: PQC. Online: EBSCO Publishing; Gale Group; ingenta.com; ScienceDirect; Swets Blackwell. Reprint: SWZ. *Indexed:* ABIn, AgeL, ArtHuCI, BAS, IBSS, JEL, PAIS, RRTA, RiskAb, SSCI, SSI, WAE&RSA. *Aud.:* Ac, Sa.

This journal aims to "contribute to the development and application of economics as a science in Europe and to improve communication and exchange between economics teachers, researchers, and students." Nine or ten articles by international authors are included in each issue. From January 2003, this journal will no longer be the official journal of the European Economic Association. See the new entry, *Journal of the European Economic Association,* for the fully owned and directly governed EEA journal. Please watch the Elsevier title for future quality. Still recommended for econometricians, theorists, and economists.

2310. *Explorations in Economic History.* Formerly: *Explorations in Entrepreneurial History.* [ISSN: 0014-4983] 1963. q. EUR 581 (Individuals, EUR 284; Students, EUR 54). Ed(s): Eugene White. Academic Press, 525 B St, Ste 1900, San Diego, CA 92101-4495; apsubs@acad.com; http://www.academicpress.com. Illus., index, adv. Refereed. Vol. ends: Oct. Online: EBSCO Publishing; Gale Group; ingenta.com; OCLC Online Computer Library Center, Inc.; RoweCom Information Quest; ScienceDirect. *Indexed:* ABS&EES, AmH&L, ArtHuCI, BAS, IBSS, JEL, PAIS, SSCI, SSI, SWA. *Aud.:* Ac, Sa.

This journal has traditionally accepted articles that apply economic analysis to historical events. Topics can include government regulation, international trade, money and finance, political economy, and technical change. The scope is wide, including "all areas of economic change, all historical periods, all geographical locations, and all political and social systems." A bonus is the "Essays in Exploration" section that surveys the recent literature. Previously an IDEAL title, it is now owned by Elsevier. The authors are economists, economic historians, demographers, geographers, and sociologists. Recommended for libraries with collection interests in history and historical economics.

Feminist Economics. See Women: Feminist and Special Interest/ Feminist and Women's Studies section.

Futures: news, analysis, and strategies for futures, options and derivatives traders. See Finance/Investment section.

2311. *Games and Economic Behavior.* [ISSN: 0899-8256] 1989. 8x/yr. EUR 841 (Individuals, EUR 121; Students, EUR 64). Ed(s): S. Neff, Ehud Kalai. Academic Press, 525 B St, Ste 1900, San Diego, CA 92101-4495; apsubs@acad.com; http://www.academicpress.com. Illus., index, adv. Refereed. Vol. ends: Nov. Online: EBSCO Publishing; ingenta.com; OCLC Online Computer Library Center, Inc.; RoweCom Information Quest; ScienceDirect; Swets Blackwell. *Indexed:* ArtHuCI, CCMJ, IBSS, JEL, MathSciNet, RiskAb, SSCI. *Aud.:* Ac, Sa.

Game theory is a very popular topic in economics and, as such, this technical and highly cited journal is very valuable for libraries with advanced programs in economics. The scope is wide, as it covers game modeling in psychology, political science, biology, computer science, and mathematical sciences. The "cross-fertilization between theories and applications" of game theory is this journal's goal, and it has consistently attracted the best papers in interdisciplinary studies. Previously an IDEAL title, it is now owned by Elsevier.

Gender and Development. See Women: Feminist and Special Interest/ Feminist and Women's Studies section.

Harvard Business Review. See Business/General section.

2312. *History of Political Economy.* [ISSN: 0018-2702] 1969. q. USD 303 includes online access (Individuals, USD 70 includes online access; USD 76 per issue). Ed(s): Craufurd D W Goodwin. Duke University Press, 905 W Main St, Ste 18 B, Durham, NC 27701; subscriptions@ dukeupress.edu; http://www.dukeupress.edu. Illus., index, adv. Refereed. Circ: 1500. Vol. ends: Winter. Microform: MIM; PQC. Online: EBSCO Publishing; Gale Group; Ingenta Select; Northern Light Technology, Inc.; OCLC Online Computer Library Center, Inc.; Project MUSE; ProQuest Information & Learning; RoweCom Information Quest; Swets Blackwell. Reprint: ISI; PQC; PSC; SCH. *Indexed:* AmH&L, ArtHuCI, BAS, IBSS, JEL, PSA, SSCI, SSI. *Bk. rev.:* 3-7, 1-3 pages. *Aud.:* Ga, Ac, Sa.

This is the leading journal in its field, and the scholarly articles focus on such topics as the development of economic thought, the historical background behind major figures, and the interpretation of economic theories. Early political economists such as Marshall, Adam Smith, Keynes, Malthus, Ricardo, and Marx are heavily featured. Each issue usually has six or seven articles and book reviews. Recommended for academic libraries.

The Independent Review. See Political Science/Comparative and American Politics section.

2313. *Indian Economic Journal.* [ISSN: 0019-4662] 1953. q. INR 200; USD 30. Ed(s): P R Brahmananda. Indian Economic Association, Delhi School of Economics, New Delhi, 110 009, India. Illus., index, adv. Refereed. Circ: 2500. Vol. ends: Jun. Reprint: PQC. *Indexed:* BAS, ForAb, IBSS, JEL, RRTA, RiskAb, SSCI, WAE&RSA. *Bk. rev.:* 15-21/yr., 150-650 words. *Aud.:* Ac, Sa.

This professional journal of the Indian Economic Association prmarily centers on economic development and the Indian economy in particular. Applied and theoretical economics are covered. An issue will typically contain five or six solid articles, notes and comments, book reviews, and a list of books received. Because this is economic journal to have for this geographic region, it is recommended for large universities, especially those with international studies programs.

2314. *International Economic Review.* [ISSN: 0020-6598] 1960. q. USD 341 print & online eds. Blackwell Publishing, Inc., Commerce Place, 350 Main St, Malden, MA 02148; subscrip@blackwellpub.com; http://www.blackwellpublishing.com. Illus., index, adv. Refereed. Circ: 2000. Vol. ends: Nov. Online: EBSCO Publishing; Gale Group; ingenta.com; JSTOR (Web-based Journal Archive); OCLC Online Computer Library Center, Inc.; RoweCom Information Quest; Swets Blackwell. *Indexed:* ABIn, ABS&EES, AgeL, AmStI, BAS, BPI, CCMJ, GeoRef, IBSS, JEL, MathSciNet, PAIS, SSCI, SSI. *Aud.:* Ac, Sa.

Published jointly by the University of Pennsylvania Economics Department and the Osaka (Japan) University Institute of Social and Economic Research Association, the *International Economic Review* focuses on quantitative economics. Issues contain about 12 articles by economics scholars worldwide. Cutting-edge articles in econometrics, economic theory, and macro and applied economics are sought for inclusion. Recommended for universities with strong econometrics programs.

2315. *International Journal of Game Theory.* [ISSN: 0020-7276] 1971. q. EUR 430 domestic; EUR 439.90 foreign; EUR 129 newsstand/cover per issue. Ed(s): D Samet. Physica-Verlag GmbH und Co., Postfach 105280, Heidelberg, 69042, Germany; physica@springer.de. Illus., adv. Refereed. Microform: PQC. Online: EBSCO Publishing; RoweCom Information Quest; ScienceDirect; Springer LINK; Swets Blackwell. Reprint: SWZ. *Indexed:* CCMJ, IBSS, JEL, MathSciNet, SSCI, ST&MA. *Aud.:* Ac, Sa.

This highly cited journal covers "game theory and its applications" in mathematical economics, management science, political science, and biology" from a methodological, conceptual, or mathematical point of view. A must for academic libraries with advanced programs in economics and other covered fields. Comparatively reasonably priced

2316. *International Monetary Fund. Staff Papers.* Formerly (until 1998): *International Monetary Fund. Staff Papers.* [ISSN: 1020-7635] 1950. q. USD 56 (Students, USD 28). Ed(s): Ian S McDonald. International Monetary Fund, Publication Services, 700 19th St, N W, Ste 12 607, Washington, DC 20431; http://www.imf.org. Illus., index, adv. Sample. Refereed. Circ: 5000. Microform: CIS; PQC. Online: Florida Center for Library Automation; Gale Group; OCLC Online Computer Library Center, Inc.; ProQuest Information & Learning. Reprint: PQC. *Indexed:* ABIn, AgeL, BAS, BPI, EIP, IBSS, IBZ, JEL, PAIS, RRTA, SSCI, SSI, WAE&RSA. *Aud.:* Ga, Ac, Sa.

This high-quality journal contains the empirical analysis of numerous macroeconomic issues that have been prepared by the International Monetary Fund staff, primarily professional economists. Topics include trade barriers and agreements, economic behavior, macroeconomic policy, fiscal analysis, devaluation of currency, tax reform, budget deficits, exchange rates, expenditures, and capital accumulation. Articles are technical but can be understood by the layperson. There is an archive of papers online organized by the JEL classification scheme. A bargain for large public and academic libraries.

2317. *International Review of Applied Economics.* [ISSN: 0269-2171] 1987. q. GBP 349 (Individuals, GBP 104). Carfax Publishing Ltd., 4 Park Sq, Milton Park, Abingdon, OX14 4RN, United Kingdom; enquiry@tandf.co.uk; http://www.tandf.co.uk/. Illus., index, adv. Refereed. Vol. ends: Jun. Online: EBSCO Publishing; Factiva; Florida Center for Library Automation; Gale Group; Ingenta Select; Northern Light Technology, Inc.; OCLC Online Computer Library Center, Inc.; ProQuest Information & Learning; RoweCom Information Quest; Swets Blackwell. Reprint: PSC. *Indexed:* ABIn, BAS, IBSS, JEL, PAIS, WAE&RSA. *Bk. rev.:* 2, several pages. *Aud.:* Ac, Sa.

This journal is "devoted to the practical applications of economic ideas . . . [It] associates itself broadly with the non-neoclassical tradition" and is not formally associated with any specific school of thought. An important feature of the papers is the cross between practical work and policy. Written in a "rigorous analytic style, yet nontechnical," the journal is suitable for large college and university libraries. Very reasonably priced.

2318. *J E I.* [ISSN: 0021-3624] 1967. q. USD 55 (Individuals, USD 45; Students, USD 15). Ed(s): Glen Atkinson. Association for Evolutionary Economics, Department of Economics, University of Nevada, Reno, NV 89507; afee@bucknell.edu; http://www.orgs.bucknell.edu/afee. Illus., index, adv. Sample. Refereed. Circ: 2000 Paid. Vol. ends: Dec. Microform: PQC. Online: bigchalk; EBSCO Publishing; Florida Center for Library Automation; Gale Group; OCLC Online Computer Library Center, Inc.; ProQuest Information & Learning; H.W. Wilson. Reprint: PQC; PSC. *Indexed:* ABIn, ABS&EES, AgeL, BPI, CJA, ForAb, IBSS, JEL, LRI, MCR, PAIS, PSA, SSCI, SSI, SociolAb, WAE&RSA. *Bk. rev.:* 15-19, 1-4 pages. *Aud.:* Ac, Sa.

Sponsored by the Association for Evolutionary Economics, this journal focuses on institutional and evolutionary economics, covering methodological topics, the organization and control of diverse economic systems, economic development, environmental/ecological issues, economic stabilization, labor relations, monetary management, and major economic policies. It is international in scope and also includes "Notes and Communications," and book reviews. The June issue contains the papers presented at the annual meeting of the Association for Evolutionary Economists. Will be of interest to university faculty and graduate students.

JASA. See Statistics section.

Journal of Accounting and Economics. See Accounting and Taxation section.

2319. *Journal of Applied Econometrics.* [ISSN: 0883-7252] 1986. 7x/yr. USD 1100. John Wiley & Sons Ltd., The Atrium, Southern Gate, Chichester, PO19 8SQ, United Kingdom; customer@wiley.co.uk; http://www.wiley.co.uk. Illus., index, adv. Sample. Refereed. Circ: 1300. Vol. ends: Dec. Reprint: SWZ. *Indexed:* ABIn, AgeL, BAS, IBSS, JEL, RiskAb, SSCI, ST&MA, WAE&RSA. *Bk. rev.:* 2, 750-3,500 words. *Aud.:* Ac, Sa.

An international journal that publishes "innovative, quantitative research in economics which cuts across areas of specialization." Econometric techniques are emphasized while covering a wide variety of problems in measurement, estimation, testing, forecasting, and policy analysis. Scholarly work is emphasized, and authors are requested to share their data sets for replicability. A typical issue contains five to nine articles followed by book and software reviews, announcements, forthcoming papers, and the call for papers. This journal is recommended for libraries that serve econometricians and interested mathematicians.

2320. *Journal of Asian Economics.* [ISSN: 1049-0078] 1990. bi-m. EUR 376 (Individuals, EUR 91). Ed(s): M. Dutta. Elsevier BV, North-Holland, Sara Burgerhartstraat 25, Amsterdam, 1055 KV, Netherlands; nlinfo-f@elsevier.nl; http://www.elsevier.nl. Illus., adv. Refereed. Microform: PQC. Online: EBSCO Publishing; ingenta.com; ScienceDirect; Swets Blackwell. *Indexed:* BAS, JEL, PAIS. *Aud.:* Ac, Sa.

Published for the American Committee on Asian Economic Studies, this journal provides a unique forum for this growing research area. Concentrating on innovative paradigms and comparative studies for Asia, it includes new models from the Soviet Union and Eastern European countries. It covers "economic theory, applied econometrics, international trade and finance, economic development, and comparative economic systems." Authors are usually academic economists from Asia, Australia, and the United States. Now owned by Elsevier, it is reasonably priced and is still recommended for large university and business libraries.

Journal of Banking and Finance. See Finance/Scholarly section.

Journal of Business. See Business/General section.

Journal of Business and Economic Statistics. See Business/General section.

Journal of Business Ethics. See Business/Ethics section.

2321. *Journal of Comparative Economics.* [ISSN: 0147-5967] 1977. q. EUR 639 (Individuals, EUR 117; Students, EUR 86). Ed(s): H. B. Bonin, John P Bonin. Academic Press, 525 B St, Ste 1900, San Diego, CA 92101-4495; apsubs@acad.com; http://www.academicpress.com. Illus., index, adv. Refereed. Vol. ends: Dec. Online: EBSCO Publishing; Gale Group; ingenta.com; OCLC Online Computer Library Center, Inc.; RoweCom Information Quest; ScienceDirect; Swets Blackwell. *Indexed:* ABS&EES, BAS, IBSS, JEL, PAIS, RRTA, SSCI, SSI, WAE&RSA. *Bk. rev.:* 2-23, 500-2,000 words. *Aud.:* Ac, Sa.

This major journal in the field of comparative economics is published for the Association for Comparative Economic Studies. It is "devoted to the analysis and study of contemporary, historical and hypothetical economic systems." Research areas include problems arising from the comparison of data from different systems and methodologies and varying institutional descriptions and systems. Each issue has at least eight articles, five or six lengthy signed book reviews, and an author index for each volume. The association owns the copyrights for the individual articles. Previously an Academic Press Ideal title, Elsevier now owns the copyright for the collective work. Recommended for universities and large institutions with international programs.

Journal of Consumer Research. See Advertising, Marketing, and Public Relations section.

2322. *The Journal of Development Economics.* [ISSN: 0304-3878] 1974. bi-m. EUR 1333 (Individuals, EUR 129). Ed(s): Pranab Bardhan, Mark R Rosenzweig. Elsevier BV, North-Holland, Sara Burgerhartstraat 25, Amsterdam, 1055 KV, Netherlands; nlinfo-f@elsevier.nl; http://www.elsevier.nl. Illus., index, adv. Sample. Refereed. Vol. ends: Oct. Microform: PQC. Online: EBSCO Publishing; Gale Group; ingenta.com; ScienceDirect; Swets Blackwell. Reprint: SWZ. *Indexed:* ABIn, BAS, GeogAbPG, H&SSA, IBSS, IBZ, JEL, PAIS, PollutAb, RRTA, RiskAb, SSCI, SSI, WAE&RSA. *Bk. rev.:* Various number and length. *Aud.:* Ac, Sa.

This journal "publishes papers relating to all aspects of economic development, from immediate policy concerns to structural problems of underdevelopment." The emphasis is on quantitative work. Issues contain eight or more articles sometimes followed by "Notes and Comments." Annually, there is an author index. There are well-written, lengthy book reviews. This journal is recommended for larger academic institutions—but review closely due to price.

2323. *Journal of Econometrics.* [ISSN: 0304-4076] 1973. m. EUR 2202 (Individuals, EUR 153). Ed(s): A. R. Gallant, T. Amemiya. Elsevier BV, North-Holland, Sara Burgerhartstraat 25, Amsterdam, 1055 KV, Netherlands; nlinfo-f@elsevier.nl; http://www.elsevier.nl. Illus., index, adv. Refereed. Microform: PQC. Online: EBSCO Publishing; Gale Group; ingenta.com; ScienceDirect; Swets Blackwell. *Indexed:* ABIn, AgeL, BAS, CCMJ, EngInd, IBSS, IBZ, JEL, MathSciNet, RRTA, RiskAb, SSCI, SSI, ST&MA, WAE&RSA. *Aud.:* Ac, Sa.

This journal provides new research in theoretical and applied econometrics and deals with estimation, application of statistical inference, application of econometric techniques, and research in traditional and developmental areas of econometrics. A new annals issue contains articles based on selected conference presentations. Extremely expensive, but very useful for econometricians and large universities.

2324. *Journal of Economic Behavior & Organization.* [ISSN: 0167-2681] 1980. m. EUR 1437 (Individuals, EUR 92). Ed(s): J. B. Rosser, Jr. Elsevier BV, North-Holland, Sara Burgerhartstraat 25, Amsterdam, 1055 KV, Netherlands; nlinfo-f@elsevier.nl; http://www.elsevier.nl. Illus., index, adv. Sample. Refereed. Vol. ends: Dec. Microform: PQC. Online: EBSCO Publishing; Gale Group; ingenta.com; ScienceDirect; Swets Blackwell. Reprint: SWZ. *Indexed:* ABIn, ArtHuCI, CJA, ForAb, IBSS, JEL, RiskAb, SSCI. *Bk. rev.:* 2-3, several pages. *Aud.:* Ac, Sa.

Written by academic economists, this journal is "devoted to theoretical and empirical research concerning economic decision, organization, and behavior and to economic change in all its aspects." The goal is to understand how humans can influence organizations and economies, how leading features of an economy can lead to macro and micro behaviors, and how changes can occur. Interdisciplinary studies using biology, psychology, law, anthropology, sociology, and mathematics are included. Issues have seven to nine articles and include longer, in-depth book reviews. Recommended for large universities and researchers.

2325. *Journal of Economic Dynamics and Control.* [ISSN: 0165-1889] 1979. m. EUR 1314 (Individuals, EUR 72). Ed(s): W. J. Den Haan, C. H. Hommes. Elsevier BV, North-Holland, Sara Burgerhartstraat 25, Amsterdam, 1055 KV, Netherlands; nlinfo-f@elsevier.nl;

http://www.elsevier.nl. Illus., index, adv. Refereed. Vol. ends: Nov. Microform: PQC. Online: EBSCO Publishing; Gale Group; ingenta.com; ScienceDirect; Swets Blackwell. Reprint: SWZ. *Indexed:* ABIn, CCMJ, GeogAbPG, IBSS, IBZ, JEL, MathSciNet, RRTA, RiskAb, SSCI, WAE&RSA. *Aud.:* Ac, Sa.

Widely recognized as the most influential journal in this field, it is organized into two parts. Section A is subtitled "Computational Methods in Economics and Finance," and Section B is subtitled "Economic Dynamics." The latter "covers theoretical and empirical aspects of dynamics and control," while the former devotes itself to "all aspects of computing, applicable to economics and finance," and may "include artificial intelligence; databases; decision support systems; genetic algorithms; modelling languages; neural networks; numerical algorithms for optimization, control and equilibria; parallel computing; qualitative reasoning." Being well-rounded in economics would be very helpful for reading this journal. Recommended for universities; but review closely due to price.

2326. *Journal of Economic Growth.* [ISSN: 1381-4338] 1996. q. USD 483 print or online ed. Ed(s): Oded Galor. Kluwer Academic Publishers, 101 Philip Dr, Assinippi Park, Norwell, MA 02061. Refereed. Online: EBSCO Publishing; ingenta.com; Kluwer Online; OCLC Online Computer Library Center, Inc.; Ovid Technologies, Inc.; RoweCom Information Quest; Swets Blackwell. Reprint: SWZ. *Indexed:* BAS, IBSS, JEL, SSCI. *Aud.:* Ac, Sa.

Started in 1996, this high-quality journal has a high impact factor in the Social Sciences Citation Index and a very decent half-life article rating. Prominent researchers on the editorial board include Robert Barro, Paul Romer, Jagdish Bhagwati, and Paul Krugman. Its scope is spelled out in its title and also includes dynamic macroeconomics. The range is wide and deals with ideas surrounding fertility, trade, money, technology, income distribution, and growth models. For academic and special libraries.

2327. *Journal of Economic History.* [ISSN: 0022-0507] 1941. q. USD 138. Ed(s): Gavin Wright, C Knick Harley. Cambridge University Press, The Edinburgh Bldg, Shaftesbury Rd, Cambridge, CB2 2RU, United Kingdom; information@cambridge.org; http://uk.cambridge.org/journals. Illus., index, adv. Refereed. Vol. ends: Dec. Microform: MIM; PQC. Online: Gale Group; JSTOR (Web-based Journal Archive); OCLC Online Computer Library Center, Inc.; Swets Blackwell. Reprint: PSC; SWZ. *Indexed:* ABS&EES, AgeL, AmH&L, ArtHuCI, BAS, BRI, CBRI, GeogAbPG, HumInd, IBSS, IBZ, JEL, PAIS, SSCI, SSI, WAE&RSA. *Bk. rev.:* 39-63, 600-1,800 words. *Aud.:* Ac, Sa.

This journal is the official publication of the Economic History Association in Great Britain. and "is devoted to the interdisciplinary study of history and economics." Of interest to economists and economic, social, and demographic historians, the journal has a broad coverage in terms of methodology and geography, covering such topics as "money and banking, trade manufacturing, technology, transportation, industrial organization, labor, agriculture, servitude, demography, education, economic growth, and the role of government and regulation." This excellent journal will appeal to the both the student and the general public. Recommended for colleges, universities, and public libraries.

2328. *Journal of Economic Literature.* Formerly (until 1968): *Journal of Economic Abstracts.* [ISSN: 0022-0515] 1963. q. USD 135 domestic; USD 160 foreign; USD 20 newsstand/cover per issue. Ed(s): John McMillan. American Economic Association, 2014 Broadway, Ste 305, Nashville, TN 37203; http://www.vanderbilt.edu/AEA/. Illus., index, adv. Refereed. Circ: 27000. Vol. ends: Dec. CD-ROM: SilverPlatter Information, Incorporated. Microform: PQC. Online: EBSCO Publishing; Gale Group; Ingenta Select; JSTOR (Web-based Journal Archive); ProQuest Information & Learning. Reprint: PQC; WSH. *Indexed:* ABIn, ABS&EES, AgeL, AmH&L, BRD, BRI, CBRI, IBSS, JEL, PAIS, SSCI, SSI. *Bk. rev.:* 40, lengthy. *Aud.:* Ac, Sa.

The *Journal of Economic Literature* is received by all members of the American Economic Association (AEA) and by numerous libraries. It contains four to six research articles written by outstanding economists, book reviews, and new book listings. The journal article index has been removed for a couple of years now, but still available via ECONLIT or at www.e-jel.org. *e-JEL*, the electronic edition of the journal, will include quarterly "citations and abstracts for current articles from the full list of journals indexed on ECONLIT." RFE (Resources for Economists), the premier web guide for economic information, is part of the AEA web site. Highly recommended for colleges, universities, and larger public and special libraries.

2329. *Journal of Economic Perspectives.* [ISSN: 0895-3309] 1987. q. Ed(s): Alan B Krueger. American Economic Association, 2014 Broadway, Ste 305, Nashville, TN 37203; http://www.vanderbilt.edu/AEA/. Illus., index, adv. Refereed. Vol. ends: Nov. Online: EBSCO Publishing; Gale Group; Ingenta Select; JSTOR (Web-based Journal Archive); ProQuest Information & Learning. *Indexed:* ABS&EES, AgeL, AmH&L, BAS, BPI, CJA, IBSS, JEL, PAIS, SSCI, SSI, WAE&RSA. *Aud.:* Ga, Ac, Sa.

This journal aims to "synthesize and integrate lessons learned from active lines of economic research; to provide economic analysis of public policy issues; to encourage cross-fertilization of ideas among fields of economics; to offer readers an accessible source for state-of-the-art economic thinking; to suggest directions for future research; to provide insights and readings for classroom use; and to address issues relating to the economics profession." A membership in this association also includes two other highly regarded journals, the *Journal of Economic Literature* and the *American Economic Review.* A typical issue contains a lecture, articles, recommendations for further reading and retrospectives, and "Notes" of association announcements and the call for papers. This journal is heartily recommended for large public and academic libraries. It's a bargain!

2330. *The Journal of Economic Psychology.* [ISSN: 0167-4870] 1981. bi-m. EUR 460 (Individuals, EUR 161). Ed(s): S. Kemp, P Earl. Elsevier BV, North-Holland, Sara Burgerhartstraat 25, Amsterdam, 1055 KV, Netherlands; nlinfo-f@elsevier.nl; http://www.elsevier.nl. Adv. Refereed. Microform: PQC. Online: Gale Group; ingenta.com; ScienceDirect; Swets Blackwell. Reprint: SWZ. *Indexed:* ABIn, FS&TA, IBSS, JEL, PsycholAb, SSCI, WAE&RSA. *Aud.:* Ac, Sa.

The study of an individual's actions and society's as a whole has made and will continue to make tremendous impact on economic theory, hence the inclusion of this journal. Published for the International Association for Research in Economic Psychology, this non-mainstream journal focuses on behavorial research, especially the socio-psychological aspects of economic events and processes such as consumption, preferences, choices, and decisions. This is a most interesting area of study, and economists, sociologists, and policy makers will appreciate this leading-edge journal. A very good selection for academic and special libraries.

2331. *Journal of Economic Theory.* [ISSN: 0022-0531] 1969. m. EUR 2878 (Individuals, EUR 113; Students, EUR 46). Ed(s): Karl Shell, Jess Benhabib. Academic Press, 525 B St, Ste 1900, San Diego, CA 92101-4495; apsubs@acad.com; http://www.academicpress.com. Adv. Refereed. Online: EBSCO Publishing; Gale Group; ingenta.com; OCLC Online Computer Library Center, Inc.; RoweCom Information Quest; ScienceDirect; Swets Blackwell. Reprint: SWZ. *Indexed:* ABIn, AgeL, CCMJ, IBSS, JEL, MathSciNet, RiskAb, SSCI, SSI. *Aud.:* Ac, Sa.

Now an Elsevier title, this heavily cited, scholarly journal publishes "original research on economic theory and emphasizes the theoretical analysis of economic models, including the related mathematical techniques." It is affiliated with the Society for the Promotion of Economic Theory. There are usually four to six articles followed by notes, comments, letters to the editor, announcements, a list of papers to appear in forthcoming issues, and an author index. An excellent journal for libraries supporting theoretical economics. It is still a must for those dealing with mathematical economics, but review closely due to price. A competitive journal, *Review of Economic Theory*, was launched in spring 2003 by ELSSS and is endorsed by SPARC.

2332. *Journal of Economics.* Formerly (until 1986): *Zeitschrift fuer Nationaloekonomie.* [ISSN: 0931-8658] 1930. 9x/yr. EUR 952 domestic; EUR 984.20 foreign; EUR 128 newsstand/cover per issue. Ed(s): D Boes. Springer-Verlag Wien, Sachsenplatz 4-6, Vienna, 1201, Austria;

journals@springer.at. Illus., index, adv. Sample. Refereed. Microform: PQC. Online: ScienceDirect; Springer LINK. Reprint: ISI; SCH; SWZ. *Indexed:* ABIn, IBSS, IBZ, JEL, PAIS, SSCI. *Bk. rev.:* 6-8, lengthy. *Aud.:* Ac.

Focusing on mathematical economic theory, this excellent journal has technical articles that cover mainly microeconomics and some macroeconomics. A typical issue has five extensive articles and six to eight lengthy book reviews. Additional supplemental issues are devoted to current issues. Authors are academic and international. For well-versed economists and readers in large academic libraries.

2333. *Journal of Environmental Economics and Management.* [ISSN: 0095-0696] 1975. 7x/yr. EUR 1091 (Individuals, EUR 120; Students, EUR 74). Ed(s): J. A. Herriges. Academic Press, 525 B St, Ste 1900, San Diego, CA 92101-4495; apsubs@acad.com; http://www.academicpress.com. Illus. Refereed. Online: EBSCO Publishing; Gale Group; ingenta.com; OCLC Online Computer Library Center, Inc.; RoweCom Information Quest; ScienceDirect; Swets Blackwell. Reprint: SWZ. *Indexed:* ABIn, ApEcolAb, BiolAb, DSR&OA, EnvAb, ExcerpMed, FPA, ForAb, GeoRef, IBSS, IndVet, JEL, PAIS, PollutAb, RRTA, S&F, SCI, SSCI, SSI, SWRA, VetBull, WAE&RSA. *Aud.:* Ac, Sa.

Regarded very highly, this is the official journal of the Association of Environmental and Resource Economists. Devoted to the worldwide coverage of theoretical and empirical research, it "concentrates on the management and/or social control of the economy in its relationship with the management and use of natural resources and the natural environment." The majority of the authors are academic economists, and it includes interdisciplinary papers from other fields of interest. This journal is recommended for university and large public libraries.

2334. *Journal of European Economic History.* [ISSN: 0391-5115] 1972. 3x/yr. Ed(s): Luigi De Rosa. Banca di Roma, Servizio Studi, Via Marco Minghetti, 17, Rome, 00187, Italy. Illus., index. Sample. Circ: 3500. Vol. ends: Winter. Reprint: SCH. *Indexed:* AmH&L, HumInd, IBSS, JEL, PAIS. *Bk. rev.:* 6-8, 600-1,750 words. *Aud.:* Ga, Ac, Sa.

This journal is "devoted to the study of the economic history of Europe and of the various European countries; to the study of the impact of the economic history of other continents, or countries, upon the history of Europe or of different countries and times; to the analysis of the problems and themes which shed light on the economic history of Europe or of its various countries; to the theory of economic history; and to European economic historiography." Each issue has three to five articles, notes, problems, debates, book reviews, and a lengthy list of books received. This journal welcomes lively discussion and accepts preliminary findings and hypotheses. The editorial board is mainly European, and the authors are international. University libraries would benefit from a subscription.

Journal of Finance. See Finance/Scholarly section.

Journal of Financial and Quantitative Analysis. See Finance/Scholarly section.

Journal of Financial Economics. See Finance/Scholarly section.

2335. *Journal of Health Economics.* [ISSN: 0167-6296] 1982. bi-m. EUR 943 (Individuals, EUR 81). Ed(s): Joseph P Newhouse, A J Culyer. Elsevier BV, North-Holland, Sara Burgerhartstraat 25, Amsterdam, 1055 KV, Netherlands; nlinfo-f@elsevier.nl; http://www.elsevier.nl. Illus., adv. Refereed. Microform: PQC. Online: EBSCO Publishing; Gale Group; ingenta.com; ScienceDirect; Swets Blackwell. Reprint: SWZ. *Indexed:* ABIn, ASG, ASSIA, AgeL, ExcerpMed, H&SSA, HRA, IBSS, JEL, MCR, PAIS, PEI, PRA, RiskAb, SCI, SFSA, SSCI. *Aud.:* Ac, Sa.

The scope of this journal is "production of health services; demand and utilization of health services; financing of health services; measurement of health; behavorial models of demanders, suppliers, and other health care agencies; manpower planning and forecasting; the prevention of sickness; cost-benefit and cost-effectiveness analyses and issues of budgeting; and efficiency and distributional aspects of health policy." An issue may have articles, and article notes. Very useful and informative for economists and students in the field, as well as for health care administrators.

2336. *Journal of Human Development.* [ISSN: 1464-9888] 2000. 3x/yr. GBP 157 (Individuals, GBP 42). Ed(s): Sakiko Fukuda-Parr. Carfax Publishing Ltd., 4 Park Sq, Milton Park, Abingdon, OX14 4RN, United Kingdom; enquiry@tandf.co.uk; http://www.tandf.co.uk/. Online: EBSCO Publishing; Ingenta Select; RoweCom Information Quest; Swets Blackwell. Reprint: PSC. *Indexed:* IBZ, PSA, SociolAb. *Aud.:* Ac, Sa.

Started in 2000, this refereed journal's contents reflect human development as a new school of thought in economics, and as such is a must purchase for academic libraries. Its scope covers the challenges dealing with development and poverty eradication, including human well-being, markets, growth, social justice, and human rights. Amartya Sen is on the editorial advisory board; he won the 1998 Nobel Prize in Economics for his "contributions to welfare economics." Affiliated with the United Nations Development Programme, this journal will be gaining circulation and respect.

Journal of Human Resources. See Management, Administration, and Human Resources/Human Resources section.

2337. *Journal of Industrial Economics.* [ISSN: 0022-1821] 1952. q. GBP 132 print & online eds. Ed(s): Luis Cabral. Blackwell Publishing Ltd., 9600 Garsington Rd, PO Box 805, Oxford, OX4 2DQ, United Kingdom; customerservices@oxon.blackwellpublishing.com; http://www.blackwellpublishing.com/. Illus., index, adv. Sample. Refereed. Circ: 1850. Vol. ends: Dec. Microform: MIM; PQC. Online: EBSCO Publishing; Gale Group; ingenta.com; JSTOR (Web-based Journal Archive); OCLC Online Computer Library Center, Inc.; RoweCom Information Quest; Swets Blackwell. Reprint: PQC; PSC. *Indexed:* ABIn, BAS, BPI, HRA, IBSS, IBZ, JEL, PAIS, PRA, SSCI. *Aud.:* Ac, Sa.

Founded to promote the analysis of modern industry, especially the behavior of firms and market functions, this widely circulated journal is primary in its field. Both theoretical and empirical works are published, covering everything from organization of industry and applied oligopoly theory to regulation, monopoly, merger, and technology policy. Large business collections and universities will want to review this important journal.

2338. *Journal of Institutional and Theoretical Economics.* Formerly: *Zeitschrift fuer die Gesamte Staatswissenschaft.* [ISSN: 0932-4569] 1844. q. EUR 214 (Individuals, EUR 164). Ed(s): Rudolf Richter. Mohr Siebeck, Wilhelmstr 18, Tuebingen, 72074, Germany; info@mohr.de; http://www.mohr.de/jite.html. Illus., index, adv. Refereed. Vol. ends: Dec. *Indexed:* AgeL, ArtHuCI, BAS, IBSS, IPSA, JEL, PAIS, PSA, SSCI, WAE&RSA. *Bk. rev.:* 10-14, 600-2,200 words. *Aud.:* Ga, Ac, Sa.

This leading and wide-ranging journal covers the "economics of property rights and of institutional evolution, transaction cost economics, contract theory, economic history and interdisplinary studies." Articles and book reviews may be in English or German, but most are in English; papers have a summary in both languages. Notable are the papers from the Symposium on New Institutional Economics, presented in a single issue annually. Recommended for very large public and university libraries.

2339. *Journal of International Economics.* [ISSN: 0022-1996] 1971. 6x/yr. EUR 1075 (Individuals, EUR 120). Ed(s): J. Eaton, C. M. Engel. Elsevier BV, North-Holland, Sara Burgerhartstraat 25, Amsterdam, 1055 KV, Netherlands; nlinfo-f@elsevier.nl; http://www.elsevier.nl. Illus., index, adv. Refereed. Vol. ends: May/Nov. Microform: PQC. Online: EBSCO Publishing; Gale Group; ingenta.com; ScienceDirect; Swets Blackwell. Reprint: SWZ. *Indexed:* ABIn, BAS, GeogAbPG, IBSS, JEL, PAIS, RRTA, RiskAb, SSCI, SSI, WAE&RSA. *Aud.:* Ac, Sa.

Articles in this solid journal pertain to "trade patterns, commercial policy, exchange rates, international institutions, open economy macroeconomics, international finance, international factor mobility." Empirical studies are encouraged for submission. Most authors are American. Each issue has seven to nine articles. Universities with studies in international economics should review the price before subscribing.

Journal of Labor Economics. See Labor and Industrial Relations section.

Journal of Law and Economics. See Law section.

2340. *Journal of Macroeconomics.* [ISSN: 0164-0704] 1979. q. EUR 250 (Individuals, EUR 50). Ed(s): Douglas McMillin, Theodore Palivos. Elsevier BV, North-Holland, Sara Burgerhartstraat 25, Amsterdam, 1055 KV, Netherlands; nlinfo-f@elsevier.nl; http://www.elsevier.nl/homepage/about/us/regional_sites.htt. Illus., index, adv. Sample. Refereed. Circ: 950. Vol. ends: Fall. Microform: PQC. Online: Gale Group; ingenta.com; Northern Light Technology, Inc.; OCLC Online Computer Library Center, Inc.; ScienceDirect. Reprint: PQC; PSC; SWZ. *Indexed:* ABIn, IBSS, IBZ, JEL, SSCI. *Bk. rev.:* 12-16, 75-100 words. *Aud.:* Ac, Sa.

The *Journal of Macroeconomics,* published for the E. J. Ourso College of Business Administration at Louisiana State University, is "devoted entirely to the broad field of macroeconomics [and] contains a variety of articles by distinguished authors on economic theory, related empirical work, and policy-oriented topics." The journal includes a list of notable and new books. Subscribers will be academic, business, and government libraries.

2341. *Journal of Mathematical Economics.* [ISSN: 0304-4068] 1974. 8x/yr. EUR 1334 (Individuals, EUR 110). Ed(s): Bernard Cornet, J. Geanakoplos. Elsevier BV, North-Holland, Sara Burgerhartstraat 25, Amsterdam, 1055 KV, Netherlands; nlinfo-f@elsevier.nl; http://www.elsevier.nl. Illus., adv. Refereed. Microform: PQC. Online: EBSCO Publishing; Gale Group; ingenta.com; ScienceDirect; Swets Blackwell. *Indexed:* ABIn, CCMJ, IBSS, JEL, MathSciNet, RiskAb, SSCI. *Aud.:* Ac, Sa.

The main goal of this journal "is to provide a forum for work in economic theory which expresses economic ideas using formal mathematical reasoning." These ideas may be in any field of economics or from any school of economic thought. A secondary goal "is to provide a forum for work which develops new mathematics inspired by economic problems." New proofs, however, must offer simplification or new insights. The authors are mainly U.S. academic economists. Review this leading specialty journal for universities and larger colleges.

2342. *Journal of Monetary Economics.* Incorporates (1978-2002): *Carnegie-Rochester Conference Series on Public Policy.* [ISSN: 0304-3932] 1975. 8x/yr. EUR 1460 (Individuals, EUR 91; Students, EUR 54). Ed(s): Robert G. King, Charles Plosser. Elsevier BV, North-Holland, Sara Burgerhartstraat 25, Amsterdam, 1055 KV, Netherlands; nlinfo-f@elsevier.nl; http://www.elsevier.nl. Illus., index, adv. Sample. Refereed. Vol. ends: Dec. Microform: PQC. Online: EBSCO Publishing; Gale Group; ingenta.com; ScienceDirect; Swets Blackwell. Reprint: ISI; SWZ. *Indexed:* ABIn, IBSS, JEL, LRI, PAIS, RiskAb, SSCI. *Aud.:* Ac, Sa.

This journal aims to publish selected papers in the growing area of monetary analysis, focusing on "the role of various institutional arrangements, the consequences of specific changes in banking structure, and the welfare aspects of structural policies." The operation of credit markets and the behavior of rates of return on assets are explored as well. The journal is published in collaboration with the University of Rochester's Graduate School of Business Administration and the Department of Economics at Boston University. Although it is expensive, libraries supporting programs in banking and finance will want to review this for their collection.

2343. *Journal of Money, Credit & Banking.* [ISSN: 0022-2879] 1969. q. USD 210. Ed(s): Stephen G Cecchetti, Paul D Evans. Ohio State University Press, 180 Pressey Hall, 1070 Carmack Rd, Columbus, OH 43210-1002; journals@osu.edu; http://www.ohiostatepress.org. Illus., index, adv. Refereed. Circ: 3200 Paid. Vol. ends: Feb/Nov. CD-ROM: ProQuest Information & Learning. Microform: PQC. Online: Florida Center for Library Automation; Gale Group; JSTOR (Web-based Journal Archive); OCLC Online Computer Library Center, Inc.; Project MUSE; ProQuest Information & Learning; Swets Blackwell; H.W. Wilson. Reprint: SCH. *Indexed:* ABIn, ATI, BLI, BPI, IBSS, JEL, PAIS, SSCI, SSI. *Bk. rev.:* 1-5, 2-4 pages. *Aud.:* Ac, Sa.

Sponsored by the Ohio State University Department of Economics, this widely read and cited journal presents "major findings in the study of monetary and fiscal policy, credit markets, money and banking, portfolio management, and related subjects." It has esteemed editors such as Alan Berger of the Board of Governors of the Federal Reserve System. There is a handy annual author-title index. Starting in 2003, there are six issues per year. Recommended for policy makers, professional and academic economists, and bankers.

2344. *Journal of Political Economy.* [ISSN: 0022-3808] 1892. bi-m. USD 275 print & online eds. (Individuals, USD 52 print & online eds.; Students, USD 33 print & online eds.). Ed(s): Fernando Alvarez, Pierre-Andre Chiappori. University of Chicago Press, Journals Division, PO Box 37005, Chicago, IL 60637; subscriptions@press.uchicago.edu; http://www.journals.uchicago.edu. Illus., index, adv. Refereed. Circ: 6100. Vol. ends: Dec. Microform: MIM; PMC; PQC. Online: EBSCO Publishing; Florida Center for Library Automation; Gale Group; JSTOR (Web-based Journal Archive); ProQuest Information & Learning. Reprint: ISI; PQC; PSC; SCH; WSH. *Indexed:* ABCPolSci, ABIn, AgeL, ArtHuCI, BAS, BLI, BRD, BRI, CBRI, CJA, GeoRef, GeogAbPG, IBSS, IBZ, IPSA, JEL, PAIS, RI-1, RRTA, SSCI, SSI, SWA, WAE&RSA. *Bk. rev.:* 1-2, 2-4 pages. *Aud.:* Ac, Sa.

Connected with the Department of Economics and the Graduate School of Business at the University of Chicago, the *Journal of Political Economy* publishes "analytical, interpretive, and empirical studies" in such traditional areas as monetary theory, fiscal policy, labor economics, planning and development, micro- and macroeconomics theory, international trade and finance, industrial organization, history of economic thought, and social economics. The journal has acquired an excellent reputation and is one of the three top journals in the field. Authors are from international academic institutions and government agencies, such as the Federal Reserve Board. Each issue includes five or six articles, occasionally followed by review articles, comments, and book reviews. Any academic or special library that deals with social economics should consider subscribing to this publication.

2345. *Journal of Post Keynesian Economics.* [ISSN: 0160-3477] 1978. q. USD 275 includes online access (Individuals, USD 89). Ed(s): Paul Davidson. M.E. Sharpe, Inc., 80 Business Park Dr, Armonk, NY 10504; custserv@mesharpe.com; http://www.mesharpe.com. Illus., index, adv. Refereed. Circ: 1700. Vol. ends: Winter. Reprint: PSC; SCH. *Indexed:* ABIn, FutSurv, IBSS, JEL, SSCI, SSI. *Aud.:* Ac, Sa.

Founded by Sidney Weintraub and Paul Davidson, this journal concentrates on post–World War II economic theory, including the "treatment of post-Keynesian economics in the history of economic thought." Each issue usually has eight technical articles, an editor's corner, and possibly a symposium. Authors are usually economics professors. The audience for this journal will be professional economists. Well worth the low price.

2346. *Journal of Public Economics.* [ISSN: 0047-2727] 1972. m. EUR 1803 (Individuals, EUR 172). Ed(s): R. Boadway, J. Poterba. Elsevier BV, North-Holland, Sara Burgerhartstraat 25, Amsterdam, 1055 KV, Netherlands; nlinfo-f@elsevier.nl; http://www.elsevier.nl. Illus., index, adv. Refereed. Vol. ends: Oct. Microform: PQC. Online: EBSCO Publishing; Gale Group; ingenta.com; ScienceDirect. *Indexed:* ABIn, ASG, AgeL, ExcerpMed, HRA, IBSS, JEL, LRI, PAIS, PRA, SSCI, SUSA. *Aud.:* Ac, Sa.

Now in its third decade, the aim of the *Journal of Public Economics* is to foster original scientific thought on the questions of public economics in such fields as education, environmental policies, and tax enforcement. The emphasis is on the application of current theory and quantitative analysis. More and more, authors in this journal are from continental Europe. Also, during the past two years, empirical papers have comprised 40 percent of the journal. The audience is generally scholars, theorists, public economists, and policy makers. A subscription is suggested for universities, but review closely due to price.

2347. ***Journal of Regulatory Economics.*** [ISSN: 0922-680X] 1989. bi-m. USD 650 print or online ed. Ed(s): Michael A Crew. Kluwer Academic Publishers, 101 Philip Dr, Assinippi Park, Norwell, MA 02061. Illus., index, adv. Refereed. Vol. ends: Dec. Microform: PQC. Online: EBSCO Publishing; ingenta.com; Kluwer Online; OCLC Online Computer Library Center, Inc.; Ovid Technologies, Inc.; RoweCom Information Quest. Reprint: SWZ. *Indexed:* IBSS, JEL, SSCI. *Aud.:* Ac, Sa.

The *Journal of Regulatory Economics* is a forum for the analysis of regulatory theories and institutions. Theoretical and applied papers are included. Topics encompass the "traditional problems of natural monopoly; deregulation and new policy instruments; and insurance, financial, health and safety, environmental, hazardous and solid waste, and consumer product regulation." Authors are international and are usually academics or professional economists. This journal will be read by researchers, policy makers, and professional economists, so large universities and special libraries will be the subscribers.

Journal of Risk and Insurance. See Finance/Insurance section.

Journal of Transport Economics and Policy. See Transportation section.

2348. ***Journal of Urban Economics.*** [ISSN: 0094-1190] 1974. bi-m. EUR 1192 (Individuals, EUR 125). Ed(s): Jan K Brueckner. Academic Press, 525 B St, Ste 1900, San Diego, CA 92101-4495; apsubs@acad.com; http://www.academicpress.com. Illus., index. Refereed. Vol. ends: May/Nov. Online: EBSCO Publishing; Gale Group; ingenta.com; OCLC Online Computer Library Center, Inc.; RoweCom Information Quest; ScienceDirect; Swets Blackwell. Reprint: SWZ. *Indexed:* AgeL, BPI, CJA, ExcerpMed, IBSS, JEL, PAIS, PRA, RiskAb, SSCI, SUSA. *Aud.:* Ac, Sa.

A respected journal in its field, the *Journal of Urban Economics* publishes scholarly work on a wide range of topics and approaches. Also featured are brief notes and an index in the last issue of a volume. This journal has some technical articles. Primarily for economists, but those interested in urban economic issues such as local public finance, transportation, and housing will also benefit. Previously an Academic Press IDEAL title, it is now owned by Elsevier.

2349. ***Kyklos: internationale Zeitschrift fuer Sozialwissenschaften.*** [ISSN: 0023-5962] 1943. q. USD 407 print & online. Ed(s): Mr. Rene L Frey. Helbing & Lichtenhahn Verlag AG (Schweiz) & Co. KG, Elisabethenstr 8, Basel, 4051, Switzerland; info@helbing.ch; http://www.helbing.ch. Illus., index, adv. Refereed. Circ: 2600. Vol. ends: Nov. Microform: PQC. Online: Gale Group; ingenta.com; RoweCom Information Quest; Swets Blackwell. Reprint: PQC; SCH. *Indexed:* ArtHuCI, BAS, ExcerpMed, GeogAbPG, IBSS, IBZ, IPSA, JEL, PAIS, PRA, RRTA, SSCI, SSI, WAE&RSA. *Bk. rev.:* 15-20, 550-1,600 words. *Aud.:* Ga, Ac, Sa.

This is one of the most widely recognized journals outside English-speaking areas and is published by an international nonprofit organization whose main purpose is "to analyze socio-economic problems of our time and to bridge the gap between scholarship and economic policy makers by means of public conferences and publications." The theoretical and empirical are covered, and unorthodox approaches are favored. Authors are from academic departments and institutions from around the world. Each article has a summary in English, German, and French, but articles are all in English. Book reviews could be written in any one of the three languages. Each issue has four to seven articles, book reviews, and a list of books received. Researchers, economists, sociologists, policy makers, and students appreciate this journal.

2350. ***Land Economics: a quarterly journal devoted to the study of economic and social institutions.*** Formerly: *Journal of Land and Public Utility Economics.* [ISSN: 0023-7639] 1925. q. USD 166 (Individuals, USD 59). Ed(s): Daniel Bromley. University of Wisconsin Press, Journal Division, 1930 Monroe St., 3rd Fl, Madison, WI 53711; journals@uwpress.wisc.edu; http://www.wisc.edu/wisconsinpress/journals. Illus., index, adv. Refereed. Circ: 2000. Vol. ends: Nov. Microform: PQC. Online: EBSCO Publishing; Florida Center for Library Automation; Gale Group; Ingenta Select; Northern Light Technology, Inc.; OCLC Online Computer Library Center, Inc.; ProQuest Information & Learning; H.W. Wilson. Reprint: PQC; PSC. *Indexed:* ABIn, AIAP, AgeL, Agr, BAS, BPI, DSR&OA, EnvAb, ExcerpMed, FPA, ForAb, GeoRef, GeogAbPG, IBSS, IBZ, JEL, LRI, PAIS, PRA, PollutAb, RRTA, RiskAb, S&F, SSCI, SSI, SUSA, WAE&RSA. *Bk. rev.:* 1-2, 1-6 pages. *Aud.:* Ac, Sa.

Land Economics is "devoted to the study of economic aspects of the entire spectrum of natural and environmental resources, emphasizing conceptual and/or empirical work with direct relevance for public policy." It is the oldest American journal dealing with the issues of land use, natural resources, public utilities, housing, and urban land. Bringing the latest results of applied research and concepts, it includes such topics as energy, transportation, environmental quality, and urban land use. Highly recommended for scholars and economists in government, business, finance, and universities.

Managerial and Decision Economics. See Management, Administration, and Human Resources/Operations Research and Management Science section.

2351. ***Manchester School.*** Formerly: *Manchester School of Economic and Social Studies.* [ISSN: 1463-6786] 1930. bi-m. GBP 256 print & online eds. Ed(s): Chris Orme, Martyn Andrews. Blackwell Publishing Ltd., 9600 Garsington Rd, PO Box 805, Oxford, OX4 2DQ, United Kingdom; customerservices@oxon.blackwellpublishing.com; http://www.blackwellpublishing.com/. Illus., index, adv. Refereed. Circ: 1300. Vol. ends: Dec. Online: EBSCO Publishing; ingenta.com; OCLC Online Computer Library Center, Inc.; RoweCom Information Quest; Swets Blackwell. Reprint: PSC. *Indexed:* ABIn, IBSS, JEL, PAIS, RRTA, RiskAb, SSCI, SSI, WAE&RSA. *Bk. rev.:* 20-30, 250-1,500 words. *Aud.:* Ac, Sa.

This international journal with an excellent reputation covers both the theoretical and applied in macroeconomics, microeconomics, labor, and econometrics. Authors are usually British, with a few Europeans and Americans. Occasionally, there are book reviews. Included is an annual supplement of papers reflecting the proceedings of the Money, Macroeconomics, and Finance Research Group. Graduate students and economists will appreciate this scholarly publication.

Meridians. See Women: Feminist and Special Interest/Feminist and Women's Studies section.

2352. ***National Institute Economic Review.*** [ISSN: 0027-9501] 1959. q. GBP 229 print & online eds. in Europe, Middle East, Africa & Australasia. Ed(s): Martin Weale. Sage Publications Ltd., 6 Bonhill St, London, EC2A 4PU, United Kingdom; info@sagepub.co.uk; http://www.sagepub.co.uk/. Illus., index, adv. Circ: 1700. Vol. ends: Nov. Online: Florida Center for Library Automation; Gale Group; ingenta.com; Northern Light Technology, Inc.; OCLC Online Computer Library Center, Inc.; ProQuest Information & Learning; RoweCom Information Quest; Swets Blackwell; H.W. Wilson. *Indexed:* ABIn, BPI, IBSS, JEL, PAIS, RRTA, WAE&RSA. *Aud.:* Ga, Ac, Sa.

From "Britain's longest established independent economic research institute," this periodical covers "quantitative research which relates directly or indirectly on economic performance, macro economies, economics of industry, trade labour markets, education, and finance." The institute receives no funding from private or public sources. There are six basic sections: Economic Overview, Commentary, The UK Economy, The World Economy, Research Articles, and Main Economic Events, which is a statistical appendix that gives series information on the GDP, output volumes, prices, unemployment, imports and exports, monthly economic indicators, and financial indicators. Sometimes a calendar of economic events follows. Strongly recommended for libraries with large economics collections or those that support international studies.

National Tax Journal. See Accounting and Taxation section.

2353. ***Netnomics.*** [ISSN: 1385-9587] 1999. 3x/yr. USD 224 print or online ed. Kluwer Academic Publishers, van Godewijckstraat 30, PO Box 17, Dordrecht, 3300 AA, Netherlands; services@wkap.nl; http://www.wkap.nl. Illus. Sample. Refereed. Online: EBSCO Publishing; ingenta.com; RoweCom Information Quest; Swets Blackwell. *Indexed:* JEL. *Aud.:* Ac.

Since 1999, this innovative journal addresses "pricing schemes for electronic services, electronic trading systems, data mining and high frequency data, real-time forecasting, filtering, economic software agents, distributed database applications, digicash-ecash systems, and many more." Available either in paper or on the web. Strongly recommended to all those dealing with these new problems and issues as a whole new field of research is emerging.

2354. ***O E C D Observer.*** [ISSN: 0029-7054] 1962. bi-m. USD 52 combined subscription print & online eds. Ed(s): Rory Clarke. Organization for Economic Cooperation and Development, 2 rue Andre Pascal, Paris, Cedex 16 75775, France; sales@oecd.org; http://www.oecd.org. Illus., index, adv. Circ: 25000. Vol. ends: Dec/Jan. Online: Chadwyck-Healey Incorporated; EBSCO Publishing; Florida Center for Library Automation; Gale Group; OCLC Online Computer Library Center, Inc.; ProQuest Information & Learning; H.W. Wilson. Reprint: PQC. *Indexed:* ABIn, BPI, CIJE, DSA, EIP, EnvAb, ExcerpMed, FutSurv, GeogAbPG, IBZ, PAIS, PollutAb, RRTA, SWA, WAE&RSA. *Bk. rev.:* 1-2. *Aud.:* Hs, Ga, Ac.

The Organisation for Economic Co-operation and Development (OECD), an international organization comprised of 29 member-countries, "is a unique forum permitting governments of the industralised democracies to study and formulate the best policies possible in all economic and social spheres." Contributing to this goal, it "collects and analyses a unique body of data that allows comparison of statistics across countries and provides macro-micro economic research and policy advice in fields that mirror policy-making ministries in governments." All of this research is made available through a large publishing mechanism, and this is one of those publications. Other excellent publications include *OECD Foreign Trade Statistics, OECD Main Economic Indicators, OECD Economic Studies,* and *OECD Economic Outlook.* The *OECD Observer* is written for a popular audience. It has a wealth of information on the member countries, and it also covers transitional economies, dynamic nonmember economies, and the developing world. It has a wide scope, encompassing "economic growth, labour markets, education, social policy, demography, industry, services, energy, finance trade, fiscal policy, public-sector management, environment, science and technology, investment and multinational enterprises, transport, agriculture and fisheries, taxation, competition and consumer policy, research and development, urban affairs, telecommunications, tourism, and rural development." Every issue has an editoral, articles on a theme, and additional titles. A very useful feature is the two to six pages of current statistics on the GDP, the consumer price index, and the leading indicators. Each year, subscribers receive a pocket book called *OECD in Figures,* a handy 60-page guide of statistics. Highly recommended for high school, academic, and public libraries.

2355. ***Oxford Bulletin of Economics and Statistics.*** Former titles (until 1973): *Oxford University. Institute of Economics and Statistics. Bulletin;* (until 1963): *Oxford University. Institute of Statistics. Bulletin.* [ISSN: 0305-9049] 1939. 5x/yr. GBP 300 print & online eds. Blackwell Publishing Ltd., 9600 Garsington Rd, PO Box 805, Oxford, OX4 2DQ, United Kingdom; jnlinfo@blackwellpublishers.co.uk; http://www.blackwellpublishing.com/. Illus., index, adv. Refereed. Circ: 1500. Vol. ends: Dec. Online: EBSCO Publishing; Gale Group; ingenta.com; OCLC Online Computer Library Center, Inc.; RoweCom Information Quest; Swets Blackwell. Reprint: PSC. *Indexed:* ABIn, FPA, ForAb, IBSS, JEL, PAIS, RRTA, RiskAb, SSCI, WAE&RSA. *Aud.:* Ac, Sa.

This bulletin's aim is to publish "international research papers on current practical issues in applied economics." An emphasis is placed on quality and the practicality of "theoretical interest and policy relevance" of each article. The journal covers applied economics very broadly, including both developed and developing countries. British economists are usually the authors, but Europeans and Americans are included as well. Academics, professionals, and students in the area of international economics will appreciate this journal.

2356. ***Oxford Economic Papers.*** [ISSN: 0030-7653] 1938. q. GBP 175. Ed(s): S. Cowan, A. Banerjee. Oxford University Press, Great Clarendon St, Oxford, OX2 6DP, United Kingdom; jnl.orders@oup.co.uk; http://www3.oup.co.uk/jnls. Illus., index, adv. Sample. Refereed. Circ: 200. Vol. ends: Oct. Microform: PQC. Online: EBSCO Publishing; Gale Group; HighWire Press; ingenta.com; Northern Light Technology, Inc.; RoweCom Information Quest; Swets Blackwell. Reprint: PQC; PSC. *Indexed:* ABIn, BAS, ExcerpMed, GeogAbPG, IBSS, JEL, PAIS, RRTA, S&F, SSCI, SSI, WAE&RSA. *Aud.:* Ac, Sa.

The *Oxford Economic Papers'* aim is to publish material in a wide range of areas in theoretical and applied economics. Contributions are accepted "in economic theory, applied economics, econometrics, economic development, economic history, and the history of economic thought." Special issues are regularly published, covering topics such as financial markets, public economics, and quantitative economic history. Although a great deal of this material centers on the United Kingdom, some of it focuses on general or other countries' problems, e.g., "The Sources of Unemployment in Canada." An issue typically has 8 to 11 articles. Recent titles include "Is There Really a European Business Cycle?," "Welfare Reform for Low Income Workers," and "Leadership and the Aggregation of International Collective Action." University and large college libraries should include this esteemed journal in their holdings.

2357. ***Petroleum Economist: the international energy journal.*** Formerly: *Petroleum Press Service.* [ISSN: 0306-395X] 1934. m. GBP 398 domestic; EUR 790 in Europe; USD 745 elsewhere. Ed(s): Derek Bamber. Euromoney Institutional Investor plc., Nestor House, Playhouse Yard, London, EC4V 5EX, United Kingdom; information@euromoneyplc.com; http://www.euromoney.com. Illus., adv. Sample. Circ: 4400. Vol. ends: Dec. Microform: PQC. Online: Florida Center for Library Automation; Gale Group; LexisNexis; Northern Light Technology, Inc.; OCLC Online Computer Library Center, Inc.; ProQuest Information & Learning; H.W. Wilson. Reprint: PQC. *Indexed:* ABIn, B&I, BPI, GeoRef, PAIS, PetrolAb. *Aud.:* Ga, Ac, Sa.

The scope of this specialized trade journal is the world oil and gas industry, but it has expanded coverage to include financial, accounting, and legal issues. Each issue has world oil and gas production and power summaries in "News in Brief" and "Analysis." As the foremost international journal in the energy industry, this title would benefit related special libraries and public, university, and government libraries.

Post-Communist Economies. See CIS and Eastern Europe section.

Post-Soviet Affairs. See CIS and Eastern Europe section.

2358. ***Public Choice.*** [ISSN: 0048-5829] 1966. 16x/yr. USD 1300 print or online ed. Ed(s): Gordon Tullock. Kluwer Academic Publishers, van Godewijckstraat 30, PO Box 17, Dordrecht, 3300 AA, Netherlands; services@wkap.nl; http://www.wkap.nl. Illus., index, adv. Sample. Refereed. Vol. ends: Dec. Microform: PQC. Online: EBSCO Publishing; ingenta.com; Kluwer Online; OCLC Online Computer Library Center, Inc.; Ovid Technologies, Inc.; RoweCom Information Quest; Swets Blackwell. Reprint: PQC; SWZ. *Indexed:* ABCPolSci, AgeL, ArtHuCI, HRA, IBSS, IBZ, IPSA, JEL, PAIS, PRA, PSA, RiskAb, SSCI, SUSA, SociolAb. *Bk. rev.:* 1-7, 500-2,000 words. *Aud.:* Ga, Ac, Sa.

Public Choice is an interdisciplinary journal of economics and political science. It was founded when economists and political scientists started to apply economic methods to problems in the realm of political science. "It has retained strong traces of economic methodology, but new and fruitful techniques have been developed which are not recognizable by economists." This journal is of value to those interested in "theoretical rigor, statistical testing, and applications to real-world problems." Editors are from the Economics Department at George Mason University, the Locke Institute, and the Center for Study of Public Choice. Each issue contains numerous articles, book reviews, and an author index for each volume. Included are book reviews, an author-volume index, and the call for papers. For large public libraries and academic collections.

2359. ***Quarterly Journal of Economics.*** [ISSN: 0033-5533] 1886. q. USD 190 print & online eds. (Individuals, USD 44 print & online eds.; Students, USD 28 print & online eds.). Ed(s): Alberto Albesina, Lawrence Katz. MIT Press, 55 Hayward St, Cambridge, MA 02142; journals-orders@mit.edu; http://mitpress.mit.edu. Illus., index, adv. Refereed. Circ: 5100 Paid. Vol. ends: Nov. Microform: PQC. Online: EBSCO Publishing; Florida Center for Library Automation; Gale Group; Ingenta Select; JSTOR (Web-based Journal Archive); OCLC Online Computer Library Center, Inc.; RoweCom Information Quest; Swets Blackwell; H.W. Wilson. Reprint: PQC; PSC. *Indexed:* ABIn, AgeL, AmH&L, BAS, BPI, CJA, ExcerpMed, GeogAbPG, HRA, IBSS, IBZ, JEL, RGPR, RRTA, RiskAb, SSCI, SSI, SUSA, SWR&A, WAE&RSA. *Aud.:* Ac, Sa.

Edited at the Department of Economics at Harvard University, this "is the oldest journal of economics in the English language." The traditional focus on microtheory has been "expanded to include both empirical and theoretical macroeconomics." Statistical methods and models are often used. A typical issue has 11 lengthy articles, sometimes controversial and always interesting. The authors are leading American economists, often affiliated with Harvard. This prestigious journal is essential for libraries serving professionals, academic economists, and well-educated students of economics.

2360. ***The Quarterly Review of Economics and Finance.*** Former titles (until 1992): *Quarterly Review of Economics and Business; Current Economic Comment.* [ISSN: 1062-9769] 1960. 5x/yr. EUR 381 (Individuals, EUR 91). Elsevier BV, North-Holland, Sara Burgerhartstraat 25, Amsterdam, 1055 KV, Netherlands; nlinfo-f@elsevier.nl; http://www.elsevier.nl. Illus., index, adv. Circ: 2000. Vol. ends: Winter. Microform: MIM; PQC. Online: EBSCO Publishing; Florida Center for Library Automation; Gale Group; ingenta.com; OCLC Online Computer Library Center, Inc.; ScienceDirect; Swets Blackwell; H.W. Wilson. Reprint: PQC; SCH. *Indexed:* ABIn, AgeL, BPI, IBSS, JEL, PAIS, PMA, RRTA, SSCI, WAE&RSA. *Aud.:* Ac, Sa.

This is the official journal of the Midwest Economic Association and the Midwest Finance Association, and it is published for the Bureau of Economic and Business Research at the University of Illinois at Urbana-Champaign by North-Holland. Covering economics, financial economics, and financial issues, this scholarly journal includes technical articles typically by American academic economists. A special feature is "Focus," where timely topics are explored. An issue could have seven to nine articles. Calls for papers, association news, and other tidbits are included. Professional and academic economists appreciate this journal.

2361. ***RAND Journal of Economics.*** Former titles (until 1984): *Bell Journal of Economics;* (until 1974): *Bell Journal of Economics and Management Science.* [ISSN: 0741-6261] 1970. q. USD 180 domestic; USD 195 foreign. Ed(s): James R Hosek. Rand Journal of Economics, 1700 Main St, Box 2138, Santa Monica, CA 90407-2138; rje@rand.org; http://www.rje.org. Illus., index. Refereed. Circ: 3000 Paid. Vol. ends: Winter. Microform: PQC. Online: EBSCO Publishing; Florida Center for Library Automation; Gale Group; JSTOR (Web-based Journal Archive); OCLC Online Computer Library Center, Inc.; ProQuest Information & Learning; H.W. Wilson. Reprint: PSC. *Indexed:* ABIn, ATI, BPI, CompR, EngInd, HRA, IBSS, JEL, PAIS, PRA, RRTA, RiskAb, SSCI, SSI, SUSA, WAE&RSA. *Aud.:* Ac, Sa.

This journal supports and encourages research "in the behavior of regulated industries, the economic analysis of organizations, and applied microeconomics." Empirical and theoretical papers in law and economics are accepted. Authors are usually connected to American universities. Highly recommended for large academic, government, business, and public libraries.

The Review of Black Political Economy. See African American section.

2362. ***The Review of Economic Studies.*** [ISSN: 0034-6527] 1933. q. GBP 167 print & online eds. Ed(s): M Armstrong, O Attanasio. Blackwell Publishing Ltd., 9600 Garsington Rd, PO Box 805, Oxford, OX4 2DQ, United Kingdom; customerservices@oxon.blackwellpublishing.com; http://www.blackwellpublishing.com/. Illus., index, adv. Sample. Refereed. Vol. ends: Oct. Online: EBSCO Publishing; Gale Group; ingenta.com; JSTOR (Web-based Journal Archive); Northern Light Technology, Inc.; OCLC Online Computer Library Center, Inc.; ProQuest Information & Learning; RoweCom Information Quest; Swets Blackwell. Reprint: PSC. *Indexed:* ABIn, AgeL, CCMJ, IBSS, JEL, LRI, MathSciNet, PAIS, RRTA, RiskAb, SSCI, SSI, WAE&RSA. *Aud.:* Ac, Sa.

This journal originated in 1933 with a group of young British and American economists. Its "object is to encourage research in theoretical and applied economics, especially by young economists." An issue may have seven or eight articles with extensive bibliographies. There is an author index in the last volume issue. This highly technical journal would be a valuable acquisition for professional and academic economists and large academic collections.

2363. ***The Review of Economic Theory.*** [ISSN: 1479-5663] 2004. q. GBP 225 (Corporations, GBP 450; Non-profit organizations, GBP 130). Ed(s): Dr. Martin J Osborne. Electronic Society for Social Scientists, University of St Andrews, Department of Economics, St. Andrews, KY16 9AL, United Kingdom; elsss@elsss.org; http://www.elsss.org/. Refereed. *Aud.:* Ac, SA.

The first journal launched by ELSSS (Electronic Learned Society for the Social Sciences), a not-for-profit organization whose aim is the wide dissemination of leading research. Its goal is "to create a premier field journal in par with other top journals in the field." The subscription cost is certainly very reasonable. Highly recommended for academic and special libraries. This new journal is funded by the Royal Economic Society, University of St. Andrews, and the Scottish Enterprise Fife. SPARC also endorses this project. The board of this journal aims to compete with Elsevier's *Journal of Economic Theory*, and with your help, it could.

2364. ***The Review of Economics and Statistics.*** [ISSN: 0034-6535] 1966. q. USD 275 print & online eds. (Individuals, USD 53 print & online eds.; Students, USD 28 print & online eds.). MIT Press, 5 Cambridge Center, Cambridge, MA 02142-1493; journals-orders@mit.edu; http://mitpress.mit.edu. Illus., index, adv. Sample. Refereed. Circ: 3500. Vol. ends: Nov. Microform: PQC. Online: EBSCO Publishing; Florida Center for Library Automation; Gale Group; Ingenta Select; JSTOR (Web-based Journal Archive); OCLC Online Computer Library Center, Inc.; RoweCom Information Quest; Swets Blackwell; H.W. Wilson. Reprint: PSC; SWZ. *Indexed:* ABIn, AgeL, Agr, BAS, BPI, ExcerpMed, GeogAbPG, HRA, IBSS, IBZ, IPSA, JEL, LRI, MCR, MagInd, PAIS, PRA, RRTA, SSCI, SSI, SUSA, SWA, WAE&RSA. *Aud.:* Ac, Sa.

Edited by the Department of Economics at Harvard University, this general journal covers "applied (especially quantitative) economics." The editorial board and the authors are academic or professional economists. Each issue has 14 to 18 articles and the "Notes" section contains one to eight papers. An important journal for university libraries, and very reasonably priced.

Review of Financial Studies. See Finance/Scholarly section.

2365. ***Review of Income and Wealth.*** Supersedes: *Income and Wealth Series.* [ISSN: 0034-6586] 1966. q. USD 200 print & online eds. Blackwell Publishing Ltd., 9600 Garsington Rd, PO Box 805, Oxford, OX4 2DQ, United Kingdom; jnlinfo@blackwellpublishers.co.uk; http://www.blackwellpublishing.com/. Refereed. Circ: 2000. Reprint: PSC. *Indexed:* AgeL, BAS, IBSS, JEL, PAIS, RiskAb, SSCI. *Aud.:* Ac, Sa.

This scholarly journal covers an increasingly studied area of economics, and it is recommended for academic libraries and institutions dealing with poverty/income issues. It is international in scope, and started in 1966. Its main objectives are "furthering research on national and economic and social accounting, including the development of concepts and definitions for the measurement and analysis of income and wealth, the development and further integration of systems of economic and social statistics, and related problems of statistical methodology." Edward Wolff, the managing editor, will be stepping down from his position in 2005.

2366. ***Review of Industrial Organization.*** [ISSN: 0889-938X] 1984. 8x/yr. EUR 594 print or online ed. Ed(s): William G Shepard. Kluwer Academic Publishers, van Godewijckstraat 30, PO Box 17, Dordrecht, 3300 AA, Netherlands; services@wkap.nl; http://www.wkap.nl. Illus., index. Sample. Refereed. Vol. ends: Dec. Microform: PQC. Online: EBSCO Publishing; ingenta.com; Kluwer Online; OCLC Online Computer Library Center, Inc.; Ovid Technologies, Inc.; RoweCom Information Quest; Swets Blackwell. Reprint: SWZ. *Indexed:* GeogAbPG, IBSS, JEL, SSCI, WAE&RSA. *Bk. rev.:* 5-7, 500-2,000 words. *Aud.:* Ac, Sa.

Published for the Industrial Organization Society, this review aims "to publish papers on all aspects of industrial organization. The main focus is on competition and monopoly in their many forms and processes and their effects on efficiency, innovation, and social conditions." Topics may range from the internal organization of enterprises to wide international comparison. Included is material on public policies dealing with antitrust, regulation, deregulation, public enterprise, privatization, economic sectors, and developed economies. This journal can benefit larger academic institutions.

2367. ***Review of Political Economy.*** [ISSN: 0953-8259] 1989. q. GBP 298 (Individuals, GBP 75). Ed(s): John Pheby. Carfax Publishing Ltd., 4 Park Sq, Milton Park, Abingdon, OX14 4RN, United Kingdom; enquiry@tandf.co.uk; http://www.tandf.co.uk/. Illus., index, adv. Refereed. Vol. ends: Oct. Online: EBSCO Publishing; Ingenta Select; Northern Light Technology, Inc.; OCLC Online Computer Library Center, Inc.; ProQuest Information & Learning; RoweCom Information Quest; Swets Blackwell. Reprint: PSC. *Indexed:* ABIn, IBSS, JEL, PSA, SociolAb. *Bk. rev.:* 2-5, 500-3,000 words. *Aud.:* Ga, Ac, Sa.

This review publishes "constructive and critical contributions in all areas of political economy, including the Post Keynesian, Sraffian, Marxian, Austrian, and Institutionalist traditions." Both theoretical and empirical research are utilized, but mathematics is limited due to editorial policy. Book reviews are also included. Highly recommended for college, university, and public libraries.

2368. ***Review of Social Economy.*** [ISSN: 0034-6764] 1948. q. GBP 129 (Individuals, GBP 54). Ed(s): John B Davis. Routledge, 11 New Fetter Ln, London, EC4P 4EE, United Kingdom; journals@routldege.com; http://www.routledge.com/routledge/journal/journals.html. Illus., adv. Refereed. Circ: 2000. Microform: PQC. Online: EBSCO Publishing; Florida Center for Library Automation; Gale Group; Ingenta Select; Northern Light Technology, Inc.; OCLC Online Computer Library Center, Inc.; RoweCom Information Quest; Swets Blackwell. Reprint: PQC; PSC; SCH. *Indexed:* ABS&EES, ASSIA, AgeL, ArtHuCI, BAS, BrHumI, CPL, IBSS, IBZ, IPSA, JEL, PAIS, PSA, RRTA, SSCI, SociolAb, WAE&RSA. *Bk. rev.:* 5-6, signed. *Aud.:* Ac, Sa.

Sponsored by the Association for Social Economics, this journal "investigates the relationship between social values and economics and the relation of economics to ethics, and focuses upon the social economy that encompasses the market economy." Themes covered include justice, need, poverty, income distribution, freedom, gender, environment, humanism, and more. Announcements and the call for papers are included. Strongly recommended for academic libraries.

2369. ***Scandinavian Journal of Economics.*** Former titles (until 1976): *Swedish Journal of Economics;* (until 1965): *Ekonomisk Tidskrift.* [ISSN: 0347-0520] 1899. q. GBP 209 print & online eds. Ed(s): Bertil Holmlund, Erling Steigum. Blackwell Publishing Ltd., 9600 Garsington Rd, PO Box 805, Oxford, OX4 2DQ, United Kingdom; jnlinfo@blackwellpublishers.co.uk; http://www.blackwellpublishing.com/. Adv. Refereed. Circ: 1100. Online: EBSCO Publishing; Gale Group; ingenta.com; OCLC Online Computer Library Center, Inc.; RoweCom Information Quest; Swets Blackwell. Reprint: SWZ. *Indexed:* ABIn, AgeL, IBSS, JEL, PAIS, SSCI. *Bk. rev.:* Number and length vary. *Aud.:* Ac, Sa.

"One of the oldest and most distinguished economic journals," this publication covers all areas of economics and related fields, and features theory and policy. The authors are international, and a special issue on a current topic is featured every year. Surveys of the work done by Nobel Memorial Prize Winners in Economics is a notable feature. Highly recommended for academic libraries and special libraries.

2370. ***Scottish Journal of Political Economy.*** [ISSN: 0036-9292] 1954. 5x/yr. GBP 150 print & online eds. Ed(s): Robert A Hart, Anton Muscatelli. Blackwell Publishing Ltd., 9600 Garsington Rd, PO Box 805, Oxford, OX4 2DQ, United Kingdom; jnlinfo@blackwellpublishers.co.uk; http://www.blackwellpublishing.com/. Illus., index, adv. Sample. Refereed. Circ: 1500. Vol. ends: Nov. Online: EBSCO Publishing; ingenta.com; OCLC Online Computer Library Center, Inc.; RoweCom Information Quest; Swets Blackwell. Reprint: PSC. *Indexed:* ABIn, AmH&L, BAS, BrHumI, GeogAbPG, IBSS, IndVet, JEL, PAIS, PSA, RRTA, SSCI, SociolAb, WAE&RSA. *Bk. rev.:* 6-9, 700-1,000 words. *Aud.:* Ga, Ac, Sa.

Sponsored by the Scottish Economic Society, this is "a generalist journal with a explicitly international reach." Contributions are from the United Kindgom, Europe, North America, Australasia, and occasionally Africa, the Middle East, and the Far East. Typically, each issue has four to eight articles followed occasionally by review articles and/or book reviews. Also, there is a special conference issue each year. An excellent journal, recommended for professional and academic economists and for large academic economics programs.

2371. ***Socio-Economic Planning Sciences: the international journal of public sector decision-making.*** [ISSN: 0038-0121] 1967. q. EUR 649 (Individuals, EUR 50). Ed(s): Barnett R Parker. Pergamon, The Boulevard, Langford Ln, East Park, Kidlington, OX5 1GB, United Kingdom. Illus., index, adv. Refereed. Circ: 1700. Microform: MIM; PQC. Online: Gale Group; ingenta.com; ScienceDirect; Swets Blackwell. *Indexed:* ABCPolSci, AIAP, AgeL, CIJE, ExcerpMed, FPA, ForAb, IBSS, IPSA, MCR, PAIS, PSA, RRTA, RiskAb, S&F, SSCI, SUSA, SociolAb, WAE&RSA. *Bk. rev.:* Various number and length. *Aud.:* Ac.

Projecting the application of plans and systems of economic improvement is the main thrust of this periodical. The whole world is the subject, no single nation. If current trends discern a favored course, this periodical will give increasing attention to a social psychology system applied to a checks-and-balances political philosophy, in concert with an economic philosophy of equitable distribution. But contrasting views can be found, for example, in an article dealing with "the applicability of the analytic hierarchy process." Authors contribute from all over the world, but are published in English. Recommended for academic audiences.

2372. ***Southern Economic Journal.*** [ISSN: 0038-4038] 1933. q. Non-members, USD 105. Ed(s): Jonathan H Hamilton. Southern Economic Association, PO Box 1897, Lawrence, KS 66044-8897; SEJ1@dale.cba.ufl.edu; http://www.okstate.edu/economics/journal/jour1.html. Illus., index, adv. Sample. Refereed. Circ: 2800 Paid. Vol. ends: Apr. Microform: MIM; PQC. Online: bigchalk; EBSCO Publishing; Florida Center for Library Automation; Gale Group; Northern Light Technology, Inc.; OCLC Online Computer Library Center, Inc.; ProQuest Information & Learning; H.W. Wilson. Reprint: PQC; PSC; SCH. *Indexed:* ABIn, ABS&EES, AgeL, ArtHuCI, BPI, CJA, GeogAbPG, IBSS, JEL, PAIS, RRTA, SSCI, SSI, SUSA, WAE&RSA. *Bk. rev.:* 24-26, 750-2,250 words. *Aud.:* Ac, Sa.

Published by the Southern Economic Association, College of Business Administrstration, Oklahoma State University at Stillwater, this solid journal typically includes 11 to 13 authoritative articles in both theoretical and applied economics. Each issue includes numerous book reviews. An cumulative index dating back to 1933 is available. Highly recommended for academic collections and professional/academic economists.

2373. ***Weltwirtschaftliches Archiv.*** [ISSN: 0043-2636] 1914. q. EUR 129.40 domestic; EUR 136.10 foreign; EUR 36. Springer-Verlag, Tiergartenstr 17, Heidelberg, 69121, Germany. Illus., index, adv. Refereed. Circ: 1800. Vol. ends: No. 4. *Indexed:* BAS, IBSS, IBZ, JEL, PAIS, SSCI. *Bk. rev.:* 10-16, 700-2,100 words. *Aud.:* Ac, Sa.

Internationally renowned and affiliated with the esteemed Kiel Institute of World Economics, *Weltwirtschaftliches Archiv* is "dedicated to the empirical application and policy relevance of international economic research." It is committed "to the study of international economics; trade in goods and services; commercial policy; currency systems and exchange rates; capital flows and migration of people; economic development, especially in nonindustrialized countries; and stabilization policies, especially in the industrialized world." Each issue has six or seven articles, shorter papers, comments, reports, book reviews, and announcements of new books. Articles are written mainly in English. This scholarly journal is an excellent choice for international economists and graduate students.

2374. *The World Bank Economic Review.* [ISSN: 0258-6770] 1986. 3x/yr. GBP 89 GBP 75 academic. Ed(s): Francois Bourguignon. Oxford University Press, 2001 Evans Rd, Cary, NC 27513; http://www3.oup.co.uk/jnls/. Illus. Refereed. Circ: 11000. Microform: PQC. Online: HighWire Press; ingenta.com; Northern Light Technology, Inc.; OCLC Online Computer Library Center, Inc.; ProQuest Information & Learning; Swets Blackwell. Reprint: PSC. *Indexed:* AbAn, BAS, FPA, ForAb, GeogAbPG, IBSS, IBZ, JEL, PAIS, PRA, S&F, SSCI, WAE&RSA. *Aud.:* Ac, Sa.

A very widely read scholarly publication, *World Bank Economic Review* is a professional journal for the dispersion of World Bank–sponsored research on policy analysis and choice. The international readers are "economists and social scientists in government, business, international universities, and development research institutions." Policy is emphasized over theoretical or methodological issues. Readers need to be familiar with economic theory and analysis but not necessarily proficient in mathematics. Six to nine articles are written by World Bank staff and economists. There are occasionally special issues by non-bank specialists. Recommended for academic libraries.

2375. *World Bank Research Observer.* [ISSN: 0257-3032] 1986. s-a. GBP 77 GBP 64 academic. Ed(s): Shantayana Devarajan. Oxford University Press, Great Clarendon St, Oxford, OX2 6DP, United Kingdom; jnl.orders@oup.co.uk; http://www3.oup.co.uk/jnls. Illus. Refereed. Circ: 5000. Microform: CIS; PQC. Online: The Dialog Corporation; HighWire Press; ingenta.com; Northern Light Technology, Inc.; OCLC Online Computer Library Center, Inc.; ProQuest Information & Learning; Swets Blackwell; H.W. Wilson. Reprint: PSC. *Indexed:* ABIn, ABS&EES, AbAn, BPI, ForAb, GeogAbPG, IBSS, JEL, PAIS, S&F, SSCI, WAE&RSA. *Aud.:* Ga, Ac, Sa.

Published by the World Bank, this journal is intended for anyone who has an interest in development issues. Written by well-established economists for the nonspecialist, key issues in development economics research and policy are examined. Surveys of the latest literature and World Bank research are included. The editorial board is drawn from the international community of economists. Each issue has six to eight articles. Highly recommended for policy makers, special libraries, and large library systems, both public and academic.

2376. *World Development.* Incorporates: *New Commonwealth.* [ISSN: 0305-750X] 1973. m. EUR 1687 (Qualified personnel, EUR 256; Students, EUR 75). Ed(s): Oliver T. Coomes, K. Molgaard. Pergamon, The Boulevard, Langford Ln, East Park, Kidlington, OX5 1GB, United Kingdom; nlinfo-f@elsevier.nl; http://www.elsevier.nl. Illus., adv. Refereed. Circ: 1600. Vol. ends: No. 29. Microform: PQC. Online: Gale Group; ingenta.com; ScienceDirect; Swets Blackwell. *Indexed:* ABCPolSci, ABIn, ABS&EES, BAS, BrHumI, DSA, FPA, FS&TA, ForAb, FutSurv, GeogAbPG, HortAb, IBSS, IPSA, JEL, PAIS, PRA, PSA, RRTA, RiskAb, S&F, SSCI, SSI, SWA, SociolAb, WAE&RSA. *Aud.:* Ac.

This multidisciplinary development studies journal is highly cited and respected. Its scope covers ways to improve the human condition, so the aspects covered are wide ranging, and include poverty, unemployment, malnutrition, disease, lack of shelter, environmental problems, and conflicts. The levels presented can range from local to national. A solid recommendation for planners, social scientists, academic and special libraries, but review closely due to price.

Electronic Journals

2377. *The B E Journals in Theoretical Economics.* 2001. a. USD 300 (Individuals, USD 35). Ed(s): Dilip Abreu, Patrick Bolton. Berkeley Electronic Press, 805 Camelia St., # 2, Berkeley, CA 94710-1417; info@bepress.com; http://www.bepress.com. *Aud.:* Ac, Sa.

The Berkeley Electronic Press initiated this project to "create a new standard in scholarly publishing." There are three web-based economics journals to peruse, each has four subsections, and all articles are peer reviewed. *The B E Journals in Theoretical Economics* cover "all areas of economic theory, including decision theory, game theory, general equilibrium theory, and the theory of economic mechanisms." *The B E Journals in Macroeconomics* "publishes in both theoretical and applied macroeconomics." A wide range of topics is covered, including business cycles, economic growth, monetary economics, labor economics, finance, development economics, political economics, public economics, and econometric theory. *The B E Journals in Economic Analysis & Policy*'s scope is microeconomics issues in business and public policy. Topics of interest include "the interaction of firms, the functioning of markets, the formulation of domestic and international policy, and the design of organizations and institutions. Articles can be on corporate finance, industrial organization, international trade, public finance, law and economics or other related fields." There is a nominal fee for the author to publish in these journals, and a small number of articles are available. I still have hope that these journals will take off.

2378. *B Quest.* [ISSN: 1084-3981] 1996. irreg. Ed(s): Dr. Carole E Scott. State University of West Georgia, Richards College of Business, 1600 Maple St, Carrollton, GA 30118-3020; cscott@westga.edu; http://www.westga.edu/~bquest. Illus. Sample. Refereed. *Aud.:* Ac.

This free web journal of applied topics in business and economics is produced by the State University of West Georgia's College of Business. Articles are written by academics and practitioners. The objective of this journal is "to serve as an interface between academic disciplines and between academicians and practitioners." Featured is a monthly economic outlook by nationally known economist and leading forecaster Donald Ratajczak. Articles are continuously published throughout the year and peer-reviewed papers are marked. Useful web links are included, such as academicians' papers and business information.

2379. *Economics Research Network.* irreg. Social Science Electronic Publishing, Michael_Jensen@ssrn.com; http://www.ssrn.com. *Aud.:* Ga, Ac, Sa.

Social Science Research Network's goal is "rapid worldwide dissemination of social science research and is composed of specialized research networks in each of the social sciences." Hal Varian is on the board of trustees. Overall, the e-library has two parts: a database containing over 52,000 scholarly working papers and an e-paper collection with over 31,800 full-text documents. It has grown quite a bit since the last edition of *Magazines for Libraries.* Also included are papers that can be purchased. *Economics Research Network* is extremely important to economists. Other networks include accounting, finance, legal, information systems, and management. Professional announcements, calls for papers, special issues of journals, and professional jobs are listed. A must for economic researchers and academic libraries. Individual and institutional pricing is offered.

2380. *The Economists' Papers Project.* irreg. Duke University, Rare Book, Manuscript, and Special Collections Library, Durham, NC 27708-0185; http://scriptorium.lib.duke.edu/. *Aud.:* Ac.

To preserve the papers of modern economists, Duke University's Rare Book, Manuscript, and Special Collections Library, with assistance from Duke's economics department, has developed *The Economists' Papers Project* (*EPP*). Currently, the *EPP* consists of the papers of 30 eminent economists. Twentieth-century economic thought is prominently featured. In July 2003, there was a History of Economics conference and the web site will be revised to reflect more papers. At least three new collections will be added: American Economic Association records and papers from Tibor Scitovsky and Lionel McKenzie. "The Kenneth Arrow Papers contain the notes he took as a student at City College of New York and Columbia University, and the notes and syllabi for the courses he later taught on Price and Allocation Theory, The Theory of Competitive Equilibrium, and The Theory of Information and Organization." Also included is material related to his roles as consultant and political advocate. Other economists included are William J. Baumol, Arthur I. Bloomfield, Martin Bronfenbrenner, Jesse Chickering, Robert Clower, Lauchlin Currie, Paul Davidson, Evsey D. Domar, Frank W. Fetter, Nicholas Georgescu-Roegen, W. M. Gorman, Earl J. Clifford Hildreth, Homer Jones, Axel Leijonhufvud, H. Gregg Lewis, Carl Menger, Karl Menger, Lloyd Metzler, Oskar Morgenstern, Douglass C. North, Vernon L. Smith, Joseph Spengler, Wolfgang F. Stolper, Sidney Weintraub, Martin Shubik, Albert E. Rees, and Don Patinkin. The Patinkin papers, the largest of the collections, consist of 80 boxes of which 44 contain correspondence. They are from his professional career and "involve almost every colleague: Kenneth Arrow, Milton Friedman, Roy Harrod, Harry Johnson, Simon Kuznets, Franco Modigliani, and Paul Samuelson, among literally hundreds of others." The papers of Mark Perlman, founder and editor from 1969 to 1981 of the *Journal of Economic Literature*, contain ten boxes of *JEL* correspondence. "A valuable resource in the history of economic thought!"

2381. ***Issues in Political Economy: undergraduate student research in Economics.*** a. Issues in Political Economy, c/o Steven Greenlaw, Professor and Chair of Economics, Fredericksburg, VA 22401; IPE@elon.edu.; http://www.elon.edu/ipe/. Refereed. *Aud.:* Ac.

An annual, this student-run journal is written by undergraduates, with oversight from faculty at Mary Washington College and Elon University, in the time-honored belief "that the best way to learn economics is to do economics." They are to be commended for keeping this project going. All papers go through a double-blind review and must be related to economics. Definitely worth a look.

2382. ***N B E R Reporter OnLine.*** q. National Bureau of Economic Research, 1050 Massachusetts Ave, 3rd Fl, Cambridge, MA 02138-5398; http://www.nber.org/reporter/. *Aud.:* Ac, Sa.

The National Bureau of Economic Research (NBER), founded in 1920, is a private, nonprofit, nonpartisan research organization. Numerous American Nobel Prize winners in economics have been researchers at the NBER. With this reputation, it is hard to pass up any information produced by them. Authors are leading university professors. The *Reporter OnLine* includes research summaries and program reports from the recent issues of the *NBER Reporter*, a print source that covers broad areas of research. Also, there are archives of two other publications, *NBER Digest* and a searchable index to over 5,000 *NBER Working Papers.* These are available at no additional cost to print subscribers (free or low-cost to begin with). A print publication and web site not to be missed for current trends, issues, and information. Also on the NBER web site are great new features: e-mail notifications of new economic releases and links to economic information such as The Economic Report of the President.

2383. ***NetEc.*** m. Ed(s): Thomas Krichel. NetEc, NetEc@mcc.ac.uk; http://netec.mcc.ac.uk. *Aud.:* Ac, Sa.

NetEc is a "collection of projects that aim to improve the scholarly commitment in economics via electronic media," and is "working towards a future with [an] exchange of academic ideas between those who generate them." Included are *WoPEc,* a database of electronic working papers; *BibEc,* a bibliography of printed working papers in economics; *WebEc,* a large set of web links of interest to economists; *CodEc,* a collection of programs for economists; *HoPEEcm,* home page papers in economics; and *JokEc,* jokes about economists and economics (one of my favorites!). *WoPEc* has access to over 55,000 economics working papers that may or may not be free. This is a major site for economic information on the Internet. Most data archives of working papers are indexed here, including the *Economics Working Paper Archive.* A link to *RFE* (*Resources for Economists on the Internet*), the premier index to economic information on the web by William Goffe and sponsored by the American Economic Association, is included. An invaluable web site for economics departments, institutes, and research centers.

2384. ***Student Economic Review.*** 1987. irreg. University of Dublin, Regents House, Trinity College, House 6, Trinity College, Dublin, 2, Ireland; http://econserv2.bess.tcd.ie/SER/. *Aud.:* Ac.

This unique journal is edited and written by third-year students from the Department of Economics, Trinity College, Dublin. It has full-text articles on a wide range of economic topics. Essays are usually chosen by professors from class assignments, but there is some independent research as well. Some recent papers are "Econometrics: Science or Pulp Fiction?," "Inflation Targeting: A New Answer to an Old Problem?," and "Theories of Distribution: Rawls versus Nozick?" Graduate thesis abstracts are available for review. Coverage is from 1994. Keep your eye on this site!

2385. ***Studies in Nonlinear Dynamics and Econometrics.*** [ISSN: 1081-1826] 1996. q. USD 140 (Individuals, USD 35). Berkeley Electronic Press, 805 Camelia St., # 2, Berkeley, CA 94710-1417; info@bepress.com; http://www.bepress.com. Refereed. *Indexed:* JEL, SSCI. *Aud.:* Ac, Sa.

This electronic journal is now published by the Berkeley Electronic Press. It is still peer reviewed, and the "editors, board, and pool of authors were unaffected by the move." The scope covers theoretical and applied papers in the fields of "statistics and dynamical systems theory that may increase our understanding of economic and financial markets." "Algorithms and rapid communications are also published." The entire back set of issues is available. Professional economists and researchers will appreciate this technical journal.

Transition Newsletter. See CIS and Eastern Europe/Electronic Journals section.

2386. ***University Avenue Undergraduate Journal of Economics.*** 1998. a. Illinois State University, College of Business, 328 William Hall, Normal, IL 61761; http://www.econ.ilstu.edu/uauje/. Illus. Refereed. *Aud.:* Ac.

Run entirely by undergraduates from Illinois State University and Illinois Wesleyan University, this electronic peer-evaluated journal has a wide scope and accepts economic papers from undergraduate students at academic institutions worldwide. Back issues are, of course, available. Definitely worth a look.

■ EDUCATION

General, K-12/Comparative Education and International/Educational Psychology and Measurement, Special Education, Counseling/Higher Education/Specific Subjects and Teaching Methods

See also Classroom Magazines; and Parenting sections.

Gladys I. Dratch, Head of Collection Development, Monroe C. Gutman Library, Harvard University, Graduate School of Education, Cambridge, MA 02138

Deborah S. Garson, Head of Research Services, Monroe C. Gutman Library, Harvard University, Graduate School of Education, Cambridge, MA 02138

Introduction

As a field, education is both interdisciplinary and inclusive of teaching and learning for pre-K to older learners. Within the social sciences, education relates particularly to the fields of psychology and sociology, as the selection of titles below indicates. By virtue of the teaching and learning components of education, however, the connections to other fields are evident, and readers may wish to examine subject-specific sections of this publication. As a discipline, the field of education is grounded in the traditional research frameworks of philosophy, theory, and methodology that form the basis for applications in many types of educational settings.

The education journals represent a broad range of publications, from the academic and scholarly to those intended for practical applications in the classroom. Journal contents reflect current educational trends and issues, as well as historical analyses of educational theory and practice. Current topics focus on educational reform, distance education, teacher and student assessment, global trends in education, international education, educational counseling, and educational technology.

Many of the printed journals indicate online availability. The online version of the publication may provide a table of contents, abstracts, full texts, or selected full-text articles. Coverage will vary and may include current issues and/or earlier archived issues. Access may be freely available or may require a subscription through a publisher or a contract with a database provider. In this section, the print journal entries indicate online availability based on web site information. Absence of a URL does not indicate the lack of an online version.

The Electronic Journals subsection contains titles available only electronically. The growth of electronic journals in every field has significant implications for research and practice. While the electronic journals listed here reflect the same educational issues and trends as in the printed journals, the electronic format in many cases offers the added value of an interactive dialogue with readers, authors, and editors.

Basic Periodicals

Ems (teachers): *The Elementary School Journal, Middle School Journal, The Reading Teacher, School Arts, Teaching Pre K-8*; Hs (teachers): *American Secondary Education, English Journal, The High School Journal, History Teacher*; Ga: *Change, The Education Digest, The ERIC Review, Phi Delta Kappan*; Ac: *Academe, American Journal of Education, The Chronicle of Higher Education, College English, Harvard Educational Review, Teachers College Record.*

Basic Abstracts and Indexes

Current Index to Journals in Education, Education Index, Resources in Education.

General, K-12

2387. *American Educational Research Journal.* [ISSN: 0002-8312] 1964. q. USD 61 (Individuals, USD 44). American Educational Research Association, 1230 17th St, N W, Washington, DC 20036-3078; http://aera.net/. Illus., adv. Refereed. Circ: 19800. Vol. ends: Winter. Microform: PQC. Online: OCLC Online Computer Library Center, Inc.; ProQuest Information & Learning; H.W. Wilson. *Indexed:* ArtHuCI, CIJE, CommAb, ECER, EduInd, HEA, IBZ, L&LBA, PsycholAb, SSCI, SWA. *Aud.:* Ac.

Within each issue this journal publishes articles in two sections under separate editorships and editorial boards: "Social and Institutional Analysis" and "Teaching, Learning, and Human Development." Addressing an audience of researchers, practitioners, and policymakers from many disciplines, the articles are lengthy and substantive, generally 20 to 30 or more pages long, representing the publication's stated focus on original empirical and theoretical studies and analyses in education. In the first section, the research centers on major political, cultural, social, economic, and organizational issues in education. This section is followed by articles that examine various aspects of teaching, learning, and human development in different types of educational settings. Eight or nine articles per issue provide in-depth research findings and analyses with extensive notes, tables, figures, and references. This is an essential resource for advanced undergraduates, graduate students, and academicians. URL: http://www.aera.net/pubs/aerj

2388. *American Educator.* [ISSN: 0148-432X] 1977. q. USD 8. Ed(s): Elizabeth McPike. American Federation of Teachers, 555 New Jersey Ave, N W, Washington, DC 20001; http://www.aft.org/. Illus., adv. Circ: 700000. Vol. ends: Fall. Reprint: PQC. *Indexed:* ABS&EES, BiogInd, CIJE, EduInd, MLA-IB, MagInd, RGPR. *Bk. rev.:* 1, 2,500 words. *Aud.:* Ga, Ac.

Addressing an audience of teachers and other school and higher education professionals, this publication of the American Federation of Teachers contains a variety of articles on topics for a wide range of reader interests. There are opinion pieces on parenting and on student attitudes, for example, practical and informational articles for applications in school settings, and discussions on the national or international school scene, covering such topics as school reform and standards. Issues often have biographical essays and tributes to important historical figures, educators, and authors that are helpful for professional development and classroom use. Recommended for public, academic, and school libraries. URL: http://www.aft.org/american_educator

2389. *American Journal of Education.* Formerly (until vol.88, Nov. 1979): *School Review.* [ISSN: 0195-6744] 1893. q. USD 111 (Individuals, USD 34; Students, USD 28). Ed(s): William Lowe Boyd. University of Chicago Press, Journals Division, PO Box 37005, Chicago, IL 60637; orders@press.uchicago.edu; http://www.journals.uchicago.edu. Illus., index, adv. Sample. Refereed. Circ: 2100 Paid. Vol. ends: Aug. Microform: PMC; PQC. Online: EBSCO Publishing; Florida Center for Library Automation; Gale Group. Reprint: PQC; PSC. *Indexed:* AmH&L, ArtHuCI, BRI, CBRI, CIJE, EduInd, IBZ, IMFL, L&LBA, PsycholAb, SSCI, SociolAb. *Bk. rev.:* 3-5, 500 words. *Aud.:* Ga, Ac.

This journal publishes scholarly articles with original approaches to a diverse range of educational topics, from the methodological and theoretical to matters of administration and policy in the schools. Historical and current perspectives for all school settings are represented. Particularly emphasized are research reports, theoretical statements, philosophical arguments, critical syntheses, and integration of educational inquiry, policy, and practice. There are generally two articles per issue. Articles have focused on immigrant Latinos and literacy development, the relationship between high school graduation and the various state policies of assessment and accountability, and research on the teaching of English with the aid of a theoretical framework. The book reviews are lengthy and most issues also have a review essay. This is a basic title for graduate students, faculty, and practitioners. URL: http://www.journals.uchicago.edu/AJE/home.html

2390. *American School Board Journal.* [ISSN: 0003-0953] 1891. m. USD 54. Ed(s): Sally Zakariya. National School Boards Association, 1680 Duke St, Alexandria, VA 22314-3493. Illus., index, adv. Sample. Circ: 40000 Paid. Vol. ends: Dec. Microform: PQC. Reprint: PQC. *Indexed:* CIJE, EduInd. *Bk. rev.:* 1, 300-1,200 words. *Aud.:* Ga, Sa.

Published by the American School Boards Association, this journal carries articles on current issues in the field and topics in the news. Authored by faculty and practitioners, articles are directed at an audience of school board members and school administrators. Some topics have been school district purchasing, school security, and issues of homework. Regular departments include letters from readers, research findings on particular topics, school law rulings on specific cases, a new section of education news and trends, and book reviews. Special supplements for subscribers of *ASBJ* are the Magna Awards, a yearly recognition of programs for major school district initiatives nationwide, and four issues of the print journal, *Electronic School*, which focuses on technology in the schools. The online edition of *Electronic School* contains all the articles in the print edition and additional material as well. Recommended for school, public, and academic libraries with an education program. URL: http://www.asbj.com

2391. *American Secondary Education.* [ISSN: 0003-1003] 1970. 3x/yr. USD 30 domestic; USD 40 foreign. American Secondary Education, c/o James A. Rycik, Ed, 401 College Avenue, Ashland, OH 44805; qvanderz@ashland.edu; http://www.ashland.edu/ase. Adv. Sample. Refereed. Circ: 400 Paid. Microform: PQC. Online: EBSCO Publishing; OCLC Online Computer Library Center, Inc.; ProQuest Information & Learning; H.W. Wilson. *Indexed:* CIJE, EduInd. *Aud.:* Ac.

Serving teachers, administrators, and all those involved in public and private secondary education, this journal examines current secondary school issues. Written by practitioners and researchers in the field, articles focus on theories, research, and practice, with discussions on such topics as controlling pupil behavior in the classroom, implementing critical-thinking instruction, the impact of school finance litigation, a qualitative study of magnet schools, and designing and implementing a peer-coaching program. Most issues have a column for an opinion or commentary and suggestions for use in the schools as techniques for handling student harassment in a high school setting. Book reviews are included. Recommended for school and academic libraries with an education program. URL: http://www.ashland.edu/journals/ase/main.htm

2392. *Childhood Education.* Incorporates (in 1991): *A C E I Exchange.* [ISSN: 0009-4056] 1924. bi-m. USD 65 non-members. Ed(s): Anne Watson Bauer. Association for Childhood Education International, 17904 Georgia Ave, Ste 215, Olney, MD 20832-2277; aceihq@aol.com; http://www.acei.org. Illus., adv. Refereed. Circ: 11500 Paid. Microform:

PMC; PQC. Online: Florida Center for Library Automation; Gale Group; OCLC Online Computer Library Center, Inc.; ProQuest Information & Learning; H.W. Wilson. Reprint: PQC. *Indexed:* BRI, CBRI, CIJE, ECER, EduInd, IMFL, MagInd, PsycholAb. *Bk. rev.:* 40-50, 75-400 words, signed. *Aud.:* Ga, Ac, Sa.

This refereed publication of the Association for Childhood Education International is focused on the development and education of children from infancy through early adolescence. It is geared toward an audience of teachers, teacher educators, parents, child care workers, administrators, librarians, and others with an interest in the field. The editors encourage articles on practices in the classroom and in other settings, international programs and practices, and reviews of research. Articles have covered a wide range of useful topics, including biracial children's development of identity, phonemic awareness, child sexual abuse, conflict resolution in a Head Start classroom, child care and education in Ghana, teaching early childhood education online, and interactive toys and children's development. Columns address issues in education, the needs of parents, and teaching strategies. Includes reviews of books for children, reviews and lists of professional books, special publications and reports, and discussions on technology in the classroom. Offers two annual theme issues, such as an international issue on schooling in countries throughout the world. This is highly recommended for school, public, and academic libraries.

2393. ***The Clearing House: a journal for middle schools, junior and senior high schools.*** [ISSN: 0009-8655] 1925. bi-m. USD 86 (Individuals, USD 45). Ed(s): Rachel Petrowsky. Heldref Publications, 1319 18th St, NW, Washington, DC 20036-1802; subscribe@heldref.org; http://www.heldref.org. Illus., index, adv. Sample. Refereed. Circ: 1500 Paid. CD-ROM: ProQuest Information & Learning. Online: bigchalk; EBSCO Publishing; Florida Center for Library Automation; Gale Group; Northern Light Technology, Inc.; OCLC Online Computer Library Center, Inc.; ProQuest Information & Learning; SoftLine Information; H.W. Wilson. Reprint: PSC. *Indexed:* ASIP, BusEdI, CIJE, ConsI, EduInd, LRI, MagInd. *Aud.:* Ac.

The content of this peer-reviewed and well-indexed journal is geared to the interests of middle level and high school teachers and administrators. The articles are based on research and school practices with a wide range of educational trends and issues, including school effectiveness, learning styles, curriculum, guidance and counseling, special education, instructional leadership, testing and measurement, and international education. Some issues have a special section with articles focusing on a special theme, such as school choice. Occasionally there are articles that present opinions on current issues of concern and debate. Articles are authored by academicians, administrators, and consultants in the field. Recommended for school libraries and academic libraries with education programs.

2394. ***Curriculum Review.*** Former titles (until Dec. 1975): *C A S Review; C S Review.* [ISSN: 0147-2453] 1960. m. USD 108 in US & Canada; USD 122 elsewhere. Ed(s): David Murray. W D & S Publishing, 1200 Tices Lane, 205, East Brunswick, NJ 08816; http://www.dealersedge.com. Illus., adv. Circ: 4800. Vol. ends: Sep/May. Microform: PQC. Online: EBSCO Publishing; Florida Center for Library Automation; Gale Group; OCLC Online Computer Library Center, Inc.; ProQuest Information & Learning; H.W. Wilson. Reprint: PQC. *Indexed:* BRI, CBRI, EduInd, MRD. *Bk. rev.:* 15-25, 150-500 words. *Aud.:* Ga, Ac.

This is a practical report issued monthly during the school year. It aims to assist K-12 teachers and administrators with ideas for the classroom, tips on resources, information about successful schools and projects, and news in the field. There are columns that present readers' ideas and experiences, offer quotations from educators that are inspiring or indicative of current education concerns, technology updates, useful techniques that point out what's working in schools and classrooms, some highlights of education news, interviews with educators, and reviews of school web sites. A section on resources for the classroom provides an abstract of useful books for students and a CD-ROM review. Available online. This is a useful publication for school libraries and libraries serving programs in undergraduate or graduate education. URL: http://www.paper-clip.com/curriculumreview/cr.asp

2395. ***Democracy & Education: the magazine for classroom teachers.*** [ISSN: 1085-3545] 1986. q. USD 40 (Individuals, USD 35; Students, USD 25). Ed(s): Jaylynne Hutchinson. Institute for Democracy in Education, Ohio University, College of Education, Athens, OH 45701-2979; democracy@ohiou.ed. Illus., adv. Refereed. Circ: 650. Vol. ends: Fall. *Aud.:* Ac.

This publication for classroom teachers is the journal of the Institute for Democracy in Education based at Ohio University, Athens, Ohio. It is written by and for teachers, administrators, faculty, students, parents, counselors, essentially all those who are involved in the educational process in K-16 and committed to democratic classroom practice. Articles and essays describe classroom experiences, projects, activities, and useful resources and discuss major issues related to practicing democratic ideals in the schools. Special *D&E* themes have focused on the legacy of Paulo Freire, democracy in the classroom, children at risk, gender and education, and lesbian, gay, transgendered and bisexual issues in education. Recommended for school and academic libraries.

2396. ***The E R I C Review.*** [ISSN: 1065-1160] 1990. a. Ed(s): Lynn Smarte. ACCESS ERIC, 2277 Research Blvd, Rockville, MD 20850; accesseric@accesseric.org; http://www.eric.ed.gov. Refereed. Circ: 50000. *Indexed:* EduInd, PAIS. *Aud.:* Ac.

Each issue of this publication focuses on a particular theme, providing information about research on the topic, resources, relevant programs, and articles. Articles are written by experts in the field and may be reprinted from other sources, such as the ERIC *Digest*. An issue discussing children's development of reading skills is directed at an audience of parents. Other issues have concentrated on urban and rural schools, school safety and the prevention of violence, K-8 science and mathematics education, and early intervention for the preparation of students for postsecondary education. Information about ERIC services is also found in each issue. A subscription to the print version of *ER* is free, and it is also available full-text online at the ACCESS ERIC web site. Early issues are also available as ERIC documents. Recommended for school, public, and academic libraries.

2397. ***Early Childhood Education Journal.*** Formerly (until 1995): *Day Care and Early Education.* [ISSN: 1082-3301] 1973. q. USD 522 print or online ed. Ed(s): Dr. Mary Jalongo. Kluwer Academic / Plenum Publishers, 233 Spring St Fl 7, New York, NY 10013-1522; http://www.wkap.nl/. Illus., adv. Sample. Refereed. Circ: 10000 Paid. Vol. ends: Summer. Microform: PQC. Online: EBSCO Publishing; ingenta.com; Kluwer Online; OCLC Online Computer Library Center, Inc.; Ovid Technologies, Inc.; RoweCom Information Quest; Swets Blackwell. Reprint: ISI; PQC. *Indexed:* BRI, CBRI, CIJE, ECER, EduInd, ExcerpMed, L&LBA, MRD, SWR&A. *Bk. rev.:* 1-5, 50-500 words, signed. *Aud.:* Ac, Sa.

A peer-reviewed publication focused on the education and care of young children from birth through age eight. Intended for early childhood practitioners such as classroom teachers and child care providers, the journal publishes articles that address the issues, trends, policies, and practices of the field. Contributors have covered topics of curriculum, child care programs, administration, staff development, equity issues, health and nutrition, facilities, and child development. Recent issues consider literacy development, family child care in the United States, social skills, and writing skills in young children. Available online. Highly recommended for academic libraries serving education programs and for libraries serving early childhood professional institutions or organizations. URL: www.kluweronline.com/issn/1082-3301/contents

2398. ***Education.*** [ISSN: 0013-1172] 1880. q. USD 33 (Individuals, USD 27). Ed(s): Lan Cassel, Dr. Russell N Cassel. Project Innovation, 1362 Santa Cruz Ct, Chula Vista, CA 91910-7114. Adv. Refereed. Circ: 3500 Paid and controlled. Microform: PMC; PQC. Online: bigchalk; EBSCO Publishing; Florida Center for Library Automation; Gale Group; Northern Light Technology, Inc.; OCLC Online Computer Library Center, Inc.; ProQuest Information & Learning; H.W. Wilson. Reprint: PQC; PSC. *Indexed:* CIJE, EduInd, L&LBA, PsycholAb, SociolAb. *Aud.:* Ac.

This journal presents a wide range of studies and theoretical papers on all areas of teaching and learning in school and university settings. Articles are both brief and lengthy, covering such topics as the learner-centered high school, gay and lesbian students, teachers' stress and TQM, role of the school psychologist for high-risk students, effective teaching, Hispanic Americans in higher education, professional development schools, and knowledge management systems. Issues have focused on school psychology, the prevention of delinquency through high school programs, and historically black colleges and universities. Recommended for school and academic libraries.

2399. ***Education and Urban Society: an independent quarterly journal of social research.*** [ISSN: 0013-1245] 1968. q. GBP 317 in Europe, Middle East, Africa & Australasia. Corwin Press, Inc., 2455 Teller Rd, Thousand Oaks, CA 91320-2218; info@sagepub.com; http://www.sagepub.com/. Illus., index, adv. Refereed. Circ: 1100 Paid. Vol. ends: Aug. Microform: PQC. Online: ingenta.com; OCLC Online Computer Library Center, Inc.; ProQuest Information & Learning; RoweCom Information Quest; Swets Blackwell. Reprint: PQC. *Indexed:* ABCPolSci, ASSIA, CIJE, CJA, EduInd, HRA, IBSS, IBZ, IMFL, L&LBA, PAIS, SFSA, SSCI, SSI, SUSA, SociolAb. *Aud.:* Ac, Sa.

This journal provides a forum for research articles that report on the role of educational institutions as they affect and are impacted by urban society. Article authors are faculty, doctoral students, and school and community administrators and professionals. Each issue focuses on a single topic, with an introduction, and is under separate editorship. These topics have covered such subjects as Catholic schools, an update on desegregation in urban schools, the urban school principalship, sexual orientation and gender identity in urban schools, and high-stakes testing. This is an important resource for academic libraries. URL: http://www.sagepub.co.uk/journals/details/j0134.html

2400. ***The Education Digest: essential readings condensed for quick review.*** [ISSN: 0013-127X] 1934. m. 9/yr., Sep.-May. USD 48 domestic; USD 58 foreign. Ed(s): Kenneth Schroeder. Prakken Publications, Inc., 3979 Varsity Dr, Ann Arbor, MI 48108. Illus., index, adv. Sample. Circ: 14000 Paid and free. Vol. ends: May. CD-ROM: ProQuest Information & Learning. Microform: PQC. Online: EBSCO Publishing; Gale Group; Northern Light Technology, Inc.; OCLC Online Computer Library Center, Inc.; ProQuest Information & Learning; H.W. Wilson. Reprint: PQC. *Indexed:* ECER, EduInd, IBZ, LRI, MagInd, RGPR. *Bk. rev.:* 4, 100 words. *Aud.:* Ga, Ac.

This publication provides a condensation of current articles on the themes chosen for the individual *ED* issues, allowing educators, students, and other interested readers an opportunity to quickly update their knowledge of particular education topics. In addition, there are regular columns such as the free-ranging discussions in "The Teachers' Lounge," capsules of education news in Washington and elsewhere, book reviews and lists, and web resources. This is a handy, pocket-sized resource that is useful for school and public libraries. URL: http://www.eddigest.com

2401. ***Education Week: American education's newspaper of record.*** [ISSN: 0277-4232] 1981. 43x/yr. USD 79.94 domestic; USD 135.94 Canada; USD 208.94 elsewhere. Ed(s): Virginia B. Edwards. Editorial Projects in Education Inc., 6935 Arlington Rd, Ste 100, Bethesda, MD 20814-5233; http://www.edweek.org. Illus., index, adv. Sample. Circ: 54000. Vol. ends: Aug. Online: EBSCO Publishing; Factiva; ProQuest Information & Learning. *Indexed:* EduInd. *Aud.:* Ga, Ac.

This weekly newspaper provides full coverage of state and national education news. There are articles on current topics and issues in the field, information about recent education reports, profiles and interviews, and weekly commentaries. It contains letters to the editor, events listings, advertisements, including books and curriculum products and services, and job postings. From time to time there is an in-depth report that appears as a series. *EW* also provides several special issues, such as the yearly review of education in the 50 states, *Quality Counts*. This is essential weekly reading for graduate education students, educators, and administrators in the field. An online edition is available. Highly recommended for school, public, and academic libraries. URL: http://www.edweek.org

2402. ***Educational Administration Quarterly.*** [ISSN: 0013-161X] 1964. 5x/yr. USD 489. Ed(s): Jim Rinehart. Corwin Press, Inc., 2455 Teller Rd, Thousand Oaks, CA 91320-2218; info@sagepub.com; http://www.corwinpress.com. Illus., index, adv. Refereed. Vol. ends: Nov. Microform: PQC. Online: ingenta.com; OCLC Online Computer Library Center, Inc.; ProQuest Information & Learning; RoweCom Information Quest; Swets Blackwell. Reprint: ISI; PQC. *Indexed:* CIJE, EduInd, IBZ, SSCI, SWA. *Bk. rev.:* 0-3, essay length. *Aud.:* Ac, Sa.

The *EAQ* seeks scholarly articles that may include empirical investigations, conceptual and theoretical perspectives, policy and legal analyses, reviews of research and practice, and analyses of methodology related to broad concepts of administration in education. The editors are especially interested in papers on education reform, governance and reform in colleges of education, teaching of educational administration, and the professional preparation of educational administrators. Faculty, principals, and teachers, national and international, have contributed research articles on the high school principalship, school superintendents, implementation of innovative programs in schools, teacher teams, and school accountability. The articles are lengthy, generally 20–30 pages, with extensive references, and with tables and figures. Some issues have a book review or review essay. There are special issues that focus on a topic, such as one devoted to research and inquiry in educational administration and another on women superintendents. This journal is published in cooperation with the University Council for Educational Administration and the University of Kentucky. Highly recommended for academic and school libraries. URL: http://www.sagepub.co.uk/journals/details/j0043.html

2403. ***Educational Evaluation & Policy Analysis: a quarterly publication of the American Educational Research Association.*** [ISSN: 0162-3737] 1979. q. USD 61 (Individuals, USD 44). Ed(s): Jane Hannaway. American Educational Research Association, 1230 17th St, N W, Washington, DC 20036-3078; http://aera.net/pubs/jebs/index.html. Illus., adv. Refereed. Circ: 6000. Vol. ends: Winter. Microform: PQC. Online: OCLC Online Computer Library Center, Inc.; ProQuest Information & Learning; H.W. Wilson. Reprint: PQC. *Indexed:* CIJE, EduInd, PsycholAb, SSCI. *Bk. rev.:* 1-2, 500-1,200 words. *Aud.:* Ac.

This journal of the American Education Research Association publishes theoretical and practical articles for the interest and benefit of researchers involved in educational evaluation or policy analysis. In brief, the editorial instructions for submission indicate that contributions should include economic, demographic, financial, and political analyses of education policies; syntheses of policy studies, evaluation theories, and methodologies; results of important evaluation efforts; and overviews of evaluation studies. Authored by faculty, graduate students, and professionals in the field, well-referenced articles have covered such topics as assessment of students with disabilities, middle school employment and effects on academic achievement, politics in the adoption of school reform models, allocation of school district resources, and enrollment practices in charter schools. This is an important resource for academic libraries. URL: http://www.aera.net/pubs/eepa

2404. ***The Educational Forum.*** [ISSN: 0013-1725] 1936. q. USD 20 domestic; USD 24 foreign. Ed(s): Grant E Mabie. Kappa Delta Pi International Honor Society in Education, 3707 Woodview Trace, Indianapolis, IN 46268-1158; gmabie@kdp.org; http://www.kdp.org. Illus., index, adv. Refereed. Circ: 7000. Vol. ends: Summer. Microform: MIM; PQC. Online: OCLC Online Computer Library Center, Inc.; ProQuest Information & Learning; H.W. Wilson. Reprint: PQC. *Indexed:* BRI, BusEdI, CBRI, CIJE, EduInd. *Bk. rev.:* 1-3, 700-1,600 words. *Aud.:* Ga, Ac.

This journal of the Kappa Delta Pi, International Honor Society in Education, has as its mission to provide scholarly inquiries on issues of importance for the improvement of education. It serves as a forum for discussion by providing differing viewpoints. The audience is university faculty and graduate students in education, educational leaders, K-12 practitioners, and the general educational community. There are themed issues, such as "Safety in Schools," with an introductory overview of the theme. Issues are generally organized into sections: a discussion forum, critical perspectives, and research in practice, with an average eight articles per issue. Includes an open forum, featuring an opinion letter to the editor, and book reviews. This is a valuable resource for undergraduate and graduate education libraries and K-12 schools. URL: http://www.kdp.org/publications_forum.asp

2405. ***Educational Foundations.*** [ISSN: 1047-8248] 1986. 4x/yr. USD 90 (Individuals, USD 50). Ed(s): William T Pink. Caddo Gap Press, 3145 Geary Blvd, Ste 275, San Francisco, CA 94118; caddogap@aol.com. Illus., adv. Sample. Refereed. Circ: 400 Paid. Vol. ends: Fall. *Indexed:* CIJE, EduInd. *Aud.:* Ac.

This journal serves as a forum for members of the American Educational Studies Association, which is composed mainly of college and university professors whose research and teaching in education is closely connected to such liberal arts disciplines as philosophy, history, politics, sociology, anthropology, economics, and comparative and international studies. The publication seeks articles and essays exploring the foundation disciplines and various aspects of the combined fields, a focus on particular topics of significance as they apply to the disciplines, methodological issues, and new research in these fields, with particular reference to the interdisciplinary aspects. Articles have discussed the implications of segregation and desegregation with respect to high-stakes testing, accountability and school reform, schooling and the rural context, women educators in the nineteenth and early twentieth centuries, foundations courses for teachers, multicultural education, and educational research in the arts. Recommended for academic libraries. URL: http://www3.uakron.edu/aesa/publications/edfound.html

2406. ***Educational Horizons.*** [ISSN: 0013-175X] 1921. q. USD 18 domestic; USD 25 foreign. Ed(s): Juli Knutson. Pi Lambda Theta, Inc., 4101 E Third St, Box 6626, Bloomington, IN 47407-6626; root@pilambda.org; http://www.pilambda.org/. Illus., index, adv. Sample. Refereed. Circ: 13000. Vol. ends: Summer. Microform: PQC. Online: OCLC Online Computer Library Center, Inc.; H.W. Wilson. Reprint: PQC. *Indexed:* CIJE, ECER, EduInd. *Bk. rev.:* 4-7, 300-500 words. *Aud.:* Ga, Ac.

This journal aims to serve as a forum for educational, social, and cultural issues that offer educators new perspectives, research findings, and scholarly essays. It is broadly directed at K-12 teachers/administrators and practitioners, as well as faculty and staff of higher education institutions. Issues generally have themes that unify the articles, such as motivation, immigrants and public education, and special education. Book reviews appear in every issue along with several regular columns that present commentaries on topics of current interest. This is a good mix of readable articles and columns for academic, public, and school libraries. URL: http://www.pilambda.org/horizons/publications%20index.htm

2407. ***Educational Leadership.*** [ISSN: 0013-1784] 1943. 8x/yr. USD 36. Ed(s): Margaret M Scherer. Association for Supervision and Curriculum Development, 1703 N Beauregard St, Alexandria, VA 22311; update@ascd.org; http://www.ascd.org. Illus., adv. Circ: 175000 Paid. Vol. ends: May. Microform: PQC. Online: EBSCO Publishing; Florida Center for Library Automation; Gale Group; OCLC Online Computer Library Center, Inc.; ProQuest Information & Learning; H.W. Wilson. Reprint: PQC. *Indexed:* AgeL, BRI, CBRI, CIJE, ECER, EduInd, IBZ, L&LBA, SSCI. *Bk. rev.:* 5, 300 words. *Aud.:* Ga, Ac, Sa.

EL's focus is on educators with leadership roles in elementary, middle, and secondary education and all those with an interest in curriculum, instruction, supervision, and leadership in the schools. Authored by teachers, administrators, higher education faculty, and other professionals in the field, articles and essays, generally three to six pages, are organized under such themes as evaluating educators, equity and opportunity, how to differentiate instruction, the science of learning, helping all students achieve, and the preparation of teacher candidates. Departments include a section on perspectives written by the editor, a research feature that provides an article/commentary, book reviews, letters to the editor, and descriptions of useful web sites. Each issue contains a wide selection of illustrated and referenced articles, and advertisements of interest to teachers and administrators. The web site for *EL* offers selected full-text articles. This is an important resource for academic, public, and school libraries. URL: http://www.ascd.org/cms/index.cfm?TheViewID=353

2408. ***Educational Researcher.*** [ISSN: 0013-189X] 1972. 9x/yr. USD 61 (Individuals, USD 44). American Educational Research Association, 1230 17th St, N W, Washington, DC 20036-3078; http://aera.net/pubs/er/index.htm. Illus., index, adv. Refereed. Circ: 23800. Vol. ends: Dec. Microform: PQC. Online: OCLC Online Computer Library Center, Inc.; ProQuest Information & Learning; H.W. Wilson. Reprint: PQC. *Indexed:* CIJE, ECER, EduInd, HEA, IBZ. *Bk. rev.:* 1-3, 1,200-2,000 words. *Aud.:* Ac.

This American Educational Research Association (AERA) journal publishes scholarly articles of significance to educational researchers from many disciplines. The features section contains articles that may report, analyze, or synthesize research inquiries or explore developments of importance to the field of research in education. The section titled "Research News and Comment" is under separate editorship and seeks articles that analyze trends, policies, and controversies regarding educational research. Responses to articles within an issue may appear, offering a dialogue highlighting divergent approaches and interpretations. Book reviews are included in every issue. Provides AERA news, with annual meeting highlights, council minutes, and meeting events. Contains advertisements for job openings. Available online. This is an important journal for graduate education students, faculty, and researchers in the field. URL: http://www.aera.net/pubs/er

2409. ***Educational Studies.*** [ISSN: 0013-1946] 1970. 6x/yr. USD 270. Ed(s): Maureen McCormack, Rebecca Martusewicz. Lawrence Erlbaum Associates, Inc., 10 Industrial Ave, Mahwah, NJ 07430-2262; journals@erlbaum.com; http://www.erlbaum.com/. Illus., index, adv. Refereed. Circ: 1300. Microform: PQC. Online: EBSCO Publishing; Ingenta Select; OCLC Online Computer Library Center, Inc.; RoweCom Information Quest; Swets Blackwell; H.W. Wilson. Reprint: PSC. *Indexed:* ABS&EES, ArtHuCI, BRD, BRI, CBRI, CIJE, EduInd, PhilInd, PsycholAb, SSCI. *Bk. rev.:* 20, essay length. *Aud.:* Ac.

Educational Studies has expanded its traditional book review format to include academic articles that focus on the interdisciplinary field of educational foundations. Articles may focus on teaching within this field, research methodologies, or report on significant findings. Articles have discussed the politics of community participation in a public school, educational biography, integrating computer technology, professional teaching standards, and social foundations of education. Each issue contains lengthy book reviews. This is a valuable journal for undergraduate and graduate education students and faculty. URL: http://www.tandf.co.uk/journals/carfax/03055698.html

2410. ***Educational Theory: a medium of expression.*** [ISSN: 0013-2004] 1951. q. USD 100 print & online (Individuals, GBP 87 print & online). Ed(s): Nicholas Burbules. Blackwell Publishing, Inc., Commerce Place, 350 Main St, Malden, MA 02148; subscrip@blackwellpub.com; http://www.blackwellpublishing.com. Illus., index, adv. Refereed. Circ: 2200 Paid. Vol. ends: Fall. Microform: PQC. Online: EBSCO Publishing; ProQuest Information & Learning. Reprint: PQC; PSC. *Indexed:* BRI, CBRI, CIJE, EduInd, IBZ, IPB, PhilInd, SSCI, SWA. *Bk. rev.:* 1-2, essay length. *Aud.:* Ac.

Founded by the John Dewey Society and the Philosophy of Education Society, this journal fosters ongoing development of educational theory and discussion of theoretical problems in the education profession. *ET* seeks scholarly articles and studies on the educational foundations of education and related disciplines that contribute to the advancement of educational theory. Issues may present articles on a single theme, such as "A Half-Century of *Educational Theory*: Perspectives on the Past, Present, and Future" and "A Symposium on Globalization and Education," or a collection of articles on a variety of topics. Topics covered have been Deweyan legacy, the uses of Foucault, education and the postmodern world, and knowledge in the postmodern university. A web site now offers full-text articles online for the years 1992-1995, with additional years to be added over time. Recommended for academic libraries.

2411. ***The Elementary School Journal.*** [ISSN: 0013-5984] 1900. 5x/yr. USD 139 (Individuals, USD 40; Students, USD 26). Ed(s): Thomas L Good. University of Chicago Press, Journals Division, PO Box 37005, Chicago, IL 60637; subscriptions@press.uchicago.edu; http://www.journals.uchicago.edu. Illus., index, adv. Refereed. Circ: 3637 Paid. Microform: PMC; PQC. Online: Gale Group. Reprint: ISI; PQC; PSC. *Indexed:* CIJE, ECER, EduInd, L&LBA, PsycholAb, SSCI. *Aud.:* Ac.

The *ESJ* seeks original studies that provide data about school and classroom processes in elementary or middle schools, as well as articles focused on educational theory and research and the implications for teaching. This publication is directed toward an audience of researchers, teacher educators, and practitioners. Articles with references, data, and tables have covered a wide range of topics, such as effective schools, school reform, process writing, school district parent involvement, and a proposal to improve classroom teaching. Themed issues are also published, such as one on social studies. This is a major title for academic and school libraries.

Gender and Education. See Women: Feminist and Special Interest/ Feminist and Women's Studies section.

2412. *Harvard Educational Review.* Formerly: *Harvard Teachers Record.* [ISSN: 0017-8055] 1931. q. USD 79 (Individuals, USD 49). Harvard University, Graduate School of Education, Gutman Library, 6 Appian Way, Ste 349, Cambridge, MA 02138; http://gseweb.harvard.edu/~hepg/her.htm/. Illus., index, adv. Refereed. Circ: 15000. Vol. ends: Nov. Microform: PQC; NRP. Online: EBSCO Publishing; Northern Light Technology, Inc.; OCLC Online Computer Library Center, Inc.; ProQuest Information & Learning. *Indexed:* AgeL, ArtHuCI, BAS, BRD, BRI, CBRI, CIJE, ECER, EduInd, IBZ, IPSA, L&LBA, PAIS, PSA, PsycholAb, SSCI, SWA, SWR&A, SociolAb. *Bk. rev.:* Number and length vary. *Aud.:* Ac.
HER, a journal of opinion and research, seeks articles on teaching and practice in the United States and international educational settings. Articles and other contributions are authored by teachers, practitioners, policy makers, scholars, and researchers in education and related fields. Authors have focused on such topics as diversity and higher education, extracurricular school activities, education for democratic citizenship, teacher unions and state testing scores, and methods for ethnographic research. An occasional feature, "Voices Inside Schools," serves as a forum for teachers, students, and others to share their research and perspectives on issues from within school settings. Contains book reviews of recent publications. *HER* is published by an editorial board of doctoral students at the Harvard Graduate School of Education. Available online. Highly recommended for academic libraries.

2413. *The High School Journal.* [ISSN: 0018-1498] 1917. bi-m. Oct.-May. USD 40 (Individuals, USD 28). Ed(s): Howard Machtinger. University of North Carolina Press, PO Box 2288, Chapel Hill, NC 27515-2288; uncpress_journals@unc.edu; http://www.uncpress.unc.edu. Illus., index. Sample. Refereed. Circ: 1500 Paid and free. Vol. ends: Apr/May. Microform: PQC. Online: bigchalk; EBSCO Publishing; Florida Center for Library Automation; Gale Group; Northern Light Technology, Inc.; OCLC Online Computer Library Center, Inc.; Project MUSE; ProQuest Information & Learning; RoweCom Information Quest; Swets Blackwell; H.W. Wilson. Reprint: PSC. *Indexed:* CIJE, EduInd, PsycholAb, SWA. *Bk. rev.:* 1, 500 words. *Aud.:* Ac.
This journal seeks reflective articles that examine the field of secondary education and report on research, informed opinions, and, occasionally, successful practices. Special issues have focused on particular topics, such as exploring the cultural worlds in schools and the use of narratives for teaching. Other issues contain a collection of topics of interest for teacher educators and other professionals and individuals interested in adolescent growth and development and secondary schools. Authors have researched secondary instruction and literacy, school principals, high school teacher attitudes about inclusion, high school course-taking, student participation in decision making, and constructivism in theory and practice. Recommended for school and academic libraries serving education programs.

2414. *History of Education Quarterly.* Formerly (until 1961): *History of Education Journal.* [ISSN: 0018-2680] 1949. q. USD 71 (Individuals, USD 40; Students, USD 20). Ed(s): Bruce C Nelson, Richard Altenbaugh. Slippery Rock University, College of Education, 220 McKay Education Building, Slippery Rock, PA 16057-1326; heq@sru.edu; http://www.sru.edu/. Illus., index, adv. Sample. Refereed. Circ: 1800. Vol. ends: Winter. Online: JSTOR (Web-based Journal Archive). Reprint: PQC. *Indexed:* AmH&L, ArtHuCI, BAS, BHA, CIJE, EduInd, IBZ, SSCI. *Bk. rev.:* 10-30, 500 words. *Aud.:* Ac.
This publication of the international and scholarly History of Education Society covers topics spanning the history of education, both formal and nonformal, including the history of childhood, youth, and the family. The articles are universal in scope and greatly vary in content and time period. Contains two or three lengthy articles per issue in addition to a historiographical essay. Research topics have included the origins of progressive education, the historiography of childhood, Bavarian schoolteachers in the 1848 revolution, Asian Americans in the history of education, a study of Amherst College from 1850 to 1880, national identity in mid-Victorian Wales, and religious schooling in America. Offers an average of 15 book reviews per issue. This is a major journal for education historians. Recommended for academic libraries.

2415. *Independent School.* Formerly: *Independent School Bulletin.* [ISSN: 0145-9635] 1941. 3x/yr. USD 17.50. Ed(s): Michael Brosnan. National Association of Independent Schools, 1620 L St, N W, Washington, DC 20036-5605. Adv. Circ: 7500. Microform: PQC. Online: EBSCO Publishing; OCLC Online Computer Library Center, Inc.; H.W. Wilson. Reprint: PQC. *Indexed:* CIJE, EduInd, MRD. *Bk. rev.:* 2. *Aud.:* Ac, Sa.
IS is published to provide an open forum for the exchange of general information about elementary and secondary education and to focus particularly on independent schools. Issues feature news and research articles reporting on such topics as the public purpose of private schools, happiness and high achievement, and sexuality education. Contains interviews, profiles, opinion pieces, and a narrative section about books. Each issue includes an insert of *The Reporter*, the independent school newsletter of the National Association of Independent Schools. Includes a classified section for job postings. Recommended for academic, public, and school libraries.

2416. *Instructor (New York, 1999).* Formed by the merger of (1996-1999): *Instructor: Primary Edition;* (1996-1999): *Instructor: Intermediate Edition;* Both of which superseded in part (1981-1996): *Instructor (New York, 1990);* Which was formerly (until 1989): *Instructor and Teacher (Cleveland);* (until 1989): *Instructor (Cleveland);* (until 1986): *Instructor and Teacher (Dansville);* Which was formed by the merger of (1931-1981): *Instructor (Dansville);* (1972-1981): *Teacher (Stamford);* Which was formerly: *Grade Teacher.* [ISSN: 1532-0200] 1981. 8x/yr. USD 9.99; USD 3 newsstand/cover per issue. Ed(s): Terry Cooper. Scholastic Inc., 555 Broadway, New York, NY 10012-0399; http://www.scholastic.com. Illus., index, adv. Sample. Circ: 200000. Vol. ends: May/Jun. Microform: PQC. Online: Gale Group; Northern Light Technology, Inc.; OCLC Online Computer Library Center, Inc.; ProQuest Information & Learning; H.W. Wilson. *Indexed:* BRI, CBRI, CIJE, CPerI, ECER, EduInd, ICM, MRD, MagInd. *Bk. rev.:* 10, 50-100 words. *Aud.:* Ga.
This resource for elementary and middle school teachers includes helpful articles with information for professional development, as well as tips, strategies, lesson plans, and activities for use in the classrooms. A section on ready-to-use material includes a poster, reproducible activities, theme units, and a variety of aids for classroom projects. Issues have featured a teacher's technology guide, with information about software, hardware, multimedia reference tools, and notes on technology products, and have also featured articles and strategies for teaching math. Issues are packed with advertisements of all types of products for classroom use. Recommended for school libraries and academic libraries serving education programs.

2417. *Journal of Classroom Interaction.* Formerly: *Classroom Interaction Newsletter.* [ISSN: 0749-4025] 1965. s-a. USD 42 (Individuals, USD 37; USD 65 combined subscription in North America for print & online). Journal of Classroom Interaction, c/o Dr H Jerome Freiberg, Ed, College of Education, University of Houston, Houston, TX 77204-5872; jci@bayou.uh.edu; http://www.coe.uh.edu/. Illus., index, adv. Sample. Refereed. Circ: 1000. Vol. ends: Winter. Microform: PQC. Online: OCLC Online Computer Library Center, Inc.; H.W. Wilson. Reprint: PQC. *Indexed:* CIJE, EduInd, PsycholAb. *Aud.:* Ac.
This semi-annual journal publishes articles on empirical research and theory dealing with observation techniques, student and teacher behavior, and other issues connected with classroom interaction. Geared for an audience of faculty, practitioners, and graduate education students, this journal has presented a range of investigations and studies authored by national and international researchers

and teacher educators. Topics have included classroom heterogeneity and instructional time in Dutch secondary schools, the development of a learning environment questionnaire, construction of science knowledge, and how classes influence the participation of students in college classrooms. Themed issues have focused on mathematics in elementary and secondary school classrooms and democratic classroom practices. Recommended for academic and school libraries.

2418. *Journal of Curriculum and Supervision.* [ISSN: 0882-1232] 1985. q. Members, USD 34; Non-members, USD 44. Ed(s): O L Davis, Jr. Association for Supervision and Curriculum Development, 1703 N Beauregard St, Alexandria, VA 22311; update@ascd.org; http://www.ascd.org. Illus., index. Refereed. Vol. ends: Summer. *Indexed:* CIJE, EduInd. *Bk. rev.:* 2, 250 words. *Aud.:* Ac.

This Association for Supervision and Curriculum Development journal publishes scholarly articles and research reports examining curriculum and supervision practices, policies, and policy issues related to teaching, learning, and leadership, representing many different viewpoints. Topics are practical or theoretical and may incorporate a variety of research methods, including interpretive, empirical, historical, critical, and analytic. Articles by scholars, school leaders, and teachers have focused on such topics as the supervision of student teachers, cultural literacy in classrooms, designing evaluation systems for professional development schools, a view from the United Kingdom and Europe of U.S. comprehensive high schools, and a forum discussing "The Educational Situation 1901-2001." Highly recommended for academic and school libraries. URL: http://www.ascd.org/cms/index.cfm?TheViewID=365&flag=365

2419. *Journal of Education.* [ISSN: 0022-0574] 1875. 3x/yr. USD 38 (Individuals, USD 35; USD 15 newsstand/cover per issue domestic). Ed(s): Dr. Edwin Delattre, Joan Dee. Boston University, School of Education, 605 Commonwealth Ave, Boston, MA 02215; bjued@bu.edu. Illus., adv. Circ: 2000. Vol. ends: Fall. Microform: PQC. Online: EBSCO Publishing; Gale Group. Reprint: PQC. *Indexed:* BRI, CBRI, CIJE, CommAb, EduInd, L&LBA, PAIS, PsycholAb, SWA. *Bk. rev.:* 1, essay length. *Aud.:* Ac.

As the new editor of this journal states in Volume 183, number 1 (2002), this is the first issue of "fundamental changes in our look, our format, our approach." With a focus on educational policy and practice for an audience of scholars and practitioners in the field, articles are considered "more in the nature of essays than scientific or scholarly studies." Authors are expected to express a range of views on topics and to promote reflection and discussion. New and regular features include "Talking about Teaching," which offers an interview with an educator; "The Latest Report," a critical examination of an important national report; "In the Public Domain," an examination of an official document relating to educational policy; and "In the Classroom," an account of a noteworthy classroom experience. This issue contains six articles by academicians and practitioners, including a teacher's reflections on learning to read in 1947, the risks and responsibilities of creative teachers, the Massachusetts Comprehensive Assessment System (MCAS), and the Department of Defense Schools and school reform. This issue offers two book reviews, and in the future there will be occasional reviews of classics in the field. Subsequent issues are expected to contain letters to the editor. This issue is a most promising new beginning for a long-established and respected journal.

2420. *The Journal of Educational Research.* [ISSN: 0022-0671] 1920. bi-m. USD 124 (Individuals, USD 62; USD 20.70 per issue). Ed(s): Jeanne Bebo. Heldref Publications, 1319 18th St, NW, Washington, DC 20036-1802; subscribe@heldref.org; http://www.heldref.org. Illus., index, adv. Refereed. Circ: 2500 Paid. CD-ROM: ProQuest Information & Learning. Microform: PMC. Online: Chadwyck-Healey Incorporated; EBSCO Publishing; Florida Center for Library Automation; Gale Group; OCLC Online Computer Library Center, Inc.; ProQuest Information & Learning; H.W. Wilson. Reprint: PSC. *Indexed:* BAS, CIJE, ECER, EduInd, HEA, IBZ, L&LBA, PsycholAb, SSCI, SWA. *Aud.:* Ac.

JER publishes research articles which are expressly relevant to educational practice in elementary and secondary schools. Articles by national and international faculty have provided studies on evaluating teacher education programs, teacher perceptions of student gender roles, the meaning of team teaching, teacher and learner perceptions of geometry programs, facilitating academic achievement in the classroom, and parents' conceptions of kindergarten readiness. Contains five or six well-illustrated and referenced articles per issue. A valuable resource for academic and school libraries.

2421. *Journal of Personnel Evaluation in Education.* [ISSN: 0920-525X] 1987. q. USD 402 print or online ed. Ed(s): Chad D Ellett. Kluwer Academic Publishers, 101 Philip Dr, Assinippi Park, Norwell, MA 02061. Illus., index, adv. Sample. Refereed. Vol. ends: Dec. Microform: PQC. Online: EBSCO Publishing; ingenta.com; Kluwer Online; OCLC Online Computer Library Center, Inc.; Ovid Technologies, Inc.; RoweCom Information Quest; Swets Blackwell. Reprint: PQC; SWZ. *Indexed:* AgeL, CIJE, HEA. *Bk. rev.:* Various number and length. *Aud.:* Ac, Sa.

JPEE offers discussion and analyses of current issues, programs, and research on personnel evaluation in education settings. This journal encourages studies that focus on the theory, research, and practice of personnel evaluation pertaining to K-12 teachers, administrators, support personnel, and faculty in colleges and universities. Articles have featured the findings of a qualitative field study of a teacher assessment system in an urban school district, a discussion of teacher evaluation and merit pay, a student survey of K-12 teachers, ethical considerations in evaluating teachers, and an assessment and evaluation of university faculty. Includes notes and reports on the annual conference of the Consortium for Research on Educational Accountability and Teacher Evaluation (CREATE). Occasional book reviews begin with Volume 14, no. 2 (2000). Recommended for academic libraries.

2422. *Journal of Thought.* [ISSN: 0022-5231] 1965. 4x/yr. USD 90 (Individuals, USD 50). Ed(s): Douglas Simpson. Caddo Gap Press, 3145 Geary Blvd, Ste 275, San Francisco, CA 94118; caddogap@aol.com. Illus., index, adv. Sample. Refereed. Circ: 300 Paid. Vol. ends: Winter. Microform: PQC. Reprint: PQC. *Indexed:* CIJE, IBZ, PhilInd, SSCI, SSI. *Aud.:* Ac.

This journal reflectively and philosophically examines worldwide educational issues and problems from the perspective of many different disciplines. It welcomes the work of scholars that represent a variety of methodologies, approaches, cultures, and nationalities. Essays that offer analyses and critiques of arguments or that report on significant research of interest to the field are encouraged. The articles are written by and directed at an audience of faculty in higher education institutions and practitioners. Issues may explore a variety of topics or offer a common thematic thread such as the achievement gap. An example of an issue with a collection of essays includes John Dewey and professional development for preservice teachers and a study of Charles Dickens. Each issue contains an essay introduction by the editor. Recommended for academic libraries.

2423. *Kappa Delta Pi Record.* [ISSN: 0022-8958] 1964. q. USD 18 domestic; USD 21 foreign. Ed(s): Kathie-Jo Arnoff. Kappa Delta Pi Publications, 3707 Woodview Trace, Indianapolis, IN 46268-1158; pubs@kdp.org; http://www.kdp.org. Illus. Refereed. Circ: 60000 Paid and controlled. Online: OCLC Online Computer Library Center, Inc.; ProQuest Information & Learning; H.W. Wilson. Reprint: PQC. *Indexed:* CIJE, ECER, EduInd. *Bk. rev.:* Number and length vary. *Aud.:* Ac.

This publication of the KDP International Honor Society in Education offers articles on current issues, classroom practices, and general educational concerns about teaching and learning. Articles are authored by faculty, teachers, administrators, parents, and others involved in the schools. Themed issues have featured articles on middle and high school topics such as flexible schedules and specific teacher preparation programs. Non-themed issues have offered articles on preservice teaching, education reform efforts, tips for publishing research findings, and the classroom environment. Includes information about Kappa Delta Pi, letters to the editor, opinion pieces, a section on programs in practice, and book reviews. Recommended for school and academic libraries.

2424. *Middle School Journal.* Formerly: *Midwest Middle School Journal.* [ISSN: 0094-0771] 1970. 5x/yr. USD 35; USD 50 foreign. Ed(s): Tom Erb. National Middle School Association, 4151 Executive Pkwy No.300,

Westerville, OH 43081-3871; http://www.mmsa.org/. Illus., index, adv. Sample. Refereed. Circ: 27000 Paid. Vol. ends: May. Microform: PQC. *Indexed:* CIJE, EduInd. *Bk. rev.:* 1-4, 500-1,800 words. *Aud.:* Ga, Ac.

The articles in this official journal of the National Middle School Association are focused on middle level education and the educational and developmental needs of youngsters aged 10-15. Written by teacher educators and professionals in the field and directed at an audience of practitioners, articles report on successful programs, discuss effective practices and research applications, and offer reflective essays. Issues may be thematic or of general interest to the readership. Coverage of topics has included mentors and community resources and success across the curriculum. Discussions have centered on advisory sessions for urban young adolescents, interdisciplinary team training for middle grades teachers, aggressive students, national board certification, and equity in mathematics classrooms. Departments include an editorial and a section on "What Research Says." Recommended for school libraries and academic libraries serving education programs.

2425. ***Momentum (Washington).*** Formerly: *Catholic School Bulletin.* [ISSN: 0026-914X] 1970. 4x/yr. USD 20. Ed(s): Patricia Feistritzer. National Catholic Educational Association, 1077 30 St, N W, Ste 100, Washington, DC 20007; nceaadmin@ncea.org; http://www.ncea.org. Illus. Circ: 25000. Microform: PQC. Online: OCLC Online Computer Library Center, Inc.; H.W. Wilson. Reprint: PQC. *Indexed:* CIJE, CPL, EduInd, PAIS. *Bk. rev.:* 3-6, 400-600 words. *Aud.:* Sa.

Geared to Catholic educators and parents, this journal offers news and articles pertinent to current issues in education, with a particular focus on Catholic schools. Each issue includes a special section that presents articles on such topics as faith and science, Catholic identity, the vocation of Catholic education, and Catholic education and public policy. Written by teachers, administrators, clergy, and professionals in the field, the articles provide practical news and information about school programs and practices for K-12 schools. Recommended for parochial school libraries and academic libraries serving education programs.

2426. ***Multicultural Education: the magazine of the National Association for Multicultural Education Planning.*** [ISSN: 1068-3844] 1993. q. USD 90 (Individuals, USD 50). Ed(s): Alan H Jones. Caddo Gap Press, 3145 Geary Blvd, Ste 275, San Francisco, CA 94118; caddogap@aol.com. Illus., adv. Sample. Refereed. Circ: 1000 Paid. Vol. ends: Summer. *Indexed:* CIJE, EduInd, L&LBA, MRD. *Bk. rev.:* 6-8, length varies. *Aud.:* Ac.

This publication provides articles on all aspects of multicultural education, innovative practices, opinion pieces, personal perspectives, reviews of books and other media, news items and announcements about conferences, events, and programs. Authored by college and university faculty, teachers, doctoral students, and administrators within schools and organizations, articles have discussed the multicultural movement, technology and multiculturalism, state requirements for the preparation of teachers working with diversity, multicultural teaching by African American faculty, promoting bilingualism, recruiting students of color to teach, and a report on the role of the arts in multicultural settings. Recommended for school and academic libraries.

2427. ***Multicultural Perspectives.*** [ISSN: 1521-0960] 1999. q. USD 190. Ed(s): Penelope L Lisi. Lawrence Erlbaum Associates, Inc., 10 Industrial Ave, Mahwah, NJ 07430-2262; journals@erlbaum.com; http://www.erlbaum.com/. Illus., adv. Reprint: PSC. *Bk. rev.:* Number and length vary. *Aud.:* Ac.

This official journal of the National Association for Multicultural Education is geared to an audience of K-12 educators, social scientists, social service personnel, teacher educators, and all those involved in multicultural education. Articles written primarily by college and university faculty have focused on multiracial and multiethnic students, multicultural lesson plans, art and multicultural education, the digital divide, bilingual and bicultural narratives for teacher research, and Latino families and special education programs. Includes reviews of books and other media. Available online. Highly recommended for school and academic libraries. URL: http://www.catchword.com/erlbaum/15210960/contp1-1.htm

2428. ***N A S S P Bulletin.*** Formerly: *National Association of Secondary School Principals. Bulletin.* [ISSN: 0192-6365] 1916. m. Sep.-May. Members, USD 185. Ed(s): Amy Ciliberto. National Association of Secondary School Principals, 1904 Association Dr, Reston, VA 22091-1598. Illus., adv. Circ: 40000 Paid. Vol. ends: Dec. Microform: PQC. Online: OCLC Online Computer Library Center, Inc.; ProQuest Information & Learning; H.W. Wilson. Reprint: PQC. *Indexed:* BRI, CBRI, CIJE, ECER, EduInd, LRI, SWA. *Bk. rev.:* 2-3 pages. *Aud.:* Ac.

This National Association of Secondary School Principals publication supports the decision making and practices of middle level and high school principals with articles that address current issues and emphasize effective administration and leadership. Issues contain research and scholarly articles authored by faculty and professionals in the field. Various themes are explored, such as implementing standards in schools, preventing school violence, developing teacher leaders, and after-school and summer programs. The editors have given priority to particular topics, for example, middle level principalship, reading to learn, and altering school start times, funding and equity, literacy in the middle level and high school, and teacher effectiveness, recruitment, and retainment. Includes book reviews. Highly recommended for school and academic libraries serving education programs. URL: http://www.nassp.org/news/bulletin.html

2429. ***N A S S P Leadership for Student Activities.*** 1988. m. USD 85. Ed(s): Lyn Fiscus. National Association of Secondary School Principals, 1904 Association Dr, Reston, VA 22091-1598. *Aud.:* Ac.

This publication of the National Association of Secondary School Principals Department of Student Activities is geared for student activities advisers and student leaders. Articles written by teachers, student council advisers, guidance counselors, and educational consultants offer practical information about successful programs for developing student leadership. Articles have discussed programs for the student council, a specific high school leadership conference, local area organizations that teach leadership, how to identify and develop leaders, and student profiles. Issues include leader resources, middle level activities, projects, national news, scholarships and awards, information about school honor societies, and an exchange of information about activities. Recommended for school libraries.

2430. ***N A S S P Newsleader.*** Formerly: *N A S S P Newsletter.* [ISSN: 0278-0569] 1971. m. Sep.-May. Free to members. Ed(s): James Rourke. National Association of Secondary School Principals, 1904 Association Dr, Reston, VA 22091-1598; http://www.nassp.org. Illus., index, adv. Sample. Circ: 42000 Controlled. Vol. ends: May. Reprint: PQC. *Bk. rev.:* 1-3, 500-1,000 words. *Aud.:* Ac.

In a newspaper format, this publication provides articles on current issues, news, and events for an audience of school leaders in middle level and high school education. It also includes coverage of the National Association of Seconary School Principals (NASSP) conferences, awards, organizational events, speeches, and elections, and available professional opportunities. This is an important resource for secondary school principals, as is the NASSP web site, which provides timely complementary information.

2431. ***Peabody Journal of Education.*** [ISSN: 0161-956X] 1923. q. USD 270. Ed(s): James W Guthrie. Lawrence Erlbaum Associates, Inc., 10 Industrial Ave, Mahwah, NJ 07430-2262; journals@erlbaum.com; http://www.erlbaum.com/. Illus., adv. Sample. Refereed. Circ: 2000 Paid. Vol. ends: Summer. Reprint: PQC; PSC. *Indexed:* AgeL, BAS, CIJE, ECER, EduInd, L&LBA, SSCI, SociolAb. *Aud.:* Ga, Ac.

PJE publishes symposia in the broad area of education and human development. Issues focus on themes with contributed articles by practitioners, academicians, policy makers, and researchers and scholars in the social sciences. The intended audience is similarly broad and diverse. Topics explored include global issues in education, the relations between schools and their constituents, and access and equity in postsecondary education. Lengthy and well-referenced articles offer in-depth examination of the selected themes. This is an important journal for academic libraries.

2432. ***Phi Delta Kappan.*** [ISSN: 0031-7217] 1915. m. Sep.-June. USD 51 (Individuals, USD 44; USD 5.50 per issue). Ed(s): Bruce M. Smith, Rise Koben. Phi Delta Kappa International, 408 N Union St, PO Box 789,

Bloomington, IN 47402-0789; kappan@kiva.net; http://www.pdkintl.org. Illus., index, adv. Circ: 95000 Paid. Vol. ends: Sep/Jun. Microform: CIS; PQC. Online: EBSCO Publishing; Florida Center for Library Automation; Gale Group; Northern Light Technology, Inc.; OCLC Online Computer Library Center, Inc.; ProQuest Information & Learning; H.W. Wilson. Reprint: PQC; PSC. *Indexed:* ABS&EES, ArtHuCI, BRD, BRI, BiogInd, CBRI, CIJE, ECER, EduInd, FutSurv, LRI, MagInd, RGPR, SSCI. *Aud.:* Ga, Ac.

PDK publishes articles on education research and leadership, with an emphasis on current issues, trends, and policy. Authored by faculty, practitioners, independent researchers, and consultants in the field, articles report on research or provide commentary on topics of concern and interest for educators at all levels. Articles have focused on testing, the standards movement, tenure in schools of education, professional certification, alternative schools, visual arts education, technological literacy, and teacher education. Departments include a Washington commentary, state news, information on current research, legal perspectives, and technology. A section titled "Backtalk" provides an opportunity for readers to submit comments on *PDK* articles. This is an important resource for educators. The web site offers selected full-text articles online. URL: http://www.pdkintl.org/kappan/kappan.htm

2433. *Principal (Alexandria).* Formerly (until Sep. 1980): *National Elementary Principal.* [ISSN: 0271-6062] 1921. 5x/yr. Non-members, USD 8. Ed(s): Leon E Greene. National Association of Elementary School Principals, 1615 Duke St, Alexandria, VA 22314-3483; lgreen@naesp.org; http://www.naesp.org/. Illus., index, adv. Circ: 29000 Paid and controlled. Vol. ends: May. Microform: PQC. Online: OCLC Online Computer Library Center, Inc.; H.W. Wilson. Reprint: PQC. *Indexed:* CIJE, ECER, EduInd. *Bk. rev.:* 350 words. *Aud.:* Ac.

Published to serve elementary and middle school educators, articles are written by teachers, principals, administrators, and other professionals to address current issues and to present ideas and information for practical applications in the schools. Regular columns include feature articles and commentaries for practitioners, a focus on the middle grades, technology trends, the reflective principal, and school law issues. Books of interest to principals are reviewed. Articles have discussed the confidentiality of student records, interviewing for the principalship, and safe schools. Issues may also have a theme, such as arts in the core curriculum and quality physical education programs. Articles have also focused on character education, geography education, and foreign language instruction. Recommended for school and academic libraries serving education programs. URL: http://www.naesp.org/comm/principl.htm

2434. *Principal Leadership (High School Edition).* Formed by the merger of (1993-2000): *The High School Magazine;* (1981-2000): *Schools in the Middle.* [ISSN: 1538-9251] 2000. m. Sep.-May. Membership. Ed(s): Patricia George. National Association of Secondary School Principals, 1904 Association Dr, Reston, VA 22091-1598. Adv. *Indexed:* BRI, CBRI, EduInd. *Aud.:* Ac.

This title is published in two separate editions, middle level and high school, and replaced two former NASSP publications, *Schools in the Middle* and *The High School Magazine*. The premiere issues began in September 2000 with the stated focus of supporting and enhancing the leadership capability of high school and middle level principals, assistant principals, and other school leaders with articles and practical information based on research and best practices. Issues have provided articles, authored by practitioners and professionals in the field, addressing educational equity, school climate, and cocurricular activities. Regular departments include a discussion of a legal problem, a focus on technology issues, an update on court decisions related to school matters, and tips for principals on various topics. The two editions of this title are nearly identical, with the exception of two to four articles specific to the editions within the contents of each of the four different issues examined. The covers are exactly the same except for the edition label. With this unusual format, the potential for confusion is unfortunate and inevitable, to say nothing of the dilemma for libraries with regard to retention of largely duplicate editions. This title is only a partial replacement for *Schools in the Middle*, which had a more direct focus on middle schools. Nonetheless, this is a title recommended for school and academic libraries serving education programs.

2435. *Radical Teacher: a news journal of socialist theory and practice.* [ISSN: 0191-4847] 1975. 3x/yr. USD 30 (Individuals, USD 15; USD 5 newsstand/cover per issue). Ed(s): Susan O'Malley. Center for Critical Education, PO Box 382616, Cambridge, MA 02238; lkampf@mit.edu; http://www.wpunj.edu/radteach. Illus., adv. Refereed. Circ: 2400 Paid. Vol. ends: Winter. *Indexed:* AltPI, CWI, EduInd, MLA-IB. *Bk. rev.:* 1-2, 1,000-2,000 words. *Aud.:* Ac, Sa.

This journal presents articles written by and for teachers at all education levels. While the majority of the articles are at the higher education level, the editors actively seek and publish the work of preschool to high school teachers. Some issues have emphasized particular themes in two parts, such as teacher education and social justice, and teaching globalization. One entire issue focuses on African American Studies and provided a dozen book and multimedia reviews. Several regular columns are reviews of books for professional reading and current education news. Recommended for school and academic libraries serving education programs. URL: http://www.wpunj.edu/radteach

2436. *Review of Educational Research.* [ISSN: 0034-6543] 1931. q. USD 61 (Individuals, USD 44). Ed(s): Kathryn Borman. American Educational Research Association, 1230 17th St, N W, Washington, DC 20036-3078; http://aera.net/. Illus., index, adv. Refereed. Circ: 18400. Vol. ends: Winter. Microform: PMC; PQC. Online: Northern Light Technology, Inc.; OCLC Online Computer Library Center, Inc.; ProQuest Information & Learning; H.W. Wilson. Reprint: PQC. *Indexed:* CIJE, CommAb, ECER, EduInd, HEA, IBZ, L&LBA, LT&LA, PsycholAb, SSCI, SociolAb. *Aud.:* Ac.

RER publishes critical reviews and interpretations of educational research literature on substantive and methodological issues. The reviews of research relevant to education may be from any discipline. Authored by faculty, doctoral students, and professionals in the field, well-referenced articles have reviewed large-scale voucher programs, the research on the teaching beliefs and practices of university academics, local school boards in their relation to students' academic achievement, postmodern perspectives on teaching freedom, the principal's role in creating inclusive schools, gender roles in school employment for over a century, and anti-oppressive education. Four to five articles per issue offer thought-provoking reviews and analyses for the American Educational Research Association (AERA) members and readers of this AERA publication. Highly recommended for academic libraries. URL: http://www.aera.net/pubs/rer

2437. *Roeper Review: a journal on gifted education.* [ISSN: 0278-3193] 1978. q. USD 75.65 (Individuals, USD 49.45). Ed(s): Ruthan Brodsky. Roeper School, PO Box 329, Bloomfield Hills, MI 48303. Illus., index, adv. Sample. Refereed. Circ: 3000 Paid. Vol. ends: Jun. *Indexed:* CIJE, ECER, EduInd, IBZ, PsycholAb. *Bk. rev.:* 4-5, 200-800 words. *Aud.:* Ga, Ac, Sa.

As the mission and contents indicate, this journal publishes articles reflecting on research, observation, experience, theory, and practice with regard to the growth, emotions, and education of gifted and talented learners. Faculty authors and professionals in the field have contributed to one issue's theme of creativity and giftedness with articles on the transition from childhood giftedness to adulthood, identifying and developing creative giftedness, defining and measuring creativity. Other issues offered articles that explored the themes of motivation and achievement and intelligence theories on gifted education. Issues generally include a section that presents one or more in-depth research articles and/or a brief research article. This is an informative and important journal in gifted education. Recommended for academic libraries serving education programs.

2438. *School Administrator: the monthly magazine for school system leaders.* Incorporates: *D C Dateline.* [ISSN: 0036-6439] 1943. m. 11/yr. USD 224 membership only. Ed(s): Jay P Goldman. American Association of School Administrators, 1801 North Moore St, Arlington, VA 22209; magazine@aasa.org; http://www.aasa.org. Adv. Circ: Controlled. Online: EBSCO Publishing; Gale Group; Northern Light Technology, Inc.; OCLC Online Computer Library Center, Inc.; ProQuest Information & Learning; H.W. Wilson. *Indexed:* CIJE, EduInd. *Bk. rev.:* Number and length vary. *Aud.:* Ac.

This American Association of School Administrators (AASA) monthly magazine for school leaders is focused on topics and news related to school district administration and is directed primarily at an audience of school superintendents. Authored by superintendents, faculty, and other professionals, articles provide practical information and discussions on important topics and often support a particular theme. Issues have offered articles on data analysis for school administration, the meaning of the new economy for education and educators, and school health isues, such as nursing needs and indoor air quality. There are guest columns on pertinent subjects, a federal-dateline column with news and perspectives by a legislative specialist, organization news, book reviews, and other resources. Issues contain an insert, the AASA *Bulletin: A Supplement to the School Administrator*, which includes organization news, conference news, calls for proposals, and job postings. An important resource for school and academic libraries serving education programs. URL: http://www.aasa.org/publications/sa/2003_04/contents.htm

2439. *Teacher Magazine.* [ISSN: 1046-6193] 1989. 8x/yr. USD 17.94 domestic; USD 27.12 Canada; USD 28.20 elsewhere. Ed(s): Virginia B. Edwards. Editorial Projects in Education Inc., 6935 Arlington Rd, Ste 100, Bethesda, MD 20814-5233; http://www.edweek.org. Illus., adv. Sample. Circ: 100000. Vol. ends: May/Jun. Online: EBSCO Publishing. *Indexed:* CIJE, EduInd. *Bk. rev.:* 4, 100-400 words. *Aud.:* Ga.

This magazine for K-12 educators contains articles on current news and education topics of interest. It includes information about programs in particular schools, profiles of teachers, interviews for reports on a particular subject, opinions, comments, and letters by the readership, and book reviews. Teachers, other education professionals, and writers contribute to this magazine. *Teacher* includes a calendar for grants, fellowships, awards and contest deadlines, as well as events information, and advertisements and general information on curriculum aids, school supplies, various products, professional development, and job postings. This is a useful K-12 resource. Available online. Recommended for school, public, and academic libraries serving education programs. URL: http://www.teachermagazine.org

2440. *Teachers College Record: a professional journal of ideas, research and informed opinion.* [ISSN: 0161-4681] 1900. m. USD 525 print & online eds. Blackwell Publishing, Inc., Commerce Place, 350 Main St, Malden, MA 02148; subscrip@blackwellpub.com; http://www.blackwellpublishing.com. Illus., index, adv. Sample. Refereed. Circ: 2500. Microform: MIM; PQC. Online: EBSCO Publishing; Gale Group; ingenta.com; OCLC Online Computer Library Center, Inc.; RoweCom Information Quest; Swets Blackwell; H.W. Wilson. Reprint: PQC. *Indexed:* AmH&L, ArtHuCI, BRD, BRI, CBRI, CIJE, ECER, EduInd, FutSurv, HEA, IBZ, MLA-IB, PsycholAb, SSCI, SWA, SociolAb. *Bk. rev.:* 6-8, 750 words. *Aud.:* Ac.

TCR is a scholarly journal of research, analysis, and commentary on a broad range of issues and topics in the field of education. Articles have focused on group learning, teacher observation of student learning, reflective journal writing, and knowledge management for school leaders. *TCR* also publishes theme issues, such as two recent ones on multicultural education that were published in two parts. Themed and non-themed issues generally contain book reviews. A recent issue, however, is entirely devoted to reviews organized topically under administration, assessment and evaluation, counseling, curriculum, diversity policy, higher education, learning, research methods, social context, teacher education, teaching, and technology. Highly recommended for academic libraries. URL: http://www.tcrecord.org

2441. *Teaching Pre K-8: the professional magazine for teachers.* Former titles: *Early Years - K-8; Early Years.* [ISSN: 0891-4508] 1971. m. 8/yr. USD 23.97 domestic; USD 33.97 foreign. Ed(s): Patricia Broderick. Early Years, Inc., 40 Richards Ave, Norwalk, CT 06854-2309; TeachingK8@aol.com; http://www.teachingk-8.com. Illus., adv. Sample. Circ: 120000. Vol. ends: May. Microform: PQC. Online: EBSCO Publishing; Northern Light Technology, Inc.; OCLC Online Computer Library Center, Inc.; ProQuest Information & Learning; H.W. Wilson. Reprint: PQC. *Indexed:* CIJE, ECER, EduInd, ICM. *Bk. rev.:* 8-12, length varies. *Aud.:* Ga.

This resource provides practical articles, tips and teaching strategies, news and classroom activities authored by teachers, education faculty, librarians, parents, and members of the teaching editorial staff. Each issue contains a section of skill-building activities, and regular departments with ideas for teaching in the middle school, teaching math, art in the curriculum, teaching reading and writing, issues in literacy and learning, and a newsletter for parents. There is information about web sites, software, and children's books. Recommended as a useful resource for school and academic libraries serving graduate and undergraduate education programs.

2442. *Theory into Practice.* Supersedes: *Educational Research Bulletin.* [ISSN: 0040-5841] 1962. q. USD 81. Ed(s): Anita Woolfolk Hoy. Ohio State University, College of Education, 341 Ramseyer Hall, 29 W Woodruff Ave, Columbus, OH 43210-1172; http://www.coe.ohio-state.edu. Illus., index, adv. Refereed. Circ: 1500. Microform: PQC. Online: EBSCO Publishing; Florida Center for Library Automation; Gale Group; Northern Light Technology, Inc.; OCLC Online Computer Library Center, Inc.; ProQuest Information & Learning; H.W. Wilson. Reprint: PSC. *Indexed:* CIJE, EduInd, PsycholAb, SFSA, SSCI. *Aud.:* Ac.

Each issue of *TIP* offers a comprehensive overview of a particular education topic, with articles representing a range of viewpoints on the subject. Articles authored by faculty and other professionals in the field are directed at an audience of teachers, education researchers, students, professors, and administrators. Editors provide an introduction to the topic for each issue. The topic of revising Bloom's taxonomy, for example, offered eight articles, including improving instruction, curricular realignment, and the role of assessment. An issue about rethinking the subject of social studies offered articles on educating democratic citizens, social action in the social studies, educating the educators by rethinking subject matter and methods, teaching from a global perspective, and gender and sexuality in the social studies. Available online. Recommended for academic libraries serving education programs. URL: http://www.coe.ohio-state.edu/TIP

2443. *Today's Catholic Teacher.* [ISSN: 0040-8441] 1967. bi-m. USD 14.95 domestic; USD 19.95 foreign. Ed(s): Mary Noschang. Peter Li, Inc., 2621 Dryden Rd., Dayton, OH 45439-1661; http://www.peterli.com. Illus., adv. Sample. Circ: 50000 Paid. Vol. ends: Apr. *Indexed:* BiolDig, CPL. *Aud.:* Ac.

Addressing K-12 Catholic school teachers, this journal provides articles on special topics such as technology in the Catholic schools and an educator development series on the vocation of teaching, as well as practical articles related to classroom activities. Includes news, ideas for class projects, resources, and other helpful aids for academic and religious lesson plans. Contains extensive advertising information on products and services for classroom use. Recommended for Catholic school libraries. URL: http://www.peterli.com/tct

2444. *Urban Education.* [ISSN: 0042-0859] 1966. bi-m. GBP 386 print & online eds. in Europe, Middle East, Africa & Australasia. Ed(s): Kofi Lomotey. Corwin Press, Inc., 2455 Teller Rd, Thousand Oaks, CA 91320-2218; info@sagepub.com; http://www.sagepub.com/. Illus., adv. Refereed. Circ: 1000 Paid. Vol. ends: Jan. Microform: PQC. Online: ingenta.com; OCLC Online Computer Library Center, Inc.; ProQuest Information & Learning; RoweCom Information Quest; Swets Blackwell. *Indexed:* BiolAb, CIJE, CJA, EduInd, HRA, SFSA, SSCI, SUSA, SWA, SociolAb. *Bk. rev.:* 2, 10 pages. *Aud.:* Ac.

This journal provides articles that examine issues of concern for city schools. Topics explored have been a study of Chicana and Chicano students in an urban setting, the depiction of Native Americans in trade books, student achievement in the Chicago schools, mentoring for urban youth, African American male students enrolled in alternative school programs, and students with special needs in three profiled high schools. Includes book reviews. A special annual issue provides in-depth coverage of an important issue in urban education, such as the issue on historical perspective on activism, empowerment, and reform in urban public schools. This journal is available online. Recommended for academic libraries.

2445. ***Vitae Scholasticae: the journal of educational biography.*** [ISSN: 0735-1909] 1982. s-a. USD 60 (Individuals, USD 40). Ed(s): Lucy F Townsend. Caddo Gap Press, 3145 Geary Blvd, Ste 275, San Francisco, CA 94118; caddogap@aol.com. Illus., index, adv. Sample. Refereed. Circ: 150 Paid. Vol. ends: Fall. *Aud.:* Ac.

As the journal of the International Society for Educational Biography, this publication offers scholarly articles on all aspects of educational biography. Articles have focused on the lives of Ella Flagg Young and Lev Vygotsky, considered the case of a nineteenth-century traveler with respect to experiential education, and explored the use and challenges of educational biography as a pedagogical tool. Issues reflect a wide range of research interests for graduate education students and faculty. Recommended for academic libraries serving education programs. URL: http://caddogap.com/journals.htm

2446. ***Voices from the Middle.*** [ISSN: 1074-4762] 1994. q. Members, USD 45. Ed(s): Kylene Beers. National Council of Teachers of English, 1111 W Kenyon Rd, Urbana, IL 61801-1096; cschanche@ncte.org. Adv. Circ: 10000 Paid. *Indexed:* EduInd. *Bk. rev.:* Number and length vary. *Aud.:* Ac.

Recognizing that middle school teachers are challenged with "a unique set of circumstances and issues," this journal is dedicated to supporting the middle school educator. Each issue provides a forum for the sharing of ideas, practices, reflections, solutions, and theories from classroom teachers and others involved with middle school students. Thematic issues consider middle school topics such as standards of learning and teaching, teaching for social justice, and social and emotional learning. Each issue has a featured theoretical article with additional articles focused on classroom practices for grades six to eight. Regular columns of professional book reviews, student book reviews, world-wide resources, and a news and notes section contribute to the journal's forum orientation. Specifically for middle schools with a professional library, as well as education libraries. URL: http://www.ncte.org/vm

2447. ***Young Children.*** [ISSN: 0044-0728] 1944. bi-m. Non-members, USD 30. Ed(s): Polly Greenberg. National Association for the Education of Young Children, 1509 16th St, N W, Washington, DC 20036-1426; http://www.naeyc.org. Illus., index, adv. Refereed. Circ: 90000. Vol. ends: Sep. Microform: PQC; NRP. Reprint: PQC. *Indexed:* AgeL, BiogInd, CIJE, ECER, EduInd, L&LBA, MRD, PsycholAb, SSCI. *Bk. rev.:* 1-8, 400-800 words. *Aud.:* Ac.

This journal of the National Association for the Education of Young Children (NAEYC) addresses an audience of teachers and directors of programs involved with children from birth through age eight within child care, preschool, Head Start, and primary grade settings. It is also directed at teacher educators, local and state decisionmakers, and researchers in child development. Practical articles provide ideas for teaching children and administering programs, and scholarly articles refer to current research and theory as a basis for practical recommendations. Articles also describe program changes that have occurred as an outcome of experts' experience and research about how young children learn. Essays discuss important issues and ideas concerning the education, care, and development of young children. Issues include NAEYC organization information, brief book reviews, letters from readers, and a calendar of conferences. Recommended for school, public, and academic libraries. URL: http://www.naeyc.org/resources/journal/default.asp

Comparative Education and International

2448. ***Adults Learning.*** [ISSN: 0955-2308] 1989. 10x/yr. GBP 56 (Individuals, GBP 34). Ed(s): Stephenie Hughes. The National Institute of Adult Continuing Education (NAICE), Renaissance House, 20 Princess Rd. W, Leicester, LE1 6TP, United Kingdom; enquiries@niace.org.uk; http://www.niace.org.uk. Illus., index, adv. Sample. Circ: 3000. Vol. ends: Jun. Online: EBSCO Publishing. Reprint: SWZ. *Indexed:* BrEdI, CIJE. *Bk. rev.:* 6-7, 500 words. *Aud.:* Ac, Sa.

This official publication of the National Institute of Adult Continuing Education (NIACE) in England and Wales provides national news of conferences and events, notes or reviews of publications, web site reviews, commentaries, and brief articles on current issues in the field. Articles by adult education consultants, university professors, and NIACE personnel have discussed the Conservative Party proposals for higher education, distance and lifelong learning, the findings of a report on attitudes of young adults concerning basic skills, language learning in the United Kingdom, skills training, and global learning. Recommended for academic and public libraries. URL: http://www.niace.org.uk/Publications/Periodicals/AdultsLearning/Default.htm

2449. ***Australian Journal of Education.*** [ISSN: 0004-9441] 1957. 3x/yr. AUD 131 (Individuals, AUD 95). Ed(s): Simon Marginson. Australian Council for Educational Research, 347 Camberwell Rd, Private Bag 55, Camberwell, VIC 3124, Australia; sales@acer.edu.au; http://www.acer.edu.au. Illus., index, adv. Sample. Refereed. Circ: 1000. Vol. ends: Nov. *Indexed:* AgeL, CIJE, HEA, IBZ, MLA-IB, PsycholAb, SSCI, SWA, SociolAb. *Bk. rev.:* 6, 800-1,500 words. *Aud.:* Ac.

AJE publishes papers on the theory and practice of education utilizing various methodologies and conceptual frameworks. Its main focus is on Australian education. Although primarily from Australia, the authors represent an international corps of scholars from a broad range of disciplines, such as philosophy, psychology, political science, economics, history, anthropology, medicine, and sociology. Articles have discussed the development of Australian teaching standards, leadership dilemmas of Hong Kong principals, programs for gifted students in Australia, and reviewed publications and citation data to evaluate the contribution of Australian educational research to major international journals. A special issue on inequality and public policy offers articles on restructuring eduational opportunity in England, curriculum policy with respect to post-compulsory education and training, and a study of mathematics achievement in the United States and Australia. Most issues contain several book reviews. Recommended for academic libraries. URL: http://www.acer.edu.au/acerpress/journals/aje.html

2450. ***British Educational Research Journal.*** Formerly (until vol.4, 1978): *Research Intelligence.* [ISSN: 0141-1926] 1975. bi-m. GBP 518 (Individuals, GBP 107). Ed(s): Ann Lewis. Carfax Publishing Ltd., 4 Park Sq, Milton Park, Abingdon, OX14 4RN, United Kingdom; enquiry@tandf.co.uk; http://www.tandf.co.uk/. Illus., index, adv. Refereed. Online: EBSCO Publishing; Ingenta Select; Northern Light Technology, Inc.; OCLC Online Computer Library Center, Inc.; ProQuest Information & Learning; RoweCom Information Quest; Swets Blackwell. Reprint: PSC. *Indexed:* BrEdI, CIJE, IBZ, L&LBA, LT&LA, PsycholAb, SFSA, SSCI, SWA, SociolAb. *Aud.:* Ac, Sa.

This major publication of the British Educational Research Association is interdisciplinary in its approach and includes reports of experiments and surveys, discussions of methodological and conceptual issues in educational research for all sectors of education, and descriptions of research in progress. Scholarly articles are primarily focused on British education although the journal's scope is international. Articles have examined differential attainment by gender for students in Wales, international comparative studies of student achievement, primary mathematics in England and Russia, ability grouping in the United Kingdom, the influence of politics in developing the curriculum. An entire issue is devoted to subject knowledge and application. Includes book reviews. Available online. Recommended for academic libraries. URL: http://www.bera.ac.uk/berj.html

2451. ***British Journal of Educational Studies.*** [ISSN: 0007-1005] 1952. q. GBP 221 print & online eds. Ed(s): Richard Pring, Geoffrey Walford. Blackwell Publishing Ltd., 9600 Garsington Rd, PO Box 805, Oxford, OX4 2DQ, United Kingdom; customerservices@oxon.blackwellpublishing.com; http://www.blackwellpublishing.com/. Illus., index, adv. Refereed. Circ: 1300. Vol. ends: Nov. Microform: PQC. Online: EBSCO Publishing; ingenta.com; OCLC Online Computer Library Center, Inc.; RoweCom Information Quest; Swets Blackwell. Reprint: SWZ. *Indexed:* ArtHuCI, BAS, BrEdI, EduInd, IBSS, IBZ, L&LBA, SSCI, SociolAb. *Bk. rev.:* 12-15, 500-1,000 words. *Aud.:* Ac.

BJES seeks articles on major education topics and principles of general interest, particularly current developments in education policy in the United Kingdom and elsewhere. Empirical research reports are not included unless they are basic to the discussion of an important topic. Articles represent a wide range of perspectives in the areas of educational philosophy, history, psychology, sociology, management, administration, and comparative studies. They are also written for an audience of nonspecialists in the field, in keeping with the journal's interest in clearly expressed and nontechnical contributions to scholarship. Articles have discussed the validity of the National Curriculum assessment in England, pedagogical practices in the workplace, secondary schooling in Germany, the writing skills and formal education needed for properly functioning in the workplace, a critical exploration of educational reforms in Western countries, and research and contemporary school leadership in England. Available online. Recommended for academic libraries. URL: http://www.soc-for-ed-studies.org.uk/journal.htm

2452. ***British Journal of Sociology of Education.*** [ISSN: 0142-5692] 1980. 5x/yr. GBP 535 (Individuals, GBP 130). Ed(s): Len Barton. Carfax Publishing Ltd., 4 Park Sq, Milton Park, Abingdon, OX14 4RN, United Kingdom; enquiry@tandf.co.uk; http://www.tandf.co.uk/. Illus., index, adv. Refereed. Online: EBSCO Publishing; Ingenta Select; Northern Light Technology, Inc.; OCLC Online Computer Library Center, Inc.; ProQuest Information & Learning; RoweCom Information Quest; Swets Blackwell. Reprint: PSC. *Indexed:* ASSIA, ArtHuCI, BrEdI, CIJE, PSA, SSCI, SWA, SociolAb. *Aud.:* Ac, Sa.

This journal publishes scholarly articles reflecting the range of current perspectives on both theory and empirical research in the sociology of education. International academic authors have contributed articles on social stratification in Zimbabwe, globalization and e-learning in higher education, the improvement of university teaching, nontraditional adult learners, and a longitudinal study of Australian secondary school students. Each issue generally contains a review essay, an extended review, and a review symposium on a major book or a collection of books. Available online. Recommended for academic libraries. URL: http://www.tandf.co.uk/journals/carfax/01425692.html

2453. ***Canadian Journal of Education.*** [ISSN: 0380-2361] 1976. q. Membership, CND 80; Non-members, CND 100; CND 25 newsstand/cover per issue. Ed(s): Samuel Robinson. Canadian Society for the Study of Education, 260 Dalhousie, Ste 204, Ottawa, ON K1N 7E4, Canada; csse@csse.ca; http://www.csse.ca. Illus., index. Sample. Refereed. Circ: 1460. Vol. ends: Fall. Microform: MML. Online: LexisNexis; Micromedia ProQuest; OCLC Online Computer Library Center, Inc.; H.W. Wilson. *Indexed:* CBCARef, CEI, CIJE, CPerI, EduInd, IBZ, L&LBA, PAIS, PsycholAb, SWA, SociolAb. *Bk. rev.:* 3-7, 600-1,500 words. *Aud.:* Ac.

CJE publishes original research primarily related to Canadian education. Included are short research notes, discussions on topics, and book reviews. Excluded in its scope are "literature reviews, applied pedagogical materials, and administrative documents." Articles are published either in English or French, with the abstracts in both languages. Other contributions are also published in either language. Topics covered have been a special education initiative in a university–school district partnership, reflections and practices in an elementary school math classroom, home schooling in Canada, pre-service teacher education, teacher education reform, Canadian educational reform and global change, and evidence of Canadians' declining confidence in public education. This is an important and well-indexed Canadian education journal. Recommended for academic libraries. URL: http://www.csse.ca/cje

2454. ***Child Education.*** [ISSN: 0009-3947] 1924. m. GBP 37.50 domestic; GBP 49.95 foreign. Ed(s): Gill Moore. Scholastic Ltd., Villiers House, Clarendon Ave, Leamington Spa, CV32 5PR, United Kingdom; enquiries@scholastic.co.uk; http://www.scholastic.co.uk. Illus., index, adv. Circ: 59926. Vol. ends: Dec. Microform: PQC. *Indexed:* EduInd. *Bk. rev.:* 15-20, 50-200 words. *Aud.:* Ac.

This publication provides lesson plans, colorful posters, and reproducible activities geared for classroom use in United Kingdom primary schools. Articles offer tips on teaching strategies and ideas to enhance the curriculum. Throughout there is useful current information about U.K. education news, publications, and resources. Each monthly issue is organized with activities under literacy, arts workshop, project, and numeracy. Book reviews include professional reading and children's books. Recommended for school and public libraries.

2455. ***Chinese Education and Society: a journal of translations.*** Formerly (until Jan. 1993): *Chinese Education.* [ISSN: 1061-1932] 1968. bi-m. USD 1150 (Individuals, USD 140). Ed(s): Stanley Rosen. M.E. Sharpe, Inc., 80 Business Park Dr, Armonk, NY 10504; custserv@mesharpe.com; http://www.mesharpe.com. Illus., index, adv. Refereed. Vol. ends: Nov/Dec. Microform: PQC. Online: EBSCO Publishing; OCLC Online Computer Library Center, Inc.; H.W. Wilson. Reprint: PSC. *Indexed:* AgeL, BAS, CIJE, EduInd, SSCI. *Aud.:* Ac, Sa.

This journal provides unabridged English translations of important articles on education in China from Chinese journals, newspapers, and collections of articles in book form. The translated names of the sources used are *Education Research, People's Education*, and *Chinese Education News*, as well as other national and local newspapers and magazines. Issues have focused on such topics as women in the teaching profession, gender equality in China, women students' culture and psychology, qualitative research, women's education and employment, education and the economy, and the brain drain, which discusses the problem of sending students abroad and then attracting them back. Recommended for academic libraries. URL: http://www.mesharpe.com/mall/results1.asp?ACR=CED

2456. ***Comparative Education: an international journal of comparative studies.*** [ISSN: 0305-0068] 1965. q. GBP 528 (Individuals, GBP 174). Ed(s): Patricia Bradfoot. Carfax Publishing Ltd., 4 Park Sq, Milton Park, Abingdon, OX14 4RN, United Kingdom; enquiry@tandf.co.uk; http://www.tandf.co.uk/. Illus., index, adv. Refereed. Circ: 1200. Vol. ends: Oct. Online: EBSCO Publishing; Ingenta Select; Northern Light Technology, Inc.; OCLC Online Computer Library Center, Inc.; ProQuest Information & Learning; RoweCom Information Quest; Swets Blackwell. Reprint: PSC. *Indexed:* BAS, BrEdI, CIJE, EduInd, L&LBA, RRTA, SSCI, SWA, SociolAb, WAE&RSA. *Aud.:* Ac, Sa.

This international journal provides current information and analyses of significant world problems and trends in the field of education, with particular emphasis on comparative studies for policy making and implementation. It also has an interest in the associated disciplines of government, management, sociology, technology, and communications with a view to the impact of these areas on educational policy decisions. The instructions to contributors have a long list of suggested themes, including educational reform, post-compulsory education, curricular content, education for the disadvantaged, higher education, and teacher preparation. Article topics have included culture and classroom reform in India, recent initiatives in school science and technology, a comparative study of educational reforms in Hong Kong and mainland China, teacher education in selected countries in the Caribbean, mathematics performance in Scotland and France, a comparative view of the National Curriculum standards in primary schools, secondary schooling in France and Australia, and the debates on education in Egypt. A recent special issue reflects on comparative and international research for the twenty-first century. Includes book reviews. Available online. Recommended for academic libraries. URL: http://www.tandf.co.uk/journals/carfax/03050068.html

2457. ***Comparative Education Review.*** [ISSN: 0010-4086] 1956. q. USD 138 print & online eds. (Individuals, USD 51 print & online eds.; Students, USD 26 print & online eds.). Ed(s): Mark Ginsburg, David Post. University of Chicago Press, Journals Division, PO Box 37005, Chicago, IL 60637; subscriptions@press.uchicago.edu; http://www.journals.uchicago.edu. Illus., index, adv. Refereed. Circ: 2400 Paid. Vol. ends: Nov. Microform: PQC. Online: East View Publications, Inc.; EBSCO Publishing; Florida Center for Library Automation; Gale Group; ProQuest Information & Learning. Reprint: ISI; PQC; PSC. *Indexed:* ABS&EES, BAS, CIJE, EduInd, IBZ, L&LBA, PAIS, RRTA, SSCI, SociolAb, WAE&RSA. *Bk. rev.:* 9-11, 800-2,000 words. *Aud.:* Ac.

The official journal of the Comparative and International Education Society, this publication seeks to advance knowledge of education policies and practices throughout the world and the teaching of comparative education studies. Articles authored by international faculty and researchers have discussed the development of education in Cambodia, equity and South Africa's education policies, the evaluation of school improvement in Indonesia, a comparative view of barriers to academic women, vocational education in eastern Germany, education and social transformation in Israel and South Africa, and educational change in the Czech Republic. Issues contain one or more essay reviews and a number of book reviews. The August issue annually offers a selective bibliography of comparative and international education journal citations published in the previous year and arranged by broad themes. In the August 2002 issue, this bibliography provided citations from over 197 journals. The 1998, 1999, and 2000 bibliographies are available online. Recommended for academic libraries. URL: http://www.journals.uchicago.edu/CER/home.html

Current Issues in Comparative Education. See Electronic Journals subsection.

2458. *Curriculum Inquiry.* Formerly: *Curriculum Theory Network.* [ISSN: 0362-6784] 1971. q. USD 237 print & online eds. Blackwell Publishing, Inc., Commerce Place, 350 Main St, Malden, MA 02148; subscrip@blackwellpub.com; http://www.blackwellpublishing.com. Illus., adv. Refereed. Circ: 1700. Vol. ends: Winter. Online: EBSCO Publishing; ingenta.com; OCLC Online Computer Library Center, Inc.; RoweCom Information Quest; Swets Blackwell. Reprint: PQC. *Indexed:* ArtHuCI, CEI, CIJE, EduInd, IBZ, SSCI, SWA. *Bk. rev.:* 1-2, essay length. *Aud.:* Ac.

This journal sponsored by the Ontario Institute for Studies in Education focuses on the study of educational research, development, evaluation, and theory. Within each issue international authors from a variety of disciplines offer articles on a wide range of issues and topics, for example, an overview of some recent research on mentoring programs in education, several case studies on preservice teachers' service learning, a collaborative relationship with teachers at an elementary school, writing as inquiry through workshops, arts and urban schools, and the selection of curricular contents of school projects in Spain. Equally important in this journal are critical book reviews, for which there are extensive instructions for in-depth essays. Editorial introductions are substantive. Available online. Recommended for academic libraries. URL: http://home.oise.utoronto.ca/~ci

2459. *Discourse: studies in the cultural politics of education.* [ISSN: 0159-6306] 1980. 3x/yr. GBP 211 (Individuals, GBP 68). Ed(s): Fazal Rizvi, Bob Lingard. Carfax Publishing Ltd., 4 Park Sq, Milton Park, Abingdon, OX14 4RN, United Kingdom; enquiry@tandf.co.uk; http://www.tandf.co.uk/. Illus., adv. Refereed. Circ: 500. Online: EBSCO Publishing; Ingenta Select; OCLC Online Computer Library Center, Inc.; RoweCom Information Quest; Swets Blackwell. Reprint: PSC. *Indexed:* L&LBA, MLA-IB, PSA, SWA, SociolAb. *Aud.:* Ac, Sa.

With its emphasis on international critical inquiry and dialogue on the cultural politics of education, this journal offers scholarly articles on a range of current topics of interest and concern. Articles have discussed reflections on Paulo Freire and education, the educational meanings and effects of 9/11, critical cultural studies, storytelling as a teaching strategy for teacher education, gifted education in South Australia, discourse though the drawings of teachers and students, Asian women's experiences in contemporary British schooling and society, and youth at risk. Includes review essays and book reviews. Available online. Recommended for academic libraries. URL: http://www.tandf.co.uk/journals/carfax/01596306.html

2460. *Economics of Education Review.* [ISSN: 0272-7757] 1982. 6x/yr. EUR 635 (Qualified personnel, EUR 174). Ed(s): Dr. Elchanan Cohn. Pergamon, The Boulevard, Langford Ln, East Park, Kidlington, OX5 1GB, United Kingdom. Illus., adv. Refereed. Circ: 525. Microform: PQC. Online: ingenta.com; ScienceDirect; Swets Blackwell. *Indexed:* ASG, BAS, CIJE, HEA, HRA, JEL, SSCI, SWA. *Bk. rev.:* 0-3, 600-1,000 words. *Aud.:* Ac.

EER provides a forum to share ideas and research findings in the economics of education. It also seeks to encourage theoretical, empirical, and policy research that points out the role of economic analysis for an improved understanding of educational problems and issues. The articles are authored by international faculty, documented with references, tables, and other data, and cover a wide range of topics. Articles have focused on an analysis of the *U.S. News & World Report* rankings of colleges and universities, how young people choose college majors, effects of school quality on income, efficiency of Australian universities, costs and other factors in year-round versus traditional school schedules, educational attainment and gender wage gap in Canada, and a merit pay model for college faculty. Includes book reviews. Recommended for academic libraries. URL: http://www.elsevier.com/inca/publications/store/7/4/3

2461. *Educational Research.* [ISSN: 0013-1881] 1958. 3x/yr. GBP 153 (Individuals, GBP 52). Ed(s): Seamus Hegarty, David Upton. Routledge, 29 W 35th St, New York, NY 10001; journals@routldege.com; http://www.routledge.com. Illus., index, adv. Refereed. Circ: 2500. Vol. ends: Nov. Microform: SWZ. Online: EBSCO Publishing; Ingenta Select; OCLC Online Computer Library Center, Inc.; RoweCom Information Quest; Swets Blackwell. Reprint: PSC; SWZ. *Indexed:* ArtHuCI, BrEdI, CIJE, EduInd, IBSS, LT&LA, PsycholAb, SSCI, SWA. *Bk. rev.:* 7, 600 words. *Aud.:* Ac.

Published by the National Foundation for Education Research in England and Wales (NFER), a major British research institution, this journal seeks articles on contemporary issues in education which convey research findings in language that is understandable for the non-expert readership. With its objective of comprehensively describing for readers the problems and the research outcomes of a wide range of concerns in all areas of education, this forum for NFER is meant to assist professionals in making practical decisions. Faculty authors and researchers have written articles on local services for special education needs (a NFER study), teachers developing a new image of themselves and their workplaces, teachers' satisfaction in working with young children, English teachers' understanding of the development of imagination in the classroom, the impact of school departments on secondary science teaching, training expert teachers, influence of television and videos on children's imagination, and classroom influences on bullying. This publication also includes short research reports and book reviews. Recommended for academic libraries. URL: http://www.tandf.co.uk/journals/routledge/00131881.html

2462. *European Education: issues and studies.* Formerly (until 1991): *Western European Education.* [ISSN: 1056-4934] 1969. q. USD 825 (Individuals, USD 140). Ed(s): Hans G Lingens. M.E. Sharpe, Inc., 80 Business Park Dr, Armonk, NY 10504; custserv@mesharpe.com; http://www.mesharpe.com. Illus., adv. Refereed. Circ: 220 Paid. Vol. ends: Dec. Reprint: PSC. *Indexed:* CIJE, EduInd, IBZ, PsycholAb. *Aud.:* Ac.

This publication contains selected articles from major journals in European countries. It also includes research reports and documents (some abridged) from various research centers and school systems. Its education scope is broad, with a particular focus on experiments and innovations. Themed issues have addressed European identity and the teaching of history, education and the future, developments in Germany, and multicultural issues in education. Recommended for academic libraries.

2463. *European Journal of Education: research, development and policies.* Formerly: *Paedagogica Europaea.* [ISSN: 0141-8211] 1964. q. USD 1110 print & online eds. Ed(s): Jean-Pierre Jallade, Jose-Gines Mora. Blackwell Publishing Ltd., 9600 Garsington Rd, PO Box 805, Oxford, OX4 2DQ, United Kingdom; customerservices@oxon.blackwellpublishing.com; http://www.blackwellpublishing.com/. Illus., index, adv. Refereed. Online: EBSCO Publishing; Ingenta Select; ingenta.com; OCLC Online Computer Library Center, Inc.; RoweCom Information Quest; Swets Blackwell. *Indexed:* BrEdI, CIJE, EduInd, HEA, IBZ, SWA. *Aud.:* Ac.

This is the journal of the European Institute for Education and Social Policy, which commissions the contributed papers from a range of specialists in the field. The aim is to offer a European perspective on policy making. The institute edits *EJE* and acts through an international board of editors. Each issue has a theme, such as challenges for citizenship education in the new Europe, new skills, higher education and graduate employment, lifelong learning in European universities, higher education and society, and vocational education training. Individual articles have focused on the changing demand for skills, multiculturalism as a pedagogical problem, an analysis of the evaluation of educational reforms in Spain, educational research in Cyprus, university research policy in Norway, Finnish higher education, and German as a second language. Recommended for academic libraries.

2464. *Higher Education: the international journal of higher education and educational planning.* [ISSN: 0018-1560] 1971. 8x/yr. EUR 717 print or online ed. Ed(s): Grant Harman. Kluwer Academic Publishers, van Godewijckstraat 30, PO Box 17, Dordrecht, 3300 AA, Netherlands. Illus., index, adv. Sample. Refereed. Vol. ends: No. 4. Microform: PQC.

Online: EBSCO Publishing; ingenta.com; Kluwer Online; OCLC Online Computer Library Center, Inc.; Ovid Technologies, Inc.; RoweCom Information Quest; Swets Blackwell. Reprint: SWZ. *Indexed:* BrEdI, CIJE, EduInd, HEA, IBSS, IPSA, LT&LA, SSCI, SWA, WAE&RSA. *Aud.:* Ac.

This publication provides a forum for the exchange of information, experiences, and research results worldwide among professionals in the field. International authors reflect on higher education problems and issues, offer comparative reviews and analyses of country policies and education systems, and consider how these contributions may impact future planning. A special issue on higher education and its clients includes articles on British education and older clients, lifelong learning, and strategies by Norwegian universities to meet market demands for continuing education. Other articles have discussed the financing of university education in Sri Lanka, internationalization of universities, the merger of non-university colleges in Norway, faculty autonomy in Taiwan, administering a multicampus university in South Africa, and the knowledge function of the university. Includes book reviews. Available online. Recommended for academic libraries.

2465. ***International Review of Education.*** [ISSN: 0020-8566] 1955. bi-m. EUR 293 print or online ed. Ed(s): Christopher McIntosh. Kluwer Academic Publishers, van Godewijckstraat 30, PO Box 17, Dordrecht, 3300 AA, Netherlands. Illus., index, adv. Sample. Refereed. Vol. ends: Dec (No. 6). Microform: PQC. Online: EBSCO Publishing; ingenta.com; Kluwer Online; OCLC Online Computer Library Center, Inc.; Ovid Technologies, Inc.; RoweCom Information Quest; Swets Blackwell. Reprint: SWZ. *Indexed:* AgeL, BAS, BrEdI, CIJE, EduInd, IBSS, L&LBA, LT&LA, SSCI, SociolAb, WAE&RSA. *Bk. rev.:* 8, 800 words. *Aud.:* Ac.

This UNESCO publication is directed at institutes of education, teacher training institutions and ministries, nongovernment organizations, and individuals throughout the world. It provides an informational forum for scholarly articles on educational policy issues, trends, and innovations in the field. Several journal issues have focused on work and learning research, literacy in the information age, and education and human rights. Article contributors have discussed rights of the child, nonformal education and distance education, multigraded schools, adult literacy, and curricula for rural areas in developing countries. A few articles within an issue may be non-English, but with an English abstract. Includes book reviews. Recommended for academic libraries.

2466. ***Irish Journal of Education.*** [ISSN: 0021-1257] 1967. a. IEP 7 per vol. in Europe; IEP 10 per vol. elsewhere. Ed(s): Thomas Kellaghan. St. Patrick's College, Educational Research Centre, Dublin, 9, Ireland. Illus., index, adv. Sample. Refereed. Circ: 1000. Vol. ends: Winter. Microform: PQC. Reprint: PQC. *Indexed:* BrEdI, L&LBA, PsycholAb, SSCI. *Aud.:* Ac.

This journal is intended for an audience of teachers at all education levels and other readers interested in the field. It presents research articles with a focus on education in Ireland, as well as developments in educational theory and practice in other countries. Subject areas covered include philosophy, history and sociology of education, educational and child psychology, comparative education, and curriculum studies. Articles have explored the college in the community, middle management in primary schools, leisure activities of pupils in relation to their reading achievement, science curriculum and policies in Ireland, Irish music education, primary school evaluation, student participation in Australian secondary school mathematics courses, and the relationship between university lecture attendance and examination performance. Recommended for academic libraries.

2467. ***J E T: Journal of Educational Thought.*** Formerly: *Journal of Educational Thought.* [ISSN: 0022-0701] 1967. 3x/yr. USD 80 (Individuals, USD 70). Ed(s): Ian Winchester. University of Calgary, Faculty of Education, 2500 University Dr NW, Calgary, AB T2N 1N4, Canada; jet@acs.ucalgary.ca; http://external.educ.ucalgary.ca/jet/jetaug.html. Illus., adv. Sample. Refereed. Circ: 575. Vol. ends: Dec. Microform: MML; PQC. Online: OCLC Online Computer Library Center, Inc.; H.W. Wilson. Reprint: PQC; PSC. *Indexed:* CEI, CIJE, EduInd, SSCI, SWA, SociolAb. *Bk. rev.:* 6-8, 700-1,500 words. *Aud.:* Ac.

This journal presents research articles on the theory and practice of education. Subject areas explored by mainly Canadian and American faculty vary widely and include administration, comparative education, curriculum, evaluation, instructional methodology, intercultural education, philosophy, psychology, and sociology. Authors have discussed native people and the social work profession, the moral dimensions of citizenship education, the relevancy of poetry in school leadership, constructivist learning, multicultural teacher education curriculum, technology and inequality in U.S. school systems, integrity within the university, vocational education in Canadian public schooling, and the portrayal of private schools in selected feature films. All articles have French and English abstracts, with occasional articles entirely in French. Each issue contains an editorial and book reviews. Recommended for academic libraries. URL: http://www.educ.ucalgary.ca/research/jet/jet.html

2468. ***Journal of Philosophy of Education.*** Formerly: *Philosophy of Education Society of Great Britain. Proceedings.* [ISSN: 0309-8249] 1966. q. GBP 395 print & online eds. Ed(s): Richard Smith. Blackwell Publishing Ltd., 9600 Garsington Rd, PO Box 805, Oxford, OX4 2DQ, United Kingdom; customerservices@oxon.blackwellpublishing.com; http://www.blackwellpublishing.com/. Illus., index, adv. Refereed. Vol. ends: No. 2. Online: EBSCO Publishing; ingenta.com; OCLC Online Computer Library Center, Inc.; RoweCom Information Quest; Swets Blackwell. *Indexed:* BrEdI, CIJE, EduInd, PhilInd, RI-1, SSCI, SWA. *Bk. rev.:* 1-2, 1,000-2,000 words. *Aud.:* Ac.

This journal is published for the Philosophy of Education Society of Great Britain. Authors discuss basic philosophical issues related to education or they may provide critical examinations of current educational practices or policies from a philosophical perspective. The authors are international, as is the editorial board. Articles have focused on such topics as faith-based schools, the funding of religious schools, school choice, the meanings of education and pedagogy, schools and moral education, schools as communities, and Nietzsche's educational legacy. Special issues devoted to a particular theme have presented articles on the philosophical problems of online education and the idea of "high culture" within education. Generally includes a book review or review article. Available online. Recommended for academic libraries.

2469. ***Prospects: quarterly review of comparative education.*** [ISSN: 0033-1538] 1969. q. EUR 100 print or online ed. UNESCO Publishing, 7 place de Fontenoy, Paris, 75352, France; http://www.unesco.org/publications. Illus. Circ: 2125. *Indexed:* CIJE, EduInd, SSCI. *Bk. rev.:* 1-2, essay length. *Aud.:* Ac.

This publication of the UNESCO International Bureau of Education provides articles on education throughout the world by scholars, practitioners, policy makers, and administrators. Themed issues have focused on school autonomy and evaluation, education in Asia, professionalism in teaching, and education for sustainable development. Each issue begins with at least one opening article that offers an opinion on a controversial topic. Some issues have a section which discusses education trends based on particular case studies, for example, modern education in Afghanistan, child rights and education in Japan, and higher education in Nigeria. Another issue provides the profile of the educator, Basil Bernstein. This journal is currently available in a number of foreign language editions: Arabic, Chinese, French, Russian, and Spanish. Recommended for academic libraries. URL: http://www.ibe.unesco.org/International/Publications/Prospects/proshome.htm

2470. ***Times Educational Supplement.*** [ISSN: 0040-7887] 1910. w. GBP 80 domestic; GBP 120 in Europe; GBP 180 elsewhere. Ed(s): Patricia Rowan. T S L Education Ltd., Admiral House, 66-68 E Smithfield, London, E1 1BX, United Kingdom; http://www.tsleducation.co.uk. Illus., index, adv. Circ: 135000. CD-ROM: Chadwyck-Healey Incorporated. Microform: RPI. Online: Gale Group; LexisNexis. *Indexed:* BNI, BRI, BrEdI, CBRI, EduInd, LT&LA. *Bk. rev.:* 8-12, 400-800 words. *Aud.:* Ac, Sa.

TES is the British version of the American publication, *Education Week*. It is the United Kingdom's major weekly publication for news concerning "primary, secondary, and further education." It includes background analyses of a wide range of current issues in education, local and national news, and a section on job openings for predominantly K-12 and also higher education positions. Provides frequent special supplements to the news edition, such as separate job advertising supplements which include international openings, a curriculum special on mathematics, a special issue on computers in education, feature supplements with a focus on human interest stories, news, and articles of interest, as well as reviews of adult and children's books, TV and radio, theater, and curriculum resources. An online version is available. Highly recommended for academic libraries. URL: http://www.tes.co.uk

2471. ***Times Higher Education Supplement.*** [ISSN: 0049-3929] 1971. w. GBP 49.95 domestic; GBP 71 in Europe; USD 79 United States. Ed(s): Auriol Stevens. T S L Education Ltd., Admiral House, 66-68 E Smithfield, London, E1 1BX, United Kingdom; http://www.tsleducation.co.uk. Illus., index, adv. Circ: 25000. CD-ROM: Chadwyck-Healey Incorporated. Microform: RPI. *Indexed:* BNI, BrEdI, BrHumI, EduInd, LT&LA, MLA-IB. *Bk. rev.:* 35, 300-1,200 words. *Aud.:* Ac.

This title is the British version of the American publication *Chronicle of Higher Education. THES* states it is "designed specifically for professional people working in higher education and research." Articles cover a range of higher education topics including governmental policy, international news and views, scientific theory, and copyright. Its review section has two distinctly British columns, Whistleblowers and Soapbox, as well as more general features as international news, opinion and letters, and book reviews. The section on teaching with theoretical and practical articles has covered the teaching of grammar, constructing a teaching portfolio, and team problem-solving. Each issue has a book review section focused on a particular area such as Cultural and Media Studies, Psychology and Psychiatry, Women's and Gender Studies, and Mathematics and Physics. As with the *Chronicle of Higher Education, THES* includes job advertisements with some international vacancies. It is also available online. This British weekly is a standard for any academic library, higher education institute, or organization. URL: http://www.thes.co.uk

Educational Psychology and Measurement, Special Education, Counseling

2472. ***Applied Measurement in Education.*** [ISSN: 0895-7347] 1988. q. USD 405. Ed(s): James C Impara, Barbara S Plake. Lawrence Erlbaum Associates, Inc., 10 Industrial Ave, Mahwah, NJ 07430-2262; http://www.erlbaum.com/. Illus., adv. Refereed. Vol. ends: No. 4. Reprint: PSC. *Indexed:* CIJE, EduInd, SSCI. *Aud.:* Ac.

Sponsored by the Oscar and Luella Buros Center for Testing, this research journal focuses on educational and psychological testing articles. The intended audience of researchers and practitioners will find articles on applied research, educational measurement problems and considered solutions, and research reviews of current issues in testing. Research studies with accompanying tables, figures, graphs, and other supporting material address topics such as selected methods of scoring classroom assessments, the assessment of graduate-level writing skills, the structure and scoring of mathematics performance assessments, an analysis of faculty evaluation data, and the use of standard calculators in testing situations. Contributors are from academic and testing institutions such as the American Council of Testing and the Education Testing System. Strongly recommended for libraries serving teachers and related education professionals.

2473. ***Counselor Education and Supervision.*** [ISSN: 0011-0035] 1961. q. USD 70 (Individuals, USD 50; Free to members). Ed(s): Marlowe H Smaby. American Counseling Association, 5999 Stevenson Ave, Alexandria, VA 22304-3300; http://www.counseling.org. Illus., adv. Refereed. Circ: 3500. Vol. ends: Jun. Microform: PQC. Online: EBSCO Publishing; Florida Center for Library Automation; Gale Group; OCLC Online Computer Library Center, Inc.; ProQuest Information & Learning; H.W. Wilson. Reprint: PQC; PSC. *Indexed:* AgeL, CIJE, EduInd, PsycholAb, SSCI. *Bk. rev.:* Occasional. *Aud.:* Ac, Sa.

This official publication of the Association for Counselor Education and Supervision (ACES) is designed for professionals engaged in the teaching and supervising of counselors. The journal's scope encompasses a broad range of workplaces, from schools to agencies to private institutions. Each issue contains about six articles written by authors predominately from academe. Articles range from pedagogical methods to practical teaching methods such as using screenwriting techniques for realistic role plays. The journal has two regularly featured sections: one on counselor preparation and the other on counselor supervision. The inclusion of ACES executive council minutes supports the professional orientation of the journal. A focused journal for a specific audience. URL: http://www.isu.edu/departments/ces/index.htm

2474. ***Educational Measurement: Issues and Practice.*** Supersedes: *National Council on Measurement in Education. Measurement News;* Formerly: *N C M E Newsletter.* [ISSN: 0731-1745] 1982. q. USD 30 (Individuals, USD 25). Ed(s): Jeffrey Smith. National Council on Measurement in Education, 1230 17th St, N W, Washington, DC 20036-3078. Illus. Refereed. Circ: 2600. Vol. ends: Winter. Reprint: PQC. *Indexed:* CIJE, EduInd, PsycholAb. *Bk. rev.:* 1, 5,000 words. *Aud.:* Ac.

A journal of the National Council on Measurement in Education (NCME) designed to both highlight and inform its professional audience as to issues and practices in the field of educational measurement. Each issue contains three articles ranging in length from five to ten pages. Journal articles cover such topics as security of web-based assessments, practice analysis for credentialing examinations, the meaning of student achievement in relation to the TIMSS international survey data, evaluation criteria for teacher certification tests, large-scale testing in other countries, and issues in large-scale writing assessments. As a membership publication, the journal also reports on NCME member activities, the annual conference, and organizational news. This journal supports practitioners in the field of testing. URL: http://www.ncme.org/pubs/emip.ace

2475. ***Educational Psychology Review.*** [ISSN: 1040-726X] 1989. q. USD 461 print or online ed. Ed(s): Kenneth A Kierwa. Kluwer Academic / Plenum Publishers, 233 Spring St Fl 7, New York, NY 10013-1522; http://www.wkap.nl/. Illus., adv. Sample. Refereed. Vol. ends: Dec. Microform: PQC. Online: EBSCO Publishing; ingenta.com; Kluwer Online; OCLC Online Computer Library Center, Inc.; Ovid Technologies, Inc.; RoweCom Information Quest; Swets Blackwell. *Indexed:* CJA, EduInd, L&LBA, PsycholAb, SSCI. *Aud.:* Ac, Sa.

An international peer-reviewed publication supporting the field of general educational psychology. Averaging four to six substantial and well-referenced articles per issue, this journal covers the history, the profession, and the issues of the educational psychology field. Two recent special issues covered intelligence and classroom motivation. A regular feature, "Reflections on the Field," provides an arena for interviews and discussion with leading educational psychologists. Article authors are predominantly from institutions of higher education. Academic libraries serving education and psychology faculty and graduate students will want this title. URL: http://www.kluweronline.com/issn/1040-726X/contents

2476. ***Journal of Educational and Behavioral Statistics.*** Formerly (until vol.19, no.3, 1994): *Journal of Educational Statistics.* [ISSN: 1076-9986] 1976. q. USD 70 (Individuals, USD 60). Ed(s): Larry Hedges. American Educational Research Association, 1230 17th St, N W, Washington, DC 20036-3078; http://aera.net/. Illus., index, adv. Refereed. Circ: 3700. Vol. ends: Winter. Microform: PQC. Online: OCLC Online Computer Library Center, Inc.; ProQuest Information & Learning; H.W. Wilson. Reprint: PQC. *Indexed:* CIJE, EduInd, PsycholAb, SSCI, ST&MA. *Aud.:* Ac.

This journal is sponsored by the American Educational Research Association and the American Statistical Association. Intended for the statistician working in the field of educational or behavioral research, the journal publishes papers on methods of analysis as well as reviews of current methods and practices. *JEBS* articles inform readers about the use of statistical methods: the "why, when, and how" of statistical methodology. Four to five articles are included per issue along with the occasional column titled "Teachers Corner," which presents brief essays on the teaching of educational and behavioral statistics. A focused journal important to those in academe, whether researcher or practitioner.

2477. ***Journal of Educational Measurement.*** Supersedes: *National Council on Measurement in Education. Yearbook.* [ISSN: 0022-0655] 1964. q. USD 60 (Individuals, USD 55). Ed(s): Rebecca Zwick. National Council on Measurement in Education, 1230 17th St, N W, Washington, DC

20036-3078; http://www.assessment.iupui.edu/NCME/NCME.html. Illus., index, adv. Refereed. Circ: 3500. Vol. ends: Winter. Microform: PQC. Online: ProQuest Information & Learning. Reprint: PQC. *Indexed:* CIJE, EduInd, HEA, IBZ, PsycholAb, SSCI. *Bk. rev.:* 2, 600-1,200 words. *Aud.:* Ac.

Published by the National Council on Measurement, this journal intends to "promote greater understanding and improved use of measurement techniques." The journal's content format is based on research studies and reports on educational measurement such as a study to investigate standard error measurement with testlets. There is a review section for books, software, and published tests and measurements. In addition, the journal asks for and publishes comments on previously published articles and reviews. The authors come from a broad range of testing and measurement backgrounds, such as the National Board of Medical Examiners, Microsoft Corporation, Research Triangle Institute, and CTB/McGraw-Hill. A scholarly research journal for those in the field of educational testing and measurement.

2478. ***Journal of Educational Psychology.*** [ISSN: 0022-0663] 1910. q. USD 300 (Members, USD 62; Non-members, USD 127). Ed(s): Dr. Michael Pressley. American Psychological Association, 750 First St, NE, Washington, DC 20002-4242; journals@apa.org; http://www.apa.org/. Illus., adv. Sample. Refereed. Circ: 4600. Vol. ends: Feb. Microform: PMC; PQC. Online: EBSCO Publishing; Gale Group; OCLC Online Computer Library Center, Inc.; Ovid Technologies, Inc.; ProQuest Information & Learning; ScienceDirect. Reprint: PQC; PSC. *Indexed:* AgeL, ArtHuCI, BiolAb, CIJE, CommAb, ECER, EduInd, HEA, IBZ, IndMed, L&LBA, LT&LA, MLA-IB, PsycholAb, SFSA, SSCI, SWA. *Aud.:* Ac.

The journal's stated purpose is to publish current research as well as theoretical and review articles in the field of educational psychology. Each issue has anywhere from 15 to 20 well-referenced research articles supported by tables, figures, and appendixes. Most articles have multiple authors. Article coverage includes learning, cognition, instruction, motivation, social issues, emotion, and special populations at all education levels. The journal has published such articles as students' perceptions of classroom activities, a comparison of five urban early childhood programs, a study which identified and described middle school students' goals, a longitudinal study of college success, and a consideration of preschool peer interactions and school success. Published by the American Psychological Association, this is an academic research journal for students, researchers, and practitioners in the field of educational psychology.

2479. ***Journal of Experimental Education.*** [ISSN: 0022-0973] 1932. q. USD 102 (Individuals, USD 52; USD 25.50 per issue). Ed(s): Jonathan Lifland. Heldref Publications, 1319 18th St, NW, Washington, DC 20036-1802; subscribe@heldref.org; http://www.heldref.org. Illus., index, adv. Sample. Refereed. Circ: 1000. CD-ROM: ProQuest Information & Learning. Microform: PMC. Online: bigchalk; Chadwyck-Healey Incorporated; EBSCO Publishing; Florida Center for Library Automation; Gale Group; OCLC Online Computer Library Center, Inc.; ProQuest Information & Learning; H.W. Wilson. Reprint: PSC. *Indexed:* CIJE, EduInd, HEA, IBZ, L&LBA, PsycholAb, SSCI. *Aud.:* Ac.

This journal publishes research studies that use quantitative or qualitative methodologies in the behavioral, cognitive, and social sciences. Intended for researchers and practitioners, the journal is dedicated to promoting educational research in areas such as teaching, learning, and schooling. Contributed articles are divided into three sections: learning and instruction; motivation and social processes; and measurement, statistics, and research design. Articles have covered such topics as motivation and self-regulation as predictors of achievement, cooperative college examinations, the effects of test anxiety on college students, and videocase construction with preservice teacher education programs. A journal intended for and useful to the professional researcher in the field of education and related social sciences. URL: http://www.heldref.org/html/body_jxe.html

2480. ***Journal of Learning Disabilities.*** [ISSN: 0022-2194] 1967. bi-m. USD 144 (Individuals, USD 56). Ed(s): Wayne P. Hresko. Pro-Ed Inc., 8700 Shoal Creek Blvd, Austin, TX 78757-6897; journals@proedinc.com; http://www.proedinc.com. Illus., adv. Refereed. Circ: 7000. Vol. ends: Dec. Microform: PQC; NRP. Online: bigchalk; EBSCO Publishing; Factiva; Florida Center for Library Automation; Gale Group; Ingenta Select; OCLC Online Computer Library Center, Inc.; ProQuest Information & Learning; H.W. Wilson. Reprint: PSC. *Indexed:* ASSIA, BRI, BiolAb, CIJE, CINAHL, ECER, EduInd, ExcerpMed, HEA, IBZ, IMFL, IndMed, L&LBA, MLA-IB, PAIS, PsycholAb, SSCI. *Aud.:* Ac, Sa.

Dedicated to the field of learning disabilities, the journal publishes articles on practice, research, and theory. Articles are organized into categories such as international studies, instructional/intervention, research, definitional issues, assessment, and special issues. Each issue averages about six to eight well-referenced articles. In covering the multidisciplinary field of learning disabilities, articles have presented topics such as learning disability asssessment across ethnic groups, impaired visual attention in children with dyslexia, inattentive behavior in young children, identifying interventions to remediate reading difficulties of children with learning disabilities, and examining an apprenticeship relationship in a collaborative writing context. A recent special issue covers IQ discrepancy and the LD diagnosis. Includes a classified advertising section with professional position postings. A professional calendar lists seminars and conferences on learning disabilities. An academic journal that covers the field. URL: http://www.proedinc.com/jld.html

2481. ***Learning Disability Quarterly.*** [ISSN: 0731-9487] 1978. q. USD 65 domestic; USD 75 foreign. Ed(s): David Edgburn. C L D, PO Box 40303, Overland Park, KS 66204; http://www.cldinternational.com. Illus., adv. Refereed. Circ: 3500. Vol. ends: Fall. Online: EBSCO Publishing; Florida Center for Library Automation; Gale Group; OCLC Online Computer Library Center, Inc.; H.W. Wilson. *Indexed:* CIJE, ECER, EduInd, PsycholAb, SSCI, SSI. *Aud.:* Ac, Sa.

Published by The Council for Learning Disabilities, an international organization, the journal's focus is on educational practices and theories as applied to disabilities. Articles cover a broad range of format including assessment or remediation reports, literature reviews, theory and issue papers, original or applied research, and professional education program models. With usually six articles an issue, the journal contents cover professional development, current issues in the field, the development of effective teaching methods, teaching in inclusive classrooms, and increasing student achievement. Figures, tables, and appendixes support the research methodology used by authors. An important journal of value to both the academician and practitioner.

2482. ***Professional School Counseling.*** Formed by the merger of (1965-1997): *Elementary School Guidance and Counseling;* (1954-1997): *School Counselor;* Which superseded (1953-1954): *Elementary Counselor.* [ISSN: 1096-2409] 1997. 5x/yr. Free to members; Non-members, USD 90. Ed(s): Kathleen M Rakestraw, Pamelia Brott. American School Counselor Association, 801 N Fairfax St, Ste 310, Alexandria, VA 22314; http://www.schoolcounselor.org/index.cfm. Illus., index, adv. Sample. Refereed. Vol. ends: May. Online: EBSCO Publishing; Florida Center for Library Automation; Gale Group; Northern Light Technology, Inc.; OCLC Online Computer Library Center, Inc.; ProQuest Information & Learning; H.W. Wilson. Reprint: PQC. *Indexed:* AgeL, CIJE, EduInd, PsycholAb, SFSA, SWR&A. *Bk. rev.:* Number and length vary. *Aud.:* Ga, Ac.

The journal is dedicated to presenting the most current theory, research, practice, techniques, materials, and ideas for school counselors. Articles are research-based, but the journal also publishes theoretical and philosophical pieces as well as literature reviews. Each issue has eight or more articles. Article topics have included school counselors and crisis intervention, multicultural group supervision, body image in the middle school, a case study in elementary school counseling, the counseling of at-risk adolescent girls, and the importance of promoting a professional identity. A regular feature, "Perspectives from the Field," gives a brief overview of current issues or practices of concern to school counselors. Books and other resources are reviewed. This is a very relevant title for school counselors or other professionals concerned with the well-being of all elementary and high school students.

2483. ***Psychology in the Schools.*** [ISSN: 0033-3085] 1964. 8x/yr. USD 469 domestic; USD 511 foreign; USD 516 combined subscription domestic for print & online eds. Ed(s): Dr. Gerald B Fuller. John Wiley & Sons, Inc., 111 River St, Hoboken, NJ 07030; uscs-wis@wiley.com;

http://www.wiley.com. Illus., index, adv. Sample. Refereed. Circ: 1700. Vol. ends: Oct. Microform: PQC. Online: EBSCO Publishing; ScienceDirect; Swets Blackwell; Wiley InterScience. *Indexed:* AgeL, CIJE, ECER, EduInd, IBZ, IMFL, L&LBA, PsycholAb, SSCI. *Bk. rev.:* 1-5, 600-2,000 words. *Aud.:* Ac.

A peer-reviewed journal intended for the school practitioner and others working in educational institutions, including psychologists, counselors, and administrators. Articles are organized into categories of evaluation and assessment, educational practices and problems, strategies for behavioral change, and general issues. Categories are indicative of article content such as evaluation and assessment focusing on testing practices and issues. Recent testing articles covered preparation of school psychologists for crisis intervention, assessing giftedness with the WISC-III and SB-IV, teacher behavior toward failing students, a review of diversity research literature in school psychology during the 1990s, predicting reading levels for low-SES English-speaking children, looking at early screening profile validity, and considering the validity of two specific measures: the Pervasive Developmental Disorders Rating Scale and the Autism Behavior Checklist. Two special issues are published annually covering current topics such as psychoeducational and psychosocial functioning of Chinese children, and school psychology in the twenty-first century. Occasional test and book reviews. An important journal for school and academic libraries.

2484. *Remedial and Special Education.* Formed by the merger of (1981-1984): *Topics in Learning and Learning Disabilities;* (1980-1984): *Exceptional Education Quarterly;* (1978-1983): *Journal for Special Educators;* Which was formed by the 1978 merger of: *Special Children; Journal for Special Educators of the Mentally Retarded;* Which was formerly: *Digest of the Mentally Retarded;* Incorporates: *Retarded Adult.* [ISSN: 0741-9325] 1984. bi-m. USD 127 (Individuals, USD 43). Ed(s): Edward Polloway. Pro-Ed Inc., 8700 Shoal Creek Blvd, Austin, TX 78757-6897; journals@proedinc.com; http://www.proedinc.com. Illus., index, adv. Sample. Refereed. Circ: 2200 Paid and free. Vol. ends: Nov/Dec. Microform: PQC. Online: EBSCO Publishing; Florida Center for Library Automation; Gale Group; Ingenta Select; OCLC Online Computer Library Center, Inc.; ProQuest Information & Learning; H.W. Wilson. Reprint: PSC. *Indexed:* ASSIA, CIJE, CJA, ECER, EduInd, IBZ, L&LBA, PsycholAb, SSCI. *Bk. rev.:* Number and length vary. *Aud.:* Ac, Sa.

A journal dedicated to the issues and practices of remedial and special education. Each issue averages five to six articles, which may be literature reviews, position papers, or research reports. Topics cover a broad range of issues concerning the population of underachieving and exceptional individuals. Recent article topics include using rewards to teach students with disabilities, social skills interventions for young children with disabilities, inclusive schooling and community-referenced learning, mediated activities and science literacy, charter school enrollment of students with disabilities, and the legal and practical issues of high school graduation for students with disabilities. A special series considered peer-mediated instruction and intervention. Contributing authors are predominantly academics, including graduate students. Book reviews and a professional calendar are regular features. A journal of importance for the special education teacher and regular classroom teacher as well as those teaching in the field.

2485. *Studies in Educational Evaluation.* [ISSN: 0191-491X] 1974. q. EUR 547. Ed(s): David Nevo. Pergamon, The Boulevard, Langford Ln, East Park, Kidlington, OX5 1GB, United Kingdom. Illus., adv. Sample. Refereed. Vol. ends: No. 3. Microform: PQC. Online: ingenta.com; ScienceDirect; Swets Blackwell. *Indexed:* BrEdI, CIJE, EduInd, HEA. *Aud.:* Ac.

An internationally authored journal publishing reports on evaluation studies for practitioners, students, and researchers. Focused on presenting both empirical and theoretical studies, the journal seeks articles that report on international educational systems, evaluation practices, and current evaluation issues of educational programs, institutions, personnel and student assessment. Additionally, the journal covers topics both general to the field and specific to a country or countries. Topics presented have included the evaluation of schools in a specific country, school composition and achievement in primary education, evaluation of an alternative teacher licensing assessment program, program evaluation using video, and Brazil's basic education evaluation system. Two thematic issues cover the findings and assessment methods of the Third International Mathematics and Science Study (TIMSS). A focused journal with international coverage recommended for libraries serving testing and education organizations or institutions.

Higher Education

2486. *A A U W Outlook.* Former titles (until 1988): *Graduate Woman;* (1962-1978): *A A U W Journal.* [ISSN: 1044-5706] 1882. q. Non-members, USD 15. Ed(s): Jodi Lipson. American Association of University Women, 1111 16th St, N W, Washington, DC 20036; ads@aauw.org; http://www.aauw.org. Illus., adv. Circ: 110000. Vol. ends: Nov/Dec. Microform: PQC. Reprint: PQC. *Indexed:* AgeL, CIJE, PAIS. *Bk. rev.:* 1-2, 200-500 words. *Aud.:* Ga, Ac, Sa.

Published by the American Association of University Women for its members, this magazine informs and promotes the organization's mission of "equity for all women and girls, lifelong education, and positive societal changes." Regular features include an equity watch and "Word Has It," which gives the history of word definitions relating to women. Illustrated throughout with photos, the magazine has classified ads including job opportunities. Featured brief articles have considered issues of women and tech-savvy, struggle for pay equity, thirty years of Title IX, AAUW members' reflections on voting experiences over eight decades, and the Violence Against Women Act. Member surveys, the President's Message, and an issue devoted to the AAUW's annual conference exemplify the outreach focus of the magazine to its members. An important magazine for academic libraries and for libraries serving women's organizations. URL: http://www.aauw.org/outlook/index.cfm

2487. *Academe.* Formed by the 1979 merger of: *Academe; A A U P Bulletin.* [ISSN: 0190-2946] 1915. bi-m. USD 64 domestic; USD 72 foreign. Ed(s): Ellen Schrecker. American Association of University Professors, 1012 14th St, N W, Ste 500, Washington, DC 20005-3465; aaup@aaup.org; http://www.aaup.org. Illus., index, adv. Refereed. Circ: 45000 Paid. Vol. ends: Nov/Dec. Microform: PMC; PQC. Online: EBSCO Publishing; Northern Light Technology, Inc.; OCLC Online Computer Library Center, Inc.; ProQuest Information & Learning. *Indexed:* AbAn, AgeL, CIJE, DSR&OA, EduInd, HEA, MLA-IB, PAIS, RI-1, SSCI. *Bk. rev.:* 3-4, 800-1,500 words. *Aud.:* Ac.

The journal of the American Association of University Professors (AAUP) is dedicated to presenting faculty views on issues concerning higher education. Each issue has a theme such as globalization and the university, ethics and higher education, professors and intellectual property, and assessment and accountability of faculty and institutions. Five or six featured articles cover such important topics as scientific misconduct, intellectual property and the AAUP, copyrighted materials and the web, diversity and affirmative action, part-time and nontenure track faculty, and Ph.D. program attrition. Regular departments report on government policy and legislation pertaining to higher education, current legal issues facing academe, book reports, and censured higher education administrations. The association provides brief reports on its committees, its council, and annual meetings. The invaluable annual report on the "economic status of the profession" keeps the higher education professional informed as to faculty economic well-being. New and noteworthy items of interest are highlighted in a regular column titled "Nota Bene." A required journal for all academic libraries and special libraries. URL: http://www.aaup.org/publications/Academe

2488. *Change: the magazine of higher learning.* Formerly: *Change in Higher Education.* [ISSN: 0009-1383] 1969. bi-m. USD 112 (Individuals, USD 55; USD 18.75 per issue). Ed(s): Nanette Wiese. Heldref Publications, 1319 18th St, NW, Washington, DC 20036-1802; subscribe@heldref.org; http://www.heldref.org. Illus., index, adv. Refereed. Circ: 3492 Paid. CD-ROM: ProQuest Information & Learning. Online: bigchalk; EBSCO Publishing; Florida Center for Library Automation; Gale Group; Northern Light Technology, Inc.; OCLC Online Computer Library Center, Inc.; ProQuest Information & Learning; SoftLine Information; H.W. Wilson. Reprint: PSC. *Indexed:* AgeL, BRI, CBRI, CIJE, EduInd, HEA, IBZ, MagInd, RGPR. *Aud.:* Ac.

With editorial guidance from the American Association of Higher Education, *Change* presents views and opinions on current higher education issues. Intended for all practitioners in higher education institutions, organizations, and government offices, the focus is on discussion and analysis of educational programs and practices. Articles have covered all aspects of higher education including teaching methods, curriculum, students, educational philosophy, economics and finance, higher education management and administration, public policy, and professional development. Each issue contains about six articles ranging from a brief point of view to a featured article. Article topics have included holistic learning, assessment-based accountability in higher education, the demographics of higher education, pay equity for faculty, academic audits, evaluating state higher education performance, and changing admissions policies. Regular departments feature an editorial and a column of items of current interest to those in the field. A title important to all those in the field of higher education from administrators to department heads to faculty. URL: http://www.aahe.org/change

2489. *The Chronicle of Higher Education.* [ISSN: 0009-5982] 1966. w. 49/yr. USD 82.50 domestic; USD 135 Canada; USD 275 elsewhere. Ed(s): Ted Weidlein, Scott Jaschik. Chronicle of Higher Education, Inc., 1255 23rd St, N W, Ste 700, Washington, DC 20037; editor@chronicle.com; http://chronicle.com/. Illus., index, adv. Sample. Circ: 100000 Paid. Vol. ends: Aug. Microform: CIS; PQC. Online: EBSCO Publishing; Gale Group; Northern Light Technology, Inc. Reprint: PQC. *Indexed:* A&ATA, ABS&EES, BRI, CBRI, CIJE, CWI, ConsI, EduInd, EngInd, LRI, MagInd, RI-1. *Aud.:* Ga, Ac.

Published weekly, *The Chronicle of Higher Education* is academe's resource for news and information. Although the journal is intended for higher education faculty and administrators, the contents are relevant for others interested in the field of higher education such as researchers, students, federal and state legislators, government policy makers, and taxpayers. The weekly is organized into sections: current developments and issues in higher education; regular features on faculty, research, money and management, government and politics, international, students, and athletics; the chronicle review, with letters to the editor and opinion articles; and the section on career network with hundreds of job listings. Additionally, twice a year *Events in Academe* indexes meetings, events, and deadlines for fellowships, grants, papers, and prizes. An annual almanac issue covers facts and statistics about U.S. higher education both at the national and state level. *CHE* is available online with a searchable archive of more than 12 years. A required standard for all academic libraries as well as higher education institutions and organizations.

2490. *College and University.* [ISSN: 0010-0889] 1925. q. Non-members, USD 50. Ed(s): Roman S Gawkoski, Saira Burki. American Association of Collegiate Registrars and Admissions Officers, One Dupont Circle, N W, Ste 520, Washington, DC 20036-1135; pubs@aacrao.org; http://www.aacrao.com. Illus., index, adv. Circ: 9500. Vol. ends: Summer. Microform: PQC. Online: bigchalk; ProQuest Information & Learning. *Indexed:* AgeL, BRI, CBRI, CIJE, EduInd, HEA, SSCI. *Aud.:* Ac.

This journal of the American Association of Collegiate Registrars and Admissions Officers publishes scholarly and educational policy articles. The journal's focus is emerging and current issues, innovative practices and techniques, and administrative information technology in the profession. Each issue contains three or four featured articles. Regular features are letters to the editor, guest commentary, and book reviews. Articles have considered doctoral student attrition, web-based registration and administrative system, admissions and applications, college choice and decision making, credential evaluation, minority application process, and a case study of transfer students' attendance patterns. Articles reflect the professional experience of the contributing academic authors. For libraries serving those working or studying in the field of higher education admissions and registration this journal is a requirement.

2491. *College Board Review.* [ISSN: 0010-0951] 1947. q. USD 25. Ed(s): Paul Barry. College Board, 45 Columbus Ave, New York, NY 10023. Illus., index. Sample. Circ: 15500. Microform: PQC. Reprint: PQC. *Indexed:* CIJE, EduInd, HEA. *Aud.:* Ga, Ac.

A journal published by the College Board offering opinions and ideas on current issues and topics in the field of education. Intended for teachers, faculty, and administrators, the *College Board Review*'s scope includes guidance, testing, financial aid, and teaching and learning. Each issue has a focus with one or more supporting articles on themes such as the SAT writing section, college admissions as big business, the affirmative action debate, and teaching as a profession. Articles are usually short opinion pieces or experience-based essays written by authors from varied higher education backgrounds, such as an education editor of a newspaper, a member of the Board of Regents of the University of California, a college president, a director of college advising, and an economist with the Consortium on Financing Higher Education. An important journal for those involved or interested in the field of higher education.

2492. *College Teaching.* Formerly: *Improving College and University Teaching.* [ISSN: 8756-7555] 1953. q. USD 93 (Individuals, USD 47; USD 23.25 per issue). Ed(s): Rachel Petrowsky. Heldref Publications, 1319 18th St, NW, Washington, DC 20036-1802; subscribe@heldref.org; http://www.heldref.org. Illus., adv. Refereed. Circ: 1873 Paid. CD-ROM: ProQuest Information & Learning. Online: bigchalk; EBSCO Publishing; Florida Center for Library Automation; Gale Group; Northern Light Technology, Inc.; OCLC Online Computer Library Center, Inc.; ProQuest Information & Learning; H.W. Wilson. Reprint: PSC. *Indexed:* CIJE, EduInd, HEA, IBZ. *Bk. rev.:* 2-4, 800-1,200 words. *Aud.:* Ac.

A journal dedicated to exploring the issues of teaching at the undergraduate and graduate level. Articles cover interdisciplinary topics that have an application focus such as active learning, teaching techniques, new classroom practices, evaluations of innovative programs and practices, and professional development. Ranging from 750 to 5,000 words, articles address such teaching issues as English literacy problems for Asian graduate students, using features films as a teaching tool, team teaching a graduate course, inclusiveness in the classroom, and Internet assignments in a political science course. Regular departments are an editorial or opinion piece and a brief column presenting a teaching idea or technique for the classroom. With a broad range of topics, this journal covers the higher education classroom. An important and informative tool for higher education instructors. URL: http://www.heldref.org/html/body_ct.html

2493. *Community College Journal.* Former titles (until 1991): *Community, Technical, and Junior College Journal; Community and Junior College Journal; Junior College Journal.* [ISSN: 1067-1803] 1930. bi-m. USD 28 domestic; USD 36 foreign. Ed(s): Cheryl Gamble. American Association of Community Colleges, One Dupont Circle, N W, Ste 410, Washington, DC 20036-1176; http://www.aacc.nche.edu/. Illus., index, adv. Sample. Circ: 11000 Paid. Vol. ends: Jun/Jul. Microform: PQC. Reprint: PQC. *Indexed:* AgeL, CIJE, EduInd, HEA. *Bk. rev.:* 4-7, 100-300 words. *Aud.:* Ac.

As the advocate for community colleges, the American Association of Community Colleges publishes this journal to support the advancement of community colleges as institutions of higher learning. The journal contents include feature articles, opinion pieces, news items, and issues in the field of higher education. Each issue is dedicated to a theme with five or six brief articles. Recent themes covered include the global workforce, directions and innovations in technology, community colleges in the post-9/11 world, and leadership development. The intended audience of presidents, board members, administrators, faculty, and staff at two-year institutions is presented with practical content. Articles focus on trends and issues in the field such as training future faculty, ethics in the curriculum, and international student enrollments. For all community college libraries and graduate education program libraries supporting those working in or preparing to work in the field. URL: http://www.aacc.nche.edu/Content/NavigationMenu/ResourceCenter/AACCPublications/CommunityCollegeJournal/Community_College_Journal.htm

2494. *Community College Review.* [ISSN: 0091-5521] 1973. q. USD 55; USD 57 Canada; USD 59 elsewhere. Ed(s): George B Vaughan. North Carolina State University, Department of Adult and Community College Education, PO Box 7801, Raleigh, NC 27695-7801; barabara_scott@ncsu.edu; http://www.ncsu.edu/ncsu/cep/ACCE/ccreview/ccreview.html. Illus. Refereed. Circ: 1325 Paid. Vol. ends: Spring. Microform: PQC. Online: EBSCO Publishing; Florida Center for Library Automation; Gale Group; OCLC Online Computer Library Center, Inc.; ProQuest Information & Learning; H.W. Wilson. *Indexed:* CIJE, EduInd, HEA, MLA-IB. *Bk. rev.:* Occasional, essay length. *Aud.:* Ac.

A refereed journal publishing articles of 12 to 24 pages in length on research and practice of interest to community college educators. Intended for a broad readership including community college presidents, administrators, graduate students, and faculty, the journal articles are primarily qualitative or quantitative research. Both scholars and practitioners contribute to the journal with topics covering professional development for community and technical college presidents, the leave-taking of community college chief academic officers, a qualitative analysis of community college faculty careers, the recruitment of community college faculty, and the ease of student transfers with state matriculation agreements. Regular features are a literature review on a specific topic and book reviews. An important title for libraries serving the higher education community. URL: http://www.ncsu.edu/cep/acce/ccr/ccreview.htm

Current Issues in Education. See Electronic Journals subsection.

2495. *Innovative Higher Education.* Formerly (until 1983): *Alternative Higher Education.* [ISSN: 0742-5627] 1976. q. USD 468 print or online ed. Ed(s): Ronald D Simpson. Kluwer Academic / Plenum Publishers, 233 Spring St Fl 7, New York, NY 10013-1522; http://www.wkap.nl/. Illus., index, adv. Sample. Refereed. Vol. ends: Summer. Microform: PQC. Online: EBSCO Publishing; ingenta.com; Kluwer Online; OCLC Online Computer Library Center, Inc.; Ovid Technologies, Inc.; RoweCom Information Quest; Swets Blackwell. Reprint: ISI; PQC. *Indexed:* CIJE, EduInd, HEA, HRA, IBZ, PsycholAb, SWA. *Aud.:* Ga, Ac.

A refereed academic journal dedicated to emerging and current trends in higher education. Its focus is to provide practitioners and scholars with current strategies, programs, and innovations to enhance the field of higher education. The publication focuses on four designated types of articles: those that consider current innovative trends and practices with application beyond the context of higher education; those that discuss the effect of innovations on teaching and students; those that present scholarship and research methods broadly defined; and those that cover practice and theory appropriate for both faculty and administrators. Recent issues feature topics relevant to the field such as interdisciplinary learning, collaborative community in a multidisciplinary environment, national trends and issues of post-tenure review, evaluation of postgraduate supervision, a case study of instructional research and development, and teaching assistants' perceptions of instructional issues. This scholarly journal is highly recommended for libraries at higher education institutions or organizations.

2496. *Journal of College Student Development.* Formerly (until 1987): *Journal of College Student Personnel.* [ISSN: 0897-5264] 1959. bi-m. USD 115 domestic; USD 127 in Canada & Mexico; USD 139.60 elsewhere. Ed(s): Gregory Blimling. Johns Hopkins University Press, Journals Publishing Division, 2715 N Charles St, Baltimore, MD 21218-4363; jlorder@jhupress.jhu.edu; http://www.press.jhu.edu/. Illus., adv. Refereed. Circ: 8000 Paid. Vol. ends: Nov. Microform: PQC. Reprint: PQC. *Indexed:* AgeL, CIJE, EduInd, HEA, PsycholAb, SSCI, SWR&A. *Bk. rev.:* 0-4, 700-1,500 words. *Aud.:* Ac, Sa.

A publication of the American College Personnel Association focused on student development, professional development, administrative issues, and innovative programs to enhance student services. Authors contribute quantitative or qualitative research articles, research reviews, and essays on theoretical, organizational, and professional topics. A regular column describes new practices related to theory and research, programs, and techniques. Each issue generally contains about seven articles with a wide range of college student topics of interest such as understanding of binge drinking behavior, a literature review of college alchohol use and sexual behavior, predicting minority academic performance, research to determine the expectations for due process in a campus disciplinary hearing, and a study that examines student perceptions of faculty teaching as an indicator of student persistence. Includes book reviews. A professional journal recommended for academic libraries. URL: http://www.jcsd.appstate.edu

2497. *Journal of Computers in Mathematics and Science Teaching.* [ISSN: 0731-9258] 1981. q. USD 95 (Individuals, USD 75). Ed(s): Ed Dubinsky. Association for the Advancement of Computing in Education, PO Box 3728, Norfolk, VA 23514; info@aace.org; http://www.aace.org. Illus., adv. Sample. Refereed. Circ: 950 Paid. Online: Florida Center for Library Automation; Gale Group; OCLC Online Computer Library Center, Inc.; H.W. Wilson. *Indexed:* CIJE, EduInd, EngInd, MicrocompInd. *Aud.:* Ac, Sa.

An academic journal providing a venue for information on using information technology in teaching mathematics and science. Published by the Association for the Advancement of Computing in Education, the journal's aim is to promote the teaching and learning of computing technologies. With an international authorship, the journal is directed to faculty, researchers, classroom teachers, and administrators. Article format includes research papers, case studies, courseware experiences, review papers, evaluations, and opinions. Issues have four to six well-referenced articles on technology and teaching, such as gender and computer-mediated communications, technology and manipulatives, the principles for design and use of simulation software in science learning, and technologies with hands-on science activities in the United States, Japan, and the Netherlands. A subject-specific journal of value to both practitioner and researcher at all education levels.

2498. *Journal of Developmental Education.* Formerly (until 1984): *Journal of Developmental and Remedial Education.* [ISSN: 0894-3907] 1978. 3x/yr. USD 32 (Individuals, USD 27). Ed(s): Milton G Spann. Appalachian State University, National Center for Developmental Education, Reich College of Education, Boone, NC 28608. Illus., index. Refereed. Circ: 5000. Vol. ends: Jan. Online: EBSCO Publishing; Northern Light Technology, Inc.; OCLC Online Computer Library Center, Inc.; ProQuest Information & Learning; H.W. Wilson. Reprint: PQC. *Indexed:* CIJE, EduInd, HEA, MLA-IB. *Aud.:* Ac, Sa.

The National Center for Developmental Education's publication is dedicated to the education of the academically at-risk college community. The intended readers are educators involved with academically at-risk college students including faculty, administrators, and others at postsecondary institutions. The editorial focus is on articles which relate educational theory to the practice of teaching, evaluative studies, and the dissemination of research and news in the field. Articles have examined program evaluation studies, comprehension monitoring for mathematical problem solving, critical thinking, basic skills education, developmental education activities, and student counseling. In addition to about four articles per issue, there are regularly featured columns listing professional conferences and workshops, and a review of computer use in the developmental classroom. An important title for all academic libraries.

2499. *Journal of Higher Education.* [ISSN: 0022-1546] 1930. bi-m. USD 110. Ed(s): Leonard L Baird. Ohio State University Press, 180 Pressey Hall, 1070 Carmack Rd, Columbus, OH 43210-1002; journals@osu.edu; http://www.ohiostatepress.org. Illus., adv. Refereed. Circ: 4200 Paid. Vol. ends: Nov/Dec. CD-ROM: ProQuest Information & Learning. Microform: PMC; PQC. Online: bigchalk; Florida Center for Library Automation; Gale Group; JSTOR (Web-based Journal Archive); Northern Light Technology, Inc.; OCLC Online Computer Library Center, Inc.; Project MUSE; ProQuest Information & Learning; Swets Blackwell; H.W. Wilson. Reprint: ISI; PQC. *Indexed:* AgeL, BRI, CBRI, CIJE, ChemAb, EduInd, HEA, MLA-IB, PsycholAb, RI-1, SSCI, SWA, SWR&A. *Bk. rev.:* 4-12, 700-1,500 words. *Aud.:* Ac.

A membership journal for several higher education associations, this is the standard title in the field of higher education. It publishes research or technical papers, professional practice papers, literature reviews, and policy papers. Article content focuses on topics of interest and importance to the higher education community. A small number of substantial articles cover the current trends and issues in the field such as women of color in academe, critical thinking through effective teaching, assessment of institutional performance, gender bias in student evaluations of teaching, faculty time allocations, dual-career couples, and racial differences in the selection of an academic major. Occasional special issues examine topics in depth, such as the faculty in the new millennium or higher education's social role in the community at large. Each issue contains several lengthy book reviews and a review essay. A highly recommended journal for all libraries serving higher education institutions and organizations.

2500. *Liberal Education.* Incorporates: *Forum for Liberal Education;* Former titles (until 1958): *Association of American Colleges. Bulletin;* (until 1939): *Bulletin of the Association of American Colleges.* [ISSN:

0024-1822] 1915. 4x/yr. Members, USD 36; Non-members, USD 42. Ed(s): Bridget Puzon. Association of American Colleges and Universities, 1818 R St, N W, Washington, DC 20009; http://www.aacu.org/. Illus., index. Circ: 5000. Vol. ends: Nov/Dec. Microform: PQC. Online: EBSCO Publishing; Florida Center for Library Automation; Gale Group; Northern Light Technology, Inc.; ProQuest Information & Learning. *Indexed:* AgeL, CIJE, EduInd, HEA, MLA-IB, SSCI. *Aud.:* Ac.

A journal of the Association of American Colleges and Universities dedicated to improving undergraduate education. As a voice of the association and a resource for the higher education community, the journal's contents highlight liberal education theory and its practical application. Three sections include a featured topic with three or four supporting articles, a perspective section with how-to pieces, and an opinion article. Featured topics have been presidential leadership in the new millennium; liberal education curriculum planning and implementation; and academic achievement theories and strategies. For all libraries serving the undergraduate education community and graduate schools of education. URL: http://www.aacu-edu.org/liberaleducation/index.cfm

2501. ***Research in Higher Education.*** [ISSN: 0361-0365] 1973. 8x/yr. EUR 709 print or online ed. Ed(s): John C Smart. Kluwer Academic / Plenum Publishers, 233 Spring St Fl 7, New York, NY 10013-1522; http://www.wkap.nl/. Illus., adv. Refereed. Vol. ends: No. 4. Microform: PQC. Online: EBSCO Publishing; ingenta.com; Kluwer Online; OCLC Online Computer Library Center, Inc.; Ovid Technologies, Inc.; RoweCom Information Quest; Swets Blackwell. Reprint: PQC; SCH. *Indexed:* AgeL, CIJE, EduInd, HEA, PsycholAb, SSCI, SWA. *Aud.:* Ac.

The journal of the Association for Institutional Research is dedicated to improving the functioning of higher education institutions. Articles are written for an audience of higher education personnel, including institutional planners, administrators, and student personnel specialists. Professional papers focus on quantitative studies of higher education procedures. Areas of focus include administration and faculty, curriculum and instruction, student characteristics, and recruitment and admissions. Each issue contains about five lengthy, well-referenced articles addressing subjects such as educational attainment for blacks and whites, research on college students' academic coping style and academic performance, evaluating MBA program admissions criteria, institutional approaches to student assessment, and a study focusing on student preference for private over public institutions. A standard journal for all academic libraries and higher education institutions and organizations. URL: http://www.kluweronline.com/issn/0361-0365/contents

2502. ***Review of Higher Education.*** Formerly (until 1978): *Higher Education Review.* [ISSN: 0162-5748] 1977. q. USD 135 (Individuals, USD 58). Ed(s): Philip Altbach. Johns Hopkins University Press, Journals Publishing Division, 2715 N Charles St, Baltimore, MD 21218-4363; http://muse.jhu.edu. Illus., adv. Refereed. Circ: 1622 Paid. Microform: PQC. Online: EBSCO Publishing; OCLC Online Computer Library Center, Inc.; Project MUSE; ProQuest Information & Learning; RoweCom Information Quest; Swets Blackwell. Reprint: PQC; PSC. *Indexed:* CIJE, HEA, SSCI. *Bk. rev.:* Occasional, essay length. *Aud.:* Ac.

The Association for the Study of Higher Education publishes this scholarly journal to report on the issues and trends affecting the field of higher education. The *RHE* contains peer-reviewed articles, essays, studies, and research findings. Issues are analyzed, examined, investigated, and described in articles focusing on topics important to the study of higher education. Recent issues have included graduate student unionization, the roles and challenges of deans of higher education, current demographics of higher education, an analysis of gender differences in faculty salaries, and fiscal ability of public universities to compete for faculty. The review essay looks at recently published titles on a topic such as a historical perspective on higher education planning. Available in an online edition. An important journal to inform all those working or interested in the field of higher education. URL: http://www.press.jhu.edu/press/journals/rhe/rhe.html

Specific Subjects and Teaching Methods

ADULT EDUCATION

2503. ***Adult Basic Education: an interdisciplinary journal for adult literacy educational planning.*** Formerly (until vol.14, no.3, 1990): *Adult Literacy and Basic Education.* [ISSN: 1052-231X] 1977. 3x/yr. USD 30 in US & Canada; USD 40 elsewhere. Ed(s): Ken Melichar. Commission on Adult Basic Education, PO Box 592053, Orlando, FL 32859-2053. Illus., index, adv. Sample. Refereed. Circ: 1500 Paid. Vol. ends: Fall. Microform: PQC. Online: EBSCO Publishing; Northern Light Technology, Inc.; ProQuest Information & Learning. *Indexed:* AgeL, CIJE, EduInd. *Bk. rev.:* 1, 10-20 pages. *Aud.:* Ac, Sa.

A peer-reviewed scholarly journal dedicated to improving educators' efforts with adult literacy. The journal's audience consists of adult educators working in volunteer-based, community-based, and institution-based literacy programs. Written for the practitioner, this journal publishes critical essays, research reviews, and theoretical or philosophical articles. With an emphasis on practical relevance, contents have considered adult numeracy education, reading strategies, a research study with resulting guidelines and practical applications for using technology in the classroom, a review process for reviewing adult literacy provision at the community provider level, and practitioner-based inquiry. A highly recommended title for libraries serving adult literacy educators.

2504. ***Adult Education Quarterly: a journal of research and theory.*** Formerly (until 1983): *Adult Education.* [ISSN: 0741-7136] 1950. q. USD 206. Ed(s): Arthur Wilson, Elizabeth Hayes. Sage Publications, Inc., 2455 Teller Rd, Thousand Oaks, CA 91320; info@sagepub.com; http://www.sagepub.com. Illus., index, adv. Sample. Refereed. Circ: 5000. Vol. ends: Summer. Microform: PQC. Online: ingenta.com; OCLC Online Computer Library Center, Inc.; ProQuest Information & Learning; RoweCom Information Quest; Swets Blackwell; H.W. Wilson. *Indexed:* AgeL, BRI, BrEdI, CBRI, CIJE, EduInd, PsycholAb, RI-1, SSCI, SWA. *Bk. rev.:* 3, 1,000 words. *Aud.:* Ac, Sa.

A refereed journal dedicated to promoting the practice and understanding of adult and continuing education. Geared for scholars and practitioners, the journal aims to be inclusive regarding adult and continuing education topics and issues. Articles cover a wide range of research, including surveys, experimental designs, case studies, ethnographic observations, theory, historical investigations, or analyses. The present editors' goal is to increase the diversity of scholarly research to include newer forms such as feminist or postmodernist research, and to include international and interdisciplinary investigations. Each issue reflects the publication's focus on research and theory with, for example, Cambodian women's participation in adult ESL programs, a focus on workplace pedagogy, an assessment study of worker education programs and globalization, and a field study of nonparticipation in literacy programs among Mayan adults. The book review policy of the journal is also inclusive, seeking to define the field of adult and continuing education as multidisciplinary and broad based. Book reviews consider publications indirectly related, such as cultural studies, work and the economy, distance learning, and international development. A standard title for academic libraries as well as adult education organizations. URL: http://www.sagepub.co.uk/journals/details/j0352.html

The Computing Teacher. See *Learning & Leading with Technology* in the Classroom Magazines/Teacher and Professional section.

Educational Media International. See Media and AV section.

2505. ***Journal of Adolescent and Adult Literacy.*** Former titles (until 1995): *Journal of Reading; Journal of Developmental Reading.* [ISSN: 1081-3004] 1957. 8x/yr. USD 122 (Individuals, USD 61; USD 12.50 in developing nations). Ed(s): Todd Goodson. International Reading Association, Inc., 800 Barksdale Rd, Newark, DE 19714-8139; journals@reading.org; http://www.reading.org. Illus., index, adv. Refereed. Circ: 15000 Paid. Vol. ends: May. Microform: PQC. Online: bigchalk; EBSCO Publishing; Florida Center for Library Automation;

Gale Group; OCLC Online Computer Library Center, Inc.; ProQuest Information & Learning; H.W. Wilson. Reprint: PQC. *Indexed:* ABS&EES, AgeL, ArtHuCI, BEL&L, BRI, CBRI, CIJE, ECER, EduInd, L&LBA, MLA-IB, MRD, SSCI. *Bk. rev.:* 3, 800 words. *Aud.:* Ac.

A peer-reviewed journal dedicated to providing a forum for educators working in the field of literacy and language arts for older learners. Published by the International Reading Association, the focus is on innovative methods of teaching and researching literacy, and the issues and concerns of literacy professionals. Original articles present practical, theoretical, or research topics such as teaching English and literature to ESL students, a survey of content area reading strategies, cross-age tutoring, a workshop format and instruction strategy for struggling adolescent readers, and adolescent vocabulary development. Regularly featured columns present opinions and viewpoints, technology issues, and literacy requirements in the current work environment. Each issue contains lengthy reviews of books for adolescents, professional materials, and classroom materials. Recommended for school and academic libraries.

Learning and Leading with Technology. See Classroom Magazines/ Teacher and Professional section.

T.H.E. Journal. See Free Magazines and House Organs section.

THE ARTS

2506. *Art Education.* Incorporates (1970-1980): *Art Teacher.* [ISSN: 0004-3125] 1948. bi-m. Non-members, USD 50. Ed(s): Paul Bolin. National Art Education Association, 1916 Association Dr, Reston, VA 20191-1590; http://www.mgi-net.com/mgilists/naea.html. Illus., index, adv. Refereed. Circ: 18000 Controlled. Vol. ends: Nov. Microform: PQC. Online: Northern Light Technology, Inc.; OCLC Online Computer Library Center, Inc.; ProQuest Information & Learning; H.W. Wilson. Reprint: PQC; PSC. *Indexed:* CIJE, EduInd, IBZ. *Aud.:* Hs, Ac.

This journal of the National Art Education Association supports the association's goal to promote art education. Articles on current issues and exemplary practices in visual arts education serve the professional needs and interests of art educators at all educational levels. Theme-focused issues have addressed topics such as defining art education as a field, secondary art education, visual culture, museum education, art education in and beyond the classroom, and art education around the world. In addition to the three or four themed articles, each issue has instructional resources including four full-color art reproductions and a lesson plan. Position advertisements are a regular item. Highly recommended for school and academic libraries.

2507. *Arts and Activities: the nation's leading arts education magazine.* [ISSN: 0004-3931] 1932. m. Sep.-June. USD 24.95; USD 3 newsstand/ cover per issue. Ed(s): Maryellen Bridge. Publishers Development Corp., 591 Camino de la Reina, Ste 200, San Diego, CA 92108; anaed@artsandactivities.com. Illus., index, adv. Sample. Circ: 22000. Microform: PQC. Online: EBSCO Publishing; Florida Center for Library Automation; Gale Group; OCLC Online Computer Library Center, Inc.; ProQuest Information & Learning; H.W. Wilson. Reprint: PQC. *Indexed:* BiogInd, EduInd, ICM, MRD. *Bk. rev.:* 2-6, 50-100 words. *Aud.:* Ems, Hs, Ga, Ac.

A magazine dedicated to providing an exchange of professional experiences, opinions, and new ideas for art educators. Contributors share strategies for art instruction, approaches to art history, techniques for engaging students in evaluating art, and programs and lessons to expand students' appreciation of art. Articles have covered a broad range of topics such as art appreciation, ceramics, computer art, drawing and painting, mixed media, papier-mache, collage, and three-dimensional design for grades K-12. A regular feature is a pullout clip-and-save art print. For the practitioner, the magazine publishes an annual buyers' guide and a listing of summer art programs. Recommended for school libraries and academic libraries with art education programs. URL: http://www.artsandactivities.com

2508. *Arts Education Policy Review.* Former titles: *Design for Arts in Education; Design.* [ISSN: 1063-2913] 1879. bi-m. USD 97 (Individuals, USD 51; USD 16.25 per issue). Ed(s): Tom O'Brien. Heldref Publications, 1319 18th St, NW, Washington, DC 20036-1802; subscribe@heldref.org; http://www.heldref.org. Illus., index, adv. Refereed. Circ: 815. CD-ROM: ProQuest Information & Learning. Microform: PQC. Online: bigchalk; EBSCO Publishing; Florida Center for Library Automation; Gale Group; Northern Light Technology, Inc.; OCLC Online Computer Library Center, Inc.; ProQuest Information & Learning; H.W. Wilson. Reprint: PSC. *Indexed:* ArtInd, BRI, CIJE, EduInd, GAA, IBZ, MagInd, RGPR. *Bk. rev.:* 1, essay length. *Aud.:* Ac.

This journal provides a forum for the discussion of arts education policy issues in grades preK-12, nationally and internationally. With a focus on presenting current and controversial ideas and issues, articles focus on the application of policy analysis to arts education topics. Contributors present a broad range of perspectives and ideas on arts education. Articles cover the arts from dance to music, and issues from the improvement of music teacher education to national theater standards. A recent issue of the journal offers a symposium on arts education from past to present. Readership includes teachers, university faculty, education students, graduate students, policymakers, and others interested in arts in education. Recommended for all school and academic libraries. URL: http://www.heldref.org/html/body_aepr.html

2509. *School Arts: the art education magazine for teachers.* [ISSN: 0036-6463] 1901. m. Sep.-May. USD 23.95 domestic; USD 32.95 foreign. Ed(s): Eldon Katter. Davis Publications, Inc. (Worcester), 50 Portland St, Printers Bldg, Worcester, MA 01608; contactus@davis-art.com; http://www.davis-art.com. Illus., index, adv. Sample. Circ: 20764 Paid. Vol. ends: May/Jun. Microform: NBI; PQC. Online: Florida Center for Library Automation; Gale Group. Reprint: PQC. *Indexed:* ASIP, BRI, CBRI, CIJE, EduInd, MRD, MagInd. *Aud.:* Ga, Ac.

A magazine dedicated to inspiring art and classroom teachers at the elementary and secondary level. Each issue has a theme such as art for life and work, which included articles on literacy learning, art criticism, bookmaking and papermaking, and art and poetry. Short focused articles present curriculum ideas and plans, art technique applications, exemplary art programs, instruction and assessment methods, teaching art to special populations, and professional development. With the practitioner as audience, the magazine contains classroom instructional materials organized by educational level and extensive advertisements for art materials. Highly recommended for all school libraries. URL: http://www.davis-art.com/schoolarts

2510. *Studies in Art Education: a journal of issues and research in art education.* [ISSN: 0039-3541] 1959. q. USD 25; USD 45 foreign. Ed(s): Janice Davenport. National Art Education Association, 1916 Association Dr, Reston, VA 20191-1590; http://www.mgi-net.com/mgilists/naea.html. Illus., index. Refereed. Circ: 3500. Vol. ends: Summer. Microform: PQC. Online: Northern Light Technology, Inc.; OCLC Online Computer Library Center, Inc.; ProQuest Information & Learning; H.W. Wilson. Reprint: PQC; PSC. *Indexed:* ABCT, ABM, CIJE, EduInd. *Bk. rev.:* 1-3, 500-1,000 words. *Aud.:* Ac.

Published by the National Art Education Association, this scholarly journal supports the association's goal to promote art education through professional development and to disseminate knowledge and information about the field. The journal reports on historical, philosophical, or empirical research in the field of art education as well as applicable research in related disciplines. An interdisciplinary approach to art education is a focus of the journal's content. Issues cover a wide variety of topics and reflect the trends and issues of art education research. Articles have examined the place of content in teaching adolescent artists, mentoring in the art classroom, and the retention of good art teachers in the public school classrooms. Highly recommended for all academic libraries.

2511. *Visual Arts Research: educational, historical, philosophical and psychological perspectives.* Formerly (until Fall 1982): *Review of Research in Visual Arts Education.* [ISSN: 0736-0770] 1973. s-a. USD 36 (Individuals, USD 25). Ed(s): Christine Thompson. University of

Illinois at Urbana-Champaign, School of Art and Design, 143 Art and Design Bldg, 408 E Peabody Dr, Champaign, IL 61820. Illus., adv. Refereed. Circ: 400. Vol. ends: Fall. *Indexed:* BHA, CIJE, EduInd, PsycholAb. *Aud.:* Ac.

A journal dedicated to research on teaching and learning in the visual arts. Article contents cover critical and cultural studies, curriculum research and development, art education history, research, and theory, aesthetics, and phenomenology. A regular column reports on dissertations published relevant to the field of visual arts instruction. Academic contributors, predominantly from the United States, present papers concerned with current issues and ideas such as aesthetic thinking of young children and adolescents, art and incarcerated women, an assessment tool for an inner-city arts program, and art education as multicultural education. A focused journal for a specific audience.

COMMUNICATION ARTS

2512. ***College Composition and Communication.*** [ISSN: 0010-096X] 1950. q. Members, USD 48. Ed(s): Marilyn Cooper. National Council of Teachers of English, 1111 W Kenyon Rd, Urbana, IL 61801-1096. Illus., index, adv. Refereed. Circ: 10000. Vol. ends: Dec. Microform: PQC. Online: JSTOR (Web-based Journal Archive); ProQuest Information & Learning. Reprint: PSC. *Indexed:* AbAn, ArtHuCI, BRI, CBRI, CIJE, EduInd, IBZ, L&LBA, MLA-IB, SSCI. *Bk. rev.:* 1, essay length. *Aud.:* Ac.

This academic journal published by the Conference on College Composition and Communication addresses the issues and concerns of college composition instructors. Articles provide a forum for critical work on the study and teaching of college level composition and reading. Article content covers all aspects of the profession including teaching practices, the historical or institutional background of an educational practice, and current issues and trends in related disciplines. Although focused on those responsible for the teaching of composition at the college level, this journal will be of interest to administrators of composition programs, community college instructors, researchers, technical writers, graduate assistants, and others involved with college writing instruction. Each issue contains featured articles, review essays, book reviews, and contributor responses to published research theory or practice. Contributors have considered visual communication in the teaching of writing, service learning programs, plagiarism in policy and pedagogy, economics of academic staffing for first-year writing courses, and the sentence-based pedagogy of the sixties and seventies. A highly recommended title for academic libraries. URL: http://www.ncte.org/ccc

2513. ***College English.*** [ISSN: 0010-0994] 1939. bi-m. Members, USD 50. Ed(s): Jeanne Gunner. National Council of Teachers of English, 1111 W Kenyon Rd, Urbana, IL 61801-1096; cnimz@ncte.org. Illus., index, adv. Circ: 15000. Vol. ends: Dec. Microform: PMC; PQC. Online: Gale Group; JSTOR (Web-based Journal Archive); OCLC Online Computer Library Center, Inc.; ProQuest Information & Learning. Reprint: PSC. *Indexed:* AbAn, ArtHuCI, BEL&L, BRI, CIJE, ECER, EduInd, HumInd, IAPV, IBZ, L&LBA, LT&LA, MLA-IB, SSCI. *Bk. rev.:* 1-3, essay length. *Aud.:* Ac.

This refereed journal of the College Section of the National Council of Teachers of English (NCTE) provides a forum for scholars on English Studies. Topics covered include but are not limited to literature, linguistics, literacy, critical theory, reading theory, rhetoric, composition, pedagogy, and professional issues. Each issue has three or four articles as well as occasional opinion pieces, book reviews, reader comments and author responses, and NCTE news and announcements. Authors have published literary articles on topics such as critiquing the anticommunist rhetoric in *Invisible Man*, exploring cultural differences through world literature, and D. H. Lawrence and the dialogical principal. Other issues have covered creative nonfiction and an empirical study on composition. A standard for all academic libraries. URL: http://www.ncte.org/ce/ce0643toc.shtml

2514. ***Education, Communications & Information.*** [ISSN: 1463-631X] 2001. 3x/yr. GBP 153 (Individuals, GBP 57). Ed(s): Jenny Leach, Stone Wiske. Routledge, 11 New Fetter Ln, London, EC4P 4EE, United Kingdom; info@routledge.co.uk; http://www.routledge.co.uk. Online: Ingenta Select. Reprint: PSC. *Bk. rev.:* Number and length vary. *Aud.:* Ac.

This journal explores the interaction of innovations in educational theory, practice, and technologies. It focuses on international research, theoretical debates, and analyses of effective practices. The editors seek "critical and comparative analyses including paradigms and methodologies that cross disciplinary and cultural boundaries." The publication addresses questions relating to the impact of Information and Communications Technology (ICT) on knowledge, learning and pedagogy, new theories of education and curriculum for the design of educational technology, and other issues for educators. The editors welcome contributions from a wide range of educators to include academicians, students, teacher educators, policy makers, librarians, and teachers from many sectors. Three to five scholarly articles per issue cover such topics as scaling up an online course for 12,000 students, quality interaction and motivation using ICT in communication, education policies for new information technologies in Latin America, a study of educational software reviews, and the use of technology in teaching eighth grade history classes. Includes book reviews, updates on current trends, major reports, initiatives, and research publications. Each volume of *ECi* offers one or more research papers that are available only in multimedia format. Recommended for academic libraries. URL: http://www.tandf.co.uk/journals/routledge/1463631X.html

2515. ***English Education: official journal of the Conference on English Education and Communication.*** Formerly: *C E E Newsletter.* [ISSN: 0007-8204] 1969. 4x/yr. Members, USD 45. Ed(s): Dana Fox, Cathy Fleischer. National Council of Teachers of English, 1111 W Kenyon Rd, Urbana, IL 61801-1096; rsmith@ncte.org. Illus., index, adv. Sample. Refereed. Circ: 3100. Vol. ends: Dec. Microform: PQC. Online: ProQuest Information & Learning. Reprint: PQC. *Indexed:* CIJE, EduInd, SSCI. *Aud.:* Ac.

Dedicated to the education of teachers of English, reading, and language arts, the Conference on English Education focuses its journal on preservice training and in-service development. Issues relevant to the profession are considered such as preservice and in-service education, professional development, student teacher evaluation, English curriculum, and trends in teacher education programs nationwide. Each issue has three or four articles covering such topics as self-motivated student literacies, intertextual composition, and preparation of English-teacher educators. Readership is aimed at a broad range of teacher education personnel, including college and university instructors of teachers, in-service educators, teacher consultants, curriculum coordinators, and classroom teachers supervising student teachers. A highly recommended journal for libraries serving education programs. URL: http://www.ncte.org/ee/index.shtml

2516. ***English Journal.*** [ISSN: 0013-8274] 1912. bi-m. Members, USD 50. Ed(s): Virginia Monseau. National Council of Teachers of English, 1111 W Kenyon Rd, Urbana, IL 61801-1096; rsmith@ncte.org. Illus., index, adv. Sample. Refereed. Circ: 45000. Vol. ends: Dec. Microform: PMC; PQC. Online: Gale Group; OCLC Online Computer Library Center, Inc.; ProQuest Information & Learning. Reprint: PQC; PSC. *Indexed:* BRI, CBRI, CIJE, ECER, EduInd, FLI, IAPV, L&LBA, LRI, LT&LA, MLA-IB, MRD, MagInd, RGPR, SSCI. *Bk. rev.:* 6, 500-700 words. *Aud.:* Ac.

A publication of the National Council of Teachers of English (NCTE), this journal serves an audience of middle school, junior high school, and senior high school teachers as well as supervisors and teacher educators. This refereed publication covers current practices and theory in teaching composition, reading skills, oral language, literature, and varied media use. Featured articles may focus on a particular issue or topic while regular columns review books and classroom material, provide a forum for the exchange of teaching suggestions and ideas, and inform as to NCTE news and activities. With fifteen or more articles per issue, the featured topic is well covered by both practical applications and theoretical perspectives. Topics have included Shakespeare for a new age, cultural issues relevant to the study of language, the issues and challenges of technology as a teaching tool, and the school and the community. A recommended journal for school and academic libraries.

2517. ***Kairos: a journal for teachers of writing in webbed environment.*** [ISSN: 1521-2300] 1996. 3x/yr. Free. Ed(s): James A. Inman, Douglas Eyman. Kairos, jinman@english.cas.usf.edu; http://129.118.38.138/kairos/default.htm. Refereed. *Indexed:* MLA-IB, OTA. *Aud.:* Ac, Sa.

A refereed "product" dedicated to exploring writing, learning, and teaching in hypertextual environments. Intended for teachers, researchers, and writing tutors at the higher education level, the journal's focus is technical and business writing, professional communication, creative writing, composition, and literature. Contributions to the journal must be written in/for hypertext or the web. The journal's contributions cover empirical research reports, sample syllabi, theoretical essays, commentary, and software reviews. Each issue has a themed focus with regular columns for news and reviews. Features have considered critical issues in computers and writing, technology and the language arts in the K-12 classroom, and hypertext fiction/hypertext poetry. A highly recommended resource for the secondary education and higher education community.

2518. ***Language Arts.*** Former titles (until 1975): *Elementary English;* (until 1946): *Elementary English Review.* [ISSN: 0360-9170] 1924. bi-m. Members, USD 50. Ed(s): Sharon Murphy, Curt Dudley Marling. National Council of Teachers of English, 1111 W Kenyon Rd, Urbana, IL 61801-1096; cschanche@ncte.org. Illus., index, adv. Sample. Refereed. Circ: 19000. Vol. ends: Dec. Microform: PQC. Online: Gale Group; OCLC Online Computer Library Center, Inc.; ProQuest Information & Learning. Reprint: PQC; PSC. *Indexed:* BRI, CBRI, CIJE, EduInd, L&LBA, LT&LA, MLA-IB, MRD. *Bk. rev.:* 30-35 children's books. *Aud.:* Ac.

A title published by the National Council of Teachers of English for elementary teachers and teacher educators of language arts. Original articles focus on all aspects of language arts learning and teaching from preschool through middle school age levels. Issues are theme focused with the exception of a single unthemed issue per volume. Recent themes consider local languages and literacies, the cross-cultural convergence with language arts, new theories and ideas on writing instruction, and the importance of a professional community for language arts educators. Each issue gives classroom strategies, methods, research reports, and opinions. Recommended for school and academic libraries serving an education program. URL: http://www.ncte.org/la/index.shtml

2519. ***Reading Improvement: a journal for the improvement of reading teaching.*** Formerly: *Reading in High School.* [ISSN: 0034-0510] 1963. q. USD 33 (Individuals, USD 27). Ed(s): Phil Feldman. Project Innovation, 1362 Santa Cruz Ct, Chula Vista, CA 91910-7114. Illus., index, adv. Sample. Refereed. Circ: 2500. Vol. ends: Winter. Microform: PQC. Online: Florida Center for Library Automation; Gale Group; OCLC Online Computer Library Center, Inc.; ProQuest Information & Learning; H.W. Wilson. Reprint: PQC. *Indexed:* CIJE, EduInd, L&LBA. *Bk. rev.:* 0-3, 200-300 words. *Aud.:* Ac.

A journal dedicated to improving the pedagogy and practice of the teaching of reading. Covering all levels of instruction, the journal publishes investigative reports and theoretical papers. Each issue contains five to seven articles with a broad range of topics including successful implementation of the America Reads Program, reading English as a foreign language, recommendations for reading improvement and achievement in multicultural settings, and computer literacy for workplace development. Recommended for school and academic libraries. URL: http://journals825.home.mindspring.com/ri.html

2520. ***Reading Research and Instruction.*** Former titles (until vol.25): *Reading World; Journal of the Reading Specialist.* [ISSN: 0886-0246] 1961. q. USD 50 domestic; USD 55 Canada; USD 58 elsewhere. Ed(s): Robert Rickelman. College Reading Association, c/o Barbara Martin Palmer, Department of Education, Emmitsburg, MD 21727. Illus., index, adv. Refereed. Circ: 1200. Vol. ends: Summer. Online: OCLC Online Computer Library Center, Inc.; ProQuest Information & Learning; H.W. Wilson. Reprint: PQC. *Indexed:* CIJE, EduInd, PsycholAb, SSCI. *Bk. rev.:* Number and length vary. *Aud.:* Ac.

A refereed journal of the College Reading Association, which publishes articles on reading research and related literacy fields. Articles include discussions of current issues, research reports, instructional practices, book reviews, and news from the field. Each issue has four or five lengthy articles on such topics as classroom spelling instruction, learning through multicultural literature, a study done to understand preservice elementary education teachers' beliefs about struggling readers, a research study to give preservice teachers a better understanding of the classroom writing process, and current findings from a study of middle school readers participating in literacy events. Highly recommended for school and academic libraries serving education programs.

2521. ***Reading Research Quarterly.*** [ISSN: 0034-0553] 1965. q. USD 122 (Individuals, USD 61). Ed(s): Donna E. Alvermann, David Reinking. International Reading Association, Inc., 800 Barksdale Rd, Newark, DE 19714-8139; journals@reading.org; http://www.reading.org. Illus., index, adv. Refereed. Circ: 13000 Paid. Vol. ends: Fall. Microform: PQC. Online: Florida Center for Library Automation; Gale Group; Ingenta Select; Northern Light Technology, Inc.; ProQuest Information & Learning. Reprint: PQC. *Indexed:* AgeL, ArtHuCI, CIJE, CommAb, ECER, EduInd, L&LBA, LT&LA, MLA-IB, PsycholAb, SFSA, SSCI. *Bk. rev.:* 1, 10 pages. *Aud.:* Ac.

Published by the International Reading Association, *RRQ* is a peer-reviewed scholarly journal dedicated to presenting and examining the issues of literacy for all learners. Articles include qualitative and quantitative research, integrative reviews, and conceptual pieces that promote and contribute to the understanding of literacy and literacy research. Each issue reflects a broad range of academic literacy research with topics and issues such as assessing narrative comprehension in young children, the tutoring of young at-risk readers by minimally trained college students, and a historical definition of social constructionism. Responding to an international readership, the journal provides a brief abstract of each featured article in six languages. Letters to the editor and commentaries contribute to the journal's dialogue on literacy research. Available online. Highly recommended for academic and school libraries. URL: http://www.reading.org/publications/rrq

2522. ***The Reading Teacher: a journal of the International Reading Association.*** [ISSN: 0034-0561] 1948. 8x/yr. USD 122 (Individuals, USD 61). Ed(s): D Ray Reutzel, Judith Mitchell. International Reading Association, Inc., PO Box 8139, Newark, DE 19714-8139; journals@reading.org; http://www.reading.org. Illus., index, adv. Refereed. Circ: 55000 Paid. Vol. ends: May. Microform: PQC. Online: EBSCO Publishing; Florida Center for Library Automation; Gale Group; Northern Light Technology, Inc.; OCLC Online Computer Library Center, Inc.; ProQuest Information & Learning; H.W. Wilson. Reprint: PQC. *Indexed:* AgeL, ArtHuCI, BRI, CBRI, CIJE, ECER, EduInd, L&LBA, MLA-IB, MRD, PsycholAb, SSCI. *Aud.:* Ga, Ac.

A peer-reviewed journal by the International Reading Association, *RT* considers practices, research, and trends in literacy education and related disciplines. This journal is published for educators and other professionals involved with literacy education for children to the age of 12. Individual issues have five or six featured articles, teaching ideas, and children's book review columns, as well as the occasional annotated bibliography of books and children's literary work. A recent themed issue covers literacy instruction in the United States and worldwide. The journal's goal to promote and affect literacy education is realized with article topics such as improving students' reading performance through standards-based school reform, measurement of attitudes toward writing, and high-stakes testing in reading. An important journal for school and academic libraries. URL: http://www.reading.org/publications/rt

2523. ***Research in the Teaching of English.*** [ISSN: 0034-527X] 1967. q. Members, USD 45. Ed(s): Peter Smagorinsky, Michael Smith. National Council of Teachers of English, 1111 W Kenyon Rd, Urbana, IL 61801-1096; rsmith@ncte.org. Illus., adv. Sample. Refereed. Circ: 4100. Vol. ends: Dec. Microform: PQC. Online: ProQuest Information & Learning. Reprint: PQC. *Indexed:* ArtHuCI, CIJE, EduInd, L&LBA, LT&LA, SSCI. *Aud.:* Ac.

RTE's definition of research in the teaching of English is broad and inclusive. The journal is dedicated to publishing multiple approaches to conducting research such as teacher-based research, historical articles, narratives, and current methodology. Additionally, the journal seeks articles that consider literacy issues regardless of language, within schools or other settings, and in other disciplines. General themes are supported with scholarly, well-referenced articles. A semi-annual selected bibliography of recent research in the teaching of English further supports *RTE*'s mission. Recommended for academic libraries. URL: http://www.ncte.org/rte

ENVIRONMENTAL EDUCATION

2524. *The Journal of Environmental Education.* Formerly: *Environmental Education.* [ISSN: 0095-8964] 1969. q. USD 107 (Individuals, USD 55; USD 26.75 per issue). Ed(s): Catherine Simon, Alison Panko. Heldref Publications, 1319 18th St, NW, Washington, DC 20036-1802; subscribe@heldref.org; http://www.heldref.org. Illus., index, adv. Sample. Refereed. Circ: 1200. CD-ROM: ProQuest Information & Learning. Online: EBSCO Publishing; Florida Center for Library Automation; Gale Group; Northern Light Technology, Inc.; OCLC Online Computer Library Center, Inc.; ProQuest Information & Learning; H.W. Wilson. Reprint: PSC. *Indexed:* AIAP, BiolAb, CIJE, DSR&OA, EduInd, EngInd, EnvAb, ExcerpMed, PollutAb, PsycholAb, RI-1, SSCI, SWRA. *Bk. rev.:* 1-2, 500 words. *Aud.:* Ac, Sa.

With a focus on environmental education, this journal publishes original articles that promote and inform on instruction, theory, methods, and practice from primary grades through college. Peer-reviewed research articles include project reports, programs, review articles, critical essays, analyses, and qualitative or quantitative studies. The emphasis is on how to instruct on environmental issues and how to evaluate existing programs. With four to six articles per issue, topics have included building environmental literacy, developing effective environmental education, considering culture as a determinant of environmental attitudes, and examining a meta-analysis of classroom interventions and improved environmental behavior. Regular columns include a review of resources and a summary of a current innovative research study. Readership consists of teachers and others involved with environmental education programs for schools, parks, camps, recreation centers, and businesses. Recommended title for schools and programs serving environmental education.

MORAL EDUCATION

2525. *Journal of Moral Education.* [ISSN: 0305-7240] 1971. q. USD 76 (Individuals, GBP 38). Ed(s): Monica Taylor. Carfax Publishing Ltd., 4 Park Sq, Milton Park, Abingdon, OX14 4RN, United Kingdom; enquiry@tandf.co.uk; http://www.tandf.co.uk/. Illus., index, adv. Sample. Refereed. Vol. ends: Dec. Online: EBSCO Publishing; Ingenta Select; Northern Light Technology, Inc.; OCLC Online Computer Library Center, Inc.; ProQuest Information & Learning; RoweCom Information Quest; Swets Blackwell. Reprint: PSC. *Indexed:* ASSIA, ArtHuCI, BrEdI, CIJE, CJA, EduInd, HEA, IBZ, PhilInd, PsycholAb, R&TA, RI-1, SSCI, SWA, SociolAb. *Bk. rev.:* 5-10, 600-1,500 words. *Aud.:* Ac.

A journal focused on all aspects of moral education and development. A multidisciplinary approach and inclusive age range contribute to the journal's broad content scope. Authors provide philosophical analyses, empirical research reports, evaluations of educational practice, and overviews of international moral education theories and practices. Five or six articles per issue cover moral education research such as character education in a public high school, a critical analysis of the meaning of dominance, an exploration of language-based socialization patterns, and children's development of moral and social knowledge. Curriculum materials and book reviews as well as special thematic issues further the academic value of the journal. Available online. A standard journal for all academic libraries. URL: http://www.tandf.co.uk/journals/archive/c-archive/jme-con.html

SOCIAL STUDIES (INCLUDING HISTORY AND ECONOMICS)

2526. *History Teacher.* [ISSN: 0018-2745] 1967. q. USD 33 (Individuals, USD 27; Students, USD 18). Ed(s): Edward A Gosselin. Society for History Education, Inc., California State University, 1250 Bellflower Blvd, Long Beach, CA 90840. Illus., index, adv. Sample. Refereed. Circ: 2000. Vol. ends: Aug. Microform: PQC. Online: EBSCO Publishing; JSTOR (Web-based Journal Archive); OCLC Online Computer Library Center, Inc.; H.W. Wilson. Reprint: PQC. *Indexed:* AmH&L, BAS, CIJE, EduInd, IBZ, MRD. *Bk. rev.:* 12-15, 600-1,200 words. *Aud.:* Ac.

A membership journal of the Society for History Education, this title is dedicated to the teaching of history in the secondary and higher education classroom. The journal focuses on professional analyses of current and innovative teaching techniques. Issues have included National History Day prize essays and articles on history teaching at the community college, digital history in the history/social studies classroom, the craft of teaching, historiography, and the state of the profession. An extensive review section covers textbooks, readers, films, computer programs, and other material. Recommended for academic libraries. URL: http://www.csulb.edu/~histeach

2527. *The Journal of Economic Education.* [ISSN: 0022-0485] 1969. q. USD 111 (Individuals, USD 57; USD 27.75 per issue). Ed(s): Rosalind Springsteen. Heldref Publications, 1319 18th St, NW, Washington, DC 20036-1802; subscribe@heldref.org; http://www.heldref.org. Illus., index, adv. Refereed. Circ: 1200. CD-ROM: ProQuest Information & Learning. Online: bigchalk; Chadwyck-Healey Incorporated; EBSCO Publishing; Florida Center for Library Automation; Gale Group; Northern Light Technology, Inc.; OCLC Online Computer Library Center, Inc.; ProQuest Information & Learning; H.W. Wilson. Reprint: PSC. *Indexed:* AgeL, BusEdI, CIJE, EduInd, IBZ, JEL, PAIS, SSCI. *Bk. rev.:* 1-2, 300-3,000 words. *Aud.:* Ac.

A journal offering original articles on innovations in and evaluations of teaching techniques, materials, and programs in economics. Designed for instructors of beginning through graduate level economics courses, issues have featured sections on research, economic instruction, and economic content. Contributed articles include theoretical and empirical studies, substantive issues, new ideas, innovations in pedagogy, interactive exemplary material, and reports on the status and events that influence academic economists. Recent article topics explore Malthus's principle of population, teaching inflation targeting, risk aversion and the value of information, graduate program ranking and job market success, high school students' opportunities for economic research, student evaluations, and the use of music to teach economics. Recommended for academic libraries. URL: http://www.indiana.edu/~econed

2528. *Social Education: the official journal of the National Council for the Social Studies.* [ISSN: 0037-7724] 1937. 7x/yr. 0 membership. Ed(s): Michael Simpson. National Council for the Social Studies, 8555 16th St, Ste 500, Silver Spring, MD 20910; ncss@ncss.org; http://www.ncss.org. Illus., index, adv. Sample. Circ: 29000. Vol. ends: Nov/Dec. Microform: PQC. Online: Factiva; Florida Center for Library Automation; Gale Group; Northern Light Technology, Inc.; OCLC Online Computer Library Center, Inc.; ProQuest Information & Learning. Reprint: PQC. *Indexed:* ABS&EES, ASSIA, AgeL, BAS, BRI, CBRI, CIJE, EduInd, LRI, MRD, SSCI. *Bk. rev.:* 1-6, 200-800 words. *Aud.:* Ac.

A journal published by the National Council for the Social Studies (NCSS) to support the council's mission "to provide leadership, service, and support" for social studies instructors. The journal's content is focused on classroom practices at all levels: elementary, middle, high school, and university. Featured articles have presented current environmental issues, a consideration of the practice and theory of instructional technology, and a ten-year study of citizenship education in five countries. Significant journal content is given to classroom curriculum such as a study unit on the Great Depression, an oral history project to explore immigration, and a critique of NCSS curriculum standards. Regularly includes book reviews, lesson plans, the Internet as an instruction tool, and a journal supplement, *Middle Level Learning*, all of which contribute to the classroom focus of this publication. Highly recommended for school and academic libraries serving education programs. URL: http://www.socialstudies.org/publications/socialed.shtml

2529. *The Social Studies.* [ISSN: 0037-7996] 1909. bi-m. USD 85 (Individuals, USD 49; USD 14.25 per issue). Ed(s): Helen Kress. Heldref Publications, 1319 18th St, NW, Washington, DC 20036-1802; subscribe@heldref.org; http://www.heldref.org. Illus., index, adv. Refereed. Circ: 1600. Microform: PQC. Online: Chadwyck-Healey Incorporated; EBSCO Publishing; Florida Center for Library Automation; Gale Group; Northern Light Technology, Inc.; OCLC Online Computer

Library Center, Inc.; ProQuest Information & Learning; SoftLine Information; H.W. Wilson. Reprint: PSC. *Indexed:* ArtHuCI, BRD, BRI, CBRI, CIJE, EduInd, IBZ, PAIS, PSA, SSCI. *Bk. rev.:* 0-1, 400 words. *Aud.:* Ac.

This peer-reviewed journal publishes articles concerned with the subjects of social studies, social sciences, history, and interdisciplinary studies for grades K-12. The journal seeks articles that give new perspectives, practical applications, and insights on issues concerning social studies curriculum and instruction. With five to seven articles per issue, *TSS* covers a broad range of topics from research based to classroom practice. Articles have focused on critical thinking for students, strategies for student-centered classroom dialogue, a review of social studies/history curriculum, 1892-1937, the use of instructional methods and curriculum in the classroom such as studying history on the Internet, a teacher's guide for a unit on Appalachia, and using student-designed oral history. Recommended for school and academic libraries. URL: http://www.heldref.org/html/body_tss.html

TEACHER EDUCATION

2530. ***Action in Teacher Education.*** [ISSN: 0162-6620] 1978. q. USD 80 (Individual members, USD 90). Ed(s): Pamela Fry. Association of Teacher Educators, 1900 Association Dr, Reston, VA 20191-1502; ate1@aol.com; http://www.siu.edu.departments/coe/ate. Illus., index, adv. Sample. Circ: 4000. Vol. ends: Winter. Microform: PQC. Online: OCLC Online Computer Library Center, Inc.; H.W. Wilson. *Indexed:* CIJE, EduInd. *Aud.:* Ac.

A refereed journal published by the Association of Teacher Educators, an organization dedicated to the improvement of teacher education for both school and higher education instructors. Intended to serve as a forum for issues, ideas, and trends concerning the improvement of teacher education, this journal is for the practitioner. Articles are focused on the theory, practice, and research of teacher education. With practitioners as audience, the content is on the applications and implications of research and practice. Issues are both thematic and nonthematic with 10 to 14 articles per issue. Themed issues have featured indigenous perspectives of teacher education, reflective practices, preparation and professional development of teachers and the impact on student learning, and three different perspectives of teaching and teacher education. Nonthemed issues have covered a broad range of issues from professional identity to writing federal grant proposals to university school district collaboration. A journal for all school and academic libraries. URL: http://www.siu.edu/departments/coe/ate/media/ate_jrn2l.htm

2531. ***Journal of Education for Teaching.*** Formerly (until 1980): *British Journal of Teacher Education.* [ISSN: 0260-7476] 1975. 3x/yr. GBP 366 (Individuals, GBP 135). Ed(s): Edgar Stones. Carfax Publishing Ltd., 4 Park Sq, Milton Park, Abingdon, OX14 4RN, United Kingdom; enquiry@tandf.co.uk; http://www.tandf.co.uk/. Adv. Refereed. Online: EBSCO Publishing; Ingenta Select; Northern Light Technology, Inc.; OCLC Online Computer Library Center, Inc.; ProQuest Information & Learning; RoweCom Information Quest; Swets Blackwell. Reprint: PSC. *Indexed:* BrEdI, CIJE, EduInd, HEA, L&LBA, LT&LA, SSCI, SWA. *Aud.:* Ac.

JET publishes original articles on the subject of teacher education. The journal's definition of teacher education is inclusive of initial training, in-service education, and professional staff development. With an international orientation, the journal seeks to promote academic discussion of issues, trends, research, opinion, and practice on teacher education. Predominantly British, authors have contributed scholarly assessment of issues such as global influences on teacher education in Scotland, teacher authority in Finnish schools, the role of higher education in the training of secondary school teachers in Great Britain, and development and change with science teachers' practice in Egyptian classrooms. Available online. Recommended for all academic libraries.

2532. ***Journal of Teacher Education: the journal of policy, practice, and research in teacher education.*** [ISSN: 0022-4871] 1950. 5x/yr. USD 322 print & online eds. Ed(s): Marilyn Cochran-Smith, David Scanlon. Corwin Press, Inc., 2455 Teller Rd, Thousand Oaks, CA 91320-2218; info@sagepub.com; http://www.corwinpress.com. Illus., adv. Sample. Refereed. Vol. ends: Nov/Dec. Microform: PQC. Online: EBSCO Publishing; Florida Center for Library Automation; Gale Group; ingenta.com; OCLC Online Computer Library Center, Inc.; ProQuest Information & Learning; RoweCom Information Quest; Swets Blackwell. Reprint: PQC. *Indexed:* ArtHuCI, BRI, CBRI, CIJE, ECER, EduInd, IBZ, PsycholAb, SSCI. *Bk. rev.:* 1-3, 1,000 words. *Aud.:* Ac.

A professional journal of the American Association of Colleges for Teacher Education, *JTE* considers teacher education as a field of study. As noted in the journal's subtitle, the focus is on policy, practice, and research in teacher education. Articles address the topics of reflective teaching, field experiences of preservice teachers, quality in preservice teacher portfolios, teacher education faculty, student teaching, and other professional interests. Themed issues have considered multicultural education, and teacher education and society with scholarly papers integrating research, practice, and theory on the topic. Highly recommended for all libraries serving teacher education programs.

2533. ***Teacher Education Quarterly.*** Formerly (until 1983): *California Journal of Teacher Education.* [ISSN: 0737-5328] 1972. 4x/yr. USD 100 (Individuals, USD 60). Ed(s): Thomas G Nelson. Caddo Gap Press, 3145 Geary Blvd, Ste 275, San Francisco, CA 94118; caddogap@aol.com. Illus., adv. Sample. Refereed. Circ: 1000 Paid. Vol. ends: Fall. Microform: CMC; PQC. Online: OCLC Online Computer Library Center, Inc.; ProQuest Information & Learning; H.W. Wilson. Reprint: PQC. *Indexed:* CIJE, EduInd. *Aud.:* Ac.

A refereed research journal that focuses on current educational research and practice as well as educational policy and reform issues. Published by the California Council on Teacher Education, an organization dedicated to supporting and promoting teacher educators. *TEQ* supports the council's mission with relevant, interesting, and challenging articles related to the field of teacher education and teacher professional development. Contributors from university researchers to teacher education practitioners cover issues such as arts-based curriculum, teacher preparation for inclusive environments, interdisciplinary team teaching as professional development, and current policy initiatives and innovative teacher education practices. Recommended for all libraries serving teacher education programs. URL: http://members.aol.com/caddogap/ccet/teq.htm

2534. ***Teaching & Teacher Education: an international journal of research and studies.*** [ISSN: 0742-051X] 1985. 8x/yr. EUR 803 (Qualified personnel, EUR 253). Ed(s): Michael J Dunkin, G Morine. Pergamon, The Boulevard, Langford Ln, East Park, Kidlington, OX5 1GB, United Kingdom. Illus., index. Sample. Refereed. Vol. ends: Nov (No. 17). Microform: PQC. Online: ingenta.com; ScienceDirect; Swets Blackwell. *Indexed:* BrEdI, CIJE, EduInd, IBZ, PsycholAb, SSCI. *Aud.:* Ac.

This international journal covers all aspects and levels of teaching and teacher education. With its broad coverage, the journal is of value to all concerned with teaching, including researchers in teacher education, educational and cognitive psychologists, and policy makers and planners. The journal is committed to promoting teaching and teacher education through the publication of theory, research, and practice. Academic authors support the journal's commitment with scholarly articles ranging from classroom practice to professional development to preservice teachers. Each issue contains seven or eight articles focused on topics such as the peer review process, a diversity study using narrative methodology, a collaborative research project exploring an innovative professional development program, and a case study of student teaching in an inner city school. Recommended for all libraries serving teacher education programs. URL: http://www.sciencedirect.com/science/journal/0742051X

2535. ***Teaching Education.*** [ISSN: 1047-6210] 1987. 3x/yr. USD 204 (Individuals, USD 68). Ed(s): Allen Luke, Carmen Luke. Taylor & Francis Inc, 325 Chestnut St, Suite 800, Philadelphia, PA 19016; info@taylorandfrancis.com; http://www.taylorandfrancis.com/. Illus., index, adv. Sample. Refereed. Circ: 1200 Controlled. Vol. ends: Spring/Summer. Online: EBSCO Publishing; Ingenta Select; OCLC Online Computer Library Center, Inc.; RoweCom Information Quest; Swets Blackwell; H.W. Wilson. Reprint: PSC. *Indexed:* CIJE, EduInd. *Bk. rev.:* 3-5, 300-500 words. *Aud.:* Ac.

Dedicated to providing a forum for innovative practice and research in teacher education, the journal's focus is on challenge and change in teacher education. Contributors address social, cultural, practical, and theoretical issues of teacher education from school to university. The journal's contents include critical and theory-based research, scholarly reflections on current teacher education issues, innovative approaches to undergraduate and graduate teaching, and new practices in the K-12 classroom. Research and scholarship topics have addressed case writing in teacher education, teaching action research to preservice teachers, the politics of pedagogy, and developing critical writing practices. Innovative approaches to curriculum have included the city as a multicultural classroom and a course on student assistance training for preservice teachers. Available online. Recommended for all academic libraries.

TECHNOLOGY

2536. ***Educational Technology: the magazine for managers of change in education.*** [ISSN: 0013-1962] 1961. bi-m. USD 139 domestic; USD 159 foreign. Ed(s): Lawrence Lipsitz. Educational Technology, 700 Palisade Ave, PO Box 1564, Englewood Cliffs, NJ 07632-0564; EdTecPubs@aol.com; http://www.bookstoread.com/etp/. Illus., adv. Sample. Circ: 3000 Paid. Vol. ends: Nov/Dec. *Indexed:* CIJE, ECER, EduInd, MRD, MicrocompInd, PsycholAb, SSCI. *Aud.:* Ac.

This magazine publishes articles that report on research and practical applications in the field of technology in education and training. It is focused on a readership of school administrators, trainers, designers, and others involved with educational technology. With nine or ten articles per issue, issues cover varied aspects of educational technology such as online collaboration, dimensions of e-learning, instructional design, interactive multimedia instruction, web-based learning, and the design of technology-based instruction. Recommended for all academic and school libraries.

2537. ***Educational Technology Research & Development.*** Incorporates (1977-1989): *Journal of Instructional Development;* (1953-1989): *Educational Communications and Technology Journal;* Formerly: *A V Communication Review.* [ISSN: 1042-1629] 1953. q. USD 75 domestic; USD 83 foreign. Ed(s): Steven M Ross, James D Klein. Association for Educational Communication and Technology (A E C T), 1800 N Stonelake Dr., Ste 2, Bloomington, IN 47404; aect@aect.org; http://www.aect.org/. Illus., index, adv. Refereed. Circ: 5000 Paid. Vol. ends: No. 4. Microform: PQC. Online: OCLC Online Computer Library Center, Inc.; ProQuest Information & Learning; H.W. Wilson. Reprint: PQC. *Indexed:* ArtHuCI, CIJE, CommAb, EduInd, L&LBA, PsycholAb, SSCI. *Bk. rev.:* 4, essay length. *Aud.:* Ac.

A publication of the Association for Educational Communications and Technology, the journal serves to promote educational technology and its application to the learning process. Each issue has five or six articles covering research and development topics. Recent topics include computer-based tools for instructional design, project-based learning with the World Wide Web, reflections on the current state of educational technology, a design theory of problem solving, and cultural connections in a distance-learning community. A regular department features issues and trends in the field of educational technology in other countries. Documents from the ERIC Clearinghouse on Educational Technology are highlighted as research abstracts. Recommended for all academic and school libraries.

2538. ***Journal of Educational Computing Research.*** [ISSN: 0735-6331] 1984. 8x/yr. USD 340 (Individuals, USD 130). Ed(s): Robert H Seidman. Baywood Publishing Co., Inc., 26 Austin Ave, Amityville, NY 11701; info@baywood.com; http://www.baywood.com. Illus., index, adv. Sample. Refereed. Vol. ends: Dec. *Indexed:* ArtHuCI, CIJE, CompLI, EduInd, IBZ, L&LBA, PsycholAb, SSCI, SWA. *Bk. rev.:* 0-2, essay length. *Aud.:* Ac.

A refereed journal publishing original articles on various aspects of educational computing: development and design of new hardware and software; interpretation and implications of research; and theory and history. Informative interdisciplinary articles are intended for a readership of practitioners, researchers, scientists, and educators from classroom teachers to faculty. Each issue's well-referenced articles advance knowledge and practice in the field of educational computing with empirical research, analyses, design and development studies, and critical reviews. Authors have presented recent research on electronic networks and systemic school reform, enabling student accomplishment online, a review of published evaluation instruments used in online formal courses, and an evaluative study of a network-based hypertext discussion tool. A special issue focuses on important issues in the K-12 environment such as digital media literacy standards. An important title for libraries serving the K-12 community and for academic libraries serving education programs.

2539. ***Tech Directions: the magazine linking education to careers.*** Former titles (until May 1992): *School Shop - Tech Directions;* (until May 1990): *New School Shop - Tech Directions;* (until May 1989): *School Shop.* [ISSN: 1062-9351] 1941. m. Aug.-May. USD 30 domestic; USD 40 foreign. Ed(s): Susanne Packham. Prakken Publications, Inc., 3979 Varsity Dr, Ann Arbor, MI 48108. Illus., index, adv. Sample. Refereed. Circ: 42784 Paid and controlled. Vol. ends: May. Microform: PQC. Online: bigchalk; EBSCO Publishing; Northern Light Technology, Inc.; OCLC Online Computer Library Center, Inc.; ProQuest Information & Learning; H.W. Wilson. Reprint: PQC. *Indexed:* CIJE, EduInd, MRD. *Bk. rev.:* 6, 150 words. *Aud.:* Ga, Ac.

A publication focused on the fields of technology, industrial, and vocational education. Contributors cover teaching techniques, school-to-work transition, industrial arts, and current issues in the field. Intended for technology and vocational technical educators at all educational levels, the magazine's articles and columns are curriculum oriented. Topics have included robot building with kits, scale model house construction, applied science, solar power, and technology concepts, as well as model school programs and an annual guide to training and certification programs. Recommended for academic and school libraries with vocational education programs. URL: http://www.techdirections.com/index.htm

2540. ***Techniques.*** Former titles (until 1996): *American Vocational Association.Techniques;* (until 1996): *Vocational Education Journal;* (until 1985): *VocEd;* (until 1978): *American Vocational Journal.* [ISSN: 1527-1803] 1926. 8x/yr. Non-members, USD 45; USD 6 newsstand/cover per issue. Ed(s): Susan Reese. Association for Career and Technical Education, 1410 King St, Alexandria, VA 22314. Adv. Circ: 38000 Paid. CD-ROM: ProQuest Information & Learning. Microform: PQC. Online: EBSCO Publishing; Florida Center for Library Automation; Gale Group; OCLC Online Computer Library Center, Inc.; ProQuest Information & Learning; H.W. Wilson. *Indexed:* BusEdI, CIJE, EduInd, MRD. *Bk. rev.:* 1, 500 words. *Aud.:* Ac, Ga, Sa.

Published by the Association for Career and Technical Education (ACTE), this magazine covers issues of career and technical education. Content is aimed at ACTE members with current news about legislation, profiles of educators, featured articles about programs and issues, and association news and events. Issues have examined career and technical education with special needs students, the history and future of school-to-career, a series on accountability and assessment, and emergency telecommunicator training for high school students. Recommended for all libraries serving career and technical education programs. URL: http://www.acteonline.org/members/techniques/index.cfm

2541. ***The Technology Teacher.*** Former titles (until 1983): *Man - Society - Technology; Journal of Industrial Arts Education.* [ISSN: 0746-3537] 1939. 8x/yr. Non-members, USD 70. Ed(s): Kathleen de la Paz. International Technology Education Association, 1914 Association Dr, Ste 201, Reston, VA 20191-1539; iteacomm@iris.org; http://www.iteawww.org. Illus., index, adv. Sample. Refereed. Circ: 7000 Paid. Vol. ends: May/Jun. Microform: PQC. Online: EBSCO Publishing; Florida Center for Library Automation; Gale Group; Northern Light Technology, Inc.; OCLC Online Computer Library Center, Inc.; ProQuest Information & Learning; H.W. Wilson. *Indexed:* CIJE, EduInd, MRD. *Bk. rev.:* 1, 100 words. *Aud.:* Ac.

As the journal of the International Technology Education Association, this publication's goal is to be a resource tool for technology education practitioners. The audience ranges from elementary school to high school classroom teachers, as well as teacher educators. Article content is focused on the sharing of classroom ideas and applications. With the practitioner as audience, article content has covered web site creation, telemedicine, computer upgrade tips, designing robots, industrial design activities, and biotechnology curriculum projects. As a membership journal, it also includes association events and news. Recommended for all school and academic libraries. URL: http://www.iteawww.org/F1.html

Electronic Journals

2542. ***Current Issues in Comparative Education (CISE).*** [ISSN: 1523-1615] 1998. s-a. Columbia University, Teachers College, 525 W 120th St, New York, NY 10027; http://www.tc.columbia.edu/cice/. *Aud.:* Ac.

An international journal dedicated to publishing scholarly debate and discussion on educational policies and comparative studies. With academic and practical experience-based contributions, the journal has a wide and diverse audience. Each themed issue has a minimum of five articles with an online commentary. Issue topics have included gender-centered theorizing, education and social exclusion, political violence and education, and HIV/AIDS education. Recommended for academic libraries. URL: http://www.tc.columbia.edu/cice

2543. ***Current Issues in Education.*** [ISSN: 1099-839X] 1998. irreg. Ed(s): Leslie Poynor. Arizona State University, College of Education, PO Box 870211, Tempe, AZ 85287-0211; cie@cie.ed.asu.edu; http://cie.ed.asu.edu/. Refereed. *Aud.:* Ac.

A peer-reviewed scholarly journal dedicated to promoting discussion, research, practice, and policy in the field of education. The journal's scope includes curriculum and instruction, policy, social and philosophical foundations, psychology, technology, school counseling, and research methodology in education. Edited by graduate students at Arizona State University's Graduate School of Education, the journal's online format facilitates an accelerated publication process. Featured articles may be linked to an online discussion. Articles cover a broad range of issues and research such as an examination of student teacher beliefs, Texas preservice teachers, teachers, and students talk about high-stakes testing, process portfolio as an assessment system in a teacher education program, and a review of an interactive program on the Holocaust. Recommended for academic libraries serving education programs. URL: http://cie.ed.asu.edu

2544. ***Education Policy Analysis Archives.*** [ISSN: 1068-2341] 1993. irreg. Free. Ed(s): Gene V Glass. Arizona State University, College of Education, PO Box 870211, Tempe, AZ 85287-0211; glass@asu.edu; http://olam.ed.asu.edu/epaa/. Refereed. *Indexed:* CIJE, HEA. *Aud.:* Ac.

A peer-reviewed journal that publishes articles on educational policy at all educational levels worldwide. Articles are in Spanish or English or both languages. Article abstracts appear at the beginning of each article. The site has a search utility to aid in finding articles of interest. Issues have covered topics of educational policy such as policymakers' online use of academic research, high-stakes testing and the history of graduation, emerging ethnocentric charter schools in Hawaii, an analysis of education policy in Portugal, financing of higher education in the Czech Republic, and the education reform process in Uruguay. Highly recommended for academic libraries. URL: http://epaa.asu.edu

2545. ***From Now On - the Educational Technology Journal.*** 1990. m. Ed(s): Jamieson McKenzie. From Now On - the Educational Technology Journal, 500 15th St, Bellingham, WA 98225-6113; mckenzie@fromnowon.org; http://fromnowon.org. *Aud.:* Ems, Hs, Ga.

A journal committed to the use of technologies for information literacy and for student learning and reasoning. Articles are written for a broad audience of parents, educators, administrators, and others involved with educational technology. Issues have covered the topics of assessment, curriculum, grants, research, staff development, technology planning, virtual museums, and web site development. Short concise articles have focused on evaluation of web information, online research modules, strategies to encourage student questioning, assessment of staff technology competencies, and the development of district technology plans. Recommended for school and academic libraries. URL: http://fromnowon.org

2546. ***International Education Webzine.*** 1996. bi-m. Knowledge Network, http://www.iteachnet.com/newsb.html. *Aud.:* Ac.

A daily magazine reporting on international education news and events. With a large number of feature stories relevant to international education (1,356 articles in 2002), the magazine is a vital resource. Sections cover book reviews, conferences, house swaps, jobs, and job seekers. Daily news is provided with links to media such as the *New York Times International* and *Science Daily*. An events calendar includes recruitment fairs. Recommended for all academic and school libraries. URL: http://iteachnet.org

2547. ***International Electronic Journal for Leadership in Learning.*** [ISSN: 1206-9620] 1997. a. w/frequent updates. Free. Ed(s): Charles F Webber. University of Calgary Press, University of Calgary, Faculty of Education ETD 722, 2500 University Dr N W, Calgary, AB T2N 1N4, Canada; http://www.ucalgary.ca/ucpress. Refereed. *Aud.:* Ems, Hs.

A refereed academic journal dedicated to promoting the study and discussion of current leadership issues related to educational communities. Articles, reviews, and commentaries focus on topics of concern to schools. Contributors have considered cognitive benefits and the community-building capacity of electronic mailing lists in an undergraduate course, skills for success in college, improving university-provided teacher in-service, and strengthening family-school relationship. A broad readership includes teachers, administrators, parents, community members, academics, and those involved with the governance of schools, such as school trustees. An important journal for all libraries serving the field of education.

2548. ***Journal of Interactive Media in Education.*** [ISSN: 1365-893X] 1996. irreg. Ed(s): Simon Buckingham Shum, Tamara Sumner. Open University, Knowledge Media Institute, Milton Keynes, MK7 6AA, United Kingdom; jime@open.ac.uk; http://www-jime.open.ac.uk. Illus. Refereed. *Bk. rev.:* Occasional, 1,600 words, signed. *Aud.:* Ac.

A journal focused on the role and contribution of interactive media to the field of learning. With an interest in the integration of technology and education, the journal publishes articles that develop theory, critique existing work, or analyze various aspects of educational technology. Articles have presented collaborative learning on the web, rhetoric in a digital media, and narrative in an information and communication technology course. Articles can have an interactive component such as examples of interactive media or access to qualitative data. Special issues focus on reusing online resources and theory for learning technologies. Book reviews include responses by authors or other readers. Recommended for academic libraries. URL: http://www-jime.open.ac.uk

2549. ***Meridian (Raleigh): a middle school computer technologies journal.*** [ISSN: 1097-9778] 1998. s-a. Ed(s): Beckey Reed. North Carolina State University, Raleigh, NC 27695; http://www.ncsu.edu/meridian/. *Aud.:* Ems, Sa.

A journal focused on the research and practice of computer technology in the middle school classroom. Journal articles feature research, practical application, commentary, and book excerpts for the middle school practitioner, administrators, and others involved with middle school students. Two issues a year consider topics and issues such as gender differences in computer technology achievement, technological literacy in middle school curriculum, virtual field trips, and technology as a resource for adolescents. A recent issue establishes an interactive forum intended to create an evolving article with readers' response on the topic of the issues in educational web design. An important journal for teachers in the middle schools.

2550. ***New Horizons in Adult Education.*** [ISSN: 1062-3183] 1987. irreg. 3-4/yr. Ed(s): Nancy Gadbow. Nova Southeastern University, Program for Higher Education, 3301 College Ave., Ft. Lauderdale, FL 33314; horizons@fcae.acast.nova.edu; http://ejournals.cic.net/journals/n/newhorizons/. Refereed. *Aud.:* Sa.

This refereed journal focuses on current research and issues in adult education and related fields. As a forum for faculty, graduate students, and adult education practitioners to share ideas and developments in the field, the journal publishes research, opinions, book reviews, point-counterpoint articles, conceptual analysis, case studies, and invitational columns. Issues cover a broad range of topics and geographic coverage is international. Topic coverage has included adult learning issues of deaf or disabled students, adult education and literacy in Nicaragua, Nigeria, and other developing countries, distance education, and ethical issues with assessment of adult learners. With its international coverage, this resource is a standard for all those working or interested in the field of adult education. URL: http://www.nova.edu/~aed/newhorizons.html

2551. *Student Affairs Journal Online.* 1996. irreg. Ed(s): Steve Eubanks. Student Affairs Journal Online, PO Box 1682, Glendora, CA 91740; connect@digiserve.com; http://www.digiserve.com/connect/sajo/. *Indexed:* HEA. *Bk. rev.:* Number and length vary. *Aud.:* Ac.

A journal focused on supporting the student affairs community. Intended for practitioners, researchers, and professionals in the field, it contributes to a better understanding of college students and how to support and serve them. Scholarly articles consider primary research, new and innovative programs, and technology issues. Contributors have written on what motivates students to enroll in online courses, the use of bulletin boards as community-building tools, the importance of utilizing technology in graduate programs, attracting prospective students and assisting new students through an institution's web site, an argument for historical research in student affairs, and Japanese students' adjustment to American colleges based on gender differences. Regular reviews cover books, software, and web resources. With a broad coverage of issues and resources, this title is highly recommended for the student affairs practitioner, researcher, and academic community. URL: http://www.studentaffairs.com/ejournal/Winter_2003

2552. *T E S L - E J.* [ISSN: 1072-4303] 1994. q. Free. Ed(s): Maggie Sokolik. T E S L - E J, University of California, Berkeley, College Writing Programs, Berkeley, CA 94720-2500; sokolik@socrates.berkeley.edu; http://www-writing.berkeley.edu/tesl-ej; http://www.kyoto-su.ac.jp/information/tesl-ej. Illus., index. Refereed. *Indexed:* BRI, CBRI, MLA-IB. *Bk. rev.:* Number and length vary. *Aud.:* Ac.

A refereed academic journal focused on the research and practice of English as a second or foreign language. *TESL-EJ* covers a broad range of issues from research to classroom practices for all education levels. Wide ranging topics covered include adult education and literacy, curriculum development and evaluation, learning theory, phonology, testing, and employment issues for EFL/ESL teachers. Issues present original articles, book or media reviews, and a forum for discussion. Featured articles range from nine to sixteen pages in length. Authors have written on such issues as an interactive information literacy course for international students, the nature of peer response variation in EFL and ESL students, and second language writing and research. A standard journal for the field of ESL. URL: http://www-writing.berkeley.edu/TESL-EJ

Women in Literature and Life Assembly. See Women: Feminist and Special Interest/Electronic Journals section.

■ ELECTRONICS

Mary Anne Hansen, Interim Associate Dean, The Libraries, Montana State University, Bozeman, MT 59717-3320; mhansen@montana.edu; FAX: 406-994-2851

Introduction

The field of electronics is advancing rapidly, as is the proliferation of periodicals about electronics and related topics. There is a wide range of users with a diversity of uses of electronics periodicals, from the amateur who studies electronics as a hobby, to the design practitioner who uses technological innovations within the industry, to students and scholarly researchers who use electronics publications as a means of keeping abreast of technological and theoretical innovations and as a publishing forum to report their own findings. Many electronics publications are trade journals that are valuable across this range of readership because they provide information on the industry in addition to technological advancements. Therefore, electronics trade publications are suitable for both the public library and the academic or research library. Collection management librarians in academic and research libraries will also want to include some scholarly refereed journals from both commercial publishers and professional associations, such as the British Institute of Electrical Engineers and the American Institute of Electrical and Electronics Engineers.

Basic Periodicals

Ga: *Electronic News, Electronics World, Popular Home Automation;* Ac, Sa: *IEEE Transactions on Consumer Electronics, IEEE Transactions on Electron Devices, IEEE Transactions on Industrial Electronics, IEEE Transactions on Power Electronics, Institute of Electrical and Electronics Engineers. Proceedings, International Journal of Electronics, Solid-State Electronics.*

Basic Abstracts and Indexes

ABI/Inform, Applied Science and Technology Index, Business and Company ASAP, Business Source Premier, Business Index, EI Compendex, INSPEC, Physics Abstracts, Science Abstracts. Section B: Electrical and Electronics Abstracts.

2553. *Audio - Video Interiors.* [ISSN: 1041-5378] 1989. m. USD 19.95 domestic; USD 34.95 foreign; USD 3.99 newsstand/cover per issue. McMullen Argus Publishing, Inc., 2400 E Katella Ave, Ste 1100, Anaheim, CA 92806; http://www.mcmullenargus.com. Adv. Circ: 56390 Paid and controlled. *Aud.:* Hs, Ga.

This consumer magazine shows readers how to combine sound and video technology with stunning home design to create their own custom entertainment centers.

2554. *AudioXpress.* Formed by the merger of (1988-2000): *Glass Audio;* (1980-2000): *Speaker Builder;* (199?-2000): *Audio Electronics;* Which was formerly (1970-199?): *Audio Amateur.* 2001. m. USD 29.95 domestic; USD 59.95 per issue foreign; USD 7 newsstand/cover per issue. Ed(s): Edward T Dell, Jr. Audio Amateur Corporation, PO Box 876, Peterborough, NH 03458-0876; custserv@audioxpress.com. Illus., adv. Sample. Circ: 16000 Paid. *Aud.:* Hs, Ga.

AudioXpress combines the types of articles, projects, tips, and technologies of the three merged publications into one monthly magazine. Includes audio construction projects, design ideas, and a review section filled with audio components.

2555. *Digital Signal Processing: a review journal.* [ISSN: 1051-2004] 1991. 6x/yr. EUR 492 (Individuals, EUR 239). Ed(s): James Schroeder, J. Campbell. Academic Press, 525 B St, Ste 1900, San Diego, CA 92101-4495; apsubs@acad.com; http://www.academicpress.com. Illus. Sample. Refereed. Online: EBSCO Publishing; ingenta.com; OCLC Online Computer Library Center, Inc.; RoweCom Information Quest; ScienceDirect. *Indexed:* EngInd, SCI. *Aud.:* Ac, Sa.

Digital Signal Processing explores the creative elements of signal processing, enabling electronics engineers, researchers, scientists, and corporate managers to stay abreast of vital information. New technologies and significant programs are broadly covered in each issue, as well as breakthroughs in the field.

2556. *E D N World: electronic technology for engineers and engineering managers.* Former titles: *E D N Magazine;* Which incorporated (2000-2002): *CommVerge;* (1962-1971): *Electronic Equipment Engineering - E E E;* (until 1961): *Electrical Design News.* 1956. bi-w. USD 149.90 domestic; USD 205.90 Canada; USD 195.90 Mexico. Ed(s): Maury Wright. Reed Business Information, 275 Washington St, Newton, MA 02458; http://www.reedbusiness.com. Illus., index, adv. Sample. Circ: 169228 Controlled. Vol. ends: No. 26. *Indexed:* ABIn, AS&TI, EngInd. *Bk. rev.:* Various number and length. *Aud.:* Ac, Sa.

Published for designers and design managers in electronics, *EDN World* features products, technology, and applications, with detailed samplings of the best designs from around the world. It also provides coverage of computers and peripherals, test and measurement equipment, data communications, semiconductor technology, and semicustom ICs.

Electronic Business. See Business/Trade and Industry section.

2557. *Electronic Design.* [ISSN: 0013-4872] 1952. fortn. USD 100 domestic (Free to qualified personnel). Ed(s): David Bursky, Roger Allen. Penton Media, Inc. (Hasbrouck Heights), 611 Rte 46 W, Hasbrouck Heights, NJ 07604; http://www.elecdesign.com; http://www.penton.com. Illus., index, adv. Sample. Circ: 165000. Vol. ends: No. 28. Microform: PQC. Online: bigchalk; The Dialog Corporation; EBSCO Publishing; Factiva; Florida Center for Library Automation; Gale Group; Northern Light Technology, Inc.; OCLC Online Computer Library Center, Inc.; ProQuest Information & Learning; H.W. Wilson. Reprint: PQC. *Indexed:* AS&TI, EngInd. *Bk. rev.:* Various number and length. *Aud.:* Ac, Sa.

Electronic Design is a trade publication that provides technical information for designers and design managers. Articles are organized by application (computers, communications, embedded systems, etc.) or by OEM product types (passive components, boards, digital ICs, etc.). Two regular sections in each issue are "EDA" (Electronic Design Automation) and "Test & Measurement." Each issue also contains either a special product-focused report or a technology-focused report of particular interest to design engineers. Occasionally, these special reports will provide conference coverage of the ISSCC, CICC, DAC, and other industry events.

2558. *Electronic Engineering Design.* Formerly (until 2001): *Electronic Engineering.* 1928. m. GBP 95.48 domestic; USD 214 foreign; GBP 10.09 newsstand/cover per issue domestic. Ed(s): Ron Neale. C M P Europe Ltd, City Reach, 5 Greenwich View Pl, Millharbour, London, E14 9NN, United Kingdom. Illus., adv. Sample. Circ: 25444. Vol. ends: Dec. Microform: PMC; PQC. Reprint: PQC. *Indexed:* AS&TI, B&I, BrTechI, CEA, ChemAb, EngInd, ExcerpMed. *Aud.:* Ac, Sa.

Targeted for design engineers, this British trade publication provides information on new products primarily from the electronics industry in the United Kingdom, but it also offers some coverage of the U.S. electronics industry. Regular items include "Updates," "Applications," "Product Focus," "New Products," "Technology Focus," and a "Features" column.

2559. *Electronic Engineering Times: the industry newspaper for engineers and technical management.* [ISSN: 0192-1541] 1972. w. USD 319 in Europe (Free to qualified personnel). Ed(s): Brian Fuller. C M P Publications, Inc., 600 Community Dr, Manhasset, NY 11030; http://www.eetimes.com. Adv. Circ: 160067 Controlled. Microform: PQC. Online: bigchalk; EBSCO Publishing; Factiva; Florida Center for Library Automation; Gale Group; LexisNexis; NewsNet; OCLC Online Computer Library Center, Inc.; ProQuest Information & Learning. *Indexed:* ABIn, B&I, CompLI, LRI. *Aud.:* Ga, Ac, Sa.

EE Times covers business and technology news in the electronics industry for engineers and technical managers. Key trends and industry developments are also covered.

Electronic House. See Home section.

2560. *Electronic News.* Former titles (until 1991): *Chilton's Electronic News; Electronic News.* [ISSN: 1061-6624] 1957. w. 51/yr. USD 119 domestic; USD 199 Canada; USD 329 elsewhere. Ed(s): Ed Sperling. Reed Business Information, 1101 S Winchester Blvd, Bldg N, San Jose, CA 95128-3901; http://www.reedbusiness.com. Illus., adv. Sample. Circ: 46250 Paid. Microform: MIM; FCM; PQC. Online: bigchalk; The Dialog Corporation; EBSCO Publishing; Factiva; Florida Center for Library Automation; Gale Group; LexisNexis; OCLC Online Computer Library Center, Inc.; ProQuest Information & Learning; H.W. Wilson. Reprint: PQC. *Indexed:* BPI, CompLI. *Bk. rev.:* 1, 700-1,000 words. *Aud.:* Ac, Sa.

A trade periodical, *Electronic News* is a weekly technology news publication for management-oriented executives working in a variety of fields: engineering, manufacturing, research and development, purchasing, marketing, communications, industrial electronics, semiconductor technology, distribution, and financial markets. Regular features include a weekly financial news column, a calendar of events, and a listing of recently awarded government contracts.

2561. *Electronics Letters.* [ISSN: 0013-5194] 1965. 25x/yr. Non-members, USD 1320 print or online. Ed(s): Eric Ash. Institution of Electrical Engineers, Michael Faraday House, Six Hills Way, Stevenage, SG1 2AY, United Kingdom; http://www.iee.org/. Illus., index, adv. Sample. Refereed. Circ: 2200. Vol. ends: No. 25. *Indexed:* C&ISA, ChemAb, DSR&OA, EngInd, ExcerpMed, IAA, SCI. *Aud.:* Ac, Sa.

The purpose of *Electronics Letters* is to provide rapid communication of new information and the results of important research in electronic science and engineering, telecommunications, and optoelectronics. Contributions of a theoretical nature are accepted if they show a specific application in one of these fields. Accepted papers are usually published within six weeks of acceptance by the referees. Issues from 1994 forward are available online to print subscribers.

2562. *Electronics World.* Former titles (until 1996): *Electronics World + Wireless World;* (until 1989): *Electronics World and Wireless World;* (until 1983): *Wireless World.* [ISSN: 1365-4675] 1911. m. Highbury Business Communications, Ann Boleyn House, 9-13 Ewell Rd, Cheam, SM3 8BZ, United Kingdom; http://www.hhc.co.uk/. Illus., adv. Sample. Circ: 21000. Microform: PMC; PQC. Online: Gale Group. *Indexed:* AS&TI, BrTechI, EngInd, IHTDI, SSCI. *Bk. rev.:* Various number and length. *Aud.:* Ga, Ac, Sa.

This British trade publication covers all areas of electronics design, including innovations, news, research, and reviews. *Electronics World* regulary publishes articles on RF engineering, CAD, electronic design, audio circuit design, electronic components, digital and DSP circuitry, communications, instrumentation and test history, analog design, and consumer electronics.

Home Theater. See Television, Video, and Radio section.

2563. *I E E E Circuits and Devices Magazine: the magazine of electronic and photonic systems.* Former titles (until 1985): *I E E E Circuits and Systems Magazine (Piscataway, 1985);* (until 1979): *Circuits and Systems.* [ISSN: 8755-3996] 197?. bi-m. USD 220 in North America; USD 255 elsewhere. Ed(s): Ronald W Waynant. Institute of Electrical and Electronics Engineers, Inc., 445 Hoes Ln, Piscataway, NJ 08854-1331; subscription-service@ieee.org; http://www.ieee.org. Illus., index, adv. Sample. Refereed. Circ: 30725. Vol. ends: Nov. Online: EBSCO Publishing; I E E E. *Indexed:* EngInd, SCI, SSCI. *Aud.:* Ac, Sa.

This publication is sponsored by a number of IEEE societies: Circuits and Systems; Components, Packaging, and Manufacturing Technology; Electron Devices; and Lasers and Electro-Optics. Coverage includes in-depth assessments of emerging technologies and their continued impact on the human-machine interface. Each issue includes four to six research articles. Regular features include software reviews, new product listings, and a conference calendar.

2564. *I E E E Electron Device Letters.* Formerly (until Jan. 1980): *Electron Device Letters.* [ISSN: 0741-3106] 1980. m. USD 535 in North America; USD 570 elsewhere. Ed(s): John R Brews. Institute of Electrical and Electronics Engineers, Inc., 445 Hoes Ln, Piscataway, NJ 08854-1331; subscription-service@ieee.org; http://www.ieee.org. Illus., index. Sample. Refereed. Online: EBSCO Publishing; I E E E. *Indexed:* AS&TI, C&ISA, ChemAb, EngInd, IAA, SCI. *Aud.:* Ac, Sa.

Published by the IEEE Electron Device Society, this journal publishes original research and significant contributions relating to the theory, design, and performance of electron and ion devices, solid state devices, integrated electronic devices, and optoelectronic devices and energy sources. Accepted papers are guaranteed to be published within two months. Issues include a calendar of events for the IEEE Electron Devices Society, notices of calls for papers, symposia, and conferences.

2565. *I E E E Journal of Quantum Electronics.* [ISSN: 0018-9197] 1965. m. USD 1030 in North America; USD 1065 elsewhere. Ed(s): Laura Vansavage. Institute of Electrical and Electronics Engineers, Inc., 445 Hoes Ln, Piscataway, NJ 08854-1331; subscription-service@ieee.org; http://www.ieee.org. Illus., index. Sample. Refereed. Online: EBSCO Publishing; Gale Group; I E E E. *Indexed:* AS&TI, ChemAb, EngInd, IAA, SCI. *Aud.:* Ac, Sa.

This scholarly journal publishes papers on optoelectronic theory and techniques, lasers, fiber optics, and the development and manufacture of systems and subsystems. Coverage includes both theoretical and experimental research. To be considered for inclusion, articles must report on state-of-the-art advance quantum electron devices, systems, or applications.

2566. *I E E E Transactions on Circuits and Systems Part 1: Regular Papers.* Formerly (until 2003): *I E E E Transactions on Circuits and Systems Part 1: Fundamental Theory and Applications;* Which superseded in part (in 1992): *I E E E Transactions on Circuits and Systems;* Which was formerly (until 1973): *I E E E Transactions on Circuit Theory;* (until 1962): *I R E Transactions on Circuit Theory;* (until 1954): *Professional Group on Circuit Theory. Transactions.* 1952. m. USD 550 in North America; USD 585 elsewhere. Ed(s): Pier Paolo Civalleri. Institute of Electrical and Electronics Engineers, Inc., 445 Hoes Ln, Piscataway, NJ 08854-1331; subscription-service@ieee.org; http://www.computer.org/. Illus., index. Sample. Refereed. Vol. ends: No. 12. Online: EBSCO Publishing; Gale Group; I E E E. *Indexed:* AS&TI, C&ISA, CCMJ, ChemAb, EngInd, MathSciNet, SCI, SSCI. *Aud.:* Ac, Sa.

This scholarly publication split into two sections in 1992 (from *IEEE Transactions on Circuits and Systems*). Part One covers analog, passive, switched-capacitor, and digital filters; electronic circuits, networks, and graph theory; system theory; discrete, IC, and VLSI circuit design; and multidimensional circuits and systems. Each issue is divided into four sections: papers, transaction briefs, express letters intended to provide rapid publication, and a circuits and systems tutorial feature on both new and old topics.

2567. *I E E E Transactions on Circuits and Systems Part 2: Express Briefs.* Formerly (until 2003): *I E E E Transactions on Circuits and Systems Part 2: Analog and Digital Signal Processing;* Which superseded in part (in 1992): *I E E E Transactions on Circuits and Systems;* Which was formerly (until 1973): *I E E E Transactions on Circuit Theory;* (until 1962): *I R E Transactions on Circuit Theory;* (until 1954): *Transactions of the I R E Professional Group on Circuit Theory.* 1952. m. USD 525 in North America; USD 560 elsewhere. Ed(s): Edgar Sanchez Sinencio. Institute of Electrical and Electronics Engineers, Inc., 445 Hoes Ln, Piscataway, NJ 08854-1331; subscription-service@ieee.org; http://www.computer.org/. Illus., index. Sample. Refereed. Vol. ends: No. 12. Online: EBSCO Publishing; Gale Group; I E E E. *Indexed:* AS&TI, C&ISA, EngInd, SCI. *Bk. rev.:* Various number and length. *Aud.:* Ac, Sa.

This scholarly publication split into two sections in 1992 (from *IEEE Transactions on Circuits and Systems*). Part Two covers analog and digital signal processing with emphasis on circuits, including neural networks, VLSI, image processing, filters, and multidimensional circuits and systems. Each issue is divided into four sections: papers, transaction briefs, express letters intended to provide rapid publication, and a circuits and systems tutorial feature on both new and old topics.

2568. *I E E E Transactions on Consumer Electronics.* Former titles (until 1974): *I E E E Transactions on Broadcast and Television Receivers;* (until 1962): *I R E Transactions on Broadcast and Television Receivers;* (until 1954): *I R E Professional Group on Broadcast and Television Receivers. Transactions.* [ISSN: 0098-3063] 1952. q. USD 215 in North America; USD 250 elsewhere. Ed(s): Wayne C Luplow. Institute of Electrical and Electronics Engineers, Inc., 445 Hoes Ln, Piscataway, NJ 08854-1331; subscription-service@ieee.org; http://www.ieee.org. Illus., index. Sample. Refereed. Vol. ends: Nov. Online: EBSCO Publishing; Gale Group; I E E E; Swets Blackwell. *Indexed:* AS&TI, ChemAb, EngInd, ErgAb, SCI, SSCI. *Bk. rev.:* Various number and length. *Aud.:* Ac, Sa.

This IEEE publication covers the design and manufacture of products and components used for educational, entertainment, and leisure activities. Accepted papers include articles that focus on either new products or new technologies. The August and November issues are devoted mainly to papers from the International Conference on Consumer Electronics, but nonconference papers appear in all four yearly issues.

2569. *I E E E Transactions on Electromagnetic Compatibility.* [ISSN: 0018-9375] 1959. 4x/yr. USD 290 in North America; USD 325 elsewhere. Ed(s): Motohisa Kanda. Institute of Electrical and Electronics Engineers, Inc., 445 Hoes Ln, Piscataway, NJ 08854-1331; subscription-service@ieee.org; http://www.ieee.org. Illus., index. Sample. Refereed. Vol. ends: Nov. Online: EBSCO Publishing; Gale Group; I E E E; Swets Blackwell. *Indexed:* AS&TI, ChemAb, EngInd, IAA, SCI. *Aud.:* Ac, Sa.

This periodical publishes papers that present the origin, control, and measurement of effects on electronic and biological systems. Coverage includes brief and longer papers in addition to correspondence from the readership. As with other IEEE transactions, tutorials are included. Topics covered include, but are not limited to, antennas/propagation, equipment/EMC, measurement technology, and shielding.

2570. *I E E E Transactions on Electron Devices.* Former titles (until 1962): *I R E Transactions on Electron Devices;* (until 1954): *I R E Professional Group on Electron Devices. Transactions.* [ISSN: 0018-9383] 1952. m. USD 910 in North America; USD 945 elsewhere. Ed(s): Renuka P Jindal. Institute of Electrical and Electronics Engineers, Inc., 445 Hoes Ln, Piscataway, NJ 08854-1331; subscription-service@ieee.org; http://www.ieee.org. Illus., index. Sample. Refereed. Vol. ends: No. 12. Online: EBSCO Publishing; Gale Group; I E E E; Swets Blackwell. *Indexed:* AS&TI, C&ISA, ChemAb, EngInd, ExcerpMed, IAA, SCI. *Bk. rev.:* Various number and length. *Aud.:* Ac, Sa.

A publication of the IEEE Electron Device Society, this periodical covers the theory, design, and applications of industrial electronics and control instrumentation science engineering. Topics include performance of devices including electron tubes, solid-state devices, energy sources, displays, and device reliability. Some issues have sections devoted to a single topic; examples include compound semiconductor devices, sensors and actuators, and silicon devices.

2571. *I E E E Transactions on Industrial Electronics.* Former titles (until 1981): *I E E E Transactions on Industrial Electronics and Control Instrumentation;* (until 1963): *I E E E Transactions on Industrial Electronics;* (until 1962): *I R E Transactions on Industrial Electronics;* (until 1959): *I R E Professional Group on Industrial Electronics. Transactions.* [ISSN: 0278-0046] 1953. bi-m. USD 550 in North America; USD 585 elsewhere. Ed(s): Joachim Holtz. Institute of Electrical and Electronics Engineers, Inc., 445 Hoes Ln, Piscataway, NJ 08854-1331; subscription-service@ieee.org; http://www.computer.org/. Illus., index. Sample. Refereed. Vol. ends: Nov. Online: EBSCO Publishing; Gale Group; I E E E; Swets Blackwell. *Indexed:* AS&TI, ApMecR, C&ISA, ChemAb, EngInd, IAA, SCI. *Bk. rev.:* Various number and length. *Aud.:* Ac, Sa.

Covers the application of electronics and electrical sciences to the control of industrial processes. Each issue includes five or six research papers. Special issues are devoted to a specific topic, such as applications of intelligent systems to industrial electronics. A guest editor oversees special issues.

2572. *I E E E Transactions on Power Electronics.* [ISSN: 0885-8993] 1986. bi-m. USD 475 in North America; USD 510 elsewhere. Ed(s): Richard G Hoft. Institute of Electrical and Electronics Engineers, Inc., 445 Hoes Ln, Piscataway, NJ 08854-1331; subscription-service@ieee.org; http://www.ieee.org. Illus., index. Sample. Refereed. Vol. ends: Oct. Online: EBSCO Publishing; Gale Group; I E E E; Swets Blackwell. *Indexed:* EngInd. *Aud.:* Ac, Sa.

Published by the Power Electronics Society of the IEEE, this journal covers research of widespread generic interest to power engineering professionals. Included are papers on new or novel device, circuit, or system issues. Papers treating device physics, conventional converter design, applications of specialized interest, etc., are not accepted, but should be submitted to other IEEE *Transactions.* Papers of a tutorial or historical nature within the scope of the publication will be considered, as will papers previously published or presented in a conference record other than that of any IEEE society.

2573. *Institute of Electrical and Electronics Engineers. Proceedings.* Former titles (until 1962): *Proceedings of the IRE;* (until 1938): *Proceedings of the Institute of Radio Engineers.* [ISSN: 0018-9219]

1913. m. USD 630 in North America for print or online ed.; USD 665 elsewhere for print or online ed.; USD 780 combined subscription in North America for print & online eds. Ed(s): J Calder. Institute of Electrical and Electronics Engineers, Inc., 445 Hoes Ln, Piscataway, NJ 08854-1331; subscription-service@ieee.org; http://www.ieee.org. Illus., index, adv. Sample. Refereed. Vol. ends: Dec. Online: I E E E. *Indexed:* AS&TI, BioEngAb, C&ISA, ChemAb, EngInd, ErgAb, ExcerpMed, GeoRef, PetrolAb, SCI, SSCI. *Aud.:* Ga, Ac, Sa.

Institute of Electrical and Electronics Engineers. Proceedings publishes invited and submitted papers on all aspects of electrical and electronic engineering and computer engineering. Papers must be comprehensive, in-depth review, tutorial, or survey papers written for technically knowledgeable readers who are not necessarily specialists in the subjects being treated. Accepted papers are of long-range interest and broad significance; emphasis is on applications, technological issues, and theory. Papers that are of general interest to the entire IEEE membership are published here.

2574. ***International Journal of Electronics.*** [ISSN: 0020-7217] 1965. m. GBP 1254. Ed(s): E M Yeatman. Taylor & Francis Ltd, 11 New Fetter Ln, London, EC4P 4EE, United Kingdom; info@tandf.co.uk; http://www.tandf.co.uk/journals. Illus., index, adv. Refereed. Online: EBSCO Publishing; Ingenta Select; OCLC Online Computer Library Center, Inc.; RoweCom Information Quest; Swets Blackwell. Reprint: PSC. *Indexed:* ApMecR, C&ISA, ChemAb, EngInd, ExcerpMed, SCI. *Aud.:* Ac, Sa.

This British research publication provides articles from the international electronics community. Coverage includes such topics as fundamental conduction processes in vacuum, gases, vapors, and semiconductors; applications of electronic devices and techniques; engineering requirements in communications, digital processing, and computing; and power regulation and measurement. Each issue provides 10 to 12 papers of original work in either experimental or theoretical fields of electronics and electronic devices.

2575. ***Journal of Electronic Materials.*** [ISSN: 0361-5235] 1971. m. USD 490 in North America; USD 525 elsewhere. Ed(s): Theodore E Harman. Institute of Electrical and Electronics Engineers, Inc., 445 Hoes Ln, Piscataway, NJ 08854-1331; subscription-service@ieee.org; http://www.ieee.org. Illus., index, adv. Sample. Refereed. Circ: 1300. Vol. ends: No. 12. Microform: PQC. Online: Ingenta Select; ProQuest Information & Learning; ScienceDirect; Swets Blackwell. Reprint: PQC. *Indexed:* AS&TI, C&ISA, CerAb, ChemAb, EngInd, IAA, SCI. *Aud.:* Ac, Sa.

This monthly publication of the Electronic Materials Committee of the Minerals, Metals & Materials Society (TMS) and the Electronic Devices Society of the IEEE covers the science and technology of electronic materials while examining new applications for semiconductors, magnetic alloys, insulators, and optical and display materials. The purpose of this publication is to appeal to both the specialists and the nonspecialists in the field. It selectively publishes invited and contributed review papers on topics of current interest to electronics professionals. Areas of focus include, but are not limited to, artificially structured materials, molecular beam epitaxy, heteroepitaxy, defects in semiconductors, ferroelectric and dielectric thin films, epitaxial growth for devices, and semiconductor and device processing.

2576. ***Microelectronics Journal.*** Incorporates (1983-1991): *Journal of Semi-Custom I Cs;* (1983-1991): *Semi-Custom I C Yearbook.* [ISSN: 0026-2692] 1967. m. EUR 1395. Ed(s): Bernard Courtois, Mohamed Henini. Elsevier Ltd., The Boulevard, Langford Ln, Oxford, OX5 1GB, United Kingdom. Illus., index, adv. Sample. Refereed. Circ: 700. Online: ingenta.com; ScienceDirect; Swets Blackwell. *Indexed:* C&ISA, ChemAb, EngInd. *Bk. rev.:* Various number and length. *Aud.:* Ac, Sa.

This British publication provides coverage of original research on solid-state technology design and applications. It publishes original papers, reviews, and informed comment by specialists from universities, institutes of technology, and industrial establishments worldwide. Accepted work includes design and application papers.

2577. ***Nuts & Volts: exploring everything for electronics.*** [ISSN: 1065-2035] m. USD 19 domestic; USD 37 in Canada & Mexico; USD 50 elsewhere. Ed(s): Larry Lemieux. T & L Publications, 430 Princeland Ct, Corona, CA 92879. Illus., adv. Sample. *Indexed:* IHTDI. *Aud.:* Hs, Ga.

This consumer publication is designed for the hobbyist. Each issue provides parts and equipment resources, as well as hard-to-find information on topics of interest to the electronics enthusiast. It includes articles on amateur radio, cellular communications, scanning, computers, amateur robotics, and lasers. Readers will also find build-it-yourself electronics projects. The web site includes a search feature for finding articles on specific topics in the online archives.

2578. ***Poptronics.*** Formed by the merger of (1989-2000): *Popular Electronics;* Which incorporated: *Hands-On Electronics;* (1929-2000): *Electronics Now;* Which was formerly (until 1992): *Radio Electronics;* (until 1948): *Radio Craft, Radio Electronics;* (until 1948): *Radio Craft.* [ISSN: 1526-3681] 1989. m. USD 19.99 domestic; USD 27.81 Canada; USD 28.99 elsewhere. Ed(s): Konstantinos Karagiannis. Gernsback Publications, Inc., 275-G Marcus Blvd, Hauppage, NY 11788; http://www.gernsback.com. Illus., adv. Sample. Circ: 74502. *Indexed:* AS&TI, IHTDI, MagInd, RGPR. *Bk. rev.:* Various number and length. *Aud.:* Hs, Ga.

For the electronics activist, *Poptronics* covers the electronics industry, technology, audio, video, computers, projects, and service. It includes building projects and product reviews. It also publishes plans or information relating to newsworthy products, techniques, and scientific and technological developments. A classified section includes ads for electronics plans and kits in addition to equipment sales.

2579. ***Popular Home Automation: hands-on solutions for better living.*** [ISSN: 1089-7925] 1996. bi-m. plus July (7 issues). USD 29.95 domestic; USD 39.95 Canada; USD 49.95 foreign. Ed(s): Rachel Cericole. E H Publishing, Inc., 526 Boston Post Rd, ste 150, Wayland, MA 01778-0340; http://www.electronichouse.com. Illus., adv. Sample. Vol. ends: No. 6. *Indexed:* IHTDI. *Aud.:* Hs, Ga.

This consumer publication reviews home technology products in every issue. Products covered include such items as home controllers, home theater systems, HVAC controls, and security cameras. Readers are also given step-by-step projects they can put together.

2580. ***Semiconductor International: the industry sourcebook for processing, assembly & testing.*** [ISSN: 0163-3767] 1978. m. USD 131.99 domestic; USD 178.90 Canada; USD 164.50 Mexico. Ed(s): Pete Singer. Reed Business Information, 2000 Clearwater Dr, Oak Brook, IL 60523; http://www.reedbusiness.com. Illus., adv. Sample. Circ: 41008 Controlled. Vol. ends: No. 14. Microform: PQC. Online: EBSCO Publishing; Gale Group; LexisNexis; OCLC Online Computer Library Center, Inc.; ProQuest Information & Learning; H.W. Wilson. *Indexed:* ABIn, AS&TI, ChemAb, EngInd. *Aud.:* Ac, Sa.

This trade publication provides five or six feature articles on key technologies in the electronics industry. In addition, it offers brief news articles on a variety of relevant topics: contamination control, industry news, assembly and packaging, inspection, measurement and test, and wafer processing. Papers accepted for publication are written by both the editorial staff and outside contributors. Editorial advisors to this publication include experts from both industry and academia.

2581. ***Semiconductor Science and Technology.*** [ISSN: 0268-1242] 1986. m. USD 2380 print & online. Ed(s): G Parry. Institute of Physics Publishing, Dirac House, Temple Back, Bristol, BS1 6BE, United Kingdom; custserv@iop.org; http://www.iop.org/. Illus., index, adv. Sample. Refereed. Circ: 689. Vol. ends: No. 12. Microform: AIP. Online: EBSCO Publishing; ingenta.com; RoweCom Information Quest; ScienceDirect; Swets Blackwell. *Indexed:* AS&TI, C&ISA, ChemAb, EngInd, SCI. *Aud.:* Ac, Sa.

This international journal publishes original research, review articles, and letters. The scope includes experimental and theoretical studies of the electrical, acoustic, and optical properties of semiconductors. Contributors include electronics engineers, chemists, physicists, and materials scientists. Also available online at no extra charge to institutional subscribers to the print version.

2582. ***Solid-State Electronics: an international journal.*** [ISSN: 0038-1101] 1960. m. EUR 2590 (Qualified personnel, EUR 253). Ed(s): Y Arakawa. Pergamon, The Boulevard, Langford Ln, East Park, Kidlington, OX5 1GB, United Kingdom. Illus., index, adv. Refereed. Circ: 2400. Vol. ends: No. 12. Microform: MIM; PQC. Online: ingenta.com; ScienceDirect; Swets Blackwell. *Indexed:* AS&TI, C&ISA, ChemAb, EngInd, ExcerpMed, IAA, SCI, SSCI. *Bk. rev.:* Various number and length. *Aud.:* Ac, Sa.

This British publication (in English, French, and German) covers research in solid-state physics, transistor technology, theory and design, crystal growth, semiconductors, and circuit engineering. Contributing authors come from both industry and academia. Also included are reviews, notes, and letters to the editor.

2583. ***Solid State Technology.*** Former titles (until 1968): *Semiconductor Products and Solid State Technology;* (until 1962): *Semiconductor Products.* [ISSN: 0038-111X] 1958. m. USD 217 domestic; USD 302 in Canada & Mexico; USD 364 elsewhere. PennWell Corp., Advanced Technology Division, 98 Split Brook Rd, Nashua, NH 03062-5737; http://www.pennwell.com. Illus., index, adv. Sample. Circ: 45000. Vol. ends: No. 12. Microform: PQC. Online: EBSCO Publishing; Florida Center for Library Automation; Gale Group; Northern Light Technology, Inc.; OCLC Online Computer Library Center, Inc. Reprint: PQC. *Indexed:* AS&TI, ChemAb, EngInd, IAA, RiskAb, SCI. *Bk. rev.:* Various number and length. *Aud.:* Ac, Sa.

The purpose of this publication is to offer technical and business information on wafer technology to the semiconductor industry. It reports on the latest process, equipment, and material technologies used in the manufacturing of integrated circuits, thin-film microelectronics, and microstructures. Primary areas of coverage are lithography, deposition, etch, diffusion and implantation, contamination control, metrology, packaging, and testing. Readership includes engineers, operators, scientists, researchers, managers, tool and materials suppliers, and professionals who manufacture and develop semiconductors, equipment, materials, instruments, and thin-film products. Archives of feature articles, a calendar of events, news, and product and job information are available online.

■ ENERGY

Sharon L. Siegler, Engineering Librarian, Lehigh University Library & Technology Services, Fairchild/Martindale Library, 8A Packer Ave., Bethlehem, PA 18015; sls7@lehigh.edu; FAX: 610-758-6524

Introduction

The energy field is huge and has many subdivisions. This section attempts to include titles that cover all of the sources of energy; consider the technical, social, and economic aspects; provide a range from lay reader to expert; and include alternative points of view. That said, there are still many titles not included here that may be of importance to specific types of libraries or specific regions of the country. In general, the journals and magazines included here discuss the energy sources in terms of their energy utilization, hence, there are no titles on petroleum geology or electricity distribution *per se.* All of the titles are published in English (although a few may accept non-English articles), and most are "U.S.-centric." Few new titles have appeared since the last edition. Aside from a few name changes, the old titles are still going strong. This edition has paid more attention to renewable sources of energy, especially wind, and a disproportionate number of titles are included for those areas. Because of the technical nature of the field, few titles are suitable for secondary students or for consumers, but the more newsy trade and professional-society magazines provide approachable material. A good energy collection requires a large budget for most academic libraries; small libraries should choose one or two areas that reflect local interest and build collections accordingly.

Basic Periodicals

Ga: *Power Engineering, U.S. Energy Information Administration. Monthly Energy Review, World Oil;* Ac: *Energy & Fuels, The Energy Journal, Fuel, Solar Energy Materials and Solar Cells, U.S. Energy Information Administration. Monthly Energy Review.*

Basic Abstracts and Indexes

Applied Science and Technology Abstracts, Engineering Index, Science Abstracts.

2584. ***Applied Energy.*** [ISSN: 0306-2619] 1975. m. EUR 2237. Ed(s): S D Probert, P Walsh. Pergamon, The Boulevard, Langford Ln, East Park, Kidlington, OX5 1GB, United Kingdom. Illus., adv. Refereed. Microform: PQC. Online: ingenta.com; ScienceDirect; Swets Blackwell. *Indexed:* ApMecR, C&ISA, ChemAb, EngInd, EnvAb, ExcerpMed, GeoRef, GeogAbPG, SCI, SSCI. *Aud.:* Ac.

Applied Energy discusses energy conversion, conservation, and management from the engineering point of view. Research here is not to develop new energy sources, but to better utilize the ones presently in use. Each issue is comprised of about half a dozen research articles; the exceptions are special thematic issues, which may have many more. Themes in recent volumes have developed "Optimization of District Heating Systems" and "Carbon Tax for Subsidizing Photovoltaic Power Generation Systems." Articles are lengthier than most, averaging more than 15 pages and often exceeding that. Authors are almost exclusively academics or from government-sponsored research institutions. With some exceptions, the lag time between receipt and publication is quite short, sometimes within two months, so that much of the work is very current. Mounted in *ScienceDirect*, searching, display, and linking (e-mail and cross-reference) features are well implemented. Unfortunately, it is a relatively expensive title in the field, with a low impact factor, and it should be considered only for an extensive academic library collection.

2585. ***Applied Thermal Engineering: design processes equipment economics.*** Former titles (until vol.16, 1996): *Heat Recovery Systems and C H P (Combined Heat and Power);* (until 1983): *Journal of Heat Recovery Systems.* [ISSN: 1359-4311] 1980. 18x/yr. EUR 1739. Ed(s): David A Reay. Pergamon, The Boulevard, Langford Ln, East Park, Kidlington, OX5 1GB, United Kingdom. Refereed. Microform: PQC. Online: ingenta.com; ScienceDirect; Swets Blackwell. Reprint: PQC. *Indexed:* ApMecR, C&ISA, CEA, ChemAb, EngInd, EnvAb, H&SSA. *Aud.:* Ac, Sa.

This journal covers thermal energy applications in depth, from the theoretical ("Artificial Neural Nets for Modeling Vapor-Compression") to extremely practical ("Modeling a Household Dryer"). Usually, though, work involves energy production and large-scale use (such as manufacturing or building heating plants). Although academic in thrust, many of the authors are from industrial concerns; the editor himself maintains a private practice as well as an academic appointment. Articles are lengthy (often more than 20 pages). The lag time between submission and publication has dropped in half (to around nine months) since this title was last reviewed; web posting of accepted articles is often within six months of receipt. Occasionally, an issue is devoted to the proceedings of a conference, but the bulk of the papers are current, independent research. Most issues include a calendar of meetings and events; others include a "Patent Alert" column. Those libraries with strong interests in energy and mechanical engineering would find this a welcome title.

2586. ***Biomass & Bioenergy.*** [ISSN: 0961-9534] 1991. m. EUR 1225. Ed(s): C P Mitchell, R POverend. Pergamon, The Boulevard, Langford Ln, East Park, Kidlington, OX5 1GB, United Kingdom. Refereed. Microform: PQC. Online: ingenta.com; ScienceDirect; Swets Blackwell. *Indexed:* BiolAb, CAPS, ChemAb, DSA, EngInd, FPA, ForAb, GeogAbPG, HortAb, S&F, WAE&RSA. *Aud.:* Ac.

As the title indicates, the coverage of this journal is very mixed. Some articles will appeal mostly to agribusiness endeavors, discussing harvesting methods, agricultural waste, pesticide runoff, and the like. Others will appeal to the energy engineer, with BTU figures and combustion problems associated with biofuels. Still others will appeal to economists and managers, with long-range forecasting of biofuel production and usage. Authors are from academia and government-sponsored research laboratories, with a wide range of backgrounds: engineering, agriculture, economics, and more. The publication lag has lengthened, averaging over 18 months from the relatively short 12 months of two years ago, although web posting of accepted articles mitigates this somewhat. Institutions with strong agriculture as well as energy collections will find this a core title. Some geographic areas will have a strong interest in this type of energy source, while others will find this a niche topic.

2587. ***Bioresource Technology.*** Incorporates (1981-1991): *Biomass;* Which incorporated (1981-1988): *Energy in Agriculture;* Former titles (until 1991): *Biological Wastes;* (until 1987): *Agricultural Wastes.* [ISSN: 0960-8524] 1979. 15x/yr. EUR 2239 (Qualified personnel, EUR 80). Ed(s): Dr. P Hobson, S C Ricke. Elsevier BV, Sara Burgerhartstraat 25, Amsterdam, 1055 KV, Netherlands; nlinfo-f@elsevier.nl; http://www.elsevier.nl. Illus., adv. Refereed. Online: ingenta.com; ScienceDirect; Swets Blackwell. *Indexed:* Agr, BioEngAb, BiolAb, CAPS, ChemAb, DSA, EngInd, EnvAb, ExcerpMed, FPA, FS&TA, ForAb, GeoRef, GeogAbPG, HortAb, IndMed, IndVet, PollutAb, RRTA, S&F, SCI, SSCI, SWRA, VetBull, WAE&RSA, WRCInf, ZooRec. *Aud.:* Ac.

Although this title is highly ranked by ISI as an Energy & Fuels journal, it is largely concerned with controlling and/or utilizing the by-products of agricultural wastes. This includes production of fuels (methane), but most of the lengthy issues deal with other matters. Only for those energy collections that also have strong agricultural chemistry programs.

2588. ***Energy.*** [ISSN: 0360-5442] 1976. 15x/yr. EUR 1875 (Qualified personnel, EUR 80). Ed(s): Dr. N Lior. Pergamon, The Boulevard, Langford Ln, East Park, Kidlington, OX5 1GB, United Kingdom. Illus., index, adv. Sample. Refereed. Circ: 1100. Vol. ends: Dec. Microform: PQC. Online: ingenta.com; ScienceDirect; Swets Blackwell. *Indexed:* AS&TI, AgeL, BAS, BrTechI, ChemAb, DSA, EnvAb, ExcerpMed, FPA, ForAb, GeoRef, GeogAbPG, HortAb, PollutAb, RRTA, S&F, SCI, SWRA, WAE&RSA. *Aud.:* Ac.

One of the first scholarly journals in the energy field, this title, published under the Pergamon imprint, covers the full spectrum: all types of energy sources, all aspects of energy production, plus economic/political/social factors. *Energy* emphasizes development, assessment, and management of energy programs. Most papers involving technical matter average fewer than eight pages; those concerned with economic issues tend to be twice as long. Technical issues still outnumber social ones, but the economic and social aspects have been seeing increased play; almost every issue has a mix. Periodically, an issue will be devoted to a theme (such as "Future Prospects of Nuclear Reactors") or a symposium (such as "Carbon Dioxide Fixation"). Bibliographies, maps, and statistics abound. Publication delay has greatly increased (from about 12 months to close to two years) since this title was last reviewed. As a ScienceDirect title, full-text searching, links to e-mail and cited/citing references, and html or pdf display are standard. A primary journal, but expensive for all except large academic or industry libraries.

2589. ***Energy and Buildings: an international journal of research applied to energy efficiency in the built environment.*** [ISSN: 0378-7788] 1978. 12x/yr. EUR 1297. Ed(s): Dr. A Meier, B B Todorovic. Elsevier S.A., PO Box 564, Lausanne, 1001, Switzerland. Illus., index, adv. Sample. Refereed. Vol. ends: No. 6. Microform: PQC. Online: ingenta.com; ScienceDirect; Swets Blackwell. *Indexed:* API, C&ISA, EngInd, EnvAb, ExcerpMed, GeoRef, PollutAb, SCI, SUSA. *Aud.:* Ac, Sa.

The emphasis here is on the "buildings," with the "energy" portion largely devoted to energy conservation, architectural design for passive energy use/savings, use of solar energy, manipulation of lighting, insulation materials, and cost/benefit analyses for energy consumption. The buildings can be anything from high-rise complexes to grass huts, from classrooms in the tropics to crawl spaces in Finland. Although scholarly in treatment, it is practical in outlook; articles have discussed energy consumption in old school buildings, low-cost insulation, pressure air-flow models for ventilation, and heat transfer in insulated concrete walls. Authorship is international. Articles tend to be short (six to ten pages). Available on the ScienceDirect site, with full-text searching, links to e-mail and cited references, article-alert service, and pdf display. Not for all collections, this title is best for libraries with interest in civil engineering or architecture as well as energy.

2590. ***Energy & Fuels.*** [ISSN: 0887-0624] 1987. bi-m. USD 931 (Individual members, USD 106; Students, USD 80). Ed(s): John W Larsen. American Chemical Society, 1155 16th St, N W, Washington, DC 20036; service@acs.org; http://pubs.acs.org. Illus., index. Refereed. Circ: 700. Vol. ends: Nov/Dec. Online: EBSCO Publishing; Swets Blackwell. *Indexed:* AS&TI, C&ISA, ChemAb, EngInd, ExcerpMed, GeoRef, SCI. *Bk. rev.:* 1, 1000 words. *Aud.:* Ac, Sa.

One of the many American Chemical Society (ACS) journals, this is a scholarly publication interested in both the discovery of non-nuclear fuels and their development as power sources. Originally concentrating on coal, it now has a broader outlook, but hydrocarbons predominate. Individual issues often contain selected papers from symposia, reviews, and "communications" (brief notes on techniques). Authorship is from academia and includes chemists and geologists as well as engineers. Publication is often within one year of receipt of manuscript. ACS has taken advantage of the wide availability of the web: Many articles have supporting material, such as extensive tabular data, that can be accessed at its web site. Tables of contents are available at the journal's web site and full text is available to subscribers, either as pdf or html documents. The html versions include thumbnails of illustrations, links to tables, and links to full text of cited ACS publications. This is a core, quality title.

2591. ***Energy Conversion and Management.*** Former titles (until 1968): *Energy Conversion; Advanced Energy Conversion.* [ISSN: 0196-8904] 1961. 20x/yr. EUR 3091. Ed(s): Jesse C. Denton, Dr. N Lior. Pergamon, The Boulevard, Langford Ln, East Park, Kidlington, OX5 1GB, United Kingdom. Illus., index, adv. Sample. Refereed. Circ: 1300. Vol. ends: No. 18. Microform: PQC. Online: ingenta.com; ScienceDirect; Swets Blackwell. Reprint: PQC. *Indexed:* AS&TI, ApMecR, CEA, ChemAb, DSA, EngInd, EnvAb, ExcerpMed, FPA, ForAb, HortAb, PollutAb, S&F, SSCI, SWRA, WAE&RSA. *Aud.:* Ac, Sa.

Another of the many energy-related scholarly publications in the Elsevier stable, this journal is concerned with technical development of all types of fuels and energy resources, ranging from hydrocarbons though biomass, solar, wind, and other renewable sources. While its sister publication, *Energy (Oxford)*, discusses large-scale management issues, *Energy Conversion* presents detailed technical papers on the ultimate production of many of the same resources. Authorship is international. Papers have become relatively lengthy (often nearly 20 pages) and are well referenced. Although one of the most expensive titles in the field, this publication has a relatively high subscription base, probably because of the emphasis on application. The ScienceDirect site includes author instructions, full-text searching, links, the highly useful "cited by" feature, and html or pdf display.

2592. ***Energy Economics: for professionals concerned with economic analysis of energy issues.*** Incorporates (in 2001): *Journal of Energy Finance and Development.* [ISSN: 0140-9883] 1979. bi-m. EUR 798 (Individuals, EUR 91). Ed(s): Derek W. Bunn, M Essayyad. Elsevier BV, North-Holland, Sara Burgerhartstraat 25, Amsterdam, 1055 KV, Netherlands; nlinfo-f@elsevier.nl; http://www.elsevier.nl. Illus., index, adv. Sample. Refereed. Vol. ends: No. 6. Microform: PQC. Online: EBSCO Publishing; ingenta.com; ScienceDirect; Swets Blackwell. *Indexed:* ABIn, EngInd, EnvAb, ExcerpMed, IBSS, JEL, PAIS, PollutAb, RiskAb, SSCI, WAE&RSA. *Aud.:* Ac.

True to its name, this scholarly journal discusses the economic issues of energy, generally on the macro scale. Recent issues feature a preponderance of petroleum-based discussion, but attention is given to coal, electricity, and "green" concerns. Definitely international in scope, the lengthy articles have covered Indian coal, oil-price sticker shock in Europe, price rigidity in the New Zealand petroleum industry, and the Colombian electricity market. Available both from Science Direct and the ECONbase system, this is a journal for larger collections with an active local interest in economics; other libraries should consider the *Energy Journal*.

2593. ***Energy Engineering.*** Former titles (until 1979): *Building Systems Design; Air Conditioning, Heating and Ventilating.* [ISSN: 0199-8595] 1904. bi-m. USD 200 in US & Canada; USD 250 elsewhere. Ed(s): Wayne C. Turner. The Fairmont Press, Inc., 700 Indian Trail, Lilburn, GA 30047; linda@fairmontpress.com; http://www.fairmontpress.com. Illus., index, adv. Refereed. Circ: 9000. Vol. ends: No. 6. Microform: PMC; PQC. Online: East View Publications, Inc.; Northern Light Technology, Inc.; OCLC Online Computer Library Center, Inc.; ProQuest Information & Learning; Swets Blackwell; H.W. Wilson. Reprint: PQC. *Indexed:* AS&TI, ChemAb, EngInd, EnvAb, ExcerpMed, GeoRef. *Aud.:* Ac, Sa.

This is the energy magazine for the plant engineer, high-rise building supervisor, and town engineer. Articles range from tips on energy auditing to surveys of energy waste minimization over several industries. Most articles are written by practitioners or consultants, but some are by academics. Some have lengthy reference lists and others are obviously "expert-advice" columns. Over the years coverage has broadened from HVAC fine-tuning and lighting system adjustments to include alternative fuels, fuel cells, cogeneration, and energy control systems. Two other journals from the same publisher (not reviewed here) are *Strategic Planning for Energy and the Environment* and *Cogeneration and Competitive Power Journal*; the former is addressed to managers and the latter discusses the technical aspects of "cogeneration" (using the byproduct of one power source to produce yet another form of energy). The publisher now has web access to all of its journals with a browsable, searchable interface. Although navigation through the interface truly is "transparent," unfortunately the response time is poor. However, users may register for an alerting service and pay-per-view of individual articles. A good choice for a large public library and/or undergraduates in an engineering curriculum.

2594. ***The Energy Journal.*** [ISSN: 0195-6574] 1980. q. USD 175 domestic; USD 200 foreign. Ed(s): David Williams. International Association for Energy Economics, 28790 Chagrin Blvd, Ste 350, Cleveland, OH 44122; iaee@iaee.org; http://www.IAEE.org. Illus., index, adv. Sample. Refereed. Circ: 3400. Vol. ends: No. 4. Microform: PQC. Online: EBSCO Publishing; Florida Center for Library Automation; Gale Group; Northern Light Technology, Inc.; OCLC Online Computer Library Center, Inc.; ProQuest Information & Learning; H.W. Wilson. *Indexed:* ABIn, BPI, BRI, CBRI, EnvAb, H&SSA, JEL, PAIS, PetrolAb, PollutAb, RiskAb, SCI, SSCI, SWRA. *Bk. rev.:* 4, 1,000 words. *Aud.:* Ac.

The journal of the International Association for Energy Economics, this is a scholarly publication covering the economic and social/political aspects of energy. Generally this means electric power, but there is some attention to oil, natural gas, and coal. Representative topics include international comparisons of carbon dioxide emissions, regional oil markets, and cointegration analysis as a tool in economic forecasting. Articles are lengthy, often more than 20 pages, with extensive bibliographies, and charts and graphs as illustrations. Authors are from the international academic and government-policy community. Announcements of association conferences and business complete the issues. There are occasional special issues (available for a modest additional price). The web site includes tables of contents and subject category indexes for the entire run of the journal, plus the option for subscribers to download issues rather than receive them by mail. This title is available full-text from several sources, the subscription price remains low, and it has one of the highest ISI impact factors in the field.

2595. ***Energy Law Journal.*** [ISSN: 0270-9163] 1980. s-a. USD 25 domestic; USD 36 Canada; USD 42 elsewhere. Ed(s): William A Mogel. Federal Energy Bar Association, 2175 K St NW #600, Washington, DC 20037-1828. Adv. Circ: 2000. Microform: WSH. Online: Gale Group; LexisNexis; ProQuest Information & Learning; West Group. Reprint: WSH. *Indexed:* CLI, ILP, LRI, PAIS. *Bk. rev.:* 2, 1000 words. *Aud.:* Ac, Sa.

As much about economics and environment as about law, the *Energy Law Journal* is a scholarly work devoted to lengthy analyses of energy issues and how they affect the law or the law affects them. Issues are not only reviewed but debated as well. Papers are written by attorneys, judges, and experts from government agencies. Most of the discussions involve U.S. law, but there are occasional works specific to other countries or international in scope. Book reviews, committee reports on energy and administrative law, and short notes (such as "Agency Conditions on the Relicensing of Hydropower Projects on Federal Reservations") round out the issues. Widely owned by law libraries, it deserves consideration by libraries with strong energy collections and public-policy collections.

2596. ***Energy Policy: international journal of the political, economic, planning and social aspects of energy.*** [ISSN: 0301-4215] 1973. 18x/yr. EUR 1418. Ed(s): Nicky France. Pergamon, The Boulevard, Langford Ln, East Park, Kidlington, OX5 1GB, United Kingdom. Illus., index, adv. Sample. Refereed. Vol. ends: No. 15. Microform: PQC. Online: Gale Group; ingenta.com; ScienceDirect; Swets Blackwell. *Indexed:* ABIn, ABS&EES, AgeL, BPI, EngInd, EnvAb, ExcerpMed, ForAb, GeoRef, GeogAbPG, IBSS, PAIS, PollutAb, RI-1, SSCI. *Aud.:* Ac.

This journal should be compared with *Energy Economics,* also from Elsevier. First, a wider range of energy forms is included (such as wind, photovoltaic, nuclear, and even renewable sources), as opposed to the primarily oil and electric power interests of its sister title. Second, the emphasis is on policy decisions, by government and by industry. Carbon dioxide and other emissions are the major topics of recent issues. Both publications have international authorship and interest, but *Energy Policy* often discusses specific countries and regions while *Energy Economics* is often global in focus.

2597. ***Energy Sources: recovery, utilization, and environmental effects.*** Incorporates (in 1994): *Energy Systems and Policy.* [ISSN: 0090-8312] 1973. m. USD 1325 (Individuals, USD 498). Ed(s): James Speight. Taylor & Francis Inc, 325 Chestnut St, Suite 800, Philadelphia, PA 19016; info@taylorandfrancis.com; http://www.taylorandfrancis.com/. Illus., index, adv. Sample. Refereed. Online: EBSCO Publishing; Ingenta Select; OCLC Online Computer Library Center, Inc.; RoweCom Information Quest; Swets Blackwell. Reprint: PSC. *Indexed:* ABIn, AS&TI, BAS, BiolAb, C&ISA, ChemAb, EngInd, EnvAb, GeoRef, PAIS, PetrolAb, PollutAb, SCI. *Aud.:* Ac.

Although the subtitle of this journal is true, it could read "extraction from biomass," "conversion of petroleum/coal processes to cleaner, more efficient methods," and "large-scale solutions to the environmental problems of day-to-day energy use." Authorship is international, and it is striking to see how many articles deal with Third World issues and energy sources that Westerners would consider "nontraditional." The chief theme, though, is hydrocarbon fuel, and the treatment is strictly engineering. Papers are generally under ten pages but are well referenced. Because of its engineering emphasis in niche areas, this title is best for comprehensive collections.

2598. ***Energy User News: energy management for commercial, industrial and institututional markets.*** [ISSN: 0162-9131] 1976. m. USD 69.50; USD 91 foreign. Ed(s): Kevin Heslin. Business News Publishing Co., 755 W Big Beaver Rd, Ste 1000, Troy, MI 48084-4903; http://www.bnp.com. Illus., index, adv. Sample. Circ: 50177 Controlled. Vol. ends: Dec. Microform: FCM. Online: The Dialog Corporation; EBSCO Publishing; Factiva; Florida Center for Library Automation; Gale Group; Northern Light Technology, Inc.; OCLC Online Computer Library Center, Inc.; ProQuest Information & Learning. Reprint: PQC. *Indexed:* C&ISA. *Aud.:* Ga, Sa.

At one time this was a thin, glossy tabloid that was mostly advertisements. Although the ads are still very much there (the reason why this is "free to qualified"), *Energy Users News* is a good example of what the web can do for what was once basically a "buyers' guide." The "users" here are businesses and industrial concerns. Their problems include high energy costs, pollution, and upgrading their power plants. Each issue has a few topical articles. The web version archives the feature articles for about two years, for free online reading. There is a fee, however, for formatted copies and the rights to add articles to a web site. Also included is a wide array of free ancillary services, such as encyclopedia-type articles on "fundamental issues" that might provide quick answers to student questions. The monthly statistics column provides regional figures for gas and electric utility prices for commercial entities. The buyers' guide is still present, with links to a lengthy list of providers. Public libraries may consider linking to the site from their catalogs; industry libraries will want to subscribe as well.

2599. ***Fuel: science and technology of fuel and energy.*** [ISSN: 0016-2361] 1922. 18x/yr. EUR 2472 (Qualified personnel, EUR 88). Ed(s): John W. Patrick, K. D. Bartle. Elsevier Ltd., The Boulevard, Langford Ln, Oxford, OX5 1GB, United Kingdom. Illus., index, adv. Sample. Refereed. Vol. ends: No. 15. Microform: PQC. Online: ingenta.com; ScienceDirect; Swets Blackwell. *Indexed:* ApMecR, BrTechI, C&ISA, ChemAb, EngInd, EnvAb, ExcerpMed, GeoRef, PetrolAb, PollutAb, SCI. *Aud.:* Ac.

One of the oldest professional journals devoted to energy sources, *Fuel* publishes highly technical articles on coal (and coal tar), petroleum (oil, oil shale, oil sands, and derivatives), natural gas, and a trace of biomass. Most of the articles concern the production of electrical energy, but there is some attention to transportation (gasoline, diesel fuel, and the like). Authorship is international and largely academic, with some coauthors from commercial enterprises. The articles are under ten pages, well referenced, and illustrated with charts, tables, and line drawings. Each issue has a meetings calendar; there are occasional short reports and calls for conference papers. The extra issues in this "monthly" are proceedings of conferences. The journal is mounted at ScienceDirect, providing a searchable interface, links to e-mail and cited/citing articles, and thumbnails of illustrations. Recently (2003) a companion service, FUELfirst.com, posts articles for *Fuel* within 31 days of acceptance, mounts supplementary data, provides an electronic submission route for authors, and includes the (searchable) archives back to 1995. This is a relatively expensive title but is useful in a number of engineering disciplines and has a proven track record.

2600. ***Fuel Processing Technology: an international journal devoted to all aspects of processing coal, oil shale, tar sands and peat.*** [ISSN: 0378-3820] 1978. 15x/yr. EUR 1862. Ed(s): G. P. Huffman. Elsevier BV, Sara Burgerhartstraat 25, Amsterdam, 1055 KV, Netherlands; nlinfo-f@elsevier.nl; http://www.elsevier.nl. Illus., index. Sample. Refereed. Microform: PQC. Online: ingenta.com; ScienceDirect; Swets Blackwell. *Indexed:* C&ISA, ChemAb, EngInd, EnvAb, ExcerpMed, GeoRef, PetrolAb, SCI. *Aud.:* Ac.

Fuel Processing Technology should be compared to its sister publication, *Fuel*. The two titles cover the same types of fuels: hydrocarbons (coal, oil, shale) and biomass. The first title emphasizes "processing" (the conversion of the raw materials to higher forms of fuels), but the second title also includes papers similar in scope. However, *Fuel Processing Technology* uses a less theoretical approach. The inclusion of patent alerts emphasizes this point. Article authorship, length, illustration, and referencing are also similar. The pair are for those libraries with strong programs in petroleum technology as well as energy.

2601. ***Fusion Science and Technology.*** Former titles (until Jul. 2001): *Fusion Technology;* (until Jun. 1984): *Nuclear Technology - Fusion.* [ISSN: 1536-1055] 1981. bi-m. plus 2 supplements. USD 1245. Ed(s): Nermin A Uckan. American Nuclear Society, 555 N Kensington Ave, La Grange Park, IL 60526; orders@ans.org; http://www.ans.org/. Illus., index. Refereed. Circ: 950 Paid. Vol. ends: No. 3. *Indexed:* AS&TI, C&ISA, ChemAb, EngInd, EnvAb, SCI. *Bk. rev.:* 1, 1,500 words. *Aud.:* Ac, Sa.

This highly technical journal has changed its name yet again to reflect the important role of science in conjunction with technology in pursuit of the practical fusion energy. By definition, work in fusion is usually confined to academia or government-sponsored installations, but this journal casts as wide a net as possible. This is still a highly technical field, but the publication's layout alleviates some of the denseness of the prose: double columns, good use of white space around illustrations, highlighted subdivisions, and keywords. Brief author biographies accompany each paper. The emphasis is on improvement of components of reactors, discussions of the theory behind some of those components, modeling, and measurement. Usually a several-page report on a major meeting is included. The web site includes tables of contents with abstracts of the papers and pay-per-view of articles. Because of the highly specialized nature of this research, this title is best for comprehensive collections, especially at sites with strong physics programs.

Geothermics. See Earth Sciences section.

2602. ***Home Energy.*** Formerly (until 1987): *Energy Auditor and Retrofitter.* [ISSN: 0896-9442] 1984. bi-m. USD 59 domestic; USD 74 elsewhere. Ed(s): Alan Meier, Jim Gunshinan. Energy Auditor and Retrofitter, Inc., 2124 Kittredge St, #95, Berkeley, CA 94704; http://www.homeenergy.org. Illus., adv. Sample. Circ: 3000 Paid. Vol. ends: Nov/Dec. Online: Florida Center for Library Automation; Gale Group. *Indexed:* EnvAb. *Aud.:* Ga, Sa.

Home Energy is published by a nonprofit organization, which states that its mission is "to provide objective and practical information for residential energy conservation." Originally intended for the professional home remodeler, since 1997 it has addressed the homeowner as well, partly with consumer guide information and partly with self-help tips. Each printed issue has a few articles that are factual in nature, cite publications or refer to web links, and include many photographs and line illustrations. Most of the issue, though, is composed of short notes, such as "Trends," "Conservation Clips," and "Field Notes." The web site is not just a reproduction of the printed product. Only subscribers have access to the current two years of the magazine, but everyone has free access to the feature articles published since 1993. Articles can be searched via keyword, and there is a complete list in pdf format as well. There is an extensive list of short, colorfully illustrated information articles for both the consumer and the contractor, plus links to sites of interest. Most of this material is free to all, subscribers or not. Libraries that subscribe will have the benefit of providing the current features and columns to their patrons.

2603. ***Home Power: the hands-on journal of home-made power.*** [ISSN: 1050-2416] 1987. bi-m. USD 22.50 domestic; USD 30 foreign. Ed(s): Richard Perez. Home Power, Inc., PO Box 520, Ashland, OR 97520-0520; hp.info@homepower.prg; http://www.homepower.com. Illus., adv. Circ: 67883. *Indexed:* ConsI. *Aud.:* Ga, Sa.

Home Power is not so much a magazine as it is an industry. Visiting its web site is as much fun as it is educational. The magazine promulgates "homemade" electric power using renewable energy resources (solar, wind, water). Regular issue features (although not in every issue) are "Things that Work" (renewable energy products that have been tested by the magazine staff), "Go Power" (alternative transportation), "Home Brew" (circuits and parts for domestic systems), "Power Politics," and several discussion columns. Many articles are success stories from the readership. The magazine is produced by desktop publishing (a full list of hardware and software is provided for the curious or the budding entrepreneur), with full-color illustrations and a crisp layout. The owners practice what they preach: The electricity for the effort comes from their own solar- and wind-powered generators. Although they use a commercial printer for the final product, even that part of the operation is environmentally friendly, using recycled, chlorine-free paper. The web site includes the full pdf version of the current issue, some useful files/data from earlier issues, links to related sites, and ads for the company's book and CD-ROM publications.

2604. ***I E E E Power & Energy Magazine.*** Formed by the merger of (1981-2003): *I E E E Power Engineering Review;* (1988-2003): *I E E E Computer Applications in Power.* [ISSN: 1540-7977] 2003. bi-m. USD 275 in North America; USD 310 elsewhere. I E E E, 445 Hoes Ln, Box 1331, Piscataway, NJ 08855-1331; http://www.ieee.org. *Bk. rev.:* 1, 1000 words. *Aud.:* Ac, Sa.

New in 2003, this is another of the highly relevant, highly useful *IEEE Magazines* series (as distinct from the often dense *IEEE Transactions*). It is designed for the "electric power professional," and the editor is careful to distinguish it from the *IEEE Power Engineering Review* and *IEEE Computer Applications in Power.* The inaugural issue featured several short, state-of-the-industry reviews; the second issue appeared more indicative of what future articles will be like, with several devoted to automation of electricity substations. Executed in the usual colorful, glossy style of the *IEEE Magazines*, articles are eight to ten pages in length, with extensive bibliographies. The remainder of the issues presents society business and book reviews. Well worth considering for many libraries, especially for those where the equivalent *IEEE Transactions* are either too expensive or too weighty.

2605. *I E E E Transactions on Energy Conversion.* Supersedes in part: *I E E E Transactions on Power Apparatus and Systems.* [ISSN: 0885-8969] 1986. q. USD 420 in North America; USD 455 elsewhere. Ed(s): James L Kirtley. Institute of Electrical and Electronics Engineers, Inc., 445 Hoes Ln, Piscataway, NJ 08854-1331; subscription-service@ieee.org; http://www.ieee.org. Refereed. Online: EBSCO Publishing; Gale Group; I E E E; Swets Blackwell. *Indexed:* AS&TI, EngInd, EnvAb, SCI. *Aud.:* Ac.

The thrust of this journal is efficient conversion of energy producing mechanisms (usually motors in small or large scale) to electrical energy. Therefore, a significant number of articles cover wind, solar, and renewable energy production problems. As usual with *IEEE Transactions* publications, the papers are written for and by academics, but there are highly practical problems under discussion. The IEEEXplore web site offers pdf versions of the papers and a reasonably sophisticated search engine for locating relevant material, and it has added links to authors' e-mail or cited references since this title was last reviewed. Large engineering collections will be pleasantly surprised to discover they have a good, economical source of material on niche energy topics. Commercial entities in solar or wind power will find this an inexpensive source of good material. It is also a good title for those electric-car enthusiasts found in engineering schools.

2606. *Institution of Mechanical Engineers. Proceedings. Part A: Journal of Power and Energy.* Formerly (until 1990): *Institution of Mechanical Engineers. Proceedings. Part A: Journal of Power Engineering;* Which superseded in part (in 1989): *Institution of Mechanical Engineers. Proceedings. Part A: Power and Process Engineering;* Which superseded in part (1847-1982): *Institution of Mechanical Engineers. Proceedings.* [ISSN: 0957-6509] 1983. bi-m. USD 824 in the Americas; GBP 514 elsewhere. Ed(s): M J Moore. Professional Engineering Publishing, Northgate Ave, Bury St Edmunds, IP32 6BW, United Kingdom; orders@pepublishing.com; http://www.pepublishing.com. Illus., index. Sample. Refereed. Circ: 1000. Vol. ends: No. 6. Microform: PMC; PQC. Online: EBSCO Publishing; Ingenta Select; OCLC Online Computer Library Center, Inc.; ProQuest Information & Learning; RoweCom Information Quest; Swets Blackwell. Reprint: PQC. *Indexed:* AS&TI, ApMecR, BrTechI, C&ISA, ChemAb, EngInd, GeogAbPG, OceAb, PollutAb. *Bk. rev.:* 3, 500 words. *Aud.:* Ac, Sa.

Normally, the journal of a professional society outside the United States would not be included in this section, especially when there are relevant titles available from U.S. equivalents (*IEEE Transactions on Energy Conversion* and *Journal of Solar Energy Engineering,* above in this section). However, this publication is well worth consideration in a broad-based energy collection. First, it covers a lot of territory: electric power, wind power, ocean wave energy, power production from coal, nuclear energy, gas, fuel cells, solar energy, in fact, everything its subtitle indicates. Second, although the publisher is a British society, the journal has an international authorship made up of a combination of academic and industry researchers. Third, it has a relatively rapid turnaround from submission to publication. Fourth, the articles are readable (it is indexed in *Applied Science and Technology Abstracts*), well referenced, and well illustrated. Even the book reviews are current. Its major shortcoming is that it is relatively expensive for a college library. Most university collections will already have it, as part of the complete IME *Proceedings,* and as such, at a cheaper rate.

2607. *International Journal of Energy Research.* [ISSN: 0363-907X] 1976. 15x/yr. USD 3895. Ed(s): J T McMullan. John Wiley & Sons Ltd., The Atrium, Southern Gate, Chichester, PO19 8SQ, United Kingdom; customer@wiley.co.uk; http://www.wiley.co.uk. Adv. Refereed. Circ: 500. Reprint: ISI; PQC; SWZ. *Indexed:* ApMecR, BrTechI, C&ISA, ChemAb, EngInd, EnvAb, ExcerpMed, GeoRef, GeogAbPG, IAA, OceAb, PollutAb, SCI, SSCI. *Aud.:* Ac.

This is an exceedingly eclectic title. According to the aims and scope information from the journal's web site, "the Editors do not wish to restrict the areas of energy research suitable for publication," and the range of topics covered in each issue verifies this statement. Article subjects range from cost-efficient control strategies for a confectionery plant (management) to fan-energy calculation in air-handling units (practical) to performance studies of combustion of gas cycle and rankine cycle engines (thermodynamics) —and these were all in one issue. Articles often run 20 or more pages. Not only are authors international, but it is not unusual to find an article co-authored by a team from three or more institutions. The Wiley web site offers html or pdf copies of articles, Boolean searching, related-article matching, and links to e-mail and cited/citing references. As it is, the price makes this a hard title to justify; the cost averages more than two dollars a page. For the comprehensive academic collection.

2608. *International Journal of Hydrogen Energy.* [ISSN: 0360-3199] 1976. 15x/yr. EUR 2200. Ed(s): T Nejat Veziroglu. Pergamon, The Boulevard, Langford Ln, East Park, Kidlington, OX5 1GB, United Kingdom. Illus., adv. Refereed. Circ: 2250. Microform: PMC; PQC. Online: ingenta.com; ScienceDirect; Swets Blackwell. Reprint: PQC. *Indexed:* C&ISA, ChemAb, EngInd, EnvAb, IAA, SCI. *Aud.:* Ac.

This may be the only journal devoted to hydrogen as an energy source, and, as such, it covers both the technical aspects and the social (economics, environment, and international impact). Most of the articles are short and highly technical, with much of the discussion concerned with fuel cells. Unusual for a scholarly journal, a regular feature is a section devoted to discussion of earlier articles. An added bonus is the quarterly bibliography of hydrogen energy articles from several sources. This is a niche area in energy research and should be considered only by those institutions with like programs.

2609. *Journal of Energy and Development.* [ISSN: 0361-4476] 1975. s-a. USD 36 (Students, USD 24; USD 44). Ed(s): Dorothea El Mallakh. International Research Center for Energy and Economic Development, 850 Willowbrook Rd, Boulder, CO 80302-7439; iceed@stripe.colorado.edu; http://www.iceed.org/. Adv. Sample. Refereed. Circ: 2000. Microform: WSH. Reprint: WSH. *Indexed:* ABCPolSci, BAS, C&ISA, CLI, EnvAb, ILP, JEL, PAIS, PSA, PetrolAb, SSCI. *Bk. rev.:* 4, 500 words. *Aud.:* Ac.

This journal is the chief contribution to the scholarly world of a tiny organization, The International Research Center for Energy and Economic Development (located at the University of Colorado at Boulder). It specializes in review articles on the economic impact of energy (chiefly oil and gas) on the large (country, world-wide) scale. For such a small publication, it has a wide readership in academia, one that cannot be attributed solely to its modest subscription price. Definitely a title to be considered for economics as well as energy collections.

2610. *Journal of Energy Finance and Development.* [ISSN: 1085-7443] 1996. s-a. NLG 1336 Combined with Energy Economics. Elsevier Ltd., The Boulevard, Langford Ln, Oxford, OX5 1GB, United Kingdom. Illus., index. Refereed. Online: ingenta.com; ScienceDirect. *Indexed:* JEL. *Aud.:* Ac.

True to its name, this scholarly journal discusses the economic issues of energy, generally on the macro scale. Recent issues feature a preponderance of petroleum-based discussion, but attention is given to coal, electricity, and "green" concerns. Definitely international in scope, the lengthy articles have covered Indian coal, oil-price sticker shock in Europe, price rigidity in the New Zealand petroleum industry, and the Colombian electricity market. Available both from Science Direct and the ECONbase system, this is a journal for larger collections with an active local interest in economics; other libraries should consider the *Energy Journal.*

2611. *Journal of Power Sources: the international journal on the science and technology of electrochemical energy systems.* [ISSN: 0378-7753] 1976. 24x/yr. EUR 3145. Ed(s): Z Ogumi, C K Dyer. Elsevier S.A., PO Box 564, Lausanne, 1001, Switzerland. Refereed. Microform: PQC. Online: ingenta.com; ScienceDirect; Swets Blackwell. *Indexed:* C&ISA, ChemAb, EngInd, EnvAb, IAA, PollutAb, SCI. *Aud.:* Ac.

Think photovoltaics: The power sources here are fuel cells and batteries for portable power supplies, electric vehicles, satellites. This journal discusses the conversion of solar, wind, and other energy sources into storage devices such as fuel cells. Much of the work involves materials properties, electrochemical reactions, and the application of photovoltaics to practical devices. Issues are lengthy, often running to 200 pages; publication lag is quite short, sometimes under four months but generally around six. This is a high impact factor journal, but quite expensive (although not on a cost-per-page basis); libraries with strong engineering collections as well as renewable-energy interests should consider it. However, it should be compared with *Progress in Photovoltaics* (below in this section).

2612. *Journal of Solar Energy Engineering.* [ISSN: 0199-6231] 1980. q. Members, USD 50 print & online eds.; Non-members, USD 230 print & online eds. Ed(s): Jane Davidson. A S M E International, Three Park Ave, New York, NY 10016-5990; infocentral@asme.org; http://www.asme.org. Illus., index. Refereed. Vol. ends: Nov. Microform: PQC. Online: EBSCO Publishing; Gale Group; Swets Blackwell. Reprint: PQC. *Indexed:* AS&TI, ApMecR, C&ISA, CEA, ChemAb, EngInd, EnvAb, SCI. *Aud.:* Ac, Sa.

This is an engineering research journal, with short articles (around six pages) on applied research into solar energy production, materials used in solar energy, and applications of solar energy to other engineering problems. Most readers are familiar with the use of solar power to dry fruits and heat water, but many will be surprised to learn that it can also be used in aluminum smelting and fullerene synthesis. The journal should really be titled "solar and wind energy"; every few issues, several articles on wind power are included. The web version displays in html (full and by sections), pdf, and PostScript, with thumbnails of illustrations and tables, plus links to e-mail and cited references; a truly user-friendly system. This is a good value for the research dollar, and it will be useful at industrial as well as academic sites.

2613. *Journal of Wind Engineering and Industrial Aerodynamics.* Formerly (until 1980): *Journal of Industrial Aerodynamics.* [ISSN: 0167-6105] 1975. 15x/yr. EUR 2313. Ed(s): N. P. Jones. Elsevier BV, Sara Burgerhartstraat 25, Amsterdam, 1055 KV, Netherlands; nlinfo-f@elsevier.nl; http://www.elsevier.nl. Refereed. Microform: PQC. Online: ingenta.com; ScienceDirect; Swets Blackwell. Reprint: SWZ. *Indexed:* ApMecR, C&ISA, EngInd, EnvAb, GeogAbPG, M&GPA, PollutAb, SCI. *Aud.:* Ac.

Billing itself as the oldest wind energy journal in English, this publication still reflects its heritage of "industrial aerodynamics." Although many of the articles in this globally oriented journal deal with wind energy generation, a sizable portion cover wind effects on structures, wind tunnel design, wind in the meteorological sense, and fluid flow and turbulence of air. Although useful and relevant, this expensive title is more suited to a mechanical or aeronautical engineering collection than to energy production. Libraries with smaller collections or more focused interests should consider the other wind power journals covered in this section.

2614. *Nuclear Energy.* Formerly: *British Nuclear Energy Society. Journal.* [ISSN: 0140-4067] 1962. bi-m. GBP 150 domestic; GBP 190 in Europe; GBP 145 elsewhere. Ed(s): V S Crocker. Thomas Telford Ltd., Thomas Telford House, 1 Heron Quay, London, E14 4JD, United Kingdom; journals@thomastelford.com; http://www.t-telford.co.uk. Illus. Refereed. Circ: 1800. *Indexed:* BrTechI, C&ISA, ChemAb, EngInd, EnvAb, ExcerpMed, PAIS. *Aud.:* Ac.

Largely a technical journal although it does include papers on the economics of the nuclear industry, this is the official journal of the British Nuclear Energy Society. Each issue contains four or five deliberately short articles (averaging six pages) on nuclear fission and fusion as energy sources. Recent articles cover decommissioning of a fusion reactor, coupling a nuclear boiler feedwater nozzle, and integrated collaboration in the global nuclear energy industry. Authors are academics, government researchers, and engineers at nuclear power plants from all over the world. On the same level as *Nuclear Technology* (below in this section), it publishes fewer articles and is more Euro-centric than its American equivalent. Libraries with extensive collections in physics as well as nuclear power will want both; others may opt for the title closest to home.

Nuclear Engineering International. See Engineering and Technology/Nuclear Engineering section.

2615. *Nuclear Technology.* Formerly: *Nuclear Applications and Technology.* [ISSN: 0029-5450] 1965. m. USD 1030 print & online eds. Ed(s): Nicholas Tsoulfanidis. American Nuclear Society, 555 N Kensington Ave, La Grange Park, IL 60526; http://www.ans.org/. Illus., index. Refereed. Circ: 1300. Vol. ends: No. 3. *Indexed:* A&ATA, AS&TI, BiolAb, C&ISA, ChemAb, EngInd, EnvAb, GeoRef, H&SSA, PollutAb, SCI, SSCI. *Aud.:* Ac, Sa.

One of several publications from the American Nuclear Society (ANS) (see also *Fusion Science and Technology*), *Nuclear Technology* publishes papers on applications of research to the nuclear energy field, as opposed to theoretical work. Each issue is subdivided into sections, such as nuclear reactor safety, fission reactors, radioactive waste management, and others as appropriate. As in its sister publication, the layout is crisp, and such features as keyword descriptors at the head of each paper help the reader target relevant papers. The authorship is international, often from industry, and publication lag averages about one year. Brief author biographies are included after the bibliographies. Papers rarely run more than ten pages. Occasionally, technical notes (one- or two-page items) are included. Book reviews are encouraged but rarely appear. Libraries with active physics researchers will probably have all of the ANS publications; others may prefer the specialized titles.

2616. *Oil & Gas Journal.* [ISSN: 0030-1388] 1902. w. USD 79 domestic; USD 84 Canada & Latin America; USD 129 elsewhere. PennWell Corp., 1421 S Sheridan Rd, Tulsa, OK 74112; http://www.pennwell.com. Illus., index, adv. Circ: 39000. Vol. ends: No. 52. Microform: PMC; PQC. Online: Florida Center for Library Automation; Gale Group; LexisNexis; Northern Light Technology, Inc.; OCLC Online Computer Library Center, Inc.; ProQuest Information & Learning. Reprint: PQC. *Indexed:* ABIn, AS&TI, BPI, C&ISA, CEA, ChemAb, DSR&OA, EngInd, EnvAb, ExcerpMed, GeoRef, GeogAbPG, OceAb, PetrolAb, PollutAb, S&F. *Aud.:* Ga, Ac, Sa.

Decade after decade, this has been a reliable source for topical industry news, special features, and lots of data. Articles comprise a large portion of the contents, either short reviews (one to three pages) by staff writers or somewhat longer referenced papers by industry specialists. Each issue follows the section format of focus articles, general interest news, exploration and development, drilling and production, and processing and transportation, with columns on equipment and statistics. There are a number of annually repeating issues, such as forecast and review or worldwide refining. Because it is a weekly, its events calendars, industry briefs, government watch items, and people columns are fresh, and the web version offers even later news. On the web site, parts of the current issue, the product guide, and the equipment exchange section are freely accessible; the complete issues and backfiles are available only to subscribers. This is also the place to find a job and to sell new or used equipment. The best section for librarians is the multi-page statistics analysis at the end of each paper issue. American Petroleum Institute data and prices (crude and refined, U.S. and world regions) are reported weekly, but other analyses pop up from time to time, such as country-by-country current/previous-year production comparison figures.

2617. *Power Engineering.* [ISSN: 0032-5961] 1896. m. USD 74 domestic; USD 82 in Canada & Mexico; USD 204 elsewhere. Ed(s): John Zink. PennWell Corp., 1421 S Sheridan Rd, Tulsa, OK 74112; Headquarters@PennWell.com; http://www.pennwell.com. Illus., index, adv. Circ: 59306. Vol. ends: Dec. Microform: PQC. Online: EBSCO Publishing; Florida Center for Library Automation; Gale Group; Northern Light Technology, Inc.; OCLC Online Computer Library Center, Inc.; ProQuest Information & Learning. *Indexed:* ABIn, AS&TI, ApMecR, C&ISA, ChemAb, EngInd, EnvAb, ExcerpMed, H&SSA, SSCI. *Aud.:* Ga, Ac, Sa.

One of those trade magazines that have been around forever, partly because it knows how to change with the times, *Power Engineering* is concerned with the electric power–producing industry with a concentration on solid fuels. In addition to short articles, it is chock-full of ads, industry briefs, and regular columns on the environment, business, and field notes (which plant is doing what about which). The articles are often by staff writers, but can also be tips from experts in the industry. Although they usually do not include references, the articles are well illustrated with color photographs, charts, tables, and line drawings. The annual buyers' guide now appears in December, but is also available on the web. Other features include the "Project of the Year" and the big industry conference, Power-Gen. Free registration at the web site provides access to the issue archives through a nice search interface.

2618. ***Power (New York).*** incorporates (1882-1883): *Steam.* [ISSN: 0032-5929] 1883. bi-m. USD 55 domestic (Free to qualified personnel). Ed(s): Robert Swanekamp. Platts, 2 Penn Plaza, 5th Fl, New York, NY 10121-2298; http://www.platts.com/. Illus., adv. Circ: 62217. Vol. ends: No. 9. Microform: PQC. Online: Dow Jones Interactive; EBSCO Publishing; LexisNexis; NewsNet; ProQuest Information & Learning. Reprint: PQC. *Indexed:* AS&TI, ApMecR, B&I, ChemAb, EngInd, EnvAb, ExcerpMed, PetrolAb, PollutAb. *Aud.:* Ga, Ac, Sa.

This "bimonthly" publication has nine issues per year; what were once special issues (such as the "Buyers' Guide") have now been transferred to the web version. Every other issue seems to have a "special report" on something, and there are annual features, such as the "Powerplant Award" and the new "Top Plants" survey. The concentration is on "traditional" power plants, which run on fossil fuels or nuclear power, but renewable energy sources are also included. Although technical, the articles are written with management in mind, which makes them approachable for the undergraduate or lay reader. Few articles have references, but the web site features links to other sites where appropriate. There are columns on fuels, labor, environment, and the latest technologies and management practices. Obviously a rival to *Power Engineering* (below) *Power* seems to have the edge on in-depth special issues, and it makes up for its (more or less) bimonthly schedule with updates at its web site. The site itself actually incorporates several McGraw-Hill publications and is free to any user, although some services require separate subscriptions.

2619. ***Progress in Energy and Combustion Science: an international review journal.*** [ISSN: 0360-1285] 1975. bi-m. EUR 1415 (Qualified personnel, EUR 90). Ed(s): Norman A Chigier. Pergamon, The Boulevard, Langford Ln, East Park, Kidlington, OX5 1GB, United Kingdom. Illus., index, adv. Refereed. Microform: PQC. Online: ingenta.com; ScienceDirect; Swets Blackwell. *Indexed:* ApMecR, C&ISA, CEA, ChemAb, EngInd, EnvAb, ExcerpMed, IAA, SCI. *Aud.:* Ac.

This is a review journal publishing papers on efficient combustion of fossil fuels, with the aim of conserving resources and protecting the environment. Articles are not for the fainthearted; the editors solicit articles from experts in the field, and they do a thorough job. It is not unusual for an issue to have only two papers, each of 50 pages or more. As such, this title is consumed by the academic market, but some papers are deliberately designed for the practicing engineer or manager. This is an expensive publication, but with a very high impact factor (as befits a review journal), and well worth considering for the complete research collection.

2620. ***Progress in Photovoltaics: research and applications.*** [ISSN: 1062-7995] 1993. 8x/yr. USD 1185. Ed(s): P A Lynn. John Wiley & Sons Ltd., The Atrium, Southern Gate, Chichester, PO19 8SQ, United Kingdom; customer@wiley.co.uk; http://www.wiley.co.uk. Adv. Refereed. Microform: PQC. Online: EBSCO Publishing; Swets Blackwell; Wiley InterScience. Reprint: SWZ. *Indexed:* ChemAb, EngInd, SCI. *Aud.:* Ac.

For "photovoltaics" in the title, the reader should substitute the term "solar cells." This journal promotes quick publication of research articles, brief communications, and short surveys, generally within a year of submission, and often less. Papers are relatively short, usually under ten pages. The articles can be quite practical, as in "Aeration of Fish Ponds by Photovoltaic Power" (a not inconsequential topic in areas of the world where food is scarce); they also can be highly theoretical, as in "Current-Voltage Characteristic of Czochralski Silicon Solar Cells." About once a year there will be a theme issue on such topics as "Photovoltaics in Rural Electrification" or "Photovoltaics in Space." The photovoltaics literature survey section, culled from other research journals in the field, began in 2000 and appears in each issue. The "Solar Cell Efficiency Tables" is an irregularly updated data survey. The Wiley web site offers Boolean searching, links to references and e-mail addresses, plus "EarlyView" of full articles in advance of the print copy. This is a good title for universities with strong interests in energy and electrical engineering.

2621. ***Public Utilities Fortnightly.*** Former titles (until Sep. 1994): *Public Utilities Reports. Fortnightly;* (until Oct. 1993): *Public Utilities Fortnightly.* [ISSN: 1078-5892] 1929. 22x/yr. USD 139 domestic; USD 190 foreign. Ed(s): Bruce W Radford. Public Utilities Reports, Inc., 8229 Boone Blvd, Ste 401, Vienna, VA 22182; pur_info@pur.com; http://www.pur.com. Adv. Circ: 6500 Paid. Microform: PQC. Online: Florida Center for Library Automation; Gale Group; Northern Light Technology, Inc.; OCLC Online Computer Library Center, Inc.; ProQuest Information & Learning; West Group. *Indexed:* ABIn, ATI, B&I, BPI, CLI, EnvAb, GeoRef, LRI, PAIS. *Aud.:* Sa.

This classic title tracks utilities news of interest to investors. Legislation, regulatory information, recycling and hazardous waste disposal, new technology, and related information are provided for specific companies, as well as for various segments of the industry, e.g., energy, telecommunications, and water. Articles evaluate coal trading futures, nuclear waste's slow boil, workforce management, and the consumer cost of renewable energy. Of special interest is the "Benchmark" data (sales by region for major utility providers) and the financial analyses that often accompany feature articles.

2622. ***Renewable and Sustainable Energy Reviews.*** [ISSN: 1364-0321] 1997. bi-m. EUR 896. Ed(s): Dr. Lawrence L Kazmerski. Pergamon, The Boulevard, Langford Ln, East Park, Kidlington, OX5 1GB, United Kingdom. *Indexed:* EngInd, SCI. *Aud.:* Ac.

As the title suggests, this is a scholarly journal that features extensive review articles. The average issue has only four articles, averaging about 20 pages and often running to over 50. Authors are either faculty at universities or researchers for government-supported organizations. The energy sources covered are biomass, geothermics, hydrogen, hydroelectric, ocean/tide, solar, and wind; treatment can be technical or a policy study. Libraries should compare this title, its sister publication *Renewable Energy*, and *Renewable Energy World* (both below) to determine which title(s) fit their collections best.

2623. ***Renewable Energy.*** Incorporates (1984-1990): *Solar and Wind Technology.* [ISSN: 0960-1481] 1985. 15x/yr. EUR 1640. Ed(s): Ali A M Sayigh. Pergamon, The Boulevard, Langford Ln, East Park, Kidlington, OX5 1GB, United Kingdom. Illus., index, adv. Sample. Refereed. Vol. ends: No. 12. Microform: PQC. Online: ingenta.com; ScienceDirect; Swets Blackwell. *Indexed:* C&ISA, EngInd, EnvAb, ExcerpMed, GeogAbPG, PollutAb, SWRA. *Bk. rev.:* 1, 1000 words. *Aud.:* Ac.

At the other end of the spectrum from such magazines as *Home Power* and *Windpower Monthly,* both in type of content and price, *Renewable Energy* is a scholarly publication. Originally emphasizing solar and wind energy (and still heavily cited in the major solar energy titles), it now includes ocean wave and geothermal material. A good number of the articles are nontechnical, covering social, political, and economic aspects of renewable energy development. The authorship is international, with a high percentage of Third World contributors, reflecting the sites that emphasize development and use of low-cost (economically and environmentally) power sources. Issues usually include a calendar, a brief review of a recent conference, and an occasional book review. The ScienceDirect version includes links to e-mail, citing/cited by references, and full-text searching.

2624. ***Renewable Energy World.*** Incorporates (1996-1998): *Sustainable Energy Industry Journal.* [ISSN: 1462-6381] 1996. bi-m. GBP 60 in Europe; GBP 70 elsewhere. Ed(s): Jackie Jones. James & James (Science Publishers) Ltd., 8-12 Camden High St, London, NW1 0JH, United Kingdom; rew@jxj.com; http://www.jxj.com/rew. Illus., adv. Circ: 15000 Controlled. *Aud.:* Ac, Sa.

A colorful trade publication with a well-designed web presence, this magazine covers all of the "renewable" energy sources: biomass, cogeneration, hydroelectric, geothermal, green, solar, wind, and tidal/wave. Each issue emphasizes one or more types in turn. Designed for the practitioner rather than the scholar, issues are crammed with current news, include ten or so articles, and have the usual conference/trade show announcements, letters, editorials, and the like. The web site includes links to suppliers, related material, and archives of selected articles from back numbers. The articles themselves often have the kinds of tables, charts, and engineering data hard to acquire elsewhere, plus sometimes lengthy bibliographies. Those on the web site are free to all, making this a good referral site for undergraduate research. Corporate libraries with interests in any renewable energy sources will want a full subscription; public and academic libraries may find the web site sufficient.

2625. *Resource and Energy Economics: a journal devoted to interdisciplinary studies in the allocation of natural resources.* Formerly (until 1993): *Resources and Energy.* [ISSN: 0928-7655] 1978. q. EUR 521 (Individuals, EUR 72). Ed(s): Charles D Kolstad, M. Hoel. Elsevier BV, North-Holland, Sara Burgerhartstraat 25, Amsterdam, 1055 KV, Netherlands; nlinfo-f@elsevier.nl; http://www.elsevier.nl/homepage/about/us/regional_sites.htt. Illus., index, adv. Sample. Refereed. Microform: PQC. Online: EBSCO Publishing; Gale Group; ingenta.com; ScienceDirect; Swets Blackwell. *Indexed:* ABIn, BiolAb, EngInd, EnvAb, ForAb, GeoRef, GeogAbPG, JEL, M&GPA, PollutAb, SSCI, WAE&RSA. *Aud.:* Ac.

This journal should be compared with its sister publication *Energy Economics* (above in this section). *Resources and Energy Economics* emphasizes use of resources, of which energy is one. The papers are scholarly and lengthy (often more than 20 pages). Recent topics include the impact of energy conservation on technology and economic growth, energy taxes in Denmark, and slow diffusion of energy-saving technologies. All of these are economic treatments rather than discussions of the technology involved. Like *Energy Economics,* this title is included in the ECONbase system. Libraries whose interest is primarily in energy will prefer *Energy Economics*; those with strong economics and/or business collections should consider both journals.

2626. *Solar Energy: international journal for scientists, engineers and technologists in solar energy and its application.* [ISSN: 0038-092X] 1957. 12x/yr. EUR 2060. Ed(s): J Luther. Pergamon, The Boulevard, Langford Ln, East Park, Kidlington, OX5 1GB, United Kingdom. Illus., index, adv. Sample. Refereed. Circ: 13000. Vol. ends: No. 6. Microform: MIM; PQC. Online: East View Publications, Inc.; Gale Group; ingenta.com; ScienceDirect. *Indexed:* API, AS&TI, ApMecR, BiolAb, C&ISA, ChemAb, DSR&OA, EngInd, EnvAb, ExcerpMed, GeogAbPG, M&GPA, SCI, SSCI. *Bk. rev.:* 1, 500 words. *Aud.:* Ac.

Solar Energy was once the premier journal in solar research, encompassing biomass and wind energy as well as the engineering and physical aspects of solar energy. It is strictly a scholarly publication, and most of its authors are academics from all of the engineering disciplines, with a few applied physicists included for good measure. Illustrations are limited to charts, tables, and line drawings, although an occasional candid photograph of field work appears. Every few months there is a topical issue (such as "Large Scale Solar Heating"), a book review, and patent reports. The subscription price continues to increase at well above the inflation rate, but the page content has remained level, as has the ISI impact factor ranking. Institutions with emphasis on materials and electronics might prefer its sister publication *Solar Energy Materials and Solar Cells* (below).

2627. *Solar Energy Materials and Solar Cells: an international journal devoted to the material science aspects of photovoltaic, photothermal, and photochemical solar energy conversion.* Formerly (until 1992): *Solar Energy Materials;* Incorporates (1979-1991): *Solar Cells.* [ISSN: 0927-0248] 1979. 20x/yr. EUR 1857. Ed(s): C. M. Lampert. Elsevier BV, North-Holland, Sara Burgerhartstraat 25, Amsterdam, 1055 KV, Netherlands; nlinfo-f@elsevier.nl; http://www.elsevier.nl/homepage/about/us/regional_sites.htt. Illus., index. Sample. Refereed. Vol. ends: No. 4. Microform: PQC. Online: ingenta.com; ScienceDirect; Swets Blackwell. *Indexed:* C&ISA, CerAb, ChemAb, EngInd, EnvAb, ExcerpMed, IAA, SCI. *Aud.:* Ac.

Aptly named, this journal publishes highly technical papers on the materials used in solar energy production and products. Aside from solar cells, it includes light control (smart windows), optical and photochemical properties of materials, and photothermal devices (used in energy storage). Recent articles discuss a thermoelectric refrigerator driven by solar cells, nanoparticles in polypyrrole thin films, and utilization of an organic polymer as a sensitizer in solid-state cells. A "Patents Alert" column appears sporadically. Mounted on ScienceDirect, this title is searchable in full-text, with links to cited/citing references and thumbnails of illustrations. This is one of the top ten most-cited journals in energy, but it is best for scholarly collections encompassing materials chemistry as well as energy.

2628. *Solar Today: today's energy choices for a cleaner environment.* Formerly: *A S E S News.* [ISSN: 1042-0630] 1987. bi-m. USD 29 domestic; USD 39 Canada; USD 49 elsewhere. Ed(s): Maureen McIntyre. American Solar Energy Society, Inc., 2400 Central Ave, Ste. G-1, Boulder, CO 80301-2843; ases@ases.org; http://www.ases.org. Illus., index, adv. Circ: 6000. Vol. ends: Nov/Dec. *Indexed:* EnvAb. *Aud.:* Ga, Sa.

This is the members' magazine for the American Solar Energy Society, the "local" for the international, which publishes *Solar Energy.* The latter is for researchers; *Solar Today* is for everybody. As is true of many magazines in the solar field, wind power is included as an also-ran. Many of the articles describe success stories on a small scale, such as "Power Solutions in Your Own Backyards." Others take the larger view, covering potential world markets for wind energy or green power. Although the topics may be technical, the treatment usually is not. The letters section is extensive, there are lots of ads (for both the contractor and the homeowner), and society news and conference programs complete the issue. The web site includes full texts of policy/position statements and links to renewable-energy sites, as well as society business and information on the annual National Tour of Solar Buildings.

2629. *U.S. Energy Information Administration. Monthly Energy Review.* Incorporates: *P I M S Monthly Petroleum Report; Monthly Energy Indicators.* [ISSN: 0095-7356] 1974. m. USD 98. U.S. Energy Information Administration, National Energy Information Center, EI-30, James Forrestal Bldg, Rm 1F 048, 1000 Independence Ave, S W, Washington, DC 20585; infoctr@eia.doe.gov; http://www.eia.doe.gov. Illus., index. Vol. ends: Dec. Microform: CIS. Online: EBSCO Publishing; Florida Center for Library Automation; Gale Group; OCLC Online Computer Library Center, Inc.; ProQuest Information & Learning. Reprint: CIS; WSH. *Indexed:* AmStI, EnvAb, GeoRef, IUSGP. *Aud.:* Ga, Ac, Sa.

A merger of print and electronic media for the transmittal of statistical data, the *Monthly Energy Review* has become entirely a creature of the web. Most issues are made up of data on specific forms of energy (coal, oil, gas, electricity, nuclear), their production, consumption, and pricing. Curiously, renewable energy sources are tabulated in the appendix section, although, beginning in 2001, some of this data was incorporated into the "Energy Overview" and "Energy Consumption" sections. Data are presented monthly for the current and previous two years, then annually for earlier years, back to 1973. Often there are accompanying illustrative charts and graphs. Each section begins with a short introduction highlighting current trends, proceeds through copious data, then ends with explanatory notes and data-source information for specific tables. The site includes conversion tables, various appendixes (such as carbon dioxide emission factors for coal), a complete list of special features published since 1975, and an extensive glossary. "Energy Plugs" became a feature in 1996; these are abstracts of lengthy reports compiled by the Energy Information Administration (EIA) that can be ordered in print or obtained, free, at the EIA web site. Individual tables may be downloaded in ASCII, Lotus (Quattro) (wk1), or Excel (xls) formats; beginning with the November 1996 issue, the entire issue is accessible in pdf format. The web site includes a broad range of other EIA data and analyses, including separate annual data compilations and an "Interactive Query" feature that helps the user produce subset reports. Add this to the Bookmark section of the reference desk browser, and, if your catalog supports it, as a direct link from the catalog record.

2630. *Wind Energy.* [ISSN: 1095-4244] 1998. q. USD 450. Ed(s): Robert Thresher. John Wiley & Sons Ltd., The Atrium, Southern Gate, Chichester, PO19 8SQ, United Kingdom; customer@wiley.co.uk; http://www.wiley.co.uk. Refereed. *Aud.:* Ac.

For many years there were only two scholarly journals covering wind sources of energy, the *Journal of Wind Engineering and Industrial Aerodynamics* and *Wind Engineering* (both reviewed in this section). *Wind Energy* was launched in 1998, evidently in direct competition to *Wind Engineering.* They both cover the technical aspects of generating power from wind sources; they both have an international scope, include papers authored largely by academic institutions and government-funded agencies, have lengthy articles and references, and include the occasional historical or economic review. They are priced about the same and average about the same number of papers and pages per year. Where they differ appears to be approach: *Wind Energy* seems to have more environmental emphasis while *Wind Engineering* includes more "mass power production" papers. *Wind Energy* also includes a running annotated bibliography of references from several other wind energy publications. Libraries with strong energy collections, especially with interests in alternative energy sources, will want both titles. Others will find *Wind Energy* useful for the bibliography and the environmental slant and *Wind Engineering* useful as a complement to a mechanical engineering collection.

2631. ***Wind Engineering.*** [ISSN: 0309-524X] 1977. 6x/yr. GBP 227 combined subscription print & online. Ed(s): John Twidell. Multi-Science Publishing Co. Ltd., 5 Wates Way, Brentwood, CM15 9TB, United Kingdom; mscience@globalnet.co.uk; http://www.multi-science.co.uk. Refereed. *Indexed:* ApMecR, C&ISA, EngInd, IAA. *Aud.:* Ac.

Wind Engineering claims to be the oldest English-language journal devoted entirely to the technical issues of wind power, which is largely true, although the *Journal of Wind Engineering and Industrial Aerodynamics* (above in this section) has been in existence longer, beginning as the *Journal of Industrial Aerodynamics*. Topics covered are wind turbines, turbine blade design, economic and historical aspects of wind energy, and a good deal of emphasis on wind farms and offshore wind energy production. It is very similar in coverage and quality to *Wind Energy* (above), and libraries with restricted budgets or tangential interest in wind power will want to carefully compare the two.

2632. ***Windpower Monthly: news magazine.*** [ISSN: 0109-7318] 1985. m. EUR 145; GBP 90; USD 140. Ed(s): Lyn Harrison. Torgny Moeller, Vrinners Hoved, Knebel, 8420, Denmark. Illus., adv. Circ: 3000. Vol. ends: No. 12. *Aud.:* Ac, Sa.

Begun in Denmark, distributed from the United States, and with a web site originating in the United Kingdom, *Windpower Monthly* is truly an international publication. The audience is wind energy businesses, investors, and power plant component manufacturers. Although each issue will have a small number of articles (one of which is the "Focus Article"), the bulk of the magazine is devoted to wind energy news reports, arranged by regions/countries of the world. Some of the news is technical ("Blades Built by Robots"), but most of it is economic or policy news. The "Windicator," a quarterly supplement, is a chart of wind power capacity worldwide, identifying industrial, political, technical, and economic trends. The *Monthly* also prepares "WindStats," a data set of wind power generation in selected regions, but at an additional cost. Issues from 1994 to the present can be searched on the web site by keyword, date, and geographic area.

2633. ***World Oil.*** Formerly: *Oil Weekly.* [ISSN: 0043-8790] 1916. m. USD 34 domestic; USD 41 foreign. Ed(s): Robert Snyder. Gulf Publishing Co., PO Box 2608, Houston, TX 77252-2608; publications@gulfpub.com; http://www.gulfpub.com. Illus., adv. Circ: 35563 Paid and controlled. Microform: PQC. Online: EBSCO Publishing; Florida Center for Library Automation; Gale Group; Northern Light Technology, Inc.; OCLC Online Computer Library Center, Inc.; H.W. Wilson. *Indexed:* AS&TI, BPI, C&ISA, ChemAb, EngInd, GeoRef, PAIS, PetrolAb, SSCI. *Aud.:* Ac, Sa.

One of the many petroleum-related trade magazines (see the *Oil & Gas Journal* above in this section), this one covers oil around the world. Each issue follows the pattern of focus articles, feature articles, columns (such as "What's New in Production" and "International Politics"), news, and departments. Focus and feature articles are short (two or three pages), but they are well illustrated in color and often have numerous references. The web site includes supplements (such as "Deepwater Technology") and case studies, plus extensive statistics (both production and price), reference tables, forecasts, and analyses. An excellent, inexpensive addition to a good energy collection.

ENGINEERING AND TECHNOLOGY

General/Biomedical Engineering/Chemical Engineering/Civil Engineering/Computer, Control, and Systems Engineering/Electrical Engineering/Manufacturing Engineering/Materials Engineering/ Mechanical Engineering/Nuclear Engineering

See also Aeronautics and Space Science; Atmospheric Sciences; Biological Sciences; Chemistry; Computer Science and Automation; Earth Sciences; Mathematics; Physics; Robotics; Science and Technology; and Systems sections.

G. Lynn Berard, Head, Science Libraries, Carnegie Mellon University, Pittsburgh, PA 15213-3890

Introduction

Engineering is the profession that deals with the properties of matter and the sources of power in nature by designing and building machines, devices, and structures useful to humans. Engineering is the product of human innovation and endeavor. In the last three decades, engineering educators and the nation's engineering schools have broadened the curriculum by adding environmental awareness to their programs. Companies are balancing their responsibilities to their shareholders and the public by supporting the incorporation of sustainable approaches to manufacturing. Industry is anticipating future hires of environmentally aware engineers and academia is preparing students to balance the tough tradeoffs in a worldwide economy of production costs versus environmental protections. Technology is a major application of engineering processes and, in a sense, is the product of engineering. The transfer of technology and engineering knowledge happens by the passing of blueprints, models, designs, patents, and education.

Less obvious, but an equal partner in the dissemination of engineering knowledge, is the formation of professional organizations and the issuing of their publications. As early as the thirteenth century, European monasteries created manuscripts showing various machines and processes. With the invention of the printing press in the fifteenth century, illustrated books and manuals were produced that depicted technical processes. The notebooks of Leonardo da Vinci, Francesco di Giorgio Martini, and Georgius Agricola were filled with sketches of futuristic inventions and were reproduced and circulated among their colleagues.

Approaching the task of building an engineering collection—whether for a special, academic, or public library—is analogous to finding yourself in an eighteenth-century garden maze working feverishly to discover the way out. This section attempts to provide a map for the selector in making purchase decisions in several areas of engineering, but it is not exhaustive by any means. I urge the reader to study carefully the preface of this book before delving into any particular discipline. The criteria for selection are carefully laid out, and they provide a basis for understanding the content of the individual sections.

Engineering has become much less departmentalized and very interdisciplinary in its approach to both practice and the design of educational curricula. This cross-pollination of the field creates a challenge for the selector, who needs to think interdisciplinarily and acknowledge that a journal that is of interest to many may stretch a limited budget. Make use of the subject index at the back of this volume and consider other sections, especially the Environment and Conservation section.

Engineering association and society publications are the bricks and mortar of a collection. Whether one chooses to enroll in a standing-order plan or simply purchase main titles produced by a pertinent society will depend in large part on the budget of the purchasing institution. Many societies offer reduced rates for institutional memberships and have flexible order plans. Engineering and technology collections are expensive. Very few U.S. libraries can afford to purchase and maintain research-level collections in engineering.

Electronic publishing is the newest innovation in providing access to periodicals in all disciplines, and now journals in electronic form are the norm. Some are free, others require a subscription fee. Formats include full-text, table of contents–only, or a combination of feature articles, advertisements, job placements, and table of contents. In the main, all the journals included in this section have some form of electronic access.

The future holds much promise for electronic publishing and the creation of true digital libraries.

Basic Periodicals

BIOMEDICAL ENGINEERING. Ac, Sa: *Biotechnology and Bioengineering.*

CHEMICAL ENGINEERING. Ga, Ac, Sa: *AIChE Journal.*

CIVIL ENGINEERING. Ac, Sa: *Civil Engineering, ENR.*

COMPUTER, CONTROL, AND SYSTEMS ENGINEERING. Ac, Sa: *Association for Computing Machinery. Journal.*

ELECTRICAL ENGINEERING. Ac, Sa: *IEEE Journals, Proceedings, and Transactions.*

MANUFACTURING ENGINEERING. Ac, Sa: *Journal of Manufacturing Systems.*

MATERIALS ENGINEERING. Ac, Sa: *Journal of Materials Research, Metallurgical and Materials Transactions A.*

MECHANICAL ENGINEERING. Ac, Sa: *American Society of Mechanical Engineers. Transactions.*

NUCLEAR ENGINEERING. Ga, Ac, Sa: *Nuclear Engineering International.*

Basic Abstracts and Indexes

Applied Science and Technology Index, ASCE Annual Combined Index, Computer & Control Abstracts (INSPEC), Electrical and Electronic Abstracts, Engineering Index, Metals Abstracts.

General

2634. ***A S E E Prism.*** Formed by the merger of (1974-1991): *Engineering Education News;* (1924-1991): *Engineering Education;* Which was formerly (until 1969): *Journal of Engineering Education (Washington).* [ISSN: 1056-8077] 1991. 10x/yr. USD 125 (Non-members, USD 75). Ed(s): Robert Black. American Society for Engineering Education, 1818 N St, N W, Ste 600, Washington, DC 20036; http://ns.asee.org/pubs/html/prism.html. Illus., index, adv. Circ: 12000. Microform: CIS; PQC. Online: OCLC Online Computer Library Center, Inc.; ProQuest Information & Learning; H.W. Wilson. Reprint: PQC. *Indexed:* ApMecR, CIJE, ChemAb, EduInd, EngInd, PsycholAb, RI-1. *Bk. rev.:* Various number and length. *Aud.:* Ac.

This journal for the academic professional presents scholarly research and teaching methods in all disciplines of engineering. It is one of the many communication tools available to the membership of the American Society for Engineering Education. Membership news, classified job ads, campaign news, and informative articles on teaching techniques are offered. Available online.

2635. ***A S H R A E Journal.*** Incorporates (1929-1959): *American Society of Heating and Air-Conditioning Engineers. Journal;* (1914-1959): *Refrigerating Engineering;* Which was formerly (until 1922): *A S R E Journal.* [ISSN: 0001-2491] 1959. m. Non-members, USD 59. Ed(s): Fred Turner. American Society of Heating, Refrigerating and Air-Conditioning Engineers, Inc., 1791 Tullie Circle, N E, Atlanta, GA 30329; comstock@ashrae.org; http://www.ashrae.org/. Illus., index, adv. Refereed. Circ: 60000 Paid. Vol. ends: Dec. Microform: PQC. Online: OCLC Online Computer Library Center, Inc.; ProQuest Information & Learning; H.W. Wilson. Reprint: PQC. *Indexed:* AS&TI, ApMecR, C&ISA, ChemAb, EngInd, EnvAb, ExcerpMed, H&SSA. *Aud.:* Ac, Sa.

The American Society of Heating, Refrigerating and Air Conditioning Engineers (ASHRAE) began this journal for their members in 1914. Their credo then and now is, "A Society like ours should be the guardian of the industry it represents; let us protect it through the Journal." In this publication, ASHRAE informs readers of changes in the HVAC&R field by providing technical papers, discussions, and news of interest. Special sections present current legal and design issues and product updates. There are classified advertisements, news regarding standards development, and a meetings and trade shows calendar. Available online.

2636. ***Graduating Engineer & Computer Careers.*** Formerly: *Graduating Engineer.* 1979. q. USD 80. Ed(s): Brandon Stahl. Career Recruitment Media, Inc., 1800 Sherman Ave, Evanston, IL 60201; info@careermedia.com; http://www.careermedia.com/. Illus., adv. Circ: 60000. *Aud.:* Ac.

This affordable journal is a must-read for engineering students. Directories abound in this publication, providing clues to which employers are hiring, engineering employers by discipline, and salary expectations. Special features include articles on career advice, how to select a graduate school, and recent graduates' experiences in the work world. Departments include "Questions with...," lots of job ads in industry and academic areas, and a campus calendar.

2637. ***Human Factors.*** [ISSN: 0018-7208] 1958. q. USD 250 domestic. Ed(s): Eduardo Salas. Human Factors and Ergonomics Society, PO Box 1369, Santa Monica, CA 90406-1369; lois@hfes.org; http://www.hfes.org. Illus., index. Refereed. Circ: 6200. Microform: PQC. Online: Florida Center for Library Automation; Gale Group; Northern Light Technology, Inc.; OCLC Online Computer Library Center, Inc.; ProQuest Information & Learning; H.W. Wilson. Reprint: PQC. *Indexed:* AS&TI, AbAn, AgeL, BiolAb, C&ISA, CommAb, EngInd, ErgAb, ExcerpMed, H&SSA, HRA, IBZ, IndMed, InfoSAb, PsycholAb, SCI, SSCI, SUSA. *Aud.:* Ac, Sa.

This journal is the official publication of the Human Factors and Ergonomics Society, an interdisciplinary organization of professional workers concerned with the role of humans in complex systems, the design of equipment and facilities, and the development of human-compatible environments. Ergonomics is the study of human capability and psychology in relation to the working environment and the equipment operated by the worker. To disseminate knowledge about human-machine-environment relationships and to promote putting this knowledge to work, the society publishes this journal. Evaluative reviews, articles on methods and quality approaches to human-machine theory, and reports of original research are presented. Free online access, with searchable index, is available at the society's web site.

2638. ***International Journal for Numerical Methods in Engineering.*** [ISSN: 0029-5981] 1969. 45x/yr. USD 7440. John Wiley & Sons Ltd. The Atrium, Southern Gate, Chichester, PO19 8SQ, United Kingdom; customer@wiley.co.uk; http://www.wiley.co.uk. Illus., index, adv. Refereed. Circ: 1500. Microform: PQC. Online: EBSCO Publishing; Wiley InterScience. Reprint: ISI; PQC; PSC; SWZ. *Indexed:* ApMecR, C&ISA, CCMJ, EngInd, GeoRef, GeogAbPG, IAA, MathSciNet, SCI. *Bk. rev.:* Various number and length. *Aud.:* Ac, Sa.

This publication provides a common platform for the presentation of papers and exchange of views on numerical methods used to solve a variety of engineering problems in such areas as heat transfer, structural analysis, fluid mechanics, network theory, electronics, and optimal system design. Available online.

2639. ***Journal of Elasticity.*** [ISSN: 0374-3535] 1971. m. EUR 1637 print or online ed. Ed(s): Roger Fosdick. Kluwer Academic Publishers, van Godewijckstraat 30, PO Box 17, Dordrecht, 3300 AA, Netherlands. Illus., adv. Refereed. Microform: PQC. Online: EBSCO Publishing; ingenta.com; Kluwer Online; OCLC Online Computer Library Center, Inc.; Ovid Technologies, Inc.; RoweCom Information Quest; Swets Blackwell. Reprint: SWZ. *Indexed:* ApMecR, CCMJ, EngInd, GeoRef, IAA, MathSciNet, SCI. *Aud.:* Ac, Sa.

Original and significant discoveries in elasticity are reported in this journal. Full articles and research notes along with occasional historical essays and classroom notes are contained within. This basic journal will be of interest to a variety of engineering professionals. Combined electronic and print access available via Kluwer Online.

2640. ***Journal of Engineering Mathematics.*** [ISSN: 0022-0833] 1966. m. EUR 1202 print or online ed. Ed(s): H K Kuiken. Kluwer Academic Publishers, van Godewijckstraat 30, PO Box 17, Dordrecht, 3300 AA, Netherlands; http://www.wkap.nl. Illus., index, adv. Refereed. Microform: PQC. Online: EBSCO Publishing; ingenta.com; Kluwer Online; OCLC Online Computer Library Center, Inc.; Ovid Technologies, Inc.; RoweCom Information Quest; Swets Blackwell. Reprint: SWZ. *Indexed:* ApMecR, C&ISA, CCMJ, EngInd, GeoRef, IAA, MathSciNet, SCI. *Bk. rev.:* Various number and length. *Aud.:* Ac, Sa.

The application of mathematics to physical problems, specifically in the general area of engineering science, is the aim of this journal. Topics include numerical analysis, ordinary and partial differential equations, and computational methods. Applied fields of interest include biomedical engineering, solid mechanics, continuum mechanics, fluid mechanics, and fracture mechanics. Available online via Kluwer.

2641. ***Journal of Fluid Mechanics.*** [ISSN: 0022-1120] 1956. s-m. USD 1890 (Individuals, USD 768). Ed(s): Stephen H Davis, T.J. Pedley. Cambridge University Press, The Edinburgh Bldg, Shaftesbury Rd, Cambridge, CB2 2RU, United Kingdom; information@cambridge.org; http://uk.cambridge.org/journals. Illus., index, adv. Refereed. Microform: PMC; PQC. Online: EBSCO Publishing; OCLC Online Computer Library Center, Inc.; RoweCom Information Quest; Swets Blackwell. *Indexed:* AS&TI, ApMecR, BiolAb, C&ISA, CCMJ, CEA, ChemAb, DSR&OA, EngInd, ExcerpMed, GeoRef, GeogAbPG, IAA, M&GPA, MathSciNet, PetrolAb, SCI, SWRA. *Bk. rev.:* 3, length varies. *Aud.:* Ga, Ac, Sa.

Offering a dozen or so full-length scholarly research papers, this interdisciplinary journal explores fundamental fluid mechanics and its application to aeronautics, astrophysics, chemical engineering, mechanical engineering, colloid science, combustion, hydraulics, and meteorology. A schedule of international conferences on fluid mechanics is listed in the June issue. Available online; free to print subscribers.

2642. ***Leadership and Management in Engineering.*** [ISSN: 1532-6748] 2001. q. Members, USD 40; Non-members, USD 60. Ed(s): Jeffrey S Russell. American Society of Civil Engineers, 1801 Alexander Graham Bell Dr, Reston, VA 20191-4400; http://www.pubs.asce.org. *Indexed:* C&ISA. *Aud.:* Ac, Sa.

A helpful, timely magazine with practical advice on leadership and management in the engineering fields. Available online at http://ojps.aip.org/leo.

2643. ***M A E S National Magazine.*** 1995. q. Ed(s): Margaret G Gonzalez. G.V.R. Public Relations Agency, PO Box 48923, Houston, TX 77258; http://www.maes-natl.org/magazine/. *Aud.:* Ac, Sa.

This is published for Hispanic engineers who want to keep up with scientific data of interest to their profession. Although technical, it does have some general interest in that it profiles prominent Hispanic personalities in engineering and related areas, and it has career information for students in both the United States and Mexico. This includes a network of data on employment, scholarships, etc. The web site is www.maesnationalmagazine.com.

Measurement Science and Technology. See Physics section.

Biomedical Engineering

2644. ***Annals of Biomedical Engineering.*** Incorporates: *Journal of Bioengineering.* [ISSN: 0090-6964] 1979. bi-m. USD 665 combined subscription domestic print & online eds.; USD 690 combined subscription in Canada, Mexico, Central and South America and Caribbean for print and online eds. ; USD 705 combined subscription in Europe, Asia, Middle East, Africa and Oceania for print & online eds. Ed(s): James B Bassingthwaighte. Biomedical Engineering Society, 8401 Corporate Dr., Ste. 110, Landover, MD 20785-2224; sslack@cc.memphis.edu; http://www.bmes.org. Illus., index, adv. Refereed. Circ: 2200. Microform: PQC. Online: EBSCO Publishing; RoweCom Information Quest; Swets Blackwell. *Indexed:* ApMecR, BiolAb, C&ISA, CPI, ChemAb, EngInd, ExcerpMed, IndMed, SCI. *Aud.:* Ac, Sa.

This is the official journal of the Biomedical Engineering Society, and its editorial board is composed mainly of U.S. academics. The journal contains scholarly articles on a wide spectrum of topics, such as bioelectric phenomena and quantitative electrophysiology, biomaterials and biomechanics, and information-systems theory applications. It is available online at ojps.aip.org/abme.

2645. ***Biotechnology and Bioengineering.*** [ISSN: 0006-3592] 1958. 28x/yr. USD 4995. Ed(s): Douglas S Clark. John Wiley & Sons, Inc., 111 River St, Hoboken, NJ 07030; uscs-wis@wiley.com; http://www.wiley.com. Illus., index, adv. Refereed. Circ: 1700. CD-ROM: The Dialog Corporation. Microform: PQC. Online: EBSCO Publishing; ScienceDirect; Wiley InterScience. *Indexed:* Agr, B&AI, BioEngAb, BiolAb, C&ISA, CEA, ChemAb, DSA, DSR&OA, EngInd, ExcerpMed, FPA, FS&TA, ForAb, HortAb, IndMed, IndVet, PollutAb, S&F, SCI, SWRA, VetBull, WAE&RSA, WRCInf. *Aud.:* Ac, Sa.

All aspects of biotechnology are explored in this journal. Topics of interest include cellular physiology, metabolism, enzyme systems and their applications, animal-cell biotechnology, bioseparations, and environmental biotechnology. Approximately ten scholarly papers are offered in each issue, as well as communications. A core journal in the biomedical engineering discipline.

2646. ***Biotechnology Progress.*** [ISSN: 8756-7938] 1985. bi-m. USD 784 (Individual members, USD 58; Students, USD 44). Ed(s): Lois Anne DeLong, Jerome S Schultz. American Chemical Society, 1155 16th St, N W, Washington, DC 20036; service@acs.org; http://pubs.acs.org. Illus., index, adv. Circ: 2800. Microform: PQC. Online: EBSCO Publishing; Swets Blackwell. Reprint: PQC. *Indexed:* AS&TI, Agr, BioEngAb, BiolAb, CAPS, ChemAb, DSA, EngInd, EnvAb, FPA, FS&TA, ForAb, HortAb, IndMed, IndVet, PollutAb, S&F, SCI, SWRA, VetBull. *Aud.:* Ac, Sa.

This journal is a joint venture of the American Chemical Society (ACS) and the American Institute of Chemical Engineers. It includes the latest research, state-of-the-art reviews, and new breakthroughs in molecular and cellular biology as applied to new processes, products, and devices. Although it focuses on the biotechnology/bioprocess industries, this interdisciplinary journal also covers aspects of the fields of chemistry, life sciences, and engineering. This journal is available online to subscribers via the ACS Web Editions program.

2647. ***Critical Reviews in Biomedical Engineering.*** Former titles: *C R C Critical Reviews in Biomedical Engineering; Critical Reviews in Bioengineering; C R C Critical Reviews in Bioengineering.* 1974. bi-m. USD 1080 (Individuals, USD 210). Ed(s): John R Bourne. Begell House Inc., 145 Madison Ave., # 6, New York, NY 10016-6717; orders@begellhouse.com; http://www.begellhouse.com. Illus., adv. Refereed. Circ: 680. *Indexed:* ApMecR, BioEngAb, BiolAb, EngInd, ExcerpMed, H&SSA, IndMed, SCI. *Aud.:* Ac, Sa.

Biomedical engineering is the application of engineering technology to the solution of medical problems. An example of this is the development of prostheses, such as artificial valves for the heart, pacemakers, and automated artificial limbs. This journal critically surveys a wide range of research and applied activities in this interdisciplinary field. One or more reviews on specific topics fill each issue. A specialty journal for the research-level collection.

2648. ***Journal of Biomechanical Engineering.*** [ISSN: 0148-0731] 1977. q. Members, USD 60 print & online eds.; Non-members, USD 350 print & online eds. Ed(s): Kenneth Diller. A S M E International, Three Park Ave, New York, NY 10016-5990; infocentral@asme.org; http://www.asme.org. Illus., index, adv. Refereed. Microform: PQC. Online: EBSCO Publishing; Gale Group; Swets Blackwell. Reprint: PQC. *Indexed:* AS&TI, ApMecR, C&ISA, CEA, ChemAb, EngInd, ExcerpMed, IndMed, SCI. *Bk. rev.:* Various number and length. *Aud.:* Ac, Sa.

The mechanics of prosthesis is a wide-open field in engineering. This refereed journal, the official publication of the Institute of Physics and Engineering in Medicine, covers all aspects of new developments in health care, including the instrumentation of function replacement, biomedical computing, clinical engineering, and biological systems. Solutions to particular patient problems are discussed and open to critical examination. Available online.

2649. ***The Journal of Biomechanics.*** [ISSN: 0021-9290] 1968. m. EUR 2370 (Individuals, EUR 295). Ed(s): Dr. Rik Huiskes, Dr. Farshid Guilak. Pergamon, The Boulevard, Langford Ln, East Park, Kidlington, OX5 1GB, United Kingdom. Illus., index, adv. Refereed. Circ: 1600. Microform: PQC. Online: ingenta.com; ScienceDirect; Swets Blackwell. Reprint: PQC. *Indexed:* AbAn, ApMecR, BioEngAb, BiolAb, C&ISA, EngInd, ErgAb, ExcerpMed, H&SSA, IAA, IndMed, PEI, SCI, SSCI. *Bk. rev.:* Various number and length. *Aud.:* Ac, Sa.

Biomechanics is the study of the mechanics of living things. From the biological side, this journal features articles dealing with the dynamics of the musculo-skeletal system, the mechanics of soft and hard tissues, the mechanics of bone and muscle, and the mechanisms of cells. From the mechanical aspect, the mechanics of prosthetics and orthotics are presented. Each issue offers research articles along with technical notes describing new techniques. Available online via ScienceDirect.

2650. ***Journal of Biomedical Materials Research. Part A.*** Supersedes in part (1966-2002): *Journal of Biomedical Materials Research;* Incorporates (1990-1995): *Journal of Applied Biomaterials.* 2003. 18x/yr. USD 5490. Ed(s): James Anderson. John Wiley & Sons, Inc., 111 River St, Hoboken, NJ 07030; uscs-wis@wiley.com; http://www.wiley.com. Illus., adv. Refereed. Circ: 2500. Reprint: PQC. *Indexed:* AS&TI, ApMecR, B&AI, BiolAb, ChemAb, EngInd, ExcerpMed, IndMed, SCI. *Aud.:* Ac, Sa.

This official journal of the Society for Biomaterials (USA), the Japanese Society for Biomaterials, the Australian Society for Biomaterials, and the Korean Society for Biomaterials covers such topics as ceramics and alloys, along with dentistry, implanted devices, and surgery. Each article contains graphs, tables, and photos and is highly readable yet scholarly. A noteworthy international effort. Available online.

Chemical Engineering

2651. ***A I Ch E Journal.*** [ISSN: 0001-1541] 1955. m. Members, USD 105; Non-members, USD 950. Ed(s): Stanley I Sandler. American Institute of Chemical Engineers, 3 Park Ave, New York, NY 10016-5901; haejh@aiche.org; http://www.aiche.org/publications. Illus., index, adv. Refereed. Circ: 3000 Paid. Vol. ends: Dec. Microform: PQC. Online: ProQuest Information & Learning; ScienceDirect; Swets Blackwell. *Indexed:* AS&TI, ApMecR, C&ISA, CEA, ChemAb, EngInd, EnvAb, ExcerpMed, GeoRef, PetrolAb, S&F, SCI, WRCInf. *Bk. rev.:* Various number and length. *Aud.:* Ac, Sa.

The main publication of the American Institute of Chemical Engineers, this journal is devoted to fundamental research and developments having immediate or potential value in chemical engineering. Each issue contains reviews, full-length research papers (both experimental and theoretical), R&D notes, and detailed book reviews. Supplemental materials are provided by contributors when they have referenced works that are not essential to the development of their article or that are not easily accessible elsewhere but are of interest to the reader. These supplemental materials are deposited on microfilm, and a footnote with an access pointer is provided. The journal is available online.

Chemical & Engineering News. See Chemistry/General section.

2652. ***The Chemical Engineer: the essential magazine for the chemical & process industries.*** Formerly: *Chemical Engineer and Transactions of the Institution of Chemical Engineers;* Which superseded in part (in 1983): *Institution of Chemical Engineers. Transactions;* Which incorporated (1922-1990): *Chemical Engineer Diary and Institution News;* Which was formerly (until 1983): *Institution of Chemical Engineers. Diary.* [ISSN: 0302-0797] 1923. m. GBP 146 domestic; EUR 166 foreign. Ed(s): Chris Webb. Institution of Chemical Engineers, George E Davis Bldg, 165-189 Railway Terr, Rugby, CV21 3HQ, United Kingdom; http://www.icheme.org/. Illus., index, adv. Refereed. Circ: 25695 Paid. Reprint: ISI. *Indexed:* AS&TI, CEA, ChemAb, EngInd, WRCInf. *Aud.:* Ac, Sa.

Published by the Institution of Chemical Engineers in the United Kingdom, this magazine is the sister publication to *Chemical & Engineering News* (see Chemistry section) in the United States. News from and about the chemical industry, feature articles, technology reports, plant and equipment developments, a literature showcase, and events of interest to the professional are provided. Great for both the general reader and the specialist. An online archive is available at www.tce-online.com/tce/mainframe.htm.

2653. ***Chemical Engineering Education.*** [ISSN: 0009-2479] 1965. q. Members, USD 25; Non-members, USD 80. Ed(s): Tim Anderson. American Society for Engineering Education, Chemical Engineering Division, 227 Chemical Engineering Bldg, Box 116005, Gainesville, FL 32611-6005; cee@che.ufl.edu. Illus., index, adv. Refereed. Circ: 2850 Paid. Microform: PQC. Reprint: PQC. *Indexed:* C&ISA, CIJE, ChemAb, EngInd, ExcerpMed. *Bk. rev.:* Various number and length. *Aud.:* Ac.

Written for the educator, *CEE* publishes papers in the broad field of chemical engineering education. Course descriptions, curriculum formats, research programs, and special instruction programs are typical subjects offered. Views on various topics of interest to the profession along with descriptions of chemical engineering departments, educators, and laboratory setups are also provided. Available only in print format.

2654. ***Chemical Engineering Progress.*** Supersedes (1908-1946): *American Institute of Chemical Engineers. Transactions.* [ISSN: 0360-7275] 1947. m. Individuals, USD 100. Ed(s): Kristine Chin. American Institute of Chemical Engineers, 3 Park Ave, New York, NY 10016-5901; xpress@aiche.org; http://www.aiche.org. Illus., index, adv. Sample. Refereed. Circ: 50000 Paid. Microform: PMC; PQC. Online: Factiva; Gale Group; Northern Light Technology, Inc.; ProQuest Information & Learning. Reprint: PQC. *Indexed:* AS&TI, BiolAb, C&ISA, CEA, ChemAb, EngInd, EnvAb, ExcerpMed, GeoRef, H&SSA, PetrolAb, PollutAb, S&F, SCI, SSCI, WRCInf. *Bk. rev.:* Various number and length. *Aud.:* Ac, Sa.

An industry news publication produced by the American Institute of Chemical Engineers. It features news on timely topics, safety and material sections, professional-development articles, and an extensive R&D update column. Classified job listings and an engineering-resource showcase are very handy. Suitable for public and academic libraries. Available online.

2655. ***Chemical Engineering Research & Design.*** Supersedes in part (in 1983): *Institution of Chemical Engineers. Transactions.* [ISSN: 0263-8762] 1923. 8x/yr. GBP 409 United Kingdom; EUR 702.24 in Euro Zone; USD 698.06 elsewhere. Ed(s): Audra Morgan. Institution of Chemical Engineers, George E Davis Bldg, 165-189 Railway Terr, Rugby, CV21 3HQ, United Kingdom; http://www.icheme.org/learning/. Illus., adv. Refereed. Circ: 800 Paid. Microform: PMC; PQC. Online: EBSCO Publishing; Ingenta Select; OCLC Online Computer Library Center, Inc.; RoweCom Information Quest; Swets Blackwell. Reprint: ISI; PQC. *Indexed:* ApMecR, BrTechI, C&ISA, CEA, ChemAb, EngInd, ExcerpMed, PetrolAb, SCI, WRCInf. *Bk. rev.:* Various number and length. *Aud.:* Ac, Sa.

This internationally renowned journal boasts a well-represented editorial board in the chemical engineering arena. Special papers, general papers, short communications, and forthcoming meetings are presented. A nice feature of these transactions is the annual listing of doctorates earned in chemical engineering at Institution of Chemical Engineers–accredited universities worldwide, listed by country.

2656. ***Chemical Engineering Science.*** [ISSN: 0009-2509] 1951. 24x/yr. EUR 4407 (Qualified personnel, EUR 388). Ed(s): John Bridgwater. Pergamon, The Boulevard, Langford Ln, East Park, Kidlington, OX5 1GB, United Kingdom. Illus., index, adv. Refereed. Circ: 2000.

Microform: PQC. Online: ingenta.com; ScienceDirect; Swets Blackwell. *Indexed:* ApMecR, BrTechI, C&ISA, CEA, ChemAb, EngInd, EnvAb, ExcerpMed, GeogAbPG, PetrolAb, PollutAb, SCI, WRCInf. *Bk. rev.:* Various number and length. *Aud.:* Ac, Sa.

The chemical, oil, pharmaceutical, and food industries will find this journal pertinent. Papers found within describe original experiments and theoretical insights. Some core topics are chemical-reaction engineering, applied catalysis, biochemical engineering, fluid mechanics, mathematical modeling and simulation, and multiphase flow. New areas of interest are environmental problems and molecular science relating to fundamental chemical engineering. Available online.

Chemical Week. See Business/Trade and Industry section.

2657. *Combustion and Flame.* [ISSN: 0010-2180] 1963. 16x/yr. EUR 1476. Ed(s): C T Bowman, A N Hayhurst. Elsevier Inc., 360 Park Ave. S, New York, NY 10010-1710; usinfo-f@elsevier.com; http://www.elsevier.com. Illus., index, adv. Refereed. Microform: PQC. Online: ingenta.com; ScienceDirect; Swets Blackwell. *Indexed:* ApMecR, BiolAb, C&ISA, CEA, ChemAb, EngInd, EnvAb, ExcerpMed, GeoRef, IAA, PollutAb, SCI. *Bk. rev.:* Various number and length. *Aud.:* Ac, Sa.

An official publication of the Combustion Institute, this general-interest journal exists for the publication of experimental and theoretical investigations of combustion phenomena and closely allied matters. The contents include scholarly articles, brief communications for the membership, a comments section for the membership, meetings calendar, and book reviews. Available online.

2658. *Computers & Chemical Engineering: an international journal of computer applications in chemical engineering.* [ISSN: 0098-1354] 1977. 12x/yr. EUR 2226 (Qualified personnel, EUR 286). Ed(s): G V Reklaitis. Pergamon, The Boulevard, Langford Ln, East Park, Kidlington, OX5 1GB, United Kingdom. Illus., adv. Refereed. Circ: 1000. Vol. ends: No. 25. Microform: PQC. Online: ingenta.com; ScienceDirect; Swets Blackwell. *Indexed:* AS&TI, C&ISA, CEA, ChemAb, EngInd, ExcerpMed, H&SSA, SCI, SSCI, WRCInf. *Bk. rev.:* Various number and length. *Aud.:* Ac, Sa.

The application of computing technology to chemical engineering problems is the focus of the professional papers published in this journal. Areas of interest include new developments, design methods for chemical engineering equipment, and the dynamic analysis and control of chemical processes and process operations (e.g., safety, scheduling, and reliability). New computer methods and programs are described. Available online.

2659. *International Journal of Multiphase Flow.* Incorporates (in 1990): *Physicochemical Hydrodynamics.* [ISSN: 0301-9322] 1974. m. EUR 2059 (Qualified personnel, EUR 88). Ed(s): G Hetsroni. Pergamon, The Boulevard, Langford Ln, East Park, Kidlington, OX5 1GB, United Kingdom. Illus., index, adv. Refereed. Circ: 1000. Microform: PQC. Online: ingenta.com; ScienceDirect; Swets Blackwell. Reprint: PQC. *Indexed:* ApMecR, C&ISA, CEA, ChemAb, EngInd, GeoRef, PetrolAb, SCI. *Aud.:* Ac, Sa.

This international journal presents articles on theoretical and experimental investigations of multiphase flow that are of relevance and permanent interest to the fluids community. Each issue includes full papers, brief communications, current investigations, discussions of previous articles, and conference announcements. Available online.

2660. *Journal of Chemical and Engineering Data.* Formerly (until 1959): *Chemical & Engineering Data Series.* [ISSN: 0021-9568] 1956. bi-m. USD 770 (Individual members, USD 81; Students, USD 61). Ed(s): Dr. Kenneth N Marsh. American Chemical Society, 1155 16th St, N W, Washington, DC 20036; service@acs.org; http://pubs.acs.org. Illus., index, adv. Refereed. Circ: 975. Online: EBSCO Publishing; Swets Blackwell. *Indexed:* AS&TI, CEA, ChemAb, EngInd, GeoRef, PetrolAb, S&F, SCI. *Aud.:* Ac, Sa.

The publication of experimental data and the evaluation and prediction of property values are the main focus of this journal. This title is the only American Chemical Society journal to report experimental data on the physical, thermodynamic, and transport properties of well-defined materials, including complex mixtures of known compositions and systems of environmental and biochemical interest. A core journal for a special collection. Available online.

2661. *Journal of Membrane Science.* [ISSN: 0376-7388] 1977. 36x/yr. EUR 5741. Ed(s): W J Koros. Elsevier BV, Sara Burgerhartstraat 25, Amsterdam, 1055 KV, Netherlands; nlinfo-f@elsevier.nl; http://www.elsevier.nl. Illus., index. Refereed. Microform: PQC. Online: ingenta.com; ScienceDirect; Swets Blackwell. *Indexed:* BioEngAb, BiolAb, C&ISA, ChemAb, DSA, EngInd, ExcerpMed, FS&TA, PollutAb, SCI, WRCInf. *Aud.:* Ac, Sa.

A highly cited journal for "membranologists," the *Journal of Membrane Science* serves to emphasize the structure and function of nonbiological membranes. Scholarly papers are accepted in the experimental and applications phases of research. This is a practical journal that aims to provide the vehicle for rapid communications among researchers. Regular features include a meetings calendar and author and subject indexes. Available online.

2662. *Plasma Chemistry & Plasma Processing.* [ISSN: 0272-4324] 1981. q. EUR 768 print or online ed. Ed(s): Emil Pfender, Stan Veprek. Kluwer Academic / Plenum Publishers, 233 Spring St Fl 7, New York, NY 10013-1522; http://www.wkap.nl/. Illus., adv. Refereed. Microform: PQC. Online: EBSCO Publishing; ingenta.com; Kluwer Online; OCLC Online Computer Library Center, Inc.; RoweCom Information Quest; Swets Blackwell. *Indexed:* C&ISA, ChemAb, EngInd, SCI. *Aud.:* Ac, Sa.

This international journal offers current scholarly reports on plasma chemistry and plasma processing as well as review articles for the plasma chemistry community. This journal will be of interest to chemists, chemical engineers, and metallurgists. Available online.

Civil Engineering

2663. *American Water Works Association. Journal.* [ISSN: 0003-150X] 1914. m. USD 85. Ed(s): Nancy M Zeilig. American Water Works Association, 6666 W Quincy Ave, Denver, CO 80235; http://www.awwa.org/journal.htm. Illus., adv. Refereed. Circ: 45000. Vol. ends: Dec. Microform: PMC; PQC. Online: ProQuest Information & Learning. *Indexed:* AS&TI, BioEngAb, BiolAb, ChemAb, DSR&OA, EngInd, EnvAb, ExcerpMed, FS&TA, GeoRef, PollutAb, SCI, SWRA, WRCInf. *Aud.:* Ga, Ac, Sa.

This is the official organ of the American Water Works Association. As in other society publications, regular departments include letters, legislation/regulations, news, business updates, product literature, meeting notices, and classified advertisements. A valuable, readable magazine that reports new testing procedures, research findings, and product information in the water/environmental arena. A must for an academic or public library. Available online.

2664. *Civil Engineering (Reston): engineered design and construction.* Former titles: *Civil Engineering - A S C E; Civil Engineering (New York).* [ISSN: 0885-7024] 1930. m. USD 160 domestic; USD 205 foreign. Ed(s): Anne Powell. American Society of Civil Engineers, 1801 Alexander Graham Bell Dr, Reston, VA 20191-4400; http://www.pubs.asce.org. Illus., index, adv. Refereed. Circ: 101210. Vol. ends: Dec. Microform: PQC. Online: EBSCO Publishing; Gale Group; OCLC Online Computer Library Center, Inc.; ProQuest Information & Learning. *Indexed:* ABIn, AS&TI, ApMecR, C&ISA, ChemAb, EngInd, EnvAb, GeoRef, GeogAbPG, SCI. *Bk. rev.:* Various number and length. *Aud.:* Ac, Sa.

This is the official news publication for the American Society of Civil Engineers (ASCE). Free to all members, it offers an up-to-date focus on what is happening in the field of civil engineering. Noteworthy departments include upcoming ASCE conferences and a calendar of events, new publications, news briefs, member news, and new products and applications. Full-length, semitechnical articles written on timely topics are offered. A necessary journal for academic and public libraries. Available online.

2665. ***Computers & Structures: an international journal.*** [ISSN: 0045-7949] 1971. 32x/yr. EUR 4921 (Qualified personnel, EUR 349). Ed(s): K J Bathe, B. H.V. Topping. Pergamon, The Boulevard, Langford Ln, East Park, Kidlington, OX5 1GB, United Kingdom. Illus., index, adv. Refereed. Circ: 1500. Vol. ends: No. 79. Microform: PQC. Online: ingenta.com; ScienceDirect. *Indexed:* ApMecR, C&ISA, CCMJ, ChemAb, CompR, EngInd, GeoRef, IAA, MathSciNet, SCI. *Aud.:* Ac, Sa.

The application of computers to the solution of scientific and engineering problems related to hydrospace, aerospace, and terrestrial structures is dealt with here. This international journal is designed for the researcher working with the practical engineering aspects of structural analysis, design, and optimization. Each issue offers highly technical articles dealing with design of structures that employ the use of analog, digital, and hybrid computers. The interdisciplinary nature of this journal, along with its internationalism, makes it a valuable addition for any technical civil engineering collection. Available online.

2666. ***E N R: the construction weekly.*** Formerly: *Engineering News-Record.* [ISSN: 0891-9526] 1874. w. USD 74 United States; USD 89 in Canada & Mexico; USD 195 elsewhere. Ed(s): Janice Lyn Tuchman. Engineering News-Record, Two Penn Plaza, 9th Fl, New York, NY 10121-2298. Illus., adv. Circ: 78011 Paid. Microform: PQC. Online: Dow Jones Interactive; EBSCO Publishing; Gale Group; LexisNexis; ProQuest Information & Learning. Reprint: PQC. *Indexed:* ABIn, AS&TI, AltPI, BPI, C&ISA, ChemAb, EngInd, ExcerpMed, GeoRef, PetrolAb. *Bk. rev.:* Various number and length. *Aud.:* Ga, Ac, Sa.

Now in its 129th year of publication, this journal is the staple of the construction industry. Very readable, it offers thoughtful articles on the environment, transportation, business, and building fronts. Mainly written for the construction industry, the articles and regular columns are easily digested by the student and professional alike. Material prices, job ads, editorials, and news from the field are all featured. Excellent for public, special, and academic libraries. Available online.

2667. ***Earthquake Engineering and Structural Dynamics.*** [ISSN: 0098-8847] 1972. 15x/yr. USD 3415. John Wiley & Sons Ltd., The Atrium, Southern Gate, Chichester, PO19 8SQ, United Kingdom; customer@wiley.co.uk; http://www.wiley.co.uk. Illus., index, adv. Refereed. Circ: 1000. Microform: PQC. Online: EBSCO Publishing; Wiley InterScience. Reprint: ISI; PQC; SWZ. *Indexed:* AS&TI, ApMecR, EngInd, EnvAb, GeoRef, H&SSA, SCI, SUSA, SWRA. *Bk. rev.:* Various number and length. *Aud.:* Ac, Sa.

Endorsed by the International Association for Earthquake Engineering, this journal is scholarly and highly technical. Articles are selected with the researcher and designer in mind and reflect the journal's international flavor. Earthquake engineering includes seismicity, ground motion characteristics, soil amplification and failure, methods of dynamic analysis, behavior of structures, seismic codes, and tsunamis. Available online.

Engineering Geology. See Earth Sciences section.

2668. ***Engineering Structures: the journal of earthquake, wind and ocean engineering.*** Incorporates (1988-1996): *Structural Engineering Review.* [ISSN: 0141-0296] 1979. 14x/yr. EUR 1824 (Qualified personnel, EUR 213). Ed(s): P L Gould. Pergamon, The Boulevard, Langford Ln, East Park, Kidlington, OX5 1GB, United Kingdom. Illus., index, adv. Refereed. Microform: PQC. Online: ingenta.com; ScienceDirect; Swets Blackwell. *Indexed:* ApMecR, C&ISA, DSR&OA, EngInd, EnvAb, GeoRef, H&SSA, SCI, SWRA. *Aud.:* Ac, Sa.

Tall buildings, bridges, cooling towers, and dams are a few of the structures under study for the dynamic effects of wind, waves, and earthquakes, and they are featured in the articles in this journal. It will be of interest to structural, environmental, and bridge engineers, as well as architects. Short communications and discussions pertaining to structural engineering are also included. Available online.

2669. ***Geotechnique: international journal of soil mechanics.*** [ISSN: 0016-8505] 1948. q. GBP 258 domestic; GBP 306 foreign. Ed(s): G Sills. Thomas Telford Ltd., Thomas Telford House, 1 Heron Quay, London, E14 4JD, United Kingdom; journals@thomastelford.com; http://www.t-telford.co.uk. Illus., index, adv. Refereed. Circ: 2500. *Indexed:* ApMecR, BrTechI, C&ISA, ChemAb, DSR&OA, EngInd, GeoRef, GeogAbPG, PetrolAb, PollutAb, S&F, SCI, SWRA. *Aud.:* Ac, Sa.

This geotechnical journal features scholarly technical articles in the fields of soil mechanics, geotechnical engineering, and engineering geology. Technical notes and discussion papers are featured in each issue. Every article contains an English and a French abstract. Available online.

2670. ***Institution of Civil Engineers. Proceedings. Civil Engineering.*** Formed by the merger of (1972-1991): *Institution of Civil Engineers. Proceedings. Part 1: Design and Construction;* (1972-1991): *Institution of Civil Engineers. Proceedings. Part 2: Research and Theory;* Formerly (1957-1972): *Institution of Civil Engineers. Proceedings;* Which was formed by the merger of: *Institution of Civil Engineers. Part 1: General;* Institution of Civil Engineers. Part 2: *Engineering Divisions. Airport, Maritime, Railway, Road;* Institution of Civil Engineers. Part 3: *Engineering Divisions. Public Health, Structural, Works Construction, Hydraulis.* [ISSN: 0965-089X] 1991. q. GBP 79 domestic; GBP 92 foreign. Ed(s): E Irwin. Thomas Telford Ltd., Thomas Telford House, 1 Heron Quay, London, E14 4JD, United Kingdom; journals@thomastelford.com; http://www.thomastelford.com/jol. Illus., index, adv. Refereed. Circ: 62475. *Indexed:* AS&TI, ApMecR, BrTechI, C&ISA, CerAb, ChemAb, EngInd, ExcerpMed, GeoRef, GeogAbPG, H&SSA, SCI, SWRA. *Bk. rev.:* Various number and length. *Aud.:* Ga, Ac, Sa.

Civil Engineering is the general part of the *Proceedings of the Institution of Civil Engineers* (ICE). Five additional journals make up the package of six journals that comprise the complete set:

Geotechnical Engineering. [ISSN: 1353-2618]
Municipal Engineer. [ISSN: 0965-0903]
Structures and Buildings. [ISSN: 0965-0911]
Transport. [ISSN: 0965-092X].
Water, Maritime and Energy. [ISSN: 0965-0946]

Civil Engineering features general articles on all aspects of civil engineering research and practice. Technical notes, discussion, and ICE activities and services are included. This journal is the British version of *Civil Engineering* (above in this section). Available online.

2671. ***International Journal of Solids and Structures.*** [ISSN: 0020-7683] 1965. 26x/yr. EUR 5992 (Qualified personnel, EUR 298). Ed(s): Charles Steele. Pergamon, The Boulevard, Langford Ln, East Park, Kidlington, OX5 1GB, United Kingdom. Illus., adv. Refereed. Circ: 1400. Microform: PQC. Online: ingenta.com; ScienceDirect; Swets Blackwell. Reprint: PQC. *Indexed:* ApMecR, C&ISA, CCMJ, ChemAb, EngInd, GeoRef, GeogAbPG, H&SSA, IAA, MathSciNet, SCI. *Aud.:* Ac, Sa.

The mechanics of solids and structures is experiencing considerable growth technologically. This field is at the crossroads of materials, life sciences, mathematics, physics, and engineering design. This journal's aim is to foster the exchange of ideas among workers internationally and among workers who emphasize different aspects of the foundations of the field. Articles are analytical, experimental, and numerical in scope. Available online.

Journal of Hydrology. See Earth Sciences section.

Computer, Control, and Systems Engineering

2672. ***Artificial Intelligence: an international journal.*** [ISSN: 0004-3702] 1970. 18x/yr. EUR 2065. Ed(s): Raymond C Perrault. Elsevier BV, North-Holland, Sara Burgerhartstraat 25, Amsterdam, 1055 KV, Netherlands; nlinfo-f@elsevier.nl; http://www.elsevier.nl. Illus., adv.

Refereed. Circ: 1100. Microform: PQC. Online: EBSCO Publishing; ingenta.com; ScienceDirect; Swets Blackwell. Reprint: SWZ. *Indexed:* AS&TI, BioEngAb, C&ISA, CCMJ, CompR, EngInd, ErgAb, GeoRef, InfoSAb, L&LBA, LISA, MathSciNet, PsycholAb, SCI, SSCI. *Aud.:* Ac, Sa.

This is the main international artificial-intelligence journal, and it presents papers in the areas of software engineering, robotics, philosophy and logic, natural languages, vision, and cognitive science. It is a very prestigious and highly cited journal in its field. Available online.

2673. *Association for Computing Machinery. Journal.* [ISSN: 0004-5411] 1954. bi-m. USD 40 student members (Members, USD 45; Non-members, USD 220). Ed(s): Roma Simon, Joseph Y Halpern. Association for Computing Machinery, Inc., One Astor Plaza, 1515 Broadway, 17th Fl, New York, NY 10036-5701; sigs@acm.org; http://www.acm.org. Illus., index. Refereed. Circ: 4000 Paid. Microform: WWS; PQC; NRP. Online: Pub.; EBSCO Publishing; Florida Center for Library Automation; Gale Group; OCLC Online Computer Library Center, Inc.; ProQuest Information & Learning. Reprint: PQC. *Indexed:* ABIn, AS&TI, BPI, C&ISA, CCMJ, CompR, EngInd, ErgAb, InfoSAb, MathSciNet, SCI, SSCI. *Aud.:* Ac, Sa.

The official publication of the Association for Computing Machinery (ACM), which endeavors to advance the science of information processing. Research papers on hardware, languages for information processing, scientific computation, operations research, and artificial intelligence are presented. Other publications by this society are *Communications of the ACM, Computing Surveys, Computing Reviews,* the annual *ACM Guide to Computing Literature, Collected Algorithms of the ACM,* and various transactions. Available online through the ACM Digital Library.

2674. *Control Engineering: covering control, instrumentation, and automation systems worldwide.* [ISSN: 0010-8049] 1954. m. USD 109.90 domestic; USD 175.20 Canada; USD 168 Mexico. Ed(s): Mark T Hoske. Reed Business Information, 2000 Clearwater Dr, Oak Brook, IL 60523; http://www.reedbusiness.com. Illus., adv. Sample. Circ: 88054. Online: EBSCO Publishing; Florida Center for Library Automation; Gale Group; LexisNexis; Northern Light Technology, Inc.; OCLC Online Computer Library Center, Inc.; ProQuest Information & Learning; H.W. Wilson. Reprint: PQC. *Indexed:* ABIn, AS&TI, C&ISA, CEA, ChemAb, CompLI, EngInd, EnvAb, SSCI. *Bk. rev.:* Various number and length. *Aud.:* Ac, Sa.

Market updates, news items in the control arena, new control products, software reviews, and business directories are all regular departments in this well-illustrated and newsy magazine. A good choice for public libraries. Available online.

2675. *I E E E Transactions on Systems, Man and Cybernetics, Part C: Applications and Reviews.* Supersedes in part (in 1996): *I E E E Transactions on Systems, Man and Cybernetics;* Which was formed by the merger of (1968-1971): *I E E E Transactions on Man-Machine Systems;* (1965-1971): *I E E E Transactions on Systems Science and Cybernetics.* [ISSN: 1094-6977] 1971. q. USD 255 in North America; USD 290 elsewhere. Ed(s): Madan G Singh. Institute of Electrical and Electronics Engineers, Inc., 445 Hoes Ln, Piscataway, NJ 08854-1331; subscription-service@ieee.org; http://www.ieee.org. Illus., index, adv. Sample. Refereed. Vol. ends: Dec. Online: EBSCO Publishing; I E E E; Swets Blackwell. *Indexed:* AS&TI, C&ISA, EngInd, ErgAb, InfoSAb, SCI. *Bk. rev.:* Occasional, 700-1,000 words. *Aud.:* Ac, Sa.

Systems engineering and science, with cybernetic and man-machine systems, comprise the areas of investigation in this journal. Headline topics of national importance bring together such areas as large-scale systems, learning and adaptive systems, and "complex hardware, behavioral, biological, ecological, educational, environment, health care, management, socio-economic, transportation, and urban systems." There are roughly five to a dozen papers of 5 to 15 pages, and 5 to 15 "Correspondences" of about three to ten pages. Theoretical inquiries join forces with pragmatic goals, for example, the uses of artificial intelligence. Articles indicate lavish use, as required, of mathematical systems, including hardware and software. The central value of this periodical is evidenced by its numerous tutorial articles. Available online.

2676. *I S A Transactions.* [ISSN: 0019-0578] 1961. q. USD 310 domestic; USD 350; USD 370. I S A (The Instrumentation, Systems and Automation Society), Publications, Dept., 67 Alexander Dr., PO Box 12277, Research Triangle Park, NC 27709; info@isa.org; http://www.isa.org. Illus., index. Refereed. Microform: PQC. Online: ingenta.com; ScienceDirect; Swets Blackwell. Reprint: ISI; PQC. *Indexed:* AS&TI, BiolAb, ChemAb, EngInd, ExcerpMed, H&SSA, IAA, IndMed, RiskAb, SCI. *Aud.:* Ac, Sa.

What's new in the field of instrumentation and control technology? This journal focuses on new developments in topics of importance in industrial measurement, control, and automation. This field is a very dynamic one, and staying current is a competitive task. Future directions and theories and applications for developing manufacturing processes and equipment are found here. Available online.

2677. *International Journal of Control.* Supersedes in part (in 1965): *Journal of Electronics and Control;* Which was formerly (1955-1957): *Journal of Electronics.* [ISSN: 0020-7179] 1965. 18x/yr. GBP 2484. Ed(s): Eric Rogers. Taylor & Francis Ltd, 11 New Fetter Ln, London, EC4P 4EE, United Kingdom; info@tandf.co.uk; http://www.tandf.co.uk/journals. Illus., adv. Refereed. Online: EBSCO Publishing; Ingenta Select; OCLC Online Computer Library Center, Inc.; RoweCom Information Quest; Swets Blackwell. Reprint: PSC. *Indexed:* ApMecR, CCMJ, ChemAb, EngInd, MathSciNet, SCI. *Bk. rev.:* Various number and length. *Aud.:* Ac, Sa.

Computer-aided design is the leading-edge technology in engineering prototype ideation. This journal promotes and reports original research in the areas of neurocontrol, robotics, automation, and adaptive control. An excellent journal choice for robotics and CAD-CAM engineering collections.

International Journal of Parallel Programming. See Computer Science and Automation/Computer Science section.

2678. *Machine Learning: an international journal.* [ISSN: 0885-6125] 1986. m. USD 1148 print or online ed. Ed(s): Thomas G Dietterich. Kluwer Academic Publishers, 101 Philip Dr, Assinippi Park, Norwell, MA 02061. Illus., adv. Refereed. Microform: PQC. Online: EBSCO Publishing; ingenta.com; Kluwer Online; OCLC Online Computer Library Center, Inc.; Ovid Technologies, Inc.; RoweCom Information Quest; Swets Blackwell. Reprint: PQC; SWZ. *Indexed:* AS&TI, BioEngAb, C&ISA, CompLI, CompR, EngInd, L&LBA, SCI, SSCI. *Aud.:* Ac, Sa.

Can machines learn? This journal provides an international forum for research on computational approaches to learning. Papers that demonstrate both theory and computer implementation are published. Learning methods of interest include inductive learning methods as applied to classification and recognition, genetic algorithms demonstrating reasoning and inference, and learning from instruction through robotic and motor control. This is a core journal for any computing, control, and systems collection. Available online.

2679. *Neural Networks.* [ISSN: 0893-6080] 1988. 10x/yr. EUR 1317 (Qualified personnel, EUR 246). Ed(s): Dr. Stephen Grossberg, Mitsuo Kawato. Pergamon, The Boulevard, Langford Ln, East Park, Kidlington, OX5 1GB, United Kingdom. Illus., adv. Refereed. Circ: 3000. Microform: PQC. Online: EBSCO Publishing; ingenta.com; ScienceDirect. *Indexed:* AS&TI, BioEngAb, BiolAb, C&ISA, CompLI, EngInd, ExcerpMed, IndMed, PsycholAb, SCI, SSCI. *Aud.:* Ac, Sa.

The modeling of the brain and behavioral processes and the application of these models to computer and related technologies are the focus of scholarly articles presented in this highly cited journal. Psychologists, neurobiologists, mathematicians, physicists, computer scientists, and engineers will find this interdisciplinary journal of value. A core journal for any computer science and systems collection. Available online.

Robotics and Autonomous Systems. See Robotics section.

Electrical Engineering

The Institute of Electrical and Electronics Engineers (IEEE) publications are vital to any engineering collection and are among the most highly cited journals in engineering. This society produces technical periodicals, conference papers, standards, reports, tutorials, and other specialized publications. The flagship journal is the *Proceedings of the IEEE* [0018-9219], a monthly that presents papers having broad significance and long-range interest in all areas of electrical, electronics, and computer engineering. Since 1913, The *Proceedings of the IEEE* has been the leading authoritative resource for in-depth research coverage, tutorial information, and reviews of electrical and computer engineering technology. More than 100 titles are available for purchase. The *Index to IEEE Publications* is an annual publication that indexes by author and subject all the publications of the society. The IEEE Computer Society also publishes materials and should be consulted for selections. A full-text electronic product called *IEEE Xplore* is available from the publisher for all of its journals, proceedings, and standards. Check for current products at http://shop.ieee.org/store.

2680. ***Institution of Electrical Engineering. Proceedings.*** Institution of Electrical Engineers, Michael Faraday House, Six Hills Way, Stevenage, SG1 2AY, United Kingdom; inspec@iee.org; http://www.iee.org/. *Aud.:* Ac, Sa.

The Institution of Electrical Engineers (IEE) is the British sister society of the Institute of Electrical and Electronics Engineers (IEEE). Its proceedings are published in 13 parts. Each part may be purchased separately. Special issues providing concentrated coverage of interesting and important subjects are published occasionally. The 13 parts of the *Proceedings* are:

Circuits, Devices and Systems [ISSN: 1350-2409]
Communications [ISSN: 1350-2425]
Computers and Digital Techniques [ISSN: 1350-2389]
Control Theory and Applications [ISSN: 1350-2379]
Electric Power Applications [ISSN: 1350-2352]
Generation, Transmission and Distribution [ISSN: 1350-2360]
Microwaves, Antennas and Propagation [ISSN: 1350-2417]
Optoelectronics [ISSN: 1350-2433]
Radar, Sonar and Navigation [ISSN: 1350-2395]
Science, Measurement and Technology [ISSN: 1350-2344]
Vision, Image and Signal Processing [ISSN: 1350-245X]
Software [ISSN: 1462-5970]
Nanobiotechnology [ISSN: 1478-1581]

2681. ***Optical Engineering.*** Formerly: *S P I E Journal.* [ISSN: 0091-3286] 1962. m. USD 550 (Members, USD 55). Ed(s): Dr. Donald C O'Shea. S P I E - International Society for Optical Engineering, 1000 20th St, PO Box 10, Bellingham, WA 98225; spie@spie.org; http://www.spie.org/. Illus., index. Refereed. Circ: 12000. Online: EBSCO Publishing; Swets Blackwell. *Indexed:* AS&TI, CPI, ChemAb, EngInd, ExcerpMed, GeoRef, IAA, PhotoAb, SCI, SSCI. *Bk. rev.:* Various number and length. *Aud.:* Ac, Sa.

This is the journal of the International Society for Optical Engineering, a technical society dedicated to the advancement of applications of optical, electro-optical, and photoelectronic instrumentation systems and technologies. Optics is the science of light and vision. The editors accept articles that report new research and development, especially new, inventive technologies. Each issue contains 40–50 short articles on such areas as lasers, imaging, holography, biomedical optics, etc. Book reviews, short courses, and a calendar of meetings are found in each issue. A great bargain for an academic or special library. Available online.

2682. ***Progress in Quantum Electronics: an international review journal.*** [ISSN: 0079-6727] 1969. bi-m. EUR 911. Ed(s): P T Landsberg, M Osinski. Pergamon, The Boulevard, Langford Ln, East Park, Kidlington, OX5 1GB, United Kingdom. Refereed. Microform: PQC. Online: ingenta.com; ScienceDirect; Swets Blackwell. *Indexed:* C&ISA, ChemAb, EngInd, SCI. *Aud.:* Ac, Sa.

An international review journal, *Progress in Quantum Electronics* is devoted to the dissemination of new, specialized topics at the forefront of quantum electronics and its applications. Theoretical and experimental articles are welcomed. Available online.

Semiconductor Science and Technology. See Electronics section.

Manufacturing Engineering

2683. ***Computers & Industrial Engineering.*** [ISSN: 0360-8352] 1977. 8x/yr. EUR 2304 (Individuals, EUR 80). Ed(s): M I Dessouky. Pergamon, The Boulevard, Langford Ln, East Park, Kidlington, OX5 1GB, United Kingdom. Illus., index, adv. Refereed. Circ: 1000. Vol. ends: No. 40 - No. 41. Microform: PQC. Online: Gale Group; ingenta.com; ScienceDirect. *Indexed:* ABIn, C&ISA, CompLI, EngInd, ErgAb, SSCI. *Bk. rev.:* Various number and length. *Aud.:* Ac, Sa.

In all forms of engineering, computers and their applications have become general tools in the profession. Software is being developed and improved that allows for computer solutions to industrial engineering problems, as well as providing new techniques for design and planning. This journal provides a forum for sharing information to all practitioners on the uses of computers and their programs in industrial applications. It features refereed articles, technical discussions, a software section, and short papers. Available online.

2684. ***Journal of Manufacturing Systems.*** [ISSN: 0278-6125] 1982. bi-m. EUR 644. Ed(s): Mrs. Ellen J Kehoe. Elsevier Ltd., The Boulevard, Langford Ln, Oxford, OX5 1GB, United Kingdom; nlinfo-f@elsevier.nl; http://www.elsevier.com. Illus., index, adv. Refereed. Circ: 1000. Online: Northern Light Technology, Inc. *Indexed:* ABIn, AS&TI, ApMecR, EngInd, SCI. *Aud.:* Ac, Sa.

The Society of Manufacturing Engineers produces this journal for its membership and all professionals interested in the manufacturing industries and R&D organizations. Decreasing plant operation costs, increasing productivity, and producing quality products are a few of the endeavors this society hopes to achieve by sharing the scientific methods developed and presented in this journal. Technical papers in robotics, machine tooling, inspection, and handling-equipment areas are accepted, along with papers that report important research and new process developments. Case studies and general surveys are offered. Available online.

2685. ***Journal of Quality Technology: a quarterly journal of methods, applications and related topics.*** Supersedes in part (in 1968): *Industrial Quality Control.* [ISSN: 0022-4065] 1944. q. USD 100 (Individuals, USD 37; Members, USD 26). Ed(s): William H Woodhall. American Society for Quality, PO Box 3005, Milwaukee, WI 53201-3005; cs@asq.org; http://www.asq.org. Illus., index. Refereed. Circ: 22000. Microform: PQC. Online: OCLC Online Computer Library Center, Inc.; ProQuest Information & Learning; H.W. Wilson. Reprint: PQC; PSC. *Indexed:* ABIn, AS&TI, C&ISA, EngInd, FS&TA, IAA, SCI. *Bk. rev.:* Various number and length. *Aud.:* Ga, Ac, Sa.

A journal suitable for practicing engineers, the *Journal of Quality Technology* publishes papers on the practical applicability of new techniques, examples of techniques in practice, and results of historical research. Departments include computer programs, technical aids, and book reviews. This journal is produced for the membership of the American Society for Quality with the goal of "dedication to the advancement of quality." Available online.

2686. ***Machine Design: magazine of applied technology for design engineering.*** [ISSN: 0024-9114] 1929. 22x/yr. USD 105 domestic; USD 135 Canada; USD 153 elsewhere. Ed(s): Ronald Khol. Penton Media, Inc., 1300 E 9th St, Cleveland, OH 44114-1503; information@penton.com; http://www.penton.com. Illus., index, adv. Circ: 186484 Paid and controlled. Microform: PQC. Online: bigchalk; The Dialog Corporation; East View Publications, Inc.; EBSCO Publishing; Florida Center for

Library Automation; Gale Group; Northern Light Technology, Inc.; OCLC Online Computer Library Center, Inc.; ProQuest Information & Learning; H.W. Wilson. Reprint: PQC. *Indexed:* A&ATA, ABIn, AS&TI, B&I, C&ISA, ChemAb, EngInd, EnvAb, ErgAb, ExcerpMed, LRI, PetrolAb. *Aud.:* Ga, Ac, Sa.

This magazine easily wins the prize for reporting on cutting-edge techno-trinkets! With color photos, graphs, and drawings, the latest whiz-kid inventions are featured here alongside many colorful ads for industry tools, software, and services. With a finger on the pulse of the field, this magazine is a must for the technologically inclined. If it's in at least the prototype stage, the device will be found here. A magazine for the "techie" in all of us. Available online.

2687. *Manufacturing Engineering.* Former titles: *Manufacturing Engineering and Management; Tool and Manufacturing Engineer.* [ISSN: 0361-0853] 1932. m. USD 100 domestic; USD 195 foreign. Ed(s): Brian Hogan. Society of Manufacturing Engineers, One SME Dr, Dearborn, MI 48121; http://www.sme.org/. Illus., adv. Circ: 110000. Microform: PQC. Online: Northern Light Technology, Inc.; OCLC Online Computer Library Center, Inc.; ProQuest Information & Learning; H.W. Wilson. Reprint: PQC. *Indexed:* ABIn, AS&TI, ApMecR, C&ISA, CompLI, EngInd, SCI, SSCI. *Bk. rev.:* Various number and length. *Aud.:* Ga, Ac, Sa.

The official publication of the Society of Manufacturing Engineers, this monthly provides feature articles on such topics as machine tools of the future, aspects of machinery (e.g., turning, milling, and cutting-tool speed limits), and the computerization of machines. Advice is given on potential tool purchases. Special departments include a tech update, shop solutions, a news desk, product reviews, and job ads. Available online.

2688. *Plant Engineering.* [ISSN: 0032-082X] 1947. 13x/yr. USD 131.99 domestic; USD 163.90 Canada; USD 156 Mexico. Ed(s): Richard L Dunn. Reed Business Information, 2000 Clearwater Dr, Oak Brook, IL 60523; http://www.reedbusiness.com. Illus., adv. Circ: 116100 Controlled. Online: The Dialog Corporation; EBSCO Publishing; Florida Center for Library Automation; Gale Group; LexisNexis; Northern Light Technology, Inc.; OCLC Online Computer Library Center, Inc.; ProQuest Information & Learning; H.W. Wilson. *Indexed:* ABIn, AS&TI, CEA, ChemAb, EngInd, ExcerpMed, H&SSA, LRI, PollutAb. *Bk. rev.:* Various number and length. *Aud.:* Ga, Ac, Sa.

Like similar Cahners publications, *Plant Engineering* is news and advertizing driven. An informative tool for industrial professionals, this magazine publishes articles on fluid handling/maintenance, facilities, coatings, HVAC, power transmission, and management topics. One will find the expected new-product news, literature updates, reader inquiry cards, and classifieds. Archives back to 1998 available at the web site.

2689. *Quality Progress.* Supersedes in part (in 1968): *Industrial Quality Control.* [ISSN: 0033-524X] 1944. m. USD 120 (Individuals, USD 60). Ed(s): Debbie Donaldson. American Society for Quality Control, 611 E Wisconsin Ave, Box 3005, Milwaukee, WI 53201-3005; http://www.asq.org. Illus., index, adv. Circ: 133000 Paid and controlled. Microform: PQC. Online: OCLC Online Computer Library Center, Inc.; ProQuest Information & Learning; H.W. Wilson. Reprint: PQC; PSC. *Indexed:* ABIn, AS&TI, C&ISA, EngInd, ExcerpMed, SSCI. *Aud.:* Ga, Ac, Sa.

This publication of the American Society for Quality Control provides information on standards, industry changes, and the society's perspective on current issues. Each issue contains eight to ten feature articles. In an effort to gain membership feedback and to improve the editorial quality of the journal, each article ends with a questionnaire requesting an opinion of the reader on the quality of the featured article. Available online, with archives back to 2001.

Materials Engineering

2690. *Acta Materialia.* Incorporates (1992-1999): *Nanostructured Materials;* Former titles (until vol.44): *Acta Metallurgica et Materialia;* (until 1990): *Acta Metallurgica.* [ISSN: 1359-6454] 1953. 20x/yr. EUR 2465. Ed(s): S Suresh. Pergamon, The Boulevard, Langford Ln, East Park, Kidlington, OX5 1GB, United Kingdom. Illus., index, adv. Refereed. Circ: 2300. Vol. ends: Dec. Microform: PQC. Online: ingenta.com; ScienceDirect; Swets Blackwell. *Indexed:* ApMecR, C&ISA, ChemAb, EngInd, GeoRef, IAA, SCI. *Bk. rev.:* Various number and length. *Aud.:* Ac, Sa.

This scholarly journal's purpose is to publish original papers that advance the understanding of the properties of such materials as metals and alloys, ceramics, high polymers, and glasses. Available online.

2691. *Advanced Materials & Processes.* Incorporates (1930-1989): *Metal Progress.* [ISSN: 0882-7958] 1983. m. Free to members; Non-members, USD 325. Ed(s): Margaret W Hunt, Donald F Baxter. A S M International, 9639 Kinsman Rd, Materials Park, OH 44073-0002; cust-srv@asminternational.org; http://www.asminternational.org. Illus., adv. Refereed. Circ: 34000 Paid. Vol. ends: Jun/Dec. Online: bigchalk; EBSCO Publishing; Florida Center for Library Automation; Gale Group; OCLC Online Computer Library Center, Inc.; ProQuest Information & Learning; H.W. Wilson. Reprint: PQC. *Indexed:* AS&TI, C&ISA, CerAb, EngInd, IAA, SSCI. *Aud.:* Ac, Sa.

Free to American Society for Metals (ASM) members, each issue includes several articles about the manufacture, R&D, and social and economic impacts of engineered materials. ASM news, technological developments, and job ads are also included. Tables of contents, an advertisers index, and an issue summary can be found online at the publisher's web site. Available online.

2692. *J O M.* Former titles (until 1989): *Journal of Metals;* (until 1977): *JOM.* [ISSN: 1047-4838] 1949. m. USD 215 (Individuals, USD 112). Ed(s): James J Robinson. T M S - The Minerals, Metals and Materials Society, 184 Thorn Hill Rd, Warrendale, PA 15086-7514; publications@tms.org; http://www.tms.org. Illus., index, adv. Refereed. Circ: 14000. Vol. ends: Dec. Microform: PQC. Online: Gale Group; Ingenta Select; ProQuest Information & Learning; ScienceDirect; Swets Blackwell. Reprint: PQC. *Indexed:* AS&TI, C&ISA, ChemAb, EngInd, GeoRef, IAA, SCI. *Bk. rev.:* Various number and length. *Aud.:* Ac, Sa.

As the primary publication of the Minerals, Metals and Materials Society (TMS), this journal covers a broad range of materials science and engineering topics and is of interest to both academic and industrial readers. Business, government, industry, and TMS news and job advertisements are regular features. Available online.

2693. *Journal of Composite Materials.* [ISSN: 0021-9983] 1967. s-m. GBP 2600 print & online eds. in Europe, Middle East, Africa & Australasia. Sage Publications Ltd., 6 Bonhill St, London, EC2A 4PU, United Kingdom; info@sagepub.co.uk; http://www.sagepub.co.uk/. Illus., index. Refereed. Circ: 790 Paid. Microform: PQC. Online: ingenta.com; OCLC Online Computer Library Center, Inc.; Swets Blackwell. Reprint: PQC. *Indexed:* AS&TI, ApMecR, ArtInd, C&ISA, ChemAb, EngInd, IAA, SCI. *Aud.:* Ac, Sa.

This journal strives to provide a permanent record of achievements in the science, technology, and economics of composite materials. The contents of upcoming and past issues are available online.

Journal of Electronic Materials. See Electronics section.

2694. *Journal of Materials Research.* [ISSN: 0884-2914] 1986. m. USD 785 domestic Incl. online subscription; USD 815 foreign Incl. online subscription. Ed(s): Gordon E Pike. Materials Research Society, 506 Keystone Dr, Warrendale, PA 15086-7573; orders@allenpress.com; http://www.mrs.org/publications/jmr/; http://www.allenpress.com. Illus., index, adv. Refereed. Vol. ends: Dec. Microform: AIP. Online: EBSCO Publishing. Reprint: PQC. *Indexed:* AS&TI, ApMecR, C&ISA, CerAb, ChemAb, EngInd, GeoRef, IAA, SCI. *Aud.:* Ac, Sa.

Focuses on original research, with occasional review articles on the theoretical description, processing, preparation, characterization, and properties of materials with new or unusual structures or properties. In addition to articles, the journal publishes communications and short submissions. Available online, where full texts of abstracts are found.

2695. ***Journal of Materials Science.*** [ISSN: 0022-2461] 1966. 24x/yr. USD 8875 print or online ed. Kluwer Academic / Plenum Publishers, 233 Spring St Fl 7, New York, NY 10013-1522; http://www.wkap.nl/. Illus., index, adv. Refereed. Vol. ends: Dec. Online: EBSCO Publishing; ingenta.com; Kluwer Online; OCLC Online Computer Library Center, Inc.; Ovid Technologies, Inc.; RoweCom Information Quest; Swets Blackwell. Reprint: ISI; PQC. *Indexed:* A&ATA, AS&TI, ApMecR, C&ISA, CerAb, ChemAb, EngInd, ExcerpMed, GeoRef, IAA, SCI. *Aud.:* Ac, Sa.

Covers interdisciplinary subjects such as metals, ceramics, glasses, polymers, and biomedical materials. Review articles are also published. Available online.

2696. ***Journal of Testing and Evaluation.*** Supersedes: *Journal of Materials. (J M L S A).* [ISSN: 0090-3973] 1966. bi-m. USD 374 (Individuals, USD 249). Ed(s): Donald Petersen. American Society for Testing and Materials, 100 Barr Harbor Dr, PO Box C700, West Conshohocken, PA 19428-2959; service@astm.org; http://www.astm.org. Illus., index, adv. Refereed. Circ: 600. Vol. ends: Nov. Microform: PMC; PQC. Reprint: ISI; PQC. *Indexed:* AS&TI, C&ISA, CerAb, ChemAb, EngInd, ExcerpMed, IAA, SCI. *Aud.:* Ac, Sa.

Published by the American Society for Testing and Materials (ASTM), this journal provides a multidisciplinary forum for the applied sciences and engineering fields. Articles feature new technical information; evaluation of materials; and new methods for testing products, services, and materials; and highlight new ASTM standards. Available online.

2697. ***Metallurgical and Materials Transactions A - Physical Metallurgy and Materials Science.*** Formerly (until 1994): *Metallurgical Transactions A - Physical Metallurgy and Materials Science;* Which superseded in part (in 1975): *Metallurgical Transactions;* Which was formed by the merger of: *American Society for Metals. Transactions Quarterly; T M S Transactions.* [ISSN: 1073-5623] 1970. 13x/yr. USD 1617 domestic; USD 1637 foreign. Ed(s): David E Laughlin. A S M International, 9639 Kinsman Rd, Materials Park, OH 44073-0002; cust-srv@asminternational.org; http://www.tms.org. Illus., index, adv. Refereed. Circ: 1450 Paid. Vol. ends: Dec. Microform: PMC; PQC. Online: Ingenta Select; ProQuest Information & Learning; ScienceDirect; Swets Blackwell. Reprint: PQC. *Indexed:* AS&TI, C&ISA, ChemAb, DSR&OA, EngInd, IAA, SCI. *Aud.:* Ac, Sa.

Published jointly by ASM International and the Minerals, Metals and Materials Society, this journal was created with the goal of transferring basic research performed in physical metallurgy and materials science from the lab to actual shop fabrication and industrial application. Available online.

Mechanical Engineering

2698. ***Acta Mechanica.*** [ISSN: 0001-5970] 1965. 28x/yr. EUR 3036 domestic; EUR 3113 foreign; EUR 130 newsstand/cover per issue. Ed(s): H Troger, F Ziegler. Springer-Verlag Wien, Sachsenplatz 4-6, Vienna, 1201, Austria; journals@springer.at. Illus., adv. Sample. Refereed. Microform: PQC. Online: EBSCO Publishing; Springer LINK. Reprint: ISI. *Indexed:* ApMecR, C&ISA, ChemAb, EngInd, GeoRef, IAA, SCI. *Aud.:* Ac, Sa.

The classic fields within theoretical and applied mechanics—such as rigid-body dynamics, elasticity, plasticity, hydrodynamics, and gas dynamics—are addressed by the original research papers presented in this journal. Special attention is given to recently developed and boundary areas of mechanics. More than a dozen papers are contributed to each issue, along with announcements of upcoming international conferences. A classic mechanical engineering journal. Available online.

2699. ***American Society of Mechanical Engineers. Transactions.*** [ISSN: 0097-6822] 1880. q. A S M E International, Three Park Ave, New York, NY 10016-5990; infocentral@asme.org; http://www.asme.org. Illus., index, adv. Refereed. *Indexed:* ApMecR, EngInd, GeoRef. *Bk. rev.:* Various number and length. *Aud.:* Ac, Sa.

The American Society of Mechanical Engineers (ASME) is the mechanical engineer's most complete single resource for the delivery of technical information. The society publishes books, transaction journals, and more than 500 codes and standards. As a general rule, engineering societies that act as their own publisher offer standing-order plans. The society has several purchase packages to choose from and offers a special package price for institutional membership to their society. ASME has several electronic, microfilm, and video products, most notably, the Worldwide Standards Service from IHS and the Boiler and Pressure Vessel Code. The transactions titles can be purchased separately. Each offers peer-reviewed articles, book reviews, technical briefs, discussion, editorials, and meetings notifications.

2700. ***Computer Methods in Applied Mechanics and Engineering.*** [ISSN: 0045-7825] 1970. 52x/yr. EUR 6940. Ed(s): T. J.R. Hughes, J. T. Oden. Elsevier BV, North-Holland, Sara Burgerhartstraat 25, Amsterdam, 1055 KV, Netherlands; nlinfo-f@elsevier.nl; http://www.elsevier.nl. Illus., index, adv. Refereed. Vol. ends: No. 190. Microform: PQC. Online: ingenta.com; ScienceDirect. *Indexed:* AS&TI, ApMecR, C&ISA, CCMJ, CompLI, CompR, EngInd, GeoRef, GeogAbPG, IAA, MathSciNet, SCI. *Aud.:* Ac, Sa.

This specialist journal publishes scholarly papers on computer applications addressing finite element and boundary element methods in applied mechanics and engineering. It is a very specialized publication, found mainly in special library and research collections. Available online.

2701. ***Engineering Fracture Mechanics: an international journal.*** [ISSN: 0013-7944] 1968. 18x/yr. EUR 3661 (Qualified personnel, EUR 262). Ed(s): R. H. Dodds, K-H Schwalbe. Pergamon, The Boulevard, Langford Ln, East Park, Kidlington, OX5 1GB, United Kingdom. Illus., index, adv. Refereed. Circ: 1600. Microform: PQC. Online: ingenta.com; ScienceDirect. *Indexed:* ApMecR, C&ISA, ChemAb, EngInd, H&SSA, IAA, SCI, SWRA. *Bk. rev.:* Various number and length. *Aud.:* Ac, Sa.

Fracture mechanics is a topic of general interest to engineers in the mechanical, material science, and civil engineering fields. This journal offers a variety of sources of fracture mechanics information to the practitioner, including book reviews, solutions, formulae, curves of data, and tables, along with full scholarly articles of a theoretical and practical nature. Available online.

2702. ***Institution of Mechanical Engineers. Proceedings.*** Price varies. Professional Engineering Publishing, Northgate Ave, Bury St Edmunds, IP32 6BW, United Kingdom; journals@pepublishing.com; http://www.imeche.org.uk. *Bk. rev.:* Various number and length. *Aud.:* Ac, Sa.

The Institution of Mechanical Engineers publishes its proceedings in 12 separate journals. Each part has its own editor and can be purchased separately.

- **A:** ***Journal of Power and Energy*** [ISSN: 0957-6509]
- **B:** ***Journal of Engineering Manufacture*** [ISSN: 0954-4054]
- **C:** ***Journal of Mechanical Engineering Science*** [ISSN: 0954-4062]
- **D:** ***Journal of Automobile Engineering*** [ISSN: 0954-4070]
- **E:** ***Journal of Process Mechanical Engineering*** [ISSN: 0954-4089]
- **F:** ***Journal of Rail and Rapid Transit*** [ISSN: 0954-4097]
- **G:** ***Journal of Aerospace Engineering*** [ISSN: 0954-4100]
- **H:** ***Journal of Engineering in Medicine*** [ISSN: 0954-4119]
- **I:** ***Journal of Systems and Control Engineering*** [ISSN: 0959-6518]
- **J:** ***Journal of Engineering Tribology*** [ISSN: 1350-6501]
- **K:** ***Journal of Multi-body Dynamics*** [ISSN: 1464-4193]
- **L:** ***Journal of Materials: Design and Application*** [ISSN: 1464-4207]

2703. ***International Journal of Heat and Mass Transfer.*** [ISSN: 0017-9310] 1960. bi-w. EUR 4553 (Qualified personnel, EUR 388). Ed(s): J P Harnett, W J Minkowycz. Pergamon, The Boulevard, Langford Ln, East Park, Kidlington, OX5 1GB, United Kingdom. Illus., index, adv. Refereed. Circ: 2500. Microform: MIM; PQC. Online: ingenta.com; ScienceDirect; Swets Blackwell. Reprint: PQC. *Indexed:* AS&TI, ApMecR, C&ISA, CEA, ChemAb, DSR&OA, EngInd, EnvAb, ExcerpMed, GeoRef, IAA, PetrolAb, SCI. *Bk. rev.:* Various number and length. *Aud.:* Ac, Sa.

This journal is one of the core titles for a collection that covers heat and mass transfer. Contents include previously unpublished scholarly articles of an analytical, numerical, and/or experimental nature; reviews of new books on heat and mass transfer; and technical notes. A companion journal, *International Communications in Heat and Mass Transfer,* is a much faster medium for notes or short papers. This volume serves as the tool for rapid dissemination of new ideas, techniques, and discussions. A joint subscription price is available. Available online.

2704. *International Journal of Mechanical Sciences.* [ISSN: 0020-7403] 1960. m. EUR 2395 (Qualified personnel, EUR 204). Ed(s): Stephen R Reid. Pergamon, The Boulevard, Langford Ln, East Park, Kidlington, OX5 1GB, United Kingdom. Illus., index, adv. Refereed. Circ: 1400. Microform: PQC. Online: ingenta.com; ScienceDirect; Swets Blackwell. Reprint: PQC. *Indexed:* ApMecR, C&ISA, ChemAb, EngInd, H&SSA, IAA, SCI. *Aud.:* Ac, Sa.

The mechanics of solids and fluids, the forming and processing of those materials, structural mechanics, and thermodynamics provide the scope for this international journal. Mechanical and civil engineers will find it valuable. Available online.

2705. *International Journal of Plasticity.* [ISSN: 0749-6419] 1985. m. EUR 1832 (Qualified personnel, EUR 210). Ed(s): A S Khan. Pergamon, The Boulevard, Langford Ln, East Park, Kidlington, OX5 1GB, United Kingdom. Illus., adv. Refereed. Microform: PQC. Online: ingenta.com; ScienceDirect; Swets Blackwell. *Indexed:* ApMecR, C&ISA, EngInd, H&SSA, IAA, SCI. *Aud.:* Ac, Sa.

A specialized plastics industry journal, the *International Journal of Plasticity* reports on original research on all aspects of plastic deformation of isotropic and anisotropic solids. Research papers, review articles, research notes, and letters to the editor are regular features. Advertisements of interest to academia are provided. Highly theoretical in nature and significant to advancing the understanding of the plastic behavior of solids. Available online.

2706. *Mechanical Engineering.* [ISSN: 0025-6501] 1906. m. Members, USD 25; Non-members, USD 123. Ed(s): Harry Hutchinson. A S M E International, Three Park Ave, New York, NY 10016-5990; infocentral@asme.org; http://www.asme.org. Illus., index, adv. Refereed. Circ: 103000 Paid. Microform: PMC; PQC. Online: EBSCO Publishing; Florida Center for Library Automation; Gale Group; OCLC Online Computer Library Center, Inc.; ProQuest Information & Learning. *Indexed:* ABIn, AS&TI, ApMecR, C&ISA, CCMJ, ChemAb, EngInd, EnvAb, ExcerpMed, H&SSA, IAA, M&GPA, PetrolAb, SWRA. *Bk. rev.:* Various number and length. *Aud.:* Ga, Ac, Sa.

Published monthly by the American Society of Mechanical Engineers (ASME), this trade publication acts as the official organ of the society. It communicates news, new products, a calendar of upcoming meetings, publications offered for sale by the society, standards and code changes, and job opportunities. Notices of articles published in the ASME Transactions series are listed, which is important to the information professional because the society ceased publishing its index in the early 1980s. *ASME News* is included as a supplement to a subscription to *Mechanical Engineering.* Necessary for all engineering collections. Available online.

Progress in Energy and Combustion Science. See Energy section.

Nuclear Engineering

2707. *Nuclear Engineering International.* Incorporates: *Nuclear Engineering; Nuclear Power.* [ISSN: 0029-5507] 1956. m. GBP 186; USD 341 in US & Canada; GBP 199 elsewhere. Ed(s): Dick Kovan. Wilmington Publishing Ltd., Wilmington House, Maidstone Rd, Footscray, Sidcup, DA14 5HZ, United Kingdom; energy@wilmington.co.uk. Illus., index, adv. Refereed. Circ: 2399. Microform: PQC. Online: Factiva; Florida Center for Library Automation; Gale Group; LexisNexis; OCLC Online Computer Library Center, Inc.; ProQuest Information & Learning. Reprint: PQC. *Indexed:* AS&TI, ApMecR, B&I, BrTechI, C&ISA, ChemAb, EngInd, EnvAb, ExcerpMed, H&SSA. *Aud.:* Ga, Ac, Sa.

Get the global perspective in nuclear engineering with the addition of this title to your collection. Features include articles, industry briefs, profiles of national nuclear programs, wall charts, and statistics pertinent to the field. Discounts are offered for three-year subscriptions. This publisher also issues the *World Nuclear Industry Handbook,* a good reference source for technical details on nuclear power plants and fuel cycle facilities. Recent issues available online at publisher's web site.

2708. *Nuclear Instruments & Methods in Physics Research. Section A. Accelerators, Spectrometers, Detectors, and Associated Equipment.* Supersedes in part (in 1984): *Nuclear Instruments and Methods in Physics Research;* Which had former titles (until 1981): *Nuclear Instruments and Methods;* (until 1958): *Nuclear Instruments.* [ISSN: 0168-9002] 1957. 60x/yr. EUR 10456 (Qualified personnel, EUR 4258). Ed(s): R Klanner, W Barletta. Elsevier BV, North-Holland, Sara Burgerhartstraat 25, Amsterdam, 1055 KV, Netherlands; nlinfo-f@elsevier.nl; http://www.elsevier.nl. Illus., index, adv. Refereed. Vol. ends: No. 456 - No. 474. Microform: PQC. Online: EBSCO Publishing; ingenta.com; ScienceDirect; Swets Blackwell. *Indexed:* A&ATA, C&ISA, ChemAb, EngInd, EnvAb, ExcerpMed, GeoRef, IAA, SCI. *Aud.:* Ac, Sa.

This highly cited international scholarly journal publishes papers on particle accelerators and other devices that produce and measure nuclear radiations. Each issue includes numerous articles on such topics as fusion, dosimetry, space radiation, and instruments and methods for high-energy physics. A meetings calendar of interest to professionals in the nuclear industry is provided. Available online.

2709. *Nuclear Instruments & Methods in Physics Research. Section B. Beam Interactions with Materials and Atoms.* Supersedes in part (in 1984): *Nuclear Instruments and Methods in Physics Research;* Which had former titles (until 1981): *Nuclear Instruments and Methods;* (until 1958): *Nuclear Instruments.* [ISSN: 0168-583X] 1957. 56x/yr. EUR 8014. Ed(s): H H Andersen, Lynn E Rehn. Elsevier BV, North-Holland, Sara Burgerhartstraat 25, Amsterdam, 1055 KV, Netherlands; nlinfo-f@elsevier.nl; http://www.elsevier.nl. Illus., index, adv. Refereed. Vol. ends: No. 173 - No. 185. Microform: PQC. Online: EBSCO Publishing; ingenta.com; ScienceDirect; Swets Blackwell. *Indexed:* ArtHuCI, C&ISA, ChemAb, EngInd, GeoRef, SCI, SSCI. *Bk. rev.:* Various number and length. *Aud.:* Ac, Sa.

This highly cited technical journal publishes experimental and theoretical papers of original research spanning all aspects of the interaction of energetic beams with atoms, molecules, and aggregate forms of matter, including ion beam analysis and modification of materials. A master cumulative index by author is a special feature of the journal. Available online.

2710. *Nuclear News.* [ISSN: 0029-5574] 1959. m. plus 3 special issues. USD 325 includes Nuclear News Buyers Guide USD 27 newsstand/cover per issue. Ed(s): Gregg M Taylor. American Nuclear Society, 555 N Kensington Ave, La Grange Park, IL 60526; http://www.ans.org/pubs/magazines/NN/. Illus., adv. Circ: 15000. *Indexed:* AS&TI, C&ISA, ChemAb. *Bk. rev.:* Various number and length. *Aud.:* Ga, Ac, Sa.

Interested in the list of scheduled outages at U.S. nuclear power plants? This nuclear industry news journal is the place to find it. Published monthly by the American Nuclear Society, this magazine includes feature articles on the power, operation, and applications within the industry; standards actions; and a calendar of meetings. Special topical issues are published annually. Archives available online back to 1999.

Electronic Journals

Electronic Green Journal. See Environment and Conservation/Electronic Journals section.

2711. *Electronic Journal of Geotechnical Engineering.* [ISSN: 1089-3032] 1996. q. USD 250 (Individuals, USD 50). Ed(s): Mete Oner. Electronic Journal of Geotechnical Engineering, oner@okway.okstate.edu; http://www. geotech.civen.okstate.edu/ejge. Refereed. *Indexed:* C&ISA, GeoRef, PollutAb, SWRA. *Aud.:* Ac, Sa.

An electronic journal created to provide an open forum for rapid, interactive, peer-reviewed information exchange in geotechnical engineering worldwide. Includes job ads, discussion forums, meetings calendar, and research papers.

2712. ***Electronic Journal of Structural Engineering.*** [ISSN: 1443-9255] 2001. irreg. E J S E International Ltd., Department of Civil and Environmental Engineering, University of Melbourne, Parkville, VIC 3052, Australia. Refereed. *Indexed:* C&ISA, H&SSA, RiskAb. *Aud.:* Ac, Sa.

This journal provides an international forum for leading research and practical applications in structural engineering. Contains research papers, discussions and comments, and news about upcoming conferences and workshops.

2713. ***InterJournal.*** [ISSN: 1081-0625] 1997. irreg. Free. Ed(s): Y Bar Yam. New England Complex Systems Institute, 24 Mount Auburn St, Cambridge, MA 02138; nesci@necsi.org. Illus. Refereed. *Aud.:* Ac, Sa.

InterJournal is a distributed, self-organizing, refereed electronic journal. Selected topics include complex systems, genetics, polymers, and complex fluids. It is published by the New England Complex Systems Institute (NECSI), an independent educational and research institution dedicated to advancing the study of complex systems. Complex systems have multiple interacting components whose collective behavior cannot be simply inferred from the behavior of components. The recognition that understanding the parts cannot explain collective behavior has led to various new concepts and methodologies that are affecting all fields of science and engineering, and they are being applied to technology, business, and even social policy. The society's web site is at www.interjournal.org.

2714. ***The Journal of Artificial Intelligence Research.*** [ISSN: 1076-9757] 1994. s-a. USD 78.95. Ed(s): Martha E Pollack. Morgan Kaufmann Publishers, Inc., 340 Pine St, 6th Fl, San Francisco, CA 94104-3205; orders@mkp.com; jair-ed@ptolemy.arc.nasa.gov; http://www.jair.org/masthead.html; http://www.cs.washington.edu/research/jair/home.html. Illus., adv. Refereed. Online: EBSCO Publishing. *Indexed:* CCMJ, EngInd, MathSciNet, SCI. *Aud.:* Ac, Sa.

This refereed electronic journal is devoted to all areas of artificial intelligence. It is indexed in INSPEC, ISI, and MathSci. It was established in 1993 as one of the first electronic scientific journals. Complete archive available online.

2715. ***Journal of Experimental Algorithmics.*** [ISSN: 1084-6654] 1996. q. USD 17 student members (Members, USD 22; Non-members, USD 149). Ed(s): Bernard M E Moret. Association for Computing Machinery, Inc., One Astor Plaza, 1515 Broadway, 17th Fl, New York, NY 10036-5701; sigs@acm.org; http://www.acm.org. Illus. Refereed. *Indexed:* CCMJ, MathSciNet. *Aud.:* Ac, Sa.

This online journal is devoted to experimental work in the design and analysis of algorithms and data structures, with two principal aims: to stimulate research in algorithms based on implementation and experimentation and to distribute programs and testbeds throughout the research community. Areas of focus include combinatorial optimization, computational biology, computational geometry, graph manipulation, graphics, heuristics, network design, parallel processing, routing and scheduling, searching and sorting, and VLSI design.

2716. ***Journal of Graph Algorithms and Applications.*** [ISSN: 1526-1719] 1997. irreg. Ed(s): Roberto Tamassia, Ioannis G Tollis. Brown University, Department of Computer Science, 115 Waterman St, Providence, RI 02912-1910; rt@cs.brown.edu; tollis@utdallas.edu; http://www.cs.brown.edu/publications/jgaa/. Illus. Refereed. *Indexed:* CCMJ, MathSciNet. *Aud.:* Ac, Sa.

A new electronic journal for the graph algorithms research community. Topics of interest include design and analysis of graph algorithms, experiences with graph algorithms, and applications of graph algorithms. Available in both print and electronic formats.

2717. ***Technology Interface: the electronic journal for engineering technology.*** [ISSN: 1523-9926] 1996. irreg. Ed(s): Jeff Beasley. New Mexico State University, MSC 3E, Box 30001, Las Cruces, NM 88003-0001; jbeasley@nmsu.edu; http://et.nmsu.edu/~etti/. *Aud.:* Ac, Sa.

News and information for engineering technology professionals, with a focus on the academic and industrial sectors. Peer reviewed.

2718. ***Ubiquity.*** [ISSN: 1530-2180] 2000. w. Free. Ed(s): John Gehl, Suzanne Douglas. Association for Computing Machinery, Inc., One Astor Plaza, 1515 Broadway, 17th Fl, New York, NY 10036-5701; sigs@acm.org; http://www.acm.org. *Bk. rev.:* Various number and length. *Aud.:* Ac, Sa.

A web-based publication fostering critical analysis and in-depth commentary on issues relating to and of interest to the information technology profession. Departments include book reviews, interviews, and reflections.

ENVIRONMENT AND CONSERVATION

See also Biological Sciences; Fishing; Hiking, Climbing, and Outdoor Recreation; Hunting and Guns; and Sports sections.

George E. Clark, Ph.D., Environmental Resources Librarian, Environmental Information Center, Cabot Science Library, Harvard University, 1 Oxford St., Cambridge, MA 02138; clark5@fas.harvard.edu; FAX: 617-495-5324

Introduction

Those new to the field of environmental studies might wonder why a listing of notable periodicals covers such a broad range of topics. That is because environmental studies is at its core a desire to understand the relationship between people and our physical surroundings. This includes relatively natural areas such as forests and oceans, cultivated landscapes such as cornfields and rice paddies, and more built-up areas such as cities and suburbs. Almost at once, even before adding in global processes such as the greenhouse effect, the purview of environmental studies covers the whole planet. At the same time, the human organism has specific health requirements relative to its surroundings, and so the field must at the same time be intimate enough to consider the needs of individual people of all ages, genders, and backgrounds.

In addition, students and researchers soon learn that oceans, forests, croplands, and the people that subsist on them are subject to the pressures of human activities and policies. Since these pressures vary by culture, government, and economy, the study of environment is necessarily a social investigation as well—similarly with cities and suburbs and the people who live in them. To top it all off, people experience environmental burdens as well as benefits. Therefore, in addition to positives such as parks, species preservation, and conservation, many environmental researchers study negatives such as pollution, disease, floods, and famines. One would be hard-pressed to name a broader field. Of course most individual library users will be interested in only a fraction of the entire field, so user needs must be considered and collections developed appropriately.

Public libraries and school libraries (as appropriate) may want to focus on issues of *metropolitan and regional planning* impacts on the environment (urban blight and suburban sprawl, development, zoning, transportation, parks, recycling, and waste management, for example), *local livelihood* impacts on and relationships to the environment (agriculture, fishing, logging, mining, manufacturing, commerce, business, and tourism), *household impacts and sustainable living*, local and regional *ecosystems and species*, the local geographic and demographic distribution of environmental threats and benefits (a field commonly called by the shorthand term of *environmental justice*), and the *capacity to deal with emergent environmental threats* (local natural and man-made hazards, public health, toxicity information, risk communication, community organizing, and environmental news). Many public libraries will already receive publications that will help users plan vacations in parks and other naturally appealing areas outside the local area. Of course, academic and special libraries will want to adapt their collections according to users' home disciplines and their local, regional, national, international, and global research questions, adding in more technical publications.

Because of the breadth of the environmental field, it is impossible to list serials that would be appropriate for each of the above topics in this section of *Magazines for Libraries*. The publications listed here include many that focus on the environment *per se*, along with a smattering that will begin to convey the true breadth of the field. Many of the other entries will have references to highly environmentally relevant journals and magazines and so should be explored by those interested in the environment.

Basic Periodicals

Conservation Ecology, Conservation in Practice, Environment, Everyone's Backyard, Global Environmental Change Part B: Environmental Hazards: Human and Policy Dimensions, Green Teacher, International Journal of Mass Emergencies and Disasters, Linkages, Local Environment, Natural Hazards Observer.

Basic Abstracts and Indexes

Academic Search Premier, Agricola, BIOSIS, Environmental Issues and Policy Index, Environmental Sciences and Pollution Management (EnvironmentS), Forestry Abstracts, GeoBase, Medline, Meteorological and Geoastrophysical Abstracts, LexisNexis Environmental, Pollution Abstracts, ProQuest Research Library, Risk Abstracts, Science Citation Index, Social Science Citation Index, TOXNET.

2719. *Ambio: a journal of the human environment.* [ISSN: 0044-7447] 1972. 8x/yr. USD 200 Print edition (Individuals, USD 72 Print edition). Ed(s): Elisabeth Kessler. Kungliga Svenska Vetenskapsakademien, Lilla Frescativaegen 4 A, PO Box 50005, Stockholm, 14005, Sweden; rsas@kva.se; http://www.kva.se. Illus., index, adv. Refereed. Circ: 4000. Vol. ends: Dec. *Indexed:* ApEcolAb, B&AI, BRI, BiolAb, CBRI, ChemAb, DSR&OA, EngInd, EnvAb, ExcerpMed, FPA, FS&TA, ForAb, FutSurv, GSI, GeoRef, GeogAbPG, HortAb, IndMed, IndVet, M&GPA, OceAb, PollutAb, RRTA, S&F, SCI, SFSA, SSCI, SUSA, SWRA, VetBull, WAE&RSA, WRCInf, ZooRec. *Aud.:* Ac.

Ambio is a peer-reviewed general environmental journal that dates from 1972 and the early consciousness of environment as a global issue. *Ambio* is sponsored by the Royal Swedish Academy of Sciences and aims to publish research perspectives that can satisfy academic scrutiny yet speak to a generalist audience. It succeeds at the former much more so than the latter. Each issue contains about a dozen articles.

American Forests. See Forestry section.

2720. *American Water Resources Association. Journal.* Formerly (until 1997): *Water Resources Bulletin.* [ISSN: 1093-474X] 1965. bi-m. Non-members, USD 165. Ed(s): Christopher Lant. American Water Resources Association, 4 W. Federal St, PO Box 1626, Middleburg, VA 20118-1626; info@awra.org; http://www.awra.org. Illus., adv. Circ: 4000. Microform: PQC. Online: ProQuest Information & Learning. *Indexed:* AS&TI, Agr, BAS, BiolAb, CAPS, ChemAb, DSA, EngInd, EnvAb, ExcerpMed, FPA, ForAb, GeoRef, GeogAbPG, HortAb, IndVet, OceAb, PollutAb, RI-1, RRTA, S&F, SCI, SSCI, SWRA, VetBull, WAE&RSA, WRCInf, ZooRec. *Aud.:* Ac, Sa.

Journal of the American Water Resources Association is the premier U.S. academic journal solely devoted to water. Water resources is broadly defined to include hydrology, watershed management, economics, engineering, groundwater, ecology, water policy, and pollution, among other topics. However, the article count runs heavily toward the physical and technical side. Includes book reviews.

The Amicus Journal. See *OnEarth.*

2721. *Audubon.* Formerly (until 1961): *Audubon Magazine.* [ISSN: 0097-7136] 1899. bi-m. USD 35; USD 45 Canada; USD 50 elsewhere. Ed(s): Lisa Gosselin. National Audubon Society, 700 Broadway, New York, NY 10003; http://www.audubon.org. Illus., adv. Circ: 453750 Paid. Vol. ends: Nov/Dec. CD-ROM: ProQuest Information & Learning. Microform: PMC; PQC. Online: Florida Center for Library Automation; Gale Group; Northern Light Technology, Inc. *Indexed:* ABS&EES, BRI, BiolAb, BiolDig, CBRI, CPerI, DSR&OA, EnvAb, GSI, GardL, MagInd, RGPR, RI-1, SWRA. *Aud.:* Hs, Ga.

Audubon is the magazine of the National Audubon Society. It's not just for birds anymore. While things with wings are strongly represented, *Audubon* branches out into critters such as fish, mushrooms, and amphibians. Watersheds, federal land management, and other broad, habitat-related concepts and issues also share the page. The magazine is packed with regular features including "Earth Almanac," "True Nature," "Incite" (a problem digest leading to "what you can do"), and "Audubon in Action." It is nicely laid out with many color photographs. A solid environmental magazine with a conservationist core.

2722. *BackHome: your hands-on guide to sustainable living.* [ISSN: 1051-323X] 1990. bi-m. USD 21.97 domestic; USD 27.97 foreign; USD 4.95 newsstand/cover per issue domestic. Ed(s): Lorna K Loveless. WordsWorth Communications Inc., PO Box 70, Hendersonville, NC 28793; info@backhomemagazine.com; http://www.backhomemagazine.com. Illus., adv. Circ: 26000 Paid. *Aud.:* Hs, Ga.

This friendly magazine bills itself as a "hands-on guide to sustainable living." Hands-on it certainly is. Want a cream cheese sandwich? Make the cream cheese yourself. Other "recipes" include beekeeping, wind power, and natural remedies for your critters. Home improvement, energy self-sufficiency, money management, animal raising, gardening, and even education are themes of this introduction to the do-it-yourself culture. *Back Home* is not a member of the chemical-free school of agriculture, but it does cater to those environmentally inclined citizens who want to "act locally."

2723. *Biodiversity and Conservation.* [ISSN: 0960-3115] 1991. m. EUR 1725 print or online ed. Ed(s): Alan T Bull, Ghillean T Prance. Kluwer Academic Publishers, van Godewijckstraat 30, PO Box 17, Dordrecht, 3300 AA, Netherlands. Illus. Refereed. Vol. ends: Dec. Online: EBSCO Publishing; ingenta.com; Kluwer Online; OCLC Online Computer Library Center, Inc.; Ovid Technologies, Inc.; RoweCom Information Quest; Swets Blackwell. *Indexed:* Agr, ApEcolAb, BiolAb, CAPS, DSA, EnvAb, FPA, ForAb, HortAb, IndVet, PollutAb, RRTA, S&F, SCI, SSCI, SWRA, VetBull, WAE&RSA, ZooRec. *Aud.:* Ac, Sa.

Biodiversity and Conservation is a peer-reviewed academic journal dealing largely with the biological side of threats to ecosystems and species. It is international in scope, and contains technical articles on species diversity, ecological communities, invasive organisms, land use impacts, ecological history, and other relevant topics. It is well illustrated with plenty of statistical analysis.

2724. *Conservation in Practice.* Formerly (until 2001): *Conservation Biology in Practice.* [ISSN: 1539-6827] 2000. q. USD 75 in US & developing nations (Individuals, USD 30 in US & developing nations). Ed(s): Kathryn A Kohm. Society for Conservation Biology, 4245 N Fairfax Dr, Arlington, VA 22203; kkohm@u.washington.edu; http://www.conservationbiology.org/SCB/index.cfm. Index. *Indexed:* ForAb, HortAb, RRTA, SWRA, WRCInf. *Bk. rev.:* Various number and length. *Aud.:* Hs, Ga, Ac, Sa.

Conservation in Practice is a general readership publication of the Society for Conservation Biology that is unafraid to tackle complex issues. Do current dolphin bycatch protections harm other marine life? Have invasive species been used in some instances to save endangered ones? *Conservation in Practice* recently carried articles on these topics. The magazine is international in scope, pleasing to read, and well illustrated, with plenty of *New Yorker*-style cartoons. It provides essays and reviews of academic journal articles, books, and web sites. Articles include a statistical feature, case studies, and critical examinations of "tools and techniques." Journal policy encourages multidisciplinary perspectives on conservation biology.

2725. *Critical Reviews in Environmental Science & Technology.* Former titles (until vol.23, 1992): *Critical Reviews in Environmental Control; C R C Critical Reviews in Environmental Control.* [ISSN: 1064-3389] 1970. q. USD 550 (Individuals, USD 110 print & online eds.). Ed(s): Terry J Logan. C R C Press, Llc, 2000 Corporate Blvd, N W, Boca Raton, FL 33431-9868; journals@crcpress.com; http://www.crcpress.com. Illus., index. Refereed. Circ: 630. *Indexed:* AS&TI, Agr, BiolAb, C&ISA, ChemAb, DSA, DSR&OA, EngInd, EnvAb, ExcerpMed, FS&TA, GeoRef, GeogAbPG, M&GPA, PetrolAb, PollutAb, RI-1, S&F, SCI, SSCI, SWRA, WRCInf. *Aud.:* Ac, Sa.

Critical Reviews in Environmental Science and Technology covers the technical processes of environmental pollution and abatement. The articles survey the literature on specific processes in great, at times ponderous, detail, with long bibliographies. There may be only a single article per issue. This can be great if the articles are directly relevant to your field, but may limit the interest of others in the publication. This is a bimonthly, peer-reviewed journal appropriate only for academic and highly specialized libraries.

2726. ***Daily Environment Report.*** [ISSN: 1060-2976] 1992. d. USD 3537. Ed(s): Larry E. Evans, Bernard S Chabel. The Bureau of National Affairs, Inc., 1231 25th St., NW, Washington, DC 20037; bnaplus@bna.com; http://www.bna.com. Illus., index. Online: Pub.; West Group. *Aud.:* Ga, Ac, Sa.

Daily Environment Report is for those with a serious interest in the processes of environmental governance in the United States. Along with concise articles on all aspects of environmental policy, this Bureau of National Affairs publication prints the Presidential and Congressional calendars, relevant new lobbyist registrations, Federal Register headlines, public comment deadlines, and an index to court cases mentioned in the day's issue.

2727. ***E Magazine: the environmental magazine.*** [ISSN: 1046-8021] 1990. bi-m. Individuals, USD 20; USD 3.95 newsstand/cover per issue. Ed(s): Jim Motavalli. Earth Action Network, 28 Knight St, Norwalk, CT 06851. Illus., adv. Sample. Circ: 50000 Paid. Vol. ends: Nov/Dec. Online: bigchalk; EBSCO Publishing; Florida Center for Library Automation; Gale Group; OCLC Online Computer Library Center, Inc.; ProQuest Information & Learning; SoftLine Information; H.W. Wilson. *Indexed:* ASIP, AltPI, BRI, BiolDig, CBRI, MagInd, RGPR, SWRA. *Aud.:* Hs, Ga.

E aims to be "a clearinghouse of information, news, and commentary on environmental issues for the benefit of the general public" and "the dedicated environmentalist." Issues are divided between news both international and domestic, feature pieces, and a guide to "Green Living" with segments on health, food (often organic and vegetarian), money, home improvement, travel, and products to buy.

2728. ***Earth First!: the radical environmental journal.*** Former titles (until 1990): *Earth First! Journal;* (until 1989): *Earth First.* [ISSN: 1055-8411] 1980. 8x/yr. USD 30 domestic; USD 40 foreign; USD 4 newsstand/cover per issue domestic. Daily Planet Publishing, PO Box 3023, Tucson, AZ 85702; collective@earthfirstjournal.org; http://www.earthfirstjouranl.org. Illus., adv. Circ: 15000. *Indexed:* AltPI, EnvAb. *Aud.:* Ga.

Earth First! is a radical magazine advocating "no-compromise" in the environmental movement. The magazine reports heavily on disobedience and action of all sorts against corporations, governments, and other entities. Traditional full names are largely not used on this publication's masthead, and the editors disclaim everything from the statements and opinions of the authors to the actions of local Earth First! groups. In addition to articles, issues feature letters, poetry, and drawings.

2729. ***Earth Island Journal: an international environmental news magazine.*** [ISSN: 1041-0406] 1986. q. USD 35 (Individuals, USD 25). Ed(s): Gar Smith. Earth Island Institute, 300 Broadway, Ste 28, San Francisco, CA 94133-3312; journal@earthisland.org; http://www.earthisland.org/ei. Illus., adv. Sample. Circ: 17000. Microform: PQC. Online: EBSCO Publishing; Florida Center for Library Automation; Gale Group; OCLC Online Computer Library Center, Inc.; ProQuest Information & Learning. *Indexed:* AltPI, EnvAb, SSCI. *Aud.:* Hs, Ga.

Earth Island Journal operates on the premise that "life on Earth is imperiled by human degradation." Published by the Earth Island Institute, the magazine is critical of the establishment and opposed to "threats to the biological and cultural diversity that sustains the environment." Unlike some publications farther from the mainstream, *Earth Island* presents serious articles, aiming toward constructive change, about news, opinion, and institute projects. Other regular features include book reviews and "Other Voices," a profile of a figure in the environmental movement.

2730. ***The Ecologist.*** Former titles (until vol.9, 1979): *New Ecologist; Ecologist Quarterly.* [ISSN: 0261-3131] 1970. 10x/yr. GBP 28 domestic; USD 52 in US & Canada; GBP 38 elsewhere. Ed(s): Zac Goldsmith. Ecosystems Ltd., 18 Chelsea Wharf, 15 Lots Rd, London, SW10 0JZ, United Kingdom. Illus., adv. Sample. Circ: 20000. Microform: PQC. Online: EBSCO Publishing; Florida Center for Library Automation; Gale Group; OCLC Online Computer Library Center, Inc.; ProQuest Information & Learning; H.W. Wilson. Reprint: PQC. *Indexed:* AltPI, BiolAb, BiolDig, BrHumI, EnvAb, ExcerpMed, ForAb, GSI, GeogAbPG, PAIS, PollutAb, S&F, SWRA, VetBull, WAE&RSA, ZooRec. *Aud.:* Hs, Ga.

The Ecologist reports environmental activism as a struggle against corporations and globalization. As such, this British publication pulls no punches. This includes punches that some might say are either below the belt or swiping at air. Features include health; politics; nature and resources; science and technology; economics; food; and society, culture, and media. Book reviews, reading lists, and web guides on selected topics are also regular features. While often entertaining and always provocative, the articles in this visually attractive publication are not well footnoted. The masthead contains a disclaimer that readers should strongly consider: "No responsibility will be accepted for any errors or omissions, or comments made by writers or interviewees."

2731. ***Ecosystems.*** [ISSN: 1432-9840] 1998. 8x/yr. USD 422; USD 62.40 per issue. Ed(s): Stephen Carpenter, Monica Turner. Springer-Verlag, Journals, 175 Fifth Ave., New York, NY 10010-7703; journals@springer-ny.com; http://www.springer-ny.com. Illus., adv. Sample. Refereed. *Indexed:* ApEcolAb, BiolAb, FPA, ForAb, GeoRef, IndVet, PollutAb, RRTA, S&F, SWRA, WAE&RSA, ZooRec. *Aud.:* Ac, Sa.

Ecosystems is a technical, peer-reviewed journal appropriate for academic libraries with users interested in ecosystem science. Rich in modelling, mapping, and remote sensing.

2732. ***Emergency Preparedness Digest.*** Formerly (until 1986): *Emergency Planning Digest;* Supersedes: *E M O National Digest.* [ISSN: 0837-5771] 1974. q. CND 20; CND 26 foreign. Ed(s): Anne Marie Demers. Canadian Government Publishing Centre, 45 Sacre Coeur Blvd, Rm A2411 E, Hull, PQ K1A 0S9, Canada. Adv. Circ: 2700. Microform: PQC. Reprint: PQC. *Indexed:* CBCARef. *Aud.:* Ga, Ac, Sa.

Emergency Preparedness Digest is the publication of Canada's civil defense and disaster management agency. Recent issues include features on businesses and disaster, drinking water, health and disaster, agency history, and case studies. It is bilingual, in English and French, and includes an events section with conference and training announcements.

2733. ***Emergency Preparedness News: contingency planning - crisis management - disaster relief.*** Incorporates (in 2003): *Port & Rail Security International.* [ISSN: 0275-3782] 1977. bi-w. USD 357 in North America; USD 373 elsewhere. Ed(s): Deborah Elby. Business Publishers, Inc., 8737 Colesville Rd, Ste 1100, Silver Spring, MD 20910-3928; bpinews@bpinews.com; http://www.bpinews.com. *Aud.:* Ga, Ac, Sa.

Emergency Preparedness News covers "contingency planning, crisis management, disaster relief." Lately it is heavy on counterterrorism and civil defense.

2734. ***Environment: where science and policy meet.*** Formerly (until 1969): *Scientist and Citizen.* [ISSN: 0013-9157] 1958. m. except Jan.-Feb., July-Aug. combined. USD 98 (Individuals, USD 48; USD 9.80 per issue). Ed(s): Barbara Richman. Heldref Publications, 1319 18th St, NW, Washington, DC 20036-1802; subscribe@heldref.org; http://www.heldref.org. Illus., adv. Refereed. Circ: 6500. CD-ROM: ProQuest Information & Learning. Online: bigchalk; EBSCO Publishing; Florida Center for Library Automation; Gale Group; Northern Light Technology, Inc.; OCLC Online Computer Library Center, Inc.; ProQuest Information & Learning; SoftLine Information; H.W. Wilson. Reprint: PSC. *Indexed:* AS&TI, B&AI, BRI, BiolAb, CBRI, CIJE, CPerI, ChemAb, DSA, DSR&OA, EnvAb, ExcerpMed, FPA, ForAb, GSI, GeoRef, GeogAbPG, IBSS, IBZ, LRI, M&GPA, MagInd, PRA, PollutAb, RGPR, RI-1, RRTA, S&F, SCI, SSCI, SSI, WAE&RSA, WRCInf, ZooRec. *Bk. rev.:* Number and length vary. *Aud.:* Hs, Ga, Ac, Sa.

Environment is probably the most stalwart mainstream environmental magazine in the English language. It is peer reviewed and well sourced, and edited by internationally recognized scholars, yet written and presented in a way that is appropriate for everyone from high school students to policy makers to members of the academy. Meaty articles are mixed with editorials, snippets of news, and book reviews. No stranger to the Internet, *Environment* has hosted the column "Bytes of Note" since at least 1996. Advertisements include a guide to graduate programs in environmental studies. Articles run towards transnational sustainable development, but regional-, country-, and issue-based studies are also common.

2735. ***Environment and Development Economics.*** [ISSN: 1355-770X] 1996. q. USD 223 (Individuals, USD 69). Ed(s): Charles Perrings. Cambridge University Press, The Edinburgh Bldg, Shaftesbury Rd, Cambridge, CB2 2RU, United Kingdom; information@cambridge.org; http://uk.cambridge.org. Illus., adv. Refereed. Online: EBSCO Publishing; OCLC Online Computer Library Center, Inc.; RoweCom Information Quest; Swets Blackwell. *Indexed:* BAS, FPA, ForAb, JEL, PAIS, PollutAb, S&F, WAE&RSA. *Aud.:* Ac.

Environment and Development Economics is a peer-reviewed, academic economics journal. It contains two types of articles, "Theory and Applications" and "Policy Options." Despite the "broad readership" that the editors seek, papers are generally quite technical. Non-economist readers will largely be confined to the helpful one- to two-page article summaries. International in scope, with a developing-country focus.

2736. ***Environmental Conservation: an international journal of environmental science.*** [ISSN: 0376-8929] 1974. q. USD 338 (Individuals, USD 128). Ed(s): Nicholas Polunin. Cambridge University Press, The Edinburgh Bldg, Shaftesbury Rd, Cambridge, CB2 2RU, United Kingdom; information@cambridge.org; http://uk.cambridge.org/journals. Illus., adv. Sample. Refereed. Vol. ends: Winter. Microform: PQC. Online: EBSCO Publishing; OCLC Online Computer Library Center, Inc.; RoweCom Information Quest; Swets Blackwell. *Indexed:* ApEcolAb, B&AI, BAS, BiolAb, BiolDig, C&ISA, ChemAb, DSR&OA, EngInd, EnvAb, ExcerpMed, FPA, ForAb, GeoRef, GeogAbPG, HortAb, IBZ, IndVet, M&GPA, OceAb, PollutAb, RRTA, S&F, SCI, SSCI, SWRA, WAE&RSA, ZooRec. *Aud.:* Ac, Sa.

Environmental Conservation is a quarterly, peer-reviewed academic publication. While the journal prominently features terrestrial and aquatic ecosciences, it also includes management and social science approaches and encourages submissions from all perspectives on the topic. Issues include "Comment" (brief articles and opinion pieces), "Papers" (longer articles), book reviews, and the occasional obituary.

2737. ***Environmental Ethics: an interdisciplinary journal dedicated to the philosophical aspects of environmental problems.*** [ISSN: 0163-4275] 1979. q. USD 50 (Individuals, USD 25). Ed(s): Eugene C Hargrove. Environmental Philosophy, Inc., Center for Environmental Philosophy, University of North Texas, Box 310980, Denton, TX 76203-0980; http://www.cep.unt.edu. Illus., index, adv. Refereed. Circ: 1900. Vol. ends: Winter. Microform: PQC. Online: Gale Group. Reprint: PQC; WSH. *Indexed:* ArtHuCI, BiolAb, EnvAb, ExcerpMed, GSI, HumInd, IPB, PSA, PhilInd, R&TA, RI-1, SSCI, SWRA, ZooRec. *Bk. rev.:* Number and length vary. *Aud.:* Ac.

Environmental Ethics is "an interdisciplinary journal dedicated to the philosophical aspects of environmental problems." It includes both normative and critical examinations of such topics as environmental justice, environmental stewardship, and environmental sustainability.

Environmental Health Perspectives. See Government Periodicals—Federal section.

Environmental History. See Forestry section.

2738. ***Environmental Protection: management and problem-solving for environmental professionals.*** [ISSN: 1057-4298] 1990. m. USD 99 domestic; USD 124 in Canada & Mexico; USD 134 elsewhere. Ed(s): Angela Neville. Stevens Publishing Corp., 5151 Beltline Rd, 10th fl, Dallas, TX 75240. Illus., index, adv. Circ: 96000. Vol. ends: Dec. *Indexed:* BPI, EnvAb, GeoRef, H&SSA, PollutAb, SWRA. *Aud.:* Sa.

Environmental Protection is an industry-focused magazine dealing with environmental regulation, compliance, and remediation. Filled with ads for chemical detection and treatment hardware, this publication contains articles that will help environmental officers and consultants deal with environmental problems (and occasionally protect the environment) while maintaining the bottom line. Each issue also contains letters, news, and columns on business trends and being an environmental manager.

2739. ***Environmental Science and Policy.*** [ISSN: 1462-9011] 1998. bi-m. EUR 597. Ed(s): Dr. J. C. Briden. Elsevier Inc., 360 Park Ave. S, New York, NY 10010-1710; usinfo-f@elsevier.com; http://www.elsevier.com. Illus. Sample. Refereed. Online: ingenta.com; ScienceDirect; Swets Blackwell. *Indexed:* ExcerpMed, GeoRef, PollutAb, WRCInf. *Aud.:* Ac.

Environmental Science and Policy is a broadly interdisciplinary scholarly journal on "environmental issues such as climate change, biodiversity, environmental pollution and wastes, renewable and non-renewable natural resources, and the interactions between these issues." Includes social science approaches.

Ethics, Place and Environment. See Geography section.

2740. ***Everyone's Backyard.*** Incorporates (1983-1990): *Action Bulletin.* [ISSN: 0749-3940] 1982. q. USD 35. Ed(s): Patty Lovera. Center for Health, Environment, and Justice, Marcoin Building, 150 South Washington St, Ste 300, Falls Church, VA 22046-6806; cchw@essential.org; http://www.essential.org/cchw; www.sustain.org/hcwh. Illus., adv. Circ: 6000. *Bk. rev.:* Number and length vary. *Aud.:* Hs, Ga.

Everyone's Backyard is the quarterly newsletter of the Center for Health, Environment, and Justice (CHEJ), a nonprofit group that offers technical help to neighborhoods and communities organizing grassroots environmental or public health campaigns. CHEJ grew out of the local response to the contamination of Love Canal in upstate New York, and it aims to help new groups have effective meetings, raise money, plan, communicate, and work with reporters and scientists. *Everyone's Backyard* contains case studies and practical tips on how to do these things, as well as book reviews and local environmental news from around the country. This magazine also has briefings about ongoing CHEJ campaigns on dioxin and making schools and childcare facilities safe from toxics. Recommended for public libraries in all communities, not just those with documented histories of environmental contamination.

2741. ***Friends of the Earth.*** Formerly (until Sep. 1990): *Not Man Apart.* [ISSN: 1054-1829] 1970. bi-m. USD 25. Ed(s): Dena Leibman. Friends of the Earth, 1025 Vermont Ave, N W, Ste 300, Washington, DC 20005. Illus., adv. Sample. Circ: 10000. *Indexed:* AltPI, EnvAb. *Aud.:* Ga.

Friends of the Earth newsmagazine is published by the environmental advocacy group of the same name. Each issue contains articles on local and international environmental actions and specific examples of the impacts of environmental pressures such as global warming. "On the Hill" reports on U.S. congressional activity. Most articles contain links to more information on the web, often at Friends of the Earth's own site.

2742. ***Global Change NewsLetter.*** [ISSN: 0284-5865] 1989. q. Free. Ed(s): Clare Bradshaw. Royal Swedish Academy of Science, International Geosphere-Biosphere Programme, IGBP Secretariat, Box 50005, Stockholm, 10405, Sweden; sec@igbp.kva.se; http://www.igbp.kva.se/. Illus. Circ: 10000 Controlled. *Indexed:* GeoRef. *Aud.:* Ac, Sa.

Global Change NewsLetter is a free color publication of the International Geosphere-Biosphere Programme (IGBP), an international research program "for the study of global change." This is a technical publication that aims to appeal to the broad range of global-change research disciplines. The focus is on IGBP research projects, meetings, and people. A calendar lists a wide range of global-change meetings and links readers to the web of global-change research organizations.

2743. ***Global Environmental Change Part B: Environmental Hazards: human and policy dimensions.*** Supersedes in part (in 1999): *Global Environmental Change.* [ISSN: 1464-2867] 1990. q. EUR 257 (Individuals, EUR 70). Ed(s): Dr. J. K. Mitchell, S. L. Cutter. Pergamon, The Boulevard, Langford Ln, East Park, Kidlington, OX5 1GB, United Kingdom. *Indexed:* ForAb, H&SSA, M&GPA, OceAb, PollutAb, S&F, SWA, SWRA, WAE&RSA. *Aud.:* Ac, Sa.

Environmental Hazards is an interdisciplinary and international peer-reviewed journal dedicated to "addressing the human and policy dimensions of hazards." Hazards covered include extreme "natural" events from earthquakes to epidemics and "technological failures and malfunctions" including fires and toxic releases. The emphasis on human and policy dimensions means that the journal focuses on rigorous studies of the social science of hazards and not exclusively on the physical and engineering parameters. This includes policy choices and other actions that cause people to be put in harm's way, the impacts of hazards on people, the differential vulnerability of certain groups, and the personal, emergency-management, and policy responses in reaction to hazardous events. The journal has a distinguished international board that includes geographers, anthropologists, and other social scientists, as well as experts from both governmental and nongovernmental organizations. Although it is relatively new, *Environmental Hazards* is poised to become a preeminent journal for "specialists from a wide range of fields who are interested in the effects of hazard events on people, property, and societies." The journal forms Part B of *Global Environmental Change*. Appropriate for academic libraries and special libraries with an interest in environmental or disaster policy.

2744. ***Green Teacher: education for planet earth.*** [ISSN: 1192-1285] 1991. q. CND 28 domestic; USD 24 United States; CND 40 rest of world. Ed(s): Tim Grant, Gail Littlejohn. Green Teacher, 95 Robert St, Toronto, ON M5S 2K5, Canada; greentea@web.net; http://www.web.net/~greentea/. Illus., adv. Sample. Circ: 6800. *Indexed:* CEI, CIJE, CPerI, EnvAb. *Aud.:* Ga, Ac.

Green Teacher is a great resource for educators, covering student populations of all school ages. Not only will traditional environmental and science educators like this illustrated publication, but also teachers of language (recent stories on nature journals and environmental literature), physical education (tracking and stalking), social sciences (ethnobotanical gardens), and integrated curricula (environmental entrepreneurship). Each issue is chock full of teaching tips, projects, activities, and readings. Also look for book reviews, Internet reviews, workshop announcements, and a listing of summer institutes for teachers. Highly recommended for elementary through high school teachers' lounges as well as educators' libraries.

2745. ***Harvard Environmental Law Review.*** [ISSN: 0147-8257] 1976. 2x/yr. USD 30 domestic; USD 38 Canada; USD 36 elsewhere. Harvard University, Law School, Publications Center, Hastings Hall, Cambridge, MA 02138; hlselr@law.harvard.edu; http://www.law.harvard.edu/studorgs/envir_law_rev/. Illus. Refereed. Circ: 1000. Microform: WSH; PMC. Online: Gale Group; LexisNexis; OCLC Online Computer Library Center, Inc.; West Group; H.W. Wilson. Reprint: WSH. *Indexed:* ABS&EES, ArtHuCI, CLI, DSR&OA, EnvAb, ILP, LRI, OceAb, PAIS, PollutAb, RI-1, SSCI, SUSA, SWRA. *Aud.:* Ac, Sa.

Harvard Environmental Law Review is a general environmental law journal containing articles on topics such as pollution, waste, the Endangered Species Act, water rights, property rights and land use, environmental regulation, and environmental legal procedure. It contains summaries of recent cases and "Notes" from Harvard law students.

2746. ***Human Ecology (New York): an interdisciplinary journal.*** [ISSN: 0300-7839] 1972. 6x/yr. USD 806 print or online ed. Ed(s): Daniel G Bates. Kluwer Academic / Plenum Publishers, 233 Spring St Fl 7, New York, NY 10013-1522; http://www.wkap.nl/. Illus., index, adv. Refereed. Online: EBSCO Publishing; Florida Center for Library Automation; Gale Group; ingenta.com; OCLC Online Computer Library Center, Inc.; Ovid Technologies, Inc.; ProQuest Information & Learning; RoweCom Information Quest; Swets Blackwell. *Indexed:* AICP, AbAn, Agr, AnthLit, ApEcolAb, BAS, BiolAb, DSA, DSR&OA, EngInd, ExcerpMed, FPA, ForAb, GeogAbPG, HortAb, IMFL, IndVet, PRA, PSA, PsycholAb, RRTA, S&F, SSCI, SSI, SUSA, SWA, SociolAb, VetBull, WAE&RSA, ZooRec. *Bk. rev.:* Number and length vary. *Aud.:* Ac, Sa.

Human Ecology is an important academic anthropology journal that is also favored by geographers and other social scientists interested in cultural and political ecology, the study of the interplay between ecosystems, cultures, and power over time and space. Articles tend to examine the present developing world, although more-developed areas and deeper historical cases are also included. A recent issue highlights the evolving use by researchers of geographic information systems and remote sensing. Producer (often subsistence) occupations such as farming, herding, and forest use feature prominently, as do the phenomena of intensification, extensification, mobility, and other coping strategies within and around land-use systems that are institutionally and biophysically constrained.

2747. ***International Journal of Mass Emergencies and Disasters.*** [ISSN: 0280-7270] 1983. 3x/yr. Institutional members, USD 48; Individual members, USD 45; Students, USD 20. Ed(s): Ronald Perry, Maureen Fordham. International Research Committee on Disasters, PO Box 425557, Women s Studies Program, Denton, TX 76204; brenda@jsucc.jsu.edu; http://www.udel.edu/drc/ircd. Adv. Refereed. *Indexed:* GeogAbPG, PSA, SociolAb. *Bk. rev.:* Number and length vary. *Aud.:* Ga, Ac, Sa.

International Journal of Mass Emergencies and Disasters is the peer-reviewed academic and professional journal of the International Sociological Association's International Research Committee on Disasters. Although sponsored by this association, the journal seeks research from all disciplines on the social and behavioral aspects of preparing for and coping with "natural," technological, and conflict-induced disasters. Recent issues include articles on the Newfoundland response to flights diverted on September 11, 2001, and divergent British and American pilot responses to safety issues surrounding secured cockpit doors, as well as more-traditional articles on hurricanes and other environmental hazards. This journal should be a core publication for emergency management and security professionals who might not otherwise have access to scientific information on the human side of disasters.

2748. ***Journal of Contingencies and Crisis Management.*** [ISSN: 0966-0879] 1993. q. USD 449 print & online eds. Ed(s): Uriel Rosenthal, Alexander Kouzmin. Blackwell Publishing Ltd., 9600 Garsington Rd, PO Box 805, Oxford, OX4 2DQ, United Kingdom; customerservices@oxon.blackwellpublishing.com; http://www.blackwellpublishing.com/. Refereed. Online: EBSCO Publishing; ingenta.com; OCLC Online Computer Library Center, Inc.; RoweCom Information Quest; Swets Blackwell. Reprint: SWZ. *Indexed:* GeogAbPG, H&SSA, IBSS, IPSA, PSA, RiskAb, SociolAb. *Bk. rev.:* Number and length vary. *Aud.:* Ac, Sa.

Journal of Contingencies and Crisis Management approaches natural, technogical, and conflict-based disasters from the perspective of the manager, and it attempts to integrate insights from all three types.

Journal of Environmental Economics and Management. See Economics section.

The Journal of Environmental Education. See Education/Subjects and Teaching Methods: Environmental Education section.

2749. ***Journal of Environmental Health.*** [ISSN: 0022-0892] 1938. 10x/yr. USD 90 (Membership, USD 75). Ed(s): Nelson Fabian. National Environmental Health Association, 720 S Colorado Blvd, S Tower, Ste 970, Denver, CO 80246; staff@neha.org; http://www.neha.org. Illus., adv. Refereed. Circ: 6000 Paid. Microform: PQC. Online: bigchalk; EBSCO Publishing; Florida Center for Library Automation; Gale Group; Northern Light Technology, Inc.; OCLC Online Computer Library

Center, Inc.; ProQuest Information & Learning; H.W. Wilson. *Indexed:* AS&TI, BiolAb, C&ISA, CIJE, CINAHL, ChemAb, DSA, EnvAb, ExcerpMed, FS&TA, GSI, GeoRef, GeogAbPG, H&SSA, IndMed, IndVet, PollutAb, RRTA, S&F, SCI, SSCI, SWRA, VetBull, WAE&RSA. *Aud.:* Ac, Sa.

Journal of Environmental Health is a magazine for professionals in the public health field. Topics run from bacteria to behavior to bioterror. Published by the National Environmental Health Association, the journal is split between peer-reviewed technical articles, columns, and news departments such as reviews, technical briefs, and legal case studies.

2750. *Journal of Environmental Systems.* [ISSN: 0047-2433] 1971. q. USD 237. Ed(s): Sheldon Reaven. Baywood Publishing Co., Inc., 26 Austin Ave, Amityville, NY 11701; info@baywood.com; http://www.baywood.com. Illus., adv. Sample. Refereed. *Indexed:* BiolAb, C&ISA, EngInd, EnvAb, ExcerpMed, GeoRef, M&GPA, PRA, PollutAb, SSCI, SUSA, SWRA. *Aud.:* Ac, Sa.

Environmental Systems is a peer-reviewed technical journal on "the often complex ecological, biological, and physical interactions that characterize environmental problems, and to the energy, economic, engineering, institutional, value, and policy systems involved." Most authors published here take a heavily statistical approach. Topics from recent issues include indoor air quality, ecological footprinting, environmental attitudes, oil spills, landfill leachate, and policy processes. Despite the range of topics, the highly technical approach makes this publication inappropriate for a general audience.

2751. *Land Letter: the newsletter for natural resource professionals.* [ISSN: 0890-7625] 1982. fortn. USD 345. Ed(s): Kevin Braun. Environmental and Energy Publishing, LLC, 122 C St, N W, Ste 722, Washington, DC 20001; pubs@eenews.net; http://www.eenews.net. Adv. Online: LexisNexis. *Aud.:* Hs, Ga, Ac, Sa.

Land Letter is a weekly news service covering natural resources, federal lands, and land management policy. From the Bureau of Reclamation to the Forest Service, *Land Letter* does for resources what its sister publications *Greenwire* and *E & E Daily* do for environmental policy and the Congress.

2752. *Liaison for Civil-Military Humanitarian Relief Collaborations.* [ISSN: 1527-7208] 1999. s-a. Ed(s): Robin Hyden. Center of Excellence in Disaster Management & Humanitarian Assistance, Tripler Army Medical Center, 1 Jarrett White Rd (MCPA-DM), Tripler AMC, HI 96859-5000; education@coe-dmha.org; http://coe-dmha.org/index.htm. *Bk. rev.:* Number and length vary. *Aud.:* Sa.

Liaison is an interesting and relatively new publication devoted to military-civilian interactions in humanitarian relief operations, and it is of obvious import to current affairs. It is published by the Center of Excellence in Disaster Management and Humanitarian Assistance (CEDMHA), a civilian- and military-staffed education, training, research, and information coordinating unit of the U.S. military. The magazine publishes training opportunities, information on publicly available educational packages, letters, acronyms, book reviews, interviews, conference reports, and feature articles. Recent topics include CEDMHA leaders, recovery from terror incidents, post-conflict reconstruction, civil-military relations, and relief operations adjunct to military operations. *Liaison* is a glossy publication with lots of photos, but it could greatly benefit from a simpler and more unified layout that would make it easier to read. It could also benefit from more information on the masthead about CEDMHA and its funders. According to its web site (www.coe-dmha.org/faqs.htm), the center, located at Tripler Army Medical Center in Honolulu, reports to the U.S. Commander-in-Chief Pacific and has been funded by the U.S. Navy, the Department of State, the Department of Health and Human Services, and the Department of Defense, among others. This publication would be of interest to special libraries covering domestic security, disaster management, international relations, and international development.

2753. *Local Environment.* [ISSN: 1354-9839] 1996. bi-m. GBP 288 (Individuals, GBP 75). Carfax Publishing Ltd., 4 Park Sq, Milton Park, Abingdon, OX14 4RN, United Kingdom; enquiry@tandf.co.uk; http://www.tandf.co.uk/. Refereed. Online: EBSCO Publishing; Ingenta Select; OCLC Online Computer Library Center, Inc.; RoweCom Information Quest; Swets Blackwell. Reprint: PSC. *Indexed:* EnvAb, GeogAbPG, IBSS, IBZ, PollutAb. *Aud.:* Ac, Sa.

Local Environment is an up-and-coming academic journal on the local facets of sustainability as components of problem solving at larger scales. It applies the insights of scholars and practitioners to practical problems. This publication is environmental in the better and broader sense: It includes economic and social as well as ecosystem sustainability. The journal is sponsored by the International Council for Local Environmental Initiatives, an international environmental agency for local governments.

2754. *Mother Earth News: the original guide to living wisely.* [ISSN: 0027-1535] 1970. bi-m. USD 12.95 domestic; USD 2.95 Canada; USD 24.95 elsewhere. Ed(s): Cheryl Long. Ogden Publications, 1503 S W 42nd St, Topeka, KS 66609-1265. Illus., index, adv. Sample. Circ: 375000. Microform: NBI; PQC. Online: bigchalk; EBSCO Publishing; Florida Center for Library Automation; Gale Group; Northern Light Technology, Inc.; OCLC Online Computer Library Center, Inc.; ProQuest Information & Learning; H.W. Wilson. *Indexed:* ASIP, CPerI, ConsI, GardL, IHTDI, MagInd, RGPR. *Aud.:* Hs, Ga.

Mother Earth News provides users with tips on how to live in an environmentally sustainable and self-reliant way. Solar, wind, and wood power feature prominently, as do building projects and gardening. Septic system care, composting toilets, and other alternatives are options for those who want to manage waste "off-grid."

National Wetlands Newsletter. See Marine Science and Technology section.

2755. *National Wildlife: dedicated to the conservation of our nation's natural resources.* [ISSN: 0028-0402] 1962. bi-m. Membership, USD 20. National Wildlife Federation, 11100 Wildlife Center Dr., Reston, VA 20190-5362; pubs@nwf.org; http://www.nwf.org. Illus., index, adv. Circ: 550000. Vol. ends: Oct/Nov. Microform: NBI; PQC. Online: bigchalk; EBSCO Publishing; Florida Center for Library Automation; Gale Group; Northern Light Technology, Inc.; OCLC Online Computer Library Center, Inc.; ProQuest Information & Learning; H.W. Wilson. Reprint: PQC. *Indexed:* BiolAb, BiolDig, CIJE, CPerI, EnvAb, GSI, ICM, MagInd, PollutAb, RGPR, RI-1, SSI, SWRA. *Aud.:* Hs, Ga.

National Wildlife covers animals, as its title would suggest. The standout feature of this magazine is its gorgeous photographs of critters of all shapes and sizes. Articles describe animal behavior, threats to animals, and the work of those who study or manage them. Editorials, letters, consumer information, news, health, and activism opportunities round out this publication.

2756. *Natural Hazards Observer.* [ISSN: 0193-8355] 1976. bi-m. USD 15 foreign. Ed(s): Sylvia C Dane. University of Colorado, Natural Hazards Center, Campus Box 482, Boulder, CO 80309; hazctr@colorado.edu; http://www.colorado.edu/hazards. Illus. Circ: 400 Paid. *Indexed:* EnvAb, GeoRef. *Aud.:* Ga, Ac, Sa.

Natural Hazards Observer is an indispensable source of information on natural and technological hazards, especially for those interested in human impacts, preparation, and response. Published by the largely federally funded Hazards Center at the University of Colorado, the *Observer* contains invited columns on current issues from floods to terror from insiders in the emergency planning profession. Each issue also includes a "Washington Update," lists of recently awarded grants and contracts, educational opportunities, and annotated bibliographies of web sites and recent publications sorted by subject. Simply designed and packed with illustrations by cartoonist Rob Pudim, *Natural Hazards Observer* is a pleasure to read and an outstanding value. Academic, government, and public libraries, particularly those in hazard-prone or high-threat areas, should rush to get this publication.

2757. *Natural Hazards Review.* [ISSN: 1527-6988] q. Members, USD 50; Non-members, USD 75. Ed(s): James E Beavers, Dennis S Mileti. American Society of Civil Engineers, 1801 Alexander Graham Bell Dr, Reston, VA 20191-4400; http://www.pubs.asce.org. Refereed. *Indexed:* C&ISA, H&SSA, RiskAb. *Bk. rev.:* Various number and length. *Aud.:* Ac, Sa.

Natural Hazards Review attempts to integrate physical science, social science, engineering, economic, and policy perspectives on disasters, including floods, earthquakes, and others. Topics include hazard mitigation and human response, land use, building design, building codes, and insurance. The journal makes important use of maps as tools to understand disasters. Published by the American Society of Civil Engineers in association with the Hazards Center at the University of Colorado at Boulder, this journal is peer-reviewed and includes book reviews.

2758. *Nature Conservancy.* Former titles (until 1990): *Nature Conservancy Magazine;* (until 1987): *Nature Conservancy News.* [ISSN: 1540-2428] 1951. q. Members, USD 50. Ed(s): Ron Geatz. Nature Conservancy, 4245 N Fairfax Dr 100, Arlington, VA 22203-1606; comment@tnc.org; http://www.tnc.org/. Illus., adv. Circ: 1000000. *Indexed:* BiolDig, EnvAb, GSI, GardL, GeoRef. *Bk. rev.:* Various number and length. *Aud.:* Hs, Ga.

The Nature Conservancy aims to protect acreage from environmental degradation. *Nature Conservancy* informs readers about important habitats and "great places." Full of lavish color photographs, ecotourism articles, and articles that would be travel articles with the addition of information on hotels and transportation, the magazine will appeal to both those who want to see nature and those who want to see pictures of nature. Deforestation, war, and overfishing are featured in recent topical articles. Book reviews, interviews, and supporter's profiles (Raffi, Dave Matthews Band) are included.

The Public Eye. See Women: Feminist and Special Interest/Feminist and Women's Studies section.

Ranger Rick. See Children section.

2759. *Wildlife Society Bulletin: perspectives on wildlife conservation and sustainable use.* [ISSN: 0091-7648] 1973. q. USD 110. Ed(s): Warren Ballard. The Wildlife Society, 5410 Grosvenor Ln, Ste 200, Bethesda, MD 20814; tws@wildlife.org; http://www.wildlife.org. Illus., index, adv. Refereed. Circ: 6400. Vol. ends: Winter. Reprint: PQC. *Indexed:* Agr, ApEcolAb, BiolAb, CAPS, ExcerpMed, FPA, ForAb, GSI, GeogAbPG, HortAb, IndVet, PollutAb, RRTA, S&F, SCI, SSCI, SWRA, VetBull, WAE&RSA, ZooRec. *Bk. rev.:* Various number and length. *Aud.:* Ga, Ac, Sa.

Wildlife Society Bulletin is a peer-reviewed research publication for wildlife managers and scholars. It carries articles on the interactions between people and habitat ("Anthropogenic Influences," "Human Dimensions") and ways to keep track of wildlife ("Techniques and Technologies," "Population Monitoring"). Other sections include physiology, waterfowl, trapping, endangered species, and statistical modeling. In addition to reviewed articles and book reviews, this publication also carries many of the features of a newsletter, including opinion pieces, regular columns, news, and lots of black-and-white photographs.

2760. *World Watch: working for a sustainable future.* [ISSN: 0896-0615] 1988. bi-m. USD 25 in North America; USD 40 elsewhere. Worldwatch Institute, 1776 Massachusetts Ave, N W, Washington, DC 20036; wwpub@worldwatch.org; http://www.worldwatch.org. Illus., index. Circ: 24000. Vol. ends: Nov/Dec. Microform: PQC. Online: bigchalk; EBSCO Publishing; Florida Center for Library Automation; Gale Group; Northern Light Technology, Inc.; OCLC Online Computer Library Center, Inc.; ProQuest Information & Learning; H.W. Wilson. *Indexed:* ABS&EES, CIJE, EnvAb, GSI, GeogAbPG, M&GPA, PAIS, RiskAb, SSCI, SSI, SWA. *Aud.:* Hs, Ga, Ac.

World Watch is a magazine published by the Worldwatch Institute, an organization dedicated to finding practical solutions to achieve an "environmentally sustainable and socially just society." Solutions are expected to come from technology, innovations in economics, and indigenous knowledge. Each issue includes feature articles (e.g., soldiers and AIDS, factory farming, biodiversity) and departments including letters, editorials, interviews, news, and book reviews. The magazine accepts no advertising; rather, it depends on foundation grants in order to publish.

Electronic Journals

2761. *Backyard Wildlife Habitat.* 1997. q. National Wildlife Federation, 11100 Wildlife Center Dr., Reston, VA 20190-5362; http://www.nwf.org/habitats/index.html. *Aud.:* Em, Hs, Ga.

Backyard Wildlife Habitat is a service of the National Wildlife Federation. This web site provides homeowners with information on how to bring nature back into the built landscape. *BWH* is a rich resource, with information on native plants and animals, networking and training on native gardening and landscaping, and how to get started. Users may log in for access to an online habitat planner. Still, there is room for improvement. When the site was reviewed in June for this edition, the regional sub-sites were still instructing users to "winterize your habitat." Regional sub-sites could use a finer level of granularity and easier searching, especially when looking for local native species. The site would also benefit from still more links to other related sites, especially those with a regional focus.

2762. *Conservation Ecology.* [ISSN: 1195-5449] 1997. 2x/yr. Free. Ed(s): Shealagh Pope. The Resilience Alliance, c/o Phil Taylor, Biology Dept., Acadia Univ., Wolfville, NS B0P 1X0, Canada; questions@consecol.org; http://www.consecol.org. Illus. Refereed. *Indexed:* ApEcolAb, BiolAb, PAIS, SWRA, ZooRec. *Bk. rev.:* Number and length vary. *Aud.:* Ac, Sa.

This is an exciting, peer-reviewed academic and professional journal that takes substantial advantage of its online format. Drawing on the vision of its esteemed founding editor, C. S. "Buzz" Holling, *Conservation Ecology* goes farthest among academic environmental publications in creating an online community of scholarly interchange. Authors include both biologists and social scientists. While articles are a mix of the technical and more readable, the "Discussion" session is highly democratic in that it allows readers to submit comments for publication. The journal also includes a useful classifieds section, which includes positions available, conferences, and announcements. One small fault is the lack of page numbers, even in the pdf versions, which makes precise citation difficult.

2763. *Electronic Green Journal.* Formerly (until 1994): *Green Library Journal.* [ISSN: 1076-7975] 1992. irreg. Free. Ed(s): Maria Anna Jankowska. University of Idaho Library, University of Idaho Library, Rayburn St, Moscow, ID 83844-2350; majordomo@uidaho.edu; http://egj.lib.uidaho.edu. Illus. Refereed. Circ: 20000 Controlled. *Indexed:* BRI, CBRI, CIJE, EnvAb, GSI, PAIS, PollutAb, ZooRec. *Bk. rev.:* Number and length vary. *Aud.:* Ga, Ac, Sa.

Electronic Green Journal is a peer-reviewed publication covering a wide range of international and regional environmental topics for researchers, professionals, and the interested public. It contains articles, opinion pieces, and reviews. The book review section is extensive for a journal and should be useful for those interested in building environmental collections.

2764. *Environment and Energy Daily.* Former titles: *Environment and Energy Weekly; U.S. Congress. Environmental and Energy Study Conference. Weekly Bulletin; Environmental and Energy Study Institute. Weekly Bulletin.* [ISSN: 1540-7896] 1975. d. while Congress is in session. USD 995. Ed(s): Kevin Braun. Environmental and Energy Publishing, LLC, 122 C St, N W, Ste 722, Washington, DC 20001; pubs@eenews.net. *Aud.:* Hs, Ga, Ac, Sa.

Appropriations and reauthorizations and hearings, oh my! *Environment and Energy Daily* provides these and more—a comprehensive online news source for Congress and the environment. From fuel economy to the Endangered Species Act, *E & E Daily* provides (yes) daily coverage of Congress's environmental maneuverings. This service complements house.gov and senate.gov because it provides the analysis and background that the Congressional web sites do not. "Committee Calendar," "Legislative Status," a story archive, and selected key documents are included.

2765. ***Environment Matters (Online).*** [ISSN: 1564-5878] World Bank Publications, 1818 H St, NW, Washington, DC 20433; http://www-esd.worldbank.org/envmat/. *Aud.:* Ga, Ac.

Environment Matters is an annual report of the World Bank, articulating the bank's assessments of global environmental needs and its approaches to environmental problems. Includes regional reviews and a list of selected available World Bank publications.

2766. ***Global Pesticide Campaigner.*** [ISSN: 1055-548X] 1990. q. USD 50 (Individuals, USD 25; Corporations, USD 100). Ed(s): Ellen Hickey. Pesticide Action Network, North America Regional Center, 49 Powell St, 500, San Francisco, CA 94102-2811; panna@panna.org; http://www.panna.org/panna. Illus. Circ: 1800. *Indexed:* AltPI. *Aud.:* Hs, Ga, Ac.

Global Pesticide Campaigner is the newsletter of the Pesticide Action Network North America. From an activist perspective, it dispenses detailed information on pesticides and genetically modified crops, the negative aspects of their effects, and their regulation. It contains domestic and international case studies, and sources are well cited.

2767. ***Greenwire.*** Former titles: *Environment and Energy Newsline; Environment and Energy Update.* [ISSN: 1540-787X] 1997. d. USD 1795 includes special reports. Ed(s): Kevin Braun. Environmental and Energy Publishing, LLC, 122 C St, N W, Ste 722, Washington, DC 20001; pubs@eenews.net. Online: Factiva; LexisNexis. *Aud.:* Hs, Ga, Ac, Sa.

Greenwire covers environment and energy policy, focusing on the national but covering many major international and state issues as well. This thorough online environmental daily includes access to a story archive, text of environmental laws, selected documents, and detailed special reports. Available also as an e-mail digest.

2768. ***Linkages.*** irreg. Free. International Institute for Sustainable Development, 161 Portage Ave. E., 6th Fl., Winnipeg, MB R3B 0Y4, Canada; info@iisd.ca; http://www.iisd.org. *Aud.:* Hs, Ga, Ac, Sa.

The online version of the *Earth Negotiations Bulletin* newspaper started at the Rio Earth Summit, *Linkages* is the leading reporter of meetings related to international environmental governance. In addition to more traditional environmental topics, *Linkages* covers "sustainable development," "human development," and "intergovernmental organizations."

■ ETHNIC STUDIES

Philip C. Howze, Social Sciences Librarian, Library Affairs, Morris Library 6632, Southern Illinois University–Carbondale, Carbondale, IL 62901-6632; phowze@lib.siu.edu; FAX: 618-453-3440

Introduction

The ability to educate oneself about specific ethnic groups, as well as social interaction in pluralistic societies, is no longer elusive. Serial publications in the area of ethnic studies range from magazines to scholarly journals. Ethnic studies is growing as a course of study, and a number of universities offer degrees in the study of ethnology. According to the *Diversity Dictionary*, ethnicity is "a quality assigned to a specific group of people historically connected by a common national origin or language. Ethnic classification is used for identification rather than differentiation." All things in the social/sociological vein are of concern to diverse ethnic groups, particularly in light of a consistently predicted decline in non-Hispanic whites as the dominant component of the U.S. population. Ethnic peoples have numerous issues, including migration, conflict and its resolution, marriage and other rites of passage, and child-rearing practices. Ethnic interests also include the teaching and preservation, through continued study and recording, of group history, archaeology, and anthropology, as well as of group language/linguistics, art, and dance. Ethnic peoples are often mobile in their search for integration. Migration is often accompanied by conflict, including racism and discrimination. Ethnic concerns, then, include assimilation or acculturation and whether one (or the other) shall be forced, induced, or voluntary (*Britannica Online*, see "Ethnic Group").

When selecting magazines for libraries, sensitivity to ethnic concerns and interests can be of great comfort to diverse groups within a community. Although many of the serials devoted to ethnic interests tend to be refereed journals of high scholarship, a sufficient number of magazines are available for the general-interest reader, including *Interracial Voice* (see Zines/Electronic Journals section) and *Migration News*.

Basic Periodicals

Ems, Hs: *Multicultural Review;* Ga: *Migration World;* Ac: *Ethnic and Racial Studies, Journal of Intercultural Studies.*

Basic Abstracts and Indexes

America History and Life, Historical Abstracts, Social Sciences Index, Sociological Abstracts.

Canadian Ethnic Studies. See Canada section.

2769. ***Ethnic and Racial Studies.*** [ISSN: 0141-9870] 1978. bi-m. GBP 202 (Individuals, GBP 63). Ed(s): Martin Bulmer. Routledge, 11 New Fetter Ln, London, EC4P 4EE, United Kingdom. Illus., index, adv. Sample. Refereed. Circ: 1550. Vol. ends: Oct. Online: EBSCO Publishing; Gale Group; Ingenta Select; RoweCom Information Quest; Swets Blackwell. Reprint: PSC. *Indexed:* ABCPolSci, AICP, ASSIA, AbAn, AmH&L, BAS, BRI, CBRI, CJA, CWI, IBSS, IBZ, IIBP, IPSA, PRA, PSA, RI-1, SSCI, SSI, SWR&A, SociolAb. *Bk. rev.:* 11-30, 500-1,000 words. *Aud.:* Ac.

This prestigious, peer-reviewed journal has an international audience. It includes works of sociological, economic, and political scholarship and commentary by prominent researchers on matters related to race and ethnicity. Review articles and book reviews are also included. This journal title can be found in numerous indexing and abstracting sources. Highly recommended for academic and research libraries.

Ethnic Groups. See *Identities: global studies in culture and power.*

2770. ***Ethnic Studies Review: ethnicity, family, and community.*** 2x/yr. Ed(s): Miguel A Carranza. National Association for Ethnic Studies (NAES), Arizona State University, Department of English, Tempe, AZ 85287-0302. *Indexed:* BAS. *Aud.:* Hs, Ac.

This scholarly journal publishes feature articles that are sociological in nature. Empirical and qualitative articles on the family, community, and cultural habits of ethnic people are studied. The journal also includes research notes, essays, and book reviews. Highly recommended for academic libraries and scholarly research centers.

2771. ***Ethnohistory: a quarterly journal relating to the past of culture and societies in all areas of the world.*** [ISSN: 0014-1801] 1954. q. USD 99 includes online access (Individuals, USD 35 includes online access; USD 25 per issue). Ed(s): Neil L Whitehead. Duke University Press, 905 W Main St, Ste 18 B, Durham, NC 27701; subscriptions@dukeupress.edu; http://www.dukeupress.edu. Illus., adv. Refereed. Circ: 1500. Vol. ends: Winter. Microform: PQC. Online: bigchalk; EBSCO Publishing; Gale Group; Ingenta Select; JSTOR (Web-based Journal Archive); Northern Light Technology, Inc.; OCLC Online Computer Library Center, Inc.; Project MUSE; ProQuest Information & Learning; RoweCom Information Quest; Swets Blackwell. Reprint: PSC; SCH. *Indexed:* ABS&EES, AICP, AbAn, AmH&L, AnthLit, ArtHuCI, BAS, BrArAb, HumInd, PRA, PSA, RI-1, SSCI, SSI, SociolAb. *Bk. rev.:* 12-27, 800-1,200 words. *Aud.:* Ac.

Articles in this scholarly journal tend to share a common theme, each treated by a different discipline, culminating in a nice merger between social sciences and humanities perspectives. Contributors are not casual; they have substantial backgrounds in ethnohistory, and it is not uncommon to find the presentation and analysis of indigenous language as discussion. Review essays and book reviews are also published with each issue. Highly recommended for academic and research libraries.

Ethnology. See Anthropology section.

2772. *Identities: global studies in culture and power.* Formerly (until 1994): *Ethnic Groups;* Incorporates: *Afro-American Studies.* [ISSN: 1070-289X] 1976. q. GBP 144 (Individuals, GBP 38). Ed(s): Jonathan D Hill. Taylor & Francis Ltd, 11 New Fetter Ln, London, EC4P 4EE, United Kingdom; info@tandf.co.uk; http://www.tandf.co.uk/. Illus., adv. Sample. Refereed. Online: EBSCO Publishing; Gale Group; OCLC Online Computer Library Center, Inc. Reprint: PSC. *Indexed:* ABS&EES, ASSIA, AbAn, AnthLit, IBSS, IBZ, IIBP, MLA-IB, SSCI, SSI, SWA, SociolAb. *Bk. rev.:* 4-5, length varies. *Aud.:* Ac.

Domination, resistance, and struggle, all constituent parts of power as they relate to race, class, and gender constitute the scope of this journal. The publication concerns itself with anthropological, economic, and political aspects of power and culture. Special thematic issues are published, as well as critical book reviews. Recommended for academic libraries.

2773. *International Migration Review: a quarterly studying sociological, demographic, economic, historical, and legislative aspects of human migration movements and ethnic group relations.* Formerly: *International Migration Digest.* [ISSN: 0197-9183] 1966. q. USD 81 (Individuals, USD 39). Ed(s): Lydio F Tomasi. Center for Migration Studies, 209 Flagg Pl, Staten Island, NY 10304-1122; http://www.cmsny.org/imr3.htm. Illus., index, adv. Refereed. Circ: 2300 Paid and free. Vol. ends: Winter. Microform: PQC. Online: Florida Center for Library Automation; Gale Group; JSTOR (Web-based Journal Archive); OCLC Online Computer Library Center, Inc.; ProQuest Information & Learning. Reprint: PQC; WSH. *Indexed:* ABS&EES, AICP, ASSIA, AbAn, AgeL, AmH&L, ArtHuCI, BAS, CIJE, HAPI, IBSS, IBZ, IMFL, LRI, PAIS, PRA, PSA, RI-1, RRTA, SFSA, SSCI, SSI, SUSA, SWA, SWR&A, SociolAb, WAE&RSA. *Bk. rev.:* 10-20, 500-1,000 words. *Aud.:* Ac.

The stated purpose of this scholarly journal is "to facilitate the study of social, demographic, historical, economic, legislative and pastoral aspects of human migration and refugee movements." It is not uncommon for some issues to present articles devoted to one topic (although manuscripts are invited). Book reviews, research notes, and conference reports are regularly featured. Highly recommended for academic libraries.

2774. *Journal of Ethnic and Migration Studies.* Former titles: *New Community;* (until 1971): *Community.* [ISSN: 1369-183X] bi-m. GBP 400 (Individuals, GBP 78). Ed(s): Malcolm Cross. Carfax Publishing Ltd., 4 Park Sq, Milton Park, Abingdon, OX14 4RN, United Kingdom; enquiry@tandf.co.uk; http://www.tandf.co.uk/. Online: EBSCO Publishing; Gale Group; Ingenta Select; RoweCom Information Quest. Reprint: PSC. *Indexed:* ASSIA, BrEdI, BrHumI, IPSA, PSA, RILM, SWA, SociolAb. *Bk. rev.:* 750 words. *Aud.:* Ac.

This scholarly journal presents research on a number of topics related to migration and cultural concerns from an international perspective. There is rigorous intellectual discussion on such topics as globalization, social polarization, and the political, economic, and social plight of immigrants around the world. Quality book reviews are also presented. Highly recommended for research-oriented and academic libraries.

2775. *Journal of Intercultural Studies.* Supersedes (in 1980): *Ethnic Studies.* [ISSN: 0725-6868] 1977. 3x/yr. GBP 196 (Individuals, GBP 72). Ed(s): Peter Lentini, Jan Van Bommel. Carfax Publishing Ltd., 4 Park Sq, Milton Park, Abingdon, OX14 4RN, United Kingdom; enquiry@tandf.co.uk; http://www.tandf.co.uk/. Illus., adv. Sample. Online: EBSCO Publishing; Florida Center for Library Automation; Gale Group; Ingenta Select; OCLC Online Computer Library Center, Inc.; RMIT Publishing; RoweCom Information Quest; Swets Blackwell. Reprint: PSC. *Indexed:* AICP, BrEdI, L&LBA, SWA, SociolAb. *Bk. rev.:* 15, 400 words. *Aud.:* Ga, Ac.

This scholarly journal, published twice a year, engages in debate and reflection on intercultural studies. One annual issue is thematic. Sample topics include multicultural citizenship and child-rearing values. Peer-reviewed articles are published, as well as theoretical papers and book reviews. It provides a forum for international research related to intercultural studies. Highly recommended for academic libraries.

Lilith. See Women: Feminist and Special Interest/Special Interest section.

MELUS. See Literature/General section.

Meridians. See Women: Feminist and Special Interest/Feminist and Women's Studies section.

2776. *Migration World.* Formerly: *Migration Today.* [ISSN: 1058-5095] 1973. 5x/yr. USD 50 (Individuals, USD 31). Center for Migration Studies, 209 Flagg Pl, Staten Island, NY 10304-1122; jfugolo@aol.com; http://www.cmsny.org/mw4.html. Illus., adv. Circ: 1800. Online: bigchalk; Florida Center for Library Automation; Gale Group; OCLC Online Computer Library Center, Inc.; ProQuest Information & Learning. *Indexed:* AbAn, CIJE, GeogAbPG, PAIS. *Bk. rev.:* Various number and length. *Aud.:* Hs, Ga, Ac.

A contemporary magazine devoted to the reporting of modern issues related to migration around the world. Laid out in a series of departments, this magazine presents discussion of such aspects of migration as religion, health, and law. The value of this magazine is that it compels the reader to want to learn more about the factual basis of migration and, related to it, the deplorable state of human rights around the world. Highly recommended for both public and academic libraries.

2777. *MultiCultural Review: dedicated to a better understanding of ethnic, racial and religious diversity.* Incorporates (1986-1992): *Journal of Multicultural Librarianship.* [ISSN: 1058-9236] 1992. q. USD 65 (Individuals, USD 29.95). Ed(s): Lyn Miller Lachmann. Greenwood Publishing Group Inc., 88 Post Rd W, PO Box 5007, Westport, CT 06881; http://www.greenwood.com/. Illus., index, adv. Sample. *Indexed:* ABS&EES, BRD, BRI, CBRI, CIJE, IBZ, MRD. *Bk. rev.:* 100, 200-500 words. *Aud.:* Hs, Ac.

An excellent reviewing tool designed to showcase and critique multicultural literature by grade level and by genre. This attractive source includes invited articles usually dealing with some aspect of diversity and librarianship. Its strength lies in the signed book reviews. Materials reviewed range from children's books to works of high fiction and drama for the adult reader. Highly recommended for public and academic libraries as well as teachers of multicultural audiences.

Race, Gender & Class. See Women: Feminist and Special Interest/Feminist and Women's Studies section.

Electronic Journals

Interracial Voice. See Zines/Electronic Journals section.

2778. *Migration News.* [ISSN: 1081-9908] 1994. m. USD 30 domestic; USD 50 foreign. Ed(s): Philip Martin. University of California at Davis, Department of Agricultural Economics, One Shields Ave, Davis, CA 95616; migrant@primal.ucdavis.edu; http://migration.ucdavis.edu. Illus. Circ: 2500. *Aud.:* Hs, Ga.

A current-awareness source for those interested in recent developments in migration. News items are presented, by continent, as well as other prominent topics related to migration. A good source for demographics as well as commentary on developing social issues. Recommended for both public and academic libraries.

■ EUROPE

General/Newspapers

See also CIS and Eastern Europe; and Latin American sections.

Sebastian Hierl, Bibliographer for English and Romance Literatures—The University of Chicago Library, JRL-363, Chicago, IL 60637; hierl@uchicago.edu

Introduction

A large and interdisciplinary section such as this is bound to be selective. The magazines, journals, newspapers, and electronic resources contained in this section focus on Western Europe, with the exclusion of Spain and Portugal. For information on Spanish and Portuguese titles, please see the Latin American section, which includes Iberian publications. For information on Eastern Europe, please see the CIS and Eastern Europe section.

This chapter aims at listing major publications that may be considered core titles for the field of European studies and for understanding European current events, economic and business trends, history, politics, and cultural events, with a focus on the arts and literature. The selection of these titles is based upon previous editions of *Magazines for Libraries* and upon recommendations by specialists in the field.

Basic Periodicals

Akzente, Central European History, L'Espresso, L'Express, Journal of European Studies, London Magazine, Magill, Merkur, La Nouvelle Revue Francaise, Scandinavian Review, Der Spiegel, Yale French Studies.

Basic Abstracts and Indexes

Annual Bibliography of English Language Literature, Arts and Humanities Citation Index, Bibliography of the History of Art, British Humanities Index, Current Contents, Francis, Humanities Index, IBZ, MLA International Bibliography, PAIS, RILM Abstracts of Music Literature, Zeitungs-Index.

General

2779. ***Airone.*** 1981. m. ITL 70000; ITL 160000 foreign. Ed(s): Nicoletta Salvatori. Editoriale Giorgio Mondadori SpA, Via Andrea Ponti, 8-10, Milan, 20143, Italy. Illus., adv. Circ: 100000. *Aud.:* Hs, Ga, Ac.

In Italian. *Airone* (Italian for "heron") is similar to *National Geographic* and *GEO*. Covering natural history, the environment, and civilization at large, *Airone* usually is comprised of six lengthy, in-depth articles and various shorter pieces. Like *National Geographic*, *Airone* derives its appeal from the combination of breathtaking photography with stories of adventure and travel. The primacy that the photographs take over the text make *Airone* a wonderful tool for beginners wishing to improve their knowledge of Italian while remaining in awe of the wonders of our world. Recommended for large public libraries.

2780. ***Akzente: Zeitschrift fuer Literatur.*** [ISSN: 0002-3957] 1954. bi-m. DEM 79.20 domestic; DEM 88.20 foreign. Ed(s): Michael Krueger. Carl Hanser Verlag, Kolbergerstr 22, Munich, 81679, Germany; info@hanser.de; http://www.hanser.de. Illus., index, adv. Sample. Circ: 3300. Reprint: SCH. *Indexed:* ArtHuCI, BHA, IBZ, MLA-IB, SSCI. *Aud.:* Ac.

In German. *Akzente* is a literary magazine steeped in tradition. First published as a poetry magazine, it now focuses on contemporary literary theory and criticism, literature, poetry, and culture in general. In recent years, it has been dedicating itself to so-called "smaller" literatures, mostly unknown beyond their national or linguistic boundaries. In some cases, *Akzente* publishes in two languages (German and the featured language) to permit translation comparisons. The magazine usually contains no illustrations and presupposes an intensive interest in literature or literary training. Contributors are generally authors and academics who focus on German literature. *Akzente* used to be distributed more widely, but it has received strong competition from newspapers such as the *Frankfurter Allgemeine Zeitung* and *Die Zeit*, whose "Feuilleton" sections haven taken over the role played by literary magazines. Nevertheless, *Akzente* is highly recommended for academic libraries supporting German studies and comparative-literature programs, as well as for large public libraries.

2781. ***Annales, Histoire, Sciences Sociales.*** Former titles (until 1946): *Annales d'Histoire Sociale;* (until 1945): *Melanges d'Histoire Sociale;* (until 1942): *Annales d'Histoire Sociale;* (until 1939): *Annales d'Histoire.* [ISSN: 0395-2649] 1929. bi-m. EUR 78.50 domestic; EUR 100 foreign; EUR 95 domestic. Armand Colin Editeur, 21 Rue du Montparnasse, Paris, 75283 Cedex 06, France; infos@armand-colin.com; http://www.armand-colin.com. Illus., adv. Sample. Refereed. Circ: 5000. Reprint: PSC; SCH. *Indexed:* AmH&L, ArtHuCI, BHA, BrArAb, IBSS, IBZ, IPSA, NumL, PAIS, PSA, SSCI, SociolAb. *Bk. rev.:* 15, length varies. *Aud.:* Ac.

In French. *Annales* was created by Lucien Febvre and Marc Bloch in Strasbourg in 1929. It was revolutionary for its time and was one of the most influential historical journals of the twentieth century. Targeted at an international audience and written in a colloquial style previously unheard of, *Annales* rejected the traditional approach of analyzing the history of politics, government, and military campaigns as official history and, instead, broadened its scope of investigation to a deeper analysis of social and economic forces. Articles are mostly in French but include English contributions. A free index and table of contents dating back to 1998 is available at http://www.ehess.fr/editions/revues/annales/Accueil.html. The journal revolutionized the way history was written, and it remains indispensable to any research library.

2782. ***Le Canard Enchaine: journal satirique paraissant le mercredi.*** [ISSN: 0088-5401] 1915. w. EUR 54.90 domestic; EUR 76.20 foreign; EUR 1.20 newsstand/cover per issue. Ed(s): Claude Angeli, Erik Emptaz. Editions Marechal, 173 rue Saint-Honore, Paris, Cedex 1 75051, France. Illus. Circ: 600000. Microform: NRP. *Bk. rev.:* Various number and length. *Aud.:* Ga, Ac.

In French. Published since 1915, *Le Canard Enchaine* is France's premier satirical magazine—and its oldest. Covering national and international politics, news, and society in general, it established a reputation of satirically uncovering corruption by politicians and other public figures in business, sports, and the media. In order to maintain its independence, *Le Canard* (literally "duck," but also a colloquial term for "newspaper" in French) does not contain any advertisements. This lack of revenue might explain why the web site, which used to contain articles and caricatures as well as an archive to previous issues, is no longer available. An important part of French culture, *Le Canard* is recommended for large research and public libraries.

2783. ***Central European History.*** [ISSN: 0008-9389] 1968. q. EUR 145 print & online eds. (Individuals, EUR 55 print & online eds.). Ed(s): Kenneth Barkin. Brill Academic Publishers, Inc., PO Box 9000, Leiden, 2300 PA, Netherlands; cs@brillusa.com; http://www.brill.nl. Illus., index, adv. Refereed. Circ: 1100. *Indexed:* ABS&EES, AmH&L, ArtHuCI, BHA, BRI, CBRI, HumInd, IBSS, SSCI. *Bk. rev.:* 15, length varies. *Aud.:* Ac.

In English. This highly regarded journal is now in its 36th year. International, scholarly, and refereed, it is published for the Conference Group for Central European History of the American Historical Association. The journal examines the social and cultural history of German-speaking Europe from the early modern period to the onset of World War II. *Central European History* includes book reviews and is available in full text online via the Ingenta search database. Recommended for research libraries.

2784. ***Contemporary French Civilization.*** [ISSN: 0147-9156] 1976. s-a. USD 60 (Individuals, USD 30). Ed(s): Lawrence R Schehr. University of Illinois at Urbana-Champaign, Department of French, c/o Professor Lawrence R. Schehr, 2090 FLB, Urbana, IL 61801. Illus., adv. Refereed. Circ: 1100. Microform: OMN. *Indexed:* AmH&L, ArtHuCI, CIJE, IPSA, PSA, SociolAb. *Bk. rev.:* various number and length. *Aud.:* Ac.

Primarily in French, but includes some English. *Contemporary French Civilization: a journal devoted to all aspects of civilization and cultural studies in France and the Francophone world* is edited by Lawrence Schehr at the University of Illinois. As the subtitle indicates, this refereed journal is particularly inclusive and covers all French-speaking cultures throughout the world. It includes research articles, interviews of famous personalities, book reviews, and scholarly, annotated bibliographies. Recommended for all libraries supporting research in French studies or for public libraries serving a French-speaking population.

Critical Quarterly. See Literary Reviews section.

2785. ***Critique: revue generale des publications francaises et etrangeres.*** [ISSN: 0011-1600] 1946. m. FRF 535 domestic; FRF 695 foreign; FRF 65 newsstand/cover per issue. Ed(s): Philippe Roger. Critique, 7 rue Bernard Palissy, Paris, 75006, France. Illus., index, adv. *Indexed:* ArtHuCI, IPB, L&LBA, MLA-IB, PSA, SSCI, SociolAb. *Bk. rev.:* 5-8, length varies. *Aud.:* Ac.

In French. Published by Editions de Minuit since 1946, *Critique* is yet another eminent French journal covering new publications on the arts, history, religion, literature, philosophy, and society. A French equivalent to the *Times Literary Supplement*, *Critique* was directed by Georges Bataille and includes Maurice Blanchot, Yves Bonnefoy, Michel Deguy, Jacques Derrida, Michel Serres, and Jean Starobinski as honorary members on its editorial board. *Critique* is an essential publication for research libraries and recommended to large public libraries.

2786. ***Le Debat: histoire, politique, societe.*** [ISSN: 0246-2346] 1980. 5x/yr. FRF 380 domestic; FRF 400 foreign; FRF 88 newsstand/cover per issue. Ed(s): Marcel Gauchet. Editions Gallimard, 15, rue Sebastien-Bottin, Paris, 75007, France. Illus. Sample. Circ: 10000. *Indexed:* BHA, IPSA, PAIS. *Aud.:* Ga, Ac.

In French. This bimonthly journal, published by the eminent publishing house Gallimard, was created by historian Pierre Nora in 1980 with the intention to provide for intellectual debate what the *Nouvelle Revue Francaise* did for literature, that is, to rally brilliant minds around one publication and generate a renewal of French critical thinking on major issues facing the contemporary world. With this rather lofty goal, topics range from discussions of political challenges to Western civilization and democracies, to religious and social challenges created by immigration and globalization, to evironmental challenges and entropy, to the latest performances at the Paris opera. Not wanting to compete with *Nouvelle Revue Francaise*, another Gallimard publication, literary topics have been largely ignored. Providing insight into the French contemporary intellectual debate, *Le Debat* is recommended for research libraries supporting French studies or political science.

2787. ***Deutschland.*** Former titles (until 1993): *Scala;* (until 1974): *Scala International.* [ISSN: 0945-6791] 1961. bi-m. DEM 24; DEM 30 foreign. Ed(s): Peter Hintereder. Frankfurter Societaets-Druckerei GmbH, Frankenallee 71-81, Frankfurt Am Main, 60268, Germany; zeitschriftenvertrieb@fsd.de; http://www.fsd.de. Illus., adv. Circ: 500000. *Indexed:* GeoRef, WAE&RSA. *Aud.:* Hs, Ga, Ac, Sa.

In English and available in 14 other languages. Published by the German federal government in an effort to promote understanding of and travel to Germany, *Deutschland* may appear to be a publicity magazine. It is more than that, however, as authors are quality journalists working for such reputable magazines as *Der Spiegel*, for example, and *Deutschland* contains a wealth of information. Readers wanting to learn more about contemporary Germany will find this magazine very appealing. Distributed in 180 countries, *Deutschland* realizes its goal: to provide an attractive overview of all things German. The web site is somewhat less successful in this and appears somewhat pale in comparison to the print edition. Yet, it is well organized and provides access to the full text of issues dating back to 1999. Available in German, English, Spanish, and French, it also provides further links on recommended web resources. In all, *Deutschland* is a valuable publication that will prove useful to teachers and students of German, as well as travelers and others wanting to learn more about Germany. Recommended for all types of libraries.

2788. ***Dutch Crossing: a journal of low countries studies.*** [ISSN: 0309-6564] 1977. s-a. GBP 25 (Individuals, GBP 16). Association of the Low Countries Studies in Great Britain and Ireland, Department of Dutch Studies, University of Hull, Hull, HU6 7RX, United Kingdom; s.drop@dutch.hull.ac.uk. Illus., index. Sample. *Indexed:* BHA, L&LBA, LT&LA, MLA-IB, PSA, SociolAb. *Bk. rev.:* 12, length varies. *Aud.:* Ac.

In English. This scholarly, multidisciplinary, peer-reviewed journal is the official publication of the Association for Low Countries Studies in Great Britain and Ireland (ALCS). *Dutch Crossing* covers the Dutch language, literature, history, politics, and art, as well as the media, culture, and society at large of the Netherlands and Vlaanderen (Flanders). Particular emphasis is given to the "relations between the Low Countries and the English-speaking world in all periods from the Middle Ages to the present day." Next to scholarly articles, it may include conference papers, translations of literary works, or book reviews. A cumulative index of the years 1977–1993 is available free from the editorial office, and the web site provides tables of contents from 1996 on. *Dutch Crossing* is highly recommended for libraries supporting research in European studies and the Low Countries.

2789. ***Elsevier.*** Incorporates (in 1998): *Elseviers Weekblad;* Formerly (until 1987): *Elseviers Magazine.* [ISSN: 0922-3444] 1944. w. NLG 274.50 domestic; NLG 321.50 Belgium; NLG 448.50 elsewhere. Ed(s): Peter Moennink. Reed Business Information bv, Van de Sande, Bakhuyzenstraat 4, Amsterdam, 1061 AG, Netherlands; info@reedbusiness.nl; http://www.reedbusiness.nl. Illus., adv. Circ: 192409 Paid. *Aud.:* Ga.

In Dutch. Upon hearing the name "Elsevier," American librarians generally think of the large, international publishing corporation. In the Netherlands, however, *Elsevier* is more commonly associated with the colorful weekly newsmagazine, which is as ubiquitous on Dutch newsstands as *Time* is in the United States. Very similar to American weekly newsmagazines, *Elsevier* covers news, politics, the economy, media, Dutch culture at large, the Internet, and sports. As the Netherlands' premier general-interest newsmagazine, *Elsevier* is a quality publication that will greatly appeal to anyone interested in Dutch current events, politics, and culture. The web site has recently changed to http://new.else4.nl/index.htm and is now purely informational, though viewers may subscribe to a free, daily newsletter sent via e-mail. Recommended for public and academic libraries with an interest in the Netherlands.

2790. ***L'Espresso: settimanale di politica, cultura, economia.*** [ISSN: 0423-4243] 1955. w. ITL 182000 domestic; ITL 208000 foreign; EUR 2.58 newsstand/cover per issue in Europe. Ed(s): Claudio Rinaldi. Editoriale l' Espresso SpA, Via Po 12, Rome, 00198, Italy; espresso@espressoedit.it; http://www.espressoedit.it. Illus., adv. Sample. Circ: 500000. Microform: PQC; NRP. Reprint: PQC. *Indexed:* PAIS. *Bk. rev.:* 3-4, length varies. *Aud.:* Ga, Ac.

In Italian. *L'Espresso* is generally considered Italy's premier general-interest magazine, and it covers national and international news, politics, the economy, the arts, media, culture, and society, including medicine, science, and technology. Very similar to *Time/Newsweek* or *L'Express* in France, *Elsevier* in the Netherlands, and *Der Spiegel* in Germany. *L'Espresso* is affiliated with the daily newspaper *La Repubblica*. The web site is mostly informational, though it contains limited full text and excerpts of select articles in past issues. An online archive is not available. Highly recommended for research libraries supporting Italian studies and public libraries.

2791. ***Esprit.*** [ISSN: 0014-0759] 1932. m. FRF 570; FRF 85 newsstand/cover per issue. Ed(s): Olivier Mongin. Esprit, 212 rue Saint Martin, Paris, 75003, France. Illus., index, adv. Circ: 10000. *Indexed:* ArtHuCI, BAS, FLI, IBSS, IPB, IPSA, MLA-IB, PAIS, RI-1. *Bk. rev.:* 10-12, length varies. *Aud.:* Ac.

In French. *Esprit* was created in 1932 by a group of intellectuals around the philosopher Emmanuel Mounier as an international magazine to promote the exchange of ideas and the dissemination of the Personalist principles. Beyond that, *Esprit* publishes widely on all contemporary philosophical issues and contains articles and commentary by international philosophers, historians, sociologists, economists, writers, literary critics, and journalists. Past contributors include Paul Ricoeur, Andre Bazin, John Rawls, and Charles Taylor, among others. *Esprit* also contains interviews and reviews of the arts and books. The web site provides a summary of the current issue and access to those of a select number of previous issues. *Esprit* is an important journal and is recommended to research libraries, public and academic.

2792. ***L'Esprit Createur: a critical quarterly of French literature.*** [ISSN: 0014-0767] 1961. 4x/yr. Ed(s): Daniel Brewer, Maria Minich Brewer. University of Minnesota, Department of French and Italian, c/o Daniel Brewer & Maria Minich Brewer, 260 Folwell Hall, 9 Pleasant St SE, Minneapolis, MN 55455; esprit@pop.uky.edu; http://www.uky.edu/. Illus., index, adv. Sample. Refereed. Circ: 950. Microform: PQC. Reprint: PQC. *Indexed:* AmHI, ArtHuCI, BRI, CBRI, IBZ, MLA-IB, SSCI. *Bk. rev.:* Various number and length. *Aud.:* Ac.

In English and French. *L'Esprit Createur* is an American publication but with a decidedly French flavor. This peer-reviewed scholarly journal contains critical essays focusing on francophone literature, criticism, and culture, as well book reviews. With such famous past contributors as Michael Butor, Jean-Paul Sartre, and Serge Doubrovsky, *L'Esprit Createur* ranks among the premier literary and critical publications and is highly recommended to academic and public research libraries.

2793. ***Europe: revue litteraire mensuelle.*** [ISSN: 0014-2751] 1923. m. EUR 73 domestic; EUR 100 foreign; EUR 19 newsstand/cover per issue. Ed(s): Pierre Gamarra. Europe, 4 Rue Marie Rose, Paris, 75014, France; europe.revue@wanadoo.fr. Illus., index, adv. Sample. Circ: 16000. *Indexed:* ArtHuCI, BEL&L, BPI, IBZ, MLA-IB. *Bk. rev.:* 20, length varies. *Aud.:* Ac.

In French. Founded in 1923 under the leadership of Romain Rolland and having counted Louis Aragon, Paul Eluard, and Elsa Triolet as past editors, as well as contemporary authors such as Gerard de Cortanze and Jean Echenoz as contributors, *Europe* is a literary review with clout. Covering not only European literature but world literature, *Europe* is nevertheless a French publication, and most authors and themes discussed in its pages are francophone. Issues are dedicated to particular themes and/or authors and include articles on a broad range of topics, such as reviews of national literatures (Turkey, Portugal, etc.) and comparative literature. *Europe* also includes short stories, poems, and reviews of contemporary theater, poetry, literature, and film. The web site was under construction during this review, but used to provide tables of contents to current and previous issues. *Europe* is highly recommended to all libraries supporting French studies and comparative literature.

2794. ***European History Quarterly.*** Formerly (until 1984): *European Studies Review.* [ISSN: 0265-6914] 1971. q. GBP 252 in Europe, Middle East, Africa & Australasia. Ed(s): R M Blinkhorn. Sage Publications Ltd., 6 Bonhill St, London, EC2A 4PU, United Kingdom; info@sagepub.co.uk; http://www.sagepub.co.uk/. Illus., index, adv. Sample. Refereed. Circ: 1150. *Indexed:* ABS&EES, AmH&L, ArtHuCI, BrHumI, HumInd, IBSS, IBZ, IPSA, NumL, PSA, RI-1, SSCI, SociolAb. *Bk. rev.:* 8-10, length varies. *Aud.:* Ac.

In English. The *European History Quarterly* covers European history from the later Middle Ages to the present. Articles are submitted by and reviewed by prominent scholars from all over Europe and North America. Review articles and book reviews in the *European History Quarterly* specifically focus on books published in European languages other than English. The journal is available electronically for print subscribers, as well as through several aggregators. For individuals not subscribing to the print edition nor affiliated with a university providing electronic access, the web site lists only tables of contents and subscription information. Recommended for academic libraries supporting European studies and history.

2795. ***L'Express.*** [ISSN: 0014-5270] 1953. w. EUR 80.50 domestic; EUR 103.30 in the European Union; EUR 129.30 in US & Canada. Ed(s): Denis Jeambar. Groupe Express-Expansion, 17 rue de l'Arrivee, Paris, Cedex 15 75733, France; http://www.groupe-expansion.com. Illus., adv. Sample. Circ: 530000. Microform: NRP. Online: Gale Group; LexisNexis. *Indexed:* PAIS. *Aud.:* Hs, Ga, Ac.

In French. Starting publication in 1953, *L'Express* was the first general-interest newsmagazine in France. Now rivaled by *Le Point* and various other publications, *L'Express* covers national and world news, politics, business and economics, the media, arts, literature, sports, and society at large. Having established its reputation on quality investigative reporting, *L'Express* is a nonpartisan, colorful, and well-designed magazine. The web site is well designed, without too many ads, and it provides access to the full text and summaries of select articles. Highly recommended for academic libraries supporting French studies and large public libraries.

2796. ***Forum Italicum: a journal of Italian studies.*** [ISSN: 0014-5858] 1967. s-a. plus irreg. Special Issues, 1-2/yr. USD 33 (Individuals, USD 23). Ed(s): Mario B Mignone. State University of New York at Stony Brook, Center for Italian Studies, Stony Brook, NY 11794-3358; mmignone@notes.cc.sunysb.edu; http://www.italianstudies.org. Illus., adv. Sample. Refereed. Circ: 850. *Indexed:* ArtHuCI, MLA-IB. *Bk. rev.:* 15-20, length varies. *Aud.:* Ac.

In Italian or English. *Forum Italicum* is published in the United States and consequently most contributors are North American, though it includes numerous Italian and European authors. *Forum Italicum* is peer reviewed, and issues usually contain five to six scholarly articles, notes, and reviews. Also included are poetry, prose, and translations. The web site contains mostly information, but it does include pdf files of the book reviews from previous issues. Highly recommended for libraries supporting Italian and European studies.

2797. ***Le Francais dans le Monde.*** [ISSN: 0015-9395] 1961. 6x/yr. EUR 77. Ed(s): Francoise Ploquin. C L E International, 27 Rue de la Glaciere, Paris, 75013, France; cle@vuef.fr; http://www.cle-inter.com/. Illus., adv. Sample. Circ: 12000. *Indexed:* CIJE, L&LBA, LT&LA, MLA-IB. *Aud.:* Hs, Ga, Ac.

In French. Published by the French Federation of Teachers of French (Federation internationale des professeurs de francais, or FIPF) and under the sponsorship of the French Foreign Ministry, *Le Francais dans le Monde* is designed for teachers of French throughout the world. The bimonthly issues cover current events and French culture and provide texts specifically designed to be read in class, with accompanying exercises. Articles usually focus on new methods of language instruction and ways to overcome teaching challenges. Also included are reviews of web sites and other multimedia tools devoted to teaching French. Readers will also find a number of advertisements for study and travel abroad, teaching aids, and correspondents. The web site is well organized and contains full texts of selected articles, as well as abstracts from 1994. *Le Francais dans le Monde* is highly recommended for academic libraries providing French-language instruction as well as school and public libraries.

2798. ***France: the quarterly magazine for Francophiles.*** [ISSN: 0958-8213] 1989. q. GBP 4.25 newsstand/cover per issue. Central Haven Ltd., Dormer House, The Square, Stow-on-the-Wold, Cheltenham, GL54 1BN, United Kingdom. Illus., adv. Sample. Circ: 53896. *Aud.:* Ga.

In English. *France* is a magazine that has the feel and look of a government-sponsored magazine to increase tourism. Yet it is actually published by a private British publisher. Similar to *France Today* and *France Magazine* (which is published by the *Maison Francaise* in Washington, D.C., and available free), *France* contains articles on French culture, culinary and other traditions, and places of interest. The magazine's layout favors large color photographs to showcase the best of France, and short articles provide "insider tips" for travelers. The web site provides summaries of articles and tables of contents back to 1992 and includes a number of tips and useful links. In particular, the "FiloF-rance" might come in handy for travelers. It includes, for example, a link to market days for every city, per department. Published for British Francophiles, the site and magazine are, nevertheless, helpful for Americans wanting to steep themselves in French (tourist) culture.

2799. ***French Cultural Studies.*** [ISSN: 0957-1558] 1990. 3x/yr. GBP 219 in Europe, Middle East, Africa & Australasia. Sage Publications Ltd., 6 Bonhill St, London, EC2A 4PU, United Kingdom; info@sagepub.co.uk; http://www.sagepub.co.uk/. Illus. Sample. *Indexed:* BrHumI, HumInd, IBSS, MLA-IB, SociolAb. *Aud.:* Ac.

In English and French. With Pierre Bourdieu on the editorial board, *French Cultural Studies* goes beyond the traditional definition of culture and emphasizes cinema, television, the press, visual arts, and popular culture over traditional areas of inquiry, such as literature. The web site is mostly informational, but it provides tables of contents from 1997 on. Highly recommended to research libraries.

2800. ***French Forum.*** [ISSN: 0098-9355] 1976. 3x/yr. USD 60 (Individuals, USD 30; USD 25 per issue). Ed(s): Gerald Prince, Lance Donaldson-Evans. University of Nebraska Press, 233 N 8th St, Lincoln, NE 68588-0255; pressmail@unl.edu; http://www.nebraskapress.unl.edu. Illus., adv. Sample. Refereed. *Indexed:* ArtHuCI, IBZ, MLA-IB, RI-1. *Bk. rev.:* 6, length varies. *Aud.:* Ac.

In English and French. *French Forum* is a peer-reviewed journal of French and francophone literature, published by the University of Nebraska and produced by the Romance Languages Department at the University of Pennsylvania. Members of the editorial board are for the most part renowned American professors of French literature and studies, and articles tend to be mostly in English, though French essays and reviews are always included. Along with articles on French literature and literary criticism, *French Forum* provides book reviews of new titles in the field, as well as a list of books received, which may be used both for receiving an overview of new publications and for potential reviewers to chose from. Recommended to research libraries.

2801. ***French Historical Studies.*** [ISSN: 0016-1071] 1958. q. USD 117 includes online access (Individuals, USD 40 includes online access). Ed(s): Eteica Spencer, Ted W Margadent. Duke University Press, 905 W Main St, Ste 18 B, Durham, NC 27701; subscriptions@dukeupress.edu; http://www.dukeupress.edu. Illus., index, adv. Sample. Circ: 1750. Online: bigchalk; Chadwyck-Healey Incorporated; EBSCO Publishing; Gale Group; Ingenta Select; JSTOR (Web-based Journal Archive); Northern Light Technology, Inc.; OCLC Online Computer Library Center, Inc.; Project MUSE; RoweCom Information Quest; Swets Blackwell. Reprint: PSC. *Indexed:* AmH&L, ArtHuCI, BHA, HumInd, IBZ, MLA-IB, SSCI. *Aud.:* Ac.

In English and French. Published by Duke University Press for the Society for French Historical Studies, *French Historical Studies*, is a refereed journal that publishes monographic articles, commentaries, research notes, and book review essays, but not book reviews. Issues also include society news, as well as bibliographies of recent publications in French history and abstracts of the articles contained in the issue, in both English and French. Occasional special issues are supervised by guest editors. The web site provides further society news and contains the table of contents for the current issue. Full texts are available through JSTOR and Project Muse. Recommended for academic libraries.

2802. ***French History.*** [ISSN: 0269-1191] 1987. q. GBP 122. Ed(s): Malcolm Crook. Oxford University Press, Great Clarendon St, Oxford, OX2 6DP, United Kingdom; jnl.orders@oup.co.uk; http://www3.oup.co.uk/jnls. Illus., adv. Sample. Refereed. Circ: 850. Reprint: PSC. *Indexed:* AmH&L, BHA, PSA, SociolAb. *Bk. rev.:* 20, length varies. *Aud.:* Ac.

In English. Published by the British Society of the Study of French History, *French History* provides a "broad perspective on contemporary debates from an international range of scholars, and covers the entire . . . range of French history from the early Middle Ages to the twentieth century." Following this statement, the editorial board is comprised of international, though mostly British, members. Issues include research articles and book reviews only. News of the society is treated in a separate publication, the *French Historian*. The web site, at Oxford University Press, provides full text in html and pdf from 2002 on (for subscribers only) and tables of contents from 1996 on. Recommended for research libraries.

2803. ***German Life and Letters.*** [ISSN: 0016-8777] 1936. q. GBP 235 print & online eds. Blackwell Publishing Ltd., 9600 Garsington Rd, PO Box 805, Oxford, OX4 2DQ, United Kingdom; customerservices@oxon.blackwellpublishing.com; http://www.blackwellpublishing.com/. Illus., index, adv. Sample. Refereed. Circ: 800. Online: EBSCO Publishing; ingenta.com; OCLC Online Computer Library Center, Inc.; RoweCom Information Quest; Swets Blackwell. Reprint: SWZ. *Indexed:* AmH&L, ArtHuCI, BrHumI, IBZ, MLA-IB, RI-1. *Aud.:* Ac.

In English and German. *German Life and Letters* was founded in England in 1936. After closing for the war, it emerged again in 1947 as a scholarly, refereed journal intended to cover "all aspects of German studies since the Middle Ages, including: literature, language, arts and culture, social history and politics." Thematic issues are published irregularly and cover a large variety of topics, ranging from German cinema to "Exilliteratur." The web site at Blackwell's provides an online cumulative index from 1932 to 2002 and tables of contents going back to 1996. Institutions with current subscriptions have access to the full text online. Recommended for academic libraries supporting research in German studies.

2804. ***The German Quarterly.*** [ISSN: 0016-8831] 1928. q. USD 75 domestic; USD 85 foreign. Ed(s): Dagmar Lorenz. American Association of Teachers of German, Inc., 112 Haddontowne Ct, Ste 104, Cherry Hill, NJ 08034; headquarters@aatg.org; http://www.aatg.org/. Index, adv. Sample. Refereed. Circ: 3500 Paid. Microform: PMC; PQC. Online: Chadwyck-Healey Incorporated; EBSCO Publishing; Gale Group; JSTOR (Web-based Journal Archive); OCLC Online Computer Library Center, Inc.; ProQuest Information & Learning; H.W. Wilson. Reprint: PQC. *Indexed:* ABS&EES, ArtHuCI, BHA, BRI, CBRI, EduInd, HumInd, IBZ, L&LBA, LT&LA, MLA-IB, SSCI. *Bk. rev.:* 35, length varies. *Aud.:* Ac.

In German and English. Published by the American Association of Teachers of German (AATG); *The German Quarterly* is a refereed journal, designed to address issues of teachers of German at all educational levels. Comprised only of academics, including eminent Germanist Paul Michael Lutzeler, *The German Quarterly* is multidisciplinary in essence and covers German cultural studies in general. Along with scholarly articles on German language, literature, history, and culture, *The German Quarterly* provides special reports and extensive book reviews of academic publications. The web site is designed to address the needs of all teachers of German and contains numerous helpful links, including a link to teaching resources. Also available through JSTOR. *The German Quarterly* should be included in any library supporting German studies.

2805. ***German Studies Review.*** [ISSN: 0149-7952] 1978. 3x/yr. USD 45 in US & Canada; USD 50 elsewhere. Ed(s): Diethelm Prowe. German Studies Association, c/o Diethelm Prowe, History Department, Northfield, MN 55057-4025; dprowe@carleton.edu; http://www.g-s-a.org. Illus., adv. Sample. Refereed. Circ: 2400. *Indexed:* ABS&EES, AmH&L, ArtHuCI, HumInd, L&LBA, MLA-IB, RI-1, SSCI, SociolAb. *Bk. rev.:* 60. *Aud.:* Ac.

In English or German. Published by the North American German Studies Association, *German Studies Review* is a refereed journal that covers interdisciplinary scholarship in German, Austrian, and Swiss history, literature, culture studies, political science, and economics. Issues generally contain about six articles and countless book reviews of academic publications. Articles and book reviews are in either English or German, but because most members of the German Studies Association are from the United States, publications are chiefly in English. The web site is mostly informational. Recommended for academic libraries supporting research in German studies.

2806. ***Germanic Review: devoted to studies dealing with the Germanic languages and literatures.*** [ISSN: 0016-8890] 1925. q. USD 107 (Individuals, USD 53; USD 26.75 per issue). Ed(s): Abigail Beckel. Heldref Publications, 1319 18th St, NW, Washington, DC 20036-1802; subscribe@heldref.org; http://www.heldref.org. Illus., index, adv. Sample. Refereed. Circ: 800 Paid. Vol. ends: Winter. CD-ROM: ProQuest Information & Learning. Microform: PQC. Online: bigchalk; Chadwyck-Healey Incorporated; EBSCO Publishing; Factiva; Florida Center for Library Automation; Gale Group; Northern Light Technology, Inc.; OCLC Online Computer Library Center, Inc.; ProQuest Information & Learning; H.W. Wilson. Reprint: PSC. *Indexed:* ABS&EES, ArtHuCI, BHA, HumInd, IBZ, MLA-IB. *Bk. rev.:* 3-9, length varies. *Aud.:* Ac.

In English and German. *Germanic Review* is a refereed journal of international scholarship in German studies. Edited at Columbia University, it contains articles on German literature, literary theory, and culture, as well as reviews of the latest publications in the field. The web page, at Heldref Publications, is purely informational. Published since 1925, *Germanic Review* is an important title for libraries supporting German studies.

2807. ***Giornale della Libreria.*** [ISSN: 0017-0216] 1888. m. ITL 109000 (Individuals, ITL 121000). Ed(s): Federico Motta. Editrice Bibliografica SpA, Via Vittorio Veneto, 24, Milan, 20124, Italy; http://www.alice.it/eb/catalogs/sommario.htm. Illus., adv. Sample. Circ: 5000. *Aud.:* Ac.

In Italian. The *Giornale della Libreria* is the official publication of the Italian publishers association. As such—and similarly to *Livres Hebdo* and *Buchreport*, which are the respective organs of the French and German publishers associations—the *Giornale della Libreria* provides the latest editorial and commercial news on the national and international publishing worlds. This includes information on the latest trends in the market and various statistical and market research information on sales per editorial segment and new products, as well as articles on particular publishing figures or houses. In addition, the *Giornale* lists new books, arranged by author, subject, and publisher and functions as an Italian *Books in Print*. Recommended to libraries as a collection development and reference tool and to stay abreast of new developments in Italian publishing.

2808. *Giornale Storico della Letteratura Italiana.* [ISSN: 0017-0496] 1883. q. ITL 165000. Editore Loescher, Via Vittorio Amedeo II, 18, Turin, 10121, Italy; mail@loescher.it; http://www.loescher.it. Illus., index. Reprint: SCH. *Indexed:* ArtHuCI, IBZ, MLA-IB. *Bk. rev.:* 20-25, length varies. *Aud.:* Ac.

In Italian. Published since 1883, the *Giornale Storico della Letteratura Italiana* is a highly reputable literary journal focusing, as the title indicates, on literary history. Issues contain scholarly articles, notes and discussions, bibliographies, and announcements, as well as a large section of books reviews. The latter, covering the latest publication in the field, constitutes a useful collection development tool. The web site at http://www.loescher.it provides tables of contents under "Riviste" from 1999. This long-standing, important publication should be made available at research libraries supporting Italian studies.

2809. *Granta.* [ISSN: 0017-3231] 1979. q. GBP 24.95 in British Isles; GBP 32.95 in Europe; USD 34 United States. Ed(s): Ian Jack. Granta Publications Ltd., 2-3, Hanover Yard, Noel Rd, London, N1 8BE, United Kingdom; http://www.granta.com. Illus., adv. Circ: 96000. Microform: PQC. Online: Gale Group. *Indexed:* HumInd. *Bk. rev.:* Various number and length. *Aud.:* Ga, Ac.

In English. *Granta* is one of the most eminent literary journals in the English-speaking world. Published at Cambridge University since 1889, *Granta* has published such world-famous authors as E. M. Forster, A. A. Milne, Ted Hughes, Sylvia Plath, Richard Ford, Salman Rushdie, Susan Sontag, John Hawkes, Paul Auster, and Milan Kundera. Each issue of *Granta* is organized around a central theme and contains original fiction, poetry, criticism, opinion, essays, and observations. The web site provides excerpts from the magazine as well as selected full text and tables of contents for all back issues. The well-organized web site is a useful place to learn more about this out-of-the-ordinary magazine. Highly recommended for all academic and public libraries.

2810. *L'Hebdo: magazine suisse d'information.* [ISSN: 1013-0691] 1981. w. CHF 198. Ed(s): Ariane Dayer. Ringier Romandie, Pont Bessieres 3, Case postale 3733, Lausanne, 1002, Switzerland; info@ringier.ch; http://www.ringier.ch. Illus., adv. Sample. Circ: 56950. *Aud.:* Ga, Ac.

In French. Similar to other general-interest newsmagazines, the Swiss *L'Hebdo* (also published in German under the title *Die Woche*) is a glossy magazine covering national and major international news, Swiss politics, the economy, arts, media, culture, and sports. Like its many European and American counterparts, *L'Hebdo* contains numerous large color photographs and an attractive layout for easy browsing. The web site includes selections and some full text as well as limited back issues. Recommended for libraries wanting to provide their users with Swiss news.

2811. *L'Histoire.* [ISSN: 0182-2411] 1978. 11x/yr. FRF 335. Societe d'Editions Scientifiques, 57 rue de Seine, Paris, Cedex 6 75280, France. Illus., adv. Sample. Circ: 76300. Reprint: ISI. *Indexed:* ArtHuCI, SSCI. *Bk. rev.:* 15, length varies. *Aud.:* Hs, Ac.

In French. *L'Histoire* is a glossy, full-color magazine, designed to bring history to the masses. Following a similar layout as a regular newsmagazine, *L'Histoire* is nevertheless a serious publication. While articles are mandatorily accompanied by large color photographs, maps, and illustrations to attract the reader and favor easy reading, they are generally accompanied by footnotes and end with a bibliography. In addition to special reports and research articles, *L'Histoire* contains a section on current events and book reviews. Clearly not a scholarly publication, *L'Histoire* is geared toward aspiring scholars, high school students, and beginning undergraduates. The web site, at http://www.histoire.presse.fr, is well organized and without advertisements. It includes free access to archival issues back to 2000, as well as a subject and author search feature. More than solely a commercial publication, though inappropriate for scholarly research, *L'Histoire* has its place on public and college library shelves.

2812. *Historische Zeitschrift.* [ISSN: 0018-2613] 1859. bi-m. EUR 307.30 domestic (Students, EUR 145.30). Ed(s): Lothar Gall. Oldenbourg Wissenschaftsverlag GmbH, Rosenheimer Str 145, Munich, 81671, Germany; vertrieb-zs@verlag.oldenbourg.de; http://www.oldenbourg.de. Illus., index, adv. Circ: 2800. Microform: OMN; PQC. Reprint: SCH. *Indexed:* AmH&L, ArtHuCI, IBZ, MLA-IB, SSCI. *Bk. rev.:* 80-100, 1-3 pages. *Aud.:* Ac.

In German. Published since 1859, *Historische Zeitschrift* is one of the premier, independent, scholarly journals in the field. Every two months, *Historische Zeitschrift* usually contains three to five articles and provides a large number of book reviews, covering most of the output in the discipline, organized by period, and ranging from ancient history to today. A wonderful tool for scholars to stay abreast of new developments in the field, *Historische Zeitschrift* also is an extremely useful tool for collection development. The web site at Oldenbourg Verlag provides access to tables of contents dating back to 1999. Highly recommended for academic libraries supporting research in German and European history.

2813. *Iceland Review.* [ISSN: 0019-1094] 1963. q. USD 29.50. Ed(s): Jon Kaldal. Iceland Review, Noatun 17, Reykjavik, 105, Iceland; iceland@icenews.is; http://www.centrum.is/icerev/ir/. Illus., adv. Sample. *Indexed:* BHA. *Aud.:* Ga.

In English. *Iceland Review* was founded in 1963 with the intention to promote the nature and culture of Iceland to the rest of the world. This travel magazine acts as an ambassador for Iceland abroad; written in English, it covers Icelandic affairs, nature, and culture for the general public. Published four times a year, it contains gorgeous photographs that will appeal to any traveler. The web site is free, but it requires registration to access featured articles. It provides tables of contents going back to 1995, and users may subscribe for access to the full text, but it is best read in print. Recommended for public libraries and academic libraries with an interest in Scandinavian studies.

2814. *In Britain.* [ISSN: 0019-3143] 1967. m. Ed(s): Andrea Spain. Romsey Publishing Company Ltd. (London), Glen House, Stag Pl, London, SW1E 5AQ, United Kingdom. Adv. Circ: 45000 Controlled. Online: EBSCO Publishing. *Aud.:* Ga.

In English. Published by the British Travel Authority (BTA), *In Britain* is a glossy, colorful magazine, filled with images designed to induce you to spend your next vacation in the U.K. *In Britain* is not without tradition, as it has been published since 1930. The layout of the magazine, however, has been updated to look like something of a *National Geographic* for Britain. There is no official web site for *In Britain*, though a web search will provide sites that include tables of contents. The BTA's web site, "visitbritain," however, is very developed and contains a wealth of information for the tourist.

2815. *L'Infini: litterature, philosophie, art, science, politique.* [ISSN: 0754-023X] 1983. q. FRF 309 domestic; FRF 365 foreign; FRF 86 newsstand/cover per issue. Ed(s): Marcelin Pleynet. Editions Gallimard, 15, rue Sebastien-Bottin, Paris, 75007, France. Illus. *Indexed:* ArtHuCI, IBZ, MLA-IB. *Aud.:* Ac.

In French. *L'Infini*, previously *Tel Quel*, joined Gallimard in 1983, under the leadership of Philippe Sollers. What differentiates *L'Infini* from Gallimard's premier literary journal, *La Nouvelle Revue Francaise*, is that *L'Infini* focuses on new, contemporary authors, whereas the more established and venerable *Nouvelle Revue* publishes the great (but also contemporary) masters. Because *L'Infini* also publishes famous authors, the main difference that it is edited by Philippe Sollers, arguably the most celebrated French author alive. The journal covers all literature, including criticism, modern poetry, interviews, and essays on philosophy, art science, and politics. *L'Infini* has published or commented on

Julia Kristeva, Philippe Roth, Milan Kundera, Vladimir Nabokov, Alain Finkielkraut, Michel Rio, Chantal Thomas, Philippe Djian, Benoit Duteurtre, and more. Academic libraries supporting French literary programs should subscribe to *L'Infini*.

2816. *Irish University Review: a journal of Irish studies.* [ISSN: 0021-1427] 1970. s-a. IEP 30 (Individuals, IEP 20; IEP 8.50 newsstand/cover per issue). Ed(s): Dr. Anthony Roche. Irish University Review, Rm. J210, Department of English, University College, Dublin, 4, Ireland. Illus., adv. Refereed. Circ: 1200. *Indexed:* ArtHuCI, MLA-IB, SSCI. *Bk. rev.:* 10, length varies. *Aud.:* Ac.

In English. The *Irish University Review: A Journal of Irish Studies* (*IUR*), established in 1970, is a refereed, scholarly, literary journal. With an emphasis on contemporary Irish literature, it includes literary essays, short fiction, poetry, a large section of book reviews, and interviews with authors, poets, and playwrights. The semiannual issues are regularly devoted to Irish authors or themes, and the book reviews are useful to stay abreast of current Irish literature. The Princess Grace Irish Library in Monaco has images of cover pages and tables of contents for all issues at http://www.pgil-eirdata.org/html/pgil_bibliogs/journals/ir_uni_rev/index.htm. Highly recommended for academic and large public libraries.

2817. *Journal of European Studies (Chalfont Saint Giles).* [ISSN: 0047-2441] 1971. q. GBP 280 print & online eds. in Europe, Middle East, Africa & Australasia. Ed(s): John Flower. Sage Publications Ltd., 6 Bonhill St, London, EC2A 4PU, United Kingdom; info@sagepub.co.uk; http://www.sagepub.co.uk/. Illus., index, adv. Sample. Circ: 550. Microform: PQC. Online: bigchalk; Chadwyck-Healey Incorporated; Florida Center for Library Automation; Gale Group; ingenta.com; OCLC Online Computer Library Center, Inc.; ProQuest Information & Learning. Reprint: PQC; SCH. *Indexed:* AmH&L, ArtHuCI, BHA, BrHumI, HumInd, L&LBA, MLA-IB, RI-1, SSCI, SociolAb. *Bk. rev.:* 30, length varies. *Aud.:* Ac.

In English. There are several journals named *Journal of European Studies* (*JES*). This quarterly, peer-reviewed journal, published by Alpha Academic, covers the literature and cultural history of Europe since the Renaissance. Published since 1971, *JES* is led by a distinguished editorial board, guaranteeing the quality of articles and review essays. Sometimes focusing on specific topics, such as "The Invasion and Occupation of France 1940-44: Intellectual and Cultural Responses," *JES* publishes mostly in English, but includes occasional contributions in French or German. The web site is mostly informational, but it provides tables of contents for previous issues back to 1997. Highly recommended for all research libraries.

2818. *Knack.* [ISSN: 0772-3210] 1971. w. BEF 3980. Ed(s): Hubert van Humbeeck, Frank de Moor. N.V. R M G, Bd Louis Schmidt 97, Brussels, 1040, Belgium; info@roularta.be; http://www.knack.be/indexkn.htm. Illus., adv. Circ: 150000 Paid. *Aud.:* Ga, Ac.

In Dutch. *Knack* is a Belgian general-interest newsmagazine written in Dutch for Flemish and Dutch readers. While *Knack* is the premier newsmagazine in Flemish-speaking Belgium, it is also widely distributed in the southern Netherlands. *Knack* covers international and national news and current events, politics, the economy, the media and the arts, culture, and sports. *Knack* also contains regular sections on multimedia trends, health news, lifestyles, gastronomy, and travel. *Knack* publishes several complements, of which *Weekend Knack* focuses on leisure and culture at large; *Focus* on the media; and *Vacature* with job ads and career tips. The *Knack* web site provides free access to the full texts of selected articles, but registration is required; the supplements, on the other hand, are available without registration, with the exception of *Vacature*. Access to complete issues as well as the archives is only available to subscribers. Recommended for large public libraries.

2819. *Kursbuch.* [ISSN: 0023-5652] 1965. 4x/yr. EUR 10 newsstand/cover. Ed(s): Ingrid Karsunke, Karl Markus. Rowohlt-Berlin Verlag GmbH, Kreuzbergstr 30, Berlin, 10965, Germany; info@rowohlt.de; http://www.rowohlt.de. Illus., adv. Sample. Circ: 6000. *Indexed:* IBZ, PAIS, PhilInd. *Aud.:* Ac.

In German. *Kursbuch* was founded by writer and leading literary critic Hans Magnus Enzensberger at Germany's renowned Suhrkamp Verlag in 1965. One of Germany's premier critical reviews, *Kursbuch* addresses contemporary issues, ranging from current social problems to literary criticism, the arts, technology, and other subjects appealing to the critical mind, through high-quality literary/philosophical essays, organized around a central theme. Contributions are usually by German writers, though *Kursbuch* regularly includes translations. Highly recommended to all academic libraries supporting German literature and studies.

2820. *Lettere Italiane.* [ISSN: 0024-1334] 1949. q. EUR 57 domestic; EUR 75 foreign. Ed(s): Vittore Branca, Carlo Ossola. Casa Editrice Leo S. Olschki, Casella Postale 66, Florence, 50100, Italy; celso@olschki.it; http://www.olschki.it. Illus., adv. Sample. Circ: 1200. *Indexed:* ArtHuCI, BHA, IBZ, MLA-IB. *Bk. rev.:* 4-6, length varies. *Aud.:* Ac.

In Italian. Edited by Vittore Branca and Carlo Ossola at the Departments of Italian Studies at the Universities of Padua and Torino and published quarterly by Leo S. Olschki since 1949, *Lettere Italiane* is one of Italy's premier scholarly, refereed literary journals. Covering Italian literature from the Middle Ages to the present, each issue contains several lengthy articles written by scholars, a news section covering literary events in the academic world, book reviews, and a list of titles received. *Lettere Italiane* is of such stature that the journal has developed two highly regarded monographic series: the *Biblioteca di Lettere Italiane* and the *Saggi di Lettere Italiane*. The web site is informational only. Indispensable to research libraries covering Italian literature, *Lettere Italiane* is recommended to all academic libraries supporting Italian studies.

2821. *Lire: le magazine des livres.* [ISSN: 0338-5019] 1975. m. EUR 27.23 domestic; EUR 41.30 foreign. Ed(s): Pierre Assouline. Groupe Express-Expansion, 17 rue de l'Arrivee, Paris, Cedex 15 75733, France; http://www.groupe-expansion.com. Illus., adv. Sample. Circ: 140000. *Bk. rev.:* Numerous. *Aud.:* Ga.

In French. Published by *L'Express*, *Lire* is a glossy magazine with the look and feel of a general-interest magazine, but devoted entirely to writing and reading. Edited by Pierre Assouline, author at Gallimard, *Lire* is an exceptional magazine to stay abreast of current French literary publications and affairs. Covering new novels, poetry, theater, as well as nonfiction, *Lire* also includes interviews with authors and large excerpts of their new works. The web site complements the magazine with full text online of numerous articles and reviews back to 1995. Also functioning as a portal to sites relevant to contemporary French literature on the web, *http://www.lire.fr* provides a free overview of current events and French literary publications. A very useful collection development tool and an important publication for research libraries and large public libraries to understand contemporary French literature.

2822. *Litterature.* [ISSN: 0047-4800] 1971. q. EUR 70 (Individuals, EUR 55). Ed(s): F Tremollieres. Larousse, 21 rue du Montparnasse, Paris, 75283 Cedex 06 , France; tleridon@larousse.fr; http://www.larousse.fr. Illus., index. Sample. *Indexed:* ArtHuCI, MLA-IB. *Bk. rev.:* 4, length varies. *Aud.:* Ac.

In French. *Litterature* is one of France's premier literary reviews. Published by the French literature department at the University of Paris VIII, *Litterature* has been published quarterly since 1971. Each issue is organized around a central theme and includes research articles, complete with thorough bibliographies of the author or topic discussed. Summaries of all articles are also provided in English at the end of the issue. Recommended for all academic libraries supporting French studies.

2823. *London Magazine (London, 1954).* [ISSN: 0024-6085] 1954. bi-m. GBP 28.50; USD 67; GBP 33.50 foreign. Ed(s): Alan Ross. London Magazine Ltd., 30 Thurloe Pl, London, SW7, United Kingdom. Illus., adv. Sample. Circ: 4000. *Indexed:* BHA, FLI. *Bk. rev.:* 20, length varies. *Aud.:* Ga, Ac.

In English. First published in 1732, the bimonthly *London Magazine* is probably one of the oldest literary magazines in existence. Now edited by Sebastian Barker and sponsored by the Arts Council England, *London Magazine* contains essays, critiques, photographs, drawings, poetry, correspondence, short stories, and reviews. The web site is purely informational. An essential publication for all research and public libraries supporting comtemporary English literature and poetry.

2824. ***Magazine Litteraire.*** [ISSN: 0024-9807] 1966. m. FRF 315 domestic; FRF 420 foreign; FRF 32 newsstand/cover per issue. Ed(s): Jean Jacques Brochier. Magazine-Expansion, 40 rue des Saints-Peres, Paris, 75007, France; magazine@magazine-litteraire.com; http://www.magazine-litteraire.com. Illus., adv. Circ: 55000. *Indexed:* IBZ, MLA-IB. *Bk. rev.:* 40+. *Aud.:* Ga, Ac.

In French. The direct competitor to *Lire* is *Magazine Litteraire*, published by the Groupe Expansion. *Magazine Litteraire* was on the market before *Lire*, but both magazines cover world literature with an emphasis on contemporary French authors. *Magazine Litteraire* is famous for its in-depth coverage of particular authors, national literatures, genres, or themes every month in its "Dossier" section. In addition, it contains news articles on the latest publications and trends, numerous brief reviews of books, and frequent interviews with contemporary authors, such as Henri Troyat and Andrei Makine. The difference with *Lire* might be that *Magazine Litteraire* focuses on literature, whereas *Lire* covers the French publishing scene as well. The web site is well organized and contains full texts of numerous articles and reviews, including a selective archive of previous "Dossiers" covering the whole span of the magazine's history (some go back as far as the 1960s). More specialized than *Lire*, *Magazine Litteraire* is highly recommended to research libraries and large public libraries as a collection development tool and to permit its users to stay abreast of the contemporary French literary scene.

2825. ***Magill: Ireland's current affairs monthly magazine.*** Incorporates (1979-1982): *Magill Digest.* [ISSN: 0332-1754] 1977. m. USD 50. Ed(s): Kevin Rafter. Magill Publications Ltd., Camden Pl, Dublin, 2, Ireland. Illus., adv. Sample. Circ: 100000 Paid and controlled. *Aud.:* Hs, Ga, Ac.

In English. A general newsmagazine, *Magill* reports on current Irish affairs, covering the news, politics, economy, technology, arts, science, literature, media, and sports. Published monthly, *Magill* also provides film, theater, and book reviews. Offering readers a window onto Irish affairs, *Magill* is recommended to research libraries with specific interest in Ireland, as well as public libraries serving a large Irish community.

2826. ***Merkur: Deutsche Zeitschrift fuer europaeisches Denken.*** [ISSN: 0026-0096] 1947. m. EUR 98 (Students, EUR 72). Ed(s): Karl Heinz Bohrer, Kurt Scheel. Verlag Klett-Cotta, Rotebuehlstr 77, Stuttgart, 70178, Germany; info@klett-cotta.de; http://www.klett-cotta.de. Illus., adv. Sample. Circ: 5300. *Indexed:* ArtHuCI, BAS, BHA, IBZ, IPSA, MLA-IB, PAIS, PhilInd, RILM, SSCI. *Aud.:* Ac.

In German. *Merkur* is not an academic journal; that is, it does not claim to be. Yet, its contributors and subscribers are all academics or intellectuals. It is not a peer-reviewed, scholarly journal, but it is one of Germany's premier cultural reviews, offering critical essays not only on politics, philosophy, history, and literature, but also any issue affecting modern society, from cloning to the Internet. With contributors such as Ralf Dahrendorf, Nathalie Sarraute, Jan Philipp Reemtsma, Richard Rorty, and Klaus von Dohnanyi—to name just a few—*Merkur* truly deserves its subtitle: A Magazine for European Thought. The web site is mostly informational, but it provides indexes for current and previous issues, dating back to 1988. It also recently started a collaboration with the Goethe-Institut to publish the *Goethe Merkur*, which provides translations of important *Merkur* articles in English, French, Spanish, and Russian, to be distributed at various branches of the Goethe-Institut throughout the world. *Merkur* is highly recommended to research libraries and large public libraries.

2827. ***Monatshefte: fuer deutschen Unterricht, deutsche Sprache und Literatur.*** Formerly: *Monatshefte fuer Deutschen Unterricht.* [ISSN: 0026-9271] 1899. q. USD 116 (Individuals, USD 47). Ed(s): Hans Adler. University of Wisconsin Press, Journal Division, 1930 Monroe St., 3rd Fl, Madison, WI 53711; http://www.wisc.edu/wisconsinpress/journals. Illus., index, adv. Sample. Circ: 1000. Microform: PMC; PQC. Reprint: PQC; PSC. *Indexed:* IBZ, L&LBA, MLA-IB. *Bk. rev.:* 15, length varies. *Aud.:* Ac.

In English and German. *Monatshefte* has been published continuously since 1899 at the University of Wisconsin, Madison. A peer-reviewed quarterly journal devoted to German literature and culture, *Monatshefte* covers topics from all periods of German literature and includes book reviews of current scholarship in German studies. Once a year, *Monatshefte* also publishes news on new hires, retirements, and visiting professors, as well as a comprehensive listing of German studies faculty and departments in North America. The web site is mostly informational, but it contains tables of contents, including abstracts of articles, from 1996. Recommended to all academic research libraries supporting German studies.

2828. ***Le Monde Diplomatique.*** [ISSN: 0026-9395] 1954. m. FRF 230 domestic; FRF 290 in Europe; FRF 350 in North America. Ed(s): Micheline Paunet. Le Monde S.A., 21 bis, rue Claude Bernard, Paris, 75005, France; http://www.ina.fr/CP/MondeDiplo. Illus., index, adv. Sample. Circ: 165000. Microform: RPI. *Indexed:* AltPI, GeoRef, PAIS. *Aud.:* Ga, Ac.

In French. Starting out as a supplement to the French daily newspaper *Le Monde*, *Le Monde Diplomatique* has successfully established itself as an independent publication, highly regarded in diplomatic and academic circles. As its name indicates, *Le Monde Diplomatique* covers the world's political, diplomatic, and economic news. Although in French, its contributors are international, and an English version is also available as a supplement to the *Guardian*. Providing lengthy, in-depth analysis of worldwide diplomatic events, the particular strength of *Le Monde Diplomatique* lies in its extensive coverage of Africa, Asia, and Latin America. Following its "parent" publication, the general editorial standpoint of *Le Monde Diplomatique* may be characterized as center-left. The web site is well organized and provides free access to the full texts of articles for the previous two years. A core title for libraries supporting international and political studies.

2829. ***Il Mondo: il settimanale economico Italiano.*** [ISSN: 0391-6855] 1949. w. 50 issues. EUR 33. Ed(s): Gianni Gambarotta. R C S Editori SpA, Periodici, Via Angelo Rizzoli, 2, Milan, 20132, Italy; ilmondo@rcs.it; http://www.ilmondo.rcs.it. Illus., index, adv. Sample. Circ: 70000 Paid. *Indexed:* PAIS. *Aud.:* Ga, Ac.

In Italian. *Il Mondo* is a business and finance magazine, published in partnership with *Business Week International.* Covering primarily business, financial markets, and the economy, *Il Mondo* also features articles on politics, society, and science and technology. The web site provides tables of contents of current issues, as well as access to the archives, with the full text of select articles. The latter is free but requires online registration. Recommended to academic libraries supporting research in international business and large public libraries.

2830. ***Neue Rundschau.*** [ISSN: 0028-3347] 1890. q. EUR 34 domestic; EUR 38 in Europe; EUR 45 elsewhere. Ed(s): Martin Bauer. S. Fischer Verlag GmbH, Hedderichstr. 114, Frankfurt am Main, 60596, Germany; verkauf@s-fischer.de; http://www.s-fischer.de. Illus., index, adv. Sample. Circ: 7000. Microform: BHP. Reprint: SCH. *Indexed:* ArtHuCI, IBZ, MLA-IB, SSCI. *Aud.:* Ac.

In German. Published since 1890 by S. Fischer Verlag, the quarterly *Neue Rundschau* is one of Germany's premier literary and cultural magazines. Each issue is organized around a theme and contains articles about or primary work from famous German and international intellectuals, such as Gunter de Bruyn, Paul Michael Lutzeler, George Steiner, Pierre Bourdieu, John Barth, Sten Nadolny, and Siegfried Unseld, to name just a few of the prominent individuals. The web site is mostly informational, but it provides tables of contents back to 1993. Highly recommended to all libraries supporting German studies and comparative literature.

2831. ***New German Critique: an interdisciplinary journal of German studies.*** [ISSN: 0094-033X] 1973. 3x/yr. USD 85 (Individuals, USD 40). Ed(s): David Bathrick. Telos Press Ltd., 431 E 12th St, New York, NY 10009; telospress@aol.com; http://www.arts.cornell.edu/ngc. Illus., index, adv. Sample. Circ: 2000. Microform: PQC. Online: EBSCO Publishing; JSTOR (Web-based Journal Archive). Reprint: PQC. *Indexed:* ABS&EES, AltPI, ArtHuCI, BHA, FLI, MLA-IB, PSA, SSCI, SociolAb. *Aud.:* Ac.

In English. The *New German Critique*, published by the Department of German Studies at Cornell University, is interdisciplinary in scope and covers all major contemporary topics pertaining to political and social theory, philosophy, literature, film, media, and the arts. Issues are organized around a theme and include up to eight lengthy scholarly articles. The web site is mostly informational, but it provides tables of contents from the first issue on. Highly recommended to all research libraries, in particular those supporting collections in contemporary criticism, philosophy, German studies, and comparative literature.

2832. *Nineteenth Century French Studies.* [ISSN: 0146-7891] 1972. s-a. USD 60 (Individuals, USD 45; USD 25 newsstand/cover per issue). Ed(s): Marshall C Olds. University of Nebraska Press, 233 N 8th St, Lincoln, NE 68588-0255; pressmail@unl.edu; http://www.nebraskapress.unl.edu. Illus., index, adv. Refereed. Microform: PQC. Online: Florida Center for Library Automation; Gale Group; OCLC Online Computer Library Center, Inc.; Project MUSE; RoweCom Information Quest; Swets Blackwell; H.W. Wilson. Reprint: PQC. *Indexed:* AmH&L, ArtHuCI, BHA, HumInd, MLA-IB. *Bk. rev.:* 10, length varies. *Aud.:* Ac.

In English and French. *Nineteenth Century French Studies* is a peer-reviewed, scholarly journal that covers all aspects of nineteenth-century French literature and criticism. The journal exmines new trends and includes reviews of promising research in a variety of disciplines in both French and English. The web site, at http://www.unl.edu/ncfs, provides information on submissions, guidelines, and subscriptions, as well as free access to the full archive of abstracts of articles published since the journal's inception. The journal is available in full text online through Project Muse and other large serials aggregators. A premier resource for nineteenth-century French literary scholarship, it is highly recommended to libraries supporting research in French literature.

2833. *Norseman: a review of current events.* Incorporates (1907-1984): *Nordmanns-forbundet.* [ISSN: 0029-1846] 1907. 5x/yr. NOK 250 (Students, NOK 200; Senior citizens, NOK 200). Ed(s): Gunnar Gran, Harry Cleven. Nordmanns-Forbundet, Radhusgata 23 B, Oslo, 0158, Norway; norseman@online.no. Illus., adv. Circ: 10000. *Bk. rev.:* 5, length varies. *Aud.:* Ga, Sa.

In English or Norwegian. *Norseman* has been published by the Nordmanns-Forbundet since 1943, with the goal of promoting "solidarity between Norway and Norwegians abroad and furthering the cause of Norwegian culture and Norwegian interest." Published half in English and half in Norwegian, the *Norseman* covers such subjects as travel, recreation, literature, and art, as well as Norwegian culture at large. Useful for tourists, exchange students, and educators, the *Norseman* provides a good introduction to Norwegian society and culture and is recommended to public libraries with an interest in Scandinavian studies.

2834. *La Nouvelle Revue Francaise.* [ISSN: 0029-4802] 1905. m. FRF 555 domestic; FRF 535 foreign; FRF 62 newsstand/cover per issue. Ed(s): Bertrand Visage. Editions Gallimard, 15, rue Sebastien-Bottin, Paris, 75007, France. Illus. Reprint: PSC. *Indexed:* ArtHuCI, BAS, MLA-IB, SSCI. *Bk. rev.:* 6, length varies. *Aud.:* Ac.

In French. *La Nouvelle Revue Francaise*, or *NRF*, is one of France's most prestigious literary reviews. *NRF* was founded in 1908 by a group of writers, among which Eugene Montfort and Andre Gide. While Gide continues to publish the review after a dissension with Montfort, the journal counts Romain Rolland, Andre Suares, Paul Claudel, Guillaume Apollinaire, Jean Giraudoux, Marcel Proust, Paul Valery, and Roger Martin of Gard among its early contributors. Currently published by novelist and critic, Michel Braudeau, the *NRF* has expanded its scope to include international figures and continues to publish established authors, among which Claudio Magris, Don deLillo, Joyce Carol Oates, Paul Auster, and Caroline Lamarche, as well as the works by new, less-known contemporary writers. Issues include critical essays, poetry, short stories, and reviews of books, art, theatre, and music. The web site at Gallimard provides tables of contents back to 1953. A key magazine, in particular for early twentieth-century French literary studies, *NRF* is highly recommended to research libraries and large public libraries.

2835. *Poetique: revue de theorie et d'analyse litteraires.* [ISSN: 0032-2024] 1970. q. FRF 370 domestic; FRF 430 foreign; FRF 95 newsstand/cover per issue. Editions du Seuil, 27 rue Jacob, Paris, Cedex 6 75261, France. Illus., adv. Sample. *Indexed:* ArtHuCI, BHA, IBZ, MLA-IB, RILM. *Aud.:* Ac.

In French. *Poetique* is published by "L'Ecole Normale Superieure" since 1970, with the support of the Centre National du Livre. With Helene Cixous, Gerard Genette, Michael Rifaterre, among other famous literary personalities, on the editorial board, *Poetique* is among France's most renowned literary periodicals. Analyzing and commenting on Western literature, drama, and film, each issue of *Poetique* contains six to nine scholarly articles. Highly recommended as a key title for libraries supporting French studies and comparative literature.

2836. *Il Politico: rivista italiana di scienze politiche.* [ISSN: 0032-325X] 1950. 3x/yr. EUR 51.65 in the European Union; EUR 77.47 elsewhere. Ed(s): Pasquale Scaramozzino. Casa Editrice Dott. A. Giuffre, Via Busto Arsizio, 40, Milan, 20151, Italy; giuffre@giuffre.it; http://www.giuffre.it. Illus., index, adv. Sample. Circ: 1100. *Indexed:* ABCPolSci, AmH&L, BAS, IBSS, IPSA, PAIS. *Aud.:* Ac.

In Italian and English. Published as a continuation of *Annali di Scienze Politiche* (*Annals of Political Sciences*), *Il Politico* is generally recognized as one of the more important periodicals in the field of political and social sciences, with an emphasis on theory. Renowned for the quality of its articles, written by internationally famous authors, and for the wealth of notes and reviews, as well as jobs ads, *Il Politico* provides English summaries at the end of each issue. The web site at http://www.giuffre.it/Riviste/Politico/Scheda.htm is purely informational. Highly recommended for academic and research libraries.

2837. *Profil: das unabhaengige Nachrichtenmagazin Oesterreichs.* [ISSN: 1022-2111] 1970. w. EUR 72.30 (Students, EUR 37.06). Ed(s): Liselotte Palme, Reinhard Tramontana. Verlagsgruppe News Gesellschaft mbH, Lindengasse 52, Vienna, 1070, Austria; http://www.news.at. Illus., adv. Sample. Circ: 91532 Paid. *Aud.:* Hs, Ga, Ac.

In German. *Profil* is a general newsmagazine, similar to *Time* or *Newsweek*. Austria's leading weekly general-interest magazine, *Profil* provides in-depth coverage of Austrian news, politics, and current events, as well as the arts, media, and cultural trends, and international news, politics, and the economy. The web site is well organized and contains numerous articles in full text, including photographs and features expected from a major news site, such as classifieds and special reports on technology, the arts, books, and more. The archives are searchable from 1994, and hits are displayed within their context, but the full text is only available to subscribers. A comprehensive source covering Austria and the world, *Profil* is highly recommended to libraries covering Austrian studies and international news.

2838. *Quinzaine Litteraire.* [ISSN: 0048-6493] 1966. fortn. FRF 425 domestic; FRF 560 foreign; FRF 25 newsstand/cover per issue. Ed(s): Maurice Nadeau. S E L I S la Quinzaine Litteraire, 135 rue Sain-Martin, Paris, Cedex 4 75194, France. Illus., adv. Sample. Circ: 20000. Microform: PQC. Reprint: PQC. *Indexed:* ArtHuCI, IBZ, MLA-IB, SSCI. *Bk. rev.:* 20, length varies. *Aud.:* Ga, Ac.

In French. The *Quinzaine Litteraire* was established in 1966 by Maurice Nadeau and quickly established itself as a serious literary journal, with a reputation for tackling the most controversial contemporary authors, both through its reviews of new publications, its essays, and its publication of original prose and poetry. Issues also include theater and cinema reviews. Contributors are among France's most well-known thinkers and writers. The web site is mostly informational, but it provides a respectable number of full-text articles and access to special issues, as well as links to selected web sites. Highly recommended to all libraries supporting research and interest in contemporary French literature.

2839. *Revue des Deux Mondes: litterature, histoire, arts et sciences.* Former titles (until 1982): *Nouvelle Revue des Deux Mondes;* (until 1972): *Revue des Deux Mondes.* [ISSN: 0750-9278] 1829. m. FRF 570; FRF 65 newsstand/cover per issue. Ed(s): Bruno de Cessole. Societe de la Revue des Deux Mondes, 54 rue Martre, Clichy, Cedex 92586, France. Illus., index, adv. Circ: 15000. Reprint: PQC; PSC; SCH. *Indexed:* BAS, HAPI, MLA-IB. *Bk. rev.:* 2, length varies. *Aud.:* Ga, Ac.

In French. The *Revue des Deux Mondes* was first published in 1829, with the objective to establish a cultural, economic, and political bridge between France and the United States. Truly multidisciplinary, the *Revue* covers all major subjects affecting our societies and is one of the primary agents of intercultural dialogue and debate between the New and Old Worlds, but also the North and South, the East and West. Providing commentary and analysis on world events from a mostly French perspective, the journal has over the years accumulated an impressive list of contributors. Truly a unique resource, the *Revue des Deux Mondes* is now also available in digital format from the *Bibliotheque Nationale*'s digital library portal, Gallica. The *Revue* is one of the few publications that may rightly claim to be a cultural institution.

2840. *Revue d'Histoire Moderne et Contemporaine.* [ISSN: 0048-8003] 1899. 4x/yr. EUR 73.18 (Individuals, EUR 58.69). Ed(s): Daniel Roche. Editions Belin, 8 Rue Ferou, Paris, 75278 Cedex 06, France; http://www.editions-belin.com. Illus., index. Sample. Refereed. Circ: 1800 Paid. Microform: PQC. Reprint: SWZ. *Indexed:* AmH&L, ArtHuCI, BAS, BHA, IBSS, IBZ, IPSA, SSCI. *Bk. rev.:* 17, length varies. *Aud.:* Ac.

In French. The *Revue d'Histoire Moderne et Contemporaine* (*RHMC*) is the official journal of the Societe d'Histoire Moderne et Contemporaine. First published by Pierre Caron in 1899, the *Revue* is supported by the Centre National de la Recherche Scientifique (CNRS) and the Centre National du Livre (CNL). Each quarterly issue of this eminent, peer-reviewed journal is comprised of six to ten lengthy research articles and detailed book reviews dealing with topics in European history from the sixteenth century to the present. Examples of recent research topics include a study of the war in Algeria and the emigration of French nobility to Germany during the French Revolution. In addition, the *Revue* contains an extensive list of books received, with summaries in both French and English. The web site at http://www.editions-belin.com is mostly informational, but it provides tables of contents of current issues back to 2001. A recommended acquisition for libraries supporting European history research.

2841. *Revue Historique.* [ISSN: 0035-3264] 1876. q. EUR 80 domestic; EUR 95 foreign. Ed(s): Claude Gauvard, J F Sirinelli. Presses Universitaires de France, Departement des Revues, 6 av. Reille, Paris, 75685 Cedex 14, France; revues@puf.com. Illus., index. Microform: PQC. Reprint: PQC; PSC. *Indexed:* AmH&L, ArtHuCI, BAS, BHA, IBZ, NumL, RILM, SSCI. *Bk. rev.:* 60, length varies. *Aud.:* Ac.

In French. Founded in 1876 by Gabriel Monod, the *Revue Historique* is published by the Presses Universitaires de France (PUF). Each issue contains several lengthy, scholarly articles; a section titled "Melanges" (Mixtures) generally consisting of new historical work expanding upon old issues; a historical bulletin; numerous reviews; calls for papers; and theses supported at French universities. The *Revue Historique* is France's main publication covering general history. The December issue contains an annual index. The web site at http://www.puf.com is informational only. Recommended to research libraries.

2842. *Rivista di Letterature Moderne e Comparate.* [ISSN: 0391-2108] 1946. q. ITL 80000; ITL 120000 foreign. Ed(s): A R Parra, A Pizzorusso. Pacini Editore, Via A. Gherardesca, Ospedaletto, 56121, Italy; pacini.editore@pacinieditore.it; http://www.pacinieditore.it. Illus., adv. Sample. Circ: 520. *Indexed:* ArtHuCI, MLA-IB. *Bk. rev.:* 13, length varies. *Aud.:* Ac.

In Italian, French, and English. Established by Carlo Pellegrini and Vittorio Santoli, the *Rivista di Letterature Moderne e Comparate* covers the whole spectrum of Western literature since the Renaissance. With about six scholarly articles and numerous book reviews in Italian, French, and English, the *Rivista* addresses comparatists in both Europe and North America. The December issue contains an index for the year. The web site at http://www.pacinieditore.it is purely informational. Recommended for research libraries supporting programs in comparative literature.

2843. *Rivista Storica Italiana.* [ISSN: 0035-7073] 1884. 3x/yr. EUR 114 (Individuals, EUR 88). Ed(s): Emilio Gabba. Edizioni Scientifiche Italiane SpA, Via Chiatamone, 7, Naples, 80121, Italy; info@esispa.com; http://www.dial.it/esi. Illus., index, adv. Sample. Circ: 1600. Reprint: SCH. *Indexed:* AmH&L, ArtHuCI, BAS, BHA, IBSS, MLA-IB, NumL, SSCI. *Bk. rev.:* 8-15, length varies. *Aud.:* Ac.

In Italian. Founded in 1884 and published by the *Edizioni Scientifiche Italiane*, the *Rivista Storica Italiana* is among Italy's premier historical journals. The comprehensive *Rivista* covers all periods of world history, albeit with a focus on Italian history. Each issue contains six to twelve lengthy scholarly articles, usually organized around a theme; a section with historiographical essays; numerous reviews of new publications; and a list of books received. This quarterly is essential to any library supporting historical research.

2844. *Scandinavian Journal of History.* Incorporates: *Excerpta Historica Nordica.* [ISSN: 0346-8755] 1976. q. GBP 102 (Individuals, GBP 52). Ed(s): Sverre Bagge. Taylor & Francis A S, Cort Adelersgt. 17, Solli, PO Box 2562, Oslo, 0202, Norway. Illus., adv. Sample. Online: EBSCO Publishing; Ingenta Select; OCLC Online Computer Library Center, Inc.; RoweCom Information Quest; Swets Blackwell. Reprint: PSC. *Indexed:* AmH&L, ArtHuCI, CJA, SSCI. *Aud.:* Ac.

In English. The *Scandinavian Journal of History* is a joint publication of the historical associations of Denmark, Finland, Norway, and Sweden. The journal contains scholarly articles and and review essays surveying themes in recent Scandinavian historical research. Although most authors are Scandinavian, all articles and reviews are published in English. It also contains a books-received section at the back of each issue. The web site at http://www.tandf.no/sjhist provides tables of contents back to 1998. Full texts are available for subscribers. Recommended for research libraries supporting Scandinavian studies.

2845. *Scandinavian Review.* Formerly (until 1975): *American Scandinavian Review.* [ISSN: 0098-857X] 1913. 3x/yr. USD 15. Ed(s): Adrienne Gyongy. American-Scandinavian Foundation, 58 Park Ave., New York, NY 10016-3007; http://www.amscan.org. Illus., index, adv. Sample. Circ: 5000. Microform: PQC. Online: bigchalk; Chadwyck-Healey Incorporated; Northern Light Technology, Inc.; OCLC Online Computer Library Center, Inc.; ProQuest Information & Learning. Reprint: PQC. *Indexed:* GeoRef, MLA-IB, PAIS, SSI. *Bk. rev.:* 2-5, 450 words. *Aud.:* Hs, Ga, Ac.

In English. *Scandinavian Review* is published by the American-Scandinavian Foundation (ASF), whose mission is to "promote an international understanding by means of educational and cultural exchange between the U.S. and Denmark, Finland, Iceland, Norway, and Sweden." The magazine covers all aspects of contemporary life in Scandinavia, with particular emphasis on art and design; industrial development; and commercial, political, economic, and social innovation. Regular features include articles on a particular theme or person, reviews of Nordic books, and a list of contributors. Subscription information and examples of articles can be found at the ASF web site at http://www.amscan.org. Leading journalists and writers on both sides of the Atlantic are contributors. Because this magazine offers information rarely found in American media about the Nordic countries, it is an excellent addition to any collection supporting European studies.

2846. *Scandinavian Studies (Provo).* [ISSN: 0036-5637] 1911. q. USD 60 (Individuals, USD 50; Students, USD 25). Society for the Advancement of Scandinavian Study, c/o Steven P Sondrup, Ed, Department of Comparative Literature, Provo, UT 84602-6118; http://www.byu.edu/sasslink. Illus., index, adv. Sample. Refereed. Circ: 1100. Microform: PQC. Online: bigchalk; Chadwyck-Healey Incorporated; EBSCO Publishing; Factiva; Gale Group; OCLC Online Computer Library Center, Inc.; ProQuest Information & Learning; H.W. Wilson. Reprint: PQC. *Indexed:* AmH&L, ArtHuCI, HumInd, LRI, MLA-IB. *Bk. rev.:* 15, lengthy. *Aud.:* Ac.

Text in English. Published by Brigham Young University, *Scandinavian Studies* is a scholarly, refereed journal covering philological and linguistic problems of Scandinavian languages, medieval and modern; Scandinavian literature; and studies of Scandinavian history, society, and culture. Although *Scandinavian Studies* accepts submissions in Scandinavian languages, all are translated into English, including the reviews. Contributors are mostly North American. Recommended to research libraries supporting Scandinavian studies.

2847. *Schweizer Monatshefte: Zeitschrift fuer Politik, Wirtschaft, Kultur.* [ISSN: 0036-7400] 1921. m. CHF 110 domestic; CHF 131 foreign. Ed(s): Robert Nef, Michael Wirth. Schweizer Monatshefte, Vogelsangstr

52, Zuerich, 8006, Switzerland. Illus., adv. Circ: 3000. Microform: PQC. Reprint: PQC. *Indexed:* BAS, IBZ, IPSA, MLA-IB, PAIS. *Bk. rev.:* Various number and length. *Aud.:* Ac.

In German and sometimes French. *Schweizer Monatshefte* is Switzerland's and one of Europe's premier critical magazines. Covering politics, the economy, and culture, *Schweizer Monatshefte* has been published since 1931 and has successfully resisted the commercial pressures of today's society. The reader will not find large color photos here; rather, *Schweizer Monatshefte* is well known for its in-depth treatment and philosophical and analytical approach to contemporary issues facing Western societies. Having published primary materials by such famous authors as Friedrich Durrenmatt and Max Frisch, and including dossiers on topics ranging from unemployment, to the ethics of modern science, to the future of higher education, *Schweizer Monatshefte* is a comprehensive, ambitious, and demanding magazine that will appeal to intellectuals in all disciplines. The web site is well organized and provides tables of contents back to 1999. Highly recommended for research institutions.

2848. ***Sinn und Form: Beitraege zur Literatur.*** [ISSN: 0037-5756] 1949. bi-m. EUR 39.90 domestic; EUR 50 foreign; EUR 9 newsstand/cover per issue. Ed(s): Sebastian Kleinschmidt. Aufbau-Verlag GmbH, Neue Promenade 6, Berlin, 10178, Germany; info@aufbau-verlag.de; http://www.aufbau-verlag.de. Adv. Refereed. Circ: 3000. *Indexed:* ArtHuCI, BHA, IBZ, MLA-IB, RILM, SSCI. *Aud.:* Ac.

In German. Published by the Deutsche Akademie der Kunste zu Berlin, *Sinn und Form* is primarily a literary magazine, focusing on literary criticism and theory, but including essays on philosophy and theology, as well as society at large. Hailed by the *Frankfurter Allgemeine Zeitung* as "possibly the best literary magazine in the German-speaking world," *Sinn und Form* boasts an exceptional list of contributors: George Steiner, Julien Green, Hans-Georg Gadamer, E. M. Cioran, Jurgen Habermas, Heiner Muller, Ernst Junger, Czeslaw Milosz, Kenzaburo Oe, Emmanuel Levinas, Jorge Semprun, Seamus Heaney, Michel Tournier, Peter Sloterdijk, and Claudio Magris—to name just a few—who have all contributed original work to the journal. Highly recommended for any library supporting research in German studies.

The Spectator. See News and Opinion section.

2849. ***Der Spiegel.*** [ISSN: 0038-7452] 1947. w. EUR 145.60 domestic; EUR 200.20 per issue in Europe; EUR 278.20 per issue elsewhere. Ed(s): Stefan Aust. Spiegel-Verlag Rudolf Augstein GmbH und Co. KG, Brandstwiete 19, Hamburg, 20457, Germany; uly_foerster@spiegel.de; http://www.spiegel.de. Illus., adv. Sample. Circ: 1122079 Paid. *Indexed:* BAS, PAIS. *Aud.:* Ga, Ac.

In German. *Der Spiegel* is Germany's premier quality newsmagazine. Covering all topics one would expect from a weekly general-interest newsmagazine, *Der Spiegel* distances itself from its more popular counterparts, such as *Focus* or *Stern*, through high-quality, in-depth reporting. Particularly strong in its coverage of German political affairs, *Der Spiegel*'s revelations on political corruption and mismanagement have, on several occasions during the magazine's history, led to the resignation of leading political figures. *Der Spiegel* is equally well known for its aggressive reporting on environmental issues and provides in-depth articles on foreign affairs. *Der Spiegel* has published several separate publications, including *Manager Magazin*, and the TV show, *Spiegel-TV*, similar to *60 Minutes*. The web site is well organized and provides countless articles in full text, including pictures and audiovisual streaming of clips. The archive (1997–) is free for the three previous months. Highly recommended to research institutions and public libraries as Germany's premier weekly magazine.

2850. ***Suomen Kuvalehti.*** [ISSN: 0039-5552] 1917. w. FIM 784. Ed(s): Tapani Ruokanen. Yhtyneet Kuvalehdet Oy, Maistraatinportti 1, Helsinki, 00015, Finland. Illus., adv. Circ: 101380. *Aud.:* Ga, Ac.

Text in Finnish. *Suomen Kuvalehti* is Finland's premier newsmagazine. Covering national and international current events; social, economic, and political news; and media, books, film, and sports, *Suomen Kuvalehti* resembles *Time*, *Der Spiegel*, and other general-interest weekly magazines. The web site contains mostly summaries, but it includes full texts of selected feature articles. The archive is freely accessible, with coverage from January 2003. Recommended to research libraries supporting Scandinavian studies and large public libraries with an interest in Finnish news.

2851. ***Les Temps Modernes.*** [ISSN: 0040-3075] 1945. bi-m. FRF 440; FRF 450 foreign. Temps Modernes, 4 rue Ferou, Paris, 75006, France. Illus., adv. Reprint: SCH. *Indexed:* AltPI, ArtHuCI, BAS, IBSS, IPSA, MLA-IB, PAIS, SSCI. *Aud.:* Ac.

In French. *Les Temps Modernes* was founded in the aftermath (1945) of World War II by Jean-Paul Sartre. The first members of the editorial board included Raymond Aron, Simone de Beauvoir, Michel Leiris, Maurice Merleau-Ponty, Albert Olivier, and Jean Paulhan. Currently published by Gallimard and edited by Claude Lanzmann, *Les Temps Modernes* is a cultural review, primarily covering politics, philosophy, and literature, but expanding its analysis to all issues facing the modern world. Over the years, it has published contributions by members of its editorial board, as well as Richard Wright, Francis Ponge, Jacques-Laurent Bost, Jean Roy, Samuel Beckett, Alberto Moravia, Carlo Levi, James Agee, Boris Vian, Raymond Queneau, Jean Genet, and Nathalie Sarraute, to name just a few. Of international stature and one of the most important publications of its type in the twentieth century, *Les Temps Modernes* is highly recommended to all research libraries.

2852. ***Text und Kritik: Zeitschrift fuer Literatur.*** [ISSN: 0040-5329] 1962. q. DEM 74. Ed(s): Heinz Ludwig Arnold. Edition Text und Kritik im Richard Boorberg Verlag, Levelingstr 6A, Munich, 81673, Germany; info@etk-muenchen.de; http://www.etk-muenchen.de. Adv. *Indexed:* ArtHuCI, BHA, MLA-IB. *Bk. rev.:* Various number and length. *Aud.:* Ac.

In German. Published since 1963, *Text und Kritik*, founded by Heinz Ludwig Arnold, is a literary review publishing contemporary authors, as well as critical essays on all of German literature. Every month, *Text und Kritik* focuses on a particular author or theme. Topics covered include, for example, the formation of the German literary canon and "pop" literature. Contributors are German literary scholars, critics, and authors, including W. G. Sebald, Jurgen Becker, and Adalbert Stifter. The web site at http://www.etk-muenchen.de/literatur is mostly informational, but it contains the tables of contents for selected back issues (1983–). Highly recommended to all research libraries supporting German studies as well as to large public libraries with an interest in German literature.

2853. ***Wespennest: Zeitschrift fuer brauchbare Texte und Bilder.*** [ISSN: 1012-7313] 1969. q. ATS 420 domestic; ATS 440 foreign. Ed(s): Walter Famler. Wespennest, Rembrandtstrasse 31, Vienna, 1020, Austria; office@wespennest.at; http://www.wespennest.at. Adv. Circ: 5000 Controlled. *Aud.:* Ga.

In German. *Wespennest* has published texts by noted authors as well as newcomers on a quarterly basis since 1969. Each issue presents a literary, essayistic, art-theoretical, or political topic. Sections include the "Wiener Portraits," which, despite its name, presents noted figures on the international cultural scene. *Wespennest* also contains interviews and reviews. The web site, unfortunately, suffers from a misuse of frames and is, at times, difficult to read, but it does provide full texts in pdf of selected articles and reviews, including some from back issues. Recommended to stay abreast of Austrian cultural events.

2854. ***Yale French Studies.*** [ISSN: 0044-0078] 1948. s-a. Ed(s): Alyson Waters. Yale University Press, PO Box 209040, New Haven, CT 06520-9040; customer.care@triliteral.org; http://www.yale.edu/yup/. Illus., adv. Sample. Circ: 2500. Microform: PQC. Online: Gale Group. Reprint: PSC. *Indexed:* ABS&EES, ArtHuCI, BHA, HumInd, MLA-IB, SSCI. *Aud.:* Ac.

One of the premier journals on French literature, thought, and civilization in the English language. Each number has a distinct title and focuses on a special topic. Althought essays are mostly contributed by North American scholars, *Yale French Studies* has included articles by the most well-known contemporary French authors and critics since its inception. The journal provides a multidisciplinary approach to literature that includes French-speaking cultures outside of France. Accessible through JSTOR with a two-year wall, and the publisher's web site (Yale University Press) provides short abstracts for each article free. Indispensable for any library supporting the study of French literature, thought, and culture.

Newspapers

Newspapers are popular among Europeans. It has been reported that an average of 31 million newspapers are sold in Germany each day and 80 percent of the German population over the age of 14 reads at least one newspaper daily. Like Germany, the rest of Western Europe has an appetite for reading newspapers. To stay competitive, newspaper publishers have created user-friendly and continuously updated web versions of their products while adding more color and innovative designs to their print editions. Although brief, this section presents newspapers that either have high international readership or are cited as the nation's newspaper of record.

See also the Newspapers section and check the index for specific titles not included here.

2855. *Aftenposten.* Formerly: *Christiania Adresseblad.* [ISSN: 0804-3116] 1860. d. NOK 2256; NOK 12 newsstand/cover per issue. Ed(s): Einar Hanseid. Aftenposten A-S, Postboks 1178, Oslo, 0107, Norway; aftenposten@aftenposten.no; http://www.aftenposten.no. Illus., adv. Circ: 279331. Online: Gale Group. *Aud.:* Ga, Ac.

In Norwegian. *Aftenposten* is Norway's main newspaper. Published in Oslo, it covers local, national, and international news, politics, business and the economy, cultural events, and sports. As the country's premier daily and paper of record, *Aftenposten* reports on and shapes the national debate, yet is full of colorful illustrations and generous white spaces that make this paper very accessible. The web site is freely accessible and provides access to a number of selected articles. Subscribers receive access to the full edition. This well-organized site provides a link to the news in English, but the ads are a bit overbearing. Recommended to all libraries wanting to cover Norwegian and international news.

2856. *Berlingske Tidende.* [ISSN: 0106-4223] 1749. d. DKK 3219; DKK 814 Sun. Ed(s): Nielse Lunde, Michael Ehrenreich. Berlingske Dagblade AS, Pilestraede 34, Copenhagen K, 1147, Denmark. Illus., index, adv. Circ: 150000 Controlled. *Aud.:* Ac.

In Danish. *Berlingske Tidende* is Denmark's main daily and newspaper of record. Founded in 1749, it is also one of the oldest newspapers in the world. *Berlingske Tidende* reports on national and international news, politics, business and economics, health and medicine, the arts, media, and sports, as well as society at large, including a lifestyle section with articles on travel, fine dining, cars, and more. The web site provides the full texts of a number of articles as well as other features one would expect from a leading newspaper. It is well organized and relatively free of ads. The archive goes back to 1990 but is reserved for subscribers only. As Denmark's premier newspaper, *Berlingske Tidende* is recommended for research collections and large public libraries.

2857. *Dagens Nyheter.* [ISSN: 1101-2447] 1864. d. SEK 2540. Ed(s): Jan Wifstrand. AB Dagens Nyheter, Gjoerwellsgatan 30, Stockholm, 10515, Sweden. Illus., adv. Circ: 360000. *Aud.:* Ga, Ac.

In Swedish. *Dagens Nyheter* is Sweden's premier daily newspaper and the paper of record. As such, it covers national and international news, politics, business and economics, culture, media, and sports. Full of photos and illustrations, including cartoons, it is a family-oriented newspaper that does not sacrifice quality. Its articles are often quoted or translated by English newspapers, such as *The Guardian* or *The Financial Times*. The web site provides free access to the text of major current articles as well as the archive from 2002. Access to articles back to 1992 is reserved to subscribers. A Sunday-only subscription is available. Recommended to all research libraries and those wanting to cover Swedish news.

2858. *Le Figaro.* [ISSN: 0182-5852] 1828. d. FRF 314.89 domestic; EUR 48 domestic; FRF 662.55 foreign. Ed(s): Baudouin Bollaert. Societe du Figaro S.A., 37 rue du Louvre, Paris, 75002, France; http://groupe.lefigaro.fr. Illus., adv. Circ: 492725 Paid. Microform: NRP. *Indexed:* GeoRef. *Aud.:* Ga, Ac.

In French. With *Le Monde*, *Le Figaro* is one of the major French newspapers, covering national and international news, politics, and cultural events. While *Le Monde* is generally perceived as the main independent French national newspaper, yet with a central-left slant, *Le Figaro* is its main contender, with a central-right slant. Published in Paris since 1828, *Le Figaro* is probably France's most ancient daily newspaper, with a long and turbulent history. Over the years, the paper has spawned several supplements, of which the *Figaro Litteraire* dates back to 1946 and counted Paul Claudel, Julien Green, and Colette, among others, as contributors. Since then, *Figaro Magazine*, *Figaro Madame*, *Le Figaro Economie*, *Le Figaro Entreprises*, and a number of other publications complement the daily newspaper. *Le Figaro* regularly shares articles with like-minded papers, such as *Die Welt* and the *Daily Telegraph*, as well as *ABC* of Spain. The freely accessible web site covers the major news stories and provides access to the archives up to 1980 on a fee-per-article basis. *Le Figaro* is recommended to libraries wanting a diversified collection and a varied take on the French news.

2859. *France - Amerique: edition international du Figaro.* [ISSN: 0747-2757] 1828. w. USD 49 domestic; USD 206 foreign; USD 1.50 newsstand/cover per issue. Ed(s): Jean-Louis Turlin. Trocadero Publishing, Inc., 1560 Broadway, Ste 511, New York, NY 10036; franceame@aol.com; http://www.france.com/france-amerique/. Illus., adv. Circ: 20000. *Aud.:* Ga, Ac.

In French. Owned by *Figaro*, *France - Amerique* is geared toward French expatriates in the United States. Covering French news, politics, business, sports, the media, culture, and society at large, *France - Amerique* relates most major stories to the French-American relationship. Also covered are French cultural events in the United States and the remnants of French culture in North America. The web site is well organized and contains full texts of selected articles. It also includes links to information about visas and other practical issues for French expatriates living in the United States. Recommended for public libraries.

2860. *Frankfurter Allgemeine: Zeitung fuer Deutschland.* [ISSN: 0174-4909] 1949. d. DEM 600; DEM 2 newsstand/cover per issue; DEM 2.50 newsstand/cover Sat. Ed(s): Hugo Mueller-Vogg. Frankfurter Allgemeine Zeitung Institut GmbH, Hellerhofstr 2-4, Frankfurt Am Main, 60327, Germany; http://www.faz.de. Illus., adv. Circ: 530443. Microform: NRP. Online: Factiva; Gale Group; LexisNexis. *Aud.:* Ga, Ac, Sa.

In German. The *Frankfurter Allgemeine Zeitung*, or *FAZ*, as it is commonly known, is generally perceived as Germany's leading newspaper. Established in 1949, in then West Germany's financial and publishing center, Frankfurt am Main, *FAZ* is a paper of exceptional quality, with carefully researched articles on national and international news, politics, business and the economy, sports, and travel. Well known for its cultural section, "Feuilleton," the *FAZ* dominates the intellectual debate and its literary critics are widely influential. The web site provides non-German speakers with an English version and includes a wide selection of articles summarized from the print version. The archive goes back to 1993 for the daily paper and 1995 for the *Rhein-Main-Zeitung*, the regional section of *FAZ*, and the *Frankfurter Allgemeinen Sonntagszeitung*, the Sunday edition. *FAZ* is indispensable for research libraries and recommended for all collections supporting German studies.

The Guardian. See Newspapers/General section.

2861. *Helsingin Sanomat.* [ISSN: 0355-2047] 1904. d. FIM 1090; FIM 10 newsstand/cover per issue. Ed(s): Janne Virkkunen. Sanoma Corporation, PL 78, Sanomat, 00089, Finland; http://www.helsinginsanomat.fi. Illus., adv. Circ: 454833. *Indexed:* MLA-IB. *Aud.:* Ga, Ac.

In Finnish. *Helsingin Sanomat* is generally considered Finland's premier newspaper. Covering national and international affairs, business, the arts and media, sports, and local events, *Helsingin Sanomat*'s evenhanded approach and balancing of views is exemplary. The paper's layout and design is attractive and includes color photographs. The web site is well organized and text-intensive. While it would benefit from large color images and more white space, the comparatively low number of ads is laudable. In addition, the web site includes a link to the *Helsingin Sanomat International Edition*, which provides a summary of the major stories in English. Access to both the *Helsingin Sanomat* and its English edition is free, as are the archives of the latter, going back to 2000. Recommended for libraries supporting Scandinavian studies.

2862. *International Herald Tribune: the world's daily newspaper.* [ISSN: 0294-8052] 1887. 6x/w. FRF 1950; USD 360; FRF 10 newsstand/cover per issue. Ed(s): Michael Getler. International Herald Tribune, 6 bis, rue des Graviers, Neuilly-sur-Seine, Cedex 92521, France; iht@iht.com; http://www.iht.com. Illus., adv. Circ: 234722 Paid. Microform: PQC; NRP. Online: bigchalk; Florida Center for Library Automation; Gale Group; LexisNexis; Northern Light Technology, Inc.; ProQuest Information & Learning. *Indexed:* B&I. *Aud.:* Ga, Ac.

In English. Published for American expatriates since 1887, the *International Herald Tribune* (*IHT*) is the product of a unique collaboration between the *New York Times* and a number of premier international newspapers, among them *El Pais*, the *Frankfurter Allgemeine Zeitung*, *Haaretz*, and others. While the *IHT* started out as being available only in select locations (Paris in the 1920s being one of them), it is now being printed in 21 locations and distributed around the world. The well-organized web site presents the news with a different emphasis according to the region of interest. It provides free access to selected full-text articles and a weekly archive. The world's most international paper, it will provide a unique summary of world news to the reader.

2863. *The Irish Times.* [ISSN: 0791-5144] 1859. d. Ed(s): Valentine Lamb. Irish Times Ltd., 10-15 D'Olier St., Dublin, 2, Ireland. Illus. Circ: 102460 Paid. Microform: NRP. Online: Gale Group; Northern Light Technology, Inc. *Indexed:* PAIS. *Aud.:* Ga, Ac.

In English. Published since 1859, the *Irish Times* established itself as Ireland's premier independent newspaper in 1974, when it established a trust to remain free "from any form of personal or party political, commercial, religious or other sectional control." With correspondents all over the world, the *Irish Times* covers international and national news, politics, the economy, technology, media, sports, the arts, and any other issue of general interest. The web site provides free access to select full text as well as an archive searchable from 1998. Recommended to research and large public libraries or those supporting a large Irish community.

2864. *Liberation.* [ISSN: 0335-1793] 1973. d. FRF 1880; FRF 7 newsstand/cover per issue. Liberation, 11 rue Beranger, Paris, Cedex 3 75154, France; espaceslibe@liberation.fr; http://www.liberation.fr. Illus., adv. Circ: 210000 Paid. Microform: NRP. Online: LexisNexis. *Bk. rev.:* Various number and length. *Aud.:* Ga.

In French. *Liberation* is one of the major French daily newspapers. Established in 1973 by Serge July in the aftermath of and in line with the student protests of May 1968, *Liberation* has an outspoken, provocative leftist slant that has not prevented the paper from becoming a serious, mainstream, and national publication. Generally read by younger generations, students, and the intellectual left, *Liberation* covers daily national and international news as well as cultural events. Geared toward younger readers, *Libe*, as it is known in France, is recommended for research libraries and for those wanting an alternative to the more established papers *Le Monde* and *Le Figaro*.

2865. *Le Monde.* [ISSN: 0395-2037] 1944. d. FRF 1980 domestic; FRF 2960 foreign; FRF 7.50 newsstand/cover per issue. Ed(s): Jean Marie Colombani. Le Monde S.A., 21 bis, rue Claude Bernard, Paris, 75005, France; redac@lemonde.fr; http://www.lemonde.fr. Illus., index, adv. Circ: 500000. Microform: RPI. Online: Telesystemes-Questel. *Aud.:* Ga, Ac.

In French. *Le Monde* is generally perceived as France's leading newspaper. Established in 1944, after France's liberation, *Le Monde* rose from the ashes of *Le Temps*, following the de Gaulle's wish for a new paper of reference. First edited by Hubert Beuve-Mery, *Le Monde* established itself as an independent newspaper through its in-depth and quality reporting on national and international news and politics, business and the economy, the arts, and media. Its political commentary and section on the arts, including a weekly literary supplement, are widely regarded as the most influential in France. Over the years, *Le Monde* has developed several supplements and sections to increase readership, for example on education and on technology. Other initiatives, such as *Le Monde Diplomatique* and the *Cahier du Cinema*, have established themselves as successful, independent publications. The free web site is one of the most complete and well organized online newspaper sites and includes full texts from a wide variety of articles. The archive, which can be searched from 1987 to the present, provides full texts for a fee. Essential to all research collections and recommended to all libraries as the major French news source.

2866. *Morgunbladid.* [ISSN: 1021-7266] 1913. d. exc. Mon. ISK 22800; ISK 125 newsstand/cover per issue. Ed(s): Matthias Johannessen, Styrmir Gunnarsson. Arvakur h.f., Kringlan 1, Reykjavik, 103, Iceland; mbl@centrum.is; http://www.mbl.is/frettir. Illus., adv. Circ: 54000 Controlled. *Aud.:* Ac.

In Icelandic. *Morgunbladid* is Iceland's premier daily newspaper. Covering national and international news, politics, the econony, arts, media, and sports, *Morgunbladid* also includes reviews of films, plays, music, and books. A Sunday-only subscription is available. The web site, well organized and easy to browse, includes an archive from 1986. Highly recommended to research libraries covering Icelandic and Scandinavian studies.

2867. *N R C - Handelsblad.* [ISSN: 0002-5259] 1970. d. Mon.-Sat. NLG 508.50; NLG 2.35 newsstand/cover per issue; NLG 3 newsstand/cover Sat. Ed(s): M Oostelaraan. P C M Uitgevers NV, N R C - Handelsblad, Postbus 8987, Rotterdam, 3009 TH, Netherlands; nrc@nrc.nl; http://www.nrc.nl. Illus., adv. Circ: 270000 Paid. *Aud.:* Ga, Ac.

In Dutch. The *NRC - Handelsblad* (*NRC*) is the Netherland's premier daily newspaper. Created in the 1970s through merger of the *Nieuwe Rotterdamse Courant* and the *Algemeen Handelsblad*, two of the country's major papers, the *NRC* is known for its independent stance and serious approach to national and international news, politics, and the economy. The *NRC* also covers cultural events in great detail and is a leading source for book reviews. The web site is well organized and provides free access to select full text. The archives are searchable for the previous three months, but require online registration. A weekend edition of the *NRC* is also available. Highly recommended to research libraries and large public libraries covering international news and Dutch studies.

2868. *Ta Nea.* 1946. d. Ed(s): Leon Karapanayiotis. Lambrakis Press SA, 10 St George Karytsis Sq, Athens, 102 37, Greece; ta-nea@dolnet.gr; http://ta-nea.dolnet.gr. Illus., adv. *Aud.:* Ac.

In Greek. *Ta Nea* is one of Greece's main daily newspapers. Published in Athens, it covers all major national and international news stories, including the arts, media, and sports. The web site provides access to selected current articles and to archival issues. Recommended for research libraries supporting contemporary Greek and international studies and for public libraries serving a large Greek community.

2869. *Neue Zuercher Zeitung.* [ISSN: 0376-6829] 1780. d. except Sun. CHF 387; CHF 2.20 newsstand/cover per issue. Ed(s): Hugo Buetler. Neue Zuercher Zeitung, Falkenstr 11, Zuerich, 8021, Switzerland. Illus., adv. Circ: 169623. Microform: RPI; NRP. Online: Factiva; Gale Group; LexisNexis. *Indexed:* B&I, BHA. *Aud.:* Ac.

In German. Published since 1780, the *Neue Zuercher Zeitung*, is one of Europe's oldest and most renowned newspapers. Switzerland's premier daily and highly regarded abroad, it provides well-written and well-researched articles on national and international news, the economy, politics, media, the arts, and sports. Particularly outstanding is its coverage of business and the economy, as well as its cultural pages. The web site is well organized and provides access to selected full texts, as well as to the archives from 1993 to date, but access to the latter is restricted. The site includes an "English Window," which includes selected full texts of articles translated into English. Should be acquired by all research libraries.

2870. ***Die Presse: unabhaengige Tageszeitungs fuer Oesterreich.*** Formerly: *Neue Freie Press.* 1848. d. Mon.-Sat. ATS 3280. Ed(s): Julius Kainz. Presse, Parkring 12 A, Vienna, 1015, Austria. Illus., adv. Circ: 104560 Paid and controlled. Microform: ALP; NRP. *Indexed:* B&I. *Aud.:* Ac.

In German. *Die Presse* is generally viewed as Austria's most reputable newspaper, though its circulation is less than that of its more popular competitors. Covering national and international news, politics, the economy, media, culture, arts, sports, technology, and local events in Vienna, *Die Presse* is available both in German and English at http://www.diepresse.at. Including full texts of selected articles, the web site provides a free newsletter service and contains numerous subsections, including one on technology. The archive is limited to subscribers to the print edition, but it is searchable online. Recommended to large research and public libraries with an interest in Austrian studies.

2871. ***La Repubblica.*** [ISSN: 0390-1076] 1976. d. Ed(s): Ezio Mauro. Editoriale la Repubblica, Piazza Indipendenza 11b, Rome, 00185, Italy; larepubblica@repubblica.it; http://www.repubblica.it. Adv. *Bk. rev.:* Various number and length. *Aud.:* Ga.

In Italian. *La Repubblica* is Italy's main independent newspaper, covering national and international news, politics, business and economics, the arts, literature, and media. The paper has several supplements, such as the highly influential literary section, published every Thursday, and the magazine *Venerdi di Repubblica*, which accompanies the paper every Friday and is similar to such American publications as *Time*. The *Repubblica*'s editorial stance is generally perceived as being on the center-left. Its main national contender is *Corriere della Sera*, which belongs to the Berlusconi empire. The web site is helpful and provides full texts of a fairly large, varied number of articles, but it is teeming with ads, which can render browsing frustrating. For subscribers, the print version is available as pdf files through http://KataWeb.it. Recommended to all research libraries and those supporting Italian studies as the primary independent Italian news source.

The Times. See Newspapers/General section.

TLS: the Times literary supplement. See Newspapers/General section.

2872. ***Die Zeit: Wochenzeitung fuer Politik, Wirtschaft, Handel und Kultur.*** [ISSN: 0044-2070] 1946. w. DEM 198.90; DEM 4.50 newsstand/cover per issue. Ed(s): Roger de Veck. Zeitverlag Gerd Bucerius GmbH, Pressehaus, Pressehaus Speersort, Hamburg, 20079, Germany; http://eunet.bda.de/bda/int/zeit. Illus., adv. Circ: 460000. Microform: NRP. *Bk. rev.:* various number and length. *Aud.:* Ga, Ac.

In German. Published, among other journals, by former chancellor Helmut Schmidt, *Die Zeit* is Germany's most prestigious weekly newspaper. Established in Hamburg in 1946, it is highly regarded in political and cultural circles and is the leading source for academic recruitment advertisements. Published every Thursday, *Die Zeit* reports on the week's national and international news, with a focus on political events, economic issues, culture, media, and academia. Because it does not cover daily events, *Die Zeit* is known for its careful analysis of the week in review. Having undergone a complete revamping at the end of the 1990s, in an effort to appeal to younger generations and to counter a dwindling subscription list, the paper has lost its former austere character by adding color, large images, and new coverage, such as sections on travel and food. It remains one of the premier sources for cultural information, and its literary section rivals that of the *Frankfurter Allgemeine*. The freely accessible web site provides full texts of a number of articles and has established itself as a portal to cultural and educational events, as well as classifieds and similar services that are common to major newspapers. Highly recommended for all libraries supporting scholarship in German studies.

Electronic Journals

Many of the resources cited in the other sections of this chapter can be found in both print and electronic format. The following is a highly selective list of news sources available on the web. They have been selected based on their authorship, the uniqueness of their information, and their price—all are free of charge.

2873. ***A E I O U.*** irreg. Bundesministerium fuer Bildung, Wissenschaft und Kultur, Minoritenplatz 5, Vienna, 1014, Austria; ministerium@bmbwk.gv.at; http://www.bmbwk.gv.at. *Aud.:* Ga.

In German and English. *AEIOU* is more a web portal than an electronic journal, but it does provide information on Austrian cultural events and it is updated regularly. Provided by the Austrian Ministry of Education, Science and Culture, it is an official site and an online "cultural window" to Austria. *AEIOU* provides access to so-called albums that are created by the AEIOU or various national cultural institutes, such as the *Institut fur Musikwissenschaft* in Graz for the music album, which contains information on instruments, composers, genres, styles, and periods. Other albums cover Sigmund Freud and video clips of historic and cultural events, as well as an encyclopedia of Austria with about 14,000 entries on Austrian history, geography, politics, economics, people, and the arts. The links to all major cultural institutions in Austria are helpful for staying abreast of the latest cultural events, but there is no online summary or newsletter detailing the latter in a quick and easy manner.

2874. ***Belgium Today.*** 1997. bi-m. Embassy of Belgium, Investments Office, 3330 Garfield St N W, Washington, DC 20008; BelgiumToday@diplobel.org ; http://www.diplobel.org/usa/. *Aud.:* Ga, Ac, Sa.

In English. Published by the Embassy of Belgium to the United States, this bimonthly newsletter is available online in pdf format. It is hardly a source of political or social commentary, but this is also not its purpose. It is designed to inform the business traveler about current events in politics, business, economics, and culture in Belgium in an easy-to-access and free manner. Very similar to *Belgium Toiday* is the *MSR Belgian* at http://www.elis.rug.ac.be/ELISgroups/speech/msr. Published by the Department of Information Science at the University of Ghent, it is available in Dutch and English and may be subscribed to via e-mail. The archives of both *Belgium Today* and the *MSR Belgian* are freely accessible.

2875. ***BioNews.*** 1999. w. Free. Ed(s): Kirsty Horsey. Progress Educational Trust, 140 Gray's Inn Rd, London, WC1X 8AX , United Kingdom; admin@progress.org.uk; http://www.progress.org.uk. *Aud.:* Ga, Ac, Sa.

In English. *BioNews* is a very specialized online journal focusing on human genetics and assisted reproduction. It is mostly directed toward researchers; but because of its coverage of the legal implications and its indexing of general and health news articles from major publications, it will appeal to anyone with a strong interest in the issues. It is published every Monday and sent to subscribers by the Progress Educational Trust, an organization working for the promotion of reproductive and genetic science. This free publication contains no images or illustrations, only ASCII text. The archive is also free and fully searchable from March 1999 to the present.

2876. ***Bollettino '900 Online.*** [ISSN: 1124-1578] bi-m. Universita degli Studi di Bologna, Dipartimento di Italianistica, Via Zamboni, 32, Bologna, 40126, Italy; boll900@iperbole.bologna.it; http://www.comune.bologna.it/iperbole/boll900/. *Indexed:* MLA-IB. *Aud.:* Ac.

In Italian. Born out of a seminar on tenth-century Italian literature, *Bollettino '900* has been published by the Department of Italian Studies at the University of Bologna since May 1995. It has broadened its scope and aims to contribute to the creation of an international research community studying contemporary Italian literature and to explore the integration of computer science in literary research. Published irregularly, it is also available in print (ISSN: 1126-7003). Some articles are translated into English. The web site indicates that an English version is in progress, but this information has not been updated since 2002. The site provides access to the complete archive without charge and includes links to useful resources for the study of Italian literature. Recommended for libraries supporting Italian studies or comparative-literature programs, as well as programs in computers in the humanities.

2877. ***Classical London.*** m. Free. Classical London, sub@classical-london.com ; http://www.classical-london.com/. *Aud.:* Ga, Ac, Sa.

Classical London is a free online classical-music newsletter distributed via e-mail. It provides CD, DVD, and concert reviews and covers classical-music news, including concerts in London. The newsletter also links to information about classical music on the Internet and contains news on competitions and job opportunities for performers and composers. Readers may sign up at the web site to stay abreast of classical-music news and events in London.

2878. ***e e ~ n.*** q. Ed(s): Walter Leal Filho. Technical University of Hamburg-Harburg, c/o Prof. Walter Leal Filho, Environmental Technology, Hamburg, D-21073, Germany; EEEN@projekte.org; http://umweltprogramme.de/eeen/index.phtml. *Aud.:* Ac.

In English. Available only electronically, the *European Environmental Education Newsletter (EEEN)* is published at the Technical University of Hamburg-Harburg, Germany. A useful source to stay up to date on environmental issues and important events, *EEEN* provides information on upcoming conferences, lists full book reviews, and provides links to environmental web sites and other resources. Back issues are available from 1998 on. A useful newsletter and web site for researchers wanting to stay abreast of current developments in the field.

2879. ***eurozine: the netmagazine.*** [ISSN: 1684-4637] 1998. irreg. Ed(s): Carl Henrik Fredriksson. eurozine, Rembrandtstr 31/10, Vienna, 1020, Austria. *Aud.:* Ga, Ac.

Published with the support of the Culture 2000 program of the European Union, *eurozine* is both a portal for European cultural journals and a multilingual magazine of its own. Created through the collaboration of European cultural journals, with *Kritika & Kontext, Mittelweg36, Ord&Bild, Revista Critica, Transit*, and *Wespennest, eurozine* provides full-text access to selected articles in various European languages, with a focus on central, northern, and eastern Europe. With the aim to open "a new space for transnational debate," *eurozine* is a nonprofit organization, with an editorial office in Vienna, and an editorial board composed of the editors of the five founding journals. The site is well organized, and all articles, including some from archival issues, may be searched by keyword and read in html or pdf. The site includes biographies of all contributors and an impressive list of all major European cultural journals, with links to their web sites. Recommended to stay abreast of the current cultural debate in Europe.

2880. ***Norway Daily.*** d. Utenriksdepartementet, Victoria Terrasse, PO Box 8114, Oalo, 0032, Norway; post@mfa.no; http://www.mfa.no. *Aud.:* Ga, Ac.

In English, French, German, and Spanish. *Norway Daily* is a daily news bulletin from Norway, based on news, editorials and commentaries from major Norwegian daily newspapers, including *Aftenposten, Dagbladet, Dagens Naeringsliv, Vart Land, Dagsavisen, Verdens Gang, Nationen, and many other. Compiled by the Nowegian Ministry of Foreign Affairs, Norway Daily* is published daily and available free of charge through various web sites of Norwegian embassies and cultural institutions, as well as through ODIN, a site providing information on Norway in English and several other European languages at http://odin.dep.no/odin/engelsk/index-b-n-a.html. ODIN's archives go as far back as January 10, 1999. Providing summaries of current events and newsstories in Norway, *Norway Daily* allows readers to stay up to date on the latest developments.

2881. ***Research in Education (Edinburgh).*** Former titles: *S C R E Newsletter;* (until 1983): *Research in Education.* 1968. s-a. Ed(s): Jon Lewin. Scottish Council for Research in Education, 15 St John St, Edinburgh, EH8 8JR, United Kingdom; scre@scre.ac.uk; http://www.scre.ac.uk/. *Aud.:* Ga, Ac, Sa.

In English. *Research in Education* is published twice a year by the Scottish Council for Research in Education at the University of Glasgow and includes lengthy articles on such topics as "Single-Sex Education for Girls: A Case Study" and "What Is Education For?" Going beyond Scotland and providing insight into the British educational system, *Research in Education* is a valuable resource for North American educators wanting to gain insight into educational issues abroad. The web site provides free access to articles in pdf and includes archives back to 1997. Also included are links to various resources in education and information about the Scottish Council's activities, fellowships, and more.

■ FAMILY AND MARRIAGE

Erin K. McCaffrey, Distance Learning Librarian, Regis Univeristy, 3333 Regis Blvd., Denver, CO 80221; emccaffr@regis.edu

Introduction

Families today represent a variety of close, intimate relationship structures, which are often very different from the traditional representation of the family. As marriage rates have decreased, the average age of first marriage has increased. Divorce rates have increased and cohabition is more common, as is single-parent child bearing and rearing. Definitions of gender roles within the family have changed. The literature in family and marriage also reflects these changes, presenting a broader representation of what constitutes "family." Gender issues, family violence, substance abuse, and cross-cultural examinations of the family are reflected in the literature.

Family and marriage periodicals tend to land in either the scholarly or the popular category. Of the scholarly journals represented here, coverage ranges from theory and research to practice and application. The popular magazines in this category are focused on self-help for couples and families. Periodicals in this category are giving greater coverage to outside influences on the family and intimate relationships.

Here, we are addressing periodicals that treat the family as a whole, focusing on family studies, family therapy, and marital therapy. Many of the periodicals in this category offer table of contents information and selected full text on their web sites. Many periodicals related to family and marriage are included in other sections of this book, such as Parenting, Women, Social Work, Sociology, and Lesbian, Gay, Bisexual and Transgender.

Basic Periodicals

Ga: *FamilyFun, Parenting, Parents;* Ac: *Family Process, Family Relations, Journal of Comparative Family Studies, Journal of Family Issues, Journal of Family Psychology, Journal of Marriage and Family;* Sa: *Families in Society, Journal of Marital and Family Therapy, Journal of Sex & Marital Therapy.*

Basic Abstracts and Indexes

Current Contents, Family & Society Studies Worldwide, Psychological Abstracts, Sage Family Studies Abstracts, Social Sciences Citation Index, Social Sciences Index.

2882. ***American Journal of Family Therapy.*** Former titles (until 1979): *International Journal of Family Counseling;* (until 1976): *Journal of Family Counseling.* [ISSN: 0192-6187] 1973. 5x/yr. USD 189 (Individuals, USD 92). Brunner - Routledge (US), 325 Chestnut St, Ste 800, Philadelphia, PA 19106; information@brunner-routledge.co.uk; http://www.brunner-routledge.com/. Illus., index, adv. Sample. Refereed. Circ: 2000. Vol. ends: Winter. Microform: PQC. Online: EBSCO Publishing; Gale Group; Ingenta Select; Northern Light Technology, Inc.; OCLC Online Computer Library Center, Inc.; ProQuest Information & Learning; RoweCom Information Quest; Swets Blackwell. Reprint: PQC; PSC. *Indexed:* AgeL, CIJE, ExcerpMed, IMFL, LRI, PsycholAb, SFSA, SSCI, SSI, SWR&A, SociolAb. *Bk. rev.:* 0-4, 600-1,200 words. *Aud.:* Ac, Sa.

The *American Journal of Family Therapy* proposes to be "the incisive, authoritative, independent voice" in family therapy. Interdisciplinary in scope, readership includes marriage and family therapists, psychiatrists, psychologists, allied health and mental health practitioners, counselors, clinical social workers, physicians, nurses, and clergy practitioners. Regular sections include Family Measurement Techniques, Family Behavioral Medicine and Health, Family Law Issues in Family Therapy Practice, Continuing Education and Training, and International Department. The journal also includes book and media reviews. Recent topics encompass forgiveness and marriage, adult attachment styles and conflict resolution in romantic relationships, and counseling with immigrants. The *American Journal of Family Therapy* is highly recommended for academic libraries seeking more than one scholarly family therapy journal.

2883. ***Child & Family Behavior Therapy.*** Formerly (until 1982): *Child Behavior Therapy.* [ISSN: 0731-7107] 1978. q. USD 575 domestic; USD 776.25 Canada; USD 833.75 elsewhere. Ed(s): Charles Diament. Haworth Press, Inc., 10 Alice St, Binghamton, NY 13904-1580; getinfo@haworthpressinc.com; http://www.haworthpress.com. Illus., adv. Sample. Refereed. Circ: 387 Paid. Vol. ends: No. 4. Microform: PQC. Reprint: HAW. *Indexed:* CIJE, CJA, ECER, EduInd, IMFL, PEI, PRA, PsycholAb, RiskAb, SFSA, SSCI, SWA, SWR&A, SociolAb. *Bk. rev.:* 1-4, 600-2,200 words. *Aud.:* Ac, Sa.

Published quarterly, *Child & Family Behavior Therapy* is aimed at counselors, family therapists, teachers, child psychologists, researchers, and others interested in utilizing behavior therapy techniques when working with difficult children and adolescents. Each issue contains three to four articles. Articles are lengthy and scientific, yet practical in approach, and include clinical applications, case studies, and original research. Recent articles include "Parent Implementation of an Oral Reading Intervention: A Case Study," "Behavioral Response Generation and Selection of Rejected-Reactive Aggressive, Rejected-Nonaggressive, and Average Status Children," and "Externalizing Disorders and the Treatment of Child Anxiety: A Preliminary Study." Researchers will find the considerable book reviews helpful. Recommended for academic libraries.

Families in Society. See Sociology and Social Work/Social Work and Social Welfare section.

Family Circle. See Women section.

Family Economics and Nutrition Review. See Home Economics section.

The Family Handyman. See Home section.

2884. ***Family Process.*** [ISSN: 0014-7370] 1962. q. USD 219 print & online. Ed(s): Carol Anderson. Blackwell Publishing, Inc., Commerce Place, 350 Main St, Malden, MA 02148; subscrip@blackwellpub.com; http://www.blackwellpublishing.com. Illus., index, adv. Sample. Refereed. Circ: 3800 Paid. Vol. ends: Dec. CD-ROM: ProQuest Information & Learning. Online: bigchalk; EBSCO Publishing; Gale Group; OCLC Online Computer Library Center, Inc.; ProQuest Information & Learning. Reprint: PQC; SWZ. *Indexed:* ASSIA, AgeL, CINAHL, CJA, CommAb, ExcerpMed, IBZ, IMFL, IndMed, PsycholAb, SFSA, SSCI, SWA, SWR&A, SociolAb. *Aud.:* Ac, Sa.

One of the foremost journals in the field, *Family Process* began publication when the field of family therapy was in its infancy. A major resource for 40 years, this multidisciplinary journal "publishes clinical research, training, and theoretical contributions in the areas of families and health." Mental health and social service professionals will find research and clinical ideas on a wide range of pyschological and behavioral problems. Recent topics include family secrecy, lived religion and family therapy, family resilience, and healing internalized racism. Subscribers can access additional material on the *Family Process* web site, and full text of their complete archives can be purchased on CD-ROM at a low price. This journal is recommended for academic libraries supporting family therapy, psychiatry, psychology, and social work programs.

2885. ***Family Relations: interdisciplinary journal of applied family studies.*** Former titles: *Family Coordinator; Family Life Coordinator.* [ISSN: 0197-6664] 1952. q. plus supp. USD 244 Print & online eds. Blackwell Publishing, Inc., Commerce Place, 350 Main St, Malden, MA 02148; subscrip@blackwellpub.com; http://www.blackwellpublishing.com. Illus., index, adv. Refereed. Circ: 4200 Paid. Vol. ends: Oct. CD-ROM: National Information Services Corp. Microform: PQC. Online: bigchalk; The Dialog Corporation; EBSCO Publishing; Gale Group; JSTOR (Web-based Journal Archive); Northern Light Technology, Inc.; OCLC Online Computer Library Center, Inc.; ProQuest Information & Learning. Reprint: PQC. *Indexed:* ASG, AgeL, BRI, CBRI, CIJE, CJA, HRA, MRD, PsycholAb, RI-1, SFSA, SSCI, SSI, SWA, SWR&A, SociolAb. *Bk. rev.:* 7-18, 500-800 words. *Aud.:* Ac, Sa.

Family Relations is one of two journals published by the National Council on Family Relations. It emphasizes "family research with implications for intervention, education, and public policy." It publishes empirical studies, conceptual analysis, and literature reviews written with the needs of pracitioners in mind. Articles are interdisciplinary in scope and focus on a diverse range of family issues including gender and family relationships, cross-cultural issues, aging, and intergenerational family relations. Recent topics include rural gay life, differential treatment of siblings, premarital prevention programs, and adoption. Readers are scholars and pracitioners, including family policy specialists, family life educators, researchers in applied family studies or with a focus on evaluation, and family practitioners. *Family Relations* is routinely cited and is an excellent resource that is highly recommended for academic libraries with programs addressing family research and family studies, psychology, or social work.

2886. ***Family Safety & Health.*** Formerly (until 1984): *Family Safety.* [ISSN: 0749-310X] 1961. q. Members, USD 16.75; Non-members, USD 21.80. Ed(s): Laura Coyne. National Safety Council, 1121 Spring Lake Dr, Itasca, IL 60143; http://www.nsc.org/pubs/fsh/. Illus., adv. Circ: 550000. Vol. ends: Winter. Microform: PQC. Reprint: PQC. *Aud.:* Hs, Ga.

Published by the National Safety Council, *Family Safety & Health* emphasizes information for living a safe and healthy life. It provides information on home, recreational, and driving safety. It also presents current nutrition news. For readers of all ages, each issue includes a "Kids' Page." Articles address topics highlighting living a safe and healthy life, such as finding time to exercise, nutrition and what to know about cholesterol, fall-proofing your home, and myths and facts about home fires. Recommended for public and high school libraries.

Family Therapy Networker. See *Psychotherapy Networker.*

FamilyFun. See Parenting section.

2887. ***Journal of Comparative Family Studies.*** [ISSN: 0047-2328] 1970. 4x/yr. USD 140 (Individuals, USD 95). Ed(s): George Kurian. University of Calgary, Department of Sociology, 2500 University Dr N W, Calgary, AB T2N 1N4, Canada; cairns@ucalgary.ca. Illus., index, adv. Refereed. Circ: 800. Vol. ends: No. 4. Microform: MIM; MML; PQC. Online: bigchalk; EBSCO Publishing; Florida Center for Library Automation; Gale Group; Micromedia ProQuest; Northern Light Technology, Inc.; OCLC Online Computer Library Center, Inc.; ProQuest Information & Learning; H.W. Wilson. Reprint: PQC. *Indexed:* ASG, ASSIA, AgeL, AnthLit, ArtHuCI, BAS, CEI, CJA, ExcerpMed, IBSS, IBZ, IMFL, PsycholAb, RRTA, SFSA, SSCI, SSI, SWA, SociolAb, WAE&RSA. *Bk. rev.:* 0-10, 400-1,300. *Aud.:* Ac.

Directed to scholars of national and international comparative family studies, this journal "tries to make a significant contribution of cross-cultural research." Abstracts are provided in English, French, and Spanish, and the editorial board and authors are international in representation. The journal publishes articles, book reviews, and research notes. Recent articles include "Divorce: Process and Correlates. A Cross-Cultural Study," and "Perceptions of Arranged Marriages by Young Pakistani Muslim Women Living in a Western Society." The *Journal of Comparative Family Studies* also publishes special issues on selected themes, such as "Immigrant and Ethnic Minority Families." The last issue of each year contains a section on books received and an index. Highly recommended for academic libraries serving anthropology, social psychology, sociology, or multicultural studies programs.

2888. ***Journal of Divorce & Remarriage: research and clinical studies in family theory, family law, family mediation and family therapy.*** Formerly (until 1990): *Journal of Divorce.* [ISSN: 1050-2556] 1977. q. in 2 vols. USD 520 domestic; USD 742.50 Canada; USD 797.50 elsewhere. Ed(s): Craig A Everett. Haworth Press, Inc., 10 Alice St, Binghamton, NY 13904-1580; getinfo@haworthpressinc.com;

http://www.haworthpressinc.com. Illus., index, adv. Sample. Refereed. Circ: 379 Paid. Vol. ends: No. 4. Microform: PQC. Online: Gale Group. Reprint: HAW; WSH. *Indexed:* ASG, ASSIA, AgeL, CIJE, CWI, GendWatch, HRA, IMFL, PsycholAb, RI-1, SFSA, SSCI, SSI, SWA, SWR&A, SociolAb. *Aud.:* Ac, Sa.

Interdisciplinary in focus, this journal publishes clinical research studies for marriage and family specialists, counselors, family therapists, social workers, and lawyers focusing in family law. Many other family journals publish articles on divorce and remarriage, but this journal serves as a practical source for these professionals. Covering "all aspects of divorce, including predivorce marital and family treatment, marital separation and dissolution, children's responses to divorce and separation, single parenting, remarriage, and stepfamilies," the emphasis is on issues of divorce within the United States. Highlights from past issues include "Some Possible Implications of Negative Stepfather Stereotypes," "Divorced Mothers: The Network of Friends Pre- and Post Divorce," and "Remarriage for Love or Money?" The *Journal of Divorce & Remarriage* is recommended for academic and special libraries as a quality secondary journal source.

2889. *Journal of Family History: studies in family, kinship and demography.* Supersedes: *Family in Historical Perspective.* [ISSN: 0363-1990] 1976. q. GBP 312 print & online eds. in Europe, Middle East, Africa & Australasia. Ed(s): Roderick Phillips. Sage Publications, Inc., 2455 Teller Rd, Thousand Oaks, CA 91320; info@sagepub.com; http://www.sagepub.com. Illus., index, adv. Sample. Refereed. Circ: 1400. Vol. ends: Oct. Online: Chadwyck-Healey Incorporated; Florida Center for Library Automation; Gale Group; ingenta.com; OCLC Online Computer Library Center, Inc.; ProQuest Information & Learning; RoweCom Information Quest; Swets Blackwell; H.W. Wilson. Reprint: PSC. *Indexed:* ABS&EES, ASG, AgeL, AmH&L, ArtHuCI, BHA, HumInd, IBSS, IBZ, IMFL, PsycholAb, SFSA, SSCI, SSI, SUSA, SWA, SociolAb. *Bk. rev.:* 4-8, 800-1,200 words. *Aud.:* Ac.

International and interdisciplinary in scope, this quarterly journal publishes scholarly research "concerning the family as a historical social form with contributions from the disciplines of history, gender studies, economics, law, political science, policy studies, demography, anthropology, sociology, liberal arts and the humanities." Contributions represent the international perspective of the research. A recent special issue focuses on "Family Law: The Present's Past and the Past's Present." Recent topics include contemporary Western family law and a European view of same-gender marriage. This journal is recommended for academic libraries.

2890. *Journal of Family Issues.* [ISSN: 0192-513X] 1980. 8x/yr. GBP 482 print & online eds. in Europe, Middle East, Africa & Australasia. Sage Publications, Inc., 2455 Teller Rd, Thousand Oaks, CA 91320; info@sagepub.com; http://www.sagepub.com. Illus., index, adv. Sample. Refereed. Circ: 1500 Paid. Vol. ends: Nov. Microform: WSH; PMC. Online: Pub.; Chadwyck-Healey Incorporated; Florida Center for Library Automation; Gale Group; ingenta.com; OCLC Online Computer Library Center, Inc.; ProQuest Information & Learning; RoweCom Information Quest; Swets Blackwell. Reprint: WSH. *Indexed:* ASG, ASSIA, AgeL, CIJE, CJA, HEA, IMFL, PsycholAb, RiskAb, SFSA, SSCI, SSI, SWR&A, SociolAb. *Aud.:* Ac, Sa.

The *Journal of Family Issues* designates two issues each year to special topics of current interest. It is "devoted to contemporary social issues and social problems related to marriage and family life and to theoretical and professional issues of current interest to those who work with and study families." Articles, advocacy pieces, and comments represent any topic related to family issues. Recent articles include "The Sibling Relationship in Young Adulthood," "The Relationship Between Marital Status and Health," and "Perceived Housework Equity, Marital Happiness, and Divorce in Dual-Earner Households." This scholarly journal is highly recommended for academic libraries.

2891. *Journal of Family Psychology.* [ISSN: 0893-3200] 1987. q. USD 169 (Members, USD 49; Non-members, USD 99). Ed(s): Ross D. Parke. American Psychological Association, 750 First St, NE, Washington, DC 20002-4242; journals@apa.org; http://www.apa.org/. Illus., index, adv. Refereed. Circ: 4800. Vol. ends: Feb. Reprint: PSC. *Indexed:* ASSIA, CJA, EduInd, IMFL, IndMed, PsycholAb, SSCI, SSI, SWA, SWR&A, SociolAb. *Aud.:* Ac, Sa.

Published by the American Psychological Association, the *Journal of Family Psychology* is regarded as a key journal in family research. It provides original scholarly articles "devoted to the study of the family system from multiple perspectives and to the application of psychological methods of inquiry to that end." The journal addresses such topics as families in transition, marital and family processes, the family and employment, cross-cultural perspectives on the family, the outcome and process of marital and family treatment, and family violence and abuse. A recent issue devotes a special section to "Family Routines and Rituals." Occasionally, the journal publishes literature reviews, case studies, or theoretical articles, but the focus of the journal is empirical research addressing behavioral, biological, cognitive, emotional, and social variables. Widely indexed, this journal is highly recommended for academic libraries.

2892. *Journal of Family Therapy.* [ISSN: 0163-4445] 1979. q. GBP 183 print & online eds. Ed(s): Ivan Eisler. Blackwell Publishing Ltd., 9600 Garsington Rd, PO Box 805, Oxford, OX4 2DQ, United Kingdom; customerservices@oxon.blackwellpublishing.com; http://www.blackwellpublishing.com/. Illus., index, adv. Refereed. Circ: 2500. Vol. ends: Nov. Online: EBSCO Publishing; ingenta.com; OCLC Online Computer Library Center, Inc.; Ovid Technologies, Inc.; RoweCom Information Quest; Swets Blackwell. *Indexed:* ASSIA, AgeL, CIJE, IMFL, PsycholAb, RiskAb, SFSA, SSCI, SWA, SociolAb. *Bk. rev.:* 1-4, 500-1,200 words. *Aud.:* Ac, Sa.

This journal is the official publication of the Association for Family Therapy in Britain. It "seeks to advance the understanding and therapy of human relationships constituted in systems such as couples, families, professional networks and wider groups." International contributions to each issue include research updates, papers, training articles, book reviews, and abstracts. Recent papers include "The presence of the third party: systemic therapy and transference analysis" and "Family-oriented treatment for people with alcohol problems in Ireland: a comparison of the effectiveness of residential and community-based programmes." Special issues have recently addressed topics such as eating disorders and the family, and the effects of parental illness on the family. The editors welcome new contributors within Europe. Recommended for academic libraries calling for original research in family therapy.

2893. *Journal of Family Violence.* [ISSN: 0885-7482] 1986. q. USD 539 print or online ed. Ed(s): Vincent B Van Hasselt, Michel Hersen. Kluwer Academic / Plenum Publishers, 233 Spring St Fl 7, New York, NY 10013-1522; http://www.wkap.nl/. Illus., index, adv. Refereed. Vol. ends: Dec. Microform: PQC. Online: EBSCO Publishing; Gale Group; ingenta.com; Kluwer Online; OCLC Online Computer Library Center, Inc.; Ovid Technologies, Inc.; RoweCom Information Quest; Swets Blackwell. *Indexed:* ASG, ASSIA, AgeL, CJA, H&SSA, IBSS, IBZ, IMFL, PRA, PsycholAb, RI-1, RiskAb, SFSA, SSCI, SSI, SUSA, SociolAb. *Bk. rev.:* 0-4, 300-1,000 words. *Aud.:* Ac, Sa.

This journal focuses on "clinical and investigative efforts concerning all forms of family violence and its precursors, including spouse-battering, child abuse, sexual abuse of children, incest, abuse of the elderly, marital rape, domestic homicide, the alcoholic marriage, and general family conflict." Interdisciplinary in scope, the clinical and research reports draw from clinical and counseling psychology, criminology, law, marital counseling, psychiatry, public health, social work, and sociology. Papers, case studies, and review articles are also included. Substance abuse, families of homicide victims, and intimate partner violence are just a few topics recently addressed, in addition to a special issue on family violence. Recommended for academic libraries, especially those supporting psychology or social work programs.

Journal of Feminist Family Therapy. See Women: Feminist and Special Interest/Feminist and Women's Studies section.

2894. *Journal of Marital and Family Therapy.* Formerly (until 1979): *Journal of Marriage and Family Counseling.* [ISSN: 0194-472X] 1975. q. USD 75 (Individuals, USD 45). Ed(s): Karen Wampler. American Association for Marriage and Family Therapy, 1133 15th St, N W, Ste

300, Washington, DC 20005. Illus., index, adv. Refereed. Circ: 20000. Vol. ends: Oct. Microform: PQC. Online: Gale Group; OCLC Online Computer Library Center, Inc.; ProQuest Information & Learning; H.W. Wilson. Reprint: PQC. *Indexed:* ASG, AgeL, BiolAb, CIJE, ExcerpMed, IMFL, IndMed, PsycholAb, SFSA, SSCI, SSI, SWA, SWR&A, SociolAb. *Bk. rev.:* 3-10, 300-1,000 words, signed. *Aud.:* Ac, Sa.

Published by the American Association for Marriage and Family Therapy, this journal "publishes articles on research, theory, clinical practice, and training in marital and family therapy." The practical articles, focused on clinical topics, are directed to marriage and family therapists, and a recent issue includes a special section on "The Effectiveness of MFT." Recent articles include "Protecting Persons in Family Therapy Research: An Overview of Ethical and Regulatory Standards" and "Values in the Role of the Family Therapist: Self Determination and Justice." Topics related to assessment, theory, and training are often included. The leading family therapy journal, this is an essential title for academic libraries serving programs in marriage and family therapy.

2895. *Journal of Marriage and the Family.* Formerly (until 1964): *Marriage and Family Living.* [ISSN: 0022-2445] 1939. q. plus supp. USD 264 print & online. Ed(s): Alexis Walker, Robert Milardo. Blackwell Publishing, Inc., Commerce Place, 350 Main St, Malden, MA 02148; subscrip@blackwellpub.com; http://www.blackwellpublishing.com. Illus., index, adv. Refereed. Circ: 6200 Paid. CD-ROM: National Information Services Corp. Microform: PQC. Online: bigchalk; The Dialog Corporation; EBSCO Publishing; Gale Group; JSTOR (Web-based Journal Archive); OCLC Online Computer Library Center, Inc.; ProQuest Information & Learning. Reprint: PQC; PSC. *Indexed:* ABS&EES, ASG, AgeL, BRD, BRI, BiogInd, BiolAb, CBRI, CIJE, CJA, CommAb, ECER, ExcerpMed, HRA, HumInd, IBSS, IMFL, MagInd, PsycholAb, RI-1, SFSA, SSCI, SSI, SUSA, SWA, SWR&A, SociolAb, WSI. *Bk. rev.:* 7-21, 600-1,000 words. *Aud.:* Ac, Sa.

The *Journal of Marriage and Family* is one of two publications of the National Council on Family Relations and a leading resource in family research. According to the *ISI Journal Citation Reports,* it is the most highly cited journal in family studies. It presents "original theory, research interpretation, and critical discussion of materials related to marriage and the family." Contributors come from a diverse array of social science fields, including psychology, anthropology, sociology, history, and economics. Here, marriage and family encompasses other forms of close relationships. All family related topics are represented, including domestic violence, families formed outside of marriage, gender and families, the changing family demography, fatherhood, remarriage, biosocial perspectives on the family, marital satisfaction, and families and social policy. Frequently cited and widely indexed, this journal is highly recommended for all academic libraries.

2896. *Journal of Sex & Marital Therapy.* [ISSN: 0092-623X] 1974. 5x/yr. GBP 145 (Individuals, GBP 65). Ed(s): Clifford J Sager, R Taylor Segraves. Brunner - Routledge (UK), 27 Church Rd, Hove, BN3 2FA, United Kingdom; information@brunner-routledge.co.uk; http://www.brunner-routledge.co.uk. Illus., index, adv. Refereed. Circ: 2000. Vol. ends: Oct/Dec. Microform: PQC. Online: EBSCO Publishing; Ingenta Select; OCLC Online Computer Library Center, Inc.; RoweCom Information Quest; Swets Blackwell. Reprint: ISI; PQC; PSC. *Indexed:* ASG, AgeL, BiolAb, ExcerpMed, IndMed, PsycholAb, SFSA, SSCI, SWA, SociolAb. *Bk. rev.:* 0-3, 400-1,000 words. *Aud.:* Ac, Sa.

This journal serves as a forum reflecting developments in the biological and psychological treatment of marital and sex disorders. The clinical and research writing adresses therapeutic techniques, special clinical and medical problems, theoretical parameters of sexual functioning, marital relatinsips, and outcome. Suggestions for improving intimacy in couples in which one partner has attention-deficit/hyperactivity disorder, factors associated with unwanted pregnancy, romantic partners use of pornography, and couple therapy for low sexual desire are just some of the topics recently addressed. Readership includes sex therapists, marriage and family therapists, psychologists, clinical social workers, physicians, nurses, clergy practitioners, and pastoral counselors. Because of its broad readership and the superior quality of its articles, as well as its low cost, you will find the journal in many academic and medical library collections. Other leading journals in the area of sex research are the *Journal of Sex Research* and the *Archives of Sexual Behavior.* The *Journal of Sex and Marital Therapy* is highly recommended for academic libraries.

2897. *Marriage Partnership.* Formerly: *Partnership.* [ISSN: 0897-5469] 1984. q. USD 19.95. Ed(s): Ginger Kolbaba. Christianity Today International, 465 Gundersen Dr, Carol Stream, IL 60188. Illus., adv. Circ: 52703. Vol. ends: Winter. Online: EBSCO Publishing; Gale Group. *Indexed:* CWI, ChrPI. *Bk. rev.:* 4-8, 100-150 words. *Aud.:* Ga.

Marriage Partnership "provides challenging practical insights into healthy Christian marriage." This self-help magazine presents practical and biblical advice from an evangelical perspective and aims to represent a realistic image of marriage and family life. While this perspective of marriage and family life may not appeal to all readers, many will find the articles useful as they try to address what couples face in day-to-day life. How-to pieces, expert interviews, couple profiles, humorous articles, and true-life stories comprise each issue, as well as hot topics such as infertility or pornography. Selected articles are available on the magazine's web site. *Marriage Partnership* is held largely in church and seminary libraries, as well as in some Christian academic libraries.

Modern Bride. See Weddings section.

2898. *Mothering: the magazine of natural family living.* [ISSN: 0733-3013] 1976. bi-m. USD 18.95 domestic; USD 23.95 Canada; USD 35.45 elsewhere. Ed(s): Peggy O'Mara. Mothering Magazine, PO Box 1690, Santa Fe, NM 87504; http://www.mothering.com. Illus., index, adv. Sample. Circ: 78000 Paid. Microform: PQC. Online: EBSCO Publishing; Gale Group; Northern Light Technology, Inc.; OCLC Online Computer Library Center, Inc. *Indexed:* AltPI. *Bk. rev.:* 10-25. *Aud.:* Hs, Ga.

Mothering is a progressive publication wishing "to provide truly helpful information upon which parents can base informed choices." Each issue addresses a diverse array of topics such as home birth, midwifery, organic foods, childhood illnesses, and homeopathy. Recent articles include "Honoring Our Cycles: Using Fertility Awareness to Achieve or Avoid Pregnancy," and "Juggling Career and Home: Albright, O'Connor and You." Published bimonthly, each issue has six regular features: "The Art of Mothering," "Health," "A Child's World," "Birth & Pregnancy," "Ways of Learning," and "Family Living." Selected articles are available at the web site, www.mothering.com. Recommended for public libraries.

Parenting. See Parenting section.

Parents. See Parenting section.

2899. *Psychotherapy Networker.* Formerly (until Mar. 2001): *Family Therapy Networker.* [ISSN: 1535-573X] 1982. bi-m. USD 24 domestic; USD 30 foreign. Ed(s): Richard Simon. Family Therapy Network, Inc., 7705 13th St, N W, Washington, DC 20012; info@psychnetworker.org; Http://www.psychotherapynetworker.org/. Illus., adv. Circ: 65000. Vol. ends: Nov. *Indexed:* AltPI, SWR&A. *Bk. rev.:* Number and length vary. *Aud.:* Ac, Sa.

Psychotherapy Networker is a trade publication aimed at therapists. The mission is to inspire therapists "with fresh ideas that keep you on the field's cutting edge" and to connect therapists with their colleagues, preventing "professional isolation and burnout." Although written for therapists, the articles also are likely to appeal to general readers interested in psychology. Family therapy is a significant subject included in this source. Feature articles, case studies, clinical methods, and career information, such as marketing your practice, coaching, and corporate consulting address this issue. Lengthy interviews with leading practitioners such as Carol Gilligan are frequently featured. Reviews of self-help and therapy books are included, as well as current popular film reviews written from a therapist's perspective. Because of its broad appeal, *Psychotherapy Networker* is recommended for academic and special libraries, as well as large public libraries.

Sexual and Marital Therapy. See *Sexual and Relationship Therapy.*

2900. ***Sexual and Relationship Therapy.*** Formerly (until vol.15): *Sexual and Marital Therapy.* [ISSN: 1468-1994] 1986. q. GBP 409 (Individuals, GBP 136). Ed(s): Dr. Kevan Wylie. Brunner - Routledge (UK), 27 Church Rd, Hove, BN3 2FA, United Kingdom; information@brunner-routledge.co.uk; http://www.brunner-routledge.co.uk. Illus., index, adv. Refereed. Vol. ends: Nov. Online: EBSCO Publishing; Ingenta Select; OCLC Online Computer Library Center, Inc.; ProQuest Information & Learning; RoweCom Information Quest; Swets Blackwell. Reprint: PSC. *Indexed:* ASSIA, BAS, CINAHL, ExcerpMed, PsycholAb, SFSA, SWA, SociolAb. *Bk. rev.:* 6-8, 200-800. *Aud.:* Ac, Sa.

This is the official journal of the British Association for Sexual and Relationship Therapy, "for everyone professionally concerned with sexual and marital function." Clinicians and therapists, psychologists, social workers, as well as academics and researchers from many different disciplines will find a diverse range of original research, case studies, subject reviews, and book reviews. Recent topics include relationships and sexuality among people with physical disability, men in love and sexual boredom, expectations of marriage, and sexual obsessions. Recommended for medical and academic libraries requiring more than one journal on sexual therapy.

Studies in Family Planning. See Medicine and Health/Family Planning section.

Working Mother. See Women section.

■ FICTION: GENERAL/MYSTERY AND DETECTIVE

General/Mystery and Detective

Laurel Bliss, Librarian for Art and Architecture, Yale University Arts Library, P.O. Box 208242, New Haven, CT 06520; laurel.bliss@yale.edu; FAX: 203-432-0549

Introduction

Magazines in this section tend either to publish original short stories by both emerging and established authors, or to focus on material geared toward a reader of fiction, such as literary analysis, reviews, and author interviews. A few ambitious publications attempt to do both. Most of the print journals have related web sites with information on subscriptions and submissions; some also feature full-text excerpts from the print edition. The most successful electronic journals take advantage of the web by having large story archives and/or well-organized links to online resources.

Basic Periodicals

GENERAL. Ga, Ac: *Fiction, Fiction International, Zoetrope.*

MYSTERY AND DETECTIVE. Ga, Ac: *ClueLass HomePage, Ellery Queen's Mystery Magazine.*

Basic Abstracts and Indexes

American Humanities Index, MLA International Bibliography, Mystery Short Fiction.

General

This category is composed primarily of journals that publish original works of fiction, usually short stories, by both emerging and established writers. Some only publish fiction, while others include book reviews or interviews. In most cases, the audience is the scholarly or general reader, and the publication has limited circulation.

2901. ***Australian Short Stories.*** [ISSN: 0810-4468] 1982. q. AUD 35; AUD 48 foreign. Ed(s): Howard Firkin. Mooltan Press, 73 Mooltan Ave, Flemington, VIC 3031, Australia. Illus., adv. Circ: 12000. *Aud.:* Ga, Ac.

This periodical presents a selection of skillfully crafted short fiction, and it is an excellent source for insight into life in Australia. It showcases, but is not limited to, Australian writers, usually presenting 10 to 20 stories in each issue of about 100 pages. Most of the writers are previously published, and some have won literary prizes. This attractively designed publication, notable for its distinctive covers and inside illustrations, is recommended for libraries with large literature collections and for those that support Australian Studies programs. Under recent new ownership and editorial direction for the first time since its founding, the magazine maintains its high standards while showing a new vitality. The magazine's web site presents a complete story from the current issue. Also included is information for subscribers and contributors.

2902. ***Canadian Fiction.*** Formerly (until 1998): *Canadian Fiction Magazine.* [ISSN: 1495-2343] 1971. 2x/yr. CND 50 (Individuals, CND 35). Ed(s): Geoffrey Hancock. Canadian Fiction, PO Box 1061, Kingston, ON K7L 4Y5, Canada. Illus., adv. Circ: 1000 Paid. Microform: MML; PQC. *Indexed:* AmHI, CBCARef, CPerI, MLA-IB. *Aud.:* Ga, Ac.

Offering 15–20 stories per issue, this rather substantial publication focuses on contemporary Canadian fiction. It uses the anthology format and its themed issues allow both well known and up-and-coming Canadian authors to showcase their work. Brief biographies of the authors appear before the short stories or excerpted materials. While of interest to a general readership, this journal is even more appropriate for academic institutions.

2903. ***Fiction.*** [ISSN: 0046-3736] 1972. 2x/yr. USD 18 (Individuals, USD 20; USD 40 foreign). Ed(s): Mark J Mirsky. Fiction, c/o City College of NY, Department of English, New York, NY 10031; http://www.ccny.cuny.edu/fiction/fiction.htm. Illus., index. Circ: 3000. Microform: PQC. Reprint: PQC. *Indexed:* AmHI. *Aud.:* Ga, Ac.

This highly respected journal focuses on innovative works of contemporary fiction. It has no letters to or from the editor, only its own ads, and no reviews; in other words, it contains just the unadorned pieces of fiction. Issues usually have around 15 short stories or excerpts. Some are by famous authors such as Joyce Carol Oates and Saul Bellow. Others are by first-time writers. To show its commitment to new authors, the journal is offering a $500 prize for writers previously unpublished in a major literary magazine. *Fiction* is a required subscription for any academic library, and very appropriate for a general readership.

2904. ***Fiction International.*** [ISSN: 0092-1912] 1973. a. USD 24 (Individuals, USD 12). Ed(s): Harry Polkinhorn, Harold Jaffe. San Diego State University Press, 5500 Campanile Dr, San Diego, CA 92182-8141; sheila.d@mail.sdsu.edu; http://www-rohan.sdsu.edu/dept/press/menu.html. Illus., adv. Circ: 500 Paid. Microform: PQC. Reprint: PQC. *Indexed:* AmHI, BRI, CBRI. *Aud.:* Ga, Ac.

This leftist magazine of arts and letters contains 20–30 works on a specific theme, such as fetish or pain. These edgy and controversial pieces take the form of short stories, nonfiction, and original art. Many contributors are well-known authors, but this journal offers a good opportunity for less-established writers to get exposure on an international level. Most appropriate for the medium-large academic library.

2905. ***Glimmer Train.*** [ISSN: 1055-7520] 1992. q. USD 32; USD 43 Canada; USD 54 elsewhere. Ed(s): Linda Suansar-Davies. Glimmer Train Press, Inc., 710 SW Madison St, Suite 504, Portland, OR 97205-2900; info@glimmertrain.com; http://www.glimmertrain.com. Sample. Circ: 16000 Paid. *Indexed:* AmHI. *Aud.:* Ga, Ac.

This quirky and creative journal, designed for "established and emerging writers," focuses on quality fiction with an emotional component. Each issue has five to ten pieces, in a variety of categories, including author interviews. The editors accept works up to 12,000 words, and have special awards for very short fiction (up to 2,000 words), new writers, and poetry. The publication's web site has useful information about submission guidelines, reading fees, and payment for accepted submissions. A good choice for most public and academic libraries.

Jacket. See Literary Reviews/Electronic Journals section.

2906. ***The Long Story.*** [ISSN: 0741-4242] 1982. a. USD 11 for 2 yrs. domestic; USD 13 for 2 yrs. foreign; USD 6 newsstand/cover per issue domestic. Ed(s): R Peter Burnham. Long Story, 18 Eaton St, Lawrence, MA 01843-1110; rpbtls@aol.com; http://www.litline.org/html/thelongstory.html. Circ: 1100. *Indexed:* AmHI. *Aud.:* Ga, Ac.

As the name says, this journal is dedicated to stories between 8,000 and 12,000 words, occasionally going up to as many as 20,000 words. The editors have very specific literary tastes, and prefer "fiction that is committed to a thematic exploration of some human issue and which is also well written and characterized by a poetic sense of both the grandeur and fragility of individuals." Issues tend to have eight to ten stories, plus an editorial prelude. While the contributors aren't household names, many have gone on to write stories for published anthologies. Appropriate for academic institutions and large public libraries.

2907. ***Other Voices (Chicago): fiction.*** [ISSN: 8756-4696] 1985. s-a. USD 28 (Individuals, USD 24; USD 7 newsstand/cover per issue domestic). Ed(s): Gina Frangello. Other Voices, Inc., University of Illinois at Chicago, Department of English, Chicago, IL 60607-7120; othervoices@listserv.uic.edu; http://www.othervoicesmagazine.org. Illus., adv. Circ: 1500. *Indexed:* AmHI. *Aud.:* Ga, Ac.

This literary journal is interested in work by both new and established writers, covering the widest possible range of contemporary fiction. It accepts short stories and self-contained novel excerts, and prefers a limit of 5,000 words. It also publishes the occasional author interview and book reviews. Its web site has the table of contents for current and back issues, with a few full-text stories. A solid choice, particularly for academic libraries.

2908. ***Quick Fiction.*** [ISSN: 1543-8376] 2002. s-a. USD 9; USD 5.50 newsstand/cover. Ed(s): Adam Pieroni, Jennifer Cande. J P Press, 50 Evergreen St., Unit 25, Jamaica Plain, MA 02130. Circ: 500 Paid and controlled. *Aud.:* Ga.

This new and emerging literary magazine focuses on short "stories and narrative prose poems that, in the space of a single page, set a scene for characters to confront conflict." It publishes 20–25 pieces per issue, with short biographies of its contributors. Its web site offers submission and subscription information, plus a table of contents for the current issue.

2909. ***Romantic Times: for readers of romantic and contemporary fiction.*** Formerly (until May 2002): *Romantic Times Magazine;* Incorporates (1986-1991): *Rave Reviews.* [ISSN: 0747-3370] 1981. m. USD 29.95 domestic; USD 44 Canada. Ed(s): Lorraine Freeney, Libby Snitzer. Romantic Times Publishing Group, 55 Bergen St, Brooklyn, NY 11201. Illus., adv. Circ: 135000. *Bk. rev.:* 120-170, 50-250 words. *Aud.:* Ga.

This glossy magazine features amusing and informative articles on popular romance and genre fiction writers. It also has an extensive book review section organized by genre, plus columns by readers, letters to the editor, and author news. The focus is certainly on romance, but this publication is a wonderful source for mystery and fantasy readers as well. Even the advertisements are informative. Its robust web site allows the user to search for book reviews, has tips on writing, and has a message board for readers, among other features.

2910. ***Short Story.*** [ISSN: 1052-648X] 1989. s-a. USD 10. Ed(s): Mary Rohrberger, Farhat Iftekharuddin. University of Texas, Brownsville, Department of English, 80 Ft Brown, Brownsville, TX 78520; http://www.uni.edu/english/shrtstry/shrtsty.htmll. Illus., adv. Sample. Refereed. Circ: 800. Vol. ends: Fall. *Indexed:* AmHI, MLA-IB. *Bk. rev.:* 3-5, 200-600 words. *Aud.:* Ga, Ac.

This journal is "dedicated to providing a publishing outlet for serious writers of short fiction and an arena for short story theorists and critics to present essays and articles." Currently based at the University of Northern Iowa and the University of Texas–Brownsville, the journal is also affiliated with the University of New Orleans. While most journals limit themselves to fiction or to criticism, *Short Story* has a mix of both that should appeal to many readers. Its web site is on the sparse side, but it does have contact information.

StoryQuarterly. See Little Magazines section.

2911. ***Zoetrope: all-story.*** [ISSN: 1091-2495] 1997. 4x/yr. USD 20 domestic; USD 26 in Canada & Mexico; USD 40 elsewhere. Ed(s): Adrienne Brodeur. A Z X Publications, 1350 Ave of the Americas 24th Fl, New York, NY 10019; info@all-story.com; http://www.all-story.com. Illus., adv. Sample. Circ: 40000 Controlled. *Aud.:* Ga, Ac.

This "quarterly literary publication founded in 1997 to explore the intersection of story and art, fiction and film" does so with great flair. Issues are jam-packed with color illlustrations, adding to its slick appeal. The content is restricted to short stories and one-act plays under 7,000 words. Each issue has a guest artist, like David Byrne, and contributors frequently are household names. The magazine's web site is just as polished, and has information on submissions, workshops, and contests.

Mystery and Detective

Magazines in this category either publish original mystery and crime fiction (usually pieces under 15,000 words) or provide articles of interest to mystery readers. These articles can be author interviews, book reviews, critical essays, and/or a calendar of events. A typical web site for the magazine will have information on subscribing and submissions and a table of contents for the current issue.

2912. ***Alfred Hitchcock's Mystery Magazine (Print edition).*** [ISSN: 0002-5224] 1956. 11x/yr. USD 33.97; USD 3.50 newsstand/cover per issue; USD 4.95 newsstand/cover per issue Canada. Ed(s): Linda Landrigen. Dell Magazines, 475 Park Ave S, 11 Fl, New York, NY 10016-6901; juliamcevoy@dellmagazines.com; http://www.dellmagazines.com. Illus., adv. Circ: 73826 Paid. Vol. ends: Dec. *Indexed:* AmHI, MSF. *Bk. rev.:* 2-7, 40-100 words. *Aud.:* Ga.

This classic mystery magazine has been in publication since 1956. Each issue contains at least seven original short stories with illustrations, plus a special reprinting of a classic tale. Other features are a story contest, puzzles, book reviews, and comments from the editor. The magazine accepts submissions on almost any kind of mystery, preferably one surrounding a crime, and they must be under 14,000 words. The web site has submission guidelines, table of contents of the current issue, and a featured story of the month. A must subscription for most public libraries.

2913. ***Baker Street Journal: an irregular quarterly of Sherlockiana.*** [ISSN: 0005-4070] 1946. q. USD 18.95; USD 21.50 foreign. Ed(s): Donald Pollock. Sheridan Press, PO Box 465, Hanover, PA 17331-0465. Illus., index, adv. Circ: 1600 Paid. Microform: PQC. Reprint: PQC. *Indexed:* AmHI, BEL&L, MLA-IB. *Bk. rev.:* 1-10, 30-90 words. *Aud.:* Ga.

This "irregular quarterly of Sherlockiana" typically contains ten or so well-researched articles on very specific topics that have to do with the fictional character of Sherlock Holmes. While not particularly scholarly in nature, these articles provide thoughtful insights of interest to the serious fan. Subjects such as "When Was the Gasfitters' Ball?" and "The Avant-Garde Sherlock Holmes" are explored in detail. As it is geared toward avid readers of the Holmes novels, this magazine also has a section for assorted announcements and a handy calendar of events.

2914. ***Clues (Bowling Green): a journal of detection.*** [ISSN: 0742-4248] 1980. s-a. USD 15 domestic; USD 19 foreign. Ed(s): Pat Browne. Clues (Bowling Green), c/o Mrs Pat Browne, Ed, Bowling Green State University, Bowling Green, OH 43403; abrowne@bgnet.bgsu.edu; http://www.bgsu.edu/colleges/library/press/pp0017.html. Illus., adv. Refereed. Circ: 700. Vol. ends: Fall/Winter. Online: Florida Center for Library Automation; Gale Group. *Indexed:* ABS&EES, MLA-IB. *Bk. rev.:* 0-60, 40-300 words. *Aud.:* Ga, Ac.

Readers interested in literary analysis will enjoy this journal. It should also appeal to the well-read mystery fan, particularly those who aren't accustomed to having their genre taken seriously as literature. A typical issue contains 10–15 articles that compare and contrast different mystery novels. Each contains a list of works cited. Author interviews also make a regular appearance. This journal is scholarly enough in nature to be appropriate for an academic audience, while still appealing to a general readership.

2915. ***Crimewave: 100% pure crime fiction.*** [ISSN: 1463-1350] 1998. s-a. GBP 11 domestic; GBP 22 foreign; GBP 3 newsstand/cover per issue domestic. Ed(s): Mat Coward, Andy Cox. T T A Press, 5 Martins Ln, Witcham, Ely, CB6 2LB, United Kingdom; ttapress@aol.com; http://www.tta-press.freewire.co.uk. Illus., adv. *Aud.:* Ga.

This edgy, thought-provoking journal attempts the "total re-creation of crime fiction . . . something entirely different [from] whatever you've read before." Issues have 10–15 short stories, many of them by up-and-coming writers. Submissions can be on any topic relating to mystery, crime, or suspense, at a maximum of 15,000 words. Stylish design and well-written content are a winning combination in this beautifully produced publication. Its web site has details on submissions and teasers from the current issue.

2916. ***Drood Review of Mystery.*** [ISSN: 0893-0252] 1982. bi-m. USD 17 domestic; USD 21 Canada; USD 27 elsewhere. Ed(s): Jim Huang. Jim Huang, Ed. & Pub., 484 E Carmel Dr 378, Carmel, IN 46032; editor@droodreview.com. Adv. Circ: 1400 Paid. Vol. ends: Dec. *Indexed:* BRI, CBRI. *Bk. rev.:* 40-50, 100-900 words. *Aud.:* Ga.

This informative and well-written magazine provides both featured and brief reviews of current mystery and detective fiction. These reviews are designed to help mystery fans determine what to read and buy. For public libraries, this is an invaluable tool for book selection. The magazine also contains author interviews and comments from the editor on the genre, all in a newsletter format. The editors accept bound galleys from authors and publicists for review, as far in advance of publication as possible. The web site has subscription and submission information, plus links to the magazine's book publishing affiliate.

2917. ***Ellery Queen's Mystery Magazine (Print Edition): the world's leading mystery magazine.*** Former titles (until 1988): *Ellery Queen;* (until 1981): *Ellery Queen's Mystery Magazine.* [ISSN: 1054-8122] 1941. 11x/yr. USD 29.97 domestic; USD 39.97 foreign. Ed(s): Janet Hutchings. Dell Magazines, 475 Park Ave S, 11 Fl, New York, NY 10016-6901; http://www.dellmagazines.com. Illus. Circ: 77270. Vol. ends: Dec. Microform: PQC. *Indexed:* AmHI, MSF. *Bk. rev.:* 8-12, 30-70 words. *Aud.:* Ga, Ac.

Established in 1941, this magazine may look like a pulp comic book, but it's really a well-known forum for every possible kind of mystery and detective short story (except true crime). Each issue contains 10–15 stories that can range in length from the very short to a short novel. Usually a few are by famous writers, although they do welcome first-time authors. Issues also contain poems, puzzles, and crosswords, as well as brief book reviews. The quality of the paper it uses is unimpressive; the content is anything but.

2918. ***Hardboiled.*** Formerly (until 1992): *Hardboiled Detective;* Which was formed by the merger of (1988-1990): *Detective Story Magazine;* (1984-1990): *Hardboiled.* 1990. q. USD 35 domestic for 5 issues; USD 55 foreign for 5 issues. Ed(s): Gary Lovisi. Gryphon Books, PO Box 290, Brooklyn, NY 11228-0209. Adv. Circ: 1000. *Indexed:* MSF. *Bk. rev.:* 8-10, 50-400 words, signed. *Aud.:* Ga.

This is described as "one tough little mag," and no holds are barred and no punches are pulled as it devotes itself to the hardboiled detective genre story. While blood and gore do not soak every page, the stories (new and some reprinted classics) are not for the squeamish. Some are not mysteries, but each delivers a jolt with hard-hitting writing style and powerful subject matter. Issues also include true crime articles, essays, and reviews of books and films, all written from the hardboiled perspective. The web site gives subscription information and highlights previous issues' contents as well as provide full-screen images of the striking artwork featured on the covers.

2919. ***Mary Higgins Clark Mystery Magazine.*** 1996. q. USD 5.99. Ed(s): Kathyrne V Sagan. Gruner + Jahr U.S.A. Publishing, 375 Lexington Ave, New York, NY 10017-5514; corpcomm@gjusa.com; http://www.gjusa.com. *Indexed:* MSF. *Aud.:* Ga.

The "Queen of Suspense" lends her name and her wildly popular talent to this slick and glossy magazine. Besides featuring stories by some top names in the mystery and suspense business, each issue has a "bonus thriller" novella by Clark herself in the form of a pull-out booklet. Also included are book reviews, interviews, articles on mystery-related topics, and a mystery quiz. Although its frequency is designated as quarterly, issues have appeared at irregular intervals. This magazine would be recommended as a popular choice for public libraries when the publisher stabilizes publication and extends distribution beyond single-copy newsstand and supermarket sales.

2920. ***Mystery Readers Journal.*** Formerly: *Mystery Readers of America Journal.* [ISSN: 1043-3473] 1985. q. USD 28 domestic; USD 40 foreign. Ed(s): Janet A. Rudolph. Mystery Readers International, P.O. Box 8116, Berkeley, CA 94707-8116; whodunit@murderonthemenu.com; http://www.mysteryreaders.org. Circ: 1500 Paid. *Bk. rev.:* 25-45, 200-900 words. *Aud.:* Ga, Ac.

Available to members of Mystery Readers International, this journal contains many articles on a specific theme, such as "Mysteries South of the Mason-Dixon Line" and "Murder Down Under." Other features include author essays of 500–2,000 words, letters to and from the editor, and a calendar of events organized by state and town. With a focus on readers' advisory and reviews, the journal does not publish any fiction. It should have the greatest appeal for the general reader because of the themed approach and the wide authorship of articles. The web site has information on subscriptions and submissions, and has sample articles.

2921. ***Mystery Review: a quarterly publication for mystery readers.*** [ISSN: 1192-8700] 1992. q. CND 21.50 domestic; USD 20 United States; USD 28 elsewhere. Ed(s): Barbara J Davey. C. von Hessert & Associates, PO Box 233, Colborne, ON K0K 1S0, Canada; mystrev@connect.reach.net; http://www.themysteryreview.com. Adv. Circ: 4500 Paid. *Aud.:* Ga.

Geared for mystery fans looking for new reading material, this publication is best known for its extensive section of book and film reviews. A typical issue will have thematic articles of 2,000–5,000 words and an author interview. Other features include poems, quotations, quizzes, a list of non-reviewed new releases, and a spotlight on a specific mystery bookshop. There's something for everyone in this thoughtful and useful magazine. Highly recommended for public libraries.

2922. ***Mystery Scene.*** [ISSN: 1087-674X] 1985. 6x/yr. USD 35; USD 65 foreign. Ed(s): Ed Gorman. Fedora, Inc., 3601 Skylark Ln SE, Cedar Rapids, IA 52403. Illus., adv. Circ: 8000. *Bk. rev.:* 10-15, 45-80 words. *Aud.:* Ga, Sa.

This comprehensive and entertaining newsmagazine is designed for both mystery authors and readers, providing industry news, author interviews, book reviews, and articles on writing. What puts this publication ahead of the pack is the high level of useful insider information, and nonfiction contributions from best-selling writers such as Lawrence Block, Donald Westlake, and Dean Koontz. The web site has details on subscribing, contributing, and advertising, as well as the table of contents of the latest issue.

2923. ***New Mystery: world's best mystery, crime, and suspense short stories.*** [ISSN: 1048-8324] 1989. irreg. USD 20 domestic; USD 37 foreign; USD 3.95 newsstand/cover per issue. Ed(s): Charles Raisch. New Mystery, Inc., 101 W 23rd St, ph 7, New York, NY 10011; editorial@newmystery.com; http://www.NewMystery.com. Illus., adv. Sample. Circ: 110000 Paid and controlled. Microform: PQC. *Indexed:* MSF. *Bk. rev.:* 6-10, 50-150 words. *Aud.:* Ga.

This magazine offers a refreshing change from the sometimes bland fare of the *Ellery Queen* and *Alfred Hitchcock* magazines. In addition to a selection of edgy, well-written stories, the magazine includes reviews of books, films, and other media. This is a quirky and vibrant publication, albeit with a somewhat amateurish, thrown-together look. It would be worth consideration by libraries as a second mystery magazine if it could achieve a regular publication schedule. The web site includes subscription information, tables of contents of back issues, writer profiles, stories from the print edition, reviews, news releases, and an index of contributors to past issues. These web features are accessible to all, but the site promises "deeper electronic access" for those subscribing to the print magazine.

2924. ***Sherlock Holmes Journal.*** [ISSN: 0037-3621] 1952. s-a. GBP 9.50; USD 21 United States; GBP 12.50 in the Middle East. Ed(s): Nicholas Utechin, Heather Owen. Sherlock Holmes Society of London, c/o R.J.

Ellis, 13 Crofton Ave, Orpington, BR6 8DU, United Kingdom; shsl221b@aol.com; http://www.sherlock-holmes.org.uk. Illus. Circ: 1600. *Bk. rev.:* 5-10, 80-700 words. *Aud.:* Ga.

Sent to members of The Sherlock Holmes Society of London, this publication is an entertaining mix of reports on social activities and serious scholarship. Issues usually contain lengthy articles on topics such as "Who was the real Dr. Watson?" and "Music inspired by Sherlock Holmes." It also has reviews of BBC productions, book reviews, and letters to the editor. Black-and-white illustrations are used to good effect. The Society's web site is comprehensive, and includes details on subscriptions, events, and obtaining back issues. Worth subscribing to for larger institutions.

Electronic Journals

Not surprisingly, this category has seen a great many publications come and go. Most print publications in the general fiction/mystery and detective area these days have a strong presence on the web. However, the electronic edition is usually an expurgated version of the original, designed to get the reader to subscribe to the print.

Digital-only publications such as *ClueLass* and InterText serve as comprehensive resources for users who are looking for fiction and for information about fiction. *ClueLass*, for instance, has multiple searchable databases for author contacts, awards, upcoming publications, etc. *InterText* has a complete archive of stories back to the first issue in 1991, and offers multiple formats for its reader. These sorts of publications really take advantage of the electronic media by means of the ease with which one can search their vast databanks.

2925. *C L F Newsletter.* [ISSN: 1084-8266] 1995. irreg. Free. Ed(s): Daniel Pearlman. Council for the Literature of the Fantastic, c/o Dept of English, Univ of Rhode Island, Kingston, RI 02881; dpe8464u@postoffice.uri.edu; http://www.uri.edu/artsci/English/clf/welcome.html. Refereed. *Bk. rev.:* 20, 200-1,500 words. *Aud.:* Ga, Ac.

This publication comes out of the Council for the Literature of the Fantastic, and was published exclusively online as of 1999.

2926. *ClueLass HomePage.* 1995. m. Ed(s): Kate Derie. Deadly Serious Press, 405 E Wetmore Rd #117-499, Tucson, AZ 85705-1700; http://www.cluelass.com. *Aud.:* Ga, Sa.

This easy-to-use web site has several robust sections of interest to the mystery fan. The "DEADline News" page contains up-to-date tidbits on award nominations for mystery writers and book festivals. The "Bloodstained Bookshelf" is a searchable database of new book releases, with links to purchasing information. The enormous "Deadly Directory Online" can be searched for information and links about mystery-related authors, independent publishers, libraries, etc. Any mystery reader will enjoy browsing through this site, and uncovering hidden treasures.

2927. *Gangway: the on-line lit mag.* [ISSN: 1327-7073] 1996. q. Free. Ed(s): Gerald Ganglbauer. Gangan Publishing, PO Box 522, Strawberry Hills, NSW 2012, Australia; books@gangan.com; http://www.gangway.net. Adv. *Aud.:* Ga.

This Australian bilingual (English and German) online literary publication contains short stories, interviews, reviews, literary news and gossip, and letters to the editor. The focus is on contemporary literature, and both contributors and content are refreshingly international in scope. According to the editor, this publication wants to "encourage authors to take advantage of interactive possibilities of this media (illustrations, hyperlinks, JavaScript, Flash 6 and so on)." The web site as a whole is fairly easy to navigate, with information in both languages.

2928. *Infinity Online: fiction, games, links, columns.* w. Ed(s): Caron Ammons. Infinite Publications, caron@infinityonline.com. *Aud.:* Hs, Ga.

Infinity Online offers three to four fiction stories, book reviews, game coverage, and at least one column. The fiction is variable, and the supporting nonfiction is sparse. *Infinity* is a free source of short fiction for librarians with an active SF and fantasy readership, and it is a market for new writers.

2929. *InterText: the online fiction magazine.* [ISSN: 1071-7676] 1991. bi-m. Ed(s): Jason Snell. InterText, jsnell@intertext.com; http://www.etext.org/zines/InterText/. Illus. Vol. ends: Dec. *Aud.:* Ga.

This online magazine accepts submissions for all genres of fiction, and encourages cross-genre writing. Each issue contains around five stories, with a maximum of 15,000 words. A helpful "Best Stories" feature allows the reader to browse back issues for acclaimed stories in three categories: mainstream, science fiction, and the fantastic. Apart from the favorite stories, all past issues are readily available in the magazine's archive. It publishes in a variety of formats, including Setext (ASCII text, which can also be read as styled text with a Setext browser), PostScript (laser printers), pdf (for Adobe's Acrobat portable document viewer), Newton Book, Palm DOC, html, and other formats.

The Richmond Review. See Little Magazines/Electronic Journals section.

■ FICTION: SCIENCE FICTION, FANTASY, AND HORROR

Carrie Donovan, Library Instruction Reference Librarian, Miller Nichols Library, University of Missouri-Kansas City, Kansas City, MO 64110, donovanc@umkc.edu

Introduction

A genre that was once considered to be the province of the occult, science fiction, along with the related genres of fantasy and horror, has experienced increasing popularity in film, television, and literature. Writers of this group of genres continue to challenge the boundaries of literary tradition by connecting the existent with the imaginative, unreal, and frightening. Science fiction has supported and cultivated publications ranging from the scholarly to the spectacular. Research-oriented publications make up a small percentage of this subject's periodicals, while resources intended for a broad readership are more common. Publishers have adapted to the web environment and online publications have been well-received. Some of the print publications have corresponding web sites that offer free access to articles, reviews, and indexes.

Basic Periodicals

Analog Science Fiction & Fact (Print edition), Asimov's Science Fiction (Print edition), Fantasy & Science Fiction, Science Fiction Studies.

Basic Abstracts and Indexes

Abstracts of English Studies, American Humanities Index, Arts & Humanities Citation Index, Book Review Index, MLA International Bibliography.

2930. *Analog Science Fiction & Fact (Print edition).* Former titles (until 1991): *Analog Science Fiction Science Fact;* (until 1965): *Analog Science Fact - Science Fiction;* (until 1961): *Astounding Science Fiction.* [ISSN: 1059-2113] 1930. 11x/yr. USD 39.97 domestic; USD 47.97 foreign; USD 3.50 newsstand/cover per issue domestic. Ed(s): Stanley Schmidt. Dell Magazines, 475 Park Ave S, 11 Fl, New York, NY 10016-6901; juliamcevoy@dellmagazines.com. Illus., index, adv. Sample. Circ: 47767 Paid. Vol. ends: Dec. Online: Gale Group; OCLC Online Computer Library Center, Inc.; ProQuest Information & Learning. Reprint: PQC. *Indexed:* ASIP, BRI, CBRI, LRI, MagInd. *Bk. rev.:* 8-12, 300-1,500 words. *Aud.:* Hs, Ga, Ac.

Analog Science Fiction and Fact is probably the foremost science fiction magazine today. The publication offers a "more realistic" approach to the genre by combining scientific articles with original fiction. The balance of fiction with fact will appeal to the realistic sensibilities of science fiction fans. Each issue includes book reviews, as well as classified advertisements and letters to and from the editor. Selected features and columns are duplicated on the publication's web site.

2931. ***Asimov's Science Fiction (Print edition).*** Former titles (until Nov. 1992): *Isaac Asimov's Science Fiction Magazine;* (until 1990): *Isaac Asimov's Science Fiction;* (until 1986): *Isaac Asimov's Science Fiction Magazine.* [ISSN: 1065-2698] 1977. 11x/yr. USD 33.97 domestic; USD 47.97 foreign; USD 3.50 newsstand/cover per issue domestic. Ed(s): Gardner Dozois, Sheila Williams. Dell Magazines, 475 Park Ave S, 11 Fl, New York, NY 10016-6901; juliamcevoy@dellmagazines.com. Illus., index, adv. Sample. Circ: 31461 Paid. Vol. ends: Dec. Microform: PQC. Reprint: PQC. *Indexed:* AmHI. *Bk. rev.:* 6-15, 50-100 words. *Aud.:* Hs, Ga, Ac.

Asimov's Science Fiction remains one of the leading magazines of the genre. It presents original works of science fiction and fantasy by well-known authors, as well as newcomers, in the form of novellas, novelettes, short stories, and poetry. Informational articles and extensive book reviews by regular contributors complete the wide scope of this publication. A calendar of events and conventions, as well as a list of classified advertisements, is also included. Selected articles and stories are duplicated on the publication's web site.

2932. ***Cemetery Dance.*** [ISSN: 1047-7675] 1988. bi-m. USD 22. Ed(s): Richard T Chizmar. Cemetery Dance Publications, PO Box 943, Abingdon, MD 21009-0943. Illus., adv. Vol. ends: Winter. *Bk. rev.:* 6-10, 200-3,000 words. *Aud.:* Ga.

This award-winning publication includes essays and artwork, as well as news and reviews. Contributions by regular columnists, aspiring writers, and well-known authors come in the form of fiction and nonfiction. Readers of horror will appreciate the six to eight original stories that are published in each issue, while fans of the broader genre of science fiction will take interest in the news articles, interviews, and reviews of movies, CDs, and books.

2933. ***Dark Side: the magazine of the macabre and fantastic.*** [ISSN: 0960-6653] 199?. m. GBP 28.80 domestic; GBP 33.36 in Europe; GBP 36.36 elsewhere. Ed(s): Allan Bryce. Ebony Media Ltd., c/o Stray Cat Publishing, Ltd., PO Box 36, Liskeard, PL14 4YT, United Kingdom; http://www.ebony.co.uk/darkside/. Illus., adv. *Aud.:* Ga, Sa.

Advertised as "Britain's best-selling horror magazine," *Dark Side* represents the genre well, with vivid photographs and uncompromising articles that focus on horror films and the people who make them. Interviews and reviews abound in this always-informative, but sometimes disturbing, magazine. A list of horror film festivals and classified advertisements are also available. Some adult content is included.

2934. ***Extrapolation.*** [ISSN: 0014-5483] 1959. q. USD 28 (Individuals, USD 18). Ed(s): Javier A Martinez. University of Texas, Brownsville, Department of English, 80 Ft Brown, Brownsville, TX 78520; jmartinez@utb.edu. Illus., index, adv. Sample. Refereed. Circ: 1000. Vol. ends: Dec. Microform: PQC. Online: bigchalk; Chadwyck-Healey Incorporated; Florida Center for Library Automation; Gale Group; Northern Light Technology, Inc.; OCLC Online Computer Library Center, Inc.; ProQuest Information & Learning. Reprint: PQC. *Indexed:* ABS&EES, ArtHuCI, BEL&L, BRI, CBRI, HumInd, IBZ, MLA-IB. *Bk. rev.:* 3-12, 50-300 words. *Aud.:* Ga, Ac.

Extrapolation is one of the foremost scholarly journals for the genre, featuring eight to ten critical articles on innovators in the field, genre studies, and thought-provoking themes. The emphasis of the journal is science fiction and fantasy and its contents include book reviews, letters, and short editorials. This publication deserves a place in any library that supports readers or scholars of science fiction.

2935. ***Fantasy & Science Fiction.*** Formerly (until 1987): *The Magazine of Fantasy and Science Fiction;* Incorporates: *Venture Science Fiction.* [ISSN: 1095-8258] 1949. m. combined Oct.-Nov. USD 44.89 domestic; USD 54.89 foreign; USD 3.99 newsstand/cover per issue. Ed(s): Gordon Van Gelder. Spilogale, Inc., P. O. Box 3447, Hoboken, NJ 07030; FandSF@aol.com; http://www.fsfmag.com. Illus., adv. Sample. Circ: 35000 Paid. Vol. ends: Jun/Dec. Microform: PQC. Online: bigchalk; EBSCO Publishing; Gale Group; OCLC Online Computer Library Center, Inc.; ProQuest Information & Learning. *Indexed:* AmHI, BRI, CBRI, MagInd. *Bk. rev.:* 5-15, 200-1,000 words. *Aud.:* Hs, Ga, Ac.

Each 160-page issue of *Fantasy & Science Fiction* features eight to ten short stories and novelettes from famous and not-so-famous authors. The magazine also includes reviews of new and forthcoming books and columns by regular contributors. This well-established publication deserves a place in libraries that support and serve readers of the genre.

2936. ***Fantasy Commentator.*** [ISSN: 1051-5011] 1943. irreg. USD 19. A. Langley Searles, Ed. & Pub., 48 Highland Circle, Bronxville, NY 10708-5909. Illus., index. Sample. Refereed. Circ: 500 Paid. *Indexed:* MLA-IB. *Bk. rev.:* 5-10, 500-3,000 words. *Aud.:* Ga, Ac.

Fantasy Commentator is a peer-reviewed journal devoted to science fiction and fantasy. It features critical articles, book reviews, and original verse by established authors. Many of the articles approach the genre from a decidedly scholarly viewpoint, making this publication most appropriate for academic libraries.

2937. ***Foundation: the review of science fiction.*** [ISSN: 0306-4964] 1972. 3x/yr. GBP 14; GBP 15 in Europe; GBP 17 elsewhere. Ed(s): Edward James. Science Fiction Foundation, University of Reading, Department of History, Faculty of Letters and Social Science, Reading, RG6 6AA, United Kingdom; e.f.james@reading.ac.uk; http://www.liv.ac.uk/~asawyer/fnd.html. Illus., index, adv. Sample. Refereed. Circ: 1000. Vol. ends: Dec. *Indexed:* MLA-IB. *Bk. rev.:* 10-20, 500-1,500 words. *Aud.:* Ga, Ac.

This British journal is published by the Science Fiction Foundation. It combines critical analysis with lively book reviews and editorials. Many well-known science fiction writers are included among the contributors. As one of the few peer-reviewed publications of the genre, *Foundation* is an excellent resource for academic and research collections.

2938. ***Interzone: science fiction and fantasy.*** Incorporates (in 1994): *Nexus;* (1991-1993): *Million.* [ISSN: 0264-3596] 1982. m. GBP 42 domestic; USD 72 United States; GBP 48 elsewhere. David Pringle Ed. & Pub., 217 Preston Drove, Brighton, BN1 6FL, United Kingdom; http://exnet.com/magsample/sf1/interzone.html. Illus., adv. Sample. Circ: 10000. *Bk. rev.:* 7-10, 100-500 words. *Aud.:* Hs, Ga, Ac.

The British publication *Interzone* features new science fiction and fantasy stories. One of the first successful British publications of the genre, *Interzone* maintains its credibility among the premier science fiction magazines of today. It has published short stories by many established science fiction writers, but its particular strength has been in the nurturing of newer writers. Interviews and reviews are also included.

2939. ***Journal of the Fantastic in the Arts.*** [ISSN: 0897-0521] 1988. q. USD 25 (Individuals, USD 20). Ed(s): William A Senior. International Association for the Fantastic in the Arts, c/o Robert A. Collins, Schmidt College of Arts and Letters, Boca Raton, FL 33431-0991; collins@fau.edu; http://iafa.org. Illus., index, adv. Sample. Refereed. Circ: 500. *Indexed:* IBZ, MLA-IB. *Aud.:* Ac.

The focus of this scholarly journal is the study of the fantastic in literature and the arts (drama, film, dance, architecture, and popular media). *JFA* includes essays on all aspects of the fantastic, as well as original artwork. Offering an interdisciplinary approach to the study of fantasy, *JFA* publishes quality papers on engaging themes, such as textual comparisons, character studies, and author analyses.

2940. ***Locus (Oakland): the newspaper of the science fiction field.*** [ISSN: 0047-4959] 1968. m. USD 55 (Individuals, USD 52). Ed(s): Kirsten Gong Wong. Locus Publications, PO Box 13305, Oakland, CA 94661; locus@locusmag.com; http://www.locusmag.com. Illus., index, adv. Sample. Circ: 9000 Paid. Vol. ends: Dec. *Indexed:* BRI, CBRI. *Bk. rev.:* 10-20, 100-500 words. *Aud.:* Hs, Ga, Ac.

Containing articles, news, and reviews, *Locus* is a critical resource for authors, publishers, and enthusiasts in the field of science fiction and fantasy. This magazine features comprehensive lists of forthcoming books, in addition to a section devoted to science fiction magazines. Also included are interviews with authors, reports of conventions and awards, and listings of events. The scope of this magazine includes the United States and Europe.

2941. ***Mythlore: a journal of J.R.R. Tolkien, C.S. Lewis, Charles Williams, and mythopoeic literature.*** Supersedes (1964-1972): *Tolkien Journal.* [ISSN: 0146-9339] 1969. q. Members, USD 18; Non-members, USD 26. Ed(s): Dr. Theodore J Sherman. Mythopoeic Society, 920 N Atlantic Blvd # E, Alhambra, CA 91801; http://www.mythsoc.org. Index, adv. Sample. Refereed. Circ: 600. Reprint: PQC. *Indexed:* AmHI, ArtHuCI, BEL&L, MLA-IB, RI-1. *Bk. rev.:* 3-15, 100-300 words. *Aud.:* Hs, Ga, Ac.

In alignment with the goals of its publishing body, *Mythlore* promotes the discussion and enjoyment of fantasy and mythic literature. This journal includes critical articles, as well as features on poetry, art, and bibliographies. The publications's title reflects the specific nature of its content.

2942. ***New York Review of Science Fiction.*** [ISSN: 1052-9438] 1988. m. USD 40 (Individuals, USD 36). Ed(s): David G Hartwell. Dragon Press, PO Box 78, Pleasantville, NY 10570; dgh@tor.com; http://www.nyrsf.com. Illus., adv. Circ: 1000 Paid. *Indexed:* MLA-IB. *Bk. rev.:* 6-12, 1,000-2,500 words. *Aud.:* Hs, Ga, Ac.

Along with extensive and thoughtful book reviews, *NYRSF* also includes articles and essays on topics related to literature in the genres of science fiction, fantasy, and horror. This publication provides an insider's view of the genres' authors and their writing. *New York Review of Science Fiction* is a must for libraries with science fiction collections of any size.

2943. ***Realms of Fantasy.*** [ISSN: 1078-1951] 1994. bi-m. USD 16.95 domestic; USD 21.95 foreign; USD 3.99 newsstand/cover per issue. Ed(s): Shawna McCarthy. Sovereign Media, 441 Carlisle Dr, Herndon, VA 20170. Illus., adv. Sample. Circ: 53000 Paid. *Aud.:* Hs, Ga, Ac.

As the title implies, *Realms of Fantasy* covers the spectrum of fantasy fiction, with six to eight short stories in each issue. Original artwork, book reviews, and coverage of computer, board, card, and role-playing games are also included. This publication is well suited to any library with moderate to large collections of science fiction and fantasy materials.

2944. ***S F X: adventures in science fiction.*** [ISSN: 0262-2971] 1981. 13x/yr. GBP 32.50 United Kingdom; GBP 35 in Europe; GBP 55 rest of world. Ed(s): Dave Golder. Future Publishing Ltd., Beauford Court, 30 Monmouth St, Bath, BA1 2BW, United Kingdom; dave.golder@futurenet.co.uk; http://www.futurenet.com/futureonline. Circ: 36710. *Bk. rev.:* 5-10, 100-500 words. *Aud.:* Hs, Ga.

SFX reviews all the latest films, DVDs, videos, and books of the genre. Biting wit and honest writing can be found on each page of this publication. Fans of popular, mainstream science fiction films and television shows will appreciate the color photographs, interviews, and behind-the-scenes coverage found in every issue of *SFX*.

2945. ***Science Fiction Chronicle: S F, fantasy & horror's monthly trade journal.*** Incorporating (as of 1984): *Starship;* Which was formerly: *Algol.* [ISSN: 0195-5365] 1979. m. USD 45 domestic; USD 56 Canada; USD 125 elsewhere. Ed(s): Warren Lapine. DNA Publications, Inc., PO Box 2988, Radford, VA 24143-2988; publisher@dnapublications.com; http://www.dnapublicvations.com. Illus., adv. Circ: 12000. Vol. ends: Sep. Microform: PQC. Online: bigchalk; Northern Light Technology, Inc.; ProQuest Information & Learning. Reprint: PQC. *Indexed:* AmHI, BRI, CBRI, MLA-IB. *Bk. rev.:* 20-50, 50-200 words. *Aud.:* Hs, Ga.

Acknowledged as the genre's only professional news magazine and trade journal, *Science Fiction Chronicle* reports on the labors of those dedicated to the literature of the fantastic. This magazine features reviews of books, young adult books, short fiction, and films. Announcements and news important to publishers, booksellers, and writers of the genre are also included.

2946. ***Science Fiction Studies.*** [ISSN: 0091-7729] 1973. 3x/yr. USD 35 (Individuals, USD 25). Ed(s): Arthur B Evans. S F - T H, Inc., EC L 06, DePauw University, Greencastle, IN 46135-0037; aevans@depauw.edu. Illus., index, adv. Sample. Refereed. Circ: 1100. Vol. ends: Dec. *Indexed:* AmHI, ArtHuCI, BRI, CBRI, HumInd, IBZ, MLA-IB. *Bk. rev.:* 10-20, 500-3,000 words. *Aud.:* Ac.

Science Fiction Studies is a necessity for any academic collection. In addition to the extensive book reviews and critical essays published in this journal, refereed articles provide readers with the scholar's approach to science fiction. The journal includes articles on topics ranging from current technologies to theories of past eras. Offering an international perspective without gender bias, *Science Fiction Studies* will complement any library's science fiction collection.

2947. ***Science Fiction Writers of America. Bulletin.*** Formerly (until 1982): *S F W A Bulletin.* [ISSN: 0192-2424] 1965. q. USD 18 domestic; USD 35 foreign. Ed(s): Mark Kreighbaum. Science Fiction and Fantasy Writers of America, Inc., PO Box 877, Chestertown, MD 21620. Illus., adv. Sample. Circ: 1500. Vol. ends: Dec. Reprint: PQC. *Bk. rev.:* 2-5, 300-1,500 words. *Aud.:* Ga, Ac.

SFWA Bulletin is geared to writers of science fiction. Published by the Science Fiction and Fantasy Writers of America (SFWA), the *Bulletin* offers reports and information useful to writers and publishers of science fiction and fantasy. Fictional essays from professional writers and book reviews are also included.

2948. ***Space and Time.*** [ISSN: 0271-2512] 1966. s-a. USD 10; USD 12 foreign. Ed(s): Gerard Houarner, Linda D Addison. Gordon Linzner, Ed. & Pub., 138 W 70th St 4 B, New York, NY 10023-4432; http://www.CITH.org. Illus., adv. Sample. Circ: 1500 Paid. *Aud.:* Hs, Ga.

With its exclusive focus on fiction, *Space and Time* introduces readers to many of the genre's new writers. It includes fiction on various topics, from supernatural horror to hard science fiction to sword and sorcery. Each issue of roughly 50 pages contains poetry, illustrations, and short stories. This magazine is a good source of short fiction for libraries with an active science fiction readership.

2949. ***Starlog: science fiction films, TV, video.*** [ISSN: 0191-4626] 1976. m. USD 49.97 domestic; USD 59.97 foreign. Ed(s): David McDonnell. Starlog Group, Inc., 475 Park Ave S, 8th Fl, New York, NY 10016. Illus., adv. Sample. Circ: 226855. *Bk. rev.:* 9-11, 50-100 words. *Aud.:* Ems, Hs, Ga.

One of the leading mass-market magazines covering science fiction, fantasy, and horror, *Starlog* caters to fans of these genres in popular media. This publication includes news, interviews, and articles on both current and past genre movies, television series, web sites, books, and the people that make them. Articles and columns are accompanied by photographs, cartoons, and humor. With the growing popularity of science fiction, fantasy, and horror in television and film, *Starlog* is an asset to libraries serving large populations.

2950. ***The Third Alternative.*** [ISSN: 1352-3783] 1994. q. USD 72. Ed(s): Andy Cox. T T A Press, 5 Martins Ln, Witcham, Ely, CB6 2LB, United Kingdom; ttapress@aol.com; http://www.tta-press.freewire.co.uk. Illus., adv. Circ: 6000 Controlled. *Indexed:* PRA. *Bk. rev.:* 15-25, 500-1,000 words. *Aud.:* Hs, Ga, Ac.

Published in the United Kingdom, *The Third Alternative* features interviews, reviews, artwork, and fiction from new and known authors and artists. With its international scope and straightforward style, this publication will satisfy science fiction fans and scholars alike. Readers of mainstream fiction will also be attracted to *The Third Alternative* for its provocative editorials and groundbreaking fiction.

2951. ***Vector: the critical journal of the British Science Fiction Association.*** Incorporates: *Paperback Inferno;* Which was formerly (until 1980): *Paperback Parlour.* [ISSN: 0505-0448] 1958. bi-m. Membership, GBP 20. Ed(s): Tony Cullen. British Science Fiction Association Ltd., c/o Estelle Roberts, Membership Secretary, 97 Sharp St, Hull, HU5 2AE, United Kingdom; bsfa@enterprise.net; http://www.bsfa.co.uk. Illus., adv. Sample. Circ: 1000. Vol. ends: Dec. *Bk. rev.:* 10-15, 100-500 words. *Aud.:* Hs, Ga, Ac.

Featuring incisive articles and in-depth book reviews, *Vector* explores the genre's literary works and discusses British science fiction of the past and present. Each issue also includes interviews and editorials. The critical tone and broad scope of this publication make it suitable for academic libraries and libraries with strong science fiction collections.

Electronic Journals

2952. ***Aphelion.*** 1997. m. Free. Ed(s): Dan Hollifield. Aphelion, vila@america.net; http://www.aphelion-webzine.com. *Aud.:* Ga.

This e-zine emphasizes new work that will introduce the public to beginning writers and introduce these first-time writers, in turn, to the criticism of editors and readers. Serialized stories and novelettes, in addition to poetry and fiction, are included. An online archive of past issues is available and searchable on the web site as well. This resource is primarily for the author trying to find his or her way, and is recommended as such.

2953. ***DargonZine: electronic magazine for the Dargon Project.*** Formerly (until 1988): *FSFnet.* [ISSN: 1080-9910] 1985. irreg. 8-12/yr. Free. Ed(s): Ornoth D A Liscomb. Dargon Project, dargon@shore.net; http://www.dargonzine.org. Illus. *Aud.:* Hs, Ga.

DargonZine is the product of the "Dargon Project," a "shared world" of amateur writers who author the fiction featured in this electronic-only resource. Many authors write in a common milieu, sharing settings and characters. Stories included in this e-zine are related to Dargon, a fantasy world that is predominantly human, at a late-medieval technology level, where magic is relatively rare. The concept is novel, and the stories are usually compelling and entertaining.

2954. ***Planet Magazine.*** [ISSN: 1526-1840] 1994. q. Ed(s): Andrew G McCann. Planet Magazine, planetmag@aol.com; http://www.planetmag.com/. *Aud.:* Hs, Ga.

One of the first science fiction e-zines, *Planet Magazine* is a good resource for anyone active in the writing community. Each issue typically includes three or four science fiction stories, three or four horror stories, one or two fantasy stories, and a few poems by emerging writers. The quality varies, ranging from good to "beginning." *Planet* offers a worthy arena for new writers and digital artists to display their work.

2955. ***Tangent Online: the science fiction and fantasy short fiction review magazine.*** Formerly (until 1997): *Tangent (Print).* 1993. bi-m. USD 5. Ed(s): David A Truesdale. Tangent, 824 Stone Arch Dr., Independence, MO 64052-1735; editor@tangentonline.com; http://www.tangentonline.com. Adv. *Bk. rev.:* 60-75, 500-2,000 words. *Aud.:* Hs, Ga, Ac.

Tangent reviews almost all the short fiction published in North American science fiction and fantasy magazines. Author profiles, regular columns, and articles are also included. Portions of this e-zine are available for free; but in order to access the most recent reviews, a $5 donation is required for a one-year subscription. This electronic-only resource will be of interest to all readers of the genres.

■ FILMS

Susan Oka, Margaret Herrick Library, Center for Motion Picture Studies – Academy of Motion Picture Arts and Sciences, 333 S. La Cienega Blvd., Beverly Hills, CA 90211; soka@oscars.org

Introduction

While researching *Velvet Light Trap* for the previous *Magazines for Libraries* edition, I came across the article, "Diverse Audiences, Changing Genres: The Evolving Landscape of Film and Television in the Age of Specialized Audiences." I still am struck by this on-target evaluation of current popular media. I also realized it is an apt assessment for serials librarians who have to make decisions on changing titles and formats for an evolving patron base.

Our library at the Academy of Motion Picture Arts and Sciences is open to the public, serving many local universities and colleges that have film programs. Industry professionals, academy members, filmmakers, and film scholars as well as the general public use our collection. They come with varying levels of cinema knowledge and a wide range of research needs. They come with class assignments; they seek information on current films and filmmakers, asking for credits and contacts; and they come for their personal research projects. I have added new titles to this section focusing on the film business and industry. Among these new titles is the weekly *Screen International*, which I feel follows the international film business more closely than the trade publication *Variety. Screen International* also provides up-to-the-minute news and developments "around the clock from around the world" through its web site. Another new title is *Film Music*, which centers around the professional in the film music industry. This particular title fills a different need from *Soundtrack!*, a publication mentioned in the last edition whose final issue was Winter 2002. A third new title, *Screentalk*, encompassing the craft of screen writing, has been added. [One title that I did not include but feel I should mention is the *Hollywood Creative Directory*, published three times a year. This directory is an indispensable resource for tracking information by giving contact and staff information along with cross-referencing indexes. It is also available online. This particular title is heavily used by our patrons.] Some publications have undergone changes. *Jump Cut*, which was previously a print publication, is now an e-zine covering television and video in addition to film. Another new title, *Animation Blast*, originally an e-zine, has turned around and is also available as a print publication. *International Documentary* has placed columns formerly included in each print issue on their web site. *Cinemaya* recently published a double issue after an eight month break. *Films in Review*, "the oldest film publication in the United States" and online since 1997, is working to bring it back to print, and another old title, *Wide Angle*, has been temporarily suspended. I am still in awe of the number of publications covering specific genres. A title not included in the last edition is *Cinefantastique*. This title recently changed publishers and plans to include "exhaustive retrospective coverage" along with the articles and interviews. *Cinescape: The Crossroads of Genre Entertainment* covers science fiction, horror, and fantasy films. The newly added e-zine title *Animation Blast* concentrates on animation and animators. There are as many publications, both print and online, to suit the needs of readers and interests. With the commercial success of "Moulin Rouge" and "Chicago," we are at the beginning of a musical-film revival, and I would not be surprised to see a title devoted to this genre. What follows is a mix of titles to serve all those "diverse audiences" out there.

Basic Periodicals

Hs: *Film Comment, Film Quarterly, Movieline's Hollywood Life, Premiere;* Ga: *Cineaste, Film Comment, Film Quarterly, Movieline's Hollywood Life, Premiere, Sight and Sound;* Ac: *Camera Obscura, Cineaste, Cinema Journal, Film Comment, Film Quarterly, Journal of Film and Video, Sight and Sound.*

Basic Abstracts and Indexes

Film Literature Index, International Index to Film Periodicals.

2956. ***American Cinematographer: the international journal of motion picture production techniques.*** [ISSN: 0002-7928] 1920. m. USD 50 domestic; USD 70 in Canada & Mexico; USD 95 elsewhere. Ed(s): Stephen Pizzello. A S C Holding Corporation, PO Box 2230, Los Angeles, CA 90078; ascmag@aol.com; http://www.cinematographer.com. Illus., adv. Circ: 32000 Paid. Vol. ends: Dec. Microform: PQC. Online: Chadwyck-Healey Incorporated; OCLC Online Computer Library Center, Inc.; H.W. Wilson. *Indexed:* ABS&EES, ArtInd, ChemAb, EngInd, FLI, IBZ, IIFP, IIPA, MRD. *Bk. rev.:* 8-10, 150 words. *Aud.:* Sa.

This monthly publication of the American Society of Cinematographers not only passes on current industry information but also provides interviews with cinematographers of current releases and a behind-the-scenes look at the technical details used to achieve a particular shot. Working cameramen can get reviews of new equipment on the market, and film buffs and burgeoning cinematographers can get detailed information about their new favorite films. Book and DVD reviews, classified ads, and an ad index are in each issue.

2957. ***Boxoffice: the business magazine of the global motion picture industry.*** [ISSN: 0006-8527] 1920. m. USD 40 domestic; USD 50 in Canada & Mexico; USD 80 elsewhere. Ed(s): Kim Williamson. R L D Communications, 155 S El Molino Ave, Ste 100, Pasadena, CA 91101-2563; editorial@boxoffice.com; http://www.boxoffice.com. Illus., adv. Circ: 6000 Paid. Vol. ends: Dec. Online: Gale Group. *Indexed:* FLI, IIPA. *Aud.:* Sa.

For almost 80 years *Boxoffice* has been required reading for every serious player in the industry, from theater owners to studio executives. There is coverage of industry news (national and international), box office grosses, production data on new Hollywood releases, and financial information on the major studios. Also included are numerous reviews of new Hollywood feature films; interviews with filmmakers, screenwriters, executives, actors, producers, and directors; and up-to-date festival information. Although it covers all areas of the film industry, it is definitely skewed towards exhibitors. It lists current and upcoming studio release charts by month. There are short reviews with "exploitips," a guide to new products, and news on concessions. Highly recommended for libraries that need complete coverage of the Hollywood film industry.

2958. ***Camera Obscura: a journal of feminism and film theory.*** [ISSN: 0270-5346] 1976. 3x/yr. USD 94 (Individuals, USD 30). Ed(s): Emily Davis. Duke University Press, 905 W Main St, Ste 18 B, Durham, NC 27701; subscriptions@dukeupress.edu; http://www.dukeupress.edu. Illus., adv. Sample. Circ: 700. Vol. ends: Sep. Online: EBSCO Publishing; Florida Center for Library Automation; Gale Group; Ingenta Select; LexisNexis; OCLC Online Computer Library Center, Inc.; Project MUSE; RoweCom Information Quest; SoftLine Information; Swets Blackwell. Reprint: ISI; PSC. *Indexed:* ABM, AltPI, ArtHuCI, ArtInd, BAS, CWI, FLI, FemPer, GendWatch, IBZ, IIFP, IIPA, MLA-IB, MRD, SSCI, SWA. *Bk. rev.:* Various number and length. *Aud.:* Ac.

This title "seeks to provide a forum for dialogue and debate on media, culture, and politics. Specifically, the journal encourages contributions in the following areas: analyses of the conjunctions among gender, race, class, sexuality, and nation, as these are articulated in film, television, popular culture, and media criticism and theory; new histories of film, television, popular culture, and media criticism and theory, as well as contemporary interventions in these fields; politically engaged approaches to visual culture, media production, and contemporary constructions of feminism—inside the academy and in popular culture." Articles are well documented and accompanied by detailed notes. This is a recommended addition to academic film collections.

2959. ***Canadian Journal of Film Studies.*** [ISSN: 0847-5911] 1990. s-a. CND 45 (Individuals, CND 35). Ed(s): William C Wees. Film Studies Association of Canada, Department of Art History and Communication Studies, McGill University, Arts Building W225, Montreal, PQ H3A 2T6, Canada; william.wees@mcgill.ca; http://www.film.queensu.ca/FSAC/CJFS.html. Illus., adv. Refereed. Circ: 300 Paid. *Indexed:* CBCARef, FLI, IIFP, IIPA, MRD. *Bk. rev.:* Various number and length. *Aud.:* Ac.

The stated aim of this publication is "to promote scholarship on Canadian film and television while . . . publishing articles, book reviews and archival materials relevant to all aspects of film and television." There are good book reviews and lengthy essays in English (or occasionally in French) covering Canadian as well as global cinema. A recent issue includes the articles "The Reel Nation: Image and Reality in Contemporary Canadian Cinema" and "Andre Tarkovsky's Madonna del Parto."

2960. ***Cineaction!: radical film criticism & theory.*** [ISSN: 0826-9866] 1985. 3x/yr. USD 35 (Individuals, USD 18). Cineaction!, 40 Alexander St, Apt 705, Toronto, ON M4Y 1B5, Canada. Illus., index, adv. Sample. Circ: 2500. Online: Florida Center for Library Automation; Gale Group. Reprint: PSC. *Indexed:* CBCARef, CPerI, FLI, IIFP, IIPA, MLA-IB, MRD. *Bk. rev.:* Various number and length. *Aud.:* Ac.

This title examines film from various differing viewpoints. Each issue focuses on a central theme, and forthcoming themes are announced, encouraging the submission of articles. In addition to scholarly articles on film theory, there are interviews with filmmakers, film reviews, book reviews, and reports from international film festivals.

2961. ***Cineaste: America's leading magazine on the art and politics of the cinema.*** [ISSN: 0009-7004] 1967. q. USD 35 (Individuals, USD 20; USD 6 newsstand/cover). Ed(s): Gary Crowdus. Cineaste Publishers, Inc., 304 Hudson St., 6th Fl, New York, NY 10013-1015; cineaste@cineaste.com; http://www.cineaste.com. Illus., index, adv. Circ: 12000 Paid. Vol. ends: Fall. Microform: PQC. Online: bigchalk; Chadwyck-Healey Incorporated; EBSCO Publishing; Factiva; Florida Center for Library Automation; Gale Group; OCLC Online Computer Library Center, Inc.; ProQuest Information & Learning; H.W. Wilson. *Indexed:* ABS&EES, AltPI, ArtHuCI, ArtInd, FLI, IBZ, IIFP, IIPA, MLA-IB, MRD, SSCI. *Bk. rev.:* Various number and length. *Aud.:* Ga, Ac.

This publication bills itself as "America's leading magazine on the art and politics of the cinema." It provides interviews with actors and filmmakers as well as film, home video, and book reviews. A recent issue contains an essay on the cinema of Akira Kurosawa, with a list of the reference sources used for the article.

2962. ***Cinefex: the journal of cinematic illusions.*** [ISSN: 0198-1056] 1980. q. USD 28 domestic; USD 42 foreign; USD 8.50 newsstand/cover per issue. Ed(s): Jody Duncan. Cinefex, PO Box 20027, Riverside, CA 92516; editor@cinefex.com. Illus., adv. Circ: 28000 Paid. Vol. ends: Dec. *Indexed:* FLI, IIFP, IIPA, MRD. *Aud.:* Sa.

"*Cinefex* is a quarterly magazine devoted to motion picture special effects. Since 1980 it has been the bible to professionals and enthusiasts, covering the field like no other publication. Profusely illustrated in color, with as many as 180 pages per issue, *Cinefex* offers a captivating look at the technologies and techniques behind many of our most popular and enduring movies." For the professional, there is a profusion of ads for services and products related to special visual effects.

2963. ***Cinema Journal.*** Formerly: *Society of Cinematologists. Journal.* [ISSN: 0009-7101] 1961. q. USD 60 (Individuals, USD 36). Ed(s): Jon Lewis. University of Texas Press, Journals Division, 2100 Comal, Austin, TX 78722; utpress@uts.cc.utexas.edu; http://www.utexas.edu/utpress/journals/journals.html. Illus., index, adv. Sample. Refereed. Circ: 2654. Vol. ends: Aug. Online: Chadwyck-Healey Incorporated; EBSCO Publishing; OCLC Online Computer Library Center, Inc.; Project MUSE; ProQuest Information & Learning; RoweCom Information Quest; Swets Blackwell. Reprint: PSC. *Indexed:* ABS&EES, ArtHuCI, ArtInd, FLI, IBZ, IIFP, IIPA, MLA-IB. *Bk. rev.:* Various number and length. *Aud.:* Ac.

This title "presents recent scholarship by Society for Cinema Studies members. The journal publishes essays on a wide variety of subjects from diverse methodological perspectives. A Professional Notes section informs . . . readers about upcoming events, research applications, and the latest published research."

2964. ***Cinema Scope.*** [ISSN: 1488-7002] 1999. q. USD 40 (Individuals, USD 20). Ed(s): Mark Peranson. Cinema Scope Publishing, 465 Lytton Blvd, Toronto, ON M5N 1S5, Canada; http://www.insound.com. Illus., adv. *Aud.:* Ac, Sc.

"An independently published quarterly jam-packed with interviews, features, and essays on film and video, CS is geared to cinephiles looking for an intelligent forum on world cinema. With unparalleled depth and breadth, CS is a real alternative in today's Canadian film scene." Includes DVD reviews, book reviews, and film festival reviews.

2965. ***Cinemaya: the Asian film quarterly.*** [ISSN: 0970-8782] 1988. q. INR 325 (Individuals, INR 175). Ed(s): Aruna Vasudev. Cinemaya, B-90 Defence Colony, New Delhi, 110 024, India; cinemaya@vsnl.com. Illus., adv. Circ: 5000 Paid and controlled. Vol. ends: Winter. *Indexed:* FLI, MRD. *Aud.:* Ga, Ac.

Official journal of the Network for the Promotion of Asian Cinema, this titles provides coverage of Asian film and filmmakers and interviews with filmmakers not commmonly found in popular movie magazines. It also provides film festival news and film reviews. Published quarterly.

2966. ***Cinescape.*** 1994. m. USD 29.95; USD 4.99 newsstand/cover. Ed(s): Anthony Ferrante. Mania Entertainment LLC, 220 Main St, Ste C, Venice, CA 90291. Illus., adv. Circ: 250000 Paid. *Aud.:* Ga.

This monthly publication concentrates on science fiction, fantasy, and horror film coverage. Most of the articles are regarding current releases, but they do have retrospective coverage as well. It includes articles on actors and filmmakers of these films. Some issues also include reviews of DVDs, soundtracks, comics, books, and games.

2967. *Classic Images.* Former titles (until 1979): *Classic Film - Video Images;* (until 1978): *Classic Film Collector; Eight MM Collector.* [ISSN: 0275-8423] 1962. m. USD 32 domestic; USD 42 foreign. Ed(s): Bob King. Muscatine Journal, 301 E Third St, Muscatine, IA 52761; classicimages@classicimages.com; http://www.classicimages.com. Illus., index, adv. Circ: 5000. Vol. ends: Dec. Microform: PQC. Reprint: PQC. *Indexed:* FLI, IIFP, IIPA, MRD. *Aud.:* Ga.

"The film fan's bible," this is the publication for people who love older, classic films. Each tabloid-format issue is approximately 80 pages in length. It has biographical articles on film stars illustrated with black-and-white production and publicity stills. There are regular monthly features: video and DVD reviews, book reviews, music in film, obituaries, and "this month in movie history." For film buffs and collectors, it has an advertisers' index for film festivals, conventions, video companies, publishers, and memorabilia merchants.

2968. *Creative Screenwriting.* [ISSN: 1084-8665] 1994. bi-m. USD 29.95 domestic; USD 34.95 Canada; USD 54.95 elsewhere. Ed(s): Erik N Bauer. Creative Screenwriting, 6404 Hollywood Blvd, Ste 415, Los Angeles, CA 90028; http://www.creativescreenwriting.com. Illus., adv. *Indexed:* IIFP, IIPA, MLA-IB. *Bk. rev.:* Various number and length. *Aud.:* Ac.

This title "publishes critical, theoretical, historical, and practical essays on all aspects of writing for feature films and television. It also publishes critical reviews of books, products, and seminars of interest to the screenwriters. In seeking to bridge the professional and screenwriting literatures, *Creative Screenwriting* welcomes contributions from diverse perspectives." This is a good addition for library collections supporting scriptwriting programs.

2969. *D G A Magazine.* Formerly: *D G A News.* 1975. bi-m. USD 30 domestic; USD 45 in Canada & Mexico; USD 60 elsewhere. Ed(s): Ted Elrick. Directors Guild of America, 7920 Sunset Blvd., Hollywood, CA 90046; http://www.dga.org. Illus., adv. Circ: 15000. *Indexed:* FLI, IIFP. *Bk. rev.:* Various number and length. *Aud.:* Sa.

This is the official magazine of the Directors Guild of America. It reports guild and industry news affecting its membership. There is a section of updates on guild members—deaths, additions, changes. Festivals are covered, and interviews with directors of upcoming major feature films and TV movies are included in each issue. Book and DVD reviews are included.

2970. *Editors Guild Magazine.* bi-m. USD 45. Ed(s): Stephanie Argy. Steven Jay Cohen, IATSE Local 700 MPEG, 7715 Sunset Blvd, Ste 200, Hollywood, CA 90046; http://www.editorsguild.com. *Aud.:* Sa.

This is the official magazine of the Editors Guild. It covers industry events impacting guild members. There are interviews with editors, assessments of new equipment and technologies, and a section on technical tips. Regular features in each issue include an index of advertisers, announcements and obituaries, and new signatories.

2971. *Encore.* Formed by the merger of (1983-1984): *Australia Film Review;* (1982-1984): *Encore Australia;* Which was formerly (1976-1982): *Encore.* [ISSN: 0815-2063] 1984. m. AUD 126.50. Ed(s): Tracy Prisk. Reed Business Information Pty Ltd, Locked Bag 2999, Chatswood, NSW 2067, Australia; customerservice@reedbusiness.com.au; http://www.reedbusiness.com.au. Illus., adv. Circ: 4426. *Indexed:* CMPI. *Aud.:* Sa.

Covering film and TV postproduction and technology, this title reports industry news at home and abroad that concerns the Australian film industry. There is a production report, including features in planning and preproduction. Current national box-office figures for Australia and internationally are listed, and video rental figures are reported. There are ads for pre- and postproduction products and services in each issue, and a calendar of upcoming film industry events.

2972. *Film & History: an interdisciplinary journal of film and television studies.* Supersedes: *Historians Film Committee Newsletter.* [ISSN: 0360-3695] 1970. s-a. USD 40 (Individuals, USD 30). Ed(s): Peter C Rollins. Historians Film Committee, Popular Culture Centre, R R 3, Box 80, Cleveland, OK 74020; RollinsPC@aol.com. Illus., adv. Refereed. Circ: 1000 Paid. *Indexed:* ABS&EES, AmH&L, FLI, IIFP, IIPA, MRD. *Aud.:* Ac.

Each issue of this semi-annual publication has a special focus or theme. Two recent issues focus on the Holocaust on film, one covering documentaries, the other covering feature films. There are television, film, and book reviews. A number of the sponsors for this title are publishers, some are university presses. This title is for academic collections.

2973. *Film & Video.* Former titles (until 1988): *Opticmusic's Film & Video Production;* (until 1987): *Optic Music.* [ISSN: 1041-1933] 1984. m. Ed(s): Peter Caranicas, Scott Lehane. Knowledge Industry Publications, Inc., 701 Westchester Ave, White Plains, NY 10604; http://www.kipinet.com. Illus., adv. *Aud.:* Ac, Sa.

This title brings the reader up to date on current technology in the film industry. A recent issue has an article spotlighting three relatively new directors who are using new technologies to complete their respective film projects, a National Association of Broadcasters' convention preview of new technologies and products, and the annual directory of stock footage sources. Advertisements for film services and equipment are included in each issue. This will be a welcome addition to any collection supporting a filmmaking program.

2974. *Film Comment.* [ISSN: 0015-119X] 1962. bi-m. USD 24.95 domestic; USD 32 in Canada & Mexico; USD 50 elsewhere. Ed(s): Doris Fellerman. Film Society of Lincoln Center, 70 Lincoln Center Plaza, New York, NY 10023-6595; http://www.filmlinc.com/fcm/fcm.htm. Illus., index, adv. Circ: 40000. Vol. ends: Nov/Dec. CD-ROM: ProQuest Information & Learning. Microform: NBI; PQC. Online: bigchalk; EBSCO Publishing; Florida Center for Library Automation; Gale Group; Northern Light Technology, Inc.; OCLC Online Computer Library Center, Inc.; ProQuest Information & Learning. Reprint: ISI; PQC. *Indexed:* ArtHuCI, ArtInd, BRI, CBRI, FLI, HumInd, IBZ, IIFP, IIPA, MRD, MagInd, RGPR. *Bk. rev.:* Various number and length. *Aud.:* Hs, Ga, Ac.

This publication by the Film Society of Lincoln Center gives excellent coverage of filmmaking in the United States as well as worldwide. A recent issue includes articles on the Dardenne brothers' film "The Son," the comedic genius of Aki Kaurismaki, and an exclusive interview with director Jin Zhangke.

2975. *Film Criticism.* [ISSN: 0163-5069] 1976. 3x/yr. USD 18 (Individuals, USD 15). Ed(s): I Lloyd Michaels. Allegheny College, 520 N Main St, Meadville, PA 16335. Illus., adv. Sample. Refereed. Circ: 500. Vol. ends: Spring. *Indexed:* ABS&EES, ArtHuCI, ArtInd, BRI, CBRI, FLI, HumInd, IIFP, IIPA, MLA-IB, MRD, SSCI. *Bk. rev.:* Various number and length. *Aud.:* Ac.

This refereed journal publishes articles that examine and re-examine films from a variety of critical, political, and aesthetic viewpoints. Unusual aspects of films and symbolism are discussed in great detail. Occasionally, the body of work by a specific filmmaker is analyzed. A recent issue focuses on French cinema of the 1990s. There are book reviews in most issues.

2976. *Film History: an international journal.* [ISSN: 0892-2160] 1987. q. USD 175. Ed(s): Richard Koszarski. John Libbey & Company Pty. Ltd., Level 10, 15-17 Young St, Sydney, NSW 2000, Australia; jlsydney@mpx.com.au. Illus., index. Sample. Refereed. Vol. ends: Dec. *Indexed:* AmH&L, IIFP, IIPA, MRD. *Bk. rev.:* Various number and length. *Aud.:* Ac.

"The subject of *Film History* is the historical development of the motion picture, and the social, technological and economic context in which this has occurred. Its areas of interest range from the technical and entrepreneurial innovations of early and pre-cinema experiments, through all aspects of the production, distribution, exhibition and reception of commercial and non-commercial motion pictures. In addition to original research in these areas, the journal will survey the paper and film holdings of archives and libraries worldwide, publish selected examples of primary documentation (such as early film scenarios) and report on current publications, exhibitions, conferences, and research in progress. Most future issues will be devoted to comprehensive studies of single themes."

2977. *Film Journal International.* Former titles (until 1996): *Film Journal; Independent Film Journal.* [ISSN: 1526-9884] 1934. m. USD 65 domestic; USD 120 foreign. Ed(s): Robert Sunshine. V N U Business Publications, 770 Broadway, New York, NY 10003; bmcomm@vnuinc.com; http://www.vnubusinessmedia.com/. Illus., index, adv. Circ: 9200. Vol. ends: Dec. Online: EBSCO Publishing; Florida Center for Library Automation; Gale Group. *Indexed:* FLI, IIPA. *Aud.:* Sa.

The intended audience for this publication is exhibitors: News, articles, and advertisements all relate to aspects of exhibition and concessions. The articles on specific film titles are written for a broader audience, but the main intent is in reporting on box-office potential. Each issue includes film reviews, film company news, new posts, new products, a buying and booking guide, trade talk, and an index of advertisers.

2978. *Film Music.* [ISSN: 1520-3891] 1998. m. USD 35 domestic; USD 45 in Canada & Mexico; USD 65 elsewhere. Film Music Network, 11601 Wilshire Blvd, Ste 500, Los Angeles, CA 90025; http://www.filmmusic.net/. *Aud.:* Ac, Sa.

The mission of *Film Music* magazine is to "promote the free flow of information about the world of film and television music for the benefit of those who work in the business and those desiring to learn more about the business." The editors state that their goals are to "promote communication, growth, education, and to empower and contribute to the success of those working in the film and television music industry."

2979. *Film Quarterly: quarterly of film, radio and television.* Formerly: *Quarterly of Film, Radio and Television.* [ISSN: 0015-1386] 1945. q. USD 112 print & online eds. USD 28 newsstand/cover. Ed(s): Ann Martin. University of California Press, Journals Division, 2000 Center St, Ste 303, Berkeley, CA 94704-1223; journals@ucop.edu; http://www.ucpress.edu/journals. Illus., index, adv. Sample. Refereed. Circ: 6450 Paid. Vol. ends: Oct. Microform: PQC. Online: EBSCO Publishing; Florida Center for Library Automation; Gale Group; Ingenta Select; Northern Light Technology, Inc.; OCLC Online Computer Library Center, Inc. Reprint: PQC. *Indexed:* ABS&EES, ASIP, ArtHuCI, ArtInd, BRD, BRI, CBRI, FLI, HumInd, IBZ, IIFP, IIPA, MLA-IB, MRD, MagInd, MusicInd, RGPR. *Bk. rev.:* Various number and length. *Aud.:* Ga, Ac.

"International in coverage and reputation, *Film Quarterly* offers lively and penetrating articles covering the entire field of film studies. Articles include interviews with innovative film- and videomakers, writers, editors and cinematographers; readable discussion of issues in contemporary film theory; definitive, thoughtful reviews of international, avant garde, national cinemas, and documentaries; and important approaches to film history." Now available online as well.

2980. *Film Score Monthly: music soundtracks for motion pictures and television.* [ISSN: 1077-4289] 1990. m. USD 36.95 domestic; USD 50 elsewhere; USD 42.95 in Canada & Mexico. Ed(s): Tim Curran, Jonathan Kopkim. Film Score Monthly, 8503 Washington Blvd, Culver City, CA 90232-7443; lukas@filmscoremonthly.com; http://www.filmscoremonthly.com. Illus., adv. Sample. Circ: 11000. *Indexed:* FLI, IIMP, IIPA. *Aud.:* Sa.

Film Score Monthly provides information for those interested in what is happening in the movie music industry: current news, record-label updates on releases, upcoming assignments (who's scoring what for whom), and CD reviews. There are feature articles on composers and behind-the-scenes looks at film music production.

2981. *Filmmaker: the magazine of independent film.* Formed by the 1992 merger of: *Off-Hollywood Report; Montage.* [ISSN: 1063-8954] 1992. q. USD 75 (Individuals, USD 18; USD 5.95 newsstand/cover per issue). Ed(s): Scott Macaulay. Filmmaker, 501 Fifth Ave, Ste 1714, New York, NY 10017; http://www.filmmakermagazine.com. Illus., adv. Sample. Circ: 42000. *Indexed:* FLI, IIPA, MRD. *Bk. rev.:* Various number and length. *Aud.:* Sa.

This title is directed toward those interested in independent, smaller-budgeted films and filmmaking. Lesser-known films currently being released are profiled in each issue, along with independent filmmaker interviews and current film festival news. There are advertisements for film products, pre- and postproduction services, and film festivals, plus a handy advertisers' index. This is a nice addition to any collection supporting a film program.

2982. *Films of the Golden Age.* [ISSN: 1083-5369] 1995. q. USD 18.80. Ed(s): Bob King. Muscatine Journal, 301 E Third St, Muscatine, IA 52761; http://www.classicimages.com/foga. Illus., adv. Vol. ends: Winter. *Indexed:* FLI, MRD. *Aud.:* Ga.

This is touted as "the magazine for film lovers." From the same publisher as *Classic Images*, this title covers films and filmmakers of the 1930s, 1940s, and 1950s. Presenting lengthy biographical articles accompanied by black-and-white production stills, this is a valentine to film's golden age. There are advertisements providing sources for stills, books, videos, and memorabilia.

2983. *Griffithiana.* [ISSN: 0393-3857] 1978. s-a. EUR 47 (Individuals, EUR 31). Ed(s): Davide Turconi, Peter Lehman. Cineteca del Friuli, Via G. Bini, Palazzo Gurisatti, Gemona, 33013, Italy; griffithiana@cinetecadelfriuli.org; http://cinetecadelfriuli.org. Illus., adv. Refereed. Circ: 2500. *Indexed:* FLI, IIFP, IIPA, MLA-IB, MRD. *Bk. rev.:* Various number and length. *Aud.:* Ac.

"An international journal of film history, *Griffithiana* is devoted to the study of animation and silent cinema. It features articles by prominent international film scholars, historians, archivists, and journalists, as well as comprehensive filmographies and reviews of international cinema books. Many issues showcase newly rediscovered and restored films presented at the Pordenone Film Festival." The articles are published in both Italian and English.

2984. *Independent Film & Video Monthly.* Formerly: *Independent (New York).* [ISSN: 1077-8918] 1978. 10x/yr. USD 75 (Individuals, USD 55; Corporations, USD 150). Ed(s): Beth Pinsker, Patricia Thompson. Foundation for Independent Video & Film, 304 Hudson St, 6th Fl, New York, NY 10013; independent@aivf.org. Illus., adv. Circ: 42000. Vol. ends: Dec. Online: ProQuest Information & Learning. *Indexed:* AltPI, FLI, MLA-IB, MRD. *Aud.:* Ac, Sa.

This monthly publication of the Foundation for Independent Video and Film (FIVF) is "dedicated to the advancement of media arts and artists." Each issue contains entertainment industry news, technology reports, and book reviews. "Distributor FAQ" and "Funder FAQ" give background information on a spotlighted company. Up-to-date information on foundation events and film festivals is provided. There are advertisements throughout for equipment and postproduction services.

2985. *International Documentary.* [ISSN: 1077-9361] 1986. m. Combined issue for Jan./Feb & Jul./Aug. USD 75 (Individuals, USD 85 for membership; Corporations, USD 700 for membership). Ed(s): Betsy A McLane. International Documentary Association, 1201 W 5th St, Ste M320, Los Angeles, CA 90017-1461; membership@documentary.org; http://www.documentary.org/. Illus., adv. Sample. Circ: 12500. Vol. ends: Nov. *Indexed:* FLI, IIFP. *Aud.:* Ac, Sa.

This publication of the International Documentary Association intends to "promote nonfiction film and video and to support the efforts of documentary makers around the world." It provides membership news and reports on festivals. Feature articles on aspects of the documentary filmmaking process are published with the doc filmmaker in mind. Ads for pre- and postproduction services, festivals, and classes in documentary filmmaking are included. Columns formerly included in each issue but now available on the web site are: North American Broadcast and Cable Premieres, Events and Screenings, Calls for Entries, Funding, and Jobs and Opportunities.

2986. ***Journal of Film and Video.*** Former titles (until 1984): *University Film and Video Association. Journal;* (until 1981): *University Film Association. Journal; University Film Producers Association. Journal.* [ISSN: 0742-4671] 1947. q. USD 35 (Individual members, USD 50). Ed(s): Suzanne Regan. University Film and Video Association, California State University, Department of Communication Studies, Los Angeles, CA 90032-8111; sregan@calstatela.edu; http://www.calstatela.edu. Illus., index, adv. Refereed. Circ: 1300. Vol. ends: Winter. Microform: PQC. Online: bigchalk; Chadwyck-Healey Incorporated; EBSCO Publishing; Gale Group; ProQuest Information & Learning. *Indexed:* ABS&EES, ArtHuCI, CIJE, CommAb, FLI, IBZ, IIFP, IIPA. *Aud.:* Ac.

This refereed journal "focuses on scholarship in the fields of film and video production, history, theory, criticism, and aesthetics." In its call for papers, it requests "articles about film and related media, problems of education in these fields and the function of film and video in society." For academic audiences.

2987. ***Journal of Popular Film and Television.*** Formerly: *Journal of Popular Film.* [ISSN: 0195-6051] 1971. q. USD 93 (Individuals, USD 48; USD 23.25 per issue). Ed(s): Page Pratt. Heldref Publications, 1319 18th St, NW, Washington, DC 20036-1802; subscribe@heldref.org; http://www.heldref.org. Illus., index, adv. Refereed. Circ: 800. CD-ROM: ProQuest Information & Learning. Online: bigchalk; Chadwyck-Healey Incorporated; EBSCO Publishing; Florida Center for Library Automation; Gale Group; LexisNexis; OCLC Online Computer Library Center, Inc.; ProQuest Information & Learning; SoftLine Information; H.W. Wilson. Reprint: PSC. *Indexed:* ABS&EES, AmH&L, ArtHuCI, ArtInd, BRI, CBRI, CWI, CommAb, FLI, HumInd, IBZ, IIFP, IIPA, MLA-IB, MRD, RI-1, SSCI. *Aud.:* Ga, Ac.

This title "is dedicated to popular film and television in the broadest sense. Concentration is upon commercial cinema and television: stars, directors, producers, studios, networks, genres, series, the audience, etc." Articles are accompanied by acknowledgements, with notes and works cited. Occasionally, an issue has a single theme—the Winter 2003 issue was devoted to the Western. Book reviews are also included.

2988. ***Movieline's Hollywood Life.*** Formerly (until Apr. 2003): *Movieline.* [ISSN: 1544-0583] 1989. 8x/yr. USD 13.75 domestic; USD 33 foreign; USD 3.99 newsstand/cover. Ed(s): Heidi Parker. Movieline, Inc., 10537 Santa Monica Blvd, Ste 250, Los Angeles, CA 90025. Illus., adv. Circ: 312000. *Indexed:* ASIP, FLI, MRD. *Aud.:* Ga.

This slick magazine presents news of current major studio releases and their stars, covering premieres, festivals, and the celebrity lifestyle. Recent video and DVD releases are showcased, along with upcoming cable TV titles. *Movieline's Hollywood Life* is aimed at general audiences.

2989. ***Moviemaker: the art and business of making movies.*** 1993. q. USD 15 domestic; USD 26 Canada; USD 48 elsewhere. Ed(s): Timothy E Rhys. Moviemaker, 2265 Westwood Blvd, Ste 479, Los Angeles, CA 90064; staff@moviemaker.com; http://www.moviemaker.com. Illus., adv. Circ: 50000 Paid and controlled. *Indexed:* FLI, IIPA. *Aud.:* Ac, Sa.

This title features articles on producers, actors, and directors. It also covers independent film industry issues, such as copyright, technical instruction, festivals, shorts, and documentaries. There are ads for film equipment and services, with an advertisers index. This is a good title for collections supporting a filmmaking curriculum.

2990. ***Outre (Evanston): entertainment from the world of ultramedia.*** Formerly (until 1995): *Filmfax.* [ISSN: 0895-0393] 1986. q. USD 20; USD 30 Canada; USD 50 elsewhere. Ed(s): Michael Stein, Ted Okuda. Filmfax, Inc., 1320 Oakton St, Evanston, IL 60202-2719; http://www.magamall.com/magazine/64791/back2/insidmag.htm. Illus., adv. *Indexed:* FLI, IIFP. *Aud.:* Ga.

This title covers science fiction, horror, and fantasy films, genres that have long attracted large groups of fans. There are biographical articles on actors who have appeared in these genres and interviews with filmmakers. For enthusiasts, there is a profusion of ads for video and movie memorabilia throughout, and a big catalog of B-movie merchandise.

2991. ***Post Script (Commerce): essays in film and the humanities.*** [ISSN: 0277-9897] 1981. 3x/yr. USD 25 (Individuals, USD 15). Ed(s): Gerald Duchovnay. Post Script, Inc., Department of Literature and Languages, Texas A & M University, Commerce, TX 75429-3011; gerald_duchovnay@tamu-commerce.edu; http://www.tamu-commerce.edu/coas/litlang. Illus., index, adv. Refereed. Circ: 400. Online: Chadwyck-Healey Incorporated; Gale Group. *Indexed:* BRI, CBRI, FLI, IIFP, IIPA, MLA-IB. *Aud.:* Ac.

This title publishes "manuscripts on film as language and literature; acting; film music; film as visual art (painting and cinematic style, set design, costuming); film and photography; film history; aesthetics; the response of film and the humanities to technology; interdisciplinary studies in theme and genre; film and American Studies; reappraisals of seminal essays; book reviews and interviews; and responses to articles appearing in *Post Script.*" Occasionally, an issue is devoted to a specific topic.

2992. ***Premiere (New York): the movie magazine.*** [ISSN: 0894-9263] 1987. 10x/yr. USD 12 domestic; USD 20 foreign. Ed(s): Peter Herbst. Hachette Filipacchi Media U.S., Inc., 1633 Broadway, New York, NY 10019; http://www.hfmus.com. Illus., index, adv. Circ: 600000 Paid. Vol. ends: Dec. Online: America Online, Inc.; Gale Group. *Indexed:* ASIP, FLI, MRD, MagInd, RGPR. *Bk. rev.:* Various number and length. *Aud.:* Hs, Ga.

Premiere is the primary publication for general audiences giving information on current major studio releases, upcoming releases, new actors, and filmmakers. Slick and readable, entertaining and informative, it will be of interest even to casual moviegoers. It is a good complement to *Movieline's Hollywood Life.*

2993. ***Quarterly Review of Film and Video.*** Formerly (until 1989): *Quarterly Review of Film Studies.* [ISSN: 1050-9208] 1976. q. GBP 299 (Individuals, GBP 67; Corporations, GBP 489). Ed(s): Wheeler Winston. Taylor & Francis Ltd, 11 New Fetter Ln, London, EC4P 4EE, United Kingdom; http://www.tandf.co.uk/journals. Illus., index. Refereed. Online: EBSCO Publishing; Gale Group. Reprint: PQC; PSC. *Indexed:* ABS&EES, ArtHuCI, ArtInd, BRI, CBRI, FLI, HumInd, IIFP, MLA-IB, MRD, SSCI. *Bk. rev.:* Various number and length. *Aud.:* Ac.

This refereed journal is international and interdisciplinary in scope. It publishes "critical, historical, and theoretical essays, book reviews and interviews in the area of moving image studies including film, video, and digital image studies." For academic institutions.

2994. ***Scenario: the magazine of screenwriting art.*** [ISSN: 1079-6851] 1995. q. USD 59.95 domestic; USD 69.95 Canada; USD 72.95 elsewhere. Ed(s): Tod Lippy. eDesign Communications, 3200 Tower Oaks Blvd, Rockville, MD 20852; info@scenariomag.com; http://www.scenariomag.com/. Illus., adv. *Indexed:* AIAP, FLI, IIFP, IIPA. *Aud.:* Sa.

This quarterly publishes complete screenplays in each issue, both recent and classic. For example, a recent issue includes "American Psycho," "The Sixth Sense," and "Rosemary's Baby." Also included are short film scripts and interviews with filmmakers. This is an excellent addition to collections supporting film studies or screenwriting programs. There was a brief period of not publishing, but according to the publisher, it has started up again.

2995. ***Screen International: the voice of the international film business.*** Former titles: *Screen International and Cinema T V Today;* (until 1975): *Cinema T V Today.* [ISSN: 0307-4617] 1912. w. GBP 98; GBP 145 in Europe; GBP 155 elsewhere. Ed(s): Boyd Farrow. Emap Media Ltd., 33-39 Bowling Green Ln, London, EC1R 0DA, United Kingdom; 74431,1401@compuserve.com; boydf@media.emap.co.uk; http://www.emap.com. Illus., adv. Circ: 10442. *Aud.:* Ac.

This weekly publication covers the "international film business" more closely than *Variety.* Published in London, it has a slight European bias to its coverage. There is production information on European and U.K. films, film reviews, statistics, and box-office roundups. This title is definitely for people needing to keep a close pulse on the worldwide film industry. The web site gives up-to-the-minute news and developments in the film industry "around the clock from around the world."

2996. ***ScreenTalk: the international voice of screenwriting.*** [ISSN: 1600-9371] 1998. bi-m. USD 39.95 in the European Union; USD 34.95 outside of the European Union; USD 8.95 newsstand/cover per issue. Ed(s): Eric Lilleor. Sommer-Lilleor Productions, Kornvej 6, Give, 7323, Denmark. Adv. *Aud.:* Ga, Ac.

Although this title is published in Denmark, it underscores the dominance of American films and television shows. There are articles on the craft of writing, such as emphasizing writing for films as opposed to writing prose or other genre writing; for example, one article addresses "the art of writing the fight scene." Interviews with filmmakers along with DVD, book, and film reviews are included in each issue.

2997. ***Scr(i)pt: where film begins.*** [ISSN: 1092-2016] 1995. bi-m. USD 29.95 domestic; USD 37.95 Canada; USD 59.95 elsewhere. Ed(s): Shelly Mellott. Scr(i)pt, 5638 Sweet Air Rd, Baldwin, MD 21013-9009; ads@scriptmag.com. Illus., adv. *Aud.:* Sa.

The explanation given for the title is, "the (i) in *Scr(i)pt* is used to honor the screenwriter . . . our message to you is that we recognize you as the genesis of film—the inspiration." This publication is for those who are beyond asking for examples of the standard script format. Interviews and articles are included of/by writers of currently released films as well, which makes it a source of practical information for both established and burgeoning screenwriters.

2998. ***Sight and Sound: the international film monthly.*** Incorporates: *Monthly Film Bulletin.* [ISSN: 0037-4806] 1932. m. GBP 45.75 domestic; GBP 54.75 foreign. British Film Institute, 21 Stephen St, London, W1T 1LN, United Kingdom; http://www.bfi.org.uk. Illus., index, adv. Circ: 26299. Vol. ends: Dec. Microform: MIM; NRP; WMP. Online: Gale Group; OCLC Online Computer Library Center, Inc.; H.W. Wilson. *Indexed:* ArtHuCI, ArtInd, BRD, BRI, BrHumI, CBRI, FLI, HumInd, IBZ, IIFP, IIPA, MLA-IB, MRD, SSCI. *Bk. rev.:* Various number and length. *Aud.:* Ga, Ac.

This publication is particularly good in the area of film reviews and credits; it consistently gives the most complete credit listings of any film periodical. Coverage includes major film festivals and filmmakers, American and foreign. It also publishes detailed articles and interviews with directors not usually found in popular movie magazines.

Variety. See Theater section.

2999. ***The Velvet Light Trap.*** [ISSN: 0149-1830] 1971. s-a. USD 48 (Individuals, USD 26). University of Texas Press, Journals Division, 2100 Comal, Austin, TX 78722; journals@uts.cc.utexas.edu; http://www.utexas.edu/utpress/journals/journals.html. Illus., index, adv. Sample. Circ: 531. Vol. ends: Sep. Microform: PQC. Online: EBSCO Publishing; Florida Center for Library Automation; Gale Group. Reprint: PQC; PSC. *Indexed:* AmH&L, AmHI, CommAb, FLI, IIFP, IIPA, MLA-IB, MRD, PRA. *Bk. rev.:* Various number and length. *Aud.:* Ac.

This publication is "devoted to investigating historical questions that illuminate the understanding of film and other media." Issues tend to have a single theme, e.g., religion and the media. Articles and interviews are of a scholarly nature and include notes. Book reviews are given in each issue. Recommended for academic collections.

3000. ***Written By.*** Former titles (until 1996): *Writers Guild of America, West. Journal;* Formerly (until 1997): *Journal.* [ISSN: 1092-468X] 1997. 10x/yr. USD 40 domestic; USD 45 Canada; USD 50 elsewhere. Ed(s): Tawn E McCarthy. Writers Guild of America, West, 7000 W Third St, W Hollywood, Los Angeles, CA 90048; writtnby@wga.org.; http://www.wga.org/WrittenBy/index.html. Illus., adv. Circ: 3000 Paid. *Indexed:* FLI. *Aud.:* Sa.

The official publication of the Writers Guild of America West, it "actively seeks material from Guild members and other writers." It covers current events and creative issues affecting screen and television writers and offers biographical articles on writers and analyses of current films. A good title for libraries supporting a screenwriting program.

Electronic Journals

There are so many web sites covering so many different aspects of film that only a few are included in this section. Some of these are of a more serious bent, and others are very genre-specific.

3001. ***24 Frames Per Second: productions on film.*** 1997. irreg. approx. bi-w. Ed(s): Kirk Hostetter. 24 Frames Per Second, khoss@earthlink.net; http://www.24framespersecond.com. *Aud.:* Ac, Sa.

This journal "provides a forum for uniquely personal reactions to films and filmmakers." A broad range of formats has been established for the participation and interaction of its readers. Whether submitting a list of favorite films, an essay on filmmaking, or an experiment in digital cinema, *24 frames per second* is offered as an alternative to all-encompassing movie web sites. The e-zine is divided into three sections: reactions to films, writings on films, and information sources.

3002. ***Animation Blast.*** 1996. a. (issue no.9 due Fall/Winter 2003). Free. Ed(s): Amid Amidi. Animation Blast, PO Box 260491, Encino, CA 91426-0491. *Aud.:* Ac, Sa.

"Animation Blast is one of the few websites in the world that has [also entered] the . . . world of print." It is a "unique blend of news and commentary—pure, unfiltered, thought-provoking." Unlike other media sources, they are "not subservient to the studios and [do not] regurgitate their press releases." It puts the focus on animation artists and their art. It is estimated that 75 percent of readers are actual animation professionals who work in the industry.

3003. ***Audience (Online Edition).*** 1998. irreg. Ed(s): Robert A Wilson, Jr. Wilson Associates, PO Box 215, Simi Valley, CA 93062; http://www.audiencemag.com/. Adv. *Aud.:* Ga, Ac.

This was a monthly print periodical from July 1968 to September 1998 and became entirely an online publication December 1998. There is an archive of articles from 1971 to 1995, book and film reviews, festival coverage, short interviews with filmmakers, and a section of films rated by staff critics.

3004. ***Bright Lights.*** [ISSN: 0147-4049] 1993. q. Free. Ed(s): Gary Morris. Bright Lights, PO Box 420987, San Francisco, CA 94142-0987; editor@brightlightsfilm.com; http://www.brightlightsfilm.com. Illus., adv. Circ: 17500. *Indexed:* IIFP, MRD. *Aud.:* Ga, Ac.

"A popular-academic hybrid of movie analysis, history and commentary, looking at classical and commercial, independent, exploitation, and international film from a wide range of vantage points from the aesthetic to the political. A prime area of focus is on the connection between capitalist society and the images that reflect, support, or subvert it—movies as propaganda." Included on this site are some highly unusual genres, such as "tranny cinema." It has feature articles, film reviews, book reviews, filmmaker interviews, and film festival coverage.

3005. ***Images (Kansas City): a journal of film and popular culture.*** q. Ed(s): Grant Tracey. Images Journal, 111 E 66th Terrace, Kansas City, MO 64113; info@imagesjournal.com; http://www.imagesjournal.com. *Aud.:* Ga.

Images "publishes articles about movies, television, video and the other popular visual arts." It is a quarterly journal, but new articles and reviews are added each week. There are also video, DVD, and book reviews.

3006. ***Journal of Religion and Film.*** [ISSN: 1092-1311] 1997. s-a. Free. Ed(s): Kathy R Schwartz, William L Blizek. University of Nebraska at Omaha, Department of Philosophy and Religion, 6001 Dodge St, Omaha, NE 68182-0265; http://www.unomaha.edu/. Adv. Refereed. *Indexed:* MLA-IB. *Aud.:* Ga, Ac.

The *Journal of Religion and Film* "examines the description, critique, and embodiment of religion in film." The editors "invite articles and discussion on a variety of film types, commercial and academic, foreign and documentary, classic and contemporary." Peer-reviewed articles and analyses of films stressing spiritual aspects are presented.

3007. ***Movie Review Query Engine.*** 1996. w. Movie Review Query Engine, http://www.mrqe.com. *Aud.:* Hs, Ga, Ac.

This web site makes available in one place a wide range of reviews (over 350,000) for over 35,000 films from leading magazines and newspapers including some foreign publications. It also provides precomputed lists of films newly released on video, festival films, current top box-office films, and American Film Institute top movie lists.

3008. ***Senses of Cinema.*** [ISSN: 1443-4059] 1999. bi-m. Free. Ed(s): Fiona A Villella. Senses of Cinema, Cinema Studies Program, School of Fine Arts, Melbourne, VIC 3010, Australia. Refereed. *Indexed:* MLA-IB. *Aud.:* Ac, Sa.

Senses of Cinema is "an online film journal devoted to the serious and eclectic discussion of cinema." It receives financial assistance from the Australian Film Commission, and it has a slight down-under, Aussie bias (the Festivals section is divided into "international festivals" and "Australian festivals"). The journal is building up a "Great Directors" database, with a critical essay on each director along with a filmography, bibliography, and web resources. It includes book and DVD reviews.

■ FINANCE

Banking/Insurance/Investment/Scholarly/Trade Journals

See also Accounting and Taxation; Business; Consumer Education; and Economics sections. For Business Valuation, see also Real Estate section.

Carol J. Elsen, Associate Academic Librarian, Andersen Library, University of Wisconsin-Whitewater, Whitewater, WI 53190

Barbara Esty, Executive Education Teaching Support Librarian, Baker Library, Harvard Business School, Boston, MA 02163 (Insurance subsection)

Introduction

Finance as a field of study encompasses the management and movement of money or its equivalent in and out of organizations and markets for the benefit of investors, organizations, and governments. Because of the international nature of financial markets, this field is taking on an increasingly global scope.

Due to the importance and broad scope of finance, titles are presented in five major sections: (1) "Scholarly" titles cover all aspects of finance, including securities markets, financial instruments, financial economics, and strategic financial management; (2) "Trade" titles are generally targeted toward professionals in various areas of finance; (3) "Banking" includes titles focusing on banks and other financial institutions that are also geared to practitioners; (4) "Insurance" titles are trade publications for insurance professionals; and (5) "Investments" includes titles that are particularly intended for individual and institutional investors and money managers.

Most of the scholarly titles are highly technical in nature and require a working knowledge of mathematics, statistics, and finance to truly appreciate the content; these are appropriate for collections that support researchers or graduate programs in finance. The trade, banking, and insurance titles are less technical and are highly practical as they are written for professionals in the field; many of these titles are appropriate for academic and public libraries. Most titles that target individual investors are reasonably priced and appropriate for all types of libraries to consider. The institutional-investing and money management titles have a scope suitable for academic and public libraries as well as any library supporting investment professionals. Investors will find that Internet sites are increasingly useful as the Securities and Exchange Commission (SEC) and an increasing number of content providers provide timely and free (or low-cost) basic financial information via the Internet.

When selecting titles for a particular patron group, keep in mind the skill level required by each title and the cost, because finance titles can be expensive.

This section embeds comments on selected Internet sites in the annotations.

Basic Periodicals

Ga: *Kiplinger's Personal Finance;* Ac, Sa: *American Banker, Euromoney, Financial Analysts Journal, Institutional Investor, Investor's Chronicle, The Journal of Finance.*

Basic Abstracts and Indexes

ABI/Inform, Business Index, Business Periodicals Index, Journal of Economic Literature, PAIS International in Print.

Banking

3009. ***A B A Bank Marketing.*** Former titles (until 2001): *Bank Marketing;* (until 1972): *Bank Marketing Management.* [ISSN: 1539-7890] 1915. m. combined Jan.-Feb & July-Aug issues. USD 150 foreign (Members, USD 80; Non-members, USD 120). Ed(s): Walt Albro. American Bankers Association, 1120 Connecticut Ave NW, Washington, DC 20036-3971; custserv@aba.com; http://www.aba.com. Illus. Circ: 4015 Paid. Microform: PQC. Online: Northern Light Technology, Inc.; ProQuest Information & Learning. *Indexed:* ABIn, BPI. *Bk. rev.:* Various number and length. *Aud.:* Ga, Ac, Sa.

This delightful glossy trade publication is filled with coverage of all aspects of retail and corporate bank marketing. Each issue includes industry news and announcements, association news, an events calendar, problems/solutions, new products/services, a half-dozen provider profiles, and special sections that focus on community heroes, brands, customer service surveys, and a wide variety of technical and related service issues, in addition to frequent practitioner-written case studies. Articles often have clever titles, such as "Portal Promises—and Perils." Some issues include an excellent "datastream" insert, which is filled with general-interest marketing and advertising statistics, quotes from the classics, and more. With its numerous interesting sidebars, this is a great title for a browsing collection.

3010. ***A B A Banking Journal.*** Incorporates: *Banking Buying Guide;* Former titles (until 1979): *Banking; American Bankers Association. Journal.* [ISSN: 0194-5947] 1908. m. USD 25 (Free to qualified personnel). Ed(s): William W Streeter, Lauren Bielski. Simmons - Boardman Publishing Corp., 345 Hudson St, 12th floor, New York, NY 10014-4502; ababj@sbpub.com; http://www.banking.com/aba. Illus., index, adv. Sample. Circ: 31302. Vol. ends: Dec. Microform: PQC. Online: Dow Jones Interactive; EBSCO Publishing; Factiva; Florida Center for Library Automation; Gale Group; LexisNexis; OCLC Online Computer Library Center, Inc.; ProQuest Information & Learning. *Indexed:* ABIn, ATI, BLI, BPI, CompLI, LRI, PAIS, RI-1, RiskAb. *Bk. rev.:* Various number and length. *Aud.:* Ac, Sa.

This industry magazine covers news, trends, and products in commercial and community banking. Columns report on community banking, compliance, mortgage lending, trusts, technology, new-product development, news and newsmakers, regulatory issues, and the general economy. A calendar of events is also included. Recent feature articles examine banking bills on Capitol Hill, the end of the mortgage boom, bank investment programs, and family-owned banks.

3011. ***American Banker.*** Incorporates (1999-2002): *Financial Services Marketing.* [ISSN: 0002-7561] 1836. d. 5/wk. USD 895 combined subscription for print & online eds. Ed(s): David Longobardi. Thomson Financial Media, One State Street Plaza, 27th Flr., New York, NY 10004-1549; http://www.americanbanker.com. Illus., index, adv. Circ: 40000. Vol. ends: Dec. CD-ROM: The Dialog Corporation. Microform: PQC. Online: bigchalk; Data-Star; EBSCO Publishing; Factiva; Florida Center for Library Automation; Gale Group; LexisNexis; NewsNet; Northern Light Technology, Inc.; OCLC Online Computer Library Center, Inc.; ProQuest Information & Learning. Reprint: PQC. *Indexed:* ATI, AgeL, B&I, BLI, LRI, NewsAb. *Bk. rev.:* Various number and length. *Aud.:* Ac, Sa.

This highly regarded daily financial paper reports on trade and industry news and newsmakers. It covers trends in banking, mortgages, investment products, debt and credit, technology, ATMs, and finance. Bank ratings, marketing, court cases, regulations, and news about movers and shakers in the banking industry are also included. Because of the in-depth coverage of banking and the concise reports of related general business and industry news, this is a must for bankers and for many libraries.

3012. ***Bank Accounting & Finance.*** [ISSN: 0894-3958] 1987. bi-m. USD 345. Ed(s): Claire Greene. Aspen Publishers, Inc., 1185 Avenue of the Americas, New York, NY 10036; customer.service@aspenpubl.com; http://www.aspenpublishers.com. Illus., index, adv. Vol. ends: No. 6. *Indexed:* ATI. *Aud.:* Ac, Sa.

This no-nonsense practitioner's magazine addresses core issues related to financial, legislative, and corporate aspects of bank management, so it is primarily of interest to bank accountants and executives. Statements of Financial Accounting Standards are analyzed and case studies are presented. Regular columns provide news on the regulatory climate, merger and acquisition strategies, taxation, SEC regulations, bank management practices, and the Financial Accounting Standards Board and the Emerging Issues Task Force. Several peer-researched feature articles focus on a specific topic, including recent ones on the new Basel Capital Accord, data warehousing, hedging for banks, and payment and settlement systems. This title provides timely, insightful information and is suitable for academic libraries that support programs in accounting and finance.

3013. ***The Banker.*** [ISSN: 0005-5395] 1926. m. GBP 215; EUR 340; USD 333. Ed(s): Stephen Timewell. Financial Times Business Information, Magazines, Tabernacle Court, 16-28 Tabernacle St, London, EC2A 4DD, United Kingdom. Illus., index, adv. Circ: 12500. Vol. ends: Dec. Microform: PQC. Online: Factiva; Florida Center for Library Automation; Gale Group; LexisNexis; OCLC Online Computer Library Center, Inc.; ProQuest Information & Learning. Reprint: SCH. *Indexed:* ABIn, B&I, BPI, PAIS, RRTA, WAE&RSA. *Bk. rev.:* Various number and length. *Aud.:* Ac, Sa.

This international banking newsmagazine provides insights into the international retail and investment banking climates. Each issue includes summary reports of economic as well as industry conditions in a dozen or more countries, along with brief reports that cover banking, capital markets, trade finance, risk analysis, and interviews. Recent contents include discussions of rebuilding investor faith in Wall Street, bank mergers, e-banks, technological innovation, investment banking in Asia, outsourcing IT, and a host of other issues for each geographic region. Ranked lists of top banks and directories of foreign banks are often provided. This is a great choice for any academic or large public library whose patrons are interested in international finance, development, and banking news.

3014. ***Banking Strategies.*** Former titles (until 1996): *Bank Management;* (until 1990): *Bank Administration; Auditgram.* [ISSN: 1091-6385] 1925. bi-m. USD 64.50 domestic (Free to qualified personnel). Ed(s): Steve Klinkerman. Bank Administration Institute, 1 N Franklin Ste. 1000, Chicago, IL 60606-3421. Illus., index, adv. Circ: 30500 Controlled. Vol. ends: Dec. Microform: PQC. Online: EBSCO Publishing; Gale Group; OCLC Online Computer Library Center, Inc. Reprint: PQC. *Indexed:* ABIn, ATI, BLI, BPI, CompLI, PAIS. *Aud.:* Ac, Sa.

Produced by the Bank Administration Institute, whose directors are executives from all areas of the banking industry, this useful practitioner's magazine reports on all aspects of banking and bank management: community banking, retail banking, lending, corporate services, operations, technology, finance/ accounting, audit/control, human resources, treasury management, regulatory issues, and strategy development. The magazine presents several 5- to 15-page articles on current topics. Departments cover trends and statistics, human resources, economic perspectives, Washington news, community banking, and the "Publisher's Perspective," which recently addressed reputational risk and financial disclosure. Large public libraries and academic libraries that support programs in finance should consider this title.

3015. ***Community Banker.*** Former titles (until 2000): *America's Community Bankers;* (until 1995): *Savings and Community Banker;* Which was formed by the merger of (1952-1993): *Savings Institution Magazine;* Which was formerly (until 1983): *Savings and Loan News;* (1983-1993): *Bottomline (Washington);* Which was formed by the merger of (1921-1983): *Savings Bank Journal;* (1974-1983): *National Savings and Community League Journal;* Incorporates: *National League Journal of Insured Savings Associations.* [ISSN: 1529-1332] m. Ed(s): Debra Cope. America's Community Bankers, 900 19th St, N W, Ste 400, Washington, DC 20006; http://www.americascommunitybankers.org. Illus., adv. Circ: 7000. Microform: PQC. Online: EBSCO Publishing; Gale Group; OCLC Online Computer Library Center, Inc.; ProQuest Information & Learning. *Indexed:* ABIn, BPI, PAIS. *Aud.:* Ac, Sa.

This trade periodical provides in-depth analysis of current legislative and regulatory developments, economic trends, national news, investment management, marketing, human resources, compliance, tax management, data processing, and personnel. A calendar and general association news and personal profiles are included. Short feature articles recently examined mystery shopping investment products programs, challenges in jumbo mortgage lending, and revving up bank web sites. Because it's primarily a practitioner's magazine, only large public libraries or academic libraries that support programs in banking and finance should consider this title.

3016. ***Corporate Finance.*** Formerly: *Euromoney Corporate Finance.* [ISSN: 0958-2053] 1984. m. 11/yr. GBP 326 combined subscription domestic; EUR 520 combined subscription in Europe; USD 485 combined subscription elsewhere. Ed(s): Angus Foote. Euromoney Institutional Investor plc., Nestor House, Playhouse Yard, London, EC4V 5EX, United Kingdom; http://www.euromoney.com. Illus., index, adv. Sample. Circ: 11200. Vol. ends: Dec. *Indexed:* ABIn, B&I, BPI. *Aud.:* Ga, Ac, Sa.

This glossy trade publication targets CFOs, corporate treasurers, and finance directors of multinational companies, with a focus on capital management and recent deals and developments. Each issue contains dozens of short articles with news, information, and analysis on all aspects of international mergers and acquisitions, corporate and industry restructuring, international capital and currency management, tax law, business regulation, deals of the year, and much more. The web site offers trial subscriptions, archives, and sneak previews of forthcoming issues.

3017. ***Credit Union Magazine: for credit union elected officials, managers and employees.*** Formerly: *Credit Union Bridge.* [ISSN: 0011-1066] 1924. m. USD 45. Ed(s): Kathryn Kuehn. Credit Union National Association, Inc., PO Box 431, Madison, WI 53701; http://www.cuna.org/. Illus., index, adv. Circ: 30983. Microform: PQC. Online: EBSCO Publishing; Northern Light Technology, Inc.; OCLC Online Computer Library Center, Inc.; ProQuest Information & Learning. Reprint: PQC. *Indexed:* ABIn, PAIS. *Aud.:* Ac, Sa.

This important trade magazine, produced by the Credit Union National Association, reports on news and newsmakers, new products and technologies, target markets, new services, and information related to credit unions in general. Recent topics have included meeting the needs of high-net-worth members, employee motivation, signature guarantee programs, and account aggregation.

3018. ***Independent Banker.*** [ISSN: 0019-3674] 1950. m. Members, USD 25; Non-members, USD 50. Ed(s): Tim Cook. Independent Community Bankers Association of America, One Thomas Circle, Ste 400, Washington, DC 20005; info@icba.org; http://www.icba.org. Illus., adv. Circ: 10000. Microform: PQC. Online: Northern Light Technology, Inc.; ProQuest Information & Learning. *Indexed:* BLI, PAIS. *Aud.:* Ac, Sa.

This "national voice of America's independent community bankers" is dedicated to the preservation of community banking. Each issue features a cover story on an executive or a timely issue. A recent cover story has reported on the congressional review of the FDIC's proposed reform recommendations. A dozen feature articles and columns provide information on investments, technology, cash management, operations, the regulatory environment, and the regional independent banking climate across the United States. There are also a calendar, news of association activities, and announcements of new products and services.

3019. *Mortgage Banking: the magazine of real estate finance managers and employees.* Former titles (until 1981): *Mortgage Banker; M B A News Review.* [ISSN: 0730-0212] 1939. m. Members, USD 60; Non-members, USD 69.96. Ed(s): Janet Hewitt. Mortgage Bankers Association of America, 1919 Pennsylvania Ave NW, Washington, DC 20006-3438; janet_hewitt@mbaa.org; http://www.mbaa.org. Illus., index, adv. Sample. Circ: 10023. Vol. ends: Sep. Microform: CIS; PQC. Online: EBSCO Publishing; Florida Center for Library Automation; Gale Group; Northern Light Technology, Inc.; OCLC Online Computer Library Center, Inc.; ProQuest Information & Learning; H.W. Wilson. *Indexed:* ABIn, ATI, BLI, BPI, PAIS. *Aud.:* Ac, Sa.

This journal is designed for anyone with an interest in mortgage banking. Articles are practical and timely and oriented to daily problems and practices. Departments cover technology, software, key people, recent books, the secondary mortgage market, statistics, sources of demographics and research, mortgage revenue bonds, and servicing. There is also a news alert page. One recent issue features several articles that discuss future trends in the serving business. Other feature articles address serving's value proposition, the delinquency dilemma, and borrower retention.

3020. *The R M A Journal.* Former titles (until Sep. 2000): *The Journal of Lending & Credit Risk Management;* (until 1996): *Journal of Commercial Lending;* (until 1992): *Journal of Commercial Bank Lending;* (until 1967): *Robert Morris Associates Bulletin.* [ISSN: 1531-0558] 1918. 10x/yr. Members, USD 40; Non-members, USD 95. Ed(s): Beverly Foster. Risk Management Association, One Liberty Place, Ste 2300, 1650 Market St, Philadelphia, PA 19103-7398; bfoster@rmahq.org. Illus., index, adv. Circ: 20000 Paid. Vol. ends: Aug. *Indexed:* ABIn, ATI, BLI, BPI, PAIS, RiskAb. *Bk. rev.:* 6-9, 150 words. *Aud.:* Ac, Sa.

The official journal of the Risk Management Association (RMA), this is a key source of information for commercial loan officers. With its new title comes an expanded scope, covering risk management issues in addition to commercial lending. Each issue contains 10 to 12 feature articles as well as regular departments on management strategies, commercial lending and risk management issues, accounting actions, and a cautionary case study. Recent article topics have included finding and mitigating faulty financial reporting, diversification, loan pricing in the twenty-first century, and retail loan portfolio dynamics.

3021. *U S Banker.* Incorporates (1997-2002): *FutureBanker;* Former titles (until 1994): *United States Banker;* (until 1977): *United States Investor - Eastern Banker;* (until 1971): *United States Investor.* 1891. m. USD 78 domestic; USD 95 foreign. Ed(s): Holly Sraeel. Thomson Financial / I M G Media, 11 Penn Plaza, 17th Fl, New York, NY 10001-2006; http://www.fgray.com/. Illus., index, adv. Sample. Circ: 39000. Vol. ends: Dec. Microform: PQC. Online: Gale Group. Reprint: PQC. *Indexed:* ABIn, B&I, BLI, BPI, LRI, PAIS. *Aud.:* Ac, Sa.

This magazine provides a good overview and update for students and practitioners who are interested in current banking issues. Profiles of companies and/or interviews with several key people are part of each issue. One or two cover stories are followed by a number of shorter articles on industry, Washington, relevant new technology, and banking news. Examples of recent topics include the "war" between banks and credit unions, Canadian bank mergers, and consumers turning to banks to protect their retirement investments. Special features include annual ranked lists, such as the 100 largest U.S. banks, the ten most profitable U.S. banks, and profitability rankings of mid-size U.S. banks. There is a directory of suppliers and professional services in each issue.

Insurance

3022. *Advisor Today.* Formerly (until January 2000): *Life Association News;* Which incorporated (1956-1986): *Probe (Rockville Centre).* [ISSN: 1529-823X] 1906. m. Non-members, USD 7. Ed(s): Jeff R Kosnett. National Association of Insurance and Financial Advisors, PO Box 12012, Falls Church, VA 22042; jkosnett@naifa.org; http://www.advisortoday.com. Illus., index, adv. Sample. Circ: 100000 Paid. Vol. ends: Dec. Microform: PQC. *Indexed:* ABIn. *Bk. rev.:* 500-1,000 words. *Aud.:* Ac, Sa.

This trade magazine has the largest circulation among insurance and financial advising magazines and is the official publication of the National Association of Insurance and Financial Advisors. News and updates on sales, law and legislation, selling strategies, managing people and technology in your office, and book reviews are accompanied by reports designed for advisors. Recent issues focus on estate planning, building strategic alliances, prospecting and selling skills, and employee benefits. Recommended for all public and academic libraries due to the excellent value for the price.

3023. *Best's Review. Insurance Issues and Analysis.* Formed by the 2000 merger of: *Best's Review. Life - Health Insurance Edition;* Which was formerly (1920-1969): *Best's Insurance News. Life - Health Edition;* (1977-2000): *Best's Review. Property - Casualty Insurance Edition;* Which was formerly: *Best's Review. Property - Liability Edition;* (1938-1969): *Best's Insurance News. Fire and Casualty.* [ISSN: 1527-5914] 2000. m. USD 25. Ed(s): Marilyn Ostermiller. A.M. Best Co., Ambest Rd, Oldwick, NJ 08858. Illus., index, adv. Vol. ends: Apr. Online: Gale Group. *Indexed:* ABIn, BPI. *Bk. rev.:* 1-10, 50-100 words. *Aud.:* Ac, Sa.

This trade magazine, formerly published as separate life/health and property/casualty editions, provides wide coverage of the insurance industry under a single title. This integrated edition includes company and industry news, political and regulatory information, new-product announcements, newsmakers in the industry, and reports of court cases in each issue. This is a core title for large public and academic libraries.

3024. *Business Insurance: news magazine for corporate risk, employee benefit and financial executives.* [ISSN: 0007-6864] 1967. w. USD 95 domestic; USD 114 in Canada & Mexico; USD 215 elsewhere. Ed(s): Paul Winston. Crain Communications, Inc., 360 N Michigan Ave, Chicago, IL 60601-3806; http://www.crain.com. Illus., adv. Circ: 50403. Microform: MIM; PQC. Online: EBSCO Publishing; Factiva; Florida Center for Library Automation; Gale Group; LexisNexis; Northern Light Technology, Inc.; OCLC Online Computer Library Center, Inc.; ProQuest Information & Learning; H.W. Wilson. Reprint: PQC. *Indexed:* ABIn, B&I, BPI, CINAHL, LRI. *Bk. rev.:* 1-5, 100-250 words. *Aud.:* Ac, Sa.

Business Insurance serves business executives who are responsible for the purchase and administration of corporate insurance/self-insurance programs, encompassing both property and liability insurance and employee benefit programs, including life, health, and pensions. Each week, this publication includes current news, editorials, and insightful feature articles that would appeal to a wide audience.

3025. *Chartered Property & Casualty Underwriters Society. Journal.* Formerly: *Society of Chartered Property and Casualty Underwriters. Annals.* [ISSN: 0162-2706] 1949. q. USD 30 domestic; USD 45 foreign. Ed(s): Barry D Smith. Chartered Property & Casualty Underwriters Society, 720 Providence Rd, PO Box 3009, Malvern, PA 19355; http://www.cpcusociety.org/. Illus., index, adv. Sample. Circ: 29000 Paid. Vol. ends: Dec. Online: EBSCO Publishing; Gale Group; OCLC Online Computer Library Center, Inc.; ProQuest Information & Learning; H.W. Wilson. *Indexed:* ABIn, BPI. *Aud.:* Ac, Sa.

The Society of Chartered Property and Casualty Underwriters is the leading professional organization in property and casualty insurance in the United States, and it has strict examination, experience, and ethical requirements for membership. This journal keeps association members informed of current issues, legal requirements, and financial aspects of property and casualty insurance. Feature articles are seven to ten pages in length; opinion pieces are slightly shorter. Articles examine insurance concepts such as professional and practitioner liability and cost containment, including alternative reinsurance, as well as specific forms of insurance, such as automobile, flood, and medical. Regular departments offer information on extended coverages, opinion pieces, and letters. Anyone interested in this area of insurance, but particularly those in academic programs or active in the insurance industry, would enjoy this publication.

3026. ***Independent Agent.*** Formerly: *American Agency Bulletin.* [ISSN: 0002-7197] 1903. m. USD 24. Ed(s): Maureen P Wall. Independent Insurance Agents of America - M S I, 127 S Peyton St, Alexandria, VA 22314; magazine@iiaa.org; http://www.iiaa.com/. Illus., adv. Sample. Circ: 55000. Vol. ends: Dec. *Aud.:* Ac, Sa.

This title serves the industry information needs of the Independent Insurance Agents of America (IIAA). Explored in each issue are reinsurance, basic coverages, liability, licensing and certification, regulatory information, finance, the competition between independent agencies and direct writers, marketing, and related topics. This magazine provides practical information for agents as well as policyholders, covering the wide scope of the independent agency system, and it should be considered both for academic libraries that support insurance education and for large public libraries.

3027. ***Insurance: Mathematics & Economics.*** [ISSN: 0167-6687] 1982. bi-m. EUR 971. Ed(s): M J Goovaerts, H. U. Gerber. Elsevier BV, North-Holland, Sara Burgerhartstraat 25, Amsterdam, 1055 KV, Netherlands; nlinfo-f@elsevier.nl; http://www.elsevier.nl. Illus., index, adv. Sample. Refereed. Circ: 1000. Vol. ends: No. 4. Microform: PQC. Online: EBSCO Publishing; ingenta.com; ScienceDirect; Swets Blackwell. Reprint: SWZ. *Indexed:* ABIn, AgeL, CCMJ, IBSS, JEL, MathSciNet, RiskAb, SSCI, ST&MA. *Aud.:* Ac, Sa.

Each issue of this journal contains six to eight papers of international interest, 10 to 15 pages long, concerned with the theory of insurance mathematics or the inventive application of it, including empirical or experimental results. Articles evaluate mathematical and economic applications related to actuarial science and a variety of insurance-related concerns. Libraries that support programs in actuarial science, mathematics, and economics will need to evaluate this journal despite its hefty price.

3028. ***Journal of Risk and Insurance.*** Formerly (until 1964): *Journal of Insurance;* Which was formed by the merger of (1954-1956): *Review of Insurance Studies;* (1933-1956): *American Association of University Teachers of Insurance. Journal;* Which was formerly (until 1937): *American Association of University Teachers of Insurance. Proceedings of the Annual Meeting.* [ISSN: 0022-4367] 1957. q. USD 243 print & online eds. Blackwell Publishing, Inc., Commerce Place, 350 Main St, Malden, MA 02148; subscrip@blackwellpub.com; http://www.blackwellpublishing.com. Illus., index, adv. Refereed. Circ: 2200. Vol. ends: Dec. Microform: PQC. Online: The Dialog Corporation; EBSCO Publishing; Florida Center for Library Automation; Gale Group; ingenta.com; JSTOR (Web-based Journal Archive); OCLC Online Computer Library Center, Inc.; ProQuest Information & Learning; Swets Blackwell; H.W. Wilson. Reprint: ISI; PQC; SCH. *Indexed:* ABIn, AgeL, BPI, JEL, LRI, MCR, PAIS, RiskAb, SSCI. *Bk. rev.:* 6-10, 500-1,000 words. *Aud.:* Ac.

Each issue generally contains an invited article, four or five refereed feature articles of roughly 20 pages in length, and a few shorter articles that present original theoretical and empirical research in insurance economics and risk management. The focus is on the organization of markets, managing pure risk, insurance finance, the economics of employee benefits, utility theory, insurance regulation, actuarial and statistical methodology, and economics of insurance institutions. Recent articles look at flexible spending accounts as insurance, no-fault insurance measures, and detection of automobile insurance fraud. There are a number of high-quality book reviews and a section of related journal abstracts that provide added value. Large public libraries and academic libraries that support business programs should consider this title.

3029. ***Life & Health Insurance Sales.*** Former titles (until 1990): *Insurance Sales; Insurance Salesman.* [ISSN: 1053-2838] 1878. bi-m. USD 17.50; USD 3.50 newsstand/cover per issue. Ed(s): Melissa Lester. Insurance Publications Inc., 9404 Reeds Rd, Overland Park, KS 66207-0000. Illus., adv. Circ: 5000 Paid. Vol. ends: Dec. *Indexed:* ABIn. *Aud.:* Sa.

This long-running publication has a highly qualified editorial board where each member has the CLU and ChFC designations. Several have LUTCF designations as well. This title reduced the number of issues by half in order to limit its dependency on advertising revenue. Feature articles are accompanied by updates on newsmakers and legal and legislative reports with an occasional lengthy book review. Large public, academic, and insurance firm libraries should consider this title.

3030. ***Life Insurance Selling.*** [ISSN: 0024-3140] 1926. m. USD 7 domestic; USD 14 Canada; USD 47 elsewhere. Pfingsten Publishing, L L C, 5700 Lombardo Center Dr, Rock Run Center, Ste 280, Seven Hills, OH 44131; info@pfpublish.com; http://www.pfpub.com. Illus., adv. Circ: 50000. Vol. ends: Dec. Microform: PQC. *Bk. rev.:* 0-2, 50 words. *Aud.:* Sa.

This is a magazine for life, health, and financial-services producers. It provides producers with practical, transferable sales ideas and information through both editorial and advertising about products they can offer to clients. Leading producers share their successful techniques in feature articles. Product survey reports that appear several times a year list characteristics of products from life and health insurance companies. Regular departments describe policies, books, sales aids, computer products, and educational programs designed for producers. This is one of the best introductions to life insurance as a career and it provides important product information for producers.

3031. ***National Underwriter. Life and Health Financial Services Edition.*** Former titles: *National Underwriter. Life and Health Life and health, financial services;* (until 1986): *National Underwriter. Life and Health Insurance Edition.* 197?. w. USD 86 domestic; USD 122 Canada; USD 191 elsewhere. Ed(s): Steve Piontek. The National Underwriter Company, 5081 Olympic Blvd, Erlanger, KY 41018; http://www.nuco.com. Illus., adv. Circ: 49419. Vol. ends: Dec. Microform: PQC. Online: Gale Group. Reprint: PQC. *Indexed:* ABIn, B&I, BPI, LRI. *Aud.:* Ac, Sa.

This is a core newspaper for the life, health, and financial-services segments of the insurance industry. Regular columns cover legislation and regulation, product news and marketing, management and benefits, agent/broker news, and more. Recent topics include annuity regulation, retirement funds, compensation, and long-term care. Convention reports, newsmakers, and political activity are reported as well. Public libraries with a balanced business collection and all academic libraries that support insurance programs should have this title.

3032. ***National Underwriter. Property & Casualty - Risk & Benefits Management Edition.*** Former titles (until 1989): *National Underwriter. Property and Casualty - Employee Benefits Edition;* (until 1986): *National Underwriter. Property and Casualty Insurance Edition.* [ISSN: 1042-6841] 1896. w. USD 98 domestic; USD 128 Canada; USD 202 elsewhere. Ed(s): Sam Friedman. The National Underwriter Company, 5081 Olympic Blvd, Erlanger, KY 41018; http://www.nuco.com. Illus., adv. Circ: 47537. Vol. ends: Dec. Microform: PQC. Online: EBSCO Publishing; Florida Center for Library Automation; Gale Group; LexisNexis; OCLC Online Computer Library Center, Inc.; ProQuest Information & Learning; H.W. Wilson. Reprint: PQC. *Indexed:* ABIn, B&I, BPI, LRI. *Aud.:* Sa.

This is a core newspaper for the international property, casualty, and risk management insurance industry. Regular columns cover legislation and regulation, product news and marketing, management and benefits, agent/broker news, the structure of the international marketplace, and financial issues such as megadeals, the faltering of Internet banner ads, health insurance reform, and insurance technology. The journal examines coverages, reinsurance programs, environmental liability, alternative markets, Internet claims, and much more. Conventions, newsmakers, and political activity are reported. Public libraries with a balanced business collection and all academic libraries that support insurance programs should have this title.

Investment

3033. ***A A I I Journal.*** [ISSN: 0192-3315] 1979. 10x/yr. USD 49 domestic; USD 64 foreign. Ed(s): Maria Crawford Scott. American Association of Individual Investors, 625 N Michigan Ave, Ste 1900, Chicago, IL 60611; members@aaii.com; http://www.aaii.com. Illus., index, adv. Sample. Circ: 180000 Paid. Vol. ends: No. 10. *Indexed:* BPI. *Bk. rev.:* Various number and length. *Aud.:* Ga, Ac, Sa.

Designed to help individuals become more effective managers of their personal investment portfolios, each issue presents regular columns on news and events related to technology, capital markets, investment technology, e-commerce, products, and special operations. A recent issue focused on portfolio strategies, including stock, bond, and fixed income strategies. There is an annual survey of discount brokerage firms that helps investors compare commissions for a range of trades. An educated general audience, as well as academicians and practitioners, will benefit from this journal.

3034. ***Better Investing.*** [ISSN: 0006-016X] 1951. m. USD 24; USD 3.95 newsstand/cover per issue. Ed(s): Donald E Danko. National Association of Investors Corp., PO Box 220, Royal Oak, MI 48067. Illus., index, adv. Sample. Circ: 327000 Paid. Microform: PQC. Online: ProQuest Information & Learning. Reprint: PQC. *Indexed:* RGPR. *Bk. rev.:* Various number and length. *Aud.:* Ga, Ac, Sa.

Each issue presents news and information related to money management, investment clubs, and NAIC events. Several feature articles provide insights and advice on such topics as teaching money management to children or long-term investment in cyclical stocks. Each issue includes an editorial, letters to the editor, "Ask Mr. NAIC," a growth fund report, a technology report, and regional notices. The stocks and funds section includes an undervalued stock, a stock to study, a contrary opinion, a "five years ago stock to study," an undervalued feature, and an 18-month undervalued review. Public and academic libraries that serve interested individual investors should certainly consider this title.

3035. ***C F A Digest.*** [ISSN: 0046-9777] 1971. q. USD 70 in US & Canada; USD 110 elsewhere. Association for Investment Management and Research, PO Box 3668, Charlottesville, VA 22903; http://www.aimr.org. Illus. Circ: 30000 Controlled. *Aud.:* Ac, Sa.

The Association for Investment Management and Research, composed of the Institute of Chartered Financial Consultants and the Financial Analysts Federation, produces this abstracting journal. Scholarly articles on investment theory, tools, valuation, equity, and derivative securities are included. A section on portfolio management research covers portfolio policies, asset allocation, fixed-income and equity portfolio management, and real estate portfolio management. Publishers' names and addresses and article order forms are included. The editor summarizes the general content and the uses of the research articles in each issue. This is a core title for academic libraries supporting programs in insurance and finance.

3036. ***Commercial Investment Real Estate.*** Former titles (until 1999): *Commercial Investment Real Estate Journal;* (until 1985): *Commercial Investment Journal.* [ISSN: 1524-3249] 1982. 6x/yr. USD 38 domestic; USD 46 foreign. Ed(s): Jennifer Norbut. C C I M Institute, 430 N Michigan Ave, Ste 800, Chicago, IL 60611-4092; http://www.ccim.com. Illus., index, adv. Circ: 15500 Paid and controlled. *Indexed:* ABIn. *Bk. rev.:* Various number and length. *Aud.:* Ac, Sa.

Real estate as an investment is the specific focus of this journal. Articles provide practical information for professionals on all aspects of commercial real estate, including management, law, legislation, and taxation. Recent articles discuss how insurance companies are tightening coverage for mold-related damages, taming your taxes, and reviewing fundamentals of section 1031 like-kind exchanges. A buyer's guide is included, as are calendars and lists of continuing-education opportunities. Public libraries that provide investment information and academic libraries with programs in real estate and finance should consider this title.

3037. ***Equities.*** Former titles (until Sep. 1990): *O T C Review;* (until Feb. 1977): *Over-the-Counter Securities Review.* [ISSN: 1053-2544] 1951. bi-m. USD 21; USD 3 newsstand/cover per issue. Ed(s): Robert J Flaherty. Equities Magazine LLC, Box 130 H, Scarsdale, NY 10583. Illus., adv. Circ: 5000 Paid. Vol. ends: Dec. Online: EBSCO Publishing; Florida Center for Library Automation; Gale Group. *Indexed:* PAIS. *Bk. rev.:* Various number and length. *Aud.:* Ac, Sa.

This trade magazine profiles small- to mid-cap public companies that offer a wide variety of unusual and unfamiliar investment opportunities, such as home-based care for organ recipients and eye sculpting. The "Equities Reporter," a special advertising section in each issue, profiles potential investment opportunities. CEO interviews, stock picks in various industry groups, and articles featuring up-and-coming companies highlight each issue. Recent articles discuss Caribbean telephony, analysis of the NASDAQ 1000, and the impact of the September 11 terrorist attacks on the U.S. security industry. Although the magazine production is somewhat amateur, it reports on topics appropriate for large public and academic libraries.

3038. ***Euromoney: the monthly journal of international money and capital markets.*** [ISSN: 0014-2433] 1969. m. GBP 329 combined subscription domestic print & online eds.; EUR 515 combined subscription in Europe print & online eds.; USD 490 combined subscription elsewhere print & online eds. Ed(s): Simon Brady. Euromoney Institutional Investor plc., Nestor House, Playhouse Yard, London, EC4V 5EX, United Kingdom; information@euromoneyplc.com; http://www.euromoney.com. Illus., index. Sample. Circ: 20674. Vol. ends: Dec. Microform: PQC. Online: The Dialog Corporation; EBSCO Publishing; Factiva; Florida Center for Library Automation; Gale Group; OCLC Online Computer Library Center, Inc.; ProQuest Information & Learning; H.W. Wilson. Reprint: PQC. *Indexed:* ABIn, B&I, BLI, BPI, IBSS, PAIS. *Bk. rev.:* Various number and length. *Aud.:* Ac, Sa.

This title monitors the global financial marketplace, including financial institutions, securities, and commodities in established and emerging economies. It provides profiles of companies, industries, and the family trees and business interests of the people who control the wealth. Related aspects of international finance are covered. Each issue provides information from a dozen or more countries and regions globally. Several supplements are issued yearly that profile individual countries. This is a core industry publication for anyone interested in international finance. As the title suggests, this journal gives a uniquely European perspective on global financial issues.

3039. ***Financial Planning.*** Formerly (until 1983): *The Financial Planner.* [ISSN: 0746-7915] 1972. m. USD 79 domestic; USD 89 foreign. Thomson Financial, 195 Broadway, 9th fl, New York, NY 10007. Adv. Circ: 100000 Paid and controlled. Online: bigchalk; EBSCO Publishing; Factiva; Gale Group; LexisNexis; OCLC Online Computer Library Center, Inc.; ProQuest Information & Learning. *Indexed:* PAIS. *Bk. rev.:* Various number and length. *Aud.:* Ga, Ac, Sa.

As you might imagine, the target audience for this journal is professional financial planners. Regular columns provide insights and advice on industry analysis, investment analysis, client strategies, effective use of human and technology resources, and behavioral finance. CFP licensees can get credits by taking the monthly continuing-education quizzes. Recent articles discuss the Eastern view of money, the dividend proposal, and using the Myers-Briggs Personality Inventory to help financial planners communicate better with customers. The web site has news, interactive tools, and the full text of many of the magazine's articles.

3040. ***Futures (Chicago): news, analysis and strategies for futures, options and derivatives traders.*** Formerly (until 1984): *Commodities;* Incorporates (in 199?): *Trends in Futures;* Which was formerly: *Commodity Closeup.* [ISSN: 0746-2468] 1972. m. USD 39 in North America; USD 92 elsewhere; USD 4.95. Ed(s): Ginger Szala. Futures (Chicago), 250 S Wacker Dr, Ste 1150, Chicago, IL 60606; jbecker@futuresmag.com; http://www.futuremag.com. Illus., index, adv. Circ: 62000 Controlled. Vol. ends: Dec. Microform: PQC. Online: EBSCO Publishing; Florida Center for Library Automation; Gale Group; OCLC Online Computer Library Center, Inc.; ProQuest Information & Learning; H.W. Wilson. *Indexed:* ABIn, BPI, PAIS. *Bk. rev.:* 0-3. *Aud.:* Ac, Sa.

This glossy trade title covers the global markets with articles and news reports about the futures/options industry. Contracts, exchanges, brokerage firms, technology, strategy, hot commodities, and trading techniques may be covered by each issue. Recent stories have discussed the crude oil market in relation to the Iraq crisis, pivot point numbers, and refining Elliott wave triangle patterns. A crucial title for libraries that support graduate business programs.

3041. ***Institutional Investor: the premier magazine of professional finance.*** Incorporates (1970-19??): *Corporate Financing.* [ISSN: 0020-3580] 1967. m. USD 445 combined subscription domestic print & online eds.; USD 475 combined subscription foreign print & online eds. Ed(s): Chris Gaudio. Institutional Investor, Inc., 225 Park Ave. S., 7th

Fl., New York, NY 10003-1605; customerservice@iinews.com; http://www.iiplatinum.com. Illus., index, adv. Sample. Circ: 101615 Paid and controlled. Vol. ends: Dec. Microform: PQC. Online: EBSCO Publishing; Florida Center for Library Automation; Gale Group; Northern Light Technology, Inc.; OCLC Online Computer Library Center, Inc.; ProQuest Information & Learning; H.W. Wilson. Reprint: PQC; PSC. *Indexed:* ABIn, ATI, AgeL, B&I, BPI, EnvAb, PAIS, SSCI. *Bk. rev.:* 1-2, 1,000-1,500 words. *Aud.:* Ac, Sa.

This practitioner's magazine is known for its benchmark rankings and ratings of analysts, asset managers, banks, and country credit globally. These rankings are designed to assist financial professionals in making sound investment decisions. The journal provides detailed coverage of commercial and investment banking and many other areas of finance and investing. It also addresses policies, strategies, and the political activities in the social arenas that influence investment decisions. A cover story and several longer feature articles look at issues such as defined contribution plans, the implications of the U.S.A. Patriot Act for money managers, and the distressed debt market. These are accompanied by many smaller pieces on international finance, travel, corporate investing, real state, mutual funds, money management, pensions, global funds, and the impact of financial accounting standards. The Internet site is a nice enhancement and well worth a visit. This publication is a must for academic and research libraries that have programs in business and finance.

3042. ***Investment Dealers' Digest: news magazine of the financial community.*** Formerly (until 1997): *I D D.* [ISSN: 0021-0080] 1935. w. USD 895 domestic; USD 945 Canada; USD 1095 elsewhere. Ed(s): Ron Cooper. Securities Data Publishing, 195 Broadway, New York, NY 10007. Illus., index, adv. Vol. ends: No. 51. Online: EBSCO Publishing; Florida Center for Library Automation; Gale Group; LexisNexis; OCLC Online Computer Library Center, Inc.; ProQuest Information & Learning. *Indexed:* ABIn, B&I, PAIS. *Aud.:* Ac, Sa.

This publication is an important tool for keeping abreast of the investment-banking and investment communities. Feature articles, usually one or two pages long, examine individuals and their trading practices, trading losses, horror stories, and successes. Each issue features "league tables" of investment banking and M&A deals by industry and also tracks new debt/equity registrations. Additional coverage is provided for news on firms and exchanges, personnel, capital markets, and aftermarket performance that serves the investment community. This newsmagazine is a must for metropolitan libraries and academic libraries with business and finance programs.

3043. ***Investor's Business Daily.*** Formerly (until 1991): *Investor's Daily.* [ISSN: 1061-2890] 1984. d.(Mon.-Fri.). USD 235. Ed(s): Wesley Mann. Investor's Business Daily, Inc., 12655 Beatrice St, Los Angeles, CA 90066. Illus., adv. Circ: 264699. *Aud.:* Ga, Sa.

This daily provides timely information for individual and institutional investors. It reports on the economic, social, and political trends that drive markets and the individuals, companies, industries, and funds that make up the competitive landscape. This newspaper is a necessity for academic libraries supporting finance programs as well as large public libraries.

3044. ***Investors Chronicle (London, 1860).*** Formerly: *Investors Chronicle and Stock Exchange Gazette;* Incorporates: *Stock Exchange Gazette; Financial World.* [ISSN: 0261-3115] 1860. w. GBP 125 domestic; GBP 4.95 newsstand/cover per issue domestic; GBP 164 in Europe. Ed(s): Matthew Vincent. Financial Times Business Ltd., Maple House, 149 Tottenham Court Rd, London, W1P 9LL, United Kingdom; ceri.jones@ft.com; http://www.ft.com. Illus., adv. Circ: 44770. Vol. ends: Dec. Microform: RPI; PQC. Online: Factiva; Gale Group; OCLC Online Computer Library Center, Inc.; ProQuest Information & Learning. Reprint: RPI. *Indexed:* ABIn, B&I, PAIS. *Bk. rev.:* Various number and length. *Aud.:* Ac, Sa.

This weekly financial news magazine reports to private and professional investors from a British perspective on international companies, exchanges, strategies for investors, and more. Articles are grouped by category under general business news, features, funds and finance, and companies. Stock tips, statistics, and a survey article appear in each issue. A number of special supplements are issued with the subscription that report on charities, management buyouts, venture capital, and other topics of interest to investors. *Datastream* and the *Financial Times* provide many of the charts for the magazine.

3045. ***Journal of Investing.*** [ISSN: 1068-0896] 1992. q. USD 350 combined subscription domestic print & online eds.; USD 425 combined subscription foreign print & online eds. Ed(s): Brian Bruce. Institutional Investor, Journals, 225 Park Ave. S., 7th Fl., New York, NY 10003-1605; info@iiplatinum.com; http://www.iijournals.com. Illus., adv. Circ: 2500 Paid. *Indexed:* ABIn, BPI. *Aud.:* Ac, Sa.

The editorial board of this journal has representatives from the major investment management and securities firms, pension funds, and universities. Although most articles address the latest developments affecting financial and investment decisions, there are some insightful historical pieces such as a recent one that discussed 300 years of stock market manipulations. Recent topics have included statistical data choice in country risk analysis, broad capitalization indexes of the U.S. equity market, and improving disclosure requirements for restated earnings per share. For a scholarly journal, these articles are highly readable, but the audience will still need a good undergraduate background in finance to appreciate them.

3046. ***Journal of Portfolio Management: the journal for investment professionals.*** [ISSN: 0095-4918] 1975. q. USD 410 combined subscription domestic print & online eds.; USD 485 combined subscription foreign print & online eds. Ed(s): Frank Fabozzi. Institutional Investor, Journals, 225 Park Ave. S., 7th Fl., New York, NY 10003-1605; info@iiplatinum.com; http://www.iijournals.com. Illus., index, adv. Sample. Refereed. Microform: PQC. Online: EBSCO Publishing; Florida Center for Library Automation; Gale Group; OCLC Online Computer Library Center, Inc.; ProQuest Information & Learning; H.W. Wilson. Reprint: PQC; PSC. *Indexed:* ABIn, ATI, BLI, BPI, JEL, PAIS, SSCI. *Bk. rev.:* Various number and length. *Aud.:* Ac, Sa.

This journal for investment professionals is particularly helpful to finance and accounting faculty, CFOs, and portfolio managers. Tightly focused articles discuss particular aspects of portfolio management in clearly written layman's English. Not longer than 20 pages each, recent articles have presented the case for whole-stock portfolios, style investing, exchange-traded funds, and fixed-weight asset allocation. Recommended for academic and large public libraries.

Journal of Real Estate Finance and Economics. See Real Estate section.

3047. ***Kiplinger's Personal Finance.*** Former titles (until 2000): *Kiplinger's Personal Finance Magazine;* (until 1991): *Changing Times.* [ISSN: 1528-9729] 1947. m. USD 23.95 domestic; USD 39.95 foreign. Ed(s): Fred Frailey. Kiplinger Washington Editors, Inc., 1729 H St, N W, Washington, DC 20006; magazine@kiplinger.com; http://www.kiplinger.com. Illus., index, adv. Circ: 1000000 Paid. CD-ROM: ProQuest Information & Learning. Microform: NBI; PQC. Online: The Dialog Corporation; EBSCO Publishing; Florida Center for Library Automation; Gale Group; LexisNexis; Northern Light Technology, Inc.; OCLC Online Computer Library Center, Inc.; ProQuest Information & Learning; H.W. Wilson. Reprint: PQC. *Indexed:* ATI, AgeL, BPI, BRI, CBRI, CINAHL, ConsI, GeoRef, MagInd, PAIS, RGPR. *Bk. rev.:* Various number and length. *Aud.:* Ga, Ac, Sa.

Indisputably the most widely circulated magazine of its kind, *Kiplinger's* takes a holistic approach to personal finance in the context of careers, lifestyles, and health. Articles present practical strategies for specific individual investors and provide information on topics ranging from cars, home mortgage options, and money management to spending and consumer advocacy. Regular departments monitor and report on mutual funds, money market funds, blue chips, and taxes. Personal-interest columns discuss travel, health, personal finances, and family finances. A handful of articles in each issue discuss general concerns related to investing. Special issues evaluate and chart mutual fund performance. The web site provides online access to selected content.

Money. See General Editorial/General section.

3048. ***Morningstar FundInvestor.*** [ISSN: 1099-0402] 1998. m. Individuals, USD 89. Ed(s): Christine Benz. Morningstar, Inc., 225 W Walker Dr, Ste 400, Chicago, IL 60606; http://www.morningstar.com. *Aud.:* Ga, Ac, Sa.

Morningstar has both stock and mutual fund investment newsletters, a clean web site with helpful free content, and an annual guide to mutual funds. The mutual fund title evaluated here provides monthly issues that contain 50 pages of full-page fund profiles, critiques and makeovers of portfolios, investing strategies, risk-adjusted ratings, and detailed statistics on performance as well as portfolio and operations data for open-end funds. There is detailed coverage on the mutual fund industry, including 500 select funds, and interviews with top financial planners and fund industry leaders, as well as news, updates, and emerging trends in the industry. All public and academic libraries that provide investment information should have this title.

3049. ***Pensions & Investments: the newspaper of corporate and institutional investing.*** Former titles: *Pensions and Investment Age; Pensions and Investments.* [ISSN: 1050-4974] 1973. bi-w. USD 225 domestic. Ed(s): Nancy Webman. Crain Communications, Inc., 711 Third Ave, New York, NY 10017-4036; http://www.crain.com. Illus., index, adv. Sample. Circ: 50000 Paid and controlled. Vol. ends: Dec. Microform: CIS; PQC. Online: EBSCO Publishing; Florida Center for Library Automation; Gale Group; LexisNexis; Northern Light Technology, Inc.; OCLC Online Computer Library Center, Inc.; ProQuest Information & Learning; H.W. Wilson. Reprint: PQC. *Indexed:* ABIn, ATI, B&I, BLI, BPI, LRI, PAIS. *Aud.:* Ga, Ac, Sa.

This weekly newsmagazine for money managers provides information, explanation, analysis, and updates on all aspects of pensions and institutional investments. Regular departments cover news, opinions, a "Pensions and Investments" index, and updates on newsmakers. Rankings of funds and managers in various categories are included regularly, including an annual "Leading Money Managers" report. Recent feature articles have addressed the FAS 87 makeover project, President Bush's proposed Employer Retirement Savings Accounts, and the SEC ruling on mutual fund proxy voting.

3050. ***Risk.*** [ISSN: 0952-8776] 1987. m. GBP 615; EUR 985; USD 985. Ed(s): Dwight Cass. Risk Waters Group, Haymarket House, 28-29 Haymarket, London, SW1Y 4RX, United Kingdom. Illus., adv. Sample. Vol. ends: Dec. *Indexed:* RiskAb. *Bk. rev.:* Various number and length. *Aud.:* Ac, Sa.

This journal provides mathematical detail in its discussions of all forms of risk, including currencies, interest rates, equities, commodities, and credit. Issues include a cover story, an organizational profile, an interview, news, and five- to ten-page articles on fund management, options, and brokers. Topics include insurance, behavioral finance, computational finance, credit risk, risk analysis, and technology. Reader polls indicate higher readership among pension fund managers than for either the *Economist* or *Institutional Investor.* Public libraries with supporting demographics and academic libraries with programs in international business, economics, or finance should consider this title for its practitioner-oriented information.

3051. ***Robb Report Worth.*** Former titles (until 2003): *Worth;* (until Jan.1992): *Investment Vision;* Which incorporated (1985-1991): *Personal Investor.* 1986. 10x/yr. USD 9.97 domestic; USD 21.97 Canada; USD 41.97 elsewhere. CurtCo Robb Media LLC., One Acton Pl, Acton, MA 01720; http://www.curtco.com/. Illus., adv. Circ: 500000. *Indexed:* ASIP, AgeL. *Aud.:* Ga, Ac, Sa.

This personal investing magazine offers the standard investment fare in a glossy, popular format. But special features on topics like the 250 wealthiest towns in America, handmade fly rods, and the world's best golf course are what lend this title its irresistible "lifestyles of the rich and famous" appeal. A recently-added "Self-Worth" section covers lifestyle investments like second homes, automobiles, and vacations. Recommended for browsing collections in all public libraries and larger academic libraries.

3052. ***SmartMoney: the Wall Street Journal magazine of personal business.*** [ISSN: 1069-2851] 1992. m. USD 15 domestic; USD 30 foreign. Ed(s): Edwin A Finn. Hearst Corporation, 1755 Broadway, 2nd Fl, New York, NY 10019; http://www.smartmoney.com. Illus., index, adv. Sample. Circ: 780909 Paid. *Indexed:* ASIP, AgeL, BPI. *Aud.:* Ga, Sa.

Along with *Kiplinger's,* this is a heavyweight title in personal finance. Published by the *Wall Street Journal,* the magazine is full of sage advice on buying cars, travel reservation systems, credit cards, employee benefits, individual investor profiles, insurance, taxes, computers and software, and family investment vehicles such as living trusts. Stock picks, industry analysis, and recommended investment vehicles are included. Feature articles, each several pages in length, provide human-interest stories on issues like retiring happy, carrying debt, and selling your home. There is a good bit of advertising related to investments and high-end consumer products. A good choice for browsing collections in public and academic libraries. The Internet equivalent is also outstanding.

3053. ***The Street.com.*** 1996. w. USD 229.95. Ed(s): Dave Kansas. TheStreet.com, Inc., 14 Wall St, New York, NY 10005; http://www.thestreet.com. *Aud.:* Ga.

Backed by *The New York Times,* this is one of the more reliable of scores of online financial-advice sites. Since 1996, it has given solid advice based on financial know-how rather than wild guesses about investments. The first-rate analysis and in-depth articles will be of interest to anyone serious about Wall Street.

Scholarly

3054. ***Applied Financial Economics.*** [ISSN: 0960-3107] 1991. m. GBP 774. Routledge, 11 New Fetter Ln, London, EC4P 4EE, United Kingdom; info@routledge.co.uk; http://www.routledge.com. Illus., index. Refereed. Online: EBSCO Publishing; Ingenta Select; OCLC Online Computer Library Center, Inc.; RoweCom Information Quest; Swets Blackwell. Reprint: PSC. *Indexed:* ABIn, BAS, BPI, IBSS, IBZ, JEL, RiskAb. *Aud.:* Ac, Sa.

This peer-reviewed journal serves as an international forum for applied research on financial markets (debt, equity, derivatives, foreign exchange) as well as corporate finance, market structure, and related areas. Each issue includes roughly a dozen articles, generally about ten pages in length, that focus on both developed markets and developing economies in Central and Eastern Europe. Topics also include econometric techniques as they relate to financial research, forecasting, and the intersection of real and financial economy. Recent articles look at risk-taking behavior in the U.S. life insurance industry and technical analysis in foreign exchange markets.

3055. ***Applied Mathematical Finance.*** [ISSN: 1350-486X] 1994. q. GBP 476 (Individuals, GBP 64). Ed(s): Pat Hagan, Jeff Dewynne. Routledge, 11 New Fetter Ln, London, EC4P 4EE, United Kingdom; info@routledge.co.uk; http://www.routledge.com. Adv. Refereed. Online: EBSCO Publishing; Ingenta Select; OCLC Online Computer Library Center, Inc.; RoweCom Information Quest; Swets Blackwell. Reprint: PSC. *Indexed:* IBZ. *Aud.:* Ac, Sa.

Aimed at financial practitioners, academics, and applied mathematicians, this title includes 15- to 20-page articles by worldwide academics that are designed to encourage the "confident use" of applied mathematics and mathematical models for finance. Papers cover such topics as economic primitives (interest rates, asset prices, etc.), market behavior, market strategy (such as hedging), financial instruments, reviews of new developments in financial engineering, general mathematical finance, models and algorithms, new products, and reviews of practical tools.

3056. ***F M.*** Formerly: *Financial Management.* [ISSN: 1087-7827] 1972. q. USD 160 (Individual members, USD 100). Ed(s): Lemma Senbet. Financial Management Association International, University of South Florida, College of Business Administration, Ste 3331, Tampa, FL 33620-5500; fma@coba.usf.edu; http://www.fma.org. Illus., index, adv. Refereed. Circ: 12000. Vol. ends: Winter. Microform: PQC. Online: Gale Group. Reprint: PQC; PSC. *Indexed:* ABIn, ATI, BPI, IBSS, JEL, PAIS, RiskAb, SSCI. *Aud.:* Ac, Sa.

This is a core publication for financial management because of its high-quality, often groundbreaking research. Editors include the most widely published scholars in the field, and each volume addresses a variety of topics related to the practical applications and economic aspects of operating large public companies. Articles report the results of empirical and survey research that examines markets, stocks, financial leverage, pricing, trading, lease-purchase options, and cash flow. Sources of data are provided, and some articles are presented as tutorials intended for classroom use. Strictly for academic and research libraries.

Finance and Development. See Free Magazines and House Organs section.

3057. *Financial Accountability & Management.* [ISSN: 0267-4424] 1985. q. GBP 252 print & online eds. Ed(s): Irvine Lapsley. Blackwell Publishing Ltd., 9600 Garsington Rd, PO Box 805, Oxford, OX4 2DQ, United Kingdom; customerservices@oxon.blackwellpublishing.com; http://www.blackwellpublishing.com/. Adv. Online: EBSCO Publishing; Gale Group; ingenta.com; OCLC Online Computer Library Center, Inc.; RoweCom Information Quest; Swets Blackwell. Reprint: PQC; SWZ. *Indexed:* ABIn, ATI, BPI, PAIS, RiskAb. *Aud.:* Ac, Sa.

This interdisciplinary journal draws from the fields of economics, social and public administration, political science, management sciences, accounting, and finance. The focus is on financial accountability, accounting, and financial and resource management for governmental and nonprofit organizations. Recent article topics include policymaking on the reserves of Dutch university hospitals, transforming an accounting system during organizational change, and a comparative study of accounting and democratic governance in a Norwegian and a Russian county. Recommended for libraries supporting upper-level finance programs or public finance professionals.

3058. *Financial History Review.* [ISSN: 0968-5650] 1994. s-a. USD 114 (Individuals, USD 53). Ed(s): Youssef Cassis, Philip Cottrell. Cambridge University Press, The Edinburgh Bldg, Shaftesbury Rd, Cambridge, CB2 2RU, United Kingdom; information@cambridge.org; http://uk.cambridge.org/journals. Illus., adv. Refereed. Reprint: ISI. *Indexed:* AmH&L, BAS, IBSS, JEL. *Bk. rev.:* 3-5, signed, 1,000-2,500 words. *Aud.:* Ac.

Founded by the European Association for Banking History, this title serves as a forum for scholars interested in the development of banking and finance. Each issue begins with article abstracts in English, French, German, and Spanish that are followed by several lengthy articles. Recent topics include the Australian banking crisis of 1893, Greek diaspora bankers of Constantinople, and ethics and options in seventeenth-century stock exchange markets. Announcements and occasional bibliographies on financial history are included.

3059. *Financial Market Trends.* [ISSN: 0378-651X] 1977. s-a. USD 96 combined subscription print & online eds. Organization for Economic Cooperation and Development, Nuclear Energy Agency, 2 rue Andre Pascal, Paris, Cedex 16 75775, France; sales@oecd.org; http://www.oecd.org. Illus., index. Vol. ends: Oct. Online: EBSCO Publishing; Florida Center for Library Automation; Gale Group; ingenta.com; Northern Light Technology, Inc.; OCLC Online Computer Library Center, Inc.; ProQuest Information & Learning; RoweCom Information Quest; Swets Blackwell. *Indexed:* ABIn, PAIS. *Aud.:* Ac, Sa.

This journal analyzes trends and developments in financial markets around the world, with special emphasis on Organization for Economic Cooperation and Development (OECD) countries. Each issue has a section in both French and English that highlights recent trends in financial markets. The remainder of each issue is in English and focuses on structural and regulatory developments in OECD countries. Financial statistics, charts, and graphs are included in each issue. Recent issues have included articles on private annuity markets, offshore financial centers, and guidelines for pension fund governance.

3060. *Financial Markets, Institutions and Instruments.* Former titles (until 1992): *Monograph Series in Finance and Economics;* (until 1990): *Salomon Brothers Center for the Study of Financial Institutions. Monograph Series; New York University Institute of Finance. Bulletin.* [ISSN: 0963-8008] 1928. 5x/yr. USD 338 print & online eds. Blackwell Publishing, Inc., Commerce Place, 350 Main St, Malden, MA 02148; subscrip@blackwellpub.com; http://www.blackwellpublishing.com. Illus., adv. Refereed. Online: EBSCO Publishing; ingenta.com; OCLC Online Computer Library Center, Inc.; RoweCom Information Quest; Swets Blackwell. *Indexed:* IBSS, JEL. *Aud.:* Ac, Sa.

This journal attempts to bridge the gap between the academic and professional finance communities by covering topics that are relevant to both groups. Contributors include both financial practitioners and academics. Each issue has in-depth articles on a single topic, while the year-end issue features the year's most significant developments in corporate finance, money and banking, derivative securities, and fixed-income securities. Recent articles have examined financial sector development in transition economies, the microfinance revolution in Bangladesh, and measuring integrated market and credit risk in bank portfolios. Recommended for academic and corporate libraries.

3061. *The Financial Review (Statesboro).* Incorporates: *Eastern Finance Association. Proceedings of the Annual Meeting.* [ISSN: 0732-8516] 1966. q. USD 225 print & online eds. Blackwell Publishing, Inc., Commerce Place, 350 Main St, Malden, MA 02148; subscrip@blackwellpub.com; http://www.blackwellpublishing.com. Illus., index, adv. Refereed. Circ: 2000. Vol. ends: Nov (No. 4). Microform: PQC. Online: Gale Group; ingenta.com; Swets Blackwell. *Indexed:* ABIn, ATI, BPI, JEL, PAIS. *Bk. rev.:* Various number and length. *Aud.:* Ac, Sa.

This refereed journal of the Eastern Finance Association publishes "empirical, theoretical and methodological articles on topics of micro- and macrofinance." Each issue contains seven to ten articles of 15–50 pages each. Recent issues have examined such topics as the use of collar offers in mergers, sponsor influence over the board of directors, and an event study of self-tender offers.

3062. *Global Finance Journal.* [ISSN: 1044-0283] 1989. 3x/yr. EUR 324 (Qualified personnel, EUR 91). Ed(s): M. Shahrokhi. Elsevier BV, North-Holland, Sara Burgerhartstraat 25, Amsterdam, 1055 KV, Netherlands; nlinfo-f@elsevier.nl; http://www.elsevier.nl. Illus., index. Refereed. Microform: PQC. Online: EBSCO Publishing; ingenta.com; ScienceDirect; Swets Blackwell. *Indexed:* ABIn, BAS, JEL, RiskAb. *Bk. rev.:* 1, 250-500 words. *Aud.:* Ac, Sa.

The School of Business and Administrative Sciences of California State University–Fresno provides the editorial direction of this journal, which focuses on theories and techniques of global finance. With a target audience of academicians and practitioners, the eight to ten articles in each issue are selected for their clarity and practicality. Recent articles have covered topics such as the impact of financial crises on international diversification, forecasting exchange rates, and trafficking in foreign tax credits.

3063. *Government Finance Review.* Formed by the merger of (197?-1985): *Government Financial Management Resources in Review;* (1926-1985): *Governmental Finance;* Which was formerly (until 1971): *Municipal Finance.* [ISSN: 0883-7856] 1985. bi-m. USD 30. Ed(s): Rowan Miranda. Government Finance Officers Association, 180 N Michigan Ave, Ste 800, Chicago, IL 60601. Illus., index, adv. Circ: 15000. Microform: PQC. Online: Florida Center for Library Automation; Gale Group; Northern Light Technology, Inc.; OCLC Online Computer Library Center, Inc.; H.W. Wilson. Reprint: PQC. *Indexed:* ABCPolSci, ABIn, ATI, BPI, LRI, PAIS. *Bk. rev.:* Various number and length. *Aud.:* Ac, Sa.

The membership magazine of the Government Finance Officers Association of the United States and Canada reflects a broad spectrum of theory and practice in finance and financial management for state and local governments. Recent article topics have included a primer for inflation-indexed bonds, tackling rising health care costs, the evolving role of government financial executives, and the ineffectiveness of the Unfunded Mandate Reform Act.

3064. *International Financial Statistics.* [ISSN: 0020-6725] 1948. m. plus annual issue. USD 495 (Students, USD 247). Ed(s): Carol Carson. International Monetary Fund, Publication Services, 700 19th St, N W,

Ste 12 607, Washington, DC 20431; http://www.imf.org. Circ: 12500. Microform: BHP; CIS; PMC; PQC. Online: National Data Corporation. Reprint: PQC. *Indexed:* PAIS. *Aud.:* Ac, Sa.

Published by the Statistics Department of the International Monetary Fund, this is considered the "standard source of statistics on all aspects of international and domestic finance." Statistics are presented monthly, quarterly, and annually in tabular form for specific countries, geographic regions, and world aggregates. Current information on exchange rates, money and banking, prices, government finance, and national accounts are just some of the contents of this important source. The annual yearbook features 30 years of annual data. Academic and large public libraries should consider this title.

3065. ***International Journal of Finance.*** [ISSN: 1041-2743] 1988. 4x/yr. USD 125 (Individuals, USD 40). Ed(s): Dilip K Ghosh. International Journal of Finance, 206 Rabbit Run Dr, Cherry Hill, NJ 08003-1427; int.journalfin@juno.com. Illus., index, adv. Refereed. Vol. ends: No. 4. *Aud.:* Ac, Sa.

This journal concentrates on publishing a half-dozen lengthy articles in each issue that are related to empirical research in the areas of corporate finance, portfolio analysis, institutions, and global finance. Recent examples of the wide variety of topics include futures and options trading on Hang Seng Index volatility, IPO betas, announcement dates in event studies, and risk diversification as a motive for bank managers. Authors are scholars and researchers from many countries. Academic libraries that support programs in international business or finance should consider this title.

3066. ***International Journal of Finance and Economics.*** [ISSN: 1076-9307] 1996. q. USD 540. John Wiley & Sons Ltd., The Atrium, Southern Gate, Chichester, PO19 8SQ, United Kingdom; customer@wiley.co.uk; http://www.wiley.co.uk. Illus., adv. Refereed. Vol. ends: Dec. *Indexed:* JEL, SSCI. *Bk. rev.:* 1, signed, 5,000 words. *Aud.:* Ac, Sa.

Each issue includes a small number of lengthy articles on topics related to some aspect of international finance. Each article has a 500-word nontechnical abstract. Occasionally, an article will be published that is academically rigorous but less technical. The content of this relatively new journal appears to be more empirical than theoretical; it is positioned as a step between practitioner and theoretical titles that focus on similar content. Recent article topics include monetary policy's effects during the financial crises in Brazil and Korea, interactions between large macro models and time series analysis, and general equilibrium analysis of foreign direct investment and the real exchange rate.

3067. ***International Review of Economics and Finance.*** [ISSN: 1059-0560] 1991. q. EUR 304 (Qualified personnel, EUR 91). Ed(s): H. Beladi, C. R. Chen. Elsevier BV, North-Holland, Sara Burgerhartstraat 25, Amsterdam, 1055 KV, Netherlands; nlinfo-f@elsevier.nl; http://www.elsevier.nl. Illus., index. Refereed. Microform: PQC. Online: EBSCO Publishing; ingenta.com; ScienceDirect; Swets Blackwell. *Indexed:* ABIn, BAS, JEL. *Bk. rev.:* Various number and length. *Aud.:* Ac, Sa.

This journal presents a truly global perspective of empirical and theoretical papers on financial and market economics. Articles in recent issues explore information content of lock-up provisions in IPOs, currency devaluation in an open shop union, globalization of labor markets, and macroeconomic equilibrium and hedging downside risk (futures vs. options). The half-dozen lengthy articles in each issue require a working knowledge of statistics to fully appreciate.

3068. ***International Review of Financial Analysis.*** [ISSN: 1057-5219] 1991. 5x/yr. EUR 324 (Individuals, EUR 91). Ed(s): Thomas A. Fetherston, C. Kearney. Elsevier BV, North-Holland, Sara Burgerhartstraat 25, Amsterdam, 1055 KV, Netherlands; nlinfo-f@elsevier.nl; http://www.elsevier.nl. Illus., index. Refereed. Microform: PQC. Online: EBSCO Publishing; ingenta.com; ScienceDirect; Swets Blackwell. *Indexed:* ABIn, BAS, JEL. *Aud.:* Ac, Sa.

This journal is focused primarily on exploring international financial markets from a "broad spectrum of cultural, spatial, institutional, historical, regulatory, and methodological" perspectives to advance the understanding of finance. Recent topics include the a comparative study of stochastic chaos or ARCH effects in stock series, contingent claims valuation of optional calling plan contracts in the telephone industry, and the information effect of economic news on SPI futures.

3069. ***Journal of Applied Corporate Finance.*** Formerly: *Continental Bank Journal of Applied Corporate Finance.* [ISSN: 1078-1196] 1988. q. USD 175 (Individuals, USD 95). Ed(s): Donald H Chew, Jr. Stern Stewart Management Services, Inc., 1345 Avenue of the Americas, 20, New York, NY 10019-5370. Illus., index. Refereed. Vol. ends: No. 4. *Indexed:* ATI, RiskAb. *Aud.:* Ac, Sa.

This journal is published by Stern Stewart, a corporate finance advisory firm, in conjunction with the Bank of America, and covers topics related to restructurings, global competition, capital management, financial innovation, and corporate governance. Recent issues highlight finance and the energy sector, corporate governance, and real options and the new economy.

3070. ***Journal of Applied Finance: theory, practice, education.*** Formerly (until 2001): *Financial Practice and Education.* [ISSN: 1534-6668] 1991. s-a. USD 40 (Individual members, USD 95). Ed(s): Raj Aggrawal. Financial Management Association International, University of South Florida, College of Business Administration, Ste 3331, Tampa, FL 33620-5500; fma@coba.usf.edu; http://www.fma.org. Adv. Refereed. Circ: 4500. Online: EBSCO Publishing. *Indexed:* BAS, JEL. *Aud.:* Ac, Sa.

This journal focuses on the theory, practice, and education of finance. Lengthy scholarly articles are geared to practitioners. Recent article topics include taxes and relative valuation of S and C corporations, exchange rate volatility and international diversification, and an improved approach to calculate the yield and duration of a bond portfolio. Recommended for academic libraries supporting finance programs.

3071. ***Journal of Banking and Finance.*** Incorporates (1985-1989): *Studies in Banking and Finance.* [ISSN: 0378-4266] 1977. m. EUR 2084 (Individuals, EUR 129). Ed(s): G. P. Szegoe. Elsevier BV, North-Holland, Sara Burgerhartstraat 25, Amsterdam, 1055 KV, Netherlands; nlinfo-f@elsevier.nl; http://www.elsevier.nl. Illus., index, adv. Sample. Refereed. Vol. ends: Dec. Microform: PQC. Online: EBSCO Publishing; ingenta.com; ScienceDirect; Swets Blackwell. Reprint: SWZ. *Indexed:* ABIn, ATI, BAS, BPI, IBSS, JEL, PAIS, RiskAb, SSCI. *Bk. rev.:* Various number and length. *Aud.:* Ac, Sa.

Each issue of this journal contains six to eight lengthy articles on topics related to financial institutions, money, and capital markets. The editorial board includes top U.S. and international finance faculty as well as some practitioners, mainly from the U.S. Federal Reserve system. Sample articles recently discussed binary choice models and corporate takeover, random walk versus breaking trend in stock prices, and whether convertible bonds are underpriced. While expensive, this is an important title for academic and research collections.

3072. ***Journal of Derivatives.*** [ISSN: 1074-1240] 1993. q. USD 365 combined subscription domestic print & online eds.; USD 440 combined subscription foreign print & online eds. Ed(s): Stephen Figlewski. Institutional Investor, Journals, 225 Park Ave. S., 7th Fl., New York, NY 10003-1605; info@iiplatinum.com; http://www.iijournals.com. Illus., index, adv. *Indexed:* ABIn, BPI. *Aud.:* Ac, Sa.

Aimed at bridging the gap between academic theory and practice, this title is marketed as the only journal that focuses exclusively on derivatives. Readers generally have some expertise in mathematics, as is demonstrated in the erratum of a recent issue. Articles range from 10 to 20 pages in length, include charts and graphs, and offer analysis and evaluative commentary on all aspects of the use of derivatives: hedging, management of foreign exchange risk, maximization of transaction costs, measuring swap exposures on a balance sheet, comparison of price models, evaluation of new products, embedded options, arbitrage between cash and futures markets, and similar themes. Recent issues have discussed the valuation of credit default swap options, no-arbitrage approach to pricing credit spread derivatives, and return and risk of CBOE buy write monthly index. Otherwise, this journal is suitable only for libraries supporting graduate work in finance and economics.

3073. ***The Journal of Finance.*** [ISSN: 0022-1082] 1946. bi-m. USD 304 except Canada & Mexico, print & online eds. USD 342 combined subscription in the Americas except Canada & Mexico, to commercial companies, print & online eds. Blackwell Publishing, Inc., Commerce Place, 350 Main St, Malden, MA 02148; subscrip@blackwellpub.com; http://www.blackwellpublishing.com. Illus., index, adv. Sample. Refereed. Circ: 8000. Vol. ends: Dec. Microform: MIM; PQC. Online: EBSCO Publishing; Gale Group; ingenta.com; RoweCom Information Quest; Swets Blackwell. Reprint: PSC. *Indexed:* ABIn, ATI, BLI, BPI, BRI, CBRI, IBSS, JEL, PAIS, RiskAb, SSCI. *Bk. rev.:* 3-4, 1,500-2,000 words. *Aud.:* Ac, Sa.

This is the official publication of the American Finance Association and is a core publication for business collections. It is one of the most highly regarded and widely cited academic journals in finance and economics. A single issue generally includes 6–10 feature articles of 20–50 pages in length plus 6–10 shorter papers that report on original scholarly research, in addition to announcements, commentaries, and lectures. Subject matter includes securities, financial institutional practices, and a variety of related topics. Recent articles have examined topics of intense interest in the field, such as clearly irrational financial market behavior, a case study of modeling sovereign yield spreads in Russia, and asset pricing with conditioning information.

3074. ***Journal of Financial and Quantitative Analysis.*** [ISSN: 0022-1090] 1966. 4x/yr. USD 120 (Individuals, USD 55; Students, USD 25). Ed(s): Jonathan Karpoff, Paul Malatesta. University of Washington, School of Business Administration, 115 Lewis Hall, Box 353200, Seattle, WA 98195. Illus., index, adv. Refereed. Circ: 3200 Paid. Vol. ends: Dec. Microform: PQC. Online: EBSCO Publishing; Gale Group; JSTOR (Web-based Journal Archive); ProQuest Information & Learning. Reprint: PQC; SCH. *Indexed:* ABIn, ATI, BLI, BPI, IBSS, IBZ, JEL, LibLit, PAIS, SSCI. *Aud.:* Ac, Sa.

Theoretical and empirical research on corporate finance, investments, financial markets, and related concepts are approached from a quantitative perspective in this academic journal. Targeted job ads may appear in some issues, as well as meeting announcements. Academic libraries with extensive programs in finance should consider this title. Recent articles have examined the option pricing in a multi-asset, complete market economy, an empirical examination of call option values implicit in U.S. corporate bonds, and daily momentum and contrarian behavior of index fund investors. A recent special issue has focused on international corporate governance. A working knowledge of finance and statistics is required to fully appreciate this journal.

3075. ***Journal of Financial Economics.*** [ISSN: 0304-405X] 1974. m. EUR 1681 (Individuals, EUR 91; Students, EUR 63). Ed(s): G. William Schwert. Elsevier BV, North-Holland, . Illus., index, adv. Sample. Refereed. Vol. ends: No. 2. Microform: PQC. Online: EBSCO Publishing; Gale Group; ingenta.com; ScienceDirect; Swets Blackwell. *Indexed:* ABIn, ATI, BPI, IBSS, JEL, RiskAb, SSCI. *Bk. rev.:* Various number and length. *Aud.:* Ac, Sa.

The focus of this journal is on reports of analytical, empirical, or clinical research in capital markets, corporate finance, corporate governance, and economics of organizations and financial institutions. Feature articles are usually 15 to 50 pages long. Recent articles have explored the personal tax advantages of equity, how family strategies affect fund performance, and cronyism and capital controls in Malaysia. Large academic libraries with graduate programs in finance and economics may be the only ones that will want to invest in this pricey journal.

3076. ***Journal of Financial Intermediation.*** [ISSN: 1042-9573] 1990. q. EUR 424 (Individuals, EUR 65). Ed(s): Anjan V Thakor, W. Christie. Academic Press, 525 B St, Ste 1900, San Diego, CA 92101-4495; apsubs@acad.com; http://www.academicpress.com. Illus. Refereed. Online: EBSCO Publishing; ingenta.com; OCLC Online Computer Library Center, Inc.; RoweCom Information Quest; ScienceDirect; Swets Blackwell. *Indexed:* IBSS, JEL, SSCI. *Aud.:* Ac.

Each issue includes a dozen scholarly articles designed to present contemporary analytical and empirical tools used to "stimulate research in the design of financial contracts and institutions." Articles also indicate a related interest in information economics and options pricing. Recent issues have included articles about the effect of decimalization on the components of the bid-ask spread, the optimal design of Ponzi schemes in finite economies, and estimating switching costs in banking.

3077. ***Journal of Financial Research.*** [ISSN: 0270-2592] 1978. q. USD 242 print & online eds. Blackwell Publishing, Inc., Commerce Place, 350 Main St, Malden, MA 02148; subscrip@blackwellpub.com; http://www.blackwellpublishing.com. Illus., index, adv. Sample. Refereed. Circ: 1900 Paid. Microform: PQC. Online: Florida Center for Library Automation; Gale Group; ingenta.com; Northern Light Technology, Inc.; OCLC Online Computer Library Center, Inc.; ProQuest Information & Learning; Swets Blackwell; H.W. Wilson. Reprint: PQC. *Indexed:* ABIn, ATI, BPI, JEL, RiskAb, SSCI. *Bk. rev.:* Various number and length. *Aud.:* Ac, Sa.

The focus of this title is on financial markets and institutions, capital market theory, and portfolio theory research that implies market characteristics and evaluates financial management of organizations. Macroeconomics and public policy are excluded. Recent issues have included articles on momentum strategies, the role of futures trading in spot market fluctuations, and forecasting emerging market exchange rates from foreign equity options. A brief summary heads each article. This is an interesting journal that would be appropriate for large public libraries that serve educated investors, as well as many academic libraries.

3078. ***Journal of Financial Services Research.*** [ISSN: 0920-8550] 1987. bi-m. USD 615 print or online ed. Ed(s): Haluk Unal. Kluwer Academic Publishers, 101 Philip Dr, Assinippi Park, Norwell, MA 02061. Illus., index. Sample. Refereed. Vol. ends: Oct. Microform: PQC. Online: EBSCO Publishing; ingenta.com; Kluwer Online; OCLC Online Computer Library Center, Inc.; Ovid Technologies, Inc.; ProQuest Information & Learning; RoweCom Information Quest; Swets Blackwell. Reprint: PQC; SWZ. *Indexed:* ABIn, IBSS, JEL, RiskAb, SSCI. *Aud.:* Ac, Sa.

The focus of this title is on theoretical and applied microeconomic analysis specifically related to financial markets and institutions. Feature articles, some 15 to 25 pages in length, cover original research on private and public policy questions that arise from the evolution of the financial-services sector. Topics in recent issues have included the dilemmas of reforming housing finance, small-business lending and profit efficiency in commercial banking, and universal banking under bilateral information asymmetry. Shadow Financial Regulatory Committee Statements are included. Academic libraries that support extensive programs in economics and finance might wish to consider this specialized title.

3079. ***Journal of Fixed Income.*** [ISSN: 1059-8596] 1991. q. USD 360 combined subscription domestic print & online eds.; USD 435 combined subscription foreign print & online eds. Ed(s): Stanley J Kon. Institutional Investor, Journals, 225 Park Ave. S., 7th Fl., New York, NY 10003-1605; info@iiplatinum.com; http://www.iijournals.com. Illus., index, adv. *Indexed:* ABIn, ATI, BPI. *Aud.:* Ac, Sa.

The associate editors represent investment firms, other financial journals, and academicians from prestigious universities. Each issue contains six to ten articles, each about 20 pages long, that report original applied research on all aspects of fixed-income investing. Articles discuss market conditions and methods of analysis of a variety of fixed-income investments. In recent issues, authors discuss Lehman Brothers swap indexes, the impact of call features on corporate bond yields, and swaps as a synthetic asset class.

3080. ***The Journal of Futures Markets.*** [ISSN: 0270-7314] 1981. m. USD 1555 domestic; USD 1675 in Canada & Mexico; USD 1777 elsewhere. Ed(s): Robert I Webb. John Wiley & Sons, Inc., 111 River St, Hoboken,

NJ 07030; uscs-wis@wiley.com; http://www.wiley.com. Illus., index, adv. Sample. Refereed. Circ: 1100. Vol. ends: Dec. Reprint: PSC. *Indexed:* ABIn, ATI, BLI, BPI, IBSS, JEL, PAIS, RiskAb, SSCI. *Aud.:* Ac, Sa.

Each issue of this highly specialized journal, affiliated with the Columbia Business School, focuses on futures, options, and other derivatives. Recent topics have included option volume and volatility response to scheduled economic news releases, the components of interest rate swap spreads, and futures hedging under mark-to-market risk. Articles include charts and tables. Recommended for academic and research libraries that support finance programs.

3081. ***Journal of International Financial Management and Accounting.*** [ISSN: 0954-1314] 1988. 3x/yr. GBP 274 print & online eds. Ed(s): Frederick Choi, Richard Levich. Blackwell Publishing Ltd., 9600 Garsington Rd, PO Box 805, Oxford, OX4 2DQ, United Kingdom; customerservices@oxon.blackwellpublishing.com; http://www.blackwellpublishing.com/. Illus. Refereed. Circ: 600. Online: EBSCO Publishing; ingenta.com; OCLC Online Computer Library Center, Inc.; RoweCom Information Quest; Swets Blackwell. Reprint: SWZ. *Indexed:* ABIn, ATI, BPI, IBSS. *Bk. rev.:* 1, 1,500 words. *Aud.:* Ac, Sa.

Each issue contains several research articles (each about 25 pages long) on topics related to financial management and accountancy, which includes banking, financial services, auditing, and taxation. Issues sometimes include an "Executive Perspective" (written by a practitioner), a case, comments concerning earlier papers, or a book review. Recent articles have discussed determinants of Internet financial reporting by New Zealand companies, and whether value stocks earn higher returns than growth stocks in emerging markets. Appropriate for academic and research libraries.

3082. ***Journal of International Money and Finance.*** [ISSN: 0261-5606] 1982. 7x/yr. EUR 890 (Individuals, EUR 85). Ed(s): James R Lothian, Michael T Melvin. Pergamon, The Boulevard, Langford Ln, East Park, Kidlington, OX5 1GB, United Kingdom. Illus., index. Refereed. Vol. ends: Dec. Microform: PQC. Online: EBSCO Publishing; Gale Group; ingenta.com; ScienceDirect; Swets Blackwell. *Indexed:* ABIn, IBSS, JEL, PAIS, RiskAb, SSCI. *Bk. rev.:* Various number and length. *Aud.:* Ac, Sa.

This publication presents research in all areas of international finance and open-economy macroeconomics. Topics include foreign exchange, balance of payments, international interactions of prices, incomes and money, multinational corporate finance, foreign aid, and international economic institutions. Articles in recent issues have examined intraday technical trading in the foreign exchange market, exchange rate intervention with options, and what can be learned about purchasing power parity from U.S. city price data. Each article is roughly 20 to 50 pages long. The price and scope make this an appropriate title for academic and research libraries.

3083. ***Managerial Finance.*** [ISSN: 0307-4358] 1975. m. EUR 5773.54 in Europe; USD 5479 in North America; AUD 4649 in Australasia. Ed(s): Richard Dobbins. Barmarick Publications, Enholmes Hall, Patrington, HU12 0PR, United Kingdom; hr24@dial.pipex.com. Sample. Refereed. Circ: 400. Reprint: PSC; SWZ. *Indexed:* ABIn, ATI, PAIS. *Aud.:* Ac, Sa.

If price is not an issue, this is a solid financial management title. The journal offers weighty articles on topics such as asset pricing, capital budgeting, corporate governance, financial forecasting, cash management, mergers, funds procurement, and investment decision making. Recommended for libraries that support finance programs or financial decision-makers.

3084. ***Mathematical Finance: an international journal of mathematics, statistics and financial economics.*** [ISSN: 0960-1627] 1991. q. USD 683 print & online eds. Blackwell Publishing, Inc., Commerce Place, 350 Main St, Malden, MA 02148; subscrip@blackwellpub.com; http://www.blackwellpublishing.com. Illus., index, adv. Sample. Refereed. Circ: 800. Vol. ends: Oct. Online: EBSCO Publishing; ingenta.com; RoweCom Information Quest; Swets Blackwell. *Indexed:* ABIn, CCMJ, IBSS, JEL, MathSciNet, SSCI, ST&MA. *Bk. rev.:* 0-2, 250-500 words. *Aud.:* Ac, Sa.

This highly specialized and technical journal is produced by scholars who represent an elite group of research universities from around the world. Issues generally include 3–6 articles of 15–20 pages on finance theory, financial engineering, and related mathematical and statistical techniques. Articles look at the mathematical and statistical basis for pricing and other activities in financial markets, present a number of pricing and hedging methods, and discuss financial markets in general from a theoretical perspective. Recent examples have included error calculus and path sensitivity in financial models, an optimal strategy for hedging with short-term futures contracts, and defaultable Levy term structure.

3085. ***Public Finance Review.*** Formerly (until 1997): *Public Finance Quarterly.* [ISSN: 1091-1421] 1973. bi-m. GBP 413 print & online eds. in Europe, Middle East, Africa & Australasia. Ed(s): J Ronnie Davis. Sage Publications, Inc., 2455 Teller Rd, Thousand Oaks, CA 91320; info@sagepub.com; http://www.sagepub.com. Illus., adv. Refereed. Circ: 800 Paid. Microform: PQC. Online: Florida Center for Library Automation; Gale Group; ingenta.com; OCLC Online Computer Library Center, Inc.; ProQuest Information & Learning; RoweCom Information Quest; Swets Blackwell. Reprint: PQC; PSC. *Indexed:* ABIn, ASG, ATI, AgeL, IBSS, JEL, PAIS, PSA, SSCI, SUSA. *Bk. rev.:* Various number and length. *Aud.:* Ac, Sa.

This scholarly economics journal explores the theory, policy, and institutions related to the allocation, distribution, and stabilization functions within the public sectors of the economy. Each issue includes five lengthy articles in which authors present theoretical and empirical studies of the positive or normative aspects of (primarily) U.S. federal, state, and local government policies. Recent article topics have included NATO peacekeeping and burden sharing, tax evasion and tax progressivity, and the impact of public investment on the performance of U.S. industries. Academic libraries that support programs in public administration and finance should consider this title.

3086. ***Quantitative Finance.*** [ISSN: 1469-7688] 2001. bi-m. USD 765 print & online (Individuals, USD 340 print only). Ed(s): Michael Dempster, Jean-Philippe Bouchaud. Institute of Physics Publishing, Dirac House, Temple Back, Bristol, BS1 6BE, United Kingdom; custserv@iop.org; http://www.iop.org/. Adv. Sample. Refereed. *Indexed:* MathSciNet. *Bk. rev.:* Various number and length. *Aud.:* Ac, Sa.

This new academic journal comes from an unlikely source: the Institute of Physics in London. It reflects the growing use of applied mathematics and physical methods to understand financial markets. Color charts, glossy photographs of contributors, book reviews, and thought pieces as well as academic research make this an exciting new title. A first-rate editorial board from universities and research institutions around the world make this a good pick for beefing up the quantitative areas in finance collections of research libraries.

3087. ***The Review of Financial Studies.*** [ISSN: 0893-9454] 1988. q. GBP 336 GBP 153 academic. Ed(s): Maureen O'Hara. Oxford University Press, Great Clarendon St, Oxford, OX2 6DP, United Kingdom; jnl.orders@oup.co.uk; http://www3.oup.co.uk/jnls. Illus., adv. Refereed. Circ: 3300. Online: EBSCO Publishing; HighWire Press; ingenta.com; RoweCom Information Quest; Swets Blackwell. Reprint: PSC; SWZ. *Indexed:* AgeL, IBSS, JEL, RiskAb, SSCI, ST&MA. *Bk. rev.:* 1, signed, 1,000-2,500 words. *Aud.:* Ac, Sa.

This scholarly journal presents a balance of new theoretical and empirical research in the form of a eight to ten lengthy articles. Recent papers have examined concepts such as the role of lockups in initial public offerings, an intraday analysis of the corporate bond market, mutual fund investment styles, and forward interest rate curves. Academic libraries should consider this a core finance title.

3088. ***Review of Quantitative Finance and Accounting.*** [ISSN: 0924-865X] 1991. 8x/yr. USD 754 print or online ed. Ed(s): Cheng-few Lee. Kluwer Academic Publishers, 101 Philip Dr, Assinippi Park, Norwell, MA 02061. Illus., adv. Sample. Refereed. Vol. ends: No. 4. Microform: PQC. Online: EBSCO Publishing; ingenta.com; Kluwer Online; OCLC Online Computer Library Center, Inc.; RoweCom Information Quest; Swets Blackwell. Reprint: SWZ. *Indexed:* IBSS, IBZ, JEL, RiskAb. *Aud.:* Ac, Sa.

The focus of this title is on quantitative theoretical and methodological research and empirical applications. Major themes trace the interaction of finance, accounting, economics, and quantitative methods. Recent articles have discussed using spinoffs to reduce capital misallocations, a trade-off model of debt maturity structure, and an empirical investigation of the option-adjusted realized return. Since a strong background in mathematics and economic statistics is required to understand these articles, only specialists and academic libraries should consider it for purchase.

Trade Journals

3089. ***A F P Exchange.*** Former titles (until 1999): *T M A Journal (Treasury Management Association);* (until Jan. 1994): *Journal of Cash Management.* [ISSN: 1528-4077] 1981. bi-m. Individuals, USD 90; Individual members, USD 120. Ed(s): John T Hiatt, Christy Kincade. Association for Financial Professionals, 7315 Wisconsin Ave, Ste 600 W, Bethesda, MD 20814; AFP@AFPonline.org; http://www.AFPonline.org. Illus., index, adv. Sample. Circ: 15000. Vol. ends: No. 6. *Indexed:* ABIn, BLI, BPI. *Aud.:* Ac, Sa.

Certified cash managers and certified public accountants are among the contributors to this association publication that provides timely, practical information and advice to cash managers in corporations and governments. Departments provide global information, a career column, a calendar, and current events. Recent features have focused on investor relations, retirement income, credit ratings, and diversifying cash. This practitioner's magazine serves as a good introduction and updating service for those interested in government, corporate, and global cash management.

3090. ***Business Credit.*** Formerly: *Credit and Financial Management.* [ISSN: 0897-0181] 1898. 10x/yr. USD 48. Ed(s): Norma Heim. National Association of Credit Management, 8840 Columbia 100 Parkway, Columbia, MD 21045; http://www.nacm.org. Illus., index, adv. Sample. Circ: 37000. Vol. ends: Dec. Microform: PQC. Online: EBSCO Publishing; Florida Center for Library Automation; Gale Group; Northern Light Technology, Inc.; OCLC Online Computer Library Center, Inc.; ProQuest Information & Learning; H.W. Wilson. Reprint: PQC. *Indexed:* ABIn, ATI, BPI, LRI. *Aud.:* Sa.

The target audience of this title is the corporate credit and financial professional, with additional emphasis on company finance in general. Each issue includes news on relevant issues, such as law and legislation, loss prevention, collections, and technology. Several ten-page feature articles present insights on such topics as web-based treasury mangement, A/R outsourcing, and lien law traps for the unwary. Columns on legal issues, personnel, and contruction provide news and updates on the legal and regulatory environment. Columns on professionals at work and member profiles present a personalized approach to industry issues. Articles in the international-affairs section give insight into the global-industry environment.

3091. ***Financial Analysts Journal.*** [ISSN: 0015-198X] 1945. bi-m. USD 220. Ed(s): Craig K Ruff. Association for Investment Management and Research, PO Box 3668, Charlottesville, VA 22903; http://www.aimr.org. Illus., index, adv. Sample. Circ: 40000. Vol. ends: Nov/Dec. Microform: PQC. Online: Gale Group; Northern Light Technology, Inc.; OCLC Online Computer Library Center, Inc.; ProQuest Information & Learning. Reprint: PQC. *Indexed:* ABIn, ATI, BPI, CompLI, IBSS, PAIS. *Bk. rev.:* 1-2, 500 words. *Aud.:* Ac, Sa.

Each issue of this title, which is aimed at academicians and practitioners, contains nearly a dozen articles of varying length on financial and investment analysis. Primary emphasis is on valuation, portfolio management, market structure, market behavior, and professional conduct and ethics. Articles also involve accounting, economics, and securities law and regulations. Recent issues include articles on global hedge funds, relative implied-volatility arbitrage with index options, and replicating default risk in a defined-benefit plan. Association content, such as speeches, commentary, and association policy statements, is also included. The editorial board has representatives from highly respected universities and capital management firms.

3092. ***Financial Executive: for today's global business leader.*** Former titles (until 1987): *F E: The Magazine for Financial Executives;* (until Jan. 1985): *Financial Executive; Controller.* [ISSN: 0895-4186] 1932. 9x/yr. USD 59 domestic; USD 75 foreign. Ed(s): Jeffrey Marshall. Financial Executives International, 200 Campus Dr, Ste 200, Florham Park, NJ 07932-0674; http://www.fei.org/. Illus., index, adv. Sample. Circ: 16000. Microform: PQC. Online: The Dialog Corporation; EBSCO Publishing; Florida Center for Library Automation; Gale Group; Northern Light Technology, Inc.; OCLC Online Computer Library Center, Inc.; ProQuest Information & Learning; H.W. Wilson. Reprint: PQC; PSC. *Indexed:* ABIn, ATI, AgeL, BPI, CompLI, PAIS. *Bk. rev.:* Various number and length. *Aud.:* Ac, Sa.

This title targets senior management, particularly chief financial officers. Topics address evolving financial, economic, strategic, and technological trends. Recent articles focus on corporate boards, the coming retirement crisis, making mergers work, B2B e-commerce, and distance education. Although aimed at the CFOs of large corporations, many medium-size businesses doing business overseas and businesses without a CFO will benefit from the practical information contained in these pages. Public libraries that serve medium to large businesses and academic libraries with programs in finance should consider this title.

3093. ***Global Finance.*** [ISSN: 0896-4181] 1987. m. USD 350. Ed(s): Paolo Panerai. Global Finance Media, Inc., 411 Fifth Ave., 7th Fl., New York, NY 10016. Illus. Circ: 50000 Controlled. Vol. ends: Dec. *Indexed:* ABIn, PAIS. *Aud.:* Ga, Ac, Sa.

Targeting corporate executives and institutional investors, this magazine features news and analysis of corporate finance, mergers and acquisitions, capital markets, banking, risk management, money management, investor relations, and other topics relevant to the global marketplace. The corporate finance news section covers foreign exchange, M&A, global ADRs, and corporate bonds. Recent feature article topics have included Europe's bourses, solving the asbestos battle, and the future of foreign exchange.

3094. ***Journal of Business Finance & Accounting.*** [ISSN: 0306-686X] 1974. 10x/yr. GBP 581 print & online. Ed(s): Richard Briston, L.A. Gordon. Blackwell Publishing Ltd., 9600 Garsington Rd, PO Box 805, Oxford, OX4 2DQ, United Kingdom; customerservices@oxon.blackwellpublishing.com; http://www.blackwellpublishing.com/. Illus., index, adv. Refereed. Circ: 1350. Vol. ends: Dec. Online: EBSCO Publishing; Gale Group; ingenta.com; OCLC Online Computer Library Center, Inc.; RoweCom Information Quest; Swets Blackwell. Reprint: PQC; SWZ. *Indexed:* ABIn, ATI, IBSS, RiskAb. *Aud.:* Ac, Sa.

This widely indexed title is a core journal in finance that addresses problems from the related disciplines of financial and management accounting and auditing. Each issue delivers 8–10 feature articles of 15–20 pages each that report on theoretical or empirical research in financial management, control, and accountability, including performance audits. Topics in recent issues include reactions of the international stock exchange to company employment announcements, a re-examination of the effectiveness of the bankruptcy process, and the effect of multinationality on security analyst underreaction. Despite the price and the U.K. focus, the large number of articles and the variety of topics make this an impressive title.

3095. ***Journal of Financial Planning.*** Formerly (until 1988): *Institute of Certified Financial Planners. Journal.* [ISSN: 1040-3981] 1979. 12x/yr. Non-members, USD 90. Ed(s): Marvin W. Tuttle. Financial Planning Association, 3801 E Florida Ave, Ste 708, Denver, CO 80210-2571; journalfp@fpanet.org; http://www.journalfp.net. Illus., index, adv. Sample. Circ: 27000 Paid. Vol. ends: No. 4. *Indexed:* ABIn, ATI, AgeL, BPI, PAIS, RiskAb. *Aud.:* Ac, Sa.

This title serves as a forum for the exchange of ideas and information related to the financial planning profession. Roughly a dozen short articles focus on professional issues, retirement, portfolio management, investment research, trends, technology, and strategies. One recent article has discussed the inroads women have made in the financial planning profession. Departments report on legal and legislative news, institutional resources, continuing education, letters to the editor, and contacts. Large public libraries and academic libraries that support programs in insurance and finance should consider this title.

3096. ***Mergers & Acquisitions (New York, 1965): the dealmakers' journal.*** Incorporated (in 1967): *Mergers and Acquisitions Monthly.* [ISSN: 0026-0010] 1965. m. USD 595 domestic; USD 7 foreign. Thomson Financial, 195 Broadway, 9th fl, New York, NY 10007. Illus., index, adv. Circ: 3000 Paid. Vol. ends: Dec. Microform: CIS; PQC. Online: EBSCO Publishing; Florida Center for Library Automation; Gale Group; LexisNexis; Northern Light Technology, Inc.; OCLC Online Computer Library Center, Inc.; ProQuest Information & Learning; H.W. Wilson. Reprint: PQC. *Indexed:* ABIn, ATI, B&I, BPI, CLI, LRI, PAIS. *Aud.:* Ac, Sa.

Corporate mergers and acquisitions (M&A) are the specialized focus of this core trade magazine from Thomson Financial. Joint ventures are reported on but are not regularly charted. Data gathered from a number of sources, including Thomson's Merger and Corporate Transaction Database, are used to develop league tables, ranking the leading financial advisers in the M&A industries, sales volumes of target companies, industries most attractive to foreign investment, countries with the largest role in M&A in the United States, and the top transactions. Quarterly rosters give data on U.S. acquisitions by SIC code, foreign acquisitions in the United States, and U.S. acquisitions overseas. There are also several five- to ten-page articles that address such issues as corporate restructuring, challenging the sale of equity carve-outs, and using pay systems as a rallying point for merged workforces. Columns address deal-making, the international climate, Washington news, trends, and the "industry's most comprehensive calendar of events," as well as a very brief case study.

3097. ***Risk Management.*** Formerly: *National Insurance Buyer.* [ISSN: 0035-5593] 1954. m. USD 59 domestic. Ed(s): Laura Sullivan. Risk Management Society Publishing, Inc., 655 Third Ave, 2nd Fl, New York, NY 10017-5637. Illus., index, adv. Circ: 15000 Paid and controlled. Vol. ends: Dec (No. 12). Microform: PQC. Online: Florida Center for Library Automation; Gale Group; Northern Light Technology, Inc.; OCLC Online Computer Library Center, Inc.; ProQuest Information & Learning; H.W. Wilson. Reprint: PQC. *Indexed:* ABIn, ATI, BPI, LRI, RiskAb. *Bk. rev.:* 6-9, 20 words. *Aud.:* Ac, Sa.

Articles in this trade journal might typically explore global growth, risk management, highly protected risks, and specific examples of companies, operations, and innovators. Regular departments include a risk reporter, emerging markets, rules and regulations, and an executive forum. A calendar and reports of society news are regular features as well. Recent feature-article topics have included global commerce, directors and officers liability, and managing risk on college campuses. Academic libraries that support business education, specifically insurance and finance, and public libraries with supporting demographics will wish to consider this title.

3098. ***Treasury & Risk Management.*** Formerly (until no.2, 1992): *Treasury;* Incorporates (1989-1992): *Corporate Risk Management.* [ISSN: 1067-0432] 1991. 10x/yr. USD 64 domestic; USD 80 foreign. Ed(s): Pat Wechsler. Wicks Business Information, 363 Reef Rd, Fairfield, CT 06430; info@wicksbusinessinfo.com; http://www.wicksbusinessinfo.com. Illus., index, adv. Sample. Circ: 46000 Controlled. Vol. ends: No. 10. Online: EBSCO Publishing; LexisNexis; OCLC Online Computer Library Center, Inc. *Aud.:* Sa.

This publication targets chief executive officers, chief financial officers, presidents, vice-presidents of treasury and finance, controllers, financial managers, cash and credit managers, and risk managers. Each issue has three or four feature articles as well as opinion pieces, news, and departments that address careers, opinions, and an executive profile. Features discuss specific solutions to practical problems of risk managers. Recent articles have included discussions of the use of expense management automation to reduce business travel expenses, the importance to companies of credit evaluation in a tough economy, and the development of EXtensible Business Reporting Language (XBRL).

3099. ***Wall Street & Technology: for senior-level executives in technology and information management in securities and investment firms.*** Formerly (until 1992): *Wall Street Computer Review;* Which Incorporated (in 1991): *Wall Street Computer Review. Buyer's Guide.* [ISSN: 1060-989X] 1983. m. USD 85 domestic; USD 105 Canada; USD 125 elsewhere. Ed(s): Kerry Massaro. C M P Media LLC, 3 Park Ave., New York, NY 10016-5902; http://www.cmp.com. Illus., index, adv. Sample. Circ: 25000 Controlled. Vol. ends: Dec. Online: EBSCO Publishing; Florida Center for Library Automation; Gale Group; LexisNexis; OCLC Online Computer Library Center, Inc.; ProQuest Information & Learning; H.W. Wilson. *Indexed:* ABIn, CompLI, LRI, MicrocompInd, PAIS. *Bk. rev.:* Various number and length. *Aud.:* Ac, Sa.

This trade newspaper is one of an important group of niche titles that provide information on the technology of financial services (others include *Insurance & Technology* and *Bank Systems & Technology*). The technology and communications aspects of the financial-services industry are discussed in articles and departments that report on trading, regulation, and money management. Significant emphasis is placed on the growing importance of the Internet, along with special attention to such tools and techniques as data mining. The "Buyer's Guide" issue includes generic software and operating systems and a list of products, hardware, materials, and services provided to the financial-services industry, divided into the type of service supported, including general quote services, securities trading by security type, portfolio accounting/management, equity research, and others. The format includes the vendor names and addresses, the products/services with which they are compatible, and product descriptions. Other regular coverage includes risk management, trading and exchange, investment technology, inside operations, m-commerce, and a calendar. Recent articles have covered document retention and storage for financial services firms as regulators increase their vigilance, the influx of new electronic trading systems for options, and the adoption of the Financial Information Exchange by small- and mid-size investment management firms.

■ FIRE PROTECTION

Lian Ruan, Director/Head Librarian, Illinois Fire Service Institute, University of Illinois at Urbana-Champaign, 11 Gerty Drive, Champaign, IL 61820; l-ruan@uiuc.edu

Introduction

Since the events of September 11, 2001, the public views firefighters and emergency responders as heroes of the highest order, leading to increased interests and information needs from the public and research worlds to the fire protection field. This section contains fire protection journals with national or international scope. The titles selected here are mainly geared toward firefighters, emergency responders, and administrators. Article topics include firefighting, fire safety, training, hazardous materials, fire management and administration, fire incidents, fire statistics, case studies, and so on. Most magazines follow a similar informative format of department sections, including such common subjects as news, politics, classifieds, and product information. This section also includes a peer-reviewed and internationally recognized scholarly journal, which will be of interest to academic programs and researchers focused on fire science. The magazines also cover a variety of topics related to fire protection, including chemistry, physics, engineering, and ergonomics.

Basic Periodicals

Ac: *Fire Chief, Fire Engineering, Fire Protection Engineering, Fire Technology, NFPA Journal;* Sa: *Advanced Rescue Technology, American Fire Journal, Fire Chief, Fire Engineering, Fire Protection Engineering, Fire Rescue Magazine, Fire Technology, Firehouse, Industrial Fire World, NFPA Journal.*

Basic Abstracts and Indexes

Chemical Abstracts, Engineering Index.

3100. ***Advanced Rescue Technology.*** Formerly: *E M S Rescue Technology.* [ISSN: 1524-0134] 1995. bi-m. USD 11.50. Ed(s): Nancy Perry. Summer Communications Inc., 7626 Densmore Ave., Van Nuys, CA 91406-2042. Circ: 40000 Controlled. *Bk. rev.:* 400-500 words. *Aud.:* Sa.

This title is geared toward emergency medical services personnel, fire service personnel, and other first responders from law enforcement, the military, and rescue. Feature articles are on hands-on rescue techniques and emergency medical care of victims. Columns include "Rescue Roundup," "Tools of the

Trade," "Media Review," "Field Report," "Hot Products," various product showcases, and classified ads. Highly recommended for fire departments, fire service personnel, emergency medical services personnel, special and large public library collections.

3101. ***American Fire Journal.*** Formerly (until 1984): *Western Fire Journal.* [ISSN: 0739-3709] 1950. m. USD 22.95; USD 42 foreign. Ed(s): Carol Carlsen Brooks. Fire Publications, Inc., c/o John A Ackerman, Pub, 9072 E Artesia Blvd, Bellflower, CA 90706. Illus., adv. Circ: 6000. *Indexed:* H&SSA. *Bk. rev.:* 400-500 words. *Aud.:* Sa.

The editor of this solution-oriented magazine focuses feature articles on the current management and technical issues in the American fire service. The magazine complements books and manuals published by Fire Publications, Inc., and provides additional training information important to fire department operations. Departments are "Looking at Books," "Hot Flashes," "Skull Session," "Equipment Directory," "What's New," and "Important Happenings." Recommended for fire officers, administrators, special library, and large public library collections.

3102. ***Fire Chief: administration, training, operations.*** Incorporates: *Volunteer Firefighter; Volunteer Fire Chief.* [ISSN: 0015-2552] 1956. m. USD 54; USD 114 foreign. Ed(s): Janet Wilmoth. Primedia Business Magazines & Media, Inc. (Atlanta), 6151 Powers Ferry Rd, N W, Atlanta, GA 30339-2941; inquiries@primediabusiness.com; http://www.primediabusiness.com/. Illus., adv. Circ: 50000. Vol. ends: Dec. Microform: PQC. Online: Gale Group; OCLC Online Computer Library Center, Inc.; ProQuest Information & Learning; H.W. Wilson. Reprint: PQC. *Bk. rev.:* 0-4, 50-300 words. *Aud.:* Ac, Sa.

This popular magazine is for progressive fire service leaders who lead and manage fire departments. Fire officers from across the country and overseas write feature articles covering a wide variety of areas in fire administration and management that are of particular importance to today's chief officers and senior officers. Subjects include fire prevention, fire suppression, incident command, public education, emergency medical response, firefighter health and safety, response to hazardous materials and terrorist acts, technology development, finance and budgeting, and training. Departments include "Product Focus," "New Deliveries," and classified ads. Each issue has an advertisers index and a timely legal column written by experienced lawyers with involvement in the fire service. The News and Columns also includes Chief Ronny J. Coleman's highly popular "Chief's Clipboard." Highly recommended for fire chiefs, senior officers, training officers, administrators, special library, large public library, and academic library collections serving fire protection and prevention programs.

3103. ***Fire Engineering: the journal of fire suppression and protection.*** [ISSN: 0015-2587] 1877. m. USD 29.50 domestic; USD 49.50 foreign; USD 5 per issue. Ed(s): William A Manning. PennWell Corp., 21-00 Rte 208 S, Fair Lawn, NJ 07410-2602; Headquarters@PennWell.com; http://www.pennwell.com. Illus., index, adv. Sample. Circ: 45000. Vol. ends: Dec. Microform: PQC. Online: EBSCO Publishing; Gale Group; LexisNexis; OCLC Online Computer Library Center, Inc. Reprint: PQC. *Indexed:* AS&TI, C&ISA, ChemAb, EngInd, ExcerpMed, H&SSA, SCI. *Aud.:* Ac, Sa.

This magazine provides practical training, education, and management information for fire and emergency services personnel worldwide. Experts in the field write feature articles and use case studies of fire and rescue incidents, which focus on lessons learned. The articles discuss real-life situations such as trench rescue, high-angle rescue, and extrication. Regular magazine departments focus on education and management issues, covering such topics as volunteers, training, news, technology product information, classifieds, and an events calendar. The online version of the magazine provides daily international business and industry-related news, current issue articles, and access to years of searchable editorial archives. Highly recommended for fire departments, fire service personnel, special library, public library, and academic library collections with fire prevention and protection programs.

3104. ***Fire Protection Engineering.*** [ISSN: 1524-900X] 1998. q. Free to qualified personnel. Society of Fire Protection Engineers, 7315 Wisconsin Ave., Ste. 1225 W, Bethesda, MD 20814; sfpehqtrs@sfpe.org; http://www.sfpe.org. *Bk. rev.:* 200-300 words. *Aud.:* Ac, Sa.

Fire Protection Engineering is a quarterly magazine published by the Society of Fire Protection Engineers (SFPE), which serves as the SFPE's information vehicle for members. There is a column on SFPE resources. The articles discuss issues on how to advance the science and practice of fire protection engineering and its allied fields. Recent topics include fire protection engineers and the design process, human capital in fire protection engineering consulting, and statistical benchmarking framework for developing stakeholder consensus. The magazine provides information on fire protection engineering education. It includes an ad index. Recommended for special library and academic library collections with fire prevention and protection programs.

3105. ***Fire Rescue Magazine.*** Formed by the merger of (1983-1997): *Firefighter's News;* (1988-1997): *Rescue;* Which was formerly (until 1989): *Rescue Magazine.* [ISSN: 1094-0529] 199?. m. USD 28.95 domestic (Students, USD 28.95). Ed(s): Lisa Dionne. Jems Communications, 525 B St., Ste 1900, San Diego, CA 92101. Adv. Circ: 43234 Paid and controlled. *Aud.:* Sa.

A well-rounded publication with bold photos and informative text, this magazine is for fire company officers and firefighters. It presents fire departments in action and focuses on problem solving with up-to-dated information and techniques that firefighters and rescuers can put to use immediately in their daily work. There are feature articles on various topics, such as fire scenes, leadership, and rescue. Each issue contains a column from a guest editor, plus "Burning Issues," "Nozzlehead," and "ToolsNewsTechniques." It also includes an advertising index, new products, classifieds, and letters to the editor. Recommended for fire departments, fire and emergency medical services professionals, special library and large public library collections.

3106. ***Fire Technology: an international journal of fire protection research and engineering.*** [ISSN: 0015-2684] 1965. q. USD 199 print or online ed. Ed(s): John Watts, Jr. National Fire Protection Association, 1 Batterymarch Park, Quincy, MA 02269; firetech@nfpa.org; http://www.nfpa.org. Illus., index. Sample. Refereed. Circ: 3000. Vol. ends: Nov (No. 4). Microform: PQC. Online: ingenta.com; Kluwer Online; Northern Light Technology, Inc.; OCLC Online Computer Library Center, Inc.; Ovid Technologies, Inc.; ProQuest Information & Learning; Swets Blackwell. Reprint: PQC. *Indexed:* AS&TI, ChemAb, EngInd, H&SSA, IAA, RiskAb, SCI. *Bk. rev.:* 1, 250-500 words. *Aud.:* Ac, Sa.

This is an internationally recognized scientific and technical peer-reviewed journal. It is the most widely read refereed journal in the fire science field. Cross-disciplinary papers from perspectives of physics, chemistry, engineering, management science, and ergonomics are included. Distinguished fire scientists discuss their studies dealing with issues like fire suppression, fire safety engineering, combustibility, and chemical reactions. The editors also encourage papers describing advances in fire technology with a strong emphasis on implementation. It also includes editorial, book, and software reviews, technical reports, and announcements of meetings. The best paper appearing in the magazine receives the Harry C. Bigglestone Award for Excellence in Communication of Fire Protection Concepts annually. Highly recommended for special library and academic library collections serving fire protection and prevention programs or allied fields with a scholarly interest in fire science, such as chemistry, physics, engineering, or ergonomics.

3107. ***Firehouse.*** [ISSN: 0145-4064] 1976. m. USD 25.97; USD 45.97 foreign. Ed(s): Harvey Eisner. Cygnus Business Media, Inc., 445 Broad Hollow Rd, Melville, NY 11747-3601. Illus., adv. Circ: 110600. Vol. ends: Dec. *Aud.:* Ga, Sa.

Firehouse is the most popular and widely read firefighter magazine, with extensive coverage of firefighting techniques, innovations, rescue operations, historic and dramatic fires, and firefighters. It appeals to all levels, career and volunteer firefighters. Feature articles are on "Major Incidents," "Training," "Firefighter Health and Safety," and "Apparatus." Under "Major Incidents," there are regular feature articles of "On the Job," reporting current fire incidents and of "Progress Report," providing news and updates of interest to firefighters. Columns include topics on safety and survival, emergency medical services, extrication, and chief concerns. Departments include forum, firefronts, hot shots, industry news, a calendar of events, new products, and an advertiser index. Highly recommended for special libraries, public library collections, fire service personnel, and fire "enthusiasts."

3108. ***Industrial Fire World.*** [ISSN: 0749-890X] 1985. bi-m. USD 29.95 domestic; USD 40 in Canada & Mexico; USD 60 elsewhere. Ed(s): Anton Riecher. Industrial Fire World, PO Box 9161, College Station, TX 77842-9161; ind@fireworld.com; http://www.fireworld.com. Adv. Sample. Circ: 31500. *Aud.:* Sa.

The articles deal with all aspects of industrial firefighting and emergency rescue, including training, techniques, prevention, and new products. The editor contributes directly to the feature articles. The regular departments include focus on Hazmat, Incident Log, New Products, Service Directory, and Classifieds. Recommended for special library and public library collections.

3109. ***N F P A Journal.*** Formed by the merger of (1907-1991): *Fire Journal;* (1984-1991): *Fire Command;* Which was formerly (until 1983): *Fire Service Today;* (1933-1970): *Fire Command.* [ISSN: 1054-8793] 1991. bi-m. Membership, USD 115. Ed(s): Stephen Murphy, John Nicholson. National Fire Protection Association, 1 Batterymarch Park, Quincy, MA 02269; dgfergason@nfpa.org; http://www.nfpa.org. Illus., index, adv. Sample. Circ: 75000 Controlled. Vol. ends: Nov/Dec. Microform: PQC. Online: ProQuest Information & Learning. Reprint: PQC. *Indexed:* AS&TI, AgeL, ChemAb, EngInd, SCI. *Aud.:* Ac, Sa.

This magazine serves as the NFPA?s official information vehicle for professional fire and life safety members. It covers major topics in fire protection and suppression and provides research and investigation reports. The unique feature is its annual NFPA statistical studies on large-loss fires, multiple-death fires, fire loss in the United States, and firefighter deaths and injuries. It also includes articles on fire protection advances and public education, and other information of interest to NFPA members. Columns provide the association's position on standards, new programs, upcoming meetings, and political issues of relevance to members. It also includes product information and classified ads in departments. Highly recommended for academic library, special library, and large public library collections.

■ FISH, FISHERIES, AND AQUACULTURE

Lenora A. Oftedahl, StreamNet Librarian, Columbia River Inter-Tribal Fish Commission, 729 NE Oregon St, Suite 190, Portland, OR 97232; OFTL@critfc.org; http://www.fishlib.org

Introduction

Fish and fisheries have become hot topics in recent years. Overfishing, in particular, is of interest to many.

Current fisheries research is reported in a number of highly technical journals written for the academic researcher or scientist. Publishers and researchers are developing new, specialized journals to meet the needs of small subject groups in the field. As more journals are developed, libraries need to review their subscriptions closely to make sure they are filling the needs of their patrons.

A few journals focus on the aquarium trade and are suitable for the general public.

Basic Periodicals

Hs, Ga: *Aquaculture Magazine, Fisheries, Freshwater and Marine Aquarium, Tropical Fish Hobbyist, AquaWorld Magazine;* Ac, Sa: *Aquaculture, Aquaculture Research, Canadian Journal of Fisheries and Aquatic Sciences, Fish Physiology & Biochemistry, Fisheries Management and Ecology, Fisheries Research, Fishery Bulletin, Journal of Fish Biology, Reviews in Fisheries Science, American Fisheries Society. Transactions.*

Basic Abstracts and Indexes

Aquatic Sciences and Fisheries Abstracts, Biological Abstracts, NISC-Aquatic Biology, Aquaculture and Fisheries Resources.

3110. ***Alaska Fishery Research Bulletin.*** Former titles (until 1994): *Alaska. Department of Fish and Game. Fishery Research Bulletin;* (until 1988): *Alaska. Department of Fish and Game. Informational Leaflet.* [ISSN: 1091-7306] 1961. s-a. Ed(s): Susan M Shirley. Alaska Department of Fish and Game, PO Box 25526, Juneau, AK 99802-5526; susan-shirley@fishgame.state.ak.us; http://www.state.ak.us/local/akpages/FISH.GAME/adfghome.htm. Illus. Sample. Circ: 700. *Indexed:* ZooRec. *Aud.:* Ac, Sa.

Although produced by the Alaska Department of Fish and Game, the *Alaska Fishery Research Bulletin* also prints general articles on fishery science and aquaculture. Many other states' departments of fish and wildlife (or equivalents) also produce fishery-related journals.

3111. ***American Fisheries Society. Transactions.*** [ISSN: 0002-8487] 1870. bi-m. USD 798. American Fisheries Society, 5410 Grosvenor Ln, Ste 110, Bethesda, MD 20814-2199; journals@fisheries.org; http://www.fisheries.org. Illus., index, adv. Refereed. Circ: 3700. Vol. ends: No. 6. *Indexed:* AnBeAb, ApEcolAb, B&AI, BiolAb, ChemAb, DSR&OA, EnvAb, ExcerpMed, FPA, ForAb, GeoRef, GeogAbPG, IndVet, OceAb, RRTA, S&F, SCI, SWRA, VetBull, WAE&RSA, WRCInf, ZooRec. *Bk. rev.:* Various number and length. *Aud.:* Ac, Sa.

The largest of the five journals published by the American Fisheries Society, this publication contains refereed technical papers on all aspects of fisheries science. A must for any fisheries scientist.

3112. ***Aquacultural Engineering.*** [ISSN: 0144-8609] 1982. 8x/yr. EUR 761. Ed(s): J Colt, Dr. J. van Rijn. Elsevier BV, Sara Burgerhartstraat 25, Amsterdam, 1055 KV, Netherlands; nlinfo-f@elsevier.nl; http://www.elsevier.nl. Illus., index, adv. Refereed. Vol. ends: No. 6. Microform: PQC. Online: ingenta.com; ScienceDirect; Swets Blackwell. *Indexed:* Agr, BioEngAb, BiolAb, EngInd, EnvAb, ExcerpMed, GeogAbPG, HortAb, IndVet, OceAb, PollutAb, S&F, SCI, SWRA, VetBull, WAE&RSA, ZooRec. *Aud.:* Ac, Sa.

An international journal written for fisheries scientists and marine biologists involved with aquaculture. It covers all aspects of engineering, including building and system designs, materials selection and utilization, construction, and studies on biological limitations.

3113. ***Aquaculture: an international journal devoted to fundamental aquatic food resources.*** Incorporates (1990-1996): *Annual Review of Fish Diseases.* [ISSN: 0044-8486] 1972. 48x/yr. EUR 3182. Ed(s): R P Wilson, B A Costa-Pierce. Elsevier BV, Sara Burgerhartstraat 25, Amsterdam, 1055 KV, Netherlands; nlinfo-f@elsevier.nl; http://www.elsevier.nl. Illus., index, adv. Refereed. Circ: 650. Microform: PQC. Online: ingenta.com; ScienceDirect; Swets Blackwell. Reprint: SWZ. *Indexed:* Agr, B&AI, BiolAb, ChemAb, DSA, DSR&OA, EnvAb, ExcerpMed, FS&TA, FoVS&M, ForAb, GeogAbPG, HortAb, IndVet, OceAb, PollutAb, S&F, SCI, SWRA, VetBull, WAE&RSA, ZooRec. *Bk. rev.:* Various number and length. *Aud.:* Ac, Sa.

This international journal is written for fisheries scientists and marine biologists. It includes research studies on aquatic life in freshwater and saltwater environments. Occasional special issues focus on one topic. About four to seven articles appear in each issue.

3114. ***Aquaculture Economics & Management.*** [ISSN: 1365-7305] 1997. irreg. 3-4/yr. Institutional members, USD 130; Individual members, USD 45; Students, USD 25. Ed(s): PingSun Leung, Clem Tisdell. International Association of Aquaculture Economics & Management, c/o School of Economics, University of Queensland, St. Lucia, QLD 4072, Australia; aqem@conomics.uq.edu.au; http://www.uq.edu.au/aem. Adv. Sample. Refereed. Circ: 400. *Indexed:* Agr, BiolAb, ForAb, OceAb, PollutAb, S&F, SWRA, WAE&RSA. *Aud.:* Ac, Sa.

A relatively new journal whose primary purpose is to publish papers on aquaculture economic analysis for managers in both the public and private sectors.

3115. ***Aquaculture Magazine.*** Former titles: *Commercial Fish Farmer and Aquaculture News; Commercial Fish Farmer; Catfish Farmer and World Aquaculture News;* Formed by the merger of: *American Fish Farmer; American Fishes and U.S. Trout News; Catfish Farmer; Catfish Farming*

Industries. [ISSN: 0199-1388] 1969. bi-m. USD 24. Ed(s): Kay Horner. Achill River Corp., PO Box 2329, Asheville, NC 28802; http://www.aquaculturemag.com. Illus., adv. Circ: 7392. Vol. ends: No. 6. *Indexed:* DSR&OA, EnvAb, FS&TA, IndVet, OceAb, VetBull, ZooRec. *Bk. rev.:* Various number and length. *Aud.:* Hs, Ga.

An international publication written for the fish farmer. Each issue contains four or five feature articles and regular features including a calendar of events, catfish production figures, a classified section, and regular columns. There is an annual buyer's guide as well. Useful for high school students researching aquaculture or for anyone else interested in the field.

3116. *Aquaculture Nutrition.* [ISSN: 1353-5773] 1995. q. GBP 319 for print & online eds. Ed(s): O Lie. Blackwell Publishing Ltd., 9600 Garsington Rd, Oxford, OX4 2ZG, United Kingdom; jnl.orders@blacksci.co.uk; http://www.blackwellpublishing.com. Illus., index, adv. Refereed. Circ: 225. Vol. ends: No. 4. *Indexed:* Agr, BiolAb, ChemAb, DSA, HortAb, IndVet, OceAb, VetBull, WAE&RSA, ZooRec. *Aud.:* Ac, Sa.

An international research publication covering the nutrition of all farmed aquatic animals. The journal accepts review and original research articles. This publication has a rather narrow focus and would be most valuable to those studying the feeding of fish.

3117. *Aquaculture Research.* Former titles (until 1995): *Aquaculture and Fisheries Management;* (until 1985): *Fisheries Management.* [ISSN: 1355-557X] 1970. m. GBP 1277 for print & online eds. Ed(s): S J de Groot, R Hardy. Blackwell Publishing Ltd., 9600 Garsington Rd, Oxford, OX4 2ZG, United Kingdom; jnl.orders@blacksci.co.uk; http://www.blackwellpublishing.com. Illus., index, adv. Sample. Refereed. Circ: 315. Vol. ends: No. 12. Microform: PQC. Online: EBSCO Publishing; ingenta.com; Munksgaard & Blackwell Science's Synergy; OCLC Online Computer Library Center, Inc.; RoweCom Information Quest; Swets Blackwell. *Indexed:* Agr, BiolAb, DSA, EnvAb, ExcerpMed, ForAb, GeogAbPG, HortAb, IndVet, OceAb, S&F, VetBull, WAE&RSA, ZooRec. *Bk. rev.:* Various number and length. *Aud.:* Ac, Sa.

An international journal covering all aspects of aquaculture in marine, freshwater, or brackish water environments. Fish species are in a broad range. Papers can be original research articles, review articles, short communications, or book reviews. Valuable for scientists working in aquaculture.

Aquatic Conservation. See Marine Science and Technology section.

3118. *Canadian Journal of Fisheries and Aquatic Sciences.* Formerly (until 1980): *Fisheries Research Board of Canada. Journal.* [ISSN: 0706-652X] 1901. m. CND 687 print ed. (Individuals, CND 187.20 online ed.). Ed(s): J C Roff, M M Ferguson. N R C Research Press, Building M 55, Ottawa, ON K1A 0R6, Canada; research.journals@nrc.ca; http://www.nrc.ca/cisti/journals/. Illus., index, adv. Refereed. Circ: 3000. Vol. ends: No. 12. Microform: PQC. Online: CISTI; EBSCO Publishing; ingenta.com; RoweCom Information Quest; Swets Blackwell. Reprint: PQC. *Indexed:* AnBeAb, ApEcolAb, B&AI, BiolAb, CBCARef, ChemAb, DSA, DSR&OA, EnvAb, ExcerpMed, FPA, FS&TA, ForAb, GeoRef, GeogAbPG, IndVet, M&GPA, OceAb, PollutAb, RRTA, S&F, SCI, SWRA, VetBull, WAE&RSA, WRCInf, ZooRec. *Aud.:* Ac, Sa.

Research publications, perspectives, and comments on the aquatic environment and all aspects of fisheries. Most articles are in English; some are in French. Very valuable to those working in fisheries.

Copeia. See Biological Sciences/Vertebrate and Invertebrate Zoology section.

3119. *Diseases of Aquatic Organisms.* [ISSN: 0177-5103] 1985. 18x/yr. EUR 1068 combined subscription domestic for print & online eds.; EUR 1084 combined subscription foreign for print & online eds. Inter-Research, Nordbuente 23, Oldendorf, 21385, Germany; marita@int-res.com; http://www.int-res.com. Refereed. *Indexed:* BiolAb, ChemAb, FoVS&M, IndMed, IndVet, OceAb, SCI, SWRA, VetBull, ZooRec. *Aud.:* Ac, Sa.

The articles in this journal will interest all biologists working with pathogens. It covers toxicology, parasites, immunology, and more. Some of the illustrations are in color. All aquatic species (vertebrate and invertebrate) and environments (freshwater, brackish, and marine) are covered.

3120. *Ecology of Freshwater Fish.* [ISSN: 0906-6691] 1992. q. USD 382 print & online eds. Ed(s): Javier Lobon Cervia, Erik Mortensen. Blackwell Munksgaard, Rosenoerns Alle 1, PO Box 227, Copenhagen V, 1502, Denmark; info@mks.blackwellpublishing.com; http://www.munksgaard.dk/. Illus., adv. Refereed. *Indexed:* ApEcolAb, BiolAb, ForAb, IndVet, S&F, SWRA, VetBull, ZooRec. *Bk. rev.:* Number and length vary. *Aud.:* Ac, Sa.

Aimed particularly at fish biologists, the journal seeks to publish relevant articles about all aspects of freshwater fish and fisheries, especially ecology. Other items on anadromous or catadromous fish will be published as long as they increase knowledge of fish biology. Short papers and book reviews are also accepted.

3121. *Environmental Biology of Fishes.* [ISSN: 0378-1909] 1976. m. EUR 1752 print or online ed. Ed(s): Eugene K Balon. Kluwer Academic Publishers, van Godewijckstraat 30, PO Box 17, Dordrecht, 3300 AA, Netherlands. Adv. Refereed. Microform: PQC. Online: EBSCO Publishing; ingenta.com; Kluwer Online; OCLC Online Computer Library Center, Inc.; Ovid Technologies, Inc.; RoweCom Information Quest; Swets Blackwell. Reprint: SWZ. *Indexed:* AnBeAb, ApEcolAb, ArtHuCI, BiolAb, CJA, ChemAb, DSR&OA, EnvAb, ExcerpMed, ForAb, GeoRef, IndVet, OceAb, S&F, SCI, SWRA, VetBull, WRCInf, ZooRec. *Aud.:* Ac, Sa.

An international journal that deals with the relationship between fishes and their external and internal environments, whether natural or unnatural. Prefers multidisciplinary papers that advance the scholarly understanding of life.

3122. *Fish and Fisheries.* [ISSN: 1467-2960] 2000. q. GBP 327 print & online eds. Ed(s): T Pitcher, P Hart. Blackwell Publishing Ltd., 9600 Garsington Rd, Oxford, OX4 2ZG, United Kingdom; customerservices@oxon.blackwellpublishing.com; http://www.blackwellpublishing.com. Refereed. Online: EBSCO Publishing; ingenta.com; Munksgaard & Blackwell Science's Synergy; OCLC Online Computer Library Center, Inc.; RoweCom Information Quest; Swets Blackwell. *Indexed:* ApEcolAb, OceAb, PollutAb, SWRA, WRCInf. *Aud.:* Ac, Sa.

"The purpose of the journal is to provide critical overviews of major physiological, molecular, ecological, and evolutionary issues in the study of fish, and to establish a forum for debate of issues of global concern in world fisheries." Controversies are inevitable, and the editors would like both sides of various issues to publish in the journal for more balanced coverage.

3123. *Fish and Shellfish Immunology.* [ISSN: 1050-4648] 1991. 10x/yr. EUR 748. Ed(s): A E Ellis, C Secombes. Academic Press, Harcourt Pl, 32 Jamestown Rd, London, NW1 7BY, United Kingdom; apsubs@acad.com; http://www.elsevier-international.com/serials/. Illus., index, adv. Refereed. Online: EBSCO Publishing; ingenta.com; OCLC Online Computer Library Center, Inc.; RoweCom Information Quest; ScienceDirect; Swets Blackwell. Reprint: SWZ. *Indexed:* BiolAb, FoVS&M, IndMed, IndVet, OceAb, SCI, VetBull, ZooRec. *Aud.:* Ac, Sa.

An international refereed journal focusing on fish and shellfish immunology. Issues contain about six papers. Review articles and short communications are regular features. This journal is available in full-text electronically as well as in print.

3124. *Fish Physiology & Biochemistry.* [ISSN: 0920-1742] 1986. 4x/yr. EUR 410 print or online ed. Ed(s): E D Stevens, J R Hazel. Kluwer Academic Publishers, van Godewijckstraat 30, PO Box 17, Dordrecht, 3300 AA, Netherlands. Illus., index. Refereed. Vol. ends: No. 4. Online: EBSCO Publishing; ingenta.com; Kluwer Online; OCLC Online Computer Library Center, Inc.; RoweCom Information Quest; Swets Blackwell. *Indexed:* BiolAb, ChemAb, ExcerpMed, IndVet, OceAb, SCI, SWRA, VetBull, ZooRec. *Aud.:* Ac, Sa.

An international journal focusing on original, experimental research articles, brief communications, review articles, editorial comments, and announcements on the physiology and biochemistry of fishes. This journal is valuable to anyone studying fish physiology.

3125. ***Fisheries.*** Supersedes (in 1976): *American Fisheries Society. Newsletter.* [ISSN: 0363-2415] 1948. m. USD 76 in North America; USD 95 elsewhere. American Fisheries Society, 5410 Grosvenor Ln, Ste 110, Bethesda, MD 20814-2199; journals@fisheries.org; http://www.fisheries.org. Illus., index, adv. Refereed. Circ: 9700 Paid. Vol. ends: No. 12. *Indexed:* B&AI, BiolAb, ChemAb, DSR&OA, EnvAb, ExcerpMed, FPA, ForAb, IndVet, OceAb, PollutAb, RRTA, S&F, SCI, SSCI, SWRA, WAE&RSA, WRCInf, ZooRec. *Bk. rev.:* Number varies, 500 words. *Aud.:* Ac, Sa.

Monthly publication from the American Fisheries Society containing news about the society, current events, editorials, book reviews, and a few feature articles that may focus on one particular topic.

3126. ***Fisheries Management and Ecology.*** [ISSN: 0969-997X] 1994. bi-m. GBP 431 print & online eds. Ed(s): I Cowx, K O'Grady. Blackwell Publishing Ltd., 9600 Garsington Rd, Oxford, OX4 2ZG, United Kingdom; customerservices@oxon.blackwellpublishing.com; http://www.blackwellpublishing.com. Illus., index, adv. Refereed. Circ: 245. Vol. ends: No. 4. *Indexed:* ApEcolAb, BiolAb, FPA, ForAb, GeogAbPG, IndVet, OceAb, RRTA, S&F, SWRA, WAE&RSA, ZooRec. *Bk. rev.:* Various number and length. *Aud.:* Ac, Sa.

An international journal covering the management, ecology, and conservation of fisheries: "The aim of this journal is to foster an understanding of how to maintain, develop and manage the conditions under which fish populations can thrive, and how they and their habitat can be conserved and enhanced."

3127. ***Fisheries Oceanography.*** [ISSN: 1054-6006] 1992. q. GBP 394 print & online eds. Ed(s): T R Parsons. Blackwell Publishing Ltd., 9600 Garsington Rd, Oxford, OX4 2ZG, United Kingdom; customerservices@oxon.blackwellpublishing.com; http://www.blackwellpublishing.com. Adv. Refereed. Circ: 430. Microform: PQC. Online: EBSCO Publishing; ingenta.com; Munksgaard & Blackwell Science's Synergy; OCLC Online Computer Library Center, Inc.; RoweCom Information Quest; Swets Blackwell. *Indexed:* BiolAb, M&GPA, OceAb, ZooRec. *Aud.:* Ac, Sa.

Sponsored by the Japanese Society for Fisheries Oceanography, this is an international journal that covers fish populations, food chains, and abundance in the marine environment. Covers species in all the oceans.

3128. ***Fisheries Research: an international journal on fishing technology, fisheries science and fisheries management.*** [ISSN: 0165-7836] 1982. 18x/yr. EUR 1705. Ed(s): A D McIntyre. Elsevier BV, Sara Burgerhartstraat 25, Amsterdam, 1055 KV, Netherlands; nlinfo-f@elsevier.nl; http://www.elsevier.nl. Illus., index, adv. Refereed. Online: ingenta.com; ScienceDirect; Swets Blackwell. *Indexed:* BiolAb, DSR&OA, EnvAb, IndVet, OceAb, RRTA, SWRA, VetBull, WAE&RSA, ZooRec. *Bk. rev.:* Various number and length. *Aud.:* Ac, Sa.

An international, multidisciplinary journal covering the science, technology, management, and economics of fisheries. The theoretical or practical papers are written for economists, administrators, policy makers, legislators, and fisheries scientists.

3129. ***Fisheries Science.*** Supersedes in part (in 1994): *Nippon Suisan Gakkaishi (Bilingual Edition).* [ISSN: 0919-9268] 1935. bi-m. GBP 265 print & online eds. Ed(s): Nobuhito Fusetani. Blackwell Publishing Asia, 550 Swanston St, Carlton South, VIC 3053, Australia; subs@blackwellpublishingasia.com; http://www.blackwellpublishing.com/. Refereed. Circ: 5400. *Indexed:* BiolAb, ChemAb, DSA, FS&TA, HortAb, IndVet, S&F, SCI, VetBull, WAE&RSA, ZooRec. *Aud.:* Ac, Sa.

An international journal sponsored by the Japanese Society of Fisheries Science, this title has a long history of quality articles in all areas of the aquatic sciences.

3130. ***Fishery Bulletin.*** [ISSN: 0090-0656] 1881. q. USD 55. Ed(s): John V. Merriner, Sharyn Matriotti. U.S. National Marine Fisheries Service, Scientific Publications Office, 7600 Sandpoint Way, N E, Bin C15700, Seattle, WA 98115; http://spo.nwr.noaa.gov. Illus. Refereed. Circ: 2000. Vol. ends: No. 4. Microform: NTI; PQC. Online: Florida Center for Library Automation; Gale Group; OCLC Online Computer Library Center, Inc.; H.W. Wilson. Reprint: NTI. *Indexed:* B&AI, BiolAb, ChemAb, EnvAb, FS&TA, GeoRef, GeogAbPG, IUSGP, IndVet, OceAb, PollutAb, SCI, SWRA, VetBull, ZooRec. *Aud.:* Ac, Sa.

This quarterly publishes original research articles or technical notes on fisheries science, engineering, and economics. Most of the contributing authors work for the National Marine Fisheries Service, but some articles from other countries appear. The publication is available free in limited numbers to libraries, research institutions, and state and federal agencies, and in exchange for other scientific publications.

Freshwater and Marine Aquarium. See Pets section.

3131. ***Journal of Applied Aquaculture.*** [ISSN: 1045-4438] 1992. q. USD 325 domestic; USD 438.75 Canada; USD 471.25 elsewhere. Ed(s): Carl D Webster. Haworth Press, Inc., 10 Alice St, Binghamton, NY 13904-1580; getinfo@haworthpressinc.com; http://www.haworthpressinc.com. Illus., adv. Sample. Refereed. Circ: 181 Paid. Vol. ends: No. 4. Reprint: HAW. *Indexed:* Agr, EnvAb, FS&TA, GeogAbPG, HortAb, IndVet, OceAb, RRTA, S&F, VetBull, WAE&RSA, ZooRec. *Aud.:* Ac, Sa.

This is a worthwhile journal and valuable to scientists in the field. However, the Haworth pricing structure discriminates against libraries. It is recommended that individuals who will use the title subscribe, rather than the library that serves them.

3132. ***Journal of Applied Ichthyology.*** [ISSN: 0175-8659] 1984. 6x/yr. GBP 392 print & online. Ed(s): H Rosenthal. Blackwell Verlag GmbH, Kurfuerstendamm 57, Berlin, 10707, Germany; verlag@blackwell.de; http://www.blackwell.de. Adv. Refereed. Circ: 340. *Indexed:* BiolAb, ChemAb, DSA, FS&TA, IndVet, OceAb, SCI, SWRA, VetBull, WAE&RSA, ZooRec. *Bk. rev.:* Various number and length. *Aud.:* Ac, Sa.

Covering all areas of aquaculture and fisheries management, the *Journal of Applied Ichthyology* publishes refereed articles on a variety of fish species. Special emphasis is given to problems occurring in developing countries.

3133. ***Journal of Aquaculture in the Tropics.*** [ISSN: 0970-0846] 1986. q. EUR 259 (Individuals, EUR 220). Ed(s): Arabindo Nath Bose. Swets & Zeitlinger BV, PO Box 800, Lisse, 2160 SZ, Netherlands; orders@swets.nl; http://www.swets.nl. Illus., adv. Refereed. Vol. ends: Nov (No. 4). *Indexed:* Agr, BiolAb, ExcerpMed, ForAb, HortAb, IndVet, OceAb, PollutAb, S&F, VetBull, WAE&RSA, ZooRec. *Aud.:* Ac, Sa.

Publishes original research and review articles on the culture of tropical species. The first international journal specializing in tropical aquaculture. Most contributions are from Asia and the Middle East with others from South America, the United States, and the South Pacific Islands.

3134. ***Journal of Aquariculture and Aquatic Sciences.*** Formerly (until 1982): *Journal of Aquariculture.* [ISSN: 0733-2076] 1980. irreg. USD 140 (Individuals, USD 70). Ed(s): John Farrell Kuhns. The Written Word, 7601 E. Forest Lake Dr., N.W., Parkville, MO 64152; JFK@compuserve.com. Illus., index, adv. Refereed. Circ: 800 Paid. Online: CompuServe Inc. *Indexed:* BiolAb, DSR&OA, PollutAb, SWRA, ZooRec. *Bk. rev.:* Various number and length. *Aud.:* Ac, Sa.

This journal publishes original research articles, correspondence, short communications, book reviews, and product reviews for the aquarium science and technology field and for the aquatic sciences. "The *Journal of Aquariculture & Aquatic Sciences* is the only peer-reviewed, international, English-language journal covering aquarium science and technology and the affiliated sciences." Published on an irregular basis.

3135. *Journal of Aquatic Animal Health.* [ISSN: 0899-7659] 1989. q. USD 195 in North America; USD 209 elsewhere; USD 209 combined subscription in North America for print & online eds. Ed(s): Vicki Blazer. American Fisheries Society, 5410 Grosvenor Ln, Ste 110, Bethesda, MD 20814-2199; journals@fisheries.org; http://www.fisheries.org. Illus., adv. Refereed. Circ: 1500. Online: EBSCO Publishing. *Indexed:* BiolAb, EnvAb, FoVS&M, HortAb, IndVet, OceAb, SWRA, VetBull, ZooRec. *Aud.:* Ac, Sa.

One of the core publications of the American Fisheries Society, this journal covers the health of fish and shellfish in all environments. Topics include disease prevention and treatment, biochemical and physiological investigations, and environmental and pathogenic causes of disease.

3136. *Journal of Fish Biology.* [ISSN: 0022-1112] 1969. m. plus supp. GBP 1284 print & online. Ed(s): J F Craig. Blackwell Publishing Ltd., 9600 Garsington Rd, PO Box 805, Oxford, OX4 2DQ, United Kingdom; customerservices@oxon.blackwellpublishing.com; http://www.blackwellpublishers.co.uk/. Illus., index, adv. Refereed. Online: EBSCO Publishing; ingenta.com; OCLC Online Computer Library Center, Inc.; RoweCom Information Quest; ScienceDirect; Swets Blackwell. Reprint: SWZ. *Indexed:* AnBeAb, ApEcolAb, BiolAb, ChemAb, DSR&OA, EnvAb, ExcerpMed, FS&TA, ForAb, GeoRef, IndVet, OceAb, RRTA, S&F, SCI, SWRA, VetBull, WAE&RSA, WRCInf, ZooRec. *Bk. rev.:* Various number and length. *Aud.:* Ac, Sa.

Published for the Fisheries Society of the British Isles by Academic Press. This international journal is intended to foster the goal of the society to develop liaisons between those active in fisheries biology. It will not publish papers that harm or kill threatened or endangered fish to gather the data.

3137. *Journal of Fish Diseases.* [ISSN: 0140-7775] 1978. 9x/yr. GBP 801 print & online eds. Ed(s): R J Roberts, R Wootten. Blackwell Publishing Ltd., 9600 Garsington Rd, Oxford, OX4 2ZG, United Kingdom; customerservices@oxon.blackwellpublishing.com; http://www.blackwellpublishing.com. Illus., index, adv. Refereed. Circ: 555. Vol. ends: No. 9. Microform: PQC. Online: EBSCO Publishing; ingenta.com; Munksgaard & Blackwell Science's Synergy; OCLC Online Computer Library Center, Inc.; RoweCom Information Quest; Swets Blackwell. Reprint: ISI. *Indexed:* BiolAb, ChemAb, ExcerpMed, FoVS&M, IndVet, OceAb, SCI, VetBull, ZooRec. *Bk. rev.:* Various number and length. *Aud.:* Ac, Sa.

This international journal publishes research papers, short communications, review articles, and book reviews focusing on the diseases of fish. This journal would be valuable in a collection serving fish pathologists or environmental researchers.

3138. *Journal of Shellfish Research.* Formerly: *National Shellfisheries Association. Proceedings.* [ISSN: 0730-8000] 1981. s-a. USD 150 (Individuals, USD 65; Students, USD 35). Ed(s): Sandra E Shumway. National Shellfisheries Association, Inc., c/o University of Connecticut, Marine Science Dept, Groton, CT 06340; http://www.shellfish.org/. Illus., index. Refereed. Circ: 950. *Indexed:* BiolAb, ChemAb, DSR&OA, HortAb, IndVet, OceAb, RRTA, SCI, VetBull, WAE&RSA, ZooRec. *Aud.:* Ac, Sa.

This society publication covers all aspects of shellfish research. Technical meeting/symposium abstracts are included in some issues.

3139. *Marine Fisheries Review.* Formerly: *Commercial Fisheries Review.* [ISSN: 0090-1830] 1939. q. USD 16. Ed(s): W L Hobart. U.S. National Marine Fisheries Service, Scientific Publications Office, 7600 Sandpoint Way, N E, Bin C15700, Seattle, WA 98115; http://spo.nwr.noaa.gov. Illus., index. Refereed. Circ: 2000. Vol. ends: No. 4. Microform: CIS; NTI. Online: bigchalk; EBSCO Publishing; Florida Center for Library Automation; Gale Group; OCLC Online Computer Library Center, Inc.; H.W. Wilson. Reprint: CIS. *Indexed:* AmStI, B&AI, BiolAb, ChemAb, EnvAb, FS&TA, GeogAbPG, IUSGP, OceAb, PAIS, SWRA, VetBull. *Aud.:* Ac, Sa.

This journal concentrates on "in-depth review articles and practical or applied aspects of marine fisheries rather than pure research." Issues usually include about six articles. Valuable for researchers working with marine fisheries. Beginning with vol. 60, no. 1, the full contents of this title are available online. The print version is running very late.

3140. *North American Journal of Aquaculture.* Formerly (until 1999): *Progressive Fish-Culturist.* [ISSN: 1522-2055] 1934. q. Members, USD 33; Non-members, USD 195. Ed(s): William L Shelton, Bruce A Barton. American Fisheries Society, 5410 Grosvenor Ln, Ste 110, Bethesda, MD 20814-2199; journals@fisheries.org; http://www.fisheries.org. Illus., index, adv. Refereed. Circ: 2600. Vol. ends: No. 4. Microform: PQC. *Indexed:* B&AI, BiolAb, ChemAb, DSA, DSR&OA, EnvAb, ExcerpMed, HortAb, IUSGP, IndVet, OceAb, RRTA, S&F, SCI, SWRA, VetBull, WAE&RSA, WRCInf, ZooRec. *Bk. rev.:* Various number and length. *Aud.:* Ac, Sa.

Produced by the American Fisheries Society, this publication reports on commercial aquaculture operations (except for the aquarium trade). Any aquaculturist or scientist working with any aquatic species would find this publication useful.

3141. *North American Journal of Fisheries Management.* [ISSN: 0275-5947] 1981. q. USD 798. Ed(s): Carolyn Griswold. American Fisheries Society, 5410 Grosvenor Ln, Ste 110, Bethesda, MD 20814-2199; journals@fisheries.org; http://www.fisheries.org. Illus., index, adv. Refereed. Circ: 3300. Vol. ends: No. 4. *Indexed:* B&AI, BiolAb, ChemAb, DSR&OA, EnvAb, FPA, ForAb, GeogAbPG, IndVet, OceAb, RRTA, S&F, SWRA, VetBull, WAE&RSA, WRCInf, ZooRec. *Aud.:* Ac, Sa.

A quarterly publication to promote information exchanges between fisheries managers. "Publishes papers on the management of finfish and exploitable shellfish in marine and fresh waters. Contributions should relate in some way to the means which species, habitats, and harvests may be managed to protect and enhance fish and fishery resources for societal benefits."

3142. *Reviews in Fish Biology and Fisheries.* [ISSN: 0960-3166] q. EUR 589 print or online ed. Ed(s): Jennifer Nielsen. Kluwer Academic Publishers, van Godewijckstraat 30, PO Box 17, Dordrecht, 3300 AA, Netherlands; services@wkap.nl; http://www.wkap.nl. Adv. Refereed. Online: EBSCO Publishing; ingenta.com; Kluwer Online; OCLC Online Computer Library Center, Inc.; RoweCom Information Quest; Swets Blackwell. *Indexed:* AnBeAb, ApEcolAb, GeogAbPG, IndVet, OceAb, S&F, SCI, VetBull, WAE&RSA, ZooRec. *Aud.:* Ac, Sa.

Publishes four to six papers per issue and book reviews, conference reports, and "Points of View." The journal caters to all those interested in fish as an organism and tries to reach all levels, from the general public to the academic researcher.

3143. *Reviews in Fisheries Science.* [ISSN: 1064-1262] 1992. q. USD 450 (Individuals, USD 110 print & online eds.). Ed(s): Robert R Stickney. C R C Press, Llc, 2000 Corporate Blvd, N W, Boca Raton, FL 33431-9868; journals@crcpress.com; http://www.crcpress.com. Illus., index. Refereed. Vol. ends: No. 4. *Indexed:* C&ISA, OceAb. *Bk. rev.:* Various number and length. *Aud.:* Ac, Sa.

This journal is co-issued by the American Fisheries Society. It covers all aspects of fisheries science and gives up-to-date coverage of the latest hot issues.

Tropical Fish Hobbyist. See Pets section.

3144. *World Aquaculture Society. Journal.* Former titles: *World Mariculture Society. Journal; World Mariculture Society. Proceedings.* [ISSN: 0893-8849] 1986. q. USD 105 domestic; USD 115 in Canada & Mexico; USD 135 elsewhere. Ed(s): Craig Tucker. World Aquaculture Society, 143 J M Parker Coliseum, Louisiana State University, Baton Rouge, LA 70803; wasmas@aol.com; http://www.was.org. Illus. Refereed. Vol. ends: No. 4. *Indexed:* Agr, BiolAb, DSA, ForAb, GeogAbPG, IndVet, OceAb, S&F, SCI, VetBull, WAE&RSA, ZooRec. *Aud.:* Ac, Sa.

This journal publishes research articles on international aquaculture geared toward fisheries scientists. Articles cover the culture of aquatic plant and animal life, and topics include diseases, economics, genetics, physiology, and reproduction.

Electronic Journals

Many of the titles listed have electronic counterparts. Most of these add to the cost of the journal. Electronic-only options tend to cost the same or more, depending on the publisher.

3145. ***Aquaworld Magazine: the aquarium world.*** 1997. q. Ed(s): Raffaele Bufo. Aquaworld Magazine, c/o Raffaele Bufo, Via Vittorio Veneto 147, Margherita di Savoia (FG), 71044, Italy; rabufo@mail4.clio.it; http://www.aquaworldnet.com/awmag.shtml. Adv. *Aud.:* Ga.

"The aquarium world magazine" covers all aspects of the hobby (and, to a lesser extent, the profession) of aquariums and fish. Articles tend to be relatively detailed, with practical suggestions. There are good illustrations and reader forums. Although some of the material is in English, often an article is in another language (either French, German, Italian, or Spanish) with a translation provided. The web site is well worth exploring for more information on aquariums as a hobby. It is the founding site for the Aquaria Web Ring.

■ FISHING

Rachel Crane, Assistant Professor and Librarian, Wichita State University Libraries, Wichita State University, Wichita, KS 67260-0068

Introduction

The magazines in this section focus on the sport of fishing, and they are appropriate for all kinds of libraries. Various fishing interests are well covered here, with titles focusing on a diversity of fishing-related activities (*Fly Tyer*), a variety of species (*Bassmaster*), and diverse fishing habitats (*Salt Water Sportsman*). A few titles incorporate other outdoor activities, notably hunting (*Fishing and Hunting News*). Although most publications listed here are not indexed, this need not be a deterrent to subscription. The following titles, being popular by nature, can often be enjoyed simply by browsing, particularly as articles are often related to seasonal changes happening on the water.

Basic Periodicals

Ems: *Field and Stream, Outdoor Life;* Hs, Ga, Ac: *American Angler, Field and Stream, Fly Rod & Reel, In-Fisherman, Outdoor Life.*

Basic Abstracts and Indexes

Access, Consumers Index to Product Evaluations and Information Sources, Magazine Index, Readers' Guide to Periodical Literature, SportsSearch.

3146. ***American Angler: the magazine of fly fishing & fly tying.*** Former titles: *American Angler and Fly Tyer; American Fly Tyer; Fly Tyer.* [ISSN: 1055-6737] 1977. bi-m. USD 19.95 domestic; USD 29.95 Canada; USD 39.95 elsewhere. Ed(s): Phil Monahan. Morris Communications Company LLC, 735 Broad St, Augusta, GA 30901; http://www.morris.com. Adv. Circ: 60000 Paid. *Aud.:* Hs, Sa.

American Angler is a wonderful publication for fly fishers and tyers of all levels. Although focusing on cold water species, articles also appear about fishing with a fly for warm water and saltwater species. Regular contributors are the tops in their field. This title recently changed the look of its cover and layout, but it still contains regular columns and departments covering entomology, casting, warm water fly fishing, knots and rigging, fly fishing techniques, fly tying, new equipment, and reflective essays. Features focus on detailed descriptions of fishing locations and fly fishing tactics. Articles are well written, enjoyable, and accompanied by fine photo illustrations. Highly recommended for all libraries serving a fly fishing population.

3147. ***Bassin': official magazine of the weekend angler.*** Formerly (until 1985): *Pro Bass.* [ISSN: 0884-4739] 1974. 7x/yr. USD 15.95. Ed(s): Jason Sowards. NatCom, Inc., 15115 S 76th E Ave, Bixby, OK 74008; cs@natcom-publications.com; http://www.natcom-publications.com. Illus., adv. Sample. Circ: 250000 Paid. Vol. ends: Dec. *Aud.:* Ems, Hs, Sa.

This magazine is directed at bass fishing the world over. Each issue is devoted to seasonal themes plus other feature and regular articles. Some of these include letters, association news, tournaments and events, tips and techniques for the young and beginning angler, tackle and boat maintenance, and lure and bait reports. The information is accurate and appropriate for readers of any age. The species most frequently discussed are are largemouth, smallmouth, and spotted bass. Periodically, information about white, stripers, Suwanee, pavon, or peacock bass is given. *Bassin'* would be well read in any library since bass fishing occurs throughout North America. The magazine has a web site, and some features are available to whet your appetite.

3148. ***Bassmaster Magazine.*** [ISSN: 0199-3291] 1968. 10x/yr. USD 20 domestic; USD 30 foreign. Ed(s): Dave Precht. B.A.S.S., Inc., PO Box 17900, Montgomery, AL 36141; bassmag@mindspring.com; http://www.bassmaster.com. Illus., adv. Circ: 600000. *Aud.:* Ga, Hs.

Bassmaster focuses on all aspects of bass fishing, but with an emphasis on bass tournament fishing. Articles cover the latest techniques, new products, tournament reports, tips from tournament professionals, conservation issues, and boating information. An annual subscription is part of a membership to the B.A.S.S. Federation, an organization dedicated to the preservation of bass fishing. *Bassmaster* would be well read in any library since bass fishing occurs throughout North America.

3149. ***Crappie World.*** Formerly (until 199?): *Crappie.* [ISSN: 1072-9011] 1989. q. USD 15.95. Ed(s): Jason Sowards. NatCom, Inc., 15115 S 76th E Ave, Bixby, OK 74008; cs@natcom-publications.com; http://www.natcom-publications.com. Illus., adv. Sample. Circ: 100000 Paid. Vol. ends: Dec. *Aud.:* Ems, Hs, Sa.

Crappie is a specialized magazine for crappie fishing. It presents information in a thorough, professional manner and covers all age groups and locations for crappie fishing. The crappie fisherperson can find information about upcoming tournaments and other events, recipes, letters, techniques for different seasons, equipment and accessory evaluations, and fishing stories. *Crappie* has good information for libraries near crappie waters, essentially all across North America.

Disabled Outdoors Magazine. See Hiking, Climbing, and Outdoor Recreation section.

Field and Stream. See Hunting and Guns section.

3150. ***Fish & Fly: for the adventure angler.*** [ISSN: 1535-6353] q. USD 15.95 domestic; USD 23.95 Canada; USD 35.95 elsewhere. Riversong Communications, LLC, PO Box 3666, Seattle, WA 98124; sales@flyandfishmagazine.com. Adv. *Aud.:* Sa.

This is a relatively new publication, and it fills a niche for the traveling angler looking for new directions to explore. Produced for the fly fisher, in-depth articles focus primarily on fishing destinations from exotic locations to neighborhood streams; as the subtitle says, this magazine is "for the adventure angler." The publication is excellently produced, with enticing feature articles accompanied by wonderful photographs, fly recipes, and local information. Departments include readers' fishing logs, letters, and reports from home waters. Although it has the look of an expensive title, its reasonable subscription price makes it an excellent publication to have in the library.

3151. ***Fishing and Hunting News: the nation's largest outdoor newspaper.*** [ISSN: 0015-301X] 1944. 24x/yr. USD 39.95; USD 2.99 newsstand/cover per issue. Ed(s): Joel Shangle, Jamie Parks. Outdoor Empire Publishing, Inc., 511 Eastlake Ave E, Box 19000, Seattle, WA 98109; advertising@fhnews.com; http://www.fishingandhuntingnews.com. Illus. Sample. Circ: 117000 Paid. Vol. ends: Dec. *Aud.:* Hs, Ga.

Fishing and Hunting News publishes seven local editions: Washington, Oregon, California, Rocky Mountain, Colorado, Great Lakes, and Mid-Atlantic, covering 15 states. The locally written articles and frequency give this magazine characteristics not found in any other periodical in this section. The photographs are well done, and many articles have charts, maps, and statistics. A publication of this quality, full of local expert advice from cover to cover, should not be ignored by libraries. The magazine's web site contains a small selection of features for each of the seven editions.

3152. ***Fly Fisherman: the leading magazine of fly fishing.*** [ISSN: 0015-4741] 1969. 6x/yr. USD 19.95 domestic; USD 30 foreign; USD 4.99 newsstand/cover per issue. Ed(s): John Randolph. Primedia Enthusiast Group, 6405 Flank Dr, Harrisburg, PA 17112; http://www.primedia.com. Illus., adv. Sample. Circ: 151774 Paid. Vol. ends: Nov. Reprint: PQC. *Bk. rev.:* 2-3; 500 words. *Aud.:* Hs, Sa.

Fly Fisherman is devoted solely to the sport of fly fishing. The articles cover fresh or saltwater fly fishing, any species of fish, and information useful to the expert or novice fly fisherperson. A unique trait of this publication is the international geographic coverage specific to fly fishing. The magazine has full-color photographs, well-written articles, and a little something for every fly fisherperson. For some feature articles in full-text, other reports, equipment, and a large database of fly patterns, go to the *Fly Fisherman's* Virtual Flyshop web site at http://www.flyfisherman.com.

3153. ***Fly Rod & Reel: the magazine of American fly-fishing.*** Formerly: *Rod and Reel.* [ISSN: 1045-0149] 1979. 6x/yr. USD 16.97 domestic; USD 26.97 foreign; USD 4.99 newsstand/cover per issue. Ed(s): Paul Guernsey. Down East Enterprise, Inc., PO Box 679, Camden, ME 04843-0370. Illus., adv. Sample. Circ: 63422 Paid. Vol. ends: Dec. *Bk. rev.:* 1-4, 500-1,500 words. *Aud.:* Sa.

Feature articles in each issue cover North, Central, and South Americas, while all subjects related to fly fishing and equipment are covered throughout the year. Regular departments explore fly tying, conservation, letters, fly casting, books, and classified ads. The features are personal stories, while the departments give more technical and how-to information. This fly fishing magazine can stand up to any of the competition, with excellent, accurate information and illustrations. For the price, *Fly Rod & Reel* is a good bargain, with information for any angler. The web site at http://www.flyrodreel.com provides an excellent preview of the printed magazine.

3154. ***Fly Tyer.*** [ISSN: 1082-1309] q. USD 21.65 domestic; USD 31.95 Canada; USD 41.95 elsewhere. Ed(s): David Klausmeyer. Morris Communications Company LLC, 735 Broad St, Augusta, GA 30901; http://www.morris.com. Adv. *Aud.:* Hs, Sa.

Fly Tyer is unique in its exclusive focus on fly tying. Flies for all species and all tying techniques are presented here. Columns cover tying history, new innovations, tips for new tyers, and materials selection. Features are in-depth pieces on fly patterns and tying methods. Patterns are presented in a clear and concise fashion with outstanding illustrations. This publication is worth the subscription price for the illustrations alone. Recommended for libraries supporting fly fishers.

3155. ***Flyfishing and Tying Journal.*** Former titles (until 199?): *Flyfishing;* (until 1997): *Western Flyfishing;* (until 1996): *Flyfishing.* 1978. q. USD 18.95 domestic; USD 23.95 foreign. Ed(s): Dave Hughes. Frank Amato Publications, Inc, PO Box 82112, Portland, OR 97282; info@amatobooks.com; http://www.amatobooks.com. Adv. Circ: 36056 Paid. *Bk. rev.:* 5, 200-500 words. *Aud.:* Hs, Sa.

Formerly known as *Western Flyfishing*, this title does emphasize Western waters in the United States, but overall coverage is international. North America is covered in each issue, and occasionally fishing locations in other countries are featured. As a publication that emphasizes both fishing and tying, the journal covers casting, fly tying, knots, places to fish, conservation, new products, and fishing news. Each issue has contributions from outstanding authors in the field, accompanied by excellent, useful illustrations. Fly fishing readers living in the West or traveling to fish in the West would get their money's worth from this publication, and so would libraries. Highly recommended.

Fur-Fish-Game. See Hunting and Guns section.

3156. ***Game & Fish.*** m. USD 14.97. Primedia Enthusiast Group, 260 Madison Ave, 8th Fl, New York, NY 10016; http://www.primedia.com. Adv. *Aud.:* Hs, Ga.

Game & Fish produces regional editions for 30 states and/or regions of the United States. This publication excels in providing timely detailed information close to home for both fishers and hunters. Contained here are feature articles covering recommended places to fish, current water conditions, suggested techniques, conservation, and new products pertaining to all species and fishing methods in the appropriate locality. Recommended for libraries serving those who wish to explore their local fishing resources. Additional information is available on the *Game & Fish* web site: http://www.gameandfishmag.com.

Gray's Sporting Journal. See Hunting and Guns section.

3157. ***In-Fisherman: the journal of freshwater fishing.*** [ISSN: 0276-9905] 1975. 8x/yr. USD 24 domestic; USD 34 Canada; USD 36 elsewhere. Ed(s): Mike Carney. Primedia Enthusiast Group, 6405 Flank Dr, Harrisburg, PA 17112; http://www.primedia.com. Illus., adv. Sample. Circ: 333040 Paid. Vol. ends: Nov. *Indexed:* ASIP. *Aud.:* Hs, Ga, Ac.

In-Fisherman coverage is complete, covering freshwater fish, lures, tactics, strategies, biology, the science of fisheries, and all kinds of waterways. Each issue of over 100 pages focuses on common fish species such as bass, walleye, pike, muskie, crappie, bluegill, perch, and catfish, with minor species covered in at least one article. Articles are well written by professional, experienced staff and have excellent illustrations. No library could go wrong with a subscription to *In-Fisherman.* It is the Cadillac of fishing magazines for older readers. Four annual guides are produced in addition to the magazine and are worth considering for purchase: *Walleye Guide, Ice-fishing Guide, Bass Guide,* and *Catfish In-sider Guide.* All this can be found at their web site: http://www.in-fisherman.com.

3158. ***Musky Hunter Magazine.*** [ISSN: 1079-3402] 1989. bi-m. USD 20.95 domestic; USD 23.95 foreign. Ed(s): Jim Saric. Esox Promotions, Inc, 7978 Hwy 70 East, St Germain, WI 54558; info@muskyhunter.com; http://www.muskyhunter.com. Adv. Circ: 32000 Paid. *Aud.:* Hs, Sa.

This is a specialized publication focusing on muskellunge and musky fishing in all areas of their range in North America. As muskies are a fish of northern regions, this title would be a particular asset to a collection serving this area of the United States or Canada. Articles focus on fishing methods, fishing history, lake profiles, angler interviews, biology, and research. Regular departments highlight reports of big fish catches, tournaments, questions answered by pro fishermen, and new gear. Informative articles are accompanied by excellent photographs that may be enough to influence any outdoors person to take up the pursuit of muskies. Recommended for public libraries residing in areas with a substantial population of muskellunge.

3159. ***North American Fisherman.*** Incorporates (1955-1996): *Fishing World.* [ISSN: 1043-2450] 1988. 7x/yr. Membership, USD 12. Ed(s): Kurt Beckstrom. North American Media Group, Inc., 12301 Whitewater Dr, Ste 260, Minnetonka, MN 55343. Illus., adv. Sample. Circ: 500000 Paid. Vol. ends: Dec. *Aud.:* Ga.

North American Fisherman is published by the fisherman for the fisherman. The North American Fishing Club provides a forum for exchanging fishing tips and information to people who fish as a pastime. Among the topics covered by this largest multispecies freshwater fishing publication are bass, panfish, trout and salmon, walleye, fly fishing, boats and accessories, and saltwater. Feature articles are more in-depth than regular columns, which include letters, conservation news, club news, Q&A, and humor. This is a fine overall fishing publication, although not at the professional level of *In-Fisherman* or *Fly Fisherman.* Look at the web site for club details.

Outdoor Life. See Hiking, Climbing, and Outdoor Recreation section.

3160. ***Salt Water Sportsman.*** [ISSN: 0036-3618] 1939. m. USD 19.97; USD 4.99 newsstand/cover per issue. Ed(s): C M Rip Cunningham. Time4 Media, Inc., Salt Water Sportsman, 263 Summer St, Boston, MA 02210-1506; editor@saltwatersportsman.com; http://www.saltwatersportsman.com. Illus., adv. Sample. Circ: 150000 Paid. Vol. ends: Jan. Online: EBSCO Publishing; Gale Group. *Indexed:* ConsI, SportS. *Aud.:* Sa.

Salt Water Sportsman is the only magazine in this section that provides international coverage for all methods of saltwater fishing including fly fishing, bottom fishing, and trolling. The full-color publication is written by professionals practicing what they preach. Excellent articles and photos present information on fish facts, tales, rigging, techniques, boats, products, destinations, offshore news, and sportfishing news. Feature articles cover more specialized topics on specific fish, equipment, management, and conservation matters. This magazine is a source of saltwater and offshore fishing information that is not found in similar periodicals.

3161. ***Saltwater Fly Fishing.*** [ISSN: 1082-1295] 1995. bi-m. USD 14.95 United States; USD 22.95 Canada; USD 34.95 rest of world. Ed(s): Art Scheck. Morris Communications Company LLC, 735 Broad St, Augusta, GA 30901; http://www.morris.com. Adv. *Aud.:* Hs, Sa.

As a specialized publication, *Saltwater Fly Fishing* caters to those who approach the seas with a fly rod and reel. Though it focuses on fly fishing on the coasts of North America, this publication is international in scope. All aspects of the sport are covered. Regular columns discuss casting, gear, fish behavior, fly tying, boating, and tactics. Features consist of regional reports, different species, new gear, and angling techniques. All articles are well written and contributed by prominent authors in the sport. Highly recommended for libraries near saltwater locations.

Tropical Fish Hobbyist. See Pets section.

3162. ***Walleye In-Sider.*** [ISSN: 1068-2112] 1989. bi-m. USD 14.97 domestic; USD 24.97 Canada; USD 26.97 elsewhere. Ed(s): Doug Stange. Primedia Enthusiast Group, 6405 Flank Dr, Harrisburg, PA 17112; http://www.primedia.com. Illus., adv. Circ: 74885 Paid. *Aud.:* Hs, Sa.

This is a specialized publication covering all aspects of walleye fishing in the United States and Canada. Articles emphasize methods and techniques used in the pursuit of walleye. Regular departments discuss fishing locations, travel, tackle, recipes, fish biology, electronic accessories, boat maintenance, best times to fish, and methods of fishing. In addition, lots of tournament information is provided. Articles are well written and provide practical information for anglers of all levels.

Women & Guns Magazine. See Women section.

Electronic Journals

3163. ***Fine Fishing.*** 1995. w. Ed(s): Louis Bignami. Fine Fishing, 1914 Conestoga St, Moscow, ID 83843; bignami@finefishing.com; http://www.finefishing.com. Adv. *Aud.:* Hs, Ga.

From the area of the best fishing in the world comes this plug for the art. The Idaho publisher has the usual mix of interviews, tips on fishing, equipment notes, where to go, what to see, etc. The articles are well written by professionals, both sportsmen and writers, and are in three categories: saltwater, freshwater, and fly fishing. A must for both expert and amateur, this is one online magazine you will want on your line.

■ FOLKLORE

Jean Piper Burton, Technical Services Librarian, FH Green Library, West Chester University of Pennsylvania, West Chester, PA 19383

Introduction

Folklore can be defined as cultural materials that are part of a group of people and are passed by oral communication, customary example, and imitation. Folk traditions can be a part of many generations or of recent developments in pop culture. Because everyone is a part of some folk-culture group, there is interest in the subject by both layperson and scholar.

To accommodate both the general reader and the researcher, there are a wide variety of publications with differing scopes. Some of the titles are concerned with a specific geographic area, some take a historical perspective, and some are research oriented. The titles reviewed here try to represent this variety. Over the past few years there have appeared more and more folklore resources on the web. Most societies and many individual folklorists have their own web site, and often these will include selected publications from the society's journal. Some of the journal titles can be found in e-format but require a paid subscription. Articles from some of the titles are available as full text through electronic indexing services. The journals listed under the electronic journals subsection are samples of e-journals in the area of folklore. They were selected as samples because they are published only in e-form by known institutions, provide free access, and indicate continuing activity.

Basic Periodicals

Hs: *The Foxfire Magazine;* Ga: *Journal of American Culture, Storytelling Magazine;* Ac: *Ethnologies, Folklore, Journal of American Folklore, Journal of Folklore Research.*

Basic Abstracts and Indexes

America: History and Life, Historical Abstracts, Humanities Index, Modern Language Abstracts.

3164. ***Asian Folklore Studies.*** Formerly (until vol.22, 1963): *Folklore Studies.* [ISSN: 0385-2342] 1942. s-a. JPY 6000 (Individuals, JPY 3000). Ed(s): Peter Knecht. Nanzan University, 18 Yamazato-cho, Showa-ku, Nagoya-shi, 466-8673, Japan; http://www.ic.nanzan-u.ac/jp/. Illus., adv. Refereed. Circ: 350. Vol. ends: No. 2. Microform: IDC. Online: EBSCO Publishing; Florida Center for Library Automation; Gale Group; Northern Light Technology, Inc.; OCLC Online Computer Library Center, Inc.; ProQuest Information & Learning; H.W. Wilson. Reprint: ISI; PQC. *Indexed:* AICP, ArtHuCI, BAS, HumInd, IBSS, IBZ, MLA-IB, RI-1, SSCI. *Bk. rev.:* 30, 1,000 words. *Aud.:* Ac.

This journal publishes scholarly research on the folklore of Asian nations, including literary works and the oral tradition; it also discusses folkloric aspects of belief, cultural customs, and art. The journal includes scholarly articles, research materials, communications, and book reviews. An example of research materials is a recent inventory of the folk-medicinal plants of Nagaland, India, including the scientific name and use of each plant. Some of the articles are purely descriptive accounts or retellings of folk tales; others are more analytic, based on research, including surveys and textual analysis or comparative study. Examples of recent topics are possible explanations for the rock sky myth of Japan, a survey on tricksters of Tibetan folklore with a recounting of important tales, and the bards and poetic forms of Saurashtra, India. Abstracts are included. Most but not all of the articles are in English; some are in French or German. The book reviews are grouped by country. Recommended for academic libraries with an interest in Asian literature or arts, folklore, or children's literature. (ChD)

3165. ***Australian Folklore.*** [ISSN: 0819-0852] 1987. a. AUD 30 (Individuals, AUD 25). Ed(s): J.S. Ryan. Australian Folklore Association, c/o Prof. J.S. Ryan, Ed., School of English Communication and Theatre,

University Of New England, NSW 2351, Australia; jryan@metz.une.edu.au; http://www.une.edu.au/arts/FolkloreJournal/AF.htm. Illus., adv. Refereed. Circ: 320 Paid. *Indexed:* IBZ, MLA-IB. *Bk. rev.:* 500-700 words. *Aud.:* Ac.

A scholarly journal devoted to mostly Australian folklore with a few articles on British and American folk subjects. Article topics cover a wide range of lore from sport to music and pop culture to traditional customs. Most articles have reference lists and/or bibliographies. Occasional issues are devoted to a single theme or to a noted folklorist and his or her work. Book reviews are split into "Australian" and "Comparative/International." Although not always an easy title to acquire, it does provide an excellent source for students of Australian folklore. Recommended for universities that support a strong folklore program.

3166. *Children's Folklore Review.* [ISSN: 0739-5558] 1979. s-a. USD 10. Ed(s): C W Sullivan, III. East Carolina University, E Fifth St, Greenville, NC 27858-4353; http://www.acls.org/afolks.htm. Circ: 150. *Indexed:* MLA-IB. *Aud.:* Ga, Ac.

Published by the Children's Folklore Section of the American Folklore Society, the scope of this title covers "all aspects of children's traditions—oral, customary, and material." Articles may also deal with the use of folklore in children's literature, education, and pop culture. Issues average two lengthy articles plus letters to the editor and section announcements. There is also a feature called "E-Contributions" that deals with e-correspondence among members. Although the format of only two feature articles may be limiting, it is a good title for those doing research in children and folklore, especially since titles that deal strictly with children's lore are not plentiful. It is also a good source for those working in critical review of children's literature as a genre.

3167. *Culture & Tradition.* [ISSN: 0701-0184] 1976. a. CND 8. Memorial University of Newfoundland, Arts and Admin. Bldg., PO Box 115, St. John's, NF A1C 5S7, Canada; CULTURE@Kean.ucs.mun.ca. Illus. Circ: 300. *Indexed:* AICP, CBCARef, CPerI, MLA-IB. *Aud.:* Ac.

Published by the graduate students of Folklore at Memorial University of Newfoundland, *Culture & Tradition* is Canada's longest running bilingual folklore journal. Published in English and French, the journal covers all aspects of folklore from traditional art and music to cultural psychology and sociological structure. Published annually, each volume contains an average of six articles, a section on book reviews, and several media reviews. In the issues with fewer book reviews, the reviews are quite lengthy. Some of the earlier volumes were edited loosely around broad themes such as music or the supernatural. A more recent issue covered the annual meeting of the Folklore Studies Association of Canada. Because it covers more than just regional topics, this is a good title for academic folklore programs.

3168. *Ethnologies.* Formerly: *Canadian Folklore.* [ISSN: 1481-5974] 1979. a. CND 65 (Individuals, CND 45; Students, CND 25). Ed(s): Nancy Schmitz. Folklore Studies Association of Canada, c/o Universite Laval, Pavillon Charles de Koninck, Quebec, PQ G1K 7P4, Canada; cfe@celat.ulaval.ca; http://www.fl.ulaval.ca/celat/acef. Illus., adv. Refereed. Circ: 500. Vol. ends: No. 2. *Indexed:* AmH&L, CBCARef, CPerI, HumInd, IBSS, MLA-IB. *Aud.:* Ac.

Published by the Folklore Studies Association of Canada, *Ethnologies* is a continuation of *Canadian Folklore/Folklore Canadien.* There seems to be little change in scope or content. Each issue of this journal is devoted to a specific topic. Themes are of a wide range, from the historic and traditional to the current trends in the field. In the several copies reviewed, the number of articles in French and in English varied, but abstracts for each article were in both languages. The review section includes both book and media titles. For academic libraries that support folk studies programs, this journal is a needed addition. Recommended for large public libraries with strong folk and culture collections.

3169. *Folklore.* [ISSN: 0015-587X] 1890. 3x/yr. GBP 185. Ed(s): Gillian Bennett. Routledge, 11 New Fetter Ln, London, EC4P 4EE, United Kingdom; journals@routldege.com; http://www.routledge.com. Illus., adv. Sample. Refereed. Circ: 1300 Paid. Microform: PMC. Online: bigchalk; Chadwyck-Healey Incorporated; EBSCO Publishing; Florida Center for Library Automation; Gale Group; Ingenta Select; Northern Light Technology, Inc.; OCLC Online Computer Library Center, Inc.; ProQuest Information & Learning; RoweCom Information Quest; Swets Blackwell; H.W. Wilson. Reprint: PSC. *Indexed:* AICP, ArtHuCI, BEL&L, BHA, BrArAb, BrHumI, HumInd, IBSS, IBZ, MLA-IB, NumL, RILM. *Bk. rev.:* 20, 500-700 words. *Aud.:* Ac.

A British publication, this scholarly journal considers itself a forum for European folk studies and culture, but most articles are on the United Kingdom. In addition to articles, some issues include papers from society meetings. Most issues include the "Topic, Notes, and Comments" section, which covers comments on articles and reviews in past issues plus reports on current meetings and conferences. Bibliographies, articles on recipients of awards in the field, and book reviews are located in the section "Review of Folklore Scholarship." This journal is for libraries that provide research materials in the area of folk studies.

3170. *Folklore Forum.* [ISSN: 0015-5926] 1968. s-a. USD 24 (Individuals, USD 15; Students, USD 10). Ed(s): Danille Christensen Lindquist. Folklore & Ethnomusicology Publications, Inc., 504 N Fess, Bloomington, IN 47408; folkpub@ucs.indiana.edu. Illus., adv. Refereed. Circ: 300 Paid. Vol. ends: No. 2. *Indexed:* ABS&EES, BAS, MLA-IB. *Bk. rev.:* 5-7, 500-600 words. *Aud.:* Ac.

Edited by graduate students at the Folklore Institute of Indiana University, this journal publishes articles that are interdisciplinary in nature. Many of the contributors are from outside the Folklore Institute. The "Open Form" section contains informal dialogue about the discipline, with short essays and responses. Issues average five to seven book reviews on a wide variety of subjects. Some volumes are devoted to a single topic. Although a good journal for cross-discipline coverage, it does have a history of delayed publication.

The Foxfire Magazine. See Teenagers section.

3171. *Journal of American Culture.* Former titles (until 2003): *Journal of American and Comparative Culture;* (until June 2001): *Journal of American Culture.* [ISSN: 1542-7331] 1978. q. USD 132 print & online eds. Ed(s): Ray Browne. Blackwell Publishing, Inc., Commerce Place, 350 Main St, Malden, MA 02148; subscrip@blackwellpub.com; http://www.blackwellpub.com. Illus. Refereed. Circ: 1200. Vol. ends: No. 4. Microform: PQC; NRP. Online: ingenta.com; Northern Light Technology, Inc. *Indexed:* ABS&EES, AmH&L, ArtHuCI, BRI, CBRI, CommAb, FLI, HumInd, IIMP, LRI, MLA-IB, PRA, PSA, RRTA, SociolAb. *Bk. rev.:* 20-30, 300-500 words. *Aud.:* Ga, Ac.

As the official journal of the American Cultural Association, the purpose of this publication is to "promote and facilitate American culture in its broadest sense." Contributors must be members of the association. There is a mix of historic and present-day material. Articles cover traditional folklore themes as well as pieces on pop culture. With the wide variety of topics and the accessible style of writing, this title will be of interest to the general reader and the student of folk studies.

3172. *Journal of American Folklore.* [ISSN: 0021-8715] 1888. q. USD 85 domestic; USD 105 foreign. Ed(s): Elaine Lawless. University of Illinois Press, 1325 S Oak St, Champaign, IL 61820-6903; uipress@uillinois.edu; http://www.press.uillinois.edu. Illus., index, adv. Refereed. Circ: 3000. Vol. ends: No. 4. Microform: MIM; PMC; PQC. Online: Chadwyck-Healey Incorporated; Gale Group; JSTOR (Web-based Journal Archive); OCLC Online Computer Library Center, Inc.; Project MUSE; ProQuest Information & Learning; RoweCom Information Quest; Swets Blackwell; H.W. Wilson. Reprint: ISI; PQC; PSC. *Indexed:* ABS&EES, AICP, AmH&L, AnthLit, ArtHuCI, BEL&L, BHA, BRI, CBRI, HumInd, IIMP, L&LBA, MLA-IB, MagInd, MusicInd, RI-1, RILM, SSCI, SociolAb. *Bk. rev.:* 10, 500-700 words. *Aud.:* Ga, Ac.

Although there is an emphasis on the United States, the scope of this journal is worldwide and varied. Articles past and present include topics such as fieldwork among the Sephardim, folklore in schools and multicultural education, or Scandinavian immigrants in the Pacific Northwest. Occasional issues are devoted to a single theme. The "Notes" section includes shorter articles on a focused topic. A new section titled "Dialogues" has been added and is designed to encourage reader response. Reviews are lengthy and cover both media reviews and book reviews. The journal has recently changed editorship and the new editor states that she wants to "push the boundaries, explore the borders, and expand the parameters of folklore." Academic libraries should select this title for their basic collection, and large public libraries will also want to consider it.

3173. ***Journal of Cultural Geography.*** [ISSN: 0887-3631] 1980. s-a. USD 25 (Individuals, USD 20). Ed(s): Louis Seig. Popular Press, Bowling Green State University, Jerome Library Room 100, Bowling Green, OH 43403; http://www.bgsu.edu/offices/press. Illus., adv. Circ: 600. Vol. ends: No. 2. Online: EBSCO Publishing; Florida Center for Library Automation; Gale Group. *Indexed:* AmH&L, BAS, MLA-IB, RI-1, RILM, WAE&RSA. *Bk. rev.:* 12, 400-500 words. *Aud.:* Ac.

This journal's articles discuss the influences of culture on the physical world. Topics vary widely, from the historic to present-day pop culture. Articles cover a wide area of folklore, from country-music radio to pilgrimages to holy sites. Some issues are thematic. Most contributors are professors or graduate students. In addition to articles, there are book reviews and occasional annotated bibliographies. This title should appeal to a variety of readers. A good pick for academic libraries and larger public libraries.

3174. ***Journal of Folklore Research: an international journal of folklore and ethnomusicology.*** Former titles: *Folklore Institute. Journal; Indiana University. Folklore Institute Journal.* [ISSN: 0737-7037] 1964. 3x/yr. USD 50; USD 70 combined subscription print & online eds. Ed(s): Mary Ellen Brown. Indiana University Press, 601 N Morton St, Bloomington, IN 47404; journals@indiana.edu; http://www.indiana.edu/~iupress. Illus., index, adv. Refereed. Circ: 700. Vol. ends: No. 3. Microform: PQC. Online: Florida Center for Library Automation; Gale Group; OCLC Online Computer Library Center, Inc.; Project MUSE; H.W. Wilson. *Indexed:* AICP, ArtHuCI, BEL&L, HumInd, IBSS, IBZ, IIMP, MLA-IB, MusicInd, SSCI. *Aud.:* Ac.

This scholarly journal is published by the Indiana University Folklore Institute. Its purpose is to provide a forum for research and theory in the field of folklore. It is international in scope. Issues cover a wide range of topics. Articles are usually related under a central theme or may highlight a noted folklorist. Most of the reviews have been moved to "Booknotes." on the institute's web site. However, more substantial ones still appear in the journal. This title is a must choice for libraries serving academic folklore research and folklore programs.

3175. ***Journal of Latin American Lore.*** [ISSN: 0360-1927] 1975. s-a. USD 45 (Individuals, USD 40). Ed(s): Colleen H Trujillo, Johannes Wilbert. University of California at Los Angeles, Latin American Center, 10343 Bunche Hall, Box 951447, Los Angeles, CA 90095-1447; lacpubs@isop.ucla.edu; http://www.isop.ucla.edu/centers/locframe.html. Illus., index, adv. Refereed. Circ: 325. Vol. ends: No. 2. *Indexed:* AICP, AmH&L, AnthLit, ArtHuCI, HAPI, HumInd, MLA-IB, RI-1. *Aud.:* Ac.

This journal is devoted to folk culture of Latin America, and its scope is from prehistoric times to the present day. Article research uses "records of ancient civilizations, indigenous groups, peasant communities, and the elite and popular sectors of modern urban society." Most pieces are scholarly in nature and most are in English. Although its publication schedule is erratic, it is a good title for academic libraries that support Latin American Studies programs. Large public libraries that serve Latino communities may want to consider it.

3176. ***Louisiana Folklore Miscellany.*** [ISSN: 0090-9769] 1958. a. USD 10 (Individuals, USD 7). Ed(s): Marcia Gaudet. Louisiana Folklore Society, c/o Dept of English, Loyola University, New Orleans, LA 70118. *Aud.:* Ga, Ac.

Published under the auspices of the Louisiana Folklore Society, *Miscellany* is described on the society's web page as a publication of "articles, notes, and commentaries on all aspects of Louisiana folklore and folklife." What makes this journal a standout in the group of southern folklore journals is its wide variety of southern cultural topics. It is an excellent source for articles on Cajun and Creole social life and customs. Issues have included topics on quilting, oral narratives, ethnicity in Louisiana product names, Christmas levee bonfires, food, Mardi Gras chase, blues/gospel music, and midwifery. The society's web page offers full text of some articles. This is a great publication for general readers interested in the traditions of the South as well as the folklore researcher. Highly recommended for a "Southern folklore" title.

3177. ***Mid-America Folklore.*** Formerly (until vol.7, 1979): *Mid-South Folklore.* [ISSN: 0275-6013] 1973. 2x/yr. USD 10. Ed(s): Robert Cochran. Mid-America Folklore Society, Center for Ozark Studies, University of Arkansas, Fayetteville, AR 72701; http://www.theology.org/APUC/hjou.html. Illus. Refereed. Circ: 200. Vol. ends: No. 2. *Indexed:* BHA, MLA-IB, RI-1, RILM. *Bk. rev.:* 16, 100-300 words. *Aud.:* Ga, Ac.

This journal is an example of a regional title. While it covers a variety of subjects, most topics involve interests in the Midwest. Articles cover traditional folklore topics as well as pop culture. It is a good source for information on the lore of the Ozark area. Signed book reviews are well written and cover a variety of materials. This is a good title for libraries within the geographic region or those interested in Midwestern folk culture.

3178. ***Mississippi Folklife.*** Formerly: *Mississippi Folklore Register.* 1967. s-a. USD 10. Ed(s): Ted Dunbyn. University of Mississippi, Center for the Study of Southern Culture, Barnard Observatory, PO Box 1848, University, MS 38677-9836; http://imp.cssc.olemiss.edu/publications/missfolf/backissues/. Illus., adv. Circ: 350. Vol. ends: No. 2. *Indexed:* MLA-IB. *Bk. rev.:* 2-3, 300-500 words. *Aud.:* Ga, Ac.

Stating that it takes "a wide view of what is folk," this title covers subjects from the historical to present-day pop culture. Some issues are thematic. Contents may include articles, photographic essays, and reviews. Reviews, both book and media, are well written. Although the scope of the journal is Mississippi and adjoining regions, it is a good title for Southern folk life in general. A must for libraries of its region and a good bet for libraries interested in Southern folk culture.

3179. ***North Carolina Folklore Journal.*** Formerly (until 1972): *North Carolina Folklore.* [ISSN: 0090-5844] 1948. 2x/yr. USD 25 (Individuals, USD 20; Students, USD 12). Ed(s): Carmine Prioli. North Carolina Folklore Society, PO Box 62271, Durham, NC 27715; newmanj@mail.ecu.edu; http://www.ecu.edu. Illus. Refereed. Circ: 500. Vol. ends: No. 2. *Indexed:* IIMP, MLA-IB, MusicInd. *Bk. rev.:* 1-2, 300 words. *Aud.:* Ga, Ac.

Published by the North Carolina Folklore Society, this title's scope is "folk culture traditions in and related to North Carolina." Topics include the historical, the traditional, and the contemporary. Issues can be thematic, delving into all aspects of a subject from geographic and occupational influences to community and domestic life. Reviews are for books and media and also for exhibits. Although not lengthy, they are well written. This journal is good not only for those interested in North Carolina folk culture, but also for those interested in the folklore of southern Appalachia and the southeastern coast. Its easy reading style makes it a title for general as well as academic library audiences.

3180. ***Now & Then: the Appalachian magazine.*** [ISSN: 0896-2693] 1984. 3x/yr. USD 25 (Individuals, USD 20 Membership contribution). Ed(s): Nancy Fischman, Jane Harris Woodside. East Tennessee State University, Center for Appalachian Studies and Services, PO Box 70556, Johnson City, TN 37614-0556; woodsidj@etsu.edu; http://cass.etsu.edu/n&t/. Circ: 1500. *Indexed:* CIJE, MLA-IB. *Bk. rev.:* 5, 500 words. *Aud.:* Ga.

Sponsored by the Center for Appalachian Studies and Services, this journal is a great source of folk culture relating to Appalachia. It is a nice mix of articles, essays, poetry, interviews, and photographs covering views of past and present folk life. Reviews are limited but additional titles are listed under "Books Worth Mentioning." Current events of the region are listed in an accompanying newsletter. An excellent title recommended for libraries of the region and for others supporting interest in its folk culture. A good general-reader publication.

3181. ***Oral Tradition.*** [ISSN: 0883-5365] 1986. s-a. USD 40 (Individuals, USD 30; Students, USD 20). Ed(s): John M Foley. Slavica Publishers, Inc., 2611 E 10th St, Bloomington, IN 47408-2603; slavica@indiana.edu; http://www.slavica.com. Illus. Refereed. *Indexed:* MLA-IB, RILM. *Bk. rev.:* 100-300 words. *Aud.:* Ac.

This journal describes its purpose as a "comparative and interdisciplinary focus for studies of oral literature and related fields by publishing research and scholarship on the creation, transmission, and interpretation of all forms of oral tradition expression." Articles are worldwide in scope, with subjects ranging from ancient epics and religious texts to modern drama and e-texts. Some issues are thematic. This scholarly title is one for academic libraries that support folk literature programs.

Parabola. See General Editorial section.

3182. ***Storytelling Magazine.*** Incorporates: *Inside Story;* Which was formerly: *Yarnspinner;* Formerly (until 1989): *National Storytelling Journal.* [ISSN: 1048-1354] 1984. bi-m. USD 29.95; USD 4.95 newsstand/cover per issue. Ed(s): Nella Tsacrios. National Storytelling Association, 101 Courthouse Sq, Jonesborough, TN 37659; nsn@naxs.net; http://www.storynet.org/Magazine/mag.htm. Illus., index, adv. Circ: 12000. *Aud.:* Hs, Ga.

Issues are a mix of articles, stories, news, and advertisements. In most issues the story section has a central theme. Bibliographies of suggested readings that accompany the articles have a mix of print, media, and Internet sources. The news section deals with all aspects of the National Storytelling Network listing conferences, awards, and call for stories. There are a fair number of advertisements in the magazine, but all are pertinent to storytellers. A good source for storytellers as well as librarians and teachers.

3183. ***Tennessee Folklore Society. Bulletin.*** [ISSN: 0040-3253] 1935. q. USD 14 (Individuals, USD 10). Ed(s): Charles K Wolfe. Tennessee Folklore Society, Box 201, Middle Tennessee State University, Murfreesboro, TN 37132; cwolfe@frank.mtsu.edu. Illus., index. Refereed. Circ: 425 Paid. Vol. ends: No. 4. Microform: TMI. *Indexed:* IIMP, MLA-IB, MusicInd, RILM. *Bk. rev.:* 2-3, 600 words. *Aud.:* Ga, Ac.

Most of the articles in this journal pertain to folk culture in Tennessee and neighboring states. However, there are occasional pieces on folklore outside the United States, and some issues are thematic. In addition to articles, there are reviews of books and media and a section listing coming events. Issues also usually contain a section listing publications available from the society. This is a must selection for Tennessee libraries and others in the geographic region surrounding Tennessee.

3184. ***Voices (Ithaca): the journal of New York folklore.*** Former titles (until 2000): *New York Folklore;* (until 1974): *New York Folklore Quarterly.* 1975. q. USD 50 (Individuals, USD 35; Students, USD 20). Ed(s): Karen Taussig Lux. New York Folklore Society, 632 W Buffalo St, 2nd Fl, Ithaca, NY 14850; nyfs@nyfolklore.org; http://www.nyfolklore.org. Illus. Refereed. Circ: 650. Vol. ends: No. 2. Microform: PQC. Reprint: PQC. *Indexed:* AmH&L, ArtHuCI, BiolAb, ChemAb, IIMP, IIPA, MLA-IB, MusicInd, RILM. *Aud.:* Ga, Ac.

Published by the New York Folklore Society, this title is a recent merging of the former *New York Folklore* and *Voices* section of the society newsletter. It covers New York State and surrounding regions. Most issues include feature articles, columns, society news, announcements, and reviews. The editors view the journal as one that publishes "peer-reviewed, research-based articles, written in an accessible style, on topics related to traditional art and life, including ethnic culture. Informative columns on subjects such as legal issues, photography, sound and video recording, archiving, ethics, and the nature of traditional art and life." For those libraries that are interested in Northeastern folklore, this is a good title.

3185. ***Western Folklore.*** [ISSN: 0043-373X] 1942. q. USD 40 domestic for membership to individuals; USD 45 foreign for membership to individuals; USD 50 domestic for membership to institutions. California Folklore Society, 9420 Carrillo Ave, Montclair, CA 91763-2412. Adv. Circ: 1200. Online: bigchalk; Chadwyck-Healey Incorporated; Gale Group; Northern Light Technology, Inc.; OCLC Online Computer Library Center, Inc.; ProQuest Information & Learning; H.W. Wilson. Reprint: PQC. *Indexed:* ABS&EES, AmH&L, ArtHuCI, BEL&L, BRI, CBRI, HumInd, IIMP, MLA-IB, MusicInd, RI-1. *Aud.:* Ga, Ac.

This title's geographic scope includes California and neighboring regions. Most issues are composed of articles and reviews. Some may take a thematic approach. Topics cover all aspects of folklore taking a wide interpretation of the subject. The concise, thorough reviews are signed. Although publication lags, this journal is a good addition for both academics and the sophisticated general reader.

Electronic Journals

3186. ***Cultural Analysis: an interdisciplinary forum of folklore and popular culture.*** 2000. irreg. Free. Ed(s): JoAnn Conrad. Cultural Analysis, University of California at Berkeley, 232 Kroeber Hall, Berkeley, CA 94720; caforum@socrates.berkeley.edu; http://socrates.berkeley.edu/~caforum/index.html. Refereed. *Aud.:* Ac.

This e-journal is an "interdisciplinary, peer-reviewed journal dedicated to investigating expressive and everyday culture." The journal includes research articles, notes, reviews, and responses. It is designed to be cross-disciplinary and international in scope. Available free on the web, the journal is produced in both html or pdf file format. Each feature article is followed by two responses. Articles cover topics such as the ethnography of listening and the image Cinderella presents to modern-day females. Each article is abstracted. Reviews average 1,500-2,000 words. One of the strengths of this publication is its diversity of authorship, with contributors from around the world. Although it has only been available for a few years, it seems to have a strong foundation. Recommended for academics with cultural studies programs.

3187. ***Folklore.*** [ISSN: 1406-0949] 1996. q. Free. Ed(s): Mare Koiva, Andres Kuperjanov. Institute of the Estonian Language, Folklore Department, Vanemuise 42-235, Tartu, 2400, Estonia; mare@haldjas.folklore.ee; cps@obs.see; http://haldjas.folklore.ee/folklore. Illus. Refereed. *Indexed:* MLA-IB. *Aud.:* Ga, Ac.

This journal is the publication of the Folklore Department of the Institute of the Estonian Language and is not to be confused with the British Folklore Society's journal of the same name. Articles cover a wide variety of topics, including "shamanism, urban legends, ethnomusicology, pareomiology, popular calendar data, and folk belief." There is a special emphasis on Estonia and neighboring regions. The real appeal is the free electronic version of this publication. Articles are done as .pdf files to provide illustrations as well as text. Access to current and back issues is through the homepage. The editorial note welcomes contributors from all countries and contributions on all aspects of folklore. Submission guidelines include a listing of software requirements. Although it has strong Eastern European emphasis, it is a worthy journal and one of the better ones with full access online. Recommended for academic and general adult readers.

3188. ***New Directions in Folklore.*** irreg. Ed(s): Camille Bacon-Smith. Temple University, Institute for the Study of Literature, Literacy, and Culture, 10th Floor, Anderson Hall, Temple University, Philadelphia, PA 19122; http://www.temple.edu/isllc. *Aud.:* Ac.

This web publication is designed to "push the envelope of folklore scholarship, particularly in the exploration of contemporary culture." Topics cover a wide variety of issues including the importance of children's folklore to children's cognitive development and the phenomenon of modern conspiracy theories. Some issues contain reviews of web sites. Others offer a section called "Notes" that includes artwork. Issues are archived and access to articles and archives is easy. There is also a searchable index. From the journal's homepage, one can join the Newfolk list, get information on the Newfolk section of the American Folklore Society, and link to other resource guides. Scholarly in nature, this e-journal will be of interest to academics. One should keep in mind that, like all "web things," Newfolk continues to change and add to its web site.

■ FOOD AND NUTRITION

See also Food and Wine section.

Heather K. Moberly, Assistant Professor, Veterinary Medicine Librarian, 102 McElroy Hall, Oklahoma State University, Stillwater, OK 74078-2013; moberlh@okstate.edu

Introduction

Food and its nutritional value continue to be featured in the forefront of media in the United States. Issues that compete for the attention of the American psyche include redefinition of the traditional "Food Pyramid" and addition of new "Food Pyramids," transition and updating of the RDAs (recommended daily allowances) to the RDIs (recommended daily intakes) by the U.S. federal government, interest in the protective and preventive medicinal values of foods, questions about genetic modifications in the food supply, and concerns about an epidemic of obesity across age groups. This section focuses on titles intended either for researchers in the fields of nutrition and the related health sciences or a general audience knowledgeable in these fields. Most of these titles are appropriate for, and will be included in, academic collections supporting these disciplines. Although several titles of interest of the casual reader are included in this section, the Food and Wine section emphasizes appropriate general titles.

Basic Periodicals

Ga: *Nutrition Action Healthletter; Nutrition News Focus, Nutrition Today, Vegetarian Journal;* Ac: *American Journal of Clinical Nutrition, Annals of Nutrition and Metabolism, The British Journal of Nutrition, Journal of Nutrition, Journal of the American Dietetic Association, Nutrition Reviews.*

Basic Abstracts and Indexes

Bibliography of Agriculture, Biological Abstracts, CAB Abstracts (primarily Human Nutrition subset); Current Contents (primarily Life Sciences section) Index Medicus, Medline, Medline Plus (Nutrition Health Topic) Nutrition Abstracts and Reviews.

3189. *American College of Nutrition. Journal.* [ISSN: 0731-5724] 1982. 6x/yr. USD 180 (Individuals, USD 90). Ed(s): David Klurfeld, Dr. Richard Caldwell. American College of Nutrition, 301 S. Duncan Ave., #225, Clearwater, FL 33755-6415; http://www.am-coll-nutr.org/jacn/jacn.htm. Illus., adv. Refereed. Circ: 1600 Paid. Online: HighWire Press. *Indexed:* Agr, BiolAb, ChemAb, DSA, ExcerpMed, IndMed, RRTA, SCI, SSCI, WAE&RSA. *Bk. rev.:* Number and length vary. *Aud.:* Ac, Sa.

This official publication of the American College of Nutrition supports the college's objective to enhance the knowledge of nutrition and metabolism, and facilitates the application of the knowledge for health maintenance and disease treatment. Emphasis is placed on novel, timely, and significant papers. Regular features include original research papers, review articles, clinical reports, laboratory reports, book reviews, and abstracts from the annual meeting of the American College of Nutrition (October issue). As of June 2003, online access, with searching capability, is available at http://www.jacn.org. The web site includes tables of contents and abstracts from 1982 to 1997 and tables of contents, abstracts, and full text from 1998 to the present. All tables of contents and abstracts are available at no charge without subscription, and the High Wire Press archive provides free full text from 1998 to the present with a one-year delay.

3190. *American Dietetic Association. Journal.* Formerly: *American Dietetic Association. Bulletin.* [ISSN: 0002-8223] 1925. m. USD 288 (Individuals, USD 208; Individual members, USD 250). Ed(s): Elaine R Monsen. Elsevier Inc., 360 Park Ave. S, New York, NY 10010-1710; usinfo-f@elsevier.com; http://www.elsevier.com. Illus., index, adv. Refereed. Circ: 67000 Paid. Microform: PMC; PQC. Online: Florida Center for Library Automation; Gale Group; ingenta.com; OCLC Online Computer Library Center, Inc.; ProQuest Information & Learning; ScienceDirect. Reprint: PQC. *Indexed:* AgeL, Agr, B&AI, BiolAb, CINAHL, ChemAb, DSA, ExcerpMed, FPA, FS&TA, GSI, H&SSA, HortAb, IndMed, PsycholAb, RRTA, S&F, SCI, SSCI, SWR&A, WAE&RSA. *Bk. rev.:* Number and length vary. *Aud.:* Ac, Sa.

This journal is essential for health sciences collections. The official research publication of the American Dietetic Association (ADA), it is targeted to professional nutritionists, however much is of interest to an educated general audience. Individual issues are primarily divided into Commentary, Research, Perspectives in Practice, Research and Professional Briefs, ADA Reports, and Of Professional Interest. Content emphasizes the broad aspects of nutrition and dietetics, diet therapy, community nutrition, education and training, and administration. As of June 2003, online access is available at http://www.adajournal.org. The web site includes tables of contents, abstracts, and full text from 1995 to the present. All tables of contents and abstracts are available at no charge without subscription. Online access includes supplements.

3191. *American Journal of Clinical Nutrition: a journal reporting the practical application of our world-wide knowledge of nutrition.* [ISSN: 0002-9165] 1952. m. USD 290 print & online eds. (Individuals, USD 155 print & online eds.; Students, USD 120 print & online eds.). Ed(s): Charles Halsted. American Society for Clinical Nutrition, Inc., 9650 Rockville Pike, Rm L-2310, Bethesda, MD 20814-3998; staff@dues.faseb.org; http://www.ajcn.org/. Illus., index, adv. Refereed. Circ: 7000. Microform: PMC; PQC. Online: EBSCO Publishing; Gale Group; HighWire Press; OCLC Online Computer Library Center, Inc.; ProQuest Information & Learning. *Indexed:* ABS&EES, AS&TI, AgeL, Agr, B&AI, BiolAb, CINAHL, ChemAb, DSA, ExcerpMed, FS&TA, H&SSA, HortAb, IndMed, IndVet, PEI, PsycholAb, RRTA, SCI, SSCI, VetBull, WAE&RSA. *Bk. rev.:* 1-4, 500-1,000 words. *Aud.:* Ac, Sa.

Published by the American Society for Clinical Nutrition with assistance from High Wire Press, this highly recommended professional core journal belongs in academic and research collections that support nutrition research. Standard journal features include editorials, review articles, original research communications, and book reviews. Catetories of research include, but are not limited to, obesity and eating disorders; lipids and cardiovascular risk; carbohydrate metabolism and diabetes; immunity; vitamins, minerals, and phytochemicals; bone metabolism; nutritional status; dietary intakes and body composition; and pregnancy and lactation. Supplements, included in the regular subscription rate or available for purchase as individual issues, publish proceedings of a variety of internationally recognized clinical nutrition conferences. Subject and author indexes appear in the July and December issues. As of June 2003, online access, with searching capability, is available at http://www.ajcn.org. The web site includes tables of contents only, 1966-1974; tables of contents and abstracts, 1975-1997; and tables of contents, abstracts, and full text, 1998 to the present. All tables of contents are available at no charge without subscription, and the High Wire Press archive provides free full text from 1998 to the present with a one-year delay. Full-text access includes both the journal and supplements.

3192. *Annals of Nutrition and Metabolism: European journal of nutrition, metabolic diseases and dietetics.* Incorporates (1947-1980): *Annales de la Nutrition et de l'Alimentation;* Former titles (until 1980): *Nutrition and Metabolism;* (until 1970): *Nutritio et Dieta.* [ISSN: 0250-6807] 1959. bi-m. CHF 1197.60 (Individuals, CHF 495). Ed(s): Ibrahim Elmadfa. S. Karger AG, Allschwilerstr 10, Basel, 4009, Switzerland; karger@karger.ch; http://www.karger.ch. Illus., index, adv. Sample. Refereed. Circ: 1250. Online: EBSCO Publishing; RoweCom Information Quest; Swets Blackwell. *Indexed:* Agr, BiolAb, ChemAb, DSA, ExcerpMed, FPA, FS&TA, ForAb, IndMed, IndVet, RRTA, SCI, VetBull, WAE&RSA. *Aud.:* Ac, Sa.

As the official journal of the Federation of European Nutrition Societies (FENS), this scholarly source emphasizes the publication of new information about the relationship between human nutrition and metabolic diseases (including their molecular genetics), recognizing that the "search for reliable dietary guidelines continues." Original research papers illuminate problems such as the "consequences of specific diets an dietary supplements, nutritional factors in the etiology of metabolic and gastrointestinal disorders, and the epidemiological association between dietary habits and disease incidence." Occasionally the journal publishes a review article. Although intended for a professional audience, an educated general audience will be interested in this title. As of June

2003, online access is available at http://www.karger.ch/journal/anm. The web site includes tables of contents, abstracts, and full text from 1998 to the present. All tables of contents and abstracts are available at no charge without subscription. They also include a link to a PubMed search for content from this title prior to 1998.

3193. ***The British Journal of Nutrition: an international journal of nutritional science.*** [ISSN: 0007-1145] 1947. m. USD 855. Ed(s): P Trayhurn. CABI Publishing, Wallingford, OC10 8DE, United Kingdom; orders@cabi.org; http://www.cabi.org. Illus., index, adv. Refereed. Microform: PMC; PQC; SWZ. Online: EBSCO Publishing; ingenta.com; OCLC Online Computer Library Center, Inc.; RoweCom Information Quest; Swets Blackwell; H.W. Wilson. *Indexed:* Agr, B&AI, BiolAb, CINAHL, ChemAb, DSA, ExcerpMed, FPA, FS&TA, HortAb, IndMed, IndVet, RRTA, SCI, VetBull, WAE&RSA. *Bk. rev.:* 1-2, 500 words, signed. *Aud.:* Ac, Sa.

The Nutrition Society, sponsor of *BJN*, strives to advance the study and application of nutrition science as it relates to maintaining human and animal health. The journal is highly technical and includes primarily original papers, review articles, short communications, and technical notes in the fields of human nutrition, clinical nutrition, general nutrition, and animal nutrition. Subject coverage includes clinical metabolism and nutritional support, obesity and body composition, international and public health nutrition, diet selection, macronutrient nutrition, malnutrition, nutrition and behavior, smoking and diet, and animal nutrition and metabolism. Topic specific supplements are included with a subscription. As of June 2003, online access is available at http://www.cabi-publishing.org/JOURNALS/BJN/Index.asp and includes table of contents, abstracts, and full text including supplements from 1998 to the present. All tables of contents and abstracts are available at no charge without subscription. Full text from Volume 80 is available at no charge without a subscription as well. Recommended for academic and research collections.

3194. ***European Journal of Clinical Nutrition.*** Formerly (until 1987): *Human Nutrition. Clinical Nutrition;* Which superseded in part (in 1981): *Journal of Human Nutrition;* Which was formerly (until 1976): *Nutrition.* [ISSN: 0954-3007] 1976. m. GBP 385 print & online eds. Ed(s): Jaap C Seidell. Nature Publishing Group, The MacMillan Building, 4 Crinan St, London, N1 9XW, United Kingdom; http://www.nature.com/. Illus., adv. Sample. Refereed. *Indexed:* Agr, BiolAb, DSA, ExcerpMed, GSI, IndMed, IndVet, RRTA, SCI, SSCI, VetBull, WAE&RSA. *Bk. rev.:* 1-3, length varies, signed. *Aud.:* Ac, Sa.

This scholarly journal, the official publication of the European Academy of Nutritional Sciences, focuses on human nutrition and does not include reports of animal studies unless it includes a parallel study of human subjects. Standard journal features include review articles, original research, and book reviews. Supplements, included with subscription, cover conference proceedings. Topics of particular emphasis include nutrition as it relates to basic theoretical, clinical, and metabolic studies; nutritional causes and effects of disease; and epidemiological and sociological aspects of nutrition, and community nutrition and education. As of June 2003, online access with search capability is available at http://www.nature.com/ecjn. The web site includes tables of contents, abstracts, and full text from 1997 to the present. All tables of contents and abstracts are available at no charge without a subscription.

International Journal of Food Sciences and Nutrition. See Food Industry section.

3195. ***Journal of Food Quality.*** [ISSN: 0146-9428] 1977. 6x/yr. USD 188. Ed(s): John J Powers. Food & Nutrition Press, Inc., 6527 Main St, PO Box 374, Trumbull, CT 06611; foodpress@worldnetatt.net; http://www.foodscipress.com. Illus., index. Sample. Refereed. *Indexed:* Agr, ChemAb, DSA, ExcerpMed, FPA, FS&TA, H&SSA, HortAb, IndVet, RiskAb, S&F, SSCI, VetBull, WAE&RSA. *Bk. rev.:* Number and length vary. *Aud.:* Ac, Sa.

This technical journal focuses on the quality assurance and regulation aspects of food and nutrition. Articles explore the intricacies and interactions between storage, stability, and preservation and food appearance and sensory perceptions. The reports of original experiments are valuable to researchers and practitioners. As of June 2003, online access is available at http://www.foodscipress.com. The web site includes tables of contents and abstracts from 2001 to the present at no charge without subscription.

3196. ***Journal of Nutrition.*** [ISSN: 0022-3166] 1928. m. USD 550 (Individuals, USD 175). Ed(s): Dr. John Suttie. American Society for Nutritional Sciences, 9650 Rockville Pike., Room L-2310, Bethesda, MD 20814; staff@faseb.org; http://www.nutrition.org. Illus., adv. Sample. Refereed. Circ: 4430. Vol. ends: Dec. Microform: PMC; PQC. Online: bigchalk; EBSCO Publishing; Gale Group; HighWire Press; Northern Light Technology, Inc.; OCLC Online Computer Library Center, Inc.; ProQuest Information & Learning; RoweCom Information Quest. Reprint: PQC. *Indexed:* AbAn, Agr, B&AI, BiolAb, BiolDig, ChemAb, DSA, ExcerpMed, FPA, FS&TA, ForAb, GSI, H&SSA, HortAb, IndMed, IndVet, RRTA, RiskAb, SCI, SSCI, VetBull, WAE&RSA, ZooRec. *Bk. rev.:* Various number and length. *Aud.:* Ac, Sa.

This research journal is the official monthly publication of the American Society for Nutritional Sciences. It publishes experimental nutrition papers, critical reviews, biographies of nutritionists, and commentaries emphasizing biochemistry, metabolism, requirements, interactions, and toxicity. Supplements provide coverage of symposia or special meetings and are included with subscription. Subject coverage includes animal and human nutrition, diet and disease, carbohydrates and fibers, community and international nutrition, energy and macronutrient nutrition, nutrient-gene interactions, metabolism and hormone regulation, pharmacology, toxicology, immunology, and epidemiology. As of June 2003, online access, with searching capability, is available at http://www.nutrition.org and includes tables of contents, abstracts, and full text from 1997 to the present. All tables of contents and abstracts are available at no charge without subscription, and the High Wire Press archive provides free full text from 1997 to the present with a one-year delay.

3197. ***Journal of Nutrition Education and Behavior.*** Formerly: *Journal of Nutrition Education.* [ISSN: 1499-4046] 1969. bi-m. USD 234 (Individuals, USD 159; USD 41 newsstand/cover per issue). Ed(s): Jane Voichick. B.C. Decker Inc., 20 Hughson St S, LCD 1, PO Box 620, Hamilton, ON L8N 3K7, Canada; info@bcdecker.com; http://www.bcdecker.com. Illus., adv. Refereed. Circ: 2856. *Indexed:* AgeL, Agr, CIJE, CINAHL, DSA, EduInd, FS&TA, GSI, SSCI, SWA, WAE&RSA. *Aud.:* Ac, Sa.

This journal publishes research about nutrition education emphasizing practice and public policy. As the official journal of the Society for Nutrition Education, it has an intended audience of society members and institutional libraries that provide access to professionals and educators in nutritional education, health promotion, and food science. Standard features include research articles, research briefs, reports, educational materials in review, viewpoints, and "gems" (short descriptions of innovative and useful nutritional education activities that can be easily replicated). As of June 2003, online access is available at http://www.jneb.org and includes only tables of contents from 2001 to the present. All tables of contents are available at no charge without subscription.

3198. ***Journal of Nutritional Biochemistry.*** Supersedes (in 1990): *Nutrition Reports International.* [ISSN: 0955-2863] 1970. m. EUR 779 (Individuals, EUR 209). Ed(s): Dr. B. Hennig. Elsevier Inc., 360 Park Ave. S, New York, NY 10010-1710; usinfo-f@elsevier.com; http://www.elsevier.com. Illus., index, adv. Sample. Refereed. Vol. ends: Dec. Microform: PQC. Online: ingenta.com; ScienceDirect; Swets Blackwell. *Indexed:* AgeL, Agr, BiolAb, ChemAb, DSA, ExcerpMed, FS&TA, HortAb, IndVet, SCI, VetBull, ZooRec. *Aud.:* Ac, Sa.

This scholarly title, recommended for academic and research collections that support both biochemistry and nutrition, is aimed at nutritionists, biochemists, physicians, dieticians, and epidemiologists. It covers experimental human and animal nutrition research as it intersects with biochemistry, neurochemistry, molecular biology, toxicology, physiology, and pharmacology. Periodic symposium reports, metabolic pathways, and rapid communications complement the regularly featured review articles, research communications, and calendar. As of June 2003, online access, with searching capability, is available at http://www.sciencedirect.com and includes tables of contents, abstracts, and full text from 1990 to the present. All tables of contents and abstracts are available at no charge without subscription.

FOOD AND NUTRITION

3199. ***Nutrition: the international journal of applied and basic nutritional sciences.*** Formerly (until 1987): *Nutrition International.* [ISSN: 0899-9007] 1985. m. EUR 436 (Individuals, EUR 238). Ed(s): Dr. Michael M. Meguid, Dr. D Labadarios. Elsevier Inc., 360 Park Ave. S, New York, NY 10010-1710; usinfo-f@elsevier.com; http://www.elsevier.com. Adv. Refereed. Circ: 20112. Vol. ends: No. 17. Online: ingenta.com; ScienceDirect; Swets Blackwell. *Indexed:* CINAHL, ChemAb, DSA, ExcerpMed, FPA, FS&TA, ForAb, IndMed, IndVet, PEI, RRTA, SCI, VetBull, WAE&RSA. *Aud.:* Ac, Sa.

This scholarly medical journal is most appropriate for libraries that serve researchers and clinicians. Subject coverage emphasizes applied and basic nutrition research including parenteral and enteral nutrition. Standard journal features include review articles about current topics, Random Bytes (nutritional statistics column), Nutrition and Epidemiology (column), Public Policy and Nutrition Practice (public policy column), Nutrition/Metabolism Classics (including prospective overviews from one original author), and book reviews. As of June 2003, information about the journal is available at http://www.upstate.edu/nutritionjournal. Online access, with searching capability, is provided through Science Direct at http://www.sciencedirect.com and includes tables of contents, abstracts, and full text 1996 to the present. All tables of contents and abstracts are available at no charge without subscription. Online access includes supplements.

3200. ***Nutrition Action Healthletter.*** Formerly: *Nutrition Action;* Incorporating (1976-1980): *Intake (New Hyde Park).* [ISSN: 0885-7792] 1974. 10x/yr. USD 24 domestic; CND 36 Canada; USD 32 elsewhere. Ed(s): Michael Jacobson, Stephen B Schmidt. Center for Science in the Public Interest, 1875 Connecticut Ave, N W, Ste 300, Washington, DC 20009-5728; cspi@cspinet.org; http://www.cspinet.org/nah. Illus., index, adv. Sample. Circ: 800000 Paid. Vol. ends: Dec. Microform: PQC. Online: bigchalk; EBSCO Publishing; Florida Center for Library Automation; Gale Group; OCLC Online Computer Library Center, Inc.; ProQuest Information & Learning. *Indexed:* Agr, AltPI, BiolDig, CINAHL, ConsI, MagInd. *Aud.:* Ga, Sa.

The Center for Science in the Public Interest (CSPI) publishes this newsletter from an unabashed advocacy viewpoint for general audiences, aiming to educate consumers about foods and nutrition. Each issue focuses on a current hot topic. Other features include "right stuff vs. food porn," food safety, and news from CSPI. As of June 2003, online access is available at http://www.cspinet.org/nah. The web site includes selected full-text articles and annual indexes from 1997 to the present and classic articles from 1989 to the present.

3201. ***Nutrition Research: the international medium for rapid publication of communications in the nutritional sciences.*** Incorporates (1975-1993): *Progress in Food and Nutrition Science;* Which was formerly: *International Encyclopedia of Food and Nutrition.* [ISSN: 0271-5317] 1981. m. EUR 1249 (Individuals, EUR 274). Ed(s): Ranjit K Chandra. Elsevier Inc., 360 Park Ave. S, New York, NY 10010-1710; usinfo-f@elsevier.com; http://www.elsevier.com. Illus., adv. Sample. Refereed. Circ: 580 Paid. Vol. ends: Dec (No. 21). Microform: PQC. Online: ingenta.com; ScienceDirect; Swets Blackwell. *Indexed:* Agr, B&AI, BiolAb, ChemAb, DSA, ExcerpMed, FPA, FS&TA, HortAb, IndMed, IndVet, RRTA, SCI, SSCI, VetBull, WAE&RSA. *Aud.:* Ac, Sa.

This scholarly journal emphasizes rapid publication of original papers covering basic and applied human and animal nutrition research. Each issue is an even division between human and animal nutrition studies, plus a review article. Interestingly, the journal reproduces the author's original manuscript. Subject areas include, but are not limited to, socioeconomic, cultural, and political influences on individual and community nutrition; food intolerance and allergy; nutrient drug interactions; work performance and behavior; nutrient requirements in health and disease; and digestion and absorption of foods. As of June 2003, online access, with searching capability, is available at http://www.sciencedirect.com. The web site includes tables of contents, abstracts, and full text from 1995 to the present. All tables of contents and abstracts are available at no charge without subscription.

3202. ***Nutrition Reviews.*** [ISSN: 0029-6643] 1942. m. USD 195 (Individuals, USD 122.50). Ed(s): Dr. Irwin H Rosenberg. International Life Sciences Institute, One Thomas Circle, 9th Fl., Washington, DC 20005; ilsi@ilsi.org; http://www.ilsi.org. Illus., index, adv. Refereed. Circ: 4400. Microform: PQC. Online: bigchalk; EBSCO Publishing; Gale Group; Ingenta Select; Northern Light Technology, Inc.; OCLC Online Computer Library Center, Inc.; Ovid Technologies, Inc.; ProQuest Information & Learning. Reprint: PQC. *Indexed:* Agr, B&AI, BiolAb, CINAHL, ChemAb, DSA, ExcerpMed, FS&TA, GSI, IndMed, IndVet, RRTA, SCI, SSCI, VetBull, WAE&RSA. *Aud.:* Ac, Sa.

This journal concentrates coverage on timely critical reviews in nutrition research, international nutrition, and science policy. Although listed as a monthly publication, many months include a second part that reports conference proceedings from a wide variety of organizations. Each issue includes a lead review, several articles, brief reviews, nutrition grand rounds, and calendar. Subscriptions include topical supplements. This title will be of interest to an educated general audience. As of June 2003, online access is available at http://www.ilsi.org/publications/reviews.html and includes tables of contents and abstracts from journal issues and supplements from 2002 to the present. All tables of contents and abstracts are available at no charge without subscription. An online Spanish-language translation is available for 2000 and 2001.

3203. ***Nutrition Today.*** [ISSN: 0029-666X] 1985. bi-m. USD 169 (Individuals, USD 69; USD 23 per issue). Ed(s): Helen Guthrie. Lippincott Williams & Wilkins, 530 Walnut St, Philadelphia, PA 19106-3621; custserv@lww.com; http://www.lww.com. Illus., index, adv. Refereed. Circ: 4780. Microform: Pub. Online: Florida Center for Library Automation; Gale Group; Northern Light Technology, Inc.; OCLC Online Computer Library Center, Inc.; H.W. Wilson. *Indexed:* AS&TI, Agr, BiolAb, DSA, FS&TA, GSI, PEI. *Aud.:* Ga, Ac, Sa.

Intended to act as a guide for professional nutritionists through the maze of "hot topic" nutrition claims, this publication balances coverage of research and policy issues. Articles include conference reports, pro/con discussions, a government-sponsored research calendar, historical discussions, and software reviews. This title will be of interest to an educated general audience. As of June 2003, online access is available at http://www.nutritiontodayonline.com. The web site includes tables of contents, abstracts, and full text from 2002 to the present. All tables of contents are available at no charge without subscription.

3204. ***Vegetarian Journal.*** Formerly: *Baltimore Vegetarians.* [ISSN: 0885-7636] 1982. q. bi-m until 2002. Members, USD 20; USD 3.50 newsstand/cover per issue domestic. Ed(s): Debra Wasserman. Vegetarian Resource Group, PO Box 1463, Baltimore, MD 21203; vrg@vrg.org; http://www.vrg.org. Illus., index. Sample. Circ: 20000. Reprint: PQC. *Bk. rev.:* Number and length vary. *Aud.:* Hs, Ga, Ac, Sa.

Published by the Vegetarian Resource Group (VRG), a nonprofit organization focused on educating the public about vegetarianism, this journal provides practical information about vegetarian and vegan lifestyles in easy-to-understand language. Topics include medical research, nutrition, travel, restaurant reviews, animal rights, ethics, and new products. All articles about nutrition are reviewed by either a registered dietician or medical doctor. VRG publishes a variety of documents, many are available as full text at their web site. As of June 2003, online access is available through http://www.vrg.org/journal and includes tables of contents, selected full-text articles, and an index to articles from 1993 to the present.

3205. ***World Review of Nutrition and Dietetics.*** [ISSN: 0084-2230] 1964. irreg. Ed(s): A P Simopoulos. S. Karger AG, Allschwilerstr 10, Basel, 4009, Switzerland; karger@karger.ch; http://www.karger.ch. Refereed. Reprint: ISI. *Indexed:* BiolAb, ChemAb, DSA, FS&TA, IndMed. *Aud.:* Ac, Sa.

This review series publishes one topical volume per year about a fundamental human or animal nutrition topic, contemporary nutritional controversy, or nutritional solution to social or preventive medical challenge. Often the articles are among the first to comprehensively address a particular topic. Recent articles include "Omega-6/Omega-3 Essential Fatty Acid Ratio: The Scientific Evidence," "Plants in Human Health and Nutrition Policy," "Nutrition and Fitness: Metabolic Studies in Health and Disease," "Mediterranean Diets," and "Street Foods." As of June 2003, online access is available at http://

www.karger.ch/bookseries/wrund and includes tables of contents, subject and author indexes, and full text from 1997 to the present. All tables of contents and indexes are available at no charge without subscription. Information about individual issues is available from 1965 to the present.

Electronic Journals

3206. ***Nutrition News Focus.*** d. Free. Ed(s): Dr. David Klurfeld. Nutrition News Focus Inc., 4426 St. Clair Ave, Studio City, CA 91604; ken@nutritionnewsfocus.com; http://www.nutritionnewsfocus.com/. *Aud.:* Ac, Sa.

Nutrition News Focus is intended to help readers understand news and news coverage about nutrition by providing a brief discussion about a current nutrition topic in a newsletter format. Each issue includes two sections: a summary of the topic and a "here's what you need to know" review of the topic. It is freely available via subscription to a daily (weekdays) e-mail or through a searchable web site at http://www.nutritionnewsfocus.com. The searchable archive includes information from 1998 to the present with a two-week delay. The sponsor, Dr. David Klurfeld, is professor and chairman of the Department of Nutrition and Food Science at Wayne State University (the publication is not affiliated with the university). He is also editor of the *Journal of the American College of Nutrition. Nutrition News Focus* is well written, timely, and will be of interest to general audiences.

■ FOOD AND WINE

See also Food and Nutrition; and Food Industry sections.

Heather K. Moberly, Assistant Professor, Veterinary Medicine Librarian, 102 McElroy Hall, Oklahoma State University, Stillwater, OK 74078-2013; moberlh@okstate.edu

Introduction

Specialty food and wine titles continue to be popular, with titles now available for almost any culinary interest and skill level. In this section you will find both general food/wine titles as well as those aimed at improving health, ethnic cuisines, and particular forms of food preparation.

Publications here tend to be popular; please see the Food and Nutrition and Food Industry sections for scholarly, commercial, and more health-related titles.

Basic Periodicals

Ga: *Bon Appetit, Cooking Light, Gourmet, Wine Spectator;* Sa: *Cook's Illustrated.*

3207. ***B B C Good Food.*** [ISSN: 0957-588X] 1989. m. GBP 25.20; GBP 2.10 newsstand/cover per issue. Ed(s): Orlando Murnin. B B C Worldwide Ltd., Woodlands, 80 Wood Ln, London, W12 0TT, United Kingdom; good.food.magazine@bbc.co.uk; http://www.bbcworldwide.com. Adv. Circ: 285125. *Bk. rev.:* Number and length vary. *Aud.:* Ga.

This title, companion to the BBC television show "Good Food," is one of the most popular food magazines in Britain. Designed for attractive access to food ideas that are both time-saving and inspirational, each issue also features ideas for foods that are in season, everyday food solutions, cookbook reviews (in a shopping section), tips, entertaining, travel, kitchen design, a guide to the top recipes from the television program, and advice columns for answering readers' questions on healthy eating. Includes a recipe index that is arranged by meal course.

3208. ***Betty Crocker Magazine.*** Formerly: *Betty Crocker Creative Recipes.* 198?. m. USD 19.95; USD 3.50 newsstand/cover per issue; USD 5.25 newsstand/cover per issue Canada. General Mills, Inc., One General Mills Blvd, Minneapolis, MN 55426; http://www.generalmills.com. *Aud.:* Ga.

This recipe-based title is a clear choice for public libraries. Each monthly issue has a topical theme such as "Simple Meals," "Potlucks," "Easy Get Togethers," "Simple Summer Grilling," "Holiday," and "Appetizers." Many recipes include color photographs and are formatted across a two-page spread. Recipes include nutritional analysis and dietary exchanges. Regular features include "Betty on Health," "Betty on What's New," and "Betty Makes It Easy." It will appeal to readers of *Better Homes and Gardens Hometown Cooking* and *A Taste of Home.*

3209. ***Bon Appetit: America's food and entertaining magazine.*** [ISSN: 0006-6990] 1956. m. USD 12 domestic; USD 30 foreign; USD 3.50 newsstand/cover per issue. Ed(s): Barbara Fairchild, William J Garry. Conde Nast Publications Inc., 4 Times Square, 5th Fl, New York, NY 10036; http://www.condenast.com. Illus., index, adv. Circ: 1300000 Paid. Vol. ends: Dec. *Indexed:* ASIP, CBCARef, ConsI, MagInd, RGPR. *Aud.:* Ga.

This colorful, classy title may be considered by some to be an old standard, however, it is not outdated! Tried and true columns such as "RSVP" (recipes from famous restaurants) are complemented by newer additions such as "Personal Taste" (profiles a cook book author and includes their favorite recipes). Expert advice is proffered in "Tools of the Trade" and "Tasting Panel." "Every Night Cooking" and "Too Busy To Cook" (reader contributed time savers) are practical. Travel, restaurants, and entertaining are also highlighted. Menu guides configure the recipes from each issue into a variety of options. There is a recipe index for each issue and some recipes include basic nutritional information. Recommended for public libraries.

3210. ***Chile Pepper: the magazine of spicy foods.*** Former titles (until Jan. 1990): *Whole Chile Pepper; Whole Chile Pepper Catalog.* [ISSN: 1069-7985] 1986. bi-m. USD 24.95 domestic; USD 34.95 Canada; USD 39.95 elsewhere. Chile Pepper, 1701 River Run Ste 702, River Plaza, Fort Worth, TX 76102; rwalsh@chilepepperhq.com. Illus., index, adv. Circ: 85000. Vol. ends: Nov/Dec. *Bk. rev.:* 5-7, 150-175 words. *Aud.:* Ga.

More than simply hot and spicy recipes, and appealing to readers who include even the smallest amount of spice in their cooking, gardens, or travels, this title provides admirably balanced coverage of the spicy, zesty lifestyle. Articles are broad in scope, including seasonally themed features about food (e.g., seafood), techniques (e.g., grilling), and entertaining (e.g., matching beverages with spicy foods), as well as non-food-related subjects (e.g., NASCAR); product reviews; cookbook reviews including sample recipes; travel features (focusing on an area and reviewing several restaurants); and gardening advice. Recipes are rated for spiciness (mild, medium, or hot) and are indexed by main ingredient and whether they are vegetarian. Other regularly included items include information on where to purchase ingredients, a cook-off calendar, world news, and spicy competition announcements.

3211. ***Chocolatier: a taste of the good life.*** [ISSN: 0887-591X] 1984. 6x/yr. USD 23.95; USD 30.95 foreign. Ed(s): Michael Schneider. Haymarket Group Ltd., 45 W 34th St, Ste 600, New York, NY 10001. Illus., index, adv. Circ: 150000. Vol. ends: Dec. *Aud.:* Ga, Sa.

Whether a spectator or an inspired chocolate cook, *Chocolatier* is the perfect choice for anyone interested in chocolate. Each issue includes three or four features about chocolate and how chocolate relates to nearly every walk of life. Recipes are luscious and provide detailed instructions so that whether beginner or expert the reader will be comfortable experimenting with this versatile ingredient. The "Latest Scoop" column presents news, products, and cookbooks that are worth watching. The "Inside Story," found inside each back cover, features amazing and unusual chocolate candies complete with ordering information. Recommended for public libraries.

3212. ***Cooking Light: the magazine of food and fitness.*** [ISSN: 0886-4446] 1987. 11x/yr. USD 22 domestic; USD 3.95 newsstand/cover per issue. Ed(s): Billy Sims, Mary Kay Culpepper. Southern Progress Corp., 2100 Lakeshore Dr, Birmingham, AL 35209; cookinglight@spc.com. Illus., index. Sample. Circ: 1425000 Paid. Online: Northern Light Technology, Inc. *Aud.:* Ga.

Lighter foods and easy-to-live-with fitness are the hallmarks of this top-notch title. Each issue includes food news, food articles (nutrition information, nutrition advice, and interviews with food personalities including chefs), fitness articles (paths to fitness, advice and reviews of equipment, and exercises), and recipes. Recipes cover a broad range of tastes and styles and include cooking with wine and healthful makeovers of some nutritionally sinful favorites. All recipes include full nutritional analysis. Unfortunately, most of the content of the magazine's web site has recently become restricted to subscribers to the print version of *Cooking Light* and to members of America Online.

3213. *Cook's Illustrated.* Former titles (until 1990): *Cook's;* (until 1985): *Cook's Magazine.* [ISSN: 1068-2821] 1980. 6x/yr. USD 29.70. Ed(s): Christopher Kimball. Boston Common Press, 17 Station St, Box 470 589, Brookline, MA 02445. Illus., index. *Indexed:* ConsI. *Bk. rev.:* 2-3, 3,350 words. *Aud.:* Ga, Ac, Sa.

Cook's Illustrated, home of "America's Test Kitchen," is simply the top of its genre. Tireless product testing produces reliable product reviews and proven techniques. The articles and technique instructions cover the spectrum from bare-bones basics to more efficient methods for common tasks and are often illustrated with black-and-white line drawings or black-and-white photographs. Many techniques and recipes are formatted across two pages. Each issue includes brand-name testing and ratings for ingredients and equipment. Recipes are indexed in each issue by meal course. One of the few drawbacks is the lack of nutritional analysis for most recipes. Although mail-order sources are included for all featured items, this title accepts no advertising. Most of their web site is restricted to members only; however, there is a free electronic monthly newsletter and access to a few free articles.

3214. *Cuisine Tours Magazine.* 2002. 9x/yr. USD 35.94. Cuisine Publishing LLC, 5800 E. Skelly Ste 707, Tulsa, OK 74135; info@cuisinemedia.com; http://www.cuisinemedia.com. *Aud.:* Ga.

This new title bears watching and deserves consideration. Although other titles (e.g., "Touring and Tasting") blur the "food and travel" topic with other specialties, *Cuisine Tours* is poised to combine the concept of touring with the lushness of the gourmand titles. Each issue focuses on one location (e.g., San Francisco, New York, Chicago) and features the restaurants, chefs, and recipes it is famous for. Restaurant and chef features include historical and biographical information. Recipes often are accompanied by commentary and techniques from the chef. The index of recipes includes color photographs of some dishes. No nutritional analysis is provided for recipes. Interestingly, a kitchen measurement chart is included.

3215. *Fine Cooking: for people who love to cook.* [ISSN: 1072-5121] 1994. bi-m. USD 29.95 in US & Canada; USD 36 elsewhere. Ed(s): Martha Holmberg. Taunton Press, Inc., 63, South Main St, PO Box 5506, Newtown, CT 06470-5506; http://www.taunton.com. Illus., index, adv. Circ: 186000 Paid. *Indexed:* ASIP. *Bk. rev.:* 4, 200-500 words. *Aud.:* Ga, Ac, Sa.

Emphasizing cooking preparation, technique, and teaching, this title will share some audience with *Cook's Illustrated*; however, the styles of the magazines are vastly different. As with *Cook's Illustrated*, recipes complement the techniques and other features rather than being the focus of the content. Standard features include "From Our Test Kitchen" (how-to techniques, recipes, ingredients), "Cooking without Recipes," "Classics Updated," "Food Science," "In Season," "World Cuisine," "Dinner with Friends," "Reader's Tips," "Q and A," and "Enjoying Wine." Menus using the recipes within each issue and comprehensive indexing are also strengths of this magazine. There are indexes for tools, techniques and ingredients, and recipes (coded for baking, make-ahead, vegetarian, or quick). Nutritional analysis is included for each recipe and summarized in one chart at the back of the issue rather than with each recipe.

3216. *Food & Wine.* Former titles (until 1983): *Monthly Magazine of Food and Wine;* (until 1981): *International Review of Food and Wine.* [ISSN: 0741-9015] 1978. m. USD 32 domestic; USD 3.95 newsstand/cover per issue; CND 4.95 newsstand/cover per issue Canada. Ed(s): Dana Cowin. American Express Publishing Corp., 1120 Ave of the Americas, New York, NY 10036; ashields@amexpub.com; http://www.foodandwine.com/. Illus., index, adv. Circ: 840101. Vol. ends: Dec. *Indexed:* ASIP. *Bk. rev.:* Number varies, 100-200 words. *Aud.:* Ga.

Food and Wine maintains its deserved place at the top of the food journal world. Although the content concentrates on food, wine, and entertaining, this title includes enough interviews, travel and restaurant information, expert advice, kitchen gadget reviews, and gardening items to satisfy the most discriminating reader. Wine reviews and food/wine pairings are always a strength. The heavy concentration of advertising in this title can be viewed as a distraction or, as in fashion magazines, as a pleasant opportunity for armchair window-shopping. Recipes do not include nutritional analysis; however, they are color-coded as fast, healthy, or make-ahead.

3217. *Gourmet: the magazine of good living.* [ISSN: 0017-2553] 1941. m. USD 15 domestic; USD 34 Canada; USD 36 elsewhere. Ed(s): Ruth Reichl, Alice S R Gochman. Conde Nast Publications Inc., 4 Times Square, 5th Fl, New York, NY 10036; http://www.epicurious.com; http://www.gourmet.com; http://www.condenast.com. Illus., index, adv. Circ: 900000 Paid. Vol. ends: Dec. Microform: PQC. Online: Gale Group. *Indexed:* ConsI, GardL, MagInd, RGPR. *Aud.:* Hs, Ga, Ac.

Gourmet continues to be at the forefront of glossy, lavishly illustrated food and travel magazines. Lifestyle articles elevate entertaining to an art. Food articles and recipes embrace the quest for sophisticated, impressive dishes and meals. Travel articles focus on international and exotic destinations, emphasizing restaurants and unusual food experiences. Regular features include "Reviews and Criticism," "Drinks," "Seasonal Kitchen," "Good Living," "Gourmet Everyday," "Kitchen Notebook," and "Recipe Tips." The "You Asked for It" column publishes reader-requested recipes from famous restaurants, similar to the "RSVP" feature in *Bon Appetit*. Recipes, although indexed, include no nutritional analysis.

3218. *Great Chefs.* 2001. q. USD 21.91 domestic; USD 24.91 foreign. Cuisine Media, PO Box 56757, New Orleans, LA 70156-6757; info@greatchefs.com. Adv. *Aud.:* Ga, Ac, Sa.

Accompanying the "Great Chefs" television program, this title blends television tie-ins and instructional recipes in a clear, easy-to-read format. Sections of each issue are color-coded (appetizers, entrees, desserts, featured ingredient, wine feature), and included is the complete schedule of the chefs and the dishes they prepare on the television show. Biographies of the chefs accompany the recipes. One-page recipes are clearly illustrated, adding to the educational quality of this not-just-for-experts magazine. No nutritional information or analysis is included. *Cook's Illustrated* and *Fine Cooking* are more highly recommended as instructional titles, but the illustration of the recipes is a strong point of *Great Chefs*.

3219. *The Magazine of La Cucina Italiana: good food for good living.* [ISSN: 1090-4484] 1996. bi-m. USD 24 domestic; USD 31.57 Canada; USD 40 elsewhere. Ed(s): Paolo Villoresi. Italian Culinary Institute, 230 Fifth Ave, Ste 1100, New York, NY 10001. Illus., index, adv. Circ: 140 Paid. Vol. ends: Nov/Dec. *Bk. rev.:* 2. *Aud.:* Ga, Sa.

Titles focusing on Italian food are a quickly proliferating area of food and wine magazines. If only one title from the genre can be included, then this English-language edition of the Italian *La Cucina Italiana* is a great choice. Wide-ranging features about Italy and culinary topics make this much more than simply a recipe magazine. Regularly covered topics include travel in and around Italy, wine reviews and announcements, cooking techniques, and gardening. A highlight of each issue is the "Glossary of Unfamiliar Terms." There are nearly 100 recipes in many issues, and although they are indexed, they include no nutritional analysis. Other, similarly themed titles include *Italian Cooking and Living* (published by the Italian Culinary Institute) and *Tastes of Italy: the Best in Italian Cooking*.

3220. *Quarterly Review of Wines.* [ISSN: 0740-1248] 1977. q. USD 14.95 domestic; USD 19.95 Canada; USD 34.95 in Europe. Ed(s): Randolph G Sheahan. Q R W, Inc., 24 Garfield Ave, Winchester, MA 01890. Illus., adv. Sample. Circ: 20000 Free. *Bk. rev.:* 2, 300-500 words. *Aud.:* Ga, Ac, Sa.

Although known widely for its reviews and buying guide, *QRW* does an admirable job covering other topics of interest to wine enthusiasts. There are more than 20 features in many issues, contributed by top wine experts. The travel articles are a strong point, whether discovering new places or revisiting classic destinations; they highlight the wine and restaurants of an entire area or feature just one restaurant. "All Things Grape and Small" is always a favorite for industry news and trivia. Also included are occasional features on spirits and the column "Cigar Talk." Particularly recommended if you are limited to only a few wine titles.

3221. *Saveur.* [ISSN: 1075-7864] 1994. 8x/yr. USD 29.95 domestic; USD 37.95 Canada; USD 45.95 elsewhere. World Publications LLC, 304 Park Ave S, 8th Fl, New York, NY 10010; info@worldpub.net; http://www.worldpub.net. Illus., index, adv. Circ: 381585 Paid. *Aud.:* Ga, Ac, Sa.

Saveur's motto, "savor a world of authentic cuisine," sets up the content quite accurately. Articles are primarily about international travel, world cuisines, and prominent food celebrities (the career of Jacques Pepin was recently reviewed) but with less emphasis on glamour than a title like *Gourmet.* Regular features are accompanied by recipes, and they provide balanced coverage of food and drink, travel, and entertaining. A comprehensive guide to selecting and purchasing the resources that are featured is included in each issue. The "Saveur Kitchen" feature includes techniques and discoveries from the editors and recipe testers. Recipes include no nutritional analysis.

3222. *Taste of Home: the magazine edited by a thousand country cooks.* [ISSN: 1071-5878] 1993. bi-m. USD 17.98 United States; USD 25.66 Canada; USD 25.98 elsewhere. Ed(s): Kathy Pohl. Reiman Publications, LLC, 5400 S 60th St, Greendale, WI 53129; http://www.reimanpub.com. Illus., index, adv. Sample. Circ: 5000000 Paid. Vol. ends: Nov/Dec. *Aud.:* Ga.

Although not exclusively about "comfort food," this is the "comfort magazine" of food periodicals. *Taste of Home* includes simple-to-prepare and practical recipes made from commonly available ingredients, contributed by a staff of 1000 people across the country. Features in each issue include "Cooking for One or Two," "Meals in Minutes," "Editor's Favorite Meal," "Mom's Best Meal," and "Late Night Snacks." A glossy "homey" picture accompanies each recipe. Few recipes include nutritional analysis or dietary exchange information. The index is arranged by meal course. Each issue includes a section of recipes formatted to "clip and save." This title has spawned a number of other magazines and its own *Taste of Home's Cookbook Collection.* (Recent titles include *Chocolate Lover's Cookbook*, *Recipe Card Collection*, and *Grandma's Best Desserts.*)

3223. *Tea: a magazine.* [ISSN: 1079-4611] 1994. bi-m. USD 17.80; USD 5 newsstand/cover per issue. Ed(s): Pearl Dexter. Olde English Tea Company, Inc., 3 Devotion Rd, PO Box 348, Scotland, CT 06264; teamag@connix.com; http://www.connix.com/~teamag. Adv. Circ: 10000 Paid. *Bk. rev.:* Number and length vary. *Aud.:* Ga, Sa.

This slim and charming title is a boon for those ensconced in the world of tea and for those just beginning to explore it. Recent articles feature teas from around the world. Each issue includes a "Directory of Tea Rooms" and book reviews. Recipes are either for tea or for food with tea as an ingredient. Few recipes include nutritional information. Advertisements are primarily for tea and tea products.

3224. *Touring and Tasting: wine, food, travel.* [ISSN: 1098-8866] 1995. s-a. USD 9. Touring and Tasting Club, 207 E Victoria St., Santa Barbara, CA 93101; wine@touringandtasting.com; http://www.touringandtasting.com. *Aud.:* Ga.

This title bridges the gap between "wine magazines" and "food and travel magazines" by striving to be the "guide to the best lodging, dinner, and recreation." It even sponsors its own wine club, advertised as America's most exciting. Readers will find no recipes in this title. It concentrates on providing articles not only about what wines to purchase but also about where to purchase them. Travel articles often focus on trips to, around, and between vineyards. This title is well worth considering for public libraries.

3225. *Vegetarian Times.* Incorporates: *Vegetarian World.* [ISSN: 0164-8497] 1974. m. USD 24 domestic; USD 36 foreign. Ed(s): Suzanne Berber. Sabot Publishing, 9 River Bend Dr S Ste 41, Stamford, CT 06907; http://www.vegetariantimes.com. Illus., adv. Circ: 340000 Paid. Vol. ends: Dec. Microform: PQC. Online: bigchalk; EBSCO Publishing; Gale Group; Northern Light Technology, Inc.; OCLC Online Computer Library Center, Inc.; ProQuest Information & Learning. Reprint: PQC. *Indexed:* MagInd. *Aud.:* Ga, Sa.

Focusing on the overall vegetarian lifestyle, this title, boasting an impressive editorial advisory board, generally includes three featured articles per issue. Articles often use a place, type of cuisine, or celebration (recent examples include Shanghai, Costa Rica, coffee, picnics, Cinco de Mayo, Mardi Gras) to frame both the article and accompanying recipes. Interviews, political issues, environmental policies, and animal rights are also commonly featured. Departments include "Vegan Gourmet," "Fast Food" (less than 30 minutes to prepare), "Wellness," and "Trends." Recipes include nutritional analysis. The index divides recipes by type of diet (egg and dairy free, egg free, dairy free, and containing dairy and eggs), low calorie, low saturated fat, and 30 minutes or less. A glossary of ingredients is also included.

3226. *Veggie Life: growing green, cooking lean, feeling good.* [ISSN: 1065-2728] 1993. q. USD 12.97; USD 3.95 newsstand/cover per issue. Ed(s): Shanna Masters. E G W Publishing Co., 1041 Shary Circle, Concord, CA 94518; support@egw.com; http://www.egw.com. Illus., index, adv. Circ: 150000 Paid. *Aud.:* Ga, Sa.

Focusing on vegetarian cuisine and health maintenance, this title boasts an impressive editorial advisory board. Each issue includes recipes submitted by readers, kitchen crafts, "Be Nourished" (Q & A column), fun fast food, goods and greens (new product information), and a pullout centerfold of recipes with illustrations and photographs designed for a three-ring binder. Recipes include nutritional analysis and vegetarian designation. The recipe index codes items by type of diet (apian, lacto, ovo, vegan) and time (greater than 45 minutes, takes additional time unattended). One drawback is that the color coding for the type of diet is subtle and could be difficult for readers who are sight-impaired or have difficulty distinguishing between colors. In late 2003, this title is scheduled to spin off a quarterly publication that will be a "best of," arranged in themed issues. It may be well worth considering also.

3227. *Wine Enthusiast.* Formerly (until 1990): *Wine Times.* [ISSN: 1078-3318] 1988. 13x/yr. USD 32.95; USD 49.95 foreign. Ed(s): Adam Strum. Wine Enthusiast, 103 Fairview Pk Dr., Elmsford, NY 10523-1553; winenthmag@aol.com; http://www.wineenthusiast.com. Adv. *Aud.:* Ga, Ac, Sa.

Wine Enthusiast covers a broader range of subjects than *QRW* and also devotes a large amount of its space to the reviews and buying guide. Articles highlight every aspect of the world of wine from specific styles of wine to vineyard reviews, from enhancing travel while keeping wine in mind to home interior design (especially wine storage and serving). The regular features "Proof Positive" (spirits review), "Vine Cuttings" (wine and vineyard news), and "Pairings" (food and wine pairing) round out the coverage. Recipes do not include nutritional analysis. Written with the comprehensive wine enthusiast in mind, this title is recommended if your collection can support several wine titles.

3228. *Wine Spectator.* [ISSN: 0193-497X] 1976. s-m. 18/yr. USD 45 domestic; USD 58.85 Canada; USD 135 overseas. Ed(s): Marvin R Shanken. M. Shanken Communications, Inc., 387 Park Ave S, New York, NY 10016; http://www.winespectator.com. Illus., adv. Vol. ends: Dec. *Indexed:* MagInd. *Aud.:* Ga, Sa.

If you can purchase only one wine magazine, this is probably the one. Comprehensively covering the wine world, *Wine Spectator* has won and continues to deserve its reputation as top wine magazine. Wine features include analysis and reviews of wines and vineyards; tasting reports and notes; and sales, auction, and industry news. The "Wine Spectator Buying Guide" in each issue is a must for wise shopping. In addition to wine coverage, the well-written articles include interviews, restaurant reviews, culinary trends, domestic and world travel (including hotel information), and a few recipes (no nutritional analysis).

3229. ***Zymurgy.*** [ISSN: 0196-5921] 1978. q. USD 33 domestic; USD 39 Canada; USD 50 elsewhere. Ed(s): Dena Niskek. American Homebrewers Association Inc., PO Box 1679, Boulder, CO 80306-1679; dena@aob.org; http://www.beertown.org. Adv. Circ: 24000 Paid. *Aud.:* Ga, Sa.

Zymurgy is defined as "the art and science of fermentation, as in brewing." Although wine titles abound, this title, published by the American Homebrewers Association, supporting their mission "to make quality beer and brewing knowledge accessible to all," fills a void in many collections: a publication for the beer enthusiast. This well-balanced magazine usually includes four uniquely themed articles (styles of beer, brewing techniques, travel, interviews), "Extract Experiments," "Quick Recipe Guide," a guide to ingredients, homebrew club news, a beer competition calendar, competition results, "Dear Professor" (Q & A), beer reviews, and product reviews.

■ FOOD INDUSTRY

Pamela Palmer, Associate Professor of Libraries, University of Memphis, Memphis, TN 38152; prpalmer@memphis.edu

Introduction

Food industry periodicals range from trade journals to scholarly publications, and their target audiences are similarly varied. Trade journals focus on trends, news, industry analysis, companies, and personalities in the industry. They are directed to a broad readership interested in corporate administration, plant operations, manufacturing equipment, and government regulation. Use of graphics, photographs, and design features make them as colorful as the products they cover.

At the other end of the spectrum, the scholarly journals are highly technical scientific reports of original research and reviews of research on food-related areas of chemistry and microbiology. Almost all the food industry titles have a web site, but online content varies widely. Some offer access to full-text articles from the current issue, while others provide only tables of contents and abstracts. Other web features offered by some titles include current news items, alerts to topics of personal interest, for-fee article access, tables of contents for older issues, and subscriptions to the online version.

Basic Periodicals

Ac: *Food Technology;* Sa: *Food Technology, Journal of Food Science, Prepared Foods.*

Basic Abstracts and Indexes

Food Science and Technology Abstracts.

3230. ***Appetite: research on eating and drinking.*** [ISSN: 0195-6663] 1980. bi-m. EUR 859 (Individuals, EUR 327). Ed(s): I L Bernstein. Elsevier BV, Life Sciences Department, Molenwerf 1, Amsterdam, 1014 AG, Netherlands. Illus., index, adv. Refereed. Vol. ends: No. 3. Online: EBSCO Publishing; ingenta.com; OCLC Online Computer Library Center, Inc.; RoweCom Information Quest; ScienceDirect; Swets Blackwell. *Indexed:* Agr, AnBeAb, BiolAb, ChemAb, DSA, ExcerpMed, FS&TA, IndMed, PsycholAb, SCI, SSCI, VetBull, WAE&RSA. *Bk. rev.:* 1, 300-400 words. *Aud.:* Ac, Sa.

Focused on behavioral nutrition and the cultural, sensory, and physiological influences on choices and intakes of food and drinks, this bimonthly journal covers normal and disordered eating and drinking, dietary attitudes and practices, and all aspects of the bases of human and animal behavior toward food. It publishes research reports, rapid communications, book reviews, and abstracts of presentations at major meetings in the social science, psychology, or neuroscience of food consumption, including the Association for the Study of Food in Society, the Society for the Study of Ingestive Behavior, and conferences on Food Choice. Sample articles indicate the international focus of the journal. Recent titles include "Effect of a carbohydrate supplement on feeding behaviour and exercise in rats exposed to hyperbaric hypoxia," "Effectiveness of trained peer models to encourage food acceptance in preschool children" from the United States, and "Proper meals in transition: young married couples on the nature of eating together" from Scotland. Target audiences include academics and other researchers in the areas of psychology, social research, neuroscience, physiology, nutrition, and sensory food science.

3231. ***Beverage Industry.*** Former titles (until 1973): *Soft Drink Industry;* (until 1966): *Bottling Industry.* [ISSN: 0148-6187] 1946. m. USD 85.05 domestic (Free to qualified personnel). Ed(s): Joan Holleran. Stagnito Communications, Inc., 155 Pfingsten Rd., Ste. 205, Deerfield, IL 60015; info@stagnito.com; http://www.stagnito.com. Illus., index, adv. Circ: 34000. Microform: PQC. Online: East View Publications, Inc.; EBSCO Publishing; Florida Center for Library Automation; Gale Group; Northern Light Technology, Inc.; OCLC Online Computer Library Center, Inc.; ProQuest Information & Learning. *Indexed:* ABIn, B&I, BPI. *Aud.:* Sa.

Beverage Industry is billed as the only feature-format tabloid serving beverage manufacturers, distributors, and retailers. This trade publication's focus is production, marketing, technology, and distribution, including coverage of obstacles facing executives in the corporate suite, on the plant floor, and in the R&D lab. Coverage is broad, including bottled water, juice/juice-type drinks, wine, liquor, alternative beverages, coffee and tea, dairy, soft drinks, and beer. Issues cover industry information—individual companies' successful sales and marketing approaches, trends and news in product safety, and product and industry issues, as well as new packaging, logistics, coverage of meetings and shows, marketing trends, and a suppliers' marketplace. One recent issue includes the Annual Soft Drink Report, complete with numerous detailed statistical charts; an in-depth look at the industry; the state of industry leaders; and new products—all presented with informative graphics. That same issue covers safety and innovation at Le-Nature's plant, experts' views on brand extension, retro aluminum packaging, research and development insights, and a special 14-page supplement on the National Soft Drink Association.

3232. ***Candy Industry: the global magazine of chocolate and confectionery.*** Former titles: *Candy and Snack Industry; Baked Snack Industry; Candy.* [ISSN: 0745-1032] 1874. m. USD 70.10 domestic (Free to qualified personnel). Ed(s): Susan Tiffany. Stagnito Communications, Inc., 155 Pfingsten Rd., Ste. 205, Deerfield, IL 60015; info@stagnito.com; http://www.stagnito.com. Illus., index, adv. Circ: 5700. Vol. ends: Dec. Microform: PQC. Online: The Dialog Corporation; EBSCO Publishing; Factiva; Florida Center for Library Automation; Gale Group; Northern Light Technology, Inc.; OCLC Online Computer Library Center, Inc.; ProQuest Information & Learning. *Indexed:* ABIn, B&I, BPI, DSA, FS&TA, LRI. *Aud.:* Sa.

A trade publication targeted to the global confectionary market, *Candy World* offers international coverage of news, key events and conferences, special reports on segments of the industry, company profiles, plant and processing technology, packaging, new products, and more. As the leading information source for the global confectionary marketplace, the magazine covers large and medium-sized confectionary manufacturers, privately owned and family-owned businesses, and smaller retail confectioners with on-premises manufacturing. Recent issues include a cover story on Ganong Bros. Ltd., a Chocolate Trendsetter column on Long Grove Confectionary Co., news items ranging from acquisitions to bankruptcies, a Category Closeup on sour candy, a special report on candy manufacturers' R&D expenditures and directions, a preview of a state association conference on technical issues, a special report on the top 100 confectionary companies with rankings by annual sales, and information on packaging innovations. An annual Buyer's Guide lists over 700 companies in 400 product areas.

3233. ***Cereal Chemistry.*** [ISSN: 0009-0352] 1924. bi-m. USD 358. Ed(s): Jon M Faubion. American Association of Cereal Chemists, Inc., 3340 Pilot Knob Rd., St. Paul, MN 55121-2097; aacc@scisoc.org; http://www.aaccnet.org. Illus., index, adv. Refereed. Circ: 2075 Paid. Vol. ends: Dec. Microform: PMC; PQC. Online: ProQuest Information & Learning. *Indexed:* Agr, B&AI, BiolAb, ChemAb, DSA, EngInd, ExcerpMed, FS&TA, HortAb, S&F, SCI. *Aud.:* Sa.

An international research journal published since 1924, *Cereal Chemistry* covers cereal science. Research areas include biochemistry, biotechnology, products, processes, and analytical procedures associated with cereals and other grain crops. The research reported here explores raw materials, processes, products utilizing cereal (corn, wheat, oats, rice, rye, etc.), oilseeds, and pulses, as well as analytical procedures, technological tests, and fundamental research in the cereals area. Articles range from comprehensive reviews to reports of original investigations. Published by the American Association of Cereal Chemists (AACC), the journal is written for a scholarly audience. Recent articles include "Effect of Particle Size and Moisture Content on Viscosity of Fish Feed," "Factors that Influence the Microwave Expansion of Glassy Amylopectin Extrudates," and "Aryl-Glycosidase Activities in Germinating Maize." On the AACC web site at www.aaccnet.org/cerealchemistry, readers have access to most of the content of the current issue, can view tables of contents from past issues, and can search the journal's abstracts from 1960 to the present, although full text is only available to subscribers to *Cereal Chemistry* online.

3234. *Cereal Foods World.* Formerly: *Cereal Science Today.* [ISSN: 0146-6283] 1956. bi-m. Nov.-Dec. combined. USD 187. Ed(s): Jody Grider. American Association of Cereal Chemists, Inc., 3340 Pilot Knob Rd., St. Paul, MN 55121-2097; aacc@scisoc.org; http://www.aaccnet.org. Illus., index, adv. Refereed. Circ: 4660 Paid and controlled. Vol. ends: Dec. Microform: PQC. Online: ProQuest Information & Learning. *Indexed:* Agr, BiolAb, ChemAb, DSA, EnvAb, FS&TA, HortAb, RRTA, S&F, SCI, WAE&RSA. *Aud.:* Sa.

Written for food industry professionals, *Cereal Foods World* focuses on industry and product information in the areas of grain-based food science, technology, and new product development. It includes high-quality feature articles and scientific research papers that focus on advances in grain-based food science and the application of these advances to product development and food production practices. Published by the American Association of Cereal Chemists (AACC), *Cereal Food World* provides tables of contents on the web site at www.aaccnet.org/cerealfoodsworld. Regular features include articles, research reports, columns on Quality Assurance, Engineering, Nutrition, and Grain Quality; news from the AACC, industry profiles, industry news, and association news. Feature articles in recent issues include "Quality Assurance for Hard Pretzel Production" and "Improving Soybean Oil for the Snack Food Industry." Research articles include "In Vitro Binding of Bile Acids by Ready-to-Eat Breakfast Cereals," and "Effects of Leavening Acids on Characteristics of Fresh and 30-Day-Old Tortillas." Each bimonthly issue has a different cereal food focus, such as baking or an ingredient update on snack foods.

3235. *Chemical Senses.* Formerly: *Chemical Senses and Flavour.* [ISSN: 0379-864X] 1974. 9x/yr. GBP 470. Ed(s): Dr. B. W. Ache, Dr. Robyn Hudson. Oxford University Press, Great Clarendon St, Oxford, OX2 6DP, United Kingdom; jnl.orders@oup.co.uk; http://www3.oup.co.uk/jnls. Illus., index, adv. Refereed. Circ: 1000. Vol. ends: No. 6. Online: EBSCO Publishing; HighWire Press; ingenta.com; RoweCom Information Quest; Swets Blackwell. Reprint: PSC; SWZ. *Indexed:* AnBeAb, ChemAb, ExcerpMed, FS&TA, IndMed, IndVet, PsycholAb, SCI, SSCI, VetBull, ZooRec. *Aud.:* Sa.

Chemical Senses publishes original research and review papers on all aspects of human and animal chemoreception. This includes the gross morphology and fine structure of receptors and central chemosensory pathways; the properties of the stimuli and the nature of the chemical-receptor interaction; and the electrical, biochemical, and behavioral correlates (both animal and human) of neural response to chemosensory stimuli. The journal covers techniques and the development and application of new methods for investigating chemoreception and chemosensory structures. It is associated with the European Chemoreception Research Organization, the Association for Chemoreception Sciences, and the Japanese Association for the Study of Taste and Smell. Geared to a scholarly/professional audience, *Chemical Senses* is international in scope and authorship. Recent articles include "Virus-mediated Transfer of Foreign DNA into Taste Receptor Cells" and "Gender Differences in the Retention of Swahili Names for Unfamiliar Odors." On the journal web site at http://chemse.oupjournals.org, users can search for articles and view abstracts from 1994. Only subscribers have no-cost access to full-text articles (1989-present); nonsubscribers can order for-fee individual articles. An e-mail alerting service also is available.

3236. *Critical Reviews in Food Science and Nutrition.* Former titles: *C R C Critical Reviews in Food Science and Nutrition; C R C Critical Reviews in Food Technology.* [ISSN: 1040-8398] 1970. 8x/yr. USD 790 (Individuals, USD 110 print & online eds.). Ed(s): Fergus M Clydesdale. C R C Press, Llc, 2000 Corporate Blvd, N W, Boca Raton, FL 33431-9868; journals@crcpress.com; http://www.crcpress.com. Illus., index. Refereed. Circ: 500. Vol. ends: Dec. *Indexed:* Agr, BiolAb, ChemAb, DSA, FS&TA, IndMed, IndVet, SCI, SSCI. *Aud.:* Ac, Sa.

Presenting critical viewpoints of current technology, food science, and human nutrition is the focus of this journal. Major areas include food safety; food processing; government regulation and policy; nutrition; fortification; new food products; food and behavior; effects of processing on nutrition; and food labeling. The application of scientific discoveries and the acquisition of knowledge, as they relate to nutrition, are thoroughly addressed in this comprehensive and authoritative information source. Reviews include issues of national concern, especially to the food science nutritionist and health professional. Bimonthly issues contain three or four authoritative critical reviews written for the scholarly or expert audience. The journal is international in both scope and authorship. Recent titles include "Wheat Protein Composition and Properties of Wheat Glutenin in Relation to Breadmaking Functionality" and "Tea Catechins and Polyphenols: Health Effects, Metabolism, and Antioxidant Functions."

3237. *Dairy Foods: innovative ideas and technologies for dairy processors.* Formerly (until 1986): *Dairy Record;* Which incorporated (in 1981): *American Dairy Review;* Which was formerly (until 1965): *American Milk Review;* (until 1959): *American Milk Review and Milk Plant Monthly;* Which was formed by the merger of (1930-1958): *Milk Plant Monthly;* (1939-1958): *American Milk Review (Year).* [ISSN: 0888-0050] 1958. m. USD 99.90 domestic; USD 141.90 Canada; USD 136.90 Mexico. Business News Publishing Co., 755 W Big Beaver Rd, Ste 1000, Troy, MI 48084-4903; http://www.bnp.com. Illus., index, adv. Circ: 18585 Controlled. Vol. ends: Dec. Microform: PQC. Online: The Dialog Corporation; EBSCO Publishing; Florida Center for Library Automation; Gale Group; Northern Light Technology, Inc.; OCLC Online Computer Library Center, Inc.; ProQuest Information & Learning. Reprint: PQC. *Indexed:* ABIn, B&I, DSA, ExcerpMed, FS&TA, RRTA, WAE&RSA. *Aud.:* Ac, Sa.

For more than a century, *Dairy Foods* has served the dairy industry by analyzing and reporting on technologies, trends, and issues and how they affect North America's processors of milk, cheese, frozen desserts, and cultured products. As the leading periodical targeting dairy processors and the companies selling to them, the monthly magazine covers News & Trends, New Products & Marketing, Ingredient Technology, Plant Operations, Departments, and Special Features. Recent issues include "Sitting Pretty: 2003 Ice Cream Outlook" and "Growth Continues—Cultured Product Trends." Departments cover an industry editorial, information on industry movers and shakers, and new products. The web site at http://dairyfoods.com includes highlights from the current issue and an archive of articles from previous issues.

3238. *Food Additives and Contaminants: analysis, surveillance, evaluation, control.* [ISSN: 0265-203X] 1984. m. GBP 1234. Ed(s): J Gilbert, P M Scott. Taylor & Francis Ltd, 11 New Fetter Ln, London, EC4P 4EE, United Kingdom; info@tandf.co.uk; http://www.tandf.co.uk/journals. Illus., index, adv. Refereed. Online: EBSCO Publishing; Ingenta Select; OCLC Online Computer Library Center, Inc.; RoweCom Information Quest; Swets Blackwell. Reprint: PSC. *Indexed:* Agr, BiolAb, ChemAb, DSA, EnvAb, ExcerpMed, FPA, FS&TA, ForAb, H&SSA, HortAb, IndMed, IndVet, S&F, SCI, VetBull, WAE&RSA. *Bk. rev.:* 2-5, 300-600 words. *Aud.:* Ac, Sa.

Publishing original research papers and reviews, *Food Additives and Contaminants* focuses on analytical methodology, occurrence, persistence, safety evaluation, detoxication, regulatory control, and surveillance of natural and man-made additives and contaminants in the food chain. Contributions cover the chemistry, biochemistry, and bioavailability of these substances; factors affecting levels of potentially toxic compounds that may arise during production, processing, packaging, and storage, and in the development of novel foods and processes; and surveillance data and exposure estimates. Readership includes scientists involved in all aspects of food safety and quality including research, analysis, safety evaluation, quality assurance, regulatory aspects, and surveillance. Recent articles include "Butyltin compounds in retail mollusc products" and "Aluminum content of Spanish infant formula." The journal's alert service for contents and keywords is available on the publisher's web site at www.tandf.co.uk/journals/online.html.

3239. ***Food and Chemical Toxicology.*** Formerly (until 1982): *Food and Cosmetics Toxicology.* [ISSN: 0278-6915] 1963. m. EUR 2211 (Qualified personnel, EUR 269). Ed(s): Joseph F. Borzelleca, Hans Verhagen. Pergamon, The Boulevard, Langford Ln, East Park, Kidlington, OX5 1GB, United Kingdom. Illus., index, adv. Refereed. Circ: 1900. Microform: PQC. Online: ingenta.com; ScienceDirect; Swets Blackwell. *Indexed:* Agr, BiolAb, C&ISA, ChemAb, DSA, ExcerpMed, FPA, FS&TA, ForAb, H&SSA, HortAb, IndMed, IndVet, PollutAb, S&F, SCI, SSCI, VetBull, WAE&RSA, WRCInf. *Aud.:* Sa.

An international journal, *Food and Chemical Toxicology* publishes original research reports and occasional interpretative reviews on the toxic effects, in animals or humans, of natural or synthetic chemicals occurring in the human environment. Other areas covered include studies relating to food, water, and other consumer products; papers on industrial and agricultural chemicals and pharmaceuticals; and new areas such as safety evaluation of novel foods and biotechnologically derived products and inter-relationships between nutrition and toxicology. Given the need for high-quality science in support of health and safety decisions, it considers publishing papers of a more regulatory nature, provided they are part of a more general scientific analysis in their Regulatory Toxicology section. Target audiences are food scientists, toxicologists, chemists, and researchers working in the pharmaceutical industry. Published since 1963, the journal is scholarly. Each issue contains a review article and several research articles. Recent titles include "Development of a urinary biomarker of human exposure to deoxynivalenol" and "Differences in ethoxyquin nephrotoxicity between male and female F344 rats."

3240. ***Food and Drug Law Journal.*** Formerly (until 1991): *Food Drug Cosmetic Law Journal.* [ISSN: 1064-590X] 1946. 3x/yr. Members, USD 299; Non-members, USD 379. Ed(s): Stephanie Scott, M Cathryn Butler. Food and Drug Law Institute, 1000 Vermont Ave, N W, Ste 200, Washington, DC 20005; http://www.fdli.org. Illus., index, adv. Refereed. Reprint: WSH. *Indexed:* CLI, ChemAb, DSA, ExcerpMed, FS&TA, H&SSA, ILP, LRI, SSCI, WAE&RSA. *Aud.:* Ac, Sa.

For over 50 years, this award-winning journal has offered readers scholarly, in-depth, analytical articles, providing insight into the actions of FDA, FTC, and USDA, how the courts interpret these actions, and the reaction of industry. Articles published in the *Food and Drug Law Journal* are heavily cited and reviewed. In 2003, the journal became a quarterly publication again, after appearing on a three-times-a-year basis. Balancing the scholarly and the practical, the journal focuses on five objectives: (1) to clarify the complex regulation and legislation affecting the food, drug, cosmetic, medical device, and healthcare technology industries; (2) to explore the possible future implications of proposed regulations and policy trends; (3) to analyze critical court decisions in food and drug law, including intellectual property, antitrust, constitutional, and criminal law issues related to the health law field; (4) to look beyond our borders to assess how food- and drug-related issues are regulated in other countries; and (5) to provide a neutral forum for intelligent discussion and debate among authors from private industry, government agencies, and academic institutions. Recent articles include "Bioterrorism: Defining a Research Agenda" and "Navigating the Hatch-Waxman Act's Safe Harbor." The journal web site at www.fdli.org/pubs/Journal%20Online/journalarticles.html provides tables of contents and article abstracts; articles may be purchased on a for-fee basis.

3241. ***Food Chemistry.*** Incorporates (1985-1991): *Journal of Micronutrient Analysis.* [ISSN: 0308-8146] 1976. 20x/yr. EUR 3190 (Qualified personnel, EUR 145). Ed(s): G. G. Birch, P. M. Finglas. Elsevier BV, Sara Burgerhartstraat 25, Amsterdam, 1055 KV, Netherlands; nlinfo-f@elsevier.nl; http://www.elsevier.nl. Illus., index, adv. Refereed. Microform: PQC. Online: ingenta.com; ScienceDirect; Swets Blackwell. *Indexed:* A&ATA, Agr, BiolAb, ChemAb, DSA, EngInd, ExcerpMed, FPA, FS&TA, ForAb, HortAb, IndVet, S&F, SCI, VetBull. *Aud.:* Ac, Sa.

Aimed at food technologists, scientists, and chemists, *Food Chemistry* publishes original peer-reviewed research papers. The focus is on six areas: the chemical analysis of food; chemical additives and toxins; chemistry relating to the microbiological, sensory, nutritional, and physiological aspects of food; structural changes in molecules during the processing and storage of foods; direct effects on foods of the use of agrochemicals; and chemical quality in food engineering and technology. In its Analytical, Nutritional, and Clinical Methods section, the journal covers the measurement of micronutrients, macronutrients, additives, and contaminants in foodstuffs and biological samples. Recent articles include "Collagen of the skin of ocellate puffer fish (*Takifugu rubripes*)" and "Variability of brewer's spent grain within a brewery."

3242. ***Food Engineering: the magazine for manufacturing management.*** Former titles (until 1998): *Chilton's Food Engineering;* (until 1977): *Food Engineering.* [ISSN: 1522-2292] 1928. 11x/yr. USD 65 in US & Canada; USD 96 foreign; USD 8 newsstand/cover per issue domestic. Ed(s): Joyce Fassl. Business News Publishing Co., 755 W Big Beaver Rd, Ste 1000, Troy, MI 48084-4903; http://www.bnp.com. Illus., index, adv. Circ: 52100. Vol. ends: Dec. Microform: CIS; PQC. Online: The Dialog Corporation; Gale Group; ProQuest Information & Learning. Reprint: PQC. *Indexed:* AS&TI, B&I, BiolAb, ChemAb, DSA, EngInd, FS&TA. *Aud.:* Ac, Sa.

Written for the manufacturing team in the food and beverage process industry, *Food Engineering* is subtitled *The Magazine for Manufacturing Management.* It covers flexible manufacturing, advanced information exchange, and the changing role of the food engineer. Now in its 75th year, the trade journal covers the full array of food industry topics, ranging from features and tech updates to issues of packaging, safety, software, R&D, and a variety of special reports. Regular special reports include "Top 100 Food and Beverage Companies," "Annual Packaging Trend Survey," and "State of Food Manufacturing." Cover articles in recent issues include "Bridging the IT/Engineering Gap" and "Food Safety: Say Goodbye to the Burn." Special reports and current issue articles are available on the journal's web site at www.foodengineeringmag.com.

3243. ***Food Reviews International.*** [ISSN: 8755-9129] 1985. 3x/yr. USD 1070. Marcel Dekker Inc., 270 Madison Ave, New York, NY 10016-0602; http://www.dekker.com. Illus., index, adv. Refereed. Circ: 350. Vol. ends: No. 4. Microform: RPI. Online: EBSCO Publishing; OCLC Online Computer Library Center, Inc.; RoweCom Information Quest; Swets Blackwell. *Indexed:* Agr, BioEngAb, ChemAb, DSA, FS&TA, H&SSA, HortAb, IndVet, S&F, SCI, WAE&RSA. *Bk. rev.:* 1-2, 300-400 words. *Aud.:* Ac, Sa.

Focused on state-of-the-art reviews concerned with food production, processing, acceptability, and health aspects of nutrition, as well as the differing problems affecting both affluent and developing nations, *Food Reviews International* offers technical solutions to critical food dilemmas and shortages. Target audiences are food scientists and technologists, food and cereal chemists, chemical engineers, agriculturists, microbiologists, toxicologists, and nutritionists. Recent articles include "Problems and Constraints of Small-Scale Irrigation (Fadama) in Nigeria" and "Modified Atmosphere and Vacuum Packaging of Meat and Poultry Products." Articles first appear on the web site (www.dekker.com/servlet/product/productid/FRI); then, four times each year, the print version is published. Subscribers can obtain complete articles online. Nonsubscribers can register for two-minute previews and purchase articles online.

3244. ***Food Technology: a publication of the Institute of Food Technologists.*** [ISSN: 0015-6639] 1947. m. Non-members, USD 82. Ed(s): John B Klis. Institute of Food Technologists, 221 N La Salle St, Chicago, IL 60601; http://www.ift.org/publ/publ_aoo.html. Illus., index, adv. Circ: 26000. Vol. ends: Dec. Microform: PQC. Online: Gale Group. Reprint: PQC. *Indexed:* AS&TI, AgeL, Agr, B&AI, BiolAb, ChemAb, DSA, EngInd, ExcerpMed, FS&TA, GSI, H&SSA, HortAb, IndVet, SCI, SSCI, VetBull, WAE&RSA. *Aud.:* Ac, Sa.

Food Technology, published by the Institute of Food Technologists, is designed to present information regarding the development of new and improved food sources, products, and processes; their proper utilization by industry and the consumer; and their effective regulation by government agencies. The monthly publication provides news and analysis of the development, use, quality, safety, and regulation of food sources, products, and processes for food scientists and other interested individuals in the food and supplier industries, government, and academia. It combines serious multidisciplinary content with top-notch photographs and graphics. Contents range from features to departments, columns, and resources. For example, a recent issue includes features on "Zoonutrients and Health" and "High Pressure Sterilization: Maximizing the Benefits of Adiabatic Heating." Departments and columns cover the interests of their audience—news, consumer trends, ingredients, packaging, laboratory, and federal government updates. A recent issue contains a 32-page "Classified Guide to Food Service Industries." Visit their web site at www.ift.org to access some articles online; the site states these can be downloaded free for a limited time.

3245. ***International Journal of Food Sciences and Nutrition.*** Former titles: *Food Sciences and Nutrition; Human Nutrition. Food Sciences and Nutrition; Journal of Plant Foods; Plant Foods for Man.* [ISSN: 0963-7486] 1973. bi-m. GBP 442 (Individuals, GBP 183). Ed(s): C J K Henry. Carfax Publishing Ltd., 4 Park Sq, Milton Park, Abingdon, OX14 4RN, United Kingdom; enquiry@tandf.co.uk; http://www.tandf.co.uk/. Refereed. Circ: 1000 Controlled. Online: bigchalk; EBSCO Publishing; Florida Center for Library Automation; Gale Group; Ingenta Select; OCLC Online Computer Library Center, Inc.; ProQuest Information & Learning; RoweCom Information Quest; Swets Blackwell. Reprint: PSC. *Indexed:* Agr, BiolAb, ChemAb, DSA, ExcerpMed, FPA, FS&TA, ForAb, GSI, HortAb, IndMed, RRTA, S&F, WAE&RSA. *Aud.:* Ac, Sa.

Designed to integrate food science with nutrition, *International Journal of Food Science and Nutrition* publishes research articles and critical reviews in the fields of food science and nutrition, with special emphasis on the emerging interface between the sciences. The journal focuses on ten major areas. These are: (1) impact of nutritional science on food product development, (2) nutritional implications of food processing, (3) bioavailability of nutrients, (4) nutritional quality of novel foods, (5) food-nutrient interactions, (6)use of biotechnology in food science/nutrition, (7) tropical food processing and nutrition, (8) food acceptability and dietary selection, (9) nutritional and physiological aspects of food, and (10) dietary requirements and nutritive value of food. Recent articles include "Nutritional aspect of zinc availability" and "Digestion rate of legume carbohydrates and glycemic index of legume-based meals." The journal alert service for contents and keywords is available on the publisher's web site at www.tandf.co.uk/journals/online.html.

3246. ***Journal of Food Protection.*** Formerly (until 1977): *Journal of Milk and Food Technology.* [ISSN: 0362-028X] 1937. m. USD 310 domestic; USD 325 in Canada & Mexico; USD 355 elsewhere. Ed(s): John Sofos, Michael Davidson. International Association for Food Protection, 6200 Aurora Ave, Ste 200W, Des Moines, IA 50322-2864; info@foodprotection.org; http://www.foodprotection.org. Illus., index, adv. Refereed. Circ: 3000 Paid. Microform: PMC; PQC. Online: Ingenta Select. Reprint: PQC. *Indexed:* Agr, B&AI, BiolAb, ChemAb, DSA, ExcerpMed, FPA, FS&TA, H&SSA, HortAb, IndMed, IndVet, PollutAb, RRTA, RiskAb, S&F, SCI, VetBull, WAE&RSA. *Aud.:* Sa.

Meeting its goal of publishing the most up-to-date, original research reports and review articles in food science and technology, the *Journal of Food Protection* publishes papers from scientists worldwide. A leader in the field of food microbiology, the journal content is scholarly and research based. Readership exceeds 11,000 scientists from 69 countries. First published in 1937, the journal is a publication of the International Association for Food Protection. In a recent issue, titles include "Recovery of *Salmonella* from Retail Broilers by a Whole-Carcass Enrichment Procedure" and "Immunological Detection of *Fusarium* Species in Cornmeal." An online subscription can be purchased separately or in conjunction with the print version.

3247. ***Journal of Food Science.*** [ISSN: 0022-1147] 1936. bi-m. Members, USD 20; Non-members, USD 100. Ed(s): Dr. Robert E Berry. Institute of Food Technologists, 221 N La Salle St, Chicago, IL 60601; http://www.ift.org/publ/publ_coo.htm. Illus., index. Refereed. Circ: 12000. Microform: PQC. Online: Gale Group. Reprint: PQC. *Indexed:* AS&TI, AbAn, Agr, B&AI, BiolAb, BiolDig, ChemAb, DSA, ExcerpMed, FS&TA, ForAb, GSI, H&SSA, HortAb, IndVet, PsycholAb, SCI, SSCI, SWRA, VetBull, WAE&RSA. *Aud.:* Ac, Sa.

The premier journal of the Institute of Food Technologists (IFT), *Journal of Food Science* contains peer-reviewed reports of original research and critical reviews of all basic and applied aspects of food sciences for food professionals. In addition to the research and review articles, a regular segment, "Industrial Aspects of Selected JFS Articles," provides short items. Each issue includes articles in these areas: Concise Reviews in Food Science, Food Chemistry and Toxicology, Food Engineering and Physical Properties, Food Microbiology and Safety, and Sensory and Nutritive Qualities of Food. Recent articles include "Oxygen Barrier Properties of Whey Protein Isolate Coatings on Polypropylene Films" and "Production of Volatiles from Fatty Acids and Oils by Irradiation." Print subscribers have online access to abstracts and full-text articles at the journal's web site, www.ift.org/publications/jfs/index.shtml, where nonsubscribers can browse abstracts and can download for-fee articles.

3248. ***Prepared Foods.*** Incorporates in 1986: *Food Plant Equipment;* Former titles (until 1984): *Processed Prepared Foods;* (1895-1977): *Canner Packer;* Incorporates in 1981: *Food Development;* Which was formerly: *Food Product Development.* [ISSN: 0747-2536] 1895. m. USD 99.90 domestic; USD 137.90 Canada; USD 136.90 Mexico. Business News Publishing Co., 755 W Big Beaver Rd, Ste 1000, Troy, MI 48084-4903; http://www.bnp.com. Illus., index, adv. Circ: 50038. Vol. ends: Dec. Microform: PQC. Online: EBSCO Publishing; Florida Center for Library Automation; Gale Group; Northern Light Technology, Inc.; OCLC Online Computer Library Center, Inc.; H.W. Wilson. Reprint: PQC. *Indexed:* B&I, BiolAb, ChemAb, DSA, FS&TA. *Aud.:* Sa.

A trade publication, *Prepared Foods* focuses on development trends and technologies for formulators and marketers. Each monthly issue includes features in the broad areas of food business and marketing, product development, and research/development, as well as special reports and news. Recent issues include articles on "Ten Trends in Nutritional Ingredient Use," "Twenty Top New Product Companies," and "Creating a Culinary Future." Special sections include Supplier Chef Profiles and Nutra Solutions—A Supplement on Solutions for the Development and Marketing of Nutritional Products. The web site at www.preparedfoods.com provides breaking news and full-text articles, and it can be browsed by ingredient, subject, and issue. Special reports, such as the "Vendor Services Report" are available online for a fee; other reports, such as "Leading 100 Food & Beverage Companies Report," are available online at no charge.

3249. ***Snack Food & Wholesale Bakery.*** Former titles (until 1996): *Snack Food;* (until 1967): *Biscuit and Cracker Baker.* [ISSN: 1096-4843] 1912. m. USD 85.06 domestic (Free to qualified personnel). Ed(s): Bernie Pacyniak. Stagnito Communications, Inc., 155 Pfingsten Rd., Ste. 205, Deerfield, IL 60015; info@stagnito.com; http://www.stagnito.com. Illus., index, adv. Circ: 18300 Paid and controlled. Vol. ends: Dec. Online: Florida Center for Library Automation; Gale Group; LexisNexis; OCLC Online Computer Library Center, Inc. *Indexed:* B&I. *Aud.:* Sa.

Covering the industry leaders in the baked goods and snack food markets, this tabloid trade publication focuses on the people, news, and trends in these growing fields. Issues include two to three features; the business and marketing editor's comments; news; market trends and new products; The SFA Section, focusing on the Snack Food Association; and Technology & Development. Recent issues include cover stories on "Awrey Bakeries" and "Executive on the Year." The publication's web site at www.snackandbakery.com lists contents of the current issue, but content is not available online.

■ FORESTRY

Bonnie E. Avery, Forestry and Natural Resources Librarian, Rm 121, The Valley Library, Oregon State University, Corvallis, OR 97331-4501; bonnie.avery@oregonstate.edu

Introduction

A broad definition of forestry would be "the study of trees, forests, and their use by people." Modern "science-based forestry" is thought to have begun in the nineteenth century when Europeans looked to specialists to address questions of wood supply and extraction both in their forests at home and in their colonies. The threat of forest loss and wood scarcity resulted in concern for increased forest growth and management techniques for improved yield. By 1891 the United States had established publicly owned forest reserves. In 1900 the

Society of American Foresters was established, as was the first School of Forestry in North American at Yale University. The U.S. Forest Service was formed three years later, and this combination of professional, scholarly, and governmental resources constitute the core of U.S. forestry research today. Since the mid-1940s the scope of forestry has grown in response to economics, demography, politics, and social change as well as developments in related fields of study. While at one time German was the primary language of forestry, since World War II most research is reported in English. Knowledge of international research and practices has grown in importance since the 1980s. In addressing global forest concerns, international and local researchers have begun to "discover" reservoirs of indigenous knowledge concerning forests and their use.

Modern forestry education has a tradition of integrating concepts from a variety of disciplines and creating new specialties. These include forest genetics, forest ecology, forest recreation, forest economics, forest engineering, urban forestry, plantation forestry, forest pathology, and wood science. The questions addressed by forestry are often interdisciplinary or require a deep understanding of a complementary discipline. As a result, a forest science collection will not be useful in isolation from access to sound collections in the natural, environmental, and agricultural sciences. Likewise, a wood science or forest engineering collection will rely on user access to collections in the physical sciences and civil, mechanical, and chemical engineering. Finally, to address the interaction of humans and "forest resources," whether looking at income generation, recreational use, traditional knowledge and practices, or conservation strategies, a forestry researcher will need access to collections in the social sciences.

Given these assumptions about access to other collections, we can define a distinct serial literature for forestry. It is defined by the history of forestry and as a result is composed largely of government document series, international, and nongovernmental organization reports as well as trade, scholarly professional, and, more recently, scholarly commercial journals.

The selected list of periodicals included here does not include government publications, although these are an important source of technical as well as scientific information. Governmental agencies such as the regional research and experiment stations of the U.S. Forest Service are vital sources of information on all aspects of forestry. Series titles such as the regional *General Technical Reports* are numerous. They are now published electronically in full-text and are available from the Forest Service web site. Canadian libraries will benefit from their easy access to this literature and that of the National Research Council of Canada's many serial publications.

Although they are important sources of information, statistical series and serials available from nongovernmental, nonprofit international organizations and research institutions have not been included in this listing. Several statistical series and *The State of the World's Forests* are available as searchable datasets and in full-text online from the Food and Agriculture Organization (FAO) Forestry Sector web site. There are numerous serial publications now available via the Internet from other nongovernmental, nonprofit agencies. These are particularly important for coverage of "international forestry." The FAO Forestry Sector web site will help identify and serve as a portal to many of these resources as will the "AgNIC Forestry" web site.

The selection of scholarly, academic, and trade journals is primarily representative and by no means exhaustive. Added to the list of forestry titles with this edition are *Agroforestry Systems* and *International Review of Forestry* as representative titles for "international forestry," as well as *Forest Policy and Economics* and the *IAWA Journal*. Deleted from the list is *Forestry Source* because the nonmember highlights are now available from the Society of American Foresters web site.

In reviewing the periodicals from the 11th edition and considering new titles, I looked for titles widely held by other libraries. In 2001, faculty members in the College of Forestry at Oregon State University were asked to list their most used or "top ten" journals. This listing provided me with evidence of the multidisciplinary underpinnings of forestry and new titles for consideration. In assessing scholarly titles, I looked for titles with high impact factors or a high journal citation half-life using the *Journal Citation Reports* from the Institute for Scientific Information. When deciding between comparable titles I took into consideration the journal subscription price, and gave preference to professional society publications over journals from commercial publishers.

In the earlier editions of this section, Carol C. Green of the University of Washington has recommended using *Literature of Forestry and Agroforestry*, published by Cornell University Press in 1996. I would like to acknowledge that I too have made use of this bibliography and to reiterate its importance to anyone managing a forestry collection. In addition to giving a useful history of forestry, it identifies both monographs and serials that have provided the foundation for "science-based forestry."

Basic Periodicals

Hs: *American Forests, Unasylva*; Ga: *American Forests, Ecoforestry, Environmental History, Journal of Forestry, Unasylva*; Ac, Sa: *Canadian Journal of Forest Research, Environmental History, Forest Ecology and Management, Forest Products Journal, Forest Science, Journal of Forestry, Wood and Fiber Science.*

Basic Abstracts and Indexes

Agricola, Bibliography of Agriculture, Biological and Agricultural Index, Forest Products Abstracts, Forestry Abstracts.

3250. *Agricultural and Forest Meteorology: an international journal.* Formerly (until 1984): *Agricultural Meteorology.* [ISSN: 0168-1923] 1964. s-m. EUR 2232. Ed(s): K T Paw U. Elsevier BV, Sara Burgerhartstraat 25, Amsterdam, 1055 KV, Netherlands; nlinfo-f@elsevier.nl; http://www.elsevier.nl. Illus., index, adv. Sample. Refereed. Microform: PQC. Online: ingenta.com; ScienceDirect; Swets Blackwell. Reprint: SWZ. *Indexed:* Agr, BiolAb, CAPS, DSA, EnvAb, ExcerpMed, FPA, ForAb, GeoRef, GeogAbPG, HortAb, IndVet, M&GPA, PollutAb, S&F, SCI, SWRA, VetBull, WAE&RSA. *Bk. rev.:* 1-3, 500-800 words. *Aud.:* Ac, Sa.

This international journal covers meteorology as it is used in the agricultural, forest, and soil sciences. Articles emphasize research relevant to the practical problems of forestry, agriculture, and natural ecosystems. Topics include the effect of weather on forests, soils, crops, water use, forest fires, the effect of vegetation on climate and weather, and canopy micrometeorology. It is heavily used by specialists working in these areas and as a result has been assigned a high impact factor by the Institute of Scientific Information. Twenty-four issues appear annually in six volumes, though it is not uncommon for issues to be combined. While this is an expensive journal, a number of thematic, special issues are available for purchase as monographs. Online access is through a separate license for *Science Direct* or through *Science Direct Web Editions* with a print subscription.

3251. *Agroforestry Systems.* Incorporates (1972-1999): *Agroforestry Forum;* Which was formerly (until 1992): *Agroforestry in the U K.* [ISSN: 0167-4366] 1982. 9x/yr. EUR 890 print or online ed.; EUR 891 print or online ed.; EUR 1068 print & online eds. Ed(s): P K Ramachandran Nair. Kluwer Academic Publishers, van Godewijckstraat 30, PO Box 17, Dordrecht, 3300 AA, Netherlands. Refereed. Microform: PQC. Online: EBSCO Publishing; ingenta.com; Kluwer Online; OCLC Online Computer Library Center, Inc.; Ovid Technologies, Inc.; RoweCom Information Quest; Swets Blackwell. Reprint: SWZ. *Indexed:* Agr, B&AI, BiolAb, CAPS, DSA, EngInd, EnvAb, FPA, ForAb, GeogAbPG, HortAb, S&F, SSCI, SWA, WAE&RSA. *Bk. rev.:* Occasional, 500-1,500 words. *Aud.:* Ac, Sa.

Sponsored in part by the World Forestry Center (formerly the International Center for Research in Agroforestry), this is an international, refereed journal. It has grown in reputation during its 20 years of publication and is currently highly cited in the research literature. Three volumes are published annually, each consisting of three issues. Included in each issue are seven to ten reports of original research, critical reviews, and short communications, with periodic book reviews and announcements. Topics include basic and applied research on indigenous species and multipurpose trees, and techniques for integrating systems of trees, crops, and livestock. For inclusion, research results and information presented must have application beyond the specific location studied. This journal would complement collections supporting agriculture and environmental studies as well as forestry, particularly those with an international development focus. Online access for an additional fee is available via *Kluwer Online*. Subscription information and the table of contents of recent issues are available on the journal web site.

3252. ***American Christmas Tree Journal.*** Formerly: *American Christmas Tree Growers' Journal.* [ISSN: 0569-3845] 1956. 5x/yr. Non-members, USD 50. Ed(s): Dennis Tompkins. National Christmas Tree Association, 1000 Executive Parkway Dr., Ste. 220, St. Louis, MO 63141-6372; info@christree.org; http://www.christree.org. Illus., index, adv. Circ: 2700. Vol. ends: Oct. *Aud.:* Ga.

This trade journal is issued five times annually. It serves as the membership journal for the National Christmas Tree Association. Feature articles are of interest to the woodlot owners who grow and market Christmas trees or related products. State chapters of the National Christmas Tree Association report and announce conferences under "Association News." Grower profiles, marketing, business and regulatory information, and silvicultural advice are covered regularly. The White House Christmas tree is featured annually, and articles with an historical perspective on Christmas trees appear regularly. This journal would be useful in general collections where this industry is part of the local economy.

3253. ***American Forests.*** [ISSN: 0002-8541] 1895. q. Membership, USD 25; USD 3 newsstand/cover per issue. Ed(s): Michelle Robbins. American Forests, PO Box 2000, Washington, DC 20013; http://www.americanforests.org. Illus., index, adv. Circ: 25000 Paid. Vol. ends: Winter. Microform: PQC. Online: bigchalk; EBSCO Publishing; Florida Center for Library Automation; Gale Group; Northern Light Technology, Inc.; OCLC Online Computer Library Center, Inc.; ProQuest Information & Learning; H.W. Wilson. *Indexed:* Agr, B&AI, BRI, BiolAb, BiolDig, CBRI, ChemAb, EngInd, EnvAb, FPA, ForAb, GSI, GeoRef, LRI, MagInd, RGPR. *Aud.:* Hs, Ga, Ac.

This magazine is the membership organ for one of the oldest conservation organizations in the United States, American Forests. Feature articles are intended for a general audience and address tree planting, tree species profiles, and current policy controversies, as well as the practical aspects of current research and how-to articles. Typical of this magazine's well-illustrated and easily read features are recent articles on the role of urban forests in urban planning and on wildfire recovery efforts in the Southwest. The organization sponsors the work of the "Global ReLeaf Center," "Forest Policy Center," and "Urban Forest Center," and maintains the "National Register of Big Trees." Editorial emphasis is placed on coverage of forests and trees located "on land where people live, work, and relax." Further explanation of sponsored programs and memberships are available on the organization's web site, as is an archive of many of the magazine's articles. This magazine is issued quarterly and would be suitable for public, school, and college libraries.

3254. ***Arborist News.*** [ISSN: 0003-7958] 1935. bi-m. Membership, USD 105. Ed(s): Peggy Currid. International Society of Arboriculture, PO Box 3129, Champaign, IL 61826-3129; isa@isa-arbor.com; http://www.isa-arbor.com. Adv. *Aud.:* Hs, Ga, Ac, Sa.

This bimonthly publication covers news of interest to the tree-care professional and is the membership publication for the International Society of Arboriculture. Regular features include the "Tree Industry Calendar," professional profiles, summaries of articles published in the *Journal of Arboriculture*, the "Climbers corner," and "European News." Continuing-education articles feature general tree-care, current tree-health problems, and business aspects of arboriculture. Selected articles are available in full text on the organization's web site, as is membership information needed for subscribing. Articles are timely, readable, and would be useful for the general homeowner as well as for the professional arborist. This publication is suitable for a general collection or public library.

3255. ***Canadian Forest Industries: Canada's only national publication serving saw and pulpwood logging, sawmilling and allied activities.*** Formed by the merger of: *Canada Lumberman; Timber of Canada.* [ISSN: 0318-4277] 1888. 6x/yr. CND 51.36 domestic; USD 55 United States; USD 75 elsewhere. Ed(s): Scott Jamieson. J C F T Forest Communications, 90 Morgan Rd., Unit 14, Baie d'Urte, PQ H9Y 3A8, Canada; http://www.forestcommunications.com/cfi/. Illus., index, adv. Sample. Circ: 12500. Vol. ends: Dec. Microform: MML; PQC. Online: Infomart Ltd.; Micromedia ProQuest. *Indexed:* CPerI, FPA, ForAb. *Aud.:* Ac, Sa.

This Canadian trade journal serves as the journal of record for the Canadian Woodlands Forum of the Forest Products Association of Canada (formerly the Canadian Pulp and Paper Association). It focuses on the full range of activities associated with logging technology and harvesting systems. Articles are of current interest, and editorial features are common and may give this publication broad appeal among those interested in industry practices suitable for North America. Topics such as environmentally sound road building, wood certification, current forest harvesting practices, and tests of new logging equipment are featured regularly and would be of interest to students in forestry or environmental policy. Regular features also include reviews of new products and literature. Subscription information for this bimonthly publication is available on its web site.

3256. ***Canadian Journal of Forest Research.*** [ISSN: 0045-5067] 1970. m. CND 732 (Individuals, CND 243). Ed(s): Doug Maynard, Cindy E Prescott. N R C Research Press, Building M 55, Ottawa, ON K1A 0R6, Canada; http://www.nrc.ca/cisti/journals/. Illus., index, adv. Sample. Refereed. Circ: 862. Vol. ends: Dec. Microform: MML; PQC. Online: CISTI; EBSCO Publishing; ingenta.com; RoweCom Information Quest; Swets Blackwell. Reprint: PQC. *Indexed:* Agr, ApEcolAb, BiolAb, CAPS, CBCARef, ChemAb, DSA, EngInd, EnvAb, ExcerpMed, FPA, ForAb, GeoRef, GeogAbPG, HortAb, IBZ, PollutAb, RRTA, S&F, SCI, SSCI, SWRA, WAE&RSA, ZooRec. *Aud.:* Ac, Sa.

Consistently in the top ten forestry journal rankings as issued by Institute for Scientific Information, this refereed journal should be a core title for any research collection in this area. International in scope, articles are in English with French summaries, report on primary research addressing an array of questions, and are accompanied by extensive bibliographies. Each issue is comprised of 15-20 articles, often authored by researchers at universities, government forestry agencies, or other research institutions. Subscription information and tables of contents are available online from the web site of the National Research of Canada. Apart from designated Canadian Depository Libraries, full-text availability requires an additional fee.

3257. ***Ecoforestry.*** Formerly (until vol.12, no.4, 1997): *International Journal of Ecoforestry.* [ISSN: 1485-8479] 1995. q. CND 60 (Individuals, CND 30). Ed(s): Bruce Whyte. Ecoforestry Institute Society, PO Box 5070, Victoria, BC V8R 6N3, Canada; journal@ecoforestry.ca; http://www.ecoforestry.ca. *Bk. rev.:* 1-2. *Aud.:* Hs, Ga, Ac.

This journal addresses the interests of those who are attempting to manage and harvest forest resources in an ecologically responsible manner. Articles do not report on research but do report on best-practice examples of private forest landowners, public and private land managers, community and nonprofit groups, and self-employed forest workers. Students will find this a useful source for articles on forest and wood certification, selective logging, horse logging, and non-wood forest-products harvesting. Selected articles are available free on the journal web site. This modestly priced publication would be useful to public, school, and academic library collections, particularly those in the western United States and Canada.

3258. ***Environmental History.*** Formed by the merger of (1976-1996): *Environmental History Review;* Which was formerly (until 1989): *Environmental Review;* (1957-1996): *Forest and Conservation History;* Which was formerly (until 1989): *Journal of Forest History;* (until 1974): *Forest History.* [ISSN: 1084-5453] 1996. q. USD 90 (Individuals, USD 45 includes membership; Students, USD 20). Ed(s): Adam Rome. Duke University Press, 905 W Main St, Ste 18 B, Durham, NC 27701; subscriptions@dukeupress.edu; http://www.dukeupress.edu. Illus., index, adv. Sample. Refereed. Circ: 2000. Vol. ends: Oct. Microform: PQC. Online: bigchalk; Northern Light Technology, Inc.; ProQuest Information & Learning. Reprint: PQC; PSC. *Indexed:* AmH&L, ArtHuCI, BHA, CIJE, EnvAb, FPA, ForAb, GeoRef, IndVet, PollutAb, RRTA, S&F, SSCI, SWRA, WAE&RSA, ZooRec. *Bk. rev.:* 15-20, 500-1,000 words. *Aud.:* Ga, Ac, Sa.

This quarterly, refereed journal provides a rich resource for those interested in the history of forestry and environmental studies. Each issue includes four or five well-documented historical articles as well as numerous book reviews. Recent issues include articles on the Forest Service and Ecosystem management, urban weed control in the early twentieth century, and a history of oaks in eighteenth- and nineteenth-century Sweden. Books, articles, theses and dissertations, and archival material added to the Forest History Society's database of "sources related to environmental history" are reported with brief annotations in the regular feature, "Biblioscope." This is a significant resource for current awareness for the researcher. Moderately priced and accessible to the general reader with an interest in history, it would be a good addition to larger public libraries as well as a standard for collections supporting both undergraduate study and graduate research in forestry and environmental studies. Tables of contents, a searchable bibliography, and subscription information are available on the journal web site.

3259. ***Forest Ecology and Management.*** [ISSN: 0378-1127] 1978. 51x/yr. EUR 3036 (Qualified personnel, EUR 404). Ed(s): R F Fisher, G M J Mohren. Elsevier BV, Sara Burgerhartstraat 25, Amsterdam, 1055 KV, Netherlands; nlinfo-f@elsevier.nl; http://www.elsevier.nl. Illus., index, adv. Sample. Refereed. Microform: PQC. Online: ingenta.com; ScienceDirect; Swets Blackwell. Reprint: SWZ. *Indexed:* Agr, ApEcolAb, B&AI, BiolAb, CAPS, ChemAb, EngInd, EnvAb, ExcerpMed, FPA, ForAb, GeoRef, GeogAbPG, HortAb, IndVet, PollutAb, RRTA, S&F, SCI, SSCI, SWRA, WAE&RSA, ZooRec. *Aud.:* Ac, Sa.

This refereed journal is perhaps most representative of the multidisciplinary nature of forestry. Each volume consists of 25 to 45 articles appearing in three issues, although these issues are often combined for publication. There are 15 to 17 volumes published annually. The journal reports on the "application of biological, ecological and social knowledge to the management of man-made and natural forests." Volumes are often thematic, and typical articles report on research related to tree growth, nutrient cycling, landscape ecology, forest as habitat, effect of logging practices, and numerous other subjects. The journal publisher's web site provides a table of contents to recent years, and a print subscription includes licensed access to the most recent 9-12 months of the journal through *ScienceDirect Web Editions.* Full online access through *ScienceDirect Digital Collections* is available for subscribers, but under a separate license and at an additional fee. The heavy use of this journal by scholars and researchers make it a core title for research-based forestry collections despite its high cost.

3260. ***Forest Landowner.*** Formerly (until 1996): *Forest Farmer.* [ISSN: 1087-9110] 1941. bi-m. USD 40. Ed(s): Paige Cash. Forest Landowners Association, PO Box 450209, Atlanta, GA 31145-0209; http://www.forestland.org/. Illus., adv. Circ: 11000 Paid. Vol. ends: Nov/Dec. *Indexed:* EnvAb. *Aud.:* Ga.

This bimonthly publication serves as the membership organ for the Forest Landowners Association and presents the issues of concern to large and small timberland owners in the southern and eastern United States. The well-illustrated trade journal provides feature articles of political as well as technical interest. Recent issues include articles on seedling mortality, riparian zones, consulting foresters, planning, and research on pest detection for forest health. Active in lobbying at the local, regional, and national level, regular columns include information on timber pricing, timber tax issues, government affairs, and hunting and wildlife, as well as new products and organization news. An annual "Seedling Nursery Directory" appears in the September/October issue, and in alternate years the "Forest Landowner Manual," a directory of dealers, mills, schools, state and federal agencies, and associations related to forestry in southern and eastern United States, is issued. In the geographic regions noted, and where the local economy includes small landowners who privately manage timberlands, this publication would be appropriate for a general library collection.

3261. ***Forest Policy and Economics.*** [ISSN: 1389-9341] 1999. bi-m. EUR 333. Ed(s): M Krott. Elsevier BV, Sara Burgerhartstraat 25, Amsterdam, 1055 KV, Netherlands; nlinfo-f@elsevier.nl; http://www.elsevier.nl. Refereed. Online: ingenta.com; ScienceDirect; Swets Blackwell. *Indexed:* BiolAb, FPA, ForAb, PollutAb, RRTA, S&F, WAE&RSA. *Aud.:* Ac, Sa.

This refereed journal is issued quarterly in collaboration with the European Forest Institute (EFI) and fills a niche in the forestry literature by addressing policy issues in an international context. It covers economics and planning as they apply to the forests and forest industries sector, and it seeks to "enhance communications amongst researchers, legislators, decision-makers, and other professionals concerned with formulating and implementing policies for the sector." Each issue consists of 7 to 12 articles as well as occasional conference announcements and EFI news. Special thematic issues have covered topics such as national forestry programs, multipurpose management of mountain forests, and forest-related rural development. As a moderately priced, scholarly forestry title, it will be an important addition to research collections but may also be a useful for large public library collections where forestry is an important part of the economy. Subscription information and table of contents for recent issues are available from the journal web site. Online access to full-text is available with paper subscriptions for an additional fee.

3262. ***Forest Products Journal.*** [ISSN: 0015-7473] 1947. 10x/yr. USD 145 domestic; USD 155 in Canada & Mexico; USD 185 elsewhere. Ed(s): Erin Bosch. Forest Products Society, 2801 Marshall Ct, Madison, WI 53705; erin@forestprod.org. Illus., index, adv. Sample. Refereed. Circ: 5000. Vol. ends: Nov/Dec. Microform: PMC; PQC. Online: EBSCO Publishing; Florida Center for Library Automation; Gale Group; Northern Light Technology, Inc.; OCLC Online Computer Library Center, Inc.; ProQuest Information & Learning. Reprint: PQC. *Indexed:* A&ATA, ABIn, Agr, B&AI, BiolAb, ChemAb, EngInd, EnvAb, ExcerpMed, FPA, ForAb, HortAb, PollutAb, RRTA, S&F, SCI, SSCI, WAE&RSA. *Bk. rev.:* 0-1, 1,000-2,000 words. *Aud.:* Ac, Sa.

Sponsored by the Forest Products Society, this refereed journal is well respected for its technical coverage of research in wood science and technology. The journal is issued ten times a year. Issues include 10 to 12 technical articles on an array of topics including management, processes, solid wood products, composites and manufactured wood products, and fundamental disciplines. To put these articles in perspective, a short statement on the relevance of each article is given under the heading, "Practicalities and Possibilities." In addition to association news and classified ads, regular feature columns report on international research literature, new publications and computer applications, patents, codes, standards, and regulatory changes. The featured article from each issue is available full text on the society web site. Although a technical publication, many articles would be useful to engineers, economists, and those wishing to keep abreast of the forest products industry.

3263. ***Forest Science: a journal of research and technical progress.*** [ISSN: 0015-749X] 1955. 6x/yr. USD 375 (Individuals, USD 130). Ed(s): Gregory S Amacher. Society of American Foresters, 5400 Grosvenor Ln, Bethesda, MD 20814; johnsonc@safnet.org; http://www.safnet.org. Illus., index, adv. Sample. Refereed. Circ: 1300. Vol. ends: Nov. Microform: PQC. Online: ingenta.com; ProQuest Information & Learning. Reprint: PQC. *Indexed:* Agr, B&AI, BiolAb, CAPS, ChemAb, EnvAb, ExcerpMed, FPA, ForAb, HortAb, PollutAb, RRTA, S&F, SCI, SSCI, ST&MA, SWRA, WAE&RSA, ZooRec. *Bk. rev.:* 2-3, 1,000 words. *Aud.:* Ac, Sa.

This bimonthly, refereed journal is one of five journals sponsored by the Society of American Foresters. Each issue includes 15 to 25 articles reporting on scientific results from both theoretical and applied research. International in scope, articles in this journal are both highly cited and consistently cited over a long period of time. It enjoys wide respect within the forestry scientific community and is heavily used by researchers, practitioners, and students alike, who consider this a core title for their work. The general format is open to a wider audience, and articles are readable, making the journal accessible to the general reader as well. Since late 2000, full-text access to articles from this journal is available to subscribers at no additional cost through *ingenta.* Subscription information is available from the web site, as is a good deal of other information concerning the society.

3264. ***Forestry Chronicle.*** [ISSN: 0015-7546] 1925. bi-m. USD 180, Libraries, CND 180 (Individuals, CND 100). Ed(s): V Nordin, B Haddon. Canadian Institute of Forestry, 151 Slater St, Ste 606, Ottawa, ON K1P 5H3, Canada; http://www.cif-ifc.org. Illus., index, adv. Sample. Refereed. Circ: 2800. Vol. ends: Nov/Dec. *Indexed:* Agr, BiolAb, CAPS, ChemAb, EngInd, EnvAb, FPA, ForAb, GeogAbPG, HortAb, IndVet, RRTA, S&F, SCI, SSCI, WAE&RSA. *Bk. rev.:* 1-10, 500-1,500 words. *Aud.:* Ac, Sa.

Published by the Canadian Institute of Forestry, this refereed journal includes both peer-reviewed articles and membership news. Bimonthly issues include 10 to 15 articles in English and, less frequently, in French with English summaries. In recent issues, the ratio of "Professional Papers" to "Scientific and Technical Papers" is two to one. Papers focus on applied and scientific research and occasionally include conference presentations. Announcements of recent publications, forestry education programs, and professional and institute news are regularly included. The intended audience for this journal is the professional forester; however, given its modest price, it is an accessible publication for collections serving undergraduates and the general public.

3265. *I A W A Journal.* Former titles (until 1993): *I A W A Bulletin; I A W A Publications.* [ISSN: 0928-1541] 1931. q. EUR 90 (Individuals, EUR 50; USD 90). Ed(s): P Baas, E A Wheeler. International Association of Wood Anatomists, PO Box 80102, Utrecht, 3508 TC, Netherlands. Refereed. Circ: 800. *Indexed:* A&ATA, BiolAb, FPA, ForAb, HortAb, S&F. *Bk. rev.:* 2-3, 500-1000 words. *Aud.:* Ac, Sa.

Published by the International Association of Wood Anatomists, this refereed journal covers topics in wood anatomy such as the micro-structure of wood, bark, and related plant products including bamboo, rattan, and palms basic to the study of forest products. Published quarterly, each issue is comprised of 8 to 10 well-documented and illustrated articles on the anatomy and properties of a variety of species, as well as association news, announcements of conferences and workshops, and two or three book reviews. For specialized and research collections, this highly cited journal is an important and inexpensive addition.

3266. *International Forestry Review.* Formerly (until 1999): *Commonwealth Forestry Review.* [ISSN: 1465-5489] 1921. q. GBP 100. Ed(s): Alan J Pottinger. Commonwealth Forestry Association, PO Box 142, Oxford, OX26 6ZJ, United Kingdom; http://cfa-international.org/publications.html. Illus., adv. Refereed. Circ: 900. *Indexed:* BiolAb, ChemAb, FPA, ForAb, GeogAbPG, HortAb, RRTA, S&F, WAE&RSA, ZooRec. *Bk. rev.:* 5-8, 300-500 words. *Aud.:* Ga, Ac, Sa.

Formerly the *Commonwealth Forestry Review*, this refereed journal is published quarterly by the Commonwealth Forestry Association (CFA). Each issue features 6 to 12 papers reporting on a wide range of research conducted, for the most part, in Asia and Africa. Also regularly featured are short opinion pieces under the heading "Comment," five to seven book reviews, and translations of article summaries in French and Spanish. Occasional issues focus on themes such as "forestry and small island developing states." One of the goals of CFA is to foster public interest in forestry. For that reason, this modestly priced and well-indexed journal is a good introduction to forestry concerns from an international as well as scientific point of view. This title would be useful for undergraduate collections supporting international programs as well as research collections.

3267. *International Journal of Forest Engineering.* Formerly (until 1999): *Journal of Forest Engineering.* [ISSN: 1494-2119] 1989. s-a. USD 125. Ed(s): Jeremy Rickards. University of New Brunswick, Faculty of Forestry and Environmental Management, PO Box 44555, Fredericton, NB E3B 6C2, Canada; jforeng@unb.co. Illus. Refereed. Circ: 350 Paid. Vol. ends: Jul. *Indexed:* FPA, ForAb, S&F, WAE&RSA. *Aud.:* Ac, Sa.

Although articles on forest engineering appear in other forestry journals, this semi-annual refereed publication sponsored by the Faculty of Forestry and Environmental Management at the University of New Brunswick is unique in being devoted to the research aspects of this field. The composition of its editorial board is representative of its international scope. Each issue contains, on average, eight technical papers along with occasional technical notes and reviews. Topics covered include forest operations, including harvesting, stand management, machine design, road design and construction, and wood engineering and processing. Beginning in 2003 a new column, "Tell us about your organization," may prove useful for librarians wishing to better acquaint themselves with this field. Modestly priced, this is an important addition to library collections supporting practitioners and researchers in forest operations.

3268. *Journal of Arboriculture.* [ISSN: 0278-5226] 1975. bi-m. USD 75. Ed(s): Robert W Miller. International Society of Arboriculture, PO Box 3129, Champaign, IL 61826-3129; http://www.isa-arbor.com. Illus., index, adv. Sample. Refereed. Circ: 8500. Vol. ends: Nov. *Indexed:* Agr, B&AI, BiolAb, FPA, ForAb, GardL, GeogAbPG, HortAb, RRTA, S&F, WAE&RSA. *Aud.:* Ac, Sa.

This is a bimonthly journal published by the International Society of Arboriculture. Each issue includes six to ten research papers intended for the practitioner, and although scientific in nature, they would be accessible to the interested layperson. Articles regularly cover topics such as green space, sustainable urban forestry, control of invasive species, and landscaping, and they would be of interest to urban policy makers as well as urban foresters and park administrators. Of interest to homeowners and gardeners are topics such as street tree inventories, effect of vegetation on energy use, and topping of trees. Included in each issue is "Arboriculture Abstracts," which summarizes relevant articles in related journals. Tables of contents with abstracts for recent issues are available on the society web site, as is subscription information.

3269. *Journal of Forestry: a journal reporting on the science, practice and profession of forestry.* [ISSN: 0022-1201] 1902. 8x/yr. USD 185 (Individuals, USD 85). Ed(s): Sally Atwater. Society of American Foresters, 5400 Grosvenor Ln, Bethesda, MD 20814; ziadia@safnet.org; http://www.safnet.org/pubs. Illus., index, adv. Sample. Refereed. Circ: 18820. Vol. ends: Dec. Microform: PMC; PQC. Online: ingenta.com; Northern Light Technology, Inc.; ProQuest Information & Learning. Reprint: PQC. *Indexed:* Agr, B&AI, BiolAb, BiolDig, ChemAb, EngInd, EnvAb, ExcerpMed, FPA, ForAb, GeoRef, GeogAbPG, HortAb, PAIS, PollutAb, RRTA, S&F, SCI, SSCI, SWRA, WAE&RSA, ZooRec. *Bk. rev.:* 5-10, 100 words; 0-1, lengthy. *Aud.:* Hs, Ga, Ac.

This is the membership journal for the Society of American Foresters. Themes for each of eight issues are available on the society web site. Current themes include forest health and ecology, international forestry and sustainable development, education and employment, and forest certification and third-party auditing, as well as two open forums and an issue devoted to technology and practice, with an annual "Professional Resource Guide." Past themes include ethics, GIS, and fire. Feature articles undergo peer review but are written for a broad audience. Regular features include member "Perspectives" and "Focus on . . . ," which features more practical information of interest to members in specific sectors of forestry. Of use to librarians for collection development is the regular column on "New Releases," which includes books, reports, and media. Both the writing and range of topics covered make this an important addition to public and college libraries as well as collections serving the professional forester and researcher. Since late 2000, full-text access to articles from this journal is available to subscribers at no additional cost through *ingenta.* Subscription information is available from the web site, as is a good deal of other information about the society.

3270. *Journal of Sustainable Forestry.* [ISSN: 1054-9811] 1993. q. USD 250. Ed(s): Graeme P Berlyn. Haworth Press, Inc., 10 Alice St, Binghamton, NY 13904-1580; getinfo@haworthpressinc.com; http://www.haworthpressinc.com. Illus., index, adv. Sample. Refereed. Circ: 152 Paid. Vol. ends: No. 4. Microform: PQC. Reprint: HAW. *Indexed:* AbAn, Agr, EngInd, EnvAb, FPA, ForAb, GeogAbPG, HortAb, PollutAb, RRTA, S&F, SWRA, WAE&RSA. *Bk. rev.:* Occasional short reviews. *Aud.:* Ac, Sa.

This international journal is refereed and focuses on research that promotes the sustainability of forests for their products (both wood and non-wood) as well as research that contributes to sustainable agroforestry. It fills a niche in the commercial journal market. Two or more of the four issues that make up each volume may be combined to serve as the record of a conference covering an unusual topic, such as a recent one on "War and tropical forests: conservation in areas of armed conflict." These multi-issue titles are often made available as monographs as well. It can be argued that more of this material is now available on the web; however, the fact that this journal is well indexed in the bibliographic databases used by students makes it particularly important for academic collections.

FORESTRY

3271. ***National Woodlands Magazine.*** [ISSN: 0279-9812] 1979. q. USD 25 includes 8 issues of Woodland Report newsletter. Ed(s): Eric Johnson. National Woodland Owners Association, 374 Maple Ave E Ste 310, Vienna, VA 22180; http://www.nationalwoodlands.org. Illus., adv. Circ: 3000. Vol. ends: Oct. *Aud.:* Ga.

This quarterly magazine serves the membership of the National Woodland Owners Association. This association monitors government activities related to its membership and works with nonprofit groups and professional societies to communicate the concerns and interests of nonindustrial, private woodlot owners. Each issue includes three to five feature articles on topics such as fire management and environmental education, as well as regular political news columns and reports from the "Forest Fire Lookout Association." Regular departments include "Timber and Taxes," "National Historic Lookout Register," and updates to the "National Directory of Consulting Foresters." Though plain in presentation, the magazine has a broad geographic focus within the United States. An inexpensive addition to a general collection, it serves to represent the point of view of the nonindustrial landowner. Membership and subscription information are available from the association web site.

3272. ***New Forests: journal of biology, biotechnology, and management of afforestation and reforestation.*** [ISSN: 0169-4286] 1986. bi-m. EUR 603 print or online ed. Ed(s): Stephen W Hallgren. Kluwer Academic Publishers, van Godewijckstraat 30, PO Box 17, Dordrecht, 3300 AA, Netherlands; services@wkap.nl; http://www.wkap.nl. Illus., index. Sample. Refereed. Microform: PQC. Online: EBSCO Publishing; ingenta.com; Kluwer Online; OCLC Online Computer Library Center, Inc.; Ovid Technologies, Inc.; RoweCom Information Quest; Swets Blackwell. Reprint: SWZ. *Indexed:* Agr, BiolAb, CAPS, EngInd, EnvAb, FPA, ForAb, HortAb, PollutAb, RRTA, S&F, SCI, WAE&RSA. *Aud.:* Ac, Sa.

This refereed journal is international in scope and is intended for an audience of scientists and practitioners. Two volumes each of three issues appear annually and contain 6-8 papers of reporting on the findings of original research. "New forests" refers to the reproduction of trees and forests by reforestation or afforestation, whether for the purposes of resource protection, timber production, or agroforestry. Topics included are silviculture, plant physiology, genetics, biotechnology, propagation methods and nursery practices, ecology, economics, and forest protection. Although relatively new, it enjoys a good reputation among researchers and should be considered a core title for a research collection. Full-text access to issues is available as an alternative to print or in addition to a print subscription for an additional fee through the publisher's web site.

3273. ***Northern Journal of Applied Forestry.*** [ISSN: 0742-6348] 1984. q. USD 136 (Individuals, USD 65). Ed(s): James W Hornbeck. Society of American Foresters, 5400 Grosvenor Ln, Bethesda, MD 20814; ziadia@safnet.org; http://www.safnet.org. Illus., index, adv. Sample. Circ: 1000. Vol. ends: Dec. Microform: PQC. Online: ingenta.com; ProQuest Information & Learning. Reprint: PQC. *Indexed:* Agr, BiolAb, ChemAb, EngInd, EnvAb, FPA, ForAb, IndVet, RRTA, S&F, ZooRec. *Aud.:* Ac, Sa.

This is one of three regional applied research journals from the Society of American Foresters. It is targeted toward the professional forester and forest landowner in the northeastern and midwestern United States and Canada and the boreal forests of these areas. Emphasis is on management practices and techniques. Quarterly issues contain six to ten peer-reviewed articles on such topics as pest and disease control, wildlife management, and harvesting practices, all focusing on practical research to help the practitioner better manage forests of the region. All three regional journals are modest in price and are important for a research and teaching collection. In areas where forests are an important part of the local economy, a general collection would be strengthened with the addition of the geographically appropriate title. Since late 2000, full-text access to articles from this journal has been available to subscribers at no additional cost through *ingenta.* Subscription information is available from the web site, as is a good deal of other information about the society.

3274. ***Southern Journal of Applied Forestry.*** [ISSN: 0148-4419] 1984. q. Individuals, USD 75. Ed(s): Ian A Munn. Society of American Foresters, 5400 Grosvenor Ln, Bethesda, MD 20814; safweb@safnet.org; http://www.safnet.org. Illus., index, adv. Sample. Refereed. Circ: 1100. Vol. ends: Nov. Microform: PQC. Online: ingenta.com; ProQuest Information & Learning. Reprint: PQC. *Indexed:* Agr, BiolAb, ChemAb, EngInd, EnvAb, FPA, ForAb, HortAb, RRTA, S&F, SWRA, WAE&RSA. *Aud.:* Ac, Sa.

This is one of three regional applied research journals from the Society of American Foresters. It is targeted toward the professional forester and forest landowner in a geographic region ranging from Oklahoma and East Texas east and south to Virginia and Kentucky. Emphasis is on management practices and techniques in this region where plantation forests are more common. Quarterly issues contain six to ten peer-reviewed articles on such topics as pest and disease control, wildlife management, and harvesting practices, all focusing on practical research to help the practitioner better manage forests of the region. All three regional journals are modest in price and are important for a research and teaching collection. In areas where forests are an important part of the local economy, a general collection would be strengthened with the addition of the geographically appropriate title. Since late 2000, full-text access to articles from this journal has been available to subscribers at no additional cost through *ingenta.* Subscription information is available from the web site, as is a good deal of other information about the society.

3275. ***Tree Physiology: an international botanical journal.*** [ISSN: 0829-318X] 1986. m. CND 1386 (Individuals, CND 252). Ed(s): Rozanne Poulson. Heron Publishing, 202-3994 Shelbourne St, Victoria, BC V8N 3E2, Canada; publisher@heronpublishing.com; http://heronpublishing.com/. Illus., index, adv. Sample. Refereed. Vol. ends: Dec. Online: The Dialog Corporation. *Indexed:* Agr, ApEcolAb, BiolAb, CAPS, ChemAb, EnvAb, FPA, ForAb, GeogAbPG, HortAb, PollutAb, S&F, SCI, SWRA. *Bk. rev.:* 0-3, 300-500 words. *Aud.:* Ac, Sa.

This refereed journal is international in scope and distribution. It is issued 18 times a year and is a medium for disseminating theoretical and experimental research results as well as occasional review articles. Each issue consists of eight to ten papers dealing with an array of topics related to tree physiology, including genetics, reproduction, nutrition, and environmental adaptation, as well as those relevant to environmental management, biotechnology, and the economic use of trees. This is an important journal for forest science and botany collections. Online access to the full text of this journal is available at no additional cost to the subscriber. The publisher's web site also provides a cumulative index for downloading.

3276. ***Trees: structure and function.*** [ISSN: 0931-1890] 1987. 6x/yr. EUR 830 domestic; EUR 846.40 foreign; EUR 166 newsstand/cover per issue. Ed(s): Robert D Guy, U E Luettge. Springer-Verlag, Tiergartenstr 17, Heidelberg, 69121, Germany. Illus., index, adv. Sample. Refereed. Vol. ends: Sep. Online: EBSCO Publishing; RoweCom Information Quest; ScienceDirect; Springer LINK; Swets Blackwell. *Indexed:* Agr, BiolAb, CAPS, FPA, ForAb, HortAb, RRTA, S&F, SCI, WAE&RSA. *Aud.:* Ac, Sa.

This international, refereed journal is narrowly focused but highly regarded among the physiologists in the scholarly community of forestry, horticulture, and botany. Each of its six annual issues includes eight to ten articles on original research in the physiology, biochemistry, functional anatomy, structure, and ecology of trees and woody plants. Review articles are included selectively, as are papers on pathology and technological problems that add to a basic understanding of the structure and function of trees. An online edition of the journal along with a table-of-contents alerting service is available from *Springer Link.*

3277. ***Unasylva: international journal of forestry and forest products.*** [ISSN: 0041-6436] 1947. q. USD 40. Ed(s): A Perlis. Food and Agriculture Organization of the United Nations, Sales and Marketing Group, Viale delle Terme di Caracalla, Rome, 00100, Italy. Illus., index. Sample. Circ: 6500. Vol. ends: Dec. Microform: CIS. *Indexed:* B&AI, BAS, BiolAb, BiolDig, DSR&OA, FPA, ForAb, HortAb, RRTA, S&F, SWA, WAE&RSA. *Bk. rev.:* 2-5, 300 words. *Aud.:* Hs, Ga, Ac.

Available in French, Spanish, and English, this international journal is published by the Food and Agriculture Organization (FAO) of the United Nations and promotes a better understanding of issues in international forestry. Articles are well illustrated and readable and will have broad appeal to an audience including students, policy makers, and professional foresters. Each quarterly issue consists of 8 to 12 articles usually addressing a theme such as conservation for biodiversity, global forest resource assessment, or forest-dependent people. Regular departments include new books, reports on FAO forestry activities, and news in the "world of forestry." This would be a good addition to general, high school, and college libraries as well as research collections. The full text of articles in each issue of the journal since 1947 is available at the FAO web site.

3278. ***Western Journal of Applied Forestry.*** [ISSN: 0885-6095] 1984. q. USD 170 (Individuals, USD 75). Ed(s): Greg M Filip. Society of American Foresters, 5400 Grosvenor Ln, Bethesda, MD 20814; safweb@safnet.org; http://www.safnet.org. Illus., adv. Sample. Refereed. Circ: 900. Vol. ends: Oct. Microform: PQC. Online: ingenta.com; ProQuest Information & Learning. Reprint: PQC. *Indexed:* Agr, BiolAb, EngInd, EnvAb, FPA, ForAb, HortAb, RRTA, S&F, WAE&RSA, ZooRec. *Aud.:* Ac, Sa.

This is one of three regional applied research journals from the Society of American Foresters. It is targeted toward the professional forester and landowner in western North America. Emphasis is on management practices and techniques. Quarterly issues contain six to ten peer-reviewed articles on such topics as pest and disease control, wildlife management, and harvesting practices, all focusing on practical research to help the practitioner better manage forests of the region. All three regional journals are modest in price and are important for a research and teaching collection. In areas where forests are an important part of the local economy, a general collection would be strengthened with the addition of the geographically appropriate title. Since late 2000, full-text access to articles from this journal has been available to subscribers at no additional cost through *ingenta*. Subscription information is available from the web site, as is a good deal of other information about the society.

3279. ***Wood and Fiber Science.*** Formerly: *Wood and Fiber.* [ISSN: 0735-6161] 1968. q. USD 250. Ed(s): Geza Ifju. Society of Wood Science and Technology, One Gifford Pinchot Dr, Madison, WI 53726-2398; http://www.swst.org. Illus., index, adv. Sample. Refereed. Circ: 1000. Vol. ends: Oct. Microform: PQC. *Indexed:* Agr, ChemAb, EngInd, FPA, ForAb, S&F, SCI, SSCI, WAE&RSA. *Bk. rev.:* 1-3, 400-600 words. *Aud.:* Ac, Sa.

This quarterly, refereed journal is the product of the Society of Wood Science and Technology in cooperation with the Forest Products Society. Typical of the range of subjects covered by the 12 to 15 articles in each issue are processing testing, modeling applied to oriented strandboard, wood adhesives, moisture movement, use of engineered wood products in Japan, and properties of wood-plastic composites, plus one or two book reviews. The journal is modestly priced and highly regarded by wood scientists and wood technologists. Particularly with the increase in international research coverage, it is also useful for those interested following new developments in these areas for product marketing. This journal is recommended for comprehensive research collections as well as those collections needing an economical representative title in this area. Tables of contents with abstracts are available on the journal web site.

■ FRATERNAL, CLUB, AND SERVICE ORGANIZATIONS

Betty K. Bryce, Reference Librarian, University of Alabama Libraries, Tuscaloosa, AL 35487-0266; bbryce@bama.ua.edu; FAX: 205-348-0760

Introduction

Service club mottos, such as the Rotary's "Service above self—He profits most who serves best," and the Lions' "No progress without service," clearly reveal the community service focus of these organizations. In the mid-twentieth century, fraternal and service clubs claimed as members half of all U.S. adults. While the numbers of participants in fraternal, club, and service organizations have declined in recent years, there are still significant numbers of civic-minded people who participate in these groups.

Many, if not all, fraternal and community organizations publish magazines to keep their readers informed. The readers of these magazines are often some of the most active civic volunteers and are a valuable asset to any community. The purpose of the magazines is to keep the members up to date on local, regional, and national events in the organization.

Many of the magazines also carry a number of feature articles of general interest that would provide intriguing reading for many library patrons. These magazines are often well written and well illustrated and contain interesting information on a variety of topics. While none of these magazines is essential to a library's serials collection, inclusion of a few of these often adds numbers and interest to the collection at little or no cost.

Basic Periodicals

Ga: *The American Legion Magazine, B'nai B'rith IJM, Kiwanis Magazine, Leader, The Rotarian, Scouting, The Torch (Norfolk);* Ac: *B'nai B'rith IJM, Kiwanis, The Rotarian, The Torch (Norfolk).*

3280. ***A M B U C S.*** 1923. q. USD 12. Ed(s): J Joseph Copeland. A M B U C S, PO Box 5127, High Point, NC 27262; ambucs@ambucs.com; http://www.ambucs.com. Adv. Circ: 7000. *Aud.:* Ga.

AMBUCS is an organization dedicated to helping people with disabilities become independent. One of their national service projects includes providing scholarships, which total five million dollars, to educate physical and occupational therapists, speech pathologists, and hearing audiologists. The magazine of the organization contains articles primarily of interest to club members and would generally not be of interest to a broader audience. The AMBUCS web site does not include the magazine in electronic form.

AAUW Outlook. See Education/Higher Education section.

3281. ***The American Legion Magazine.*** [ISSN: 0886-1234] 1919. m. Non-members, USD 15. Ed(s): John B Raughter. American Legion Magazine, PO Box 1055, Indianapolis, IN 46206; http://www.legion.org. Illus., adv. Circ: 2700000. Vol. ends: Jun/Dec. Reprint: PQC. *Indexed:* LRI, MagInd, PAIS. *Aud.:* Ga.

The American Legion has more than 15,000 posts around the world, and counts some three million men and women as members. While the articles in the organization's magazine are written from a decidedly conservative point of view, there are many articles of interest to veterans and to older people in general. Recent issues have included an article on the threats of nuclear and biological warfare, an essay by Supreme Court Justice Clarence Thomas, and a story about World War II orphans. One of the most engaging parts of the magazine is a column that asks two members of Congress of opposing views to address a particular issue of national interest. Some of the feature articles from the past four years of the magazine are available on the organization's web site. Recommended.

3282. ***The B'nai B'rith I J M.*** Former titles (until 2001): *B'nai B'rith International Jewish Monthly;* (until 1981): *National Jewish Monthly;* (until 1939): *B'nai B'rith National Jewish Monthly.* 1886. bi-m. USD 18; USD 3 newsstand/cover per issue. Ed(s): Eric Rozenman. B'nai B'rith International, 1640 Rhode Island Ave, N W, Washington, DC 20036; ijm@bnaibrith.org; http://www.bbinet.org. Illus., index, adv. Circ: 45000 Paid and controlled. Vol. ends: Jun/Jul. *Indexed:* ABS&EES, IJP, PAIS. *Aud.:* Ga, Ac.

The B'nai B'rith I J M informs its readers on B'nai B'rith activities and contains other articles that are of interest to English-speaking Jews. Though the magzine is written from a Jewish perspective, many articles are well written and well illustrated, and touch upon a variety of subjects that a more general audience would find of interest. In a recent issue there were articles on Jews of Ireland, an orthodox Jewish guitarist, and the return visit home of a group of Cuban Jews. There is an online edition of the magazine on the organization's web site but it is different from the print version. There is also an online index of the periodical from 1886. Recommended.

FRATERNAL, CLUB, AND SERVICE ORGANIZATIONS

3283. ***Catholic Forester.*** [ISSN: 0008-8048] 1893. q. Membership. Ed(s): Mary Anne File. Catholic Order of Foresters, 355 Shuman Blvd, Box 3012, Naperville, IL 60566-7012; cofpr@aol.com; http://www.catholicforester.com. Illus. Circ: 100000 Controlled. Vol. ends: Dec. *Aud.:* Ga.

The Catholic Order of Foresters is a fraternal insurance company for members of all ages. The magazine contains news of the company as well as feature articles on such general topics as aging, sports, and insurance. The magazine is very family-oriented and includes, among other sections, a children's page, a crossword puzzle, and a food section. The magazine is not available on the company's web site. While this magazine is not a recommended title, it is a good family magazine with nice reading and activities for the entire family.

3284. ***Columbia (New Haven): America's largest Catholic family magazine.*** [ISSN: 0010-1869] 1921. m. USD 6 domestic. Ed(s): Tim Hickey. Knights of Columbus, 1 Columbus Plaza, New Haven, CT 06510-3326; thickey@kofc-supreme.com; http://www.kofc.org. Illus., adv. Circ: 1500000. Vol. ends: Dec. *Indexed:* CPL. *Aud.:* Ga.

The Knights of Columbus is an organization that was founded in 1882 to support Catholic Church programs. There are currently 1.6 million Knights of Columbus. The magazine is chiefly devoted to news of the organization. The articles and columns are written from a decidedly Roman Catholic point of view and thus will appeal primarily to members of the Roman Catholic Church or those who subscribe to its views. The magazine is not presently available on the organization's web site.

3285. ***The Elks Magazine.*** [ISSN: 0013-6263] 1922. 10x/yr. Non-members, USD 18.50. Ed(s): Fred D Oakes. Benevolent and Protective Order of Elks of the United States of America, 425 W Diversey, Chicago, IL 60614-6196; fredo@elks.org; http://www.elks.org/elksmag. Illus., adv. Circ: 1650679. Vol. ends: May. *Aud.:* Ga.

The Benevolent and Protective Order of Elks is one of the oldest and largest fraternal organizations in the United States. It has some 1.2 million members in over 2,000 communities. The magazine of the organization is devoted to activities of the national organization and news of the local chapters. There are generally one or two articles of general interest for older, conservative citizens. One article in each issue focuses on a travel spot, with detailed information about the locale and many full-color photographs. Part of the magazine is featured online and is available back to September 1997.

Futurist. See Cultural-Social Studies section.

3286. ***G F W C Clubwoman: magazine of the General Federation of Women's Clubs.*** Former titles (until 1978): *Clubwoman News;* (until 1976): *General Federation Clubwoman.* [ISSN: 0745-2209] 1897. bi-m. USD 6 domestic; USD 12 foreign. Ed(s): Sarah Dustin Wees. General Federation of Women's Clubs, 1734 N St, N W, Washington, DC 20036; http://www.gfwc.org/. Illus., adv. Circ: 15000. Vol. ends: Aug/Sep. *Aud.:* Ga.

The General Federation of Women's Clubs represents the world's largest and oldest women's organization. Notable clubwomen of the past include Eleanor Roosevelt and Margaret Chase Smith. The magazine of the organization includes news of the local clubs and their projects. Of more general interest is a section entitled "Program Updates," which contains information about national events in the arts, education, international affairs, and other major themes. Another column is an update on events in Congress that affect issues related to women and women's interests. The table of contents of the most recent magazine is available on the organization's web site.

3287. ***I O O F News.*** bi-m. USD 5. Ed(s): Arthur A Craig, Harry V. Lohman. Independent Order of Odd Fellows, 422 Trade St. N W, Winston-Salem, NC 27101-2830; ioofsgl@aol.com. Illus. Sample. Circ: 412000. *Aud.:* Ga.

The Independent Order of Odd Fellows, one of the largest and oldest fraternal orders in the United States, came to America from England in 1819. The organization does good works through its lodges in local communities. The magazine of the organization is almost entirely geared to news and activities of its member lodges, of which there are over 9,000 worldwide. It would not, therefore, be of much interest to the general reader. The organization's web site does not contain an electronic copy of the magazine.

3288. ***Kiwanis Magazine: published for community leaders.*** [ISSN: 0162-5276] 1917. 10x/yr. Members, USD 10; Non-members, USD 20. Ed(s): Chuck Jonak. Kiwanis International, 3636 Woodview Trace, Indianapolis, IN 46268; kiwanismail@kiwanis.org; http://www.kiwanis.org. Illus., adv. Circ: 239452 Paid. Vol. ends: Dec. Microform: PQC. *Aud.:* Ga, Ac.

Kiwanis International has chapters in over 8,000 communities throughout the world and has members representing all professions. The organization is dedicated to service for the advancement of the welfare of the individual, the community, and the nation. The magazine of the organization contains a little news and activity reports of the chapters but primarily has well-written articles of general interest accompanied by many colorful photographs. A recent issue contained articles on Romania and a bone marrow transplant program. The organization's web site offers an online version of the magazine from 1999 to the present. Recommended. Kiwanis also publishes *Keynoter* for the high school key clubs and *Circle K Magazine* for the college chapters of the organization.

3289. ***Leader: for adults in girl scouting.*** Formerly (until 1999): *Girl Scout Leader.* 1923. q. USD 5 domestic; USD 7.50 foreign. Ed(s): Janet Lombardi. Girl Scouts of the U.S.A., 420 Fifth Ave, New York, NY 10018-2798; http://www.girlscouts.org. Illus. Circ: 800000 Controlled. Vol. ends: Winter. *Bk. rev.:* Various number and length. *Aud.:* Ga.

The primary purpose of this magazine is to guide the scouting leaders in helping the Girl Scouts with their activities. There are many suggested activities to keep girls interested and involved as well as recommended supplemental material of books, magazines, and web sites that leaders can turn to for more information on many topics. Though the magazine is written specifically to help Scout leaders with their troops, anyone working with children would find this magazine helpful in its suggested activities and information. The magazine also contains book reviews on books related to scouting interests and articles of general interest such as fitness. The magazine is not currently available on the organization's web site. Recommended.

3290. ***The Lion (Oak Brook): an international magazine for service-minded individuals.*** [ISSN: 0024-4163] 1918. m. Non-members, USD 6. Ed(s): Winthrop W Hamilton, Gary LaPetina. International Association of Lions Clubs, 300 22nd St., Oak Brook, IL 60523-8842; http://www.lionsclubs.org/. Illus., adv. Circ: 600000 Controlled. Vol. ends: Jun. *Aud.:* Ga.

Lions International has 44,000 clubs in 185 countries and is an organization recognized worldwide for its service to the blind and visually impaired. With 1.4 million members, the Lions represent the world's largest service organization. The magazine of the organization is available in 20 languages and contains articles on club activities from all over the world. Because the magazine's contents are limited to member activities, however, it has no appeal to general readers. There is currently no electronic version on the organization's web site.

3291. ***Modern Woodmen: a family and financial resource for Modern Woodmen members.*** [ISSN: 0279-8670] q. Free to libraries. Ed(s): Glough Bergh. Modern Woodmen of America, 1701 First Ave, Rock Island, IL 61204-2005; http://www.modern-woodmen.org/. Illus. Circ: 400000 Controlled. *Aud.:* Ga.

Modern Woodmen of America is the nation's fifth largest fraternal life insurance society. It provides financial security for its members through life insurance and annuities. The magazine of the organization contains feature articles primarily on insurance issues. The articles are well illustrated and well written but limited to family life, community service, and financial security. The Modern Woodmen web site does not contain the magazine in electronic form.

3292. ***The Optimist (Saint Louis).*** Formerly: *Optimist Magazine.* [ISSN: 1085-5017] 1919. bi-m. Members, USD 4.50; Non-members, USD 5. Ed(s): Al Schon. Optimist International, 4494 Lindell Blvd., St. Louis, MO 63108-2404; magazine@optimist.org; http://optimist.org. Illus., adv. Circ: 122000 Paid. Vol. ends: Jan. *Aud.:* Ga.

The Optimist International has 3,800 clubs in communities in the United States, Canada, and the Caribbean. Its mission is to provide educational opportunities and charitable assistance primarily through scholarships for boys and girls who are involved in Optimist programs such as oratorical and essay contests. The magazine reports on club activities to promote optimism, patriotism, and respect for the law. The magazine is of interest primarily to club members.

A French-language version is published for the club's members in Quebec. There is currently not an electronic version of the Optimists' web site.

3293. ***The Rotarian.*** [ISSN: 0035-838X] 1911. m. USD 12. Ed(s): Charles W Pratt. Rotary International, 1560 Sherman Ave, Evanston, IL 60201; http://www.rotary.org. Illus., adv. Circ: 515000 Paid. Vol. ends: Jun/Dec. Microform: PQC. Reprint: PQC. *Indexed:* AgeL, MagInd. *Aud.:* Ga, Ac.

Rotary International is an organization of business and professional leaders in 160 countries worldwide who are involved in humanitarian service. One recent project has been to eradicate polio worldwide by raising millions of dollars to immunize children all over the world. Each issue of the magazine contains well-written and illustrated feature articles on a wide variety of topics of general interest. An online version of the magazine is available on the organization's web site. Recommended.

3294. ***Scouting: a family magazine.*** [ISSN: 0036-9500] 1913. 6x/yr. Non-members, USD 15. Ed(s): Jon C Halter. Boy Scouts of America, PO Box 152079, Irving, TX 75015-2079; http://www.scoutingmagazine.org. Illus., index, adv. Circ: 1000000 Paid. Vol. ends: Dec. Microform: PQC. Reprint: PQC. *Indexed:* MagInd. *Aud.:* Ga.

This magazine is designed for use by the adults who work as leaders of male Scouts, including Cub Scouts, Boy Scouts, and Explorer Scouts. It provides information on ideas for activities for young people. There are many articles of general interest such as safe driving skills, changing television viewing habits, and swimming safety. Any adult working with young people will find this magazine informative and helpful. There is an online version of the magazine that contains issues back to 1999. There is also an online index for issues back to 1993 and a means of requesting them over the Internet. Recommended.

3295. ***Soroptimist.*** [ISSN: 0097-9562] 1931. 7x/yr. USD 11 in US & Canada; USD 15 elsewhere. Ed(s): Darlene Friedman. Soroptimist International of the Americas, Two Penn Center, Ste 1000, Philadelphia, PA 19102; siahq@soroptimist.org; http://www.soroptimist.org. Illus., adv. Circ: 45000. Vol. ends: Jul/Aug. *Aud.:* Ga.

The Soroptimist Club's mission is "to make a difference for women" through service in the community. Formed in 1921, and now with some 100,000 members in 119 countries around the world, the organization regards its top priority as speaking out on behalf of women. The magazine of the organization contains information that will primarily be of interest to members. There is usually, however, a feature article about a topic that would be of general interest to women and a list of recommended books for further reading. A recent issue contained an article on the state of the world's fresh water. Feature articles from each issue since 1999 are available on the organization's web site.

3296. ***The Torch (Norfolk).*** [ISSN: 0040-9448] 1928. 3x/yr. USD 7.50 (Non-members, USD 20). Ed(s): Patrick Deans. International Association of Torch Clubs, c/o R Patrtick Deans, Ed, Strickland & Jones PC, Norfolk, VA 23510-1517; http://www.torch.org. Illus. Circ: 2850 Controlled. Vol. ends: Spring. *Aud.:* Ga, Ac.

There are 75 local Torch clubs in the United States and Canada. They provide a forum for professional men and women to present and discuss papers related to their fields of expertise. The organization's magazine contains the best of these papers. Each issue has some six or seven articles on a variety of topics. Recent issues have included articles on gun control, American foreign policy, and home schooling. Local club news takes up a small section of each issue. The organization's web site has several back issues of each year available electronically. Recommended.

3297. ***V F W Magazine: ensuring rights, recognition, and remembrance.*** [ISSN: 0161-8598] 1912. 11x/yr. Non-members, USD 10. Ed(s): Richard Kolb. Veterans of Foreign Wars of the United States, 406 W 34th St, Kansas City, MO 64111; http://www.vfw.org. Illus., adv. Circ: 2000000. Vol. ends: Aug. Microform: PQC. Online: Gale Group; ProQuest Information & Learning. *Aud.:* Ga, Ac.

While this magazine's primary focus is on topics related to the military, it is nevertheless a magazine with broad appeal. It contains articles of general interest on such varied topics as historical battles, terrorism, and patriotic music. News of the organization takes up a few of the pages but the rest of the magazine contains well-written, informative articles that would be worthwhile for anyone interested in military subjects. The organization's web site contains the magazine's feature articles back to 1996. Recommended.

3298. ***Woodmen.*** Formerly: *Woodmen of the World Magazine.* [ISSN: 1069-1790] 1890. bi-m. USD 3. Ed(s): Scott J Darling. Woodmen of the World - Omaha Woodmen Life Insurance Society, c/o Billie Jo Foust, Asst Ed, 1700 Farnam St, Omaha, NE 68102; service@woodmen.com. Illus. Sample. Circ: 500000 Controlled. Vol. ends: Nov/Dec. *Aud.:* Ga.

Woodmen of the World is a fraternal insurance society. The organization's magazine contains primarily reports of local chapter activities, although it does contain a few short articles of general interest on such topics as insurance, family, and history. It is not a recommended acquisition for libraries, however, as it is mainly of interest to members. The magazine is not available on the organization's web site.

■ FREE MAGAZINES AND HOUSE ORGANS

Kathleen M. Conley, Head, General Reference and Documents, Milner 8900, Illinois State University, Normal, IL 61790-8900; kcconle@ilstu.edu; FAX: 309-438-3676

Introduction

Free magazines need no explanation, but the definition of house organs might need some amplification. Generally, house organs are targeted to internal communities of particular corporations, agencies, or associations and report technical information, research or development initiatives, and personnel or other insider news of interest. External house organs seek a broader audience, frequently presenting a positive public relations message through objective reporting of research initiatives, foundation activities, or examples of creative problem-solving. Many house organs are from the manufacturing, banking, or service industries. Free magazines, which can include house organs, are often issued by governmental agencies, research foundations, colleges and universities, or other nonprofit organizations.

In an online environment, the line between free and "somebody's paying for it" is becoming less of a demarcation and more of a virtual afterthought. A majority of the paid-subscription magazines, periodicals, or newsletters that libraries offer to their users have web sites with the text of current issues, archives, ability to do keyword searches in those archives, and enhancements. Increasingly, one can access full content, colorful and interactive. Yet, a significant number of magazines offer free print or online subscriptions. Some publications are free and only available online.

Uncertain financial times and trends dictate that libraries spend judiciously for their resources, acknowledging their often diverse communities of users as they try to balance their budgets. To offer free print resources that complement collections, or balance perspectives that are offered by paid subscriptions, seems like a good and practical undertaking. Additionally, free print publications provide good vertical file or browsing material. Selected e-journals for leisure or education can be linked from libraries' homepages; often the reader will have an opportunity to subscribe to those found to be enlightening or interesting. Libraries might want to change links or highlight new titles monthly.

To preview and select useful and appropriate electronic publications, the reader can browse *NewJour,* the Internet list for new journals and newsletters available on the Internet (http://gort.ucsd.edu/newjour/). *Serials in Cyberspace* (http://www.uvm.edu/~bmaclenn/#ejour) comprises selective listings of web sites with electronic journal collections and services both inside and outside the U.S., miscellaneous collections and resources, selected e-journal titles, and other web pages concerning serials that may be of interest to librarians.

The following annotated selections are thematic in the broadest sense only, but address, for the most part, quality of life issues. These publications stress the need for cooperation and problem solving, often present a multicultural or global perspective, assist in informed decision-making by consumers, and attempt to demystify or explain omnipresent technology. In the contexts of mission statements and assessments of primary clientele, libraries should find free publications, whether they are entertaining or elucidating, to acquire and promote.

Basic Periodicals

Ems: *Saudi Aramco World;* Hs: *Talking Book Topics, Refugees*; Ga: *Consumer Information Catalog, Law Matters*; Ac, Sa: Select as needed.

Affirmative Action Register. See Occupations and Careers section.

American Baby: for expectant and new parents. See Parenting section.

3299. *Appalachia.* Formerly: *Appalachian Digest.* [ISSN: 0003-6595] 1967. 3x/yr. Ed(s): Diane Bowker Smith. U.S. Appalachian Regional Commission, 1666 Connecticut Ave N W, Washington, DC 20235. Illus., index. Sample. Circ: 20000. Vol. ends: Dec. *Indexed:* Agr, BRI, BiolAb, CBRI, CIJE, EnvAb, GeoRef, IUSGP, PAIS, SportS. *Aud.:* Hs, Ga, Ac, Sa.

Several feature articles detail aspects of Appalachian regional development from infrastructure to information technology. Areas covered include child development, education, entrepreneurship, health, strategic planning, telecommunications, and workforce training. Emphasis is on collaboration and partnering among agencies, individuals, and institutions. "Appalachian Scene" profiles individuals who work to improve the quality of life for inhabitants. "Inside Information" highlights activities of the Appalachian Regional Commission (ARC) and relevant legislative updates. Brief reports cover programs and activities of the ARC. Issues are profusely illustrated with black-and-white photographs and maps. This colorful magazine is of paramount importance to libraries in Appalachia; others will find it effective for its positive presentation of local initiatives and individual successes.

3300. *Appliance Manufacturer.* [ISSN: 0003-679X] 1953. m. USD 55 domestic (Free to qualified personnel). Ed(s): Joe Jancsurak. Business News Publishing Co., 755 W Big Beaver Rd, Ste 1000, Troy, MI 48084-4903. Illus., adv. Circ: 36141 Paid and controlled. Vol. ends: Dec. Online: The Dialog Corporation; EBSCO Publishing; Florida Center for Library Automation; Gale Group; Northern Light Technology, Inc.; OCLC Online Computer Library Center, Inc.; ProQuest Information & Learning. *Indexed:* ABIn, BPI. *Aud.:* Ac, Sa.

The stated objective of *AM* is "providing solutions for design and engineering teams in the global, commercial, and medical appliance/durable goods industry." Case histories, information on new products and technologies, and news about major appliances, housewares, medical/lab, lawn and garden, commercial vending, electronics/communications, and computer/business equipment are provided; news about industry personnel or leaders is sparse. Industry news briefs comprise the "Manager's Update." "Lit/Facts" lists and describes new-product brochures that can be ordered. Each article is coded so that readers can obtain additional information through a reader service card. The online site features full-text feature articles from 2000 to date, association links, and a calendar of events in addition to subscription, advertising, and editorial information. Although this is a trade publicaton, consumers with a penchant for the latest in home appliances and technology will find something of interest here.

The AV Magazine. See Animal Welfare section.

3301. *Berkeley Lab Research Review.* Former titles: *L B L Research Review;* (until 1985): *L B L News Magazine.* 1985. 3x/yr. Free to qualified personnel. Ed(s): Pam Patterson. Ernest Orlando Lawrence Berkeley National Laboratory, Public Information Department, 1 Cyclotron Rd MS-65, Berkeley, CA 94720; http://www.lbl.gov. Illus. Sample. Circ: 8000. Vol. ends: Fall/Winter. *Aud.:* Hs, Ga, Ac, Sa.

Research at the Ernest Orlando Lawrence Berkeley Laboratory is managed by the University of California for the United States Department of Energy. This publication supports energy-related research in the fields of engineering, mathematics, and computer and natural sciences. Six to eight feature articles report, in nontechnical language, research activities conducted at the lab and are liberally illustrated with charts, photographs, and drawings. Accomplishments of lab personnel, honors accorded, and patents awarded are included. The online version includes a news archive that lists articles by subject and ability to search by keyword. This review should have wide appeal to libraries that support interest in current scientific research.

3302. *Bio-IT World.* m. USD 199 domestic (Free to qualified personnel). Bio-It World, Inc, 500 Old Connecticut Path, Framingham, MA 01701; http://www.bio-itworld.com/. *Aud.:* Ac, Sa.

Bio-IT World explores the convergence of information technology and the life sciences. The audience for this cutting-edge publication is senior IT/scientific management or academics. Coverage spans life sciences and research organizations, and includes pharmaceuticals, biotechnology, drug discovery and development, genomics and preteomics—the large scale study of proteins. Available both in print and online, a current issue, which coincides with the fiftieth anniversary of the discovery of the double helix, has several articles on DNA and an interview with James Watson. The web version (http://www.bio-itworld.com) includes industry news, archives of all past issues, a section on new products, case studies, an events calendar, links to info technology resources, life sciences resources, and career centers.

Braille Book Review. See Large Print section.

3303. *California Agriculture: reports of progress in research.* [ISSN: 0008-0845] 1946. bi-m. USD 18 foreign. Ed(s): Jane White, Pam Kan-Rice. University of California at Oakland, Division of Agriculture and Natural Resources, 1111 Franklin St, 6th Fl, Oakland, CA 94607-5200; calag@ucop.edu; http://danr.ucop.edu/calag/. Illus., index. Sample. Refereed. Circ: 18484. Vol. ends: Dec. *Indexed:* BiolAb, ChemAb, DSA, EnvAb, ExcerpMed, FPA, FS&TA, ForAb, HortAb, IndVet, PollutAb, RRTA, S&F, SWRA, VetBull, WAE&RSA, ZooRec. *Aud.:* Ac, Sa.

This publication is one of the oldest continuously published land grant university research publications. Each issue has five or six research and review articles that deal with economic and public policy, food and nutrition, pest management, or land, air, and water sciences. The articles are peer-reviewed with full citations. Authors are primarily UC faculty, UC Cooperative Extension specialists, advisors, and associated staff. The research articles contain new data that represent advances in particular fields. Reviews analyze recent research developments that strongly impact agricultural, natural, or human resources in California and express future directions for research. Occasional special issues focus on single subjects that have supported significant interdisciplinary research and/or extension efforts at the university. Color photographs, charts, and tables illustrate each issue. Libraries that serve academic researchers, agribusiness, or farming communities will find this a valuable edition to their collections.

3304. *Carnegie Reporter.* Former titles: *Carnegie Quarterly; Carnegie Corporation of New York Quarterly; Carnegie Corporation of New York. Quarterly Report.* 1953. 2x/yr. Free. Ed(s): Eleanor Lerman. Carnegie Corporation of New York, 437 Madison Ave, New York, NY 10022. Illus. Sample. Circ: 38500. Vol. ends: Winter. Reprint: PQC. *Indexed:* AbAn, PAIS. *Bk. rev.:* 4-5, length varies. *Aud.:* Ga, Ac, Sa.

The Carnegie Foundation initially sought to "promote the advancement and diffusion of knowledge and understanding among the people of the United States." Subsequently, its purpose was broadened to include countries that have been members of the British Commonwealth. Continuing the integrity of the

Carnegie Quarterly, the *Carnegie Reporter,* initiated in 2000, focuses on each of the foundation's four main areas of work—education, international peace and security, international development, and democracy. "Foundation Roundup" details Carnegie as well as other foundation-sponsored initiatives, surveys, and reports. A few illustrations enhance the well-written text. The *Carnegie Reporter* avows that its purpose is "to challenge you with insights, intellectual questions and tested observations."

3305. *Connected Home.* 2002. 8x/yr. USD 29.95 domestic; USD 35.95 Canada; USD 59.95 elsewhere. Penton Media, Inc., 1300 E 9th St, Cleveland, OH 44114-1503; http://www.penton.com. Adv. *Aud.:* Ga, Sa.

This publication asks the question, "Are you ready to live like the Jetsons?" It covers home computing networks for telecommuting, home entertainment equipment, multimedia and gaming components, personal digital assistant devices, Internet appliances, cellular phones, and home office equipment. "Connected Home EXPRESS," which is offered on the web site, is a free bimonthly online newsletter that provides advice, tips, and news for individuals that need some help keeping up-to-date with the latest high-tech products. The web site (http://www.connectedhome.com/) also offers free special supplements of *Connected Home Magazine* that include groundbreaking how-to articles and other resources to assist in readers attaining their dream wired environments.

3306. *Consumer Information Catalog.* Formerly: *Consumer Information.* 1971. q. Free. Ed(s): Christine Stevenson. U.S. General Services Administration, Consumer Information Center, 1800 F Sts, N W, Rm G 142, Washington, DC 20405; cic.info@pueblo.gsa.gov; http://www.pueblo.gsa.gov. Circ: 12000000. *Aud.:* Ga.

More than 200 free or low-cost publications are listed in each issue of this catalog. Topics include cars, children, computers, education, employment, federal programs, food, health, housing, money, small business, and travel. Each entry is briefly annotated. Featured publications are suitable for vertical files. Copies can be requested from Consumer Information Catalog, Pueblo, CO 81009. The latest catalog is published online with full-text versions of hundreds of the best federal consumer publications available, including the latest *Consumer Action Handbook.* This publication provides consumer tips and suggests ways to resolve marketplace problems. One can also find links to recalls and scams/frauds. An excellent source of information.

3307. *D - Lib Magazine.* [ISSN: 1082-9873] 1995. m. Ed(s): Bonita Wilson. Corporation for National Research Initiatives, 1895 Preston White Dr, Reston, VA 20191; dlib@cnri.reston.va.us; http://www.dlib.org. *Indexed:* CIJE, InfoSAb, LISA, LibLit, PAIS. *Aud.:* Ac, Sa.

This monthly electronic magazine is about innovation and research in digital libraries, directed to technical and professional audiences. The overall objective of *D-Lib Magazine* is "to help digital libraries be a broad interdisciplinary field, and not a set of specialties that know little of each other." Each issue features four to six articles that highlight individual or institutional digital initiatives or research trends in digital library development. An entire recent issue was devoted to digital reference. Each issue links to short current awareness items, recent press releases, and a calendar of activities; the "Clips & Pointers" section notes documents, deadlines, and calls for participation. The entire archive of back issues is accessible through alphabetical title and author indexes, selection by date, or searching by keyword. "Ready Reference" links to other digital library sites. Especially notable is the "Featured Collection" section, which has showcased "Mark Twain in His Times," the American Numismatic web site, and "Digital Morphology" among many others. This publication is an excellent way for educators, researchers, and those with an interest in information technology to keep up-to-date.

3308. *Design News: news for OEM design engineers.* [ISSN: 0011-9407] 1946. s-m. USD 139.90 domestic; USD 184.90 Canada; USD 172.90 Mexico. Ed(s): Karen Auguston Field. Reed Business Information, 275 Washington St, Newton, MA 02458; http://www.reedbusiness.com. Illus., index, adv. Sample. Circ: 180000. Vol. ends: Nov. Online: bigchalk; EBSCO Publishing; Florida Center for Library Automation; Gale Group; LexisNexis; Northern Light Technology, Inc.; OCLC Online Computer Library Center, Inc.; ProQuest Information & Learning; H.W. Wilson. Reprint: PQC. *Indexed:* AS&TI, C&ISA, ChemAb, EngInd, EnvAb, LRI, MagInd. *Aud.:* Ac, Sa.

"America's best-read design engineering magazine" covers the latest tools, components, and materials used in industrial design. Articles emphasize the latest successful engineering products and technologies that can be used to jump-start thinking about innovative product development. Each issue presents two or three feature articles, new product listings, news briefs, and guest commentaries. The editorial staff, many of whom are engineers, writes all feature articles. The text is liberally sprinkled with advertisements, photographs, and drawings. *Design News Online* offers back issue content from 1995. The online version adds value to the print version, including a "Career Center" an "OEM Directory" and a recently added "Spec Search" for products, supplies, and service companies. The very busy web site also offers access to market- and technology-specific news, magazine articles, corporate bulletins, engineering technical papers, and additional web sites.

3309. *Elderhostel Catalog.* 1978. 8x/yr. Free. Elderhostel, Inc., 11 Avenue de Lafayette, Boston, MA 02111-1746; http://www.elderhostel.org. Circ: 900000. *Aud.:* Ga, Sa.

Elderhostel is a not-for-profit organization that offers high-quality, affordable, educational adventures to adults 55 and older. This tabloid-format catalog describes extensive programs of study offered in classrooms, in labs, aboard ship, and in rural or urban areas in the United States or in foreign countries. Programs are listed by type and geographic location. Each program listing describes the itinerary, accommodations, and course of study. Interested individuals can create an account online that allows one to enroll in programs, set and record personal preferences, request free catalogs and e-mailings, and view and manage Elderhostel payment records. This publication should engender strong interest as baby boomers attain the requisite age for participation.

3310. *Federal Reserve Bank of New York. Economic Policy Review.* Formerly (until 1995): *Federal Reserve Bank of New York. Quarterly Review;* Supersedes (with vol.58, no.10): *Federal Reserve Bank of New York. Monthly Review.* 1976. q. Free. Federal Reserve Bank of New York, Public Information, 33 Liberty St, New York, NY 10045-0001. Circ: 38000. Microform: CIS; PQC. Online: The Dialog Corporation. Reprint: CIS; PQC; SCH. *Indexed:* ABIn, AgeL, AmStI, BLI, BPI, IBSS, JEL, PAIS, SUSA. *Aud.:* Ga, Ac, Sa.

Selected topics in macroeconomics, banking, and financial marketing are featured in this policy-oriented research journal. Both domestic and international arenas are covered. Conference volumes, reflecting a growing public interest in conferences sponsored by the Federal Reserve Bank of New York, cover a single theme. Articles are signed, fully cited, and usually illustrated with charts or graphs. Subscribers receive the reserve bank's annual report. Some knowledge of economics on the part of readers is assumed, but this publication should find an audience among policymakers, business and banking professionals, and the general public. Information about the Federal Reserve Bank of New York can be found on the organization's web site.

3311. *Federal Reserve Bank of Philadelphia. Business Review.* [ISSN: 0007-7011] 1918. q. Free. Ed(s): Sarah Burke. Federal Reserve Bank of Philadelphia, PO Box 66, Philadelphia, PA 19105; http://www.phil.frb.org. Illus. Sample. Circ: 10000. Vol. ends: Spring/Winter. Microform: MIM; CIS; PQC. Online: EBSCO Publishing; Florida Center for Library Automation; Gale Group; OCLC Online Computer Library Center, Inc.; ProQuest Information & Learning; H.W. Wilson. Reprint: CIS; PQC. *Indexed:* ABIn, AmStI, BLI, BPI, JEL, PAIS. *Aud.:* Ga, Ac, Sa.

Each issue features three well-researched, understandable, and clearly written articles that cover topics of current national and international interest in economic policy, financial economics, banking, and monetary policy. The articles are signed and fully cited. Color maps, charts, and tables contribute to a pleasing format. High-quality paper and lively covers set this publication apart from other Federal Reserve Bank publications. The web site presents text of the current issue and issues back approximately seven years. Additionally, online links to regional data, consumer information, economic education, news for financial institutions, money topics, and research publications supplement the print issues. Content in *The Business Review* can engender college-level discussions of current economic themes, and readers with a serious concern for economics and finance will find this publication of interest.

3312. ***Finance and Development (Print Edition).*** Formerly (until 1967): *Fund and Bank Review.* [ISSN: 0145-1707] 1964. q. Free. Ed(s): Laura Wallace. International Monetary Fund, Publication Services, 700 19th St, N W, Ste 12 607, Washington, DC 20431; http://www.imf.org. Illus., index, adv. Sample. Circ: 121000. Vol. ends: Dec. Microform: CIS; PQC. Online: Gale Group. Reprint: PQC. *Indexed:* ABIn, ATI, BAS, BPI, EIP, IBSS, JEL, PAIS, SSI, WAE&RSA. *Bk. rev.:* 2-6, 300-800 words. *Aud.:* Ga, Ac, Sa.

This magazine is published quarterly by the International Monetary Fund in English, Arabic, Chinese, French, Russian, and Spanish and presents articles on a wide variety of topics in international economics and finance, with special emphasis on economic development. The online version is available in English, French, and Spanish. Relational aspects of government and social policy are explored in the areas of environmentalism, government reform, urban and rural development, banking, and inflation. Many charts, graphs, tables, and photographs enhance the text. Articles are aimed at nonspecialist readers. Substantive reviews of books in economics and finance are presented in each issue. An annual index of articles and reviews is carried in the December issue. Because the format supports breadth of coverage, this appealing publication could serve as a core title in the field of international finance for academic or public libraries.

First Monday. See Internet-World Wide Web/Electronic Journals section.

3313. ***Folklife Center News.*** [ISSN: 0149-6840] 1978. q. Free. Ed(s): James Hardin. U.S. Library of Congress, American Folklife Center, 101 Independence Ave, S E, Washington, DC 20540; http://lcweb.loc.gov/folklife. Illus. Sample. Circ: 14000. Vol. ends: Fall. *Indexed:* IUSGP, MLA-IB, RILM. *Aud.:* Ga, Ac, Sa.

Programs and activities of the American Folklife Center—including research, documentation, archival presentation, live performance, exhibitions, publications, and training—are emphasized, although other articles on traditional expressive culture are sometimes published. This newsletter is not, however, a forum for discussion of folklore or folklife in general. Reviews of books published by the Library of Congress are included in topical essays. With generally fewer than 24 pages, this publication's length allows for easy locating of information even though issues lack tables of contents. Libraries that support folklife collections for the amateur or the enthusiast will find this title of interest. The electronic edition provides full text of current and back issues to 1992, but no graphics; the print publication is more appealing.

3314. ***Ford Foundation Report.*** Formerly: *Ford Foundation Letter.* [ISSN: 1063-7281] 1970. 3x/yr. Free. Ed(s): Thomas Quinn. Ford Foundation, Office of Communications, c/o Mary Loftus, 320 E 43rd St, New York, NY 10017; http://www.fordfound.org. Illus., index. Sample. Circ: 35000. Vol. ends: Winter. Microform: PQC. Reprint: PQC. *Indexed:* ABS&EES. *Aud.:* Ac, Sa.

Articles in this report describe the Ford Foundation's activities and interests in the United States and abroad. Goals of the foundation include strengthening democratic values, reducing poverty and injustice, promoting international cooperation, and advancing human achievement. Areas covered include education, public policy, community involvement, and culture and the arts. Also noted are grant announcements, new appointments, and publications. Emphasis is on the development of social programs and individual and community successes. Libraries that offer resources on social issues will want to include this title.

3315. ***Furrow: a journal of popular farm science and rural life.*** [ISSN: 0016-3112] 1895. 8x/yr. Free to qualified personnel. Ed(s): Fred Wolf. Deere & Company, John Deere Publishing, 11145 Thompson Ave., Lenexa, KS 66219. Illus. Circ: 550000 Controlled. Microform: PQC. Reprint: PQC. *Indexed:* CPL. *Aud.:* Ga, Sa.

Furrow is a "United States edition of the *Worldwide Farm Magazine* published in 12 languages by Deere & Co. and its subsidiaries." Color illustrations enhance the six to eight feature articles, which showcase recent developments in crop production and marketing, agribusiness initiatives, or creative and successful individual farming efforts. Regular features include "Farm Facts and Fantasies," which briefly covers news items, and "Fun and Philosophy," a compendium of quotations, words of wisdom, and short jokes, not necessarily with a rural flavor.

3316. ***The Future of Children.*** [ISSN: 1054-8289] 1991. 2x/yr. Free. Ed(s): Richard E Behrman. David and Lucile Packard Foundation, Center for the Future of Children, 300 Second St, Ste 102, Los Altos, CA 94022; http://www.futureofchildren.org. Illus. Refereed. Circ: 50000. Vol. ends: Winter. Online: bigchalk; Gale Group; Northern Light Technology, Inc.; ProQuest Information & Learning. *Indexed:* CIJE, CINAHL, CJA, ExcerpMed, IMFL, IndMed, SSCI, SWR&A, SociolAb. *Aud.:* Ga, Ac, Sa.

The primary purpose of this journal is to "to promote effective policies and programs for children by providing policymakers, service providers, and the media with timely, objective information based on the best available research." The journal purports to complement, not duplicate, the information presented in academic journals. Abstracts precede the articles, which are written by doctors or other professionals. Each issue has a particular theme such as "Children and Poverty" or "Children and Computer Technology." Electronic access provides full text of current and back issues, subjects of forthcoming issues, and ordering information for print copies. A new online feature allows readers to participate in conversations with authors and editors related to issues covered in the journal. "My Journal Library" invites visitors to compile and save links to articles in published selections. Libraries with an interest in children's issues will find this journal indispensable.

3317. ***H H M I Bulletin.*** q. Free. Ed(s): Stephen Pelletaer. Howard Hughes Medical Institute, 4000 Jones Bridge Rd., Chevy Chase, MD 20815-6789; webmaster@hhml.org; http://www.hhmi.org. *Aud.:* Hs, Ga, Ac, Sa.

The Howard Hughes Medical Institute is a nonprofit organization of leading biomedical scientists. Through its grants program, HHMI enhances science education at all levels. The online *Bulletin* features five articles of interest to both scientists and laypersons. The format is colorful and appealing, and the articles, available in full text or as PDF files, address research at HHMI. Recent topics explored have included stem cell research, the obesity drug leptin, and the war on malaria. Especially notable are the sidebars with links that supplement the main topics. Scientists or researchers noted in the articles have links to their research abstracts. The issues are archived back to January 2001. The complete HHMI web site, news articles, investigator abstracts, or the complete grants index can be searched. Subscribers can receive e-mail notification when a new issue of the *Bulletin* appears on the web, and can opt to receive a print version of the bulletin with additional articles and features at no cost.

3318. ***Imprimis.*** [ISSN: 0277-8432] 1972. m. Free. Ed(s): Douglas A Jeffrey, Timothy W Caspar. Hillsdale College Press, Center for Constructive Alternatives, 33 East College St, Hillsdale, MI 49242-0000; imprimis@hillsdale.edu; http://www.hillsdale.edu. Adv. Circ: 1117000 Free. *Indexed:* PAIS. *Aud.:* Ga, Ac.

Each issue of this periodical publishes a paper given at Hillsdale College's Center for Constructive Alternatives, its Ludwig von Mises seminars, or its Shavano Institute for National Leadership. Topics cover political, economic, cultural, or moral issues and are presented by leading conservative thinkers such as William J. Bennett, Midge Dector, or James Buchanan. In addition to the text of the paper, a photograph and background information is given for each author. The college promotes the political ideas of natural rights, free enterprise, limited government, and moral responsibility. An online version of the papers and subscription information is available. This publication could be included by libraries that desire a conservative point of view to balance collections.

3319. ***Institute for Studies in American Music. Newsletter.*** [ISSN: 0145-8396] 1971. s-a. Free. Ed(s): Ray Allen. Institute for Studies in American Music, Conservatory of Music, Brooklyn College, Brooklyn, NY 11210. Illus., adv. Sample. Circ: 4200. Vol. ends: Spring. *Indexed:* IIMP, MusicInd. *Bk. rev.:* 3-4, lengthy. *Aud.:* Ga, Ac, Sa.

The Institute for Studies in American Music (ISAM) is a research and information center. The *Newsletter* includes essays, profiles of composers from Aaron Copland to Frank Zappa, and signed reviews of books, music, and recordings. Bibliographic essays survey important books in particular genres. Topics address the history, state of the art, and emerging trends in country, gospel, jazz, and popular American music. Photographs of performers comprise the majority of illustrations. The informative articles can be understood and enjoyed by the nonspecialist who has a love for music. The detailed reviews will be welcomed by librarians.

3320. *Insurance Institute for Highway Safety. Status Report.* Formerly: *I I H S Report.* [ISSN: 0018-988X] 1961. 10x/yr. Free. Ed(s): Anne Fleming, Kim Stewart. Insurance Institute for Highway Safety, 1005 North Glebe Rd, Arlington, VA 22201. Circ: 17000. Microform: PQC. Reprint: PQC. *Indexed:* ConsI. *Aud.:* Hs, Ga, Ac.

The Insurance Institute for Highway Safety, an independent, nonprofit, scientific, and educational organization, is "dedicated to reducing the losses—deaths, injuries, and property damage—from crashes on the nation's highways." The institute is wholly supported by automobile insurers. This newsletter provides up-to-date technological innovations, legislation, and policy issues that affect driving and highway safety. Several special issues each year address such topics as highway safety versus other public heath issues or older drivers. Colorful photographs, charts, and graphs enhance each report. Vehicle safety ratings, fatality facts, news releases, and listings of consumer publications and videos can be found on the companion web site. The online site also includes a substantial bibliography of research reports by IIHS as well as journal articles. The continuously updated web section on state law facts is an excellent source for comparative and current statistics. This periodical should prove quite useful in public, high school, and academic libraries.

3321. *Items & Issues.* Formerly (until 2000): *Items.* 1947. q. Free. Ed(s): Elsa Dixler. Social Science Research Council, 810 Seventh Ave, 31st Fl, New York, NY 10019-5818; dixler@ssrc.org; http://www.ssrc.org. Illus. Sample. Circ: 8500. Vol. ends: Dec. *Indexed:* ABS&EES, AICP, AnthLit, PRA. *Bk. rev.:* 2-4; length varies. *Aud.:* Ac.

The Social Science Research Council's purpose is "to advance social sciences throughout the world and support research, education and scholarly exchange on every continent." Three to five signed research articles by distinguished members of the council appear in each issue and focus on innovations in the social sciences. Past articles have explored current trends and future directions in sexuality research and political and social action in Iraq. Notices of research activities, fellowships, conferences, symposia, grant-supported council activities, book reviews, and recent council and staff publications are included. The online version archives issues back to 1995 and includes an index to articles published from 1947 to 1997. This journal offers thought-provoking pieces on contemporary social issues and is suitable for academic libraries.

3322. *Japan Foundation Newsletter.* [ISSN: 0385-2318] 1973. q. Free. Japan Foundation, Ark-Mori Bldg 20th Fl, 1-12-32 Akasaka, Tokyo, 107-0052, Japan; jfnl@jpf.go.jp. Illus., index. Sample. Circ: 4000. Vol. ends: Mar. *Indexed:* BAS. *Bk. rev.:* 1-2 lengthy. *Aud.:* Ac, Sa.

Directed to "individuals and organizations interested in Japanese Studies and international cultural exchange," mainly those overseas individuals and organizations, this newsletter reports on contemporary issues in Japanese culture. Featured topics have been studied or investigated by the foundation. Also presented are highlights from the Japanese press, research reports, reviews of books in Japanese and other languages, and a brief report of foundation activities. The web site allows full-text access to issues dating back to 1997. Although aimed at an academic audience, the reports are accessible and eclectic enough to engage any reader with a serious interest in Japanese culture.

3323. *Law Matters.* Formerly (until 1995): *Passport to Legal Understanding.* [ISSN: 1083-6225] 1983. 3x/yr. Free. Ed(s): R Gary Alexander. American Bar Association, Division on Public Understanding About the Law, 541 N Fairbanks, Chicago, IL 60611. Illus., adv. Sample. Circ: 10000. Vol. ends: No. 3. *Bk. rev.:* irregular; one per issue. *Aud.:* Hs, Ga, Ac, Sa.

This informative newsletter affirms that "law matters in everyone's life." Each issue includes a focus on a contemporary legal issue, notice of important developments in law and education, and reviews/updates of print, video, multimedia, and online resources. Recent newsletters have dealt with such issues as e-mail online ordering, the future of immigration, and the child care choices that working parents must consider. The style is concise and accessible, and the content is pertinent to both classroom discussion and the general adult public.

3324. *N A T O Review.* Formerly: *N A T O Letter.* [ISSN: 0255-3813] 1953. q. Ed(s): Christopher Bennett. North Atlantic Treaty Organization, Office of Information and Press, Brussels, 1110, Belgium; natodocs@hq.nato.int. Illus., index. Sample. Vol. ends: Nov. Microform: PQC. Online: bigchalk; ProQuest Information & Learning. Reprint: PQC. *Indexed:* ABCPolSci, GeoRef, PAIS. *Bk. rev.:* 2-3 per issue. *Aud.:* Ga, Ac, Sa.

The *NATO Review* is "intended to contribute to a constructive discussion of Atlantic problems" and claims that it does not necessarily represent the official opinion or policy of member governments or NATO. Defense and security issues are the focus. A strength is the variety of viewpoints that are clearly and succinctly presented in the six to eight feature articles written by government officials, NATO officials, or other international opinion leaders. Black-and-white photographs identify key diplomats, show troop placements, or capture the emotions of ordinary citizens. "Focus on NATO" sidebars report short news items or updates. A documents section includes official statements and graphs and charts. An interview feature and a statistics page are recent innovations. This periodical is available in 17 languages and would be a good choice for general reading about this organization. Its web site offers texts of current and back issues and information about NATO's structure and membership. Links to policy centers, institutes, and commissions and a brief preview of the forthcoming issue are included.

3325. *N L M Newsline.* Formerly: *National Library of Medicine News.* [ISSN: 1094-5970] 1945. q. Free. Ed(s): Melanie Modlin. U.S. National Library of Medicine, Bldg 38, 8600 Rockville Pike, Bethesda, MD 20894; mm354i@nih.gov; http://www.nlm.gov. Illus. Sample. Circ: 6000. Vol. ends: Dec. Microform: PQC. Reprint: PQC. *Indexed:* CINAHL. *Aud.:* Ac, Sa.

The National Library of Medicine's *NLM Newsline* is "published for institutions and individuals interested in health science communications." Advancements in information access, new initiatives, NLM-sponsored programs, and staff news keep readers apprised of the work of the world's largest medical library. New products and programs are highlighted. This newsletter is an important link between the NLM and medically-related libraries and college or university libraries that support medical or health curricula. Notably, the web NLM Gateway allows users to search in multiple retrieval systems at the U.S. National Library of Medicine (NLM). The Gateway searches MEDLINE/PubMed, OLDMEDLINE, LOCATORplus (catalog of books, journals, and audiovisuals in the NLM collections), MEDLINEplus, ClinicalTrials.gov, DIRLINE (Directory of health organizations), Meeting Abstracts, and HSRPro. Additional links to information on broad health subjects from AIDS to toxicology, library services, and research programs make this a useful site for both consumers and practitioners.

National Institute of Justice Journal. See Criminology and Law Enforcement section.

3326. *Public Health and the Environment.* Formerly: *Hazardous Substances & Public Health.* 1990. q. Free. Ed(s): Georgia Moore. U.S. Department of Health and Human Services, Agency for Toxic Substances and Disease Registry, 1600 Clifton Rd, N E, Mail Stop E 33, Atlanta, GA 30333; GBM7@cdc.gov; http://atsdr1.atsdr.cdc.gov:8080/HEC?hsphhome.html. Illus., adv. Sample. Circ: 10000. Vol. ends: Winter. *Indexed:* CINAHL, EnvAb. *Aud.:* Hs, Ga, Sa.

Articles in this redesigned newsletter, formerly *Hazardous Substances and Public Health,* aim to identify public health hazards, inform the public at risk, and propose corrective measures. Each issue features a lead article that addresses such issues as asbestos or children and the environment. Resources available, and a calendar of forthcoming conferences and symposia, are included. The online version has numerous pertinent links to both governmental and nongovernmental sources. Recent publications, some downloadable, provide additional venues for exploration. The concise but useful information presented here will be welcomed by readers who are interested in health and environmental issues.

3327. *Refugees.* Incorporates (1982-1983): *Refugees Magazine;* Former titles (until 198?): *U N H C R; H C R Bulletin.* [ISSN: 0252-791X] 1972. q. Free. Ed(s): Ray Wilkinson. United Nations High Commissioner for Refugees, Public Information Section, PO Box 2500, Geneva, 1211, Switzerland; http://www.unhcr.ch/. Illus. Circ: 227500. Microform: CIS. *Indexed:* PRA. *Aud.:* Hs, Ga, Ac.

The United Nations High Commissioner for Refugees (UNHCR) is mandated by the U.N. to "lead and coordinate international action for the world-wide protection of refugees and the resolution of refugee problems." This publication, postulating that each individual has the right to seek asylum and find secure refuge in another state or return home safely, features the plight of people left abandoned or displaced because of war, persecution, human rights abuses, or such scourges as drought or AIDS. Each issue has a theme; recent issues have covered the Somali Bantu, the environment, and the global impact of September 11. Exquisite photographs poignantly illustrate the feature articles. The companion UNHCR web site is a rich source for statistics on refugees and agency policy issues. Also included are maps and country-specific information, and teaching tools for elementary and secondary school teachers on how to integrate refugee studies into subject disciplines.

3328. *Resources (Washington).* [ISSN: 0048-7376] 1959. q. Free. Ed(s): Felicia Day. Resources for the Future, Inc., 1616 P St, N W, Washington, DC 20036; info@rff.org; http://www.rff.org. Illus., index. Sample. Circ: 14000 Controlled. Vol. ends: Fall. Microform: PQC. Reprint: PQC. *Indexed:* EnvAb, ForAb, GeoRef, PAIS, PollutAb, RRTA, S&F, SWRA, WAE&RSA. *Aud.:* Ga, Ac, Sa.

Resources "contains news of research and policy analysis regarding natural resources and the environment" and claims that it brought into existence the subdiscipline of environmental and resource economics and applied it to emerging policy issues. Three to five feature articles written by Resources for the Future (RFF) researchers or senior fellows propose speculative, creative approaches to problem solving. Shorter news items focus on the "people side" of problem solving, RFF announcements, and gift fund information. This established publication is for libraries that maintain resources in policy and social issues. Its up-to-date, excellent web site contains information about RFF, conferences and workshops, discussion papers, publications from the RFF press, testimony from the RFF staff before Congressional committees, educational seminars, employment opportunities, fellowships and internships, and back and current issues of *Resources.* The web site also lists relevant topics under its "Research Areas."

3329. *Saudi Aramco World.* Former titles (until 2000): *Aramco World;* (until 1987): *Aramco World Magazine;* (until 1968): *Aramco World.* [ISSN: 1530-5821] 1949. bi-m. Free. Ed(s): Robert Arndt. Aramco Services Company, PO Box 2106, Houston, TX 77252-2106. Illus., index. Sample. Circ: 180000 Controlled. Vol. ends: Nov/Dec. *Indexed:* API, EnvAb, GeoRef, NumL, PAIS. *Aud.:* Ems, Hs, Ga.

Beautiful color photographs and appealing illustrations embellish this 40- to 60-page publication, which features articles on the culture, history, geography, and economy of the Arab and Muslim worlds. The information is presented without political bias or industry advocacy. Authoritative signed articles delineate cross-cultural influences. Included is a calendar of international events and exhibitions related to the history and culture of the Middle East. Annual and cumulative indexes increase the publication's utility. Libraries that need cultural material on this area of the world will find this magazine a worthy addition.

3330. *Smithsonian Institution Research Reports.* Formerly: *Smithsonian Research Reports.* [ISSN: 0364-0175] 1972. q. Free. Ed(s): Jo Ann Webb. Smithsonian Institution, Office of Public Affairs, 900 Jefferson Dr, Rm 2410, Washington, DC 20560. Illus. Sample. Circ: 67000. Vol. ends: Autumn. *Indexed:* BiolDig, EnvAb, GeoRef, IUSGP. *Aud.:* Hs, Ga, Ac, Sa.

This newsletter is directed to contributing members, scholars, educators, museum and library personnel, and journalists. Behind-the-scenes glimpses into collections in the areas of natural history, ecology, air-and-space history, or popular culture make for fascinating reading. Smithsonian awards and research highlights are noted. The back of each issue is devoted to briefly described series publications, books, and recordings issued by the Smithsonian Institution Press. The web site for this publication offers the text of issues dating from 1995; latest issues are available in pdf only. Researchers and teachers, as well as general readers interested in science or history, will find this publication of value.

3331. *Syllabus (Sunnyvale): new directions in educational technology.* Incorporates (1991-199?): *Higher Education Product Companion;* (1992-1993): *Computer Science Syllabus.* [ISSN: 1065-2051] 1988. 10x/yr. Free. Ed(s): Mary Grush. Syllabus Press, 9121 Oakdale Ave., Ste. 101, Chatsworth, CA 91311-6526; mgrush@syllabus.com; http://www.syllabus.com. Illus., adv. Sample. Circ: 55000. Vol. ends: May. *Aud.:* Ac, Sa.

Syllabus is the only monthly publication that focuses on the role of technology in higher education. "To inform educators on how technology can be used to support their teaching, learning and administrative activities" is the mission of this publication. It includes feature articles, case studies, and product reviews, and profiles technology use. Topics addressed include distance learning, multimedia, the Internet, quantitative tools, and publishing and administrative technology. The web site includes conference information, news for campus and industry professionals, a calendar, fora, and a job board. This publication would appear to be mandatory reading for those who implement or use technology on campus.

3332. *T H E Journal.* [ISSN: 0192-592X] 1973. m. 11/yr. USD 29; USD 95 foreign. Ed(s): Sylvia Charp. Ed Warnshuis Ltd., 17501 17th St, Ste 230, Tustin, CA 92680; cedwards@thejournal.com; charp@eniac.seas.upenn.edu; http://www.thejournal.com. Illus., adv. Circ: 165500 Controlled. Microform: PQC. Online: bigchalk; EBSCO Publishing; Florida Center for Library Automation; Gale Group; OCLC Online Computer Library Center, Inc.; ProQuest Information & Learning; H.W. Wilson. *Indexed:* CIJE, CompLI, ConsI, EduInd, LRI, MicrocompInd. *Aud.:* Hs, Ac, Sa.

T.H.E. Journal disseminates information on the use of technology in education. The focus is on American educational initiatives, but international endeavors are occasionally highlighted. Two feature articles describe creative applications of technology in the classroom. Other articles include a description of applications, e-learning activities, selected educational web sites, news items, and a "Product Watch." The journal's web site adds "T.H.E. Source," a new area that provides educators with information about new technology and a "Roadmap to the Internet," a directory of catalog resources. Libraries that support media technology or are affiliated with educational institutions will want to include this journal.

3333. *Talking Book Topics.* [ISSN: 0039-9183] 1935. bi-m. Free. Ed(s): Edmund O'Reilly. U.S. Library of Congress, National Library Service for the Blind and Physically Handicapped, 1291 Taylor St, NW, Washington, DC 20011; nls@loc.gov; http://www.loc.gov/nls/. Index. Sample. Circ: 330000. Vol. ends: Nov/Dec. *Aud.:* Ems, Hs, Ga, Ac, Sa.

Talking Book Topics is published in large-print, cassette, audio disc, and computer diskette and distributed free of charge to the blind and physically handicapped who participate in the Library of Congress National Free Reading Program. Recent fiction and nonfiction additions to the program are featured, as well as foreign language and magazine selections for adults and children. Annotations are descriptive and identify the targeted reader. An author-title index and order forms are included in each issue.

3334. *Teaching Tolerance.* [ISSN: 1066-2847] 1991. s-a. Ed(s): Jim Carnes, Elsie Williams. Southern Poverty Law Center, 400 Washington Ave., Montgomery, AL 36104; http://www.teachingtolerance.org/. Circ: 600000 Controlled. *Indexed:* CIJE, EduInd, MRD. *Bk. rev.:* 4-5 (50-60 words). *Aud.:* Hs, Ac, Sa.

This 64-page, full-color magazine provides a forum for educators to share new techniques and ideas in the areas of tolerance, diversity, and justice. Each issue includes features on topics such as sexual harassment, religious and gender diversity, race relations, and strengthening classroom community. Grant intiatives in the field of toleration are showcased, as are recommended teaching tools and primarily relevant and recommended books. Articles address concerns from preschool through secondary education. The web version includes archives from 1996. Subscriptions are available free to "teachers, religious and community leaders, healthcare providers and other educators upon written request on school or organization letterhead." This publication would also find utility in teacher education programs.

3335. ***U.S. Library of Congress. Information Bulletin.*** [ISSN: 0041-7904] 1942. 11x/yr. Free to libraries, the media and institutions. Ed(s): Helen Dalrymple. U.S. Library of Congress, Office of Public Affairs, Washington, DC 20540-8610; http://lcweb.loc.gov/. Illus., index. Sample. Circ: 14000. Vol. ends: No. 24. Microform: LCP. *Indexed:* A&ATA, ABS&EES, IUSGP, LibLit, PAIS, RI-1. *Aud.:* Ga, Ac, Sa.

Although this newsletter is restricted to news about the Library of Congress and its staff, that restriction nevertheless encompasses the whole of American history and its citizens at home or abroad. Treasures highlighted in past issues range from the work of Ansel Adam's photo documentation of World War II Japanese internment to a preview of a Lewis and Clark exhibition commemorating their epic journey of discovery. The Library and OCLC have developed QuestionPoint, a new collaborative online reference service, and considerable content has been devoted recently to virtual reference. News from the Center for the Book, notices of conferences, displays, acquisitions, and a calendar of events that are open to the public complete this publication.

3336. ***Utah Science.*** Formerly: *Utah Farm and Home Science.* [ISSN: 0042-1502] 1940. q. Free. Ed(s): Lynnette F Harris. Utah Agricultural Experiment Station, Utah State University, Logan, UT 84322; http://www.agx.usu.edu. Illus., index. Sample. Circ: 4000. Vol. ends: Winter. *Indexed:* BiolAb, DSA, FS&TA, GeoRef, IndVet, PollutAb, SWRA, VetBull, ZooRec. *Aud.:* Hs, Ga, Ac, Sa.

The content of this publication is devoted primarily to experiment station research in agriculture and related areas. Brief, readable articles address issues in human nutrition, consumer marketing and product development, animal and dairy management, and crop production. Articles range beyond regional interests and are written for the nonspecialist. Contributors' e-mail addresses and telephone numbers are included with each article, so that readers can get in touch with an expert or glean additional information. Photographs and subtle graphics illustrate the text. University research grants, contracts received, and student study and research are noted. A photo quiz challenges readers to identify by name and purpose objects related to agricultural research. The format invites browsing and should appeal to readers in all types of libraries.

Electronic Journals

3337. ***Ed. Net Briefs.*** 1995. w. Free. Ed(s): Steven W Simpson. Simpson Communications, info@edbriefs.com. *Aud.:* Ac, Sa.

This newsletter is directed at educators short on time who want to be apprised of the rapid changes in education and educational technology. Approximately eight feature article abstracts allow the reader to receive a "reasonably complete overview of the week's important or interesting education news" in about ten minutes. A complete source citation accompanies each abstract, including a linkable URL if available. Ostensibly, the newsletter provides useful information that will improve the quality of classroom instruction, schools, and educators' decisions in general. "The Educators' Bookstore" in association with Amazon.com allows readers to select and order from preschool to secondary level and discipline categories. A large selection of education sites and resources with brief annotations is included. Archives, searchable by keyword, date from 1996. This publication would be quite useful not only for teachers, but also for education majors or citizens who want to be conversant in pertinent educational issues.

3338. ***Fine Travel.*** Formerly: *Fine Food & Travel Magazine.* 1995. d. Ed(s): Louis Bignami. Fine Travel, 1914 Conestoga St, Moscow, ID 83843; bignami@finefishing.com; http://www.finetravel.com. *Bk. rev.:* Number varies. *Aud.:* Ga.

This Internet journal should appeal to those who disdain the mundane as well as armchair travelers who enjoy reading about the art of travel as opposed to perusing a guidebook. More than 250 articles written by professional writers cover "posh" resort, cruise, and charter travel. Fine restaurants and upscale hotels are also showcased. Five or six new articles and a featured area are introduced each month. In addition to selecting from various geographic areas—the U.S., Canada, Mexico, Europe, Africa, Asia and Australia, Central and South America, the Bahamas, and the Caribbean—the reader can search the categories of Hotels and Restaurants, Golf, Skiing, and Oddments; the latter offers such fare as flyfishing stories by women, renting exotic automobiles for Southern California drivers, and advice on horsepacking trips as a summer option. Recent articles selected from the geographic categories have included "Milan's Best Hotels," "Where to see Nesting Sea Turtles," and "Roughing it on the Australian Coast." A geographical hierarchical table of contents is available. Readers can receive notice of new articles and travel tips by submitting their e-mails to the site.

■ GAMES

See also Computer Science and Automation; and Sports sections.

Patrick Jose Dawson, Head, Information Services, Davidson Library, University of California, Santa Barbara, CA 93107; dawson@library.ucsb.edu

Introduction

Game magazines cover a broad spectrum, attempting to capture all that is classified as a "game." As games and the means to play them have changed, so, too, have game magazines. There are still the traditional magazines dealing with time-tested games such as chess and bridge, while the publication explosion of electronic-games magazines reflects the huge increase in the number and types of electronic games. More-traditional game magazines tend to use print, while electronic and computer games opt for online publishing.

Games and game magazines fall into four basic types: (1) games of chance, (2) adventure games, (3) computer or electronic games, and (4) traditional games. The majority of game magazines in print today are devoted to traditional games like chess, checkers, and bridge, due mostly to the large number of worldwide associations that are devoted to these traditional games. As role-playing games—a type of adventure game—have become more prevalent, there has also been an increase in the number of these magazines. Many of them deal with the games themselves (e.g., "Dungeons and Dragons"), while some are concerned with the collections of cards and figures associated with these games, and this has become quite lucrative and popular. Another type of adventure game is "Paintball," which gives participants the opportunity to hunt, "kill," and "be killed" in a rather safe environment. There has been an increase, both in print and online, in the number of lottery and game-of-chance magazines as more states conduct lotteries and the number of casinos has increased, with legalized gambling no longer confined to Las Vegas and Atlantic City. Computer and electronic games are extremely popular, and the number of electronic publications for these games has dramatically increased.

Electronic publication of game magazines is becoming the means of choice for many publishers, especially those that deal with computer and electronic games. Use your preferred search engine with the terms "games" or "gaming" and you will find a multitude of titles, including many self-published works. However, many of the hits you do get will not be established publications, most lacking ISSN numbers or any affiliation with a recognized publisher. Many of the print publishers also offer an online equivalent; however, it is either included in the cost of the print edition or is an abridged version of the print. The advantages to publishing on the web are that it allows for real-time updates, changing calendars of game events, buying and selling of games, and interactive tutorials and problem solving, not to mention copious "cheats" for winning, and it is a more economical means of publishing, especially for individuals. While many of these titles are free, they do require that a "profile" be established so that the sponsors of the magazine or web site are able to send e-mail advertising.

Basic Periodicals

Ga: *ACF Bulletin, Bridge World, Chess Life, Games.*

3339. ***A C F Bulletin.*** [ISSN: 1045-8034] 1952. bi-m. USD 25. Ed(s): Charles C Walker. American Checker Federation, PO Box 365, Petal, MS 39465. Illus. Circ: 1000. *Aud.:* Ems, Hs, Ga, Ac.

The *ACF Bulletin* is the official periodical of the American Checker Federation (ACF). It covers checkers-related news at state, district, national, and international levels. It reports the results of ACF and affiliated tournaments, including annotated accounts of national tournament games. The "Mail Play News" caters to the correspondence checker player, including news of mail games between Great Britain and the United States as well as local matches. There is a problem-and-solution article each month, and the "Swap Shop" page features books for sale on checkers and checker boards. The ACF web site is worth checking out for its archived problems, games, and interviews. Available online at http://www.acfcheckers.com.

3340. ***A P C T News Bulletin.*** 1967. 6x/yr. USD 18; USD 36 foreign. Ed(s): Helen Warren. American Postal Chess Tournaments, PO Box 305, Western Springs, IL 60558-0305; apct@aol.com. Adv. Circ: 1000. *Bk. rev.:* 3, 50 words. *Aud.:* Hs, Ga, Ac.

American Postal Chess Tournaments (APCT) is geared toward correspondence chess players, offering postal and e-mail events. Currently, the APCT has over 1,000 "Postalities" in 50 states and 8 foreign countries. The APCT offers 11 distinctive tournaments, ranging from the Pawn Tournaments for more sociable play to the more competitive Queen Tournaments. The bulletin includes game results, ratings, annotated and nonannotated games, "how to improve" articles, and a listing of new and out-of-print chess books. A new area of writing deals with theory as well as computer chess. The book reviews are particularly good and of interest to all chess players. The APCT is an affiliate of the U.S. Chess Federation.

Action Pursuit Games. See Military Games section.

3341. ***Blitz Chess.*** [ISSN: 1053-3087] 1988. q. USD 4 newsstand/cover per issue domestic; USD 4.50 newsstand/cover per issue in Canada & Mexico; USD 5 newsstand/cover per issue elsewhere. Ed(s): Walter S Browne. World Blitz Chess Association, 8 Parnassus Rd, Berkeley, CA 94708; wbcablitz@aol.com. Illus., adv. Circ: 1200 Paid. *Aud.:* Ga, Ac.

This magazine is devoted to blitz chess, the fastest form of the game, with a five-minute time limit per player. There is coverage of chess events, including where to play, annotated games, articles about players, articles on blitz tactics, and announcements of tournaments with end-game articles by Pal Benko. The contents are not limited to blitz chess, however. Top international chess events are covered, and there are interesting historical chess problems to solve as well as information on the grand masters. Each issue includes a complete list of members and a quarterly rating list.

3342. ***The Bridge Bulletin.*** Former titles: *American Contract Bridge League. Bulletin;* (until 1993): *Contract Bridge Bulletin.* [ISSN: 1089-6376] 1935. m. Non-members, USD 20. Ed(s): Paul Linxwiler, Brent Manley. American Contract Bridge League, 2990 Airways Blvd, Memphis, TN 38116-3847; acbl@acbl.org. Illus., adv. Sample. Circ: 147000 Controlled. *Bk. rev.:* 3, 50 words. *Aud.:* Ga.

The Bridge Bulletin is the major source for news and information about contract bridge, including duplicate bridge. The *Bridge Bulletin* publishes articles on strategy, contains interviews with players, and includes a calendar of national and world events. Included are a listing of tournament schedules and results, miscellaneous bridge news, and special instructional sections devoted to novice and intermediate players.

3343. ***Bridge (London).*** Former titles: *Bridge International; Bridge Magazine;* Incorporates: *British Bridge World.* [ISSN: 0958-6768] 1926. m. GBP 34.95 domestic; GBP 44.95 in Europe; USD 70 in US & Canada. Ed(s): Mark Horton. Chess & Bridge Ltd., 369 Euston Rd, London, NW1 3AR, United Kingdom; chesscentre@easynet.co.uk; http://www.bridgemagazine.co.uk. Illus., adv. Circ: 10000. *Bk. rev.:* Each issue. *Aud.:* Ga, Ac, Sa.

This magazine has a long publishing history, having survived for over 70 years. It has a substantial circulation worldwide for a magazine that only deals with the game of bridge. It contains all that a good magazine on bridge should: articles on bidding and play as well as instruction articles for playing or learning bridge. It also contains information on competitions, reports on tournaments, and humor related to bridge.

3344. ***Bridge Today: the magazine for people who love to play bridge.*** [ISSN: 1043-6383] 1988. 6x/yr. USD 24 domestic; USD 29 Canada; USD 34 elsewhere. Ed(s): Matthew Granovetter. Granovetter Books, 3329 Spindletop Dr NW, Kennesaw, GA 30144-7336. Illus., adv. Sample. Circ: 6000. *Aud.:* Ga.

This title offers game analyses, problems, and articles on specific aspects of bridge. The distinguishing feature of *Bridge Today* is the clear and entertaining annotations. Each article is a bridge lesson in itself. A list of books available from the Bridge Today Bookshop is also included. An excellent complement to *The Bridge Bulletin* and *Bridge World.*

3345. ***Bridge World.*** [ISSN: 0006-9876] 1929. m. USD 52; USD 62 foreign. Ed(s): Jeff Rubens. Bridge World Magazine Inc., 717 White Plains Rd., White Plains, NY 10583-5009; mail@bridgeworld.com; http://www.bridgeworld.com. Illus., adv. Circ: 7800. *Aud.:* Ga.

This title is aimed at the dedicated player. That said, it offers a wide variety of articles, problems, bridge news, and instructional features. The articles, written by a number of well-known bridge analysts, are rather technical but generally informal in style. There is also a section of book reviews, which is of use to the serious player. *Bridge World* will be appreciated where there is a significant population of serious bridge players.

3346. ***British Chess Magazine.*** [ISSN: 0007-0440] 1881. m. GBP 28; GBP 30 in Europe; GBP 34 elsewhere. Ed(s): Murray Chandler. British Chess Magazine Ltd., The Chess Shop, 69 Masbro Rd, London, W14 0LS, United Kingdom; 100561.3121@compuserve.com; http://www.bcmchess.co.uk. Illus., adv. Circ: 4000. Vol. ends: Dec. *Bk. rev.:* 8, 50 words. *Aud.:* Ga, Ac.

This is the leading chess magazine in Great Britain, with a substantial circulation worldwide. It has something for every chess player: reports of current tournaments, historical features, problems and studies, correspondence chess, and opening theory. The *British Chess Magazine* is particularly famous for its deeply annotated games, chosen for instruction and enjoyment. The magazine is written for players at every strength level.

3347. ***Card Player: the magazine for those who play to win.*** [ISSN: 1089-2044] 1988. fortn. USD 49; USD 159 foreign. Ed(s): Steve Radulovich. Card Player, 3140 S Polaris Ave, Las Vegas, NV 89102; cpljda@aol.com; http://cardplayer.com. Illus., adv. Circ: 5000 Paid. *Aud.:* Ga.

This magazine, published in Las Vegas and host to major poker tournaments, is devoted to poker throughout the world. It includes articles on strategy, interviews, poker stories, poker-themed travel, and tournament schedules and results.

3348. ***Casino Chronicle: a weekly newsletter focusing on the gaming industry.*** [ISSN: 0889-9797] 1983. w. 48/yr. USD 175 domestic; USD 190 in Canada & Mexico; USD 190 Mexico. Ed(s): Ben A Borowsky. Casino Chronicle, P.O. Box 740465, Boynton Beach, FL 33474-0465. Illus., adv. Sample. Circ: 1500 Paid and controlled. *Aud.:* Sa.

This newsletter is aimed at executives in the casino industry and companies and individuals engaged in business with casino hotels. It gives concise, thorough coverage of everything from legislation, company news, and construction to financial information. The major emphasis is on Atlantic City, but it also covers Las Vegas and other gambling operations nationwide.

3349. ***Chess Correspondent.*** [ISSN: 0009-3327] 1926. 6x/yr. USD 16. Ed(s): Joe Ganem. C C L A, PO Box 59625, Schaumburg, IL 60159-0625. Illus., adv. Sample. Circ: 1000. *Aud.:* Ac, Sa.

This is the official publication of the Correspondence Chess League of America, a nonprofit organization founded in 1909. It features annotated games, articles on chess fundamentals, book reviews, and ratings, all with an emphasis on correspondence chess. The league sponsors postal and e-mail tournaments. This publication won the 1993 award from the Chess Journalists Association for the Best Magazine on Postal Chess.

3350. ***Chess Life.*** Formerly (until 1980): *Chess Life and Review;* Incorporates: *Chess Review.* [ISSN: 0197-260X] 1933. m. USD 45; USD 3.75 newsstand/cover per issue; USD 51 Canada. Ed(s): Glenn Petersen. United States Chess Federation, 3054 NYS Rte 9W, New Windsor, NY 12553; http://www.uschess.org. Illus., adv. Sample. Circ: 70000. Vol. ends: Dec. Microform: PQC. *Bk. rev.:* 2-3, 250 words. *Aud.:* Hs, Ga, Ac.

This official publication of the U.S. Chess Federation provides exhaustive coverage of chess-related news for federation members: workshops, tournaments, and a calendar of national and state events. It covers all aspects of chess: carefully annotated games, interviews, puzzles, and advice. Also included are columns on historical topics, personality profiles (the emphasis is on American players), and short stories. This is a basic chess title, recommended for most libraries. The U.S. Chess Federation also publishes *School Mates,* aimed at young chess players.

3351. ***Dragon Magazine.*** [ISSN: 0279-6848] 1976. m. USD 36.95. Ed(s): Chris Thomasson. Paizo Publishing LLC, 3245 146 Pl SE, Ste 110, Bellevue, WA 98007; customer.service@paizo.com; http://www.paizopublishing.com. Illus., adv. Sample. Circ: 70000. *Aud.:* Ems, Hs, Ga.

Dragon Magazine is dedicated to role-playing games, not exclusively to Dungeons and Dragons. It is a profusely illustrated publication, full of practical advice on designing scenarios, characters, and environments. It has an exhaustive calendar of events and lists sources for role-playing equipment. Also published by TSR is the popular *Dungeon: Adventures for TSR Role-Playing Games.*

3352. ***The Duelist: the official trading card magazine from Wizards of the Coast.*** [ISSN: 1082-8621] 1994. m. USD 24.95; GBP 24.95 in Europe; GBP 34.95 elsewhere. Ed(s): Will McDermott. Wizards of the Coast, Inc., 1801 Lind Ave, PO Box 707, Renton, WA 98057; duelist@wizards.com; http://www.wizards.com/Duelist_Online. Illus., adv. Circ: 100000 Paid. *Aud.:* Ems, Hs, Ga.

Duelist is devoted to "Magic: The Gathering" (the popular trading card game) and other trading-card games. It contains reviews of new games, articles on the use of individual cards, articles on deck building, and strategy advice. Many of the articles utilize the expertise of top players as well as game designers and developers. The magazine is branching out to cover other, related electronic games.

3353. ***Electronic Gaming Monthly.*** [ISSN: 1058-918X] 1986. m. USD 19.97 domestic; USD 35.97 foreign. Ed(s): Joe Fielder. Ziff Davis Media Game Group, 28 East 28th St, New York, NY 10016-7930; info@ziffdavis.com; http://www.ziffdavis.com. Illus., adv. Circ: 398219 Paid. Online: EBSCO Publishing; Factiva; Gale Group; ProQuest Information & Learning. *Aud.:* Ems, Hs, Ga.

Electronic Gaming Monthly covers electronic games on all the major game systems. Networked online games are covered by *Computer Gaming World,* another Ziff-Davis publication. Most of the magazine is devoted to game previews and reviews. The evaluations are detailed and objective and provide a good source of consumer information. Libraries should be aware of occasional lurid covers and ads. The web site offers an abbreviated free version of the magazine.

3354. ***En Passant: Canada's chess magazine.*** Former titles: *Chess Canada Echecs; Chess Federation of Canada. Bulletin.* [ISSN: 0822-5672] 1973. 6x/yr. CND 15; CND 18 foreign. Ed(s): Hal Bond. En Passant Publishers Ltd., 2212 Gladwin Cres E 1, Ottawa, ON K1B 5N1, Canada. Illus., adv. Circ: 3000. *Bk. rev.:* 10, 25 words. *Aud.:* Ga, Ac.

This is the official journal of the Chess Federation of Canada (CFC). The mandate of the CFC is to promote and encourage the knowledge, study, and play of chess in Canada. The magazine is aimed at players of all strengths. Regular features include a calendar of events, analysis of major games, interviews, book reviews, listings of other Canadian chess associations and local clubs, reports from the clubs, and ratings of players.

3355. ***Gambling Times Magazine.*** Former titles: *Win Magazine;* (until 1990): *Gambling Times.* [ISSN: 1533-6603] 1977. m. USD 44; USD 51 foreign. Gambling Times, Inc., 3883 W. Century Blvd., # 608, Inglewood, CA 90303-1003. Illus., adv. Circ: 125000 Paid and free. Vol. ends: Feb. *Aud.:* Ac, Sa.

This is the basic title for those who make gambling a serious pursuit. It offers articles on gambling systems, various betting procedures and games, and features on gambling personalities. Other features include advice, strategy, statistics, betting guides, reviews on casino conditions, and information on the casino and hotel entertainment scene. Recommended for libraries in areas where there is a strong interest in gambling.

3356. ***Games.*** [ISSN: 0199-9788] 1977. 9x/yr. USD 26.95 domestic; USD 34.95 Canada; USD 41.97 elsewhere. Ed(s): R Wayne Schmittberger. Games Publications, Inc., 7002 West Butler Pike, Ambler, PA 19002; gamespub@tidalwave.com. Illus., adv. Circ: 190000. *Indexed:* BRI, CBRI. *Bk. rev.:* Number varies, 100 words. *Aud.:* Hs, Ga.

Games includes something for everyone, including its own games, which are some of the most challenging and original puzzles around, and games for one or several players. Puzzle types range from photo identification to intellectual problem solving. Games are rated for level of difficulty. Features include contests, short articles, and book and game reviews.

3357. ***GameWEEK: the newspaper of the interactive entertainment industry.*** Formerly (until 1998): *Videogame Advisor.* [ISSN: 1097-394X] 1985. 44x/yr. USD 99 domestic; USD 149 in Europe; USD 200 elsewhere. Ed(s): Mike Davila. CyberActive Publishing, 64 Danbury Rd, Ste 500, Wilton, CT 06897; jim@gameweek.com; http://www.gameweek.com/. Illus., adv. Online: America Online, Inc. *Aud.:* Ga, Sa.

This large-format trade magazine covers industry news, trade shows, and financial news and projections, using a clear, visually oriented format. There are some game previews and reviews, but far more space is devoted to evaluations of new software and hardware, sales rankings, company profiles, and long interviews. The web site complements the print publication with daily industry-related press releases and "GameJobs," a listing of job openings in the game industry. Should be of interest in areas where the gaming industry is a significant factor in the local economy.

3358. ***Go World.*** [ISSN: 0286-0376] 1977. q. USD 32; USD 50 in Europe. Ed(s): Richard Bozulich. Kiseido Publishing Company, C.P.O. Box 1140, Tokyo, Japan; kiseido@yk.rim.or.jp; http://www.kiseido.com. Illus., adv. Circ: 10500. *Aud.:* Hs, Ga.

This quarterly offers instructional articles for beginners and more-advanced players, commentary, news, and articles of general interest about the game Go. Go is an ancient board game that uses simple materials and concepts to generate complex strategies and tactics. The major Go tournaments in Japan, Korea, and China are also covered.

3359. ***Lottery & Casino News.*** Formerly: *Lottery Player's Magazine.* [ISSN: 1088-727X] 1981. bi-m. USD 17.75; USD 35.50 foreign. Ed(s): Samuel W Valenza, Jr. Regal Publishing Corporation, PO Box 487, Marlton, NJ 08053-0487; regalpub@lottery-casino-news.com; http://www.lottery-casino-news.com. Illus., adv. Circ: 150000 Paid. *Aud.:* Ga.

Coverage in this publication is not limited to lotteries. There are also features about other gambling games, ranging from bingo and racing to casino action. The main emphasis is on lotteries, with numerous articles, features, and short pieces giving background information on the subject. Upcoming lotteries and winning numbers in the states that sponsor the games are also provided. Of interest is information provided on legislation concerning lotteries and gaming. Back issues are available.

3360. ***LottoWorld: America's lottery magazine.*** [ISSN: 1077-1840] 1993. m. USD 29.95. Ed(s): Dennis Schroeder. Lottoworld Inc., 201 8th St S Ste 107, Naples, FL 33940-4811; rholman@coconet.com; http://www.lottoworldmagazine.com. Illus., adv. Circ: 250000 Paid. *Aud.:* Ga.

This national lottery magazine has eight regional or state editions as well as a national edition. It includes features on winning strategies, lottery statistics, and interviews. The web site has an abbreviated version of the print magazine.

3361. ***New in Chess Magazine.*** [ISSN: 0168-8782] 1984. 8x/yr. USD 79. Ed(s): J H Timman, D J Ten Geuzendam. Chess Combination, Inc., PO Box 2423, Bridgeport, CT 06608-0423; http://www.chessnic.com/. Illus., adv. Sample. Vol. ends: Jan. *Bk. rev.:* 3, 100 words. *Aud.:* Hs, Ga, Ac.

This is one of the newer chess titles. There is more of a European focus than in *Chess Life* or other U.S. chess magazines. There are articles on world chess tournament play with detailed game analyses, as well as interviews and articles on the history of chess that may be of interest to the lay reader. There is a supplement (issued four times per year) available for an additional $129. Subscribers may also obtain data disks on the more than 16,000 games that are discussed or cited in the yearbook. Special Nicbase software is required to read the data and replay the games.

3362. ***P C Gamer.*** Former titles (until May 1994): *Game Player's P C Entertainment;* (until 1991): *Game Player's P C Strategy Guide; Game Player's M S - D O S Strategy Guide.* [ISSN: 1080-4471] 1988. m. USD 29.95 includes m. CD-ROM; USD 7.99 newsstand/cover per issue domestic; CND 8.99 newsstand/cover per issue Canada. Ed(s): Rob Smith. Imagine Media, Inc., 150 North Hill Dr, Brisbane, CA 94005; webmaster@imaginemedia.com; http://www.imaginemedia.com. Adv. Circ: 250000 Paid. *Aud.:* Hs, Ga, Ac.

This publication, originally evaluating educational products for IBM PC and compatible computers, has come to focus more on PC-compatible games. Sections include hints to improve scores, announcements of new games, interviews with game creators, and downloadable previews to new games. There is a companion web site at http://www.pcgamer.com.

3363. ***Scrye.*** 1994. m. USD 29.98; USD 5.50 newsstand/cover per issue. Ed(s): Joyce Greenholdt. Krause Publications, Inc., 700 E State St, Iola, WI 54990-0001; info@krause.com; http://www.krause.com. Adv. Circ: 47015 Paid and free. *Aud.:* Hs, Ga.

A price and buying guide for collectors of miniatures and card games, with a section for trading, listing your collectibles, and searching for dealers. There is also news on nationwide conventions, a tournament calendar for deck games, and tournament winners.

3364. ***White Dwarf.*** [ISSN: 0265-8712] 1977. m. GBP 35 domestic; GBP 45 in Europe; GBP 75 elsewhere. Ed(s): Jake Thornton. Games Workshop Ltd., Willow Rd, Lenton, NG7 2WS, United Kingdom; http://www.games-workshop.com. Circ: 60968. *Aud.:* Hs, Ga.

This monthly hobby magazine of Games Workshop is intended to keep the reader informed of new game releases, upcoming games, and what is going on with the workshop. Included are photos of new minatures and information on trading and prices of miniatures.

Electronic Journals

3365. ***Game Report Online.*** 1994. q. Ed(s): Peter Sarrett. Game Report Online, 1920 N 49th St., Seattle, WA 98103; editor@gamereport.com; http://www.gamereport.com. *Aud.:* Hs, Ga.

The editor of this first-class review of games has definite opinions about what is good and what is bad, and he says so without any "ifs" or "buts." The result is a reliable place to turn for information about all types of games, from board games to dice, family games, and strategy games. There are a few features and articles, but most of the focus is on reviews, covering material for all age groups. The site also allows for posting anything from news to advertising. (BK)

3366. ***Game Zero Magazine.*** 1997. irreg. Game Zero Magazine, http://www.vol.it/team-0/contents.html. *Aud.:* Ga.

Here the emphasis is on reviews of video games, with a nod to other types of games found on the web. The reviews are more descriptive than critical, but at least they keep the fan current on what is being released. Of particular value are links to related sites. (BK)

3367. ***Games Domain Review.*** 1994. w. Ed(s): Rich Greenhill. Games Domain Review, 435 Lichfield Rd., Aston, Birmingham, B67 SS, United Kingdom; http://www.gamesdomain.co.uk/help/newsletter.html. *Aud.:* Ga.

Published in England, this magazine has a broader interest for Americans than one might suspect. True, a few news items and reviews of electronic games are of interest only to the British, but many will be valued by those in North America. In a typical issue, one finds short pieces on such items of universal interest as Star Wars, Starship Titanic, and Alluds: Sealed Mystery, as well as reviews of the latest games. There is an archive of over 1,400 reviews that are as evaluative as they are descriptive. For this reason alone, anyone involved with electronic games should turn to this site for advice. (BK)

3368. ***I M P Bridge Magazine.*** 1995. m. Ed(s): Jan Van Cleeff. I M P Bridge Magazine, 2512 GA, The Hague, Netherlands; http://www.imp-bridge.nl. *Aud.:* Ga, Ac.

This has flourished as a print magazine since 1989. While published in The Netherlands, its text is in English and meant for an international group of bridge players. The primary focus is on tournaments, but it also has numerous features on methods of play and defense. The primary audience is the near-expert, not the beginner. However, there are numerous links to other bridge web sites and related bridge magazines that can be used by the person first being introduced to the game. (BK)

3369. ***NOSTalgia (Victorville, E-mail Edition).*** Formerly: *Nost-Algia (Print Edition).* 1960. q. Membership, USD 20; Members, USD 10. Ed(s): Don Cotten. Knights of the Square Table, c/o Donald Cotten, 13393 Mariposa Rd 248, Victorville, CA 92392-5324; http://www.nostgames.com/. Adv. Circ: 350. *Aud.:* Ga, Ac.

NOSTalgia stands for Knights of the Square Table and is a postal games club, primarily chess, but also checkers, shogi, and go. Regular features include an editorial, chess problems, chess results, checkers problems, a calendar of conventions, and news about members. Secret word ladders, a word game, is also featured in the bulletin. The NOST has been accepted as a member of the U.S. Postal Chess Federation. Includes book reviews.

3370. ***Rolling Good Times Online.*** 1995. d. Free. Ed(s): Sue Schneider. R G T Online Inc., 205 S. Main St., St. Charles, MO 63301-2804; rgt@rgtonline.com; http://www.rgtonline.com. Adv. *Aud.:* Ga.

This gamblers' magazine covers a wide spectrum, from where professional gambling is taking place to interviews and comments by the same professionals. The tips on how to win, strategies to follow, and games to watch may or may not be valid, depending on the viewpoint of the reader and the person giving the help. Be that as it may, the magazine does pretty well covering the field. (BK)

■ GARDENING

See also Agriculture; and Home sections.

Barbara Halporn, Head of the Collection Development Dept., Widener Library, Harvard University, Cambridge, MA 02138; bhalporn@fas.harvard.edu

Chip Robinson, Germanic Division, Harvard College Library Technical Services, 625 Massachusetts Avenue, Cambridge, MA 02139; crobins@fas.harvard.edu

Introduction

To garden is to participate in life. To read about gardening and gardens is to participate in the life of the imagination. Reading gives us inspiration to survive winter's desolation and summer's disappointments and to plan next year's (always better) garden. Magazines offer a wide variety of current information and delightful, inspirational reading that libraries will want to make available for their users.

This list offers a representative selection from the dozens of garden magazines published. Space and our desire to present a core of publications aimed at a climatologically diverse, national readership prevent us from covering this extensive literature comprehensively. In addition to these general magazines, many others are published on gardening for specific regions and special types of gardening. We include only a few of these. Many shelter and lifestyle magazines also contain excellent articles on gardening, but this list concentrates on magazines for which gardens and gardening are the primary focus.

Gardeners are insatiable in their desire for information, ideas, advice, practical plans, and beautiful pictures. Books, magazines, and increasingly the burgeoning sites on the Internet feed that harmless gluttony. Although some electronic garden magazines are being published, the distinction between them and the many gardening web sites is increasingly fuzzy. Gardening Internet sites have become a new species; they expand on the magazine concept and take advantage of the web to continually update information and link gardeners to related sites. These e-resources complement, but do not replace, print magazines as sources of information and pleasure. Noteworthy sites that librarians will want to alert users to are these: www.gardenweb.com, www.gardeninglaunchpad.com, and www.garden-gate.prairienet.org.

Many publishers of gardening books and magazines also publish special seasonal issues that may be acquired more easily on the newsstand than through standard subscriptions. These seasonal series often contain excellent articles that will be of great interest to gardening patrons.

We also draw attention to *Garden Literature: An Index to Periodical Articles and Book Reviews* [ISSN 1061-3722], which will be invaluable to readers who want to pursue a subject in numerous publications or to locate an article once read and now lost in bibliographic oblivion.

Gardening magazines help bridge the gap between fantasy and reality and represent the triumph of hope over experience.

Basic Periodicals

Ga: *The American Gardener, BBC Gardeners' World Magazine, Fine Gardening, The Garden, Garden Design, The Herb Companion, Horticulture, HortIdeas, OG, Plants & Gardens News.*

Basic Abstracts and Indexes

Horticultural Abstracts; Garden Literature: An Index to Periodical Articles and Book Reviews.

3371. *Alpine Gardener.* Formerly (until vol.68, 2000): *Alpine Garden Society Quarterly Bulletin;* Incorporates: *Alpine Gardening.* [ISSN: 1475-0449] 1930. q. Membership, GBP 18. Ed(s): Dr. C Grey-Wilson. Alpine Garden Society, A G S Centre, Avon Bank, Pershore, WR10 3JP, United Kingdom; ags@alpinegardensociety.org; http://www.alpinegardensociety.org. Illus., index, adv. Circ: 11500 Paid. Vol. ends: Dec. *Indexed:* GardL. *Bk. rev.:* Occasional, 600 words. *Aud.:* Ga.

The goal of *Alpine Gardener* is to publish "authoritative articles for experts and beginners on plants in the wild, cultivation, and conservation." It encourages an appreciation of the astonishing variety of plants that decorate the lush meadows and precarious slopes of higher elevations. The bulletin highlights plant species from all over the world in articles whose style invites the reader to stroll along with the author. Emphasis is given to descriptions of species found during contributors' explorations of alpine locations from New Zealand to central Asia to California. The first part of an issue usually concentrates on practical advice, such as how to become an alpine garden enthusiast, raise a hybrid, select pots, and propagate bulbs. Color photographs feature plant close-ups and natural surroundings. It also includes the complete Alpine Garden Society newsletter. The magazine lists award-winning plants and includes a section on seed and plant sources in nursery advertisements.

3372. *The American Gardener.* Former titles: *American Horticulturist; American Horticultural Magazine;* Incorporates: *American Horticultural Society News and Views; Gardeners Forum.* [ISSN: 1087-9978] 1922. bi-m. USD 35 domestic; USD 4.95 newsstand/cover per issue. Ed(s): David J Ellis. American Horticultural Society, 7931 E Boulevard Dr, Alexandria, VA 22308; editor@ahs.org; http://www.ahs.org. Illus., adv. Circ: 25000 Paid and controlled. Vol. ends: Nov/Dec. Microform: PQC. Online: Gale Group. Reprint: PQC. *Indexed:* B&AI, BiolDig, GSI, GardL, HortAb. *Bk. rev.:* 3, 500 words. *Aud.:* Ga, Ac.

As a publication of the American Horticultural Society, this magazine lives up to its national scope and covers gardening issues for all areas of the country. Each issue includes at least four substantial and informative articles on such topics as incorporating native plants into a landscape design; edible ornamentals; and using stone or elements of natural landscaping in one's garden. Informative sidebars and source boxes for additional print resources and addresses of suppliers accompany most articles. Regular departments feature an entertaining guest essay, "Conservationist's Notebook," a substantial Q&A section, advice for the urban gardener, and a plant or seed mail-order service. "Focus" highlights practical ideas like finding great nursery bargains at the end of the season or coping with weather extremes. Book reviews, a calendar of regional garden events, a pronunciation guide to plants found in the issue, and selective advertising complete each issue.

3373. *American Nurseryman.* [ISSN: 0003-0198] 1904. s-m. USD 48 domestic; USD 80 foreign. Ed(s): Sally D Benson. American Nurseryman Publishing Co., 77 W. Washington St, Ste 2100, Chicago, IL 60602-2904; subscriptions@amerinursery.com; http://www.amerinursery.com. Illus., index, adv. Sample. Circ: 13913 Paid. Vol. ends: Jun. Microform: PQC. Reprint: PQC. *Indexed:* B&AI, ChemAb, ForAb, GardL, HortAb. *Aud.:* Sa.

This attractive trade publication calls itself the "No. 1 trade magazine for the United States commercial horticulture industry, serving the business and technical needs of growers, landscapers and garden center owners and operators." The articles, written by researchers and industry experts, cover important aspects of the retail garden business such as attracting customers, management/employee issues, and keeping up with market and consumer trends. Advertising and articles provide wholesale sources for equipment and plants. The reviews of new plants introduced to the market each year enable the retailers to answer customers' questions about how this variety differs from other species/cultivars. Although the primary audience for this magazine is the retail horticulturalist, the articles are accessible and interesting to the home gardener. Equally helpful are the announcements of new products and the reader-contributed "Field Notes," which feature a plant or tree that deserves more use in the garden. The section devoted to seed sources and plant suppliers is useful, as is the pest control page.

3374. *The Avant Gardener.* [ISSN: 0005-1926] 1968. m. USD 24 domestic; USD 30 foreign. Ed(s): Thomas Powell. Horticultural Data Processors, PO Box 489, New York, NY 10028. Index. Sample. Vol. ends: Oct. *Indexed:* GardL. *Bk. rev.:* 3, 50 words. *Aud.:* Sa.

This "unique horticultural news service" emphasizes what's new in plants, products, and techniques. Its "news briefs" carry information about a variety of horticultural issues such as leafcutter bees, new tools and equipment, and ecology action groups. Special issues cover currently hot industry topics, such as climbing plants. The newsletter supplies sources for plants and studies mentioned and leaves responsibility for obtaining details with the reader. There are no illustrations, but in eight or so pages, this publication highlights unusual varieties of vegetables, fruit, or flowers and useful gardening methods. Issues have covered such topics as Asian long-horned beetles, zelkovas as recommended substitutes for the American elm, and the use of textured plants to add visual appeal to a landscape. It is written in a clear, often conversational style, easily understood by even inexperienced gardeners.

3375. *B B C Gardeners' World Magazine.* [ISSN: 0961-7477] 1991. m. GBP 32.40 domestic; GBP 61.35 foreign. Ed(s): Adam Pasco. B B C Worldwide Ltd., Woodlands, 80 Wood Ln, London, W12 0TT, United Kingdom; http://www.bbcworldwide.com. Illus., index, adv. Sample. Circ: 382816 Paid. Vol. ends: Feb. *Aud.:* Ga.

The British are legendary gardeners, and readers on this side of the Atlantic are always interested in how they do it. This magazine, linked to the numerous BBC gardening programs and the expert gardeners who present them, is packed with short, informative, illustrated articles with enough variety to appeal to every taste. No equivalent magazine for North America exists, and American gardeners may well envy the broad and rich coverage it presents. Lively and unpretentious, each issue features noteworthy gardens, a practical guide to the essential gardening chores of the month, a garden wildlife section, news about future horticultural developments, and fun gardening suggestions for children. Although its subjects and departments are to be found in nearly all of the general garden magazines, this magazine goes all of them one better. Despite its fairly hefty subscription price, this garden magazine is an excellent value. Even if you take into account the vast differences in climate and growing conditions between Britain and America, the wealth of ideas and geographically boundless spirit of the magazine make it a welcome addition to general library collections in the U.S.

Canadian Gardening. See Canada section.

3376. *Country Gardens.* [ISSN: 1068-431X] 1992. bi-m. USD 19.97. Ed(s): Luann Brandsen, Carol Sheehan. Meredith Corp., 1716 Locust St, Des Moines, IA 50309-3023; http://www.meredith.com. Illus., adv. Circ: 325000 Paid. Vol. ends: Fall. *Indexed:* GardL. *Bk. rev.:* 500 words. *Aud.:* Hs, Ga, Ac.

From the publishers of *Country Home* comes a richly diverse *Country Gardens.* Fully illustrated, it contains a wide selection of garden concerns centering on design, decorating, and plantings. Articles have addressed a grandmother's influence on a garden and gardener, Asian ideas, dwarf plants in an old trunk, and pelargoniums. Smaller rubrics bring attention to garden awards, recommended tools, and even recipes. The large staff of contributors, photographers, and off-site editors means that there is generous attention to regional topics. This magazine is not burdened by advertising, and it also has a marketplace and product literature section toward its end.

3377. *Country Living Gardener.* [ISSN: 1086-3753] 1993. bi-m. USD 19.97 domestic; USD 28.97 foreign; USD 4.50 newsstand/cover per issue domestic. Ed(s): Diana Gold Murphy. Hearst Corporation, 1790 Broadway, 14th Fl, New York, NY 10019. Illus., adv. Circ: 475000 Paid. Online: EBSCO Publishing; Gale Group. *Bk. rev.:* 8-10, 100-200 words. *Aud.:* Ga.

This magazine blends garden and shelter articles with the intention of helping readers integrate a "love of gardening in other aspects of [their] life." Each issue includes features on "Gardening," "Decorating, Building, and Crafts," and "Food and Entertaining." "Plant Portraits" highlights unusual cultivars or species. Articles lavishly illustrate every aspect of gardening, including starting a garden from scratch, 50 ways to wake up your winter garden, and gardens to visit. "Grapevine," the product section, features garden-motif gift items; "Tools of the Trade" reviews new garden gadgets and equipment. Although most articles contain minimal coverage of cultivation techniques, an excellent practical feature, "Mapping a Garden," offers detailed advice, enhanced by excellent illustrations, on a particular garden subject, such as growing roses or installing a garden water feature. Readers will find many tempting ideas to try indoors and out.

3378. *Fine Gardening.* [ISSN: 0896-6281] 1988. bi-m. USD 29.95 in US & Canada; USD 36 elsewhere. Ed(s): Marc Vassallo. Taunton Press, Inc., 63, South Main St, PO Box 5506, Newtown, CT 06470-5506; http://www.taunton.com. Illus., index, adv. Circ: 193134 Paid. *Indexed:* ASIP, BRI, CBRI, GardL, IHTDI. *Bk. rev.:* 4, 250 words. *Aud.:* Ga.

This high-quality publication more than lives up to its title. *FG* aims to help readers learn about tools, techniques, plant materials, and garden design in order to create personalized garden spaces for themselves. Practical and easily understood articles address a wide variety of gardening concerns, problems, and projects relevant to all areas of the United States. Specific plant varieties, site plans for landscaping small and large properties, propagation techniques, and pest control are examples of topics covered. The letters from readers section is packed with tips, caveats, and information. Excellent drawings and diagrams and exceptional color photography; lists of plant sources for each article; an excellent Q&A section; a regular "gardening basics" feature; and an entertaining essay on the last page make this magazine a garden of delights.

3379. *Fruit Gardener.* [ISSN: 1049-4545] 1969. 6x/yr. USD 21 domestic; USD 27 foreign; USD 4 newsstand/cover per issue. Ed(s): Ronald M Couch. California Rare Fruit Growers, Inc., Fullerton Arboretum CSUF, Box 6850, Fullerton, CA 92834-6850; info@crfg.org; http://www.crfg.org. Adv. Circ: 3500 Paid. *Aud.:* Ga, Ac, Sa.

Published by the California Rare Fruit Growers, Inc., and devoted to amateurs, *Fruit Gardener* "is focused on species not native to nor grown commercially in any given area" although it deals with any and every edible plant, and its contributors are anything but simple amateurs. From botanical history ("Fruits dispersed by extinct mammals") to practical growing ("Understanding soil preparation"), the magazine presents vast subjects to inform growers. Departments include book reviews, Seed Bank, organic and container gardening, and Ask the Experts. Diagrams and illustrations serve the information. There are news and notices, ads, and a marketplace, which is rich with book selections.

3380. *The Garden.* Formerly (1846-1975): *Royal Horticultural Society. Journal;* Which superseded (1838-1843): *Royal Horticultural Society. Proceedings.* [ISSN: 0308-5457] 1804. m. Ed(s): Ian Hodgson. Emap Active Ltd. (Apex House), Apex House, Oundle Rd, Peterborough, PE2 9NP, United Kingdom; subs@ecm.emap.com. Illus., index, adv. Sample. Circ: 265906. Vol. ends: Dec. *Indexed:* B&AI, BiolAb, BiolDig, ChemAb, DAAI, ForAb, GardL, HortAb. *Bk. rev.:* 8-10, 200 words. *Aud.:* Ga, Ac.

The Garden offers an enormous amount of information written by specialists, all well within the grasp of any gardener. The magazine presents a good mix of general articles about plants, gardens, and practical growing techniques. Some articles have a historic facet such as the history of a plant and its uses or historic gardens. Noteworthy gardens both in Great Britian and in other areas of the world are featured. Book reviews, sources and advertisements for plants and products, and reports of the society's activities and flower shows are helpful. This is a valuable title for an academic library with a horticulture program to support, as well as a magazine to be enjoyed by avid gardeners everywhere.

3381. *Garden Design: the fine art of residential landscape architecture.* [ISSN: 0733-4923] 1982. bi-m. USD 23.95 domestic; USD 29.95 Canada; USD 35.95 elsewhere. World Publications LLC, 460 N Orlando Ave, Ste 200, Winter Park, FL 32789; info@worldpub.net; http://www.worldpub.net. Illus., adv. Circ: 339725 Paid. Vol. ends: Nov/Dec. *Indexed:* AIAP, ArtInd, DAAI, GardL. *Bk. rev.:* 3-5, 300 words. *Aud.:* Ga.

Garden Design is directed to the "upscale, design-conscious reader who is serious and passionate about...gardening,...fine design, decorating, and all the pleasures of outdoor living." Although most of the trendy and imaginative gardens are beyond the resources of the average gardener, what reader does not like to peek into a world of garden chic, where city rooftops are turned into penthouse gardens and a tiny eighteenth-century cottage becomes a lovely twenty-first-century pool house and garden? Lavish photographs of landscapes dotted with ancient trees, pergolas, follies, dovecotes, and dappled light on the greensward fill the pages of this magazine. The splendid coverage of luxurious garden creations is balanced with the practical and attainable advice. Departments offering useful and interesting information are "Sage Advice," a Q&A column; "Leaves," a lengthy excerpt from a garden literature classic; and "Dirt," a section on hot gardening topics and news. Readers can go to the "Green Market" advertising section and address book for products to try to turn the magazine's imaginative suggestions for garden elegance into reality.

3382. *Garden History.* [ISSN: 0307-1243] 1973. s-a. Membership, GBP 25. Ed(s): Jan Woudstra. Garden History Society, 70 Cowcross St, London, ECIM 6EJ, United Kingdom; enquiries@gardenhistorysociety.org; http://www.gardenhistorysociety.org. Illus., index. Refereed. Circ: 2750. Vol. ends: Winter. *Indexed:* AIAP, API, BHA, BrArAb, GardL, NumL. *Bk. rev.:* 6, 500-1,000 words. *Aud.:* Ac.

This scholarly journal presents an eclectic collection of articles relating garden and landscape design to architecture, art, literature, philosophy, and society. Although the focus of the journal is decidedly British, numerous articles deal with gardens in other areas of the world, e.g., the garden in prehistoric Mexico. References, photographs, drawings, and diagrams accompany the articles. Substantial book reviews reflect the wide-ranging scholarly interests of the society. Browsers will find valuable tidbits of information about the long and varied history of gardening, and scholars will find a rich source of details on numerous topics. Society news and announcements of seminars or conferences are restricted to a separate newsletter, so the journal itself can be enjoyed as a distinct entity.

3383. ***Gardens Illustrated.*** [ISSN: 0968-8927] 1993. 10x/yr. GBP 37.50; USD 79.50; GBP 3.75 newsstand/cover per issue United Kingdom. B B C Worldwide Ltd., Woodlands, 80 Wood Ln, London, W12 0TT, United Kingdom; bbcworldwide@bbc.co.uk; http://www.bbcworldwide.com. *Indexed:* DAAI, GardL. *Aud.:* Hs, Ga, Ac, Sa.

Gardens Illustrated, part of the BBC family of publications, has a wide international readership and is popular in the United States. Known for its stunning photography and high standard of journalism, it also includes regular contributions by renowned designers. Its main entries are People, Plants, and Places, and they contain a wealth of personal horticultural profiles and detailed and specific plant care, and they look at various gardens in every climate. Regular aspects of the contents are devoted to news, lecture announcements, book reviews, properties for sale, and new skills. Past issues have interviewed designer Mary Keen, focused on abundantly blooming Helleborus x sternii, and traveled to a naturalistic Jamaican garden.

3384. ***The Heirloom Gardener Magazine.*** 2003. q. USD 12. Ed(s): Jeremiath Gettle. Hill Folk's Publishing, 2278 Baker Creek Rd, Mansfield, MO 65704; heirloomgardener@getgoin.net. *Aud.:* Hs, Ga, Ac.

The Heirloom Gardener is new on the scene and fills the need to connect with the past, both in the garden and in the publication. But why glimpse the past if not to plan a better future? One of the goals of the magazine is to promote heirloom crops and alternatives to genetically modified plants for a healthier food supply. Without being anachronistic, the layout does include charmingly retro color drawings and fonts as well as current photographs, diagrams, and ads. A typical issue features heirloom pears, bottle beds, a trip to Thailand, tomatoes, and bachelor's buttons. Regular columns are "Frankenfood" (alerting readers to genetic pollution), "Historical Clippings" (from old publications), and "Recipes." News, events, and vignettes are interspersed.

3385. ***The Herb Companion: in celebration of the useful plants.*** [ISSN: 1040-581X] 1988. bi-m. USD 21.95 domestic; USD 31.95 foreign. Ed(s): K.C. Compton. Ogden Publications, 1503 S W 42nd St, Topeka, KS 66609-1265; http://www.ogdenpubs.com. Illus., adv. Circ: 125000. *Indexed:* GardL, IHTDI. *Bk. rev.:* 3-8, 600 words. *Aud.:* Ga.

The subtitle of this journal, *in celebration of the useful plants,* accurately expresses the overall intent of this publication. It defines its readership as "avocational herb gardeners, cooks, crafters, and general enthusiasts." Full-color photographs and articles on culinary, medicinal, and craft uses of herbs appeal to the senses of sight, taste, and smell. A typical feature article includes sources, growing information, medicinal uses, folklore, and suggested further reading. Regular features include mail-order sources, book reviews, a round-robin discussion of observations and suggestions from herb gardeners, and a spotlight on "An Herb to Know." The "Herbs for Health" section contributed by the American Botanical Council and Herb Research Foundation presents alternatives to pharmacy and over-the-counter medications. The magazine's high-quality, easy-to-read, enthusiastic articles and its wide variety of topics make it a valuable and appealing periodical for a wide audience.

3386. ***Herb Quarterly.*** [ISSN: 0163-9900] 1978. q. USD 19.95 domestic; USD 24.95 in Canada & Mexico; USD 26.95 foreign. Ed(s): Jennifer Barrett. E G W Publishing Co., 1041 Shary Circle, Concord, CA 94518; support@egw.com; http://www.egw.com. Illus., index, adv. Circ: 56000 Paid. Vol. ends: Winter. *Indexed:* GardL. *Bk. rev.:* 5-6, 1 column. *Aud.:* Ga.

The articles in this delightful quarterly remind one of a chat over the backyard fence with a neighborly gardener wise in the ways of plants for medicine, health, food, and pleasure. Attractive drawings accompany most articles, which are more informative and inspirational than technical or hands-on. The collection of folklore, recipes, history, and descriptions of gardens to visit will interest any herb enthusiast. Each issue features a centerfold layout diagram with plant suggestions for themes such as a courtyard garden bounded by walls or a Puritan-era herb garden of "useful plants." Issues regularly contain articles on the use of herbs for treating such problems as depression or the discomforts of chicken pox; the articles also supply suggested reading for additional research and information. Recipes range from the edible (horseradish, rose petals) to the practical (composting) and the medicinal (for treating varicose veins). There are numerous ideas and directions for gifts, and the source list of books and catalogs is helpful.

3387. ***Herbarist.*** [ISSN: 0740-5979] 1935. a. Non-members, USD 10. Ed(s): Robin A Siktberg. Herb Society of America, Inc., 9019 Kirtland Chardon Rd, Mentor, OH 44060; http://www.herbsociety.org. Illus., index, adv. Circ: 3000. *Indexed:* GardL. *Bk. rev.:* 10, 200 words. *Aud.:* Ga.

The cultivation of herbs has a special place in the horticultural scene and attracts the attention of gardeners, botanists, folklorists, and medical researchers. Published by the Herb Society of America, this journal presents the "latest findings, writings, and information on herbs." Naturalists, landscape architects, biologists, botanists, and freelance writers interested in herb cultivation are represented in this attractive annual. This publication blends "scholarly and popular approaches to dissemination of information on herbs." Typically, the collection of essays includes discussions of the basics of growing herbs, history, folklore, and medicinal uses of herbs in the past and present. Most articles are unobtrusively footnoted and have a bibliography or list of references for further study. An advertising section, restricted to the end of the publication, offers a broad selection of plant, seed, gift, and literature sources.

3388. ***Historic Gardens Review: the voice of historic parks and gardens worldwide.*** Formerly (until 1996): *European Gardens.* [ISSN: 1461-0191] 1995. 3x/yr. USD 45. Ed(s): Gillian Mawrey. The Historic Gardens Foundation, 34 River Court, Upper Ground, London, SE1 9PE, United Kingdom; office@historicgardens.org; http://www.historicgardens.org. *Aud.:* Ga, Ac, Sa.

Historic Gardens Review is delivered by the Historic Gardens Foundation in the United Kingdom, whose aim is to ensure that historic gardens receive the same attention and support as historic sites or buildings. Further, it seeks to serve as a link for those interested in the preservation of historic parks and gardens. The review has considered the contributions of Frederick Law Olmsted, surveyed a monastic garden in Greece, and covered the restoration of a Japanese garden in England. With few or no ads, the color-illustrated review adds letters, book reviews, a bibliography, and profiles of gardens recommended for visiting. The novel Optimist/Pessimist section offers news of sites in the spotlight.

3389. ***Horticulture: gardening at its best.*** [ISSN: 0018-5329] 1904. bi-m. USD 19.95; USD 4.99 newsstand/cover per issue. Ed(s): Patricia Wesley Umbrell. Krause Publications, Inc., 700 E State St, Iola, WI 54990-0001; info@krause.com; http://www.krause.com. Illus., index, adv. Sample. Circ: 280936 Paid and controlled. Vol. ends: Nov/Dec. Microform: MIM; PQC. Online: EBSCO Publishing; Florida Center for Library Automation; Gale Group; OCLC Online Computer Library Center, Inc.; H.W. Wilson. Reprint: PQC. *Indexed:* ASIP, B&AI, BRI, BiolAb, BiolDig, CBRI, ConsI, ExcerpMed, GSI, GardL, IHTDI, MagInd, RGPR. *Bk. rev.:* 3, 500 words. *Aud.:* Ga, Ac.

Horticulture is one of those magazines from which a reader might save articles for future reference. Every issue contains "a rich assortment of technique pieces, profiles of plants and people, and discussions of dazzling designs." Generously illustrated with color photographs, the features address central concerns such as choosing the right mulch for a garden, as well as exploratory articles such as on the restoration of an Italianate garden in Florida. Regular departments include "Field Notes" (the regional guide), "Unearthed" (news of gardeners and tips on tulips), "Pest Watch," and "Tool Shed." Every issue contains a reader-expert Q&A exchange, book reviews, Horticulture Tours & Symposia Reviews, Plant Index and Pronunciation Guide and Sources, and a shopping guide. The editors of *Horticulture* also put out the quarterly *Garden Style.* Each issue focuses on an area of gardening as its focus, including kitchen gardens, container gardening, basic garden design, and shade gardens.

3390. ***HortIdeas.*** [ISSN: 0742-8219] 1984. m. USD 25 domestic; USD 32 in Canada & Mexico; USD 42 elsewhere. Ed(s): Gregory Williams, Patricia Williams. HortIdeas Publishing, 750 Black Lick Rd, Gravel Switch, KY 40328; gwill@mis.net; http://www.users.mis.net/~gwill. Index. Sample. Circ: 1200 Paid and free. Vol. ends: Dec. *Indexed:* ExcerpMed, GardL. *Bk. rev.:* 3, 500 words. *Aud.:* Ga.

Black-and-white, three-hole-punched, and ad free, *HortIdeas* summarizes and reports on the "latest research, methods, tools, plants and books gathered from hundreds of popular and technical sources worldwide." Article topics include tree roots, a seawater greenhouse, aphids, soil carbon tests, and roses. The editors examine a wide variety of sources to provide the busy professional horticulturalist or the experienced home gardener with brief articles of abstracted news and research. References are provided at the end of each report for those seeking to explore a subject further. The humorous style is appreciated by hundreds of devoted readers. Issues include such regular sections as perennial plant of the year, internship opportunities, reviews of new gardening books, and technical topics.

3391. ***Hortus: a gardening journal.*** [ISSN: 0950-1657] 1987. q. GBP 32 United Kingdom; GBP 37 in Europe; USD 68 United States. Ed(s): David Wheeler. The Bryansground Press, Bryan's Ground, Stapleton, Presteigne, LD8 2LP, United Kingdom; all@hortus.co.uk; http://www.hortus.co.uk. Illus., index, adv. Sample. Circ: 3000 Paid. Vol. ends: Winter. *Indexed:* GardL. *Bk. rev.:* various number, 1,000 words. *Aud.:* Ga.

Hortus is the gardener's magic carpet ride. Beautifully bound, with cream-colored pages, the publication focuses on literary description, encounters with great figures of horticulture, and visits to historic and contemporary gardens around the world. Balancing the substantial offerings are fine drawings, notes, and book reviews. Previous adventures have included "An Artist's Garden in Tuscany," "What Makes a Space a Place?," and "Gardens and Russian Writers." The extensive range of topics, unique presentation, and appeal to the intellect and imagination make *Hortus* an enticing complement to the gardening journal repertoire.

Journal of Arboriculture. See Forestry section.

3392. ***New England Garden History Society. Journal.*** [ISSN: 1053-2617] a. USD 35. New England Garden History Society of the Massachusetts Horticultural Society, 300 Massachusetts Ave, Boston, MA 02115. Illus. *Indexed:* AmH&L. *Bk. rev.:* 750-1,000 words. *Aud.:* Ga, Ac, Sa.

With a scope beyond its title, the *Journal of the New England Garden History Society* covers topics in North America. The scholarly but accessible writing takes up the heritage of landscapes, designers, authors, and special gardens. Simple, focused in design, and finely printed and bound, the publication has given mention to the neoclassical Meridian Hill Park in Washington, D.C., to Southern garden writing, and Parmentier and Upper Canada. The superb documentation is accompanied by laudable book reviews.

3393. ***O G.*** Former titles (until 2003): *Organic Gardening;* (until 1988): *Rodale's Organic Gardening;* (until 1985): *Organic Gardening;* (until 1978): *Organic Gardening and Farming.* [ISSN: 1536-108X] 1942. bi-m. USD 24.96 domestic; CND 34.96 Canada; USD 42 elsewhere. Rodale, 33 E Minor St, Emmaus, PA 18098; info@rodale.com; http://www.rodale.com. Illus., index, adv. Circ: 300000 Paid. Vol. ends: Dec. Microform: NBI; PQC. Online: bigchalk; EBSCO Publishing; Florida Center for Library Automation; Gale Group; OCLC Online Computer Library Center, Inc.; ProQuest Information & Learning. Reprint: PQC. *Indexed:* Agr, B&AI, BiolDig, GardL, IHTDI, MagInd, RGPR. *Aud.:* Ga.

Still a singular voice in the natural cultivation of fruits, vegetables, and flowers, *OG* guides readers through the processes needed to arrive at garden environments that are safe and healthy. Each issue reinforces the theme of dispensing with the use of pesticides and fertilizers in favor of maximizing existing resources such as water, soil, and insects. Articles bring light to those things the gardener adds, drawing on the cycle of natural organic waste like the garden's own discards, fruit and vegetable refuse, and grass and leaves. These and regular items inform readers to mind such things as those plants that best thrive in the gardener's climate and soil conditions. Past features have discussed parsley varieties, seed starting, composting, and tomato disease-fighting secrets.

3394. ***Plants & Gardens News.*** 1986. 4x/yr. Ed(s): Janet Marinelli. Brooklyn Botanic Garden, 1000 Washington Ave, Brooklyn, NY 11225. Circ: 25000. *Indexed:* GardL. *Aud.:* Ga.

Plants & Gardens News flows directly from the mission of the Brooklyn Botanic Garden (BBG), which seeks to serve widely in the practice of horticulture, the pursuit of research, the instruction of children and adults, and outreach locally and globally. Readers will find articles on horticulture in cinema, cut-flower care, tips on snails, and a what's-new and where-to-get guide. Members of BBG will get much more than *Plants & Gardens News*. Beyond the benefits of membership, there are the attractive and useful All-Region Guides, gardening handbooks that are also known as the 21st-Century Gardening Series. These have covered sunny and shady borders, indoor landscaping, and bird gardens.

3395. ***Rock Garden Quarterly.*** Formerly (until 1995): *American Rock Garden Society Bulletin.* [ISSN: 1081-0765] 1934. q. Free to members. Ed(s): Jane McGary. North American Rock Garden Society, c/o Jacques Mommens, Box 67, Millwood, NY 10546; http://www.nargs.org. Illus., index, adv. Circ: 4500 Paid. Vol. ends: Fall. *Indexed:* GardL. *Bk. rev.:* 3-4, 1 page. *Aud.:* Ga, Sa.

An annual subscription to the North American Rock Garden Society (NARGS) provides *Rock Garden Quarterly*. Member contributors offer articles on a variety of topics such as wildflowers, propagation methods, and regional features like the Rocky Mountains, the Netherlands, and Appalachia. Through its publication, the society encourages the beginner and the specialist to work with alpine and other perennials that thrive in high and low altitudes and rocky conditions. Special interests are always addressed, such as container and woodland gardens and even walls. Illustrations, diagrams, and plates are helpful, as are the references. Ads are restricted to the back of the bulletin, where NARGS contact information and resources can also be found.

3396. ***Studies in History of Gardens & Designed Landscapes.*** Formerly (until 1997): *Journal of Garden History.* [ISSN: 1460-1176] 1981. q. GBP 351 (Individuals, GBP 144). Ed(s): John Dixon Hunt. Taylor & Francis Ltd, 11 New Fetter Ln, London, EC4P 4EE, United Kingdom; info@tandf.co.uk; http://www.tandf.co.uk/journals. Illus., index, adv. Sample. Refereed. Vol. ends: Winter. Reprint: PSC. *Indexed:* A&ATA, AIAP, API, ArtHuCI, ArtInd, BHA, BrArAb, BrHumI, GardL, NumL. *Aud.:* Ac.

Whether covering central themes, such as the documentation of a significant location, or providing information on related matters, such as issues of restoration, *Studies in the History of Gardens and Designed Landscapes* is a major source for scholarly attention to garden history. Predominantly in black-and-white with some color illustrations and layouts, the journal has featured Asian garden history and nineteenth-century garden function. It is costly but suited for landscape design programs and cultural historians who can count on documentation of gardens worldwide and such factors as economic history, aesthetics, and technology. Excellent book reviews are found in every issue.

3397. ***Water Gardening.*** [ISSN: 1090-6827] 1996. bi-m. USD 20; USD 25; USD 30. Ed(s): Sue Speichert. Water Gardeners, PO Box 607, St John, IN 46373. *Aud.:* Hs, Ga, Ac, Sa.

Water Gardening has a commitment to sound pond-keeping education. Experts advise on tips, tricks, and respect for Mother Nature. The staff attempts to appeal to all ages and backgrounds and to promote an appreciation not just for the art of water gardening itself but also for the eco-culture of which it is a part. Their passion comes through on every page. Regular articles cover care of fish and plants, setting design, and even filtration. Specific varieties of plant and animal life as well as supplies get sharper focus. Find out how to keep your pond free of debris, learn what you can create indoors, or how water and electricity work together safely. Behind the appealing covers are also letters, products, reviews, club information, and whimsical interest pieces.

Electronic Journals

3398. ***The Virtual Gardener.*** 1996. q. USD 11.95. Ed(s): Clyde Snobelen. Virtual Gardener, Inc., PO Box 195, Brentwood Bay, BC V8M 1R3, Canada; csnobelen@gardenmag.com; http://www.gardenmag.com. *Aud.:* Ga.

Once free and now fee-based, *The Virtual Gardener* hopes to make its content worth the subscription price. For those who like to pick, choose, and download, this site provides clearly delineated sections and downloadable "Virtual Books." The Cover Story includes the main offering of the quarter, and "In the Features" presents, among other things, organic means of dealing with mildew and fungus. "Tips and Tales" delves into feeding birds or heirloom comebacks, while "Plant Profiles" enlightens on Veronica spicata and Vinca minor. "Talk Back" allows readers to send questions and get expert answers, and Classifieds provides numerous, varied ads and announcements. Canadian and other international postings are a plus.

■ GENEALOGY

Computers and Genealogy/International and Ethnic-Interest Journals/ National and Regional Journals/State—Alphabetical by State

See also Canada; City and Regional; Europe; and History sections.

Scott Andrew "Drew" Bartley, former archivist and reference librarian at the New England Historic Genealogical Society, now researcher, consultant, editor of the Mayflower Descendant *and the Vermont Families in 1791 project, Boston, Massachusetts; www.yourgenealogist.com*

Introduction

Genealogy has exploded on the Internet and claims the largest single database: census images and indexes from 1790 to 1930. There are many more data sites that make it the most important general source for genealogical research. *Time* magazine proclaimed it to be America's latest obsession. With that comes the responsibility for libraries to support their patrons' interest.

Every library needs an adequate genealogical collection. Part of any good collection is access to the latest articles written on the subject.

Genealogical periodicals cover the gamut of topics across geographical locations, ethnicities, and time periods. There are scholarly journals, commercial publications, how-to manuals, society newsletters, and a mixture of all of these. There are so many genealogical periodicals in print today that not all could be presented here. No surname-based journals are presented (e.g., the *Smith Family Journal*). Only a few county or local journals are presented when no statewide journal exists. (For a list of those journals, see *Printed Sources: A Guide to Published Genealogical Records* by Kory L. Meyerink [*Ancestry*, 1998], pp. 742–750). One representative journal from each U.S. state was solicited, and 46 out of 50 states are represented either by their own journal or by a regional journal. Some states have more than one journal, but limited space requires that each state have but one entry with two exceptions. Journals based on ethnicity were selected from those published in English. Recently, the leading Irish journal ceased publication. There are no comprehensive journals for Hispanic or Italian genealogy. Some of these are international publications, but no other international journals were solicited.

Journals on computers and genealogy, as well as e-journals, have undergone major changes since the last edition, demonstrating how new and volatile the Internet is. The best meta-site for all things genealogical continues to be found at www.CyndisList.com.

As used herein, the term *scholarly* should not be thought of as applying to an arcane, intellectual journal meant only for the elite. I use the term to qualify those journals that properly footnote each genealogically significant event to a primary source so that a reader may go directly to that source. *Solid* journals are those that footnote a majority of their work, although not completely. In many instances secondary print sources are cited, which forces a researcher to do a double look-up. *Basic* journals do not cite sources; and although they publish worthy material, it is left to the reader to follow up on the journal's research. The term *FASG,* which stands for Fellow of the American Society of Genealogists, follows several of the editors' names in this section. The ASG is the leader in genealogical scholarship, and the journals edited by fellows of that society should be looked upon as models in this field. *Primary-source transcriptions* refers to printed lists of original records for genealogy, such as tax lists, marriage records, Bible records, freeman lists, etc.

Computers and Genealogy

3399. ***Genealogical Computing.*** [ISSN: 0277-5913] 1981. q. USD 25 domestic; USD 30 in Canada & Mexico; USD 35 elsewhere. Ed(s): Elizabeth Kelley Kerstens. MyFamily.com Inc., PO Box 990, Orem, UT 84059-0990; gceditor@ancestry-inc.com; http://www.ancestry.com. Illus., index, adv. Circ: 11000. Vol. ends: Apr. *Indexed:* GPAI. *Aud.:* Ga.

From the publishers of *Ancestry,* this journal focuses on the use of computers to enhance genealogical research. Software, CD-ROMs, scanners, and the Internet are all well-covered topics. Software and CD-ROM reviews are regular features. An annual directory of genealogy software is comprehensive and supplies all the information needed for this field. Recommended for all libraries.

International and Ethnic-Interest Journals

3400. ***Acadian Genealogical Exchange Newsletter.*** [ISSN: 0199-9591] 1972. s-a. USD 17 domestic; USD 20 foreign. Ed(s): Janet B Jehn. Acadian Genealogical Exchange, 3265 Wayman Branch Rd, Covington, KY 41015; janjehn@aol.com; http://www.acadiangenexch.com. Illus., adv. Circ: 600. Vol. ends: Oct. *Indexed:* GPAI. *Bk. rev.:* 20/yr. *Aud.:* Ga.

A journal dedicated to Acadian, French Canadian, and Cajun ancestry. Its articles run the gamut from genealogical help on the Internet to family genealogies. Ancestor tables and queries are published. The April and July issues are combined into one magazine.

3401. ***Afro-American Historical and Genealogical Society. Journal.*** [ISSN: 0272-1937] 1980. s-a. USD 45 (Individuals, USD 35). Ed(s): Sylvia Polk-Burriss. Afro-American Historical and Genealogical Society, PO Box 73086, Washington, DC 20056-3086. Illus., index, adv. Circ: 900. Vol. ends: Summer/Fall. *Indexed:* GPAI, IIBP. *Bk. rev.:* 10/yr. *Aud.:* Ga, Ac.

This scholarly journal provides in-depth methodology for the research of African American ancestry. Primary source transcriptions are included, as well as analyses of such data for research. Family genealogies are published, as are reports of archives with depository materials for African American genealogy. A cumulative index for 1980–1990 is available.

3402. ***Augustan.*** Former titles: *Augustan Society Omnibus; Augustan Society Information Bulletin; Forbears; Augustan;* Incorporates: *Royalty and Monarchy; Genealogical Library Journal; Colonial Genealogist; English Genealogist;* Which was formerly: *English Genealogist Helper;* Incorporates: *Germanic Genealogist;* Which was formerly: *Germanic Genealogist Helper;* Incorporates: *Heraldry; Chivalry.* 1957. q. USD 24. Ed(s): Rodney Hartwell. Augustan Society, Inc., PO Box 75, Daggett, CA 92327-0075; http://www.augustansociety.org. Illus., index, adv. Vol. ends: No. 4. *Indexed:* GPAI. *Bk. rev.:* 10/yr. *Aud.:* Sa.

A scholarly journal that focuses on ancient, medieval, and royal European ancestry. A cumulative index for 1959–1975 is available.

3403. ***Avotaynu: the international review of Jewish genealogy.*** [ISSN: 0882-6501] 1985. q. USD 35 in North America; USD 43 elsewhere. Ed(s): Sallyann Admur Sack. Avotaynu Inc., 155 N Washington Ave, Bergenfield, NJ 07621. Illus., adv. Circ: 3000 Paid. Vol. ends: Winter. *Indexed:* IJP. *Bk. rev.:* 15/yr. *Aud.:* Ga, Ac.

A scholarly journal that focuses on Jewish genealogy. Articles concentrate on resources, both in the United States and abroad, to aid the researcher, as well as methodology suggestions. Queries, "Ask the Experts," and Internet help are regular features.

3404. ***Family History.*** [ISSN: 0014-7265] 1962. q. GBP 15. Ed(s): Cecil R Humphery Smith. Institute of Heraldic and Genealogical Studies, 79-82, Northgate, Canterbury, CT1 1BA, United Kingdom; ihgs@ihgs.ac.uk; http://www.ihgs.ac.uk. Illus., adv. Circ: 1300. Vol. ends: Oct. Microform: PQC. Reprint: PQC. *Indexed:* ABS&EES, BrArAb, NumL. *Bk. rev.:* 35/yr. *Aud.:* Ga, Ac.

This scholarly journal reflects the mission of the institute, which is to study the history and structure of the family. The articles focus on British genealogy, much of which is medieval and contains heraldic information. The institute's news and upcoming events are also published.

3405. ***The Genealogist.*** [ISSN: 0311-1776] 1974. q. Ed(s): Margaret Rowe-Keys. Australian Institute of Genealogical Studies, 1-41 Railway Rd, Blackborn, VIC 3782, Australia. Circ: 4000. *Aud.:* Ga.

This basic journal features how-to articles, society news, library acquisitions, surname interest lists, and a column on web sites.

3406. ***Genealogists' Magazine.*** [ISSN: 0016-6391] 1925. q. GBP 12; USD 19.80. Ed(s): Michael Gandy. Society of Genealogists, 14 Charterhouse Bldgs, Goswell Rd, London, EC1M 7BA, United Kingdom; http://www.sog.org.uk. Illus., index, adv. Sample. Circ: 16000. Vol. ends: Dec. Reprint: PQC. *Indexed:* GPAI. *Bk. rev.:* 50/yr. *Aud.:* Ac, Sa.

The national scholarly journal for genealogy in the United Kingdom. Articles are well cited and focus on methodology and primary sources rather than actual family genealogies. Queries, library updates, obituaries, and society news appear in each issue.

3407. ***German Genealogical Digest.*** [ISSN: 1085-2565] 1985. q. USD 22. Ed(s): Larry Jensen. Jensen Publications, PO Box 780, Pleasant Grove, UT 84062. Adv. Circ: 1300. *Indexed:* GPAI. *Bk. rev.:* 10/yr. *Aud.:* Ga.

A well-written scholarly journal for German genealogy written in English. The articles are well cited and focus on methodology. An "Ask the Experts" section and queries are regular features. Because more Americans are ethnically German than anything else, this is an important journal for all libraries.

3408. ***Mennonite Family History.*** [ISSN: 0730-5214] 1982. q. USD 18. Ed(s): J Lemar Mast. Masthof Press, 220 Mill Rd, Morgantown, PA 19543; mast@masthof.com. Illus., adv. Circ: 1850. *Indexed:* GPAI. *Aud.:* Ga, Ac.

A scholarly journal featuring primary source and genealogy for Mennonite, Amish, and Brethren family history. The annual index is published separately.

3409. ***Nase Rodina.*** [ISSN: 1045-8190] 1989. q. Membership, USD 20 individuals. Czechoslovak Genealogical Society, Intl., PO Box 16225, St. Paul, MN 55116-0225; http://www.cgsi.org. *Aud.:* Ga.

Nase Rodina, a scholarly journal, promotes genealogy of the ethnic groups that comprise Czechoslovakia as it was formed in 1918. Those groups include Czech, Bohemian, Moravian, Slovak, German, Hungarian, Jewish, Rusyn, and Silesian genealogy. Each issue has a single theme or topic for all articles. Each include queries and a calendar of events.

3410. ***New Netherland Connections.*** [ISSN: 1087-4542] 1996. q. USD 15. Ed(s): Dorothy A Koenig. New Netherland Connections, 1232 Carlotta Ave, Berkeley, CA 94707-2707; dkoenig@library.berkeley.edu. Illus., index. Sample. Circ: 500. Vol. ends: Nov. *Indexed:* GPAI. *Bk. rev.:* 4/yr. *Aud.:* Ga.

This journal focuses on the families of the New Netherland Colony (New York and New Jersey) in the colonial period, 1624–1664. Articles include family genealogies and methodology. Ancestor tables are not published, but queries and answers are. Corrections to errors in printed genealogies are also a focus of this journal.

3411. ***Palatine Immigrant: Researching German-speaking ancestry.*** [ISSN: 0884-5735] 1975. q. Individuals, USD 28. Ed(s): John T Golden. The Palatines to America Society, Capital University, Columbus, OH 43209-2394; pal-am@juno.com; http://www.palam.org. Illus., index. Circ: 3000 Paid. Vol. ends: Dec. *Indexed:* GPAI. *Bk. rev.:* 80/yr. *Aud.:* Ga, Ac.

A scholarly journal for German-speaking ancestry, not just Palatine research. Articles on methodology and primary source transcriptions appear in English. An immigrant ancestor register is a regular feature, along with upcoming events for the society.

3412. ***Polish Genealogical Society of America. Bulletin.*** [ISSN: 0735-9349] 1979. q. USD 7.50 (Individuals, USD 15). Ed(s): William Hoffman. Polish Genealogical Society of America, Inc., 984 N Milwaukee Ave, Chicago, IL 60622; pgsamerica@aol.com; http://www.pgsa.org. Illus., index, adv. Circ: 1500. Vol. ends: Dec. *Indexed:* ABS&EES. *Aud.:* Ga.

These companion journals focus on Polish American ancestry. *Rodziny* is published semiannually (May and August) and is the more scholarly of the two. The *Bulletin* provides society news, queries, and upcoming events and is published quarterly. All aspects of Polish genealogy are covered.

3413. ***The Scottish Genealogist.*** [ISSN: 0300-337X] 1954. q. GBP 16 (Individuals, GBP 16). Ed(s): Stuart E Fleming. Scottish Genealogy Society, 15 Victoria Terr, Edinburgh, EH1 2JL, United Kingdom; info@scotsgenealogy.com; http://www.scotsgenealogy.com. Illus., index. Circ: 2000. Vol. ends: Dec. *Bk. rev.:* 20/yr. *Aud.:* Ga, Ac.

The national scholarly journal for genealogy in Scotland. Articles focus on methodology and primary source suggestions rather than family genealogies. Queries, library news, Scottish genealogies in progress, and society news are also included.

3414. ***Swedish American Genealogist: a quarterly journal devoted to Swedish American biography, genealogy and personal history.*** [ISSN: 0275-9314] 1981. q. USD 25. Ed(s): James E Erickson. Swenson Swedish Immigration Research Center, Augustana College, 639 38th St, Rock Island, IL 61201-2296; swseaholm@augustana.edu; http://www.augustana.edu/administration/swenson/. Illus., index, adv. Circ: 900. Vol. ends: Dec. *Indexed:* GPAI. *Bk. rev.:* 10/yr. *Aud.:* Ga, Ac.

The scholarly journal is subtitled "devoted to Swedish American biography, genealogy and personal history," and all these areas are covered. It provides methodology articles and primary source materials on Swedes in both the United States and Sweden. Family genealogies, ancestor tables, and queries are included.

National and Regional Journals

3415. ***American Genealogist.*** Formerly (until 1932): *New Haven Genealogical Magazine.* [ISSN: 0002-8592] 1922. q. USD 30. Ed(s): A Jane McFerrin, David L Greene. David L. Greene, Pub., PO Box 398, Demorest, GA 30535-0398; amgen@alltel.net; http://www.amgen.alltel.net/. Illus., index. Refereed. Circ: 1920 Paid and free. Vol. ends: Oct. Microform: PQC. Online: bigchalk; Northern Light Technology, Inc.; ProQuest Information & Learning. Reprint: PQC. *Indexed:* BRI, CBRI, GPAI. *Bk. rev.:* 40/yr. *Aud.:* Ga, Ac.

This scholarly journal focuses on genealogical methodology and problem solving in the context of colonial American families. European origins and some medieval and royal-ancestry articles are also included. There is a query section, but ancestor tables are no longer published. There is a yearly index and a published index of the first 60 volumes (currently out of print). *Periodical Contents Index* includes this journal through the year 1960 (volume 36). Recommended for both academic and public libraries.

3416. ***American Genealogy Magazine.*** [ISSN: 1049-6696] 1986. bi-m. USD 22.50. Ed(s): Jamese Pylant. Datatrace Systems, 378 S Baxter, Box 1587, Stephenville, TX 76401. Illus., adv. Circ: 1200 Paid. *Indexed:* GPAI. *Aud.:* Ga.

A scholarly journal featuring how-to articles and abstracts of primary sources. Each issue includes a surname-only index.

3417. ***Ancestry Magazine.*** Formerly: *Ancestry Newsletter.* [ISSN: 1075-475X] 1983. bi-m. USD 24.95 domestic; USD 29.95 in Canada & Mexico; USD 34.95 elsewhere. Ed(s): Jennifer Utley. MyFamily.com Inc., PO Box 990, Orem, UT 84059-0990; ameditor@ancestry-inc.com; http://www.ancestry.com. Illus., adv. Circ: 33000 Paid. Vol. ends: Nov/Dec. *Aud.:* Ga.

This is a sleek, visually beautiful magazine and one of the few genealogy publications found on newsstands. Articles by experts in the field focus on methodology, top research areas, etc., and the scope is national. The publisher also hosts a popular web site on genealogy.

3418. ***Association of Professional Genealogists Quarterly.*** Former titles (until 1991): *A P G Quarterly; A P G Newsletter;* Supersedes (1975-1979, vol.5, no.3): *Professional Genealogists' News Bulletin.* [ISSN: 1056-6732] 1979. q. USD 50 domestic; USD 55 Canada; USD 70 elsewhere. Ed(s): Pamela Boyer Porter. Association of Professional Genealogists, PO Box 350998, Westminster, CO 80035-0998. Illus., adv. Circ: 1400. Vol. ends: Dec. *Indexed:* GPAI. *Bk. rev.:* 25/yr. *Aud.:* Sa.

This journal provides articles aimed at the professional genealogist, including software reviews, research tips, and writing and editing suggestions. Society news and upcoming events are features. A 20-year (1979–1999) cumulative article index is available online at www.apgen.org/qindex.html.

3419. ***Family Chronicle: the magazine for families researching their roots.*** bi-m. CND 28; USD 24. Ed(s): Halvor Moorshead. Moorshead Magazines Ltd., 505 Consumers Rd, Ste 500, Toronto, ON M2J 4V8, Canada; famchron@moorshead.com. Adv. *Indexed:* CBCARef, GPAI. *Aud.:* Ga.

A slick news journal–like magazine with how-to and computer-topic articles and many business advertisements. This is the perfect magazine for a general public library collection.

3420. ***Family Tree Magazine: discover, preserve and celebrate your family history.*** [ISSN: 1529-0298] 1999. bi-m. USD 27 domestic; USD 34 foreign; USD 4.99 newsstand/cover per issue. Ed(s): David A Fryxell. F & W Publications, Inc., 1507 Dana Ave, Cincinnati, OH 45207; ftmletters@; http://www.fwpublications.com. Adv. Circ: 145000 Paid. *Bk. rev.:* 20/yr. *Aud.:* Ga.

This is the latest slick news magazine–like journal for a general audience. It is ideal for a general public library collection. It is also available at newsstands.

3421. ***Federation of Genealogical Societies Forum.*** Formerly (until 1989): *Federation of Genealogical Societies Newsletter.* 1976. q. Members, USD 11; Non-members, USD 17. Ed(s): Sandra H Luebking. Federation of Genealogical Societies, PO Box 200940, Austin, TX 78720-0940; fgs-office@fgs.org; vhwc10@prodigy.com; http://www.fgs.org. Illus., adv. Circ: 25000. Vol. ends: Winter. *Bk. rev.:* 60/yr. *Aud.:* Ga.

This journal provides society news, upcoming events, software reviews, book reviews, etc., to its constituent audience: genealogical societies and libraries. Some methodology articles appear, and regular features include records access, state by state, and a family associations update. The *Forum* was a newsletter from 1976 to 1988.

3422. ***Genealogical Helper: for those who wish to do their own genealogical research.*** [ISSN: 0016-6359] 1947. bi-m. USD 24; USD 26.10 foreign. Ed(s): Valarie N Chambers. Everton Publishers Inc., PO Box 368, Logan, UT 84323-0368; customer_service@everton.com; http://www.everton.com. Illus., index, adv. Circ: 48000. Vol. ends: Nov/Dec. Microform: PQC. *Indexed:* GPAI. *Aud.:* Ga.

Often called *Genealogical Helper* or *Genie Helper,* this magazine is "dedicated to helping genealogists." Although there are still large sections devoted to queries and book advertisements, more-substantive articles also appear in each issue. A column for upcoming genealogical events is included, as are over 40 pages in the "Everton's Computer Helper" section. Software reviews, web site URL listings, and computer tips are given. Each issue is separately indexed for subject, locality, and surname. A very useful all-around magazine for genealogy and appropriate for all public libraries. The online version provides the table of contents of the current print issue and a snippet of each article. For the entire article, one must subscribe.

3423. ***The Genealogist.*** [ISSN: 0197-1468] 1980. 2x/yr. USD 25 domestic; USD 33 foreign. Ed(s): Charles M Hansen, Gale Ion Harris. Picton Press, PO Box 250, Rockport, ME 04856-0250; sales@pictonpress.com; http://www.pictonpress.com. Index, adv. Refereed. Circ: 500. Vol. ends: Fall. *Indexed:* AmH&L, GPAI. *Aud.:* Ac, Sa.

The Genealogist is a highly respected scholarly journal that deals with European origins, royal and medieval ancestry, knotty genealogical problems, complete descendant genealogies, and related studies that are deemed too lengthy by other scholarly journals in the field. Founded in 1980 as a private enterprise with an irregular publishing schedule, it became the official journal of the American Society of Genealogists (ASG) in 1997 (volume 11). Under the aegis of ASG, it has consistently maintained its semiannual publication, as well as its longstanding quality. This is a journal for all academic libraries and libraries with a major genealogical focus.

3424. ***Great Migration Newsletter.*** [ISSN: 1049-8087] 1990. q. USD 15. Ed(s): Robert Charles Anderson. New England Historic Genealogical Society, 101 Newbury St, Boston, MA 02116. Illus., adv. Circ: 4000. *Indexed:* GPAI. *Bk. rev.:* 40/yr. *Aud.:* Ac, Sa.

This newsletter provides ongoing information from the Great Migration Study Project. This project has already produced a valuable study of all the immigrants for the years 1620–1633 (available from the New England Historic Genealogical Sociey), surnames A to F for 1634–1635, and it plans to continue through to 1640, encompassing more than 15,000 people. Articles provide research methodology and analysis of primary source records of each early New England town. Recent literature, including articles, is reviewed by the editor. The first five volumes of this newsletter can be purchased as a monograph for $19.50 from the society.

3425. ***Heritage Quest Magazine.*** Formerly: *Heritage Quest;* Incorporates: *Pastime & Heritage Quest News.* [ISSN: 1074-5238] 1985. bi-m. USD 28 domestic; USD 40 foreign; USD 6.95 newsstand/cover per issue. Ed(s): Patty Meitzler, Leland K Meitzler. Heritage Quest, 669 West 900 North, North Salt Lake, UT 84054; Leland@heritagequest.com; http://www.heritagequest.com. Adv. Circ: 14000 Paid. *Indexed:* GPAI. *Aud.:* Ga.

This journal is designed for a general audience and brings together how-to articles. It is available on CD-ROM for volumes 1–15 (1985–1999).

3426. ***Mayflower Descendant: a magazine of Pilgrim genealogy and history.*** [ISSN: 8756-3959] 1985. s-a. USD 25. Ed(s): Scott Andrew Bartley. Massachusetts Society of Mayflower Descendants, Drew Bartley, 100 Boylston St Ste 750, Boston, MA 02116-4610; msmd@tiac.net; http://www.massmayflowersociety.com. Illus., index. Circ: 600. Vol. ends: Jul. *Bk. rev.:* 30/yr. *Aud.:* Ga, Ac.

This scholarly journal was resurrected after a nearly 50-year hiatus (volumes 1–34; 1899–1937). Membership in the Mayflower Society is not necessary to subscribe. Articles focus on Pilgrim families (not just *Mayflower* families), transcriptions of primary source material, methodology, published genealogies, and corrections to the five generations project. Volume 35 to 48 was in an 8 1/2" x 11" format. With volume 49 (2000), the 6" x 9" format and scholarly footnoting started.

3427. ***National Genealogical Society Quarterly.*** [ISSN: 0027-934X] 1912. q. USD 30 (Members, USD 40). Ed(s): Elizabeth Shown Mills. National Genealogical Society, 4527 17th St N, Arlington, VA 22207; membership@ngsgenealogy.org; ngsgenealogy@ngsgeneology.org; http://www.ngsgenealogy.org. Illus., index, adv. Refereed. Circ: 18000 Paid. Vol. ends: Dec. Microform: PMC. *Indexed:* BRI, CBRI, GPAI. *Bk. rev.:* 50/yr. *Aud.:* Ga, Ac.

This scholarly journal includes articles that truly run the gamut of American genealogy—all ethnicities, all locales, and all time periods, including the twentieth century. The focus of most are particularly well-written methodology articles that point to hidden and very helpful resources. Updates and corrections to articles appear, as does some primary source material (mostly Bible records). Review essays and regular book reviews are in each issue. The journal's editorial base since 1987 has been the Department of History, University of Alabama. The journal is available on CD-ROM that includes volumes 1–85 (1912–1997).

3428. ***New England Ancestors.*** Formerly (until Jan. 2000): *N E H G S Nexus.* 1984. 5x/yr. USD 40 domestic; USD 50 foreign. Ed(s): Carolyn Oakley. New England Historic Genealogical Society, 101 Newbury St, Boston, MA 02116. Illus., index. Circ: 19000. Vol. ends: Dec. *Indexed:* GPAI. *Bk. rev.:* 5/yr. *Aud.:* Ga.

This companion journal to the society's *Register* provides society news and updates to the society's premier New England library. The well-cited articles focus on topics of interest to all genealogists. Regular columns appear on what's new, computer interests, a pocket librarian (surveying collections across the country), and pilgrim life (a special project focusing on the Mayflower passenger). Recent feature article topics have included genetics and genealogy, ancient lineages, pioneers in computer genealogy, and research in Boston. Family associations, genealogies in progress, and notable kin are highlighted in each issue. There is a query section, with answers, and a section for corrections to genealogies in print.

3429. ***New England Historical and Genealogical Register.*** [ISSN: 0028-4785] 1847. q. USD 40; USD 50 foreign. Ed(s): Henry Hoff. New England Historic Genealogical Society, 101 Newbury St, Boston, MA 02116. Illus., index, adv. Circ: 19000. Vol. ends: Oct. Microform: PQC. *Indexed:* AmH&L, GPAI. *Bk. rev.:* 50/yr. *Aud.:* Ga, Ac.

The doyenne of scholarly genealogical journals, this remains the model against which other journals are judged. The *Register*'s primary focus is colonial New England families, the European origins of those families, and some medieval and royal ancestry for New Englanders. New England primary source material is also abstracted and published. Book reviews are detailed and scholarly. There is a yearly index and cumulative indexes for volumes 1–50 and 51–148. The CD-ROM of the first 148 volumes is full-text and searchable. Microfilms have been created in blocks of five years per reel. Recommended for both academic and public libraries.

3430. ***Southern Genealogist's Exchange Quarterly.*** [ISSN: 0584-4487] 1957. q. USD 20 domestic; USD 27 in Canada & Mexico; USD 35 elsewhere. Ed(s): Mary Louise Howard. Southern Genealogist's Exchange Society, Inc., PO Box 2801, Jacksonville, FL 32203-2801; sges@juno.com; http://sgesjax.tripod.com. Illus., index, adv. Circ: 300. Vol. ends: Dec. *Indexed:* GPAI. *Bk. rev.:* 150/yr. *Aud.:* Ga.

A regional journal that covers the 12 southern states of Virginia, West Virginia, North Carolina, South Carolina, Georgia, Florida, Kentucky, Tennessee, Alabama, Mississippi, Arkansas, and Louisiana and may extend into any of the other states. Articles cover primary source transcriptions and, to a lesser extent, methodology and family genealogies. Queries are published.

State—Alphabetical by State

ALABAMA

3431. ***Alabama Genealogical Society Magazine.*** [ISSN: 0568-806X] 1967. s-a. Institutional members, USD 15; Individual members, USD 20. Ed(s): Marcia K Smith Collier. Alabama Genealogical Society, Samford University, Box 2296, Birmingham, AL 35229; jylhardy@bellsouth.net; http://www.archives.state.al.us/ags. Illus., index. Circ: 400 Paid. Vol. ends: Winter. *Indexed:* GPAI. *Bk. rev.:* 20/yr. *Aud.:* Ga.

A solid genealogical journal. The lengthy and substantive articles are well footnoted and scholarly. Primary source transcriptions such as Bible records and census listings are included, and society news and queries are regular features.

ALASKA

3432. ***Anchorage Genealogical Society. Quarterly Report.*** q. Membership, USD 18 individual. Anchorage Genealogical Society, PO Box 242294, Anchorage, AK 99524-2294; ags@ak.net; http://www.rootsweb.com/~akags/. *Bk. rev.:* 10/yr. *Aud.:* Ga.

A basic journal that publishes abstracts of primary sources from the Anchorage area and society news.

ARIZONA

3433. ***Copper State Journal.*** Formerly: *Copper State Bulletin.* 1965. q. USD 14. Ed(s): Rondie R Yancey. Arizona State Genealogical Society, PO Box 42075, Tucson, AZ 85733-2075. Illus., index, adv. Circ: 500. Vol. ends: Winter. *Indexed:* GPAI. *Bk. rev.:* 20/yr. *Aud.:* Ga.

A basic journal that focuses on the publication of primary source material and methodology tips for genealogy in southern Arizona and Pima County. Society news, additions to the society's library, and queries are regular features. Each issue is separately indexed. Selected articles back to 1996 are on the society's web page.

ARKANSAS

3434. ***Arkansas Family Historian.*** [ISSN: 0571-0472] 1962. q. USD 20. Ed(s): Margaret Harrison Hubbard. Arkansas Genealogical Society, Inc., PO Box 908, Hot Springs, AR 71902-0908. Illus., index. Circ: 1000. Vol. ends: Dec. *Indexed:* GPAI. *Bk. rev.:* 60/yr. *Aud.:* Ga.

A basic journal that focuses on the publication of primary source material and methodology tips for genealogy in Arkansas. Society news and queries are regular features. Each issue is separately indexed.

COLORADO

3435. ***Colorado Genealogist.*** [ISSN: 0010-1613] 1939. q. USD 20 (Individuals, USD 15). Ed(s): Juanita Moston. Colorado Genealogical Society, PO Box 9218, Denver, CO 80209. Illus., index, adv. Circ: 650. Vol. ends: Nov. *Indexed:* GPAI. *Bk. rev.:* 15/yr. *Aud.:* Ga.

A solid genealogical journal. An extensive index to the most recently received periodical issues at the society's library is a wonderful feature.

CONNECTICUT

3436. ***Connecticut Nutmegger.*** Formerly (until 1970): *Nutmegger (West Hartford).* [ISSN: 0045-8120] 1968. q. USD 15. Ed(s): Patricia Morrissey. Connecticut Society of Genealogists Inc., PO Box 435, Glastonbury, CT 06033. Illus., adv. Circ: 5000 Paid. Vol. ends: Mar. *Indexed:* GPAI. *Bk. rev.:* 100/yr. *Aud.:* Ga.

A solid genealogical journal for research in Connecticut. Methodology and family genealogies are included. Ongoing transcriptions of primary source material are a mainstay of this journal. They are publishing the Barbour Collection of vital records for the state (now being published by GPC). Queries (and a wonderful index to the names in the queries), family Bible records, and an ongoing list of families for which information has been sent in by members (ancestry service) are all published.

DELAWARE

3437. ***Delaware Genealogical Society. Journal.*** [ISSN: 0731-3896] 1980. 2x/yr. Institutional members, USD 18; Individual members, USD 14.50. Ed(s): Mary Fallon Richards. Delaware Genealogical Society, 505 N Market St, Wilmington, DE 19801-3091; mfallonr@ix.netcom.com; http://www.delgensoc.org. Illus., index, adv. Circ: 700. Vol. ends: Oct. *Indexed:* GPAI. *Aud.:* Ga.

This semiannual journal mainly provides primary sources in Delaware genealogy: marriage bonds, cemetery listings, Bible records, church, court, and newspaper death abstracts. Each issue is separately indexed.

FLORIDA

3438. ***Florida Genealogist.*** [ISSN: 0161-4932] 1977. q. USD 25. Ed(s): Jackie Hufschmid. Florida State Genealogical Society, Inc., PO Box 10249, Tallahassee, FL 32302-2249. Illus., index. Circ: 800. Vol. ends: Winter. *Indexed:* GPAI. *Bk. rev.:* 5/yr. *Aud.:* Ga.

A basic journal that focuses on the publication of primary source material and methodology tips for genealogy in Florida. Additions to the society's library and queries are regular features. Each issue is indexed separately. The first ten volumes (1978–1988) have a cumulative index available in print or microfiche.

GEORGIA

3439. ***Georgia Genealogical Society Quarterly.*** [ISSN: 0435-5393] 1964. q. USD 25. Georgia Genealogical Society, Inc., PO Box 54575, Atlanta, GA 30308-0575. Illus., index, adv. Circ: 1100 Paid. Vol. ends: Winter. *Indexed:* GPAI. *Bk. rev.:* 60/yr. *Aud.:* Ga, Ac.

A solid genealogical journal devoted to the state of Georgia. Most articles present primary source transcriptions, with some methodology articles also included. Queries and additions to the society's library are published. Each issue is separately indexed, and a cumulative index for 1964–1980 ($25) is available from the society.

IDAHO

3440. ***Idaho Genealogical Society Quarterly.*** [ISSN: 0445-2127] 1958. q. Membership, USD 20. Ed(s): Steve Barrett. Idaho Genealogical Society, PO Box 1854, Boise, ID 83701-1854; http://www.lili.org/idahogenealogy. Illus., adv. Circ: 400. *Bk. rev.:* 10/yr. *Aud.:* Ga.

A basic journal that focuses on the publication of primary source material and methodology tips for genealogy in Idaho. Society news, additions to the society's library, and queries are regular features.

ILLINOIS

3441. ***Illinois State Genealogical Society Quarterly.*** [ISSN: 0046-8622] 1969. q. Individual members, USD 25. Ed(s): David D Brown. Illinois State Genealogical Society, PO Box 10195, Springfield, IL 62791-0195; http://www.tbox.com/ISGS. Illus., index, adv. Circ: 2300. Vol. ends: Winter. *Indexed:* GPAI. *Bk. rev.:* 75/yr. *Aud.:* Ga, Ac.

This solid journal focuses on the publication of primary source material and methodology for genealogy in Illinois. Family genealogies are also included. Additions to the society's library and queries are regular features. Each issue is separately indexed. A 25-year cumulative index is available for 1969–1993 as a county-subject, author-title, and table of contents index. A five-year cumulative index is available for 1969–1973 as a subject–title and name index.

INDIANA

3442. ***The Hoosier Genealogist.*** [ISSN: 1054-2175] 1961. q. Members, USD 35. Ed(s): Teresa Baer. Indiana Historical Society, 450 W. Ohio St., Indianapolis, IN 46202-3269; pr@indianahistory.org; http://www.indianahistory.org. Illus., index. Circ: 6000 Paid and controlled. Vol. ends: Dec. *Indexed:* GPAI. *Aud.:* Ga, Ac.

This solid journal focuses on the publication of primary source material for genealogy in Indiana broken down by regions (northern, central, southern), genealogies, family records, and three feature articles. Queries are included.

IOWA

3443. ***Hawkeye Heritage.*** [ISSN: 0440-5234] 1966. q. Members, USD 25. Ed(s): Tami Foster. Iowa Genealogical Society, PO Box 7735, Des Moines, IA 50322; igs@iowagenealogy.org; http://www.iowagenealogy.org/. Illus., index, adv. Circ: 3000. Vol. ends: Winter. *Indexed:* GPAI. *Aud.:* Ga.

A basic journal that focuses on the publication of primary source material and methodology tips for genealogy in Iowa. Some family genealogies are also published. Society news, additions to the society's library, and queries are regular features.

KANSAS

3444. ***The Treesearcher.*** 1959. q. USD 12 (Individuals, USD 15; USD 20 families). Kansas Genealogical Society, Inc., 2601 Central, Village Square Mall, PO Box 103, Dodge City, KS 67801-0103; http;//www.dodge.city.net/kgs. Circ: 525. *Indexed:* GPAI. *Bk. rev.:* 25/yr. *Aud.:* Ga.

A basic journal that contains some primary material as well as information about genealogical lectures in the area, including the speakers' handouts. Queries are published.

KENTUCKY

3445. ***Kentucky Ancestors.*** [ISSN: 0023-0103] 1965. q. USD 25. Ed(s): Thomas Stephens. Kentucky Historical Society, 100 W. Broadway St., Frankfort, KY 40601-1931. Illus., index. Circ: 4800. Vol. ends: Spring. *Indexed:* GPAI. *Bk. rev.:* 50/yr. *Aud.:* Ga, Ac.

Some states are lucky to have one genealogical journal, while Kentucky can boast of four. This is the most comprehensive of the four, covering the entire state, while the others concentrate on the western, central, and eastern portions of the state. A solid journal, *Kentucky Ancestors* includes articles on methodology and local history as well as primary source transcriptions. Society news, queries, and additions to the society's library are regularly published.

LOUISIANA

3446. ***Louisiana Genealogical Register.*** [ISSN: 0148-7655] 1954. q. USD 25 domestic; USD 35 Canada; USD 45 elsewhere. Ed(s): David Howell. Louisiana Genealogical and Historical Society, PO Box 82060, Baton Rouge, LA 70884-2060; bcomeaux@aol.com. Illus., index. Circ: 650. Vol. ends: Dec. *Bk. rev.:* 40/yr. *Aud.:* Ga.

This solid journal provides primary source records and family genealogies for Louisiana. Some but not all articles are footnoted. Ancestor tables, additions to the society's library, and queries are published.

MAINE

3447. ***Maine Genealogist.*** Formerly: *Maine Seine.* [ISSN: 1064-6086] 1978. q. USD 20. Ed(s): Joseph Anderson, Lois Ware Thurston. Maine Genealogical Society, PO Box 221, Farmington, ME 04938-0221. Illus., index. Circ: 1000 Paid. Vol. ends: Nov. *Indexed:* GPAI. *Bk. rev.:* 15/yr. *Aud.:* Ga, Ac.

This journal is a scholarly publication that deserves its place among the best in the country. Articles focus on Maine families and primary source materials. Includes articles on methodology and queries.

MARYLAND

3448. ***Maryland Genealogical Society Bulletin.*** [ISSN: 0542-8351] 1960. q. USD 20. Ed(s): Martha Reamy. Maryland Genealogical Society, 201 W Monument St, Baltimore, MD 21201. Illus., index, adv. Circ: 1200. Vol. ends: Fall. *Indexed:* GPAI. *Bk. rev.:* 30/yr. *Aud.:* Ga, Ac.

A scholarly journal that focuses on Maryland families and source materials. Articles are well cited by end notes, and those dealing with family genealogies are given for many generations. Queries and letters to the editor are featured. Each issue indexed separately.

MICHIGAN

3449. ***Detroit Society for Genealogical Research. Magazine: containing records of Michigan and Michigan source states.*** [ISSN: 0011-9687] 1937. q. USD 20 domestic; USD 25 Canada; USD 30 elsewhere. Ed(s): Patricia Ibbotson. Detroit Society for Genealogical Research, Inc., c/o Detroit Public Library, Burton Historical Collection, Detroit, MI 48202; http://www.dsgr.org. Illus., index. Circ: 1000. Vol. ends: Summer. Microform: PQC. *Indexed:* GPAI. *Bk. rev.:* 50/yr. *Aud.:* Ga.

This solid journal devotes each issue to records of Michigan and Michigan source states. Short family genealogies and queries are published, although ancestor tables are not. Newspaper abstracts, cemetery records, Bible records, court records, and other specialized resources comprise the bulk of this journal. A cumulative index is available for volumes 1–10, 11–15, 16–20, 21–25, 26–30, and annually after that.

MINNESOTA

3450. ***Minnesota Genealogical Journal.*** [ISSN: 0741-3599] 1984. 2x/yr. USD 20 domestic; USD 22 Canada; USD 25 elsewhere. Ed(s): Mary Hawker Bakeman. Park Genealogical Books, PO Box 130968, Roseville, MN 55113-0968; mbakeman@parkbooks.com; http://www.parkbooks.com/mgjbroch.html. Adv. Circ: 600 Paid. *Aud.:* Ga.

This solid journal focuses on the transcription of primary material or indexes to the same. The material is arranged by county.

3451. ***Minnesota Genealogist.*** [ISSN: 0581-0086] 1969. q. Members, USD 25. Ed(s): Erv Chorn. Minnesota Genealogical Society, 5768 Olson Memorial Highway, Golden Valley, MN 55422; mgsdec@mtn.org; http://www.mtn.org/mgs. Illus., adv. Circ: 1800 Paid. *Indexed:* GPAI. *Bk. rev.:* 10/yr. *Aud.:* Ga.

A solid genealogical journal for the state of Minnesota. Articles cover methodology, including Internet research, primary source transcriptions, and some family genealogies. A column for Minnesota connections in printed works, queries, and society news are all featured. A cumulative 30-year index is available.

MISSOURI

3452. ***Missouri State Genealogical Association Journal.*** [ISSN: 0747-5667] 1981. q. USD 15; USD 25 foreign. Ed(s): Jerry R Ennis. Missouri State Genealogical Association, PO Box 833, Columbia, MO 65205-0833; bdoerr@rollanet.org; http://www.rollanet.org/~bdoerr/state.htm. Illus., index. Circ: 1000. Vol. ends: No. 4. *Indexed:* GPAI. *Bk. rev.:* 40/yr. *Aud.:* Ga.

A basic journal that focuses on the publication of primary source material and methodology tips for genealogy in Missouri. Editorials and queries are regular features.

MONTANA

3453. ***Treasure State Lines.*** [ISSN: 1060-0337] 1976. q. USD 20. Ed(s): Alice L Heisel. Great Falls Genealogy Society, 422 2nd St S., Great Falls, MT 59405-1816; gfgs@mcn.net. Illus., index, adv. Circ: 200. Vol. ends: Nov. *Indexed:* GPAI. *Aud.:* Ga.

This basic journal includes primary source transcriptions and methodological articles. Queries are included. A subject index for volumes 1–22 (1976–1998) and a surname index for volumes 1–20 (1976–1996) are available from the society.

NEBRASKA

3454. ***Nebraska Ancestree.*** 1978. q. USD 15. Ed(s): Mary Bergsten. Nebraska State Genealogical Society, Box 5608, Lincoln, NE 68505-0608. *Aud.:* Ga.

A solid genealogical journal that focuses on Nebraska families. Society news and queries are regularly featured, with a few methodological articles and primary-source transcriptions.

NEVADA

3455. ***The Nevada Desert.*** 1981. 9x/yr. USD 10. Ed(s): Dee Clem. Nevada State Genealogical Society, 8044 Moss Creek Dr, Reno, NV 89506-3121. *Aud.:* Ga.

This basic society newsletter includes articles on guest speakers, new additions to local family history centers, methodology, and sources.

3456. ***The Prospector.*** [ISSN: 1085-3707] 1980. q. Membership, USD 16 individual. Clark County Nevada Genealogical Society (CCNGS), PO Box 1929, Las Vegas, NV 89125-1929; ccngs@juno.com; http://www.lvrj.com/communitylink/ccngs/. *Bk. rev.:* 10/yr. *Aud.:* Ga.

A basic journal that publishes abstracts statewide, queries, and society news.

NEW HAMPSHIRE

3457. ***New Hampshire Genealogical Record.*** [ISSN: 1055-0763] 1903. q. Non-members, USD 20. Ed(s): Ann Theopold Chaplin. New Hampshire Society of Genealogists, PO Box 2316, Concord, NH 03302-2316; acnack@aol.com. Illus., index, adv. Circ: 925. Vol. ends: Oct. *Indexed:* GPAI. *Bk. rev.:* 20/yr. *Aud.:* Ga, Ac.

Resurrected in 1990, this scholarly journal focuses on New Hampshire families and source materials. Articles are well cited, and those dealing with family genealogies are given for many generations. The first seven volumes (1903–1910) are available for purchase as a set.

NEW JERSEY

3458. ***Genealogical Magazine of New Jersey.*** [ISSN: 0016-6367] 1925. 3x/yr. USD 15. Ed(s): Roxanne K Carkhuff, Janet T Riemer. Genealogical Society of New Jersey, PO Box 1291, New Brunswick, NJ 08903. Illus., index. Circ: 875 Paid. Vol. ends: Sep. *Indexed:* GPAI. *Aud.:* Ga, Ac.

This scholarly journal focuses on the publication of primary source material for genealogy in New Jersey. Selected Bible and family records are also published when received by the society.

NEW MEXICO

3459. ***New Mexico Genealogist.*** [ISSN: 0545-3186] 1962. q. USD 20. Ed(s): Karen S. Daniel. New Mexico Genealogical Society, PO Box 8283, Albuquerque, NM 87198-8283; info@nmgs.org; http://www.nmgs.org. Index. *Aud.:* Ga.

A solid genealogical journal for New Mexico, whose history predates New England's by 22 years. Methodological articles and genealogies are well footnoted and well written. Primary source transcriptions and queries also are included. There is a cumulative subject and surname index for volumes 1–33 (1962–1994). Tables of contents for 1996 to the present appear on the web site of the society.

NEW YORK

3460. ***New York Genealogical and Biographical Record.*** [ISSN: 0028-7237] 1869. q. USD 30 includes NTG&B Newsletter USD 50 individual membership. Ed(s): Harry Macy. New York Genealogical and Biographical Society, 122 E 58th St, New York, NY 10022-1939; mhartsoe@nygbs.org; http://www.nygbs.org. Illus., adv. Refereed. Circ: 3000 Paid. Vol. ends: Oct. Microform: PQC. Reprint: PQC. *Indexed:* GPAI. *Bk. rev.:* 60/yr. *Aud.:* Ga, Ac.

The second oldest genealogical journal in the United States, *NYGBR* upholds high scholarly standards in dealing with the subject matter of New York State and the Dutch and English colonies that preceded it. Articles span the gamut of transcriptions of source materials, both U.S. and Dutch, to family genealogies. It is a state journal with regional and national importance. Regular features include additions to the society's library and society notes. A subject index was complied by Jean D. Worden for 1870 to 1982 and published independently. This is out of print. The journal is indexed annually with a separate index mailed with the January issue of the following year. There are plans to create a CD-ROM version of the journal.

NORTH CAROLINA

3461. ***North Carolina Genealogical Society Journal.*** [ISSN: 0360-1056] 1975. q. USD 30. Ed(s): Raymond A Winslow, Jr. North Carolina Genealogical Society, PO Box 1492, Raleigh, NC 27602; ncgs@earthlink.net; http://www.ncgenealogy.org. Illus., index, adv. Circ: 1900. Vol. ends: Nov. *Indexed:* GPAI. *Bk. rev.:* 90/yr. *Aud.:* Ga, Ac.

This scholarly journal focuses on the publication of primary source material for genealogy in North Carolina. Queries and a lengthy "document review" (i.e., book) section are included in each issue, which is separately indexed. A 20-year cumulative index to articles (1975–1995) is available from the society.

NORTH DAKOTA

3462. ***North Central North Dakota Genealogical Record.*** [ISSN: 0736-5667] 1978. q. USD 15. Mouse River Loop Genealogy Society, PO Box 1391, Minot, ND 58702-1391. *Bk. rev.:* 10/yr. *Aud.:* Ga.

A basic journal publishing abstracts of primary sources, queries, and society news.

OHIO

3463. ***Ohio Records & Pioneer Families: the cross road of our nation.*** [ISSN: 1063-4649] 1960. q. Members, USD 15; Non-members, USD 20. Ed(s): Susan Dunlap Lee. Ohio Genealogical Society, 713 S Main St, Mansfield, OH 44907-1644; ogs@ogs.org; http://www.ogs.org. Illus., index. Circ: 1600. Vol. ends: No. 4. *Indexed:* GPAI. *Aud.:* Ga.

Ohio is a critical state for anyone pursuing pioneer genealogy. This basic journal focuses on the publication of primary source material and pioneer family genealogies in Ohio. Queries appear in each issue. A ten-year (1985–1994) surname index is available from the society. The society also publishes *Ohio Civil War Genealogy Journal, The Report,* and a society newsletter.

OKLAHOMA

3464. ***Oklahoma Genealogical Society Quarterly.*** [ISSN: 0474-0742] 1955. q. Members, USD 15. Ed(s): Tracy Jackson. Oklahoma Genealogical Society, PO Box 12986, Oklahoma City, OK 73157. Illus., index. Circ: 1150. Vol. ends: Dec. *Indexed:* GPAI. *Bk. rev.:* 20/yr. *Aud.:* Ga.

A basic journal that focuses on the publication of primary source material and methodology tips for genealogy in Oklahoma. Society news, additions to the society's library, and queries are regular features. Each issue is separately indexed, and a subject index from 1955 to 1990 is available from the society. The journal is also on microfilm from 1955 to 1990.

OREGON

3465. ***Oregon Genealogical Society Quarterly.*** [ISSN: 0738-1891] 1962. q. USD 25 domestic; USD 30 foreign. Linda Forrest, Ed. & Pub., PO Box 10306, Eugene, OR 97440-2306. Illus., index, adv. Circ: 475. Vol. ends: Winter. *Indexed:* GPAI. *Bk. rev.:* 30/yr. *Aud.:* Ga.

A basic journal that focuses on the publication of primary source material and methodology tips for genealogy in Oregon. Ancestor tables and queries are regular features.

PENNSYLVANIA

3466. ***Pennsylvania Genealogical Magazine.*** Formerly (until 1948): *Genealogical Society of Pennsylvania. Publications.* [ISSN: 0882-3685] 1895. s-a. Membership, USD 25. Ed(s): Marion F Egge. Genealogical Society of Pennsylvania, 215 S. Broad St., 7 th floor, Philadelphia, PA 19107; gappa@aol.com; http://www.libertynet.org/gspa/. Illus., adv. Refereed. Circ: 1600. Vol. ends: Fall/Winter. *Indexed:* GPAI. *Bk. rev.:* 25/yr. *Aud.:* Ga, Ac.

This scholarly journal focuses on the publication of primary source material for genealogy in Pennsylvania. Methodology articles, library updates, and queries are also included. Pennsylvania was a major entry port for immigration, making this journal an important one nationally as well as locally. There is a query section.

RHODE ISLAND

3467. ***Rhode Island Roots.*** Formerly (until 1981): *R.I. Roots.* [ISSN: 0730-1235] 1976. q. USD 10. Ed(s): Jane Fletcher Fiske. Rhode Island Genealogical Society, 13 Countryside Dr, Cumberland, RI 02864. Illus., index, adv. Circ: 800 Controlled. Vol. ends: Dec. *Indexed:* GPAI. *Bk. rev.:* Number varies. *Aud.:* Ga, Ac.

This scholarly journal publishes articles on the families of and research in Rhode Island. Primary source transcriptions as well as methodology articles are published. News of the society and queries are regular features. A cumulative index of the first five volumes is available.

SOUTH CAROLINA

3468. ***South Carolina Magazine of Ancestral Research.*** [ISSN: 0190-826X] 1973. q. USD 27.50; USD 30. Brent H. Holcomb, Ed. & Pub., PO Box 21766, Columbia, SC 29221. Illus., adv. Circ: 750. Vol. ends: Fall. *Indexed:* GPAI. *Bk. rev.:* 25/yr. *Aud.:* Ga.

A solid genealogical journal that focuses on primary source material and methodology for research in South Carolina. Queries are published.

TENNESSEE

3469. ***Tennessee Ancestors.*** [ISSN: 0882-0635] 1985. 3x/yr. USD 15. Ed(s): Rene Jordan. East Tennessee Historical Society, 600 Market Street, PO Box 1629, Knoxville, TN 37902. Illus., index. Circ: 2200. Vol. ends: Dec. *Bk. rev.:* 60/yr. *Aud.:* Ga, Ac.

This scholarly journal focuses on methodology articles on research in Tennessee. Primary source transcriptions and updates to the membership of the First Families of Tennessee Society are included. Queries are published in each issue.

3470. ***Tennessee Genealogical Magazine: Ansearchin News.*** Formerly: *Ansearchin' News.* 1954. q. Members, USD 20. Ed(s): Dorothy Roberson. Tennessee Genealogical Society, Davies Plantation, 9114 Davies Plantation Rd, Brunswick, TN 38014-0247. Circ: 1200 Paid. *Aud.:* Ga.

A solid journal that features abstracts of primary sources, queries, book reviews, and society news. The annual index is published separately.

TEXAS

3471. ***Stirpes.*** [ISSN: 0039-1522] 1961. q. USD 22. Ed(s): Frances Pryor. Texas State Genealogical Society, 3219 Meadow Oaks Dr, Temple, TX 76502-1752; wdonaldsn@aol.com; http://www.rootsweb.com/~txsgs/. Illus., index, adv. Circ: 850 Controlled. Vol. ends: Dec. *Indexed:* GPAI. *Bk. rev.:* 15/yr. *Aud.:* Ga.

A solid genealogical journal for Texas with primary source transcription, well-footnoted articles, and queries. The index is published separately. A cumulative index (1961–1985) is available from the society. The journal is available on microfilm for 1961 to 1994.

UTAH

3472. ***Utah Genealogical Association. Genealogical Journal.*** [ISSN: 0146-2229] 1972. q. USD 45 (Individuals, USD 35). Ed(s): Judith W Hansen. Utah Genealogical Association, PO Box 1144, Salt Lake City, UT 84110; uga@softsolutions.com; http://www.infouga.org. Illus., index. Refereed. Circ: 1000. Microform: PQC. *Indexed:* GPAI. *Bk. rev.:* 20/yr. *Aud.:* Ga.

Aimed at a Utah audience, this solid journal covers all geographic areas of the United States and provides methodology help and support for the collections at the Family History Library in Salt Lake City, the largest genealogical library in the world. Other articles focus on Utah's families, research sources, primary source abstracts, and Mormon genealogy. A ten-year (1985–1995) cumulative article index is available at the society's web site.

VERMONT

3473. ***Vermont Genealogy.*** Formerly (until 1996): *Branches and Twigs.* [ISSN: 1086-2439] 1972. q. USD 20 domestic; USD 25 in Canada & Mexico; USD 30 elsewhere. Ed(s): Robert H Rodgers. Genealogical Society of Vermont, PO Box 1553, St. Albans, VT 05478-1006; http://www.rootsweb.com/~vtgsv. Illus., index, adv. Circ: 11300 Paid. Vol. ends: Oct. *Indexed:* GPAI. *Bk. rev.:* 25/yr. *Aud.:* Ga, Ac.

A scholarly journal that focuses on well-cited articles on Vermont families, primary source materials, and methodologies. Queries are still part of this journal, but all society news can now be found in the society's newsletter.

VIRGINIA

3474. ***Virginia Genealogist.*** [ISSN: 0300-645X] 1957. q. Individuals, USD 25. Ed(s): John Frederick Dorman. Virginia Genealogist, PO Box 5860, Falmouth, VA 22403-5860. Illus., index. Circ: 715 Paid. Vol. ends: Oct/Dec. *Indexed:* GPAI. *Bk. rev.:* 30/yr. *Aud.:* Ga, Ac.

A scholarly journal that focuses on Virginia families and source materials. The well-cited articles deal with European origins and medieval and royal lineages for Virginia immigrants. There is a query section in each issue. Virginia is to Southern genealogy what Massachusetts is to New England genealogy, so this is an important journal with national appeal. Two consolidated indexes are available from the editor for volumes 1–20 and volumes 21–35. Genealogies are numbered using the Henry system.

WASHINGTON

3475. ***Seattle Genealogical Society Bulletin.*** 1952. q. USD 20. Seattle Genealogical Society, PO Box 75388, Seattle, WA 98125-0388. Adv. Circ: 1700 Paid. *Indexed:* GPAI. *Bk. rev.:* 30/yr. *Aud.:* Ga.

A basic journal for genealogy. Articles are not limited to the state of Washington (one recent article focused on New York, another on California). A listing of recent acquisitions in the Seattle Public Library is a regular feature. Queries are included.

WEST VIRGINIA

3476. ***Kanawha Valley Genealogical Society. Journal.*** [ISSN: 0270-4064] 1977. q. USD 15. Kanawha Valley Genealogical Society, PO Box 8555, South Charleston, WV 25303. *Aud.:* Ga.

A basic journal featuring abstracts of primary sources, queries, and society news.

WISCONSIN

3477. ***Wisconsin State Genealogical Society Newsletter.*** [ISSN: 1094-9445] 1954. q. USD 20 (Individuals, USD 18). Ed(s): Virginia V Irvin. Wisconsin State Genealogical Society, Inc., 2109 20 Ave, Monroe, WI 53566; md2609@tds.net; http://www.rootsweb.com/~wsgs/. Circ: 1600 Paid. *Indexed:* GPAI. *Aud.:* Ga.

A basic journal that focuses on the publication of primary source material and methodology for genealogy in Wisconsin. Society news, additions to Wisconsin genealogical libraries, upcoming events, and queries are all regular features. Materials are arranged county by county and designed to be taken apart. There is a second pagination unique to each county.

Electronic Journals

3478. ***Eastman's Online Genealogy Newsletter.*** w. Ed(s): Richard Eastman. MyFamily.com Inc., PO Box 990, Orem, UT 84059-0990; http://www.myfamilyinc.com/. *Aud.:* Ga.

Now part of the Ancestry.com web site, this newsletter is still thriving under Eastman's editorship. Everything is discussed, from new books and electronic products to genealogically interesting news items and upcoming events. An archive of columns from May 1998 to September 1999 is available on the web site. Newsletters from April 1999 to the present are found at www.ancestry.com/library/view/columns/eastman/eastman.asp under the archives section. Access to this part of Ancestry.com is still free, although membership gives the viewer access to many databases from this company.

3479. ***Journal of Online Genealogy.*** 1996. m. Free. Ed(s): Matthew Helm. Journal of Online Genealogy, mhelm@tbox.com; http://www.onlinegenealogy.com. *Aud.:* Ga.

This is the best of the genealogical e-journals. It features methodology articles for pursuing research online and other news, successful research stories, and press releases of new products. Articles discuss usenet newsgroups, discussion lists, and new web sites. The last year's issues are archived on the site.

■ GENERAL EDITORIAL

General/Tabloids

See also Alternatives; Canada; City and Regional; Europe; and News and Opinion sections.

Susan G. Baird, Patron Services Department Head, Oak Lawn Public Library, 9427 S. Raymond, Oak Lawn, IL 60453

Introduction

The wonderful magazines in this section are welcome companions at any time. However, with a weakened economy and worldwide threats of war and terrorism, the world of magazines will become even more important and enriching. Fewer magazines have ceased during this period, but fewer new titles have come forth as well. Fortunately, what we still have is an excellent range of publications to satisfy a variety of tastes, education levels, and requirements.

Basic Periodicals

Ems: *National Geographic;* Hs: *National Geographic, Smithsonian, World Press Review;* Ga: *National Geographic, The New Yorker, Smithsonian, World Press Review;* Ac: *American Scholar, Smithsonian, The Wilson Quarterly.*

Basic Abstracts and Indexes

Access, American Humanities Index, Magazine Article Summaries, Magazine Index, Readers' Guide to Periodical Literature.

General

3480. ***A I M.*** 1974. q. USD 12. Ed(s): Myron Apilado. A I M Publishing Association, 7308 Eberhart, Chicago, IL 60619. Illus. Circ: 10000. *Aud.:* Ga, Ac.

This fantastic magazine has the perfect motto, "To Purge Racism from the Human Bloodstream." Everything the magazine runs supports this premise, whether it's poetry titled "To Amadou Diallo," news like the political views of the Presidential election, or cover stories such as "Of These Who Would Address Racial Issues?" or "Carl Gorman: Navajo Code Talker." Articles and fiction vary from short to mid-length and are contributed from all over the United States. The magazine's call for a short story contest's requirements perfectly describe the magazine itself: "Prove that people from different racial/ethnic backgrounds are more alike than different and no moralizing." The letters to the editor are also outstanding, and they are quite participatory and activist! A wonderful addition to all sizes and types of collections.

African American Review. See African American section.

3481. ***American Scholar.*** [ISSN: 0003-0937] 1932. q. USD 30 (Individuals, USD 25; USD 6.95 newsstand/cover per issue domestic). Ed(s): Anne Fadiman. Phi Beta Kappa Society, 1785 Massachusettts Ave, N W, 4th Fl, Washington, DC 20036-2117; http://www.pbk.org. Illus., adv. Sample. Refereed. Circ: 27000 Paid. Vol. ends: Fall. Microform: PMC; PQC. Online: Chadwyck-Healey Incorporated; EBSCO Publishing; Florida

Center for Library Automation; Gale Group; OCLC Online Computer Library Center, Inc.; ProQuest Information & Learning; H.W. Wilson. *Indexed:* ABS&EES, AmH&L, ArtHuCI, BHA, BRD, BRI, BiogInd, CBRI, CIJE, FLI, HumInd, IAPV, IBZ, IPSA, LRI, MLA-IB, MagInd, PAIS, PSA, PsycholAb, RGPR, RI-1, SSCI, SWR&A. *Bk. rev.:* 5-9, essay-length. *Aud.:* Hs, Ga, Ac.

American Scholar carries a surprisingly varied range of pieces, and not all are strictly scholarly. For example, one issue contains "The End of Linguistics," "The Worldly Stendhal," and "Elvis Movies." The latter article is brimming with sad truths and surprising facts of interest even to non-Elvis-fan readers. Articles and poetry sit side by side and are the products of knowledgeable professors, experts, and other luminaries. Books reviewed are generally quite scholarly. Medium-sized and large public, university, and special libraries should contain *American Scholar.*

3482. ***The Atlantic Monthly.*** Former titles (until 1993): *Atlantic;* (until 1981): *Atlantic Monthly;* (until 1971): *Atlantic;* (until 1932): *Atlantic Monthly.* [ISSN: 1072-7825] 1857. 11x/yr. USD 29.95 United States; USD 37.95 Canada includes surcharge; USD 44.95 rest of world. Ed(s): Cullen Murphy. Atlantic Monthly Co., 77 N Washington St, Ste 5, Boston, MA 02114-1908; wen@theatlantic.com; http://www.theatlantic.com. Illus., adv. Circ: 457343 Paid. Vol. ends: Jun/Dec. CD-ROM: ProQuest Information & Learning. Microform: PMC; PQC; NRP. Online: EBSCO Publishing; Florida Center for Library Automation; Gale Group; ProQuest Information & Learning. *Indexed:* ABS&EES, AgeL, BAS, BRD, BRI, CBCARef, CBRI, CJA, CPerI, FLI, FutSurv, GeoRef, IAPV, MagInd, PAIS, PRA, RGPR, RI-1. *Bk. rev.:* 2-3, 500 words. *Aud.:* Hs, Ga, Ac.

Renowned writers contribute an array of interesting articles on many subjects in this attractive publication. One issue examined includes "Russia is Finished," written by an author of travel books who lived in Russia. The accompanying pictures are amazing and visually support the story. Another delightful article covers the lost-and-found department at New York City's Grand Central Terminal, revealing that 15,000 items are turned in annually with 56 percent being recovered. Short stories, poetry, the arts, and travel are also covered. *The Atlantic Monthly* should be offered in high school and in most other libraries.

3483. ***AudioFile: the magazine for people who love audiobooks.*** [ISSN: 1063-0244] 1992. 6x/yr. USD 48. Ed(s): Robin F Whitten. AudioFile, 37 Silver St, Box 109, Portland, ME 04112-0109; info@audiofilemagazine.com. Illus., adv. Circ: 10000. *Indexed:* MRD. *Bk. rev.:* 100 per issue. *Aud.:* Ac, Ga, Hs.

AudioFile is a dream come true for any audiobook lover. Reviews of abridged and unabridged books and a wide range of other audio products are given well-balanced treatment. The audiobook's narration is always the focus. In addition to reviews, there are well-written and very interesting articles, such as one about a meeting between author Sue Grafton and the narrator of her books, Judy Kaye (including pictures). Regular columns include Editor's Notes, Hear Here (tidbits and newsy items about audiobooks), AudiOpinion, Letters, Listening Librarian (librarians and teachers sharing ideas about audiobooks), and Listening With, which has a picture and brief information about an actual audiobook listener. An outstanding title that should be in all collections.

3484. ***Australian Women's Weekly.*** [ISSN: 0005-0458] 1933. m. AUD 66; AUD 5.50 newsstand/cover. Ed(s): Deborah Thomas. A C P Women's Lifestyle Group, GPO Box 4178, Sydney, NSW 1028, Australia; http://www.acp.com.au/. Illus., adv. Circ: 696530. *Aud.:* Ga.

This charming magazine can be enjoyed by women everywhere but probably is a unique glimpse for Westerners of a lifestyle like and yet quite unlike ours. Contents are identical to "our" female-oriented publications, but with fashions revealing an Asian flair. Food ads and recipes are unusual, such as honey leg ham and Yakult, which is fermented milk! The usual celebrities are covered, with Aussie Nicole Kidman getting lots of exposure. An unusual piece on the Dalai Lama was written by Sarah Ferguson ("Fergie"), and she's pictured with him in some gorgeous photos. "Wedding Belles" includes very unusual wedding pictures of couples of all types and ages. There is a section on gardening by the stars (horoscope—not at night!) and a great selection of puzzles. An excellent resource for large libraries of all types and for collections that aim for the unusual.

3485. ***B B C on Air.*** Supersedes (in 1996): *B B C Worldwide;* Which was formerly (until 1992): *London Calling.* [ISSN: 1365-1978] 1996. m. GBP 20; USD 32; GBP 2 newsstand/cover per issue. Ed(s): Kirsty Cockburn. British Broadcasting Corp., Bush House NW, Rm 310, London, WC2B 4PH, United Kingdom; on.air.magazine@bbc.co.uk; http://www.bbc.co.uk/worldservice/onair. Illus., adv. Vol. ends: Dec. *Aud.:* Ga.

This outstanding publication is the BBC's international magazine and program guide. And what a guide it is! It is filled with wonderful details and revelations on how particular programs came to be adapted for the air. Highlights and weekend schedules are well covered, with the continents of the world in one inclusive listing. Television is also included. Article topics fit the month's offerings, for example, the new face of leprosy or being Muslim in England. Educational shows and other programs that are offered in several segments (such as mini-courses) are explained. The schedules are easy to read and include cable and satellite listings. There is nothing else like the BBC—or this guide. The perfect choice for large or communications-oriented collections or international institutions.

The Baffler. See Alternatives section.

Better Homes and Gardens. See Home section.

3486. ***Bomb: interviews with artists, writers, musicians, directors and actors.*** [ISSN: 0743-3204] 1981. q. USD 18 domestic; USD 40 foreign. Ed(s): Betsy Sussler. New Art Publications, Inc., 594 Broadway, 905, New York, NY 10012-3233; bombmag@bombsite.com; http://www.bombsite.com. Illus., adv. Sample. Circ: 25000. *Indexed:* ABM, AmHI, FLI, HumInd, IAPV, MRD. *Aud.:* Hs, Ga, Ac.

This unique publication is celebrating its twentieth anniversary of pairing artists and writers with their peers for compelling, thoughtful interviews. Illustrations, pictures, sketches, etc., are wonderful to behold. The major interviews are lengthy and are in a Q & A format. In one issue, for example, a piece on Madison Smartt Bell is done by a college professor who uses Bell's first book as required reading for class. In another piece, Miriam Makeba is interviewed by a woman who is a community activist and theater director in Manhattan and South Africa. The online version of the magazine provides access to many of the interviews and illustrations to be found in the print version. An excellent choice for high school, large public, and academic libraries, and any collection with modern arts emphasis.

3487. ***The City Journal.*** Formerly (until 1992): *N Y.* [ISSN: 1060-8540] 1990. q. USD 23. Ed(s): Myron Magnet. Manhattan Institute, Inc., 52 Vanderbilt Ave, New York, NY 10017-3808; http://www.city-journal.org. Adv. Circ: 10000 Paid. *Indexed:* CJA, PAIS. *Aud.:* Hs, Ga, Ac.

The Manhattan Institute puts out this magazine dedicated to rebuilding the urban area. The publication committee includes people from *Fortune* magazine, the Philip Morris company, the State University of New York, and the like. A page advertising the publication has quotes of praise from George Will, Bill Moyers, and Rudy Giuliani. Excellent black-and-white pictures illustrate articles written by experts from the United States and England. Articles focus on national topics (Bush's urban problems or the U.S. bishops' crime report) and local topics ("How to Run the Mob out of Gotham" or Philadelphia teachers and discipline). Excellent cartoons from other publications are run with a tiny number of ads gracing the front and back. The perfect choice for large public, high school, and urban libraries.

Commentary. See News and Opinion section.

Consumer Reports. See Consumer Education section.

3488. ***Country (Greendale): for those who live in or long for the country.*** [ISSN: 0895-0377] 1987. bi-m. USD 17.98 domestic; USD 23.98 Canada; USD 25.98 elsewhere. Ed(s): Jerry Wiebel. Reiman Publications, LLC, 5400 S 60th St, Greendale, WI 53129; subscriberservices@reimanpub.com; http://www.reimanpub.com. Illus., adv. Circ: 1500000 Paid. *Aud.:* Ga, Ac.

This wonderfully upbeat publication is a combination of *Reader's Digest* and *Grit* in a traditional glossy format. The photography is stupendous, and many of the pictures and articles come from the readers themselves. Specific sections include Country People, Animal Tales, Getting to Know Nature, Country Scenery, and Photo Tours. Everything has a rural emphasis, and there are quite a few e-mail addresses should a reader want to know more or contact a contributor. Every article or picture (there are many photo-essays) specifically notes the town and state covered. Not to be overlooked is a delicious "Taste of the Country" section complete with clip-out recipes. An excellent addition to Americana collections or to illustrate less-often-covered areas of our country.

3489. *Culture Change.* Former titles (until 2001): *Auto-Free Times; Paving Moratorium Update - Auto-Free Times; Fossil Fuels Action Update; Ecodemocracy.* 1989. s-a. USD 20. Ed(s): Jan Lundberg. Sustainable Energy Institute, PO Box 4347, Arcata, CA 95518. Adv. Circ: 15000. *Indexed:* AltPI. *Bk. rev.:* 2-3, 500 words, signed. *Aud.:* Hs, Ga, Ac.

This publication is a fine example of simplicity, with its pulplike paper, basic cover art, black-and-white pictures, and, of course, subject matter. However, the *A-FT* is bursting with an experienced and concerned advisory board that includes doctors, teachers, authors, and energy experts. Full-length articles cover subjects like bikes versus cars, a sermon and pictures on a car burial, and the joys of carlessness. Letters to the editor are titled "Backfire" and can be quite spirited. "Blubs" is a section filled with auto-related snippets from national and international sources. Web addresses at the end of articles and from a column called "Making Contact" firmly ground the publication in the twenty-first century. This very thoughtful publication should be in most library collections.

3490. *Daedalus.* Formerly (until 1955): *American Academy of Arts and Sciences. Proceedings.* [ISSN: 0011-5266] 1950. q. USD 49.50 (Individuals, USD 33). Ed(s): Stephen R Graubard. American Academy of Arts and Sciences, 136 Irving St, Cambridge, MA 02138; daedalus@amacad.org. Illus., index. Sample. Refereed. Circ: 20000. Vol. ends: Fall. Microform: PQC. Online: Florida Center for Library Automation; Gale Group; Northern Light Technology, Inc.; OCLC Online Computer Library Center, Inc.; ProQuest Information & Learning. Reprint: PQC. *Indexed:* ABCPolSci, AmH&L, ArtHuCI, BAS, BHA, BRI, BiolAb, BrArAb, CBRI, ChemAb, DSR&OA, FutSurv, GeoRef, HumInd, IBSS, IPSA, LRI, MLA-IB, MagInd, PAIS, PSA, PsycholAb, RGPR, RI-1, SSCI, SociolAb. *Aud.:* Ga, Ac.

Each issue of this impressive magazine focuses on a major topic. All articles are by experts in their fields and support the cover topic. An international array of authors is represented, and many articles are by several authors. The endnotes are most impressive (one article alone had 112!) and offer many additional sources. A recent issue on "Why South Africa Matters" has interspersed excerpts from earlier *Daedalus* issues on the same subject. This scholarly journal should be included in large and academic collections.

Ebony. See African American section.

3491. *Esquire: the magazine for men.* Former titles (until 1979): *Esquire Fortnightly;* (until 1978): *Esquire.* [ISSN: 0194-9535] 1933. m. USD 8.97 domestic; USD 20.97 Canada; USD 39.94 elsewhere. Ed(s): David Granger. Hearst Corporation, 250 W 55th St, 5th Fl, New York, NY 10019; hearstlink@hearst.com; http://www.hearstcorp.com. Illus., adv. Circ: 650000 Paid. Vol. ends: Dec. Microform: PQC. Online: EBSCO Publishing; Florida Center for Library Automation; Gale Group; OCLC Online Computer Library Center, Inc.; ProQuest Information & Learning. Reprint: PQC. *Indexed:* BEL&L, BRI, CBRI, FLI, MLA-IB, MRD, MagInd, RGPR. *Aud.:* Ga, Ac.

This magazine is predictable and changes little year after year. A few current events are covered and contributors are often well known. For example, a piece by Paul Begala called "What does W Stand For?" quotes Sen. John McCain, Sen. Edward Kennedy, and Rep. Robert Wexler. Other in-depth articles include a "Desire Survey" that focuses on the libido. Pictures are both in black and white and in color and are excellent. Movies, books, and men's fashions are highlighted, and ads fit the reader profile. *Esquire* should be most at home in libraries that offer leisure reading for men.

Futurist. See Cultural-Social Studies section.

3492. *Gadfly: culture that matters.* [ISSN: 1099-2197] 1997. bi-m. USD 19.95 domestic; USD 47.40 foreign; USD 4.95 newsstand/cover per issue. Ed(s): John Whitehead. Gadfly Productions, PO Box 7926, Charlottesville, VA 22906-7926. Illus., adv. Sample. Vol. ends: Dec. *Indexed:* RGPR. *Aud.:* Hs, Ga, Ac.

This fun magazine lives up to its subtitle, "culture that matters." Its lists of top films and songs are more atypical than those found in most mainstream publications and are rewarding. Articles have included a piece on Lenny Bruce by Nat Hentoff discussing the barriers Bruce broke down for comedians who followed him. The ads for music and books are quite complete and include information on where the material can be found. Reviews are both long and short. One typical article, "Ten Great Books that Could, Should or Did Cause a Revolution," is worthwhile and unique. The only shortcoming (a minor one) is that pictures are of a rather poor quality. The magazine is rounded out with information and articles on literature, television, the arts, and film. An excellent addition for medium-sized libraries of all kinds and all contemporary collections.

3493. *German Life.* [ISSN: 1075-2382] 1994. bi-m. USD 22.95 domestic; USD 32 foreign. Ed(s): Carolyn Cook. Zeitgeist Publishing, 1068 National Hwy, Lavale, MD 21502-7501. Illus., adv. Sample. Circ: 40000 Paid and controlled. Online: Northern Light Technology, Inc.; ProQuest Information & Learning. *Indexed:* ENW. *Aud.:* Hs, Ga.

This magazine gives readers a chance to experience a little bit of Germany regardless of their locale. Articles present German subjects, profile famous German people, and describe German travel destinations. An excellent feature is the inclusion of some German words beside their English counterparts. Ads are glorious, delicious, endlessly tempting, and many are mail-order for armchair travelers. All things German are covered, traditions are explained, and international locations influenced by Germany are presented with photos. Probably the food articles and pictures are the best feature. These offer clear explanations and provide various methods of preparing a recipe. An excellent purchase for large public libraries and all German-oriented collections.

Good Housekeeping. See Women section.

Gray Areas. See Alternatives/General section.

3494. *Grit: American life & traditions.* [ISSN: 0017-4289] 1882. 20x/yr. USD 12.95 domestic; USD 15.45 foreign. Ed(s): Ann Crahan. Ogden Publications, 1503 S W 42nd St, Topeka, KS 66609-1265; grit@cjnetworks.com; http://www.ogdenpubs.com. Illus., adv. Sample. Circ: 120000 Paid. *Aud.:* Ems, Hs, Ga.

Despite a change in its subtitle, *Grit* remains an American institution and an excellent example of Americana. The pictures are excellent, every bit as fine as those found in more glitzy publications. The emphasis is on the outdoors via gardening, parks, and recreation. Human-interest articles abound, such as a recent one about a Branson, Missouri, crossing guard who brings joy to students, teachers, and parents. Regular inclusions relate to food, recipes, and questions and answers (all from readers). An inclusive page offers all sorts of puzzles and the Wishing Well, an almost unbelievable sight in the twenty-first century! A regular Billy Graham column sits beside Hometown Kitchen dealing with Amish cooking. The ads are wonderful; "Kill Foot Pain Dead" says it all.

3495. *Harper's.* Former titles (until 1976): *Harper's Magazine;* (until 1913): *Harper's Monthly Magazine;* (until 1900): *Harper's New Monthly Magazine;* Which incorporated (1850-1852): *International Magazine of Literature, Art, and Science.* [ISSN: 0017-789X] 1850. m. USD 14 domestic; CND 24 Canada; USD 41 elsewhere. Ed(s): Lewis H Lapham. Harpers Magazine, 666 Broadway, 11th Fl, New York, NY 10012-2317; http://www.harpers.org/. Illus., adv. Circ: 175000 Paid. Vol. ends: Jun/Dec. CD-ROM: ProQuest Information & Learning. Microform: NBI; PMC; PQC. Online: bigchalk; EBSCO Publishing; Florida Center for Library Automation; Gale Group; Northern Light Technology, Inc.;

OCLC Online Computer Library Center, Inc.; ProQuest Information & Learning; H.W. Wilson. Reprint: PQC. *Indexed:* ABS&EES, BEL&L, BRD, BRI, BiogInd, CBCARef, CBRI, CPerI, FLI, FutSurv, IAPV, LRI, MLA-IB, MRD, MagInd, PRA, RGPR, RI-1. *Aud.:* Hs, Ga, Ac.

Despite being rather scholarly, *Harper's* contains a few surprises. Articles can cover "unlikely" subjects. For example, one describes the "World Series of poker" accompanied by amazing pictures and a glossary of poker terms. In another piece, affecting photographs illustrate the drug war in Colombia. Articles are well written by experts. There are some ads that would seem to be more appropriate for a tabloid publication. Noteworthy is the popular "Harper's Index," a fascinating-facts-and-figures column. An excellent inclusion for most large public and academic library collections.

3496. ***Harvard Magazine.*** Formerly (until 1973): *Harvard Bulletin.* [ISSN: 0095-2427] 1898. bi-m. USD 30 domestic; USD 35 in Canada & Mexico; USD 55 elsewhere. Ed(s): John S Rosenberg. Harvard Magazine, Inc., 7 Ware St, Cambridge, MA 02138. Illus., adv. Sample. Circ: 218491. Vol. ends: Jul/Aug. *Indexed:* AIAP, ASIP, BHA, EnvAb, GeoRef, RiskAb. *Bk. rev.:* 5-7, 200-650 words. *Aud.:* Ac.

The emphasis of this magazine is naturally on all things Harvard, past and present. Articles are interesting and well written. Issues have included, for example, a piece by *Bartlett's Familiar Quotations* editor Justin Kaplan. Another article describes a 60-year study of the "greatest generation" and its talent for aging well. Schedules of upcoming events are included. A favorite section is "Crimson Classifieds," where one can find ads like "Date somebody who knows The Magic Mountain is not a theme park." A worthy addition to large collections or those that serve a large number of Harvard graduates.

3497. ***Hello!*** [ISSN: 0214-3887] 1988. w. GBP 48 for 6 mos. domestic; GBP 65 for 6 mos. in Europe; GBP 100 for 6 mos. elsewhere. Hello! Ltd., Wellington House, 69-71 Upper Ground, London, SE1 9PQ, United Kingdom. Illus., adv. Circ: 546952 Paid. *Aud.:* Ga.

This fun magazine is kind of a union of *People Weekly* and *Town and Country.* Wonderful celebrity-related pictures of all of the places and things "outsiders" would love to see grace each issue. The focus is international, with an emphasis on Britain and the United States. An impressive insert titled "Seven Days" includes anything and everything about London (worth the price alone). It is very timely, but there is little "real news." There are also sections on fashion, beauty, and cookery, and a travel section surprisingly includes prices. There is, however, a slant on charity that differentiates it from its American cousins. A "frivolous" and fun inclusion for large public libraries and any that focus on the United Kingdom.

Hope Magazine. See Alternatives/General section.

3498. ***In Touch (Englewood Cliffs).*** [ISSN: 1540-8280] 2002. w. USD 77.48 domestic; USD 129.48 foreign; USD 1.49 newsstand/cover. Ed(s): Richard Spencer. Bauer Publishing Company, L.P., 270 Sylvan Ave, Englewood, NJ 07632-2513. Illus., adv. *Aud.:* Ga.

In Touch is another celebrity vehicle in which photos seem to be large and abundant. Sections include Celebrity, Body, Style, Lifestyle, and Stars Above (Astrology), and deal with celebrities exclusively. The News section is two pages covering only famous names in minor news items. The Best of the Week consists of three pages of TV, Books, Music, Movies, and Events, with an emphasis on events. Add this to your leisure collection if you have extra money to spend.

3499. ***Intelligence Report.*** Supersedes (in 1996): *Klanwatch Intelligence Report.* 1981. q. Ed(s): Mark Potok. Southern Poverty Law Center, Intelligence Project, PO Box 548, Montgomery, AL 36104-0548; http://www.splcenter.org. Illus. Circ: 380000 Controlled. *Aud.:* Ga.

A donation gets the donor, law enforcement agencies, and police officers copies of this unique and outstanding publication. Excellent in-depth articles, often enhanced by detailed timelines, grace each issue. There are also brief snippets on U.S. hate groups, neo-Nazis, Klan activities, and other groups and individuals who dedicate themselves to racism, hate crimes, anti-immigration activities, and the like. National and international events are included. Regular departments include "Hate Group Map," "Hate Group List," and "Hate Site List." Also, "For the Record" includes dates and locations of incidents. A recent article on the anti-gay Rev. Fred Phelps well illustrates this publication's vital work. Note that the magazine's articles may be reprinted by government agencies provided the Southern Poverty Law Center is credited. A must for all American libraries.

3500. ***International Express (US Edition).*** w. USD 69 for 6 mos. Express Newspaper Ltd., Hamilton House, 1 Temple Ave, London, EC4, United Kingdom; http://www.express.co.uk. *Bk. rev.:* 10-15, 40-250 words. *Aud.:* Hs, Ga, Ac.

"Have the week's news delivered to your door" and "read in over 100 countries" are claims that accompany subscription information for this enjoyable and informative weekly. The emphasis is on the U.K., but there is also coverage of international affairs. Subjects run the gamut from politics, sports, and the arts to motoring, money, and royalty. It's fascinating to see how this paper differs from its American counterparts. For instance, there is less hesitation to deal directly with age. One article notes that the majority of top earners in pop music in Great Britain are over 50 years old, and another piece profiles a fitness expert known as the Green Goddess who is now 60 and campaigning for the mature. There are excellent profiles of the famous, short and gossipy pieces about "everyone," and an excellent column by Boy George. The *Express* belongs in large and international library collections.

Interview. See News and Opinion section.

Jet. See African American section.

Lilith. See Women: Feminist and Special Interest/Special Interest section.

3501. ***Long Term View: a journal of informed opinion.*** [ISSN: 1066-1182] 1992. q. USD 10; USD 3.95 newsstand/cover per issue. Ed(s): Lawrence Velvet, Nancy E Bernhard. Massachusetts School of Law at Andover, 500 Federal St, Woodland Park, Andover, MA 01810; neb@mslaw.edu; http://www.mslaw.edu. Illus. Sample. Circ: 5000. Vol. ends: Oct/Nov. *Aud.:* Hs, Ga, Ac.

Each issue devotes itself to one topic that is presented in many formats, such as essays, analytical articles, interviews, speeches, and book excerpts. Contributors are well qualified and are international. Recent topics include legacies of Vietnam, medicine in transition, and history in the United States. Articles vary in length, beginning with a synopsis and closing with the author's biography and credits. Highlighted quotes and an appealing format make for easy reading. *LTV* welcomes submissions in each issue. An outstanding inclusion for large public and academic libraries and all that serve a community of lawyers and related professions.

Lumpen Magazine. See Zines section.

3502. ***Mental Floss: feel smart again.*** [ISSN: 1543-4702] 2001. bi-m. USD 19.97 domestic; USD 25 Canada; USD 40 elsewhere. Ed(s): William Pearson, Mangesh Hattikudur. Mental Floss L L C, PO Box 2730, Durham, NC 27715. Illus. *Aud.:* Hs, Ga, Ac, Sa.

Everything about this delightful magazine is fun and enlightening. Even the accomplished contributors' bios are humorous. In a recent issue, the book section tackles James Joyce's "Portrait of an Artist as a Young Man," and tells you what your teacher never taught you about Joyce, that he swore a lot as a youth but gave it up entirely as an older man. An excellent article on Edgar Degas quotes the artist: "A painting requires as much fraudulence, trickery and deception as the perpetration of a crime." The cover story, "What's the Difference?," tackles such timeless questions as Coke-Pepsi, woodchuck-groundhog, Monet-Manet, and diamonds-fakes. Another in-depth article is "20-30 Things You Might Not Know about the Czech Republic." An excellent purchase for most libraries.

3503. ***Moment: the magazine of Jewish culture, politics, and religion.*** [ISSN: 0099-0280] 1975. bi-m. USD 14.97 domestic; USD 20.97 foreign. Ed(s): Hershel Shanks. Moment Magazine, 4710 41st St, N W, Washington, DC 20016. Illus., adv. Sample. Circ: 65000. Vol. ends:

Jan/Feb. Microform: PQC. Online: EBSCO Publishing; Northern Light Technology, Inc.; OCLC Online Computer Library Center, Inc.; ProQuest Information & Learning; SoftLine Information. *Indexed:* ABS&EES, ENW, IJP. *Bk. rev.:* 2-3, 750-1,500 words. *Aud.:* Ga.

Moment is like a mini-reference book that could satisfy the curiosity of most Jews and non-Jews. Contemporary issues such as "the gay orthodox underground" and "Hooking Jews on Jesus" are addressed in thorough, well-written articles by experts. Historical issues also receive their due, and a calendar presents historical tidbits. Articles cover such subjects as the Holocaust, Niger Jews, and marriage to non-Jews. Opinions are varied and quite feisty. "Forum," "Readers React," and various surveys enable participants to really get something off their chest. Excellent ads, guides to retreats, and higher-learning opportunities can all be found here. Reviews of books, music, and videos round out the worthwhile contents. A favorite is a listing of books for potential review that have been received by *Moment*. A wonderful addition for libraries serving the Jewish community and for large public libraries.

3504. ***Money (New York).*** [ISSN: 0149-4953] 1972. 13x/yr. USD 19.95 domestic; USD 37 Canada. Ed(s): Robert Safian. Time, Inc, Time & Life Bldg, Rockefeller Center, 1271 Ave of the Americas, New York, NY 10020-1393; http://www.money.cnn.com. Illus., index, adv. Circ: 1900000 Paid. Vol. ends: Dec. CD-ROM: ProQuest Information & Learning. Microform: CIS; PQC. Online: bigchalk; The Dialog Corporation; EBSCO Publishing; Factiva; Florida Center for Library Automation; Gale Group; LexisNexis; MediaStream, Inc.; OCLC Online Computer Library Center, Inc.; ProQuest Information & Learning; H.W. Wilson. *Indexed:* ABIn, ATI, BLI, BPI, BRI, CBRI, ConsI, EnvAb, LRI, MagInd, PAIS, RGPR. *Bk. rev.:* 500-700 words, number varies. *Aud.:* Ga, Ac.

Money presents the ups and downs and uncertainties of everything related to buying and selling, profit and loss. There is an array of excellent sections on investing, saving and spending, and e-money. Brief pieces on books and travel accompany feature stories. There is a heavy emphasis on presenting web sites, but also a commitment to reporting the demise of dot-com addresses. Charts, timelines, and comparisons support and enhance many articles. A recent feature, "Best Places to Live," challenges a *Business Week* contention that Chicago is losing its edge. *Money* should be in any library that serves investors (big and small) and in specialty libraries.

3505. ***Mother Jones: exposes & politics.*** [ISSN: 0362-8841] 1976. bi-m. USD 18 domestic; USD 28 foreign; USD 4.94 newsstand/cover per issue. Ed(s): Roger Cohn. Foundation for National Progress, 731 Market St, Ste 600, San Francisco, CA 94103. Illus., adv. Circ: 148000 Paid. Vol. ends: Dec. CD-ROM: ProQuest Information & Learning. Microform: NBI; PQC. Online: bigchalk; CompuServe Inc.; The Dialog Corporation; EBSCO Publishing; Florida Center for Library Automation; Gale Group; Northern Light Technology, Inc.; OCLC Online Computer Library Center, Inc.; ProQuest Information & Learning; H.W. Wilson. Reprint: PQC. *Indexed:* ASIP, AltPI, BRI, CBRI, CWI, EnvAb, FutSurv, GeoRef, MRD, MagInd, PAIS, RGPR, WSA. *Bk. rev.:* 3, 100-400 words. *Aud.:* Ga, Ac.

Mother Jones is one of the most uplifting reads on the market. Everything is somewhat irreverent but on target. Alternative Press has presented *Mother* with its Best Magazine of the Year Award. Celebrity authors like Molly Ivins and Pete Hamill are counted among the magazine's contributors, and Hamill did a great piece on Northern Ireland replete with funeral pictures. The "Media Jones" section encompasses film, books, music, and interviews. Laughs abound in comics and spoofs. Advertisers include Ben and Jerry, Green Century Funds, and Smithsonian Folkways. Any magazine that sports a picture with the caption "Mary Harris - Mother Jones (1830-1930) - orator, union organizer and hellraiser" should be found in all American libraries that want to present multiple viewpoints.

3506. ***National Geographic.*** [ISSN: 0027-9358] 1888. m. Membership, USD 34. Ed(s): William L Allen, Robert L Booth. National Geographic Society, 1145 17th St, N W, Washington, DC 20036; http://www.nationalgeographic.com/. Illus., index, adv. Circ: 9000000. Vol. ends: Jun/Dec. Microform: PMC; PQC. Online: America Online, Inc.; EBSCO Publishing; Florida Center for Library Automation; Gale Group; OCLC Online Computer Library Center, Inc.; ProQuest Information & Learning; H.W. Wilson. Reprint: PQC; WSH. *Indexed:* A&ATA, ABS&EES, AICP, AbAn, AnthLit, BEL&L, BiolAb, BiolDig, CBCARef, CPerI, DSR&OA, EnvAb, GardL, GeoRef, ICM, LRI, MagInd, RGPR, RI-1. *Aud.:* Ems, Hs, Ga, Ac.

National Geographic is almost an institution, and yet it simply continues to improve. The content and photos are spectacular, and some subjects are rarely covered elsewhere. Helpful timelines, maps, lineages, and a dimensional globe viewed from the side accompany articles. One recent issue covered Egyptian pharaohs, Harlem, African bushmen, and a profile of gypsies. What other magazine has such scope? Most libraries cannot afford not to subscribe to this magazine.

3507. ***New Internationalist.*** Formerly: *Internationalist.* [ISSN: 0305-9529] 1970. 11x/yr. Individuals, GBP 28.85. Ed(s): Katherine Ainger, Chris Richards. New Internationalist Publications Ltd., 55 Rectory Rd, Oxford, OX4 1BW, United Kingdom; mazine@indas.on.ca; http://www.newint.org/. Illus., index, adv. Sample. Circ: 75000. *Indexed:* AltPI, BrHumI, CBCARef, CPerI, CWI, PRA, RRTA, WAE&RSA. *Bk. rev.:* 2-3, 250-300 words. *Aud.:* Hs, Ga, Ac.

Everything including the ads (volunteer opportunities, global exchanges, coffee with a conscience) works together to support social justice. Each issue covers a theme, and much material is supplied by the United Nations. An excellent regular feature is "Worldbeaters," which "mostly meanders around the morals of the rich and famous." This worthy publication should be found in all libraries desiring to present unusual and possibly unpopular issues.

3508. ***The New Yorker.*** [ISSN: 0028-792X] 1925. w. USD 49.95 domestic; USD 87.95 Canada; USD 109.95 elsewhere. Ed(s): David Remnick. Conde Nast Publications Inc., 4 Times Square, 5th Fl, New York, NY 10036; http://www.newyorker.com; http://www.condenast.com. Illus., adv. Circ: 813434 Paid. Vol. ends: Dec. Microform: PQC. Online: Florida Center for Library Automation; Gale Group; LexisNexis; ProQuest Information & Learning. *Indexed:* ABS&EES, AgeL, BEL&L, BHA, BRD, BRI, CBRI, DSR&OA, FLI, GardL, GeoRef, IAPV, IDP, IIMP, IIPA, LRI, MLA-IB, MRD, MagInd, MusicInd, RGPR, RI-1, RILM. *Bk. rev.:* 0-9, 200-3,000 words. *Aud.:* Hs, Ga, Ac.

This magazine covers the largest city in the United States with all its depth and diversity. Lavish pictures and an impressive array of writers do both the city and the magazine proud. Even the advertisements are outstanding. The content of this publication is among the best anywhere. Ads for wonderful books, travel, jewelry, and even the American Civil Liberties Union can be found. Articles are brief as well as in-depth and are written by knowledgeable authors. For instance, one issue includes a profile of August Wilson by John Lahr. Other articles support New York City's current theater, art, movies, et al. Local issues (such as "After Welfare") are also covered to round out this fine publication. All New York libraries, medium-sized and larger public libraries, and other libraries that collect arts or related subjects should own *The New Yorker*.

Newsweek. See News and Opinion section.

3509. ***The Oxford American: the Southern magazine of good writing.*** [ISSN: 1074-4525] 1992. 8x/yr. USD 29.95. Ed(s): Marc Smirnoff. Oxford American, 303 President Clinton Ave., Little Rock, AR 72201; oamag@oxfordamerican.com; http://www.oxfordamericanmag.com. Illus., adv. Circ: 62500 Paid. *Indexed:* AmHI. *Bk. rev.:* 3-4 reviews, 250-300 words. *Aud.:* Hs, Ga, Ac.

OA is a very special publication. It is literate and impressive without being in the least stuffy. Whether or not the intent is to remind the rest of the country of the South's many contributions, that is partly what is accomplished. Here's a sampling of things *Oxford American*: The real Peggy Sue writes about Buddy Holly; country musician Marty Stuart presents a photo essay of clothing from Opryland; an article on Dr. Martin Luther King is supported by the text of an early sermon of his and a poem about his assassination; "Departures" notes the death of singer Jeff Buckley in essays written by ordinary people who were his friends. There are long and short book and music reviews, columns by Southern luminaries, and spirited letters to the editor. A must for most Southern, high school, mid- and large-sized public, and related academic libraries.

3510. ***Parabola: myth, tradition, and the search for meaning.*** [ISSN: 0362-1596] 1976. q. USD 24 domestic; USD 30 foreign; USD 7.50 newsstand/cover per issue. Ed(s): David Appelbaum. Society for the Study of Myth and Tradition, 656 Broadway, New York, NY 10012-2317; editors@parabola.org; http://www.parabola.org. Illus., index, adv. Sample. Circ: 41000 Paid. Vol. ends: Winter. Microform: PQC. Online: Gale Group; Northern Light Technology, Inc. *Indexed:* AmHI, ArtHuCI, BRI, CBRI, HumInd, LRI, MLA-IB, R&TA, RI-1, SSCI. *Bk. rev.:* 5-8, 600-1,200 words. *Aud.:* Hs, Ga, Ac.

For 25 years *Parabola* has been presenting "a wealth of timeless resources to inform, inspire and guide you on your inner journey." Each issue covers one topic from a range of perspectives, times, and places. Book excerpts, articles, and interviews contribute to subjects such as "Women, Death or Addiction." Letters to the editor invite readers to "share the riddles and mysteries you have encountered on the road to understanding." This wonderful invitation results in unique letters that run from one line to many paragraphs. *Parabola* should be part of specialty collections and large public and selected academic libraries.

People. See News and Opinion section.

3511. ***Popular Mechanics.*** [ISSN: 0032-4558] 1902. m. USD 21.97 domestic; USD 37.97 foreign; USD 2.95 newsstand/cover per issue. Ed(s): Joe Oldham. Hearst Corporation, Popular Mechanics, 810 Seventh Ave., New York, NY 10019; popularmechanics@hearst.com; http://www.popularmechanics.com. Illus., index, adv. Circ: 1586000 Paid. Vol. ends: Dec. CD-ROM: ProQuest Information & Learning. Microform: NBI; PQC. Online: EBSCO Publishing; Florida Center for Library Automation; Gale Group; Northern Light Technology, Inc.; OCLC Online Computer Library Center, Inc.; ProQuest Information & Learning. *Indexed:* A&ATA, BiogInd, CBCARef, CPerI, ConsI, GeoRef, ICM, IHTDI, MagInd, RGPR. *Aud.:* Hs, Ga.

The name of this magazine is somewhat misleading because *Popular Mechanics* also includes a fair amount of science and even science fiction. This very inclusive publication covers the outdoors, technology, home improvement, and automotive topics. Feature articles include impressive photographs and detailed sketches with specifications. There are excellent in-depth articles, such as one on airplanes of the future that will contain a mall, restaurant, showers, and beds; and on the U.S. Air Force's nuclear flying saucers (which may explain decades of sightings!). "How to" articles are complete with very specific and graphic directions and cover projects like building a five-string banjo or installing gutters. A splendid addition to all public, junior and senior high school, and other libraries serving a do-it-yourself clientele.

Popular Science. See Science and Technology section.

Rapport. See Music/Popular section.

3512. ***Reader's Digest.*** [ISSN: 0034-0375] 1922. m. USD 26.98 domestic; USD 38.95 foreign; USD 2.99 per issue. Ed(s): Jacqueline Leo, Kenneth Y Tomlinson. Reader's Digest Association, Inc, Reader's Digest Rd, Pleasantville, NY 10570-7000; http://www.rd.com. Illus., index, adv. Sample. Circ: 15000000. Vol. ends: Dec. Microform: PQC. Online: Gale Group. *Indexed:* CINAHL, CPerI, LRI, MagInd, RGPR, RI-1. *Aud.:* Ems, Ga, Hs.

Reader's Digest continues to be a wonderful little magazine that truly caters to every type of reader. Included are many anecdotes, jokes, and witticisms that the readers themselves contribute to the magazine (some even get paid). It publishes a wide range of excerpts from national magazines and newspapers on such topics as smoking, parents ruining kids' sports, and health. It also presents its own impressive articles, such as one naming the country's worst judges. On the whole, the magazine offers its readers a sense of hope, a concept often sadly lacking today. Along with this "old-fashioned" optimism, there are plenty of signs of technology, and web sites are highlighted throughout the magazine. All public libraries should own *Reader's Digest.*

3513. ***Red Pepper: raising the political temperature.*** [ISSN: 1353-7024] 1994. m. USD 60. Ed(s): Hillary Wainwright. Socialist Newspaper (Publications) Ltd., 1b Waterlow Rd, London, N19 5NJ, United Kingdom; redpepper@onlne.rednet.co.uk; http://www.redpepper.org.uk/. Illus., adv. *Indexed:* AltPI. *Aud.:* Hs, Ga, Ac.

This wonderful publication offers clear reporting, commentary, and analysis of international and U.K. politics, economics, ecology, consumer issues, culture, and society. It tackles the stories behind the headlines, for example, "vote nobody" as a display of voter disillusionment, an interview with a Soweto radical teacher/activist, and a world without Microsoft. Further examples include a book of the month by Noam Chomsky and a featured film, *Blackboards*, about Iranian teachers who have to seek pupils. The format is easy to read with small columns and color highlights. Pictures are simple and very effective. *RP* is also available as talking pages and electronically. The perfect choice for high school, medium-sized, and larger public libraries and all wishing to present diverse viewpoints.

Redbook. See Women section.

3514. ***Reunions Magazine.*** [ISSN: 1046-5235] 1990. bi-m. USD 24 domestic; USD 42 foreign. Ed(s): Edith Wagner. Reunions, PO Box 11727, Milwaukee, WI 53211-0727; reunions@execpc.com; http://www.reunionsmag.com. Illus., adv. Sample. Circ: 18000. *Aud.:* Ga.

This valuable magazine has no competitor but continues to do an outstanding job. In addition to magazine staff, contributors include many "ordinary" people who enjoy sharing their expertise. All sorts of reunions are covered: family, school, military, and social. Pictures are very effective and are also contributed by readers. A very large percentage of the publication consists of resources and classifieds. Reunion planners can find anything they want, as well as many things they didn't think about. *Reunions* also produces and sells a helpful "Workbook and Catalog" that simplifies the process further. Large public libraries should include this in their collections.

Rolling Stone. See Music/Popular section.

Russian Life. See CIS and Eastern Europe section.

3515. ***Saturday Evening Post.*** [ISSN: 0048-9239] 1971. bi-m. USD 14.97 domestic; USD 19.97 foreign; USD 2.95 newsstand/cover per issue. Ed(s): Ted Kreiter. Benjamin Franklin Literary and Medical Society, Inc., 1100 Waterway Blvd, PO Box 567, Indianapolis, IN 46206; drsutton@tcon.net; http://www.satevepost.org. Illus., adv. Sample. Circ: 400000. Vol. ends: Dec. Microform: NBI. Online: The Dialog Corporation; EBSCO Publishing; Florida Center for Library Automation; Gale Group; Northern Light Technology, Inc.; OCLC Online Computer Library Center, Inc.; ProQuest Information & Learning; H.W. Wilson. Reprint: PQC. *Indexed:* BRI, BiogInd, CBRI, CINAHL, GeoRef, MagInd, RGPR. *Aud.:* Ems, Ga, Hs.

This long-lived magazine looks just as it should! There are lots of articles on health, pictures are bright but old-fashioned looking, and recipes promote a healthy heart. There is a multitude of cartoons and many letters to the editor. Ads are amusing and are oriented to the elderly. Unique features include "Wordwatch," which traces word derivations or explains words that have ceased being used. The "Medical Mailbox" is a Q & A column presented by the editor himself. Most libraries should add *Saturday Evening Post* to round out their collections.

Scientific American. See Science and Technology section.

3516. ***Seed (Montreal): beneath the surface.*** [ISSN: 1499-0679] 2001. bi-m. USD 14.85; USD 4.95 newsstand/cover per issue; USD 5.95 newsstand/cover per issue Canada. Ed(s): Adam Bly. Seed Magazine, PO Box 4009, Montreal, PQ H2Z 2X3, Canada. Illus., adv. *Aud.:* Hs, Ga, Ac.

Seed is an unusual combination that mixes science with pop culture, celebrity, and current events. It has been called "*Scientific American* meets *Vanity Fair.*" It sports a Scene Calendar much like that of *The New Yorker.* In one issue, "Scene Nightlife" includes photos of dolled-up guests attending an American

Museum of Natural History event, while "Library" includes one long and eight short book reviews. In one long feature titled "Dear Mr. President," scientists share their views and offer brilliant advice on pressing international concerns. A true-crime piece about prostitutes murdered on a Canadian pig farm brings a strong dose of sobering everyday life. Another article discusses the demise of science fiction as it more closely approaches reality. This excellent publication, for more selective audiences, would be at home in large public and large academic libraries.

Self. See Women section.

Seventeen. See Teenagers section.

Skeptic. See Parapsychology section.

3517. *Smithsonian.* [ISSN: 0037-7333] 1970. m. USD 28 domestic; USD 41 foreign; USD 4 newsstand/cover per issue. Ed(s): Carey Winfrey. Smithsonian Magazine, 900 Jefferson Dr, S W, Washington, DC 20560-0406; http://www.smithsonianmag.si.edu. Illus., index, adv. Circ: 7142000. Microform: PQC. Online: EBSCO Publishing; Florida Center for Library Automation; Gale Group; OCLC Online Computer Library Center, Inc.; ProQuest Information & Learning; H.W. Wilson. *Indexed:* ABS&EES, AIAP, AbAn, AmH&L, AnthLit, ArtHuCI, BEL&L, BHA, BRD, BRI, BiolDig, CBCARef, CBRI, CPerI, DSR&OA, EngInd, EnvAb, GardL, GeoRef, IBZ, LRI, MagInd, RGPR, RI-1, SSCI. *Bk. rev.:* 4, 500 words. *Aud.:* Hs, Ga, Ac.

Picking up a *Smithsonian* magazine is much like taking a grand trip, at least to a museum if not around the world. This glorious publication is beautifully put together and well written by experts. Features are accompanied by outstanding pictures, whether they are illustrating art nouveau or Australian camels. Naturally, many articles supplement exhibits at the Smithsonian. However, current events (some with a historical viewpoint) are featured. International topics are also included, such as "Inside Bollywood," an interesting article about the Indian film industry. Marvelous advertisements (many Smithsonian-related) add to the timeless and international feel of the magazine. All libraries should have this unique and outstanding periodical.

3518. *Southern Living.* [ISSN: 0038-4305] 1965. m. USD 19.97 domestic; USD 34.97 foreign; USD 4.99 newsstand/cover. Ed(s): John Alex Floyd, Jr. Southern Progress Corp., 2100 Lakeshore Dr, Birmingham, AL 35209; southernliving@spc.com; http://southern-living.com/. Illus., adv. Sample. Circ: 2450000 Paid. Online: bigchalk; Gale Group; Northern Light Technology, Inc.; OCLC Online Computer Library Center, Inc.; ProQuest Information & Learning. Reprint: PQC. *Indexed:* BRI, CBRI, ConsI, GardL, MagInd, RGPR. *Aud.:* Hs, Ga.

This glorious magazine emphasizes Southern food and travel but also covers gardens, homes, books, Southerners, and the outdoors. Each subject is well covered with details, costs, sources, and even sketches. Every issue includes a monthly calendar of events. Excellent pictures accompany all articles. The ads and classified sections are wide ranging and very helpful. Details for online access to the magazine, television, and even telephone numbers are included in general information. A must for all Southern, medium-sized, and larger public libraries.

The Spectator. See News and Opinion section.

Sports Illustrated. See Sports/General section.

3519. *Success: for the innovative entrepreneur.* Formerly (until 1981): *Success Unlimited.* [ISSN: 0745-2489] 1895. 10x/yr. USD 19.97 domestic; USD 33.97 foreign; USD 3.95 newsstand/cover per issue domestic. Ed(s): Ripley Hotch. Success Holdings Company LLC, 150 Fayetteville St., Mall, Ste. 1110, Raleigh, NC 27601; letters@successmagazine.com; http://www.successmagazine.com. Illus., adv. Refereed. Circ: 275000 Paid. Vol. ends: Dec. Online: Florida Center for Library Automation; Gale Group; Northern Light Technology, Inc.; OCLC Online Computer Library Center, Inc. *Indexed:* ABIn, BPI, RGPR. *Bk. rev.:* 1, 500 words. *Aud.:* Ga, Sa.

An array of ideas is presented in "Trends," as well as sections such as marketing, legal, finance, and cyber success. Cover stories and feature articles include one on an Alaskan brewing company, top franchises, and a marketing guru who uniquely hypes Chinese New Year rather than the traditional Christmas season. The magazine is appealingly arranged, well divided, and rich in resources at the end of articles. Even the ads are convenient for those looking for seminars, the latest technology, and books. However, the magazine remains very white-male oriented. A good purchase for most libraries, but it should be supplemented to represent the rest of the population that also wants to attain "success."

3520. *Sunset: the magazine of Western living.* [ISSN: 0039-5404] 1898. m. USD 21 domestic; USD 4.50 newsstand/cover per issue domestic. Ed(s): Carol Hoffman. Sunset Publishing Corp., 80 Willow Rd, Menlo Park, CA 94025-3691; http://www.sunset.com. Illus., adv. Circ: 1425000 Paid. Vol. ends: Dec. Microform: PQC. Online: The Dialog Corporation; Gale Group; Northern Light Technology, Inc.; OCLC Online Computer Library Center, Inc.; ProQuest Information & Learning; H.W. Wilson. Reprint: PQC. *Indexed:* ConsI, GardL, IHTDI, MagInd, RGPR. *Aud.:* Ga, Sa.

Sunset is a beautiful magazine. The covers are so memorable, and readers may even buy a poster of century covers. Everything connected to Western living can be found from travel to recipes to gardening to remodeling. Each subject area is exhaustively covered, ads are very helpful and encompass Western-oriented travel, house plans, schools/camps, and a shopping directory. The perfect choice for most Western libraries and mid-sized to large public libraries.

3521. *T V Guide.* [ISSN: 0039-8543] 1953. w. USD 46.28; USD 1.99 newsstand/cover. Ed(s): Michael LaFavore. Gemstar - TV Guide International, 1211 Ave of the Americas, New York, NY 10036; http://www.tvguide.com. Illus., index, adv. Circ: 9900000 Paid. Online: Gale Group. *Indexed:* ASIP, LRI, MagInd, RGPR. *Aud.:* Ga.

No one can have an excuse for missing a TV program if they have "the guide" and a VCR! There are reviews and program lists for all interests. Subjects covered in articles run the gamut from Dale Evans to Janet Jackson to *The Sopranos.* Advertisements mostly feature food, food, food. We are promised more in-depth information on the web. Finally, most helpfully, there is a multi-page cable conversion chart and a guide for the premium channels. *TV Guide* should be at home in all libraries that support leisure collections.

Time. See News and Opinion section.

3522. *Tokion.* bi-m. JPY 48000 domestic; USD 25 United States; USD 40 Canada. Ed(s): Kaori Sakurai. Knee High Media, 1-23-3 Higashi Shibuya-ku, Tokyo, 150-0011, Japan; http://www.tokion.com/. *Aud.:* Hs, Ga, Ac, Sa.

At first glance *Tokion* appears to be just another lightweight, frothy confection. It is very heavy on advertisements and includes a large number of both excellent and quirky photographs. It also offers the usual regulars such as very short pieces on fashion, books, music, and photography. Then it really gets down to business with feature articles such as these: "Borderline," which defines what borders mean depending upon who and where you are; "City of God," which follows film director Fernando Meirelles as he shoots a movie in Brazil's slums ("tragic to watch and an inspiring achievement"); "Urban Caballero," which is a photo-essay about Mexican music in East Los Angeles. CD reviews cover unique subjects such as Trinidadian calypso in London, 1950-1956. *Tokion* offers a wide range of worthwhile goodies for discerning readers.

3523. *Town & Country.* Incorporates (1901-1992): *Connoisseur.* [ISSN: 0040-9952] 1846. m. USD 28 domestic; USD 56 foreign; USD 4 newsstand/cover per issue domestic. Ed(s): Pamela Fiori, Linda Nardi. Hearst Corporation, Town and Country, 1700 Broadway, New York, NY 10019; http://www.hearstcorp.com/. Illus., adv. Circ: 480000 Paid. Vol. ends: Dec. *Indexed:* AIAP, ASIP, ArtInd, BAS, BHA, BRI, DAAI, GeoRef, MagInd. *Aud.:* Ga.

This is the perfect magazine for dreaming. Where else would most of us find ads for Worth gowns, Harrod's, or intuitive counseling? Pictures illustrating articles and advertisements are gorgeous. Features such as "Connoisseur's World," "Town and Country Scene and Be Seen," or "Parties" can be frustratingly shallow. However, the "Personal Opinion" column restores faith when "What Is Luxury?" elicits answers like "unscheduled time" or "cozy with family and friends." A logical purchase for wealthy communities or large public libraries.

3524. ***Troika: wit, wisdom & wherewithal.*** [ISSN: 1083-2335] 1993. q. USD 20. Ed(s): Celia Meadow. Lone Tout Publications, PO Box 1006, Weston, CT 06883; etroika@aol.com; http://www.troikamagazine.com. Illus., adv. Circ: 120000 Paid. Vol. ends: Dec. *Aud.:* Ga.

Troika includes articles on music, religion, family life, and travel, for example, "Modern Life and Lent"; a piece showing the parallels between the *Wizard of Oz* and *Harry Potter* (including ALA intellectual freedom issues); a profile on tuberous sclerosis (with excellent resources ending the article); and "Voluntary Simplicity," suggesting ways to put such a change into action. Unusually, illustrators and authors have equal billing, and the illustrations are very distinctive. *Troika* belongs in mid-sized and large public libraries, high schools, and any collection that aims for special and unique offerings.

U.S. News & World Report. See News and Opinion section.

Us Weekly. See News and Opinion section.

3525. ***Vanity Fair.*** [ISSN: 0733-8899] 1983. m. USD 18 domestic; USD 38 Canada; USD 43 elsewhere. Ed(s): Graydon Carter. Conde Nast Publications Inc., 4 Times Square, 5th Fl, New York, NY 10036; http://www.condenast.com. Illus., adv. Circ: 1052290 Paid. Vol. ends: Dec. *Indexed:* ASIP, DAAI, MRD, MagInd, MusicInd, RGPR, RILM. *Aud.:* Ga.

There is always something titillating or at least interesting in *Vanity Fair*, if the reader can endure all the pages of ads before even reaching the table of contents. Covers and inside artwork are unfailingly wonderful and sometimes eye-popping. Subjects are covered in depth, including Hollywood types and celebrities, along with serious subjects like Holocaust-heroine Ruth Gruber, exposing the dubious sugar kings of Florida, and the sad truth about North Korea. Photographers are first-rate: Annie Leibovitz, Lord Snowdon, and Helmut Newton, among others. Writers include Maureen Orth, Dominick Dunne, the ever-angry Christopher Hitchens, and other luminaries. An excellent choice for high school, academic, and public libraries.

3526. ***The Village Voice.*** [ISSN: 0042-6180] 1955. w. Free in New York City. Ed(s): Donald H Forst, Doug Simmons. Village Voice Media, Inc., 36 Cooper Sq, New York, NY 10003. Illus., adv. Circ: 253000. Vol. ends: Dec. Microform: PQC. Online: Chadwyck-Healey Incorporated; Dow Jones Interactive; LexisNexis; Northern Light Technology, Inc.; OCLC Online Computer Library Center, Inc.; ProQuest Information & Learning. *Indexed:* ASIP, BRI, CBRI, FLI, IIMP, IIPA, MRD, MusicInd. *Bk. rev.:* 1-7, 500-4,000 words. *Aud.:* Ga, Ac.

The Village Voice is a big, sprawling weekly journal with a rather liberal bent that covers a surprisingly large number of subjects. In addition to its international coverage, a goodly number of local issues are discussed in the City/State section, giving the magazine a wide-ranging scope. There are long and short reviews for books, film, theater, etc. An interesting section called "Machine Age" reports on technology in its various guises. The content is excellent, and ads are inclusive and entertaining, for example, John Waters at a DVD signing, the amazing five-minute face-lift, and, in a piece on Larry Flint, "Doesn't the biggest hustler for free speech deserve the Hugh Hefner First Amendment Award?" An excellent read for people with open minds.

3527. ***The Week: all you need to know about everything that matters.*** [ISSN: 1533-8304] 2001. w. USD 38.94 domestic; USD 39 Canada; USD 127.50 elsewhere. Ed(s): William Falk. Dennis Publishing, Inc., 1040 Ave of the Americas, 23rd Fl, New York, NY 10018; adsales@theweekmagazine.com. Adv. Circ: 100000 Paid and controlled. *Aud.:* Hs, Ga, Ac.

This wonderful new publication includes news, comment, entertainment, sports, travel, and financial news from more than 100 national and international newspapers. These sources and their URLs are listed. Each page is packed with information. Pictures are minimal, but excellent maps (World at a Glance) and charts supplement articles. Pleasant, nonsensical, and controversial topics are covered. Both sides of an issue are included, e.g., a piece on global warming ends with "should we worry about global warming?" The format is very readable with colorful and appealing columns. This extremely worthwhile magazine should be found in junior high school and most other libraries whether public, academic, or specialized.

3528. ***Weight Watchers Magazine.*** [ISSN: 0043-2180] 1968. bi-m. USD 13.95 domestic; USD 20.95 Canada; USD 23.95 elsewhere. Ed(s): Nancy Galiardi. Weight Watchers Publishing Group, 747 3rd Ave., New York, NY 10017-2803; http://www.weightwatchers.com/. Illus., index, adv. Circ: 1060000 Paid. Vol. ends: Dec. Microform: PQC; NRP. Online: Gale Group. *Indexed:* MagInd. *Bk. rev.:* Notes. *Aud.:* Hs, Ga, Ac.

Weight Watchers is back and seems even better after a short interruption in publication. The advertisements make low-calorie foods look quite appealing. All aspects of healthy living are covered: mind and body, food and cooking, beauty and fashion, and fitness. A multitude of success stories with before-and-after pictures help struggling dieters. Sarah Ferguson ("Fergie") is to be found in ads and contributing short articles. The most prominent feature is "Winning Points," Weight Watchers' new approach to tailoring a personal diet that fits one's needs and tastes. An excellent magazine for all public, middle school, and high school libraries and any collection covering health and physical education.

3529. ***The Wilson Quarterly: surveying the world of ideas.*** [ISSN: 0363-3276] 1976. q. Membership, USD 24; USD 6 newsstand/cover per issue domestic. Ed(s): Steven Lagerfeld. Woodrow Wilson International Center for Scholars, 1 Woodrow Wilson Plaza, 1300 Pennsylvania Ave, N W, Washington, DC 20004-3027. Illus., index, adv. Sample. Circ: 60000. Vol. ends: Nov. Microform: PQC. Online: bigchalk; EBSCO Publishing; Florida Center for Library Automation; Gale Group; Northern Light Technology, Inc.; OCLC Online Computer Library Center, Inc.; ProQuest Information & Learning; H.W. Wilson. *Indexed:* ABS&EES, AmH&L, AmHI, BRI, CBRI, GeoRef, HumInd, LRI, PAIS, RGPR, RI-1, SSI. *Bk. rev.:* 11-16, 1,500 words. *Aud.:* Ga, Ac.

This impressive publication includes a calendar of events for the Woodrow Wilson Center for Scholars and ads for fellowships it offers. Each article packs lots of information into mid-sized pieces. Authors are outstanding in their fields. Also, helpfully, authors' current and upcoming works are described. The magazine's stated purpose is to present essays in the spirit of public debate rather than to further an opinion. For example, in its 25th anniversary edition, experts shared how the world views America. Africa, France, the Middle East, China, Mexico, and Russia were the areas covered. Other sections include "Periodical Observer," which reviews mostly American publications, and "Research Reports," which discusses new research at public agencies and private institutions. "Current Books" profiles new releases. *WQ* should find a home in all scholarly collections and in large public libraries.

Wired. See Internet-World Wide Web section.

3530. ***Workbench: woodworking to improve your home.*** [ISSN: 0043-8057] 1954. bi-m. USD 22 domestic; USD 4.99 newsstand/cover per issue. Ed(s): Tim Robertson. August Home Publishing Co., 2200 Grand Ave, Des Moines, IA 50312-5306; workbench@workbenchmag.com; http://www.augusthome.com. Illus., adv. Circ: 375000 Paid. *Indexed:* ConsI, IHTDI, MagInd, RGPR. *Bk. rev.:* 1-3, 200-400 words. *Aud.:* Hs, Ga.

This nifty magazine is brimming not only with great suggestions and question-and-answer columns but puns aplenty, such as "Cutting to the Core of Plywood" and "First Class Mail" (an article on making your own mailbox). Pictures either illustrate products or clearly guide the reader on a project. There is also a multitude of charts that outline the differences between similar items. The magazine's web site is promoted, and many items are found in both places. Particularly helpful are the features that do in-depth comparisons of items such as tool kits or miter saws. The pros and cons of items, including prices, are discussed before you need to set foot in a store. *Workbench* would be at home in public or high school libraries and in browsing or leisure collections.

3531. ***The World & I: the magazine for lifelong learners.*** [ISSN: 0887-9346] 1986. m. USD 45 for print & online eds.; USD 69 Canada for print & online eds.; USD 117 elsewhere for print & online eds. Ed(s): Michael Marshall. News World Communications, Inc., 2800 New York Ave., N.E., Washington, DC 20002; online@worldandi.com. Illus., index, adv. Sample. Circ: 15000 Paid and free. Vol. ends: Dec. *Indexed:* ABS&EES, AgeL, BRI, CBRI, EnvAb, PAIS. *Bk. rev.:* 10-12 essay length, signed. *Aud.:* Hs, Ga, Ac.

This excellent publication is probably an ideal choice if you were permitted just one magazine for a long airplane trip. The broad subject areas include Current Issues, Arts, Life, Natural Science, Culture, Book World, and Modern Thought. Authors are experts in their subjects but write in a style understandable to most readers. The following represent a sampling of topics from a recent issue: A profile of Nobel laureate Harold Varmos, who discovered cancer-causing genes, illustrates that he is also a lover of literature and the fine arts. "Is PBS a Necessity or Anachronistic?" presents an excellent argument representing both sides of the question and allows readers to draw their own conclusions. The book review section is outstanding; it includes an excerpt, a commentary, and about six inclusive reviews on a wide range of subjects. There is also a Writers and Writing section that profiles authors of any period or nationality. The issue concludes with Currents in Modern Thought, discussing "The Retreat of Recess," an essay on the necessity of breaks for workers and students of all ages. *The World and I* should comfortably fit into nearly all library settings.

3532. ***World Press Review: news and views from around the world.*** Former titles (until 1980): *Atlas World Press Review;* (until 1972): *Atlas.* [ISSN: 0195-8895] 1961. m. USD 26.97 domestic; USD 34.97 Canada; USD 46.97 foreign. Ed(s): Alice Chasan. Stanley Foundation (New York), 700 Broadway 3rd Fl, New York, NY 10003-9536. Illus., adv. Sample. Circ: 51000 Paid. Vol. ends: Dec. Reprint: PQC. *Indexed:* BAS, CPerI, HumInd, MagInd, PAIS, PRA, RGPR, SSI. *Bk. rev.:* 1-2, 1,000 words. *Aud.:* Hs, Ga, Ac.

Opening a copy of *World Press Review* is like finding a trove of current information from a multitude of perspectives; the reader can choose which view to accept. Each issue features an international viewpoint on a cover topic; for example, an article on Putin contains clips from liberal, centrist, conservative, and official media throughout Europe. There are sections on the arts, science and technology, the world in cartoons, and regional reports by continent. Splendid pictures enliven each story. A World Literature Edition includes reports on a Tel Aviv scholar, a camel mobile library in Kenya, and a floating library in Thailand. This is a wonderful source for readers who desire more than a view of the status quo.

Yankee. See City, State, and Regional section.

Tabloids

These titles may serve a greater purpose than they have in the past as the economy tanks and war surrounds us. More than ever we all need to escape into the world of glitter, celebrities, and sometimes even fantasy! The selection remains constant with the six "basic" titles. However, it seems a growing number of magazines are competing with tabloid journalism having similar offerings in titles such as *In Touch* (see General subsection).

3533. ***Globe (Boca Raton).*** Former titles: *Midnight Globe; Midnight.* [ISSN: 1094-6047] 1954. w. USD 49.96 United States; USD 69.96 Canada; USD 89.96 elsewhere. Ed(s): Brian Williams. American Media, Inc., 5401 NW Broken Sound Blvd, Boca Raton, FL 33487. Illus., adv. Sample. Circ: 800000 Paid. Vol. ends: Dec. *Aud.:* Ga.

Sensational pictures probably take up as much space as does text. Regular features include "Hollywood Gossip," which is loaded with celebrity photos. Ads are tempting: Techno Scout allows the lucky buyer to tone his muscles while lying on the couch. Books are not overlooked. For example, a recent issue contained sensational excerpts from biographies of Natalie Wood and Howard Hughes. A fun addition to casual or leisure collections.

3534. ***National Enquirer.*** [ISSN: 1056-3482] 1952. w. USD 56.96 domestic; USD 76.96 Canada; USD 96.96 newsstand/cover per issue elsewhere. Ed(s): Steve Coz. American Media, Inc., 5401 NW Broken Sound Blvd, Boca Raton, FL 33487. Illus., adv. Sample. Circ: 2300000. Vol. ends: Dec. *Aud.:* Ga.

The *Enquirer* continues to promote its recent, more legitimate status due to helping solve Bill Cosby's son's murder and assisting with the success of O.J. Simpson's civil case. Whether you take some, all, or none of the *Enquirer* seriously, it is a barometer of our changing society. It reports, for example, that more people recognize one of the "stars" of the television show "Survivor" than recognize Vice President Cheney. There is also a helpful section called "Video Head" that includes video reviews and announcements of upcoming releases. Most public libraries should own at least one tabloid, and this is it.

3535. ***National Examiner.*** [ISSN: 1094-6055] w. USD 39.95; USD 1.39 newsstand/cover per issue. Ed(s): Ray Zillowck. American Media, Inc., 5401 NW Broken Sound Blvd, Boca Raton, FL 33487. Illus., adv. Circ: 420000 Paid. Vol. ends: Dec. *Aud.:* Ga.

The *Examiner* emphasizes bizarre stories both national and international. In addition to sensationalistic text, unflattering photographs are used to illustrate stories about the rich and infamous. There is an emphasis on psychics. This tabloid is best left in the convenience store rather than on your library's shelf.

3536. ***Star (Boca Raton): nobody knows the stars like the Star.*** Formerly: *National Star.* [ISSN: 1052-875X] 1974. w. USD 56.96 domestic; USD 76.96 Canada; USD 96.96 elsewhere. Ed(s): Tony Frost. American Media, Inc., 5401 NW Broken Sound Blvd, Boca Raton, FL 33487. Illus., adv. Sample. Circ: 1752557 Paid. Vol. ends: Dec. *Bk. rev.:* 3, 20-40 words. *Aud.:* Ga.

The *Star* probably is in second place (after the *National Enquirer*) as a "reputable" tabloid. This idea seems to be furthered by an offer to potential subscribers—you can subscribe to both and save 57 percent! The magazine's content is entertaining. For example, there is a piece on a surprisingly humble Anne Robinson, who admits she was her marriage's "weakest link." There are many plays on words in each issue, such as "this is Gladys' fourth wedding knight." It is gratifying to see that the rich and famous look as ridiculous as the rest of us when using cell phones in public! An excellent addition to large or leisure library collections.

3537. ***Sun (Montreal).*** 1983. w. CND 29.95. Ed(s): John Vader. Globe International, Inc., 1350 Sherbrooke St. W., Ste 600, Montreal, PQ H3G 2T4, Canada. Illus. *Aud.:* Ga.

The *Sun* gives readers the opportunity to be an editor from home by rating levels of interest for the following: Edgar Cayce, Nostradamus, Our Lady of Lourdes (or Fatima), predictions, horoscopes, UFOs, and medical breakthroughs. This list almost completely sums up the tabloid's contents. Articles frequently mention universities and doctors to create a dubious authenticity. Sensational pictures and vocabulary enhance the stories. The *Sun* needn't take up library space or money. Patrons can buy or read it at the grocery or convenience store.

3538. ***Weekly World News.*** [ISSN: 0199-574X] 1979. w. USD 39.96 domestic; USD 59.96 Canada; USD 79.96 elsewhere. Ed(s): Derek Colntz, Leskie Pinson. American Media, Inc., 5401 NW Broken Sound Blvd, Boca Raton, FL 33487. Illus., adv. Sample. Circ: 385000. *Aud.:* Ga.

Prominently next to this tabloid's name, "more than 130 exciting stories and features inside" are promoted. In addition to this strong selling point, the cover photo is usually irresistibly sensational. The subjects covered are decidedly over the top, and there are two regular gossip columnists, as well as "Serena Salbak, America's Sexiest Psychic." Let your patrons buy their own copy or take a quick look at the grocery store check-out counter.

■ GENERAL EDITORIAL-INTERNET

See also General Editorial section.

Chris F. Neuhaus, Library Instruction Coordinator, University of Northern Iowa, Cedar Falls, IA 50613-3675; chris.neuhaus@uni.edu; FAX: 319-273-2913

Ellen E. Neuhaus, Reference Librarian, University of Northern Iowa, Cedar Falls, IA 50613-3675; ellen.neuhaus@uni.edu; FAX: 319-273-2913

Introduction

The litmus test for general editorial Internet magazines remains the willingness of the publisher to place the majority of its magazine on the web. However, unless access to the e-zine is restricted, the magazine will then be free to the subscriber and nonsubscriber alike. Without revenue from subscriptions, publishers must rely on advertising alone to support their endeavors. As a result, many web versions of general editorial magazines have evolved into sites rife with advertising, but containing very little of the material found in the print edition. While many of these general editorial electronic magazines offer a wide array of eye-catching pages, most prove to be insubstantial on closer inspection. The bursting of the dot-com bubble delivered a severe financial shock to publishers of Internet-hosted magazines. Under mounting economic pressures, many online general editorial magazines placed pay-per-view restrictions on much or all of their content. Unable to attract enough advertising revenue or convince readers to pay for online content, other well-loved electronic magazines either found larger corporate sponsors or simply ceased publication.

The following somewhat diminutive set of general editorial web magazines was created with three criteria in mind: popularity, substantial full-text, and free accessibility. The general editorial web magazines selected for this section were primarily those with popular print equivalents (based on circulation figures for the print editions). The majority of magazines in this section also contain a substantial offering of full text. All of the electronic magazines here are free. Thus, the following titles can serve as a core for building inexpensive general editorial Internet magazine collections.

Basic Periodicals

Select as needed for particular audience.

Atlantic Unbound. See Internet-World Wide Web/Electronic Journals section.

3539. *Business 2.0 Online.* Ed(s): Ned Desmond. Time Inc., Fortune Group, 1 California St., San Francisco, CA 94111; http://www.business2.com. *Aud.:* Hs, Ga, Ac.

Business 2.0 is not just a business magazine; it is a general-interest magazine about business in, on, and around the Internet. The electronic-magazine version of *Business 2.0* practices what it preaches and employs web technology to full advantage. There is plenty of full text creatively displayed and tastefully arranged. The most recent e-zine issue contains a number of full-text articles in html format laced with links to relevant web sites. All past editions of this magazine are archived and feature the full content of the print edition. Extras provided by *Business 2.0* on the web include the "Web Guide" to business links on the Internet, a calendar of upcoming business conferences, and a host of newsletters and columns such as "Future Boy," "Gizmos Weekly," and "Talent Monger." *Business 2.0* should interest anyone planning to do business in a high-technology environment. It should be included in all general editorial Internet magazine collections.

3540. *BusinessWeek Online.* McGraw-Hill Companies, Inc., 1221 Ave of the Americas, New York, NY 10020. *Aud.:* Hs, Ga, Ac.

This multifaceted electronic magazine offers more components than are found in the print version of *Business Week.* Many of the *BusinessWeek Online* features can be accessed free, although there are some functions that require a payment before access. *BusinessWeek Online* offers free access to the table of contents of the most recent issue of all editions of *Business Week*, including international editions. The actual articles and related charts, photos, tables, and sidebars in the latest issue are available only to paid *BusinessWeek Online* subscribers. However, selected stories and their related items are made available to nonpaying users. The news articles, arrayed under the headings "Daily Briefing," "Investing," "Global Business," "Technology," "Small Business," "B-Schools," and "Careers," can also be viewed without charge. This online resource provides an extensive archive containing more than 40,000 *Business Week* articles dating back to 1991. The archive offers search and browse functions. The archive—although somewhat hidden from view—is accessed via the *BW Magazine* option and then through the *Search and Browse* option towards the bottom left-hand portion of the page. Articles found within the archives are arranged chronologically, but they can also be found using the search and browse functions. Some of the stories located in the archive can be read at no charge. Other articles require the user to be a paid subscriber. Still others require the viewer to pay an access fee for the article in question before full access is permitted. The "B-Schools" section offers MBA program profiles and rankings, recommended online readings, and useful utilities for calculating cost-of-living and salary information. Investment information—including information concerning the stock market, mutual funds, investment research tools, economy, and banking—can be found in the "*Business Week* Investment" section. *BusinessWeek Online* also provides a "Tools & Scoreboards" section that features numerous utilities such as "Personal Finance Calculators" and "Benefit Benchmarks." Additional resources offered include the sections "Global Business," "Small Business," and "Technology." There is an extensive array of free online video and audio business pieces under the "Video Views." A remarkable reference tool and electronic magazine, *BusinessWeek Online* is an important resource for all Internet collections.

3541. *Car and Driver.com.* Hachette Filipacchi Media U.S., Inc., 1633 Broadway, 41st Fl, New York, NY 10019. *Aud.:* Hs, Ga.

Car and Driver.com is the monthly web near-equivalent of the print *Car and Driver*, with daily news updates. It offers news, previews of new car models, auto show announcements, and reviews under the headings "C/D Content," "Car News," "Driver's Center," and "Auto Shows." Vehicular editorials are to be found in the "Columns" section. The "Buyer's Guide" allows the viewer to access both a "New Cars" guide and a "Used Cars" guide as well as online utilities such as "Reviews/Rod Tests," "User's Road Tests," and "Get a Free Quote." Both guides provide information based on make, model, vehicle type, price range, and—in the case of the "Used Cars" guide— year back to 1991. A "Special Section" features text, video clips, and audio clips of the ten best cars and five best trucks of the year. Finally a "Community" section offers articles on "Classic Cars" and provides for viewer feedback via "Chat" and "Forums." An extensive "Automotive Glossary" helps clarify everything from beam axles and bevel gears to valve trains and viscous couplings. Very high-tech and graphics-intensive, *Car and Driver.com* should be included in all library Internet collections.

3542. *CNN/Money.* Time, Inc, Time & Life Bldg, Rockefeller Center, 1271 Ave of the Americas, New York, NY 10020-1393; cnnmoney@money.com; http://www.money.cnn.com. *Aud.:* Ga, Ac.

As more people take financial planning into their own hands, information resources such as *Money* magazine and *CNN/Money* on the web are likely to gain in popularity. *CNN/Money*, formerly *Money.com*, offers only a fraction of the articles found in the print *Money* magazine. It is the many other financial-advice tools and features that will attract viewers to this web site. *CNN/Money* provides a wealth of market data associated with the Dow Jones, the NASDAQ, the S&P 500, and international markets. Articles and essays on investment located under "Money 101" are a counterbalance to the statistical offerings. *CNN/Money* provides market-related news briefs from *CNNfn* under its "Services" category. Additional multifaceted resources provide news and advice under "Markets & Stocks," "Company News," "Economy," "World Biz," "Technology," "Personal Finance," "Mutual Funds," and "Commentary." For libraries that regularly receive questions dealing with personal finance, *CNN/Money* should be among the featured electronic resources of a well-maintained virtual library.

3543. *The Economist.* Economist Newspaper Ltd, 25 St James's St, London, SW1A 1HG, United Kingdom; letters@economist.com; http://www.economist.com. *Bk. rev.:* 1, 800-1200 words. *Aud.:* Ga, Ac.

The traditionally independent and straightforward reporting of *The Economist* is now also to be found at http://economist.com. Although the free version of this online magazine features only a fraction of the current and archived articles found in the print edition, an individual subscription to *Economist.com* provides all the articles featured in the print version since 1997 for a cost of $69 per year or $19.95 per month (and both single and multiple articles can be purchased via a pay-per-view option). News, opinion, reviews, and financial information are succinctly arrayed in such categories as "The Global Agenda," "Opinion," "Markets & Data," and "Science & Technology." Special features include a "Cities Guide" to major international cities, an extensive "Country Briefings" information center, a guide for international business people called "Global Executive," and "Backgrounders," a geographically and thematically arranged current-conditions encyclopedia that provides ready background information on countries and issues. The "Research Tools" section offers access to surveys, a style guide, and a business encyclopedia. "From the Web" provides ready access to late-breaking news as reported on newswires such as CNN and the BBC. *Economist.com* is an essential online magazine for all Internet library collections.

3544. *EW.com.* Ed(s): Mark Bautz, Michael Small. Entertainment Weekly Inc., Time-Life Building, Rockefeller Plaza, New York, NY 10020. *Bk. rev.:* Occasional, 100-200 words. *Aud.:* Hs, Ga.

EW.com, also known as *Entertainment Weekly Online*, provides its full content only to AOL members and subscribers of *Entertainment Weekly* in print. However, as a media-review website *EW.com* provides movie reviews, ratings, and biographical snippets of some of Hollywood's well-known denizens. It offers a search engine for movie, music, book, and video reviews back to 1990, and also features daily news updates. Information is arranged under the categories "Movies," "Video & DVD," "TV," "Music," "Books," and "Pop Culture," with regularly updated pieces covering the many branches of the entertainment industry. Other offerings such as "Today's Highlights," "Photo Gallery," and "Commentary" provide visual coverage of celebrities. Online opinion polls and message boards are also featured. Though *Entertainment Weekly Online* can only fully be enjoyed via subscription— *EW.com* can still prove useful for those looking for advice on that new movie, or perhaps a scoop on the latest Hollywood scuttlebutt.

3545. *Forbes.com.* Ed(s): Paul Maidment. Forbes, Inc., 28 W 23rd St, 11th fl, New York, NY 10010; letters@forbes.net; http://www.forbes.com. *Aud.:* Hs, Ga, Ac.

Forbes.com is an exceptional resource offering much more than just the online version of *Forbes* magazine. The user has access to articles from the current issue of *Forbes* along with associated charts, tables, and sidebars. In addition, there is an archive that includes the full texts of articles going back to 1997. The user also has access to the resources "Forbes Global," "Forbes.com Best of the Web," and "Forbes FYI," all to be found under the heading "Magazines." The web site features a number of categories from which the user can select, including "Business," "Columnists," "Technology," "Markets," "Work," "Personal Finance," and "Lifestyle." Each category supplies a multitude of articles, financial utilities, online slide shows and videos. "Lists" provides charts and statistics on companies, the financial worth of the rich and famous, and best and worst cities, city guides and other geographical/demographical ratings. "Inside *Forbes.com*" features "Premium Tools" for monitoring the market, "Investment Newsletters," "Polls and Discussions," "Special Reports," the statistical-chronological and very graphical reporting option "Watchlist," and online videos and commentaries via the "Audio and Video" section. A "Tools" category offers a variety of items, including various calculators, calendars, and surveys. In addition, *Forbes.com* contains a number of information centers for mortgages, careers, small businesses, and mutual funds. This outstanding site should serve as an essential ingredient in an electronic-magazine collection.

3546. *Fortune.com.* Time Inc., Business Information Group, 1271 Ave of the Americas, New York, NY 10020; letters@fortune.com; http://www.fortune.com. Adv. *Aud.:* Ga, Ac.

Fortune.com offers a panoply of articles, news, advice, investment tools, market reports, and ready access to corporate information. This electronic magazine offers the full texts of some of the articles to be found in the print edition of *Fortune*. Articles are arranged under categories such as "Investing," "Careers," and "Technology." A modest "Archives" section allows for access to selected articles from the past two years. Sections such as "Company Profiles," "Fortune 500," and "Global 500" provide financial reviews of business-world movers and shakers, and an abundance of charts, graphs, tables, and statistics is included. *Fortune.com* provides rich, multilayered interaction with the world of business information, and it should be found in any well-organized electronic-magazine collections.

3547. *GolfDigest.com.* Ed(s): John Barker. The Golf Digest Companies, 20 Westport Rd, Wilton, CT 06897. *Aud.:* Hs, Ga.

GolfDigest.com provides articles focusing on top golfers, equipment, and improving your game, in addition to reviews of the classic golf courses of the world. It offers a number of articles from the print magazine *Golf Digest*. The "Daily Digest" provides daily editorials such as "This Week in Golf," "Tour Insider," "Equipment Extra," and "Course Critic." The companion online magazines *Golf for Women* and *Golf World* are also found at this site, providing still more feature articles, statistics, and upcoming golfing events under the headings "Features," "Departments," "The Bunker," "Tour Talk," "Columns," "Equipment," and "Golf World Business Weekly." *Golf World* online articles going back to January 2001 are easily accessed, and access to archived articles back to 1999 can be found in the 2001 issues. *Golf for Women* offers archives back to 2002. The popularity of this sport and the high quality of this resource make *GolfDigest.com* and the associated magazines *Golf for Women* and *Golf World* a must for all general electronic-magazine collections.

3548. *MotherJones.com.* Foundation for National Progress, 731 Market St, Ste 600, San Francisco, CA 94103; backtalk@motherjones.com; http://www.motherjones.com. *Aud.:* Hs, Ga, Ac.

MotherJones.com is the full-text web version of the print bimonthly *Mother Jones*, and it offers most of the content found there. This electronic magazine provides a politically liberal counterpoint to other, more conservative media outlets. *Mother Jones* and *MotherJones.com* are published by the Foundation for National Progress, "a nonprofit activist organization dedicated to advancing progressive causes through the media." *MotherJones.com* offers substantially more full-text articles and significantly more hyperlinks per article than most other electronic news magazines. Portions of the bimonthly print version appear logically under "In the Current Issue." Large quantities of muck are raked in the sections "Commentary" and "News." "Humor" features satire in various multimedia formats, and "Arts" presents reviews of recent books, films, and music. A sophisticated search engine with a browsing option offers access to an archive of articles back to 1993. Any library wishing to provide balance to their electronic-magazine collection should consider *MotherJones.com*.

3549. *The Nation.* The Nation Company, L.P., 33 Irving Pl, 8th Fl, New York, NY 10003; info@thenation.com; http://www.thenation.com. *Bk. rev.:* 2-4, 2,000-3,500 words. *Aud.:* Hs, Ga, Ac.

The web version of this journal, the oldest weekly magazine in the United States, offers roughly two-thirds of the articles, columns, and editorials in the print version of *The Nation*. It provides a liberal viewpoint on politics and policy. In the words of publisher Victor Navasky, *The Nation* is "a dissenting, independent, trouble-making, idea-launching journal of critical opinion." Articles and editorials generally offer additional links to related information and additional works by the author. Many of the reviews of books, films, music, and other art forms appearing in *The Nation* are also presented here in electronic form. Chronologically arranged archives allow the reader to browse electronic issues back to 1999, while a keyword search engine provides direct connections to specific topics mentioned in disparate articles, columns, or editorials. Libraries may purchase a complete (1865-present) digital archive of *The Nation*. A special feature of the web version of this magazine includes a link to the weekly news radio show *RadioNation*. The online version of *The Nation*, a longtime standard-bearer for liberal ideals, is an essential addition to all electronic-magazine collections.

3550. *National Geographic Online.* 1996. Ed(s): M. Ford Cochran. National Geographic Society, 1145 17th St, N W, Washington, DC 20036; http://www.nationalgeographic.com/. Adv. *Aud.:* Hs, Ga.

National Geographic Magazine Online, while not matching the content of the revered print edition, nevertheless merits serious consideration. Although most articles provide only a summary and offer only a few of the many photographs accompanying articles in the print edition, some feature very sophisticated and often interactive graphics, audio clips, and video clips not found in the print version. Also, links to a wealth of other related web resources and forums make *National Geographic Magazine Online* a fine complement to the print edition. Perhaps the best point of entry to this magazine is from the archives page (http://www.nationalgeographic.com/ngm/archives.html), where all the monthly electronic offerings back to 1996 are arrayed. The *National Geographic* publications index (http://www.nationalgeographic.com/publications/explore.html) is an indispensable guide to all *National Geographic* articles in print. The National Geographic Society home page (http://www.nationalgeographic.com) provides additional features, such as a *National Geographic* television guide, access to the child-oriented *National Geographic World Online*, and links to the online versions of the magazines *National Geographic Traveler* and *National Geographic Adventure*. A host of other educational offerings provided by the society can also be accessed here. Although *National Geographic Magazine Online* is no substitute for the print edition, this electronic version and the substantial National Geographic Society web site will likely attract many visitors.

3551. *National Review.* National Review, Inc., 215 Lexington Ave, New York, NY 10016; nronline@nationalreview.com; http://www.nationalreview.com/. *Bk. rev.:* 1, 500-1,500 words. *Aud.:* Hs, Ga, Ac.

National Review online, a.k.a. *NRO*, provides a constantly updated conservative counterpoint to many of the other newsmagazines in this section. This web version of *National Review* includes only a small fraction of the articles found in print. Electronic news briefs or columns provide the bulk of the available text. "Washington Bulletin" offers a short week-in-review of political intrigue and blunders. "The Goldberg File" provides no-holds-barred commentary from Jonah Goldberg that focuses on society and politics. "NRO Weekend" presents commentary on American culture as well as reviews of books, art, poetry, history, and television. Additional features include "NRO Financial" and "NRO Culture Watch." *NRO* also provides a forum for a host of columnists ranging from William F. Buckley, Jr. and John Derbyshire to Kate O'Beirne and Byron York. This online magazine, although offering fewer full-text articles, could nevertheless serve as an ideological counterpoint to electronic magazines such as *MotherJones.com* and *The Nation*.

3552. *New Internationalist Online.* New Internationalist Publications Ltd., 55 Rectory Rd, Oxford, OX4 1BW, United Kingdom; http://www.newint.org/. *Bk. rev.:* 8, 200-400 words. *Aud.:* Hs, Ga, Ac.

The *New Internationalist* reports on issues of world poverty, oppression, inequality, injustice, and international trends. This online version provides ample access to free full-text articles arranged either by issue or by topic via "NI Themes." An extensive archive dating back to 1983 can be accessed through "NI Back Issues," browsed by topic via the "Topic Index" or the even-more-extensive "Mega Index," or explored via "Search this Website." Featured in "Mixed Media—Reviews" is a large collection of book, film, and music reviews. "Country Profiles" provides a brief synopsis of recent history for nearly every country, with accompanying statistics and ratings for income distribution, self-reliance, the position of women, literacy, freedom, and life expectancy. "NI Action" offers summaries and links to hundreds of thematically arranged action groups. Audio clips are provided for "Editor's Letters," "Interviews," and "NI Press Releases." *New Internationalist Online* is a vast and extensive web site that provides a counterpoint to online publications from the mainstream.

3553. *The New Republic Online.* New Republic, 1331 H St NW, Ste 700, Washington, DC 20005-4737; tnr@aol.com; http://www.thenewrepublic.com. *Bk. rev.:* 2-3, essay length. *Aud.:* Hs, Ga, Ac.

The web edition of *The New Republic* provides very readable, nonpartisan articles corresponding to those in the print edition. It offers access to approximately one-third of the highly articulate articles written for the print version. Offerings in each online edition focus on national and international events, foreign policy concerns, and societal and cultural issues. "Politics," a regular column, dwells upon the nature and recurring themes of politics, with occasional forays into social concerns, ethics, business and finance, and other topics. This electronic journal also offers reviews of film, theater, and literature under the heading "Books & the Arts." "This Week in Print" provides a table of contents and a brief description of the articles found only in the print edition, while the "View Other Issues" option provides similar access for issues from the past three months. Although much is missing from the web version of *The New Republic* that can only be found in the print edition, what remains is high-quality reading. It belongs in every virtual library.

3554. *PopSci.com.* Time4 Media, Inc., 2 Park Ave, New York, NY 10016; http://www.popsci.com. *Aud.:* Hs, Ga.

When is science popular? When it's *Popular Science. PopSci.com* continues, via the web, the 125-year tradition of bringing scientific discoveries and facts to the layperson. *PopSci.com* provides applied and pure science information from the full spectrum of science. The categories "Science," "Internet," "Medicine & Biotechnology," "Computers," "Consumer Electronics," "Aviation & Space," "Home Tech," and "Auto" offer updates of varying length on new gadgetry and scientific events. Other features include forums, a newsletter, and a "PopSci Shop." Although *PopSci.com* includes a mere fraction of the articles found in the print edition of *Popular Science*, plentiful daily scientific news updates make this online magazine a useful science information resource for the general public.

3555. *Popular Mechanics PMZone.* Hearst Corporation, Popular Mechanics, 810 Seventh Ave., New York, NY 10019; popularmechanics@hearst.com; http://www.popularmechanics.com. *Aud.:* Hs, Ga.

The web version of *Popular Mechanics, Popular Mechanics PMZone* features dozens of articles focusing on science, cars and trucks, home improvement, and technology. A daily feature, "Today's News," provides brief news releases that are updated every 20 minutes. Regular features include "Automotive," "Technology," "Home," "Science," and "Outdoors." These features offer limited access to archival material. The *PMZone* "Automotive" section provides links to "Popular Mechanics New Cars & Trucks" and "Popular Mechanics Used Cars & Trucks," which are buyer's guides to hundreds of makes and models. They include detailed descriptions, pricing, and a car cost calculator. A "Popular Mechanics Electronic Buyer's Guide" includes information on electronic products, components, and accessories. The "Home" section covers everything from gardening and consumer tips to advice on tools and the workshop, and it also features the monthly "Homeowners Clinic." The "Science" section focuses heavily on the physical sciences and provides access to old *Popular Mechanics* articles, dating back to 1900, through the "PM Time Machine." The "Technology" section focuses on computers, telecommunications, and a variety of electronic media. Although additional information can be found in the print edition of the magazine, *Popular Mechanics PMZone* is a must-read for the mechanically inclined, and it should be included in most electronic-magazine collections.

3556. *rd.com.* Reader's Digest Association, Inc, Reader's Digest Rd, Pleasantville, NY 10570-7000; http://www.rd.com. *Aud.:* Ga.

The online *Reader's Digest*, or *rd.com*, offers the visitor a small sampling of the articles found in the traditional print publication. Articles often feature links to a number of web sites featuring related information. Where applicable, the links also lead to varied, sometimes opposing viewpoints on a particular issue. Under the section "Community Talk," the reader may participate in e-mail discussions on many topics. Offerings are arranged under the headings "Health," "Money," "Family," "Home," "Inspiration," and "Fun." Modest archives are located under each heading and can be browsed by topic. Past articles can also be found by using a keyword search feature. "Tools & Quizzes" provides calculators and online utilities for determining and planning for your physical, emotional, and financial health. Although *rd.com* does not include the full complement of articles and features found in the traditional print magazine, this web edition provides enough full-length stories and other electronic features to win many adherents.

3557. *Salon.* 1995. d. Mon.-Fri. USD 30. Ed(s): David Talbot. Salon Media Group, 22 4th St. 16th Fl, San Francisco, CA 94103; salon@salon.com; http://www.salon.com. Adv. Circ: 41500. *Bk. rev.:* 2-7, 500-2,000 words. *Aud.:* Hs, Ga, Ac.

A sophisticated and diverse electronic magazine, *Salon.com* offers an abundance of news, views, and reviews. Roughly two dozen daily offerings—articles, cartoons, and columns—transport the reader to both the surreal and the all-too-real. *Salon.com* features national and international events, cultural and social musings, insights into business and technology, reflections on human behavior and political misbehavior, tales of travel and health, reviews of entertainment and sports, regular reflections on literature and the arts, and a good dose of satire and humor. Items are located under various headings such as "News & Politics," "Tech & Business," "Arts & Entertainment," and the more visceral "Life," "Sex," and "Opinion." Entire collections of related articles are packaged together and provide comprehensive coverage of various issues under "Hot Topics." As if this multifaceted journalistic approach weren't enough, *Salon.com* also hosts a series of online discussion groups and provides a number of free daily and weekly e-mail newsletters. A sophisticated search engine allows the web wanderer to quickly locate specific items of interest. A chronologically arranged archive allows readers to browse by date, issue, or subject back to 1995. Although a number of the archived and current articles are free, additional articles are available only with a "premium content" subscription. One of the finest publications on the web, this outstanding resource is a must for all electronic-magazine collections.

3558. *SI.com.* Time Inc., Sports Illustrated Group, Sports Illustrated Bldg, 135 W 50th St, 4th Fl., New York, NY 10020-1393; http://sportsillustrated.cnn.com/si_online/. *Aud.:* Ga.

SI.com, the web version of *Sports Illustrated* and a product of CNN, provides daily news updates for a universe of professional and amateur sports. Articles varying in length from 300 to 1,200 words offer numerous hyperlinks to additional stories. Each article is followed by hyperlink options to related articles. Coverage includes baseball, pro and college football, pro and college basketball, hockey, tennis, golf, soccer, and motor sports. The options "More Sports," "U.S. Sports," and "World Sport" lead to coverage of additional sporting events and stories. *SI.com* also offers plenty of editorials, scores from recent sporting events, draft and recruiting proceedings, and schedules of upcoming events. Statistics and tables abound throughout, with links to polls, schedules, conference and team archives, and a multitude of specific stats for each league, team, and many players. An archive allows browsing of *SI.com* back to 1998. Most video and audio clips are no longer free but can be accessed with a subscription. Many additional links allow browsers to access online games, shopping, chat rooms, bulletin boards, schedules for televised sporting events, and photo galleries. *SI Adventure* (http://sportsillustrated.cnn.com/siadventure) provides in-depth coverage of outdoor sports including winter and extreme sports, fishing, hunting, and boating. *Sports Illustrated for Kids* (http://www.sikids.com) is tailored for a grade school audience. *SI.com* is a tremendous electronic magazine for locating recent facts and figures from the world of sports.

3559. *Slate.* [ISSN: 1091-2339] 1996. d. USD 19.95. Ed(s): Michael Kinsley. Microsoft Corporation, One Microsoft Way, Redmond, WA 98052-6399; slate@msn.com; http://www.slate.com/. Illus., adv. *Indexed:* ABS&EES. *Aud.:* Hs, Ga, Ac.

Slate is an online newsmagazine covering entertainment and culture, business and finance, politics and policy, satire, and national news. News and commentary are dispensed in many forms: essays, reviews (art, book, journal, movie, music, theater, television), dispatches, and cartoons, all organized under the categories "News & Politics," "Arts & Life," "Business," "Sports," "Technology," and "Travel & Food." A rich blend of daily offerings and editorials can be found under headings such as "Culturebox," "Chatterbox," "Moneybox," "Sports Nut," "Dialogue," "Frame Game," "Cartoon Index," and "Today's Papers." This oft-mentioned publication offers a number of special features, such as "The Fray," an online reader forum, "eBooks," a collection of electronic books, and "Handheld Devices," which includes instructions on how to download *Slate* to a Pocket PC or Palm. The *Slate* archive—containing material dating back to 1996—may be searched by keyword, topic, department, author, or publication date. The "Output Options" section provides advice on printing *Slate*, converting *Slate* to various electronic formats, creating content alerts, and on creating a personalized version of *Slate*—"Build Your Own Slate." A rich and sophisticated periodical, *Slate* should grace the virtual bookshelves of all libraries.

3560. *Smithsonian Magazine Web.* Smithsonian Magazine, 900 Jefferson Dr, S W, Washington, DC 20560-0406; email@simag.si.edu; http://www.smithsonianmag.si.edu. *Bk. rev.:* 1, 400-600 words. *Aud.:* Hs, Ga.

Smithsonian Magazine offers a potpourri of articles covering everything from archaeology and geography to scientific discoveries, history, and tourism. This online magazine includes the full texts of feature articles from the current print issue. Each provides a link to an "Additional Sources" page that includes links to web sites related to the topic at hand. *Smithsonian Magazine* offers the full texts of various columns from the current issue, including "Letters," "Additional Sources," and "Highlights Calendar." A search function allows the user to identify past articles on specific topics using a keyword or a search feature called "Issues by Date." The reader can access a list of articles that were published from 1995 to the present. While articles in the past few issues are available full-text at this site, older articles must be purchased. In addition, there is an "Image Gallery" feature that includes the online portfolios of contributing photographers and illustrators. There is also a feature called "Journeys," where *Smithsonian* writers and photographers explore fascinating corners of the world to help you design your own adventure!

3561. *Time.com.* Time, Inc, Time & Life Bldg, Rockefeller Center, 1271 Ave of the Americas, New York, NY 10020-1393; http://www.time.com/time/. *Aud.:* Hs, Ga, Ac.

Time.com provides a blend of lengthy weekly and daily articles that cover national and international news. While many current articles are free, others are available only with a "premium archive article" subscription. Although *Time.com* does not provide the full text of *Time*, there is much additional information that warrants its inclusion in any electronic-magazine collection. Articles are arrayed under the headings "Nation," "World," "Business & Tech," "Entertainment," "Science & Health," and "Special Reports." The "Photos" section offers access to a vast photo-essay library, and the "Columnists" section provides links to the work of at least half a dozen *Time* columnists. The "Current Issue" section features a few articles from the print edition of *Time*. There is an archive of article titles and abstracts back to 1985. The well-crafted *Time.com* should be a regular feature on all web magazine stands.

3562. *T V Guide.* Gemstar - TV Guide International, 1211 Ave of the Americas, New York, NY 10036; http://www.tvguide.com. *Aud.:* Hs, Ga.

TV Guide Online, like its counterpart in print, offers program schedules for major television broadcasters and cable and satellite providers throughout the United States and several other North and South American countries. To view the offerings for a particular region and delivery system (broadcast, cable, satellite), one selects "TV Listings" and enters the appropriate ZIP code. Viewers are then treated to an interactive menu that includes brief summaries of scheduled programs. As with the print *TV Guide*, readers can peruse a brief synopsis of sitcom, soap, and movie programming or catch up on the latest Hollywood gossip. There are a multitude of links to movie reviews, cast and credit listings, and news (both text and audio). A sophisticated search engine allows for keyword searching of the upcoming week's TV programming, or one can search by category. The "Movie Guide" offers a search engine that can be set to either film title or person's name (e.g., actor, actress, director). With articles, audio interviews, box office statistics, video reviews, photo galleries, online shopping, previews, crossword puzzles, and horoscopes, *TV Guide Online* provides the viewer with a near carnival-like information-gathering experience. It is an integral resource for any general electronic-magazine collection.

3563. *U S News.com.* 1933. U S News & World Report Inc., 1050 Thomas Jefferson St, NW, Washington, DC 20007; letters@usnews.com; http://www.usnews.com. *Aud.:* Hs, Ga, Ac.

U S News.com provides an online version of *U.S. News & World Report* and more via categories: "Money & Business," "Education," "Health," "News Briefings," "Opinion," "Photography," "Technology," "Washington Whispers," and "Work & Career." "Money & Business" includes both national and international business news, business statistics, and market summaries. "Education" features articles and a wealth of online utilities useful for rounding up financial aid, comparing colleges and graduate schools, and entering the job market. "Health" offers the latest medical news via "Pulse" and provides essays focusing on children's health, women's health, men's health, health after 50, heart disease, and wellness. "Opinion" provides editorials from Jodie Allen,

Michael Barone, Gloria Borger, Lou Dobbs, David Gergen, John Leo, and Mortimer Zuckerman. "Photography" offers a series of photo-essays on a wide range of topics. "Technology" provides a tour of new technology including new games, new inventions in the world of audio, advances in robotics, and the latest in home computing. "Washington Whispers" provides regular coverage of inside-the-beltway happenings. "Work & Career" includes articles, advice, and statistics concerning finding a new job and surviving or retiring from a current career. *USNews.com* provides free access to issues from the past two years and hosts a fee-based archive back to 1992. A robust and wide-ranging electronic magazine, *USNews.com* is an important online news source for any electronic library.

■ GEOGRAPHY

See also Population Studies section.

Fred Burchsted, Reference Librarian, Research Services Dept., Widener Library, Harvard University, Cambridge, MA 02138; burchst@fas.harvard.edu

Introduction

Geography is the study of spatial patterns on the surface of the earth. Geography is traditionally divided into physical geography, concerned especially with the origin of landscapes, and human geography, dealing with human settlement patterns and the influence of people upon place and of place upon people. Geography has recently come to overlap broadly with environmental studies. It has also increasingly come to be seen less as a subject than as a spatial perspective on other fields. Geography has traditionally been closely associated with geology and with economics, but recently there has been a surge of interest in the spatial aspects of many other fields, including archaeology, ethics, political science, and literature, as well as population, urban, women's, cultural, and environmental studies.

Geography's traditional applied division, cartography, has been joined by new technologies, including geographical information systems (GIS), global positioning systems (GPS), remote sensing, and other systems. These new geographic technologies have wide applications both in science and in many practical monitoring and management uses. GIS, in which spatial data are digitized and then analyzed and displayed by computer techniques, has many and diverse applications in scientific research, environmental monitoring and management, urban and regional planning, marketing, and other fields. All these changes in geography are reflected in its periodical literature.

A comprehensive list of journals, print and electronic, may be found at Geosource: Web Resources for Human Geography, Physical Geography, Planning, Geoscience and Environmental Science (www.library.uu.nl/geosource/).

The following is a selection of the most important general interest, scholarly/research, and trade periodicals in geography.

Basic Periodicals

Hs: *Geographical, National Geographic;* Ga: *Explorers Journal, Geographical, National Geographic;* Ac: *Association of American Geographers. Annals, Cartography and Geographic Information Science, Geographical Review, Institute of British Geographers. Transactions, The Professional Geographer.*

Basic Abstracts and Indexes

Geographical Abstracts.

3564. ***Antipode: a radical journal of geography.*** [ISSN: 0066-4812] 1969. 5x/yr. USD 533 print & online eds. Ed(s): Jane Wills, Jamie Peck. Blackwell Publishing Ltd., 9600 Garsington Rd, PO Box 805, Oxford, OX4 2DQ, United Kingdom; jnlinfo@blackwellpublishers.co.uk; http://www.blackwellpublishers.co.uk/. Illus., index, adv. Sample. Refereed. Circ: 1050. Vol. ends: Oct. Online: EBSCO Publishing; ingenta.com; OCLC Online Computer Library Center, Inc.; RoweCom Information Quest; Swets Blackwell. *Indexed:* AltPI, AmH&L, ArtHuCI, IBSS, M&GPA, PRA, PSA, RI-1, SSCI, SWRA, SociolAb, WAE&RSA. *Bk. rev.:* 3-6, 1,200-2,400 words, signed. *Aud.:* Ac.

Antipode publishes articles from a variety of radical ideological positions, offering dissenting perspectives on environmentalism, feminism, postcolonialism, postmodernism, race, urbanism, war, and other topics. Frequently, issues are devoted to special topics. This journal is devoted to fostering social and political change through activist scholarship and free discussion. The editorship is U.S./U.K. with an international editorial board. Authorship is U.S./U.K. with some international. This journal is important for academic libraries that support geography and political science departments.

3565. ***Applied Geography.*** [ISSN: 0143-6228] 1981. q. EUR 521 (Individuals, EUR 154). Ed(s): Robert Rogerson. Pergamon, The Boulevard, Langford Ln, East Park, Kidlington, OX5 1GB, United Kingdom. Illus., index. Sample. Refereed. Vol. ends: Oct. Microform: PQC. Online: ingenta.com; ScienceDirect; Swets Blackwell. *Indexed:* EnvAb, FPA, ForAb, GeoRef, GeogAbPG, HortAb, RRTA, S&F, SSCI, SUSA, SWRA, WAE&RSA. *Bk. rev.:* 6-8, 400-700 words, signed. *Aud.:* Ac, Sa.

Applied Geography applies geographical thought and methods to human problems that have a spatial component by fostering an understanding of the underlying systems, human or physical. Coverage includes resource management, environmental problems, agriculture, and urban and regional planning. The target audience is planners and policymakers as well as academics. The editorship is U.K. with a U.K./U.S./international editorial board. Authorship is international with a U.K. emphasis. Important for libraries that support academic geography departments or agencies concerned with policy and planning.

3566. ***Arab World Geographer.*** [ISSN: 1480-6800] 1998. q. USD 134 (Individuals, USD 48). Ed(s): Ghazi Falah. Centre for Urban and Community Studies, Department of Geography and Planning, Butchtel College of Arts and Sciences, Akron, OH 44325-5005. Refereed. *Bk. rev.:* 1-2, 400-800 words, signed. *Aud.:* Ac, Sa.

Arab World Geographer publishes articles on geographical research, both theoretical and applied, on all aspects, cultural and physical, of the human environment in the Arab countries. There is an emphasis on application of research to policy and on the publication of work by Arab geographers. The editorship is Canadian and American with an international editorial board. Authorship is international. Important for academic libraries that support geography departments or area studies programs with Middle Eastern interests.

3567. ***Arctic, Antarctic, and Alpine Research.*** Formerly: *Arctic and Alpine Research.* [ISSN: 1523-0430] 1969. q. USD 140 (Individuals, USD 85; Students, USD 60). Ed(s): Ms. Connie Oehring, Dr. Mark W Williams. University of Colorado, Institute of Arctic and Alpine Research, UCB 450, Boulder, CO 80309-0450; http://instaar.colorado.edu/. Illus., index, adv. Sample. Refereed. Circ: 800. Vol. ends: Nov. Microform: PQC. Online: BioOne. *Indexed:* AbAn, Agr, ApEcolAb, BiolAb, ChemAb, DSR&OA, EnvAb, FPA, ForAb, GeoRef, GeogAbPG, HortAb, M&GPA, PollutAb, RRTA, S&F, SCI, SWRA, WAE&RSA, ZooRec. *Aud.:* Ac.

Arctic, Antarctic, and Alpine Research publishes research of interdisciplinary interest on all aspects, human and physical, of alpine, Arctic, and Antarctic as well as subalpine, subarctic, and subantarctic environments, past and present. It includes research papers, short communications, comments on papers, and book reviews. Special topically focused issues are occasionally published. The journal is edited at the University of Colorado with an international editorial board. About half the articles are by American authors. Important for libraries that support geography, biology, and geology departments with cold climate interests.

3568. ***Area.*** [ISSN: 0004-0894] 1969. q. USD 190 print & online eds. Ed(s): Mike Bradshaw. Blackwell Publishing Ltd., 9600 Garsington Rd, PO Box 805, Oxford, OX4 2DQ, United Kingdom. Illus. Refereed. Circ: 2500. Vol. ends: Dec. *Indexed:* AIAP, ArtHuCI, BAS, BrArAb, CJA, GeoRef, GeogAbPG, IBSS, IBZ, NumL, RRTA, SSCI, SWA, WAE&RSA. *Bk. rev.:* 6-20, 1,000-2,000 words, signed. *Aud.:* Ac.

Area is a scholarly journal that features short research and discussion articles on topics of current professional interest and expressions of opinion by geographers on public questions. Groups of several articles that focus on special subjects are often published. The "Observations" section features short reviews and opinion pieces on subjects of current debate. This journal aims at a free discussion of geographical ideas, results, and methodology. Authorship and editorship are British. Important for libraries that support a geography department.

3569. *Association of American Geographers. Annals.* [ISSN: 0004-5608] 1911. q. USD 614 print & online eds. Ed(s): Basil Gomez, Roger E Kasperson. Blackwell Publishing, Inc., Commerce Place, 350 Main St, Malden, MA 02148; subscrip@blackwellpub.com; http://www.blackwellpublishing.com. Illus., index, adv. Sample. Refereed. Circ: 9000 Paid. Vol. ends: Dec. Microform: PQC. Online: EBSCO Publishing; Gale Group; ingenta.com; JSTOR (Web-based Journal Archive); OCLC Online Computer Library Center, Inc.; RoweCom Information Quest; Swets Blackwell. *Indexed:* ABS&EES, AbAn, AmH&L, BAS, BRI, BiolAb, CBRI, CJA, DSR&OA, GeoRef, GeogAbPG, IBSS, IBZ, IPSA, LRI, M&GPA, PRA, PollutAb, RI-1, RRTA, S&F, SSCI, SSI, SUSA, SWRA, WAE&RSA. *Bk. rev.:* 10-20, 750-2,000 words, signed. *Aud.:* Ac.

The *Annals* is often considered the leading American research journal in geography. Covering all areas of geography worldwide, it offers research articles, commentaries on published articles, book review forums, and occasional review articles and map supplements. Editorship/authorship is largely American with some international editors and contributors. Important for all academic and for large public libraries.

3570. *Australian Geographer.* [ISSN: 0004-9182] 1928. 3x/yr. GBP 161 (Individuals, GBP 83). Ed(s): Graeme Aplin. Carfax Publishing Ltd., 4 Park Sq, Milton Park, Abingdon, OX14 4RN, United Kingdom; enquiry@tandf.co.uk; http://www.tandf.co.uk/. Illus., index, adv. Sample. Refereed. Circ: 1200. Vol. ends: Nov. Online: bigchalk; EBSCO Publishing; Ingenta Select; OCLC Online Computer Library Center, Inc.; ProQuest Information & Learning; RMIT Publishing; RoweCom Information Quest; Swets Blackwell. Reprint: PSC. *Indexed:* BAS, BiolAb, DSA, FPA, ForAb, GeoRef, GeogAbPG, HortAb, IBSS, IBZ, PAIS, PollutAb, RRTA, S&F, SSCI, SWRA, WAE&RSA. *Bk. rev.:* 5-7, 600-900 words, signed. *Aud.:* Ac.

Published under the auspices of the Geographical Society of New South Wales, *Australian Geographer* offers research articles on human and physical geography, focusing on environmental studies. There is a strong Australian concentration with some articles on the broader Asia-Pacific region (and more coverage of the Asia-Pacific region is planned). Occasional collections of short papers on focused topics are published. Editorship/authorship is largely Australian. Important for academic libraries that support geography departments, and environmental or area studies programs with Australasian interests.

3571. *Base Line.* [ISSN: 0272-8532] 1980. 6x/yr. Non-members, USD 15. Ed(s): Mark Thomas. American Library Association, 50 E Huron St, Chicago, IL 60611-2795; http://www.ala.org. Adv. Circ: 500. *Bk. rev.:* 1-6, 500-1,500 words, signed. *Aud.:* Ac, Sa.

Published by the American Library Association's Map and Geography Round Table (MAGERT), this newsletter offers articles of interest to map librarians and often of wide cartographic interest. There is extensive news of events, publications, and web sites. Important for academic libraries that support a geography department or map collection.

3572. *Cartographic Perspectives.* Former titles (until 1989): *Cartographic Information; Map Gap.* [ISSN: 1048-9053] 1981. 3x/yr. USD 72 (Individuals, USD 42; Students, USD 20). Ed(s): Scott Freundschuh. North American Cartographic Information Society, PO Box 399, Milwaukee, WI 53201; sfreunds@d.umn.edu. Refereed. Circ: 400 Paid. *Indexed:* GeoRef. *Bk. rev.:* 5-8, 500-750 words, signed. *Aud.:* Ac, Sa.

Cartographic Perspectives addresses a wide audience, including map publishers and designers, map curators, academics, and amateurs. It contains authoritative articles and papers that deal with all aspects of cartography and related topics. The journal also includes cartographic news and reviews of recent books and software. Important for academic libraries that support a geography department or map collection and for special libraries that support cartographic work.

3573. *Cartography and Geographic Information Science.* Former titles (until Jan. 1999): *Cartography and Geographic Information Systems;* (until 1990): *American Cartographer.* [ISSN: 1523-0406] 1974. q. Non-members, USD 110. Ed(s): Ilse Alipui. American Congress on Surveying and Mapping, 6 Montgomery Village Ave., Ste 403, Gaithersburg, MD 20879; infoacsm@acsm.net; http://www.acsm.net. Illus., adv. Sample. Refereed. Circ: 3500. Vol. ends: Oct. *Indexed:* ABS&EES, GeoRef, GeogAbPG, SSCI. *Bk. rev.:* 3-5, 400-600 words, signed. *Aud.:* Ac, Sa.

Published by the American Congress on Surveying and Mapping in collaboration with the Cartography and Geographic Information Society, *Cartography and Geographic Information Science* publishes research papers, technical notes, software reviews, and lists of current literature on traditional cartography, GIS, and other digital mapping technologies. The emphasis is on extending cartographic methodology. There are frequent special issues. Editors are largely American, as are the authors, with a significant representation of foreign authors. Important for any library, academic, public, or special, that supports work in any of the numerous applications of GIS and related technologies.

3574. *Cultural Geographies: a journal of cultural geographies.* Formerly (until 2001): *Ecumene.* [ISSN: 1474-4740] 1994. q. GBP 207 (Individuals, GBP 54; Members, GBP 49 American Sociological Association). Ed(s): Phil Crang. Arnold Publishers, 338 Euston Rd, London, NW1 3BH, United Kingdom; http://www.arnoldpublishers.com/journals/. Illus., index, adv. Sample. Refereed. Circ: 900. Vol. ends: Oct. Online: EBSCO Publishing; OCLC Online Computer Library Center, Inc.; RoweCom Information Quest; Swets Blackwell. *Indexed:* BrHumI, GeogAbPG, IBZ, PSA, SSCI, SociolAb. *Bk. rev.:* 4-8, 700-1,300 words, signed. *Aud.:* Ac.

Drawing on contributors from a wide range of disciplines, *Cultural Geographies* explores thought on the perception, representation, and interpretation of the earth and on "the cultural appropriation of nature, landscape, and environment." Interest in these themes comes from a variety of artistic, humanistic, environmental, and geographical communities. The editorship is U.S./U.K. with international editorial/advisory boards. Authorship is international, with the U.S./Canada/U.K. most heavily represented. Important for libraries that support geography departments and environmental and cultural studies programs.

3575. *Current Geographical Publications.* [ISSN: 0011-3514] 1938. m. USD 70. Ed(s): Christopher Baruth, Susan M. Peschel. University of Wisconsin at Milwaukee Library, Current Geographical Publications, PO Box 399, Milwaukee, WI 53201; http://leardo.lib.uwm.edu/. Illus., adv. Circ: 1200. Vol. ends: Dec. Microform: PQC. Reprint: PQC. *Indexed:* GeoRef. *Aud.:* Ac, Sa.

Current Geographical Publications lists the publications, including books, periodical articles, pamphlets, maps and atlases, and government documents received by the American Geographical Society Collection at the University of Wisconsin-Milwaukee. Publications are arranged by subject under four general headings: Topical, Regional, Maps, and Selected Books and Monographs. It is a very comprehensive list. Since it has not been cumulated since 1976, this periodical is more useful for current-awareness browsing than as a periodical index. Issues since April 2002 are available free on the publication's web site. Important for any academic library that supports a geography department or area studies program.

Earth Interactions. See Atmospheric Sciences/Electronic Journals section.

3576. *Earth Observation Magazine: the magazine for geographic mapping, earth information.* [ISSN: 1076-3430] 1992. m. USD 52; USD 107 foreign. Ed(s): Roland Mangold. Professional Surveyors Publishing Co., Inc., 100 Tuscanney Dr, Ste B-1, Frederick, MD 21702. Illus. Sample. Circ: 30000. Vol. ends: Dec. *Indexed:* GeoRef, GeogAbPG. *Bk. rev.:* Occasional, 150-450 words, signed. *Aud.:* Sa.

EOM is a trade journal aimed at professionals in the fields of GIS, aerial photography, remote sensing, mapping, orthophotography, photogrammetry, and related fields. It aims to keep practitioners in these fields abreast of current projects, applications, and technical developments. There are articles that review current technical and business trends, and new projects and systems, together with editorials, new product information, vendor directories, and the like. Important for any library, academic, public, or special, that supports work in any of the numerous applications of GIS, remote sensing, and related technologies.

Earth Surface Processes and Landforms. See Earth Sciences section.

3577. *Economic Geography.* [ISSN: 0013-0095] 1925. q. USD 73. Ed(s): David Angel. Clark University, 950 Main St, Worcester, MA 01610; econgeography@clarku.edu; http://www.clarku.edu/. Illus., index, adv. Refereed. Circ: 1700. Vol. ends: Oct. Microform: PMC; PQC. Online: bigchalk; East View Publications, Inc.; Florida Center for Library Automation; Gale Group; JSTOR (Web-based Journal Archive); Northern Light Technology, Inc.; OCLC Online Computer Library Center, Inc.; ProQuest Information & Learning. *Indexed:* ABS&EES, AgeL, AmH&L, BAS, BRI, BiolAb, CBRI, DSA, GeogAbPG, IBSS, IBZ, IPSA, JEL, PAIS, PSA, RRTA, SSCI, SSI, SWA, WAE&RSA. *Bk. rev.:* 7-10, 800-1,800 words, signed. *Aud.:* Ac.

Economic Geography publishes theoretical articles and empirical papers that make a contribution to theory. Topics include land use, agriculture, and urban and regional development, with an emphasis on recent approaches that involve gender and environmental issues, and industrial change. The editors wish to make *EG* a focus for debate on the current diversity of theories in economic geography. The editorship/authorship is largely U.S./U.K./Commonwealth. Important for libraries that support academic geography and economics departments or urban and regional planning programs.

3578. *Ethics, Place and Environment.* [ISSN: 1366-879X] 1998. 3x/yr. GBP 176 (Individuals, GBP 63). Ed(s): Tim Unwin. Carfax Publishing Ltd., 4 Park Sq, Milton Park, Abingdon, OX14 4RN, United Kingdom; enquiry@tandf.co.uk; http://www.tandf.co.uk/. Illus., index, adv. Sample. Refereed. Vol. ends: Oct. Online: EBSCO Publishing; Ingenta Select; RoweCom Information Quest; Swets Blackwell. Reprint: PSC. *Indexed:* IBZ, SociolAb. *Bk. rev.:* 4-8, 600-2,000 words, signed. *Aud.:* Ac.

Here is a scholarly journal of geographical and environmental ethics that is concerned with human behavior in social/cultural as well as physical/biological environments. Emphases are on ethical problems of geographical and environmental research, ethical implications of environmental legislation, and business ethics from a geographical/environmental perspective. Both research and review articles are published together with sets of short communications on special topics, including debates, conference reports, commentaries on published papers, opinions, and book reviews. The editorial board and authorship is largely U.S./U.K./Commonwealth, with some broader international representation. Important for academic libraries that support geography or philosophy departments and for any library that supports an environmental studies program.

Eurasian Geography and Economics. See CIS and Eastern Europe section.

3579. *Explorers Journal.* [ISSN: 0014-5025] 1921. q. USD 24.95. Ed(s): Angela Schuster. Explorers Club, 46 E 70th St, New York, NY 10021; http://www.explorers.org/. Illus., index, adv. Refereed. Circ: 3500. Vol. ends: Dec. Microform: PQC. Reprint: PQC. *Indexed:* BiolAb, GeoRef, ZooRec. *Bk. rev.:* 5-7, 100-400 words, signed. *Aud.:* Hs, Ga, Ac.

The Explorers Club, a learned society devoted to the advancement of exploration, promotes all areas of field research by publishing in its journal scholarly articles of high literary and aesthetic quality that communicate the excitement of exploration and field research. Articles are accessible to nonspecialist readers and feature high-quality color illustrations. Also included are brief notes on new discoveries and news of exploration and explorers. Useful for public libraries and for libraries that support institutions that undertake overseas field research.

3580. *Gender, Place and Culture: a journal of feminist geography.* [ISSN: 0966-369X] 1994. q. GBP 275 (Individuals, GBP 86). Ed(s): Lynn A Staeheli, Gill Valentine. Carfax Publishing Ltd., 4 Park Sq, Milton Park, Abingdon, OX14 4RN, United Kingdom; enquiry@tandf.co.uk; http://www.tandf.co.uk/. Illus., index, adv. Sample. Refereed. Vol. ends: Dec. Online: EBSCO Publishing; Ingenta Select; OCLC Online Computer Library Center, Inc.; ProQuest Information & Learning; RoweCom Information Quest; Swets Blackwell. Reprint: PSC. *Indexed:* AltPI, BrHumI, CWI, FemPer, IBSS, IBZ, SWA, SociolAb. *Bk. rev.:* 8-12, 900-1,500 words, signed. *Aud.:* Ac.

Gender, Place and Culture provides a forum for research and debate concerning the connections of geography and gender issues. Topics include spatial aspects of gender relations; oppression structures; gender construction and politics; and relations between gender and ethnicity, age, class, and other social categories, and so on. Articles are theoretical or empirical but with implications for theory. The journal emphasizes the relevance of its subject area for feminism and women's studies. The "Viewpoints" feature offers commentaries on published papers, debates, and other short items. Editorship/authorship is largely U.S./U.K./Commonwealth. Important for academic libraries that support geography departments or programs in women's or cultural studies.

3581. *Geo World.* Formerly (until 1998): *G I S World;* Which incorporated (1997-1997): *GeoDirectory. Vol. 1 Products and Services;* Which superseded in part (1989-1997): *G I S World Sourcebook;* Which was formerly (until 1995): *International G I S Sourcebook;* (until 1992): *G I S Sourcebook.* [ISSN: 1528-6274] 1988. m. USD 72 domestic; USD 90 Canada; USD 108 elsewhere. Ed(s): John R Hughes. Adams Business Media, 2101 S Arlington Heights Rd, Ste 150, Arlington Heights, IL 60005-4142; cwilliams@mail.aip.com; http://www.geoplace.com. Illus., adv. Circ: 20480. *Indexed:* AS&TI, CompLI, EnvAb, GeoRef, GeogAbPG. *Aud.:* Sa.

Geo World offers articles on recent technological and applications developments in geographic information systems. Articles also describe new and ongoing projects involving GIS, and management and policy implications. Several columns and departments present unusual uses of GIS, business trends, news of the profession, software and web site reviews, schedules of events, and government geospatial data activities. Important for any library, academic, public, or special, that supports work in any of the numerous applications of GIS.

3582. *Geoforum: the international multi-disciplinary journal for the rapid publication of research results and critical review articles in the physical, human and regional geosciences.* [ISSN: 0016-7185] 1970. bi-m. EUR 902 (Qualified personnel, EUR 82). Ed(s): Andrew Leyshon, Jennifer Robinson. Pergamon, The Boulevard, Langford Ln, East Park, Kidlington, OX5 1GB, United Kingdom. Illus., adv. Sample. Refereed. Circ: 600. Vol. ends: Nov. Microform: PQC. Online: ingenta.com; ScienceDirect; Swets Blackwell. Reprint: PQC. *Indexed:* AgeL, BAS, CJA, DSR&OA, EnvAb, ExcerpMed, FPA, ForAb, GeoRef, GeogAbPG, HortAb, IBSS, IndVet, PSA, PollutAb, RRTA, S&F, SSCI, SWA, SociolAb, WAE&RSA. *Aud.:* Ac, Sa.

Geoforum addresses the management of the physical and social human environment by focusing on the spatial organization of economic, environmental, political, and social systems at scales from the global to the local. It emphasizes international, interdisciplinary, and integrative approaches and applications to policy. Issues generally focus on special subjects. Appropriate for libraries that support programs in urban/regional planning and environmental programs as well as academic geography.

3583. *Geographical.* Former titles (until 2000): *The Royal Geographical Society Magazine;* (until 1997): *Geographical Magazine.* 1935. m. GBP 33 United Kingdom; GBP 39 in Europe; USD 69 in US & Canada. Ed(s): Carolyn Fry. Royal Geographical Society, PO Box 285, Sittingbourne, ME9 8PF, United Kingdom; http://glacier.gg.rhbuc.ac.uk. Illus., adv. Circ: 30000. Vol. ends: Dec. Microform: WMP. Online: Gale Group. *Indexed:* BAS, BrHumI, GSI, GeoRef, PAIS, SSI. *Bk. rev.:* 3-5, 150-300 words, signed. *Aud.:* Ga.

Geographical publishes colorfully illustrated popular but scholarly articles on field research in geography, anthropology, environmental studies, and natural history, and on subjects of geographical interest worldwide. Regular features include "CountryFile," profiling a country in each issue; "GeoJobs," interviewing persons in geographically related professions; and "Healthwise," presenting health items of interest to travelers. Editorship/authorship is largely from the United Kingdom. Useful for public libraries and for libraries that support institutions that undertake overseas field research.

3584. ***Geographical Analysis: an international journal of theoretical geography.*** [ISSN: 0016-7363] 1969. q. USD 135. Ed(s): Alan T Murray. Ohio State University Press, 180 Pressey Hall, 1070 Carmack Rd, Columbus, OH 43210-1002; journals@osu.edu; http://www.ohiostatepress.org. Illus., index, adv. Refereed. Circ: 1000 Paid. Vol. ends: Jan/Oct. Microform: PQC. Online: Florida Center for Library Automation; Gale Group; OCLC Online Computer Library Center, Inc.; Project MUSE; Swets Blackwell. Reprint: ISI; PQC. *Indexed:* BAS, GeoRef, GeogAbPG, IBSS, IBZ, RRTA, SSCI, SUSA, SWA, WAE&RSA. *Bk. rev.:* Number varies, 700-1,200 words, signed. *Aud.:* Ac.

Geographical Analysis publishes methodological articles and new applications of mathematical and statistical methods in geographical analysis, including spatial data analysis and spatial econometrics. Editorship is largely U.S./U.K.; authorship is international. Appropriate for college/university libraries with programs in quantitative social science research, as well as in geography.

3585. ***The Geographical Journal.*** Formerly (until 1892): *Royal Geographical Society and Monthly Record of Geography. Proceedings.* [ISSN: 0016-7398] 1879. q. USD 180 print & online eds. Ed(s): A Millington. Blackwell Publishing Ltd., 9600 Garsington Rd, PO Box 805, Oxford, OX4 2DQ, United Kingdom; customerservices@oxon.blackwellpublishing.com; http://www.blackwellpublishers.co.uk/. Illus., index, adv. Refereed. Circ: 8250. Vol. ends: Nov. CD-ROM: ProQuest Information & Learning. Microform: PQC. Online: EBSCO Publishing; Florida Center for Library Automation; Gale Group; ingenta.com; JSTOR (Web-based Journal Archive); Northern Light Technology, Inc.; OCLC Online Computer Library Center, Inc.; ProQuest Information & Learning; Swets Blackwell. Reprint: PQC. *Indexed:* AICP, AmH&L, ArtHuCI, BAS, BRI, BrArAb, BrHumI, CBRI, DSR&OA, ExcerpMed, GeoRef, GeogAbPG, IBSS, IBZ, IPSA, M&GPA, NumL, PAIS, S&F, SCI, SSCI, SSI, SUSA, SWRA, WAE&RSA. *Bk. rev.:* 15-20 short, 70-150 words; 8-15 long, 400-600 words, signed. *Aud.:* Ga, Ac.

A journal of the Royal Geographical Society, *The Geographical Journal* publishes articles on all aspects of geography with an emphasis on environment and development. Book reviews, society news, meeting reports, and a substantial section on news of the profession are included. There is an annual special issue on cartography, including GIS and remote sensing. Editorship is British; authors are increasingly international. Important for any library that supports geography or area studies departments.

3586. ***Geographical Review.*** Former titles (until 1916): *American Geographical Society. Bulletin;* (until 1901): *American Geographical Society of New York. Journal;* (until 1872): *American Geographical and Statistical Society. Journal.* [ISSN: 0016-7428] 1859. q. USD 126 (Individuals, USD 76). Ed(s): Douglas L Johnson, Viola Haarmann. American Geographical Society, 120 Wall St., Ste. 100, New York, NY 10005-3904; http://www.amergeog.org. Illus., index, adv. Refereed. Circ: 3000. Vol. ends: Oct. Microform: PMC; PQC. Online: bigchalk; EBSCO Publishing; Florida Center for Library Automation; Gale Group; JSTOR (Web-based Journal Archive); Northern Light Technology, Inc.; OCLC Online Computer Library Center, Inc.; ProQuest Information & Learning; H.W. Wilson. Reprint: PQC. *Indexed:* ABS&EES, AbAn, AgeL, AmH&L, ArtHuCI, BAS, BHA, BRI, BiolAb, BrArAb, CBRI, ChemAb, DSR&OA, EngInd, GeoRef, GeogAbPG, HAPI, IBSS, IPSA, PAIS, PRA, PollutAb, RRTA, S&F, SSCI, SSI, SWA, WAE&RSA. *Bk. rev.:* 14-16, 600-2,000 words, signed. *Aud.:* Ga, Ac.

A publication of the American Geographical Society, *Geographical Review* publishes research articles and numerous book reviews. Regular features include "Geographical Record," short, sharply focused review articles, and "Geographical Field Note," short local case studies. This journal is designed to present the results of geographical research to the interested nonprofessional as well as to academics. Authorship is largely American and Canadian. Appropriate for most academic and large public libraries.

3587. ***Geography: an international journal.*** [ISSN: 0016-7487] 1901. q. GBP 67. Ed(s): Dr. Kenneth Lynch. Geographical Association, 160 Solly St, Sheffield, S1 4BF, United Kingdom; http://www.geography.org.uk. Illus., index, adv. Refereed. Circ: 5000. Vol. ends: Oct. *Indexed:* AmH&L, BAS, BiolAb, BrArAb, BrEdI, BrHumI, EIP, ForAb, GeoRef, GeogAbPG, IBSS, IBZ, NumL, PollutAb, RRTA, S&F, SSCI, SSI, SWA, SWRA, WAE&RSA. *Bk. rev.:* 10-15, 250-500 words, signed. *Aud.:* Ac.

This is the major journal of the Geographical Association, the society devoted to the teaching of geography in Britain at the college and secondary levels. Articles present research results with classroom applications, report on ongoing changes in the earth's human and physical geography, and discuss environmental, policy, and quality issues in geographical education. "Case Studies" are articles on geographical subjects focused on individual locations. There are reviews of new educational resources. Editorship/authorship is U.K. Useful in any library that supports a geography department or teacher education program.

3588. ***GeoJournal: an international journal on human geography and environmental sciences.*** [ISSN: 0343-2521] 1977. m. EUR 1723 print or online ed. Ed(s): Herman van der Wusten, O Gritsai. Kluwer Academic Publishers, van Godewijckstraat 30, PO Box 17, Dordrecht, 3300 AA, Netherlands. Illus., index, adv. Refereed. Vol. ends: No. 4. Microform: PQC. Online: EBSCO Publishing; ingenta.com; Kluwer Online; OCLC Online Computer Library Center, Inc.; Ovid Technologies, Inc.; RoweCom Information Quest; Swets Blackwell. Reprint: SWZ. *Indexed:* BAS, BiolAb, CAPS, EngInd, FPA, ForAb, GeoRef, GeogAbPG, HortAb, IBSS, IBZ, M&GPA, OceAb, PollutAb, RRTA, S&F, SWRA, WAE&RSA. *Bk. rev.:* 0-8, 800-1,000 words, signed. *Aud.:* Ac, Sa.

GeoJournal applies the methods and results of human geography and allied fields to problems of social/environmental change and technological development. Applications to forecasting and planning are emphasized. There are frequent special issues with guest editors and occasional review articles. *GJ* communicates news of the International Geographical Union (IGU) activities and of discussion within the IGU. Editorship/authorship is international. Important for libraries that support geographical/environmental research or management/planning with a spatial emphasis.

3589. ***Imago Mundi: the international journal for the history of cartography.*** [ISSN: 0308-5694] 1935. a. USD 80 (Individuals, GBP 30). Ed(s): Catherine Delano Smith. Imago Mundi Ltd., c/o the Map Library, The British Library, 96 Euston Rd, London, NW1 2DB, United Kingdom. Illus., index, adv. Refereed. Circ: 700. *Indexed:* AmH&L, BHA, BrHumI, GeoRef, GeogAbPG. *Bk. rev.:* 10-15, 400-1,000 words, signed. *Aud.:* Ac, Sa.

Imago Mundi is a scholarly journal on the history of maps worldwide in all periods, publishing research and occasional review articles and obituaries. Each issue includes book reviews, an indexed bibliography of current literature, and an extensive news and notices section on conferences, exhibits, map acquisitions, and so on. The editorship is largely U.S./U.K. with an international editorial board. Important for academic libraries that support a geography department or map collection.

3590. ***Institute of British Geographers. Transactions.*** [ISSN: 0020-2754] 1933. q. USD 355 print & online eds. Blackwell Publishing Ltd., 9600 Garsington Rd, PO Box 805, Oxford, OX4 2DQ, United Kingdom; jnlinfo@blackwellpublishers.co.uk; http://www.blackwellpublishing.com/. Illus., index. Refereed. Circ: 2600. Vol. ends: No. 4. Online: EBSCO Publishing; ingenta.com; JSTOR (Web-based Journal Archive); RoweCom Information Quest; Swets Blackwell. *Indexed:* AgeL, BAS, BrArAb, CJA, GeoRef, GeogAbPG, IBSS, IBZ, NumL, PAIS, RRTA, S&F, SSCI, SWA, WAE&RSA. *Bk. rev.:* 4-6, 900-1,200 words, signed. *Aud.:* Ac.

The major journal of the leading British research-oriented geographical society, now joined with the Royal Geographical Society, and one of the leading geographical journals. Editorials discuss current trends in geographical research. Although general in scope, it publishes more human than physical geography. Important for any library that supports a geography department.

3591. *International Journal of Geographical Information Science.* Formerly (until 1997): *International Journal of Geographical Information Systems.* [ISSN: 1365-8816] 1987. 8x/yr. GBP 544 (Individuals, GBP 257). Ed(s): Peter Fisher. Taylor & Francis Ltd, 11 New Fetter Ln, London, EC4P 4EE, United Kingdom; info@tandf.co.uk; http://www.tandf.co.uk/journals. Illus., index, adv. Sample. Refereed. Circ: 1150. Vol. ends: Dec. Online: EBSCO Publishing; Ingenta Select; OCLC Online Computer Library Center, Inc.; RoweCom Information Quest; Swets Blackwell. Reprint: PSC. *Indexed:* AgeL, BrArAb, CompLI, ErgAb, GeoRef, GeogAbPG, InfoSAb, NumL, PollutAb, SCI, SSCI, SWRA, WRCInf. *Bk. rev.:* 0-4, 400-1,200 words, signed. *Aud.:* Ac, Sa.

Publishes research articles on new geographical information technology and on new applications in such fields as environmental and social monitoring, planning, and policy making. It is aimed at information technology developers and users. The editorship and authorship are largely U.K./Commonwealth/U.S., with an international editorial board. Important for any library, academic, public, or special, that supports work in any of the numerous applications of GIS and related technologies.

3592. *Journal of Geography.* [ISSN: 0022-1341] 1917. 6x/yr. USD 65 domestic; USD 73 foreign. Ed(s): Elizabeth J Leppman. National Council for Geographic Education, 206-A Martin Hall, Jacksonvile State University, Jacksonville, AL 36265-1602; levasseu@jsucc.jsu.edu; http://www.ncge.org. Illus., index, adv. Refereed. Circ: 3900 Paid. Vol. ends: Dec. Microform: PQC. Online: bigchalk; Chadwyck-Healey Incorporated; OCLC Online Computer Library Center, Inc.; ProQuest Information & Learning; H.W. Wilson. Reprint: PQC. *Indexed:* AgeL, BAS, BHA, CIJE, EduInd, EnvAb, GeoRef, GeogAbPG, IBZ, MRD, PRA, SSCI, SUSA. *Bk. rev.:* 2-5, 500-600 words, signed. *Aud.:* Ac.

Published by the National Council for Geographic Education, *Journal of Geography* is concerned with geographical teaching at all levels. It offers articles on teaching methods and strategies as well as educational policy, and it contains teaching resources and news of the profession. In "Review Symposia," authors offer reviews of important new publications. Occasional special theme issues are published. Editorship and authorship are largely American. Useful in any library that supports a geography department or teacher education program.

3593. *Journal of Geography in Higher Education.* [ISSN: 0309-8265] 1977. 3x/yr. GBP 516 (Individuals, GBP 36). Ed(s): Hugh Matthews, Ian Livingstone. Carfax Publishing Ltd., 4 Park Sq, Milton Park, Abingdon, OX14 4RN, United Kingdom; enquiry@tandf.co.uk; http://www.tandf.co.uk/. Illus., index, adv. Sample. Refereed. Online: EBSCO Publishing; Ingenta Select; Northern Light Technology, Inc.; OCLC Online Computer Library Center, Inc.; ProQuest Information & Learning; RoweCom Information Quest; Swets Blackwell. Reprint: PSC. *Indexed:* BrEdI, CIJE, GeogAbPG, SSCI, SWA. *Aud.:* Ac.

Journal of Geography in Higher Education offers research articles along with teaching resources and discussions of methods, policy, and standards. Occasional symposia on special subjects are published. Useful in any library that supports a geography department or teacher education program.

3594. *Journal of Historical Geography.* [ISSN: 0305-7488] 1975. q. EUR 395 (Individuals, EUR 100). Ed(s): Mike Heffernan, D. Robinson. Academic Press, Harcourt Pl, 32 Jamestown Rd, London, NW1 7BY, United Kingdom; apsubs@acad.com; http://www.elsevier-international.com/serials/. Illus., index, adv. Sample. Refereed. Vol. ends: Oct. Online: Chadwyck-Healey Incorporated; EBSCO Publishing; Gale Group; ingenta.com; OCLC Online Computer Library Center, Inc.; RoweCom Information Quest; ScienceDirect; Swets Blackwell. Reprint: SWZ. *Indexed:* AbAn, AmH&L, ArtHuCI, BAS, BRI, BrArAb, CBRI, GeoRef, GeogAbPG, NumL, RI-1, SSCI, SSI. *Bk. rev.:* 15-30, 500-750 words, signed. *Aud.:* Ac.

Journal of Historical Geography publishes research papers, methodological contributions, commentaries on published papers, news of the specialty, and occasional review articles. Subjects treated include reconstruction of past human environments and instances of environmental change, geographical aspects of imagination and culture in the past, and historical methodology. Applications to historic preservation are discussed. Editorship and authorship are U.S./U.K./Commonwealth. Important for academic libraries that support geography or history departments.

Journal of Transport Geography. See Transportation section.

National Geographic. See General Editorial/General section.

3595. *Physical Geography.* [ISSN: 0272-3646] 1980. 6x/yr. USD 294 in North America; USD 299 elsewhere. Ed(s): Antony R Orme. V.H. Winston & Son, Inc., c/o Bellwether Publishing, Ltd, 8640 Guilford Rd, Ste 200, Columbia, MD 21046; bellpub@bellpub.com; http://www.bellpub.com. Illus., index. Sample. Refereed. Circ: 400. Vol. ends: Dec. *Indexed:* GeoRef, GeogAbPG, M&GPA, SWRA. *Aud.:* Ac.

Physical Geography carries research papers on geomorphology, climatology, soil science, biogeography, and related subjects. Subject coverage is worldwide. Review articles and methodological and discussion papers are also published. The editors and editorial board are American/Canadian. Important for academic libraries that support geography, geology, or environmental studies departments.

3596. *Political Geography.* Formerly (until 1992): *Political Geography Quarterly.* [ISSN: 0962-6298] 1982. 8x/yr. EUR 886 (Individuals, EUR 201). Ed(s): John O'Loughlin, David Slater. Pergamon, The Boulevard, Langford Ln, East Park, Kidlington, OX5 1GB, United Kingdom. Illus., index, adv. Sample. Refereed. Vol. ends: No. 8. Microform: PQC. Online: Gale Group; ingenta.com; ScienceDirect; Swets Blackwell. *Indexed:* ABCPolSci, AmH&L, ArtHuCI, CJA, GeogAbPG, IBSS, IBZ, IPSA, PAIS, PSA, SSCI, SSI, SWA, SociolAb. *Aud.:* Ac.

Covers traditional approaches, quantitative studies, and studies based on alternative theories of the state and world-systems approaches. Contributions from non-geographers on spatial aspects of politics are encouraged. Debates on topics of wide interest are published, as are special issues. Editorship and authorship are largely U.K./U.S. Important for academic libraries that support geography, political science, or international relations departments.

3597. *Population Space and Place.* Formerly (until 2003): *International Journal of Population Geography.* [ISSN: 1544-8444] 1995. bi-m. USD 735. John Wiley & Sons Ltd., The Atrium, Southern Gate, Chichester, PO19 8SQ, United Kingdom; customer@wiley.co.uk; http://www.wiley.co.uk. Illus., index, adv. Sample. Refereed. Vol. ends: Dec. Microform: PQC. Online: EBSCO Publishing; ScienceDirect; Swets Blackwell; Wiley InterScience. Reprint: PSC. *Indexed:* RRTA, S&F, SWA, WAE&RSA. *Bk. rev.:* 3-4, 800-1,500 words, signed. *Aud.:* Ac.

Population Space and Place publishes research and review articles, book reviews, and articles on current debates. Topics covered include migration, the geography of fertility/mortality, population modeling and forcasting, environmental issues, spatial aspects of labor, housing, minority groups, and historical demography. Planning and policy implications of population research are emphasized. Articles originating in allied disciplines are published. The editorship is largely U.K. with an international advisory board; the authorship is international. Important for any library that supports research in geography or population studies, or in social science generally.

3598. *The Professional Geographer.* [ISSN: 0033-0124] 1949. q. Ed(s): Truman Hartshorn. Blackwell Publishing, Inc., Commerce Place, 350 Main St, Malden, MA 02148; subscrip@blackwellpub.com; http://www.blackwellpublishing.com. Illus., index, adv. Refereed. Circ: 9000 Paid. Vol. ends: Nov. Microform: PQC; NRP. Online: EBSCO Publishing; Gale Group; ingenta.com; OCLC Online Computer Library

Center, Inc.; RoweCom Information Quest; Swets Blackwell. *Indexed:* ABS&EES, AbAn, AgeL, ArtHuCI, BAS, CJA, ForAb, GeoRef, GeogAbPG, IBSS, IBZ, M&GPA, PRA, PollutAb, RRTA, S&F, SSCI, SSI, SUSA, SWA, WAE&RSA. *Bk. rev.:* 4-7, 700-1,200 words, signed. *Aud.:* Ac.

A publication of the Association of American Geographers, *The Professional Geographer* publishes short research papers and essays on all aspects of geography. New approaches and alternative perspectives are emphasized. "Focus" is a section for collections of short articles on special topics. Important for all academic and for large public libraries.

3599. ***Progress in Human Geography: an international review of geographical work in the social sciences and humanities.*** [ISSN: 0309-1325] 1977. bi-m. GBP 256 (Individuals, GBP 96; Members, GBP 79 IBG, RGS, KNAG, SAGS, IAG, ASA (American Sociological Association), and AAG). Ed(s): Kay Anderson, Peter Dicken. Arnold Publishers, 338 Euston Rd, London, NW1 3BH, United Kingdom; http://www.palliativemedjournal.com. Illus., index, adv. Sample. Refereed. Circ: 1200. Vol. ends: No. 4. Online: EBSCO Publishing; OCLC Online Computer Library Center, Inc.; RoweCom Information Quest; Swets Blackwell. *Indexed:* ASSIA, AgeL, ArtHuCI, BAS, BrArAb, GeogAbPG, H&SSA, IBSS, PSA, PollutAb, SSCI, SUSA, SWRA, SociolAb. *Bk. rev.:* 9-21, 700-1,600 words, signed. *Aud.:* Ac.

Publishes review articles on trends and developments in human geography and related work in other disciplines. Articles cover the full international literature and discuss possible applications. The "Classics" section comprises short commentaries on older books answered by the book's author. "Progress Reports" are short essay reviews of several new books in particular areas. Editorship and authorship are largely U.K./Commonwealth/U.S. This journal is important for academic libraries that support social science research and geography departments as well as large public libraries. Arnold also issues a similar title, *Progress in Physical Geography* (ISSN: 0309-1333), which is appropriate for libraries that serve geography and geology departments and environmental studies programs.

Progress in Physical Geography. See under *Progress in Human Geography.*

3600. ***Singapore Journal of Tropical Geography.*** Supersedes in part: *Journal of Tropical Geography.* [ISSN: 0129-7619] 1980. 3x/yr. USD 171 print & online eds. Ed(s): Shirlena Huang. Blackwell Publishing Asia, 550 Swanston St, Carlton South, VIC 3053, Australia; subs@blackwellpublishingasia.com; http://www.blackwellpublishing.com/. Illus. Sample. Refereed. Circ: 660. Online: EBSCO Publishing; ingenta.com; OCLC Online Computer Library Center, Inc.; RoweCom Information Quest; Swets Blackwell. Reprint: PSC. *Indexed:* BAS, BiolAb, EIP, GeoRef, GeogAbPG, IBSS, PSA, RRTA, S&F, SSCI, SociolAb, WAE&RSA. *Bk. rev.:* 4-6, 400-600 words, signed. *Aud.:* Ac.

Edited at the Department of Geography of the University of Singapore, this journal treats human and physical geography and spatial aspects of development from an interdisciplinary perspective. Papers from scholars outside of geography are welcome. It contains more on the Asian tropics than on Africa or South America. Authorship is international. Important for academic libraries that support geography departments or area studies programs with interests in the Old World tropics.

3601. ***Social & Cultural Geography.*** [ISSN: 1464-9365] 2000. q. GBP 224 (Individuals, GBP 60). Ed(s): Rob Kitchin, Cindi Katz. Routledge, 11 New Fetter Ln, London, EC4P 4EE, United Kingdom; http://www.tandf.co.uk/journals/. Sample. Refereed. Reprint: PSC. *Indexed:* PSA, SociolAb. *Bk. rev.:* Various number and length. *Aud.:* Ac.

Publishes theoretically based empirical articles on spatial patterns in social and cultural life. Examples include language, shopping, tourism, race, burial, disability, etc. The journal features special thematic sections, book reviews, and lists of recently completed doctorates. The editorial board and, largely, the authorship are U.K./Irish/Australian/U.S.; subject coverage is worldwide. Important for academic libraries that support social science.

3602. ***Space and Polity.*** [ISSN: 1356-2576] 1997. 3x/yr. GBP 191 (Individuals, GBP 71). Ed(s): Ronan Paddison. Carfax Publishing Ltd., 4 Park Sq, Milton Park, Abingdon, OX14 4RN, United Kingdom; enquiry@tandf.co.uk; http://www.tandf.co.uk/. Illus. Refereed. Vol. ends: Nov. Online: EBSCO Publishing; Ingenta Select; OCLC Online Computer Library Center, Inc.; RoweCom Information Quest; Swets Blackwell. Reprint: PSC. *Indexed:* IBZ. *Bk. rev.:* 3-5, 1,000-1,400 words, signed. *Aud.:* Ac.

Space and Polity deals with spatial aspects of politics, emphasizing the relation between the state and regional/local politics and the relation to globalization during the current period of rapid change in these relationships. The emphasis is on publishing work, both theoretical and empirical, from a wide range of social science disciplines. There are occasional review articles. The editors are U.K./U.S. with an international advisory board; authorship is international with a U.K./U.S. majority. Important for academic libraries that support political science, economics, and sociology as well as geography departments.

3603. ***Surveying and Land Information Science: an official journal of ACSM devoted to the science of surveying and mapping, land information, and related fields.*** Former titles (until 2002): *Surveying and Land Information Systems;* (until 1990): *Surveying and Mapping.* [ISSN: 1538-1242] 1941. q. Non-members, USD 110. Ed(s): Joseph C. Loon. American Congress on Surveying and Mapping, 6 Montgomery Village Ave., Ste 403, Gaithersburg, MD 20879; infoacsm@acsm.net; http://www.acsm.net. Illus., index, adv. Sample. Refereed. Circ: 9000. Vol. ends: Dec. Microform: PQC. Online: ProQuest Information & Learning; H.W. Wilson. Reprint: PSC. *Indexed:* AS&TI, EngInd, GeoRef, GeogAbPG. *Bk. rev.:* 1-2, 800-2,400 words, signed. *Aud.:* Ac, Sa.

This official journal of the American Congress on Surveying and Mapping keeps its readers up-to-date on theoretical, technical, and policy developments in surveying, mapping, and land information systems, including geodesy and hydrography, through research articles, book reviews, current literature lists, and comments and discussion. Topics of current interest, such as global positioning systems and total stations, are emphasized. There is a regular section on surveying and mapping education. Issues on special topics are occasionally published. Important for any library, academic, public, or special, that supports research or teaching in any of the numerous applications of GIS and related technologies.

3604. ***Terrae Incognitae: the journal for the history of discoveries.*** [ISSN: 0082-2884] 1969. a. USD 30 in US & Canada; USD 35 foreign. Ed(s): David Buisseret. Society for the History of Discoveries, c/o Dr. Sanford H. Bederman, Sec.-Treas., 5502 Laurel Ridge Drive, Alpharetta, GA 30005; buisser@uta.edu; http://www.sochistdisc.org/. Illus., index. Refereed. Circ: 600. *Indexed:* AmH&L. *Bk. rev.:* 4-5, 300-1,000 words, signed. *Aud.:* Ac.

This is a scholarly journal that covers the worldwide history of discovery and exploration. It publishes research articles, book reviews, and a bibliography of current literature. Editorship is American, Canadian, and British; authorship is international. Important for academic libraries that support geography and history departments.

3605. ***Tijdschrift voor Economische en Sociale Geografie.*** [ISSN: 0040-747X] 1910. q. GBP 162 print & online eds. Ed(s): Jan van Weesep. Blackwell Publishing Ltd., 9600 Garsington Rd, PO Box 805, Oxford, OX4 2DQ, United Kingdom; customerservices@oxon.blackwellpublishing.com; http://www.blackwellpublishing.com/. Illus., index, adv. Sample. Refereed. Circ: 1150 Paid. Vol. ends: No. 5. Online: EBSCO Publishing; ingenta.com; OCLC Online Computer Library Center, Inc.; RoweCom Information Quest; Swets Blackwell. *Indexed:* ExcerpMed, FS&TA, ForAb, GeoRef, GeogAbPG, IBSS, PAIS, PSA, RRTA, S&F, SSCI, SWA, SociolAb, WAE&RSA. *Aud.:* Ac.

Published under the auspices of the Royal Dutch Geographical Society, *TESG* offers scholarly articles and subject-focused issues in human geography, emphasizing new approaches emanating from both continental and Anglo-American traditions. Special sections discuss Dutch and European geographical trends.

Each issue carries maps illustrating Netherlands human geography. Editorship is largely Dutch; authorship is international. Important for academic libraries that support geography departments or area studies programs with interests in Western Europe.

Urban Geography. See Urban Studies section.

Electronic Journals

3606. ***CyberGEO.*** [ISSN: 1278-3366] 1996. irreg. Ed(s): Christine Kosmopoulos. CyberGeo, 13 rue du Four, Paris, 75006, France; vanky@parisgeo.cnrs.fr; http://www.cybergeo.presse.fr/. *Bk. rev.:* 10-20/year, 200-800 words, signed. *Aud.:* Ac.

This is a free online journal that publishes articles on the whole range of geography. It offers authors quick publication and immediate reader feedback. Results of reader feedback may be incorporated into or added to articles. There is an associated discussion mailing list. The web page has an English version. Articles have English summaries and are in French, English, and other languages. The editorial board is European, largely French.

■ GOVERNMENT PERIODICALS—FEDERAL

Rosemary L. Meszaros, Coordinator, Government Information and Law, Western Kentucky University, Bowling Green, KY 42101; rosemary.meszaros@wku.edu; 270-745-7175

Introduction

Government periodicals cover every subject imaginable. Publications of the federal government, from the many federal agencies in the executive branch to the Congress and its agencies and the Supreme Court, offer something for every interest. Law, military, politics, education, environment, business, economics, agriculture, weather, science, demographics, large print, audio and braille bibliographies, consumer information, statistics—all are represented in the array of magazines and journals published, distributed, and sold by the U.S. Government Printing Office (GPO). Unless otherwise noted, all information from the federal government is copyright free. That is the reason much of the information produced by the government is repackaged and vended by private companies.

The Government Printing Office provides free electronic access to the wealth of important information products produced by the federal government through its *GPO Access* database. This free service is funded by the Federal Depository Library Program and has grown out of Public Law 103-40, known as the Government Printing Office Electronic Information Enhancement Act of 1993 (http://www.gpoaccess.gov/). In addition, some of the individual federal agencies post their own publications on their web sites. GPO has stepped into the role of preserver, maintainer, and vendor of government information. Through its network of Federal Depository Libraries—there's one in your neighborhood—(see http://www.gpoaccess.gov/libraries.html), over 1,300 libraries nationwide and in the U.S. Commonwealths and Territories receive GPO materials. Dedicated librarians staff these depository library collections and stand ready to assist. GPO is maintaining electronic publications through a Persistent Uniform Resource Locator or PURL system (see http://purl.access.gpo.gov/). Finally, GPO fulfills its role as vendor of federal government publications through its GPO Bookstores. See a list of bookstores at http://bookstore.gpo.gov/locations/index.html. For online ordering convenience, see http://bookstore.gpo.gov/.

Many federal government periodicals have migrated to the Internet or have both print and online formats available. Keeping track of them is a great web site produced by the University of Memphis, appropriately titled "Uncle Sam Migrating Government Publications" at http://www.lib.memphis.edu/govpubs/mig.htm. This list is browsable by Superintendent of Documents number or by publication title.

A very useful, alphabetical list of federal government periodicals with clickable links is maintained by the University of Louisville Libraries at http://library.louisville.edu/government/periodicals/periodall.html.

Two other gateways have made their debut and aim to facilitate access to Web-based information: *FirstGov.gov* from the General Services Administration (http://www.firstgov.gov), which describes itself as "The U.S. Government's Official Web Portal," and *GovSpot* from the Library of Congress (http://www.govspot.com). In addition, the consumer publications from the Federal Citizen Information Center in Pueblo, Colorado, (http://www.pueblo.gsa.gov/) continues to provide quick and easy access to their publications.

Congressional Information Service was purchased by Lexis/Nexis, so their very worthwhile indexes, e.g., *American Statistics Index, CIS Index,* and *U.S. Government Periodicals Index,* have become part of *LexisNexis Statistical, LexisNexis Congressional,* and *LexisNexis Government Periodicals Index,* respectively.

Basic Periodicals

Ga: *U.S. Congress. Congressional Record, U.S. Office of the Federal Register. Weekly Compilation of Presidential Documents;* Ac: *U.S. Congress. Congressional Record, Morbidity and Mortality Weekly Report, U.S. Office of the Federal Register. Weekly Compilation of Presidential Documents;* Sa: *Morbidity and Mortality Weekly Report.*

Basic Abstracts and Indexes

LexisNexis Government Periodicals, LexisNexis Statistical, Public Affairs Information Service International.

3607. ***AgExporter.*** Formerly (until 1989): *Foreign Agriculture.* [ISSN: 1047-4781] 1937. m. USD 44. U.S. Department of Agriculture, Foreign Agricultural Service, Information Division, Rm 4638 S, Washington, DC 20250-1000; http://ffas.usda.gov/info/agexporter/agexport.html. Illus., index. Sample. Circ: 1800. Vol. ends: No. 12. Microform: MIM; CIS; PQC. Online: Florida Center for Library Automation; Gale Group; Northern Light Technology, Inc.; OCLC Online Computer Library Center, Inc.; ProQuest Information & Learning; H.W. Wilson. Reprint: CIS; PQC. *Indexed:* ABS&EES, Agr, AmStI, B&AI, BiolAb, DSA, HortAb, IUSGP, PAIS, RRTA, WAE&RSA. *Aud.:* Sa.

Written by USDA staff for businesses selling farm products overseas, providing tips on exporting, descriptions of markets with the greatest sales potential, and information on export assistance available from the U.S. Department of Agriculture. The audience is U.S. agricultural producers, exporters, trade organizations, state departments of agriculture, and any other export-oriented organization. Issues are 20–30 pages long and focus on the practical.

Agricultural Research. See Agriculture section.

Airman: magazine of America's Air Force. See under *Marines,* Military section.

Airpower. See Military section.

3608. ***Alcohol Research & Health.*** Formerly (until 1999): *Alcohol Health & Research World.* [ISSN: 1535-7414] 1975. q. USD 22 domestic. Ed(s): Dianne M Welsh. U.S. National Institute on Alcohol Abuse and Alcoholism, 6000 Executive Blvd, Bethesda, MD 20892-7003; http://www.niaaa.nih.gov. Illus., index. Refereed. Circ: 3700 Paid. Vol. ends: No. 4. Online: EBSCO Publishing; Florida Center for Library Automation; Gale Group; ProQuest Information & Learning. *Indexed:* AgeL, AmStI, CINAHL, ChemAb, IUSGP, IndMed, MagInd, PAIS, PsycholAb, SSCI, SSI, SWR&A. *Aud.:* Ac, Sa.

Each issue is devoted to a particular topic in alcohol research, e.g., children of alcoholics, chronobiology, circadian rhythms, and alcohol use; and alcohol and comorbid mental health disorders. This quarterly, peer-reviewed scientific journal is available in full text from 1997 to date on the National Institute on Alcohol Abuse and Alcoholism's web site.

All Hands. See under *Marines,* Military section.

Amber Waves. See Agriculture section.

American Rehabilitation. See Disabilities section.

Appalachia. See Free Magazines and House Organs section.

The Astronomical Almanac. See Astronomy section.

3609. *Consumer Product Safety Review.* Former titles (until 1996): *N E I S S Data Highlights; N E I S S News.* 1976. q. USD 16 domestic; USD 20 foreign. Ed(s): Nancy Sachs. U.S. Consumer Product Safety Commission, Washington, DC 20207. Circ: 1300 Paid. *Indexed:* AmStI. *Aud.:* Ga, Sa.

This quarterly journal offers an in-depth look at the latest hazards associated with 15,000 types of consumer products under the agency's jurisdiction, both home and recreational products, as well as the most significant current product recalls. Available in full text on the Consumer Products Safety Commission's web site from its first issue in 1997—whose feature article was about the reduction of baseball injuries by using protective equipment—to its current issue.

Daily Weather Maps. See Atmospheric Sciences section.

3610. *Emerging Infectious Diseases (Print Edition).* [ISSN: 1080-6040] 1995. m. Free. Ed(s): Peter Drotman. U.S. National Center for Infectious Diseases, 1600 Clifton Rd, Mailstop D61, Atlanta, GA 30333; eideditor@cdc.gov; http://www.cdc.gov/. Illus. Refereed. Circ: 23500. Vol. ends: No. 4. Online: Gale Group. *Indexed:* BiolAb, DSA, ExcerpMed, ForAb, GSI, H&SSA, IndMed, IndVet, RRTA, RiskAb, S&F, SCI, SWRA, VetBull, WAE&RSA, ZooRec. *Aud.:* Ga, Sa.

This is a monthly peer-reviewed journal tracking and analyzing disease trends. It has a very high citation rate and ranking in its field. In addition to dispatches on the latest epidemiology of infectious diseases, the issues contain research articles, columns, letters, commentary, and book reviews. Available in full text beginning with its inaugural issue in 1995 from the Centers for Disease Control and Prevention web site.

3611. *Endangered Species Bulletin.* Formerly (until 1994): *Endangered Species Technical Bulletin.* [ISSN: 1091-7314] 1976. 6x/yr. Ed(s): Mike Bender. U.S. Fish and Wildlife Service, Division of Endangered Species, 452 Arlington Sq, Washington, DC 20240; http://www.fws.gov. Illus. *Indexed:* EnvAb, GardL. *Aud.:* Ga, Ac.

The *Endangered Species Bulletin* was created in 1976 to meet the growing demand for news of developments in the endangered-species program. The *Bulletin* is the primary means by which the U.S. Fish and Wildlife Service disseminates information on rule makings (listings, reclassifications, and delistings), recovery plans and activities, regulatory changes, interagency consultations, changes in species' status, research developments, new ecological threats, and a variety of other issues. It is published bimonthly with an annual index. The Fish and Wildlife Service distributes the *Bulletin* free to federal, state, and local agencies and official contacts of the endangered-species program. The *Bulletin* also is reprinted by the University of Michigan as part of its own publication, *The Endangered Species UPDATE.*

3612. *English Teaching Forum: a journal for the teacher of English outside the United States.* Former titles: *Forum; English Teaching Forum.* 1963. q. USD 17. Ed(s): Damon Anderson. U.S. Department of State, Bureau of International Information Programs, 301 4th St, S W, Washington, DC 20547; http://usinfo.state.gov/homepage.htm. Illus. Circ: 100000. *Indexed:* IUSGP, LT&LA. *Bk. rev.:* 4, one-half page in length. *Aud.:* Ga, Ac, Sa.

A quarterly journal published by the U.S. Department of State for Teachers of English as a Foreign or Second Language. Over 60,000 copies of the magazine are distributed in 100 countries. In 2002, the *Forum* celebrated its 40th anniversary. Most of the authors published in the journal are classroom teachers and regular readers of the journal. Submissions from English-language teachers around the world are welcomed. Articles from issues of the *Forum* dating back to 1993 are available online through *GPO Access.*

3613. *Environmental Health Perspectives.* Supersedes in part (in 1993): *E H P.* 1993. m. USD 1369 Corporate Institutions (Individuals, USD 249; Students, USD 45). Ed(s): Gary E R Hook. U.S. Department of Health and Human Services, National Institute of Environmental Health Sciences, PO Box 12233, Research Triangle Park, NC 27709; ehis@niehs.nih.gov; http://ehis.niehs.nih.gov/. Illus., adv. Refereed. Circ: 6500. Vol. ends: Dec (No. 12). *Indexed:* ChemAb, DSA, EnvAb, ExcerpMed, FPA, FS&TA, ForAb, GSI, IndMed, IndVet, S&F, SCI, SSCI, WAE&RSA, ZooRec. *Aud.:* Ac.

This peer-reviewed journal dedicated to the discussion of the effects of the environment on human health contains articles, commentary, news, editorials, and a research forum. *EHP* publishes 17 issues annually, monthly sections devoted to children's health and environmental medicine, a toxicogenomics research section published with toxicogenomics news in separate quarterly issues, and an annual review issue. They also publish a quarterly Chinese-language edition and occasional special issues. Full text is available online since April 1993.

F B I Law Enforcement Bulletin. See Criminology and Law Enforcement section.

FDA Consumer. See Medicine and Health/Consumer Health section.

Federal Probation. See Criminology and Law Enforcement section.

3614. *Federal Reserve Bulletin.* [ISSN: 0014-9209] 1915. m. USD 25; USD 35 foreign. U.S. Federal Reserve System, Board of Governors, Publications Services, Rm MS 138, Washington, DC 20551. Circ: 26000. Microform: MIM; CIS; PMC; PQC. Online: bigchalk; The Dialog Corporation; EBSCO Publishing; Florida Center for Library Automation; Gale Group; Northern Light Technology, Inc.; OCLC Online Computer Library Center, Inc.; ProQuest Information & Learning; H.W. Wilson. Reprint: CIS; PQC; PSC; WSH. *Indexed:* ABIn, AgeL, AmStI, BLI, BPI, CLI, IBSS, ILP, IUSGP, JEL, PAIS, WAE&RSA. *Aud.:* Ac, Sa.

Staff members of the Board of Governors of the Federal Reserve prepare the articles for this publication. In general they report and analyze economic developments, discuss bank regulatory issues, and present new data. Available in full text online since 1997 from the Federal Reseve Board web site.

Fishery Bulletin. See Fish, Fisheries, and Aquaculture section.

3615. *Health Care Financing Review.* [ISSN: 0195-8631] 1979. q. USD 48. Ed(s): Linda F Wolf. U.S. Health Care Financing Administration, C 3 24 07, 7500 Security Blvd, Baltimore, MD 21244-1850; http://www.hcfa.gov/. Illus. Vol. ends: Summer (No. 4). Microform: CIS; PQC. Online: EBSCO Publishing; Florida Center for Library Automation; Gale Group; Northern Light Technology, Inc.; OCLC Online Computer Library Center, Inc.; ProQuest Information & Learning; H.W. Wilson. Reprint: CIS. *Indexed:* ABIn, ASG, AgeL, AmStI, BPI, ExcerpMed, IUSGP, MCR, PAIS, SCI, SSCI, SSI, SWR&A. *Aud.:* Ac, Sa.

The Health Care Financing Administration was renamed the Centers for Medicare and Medicaid Services in 2001, but the journal retains the familiar name. It highlights the results of policy-relevant research and provides a forum for a broad range of viewpoints to stimulate discussion among a diverse audience that includes policy makers, planners, administrators, insurers, researchers, and health care providers. Topics include managed and community-based care, Medicaid reform, and prescription drugs. Many articles include statistics. Available in full text online since the spring 1999 issue from the Centers for Medicare and Medicaid web site.

Humanities: the magazine of the national endowment for the humanities. See Cultural-Social Studies section.

Job Safety and Health Quarterly. See Safety section.

Journal of Rehabilitation. See Disabilities section.

Marine Fisheries Review. See Fish, Fisheries, and Aquaculture section.

Marines. See Military section.

Military History. See Military section.

Military Review. See Military section.

Monthly Climatic Data for the World. See Atmospheric Sciences section.

3616. *Morbidity and Mortality Weekly Report.* Formerly (until 1976): *U.S. National Communicable Disease Center. Morbidity and Mortality;* Formerly: *U.S. Centers for Disease Control, Morbidity and Mortality Weekly Report.* [ISSN: 0149-2195] 1951. w. USD 255. Ed(s): Dr. John W Ward. U.S. Department of Health and Human Services, Centers for Disease Control and Prevention, Epidemiology Program Office MS C-08, 1600 Clifton Rd NE, Atlanta, GA 30333; http://www.cdc.gov/. Illus., index. Circ: 30000 Paid. Microform: CIS; PQC. Online: EBSCO Publishing; Florida Center for Library Automation; Gale Group; LexisNexis; NewsNet; OCLC Online Computer Library Center, Inc.; ProQuest Information & Learning. Reprint: CIS. *Indexed:* AmStI, BiolAb, CINAHL, CJA, CWI, DSA, EnvAb, FS&TA, H&SSA, IndMed, IndVet, PEI, RRTA, RiskAb, VetBull, WAE&RSA. *Aud.:* Ac, Sa.

Morbidity and Mortality Weekly Report (*MMWR*) went totally electronic in 2001. Issues from 1982 are available online in full text through *GPO Access* and through the Centers for Disease Control's own web site. The *MMWR* weekly contains data on specific diseases as reported by state and territorial health departments and reports on infectious and chronic diseases, environmental hazards, natural or human-generated disasters, occupational diseases and injuries, and intentional and unintentional injuries. Also included are reports on topics of international interest and notices of events of interest to the public health community.

3617. *National Institute of Standards and Technology. Journal of Research.* Former titles (until 1988): *U.S. National Bureau of Standards. Journal of Research;* Formed by the 1977 merger of: *U.S. National Bureau of Standards. Journal of Research. Section A. Physics and Chemistry; U.S. National Bureau of Standards. Journal of Research. Section B. Mathematical Sciences;* Which was formerly (until 1967): *U.S. National Bureau of Standards. Journal of Research. Section B. Mathematics and Mathematical Physics;* Which superseded in part (in 1959): *U.S. National Bureau of Standards. Journal of Research.* [ISSN: 1044-677X] 1927. bi-m. USD 31; USD 38.75. Ed(s): Theodore V Vorburger. National Institute of Standards and Technology, 100 Buvean Dr, Stop 8401, Gaithersburg, MD 20899-8401; http://www.nist.gov/. Illus., index. Refereed. Circ: 2000 Paid and controlled. Vol. ends: Nov/Dec. Microform: PQC. Online: Florida Center for Library Automation; Gale Group; OCLC Online Computer Library Center, Inc.; ProQuest Information & Learning; H.W. Wilson. Reprint: PQC. *Indexed:* AS&TI, ApMecR, BiolAb, C&ISA, CerAb, ChemAb, DSR&OA, EngInd, FS&TA, ForAb, GeoRef, IAA, IUSGP, SCI. *Aud.:* Ac, Sa.

This journal reports National Institute of Standards and Technology (NIST) research and development in metrology and related fields of physical science, engineering, applied mathematics, statistics, biotechnology, and information technology. Papers cover a broad range of subjects, with major emphasis on measurement methodology and the basic technology underlying standardization. Also included, on occasion, are articles on topics closely related to the institute's technical and scientific program. NIST was formerly the National Bureau of Standards. Full text of all articles since 1995 are available from the NIST web site.

Occupational Outlook Quarterly. See Occupations and Careers section.

Parameters. See Military section.

3618. *Peace Watch.* Formerly (until 1994): *United States Institute of Peace. Journal.* [ISSN: 1080-9864] 1988. bi-m. Ed(s): Renee Storteboom. U.S. Institute of Peace, 1200 17th St NW, Ste 200, Washington, DC 20036-3011; http://www.usip.org. Illus. Circ: 15000. Vol. ends: Oct (No. 6). *Indexed:* ABS&EES. *Aud.:* Ga, Ac, Sa.

The Institute of Peace is an independent, nonpartisan federal institution created by Congress to promote the prevention, management, and peaceful resolution of international conflicts. Articles written by the institute's staff focus on news of conflicts worldwide and reports on symposia held under the sponsorship of the institute. Full text is available online at its web site since June 1996.

Prologue. See Archives and Manuscripts section.

Public Health Reports. See Medicine and Health/Public Health section.

Public Roads. See Transportation section.

3619. *Schizophrenia Bulletin.* [ISSN: 0586-7614] 1969. q. USD 28 domestic; USD 39.20 foreign. Ed(s): John K Hsiao, David Shore. U.S. Public Health Service, National Institute of Mental Health, 6001 Executive Blvd, Rm 8184, Bethesda, MD 20892-9663; lalberts@nih.gov; http://www.nimh.nih.gov/. Illus. Circ: 7000. Vol. ends: No. 4. Microform: MIM; PQC. Online: Northern Light Technology, Inc.; ProQuest Information & Learning. Reprint: PQC. *Indexed:* AgeL, BiolAb, CINAHL, CJA, ECER, ExcerpMed, IBZ, IUSGP, IndMed, PsycholAb, SCI, SSCI. *Aud.:* Sa.

A scientific journal prepared by the Office of Communications and Public Liaison of the National Institute of Mental Health (NIMH), its articles are concerned with all facets of schizophrenia research and treatment. About half of the issues focus on a single critical topic, such as treatment, genetics, or etiology. Special emphasis is placed on exhaustive state-of-the-art reviews of critical areas in the study of schizophrenia. In addition to containing full-length articles, the *Bulletin* features shorter pieces on topical issues in an "At Issues" section and reports of scientific meetings related to schizophrenia (particularly those sponsored by the NIMH). A "Letters to the Editor" section facilitates timely exchanges of ideas. There is also a section devoted to first-person accounts in which patients, family members, and others share their experiences so that readers may better understand the issues and difficulties confronted by individuals with this illness. Featured on the cover of each issue is artwork by different individuals with schizophrenia.

Science & Technology Review. See Science and Technolony section.

Social Security Bulletin. See Aging section.

Soldiers. See under *Marines,* Military section.

3620. *Sotsialisticheskii Trud.* [ISSN: 0037-8216] 1956. m. Ed(s): P M Loznevoi. Gosudarstvennyi Komitet Soveta Ministrov po Voprosam Truda i Zarabotnoi Platy, Pl Kuibysheva 1, Moscow, Russian Federation. Illus. Circ: 65000. *Indexed:* IBSS. *Aud.:* Ga, Ac, Sa.

This award-winning magazine from the National Parks Service archaeology program has had two name changes: from *Common Ground: Archeology and Ethnography in the Public Interest* and prior to that *Federal Archaeology.* Expanding its scope beyond archaeology and ethnography, *Common Ground* now offers an in-depth look at the nationwide effort to preserve our heritage in all its forms. Stories focus not only on preservation, but on the people making it happen—on public and tribal lands and in cities, towns, and neighborhoods across the nation. Readers will find a wealth of useful information—from the nuts and bolts of approaches that work, to where to get grants, to the latest research findings. It is written in a style that is jargon-free and to-the-point. Quality artwork and photography provide an intimate portrait of America's heritage.

Storm Data. See Atmospheric Sciences section.

Survey of Current Business. See Business section.

U.S. Bureau of Labor Statistics. Monthly Labor Review. See Labor and Industrial Relations section.

3621. *U.S. Congress. Congressional Record: proceedings and debates of the Congress.* [ISSN: 0363-7239] 1873. d. when Congress is in session. USD 393. U.S. Government Printing Office, Superintendent of Documents, PO Box 371954, Pittsburgh, PA 15250-7954; http://www.access.gpo.gov. Illus., index. *Aud.:* Ac, Sa.

The *Congressional Record* is the most widely recognized published account of the debates, proceedings, and activities of the United States Congress. Currently averaging over 200 pages a day, it is a substantially verbatim account of the proceedings of Congress. It is published daily when either or both Houses of Congress are in session. It may be thought of as the world's largest daily newspaper because it contains an account of everything that is said and done on the floors of the House and Senate, extensive additional reprinting of inserted materials, and, since 1947, a resume of congressional activity (the *Daily Digest*). Available and searchable online through *GPO Access* from 1994 to 1995 (103rd Congress) and through the Library of Congress's *THOMAS* database from 1989 to 1990 (101st Congress).

U.S. Energy Information Administration. Monthly Energy Review. See Energy section.

3622. *U.S. Office of the Federal Register. Weekly Compilation of Presidential Documents.* [ISSN: 0511-4187] 1965. w. USD 80 domestic; USD 93.75 foreign. U.S. Office of the Federal Register, National Archives and Records Administration, Eighth St and Pennsylvania Ave, N W, Washington, DC 20408; http://www.access.gpo.gov/nara/nara003.html. Illus., index. Circ: 7000. Vol. ends: No. 52. Reprint: WSH. *Indexed:* PAIS. *Aud.:* Ga, Ac, Sa.

Issued every Monday from the White House, this journal contains statements, messages, proclamations, executive orders, radio addresses, speeches, press conferences, communications to Congress and federal agencies, statements regarding bill signings and vetoes, appointments, nominations, reorganization plans, resignations, retirements, acts approved by the president, nominations submitted to the Senate, and White House announcements and press releases. Available in full text online since 1993 and searchable through *GPO Access*.

■ GOVERNMENT PERIODICALS—STATE AND LOCAL

General/State and Municipal Associations

See also City and Regional; Political Science; and Urban Studies sections.

Rosemary L. Meszaros, Coordinator, Government Information and Law, Western Kentucky University, Bowling Green, KY 42101; rosemary.meszaros@wku.edu; FAX: 270-745-6175

Introduction

Unlike the U.S. government's Federal Depository Library Program, each state does not replicate this system of depositing a copy of its publications in designated libraries in that state. Some states—Alaska, California, Missouri, New Hampshire, and Texas, among others—have established such a state depository system. For the other state-document librarians, constant vigilance is required to keep up with materials produced by their state and local governments. Often this information is essential to the researcher and difficult to find. With the advent of the Internet, many states and localities have taken advantage of web-based publication. The two-edged sword is that easy access does not mean permanent access. That would indeed be a loss. State and local periodicals are focused and give the home-grown touch that national periodicals cannot. Inconsistent indexing of these periodicals puts data and details at the state and local levels at risk.

The periodicals in this section offer a variety of coverage of local and state issues. Some may be of interest primarily to state and local officials, but most are of interest to residents of the areas. The focus is on state or local policy issues or how the federal government's policies may impact them, on profiles of officials, or on comparative governmental issues. Budgeting, the environment, infrastructure, technology, telecommunications, health care, etc. are topics of commonality. Some magazines offer a smorgasbord of features about state and local issues that aim at a national audience. Companion sections include City and Regional and Urban Studies.

Basic Periodicals

Ga: *Nation's Cities Weekly, State Government News;* Ac: *Governing, Spectrum, State and Local Government Review, State Legislatures.*

Basic Abstracts and Indexes

Political Science Abstracts, Public Affairs Information Service. Bulletin, Sage Urban Studies Abstracts, Urban Affairs Abstracts.

General

American City & County. See Urban Studies section.

3623. *California Journal: the monthly analysis of state government and politics.* [ISSN: 0008-1205] 1970. m. USD 59 (Individuals, USD 39.95; Corporations, USD 95). Ed(s): Cynthia H Craft. Information for Public Affairs, Inc., 2101 K St, Sacramento, CA 95816. Illus., adv. Circ: 12000. Vol. ends: Dec. Microform: LIB. Online: Gale Group; LexisNexis. *Indexed:* PAIS, SUSA. *Aud.:* Ga, Ac.

Launched in 1970 to provide a source of authoritative information on state government and politics from a nonpartisan, independent viewpoint, this magazine is written and edited by journalists with decades of first-hand experience in covering inside news from the state capitol and the campaign trail. Available through StateNet.

3624. *Common Wealth.* 1996. q. USD 50. Ed(s): Robert Keough. The Massachusetts Institute for a New Common Wealth, 18 Tremont St., Ste 1120, Boston, MA 02108; info@massinc.org; http://www.massinc.org. *Bk. rev.:* Number and length vary. *Aud.:* Ga, Ac, Sa.

The mission of MassINC, publisher of *CommonWealth* is to develop a public agenda for Massachusetts that promotes the growth and vitality of the middle class. MassInc has four primary initiatives: economic prosperity, lifelong learning, safe neighborhoods, and civic renewal. It includes articles, interviews, news, and book reviews. *CommonWealth* calls itself the Bay State's leading political magazine. A *Boston Globe* journalist has called it "snazzy and fair-minded." Web access has been available since summer 1996.

3625. *County News.* Formerly: *N A C O News and Views.* [ISSN: 0744-9798] 1970. fortn. USD 82.50. Ed(s): Beverly Schlotterbeck. National Association of Counties, 440 First St, N W, Washington, DC 20001. Illus., adv. Circ: 27000 Controlled. Vol. ends: Dec. *Aud.:* Sa.

Published by the National Association of Counties (NACo), this journal evaluates issues and policies of interest to county officials nationwide. Sections include "Financial Services News," "HR (Human Resources) Doctor," "Job Market," "News from the Nation's Counties," "Notices," "NACo On the Move," "Profiles in Service" (profiles of county officials), "Research News," and "Web Watch." Full text available online since February 1994 at NACo's web site.

3626. *Empire State Report: the magazine of politics and public policy in New York State.* Former titles: *Empire State Report Weekly; Empire State Report.* [ISSN: 0747-0711] 1982. m. USD 19.95 domestic; USD 45 foreign; USD 4.50 newsstand/cover per issue. Ed(s): Mary Caroline Powers. Empire State Report Inc, 25-35 Beechwood Ave, Mount Vernon, NY 10553; epire@cinn.com. Adv. Circ: 10000 Paid and controlled. *Indexed:* PAIS. *Bk. rev.:* Number and length vary. *Aud.:* Ga, Ac, Sa.

The magazine of politics, policy, and the business of government in New York State reaches the state's senior municipal and town executives and financial decision makers (mayors, town supervisors, village managers, comptrollers, etc.) Readers also include statewide elected officials, state agency and authority heads, state government managers and senior staff, local and town government officials, public school and college/university administrators, private association executives, and business leaders across the state. *Empire State Report* dissects legislative issues from all angles and presents ideas in an objective fashion to incite balanced and beneficial change.

3627. ***Governing: the states and localities.*** [ISSN: 0894-3842] 1987. m. USD 39.95; USD 59.95 foreign; USD 19.95 govt. employees. Ed(s): Peter A Harkness. Governing, 1100 Connecticut Ave, N W, Ste 1300, Washington, DC 20036; http://www.governing.com. Illus., adv. Circ: 86000 Paid and controlled. Vol. ends: Sep. Online: Gale Group; LexisNexis; OCLC Online Computer Library Center, Inc.; H.W. Wilson. *Indexed:* AgeL, LRI, MagInd, PAIS, RGPR. *Aud.:* Ac, Sa.

The men and women who set policy for and manage the day-to-day operations of cities, counties, and states, as well as such governmental bodies as school boards and special districts, are the primary audience for *Governing*, published by Congressional Quarterly. A past recipient of a *Folio* magazine Editorial Excellence Award, *Governing* also has been nominated several times for National Magazine Awards in the public-interest category and for general excellence in the under-100,000 circulation category. *Governing* posts stories from leading newspapers nationwide on management, policy, technology, and current news, along with links to web sites of interest, such as on city planning, deregulation, tourism, and more.

3628. ***Government West: discussing the business of government in the West.*** [ISSN: 1520-8273] 1985. bi-m. USD 24. Ed(s): Katherine Gallia. Colt Stewart, Inc., 1005 12th St, Ste H, Sacramento, CA 95814; info@govwest.com. Adv. Circ: 19853 Controlled. *Aud.:* Sa.

Government West is written for state and local government officials who set policy and manage the day-to-day operations of cities, counties, and states, as well as such governmental bodies as special districts in the western United States: governors, legislators, county commissioners, mayors, city managers, council members, and other elected, appointed, and career officials. It boasts of its "Western perspective" on issues such as population growth, water, energy, the environment, land use planning, and immigration. The majority of the editorials and features are written by their readers: government officials. The 14 Western states covered are Alaska, Arizona, California, Colorado, Hawaii, Idaho, Montana, Nevada, New Mexico, Oregon, Texas, Utah, Washington, and Wyoming. It is a trade magazine devoted to the business of government in the West.

3629. ***Illinois Issues: a magazine of government and politics.*** [ISSN: 0738-9663] 1975. m. USD 35.95; USD 94.95 foreign. Ed(s): Peggy Boyer Long. University of Illinois at Springfield, PO Box 19243, Springfield, IL 62794-9243; http://www.uis.edu. Illus., adv. Circ: 6500. Vol. ends: Dec. *Indexed:* PAIS. *Bk. rev.:* 1, 1,000 words. *Aud.:* Ga, Ac.

Its mission is dedicated to providing fresh, provocative analysis of public policy in Illinois. With a special focus on Illinois government and politics, the magazine pays close attention to current trends and legislative issues and examines the state's quality of life. The magazine also engages its readers in dialogue, enhancing the quality of public discourse in Illinois. A not-for-profit monthly magazine published by the University of Illinois at Springfield, *Illinois Issues* also sponsors and promotes other appropriate public affairs educational activities. Available in full text online since March 2002.

3630. ***Maine Policy Review.*** [ISSN: 1064-2587] 1991. 3x/yr. 0 Donation. Ed(s): Greg Gallant, Jonathan Rubin. Margaret Chase Smith Center for Public Policy, 15 Coburn Hall, University of Maine, Orono, ME 04469-5715; mcsc@umit.maine.edu; http://www.umaine.edu/mcsc/mpr.htm. *Aud.:* Ga, Ac, Sa.

A joint publication of the Margaret Chase Smith Center for Public Policy at the University of Maine and the Margaret Chase Smith Library. The majority of articles in *Maine Policy Review* are written by Maine citizens, many of whom are readers of the journal. It publishes independent analyses of public policy issues relevant to Maine by providing accurate information and thoughtful commentary. Issues range from snowmobiling to housing. Most issues are on the web site since 1994.

3631. ***N A T A T's Reporter.*** Formerly: *N A T A T's National Community Reporter.* [ISSN: 0735-9691] 1977. bi-m. USD 36. Ed(s): Ronnie J Kweller. National Association of Towns and Townships, National Center for Small Communities, 444 N Capitol St, N W, Ste 294, Washington, DC 20001-1512. Illus., adv. Circ: 15000. Vol. ends: Dec. *Aud.:* Ga, Sa.

This periodical is designed to keep local officials informed of federal affairs with particular significance to smaller local governments. From as few as six to over two dozen news articles are featured in each issue. On occasion, there are links provided to additional sources of information. Available in full text online since 2001; highlights are available for 2000.

3632. ***Nation's Cities Weekly.*** Incorporates (in 1978): *City Weekly;* Supersedes (1963-1978): *Nation's Cities.* [ISSN: 0164-5935] 1978. w. USD 96. Ed(s): Julianne Ryan Ryder. National League of Cities, 1301 Pennsylvania Ave, N W, Washington, DC 20004; http://www.nlc.org. Illus., adv. Circ: 30610 Paid and free. Vol. ends: Dec. Microform: PQC. Online: Florida Center for Library Automation; Gale Group; Northern Light Technology, Inc. Reprint: PQC. *Indexed:* AIAP, LRI, MagInd, PAIS, SSI. *Aud.:* Ga, Sa.

This tabloid provides up-to-the-minute news on how national developments will affect cities, in-depth reports and case studies on how local governments are finding innovative solutions to today's municipal problems, and special editorial features by urban affairs experts. It includes regular reporting on developments in Congress and the Bush administration, the courts, and state government. To supplement this extensive coverage, *The Nation's Cities Weekly* provides special reports throughout the year on key topics of interest to local government leaders on finance, the environment, housing, technology, economic development, and telecommunications,- as well as extensive coverage of the National League of Cities' two annual conventions. Regular monthly columns feature news about technologies, products, and services of interest to local governments and a roundup of news about how cities are solving today's problems and improving services to citizens.

3633. ***New Rules.*** [ISSN: 1521-9917] 1999. q. USD 15. Ed(s): David Morris. Institute for Local Self-Reliance, 1313 Fifth St, S E, Minneapolis, MN 55414; dmorris@ilsr.org; http://www.newrules.org. *Indexed:* AltPI. *Aud.:* Hs, Ga, Ac.

"Designing rules as if community matters" is the slogan of the New Rules Project from the Institute for Local Self-Reliance (ILSR). Espousing the principles of the "new localism," ILSR proposes a set of new rules that builds community by supporting humanly scaled politics and economics. The publication is aimed at policy makers, organizations, and activists looking for innovative public policies. Articles are divided into 11 sections: Agriculture, Business, Electricity, Environment, Equity, Finance, Governance, Information, Retail, Sports, and Taxation. Sample topics include mail order and Internet taxation, health care, living wages, community-owned professional sports teams, ethanol, and agricultural subsidies, to name a few.

3634. ***Pennsylvania Township News.*** [ISSN: 0162-5160] 1948. m. USD 32. Ed(s): Ginni Linn. Pennsylvania State Association of Township Supervisors, 3001 Gettysburg Rd, Camp Hill, PA 17011; http://www.psats.org. Illus., adv. Circ: 12000. Vol. ends: Dec. *Aud.:* Sa.

Regular features of *Pennsylvania Township News* are the following: "Legislative Update," "Environmental Digest," "Newsworthy Items," "One Source Municipal Training?" (a listing and description of courses offered to township officials), and a "Questions & Answers" column. Articles deal with common interests to the over 1,450 Pennsylvania member townships: stormwater drainage, animal control, recycling, etc. There are also interviews with top-ranking township officials.

3635. ***Popular Government.*** [ISSN: 0032-4515] 1931. q. USD 20. Ed(s): Carol Offen, Margo Johnson. University of North Carolina at Chapel Hill, Institute of Government, Campus Box 3330, Knapp Bldg, Chapel Hill, NC 27599-3330; khunt@iogmail.iog.unc.edu; http://ncinfo.iog.unc.edu. Illus., index. Circ: 7700 Paid and free. Vol. ends: Summer. Microform: PQC. *Indexed:* CJA, PAIS. *Bk. rev.:* 1, 2,000 words. *Aud.:* Ga, Ac.

Directed to approximately 7,500 North Carolina state and local public officials, *Popular Government* contains articles on tax and finance, budgeting and purchasing, management and personnel, social services, education, justice and corrections, environmental protection, land use, and other topics of importance to governmental administration and public policy. Many of the articles are written by members of the faculty of the Institute of Government of the University of North Carolina at Chapel Hill. Others are written by specialists and practitioners in appropriate fields. Available in full text online through its web site since summer 1999; some articles are available from 1996 through spring 1999.

3636. *Privatization Watch.* Formerly (until 1988): *Fiscal Watchdog.* 1976. m. USD 135 (Individuals, USD 135; Non-profit organizations, USD 75). Ed(s): Robin Johnson. Reason Foundation, 3415 S Sepulveda Blvd, Ste 400, Los Angeles, CA 90034-6060; chrism@reason.com; http://www.reason.org/pwatch.html. Adv. Circ: 1000. *Aud.:* Ga, Ac.

Each issue is about a different topic: education, environment, corrections, public safety, and other subjects of interest. Published by the Public Policy Institute of the Reason Foundation, a public policy think tank promoting choice, competition, and a dynamic market economy as the foundation for human dignity and progress. Coverage of public-private partnerships is worldwide. Some of the articles in each issue are available online.

3637. *Public Management: devoted to the conduct of local government.* [ISSN: 0033-3611] 1918. m. USD 34 domestic; USD 50 foreign. Ed(s): Beth Payne. International City/County Management Association, 777 North Capitol St, N E Ste 500, Washington, DC 20002-4201. Illus., adv. Circ: 14000 Paid. Vol. ends: Dec. Microform: MIM; PQC. Online: bigchalk; EBSCO Publishing; Florida Center for Library Automation; Gale Group; Northern Light Technology, Inc.; OCLC Online Computer Library Center, Inc.; ProQuest Information & Learning; H.W. Wilson. *Indexed:* ABIn, BPI, MagInd, PAIS, PRA, SSI. *Aud.:* Ga, Sa.

The International City/County Management Association (ICMA) is the publisher of *Public Management*. ICMA is the professional and educational organization for chief appointed managers, administrators, and assistants in cities, towns, counties, and regional entities throughout the world. Feature articles are written from the local government manager's point of view. The intent of the articles is to allow other local government managers to adapt solutions to fit their own situations. Regular sections include letters to the editor, profiles of individual officials and corporate entities, book reviews, an ethics column, and FYI news briefs.

3638. *Spectrum (Lexington).* Former titles (until 1992): *The Journal of State Government;* (until 1986): *State Government.* [ISSN: 1067-8530] 1927. q. USD 49.99. Ed(s): Howard Mayes. Council of State Governments, 2760 Research Park Dr, Box 11910, Lexington, KY 40578-1910; info@csg.org; http://www.csg.org/. Illus. Circ: 9000. Vol. ends: Fall. Microform: WSH; PMC. Online: EBSCO Publishing; Florida Center for Library Automation; Gale Group; OCLC Online Computer Library Center, Inc.; ProQuest Information & Learning; H.W. Wilson. Reprint: PSC; WSH. *Indexed:* ABCPolSci, ABIn, FutSurv, LRI, PAIS, SSCI, SSI. *Bk. rev.:* 1, 1,000 words. *Aud.:* Ac, Sa.

Spectrum's mission is to provide reliable information on and insightful analysis of public policy issues to anyone whose interest in state government stretches beyond the limited, short-term goals of the status quo. It seeks to develop common ground among entities and individuals who are interested in improving state government, from the practitioners to the academics to the media. The focus is on emerging trends, perspectives, solutions, and papers from the Council of State Governments symposia. Some excerpts are available online.

3639. *State and Local Government Review: a journal of research and viewpoints on state and local government issues.* Supersedes: *Georgia Government Review.* [ISSN: 0160-323X] 1968. 3x/yr. USD 24 (Individuals, USD 16). Ed(s): Richard W Campbell. University of Georgia, Carl Vinson Institute of Government, 201 N Milledge Ave, Athens, GA 30602; http://www.cviog.uga.edu/projects/slgr. Illus., index. Refereed. Circ: 1000. Vol. ends: Fall. *Indexed:* ABCPolSci, HRA, IBZ, IPSA, PAIS, PRA, PSA, SUSA. *Bk. rev.:* 1, 1,000 words. *Aud.:* Ac, Sa.

State and Local Government Review is jointly sponsored by the Carl Vinson Institute of Government of the University of Georgia and the Section on Intergovernmental Administration and Management (SIAM) of the American Society for Public Administration (ASPA). SIAM is the section of ASPA dedicated to state and local as well as intergovernmental teaching and research. Membership in SIAM includes a subscription to *State and Local Government Review.* Issues include feature stories and the "Practitioner's Corner," offering practical advice for government officials on issues such as local government, federalism, telecommunications, utility deregulation, etc. This is one of the few scholarly journals in this field. Available online since 1993 through the Carl Vinson Institute of Government.

3640. *State Government News: the monthly magazine covering all facets of state government.* [ISSN: 0039-0119] 1958. m. USD 39 domestic; USD 45 foreign. Ed(s): Elaine Stuart. Council of State Governments, 2760 Research Park Dr, Box 11910, Lexington, KY 40578-1910; info@csg.org; http://www.csg.org/. Illus., adv. Circ: 17000. Vol. ends: Nov/Dec. Microform: WSH. Reprint: WSH. *Indexed:* AgeL, PAIS, SUSA. *Aud.:* Ga, Sa.

For more than 40 years, *State Government News* magazine has been a source of nonpartisan information. It offers updates and in-depth analyses of state programs, policies, and trends in the executive, legislative, and judicial branches, in areas such as health and human services, environment and natural resources, agriculture and rural policy, public safety and justice, education, energy, transportation, telecommunications, digital government, fiscal policy, economic development, state leadership, state management and administration, federalism and intergovernmental relations, interstate relations, election coverage, emergency management, and more. Each issue is devoted to a single subject, with highlights of meetings, conferences, and new publications from the Council of State Governments and affiliated organizations, plus "Perspective" columns from experts and state officials and a conference calendar to inform readers of upcoming events.

3641. *State Legislatures.* [ISSN: 0147-6041] 1975. m. USD 49 domestic; USD 51.50 Canada. Ed(s): Karen Hansen. National Conference of State Legislatures, 7700 E First Pl, Denver, CO 80230; http://www.ncsl.org. Illus., adv. Circ: 18208. Vol. ends: Dec. Online: bigchalk; EBSCO Publishing; Florida Center for Library Automation; Gale Group; LexisNexis; Northern Light Technology, Inc.; ProQuest Information & Learning. *Indexed:* PAIS, SUSA. *Aud.:* Ga, Ac.

The trends, issues, solutions, personalities, innovations, and challenges of managing a state—they will all be found in *State Legislatures* magazine, published by the National Conference of State Legislatures. This national magazine of state government and policy provides lively, insightful articles encompassing vital information on public policies. From agriculture to cloning to transportation, a wide variety of topics are covered.

3642. *State Net Capitol Journal.* [ISSN: 1521-8457] 1998. w. USD 1800. State Net, 2101 K St, Sacramento, CA 95816; statenet@statenet.com; http://www.statenet.com. *Aud.:* Ga, Ac, Sa.

State Net produces two publications devoted to government and politics: *California Journal* (see above) and *State Net Capitol Journal.* The latter provides a comprehensive look at the issues and politics driving state governments all over the country. The 50-state edition covers major trends in the spotlight, from Augusta to Honolulu, featuring original reporting from its team of editors, from governors' agendas to legislative hot topics. It also provides an entertaining and informative array of notes and quotes, selecting information from numerous publications around the country.

3643. *Virginia Review.* Formerly (until 1981): *Virginia Municipal Review.* [ISSN: 0732-9156] 1924. bi-m. USD 19. Ed(s): Alyson L Taylor White. Review Publications, Inc., PO Box 860, Chester, VA 23831-0860; rhabeck@mindspring.com; http://www.reviewnet.com. Illus., adv. Circ: 5000 Paid and controlled. Vol. ends: Nov/Dec. *Aud.:* Sa.

A professional journal for officials at all levels of government in the Commonwealth of Virginia, *Virginia Review* prints articles describing specific problems faced by localities and how the problems were solved, as well as employee relations, planning for growth, and economic development, among other topics. Each issue focuses on a specific theme. The journal does not include political articles or those that have the sole purpose of selling a product or concept.

State and Municipal Associations

These periodicals offer a forum for discussion and a medium for the exchange of ideas and information on municipal matters for local officials. Similar in pattern to magazines in the State and Local/General section, the periodicals in this category generally have several feature articles in each issue, in addition to a calendar segment, a solutions column, and a legal advice column. While some have a rosy-colored outlook, most write of issues to be confronted and solved, urban sprawl, mosquito control, traffic, crime, saving energy, and revitalizing downtown areas, to name a few topics. Of interest to practitioners and observers of municipal government.

3644. ***Alabama Municipal Journal.*** [ISSN: 0002-4309] 1943. m. USD 12. Ed(s): Ann Christensen. Alabama League of Municipalities, 535 Adams Ave, Box 1270, Montgomery, AL 36102. Illus., adv. Circ: 4500. Vol. ends: Jun. *Aud.:* Sa.

From the Alabama League of Municipalities, the articles in this periodical highlight the practical issues faced by local governments in Alabama and spotlight common problems, solutions, trends, and legal information. It offers reprints of speeches and articles from other publications from time to time. Unrestricted Internet access includes select recent articles.

3645. ***City & Town.*** Formerly: *Arkansas Municipalities.* [ISSN: 0193-8371] 1947. m. USD 15; USD 1.50 newsstand/cover per issue. Ed(s): John K Woodruff. Arkansas Municipal League, PO Box 38, North Little Rock, AR 72115; jkw@arml.org; http://www.arml.org. Illus., index, adv. Circ: 7000 Paid and free. Vol. ends: Dec. *Aud.:* Sa.

Designed to provide a forum for municipal officials to exchange ideas and compare notes on accomplishments and problems in Arkansas, *City & Town* is sent to elected officials, city administrators and managers, police chiefs, fire chiefs and other department heads, and state officials, local newspapers, chambers of commerce, and other offices and persons who are interested in municipal affairs. Employment opportunities and classified ads are spotlighted in the Municipal Mart section. Selected articles appear online.

3646. ***Cityscape.*** [ISSN: 1088-5951] 1995. m. USD 18 in state. Ed(s): Mindy Kralicek. Iowa League of Cities, 317 Sixth Ave, Ste. 1400, Des Moines, IA 50309-4111. Illus., adv. Circ: 5500 Paid. Vol. ends: Jun. *Indexed:* AmStI, CJA, JEL. *Aud.:* Sa.

Cityscape is part of the membership benefits of the Iowa League of Cities. The publication contains articles about city government issues in Iowa and serves as a communication tool for local government officials. Not available online.

3647. ***Colorado Municipalities.*** [ISSN: 0010-1664] 1925. bi-m. Non-members, USD 25. Ed(s): Alison Lockwood. Colorado Municipal League, 1144 Sherman St, Denver, CO 80203-2207; http://www.cml.org. Illus., adv. Circ: 4900. *Indexed:* PAIS. *Bk. rev.:* Number and length vary. *Aud.:* Ga, Ac, Sa.

This is the flagship magazine of the Colorado Municipal League. Its target audience is Colorado municipal government officials. Each issue runs to about 30 pages and is packed with in-depth coverage of the topics and issues important to those officials. Not available online.

3648. ***Delaware Capitol Review.*** Formerly: *Delaware Business Review.* [ISSN: 1093-0736] 1978. w. USD 78 domestic; USD 90 in the Americas. Ed(s): Diane Cook. Independent Newspapers, Inc., PO Box 737, Dover, DE 19903. Adv. Circ: 10100. Online: Northern Light Technology, Inc.; OCLC Online Computer Library Center, Inc.; ProQuest Information & Learning. *Aud.:* Ga, Ac, Sa.

This tabloid weekly newspaper describes itself as the only public affairs journal devoted to state government, politics, and issues affecting all Delawareans. It also holds the exclusive contract to publish state invitations to bid and legal ads. Not available online.

3649. ***Illinois Municipal Review: the magazine of the municipalities.*** [ISSN: 0019-2139] 1922. m. USD 10 (Free to members). Ed(s): Gary Koch. Illinois Municipal League, PO Box 5180, Springfield, IL 62705-5180; gkoch@iml.org; http://www.iml.org. Illus., adv. Circ: 13500. Vol. ends: Dec. *Aud.:* Sa.

A legal Q&A, municipal calendar, exchange column, editorials, and a variety of articles of interest to local Illinois government officials make up this magazine. Available online and searchable back to 1997.

3650. ***Kansas Government Journal.*** [ISSN: 0022-8613] 1914. m. USD 28. Ed(s): Kim Gulley. League of Kansas Municipalities, 300 S W Eighth St, Topeka, KS 66603-3912; http://www.ink.org/public/kmin/league/mission.html. Illus., index, adv. Circ: 6050. Vol. ends: Dec. *Aud.:* Sa.

This periodical keeps Kansas officials up to date on federal and statewide legislation as well as economic developments and budgetary procedures impacting municipalities. It also focuses on new ways of solving problems and assisting citizens. A subject index appears in the December issue. Not available online.

3651. ***Louisiana Municipal Review.*** [ISSN: 0164-3622] 1938. m. USD 12. Ed(s): L Gordon King. Louisiana Municipal Association, PO Box 4327, Baton Rouge, LA 70821; lamunicipalassociation@compuserve.com; http://www.lamunis.org. Adv. Circ: 3300 Paid and controlled. *Aud.:* Ga, Ac, Sa.

The official publication of the Louisiana Municipal Association, a statewide league of villages, towns, and cities in Louisiana, *Louisiana Municipal Review* serves as a medium of exchange of ideas and information on municipal affairs for the public officials of Louisiana. It includes news articles, features, obituaries, and a column written by the state's governor.

3652. ***Michigan Municipal Review.*** [ISSN: 0026-2331] 1928. 10x/yr. USD 24. Ed(s): Judi L Campbell. Michigan Municipal League, 1675 Green Rd, Box 1487, Ann Arbor, MI 48106; http://www.minl.org/. Illus., adv. Circ: 9200. Vol. ends: Dec. Microform: PQC. Reprint: PQC. *Indexed:* PAIS. *Aud.:* Sa.

This periodical aims to provide a forum to Michigan officials for the exchange of ideas and information. Municipal officials, consultants, legislators, and staff members of the Michigan Municipal League contribute to the publication. Want ads, a marketplace column, municipal calendar, and legal spotlights round out the issues. Selected articles appear online.

3653. ***Minnesota Cities.*** Formerly: *Minnesota Municipalities.* [ISSN: 0148-8546] 1916. m. USD 20. Ed(s): Erica Noris. League of Minnesota Cities, 145 University Ave. W., St. Paul, MN 55103-2044; http://www.lmnc.org. Illus., adv. Circ: 9900. *Indexed:* PAIS. *Aud.:* Ga, Ac, Sa.

The League of Minnesota Cities' monthly magazine includes articles on a wide range of city-related topics. Each issue is based on a theme—for example, human resources, technology, and winter. Highlights on the current issue are on their web site.

3654. ***Municipality.*** [ISSN: 0027-3597] 1900. m. Members, USD 18. Ed(s): Jean Staral. League of Wisconsin Municipalities, 202 State Street, Ste 300, Madison, WI 53703. Illus., index, adv. Circ: 9682. Vol. ends: Dec. *Indexed:* PAIS. *Aud.:* Sa.

From mosquito control to complex legal matters, this periodical showcases issues of interest to local government officials in Wisconsin. News about local officials, web links of interest, and a calendar are also included. Full text on the web.

3655. ***New Jersey Municipalities.*** [ISSN: 0028-5846] 1917. m. Oct.-Jun. Members, USD 14; Non-members, USD 16. Ed(s): William G Dressel, Jr. New Jersey State League of Municipalities, 407 W State St, Trenton, NJ 08618. Illus., index, adv. Circ: 8200. Vol. ends: Dec. *Indexed:* PAIS, SFSA, SUSA. *Aud.:* Sa.

Typical lead articles have been on public-private partnerships, energy, and urban sprawl. Columns include "Legal Q&A," "Legislative Update," "Labor relations," "Washington Watch," job notices, and a calendar. Selected articles available online.

3656. ***Quality Cities.*** Formerly: *Florida Municipal Record.* [ISSN: 0892-4171] 1928. m. 11/yr. USD 20. Ed(s): Beth Mulrennan. Florida League of Cities, Inc., PO Box 1757, Tallahassee, FL 32302. Illus., adv. Circ: 4900. Vol. ends: May. *Aud.:* Ga, Sa.

Quality Cities serves as a medium of exchange of ideas and information for Florida's municipal officials. Reporting addresses legislation affecting cities, current municipal issues, and innovative local government ideas. The two summer numbers cover the post-legislative session report and the Florida League of Cities' conference.

3657. ***Small Community Quarterly.*** 2001. q. Free. Ed(s): Robert Neidlinger. National Center for Small Communities, 444 N Capitol St., NW, Ste 397, Washington, DC 20001-1202; ncsc@sso.org; http://www.smallcommunities.org. *Aud.:* Ga, Ac, Sa.

The newsletter of the National Center for Small Communities (NCSC), the *Small Community Quarterly*, concentrates on issues of importance to small and rural towns. It features interviews with public policy and opinion leaders and articles on economic development, financial management, revenue generation, telecommunications, environmental concerns, and more. The *Quarterly* also includes helpful resources and updates on the NCSC's publications and activities. Subscriptions are available with NCSC membership. Each issue online features brief summaries of all articles with links to longer versions. Announcements of funding opportunities and resource publications are followed by direct links to follow-up on application or ordering details. Available free on the Web since the winter 2001 issue.

3658. ***Virginia Town & City.*** [ISSN: 0042-6784] 1966. m. USD 8. Ed(s): Christine A Everson. Virginia Municipal League, PO Box 12164, Richmond, VA 23241-0164. Illus., adv. Circ: 5000. *Bk. rev.:* Number and length vary. *Aud.:* Ga, Ac, Sa.

Each issue is devoted to a single theme. Typical themes have been terrorism, budgets, urban planning, and records managment. Selections have been available on the web since 2002.

3659. ***Western City.*** [ISSN: 0279-5337] 1925. m. USD 39 domestic (Students, USD 26.50). Ed(s): Jude Hudson. League of California Cities, 1400 K St, 4th Floor, Sacramento, CA 95814-3916; maxwellp@cacities.org; http://www.westerncity.com. Illus., index, adv. Circ: 10800 Paid and controlled. Vol. ends: Dec. *Indexed:* PAIS. *Aud.:* Sa.

Both practical ideas and bigger-picture policy issues and trends are the twin goals of *Western City*. The magazine's stated mission is to support and serve elected and appointed city officials (and those interested in local government), and to examine the policy, process and fiscal issues that affect local government and to do so from a number of angles, including individual city success stories, legal analyses, and statewide perspectives. The current issue and issues from the previous six months are available online, with tables of contents available back to 1996.

■ HIKING, CLIMBING, AND OUTDOOR RECREATION

General/Association Magazines/Association Newsletters

Pauline Baughman, Reference Librarian, Multnomah County Library, 801 S.W. Tenth Ave., Portland, OR 97205-2597; paulineb@multcolib.org; FAX: 503-988-5226

Introduction

No matter the season, outdoor recreation, in its many forms, is popular. Most publications focus on specific activities, with publishers concentrating on specific audiences for their publications rather than focusing on outdoor recreation in general. While a number of the titles below will be enjoyed by a general audience, many of them are specialized and will be of interest only to those who participate in the activity involved. Many of the titles included in this section have web sites that contain one or more articles from the print publication.

Outdoor magazines included in this section focus on a broad range of issues and activities, including conservation and environmental issues, and will appeal to a broad range of people. Aimed at the general consumer, they are attractive and contain many color photographs.

The commercial climbing magazines listed here focus primarily on the United States, with some international coverage. Most titles include equipment reviews, climbing tips, and maps and route information, along with stunning color photos. Association magazines, on the other hand, primarily contain accounts of trips and expeditions, together with some general interest or regional articles.

Like commercial climbing magazines, commercial hiking publications cover wide geographic regions and have articles that will be of interest to many hikers. Association magazines, however, fill the local and regional information gap left by commercial publishers by focusing on specific regions and trails.

In addition to the annotated list of commercial publications and association magazines below, there is an unannotated sample of hiking, climbing, and outdoor recreation association newsletters. Most association magazines and newsletters focus on the particular geographic region in which the organization is based and are a good supplement to the commercial titles available. Librarians are advised to seek out and collect publications from those local organizations that will be of most interest to their patrons.

Basic Periodicals

Hs: *Backpacker;* Ga: *American Hiker, Backpacker, Climbing, Outside (Santa Fe), Rock & Ice;* Ac: *Alpine Journal, American Alpine Journal, Backpacker, Canadian Alpine Journal, Climbing, Outside (Santa Fe), Rock & Ice.*

Basic Abstracts and Indexes

Ingenta.

General

3660. ***Backpacker: the magazine of wilderness adventure.*** Former titles (until 1980): *Backpacker Including Wilderness Camping;* (until 1979): *Backpacker (1973);* Incorporates (1971-19??): *Wilderness Camping.* [ISSN: 0277-867X] 1973. 9x/yr. USD 29.98 domestic; USD 42.98 Canada; USD 41.98 elsewhere. Ed(s): Jonathan Dorn. Rodale, 33 E Minor St, Emmaus, PA 18098; info@rodale.com; http://www.rodale.com. Illus., adv. Sample. Circ: 295000 Paid. Vol. ends: Nov/Dec. Microform: PQC. Online: bigchalk; EBSCO Publishing; Florida Center for Library Automation; Gale Group; Northern Light Technology, Inc.; OCLC Online Computer Library Center, Inc.; ProQuest Information & Learning; H.W. Wilson. *Indexed:* ASIP, ConsI, MagInd, PEI, RGPR, SportS. *Bk. rev.:* 2-3, 100-200 words. *Aud.:* Hs, Ga, Ac.

Backpacker focuses primarily on hiking and backpacking, but it is a magazine that will appeal to many outdoor enthusiasts. Along with detailed information on planning trips, this magazine contains articles on nature, health and nutrition, and first aid and safety, as well as recipes and product reviews. The annual "gear guide" contains equipment and clothing reviews. *Backpacker*'s web site, *BaseCamp,* does not contain articles from the print edition of the magazine, but it features daily news items, a weekend wilderness guide, and an online version of the annual gear guide.

3661. ***Climber.*** Former titles (until 1995): *Climber and Hillwalker; Climber; Climber and Rambler; Climber.* [ISSN: 1358-5207] 1961. m. GBP 32 domestic; GBP 45 in Europe; GBP 58 elsewhere. Ed(s): Bernard Newman. Warners Group Publications Plc, The Maltings, West St, Bourne, PE10 9PH, United Kingdom; subscriptions@warnersgroup.co.uk; http://www.warnersgroup.co.uk. Illus., adv. Sample. Circ: 15549. Vol. ends: Dec. *Indexed:* SportS. *Bk. rev.:* 2-4, 300-800 words. *Aud.:* Ac, Sa.

This magazine has very limited coverage of North America, but it will be of interest to those who climb internationally. Each issue contains news items, route descriptions, profiles of climbers, and gear reviews. Primary coverage is of rock and ice climbing.

3662. *Climbing.* [ISSN: 0045-7159] 1970. 9x/yr. USD 29.95 domestic; USD 39.95 Canada; USD 44.95 elsewhere. Primedia Enthusiast Group, 0326 Hwy 133, Ste 190, Carbondale, CO 81623; http://www.primedia.com. Illus., adv. Sample. Circ: 50422 Paid. Vol. ends: Dec/Jan. *Indexed:* SportS. *Bk. rev.:* 4-5, 100-300 words. *Aud.:* Ac, Sa.

Climbing contains a variety of articles related to sport, traditional, alpine, and ice climbing in the United States, with some international coverage. Each issue contains interviews, news, a detailed expedition plan to a particular area, equipment reviews, competition results, and spectacular photos. One issue a year is dedicated to gear and product reviews. The web site contains much of the full text of the print magazine and includes news, an events calendar, and an index to past issues of *Climbing.*

3663. *The Climbing Art: literature, poetry, art, and information for and about the spirit of climbing.* [ISSN: 1073-4988] 1986. s-a. USD 18 domestic; USD 30 foreign. Ed(s): Ron Morrow. Ron Morrow, Ed. & Pub., 6390 E Floyd Dr, Denver, CO 80222-7638; rmorrow@dnor.uswest.net. Illus., adv. Sample. Circ: 1200. Vol. ends: Dec. *Bk. rev.:* 10-15, length varies. *Aud.:* Ga, Ac, Sa.

This literary climbing magazine is unlike any of its counterparts. It is international in scope and presents small stories about the world of climbing. Each issue contains essays, personal narratives, stories, and poems, as well as black-and-white drawings, cartoons, and photographs.

3664. *Disabled Outdoors Magazine.* [ISSN: 1067-098X] 1987. q. USD 14; USD 20 Canada. Ed(s): Carolyn Dohme. John Kopchik, Jr., HC 80, Box 395, Grand Marais, MN 55604. Illus., adv. Circ: 7800. Vol. ends: Dec. *Bk. rev.:* 1-4, 500-1,500 words. *Aud.:* Ems, Hs, Ac, Sa.

Disabled Outdoors is the only magazine in the United States dedicated specifically to the outdoors and the disabled person. Articles are written by people with disabilities for people of all ages and with all types of disabilities. Topics cover the United States and Canada and include camping, mountaineering, hunting, fishing, boating, and snow and water skiing.

Field & Stream. See Hunting and Guns section.

3665. *High Mountain.* Former titles: *High Mountain Sports; High Magazine.* 1982. m. GBP 28 domestic; GBP 45 foreign; GBP 2.99 newsstand/cover per issue. Ed(s): Geoff Birtles. Greenshires Publishing Limited, Telford Way, Kettering, NN16 8UN, United Kingdom; http://www.greenshirespublishing.com. Illus., adv. Sample. Circ: 14000. Vol. ends: Dec. *Bk. rev.:* 2-4, 400-1,200 words. *Aud.:* Ac, Sa.

Focusing primarily on Britain, *High Mountain* is a commercial journal that publishes the British Mountaineering Council's news and notes. Each issue contains articles related to rock climbing and mountaineering as well as interviews and equipment reviews.

3666. *Outdoor Life.* [ISSN: 0030-7076] 1898. m. USD 11.95 domestic; USD 19.95 Canada; USD 3.99 newsstand/cover per issue. Ed(s): Todd Smith. Time4 Media, Inc., 2 Park Ave, New York, NY 10016; steve.clow@tmm.com; http://www.outdoorlife.com. Illus., adv. Sample. Circ: 1350000 Paid. Vol. ends: Dec. CD-ROM: ProQuest Information & Learning. Microform: NBI; PQC. Online: The Dialog Corporation; EBSCO Publishing; Gale Group; Northern Light Technology, Inc.; OCLC Online Computer Library Center, Inc.; ProQuest Information & Learning. Reprint: PQC. *Indexed:* ConsI, MagInd, RGPR. *Aud.:* Ems, Hs, Ga, Ac.

Outdoor Life has been providing readers with articles on hunting and fishing for over 100 years. There are four regional editions: East, Midwest, South, and West; the edition received is determined by address. Topics include techniques, gear and product reviews, and the occasional article on conservation and the environment. Coverage is primarily North America and Canada. The web site, which is also the web site for *Field & Stream,* will be of interest to fans of either magazine.

3667. *Outside (Santa Fe).* Formerly (until 1980): *Mariah - Outside;* Which was formed by the merger of (1976-1979): *Mariah;* (1977-1979): *Outside (San Francisco).* [ISSN: 0278-1433] 1976. m. USD 18 domestic; USD 38.97 Canada; USD 45.97 elsewhere. Ed(s): Sarah Friedman. Mariah Media Inc., Outside Plaza, 400 Market St, Santa Fe, NM 87501; http://www.outsidemag.com/. Illus., adv. Circ: 575000. Microform: PQC. Reprint: PQC. *Indexed:* ASIP, RI-1, SportS. *Aud.:* Hs, Ga.

Outside magazine covers all aspects of outdoor activities, including camping, climbing, hiking, cycling, and fishing. Included are articles that cover the United States and the globe, as well as photographs, gear reviews, and fitness tips. The advertising section "Active Traveler Directory" lists recreational opportunities across the world. *Outside* won the National Magazine Award for General Excellence 1996–1998.

3668. *Rock & Ice: the climber's magazine.* [ISSN: 0885-5722] 1984. 8x/yr. USD 29.95; USD 4.95 newsstand/cover. Ed(s): Tyler Stableford. Big Stone Publishing, 1101 Village Rd, Ste UL-4D, Carbondale, CO 81623. Illus., adv. Sample. Circ: 37000 Paid. Vol. ends: Nov/Dec. *Bk. rev.:* 5-8, 300-500 words. *Aud.:* Ac, Sa.

Aimed at the serious climber, *Rock & Ice* provides general articles on climbing and climbers as well as detailed information on climbing areas, primarily in the United States, including locations, routes, and interviews. There are also articles on techniques, product reviews, and an impressive photo gallery. Special issues include an annual guide to road trips and a "SuperGuide" that covers international climbing. *Rock & Ice Online* features news, notice of climbing events, technical tips, and reader responses to controversial climbing topics.

3669. *Sierra: exploring, enjoying and protecting the planet.* Formerly: *Sierra Club Bulletin.* [ISSN: 0161-7362] 1893. bi-m. USD 12 (Membership, USD 39). Ed(s): Joan Hamilton. Sierra Club, 85 Second St, San Francisco, CA 94105-3441; sierra.magazine@sierraclub.org; http://www.sierraclub.org/sierra/. Illus., index, adv. Circ: 550000. Vol. ends: Nov/Dec. Microform: PQC. Online: bigchalk; EBSCO Publishing; Florida Center for Library Automation; Gale Group; Northern Light Technology, Inc.; OCLC Online Computer Library Center, Inc.; ProQuest Information & Learning; H.W. Wilson. Reprint: PQC. *Indexed:* AltPI, BAS, BRI, BiogInd, BiolAb, BiolDig, CBRI, CIJE, EnvAb, GSI, GeoRef, LRI, M&GPA, MagInd, RGPR. *Aud.:* Hs, Ga, Ac.

The Sierra Club, founded in 1892, is well known for its commitment to protecting the earth's ecosystems. *Sierra,* the official publication of the club, contains well-researched articles that are usually written by freelance journalists or Sierra Club members, combined with numerous color photographs. The "Mixed Media" feature reviews selected environmental books, web sites, and videos. Many of the articles found in *Sierra* are available on the web site.

3670. *Summit: The Mountain Journal.* [ISSN: 0039-5056] 1955. bi-m. USD 24.95. Ed(s): John Harlin, III. Summit Publications, PO Box 1341, Eagle, ID 83616-1341. Illus., index, adv. Circ: 35000. Vol. ends: Nov/Dec. *Indexed:* SportS. *Bk. rev.:* 2-4, 100-400 words. *Aud.:* Ga, Ac.

This journal, which attempts to capture the spirit of mountaineering, will appeal to the reader with a casual interest in the topic. It does not focus on the activity of climbing, but each issue contains general-interest articles on adventure, history, and individuals. Issues occasionally contain fiction and gear reviews. Each issue includes a bibliography of suggested further readings.

Association Magazines

3671. *A M C Outdoors.* Formerly: *Appalachia Bulletin;* Which superseded: *A M C Times.* [ISSN: 1067-5604] 1907. 10x/yr. Members, USD 40. Ed(s): Madeleine Eno, Jane Roy Brown. Appalachian Mountain Club, 5 Joy St, Boston, MA 02108; http://www.outdoors.org. Illus., adv. Sample. Circ: 68000 Paid. *Bk. rev.:* 2-4, 400-1,200 words. *Aud.:* Ac, Sa.

Published by the Appalachian Mountain Club (see annotation below for *Appalachia Journal,* the club's journal), this magazine features articles on hiking areas and conservation issues in the Northeast. Each issue contains club news and information on club activities, profiles of members, and technique and equipment tips.

3672. *Adirondac.* [ISSN: 0001-8236] 1945. 6x/yr. Non-members, USD 20. Ed(s): Neal Burdick. Adirondack Mountain Club, Inc., 814 Goggins Rd, Lake George, NY 12845-4117; pubs@adk.org; http://www.adk.org. Illus., index, adv. Sample. Circ: 18500 Controlled. Vol. ends: Nov/Dec. *Indexed:* BHA, EnvAb. *Bk. rev.:* 2-3, 200-400 words. *Aud.:* Ga.

This magazine is dedicated to "promoting the protection and enlightened use of state park and forest preserve lands." Focusing on the Adirondack and Catskill mountain regions, this title contains articles on current environmental topics, personal accounts of hiking, climbing, and canoeing trips, and club news and programs.

3673. *Alpine Journal: a record of mountain adventure and scientific observation.* Incorporates (in 1982): *Alpine Climbing;* (in 1977): *Ladies Alpine Club. Journal.* [ISSN: 0065-6569] 1863. a. GBP 18.50. Ed(s): Johanna Merz. Cordee Books & Maps, 3a De Montfort St, Leicester, LE1 7HD, United Kingdom. Illus., index, adv. Sample. Circ: 1500. *Indexed:* GeoRef, SportS. *Bk. rev.:* 30-45, 50-1,500 words. *Aud.:* Ac, Sa.

International in scope, this annual publication presents detailed accounts of expeditions and climbs throughout the world, recording all aspects of mountains and mountaineering, including art, literature, geography, history, geology, medicine, and ethics in the mountain environment. *Alpine Journal* contains numerous illustrations and maps, amid its general-interest articles and club notes.

3674. *American Alpine Journal.* [ISSN: 0065-6925] 1929. a. USD 30. Ed(s): Christian Beckwith. American Alpine Club, 710 10th St, Ste 100, Golden, CO 80401-1022; aaj@americanalpineclub.org; http://www.americanalpineclub.org. Illus., index. Circ: 8000. Microform: PQC. Reprint: PQC. *Indexed:* GeoRef. *Bk. rev.:* 20-30, 200-1,200 words. *Aud.:* Ac, Sa.

Each issue of this journal features 15–20 personal narratives of mountaineering expeditions around the world. Most articles include photos and maps of routes and a summary of area and new-route statistics. Each issue contains a lengthy "Climbs and Expeditions" section, which gives details of major climbs and attempts throughout the world, and concludes with summaries of club activities and member obituaries.

3675. *American Alpine News.* Formerly: *A A C News.* [ISSN: 0147-9288] 1950. q. USD 5 domestic; USD 10 foreign. Ed(s): Hilary Maitland, Gene Ellis. American Alpine Club, 710 10th St, Ste 100, Golden, CO 80401-1022; getinfo@americanalpineclub.org; http://www.americanalpineclub.org. Illus., adv. Sample. Circ: 6000. Vol. ends: Dec. Reprint: PQC. *Indexed:* CINAHL, SportS. *Bk. rev.:* 1-2, 200-250 words. *Aud.:* Ac, Sa.

Like most of the other association magazines in this section, *American Alpine News* contains club and expedition news, a calendar of events, and features on club members. It includes articles on topics of interest to climbers, reports of climbs, and classified ads.

3676. *American Hiker: the magazine of American Hiking Society.* Formerly (until 1993): *American Hiker News.* [ISSN: 0279-9472] 1977. bi-m. USD 25. Ed(s): David Lillard. American Hiking Society, PO Box 20160, Washington, DC 20041-2160; info@americanhiking.org; http://www.americanhiking.org. Illus., adv. Sample. Circ: 10000. Vol. ends: Dec. *Aud.:* Ga, Ac, Sa.

The American Hiking Society, a nonprofit organization, is dedicated to preserving America's hiking trails. Its magazine covers a wide geographic area and contains general interest articles on hiking and features trail and equipment information as well as society news.

3677. *Appalachia Journal.* [ISSN: 0003-6587] 1876. s-a. USD 10. Ed(s): Lucille Daniel. Appalachian Mountain Club, 5 Joy St, Boston, MA 02108. Illus., index, adv. Sample. Circ: 13000. Vol. ends: Winter. *Indexed:* BiolAb, GeoRef. *Bk. rev.:* 5-10, 200-400 words. *Aud.:* Ga, Ac, Sa.

Because of its broad geographic scope, *Appalachia Journal* will appeal to many hikers and climbers. Described as "America's oldest journal of mountaineering and conservation," it contains articles on hiking and climbing experiences, conservation, and natural history. Also included are club notes, obituaries, and analyses of hiking and climbing accidents.

3678. *Appalachian Trailway News.* [ISSN: 0003-6641] 1939. 5x/yr. USD 15. Ed(s): Judith Jenner. Appalachian Trail Conference, PO Box 807, Harpers Ferry, WV 25425; http://www.atconf.org. Illus. Circ: 29000 Paid. Vol. ends: Nov/Dec. *Indexed:* GeoRef. *Bk. rev.:* 1-2, 200-400 words. *Aud.:* Ga.

Focusing primarily on preserving and maintaining the Appalachian Trailway, this magazine covers conservation and environmental issues, trail-building efforts, hiking experiences, and club news.

3679. *British Columbia Mountaineer.* [ISSN: 0045-2998] 1917. biennial. CND 12. Ed(s): M C Feller. British Columbia Mountaineering Club, PO Box 2674, Vancouver, BC V6B 3W8, Canada. Illus., adv. Circ: 500. *Aud.:* Ac, Sa.

British Columbia Mountaineer, the club journal, reports on recent climbs in British Columbia, camps, and expeditions. It is illustrated with black-and-white photos and maps. The newsletter, published ten times a year, contains club news, trip schedules, and access information.

3680. *Bruce Trail News.* [ISSN: 0383-9249] 1963. q. CND 12; USD 12. Ed(s): Norman Day. Trail News Inc., 17 Marlborough Ave, Toronto, ON M5R 1X5, Canada. Illus., adv. Sample. Circ: 10000 Controlled. *Bk. rev.:* 2-4, 100-500 words. *Aud.:* Ga.

The Bruce Trail consists of more than 800 kilometers of hiking trails on the Niagara Escarpment between Niagara Falls and Tobermory, Canada. This publication offers club news, trail updates, personal narratives related to the trail, and general interest articles related to the environment and nature. The association's web site provides general information about the trail as well as publication and membership information.

3681. *Canadian Alpine Journal.* [ISSN: 0068-8207] 1907. a. CND 28.95. Ed(s): Geoff Powter. Alpine Club of Canada, PO Box 8040, Canmore, AB T1W 2T8, Canada; alpclub@teluspianet.net; http://www.AlpineClubfCanada.ca. Illus., index, adv. Sample. Circ: 3500. *Indexed:* GeoRef, SportS. *Bk. rev.:* 3-4, 500-800 words. *Aud.:* Ac, Sa.

The *Canadian Alpine Journal* features accounts of mountaineering expeditions in Canada and of Canadian mountaineers. Also included are adventures in other countries, essays, stories, club news, and obituaries.

3682. *Mountaineer (Seattle): to explore, study, preserve and enjoy the natural beauty of the Northwest and beyond.* [ISSN: 0027-2620] 1907. m. plus special issues. USD 20. Ed(s): Brad Stracener. Mountaineers, Inc., 300 Third Ave W, Seattle, WA 98119-4117. Illus., adv. Sample. Circ: 15000. Vol. ends: Dec. *Indexed:* GeoRef. *Bk. rev.:* 1-3, 200-400 words. *Aud.:* Ac, Sa.

Mountaineer is the monthly publication of the Seattle Mountaineers club. Issues consist primarily of information about club activities, trips, and classes. Each issue contains four to five articles related to local issues of interest and reports of legislative news related to the environment.

3683. *Signpost for Northwest Trails.* Formerly: *Signpost for Northwest Hikers.* [ISSN: 8750-1600] 1966. m. USD 25. Ed(s): Dan Nelson. Washington Trails Association, 1305 4th Ave, 512, Seattle, WA 98101-2401; http://pasko.physiol.washington.edu/wta/. Illus., index, adv. Sample. Circ: 3500 Paid. Vol. ends: Dec. *Aud.:* Ga.

Focusing on the Pacific Northwest, this magazine includes descriptions of hikes, hiking techniques, environmental legislation news, and activity reports of the Washington Trails Association. It is most useful for its reader-contributed trail-condition reports.

3684. ***Trail and Timberline.*** [ISSN: 0041-0756] 1918. m. Non-members, USD 15. Ed(s): Scott Stebbinson. Colorado Mountain Club, 710 10th St, Ste 200, Golden, CO 80401-1022. Illus., index, adv. Circ: 7500. Vol. ends: Dec. *Bk. rev.:* 1-2, 100-400 words. *Aud.:* Ga.

This association magazine reports the activities and news of the Colorado Mountain Club. It includes personal narratives of club members and includes occasional articles on environmental issues and natural history.

Association Newsletters

Access Notes. q. Free to members. Sally Moser, Access Fund, P.O. Box 17010, Boulder, CO 80308.

Adirondack Forty-Sixer Peeks. 1948. s-a. Free to members. P.O. Box 180, Cadyville, NY 12918-0180.

Adirondack Trail Improvement Society Newsletter. 1897. s-a. Free to members. Tony Goodwin, Adirondack Trail Improvement Soc., P.O. Box 565, Keene Valley, NY 12943.

American Alpine News. [ISSN: 0147-9288] 1950. 4/yr. $10. Hilary Maitland, Amer. Alpine Club Press, 710 Tenth St., Ste. 100, Golden, CO 80401; http://www.americanalpineclub.org.

American Hiker. [ISSN: 0164-5722] 1979. bi-m. Free to members (Nonmembers, $25). Sue Dodge, Amer. Hiking Soc., 1422 Fenwick Ln., Silver Spring, MD 20910-3328.

Apex to Zenith. q. Free to members. Highpointers Club, P.O. Box 70, Arcadia, MO 63621.

B.C. Mountaineer Newsletter. [ISSN: 0045-2998] 1917. 10/yr. Free to members. M. C. Feller, British Columbia Mountaineering Club, P.O. Box 2674, Vancouver, BC, Canada V6B 3W8.

Buckeye Trailblazer. bi-m. James W. Sprague, Buckeye Trail Association, P.O. Box 254, Worthington, OH 43085.

California Explorer. [ISSN: 0164-8748] 1974. bi-m. $28.50. Kay Graves, JBK Enterprises, 1135 Terminal Way, Suite 209, Reno, NV 89502.

Chicago Mountaineer. 1945. m. Free to members (Nonmembers, $10). David L. Harrison, Chicago Mountaineering Club, 3239 N. Kenmore Ave. #5, Chicago, IL 60657.

Desert Trails. 1975. q. Free to members. Anne Garrison, Desert Trail Assn., P.O. Box 34, Madras, OR 97741.

DIVIDEnds. [ISSN: 1069-6660] 1980. s-a. $7.50. Gary Grey, Continental Divide Trail Soc., 3704 N. Charles St. #601, Baltimore, MD 21218; http://www.gorp.com/dcts/.

FLT News. q. Free to members. Dorothy J. Beye, Finger Lake Trail Conference, P.O. Box 18040, Rochester, NY 14618.

Footprint. [ISSN: 1064-0681] 1966. bi-m. Free to members. Peter Durnell, Florida Trail Assn., 5415 SW 13th St., Gainesville, FL 32608.

Gazette of the Alpine Club of Canada. [ISSN: 0833-0778] 1986. q. Free to members. Zac Bolan, Alpine Club of Canada, P.O. Box 8040, Indian Flats Rd., Canmore, AB, Canada T1W 2T8.

Iowa Climber. 1940. s-a. Free to members. John Ebert, Iowa Mountaineers, P.O. Box 163, Iowa City, IA 52244.

Lincoln Heritage Trail Foundation. 1963. 5/yr. Free to members. Bryan Marshall, Lincoln Heritage Trail Foundation, P.O. Box 1507, Springfield, IL 62705.

Long Trail News. 1922. q. Free to members (Nonmembers, $24). Sylvia Plumb, Green Mountain Club, Inc., Route 100, R.R. 1 Box 650, Waterbury Center, VT 05677.

Mazama. [ISSN: 0275-6226] 1896. m. $15. John Salisbury, The Mazamas, 909 N.W. 19th Ave., Portland, OR 97209.

Mountaineer: to explore, study, preserve and enjoy the natural beauty of the Northwest and beyond. 1907. m. $15. Brad Stracener. Mountaineers, Inc., 300 Third Ave. W., Seattle, WA 98119-4117.

North Star: the newsletter of the North Country Trail Association. 1981. q. Free to members. Robert Papp, North Country Trail Assn., 49 Monroe Center, Suite 200B, Grand Rapids, MI 49503.

Outdoor Report. [0826-3019] 1977. q. $10. Norma Wilson, Outdoor Recreation Council of B.C., 334-1367 W. Broadway, Vancouver, BC, Canada V6H 4A9; http://www.orcbc.bc.ca.

Ozark Highlands Trail Association Newsletter. m. Tim Ernst, HC 33, Box 50-A, Pettigrew, AR 72752; http://wilderness.arkansasusa.com/ohta.html.

Pathways Across America. 1988. q. Free. Sue Dodge, Gary Werner, Amer. Hiking Soc., 1422 Fenwick Lane, Silver Spring, MD 20910.

Potomac Appalachian. [ISSN: 0092-2226] 1932. m. $6. Linda Shannon-Beaver, Potomac Appalachian Trail Club, 118 Park St. S.E., Vienna, VA 22180; http://www.patc.net.

Prairie Club Bulletin. [ISSN: 0032-6607] 1908. 6/yr. Free to members (Nonmembers, $15). Susan Messer, The Prairie Club, 533 W. North Ave., No. 10, Elmhurst, IL 60126.

Ridgeline. 1987. bi-m. Free to members (Nonmembers, $1). Superior Hiking Trail Assoc., P.O. Box 4, Two Harbors, MN 55616; http://www.shta.org.

Skyliner. 1933. m. Free to members. Skyline Hikers of the Canadian Rockies, P.O. Box 3514, Postal Sta. B., Calgary, AB, Canada T2M 4M2.

Trail Tracks. [ISSN: 1082-8308] 1971. q. Free to members (Nonmembers, $35). Stuart Macdonald, American Trails, 1400 16th St. N.W., Washington, DC 20036; http://www.americantrails.org/trailtracks/index.html.

Trail Walker: news of hiking and conservation. [ISSN: 0749-1352] 1963. bi-m. $15. New York-New Jersey Trail Conference, 156 Ramapo Valley Rd., Mahwah, NJ 07430.

Trailblazer. 1985. q. Free to members. Rails-to-Trails Conservancy, 1100 17th St. N.W., 10th Floor, Washington, DC 20036.

Trailhead. 1974. bi-m. Free to members (Nonmembers, $10). Bernice E. Paige, Idaho Trails Council, P.O. Box 1629, Sun Valley, ID 83353.

Trails Advocate. q. $15. Tom Neenan, Iowa Trails Council, Inc., P.O. Box 131, Center Point, IA 52213.

Up Rope. 1944. m. $15. T. Isaacson, Potomac Appalachian Trail Club, 118 Park St. S.E., Vienna, VA 22180.

Voyageur Trail News. [ISSN: 1040-8541] 3/yr. Free to members. Cheryl Landmark, 150 Churchill Blvd., P.O. Box 20040, Sault Sainte Marie, ON, Canada P6A 6W3; http://www3.sympatico.ca/voyageur.trail.

Whoop 'n' Holler. q. Free to members. George Rosier, West Virginia Scenic Trails Assoc., 633 W.V. Ave., Morgantown, WV 26505.

■ HISTORY

Ellen Fladger, Head of Special Collections, Schaffer Library, Union College, Schenectady, NY 12308

Lorraine Wies, Periodicals/Acquisitions Library, Schaffer Library, Union College, Schenectady, NY 12308

Introduction

Historical writing is more than a simple chronological record of the events of a country or other geographical area, a people, an institution, or even natural phenomena. Analysis of the events associated with the historical subject, detection of patterns in those events, and the relationship of those events to other aspects of culture or nature may all be reflected in writing about history. The journals included in this section reflect the increasingly interdisciplinary nature of historical writing. Titles such as *Journal of Interdisciplinary History, Journal of Social History,* and *Journal of the History of Sexuality* are among the publications whose purpose is to link the work of historians with the work of other social scientists and present it to the public. Topics in philosophy, literature, and sociology intersect with aspects of history and have historical components. This section includes titles on historical subjects in each of those disciplines and others. All of the journals chosen, however, focus primarily on historiography, or a facet of history. All periodicals selected have English as the primary language because they will be the most useful to the greatest number of libraries. Journals were evaluated on features such as scholarly apparatus, scope, presentation, and authority. Other features such as readability, application, and use of illustrations were also considered.

The two online titles included are available to libraries at no cost and only in electronic format. Fee-based resources such as Project Muse and JSTOR make collections of journals, including many history titles, available only to subscribers. Many of the titles included in this section have web sites that provide basic information about the titles, such as guidelines for authors, contact information, subscription information, and tables of contents. However, these titles rarely provide full-text content files and, if these are provided, they are accessible only to subscribers. Users of electronic titles will be wise to check the URLs as they are subject to frequent change.

Basic Periodicals

Ems: *American Heritage, American History (Leesburg);* Hs: *American Heritage, American History, History Today;* Ga: *American Heritage, American History (Leesburg), History News, History Today;* Ac: *American Heritage, American Historical Review, English Historical Review, Hispanic American Historical Review, The Historian (East Lansing), History, History Today, Journal of American History, Journal of Contemporary History, Journal of Modern History, Journal of Urban History, William and Mary Quarterly.*

Basic Abstracts and Indexes

America: History and Life, The Arts and Humanities Citation Index, Historical Abstracts.

3685. *Alaska History: a publication of the Alaska Historical Society.* [ISSN: 0890-6149] 1984. s-a. Non-members, USD 12. Ed(s): James H Ducker. Alaska Historical Society, PO Box 100299, Anchorage, AK 99510-0299; ahs@alaska.net; http://www.alaska.net/~ahs. Illus. Sample. Refereed. Circ: 700. *Indexed:* AmH&L. *Bk. rev.:* 6-20, 350-600 words. *Aud.:* Ga, Ac.

Various aspects of the history of the state of Alaska are covered in this semi-annual journal published by the Alaska Historical Society. The authors are laypersons as well as academics. Illustrations, especially photographs, are plentiful and useful. Maps are also included when relevant. The book reviews cover titles about the northwestern United States as well as Alaska. In addition, the section on Alaskana provides basic bibliographic information about new works on Alaskan history and culture. Articles such as "The Kaiury: Slaves of Russian America" and "Northern Alaska's First Printing Press and its Sometimes Curious History" are in recent issues.

3686. *Albion: a quarterly journal concerned with British studies.* [ISSN: 0095-1390] 1969. q. USD 85 (Individuals, USD 40). Ed(s): Michael J Moore. Appalachian State University, Department of History, PO Box 32072, Boone, NC 28608-2072; albion@appstate.edu; http://www.albion.appstate.edu. Illus., adv. Sample. Refereed. Circ: 1500. Vol. ends: Winter (No. 4). Microform: PQC; NRP. Online: Gale Group. *Indexed:* AmH&L, ArtHuCI, BAS, BRI, BrArAb, CBRI, IBZ, NumL. *Bk. rev.:* 50-60, length varies. *Aud.:* Ac, Sa.

This academic journal of British Studies is published in the United States. Most of the content is devoted to book reviews covering numerous aspects of British social, intellectual, cultural, literary, and military history from the thirteenth century to the present. In each issue the reviews are preceded by two to four major articles by academic, usually American authors. Articles such as "King John, the Braoses, and the Celtic Fringe, 1207–1216," "English Funeral Sermons as Sources," and "Impressions of a Century of Historiography" are included in recent issues. Book reviews are well written and cover an unusually broad range of topics such as homosexuality and women's studies. Anyone interested in any topic of British Studies will find this title useful.

3687. *American Heritage.* [ISSN: 0002-8738] 1954. 8x/yr. USD 32 domestic; USD 38 foreign. Ed(s): Richard Snow. American Heritage, 90 Fifth Ave, New York, NY 10011; http://www.americanheritage.com. Illus., index, adv. Circ: 340000. Online: bigchalk; The Dialog Corporation; EBSCO Publishing; Florida Center for Library Automation; Gale Group; OCLC Online Computer Library Center, Inc.; ProQuest Information & Learning. *Indexed:* ABS&EES, AmH&L, ArtHuCI, BEL&L, BHA, BRI, CBRI, LRI, MLA-IB, MagInd, RGPR, SSCI. *Aud.:* Ems, Hs, Ga, Ac.

This popular magazine of American history is, and should be, a standard found in most public and academic libraries. The articles cover a broad range of topics in American Studies and history. Well-known writers of history such as Stephen Ambrose and David McCullough are frequently the authors of the articles. Topics as wide-ranging as Mae West, the B-24 bomber, Pearl Harbor, and standard time are included in recent issues. The writing style is informative and appealing without pandering to the audience. The departments included, such as "Time Machine" and "History Now," further enhance the appeal of the magazine. Most articles and columns are amply illustrated, and the illustrations are another means to enhance the study of history. This well-loved magazine has made a successful transition to the twenty-first century.

3688. *American Historical Review.* [ISSN: 0002-8762] 1895. 5x/yr. USD 120 (Individuals, USD 48). Ed(s): Michael Grossberg. American Historical Association, 400 A St, S E, Washington, DC 20003-3889; aha@theaha.org; http://www.theaha.org. Illus., index, adv. Refereed. Circ: 23000. Vol. ends: Dec. Microform: PQC. Online: EBSCO Publishing; JSTOR (Web-based Journal Archive); ProQuest Information & Learning. Reprint: PQC; PSC. *Indexed:* ABS&EES, AbAn, AmH&L, ArtHuCI, BAS, BHA, BRD, BRI, BrArAb, CBRI, CIJE, FLI, HumInd, IBSS, IBZ, IPSA, JEL, MagInd, NumL, PRA, RGPR, RI-1, SSCI, SUSA, SWA. *Bk. rev.:* 250-275, 450 words. *Aud.:* Ac, Sa.

Study of the full range of history would not be possible without this journal, which is the official publication of the American Historical Association. The articles in *American Historical Review* represent the leading edge in scholarly writing on American and world history. Each issue contains from two to six major articles and numerous book reviews. Special features such as "AHR Forum" and "Forum Essay" discuss topics such as a comparison of the role played by Asia and Europe in the world economy and an examination of the impact of the print revolution. Each issue has a topical table of contents, a useful feature for those seeking to browse the subject contents. Another useful section is "In This Issue," which presents a brief description of each of the major articles and an overview of the entire issue. A section of film reviews is regularly provided. Additionally, a supplement listing the table of contents for all volumes published for the year is also included.

3689. *American History (Leesburg).* Formerly (until 1995): *American History Illustrated.* [ISSN: 1076-8866] 1966. bi-m. USD 19.95. Primedia Enthusiast Group, 741 Miller Dr, SE, Ste D-2, Leesburg, VA 20175; http://www.primedia.com. Illus., index, adv. Circ: 100000 Paid. Microform: NBI; PQC. Online: bigchalk; EBSCO Publishing; Florida Center for Library Automation; Gale Group; OCLC Online Computer Library Center, Inc.; ProQuest Information & Learning. Reprint: PQC. *Indexed:* AmH&L, ArtHuCI, MagInd, RGPR, SSCI. *Bk. rev.:* 2-29, 200-300 words. *Aud.:* Ems, Hs, Ga.

This is one of the better publications of the Primedia Enthusiast Group. *American History* is aimed at a general audience and makes extensive use of accompanying illustrations to supplement the articles on various topics in American history. Recent issues include such articles as "Pearl Harbor Submarine Discovered" and "The Lewis and Clark Expedition." Special features such as "History Today" and "Museum Spotlight" add interest and color to this publication. A few books and other historical media are reviewed in each issue. This journal is a good place for students researching topics in history to begin, and a good source of information for adults with interest in topics in American history.

3690. *American Jewish History.* Former titles: *American Jewish Historical Society. Publications; American Jewish Historical Quarterly.* [ISSN: 0164-0178] 1893. q. USD 108 (Individuals, USD 50). Ed(s): Eli Faber. Johns Hopkins University Press, Journals Publishing Division, 2715 N Charles St, Baltimore, MD 21218-4363; http://www.press.jhu.edu/. Illus., index, adv. Refereed. Circ: 2540. Vol. ends: Dec. Microform: NRP. Online: EBSCO Publishing; Gale Group; Northern Light Technology, Inc.; RoweCom Information Quest; Swets Blackwell. Reprint: ISI; PSC. *Indexed:* ABS&EES, AmH&L, ArtHuCI, FLI, HumInd, IJP, MLA-IB, PSA, RI-1, SSCI, SociolAb. *Bk. rev.:* 5-10, 1 page. *Aud.:* Ga, Ac.

The American Jewish Historical Society is the sponsor of this journal, and examination of the full range of American Jewish Studies is the goal of the organization and the publication. This scholarly journal is published quarterly. Whole issues are often devoted to the discussion of a single topic. A recent issue presents six essays discussing "The Americanization of the Synagogue, 1820–1870." Regular features in each issue include several book reviews and an occasional review essay. Contributor profiles, located at the beginning of each issue, are a helpful addition. The wide range of topics in this journal broadens its appeal to laypersons in addition to academics.

3691. ***The American Neptune: a quarterly journal of maritime history & arts.*** [ISSN: 0003-0155] 1941. q. USD 45 (Individuals, USD 39). Ed(s): Barry Gough. Peabody Essex Museum of Salem, East India Sq, Salem, MA 01970-3783; will_lamoy@pem.org; http://www.pem.org/Neptune. Illus., index, adv. Circ: 1500. Vol. ends: Fall. Microform: PQC. *Indexed:* AmH&L, ArtHuCI, BAS, IBZ. *Bk. rev.:* 7-13, length varies. *Aud.:* Ga, Sa.

The glossy appearance of *The American Neptune* does not diminish the depth of its contents. This quarterly journal published by the Peabody Essex Museum covers virtually all aspects of international maritime history and the maritime arts. Recent articles include "Methodists to the California Gold Fields in 1849" and "The Right to Unrestricted Navigation on the Mississippi, 1812–1818." Articles are amply documented and appropriately illustrated. Authors are knowledgeable laypersons and nautical personnel as well as academics. The articles in this publication will be interesting to the layperson and helpful to the scholar.

3692. ***The Annals of Iowa: a quarterly journal of history.*** [ISSN: 0003-4827] 1863. q. USD 19.95. Ed(s): Marvin Bergman. State Historical Society of Iowa, 402 Iowa Ave, Iowa City, IA 52240; mbergman@blue.weeg.uiowa.edu; http://www.culturalaffairs.org. Illus., index. Circ: 1200. Microform: PQC. Reprint: PQC. *Indexed:* AmH&L, GeoRef, IBZ, RGPR. *Bk. rev.:* 17-19, 500-2,750 words. *Aud.:* Ac, Sa.

Although the history of Iowa is the primary focus of the articles in this publication, the book reviews included in each issue cover a much wider geographic area and a broader range of topics. Contributors include both academics and informed laypersons. A recent issue includes an article on the Quaker community. Articles are informative, scholarly, and well written, and lack the density seen in some similar publications.

3693. ***Arkansas Historical Quarterly.*** [ISSN: 0004-1823] 1942. q. USD 16. Ed(s): Jeannie M Whayne. Arkansas Historical Association, University of Arkansas, Department of History, Fayetteville, AR 72701; http://www.uark.edu/depts/histinfo/public_html/ARKQuart/index.html. Illus., index, adv. Refereed. Circ: 1600. Microform: PQC. Online: ProQuest Information & Learning. Reprint: PSC. *Indexed:* AmH&L, ArtHuCI, BEL&L, IBZ, SSCI. *Bk. rev.:* 1-26, 450 words. *Aud.:* Ac, Sa.

As with many other state historical journals, one state is the focus of this publication—Arkansas, in this case. The book reviews cover a wider territory of subjects and geography. Recent articles include "On the Shore Beyond the Sea: Black Missionaries from Arkansas in Africa during the 1890's," and "The Great Flood of 1927: A Portfolio of Photographs." Other regular features of the journal are book reviews; "Arkansas Listings in the National Register of Historic Places"; and "Resources in Arkansas History," information on primary source materials about Arkansas in various repositories. This is an important bibliographical resource for those interested in the history of one of the more colorful Southern states.

3694. ***Biography (Honolulu): an interdiscliplinary quarterly.*** [ISSN: 0162-4962] 1978. q. USD 50 (Individuals, USD 30). Ed(s): Craig Howes. University of Hawaii Press, Journals Department, 2840 Kolowalu St, Honolulu, HI 96822-1888; biograph@hawaii.edu; http://www.uhpress.hawaii.edu/. Illus., index. Sample. Refereed. Circ: 450. Vol. ends: Fall (No. 4). Online: bigchalk; Chadwyck-Healey Incorporated; EBSCO Publishing; Florida Center for Library Automation; Gale Group; OCLC Online Computer Library Center, Inc.; Project MUSE; ProQuest Information & Learning; RoweCom Information Quest; Swets Blackwell. Reprint: ISI; PQC; PSC. *Indexed:* AmH&L, ArtHuCI, BRI, CBRI, IBSS, IBZ, MLA-IB, SSCI. *Bk. rev.:* Number varies, 2-4 pages, signed. *Aud.:* Ac.

This scholarly journal publishes articles of significant length on theoretical, generic, historical, and cultural dimensions of life-writing, encompassing biography, autobiography, diary writing, and other forms. Recent issues feature essays on such topics as autobiography and geography, Edgar Allan Poe, and the traditions of Victorian women's autobiography. Each issue provides approximately 100 excerpted reviews of life-writing works published elsewhere, and a "Lifelines" section announcing publishing, conference, and grant opportunities. An annual bibliography of recent biographical writing appears in the fall issue. Recommended for all academic collections, especially those that specialize in literature, history, or life-writing. Tables of contents and abstracts back to the winter 1995 issue are on the University of Hawaii Press web site.

3695. ***British Heritage.*** Incorporates: *British History Illustrated.* [ISSN: 0195-2633] 1974. 6x/yr. USD 25.90 domestic; USD 36.95 Canada; USD 4.99 newsstand/cover per issue. Ed(s): Gail Huganir. PRIMEDIA Special Interest Publications, History Group, 6405 Flank Dr., Harrisburg, PA 17112; gailh@cowles.com. Illus., index, adv. Circ: 104481 Paid. Microform: PQC. Online: bigchalk; EBSCO Publishing; Factiva; Florida Center for Library Automation; Gale Group; ProQuest Information & Learning. Reprint: PQC. *Bk. rev.:* 3-4, 300-400 words. *Aud.:* Hs, Ga.

Any library serving the general public and any academic library serving an undergraduate population will find *British Heritage* a valuable addition to their collections. This colorful magazine includes articles on all periods and eras of British history. Elizabethan festivals, the QE2, and London street markets are just some of the topics in recent issues. Articles are heavily illustrated, but not to the detriment of the text. Regular departments such as "Brit Tips" and "Notable Britons" provide further information. "Brit Tips" is particularly useful for those contemplating a trip to the British Isles. A thoroughly enjoyable magazine for laypersons. Even scholars will find useful material here.

3696. ***California History (San Francisco).*** Former titles: *California Historical Quarterly; California Historical Society Quarterly.* [ISSN: 0162-2897] 1922. q. USD 50 domestic; USD 60 foreign. Ed(s): Janet R Fireman. California Historical Society, 678 Mission St, San Francisco, CA 94105; info@calhist.org; http://www.calhist.org. Illus., index, adv. Refereed. Circ: 6000. Microform: LIB. Online: Florida Center for Library Automation; Gale Group. *Indexed:* AmH&L, ArtHuCI, BAS, MLA-IB, SSCI. *Bk. rev.:* 8-12, length varies. *Aud.:* Ga, Ac.

Although its primary geographic focus is the state of California, this journal has a much broader cultural view. Subjects as diverse as the writers Raymond Carver and Richard Brautigan, California in contemporary rap music, and car culture are found in recent issues. One issue is devoted entirely to various aspects of the California gold rush. The separation of endnotes from their articles in a section toward the back of the journal is workable, but not helpful. "California Checklist" is a useful bibliographic feature; it lists recent publications on all aspects of the history of California. The activities of the California Historical Society are fully reported. Article authors may be academics, laypersons, or staff members of the society. A well-written and recommended addition to general and academic libraries.

3697. ***Canadian Journal of History.*** [ISSN: 0008-4107] 1966. 3x/yr. CND 40 (Individuals, CND 32; Students, CND 15). Ed(s): Linda Dietz, Larry Stewart. University of Saskatchewan, Dept of History, 9 Campus Dr, 707 Arts Bldg, Saskatoon, SK S7N 5A5, Canada; cjh@duke.usask.ca; http://www.usask.ca/history/cjh. Illus., adv. Refereed. Circ: 700. Vol. ends: Dec. CD-ROM: H.W. Wilson. Microform: MML. Online: bigchalk; EBSCO Publishing; Florida Center for Library Automation; Gale Group; LexisNexis; Micromedia ProQuest; Northern Light Technology, Inc.; OCLC Online Computer Library Center, Inc.; ProQuest Information & Learning; H.W. Wilson. Reprint: PQC; PSC. *Indexed:* ABS&EES, AmH&L, ArtHuCI, BAS, CBCARef, CPerI, HumInd, LRI, MLA-IB, PSA, SociolAb. *Bk. rev.:* 50, 1,000 words. *Aud.:* Ac, Sa.

The articles in this scholarly journal are generally about some historical aspect of British or European history. In spite of the title, Canada itself seems rarely to be the subject of the articles. Articles such as "The Birching of Young Scottish Offenders," "The London YMCA," and "From Law Student to Einsatzgruppe Commander: The Career of a Gestapo Officer" are found in recent issues. Book reviews and review essays are regular features in each issue. Article abstracts are in French and English, although the text is in English. Given the chronological and geographic scope of this publication, it is recommended for most academic libraries.

3698. ***Catholic Historical Review.*** [ISSN: 0008-8080] 1915. q. Jan., Apr., Jul. & Oct. USD 50 (Individuals, USD 45). Ed(s): Robert Trisco. Catholic University of America Press, 620 Michigan Ave, NE, 240 Leahy Hall, Washington, DC 20064; cua-press@cua.edu; http://cuapress.cua.edu. Index, adv. Refereed. Circ: 900. Microform:

PMC; PQC. Online: EBSCO Publishing; Gale Group; Northern Light Technology, Inc.; OCLC Online Computer Library Center, Inc.; Project MUSE; ProQuest Information & Learning; RoweCom Information Quest; Swets Blackwell; H.W. Wilson. Reprint: PQC; PSC. *Indexed:* ABS&EES, AmH&L, ArtHuCI, BEL&L, BHA, BRI, CBRI, CPL, HumInd, IBZ, MLA-IB, OTA, R&TA, RI-1, SSCI. *Bk. rev.:* 30-50, 1-2 pages. *Aud.:* Ac, Sa.

The Catholic Church and its missionaries have had a significant impact on the historical development of numerous countries and population groups. This scholarly journal published by the American Catholic Historical Association covers not only the history of the Roman Catholic Church, but also its social, political, cultural, and historical impact. Book reviews and a periodical listing of relevant journal articles are included in each issue. Given the scope of topics covered here, this journal is recommended for academic libraries.

3699. ***Civil War History: a journal of the middle period.*** [ISSN: 0009-8078] 1955. q. USD 35 (Individuals, USD 25). Ed(s): William Blair. Kent State University Press, 307 Lowry Hall, PO Box 5190, Kent, OH 44242-0001; sclarki@kent.edu; http://www.kent.edu:80/history/. Illus., index, adv. Refereed. Circ: 1800. Microform: MIM; PQC. Online: bigchalk; Florida Center for Library Automation; Gale Group; Northern Light Technology, Inc.; OCLC Online Computer Library Center, Inc.; Project MUSE; ProQuest Information & Learning; RoweCom Information Quest; Swets Blackwell; H.W. Wilson. Reprint: PQC. *Indexed:* AmH&L, ArtHuCI, BEL&L, HumInd, RI-1, SSCI. *Bk. rev.:* 7-13, 1-2 pages. *Aud.:* Ga, Ac.

The Civil War continues to be a topic of strong interest for scholars and laypersons. This journal has three or four major articles and 10–15 book reviews in each issue. Although this is the scholarly companion to *Civil War Times*, the information contained herein will be useful to anyone who desires more in-depth knowledge of Civil War topics. Articles cover many aspects of the war such as "The Irish Brigade," and "Southerners Against Secession." Although probably not for the casual reader, this journal should be included in academic and general library collections.

3700. ***Civil War Times Illustrated: a magazine for persons interested in the American Civil War, its people, and its era.*** [ISSN: 0009-8094] 1959. 7x/yr. USD 27.95 domestic; USD 34.95 Canada; USD 3.99 newsstand/cover per issue. Ed(s): James P Kushlan. PRIMEDIA Special Interest Publications, History Group, 6405 Flank Dr., Harrisburg, PA 17112; cwt@cowles.com; http://www.thehistorynet.com. Illus., index, adv. Circ: 163352 Paid. Online: bigchalk; EBSCO Publishing; Florida Center for Library Automation; Gale Group; ProQuest Information & Learning. Reprint: PQC. *Indexed:* AmH&L. *Bk. rev.:* 2-3, length varies. *Aud.:* Hs, Ga.

Another of the publications produced by the Primedia Enthusiast Group. Civil War publications have an avid readership, and *Civil War Times Illustrated* is one of the most popular. The extensive use of illustrations supplement such topics as ironclads, John Brown, the YMCA, and President Rutherford B. Hayes. Regular features such as "Gallery," "Travel," and "My War" add to the appeal of this magazine. Intended primarily for the general reader and Civil War enthusiast, this publication would also be helpful to high school and junior college students beginning research on a Civil War topic.

3701. ***Clio (Ft. Wayne): a journal of literature, history, and the philosophy of history.*** [ISSN: 0884-2043] 1971. q. USD 60 (Individuals, USD 27). Ed(s): Lynette Felber. Indiana University, English Department, 316 N Jordan, Bloomington, IN 47405; clio@ipfw.edu; http://www.ipfw.edu. Illus., index, adv. Refereed. Circ: 800. Microform: PQC. Online: bigchalk; Chadwyck-Healey Incorporated; Factiva; Florida Center for Library Automation; Gale Group; OCLC Online Computer Library Center, Inc.; ProQuest Information & Learning; H.W. Wilson. *Indexed:* AmH&L, ArtHuCI, BRI, CBRI, HumInd, MLA-IB, PhilInd. *Bk. rev.:* 10-12, 2-3 pages. *Aud.:* Ac, Sa.

This quarterly, published by Indiana and Purdue Universities, takes an unusual approach to the study of history. History as it impacts, and is influenced by, both literature and the philosophy of history is the focus. This view is reflected in recent articles such as "Putting History to the Question: Power, Politics and Society in English Renaissance Drama," and "Dream a Little: Land and Social Justice in Modern America." Book reviews and review essays cover a broad range of eras and literary genres. This publication is most suited for academic and special libraries and for advanced readers and scholars.

3702. ***Comparative Studies in Society and History: an international quarterly.*** [ISSN: 0010-4175] 1959. q. USD 130 (Individuals, USD 51). Ed(s): Thomas R Trautmann. Cambridge University Press, The Edinburgh Bldg, Shaftesbury Rd, Cambridge, CB2 2RU, United Kingdom; information@cambridge.org; http://uk.cambridge.org/journals. Illus., index, adv. Refereed. Vol. ends: Nov. Microform: PQC. Online: EBSCO Publishing; Gale Group; JSTOR (Web-based Journal Archive); OCLC Online Computer Library Center, Inc.; RoweCom Information Quest; Swets Blackwell. Reprint: SWZ. *Indexed:* ABCPolSci, ABS&EES, AICP, AmH&L, AnthLit, ArtHuCI, BAS, DSA, ForAb, HumInd, IBSS, IBZ, IMFL, IPSA, PRA, PSA, RI-1, RRTA, SSCI, SWA, SociolAb, WAE&RSA. *Aud.:* Ac, Sa.

This quarterly journal is "a forum for new research and interpretation concerning problems of recurrent patterning and change in human societies through time and in the contemporary world." The article topics cover either historical or other social science aspects. Each issue contains articles on themes such as "Globalizations," "Rural Economies," "Competing Histories," and "Reading Religions." The authors are usually academics from North American and European institutions. Articles are well documented, and abstracts are located at the front of each issue. The interdisciplinary nature of this journal makes it particularly useful for those concerned with the study of history as it interconnects with other disciplines. Strongly recommended for academic libraries

3703. ***Continuity and Change: a journal of social structure, law and demography in past societies.*** [ISSN: 0268-4160] 1986. 3x/yr. USD 154 (Individuals, USD 64). Ed(s): Lloyd Bonfield, Steven Hoch. Cambridge University Press, The Edinburgh Bldg, Shaftesbury Rd, Cambridge, CB2 2RU, United Kingdom; information@cambridge.org; http://uk.cambridge.org/journals. Illus., adv. Sample. Refereed. Microform: PQC. Online: EBSCO Publishing; OCLC Online Computer Library Center, Inc.; RoweCom Information Quest; Swets Blackwell. Reprint: SWZ; WSH. *Indexed:* AgeL, AmH&L, BAS, BrHumI, CJA, IBSS, IBZ, PSA, SSCI, SociolAb. *Bk. rev.:* 5, 600 words to essay length. *Aud.:* Ac, Sa.

This publication emphasizes the "long-term continuities and discontinuities in the structure of past societies." Articles focus on comparative and historical aspects of social issues. Recent issues include articles on "Landholdings and the Family Lifecycle," "Images of the Poor in an Official Survey of Osaka," and "The Gender Division of Labour: The Case of Tuscan Smallholders." The choice of international subjects is further emphasized by the inclusion of article abstracts in English, French, and German. This is a very scholarly journal and best suited for upper-level academic and special libraries.

3704. ***Delaware History.*** [ISSN: 0011-7765] 1946. s-a. Non-members, USD 15. Ed(s): Carol Hoffecker. Historical Society of Delaware, 505 Market St, Wilmington, DE 19801; http://www.hsd.org. Illus., index. Refereed. Circ: 1600 Paid. Reprint: PSC. *Indexed:* AmH&L. *Aud.:* Ga, Ac.

This twice-yearly publication by the Historical Society of Delaware is typical of many state historical journals. Each issue usually has three lengthy articles on some aspect of Delaware history, and the fourth issue in each volume has a bibiography of Delaware history. The activities of the society are reported here as well. Occasionally, issues focus on one topic, such as the Delaware artist Ethel Pennewill Brown Leach in the combined 1998–1999 issue. Articles are accompanied by illustrations and often make extensive use of primary source materials. This journal is primarily for those with an interest in Delaware history.

3705. ***Diplomatic History.*** [ISSN: 0145-2096] 1977. q. USD 208 print & online eds. Blackwell Publishing, Inc., Commerce Place, 350 Main St, Malden, MA 02148; subscrip@blackwellpub.com; http://www.blackwellpublishing.com. Illus., adv. Refereed. Circ: 1750.

Vol. ends: Oct. Online: EBSCO Publishing; Gale Group; ingenta.com; OCLC Online Computer Library Center, Inc.; RoweCom Information Quest; Swets Blackwell. *Indexed:* ABS&EES, AmH&L, ArtHuCI, BAS, HumInd, IBSS, IBZ, IPSA, PRA, PSA, SSCI. *Bk. rev.:* 4-5, 3-8 pages. *Aud.:* Ac, Sa.

This scholarly journal contains articles on U.S. diplomatic history from the country's founding to the present day. Issues focus on themes such as "International Dimensions of the Vietnam War" and "The Road To and From September 11th: A Roundtable." In addition, there is also a review essay and four or five signed book reviews in each issue. Recent issues include articles on "Invisible by Design: U.S. Policy in the Middle East," "The Logic of Soviet Cultural Diplomacy,"and "Jimmy Carter, Human Rights and Cambodia." This journal is of particular interest to those involved with this aspect of American history and will be most useful in academic and special libraries.

3706. *English Historical Review.* [ISSN: 0013-8266] 1886. 5x/yr. GBP 150. Ed(s): Dr. Jean Dunbabin. Oxford University Press, Great Clarendon St, Oxford, OX2 6DP, United Kingdom; jnl.orders@oup.co.uk; http://www3.oup.co.uk/jnls. Illus., index, adv. Refereed. Circ: 2550. Vol. ends: Nov. Microform: IDC; PMC; PQC. Online: Florida Center for Library Automation; Gale Group; ingenta.com; JSTOR (Web-based Journal Archive); Northern Light Technology, Inc.; Swets Blackwell. Reprint: PQC; PSC. *Indexed:* AmH&L, ArtHuCI, BAS, BHA, BRD, BRI, BrArAb, BrHumI, CBRI, HumInd, IBZ, MLA-IB, NumL, PSA, RI-1, SSCI, SociolAb. *Bk. rev.:* numerous reviews of varying length. *Aud.:* Ac, Sa.

The articles in *English Historical Review* cover a range of topics in English medieval and modern history. Articles are generally quite dense with the usual scholarly apparatus. Each issue has a "Notes and Documents" section with one or two articles analyzing one or multiple archival documents. Numerous book reviews, of varying lengths, are also included. Recent issues include articles such as "Urban Conflict in Late Fourteenth-Century England: The Case of York in 1380-81," and "Imperial Policies and Nationalism in the Decolonization of Somaliland, 1954-1960." This is certainly one of the best journals on the subject of British history and is recommended for all academic libraries.

3707. *Filson History Quarterly.* Formerly: *Filson Club History Quarterly.* [ISSN: 1536-0490] 1926. q. Members, USD 40. Ed(s): Nelson L Dawson. Filson Historical Society, 1310 S Third St, Louisville, KY 40208-2306; wallace@filsonhistorical.org; http://www.filsonhistorical.org. Illus., index, adv. Refereed. Circ: 4000. Vol. ends: Oct. Microform: PQC. Reprint: PQC. *Indexed:* AmH&L. *Bk. rev.:* 26, 1-2 pages. *Aud.:* Ga, Ac.

This publication, named for John Filson, Kentucky's first historian, includes articles on the history of Kentucky, the Ohio Valley, and the Upper South. As such, it is truly a magazine of regional history. The average issue has three lengthy articles and perhaps a dozen book reviews of varying lengths. Recent issues include articles such as "In Pursuit of Freedom: Slave Law and Emancipation in Louisville," "Pioneer Routes in Central Kentucky," and "Kentucky's 1944 Polio Epidemic." The authors come from a variety of backgrounds, and all of the feature articles are well documented. The regional nature of this journal makes it useful for general and academic libraries with a specialty or interest in this subject.

3708. *Florida Historical Quarterly.* [ISSN: 0015-4113] 1908. q. USD 55 (Members, USD 40). Ed(s): Craig Thompson Friend. Florida Historical Society, 1320 Highland Ave, Melbourne, FL 32935; wynne@metrolink.net; http://www.florida-historical-soc.org. Illus., index. Circ: 2500. *Indexed:* AbAn, AmH&L. *Bk. rev.:* 14-18, 1-2 pages. *Aud.:* Ac, Sa.

The state of Florida played an important role in the early history of the United States. Hence, this journal is particularly recommended for those libraries with in-depth collections in American history. Each issue has three or four major articles plus book reviews, book notes, and a section on recent primary source acquisitions by Florida institutions. The major articles generally involve some aspect of Florida history while the book reviews cover a broader geographic area. Recent articles include "Booker T. Washington's Tour of the Sunshine State, March 1912," "The Icelandic Man Cometh: North Dakota State Attorney Gudmunder Grimson and a Reassessment of the Martin Tabert Case," and "Daytona Beach: A Closed Society." This is a very useful research and bibliographic tool for those interested in Florida history or the impact of broader topics in Southern history on the state of Florida.

Gender and History. See Women: Feminist and Special Interest/Feminist and Women's Studies section.

3709. *Georgia Historical Quarterly.* [ISSN: 0016-8297] 1917. q. USD 40, Libraries, USD 40 (Individuals, USD 35). Ed(s): Anne J Bailey. Georgia Historical Society, 501 Whitaker St, Savannah, GA 31499; ghs@georgiahistory.com; http://www.georgiahistory.com. Illus., index, adv. Refereed. Circ: 3200. Vol. ends: Winter. Microform: MIM; PMC; PQC. Reprint: PQC. *Indexed:* AmH&L, BEL&L. *Bk. rev.:* 8-24, 1-2 pages. *Aud.:* Ac, Sa.

This quarterly publication of the Georgia Historical Society generally covers historical matters pertaining to the state of Georgia. The book reviews in each issue are geographically broader in scope. Articles analyzing primary source materials are also included in some issues. Although this journal is intended for those interested in Georgia historical subjects, there are occasionally articles and topics with relevance to students pursuing other research.

3710. *Hispanic American Historical Review.* [ISSN: 0018-2168] 1921. q. USD 242 includes online access (Individuals, USD 44 includes online access; USD 61 per issue). Ed(s): Kathryn Litherland. Duke University Press, 905 W Main St, Ste 18 B, Durham, NC 27701; subscriptions@dukeupress.edu; http://www.dukeupress.edu. Illus., index, adv. Refereed. Circ: 2300. Microform: MIM; PMC; PQC. Online: EBSCO Publishing; Gale Group; Ingenta Select; JSTOR (Web-based Journal Archive); Northern Light Technology, Inc.; OCLC Online Computer Library Center, Inc.; Project MUSE; ProQuest Information & Learning; RoweCom Information Quest; Swets Blackwell. Reprint: ISI; PQC; PSC. *Indexed:* AmH&L, ArtHuCI, BRI, CBRI, HAPI, HumInd, IBSS, IBZ, MLA-IB, NumL, SSCI. *Bk. rev.:* Numerous, 1 page. *Aud.:* Ac, Sa.

This scholarly journal covers the field of Latin American history from the colonial era to the present. Articles in recent issues include "The Vanguard Landowners of Buenos Aires: A New Production Model," and "The Upper Classes and Their Upper Stories: Architecture and the Aftermath of the Lima Earthquake of 1746." Each issue usually has three lengthy articles and many book reviews. The book reviews are arranged chronologically by historical period and are very helpful for the compilation of bibliographies. This is one of the major publications in English on the topic of Latin American history and, as such, it is highly recommended for all academic libraries and for those general libraries whose clientele may require this source.

3711. *The Historian (East Lansing): a journal of history.* [ISSN: 0018-2370] 1938. q. USD 105 print & online eds. Ed(s): Kathleen Paul. Blackwell Publishing, Inc., Commerce Place, 350 Main St, Malden, MA 02148; subscrip@blackwellpub.com; http://www.blackwellpublishing.com. Illus., adv. Refereed. Circ: 18000. Vol. ends: Aug. Microform: PQC. Online: Gale Group; ingenta.com. Reprint: PQC. *Indexed:* ABS&EES, AmH&L, ArtHuCI, BAS, BRI, BrArAb, CBRI, HumInd, LRI, MagInd, NumL, PRA, PSA, RI-1. *Bk. rev.:* 40-60, 400-500 words. *Aud.:* Ga, Ac.

This publication from Phi Alpha Theta, the International Honor Society in History, is issued quarterly and contains five to ten lengthy articles, an interview with a well-known historian, book reviews arranged by geographic area, and, occasionally, a review essay in each issue. Recent issues include such articles as "Bede's Ecclesiastical History of the English People" and "More Than Nuts and Bolts: Technology and the German Army." It is evident that the range of historical topics covered in this journal is very broad. Given the nature of its contents and their relevance to readers and scholars of all levels, *The Historian* is recommended for all libraries.

3712. *Historical Journal.* Formerly (until 1957): *Cambridge Historical Journal.* [ISSN: 0018-246X] 1923. q. USD 250 (Individuals, USD 99). Ed(s): Peter Mandler, Robert Tombs. Cambridge University Press, The Edinburgh Bldg, Shaftesbury Rd, Cambridge, CB2 2RU, United Kingdom; information@cambridge.org; http://uk.cambridge.org/journals.

Illus., index, adv. Circ: 1500. Vol. ends: Dec. Microform: PQC. Online: EBSCO Publishing; Gale Group; JSTOR (Web-based Journal Archive); OCLC Online Computer Library Center, Inc.; RoweCom Information Quest; Swets Blackwell. Reprint: PSC; SWZ. *Indexed:* AmH&L, ArtHuCI, BAS, BEL&L, BrArAb, BrHumI, GeogAbPG, HumInd, IBSS, IBZ, LRI, NumL, PRA, RI-1, SSCI. *Bk. rev.:* 5-28, lengthy. *Aud.:* Ac, Sa.

Officially, this publication "covers all aspects of European and world history since the 15th century." In practice, the principal focus is Great Britain. The contents consist of lengthy book review essays and six or seven scholarly and generally esoteric articles.

3713. *Historical Methods: a journal of quantitative and interdisciplinary history.* Formerly (until 1977): *Historical Methods Newsletter.* [ISSN: 0161-5440] 1967. q. USD 131 (Individuals, USD 60; USD 32.75). Ed(s): Barbara Kahn. Heldref Publications, 1319 18th St, NW, Washington, DC 20036-1802; subscribe@heldref.org; http://www.heldref.org. Illus., index, adv. Refereed. Circ: 550. Vol. ends: Winter. CD-ROM: ProQuest Information & Learning. Online: bigchalk; Chadwyck-Healey Incorporated; EBSCO Publishing; Florida Center for Library Automation; Gale Group; Northern Light Technology, Inc.; OCLC Online Computer Library Center, Inc.; ProQuest Information & Learning; H.W. Wilson. Reprint: PSC. *Indexed:* ABS&EES, AmH&L, ArtHuCI, BAS, CIJE, ExcerpMed, IBZ, PSA, SSCI, SociolAb. *Aud.:* Ac, Sa.

The title is descriptive of the scope and purpose. There usually are three or four lengthy articles that stress the joys and hazards of historical methodology, e.g., "Missing, Biased and Unrepresentative: The Quantitative Analysis of Multi-source Biographical Data." "Identifying Celts in the Past: A Methodology" indicates the international aspects of the journal. The articles are typically filled with graphs, tables, and/or mathematical formulas. The contents principally focus on economic and social issues. Book reviews are not included, but there are occasional lengthy criticisms of methodologically important works.

3714. *Historical Research.* Formerly (until 1987): *University of London. Institute of Historical Research. Bulletin.* [ISSN: 0950-3471] 1923. q. GBP 118 print & online eds. Ed(s): Prof. David N. Cannadine. Blackwell Publishing Ltd., 9600 Garsington Rd, PO Box 805, Oxford, OX4 2DQ, United Kingdom; customerservices@oxon.blackwellpublishing.com; http://www.blackwellpublishing.com/. Illus., adv. Refereed. Circ: 1400. Vol. ends: Nov. Microform: IDC. Online: EBSCO Publishing; ingenta.com; OCLC Online Computer Library Center, Inc.; RoweCom Information Quest; Swets Blackwell. Reprint: PQC; PSC. *Indexed:* AmH&L, ArtHuCI, BHA, BrArAb, BrHumI, HumInd, IBZ, NumL, PSA, RI-1, SSCI, SociolAb. *Aud.:* Ac, Sa.

Sponsored by the Institute of Historical Research at the University of London, this journal concentrates on medieval and modern history in most parts of the world, but particularly in Britain, the Commonwealth, and the United States. Four or five articles of 15 to 20 pages each present such topics as "Whig History and Puritan Politics: The Memoirs of Edmund Ludlow Revisited" and "Discord in Drogheda: A Window on Irish Church-State Relations in the Sixteen Forties." Recommended because it serves both students and scholars as a basic source of research ideas.

3715. *History.* [ISSN: 0018-2648] 1912. q. GBP 206 print & online eds. Ed(s): Joseph Smith. Blackwell Publishing Ltd., 9600 Garsington Rd, PO Box 805, Oxford, OX4 2DQ, United Kingdom; customerservices@oxon.blackwellpublishing.com; http://www.blackwellpublishing.com/. Illus., adv. Sample. Refereed. Circ: 5300. Vol. ends: Oct. Microform: MIM; IDC; PQC. Online: EBSCO Publishing; Gale Group; ingenta.com; OCLC Online Computer Library Center, Inc.; RoweCom Information Quest; Swets Blackwell. Reprint: PQC; PSC. *Indexed:* AmH&L, ArtHuCI, BAS, BHA, BRD, BrArAb, BrEdI, BrHumI, HumInd, IBSS, IBZ, IPSA, NumL, PSA, SSCI, SociolAb. *Bk. rev.:* 36-95, lengthy. *Aud.:* Ac, Sa.

This is the official journal of England's prestigious Historical Association. Three or four research and review articles normally comprise about half of each issue. The other half is devoted to book reviews. The focus of the articles is largely on modern European (particularly British) events, while the reviews cover a wider geographic range. For example, a typical issue may include such articles as "English University Benefactors in the Middle Ages," "Love-Making and Diplomacy: Elizabeth I and the Anjou Marriage," "The Church Settlement of Oliver Cromwell," and "Sleeping With the Enemy: Britain, Japanese Troops and the Netherlands East Indies, 1945–46." Considering the large number of evaluative book reviews, *History* is a valuable tool for the bibliographer.

3716. *History and Theory: studies in the philosophy of history.* [ISSN: 0018-2656] 1960. q. USD 161 print & online eds. Blackwell Publishing, Inc., Commerce Place, 350 Main St, Malden, MA 02148; subscrip@blackwellpub.com; http://www.blackwellpublishing.com. Index, adv. Refereed. Vol. ends: Dec. Microform: PQC. Online: EBSCO Publishing; Gale Group; ingenta.com; JSTOR (Web-based Journal Archive); OCLC Online Computer Library Center, Inc.; RoweCom Information Quest; Swets Blackwell; H.W. Wilson. *Indexed:* ABS&EES, AmH&L, ArtHuCI, BAS, BHA, BRI, CBRI, HumInd, IBSS, IBZ, IPB, IPSA, PSA, PhilInd, RI-1, SSCI, SociolAb. *Bk. rev.:* Number varies, essay length. *Aud.:* Ac, Sa.

Articles, review essays, and summaries of books mainly in the areas of "critical philosophy of history . . . speculative philosophy of history . . . history of historiography . . . historical methodology . . . critical theory . . . time and culture," and "related disciplines" are the proclaimed focus of this quarterly. Four articles, four lengthy book review essays, and shorter book reviews appear in a typical issue. The fourth issue of each volume is a "theme issue" or, every few years, a bibliography of books and articles on the philosophy of history. The scholarly quality and reputation of this journal are outstanding. It has an interdisciplinary appeal for historians and philosophers, as well as for social scientists interested in questions of methodology.

3717. *History News: the magazine of the American Association for State and Local History.* [ISSN: 0363-7492] 1940. q. USD 75 (Individuals, USD 50). Ed(s): Harry Klinkhamer. American Association for State and Local History, 1717 Church St, Nashville, TN 37203-2921; http://www.aaslh.org. Illus., index, adv. Circ: 7000. *Indexed:* A&ATA. *Bk. rev.:* Occasional. *Aud.:* Ga, Ac.

Described as "the magazine for historical agency and museum professionals and volunteers." The aim of the association responsible for this important information source is "advancing knowledge, understanding and appreciation of local history in the U.S. and Canada." *History News* participates in this goal by providing news on local or, to use the broader term, "nearby history" activities. Each issue contains "Faces and Places," focusing on happenings of interest to the preservationist, curator, educator, archivist, local historian, or administrator. An irregular feature is "The Bookshelf," consisting of reviews of a few books relevant to local history and historical associations. This is an attractive, readable publication filled with photographs.

3718. *History Today.* [ISSN: 0018-2753] 1951. m. GBP 33.05 United Kingdom; GBP 48.95 rest of Europe; USD 62 United States. Ed(s): Peter Furtado. History Today Ltd., 20 Old Compton St, London, W1D 4TW, United Kingdom; admin@historytoday.com; http://www.historytoday.com. Illus., index, adv. Refereed. Circ: 35000 Paid. Vol. ends: Dec. CD-ROM: ProQuest Information & Learning. Microform: NBI. Online: bigchalk; Chadwyck-Healey Incorporated; EBSCO Publishing; Florida Center for Library Automation; Gale Group; Northern Light Technology, Inc.; OCLC Online Computer Library Center, Inc.; ProQuest Information & Learning; H.W. Wilson. Reprint: PQC. *Indexed:* AmH&L, ArtHuCI, BAS, BEL&L, BRD, BRI, BrArAb, BrHumI, CBRI, HumInd, IndVet, LRI, MagInd, NumL, PRA, RGPR, RI-1, SSCI. *Aud.:* Ga, Ac.

This is somewhat the English equivalent of *American Heritage,* although with considerably more claim to scholarship. *History Today* is suitable for both the layperson and the professional historian who wishes to wander outside his or her field of interest. The half-dozen articles are written in a journalistic, popular fashion, although always accurate and sometimes supported with bibliographic data. Most of the emphasis is on England, although from time to time the authors wander to other parts of the world, e.g., "Deep Time and Australian History." Features, which run from a paragraph to a page, include columns and news notes. Handsomely illustrated.

3719. ***History (Washington): reviews of new books.*** [ISSN: 0361-2759] 1972. q. USD 130 (Individuals, USD 65; USD 32.50 per issue). Ed(s): Jessica Palmer. Heldref Publications, 1319 18th St, NW, Washington, DC 20036-1802; subscribe@heldref.org; http://www.heldref.org. Illus., index, adv. Refereed. Circ: 450. CD-ROM: ProQuest Information & Learning. Online: EBSCO Publishing; Florida Center for Library Automation; Gale Group; Northern Light Technology, Inc.; ProQuest Information & Learning. Reprint: PSC. *Indexed:* ABS&EES, ArtHuCI, BRI, BiogInd, CBRI. *Bk. rev.:* Number varies, 400 words. *Aud.:* Hs, Ga, Ac.

This book review source provides an authoritative and helpful selection tool for any library acquiring historical works. It provides reasonably current "informative evaluations" of books 1 to 12 months after publication. The reviews, written and signed by specialists, discuss content, strengths and weaknesses, authors' credentials, and audience addressed. Complete bibliographic information is also given. The 100 reviews that are published each quarter average approximately 450 words each and cover all geographic areas and chronological eras. There is an author index plus a lengthy "feature review" in each issue. Book selectors solely interested in U.S. history should also be aware of *Reviews in American History* (below in this section).

3720. ***History Workshop Journal.*** Formerly: *History Workshop.* [ISSN: 1363-3554] 1975. s-a. GBP 72. Ed(s): Matt Cook. Oxford University Press, Great Clarendon St, Oxford, OX2 6DP, United Kingdom; jnl.orders@oup.co.uk; http://www3.oup.co.uk/jnls. Illus., adv. Refereed. Circ: 1730. Online: ingenta.com; Swets Blackwell. Reprint: PSC. *Indexed:* AltPI, AmH&L, ArtHuCI, BHA, PSA, SSCI, SWA, SociolAb. *Bk. rev.:* 10-20, length varies. *Aud.:* Ga, Ac, Sa.

This journal concerns itself with "the fundamental elements of social lifework and material culture, close relations and politics, sex divisions, family, school and home." True to the "workshop" aim of demystifying historical production, the editors encourage critical dialogue and debate through a variety of features. The editors also insist that contributors write in a clear, accessible style, avoid jargon, and not assume prior knowledge or specialized interest among the readership. There are generally four or five articles and essays with such titles as "Mona Lisa: The Best Known Girl in the Whole Wide World" or "A Place Called Sex: Gender, Space and Modernity in Eighteenth-century England." This is an outstanding journal for both expert and layperson.

3721. ***Indiana Magazine of History.*** [ISSN: 0019-6673] 1905. q. USD 15. Ed(s): Bernard W Sheehan. Indiana University, Department of History, Ballantine Hall 742, Bloomington, IN 47405; http://www.indiana.edu/~imaghist/. Illus., adv. Refereed. Circ: 11000. Reprint: PSC. *Indexed:* AmH&L, BEL&L, BRI. *Bk. rev.:* 12-18, 500-750 words. *Aud.:* Ac, Sa.

Published by the Indiana University Department of History in cooperation with the Indiana Historical Society, this is a mixture of scholarly and popular articles. Some issues focus on a special topic, e.g., "Thomas Jefferson," with a series of viewpoints, some of which are highly controversial. Typical articles of interest are "Hoosier Women and the Civil War Home Front" and "A Truly Midwestern City: Indianapolis on the Eve of the Great Depression." Lively, well edited, and usually much broader in scope than Indiana interests, this is a good general title for large and medium-to-large libraries in the region.

3722. ***The International History Review.*** [ISSN: 0707-5332] 1979. q. USD 150 (Individuals, USD 45). Ed(s): Terence Ollerhead, Edward Ingram. International History Review, EAA 2010, Simon Fraser Univ, Burnaby, BC V5A 1S6, Canada. Illus., adv. Refereed. Circ: 900. *Indexed:* ABS&EES, AmH&L, ArtHuCI, BAS, CBCARef, CPerI, HumInd, IBSS, IBZ, IPSA, PRA, SSCI. *Bk. rev.:* 70-80, length varies. *Aud.:* Ac.

An impressive overview of world history is found here, matched only by the extensive book reviews, which may run from a page to several pages. Coverage, ranging from Rome and Byzantium to modern times, is truly international and for all periods. This is both a bibliographer's dream and an ideal source of reliable and often imaginative new ideas about world history. Each issue is 256 pages long, contains four scholarly articles, at least one review article, "Notes with Documents," often an "Essay and Reflection," and about 80 book reviews. Required for any large history collection.

3723. ***Irish Historical Studies.*** [ISSN: 0021-1214] 1938. s-a. USD 45 (Students, IEP 14.50; IEP 29). Ed(s): Ciaran Brady, David Hayton. Irish Historical Society, Department of Modern History, Trinity College, Dublin, 2, Ireland. Index, adv. Refereed. Circ: 900. *Indexed:* AmH&L, ArtHuCI, BrArAb, BrHumI, IBZ, MLA-IB, NumL, SSCI. *Bk. rev.:* 15-23, length varies. *Aud.:* Ac, Sa.

Although published in Dublin, this semi-annual journal is co-sponsored by the Ulster Society for Irish Historical Studies. Five or more learned articles in each issue cover most periods of Ireland's turbulent past from medieval times through the early twentieth century. Contemporary history is not often covered. The tone is one of scholarly detachment when dealing with such issues as famine and land settlements. Considering that the interpretation of Irish history is a burning political controversy, such detachment makes the journal a unique forum. One number of each volume provides a classified list of theses written in Irish universities. As "the only scholarly journal exclusively devoted to the study of Irish History," this journal belongs in any collection seeking serious treatment of this subject.

3724. ***Journal of American History.*** Formerly (until 1964): *Mississippi Valley Historical Review.* [ISSN: 0021-8723] 1914. q. USD 170 (Individuals, USD 45). Organization of American Historians, 112 N Bryan Ave, Bloomington, IN 47408; http://www.oah.org. Illus., index, adv. Refereed. Circ: 12000. Vol. ends: Dec. Microform: PMC; PQC. Online: Gale Group; JSTOR (Web-based Journal Archive); Northern Light Technology, Inc.; OCLC Online Computer Library Center, Inc.; ProQuest Information & Learning. Reprint: PQC; PSC. *Indexed:* ABS&EES, AmH&L, ArtHuCI, BAS, BRD, BRI, CBRI, CIJE, HumInd, IBZ, LRI, MLA-IB, MagInd, RI-1, SSCI, SociolAb. *Bk. rev.:* 100, 1-5 pages. *Aud.:* Ac, Sa.

The publisher of this important title is the primary scholarly organization for American history specialists. Unlike *The American Historical Review* (above in this section), the *Journal* is exclusively devoted to America's past. The scholarly articles presuppose some knowledge of American history. In addition to numerous book reviews and book notes, each issue provides a list of recent dissertations and published bibliographies and a classified listing of recent articles. Thoughtful reviews of films that touch on America's past are a valuable new feature. Recent articles include such topics as the impact of digital technology on the teaching of history. This is a substantive bibliographic source and a basic journal for any library collecting in the field. Institutional subscribers also receive *OAH Newsletter* and the *Magazine of History* (below in this section), which is aimed at history teachers.

3725. ***Journal of Contemporary History.*** [ISSN: 0022-0094] 1966. q. GBP 285 print & online eds. in Europe, Middle East, Africa & Australasia. Ed(s): Walter Laqueur, Richard J Evans. Sage Publications Ltd., 6 Bonhill St, London, EC2A 4PU, United Kingdom; info@sagepub.co.uk; http://www.sagepub.co.uk/. Illus., adv. Refereed. Circ: 2000. Microform: PQC. Online: bigchalk; Chadwyck-Healey Incorporated; Gale Group; ingenta.com; JSTOR (Web-based Journal Archive); Northern Light Technology, Inc.; OCLC Online Computer Library Center, Inc.; ProQuest Information & Learning; RoweCom Information Quest; Swets Blackwell. Reprint: PQC. *Indexed:* ABCPolSci, ABS&EES, AmH&L, ArtHuCI, BAS, BrHumI, HumInd, IBSS, IBZ, IPSA, PRA, PSA, SSCI, SUSA, SociolAb. *Bk. rev.:* 6-12. *Aud.:* Ga, Ac.

Europe is the primary (although not exclusive) focus of this "international forum for the analysis of twentieth century European history." Occasionally, there are special theme issues, e.g., "Medicine, History and Society," "Working-Class and Left-Wing Politics," and "Bolshevism and the Socialist Left." This scholarly quarterly consciously attempts to bridge the gap between the professional historian and the general student of history. Although the subject matter of the journal is relatively narrow, it includes topics of wide appeal, since accessibility to a broad audience is one of its hallmarks.

Journal of Ecclesiastical History. See Religion section.

3726. ***The Journal of Imperial and Commonwealth History.*** [ISSN: 0308-6534] 1972. 3x/yr. GBP 192 print & online eds. Ed(s): A J Stockwell, Peter Burroughs. Frank Cass Publishers, Crown House, 47 Chase Side, Southgate, London, N14 5BP, United Kingdom; jnlsubs@

frankcass.com; http://www.frankcass.com/jnls/. Illus., index, adv. Refereed. Vol. ends: Sep. Microform: PQC. Online: Ingenta Select. *Indexed:* AmH&L, ArtHuCI, BAS, BrHumI, IBSS, IBZ, PSA, SSCI, SociolAb. *Bk. rev.:* Number varies, 350-600 words. *Aud.:* Ac.

This title is an important, although pricey, source for the scholar or layperson interested in the history of British colonialism. Four or five studies in each issue, written by academics, deal with such topics as imperial policy and diplomacy, the growth of nationalism, decolonization, and the evolution of the Commonwealth. Considering the length and geographical extent of British rule, this journal touches on the history of the entire world, including, of course, today's developing nations. The bibliographic and historical information provided in each volume offers complete coverage of this field. Recent articles have included such topics as orphans in early colonial India, the Welsh and the British Empire, and propaganda on the BBC.

Journal of Interdisciplinary History. See Interdisciplinary Studies section.

3727. *Journal of Medieval and Early Modern Studies.* Formerly: *Journal of Medieval and Renaissance Studies.* [ISSN: 1082-9636] 1971. 3x/yr. USD 176 includes onlines access (Individuals, USD 38 includes online access; USD 59 per issue). Ed(s): Annabel Wharton, Sarah Beckwith. Duke University Press, 905 W Main St, Ste 18 B, Durham, NC 27701; subscriptions@dukeupress.edu; http://www.dukeupress.edu. Illus., adv. Refereed. Circ: 1100. Vol. ends: Fall. Microform: PQC. Online: EBSCO Publishing; Gale Group; Ingenta Select; OCLC Online Computer Library Center, Inc.; Project MUSE; ProQuest Information & Learning; RoweCom Information Quest; Swets Blackwell. Reprint: ISI; PQC; PSC. *Indexed:* AmH&L, ArtHuCI, BEL&L, BHA, HumInd, IBZ, MLA-IB, RI-1, SSCI. *Aud.:* Sa.

The purpose of this title is to publish "work across the disciplines on topics ranging from late antiquity to the seventeenth century, work that is both historically grounded and informed by the broad intellectual shifts that have occurred in the academy." Each issue is usually devoted to a special topic such as "Gender and Empire in the Early Medieval World," or "Marxist Premodern." The geographic coverage remains overwhelmingly that of Western Europe. There are no book reviews.

3728. *Journal of Medieval History.* [ISSN: 0304-4181] 1975. q. EUR 466 (Individuals, EUR 180). Ed(s): A E Curry. Elsevier BV, Sara Burgerhartstraat 25, Amsterdam, 1055 KV, Netherlands; nlinfo-f@elsevier.nl; http://www.elsevier.nl. Illus., index. Refereed. Microform: PQC. Online: ingenta.com; ScienceDirect; Swets Blackwell. Reprint: SWZ. *Indexed:* ArtHuCI, BHA, BrArAb, GeogAbPG, NumL, SSCI. *Aud.:* Ac, Sa.

The *Journal of Medieval History* "aims at meeting the need for a major publication devoted exclusively to the history of Europe in the Middle Ages." Medieval Europe, including Britain and Ireland, from the fall of the Roman Empire to the Renaissance, comprises the subject matter of this publication. The editorial goal is to make "continental work in medieval history better known and more accessible, especially in Britain and North America." Most of the three to five articles in each issue are in English, with English summaries provided for articles in French or German. Each issue also contains a review article or essay on the historiography of the Middle Ages.

3729. *Journal of Mississippi History.* [ISSN: 0022-2771] 1939. q. USD 25 domestic; USD 35 foreign. Ed(s): Elbert R Hilliard, Kenneth McCarty. Mississippi Historical Society, PO Box 571, Jackson, MS 39205; http://www.mdah.state.ms.us/admin/jmh.html. Illus., index, adv. Refereed. Circ: 1500. Microform: PQC. Reprint: PQC. *Indexed:* AmH&L, GeoRef. *Bk. rev.:* 6-10, 1-2 1/2 pages. *Aud.:* Ac, Sa.

This title is published jointly by the Mississippi Department of Archives & History and the Mississippi Historical Society. It follows the typical pattern of regional historical journals; first, three or four articles such as "Sectional Contrasts and the Demise of Old South Jackson's White Residential Areas" and "Elizabeth Croom Bellamy, the Delta, and the Enduring Importance of Family"; the articles are followed by a section on "Historical News and Notices" and a section of book reviews that are well written although not all that current. An annual bibliography of dissertations relating to Mississippi history is included in the first issue of each volume.

3730. *Journal of Modern History.* [ISSN: 0022-2801] 1929. q. USD 189 print & online eds. (Individuals, USD 40 print & online eds.; Students, USD 31 print & online eds.). Ed(s): John W Boyer, Sheila Fitzpatrick. University of Chicago Press, Journals Division, PO Box 37005, Chicago, IL 60637; subscriptions@press.uchicago.edu; http://www.journals.uchicago.edu. Illus., index, adv. Refereed. Circ: 3000 Paid. Vol. ends: Dec. Microform: PMC; PQC. Online: EBSCO Publishing; Florida Center for Library Automation; Gale Group; JSTOR (Web-based Journal Archive); ProQuest Information & Learning. Reprint: ISI; PQC; PSC. *Indexed:* ABS&EES, AmH&L, ArtHuCI, BAS, BEL&L, BHA, BRI, CBRI, HumInd, IBSS, IBZ, IPSA, PRA, PSA, RI-1, SSCI. *Bk. rev.:* 40-50, 1-2 pages. *Aud.:* Ac, Sa.

The perceived need by the American Historical Association for a journal exclusively devoted to modern history brought about this publication in 1929. It is published in cooperation with the association's Modern European History Section, and its scope was originally confined generally to modern Europe since the Renaissance, with a distinct emphasis on Western Europe. Today, it is devoted to "historical analysis from a global point of view," and it "features comparative and cross-cultural scholarship." An average issue contains four or five articles that can run as much as 50 pages each, plus review articles and lengthy book reviews. Typical topics include "Ordinary Stalinism: The Council of Ministers and the Soviet Neopatrimonial State, 1946-1953," and "History Is the Opposite of Forgetting: The Limits of Memory and the Lessons of History in Interwar France."

3731. *Journal of Social History.* [ISSN: 0022-4529] 1967. q. USD 97; USD 135.80 combined subscription. Ed(s): Peter N. Stearns. George Mason University, 4400 University Dr, Fairfax, VA 22030. Illus., adv. Refereed. Circ: 1500. Vol. ends: Summer. Microform: MIM; PQC. Online: bigchalk; Chadwyck-Healey Incorporated; EBSCO Publishing; Florida Center for Library Automation; Gale Group; Northern Light Technology, Inc.; OCLC Online Computer Library Center, Inc.; Project MUSE; ProQuest Information & Learning; RoweCom Information Quest; Swets Blackwell; H.W. Wilson. Reprint: PQC; PSC. *Indexed:* ABS&EES, AgeL, AmH&L, ArtHuCI, BAS, BRI, CBRI, CJA, HumInd, IBSS, IBZ, PSA, RI-1, SFSA, SSCI, SSI, SWA, SociolAb. *Bk. rev.:* 25-30, lengthy. *Aud.:* Ac, Sa.

The content is a reflection of the impact the social sciences have had on contemporary historical research. Articles are often replete with statistical tables and graphs. The nineteenth and twentieth centuries are the typical (although not exclusive) focus of most of the research published in this journal. A typical issue includes six or more articles, review essays, and relevant book reviews. Recent articles include "The Uneven Rewards of Professional Labor: Wealth and Income in the Chicago Professions, 1870–1920" and "Learning and Earning: Schooling, Juvenile Employment, and the Early Life Course in Late Nineteenth-Century New Haven." A journal of interdisciplinary scholarly value, particularly for the academic library collection.

3732. *Journal of Southern History.* [ISSN: 0022-4642] 1935. q. USD 35 (Individuals, USD 25). Ed(s): John B Boles. Southern Historical Association, Rice University, Box 1892, Houston, TX 77251; jinscoe@arches.uga.edu; http://www.uga.edu/~sha. Illus., index, adv. Refereed. Circ: 5000 Paid. Vol. ends: Nov. Online: Florida Center for Library Automation; Gale Group; JSTOR (Web-based Journal Archive); ProQuest Information & Learning. Reprint: PQC. *Indexed:* AbAn, AmH&L, ArtHuCI, BRI, BiogInd, CBRI, HumInd, IIBP, RI-1, SSCI. *Bk. rev.:* 30-40, 500-600 words. *Aud.:* Ac, Sa.

The distinguished scholarly journal for students of the South's rich history. Each issue features four research articles written by history professors from all over the United States. No topic or time period is ignored, from the culture of slavery to the modern civil rights movement. An annual feature is a bibliography of articles about Southern history. Such special features, together with the numerous book reviews, make the journal a convenient bibliographic source for the study of the South. One of the finest regional journals, it is highly recommended, particularly for the academic library.

3733. *Journal of the Early Republic.* [ISSN: 0275-1275] 1981. q. USD 60. Ed(s): John L Larson, Michael A Morrison. Society for Historians of the Early American Republic, Purdue University, Department of History, West Lafayette, IN 47907-1358; jer@sla.purdue.edu; http://www.sla.purdue.edu/jer/. Illus., index, adv. Refereed. Circ: 1500 Paid. Online: bigchalk; Gale Group; Northern Light Technology, Inc.; ProQuest Information & Learning. Reprint: PQC. *Indexed:* AmH&L, ArtHuCI, CJA, HumInd, IBZ, LRI, RI-1. *Bk. rev.:* 15-20, 1-3 pages. *Aud.:* Ac, Sa.

"Committed to the history and culture of the United States from 1789 to 1850." According to editorial policy, "the terms history and culture are interpreted broadly, and contributions in political, economic, social, cultural and other fields are welcome." Four articles typically appear in each issue. Annual features include listings of recent dissertations and articles in other journals about the early American republic. The journal is scholarly, and it is aimed at the professional historian who has a particular interest in this period. Such individuals will also be interested in *William and Mary Quarterly* (see below in this section).

3734. *Journal of the History of Sexuality.* [ISSN: 1043-4070] 1990. q. USD 130 (Individuals, USD 43). Ed(s): Barbara Loomis, William Bonds. University of Texas Press, Journals Division, 2100 Comal, Austin, TX 78722; utpress@uts.cc.utexas.edu; http://www.utexas.edu/utpress/journals/journals.html. Illus., adv. Sample. Refereed. Circ: 746. Vol. ends: Nov. Reprint: PSC. *Indexed:* ABS&EES, AgeL, AmH&L, ArtHuCI, BHA, CJA, HumInd, IBSS, IPSA, MLA-IB, RI-1, SSCI, SWA, SociolAb. *Bk. rev.:* 11-16, 2-3 pages. *Aud.:* Ac, Sa.

This journal seeks to illuminate sexuality "in all its expressions, recognizing differences of class, culture, gender, race, and sexual preference" within a scope transcending "temporal and geographic boundaries." Articles include studies on the World League for Sexual Reform, psychoanalysis, sex lives of early Catholic saints, the history of treatment of sexually transmitted diseases, and "sexuality and German fascism." The entire content is a reflection of first-rate scholarship. Occasionally, there is a critical commentary or debate relevant to a previous article. The book reviews, book lists, and review essays provide a comprehensive bibliographic source.

3735. *Journal of the Southwest.* Formerly: *Arizona and the West.* [ISSN: 0894-8410] 1959. q. USD 24 (Individuals, USD 18). Ed(s): Joseph C Wilder. University of Arizona, Southwest Center, 1052 N Highland, Tucson, AZ 85721-0185; http://www.uapress.arizona.edu/. Illus., index, adv. Refereed. Circ: 900. Microform: PQC. Online: Florida Center for Library Automation; Gale Group; OCLC Online Computer Library Center, Inc.; H.W. Wilson. Reprint: PSC. *Indexed:* AmH&L, ArtHuCI, HumInd, MLA-IB, SSCI. *Bk. rev.:* 9-15, 500 words. *Aud.:* Ga, Ac, Sa.

Scholarly articles related to all areas of the greater Southwest, including northern Mexico, make up the content of this journal. Its stated mission is to publish "broadly across disciplines, including: intellectual and social history, anthropology, literary studies, folklore, historiography, politics, borderlands studies, and regional natural history." Photographs and other illustrations add to the overall appeal of this well-edited journal. The book reviews comprise a useful bibliographical source for the study of the region.

3736. *Journal of the West: an illustrated quarterly of Western American history and culture.* [ISSN: 0022-5169] 1962. q. USD 60 (Individuals, USD 45). Ed(s): Dr. Robin Higham. Journal of the West, Inc., 1531 Yuma, Box 1009, Manhattan, KS 66505-1009; pub@sunflower-univ-press.org; http://www.sunflower-univ-press.org. Illus., index, adv. Refereed. Circ: 4500. Vol. ends: Oct. *Indexed:* AmH&L, ArtHuCI, GeoRef, HumInd, SSCI. *Bk. rev.:* 30-50, 250-500 words. *Aud.:* Ga, Ac.

This quarterly is aimed at both the layperson and the historian. Its contents are well documented and, somewhat unusually, written in a popular style. Each issue consists of 100–125 pages, with numerous black-and-white illustrations to support the dozen or so articles. A wide range of subject matter is considered, and each issue is given over to a single topic such as "Mining, Natural Resources, and The Victorian West." The "Western Forum" column in each issue provides a space for historians and others to discuss particular, provocative topics. This is a general-interest publication that should be considered by many different types of libraries, particularly in the western United States.

3737. *Journal of Urban History.* [ISSN: 0096-1442] 1974. bi-m. GBP 413 print & online eds. in Europe, Middle East, Africa & Australasia. Ed(s): David R Goldfield. Sage Publications, Inc., 2455 Teller Rd, Thousand Oaks, CA 91320; info@sagepub.com; http://www.sagepub.com. Illus., index, adv. Refereed. Circ: 1350. Vol. ends: Sep. Online: Chadwyck-Healey Incorporated; EBSCO Publishing; Florida Center for Library Automation; Gale Group; ingenta.com; OCLC Online Computer Library Center, Inc.; ProQuest Information & Learning; RoweCom Information Quest; Swets Blackwell. *Indexed:* ABCPolSci, ABS&EES, AIAP, AmH&L, ArtHuCI, BAS, BHA, BRI, CBRI, GeogAbPG, HumInd, IBSS, IIBP, PSA, SSCI, SUSA, SociolAb. *Bk. rev.:* 3-4, essay length. *Aud.:* Ac.

Devoted to "the history of cities and urban societies throughout the world in all periods of human society," this journal pays special attention to studies "offering important new insights or interpretations; utilizing new research techniques or methodologies; comparing urban societies over space and/or time." The contents of each volume generally meet these demanding editorial criteria, although there is an overall emphasis on modern history. There are three or four articles per issue, treating such topics as city planning history, migration, and urban growth. Books are critically reviewed in three or four lengthy review essays. This is a fine scholarly journal of interdisciplinary value that does justice to a crucial subject of international importance.

Journal of Women's History. See Women: Feminist and Special Interest/Feminist and Women's Studies section.

3738. *Journal of World History: official journal of the World History Association.* [ISSN: 1045-6007] 1990. s-a. USD 75; USD 105 combined subscription print & online eds. Ed(s): Jerry H Bentley. University of Hawaii Press, Journals Department, 2840 Kolowalu St, Honolulu, HI 96822-1888; uhpjourn@hawaii.edu; http://www.uhpress.hawaii.edu/. Illus., adv. Sample. Refereed. Circ: 1800. Online: bigchalk; EBSCO Publishing; Florida Center for Library Automation; Gale Group; Northern Light Technology, Inc.; OCLC Online Computer Library Center, Inc.; Project MUSE; ProQuest Information & Learning; RoweCom Information Quest; Swets Blackwell. Reprint: PQC; PSC. *Indexed:* AmH&L, ArtHuCI, CIJE, GeogAbPG, IBSS, PSA, SociolAb. *Bk. rev.:* 10, 1-4 pages. *Aud.:* Ac, Sa.

This title is "devoted to historical analysis from a global point of view." The journal recognizes the limitations of the predominant national focus of historical scholarship on such topics as movements in population, climate change, imperial expansion, spread of religion and ideas, etc. Volumes of this title offer a wide variety of relevant scholarly articles and essays on such subjects as the rise of "prehistory," culture contact, and the concept of "early modernity." This journal is an important addition to scholarly publishing and should be considered for inclusion in all college and university libraries.

3739. *Kansas History.* Supersedes (1931-1977): *Kansas Historical Quarterly.* [ISSN: 0149-9114] 1978. q. Members, USD 30. Ed(s): Virgil W Dean. Kansas State Historical Society, Center for Historial Research, 6425 S W 6th Ave, Topeka, KS 66615-1099; vdean@kshs.org; http://www.kshs.org. Illus., index. Refereed. Circ: 3800 Paid. Microform: PQC. *Indexed:* ABS&EES, AmH&L, GeoRef, IBZ. *Bk. rev.:* 5-26, 300-2,600 words. *Aud.:* Ga, Ac, Sa.

The editors of this well-illustrated journal publish "political, social, intellectual, cultural, economic and institutional histories," and "biographical and historiographical interpretations and studies of archeology, the built environment and material culture." The subtitle notwithstanding, the contents are primarily concerned with the "Sunflower State" and focus on all eras from the prehistoric period to the present time. This is a local-history title with some imagination. Although the feature articles are chiefly on Kansan historical topics, the book reviews cover a broader geographical area. Noteworthy are the personal journals and memoirs that are occasionally published here. Numerous photographs add to the appeal.

3740. ***Literature & History.*** [ISSN: 0306-1973] 1975. s-a. GBP 65 (Individuals, GBP 26). Ed(s): John King, Alan Armstrong. Manchester University Press, Oxford Rd, Manchester, M13 9NR, United Kingdom; http://www.manchesteruniversitypress.co.uk/. Illus., adv. Refereed. Circ: 600. Online: EBSCO Publishing. *Indexed:* ArtHuCI, BRI, CBRI, MLA-IB. *Bk. rev.:* 3-4, essays and short notices. *Aud.:* Ac.

The aim of this scholarly semi-annual journal is to explore "the relations among writing, history and ideology." Issues contain such articles as "Thackeray's Waterloo: History and War in 'Vanity Fair,'" "The Politics of Cultural Nostalgia: History and Tradition in Ford Madox Ford's 'Parade's End,'" and "Writing and Re-writing the English Civil Wars." Analyzing the political and ideological content of literary texts is a current trend in many academic institutions, and this journal undoubtedly has a niche in such places.

3741. ***Louisiana History.*** [ISSN: 0024-6816] 1960. q. USD 25. Ed(s): Carl A Brasseux. Louisiana Historical Association, PO Box 42808, Lafayette, LA 70504. Illus., index, adv. Circ: 1400. *Indexed:* AmH&L. *Bk. rev.:* 5-15, 1-3 pages. *Aud.:* Ga, Ac, Sa.

Amateur and professional historians are contributors to this solid local publication. The four or five documented studies in a typical issue deal with all conceivable aspects of Louisiana's rich history, including the periods of Spanish and French colonization. Much of the content emphasizes the antebellum and Civil War periods. This is a scholarly and readable journal that should be considered by public and academic libraries in the South as well as libraries with geographically broader historical collections.

3742. ***Magazine of History: for teachers of history.*** [ISSN: 0882-228X] 1985. q. Members, USD 15; Non-members, USD 25; Students, USD 12. Organization of American Historians, 112 N Bryan Ave, Bloomington, IN 47408; magazine@oah.org; http://www.oah.org. Illus., adv. Refereed. Circ: 6500. Microform: PQC. Online: bigchalk; ProQuest Information & Learning. Reprint: PQC. *Indexed:* AmH&L, CIJE, EduInd, IBZ. *Bk. rev.:* 2-4, 1/2-1 page. *Aud.:* Hs, Ga, Ac.

This publication is directed to high school, middle school, and college history and social studies teachers. Its editorial guidelines call for articles on recent scholarship, curriculum, and education methodology "written in a style that is readable and accessible" to this audience. Issues are devoted to special themes. Specifics of these subjects are further illustrated with model lesson plans. The editors particularly welcome material of multicultural interest. This title is highly recommended, particularly for curriculum collections or other library collections supporting teacher training. The Organization of American Historians also publishes the highly regarded scholarly *Journal of American History* (see above in this section). Institutional subscribers to that publication also receive this one, as well as the *OAH Newsletter.*

3743. ***Maryland Historical Magazine.*** [ISSN: 0025-4258] 1906. q. USD 30 (Individual members, USD 40). Ed(s): Robert I Cottom. Maryland Historical Society, 201 W Monument St, Baltimore, MD 21201; press@mdhs.org; http://www.mdhs.org. Illus., index, adv. Circ: 5300. Vol. ends: Dec. Microform: MIM; WWS; NRP. *Indexed:* AIAP, AmH&L, GPAI, PSA, SociolAb. *Bk. rev.:* 4-10, 500-1,000 words. *Aud.:* Ga, Ac.

This covers Maryland from a "Picture Puzzle" and "Books in Brief" on the the state to such articles as "'Maryland's Shame': Photojournalism and Mental Health Reform, 1935–1949," "A Quiet Partnership: Clara Barton, Julian Hubbell, and the Forging of the American Red Cross," and "Prodigies and Portents: Providentialism in the Eighteenth-Century Chesapeake." Although the focus is primarily on Maryland history, some article topics involve broader, national issues. There are book reviews of a page or more and sometimes excerpts from one of the titles reviewed. Useful for both the scholar and the layperson.

3744. ***Minnesota History.*** [ISSN: 0026-5497] 1915. q. USD 20. Ed(s): Anne R Kaplan, Marilyn Ziebarth. Minnesota Historical Society, 345 Kellogg Blvd W, St Paul, MN 55102; http://www.mnhs.org/market/mhspress/mnhistory.html. Illus., index. Refereed. Circ: 15000. Microform: MIM; PQC. *Indexed:* ABS&EES, AmH&L. *Bk. rev.:* 5-25, 450 words. *Aud.:* Ga, Ac.

This journal emphasizes the history of the state of Minnesota and the history of the Upper Midwest. It is published by the Minnesota Historical Society, and the authors of the refereed articles range from academics to well-informed amateurs. The large number of illustrations included in each issue richly supplement the prose but do not overwhelm it. Recent topics include mandolin orchestras, the role of flour milling, and the Minnesota hydroelectric power industry. Special sections in each issue discuss artifacts from the Minnesota Historical Society's collections. A well-written regional journal with broad appeal.

3745. ***Montana: the magazine of western history.*** [ISSN: 0026-9891] 1951. q. USD 37 foreign (Non-members, USD 29). Ed(s): W Clark Whitehorn. Montana Historical Society, 225 N Roberts St, Helena, MT 59620; tryanmhs@aol.com; http://www.montanahistoricalsociety.org. Illus., adv. Refereed. Circ: 10000 Paid and free. *Indexed:* AmH&L, ArtHuCI, SSCI. *Bk. rev.:* 10-20, 500-1,000 words. *Aud.:* Ga, Ac.

This handsome and entertaining magazine contains information not geographically confined to the borders of "The Treasure State." Such regular features as "Historical Commentary" and "Montana Episodes" are particularly interesting. Each issue consists largely of four interpretive, documented articles presented in an attractive format supplemented by numerous photographs and other illustrations. This title has both academic and popular appeal, and it would enhance almost any general library collection in the Western states or collections elsewhere with a collecting strength in that area.

3746. ***New England Quarterly: a historical review of New England life and letters.*** [ISSN: 0028-4866] 1928. q. USD 25 (Individuals, USD 20; USD 7 newsstand/cover per issue). Ed(s): Linda Smith Rhoads. New England Quarterly, Inc., 241 Meserve Hall, Northeastern University, Boston, MA 02115; neq@lynx.neu.edu; http://www.newenglandquarterly.org. Illus., index, adv. Refereed. Circ: 2500 Paid. Vol. ends: Dec. Microform: PMC; PQC. Online: Chadwyck-Healey Incorporated; Gale Group; JSTOR (Web-based Journal Archive); Northern Light Technology, Inc.; ProQuest Information & Learning. Reprint: PQC. *Indexed:* AmH&L, ArtHuCI, BEL&L, BRD, BRI, CBRI, HumInd, IBZ, MLA-IB, R&TA, RI-1. *Bk. rev.:* 6-20, 2-4 pages. *Aud.:* Ac, Sa.

The focus of this highly regarded journal is the history and culture of a single region. Many of the articles are about famous New Englanders, and some actually fall into the category of literary criticism. The contents are not limited to any time period, but the colonial period and the nineteenth century receive the most emphasis. Among the six or seven features per issue are an occasional review essay and "Memoranda and Documents," featuring short articles or a historical document with commentary. Considering the importance of New England's history and culture through all periods of American history, this is a journal whose appeal extends beyond the region. A key title for both American history and literature collections.

3747. ***New Jersey History: a magazine of New Jersey history.*** Formerly (until 1967): *New Jersey Historical Society. Proceedings.* [ISSN: 0028-5757] 1845. s-a. USD 30 (Members, USD 15). Ed(s): Kathryn Grover. New Jersey Historical Society, 52 Park Pl, Newark, NJ 07102-4302. Illus., adv. Refereed. Circ: 1200 Paid. Microform: BHP; PQC. Reprint: PQC. *Indexed:* AmH&L, BEL&L, GeoRef, MLA-IB. *Bk. rev.:* 3-30, length varies. *Aud.:* Ga, Sa.

Amateur and professional historians are among the contributors to this publication, which publishes original contributions about New Jersey's rich history. Two to four articles appear in each issue. The "Notes and Documents" section often contains an edited document illuminating some aspect of New Jersey's past. Recent articles include "In Search of Robins Tavern," "Doctors, Chauffeurs, and Soldiers: The First New Jersey Ambulance Company in World War I," and "Charter Change and Civic Reform in Newark, 1953–1954."

3748. ***The New Mexico Historical Review.*** [ISSN: 0028-6206] 1926. q. USD 50 (Individuals, USD 30; Students, USD 20). Ed(s): Durwood Ball. University of New Mexico, 1013 Mesa Vista Hall, Albuquerque, NM 87131-1186; nmhr@unm.edu; http://www.unm.edu/~nmhr/. Illus., index, adv. Refereed. Circ: 1500 Paid. Microform: BHP; PQC. Reprint: PQC. *Indexed:* AICP, AmH&L, ArtHuCI, CJA. *Bk. rev.:* 9-25, 1 page. *Aud.:* Ga, Sa.

This quarterly journal publishes "original articles dealing with Southwestern history and culture from the earliest pre-history to the present." Much of the content deals with what is today the state of New Mexico and the area of northern Mexico. The style is scholarly but the contents also have a high degree of popular appeal. Book reviews and review essays supplement the information in this distinguished journal.

3749. ***New York History: quarterly journal of the New York State Historical Association.*** [ISSN: 0146-437X] 1919. q. Individuals, USD 50 membership; Students, USD 25 membership. Ed(s): Daniel Goodwin. New York State Historical Association, Lake Rd, Box 800, Cooperstown, NY 13326; http://www.nysha.org/. Illus., index. Circ: 4000. Vol. ends: Oct. Microform: PQC. *Indexed:* AIAP, AmH&L, ArtHuCI, BHA, MLA-IB, RI-1, SSCI. *Bk. rev.:* 8-10, 1-2 pages. *Aud.:* Ac.

In spite of its long history, this journal has consistently demonstrated quality in both scholarship and writing. Members of the New York State Historical Association receive this journal as part of their membership benefits. A typical issue will feature three scholarly articles. In addition to the lengthy book reviews, the "Books-in-Brief" section provides shorter critiques of relevant publications. Highly recommended for academic and public library collections, even those outside the Empire State.

3750. ***North Dakota History: journal of the Northern Plains.*** [ISSN: 0029-2710] 1926. q. USD 35 domestic; USD 42 Canada; USD 50 elsewhere. Ed(s): Susan Dingle. State Historical Society of North Dakota, North Dakota Heritage Center, Bismarck, ND 58505. Illus., index. Refereed. Circ: 2000. Microform: PQC. Reprint: PQC. *Indexed:* AmH&L, BiolAb. *Bk. rev.:* 4-16, 1-2 pages. *Aud.:* Ga, Ac.

A regional history journal whose scope extends beyond the state of North Dakota to include the northern plains. Recent articles include "Quest for Empire: Historical and Ideological Underpinnings for the Lewis and Clark Expedition," "Dr. Orin G. Libbey: A Centennial Commemoration of the Father of North Dakota History," and "The ~March King' John Philip Sousa in North Dakota." This title is amply illustrated and includes book reviews. Well written and suitable for laypersons and professional alike.

3751. ***Ohio History.*** [ISSN: 0030-0934] 1887. 2x/yr. USD 30 (Members, USD 5; Non-members, USD 18). Ed(s): Robert Daugherty. Ohio Historical Society, 1982 Velma Ave, Columbus, OH 43211-2497; ohiohistory@ohiohistory.org; http://www.ohiohistory.org. Illus., index. Circ: 3500. Microform: BHP; PMC; PQC. Reprint: PQC. *Indexed:* AmH&L, BHA, IBZ, MLA-IB. *Bk. rev.:* 18-24, 1,000 words. *Aud.:* Ga, Ac.

The political, social, economic, and cultural history of the "Buckeye State" is subject of the three or four lengthy articles published in each issue. In a typical issue, articles cover such topics as Jewish settlement in the Ohio River Valley, women's suffrage, and progressive leadership in Cleveland. There are book review and book notes sections in each issue. The authors are professional historians and the style is scholarly, but there is much here for the educated general reader interested in American history. This is a regional history journal whose topics are frequently relevant to other geographic areas.

3752. ***Oregon Historical Quarterly.*** [ISSN: 0030-4727] 1900. q. Individuals, USD 30; Students, USD 25. Ed(s): Marianne Keddington-Lang. Oregon Historical Society, 1200 S W Park Ave, Portland, OR 97205. Illus., index. Refereed. Circ: 7500. Microform: PMC. Online: Florida Center for Library Automation; Gale Group. Reprint: ISI. *Indexed:* ABS&EES, AmH&L, ArtHuCI, GeoRef, SSCI. *Bk. rev.:* 2-28, 250-800 words. *Aud.:* Ga, Ac.

This is a "popular historical publication containing research and essays on the history and culture of the Pacific Northwest, particularly the state of Oregon." Amateur and professional historians alike are the authors and book reviewers, and the writing is exceptionally good. Three or four articles with illustrations appear in each issue. Typical articles include "Beavers, Firs, Salmon, and Falling Water: Pacific Northwest Regionalism and the Environment," "Replacing Salmon: Columbia River Indian Fishing Rights and the Geography of Fisheries Mitigation," and "~The School Is Under My Direction': The Politics of Education at Fort Vancouver, 1836–1838." Perhaps the most interesting aspect is the number of personal reminiscences published here. Recommended particularly for public and academic libraries in the Pacific Northwest.

3753. ***Pacific Historical Review.*** [ISSN: 0030-8684] 1932. q. USD 115 print & online eds. USD 28 newsstand/cover. Ed(s): David A Johnson, Carl Abbott. University of California Press, Journals Division, 2000 Center St, Ste 303, Berkeley, CA 94704-1223; journals@ucop.edu; http://www.ucpress.edu/journals. Illus., adv. Refereed. Circ: 1500 Paid. Vol. ends: Nov. Microform: PQC. Online: EBSCO Publishing; Florida Center for Library Automation; Gale Group; Ingenta Select; OCLC Online Computer Library Center, Inc. Reprint: PQC. *Indexed:* ABS&EES, AmH&L, ArtHuCI, BAS, BRI, CBRI, HumInd, IBSS, SSCI. *Bk. rev.:* 25-30, 1-5 pages. *Aud.:* Ac, Sa.

The scope of this review is "the history of American expansionism to the Pacific and beyond, and the post-frontier developments of the twentieth century American West." Articles are also published on "historians' methodologies and philosophies." There are usually three or four major features in each issue, e.g., "Red Rock and Gray Stone: Senator Reed Smoot, the Establishment of Zion and Bryce Canyon National Parks, and the Rebuilding of Downtown Washington, D.C.," "New Deal Public Works at War: The WPA and Japanese American Internment," and "From Intellectual Deficiency to Cultural Deficiency: Mexican Americans, Testing, and Public School Policy in the American Southwest, 1920–1940." Articles are followed by research notes and detailed book reviews. This is the official publication of the Pacific Coast Branch of the American Historical Association. As such, it is one of the more important scholarly publications devoted to U.S. history and is a valuable tool for the serious student of the American West and the Far East. Recommended for all academic libraries.

3754. ***Past and Present: A Journal of Historical Studies.*** [ISSN: 0031-2746] 1952. q. GBP 104. Ed(s): Lyndal Roper, Chris Wickham. Oxford University Press, Great Clarendon St, Oxford, OX2 6DP, United Kingdom; jnl.orders@oup.co.uk; http://www3.oup.co.uk/jnls. Illus., index, adv. Sample. Refereed. Circ: 3300. Reprint: PSC. *Indexed:* AmH&L, ArtHuCI, BAS, BEL&L, BrArAb, BrHumI, CJA, GeogAbPG, HumInd, IBSS, IBZ, NumL, PSA, SSCI, SociolAb. *Aud.:* Ac, Sa.

Published on behalf of the Past and Present Society, this journal is associated with the British academic left wing. In terms of its readability and intellectual level, it is a scholarly publication of quality oriented toward the historian and the educated layperson. One of the journal's aims is to present material that can be the subject of debate and controversy. The content of each volume, regarding time and place, is eclectic, with a certain emphasis on social history. The half-dozen articles range from "Forgery and Miracles in the Reign of Henry VIII," "Mosquitoes, Quinine, and the Socialism of Italian Women, 1900–1914," and "Queenship, Nunneries, and Royal Widowhood in Carolingian Europe." Book reviews do not appear regularly, but there are occasional lengthy review articles.

3755. ***Pennsylvania History: a journal of Mid-Atlantic studies.*** [ISSN: 0031-4528] 1933. q. USD 30 (Individuals, USD 20). Ed(s): Brian Black. Pennsylvania Historical Association, 108 Weaver Bldg, Penn State University, State College, PA 16802; jbf2@psu.edu; http://www3.la.psu.edu/histrlst/journals/ph.htm. Illus., index, adv. Refereed. Circ: 850 Paid. Vol. ends: Fall. Microform: PQC. Reprint: PQC. *Indexed:* AmH&L, BHA, RI-1. *Bk. rev.:* 8-12, 1-2 pages. *Aud.:* Ga, Ac.

The official publication of the Pennsylvania Historical Association, *Pennsylvania History* contains two to four studies in each issue "dealing with the social, intellectual, economic, political and cultural history of Pennsylvania and the Middle Atlantic region." A feature of this publication is the regular inclusion of edited documentary material. The contributors are mostly academics, but the well-documented articles are selected for their appeal to both the specialist and the general reader.

Readers should also be aware of *The Pennsylvania Magazine of History and Biography,* another scholarly quarterly, published since 1877 by the Historical Society of Pennsylvania (1300 Locust St., Philadelphia, PA 19107).

3756. ***Review (Binghamton).*** [ISSN: 0147-9032] 1977. q. USD 98 (Individuals, USD 28). Ed(s): Immanuel Wallerstein. Fernand Braudel Center for the Study of Economies, Historical Systems, and Civilizations, Binghamton University, P.O. Box 6000, Binghamton, NY 13902-6000; http://fbc.binghamton.edu. Illus., adv. Refereed. Circ: 1100. *Indexed:* AltPI, AmH&L, GeogAbPG, IBSS, PSA, SociolAb. *Aud.:* Ac.

"We hope to make our journal a forum that will reflect the true diversity of contemporary world scholarship." Committed to "the primacy of analysis of economies over long historical process, and the transitory (heuristic) nature of theories," the journal features five or six articles in each issue with such titles as "Why Is Europe's South Poor? A Chain of Internal Peripheries along the Old Muslim-Christian Borders" and "The Weakness of Well-Ordered Societies: Gypsies in Western Europe, the Ottoman Empire, and India, 1400–1914." All are scholarly, original, and well written.

3757. ***Reviews in American History.*** [ISSN: 0048-7511] 1973. q. USD 112 (Individuals, USD 30). Ed(s): Louis P Masur. Johns Hopkins University Press, Journals Publishing Division, 2715 N Charles St, Baltimore, MD 21218-4363; http://www.press.jhu.edu/. Illus., index, adv. Circ: 3205 Paid. Vol. ends: Dec. Microform: PQC. Online: EBSCO Publishing; Florida Center for Library Automation; Gale Group; JSTOR (Web-based Journal Archive); OCLC Online Computer Library Center, Inc.; Project MUSE; ProQuest Information & Learning; RoweCom Information Quest. Reprint: PQC; PSC. *Indexed:* ABS&EES, AmH&L, ArtHuCI, BRD, BRI, CBRI, HumInd, SSCI. *Bk. rev.:* 30-40, lengthy. *Aud.:* Ac, Sa.

Each quarterly issue "presents more than 20 comparative and interpretive essays analyzing recent research published on all specialties of American history, including economics, military history, women in American history, law, political philosophy, and religion." References are made to earlier works, and complete bibliographic information is provided. Retrospective essays that examine landmark works by major historians are also regularly featured. This is a convenient, authoritative source for keeping abreast of important scholarship in the field of American history, and a useful tool for any library ordering selectively in this subject area. Also useful for colleges where students are required to produce research-length papers on topics in American history.

3758. ***Scottish Historical Review.*** [ISSN: 0036-9241] 1903. s-a. GBP 62. Ed(s): Colin Kidd, Roger A Mason. Edinburgh University Press, 22 George Sq, Edinburgh, EH8 9LF, United Kingdom; http://www.eup.ed.ac.uk. Illus., index, adv. Refereed. Circ: 900. Vol. ends: Oct. Microform: IDC; PQC. Online: Chadwyck-Healey Incorporated; EBSCO Publishing. Reprint: PSC. *Indexed:* AmH&L, ArtHuCI, BHA, BrArAb, BrHumI, NumL, RI-1. *Bk. rev.:* 10-20, length varies. *Aud.:* Ac, Sa.

Intended as an equivalent to the *English Historical Review* (above in this section), this review covers all aspects of Scotland's long and often tumultuous history. Few of the scholarly studies in each issue, however, go beyond the nineteenth century. Special features include a classified bibliography of articles on the history of Scotland published each year and occasional "Notes and Comments" regarding relevant documentary sources. This is the only learned journal exclusively devoted to this subject. It is also a useful tool for the bibliographer collecting in this area. Most appropriate for academic libraries with collections and curriculum in this area.

3759. ***Social History.*** [ISSN: 0307-1022] 1976. 3x/yr. GBP 173 (Individuals, GBP 50). Ed(s): Janet Blackman, Keith Nield. Routledge, 11 New Fetter Ln, London, EC4P 4EE, United Kingdom; journals@routldege.com; http://www.routledge.com/routledge/journal/journals.html. Illus., index, adv. Circ: 1000. Online: EBSCO Publishing; Gale Group; Ingenta Select; OCLC Online Computer Library Center, Inc.; RoweCom Information Quest; Swets Blackwell. Reprint: PSC. *Indexed:* ABS&EES, AmH&L, ArtHuCI, BrHumI, CBCARef, HumInd, IBSS, IBZ, PSA, SSCI, SSI, SociolAb. *Bk. rev.:* 10-13, lengthy. *Aud.:* Ac, Sa.

"Articles, reviews and debates of high quality historical analysis without restriction on place, period or viewpoint" is the editorial description of this journal. Years ago, the editors also proclaimed that "*Social History* has established a firm and stable place among the handful of English-language journals publishing historical material of the highest quality." Indeed, the editors have successfully published studies that "encourage an interdisciplinary approach to historical questions, and are concerned to provide an opportunity for critical analysis of the concepts and methods of the social sciences as they bear on the work of the social historian." British social history receives the most attention. In addition to the original research articles, there are several regular features and review essays. The latter, together with the excellent book reviews and a list of books received, provide an inclusive bibliographical source.

3760. ***The South Carolina Historical Magazine.*** Formerly (until 1951): *The South Carolina Historical and Genealogical Magazine.* [ISSN: 0038-3082] 1900. q. USD 55 domestic; USD 75 foreign. Ed(s): W. Eric Emerson. South Carolina Historical Society, Fireproof Bldg, 100 Meeting St, Charleston, SC 29401-2299; info@schistory.org; http://www.schistory.org. Illus., index. Circ: 5500. Vol. ends: Oct. Microform: PQC. Reprint: PQC. *Indexed:* AmH&L. *Bk. rev.:* 5-10, 1-2 pages. *Aud.:* Ac, Sa.

The South Carolina Historical Society was founded in 1855 for the purpose of collecting "information respecting every portion of the state, to preserve it and when deemed advisable, to publish it." The society's scholarly journal successfully meets this worthy mandate in service of a state that was in many respects a crucible of the South's and the nation's development. In addition to one- to two-page book reviews, the journal covers such topics as "South Carolina and Irish Famine Relief, 1846-47," and "Toward Humanitarian Ends? Protestants and Slave Reform in South Carolina, 1830–1865." Other pieces originate in memoirs and biography. Among the features are "recently processed manuscripts."

3761. ***Southwestern Historical Quarterly.*** [ISSN: 0038-478X] 1897. q. USD 100 (Individuals, USD 50). Ed(s): Ron Tyler. Texas State Historical Association, 2-306 Richardson Hall, University Station, Austin, TX 78712; http://www.tsha.utexas.edu. Illus., index, adv. Circ: 3430 Paid and free. Vol. ends: Apr. Microform: PQC. Online: Gale Group. *Indexed:* AbAn, AmH&L, ArtHuCI, HumInd, SSCI. *Bk. rev.:* 1-12, 1-5 pages. *Aud.:* Ac, Sa.

"Scholarly research on the history of Texas and the Southwest is the focus of *SHQ.*" This journal of the highest caliber typically features three articles, an edited contemporary document, and a book review essay. It is somewhat misnamed because the contents deal largely with Texas history and the contributors are mostly Texas historians. Special-topic issues over the years have included one on the University of Texas at Austin, five on Texas and its sesquicentennial, and three award-winning issues on the Texas state capitol, J. Frank Dobie and Walter Prescott Webb, and the Alamo. Recent issues deal with archaeology in the Texas panhandle, Texans in the Spanish-American War, and Texas constitutional history. Because of the attractive layout, typography, and accompanying photographs, this is a handsome publication compared with similar scholarly titles.

3762. ***True West.*** Incorporates (1923-1981): *Frontier Times.* [ISSN: 0041-3615] 1953. 8x/yr. USD 29.95; USD 4.99 newsstand/cover per issue. Ed(s): Bob Boze Bell, R G Robertson. True West Publications, PO Box 8008, Cave Creek, AZ 85327-8008; truepublications@aol.com; http://www.truewestmagazine.com. Illus., index, adv. Sample. Circ: 30000 Paid. Vol. ends: Dec. *Bk. rev.:* 4-25, 300-600 words. *Aud.:* Hs, Ga.

A magazine that attempts to provide a feeling of the Wild West by covering Western history and culture from pre–Civil War days to the present. This magazine is easy reading, with good, authentic photographs and illustrations. Aimed at a general audience, it is suitable for high schools and public libraries. The style is popular, the illustrations are excellent, and the material is nicely presented. The scope is obvious from the title. *True West* includes factual accounts, reviews of nonfiction books, columns on Western films and travel, family history, cooking, and a section of queries asking readers to share information. In addition to the eight issues per year, the magazine publishes two special issues, a travel issue and a "Best of the West" issue that are included with an annual subscription.

3763. ***Virginia Magazine of History and Biography.*** [ISSN: 0042-6636] 1881. q. Individuals, USD 38; Students, USD 25. Ed(s): Nelson D Lankford. Virginia Historical Society, PO Box 7311, Richmond, VA 23221; http://www.vahistorical.org. Illus., index, adv. Circ: 8100. Vol.

ends: Oct. Microform: PMC; PQC. Online: EBSCO Publishing; Gale Group; OCLC Online Computer Library Center, Inc.; ProQuest Information & Learning. Reprint: PQC; PSC. *Indexed:* AmH&L, ArtHuCI, HumInd, MLA-IB, SSCI. *Bk. rev.:* 4-40, 200-500 words. *Aud.:* Ac, Sa.

Because of Virginia's importance in the colonial and Civil War periods in American history, a significant portion of the studies in this quarterly fall in the period from the seventeenth through the nineteenth centuries. Many of the heavily footnoted articles and other features in each issue are biographical or contain biographical aspects. Occasionally, an issue is devoted to one topic. A recent issue contains articles on "'Richmond Again Taken': Reappraising the Brady Legend through Photographs by Andrew J. Russell," and "Flag-Waving Wahoos: Confederate Symbols at the University of Virginia 1941–1951." The contents are nicely illustrated with numerous black-and-white photographs. A valuable addition to academic libraries supporting courses in early American history.

3764. ***Western Historical Quarterly.*** [ISSN: 0043-3810] 1969. q. USD 70. Ed(s): Anne M Butler. Western History Association, Utah State University, 0710 Old Main Hill, Logan, UT 84322-0740; whq@hass.usu.edu; http://www.usu.edu/~history/text/whq.htm. Illus., index, adv. Circ: 3000. Vol. ends: Winter. Online: Gale Group. *Indexed:* ABS&EES, AUNI, AmH&L, ArtHuCI, BRI, CBRI, HumInd, RI-1, SSCI. *Bk. rev.:* 30-40, 375 words. *Aud.:* Ga, Ac, Sa.

This title's purpose "shall be to promote the study of the North American West in its varied aspects and broadest sense." Recent articles include "Restructuring Race," "Falling into History: The Imagined Wests of Kim Stanley Robinson in the 'Three Californias' and Mars Trilogies," and "Cody's Last Stand: Masculine Anxiety, the Custer Myth, and the Frontier of Domesticity in Buffalo Bill's Wild West." Book reviews—often extensive—book notices, and similar features make good the boast that this journal, both for scholars and laypersons, offers a wide variety of information about the West from a variety of social science disciplines.

3765. ***William and Mary Quarterly: a magazine of early American history and culture.*** [ISSN: 0043-5597] 1892. q. USD 75 (Individuals, USD 35; Students, USD 15). Ed(s): Christopher Grasso. Omohundro Institute of Early American History & Culture, PO Box 8781, Williamsburg, VA 23187-8781; ieahc1@wm.edu; http://www.wm.edu/oieahc. Illus., index, adv. Refereed. Circ: 3700. Vol. ends: Oct. Microform: PQC. Online: Gale Group. Reprint: PQC; PSC. *Indexed:* AmH&L, ArtHuCI, BRI, CBRI, HumInd, IBZ, MLA-IB, R&TA, RI-1, SSCI. *Bk. rev.:* 13-20, 1,000 words. *Aud.:* Ac, Sa.

Although American history before 1815 is the chief focus of this well-established and respected quarterly, the editors also encourage contributions in the areas of literature, ethnohistory, and the arts. Its articles, notes and documents, and reviews range from British North America and the United States to Europe, West Africa, the Caribbean, and the Spanish American borderlands. Forums and topical issues, including a recent one on "Sexuality in Early America," address topics of active interest in the field. An important journal for all levels of academic libraries and for public libraries with an emphasis on American history.

3766. ***Wisconsin Magazine of History.*** [ISSN: 0043-6534] 1917. q. USD 55 membership (Individuals, USD 37.50 membership). Ed(s): Kent J Calder. Wisconsin Historical Society, 816 State St, Madison, WI 53706; http://www.shsw.wisc.edu. Illus., index. Circ: 7000. Microform: MIM; PQC. Reprint: PQC; PSC. *Indexed:* ABS&EES, AmH&L, MLA-IB. *Bk. rev.:* 12-15, 500-1,000 words. *Aud.:* Ac, Sa.

"Collecting, advancing and disseminating knowledge of Wisconsin and of the trans-Allegheny West" is the mission of the historical society that publishes this fine scholarly journal. *Wisconsin Magazine of History* does much to carry out this responsibility. The articles are written by both amateur and professional historians, and the contents frequently go beyond regional interests. A recent issue with four lead articles includes "New Cases and Changing Faces: the Wisconsin Supreme Court in 2003," "Married to the Job: Wisconsin's Women Sheriffs," and "Politics in Play: Socialism, Free Speech, and Social Centers in Milwaukee." Each number also contains "Wisconsin History Checklist," materials added to the society's library, and a detailed listing of new manuscript accessions. Selected articles are available online at their web site. A valuable addition to all research collections in the area of American history.

Women's History Review. See Women: Feminist and Special Interest/Feminist and Women's Studies section.

Electronic Journals

3767. ***Essays in History.*** [ISSN: 0071-1411] 1954. a. USD 5. Ed(s): Edward George Lengel. University of Virginia, Corcoran Department of History, Randall Hall, PO Box 400180, Charlottesville, VA 22904; egl2r@faraday.clas.virginia.edu; http://wwww.lib.virginia.edu/journals/EH/EH.html. Refereed. Circ: 250. Reprint: PQC. *Indexed:* AmH&L. *Aud.:* Ac.

Although this electronic journal is produced by graduate students at the University of Virginia, article authors may range from undergraduates to tenured faculty members. It is divided into two parts. The first (four to five articles) covers current historical studies from Mexico and Eastern Europe to Japan. The second part consists of essay-length book reviews, usually about a half dozen. The reviews, as is standard for such publications, are about a year to 18 months after publication. Note that this scholarly title is free, which is highly unusual.

3768. ***Essays in Medieval Studies.*** [ISSN: 1043-2213] 1984. a. USD 35 (Individuals, USD 25). Ed(s): Allan J. Frantzen. West Virginia University Press, PO Box 6295, Morgantown, WV 26506; press@wvu.edu; http://www.as.wvu.edu/press. Refereed. *Aud.:* Ac.

An annual publication that features scholarly articles on all aspects of medieval history and culture, representing the proceedings of the Illinois Medieval Association. Each volume is dedicated to a theme; recent themes have included children and the family, medieval communities, and emotions in the Middle Ages. All electronic issues of *EMS* are also available in print. What is remarkable about this journal is that it is a high-quality, refereed title that is free.

Intersections. See Women: Feminist and Special Interest/Electronic Journals section.

■ HOME

See also Interior Design and Decoration; and Women sections.

Pamela Matz, Reference Librarian, Widener Library, Harvard University, Cambridge, MA 02138

Introduction

Many readers value the stability and serenity that can be found at home as a solace in uncertain times, and most magazines devoted to the home have survived, despite decreasing ad revenues. Traditional home magazines continue to dominate the field, offering a wealth of beautifully illustrated glimpses of the way others live. (Readers may want to know that many of the larger home magazines offer extensive selections on their web sites, without charge.) A trend to niche marketing also continues, with smaller-circulation magazines (such as *Backwoods Home*, *Natural Home*, and *Victorian Homes*) targeting specialty groups. Libraries will select among such titles based on the degree of do-it-yourself interest and style aspirations of the community.

Newer entrants in the field, such as *Real Simple* and this year's *Budget Living*, offer a different slant on the scope of the home magazine, including some topics more commonly found in publications focused on women, lifestyles, or shopping. Some of these newer entrants too recent to recommend but worth watching are *Organic Style*, *LivingRoom*, and *Chic Simple*.

Basic Periodicals

Hs: *Better Homes and Gardens;* Ga: *Better Homes and Gardens, The Family Handyman, House Beautiful, Martha Stewart Living;* Ac: *Electronic House, Traditional Home, Victorian Homes.*

Basic Abstracts and Indexes

Magazine Index, Periodical Abstracts, Readers' Guide to Periodical Literature.

3769. *Backwoods Home Magazine: practical ideas for self reliant living.* [ISSN: 1050-9712] 1989. bi-m. USD 21.95. Ed(s): Dave Duffy. David J. Duffy, Ed. & Pub., PO Box 712, Gold Beach, OR 97444; http://www.backwoodshome.com. Illus., adv. Circ: 60000. Vol. ends: Dec. *Bk. rev.:* 1, 200 words. *Aud.:* Ga.

Backwoods Home offers features on owner-built housing, independent energy, gardening, health, self-employment, and country living, advocating a self-reliant lifestyle. A series on hydroelectric power, for example, discusses how to evaluate the potential of generating power from the water flow across one's land; and an article on the perfect cup of coffee gives instructions for roasting one's own coffee beans. Readers interested in an independent, rural lifestyle will find *Backwoods Home* valuable.

3770. *Better Homes and Gardens.* [ISSN: 0006-0151] 1922. m. USD 22 domestic; USD 35 foreign. Ed(s): Jean Lenmon. Meredith Corp., 1716 Locust St, Des Moines, IA 50309-3023; http://www.meredith.com. Illus., adv. Circ: 7600000. Vol. ends: No. 12. Microform: PQC. Online: bigchalk; Factiva; Gale Group; OCLC Online Computer Library Center, Inc.; ProQuest Information & Learning. Reprint: PQC. *Indexed:* CINAHL, ConsI, IHTDI, MagInd, RGPR. *Aud.:* Hs, Ga, Ac.

There is a strong chance that whatever home project readers are planning, it will be covered by *Better Homes and Gardens*. The magazine's strength is its combination of extensive scope and fine detail. Each issue includes features on gardening, interior design, building, family matters, food, and health; and across the range of topics, articles include precise technical information. This magazine would be a good choice for most public libraries. *Better Homes and Gardens* also publishes titles focusing on particular aspects of the home and home ownership.

3771. *Budget Living: spend smart, live rich.* [ISSN: 1541-3675] 2002. bi-m. USD 14.95; USD 3.99 newsstand/cover per issue; USD 4.99 newsstand/cover per issue Canada. Ed(s): Sarah Gray Miller. Budget Living Media, 317 Madison Ave., Ste. 2300, New York, NY 10017. Adv. Circ: 300000. *Aud.:* Ga.

AdWeek Magazine's "2003 Startup Magazine of the Year," *Budget Living* is targeted at relatively young, relatively affluent readers who want to live well but not spend too much. *Budget Living* doesn't advocate penny-pinching; it suggests that readers can enjoy the good life even more when they're clever enough to get it for less. Money-saving ideas range from home improvement (a $3,000 kitchen makeover) to travel (Paris on $100 a day) to clothes (buy at Gap Kids instead of adult Gap). A busy layout, with retro styling, gives *Budget Living* the good-natured air of a fun flea market or consignment shop—but the goods are all new.

3772. *Country Almanac.* [ISSN: 1058-3734] 1981. q. USD 17.97 for 2 yrs. domestic; USD 23.36 for 2 yrs. Canada; USD 35.94 elsewhere. Ed(s): Jodi Zucker. Harris Publications, Inc., 1115 Broadway, 8th Fl, New York, NY 10010-2803; countryalmanac@harris-custsvc.com; http://www.countryalmanacmag.com. Illus., adv. Circ: 400000. Vol. ends: No. 4. *Bk. rev.:* Various number and length. *Aud.:* Ga.

Each issue of *Country Almanac* includes articles on collecting and decorating with country details (both original and reproduction), tours of charming houses with a country look, and do-it-yourself projects. *Country Almanac* emphasizes the affordability and ease of projects, and it praises country style for providing both cozy, "down-home" qualities and forms of creative self-expression.

3773. *Country Home.* [ISSN: 0737-3740] 1979. 10x/yr. USD 21.97 domestic; USD 29.97 foreign; USD 4.95 newsstand/cover domestic. Ed(s): Carol Sheehan. Meredith Corp., 1716 Locust St, Des Moines, IA 50309-3023; http://www.meredith.com. Illus., index, adv. Circ: 1200000. Vol. ends: No. 6. Microform: NBI. *Indexed:* ASIP, GardL. *Aud.:* Ga.

Country Home is aimed at readers who want to draw on traditional artifacts and customs to enrich contemporary homes and lifestyles. Articles focus on homeowners' experiences creating beautiful country homes; decorating and gardening suggestions; and tips on choosing and caring for antiques. Targeted at an upper-middle-class audience, *Country Home* is richly illustrated and full of reports of life's potential pleasures, from the complex flavors of bread at regional artisan bakeries to the beauties of vintage game boards.

3774. *Country Living (New York).* Formerly: *Good Housekeeping's Country Living.* [ISSN: 0732-2569] 1978. m. USD 12 domestic; USD 28 foreign. Ed(s): Nancy Mernit Soriano. Hearst Corporation, Country Living, 224 W 57th St, New York, NY 10019; hacl@hearst.com; http://countryliving.com; http://www.hearstcorp.com. Illus., adv. Circ: 350000 Paid. Vol. ends: Dec. *Indexed:* GardL, MagInd. *Aud.:* Ga.

Like other country periodicals, *Country Living* discusses decorating, antiques, cooking, travel, home building, gardens, and crafts. Its distinctive features include an emphasis on items just becoming collectible—such as nineteenth- and twentieth-century lawn games and giveaway juice glasses—and do-it-yourself projects in a range of budget categories.

3775. *Dwell: at home in the modern world.* [ISSN: 1530-5309] 2000. 8x/yr. USD 19.95 domestic; USD 29.95 Canada; USD 35.95 elsewhere. Ed(s): Allison Arieff. Pixie Communications, 99 Osgood Pl., San Francisco, CA 94133; http://www.dwellmag.com. Illus., adv. Circ: 100000 Paid. *Indexed:* ASIP. *Aud.:* Ga.

One of *Library Journal*'s best new magazines of 2000, *Dwell* showcases home architecture of surprising kinds in surprising locations. A recent issue includes a weekend getaway in Milanville, Pennsylvania, and an affordable, architect-designed house in East Austin, Texas. *Dwell* readers are likely to be younger than followers of *Better Homes and Gardens* or the various country journals. The magazine has an environmentally conscious slant; a hip, contemporary look; and an imaginative way of marrying design consciousness to practical information.

3776. *Electronic House: enhanced lifestyle through home automation.* [ISSN: 0886-6643] 1986. 12x/yr. USD 29.95 domestic; USD 955 foreign. Ed(s): Melisa Mielke, Amanda Finch. E H Publishing, Inc., 526 Boston Post Rd, ste 150, Wayland, MA 01778-0340; http://www.electronichouse.com. Illus., adv. Circ: 31000. Vol. ends: No. 6. *Indexed:* IHTDI. *Aud.:* Ga, Sa.

Written for consumers who enjoy technology but aren't necessarily engineers, *Electronic House* includes articles on both extravagant and affordable smart homes. Some electronic controls cover a whole house, while others manage subsystems such as lighting, security, home theater, energy use, and telecommunications. *Electronic House* evaluates products and provides tips and guidelines.

Elle Decor. See Interior Design and Decoration section.

3777. *The Family Handyman: tons of projects, tips and tools.* Incorporates: *Home Garden.* [ISSN: 0014-7230] 1951. 10x/yr. USD 19.97 domestic; USD 28.97 foreign; USD 2.99 newsstand/cover per issue domestic. Ed(s): Gary Havens. Reader's Digest Association, Inc, Reader's Digest Rd, Pleasantville, NY 10570-7000; http://www.rd.com. Illus., index, adv. Circ: 1150000 Paid. Vol. ends: Dec. *Indexed:* ConsI, IHTDI, MagInd, RGPR. *Aud.:* Ga.

The Family Handyman covers home remodeling and repairs for people who enjoy taking on most of the tasks themselves. Regular columns answer readers' questions, give directions for fixing common home problems, advise on tool use, etc. Features address woodworking, gardening, remodeling, auto and appliance repairs, and new-product reviews. Step-by-step, illustrated instructions seem especially valuable. Recommended for libraries with do-it-yourselfers in their communities.

3778. *Home: the remodeling and decorating resource.* Former titles (until 1981): *Hudson Home Magazine;* (until 1980): *Hudson Home Guides;* Incorporates: *Home Building and Remodeling; Home Planning and Design; Home Improvement and Repair; Home Plans and Ideas; Kitchens, Baths and Family Rooms.* [ISSN: 0278-2839] 1955. 10x/yr.

USD 12 domestic; USD 22 foreign. Ed(s): Gale Steves. Hachette Filipacchi Media U.S., Inc., 1633 Broadway, New York, NY 10019; http://www.hfmus.com. Illus., adv. Circ: 1000000 Paid. Vol. ends: No. 10. Online: America Online, Inc. *Aud.:* Ga.

Home emphasizes home design and renovation and is aimed primarily at middle-income homeowners. It provides descriptions of whole-house renovations and of smaller room-by-room redos, with detailed product evaluations. This magazine focuses less than others in this category on lifestyle but emphasizes practical aspects of home ownership, such as financing and insuring. Recommended for libraries in communities where many homeowners are remodeling.

3779. *House Beautiful.* [ISSN: 0018-6422] 1896. m. USD 12 domestic; USD 28 foreign. Ed(s): Mark Mayfield. Hearst Corporation, 1700 Broadway, Ste 2801, New York, NY 10019; http://www.housebeautiful.women.com. Illus., adv. Circ: 865000. Vol. ends: No. 12. Microform: NBI; PQC. Online: bigchalk; EBSCO Publishing; Gale Group; Northern Light Technology, Inc.; OCLC Online Computer Library Center, Inc.; ProQuest Information & Learning. Reprint: PQC. *Indexed:* AIAP, ASIP, ConsI, GardL, MagInd, RGPR. *Aud.:* Ga.

New editor Mark Mayfield took over at *House Beautiful* in 2002, indicating a return to the magazine's traditional mainstream focus, after a brief experiment with a bolder, more up-scale image. As in the past, *House Beautiful* features articles on home decorating and remodeling, architecture, entertaining, and gardening that guide readers in creating comfortable homes expressing their personal styles. Projects primarily draw on high-end materials, with some more cost-conscious features.

3780. *Martha Stewart Living.* [ISSN: 1057-5251] 1990. m. USD 28 domestic; CND 38 Canada; USD 54 elsewhere. Ed(s): Margaret Roach. Martha Stewart Living Omnimedia LLC, 20 W 43rd St, 25th Fl, New York, NY 10036; mstewart@marthastewart.com; http://www.marthastewart.com. Illus., adv. Circ: 2430000 Paid. Vol. ends: No. 12. *Indexed:* RGPR. *Aud.:* Ga.

Allegations of insider trading have somewhat dimmed the popularity of founder Martha Stewart, but *Martha Stewart Living* continues to provide a beautifully illustrated set of directions for creating a home that is gracious, comfortable, and orderly. Each issue includes ideas for gardening, cooking, collecting, decorating, and crafts. The magazine explains both basic tasks (how to paint a window frame) and more-complicated projects (how to marbleize Easter eggs).

3781. *Mary Engelbreit's Home Companion.* [ISSN: 1096-5289] 1996. bi-m. USD 19.95 domestic; USD 36.95 foreign; USD 4.95 newsstand/cover per issue. Ed(s): Mary Engelbreit. Universal Engelbreit Cox LLC, 317 Madison Avenue, 1606, New York, NY 10017; edquestions@mehc.com. Illus., adv. Circ: 363575. *Aud.:* Ga.

Founded and edited by Mary Engelbreit, whose whimsical drawings are a familiar sight on greeting cards and other products, *Home Companion* is aimed at middle-class baby-boomers with a creative streak. Issues include do-it-yourself crafts, recipes, and visits to artists' and collectors' homes. However, this standard fare is presented with surprising twists. A home renovation, for example, is treated as a "beauty makeover," and summer recipes are linked to American literary classics. The look is bright, the attitude is cheerful and easy-going, and Engelbreit's drawings are sprinkled throughout.

3782. *Metropolitan Home: style for our generation.* Former titles (until 1981): *Apartment Life;* (until 1970): *Apartment Ideas.* [ISSN: 0273-2858] 1969. bi-m. USD 9.97; USD 19.97. Ed(s): Donna Warner. Hachette Filipacchi Media U.S., Inc., 1633 Broadway, New York, NY 10019; http://www.hfmus.com. Illus., adv. Circ: 613613 Paid. Vol. ends: Dec. Microform: PQC. Online: America Online, Inc.; Gale Group. *Indexed:* AIAP, ASIP, ArtInd, DAAI, IHTDI, MagInd. *Aud.:* Ga.

Like other home magazines, *Metropolitan Home* includes articles on decorating, remodeling, collecting, cooking, designing, and entertaining, but its look and focus are decidedly urban, upscale, contemporary, and clean. Articles focus on design-conscious elegance in a variety of metropolitan settings, including one or two international locations per issue. *Metropolitan Home* would be welcome in libraries where readers are likely to pursue sophisticated home styles.

3783. *Natural Home.* [ISSN: 1523-9837] 1998. bi-m. USD 19.95. Ed(s): Robyn Griggs. Natural Home L L C, 201 E 4th St, Loveland, CO 80537-5565; naturalhome@interweave.com; http://www.interweave.com. Illus., adv. *Aud.:* Ga.

Natural Home addresses home and lifestyle issues for a middle-class, environmentally conscious readership. It aims to inspire and inform a mainstream audience, with the message that what is good for the planet can also be delightful, convenient, and comfortable. Topics include innovative homebuilding, cooking, gardening, uses of salvaged materials, and responsible product choices. Useful for libraries within environmentally active communities.

3784. *Real Simple: the magazine for a simpler life - home - body - soul.* [ISSN: 1528-1701] 2000. 10x/yr. USD 19.95 domestic; USD 29.95 Canada. Ed(s): Susan Wyland. Time, Inc, Time & Life Bldg, Rockefeller Center, 1271 Ave of the Americas, New York, NY 10020-1393; letters@realsimple.com; http://www.realsimple.com/. Illus., adv. Sample. Circ: 400000 Paid. *Aud.:* Ga.

Named one of the ten best new magazines of 2000 by *Library Journal*, *Real Simple* aims at providing realistic solutions for simplifying complex lives. The design is distinctive: muted colors, large pictures, a lucid layout. Short features with a friendly, authoritative tone offer information on a range of home problems, from how to sort and store children's artwork to how to invest. Active, middle-class women are the target audience, and the focus is on fashion and beauty articles, but men striving to manage personal, professional, and community commitments may be interested as well.

3785. *Romantic Homes.* Formerly: *Victorian Sampler.* [ISSN: 1086-4083] 1983. m. USD 29.95 domestic; USD 3.99 newsstand/cover per issue. Ed(s): Catherine Yarnovich, Eileen Paulin. Y-Visionary Publishing, 265 S Anita Dr, Ste 120, Orange, CA 92868. Illus., adv. Circ: 130000 Paid. Vol. ends: No. 12. *Aud.:* Ga.

Romantic Homes is aimed at readers who want to create a warm, casually elegant, home haven. It emphasizes using items from other cultures or periods (original or reproduction) to bring a special flair to home decorating. Most issues focus on a particular "romantic" style, such as British Colonial, Caribbean Island, or Country Life.

Southern Accents. See Interior Design and Decoration section.

Sunset. See General Editorial/General section.

3786. *This Old House.* Incorporates (in 2001): *Today's Homeowner Solutions;* Which was formerly (until 2001): *Today's Homeowner;* (until 1996): *Home Mechanix;* (until 1984): *Mechanix Illustrated;* Which incorporated: *Electronics Illustrated.* [ISSN: 1086-2633] 1995. 10x/yr. USD 15.96 domestic; USD 25.96 Canada; USD 29.95 elsewhere. Ed(s): Donna Sapolin. Time4 Media, Inc., 1185 Ave of the Americas, 27th Fl, New York, NY 10035; http://www.thisoldhouse.org. Illus., adv. Circ: 672754 Paid. Online: EBSCO Publishing. *Aud.:* Ga.

This Old House includes columns by the staff of the popular television show and articles on the show's remodeling projects, but it has strong stand-alone value also. For anyone interested in renovating vintage homes, *This Old House* is a good resource for real-world information, with discussions that document how the construction and design decisions get made and photographic sequences that illustrate how the work gets done. Like the television show, the magazine emphasizes old-fashioned craftsmanship enhanced by contemporary materials and technology.

3787. *Traditional Home.* Formerly (until 1985): *Traditional Home Ideas.* [ISSN: 0883-4660] 1978. 8x/yr. USD 22 domestic; USD 30 foreign. Ed(s): Karol DeWolf Nickell. Meredith Corp., 1716 Locust St, Des Moines, IA 50309-3023; http://www.meredith.com. Illus., adv. Circ: 925000. Vol. ends: No. 6. Microform: NBI. *Indexed:* DAAI. *Aud.:* Ga.

Like *Country Home* and *Romantic Homes* (above in this section), *Traditional Home* addresses the technique of combining elements of classic decor with realities of contemporary life in renovating, decorating, and entertaining. However, it is more substantial and upscale than *Romantic Homes*, combining rich pictorials with detailed text; and *Traditional Home*'s featured designs include both country styles and more classic and formal examples. Offers expert advice on antiques; art; and, uniquely, etiquette. Worth consideration by libraries with strong home collections.

3788. ***Veranda: a gallery of fine design.*** [ISSN: 1040-8150] 1987. bi-m. USD 24 domestic; USD 52 foreign; USD 5.50 newsstand/cover per issue. Ed(s): Lisa Newsom. Veranda, 455 E Paces Ferry Rd, Ste 216, Atlanta, GA 30305; http://www.veranda.com. Illus., adv. Circ: 340220 Paid. Vol. ends: No. 4. *Aud.:* Ga.

Acquired by the Hearst Corporation in May 2002, *Veranda* has dropped the word "Southern" from its subtitle, indicating an even more national focus. *Veranda* features beautiful (and, doubtless, expensive) homes throughout the United States in a variety of lush styles. The magazine is gorgeous, featuring artful photography of interiors, gardens, table settings, and floral arrangements. Articles focus on decorative arts, books, collectibles, luxury goods, unusual travel destinations, art exhibitions, architects, and the latest in furnishings. There is no discussion of remodeling or renovating.

3789. ***Victorian Decorating & Lifestyle.*** Former titles (until 1994): *Country Victorian Decorating and Lifestyle;* (until 1991): *Country Victorian Accents; Country Victorian Decorating; Victorian Accents.* [ISSN: 1076-0075] 1989. bi-m. USD 19.97; USD 25.97 foreign; USD 3.99 newsstand/cover per issue. Ed(s): Florine McCain. Goodman Media Group, Inc., 1700 Broadway, 34th Fl, New York, NY 10019; http://www.goodmanmediagroup.com. Illus., adv. Circ: 130000. Vol. ends: No. 6. *Bk. rev.:* Various number and length. *Aud.:* Ga, Sa.

Victorian Decorating & Lifestyle is a resource for readers who consider themselves "Victorian at heart." The magazine is aimed at those who want to re-create the ambience of the Victorian era, whether on a budget, using replicas, or with less limited funds and a commitment to authenticity. Evocative articles highlight Victorian architecture, art, and culture, with emphasis on the period's way of life and the uses of particular objects in everyday pursuits.

3790. ***Victorian Homes.*** [ISSN: 0744-415X] 1982. bi-m. USD 19.95; USD 3.99 newsstand/cover per issue. Ed(s): Erika Kotite. Y-Visionary Publishing, 265 S Anita Dr, Ste 120, Orange, CA 92868. Illus., adv. Circ: 100000 Paid. Vol. ends: No. 6. *Indexed:* AIAP, GardL. *Aud.:* Ga, Sa.

Victorian Homes combines well-illustrated articles with instructive text, cultivating understanding and appreciation of Victorian architecture and artifacts and the culture that gave them life. Included are discussions of Victorian building materials, ways to shop for and care for particular kinds of antiques, and guides for choosing period fixtures and replicas. An annual sourcebook of companies offering products and services for the Victorian revival market may be especially useful to owners of nineteenth- and early-twentieth-century homes.

Electronic Journals

Many print home magazines both showcase features from current issues on their web sites and offer other resources that are only available electronically. These web sites are worth noting. *Better Homes and Gardens*, for example, offers a "Home Care Tracker" and a "Stain Solver," while the *Martha Stewart Living* web site provides a weekly calendar of household activities with directions, and the *This Old House* web site includes a resource directory of products, supplies, and services used in the show.

3791. ***Living Home.*** 1995. irreg. Ed(s): Kim Garretson. Novo Media Group, http://www.livinghome.com. *Aud.:* Ga.

Living Home is an interesting—and free—compendium of home and garden information, including a useful "tool chest" with tile and paint estimators and a window design planner. Unfortunately, a cluttered site design can make it difficult to find a particular topic, and links to commercial products sometimes seem to blur editorial boundaries, but the site offers lively writing and a fresh approach to home-related topics. It is fun to browse.

3792. ***Remodeling Online.*** Hanley-Wood, Llc., One Thomas Circle, N W, Ste 600, Washington, DC 20005-5701. *Aud.:* Ga.

Remodeling Online serves and promotes the community of remodelers. It offers content from the print magazine, *Remodeling*, from other publications of the parent company Hanley-Wood, and articles from other remodeling sources. Do-it-yourself remodelers will find useful information, such as the annual report on returns related to the cost of remodeling projects. As in other vendor-sponsored electronic journals, editorial and advertising content are not strictly separated.

■ HORSES

Linda Collins, Head of Access Services, Lamont Library, Harvard University, Cambridge, MA 02138

Introduction

The horse plays an important role in the American economy. Diverse equine interests represent a 25 billion-dollar industry. From the Western ranges to Virginia's Hunt Country and in suburban communities across the nation, we continue our love affair with this noble beast. The recreational uses of the horse cannot be clearly defined by region. The country is a melting pot of equine activity, from horse racing and show jumping to Western reining and dressage. Across the country, 4-H and Pony Clubs continue to introduce children to riding, showing, and the basics of horse care and management.

From general-interest to breed-specific titles, there are many journals that support all types of equine involvement. The nonprofit American Horse Publications Association (www.americanhorsepubs.org) is a great source of information about equine publications. Another excellent resource is the American Horse Council (www.horsecouncil.org), the national trade association representing the horse industry in Washington, D.C. The following is a selection of the major equine publications in the field.

Basic Periodicals

Ga: *Equus, Horse & Rider, Horse Illustrated, Practical Horseman, Western Horseman.*

3793. ***The American Quarter Horse Journal.*** Formerly (until Jun. 2001): *Quarter Horse Journal.* 1948. m. USD 25 domestic; USD 50 Canada; USD 80 foreign. Ed(s): Lesli Groves. American Quarter Horse Association, 1600 Quarter Horse Dr, Amarillo, TX 79168; http://www.aqha.com. Illus., index, adv. Sample. Circ: 74000. Vol. ends: Sep. Microform: PQC. *Bk. rev.:* 3, 250 words. *Aud.:* Sa.

This comprehensive journal is the official publication of the American Quarter Horse Association. Covering all disciplines, it speaks to the versatility of this popular horse. With more registered quarter horses than any other breed, this journal has a strong following. Because the quarter horse plays an important and influential role in many cross-breeding programs, the stallion issue is of interest to horsemen across the country.

3794. ***The American Saddlebred.*** [ISSN: 0746-6153] 1983. bi-m. Non-members, USD 25. Ed(s): Mary Kirkman. American Saddlebred Horse Association, 4093 Iron Works Pike, Lexington, KY 40511. Illus., adv. Sample. Circ: 7200. Vol. ends: Dec. *Bk. rev.:* 2, 150 words. *Aud.:* Sa.

The official journal of the American Saddlebred Horse Association, this publication does not stray far from its primary focus, the breeding, training, showing, and promotion of these flashy, charismatic horses. The journal is the primary communication tool of the association and serves as a platform for interesting and continued discussions. The articles are well written and educational, including everything from legal responsibilities to understanding the direction of the breed past and present. Exceptional color photographs enhance the cover, but most photos accompanying the articles are black-and-white. Included are a calendar of events, classified ads, a listing of breeders by state, and association notes and updates. A must for all American Saddlebred enthusiasts and libraries where this style of horsemanship is prevalent.

3795. ***Appaloosa Journal.*** Formerly: *Appaloosa News.* [ISSN: 0892-385X] 1946. m. USD 29.95 domestic; USD 39.95 Canada; USD 49.95 elsewhere. Ed(s): Robin Hendrickson. Appaloosa Horse Club, 2720 West Pullmann Rd, Moscow, ID 83843-0903; journal@appaloosa.com; http://www.appaloosa.com. Adv. Sample. Circ: 21341 Paid and free. Vol. ends: Dec. Microform: PQC. *Aud.:* Sa.

Appaloosa Journal is the official publication of the national breed association and registry for Appaloosa horses. Its stated mission is to advance and improve the breeding and performance of the Appaloosa horse. To this end, the journal includes information on Appaloosa breeding, listing leading sires and incentive programs. An extensive show calendar includes class lists for each event and current national standings. Feature articles on training help to improve the performance of the horse. Each issue includes information on Appaloosa stakes racing and news from the regional associations.

3796. ***Arabian Horse World: the magazine for owners, breeders and admirers of fine horses.*** [ISSN: 0003-7494] 1960. m. USD 40 domestic; USD 72 Canada; USD 88 elsewhere. Ed(s): Mary Jane Parkinson, Lynn Anderson. Primedia Enthusiast Group, 1316 Tamson Dr., Ste 101, Cambria, CA 93428; http://www.primedia.com. Illus., adv. Sample. Circ: 11000. Vol. ends: Dec. *Aud.:* Sa.

Arabians are one of the oldest, purest breeds and have been admired for centuries for their classic beauty, strength, and stamina. *Arabian Horse World* is a publication as exquisite as the breed it represents. Artistic color photographs enhance every issue. Profiles of top breeders, leading sires, and prominent Arabian farms are featured. The versatility of the Arab is apparent, with articles on racing and endurance riding. This comprehensive journal often has over 300 pages and is of particular interest to those involved in the breeding of these lovely horses.

3797. ***The Blood-Horse.*** [ISSN: 0006-4998] 1916. w. USD 89 domestic; USD 94.34 in Kentucky; USD 164.78 Canada. Ed(s): Raymond S Paulick. The Blood-Horse, Inc., 1736 Alexandria Dr, PO Box 4680, Lexington, KY 40544-4038; http://www.bloodhorse.com. Illus., index, adv. Sample. Circ: 24635 Paid. Vol. ends: Dec. Microform: PQC. *Aud.:* Sa.

The Blood-Horse is the primary publication of the international thoroughbred industry. Published for 85 years, this weekly journal dedicates itself to the improvement of thoroughbred breeding and racing. This is the bible of the sport of horseracing. It is of interest to racing professionals, those involved in breeding programs, handicappers, and fans. Race results, statistics, information on top lineage, sales, and biographies fill each issue. A must for all communities with ties to the thoroughbred industry. The electronic version of *The Blood-Horse* includes news, racing results, sales and breeding information, and links to stud farms. There is a 12-month archive for subscribers. The web site is http://www.bloodhorse.com/.

3798. ***Carriage Journal.*** [ISSN: 0008-6916] 1963. 5x/yr. Membership, USD 45. Ed(s): Jill Ryder. Carriage Association of America, Inc., 177 Pointers Auburn Rd, Salem, NJ 08079. Illus., index, adv. Sample. Circ: 3200. Vol. ends: Spring. *Indexed:* SportS. *Bk. rev.:* 3-4, 500 words. *Aud.:* Sa.

Published by the Carriage Association of America, this journal has a very international feel, with reports from England, South Africa, Germany, Argentina, and many other countries. It is apparent that carriage horse enthusiasts will travel great distances in pursuit of their sport. Articles are extremely well researched and authoritative, and cover a vast array of topics in great detail. Black-and-white photographs accompany most articles. An updated calendar lists events, trips, shows, and sales. Classified ads include everything from harnesses to horses to carriages. Because of its commitment to carriages from Roman times to the present, this publication may be of to historians as well as to driving enthusiasts.

3799. ***The Chronicle of the Horse.*** [ISSN: 0009-5990] 1937. w. USD 52 domestic; USD 72 foreign. Ed(s): Tricia Booker, John Strassburger. Chronicle of the Horse, Inc., PO Box 46, Middleburg, VA 20118. Illus., index, adv. Sample. Circ: 22000 Paid. Vol. ends: Dec. Microform: PQC. *Bk. rev.:* Occasionally, 3-4, 300 words. *Aud.:* Ga, Sa.

This weekly publication is to the show-horse crowd what *The Blood-Horse* is to thoroughbred racing enthusiasts, a primary source for events, results, and the participants. Focusing on show jumping, dressage, eventing, driving, and hunter jumpers, this is a first-rate professional publication. The extensive classified ads offer horses, ponies, real estate, jobs, vans, and trailers. Each issue is packed with interesting feature articles on the personalities involved in the sport. The online version provides access to the same reliable source of current news and results for the entire sport horse community. The web site: http://www.chronofhorse.com/.

3800. ***Cutting Horse Chatter.*** Former titles (until Apr. 1993): *Cutting Horse;* (until 1991): *Cuttin' Hoss Chatter.* [ISSN: 1081-0951] 1948. m. USD 5 newsstand/cover per issue. Ed(s): Peggy Riggle. National Cutting Horse Association, 4704 Hwy. 377, S., Ft. Worth, TX 76116-8805. Illus., adv. Sample. Circ: 12000. Vol. ends: Dec. *Aud.:* Sa.

Cutting Horse Chatter is the official publication of the governing body of the sport of cutting, a competition that comes from the Western tradition of cattle handling. Much of the business of the National Cutting Horse Association is carried in the journal. Half of the almost 400 pages are devoted to show results, standings, upcoming events, and issues related to association management. Feature article topics include training, personality profiles, and cattle management. Interest in the sport of cutting is definitely on the increase, with events and clinics being held regularly in such unlikely locations as New England.

3801. ***The Draft Horse Journal.*** [ISSN: 0012-5865] 1964. q. USD 27 domestic; USD 32 Canada; USD 37 elsewhere. Ed(s): Lynn Telleen. Draft Horse Journal, PO Box 670, Waverly, IA 50677; http://www.horseshoes.com. Illus., index, adv. Sample. Circ: 21000 Paid and controlled. Vol. ends: Winter. *Bk. rev.:* 1, 200 words. *Aud.:* Sa.

This quarterly publication represents the heavyweight division: Belgians, Percherons, Clydesdales, and Shires. Focusing on breeding and sales, it also covers the draft horse shows and the county fair circuit of horse pulls. Feature articles discuss the nuances of the eight-horse hitch, harness and tack, and the history and use of these big horses in logging, agriculture, and transportation. *The Draft Horse Journal* is a unique and important resource.

3802. ***Dressage Today.*** [ISSN: 1079-1167] 1994. m. Primedia Enthusiast Group, 656 Quince Orchard Rd, Gaithersburg, MD 20878; http://www.primedia.com. Illus., adv. Sample. Circ: 33353 Paid. Vol. ends: Aug. *Bk. rev.:* 1-2, 300 words. *Aud.:* Ga, Sa.

Dressage brings the training of the horse to an art form. At the most advanced levels, it is the pinnacle of harmony between horse and rider, but more basic levels of dressage training can serve as the foundation for all other styles of riding. *Dressage Today* features articles related to the sport of dressage but also includes a wealth of training information that easily relate to other disciplines. Interviews with leaders in the sport, information on national and international competitions, and articles on the selection and care of the dressage horse are just some of the contents. As the nationwide interest in dressage grows, this journal enjoys increased popularity.

3803. ***Equine Images: reflections of the equestrian lifestyle.*** [ISSN: 1044-0224] 1986. bi-m. USD 29.95 domestic; USD 39.95 Canada; USD 41.95 foreign. Heartland Construction Group, Inc., 1003 Central Ave, Fort Dodge, IA 50501; amy@hlipublishing.com; http://www.equineimages.com. Illus., adv. Sample. Vol. ends: Dec. *Aud.:* Ga.

Equine Images is an art magazine with a mission to understand the art world as it is inspired by the horse. This 14-year-old publication is a recent acquisition of The Blood-Horse, Inc., which ensures continued quality and a commitment to celebrating the art and culture of the horse. Feature articles spotlight equine art, artists, patrons of the arts, and galleries and museums that bring this art to the public. Travel notes include popular destinations for collectors and aficionados. "Behind the Image" is a regular column that explores the artist's creative process. A unique publication of interest to artists, collectors, and all those with an appreciation for the beauty of the horse.

Equine Veterinary Journal. See Veterinary Science.

3804. *Equus.* [ISSN: 0149-0672] 1977. m. USD 19.95 domestic; USD 31.95 foreign. Primedia Enthusiast Group, 1316 Tamson Dr., Ste 101, Cambria, CA 93428; http://www.primedia.com. Illus., index, adv. Sample. Circ: 150328 Paid. Microform: PQC. Reprint: PQC. *Indexed:* SportS, ZooRec. *Aud.:* Ga.

If you were to select only one general horse publication, this is the classic. A repeat winner of the American Horse Publications Awards, *Equus* provides horsemen with sound advice on horse health. Feature articles by leaders in the industry are consistently well written and researched. "The Medical Front" is a monthly column describing the latest therapies, drugs, and procedures in laymen's terms. "Case Reports" are particularly good horse/human-interest stories. *Equus* has a licensed veterinarian on its editorial board to ensure the accuracy of its medical reports. This publication has wide appeal to a broad range of horse enthusiasts.

3805. *Hoof Beats.* [ISSN: 0018-4683] 1933. m. Non-members, USD 32.50. Ed(s): Dean A Hoffman. United States Trotting Association, 750 Michigan Ave, Columbus, OH 43215; dhoffman@ustrotting.com; http://www.ustrotting.com. Illus., index, adv. Sample. Circ: 15500. Vol. ends: Feb. *Bk. rev.:* 1, 300 words. *Aud.:* Sa.

Hoof Beats is as important to the standardbred racing industry as *The Blood-Horse* is to thoroughbred racing. The official publication of the United States Trotting Association, this monthly publication carries features about leading drivers and winning trotters and pacers. Also included are regular articles on the business of the sport, including legislative changes that affect parimutuel wagering and taxes. Information on top stallions, successful breeding lines, and statistics round out the offerings. This is an important publication for anyone with ties to the harness racing community.

3806. *Hoofcare & Lameness: the journal of equine foot science.* Former titles (until 1992): *Hoofcare and Lameness Quarterly Report;* (until 1991): *F Y I.* [ISSN: 1076-4704] 1985. q. USD 59 domestic; USD 65 Canada; USD 75 elsewhere. Ed(s): Fran Jurga. Hoofcare Publishing, 19 Harbor Loop, PO Box 660, Gloucester, MA 01930. Illus., adv. Circ: 1500 Paid. *Bk. rev.:* 3-4, 250 words. *Aud.:* Ac, Sa.

This journal of equine foot science is a very focused quarterly publication for the professional farrier, veterinarian, or those involved with the care of the performance horse. "No hoof, no horse" is the popular saying that this publication addresses, with an international board of consulting editors who are not shy about challenging conventional practice and hoof care theory. This scholarly journal's 15-year index is a virtual Who's Who and what's what in the history of horseshoeing and lameness. If you are interested in examining the horse from the ground up, this is an excellent place to begin. *Hoofcare & Lameness* also has a web presence, with access to news and events, book and video reviews, and some past articles. http://www.hoofcare.com/

3807. *The Horse.* Formerly (until 1995): *Modern Horse Breeding.* [ISSN: 1081-9711] 1984. m. 10/yr. plus a. edition. USD 24 domestic except KY; USD 25.44 KY State; USD 40.45 Canada. Ed(s): Kimberly Graetz. The Blood-Horse, Inc., 1736 Alexandria Dr, PO Box 4680, Lexington, KY 40544-4038; http://www.bloodhorse.com. Adv. Circ: 41334. *Indexed:* IndVet. *Aud.:* Ga, Ac, Sa.

Published by The Blood-Horse, this independent journal relies on the expertise of the American Association of Equine Practitioners. Focusing on health, it has regular features on sports medicine, nutrition, and equine behavior. It includes reports from recent symposiums, association meetings, and current research. This is an important publication of interest to equine practitioners as well as horse owners who want to stay informed on veterinary science, particularly as it pertains to the horse.

3808. *Horse & Rider.* Incorporates (1981-1991): *Performance Horseman.* [ISSN: 0018-5159] 1968. m. USD 15.95 domestic; USD 27.95 foreign. Primedia Enthusiast Group, 656 Quince Orchard Rd, Gaithersburg, MD 20878; http://www.primedia.com. Illus., index, adv. Circ: 175104 Paid. Vol. ends: Dec. *Indexed:* SportS. *Bk. rev.:* 1, 50 words. *Aud.:* Ga.

Horse & Rider is a self-proclaimed magazine for the Western rider, but its broad scope makes it so much more. Articles include training tips from professionals across the disciplines, the latest information on horse care, and regular features on horse people from chiropractors to authors. This is a high-quality publication with wonderful photographs enhancing the feature articles. It is well written and researched. A comprehensive index published annually in the January issue is an extremely useful tool, making this a publication well worth collecting.

3809. *Horse Illustrated: your complete guide to owning and caring for your horse.* [ISSN: 0145-9791] 1976. m. USD 23.97; USD 34.47 Canada; USD 39.97 elsewhere. Ed(s): Moira Harris. Fancy Publications, Inc., 3 Burroughs, Irvine, CA 92618-2804; http://www.animalnetwork.com. Illus., index, adv. Circ: 183000 Paid. Vol. ends: Dec. *Bk. rev.:* 2, 150 words. *Aud.:* Ga.

This general-interest horse magazine does an exceptional job of providing articles of interest to all disciplines. Whether the focus is Western pole bending or top-level dressage, the articles always find the common ground. They are accompanied by rich color photographs. The quality of writing aside, this publication beats the other general-interest magazines in its sheer size. A most recent issue was a full 140 pages with nine feature articles of six to eight pages each. Regular columns include the latest industry news and guest editorials on controversial topics. This is a great all-around publication that will be of interest to all horse owners and enthusiasts.

3810. *Michael Plumb's Horse Journal.* [ISSN: 1073-5704] 1994. m. USD 45; USD 57 foreign. Belvoir Publications, Inc., 75 Holly Hill Ln, Box 2626, Greenwich, CT 06836-2626. Illus., index. Sample. Vol. ends: Dec. *Aud.:* Ga.

This publication describes itself as the product, care, and service guide for people who love horses. It is the *Consumer Reports* of the equine crowd, accepting no commercial advertising. The product recommendations are unbiased and firmly based on field trials and experience. In the same authoritative, no-nonsense style, articles inform readers on nutrition, health care, training, and the latest technological advances. The subscription rates are a little high, but each issue is packed with valuable advice.

3811. *The Morgan Horse.* [ISSN: 0027-1098] 1941. m. USD 31.50. Ed(s): Christina Kollander. American Morgan Horse Association, PO Box 960, Shelburne, VT 05482-0960; info@morganhorse.com. Illus., index, adv. Sample. Circ: 9000. Vol. ends: Jan. *Bk. rev.:* 2, 100 words. *Aud.:* Sa.

The official journal of the Morgan Horse Breed Association, this publication has all the information one needs for breeding, showing, or just enjoying this versatile horse. Articles include information about the Morgan in harness, as a park horse, and in the hunter division; English and Western pleasure; and dressage. There are extensive show results and regional reports. Leading personalities, past and present, are profiled, as well as prominent Morgan horse farms. The popularity of this breed has spread from its origins in Vermont and enjoys a strong following across the country.

3812. *N A R H A Strides.* 1995. 4x/yr. Membership, USD 40. North American Riding for the Handicapped Association, Inc., PO Box 33150, Denver, CO 80233; http://www.narha.org. Illus., adv. Circ: 4500. *Aud.:* Sa.

The official publication of the North American Riding for the Handicapped Association, this nonprofit journal concerns itself with industry standards, program accreditation, and certification of instructors. Articles include a wide range of topics, such as the correct training of horses for use in these types of programs, insurance policy limitations and general liability, crisis management, and a definition of terms used in therapeutic applications. It also features very heartwarming success stories of young riders who gain increased confidence and physical ability as a direct result of their participation in the riding program.

This publication would be of interest to administrators of handicapped riding facilities, mental health professionals, instructors, barn managers, volunteers, fundraisers, sponsors, and the participants and their parents.

3813. ***N R H A Reiner.*** [ISSN: 0199-6762] 1980. bi-m. Members, USD 40. Ed(s): Sharon Barr. National Reining Horse Association, 3000 N.W. Tenth St., Oklahoma, OK 73107-5302. Illus., adv. Sample. Circ: 6000. Vol. ends: Mar. *Aud.:* Sa.

The National Reining Horse Association (NRHA) is the governing body of the sport of reining. Its mission is to enforce the standards of competition and educate the public on the proper performance of a reining horse. *NRHA Reiner,* the association's official publication, presents association news and regional reports and highlights the major reining events across the country. Proper training is emphasized, as well as communication between horse and rider. The sport of reining is growing, with enthusiasts nationwide and over 350 sanctioned events.

3814. ***Paint Horse Journal.*** [ISSN: 0164-5706] 1962. m. Members, USD 35; Non-members, USD 30. Ed(s): Tracy Gantz, Darrell Dodds. American Paint Horse Association, PO Box 961023, Ft. Worth, TX 76161-0023. Illus., index, adv. Sample. Circ: 29227 Paid. Vol. ends: Dec. *Bk. rev.:* 1-3, 200 words. *Aud.:* Sa.

The official publication of the American Paint Horse Association, this is the magazine for owners and breeders who appreciate a little splash of color in their barn. The breeding of paints is a study in genetics and this journal is an important resource. Covering all aspects of breeding, training, showing, and racing, it is a must for paint horse enthusiasts.

3815. ***Polo Players' Edition.*** m. Ed(s): Gwen Rizzo. Rizzo Management Corp., 3500 Fairlane Farms Rd, Ste 9, Wellington, FL 33414. Circ: 6500 Paid. *Aud.:* Sa.

This is a magazine by polo players for polo players. Articles include advice on training for players and their horses, reports on events, and features on celebrity players. More important are tournament results, the calendar of upcoming matches, and news from the polo scene. The polo community's commitment to philanthropy is evidenced by the number of articles reporting on fundraising and other charitable events. Published within *Polo Players' Edition* is the *USPA Bulletin*: the official publication of the U.S. Polo Association.

3816. ***Practical Horseman.*** [ISSN: 0090-8762] 1973. m. USD 24.95; USD 2.95 newsstand/cover per issue. Primedia Enthusiast Group, 656 Quince Orchard Rd, Gaithersburg, MD 20878; http://www.primedia.com. Illus., adv. Sample. Circ: 81500. Vol. ends: Dec. *Indexed:* SportS. *Aud.:* Ga.

Practical Horseman bills itself as the "number one resource for English riders," and there is no better in its class. The articles on training of both horse and rider are comprehensive and accompanied by exceptional color photographs. The monthly jumping clinic is a great exercise in developing a keen eye for evaluating the athleticism of both horse and rider. The journal is packed full of sage advice for beginners to seasoned professionals. It also serves as a platform for discussion on topics that affect the industry. Valuable for those involved in all aspects of English riding, from the trail to the show ring.

3817. ***Trail Rider Magazine.*** [ISSN: 0892-3922] 1970. m. USD 18. Trail Rider Magazine, PO Box 2038, Medford, NJ 08055. Adv. Circ: 3000 Paid. *Aud.:* Sa.

This publication is as rough and ready as the horsemen it's written for. Billed as America's premier trail riders' information source, it concerns itself with recreational and competitive trail riding and the horses bred and sold for this purpose. The protection of the land and trails they ride on is a major focus, as well as popular destinations for trail-riding adventures.

3818. ***Western Horseman.*** [ISSN: 0043-3837] 1936. m. USD 22 domestic; USD 29 foreign; USD 3.99 newsstand/cover per issue. Ed(s): A J Mangum. Western Horseman, Inc., PO Box 7980, Colorado Springs, CO 80933-7980. Illus., index, adv. Sample. Circ: 223000 Paid. Vol. ends: Dec. Microform: PQC. Reprint: PQC. *Indexed:* ASIP, B&AI, SportS. *Bk. rev.:* 3-4, 300 words. *Aud.:* Ga.

This granddaddy of the industry bills itself as "the world's leading horse magazine since 1936" and has the readership to prove it. A tremendously popular general-interest horse magazine with a decidedly Western slant, this publication features a wide array of articles that cover training, health care, equipment, events, ranching, and personality profiles. There is something here for everyone, including a column for young horsemen; a "Political Watch," which informs readers of legislative changes effecting them; and even a column on Western art. Every issue includes product reviews, a cartoon of the month, a calendar of events, show results, and classified ads. The *Western Horseman* online includes a search engine for equestrian events across the country, current point standings, and a link to numerous breed registries. http://www.westernhorseman.com/

3819. ***Young Rider: the magazine for horse and pony lovers.*** [ISSN: 1098-2442] 1995. bi-m. USD 15 domestic; USD 20.25 Canada; USD 23 elsewhere. Ed(s): Lesley Ward. Fancy Publications, Inc., 2401 Beverly Blvd, Los Angeles, CA 90057-0900; lward@fancypubs.com; http://www.animalnetwork.com. Illus., adv. Circ: 26603 Paid. *Bk. rev.:* 1, 100 words. *Aud.:* Ems.

Young Rider is arguably the best equine publication for young people. Directed toward 8- to 14-year-old readers, the articles are informative, interesting, and intelligent. The magazine is valuable to children who ride at public stables; English riders; Western riders; those who show; those who compete in gymkhanas; and those who just plain like horses. The articles are colorfully presented and accompanied by many photographs. There is an ever-present emphasis on safety and responsible behavior. Each edition includes large, removable color posters. It is not heavy with advertisements, and those found are age-appropriate. Overall, this is a wonderful publication for young people who are interested in horses.

Electronic Journals

The highest-quality electronic journals are related to the major publishers of standard equine publications. Primedia, Inc., publisher of *Equus, Practical Horseman, Arabian Horse World,* and *Horse Illustrated,* also publishes two electronic journals: *EquiSearch* (www.equisearch.com) and *Arabian Horse World* (www.AHW.com), both worth a visit. The Blood-Horse, Inc., publisher of *The Blood-Horse, Equine Images,* and *The Horse—Your Guide to Equine Health,* also has a wonderful e-journal, *The Horse Interactive* (www.thehorse.com). There are other, more specialized web journals such as *DRF.com* (www.drf.com), published by the *Daily Racing Form.* The Equestrian Times (www.equestriantimes.com) specializes in international competition. To find other sites, visit *The HayNet* (www.haynet.net), published by The Blood-Horse, Inc. This is an excellent resource.

3820. ***The Equestrian Times.*** 1995. d. USD 40. Ed(s): Nicole Graf. International Equestrian News Network, PO Box 227, Marshfield Hills, MA 02051; info@ienn.com; http://www.ienn.com/ienn/contact.html. *Aud.:* Ga, Sa.

The Equestrian Times is an online publication of the International Equestrian News Network, covering international equestrian events, show results, reports, feature articles, interviews, and photos. Available by subscription only, it provides a wealth of information, with archives going back to January 1997. Very comprehensive coverage of the international world of equine sport. http://www.equestriantimes.com/

■ HOSPITALITY/RESTAURANT

Judith Ohles Kooistra, Collection Development Librarian, Stark Campus Library, Kent State University, 6000 Frank Ave., Canton, OH 44720; jkooistra@stark.kent.edu

Introduction

The hospitality industry has suffered some setbacks in the past couple of years due to 9/11 and tough economic times. Hospitality and tourism magazines reflect these concerns and attempt to provide forecasts for the future. For a time, professionals in the industry were cautiously optimistic and predicting a turnaround in the near future. With the ongoing fear of terrorism and of health concerns like SARS, they seem to be more guarded in their predictions. In a recent issue of *Hotel & Motel Management*, Editor Jeff Higley reported on a conference, saying that hotel management and owners are dealing with stress as "the U.S. lodging industry muddles through the most unpredictable time in its history." With the continuing uncertainty about international politics, the economy, and health issues, it is difficult to currently assess how soon a turnaround for the hospitality industry might happen. Magazines in this section reflect this uncertainty as they continue to provide research and practical advice for professionals in the industry.

These publications cover the spectrum of the hospitality and tourism industry, and issues such as management, finance, future trends, technology, food service, and human resources are addressed. Also included are weekly newsmagazines and scholarly, refereed journals. All titles in this section have corresponding web sites with varying degrees of access to the same information as in the print version. Sometimes the web sites also include daily updates on developments in the industry.

A Literature Guide to the Hospitality Industry (Greenwood Press, 1990) is still a basic source of information about hospitality publications. Despite the need for an update, it remains a source for further information about journals, databases, and abstracts in the hospitality field. Libraries supporting hospitality education will want to include the titles in this section to reflect both scholarly research and practical application.

Basic Periodicals

Ac: *The Cornell Hotel & Restaurant Administration Quarterly;* Sa: *Nation's Restaurant News, Restaurant Business, Restaurants and Institutions.*

Basic Abstracts and Indexes

Lodging, Restaurant and Tourism Index.

3821. *The Cornell Hotel & Restaurant Administration Quarterly.* [ISSN: 0010-8804] 1960. q. GBP 220 in Europe, Middle East, Africa & Australasia (Individuals, USD 113). Sage Publications, Inc., 2455 Teller Rd, Thousand Oaks, CA 91320; info@sagepub.com; http://www.sagepub.com. Illus., index. Sample. Refereed. Circ: 8000. Vol. ends: Nov/Dec (No. 42). Online: Florida Center for Library Automation; Gale Group; ingenta.com; OCLC Online Computer Library Center, Inc.; ProQuest Information & Learning; ScienceDirect; Swets Blackwell. Reprint: PQC. *Indexed:* ABIn, ABS&EES, ATI, BAS, BPI, FS&TA, LR&TI, LRI, PAIS, RRTA, S&F, WAE&RSA. *Aud.:* Ac, Sa.

Published by The Cornell School of Hotel Administration, *The Cornell Hotel & Restaurant Administration Quarterly* is a highly respected, scholarly publication in the hotel and restaurant industry. The journal describes its intended audience as "executives, mid-level Managers, and Consultants in the lodging, resort and food service industry, as well as Academics and Students in business and hotel and restaurant management schools." It offers lengthy, well-researched articles covering various topics in the hospitality industry. Boasting an impressive editorial board, *The Cornell Hotel & Restaurant Administration Quarterly* offers articles based on research and reviews of case studies. Each issue offers "In Brief," which summarizes the feature articles of that issue and provides a useful way to browse the contents of issues. Considered an extremely important, valuable, and scholarly title, it is highly recommended for libraries that serve hospitality professionals and scholars.

3822. *Hotel and Motel Management: the global news magazine of the hospitality industry.* Incorporates: *Motor Inn Journal.* [ISSN: 0018-6082] 1875. 21x/yr. USD 49.90 US & Possessions; USD 69 in Canada & Mexico; USD 121.50 elsewhere. Ed(s): Jeff Higley. Advanstar Communications Inc., Healthcare Group, 7500 Old Oak Blvd, Cleveland, OH 44130-3369; info@advanstar.com; http://www.advanstar.com. Illus., index, adv. Circ: 60000 Controlled. Vol. ends: Dec. Microform: PQC. Online: The Dialog Corporation; EBSCO Publishing; Florida Center for Library Automation; Gale Group; OCLC Online Computer Library Center, Inc.; ProQuest Information & Learning; H.W. Wilson. *Indexed:* ABIn, ATI, B&I, BPI, LR&TI. *Aud.:* Sa.

With a focus on practical advice, *Hotel and Motel Management* is a biweekly tabloid appealing to hotel professionals. Several articles per issue discuss current events and trends in the hospitality industry. In addition, several departments cover many aspects of hotel management including technology, operations, design and decor, sales and marketing, finance, real estate, human resources, and timeshare. In addition, the "People" department identifies changes of position for prominent people and positions in the hotels. The magazine's web site, at www.hotelmotel.com, includes extras such as a franchise fee calculator and an e-directory, which is "an online source of the best providers of services and goods to the hotel industry." The e-directory allows searching by keyword and could provide valuable information to hotel management. Altogether, an interesting, news-packed publication that is an important read for those in the hotel industry.

3823. *Hotels: the magazine of the worldwide hotel industry.* Formerly (until Oct. 1989): *Hotels and Restaurants International;* Which incorporated (in 1982): *International Hotel Review;* Which was formerly: *Service World International.* [ISSN: 1047-2975] 1966. m. USD 99.90 domestic; USD 136.90 Canada; USD 125.90 Mexico. Ed(s): Jeff Weinstein. Reed Business Information, 2000 Clearwater Dr, Oak Brook, IL 60523; http://www.reedbusiness.com. Illus., index, adv. Sample. Circ: 59300. Vol. ends: Dec. *Indexed:* BPI, FS&TA, LR&TI. *Aud.:* Sa.

Hotels: the Magazine of the Worldwide Hotel Industry is meant for hotel professionals, and many aspects of the industry are covered, including hotel management, operations, sales, marketing, investment, food service, and design. Sample cover stories include a forecast for the international hotel industry, timeshares in international hotel franchises, and hotel development in Asia. Regular features include "Food and Beverage," "Design," "Technology," "Global Update," and "World Construction News." The online version of *Hotels*, found at www.hotelsmag.com, is updated daily and includes an editorial archive and a feature called "Product Showcase." The online site is searchable and offers a great deal of information. Subscribers can now receive either a print or a digital version of *Hotels*. This title is recommended for libraries that support hospitality programs.

3824. *International Journal of Hospitality and Tourism Administration.* Supersedes (in 2000): *Journal of International Hospitality, Leisure and Tourism Management.* [ISSN: 1525-6480] 1997. q. USD 200 domestic print & online eds.; USD 270 Canada print & online eds.; USD 290 elsewhere print & online eds. Ed(s): Clayton W Barrows. Haworth Press, Inc., 10 Alice St, Binghamton, NY 13904-1580; getinfo@haworthpressinc.com; http://www.haworthpressinc.com. Adv. Refereed. Circ: 173 Paid. Microform: PQC. Reprint: HAW. *Indexed:* IBZ, LR&TI, PAIS, PEI, RRTA, S&F, WAE&RSA. *Aud.:* Ac, Sa.

A relatively new publication begun in 1997, the *International Journal of Hospitality and Tourism Administration* is "an applied, internationally oriented hospitality and tourism management journal designed to help practitioners and researchers stay abreast of the latest developments in the field as well as facilitate the exchange of ideas." International in scope and with a distinguished editorial board, this journal typically includes four to six feature articles about various topics in the hospitality and tourism industry. The articles are well-researched and written by scholars in the field. Covering topics such as industry trends, technological advances, consumer behavior, workplace diversity, and security issues, the journal is published by the University of Guelph (Ontario, Canada) School of Hospitality & Tourism Management. This title is a nice addition to the literature of hospitality and tourism. Recommended for libraries that support studies in this area.

3825. *Journal of Hospitality & Tourism Research.* Formed by the merger of (1989-1997): *Hospitality and Tourism Educator;* (1990-1997): *Hospitality Research Journal;* Which was formerly: *Hospitality Education and Research Journal;* (1976-1983): *Journal of Hospitality Education.* [ISSN: 1096-3480] 1997. q. USD 306. Ed(s): Kaye Chon. Sage Publications, Inc., 2455 Teller Rd, Thousand Oaks, CA 91320; info@sagepub.com; http://www.sagepub.com. Illus., adv. Refereed. Circ: 1300. *Indexed:* LR&TI, SUSA. *Bk. rev.:* Various number and length. *Aud.:* Ac, Sa.

This journal "publishes high-quality, refereed articles that advance the knowledge base of the hospitality and tourism field." With an impressive editorial board, the journal is focused on presenting research articles and book and software reviews, conference reviews, and research notes. There are typically five or six major research articles provide interesting, in-depth reading. Recent articles include "Diversity Training Management Initiatives in the Lodging Industry;" "Job Satisfaction of Restaurant Employees: An Empirical Investigation Using the Minnesota Satisfaction Questionnaire;" and "The Competitive Market Efficiency of Hotel Brands: An Application of Data Envelopment Analysis." This journal is international in scope and is geared towards scholars in the fields of hospitality and tourism. It is published by The International Council on Hotel, Restaurant, and Institutional Education (CHRIE), "a unique non-profit international organization dedicated to building professionalism in the hospitality and tourism industry." CHRIE has a membership of more than 2,200 in 53 countries. From the web site, www.sagepub.com, one can view a journal sample online and review tables of contents for recent issues. Similar in scope to *The Cornell Hotel & Restaurant Administration Quarterly* (above in this section), this journal provides important research to professionals in the field.

3826. *Lodging.* Former titles (until 1993): *Lodging Magazine;* (until 1990): *Lodging.* [ISSN: 1078-5795] 1975. 11x/yr. Free to members. Ed(s): Philip Hayward. American Hotel and Lodging Association, 1201 New York Ave, N W, Ste 600, Washington, DC 20005-3931; http://www.ahma.com. Illus., adv. Circ: 28194 Paid. *Indexed:* LR&TI. *Aud.:* Ga, Sa.

The official publication of the American Hotel and Lodging Association, *Lodging* is geared toward staff of lodging establishments, particularly management staff. Covering topics in marketing, future trends, technology, operations, human resources, and food and beverage, law, and finance, among others, *Lodging* offers a great deal of information for hotel professionals. Departments include "Celebrity Check-In," "Where Are They Now?," and "Profile." The online version, found at www.lodgingmagazine.com, includes an archive of past articles as well as daily updates of newsworthy items. This title is an important one for professionals in the lodging industry.

3827. *Lodging Hospitality.* Former titles: *Hospitality Lodging; Hospitality-Food and Lodging; Hospitality-Restaurant and Lodging; American Motel Magazine.* [ISSN: 0148-0766] 1949. m. bi-m. in Mar., May, Jul., Sep. USD 70 domestic; USD 90 Canada; USD 140 elsewhere. Ed(s): Ed Watkins. Penton Media, Inc., 1300 E 9th St, Cleveland, OH 44114-1503; information@penton.com; http://www.penton.com. Illus., index, adv. Sample. Circ: 50976 Controlled. Vol. ends: Dec. Microform: CIS; PQC. Online: bigchalk; The Dialog Corporation; EBSCO Publishing; Florida Center for Library Automation; Gale Group; Northern Light Technology, Inc.; OCLC Online Computer Library Center, Inc.; ProQuest Information & Learning; H.W. Wilson. Reprint: PQC. *Indexed:* ABIn, ATI, B&I, BPI, LR&TI. *Aud.:* Sa.

This polished monthly magazine is geared toward professionals in the lodging field. It offers articles on such topics as timeshares, corporate ethics, hotel investment, and security in hotels. Pieces often discuss improvements in the field and future developments in lodging. Also included are practical tidbits such as "How To Stretch Your Laundry Dollar." Monthly departments include "Lodging Today," "Timeshare," "Technology Today," "Design Side," and "Supply Side." Editor Ed Watkins provides "The Forum," which discusses issues of topical importance in the U.S. lodging industry. The magazine's web version is billed as "the industry's number one on-line resource, exclusively reserved for owners, managers and operators of lodging businesses." Items of particular interest to professionals include the "Buyer's Guide," "Franchise Calculator," and "Free Classifieds." "Article Archive" and "Industry Events" round out the offerings of the web site. This is a very useful title for collections covering the lodging industry, and it offers important information for professionals wanting to keep abreast of changes in the field.

3828. *Nation's Restaurant News: the newspaper of the food service industry.* [ISSN: 0028-0518] 1967. w. 50/yr. USD 39.95; USD 5 newsstand/cover. Lebhar-Friedman, Inc., 425 Park Ave, New York, NY 10022; http://www.nrn.com. Illus., index, adv. Circ: 90000. Vol. ends: Dec. Microform: CIS; PQC. Online: EBSCO Publishing; Factiva; Florida Center for Library Automation; Gale Group; LexisNexis; Northern Light Technology, Inc.; OCLC Online Computer Library Center, Inc.; ProQuest Information & Learning; H.W. Wilson. Reprint: PQC. *Indexed:* ABIn, B&I, BPI, LR&TI, LRI. *Aud.:* Ga, Sa.

This is a weekly newsmagazine with many brief articles covering all aspects of the restaurant business. Heavily illustrated with photos, it is an eye-catching publication geared toward keeping restaurant professionals up to date on industry news. Regular departments include "Finance," "Marketing," "Editorial," "Opinion," "Supplier News," and "Coast to Coast." An online version, www.nrn.com, provides daily news updates. It also offers a recipe index and an archives search mechanism among other features. This magazine and its companion web site will keep foodservice professionals abreast of current industry developments. Highly recommended as an important title for libraries with an interest in the restaurant industry.

3829. *Restaurant Business.* Formerly: *Fast Food.* [ISSN: 0097-8043] 1902. bi-w. USD 119 domestic (Free to qualified personnel). Ed(s): Peter Romeo. V N U Business Publications, 770 Broadway, New York, NY 10003; bmcomm@vnuinc.com; http://www.vnubusinessmedia.com/. Illus., adv. Circ: 130112. Microform: CIS; PQC. Online: bigchalk; EBSCO Publishing; Factiva; Florida Center for Library Automation; Gale Group; Northern Light Technology, Inc.; OCLC Online Computer Library Center, Inc.; ProQuest Information & Learning; H.W. Wilson. Reprint: PQC. *Indexed:* ABIn, BPI, FS&TA, LR&TI, LRI. *Aud.:* Sa.

This colorful biweekly "serves the information needs of owners and operators of commercial foodservice locations including restaurants, hotels, resorts, clubs and catering." Focusing on all aspects of the restaurant industry, this title is an important read for industry professionals. It provides timely and interesting information on such topics as menu planning, food preparation, trends, regulations, labor, taxes, technology, and equipment. Several issues have profiled the industry's most notable women. Recent cover stories discuss controversial issues like employee theft and smoking policies in restaurant establishments. The online version of *Restaurant Business* provides more frequent updates of restaurant news and a list of industry web sites. In addition, it offers a link to Food Industry Research Center, a searchable archive of five industry publications, *Food Service Director, ID Magazine, Progressive Grocer, Restaurant Business*, and *Supermarket Business*. This is an important publication for libraries with patrons who have an interest in the foodservice industry.

3830. *Restaurant Hospitality.* Former titles (until 1976): *Hospitality, Restaurant;* (until 1967): *American Restaurant Hospitality;* (until 1962): *American Restaurant Magazine;* (until 1928): *American Restaurant.* [ISSN: 0147-9989] 1919. m. USD 70 domestic; USD 85 Canada; USD 135 elsewhere. Ed(s): Michael Sanson. Penton Media, Inc., 1300 E 9th St, Cleveland, OH 44114-1503; http://www.penton.com. Illus., adv. Circ: 122991 Controlled. Vol. ends: Dec. Microform: PQC. Online: bigchalk; EBSCO Publishing; Florida Center for Library Automation; Gale Group; Northern Light Technology, Inc.; OCLC Online Computer Library Center, Inc.; ProQuest Information & Learning; H.W. Wilson. Reprint: PQC. *Indexed:* ABIn, ATI, B&I, BPI, FS&TA, LR&TI. *Bk. rev.:* 2, length varies. *Aud.:* Sa.

From menus and recipes to articles about the future of the restaurant industry, *Restaurant Hospitality* is an important source of information for foodservice professionals. There are generally two to five feature articles covering topics such as restaurant interior design, top chain restaurants, restaurant equipment, casual dining, and food safety. Regular departments include "Debut," which profiles new restaurants; "Rising Star," which provides a brief synopsis of an up-and-coming chef's career; "Heroes," which indicates how the restaurant industry gives to communities and charities; and the whimsical "Fridge Raid," which provides a photographic glimpse into a top chef's refrigerator along with a brief interview about its contents. The web site that accompanies this title, *FoodServiceSearch.com*, includes a "Recipe of the Month," a keyword-searchable recipe archive, "Buyer's Guide," "Events Calendar," and sections on equipment and food safety. The online magazine provides free registration to foodservice professionals. Libraries with clientele interested in the food service industry will want to subscribe to this title.

3831. ***Restaurants and Institutions.*** Incorporates (in 1986): *Bar Business;* Former titles: *Institutions; Institutions - Volume Feeding; Institutions - Volume Feeding Management.* [ISSN: 0273-5520] 1937. s-m. USD 149.90 domestic; USD 194.90 Canada; USD 184.90 Mexico. Ed(s): Patricia B Dailey. Reed Business Information, 2000 Clearwater Dr, Oak Brook, IL 60523; http://www.reedbusiness.com. Illus., index, adv. Circ: 167508. Microform: CIS. Online: EBSCO Publishing; Florida Center for Library Automation; Gale Group; OCLC Online Computer Library Center, Inc.; ProQuest Information & Learning; H.W. Wilson. *Indexed:* ABIn, AgeL, BPI, LR&TI, LRI. *Aud.:* Sa.

This publication bills itself as "the leading source for food and beverage trends, exclusive industry research and reports, marketing and operations information among both commercial and noncommercial operators." It provides a great deal of food coverage, typically offering readers six to ten feature articles on such topics as menus, consumers' opinions, and restaurant profitability. Issues focus on the most important aspects of the restaurant industry, food and business. Of particular interest are the occasional reports on consumer research regarding the restaurant industry. An advertiser's index and a recipes index are very welcome aspects of the magazine. The web site provides archives of back issues, a searchable recipe database, and a gallery of industry products. *Restaurants and Institutions* is an extremely valuable title for all foodservice professionals.

■ HUMOR

Michael J. Hemment, Research Librarian and Coordinator of E-Texts in the Humanities, Harvard College Library, Widener Library, Harvard University, Cambridge, MA 02138; hemment@fas.harvard.edu

Introduction

I slapped many knees while researching these magazines—and most weren't mine. There are some truly laugh-worthy publications on the market that deserve consideration by libraries. Some parody politics, pop culture, and well-known figures, while others treat humor as a subject of serious scientific and literary study. Online humor magazines come in several flavors: college satire rags, fake news sites, digital joke archives, electronic comic strips, etc. The funniest thing about many humor sites is that they have the shelf life of brie on a warm summer day. Indeed, several electronic journals have disappeared or have been abandoned by their creators since the last edition of *MFL*, and a few others deemed to have "staying power" have been added. There have not been many significant additions to this genre in print. Nevertheless, you are guaranteed to find something here to tickle your patrons' funny bones.

Basic Periodicals

Hs: *Mad;* Ga: *Mad, The Onion;* Ac: *The Annals of Improbable Research;* Sa: *Journal of Polymorphous Perversity.*

3832. ***The Annals of Improbable Research: the journal of record for inflated research and personalities.*** [ISSN: 1079-5146] 1995. 6x/yr. USD 29 domestic; USD 33 in Canada & Mexico; USD 45 elsewhere. Ed(s): Marc Abrahams. Annals of Improbable Research, PO Box 380853, Cambridge, MA 02238; info@improbable.com; http://www.improbable.com. Illus. Refereed. *Aud.:* Ac, Sa.

With articles like "Courtship Behaviour of Ostriches Towards Humans Under Farming Conditions in Britain," *AIR* satirizes the often obtuse and jargon-filled landscape of modern scholarship and scientific research. Produced by the same gang who from 1955 to 1994 founded and edited the *Journal of Irreproducible Results*, this magazine has two goals: one, to be funny, and two, to raise the question: "How do you figure out what's important and what's not, and what's real and what's not—in science and everywhere else?" *AIR*'s editorial board consists of fifty-odd eminent scientists, doctors, etc., from around the world, including several Nobel Prize winners and a convicted felon. A must-have item for research libraries as well as large public libraries.

3833. ***Comic Relief: the monthly topical humor review.*** [ISSN: 1055-9639] 1989. m. USD 28. Ed(s): Michael Kunz. Page One Publishers and Bookworks, Inc., PO Box 6606, Eureka, CA 95502. Illus., adv. Circ: 13000 Paid. *Aud.:* Hs, Ga.

A superb collection of timely comic strip reprints, political satires, and other humor. *Comic Relief* pokes fun at social, political, and religious institutions, as well as cultural icons. Features include columns by Dave Barry and Ian Shoales and "This Month In Cartoons." Recommended for all libraries whose patrons can take a joke.

The Door Magazine. See Zines section.

3834. ***Funny Times.*** [ISSN: 1045-0491] 1985. m. USD 23 domestic; USD 33 foreign; USD 2.95 newsstand/cover per issue. Ed(s): Raymond Lesser, Susan Wolpert. Susan Wolpert & Raymond Lesser, Eds. & Pubs., PO Box 18530, Cleveland, OH 44118; ft@funnytimes.com; http://www.funnytimes.com. Illus. Sample. Circ: 60000 Paid. *Aud.:* Hs, Ga, Ac.

The *Funny Times* is America's leading liberal monthly humor review. It employs some of America's best cartoonists and writers to bring their humorous perspectives to a variety of topics, including politics, the environment, and pop culture. The comedic goal is to be "poignant" but not "mean-spirited, sexist, or boring." Each issue contains over a hundred cartoons, humor columns, and regular features like "News of the Weird," "Harper's Index," "Dr. Science," and "Jon Winokur's Curmudgeon." Recommended for both public and academic libraries.

3835. ***Humor: international journal of humor research.*** Former titles: *World Humor and Irony Movement Serials Yearbook; World Humor and Irony Membership Serial Yearbook; Western Humor and Irony Membership Serial Yearbook.* [ISSN: 0933-1719] 1988. q. EUR 169.10 domestic; EUR 174.20 foreign; EUR 41 newsstand/cover. Ed(s): Lawrence E. Mintz. Mouton de Gruyter, Genthiner Str 13, Berlin, 10785, Germany; mouton@degruyter.de; http://www.degruyter.de. Illus., index, adv. Refereed. Reprint: PSC; SCH. *Indexed:* AgeL, ArtHuCI, BRI, CBRI, IBSS, IBZ, L&LBA, MLA-IB, PsycholAb, SSCI. *Bk. rev.:* 2-4, 350-400 words. *Aud.:* Ac.

Published in Germany, this journal is intended for a scholarly audience who views humor as an important and universal human faculty. The articles are predominantly high-quality research papers on humor, covering topics such as interdisciplinary humor research, humor theory and methodologies, technology, and more. Not likely to tickle anyone's funny bone, this journal is still useful for scholars serious about investigating the genre. Primarily for an academic audience.

3836. ***Journal of Irreproducible Results.*** [ISSN: 0022-2038] 1955. bi-m. USD 32 (Individuals, USD 19.85; USD 3.50 newsstand/cover per issue domestic). Journal of Irreproducible Results, PO Box 234, Chicago, IL 60411; jir@interaccess.com; http://www.jir.com. Illus., index, adv. Refereed. Circ: 9000. Vol. ends: No. 6. *Indexed:* BiolAb. *Aud.:* Ac, Sa.

Scientists with a taste for humor will embrace this journal that has been making light of heavy research since 1955. Described as a "corrective to academics who take themselves too seriously and to the overly credulous who believe anything that scientists tell them," *JIR* features articles like "How Dead Is a Doornail?," "Furniture Airbags," and "The Medical Effects of Kissing Boo-Boos." Also includes a list of the Ig Nobel Prize winners, annually awarded "for scientific achievements which cannot or should not be reproduced." Recommended for both large public, academic, and science libraries.

3837. ***Journal of Polymorphous Perversity.*** [ISSN: 0737-1195] 1984. s-a. USD 25 (Individuals, USD 14.95). Ed(s): Glenn Ellenbogen. Wry-Bred Press, Inc., PO Box 1454, New York, NY 10159-1454; info@psychhumor.com; http://www.psychhumor.com. Illus., index, adv. Circ: 4125. Vol. ends: Fall. *Aud.:* Ac, Sa.

A humor magazine, now in its 14th year of publication, that spoofs psychology, psychiatry, and medicine. Where else will you find an article on deja vu that appears twice in the same issue? This is a social scientist's version of the *AIR*, containing knee-slapping treats like "Psychotherapy of the Dead," "Oral Sadism and the Vegetarian Personality," and "The Relationship of Country Music to Psychopathology." Highly recommended for academic libraries.

3838. ***Light Quarterly.*** Formerly: *Light (Chicago).* 1992. q. USD 20 domestic; USD 34 foreign; USD 6 newsstand/cover per issue. Ed(s): John Mella. Light Quarterly, PO Box 7500, Chicago, IL 60680-7500; lightquarterly@cs.com; http://www.litline.org/html/lightquarterly.html. Illus., adv. Circ: 1100 Paid. *Indexed:* IAPV. *Aud.:* Ga.

A recent poem by Pat D'Amico in *Light Quarterly* titled "Theoretically Speaking" goes like this: "A fat free meal / Has a lot of appeal / And it needn't be boring or dreary. / The truth is, in practice, I'd rather eat cactus. / However, I'll stand by my theory." It is the only American magazine devoted exclusively to light verse and "unserious" poets, and contributors have included literary greats like John Updike as well as exciting new talent. The journal's stated mission is to discard what is "obscure and dreary" and to restore "lightness, understandability, and pleasure" to the reading of poems. Recommended for academic libraries and large public libraries serving literary-minded patrons.

3839. ***Mad.*** [ISSN: 0024-9319] 1952. m. USD 24 domestic; USD 30 foreign; USD 2.99 newsstand/cover per issue. Ed(s): Nick Meglin, John Ficarra. E.C. Publications, Inc., 1700 Broadway, New York, NY 10019; http://www.modmag.com. Illus. Circ: 500000. *Aud.:* Hs, Ga.

No one is safe! Politics, TV, movies, music, and current affairs are all fair game for America's foremost magazine of biting social parody, political humor, and general kookiness. Now in color and celebrating its 50th year, *MAD* continues to be the wiggling feather under America's armpit, with outrageous movie and television parodies, the slapstick action of Spy vs. Spy, and Al Jaffee's famous Fold-In! Bound to be requested by library patrons of all shapes and sizes.

3840. ***The Old Fart: a magazine for and by curmudgeons.*** [ISSN: 1192-6562] 1993. q. CND 10. Ed(s): John Brinckman. Old Fart, 191 St George St, Toronto, ON M5R 2M6, Canada. Illus., adv. Circ: 3000. *Aud.:* Ga.

The Oxford English Dictionary defines "curmudgeon" as "An avaricious churlish fellow; a miser, a niggard"—if this is you, you'll love *The Old Fart.* Created by former Canadian apple farmer John Brinckman (without a doubt, a world-class "curmudgeon" himself), this journal denounces concepts like progress and innovations like electric toothbrushes, personal organizers, and the Internet. In fact, you won't even find an *Old Fart* web site. Lighthearted fare for your library's older (and smellier) patrons.

3841. ***The Onion.*** w. USD 39.95 domestic; USD 110 Canada; USD 200 elsewhere. Ed(s): Robert Siegel. Onion, Inc., 33 University Sq, Ste 270, Madison, WI 53715; infomat@theonion.com; http://www.theonion.com. *Aud.:* Ga.

No cryin' from this onion, unless we're taking about giggle tears! Starting out as an alternative weekly newspaper for University of Wisconsin students, *The Onion* has become the web's premier source of political and cultural humor. Stories like "Casual One-Nighter Gives Strom Thurmond Change of Heart on Gay Issue" and "Secondhand Smoke Linked to Secondhand Coolness" cater to a young, hip crowd. *The Onion*'s site serves as a welcome antidote to CNN-style news web sites, with political incorrectness and parodies of breaking news items at every turn. The humor is often crude and biting, but consistently funny. Headlines have included: "Mother Teresa Sent to Hell in Wacky Afterlife Mix-Up," "Fisherman's Four-Year-Old Son Liberates Bait," and "Are All Women Nutso, Or Just The Ones I Cheat On My Wife With?" Intended for a college and adult audience at public and academic libraries.

3842. ***Studies in American Humor.*** Incorporates (1974-1984): *American Humor.* [ISSN: 0095-280X] 1974. a. Membership, USD 20. Ed(s): Michael Kiskis. American Humor Studies Association (New Haven), c/o Joseph Alvarez, Sec, Box 35009, Charlotte, NC 28235-5009; joe_alvarez@cpcc.cc.nc.us. Illus., index, adv. Refereed. Circ: 500. *Indexed:* AmH&L, HumInd, MLA-IB. *Bk. rev.:* 2-4, 400-600 words. *Aud.:* Ac.

Founded in 1974, *Studies in American Humor* publishes scholarly essays and book reviews on all aspects of American humor, including belles lettres, popular comic papers, and various sub-literary media. Topics have included everything from "Woody Allen and the Comic Tradition in America" to "Benjamin Franklin as Founding Father of American Humor." Recommended for academic libraries and large public libraries with literary-minded patrons.

3843. ***Thalia: a journal of studies in literary humor.*** [ISSN: 0706-5604] 1978. s-a. CND 27 (Individuals, CND 25). Ed(s): Janice McIntire-Strasburg. Association for the Study of Humor, c/o Janice McIntire-Strasburg, Man. Ed., St Louis University, Department of English, St Louis, MO 63108; mcintire@slu.edu; http://www.slu.edu/colleges/AS/ENG/thalia/thalia.html. Illus., index. Refereed. Circ: 500. Vol. ends: Fall/Winter. Reprint: ISI. *Indexed:* ArtHuCI, IBZ, MLA-IB. *Bk. rev.:* 5-7, 300 words. *Aud.:* Ac.

Covering everything from phony interviews with major literary figures to fictitious works and serious scholarship, *Thalia* is a journal dedicated to the study of literary humor. Traditional scholarly articles, like "Nonsense, Satire, and Language Art: George V. Hobart's German-American Dialect Writing," examine the numerous ways literary humor has evolved over time. Often, the articles presented in each journal share common themes such as literary satire or a study of dark comedy. *Thalia* invites contributions of scholarly articles as well as creative works of humorous fiction, poetry, or art work. Published twice a year or once in a double issue. Primarily for academic libraries.

Electronic Journals

3844. ***Fade to Black Comedy Magazine.*** w. Ed(s): Michael Page. Fade to Black, PO Box 826, Ramsey, NJ 07446; f2b@fadetoblack.com; http://www.fadetoblack.com. *Aud.:* Hs, Ga, Ac.

The goal of this online comedy magazine, started by Michael Page, is to utilize the unique medium of the Internet to bring thoughts, ideas, and comedy that cannot be delivered through traditional stand-up, television, or print. The publication's dark tone is captured by the following: "The Fade to Black staff would like to thank the following people, things, and intangible objects, that have really helped us along the way: Our parents, for being emotionally absent for most of our childhood thus instilling in us a cynical outlook and dark sense of perception and humor, along with the other flaws yet to be discovered. Most comedy shows and sitcoms on television for showing us what NOT TO DO to be funny. All people whose ignorance we can mock and laugh at, thus alleviating our own low self-esteem and feelings of self loathing." Includes daily comic strips, stories, online discussions, and funny lists galore. Librarians should be aware that this site contains some "adult" humor.

3845. ***Gracies Dinnertime Theatre.*** 1995. w. Gracies Dinnertime Theatre, 472 French Rd, Rochester, NY 14623; http://www.csh.rit.edu/~diablo/gdt. *Aud.:* Ga, Ac.

Serving up a rich menu of snickers and smiles, *Gracies Dinnertime Theatre* features sophisticated humor for the literate reader. Created by students at the Rochester Institute of Technology, most of the articles are inspired by the humor in daily life, however, they admittedly "make excursions into serious issues or purely creative arenas from time to time." Each issue features regular columns, cartoons, and miscellaneous articles. Mostly intended for a college audience.

3846. ***The Specious Report: America's oldest news magazine, spreading rumours, half truths and misinformation since 1789.*** irreg. Free. Specious World News Organization, . *Aud.:* Hs, Ga, Ac.

An *Onion*-like pseudo-news site "spreading rumors, half-truths and misinformation since 1789." Highlights include a hilarious classifieds section, in-brief and in-depth reports, a Newsjunkie Daily Roundup, and a Reader's Choice of the most frequently e-mailed articles. Many library patrons will find this worth a click.

3847. ***The Toque: Canada's source for humour and satire.*** w. Free. The Toque Entertainment, . *Aud.:* Hs, Ga, Ac, Sa.

The self-proclaimed world leader in Canadian satire, *The Toque* is published every Tuesday and features original stories written by its own staff. They offer unique and humorous perspectives on current events and American culture. Although it satirizes any subject matter, it is typically less biting and dark than other online news parodies like *The Onion*. Recommended for public and academic libraries everywhere.

3848. *Toxic Custard Workshop Files.* 1990. w. Ed(s): Daniel Bowen. Toxic Custard Workshop Files, tcwf@gnu.ai.mit.edu; http://www.toxiccustard.com. *Aud.:* Ga, Ac.

Pathetic. Irresponsible. Shameful. Worthless. It's Australia's premier online humor magazine! With features like "A Toxic History of the World" and "Great Vomits of the 20th Century," these Aussies are fit to be tied. Witty, clever, and often tasteless, this one's a keeper—perfect for American library patrons interested in comparative humor.

■ HUNTING AND GUNS

Clifton W. Boyer, Assistant Librarian, University of South Carolina Spartanburg, 800 University Way, Spartanburg, SC 29303; 864-503-5620; cboyer@gw.uscs.edu

Karen L. Swetland, Assistant Librarian, University of South Carolina Spartanburg, 800 University Way, Spartanburg, SC 29303; 864-503-5620; kswetland@gw.uscs.edu

Introduction

The Hunting and Guns section of *Magazines for Libraries* represents a broad range of magazines, journals, and newsprints devoted to the closely linked world of hunting and shooting. These publications will address one or all of the following: the instruments and equipment used for the sport, methods or techniques, and the target or intended quarry. Due to the diversity of this group, librarians building a collection in hunting or guns should consider the sporting endeavors of patrons based on either interest or geographic locality. While some of the publications that follow take a comprehensive look at either hunting or guns, most are specialized and devoted to one unique aspect of the sport. For example, in hunting, some magazines are centered on the tool used such as a bow, knife, trap, or choice of firearm. They can be further delineated by the intended game such as deer, turkey, and waterfowl. Due to specificity of some publications, many are not included in standard library periodical indexes. Collectively, the titles found in this chapter have more to offer than just procedural articles. There is a wealth of information related to conservation, history, hunter and shooter education, equipment safety, animal biology and behavior, news and legislation, wildlife art and literature, and even the occasional game dish recipe. The hunting and shooting community is also striving to expand its population base by making it more diverse. There are a growing number of titles for specific demographic groups such as women and the disabled. Other magazines include regular features that discuss the needs and issues specific to women, the disabled, and adolescent sportsmen. Almost all of the titles in this section have corresponding web sites that provide selective articles and information. Libraries should be aware that some publications are venturing into television and radio markets, which will likely increase patron awareness of these magazines.

Basic Periodicals

Ems: *American Hunter, Field & Stream, Outdoor Life;* Hs, Ga, Ac: *American Hunter, American Rifleman, Blade, Bow and Arrow Hunting, Bowhunting World, Field & Stream, Fur-Fish-Game, Guns & Ammo, Muzzle Blasts, Outdoor Life, Petersen's Hunting, Shotgun Sports.*

Basic Abstracts and Indexes

Access, Magazine Index, Readers' Guide to Periodical Literature.

3849. *American Hunter.* [ISSN: 0092-1068] 1973. m. Membership, USD 35; USD 2 newsstand/cover per issue domestic. Ed(s): John Zent. N R A Publications, 11250 Waples Mill Rd, Fairfax, VA 22030-9400; membership@nrahq.org; http://www.nrahq.org/. Illus., adv. Sample. Circ: 1000000 Paid. Vol. ends: Dec. *Indexed:* ConsI. *Bk. rev.:* 1-4, 500 words. *Aud.:* Hs, Ga, Ac.

This NRA publication holds the reader's attention by offering a wide variety of columns and solid hunting discussions. Besides the familiar NRA columns such as "Armed Citizens," "Standing Guard," and "President's Column," the reader can explore columns about hunting equipment within the "Hardware" and "Gear & Gadgets" columns. Wildlife management and the Second Amendment are representative topics of discussion. Feature articles are written by skilled writers and cover a wide variety of hunting topics. Some feature articles include studies, graphs, and proven techniques. In addition, there are letters to the editor, Q&A interviews with experts, personal hunting narratives, and a member online survey (http://www.nrahq.org/ahsurvey) each month with results. Advertisements for additional hunting equipment and events are found throughout the publication. Every nook and cranny of the periodical is full of information useful to those hunting pheasants, turkey, deer, bear, and other game. In 2003, this periodical launched an accompanying television program, *The American Hunter*, on The Outdoor Channel.

3850. *American Rifleman.* [ISSN: 0003-083X] 1885. m. USD 35 domestic; USD 45 foreign. Ed(s): Mark A Keefe, IV. N R A Publications, 11250 Waples Mill Rd, Fairfax, VA 22030-9400; membership@nrahq.org; http://www.nrahq.org/. Illus., adv. Sample. Circ: 1600000. Vol. ends: Dec. Microform: PQC. Online: bigchalk; Gale Group; Northern Light Technology, Inc.; OCLC Online Computer Library Center, Inc.; ProQuest Information & Learning. *Indexed:* ConsI, MagInd, SportS. *Bk. rev.:* 3-7, 150-250 words. *Aud.:* Hs, Ga, Ac.

This National Rifle Association publication is perfect for gun enthusiasts. The periodical is divided into feature articles, special reports, "Dope Bag," 12 departments, and "Inside NRA." Each issue offers approximately six feature articles covering history, current topics, and upcoming developments within the shooting world. For history buffs, there are feature articles detailing the role of rifles in U.S. history. Special reports display many of the familiar NRA columns such as "Standing Guard" and "The President's Column." The "Dope Bag: Data & Comment" section gives gun owners detailed reviews of current manufactured products. The departments cover Q&A, letters by the editor, book reviews, and much more. Recently, women and guns was added as a permanent fixture. NRA members will find special membership benefits, gun championships, and national NRA news. *American Rifleman* is fundamental to any hunting magazine collection.

3851. *American Trapper.* [ISSN: 1050-4036] 1955. bi-m. USD 25. Ed(s): Tom Krause. National Trappers Association, 3200 Lewis Rd, PO Box 513, Riverton, WY 82501-0513; TKrause@wyoming.com. Illus., adv. Sample. Circ: 20000 Paid. Vol. ends: Dec. *Aud.:* Sa.

American Trapper is the official publication of the National Trapper's Association. Each issue includes organizational reports from the President, Vice President, General Organizer, Director of National & International Affairs, and the Editor. Other news includes letters to the editor, "In Passing," and "Classified Ads." The periodical presents a straightforward layout and a simple mission to educate and share information among trappers. Information on conventions and specialized trapper merchandise is found throughout the pages. The biggest strength of the periodical is the down to earth "Exclusive Stories" from member trappers. These personal narratives include photos and adventures in trapping rats, bears, raccoons, bobcats, beavers, foxes, and other animal life. *American Trapper* is a good network of resources for trappers throughout the U.S.

3852. *Blade.* Formerly: *Blade Magazine;* Which incorporated: *Edges;* Formerly (until 1982): *American Blade.* [ISSN: 1064-5853] 1973. m. USD 25.98 domestic; USD 52.98 foreign; USD 4.99 newsstand/cover per issue. Ed(s): Steve Shackleford. Krause Publications, Inc., 700 E State St, Iola, WI 54990-0001; info@krause.com; http://www.krause.com. Illus., adv. Circ: 39169 Paid and free. *Indexed:* CBCARef. *Aud.:* Hs, Ga, Ac.

Blade offers the bladesmith community a wealth of information. This periodical presents a global perspective about the importance and history of blades. Feature articles may be presented in a single-issue format or in a series format. The latter allows a given topic room for more content and depth. Calendars detail conventions, knife shows, and even bladesmith classes and training. The "Blades In The Movies" section discusses the accuracy of blade usage in films. The advertiser's index is a bonus to the substantial knifemaking supply advertisements. This magazine is for the true enthusiast interested in the artistry of hunting knives, military knives, swords, axes, pocket knives, or other blades.

3853. *Bow and Arrow Hunting: the world's leading archery magazine.* Formerly (until 1985): *Bow and Arrow.* [ISSN: 0894-7856] 1963. 9x/yr. USD 20.97 domestic; USD 29.97 Canada; USD 39.97 elsewhere. Ed(s): Joe Bell. Y-Visionary Publishing, 265 S Anita Dr, Ste 120, Orange, CA 92868. Illus., adv. Circ: 98000. *Indexed:* SportS. *Bk. rev.:* 1-3, 200-500 words. *Aud.:* Hs, Sa.

With nine issues per year, this subscription offers a little bit of everything. Each issue hosts nearly 20 features/columns written by men and women. Topics include shooting techniques, equipment and supplies, weather survival, safety measures, terrain strategies, and other helpful tips. Full-color illustrations show the hunting of deer, bear, moose, boar, pig, deer, turkey, elk, and other animals. The "Bow Report" reviews equipment in the field. For those that choose to hunt using a bow and arrow, this magazine is a perfect match.

3854. *Bowhunting World: the archery equipment authority.* Formerly (until 1989): *Archery World.* [ISSN: 1043-5492] 1952. 9x/yr. USD 20 domestic; USD 29 foreign. Ed(s): Mike Strandlund. Ehlert Publishing Group, Inc., 601 Lakeshore Parkway, Ste 600, Minnetonka, MN 55305-5215. Illus., index, adv. Sample. Circ: 88167. Vol. ends: Dec. Reprint: PQC. *Indexed:* ConsI, MagInd, PEI, SportS. *Aud.:* Sa.

Bowhunting World supports the development of archery and its equipment. Articles include interviews with experts, "Tech Talk," "Cutting Edge," and studies about equipment complete with graphs and charts. Calendars give tournament schedules, championship competitions, training opportunities, and other events. For bowhunters wanting to perfect their equipment care and knowledge, this magazine is a pillar.

3855. *Bugle (Missoula): journal of elk and the hunt.* [ISSN: 0889-6445] 1984. bi-m. USD 30 domestic; USD 35 foreign. Ed(s): Dan Crockett. Joy Publications, LLC, 2291 W Broadway, PO Box 8249, Missoula, MT 59807-8249; http://www.elkfoundation.org. Illus., adv. Sample. Circ: 195000 Paid. Vol. ends: Dec. *Aud.:* Ga, Ac.

Bugle is one of the highest-quality hunting magazines to be found in any collection. The Rocky Mountain Elk Foundation, an "international, non-profit wildlife habitat conservation organization," produces this magazine. The hunt of choice for the organization is elk. The lengthy articles are written by ecologists, rangers, and other qualified experts. The photographs are simply breathtaking. Reports include conservation and wildlife management efforts within schoolrooms, land developments, the oil and gas industry, water reserves, and other fronts. An accompanying television program, *Elk Country Journal,* is on the Outdoor Life Network.

3856. *The Chase: a full cry of hunting.* [ISSN: 0009-1952] 1920. 11x/yr. USD 24 domestic; USD 26 Canada; USD 28 elsewhere. Ed(s): JoAnn Stone. Chase Publishing Co., Inc., 1150 Industry Rd, PO Box 55090, Lexington, KY 40555; chasepubl@aol.com. Illus., adv. Sample. Circ: 3450 Paid. Vol. ends: Jun. *Aud.:* Sa.

Since 1920, *The Chase* has supported networking among foxhunters. The oversize issues offer events and past results of field trials and bench shows. Photos and full descriptions of hounds for sale are included. Articles are written and submitted by readers at large. Issues provide over 100 pages of meticulously rendered details that are perfect for foxhunters.

3857. *Deer & Deer Hunting: practical & comprehensive information for white-tailed deer hunters.* [ISSN: 0164-7318] 1977. 9x/yr. USD 19.95; USD 3.95 newsstand/cover per issue. Ed(s): Daniel E Schmidt. Krause Publications, Inc., 700 E State St, Iola, WI 54990-0001; info@krause.com; http://www.krause.com. Illus., adv. Sample. Circ: 212500 Paid. Vol. ends: Aug. *Bk. rev.:* Occasional, up to 2,000 words. *Aud.:* Hs, Sa.

White-tail-deer hunters cannot go wrong with this periodical. The issues are tailored to their specific needs and concerns and cover pressing topics such as hunting guidelines, ethics, art and wildlife images, and animal education. Deer biologists present information along with editors, columnists, and guest writers. Some articles span multiple issues. Libraries should expect eight topical issues and one *Fall Equipment Guide* each year.

Disabled Outdoors Magazine. See Hiking, Climbing, and Outdoor Recreation section.

3858. *Field & Stream. Northeast Edition.* Supersedes in part (in 1984): *Field and Stream;* Incorporates: *Living Outdoors.* [ISSN: 8755-8580] 1895. m. USD 11.97 domestic; USD 19.97 Canada; USD 3.99 newsstand/cover per issue. Ed(s): Sid Evans. Time4 Media, Inc., 2 Park Ave, New York, NY 10016; info@fieldandstream.com; http://www.fieldandstream.com. Illus., adv. Circ: 1790251 Paid. Microform: NBI; PQC. Online: EBSCO Publishing; Gale Group. Reprint: PQC. *Indexed:* ConsI, MagInd, RGPR. *Bk. rev.:* 4-6, 200-300 words. *Aud.:* Ems, Hs, Ga.

Field & Stream is outstanding. For over 100 years, readers have benefited from quality hunting and fishing articles. Each issue is a feast of nearly 10 feature articles and 20 columns, offering something for everyone. Topics include product reviews, book reviews, animal life and habits, environmental concerns, and overall hunting themes. Some articles appear in a series. Whether hunters are looking for their game in air, land, or water, this is a fundamental serial. The Outdoor Life Network offers an accompanying *Field & Stream* television program. For radio listeners, The Outdoor Channel offers *Field & Stream Radio.*

Fishing and Hunting News. See Fishing section.

3859. *Full Cry: published exclusively for the American coon hound and trail hound enthusiast.* [ISSN: 0016-2620] 1939. m. USD 23 domestic; USD 31 foreign. Ed(s): Seth R Gault. C & H Publishing, PO Box 777, Sesser, IL 62884. Illus., adv. Sample. Circ: 19721 Paid. Vol. ends: Jan. *Aud.:* Sa.

The ultimate publication for coonhound and tree dog hunters is *Full Cry.* Serving the hunting population since 1939, this serial offers articles, news, calendar updates, and product advertisements. The nearly 20 articles per issue run the gamut from personal stories and breeding news to legislative updates and animal rights discussions. The strength of the publication is the 70+ news entries from national, regional, state, and local associations. These entries and monologues are true testimonies and lessons shared among tree dog hunters. The internal indexes to product advertisements and tree dog "Coming Events" are a librarian's dream. The latter lists city, date, periodical page, and type of event. This publication is a real jewel for its audience.

3860. *Fur - Fish - Game. Harding's Magazine.* [ISSN: 0016-2922] 1925. m. USD 16.95 domestic; USD 23.95 foreign. Ed(s): Mitch Cox. A.R. Harding Publishing Co., 2878 E Main St, Columbus, OH 43209; ffgservice@ameritech.net. Illus., adv. Sample. Circ: 112000 Paid. Vol. ends: Dec. *Aud.:* Hs, Ga, Ac.

The focus of this periodical is an honest hands-on approach to hunting. Issues include 11 regular columns, seven feature articles by guest writers, and five or more additional articles. Within the columns are calendars of upcoming events, Q&A for hunting questions, and new product reviews. In theme with fur-fish-game, specialty columns include "Fish & Tackle," "The Gun Rack," and "The Trapline." Readers interested in fur trading will be delighted with the column "Fur Market Report." Feature articles discuss pike, trout, sled dogs, turkeys, boar, beaver, bobcats, coyotes, and other wildlife. This serial is perfect for all types of hunting.

3861. ***Gray's Sporting Journal.*** [ISSN: 0273-6691] 1975. 7x/yr. USD 36.95 domestic; USD 46.95 Canada; USD 56.95 elsewhere. Ed(s): David C Foster. Morris Communications Company LLC, 735 Broad St, Augusta, GA 30901; http://www.morris.com. Illus., adv. Sample. Circ: 35000. Vol. ends: Jan. *Bk. rev.:* 1-3; 500+ words. *Aud.:* Ac, Sa.

This affluent periodical is a perfect fit for those hunters intrigued by artistic works and high-quality articles. The photographs show Mother Nature at her best. Subject matter includes recipes, history, tradition, poems, and other hunting entries. The dedicated book section with multiple book reviews is a collection development dream. The calendar of outfitters and lodges is listed alphabetically by state or international territory, making it a wonderful tool for those wanting to experience hunting on guided tours. Advertisements include paintings, sculptures, and fine art pieces all with an outdoor theme. There is an accompanying television program, *Gray's Sporting Journal Television,* seen on the Outdoor Life Network.

3862. ***Gun Dog: upland bird and waterfowl dogs.*** [ISSN: 0279-5086] 1981. bi-m. USD 29.97 domestic; USD 42.97 Canada; USD 44.97 elsewhere. Ed(s): Rick Van Etten. Stover Publishing Co., Inc., PO Box 2086, Marion, OH 43306-8186. Illus., adv. Sample. Circ: 52971. Vol. ends: Dec/Jan. *Aud.:* Hs, Sa.

Gun Dog proclaims itself as "North America's only magazine devoted totally and exclusively to the world of upland bird and waterfowl hunters and their dogs." Feature articles discuss the history of hunting and breeds, health of dogs, habits and education of animals, and the handling and training of dogs. Nearly ten columns follow similar themes. Four notable columns are "News & Views," "Bird Hunter's Diary," "Veterinary Clinic," and "Training Q&A." With a clear message, this serial offers a solid approach for any upland bird and waterfowl hunter.

3863. ***Gun-Knife Show Calendar.*** Formerly: *Gun Show Calendar.* [ISSN: 1522-9572] 1979. q. USD 14.95 domestic; USD 25.95 in Canada & Mexico; USD 44.95 elsewhere. Krause Publications, Inc., 700 E State St, Iola, WI 54990-0001; info@krause.com; http://www.krause.com. Illus., adv. Sample. Circ: 6802 Paid and free. Vol. ends: Dec. *Aud.:* Sa.

The newsprint pages are a combination of submitted show entries and paid advertisements. Show entries can be submitted free of charge to the publisher. Arranged chronologically, show entries list hours, admission fee, city, state, number of dealers, admission age, and additional contact information. Added notes about reading entry information and listings make this publication easy to use. Knife shows are listed on the "Blade Show Calendar." Paid advertisements include detailed show promotions, consignment contacts, buying-selling-trading establishments, auctioneers, and so much more. The 90 pages are an itinerary dream for collectors wanting to experience U.S. gun and knife shows.

3864. ***Gun List: the indexed firearms paper.*** [ISSN: 0894-8119] 1984. bi-w. USD 36.98; USD 20.98 for 6 mos.; USD 5.50 newsstand/cover per issue. Krause Publications, Inc., 700 E State St, Iola, WI 54990-0001; info@krause.com; http://www.krause.com. Illus., index, adv. Sample. Circ: 72553 Paid and free. Vol. ends: Dec. *Aud.:* Sa.

This oversize newsprint publication hosts thousands of guns to buy-sell-trade. This serial is an excellent tool for Americans transferring gun ownership. While there are listings for knives, accessories, and gun show advertisements, the primary focus is the classified gun ads. The index on the front cover is a librarian's compass. Perfect for libraries that serve a large gun-owner population.

3865. ***Gun World: for the firearms & hunting enthusiast.*** [ISSN: 0017-5641] 1960. m. USD 21.95 domestic; USD 33.95 Canada; USD 45.95 elsewhere. Ed(s): Jan Libourel. Y-Visionary Publishing, 265 S Anita Dr, Ste 120, Orange, CA 92868. Illus., adv. Circ: 130000. Vol. ends: Dec. Reprint: PQC. *Bk. rev.:* 1, 200-300 words. *Aud.:* Ga.

This magazine dazzles gun owners with informative articles, product reviews, and firearm discussions. Topics range from handguns, rifles, shotguns, barrels, holsters, and ammunition to gun performances, designs, and hunting success. Each month the magazine provides 80 pages of gun insights. Perfect for any library that serves a strong gun-owner population.

3866. ***Guns & Ammo.*** Incorporates (1995-1996): *Performance Shooter.* [ISSN: 0017-5684] 1958. m. USD 17.94; USD 30.94 Canada; USD 32.94 elsewhere. Ed(s): Lee Hoots. Primedia Consumer Media & Magazine Group, 200 Madison Ave, New York, NY 10016; http://www.primedia.com. Illus., index, adv. Circ: 590238 Paid. Vol. ends: Dec. Microform: PQC. Online: The Dialog Corporation; Gale Group. Reprint: PQC. *Indexed:* ConsI, MagInd. *Aud.:* Hs, Ga, Ac.

Guns & Ammo covers a broad range of issues related to firearms for anyone with an interest in guns or the outdoors whether they are a novice or an expert. Articles include product reviews and coverage of firearms safety, hunting, shooting, reloading, collecting, technical information, and legislative news related to gun ownership. This is a great title for any library that needs a general magazine on guns.

3867. ***Hunter Education Journal.*** Former titles (until 1998): *Hunter Education Instructor;* (until 1989): *Hunter Safety Instructor;* (until 1983): *Hunter Safety News.* [ISSN: 1521-5970] 1973. 3x/yr. Free to members. Focus Group, Inc., 1800 Westlake Ave N, Ste 206, Seattle, WA 98109. Illus., adv. Circ: 65000 Controlled. *Aud.:* Ems, Hs, Ga.

Published by the International Hunter Education Association, *Hunter Education Journal* strives to increase safe responsible hunting through developing quality hunter education. Most of the articles focus on hunter safety issues related to firearms, equipment and accessories, and hunting techniques. In addition, there are well-written articles on teaching hunter and firearms safety, opinion pieces, and game recipes. This title should be considered for any library that maintains a large hunting collection.

3868. ***Muzzle Blasts.*** [ISSN: 0027-5360] 1939. m. Membership, USD 35. Ed(s): Terri Trowbridge. National Muzzle Loading Rifle Association, PO Box 67, Friendship, IN 47021; nmlra@nmlra.org. Illus., adv. Sample. Circ: 25000 Controlled. Vol. ends: Aug. *Bk. rev.:* 1, 1,000 words. *Aud.:* Hs, Sa.

Muzzle Blasts, the official publication of the National Muzzle Loading Rifle Association, publishes association news and articles related to muzzle-loading firearms, accoutrements, and historical data from the eras of black powder firearms. This highly informative publication covers the history of specific weapons, people, and accessories associated with using muzzle loaders. In addition, there are updates about impacting legislation and "how-to" articles on making authentic period reproductions of items such as powder horns, patch knives, and gunstocks.

3869. ***Muzzleloader: publication for black powder shooters and American History.*** [ISSN: 0274-5720] 1974. bi-m. USD 20 domestic; USD 25.50 foreign. Ed(s): Bill Scurlock. Scurlock Publishing Co., Inc., R R 5, Box 347M, Texarkana, TX 75503-9403; jason@scurlockpublishing.com; http://www.muzzleloadermag.com. Illus., index, adv. Sample. Circ: 15000 Paid. Vol. ends: Feb. *Bk. rev.:* 2-4, 500-1,500 words. *Aud.:* Hs, Sa.

Muzzleloader is more than a black powder shooting magazine. This publication will be enjoyed by anyone with an interest in eighteenth- and early nineteenth-century American history. *Muzzleloader* has well-written and documented articles that explore multiple aspects of life in early America, especially along the frontiers. In addition to great history articles, there are features on hunting, shooting, product and book reviews, and do-it-yourself projects, along with tips and advice for anyone who shoots muzzleloading firearms. While *Muzzleloader* is written primarily for black powder enthusiast and American history reenactors, this title could benefit almost any library's history collection.

3870. ***North American Whitetail: the magazine devoted to the serious trophy deer hunter.*** [ISSN: 0746-6250] 1982. 8x/yr. USD 14.97; USD 2.99 newsstand/cover per issue domestic; USD 3.99 newsstand/cover per issue Canada. Primedia Enthusiast Group, 2 News Plaza, PO Box 1790, Peoria, IL 61656. Illus., adv. Sample. Circ: 157130. Vol. ends: Feb. *Aud.:* Hs, Sa.

At the conception of *North American Whitetail* in 1982, three of the basic goals of the publication were to profile the greatest bucks harvested across the continent, the places where these deer were being taken, and the sportsmen who claimed them. This magazine continues to deliver on these goals and surpasses them by publishing articles designed to help deer hunters take trophy bucks.

Both bow and gun hunters will benefit from the informative features related to techniques, methods, and deer conservation. In view of the popularity of whitetail deer hunting, this magazine could be considered by any library that maintains a collection for hunters.

Outdoor Life. See Hiking, Climbing, and Outdoor Recreation section.

3871. *Petersen's Hunting.* [ISSN: 0146-4671] 1973. 10x/yr. USD 14.97 domestic. Ed(s): Scott Rupp. Primedia Consumer Media & Magazine Group, 200 Madison Ave, New York, NY 10016; http://www.primedia.com. Illus., adv. Circ: 380798 Paid. Microform: PQC. Online: Gale Group. *Bk. rev.:* Occasional. *Aud.:* Hs, Ga, Ac.

Petersen's Hunting is a comprehensive hunting magazine intended to cover the many aspects of the sport. This publication is expertly written and provides informative articles on hunting techniques, methods, product reviews, and evaluations along with news that impacts hunting and sportsmen. Most of the articles are accompanied by illustrations, photographs, or charts. *Petersen's Hunting* includes articles on hunting large game, turkey, waterfowl, and small game, and covers hunting expeditions from around the world. An excellent title to consider if only one hunting magazine is needed.

3872. *Pheasants Forever: journal of upland game conservation.* [ISSN: 1079-7041] 1982. 5x/yr. USD 25. Ed(s): Mark Herwig. Pheasants Forever Inc., 1783 Buerkle Circle, St. Paul, MN 55110-5254. Illus., adv. Circ: 100000. *Aud.:* Ac, Sa.

Pheasants Forever is more than a hunting magazine. Published by the organization Pheasants Forever, Inc., this magazine delivers articles related to the many aspects of upland game bird habitat conservation including restoration, development and maintenance, land and water management policies, and public awareness and education. There are also articles directly related to the sport, including on shooting, gun dogs, equipment, and the habits and biology of pheasants. This high-quality journal is beautifully illustrated with color photographs and graphics. *Pheasants Forever* should be in any library that serves upland game bird hunters.

3873. *Precision Shooting: dealing exclusively with extreme rifle accuracy.* [ISSN: 0048-5144] 1956. m. USD 37; USD 3.95 newsstand/cover per issue. Ed(s): David D Brennan. Precision Shooting, Inc., 222 McKee St, Manchester, CT 06040. Illus., adv. Sample. Circ: 20000 Paid. *Indexed:* SportS. *Aud.:* Ac, Sa.

Precision Shooting is a magazine for the shooting enthusiast devoted to improving his or her accuracy. This is a highly authoratative and technical publication that covers many different shooting sports. Articles address technique, equipment and accessories, ammunition, and coverage of shooting competitions. This magazine is an excellent choice for libraries with collections on firearms and shooting.

3874. *Rifle: the sporting firearms journal.* Formerly: *Rifle Magazine.* [ISSN: 0162-3583] 1968. bi-m. USD 22; USD 28 foreign. Ed(s): Dave Scovill. Wolfe Publishing Co., 2625 Stearman Rd., Ste. A, Prescott, AZ 86301-6155. Illus., adv. Sample. Circ: 100000. Vol. ends: Dec. *Bk. rev.:* 3-5, 250-500 words. *Aud.:* Hs, Sa.

One of the strengths of *Rifle* is the in-depth articles written by knowledgable and experienced shooters. Topics of articles range from extensive reviews of the latest firearms and accessories, gunsmithing, ammunition, optics, book reviews, and profiles of historic firearms. This magazine will appeal to a diverse group of shooters regardless of whether they are primarily interested in hunting or target shooting. *Rifle* should be considered by any library that has a hunting or guns collection.

3875. *Rifle's Handloader: ammunition reloading journal.* Formerly: *Handloader.* 1966. bi-m. USD 19.97 domestic; USD 26 foreign. Ed(s): Dave Scovill. Wolfe Publishing Co., 2625 Stearman Rd., Ste. A, Prescott, AZ 86301-6155. Illus., index, adv. Sample. Circ: 100000. Vol. ends: Jan. *Aud.:* Ac, Sa.

Rifle's Handloader is a unique journal that publishes articles related to the reloading of centerfire and shotgun ammunition, including the casting of bullets. There are well-written and illustrated technical articles about specific cartridges, special loads, and other components for rifles, handguns, and shotguns. *Rifle's Handloader* is an excellent publication and should be included in any library that has a focused collection on firearms or hunting.

3876. *S H O T Business: shooting, hunting & outdoor trade.* [ISSN: 1081-8618] 1993. m. USD 25. Ed(s): Slaton White. Time4 Media, Inc., 1185 Ave of the Americas, 27th Fl, New York, NY 10035. Illus., adv. Circ: 20500 Controlled. Vol. ends: Dec. *Bk. rev.:* 6-8, 500-1,000 words. *Aud.:* Ac, Sa.

S H O T Business is the official publication of the National Shooting Sports Foundation and focuses on individuals and businesses involved in the shooting industry. This is an excellent publication in regard to content and layout. The articles address topics that help large and small businesses flourish in the market by providing practical ideas and solutions related to inventory control, retail, human resources, customer relations management, and marketing and promotions. In addition, this magazine highlights legislation and industry news that will have an impact on business.

3877. *Shotgun Sports: America's leading shotgun magazine.* [ISSN: 0744-3773] 1976. m. USD 31 domestic; USD 38 foreign. Ed(s): Frank Kodl. Shotgun Sports, PO Box 6810, Auburn, CA 95604. Illus., adv. Sample. Circ: 108000. Vol. ends: Dec. *Aud.:* Hs, Sa.

Shotgun Sports could easily be considered the magazine of choice for shotgun enthusiast. This publication covers a wide range of shotgun shooting including trap, sporting clays, skeet, and hunting. Along with extensive reviews of shotguns, both new and classic models, there are useful articles relating to shooting techniques and ammunition. While the articles are written by authors who are highly knowledgeable on the sport, they can easily be enjoyed by beginners or experts alike. *Shotgun Sports* is a title that most libraries should consider having in their guns and hunting collections.

3878. *Trap & Field: the official publication of the Amateur Trapshooting Association.* [ISSN: 0041-1760] 1890. m. USD 25 domestic; USD 37 foreign. Ed(s): Terry Ewing. Curtis Magazine Group, Inc., 1000 Waterway Blvd, Indianapolis, IN 46202-2157. Illus., adv. Sample. Circ: 14000 Paid. Vol. ends: Dec. *Indexed:* SportS. *Aud.:* Ems, Hs, Sa.

Trap & Field is published by the Amateur Trap Association (ATA) and focuses on ATA regional and national news, firearms and equipment, domestic and international gun news and legislation, and scores and reports from trap shoots across the nation. Each issue also has one or two feature articles that profile people or events.

3879. *Trapper & Predator Caller: practical information for experienced dedicated trappers & predator callers.* Formerly (until 1984): *Trapper.* [ISSN: 8750-233X] 1975. 10x/yr. USD 18.95 domestic; USD 38.95 foreign; USD 3.50 per issue. Ed(s): Paul Wait. Krause Publications, Inc., 700 E State St, Iola, WI 54990-0001; info@krause.com; http://www.krause.com. Illus., adv. Sample. Circ: 38740 Paid and free. Vol. ends: Dec. *Aud.:* Ems, Hs, Sa.

Trapper & Predator Caller covers news and information related to trapping. Regular features include reports on the fur market, calendar of events, state association news, animal behavior, and advice for the expert or novice trapper. Feature articles cover techniques and methods, product information, and how-to's related to different aspects of trapping and the fur trade. This magazine also publishes feature articles on the hunting of predator animals.

3880. *Turkey & Turkey Hunting: practical & comprehensive information for wild turkey hunters.* Incorporates (in 1992): *Turkey Hunter;* Which was formerly (1984-198?): *Turkey.* [ISSN: 1067-4942] 1983. 6x/yr. USD 14.95 domestic; USD 22.95 foreign; USD 3.95 newsstand/cover per issue. Ed(s): James Schlender. Krause Publications, Inc., 700 E State St, Iola, WI 54990-0001; info@krause.com; http://www.krause.com. Illus., adv. Sample. Circ: 81342 Paid and free. Vol. ends: Winter. *Bk. rev.:* 1, 5,000 words. *Aud.:* Hs, Sa.

Turkey & Turkey Hunting is an outstanding publication for both gun and bow hunters. Articles focus on various aspects of turkey hunting, including strategies, calling, turkey behavior and biology, firearms, bows, and accessories. The articles are not only informative, but well written and illustrated. *Turkey & Turkey Hunting* should be considered by any library with a hunting collection.

3881. ***Wheelin' Sportsmen.*** [ISSN: 1538-1218] 2002. q. National Wild Turkey Federation, Inc., 770 Augusta Rd, PO Box 530, Edgefield, SC 29824-0530; kroop@nwtf.net; http://www.nwtf.net. Adv. *Bk. rev.:* 2-4, 200-400 words. *Aud.:* Hs, Ga, Sa.

While the National Wild Turkey Federation produces *Wheelin' Sportsmen,* the focus is not strictly turkey hunting. In actuality, the magazine is "dedicated to the education and entertainment of disabled outdoors enthusiasts...." Articles include equipment modification, hunting experiences, product advertisements, survival techniques, and wilderness opportunities for the disabled. Hunting and outdoor topics of interest to any hunter are also present. It is refreshing to see an outdoor magazine for a forgotten population.

3882. ***Wildfowl: the magazine for duck & goose hunters.*** [ISSN: 0886-0637] 1985. bi-m. USD 27.97 domestic; USD 42.97 Canada; USD 39.97 elsewhere. Ed(s): Richard Jacobsen. Primedia Enthusiast Group, PO Box 2087, Marion, OH 43306-8187; http://www.primedia.com. Illus., adv. Sample. Circ: 40553. Vol. ends: Jul. *Bk. rev.:* Various number and length. *Aud.:* Hs, Sa.

Wildfowl is the "where to, how to" magazine for waterfowlers. This publication will provide duck and goose hunters with excellent information on a wide range of issues and topics relevant to the sport. Article coverage includes product information on the latest gear and gadgets, conservation, shooting techniques, hunting methods, dog training, recipes for harvested game, and profiles of places to hunt. *Wildfowl* has knowledgable writers and excellent photography, and would be an excellent addition to any hunting collection.

3883. ***Wildlife Harvest: the magazine for gamebird production & improved hunting.*** [ISSN: 0886-3458] 1970. m. USD 60. Ed(s): Peggy Boehmer. Wildlife Harvest Publications, PO Box 96, Goose Lake, IA 52750. Illus., adv. Sample. Circ: 2943 Paid. Vol. ends: Dec. *Bk. rev.:* 1-3, 100-200 words. *Aud.:* Hs, Ga.

Wildlife Harvest provides news and information to those who produce and purchase game birds. The articles in this magazine cover various topics related to farming techniques and practices, current issues in legislation, and conservation. This title may not be suitable for all libraries, but should be considered for collections that support large agriculture communities or academic programs.

3884. ***Women in the Outdoors.*** [ISSN: 1526-8217] q. National Wild Turkey Federation, Inc., 770 Augusta Rd, PO Box 530, Edgefield, SC 29824-0530; kroop@nwtf.net; http://www.nwtf.net. *Aud.:* Hs, Ga, Sa.

The National Wild Turkey Federation Women in the Outdoors Program hosts this magazine for women outdoor enthusiasts. Topics include sports, wildlife interests, and overall outdoor education. Women are depicted in sports from snow skiing to rock climbing, in wildlife interests from fishing to nature photography, and in outdoor education from gardening to animal profiles. The 80 pages encourage and promote women to experience outdoor activities.

■ INTERDISCIPLINARY STUDIES

Courtney L. Young, Social Sciences Librarian, Selector for Race, Gender, Ethnicity, and Sexuality, The Pennsylvania State University, University Park, PA 16802

Introduction

The creation and inclusion of a section titled Interdisciplinary Studies reflects both the increase in scholarship that employs the use of multiple approaches and the scholastic conversations taking place across disciplines. In many ways, this section is a complement to sections that focus on racial, gender, and sexual diversity. It focuses on cross-disciplinary education and the facilitation of conversations among educators in a variety of fields. The emphasis of the journals included here is on science, approaches to education, and the understanding that one approach is really a strategy among many approaches. A large number of journals include "interdisciplinary" as a subtitle but are better suited for other sections. Another challenge in writing this section was the large number of journals with a sporadic publishing history or journals that had simply ceased. While you are encouraged to explore the many sections that more directly focus on specific disciplines and types of diversity, consider these periodicals as a starting point when building collections to integrate these important types of resources. Suggestions for expanding this list are encouraged.

Basic Periodicals

Ac: *Issues in Integrative Studies.*

Basic Abstracts and Indexes

EBSCO Academic Premiere; ProQuest Research Library.

American Quarterly. See Cultural-Social Studies section.

American Studies. See Cultural-Social Studies section.

3885. ***Interdisciplinary Environmental Review.*** [ISSN: 1521-0227] 1999. a. USD 60 (Individuals, USD 30; Students, USD 20). Ed(s): Kevin Hickey, Demetri Kantarelis. Interdisciplinary Environmental Association, Department of Economics and Foreign Affairs, Assumption College, Worcester, MA 01615-0005; http://www.desu.edu/mreiter/iea.htm. *Bk. rev.:* Number and length varies; signed. *Aud.:* Ac.

Published by the Interdisciplinary Environmental Association, *IER* publishes "research and survey papers" in all disciplines concerning the "natural environment." Each annual issue features seven to eight articles. Scholarship on ethics, religion, gender, and globalization as they relate to the environment are but a handful of diverse topics included in each publication. Submission information encourages authors to write their manuscripts in a manner that will "facilitate communication between disciplines." A journal sure to serve a variety of researchers.

3886. ***Interdisciplinary Literary Studies: a journal of criticism and theory.*** [ISSN: 1524-8429] s-a. USD 35 (Individuals, USD 25). Ed(s): Kenneth Womack. Interdisciplinary Literary Studies, c/o Kenneth Womack, Penn State Altoona, Altoona, PA 16601-3760. *Indexed:* MLA-IB. *Bk. rev.:* Number and length varies; signed. *Aud.:* Ac.

This journal publishes research exploring "the interconnections between literary studies and other disciplines, ideologies, and cultural methods of critique." Scholarship focuses on discussing the "pedagogical possibilities of interdisciplinary literary studies." Book reviews and interviews with important scholars in the field are included.

3887. ***Interdisciplinary Science Reviews.*** [ISSN: 0308-0188] 1976. q. USD 517 (Individuals, USD 49). Ed(s): Howard Cattermole, J E Harris. Maney Publishing, Hudson Rd, Leeds, LS9 7DL, United Kingdom; maney@maney.co.uk; http://www.maney.co.uk. Adv. Refereed. Circ: 400 Paid. *Indexed:* C&ISA, ChemAb, EngInd, GeoRef, SSCI. *Bk. rev.:* Number and length varies; signed. *Aud.:* Ac.

Founded in 1976, *ISR* aims to "foster inclusive pluralistic appreciation and understanding of scientific activity." This is accomplished through the submissions of scholars with diverse research interests, including the physical and biological sciences, social sciences, and humanities. Faculty and research from around the world contribute frequently. Special issues are often published, with themes including "Science and Theatre" and "Radioactive Waste." Most issues are heavily illustrated. Book reviews and letters to the editor round out each issue. A fascinating and essential journal for interdisciplinary collections.

3888. ***Interdisciplinary Studies in Literature and Environment.*** [ISSN: 1076-0962] 1993. s-a. USD 25 (Individual members, USD 25). Ed(s): Scott Slovic. Association for the Study of Literature and Environment, c/o Annie Merrill Ingram, Davidson College, Dept. of English, Davidson, NC 28036-6961; aningram@davidson.edu; http://www.asle.umn.edu. Adv. *Indexed:* MLA-IB. *Bk. rev.:* Number and length varies; signed. *Aud.:* Ac.

Another journal with a focus on the increasing research and scholarship on the environment, *ISLE* "seeks to bridge the gap between scholars, artists, students, and the public." Produced by the Association for the Study of Literature and Environment since 1993, *ISLE* bridges the gap with scholarship on advertising, poetry, religion, the environment, and representations of nature in literature. Book reviews and an annotated list of recent books are included.

3889. ***Issues in Integrative Studies.*** [ISSN: 1081-4760] 1982. a. Institutional members, USD 100; Individual members, USD 40; Students, USD 15. Ed(s): Stanley Bailis. Association for Integrative Studies, c/o Prof William Newell, Ed, School of Interdisciplinary Studies, Oxford, OH 45056; newellwh@muohio.edu; http://www.muohio.edu/ais. Adv. Refereed. Circ: 550 Paid. *Indexed:* HEA. *Bk. rev.:* Number and length varies; signed. *Aud.:* Ac.

While other journals take an interdisciplinary approach to the study of disciplines, research in *Issues in Integrative Studies* explores what exactly interdisciplinary studies is all about. Each publication examines the challenges of exploring this area of study including "interdisciplinary theory and methodology; the nature, means, and problems of integrative research, especially on the human experience; and special pedagogical approaches for enhancing interdisciplinary/integrative comprehension, perspectives, knowledge, and utilization." An impressive, key journal for institutions with interdisciplinary studies programs, with applications for education programs.

Journal of Interdisciplinary Gender Studies. See Women: Feminist and Special Interest section.

3890. ***Journal of Interdisciplinary History.*** [ISSN: 0022-1953] 1969. q. USD 198 (Individuals, USD 48; Students, USD 28). Ed(s): Robert I Rotberg, Theodore K Rabb. MIT Press, 5 Cambridge Center, Cambridge, MA 02142-1493; journals-orders@mit.edu; http://mitpress.mit.edu/JIH. Illus., index, adv. Refereed. Circ: 1700. Microform: PQC. Online: EBSCO Publishing; Gale Group; Ingenta Select; RoweCom Information Quest. Reprint: PQC; SCH. *Indexed:* ABCPolSci, ABS&EES, AmH&L, ArtHuCI, BAS, BHA, BRI, BrArAb, CBRI, HumInd, IBSS, IPSA, NumL, PRA, PSA, SSCI, SUSA, SWA, SociolAb. *Bk. rev.:* 30-45, 2-3 pages, signed. *Aud.:* Ac, Sa.

Incorporating "contemporary insights on the past," articles in this journal employ a diverse approach to analysis and methodology in historical scholarship. Sample titles of articles clearly influenced by an interdisciplinary approach to research include "The Mulatto Advantage: The Biological Consequences of Complexion in Rural Antebellum Virginia"; "Nutritional Success on the Great Plains: Nineteenth-Century Equistrian Nomads"; and "Urban Identity in Medieval English Towns." Book reviews, research notes, and review essays continue to be a strength of the journal. While remaining an important journal in the discipline of history, the *Journal of Interdisciplinary History* is a solid contributor for interdisciplinary studies.

Studies in the Decorative Arts. See Art section.

■ INTERIOR DESIGN AND DECORATION

See also Home section.

Holly Stec Dankert, Reference Instruction Librarian, DePaul University Libraries, 2350 N. Kenmore, Chicago, IL 60614; hdankert@depaul.edu; FAX: 773-325-7870

Introduction

Trade magazines aimed at professional designers provide the backbone of interior design publications; however, consumer-oriented titles play an important role in providing product information and consumer trends to practitioners while bringing design principles to the masses. Both types of magazines are central to interior design.

Trade publications serve to inform decorators, designers, and architects of current practices, trends, and new products and services in both commercial and residential interiors. Most of these trade titles include reader service information, professional development opportunities, new technology advancements in furnishings and materials, calendars of professional events, and reviews of new publications in interior design. In addition, these publications provide many full-color illustrations of interiors and the materials used for their creation. Professional literature is best suited for academic libraries offering degrees in interior design or decorating and public libraries that support their local design community.

Consumer-oriented titles target the affluent buyer as well as the professional decorator or designer, and generally devote a great deal more copy space to photography of the featured interiors and to advertisements that highlights furnishings, wall coverings, textiles, flooring, and interior architecture. Many from this second group focus on the homes of celebrities and renowned designers or collections of art, antiques, and custom furnishings, and are almost exclusively devoted to residential interiors.

The hallmark of all titles in this section is the extensive use of lush, full-color illustrations. The web sites of the trade titles continue to provide more relevant content to their constituents than do the consumer titles, which typically provide subscriber services and little more. Magazines in this section will appeal to all library users but are aimed at working designers and a clientele in search of professional design services.

Basic Periodicals

Ga: *Architectural Digest, House & Garden;* Ac: *Architectural Digest, Contract, ID (Cincinnati), Interior Design, Interiors & Sources, Journal of Interior Design.*

Basic Abstracts and Indexes

Art Abstracts/Index, Avery Index to Architectural Periodicals.

3891. ***American Style: the art of living creatively.*** [ISSN: 1078-8425] 1995. q. USD 18.74 domestic; USD 33.78 Canada; USD 48.78 foreign. Ed(s): Hope Daniels. Rosen Group, 3000 Chestnut Ave, Baltimore, MD 21211-2743; http://www.americanstyle.com. Illus., adv. Sample. Circ: 60000. Vol. ends: Summer. *Aud.:* Ga, Sa.

This magazine provides collectors, decorators, and designers with beautifully photographed residential interiors highlighting American craft art: pottery and ceramic sculpture, art glass, jewelry and wearable art, and fine gifts. Showcasing artists, each issue features the homes of collectors, artists, and gallery owners giving prominence to the objects they collect or create. Regular departments spotlight special attractions, segments highlighting an artist or location, "Datebook," and "Showtime," the latter two providing information on gallery shows, museum exhibitions, craft fairs, and arts festivals throughout the United States. Blending art and interior design, *American Style* is recommended for all public and academic libraries that serve collectors or the design community.

3892. ***Architectural Digest: the international magazine of interior design.*** [ISSN: 0003-8520] 1920. m. USD 39.95 domestic; USD 59.95 Canada. Ed(s): Paige Rense. Conde Nast Publications Inc., 4 Times Square, 5th Fl, New York, NY 10036; http://www.condenast.com. Illus., adv. Circ:

835563 Paid. Vol. ends: Dec. Microform: PQC. Online: Gale Group; OCLC Online Computer Library Center, Inc.; H.W. Wilson. *Indexed:* A&ATA, ABS&EES, AIAP, ASIP, ArtHuCI, ArtInd, GardL, IIFP, MagInd, RGPR. *Aud.:* Ga, Ac.

Lavish homes decorated by renowned interior designers are captured in this classic interior design magazine. International in scope, each issue features condominiums, co-ops, and houses exquisitely furnished with expensive, often one-of-a-kind, antiques, objets d'art, and premium designer furniture. Occasional issues are devoted to a particular style or period and feature luxurious hideaways around the world; not to be missed is the summer issue devoted to American country houses. With its glossy advertising of luxury products, showcase for antiques, designer, and collector items, and sophisticated international locations, *Architectural Digest* is aimed at the rich and cosmopolitan. Many readers, regardless of income, will find it appealing. A standard design magazine recommended for all libraries.

3893. *Contract.* Former titles (until 2000): *Contract Design;* (until 1990): *Contract.* [ISSN: 1530-6224] 1960. m. USD 79 domestic (Free to qualified personnel). Ed(s): Diana Mosher. V N U Business Publications, 770 Broadway, New York, NY 10003; bmcomm@vnuinc.com; http://www.vnubusinessmedia.com/. Illus., adv. Sample. Circ: 30000. Vol. ends: Dec. Microform: PQC. Online: EBSCO Publishing; Gale Group; OCLC Online Computer Library Center, Inc.; ProQuest Information & Learning. *Indexed:* ArtInd. *Bk. rev.:* Various number and length. *Aud.:* Ac, Sa.

Focusing on commercial interiors artfully photographed, this premier trade magazine offers the design professional important industry information. *Contract* features trends in corporate, retail, educational, hospitality, health care, entertainment, government, and institutional design, plus new product information on floor and wall coverings, textiles, lighting, and furniture. Practitioners will value the industry news and resource departments in each issue, plus the "Annual Source Guide" in December of each year. Most useful is the web site, www.contractmagazine.com, which offers links to current design projects, industry updates, vendors, conferences, trade shows, and professional associations—everything needed to stay current in nonresidential design, plus the table of contents and some articles from the current issue. Aimed at the architect and design community, this core title is a must-have for all libraries serving architect and design professionals and students.

Dwell. See Home section.

3894. *Elle Decor.* [ISSN: 1046-1957] 1989. 8x/yr. USD 14.97 domestic; USD 24.97 foreign. Hachette Filipacchi Media U.S., Inc., 1633 Broadway, New York, NY 10019; http://www.hfmus.com. Illus., adv. Sample. Circ: 450000 Paid. Vol. ends: Nov. *Indexed:* AIAP, ASIP. *Aud.:* Ga.

Elle Decor exudes a younger and more spirited tone than other magazines in this section. Popular interior design, posh retreats, country homes, and trendy gadgets are the focus of the dozen or so articles featuring artists and designers and their affluent twenty- and thirtysomething clients. Each issue includes trend-setting designs that are inspirational and attainable. Resource contacts and reader services make this title valuable for both professionals and do-it-yourself decorators. Elledecor.com is a wonderful new edition to the web and highlights some print content plus fun sections on "What's Hot," "Trend Alert," "Truth in Decorating," "Elle Decor Style," and "Promo/Events." Suitable for public libraries.

3895. *House & Garden.* Former titles (until Sep. 1996): *H G;* (until 1987): *House and Garden;* Incorporating: *Living for Young Homemakers.* [ISSN: 1087-9528] 1901. m. USD 15 domestic; USD 33.97 Canada; USD 38.97 elsewhere. Ed(s): Dominique Browning. Conde Nast Publications Inc., 4 Times Square, 5th Fl, New York, NY 10036; http://www.condenast.com. Illus., adv. Sample. Circ: 770325 Paid. Vol. ends: Dec. Microform: PQC. Reprint: PQC. *Indexed:* AIAP, API, BiogInd, DAAI, GardL, MagInd, RGPR. *Aud.:* Ga.

Monothematic treatments predominate each month in the quintessential *HG*, which provides an astonishing array of gadgets for the home, culinary foodstuffs, fabrics, flora, and outdoor furnishings to tempt consumers and decorators alike in its regular departments. Offering a range of mid-priced objects, this Conde Nast publication is a foil for its more upscale *Architectural Digest.* Feature articles highlight apartments, houses, estates, gardens, and collections owned or designed by famous folks. Although aimed at the consumer, *HG* is of value to professional residential designers, too. Recommended for public libraries.

3896. *I D (Cincinnati).* Former titles (until 1984): *Industrial Design;* (until 1983): *Industrial Design Magazine;* (until vol. 26, 1979): *Industrial Design.* [ISSN: 0894-5373] 1954. 8x/yr. USD 60; USD 75 Canada. Ed(s): Jenny Wohlfarth. F & W Publications, Inc., 1507 Dana Ave, Cincinnati, OH 45207. Illus., adv. Sample. Circ: 38839. Vol. ends: Dec. Microform: PQC. Online: Gale Group; ProQuest Information & Learning. Reprint: PQC. *Indexed:* AIAP, AS&TI, ArtInd, DAAI. *Bk. rev.:* 2-3, 300 words. *Aud.:* Ac, Sa.

The self-professed "leading critical magazine for covering the art, business and culture of design," *ID* introduces new products to industrial, interior, and contract designers. Features include current business practices, technology and book reviews, notable products, and an exposition and events calendar making it valuable for the professional design community. Not to be missed is the annual December issue, "Design Sourcebook," which is a directory/buyer's guide to the design world, and the "Annual Design Review," *ID*'s prestigious, juried design recognition program, displaying international premium consumer products, furniture, equipment, environmental designs, packaging, and graphic design. Its web site, www.id-mag.com, offers the table of contents and some articles from the print version. Winning numerous design awards itself, this magazine provides a rich source of ideas and is a welcome addition to libraries with art and design collections and those serving design professionals and students.

3897. *I S Magazine.* Formerly: *Interiors & Sources.* [ISSN: 1542-4219] 1990. bi-m. USD 27 domestic; USD 50 in Canada & Mexico. Ed(s): Katie Sosnowchick. L.C. Clark Publishing Co., Inc., 840 US Highway 1, Ste. 330, No Palm Beach, FL 33408-3878; ksosnowchik@lcclark.com; http://www.isdesignet.com. Illus., index, adv. Sample. Circ: 26987. Vol. ends: Nov/Dec. *Indexed:* ArtInd. *Aud.:* Ac, Sa.

Catering to the professional designer and architect, *IS* concentrates on commercial interiors. The novel approach of featuring an individual designer or design team and their current projects on the cover, plus additional articles on noteworthy commercial and residential interiors, coverage of professional events, conferences, industry news, troubleshooting tips, and fairly extensive product sources, allows *IS* to live up to its mission "to deliver relevant and timely information which supports the advanced professionalism and long-term growth of the design field." Practitioners will appreciate "ASID Update," "IIDA Notes," "IDEC Report," and "NCIDQ News," plus sections on health and green design. The web site provides professional trade news and information including an archive dating back to 1995. Recommended for academic libraries with a design focus and public libraries serving the local interior design/architecture community.

3898. *Interior Design.* [ISSN: 0020-5508] 1932. m. USD 64.95 domestic; USD 87 Canada; USD 187 elsewhere. Ed(s): So Chung Shinn. Reed Business Information, 360 Park Ave South, New York, NY 10010; http://www.reedbusiness.com. Illus., adv. Circ: 55420. Vol. ends: Dec. Microform: CIS; PQC. Online: EBSCO Publishing; Florida Center for Library Automation; Gale Group; Northern Light Technology, Inc.; OCLC Online Computer Library Center, Inc.; ProQuest Information & Learning; H.W. Wilson. Reprint: PQC. *Indexed:* AIAP, ArchI, ArtInd, DAAI. *Bk. rev.:* 4-5, 150 words. *Aud.:* Ac, Sa.

Interior Design is arguably the leader in the interior design press and is renowned for its extensive coverage of commercial and residential interior design projects. It has the largest circulation and is probably the most widely read trade magazine by interior designers. The recent web initiative, www.interiordesign.net, serves the professional interior design community with bountiful offerings in new products, industry news, and topical features. The print edition offers lengthy (10–15 pages) feature articles focusing on notable projects or design firms, primarily in the United States. "Forums" includes industry awards news, new projects, technology, and the latest innovations in furnishings from international manufacturers. Extensive advertising space is given to premier U.S. and European design manufacturers. A subscription includes fall and spring "Market" issues and the annual "Interior Design Buyers Guide." Recommended for all libraries.

3899. ***Journal of Interior Design.*** Formerly: *Journal of Interior Design Education and Research.* [ISSN: 1071-7641] 1976. s-a. USD 80 (Individuals, USD 50; Students, USD 25). Ed(s): Susan Zavotka. Interior Design Educators Council, Inc., c/o Susan Zavotka, Ed, Ohio State University, Columbus, OH 43210; dguerin@che2.che.umn.edu. Illus., index, adv. Sample. Refereed. Circ: 700. *Indexed:* ABM, ErgAb. *Bk. rev.:* 4-5, 500 words. *Aud.:* Ac.

JID has the distinction of being the only scholarly title for the interior design profession. Published by the Interior Design Educators Council, it focuses on education, practice, research, and theory, providing scholars and teachers with a forum for "scientific applications of design principles," historical research, and design processes in theory and practice. Regular reports give readers current practices and techniques for classroom and studio education plus reviews of new books, technology, and other media. The council's web site, www.idec.org, provides annual conference, membership, graduate program and other information pertinent to design educators. Recommended for all academic collections with design programs.

3900. ***Nest: a quarterly of interiors.*** [ISSN: 1098-4585] 1998. q. USD 34 domestic; USD 54 foreign; USD 12.50 newsstand/cover. Ed(s): Paul Franklin. Nest LLC, PO Box 2033, Marion, OH 43306-8133. Adv. *Aud.:* Ga, Sa.

International fashion design sensibilities inform this strikingly different publication that strives to raise awareness of the meaning of "spaces" as opposed to traditional interior design. *Nest*'s eclectic mix of visual and literary offerings venture far from the typical titles in this section. Covering all varieties of dwellings created by mankind, *Nest* bills itself as "a unique shelter magazine...where high-style London and Paris meet igloos and prison cells on equal terms." Written in breezy, tongue-in-cheek fashion and filled with lush photography, this magazine is a treat for the senses. Article summaries in French, Italian, and Japanese are included in each issue. The web site offers a handful of quirky fabrics and wall coverings for sale and table of contents listings for current and back issues. Recommended for all libraries.

3901. ***Southern Accents: the magazine of fine Southern interiors and gardens.*** [ISSN: 0149-516X] 1977. bi-m. USD 28 domestic; USD 34 foreign; USD 5.50 newsstand/cover per issue. Ed(s): Candace Schlosser, Mark Mayfield. Southern Progress Corp., 2100 Lakeshore Dr, Birmingham, AL 35209. Illus., adv. Circ: 370653 Paid. Vol. ends: Nov/Dec. *Indexed:* AIAP, GardL. *Aud.:* Ga.

Featuring elegant gardens and homes located in the southern United States, this publication caters to decorators and clients of a traditional sensibility. Six to seven articles illustrate classic and traditional interiors decorated by professionals. Tips on entertaining, antiques, flowers, travel, gardening, and collecting are regular departments, with a calendar, sourcebook, and trade show listings rounding out each issue. More entertaining and decorating ideas are available at www.southernaccents.com for subscribers only. Recommended for public libraries and academic design collections.

3902. ***V M & S D.*** Former titles: *Visual Merchandising & Store Design;* (until 1982): *Visual Merchandising;* (until 1973): *Display World.* [ISSN: 1072-9666] 1922. m. USD 39. Ed(s): Janet Groeber. S T Publications Inc., 407 Gilbert Ave, Cincinnati, OH 45202; cwinters@stpubs.com; http://www.visualstore.com. Illus., adv. Sample. Circ: 30859. Vol. ends: Dec. *Indexed:* BPI, DAAI. *Aud.:* Ac, Sa.

VM&SD is the trade magazine for interior designers, owners, managers, and marketers of retail establishments. Typical of most trade magazines, it provides a wealth of industry related news and feature articles, frequently with a single-topic theme. Other industry content—calendar of events, annual survey of top fixture manufacturers of signage, graphics, and props, plus the annual buyers' guide (January issue)—round out this important resource to merchandisers. Not to be missed is the accompanying web site, www.visualstore.com, that serves the retail profession. Recommended for academic libraries with interior design programs or public libraries catering to local retailers.

Veranda: a gallery of fine design. See Home section.

3903. ***The World of Interiors.*** [ISSN: 0264-083X] 1981. m. GBP 25 domestic; GBP 54 foreign; GBP 3.20 newsstand/cover per issue. Ed(s): Min Hogg. Conde Nast Publications Ltd., Vogue House, Hanover Sq, London, W1R 0AD, United Kingdom; http://www.worldofinteriors.co.uk. Illus., adv. Circ: 71691. Vol. ends: Dec. *Indexed:* AIAP, ArtInd, DAAI. *Bk. rev.:* 5-6, 500 words. *Aud.:* Ga, Sa.

This lush British monthly offers international coverage of residential interior design. Regular departments with catchy titles provide design trends, auction and fair dates, merchandise, and suppliers for the U.K. market. Articles often feature renowned personalities, showcasing royal abodes, historic homes, modern penthouses, and whimsical to formal gardens throughout the world, but predominantly in Britain. Fine art and antiques collections are also featured. Aimed at designers in the United Kingdom and their clients, it is best suited to large libraries serving the design community.

■ INTERNET-WORLD WIDE WEB

See also Business; Communications; Computer Science and Automation; Electronics; Engineering and Technology; and Library Periodicals sections.

Xiaochang Yu, Systems Librarian, VCU Libraries, Virginia Commonwealth University, Richmond, VA 23284-2033; FAX: 804-828-0151; xyu@vcu.edu

Introduction

The Internet and World Wide Web have penetrated almost all areas. Today, most magazines deal with the Internet and the web in some way, and most of them have some web presence. However, while few titles in other sections treat the Internet and the web as the primary topic, it is the subject per se of titles in this section.

Magazines reviewed here can be roughly grouped into three categories. There are scholarly journals aimed at researchers and educators who study various aspects of the Internet and the web. Other magazines tend to serve mainly technical professionals such as computer programmers and applications developers specializing in various Internet and web technologies. Still others appeal to a broad audience—the general public or ordinary web users who are more interested in using the Internet and exploring the web.

The setback of Internet companies and their declining stock prices since the year 2000 seem to have had a direct impact on the number of magazines in this field, with dramatic decreases. About half of all the print titles covered in the last edition of *MFL* have either ceased publication altogether or are now available online only. Given the principle of survival of the fittest, the quality of the remaining titles should be fairly high. In a way, this has made selecting magazines in this field somewhat easier.

Basic Periodicals

IEEE Internet Computing, Internet Research.

Basic Abstracts and Indexes

Computer Literature Index, INSPEC, Microcomputer Index.

3904. ***Boardwatch Magazine: guide to Internet access and the World Wide Web.*** Incorporates (1999-2000): *C L E C Magazine;* Formerly (until 1989): *Denver P C Boardwatch.* [ISSN: 1054-2760] 1987. m. USD 72 in US & Canada; USD 128 foreign; USD 7 newsstand/cover per issue domestic. Ed(s): Todd Erickson. Penton Media, Inc. (Golden), 13949 W Colfax Ave, Ste 250, Golden, CO 80401-3209; http://www.penton.com. Illus., adv. Sample. Circ: 11200. Vol. ends: Dec. Online: EBSCO Publishing; Gale Group; OCLC Online Computer Library Center, Inc.; ProQuest Information & Learning. *Indexed:* CompLI. *Bk. rev.:* 2-3, 200 words. *Aud.:* Ga, Sa.

This magazine provides comprehensive information for Internet service providers (ISPs). Each issue has two major components: columns and feature articles. Columns offer timely information on a variety of topics such as Internet standards watch and ISP market report. Feature articles address ISP-related new technologies, government policies, industry standards, and business practices. Recent themes include mobile wireless access, peer-to-peer networking, and Internet voting. Articles and columns are very well written and often fun to read. Although its main audience is ISPs (over 7,000 in the United States alone), *Boardwatch* appeals to many readers interested in the Internet as well.

3905. ***The CyberSkeptic's Guide to Internet Research.*** [ISSN: 1085-2417] 1995. 10x/yr. USD 159 domestic (Non-profit organizations, USD 104). Information Today, Inc., 143 Old Marlton Pike, Medford, NJ 08055-8750; custserv@infotoday.com; http://www.infotoday.com. Illus. Sample. *Indexed:* CINAHL, InfoSAb. *Aud.:* Ga, Sa.

This newsletter is primarily for information professionals. It reviews selected web sites and tools. A typical issue includes a discussion of the "site of the month," brief introductions to various web sites, evaluations or comparisons of web sites, and analyses of search engines or other web tools. The newsletter maintains a healthy skeptical view of cyberspace.

3906. ***e-Service Journal.*** [ISSN: 1528-8226] 2001. 3x/yr. Individuals, USD 45. Ed(s): Laku Chidambaram, Carol Saunders. Indiana University Press, 601 N Morton St, Bloomington, IN 47404; http://www.indiana.edu/~iupress/journals/. Illus. Sample. Refereed. Circ: 200 Paid. *Aud.:* Ga, Ac, Sa.

This peer-reviewed journal covers various aspects of electronic services, from methods and infrastructures to policies and social impacts. It combines both private sector and public sector perspectives regarding electronic services. The articles, including both research articles and case studies, are mainly intended for researchers and practitioners involved in developing e-government and e-business. Authors are knowledgeable and topics are interesting. It is a very decent publication.

3907. ***Educause Review.*** Former titles (until 1999): *Educom Review;* (until 1989): *Educom Bulletin;* (until 1984): *Educom.* [ISSN: 1527-6619] 1966. bi-m. USD 24 in US & Canada; USD 48 elsewhere. Ed(s): Teddy Diggs. Educause, 4772 Walnut St, Ste 206, Boulder, CO 80301-2536. Illus., index, adv. Sample. Refereed. Circ: 20000. Vol. ends: Dec. *Indexed:* CIJE, CompLI, EduInd, HEA. *Aud.:* Ga, Ac.

This publication was a consolidation of *Educom* and *Cause* in 1998. The journal explores various challenging issues related to the development and deployment of the Internet and information technology in higher education. It addresses such topics as the digital divide in higher education, the use of wireless and other new technologies in teaching and learning, and library and information services in the digital environment. The focus is often on the policy, management, and infrastructure sides. Many articles are by college and university administrators.

eWEEK. See Business/General section.

3908. ***I E E E Internet Computing.*** [ISSN: 1089-7801] 1997. bi-m. USD 650 in North America; USD 685 elsewhere. Ed(s): Munindar P Singh. Institute of Electrical and Electronics Engineers, Inc., 445 Hoes Ln, Piscataway, NJ 08854-1331; subscription-service@ieee.org; http://www.ieee.org. Illus., index, adv. Refereed. Circ: 17771 Paid. Vol. ends: Dec. Online: EBSCO Publishing; I E E E. *Indexed:* C&ISA, CompLI, EngInd, MicrocompInd, RiskAb. *Aud.:* Ac, Sa.

With a very attractive appearance, this IEEE journal is actually highly technical in nature. It is mainly concerned with the engineering side of the Internet. A sample of recent topics illustrates the focus of the journal: XML and web services, virtual private networks and web securities, and web search using a genetic algorithm. Articles are well written and are at the frontier of study. One of the unique features is its "Elsewhere" department, which lists and abstracts research articles on the Internet that are newly published in other important journals. It is a simple thing that any journal can do, yet to actually do it demonstrates the self-confidence of *Internet Computing*. Recommended.

3909. ***I-Ways: digest of electronic commerce policy and regulation.*** Formerly (until Mar 1995): *Transnational Data and Communications Report;* Which was formed by the merger of (1980-1984): *Chronicle of International Communication;* (1978-1984): *Transnational Data Report.* [ISSN: 1084-4678] 1984. q. EUR 358. I O S Press, Nieuwe Hemweg 6B, Amsterdam, 1013 BG, Netherlands; order@iospress.nl; http://www.iospress.nl. Illus., index, adv. Sample. Vol. ends: Dec. *Indexed:* CommAb, CompLI, PAIS. *Bk. rev.:* 4-5, 175 words. *Aud.:* Ac, Sa.

The new title of this authoritative publication captures exactly its main focus: reports and digests of electronic commerce policies and regulations. It addresses such issues as transborder data privacy, Internet taxing, encryption regulations, and important developments in e-commerce and e-government. It covers individual country as well as regional and worldwide organizations. The contributors are truly international in scope. Some of the recent reports and digests concern the newly passed Internet privacy laws in China, Canada, and several other countries, Europe's commitment to combatting computer crimes, an African telecommunications conference, and United States electronic-signature law.

3910. ***Information Superhighways.*** [ISSN: 1078-6589] 1993. m. USD 695 in US & Canada; USD 745 elsewhere. Ed(s): Tony Carmona. Information Gatekeepers, Inc., 214 Harvard Ave, Ste 200, Boston, MA 02134; info@igigroup.com; http://www.igigroup.com. Illus., adv. Vol. ends: Dec. Online: Florida Center for Library Automation; Gale Group. *Indexed:* CompLI. *Aud.:* Sa.

This monthly is one of 45 or so newsletters published by Information Gatekeepers, Inc. It addresses worldwide developments in information technologies and e-commerce practices. It covers government policies and regulations, new products and services, business and market activities, and other topics. It is current, straightforward, and concise. The high price may keep some potential subscribers away.

3911. ***Internet Research.*** Formerly (until 1993): *Electronic Networking.* [ISSN: 1066-2243] 1991. 5x/yr. EUR 2010.79 in Europe; USD 1839 in North America; AUD 2069 in Australasia. Ed(s): Dr. David G Schwartz. Emerald, 60-62 Toller Ln, Bradford, BD8 9BY, United Kingdom; info@emeraldinsight.com; http://www.emeraldinsight.com/journals/. Illus., index, adv. Refereed. Vol. ends: Dec. Online: Pub.; EBSCO Publishing; OCLC Online Computer Library Center, Inc.; ProQuest Information & Learning; RoweCom Information Quest; Swets Blackwell. Reprint: PSC. *Indexed:* CIJE, CommAb, HRA, InfoSAb, LISA, LibLit, MicrocompInd, PAIS, PRA, RiskAb, SSCI. *Aud.:* Ac, Sa.

International in scope, this scholarly journal has the goal of describing, evaluating, and understanding the role of the Internet and other information networks. Most of the contributors are researchers and college and university professors worldwide. It tends to emphasize the foundational, methodological, and other significant aspects of information networks rather than specific issues. The journal is very well organized and the contents are current. Many of the papers try to provide solutions to real concerns of Internet researchers, developers, and users. It is one of the premier journals on the Internet. Recommended.

3912. ***Internet Week: news and analysis of internet business opportunities.*** Incorporates (1993?-1995): *Internet Letter.* [ISSN: 1081-2474] 1995. 53x/yr. USD 175; USD 395 in Europe; USD 425 in Asia. C M P Media LLC, 600 Community Dr, Manhasset, NY 11030; http://www.cmp.com. Illus., adv. Sample. Online: LexisNexis; Northern Light Technology, Inc. *Aud.:* Ga, Sa.

This weekly publication offers timely news to Internet users and the business community. Although it reports on a broad range of network related subjects, such as emerging technologies, the focus is clearly on the business and market aspects. Besides the news items, each issue also contains a couple of detailed reports and a column of new product reviews. Surprisingly, this decent publication is free to qualified management and professional personnel at companies involved in the communications industry.

3913. ***Internet World (New York): the voice of e-business and internet technology.*** Former titles (until 1997): *Web Week; World-Wide WebWeek.* [ISSN: 1097-8291] 1995. m. Free. Ed(s): Tony Rizzo, Thomas J DeLoughry. Internet World Media, 250 Park Ave S, 10th Fl, New York, NY 10003; http://www.iw.com/. Illus., adv. Sample. Circ: 182233. *Indexed:* BPI, CompLI, MicrocompInd. *Aud.:* Ga, Ac.

Although it addresses many aspects of the Internet, the main focus is on the business side of Internet development. It covers various topics such as electronic customer relationship management, dynamic pricing in the online world, and online advertising. Each issue includes such topics as policy watch, news analyses, companies to watch, and interviews. Items are short and to the point.

3914. ***Java Developer's Journal.*** [ISSN: 1087-6944] 1996. m. USD 69.99 domestic; USD 89.99 in Canada & Mexico; USD 99 elsewhere. Ed(s): M'lou Pinkham, Sean Rhody. SYS-CON Media, Inc., 135 Chestnut Ridge Rd, Montvale, NJ 07645; info@sys-con.com; http://www.sys-con.com. Illus., adv. Circ: 110000 Paid. Vol. ends: Dec. Online: Factiva; Florida Center for Library Automation; Gale Group. *Bk. rev.:* 2-3, 300 words. *Aud.:* Ga, Ac, Sa.

This journal is clearly for Java programmers and developers. It covers applications, tools, innovations, and programming issues. The scope ranges from relatively basic topics such as dynamically extracting data from a database into a JSP file to more advanced topics such as developing voice portals with Java. Its feature articles are substantial. Its columns include, among other items, brief news, industry watches, product reviews, and interviews. The journal is well designed and organized.

3915. ***Network World.*** Incorporates (in 1991): *Connect;* Former titles (until 1986): *On Communications; Computerworld on Communications.* [ISSN: 0887-7661] 1983. w. Mon. USD 129 domestic; USD 160.50 Canada; USD 150 in South America. Ed(s): John Gallant. Network World Inc., 118 Turnpike Rd, Southborough, MA 01772; http://www.nwfusion.com. Illus., adv. Sample. Circ: 157000 Controlled. Vol. ends: Dec. Online: EBSCO Publishing; Factiva; Florida Center for Library Automation; Gale Group; LexisNexis; Northern Light Technology, Inc.; OCLC Online Computer Library Center, Inc.; ProQuest Information & Learning. *Indexed:* ABIn, B&I, CompLI, LRI, MicrocompInd. *Bk. rev.:* 3-4, 200 words. *Aud.:* Ga, Sa.

This trade magazine reports on trends and news, applications and technologies, companies and products, key personnel and remarkable events, business and marketing, policies and politics, and other topics in the Internet and networking fields. Its annual special issues are outstanding. For example, in "The Power Issue," it rates and profiles, among others, the most powerful companies, the most powerful people, and the most significant power struggles in networking. The advertisements are extensive. Qualified readers may get a free one-year subscription.

3916. ***Wired.*** [ISSN: 1059-1028] 1993. m. USD 10. Ed(s): Chris Anderson. Conde Nast Publications Inc., Wired Ventures Ltd., 520 Third St, 4th Fl, San Francisco, CA 94107-1815; editor@wired.com; http://www.wired.com/. Illus., adv. Sample. Circ: 468905 Paid. Vol. ends: Dec. *Indexed:* ABS&EES, ASIP, BrArAb, CompLI, FutSurv, LISA, MicrocompInd, RGPR. *Bk. rev.:* 5-8, 100 words. *Aud.:* Hs, Ga.

This magazine covers the Internet and other areas of science and technology of interest to the public. The coverage is very broad. It publishes detailed reports and analyses as well as brief news and reviews on a variety of topics, from digital games to DNA to international businesses. Regular departments include "Start," "Play," "Rants and Raves," and "View." The magazine, including its extensive advertisements, is very beautifully designed.

3917. ***X M L Journal.*** [ISSN: 1534-9780] 2000. m. USD 69.99 domestic; USD 89.99 in Canada & Mexico; USD 99.99 elsewhere. Ed(s): Ajit Sagar. SYS-CON Media, Inc., 135 Chestnut Ridge Rd, Montvale, NJ 07645; info@sys-con.com; http://www.sys-con.com. Adv. Circ: 55000 Paid. *Aud.:* Ga, Ac, Sa.

This journal covers all aspects of XML technology, such as XSLT, XPath, XLink, XForms, and XML documents. In addition to editorials, news, product reviews, and interviews, it has articles addressing novel applications, parsing, encoding, editing tools, and trends in industry standards, among other topics. Since XML is mainly an enabling technology, this journal also addresses a variety of other closely related programming languages and technologies, such as Java, Cobra, SQL, databases, and web services. Authors are knowledgeable and topics are interesting. The publication is well designed and organized.

Electronic Journals

3918. ***Apache Week.*** 1999. w. Free. Apache Week, Red Hat Europe, 10 Alan Turing Way, Guildford, GU2 7YF, United Kingdom; editors@apacheweek.com. *Aud.:* Sa.

This electronic newsletter is solely devoted to Apache servers. It provides timely information, mainly new product releases and bug fixes, to the Apache community. Besides the news column, the regular columns also include security reports and featured articles. The featured articles are basically abstracts of some of the publications on the web that are of interest to Apache users. The publication is also sent to subscribers by e-mail weekly. *Apache Week* is one of the essential resources for anyone running an Apache server or running Apache-based services.

3919. ***Atlantic Unbound.*** 1993. m. Ed(s): Wen Stephenson. Atlantic Monthly Co., 77 N Washington St, Ste 5, Boston, MA 02114-1908; wen@theatlantic.com; http://www.theatlantic.com. *Bk. rev.:* 4-6, 2,000-3,000 words. *Aud.:* Hs, Ga, Ac.

The Internet plays host to *The Atlantic Online*—a web site offering both portions of *The Atlantic Monthly* and the web-only creations of the *Atlantic Unbound.* Though most of the articles found in *The Atlantic Monthly* are available only through various payment plans, the majority of reviews and editorials are freely accessible. In addition *The Atlantic Unbound* provides a rich selection of free online reading. *The Atlantic Unbound* is accessed directly from *The Atlantic Online* and offers readings, reviews, poetry, satirical cartoons and a look at articles from past issues under various headings, such as "Corby's Table," "Fallows@Large," "Flashbacks," "Interviews," "Poetry Pages," "Politics & Prose," "Sage, Ink," "Soundings," and "Unbound Fiction." *The Atlantic Online* and *The Atlantic Unbound* are sophisticated and scintillating choices for any electronic-magazine collection.

3920. ***EFFector.*** [ISSN: 1062-9424] 1991. irreg. 1-4/mo. Free. Ed(s): Stanton McCandlish. Electronic Frontier Foundation, 454 Shotwell St., San Francisco, CA 94110-1914; editor@eff.org; http://www.eff.org/effector. Circ: 20000. *Aud.:* Ga, Ac, Sa.

This newsletter of the Electronic Frontier Foundation is one of the best free online publications on the Internet. While many free online publications these days serve mainly as portals to online resources on other web sites, *EFFector* still publishes its own materials. Its mission is clear and very focused: defending freedom in the digital world. It covers mainly news, alerts, and commentaries on issues related to free speech on the Internet. Recent issues cover such topics as the foundation's support for the Wyden-Feinstein measure to stop the Total Information Awareness program, discussions on the Digital Media Consumers' Rights Act, and legal battles over an e-book copyright case. All the back issues since 1990 are available. The newsletter is also sent to subscribers by e-mail weekly.

3921. ***First Monday.*** [ISSN: 1396-0466] 1996. m. Ed(s): Edward J Valauskas. First Monday Editorial Group, c/o Edward Valauskas, Chief Editor, PO Box 87636, Chicago, IL 60680-0636; http://www.firstmonday.org. Illus. Refereed. Circ: 314559. *Indexed:* BRI, CBRI, InfoSAb, LISA, PAIS. *Bk. rev.:* 5-10, 500-1500 words. *Aud.:* Ga, Ac.

This is one of the first refereed online journals on the web and is published regularly on the first Monday of every month since 1996. The journal explores a variety of Internet issues, from the political, cultural and regulatory impacts on the Internet to the technical ones. Articles are indexed by authors and by titles. The journal database is easily searchable. *First Monday* is one of the best electronic journals devoted to the Internet.

3922. *JavaWorld: fueling innovation.* [ISSN: 1091-8906] 1996. m. Ed(s): Carolyn Wong. Web Publishing Inc, 501 Second St, Ste 310, San Francisco, CA 94107; http://www.javaworld.com. Illus., adv. Circ: 140000. Vol. ends: Dec. *Bk. rev.:* 5-8, 100 words. *Aud.:* Ga, Sa.

This web-based magazine covers Java programming language and the related technologies. It aims at Java beginners as well as experienced developers. Besides in-depth articles, it also features news, reports, reviews, and other items of interest to the Java community. The web site is well organized and searchable. Its weekly version is available through e-mail. This is a solid publication.

3923. *Netsurfer Digest.* 1994. w. Free. Ed(s): Arthur Bebak, Lawrence Nyveen. Netsurfer Digest, 333 Cobalt Way, Ste 107, Sunnyvale, CA 94086; editor@netsurf.com; http://www.netsurf.com/nsd/. *Aud.:* Ga.

Published since 1994, this weekly publication is one of the oldest existing web-based magazines. It features news, reviews, analyses, and other items of interest to the public. It is mainly a gateway to selected online resources. In most cases, it summarizes and classifies external resources and provides hyperlinks to them. In its own words, it provides "an informative and entertaining snapshot of the vast wired world." The publication is well organized and current. All back issues are available online and searchable. The publication is also delivered freely via e-mail to subscribers.

3924. *The Perl Journal (Online Edition).* Formerly: *The Perl Journal (Print Edition).* [ISSN: 1545-7567] 1996. m. USD 12. Ed(s): Jon Orwant. C M P Publications, Inc., 600 Community Dr, Manhasset, NY 11030; http://www.cmp.com. Adv. Circ: 16000 Paid. *Aud.:* Ga, Ac, Sa.

The print version of this journal has ceased publication, and now it is available online only. It is by and for Perl programmers. Most articles seek to cover new developments of Perl programs, including modules, packages, tool kits, and applications. Still others explore more basic issues, such as patterns in Perl and object-oriented Perl. Coding is extensive. The journal also includes a news column, which covers news about the Perl community. This is a very solid journal of one of the most important web programming languages.

3925. *The Scout Report.* [ISSN: 1092-3861] w. University of Wisconsin at Madison, Computer Sciences Department, 5355a Computer Sciences and Statistics, 1210 West Dayton St, Madison, WI 53706; scout@cs.wisc.edu; http://scout.wisc.edu/. *Aud.:* Ems, Hs, Ac.

This well-respected publication of the Internet Scout Project highlights current Internet resources of interest to educators and researchers. It covers news, tools, and research articles. Although most materials are external resources on other web sites, they are very well selected, annotated, cataloged, and organized. Due to a lack of funding, the project has decided to cease publishing all its subject reports, e.g., *Scout Reports for Social Sciences and Humanities.* Its flagship publication, namely *Scout Report* itself, will still be published regularly. The web site provides a sophisticated search engine. All materials are searchable by Library of Congress subject headings, among other fields. This search feature is rare in freely available online resources.

■ JOURNALISM AND WRITING

Journalism/Writing

Caroline M. Kent, Head of Research Services, Widener Library, Harvard University, Cambridge, MA 02138, cmkent@fas.harvard.edu

Gary B. Thompson, Director of Library and Audiovisual Services, Siena College, Loudonville, NY 12211-1462

Catherine Crohan, Serials Librarian and Coordinator of Instruction, Siena College, Loudonville, NY 12211-1462

Introduction

Journalism and writing are in an interesting state of transition: the web has certainly wrought vast changes in reporting and our expectations of access to news. Journalistic web sites provide sound bites of breaking news along with full coverage of in-depth stories: witness the immediate updates from the latest conflict with Iraq, including gruesome pictures posted on the web to prove the deaths of Saddam Hussein's sons. Meanwhile, the increasing popularity and use of blogs and wikis are challenging our conceptions of what journalism, writing, and editing are. At the same time, we're witnessing stunning developments at more traditional institutions: the 2003 scandal at *The New York* involving a young reporter who apparently plagiarized and made up many stories at the country's paper of record caused top-level editorial resignations and a fundamental reexamination of journalistic conduct and ethics.

The journals in this section concentrate on conventional journalism and writing as we have known them, although you'll find that many of the articles in them explore new global and cooperative venues for self-expression (blogging) and community creation of documents (wikis). Writing journals listed here are directed more to individual practitioners, while the journalism titles tend more toward the academic. But it seems very possible that current trends may make the boundaries between these two areas less distinguishable: with Google buying Blogger.com earlier this year, it seems likely that more writers and reporters will be taking to the web both to read and report the news and their thoughts, minute by minute, byte by byte.

Basic Periodicals

JOURNALISM. Hs: *Communication: Journalism Education Today;* Ga: *American Journalism Review, Columbia Journalism Review, Editor & Publisher, Online Journalism Review;* Ac: *Columbia Journalism Review, Editor & Publisher, The Harvard International Journal of Press - Politics, Journalism and Mass Communication Educator, Newspaper Research Journal, Online Journalism Review.*

WRITING. Hs: *Writer's Digest;* Ga: *Poets & Writers Magazine, Writer's Block, Writer's Digest;* Ac: *Technical Communication, The Writing Center Journal.*

Basic Abstracts and Indexes

JOURNALISM. *Communication Abstracts, Humanities Index.*

WRITING. *Readers' Guide to Periodical Literature.*

Journalism

3926. *American Editor.* Formerly (until 1995): *American Society of Newspaper Editors. Bulletin.* [ISSN: 1083-5210] 1926. 9x/yr. USD 29; USD 34.50 Canada; USD 44 elsewhere. Ed(s): Craig Branson. American Society of Newspaper Editors, 11690 Sunrise Valley Dr, No B, Reston, VA 20191-1409; http://www.asne.org/. Illus. Sample. Circ: 2500. *Indexed:* ABIn. *Aud.:* Ac, Sa.

This publication of the American Society of Newspaper Editors is designed to convey useful information, to put forward new ideas, and to promote debate among newspaper journalists. Articles report on successes and failures of editors facing challenges from technology, ethics, government regulation, legal cases, management, and social responsibility. Brief news items keep editors current on the latest trends and people in the industry. Online access is available to noncurrent articles back to 1996. Most useful to libraries serving prospective and practicing newspaper editors.

3927. *American Journalism Review.* Former titles (until Mar. 1993): *Washington Journalism Review;* (until 1983): *W J R;* (until 1981): *Washington Journalism Review.* [ISSN: 1067-8654] 1977. m. USD 24 domestic; USD 29.50 foreign. Ed(s): Rem Rieder. American Journalism Review, 1117 Journalism Bldg, University of Maryland, College Park, MD 20742-7111; editor@ajr.umd.edu; http://www.ajr.org. Illus., index, adv. Sample. Circ: 25000. Vol. ends: Dec. Microform: PQC. Online: EBSCO Publishing; Factiva; Florida Center for Library Automation; Gale Group; LexisNexis; Northern Light Technology, Inc.; OCLC Online Computer Library Center, Inc.; ProQuest Information & Learning; H.W. Wilson. *Indexed:* ABS&EES, ASIP, AgeL, BRI, CBRI, FLI, HumInd, PAIS, RGPR. *Bk. rev.:* 1-2, 700-1000 words. *Aud.:* Hs, Ga, Ac.

This glossy little journal has broad coverage of the American news scene. Its articles are interesting, newsy, and accessible to most readers. It basically consists of reporters reporting on reporting. There are regular columns, such as "Free Press," "Online Frontier," "First Amendment Watch," and "Books." Some recent articles titles include "Media Mood Swings," "Free to Blog?" and "The Television War." This is a good choice for high school libraries, college and university libraries, and public libraries serving the needs of active news journalists.

3928. ***Columbia Journalism Review.*** Incorporates: *More Magazine; Public Interest Alert; Media and Consumer.* [ISSN: 0010-194X] 1961. bi-m. USD 19.95 domestic; USD 4.95 newsstand/cover per issue. Ed(s): Michael Hoyt, Gloria Cooper. Columbia University, Graduate School of Journalism, Journalism Bldg, 2950 Broadway, New York, NY 10027; http://www/cjr.org. Illus., index, adv. Sample. Circ: 31000. Vol. ends: No. 6. Microform: PQC. Online: bigchalk; Chadwyck-Healey Incorporated; EBSCO Publishing; Florida Center for Library Automation; Gale Group; LexisNexis; Northern Light Technology, Inc.; OCLC Online Computer Library Center, Inc.; ProQuest Information & Learning; H.W. Wilson. Reprint: PQC; WSH. *Indexed:* ABIn, ABS&EES, BRD, BRI, CBRI, CLI, FLI, HumInd, ILP, PAIS, RGPR, SSCI. *Bk. rev.:* 4-6, 100-300 words; 1-2 1,000-2,000 words. *Aud.:* Hs, Ga, Ac.

This is a wonderfully accessible, well-edited journal full of interesting, well-written articles. It also has an excellent web site on which many of its articles are archived in full text. Its coverage ranges from journalistic practice to articles of both national and international newsworthiness. Some recent titles include "Special Report: Perspectives on the *Times*," "Rebuilding Iraq's Media," and "News in Mormon Country." The book review section is a particularly rich one. Each issue not only contains 4-6 short (100-300 word) "reports" on books, but also 1-2 very extensive and in-depth reviews. Despite its high academic pedigree, this magazine would be a very good choice not only for college and university libraries but also for high school libraries (at an excellent price!). Public libraries serving populations with high interest in current events should also consider its purchase.

3929. ***Communication: Journalism Education Today.*** [ISSN: 0010-3535] 1967. q. USD 45, Libraries, USD 30 (Students, USD 35). Ed(s): Bradley Wilson. Journalism Education Association, Inc., Kedzie Hall 103, Kansas State University, Manhattan, KS 66506; jea@spub.ksu.edu; http://www.jea.org. Illus., adv. Circ: 1900. Microform: PQC. *Indexed:* CIJE. *Aud.:* Hs, Ac.

Published by the Journalism Education Association, *Communication: Journalism Education Today* is intended for high school journalists, journalism teachers, and newspaper advisors. Articles are written by college and university faculty, practicing journalists, and high school teachers/advisors. Topics have included the necessity of math for journalists, what to look for in a college journalism program, and video journalism. Short "how I do it" articles by professionals give students a look at real-life journalism. Some articles are aimed primarily at instructors. Practical exercises for students are included in each issue. Recommended for high school libraries and academic libraries with journalism and/or teacher education programs.

3930. ***Editor & Publisher: the newsmagazine of the fourth estate since 1894.*** [ISSN: 0013-094X] 1884. 46x/yr. USD 99 combined subscription domestic print & online eds.; USD 159 combined subscription Canada print & online eds.; USD 320 combined subscription elsewhere print & online eds. Ed(s): Sidney Holt, J. J. McGrath. Editor & Publisher Co., Inc., 770 Broadway, New York, NY 10003-9595. Illus., index, adv. Sample. Circ: 20566 Paid and controlled. Vol. ends: Dec. Online: bigchalk; EBSCO Publishing; Factiva; Florida Center for Library Automation; Gale Group; OCLC Online Computer Library Center, Inc.; ProQuest Information & Learning; H.W. Wilson. Microform: PQC. Reprint: PQC. *Indexed:* ABIn, BPI, LRI. *Aud.:* Ac, Sa.

This magazine fairly claims to be "America's oldest journal covering the newspaper industry." Its format is glossy, and its articles are newsy and directed at industry members. There are many short columns and departments. Recent article titles include "Can't We All Just Get Along?" (about newspaper union issues), "The *Sun* Comes Out, but Storm Clouds Remain," and "AP Counts the Civilian Toll." University libraries, addressing the needs of future journalists, should consider purchasing this magazine. It would also be appropriate for some special industry libraries.

3931. ***Extra!*** [ISSN: 0895-2310] 1987. bi-m. USD 21 domestic; USD 31 foreign; USD 3.95 newsstand/cover domestic. Ed(s): Jim Naureckas. Fairness & Accuracy In Reporting (F.A.I.R.), 112 W. 27th St, New York, NY 10001; fair@fair.org; http://www.fair.org. Adv. Circ: 13000. *Indexed:* AltPI, PRA. *Aud.:* Ga, Ac.

FAIR (Fairness and Accuracy In Reporting) is an anti-censorship watch-group, working to create balance in media reporting. Its main publication, *Extra!*, is edgy and fascinating. Recent articles include such titles as "Department of Spin: Will Homeland Security Bureau Bottle Up News?," "Let Them Eat Cake: TV Blames Africans for Famine," and "White Noise: Voices of Color Scarce on Urban Public Radio." Like most news reporting, it is not scholarly in nature, but the publication should be added to any library collection serving the needs of journalists or journalism students.

3932. ***The Harvard International Journal of Press - Politics.*** [ISSN: 1081-180X] 1996. q. USD 302. Ed(s): Pippa Norris, Alex Jones. Sage Publications, Inc., 2455 Teller Rd, Thousand Oaks, CA 91320; info@sagepub.com; http://www.sagepub.com. Illus., adv. Refereed. Vol. ends: Fall. Online: Pub.; Ingenta Select; ingenta.com; OCLC Online Computer Library Center, Inc.; Project MUSE; RoweCom Information Quest. *Indexed:* CommAb, HRA, IPSA, PAIS, PRA, PSA, SSCI, SociolAb. *Bk. rev.:* 4-6, 100-250 words, signed. *Aud.:* Ac.

This journal, edited and published by Harvard's Kennedy School of Government, strives to address the academic needs of journalists, politicians, and political scientists. It is heavily academic, with well-written, well-referenced, refereed articles. Recent article titles include "Private and Government Sides of Tanzanian Journalists," "Is Negative Advertising Effective for Female Candidates?," and "The Political Content of Late Night Comedy." In addition to the feature articles, issues often lead off with a substantive interview with a well-known practitioner. Academic libraries in colleges or universities with strong political science, communication, or journalism programs will want this journal.

3933. ***I P I Global Journalist.*** Formerly: *I P I Report.* 1952. q. CHF 250. Ed(s): Stuart Loory. International Press Institute, Spiegelgasse 2, Vienna, 1010, Austria; http://www.freemedia.at. Illus., adv. Sample. Circ: 4000. *Aud.:* Ga, Sa.

Funded in part by the nonpartisan international foundation Freedom Forum, this journal is dedicated to the journalists of the world who defend freedom of the press and the free exchange of ideas. It is truly international in scope, with substantial reports in each issue about press freedom in four to six nations plus regular accounts of attacks on journalists around the world. The magazine consists of human-interest stories, photographs, special reports, and feature stories. Its attractive layout and readable text make it easily accessible to a wide audience. Two special issues are published: the "World Press Freedom Review" and the "IPI Congress Report." For public and academic libraries with comprehensive journalism collections or serving large international populations.

3934. ***I R E Journal.*** [ISSN: 0164-7016] 1978. 6x/yr. USD 70 (Non-members, USD 60; USD 75 foreign). Ed(s): Steve Weinberg. Investigative Reporters & Editors, Inc., 138 Neff Annex, School of Journalism, Columbia, MO 65211; journal@ire.org; http://www.ire.org. Illus., index, adv. Sample. Circ: 3500 Paid. Vol. ends: Nov/Dec. Microform: PQC. Online: EBSCO Publishing; Gale Group; OCLC Online Computer Library Center, Inc.; ProQuest Information & Learning. *Aud.:* Sa.

The *I R E Journal* is the organ of the organization Investigative Reporters and Editors. It includes member news, discussions of professional issues, awards, and conference notifications. Each issue also includes several articles, sometimes as short as a column, sometimes several pages long. Recent titles include "Following the Faithful: Investigative Reporting and Religion,"

"Torture: Iraqi Athletes Report Regime's Cruelties," and "Silent Abuse: Records, Sources Prove Long-Running Sex Abuse at State School for Deaf." This publication should be considered for any academic library serving a journalism program.

Index on Censorship. See Civil Liberties/Freedom of Expression and Information section.

3935. ***Journal of Mass Media Ethics: exploring questions of media morality.*** [ISSN: 0890-0523] 1985. q. USD 340. Ed(s): Deni Elliot, Ralph D Barney. Lawrence Erlbaum Associates, Inc., 10 Industrial Ave, Mahwah, NJ 07430-2262; journals@erlbaum.com; http://www.erlbaum.com/. Illus., adv. Sample. Refereed. Microform: PQC. Online: EBSCO Publishing; Gale Group; Ingenta Select; OCLC Online Computer Library Center, Inc.; RoweCom Information Quest; Swets Blackwell. Reprint: PSC. *Indexed:* CommAb, HumInd, PAIS, RI-1, RiskAb. *Bk. rev.:* Various number and length. *Aud.:* Ac.

Written by university faculty, the medium-length to long articles in this quarterly research journal delve into the larger ethical problems and issues confronting the mass media. Some articles are heavily philosophical and theoretical, while others report the results of surveys, case studies, and other social science research relating to the professional rights and responsibilities of journalists. Many of the articles include charts, tables, and lists of references. The targeted audience is faculty and students interested in the ethical considerations of reporting the news and the use of mass communication to inform the public on important topics. The "Case Studies and Commentaries" feature elucidates the moral dilemmas of news reporting. Most appropriate for academic libraries serving comprehensive mass communication and journalism departments.

3936. ***Journalism and Mass Communication Educator.*** Formerly: *Journalism Educator.* [ISSN: 1077-6958] 1945. q. USD 60 (Individuals, USD 35; USD 15 newsstand/cover per issue). Ed(s): Jim A Crook. Association for Education in Journalism and Mass Communication, 234 Outlet Pointe Blvd Ste A, Columbia, SC 29210-5667. Illus., index, adv. Sample. Refereed. Circ: 2500. Vol. ends: Winter. Microform: CIS; PQC. Online: Gale Group; OCLC Online Computer Library Center, Inc.; ProQuest Information & Learning. Reprint: PQC. *Indexed:* CIJE, CommAb, EduInd. *Bk. rev.:* 10-12, 250-500 words. *Aud.:* Ac.

The purpose of this journal is to provide a forum for professors of journalism and mass communication to discuss teaching philosophy and methods and the role of faculty and administrators in curriculum design and education. The journal accepts research reports, commentary, interpretive articles, and critical reviews of books, videos, software, and other teaching materials. Articles have focused on such topics as magazine design, student press law, teaching research skills, course development, and multicultural issues. There is also a section on news from the association and its members. Journalism faculty could gain new insights into teaching from this source. Recommended for college and university libraries with journalism programs.

3937. ***Journalism and Mass Communication Quarterly: devoted to research and commentary in journalism and mass communication.*** Former titles: *Journalism Quarterly;* (until 1928): *Journalism Bulletin.* [ISSN: 1077-6990] 1924. q. USD 70 (Individuals, USD 50; USD 20 newsstand/cover per issue foreign). Ed(s): Jean Folkerts. Association for Education in Journalism and Mass Communication, 234 Outlet Pointe Blvd Ste A, Columbia, SC 29210-5667. Illus., adv. Sample. Refereed. Circ: 4500 Paid. Vol. ends: Winter. Microform: PQC. Online: Gale Group; OCLC Online Computer Library Center, Inc.; ProQuest Information & Learning. *Indexed:* ABIn, ABS&EES, AgeL, AmH&L, ArtHuCI, BAS, BRI, CBRI, CIJE, CJA, CommAb, HRA, HumInd, IJCS, IPSA, LISA, LRI, MLA-IB, PAIS, PRA, PSA, PsycholAb, SFSA, SSCI, SUSA, SociolAb. *Bk. rev.:* 12-25, 700-1200 words. *Aud.:* Ac.

This scholarly journal "strives to be the flagship journal of the Association for Education in Journalism and Mass Communication." Its articles develop theory, introduce new ideas, and work to challenge the boundaries of the existing bodies of research. Its issues often contain themes, such as "Advertising Effects," "Copyright Law," and "Research Methodology." Recent articles include "Sex and Violence in Slasher Films: Re-examining the Assumptions," "Going Negative: Candidate Usage of Internet Websites during the 2000 Presidential Campaign," and "Looking Beyond Hate: How National and Regional Newspapers Framed Hate Crimes in Jasper, TX, and Laramie, WY." It is a intersting journal, filled with thoughtful, well-research articles. Any library serving academic programs in communication and journalism should include this journal in its collection.

3938. ***Journalism Studies.*** [ISSN: 1461-670X] 2000. q. GBP 176 (Individuals, GBP 48). Ed(s): Bob Franklin, Judy Van Slyke Turk. Routledge, 11 New Fetter Ln, London, EC4P 4EE, United Kingdom; journals@routldege.com; http://journals.routledge.com. Online: EBSCO Publishing; Ingenta Select; RoweCom Information Quest; Swets Blackwell. Reprint: PSC. *Indexed:* CommAb. *Bk. rev.:* 8-12, 800-1200 words. *Aud.:* Ac.

One of the ongoing complaints about Americans is that we know too little about how our nation and its actions are seen abroad. Certainly the community of journalists is more aware of contemporary foreign opinion, but there is also value in the closer looks given us by authors publishing in journals like *Journalism Studies.* This British journal, published in association with the European Journalism Training Association, is geared to serious journalists and journalism historians. It contains regular columns, such as "Debate," "Website Review," and "Feature Review." Titles of recent feature articles include "The 2000 U.S. Presidential Election in Salon.com and the *Washington Post,*" "Mourning in America: Ritual, Redemption, and Recovery in News Narrative After Sept.11," and "New Relationships: Eastern European Media and the Post-Communist Political World." Yes, this *is* a relatively expensive journal—expensive enough that some academic libraries will make the decision to not purchase it. But for university libraries serving strong journalism programs, it is invaluable. Full text is available online.

3939. ***News Media and the Law.*** Supersedes (in 1977): *Press Censorship Newsletter.* [ISSN: 0149-0737] 1973. 4x/yr. USD 30 domestic; USD 45 foreign. Ed(s): Gregg Leslie. Reporters Committee for Freedom of the Press, 1815 N Fort Myer Dr Ste 900, Arlington, VA 22209. Illus., index, adv. Sample. Circ: 3500. Vol. ends: Fall. Microform: PQC. Online: EBSCO Publishing; Gale Group; ProQuest Information & Learning. Reprint: PQC; WSH. *Indexed:* CLI, ILP, LRI. *Aud.:* Sa.

The Reporters Committee for the Freedom of the Press (RCFP) has created this journal as a resource for reporters and editors in the defense of their legal rights and professional obligations. Regular columns give an overview and a roundup of national and state legislation and cases dealing with freedom of information, confidentiality, libel, privacy, prior restraint, broadcasting, and copyright. Each issue has a cover story discussing the rights and responsiblities of the press. There are important tips for reporters facing legal action relating to disclosure of sources and subpoenas, with appropriate legal citations. The "Sources & Citations" section at the back of each issue lists all court cases, bills, and statutes cited in the issue, with page-number referencing. A vital source for libraries serving preprofessional and practicing journalists. The RCFP also maintains a daily web site and a toll-free hotline to provide information on news concerning threats to press freedom and advice on how to handle first amendment and freedom-of-information issues.

News Photographer. See Photography section.

3940. ***Newspaper Research Journal.*** [ISSN: 0739-5329] 1979. q. USD 50, Libraries, USD 40 (Individuals, USD 40). Ed(s): Ralph Izard. Association for Education in Journalism and Mass Communication, 234 Outlet Pointe Blvd Ste A, Columbia, SC 29210-5667. Illus. Refereed. Circ: 900. Vol. ends: Fall. Microform: PQC. Online: bigchalk; EBSCO Publishing; Florida Center for Library Automation; Gale Group; Northern Light Technology, Inc.; OCLC Online Computer Library Center, Inc.; ProQuest Information & Learning. Reprint: PQC. *Indexed:* CommAb, PRA, SUSA. *Bk. rev.:* 3-5, 500-750 words. *Aud.:* Ac.

This scholarly journal is intended to address both the needs of the academic journalism student and the serious practitioner. Its articles are well written, interesting, and often practical. Sometimes an entire issue will be dedicated to a particular topic, such as a recent one on September 11th. In others, a wide selection of articles is present, titles such as "Combat, Political Violence: Top International News Catagories." Libraries supporting serious journalism programs should consider this journal.

3941. ***Nieman Reports.*** [ISSN: 0028-9817] 1947. q. USD 20 domestic; USD 30 foreign. Ed(s): Melissa Ludtke. Nieman Foundation, Harvard University, 1 Francis Ave, Cambridge, MA 02138. Illus., index, adv. Circ: 6022. Vol. ends: Dec. CD-ROM: ProQuest Information & Learning. Online: bigchalk; EBSCO Publishing; Florida Center for Library Automation; Gale Group; Northern Light Technology, Inc.; OCLC Online Computer Library Center, Inc.; ProQuest Information & Learning; SoftLine Information. Reprint: PQC. *Indexed:* ABIn, BEL&L, RI-1. *Bk. rev.:* 3-6, 700-1,500 words, signed. *Aud.:* Ga, Ac.

This journal provides thought-provoking articles on the wider economic, political, and technological issues impacting the American and worldwide press. Recent issues present forums of journalists, public advocates, and experts discussing the Internet and the media, "watchdog" journalism, and photojournalism. "Journalist's Trade" includes interviews and commentaries from leading journalists about changes in news gathering and reporting. As a communication medium for the Nieman Foundation at Harvard, issues contain letters to the editors, international field reports from Nieman fellows, and obituaries of Nieman fellows. With a readable text on important public debates faced by journalists, it is suitable for academic libraries with journalism programs and for public libraries.

3942. ***Presstime.*** Supersedes (in 1979): *American Newspaper Publishers Association, Research Institute. R I Bulletins.* [ISSN: 0194-3243] 1979. m. USD 140 domestic; USD 150 foreign. Ed(s): Terence Poltrack. Newspaper Association of America, 1921 Gallows Rd, Ste 600, Vienna, VA 22182-3900; http://www.naa.org. Illus., adv. Circ: 16800. Microform: CIS. Online: LexisNexis. *Indexed:* AgeL, EngInd. *Aud.:* Ac,Sa.

This glossy, newsy magazine is intended for newspaper professionals. It covers all aspects of the newspaper biz, from production issues to staffing to writing and marketing. There are regular departments, such as "Public Policy," "Workforce," "Marketing," and "Digital Edge." Recent articles include such titles as "Trends and Numbers: Circulation Survey Finds New Emphasis on Customer Services," "World Press Outlook," and "Pring and Online Synergy." This is not an academic journal, but academic libraries serving active journalism programs should consider it. Any special library serving newspaper professionals should purchase it.

3943. ***Quill (Greencastle): the magazine for journalists.*** [ISSN: 0033-6475] 1912. m. USD 35 domestic; USD 54 foreign. Ed(s): Jeff D Mohl. Society of Professional Journalists, Eugene S. Pullman National Journalism Center, 3909 N Meridian St, Indianapolis, IN 46208; spj@spj.org; http://www.spj.org. Illus. Sample. Circ: 18000 Paid. Vol. ends: Dec. Microform: PQC. Online: bigchalk; The Dialog Corporation; EBSCO Publishing; Florida Center for Library Automation; Gale Group; OCLC Online Computer Library Center, Inc.; ProQuest Information & Learning; H.W. Wilson. *Indexed:* ABIn, HumInd. *Aud.:* Sa.

As the official publication of the Society of Professional Journalists (SPJ), *Quill* publishes articles and commentary that deal with developments in print and electronic journalism, including discussions of technology, laws and regulations, diversity, freedom of information, professional standards, and education. The articles are accessible to a wide range of readers. "People & Places" reports on news of the membership. Each issue also incorporates the *SPJ Report*, which reports news of the society's regional chapters. Libraries serving practicing journalists will want this publication.

Writing

3944. ***The Author.*** [ISSN: 0005-0628] 1890. q. Non-members, GBP 24. Ed(s): Derek Parker. Society of Authors, 84 Drayton Gardens, London, SW10 9SB, United Kingdom; info@societyof authors.org; http://www.societyofauthors.org. Adv. Circ: 7500. Microform: PQC. Reprint: PQC. *Indexed:* BrHumI. *Aud.:* Ga,Ac.

There are many areas where British and American writers have little in common, such as their countries' publishing practices. However, there are constants in the life of writing that have no geographic boundaries. *The Author* is an old, particularly thoughtful journal on writing for writers. Its coming events, conferences, and classifieds may not hold much interest for all American writers, but its articles make the journal well worth purchasing. A couple of recent article titles are "The Grateful Dead: The World of Obituary Writing" and "A Room with No View—Where I Work." Any academic library with a community of writers or with a writing program should acquire this journal.

3945. ***Computers and Composition: an international journal for teachers of writing.*** [ISSN: 8755-4615] 1983. 4x/yr. EUR 251 (Individuals, EUR 61). Ed(s): Dr. Gail E. Hawisher, Cynthia L Selfe. Elsevier Ltd., The Boulevard, Langford Ln, Oxford, OX5 1GB, United Kingdom. Refereed. Vol. ends: No. 18. *Indexed:* CIJE, EduInd, MLA-IB. *Bk. rev.:* 1-4, 2,500-3,000 words. *Aud.:* Ac.

As the official journal for the Alliance for Computers and Writing, this scholarly publication "is devoted to exploring the use of computers in writing classes, writing programs, and writing research." Among the many themed issues are "Computers, Composition and Gender," "Tenure 2000," and "Digital Rhetoric, Digital Literacy, and Computers and Composition." Each issue contains one to four lengthy book reviews. There is an excellent web version with the complete archives searchable by contents keyword, chronological order, and alphabetically by author. Recommended for academic libraries.

3946. ***Issues in Writing: education, government, arts and humanities, business and industry, science and technology.*** [ISSN: 0897-0696] 1988. s-a. USD 24; USD 28 foreign. Ed(s): M Wade Mahon. University of Wisconsin at Stevens Point, Department of English, 2100 Main St, Stevens Point, WI 54481; wmahon@uwsp.edu; http://www.uwsp.edu/acad/eng/iw/. Adv. Refereed. *Indexed:* EduInd, L&LBA. *Bk. rev.:* 6-7 per issue, 1,500-4,000 words. *Aud.:* Ac.

There are simply not many journals that are directed at teaching writing across the disciplines. This nice little journal published out of the University of Wisconsin—Stevens Point was designed to "provide insight for teachers in all desciplines who must prepare students to write effectively." Recent article titles include "Rethinking Plagiarism: What Our Students Tell Us When They Cheat" and "An Informal Survey of College Writing Instruction in the Philippines." Each issue also contains several authoritative and substantive book reviews. Recommended for colleges and universities where teaching writing is regarded as an important faculty activity.

3947. ***Journal of Technical Writing and Communication.*** [ISSN: 0047-2816] 1971. q. USD 237 (Individuals, USD 60). Ed(s): Charles H Sides. Baywood Publishing Co., Inc., 26 Austin Ave, Amityville, NY 11701; info@baywood.com; http://www.baywood.com. Illus., index. Sample. Refereed. Vol. ends: No. 4. *Indexed:* ArtHuCI, CIJE, CommAb, EngInd, IAA, L&LBA, SSCI. *Bk. rev.:* Various number and length. *Aud.:* Ac, Sa.

Designed for practitioners and teachers, this journal explores a wide range of topics related to business, scientific, and technical communication, including conceptual frameworks, mechanics, technology, and pedagogy. Contributors are mainly university professors representing departments of technical writing, English, business, and the sciences. The lengthy articles present social science research findings, historical studies, new theoretical constructs, and reviews and commentaries on the current practice of technical writing. For academic and special libraries.

3948. ***Poets & Writers Magazine.*** Formerly (until 1987): *Coda: Poets and Writers Newsletter.* [ISSN: 0891-6136] 1972. bi-m. USD 19.95 domestic; USD 29.95 Canada; USD 35.95 elsewhere. Ed(s): Therese Eiben. Poets & Writers, Inc., 72 Spring St, New York, NY 10012; http://www.pw.org. Illus., adv. Circ: 71000. Microform: PQC. Online: Gale Group. Reprint: PQC. *Indexed:* HumInd. *Aud.:* Ga, Ac.

Poets and Writers Magazine, published since 1973, is considered the premier writers-on-writers journal. It often contains extensive interviews with well-known and thoughtful writers. Other articles cover historical issues, publishing-industry news, and genre writing. Some recent article titles include "Living

Large: A Conversation with Nadine Gordimer," "Translation, Please: Why We Need It More than Ever," and "From Bosnia with Love: An Interview with Aleksandar Hemon." There are also regular columns, such as "The Practical Writer" and "The Literary Life." The "Resources" section has huge listings of grants, awards, fellowships, and other classifieds. Any public library serving a community of writers should purchase this title, and academic libraries serving writing programs should include it in their collection.

3949. ***Technical Communication.*** [ISSN: 0049-3155] 1953. q. USD 60. Ed(s): George Hayhoe. Society for Technical Communication, 901 N Stuart St, Ste 904, Arlington, VA 22203-1822; http://www.stc-va.org/publicationsframe.html. Illus., index, adv. Refereed. Circ: 17000. Vol. ends: No. 4. Microform: MIM; PMC; PQC. Online: EBSCO Publishing; Florida Center for Library Automation; Gale Group; Northern Light Technology, Inc.; OCLC Online Computer Library Center, Inc.; ProQuest Information & Learning. Reprint: PQC. *Indexed:* AbAn, BPI, CIJE, CommAb, IAA, InfoSAb, LISA, MagInd, SSCI. *Bk. rev.:* 10-12, 500-800 words each. *Aud.:* Ac, Sa.

This is a professional journal for technical writers, being the major publication of the Society for Technical Communication. Regular departments include correspondence, editorials, technology, and association news. Two other departments provide substantial book reviews and shorter abstracts of articles appearing in other professional journals. Major articles appear under the following topics: "Applied Theory," "Case History," "Review of Research," "Tutorials," "The Practice," and "Global Perspectives." Recent issues focus on special topics of professional interest, such as information design, heuristics, and knowledge management. Contributors are affiliated with corporations, universities, communication firms, vendors, and research laboratories. For academic and special libraries serving technical writers.

3950. ***The Writer.*** [ISSN: 0043-9517] 1887. m. Individuals, USD 29; USD 4.95 newsstand/cover per issue. Ed(s): Elfrieda Abbe. Kalmbach Publishing Co., PO Box 1612, Waukesha, WI 53187-1612; http://www.kalmbach.com. Illus., index, adv. Circ: 37000 Paid. Vol. ends: Dec. *Indexed:* IAPV, MagInd, RGPR. *Aud.:* Hs, Ga.

This long-established magazine has undergone some major changes. Longtime editor and publisher Sylvia K. Burack retired, selling *The Writer* to Kalmbach Publishing. The publication now sports a glossy cover, color illustrations, and photographs. The quality of the information remains high, providing how-to articles on all types of writing including children's fiction, screenwriting, poetry, fillers, and travel writing. There are interviews with established authors. The "Market Focus" section advises writers of publication opportunities, and "Dear Writer" provides commonsense answers to writers' questions. There are additional market listings, and contest and conference announcements. Although all writers will find this publication useful, *The Writer* is especially useful for beginning writers. Recommended for high school libraries and libraries that serve the general public.

3951. ***The Writer's Chronicle.*** Formerly (until 1998): *A W P Newsletter.* [ISSN: 1529-5443] 1970. 6x/yr. USD 20 domestic; USD 25 Canada; USD 3.95 newsstand/cover per issue domestic. Ed(s): David W Fenza. Associated Writing Programs, Tallwood House, Mail Stop 1E3, Fairfax, VA 22030; awpchron@mason.gmu.edu; http://awpwriter.org. Adv. Circ: 20000. *Aud.:* Ga, Ac.

Published by the Associated Writing Programs (AWP), a nonprofit literary and educational organization, *The Writer's Chronicle* should be of interest to all creative writers. "AWP's mission is to foster literary talent and achievement, to advance the art of writing as essential to a good education, and to serve the makers, teachers, students, and readers of contemporary writing." Each issue features one or two interviews with established authors. Articles titles include "The Yin & Yang of Teaching Creative Writing," "The Electronic Marketplace for Writers," and "Breaking into Book Publishing." This tabloid publication regularly lists opportunities for grants and awards, as well as conferences. Advertisements promote degree programs. Free to AWP members, it is recommended for large public libraries and academic libraries supporting creative writing programs.

3952. ***Writer's Digest.*** [ISSN: 0043-9525] 1920. m. USD 19.96 domestic; CND 29.96 Canada; USD 54.96 elsewhere. Ed(s): David A Fryxell. F & W Publications, Inc., 1507 Dana Ave, Cincinnati, OH 45207; http://www.fwpublications.com. Illus., index, adv. Sample. Circ: 170000 Paid. Vol. ends: Dec. Microform: MIM; PQC. Online: bigchalk; Gale Group; OCLC Online Computer Library Center, Inc.; ProQuest Information & Learning. Reprint: PQC. *Indexed:* ASIP, IHTDI, MagInd, RGPR. *Aud.:* Hs, Ga, Ac.

Writer's Digest continues to offer high-quality practical information for all types of writers. There are regular columns on fiction, nonfiction, electronic publishing, and zines (both print and electronic). Each issue usually includes an interview with or an article by a well-known author. Feature articles discuss such topics as freelancing, copyright, computer issues, and self-promotion. Each issue includes a writing assignment challenging the reader to submit entries for a small prize. "The Markets" lists various potential markets for selling fiction, articles, poetry, and other forms of marketable writing. There are pages of advertising and classifieds. *Writer's Digest* is enjoyable to read and is recommended for most libraries. A companion e-mail newsletter, *Tips & Updates from Writer's Digest*, is available free of charge.

3953. ***The Writing Center Journal.*** [ISSN: 0889-6143] 1979. 2x/yr. USD 10 domestic; USD 15 foreign. Ed(s): Albert De Ciccio, Joan Mullin. National Writing Centers Association, c/o Albert De Ciccio, Rivier College, Nashua, MA 03060-5086; jmullin@uoft02.utoledo.edu. Adv. Refereed. Circ: 800. *Indexed:* CIJE, MLA-IB. *Bk. rev.:* 2, 1,200-1,500 words. *Aud.:* Ac.

This refereed publication of the National Writing Centers Association is a key journal for administrators and faculty of college and university writing centers. Articles cover the theoretical and the practical. Recent articles examine tutor training, the viability of writing centers on academic campuses, and the "Confessions of a First-Time Writing Center Director." There is an occasional article about writing centers in secondary education. Each issue contains two lengthy book reviews, plus calls for papers and conference proposals. "News from the Association" includes the minutes of the semi-annual meetings. An important journal for academic libraries.

Electronic Journals

3954. ***The Internet Writing Journal.*** [ISSN: 1095-3973] 1997. m. Writers Write, Inc., 8214 Westchester Ste 500, Dallas, TX 75225; journal@writerswrite.com; http://www.writerswrite.com/journal. Illus., adv. *Bk. rev.:* Numerous, 150-200 words. *Aud.:* Ga.

The Internet Writing Journal is billed as "The Online Monthly Magazine for Writers and Book Lovers since 1997." Both will find much to enjoy. Each issue includes at least two interviews with established authors, feature articles, and news of contests and conferences. Sample topics include the how-to of songwriting, how to get a book contract, publicity, and e-book publishing. The book review section is not limited to nonfiction writing resources; there are reviews of all types of fiction including fantasy/science fiction, mystery, romance, and children's books. All back issues are archived. Excellent use of format and graphics makes this an easily read publication. Highly recommended for public library audiences.

Kairos. See Education/Specific Subjects and Teaching Methods/Communication Arts section.

3955. ***Online Journalism Review.*** [ISSN: 1522-6883] 1998. w. Ed(s): Joshua S Fouts. Annenberg School for Communication, University Park Campus, Los Angeles, CA 90089; fouts@usc.edu; http://www.ojr.org/. Illus. *Aud.:* Ga, Ac.

Online Journalism Review is produced by the Annenberg School for Communication in Los Angeles. The intended audience is "journalists and anyone interested in where journalism is going in cyberspace," and there aren't many of us who don't fit into the latter category. The site contains columns and sections on business, law, and ethics, to name a few, plus web site reviews. Recent article titles include "Moblogs Seen as a Crystal Ball for a New Era in Online Journalism," "Afghans' Thirst for Web Access," and "Are Online Search Tools Lulling Journalists Into Laziness?" Like many effective e-zines, the content shifts quickly, and the site contains some non-journal-like content such as online forums. However, material is archived and dated, and web site interactivity is simply part of the newly emerging format. Any academic library, with or without journalism or communications programs, should link to this resource. In addition, many public libraries with technologically savvy patrons should provide a link to it.

3956. ***Writer On Line.*** 1998. m. Ed(s): Terry Boothman. Novation Learning Systems, Incorporated, 190 Mount Vernon Ave., Rochester, NY 14620; email@novalearn.com; http://www.novalearn.com/wol. Circ: 35000. *Aud.:* Ga.

This electronic journal is a practical source of information and inspiration for all types of writers, including practitioners of creative nonfiction, business writing, and technical writing. It contains a small section of short fiction and poetry. There are links to publisher news, courses for writers, conference and contest information, and classifieds. Searching the archives is eased by subject arrangement. It is tied closely to the Write/Read.com web site. Recommended for public libraries.

3957. ***Writer's Block: the Canadian E-zine for the writing trade.*** [ISSN: 1488-4801] 1995. irreg. Ed(s): Dalya Goldberger. NIVA Inc., 500-1145 Hunt Club Rd, Ottawa, ON K1V 0Y3, Canada; dgoldberger@niva.com; http://www.writersblock.ca/. *Bk. rev.:* 1, 700-1,200 words. *Aud.:* Ga, Sa.

This electronic publication is oriented toward professional writers, editors, and publishers. Feature stories cover such topics as the necessary talents needed to be a creative writer, interviewing techniques, and how to work as part of a creative team. Other sections focus on the business aspects of creative writing, the changing uses of technology, and the use of words. There is usually one book review per issue plus a short essay, story, or poem. This publication makes good use of graphics. The archives include all back issues. Although this publication is "aimed at Canadians in the writing trade," most articles are suitable for a wider audience. A good offering for public and special libraries.

3958. ***Writing for Money (Online Edition): the Internet newsletter that shows you how to make money and live a great life as a freelance writer.*** 1993. d. USD 99. Ed(s): John Clausen. Newmarket Media, Inc., PO Box 6124, Hendersonville, NC 28793; http://www.writingformoney.com. *Aud.:* Ga.

This electronic newsletter focuses on the business side of freelance writing. Sample articles include information on contract negotiation, finance, marketing one's writing, and ghostwriting. Unfortunately, the articles are not dated—this would be helpful. "Who's Buying What" lists specific markets for freelancers (magazines, book publishers, agents, commercial and technical writing, etc.) with their requirements and payment information. These market listings are useful and are added to frequently, but publications such as *The Writer* and *Writer's Digest* provide more extensive market listings. The "Market Reports" section does a nice job reviewing the opportunities available in specific writing fields such fitness writing, travel writing, greeting cards, and romance writing. Available by paid subscription, *Writing for Money* also has a free version available from the same web site. The current articles and complete market listings are available only from the subscriber site, but the complete archives of past articles is available from both. Public libraries will want to provide a link to the site so that patrons can access the free version.

3959. ***The Writing Instructor (Online Edition).*** 2001. irreg. Ed(s): Dawn Formo, David Blakesley. The Writing Instructor, c/o Dawn Formo, ed., Literature & Writing Studies Program, San Marcos, CA 92096-0001. Refereed. *Bk. rev.:* 1-2 1,500 words. *Aud.:* Ac.

This journal is targeted at teachers and professors of writing and covers a broad range of topics related to educational theories and practical experience at the college level. The emphasis is on general concepts of composition. Conferences, calls for manuscripts, and book reviews of interest to writing instructors are included. *The Writing Instructor* is now published exclusively as a web-based journal. A specialized journal for college and university libraries supporting writing programs.

■ LABOR AND INDUSTRIAL RELATIONS

See also Business; Disabilities; Economics; and Occupations and Careers sections.

Jane Cramer, Government Publications, Periodicals and Microforms Librarian, Brooklyn College Library, 2900 Bedford Ave., Brooklyn, NY 11210; janec@brooklyn.cuny.edu

Introduction

One of the magazines included here is aptly named: *World of Work.* That sums up the focus of this section fairly well. The workplace is changing as companies are downsizing, the population is aging, computers are allowing workers to move out of the office, and less costly part-time workers are replacing full-time employees. Globalization has become an increasingly important issue, as has the effort to organize white-collar and part-time workers. New laws, regulations, and international agreements have all changed the workplace.

That said, the nature of the publications in this area stays fairly constant. There is an interesting mix of pragmatic how-to journals both for workers and management. The human resources/benefits journals are well organized, concise, accessible to both managers and recipients, and mostly free of jargon. Articles are most often written by practitioners. The discipline also has a substantial body of scholarly literature covering labor history, labor law, and labor economics. In addition, there are industrial relations journals, many of which are interdisciplinary and representing almost all areas of scholarship. Notably, they draw from the fields of economics, sociology, psychology, and history, although even mathematics and philosophy appear. The union publications are vastly different in opinion and style, from the IWW, the old-timer on the scene, to the AFL-CIO with its slick online publications. In between, there are grassroots organizers operating on a shoestring, international movements organizing globally, organizations devoted solely to opening the eyes of workers to union abuses, as well as the loyal opposition composed of union members who simply want the system to work better. The International Labor Organization (ILO) supports its mission by publishing both reliable statistics about workers worldwide and educational materials.

Unions are finding it necessary to reinvent themselves in order to remain viable in this changed environment. Classes of workers who had not considered themselves union material are finding that there may be advantages to collective bargaining. In less developed parts of the world, unions often find themselves involved in more than workplace issues as they join with larger social and environmental movements. New players such as the Anarchist movement and grassroots organizers who are not fans of big unionism are also asserting themselves.

Globalization of industries and economies is an increasingly important factor in the interaction between labor and management. Western nations are finding that many of their heavy industries are gone. There are gaps in the workforce where skilled labor is being forced out and service industries are having trouble recruiting. Business and educational institutions are finding that they need to forge partnerships to produce workers with the necessary skills for an evolving workplace. Workers in less developed parts of the world want the benefits and advantages of similar workers in more developed countries. NAFTA has had a huge impact on North American workers, and this shows up in the study of industrial relations.

The United States is an extremely litigious society, and the workplace is fertile ground for lawsuits. The maze of new laws and regulations can begin to sound to like something from Alice in Wonderland. Publications that offer sound legal analysis and regulations are essential, particularly with regard to the Americans with Disabilities Act and the rising tide of sexual harassment litigation. *Labor Law Journal, Labor Notes, Employee Benefits Journal,* and the *Berkeley Journal of Employment and Labor Law* are all excellent resources for making sense of a very complicated area of law and regulation. Most offer updates on legislation, regulatory changes, and judicial rulings. The ILO's online database, NATLEX, which has "bibliographic references to and full texts of national laws on labour, social security and related human rights," helps users keep up with international law on the subject. It is a wonderful resource for anyone working with foreign labor law.

Although publications from specific unions are not included here, many can be found online. Two good sources of links are *Laborhood* (www.people-link.org/neighborhoods/index.html) and *LaborNet* (www.labornet.org/links/directory.html). Publications by larger trade union associations such as the AFL-CIO, IWW, ILO, and ICFTU attempt to cover both the concerns of specific unions and broader issues confronting labor at large. Along with alerts of strikes, boycotts, and newly organized shops, these publications reflect the growing sophistication of the movement in the twenty-first century. The ILO focuses particularly on the developing world and labor trends there. This fills an important niche, particularly at a time when world debt and globalization are major economic issues worldwide.

A few standout web sites include *Workindex, LabourStart, LaborNet,* and the ILO's *World of Work.*

Most titles are now available online; however, many are no longer freely available to nonsubscribers. The larger aggregators provide good coverage of the discipline, and whatever package your library chooses, you should find a good selection of reputable titles in this area. All aspects of labor and industrial relations are vital and fascinating areas of study, with a large audience of both administrators and workers.

Basic Periodicals

Hs: *Bulletin of Labour Statistics;* Ga: *America at Work, LaborNet, Labor's Heritage, U.S. Bureau of Labor Statistics. Monthly Labor Review;* Ac: *Bulletin of Labour Statistics, Industrial and Labor Relations Review, Labor History, LaborNet, Workindex, World of Work;* Sa: *Benefits Quarterly, Employee Benefits Journal, Employee Relations Law Journal, Japan Labour Bulletin.*

Basic Abstracts and Indexes

ABI/INFORM, America: History and Life, Business Periodicals Index, PAIS, Social Sciences Index, Work Related Abstracts.

3960. ***America at Work.*** Formerly (until 1996): *A F L - C I O News.* [ISSN: 1091-594X] 1955. m. Members, USD 14.95. Ed(s): Tula Cornell. American Federation of Labor - Congress of Industrial Organizations, Public Affairs Department, 815 16th St, N W, Washington, DC 20006; atwork@aflcio.org; http://www.aflcio.org/. Illus. Circ: 55000. Vol. ends: Dec. Microform: PQC. *Indexed:* MCR. *Bk. rev.:* Occasional, short. *Aud.:* Ga, Ac, Sa.

This glossy, 24-page, heavily illustrated monthly, in conjunction with the online newsletter *Work in Progress,* replaces the tabloid *AFL-CIO News. America at Work* features brief news articles on labor activists and issues and workforce trends. An official AFL-CIO publication, it presents the unionist viewpoint in the United States, although the magazine covers international work and union issues and events as well. Many of the articles focus on the concerns and needs of working families. The content is attractively presented, half in short news items and the rest in a few more substantive pieces per issue. "Voices" prints letters from readers, and "Currents" consists of short articles on union concerns and activities. A roundup at the end gives updates on union leaders and actions. Short reviews of books, music, art, and events of interest to union members are also included. The stated goal is to provide organizers and activists "creating change for working families with ideas, info, and ammo" to carry on their work. Good for libraries supporting labor relations, business, or economics programs, or for libraries with union members as patrons.

3961. ***Benefits Quarterly.*** [ISSN: 8756-1263] 1985. q. USD 100. Ed(s): Jack L Vanderhei. International Society of Certified Employee Benefit Specialists, Inc., PO Box 209, Brookfield, WI 53008-0209; iscebs@ifebp.org. Illus., index, adv. Sample. Circ: 17000. Vol. ends: Dec. Online: Northern Light Technology, Inc.; OCLC Online Computer Library Center, Inc.; ProQuest Information & Learning. *Indexed:* ABIn, AgeL, PAIS. *Bk. rev.:* 6-8, 200-500 words. *Aud.:* Sa.

This sleek, streamlined journal gets right to point. Anyone working in or studying human relations or any aspect of benefits and compensation needs to have this magazine at hand. Articles offer an opening precis and guide the reader quickly to main points using bold-faced subheadings; major concepts are summarized in the margins, and readers can quickly locate the information they need most. Articles focus on introducing new trends and innovations in the field, often offering new techniques or approaches to problems. There are also analytical articles on the impact of new legislation or judicial rulings as well. Most issues deal with one topic in depth, such as prescription drugs, health and retirement, outsourcing, executive compensation, and defined-contribution health plans. Each issue also includes an overview of legal developments, a book abstract section, and the extremely helpful "Review of Current Literature," which alerts readers to significant articles in other publications. While this journal's audience is limited, it is a must-have for its niche. Information about the journal, including summaries of articles in the current and previous issues, upcoming special topics, a subject index covering 1995 to the present, and guidelines for authors, can be found at the International Society of Certified Employee Benefit Specialists web site (http://www.iscebs.org/BQinfo). New subscribers receive a CD-ROM of the past six years' issues. Members of the organization have full-text access online.

3962. ***Berkeley Journal of Employment and Labor Law.*** Formerly (until 1993): *Industrial Relations Law Journal.* [ISSN: 1067-7666] 1976. biennial. USD 47 (Individuals, USD 36). Ed(s): Paul More. University of California, Berkeley, School of Law, Boalt Hall, Berkeley, CA 94720-7200. Illus., index, adv. Refereed. Circ: 650 Paid. Vol. ends: Dec. Microform: WSH; PQC. Online: EBSCO Publishing; Florida Center for Library Automation; Gale Group; LexisNexis. Reprint: PQC; WSH. *Indexed:* ABIn, CJA, CLI, ILP, LRI, PAIS, SSCI. *Bk. rev.:* Various number and length. *Aud.:* Ac, Sa.

Edited by law school students, this journal keeps pace with the pulse of the law. The stated goal is to provide "a source of scholarly materials" for the legal profession. Articles are well researched and, significantly, written to be useful to nonspecialists as well as legal practitioners. They cover the full spectrum of employment law including "discrimination, traditional labor law, the public sector, international and comparative labor law, benefits, and wrongful termination." An effort is made to explore topics from both a management and a labor perspective. It offers scholarly analysis of recent legal developments while also featuring articles that analyze the long-term effects of older decisions and legislation. Issues feature several scholarly research articles mixed with topical essays. Some issues deal with a single topic, such as the impact of ADA and an analysis of recent legislation and case law. Student contributions are encouraged. A very valuable section is the survey of literature containing abstracts of important articles in other journals. The "Abstracts" and "Recent Publications" sections provide an extensive listing of articles, decisions, and legislation. The overview of developments in the area of employment and labor law makes this journal worth consulting. Academic libraries should have this title.

3963. ***British Journal of Industrial Relations.*** [ISSN: 0007-1080] 1963. q. GBP 230 print & online eds. Ed(s): Stephen Wood. Blackwell Publishing Ltd., 9600 Garsington Rd, PO Box 805, Oxford, OX4 2DQ, United Kingdom; customerservices@oxon.blackwellpublishing.com; http://www.blackwellpublishing.com/. Illus., index, adv. Refereed. Circ: 2000. Vol. ends: Dec. Online: EBSCO Publishing; Gale Group; ingenta.com; OCLC Online Computer Library Center, Inc.; RoweCom Information Quest; Swets Blackwell. Reprint: PQC; SWZ. *Indexed:* ABIn, ArtHuCI, BAS, BPI, BrHumI, ErgAb, H&SSA, IBSS, IBZ, IPSA, JEL, PAIS, PSA, RiskAb, SSCI, SociolAb. *Aud.:* Ac, Sa.

This well-respected journal has shown its intention to keep its place as a leader in the field by changing its content to reflect recent changes in the discipline. Recognizing that collective bargaining and trade unions now share the field with "new forms of management, new methods of pay determination, and changes in government policies," they have broadened the scope of the content to include greater coverage of transnational matters and internationalization, encouraging contributors from a broader range of disciplines and offering readers articles on topics often overlooked. The journal addresses a broad spectrum of development in the field of industrial relations. Articles are a mix of empirical studies and theoretical papers spanning the full range of the field. Most articles cover developments in advanced industrial nations, but developing nations are also represented as globalization becomes increasingly important. Each issue has four or five substantive articles along with several shorter pieces, often with accompanying tables and charts. Recent article topics include declining union membership in the United States and other nations, union organizing and information technology, labor-management partnership in the workplace, production incentives in Spain, and a study of Israeli judicial discretion in dealing with strikers. Due to the theoretical nature of many of the articles, a familiarity with the field is helpful for a full appreciation. The journal draws well-known scholars from a wide range of fields and presents solid scholarly work that has a place in any academic collection dealing with industrial relations. A tiered subscription plan allows subscribers a variety of online access options in addition to the print copies, and nonsubscribers can use Blackwell's service to purchase individual articles from their web site.

3964. *Bulletin of Labour Statistics: supplementing the annual data presented in the Year Book of Labour Statistics.* [ISSN: 0007-4950] 1965. 4x/yr. CHF 105; USD 84. I L O Publications, PO Box 6, Geneva, 1211, Switzerland. Illus., index. Vol. ends: No. 4. *Indexed:* PAIS. *Aud.:* Ac, Sa.

An essential publication for anyone doing statistical work in this field. The ILO now makes metadata from this publication available via the Internet at laborsta.ilo.org. The country-level data on employment, unemployment, hours of work, wages, and the consumer price index allows worldwide comparison by pulling together official figures from national statistical services. The addition of statistics for Eastern European and the former Soviet republics makes this an even more valuable tool. Most countries include statistics by gender or other designations, making this useful to sociologists and others outside labor and economics. Each issue features a few substantive pieces about data and data collection or research in the field. Quarterly issues are updated by statistical supplements that can be discarded when the next quarterly issue arrives. Time series data is included semiannually for four- or five-year spans. In keeping with the multinational base of the ILO, articles are presented in English, French, and Spanish. Necessary for academic collections and large public libraries.

3965. *Dispute Resolution Journal.* Formerly (until 1993): *Arbitration Journal.* [ISSN: 1074-8105] 1937. q. USD 125. Ed(s): Susan Zuckerman. American Arbitration Association, 335 Madison Ave, New York, NY 10017; http://www.adr.org/. Illus., index. Circ: 10000. Vol. ends: Dec. Microform: PQC. Online: EBSCO Publishing; Gale Group; Northern Light Technology, Inc.; OCLC Online Computer Library Center, Inc.; ProQuest Information & Learning; H.W. Wilson. Reprint: WSH. *Indexed:* ABIn, BPI, CLI, ILP, LRI, RiskAb, SSCI. *Aud.:* Ga, Ac, Sa.

In an increasingly litigious society, alternative dispute resolution (ADR) has become more important in all areas of human endeavor but is especially crucial in the field of labor/employment law. This is a top-notch publication highlighting new developments in the field and innovative ways to use dispute resolution in the workplace, with the emphasis on alternative dispute resolution. Articles deal with the usual union/management issues but give examples of negotiation, mediation, arbitration, and other alternatives to deadlock or litigation in a wide variety of situations. However, keeping up with changes in the field, the journal is now including material dealing with "construction, technology, labor/employment, commercial, and health care, both domestic and international," as well as more traditional areas. A great deal of emphasis is given to its use in the public sector, particularly in light of federal law that guarantees public employees recourse to alternative dispute resolution. Most articles deal with the workplace and the various and new ways that dispute resolution techniques can be applied to problems. There are also interesting articles advocating the use of mediation where it may not be an obvious solution, such as in schools or in resolving cross-border trade disputes. The Americans with Disabilities Act and other subsequent legislative and regulatory changes necessitate rethinking workplace policies and practices. It has proven to be an area where dispute resolution is especially useful and productive as a means of resolving issues. Contributors are drawn from experts in international relations, business, finance, labor relations, construction, law, insurance, health care, and technology. The articles are thorough and insightful, including notes for further research. Some articles on arbitration practices abroad are included as well. In addition to the articles, important features of the magazine include ADR news, court decisions, and book reviews. This journal is essential reading for anyone involved in or studying conflict resolution, no matter which side of the table they are on.

3966. *Employee Benefit Plan Review.* [ISSN: 0013-6808] 1946. m. USD 302. Ed(s): Bruce F Spencer. Charles D. Spencer & Associates, Inc., 250 S Wacker Dr, Ste 600, Chicago, IL 60606-5834; editor@spencernet.com; http://www.spencernet.com. Illus., index, adv. Circ: 25000 Paid and controlled. Vol. ends: Jun. Microform: PQC. Online: Northern Light Technology, Inc.; OCLC Online Computer Library Center, Inc.; ProQuest Information & Learning. Reprint: PQC. *Indexed:* ABIn, AgeL, BPI, CINAHL, LRI. *Aud.:* Ga, Ac, Sa.

In addition to its primary audience of practitioners in the employee benefits field, this well-organized and frequently cited publication is also useful to academics attempting to track real-world trends and developments in the field. The whole gamut of benefits issues is included in the coverage. This publication is effective because it not only covers current practice but actively pursues information about new developments and trends. Each issue offers a collection of articles on a single topic along with reports on laws, regulations, and new practices. Articles analyze their impact and offer readers new ideas and strategies on how to use or cope with these developments. Topics featured recently include COBRA, pensions, prescription drug plans, and disability benefits. International trends and events pertinent to the field are covered, as well as U.S. practices. Other sections use short news items to update practitioners on "Reporting and Disclosure," "Health Care," "Rules and Laws," and "Courts." The legal reporting is written for the layperson without being overly simplified. Legislative updates, regulatory changes, recent rulings, and pending legislation are all covered. Contributors are drawn from the HR community, supplemented by academics from time to time. This journal is practical rather than theoretical. A skillful use of graphics with the text guides readers to the gist of the article quickly. A must for everyone who needs to stay current with the field. It is still a product of Spencer and Associates, but is now distributed by Aspen Publishing.

3967. *Employee Benefits Journal.* [ISSN: 0361-4050] 1975. q. USD 80. Ed(s): Mary Jo Brzezinski. International Foundation of Employee Benefit Plans, 18700 W Bluemound Rd, Box 69, Brookfield, WI 53008-0069; books@ifebp.org; http://www.ifebp.org. Illus., index, adv. Circ: 36000. Vol. ends: Dec. Microform: PQC. Online: EBSCO Publishing; Northern Light Technology, Inc.; OCLC Online Computer Library Center, Inc.; ProQuest Information & Learning; H.W. Wilson. *Indexed:* ABIn, AgeL, BPI. *Bk. rev.:* Notes. *Aud.:* Ga, Ac, Sa.

This journal offers substantive, definitive articles for practitioners who need to keep up with benefits issues and trends. It is hands-on rather than theoretical. "Practical articles by benefits experts" are what it claims to provide, and it does. Articles analyze trends and events as well as simply report news from the field. Some articles are technical in their exploration of increasingly complex issues. Clear writing and good use of graphics makes the material as accessible and comprehensible to nonexpert readers as to HR professionals. This is a nuts-and-bolts publication with only an occasional theoretical discussion of HR developments. Recent articles cover a range of ways of dividing scarce resources among employees, dividing health care costs between high and low risk employees, managing drug plan costs, reporting of post-employment benefits to the government, credibility in the accounting profession, and HIPP rules and compliance. The evaluation of various benefit-plan software packages should be very helpful to HR professionals. Legal aspects of benefits programs are well covered, and the "Literature Review" offers brief annotations on recent articles and books in the field. This journal is more useful than ever because it provides complete and accurate coverage of the field for professionals while maintaining its readability for students and others. A solid addition for large collections wishing to cover this aspect of labor relations.

3968. *Employee Relations Law Journal.* [ISSN: 0098-8898] 1975. q. USD 302. Ed(s): William J Kilberg, Dianne C Scent. Aspen Law & Business, 1185 Ave of the Americas, 37th Fl, New York, NY 10036; customer.service@aspenpubl.com; http://www.aspenpub.com. Illus., index, adv. Vol. ends: Spring. Microform: WSH; PMC; PQC. Online: The Dialog Corporation; EBSCO Publishing; Florida Center for Library Automation; Gale Group; Northern Light Technology, Inc.; ProQuest Information & Learning. Reprint: PQC; WSH. *Indexed:* ABIn, AgeL, BLI, BPI, CLI, ILP, LRI, PAIS, SFSA, SSCI. *Aud.:* Ac, Sa.

This very focused journal offers concise, well-organized, comprehensive coverage of developments in law and legislation pertaining to labor. For a quarter century it has provided a means for high-level HR managers, in-house counsel, and employment law specialists to keep up with the barrage of changes in the field easily and quickly. Articles are informative, analytical, and practical, but not overly technical. The "Literature Review" has signed essays. Focusing primarily on personnel management techniques, legal compliance, and court cases, recent articles address such topics as the ADA, family medical leave, sexual harassment, termination and RIFs, age discrimination, alternative dispute resolution, NLRB decisions, benefits cost management, and employment law trends. The "Update" section's columnists report regularly not only on the status but the implications of pending and recent legislation, federal regulatory agency actions, new case law affecting benefits, and labor-management decisions, making this journal especially valuable for busy executives and practicing lawyers. Contributors are practitioners, not academics, for the most part. For this aspect of law, this is the journal to chose.

3969. ***Government Union Review and Public Policy Digest: quarterly journal on public sector labor relations.*** Formerly (until 2001): *Government Union Review.* 1980. q. USD 20. Ed(s): David Y Denholm. Public Service Research Foundation, 320 Maple Ave E, Ste 4, Vienna, VA 22180-4742; info@psrf.org; http://www.psrf.org. Illus. Circ: 5000. Microform: PQC. Online: Gale Group; Northern Light Technology, Inc. Reprint: PQC; WSH. *Indexed:* ABIn, CIJE, CLI, LRI, PAIS, PSA. *Aud.:* Ac.

The nonprofit Public Service Research Foundation publishes this journal to increase awareness of why public employees' union contracts should not be merely "regarded as problems between labor and management, rather than the important questions of public policy." It provides a seldom-seen perspective on this issue. Education and teachers unions are of particular interest to the group. Articles are empirical and scholarly, often case studies based on actual events. Cost cutting in government by controlling unions is a recurring theme. Authors are from academia, think tanks, and the private sector. Issues are organized around two or three major articles, frequently on related subjects. Articles have discussed privatization of public transit, teachers unions, the use of permanent striker replacements, and workers' compensation and OSHA. Its international coverage, particularly of other industrialized nations, is quite extensive. Good for large academic libraries, and necessary for institutions with programs in industrial relations or public administration. A significant number of full-text articles are available on their web site, and even if your library does not elect to subscribe, the site should be bookmarked.

3970. ***Industrial and Labor Relations Review.*** [ISSN: 0019-7939] 1947. q. USD 52 (Individuals, USD 32; Students, USD 16). Ed(s): Tove Hammer. Cornell University, New York State School of Industrial and Labor Relations, 158 Ives Hall, Ithaca, NY 14853-3901; blk5@cornell.edu; http://www.ilr.cornell.edu/depts/ilrrev/. Illus., index, adv. Refereed. Circ: 2500. Vol. ends: Jul. Microform: WSH; PQC. Online: Chadwyck-Healey Incorporated; The Dialog Corporation; EBSCO Publishing; Florida Center for Library Automation; Gale Group; JSTOR (Web-based Journal Archive); LexisNexis; OCLC Online Computer Library Center, Inc.; ProQuest Information & Learning; West Group; H.W. Wilson. Reprint: PQC; PSC; WSH. *Indexed:* ABCPolSci, ABIn, ABS&EES, ASG, AgeL, ArtHuCI, BAS, BPI, BRD, BRI, CBRI, CIJE, CJA, CLI, HRA, IBSS, IBZ, ILP, IPSA, JEL, LRI, PAIS, PMA, PRA, PSA, PsycholAb, SSCI, SSI, SUSA, SociolAb, WSA. *Bk. rev.:* Various number and length. *Aud.:* Ac, Sa.

Published by the well-respected Cornell School of Industrial and Labor Relations this multidisciplinary journal maintains high standards for the scholarly study of industrial relations. Its empirical studies reflect all aspects of industrial relations. Articles are quantitative, very dense, and heavily statistical. The content is international in scope. Articles reflect "all aspects of the employment relationship, including collective bargaining, labor law, labor markets, social security and protective labor legislation, management and personnel, human resources, worker participation, workplace health and safety, organizational behavior, comparative industrial relations, and labor history." A thorough grounding in statistics and economic theory is required to interpret much of the material included. Research topics are international in scope; recent issues present research on Mexico, Germany, and South Africa. Book reviews are conveniently grouped by subject, and in-depth, subject-based literature reviews are included. This scholarly journal is required for serious academic collections. The web site offers tables of contents back to 1994, abstracts of articles, reports on research in progress, and subscription information.

3971. ***Industrial Relations: a journal of economy and society.*** [ISSN: 0019-8676] 1961. q. USD 185 print & online eds. Blackwell Publishing, Inc., Commerce Place, 350 Main St, Malden, MA 02148; subscrip@blackwellpub.com; http://www.blackwellpublishing.com. Illus., index, adv. Refereed. Circ: 2300. Vol. ends: Fall. Microform: PQC. Online: EBSCO Publishing; Gale Group; ingenta.com; OCLC Online Computer Library Center, Inc.; RoweCom Information Quest; Swets Blackwell. Reprint: SCH. *Indexed:* ABIn, AgeL, BPI, CBCARef, CJA, CLI, ErgAb, H&SSA, IBSS, IPSA, JEL, LRI, PAIS, PMA, PSA, RiskAb, SSCI, SWR&A, SociolAb. *Bk. rev.:* Brief. *Aud.:* Ac.

The substantive and wide-ranging articles in this journal deal with all aspects of employee-employer relationships. The articles are heavy on economic analysis, so a good working knowledge of economic theory and practice is needed to grasp the finer points of the material. Much of the focus of the journal is on how theory can be brought into practice. Many articles show how theory explains real-world events. A recent article considers how race affects the length of time it requires for baseball players to be elected to the hall of fame. Another looks at how judicial decisions related to the Americans with Disabilities Act have affected the economy and discusses unresolved issues related to it. Yet another considers the effect on research productivity among university professors and early retirement decisions. Articles on the impact of race on employment and well-being, as well as considerations of public- and private-sector workplace situations are often presented in the research. Each issue has a column on Internet resources and a survey of recent publications. Contributors come from a variety of disciplines. The scope of the articles is international, although most deal with American scenarios. In addition to economics, articles may be using sociological, psychological, political, historical, or legal considerations to analyze a topic. Even for those whose grasp of economic theory is not at an advanced level, the well-written text and clear tables allow lay readers to work around the formulae and understand the point. This is a valuable journal in the field and should be part of academic collections and large public libraries.

3972. ***Industrial Worker.*** [ISSN: 0019-8870] 1909. m. USD 20 (Individuals, USD 15). Ed(s): Jon Bekken. Industrial Workers of the World, PO Box 13476, Philadelphia, PA 19101-3476; http://iww.org. Illus. Circ: 4300 Paid. Vol. ends: Dec. Microform: BHP; PQC; NRP. Reprint: PQC. *Indexed:* AltPI. *Aud.:* Ga, Ac.

Industrial Worker is the IWW's official newspaper. It shows that although Joe Hill may indeed be dead, the Industrial Workers of the World have lost none of their fervor for his goals. This tabloid-style newspaper familiar to IWW members and scholars continues to spread the word and keep up the struggle. Certainly the most radical of American union newspapers or journals, it brings a unique perspective to any collection. World labor news is covered in depth, as is news from U.S. locals. There are many features about organizing initiatives, law and legal developments, specific strike actions, and other topics of interest to members. Articles are actively solicited from union activists and other workers. The editor is elected from the IWW membership for a two-year term. An unofficial archive, searchable back to 1995, is available at the Boston office's web site (www.iww.org/~iw).

3973. ***International Labor and Working Class History.*** Former titles: *Labor and Working Class History Newsletter; European Labor and Working Class History Newsletter.* [ISSN: 0147-5479] 1972. s-a. USD 68 (Individuals, USD 34). Ed(s): Michael Hanagan, Joshua Freeman. Cambridge University Press, The Edinburgh Bldg, Shaftesbury Rd, Cambridge, CB2 2RU, United Kingdom; information@cambridge.org. Illus., index, adv. Refereed. Circ: 1000. *Indexed:* ABS&EES, AltPI, AmH&L, ArtHuCI, BAS, PSA, SociolAb. *Bk. rev.:* Number varies, essay length. *Aud.:* Ac.

This journal's nontraditional approach to its subject adds a unique perspective to the study of labor and working-class history. Its essays are dense and scholarly, intended to "change the character of historical conversation by expanding its scope, enlarging its scope and changing its terms." Each issue features a series of essays exploring a common subject from a variety of viewpoints or multiple aspects of a issue. Contributors are routinely drawn from disciplines beyond the industrial relations community including political scientists, sociologists, and historians, among others. One of the most useful features in the journal is the extensive coverage of material presented at academic meetings, allowing readers to keep up with new scholarship in the field. Topics such as globalization's impact on workers' rights, class and consumption, national and international labor movements, class identity, unions, and working-class politics all receive coverage. Recent issues deal with the impact of natural disasters and man-made calamities on workers, and "Workers and Film as Subject and Audience." These are complemented by reports of work in progress, short papers, and critical commentary on material presented in earlier issues as well as numerous book reviews. There is excellent coverage of international events. Occasional special-theme issues focus on specific aspects of the class struggle and labor history. The journal is worldwide in scope, and its focus on the family makes it different from other labor history journals. It should be in academic collections.

3974. ***International Labour Review.*** [ISSN: 0020-7780] 1921. q. CHF 99 domestic; GBP 48 in Europe; EUR 60 in Europe. Ed(s): Iftikhar Ahmed. I L O Publications, PO Box 6, Geneva, 1211, Switzerland; publns@ilo.org; http://www.ilo.org/publns. Illus., index, adv. Refereed. Circ: 5300. Vol. ends: Nov/Dec. Microform: ILO; CIS; PMC; PQC. Online: bigchalk; EBSCO Publishing; Florida Center for Library Automation; Gale Group; Ingenta Select; Northern Light Technology, Inc.; OCLC Online Computer Library Center, Inc.; ProQuest Information & Learning; H.W. Wilson. Reprint: SCH. *Indexed:* ABIn, ASG, ASSIA, AgeL, BAS, BPI, BRI, CBRI, CIJE, EIP, ErgAb, FutSurv, HRA, HumInd, IBSS, JEL, MCR, PAIS, PMA, PRA, PSA, RRTA, RiskAb, SFSA, SSCI, SSI, SWA, SociolAb, WAE&RSA. *Bk. rev.:* Various number and length. *Aud.:* Ac, Sa.

The International Labor Organization (ILO) publishes extensively about industrial relations and trade union movement, focusing in large part on developing countries often underrepresented in the literature. The ILO's only agenda is the promotion of social justice, and they remain staunchly apolitical. Their approach to the subject is rooted in the belief that countries resolve their economic problems as part of the world community and solutions must be sought in that arena. This journal is dedicated to furthering this goal by presenting "reasoned views of experts in different disciplines, cultures and perspectives." The contributor pool is drawn from academia, labor leaders, government officials, and technical experts, who provide a wide range of expertise and varied points of view on events. The articles may discuss specific issues such as the economics of child labor or a comparison of unemployment compensation systems, or present a study of wider-ranging topics such as new standards for assessing employment protection or concepts of work in the global economy. A very useful literature review is included in each issue. For anyone interested in developing countries, this is an important journal. Tables of contents with article abstracts are available from 1996 to the present, and subscribers to the print edition have full online access as well.

3975. ***Japan Labour Bulletin.*** [ISSN: 0021-4469] 1962. m. JPY 4320 domestic. Ed(s): H. Sakashita. Japan Institute of Labour, Shinjuku Monolith, P.O. Box 7040, Tokyo, 163-0926, Japan; http://www.jil.go.jp. Illus., index. Circ: 3100. Vol. ends: Dec. *Aud.:* Ac, Sa.

Published by the Japanese Institute of Labour, a division of the Japanese Ministry of Labour, this compact English-language newsletter offers nearly comprehensive coverage of working life in Japan. Its short, well-written, and to-the-point articles provide a picture of working and living conditions for all types of workers in this important industrialized nation. Articles report on major topics such as the trends in industrial relations, human resources management, working conditions, labor economy, and labor policy. Many issues feature a special topic to be explored in detail in addition to other short articles. Recent special topics include labor law and social policy, young workers, the labor market and employment, social security, and human resource developments. The journal also participates in a consortium with labor law journals from around the world to expand its coverage of international materials. For a Japanese perspective on labor relations, this is the source. The web site provides full texts and indexing for the bulletin from 1992 to the present.

3976. ***Journal of Collective Negotiations in the Public Sector.*** [ISSN: 0047-2301] 1971. q. USD 237 (Individuals, USD 60). Ed(s): David A Dilts. Baywood Publishing Co., Inc., 26 Austin Ave, Amityville, NY 11701; info@baywood.com; http://www.baywood.com. Illus., index, adv. Sample. Vol. ends: Dec. *Indexed:* ABIn, BPI, CIJE, CJA, CLI, HRA, LRI, PAIS, PRA, PSA, SSCI. *Aud.:* Ac, Sa.

With the growth of public-sector unions and public-sector financial problems, this area of labor relations has become increasingly critical and complex in light of new legislation and regulations. Public officials, policy makers and analysts, academics, public employees, and concerned taxpayers are all concerned with the outcome of this process. Articles analyze "problems encountered during contracts negotiations, techniques for resolving impasses, strike resolution, grievance procedures, and ways of administering contracts for various areas of the public sector." The journal recognizes that to be successful in this area, a grasp of current legislation and regulation, in addition to an awareness of public opinion, government projections, and attitudes and employee expectations is necessary. Contributors include active negotiators, public officials, and academics. Articles focus on the United States, but developments in other countries are covered as well. This journal provides an active forum for the exchange of ideas between people who often only meet as adversaries, and suggests practical techniques that can be used in negotiations. Articles offer constructive approaches to problem solving amid the complexities of the public sector. No other journal covers public sector issues this completely or this pragmatically. Subscribers have online access to full texts of the entire contents of the journal, and nonsubscribers may purchase individual articles online.

3977. ***Journal of Labor Economics.*** [ISSN: 0734-306X] 1983. q. USD 241 print & online eds. (Individuals, USD 54 print & online eds.; Students, USD 40 print & online eds.). Ed(s): Derek A Neal. University of Chicago Press, Journals Division, PO Box 37005, Chicago, IL 60637; subscriptions@press.uchicago.edu; http://www.journals.uchicago.edu. Illus., index, adv. Refereed. Circ: 2000. Vol. ends: Oct. Microform: PQC. Online: EBSCO Publishing; Florida Center for Library Automation; Gale Group; JSTOR (Web-based Journal Archive); OCLC Online Computer Library Center, Inc.; ProQuest Information & Learning. Reprint: PSC. *Indexed:* ABIn, AgeL, BPI, H&SSA, IBSS, JEL, RiskAb, SSCI, SSI. *Bk. rev.:* Various number and length. *Aud.:* Ac, Sa.

During the past two decades, the *Journal of Labor Economics* has built a solid reputation for first-rate scholarship. It "examines issues affecting the economy as well as social and private behavior" in long studies that may be either theoretical or may use applied research as the basis of their conclusions. Topics cover a wide range of labor economics issues including changes in the supply and demand of labor services, the distribution of income, collective bargaining, the economic impact of evolving personnel issues, demographics, and the impact of public policy decisions. A good grounding in economics is needed to fully use this journal. Recent articles examine how high- and low-wage jobs coexist in parallel markets; how race differences in school and labor market success might be addressed by various theorists; whether school or family has a greater impact on student success rates; a psychological study of unemployment as a social norm; a study of child labor laws and their impact on school achievement; and a study of younger workers' interpretation of gender as an advantage or disadvantage in the workplace. The quality of the scholarship and the diversity of the material covered make this an excellent addition to academic collections.

3978. ***Journal of Labor Research.*** [ISSN: 0195-3613] 1979. q. USD 110 (Individuals, USD 35). Transaction Publishers, 35 Berrue Circle, Rutgers University, Piscataway, NJ 08854-8042; trans@transactionpub.com; http://www.transactionpub.com. Illus., index, adv. Refereed. Circ: 600. *Indexed:* ABIn, AgeL, CJA, CommAb, H&SSA, HRA, IBSS, JEL, PAIS, PRA, PSA, RiskAb, SFSA, SSCI, SSI, SociolAb. *Aud.:* Ac, Sa.

This first-rate journal offers complex analysis of "workplace issues and employment relationships." Contributors are primarily academics and practitioners, so readers need a good working knowledge of economic theory and statistical analysis. The lengthy articles are devoted to the study of the economic behavior of unions and their impact on political and social conditions. It is now published jointly by the George Mason University economics department and the Locke Institute, dedicated to the principles of John Locke. Its primary focus is on the United States, however international studies are sometimes included. Most issues feature a symposium bringing together several articles presenting a variety of viewpoints on a trend or new policy issue. Recent topics include "Nonunion Employee Representation," "The Transition from Welfare to Work: Problems and Policies," and "Flexible Employment and Alternate Work Arrangements." Interdisciplinary studies are encouraged. Recent issues focus on technology and privacy in the workplace, union involvement in the management process, labor exemptions and antitrust law, recent activities of the NLRB, and the effect of the Internet on union campaigns. Full text of this journal is included in Ebsco's Business Source Premier. This journal is primarily for serious scholars and labor economists.

3979. *Labor History.* Formerly: *Labor Historian's Bulletin.* [ISSN: 0023-656X] 1960. q. GBP 153 (Individuals, GBP 45). Ed(s): Dan J Leab. Carfax Publishing Ltd., 4 Park Sq, Milton Park, Abingdon, OX14 4RN, United Kingdom. Illus., index. Refereed. Circ: 1800 Paid. Vol. ends: Fall. Online: bigchalk; EBSCO Publishing; Florida Center for Library Automation; Gale Group; Ingenta Select; Northern Light Technology, Inc.; OCLC Online Computer Library Center, Inc.; ProQuest Information & Learning; RoweCom Information Quest; Swets Blackwell. Reprint: PSC. *Indexed:* ABS&EES, AltPI, AmH&L, ArtHuCI, BPI, HRA, HumInd, IBZ, JEL, LRI, PRA, PSA, RI-1, SSCI, SociolAb. *Aud.:* Ac, Sa.

Affiliated with the Tamiment Institute / Wagner Archive, *Labor History*'s stated aim is to publish original research in "history of work and its representation, labor systems, social reproduction of labor, social class, occupational culture and folklore, and worker migration, as well as new research and argument on the history of the labor movement, labor politics, and industrial conflict and regulation." Focusing primarily on American labor, it also strives to document transnational movements and global trends. Contributors are drawn from a wide range of disciplines outside labor studies. This journal is a major contributor of new ideas in labor history. The journal's reputation is built on its solid scholarly research and writing without becoming too narrowly focused. Recent articles include studies of the coal strikes in the 1930s, the treatment of guestworkers, the contemporary living wage movement, and transnational labor solidarity in light of NAFTA. As the standard journal for this area of study, it belongs in large public libraries and academic collections. *Labor History* participates in the CrossRef project and is available online to subscribers at www.catchword-.co.uk.

3980. *Labor Law Journal: to promote sound thinking on labor law problems.* [ISSN: 0023-6586] 1949. q. USD 219; USD 42.25 newsstand/cover. C C H Inc., 2700 Lake Cook Rd., Riverwoods, IL 60015; cust_serv@cch.com; http://www.cch.com. Illus., index. Vol. ends: Dec. Microform: PQC. Online: EBSCO Publishing; Gale Group; OCLC Online Computer Library Center, Inc.; H.W. Wilson. Reprint: WSH. *Indexed:* AgeL, BPI, CLI, ILP, LRI, PAIS, RI-1, SSCI. *Aud.:* Ac, Sa.

This well-organized and accessible journal features substantive articles written by labor law specialists, mediators, and academics. Contributors are encouraged to use clear, jargon-free language and subtitles to assist readers in finding pertinent information in articles quickly. Citations are in the endnotes, leaving the text cleaner. Recent articles explore white-collar workers and unpaid overtime under FLSA, e-mail policies, international employment and labor law, administrative dispute resolution, ADA issues, and sexual harassment. Some issues offer more than one article on a single aspect or ruling in labor law, and occasionally articles dealing with international events are included. All articles provide detailed citations for supporting case law. "Who's What in Labor" gives up-to-date information on important players in the field. This journal offers well-thought-out analytical examination of employment law. Recent issues cover the impact of the Supreme Court rulings on labor and employment law, several articles on the Weingarten ruling, and a study of child labor law in the United States. This is an important journal for serious students and users of employment law.

3981. *Labor Notes.* [ISSN: 0275-4452] 1979. m. USD 30 (Individuals, USD 20). Ed(s): Jim West, Martha Gruelle. Labor Education & Research Project, 7435 Michigan Ave, Detroit, MI 48210; labornotes@labornotes.org; www.labornotes.org. Illus. Circ: 11000. Reprint: PQC. *Indexed:* AltPI. *Aud.:* Ga, Ac, Sa.

The goal of this nonprofit organization is to provide tools for labor activists through its publications, schools, and conferences. An unabashed worker advocate, *Labor Notes* is equally critical of big labor and management when they act to the detriment of working people. The articles provide practical and accessible ideas and strategies for organizing and dealing with workplace issues; this is not a theoretical journal. There is heavy coverage of union issues including contracts, ongoing negotiations, strikes, boycotts, and working conditions. Grassroots labor activity is also featured. Its editorial stance is that if organized labor is to remain a viable player in the American workplace, it must admit that some of the difficulties it faces are the fault of unions having not faced difficult issues head-on. Editorial policy is just as unrelenting in dealing with management's part of the equation. It also covers movements in Canada and Mexico, especially with regard to NAFTA. The problems encountered by women and minorities gets wide coverage as well. Recent articles discuss the privatization of health care workers in British Columbia, Florida farm workers, how to find out more about your employer, unions mobilizing against war, and a roundtable on what is needed to successfully organize a new shop. Legislation, judicial rulings, and statistical briefs, plus a survey of labor news from other publications, are included. "Solidarity Notes" gives updates on current actions. This journal presents a clear picture of union activities in the United States today from an independent perspective. The most recent issues of the newsletter are available on their web site.

3982. *Labor Relations Bulletin.* Former titles (until 1994): *Discipline and Grievances. White Collar Edition;* (until 1993): *Discipline and Grievances.* [ISSN: 1080-3211] 1950. m. Individuals, USD 219; USD 21 newsstand/cover per issue. Ed(s): Robert Halprin. Aspen Law & Business, 1185 Ave of the Americas, 37th Fl, New York, NY 10036; http://www.aspenpub.com. Illus., index. Online: EBSCO Publishing; Florida Center for Library Automation; Gale Group. *Aud.:* Ac, Sa.

This compact and well-organized newsletter is aimed at management in unionized shops and union leaders. "Discipline and Grievances" features short, two-to four-page case studies dealing with actual cases and decisions. The advice to employers on how to handle similar situations is easy to understand and apply. Each issue contains several of these on various topics. Shorter pieces in the "Perspectives on Discipline" section reports cases. New case law and legislation pertaining to labor relations, NLRB decisions, trends, and emerging concerns in the field are all reported. Recent case studies deal with insubordination, protected speech, overtime, absenteeism, e-mail, and sexual harassment policy enforcement. This extremely pragmatic approach, bolstered by concrete examples of sound practice, makes the newsletter an asset to those in the rapidly changing area of industrial/labor relations. The title is included in EBSCO's Business Source Premier. It should be available in academic collections supporting a business, labor, or industrial relations program.

3983. *Labor Studies Journal.* [ISSN: 0160-449X] 1976. q. USD 120 (Individuals, USD 45). Ed(s): Paul Jarley, Bruce Nissan. West Virginia University Press, PO Box 6295, Morgantown, WV 26506; press@wvu.edu; http://www.as.wvu.edu/press. Illus., adv. Refereed. Circ: 800. Vol. ends: Winter. Microform: PQC. Online: EBSCO Publishing; Florida Center for Library Automation; Gale Group; OCLC Online Computer Library Center, Inc.; Project MUSE; Swets Blackwell. Reprint: PQC; PSC. *Indexed:* ABS&EES, AmH&L, BPI, IBZ, IPSA, LRI, PAIS, PSA, SociolAb. *Bk. rev.:* 7-12, 400-2,700 words. *Aud.:* Ac, Sa.

Although *Labor Studies Journal* is the official journal of the University and College Labor Education Association, its target audience is not just academics but also unions, community-based labor educators, and activists. The scholarly articles, a mix of qualitative and quantitative research, are also very accessible to laypersons. They focus on "research about work, workers, labor organizations, and labor studies and worker education." By applying a multidisciplinary approach to the study of the philosophy, content, and history of worker/labor education; legal aspects of union activity; and labor history incorporating international union events, the journal presents a well-rounded view of the subject. Articles vary from empirical studies of current events to historical or even theoretical studies. The journal attracts scholars from all aspects of the discipline and encourages a free exchange of ideas. Occasional theme issues examine topics in detail; one recent theme is communication between labor and management, within unions, and within the workplace. The journal also includes reviews of books and audiovisual and electronic materials. It is included in Project Muse and EBSCO's Business Source Premier collections. A good addition to academic libraries.

3984. ***Labor's Heritage.*** [ISSN: 1041-5904] 1989. q. USD 19.95 domestic; USD 24.95 Canada; USD 29.95 elsewhere. Ed(s): Michael Merrill. George Meany Center for Labor Studies, 10000 New Hampshire Ave, Silver Spring, MD 20903; blevins@georgemeany.org. Illus., index. Refereed. Circ: 8000 Paid. Vol. ends: Oct. *Indexed:* AmH&L. *Aud.:* Ga, Ac.

The George Meany Center for Labor Studies, the parent organization of the George Meany Archives, is now also home to the National Labor College. *Labor's Heritage*, in order to reflect the needs and goals of both organizations, has expanded its scope. Although it will still include articles about significant events and individuals in the labor movement, there will also be interpretive essays that are intended to "teach and inspire." It maintains a high level of scholarship without sacrificing accessibility. Articles are well researched and written, but the eye-catching photos make this one of the most attractive and appealing journals in the field. The lavish use of photography and other visual art adds to the impact of the text. The journal's goal of bringing public attention to the rich and varied heritage of American workers is amply realized in its articles, which frequently feature the experiences of women and minorities. Exhibits, collections, research projects, conferences, and other resources in the field of labor history are listed in its news section. The centerfold of each issue displays labor-themed artwork. Contributors include historians, archivists, museum directors, art historians, or anyone with a story to tell about work life. Recent articles deal with labor during wartime. Buy it for the articles, but you will linger over the pictures. Public and academic libraries should strongly consider adding this title to their collections.

3985. ***Labour Education.*** [ISSN: 0378-5467] 1964. q. CHF 55; USD 44. Ed(s): Clara Foucault Mohammed. I L O Publications, PO Box 6, Geneva, 1211, Switzerland; publns@ilo.org; http://www.ilo.org/publns. Illus. Circ: 2500. Vol. ends: No. 4. Microform: ILO. Reprint: PQC. *Indexed:* CIJE. *Aud.:* Ac, Sa.

This magazine attempts both to educate trade union members and nonunion workers and to facilitate the development of local and regional education programs providing training and information for union members. Information on current events, trade union rights, legislation, and methods are covered. Articles on collective bargaining, communications, training, and grievance mediation are standard; others may outline programs for social, political, and economic education. Media for worker education such as software, video, and other formats are reviewed. Geared toward workers and unions, the articles are outlines for action; the journal is theoretical. As with many ILO publications, the needs of workers in developing nations get significant coverage due to the role trade unions often play in their social and economic development. Gender issues, the plight of rural workers, suppression of the right to free association, and trade union rights receive significant attention. Material is presented to "assist trade unions in their endeavors to strengthen their structure, modernize their methods of action and enhance their capacity to participate in social dialogue" in their efforts to improve working and living conditions. New methodologies may be discussed, and important documents in labor rights are reproduced. Some issues are devoted to a single theme. It is intended for readers who are in a position to make use of the information, although theorists studying the social process and the results of labor activism might use it.

3986. ***National Right to Work Newsletter.*** [ISSN: 0197-7032] 1955. m. Free. Ed(s): Stanley Greer. National Right to Work Committee, 8001 Braddock Rd, Ste 500, Springfield, VA 22160. Illus. Circ: 150000. Vol. ends: Dec. *Aud.:* Ga, Ac, Sa.

There is no mistaking the goal of this publication. It is to work in "Congress and in the state legislatures across the country to safeguard and extend the Right to Work protections" by repealing sections of federal labor law that permit union bosses to force workers to pay union dues or "fees" as a condition of employment. The articles are short and to the point and pull no punches. Words like "henchmen," "squads," and "czar" appear regularly in reference to union members and leaders. A founding member and the first president of the committee was Fred A. Hartley, Jr., one of the authors of the Taft-Hartley Act. The eight-page newsletter strives to raise awareness about its concerns, tells members how to assist the cause, and offers updates on state and federal legislative initiatives. Articles stress the disadvantages of unions for workers and the inequity of the closed-shop workplace, as well as misconduct by union officials and members, especially during strikes or organizing drives. Public-employee unions are excoriated as a special menace and costly to the nation as a whole. Also included are news updates and legal developments appropriate to the subject, coverage of PAC activities, and legislative alerts to members when letters to elected representatives are required. This journal espouses a point of view seldom represented in labor literature and should be included in larger collections for balance. A free online pdf version of the newsletter from September 1999 to the present is available (www.nrtwc.org/nl.html).

3987. ***New Labor Forum.*** [ISSN: 1095-7960] 1997. s-a. USD 50 (Individuals, USD 14; USD 20 domestic). Ed(s): Geoffrey Jacques, Paula Finn. Queens College Labor Resource Center, Queens College, City University of New York, 25 W 43rd St, 19th Fl, New York, NY 10036. Illus., adv. Refereed. Circ: 3000. *Indexed:* PAIS, PSA, SociolAb. *Bk. rev.:* Number and length varies. *Aud.:* Ga, Ac.

New Labor Forum aims to provide just that, a place where union members and organized labor can interact with academicians and others who are interested in the movement and its goals. Its articles deal with the history of the labor movement, recent developments, and the impact of economic and international events, often discussing methodologies and strategies for responding to them. The journal recognizes that the challenges facing organized labor today are very different from those historically addressed by unions. There exist different economic conditions, globalization, and increasing numbers of white- and pink-collar workers in addition to the traditional blue-collar base membership. The lively but scholarly articles are topical and practical as well as theoretical. Articles are not afraid to challenge the conventional wisdom about organized labor. A recent article considers the long-term relationship between organized labor and the Democratic Party; another questions the lack of humor in the movement in an examination of labor-related cartooning; and another focuses on the depiction of working-class culture in *The Simpsons*. Another series of articles deals with organized labor in recent fiction, and others discuss the impact of Chinese labor on U.S. workers, how to organize a new shop, and labor and the "global justice movement." This young journal is an excellent example of the new and innovative thinking in this field. Academic libraries who haven't yet considered it, should.

Occupational Outlook Quarterly. See Occupations and Careers section.

3988. ***Relations Industrielles.*** [ISSN: 0034-379X] 1945. 4x/yr. CND 70 (Individuals, CND 35). Ed(s): Sylvie Montreuil. Laval University, Department of Industrial Relations, Cite Universitaire, Quebec, PQ G1K 7P4, Canada; relat.ind@rlt.ulaval.ca; http://www.rlt.ulaval.ca/ri-ir/. Illus., index, adv. Refereed. Circ: 1200. Microform: BNQ; PQC. Online: EBSCO Publishing; Florida Center for Library Automation; Gale Group; OCLC Online Computer Library Center, Inc.; ProQuest Information & Learning. Reprint: PQC. *Indexed:* ABIn, AgeL, CLI, CPerI, HRA, IBZ, LRI, PAIS, PRA, SFSA, SSCI, SUSA, SociolAb. *Aud.:* Ac, Sa.

One of the first journals in this field and the only Canadian one, this publication has presented authoritative research articles covering all "aspects of the world of work" for more than 50 years. Articles are in either French or English with complete summaries in the other language, supplemented with brief summaries in Spanish as well. Articles are drawn from a wide variety of fields and all are refereed. Using a variety of social science methodologies, articles study the impact of working conditions on workers and society and the effect of unions on workers, the workplace, and society as a whole. There are also theoretical discussions of industrial relations. While Canadian topics predominate, the journal is not exclusively Canadian in scope. The articles are clearly written and free of jargon while maintaining high standards of scholarship. The journal will be publishing thematic issues dealing with globalization, union renewal, ergonomics as a concern of industrial relations, and a number of workplace surveys. Tables of contents and abstracts of articles are available back to 1996 on the web site. Full-text access is available online through EBSCO Business Source Premier.

Social Security Bulletin. See Aging section.

3989. ***Trade Union World.*** Formerly: *Free Labour World.* 1950. m. EUR 46.20 domestic; USD 60 foreign. Ed(s): Louis Bellanger, Natacha David. International Confederation of Free Trade Unions (ICFTU), Bd Emile

Jacqmain 155, Bte 1, Brussels, 1210, Belgium; internetpo@icftu.org; http://www.icftu.org. Illus., index. Circ: 16000. Vol. ends: Dec. *Indexed:* BAS, PAIS. *Bk. rev.:* Occasional, length varies. *Aud.:* Ac, Sa.

This slim journal packs a lot of information for activists and reformers into each issue. The International Confederation of Free Trade Unions (ICFTU) slogan, "Bread, Peace, Freedom," clearly reflects its goals. Although the journal is based in Europe, the content is global in scope, covering trade unionism worldwide. There are reports on trade union issues, inequalities within and between countries, human rights, and the problems of developing nations and the role of trade unions in these struggles. Issues such as child labor, forced labor, and gender disparities are also addressed. The journal promotes and defends trade union rights through international campaigns, encouraging governments and unions in developed nations to support efforts to organize workers. Reports on the work of trade unions in Europe, South America, and Africa are informative and provide an international perspective. Many articles report on the role that labor plays in the struggle for democracy. Other articles explore the situation of migrant workers and the conditions of women and ethnic minorities in various host countries. The ICFTU, despite its advocacy of political action, is not affiliated with any specific party or program. The web site offers articles, editorials, and briefings free online, which can be sorted by date, country, subject, or type. Readers may also find further information about recent developments in trade unionism and about the organization there. Although outside the range of many libraries, this is a good addition to large collections.

3990. *Union Democracy Review.* Supersedes: *Union Democracy in Action.* [ISSN: 1077-5080] 1972. bi-m. USD 15. Ed(s): Herman Benson. Association for Union Democracy, Inc., 500 State St, Brooklyn, NY 11217; aud@igc.apc.org; http://www.uniondemocracy.com. Circ: 3000. *Indexed:* AltPI. *Aud.:* Ga, Ac, Sa.

Union Democracy Review is the official publication of the Association for Union Democracy, "a pro-labor, nonprofit organization dedicated to advancing the principles and practices of democratic trade unionism in the North American labor movement." The newsletter offers short, insightful articles about workers and unions. Although the focus is on problems of workers with their unions in maintaining true democratic conditions and working out problems that arise, the tone of the newsletter is pro-labor and pro-union. Unlike other publications covering problems within big labor, this one believes in the process and seeks to support union membership as a force working for the good of workers in particular, and the unions as a force for workers in a democracy. Longer articles may run a page or more, and there are many short, paragraph-length news items sprinkled throughout the 12-page publication. Writing is clear and to the point, the coverage of events across the United States and North American is good, and no subject is out of bounds, even the U.S. Department of Labor gets mentioned if they fail, in the reporter's opinion, to follow the rules. All in all, this is an interesting addition to large collections, or to any collection on labor and industrial relations.

3991. *United States N L R B Online.* w. National Labor Relations Board, 1099, 14th St, Washington, DC 20570-0001; david.parker@nlrb.gov. *Aud.:* Ga, Ac, Sa.

Created in 1935 to enforce the National Labor Relations Act, this independent federal agency holds secret-ballot elections to determine whether employees want union representation and investigates and remedies unfair labor practices by employers and unions. This site expedites the process for users wanting to access the many resources and services of this agency that is central to labor and industrial relations in the United States. Users can get help finding out more about rights and obligations for workers and management under the act (as well as other labor laws) and how to file a charge or election petition here. This well-organized and very straightforward site offers weekly summaries of new decisions, press releases, public notices, forms, rules and regulations, pdf and html versions of their manuals, text of decisions back to Vol. 272 (a very handy resource for libraries not able to keep up with the massive looseleaf publications previously required), and FOIA information. This site should be useful for scholars, workers, students, and unions—anyone who works or studies work. A well-done web site that should be bookmarked widely.

3992. *U.S. Bureau of Labor Statistics. Monthly Labor Review.* Supersedes: *U.S. Bureau of Labor Statistics. Monthly Review.* [ISSN: 0098-1818] 1915. m. USD 45 domestic; USD 63 foreign. Ed(s): Deborah Klein. U.S. Bureau of Labor Statistics, 2 Massachusetts Ave, N E, Washington, DC 20212; mlr@bls.gov; http://www.bls.gov/mlr/opub/mlrhome.htm. Illus., index. Refereed. Circ: 9000. Vol. ends: Dec. Microform: CIS; PMC. Online: bigchalk; The Dialog Corporation; EBSCO Publishing; Florida Center for Library Automation; Gale Group; Northern Light Technology, Inc.; OCLC Online Computer Library Center, Inc.; ProQuest Information & Learning; H.W. Wilson. Reprint: CIS; WSH. *Indexed:* ABIn, ASG, ATI, AgeL, AmStI, B&I, BPI, BRD, BRI, CBRI, CIJE, CLI, IUSGP, JEL, LRI, MagInd, PAIS, RGPR, SSCI, SSI, SWR&A, WAE&RSA. *Aud.:* Ga, Ac, Sa.

This invaluable publication is now even more accessible. Their online version is now available in full-text pdf format at the Bureau of Labor Statistics (BLS) web site (www.bls.gov/opub/mlr/mlrhome.htm). Many of the tables can be downloaded, not just as they appear in the magazine, but also as data files ready to use in a database or spreadsheet. The extensive statistical tables have long been the core of this government publication, but it would be foolish to overlook the excellent articles combining theory with analysis and hard information by BLS specialists. Each issue contains three or four substantive articles, frequently grouped to explore different aspects of a single topic. One recent issue featured an overview of state-labor-related legislation, changes in federal workers compensation laws, and unemployment insurance during the previous year. Statistical data include labor force, compensation, price, productivity, international comparison, and illness and injury figures. Explanatory material offering background on how the data is derived is included in each issue. Significant regular features are "Major Agreements Expiring Next Month" and "Significant Decisions" (in labor cases). All libraries should have this publication, or at least bookmark it prominently. The *MLR* archives provide full-text articles back to 1989, and there are time series and other data available.

Electronic Journals

3993. *Labor Watch.* bi-w. Labor Watch, http://www.zmag.org/LaborWatch.htm. *Aud.:* Ga, Ac, Sa.

Znet is an independent, counterculture-oriented site with a global scope, although much of the content focuses on cultural, social, and economic events in the United States. *Labor Watch* is the section of the vast Znet web site devoted to tracking events relating to work and workers. In addition to reprinting labor-related articles from *Z Magazine* and other left-oriented publications, it reports news, events, and other information. One of the site's goals is to act as a meeting place and clearing house for activists helping to develop strategies and programs. Links to other labor- and left-oriented web sites are provided as well. It has good coverage of alternative viewpoints to big labor. An interesting bookmark to add to collections that aim for wide coverage of all aspects of working life.

3994. *LaborNet.* d. LaborNet, http://www.labornet.org. *Aud.:* Ga, Ac, Sa.

LaborNet, now in its second decade, uses new technologies to "revitalize and rebuild the labor movement." Their motto is "Global online communication for a democratic, independent labor movement." Unaffiliated with a union, it is as often critical of big labor as of management and government when workers' best interests are not being represented. It was the first labor news site in the United States, and in recent years it has inspired *LaborNet* sites in Canada, the United Kingdom, Austria, Germany, and Korea, working in conjunction with the Association of Progressive Communication. It takes its news from both mainstream sources like the *New York Times* and a variety of independent sources such as labor publications, the alternative press, and other web sites. The site offers news, strike alerts, and papers from the last LaborTech conference offering tools for activists. In the "Viewpoints" section, essays by activists and journalists who have covered the labor movement are available to supplement the more straightforward news on the main pages. Also offered are forums where users can exchange ideas. There is an interesting selection of links about work, politics and current events. In addition to presenting labor news, *LaborNet*'s founders are active in fighting Internet censorship and the growing privatization of information. This site is an excellent source of labor news not filtered through big unions and should be bookmarked by students of the movement. Public libraries and academic libraries with labor relations programs will find it useful.

3995. ***LabourStart.*** d. Ed(s): Eric Lee. Labour and Society International, ITF Bldg, Third Fl, 49-60 Borough Rd, London, SE1 1DS, United Kingdom; http://www.labourstart.org. *Aud.:* Ga, Ac, Sa.

Describing itself as "where trade unionists start their day on the net," *Labour Start* is truly international. Not only does it gather news from every corner of the globe, it is available in ten languages. Articles are drawn from the international press, independent publications, unions, and activists, and the site is updated constantly. A news ticker you can add to your site is available as well. Subject searching is offered, and news can be sorted by country. Editorials discuss the condition of labor and tools that activists may need, language barriers to organizing, and technology issues. It has an interesting mix of news and tools for those involved in the trade union movement. The site also has links to the Global Labour Calendar, radio and television webcasts, articles on labor and the Internet, and an extensive list of online labor forums. Free e-mail for trade unionists is provided. There is an extensive section on how to build a better web site, presumably to further labor causes. The web site fully realizes the goals of its parent organization, Labour and Society International, an independent group that supports human rights activism in the global workplace through "advocacy, education and research" by working with "trade unions and civil society organizations." If you have an interest in the trade union movement, especially internationally, this is a valuable web site.

3996. ***NATLEX.*** 1984. irreg. continuously-updated. International Labour Organization, 4, route des Morillons, Geneva 22, CH-1211, Switzerland; ilo@ilo.org; http://www.ilo.org/. *Aud.:* Ac, Sa.

NATLEX is an electronic database of bibliographic citations for and full-text coverage of national laws on labor, social security, and related human rights covering nearly 175 countries and 50 other authorities. It now has over 55,000 bibliographic records and more than 300 full-text laws. Content is derived from the official gazettes, legislative databases, ILO field offices, and various other publications. Records provide bibliographic information, abstracts and keywords, and legal relationships between other citations are noted. Records by ILO specialists are written in the three working languages of the ILO (English, French, and Spanish). The database is searchable by country, subject, year, or keyword. This database should be useful to anyone working with labor law in the United States or with laws of other nations. The browse mode and subject profiles are especially useful, as is the legislative information section that allows users to see the most recent additions to the database. Recommended for public, academic, and special libraries.

3997. ***Work in Progress: this week with America's unions.*** w. American Federation of Labor - Congress of Industrial Organizations, Public Affairs Department, 815 16th St, N W, Washington, DC 20006; http://www.aflcio.org/. *Aud.:* Ga, Ac, Sa.

Work in Progress, the online weekly newsletter of the AFL-CIO, offers pared-down, no-frills nuggets of labor news. There is now a keyword index that can be limited by date or searched cumulatively. Because there is no table of contents or other index, it is advisable to use this option if specific topics are needed. As a way of quickly getting an overview of the week's developments in the field of labor, it's a good tool. Reports on current strikes, new shops, organizing efforts, new legislation, and action alerts for both legislation and regulations are included. The focus is on the United States, but international events, especially matters pertaining to NAFTA, get good coverage. Many items include relevant contact information for more in-depth coverage of events. Recent issues include several items on child labor in China, OSHA rulings, and a photo exhibit at the George Meany Archives, as well as many items about legislation and government policy. Users can also have the newsletter e-mailed to them directly. An archive back to its 1995 debut is available online. The newsletter will mainly interest labor activists, those studying the movement, and perhaps policy makers. The main AFL-CIO web site at www.afl-cio.org should not be overlooked by anyone seeking information on unions in the United States.

3998. ***Workindex.*** 1997. d. Ed(s): Michelle Liberatore. Human Resources Executive, 747 Dresher Rd, Horsham, PA 19044; http://www.workindex.com/. Illus. *Bk. rev.:* Number varies, brief. *Aud.:* Ac, Sa.

This award winning web resource is produced jointly by the ILR school at Cornell and Human Resources Executive. It offers a mix of current scholarship and a practitioner's eye for getting to the heart of the matter. This is a powerful tool for both students and practitioners in the field. An extensive list of refereed links to goods and services in the field is a huge asset. A good subject index is supplemented by keyword searching. Feature articles are easy to read and reflect a variety of views about the workplace. The site has invaluable material for anyone looking for workplace information, including human resources, labor relations, benefits, training, technology, staffing, recruiting, leadership, motivation, insurance, relocation, and legal issues. Bonus features include a salary calculator, software tester, and a legal clinic. The editors review both books and web sites, and books are linked to Amazon.com. If you are a student of human resources or a practitioner this should be bookmarked.

3999. ***World of Work: the magazine of the ILO.*** Formerly (until 1992): *I L O Information.* [ISSN: 1020-0010] 1965. 5x/yr. Free. Ed(s): Thomas Netter. International Labour Office, Department of Communication, 4 Route des Morillons, Geneva 22, CH-1211, Switzerland; communication@ilo.org; http://www.ilo.org/communication. Illus. Circ: 50000. Vol. ends: Dec. *Indexed:* BRI, CBRI, CIJE, ErgAb, FPA, ForAb. *Bk. rev.:* Number varies, brief. *Aud.:* Hs, Ga, Ac, Sa.

This wide-ranging magazine is not an official publication of the International Labor Organization, and articles do not always present ILO views. Its extensive reporting on such things as the conditions in specific countries, or its analytical articles about the global impact of technology, or items on trade unions and democratic movements make it an asset to any collection supporting labor or the growing field of global studies. The web edition is readily accessible, offering individual articles in text format or the entire magazine in pdf format, preserving the visual impact of the heavily illustrated original. It offers the same global coverage as other ILO publications, but in a less formal format. Issues normally contain several multi-page articles, along with brief news items and regular columns covering "Around the Continents," "Working World," and "Media Shelf." Many pieces include URLs for further information online. The content, while not exclusively devoted to developing nations, does focus on events there, and much of the information is presented to meet the needs of labor activists. The elimination of child labor, women's issues, international solidarity, and minimum-wage laws are among topics addressed in recent issues. The newspaper-style writing makes it accessible to readers from any background. In keeping with the ILO's nonpartisan stance, the articles represent a wide range of political perspectives and points of view and show a great diversity in the reporting. An archive back to 1996 is available. The magazine is now published in Chinese, Czech, Danish, English, Finnish, French, German, Hindi, Hungarian, Japanese, Norwegian, Russian, Slovak, Spanish, and Swedish. Recommended for most libraries. Bookmark this site.

■ LANDSCAPE ARCHITECTURE

Thomas P. Gates, Architecture Library, Kent State University, Kent, OH 44242; tgates@lms.kent.edu

Introduction

The profession and practice of landscape architecture encompasses a wide range of specialized talents and—in more cases than not—projects involve collaboration with other design professionals in architecture, environmental studies, landscape conservation, urban design, and fine arts. Today's international landscape architecture journals, although limited to less than 20, document the breadth of many exciting landscape design projects. The projects represent the gamut of the landscape architecture profession and often include theoretical and critical discussion and documentation in the form of photographs, drawings, and charts in numerous areas, among them city and town planning, landscape design for industrial parks, rooftop and interior gardens for commercial buildings, planning for sports facilities, and design for recreational and amusement parks.

The scientific study related to landscape architecture falls into the categories of environmental studies and land conservation. Two journals in these areas, *Landscape and Urban Planning* and *Landscape Research,* have been included because of their international importance to the field.

Landscape architecture also involves the artist—quite often the sculptor—who manipulates land forms, natural materials, and plant and tree species for a purely aesthetic effect. From this impulse arise highly individualistic and often socially and environmentally conscious designers who create unusual ecosystems or controversial and fantastic configurations.

The more pragmatic aspects of landscape architecture are found in journals published by professional societies, exemplified by the American Society of Landscape Architects (ASLA), which produces *Landscape Architecture*, or the Australian Institute of Landscape Architects (AILA), which publishes *Landscape Australia.* These journals usually follow a standardized format, have occasional thematic issues, and provide information about events, awards, competitions, current projects, new products, reports on soils, new technologies, and book reviews. The publications of the professional societies usually are produced by the membership and include relevant advertising as well as drawings, photographs, maps, charts, and reference notes.

In addition to the journals published by professional societies with their more pragmatic and product-oriented content, more esoteric publications appear irregularly, are thematic in nature, and are classed as "monographic series." One cited here is *Landscape Architecture and Town Planning in the Netherlands.* This glossy title is edited by academicians, practitioners, and theorists and is oversize in format with exceptional graphic layout, stunning color illustrations, and meticulous drawings. This publication is included not only because of its quality but because of the well-written articles that document important international public and private projects and include discussions of contemporary landscape and urban design. International journals often contain summaries in English or text in two or three languages including English.

Landscape architecture journals are usually written by academics, practitioners, and historians, by and for a highly specialized audience, more than likely those in the landscape profession. But this does not preclude appreciating their important contributions to the design profession as a whole. Many landscape architecture journals are appropriate for a public library with a strong architecture collection. Certainly universities with programs in landscape architecture, horticulture, urban design, art history, and environmental studies would benefit by acquiring many of the titles listed.

Because landscape architecture is a specialized field with a narrow audience range, the majority of titles listed here would appeal to academic and specialized readerships. A title such as *Land Marks* would appeal to a more general public library clientele.

Basic Periodicals

Ac: *Landscape Architecture, Landscape Design, Landscape Journal;* Ga: *Land Marks;* Sa: *Landscape and Urban Planning, Landscape Research, Topos.*

Basic Abstracts and Indexes

Avery Index to Architectural Periodicals; Garden Literature; Geographical Abstracts; ICONDA, International Construction Database.

4000. ***Anthos: vierteljahres-Zeitschrift fuer Freiraumgestaltung, Gruen und Landschaftsplanung.*** [ISSN: 0003-5424] 1962. q. CHF 59. Ed(s): Felix Guhl. Verlag Niggli AG, Steinackerstr 8, Sulgen, 8583, Switzerland; http://www.niggli.ch. Illus., adv. Circ: 5000. Vol. ends: Dec. *Indexed:* AIAP, API, GardL, IBZ, RRTA, WAE&RSA. *Bk. rev.:* 10. *Aud.:* Ac, Sa.

Anthos ("the bloom" in Greek) is the official organ of the International Federation of Landscape Architects (IFLA). It was at first published for a trilingual readership (German, French, and English), but since 1996 has eliminated English; the text now appears only in the two other languages. Its scope is international, with subscribers in more than 40 countries. The thematic nature of each issue can be exemplified by one titled "Une Ecologie pour l'Architecture" containing eight essays illuminating various designs for contemporary gardens such as those for Norman Foster's bank in Frankfurt. Other interesting and timely international projects are documented, such as an industrial park in California's Silicon Valley or the preservation of a historic landscape in Hungary. Information about the worldwide activities of IFLA, descriptions of landscape projects, and book reviews (most in German) allow the reader to gain an overview of developments in the profession from an international perspective. Although *Anthos* is directed toward an academic Franco-German audience, it is deemed important enough to be considered for an architecture library collection in the United States.

4001. ***Colloquium on the History of Landscape Architecture. Papers.*** 1972. irreg. Dumbarton Oaks, 1703 32nd St, N W, Washington, DC 20007; http://www.doaks.org/publications.html. Refereed. Circ: 1000. *Aud.:* Ac.

This publication is a scholarly compilation of papers presented at the annual colloquium at Harvard University's Dumbarton Oaks in Washington, D.C. The series was instituted in 1971, and essays from the papers are usually published annually in a monographic format. The series began "to further the objectives of scholarship in areas relating to the Garden Library collection. The series is designed to bring together leading scholars who have undertaken research in selected aspects of the history of landscape architecture and, through the publication of their papers to make the results of their research available to a wider audience." Each colloquium focuses on a topic of landscape architectural research, e.g., *Environmentalism In Landscape Architecture* (2000) and *Places of Commemoration: Search for Identity and Landscape Design* (2001). International scholars of landscape architectural history contribute in-depth essays, enhanced by prints, drawings, photographs, and bibliographic footnotes. This monographic series is essential for an academic architecture library.

Fine Gardening. See Gardening section.

Garden History. See Gardening section.

4002. ***Garten und Landschaft: journal of landscape architecture and landscape planning.*** [ISSN: 0016-4720] 1890. m. Individuals, DEM 205; Students, DEM 154.80. Callwey Verlag, Postfach 800409, Munich, 81604, Germany; http://www.garten-landschaft.de. Illus., index, adv. Circ: 8800. Vol. ends: Dec. *Indexed:* AIAP, ExcerpMed, IBZ. *Bk. rev.:* 4. *Aud.:* Ac, Sa.

Garten und Landschaft is a medium-sized format journal published by the Deutsche Gesellschaft fuer Gartenkunst und Landschaftspflege (German Society for Garden Design and Landscape Architecture). The journal, which includes English summaries, follows the usual format and contains information similar to other professional landscape society publications. It also includes articles of local interest and information about notable landscape architects of the past; current professional issues of interest, such as projects in the countryside and urban areas; and information about lectures, symposia, exhibitions, programs, and special events occurring in Germany. Each monthly issue is thematic and includes such topics as "Wasser in der Stadt," providing discussion about the ecology of water sources and solutions to regional water shortages. The articles are written by landscape architects, usually authorities in specific fields. Brief biographical sketches about each author are included. Frequently projects in other European countries are discussed. The graphic layout of the journal is well organized, with advertisements not interfering with the text and illustrations. The journal would be a useful addition to an academic library collection supporting a landscape architecture curriculum and for a special audience such as landscape architects interested in German projects.

4003. ***GruenForum.LA: Branchenmagazin fuer GaLaBau und Landschaftsarchitektur.*** Former titles (until 2002): *Landschaftsarchitektur;* (until 1972): *Deutsche Gartenarchitektur.* [ISSN: 1610-4730] 1962. m. EUR 78 domestic; EUR 86.40 foreign. Ed(s): Matthias Hinkelammert. Thalacker Medien, Bernhard Thalacker Verlag GmbH und Co. KG, Postfach 8364, Braunschweig, 38133, Germany; info@thalackermedien.de; http://www.thalackermedien.de. Illus., adv. Sample. Circ: 5527 Controlled. *Bk. rev.:* 7. *Aud.:* Ac, Sa.

This is a lively trade publication that provides information about the landscape architecture profession in Germany, new products, and current events. The contents focus regularly on such topics as interior landscaping, garden furniture, and new machinery. There are also book reviews. Readership is limited to those who read German, but an academic architecture library with a scope of collecting international landscape journals would benefit from acquiring this title.

4004. ***Land Marks.*** 1997. bi-m. Spacemaker Press, PO Box 898, Marshall, VA 20116-0898. *Aud.:* Ac, Ga.

Land Marks is a monographic series published with separate titles for each issue. Its content focuses on major projects by architects, planners, sculptors, and landscape architects. The scope of the publication encompasses projects by United States designers and stresses the interrelationship of landscape design with art, architecture, and the environment. Two recent titles of *Land Marks* are "The Offices of Hideo Sasaki: A Corporate History" (2001) by Melanie Louise Simo and "Thomas Balsley, the Urban Landscape" (2000). *Land Marks* is consistently of high quality, and it is illustrated with a portfolio of stunning full-page color photographs, conceptual drawings, models, and sections. The monographic series is helpful in understanding, in detail, important landscape and planning projects. Because of the substantial research, well-written text, and excellent graphic design and illustrations, the series would be an important addition for an academic architecture library as well as for a public library's architecture collection.

4005. ***Landlines.*** Formerly (until 1998): *Landscape Design Extra.* [ISSN: 1469-0985] 1990. m. 11/yr. GBP 15 in UK & Ireland (Students, GBP 10 in UK & Ireland). Landscape Design Trust, 13a West St, Reigate, RH2 9BL, United Kingdom; info@landscape.co.uk; http://www.landscape.co.uk. Adv. *Indexed:* AIAP. *Aud.:* Ga, Ac.

Landlines, published in newspaper format, replaced *Landscape Design Extra* in 1998. It is a free supplement with a subscription to *Landscape Design* and can also be purchased separately. The newspaper provides timely information about recent developments in Europe and the United Kingdom regarding landscape and urban policy and important related issues.

4006. ***Landscape and Urban Planning: an international journal on landscape design, conservation and reclamation, planning and urban ecology.*** Incorporates (in 1988): *Reclamation and Revegetation Research;* (in 1986): *Urban Ecology;* Formerly: *Landscape and Planning.* [ISSN: 0169-2046] 1974. 16x/yr. EUR 1375. Ed(s): J R Rodiek. Elsevier BV, Sara Burgerhartstraat 25, Amsterdam, 1055 KV, Netherlands; nlinfo-f@elsevier.nl; http://www.elsevier.nl. Illus., index, adv. Refereed. Online: ingenta.com; ScienceDirect; Swets Blackwell. Reprint: SWZ. *Indexed:* AIAP, ApEcolAb, BiolAb, CJA, EngInd, EnvAb, ExcerpMed, FPA, ForAb, GeoRef, GeogAbPG, HortAb, PollutAb, RRTA, S&F, SSCI, SUSA, SWRA, WAE&RSA, ZooRec. *Bk. rev.:* 2-4. *Aud.:* Ac, Sa.

The primary concern of *Landscape and Urban Planning* is "with conceptual, scientific, and design approaches to land use. Emphasis is on a multi-disciplinary approach to analysis and planning and design." This scientific/academic journal deals with such topics as wildlife conservation and environmental ecology, issues relevant to the study of landscape design. Most of the articles are by international scholars representing the physical and environmental sciences. They discuss such research methods as data collection, GIS-based analysis and problems, and issues of management ecology. Thematic issues appear occasionally. Because of the cross-disciplinary scope of the subjects discussed in the journal, it would be directed toward an academic and specialized architecture library audience. A computer file to the journal has been available since 1998 on the web. For access, a subscription and registration are required. Full-text issues of the journal are archived on the site from February 1995 to the present, and diagrams, charts, and other illustrations are provided online.

4007. ***Landscape Architectural Review.*** [ISSN: 0228-6963] 1980. 4x/yr. CND 25; USD 25. Ed(s): Nick Van Vliet. Landscape Architectural Review, 24 Kensington Ave, Willowdale, ON M2M 1R6, Canada. Illus., index, adv. Circ: 1400. Vol. ends: Dec. *Indexed:* AIAP, GardL. *Bk. rev.:* 2. *Aud.:* Ac.

This publication is the Canadian equivalent of the U.S. journal *Landscape Architecture.* It is the official publication of the Canadian Society of Landscape Architects and describes itself as a Canadian forum for the exchange, discussion, and review of a broad range of ideas and topics related to the theory and practice of landscape architecture, the environmental sciences, and related professions. The articles, written primarily by academics and practitioners, include information about projects in Canada, the United States, and other countries. They range from more scholarly case studies to discussions of a pragmatic nature. Examples of article titles include "The Community Park Users Survey" and "Canadian Community Gardens, a Sustainable Landscape Legacy." Some articles are in French with summaries in English, and all of the English articles are summarized in French. The journal's format is not as glitzy as some of the European journals, but the articles are timely and they provide a glimpse of Canada's landscape architecture scene across its far-reaching provinces. The journal is full of advertisements. Illustrations for the articles are in color and black and white. The contents are neatly arranged into "Articles" and "Departments." The latter include a "Message from the Editor," "Book Reviews," a list of recent "Publications," "Letters," "New Products," "New Plants," and "Coming Events." An academic audience would certainly benefit from the publication, as would a general adult audience using a public library.

4008. ***Landscape Architecture.*** [ISSN: 0023-8031] 1910. 12x/yr. USD 49. American Society of Landscape Architects, 636 Eye St, N W, Washington, DC 20001-3736; scahill@asla.org; http://www.asla.org. Illus., index, adv. Sample. Circ: 26000. Vol. ends: Dec. *Indexed:* AIAP, API, ArchI, ArtHuCI, ArtInd, EIP, GardL, IBZ, SSCI. *Bk. rev.:* 4. *Aud.:* Ac, Sa.

Landscape Architecture, published by the American Society of Landscape Architects (ASLA), is described as "an international magazine of landscape design, planning, and management." The publication serves the ASLA mission "to lead, to educate, and to participate in the careful stewardship, wise planning, and artful design of our cultural and natural environments." A range of short but succinctly written articles with good color illustrations and drawings discuss international landscape projects, urban design, and land conservation. One issue a year is dedicated to the annual ASLA Awards in such categories as "Design," "Research," and "Communication." This professionally directed journal contains timely information and is recommended for an academic or a specialized audience.

4009. ***Landscape Architecture and Town Planning in the Netherlands.*** 1993. irreg. Ed(s): Harry Harsema. Uitgeverij Thoth, Prins Hendriklaan 13, Bussum, 1404 AS, Netherlands. *Aud.:* Ac, Ga.

This biennial serial is included here because of its outstanding graphics and timely content. The publication's stated purpose is to provide an impression of current Dutch landscape design and urban planning projects, with the first series covering the years 1993–1995. The text is in adjacent Dutch and English, and the plentiful articles document a variety of interesting solutions to planning and landscape architecture. Sites are described with accompanying photographs and line drawings. The publication contains no advertising or book reviews, but does include "Nominations" for landscape and urban planning projects and in-depth essays with such titles as "Designing for Ambivalence." The excellent quality of the color photographs, the beautiful graphic layout, and the inclusion of fine line drawings puts this magazine on a par with the German annual *Topos.* It would certainly be a useful addition to an academic architecture library or a public library with a specialized clientele seeking landscape and urban design source material of an "inspirational" nature.

4010. ***Landscape Australia.*** [ISSN: 0310-9011] 1979. q. AUD 48.40 domestic (Students, AUD 39.60). Ed(s): Marion Pennicuik. Landscape Publications, PO Box 356, Mont Albert, VIC 3127, Australia; landaust@landaust.com.au; http://www.landaust.com.au. Illus., index, adv. Circ: 2858. Online: RMIT Publishing. *Indexed:* AIAP, API, GardL. *Bk. rev.:* 2. *Aud.:* Ac.

Landscape Australia is a publication of the Australian Institute of Landscape Architects and covers the profession in the broadest sense as it delves into Australian urban and landscape design, land use planning, and landscape construction. Full of information, it includes a regular features section with short articles on people, environmental policy, forthcoming events, current projects, and contractor news. More in-depth articles focus on a variety of topics such as tree specifications, public gardens, and planning for major urban development projects. An academic architecture library readership interested in international landscape architecture projects and professional developments would find the informal and down-to-earth tone of the publication appealing—and so Aussie!

4011. ***Landscape Design.*** Formerly: *Institute of Landscape Architects. Journal.* [ISSN: 0020-2908] 1934. 10x/yr. GBP 49 in UK & Ireland (Students, GBP 30 in UK & Ireland). Ed(s): Ken Fieldhouse. Landscape Design Trust, 13a West St, Reigate, RH2 9BL, United Kingdom;

info@landscape.co.uk; http://www.landscape.co.uk. Illus., index, adv. Sample. Circ: 6500. Vol. ends: Jun. *Indexed:* AIAP, API, ArtInd, RRTA, WAE&RSA. *Bk. rev.:* 2-6. *Aud.:* Ac, Ga.

This is the professional journal of the Landscape Institute, published by the Landscape Design Trust of the United Kingdom. It can be compared in scope, content, and format to similar professional landscape architecture societies' publications from the United States, Canada, and Australia. Illustrated articles cover urban, environmental, and planning policies as well as European Community environmental and land-conservation concerns. There is a regular section that provides information about products, reports, new books, services, and forthcoming events. The supplement, *Landlines, an Eye on Landscape* [1469-0985], is described as a "newspaper" and is free to subscribers. The supplement provides a good overview of British landscape design projects and government policies in a capsule format. *Landscape Design* is invaluable for a general public library readership as well as an academic audience seeking information in English about British and European landscape architecture events and issues.

4012. *Landscape Journal: design, planning, and management of the land.* [ISSN: 0277-2426] 1981. s-a. USD 135 (Individuals, USD 42). Ed(s): Kenneth Helphand. University of Wisconsin Press, Journal Division, 1930 Monroe St., 3rd Fl, Madison, WI 53711; http://www.wisc.edu/wisconsinpress/journals. Illus., index, adv. Sample. Refereed. Microform: PQC. Reprint: PQC; PSC. *Indexed:* AIAP, API, ArtInd, BHA, GardL, SUSA. *Bk. rev.:* 8. *Aud.:* Ac.

Sponsored by the Council of Educators in Landscape Architecture, *Landscape Journal* is "dedicated to the dissemination of the results of academic research and scholarly investigation of interest to practitioners, academicians, and students of landscape architecture." The journal contains engaging research articles by educators in the landscape field. Each article is preceded by an abstract and illustrated with black-and-white photographs and drawings. Topics of the articles are varied and deal with historical figures in the landscape profession as well as current issues and theory, including some new areas of study. Because of its research direction, *Landscape Journal* would be appropriate for an academic architecture library.

4013. *Landscape Research.* Formerly (until 1976): *Landscape Research News.* [ISSN: 0142-6397] 1968. q. GBP 257 (Individuals, GBP 95). Ed(s): Paul Selman. Carfax Publishing Ltd., 4 Park Sq, Milton Park, Abingdon, OX14 4RN, United Kingdom; enquiries@carfax.co.uk/; http://www.tandf.co.uk/. Illus., index, adv. Sample. Refereed. Circ: 650. Vol. ends: Nov. Online: EBSCO Publishing; Ingenta Select; Northern Light Technology, Inc.; OCLC Online Computer Library Center, Inc.; ProQuest Information & Learning; RoweCom Information Quest; Swets Blackwell. Reprint: PSC. *Indexed:* API, BHA, BiolAb, BrArAb, ForAb, GardL, GeogAbPG, HortAb, IBZ, NumL, RRTA, S&F, SWRA, WAE&RSA. *Bk. rev.:* 4, 600-800 words. *Aud.:* Ac, Sa.

This is an interdisciplinary, international publication dealing with such environmental and ecological topics as cultural landscapes, landscape surveys, and land conservation and protection. The articles are well researched by noted scholars and presented with an abstract and keywords related to their content; they are also enhanced with footnotes, bibliographies, diagrams, charts, and illustrations. The book reviews are well done and serve to "titillate" rather than overwhelm the reader. Because of the scholarly nature of *Landscape Research,* it is recommended for an academic audience with specialized interests not only in landscape architecture but also in physical geography and environmental studies.

4014. *Landskab: tidsskrift for planlaegning af have og landskab, review for garden and landscape planning.* Formerly (until 1968): *Havekunst.* [ISSN: 0023-8066] 1923. 8x/yr. DKK 645 domestic; DKK 516 foreign excl. tax and postage; DKK 68 newsstand/cover per issue. Ed(s): Annemarie Lund. Arkitektens Forlag, Strandgade 27 A, Copenhagen K, 1401, Denmark; info@arkfo.dk; http://www.arkfo.dk. Illus., index, adv. Sample. Circ: 1561. Vol. ends: Dec. Reprint: PQC. *Indexed:* AIAP, API, BHA. *Bk. rev.:* 2-4. *Aud.:* Ac, Sa.

Landskab is a publication of the Association of Danish Landscape Architects. Although the text is in Danish, there are captions and summaries of articles in English. The reader benefits from the discussion of landscape and urban design projects of Denmark and other Scandinavian countries. Good graphic design, color photographs, and black-and-white site plans and details also contribute to *Landskab*'s appeal. Students studying landscape design would benefit from this nicely illustrated professional journal.

Studies in History of Gardens & Designed Landscapes. See Gardening section.

4015. *Topos: European landscape magazine.* [ISSN: 0942-752X] 1992. q. DEM 216 (Students, DEM 168). Callwey Verlag, Postfach 800409, Munich, 81604, Germany; http://www.topos.de. Illus., index, adv. Circ: 4000. *Indexed:* AIAP, API. *Aud.:* Ac, Sa.

Each quarterly issue of *Topos* has text in both German and English and covers 15 to 19 landscape design projects. Examples of themes include "Visionary Landscape," "Wedge Pathways," and "Nightscape." The format is folio, and the color photographs and drawings are carefully juxtaposed to the corresponding text. A section at the back of each issue termed "Short Cuts" provides the reader with information about European landscape architecture competitions, winners of awards, conference news, exhibitions, current projects, and news of the International Federation of Landscape Architects. Brief biographical sketches of contributing authors reveal that most are European and are practicing landscape architects, academicians, journalists, or urban planners. This journal would be a worthy acquisition for the collection of an architecture library because it is not only of superb quality but provides well-documented information about important landscape and urban design projects all over Europe.

■ LARGE PRINT

See also Disabilities section.

Camille McCutcheon, Coordinator of Library Instruction/Assistant Librarian, University of South Carolina Spartanburg, 800 University Way, Spartanburg, SC 29303, CMcCutcheon@uscs.edu, FAX: 864-503-5601

Introduction

Many periodicals are now available to address the needs of blind and visually impaired individuals, their family members, and the professionals who serve them. The intended audience of these publications varies, from individuals with low vision to the parents of blind children, to diabetics who have vision-related diseases, to blinded veterans of the U.S. Armed Forces. The subject matter of these periodicals includes information ranging from tips on day-to-day living with blindness or visual impairments; poetry or prose submitted by blind and visually impaired individuals; ways to adjust to vision loss late in life; and improvements in adaptive technology, as well as accessibility issues and the Internet. Other titles contain reprints and compilations of articles from mainstream magazines and newspapers.

Several of these publishers, such as National Braille Press, Inc. and The American Printing House for the Blind (APH), Inc., produce books in Braille. Clovernook and APH produce Braille and other accessible formats such as electronic Braille or "talking" cassettes, of mainstream titles like *Reader's Digest* and *Newsweek.*

All of the publishers of these magazines included in this chapter have web sites, and many can be contacted via e-mail. Almost all of them have current and back issues that can be accessed online via the Internet. Most of these magazines and newsletters are in large print, and most are 14-point type or larger. In addition to large type and online, other available formats of these titles include "talking" cassettes, inkprint, ASCII text, e-mail, and Braille.

Basic Periodicals

FOR THE BLIND AND VISUALLY IMPAIRED. *Braille Book Review, Dialogue, The New York Times Large Type Weekly, Reader's Digest Large Edition for Easier Reading, Syndicated Columnists Weekly, Talking Book Topics. Many of the organizations listed below also have catalogs of mainstream magazines that are reprinted for the visually impaired.*

ABOUT THE BLIND AND VISUALLY IMPAIRED. *Braille Monitor, Journal of Visual Impairment and Blindness, Review.*

Basic Reference Materials

Library of Congress. National Library Service for the Blind and Physically Handicapped.

Organizations

American Council of the Blind, 1155 15th Street, NW, Suite 1004, Washington, DC 20005, http://www.acb.org/, info@afb.org.

American Foundation for the Blind, 11 Penn Plaza, Suite 300, New York, NY 10001-2017, http://www.afb.org/, afbinfo@afb.net.

American Printing House for the Blind, Inc., P.O. Box 6085, Louisville, KY 40206-0085, http://www.aph.org/, info@aph.org.

Clovernook Center for the Blind, 7000 Hamilton Ave, Cincinati, OH 45321-5297, http://www.clovernook.org/,clovernook@clovernook.org.

Helen Keller National Center for Deaf-Blind Youths and Adults, 111 Middle Neck Rd., Sands Point, NY 11050, http://www.helenkeller.org/national/, hkncdir@aol.com.

Lighthouse International, 111 East 59th Street, New York, NY 10022, http://www.lighthouse.org/, info@lighthouse.org.

National Association for Visually Handicapped, 22 W. 21st St., New York, NY 10010, http://www.navh.org/, staff@navh.org.

National Federation of the Blind, 1800 Johnson St., Baltimore, MD 21230, http://www.nfb.org/, nfb@nfb.org.

Basic Abstracts and Indexes

The only index specific to this subject, *Rehabilitation Literature,* ceased publication in 1986. General indexes provide some guidance.

4016. *A F B Directory of Services for Blind and Visually Impaired Persons in the United States and Canada.* Former titles: *A F B Directory of Services for Blind and Visually Impaired Persons in the United States; A F B Directory of Agencies Serving the Visually Handicapped in the U S.* [ISSN: 1067-5833] biennial. USD 69.95 print & online eds. American Foundation for the Blind Press, 11 Penn Plaza, Suite 300, New York, NY 10001; afbinfo@afb.net; http://www.afb.org. *Aud.:* Ga, Sa.

This publication provides information on organizations and agencies in the United States and Canada that serve the needs of blind and visually impaired individuals. Section One of the directory is organized by the following categories: federal agencies, national organizations, national membership organizations, types of organizations, types of services, computer training, and products. Section Two includes U.S. organizations; Section Three, Canadian organizations; Section Four, U.S./Canadian publishers of Braille, audio, and other non-print formats; Section Five, U.S./Canadian sources of adapted products for persons with visual impairments; and Section Six, an alphabetical index to the entire directory. This directory is available in standard print. With the purchase of the print directory, access to the online version is included. An excellent reference source.

4017. *A F B News.* Former titles: *American Foundation for the Blind News; American Foundation for the Blind Newsletter.* 1966. s-a. Free. American Foundation for the Blind Press, 11 Penn Plaza, Suite 300, New York, NY 10001; afbinfo@afb.net; http://www.afb.org. Adv. Circ: 7500. *Aud.:* Ga.

This general readership newsletter provides information to individuals who are blind or have visual impairments. It includes updates and articles regarding national legislative activities and AFB's services, people, activities, and programs. Announcements of books recently published by the AFB Press are also included. The text of the newsletter for Summer 2002 and Winter 2003 can be accessed from AFB's web site. It is also available in standard print.

4018. *A P H Slate.* [ISSN: 1081-5198] 1985. s-a. Free. Ed(s): Scott Blome. American Printing House for the Blind, Inc., 1839 Frankfort Ave, Louisville, KY 40206; info@aph.org; http://www.aph.org/. Illus. Sample. Circ: 8700. Vol. ends: Spring/Fall. *Aud.:* Ga, Sa.

This newsletter provides information on APH's current projects and activities. Also included are profiles on products that are innovations created or distributed by APH. The current issue of the newsletter, along with issues dating back to 2000, can be accessed via APH's web site. This publication is also available on diskette, in Braille, and in 16-point large type.

4019. *AccessWorld (Print Edition): technology and people with visual impairments.* Incorporates: *Tactic.* [ISSN: 1526-9582] 2000. bi-m. USD 39.95 domestic; USD 54.95 foreign. Ed(s): Jay Leventhal. American Foundation for the Blind Press, 11 Penn Plaza, Suite 300, New York, NY 10001; http://www.afb.org. Illus., adv. Circ: 1100. Vol. ends: Nov. *Aud.:* Ga.

AccessWorld provides news and presents articles on assistive technology and visual impairment. It also includes information on accessibility issues and product reviews. *AccessWorld Extra* is a bi-monthly e-mail newsletter of additional content that is free to *AccessWorld* subscribers. A sample issue of *AccessWorld* can be accessed from AFB's web site. This publication is also available in the following formats: 14-point large type, cassette, ASCII disk, and Braille.

4020. *Aging & Vision: a publication for practitioners, researchers and educators.* 1998. q. Free. Ed(s): Sarah Lloyd. Lighthouse International, 111 E 59th St, New York, NY 10022; info@lighthouse.org; http://www.lighthouse.org. Circ: 20000. *Aud.:* Sa.

Lighthouse International is a "leading resource worldwide on vision impairment and vision rehabilitation." Its newsletter provides information for practitioners, researchers, and educators who work with individuals who are blind or visually impaired. Articles included range from news about Lighthouse International, health issues related to aging and vision, accessibility issues and the Internet, to living with and adjusting to vision loss late in life. The current issue, along with selected issues dating back to 1998, can be access via Lighthouse International's web site. Although the newsletter is currently available in standard print, beginning in fall 2003, *Aging & Vision* only will be available online. Upon request, it is also available in Braille.

4021. *The B V A Bulletin.* [ISSN: 0005-3430] 1946. bi-m. Free. Ed(s): Stuart Nelson. Blinded Veterans Association, National Board of Directors, 477 H St, NW, Washington, DC 20001; bva@bva.org; http://www.bva.org. Illus. Circ: 13800 Controlled. Online: ProQuest Information & Learning. *Aud.:* Ga, Sa.

Information in *The BVA Bulletin* is written by blinded veterans for blinded veterans. The publication covers legislation, news, feature articles, information from the President of the BVA, recent and upcoming activities of the association, letters to the editor, and an "in remembrance" section for blinded veterans who have recently died. The most recent issue can be accessed via the BVA web site, along with issues dating back to 2001. This publication also is available in 14-point large type and on cassette.

4022. *Braille Book Review.* [ISSN: 0006-873X] 1932. bi-m. Free. Ed(s): Edmund O'Reilly. U.S. Library of Congress, National Library Service for the Blind and Physically Handicapped, 1291 Taylor St, NW, Washington, DC 20011; nls@loc.gov; http://www.loc.gov/nls/. Illus., index. Sample. Circ: 5000. Vol. ends: Nov/Dec. *Aud.:* Ems, Hs, Ga, Sa.

Braille Book Review contains annotated lists of the most recent nonfiction and fiction titles produced in Braille for adults and children that are available through the National Library Service for the Blind and Physically Handicapped and its network of cooperating libraries. Genres represented include mysteries, classics, biographies, gothics, and how-to and self-help guides. In each issue of *BBR,* books that have been recently added to the national collection are listed and announcements and news about NLS are included. *BBR* lists Braille magazines that are available through the network as well. The Braille edition of *BBR* includes recorded books, with abbreviated annotations. The current issue of *BBR,* along with back issues to 1994, can be accessed via the NLS web site. *BBR* is also available in 14-point large type, in Braille, and on diskette.

4023. ***The Braille Forum.*** [ISSN: 0006-8772] 1962. m. USD 25 Free to members. Ed(s): Penny Reeder. American Council of the Blind, 1155 15th St, N W, Ste 1004, Washington, DC 20005; http://www.acb.org. Illus., adv. Sample. Circ: 26000. Vol. ends: Jun. Online: ProQuest Information & Learning; SoftLine Information. *Aud.:* Sa.

The Braille Forum's intended audience includes blind and visually impaired individuals. It publishes poetry along with topics such as news, legislation, employment, health, new products and services, human interest stories, and sports and leisure activities. The current issue, along with issues dating back to 1990, can be accessed via ACB's web site. *The Braille Forum* is also available in Braille, 16-point large type, half-speed four-track cassette, and computer diskette, as well as via e-mail.

4024. ***Braille Monitor: voice of the nation's blind.*** [ISSN: 0006-8829] 1956. m. Non-members, USD 25. Ed(s): Mrs. Barbara Pierce. National Federation of the Blind, 1800 Johnson St, Baltimore, MD 21230; nfb@nfb.org; http://www.nfb.org. Illus., index, adv. Sample. Circ: 38000. Vol. ends: Dec. *Indexed:* ECER. *Aud.:* Sa.

The leading publication of the NFB, the *Braille Monitor* is read by the blind, their families, and the professionals who serve them. Information in the *Braille Monitor* includes recipes, human interest stories, profiles of blind individuals, and highlights of NFB's activities and programs. This title addresses issues of the blind, such as civil rights, social concerns, legislation, employment, and education, and it provides information on technology and aids/appliances used by the blind. The current issue, as well as back issues to 1987, can be accessed via the NFB's web site. The *Braille Monitor* also is available in 14-point large type, in Braille, on cassette, in inkprint, or via e-mail.

4025. ***Deaf - Blind Perspectives.*** [ISSN: 1526-9841] 1993. 3x/yr. Free. Western Oregon University, Teaching Research Division, 345 N Monmouth Ave, Monmouth, OR 97361; kenyond@wou.edu; http://www.tr.wou.edu/. Circ: 4000. *Bk. rev.:* various number and length. *Aud.:* Sa.

This publication provides information on topics relating to deaf-blind individuals and includes announcements, articles, and essays about the deaf-blind, their family members, and the professionals who serve them. Persons affiliated with DB-LINK (National Information Clearinghouse on Children Who Are Deaf-Blind) and NTAC (National Technical Assistance Consortium for Children and Young Adults Who Are Deaf-Blind) regularly contribute to this publication. The current issue of *Deaf-Blind Perspectives,* as well as back issues to 1993, can be accessed via the web site for *Deaf-Blind Perspectives.* This publication also is available in Braille, 16-point large type, standard print, and ASCII via e-mail or diskette.

4026. ***Dialogue (Salem): a world of ideas for the visually impaired of all ages.*** Incorporates (1983-1995): *Lifeprints.* [ISSN: 1069-6857] 1961. q. USD 40; USD 28 for visually impaired. Ed(s): Carol M McCarl. Blindskills, Inc., PO Box 5181, Salem, OR 97304-0181; blindskl@teleport.com; http://www.blindskills.com. Illus., adv. Sample. Circ: 1100 Paid. Vol. ends: Winter. *Aud.:* Ga, Sa.

Dialogue contains poetry, prose, and informative articles that are written by people who are blind or visually impaired. Technology, spotlights on families of visually impaired individuals, information for visually impaired students, sports and recreation, travel destinations, cooking, gardening, and health are just some of the topics covered in *Dialogue.* There is also a book review section, news, and information on ways to obtain new products and services, computer-related and otherwise. This publication is available in 18-point large type, on cassette, on diskette, and in Braille.

4027. ***EnVision: a publication for parents and educators of children with impaired vision.*** 1993. s-a. Free. Ed(s): Sarah Lloyd. Lighthouse International, 111 E 59th St, New York, NY 10022; info@lighthouse.org; http://www.lighthouse.org. Circ: 10000. *Aud.:* Sa.

EnVision is a newsletter that contains information for parents and educators of children with impaired vision. The current issue of *EnVision,* as well as back issues to 1999, can be accessed via Lighthouse International's web site. Although the newsletter is currently available in standard print, beginning in fall 2003, *EnVision* only will be available online. Upon request, it is also available in Braille.

4028. ***Future Reflections.*** [ISSN: 0883-3419] 1981. q. Members, USD 8; Non-members, USD 15. Ed(s): Barbara A Cheadle. National Federation of the Blind, 1800 Johnson St, Baltimore, MD 21230; nfb@nfb.org; http://www.nfb.org. Circ: 13000. *Aud.:* Sa.

Parents and educators of blind children are the target audience of *Future Reflections.* This work publishes poetry and prose submitted by blind children and profiles blind children and their parents and educators. Also included are articles on educational programs for blind students and resources for parents and teachers. The current issue of *Future Reflections,* as well as back issues to 1991, can be accessed via the NFB's web site. It also is available on cassette and in 14-point large type.

4029. ***Guideposts: a practical guide to successful living.*** [ISSN: 0017-5331] 1945. m. 11/yr. USD 14.97 domestic; USD 20.97 Canada; USD 22.97 elsewhere. Ed(s): Edward Grinnan. Guideposts Associates, Inc., 39 Seminary Hill Rd, Carmel, NY 10512; http://www.guideposts.org. Illus., index, adv. Sample. Circ: 4500000. Vol. ends: Mar. *Aud.:* Ga, Sa.

A "guide for practical living," *Guideposts* is an inspirational, interfaith publication that presents first-person narratives that encourage readers to achieve their maximum personal and spiritual potential. Selected departments and stories from the current issue of the magazine can be accessed from the *Guideposts* web site. This publication is available on cassette and computer diskette, in a talking book edition, in 18-point large type, and in Braille.

Journal of Visual Impairment & Blindness. See Disabilities section.

4030. ***Library Resources for the Blind and Physically Handicapped.*** Formerly: *Directory of Library Resources for the Blind and Physically Handicapped.* [ISSN: 0364-1236] 1968. a. Free to qualified personnel. U.S. Library of Congress, National Library Service for the Blind and Physically Handicapped, 1291 Taylor St, NW, Washington, DC 20011; nls@loc.gov; http://www.loc.gov/nls/. Illus. Sample. *Indexed:* CIJE. *Aud.:* Ga, Ac, Sa.

The National Library Service for the Blind and Physically Handicapped (NLS) administers a free program that provides music scores in Braille and large print, books and magazines in recorded and Braille formats, and specially designed playback equipment linked to a cooperating network of regional and subregional libraries. These network libraries, in turn, circulate these materials, via postage-free mail, to eligible borrowers who are unable to read them in standard print format. This publication includes information on the NLS and its services and a directory of the network libraries and machine-lending agencies arranged alphabetically by state. This directory, excluding the appendices, can be accessed via the NLS web site. It is also available in standard print. An excellent reference source.

4031. ***Musical Mainstream (Large Print Edition).*** Former titles (until Dec. 1976): *New Braille Musician; Braille Musician.* [ISSN: 0364-7501] 1942. q. Free. Ed(s): Irene Kost. U.S. Library of Congress, National Library Service for the Blind and Physically Handicapped, 1291 Taylor St, NW, Washington, DC 20011; nls@loc.gov; http://www.loc.gov/nls/. Sample. Circ: 300. Vol. ends: Oct/Dec. *Bk. rev.:* Various number and length. *Aud.:* Ga, Sa.

Published by the Music Section of the National Library Service for the Blind and Physically Handicapped, *Musical Mainstream* contains reprints of articles on classical music and music education from national publications such as *Opera News, Billboard, Piano Today,* and *American Record Guide.* According to the inside cover, some of the issues include articles of interest to blind and physically handicapped persons as well as current information about the music program of the NLS and recent additions to its collections. This publication is available in 16-point large type, in Braille, and on diskette.

4032. ***N A V H Update.*** 1997. q. Free. Ed(s): Dr. Lorraine H Marchi. National Association for Visually Handicapped, 22 W 21st St, 6th Fl, New York, NY 10010; staff@navh.org; http://www.navh.org. Circ: 13000. *Aud.:* Ga, Sa.

This newsletter contains brief articles on nutrition and health as well as on technological advances; an update on NAVH's Large Print Loan Library; news; gift ideas; and many other tips and items of interest. It also includes announcements of recently published titles of interest to blind and visually impaired individuals. It is available in 16-point-type large print.

4033. ***Nat-Cent News.*** 3x/yr. Free to libraries and visually and hearing impaired. Ed(s): Robert J Smithdas. Helen Keller National Center for Deaf - Blind Youths and Adults, 111 Middle Neck Rd., Sands Point, NY 11050; info@helenkeller.org; http://www.helenkeller.org/national. Circ: 3000. *Aud.:* Sa.

This publication includes poetry written by and profiles of deaf-blind persons, announcements of new products, technological advances, and news and feature articles that are of interested to deaf-blind individuals. *Nat-Cent News* is available in 24-point large type and in Braille.

4034. ***New York Times Large Type Weekly.*** [ISSN: 0028-7814] 1967. w. USD 78; USD 1.50 per issue. Ed(s): Tom Brady. New York Times Company, 229 W 43rd St, New York, NY 10036; wedemeye@nytimes.com; http://www.nytimes.com. Illus. Sample. Vol. ends: Feb. *Aud.:* Ga, Sa.

The New York Times Large Type Weekly includes selected articles that have appeared throughout the past week in *The New York Times*. Graphics and color photographs enhance stories on national and international news, science and health, business, the arts, sports, and editorials. A crossword puzzle is also included. This publication is available in 16-point large type and in Braille.

4035. ***Our Special: magazine devoted to matters of interest to blind women.*** [ISSN: 0030-6959] 1927. bi-m. USD 15. Ed(s): Dana Nichols. National Braille Press, Inc., 88 St Stephen St, Boston, MA 02115; orders@nbp.org; http://www.nbp.org. Circ: 850. *Aud.:* Sa.

This publication for blind women contains articles originally written especially for this publication along with ones reprinted from women's magazines such as *Good Housekeeping* and *Redbook,* and from newspapers such as *The New York Times, The Christian Science Monitor,* and *The Wall Street Journal*. Topics featured in *Our Special* include career issues, family life, health, dating, cooking, travel, and fashion. This publication is only available in Braille.

4036. ***Reader's Digest Large Edition for Easier Reading.*** Formerly: *Reader's Digest Large Type Edition.* [ISSN: 1094-5857] 1964. m. USD 27.96 domestic. Ed(s): Jacqueline Leo. Reader's Digest Association, Inc, Reader's Digest Rd, Pleasantville, NY 10570-7000; http://www.rd.com. Adv. Circ: 510203 Paid. *Bk. rev.:* Various number and length. *Aud.:* Ga.

Printed on non-glare paper, *Reader's Digest Large Edition for Easier Reading* contains in-depth feature articles and departments such as "Word Power," "Humor in Uniform," "Life in the United States," "Drama in Real Life," "Laughter is the Best Medicine," and the book-length feature. It is available in 21-point large type from Reader's Digest, Inc. This periodical is also available from The American Print House for the Blind (APH), Inc. in the following formats: 4-track ips cassette, in Braille, and on electronic Braille/diskette. The advertising has been removed from these APH formats.

Re:View. See Disabilities section.

4037. ***Sharing Solutions: a publication for people with impaired vision and their support networks.*** s-a. Free. Ed(s): Sarah Lloyd. Lighthouse International, 111 E 59th St, New York, NY 10022; info@lighthouse.org; http://www.lighthouse.org. Circ: 20000. *Aud.:* Ga, Sa.

Sharing Solutions is for individuals with impaired vision and their support networks. Topics vary, from news, legislation, Medicare, exercise, health, eye diseases, and adaptive computer technology, to articles of interest on solutions to life's everyday problems. The current issue, along with some issues dating back to 1998, can be accessed via Lighthouse International's web site. This newsletter is also available in 16-point large type and on cassette. Upon request, it is also available electronically and in Braille.

4038. ***Syndicated Columnists Weekly.*** 1984. w. USD 24. National Braille Press, Inc., 88 St Stephen St, Boston, MA 02115; orders@nbp.org; http://www.nbp.org. Circ: 380. *Aud.:* Sa.

The *Syndicated Columnists Weekly* newspaper contains the best editorials written by syndicated columnists that have appeared that week in major U.S. newspapers such as *The Wall Street Journal, The New York Times, The Washington Post,* and *The Boston Globe*. *SCW* is only available in Braille.

Tactic. See *AccessWorld.*

4039. ***Vision Enhancement.*** [ISSN: 1094-8635] 1996. q. USD 25 in US & Canada; USD 50 elsewhere. Ed(s): Patricia Price. Vision World Wide, Inc., 5707 Brockton Dr, 302, Indianapolis, IN 46220-5481; info@visionww.org; http://www.visionww.org. Adv. *Bk. rev.:* Various number and length. *Aud.:* Ga, Sa.

Published by Vision World Wide, Inc., *Vision Enhancement*'s intended audience includes individuals experiencing vision loss, their families, and the professionals who serve them. A typical issue includes a section which answers questions from readers; feature articles addressing vision loss; news and events occurring in the visually impaired community; articles on consumer protection; profiles of accomplishments of people with vision loss; articles on eye diseases, conditions, and treatments; creative ideas to benefit the visually impaired; latest assistive devices to promote independence; information on libraries and related reading materials; books, magazines, and videos for the visually impaired and their caregivers; earning opportunities for the visually impaired; items of interest to visually impaired computer users; news about Vision World Wide, Inc.; and a directory of resources, programs, and services featured in the issue. A few issues along with sample contents of past issues can be accessed via Vision World Wide's web site. This publication also is available in 16-point large type; on standard two-track, tone-indexed cassette; in enhanced letter format (ELF) computer diskette; electronically via e-mail; and on computer diskette (ASCII format). Both the e-mail and the computer diskette (ASCII format) versions contain a special file for Braille output.

4040. ***Voice of the Diabetic: a support and information network.*** [ISSN: 1041-8490] 1986. q. Non-members, USD 20. Ed(s): Ed Bryant. National Federation of the Blind, Diabetes Action Network, 1412 I70 Dr SW, C, Columbia, MO 65203; http://www.nfb.org/voice.htm. Adv. Circ: 320000. *Aud.:* Ga, Sa.

This newspaper includes articles pertaining to diabetes and blindness and promotes "good diabetes control, diet, and independence." Included are profiles of diabetics, recipes, a resource column, and informational articles on topics ranging from diabetes education, physical exercise, and Social Security disability to medical questions answered by an insulin-dependent physician. This publication is available in standard print, via e-mail, and on 15/16 ips audiocassette, "talking book" speed.

■ LATIN AMERICAN

Joseph R. Diaz, Associate Librarian, University of Arizona Library, 1510 E. University Blvd., Tucson, AZ 85721-0055; diazj@u.library.arizona.edu; FAX: 520-621-9733

Olivia Olivares, Assistant Librarian, University of Arizona Library, 1510 E. University Blvd., Tucson, AZ 85721-0055; olivareso@u.library.arizona.edu; FAX: 520-621-9733

Veronica Reyes, Assistant Librarian, University of Arizona Library, 1510 E. University Blvd., Tucson, AZ 85721-0055; reyesv@u.library.arizona.edu; FAX: 520-621-9733

Introduction

This section focuses on scholarly journals and popular magazines about and/or from Latin America, published either in English or Spanish or both. Covering huge geographical and cultural areas, these titles are published worldwide, ample evidence that there is a global interest in things Latin American. The academic titles are concentrated in the social sciences and humanities—disciplines that have traditionally focused on Latin American Studies. While some of the titles included are not comprehensively indexed, most are indeed indexed in a variety of sources, including electronic databases, such as the Hispanic American Periodicals Index. This list is not intended to be comprehensive; rather, it should serve as a guide in developing library collections relevant to this area.

Tackling such a large region has been challenging. We have attempted to include representative titles from throughout Latin America, but we have emphasized inclusion of materials that are readily available in the United States. Rather than focus on a particular country, most titles cover either a region of Latin America, such as Central America or the Caribbean region, or more broadly, the entire Hispanic world. Ordering titles directly from publishers in Latin America can prove to be a slow, cumbersome process. Therefore, we strongly suggest that selectors of Spanish-language periodicals and other materials find vendors or distributors that are willing to help identify and provide titles that are readily available.

Basic Periodicals

Hs: *The Americas, Eres, Geomundo, Tu;* Ga: *The Americas, Buenhogar, Contenido, Hola, Impacto;* Ac: *Historia Mexicana, Review (Americas Society).*

Basic Abstracts and Indexes

Hispanic American Periodicals Index.

4041. *America Indigena.* [ISSN: 0185-1179] 1941. q. USD 75; USD 80 in Latin America; USD 80 in North America. Instituto Indigenista Interamericano, Apdo. Postal 20315, Mexico City, 01001, Mexico. Illus., index. Reprint: SWZ. *Indexed:* AICP, AmH&L, AnthLit, HAPI, IBSS, IBZ, RI-1. *Aud.:* Ac.

The stated focus of this longstanding quarterly publication is on the "scientific analysis of the problems, processes and tendencies of the native peoples of Latin America." Broad in scope, with articles written in English, Spanish, and Portuguese, it covers anthropological, legal, and historical aspects of native culture as well as the relationship between native and non-native societies in Latin America. Recent issues provide extensive coverage of native peoples' legal rights in the Americas, with a heavy emphasis on Central America. Recommended for academic libraries. (JRD)

4042. *The Americas: a quarterly review of Inter-American cultural history.* [ISSN: 0003-1615] 1944. q. USD 105 (Individuals, USD 40; Students, USD 25 post-secondary only). Ed(s): Judith Ewell. Academy of American Franciscan History, 1712 Euclid Ave, Berkeley, CA 94709-1208; acadafh@aol.com; http://www.aafh.org. Illus., index, adv. Refereed. Circ: 1000. *Indexed:* ABS&EES, AmH&L, ArtHuCI, BRI, CBRI, HAPI, HumInd, IBZ, MagInd, SSCI, SSI. *Bk. rev.:* 15, 500-700 words. *Aud.:* Ac.

This is a well-established scholarly journal that focuses on the social and cultural history of Latin America and inter-American affairs, with a slant toward the study of the history and influence of the Catholic Church in the Americas. Each issue contains five to ten in-depth articles on very narrow aspects of Latin American sociocultural history, as well as an extensive book review section. A section titled "InterAmerican Notes" highlights upcoming professional conferences, calls for papers, and forthcoming publications. Not to be confused with the Organization of American States magazine by the same title, this refereed journal is intended for academic audiences. (JRD)

4043. *Americas (English Edition).* [ISSN: 0379-0940] 1949. bi-m. USD 18. Ed(s): James Patrick Kiernan. Americas Magazine, 19th St & Constitution Ave, N W, Ste 300, Washington, DC 20006; jkiernan@oas.org; http://www.oas.org/. Illus. Sample. Circ: 50000 Paid. Microform: PQC. Online: EBSCO Publishing; Florida Center for Library Automation; Gale Group; OCLC Online Computer Library Center, Inc.; ProQuest Information & Learning; H.W. Wilson. *Indexed:* ArtHuCI, BAS, BRI, HAPI, HumInd, MLA-IB, MagInd, PRA, RGPR, RI-1, SSCI. *Bk. rev.:* 2-3, 600-1,200 words. *Aud.:* Ga, Ac.

A lavishly illustrated bimonthly magazine published by the Organization of American States (OAS), *Americas* is a general-interest periodical that features articles and photo essays on a variety of topics, including art, nature, travel, biography, and cultural anthropology, as well as regular columns on music, food, literature, and dance in Latin America. There is also a column on OAS news, issues, and activities. A staple in the genre of general-interest periodicals on Latin America since 1949, this colorful and informative publication is available in both English and Spanish. It would make a welcome addition to any high school, public, or academic library collection. (JRD)

Ancient Mesoamerica. See Archaeology section.

4044. *Anuario de Estudios Centroamericanos.* [ISSN: 0377-7316] 1974. 2x/yr. USD 30. Ed(s): Oscar Fernandez. Editorial de la Universidad de Costa Rica, Apdo. 75-2060, Ciudad Univ. R. Facio, San Jose, 2050, Costa Rica; cmmoreno@cariari.ucr.ac.cr. Adv. Circ: 1000. Microform: OMN. *Indexed:* HAPI, IBSS, PAIS. *Bk. rev.:* Various number and length. *Aud.:* Ac.

This refereed scholarly journal, published twice a year, focuses on all aspects of the social sciences. Coverage is limited to the Central American region, with heavy emphasis on the study of the history and culture of Costa Rica. Recent submissions cover such topics as rural development and poverty in Central America in the 1990s and Spaniards in the City of San Jose, Costa Rica, at the end of the nineteenth century. A longstanding publication that belongs in academic libraries with programs in Latin American Studies. (JRD)

4045. *Buenhogar.* [ISSN: 0186-422X] 1966. m. USD 53.70; USD 2.95 newsstand/cover per issue. Ed(s): Paolo Merigo. Editorial Televisa, 6355 N W 36th St, Miami, FL 33166; subscriptions@editorialtelevisa.com. Illus., adv. Circ: 150000. Online: Gale Group. *Aud.:* Ga.

As the Spanish-language edition of *Good Housekeeping,* this magazine offers the standard fare of short but informative articles for women on any number of topics, including advice on relationships, recipes, new cosmetic and household products, decorating tips, exercise advice, and a regular horoscope column. Filled with glossy full-page ads, it includes interviews with American celebrities such as Tom Cruise and Richard Gere and a regular column by Dr. Joyce Brothers. While everything in this publication is in Spanish, the focus is on the culture and products of the United States. Even so, this is sure to be a popular item. Recommended for public libraries. (JRD)

4046. *Caribbean Quarterly.* [ISSN: 0008-6495] 1949. q. JMD 200; USD 35. Ed(s): Rex Nettleford. University of the West Indies, School of Continuing Studies, PO Box 42, Kingston, 7, Jamaica. Index, adv. Circ: 1500. Microform: PQC. Reprint: PSC. *Indexed:* ASSIA, AmH&L, HAPI, IBSS, IIBP, PAIS, RRTA, WAE&RSA. *Bk. rev.:* Various number and length. *Aud.:* Ac.

This journal, published in Jamaica, has been in existence for over 50 years. Its focus is on the literature, politics, and history of the Caribbean region and includes scholarly articles, book reviews, fiction, and poetry. Sample articles focus on the Caribbean as multi-ethnic, as dispossessed, and as independent and attaining selfhood. For academic libraries with programs in Latin American/ Caribbean Studies. (JRD)

4047. ***Casa y Estilo Internacional.*** [ISSN: 1521-8287] bi-m. Ed(s): Alfonso Nino. Linda International Publishing, 12182 SW 128th St, Miami, FL 33186; info@estilonet.com. Adv. *Aud.:* Ga.

This glossy, Spanish language lifestyle magazine is aimed specifically at the upscale Hispanic market. Topics covered include art design, profiles of custom-made homes and interiors, interviews with trend setting personalities, a section on cooking, restaurant reviews, and a travel section. This publication is sure to be a winner with those interested in keeping up with the latest styles and trends in interior design and other aspects of "fine living." Recommended for public libraries. (JRD)

4048. ***Chasqui.*** [ISSN: 0145-8973] 1972. s-a. USD 25 (Individuals, USD 15). Ed(s): David W Foster. Arizona State University, Languages and Literatures, University Dr & Mill Ave, Tempe, AZ 85287; david.foster@asu.edu; http://www.wm.edu/. Illus., adv. Refereed. Circ: 400 Paid. Reprint: ISI. *Indexed:* ArtHuCI, HAPI, MLA-IB, SSCI. *Bk. rev.:* 25-30, 500-3,000 words. *Aud.:* Ac.

A literary journal with articles published in Spanish, English, and Portuguese, this publication features literary criticism (six to eight articles per issue), bibliographic essays, original works of creative writing, interviews with writers, and plenty of book reviews of works by well-known and lesser-known authors. It encourages the submission of manuscripts that focus on interdisciplinary approaches, the bridging of national and linguistic divisions, subaltern studies, feminism, queer theory, popular culture, and minority topics. One of many in the genre of "revista de literatura latinoamericana," it is appropriate for academic libraries with large Latin American collections. (JRD)

4049. ***Clara: mensual con mil ideas.*** m. MXP 108; USD 71. Ed(s): Perla Carreto. Consorcio Sayrols, Mier y Pesado 126, Mexico, Col del Valle, Mexico City, 03100, Mexico; beatrizc@spin.com.mx; http://www.sayrols.com.mx. Circ: 150000. *Aud.:* Ga.

This magazine is one of many popular women's magazines from Latin America that focus on health, fashion, beauty, relationships, travel, and leisure. It is unique in that it is published in Mexico and not in Miami as so many others are. Reminiscent of American magazines such as *Good Housekeeping* and *Family Circle, Clara* is widely circulated and appears monthly. Each issue contains many glossy, full-page ads, recipes, advice on health and relationships, and other standard fare found in women's magazines. Occasionally, an interview with an important cultural or political figure will be included. A popular title in Latin America, this publication will find a welcome home in any public library that serves a Spanish-speaking clientele. (JRD)

4050. ***Colonial Latin American Review.*** [ISSN: 1060-9164] 1992. s-a. GBP 164 (Individuals, GBP 47). Ed(s): Raquel Chang Rodriguez. Carfax Publishing Ltd., 4 Park Sq, Milton Park, Abingdon, OX14 4RN, United Kingdom; enquiry@tandf.co.uk; http://www.tandf.co.uk/. Illus., index. Refereed. Online: EBSCO Publishing; Ingenta Select; OCLC Online Computer Library Center, Inc.; RoweCom Information Quest; Swets Blackwell. Reprint: PSC. *Indexed:* AICP, AmH&L, HAPI, MLA-IB, PSA, SociolAb. *Aud.:* Ac.

This interdisciplinary journal focuses on the colonial period in Latin America. Included are articles, review essays, research notes, book reviews, conference announcements, and even obituaries in English, Spanish, and Portuguese. *CLAR* is intended to provide a forum for critical analysis and scholarship in the disciplines of art, anthropology, geography, history, and literature, with the goal of fostering dialogue among these disciplines. Articles are from international contributors and are the work of both emerging and established scholars. Recommended for libraries with comprehensive Latin American collections. (JRD)

4051. ***Contenido.*** [ISSN: 0010-7581] 1963. m. MXP 220; MXP 20 newsstand/cover per issue; USD 45 foreign. Ed(s): Armando Ayala Anguiano. Editorial Contenido S.A., BUFFON 46, esq. Ejercito Nacional 9o piso, Mexico, Col Anzures, Mexico City, 11590, Mexico; ecsa@data.net.mx; http://www.contenido.com.mx. Illus., adv. Circ: 200000. Online: EBSCO Publishing; Gale Group. *Aud.:* Ga.

Very similar in format to *Reader's Digest,* this monthly publication contains many brief, general-interest articles on topics such as health, science, technology, food, recipes, and humor, all from a Mexican perspective. Also included are articles on popular Mexican celebrities and well-known international figures, and features on geography and history. Every issue also contains a condensed book by a well-known Latin American author. Sure to be popular with a variety of readers, this magazine is recommended for public libraries. (JRD)

4052. ***Cosmopolitan en Espanol.*** [ISSN: 0188-0616] 1973. m. USD 21.95 domestic; USD 45.35 foreign; USD 2.95 newsstand/cover per issue domestic. Editorial Televisa, 6355 N W 36th St, Miami, FL 33166; subscriptions@editorialtelevisa.com. Illus., adv. Circ: 52630 Paid. Microform: PQC. Online: Gale Group. *Aud.:* Ga.

Appealing primarily to women, the Spanish-language version of *Cosmopolitan* is quite popular in Mexico and other parts of Latin America. While it offers nothing unique as far as popular women's magazines in Spanish are concerned, it does manage to hold its own, perhaps because of its titillating focus on sex and male/female relationships. Included in each issue are articles focusing on fashion, beauty, self-help, and home decorating. Also featured are lots of photographs and interviews with Hollywood celebrities and regular columns on music, travel, health, and astrology. Recommended for public libraries. (JRD)

4053. ***Cristina: la revista.*** [ISSN: 1067-2575] 1991. m. USD 14.95; USD 3.95 newsstand/cover per issue. Ed(s): Wanda Negron Cruz. Editorial America, S.A., 6355 NW 36th St, Miami, FL 33166. Adv. *Aud.:* Ga.

Founded in November 1991 and published by Cristina Saralegui, the well-known Latina television talk-show host based in Miami, *Cristina* is a Spanish-language monthly. Each issue contains approximately 80 full-color pages entirely devoted to the Latin world and its people. This periodical includes celebrity news, exclusive interviews, and success stories. Most of the articles are on Latin American actors, musicians, or others who have found fame in the popular arts. Recommended for public libraries. (JRD)

4054. ***Critica Hispanica.*** [ISSN: 0278-7261] 1979. s-a. USD 35 domestic; USD 45 foreign. Ed(s): Gregorio C Martin. Critica Hispanica, Department of Modern Language, Duquesne University, Pittsburgh, PA 15282. Illus., adv. Refereed. Circ: 500. *Indexed:* ArtHuCI, MLA-IB. *Bk. rev.:* 6-10, 400-800 words. *Aud.:* Ac.

This is a scholarly literary and linguistics journal. Each issue is devoted to a specific theme or author, such as the Caribbean character in literature, the Cuban political novel, or Pablo Neruda. Each volume contains nine or ten lengthy articles accompanied by notes and bibliographies, and it may include interviews and book reviews. Articles are in Spanish or English. Recommended for academic libraries supporting Latin American literature and literary studies programs. (VR)

4055. ***Cuadernos Hispanoamericanos: revista mensual de cultura hispanica.*** [ISSN: 0011-250X] 1948. m. EUR 51.09 domestic; USD 140 in Europe; USD 170 in the Americas. Ed(s): Felix Grande. Instituto de Cooperacion Iberoamericana, Avda Reyes Catolicos, 4, Ciudad Universitaria, Madrid, 28040, Spain; cuadernos.hispanoamericanos@aeci.es. Illus. Circ: 2000. *Indexed:* ArtHuCI, BHA, HAPI, MLA-IB, RI-1, SSCI. *Aud.:* Ac.

Cuadernos hispanoamericanos is a fascinating review of current literary and cultural thought from some of Latin America's leading intellectuals. Each issue includes a "Dossier" or collection of essays on a particular aspect of Latin American culture or the culture of a particular country or geographic region; a "Punto de vista" section with viewpoint essays and occasionally poetry and fiction; and a book review section, "Biblioteca." This excellent journal is recommended for academic libraries. (OO)

4056. *Eres.* s-m. USD 36.50. Editorial Televisa, 6355 N W 36th St, Miami, FL 33166; subscriptions@editorialtelevisa.com. Adv. *Aud.:* Hs, Ga.

Reminiscent of many American teen magazines, *Eres* is full of gossip and glossy photos of the most popular young movie stars, musicians, and other celebrities in the Latin world. Included in each issue is a photo-filled interview with a popular celebrity such as Ricky Martin, an astrology section, and a section on American music. Also included are articles and photos of the latest fashions, and features on topics of concern to teens such as anorexia nervosa, relationships, and personal hygiene. Sure to appeal to the young-adult crowd. For public libraries. (JRD)

4057. *Fem.* [ISSN: 0185-4666] 1976. m. USD 60. Ed(s): Esperanza Brito de Marti. Difusion Cultural Feminista A.C., Ave. Insurgentes Sur 598-302, Mexico, D.F., 03100, Mexico. Illus., adv. Circ: 15000. *Indexed:* BAS, HAPI. *Aud.:* Ac, Ga.

Looking for a Latin American counterpart to *Ms.* magazine? *Fem* is it. This progressive news, opinion, and cultural monthly is a refreshing alternative to most Latin American publications for women. Coverage includes features on critical social issues such as AIDS, mental health, child welfare, and abortion, plus articles on Mexican politics written from a feminist perspective. Also included are short stories, poetry, and other creative writing by women. For public and academic libraries. (JRD)

4058. *Feminaria.* 1988. s-a. USD 40 (Individuals, USD 24). Ed(s): Lea Fletcher. Feminaria Editora, C.C. 402, Buenos Aires, 1000, Argentina; feminaria@fibertel.com.ar; http://www.latbook.com.ar. Refereed. Circ: 1000. *Indexed:* HAPI, MLA-IB. *Aud.:* Ac, Sa.

Published in Argentina, this magazine focuses on feminist theory, feminist literary theory, and criticism. While most of the articles are about women and Latin American literature, coverage also includes scholarly works on the social, political, and cultural aspects of modern life. Artwork, interviews, and poetry are also featured, as is a bibliographic section highlighting recent publications from Latin America. Not limiting itself to any one form of feminism, the magazine considers for publication "any work that is not sexist, racist, [or] homophobic or that expresses any other type of discrimination." For collections that seek a balance between popular and scholarly reading materials for women in Spanish. (JRD)

4059. *Frontera Norte.* [ISSN: 0187-7372] 1989. s-a. MXP 200 domestic; USD 35 foreign. Ed(s): Erika Moreno. Colegio de la Frontera Norte, Publications Department, Blvd Abelardo L Rodriguez 2925, Zona del Rio, Tijuana, 22350, Mexico; publica@colef.mx. Illus. Refereed. Circ: 2000. *Indexed:* HAPI. *Aud.:* Ac.

This Spanish-language scholarly journal publishes extensively researched articles by Mexicans and Americans who specialize in issues confronting the U.S.-Mexico border region. Each issue includes five to six articles on political, social, economic, and environmental issues and trends, a section of book reviews, and a position paper, "Nota critica." Articles are extensively researched and annotated. For academic libraries with border studies collections. (OO)

4060. *Furia Musical.* 1993. fortn. MXP 4 newsstand/cover per issue; USD 1.50 newsstand/cover per issue. Ed(s): Jesus Gallegos. Provenemex, S.A. de C.V., Lucio Blanco 435, Azcapotzalco, Mexico City, 02400, Mexico. *Aud.:* Ga.

Remember *Tiger Beat* and *Teen Beat* magazines? This Spanish-language publication is somewhat reminiscent of these old teeny bopper music rags. Included are lots of celebrity photos of musicians and actors and a feature or two on a major singing star or musical group. While there isn't a lot of written content, the photos alone are enough to make a fan of Mexican popular music swoon with delight. Recent issues have featured musicians such as Pepe Aguilar and Alejandro Fernandez. Pullout posters of a major musical group are usually included. For public libraries with Spanish-speaking populations. This magazine will appeal mostly to youth. (JRD)

4061. *Geomundo: la guia practica para explorar tu mundo.* [ISSN: 0256-7253] 1977. m. USD 27. Ed(s): Gabriel Gonzalez. Editorial Televisa, 6355 N W 36th St, Miami, FL 33166; subscriptions@editorialtelevisa.com. Illus., adv. Circ: 116000. *Aud.:* Hs, Ga, Ac.

Very similar in format and content to *National Geographic* magazine, this publication is filled with interesting in-depth articles and beautiful photographs of everything from bugs and plants to art and food to features on exotic peoples and places worldwide. Also included are articles on environmental and social concerns. There is an annual issue that highlights the works of many amateur photographers. Sure to be a popular item, this publication is recommended for all libraries. (JRD)

4062. *Gestos: teoria y practica del teatro hispanico.* [ISSN: 1040-483X] 1986. s-a. USD 40 (Individuals, USD 22.50). Ed(s): Juan Villegas. University of California at Irvine, Department of Spanish and Portuguese, Humanities Hall, Irvine, CA 92697; gestos@uci.edu; http://www.hnet.uci.edu/gestos. Illus. Refereed. Circ: 700 Paid. *Indexed:* MLA-IB. *Bk. rev.:* 8-10, 500-1,000 words. *Aud.:* Ac.

This is an academic publication devoted to the study of Hispanic drama and the theater. Each issue includes six to eight scholarly essays, in English or Spanish, on various aspects of playwriting and the theater, plus interviews with well-known and lesser-known playwrights and reviews of recent dramatic productions. Also contained in each issue is an original play. Coverage includes all of Latin America, Spain, and the United States, making *Gestos* a well-rounded, global source for criticism, interpretation, and news about *el teatro hispano.* For academic libraries. (JRD)

4063. *Harper's Bazaar en Espanol.* [ISSN: 0890-9598] 1949. m. USD 18.90; USD 2.95 newsstand/cover per issue. Ed(s): Carols Mendez. Editorial Televisa, 6355 N W 36th St, Miami, FL 33166; subscriptions@editorialtelevisa.com. Illus., adv. Circ: 52000. *Aud.:* Ga.

Very much like its English-language counterpart, this glossy high-fashion and beauty magazine is filled with page after page of elegant and beautiful models showing off the latest styles by today's most popular designers. Included in each issue are two or three feature interviews with the royalty of fashion and film, a horoscope column, and a number of short pieces on travel and food. Lavishly illustrated, this magazine will appeal primarily to girls and young women who are interested in keeping up with the latest trends. For public libraries. (JRD)

4064. *Hemisphere: a magazine of Latin American and Caribbean affairs.* [ISSN: 0898-3038] 1988. 3x/yr. USD 20; USD 27 foreign. Ed(s): Eduardo Gamarra. Latin American and Caribbean Center, Florida International University, University Park, Miami, FL 33199; newmana@fiv.edu; http://lacc.fiv.edu/hemisphere/hemisphere.html. Illus., adv. Circ: 2000. *Indexed:* ABS&EES, BAS, HAPI. *Aud.:* Ga, Ac.

The masthead of this magazine states that it is "dedicated to provoking debate on the problems, initiatives and achievements of Latin America and the Caribbean." Issues include excellent photo essays as well as articles on government, economics, politics, and social issues. The magazine also features literature reviews and a news-in-brief section. Contributors are from varied backgrounds and include university faculty, intergovernmental agency officials, and relief agency workers. For general audiences and public and academic libraries. (OO)

4065. *Hispamerica: revista de literatura.* [ISSN: 0363-0471] 1972. 3x/yr. USD 36 (Individuals, USD 27; USD 32.40 Agencies). Ed(s): Saul Sosnowski. Hispamerica, c/o Latin American Studies Center, University of Maryland, College Park, MD 20742; SS55@umail.umd.edu. Illus., adv. Refereed. Circ: 1000. Vol. ends: Dec. *Indexed:* ArtHuCI, HAPI, MLA-IB, SSCI. *Bk. rev.:* 7-15, 300-2,500 words. *Aud.:* Ac.

This Spanish-language journal provides a broad review of issues and perspectives in contemporary Latin American literature. Each issue includes critical essays, short stories and poetry, interviews with Latin American authors, and book reviews. This periodical is of interest primarily to academic libraries that support Latin American literature collections, although public libraries with a large Spanish-speaking clientele might also benefit. (OO)

Hispanic Business Magazine. See Latino Studies section.

4066. *Hispanic Journal (Indiana).* [ISSN: 0271-0986] 1979. s-a. USD 40 (Individuals, USD 20). Ed(s): David Foltz. Indiana University of Pennsylvania, Department of Spanish and Classical Languages, 462 Sutton Hall, Indiana, PA 15705; dafoltz@grove.iup.edu; http://www.chss.iup.edu/spanish/. Adv. Refereed. Circ: 450 Paid. *Indexed:* HAPI, MLA-IB, RI-1. *Aud.:* Ac.

The introduction to this excellent scholarly journal states that its purpose is "to publish research and criticism of the highest quality in the areas of Spanish, Portuguese and Catalan literatures, language and linguistics." Articles may be written in English, Spanish, Portuguese, or Catalan. All are annotated and include bibliographies. Recommended for academic libraries. (OO)

Hispanic Journal of Behavioral Sciences. See Psychology section.

4067. *Hispanic Review: a quarterly journal devoted to research in the Hispanic languages and literatures.* [ISSN: 0018-2176] 1933. q. USD 37.50 (Individuals, USD 27.50; Students, USD 17). Ed(s): Ignacio Javier Lopez. University of Pennsylvania, Department of Romance Languages, 512 Williams Hall, Philadelphia, PA 19104-6305; hisprev@mail.sas.upenn.edu; http://www.upenn.edu/. Illus., adv. Refereed. Circ: 1600. Vol. ends: Fall. Online: bigchalk; Chadwyck-Healey Incorporated; EBSCO Publishing; Gale Group; JSTOR (Web-based Journal Archive); Northern Light Technology, Inc.; OCLC Online Computer Library Center, Inc.; ProQuest Information & Learning; H.W. Wilson. *Indexed:* AmH&L, ArtHuCI, BHA, HAPI, HumInd, IBZ, MLA-IB, SSCI. *Aud.:* Ac.

This scholarly journal's masthead states that it is "devoted to research in the Hispanic languages and literatures." It features articles by noted scholars of literary analysis and criticism. There is a monthly section of book reviews as well. Articles and reviews may be in Spanish or English. The last issue of the year provides a list of articles and book reviews that appeared during the year. In format, content, and style, this journal is quite similar to *Hispanofila, Hispanic Review,* and other university-published literary journals. Recommended for academic libraries that support programs in Spanish language and literature. (OO)

4068. *Hispanofila.* [ISSN: 0018-2206] 1957. 3x/yr. USD 35 (Individuals, USD 25; Students, USD 11). Ed(s): Fred M Clark. University of North Carolina at Chapel Hill, Department of Romance Languages, CB 3170, 238 Dey Hall, Chapel Hill, NC 27599-3170. Illus., index, adv. Refereed. Circ: 500. Vol. ends: May. Microform: PQC. Reprint: PQC. *Indexed:* ArtHuCI, MLA-IB. *Aud.:* Ac.

This academic journal publishes research articles and essays by noted scholars on issues in Spanish-language literature and linguistics, although the emphasis is on literature. Articles are footnoted, include bibliographies, and may be written in English or Spanish. Each issue includes an extensive book review section. Recommended for academic libraries. (OO)

4069. *Historia Mexicana.* [ISSN: 0185-0172] 1951. 4x/yr. USD 104. Ed(s): Francisco Gomez Rulz. Colegio de Mexico, A.C., Departamento de Publicaciones, Camino al Ajusco 20, Col. Pedregal Santa Teresa, Mexico City, 10740, Mexico; http://www.colmex.mx. Illus., index, adv. Circ: 1500. Vol. ends: Jun. *Indexed:* AICP, AmH&L, ArtHuCI, BAS, HAPI, MLA-IB, PSA, SSCI, SociolAb. *Bk. rev.:* 2-8, 500-2,000 words, signed. *Aud.:* Ac.

Produced by the Centro de Estudios Historicos of the Colegio de Mexico and written in Spanish, this is one of the premier journals in Mexican history. Its contributors include the leading historians working in the field. All articles are extensively footnoted and annotated, and include bibliographies. Each issue also includes a book review section, a section of summaries of recent publications, and a section of English-language abstracts. Recommended for academic libraries that support Latin American Studies programs and history departments with an interest in Mexican or Latin American history. (OO)

4070. *Hola.* [ISSN: 0214-3895] 1944. w. EUR 84 domestic. Ed(s): Eduardo Sanchez Junco. Empresa Editora Hola, S.A., Miguel Angel 1, Madrid, 28010, Spain. Illus., adv. Sample. Circ: 582778. *Aud.:* Ga.

Similar to *People* or *Us* magazines in content and format, *Hola* features articles about the rich and famous of Spain, Europe, and to a lesser extent, the United States. European (mainly Spanish) royalty gets the greatest amount of coverage, followed by the wealthy of Europe, European heads of state, and American movie stars. The articles are lavishly illustrated with large color photographs, and indeed the photographs are more numerous and more prominent than the text. There are also shorter, regular sections on food, beauty, health, and fashion. Of interest to public libraries with Spanish-speaking patrons. (OO)

4071. *Impacto.* [ISSN: 0019-2880] 1950. w. MXP 8 per issue. Ed(s): Carlos Moncada Ochoa. Impacto, Av. Ceylan 517, Apdo. 2986, Mexico City, 23000, Mexico. Illus., adv. Circ: 115000. *Aud.:* Ga.

This large-format Mexican publication is reminiscent of *Life* magazine. It deals largely with political, economic, and social issues in Mexico, with some attention paid to international affairs. Articles cover religion, health, and ecology, as well as the arts and in-depth analysis of Mexican political issues. All articles are in Spanish and are well illustrated. This magazine will appeal to public libraries that serve Spanish-speaking populations. (JRD)

4072. *Journal of Latin American Cultural Studies.* Formerly (until 1995): *Travesia.* [ISSN: 1356-9325] 1992. 3x/yr. GBP 266 (Individuals, GBP 65). Ed(s): Catherine Boyle. Carfax Publishing Ltd., 4 Park Sq, Milton Park, Abingdon, OX14 4RN, United Kingdom; enquiry@tandf.co.uk; http://www.tandf.co.uk/. Illus. Vol. ends: Nov. Online: EBSCO Publishing; Ingenta Select; OCLC Online Computer Library Center, Inc.; RoweCom Information Quest; Swets Blackwell. Reprint: PSC. *Indexed:* HAPI, MLA-IB, PSA, SociolAb. *Bk. rev.:* 3-5, 500-2,000 words. *Aud.:* Ac.

This scholarly journal's primary goals are to stimulate "interdisciplinary work on Latin American culture and cultural history and [to encourage] debate on the teaching and reception of Latin American cultural materials." This well-known title focuses primarily on Latin American culture after 1492, and it covers anthropology, communication, history, and literature. Included in each issue is a section that provides authoritative overviews of the current state of those disciplines that fall within the framework of Latin American cultural studies, including literature, film studies, music, and communication studies. Recent issues included articles on Cuban music, as well as Miami as portrayed in telenovelas. Articles are well written, annotated, and include bibliographies. Recommended for academic libraries. (OO)

4073. *Journal of Latin American Studies.* [ISSN: 0022-216X] 1969. q. USD 218 (Individuals, USD 80). Ed(s): Paul Cammack, Rachel Sieder. Cambridge University Press, The Edinburgh Bldg, Shaftesbury Rd, Cambridge, CB2 2RU, United Kingdom; information@cambridge.org; http://uk.cambridge.org/journals. Illus., adv. Refereed. Vol. ends: Nov. Microform: PQC. Online: EBSCO Publishing; Florida Center for Library Automation; Gale Group; JSTOR (Web-based Journal Archive); OCLC Online Computer Library Center, Inc.; RoweCom Information Quest; Swets Blackwell. Reprint: SWZ. *Indexed:* ABCPolSci, AICP, AmH&L, AnthLit, ArtHuCI, BrHumI, ForAb, GeogAbPG, HAPI, IBSS, IBZ, IPSA, LRI, MLA-IB, PAIS, PRA, PSA, RI-1, S&F, SSCI, SSI, SociolAb, WAE&RSA. *Bk. rev.:* 22-28, 350-2,000 words. *Aud.:* Ga, Ac.

This English-language scholarly journal covers issues and trends in Latin America with an emphasis on sociology, history, anthropology, sociology, economics, and international relations. The articles and reviews are written by leading scholars and researchers. Issues may be dedicated to one particular country or question or may reflect this excellent journal's broad coverage of Latin America. Each issue also includes book reviews. Recommended for academic libraries that support programs in Latin American Studies, political science, and economics, and large public research libraries. (OO)

4074. *Kena.* 1964. fortn. MXP 15 per issue. Ed(s): Liliana Moreno. Grupo Juventud S.A., Ave. INSURGENTES SUR 605-906, Col Napoles, Mexico City, 03810, Mexico. Adv. Circ: 86349. *Aud.:* Ga.

Kena offers a wide range of material aimed at the modern women and her younger sisters. Included in each issue are features on health and beauty, crafts, homemaking, and fashion; advice on relationships and careers; entertainment news from Hollywood; and photo-filled feature stories on such locales as

Guadalajara, Mexico. There is also a lengthy section of photos of popular Mexican and American celebrities in the news and a section highlighting new consumer products. Although there are a number of publications in this genre, *Kena*'s focus is on new products and ideas. For public libraries. (JRD)

4075. *Latin American Indian Literatures Journal: a review of American Indian texts and studies.* Supersedes (in 1985): *Latin American Indian Literatures.* [ISSN: 0888-5613] 1977. s-a. USD 49 (Individuals, USD 29; USD 28 per issue). Ed(s): Mary H Preuss. Penn State University, McKeesport, 4000 University Dr, McKeesport, PA 15132-7698; mhp1@psu.edu. Illus., adv. Refereed. Circ: 300 Paid. *Indexed:* AICP, AnthLit, ArtHuCI, HAPI, IBSS, MLA-IB, RI-1. *Bk. rev.:* 3-5, 500-1,500 words. *Aud.:* Ac.

This scholarly journal focuses exclusively on the native aboriginal languages of Latin America. Each issue contains informative and thoroughly researched articles and studies of these languages, as well as book reviews, article abstracts, and bibliographies. Many articles include excerpts of transcriptions of native aboriginal-language poetry or stories in the original, with English-language translations. Some articles include photos of illustrations from codices and other historical documents of interest to linguists and researchers. Highly recommended for academic libraries that support Latin American Studies programs and graduate linguistics programs. (OO)

4076. *Latin American Literary Review.* [ISSN: 0047-4134] 1972. s-a. USD 40 (Individuals, USD 24). Ed(s): Yvette E Miller. Latin American Literary Review, PO Box 17660, Pittsburgh, PA 15235; lalrp@angstrom.net; http://www.lalrp.org. Illus., index, adv. Refereed. Circ: 1500 Paid. Microform: PQC. Online: bigchalk; Gale Group; Northern Light Technology, Inc.; ProQuest Information & Learning. *Indexed:* AmHI, ArtHuCI, HAPI, HumInd, MLA-IB. *Bk. rev.:* 4-6, 90-100 words. *Aud.:* Ga, Ac.

This scholarly journal's editorial board includes some of the most prominent Latin American Studies scholars of the United States. Its stated purpose is to publish "scholarly essays and book reviews on the literatures of Spanish America and Brazil." Articles may be in English, Spanish, or Portuguese. The journal's contributors are as illustrious as its editorial board. This publication makes a very important contribution to the understanding of the literature of Latin America. Past issues included excerpts of creative works, but more recent issues have not, with articles in recent issues being of a critical or analytical nature. Highly recommended for academic libraries and large public libraries. (OO)

4077. *Latin American Perspectives: a journal on capitalism and socialism.* [ISSN: 0094-582X] 1974. bi-m. USD 491 print & online eds. Ed(s): Ronald H Chilcote. Sage Publications, Inc., 2455 Teller Rd, Thousand Oaks, CA 91320; info@sagepub.com; http://www.sagepub.com. Illus., adv. Refereed. Circ: 1000 Paid. Microform: PQC. Online: bigchalk; EBSCO Publishing; Florida Center for Library Automation; Gale Group; ingenta.com; JSTOR (Web-based Journal Archive); OCLC Online Computer Library Center, Inc.; ProQuest Information & Learning; Swets Blackwell. Reprint: PSC. *Indexed:* ABCPolSci, AltPI, AmH&L, GeogAbPG, HAPI, IBSS, IPSA, PAIS, PRA, PSA, SFSA, SSCI, SSI, SUSA, SociolAb, WAE&RSA. *Aud.:* Ga, Ac.

Each issue of this scholarly journal offers extensive, well-researched, and annotated articles that discuss a single topic of pressing importance in Latin America. Recent issues have dealt with the civil war in Columbia; the struggle of the indigenous peoples of Chiapas; and political, economic, and social turmoil in Mexico. The articles are written by well-known scholars and researchers and offer diverse perspectives on the issue they treat. Some issues feature excellent book reviews. This journal is highly recommended for academic libraries that support research programs in Latin American Studies, economics, sociology, and political science, as well as large public libraries with a research focus. (OO)

4078. *Latin American Research Review: a journal to achieve greater and more systematic communication among individuals and institutions concerned with scholarly studies of Latin America.* [ISSN: 0023-8791] 1965. triennial. USD 60 (Individuals, USD 40). Ed(s): Peter Ward. University of Texas Press, Journals Division, 2100 Comal, Austin, TX 78722; utpress@uts.cc.utexas.edu; http://www.utexas.edu/utpress/journals/journals.html. Illus., index. Sample. Refereed. Circ: 5000 Paid. Microform: PQC. Online: bigchalk; Chadwyck-Healey Incorporated; EBSCO Publishing; Florida Center for Library Automation; Gale Group; JSTOR (Web-based Journal Archive); Northern Light Technology, Inc.; OCLC Online Computer Library Center, Inc.; ProQuest Information & Learning. Reprint: PSC. *Indexed:* ABCPolSci, ABS&EES, AmH&L, AnthLit, ArtHuCI, FLI, GeogAbPG, HAPI, IBSS, IBZ, IIBP, IPSA, PAIS, PRA, SSCI, SSI, WAE&RSA. *Aud.:* Ga, Ac.

The *Latin American Research Review* was established to achieve "a better understanding and a more systematic communication among individuals and institutions concerned with scholarly studies of Latin America." Each issue includes articles on politics, economics, history, sociology, or culture, all extensively footnoted and with bibliographies appended. There is also an extensive review essay section that examines issues in the light of recently published scholarship. Articles and essays may be in English or Spanish. This journal is highly recommended for large public libraries with a research focus and academic libraries that support Latin American Studies programs. (OO)

Latin American Theatre Review. See Theater section.

Latina (New York). See Women section.

4079. *Letras Femeninas.* [ISSN: 0277-4356] 1974. 2x/yr. USD 40 (Individuals, USD 25). Asociacion de Literatura Femenina Hispanica, Department of Modern Languages, University of Nebraska, Lincoln, NE 68588-0315. Illus., adv. Circ: 600. *Indexed:* HAPI, IAPV, MLA-IB. *Aud.:* Ac.

This journal is dedicated to the study and critique of women's literature in the Hispanic world from a distinctly feminist viewpoint. The journal publishes the work of prominent, established female writers and scholars from Spain, Latin America, and the United States. Articles are in Spanish, English, or Portuguese. Regular sections include review articles, book reviews, interviews, poetry, essays on issues in literature and writing, and news and announcements. Recommended for academic libraries that support women's studies and literature programs. (OO)

4080. *Libros de Mexico.* [ISSN: 0186-2243] 1985. q. USD 40 in the Americas; USD 50 elsewhere. Ed(s): Federico Krafft Vera. Camara Nacional de la Industria Editorial Mexicana, Holanda 13, Col. San Diego Churubusco, Coyoacan, 04120, Mexico; ciecprom@inetcorp.net.mx; http://www.libromex.com.mx. Illus., adv. Circ: 5000. *Indexed:* IBZ. *Aud.:* Hs, Ga, Ac.

This publication, written completely in Spanish, is an excellent selection tool for librarians in charge of acquiring current material from Mexico. It offers up-to-date information on the Mexican book trade industry. The "Profile" section presents a different publisher in each issue. Additional regular sections include serials, news, interviews, and editorial news. This last section lists new publications by publisher and groups them by Dewey classification number. (JRD)

4081. *Luzo - Brazilian Review: devoted to the culture of the Portuguese-speaking world.* [ISSN: 0024-7413] 1963. s-a. USD 140 (Individuals, USD 48). University of Wisconsin Press, Journal Division, 1930 Monroe St., 3rd Fl, Madison, WI 53711; journals@uwpress.wisc.edu; http://www.wisc.edu/wisconsinpress/journals. Illus., adv. Refereed. Circ: 600. Microform: PQC. Reprint: PSC. *Indexed:* AmH&L, HAPI, IBZ, L&LBA, MLA-IB, PSA, SociolAb. *Bk. rev.:* 5, 700 words. *Aud.:* Ac.

This is an important scholarly journal, published twice a year, that provides a multidimensional look at the Portuguese-speaking world. Includes articles in English or Portuguese on a variety of topics, from studies of immigrant communities in Brazil to a study of slavery in Bahia. A typical issue includes about six articles, a book review section, a list of books received, and segments with announcements, brief contributors' profiles, and a report on research in progress. This publication makes a significant contribution to the understanding of Luso-Brazilian culture. Recommended for academic libraries that support Latin American Studies programs. (JRD)

4082. ***Marie Claire en Espanol.*** [ISSN: 0188-2724] 1954. m. Ed(s): Louise Gras Mereles. Editorial Televisa, Vasco de Quiroga 2000 Edificio E, Col Santa Fe, Mexico City, 01210, Mexico. Illus., adv. Sample. *Aud.:* Ga.

The Spanish edition of the well-known international magazine covers topics considered of interest to women. Like its competitors *Harper's Bazaar* and *Vogue,* it has articles on fashion and beauty and columns dealing with current issues, especially health topics. Interviews with notable figures in the arts, literature, and music are also frequently included. Each issue devotes several pages to the latest trends in fashion and the culinary arts plus a monthly horoscope. This magazine will find a place in any public library that serves a Spanish-speaking audience. (JRD)

4083. ***Mexican Studies.*** [ISSN: 0742-9797] 1985. s-a. USD 100 print & online eds. USD 50 newsstand/cover. Ed(s): Jaime E Rodriguez. University of California Press, Journals Division, 2000 Center St, Ste 303, Berkeley, CA 94704-1223; journals@ucop.edu; http://www.ucpress.edu/journals. Illus., index, adv. Refereed. Circ: 1300 Paid. Microform: PQC. Online: EBSCO Publishing; Florida Center for Library Automation; Gale Group; Ingenta Select; OCLC Online Computer Library Center, Inc. *Indexed:* AICP, AmH&L, ArtHuCI, HAPI, HRA, HumInd, IPSA, PSA, SSCI, SSI, SociolAb. *Aud.:* Ac.

This interdisciplinary, scholarly publication focuses on research on Mexico and its people. It draws scholars from all disciplines and offers lengthy articles in English or Spanish on cultural, historical, political, social, economic, and scientific factors that affect the country's growth and development. It also offers review essays and sections such as "Other Books Received" and "Notes on Contributors." The journal is a joint effort of the University of California Institute for Mexico and the United States and the Universidad Nacional Autonoma de Mexico. It is now available electronically. Recommended for academic libraries that support teaching and research on Mexico. (VR)

4084. ***Mexico Desconocido.*** [ISSN: 0187-1560] 1976. m. MXP 240 domestic; USD 60 United States; USD 70 in Europe. Ed(s): Beatriz Quintanar Hinojosa. Editorial Mexico Desconocido S.A.de C.V., Monte Pelvoux 110, Planta Jardin, Lomas de Chapultepec, Mexico City, 11000, Mexico. Illus., index, adv. Circ: 64000. *Aud.:* Ga.

This is a beautifully designed magazine that features articles on the artistry, culture, cuisine, and hidden wonders of Mexico, covering a wide range of geographic areas. Topics have included the artisan work of San Salvador Huixcolotla and hidden caves in Guerrero. Color photographs of natural and architectural design complement the lengthy and informative pieces. Each issue offers eight to ten engaging articles from seven to ten pages in length. Selected articles are available online in Spanish and English versions. (VR)

4085. ***N A C L A Report on the Americas.*** Former titles: *Report on the Americas; N A C L A Report on the Americas; N A C L A's Latin America and Empire Report; N A C L A News.* [ISSN: 1071-4839] 1967. bi-m. USD 55 (Individuals, USD 32; USD 4.95 newsstand/cover per issue). Ed(s): Jo Ann Kawell. North American Congress on Latin America, Inc., 475 Riverside Dr, Rm 454, New York, NY 10115; nacla@nacla.org; http://www.nacla.org. Illus., adv. Refereed. Circ: 11000. Vol. ends: Jul/Jun. Microform: PQC. Online: EBSCO Publishing; Florida Center for Library Automation; Gale Group; OCLC Online Computer Library Center, Inc.; ProQuest Information & Learning; H.W. Wilson. Reprint: PQC. *Indexed:* AltPI, HAPI, PAIS, PRA, SSI. *Aud.:* Ga, Ac.

The *NACLA Report* provides articles on major trends in Latin America written by scholars, journalists, and others. They offer detailed analyses of internal and external political and social developments. Each issue covers a specific topic, such as "Gender in the New World Order," "Race and Racism in the Americas," or "Central America after Mitch." Also included are sections for brief news updates, short book reviews, and research notes. *NACLA Report* offers well-researched news items. The web site contains the full text in Spanish for the current issue. This is an important magazine for both academic and public libraries. (VR)

4086. ***Newsweek en Espanol.*** [ISSN: 1091-3416] 1996. w. USD 89 domestic; USD 100 Canada; MXP 889 Mexico. Ed(s): Jose Forteza. Ideas Publishing Group, 1101 Brickell Ave, 15th Fl, Miami, FL 33131; newsesp@gate.net; http://www.ideaspublishinggroup.com. Illus., adv. Sample. Circ: 52000 Paid. *Aud.:* Ga, Ac.

Like its English-language equivalent, this magazine covers international issues such as politics, health, and medicine, as well as science and technology. In addition to its traditional coverage of world events and editorial commentary, it covers sports, the world economy, arts, and entertainment. The Spanish-language edition provides the same high-caliber journalism as its English-language counterpart. It also includes literature, music, theatre, and cinema reviews. Highly recommended for academic libraries and public libraries that serve Hispanic communities. (VR)

4087. ***Padres e Hijos.*** [ISSN: 0188-0667] 1980. m. Ed(s): Alejandra Pastrana Lopez. Editorial Televisa, Vasco de Quiroga 2000 Edificio E, Col Santa Fe, Mexico City, 01210, Mexico; http://www.televisa.com.mx. Illus., adv. Sample. Circ: 105000. *Aud.:* Ga.

This publication is geared toward future parents, new parents, and parents of young children up to eight years of age. Entirely in Spanish, each issue includes regular columns that address health and nutrition. It also offers articles discussing, in plain language, educational and psychological issues that parents may face while caring for their children. New products and recent literature for and about children are highlighted and rated in short paragraphs. Recommended for public libraries. (VR)

4088. ***People en Espanol.*** 1997. 10x/yr. USD 14.97 domestic; USD 20.95 Canada; USD 2.49 domestic. Ed(s): Angelo Figueroa. Time, Inc, Time & Life Bldg, Rockefeller Center, 1271 Ave of the Americas, New York, NY 10020-1393; espanol@people.com; http://www.people.com/. Adv. Circ: 356000 Paid. *Aud.:* Ga.

This product of Time, Inc., is closely modeled after its parent publication, *People,* but is in Spanish and is focused on news, people, and events throughout the Latin world. It includes lots of news and information on the arts and entertainment world, with a heavy dose of celebrity photographs. Features on many other topics of interest ranging from the literary to the political are also included. A very popular title, this magazine is best suited for public libraries. (JRD)

4089. ***Problemas del Desarrollo: revista latinoamericana de economia.*** [ISSN: 0301-7036] 1969. q. MXP 120; USD 40. Ed(s): Salvador Rodriguez Y Rodriguez. Universidad Nacional Autonoma de Mexico, Instituto de Investigaciones Economicas, Torre II de Humanidades 5o Piso, Ciudad Universitaria, Mexico City, 04510, Mexico; revprode@servidor.unam.mx; http://serpiente.dgsca.unam.mx/iie. Illus., index, adv. Refereed. Circ: 2000. *Indexed:* HAPI, PAIS. *Bk. rev.:* 1-10, 800-1,500 words. *Aud.:* Ac.

This publication offers critical analysis of economic and socio-economic issues that affect Latin America, specifically Mexico. It presents five or six full-length, scholarly articles with research notes and references. Each article is preceded by an abstract in Spanish, English, and French. It also includes a section titled "Conyuntura y dabate," with discussions of such topics as neoliberalism in Mexico and indigenous autonomy. This journal is recommended for academic libraries with graduate programs in Mexican or Latin American Studies with concentrations in economic or socio-economic development. Also useful for libraries with substantial Latin American collections. (VR)

4090. ***Proceso: semanario de informacion y analisis.*** [ISSN: 0185-1632] 1976. w. MXP 660; USD 150 United States; USD 350 in Europe. Ed(s): Rafael Rodriguez Castaneda. Comunicacion e Informacion S.A. de C.V. (CISA), Fresas 13, Col Del Valle, Mexico City, 03100, Mexico; buzon@proceso.com.mx; http://www.proceso.com.mx/. Illus., adv. Sample. Online: Gale Group. *Indexed:* AltPI. *Bk. rev.:* 1, lengthy. *Aud.:* Ga, Ac.

Similar in format to *Newsweek* and *Time,* this Spanish-language magazine focuses on current issues in politics, economics, labor, and human rights in Mexico. A section is dedicated to covering international politics with a focus on Latin American countries. This magazine includes color photographs and political cartoons and regular commentary on theater, culture, art, and music. It belongs in all large public and academic libraries that support Latin American collections and researchers in the area of Latin American politics. The current issue is available online. (VR)

4091. ***Review (Americas Society).*** Formerly (until 1987): *Review - Center for Inter-American Relations.* [ISSN: 0890-5762] 1968. 2x/yr. USD 29.95 (Individuals, USD 19.95). Ed(s): Alfred J MacAdam. Americas Society, 680 Park Ave, New York, NY 10021. Illus., adv. Sample. Circ: 6000. Microform: PQC. *Indexed:* AmHI, ArtHuCI, HAPI, MLA-IB. *Bk. rev.:* 9-12, 900-1,200 words. *Aud.:* Ga, Ac, Sa.

This publication from The Americas Society is dedicated to the arts, culture, and literature of Latin America. Entirely in English, *Review* includes excerpts from literary works such as Vargas Llosa's *La Fiesta del Chivo.* It also features interviews, articles, essays, short fiction, and poetry, as well as art, music, film, and theatre reviews. Often, the magazine focuses on a specific topic, such as Latin American Writing and Music. This is a sophisticated publication that provides access to significant Latin American literary, art, and cultural commentary. Recommended for art and museum libraries and large academic and public libraries. (VR)

4092. ***Revista Canadiense de Estudios Hispanicos.*** Former titles (until 1976): *Reflexion Two; Reflexion.* [ISSN: 0384-8167] 1970. 3x/yr. CND 45 (Individuals, CND 30). Ed(s): Richard Young. Revista Canadiense de Estudios Hispanicos, Carleton University, ICLACS, Rm 1423, Dunton Tower, Ottawa, ON K1S 5B6, Canada. Illus., index, adv. Refereed. Circ: 800. Vol. ends: Spring. Reprint: PSC. *Indexed:* HAPI, IBZ, MLA-IB. *Bk. rev.:* 10-15, 500-1,500 words. *Aud.:* Ac.

This publication offers scholarly articles on the study of language, literary criticism, philosophy, and the cultural history of the Spanish-speaking world. Articles are written in Spanish, French, and English, with short abstracts in Spanish. Also offering research notes and an extensive book review section, this is a substantial journal that makes an important contribution to Hispanic and Latin American Studies. Recommended for libraries with strong collections in this subject area. (VR)

4093. ***Revista de Critica Literaria Latinoamericana.*** [ISSN: 0252-8843] 1975. s-a. USD 60 (Individuals, USD 35). Ed(s): Antonio Cornejo Polar. Latinoamericana Editores, 5319 Dwinelle Hall, University of California, Berkeley, CA 94720-2590; acorpol@socrates.berkeley.edu. Adv. Refereed. Circ: 1000. *Indexed:* ArtHuCI, HAPI, IBZ, MLA-IB. *Bk. rev.:* Various number and length. *Aud.:* Ac.

First published in 1975 in Lima by founder Antonio Cornejo Polar, this important peer-reviewed publication has been based at the University of Pittsburgh, in Berkeley, and since 1998, at Dartmouth College. The journal has only grown stronger with all of its changes. It is now online, with most articles available in full text from 1999 forward. A general index is in its final stages. *RCLL* includes literary criticism, cultural commentary within its social and historical context, and a substantial book review section. Recommended for academic and public research libraries. (VR)

4094. ***Revista de Historia de America.*** [ISSN: 0034-8325] 1938. s-a. USD 42 in Central America; USD 42 in North America; USD 47 in South America. Ed(s): Francisco Enriquez Solano. Instituto Panamericano de Geografia e Historia, Ex-Arzobispado 29, Col Observatorio, Mexico City, 11860, Mexico; ipgh@laneta.apc.org. Illus., adv. Circ: 1500. Microform: PQC. Reprint: PQC. *Indexed:* AmH&L, ArtHuCI, BHA, HAPI, IBZ. *Bk. rev.:* 2-4, 1,500-2,500 words. *Aud.:* Ac, Sa.

Published by the Instituto Panamerican de Geografia e Historia (IPGH), this journal offers articles in Spanish, Portuguese, or English that cover important issues in the history of Latin America and the Caribbean, specifically from pre-Hispanic occupation through the National period. It includes five to eight scholarly articles with abstracts in English and Spanish. Book reviews are also included. The table of contents and article summaries are on the IPGH web site, spin.com.mx/~ipgh. Although published only once or twice a year, this is a useful source for students and researchers in Latin American Studies. Recommended for academic libraries and libraries with strong Latin American holdings. (VR)

4095. ***Revista de Indias.*** [ISSN: 0034-8341] 1940. 3x/yr. ESP 6700; ESP 11100 foreign. Ed(s): Consuelo Naranjo Orovio. Consejo Superior de Investigaciones Cientificas, Departamento de Publicaciones, Centro de Estudios Historicos, Vitruvio 8, Madrid, 28006, Spain; publ@orgc.csic.es; http://www.csic.es/publica. Illus., index. Circ: 1500. Reprint: SCH. *Indexed:* AICP, AmH&L, ArtHuCI, BAS, BHA, HAPI, IBZ, RI-1, SSCI. *Bk. rev.:* Various number and length. *Aud.:* Ac.

This well-respected and longstanding journal features articles on everything from pre-Hispanic themes to today's Iberoamerican culture and literature. Its multidisciplinary approach allows for a variety of themes in each volume. One volume a year is dedicated to one or two specific themes, resulting in a sort of monograph or dossier. Each volume offers approximately six full-length articles written in Spanish, English, or Portuguese, each with abstracts in Spanish and English. There is an extensive section for research notes and book reviews. This is an essential journal for academic libraries and collections that focus on Latin American Studies. (VR)

4096. ***Revista de Occidente.*** [ISSN: 0034-8635] 1923. m. EUR 67 domestic; EUR 85 in Europe; USD 110 elsewhere. Ed(s): Soledad Ortega. Fundacion Jose Ortega y Gasset, Fortuny, 53, Madrid, 28010, Spain; fogrocci@accessnet.es; http://www.ortegaygasset.edu/. Illus., index, adv. Circ: 20000. Reprint: PSC. *Indexed:* ArtHuCI, BHA, MLA-IB, SSCI. *Bk. rev.:* 1-3, 500-1,250 words. *Aud.:* Ga, Ac.

This journal is widely recognized in academic circles as a forum where intellectuals share their thoughts on the most relevant topics of the time. *Revista de Occidente,* founded by Jose Ortega y Gasset in 1923, offers articles on the social sciences and the humanities. Five or six full-length essays in Spanish on a wide range of topics are accompanied by literary and art criticism. The journal also includes research notes, book reviews, a listing of current publications, and brief profiles for each contributor. Occasionally, an issue is dedicated to a specific theme, such as "Knowledge in the Digital Universe," "Art and Esthetic Thought in France," or "Ortega and European Thought." Recommended for academic libraries and libraries with substantial Latin American collections. (VR)

4097. ***Revista Iberoamericana.*** [ISSN: 0034-9631] 1938. q. USD 100 (Individuals, USD 65). Ed(s): Mabel Morana. International Institute of Ibero-American Literature, 1312 C L, University of Pittsburgh, Pittsburgh, PA 15260; iilit@pitt.edu; http://www.pitt.edu/~illi. Illus., adv. Circ: 2000. Microform: PQC. Reprint: PQC; PSC. *Indexed:* ArtHuCI, HAPI, MLA-IB. *Bk. rev.:* 15-20, 500-3,500 words. *Aud.:* Ac.

In publication for over 60 years, this well-recognized journal has been the vehicle for publishing scholarly studies on Iberoamerican culture and literature. It is often devoted to a single author, such as Ruben Dario, Cesar Vallejo, Vicente Huidobro, Miguel Angel Asturias, Pablo Neruda, or Jorge Luis Borges. There have also been volumes dedicated to the literature of specific countries, such as Brazil, Mexico, Nicaragua, Bolivia, and Colombia. The journal offers essays by scholars, an extensive book review section, and interviews. Articles are published in Spanish and Portuguese. Essential for academic libraries and libraries with extensive Latin American holdings. (VR)

4098. ***T V y Novelas.*** [ISSN: 0188-0683] 1982. bi-w. USD 40.95 domestic; USD 137.25 foreign; USD 2.25 newsstand/cover per issue. Ed(s): Gloria Calzada. Editorial Televisa, 6355 N W 36th St, Miami, FL 33166; subscriptions@editorialtelevisa.com. Adv. Circ: 144994 Paid. *Aud.:* Ga.

A rank lower than *People Magazine,* this publication serves as a supplement for those who watch Spanish-language television stations. It consists of gossip on TV celebrities from Mexico and Latin America for the most part, with some mention of U.S. celebrities. Lots of color photographs fill the pages of this popular magazine. Recommended for public libraries with big budgets. (VR)

4099. ***Tu.*** Former titles: *Tu Internacional; Tu.* 1980. m. USD 22.50 domestic; USD 2.50 newsstand/cover per issue. Ed(s): Ana Maria Echevarria. Editorial Televisa, 6355 N W 36th St, Miami, FL 33166; subscriptions@editorialtelevisa.com. Illus., adv. Circ: 190000. *Indexed:* ChemAb. *Aud.:* Ga.

This teen magazine is published in Mexico but is read in many Latin American countries. It dedicates two or three pages to the questions of teens that write from their native countries. Similar in format to *Seventeen,* this magazine includes regular features such as reviews of film, music, and videos, and includes celebrity gossip, fashion, health, nutrition, and beauty advice. Three or four articles discuss such topics as eating disorders, relationships, and peer pressure. Recommended for public and school libraries. (VR)

4100. ***Vanidades Continental.*** [ISSN: 0505-0146] 1961. bi-w. USD 45 domestic; USD 96.20 foreign; USD 3.50. Ed(s): Sara Castany. Editorial Televisa, 6355 N W 36th St, Miami, FL 33166; subscriptions@editorialtelevisa.com. Illus., adv. Sample. Circ: 89108 Paid. *Aud.:* Ga.

Geared toward educated, professional women between the ages of 20 and 40, this magazine features articles on health, beauty, fashion, entertainment, relationship advice, and the workplace. Each issue features a current international personality like Tom Cruise, Nicole Kidman, or Salma Hayak. It includes short articles on travel, food, home decorating, and a horoscope section. Highly recommended for public libraries. (VR)

Electronic Journals

The Internet is becoming a more established source of information on Latin America and Latinos in the United States. An increasing number of journals and newspapers are available electronically. They are not included in this section because they are available in paper format as well. Do not be deterred by the low numbers of entries below. Retrieving information about journals and newspapers from the Internet can be a challenging but rewarding undertaking. A vast amount of information is available for those who have access to the technology and are willing to try.

One efficient way to search for this information is through mega-sites such as the Latin America information server at the University of Texas at Austin. This site (known as LANIC) provides a gateway to information about Latin America, including information about journals, magazines, and newspapers. Other specialized directories are available as well. What one will find at these sites will vary. For some titles the user will find the full text of the current issue of a magazine or newspaper; other sites will provide only subscription information; others will offer the tables of contents for current and occasionally for past issues. In general, the titles available on the Internet tend to cover business and current-events themes. Magazines for the general public are in abundance as well. Examples of such mega-sites are the Latin American Network Information Center (LANIC) (lanic.utexas.edu), electronic journals from the WWW Virtual Library (www.edoc.com/ejournal), and the Association of Research Libraries Directory of Electronic Journals, Newsletters, and Academic Discussion Lists (arl.cni.org/scomm/edir/index.html).

4101. ***Planeta.com.*** Formerly: *El Planeta Platica.* [ISSN: 1089-8395] 1994. q. USD 7 newsstand/cover per issue. Ed(s): Ron Mader. Talking Planet, 1511 Twin Springs Ct, Henderson, NV 89014-0320; ron@greenbuilder.com; http://www.planeta.com. Illus., adv. Circ: 90000. *Bk. rev.:* 10-15, 25-50 words. *Aud.:* Ga.

This online newsletter provides information on the ecological situation in Latin America. The site focuses on environmental news and travel in the Americas and is updated several times a month. It includes sections such as recommended readings, book reviews, and Spanish-language schools in Latin America. Planeta.com, as it is now known, has received praise from *The New York Times* and President Vicente Fox. The newsletter also serves as a clearinghouse for other web sites on environmental news and travel in the Americas. Recommended for those interested in current environmental and travel issues in Latin America. (VR)

4102. ***Sincronia: revista electronica de estudios culturales.*** [ISSN: 1562-384X] 1997. q. Free. Universidad de Guadalajara, Centro Universitario de Ciencias Sociales y Humanidades, Depto de Letras, Centro Universitario de Ciencias Sociales y Humanidades, Jalisco, 44210, Mexico; sgilbert@udgserv.cencar.udg.mx; http://fuentes.csh.udg.mx/CUCSH/Sincronia/index.html. Refereed. *Aud.:* Ga, Ac.

This scholarly journal publishes articles in Spanish, or in English relating to Latin America, in the areas of social sciences and the humanities by scholars such as Noam Chomsky. It covers various topics in one issue, such as the philosophy of age in certain societies, Pablo Neruda's poetry, communication in a global economy, and Saramago's female characters. All articles go through a review process. Although this journal is geared toward academics, others interested in the humanities and social sciences may find it useful. (VR)

■ LATINO STUDIES

Joseph R. Diaz, Associate Librarian, University of Arizona Library, 1510 E. University Blvd., Tucson, AZ 85721-0055; diazj@u.library.arizona.edu; FAX: 520-621-9733

Olivia Olivares, Assistant Librarian, University of Arizona Library, 1510 E. University Blvd., Tucson, AZ 85721-0055; olivareso@u.library.arizona.edu; FAX: 520-621-9733

Veronica Reyes, Assistant Librarian, University of Arizona Library, 1510 E. University Blvd., Tucson, AZ 85721-0055; reyesv@u.library.arizona.edu; FAX: 520-621-9733

Introduction

The authors have chosen to use "Latino Studies" as the title for this section of *Magazines for Libraries.* We define Latinos, now the country's largest group, as including Puerto Ricans, Americans of Mexican descent, Cubans, and others from throughout Latin America and the Caribbean who now make the United States their home. (For information on magazines from and/or about Latin America, please see the Latin American section.)

Included in this section are all types of popular magazines and scholarly journals that focus on the Latino experience in the United States. While the list is small, that is partly because we have limited inclusion to magazines, journals, and a select number of online publications. If one adds the number of newsletters, newspapers, and other online sources available that are by or about Latinos, one can come up with a nice-sized list of reading material.

Unfortunately, the list could still be longer. While there do exist magazines and journals that have longstanding publication records and are still in business, many new publications only manage to survive for short periods of time. Librarians whose job it is to build collections on Latinos need to keep a vigilant eye out for new publications, as the number is bound to increase with the increasing size of the Latino population.

Those selecting information and recreational materials needed by Latinos should also supplement collections with local sources in their region. Reaching out to the community and assessing its needs will provide a more accurate picture of what materials to purchase. This is especially true for the Latino population because of its great diversity. Within particular communities there are local newsletters and newspapers as well as publications by special-interest groups. In addition, there are several Spanish-language newspapers that cover various regions of the United States: *La Opinion,* published in Los Angeles; *La Prensa,* in San Diego; *El Hispano News,* in Albuquerque; *El Nuevo Herald,* in Miami, and *El Diario,* in New York. These well-known newspapers cover issues and topics of interest to the Latino community as well as national and international news. A newspaper from the local vicinity would be a valuable addition to individual library collections and might attract new readers. (For more information on these types of resources, see Guerena et al., *Latino Periodicals: A Selection Guide.*)

Basic Periodicals

El Andar, Aztlan, Hispanic.

Basic Abstracts and Indexes

Alternative Press Index, Chicano Database, Ethnic Newswatch, Hispanic American Periodicals Index.

4103. ***El Andar: a Latino magazine for the new millennium.*** [ISSN: 1525-4194] 1998. q. USD 30 (Individuals, USD 18; USD 42 foreign). Ed(s): Julia Reynolds. El Andar Publications, PO Box 7745, Santa Cruz, CA 95060; info@elandar.com; http://www.elandar.com. *Aud.:* Hs, Ga, Ac.

One of only a handful and one of the best Latino-oriented publications available today, *El Andar* is a treasure trove of contemporary Latino thought and culture. Published quarterly, this well-designed and informative magazine includes in-depth essays, poetry and other fiction, investigative journalism, photoessays, reviews of all sorts, and biographical pieces on Latinos from all walks of life, with an emphasis on famous Latino writers, musicians, politicians, and actors. Contributors include big names like Gabriel Garcia Marquez, Gary Soto, and Rosario Ferre. A must for all libraries that serve a Latino/a clientele. (JRD)

4104. ***Aztlan: a journal of Chicano studies.*** [ISSN: 0005-2604] 1970. s-a. USD 50 in US & Mexico (Individuals, USD 25 in US & Mexico). Ed(s): Chon Noriega. University of California at Los Angeles, Chicano Studies Research Center Publications, 193 Haines Hall, Box 951544, Los Angeles, CA 90095-1544; aztlan@csrc.ucla.edu; http://www.sscnet.ucla.edu/esp. Illus., adv. Refereed. Circ: 600 Paid. Microform: LIB. Online: Gale Group; Swets Blackwell. Reprint: PQC. *Indexed:* AmH&L, BRI, CBRI, CIJE, HAPI, IBZ, L&LBA, MLA-IB, PAIS, PSA, RI-1, SSI, SociolAb. *Bk. rev.:* 1-7, 350-1,000 words. *Aud.:* Ac.

One of the first and currently one of the few existing scholarly journals devoted solely to Chicano Studies, *Aztlan* is an interdisciplinary journal that focuses on critical analysis, research, theory, and methodology as they relate to the study of Mexican Americans. Many of the articles are original works of research with extensive footnotes and bibliographical references. Topics covered range from sociology to history to art to women's studies to literature. Recent issues have provided a section where scholars can state their theoretical views and participate in a dialogue whereby they receive critical feedback from others in their field in subsequent journal issues. This title should find a place in all collections that deal with Chicano/Mexicano Studies. (JRD)

4105. ***Bilingual Research Journal.*** Former titles (until 1992): *N A B E Journal;* (until 1979): *N A B E.* [ISSN: 1523-5882] 1975. q. Ed(s): Josue Gonzales. National Association for Bilingual Education, 1030 15th St N W, Ste 470, Washington, DC 20005; http://www.ed.arizona.edu/departs/lrc/journal.htm. Illus., adv. Refereed. *Indexed:* CIJE, EduInd, LT&LA, MLA-IB. *Bk. rev.:* 4-6, 80-100 words. *Aud.:* Ga, Ac.

This is a scholarly, peer-reviewed journal published by the National Association for Bilingual Education. Its primary focus is on issues surrounding bilingualism and schooling in the United States. It serves as a forum for discussion of policy issues, instruction, and methodology, and it attempts to connect theoretical with practical aspects of issues, with an emphasis on applied results. Included are feature articles, essays, research summaries, and book reviews. Recent issues have taken a thematic approach and have covered such topics as the implementation of California's Proposition 227 and case studies on the implementation of bilingual education in the classroom. Researchers, students, practitioners, and the general public concerned with these topics should benefit from the analyses offered in this publication. Recommended for academic libraries of all sizes, and public libraries that serve a diverse population. (JRD)

4106. ***Bilingual Review.*** [ISSN: 0094-5366] 1974. 3x/yr. USD 38 (Individuals, USD 23). Ed(s): Gary D Keller. Bilingual Review Press, Hispanic Research Center, Arizona State University, Box 872702, Tempe, AZ 85287-2702; brp@asu.edu; http://www.asu.edu/brp. Illus., adv. Refereed. Circ: 1500. Microform: PQC. Reprint: PQC. *Indexed:* ArtHuCI, CIJE, EduInd, HAPI, IAPV, L&LBA, MLA-IB. *Aud.:* Ac.

Primarily a literary journal, but promoted as one that focuses on the linguistics and literature of bilingualism and bilingual education in the United States, this scholarly publication offers the reader a generous helping of original short stories, poetry, interviews, literary criticism, essays, and scholarly book reviews—all focused primarily on Chicano, Puerto Rican, and Cuban American literature. Recent issues, however, have diverged a bit and focus on a single theme, such as the legal, literary, and historic perspectives of the legacy of the Mexican-American and Spanish-American wars. The journal also contains a professional announcements section that includes notices of upcoming conferences, literary prizes, and other information of interest. Highly recommended for libraries with Latino literature collections. (JRD)

4107. ***La Herencia: our past, our present, our future.*** Formerly: *La Herencia del Norte.* [ISSN: 1531-0442] 1994. q. USD 19.99. Ed(s): Walter Lopez. Gran Via, Inc., PO Box 22576, Santa Fe, NM 87502. Illus., index, adv. *Bk. rev.:* 2-3, 400-500 words. *Aud.:* Ga, Sa.

La Herencia is a joyous celebration of Hispanic culture in New Mexico. It is lavishly illustrated and lovingly written, and its contributors range from noted scholars to longtime New Mexicans, all fascinated with the culture, history, and heritage of the *Hispanos* of New Mexico, Latinos who can trace their lineage and heritage to the Spanish *conquistadores* and who have lived in New Mexico for generations. Past articles have discussed the 400th anniversary of Spain's settlement of New Mexico, the Santuario de Chimayo, and the Roman Catholic Church in New Mexico. Highly recommended for public libraries, and for collections that focus on Mexican Americans or the Southwest. (OO)

4108. ***Hispanic: the magazine for and about Hispanics.*** [ISSN: 0898-3097] 1988. m. 11/yr. USD 18 (Free to qualified personnel). Ed(s): Alfredo Estrada. Hispanic Publishing Corp., 999 Ponce De Leon Ave, 600, Coral Gables, FL 33134-3037; http://www.hispaniconline.com. Illus., adv. Online: bigchalk; EBSCO Publishing; Gale Group; Northern Light Technology, Inc.; OCLC Online Computer Library Center, Inc.; ProQuest Information & Learning; SoftLine Information; H.W. Wilson. *Indexed:* AgeL, CIJE, ENW, MagInd, SSI. *Bk. rev.:* 1,500 words. *Aud.:* Ga, Ac.

This highly popular magazine covers a wide range of issues important to the Hispanic community in the United States, from business and investment advice, to politics (American and Latin American), to health and fitness, and to education and society. Regular features include the "Hispanic Calendar," with news of events hosted by and for Hispanics around the country, and "Forum," which presents a reader-contributed essay. *Hispanic* also features much-awaited annual lists of best communities for Latinos, best corporations for Latino employees, and the top 25 best colleges and universities for Latinos. This glossy magazine is highly recommended for public libraries, but academic libraries that serve Latino student populations will also find it useful. (OO)

4109. ***Hispanic Business Magazine.*** [ISSN: 0199-0349] 1979. m. USD 10 domestic; USD 30 foreign. Ed(s): Vaughn Hagerty. Hispanic Business Inc., 425 Pine Ave, Santa Barbara, CA 93117-3700; hbinfo@hninc.com; http://www.hispanstar.com. Illus., adv. Circ: 215000 Paid and controlled. *Indexed:* BPI, MagInd, PAIS. *Aud.:* Ga, Ac.

This journal is one of the best and most informative magazines available for Latino entrepreneurs and businesspersons. The articles provide important information on all aspects of business in the United States from entrepreneurship to small businesses to corporate finance. Recent issues have featured cover stories on the top Hispanic women in business in the United States and Latinos in tech-oriented businesses. Regular features include "Market Watch," with news on trends and prominent businesspersons; "Money Matters," with tax and investment advice; and "BizWare," with office computing advice. Highly recommended for public and academic libraries. (OO)

4110. ***Hispanic Journal (Dallas).*** Formerly: *Texas Hispanic Business Journal.* 1997. m. USD 24. Ed(s): Denise Nuno. Hispanic Journal, PO Box 810650, Dallas, TX 75381; sales@hispanicjournal.com; http://www.hispanicjournal.com. *Aud.:* Ga.

Founded in 1994 and published as the *Texas Hispanic Business Journal,* this glossy magazine became incorporated as *Hispanic Journal* in 1997. *Hispanic Journal*'s stated goal is to serve "the unique needs of the Hispanic business and professional community." The magazine features articles on Latino business ownership and development, the promotion of Latino leadership in business and government, and selected aspects of Latino culture in the United States. There are annual special issues on higher education and Latinas in business. Highly recommended for public libraries, although academic libraries will also find it useful for Latino college students studying business. (OO)

4111. ***Hispanic Outlook in Higher Education.*** [ISSN: 1054-2337] 1990. bi-w. USD 29.99; USD 3.75 newsstand/cover. Ed(s): Adalyn Hixson. Hispanic Outlook in Higher Education Publishing Company, Inc., 210 Rt 4 E Ste 310, Paramus, NJ 07652; outlook@aol.com;

http://www.hispanicoutlook.com. Illus., adv. Sample. Refereed. Circ: 28000. Online: EBSCO Publishing; Northern Light Technology, Inc.; OCLC Online Computer Library Center, Inc.; ProQuest Information & Learning; SoftLine Information. *Indexed:* ENW. *Aud.:* Ac.

This monthly English-language magazine covers issues and trends in higher education as they affect Latinos in the United States. Each issue has a cover story and five or six feature articles on prominent Latinos in higher education, programs for Latinos in higher education, or Latino advocacy groups. It includes regular departments such as "Outlook on Washington," "FYI," and a back-cover, reader-contributed opinion essay, "Punto Final!" There is also a section with job openings in academia. Recommended for academic libraries. (OO)

4112. ***Hispanic Times Magazine: the nation's only career and business magazine for Hispanics, American Indians and Native Americans.*** [ISSN: 0892-1369] 1978. 5x/yr. USD 30 domestic; USD 47.50 foreign. Ed(s): Gloria J Davis. Hispanic Times Enterpriser, PO Box 579, Winchester, CA 92596; ep@epnet.con; http://www.epnet.com. Illus., adv. Circ: 35000. Vol. ends: Oct/Nov (No. 5). *Indexed:* ENW. *Aud.:* Ga.

This is an excellent resource for job-seeking Latinos. The journal's goal is to cover "all level of Hispanic interests—from selecting career objectives and methods of fulfillment to how-to articles." Written in clear and concise prose, the articles are easy to read and always highly informative. Regular features include sections on resume writing, business news, careers in engineering and the health professions, book reviews, and job market information. Highly recommended for public, high school, and academic libraries. (OO)

4113. ***Hispanic Trends: the magazine for Latin business and political leaders.*** [ISSN: 1538-9928] 2002. m. Free to qualified personnel. Ed(s): Joe Vidueira. Hispanic Publishing Corp., 999 Ponce De Leon Ave, 600, Coral Gables, FL 33134-3037; rperez@hisp.com; http://www.hispaniconline.com. Adv. *Aud.:* Ga.

Similar to *Hispanic Business* in coverage and format, this recent creation from the publishers of *Hispanic* tracks developing trends in business, politics, and Latino culture. Issues include a section called "Briefcase," which covers the most active trends in business in the United States and their effects on Latinos; a section called "Trends Portfolio," which tracks the stock performance of the top 100 companies in the United States with significant Latino leadership; and a column on prominent Latino leaders in business and politics. Highly recommended for public libraries with a large Latino clientele and academic libraries that support business programs.

In Motion Magazine. See Alternatives/Electronic Journals section.

4114. ***Latin Beat Magazine: salsa, afro-antillana, latin jazz and more.*** 1991. m. 11/yr. USD 20; USD 35 Canada; USD 50 elsewhere. Latin Beat Magazine, 15900 Crenshaw Blvd, Ste 1-223, Gardena, CA 90249. Adv. *Indexed:* IIMP. *Aud.:* Ac, Ga.

This magazine focuses on Latin music, with a decided emphasis on salsa, Latin jazz, and other forms of music that come from the Caribbean region. It has a decade-long reputation as the premier publication in this genre. Included are feature articles about prominent musicians, recording and concert reviews, and interviews. While contemporary music and musicians are featured, the magazine also does an excellent job of looking at the history of Latin music, with features on such legendary greats as Machito, Tito Puente, and Celia Cruz. Contributors include music professors, disc jockeys, and former band leaders. Because there are so few publications on Latin music, this one is indispensable and will be a welcome addition to any high school or public library, or college libraries that serve Latinos or support good music programs. (OO)

4115. ***Latin Style: the Latin arts and entertainment magazine.*** [ISSN: 1525-7851] 1994. m. 11/yr. USD 24; USD 2.50 newsstand/cover per issue. Ed(s): Walter Martinez. Latin Style Magazine, 244 5th Ave, 2073, New York, NY 10001. Illus., adv. *Aud.:* Ga.

Latin Style Magazine is a glossy, lavishly illustrated, high-quality magazine that covers the areas of entertainment, the arts, literature, and politics, from a Latino perspective. Written entirely in English, this one-of-a-kind magazine provides in-depth coverage of current issues and provides biographical profiles of Latino personalities involved in all aspects of the arts and other arenas of contemporary culture. For public libraries. (JRD)

4116. ***Latina Style: a national magazine for the contemporary Hispanic woman.*** [ISSN: 1531-0868] 1994. 5x/yr. USD 20 for 2 yrs.; USD 2.95 newsstand/cover per issue. Latina Style, Inc., 1730 Rhode Island Ave, N W 1207, Washington, DC 20036-3102. Illus., adv. Circ: 150000. *Aud.:* Ga.

Latina Style is an excellent magazine for Hispanic women by Hispanic women. Entirely in English, this hefty publication includes six feature articles in each issue on a variety of topics, such as Latina artists, Latinas at work, Latinas' battle with AIDS, and Latina boxers in the ring. Regular columns include politics, home, business sense, beauty, money, fashion, food and entertainment, family values, and career moves. Film, music, and book reviews add to the mix. A bit of celebrity gossip gives a light touch to this engaging, no-nonsense publication. One column is dedicated to the male point of view. Highly recommended for public libraries. Academic libraries that support women's studies programs may want to consider this. (VR)

4117. ***Latino Leaders: the national magazine of the successful Hispanic American.*** [ISSN: 1529-3998] 1999. bi-m. Ed(s): Adam Garst. Ferraez Publications of America, Corp., Invierno 16, Merced Gomez, 01600, Mexico. Circ: 100000. *Aud.:* Ga.

This relatively new, glossy publication aims to highlight the careers and success of prominent Latinos in the United States. The editors state that their purpose is to discuss "the most important aspects of these leaders' lives—the moments, experiences, and achievements that reveal who they are and how they got there." Regular features include "Mundo Latino," a section on news and events in the Latino community; a "Leader of the Past" profile of a historically prominent or important Latino; and a "Leader of the Future" profile of a successful Latino in business, politics, or education. While profiles of Latinos in entertainment are occasionally included, the magazine's emphasis is on white-collar Latinos working in the United States today. Highly recommended for public libraries with a large Latino clientele, although academic libraries might also find this publication useful for business students. (OO)

4118. ***Latino(a) Research Review.*** Formerly (until 2000): *Latino Review of Books.* 1995. q. USD 35 (Individuals, USD 25). State University of New York at Albany, Center for Latino, Latin American, and Caribbean Studies (CELAC), SS 247, Albany, NY 12222; lrr@cnsunix.albany.edu; http://www.albany.edu/celac/docs.lrb. Illus., adv. Refereed. *Indexed:* MLA-IB. *Bk. rev.:* 10-15, 1,000-1,500 words. *Aud.:* Ga, Ac.

This journal, formerly known as the *Latino Review of Books,* publishes scholarly articles, research notes, review articles, and book reviews that focus primarily on the Latino experience in the United States. In the introduction to the first issue carrying the new title, the editors state their intent to make *LRR* "one of the leading journals in promoting scholarly research and dissemination of publications and materials on the U.S. Latino(a) experience and on the transnational connections that these groups maintain with their respective Latin American and Caribbean countries of origin." Of interest to academic libraries and large public libraries that serve a large Spanish-speaking clientele. (OO)

4119. ***Lowrider.*** [ISSN: 0199-9362] 1978. m. USD 35 domestic; USD 55 Canada; USD 110 elsewhere. McMullen Argus Publishing, Inc., 2400 E Katella Ave, Ste 1100, Anaheim, CA 92806. Illus., adv. Sample. Circ: 23300. *Aud.:* Ga.

Written in English peppered with Calo words and slang, this magazine is aimed at Latino low-rider car-club members. While low riding started as a Mexican-American/Chicano hobby and continues to be dominated by Chicanos and men, low riding is gaining in popularity among other Latino groups and among women, a development reflected in the magazine's text if not its layout, which continues to feature scantily clad Latina models. *Lowrider* has recently begun to publish issues for Europe and Latin America, reflecting a growing interest in the culture and hobby around the world. Each issue features several "special" low-rider cars. This magazine provides information on current events and car shows and articles on car customizing techniques. Predictably, each issue is packed with advertisements for car accessories. *Lowrider* covers a prominent and important aspect of Chicano and Latino culture in the United States. Recommended for public libraries. (OO)

Q V Magazine. See Lesbian, Gay, Bisexual, and Transgender section.

4120. *Urban Latino.* [ISSN: 1521-1487] 1994. bi-m. USD 14 domestic; USD 30 foreign; USD 2.99 newsstand/cover per issue. Urban Latino, 44-45 21st St, 3rd Fl, Long Island City, NY 11101. Adv. *Aud.:* Hs, Ga, Ac.

This affordable and colorful bimonthly magazine is an all-purpose publication intended for young Latinos interested primarily in the contemporary hip hop and Latino music scene from an East Coast perspective. While it does an excellent job of this, it also contains columns that feature celebrity news and behind-the-scenes gossip, interviews with prominent and up-and-coming Latino writers, a horoscope section, columns devoted to beauty advice and health trends, and features on fashion and home decorating. It also contains short profiles of what is hot around the country, including dance clubs and restaurants. Sure to appeal to teen and college-age Latinos, this is suitable for high school, public, and college libraries. (JRD)

Electronic Journals

4121. *Contacto (Burbank): a magazine for today's Latinos.* 1994. unknown. Ed(s): Jesus Hernandez Cuellar. Contacto Magazine, 1317 N San Fernado Blvd, PMB 246, Burbank, CA 91504; editor@contactomagazine.com. *Aud.:* Ga.

First published in 1994 in print format, this well-organized publication has been available online since 1998, and is devoted to addressing Latino and Latin American related topics, including politics, education, business, and entertainment. It features in-depth news articles, including pieces on media-related issues and human rights issues. Recent coverage of the war in Iraq has included articles written by former President Jimmy Carter and Noam Chomsky. This is a very useful, easy-to-navigate, electronic journal that covers a wide array of current topics. (JRD)

4122. *El Cuarto del Quenepon.* 1995. bi-m. Ed(s): Marma O'Neill, Rosa Irigoyen. El Cuarto del Quenepon, PMB 205, #667 Ponce de Leon, San Juan, 00907, Puerto Rico; quenepas@caribe.net; http://cuarto.quenepon.org/. *Aud.:* Ga, Ac.

This groundbreaking Spanish-language interactive magazine, originating in Puerto Rico, focuses on the arts in cyberspace. In addition to the editor's work, a single artist in various media is featured. Prose and imaginative writings by others in the community are also included. The magazine has sponsored online conferences on the arts and welcomes creative works in various media that serve to preserve Puerto Rican culture. There is a summary in English, but the art itself scarcely requires explanation. (JRD)

4123. *L A Ritmo.com: Latin American Rhythm & Sound Magazine.* [ISSN: 1525-853X] 1998. bi-w. Free. Ed(s): Sounni de Fontenay. Tag It, 1814 Astoria Blvd., Astoria, NY 11102; info@taggin.com; http://www.laritmo.com. Adv. Circ: 1300. *Aud.:* Ga.

Published in New York, a hotbed for salsa and other forms of contemporary, urban Latin music, this very useful online magazine is devoted to reporting the news as it pertains to what is happening musically not only in New York but in all the Latin world. Included in this incredible treasure trove are record reviews of the works of a variety of artists, the latest hit charts, interviews with Latin musicians, photo galleries, an archive to previous issues, and links to individual artists' web pages. A great, free resource useful to anyone who enjoys listening to or collecting Latin music. (JRD)

4124. *LatinoLA.* irreg. LatinoCities, Inc., 15115 1/2 W Sundset Blvd #B, Pacific Palisades, CA 90272-3721; info@latinola.com; http://www.latinola.com/. Adv. *Aud.:* Ga.

This is an online magazine that is chock-full of all kinds of information of interest to Latinos everywhere. While it showcases news and events from the Los Angeles area, it goes far beyond that to provide worldwide news coverage on a variety of issues. It includes a calendar section, an arts and entertainment section, a section on people, and a forum section plus an online mercado. Recent features have focused on such topics as the Zapatista movement, the legacy of Bert Corona, and a review of the movie *Bread and Roses*. Some fiction and poetry are also included. This web site is a welcome addition to the many new online publications that are available on Latinos. (JRD)

■ LAW

Donald J. Dunn, Dean & Professor of Law, University of La Verne College of Law, 320 East D Street, Ontario, CA 91764

Introduction

Over the last 30 years there has been a proliferation of legal periodical titles, with the total now well into the thousands. Typical academic law libraries subscribe to at least 1,000 titles. Legal periodicals can usually be grouped into six categories: (1) law-school reviews (*Florida Law Review*), (2) subject specialty journals (*Ecology Law Journal*), (3) bar association journals, (4) interdisciplinary journals (*Harvard Journal of Law and Public Policy*), (5) news, general-interest, and current-events publications (*ABA Journal*), and (6) foreign legal periodicals (*Cambridge Law Journal*). They can also be assorted by publisher (law school, commercial, and professional association or learned society).

Law-school reviews are a tradition in legal education. Because at least 50 law schools would argue that they should be included among the top 20 in the country, it is difficult to make recommendations as to which are most appropriate for a particular collection. The so-called traditional ones included in this section were selected because of the reputation of the schools, the quality of the publications, geographic locations, and the frequency with which they are cited by others. When selecting law-school reviews for purchase, it is often good practice to begin with those published by the law school(s) in your state.

Commercial publishers, learned societies, and professional associations generally publish subject specialty journals. As soon as a "hot" topic or a major area of expertise develops, a journal will be launched to cover it. As a general rule, society and association publications are scholarly, of high quality, and distributed as part of a membership fee. Commercial publications tend to be more practitioner-oriented, to be published more frequently, and to rely on advertising for support.

Although no state bar association publications are included in the list that follows, this does not imply that they should not be acquired. It is wise to obtain the bar journal for your state and the county or city bar journal, if one exists, for your locale. These are almost entirely practitioner-oriented, provide how-to advice, and often discuss members of the state's legal community.

When selecting law journals for your collection, it is important to bear in mind your type of library and the constituency you serve. Academic law libraries may acquire almost all law-school reviews and learned-society publications as well as those of the American Bar Association and other law-related professional groups. Other libraries will have a more limited scope: A business school will focus on materials germane to its discipline; a library in Florida might want more materials on estate planning and probate; a Midwestern state may require more on agriculture; and a general academic or public library may be more interested in subject specialty and interdisciplinary titles.

Basic Periodicals

Ga: *ABA Journal, National Law Journal, The Practical Lawyer, Trial;* Ac: *ABA Journal, Business Lawyer, Columbia Law Review, Harvard Law Review, Law and Contemporary Problems, National Law Journal, University of Chicago Law Review, Yale Law Journal.*

Basic Abstracts and Indexes

Current Law Index, Index to Legal Periodicals, Legal Resource Index, LegalTrac.

4125. ***A B A Journal: the lawyer's magazine.*** Formerly (until 1983): *American Bar Association Journal.* 1915. m. USD 120 (Individuals, USD 75; USD 7 newsstand/cover). Ed(s): Debra Cassens, Danial Kim. American Bar Association, 750 N Lake Shore Dr, Chicago, IL 60611; service@abanet.org. Illus., index, adv. Sample. Refereed. Circ: 387632 Paid. Vol. ends: Dec. Microform: WSH; PQC. Online: EBSCO Publishing; Gale Group; LexisNexis; OCLC Online Computer Library Center, Inc.; ProQuest Information & Learning; West Group. Reprint: WSH. *Indexed:* ABIn, ABS&EES, ATI, AgeL, ArtHuCI, BAS, BRI, CBRI, CJA, CJPI, CLI, ILP, LRI, PAIS, SSCI. *Bk. rev.:* 2-4, 2,000 words. *Aud.:* Ga, Ac, Sa.

With by far the largest circulation of all the legal publications, due mainly to its distribution to members of the American Bar Association, this magazine is designed to be of interest to all segments of the legal profession. It can perhaps best be described as *Time* for lawyers. In addition to containing several timely feature articles of four to six pages in length, several "departments" address different aspects of law and law practice. For example, the "President's Message" discusses the ABA president's thinking on major legal concerns; the "Letters" section provides for reader exchanges; the "Substantive Law" department analyzes trends in the law; while the "Supreme Court Report" speculates about the outcome of cases not yet decided by the U.S. Supreme Court and reports on recent rulings; and "Practice Strategies" contains information on litigation techniques, solo practice, technology, and other topics of broad interest. From time to time, interviews with prominent legal figures provide insights unavailable elsewhere. The *Journal*'s attractive layout, color illustrations, and timeliness contrast remarkably with more traditional, staid legal publications.

4126. ***Administrative Law Review (Chicago).*** [ISSN: 0001-8368] 1973. q. Non-members, USD 35. Ed(s): Charles H Koch, Jr. American Bar Association, Administrative Law and Regulatory Practice Section, 750 N Lake Shore Dr, Chicago, IL 60611; http://www.lexis.nexis.com/lncc/sources/libcont/aloa.html. Illus., index, adv. Refereed. Circ: 8000. Vol. ends: Fall. Microform: WSH. Online: Gale Group. Reprint: WSH. *Indexed:* AgeL, CLI, ILP, LRI, SSCI. *Bk. rev.:* Occasional, length varies. *Aud.:* Ac, Sa.

Administrative law is concerned with government authorities other than courts and legislative bodies. Administrative agencies—national, state, and local—promulgate rules and regulations and issue decisions that govern our daily lives. Consequently, the power wielded by these agencies is often immense. This journal, published jointly by the Section of Administrative Law and Regulatory Practice of the American Bar Association and its student staff members at the Washington College of Law of American University, discusses all aspects of administrative law, including such topics as consumer protection regulation, administrative rule making, immigration law, banking and currency regulation, and energy and environmental, insurance, and postal regulations. This title has the widest distribution of all journals devoted to administrative law. A recent issue is devoted to a colloquy regarding a cost-benefit analysis of the government control of environmental risk. An annual review of administrative law cases is contained in one issue each year.

Air & Space Law. See Aeronautics and Space Science section.

4127. ***American Business Law Journal.*** [ISSN: 0002-7766] 1963. q. USD 28; USD 27 foreign. Ed(s): Jere Morehead. Academy of Legal Studies in Business, c/o Daniel J Herron, Dept of Finance, 120 Upham Hall, Oxford, OH 45056; http://miavx1.muohio.edu/~herrondj/. Illus., index, adv. Refereed. Circ: 2000. Vol. ends: Winter. Microform: PQC. Online: bigchalk; EBSCO Publishing; Florida Center for Library Automation; Gale Group; LexisNexis; Northern Light Technology, Inc.; OCLC Online Computer Library Center, Inc.; ProQuest Information & Learning; H.W. Wilson. Reprint: WSH. *Indexed:* ABIn, ATI, BPI, CLI, ILP, LRI, RI-1, RiskAb, SSCI. *Bk. rev.:* Occasional. *Aud.:* Ac, Sa.

The American Business Law Association is a professional organization with a membership consisting primarily of professors who teach in undergraduate and graduate programs. The authors of the articles are usually associated with these types of institutions or programs. A typical issue contains four to six articles. Recent articles address consumers' rights with respect to direct shipment of wine and the state of state whistleblower protection.

4128. ***American Criminal Law Review.*** Formerly: *American Criminal Law Quarterly.* [ISSN: 0164-0364] 1962. q. USD 30 domestic; USD 40 foreign; USD 10 newsstand/cover per issue. Georgetown University Law Center, 600 New Jersey Ave, NW, Washington, DC 20001; http://www.ll.georgetown.edu/. Illus., index, adv. Refereed. Circ: 2153. Vol. ends: No. 4. Microform: WSH; PQC. Online: EBSCO Publishing; Florida Center for Library Automation; Gale Group; LexisNexis; Northern Light Technology, Inc.; OCLC Online Computer Library Center, Inc.; ProQuest Information & Learning; West Group; H.W. Wilson. Reprint: PQC; WSH. *Indexed:* ABS&EES, CJA, CJPI, CLI, ILP, LRI, RiskAb, SSCI. *Bk. rev.:* Occasional, lengthy. *Aud.:* Ac, Sa.

Criminal law is an area that is changing dramatically with the more conservative nature of the U.S. Supreme Court. This student-edited journal includes articles, notes, project reports, and symposia that focus on some of the more complicated issues in the criminal law area, with recent issues addressing the exclusionary rule, capital punishment, and the prison industry. A regular though not annual feature is a survey of white-collar crime. Representative articles include "The Case for the Contingent Exclusionary Rule" and "Don't Let Sleeping Lawyers Lie: Raising the Standard for Effective Assistance of Counsel."

American Indian Law Review. See Native Americans section.

4129. ***American Journal of Comparative Law.*** [ISSN: 0002-919X] 1952. q. USD 30 domestic; USD 32 foreign; USD 10 newsstand/cover per issue. Ed(s): Richard M Buxbaum. American Society of Comparative Law, University of California, 394 Boalt Hall, Berkeley, CA 94720-7200; http://www.comparativelaw.org. Illus., index, adv. Refereed. Circ: 2100. Vol. ends: Fall. Microform: PQC. Online: Gale Group; LexisNexis. Reprint: ISI; PQC; WSH. *Indexed:* ABCPolSci, ABS&EES, BAS, CJA, CLI, IBSS, ILP, LRI, PAIS, PSA, SSCI. *Bk. rev.:* 6-10, 1,200-5,000 words. *Aud.:* Ac, Sa.

Comparative law, as the topic suggests, compares the laws of one or more nations with those of another or discusses one jurisdiction's law in order for the reader to understand how it might differ from that of the United States or some other country. This widely respected publication features articles by major scholars and comments by law student writers. The diversity of coverage is illustrated by "Company Law Theory-England and France." The annual "Bulletin" section contains the membership list of the American Foreign Law Association and the association president's annual report.

4130. ***American Journal of International Law.*** [ISSN: 0002-9300] 1907. q. USD 140; USD 175 foreign. Ed(s): Jonathan Charney, Michael Reisman. American Society of International Law, 2223 Massachusetts Ave, N W, Washington, DC 20008-2864; http://www.asil.org. Illus., index, adv. Refereed. Circ: 7000. Vol. ends: Oct. Microform: WSH; IDC; PQC. Online: Factiva; Gale Group; JSTOR (Web-based Journal Archive); LexisNexis; Northern Light Technology, Inc.; OCLC Online Computer Library Center, Inc.; ProQuest Information & Learning. Reprint: WSH. *Indexed:* ABCPolSci, ABS&EES, ArtHuCI, BAS, CLI, DSR&OA, IBSS, IBZ, ILP, IPSA, LRI, PAIS, PRA, RiskAb, SSCI, SSI, SWRA. *Bk. rev.:* 15-20. *Aud.:* Ac, Sa.

This highly respected English-language journal featuring a prestigious board of editors focuses on all aspects of private and public international law. An annual volume averages over 1,000 pages and contains discussions of international organizations, foreign-relations law, and international conventions and protocols. In addition to the major articles and numerous book reviews, the "Current Developments" section addresses major news events, and recent cases are discussed in "International Decisions." This is often the first journal to publish selected treaties and other international documents. "Contemporary Practice of the United States Relating to International Law," which analyzes international issues by subject, is arranged according to the *Annual Digest of United States Practice in International Law,* published by the U.S. Department of State.

4131. ***American Journal of Jurisprudence: an international forum for legal philosophy.*** Formerly: *Natural Law Forum.* [ISSN: 0065-8995] 1956. a. USD 40 (Individuals, USD 25). Ed(s): Gerard Bradley. University of Notre Dame, Law School, Notre Dame, IN 46556; aberreth@earthlink.net; http://www.nd.edu/. Illus., index, adv. Circ: 1000.

Microform: WSH; PMC; PQC. Online: Gale Group; LexisNexis; OCLC Online Computer Library Center, Inc.; H.W. Wilson. Reprint: PQC; WSH. *Indexed:* ABCPolSci, CLI, CPL, IBZ, ILP, LRI, PSA. *Bk. rev.:* 3-5, 2,000-7,000 words. *Aud.:* Ac, Sa.

Jurisprudence, the philosophy of law or the formal science of law, is frequently a "heady" topic, often drawing heavily on the works of such luminaries as Rawls, Hegel, Habermas, Kant, Aquinas, Mill, Kelsen, Unger, Dworkin, and Bentham. However, if one is seeking a broad-based collection—a little of this and a little of that—a publication on jurisprudence fills in a small but important segment of legal scholarship. While jurisprudence articles are frequently found in other journals, this annual volume, published by the Natural Law Institute of the Notre Dame Law School, is the only one in the nation by a law school that is devoted exclusively to legal philosophy. Volume 45 (2000) contains an index to volumes 1-40 (1956-1995). Also published by the School is the *Notre Dame Law Review, Notre Dame Journal of Law, Ethics & Public Policy,* and *Journal of College and University Law.*

4132. ***American Journal of Law & Medicine.*** [ISSN: 0098-8588] 1975. q. USD 195 (Individuals, USD 105). Ed(s): Frances Miller. American Society of Law, Medicine & Ethics, 765 Commonwealth Ave, Ste 1634, Boston, MA 02215; aslme@bu.edu; orders@allenpress.com; http://www.aslme.org. Illus., index, adv. Refereed. Circ: 4000. Vol. ends: Winter. Microform: WSH; PMC. Online: EBSCO Publishing; Florida Center for Library Automation; Gale Group; LexisNexis; Northern Light Technology, Inc.; OCLC Online Computer Library Center, Inc.; ProQuest Information & Learning; West Group; H.W. Wilson. Reprint: WSH. *Indexed:* AgeL, BiolAb, CLI, ExcerpMed, H&SSA, ILP, IMFL, IndMed, LRI, MCR, RI-1, RiskAb, SSCI. *Bk. rev.:* Occasional, 3, 600 words. *Aud.:* Ac, Sa.

As issues such as the right-to-life, abortion, AIDS, genetic engineering, and medical malpractice proliferate, the interrelationship of law and medicine has become increasingly complex. This interdisciplinary journal, among the earliest to be devoted to law and medicine, has established itself as one of the more scholarly and thoughtful publications of its type. Published in connection with the Boston University School of Law, it contains lead articles and student pieces. "Recent Developments in Health Law" contains annotations of recent court cases and various types of announcements.

4133. ***American Journal of Legal History.*** [ISSN: 0002-9319] 1957. q. USD 40 (Individuals, USD 30). Ed(s): Diane Maleson. Temple University, School of Law, 1719 N Broad St, Philadelphia, PA 19122; http://www.temple.edu/departments/lawschool/. Illus., index, adv. Refereed. Circ: 1200. Vol. ends: Oct. Microform: WSH. Online: Gale Group; West Group. Reprint: WSH. *Indexed:* ABCPolSci, AmH&L, ArtHuCI, CJA, CLI, IBZ, ILP, LRI, SSCI. *Bk. rev.:* 7-20, length varies. *Aud.:* Ac, Sa.

Historical underpinnings are often important to an understanding of current-day law. Similarly, a sense of perspective enhances an appreciation of our legal system. Although numerous journals occasionally feature an article on legal history, this journal is devoted exclusively to the topic. Each issue is small, approximately 115 pages, and usually contains three or four feature articles and numerous book appraisals. Historians are important for all disciplines; there is usually at least one legal historian on each law school faculty. This journal provides interesting insights into people, places, and events that have shaped our system of justice and offers a nice respite for students and members of the bar. Temple also publishes *Temple Law Review, Temple Environmental Law & Technology Journal,* and *Temple International and Comparative Law Journal.*

4134. ***The American Lawyer.*** [ISSN: 0162-3397] 1979. m. 10/yr. USD 298 domestic; USD 350 foreign. Ed(s): Aric Press. American Lawyer Media, Inc., 105 Madison Ave, New York, NY 10016; catalog@amlaw.com; http://www.americanlawyermedia.com. Illus., index, adv. Circ: 17000. Vol. ends: Dec. Reprint: WSH. *Indexed:* ASIP, CLI, ILP, LRI. *Bk. rev.:* Usually 1. *Aud.:* Ga, Ac, Sa.

When this newspaper first hit the scene, it was often viewed as a legal tabloid and not serious journalism. While its focus is still sometimes sensational, its reputation for investigative reporting has improved. It is a glossy, well-illustrated publication featuring bold headlines and snappy captions. In addition to feature articles, there are regular departments including "Headnotes," "Bar Talk," "Big Deals," "Big Suits," "Heavy Hitter," "IP Land," and "In the News." There are frequent special pull-out sections and supplements, for example, an annotated list of the top 100 law firms; corporate mergers and acquisitions; and a legal-recruiters directory. Although this publication may not be prominently displayed in a law firm's waiting room, its large subscription base suggests it is widely read in private.

Animal Law. See Animal Welfare section.

Berkeley Journal of Employment and Labor Law. See Labor and Industrial Relations section.

4135. ***Berkeley Technology Law Journal.*** Formerly (until vol.11, 1996): *High Technology Law Journal.* [ISSN: 1086-3818] 1986. 3x/yr. USD 65; USD 27 per issue. Ed(s): Sonal N. Mehta, Sarah Ratcliffe. University of California, Berkeley, School of Law, Boalt Hall, Berkeley, CA 94720-7200; btlj@law.berkeley.edu. Illus., index, adv. Refereed. Circ: 450. Vol. ends: Fall. Microform: WSH; PQC. Online: EBSCO Publishing; Florida Center for Library Automation; Gale Group; LexisNexis. Reprint: WSH. *Indexed:* ABIn, CLI, IBSS, ILP, LRI, PAIS, RiskAb. *Bk. rev.:* Occasional, 2,500 words. *Aud.:* Ac, Sa.

As novel legal issues were being posed by advancing technologies, the language of technology was foreign to legal discourse. This journal was launched with the goal of bridging the gap between law and science. It quickly became a respected source for discussions of cutting-edge issues in the law. Recent articles address such eclectic topics as the idea of "scientific knowledge," patent disputes, printing presses, information services, intellectual property and contract law, and e-mail privacy. One issue is an annual review of law and technology.

4136. ***Boston University Law Review.*** [ISSN: 0006-8047] 1897. 5x/yr. USD 30 domestic; USD 35 foreign. Ed(s): Howard A. Lipton, Brett Budzinski. Boston University, School of Law, Law Review, 765 Commonwealth Ave, Boston, MA 02215; http://web.bu.edu/law/. Illus., index, adv. Refereed. Circ: 3000. Vol. ends: Dec. Microform: WSH. Online: Gale Group; LexisNexis; West Group. Reprint: WSH. *Indexed:* CJA, CLI, ILP, LRI, PAIS, SSCI. *Bk. rev.:* Occasional, lengthy. *Aud.:* Ac, Sa.

Among the older law reviews in the country, this student-edited journal is traditional in coverage and format. It features consistently high-quality articles on a wide cross-section of topics by noted authorities, notes by student members of the *Review,* and occasional book reviews. Recent issues cover such diverse topics as impeachment, rape, legal ethics, and trusts. It has one of the highest circulations of all the law school's reviews. An average issue is approximately 250 pages. Boston University School of Law also publishes *The American Journal of Law & Medicine* (jointly with the American Society of Law and Medicine) (see above this section), *Annual Review of Banking Law, Boston University International Law Journal, Journal of Science & Technology Law,* and *Public Interest Law Journal.*

4137. ***Business Lawyer.*** [ISSN: 0007-6899] 1946. q. Members, USD 99; Non-members, USD 149. Ed(s): Maury B Poscover. American Bar Association, Business Law Section, 750 N Lake Shore Dr, Chicago, IL 60611; http://www.lexis-nexis.com/lncc/sources/libcont/aba.html. Illus., index, adv. Circ: 55000. Vol. ends: Aug. Microform: MIM; WSH. Online: Florida Center for Library Automation; Gale Group; LexisNexis; Northern Light Technology, Inc.; OCLC Online Computer Library Center, Inc.; ProQuest Information & Learning; West Group. Reprint: WSH. *Indexed:* ABIn, ATI, CLI, IBZ, ILP, LRI, PAIS, SSCI. *Bk. rev.:* 1-2, 2,400 words. *Aud.:* Ac, Sa.

This journal's extensive circulation is due in large part to the tremendous number of members in this American Bar Association (ABA) section. A typical issue of this highly esteemed and often-cited publication contains eight to ten articles and 425 pages. A volume includes special reports; surveys, such as the "Annual Survey of Consumer Financial Services Law" changes in model acts; and task-force reports. Because the topic "business law" encompasses so many issues—for example, constitutional, banking, commercial, financial institutions, business financing, securities, partnership, bankruptcy, and environmental law—current developments are the principal focus.

4138. *California Law Review.* [ISSN: 0008-1221] 1912. bi-m. USD 45 USD 11 per issue. Ed(s): Jason Snyder, Brian McDonald. University of California, Berkeley, School of Law, Boalt Hall, Berkeley, CA 94720-7200. Illus., index, adv. Refereed. Circ: 1650 Paid. Vol. ends: Dec. Microform: WSH; PQC. Online: EBSCO Publishing; Florida Center for Library Automation; Gale Group; LexisNexis; Northern Light Technology, Inc. Reprint: WSH. *Indexed:* ABCPolSci, ABIn, ArtHuCI, CJA, CLI, CommAb, ILP, LRI, PAIS, RiskAb, SSCI. *Bk. rev.:* Occasional, length varies. *Aud.:* Ac, Sa.

Among the most prestigious of all the student-edited law reviews and the oldest from the West Coast law schools, this University of California School of Law at Berkeley publication includes a wide assortment of provocative articles by legal professionals and law students. A typical six-issue volume will contain approximately 1,500 to 2,000 pages. Although most articles are of a traditional, stodgy nature, some are quite creative. Each volume typically contains a symposium issue illustrated by "Law in the Twentieth Century" and "Intellectual Property and Contract Law for the Information Age." This school also publishes *Berkeley Women's Law Journal, Ecology Law Quarterly,* and *Berkeley Technology Law Journal* (see above and below in this section), as well as *African-American Law & Policy Report, Asian Law Journal, Berkeley Journal of Employment and Labor Law, International Tax and Business Lawyer,* and *La Raza Law Journal.*

4139. *Cambridge Law Journal.* [ISSN: 0008-1973] 1921. 3x/yr. USD 89. Ed(s): M J Prichard. Cambridge University Press, The Edinburgh Bldg, Shaftesbury Rd, Cambridge, CB2 2RU, United Kingdom; information@cambridge.org; http://uk.cambridge.org/journals. Illus., index, adv. Circ: 1600. Vol. ends: Nov. Microform: PQC. Online: EBSCO Publishing; Gale Group; OCLC Online Computer Library Center, Inc.; RoweCom Information Quest; Swets Blackwell. Reprint: WSH. *Indexed:* CJPI, CLI, IBSS, ILP, LRI, PSA, SWR&A, SociolAb. *Bk. rev.:* 30, 1,200-1,500 words. *Aud.:* Ac, Sa.

Considered by most legal scholars to be the best British legal periodical, this publication reverses the format used by its American counterparts—that is, the student case notes and comments precede the longer scholarly articles. World-renowned legal scholar Glanville Williams contributed "The Fetus and the 'Right to Life.'" The book reviews, both cogent and forceful, serve as excellent aids in collection development for materials from the United Kingdom.

4140. *Chicano - Latino Law Review.* Formerly: *Chicano Law Review.* [ISSN: 1061-8899] 1972. a. USD 15; USD 19 foreign. Ed(s): Carmen Santana, Salvador Mendoza. University of California, Los Angeles, James S. Coleman African Studies Center, 405 Hilgard Ave, Los Angeles, CA 90024; clr@law4.law.ucla.edu; http://www.ucla.edu/. Illus., index, adv. Circ: 600. Microform: LIB. Online: Gale Group; LexisNexis; West Group. Reprint: WSH. *Indexed:* CLI, ILP, LRI. *Bk. rev.:* Occasional, essay length. *Aud.:* Ac, Sa.

This publication of Chicano-Latino law students at UCLA School of Law, like *La Raza Law Journal* from UC Berkeley, is a law-related publication specifically established to address issues concerning the Mexican American community and the broader-based Latino community. It is supposed to be an annual, but its schedule is less than admirable, with only 21 volumes being published since its establishment in 1972. Even so, as a forum for an underrepresented minority in the legal community, this publication is important because of its particular perspective. It identifies and analyzes legal issues affecting the Latino community and focuses on how these legal issues impact on the political and cultural interaction of the United States and Latin America. A recent symposium issue focuses on hate crimes.

Children's Legal Rights Journal. See Sociology and Social Work/General section.

4141. *Clearinghouse Review: journal of poverty law and policy.* [ISSN: 0009-868X] 1969. bi-m. USD 125 (Individuals, USD 95). Ed(s): Rita McLennon. National Clearinghouse for Legal Services, Inc., 205 W Monroe, 2nd Fl, Chicago, IL 60606; http://www.povertylaw.org/. Illus., index. Circ: 10000. Vol. ends: Apr. Microform: PQC. Online: Gale Group. Reprint: WSH. *Indexed:* AgeL, CLI, ILP, LRI, MCR, PAIS, SWR&A. *Aud.:* Ga, Ac, Sa.

Legal services and poverty law are the focus of this publication. Articles, averaging between 8 and 15 per issue, are straightforward, readable, and "how-to" in nature. The orientation is toward assisting legal-services attorneys in the day-to-day practice of law, with contributions from a variety of individuals in the poverty law field. Topics frequently addressed include housing, civil rights, welfare reform, consumer protection, and senior citizens. Case reports, a regular feature, provide abstracts of cases submitted to the National Center on Poverty Law Library. The "Annual Review of Poverty Law" is the subject of each January issue.

4142. *Clinical Law Review: a journal of lawyering and legal education.* [ISSN: 1079-1159] 1994. s-a. USD 20 domestic; USD 26 foreign; USD 14 newsstand/cover per issue. Ed(s): Randy Hertz. New York University School of Law, 40 Washington Square South, Vanderbilt Hall, New York, NY 10012; http://www.law.nyu.edu/. Refereed. *Indexed:* CLI, ILP. *Aud.:* Ac, Sa.

"Practical skills," "hands-on," "lawyering," and "real world," are words that help describe clinical legal education. It's a fairly recent phenomenon in law schools, but it has quickly become commonplace. This journal, jointly sponsored by NYU School of Law, the Clinical Legal Education and the Association of American Law Schools, fills a need by discussing the special forms of academic pedagogy required for successful clinical education experiences.

Columbia Journal of Gender and the Law. See Women: Feminist and Special Interest/Feminist and Women's Studies section.

4143. *Columbia Journal of Law & the Arts: a quarterly journal of law and the arts, entertainment, communications and intellectual property.* Former titles (until 2001): *Columbia - V L A Journal of Law & the Arts;* (until 1985): *Art and the Law.* 1974. q. USD 45 in North America; USD 53 elsewhere. Columbia University School of Law, Jerome Greene Hall, 435 W 116th St, New York, NY 10027; http://www.columbia.edu/. Illus., index, adv. Circ: 750. Vol. ends: Summer. Microform: WSH. Online: Gale Group. Reprint: WSH. *Indexed:* CLI, ILP, LRI. *Aud.:* Ac, Sa.

As the subtitle of this publication indicates, coverage is sufficiently broad to include a multitude of issues relating to the arts and entertainment industry. The four to six articles in each issue present enlightening, out-of-the-mainstream legal scholarship devoted to the interests of artists and attorneys whose specialty is serving artists. A recent issue includes articles on applying copyright protection to sports moves and regulating electronic junk mail. The *Hastings Communications and Entertainment Law Journal* is of the same genre and also worth consideration.

4144. *Columbia Law Review.* [ISSN: 0010-1958] 1901. m. Oct.-Jan., Mar.-Jun. USD 49 domestic; USD 70 foreign. Ed(s): Bryan Diederich. Columbia Law Review Association, 435 W 116th St, New York, NY 10027. Illus., index, adv. Refereed. Circ: 2500 Paid. Vol. ends: Dec. Microform: WSH. Online: Gale Group; LexisNexis; West Group. Reprint: WSH. *Indexed:* ABCPolSci, ABIn, ABS&EES, ATI, AgeL, ArtHuCI, BRI, CBRI, CJA, CLI, IBSS, ILP, IPSA, LRI, PAIS, RiskAb, SSCI. *Bk. rev.:* occasional, essay length. *Aud.:* Ac, Sa.

A prestigious law review from an equally prestigious law school with a long and distinguished history, this publication follows the traditional model of lead articles by professionals, comments and notes by students, and occasional scholarly book review essays. Recent issues address such diverse topics as taxation, transgender rights, and child pornography. Columbia University School of Law publishes 14 separate journals, more than any other law school in the nation. The others are *American Review of International Arbitration, Columbia Business Law Review, Columbia Human Rights Law Review, Columbia Journal of Environmental Law, Columbia Journal of Law & the Arts* (see above in this section), *Columbia Journal of Law and Social Problems, Columbia Journal of Transnational Law, Columbia Journal of Gender and Law, Columbia Journal of Asian Law, Columbia Journal of East European Law, Columbia Science and Technology Law Review, National Black Law Journal,* and *Columbia Journal of European Law.*

Constitutional Commentary. See Civil Liberties/General section.

4145. *Cornell Law Review.* Formerly: *Cornell Law Quarterly.* [ISSN: 0010-8847] 1915. 6x/yr. USD 35; USD 39 foreign. Ed(s): Alison Nathan. Cornell University, Cornell Law School, Myron Taylor Hall, Ithaca, NY 14853; http://www.law.cornell.edu/. Illus., index, adv. Refereed. Circ: 3500. Vol. ends: No. 6. Microform: WSH. Online: Florida Center for Library Automation; Gale Group; LexisNexis; West Group. Reprint: WSH. *Indexed:* ABCPolSci, ATI, ArtHuCI, BLI, CJA, CLI, ILP, LRI, PAIS, SSCI. *Aud.:* Ac, Sa.

Another traditional, student-edited law review that features lengthy, heavily researched articles by preeminent scholars and shorter pieces by student authors, this journal conforms to the law school's mission of preparing lawyers to understand the interactions between legal and social process in service to their clients. Recent articles illustrative of the breadth of coverage include "Middle-Class Black Suburbs and the State of Integration: A Post-Integrationist Vision for Metropolitan America" and "Inside the Judicial Mind." Cornell Law School also publishes the *Cornell International Law Journal* and *Cornell Journal of Law and Public Policy.*

4146. *Duke Law Journal.* Formerly (until 1957): *Duke Bar Journal.* [ISSN: 0012-7086] 1951. 6x/yr. USD 39; USD 45 foreign. Duke University, School of Law, PO Box 90364, Durham, NC 27708-0364; tom@faculty.law.duke.edu; http://www.law.duke.edu/. Illus., index, adv. Refereed. Circ: 1400. Vol. ends: Dec. Microform: WSH; PMC. Online: Florida Center for Library Automation; Gale Group; LexisNexis; West Group. Reprint: WSH. *Indexed:* CJA, CLI, CommAb, ILP, LRI, RI-1, RiskAb, SSCI. *Bk. rev.:* Occasional, lengthy. *Aud.:* Ac, Sa.

This student-edited review, national in scope, consistently has high-quality articles on a wide range of legal topics. A recent issue includes articles on conflict of laws in litigation between original owners and good faith purchasers of stolen art and on law and policy in the age of the Internet. The highly respected "Annual Administrative Law Issue" discusses and evaluates recent developments in administrative law. The Duke University School of Law also publishes the influential *Law and Contemporary Problems* (see below in this section), *Duke Journal of Comparative & International Law, Duke Environmental Law & Policy Forum, Duke Journal of Gender Law & Policy, Duke Law & Technology Review,* and the *Alaska Law Review* (because Alaska has no law school, yet has among the highest number of lawyers per capita of any state, an agreement between Duke and the Alaska Bar Association enables this journal to be responsive to the needs of Alaska's diverse legal community).

4147. *Ecology Law Quarterly.* [ISSN: 0046-1121] 1971. q. USD 54 (Individuals, USD 30; Students, USD 22). Ed(s): Cinnamon Gilbreath, Kari Krogseng. University of California, Berkeley, School of Law, Boalt Hall, Berkeley, CA 94720-7200. Illus., index, adv. Refereed. Circ: 1150 Paid. Vol. ends: No. 4. Microform: WSH; PMC. Online: EBSCO Publishing; Florida Center for Library Automation; Gale Group; LexisNexis. Reprint: WSH. *Indexed:* CLI, DSR&OA, EnvAb, ExcerpMed, GeoRef, ILP, LRI, OceAb, PAIS, PollutAb, RI-1, SCI, SSCI, SUSA, SWRA. *Bk. rev.:* Occasional, 500-1,000 words. *Aud.:* Ac, Sa.

When the environment became a major concern following Earth Day in 1970, the law students at Boalt Hall were among the first to address law-related ecological issues via a law review. They are to be commended for their long-standing commitment to these matters. Throughout its history, this journal has featured consistently high-quality pieces by scholars and students covering such diverse topics as biodiversity, global warming, and wastewater discharge. Consistent with the theme of preserving the environment and its natural beauty and resources, the cover of each issue is enhanced by an Ansel Adams photograph.

4148. *The Elder Law Journal.* [ISSN: 1070-1478] 1993. s-a. USD 25 domestic; USD 35 foreign. Ed(s): Joanna Grama. University of Illinois at Urbana-Champaign, College of Law, 504 E Pennsylvania Ave, Champaign, IL 61820; http://www.law.uinc.edu/publish/elderlaw. Adv. *Indexed:* AgeL, CLI, ILP, LRI. *Aud.:* Ac, Sa.

As the population continues to age, increased attention is being paid to the legal needs of the elderly. This journal addresses the plethora of legal issues relating to senior citizens, such as guardianship proceedings, spending down for Medicaid eligibility, long-term health care, financial management of continuing-care retirement communities, and reverse mortgages. Representative articles include "Reforming Our Ailing Social Security System: The State of the Current System and Its Impact on African Americans" and "Federal and State Initiatives to Jump Start the Market for Private Long-Term Care Insurance." The journal will likely increase in importance parallel with the growth in elder law. The school's primary journal is the highly respected *University of Illinois Law Review.*

4149. *Emory Law Journal.* Formerly (until 1974): *Journal of Public Law.* [ISSN: 0094-4076] 1952. q. USD 30; USD 34 foreign. Ed(s): Christopher Hunber. Emory University, School of Law, Gambrell Hall, Atlanta, GA 30322; http://www.law.emory.edu. Illus., index, adv. Circ: 1100. Vol. ends: No. 4. Microform: WSH; PMC; PQC. Online: Gale Group; LexisNexis; Northern Light Technology, Inc.; OCLC Online Computer Library Center, Inc.; ProQuest Information & Learning; West Group; H.W. Wilson. Reprint: WSH. *Indexed:* CLI, ILP, LRI, SSCI. *Bk. rev.:* Occasional, lengthy. *Aud.:* Ac, Sa.

The School of Law of Emory University has a national reputation with a national and international focus. Its long-standing primary journal, traditional in nature, reflects the school's scholarly bent. Articles and student notes and occasional review essays address any legal topic. Because this journal is increasingly cited by other reviews, it has an important place on library shelves. Recent articles have been devoted to issues regarding bankruptcy reform, due process concerns, and interstate class actions. Also published by the school are *Georgia Journal of International and Comparative Law* and *Bankruptcy Developments Journal.*

Employee Relations Law Journal. See Labor and Industrial Relations section.

4150. *Environmental Law (Portland).* [ISSN: 0046-2276] 1970. q. USD 40 domestic; USD 48 foreign; USD 12 newsstand/cover per issue. Ed(s): Stacy D Harrop. Lewis and Clark College, Northwestern School of Law, 10015 S W Terwilliger Blvd, Portland, OR 97219; http://www.lclark.edu/. Illus., index, adv. Circ: 1100. Vol. ends: Oct. Microform: WSH; PQC. Online: Florida Center for Library Automation; Gale Group; LexisNexis; West Group. Reprint: PQC; WSH. *Indexed:* CLI, DSR&OA, EnvAb, ExcerpMed, GeoRef, IBSS, ILP, LRI, OceAb, PollutAb, RI-1, SWRA. *Bk. rev.:* Occasional, lengthy. *Aud.:* Ac, Sa.

Environmental law is one of the most rapidly developing and frequently changing areas of the law. The Northwestern University School of Law of Lewis and Clark College has built as its specialty environmental law. Its program is consistently rated at or near the top. The school's journal is consistent with the school's focus, and it is the oldest legal journal devoted exclusively to issues of environmental concern, such as ecosystems, endangered species, and the Clean Water Act. While each issue is hefty, often exceeding 300 pages, it is printed on unbleached, 100 percent recycled, 50 percent post-consumer paper with soy ink.

4151. *Family Law Quarterly.* [ISSN: 0014-729X] 1967. q. Non-members, USD 49.95. Ed(s): Linda D Elrod. American Bar Association, Family Law Section, 750 N Lake Shore Dr, Chicago, IL 60611; http://www.lexis-nexis.com/lncc/sources/libcont/aba.html. Illus., index, adv. Refereed. Circ: 16000. Vol. ends: Winter. Microform: WSH; PMC; PQC. Online: Gale Group; West Group. Reprint: WSH. *Indexed:* AgeL, CJA, CJPI, CLI, ILP, LRI, SSCI. *Bk. rev.:* Occasional, 500-1,500 words. *Aud.:* Ac, Sa.

The American Bar Association's (ABA) Section of Family Law has as its purpose "to promote the objectives of the American Bar Association by improving the administration of justice in the field of family law by study, conferences, and publication of reports and articles with respect to both legislation and administration." This publication, under editorship of students at Washburn University School of Law, is one of the principal means toward that end. Issues discuss such topics as divorce, parentage, child custody and support, property rights, domestic torts, and adoption. The annotated "Summary of the Year in Family Law" is contained in the Winter issue. *The Family Advocate,* also published by this ABA section, is a more basic magazine offering practical advice for attorneys practicing family law.

4152. *Florida Law Review.* Formerly: *University of Florida Law Review.* [ISSN: 1045-4241] 1948. 5x/yr. USD 30. Ed(s): John Simons. University of Florida, Levin College of Law, 141 Bruton Geer, Gainesville, FL 32611; http://www.ufl.law.edu/. Illus., index, adv. Circ: 1000. Vol. ends: Dec. Microform: WSH. Online: Gale Group; West Group. Reprint: WSH. *Indexed:* CJA, CLI, ILP, LRI. *Bk. rev.:* Occasional, lengthy. *Aud.:* Ac, Sa.

Founded in 1909, the University of Florida is among the oldest law schools in the South and so, too, is its primary law review. This publication is traditional in format, with feature articles by scholars and notes and case comments by students. As such, readers can expect to find contributions on any legal subject. For example, recent issues address the intersection of cyberspace and patent law, racial segregation in American churches, and insurer insolvency. Students here also publish the *Florida Journal of International Law, Journal of Entertainment, Art and Sports Law, Journal of Technology Law & Policy* and the *Journal of Law & Public Policy.* The *Florida Tax Review* is a faculty-edited publication of the school.

Food and Drug Law Journal. See Food Industry section.

4153. *Fordham Law Review.* [ISSN: 0015-704X] 1914. bi-m. USD 40; USD 50 foreign. Fordham University, School of Law, Lincoln Center, 140 W 62nd St, New York, NY 10023; http://www.fordham.edu. Adv. Refereed. Circ: 2800. Microform: WSH; PQC. Online: Gale Group; LexisNexis; OCLC Online Computer Library Center, Inc.; West Group; H.W. Wilson. Reprint: PQC; WSH. *Indexed:* ABS&EES, AgeL, ArtHuCI, BLI, CJA, CLI, ILP, LRI, PSA, SSCI. *Aud.:* Ac, Sa.

The *Fordham Law Review* places special emphasis on its "Essays" as well as "Articles and Responses" sections. Many of the topics covered in the *Review* include regulatory issues. Recent articles include "Professional Liability Insurers as Regulators of Law Practice" and "The Chaos of 12 U.S.C. Section 1821(k): Congressional Subsidizing of Negligent Bank Directors and Officers." Student notes are usually limited to one per issue. Fordham also publishes the *Fordham Environmental Law Journal, Fordham Intellectual Property, Media & Entertainment Law Journal, Fordham International Law Journal, Fordham Journal of Corporate and Financial Law,* and *Fordham Urban Law Journal.*

4154. *G P Solo.* Formerly (until 2000): *General Practice, Solo, and Small Firm Lawyer: The Complete Lawyer;* Which was formed by the merger of (1984-1998): *Compleat Lawyer;* (1997-1998): *Best of A B A Sections. General Practice, Solo & Small Firm Section;* (1997-1998): *Technology and Practice Guide.* [ISSN: 1528-638X] 1998. 8x/yr. USD 48 domestic; USD 72 foreign. Ed(s): Robert M Salkin. A B A Publishing, 750 N Lake Shore Dr, Chicago, IL 60611; service@abanet.org; http://www.abanet.org. Illus., index, adv. Circ: 19000. *Indexed:* CLI, LRI. *Aud.:* Ga, Ac, Sa.

Although law is becoming more and more specialized, there are still a substantial number of attorneys engaged in general practice. This magazine caters to the needs of the general practitioner by providing timely, concise articles on all aspects of substantive law, news of the American Bar Association (ABA) section and committee activities, and updates relating to legislation, ethics, taxes, and solo practice. A recent issue is devoted exclusively to elder law. This publication is a good companion to the ABA's *Law Practice Management* (see below in this section).

4155. *George Washington Law Review.* [ISSN: 0016-8076] 1932. 6x/yr. USD 34; USD 38 foreign. Ed(s): Jonathan Gottlieb. George Washington Law Review, 2008 G St, N W, 2nd Fl, Washington, DC 20052; GWLR@gwu.edu; http://www.law.gwu.edu/lawrev/. Illus., index, adv. Refereed. Circ: 2000. Vol. ends: Aug. Microform: WSH; PMC. Online: Gale Group; LexisNexis; West Group. Reprint: WSH. *Indexed:* AgeL, ArtHuCI, BAS, CLI, ILP, LRI, PAIS, PSA, RiskAb, SSCI, SociolAb. *Bk. rev.:* Occasional, lengthy. *Aud.:* Ac, Sa.

The *Review* tends to contain three or four articles, often with an emphasis on federal law. A review of D.C. Circuit Court opinions is published annually. The school also publishes the *George Washington International Law Review, Environmental Lawyer* (with the ABA), *American Intellectual Property Law Association Quarterly Journal* (with the AIPLA), and the *Public Contact Law Journal* (with the ABA).

4156. *Georgetown Journal of Legal Ethics.* [ISSN: 1041-5548] 1987. q. USD 35 domestic; USD 12.50 newsstand/cover per issue foreign. Georgetown University Law Center, 600 New Jersey Ave, NW, Washington, DC 20001; http://www.law.gwu.edu/. Illus., index. Vol. ends: Spring. Microform: WSH. Online: EBSCO Publishing; Gale Group; LexisNexis; OCLC Online Computer Library Center, Inc.; ProQuest Information & Learning; H.W. Wilson. Reprint: WSH. *Indexed:* ABIn, CLI, ILP, LRI. *Bk. rev.:* Occasional, lengthy. *Aud.:* Ac, Sa.

Ours is a litigious society, and the bad acts of a few reflect adversely on many. Every law school in the country is required to offer a course in professional responsibility, sometimes called legal ethics. Professional responsibility is a separate requirement on the multistate bar examination. This student-edited journal endeavors to heighten awareness of ethical issues within the legal community by providing scholarly articles, student notes and comments, and other information of interest to members of the bar. Recent writings address such diverse issues as representing children in abuse and neglect cases, civil commitment hearings, and questioning judicial impartiality.

4157. *Georgetown Law Journal.* [ISSN: 0016-8092] 1912. 8x/yr. USD 45 domestic; USD 55 foreign; USD 15 newsstand/cover per issue. Georgetown University Law Center, 600 New Jersey Ave, NW, Washington, DC 20001; http://www.law.gwu.edu/. Illus., index, adv. Refereed. Circ: 1319. Vol. ends: Jul. Microform: WSH. Online: EBSCO Publishing; Gale Group; LexisNexis; Northern Light Technology, Inc.; OCLC Online Computer Library Center, Inc.; ProQuest Information & Learning; West Group; H.W. Wilson. Reprint: WSH. *Indexed:* ArtHuCI, BLI, CJA, CLI, CPL, ILP, LRI, PAIS, RiskAb, SSCI. *Aud.:* Ac, Sa.

The Georgetown Law Center, located in our nation's capital, has the largest enrollment and among the highest academic standards of any law school in the country. This journal, the oldest from the District of Columbia law schools, is among eight published by Georgetown and has an outstanding reputation for producing traditional legal scholarship. Articles by noted authorities and student research pieces are lengthy, well documented, and influential. Its "Annual Review of Criminal Procedure," also known as the "Criminal Procedure Project" and a team effort of the journal staff is monumental in scope and depth. For example, the 1999–000 "Project" contained over 900 pages and over 2,900 footnotes. This journal is among the more frequently cited—by courts and other legal journals—in the country. The school also publishes *American Criminal Law Review, Law and Policy in International Business,* and *The Tax Lawyer* (see above and below in this section), as well as *Georgetown Immigration Law Journal, Georgetown International Environmental Law Review, Georgetown Journal of Legal Ethics, Georgetown Journal on Poverty Law & Policy,* and *Journal of Law and Technology.*

Harvard Civil Rights—Civil Liberties Law Review. See Civil Liberties/General section.

Harvard Environmental Law Review. See Environment and Conservation section.

4158. *Harvard Journal of Law and Public Policy.* [ISSN: 0193-4872] 1978. 3x/yr. USD 35 (Students, USD 20). Ed(s): Susanna Dokupil. Harvard Society for Law and Public Policy, Inc., Harvard Law School, Cambridge, MA 02138; jlpp@law.harvard.edu. Illus., index, adv. Refereed. Circ: 6500. Vol. ends: No. 3. Microform: WSH; PMC. Online: EBSCO Publishing; Florida Center for Library Automation; Gale Group; LexisNexis; OCLC Online Computer Library Center, Inc.; ProQuest Information & Learning; West Group; H.W. Wilson. Reprint: WSH. *Indexed:* ABCPolSci, ArtHuCI, CLI, ILP, LRI, PAIS, RI-1, RiskAb, SSCI. *Bk. rev.:* Occasional. *Aud.:* Ac, Sa.

Mainstream law reviews often have a liberal bent. This one, exceeding 1,000 pages and published without any financial support from Harvard, is prepared by law students in the Federalist Society, a conservative and libertarian group. Issues of this journal are usually symposia, such as the recent one somewhat presumptively entitled "Advice to the New American President." Contributors over the years have included Charles Freed, Edwin Meese III, Orrin Hatch, and George Bush. This is a good source for viewpoints alternative to those often found in student-edited law reviews.

4159. ***Harvard Journal on Legislation.*** [ISSN: 0017-808X] 1964. 2x/yr. USD 30 domestic; USD 38 Canada; USD 36 elsewhere. Harvard University, Law School, Publications Center, Hastings Hall, Cambridge, MA 02138; http://www.law.harvard.edu/. Illus., index, adv. Refereed. Circ: 800. Vol. ends: Summer. Microform: WSH; PQC. Online: Gale Group; LexisNexis; OCLC Online Computer Library Center, Inc.; West Group; H.W. Wilson. Reprint: PQC; WSH. *Indexed:* ABCPolSci, AgeL, CLI, IBZ, ILP, LRI, PAIS, PSA, RiskAb, SSCI. *Bk. rev.:* Occasional. *Aud.:* Ac, Sa.

This is the second oldest of Harvard Law School's 12 student-edited reviews. According to the journal's publication policy, it specializes in the analysis of legislation and the legislative process by focusing on legislative reform and on organizational and procedural factors that affect the efficacy of legislative decision-making. The journal publishes articles that examine a public-policy problem of nationwide significance and propose legislation to resolve it. A recent symposium is "Social Reform Through the Class Action." A section devoted to recent legislation provides analysis of recent statutory interpretations and discussions of recent statutory enactments.

4160. ***Harvard Law Review.*** [ISSN: 0017-811X] 1887. m. 8/yr. USD 45; USD 51 foreign. Ed(s): Kenneth Damberger. Harvard Law Review Association, Gannett House, Cambridge, MA 02138; http://gannett-netserv.law.harvard.edu/. Illus., index, adv. Refereed. Circ: 7500. Vol. ends: Jun. Microform: WSH; PQC. Online: EBSCO Publishing; Gale Group; LexisNexis; West Group. Reprint: PQC; WSH. *Indexed:* ABCPolSci, ABIn, ABS&EES, ATI, AgeL, ArtHuCI, BLI, BRI, CBRI, CJA, CLI, IBSS, ILP, IPSA, LRI, PAIS, RI-1, RiskAb, SSCI. *Bk. rev.:* Occasional, essay length. *Aud.:* Ac, Sa.

When it comes to tradition, Harvard is steeped in it; so, too, is its primary journal. It is by far the most widely subscribed to of all the law school reviews. To be selected for the *Harvard Law Review* is almost always a prediction of greater things to come. Articles are selected from a massive pool of submissions and frequently are in the forefront of legal thinking. A typical volume contains approximately 2,000 pages. Each year, the *Review* publishes an evaluation, complete with charts and statistical analyses, of the U.S. Supreme Court decisions during the recently completed term. The ten other journals edited by students at the school are *Harvard Journal on Legislation* and *Harvard Journal of Law & Public Policy* (see above in this section); *Harvard BlackLetter Journal,* and *Harvard Civil Rights—Civil Liberties Law Review* (see Civil Liberties section); *Harvard Environmental Law Review; Harvard Human Rights Journal; Harvard International Law Journal; Harvard Journal of Law & Technology; Harvard Latino Law Review* and *Harvard Women's Law Review.*

4161. ***Hastings Law Journal.*** [ISSN: 0017-8322] 1949. bi-m. USD 30 domestic; USD 35 foreign; USD 12 newsstand/cover per issue domestic. University of California at San Francisco, Hastings College of the Law, 200 McAllister St, San Francisco, CA 94102-4978; http://www.uchastings.edu/. Illus., index, adv. Refereed. Circ: 1500 Paid and controlled. Microform: WSH; PMC; PQC. Online: Gale Group; LexisNexis; West Group. Reprint: PQC; WSH. *Indexed:* AgeL, CJA, CLI, HRA, IBZ, ILP, LRI, PRA, SSCI. *Bk. rev.:* Occasional, essay length. *Aud.:* Ac, Sa.

Established in 1878, Hastings College is the oldest and largest law school in the western United States. Hastings is known for its prestigious "65-Club"—a group of outstanding law professors who have retired from other institutions and now teach at this school. As a result of having this pool of great legal scholars available, the San Francisco location, and the overall quality of the academic program, the school has a student body with some of the best academic credentials in the country. The *Journal* is traditional, having a lengthy major article or two by a prominent scholar followed by student comments and notes. Even the book reviews are highly substantive. This journal is well respected and among the most frequently cited. Hastings also publishes the *Hastings Constitutional Law Quarterly, Hastings International and Comparative Law Review, Hastings West-Northwest Journal of Environmental Law and Policy, Hastings Communications and Entertainment Law Journal* (COMM/ENT), and *Hastings Women's Law Journal.*

Hastings Women's Law Journal. See Women: Feminist and Special Interest/Feminist and Women's Studies section.

4162. ***Howard Law Journal.*** [ISSN: 0018-6813] 1955. s-a. USD 22; USD 25 foreign. Ed(s): Ardrelle Bahar. Joe Christensen, Inc., 1540 Adams St, Box 81269, Lincoln, NE 68501. Illus., index, adv. Circ: 1100. Vol. ends: No. 3. Microform: WSH; PMC. Online: Chadwyck-Healey Incorporated; Gale Group; LexisNexis; West Group. Reprint: WSH. *Indexed:* CLI, IIBP, ILP, LRI, PAIS, RiskAb. *Bk. rev.:* 1-2, lengthy. *Aud.:* Ac, Sa.

Howard University is the second oldest law school in our nation's capital, and its student body is predominantly African American. The format of its *Journal* is rather traditional, although the focus of the articles tends to be directed toward the interests of minorities. For example, one recent article is entitled "Thinking Outside of the Box: The Multiracial Category and its Implications for Race Identity Developments."

Human Rights Quarterly. See Civil Liberties/General section.

4163. ***International Lawyer.*** Formerly: *American Bar Association. Section of International and Comparative Law. Journal and Proceedings.* [ISSN: 0020-7810] 1966. q. Non-members, USD 60. Ed(s): Christine Szaj. American Bar Association, International Law and Practice Section, 740 15th St, N W, Washington, DC 20005; http://www.lexis-nexis.com/lncc/. Index, adv. Refereed. Circ: 13000. Microform: WSH. Online: Gale Group; LexisNexis; West Group. Reprint: WSH. *Indexed:* ABS&EES, BAS, CLI, ILP, LRI, PRA, RiskAb, SSCI, SWRA, WAE&RSA. *Bk. rev.:* Occasional, length varies. *Aud.:* Ac, Sa.

Published under the auspices of the American Bar Association's Section of International Law and Practice, this journal has as its primary focus practical issues facing lawyers engaged in international practice. Topics concerning international trade, licensing, direct investment, finance, taxation, and litigation and dispute resolution are preferred. It provides information on significant current legal developments throughout the world using articles and recent developments, regional development, and case notes. A recent symposium issue convers borderless electronic commerce. Contributions are by professors and practicing attorneys.

4164. ***Iowa Law Review.*** [ISSN: 0021-0552] 1915. 5x/yr. USD 43 domestic; USD 50 foreign; USD 10 newsstand/cover per issue. Ed(s): Trystan Phifer O'Leary. University of Iowa, College of Law, 190 Boyd Law Bldg, Iowa City, IA 52242-1113; ilr@blue.weeg.uiowa.edu; http://www.law.uiowa.edu/. Illus., index, adv. Refereed. Circ: 1800. Vol. ends: No. 5. Microform: WSH; PMC. Online: Gale Group; LexisNexis; West Group. Reprint: WSH. *Indexed:* ATI, CLI, ILP, LRI, PAIS, SSCI. *Bk. rev.:* Occasional, essay length. *Aud.:* Ac, Sa.

It may surprise some to learn that the University of Iowa College of Law, founded in 1865, is the oldest law school west of the Mississippi. The standards used to select the students for the *Review* are among the most rigorous in the country. Due to the College of Law's academic excellence and its longevity, its primary journal has a well-deserved reputation for publishing outstanding legal scholarship. Articles are well researched, heavily documented, and widely cited. The law students also edit the *Journal of Corporation Law* (below in this section), *Journal of Gender, Race & Justice* and *Transnational Law & Contemporary Problems.*

Issues in Law and Medicine. See Civil Liberties/Bioethics: Reproductive Rights, Right-to-Life, and Right-to-Die section.

The Journal of Air Law and Commerce. See Transportation section.

Journal of Criminal Justice. See Criminology and Law Enforcement section.

4165. ***Journal of Criminal Law & Criminology (Chicago, 1973).*** Supersedes in part (in 1972): *Journal of Criminal Law, Criminology and Police Science;* Which had former titles (until 1951): *Journal of Criminal Law & Criminology (Chicago, 1931);* (until 1940): *American Institute of Criminal Law and Criminology. Journal.* [ISSN: 0091-4169] 1910. q. USD 45 domestic; USD 50 foreign; USD 9 newsstand/cover domestic. Ed(s): Matthew Burke. Northwestern University, School of Law, 357 E Chicago Ave, Chicago, IL 60611; http://www.nwu.edu/

lawschool/. Illus., index. Refereed. Circ: 2700. Vol. ends: Winter. Microform: WSH; PQC. Online: EBSCO Publishing; Florida Center for Library Automation; Gale Group; LexisNexis; Northern Light Technology, Inc.; OCLC Online Computer Library Center, Inc.; ProQuest Information & Learning; West Group; H.W. Wilson. Reprint: WSH. *Indexed:* ABCPolSci, CJA, CJPI, CLI, ExcerpMed, IBSS, ILP, LRI, PAIS, PSA, PsycholAb, SSCI, SSI, SociolAb. *Bk. rev.:* 0-4, lengthy. *Aud.:* Ac, Sa.

This journal dates back over 80 years and is among the first of the subject specialty law school reviews. Both its long history and the quality of its content make it a leader in the field and among the most frequently cited legal journals. Edited by students of Northwestern University School of Law, the journal is divided into "Criminal Law" and "Criminology" sections, written by law professionals and social scientists respectively, with a separate section of student-written "Comments." The winter issue contains a highly respected, heavily analytical review of U.S. Supreme Court decisions pertaining to criminal law and criminal procedure.

4166. *Journal of Dispute Resolution.* Formerly (until 1987): *Missouri Journal of Dispute Resolution.* [ISSN: 1052-2859] 1984. s-a. USD 21 domestic; USD 26 Canada; USD 28 elsewhere. Ed(s): Ryan O'Dell. University of Missouri at Columbia, School of Law, 206 Hulston Hall, Columbia, MO 65211; http://www.law.missouri.edu/csdr/jdr.html. Illus., index, adv. Circ: 700 Paid. Vol. ends: No. 2. Microform: WSH. Online: Gale Group; LexisNexis. Reprint: WSH. *Indexed:* CLI, ILP, LRI. *Bk. rev.:* 1, 2,000-4,000 words. *Aud.:* Ac, Sa.

Very few cases actually go to trial. This interdisciplinary journal, published in conjunction with the Center for the Study of Dispute Resolution, fills an important gap in the legal literature in that it discusses the means to avoid the high costs of litigation, such as negotiation, settlement, mediation, and arbitration. Articles, contributed by major legal scholars, address philosophical, practical, and political aspects of dispute processing and at times are the result of empirical research. Some writings relate to the teaching of dispute resolution, while others concern the legal aspects of dispute resolution processes. Comments, case notes, surveys, and studies analyze individual disputes or transactions in detail. An annual student project is an examination of developments pertaining to the Uniform Arbitration Act. The *Missouri Law Review* is also published by this law school.

4167. *Journal of Health Law.* Former titles: *Journal of Health and Hospital Law;* (until 1988): *Hospital Law.* [ISSN: 1526-2472] 1969. q. USD 150. American Health Lawyers Association, 1025 Connecticut Ave NW, Ste. 600, Washington, DC 20036-5428; info@healthlawyers.org; http://www.healthlawyers.org. Illus. Circ: 3000 Paid. *Indexed:* ILP, LRI. *Aud.:* Ac, Sa.

Health and legal issues related to it is one of the most rapidly growing areas of law. A number of journals have emerged discussing different aspects of health care law. This journal, a collaborative effort among the American Health Lawyers Association and Saint Louis University School of Law, is the oldest. It is also the most expensive. Other similar publications are *Berkeley Journal of Health Care Law,* Catholic University's *Journal of Contemporary Health Law and Policy,* Duke's *Journal of Health Politics, Policy and Law,* DePaul's *Journal of Health Care Law,* Case Western's *Health Matrix,* and Cleveland State's *Journal of Law and Health.*

4168. *Journal of Law and Economics.* [ISSN: 0022-2186] 1958. s-a. USD 68 (Individuals, USD 25; Students, USD 15). Ed(s): Dennis W Carlton, Sam Peltzman. University of Chicago Press, Journals Division, PO Box 37005, Chicago, IL 60637; subscriptions@press.uchicago.edu; http://www.journals.uchicago.edu. Illus., index, adv. Refereed. Circ: 2800. Vol. ends: Oct. Microform: WSH; PQC. Online: LexisNexis; West Group. Reprint: WSH. *Indexed:* ABCPolSci, ABIn, AgeL, AmH&L, BAS, BLI, CJA, CLI, DSR&OA, ExcerpMed, IBSS, ILP, IPSA, JEL, LRI, PAIS, RiskAb, SSCI, SSI. *Aud.:* Ac, Sa.

This highly regarded, widely referenced, interdisciplinary journal is intended for a true specialist who is concerned with the influence of regulation and legal institutions on the operation of economic systems, especially the behavior of markets and the impact of government institutions on markets. Use of charts, graphs, and other forms of statistical analyses is commonplace, and plodding through an article can be quite a chore. Each issue has 8 to 12 articles, together totaling approximately 300 pages. The University of Chicago Law School is known for its law and economics orientation, and this publication is true to the school's mission.

Journal of Law and Religion. See Civil Liberties/Freedom of Thought and Belief section.

Journal of Law, Medicine, and Ethics. See Medicine and Health/Medicine and Society section.

4169. *Journal of Legal Education.* Formerly (until 1940): *National Journal of Legal Education.* [ISSN: 0022-2208] 1937. q. USD 38; USD 42 foreign; USD 15 per issue. Association of American Law Schools, 1201 Connecticut Ave, N W, Ste 800, Washington, DC 20036-2605; http://www.aals.org. Illus., index, adv. Sample. Refereed. Vol. ends: Dec. Microform: PQC. Online: Gale Group. Reprint: PQC; WSH. *Indexed:* ABS&EES, CIJE, CLI, HEA, IBZ, ILP, LRI, SSCI. *Bk. rev.:* 0-4, 500-10,000 words. *Aud.:* Ac, Sa.

The Association of American Law Schools is a membership organization, and this, its professional journal, is distributed to all law professors in the country. Its primary purpose is to foster a rich interchange of ideas and information about legal education and related matters, including, but not limited to, the legal profession, legal theory, and legal scholarship. The *Journal* features general articles, shorter discussions of developments in legal education, an occasional symposium, and from time to time even a poem or a short story. Because all law professors receive it automatically, it is probably the most widely read of all journals in legal academia.

4170. *The Journal of Legal Studies.* [ISSN: 0047-2530] 1972. s-a. USD 68 (Individuals, USD 25; Students, USD 15). Ed(s): William M Landes, J Mark Ramseyer. University of Chicago Press, Journals Division, PO Box 37005, Chicago, IL 60637; subscriptions@press.uchicago.edu; http://www.journals.uchicago.edu. Illus., index, adv. Refereed. Circ: 1694 Paid and free. Vol. ends: Jun. Microform: WSH; PQC. Online: Gale Group; LexisNexis. Reprint: PQC; WSH. *Indexed:* AUNI, CJA, CJPI, CLI, IBSS, ILP, IPSA, JEL, LRI, PSA, SSCI, SociolAb. *Aud.:* Ac, Sa.

Like other law-related publications from the University of Chicago, this title ranks among the most frequently cited of the legal literature. It provides a forum for basic theoretical, empirical, historical, and comparative research into the operation of legal systems and institutions, relying on contributions from economists, political scientists, sociologists, and other social scientists, as well as legal scholars, for its content. Occasionally, an issue is published in two parts or has a special focus. The number and length of articles are consistent with its companion journal, *The Journal of Law & Economics* (see above in this section).

Journal of Maritime Law and Commerce. See Transportation section.

4171. *Journal of Supreme Court History.* Formerly (until 1989): *Supreme Court Historical Society. Yearbook.* [ISSN: 1059-4329] 1976. 3x/yr. USD 103 print & online eds. Blackwell Publishing, Inc., Commerce Place, 350 Main St, Malden, MA 02148; subscrip@blackwellpub.com; http://www.blackwellpublishing.com. Illus., adv. Refereed. Circ: 5000. Reprint: WSH. *Indexed:* AmH&L, CLI, ILP, LRI. *Bk. rev.:* 5-7, 500-1,000 words. *Aud.:* Ga.

The recent acrimony associated with the confirmation process for a seat on the Supreme Court, along with a number of cases decided by a deeply divided court, has heightened interest in our nation's most powerful judicial body. Established in 1974, the Supreme Court Historical Society is dedicated to the collection and preservation of the history of the Supreme Court of the United States. Its *Journal* reflects this commitment. Initially published as an annual, it expanded to three issues per year in 1999. Articles are brief, historical in nature, and highly illustrated from archival sources, and they discuss all aspects of the court, including justices, cases, and themes. The cost, scope, and interesting coverage make this a nice addition to any type of library collection or even a coffee table.

4172. *Journal of the Legal Profession.* [ISSN: 0196-7487] 1976. a. USD 14. University of Alabama, School of Law, PO Box 870382, University, AL 35487-0382; http://boots.law.ua.edu/. Illus., index. Microform: WSH. Online: Gale Group; LexisNexis. Reprint: WSH. *Indexed:* CLI, ILP, LRI. *Aud.:* Ac, Sa.

This publication is unique in that it is the only student-edited journal devoted to the legal profession in general. While the focus of the student pieces is frequently on legal ethics, the 10 to 12 articles in a volume, averaging about 15 pages each, are much more diverse. The *Journal* is intended as a forum for the explanation and exposition of the legal profession's problems, shortcomings, and achievements, as well as a legal ethics and law publication for lawyer and judge. The content is clear, concise, and readable enough to be enjoyed by any segment of the legal community. Each annual volume contains an annotated bibliography of law review articles about the legal profession and abstracts of selected ethics opinions. The students at the University of Alabama School of Law also edit the *Alabama Law Review* and *Law and Psychology Review.*

Journal of Transportation Law, Logistics, and Policy. See Transportation section.

4173. *Judicature: journal of the American Judicature Society.* Formerly: *American Judicature Society Journal.* [ISSN: 0022-5800] 1917. bi-m. USD 54 domestic; USD 66 foreign. Ed(s): David Richert. American Judicature Society, 2700 University Ave, Des Moines, IA 50311; http://www.ajs.org/. Illus., index, adv. Refereed. Circ: 6000 Paid and controlled. Vol. ends: Apr/May. Microform: PQC. Online: Gale Group; OCLC Online Computer Library Center, Inc.; West Group; H.W. Wilson. Reprint: ISI; PQC; WSH. *Indexed:* ArtHuCI, CJA, CJPI, CLI, ILP, LRI, PAIS, PSA, SSCI, SociolAb. *Bk. rev.:* 2-3, 500-5,000 words. *Aud.:* Ga, Ac, Sa.

The American Judicature Society has as its purpose the promotion of the effective administration of justice and is open to all persons interested in working toward court improvement. This publication is intended as a forum for fact and opinion relating to the administration of justice and its improvement. The four to eight articles per issue are short, entertaining, and of current interest. The use of graphics, cartoons, and photographs contributes to overall readability.

4174. *Jurimetrics: journal of law, science and technology.* Former titles (until 1978): *Jurimetrics Journal; Modern Uses of Logic in Law (MULL).* [ISSN: 0897-1277] 1959. q. Non-members, USD 40. Ed(s): David Kaye. American Bar Association, Science and Technology Section, 750 N Lake Shore Dr, Chicago, IL 60611; http://www.lexis-nexis.com/lncc/sources/libcont/aba.html. Illus., index, adv. Circ: 6200. Vol. ends: Summer. Microform: WSH. Online: Gale Group. Reprint: WSH. *Indexed:* CJA, CJPI, CLI, CompLI, CompR, ILP, LRI. *Aud.:* Ac, Sa.

Co-published by the Section of Science and Technology of the American Bar Association and the Arizona State University College of Law, this journal traces its roots to Yale Law School and a previous title. It is the oldest journal of law and science in the United States. Articles relate to computer law, law and medicine, the legal reception of scientific evidence, the legal regulation of science or advanced technology, issues relating to new communications technologies, and the use of technology in the administration of justice. A recent volume contains a two-part symposium on "Legal Liabilities at the Frontier of Genetic Testing." A typical issue will often contain articles, technical notes, and an annotated literature review.

Labor Law Journal. See Labor and Industrial Relations section.

4175. *Labor Lawyer.* [ISSN: 8756-2995] 1985. 3x/yr. Non-members, USD 45. Ed(s): Robert J Rabin. American Bar Association, Labor and Employment Law Section, 750 N Lake Shore Dr, Chicago, IL 60611; abasveetr@abanet.org; http://www.lexis-nexis.com/lncc/. Illus., index. Circ: 20700. Vol. ends: Fall. Microform: WSH. Online: Gale Group. Reprint: WSH. *Indexed:* CLI, ILP, LRI. *Bk. rev.:* Occasional, lengthy. *Aud.:* Ac, Sa.

Another of the many American Bar Association section publications, this journal is devoted to labor and employment law and is intended to provide practitioners, judges, administrators, and the interested public with balanced discussions of topical interest within the parameters of the journal's scope. Each issue contains 8 to 12 articles covering diverse topics, such as sexual harassment, labor unions, and employment law. Most articles are written by those practicing in the field and are practitioner oriented. The summer issue is devoted exclusively to reports of section committees.

4176. *Law and Contemporary Problems.* [ISSN: 0023-9186] 1933. q. USD 48 domestic; USD 54 foreign. Ed(s): Theresa N Glover. Duke University, School of Law, PO Box 90364, Durham, NC 27708-0364; tom@faculty.law.duke.edu; http://www.law.duke.edu/. Illus., index, adv. Circ: 2100. Vol. ends: Sep. Microform: WSH. Online: Florida Center for Library Automation; Gale Group; LexisNexis; OCLC Online Computer Library Center, Inc.; H.W. Wilson. Reprint: PSC; WSH. *Indexed:* ABCPolSci, ATI, BAS, CJA, CLI, CommAb, IBSS, IBZ, ILP, IPSA, JEL, LRI, PAIS, PSA, RI-1, SSCI, SSI, SociolAb. *Aud.:* Ac, Sa.

If one could only select a few titles from this section, this journal should be among them. Each issue is in a symposium format devoted to a current legal topic of interest. A special editor for each issue solicits the articles and writes the foreword. Over the years, this publication has earned its well-deserved reputation as among the most distinguished in the country and is generally among the most frequently cited legal publications. A recent symposium concerns "The United States and the International Criminal Court." When one finds a *Law and Contemporary Problems* issue in an area of interest, it represents a veritable gold mine of information.

4177. *Law and History Review.* [ISSN: 0738-2480] 1983. 3x/yr. USD 85 (Individuals, USD 50). Ed(s): Christopher Tomlins. University of Illinois Press, 1325 S Oak St, Champaign, IL 61820-6903; uipress@uillinois.edu; http://www.press.uillinois.edu. Illus., index, adv. Refereed. Circ: 1200. Vol. ends: Fall. Microform: WSH; PQC. Online: Gale Group; LexisNexis. Reprint: WSH. *Indexed:* AmH&L, CLI, ILP, LRI. *Bk. rev.:* 10-15, 1,000-2,000 words. *Aud.:* Ac, Sa.

This is the official publication of the American Society of Legal History, a membership organization dedicated to further research and writing in the fields of social history of law and the history of its legal ideas and institutions. Articles are scholarly and refereed. Its editorial board consists of preeminent scholars throughout the country. As an interdisciplinary journal, it spans the interplay between law and history. A recent example is "Settlement and the Decline of Private Prosecution in Thirteenth-Century England."

Law and Human Behavior. See Psychology section.

Law & Inequality: a journal of theory and practice. See Civil Liberties/General section.

4178. *Law and Literature.* Formerly (until 2002): *Cardozo Studies in Law and Literature.* [ISSN: 1535-685X] 1989. 3x/yr. USD 145 print & online eds. USD 50 newsstand/cover. Ed(s): Richard H Weisberg. University of California Press, Journals Division, 2000 Center St, Ste 303, Berkeley, CA 94704-1223; journals@ucop.edu; http://www.ucpress.edu/journals. Illus., index, adv. Refereed. Circ: 700. Vol. ends: Winter. Online: Gale Group; Ingenta Select. Reprint: WSH. *Indexed:* CLI, ILP, LRI, MLA-IB. *Aud.:* Ga, Ac.

Published under the auspices of the Jacob Burns Institute for Advanced Legal Studies, this journal features contributions by practitioners and scholars, poets and playrights, artists, and technicians of all kinds. The list of noted contributors is impressive, and the content is a delightful diversion from the traditional, often dry law reviews. "Theaters of Justice and Fictions of Law" is the topic of a recent symposium. A somewhat similar journal is the *Yale Journal of Law & the Humanities* (see below).

Law and Philosophy. See Philosophy section.

4179. *Law and Policy in International Business.* [ISSN: 0023-9208] 1969. q. USD 35 domestic; USD 12.50 newsstand/cover per issue foreign. Georgetown University Law Center, 600 New Jersey Ave, NW, Washington, DC 20001; http://www.law.gwu.edu/. Illus., index, adv. Circ: 861. Vol. ends: Dec. Microform: WSH; PQC. Online: EBSCO Publishing;

Factiva; Florida Center for Library Automation; Gale Group; LexisNexis; OCLC Online Computer Library Center, Inc.; ProQuest Information & Learning; West Group; H.W. Wilson. Reprint: PQC; WSH. *Indexed:* ABIn, ABS&EES, BAS, CLI, ILP, LRI, PAIS, RiskAb. *Bk. rev.:* Occasional, length varies. *Aud.:* Ac, Sa.

International business is an important subspecialty in law and has become even more so with the realization of a unified Europe. This journal's purpose is to analyze the law and policies of governments and organizations with respect to transnational business and economics. It is a student-edited review with the traditional lead article and student note and comments sections. Focus is on antitrust, environment, foreign investment, intellectual property, international trade, labor, and taxes. Articles cover topics of international importance, from multinational patent enforcement to emerging markets. This journal has the largest circulation of all international law publications edited entirely by law students.

4180. ***Law and Social Inquiry.*** Formerly: *American Bar Foundation Journal.* [ISSN: 0897-6546] 1976. q. USD 130 (Individuals, USD 42; Students, USD 29). Ed(s): John Hagan, Victoria Saker Woeste. University of Chicago Press, Journals Division, PO Box 37005, Chicago, IL 60637; subscriptions@press.uchicago.edu; http://www.journals.uchicago.edu. Illus., adv. Refereed. Circ: 6700. Vol. ends: Fall. Microform: WSH; PQC. Online: EBSCO Publishing; Gale Group; LexisNexis; ProQuest Information & Learning. Reprint: PSC; WSH. *Indexed:* ABS&EES, ArtHuCI, CJA, CJPI, CLI, CommAb, ILP, JEL, LRI, PSA, PsycholAb, RI-1, SSCI, SociolAb. *Aud.:* Ac, Sa.

Empirical research is rare in legal scholarship. The American Bar Foundation is an independent research institute committed to sociolegal research. Its professional journal, a significant contribution to the legal literature, is refereed and its content is empirical and theoretical. The journal is typically in three sections: The first contains lengthy articles of an empirical nature directed at legal institutions, lawyers, and law; the second is a series of critical review essays of books that impact on law and society; and the third is shorter book notes. Frequently, an issue or part of an issue will have a particular focus, as illustrated by a symposium in a recent issue on "The Common Place of Law."

4181. ***Law & Society Review.*** [ISSN: 0023-9216] 1966. q. USD 222 print & online eds. Ed(s): Susan Silbey. Blackwell Publishing, Inc., Commerce Place, 350 Main St, Malden, MA 02148; subscrip@blackwellpub.com; http://www.blackwellpub.com. Illus., index, adv. Refereed. Circ: 2400. Vol. ends: Dec. Microform: WSH; PQC. Online: bigchalk; Chadwyck-Healey Incorporated; EBSCO Publishing; Factiva; Gale Group; ingenta.com; Northern Light Technology, Inc.; OCLC Online Computer Library Center, Inc.; ProQuest Information & Learning; H.W. Wilson. Reprint: ISI; WSH. *Indexed:* ABCPolSci, ASSIA, AgeL, AmH&L, AnthLit, ArtHuCI, BAS, CJA, CLI, CommAb, IBSS, IBZ, ILP, IMFL, IPSA, LRI, PAIS, PRA, PSA, PsycholAb, RI-1, SSCI, SSI, SUSA, SWR&A, SociolAb. *Bk. rev.:* 3-4, essay length. *Aud.:* Ac, Sa.

The Law and Society Association is an international group drawn primarily from the legal and social science professions, whose purpose is the stimulation and support of research and teaching on the cultural, economic, political, psychological, and social aspects of law and legal systems. Contributions are drawn from law professors, sociologists, and political scientists. Big names in these various disciplines are frequent writers for this interdisciplinary, refereed journal. Included in a recent issue are such diverse articles as "Judicial Rhetoric Meaning-Making, and the Institutionalization of Hate Crimes" and "The Shifting Rhetoric of Insurance Denial."

Law Library Journal. See Library and Information Science section.

4182. ***Law Practice Management: the magazine of law office management.*** Formerly: *Legal Economics.* [ISSN: 1045-9081] 1975. 8x/yr. Non-members, USD 48. Ed(s): Delmar L Roberts. American Bar Association, Law Practice Management Section, 750 N Lake Shore Dr, Chicago, IL 60611; http://www.lexis-nexis.com/lncc. Illus., index, adv. Sample. Circ: 23817. Vol. ends: Nov. Microform: WSH. Online: Gale Group; LexisNexis; West Group. Reprint: WSH. *Indexed:* ABIn, ATI, CLI, LRI, PAIS. *Aud.:* Ac, Sa.

This magazine's purpose is to assist the practicing lawyer in operating and managing the office in an efficient and economical manner. It provides, in an easy-to-read, straightforward style, practical tips and how-to advice on a panoply of topics ranging from how to store files to how to design office space and then plan for the move into it. More and more of the articles pertain to law office computer applications. The April issue is devoted to finance and billing. The advertising highlights the newest in office furniture, equipment, law books, and technology. An occasional cartoon or poem, color illustrations, and notice of events of general interest to the practicing bar contribute to its popularity.

4183. ***Legal Times: law and lobbying in the nation's capital.*** Former titles: *Legal Times of Washington;* (until 1982): *Legal Times.* [ISSN: 0732-7536] 1978. w. Individuals, USD 318. Ed(s): Richard Barbieri. American Lawyer Media, L.P., 1730 M St, N W, Ste 800, Washington, DC 20036. Illus., index, adv. Circ: 10000 Paid. Vol. ends: May. Online: EBSCO Publishing; Factiva; Gale Group; LexisNexis. *Indexed:* BLI, CLI, LRI. *Bk. rev.:* 2-3, length varies. *Aud.:* Ga, Ac, Sa.

This weekly legal newspaper, self-described as covering "law and lobbying in the nation's capital," is frequently national in scope. A typical issue contains from 48 to 80 pages. The staff of editors and reporters write about a host of legal topics, including the U.S. Supreme Court, the federal bureaucracy, major law firms, scandals, and controversial cases. Regular features are especially useful in a variety of ways. For example, "Inadmissible" is something of a gossip column; "Lobby Talk" discusses how particular groups are attempting to influence legislation and the outcome of court cases; "Analysis" looks at a thorny legal issue in some depth; "Points of View" is an opinion and commentary section; and "After Hours" focuses on books, arts, and leisure. Professional and classified ads are included.

4184. ***Litigation (Chicago).*** [ISSN: 0097-9813] 1975. q. Non-members, USD 40. American Bar Association, Litigation Section, 750 N Lake Shore Dr, Chicago, IL 60611; http://www.lexis-nexis.com/lncc/. Illus., index. Sample. Circ: 63000. Vol. ends: Summer. Microform: WSH; PMC. Online: Gale Group; West Group. Reprint: WSH. *Indexed:* CLI, ILP, LRI. *Bk. rev.:* Occasional, 500-600 words. *Aud.:* Ac, Sa.

This journal is designed for the trial bar and trial judges, with a series of short articles written by members of the practicing bar. Each issue is organized around a theme, such as evidence, appeals, strategy, or surprises. Often the articles are argumentative and challenging, typical of the seasoned litigator likely to read this publication. However, articles are also straightforward and entertaining enough to be enjoyed by a much wider audience. For the traditional, scholarly law review approach to this subject, the best choice is the University of Texas's *The Review of Litigation.*

4185. ***Marquette Sports Law Review.*** Formerly (until 2000): *Marquette Sports Law Journal.* [ISSN: 1533-6484] 1990. s-a. USD 25 (Membership, USD 100). Ed(s): Andrew Rhim. Marquette University, 1212 Building, Rm 315, Box 1881, Milwaukee, WI 53201-1881; http://www.mu.edu/law/. Illus., index, adv. Vol. ends: Spring. Reprint: WSH. *Indexed:* CLI, ILP, LRI, PEI. *Bk. rev.:* Occasional, lengthy. *Aud.:* Ac, Sa.

In response to the growing importance of the relationship between sports and the law, in 1989 Marquette University Law School established the National Sports Law Institute. The institute's principal purpose is "to promote the development of ethical practices in all phases of amateur and professional sports." This journal, a product of the institute, covers a panoply of legal issues in the sports industry and is aimed at attorneys and sports industry professionals. Because sports are so ingrained in the American tradition, this journal provides coverage of an increasingly important area of specialized legal representation. The *Marquette Law Review,* however, is the primary journal of the school.

4186. ***Mental and Physical Disability Law Reporter: covers all aspects of handicapped law.*** Formerly (until 1984): *Mental Disability Law Reporter.* [ISSN: 0883-7902] 1976. bi-m. USD 299 (Individuals, USD 239). Ed(s): John W Parry. American Bar Association, Commission on

Mental & Physical Disability Law, 740 15th St, N W, Washington, DC 20005-1022; cmpdl@abanet.org; http://www.lexis-nexis.com/lncc/sources/libcont/aba.html. Illus., index, adv. Circ: 1000 Paid. Vol. ends: Nov/Dec. Reprint: WSH. *Indexed:* CJA, CLI, ILP, IndMed, LRI, PsycholAb. *Aud.:* Ac, Sa.

This publication is quite different from and more expensive than other publications in this section, but its unique subject matter justifies its inclusion. The American Bar Association's Commission on Mental & Physical Disability Law is composed of lawyers, psychiatrists, psychologists, consumer advocates, and mental health administrators concerned with promoting multidisciplinary solutions to legal problems of persons with mental and physical disabilities. Each issue starts with a subject "Directory of Cases & Legislation" discussed in that issue. This is followed by "Highlights & Trends," "Summary of U.S. Supreme Court Action," "Case Law Developments," and "Legislation and Regulations." A feature article usually concludes the issue. There is a "Subject Key" at the end of the publication.

Michigan Journal of Gender & Law. See Women: Feminist and Special Interest/Feminist and Women's section.

4187. *Michigan Law Review.* [ISSN: 0026-2234] 1902. 8x/yr. USD 50 domestic; USD 60 foreign; USD 8 newsstand/cover per issue. Ed(s): Eric R Olson. Michigan Law Review Association, 625 South State St, Hutchins Hall, Ann Arbor, MI 48109-1215; dkz@umich.edu; http://www.law.umich.edu/pubs/journals/mlr. Illus., index, adv. Refereed. Circ: 2138. Vol. ends: Aug. Microform: WSH; PMC; PQC. Online: EBSCO Publishing; Florida Center for Library Automation; Gale Group; LexisNexis; Northern Light Technology, Inc.; OCLC Online Computer Library Center, Inc.; ProQuest Information & Learning; West Group; H.W. Wilson. Reprint: WSH. *Indexed:* ABIn, ATI, AgeL, ArtHuCI, BLI, CJA, CLI, ILP, JEL, LRI, PAIS, SSCI. *Bk. rev.:* Occasional, essay length. *Aud.:* Ac, Sa.

Regardless of which of the numerous ratings of law reviews one might consult, this title is always in the top ten. That recognition is gained from the consistently high-level articles from leading scholars, quality and in-depth student research pieces, and an overall adherence to fine legal scholarship. In publishing lengthy lead articles and student notes, this review is quite traditional. It varies from other reviews because of several different practices. Occasionally, "Correspondence" responds to or takes issue with an item published earlier in the journal; the "Essay" section may contain more down-to-earth writings, such as an article by a judge on how he or she selects a law clerk; an annual issue devoted to lengthy, critical book reviews serves as an excellent selection guide; and the regular, subject-arranged "Periodical Index" of materials from leading law reviews provides an access point to significant legal literature. The school also publishes *Michigan Journal of Law Reform, Michigan Journal of Gender & Law, Michigan Journal of International Law, Michigan Telecommunications and Technology Law Review,* and *Michigan Journal of Race & Law.*

4188. *Military Law Review.* [ISSN: 0026-4040] 1958. q. USD 17 domestic; USD 21.25 foreign. Ed(s): Capt. Todd S Milliard. U.S. Army Judge Advocate General's Corps., c/o JAGS-ADL-P, Charlottesville, VA 22903-1781. Illus., index. Circ: 8000. Microform: MIM; PQC. Online: Gale Group; LexisNexis; OCLC Online Computer Library Center, Inc.; West Group; H.W. Wilson. Reprint: WSH. *Indexed:* ABCPolSci, ABS&EES, ArtHuCI, CLI, ILP, IUSGP, LRI, PAIS, PRA, PSA, SSCI. *Aud.:* Ac, Sa.

Published at the Judge Advocate General's School, U.S. Army, Charlottesville, Virginia, the *Review* provides a forum for those interested in military law to share the products of their experience and research and is designed for use by military attorneys in connection with their official duties. Each quarterly issue is a complete, separately numbered volume. One can frequently gain a different insight on issues, as evidenced by "the Concept of Belligerency in International Law."

4189. *Minnesota Law Review.* [ISSN: 0026-5535] 1917. 6x/yr. USD 24. University of Minnesota, Law School, 229 19th Ave S, Minneapolis, MN 55455. Illus., index, adv. Circ: 1486. Vol. ends: Jun. Microform: WSH; PMC. Online: Gale Group; LexisNexis; OCLC Online Computer Library Center, Inc.; West Group; H.W. Wilson. Reprint: WSH. *Indexed:* BLI, CJA, CLI, ILP, LRI, PAIS, SSCI. *Bk. rev.:* Occasional, length varies. *Aud.:* Ac, Sa.

This is another of the frequently cited traditional law reviews publishing articles and student pieces on a myriad of legal topics. The contents are always thoughtful, heavily documented, and influential. Volumes contain articles representing a wide cross-section of legal thinking that is both provocative and challenging. A recent issue includes articles on "Transforming the Internet into a Taxable Forum: A Case Study in E-Commerce Taxation," and "Preferential Treatment: The Varying Constitutionality of Private Scholarship Preferences at Public Universities." *Constitutional Commentary, Law and Inequality: A Journal of Theory and Practice, Minnesota Intellectual Property Review,* and *Minnesota Journal of Global Trade* are also published by this law school.

4190. *National Black Law Journal.* Formerly (until 1987): *Black Law Journal.* [ISSN: 0896-0194] 1971. 3x/yr. Ed(s): Allison James. Columbia University, Columbia Law School, 435 West 116th St, New York, NY 10027; http://www.law.columbia.edu/. Illus., index, adv. Circ: 650. Vol. ends: No. 3. Microform: WSH; PMC; PQC. Online: Factiva; Gale Group; Northern Light Technology, Inc.; ProQuest Information & Learning. Reprint: PQC; WSH. *Indexed:* CLI, IIBP, ILP, LRI, RI-1, RiskAb. *Bk. rev.:* 2, 600-2,500 words. *Aud.:* Ac, Sa.

This journal and *Harvard BlackLetter Journal* are the only legal journals devoted exclusively to discussing and analyzing issues involving the Black community. Issues often have a theme, such as voting rights, affirmative action, or race relations in the South. While the *Journal*'s base of operations is at Columbia Law School, a consortium agreement with other law schools enables another school to have editorial responsibility for a particular issue. The use of the word *national* in the title, therefore, is entirely appropriate. In recent volumes, law students from a wide variety of schools have prepared issues of the *Journal.*

4191. *National Law Journal: the weekly newspaper for the profession.* [ISSN: 0162-7325] 1978. w. USD 158 domestic; USD 233 foreign. Ed(s): Charles Carter. American Lawyer Media, Inc., 105 Madison Ave, New York, NY 10016; catalog@amlaw.com; http://www.americanlawyermedia.com. Illus., index, adv. Circ: 39500. Vol. ends: Aug. Microform: NYL. Online: Gale Group; LexisNexis. *Indexed:* ATI, BLI, CLI, EnvAb, LRI. *Aud.:* Ga, Ac, Sa.

With by far the largest subscription base of the several national legal newspapers and considering its pass-along readership in firms and law libraries, this publication reaches an estimated 200,000 members of the legal community. It offers something for just about everyone involved with law, but its real value is in the timely coverage of people, places, and events. With bureau chiefs in New York, Los Angeles, San Francisco, and Washington, D.C., and contributors from a host of states, this publication is the best single source for fast-breaking legal developments. Frequently, supplements enhance the publication's overall popularity. The "Annual Guide to the Legal Search Profession" (a survey of recruiters), "What Lawyers Earn" (national salary survey), and a listing of the nation's largest law firms (with billing rates) are anxiously awaited.

New York Law School Journal of Human Rights. See Civil Liberties/General section.

4192. *New York University Law Review (New York, 1950).* Former titles (until 1949): *New York University Law Quarterly Review;* (until 1929): *New York University Law Review (New York, 1924).* [ISSN: 0028-7881] 1924. 6x/yr. USD 35 domestic; USD 40 foreign. Ed(s): Carol M Kaplan. New York University School of Law, 110 W Third St, New York, NY 10012; http://www.law.nyu.edu/. Illus., index, adv. Refereed. Circ: 2050. Vol. ends: Dec. Microform: WSH. Online: Gale Group; LexisNexis; West Group. Reprint: WSH. *Indexed:* ATI, AgeL, CJA, CLI, IBZ, ILP, IPSA, LRI, PAIS, SSCI. *Aud.:* Ac, Sa.

New York University (NYU) School of Law, founded in 1835, is one of the oldest law schools in the United States. This student-edited journal contains in its lead articles some of the finest legal scholarship from some of the best legal minds in the country on just about any legal topic. Student pieces are likewise of high quality, e.g., "The Role of Gender and Relationship in Reforming the Rockefeller Drug Laws." Also published by NYU School of Law are the *Annual Survey of American Law* and *Clinical Law Review* (see above in this section), as well as *East European Constitutional Review, Journal of International Law and Politics, New York University Review of Law & Social Change, Journal on Legislation and Public Policy, New York University Environmental Law Journal,* and the *Tax Law Review* (see below in this section).

News Media and the Law. See Journalism and Writing/Journalism section.

4193. *North Carolina Law Review.* [ISSN: 0029-2524] 1922. bi-m. USD 32 domestic; USD 36 foreign; USD 8 newsstand/cover per issue. Ed(s): Mitch Ambruster. North Carolina Law Review Association, University of North Carolina, School of Law, Chapel Hill, NC 27599-3380; nclrev@unc.edu; http://www.unc.edu/stud. Adv. Refereed. Circ: 950. Microform: BHP; WSH. Online: Gale Group; LexisNexis; West Group. Reprint: WSH. *Indexed:* AgeL, CLI, ILP, LRI, PAIS, RiskAb. *Bk. rev.:* Occasional, lengthy. *Aud.:* Ac, Sa.

Consistently considered one of the top law schools in the country, this school's law review has an 80-year history of publishing quality legal scholarship. The format is traditional with articles, comments, and notes on any type of topic. A recent issue covers employment, sodomy, charter schools, and union-financed legal services. Other journals from this school are *North Carolina Banking Institute Journal, North Carolina Journal of International Law and Commercial Regulation* and *North Carolina Journal of Law and Technology.*

4194. *Northwestern University Law Review.* Formerly (until 1952): *Illinois Law Review.* [ISSN: 0029-3571] 1906. q. USD 40; USD 45 foreign. Northwestern University, School of Law, 357 E Chicago Ave, Chicago, IL 60611; http://www.nwu.edu/lawschool/. Illus., index, adv. Refereed. Circ: 1200. Vol. ends: No. 4. Microform: BHP; WSH; PQC. Online: Gale Group; LexisNexis; ProQuest Information & Learning; West Group. Reprint: WSH. *Indexed:* ABCPolSci, CJA, CLI, ILP, LRI, PAIS, RI-1, SSCI. *Bk. rev.:* Occasional, length varies. *Aud.:* Ac, Sa.

Dating back almost to the turn of the century, this publication has a rich tradition of providing sophisticated legal analysis on innumerable topics of legal significance. The various pieces are grouped under several headings, although each heading is not used in each issue. This publication sometimes contains articles that are followed by commentaries on the same subject. Student comments and notes and lengthy book review essays occupy other sections. The prestigious *Journal of Criminal Law and Criminology* (see above in this section) and the *Northwestern Journal of International Law & Business* are the other review-type publications of this law school.

4195. *The Practical Lawyer.* [ISSN: 0032-6429] 1955. bi-m. 8/yr. until 2002. USD 49. Ed(s): Mark T Carroll. American Law Institute - American Bar Association, Committee on Continuing Professional Education, 4025 Chestnut St, Philadelphia, PA 19104-3099; publications@ali-aba.org; http://www.ali-aba.org. Illus., index, adv. Circ: 3500 Paid. Vol. ends: Dec. Microform: WSH; PQC. Online: Gale Group; Northern Light Technology, Inc.; ProQuest Information & Learning. Reprint: PQC; WSH. *Indexed:* ATI, AgeL, BLI, CLI, ILP, LRI. *Aud.:* Ga, Ac, Sa.

This wonderful little magazine provides a nuts-and-bolts approach to the practice of law with information about continuing legal education programs. Articles are, as the title suggests, practical. Examples illustrative of the diversity of information found in it are "How To Prevent and Solve Operating Problems in the Family Business" and "Licensing in the Cyberspace World." Articles are accompanied by practice checklists to be used to ensure that the germane matters are covered. A regular column on writing and style, "The Grammatical Lawyer," has been compiled and published as a book. Newer titles by the same publisher, but subject specific, are *The Practical Real Estate Lawyer, The Practical Tax Lawyer,* and *The Practical Litigator.*

4196. *Preview of United States Supreme Court Cases.* [ISSN: 0363-0048] 1963. 8x/yr. USD 130 (Individuals, USD 105). Ed(s): Charles Williams. American Bar Association, Public Education Division, 541 N Fairbanks Ct, Chicago, IL 60611-3314; http://www.lexis-nexis.com/lncc/sources/libcont/aba.html. Illus. Sample. Circ: 3000. Vol. ends: May. Online: West Group. *Indexed:* CJPI. *Aud.:* Ga, Ac, Sa.

This publication is a departure from other titles described in this section. As its title indicates, each issue, monthly during the U.S. Supreme Court term, provides a discussion of cases soon to be decided by the court. After a case is calendared for oral argument, but before a decision is rendered, a legal professional in the subject field of the case presents the issues, gives the facts, analyzes the background and significance of the case, lists the counsel for each side and their legal arguments, and indicates the parties who have filed *amicus* briefs. The advisory board is composed of heavyweights; and 20 legal scholars write the "previews." For those interested in some advance warning about what the nation's Supreme Court is considering, this current-awareness source serves this important purpose exceedingly well. A calendar of scheduled oral arguments is included.

4197. *Real Property, Probate and Trust Journal.* [ISSN: 0034-0855] 1966. q. Non-members, USD 23. Ed(s): Amy Morris Hess. American Bar Association, Real Property, Probate and Trust Law Section, 750 N Lake Shore Dr, Chicago, IL 60611; http://www.lexis-nexis.com/lncc/sources/libcont/aba.html. Illus., index. Circ: 37970. Vol. ends: Winter. Microform: WSH; PQC. Online: Gale Group; ProQuest Information & Learning; West Group. Reprint: PQC; WSH. *Indexed:* ATI, AgeL, CLI, ILP, LRI, SSCI. *Bk. rev.:* Occasional, lengthy. *Aud.:* Ac, Sa.

The *Journal*'s focus is principally scholarly, and it is edited by law students at the University of South Carolina School of Law. Each issue contains three to five heavily researched, substantive articles. One issue annually includes a discussion of the previous year's developments in probate and trust law; another contains an annotated, subject-arranged bibliography, "Significant Real Property Literature." Much of the section materials once found in this publication, as well as shorter, more practice-oriented articles, are contained in *Probate & Property,* published by the same ABA section.

4198. *Scribes Journal of Legal Writing.* [ISSN: 1049-5177] 1990. a. USD 65. Ed(s): Glen Peter Ahlers. American Society of Writers on Legal Subjects, Scribes Administrative Office, University of Arkansas School of Law, Fayetteville, AR 72701-1201. Illus. Circ: 3900 Controlled. Online: Gale Group; LexisNexis; OCLC Online Computer Library Center, Inc.; H.W. Wilson. Reprint: WSH. *Indexed:* CLI, ILP, LRI. *Bk. rev.:* 5, 1,500-3,000 words. *Aud.:* Ac, Sa.

After years of criticism of lawyers' use of "legalese," this scholarly journal seeks to promote better legal writing within the legal community. The *Journal*'s goals are refreshing. It advocates "lucidity, concision, and felicity of expression" and hopes "to spread the growing scorn for whatever is turgid, obscure, or needlessly dull." Leading legal scholars who are equally good writers and grammarians contribute up to a dozen 6- to 20-page articles in each issue. Student essays are published, and all contributions are first-rate. Also included is a section titled "Notes and Queries" that contains brief (approximately 1,500 words) attempts to correct common mistakes in, or misjudgments about, legal writing. Membership in the Scribes is open to members of the legal profession who are authors of a book or two or more articles, or who have served as editor of a legal journal, and judges who have written opinions published in an official reporter.

4199. *Southern California Law Review.* [ISSN: 0038-3910] 1927. bi-m. USD 36 domestic; USD 45 foreign; USD 12.50 newsstand/cover per issue. Ed(s): Annagvey Marybeth. University of Southern California, Law School, Room 330, University Park, Los Angeles, CA 90089-0071; http://www.usc.edu/. Illus., index, adv. Refereed. Circ: 1500. Vol. ends: No. 6. Microform: WSH; PMC. Online: Gale Group; LexisNexis. Reprint: WSH. *Indexed:* AgeL, BAS, CJA, CLI, ILP, IPSA, LRI, PSA, SSCI, SUSA. *Aud.:* Ac, Sa.

The law school of the University of Southern California (USC) focuses on the law as an expression of social values and as an instrument for implementing social goals. It is an exemplary law review in the traditional mold and is among the most frequently cited. Articles, two or three per issue and consistent with the aims of the institution, are written by scholars and probe deeply into a particular legal issue—for example, "Toward a Coherent Theory of Strict Tort Liability for Trademark Licensors." USC law students also publish the *Southern California Interdisciplinary Law Journal,* and *Southern California Review of Law and Women's Studies.*

Southern California Review of Law and Women's Studies. See Women: Feminist and Special Interest/Feminist and Women's Studies section.

4200. *Stanford Law Review.* Formerly: *Stanford Intramural Law Review.* [ISSN: 0038-9765] 1948. bi-m. USD 40; USD 14 newsstand/cover per issue; USD 45 foreign. Ed(s): Stephanie Plasse. Stanford Law Review, Crown Quadrangle, Stanford, CA 94305-8610; http://www.leland.stanford.edu/group/law. Illus., index, adv. Refereed. Vol. ends: Jul. Microform: WSH. Online: Florida Center for Library Automation; Gale Group; LexisNexis; West Group. Reprint: WSH. *Indexed:* ABCPolSci, ATI, AgeL, ArtHuCI, BAS, CJA, CLI, ILP, LRI, PAIS, SSCI. *Bk. rev.:* 1-2, 4,000-8,000 words. *Aud.:* Ac, Sa.

No self-respecting library, even one seeking to have only a minimal legal collection, would be without this publication. Stanford's admission requirements are among the highest in the nation, and its faculty members are among the most prestigious. Its *Review* reflects the overall quality of the institution. Articles can be broad, such as "The First Amendment's Purpose." Occasional essays examine a legal issue of current interest, often in response to an earlier piece in the *Review.* Student notes and lengthy book review essays round out an issue. Students also edit the *Stanford Agora: An Online Journal of Legal Perspectives, Stanford Environmental Law Journal, Stanford Journal of International Law, Stanford Journal of Legal Studies, Stanford Law & Policy Review, Stanford Journal of Law, Business, and Finance,* and *Stanford Technology Law Review.*

4201. *Student Lawyer (Chicago).* Supersedes: *Student Lawyer Journal.* [ISSN: 0039-274X] 1972. 9x/yr. Non-members, USD 22. Ed(s): Ira Pilchen. American Bar Association, Law Student Division, 750 N Lake Shore Dr, Chicago, IL 60611; http://www.lexis-nexis.com. Illus., index, adv. Sample. Circ: 35000 Paid. Vol. ends: May. Microform: WSH. Online: Gale Group. Reprint: PQC; WSH. *Indexed:* CLI, LRI. *Aud.:* Ga, Ac, Sa.

All law students who are attending American Bar Association (ABA)–accredited law schools are eligible for membership in the ABA's Law Student Division. Relevant, lively, and informative articles on legal education, social/legal issues, careers, the practice of law, and Law Student Division news comprise the contents of this popular magazine. Often it presents a "what's on my mind" article from a law student's point of view or provides entertaining anecdotes, and sometimes "survival techniques," for the study-weary student. There is advertising, information on bar review courses, an annual guide to summer-abroad law programs, and miscellaneous tidbits for students, prospective students, and the general reader.

4202. *Tax Law Review.* [ISSN: 0040-0041] 1945. q. Ed(s): Deborah Schenk. New York University, School of Law, 40 Washington Sq S, Rm 430, New York, NY 10012-1099; http://www.law.nyu.edu/. Illus., index, adv. Vol. ends: Summer. Microform: WSH. Online: Gale Group; West Group. Reprint: PQC; WSH. *Indexed:* ABIn, ATI, BLI, CLI, ILP, LRI, PAIS. *Aud.:* Ac, Sa.

This faculty-edited publication of the New York University School of Law is widely regarded as the most prestigious scholarly publication in the field of taxation. Articles include survey pieces as illustrated by "Income Tax Discrimination Against International Commerce" as well as attempts to explain a complex tax law. Libraries wanting materials on taxation would certainly acquire this publication.

4203. *Tax Lawyer.* [ISSN: 0040-005X] 1947. q. Non-members, USD 83. Ed(s): Gersham Goldstein. American Bar Association, Taxation Section, 740 15th St, N W, Washington, DC 20005-1009; http://www.lexis-nexis.com/lncc/sources/libcont/aba.html. Illus., index, adv. Circ: 24000. Vol. ends: Summer. Microform: WSH; PQC. Online: Gale Group; West Group. Reprint: WSH. *Indexed:* ABIn, ATI, BLI, CLI, ILP, LRI. *Aud.:* Ac, Sa.

This is a joint publishing endeavor of the American Bar Association's Section of Taxation and the students at the Georgetown University Law Center. The section's editorial board is responsible for the scholarly articles—typically three or four of approximately 35 pages each in each issue. A student editorial board is responsible for student notes. The articles and notes are of high quality and run the gamut of issues involving taxation. The winter issue contains a review of decisions on taxation from the previous year. The summer issue carries "Important Developments during the Year." This developments section analyzes, categorized under more than 30 subject headings, significant events involving taxation that have occurred since the previous summer issue.

4204. *Texas Law Review.* [ISSN: 0040-4411] 1922. 7x/yr. USD 44 domestic; USD 50 foreign. Ed(s): Paul Goldman. University of Texas at Austin, School of Law Publications, 727 E Dean Keeton St, Austin, TX 78705-3299; Publications@mail.law.utexas.edu; http://www.texaslawpublications.com/. Illus., index, adv. Refereed. Circ: 1600. Vol. ends: Jun. Microform: WSH. Online: EBSCO Publishing; Factiva; Gale Group; LexisNexis; Northern Light Technology, Inc.; OCLC Online Computer Library Center, Inc.; ProQuest Information & Learning; H.W. Wilson. Reprint: WSH. *Indexed:* ABCPolSci, ABIn, ArtHuCI, CLI, ILP, LRI, SSCI. *Bk. rev.:* Occasional, lengthy. *Aud.:* Ac, Sa.

There is the South, North, East, and West, and then there is Texas. The University of Texas, with its 50,000-member student body and capital city Austin location, is considered to have one of the finest law schools and law reviews in the nation. Like other student-edited law school publications, this one contains two or three major articles by legal scholars on an array of legal topics, student notes relating to recent legislation or cases, and essay-length book reviews. A volume will contain approximately 1,500 pages and be among the most frequently cited in the country. Other publications by University of Texas law students are the *American Journal of Criminal Law, Texas Forum on Civil Liberties & Civil Rights, Texas Hispanic Journal of Law and Policy, The Review of Litigation, Texas Environmental Law Journal, Texas Intellectual Property Law Journal, Texas International Law Journal, Texas Journal of Business Law, Texas Review of Entertainment and Sports Law, Texas Review of Law & Politics,* and *Texas Journal of Women and the Law.*

4205. *Tort Trial & Insurance Practice Law Journal.* Former titles (until 2003): *Tort & Insurance Law Journal;* (until 1985): *Forum (Chicago, 1965).* 1965. q. Non-members, USD 50. Ed(s): Wendy Smith. American Bar Association Publishing, Tort and Insurance Practice Section, 750 N Lake Shore Dr, Chicago, IL 60611; http://www.lexis-nexis.com/lncc/sources/libcont/aba.html. Illus., index. Circ: 35000. Vol. ends: Summer. Microform: WSH; PQC. Online: Gale Group; LexisNexis; West Group. Reprint: WSH. *Indexed:* CLI, ILP, LRI, PAIS. *Aud.:* Ac, Sa.

Because of the myriad of issues associated with tort law and insurance law, this is one of the largest sections of the American Bar Association. This publication mirrors the interests of the section, which spans 33 general substantive and procedural areas involved in or affecting the law of torts and insurance. An issue will typically contain six or seven articles of approximately 20 pages each addressing such topics as product liability, automotive law, aviation and space law, workers' compensation, media and defamation torts, health and life insurance, medicine, damages, and commercial torts. The entire winter issue is devoted to the "Annual Survey of Tort and Insurance Law." Because both torts and insurance cut across all disciplines and impact on our daily lives, this is an especially important publication.

Transportation Law Journal. See Transportation section.

4206. *Trial.* Formerly: *National Legal Magazine.* [ISSN: 0041-2538] 1965. m. USD 79. Ed(s): Elizabeth E Yeary. Association of Trial Lawyers of America, 1050 31st St, N W, Washington, DC 20007-4499; http://www.atla.org. Illus., index, adv. Circ: 55000. Vol. ends: Dec. Microform: WSH; PQC. Online: Florida Center for Library Automation; Gale Group; Northern Light Technology, Inc.; OCLC Online Computer Library Center, Inc.; ProQuest Information & Learning. Reprint: WSH. *Indexed:* AgeL, CJA, CJPI, CLI, ILP, LRI, SSCI, SSI. *Bk. rev.:* 2-7, 300-1,500 words. *Aud.:* Ga, Ac, Sa.

The purpose of this attractive magazine is to provide information that is timely, practical, and readable and that will serve the large membership of the American Trial Lawyers Association. Approximately a dozen articles appear in each issue. Most articles are how-to in nature. A recent article looks at "Techniques for Arguing Damages to a Juror." Certain regular columns offer practical information. Other sections are intended for current awareness and for professional-services advertising.

4207. *Trusts and Estates (Atlanta).* [ISSN: 0041-3682] 1904. m. USD 139 domestic; USD 159 foreign. Ed(s): Michael S Klim. Primedia Business Magazines & Media, Inc. (Atlanta), 6151 Powers Ferry Rd, N W, Atlanta, GA 30339-2941; inquiries@primediabusiness.com; http://www.primediabusiness.com/. Illus., index, adv. Circ: 14723. Vol. ends: Dec. Microform: CIS; PQC. Online: bigchalk; Florida Center for Library Automation; Gale Group; OCLC Online Computer Library Center, Inc.; ProQuest Information & Learning. Reprint: PQC; WSH. *Indexed:* ABIn, ATI, AgeL, BPI, CLI, ILP, LRI, PAIS. *Aud.:* Ga, Ac, Sa.

Planning for one's death during life, dealing with the myriad issues that arise after death, and capitalizing on the available options to maximize tax benefits during one's lifetime are the principal focuses of this publication. Prudent tax planning, wise use of trusts, insurance options, and issues involving divorce and separation are examples of the type of coverage. While this title is intended for lawyers, trust officers, and others involved in estate planning and administration, there is sufficient information, presented clearly and concisely, to warrant a far wider readership. As the population ages, this publication will undoubtedly grow in popularity. A thirteenth issue arriving in December as part of the subscription is the *Directory of Trust Institutions.*

4208. *U C L A Law Review.* [ISSN: 0041-5650] 1953. bi-m. USD 35; USD 40 foreign. Ed(s): Laura Reider. University of California at Los Angeles, School of Law, 405 Hilgard Ave, Rm 2410, PO Box 951476, Los Angeles, CA 90095-1476; http://www.law.ucla.edu/. Illus., index, adv. Refereed. Circ: 1000. Vol. ends: Aug. Microform: WSH. Online: Gale Group; LexisNexis; West Group. Reprint: WSH. *Indexed:* ABIn, CJA, CLI, CommAb, ILP, LRI, PAIS, SSCI. *Aud.:* Ac, Sa.

Located on the university campus in the foothills of the Santa Monica Mountains, this law school recruits one of the finest student bodies in the country. Its primary journal reflects the same high qualities. One to three lead articles on any legal topic, some exceeding 100 pages in length, are written by legal professionals. Student comments frequently examine cutting-edge issues in the law. Student notes on recent cases are rare. The UCLA law students also edit *Chicano-Latino Law Review* (see above in this section), *Federal Communications Law Journal, UCLA Pacific Basin Law Journal, UCLA Women's Law Journal, UCLA Asian Pacific American Law Journal, UCLA Journal of International Law and Foreign Affairs, Journal of Law and Technology, Entertainment Law Review, UCLA Journal of Legal Scholarship, UCLA Journal of Islamic and Near Eastern Law,* and *UCLA Journal of Environmental Law and Policy.*

4209. *University of Chicago Law Review.* [ISSN: 0041-9494] 1933. q. USD 38 domestic; USD 41 in Canada & Mexico; USD 44 elsewhere. University of Chicago, Law School, 1111 E 60th St, Chicago, IL 60637; http://www.journals.uchicago.edu/pub-alpha.html. Illus., index, adv. Refereed. Circ: 2400. Vol. ends: Fall. Microform: WSH; PMC; PQC. Online: Chadwyck-Healey Incorporated; Factiva; Gale Group; LexisNexis; Northern Light Technology, Inc.; OCLC Online Computer Library Center, Inc.; ProQuest Information & Learning. Reprint: WSH. *Indexed:* ABCPolSci, ABIn, ArtHuCI, BLI, CJA, CLI, ILP, LRI, SSCI. *Bk. rev.:* 1-2, essay length. *Aud.:* Ac, Sa.

Recent studies suggest that, in terms of publishing, the University of Chicago Law School faculty is the most prolific in the nation. The law school's curriculum stresses the interdependence of legal and social studies in the training of lawyers. A significant fraction of the faculty represent disciplines other than law, including economics, history, sociology, philosophy, and political science. Certainly the *Review,* at times reaching more than 1,500 pages, is among the most highly respected and most often cited of all legal periodicals. A representative issue contains a major article or two; a refreshing correspondence section of moderate length in which legal scholars respond to articles, essays, and book reviews previously published in the *Review*; student comments; and essay-length book reviews. The school is also the home of the *Supreme Court Review, Journal of Law & Economics,* and *Journal of Legal Studies* (see above in this section); as well as the *University of Chicago Legal Forum, Chicago Journal of International Law,* and *University of Chicago Law School Roundtable.*

4210. *University of Michigan Journal of Law Reform.* Former titles: *Journal of Law Reform; Prospectus.* [ISSN: 0363-602X] 1968. q. USD 35; USD 40 foreign. University of Michigan, Law School, 625 South State St, Ann Arbor, MI 48109-1215; http://www.law.umich.edu/pubs/journals/mju.html. Illus., index, adv. Vol. ends: Summer. Microform: WSH; PMC. Online: Gale Group. Reprint: WSH. *Indexed:* CJA, CLI, ILP, LRI, PAIS. *Aud.:* Ac, Sa.

The *Journal* seeks to improve the law and its administration by providing a forum for discussion that identifies contemporary issues for reform efforts, proposes concrete means to accomplish change, and evaluates the impact of law reform. Faculty members and other legal professionals contribute the articles; students write the comments and notes. A recent symposium covers "Competing in the 21st Century: Title IX, Gender Equity, and Athletics."

4211. *University of Pennsylvania Law Review.* Former titles (until 1944): *University of Pennsylvania Law Review and American Law Register;* (until 1907): *American Law Register (Philadelphia, 1898);* (until 1897): *American Law Register and Review;* (until 1891): *American Law Register (Philadelphia, 1852).* [ISSN: 0041-9907] 1852. bi-m. USD 42; USD 48 foreign. Ed(s): Daniel Garodnick. University of Pennsylvania Law Review, 3400 Chestnut St, Philadelphia, PA 19104-6204; http://www.law.upenn.edu/lrev. Illus., index, adv. Refereed. Circ: 1850. Vol. ends: Jun. Microform: WSH. Online: EBSCO Publishing; Gale Group; LexisNexis; West Group. Reprint: WSH. *Indexed:* ABCPolSci, CIJE, CJA, CLI, IBZ, ILP, LRI, PAIS, PSA, SSCI. *Bk. rev.:* Occasional, essay length. *Aud.:* Ac, Sa.

This is one of the oldest law reviews in the nation, dating from 1886; and if tracked to its lineal successor (the *American Law Register,* which originated in 1852), the *University of Pennsylvania Law Review* has the highest volume number of all existing reviews. It is influential, traditional in format, diverse in the type of subjects discussed, and edited by a student board of editors with first-rate academic credentials. Contributions concentrate mainly on everyday issues such as bankruptcy, constitutional law, intellectual property, and commercial paper. Other journals edited by the law students at the University of Pennsylvania are the *Journal of Labor and Employment, Journal of Constitutional Law,* and the *Journal of International Economic Law.*

4212. *University of Toronto Law Journal.* [ISSN: 0042-0220] 1937. q. CND 85. Ed(s): Bruce Chapman. University of Toronto Press, Journals Department, 5201 Dufferin St, Toronto, ON M3H 5T8, Canada; journals@utpress.utoronto.ca; http://www.utpjournals.com. Illus., index, adv. Sample. Refereed. Circ: 700. Vol. ends: Fall. Microform: MML; PQC. Online: EBSCO Publishing; LexisNexis. Reprint: WSH. *Indexed:* CBCARef, CLI, IBZ, ILP, LRI, PAIS, PSA, SSCI, SociolAb. *Bk. rev.:* Occasional, lengthy. *Aud.:* Ac, Sa.

Our neighbor to the north deserves to have some representation in this law listing. That distinction goes to this highly regarded journal. Edited by members of the faculty of the prestigious University of Toronto Faculty of Law, the *Journal* provides a heavy dose of analysis of Canadian law and Canadian legal history. Unlike in the United States, where faculty members prefer to publish anywhere but in their own review, most articles in this publication are by faculty members from the law school. Student pieces are published in a separate journal, the semiannual *University of Toronto Faculty of Law Review.* Libraries with a special interest in Canadian materials would certainly want to consider either or both of these titles. For libraries seeking materials on the relationship of the United States and Canada, the *Canada–United States Law Journal,* published annually by the law students at Case Western Reserve University, is a better choice.

4213. *The Urban Lawyer: the national quarterly on urban law.* [ISSN: 0042-0905] 1969. q. USD 130 (Individuals, USD 69). Ed(s): Robert M Vercruck, Julie M Cheslik. A B A Publishing, 750 N Lake Shore Dr, Chicago, IL 60611; service@abanet.org; http://www.abanet.org. Illus., index. Refereed. Circ: 6500. Vol. ends: Fall. Microform: WSH; PMC. Online: Gale Group. Reprint: WSH. *Indexed:* ABS&EES, AgeL, ArtHuCI, CJA, CLI, ILP, LRI, SSCI, SUSA. *Aud.:* Ac, Sa.

Local government law is wide ranging and far reaching. This publication of the American Bar Association's Section of Urban, State and Local Government Law has a student editorial board based at the University of Missouri–Kansas City School of Law. Articles run the gamut of the scope of the section and cover such issues as gerrymandering, Superfund cleanups, sales tax incentive programs, governmental tort liability, airports, land use planning and zoning, labor relations, and HUD housing. Each issue contains four or five articles; a section discussing cases, statutes, and recent developments; and book reviews. The entire fall issue discusses developing issues in urban, state, and local government law and contains a section directory.

4214. *Vanderbilt Law Review.* [ISSN: 0042-2533] 1947. 6x/yr. USD 42 United States; USD 48 elsewhere. Ed(s): Jason Hall. Vanderbilt University, Law School, 131 21st Ave South, Nashville, TN 37203-1181; mwaggone@law.vanderbilt.edu. Adv. Refereed. Circ: 1300. Microform: WSH; PMC; PQC. Online: Factiva; Gale Group; LexisNexis; Northern Light Technology, Inc.; OCLC Online Computer Library Center, Inc.; ProQuest Information & Learning; West Group. Reprint: PQC; WSH. *Indexed:* ABIn, ATI, ArtHuCI, CJA, CLI, CommAb, ILP, LRI, SSCI. *Aud.:* Ac, Sa.

Vanderbilt University Law School is among the most respected in the nation, and its review enjoys the same reputation. Having one's work published in this source is a real badge of honor. Articles and student notes cover the gamut of legal scholarship, with a recent issue addressing bankruptcy, constitutional criminal procedure, Medicaid, employment discrimination, judges, and arbitration. Other Vanderbilt legal journals are *Vanderbilt Journal of Entertainment Law and Practice* and *Vanderbilt Journal of Transnational Law.*

4215. *Virginia Law Review.* [ISSN: 0042-6601] 1913. 8x/yr. USD 44. Ed(s): Bryan J Rose. Virginia Law Review Association, University of Virginia, School of Law, Charlottesville, VA 22903-1789; lawrev@virginia.edu; http://www.scs.student.virginia.edu/~lawrev. Illus., index, adv. Refereed. Circ: 2200. Vol. ends: Nov. Microform: WSH. Online: Gale Group; LexisNexis; National Data Corporation; West Group. Reprint: WSH. *Indexed:* ABIn, ATI, AgeL, ArtHuCI, CJA, CLI, ILP, LRI, PAIS, RiskAb, SSCI. *Bk. rev.:* Occasional, essay length. *Aud.:* Ac, Sa.

The University of Virginia School of Law has produced many of the great lawyers of this country. It is an institution rich in tradition, and its *Review* ranks among the best of all those published. With the standard professional articles and student notes and comments, this publication is as widely regarded for the content of the articles as it is for the contributors. Other journals published by University of Virginia law students are *Virginia Journal of International Law, Virginia Environmental Law Journal, Virginia Journal of Law and Technology, Virginia Sports and Entertainment Law Journal, Journal of Law and Politics, Virginia Journal of Social Policy & the Law,* and *Virginia Tax Review.*

4216. *Washington and Lee Law Review.* [ISSN: 0043-0463] 1939. 4x/yr. USD 32.50 per vol. domestic for vol.60; USD 36 per vol. overseas for vol.60. Ed(s): Brian Williams, Carter Williams. Washington and Lee University, School of Law, Lewis Hall, Lexington, VA 24450-1799; http://law.wlu.edu/. Illus., index, adv. Circ: 1100. Vol. ends: No. 4. Microform: WSH. Online: Factiva; Gale Group; LexisNexis; ProQuest Information & Learning; West Group. Reprint: WSH. *Indexed:* ATI, BLI, CLI, ILP, LRI. *Bk. rev.:* Occasional, essay length. *Aud.:* Ac, Sa.

With one of the smallest enrollments and lowest student-faculty ratios of any law school in the country, this delightful little school produces a national journal discussing important legal problems. Special funding enables the school to attract outstanding scholars for lectures, and their papers often appear in the *Review.* The spring issue features "The Annual Review of Securities and Commodities Law" and in the summer issue is the "Fourth Circuit Review." Often an issue will focus on a special topic, such as the symposium on "The Future of International Human Rights."

4217. *Washington Law Review.* [ISSN: 0043-0617] 1926. 4x/yr. USD 32 domestic; USD 38 foreign. Ed(s): Rebecca Harrison. Washington Law Review Association, University of Washington, School of Law, Seattle, WA 98105-6617; wlr@r.washington.edu; http://www.law.washington.edu/~wlr/. Illus., adv. Refereed. Circ: 1300 Paid. Vol. ends: Sep. Microform: WSH. Online: Gale Group; LexisNexis; West Group. Reprint: WSH. *Indexed:* ATI, AgeL, CJA, CLI, CommAb, ILP, LRI, RiskAb, SSCI. *Bk. rev.:* Occasional, lengthy. *Aud.:* Ac, Sa.

Established in 1899, the University of Washington in Seattle is one of the oldest West Coast law schools. The school has a relatively small but highly diverse student enrollment and an excellent student-faculty ratio. Its law review is traditional in nature, organized around lead articles and student notes and comments, and is national in scope. An example of a representative article is "Rights, Rights of Action, and Remedies: An Integrated Approach." The school also publishes the *Pacific Rim Law & Policy Review.*

4218. *Washington University Law Quarterly.* Formerly: *St. Louis Law Review.* [ISSN: 0043-0862] 1915. q. USD 40 domestic; USD 44 foreign. Ed(s): John Shively. Washington University, School of Law, 1 Brookings Dr, Campus Box 1120, St Louis, MO 63130-4899; http://law.wustl.edu. Adv. Circ: 800. Microform: WSH; PMC. Online: Gale Group; LexisNexis; OCLC Online Computer Library Center, Inc.; West Group; H.W. Wilson. Reprint: WSH. *Indexed:* CLI, ILP, LRI. *Aud.:* Ac, Sa.

This review and its law school has a long-standing and well deserved standard of excellence. The facility is outstanding thanks to a significant contribution by Anheuser-Busch. The journal is traditional, with articles, notes, and discussions of recent developments. A recent article deals with "Natural Born Copyright Killers and the Law of Shock Torts." Other journals prepared by students at this school are *Washington University Journal of Law and Policy* and *Washington University Global Studies Law Review.*

4219. *Wisconsin Law Review.* [ISSN: 0043-650X] 1920. bi-m. USD 36; USD 40 foreign. Ed(s): Laura Katers. University of Wisconsin at Madison, Law School, 975 Bascom Mall, Madison, WI 53706-1399; http://www.law.wisc.edu/. Illus., index, adv. Refereed. Circ: 2150. Vol. ends: No. 6. Microform: WSH; PQC. Online: Gale Group; LexisNexis; OCLC Online Computer Library Center, Inc.; West Group; H.W. Wilson. Reprint: WSH. *Indexed:* AgeL, ArtHuCI, CJA, CLI, ILP, LRI, PAIS, PSA, RiskAb, SSCI, SociolAb. *Bk. rev.:* 1, length varies. *Aud.:* Ac, Sa.

This outstanding law school was a pioneer in articulating the view that law must be studied in its relationship to society, often in its historical context. Some of the major national social legislation has originated with Wisconsin law professors. While the *Review* carries articles by law professionals on any legal topic, it also remains true to the school's social concerns by publishing such articles as "Will the Death Penalty Remain Alive in the Twenty-First Century?" Student notes and comments likewise are eclectic, with the notes focusing more on Wisconsin law. Remaining true to its mission, the law school also publishes the *Women's Law Journal, Graven Images: A Journal of Culture, Law and the Sacred, Wisconsin Environmental Law Journal, Multi Cultural Law Journal,* and the *Wisconsin International Law Journal.*

4220. *Yale Journal of Law & the Humanities.* [ISSN: 1041-6374] 1988. s-a. USD 34 (Individuals, USD 18). Yale University, School of Law, PO Box 208215, New Haven, CT 06520; http://www.yale.edu/lawweb/lawschool/pub.htm. Illus., index, adv. Sample. Circ: 525. Vol. ends: No. 2. Microform: WSH. Online: Gale Group; LexisNexis; OCLC Online Computer Library Center, Inc.; H.W. Wilson. Reprint: WSH. *Indexed:* AmH&L, CLI, ILP, LRI, MLA-IB. *Bk. rev.:* Occasional, essay length. *Aud.:* Ga, Ac, Sa.

Just when it seemed that all law reviews were drab and boring, here is one that intertwines the law and the liberal arts. Perhaps reacting to the law and economics focus prevalent at Yale, this journal eschews the scientific and embraces philosophy, literature, anthropology, social and political science, and the fine arts. Boasting an outstanding, nationally drawn editorial advisory board and an equally well-recognized group of writers, the *Journal* is a welcome and important departure from traditional legal scholarship. A recent issue includes "Reading Texts, Reading Traditions: African Masks and American Law." The semi-annual *Cardozo Studies in Law and Literature,* launched in the same year as this publication, has a similar focus. Let us hope there are more to come.

4221. ***Yale Law Journal.*** [ISSN: 0044-0094] 1891. 8x/yr. USD 40; USD 46 foreign. Yale Journal Co. Inc., PO Box 208215, New Haven, CT 06520-8215; http://www.yale.edu/yalelj/. Illus., index, adv. Circ: 4500. Vol. ends: Jul. Microform: WSH. Online: Florida Center for Library Automation; Gale Group; LexisNexis; Northern Light Technology, Inc.; OCLC Online Computer Library Center, Inc.; ProQuest Information & Learning. Reprint: ISI; WSH. *Indexed:* ABCPolSci, ABIn, ATI, AgeL, ArtHuCI, BAS, BLI, BRI, CBRI, CJA, CLI, IBSS, ILP, IPSA, JEL, LRI, PAIS, RiskAb, SSCI. *Bk. rev.:* Occasional, essay length. *Aud.:* Ac, Sa.

Regardless of whom one asks or what survey one reads, the *Yale Law Journal* will always be among the very first law reviews mentioned for outstanding legal scholarship and influential content. It is simply among the best there is, and its importance cannot be overstated. Yale sees the study of law as interrelated with other intellectual disciplines and includes prominent scholars from economics, philosophy, and psychoanalysis among its faculty. The school's much ballyhooed centennial issue (March 1991) included "The Most-Cited Articles from *The Yale Law Journal.*" More-recent issues include articles on federal regulation of state court procedures and on citizen suits. Six other journals are edited by the Yale law students: *Yale Law & Policy Review, Yale Journal of Law & the Humanities* (see above in this section), *Yale Journal of International Law, Yale Journal of Law & Feminism, Yale Journal of Health Policy, Law, and Ethics, Yale Journal on Regulation;* there are also *Yale Human Rights & Development Law Journal* and *Yale Sumposium on Law and Technology* (both electronic only).

Electronic Journals

4222. ***Law and Politics Book Review.*** [ISSN: 1062-7421] 1991. m. American Political Science Association, 1527 New Hampshire Ave, N W, Washington, DC 20036-1206; http://www.apsanet.org. *Indexed:* BRI, CBRI. *Aud.:* Ac.

Law and Politics Book Review publishes academic book reviews for those who teach law and political science. Publication on the web has two major benefits: The reviews tend to be relatively current, usually within months rather than years after the title is published. Second, the reviews bind law and political science together in such a way that the relevancy of the two is shown. This means that a book tied to the law or one bound to political science may be seen as of benefit to the political scientist and/or the lawyer, which may not be immediately evident by the title, author, or publisher. The reviews are generally essay length. A must for librarians with large political science–law related collections, as well as for individual teachers. (BK)

4223. ***The Richmond Journal of Law & Technology.*** [ISSN: 1091-7322] 1995. s-a. University of Richmond, T.C. Williams School of Law, Richmond, VA 23173; http://www.urich.edu/jolt. *Indexed:* ILP, RiskAb. *Aud.:* Ac, Sa.

This is the first exclusively online law review. It contains articles, notes, comments, essays, and an occasional book review. Recent articles include "State Cybercrime Legislation in the United States of America: A Survey" and "Encryption and the Discovery of Documents." While there are a few other law journals that are exclusively electronic, their publication schedule has not had the consistency this publication enjoys. Accessing this title will provide links to other legal periodicals online.

■ LESBIAN, GAY, BISEXUAL, AND TRANSGENDER

Amy Kautzman, Head, Research, Reference, and Collections, Doe/Moffitt Libraries, 212 Doe Library, #6000; University of California, Berkeley, CA 94720-6000; akautzma@library.berkeley.edu

Michael J. Rogan, Music Librarian, Tufts University, 026 Aidekman Arts Center, Medford, MA 02155; michael.rogan@tufts.edu; FAX: 617-627-3684

Introduction

America is schizophrenic when it comes to gays, lesbians, bisexuals, and transgender people. Showtime and HBO feature explicitly gay-friendly television while NBC follows with the nonexplicit "Will & Grace." GLBT issues are seriously covered by major news organizations in a mostly respectful manner and more people are accepting of alternative lifestyles. The lessening stigma alongside the gay/lesbian baby boom has pushed our families into the PTA and mainstream community in a fashion that cannot be denied. However, like racism, pockets of gay bashing and transphobic behavior regularly make the news in both cities and rural areas.

If the GLBT community has more visibility and political/economic clout than ever, why does it appear that our magazines are becoming less interesting, less innovative, and less political? An overview of titles for this edition's entries reflects the same issues and problems that affect the dominant media industry. The magazine industry is biting its nails as it watches the relevancy and influence of weekly and monthly newsmagazines wane. As the influence of *Time* and *Newsweek* has diminished during the past 25 years, so, too, has *The Advocate*'s ability to provide cutting-edge criticism of our society and culture diminished.

Another reason for the shrinking number of politically relevant titles in this section is the continuing focus on "lifestyle" magazines. Operating under the stereotype of gays as DINKS (double income, no kids) advertisers are drooling to sell their goods to the "alternative audience." Magazines that benefit from the presence of major advertisers tend to have milquetoast content and slick designs. These are wonderfully fun titles to thumb through. In this sea change, there is little room for strong editorials, nudity, and leftist politics; the hallmarks of earlier GLBT publications. Also left out of the content mix are women and racial and sexual minorities who, while still higher earners than their heterosexual peers, are generally not included in the marketing plan for expensive alcohol, clothing, vacations, etc.

There are many reasons for this downturn of originality and lack of overt politics. First and foremost, the nation is in a financial quandary. Just as the conformist era of the 1950s maimed radical politics, so has the bust following the dot-com boom. Also, gays and lesbians are more entrenched in a sort of cultural normalcy than ever before. It has become easier to deny the existence of real legal and social issues, such as no marriage rights, uneven adoption laws, employment discrimination, or hate crimes. Bisexuals still run under the radar of most people's experiences, and transsexuals are only starting down the long road to public acceptance. There has never been a time in our history when so many people, especially young people, are out and proud, and with this acceptance comes complacency and comfort over activism. Some of our news journals are so busy highlighting celebrities they fail to put the spotlight on life-and-death issues.

One has to ask why should any library purchase GLBT titles? That is not a difficult question to answer. The 2000 U.S. Census brought to life the fact that 600,000+ same-sex couples were willing to be noted as cohabiting. While the breakdown between genders was evenly split, the concentration of populations could not be more different. Male couples were drawn to urban centers, while the women chose suburbs and small towns. Meaning that we truly are found everywhere. In most every library, every community, and every social stratum there are GLBT people who are looking for representation, information, and even entertainment in journals.

The biggest titles tend to have a lack of true diversity, with their attention to the bottom line, and a gentrified middle-of-the-road editorial approach that threatens to represent only the white gay man with significant disposable income. The number of titles directed toward people of color continues to decline; the representation of women and their politics of inclusion is undermined, while slick, materialistic titles remain the one genre that is profitable.

The jury is out on how assimilation will affect the GLBT community. At this juncture, we will venture to speak only about collection development and magazines. The importance of these titles cannot be overstated. Although it has become easier for GLBT people to obtain information, the community is still stigmatized.

Our biggest concern is that the fiscal crisis facing all libraries will be the excuse for not subscribing to GLBT titles. While we can't dictate what any library purchases, we feel compelled to push the importance of these journals to a sometimes hidden population. It is imperative that every library offer national titles such as *The Advocate* and/or *Out.* But even more necessary is the inclusion of local newspapers (even if they are sometimes less sophisticated), as well as magazines that represent *your* community's diversity. Depending on your patrons, this could be *Noodle* or *Venus, and baby, Transgender/Tapestry* or *qvMagazine, Trikone* or *RFD.* What is important is that we dig deeper to find the titles that best serve the full spectrum of people who walk through our library doors. Membership organizations often produce regular newsletters full of specific information and support; these are not included in this section. If you need more than what is presented here to reach out to a particular population, remember that the *Encyclopedia of Associations* (Gale Research, 39th ed., 2003, ISSN: 0071-0202) contains Gay/Lesbian subsections within major sections, such as Social Welfare Organizations (PFLAG, SAGE) and Religious Organizations (Dignity/USA, Evangelicals Concerned). Connecting a minoritized individual with a supportive community doesn't have to be relegated to the web; it can still happen in the library. (AMK, MJR)

Basic Periodicals

Hs: *The Advocate, Lambda Book Report, Oasis (electronic), Out, XY Magazine;* Ga: *The Advocate, and baby, Curve, The Gay & Lesbian Review Worldwide, GMHC Treatment Issues, James White Review, Lambda Book Report, Lambda Update, Noodle, Out, Out & About, Venus Magazine;* Ac: *The Advocate, Blithe House Quarterly (electronic), Curve, The Gay & Lesbian Review Worldwide, Gay Theological Journal, GLQ, The Harrington Gay Men's Fiction Quarterly, Harrington Lesbian Fiction Quarterly, ILGA Bulletin, James White Review, Journal of Bisexuality, Journal of Homosexuality, Journal of Lesbian Studies, Lambda Book Report, Lambda Update, LGSN.*

Basic Abstracts and Indexes

Alternative Press Index, Expanded Academic ASAP, Gay and Lesbian Abstracts, GenderWatch, Sexual Diversity Studies.

4224. ***A & U: America's AIDS magazine.*** Formerly (until 1996): *Art & Understanding.* [ISSN: 1545-0554] 1991. m. USD 80 (Individuals, USD 24.95; USD 3.95 newsstand/cover per issue). Ed(s): David Waggoner. Art & Understanding, Inc., 25 Monroe St, Ste 205, Albany, NY 12210-2743; mailbox@aumag.org; http://www.aumag.org. Illus., adv. Circ: 205000. *Indexed:* IAPV. *Bk. rev.:* 2, 600-1,000 words. *Aud.:* Ga.

A common thread, dealing with AIDS, runs through the contents of each issue, which includes poetry and fiction, artwork (painting and photography), book and music reviews, a media-watch column, treatment issues, opinion pieces, and celebrity interviews. Glossy and informative, the publication presents an interesting variety of writers. Recommended for any library with any HIV+ constituents. (MJR)

4225. ***The Advocate (Los Angeles, 1967): the national gay & lesbian newsmagazine.*** [ISSN: 0001-8996] 1967. bi-w. m. in Jan, Aug. USD 39.95 domestic; USD 3.95 newsstand/cover per issue domestic. Ed(s): Judy Wieder, John Jameson. Liberation Publications Inc., 6922 Hollywood Blvd, 10th Fl, Ste 1000, Los Angeles, CA 90028; http://www.advocate.com. Illus., adv. Circ: 94000 Paid. Online: EBSCO Publishing; Florida Center for Library Automation; Gale Group; LexisNexis; OCLC Online Computer Library Center, Inc.; ProQuest Information & Learning; SoftLine Information; H.W. Wilson. *Indexed:* AltPI, BRI, CBRI, LRI, MagInd, RGPR. *Bk. rev.:* 1-5, 50-100 words. *Aud.:* Hs, Ga, Ac.

The Advocate is akin to a gay and lesbian *Time,* successfully reporting on the gay and lesbian communities' political issues, social concerns, and entertainment interests for over 30 years. It has a Washington correspondent on staff, as well as a parade of sometimes witty, sometimes wise, sometimes angry columnists. If your library can only subscribe to one gay and lesbian magazine, choose *The Advocate*—and rethink that policy! Recommended for all collections. (MJR)

And Baby. See Parenting section.

4226. ***Arise Magazine: for diverse people of african descent.*** [ISSN: 1534-2174] 2000. m. USD 35; USD 4 newsstand/cover per issue. Arise Magazine, 1533 41st St, Sacramento, CA 95819. Adv. *Aud.:* Ga.

The *Arise* mission is to "challenge the mind, encourage the spirit, and affirm the value of all sexually diverse people of African descent." *Arise* targets both men and women readers who are achievers, and admits a "commitment to a distinct quality as well as a comfortable standard of living." Reflected throughout the journal are articles on health, wellness, travel, literature, the arts, entertainment, technology, professional growth, entrepreneurialism, and financial success. Yet, importantly, the common thread is not consumerism but enlightenment. "To ARISE, one must be willing to move higher in the knowledge of self and the world around us. *Arise* magazine is here to articulate the message of success, hope, and courage embodied in the spirit of African-American people who are accomplishing prodigious feats in spite of the odds." The glossy layout and fashionable photography capture the eye, while the text, sometimes thoughtful, sometimes political, engages the mind and uplifts the spirit. Recommended for all libraries that serve diverse populations. (MJR)

4227. ***Bay Area Reporter.*** 1971. w. USD 125. Ed(s): Mike Salinas. Benro Enterprises, Inc., 395 Ninth St, San Francisco, CA 94103-3831. Circ: 37500 Controlled. *Bk. rev.:* 2, 200-500 words. *Aud.:* Ga.

The *Bay Area Reporter* is the only weekly newspaper for San Francisco's lesbian, gay, bisexual, transgender, queer, and questioning community. It is now in its 29th year of uninterrupted publication. Local, national, and international news, events, reviews, and interviews fill its pages and keep Bay Area residents (and those interested in San Francisco news) up to date. A strong addition for California libraries and libraries looking for regional representation. (AMK)

4228. ***Curve: the best-selling lesbian magazine.*** Formerly (until vol.6, 1996): *Deneuve.* [ISSN: 1087-867X] 1991. 8x/yr. USD 21.95 domestic; USD 33.95 Canada; USD 43.95 elsewhere. Ed(s): Gretchen Lee. Outspoken Enterprises, Inc., 1550 Bryant St. Ste 510, San Francisco, CA 94103. Illus., adv. Circ: 68400. Online: Florida Center for Library Automation; Gale Group; LexisNexis. *Indexed:* AltPI. *Bk. rev.:* 4-6, 100-400 words. *Aud.:* Hs, Ga, Ac.

This fun, glossy title is one of the strongest national lesbian magazines. In its 12th year *Curve* is a popular-culture journal with fashion, music, interviews, soft politics, and book reviews. The articles examine all aspects of lesbian life. A recent issue featured interviews with Rosie O'Donnell and Ani DiFranco. Funny, ironic, always interesting, and highly recommended to balance the male bias of most gay titles. (AMK)

4229. ***G L Q: a journal of lesbian and gay studies.*** [ISSN: 1064-2684] 1993. q. USD 143 includes online access (Individuals, USD 38 includes online access; USD 36 per issue). Ed(s): Carolyn Dinshaw, David M Halpern. Duke University Press, 905 W Main St, Ste 18 B, Durham, NC 27701; subscriptions@dukeupress.edu; http://www.dukeupress.edu. Illus., adv. Refereed. Circ: 850. Online: EBSCO Publishing; Gale Group; Ingenta Select; OCLC Online Computer Library Center, Inc.; Project MUSE; RoweCom Information Quest; Swets Blackwell. Reprint: PSC. *Indexed:* AltPI, AmHI, ArtHuCI, HumInd, IBZ, MLA-IB, SSCI, SWA, SociolAb. *Bk. rev.:* 1-2, 1,200 words. *Aud.:* Ac.

The most intellectually challenging GLBT title around, *GLQ* has many big-name scholars on its diverse editorial and advisory boards. Authors include Judith Butler, Inderpal Grewal, and Jonathan Freedman. Excellent writing and editing help to make *GLQ* a truly cutting-edge theoretical journal. "*GLQ* proposes to illuminate the complex interplay among sexual and social meanings, individual and collective practices, private fantasies and public institutions, erotics and politics." It features in-depth book and film reviews and a "Gallery" featuring photography. A fascinating addition is the inclusion of "GLQ Archives," featuring primary materials, usually of historical significance, that have never been published. These primary materials often take the forms of legal documents, manuscripts, commentaries, correspondence, interviews, roundtables, or keynote addresses. No academic library should be without this title. (AMK)

4230. ***G M H C Treatment Issues: newsletter of experimental AIDS therapies.*** Formerly: *Treatment Issues.* [ISSN: 1077-1824] 1987. m. USD 95 (Individuals, USD 55). Ed(s): David Gilden. Gay Men's Health Crisis, Inc., Treatment Education and Advocacy, 119 W 24th St, New York, NY 10011; fredg@gmhc.org; http://www.gmhc.org. Illus. Circ: 18000. *Aud.:* Ga, Ac.

The Gay Men's Health Crisis (GMHC), since the discovery of AIDS, has been on the cutting edge of treatment options. This newsletter is an important supplement to any library collection that serves the populations affected by AIDS. The newsletter offers no-nonsense medical reporting for AIDS patients and their loved ones who need a source where they can read honest assessments of experimental health treatments. All articles are fully documented; and while they may not recommend a specific treatment, they do place facts in the public realm. Recommended for libraries that serve diverse, large, or medical constituents. (AMK)

4231. ***Gay and Lesbian Medical Association. Journal.*** [ISSN: 1090-7173] 1997. q. USD 261 for print or online ed. Ed(s): Mark H Townsend, Jocelyn C White. Kluwer Academic / Plenum Publishers, 233 Spring St Fl 7, New York, NY 10013-1522; http://www.wkap.nl/. Adv. Refereed. *Indexed:* ExcerpMed. *Bk. rev.:* 1, 100-200. *Aud.:* Ac, Sa.

According to its blurb, this title "is the world's first peer-reviewed, multidisciplinary journal dedicated to lesbian, gay, bisexual, and transgender health." Written by doctors for doctors, this journal examines clinical and research issues with a GLBT perspective. With recent studies showing bias in health care against lesbians and transgendered people, this title is a necessary addition to any medical research library. (AMK)

4232. ***The Gay & Lesbian Review Worldwide.*** Formerly (until 2000): *Harvard Gay & Lesbian Review.* [ISSN: 1532-1118] 1994. bi-m. USD 60 (Individuals, USD 19.75; USD 10 newsstand/cover). Ed(s): Richard Schneider, Jr. Harvard Gay & Lesbian Review Inc., PO Box 180300, Boston, MA 02118; hglr@aol.com. Illus., adv. Circ: 9000 Paid. *Indexed:* AltPI, AmHI, CWI, GendWatch, HumInd. *Bk. rev.:* 10-15, 500-1000 words. *Aud.:* Ac, Ga.

If your coffee table features *The New Yorker* and *The Nation*, you need to immediately acquire the *Gay & Lesbian Review.* This title is the thinking-queer's magazine. It addresses legal wrangles, literature, film criticism, culture wars, politics, and so much more. Serious, ironic, and learned, this is a trove of thought-inducing material. Necessary for all academic and public libraries. (AMK)

4233. ***Gay Theological Journal: homosexual hermeneutics on religion & the Scriptures.*** [ISSN: 1521-1258] 1997. 3x/yr. USD 30. Ed(s): James D Anderson. Publishing Partners, 8571-B Sudley Rd, Manassass, VA 20110-3811. *Bk. rev.:* 300-1,200 words, signed. *Aud.:* Ga.

Gay Theological Journal covers the entire spectrum of spiritual issues in feature articles, commentaries, reviews, and resources for ministering to people of faith in the gay and lesbian community. The publisher welcomes submissions from all faiths, and many of the items are reprinted from elsewhere. Each issue includes a list of "Religious Organizations Working for Gay and Lesbian Inclusion." Casting the net so widely means that there is a broad variety of style and content within the journal's deceptively simple design, which makes this a useful title in an equally broad variety of library settings. (MJR)

4234. ***Genre Magazine.*** [ISSN: 1074-5246] 1991. 12x/yr. USD 19.95 domestic; USD 31.95 Canada; USD 43.95 elsewhere. Ed(s): Tom Eubanks. Genre Magazine, Empire State Bldg, Ste 6917, New York, NY 10118. Illus., adv. Circ: 50000 Paid. *Bk. rev.:* 3-8, 50-150 words. *Aud.:* Ga.

Genre is the enduring entertainment, celebrity, travel magazine for young gay men in a field with constant new competition and, increasingly, market fragmentation (*Noodle, qvMagazine, XY*). Interviews, fashion shoots, music, film, and book reviews are accompanied by lifestyle articles and travel pieces on fabulous destinations. There's also an occasional piece of fiction. Editor in Chief Andy Towle has written, "Somebody joked to me that *Genre* was for shiny happy gay people. If that is the impression people are getting, I hope it continues." (MJR)

4235. ***Girlfriends: lesbian culture, politics, and entertainment.*** [ISSN: 1078-8875] 1994. m. USD 29.95 domestic; USD 39.95 Canada; USD 44.95 elsewhere. Ed(s): Heather Findlay. H A F Publishing, 3415 Cesar Chavez, Ste 101, San Francisco, CA 94110; staff@girlfriendsmag.com; http://www.girlfriendsmag.com. Illus., adv. Sample. Circ: 30000. *Bk. rev.:* 6-9, 80-500 words. *Aud.:* Ga, Ac.

Girlfriends is one of my favorite "fun" lesbian titles. It features interviews with fascinating women (and some celebrities) along with articles on health, spirituality, money matters, cultural criticism, and reviews of books, movies, and more. Imagine *People* magazine, only more interesting and better written. This title covers the full spectrum of lesbian life. Recommended for public libraries and research libraries with pop culture, feminist collections. (AMK)

4236. ***The Guide: gay travel, entertainment, politics and sex.*** Formerly: *Guide to the Gay Northeast.* [ISSN: 1047-8906] 1980. m. USD 30 domestic; CND 45 Canada; USD 75 elsewhere. Ed(s): French Wall. Fidelity Publishing, PO Box 990593, Boston, MA 02199; theguide@guidemag.com; http://www.guidemag.com. Illus., adv. Circ: 30000 Paid and controlled. *Bk. rev.:* 2, 1,000-1,500 words. *Aud.:* Ga.

If a typical "bar rag" covers a local scene, has a lot of ads, and includes some local news (in that order), then *The Guide* is a bar rag on steroids. The coverage of this monthly magazine for gay men is beefed up to include most major cities and gay hot spots across the nation—complete with maps, columns, and classifieds showing where to stay and where to play. Canada, Europe, and Australia are regularly represented. Much of the writing is meatier, too, than the typical bar rag—whether editorials, articles, reviews, or erotica. The web site includes a listing of travel articles by destination. (MJR)

4237. ***The Harrington Gay Men's Fiction Quarterly.*** [ISSN: 1522-3140] 1998. q. USD 75 domestic; USD 101.25 Canada; USD 108.75 elsewhere. Ed(s): Thomas Long. Haworth Press, Inc., 10 Alice St, Binghamton, NY 13904-1580; getinfo@haworthpressinc.com; http://www.haworthpressinc.com. Adv. Sample. Circ: 201 Paid. *Aud.:* Ga, Ac.

Gay writing has been assimilated into undergraduate literature seminars and *The New Yorker.* Even as we celebrate diverse voices in major magazines, there is a place for smaller literary quarterlies. According to their web site, "*HGMFQ* is devoted to the latest names and innovations in gay men's fiction and serves as a forum for discovering new talents. You'll get exclusive 'sneak peeks' of the latest works in progress from such prominent writers as Andrew Holleran, Scott Heim, and Bernard Cooper, and new critical examinations of 'lost' gay novels." The focus is on short stories with some artwork. Libraries supporting writing programs or voracious readers need to consider *HGMFQ.* (AMK)

4238. ***Harrington Lesbian Fiction Quarterly.*** [ISSN: 1522-8894] 2000. q. USD 75 domestic; USD 101.25 Canada; USD 108.75 elsewhere. Ed(s): Judith P Stelboum. Haworth Press, Inc., 10 Alice St, Binghamton, NY 13904-1580; getinfo@haworthpressinc.com; http://www.haworthpressinc.com. Adv. Sample. Circ: 111 Paid. *Indexed:* MLA-IB. *Aud.:* Ac, Ga.

The lesbian writing community has always sustained itself with a vibrant press. Literary magazines that mix short stories and politics have educated generations of women. *HLFQ* continues this powerful literary tradition. With stellar authors such as Donna Allegra, Achy Obejas, Ruthann Robson, and Sarah Schulman this could become the best place to find great reading and wonderful new writers. *HLFQ* features a nice mix of short stories, poetry, and art. Strongly recommended for libraries supporting writing programs and literature collections. (AMK)

4239. ***I L G A Bulletin.*** [ISSN: 0281-627X] 1981. q. GBP 30 domestic; USD 50 domestic; GBP 60 foreign. International Lesbian and Gay Association, Rue Marche-au-Charbon 81, Brussels, 1000, Belgium; ilga@ilga.org; http://www.ilga.org. Illus. Circ: 800. *Aud.:* Hs, Ga, Ac.

The *ILGA Bulletin* reflects its parent organization, the International Lesbian and Gay Association, the only general GLBT global organization, which operates in a democratic and decentralized manner as a federation of national and local groups. The *Bulletin*'s content is gathered from various "Information Pools" (Africa, Latin America, Euro Working Party, Christian churches, youth, health), "Project Groups" (AIDS, Amnesty International, trade unions), and the association's "Secretariats" (financial, Asian, regional, women's). In addition to reports, news, and action alerts, there are announcements of events and conferences and new publications. Although often brief, *ILGA Bulletin* more than makes up for it in breadth. Recommended for all GLBT collections. (MJR)

4240. *Instinct.* [ISSN: 1096-0058] 10x/yr. USD 14.95 domestic; USD 38.95 foreign. Ed(s): Ben R Rogers. Instinct Publishing, 15335 Morriston St, Ste 325, Sherman Oaks, CA 91403-1590. Adv. *Aud.:* Ga.

Launched in 1997, *Instinct* prides itself as "the first gay magazine to focus on humor as the cornerstone of its editorial... a clever mix of *Cosmo* and *Maxim*" for young gay men. Billed as "America's #1 Gay Men's Magazine" (achieved in just 5 years), it provides the customary glossy/prettyboy mix of travel, entertainment, fashion and home, cars, and health and fitness. *Instinct* attempts to entertain and enlighten while providing "readers with a much-needed vacation from the politically correct world." With more attitude than substance, it will appeal more to certain (young smartass) audiences than *Genre* or *Out* and much less to other audiences, such as those who seek political awareness (*The Advocate*) or seek stronger community identity (*qvMagazine, Trikone*). (MJR)

4241. *James White Review: a gay men's literary quarterly.* [ISSN: 0891-5393] 1983. q. USD 17.50 domestic; USD 20 in Canada & Mexico; USD 30 elsewhere. Ed(s): Patrick Merla. James White Review Association, PO Box 73910, Washington, DC 20056-3910; lbreditor@aol.com. Illus., index, adv. Circ: 7000 Paid. Online: EBSCO Publishing. *Indexed:* AmHI, IAPV, MLA-IB. *Bk. rev.:* 10-15, 800-2,800 words. *Aud.:* Ga, Ac.

The *James White Review* is the premier gay men's literary magazine, with fiction, poetry, photography, art, essays, and reviews by the community's finest writers. In existence for over 20 years, it has been published by the Lambda Literary Foundation since 1998, the same foundation that produces the *Lambda Book Report.* This quarterly's importance to gay and lesbian studies and literature collections cannot be overstated. Strongly suggested for libraries with liberal arts collections. (AMK)

4242. *Journal of Bisexuality.* [ISSN: 1529-9716] 2000. q. USD 225 domestic print & online eds.; USD 303.75 Canada print & online eds.; USD 326.25 elsewhere print & online eds. Ed(s): Fritz Klein. Haworth Press, Inc., 10 Alice St, Binghamton, NY 13904-1580; getinfo@haworthpressinc.com; http://www.haworthpressinc.com. Adv. Sample. Refereed. Circ: 122 Paid. *Indexed:* PAIS, SFSA. *Bk. rev.:* Various number and length. *Aud.:* Ac.

The *Journal of Bisexuality* is the first professional quarterly to publish both scholarly articles and serious essays on bisexuality and its meaning for the individual, the community, and society. As a group, bisexuals are often invisible, on the outskirts of the gay, lesbian, and heterosexual communities. This journal is an academic, refereed title that will explore bisexuality in history, film, culture, health, and more. This journal will help academics and interested readers explore a population not represented well elsewhere. Recommended for academic libraries. (AMK)

4243. *Journal of Gay & Lesbian Issues in Education: an international quarterly devoted to research, theory, and practice.* [ISSN: 1541-0889] 2003. q. USD 250 domestic print & online eds.; USD 337.50 Canada print & online eds.; USD 362.50 elsewhere print & online eds. Ed(s): James T. Sears. Haworth Press, Inc., 10 Alice St, Binghamton, NY 13904-1580; getinfo@haworthpressinc.com; http://www.haworthpressinc.com. Adv. Refereed. *Aud.:* Ac, Sa.

The *Journal of Gay & Lesbian Issues in Education* contains cutting-edge research studies, articles from frontline practitioners, and scholarly essays, as well as reviews, bibliographies, and ongoing columns. International in scope, this peer-reviewed journal is intended to provide current information in educational policy, curriculum development, professional practice, and pedagogy. In addition to general issues, there is at least one in-depth themed feature in every other issue, such as "Gay-Straight Alliances & GLBT Student Support Groups" or "Issues in Education & Globalization." The concise, jargon-free writing style makes this journal useful for a wider audience including researchers, teachers, teacher educators, and policy makers. (MJR)

4244. *Journal of Gay & Lesbian Politics.* [ISSN: 1537-9426] 2005. q. Haworth Press, Inc., 10 Alice St, Binghamton, NY 13904-1580; getinfo@haworthpressinc.com; http://www.haworthpressinc.com. Adv. *Aud.:* Ga, Ac, Sa.

The *Journal of Gay & Lesbian Politics* has been launched to "facilitate discourse on the politics of sexual orientation and help to stimulate academic discussion on all aspects of sexual minority politics including bisexuality, transvestitism, and transgendered identity." Intended to appeal to both scholars and activists, the journal publishes submissions from across the spectrum of political science: "comparative and international studies, political theory, public policy, and American national, state, and local politics," as well as contributions from "political activists whose experiences and insights offer valuable help in understanding movement politics." This title will appeal to both academic and public libraries where there is community activism. (MJR)

4245. *Journal of Gay & Lesbian Psychotherapy.* [ISSN: 0891-7140] 1988. q. USD 180 domestic; USD 243 Canada; USD 261 elsewhere. Ed(s): Dr. Jack Drescher. Haworth Press, Inc., 10 Alice St, Binghamton, NY 13904-1580; getinfo@haworthpressinc.com; http://www.haworthpressinc.com. Illus., adv. Sample. Refereed. Circ: 314 Paid. Microform: PQC. Online: Gale Group. Reprint: HAW; ISI. *Indexed:* AbAn, CWI, GendWatch, IMFL, PsycholAb, SWR&A, SociolAb. *Aud.:* Ac.

A title for and by professionals, the *Journal of Gay & Lesbian Psychotherapy* is the official journal of the Association of Gay and Lesbian Psychiatrists. Each issue features a guest editor and focuses on the concerns of psychologists, social workers, nurses, clergy, and other mental-health providers. The articles are academically dense, with abstracts and supporting charts and tables. Methodology, solid scholarship, and extensive bibliographies make this a useful title for people in the psychotherapy field. Recommended for libraries that support a psychology collection. (AMK)

4246. *Journal of Gay & Lesbian Social Services: issues in practice, policy & research.* [ISSN: 1053-8720] 1994. q. USD 225 domestic; USD 303.75 Canada; USD 326.25 elsewhere. Ed(s): James J Kelly, Raymond M. Berger. Haworth Press, Inc., 10 Alice St, Binghamton, NY 13904-1580; getinfo@haworthpressinc.com; http://www.haworthpressinc.com. Illus., adv. Sample. Refereed. Circ: 280 Paid. Microform: PQC. Online: Northern Light Technology, Inc. Reprint: HAW. *Indexed:* AgeL, CJA, CWI, IBZ, IMFL, PAIS, RiskAb, SFSA, SWA, SWR&A, SociolAb. *Bk. rev.:* 0-3, 1,000-2,500 words. *Aud.:* Ac, Sa.

This journal "aims to promote the well-being of homosexuals and bisexuals in contemporary society through disseminating information on innovative approaches to the design, evaluation, and delivery of social services to lesbians and gays." It serves as a resource for professionals who work with individuals, groups, families, and communities; programs and services; and social policy. Issues often have themes, such as "the proceedings of the SAGE Conference on Aging," "educational issues in Australia," and "multicultural competence." All articles have abstracts and references. Necessary for libraries that support social-services collections. (MJR)

4247. *Journal of Homosexuality.* [ISSN: 0091-8369] 1974. q. in 2 vols. USD 480 domestic; USD 648 Canada; USD 696 elsewhere. Ed(s): John P De Cecco. Haworth Press, Inc., 10 Alice St, Binghamton, NY 13904-1580; getinfo@haworthpressinc.com; http://www.haworthpressinc.com. Illus., adv. Sample. Refereed. Circ: 811 Paid. Microform: PQC. Online: Gale Group. Reprint: HAW. *Indexed:* ASSIA, AbAn, AgeL, AltPI, ArtHuCI, BRI, BiolAb, CBRI, CJA, CWI, ExcerpMed, GendWatch, H&SSA, HEA, HRA, IMFL, IndMed, LRI, MagInd, PAIS, PsycholAb, RI-1, RiskAb, SFSA, SSCI, SSI, SWA, SWR&A, SociolAb, WSA. *Bk. rev.:* 4, 2,000-5,000 words. *Aud.:* Ac.

The *Journal of Homosexuality* is devoted to "scholarly research on homosexuality, including sexual practices and gender roles and their cultural, historical, interpersonal, and modern social contexts." It is peer reviewed, with over 120 scholars from all over the world on its editorial board. The wide variety of subjects in the journal includes anthropology, art, history, law, literature, philosophy, politics, religion, sociology, biologicial sciences, medicine, psychiatry, and psychology. In addition to being a vehicle to bring together scholarly research on homosexuality and to support lesbian and gay studies programs, it aims "to confront homophobia through the encouragement of scholarly inquiry and the dissemination of sound research." Recommended for all academic libraries. (MJR)

Journal of Interdisciplinary Gender Studies. See Women: Feminist and Special Interest/Feminist and Women's Studies section.

4248. *Journal of Lesbian Studies.* [ISSN: 1089-4160] 1997. q. USD 215 domestic; USD 290.75 Canada; USD 311.75 elsewhere. Ed(s): Esther D Rothblum. Haworth Press, Inc., 10 Alice St, Binghamton, NY 13904-1580; getinfo@haworthpressinc.com; http://www.haworthpressinc.com. Illus., adv. Sample. Refereed. Circ: 220 Paid. Microform: PQC. Online: LexisNexis. Reprint: HAW. *Indexed:* CJA, FemPer, GendWatch, PAIS, SWA, SociolAb. *Bk. rev.:* Various number and length. *Aud.:* Ac.

The *Journal of Lesbian Studies* is the only academic journal devoted exclusively to the lesbian experience, according to its publisher. The journal produces articles that are informative, practical, research based, and theoretical. The publication functions as a vehicle for the promotion of scholarship and commentary on lesbianism from an international, multicultural perspective. Guest editors focus on such themes as "From Nowhere to Everywhere: Lesbian Geographies" or "Sexual Behaviors and Sexually Transmitted Diseases of Lesbians: Results of the Boston Lesbian Health Project." Recommended for academic collections. (AMK)

4249. *L G S N: Lesbian and Gay Studies Newsletter.* Formerly: *G S N.* [ISSN: 1064-5950] 1973. 3x/yr. USD 40 (Individuals, USD 22; Students, USD 12). Ed(s): Jack Richtman. Duke University Press, 905 W Main St, Ste 18 B, Durham, NC 27701; subscriptions@dukeupress.edu; http://www.dukeupress.edu. Illus., adv. Circ: 350. *Bk. rev.:* 8-18, 750-1,400 words. *Aud.:* Ac.

An official vehicle of the Modern Language Association's Gay and Lesbian Caucus, this newsletter not only features information of professional interest to caucus members (about job offers, conferences, and people in the field) but offers many excellent, substantive book reviews. An absolutely necessary acquisition for any academic library supporting literary studies. (AMK)

4250. *Lambda Book Report: a review of contemporary gay and lesbian literature.* Formerly (until 1991): *Lambda Rising Book Report.* [ISSN: 1048-9487] 1987. bi-m. Individuals, USD 34.95. Ed(s): Greg Herren. Lambda Literary Foundation, PO Box 73910, Washington, DC 20056-3910; lbreditor@aol.com; http://www.lambdalit.org. Illus., adv. Circ: 11000. Microform: PQC. Online: bigchalk; EBSCO Publishing; Florida Center for Library Automation; Gale Group; LexisNexis; Northern Light Technology, Inc.; OCLC Online Computer Library Center, Inc.; ProQuest Information & Learning; SoftLine Information. *Indexed:* AltPI, BRI, CBRI, CWI, GendWatch. *Bk. rev.:* 55-60, 300-3,000 words. *Aud.:* Hs, Ga, Ac.

Lambda Book Report is a monthly magazine devoted to reviewing books, interviewing authors, and following the trends in lesbian, gay, bisexual, and transgender publishing. Every issue contains provocative discussion and criticism of the latest books and topics affecting our readers. The magazine is carried by a large number of university and public libraries and is indispensable reading for professional booksellers. It is a necessary collection development tool for all libraries. (AMK)

4251. *Lambda Update.* [ISSN: 1058-949X] 1976. 3x/yr. USD 40. Ed(s): Joneil Adriano. Lambda Legal Defense & Education Fund, Inc., 120 Wall St, Ste 1500, New York, NY 10005-3904; lambdalegal@lambdalegal.org; http://www.lambdalegal.org. Illus., adv. Circ: 20000. *Aud.:* Ga, Ac.

Under the auspices of the Lambda Legal Defense and Education Fund working to "achieve full recognition of the civil rights of lesbians, gay men and people with HIV/AIDS through impact litigation, education and public policy work," *Lambda Update* is an excellent tool for following national legal battles and evolving public policy. The articles provide analysis and legal and political information on a variety of fronts. Updates from around the nation track anti- or pro-gay legislation as well as specific cases on the docket. Much of the information is searchable on its excellent web site. Necessary for all legal collections, academic or public. (AMK, MJR)

4252. *Lesbian Connection.* [ISSN: 1081-3217] 1974. bi-m. Free to Lesbians worldwide. Elsie Publishing Institute, PO Box 811, E Lansing, MI 48826; elsiepub@aol.com. Illus., adv. Sample. Circ: 23000. *Bk. rev.:* 2-4, 200-300 words. *Aud.:* Hs, Ga.

A truly grassroots publication, *Lesbian Connection* is more connected to the pulse of American lesbianism than most titles. Written by its audience, it began as a mimeographed publication sent to all who requested a copy. Thanks to technology, it has progressed into a better designed newsletter. Still a product of audience participation, it serves as a wide-ranging lesbian forum on such issues as gender, class, homophobia, legal issues, and whatever else is in the air. A listing of "Contact Dykes" acts as a "welcome wagon" all over the world. Especially good for keeping up on lesbian events, businesses, groups, and services throughout the United States. This is the one magazine where historians will find lesbian issues discussed in unadulterated fashion by the people directly affected by them. Fascinating. Recommended for libraries with feminist collections. (AMK)

4253. *Lesbian - Gay Law Notes.* [ISSN: 8755-9021] 1980. m. except Aug. USD 55 domestic; USD 60 in Canada & Mexico; USD 70 elsewhere. Ed(s): Arthur S Leonard. Lesbian & Gay Law Association Foundation of Greater New York, 799 Broadway, Ste 340, New York, NY 10003-6811; le-gal@interport.net; http://www.le-gal.org. *Aud.:* Ga, Ac.

Lesbian/Gay Law Notes is a useful compendium of recent legal decisions affecting the GLBT community in the United States and worldwide. Typical categories in each issue include "Lesbian/Gay Legal News," "Litigation Notes," "Legislative Notes," "Law & Society Notes," "International Law Notes," "AIDS & Related Legal Notes," and "Publications Noted." A very useful addition to public library collections and law school collections. (AMK)

4254. *Lesbian News.* [ISSN: 0739-1803] 1975. m. USD 35 domestic; USD 55 foreign; USD 3.96 newsstand/cover per issue. Ed(s): Claudia Piras. L N Publishing Inc., PO Box 55, Torrance, CA 90507; theln@earthlink.net; http://www.lesbiannews.com. Illus., adv. Circ: 39000 Paid and free. Online: EBSCO Publishing. *Indexed:* AltPI. *Bk. rev.:* 8-10, 300-500 words. *Aud.:* Hs, Ga.

Featuring a glossy cover with a newsprint interior, *LN* is an interesting, chatty magazine. Covering politics, current news, arts, entertainment, and local California events, it claims to be "a national monthly magazine" but is basically a Southern California news source. However, this should not detract from its importance as a long-standing (28 years) title nor as an excellent community resource. A good resource for all Southern California libraries. (AMK)

4255. *Metro Source: a celebration and exploration of urban gay life.* [ISSN: 1529-935X] 1990. 5x/yr. USD 16.95. Ed(s): Richard Walsh. Metrosource Publishing, Inc., 180 Varick St, 5th Fl, New York, NY 10014-4606; metrosourc@aol.com; http://www.metrosource.com/. Illus., adv. Circ: 15018 Paid. *Bk. rev.:* 6, 240-360 words. *Aud.:* Ga.

Yet another lifestyle magazine for gay men, *Metro Source* in its national guise is an offshoot of a New York City–based publication of the same name that has been around for over a decade. Like the other lifestyle magazines in this section (e.g., *Genre, qvMagazine*), it is a slick production, with plenty of photos of beautiful men (both in features and in advertising), and it includes celebrity interviews, fashion, travel, and health/fitness features, and music, art, book, and entertainment reviews. (MJR)

Michigan Journal of Gender & Law. See Women: Feminist and Special Interest/Feminist and Women's Studies section.

4256. *New York Blade News.* 1997. w. USD 35 for 6 mos. Ed(s): Lisa Keen, Inga Sorenson. Window Media LLC, 242 W 30th St, 4th Fl, New York, NY 10001; http://www.nyblade.com. Adv. Circ: 50000. *Aud.:* Ga.

Although obviously a local newspaper, the *Blade* not only covers the Big Apple for gays and lesbians, but it regularly includes items about the national scene, particularly concerning politics and following the actions of national gay and lesbian organizations. An important regional resource. (MJR)

4257. *Noodle: it's all in your head.* [ISSN: 1540-1774] 2002. q. USD 17.95. M L Productions, 944 Market St., Ste. 704, San Francisco, CA 94102; info@noodlemagazine.com. *Bk. rev.:* 1, 1000-1500. *Aud.:* Hs, Ga, Ac, Sa.

Noodle is my favorite new title. It is a slick lifestyle magazine with an Asian American focus. Supporting and representing its target audience, *Noodle* is humorous, well written, beautifully designed, a little bit political and a bit practical. Yes, it is eye candy, but what fun and positive candy it is. The writing matches *Out*, but the images of Asians on every page makes for a dynamic, representational read. Included are articles on sports, fashion, books, films, health, and more. The only downside is the lack of female representation (it is a gay-male title, after all). This is a necessary magazine for any public or university library with an Asian clientele. (AMK)

4258. *Our World: the international gay and lesbian travel magazine.* [ISSN: 1044-6699] 1989. 10x/yr. USD 35 domestic; USD 45 Canada; USD 60 elsewhere. Ed(s): Wayne Whiston. Our World Publishing, 1104 N Nova Rd, Ste 251, Daytona Beach, FL 32117. Illus., adv. Circ: 55000 Paid. *Aud.:* Ga.

Whether you are looking for New York or Naples, Vermont or Vienna, Key West or Katmandu, *Our World* has been a global guide for gay and lesbian travel interests since 1989. Heavily illustrated with beautiful photography, it includes information on cruises and group tours, not just individual locations. Directed to both gay men and lesbians, this glossy magazine is filled with ads and articles that pique interest in a wide variety of alluring destinations. (MJR)

4259. *Out.* [ISSN: 1062-7928] 1992. 11x/yr. USD 19.95 domestic; USD 34.95 foreign. Ed(s): Brendan Lemon. Liberation Publications Inc., 80 8th Ave, Ste 315, New York, NY 10011. Illus., adv. Circ: 115429 Paid. Microform: PQC. *Indexed:* PAIS. *Bk. rev.:* 6-9, 50-400 words. *Aud.:* Hs, Ga, Ac.

A successful glossy lifestyle magazine, *Out* attracts major advertisers and writers. The cover can as easily show a political figure as a movie star, with the stories running the gamut from theater and book reviews to cutting-edge fashion to mindless pabulum. Owned by the publishers of *The Advocate*, the content is "gay lite." It is a necessary purchase for all public and academic libraries that cover pop culture and subscribe to *Vanity Fair* and *People* magazine. (AMK)

4260. *Out & About.* [ISSN: 1066-7776] 1992. 10x/yr. USD 49 domestic; USD 59 in Canada & Mexico; USD 69 elsewhere. Out & About, Inc., PO Box 500, San Francisco, CA 94104-0500. Illus., adv. Sample. Circ: 11000. *Aud.:* Ga, Ac.

Addressing the needs of gay and lesbian travelers, *Out & About* is a succinctly written magazine that is informative, upbeat, and dream inducing. Focusing on one to three cities per issue, the magazine covers pleasure and business trips with lots of useful tidbits thrown in. Issues have featured visits to the Netherlands and Hong Kong as well as articles about food and wine. U.S. cities are highlighted in each edition, addressing sites of interest, restaurants, hotels, and clubs (including prices, addresses, and phone numbers). This title accepts no advertising, which allows for honest travel reportage. *Out & About* is a useful planning guide that should be held by any library with a travel collection. (AMK)

4261. *Passport.* 2000. bi-m. USD 19.95 United States; USD 25.95 in Canada & Mexico; USD 35.95 elsewhere. Ed(s): Reed Ide. Q Communications, Inc., 584 Castro St, Ste 521, San Francisco, CA 94114. Adv. *Aud.:* Ga.

The "gay and lesbian travel resource" *Passport* reflects the fact that travel—or at least reading glossy travel magazines—has become quite popular with gays and lesbians, for whom "new cultural experiences and interactions add depth to our lives." The editors encourage readers to write about their own travel experiences, good and bad. Similarly, feature authors present very personal narratives as they recount their adventures. Although *Passport* intends to be a "lively resource for gay and lesbian travelers who have the spirit for adventure and discovery in their blood," probably the most useful regular column is "Business Class," a brief guide to accommodations, restaurants, and entertainment in various U.S. cities for the gay business traveler. Part of any well-rounded travel collection. (MJR)

4262. *Q V Magazine: gay Latino men's journal.* [ISSN: 1522-7588] 1997. bi-m. USD 29.95; USD 4 newsstand/cover per issue. Ed(s): Demetrio Roldan. Q V Magazine, Box 9700, Long Beach, CA 90810. Adv. *Aud.:* Ga.

Q V Magazine advertises itself as "the nation's largest and most respected gay Latino magazine, a men's journal of style, culture, and entertainment, providing celebrity interviews, thought-provoking stories, and personal viewpoints—all creatively and uniquely written from the gay Latino perspective." Written entirely in English, it represents more of a fragmentation of the lifestyle magazine market than an expansion. It also includes music reviews, club listings, gay Latino resources (including the "qv website of the month"), and "qv Pen Papiz" (personal ads, with photos). If your library serves a Latino population, this title could be more appropriate than *Instinct* or *Genre*. (MJR)

Queerzine Explosion. See Zines section.

4263. *R F D: a country journal for gay men everywhere.* [ISSN: 0149-709X] 1974. q. USD 25 domestic; USD 40 foreign; USD 7.75 newsstand/cover per issue. RFD Press, PO Box 68, Liberty, TN 37095; mail@rfdmag.org. Illus., adv. Circ: 1500 Paid. *Indexed:* AltPI. *Bk. rev.:* 1-2, 400-1,000 words. *Aud.:* Ga.

RFD is as far from the urban gay scene as you can get. It reflects the collective spirit that started the journal in 1974 by offering a mix of reader-written articles on homesteading, sexuality, spirituality, and gardening, along with recipes, poetry, book reviews, and letters. The unofficial journal of the radical-faerie movement in the United States, *RFD* contains announcements and reports of faerie gatherings, "the building of a sense of community," and articles about care for the environment. The title *RFD* (from "Rural Free Delivery") is amusingly reinterpreted with each issue. Reader photos (often nude) and artwork illustrate each issue. (AMK)

Sexualities. See Sexuality section.

4264. *Transgender Community News.* [ISSN: 1523-293X] 1999. m. Individuals, USD 45; Senior citizens, USD 20; USD 8 newsstand/cover per issue domestic. Ed(s): Ms. Angela Gardner. The Renaissance Transgender Association, Inc., 987 Old Eagle School Rd, Ste 719, Wayne, PA 19087. *Aud.:* Ga.

I was immediately impressed that this newsletter contains the regular column "TG in History" by Michelle Moore, Renaissance Transgender Association Librarian. It speaks to the dual nature of *Transgender Community News,* which strives to offer both education and support. Other columns and regular features include medical advice from an M.D., shopping advice, commentary on other transgender publications, news from Renaissance chapters and affiliated support groups, and notices of newsworthy transgender events. Features may provide a lengthy review of a web site or a book, cover a social or political event, or provide a few glamorous photos. This is the product of a community definitely out to help its own. An excellent choice for libraries to support what is often a hidden population. (MJR)

4265. *Transgender Tapestry: the journal for persons interested in crossdressing & transsexualism.* Formerly: *T V - T S Tapestry.* 1978. q. USD 40; USD 55 foreign. Ed(s): Jean Marie Stine. International Foundation for Gender Education, Inc., PO Box 229, Waltham, MA 02254; IFGE@World.STD.COM. Illus., adv. Circ: 10000 Paid. *Bk. rev.:* 300-1,200 words, signed. *Aud.:* Ga.

Slickly produced, *Transgender Tapestry* is a magazine for crossdressers, transsexuals, and "anyone who does not identify with traditional gender roles or who supports freedom of gender expression." Full of pictures, helpful articles, and advice, this magazine provides a link to a community rarely represented by popular-culture titles. An issue may include an article on transgender history or child custody issues, or in-depth interviews with transgender people successfully living their lives. Especially useful are the regular columns and departments, such as "Professional Listings" and "Support Groups." This is a necessary addition for libraries that choose to represent the full spectrum of their clientele. (AMK)

4266. *Trikone Magazine: bisexual, gay and lesbian South Asians.* Formerly (until 1987): *Trikon.* [ISSN: 1042-735X] 1986. q. USD 12.95 domestic; USD 19.95 foreign; USD 3.95 newsstand/cover per issue. Ed(s): Sandip Roy. Trikone Magazine, PO Box 21354, San Jose, CA 95151-1354; trikone-web@trikone.org; http://www.trikone.org. Illus., adv. Circ: 1200 Paid. Online: OCLC Online Computer Library Center, Inc.; SoftLine Information. *Indexed:* GendWatch. *Aud.:* Hs, Ga, Ac, Sa.

Trikone (Sanskrit for "triangle") is a California-based support and social group for lesbian, gay, and bisexual South Asians. (South Asia includes Afghanistan, Bangladesh, Bhutan, Burma, India, the Maldives, Nepal, Pakistan, Sri Lanka, and Tibet.) *Trikone Magazine*, now in its second decade of publication, features articles by and about women and men of South Asian heritage in North America as well in as South Asia. Each quarterly issue includes articles exploring aspects of gay and South Asian identity, poetry and fiction, lists of resources and contacts, classified ads, and a calendar of events of interest in U.S. cities. Founded by men in San Francisco, the organization has worked toward achieving gender parity in recent years with the increased presence of women on its board of directors and coverage of women's issues. Necessary for all libraries that serve diverse populations. (MJR)

4267. *Velvet Park: dyke culture in bloom.* [ISSN: 1540-3777] bi-m. USD 21. Velvet Park Magazine, 210 Cook St., #311, Brooklyn, NY 11206; info@velvetparkmagazine.com. *Bk. rev.:* 1, 1,000 words. *Aud.:* Ga.

The tag line for *Velvet Park* is "Dyke culture in bloom." This new, stylish glossy magazine is intended for "urban lesbians, feminists, and the gay men who adore them." It presents an interesting mix of short articles, columns, and reviews (all with chic photos), covering "culture" rather broadly defined—and with some unusual choices: music (cover interview with singer-songwriter Toshi Reagon, the Michigan Womyns Music Festival), art (Kiki Smith, Elizabeth Murray, Maria Elena Gonzalez), film (film maker Ileana Pietrobruno, an interview with the cast of Almodovar's "Talk to Her"), theater (GOGA—all girl improv), culture/society (pro-anorexia web sites, female aggression, the "evolution of femme"), and even politics (Log Cabin Republicans, lesbian and gay rights to marriage). Other featured cover interviews have included comedian Margaret Cho, singer Joan Osborne, and activist-playwright Eve Ensler. Not your average glossy, *Velvet Park* deserves attention for its bold start. Particularly useful for collections needing to balance their gay male lifestyle magazine subscriptions. (MJR)

4268. *Venus Magazine.* 6x/yr. USD 19.95; USD 34.95 foreign. Cothran Publications, Inc., PO Box 150, Hastings, NY 10706; editor@venusmagazine.com; http://www.venusmagazine.com. Adv. *Bk. rev.:* 1-3, 25-100 words. *Aud.:* Hs, Ga.

Venus claims to be "the nation's only lifestyles magazine specifically for Gay and Lesbian People of African Descent." A slick, full-color, well-written product, *Venus* helps address the void of GLBT titles that represent people of color. As the web site states, "This is where People of African Descent in the Life come together to explore national events, community news, entertainment news, theater, film and literature reviews, gay travel destinations, conference updates, cocktail lounges, gossip, advice and much more." Necessary for all libraries that serve diverse populations. (AMK)

4269. *The Washington Blade: the gay weekly newspaper of the nation's capital.* [ISSN: 0278-9892] 1969. w. USD 45. Ed(s): Kristina Campbell. Window Media LLC, 1408 U St, N W, 2nd Fl, Washington, DC 20009-3916; webmaster@washblade.com; http://www.washblade.com. Illus., adv. Sample. Circ: 44000. Microform: PQC. Reprint: PQC. *Bk. rev.:* 6-8, 400-600 words. *Aud.:* Hs, Ga, Ac.

The "gay weekly of the nation's capital" is the best source of information for the gay and lesbian community of the metropolitan D.C. area. Each issue includes reports of news (politics, health, and entertainment) from around the United States and the world, as well as local news and advertising. *The Blade* provides excellent coverage of national politics as it affects the gay community, but its international coverage is equally impressive. In a surge of newspaper consolidation, the parent company of *Southern Voice* purchased *The Washington Blade*, the nation's oldest, largest gay newspaper, and its New York City counterpart *The New York Blade*. The Washington Blade Online presents selected articles free on the web, and archives for the previous three months can be searched. (AMK, MJR)

4270. *White Crane Journal: a journal exploring gay men's spirituality.* Formerly: *White Crane Newsletter.* [ISSN: 1070-5430] 1989. q. USD 14 in US & Canada; USD 20 elsewhere; USD 4 newsstand/cover per issue. Ed(s): Toby Johnson. White Crane Journal, PO Box 2762, Wimberley, TX 78676-2762; editor@whitecranejournal.com; http://www.whitecranejournal.com. Illus., adv. Sample. Circ: 425 Paid. *Bk. rev.:* 2, 150-650 words. *Aud.:* Ga.

White Crane is intended as a forum for exploring and enhancing gay men's spirituality and invites reader submissions as they "use many paths to grow spiritually and enhance their experience of life, [including] meditation, prayer, psychotherapy, service, religion, music, drugs, yoga, breathing, ritual, dream study, dressing up, dressing down, role-playing, relationships, gardening, sex, sex rituals, dancing, and more." Each issue has a number of items on a featured subject (pilgrimage, gay priests, altered states), as well as other articles, reviews, and sometimes poetry. (MJR)

4271. *Windy City Times.* [ISSN: 1049-698X] 1985. w. USD 150. Ed(s): Tracy Baim. Lambda Publications, Inc., 1115 W Belmont Ave, Ste 2D, Chicago, IL 60657-3312; outlines@suba.com; http://outlineschicago.com. Adv. Circ: 24000 Controlled. Microform: MMP. *Aud.:* Hs, Ga, Ac.

An award-winning leader in the gay and lesbian press, the *Windy City Times* merged with and incorporated *Outlines*, which has become a section focusing on viewpoints, essays, family issues, and features. The new owner, Lambda Publications, also produces *BLACKlines* and *En La Vida*. These potent combined forces report on Chicago, Midwestern, national, and world politics, events, news, and nearly everything else of interest to a general lesbian and gay community. One of the top gay and lesbian local news organizations in the country, recommended for all libraries everywhere. (MJR)

4272. *Women in the Life.* [ISSN: 1526-7202] 1993. q. USD 20. Ed(s): Sheila Alexander-Reid. Women in the Life, 1623 Connecticut Ave NW, Rear Carriage House, Washington, DC 20009. *Aud.:* Hs, Ga, Ac, Sa.

Women in the Life is a vibrant title that represents the power, the poetry, and the day-to-day concerns of our African American sisters. Articles run the spectrum from Florida's vote-count problems to Iraq war critiques to poems and short stories. A rich mix of good and good-for-you articles focused on the concerns of African American lesbians, this title is affordable enough to be included in all public libraries with a diverse audience. (AMK)

4273. *XY Magazine.* 1996. 10x/yr. USD 40 domestic; CND 75 Canada; USD 65 Mexico. Ed(s): Peter Ian Cummings. XY Media, Ltd., 4104 24th St, Ste 900, San Francisco, CA 94114-3615; xypost@xy.com; http://www.xy.com. Illus., adv. *Bk. rev.:* 7-12, 50-500 words. *Aud.:* Hs, Ga, Ac.

XY Magazine is a provocative and stylish publication intended for gay men in their teens and twenties (less than 25 percent of its readers are under 18, according to the editor). Written for, and often by, the youth culture, the influence of the Internet is all over this magazine, both in content and design. Diverse and provocative (meaning both titillating and confrontational), the glossy, photo-heavy pages have a high-energy, irreverent style, whatever issues are being addressed: coming out, sex, relationships, health, fashion, or music. The tone consistently borders on impatience with "the socially repressive superstructure." Public libraries should expect this magazine to be challenged by (some) adults and stolen by youths. (MJR)

Electronic Journals

4274. *BLACKlines: expressions from black gay, lesbian, bisexual & transgendered life.* 1994. m. Free in Chiago. Ed(s): Tracy Baim. Lambda Publications, Inc., 1115 W Belmont Ave, Ste 2D, Chicago, IL 60657-3312; outlines@suba.com; http://outlineschicago.com. *Aud.:* Ga.

In addition to covering local Chicago news and events, *BLACKlines* includes arts, entertainment, political, and black GLBT community news and reviews from around the country. The association with *Windy City Times* and the transfer of this periodical to the web help to continue its much-needed outreach, as this community is underserved in most other periodicals in this section. (MJR)

4275. *Blithe House Quarterly: a site for gay short fiction.* 1997. q. Free. Ed(s): Aldo Adalvarez. Blithe House Quarterly, adalvarez@aol.com; http://www.blithe.com. *Aud.:* Ga.

Blithe House Quarterly publishes six to ten short stories of 1,500 to 7,500 words in each issue. The web site showcases a diversity of style, tone, point of view, and subject, by gay, lesbian, bisexual, or transgendered authors, established or emerging. In addition to its interest in fiction, it is also seeking "critical essays on the lesbigay short story." While not everyone will like every story, there should be something here for just about anyone. As the web site proclaims, "We publish lesbian, gay, bisexual and transgendered fiction not as a genre or ghetto, but as a literature that can stand by any other in its quality and innovation." (AMK, MJR)

4276. *Electronic Gay Community Magazine.* 1988. d. Free. Electronic Gay Community Magazine, http://www.awes.com/egcm. *Aud.:* Hs, Ga, Ac.

"Reaching thousands of gay men and lesbian women with the speed of electronic communications, the goal of the *Electronic Gay Community Magazine* has been to entertain, educate and inform." The initial idealism of the web survives here in that there is no subscription fee, anyone may submit an article, and there is no copyright fee. It also features the unfortunate design elements of earlier web sites, even as the content perseveres. The magazine has departments that feature politics, legal news, editorials, campus news, and more. Published since 1988, it is the world's longest running electronic publication for the GLBT community. This site is more like an unsubstantiated newspaper in the breadth and length of its articles. Very informative and (particularly for the price) nearly perfect—if only they'd date the articles. (AMK)

4277. *En La Vida: voces de lesbians, gays, bisexuales y transgeneros latinos.* 8x/yr. USD 8. Ed(s): Jean Albright. Lambda Publications, Inc., 1115 W Belmont Ave, Ste 2D, Chicago, IL 60657-3312; http://www.outlineschicago.com/enlavida.html. *Aud.:* Ga.

Like its sister web site *BLACKlines*, *En La Vida* provides news, features, entertainment, and community resources for the Latino/a community. It is also based in Chicago and associated with *Windy City Times*. It is an important outreach to an underserved community. (MJR)

4278. *Gay Law Net.* Formerly: *Gay Law News.* m. Free. Ed(s): David B Allan. Gay Law Net, gaylawnet@labyrinth.net.au; http://www.gaylawnet.com/. *Aud.:* Hs, Ga, Ac.

Gay Law Net is where I would send anybody beginning a search for legal help. The inclusive web site has an FAQ section, current news, and information on a multitude of legal issues, legislation, links, and more. Most helpful are the worldwide attorney listings. They are marked as being lesbian, gay, etc., themselves or as gay-friendly. As the web site claims, "*Gay Law Net* is dedicated to providing general information and resources concerning the law as it affects the global gay, lesbian, bisexual, transsexual and intersex (GLBTI) community." While a redesign would be wonderful, the content transgresses the sickly pink design elements. (AMK)

Genders. See Women: Feminist and Special Interest/Electronic Journals section.

Intersections. See Women: Feminist and Special Interest/Electronic Journals section.

4279. *Oasis.* 1995. m. Free. Ed(s): Jeff Walsh. Oasis, PO Box 626, Largo, FL 33779-0626; jeff@oasismag.com; http://www.oasismag.com. *Aud.:* Hs, Ga.

Profiles, news, events, arts, entertainment, interviews, advice, and regular columns written by high school and college students from all across the United States—*Oasis* has it all, as "a writing community for queer and questioning youth." Young adults will want—and deserve to have—this resource clearly focused on their issues and in their language. (MJR)

Sexing the Political. See Women: Feminist and Special Interest/ Electronic Journals section.

4280. *Trans-Health: the online magazine of health and fitness for transsexual and transgendered people.* 2001. q. Trans-Health, info@trans-health.com; http://www.trans-health.com. *Aud.:* Hs, Ga, Ac, Sa.

Trans-Health, the quarterly online magazine devoted exclusively to the health and fitness concerns of transgendered people, began when three people came together to write a journal that would present articles similar to those seen in men's and women's fitness magazines. The twist is that this title is aimed specifically at the concerns of transgendered people. The journal raises important issues and supports a core audience that is not always welcomed in gyms or HMOs. (AMK)

4281. *Whosoever: an online magazine for gay, lesbian, bisexual and transgendered christians.* 1996. bi-m. Free. Ed(s): Candace L Chellew. Whosoever, editor@whosoever.org; http://www.whosoever.org. *Aud.:* Hs, Ga, Ac.

Whosoever "is an online magazine dedicated to the spiritual growth of gay, lesbian, bisexual and transgendered Christians. Every other month, *Whosoever* takes a look at issues affecting gay, lesbian, bisexual, and transgendered Christians, and how they can respond to the world with the love of Christ." It includes links to other resources, prayer requests, action alerts, a bookstore, and more. This site will be of great interest to religious collections and Christian patrons. (AMK, MJR)

■ LIBRARY AND INFORMATION SCIENCE

See also Archives and Manuscripts; Bibliography; Books and Book Reviews; Printing and Graphic Arts; and Serials sections.

Miriam Tuliao, Senior Librarian, Office of Adult Services, New York Public Library, New York, NY 10016; mtuliao@nypl.org

Cheryl LaGuardia, Head of Instructional Services for the Harvard College Library, Widener Library, Research Services, Harvard University, Cambridge, MA 02138; claguard@fas.harvard.edu

Introduction

The aim of this section is to present a core collection of library journals for professionals working in various arenas, such as public libraries, school library media centers, information centers, and academic libraries. The majority of publications focus on one of three primary aspects of library work: user services, technical services, and administrative services. Many publications follow developments in information technology, publishing, and the media. Additionally, most journals address professional priorities, including the development of resource sharing; the development of library professionals; and the promotion of standards, guidelines, and best practices. Only English-language publications are included.

Basic Periodicals

Ems: *Library Media Connection, School Library Journal, School Library Media Research, Teacher Librarian Journal;* Hs: *School Library Journal, Teacher Librarian Journal, Young Adult Library Services;* Ga: *ALCTS Newsletter Online, American Libraries, Library Journal;* Ac: *American Libraries, College & Research Libraries, College & Research Libraries News, Journal of Academic Librarianship, Library Journal, Library Resources & Technical Services.*

Basic Abstracts and Indexes

Information Science Abstracts, Library and Information Science Abstracts, Library Literature.

4282. ***A R L: a bimonthly report on research library issues and actions.*** Formerly (until 1990): *A R L Newsletter.* [ISSN: 1050-6098] 1965. bi-m. Members, USD 25; Non-members, USD 50. Ed(s): Jaia Barrett. Association of Research Libraries, 21 Dupont Circle, Ste 800, Washington, DC 20036; pubs@arl.org; http://www.arl.org/newsltr. Illus. Circ: 1000. Online: H.W. Wilson. *Indexed:* LibLit, PAIS. *Aud.:* Ac, Sa.

This resource reports on news and developments affecting higher education and the library world. Issues present articles on scholarly communication, copyright, collection management, access and delivery services, cultural diversity, and federal relations. The publication fully articulates and promotes the professional concerns of research librarians and administrators. Recommended for academic and special libraries.

4283. ***Against the Grain: linking publishers, vendors and librarians.*** [ISSN: 1043-2094] 1989. bi-m. USD 40 domestic; USD 50 Canada; USD 60 elsewhere. Ed(s): Katina Strauch. Against the Grain, LLC, 209 Richardson Ave., MSC 98, The Citadel, Charleston, SC 29409. Illus., adv. Sample. Circ: 2100. Vol. ends: Dec/Jan. *Indexed:* CIJE, InfoSAb, LibLit. *Bk. rev.:* 10-20, 100-500 words. *Aud.:* Ga, Ac, Sa.

This unique journal publishes current news about libraries, book jobbers, publishers, and subscription agents. Each bimonthly issue includes book reviews, relevant reports on legal issues, bookselling, technology, international news, and lively profiles and interviews. Recent articles consider digital scholarship, copyright, outsourcing, marketing, collection development, and customer service. Full of information about the publishing industry and acquisition business, this magazine is recommended for academic and public libraries.

4284. ***American Libraries.*** Formerly: *A L A Bulletin.* [ISSN: 0002-9769] 1907. m. 11/yr. USD 60. Ed(s): Leonard Kniffel. American Library Association, 50 E Huron St, Chicago, IL 60611-2795; http://www.ala.org. Illus., index, adv. Circ: 64872 Paid and controlled. Vol. ends: Jan. Microform: NBI; PMC; PQC. Online: bigchalk; The Dialog Corporation; EBSCO Publishing; Florida Center for Library Automation; Gale Group; OCLC Online Computer Library Center, Inc.; ProQuest Information & Learning; H.W. Wilson. Reprint: PQC. *Indexed:* ABS&EES, ASIP, AgeL, BEL&L, BRI, CBRI, CIJE, CINAHL, ConsI, EduInd, IBZ, InfoSAb, LISA, LRI, LibLit, MRD, MagInd, PAIS, RGPR, RI-1. *Aud.:* Ga, Ac, Sa.

This journal of the American Library Association (ALA) publishes practical articles and news of interest to its members and other library and information professionals. The monthly provides extensive coverage of the association's activities and goals. Issues relevant to the profession are considered, such as intellectual freedom, collection development, technology, pay equity, and library education. Regular columns review books and professional literature, provide a readers' forum, report on national and international library news, and list sources for library job openings. The journal provides information about ALA-sponsored events and conferences. An essential publication for all libraries.

4285. ***American Society for Information Science and Technology. Journal.*** Former titles (until 2000): *American Society for Information Science. Journal;* (until 1970): *American Documentation;* (until 1942): *Journal of Documentary Reproduction.* [ISSN: 1532-2882] 1938. 14x/yr. USD 1650 domestic; USD 1790 in Canada & Mexico; USD 1909 elsewhere. Ed(s): Donald H Kraft. John Wiley & Sons, Inc., 111 River St, Hoboken, NJ 07030; uscs-wis@wiley.com; http://www.wiley.com. Illus., index, adv. Refereed. Circ: 4800. Microform: PQC. Online: EBSCO Publishing; Gale Group; Wiley InterScience. Reprint: PSC; RPI. *Indexed:* ABIn, ABS&EES, AgeL, C&ISA, CIJE, ChemAb, CompR, EngInd, ExcerpMed, GeoRef, InfoSAb, LISA, LibLit, MLA-IB, PAIS, PollutAb, SCI, SSCI, SWR&A. *Aud.:* Ga, Ac, Sa.

The official journal of the American Society for Information Science and Technology (ASIST) provides scholarly research articles to its members and other professionals in the information science field. Theme issues have addressed such topics as the history of documentation and information science, emerging information systems applications, social informatics, and human-computer interaction. The publication includes book reviews, opinion papers, European research letters, and student papers. Recommended for information science professionals.

4286. ***American Society for Information Science. Bulletin.*** Supersedes: *A S I S Newsletter;* Former titles: *American Documentation Institute. Newsletter; American Society for Information Science. Newsletter.* [ISSN: 0095-4403] 1974. bi-m. Members, USD 19; Non-members, USD 60; USD 10 newsstand/cover per issue. Ed(s): Irene Travis. American Society for Information Science & Technology, 1320 Fenwick Ln, Ste 510, Silver Spring, MD 20910; http://www.asis.org. Illus., adv. Circ: 4500. Microform: PQC. Online: Gale Group; OCLC Online Computer Library Center, Inc.; ProQuest Information & Learning. Reprint: PQC. *Indexed:* ABIn, ABS&EES, CIJE, CINAHL, EngInd, GeoRef, InfoSAb, LISA, LRI, LibLit, MagInd, PAIS, SSCI, SWR&A. *Aud.:* Ga, Ac, Sa.

This news magazine of the American Society for Information Science and Technology (ASIST) publishes articles of interest to its members, including concentrated coverage of the association's activities and its annual conference. Each issue is dedicated to a particular topic, such as telecommunications, law, digital libraries, and the knowledge network. Recent articles include "The Semantic Web: More than a Vision," "Metadata: A Fundamental Component of the Semantic Web," and "An Overview of W3C Semantic Web Activity." Recommended for information science and technology professionals in academic and special libraries.

4287. ***Art Documentation: bulletin of the Art Libraries Society of North America.*** Supersedes (in 1981): *A R L I S - N A Newsletter.* [ISSN: 0730-7187] 1972. s-a. USD 80 (Individuals, USD 65). Ed(s): Stephanie Sigala, Elizabeth Peck Learned. Art Libraries Society of North America, 329 March Rd., Ste 232, Box 11, Kanata, ON K2K 2E1, Canada; arlisna@igs.net; http://afalib.uflib.edu/arlis/publications/publications-print.html. Illus., adv. Refereed. Circ: 1400. Microform: PQC. Online: OCLC Online Computer Library Center, Inc.; H.W. Wilson. *Indexed:* ABM, BHA, DAAI, LISA, LibLit. *Aud.:* Ga, Ac, Sa.

The Arts Libraries Society of North America (ARLIS/NA) publishes this journal to report on the issues and trends affecting the field of art librarianship. It provides a forum for the discussion of art documentation issues and topics relevant to art librarianship and visual resources curatorship. Recent articles consider digital projects, archived architectural records, and American museum and university collections. The book reviews are cogent and helpful with collection development. A highly recommended art publication for public, academic, and special libraries.

4288. ***The Bottom Line: managing library finances.*** [ISSN: 0888-045X] q. EUR 1129.91 in Europe; USD 1039 in North America; AUD 1299 in Australasia. Ed(s): James H Walther. Emerald, 60-62 Toller Ln, Bradford, BD8 9BY, United Kingdom; info@emeraldinsight.com; http://www.emeraldinsight.com/journals/. Sample. Refereed. Online: Pub.; EBSCO Publishing; Gale Group; LexisNexis; Northern Light Technology, Inc.; OCLC Online Computer Library Center, Inc.; ProQuest Information & Learning; RoweCom Information Quest; Swets Blackwell. Reprint: PSC. *Indexed:* InfoSAb, LISA, LibLit. *Aud.:* Ga, Ac, Sa.

This journal serves an audience of librarians and library trustees and managers. The publication addresses issues related to the finance of library operations, including cost measurement, development, resource allocation, and fiscal policies and procedures. Recent articles consider government agencies, lobbying, human resources management, academic libraries, and management techniques. Regular departments focus on economics, fund raising, financial issues, and book reviews. Highly recommended for all types of libraries.

4289. ***The Charleston Advisor: critical reviews of Web products for information professionals.*** [ISSN: 1525-4011] 1999. q. USD 295 (Individuals, USD 295; USD 495 others). Ed(s): Rebecca T Lenzini. The Charleston Company, 618 South Monroe Way, Denver, CO 80209; rlenzini@charlestonco.com; http://www.charlestonco.com. Adv. Sample. Circ: 750 Paid. *Indexed:* InfoSAb. *Aud.:* Ga, Ac, Sa.

The Charleston Advisor provides exceptional reviews of web-based electronic resources. Every online product is critically examined based on four elements: content, searchability, price, and contract provisions. Its comparative reviews on journal and research databases are thorough and informative. As libraries continue to make greater use of electronic resources, this publication will become an essential selection tool for web-based and other electronic information sources.

4290. ***Collection Building.*** [ISSN: 0160-4953] 1978. q. EUR 1129.91 in Europe; USD 1039 in North America; AUD 1299 in Australasia. Ed(s): Kay Ann Cassell. Emerald, 60-62 Toller Ln, Bradford, BD8 9BY, United Kingdom; info@emeraldinsight.com; http://www.emeraldinsight.com/journals/. Refereed. Online: Pub.; EBSCO Publishing; OCLC Online Computer Library Center, Inc.; ProQuest Information & Learning; RoweCom Information Quest; Swets Blackwell. Reprint: PSC. *Indexed:* InfoSAb, LISA, LibLit. *Aud.:* Ga, Ac, Sa.

This journal's stated purpose is to publish authoritative and practical information on collection development and maintenance. Feature articles are timely, thoughtful, and well researched. Topics include electronic publishing, distance learning, funding, reference linking, and digital preservation. Regular departments feature conference reports and reviews of books and online resources. A focused journal and essential management tool for all library professionals who build or maintain resource collections.

4291. ***College & Research Libraries.*** [ISSN: 0010-0870] 1939. bi-m. USD 60 domestic; USD 65 in Canada & Mexico; USD 70 elsewhere. Ed(s): William Gray Potter. Association of College and Research Libraries, 50 East Huron St, Chicago, IL 60611; acrl@ala.org; http://www.ala.org/acrl. Illus., index, adv. Sample. Refereed. Circ: 13000. Vol. ends: Nov. Microform: PQC. Online: bigchalk; OCLC Online Computer Library Center, Inc.; H.W. Wilson. Reprint: PQC; PSC. *Indexed:* ArtHuCI, BEL&L, BRD, BRI, CBRI, CIJE, ChemAb, EduInd, HEA, IBZ, InfoSAb, LISA, LibLit, LingAb, MLA-IB, MusicInd, PAIS, SCI, SSCI. *Aud.:* Ac, Sa.

A publication of the American Library Association's Association of College Research and Libraries, *C&RL* presents thoughtful discussions of the issues affecting academic and research librarians. With usually six articles per issue, the journal covers professional education program models, case studies, and descriptive narratives about policies and programming. Figures, tables, and notes support the research methodology. Recent articles consider database vendors, library instruction, collection management, electronic journals, and faculty/librarian partnerships. An important title for academic and special libraries.

4292. ***College & Research Libraries News.*** [ISSN: 0099-0086] 1966. m. 11/yr. Non-members, USD 40; USD 6.50 newsstand/cover per issue. Association of College and Research Libraries, 50 East Huron St, Chicago, IL 60611; acrl@ala.org; http://www.ala.org/acrl. Illus., adv. Sample. Circ: 10500. Vol. ends: Dec. Online: OCLC Online Computer Library Center, Inc.; H.W. Wilson. Reprint: PQC. *Indexed:* A&ATA, ABS&EES, CIJE, ConsI, InfoSAb, LISA, LibLit, PAIS, RI-1, SCI. *Aud.:* Ac, Sa.

As the official publication of record of the Association of College & Research Libraries (ACRL), *CR&L News* provides a forum for the discussion of issues affecting the management of academic and research libraries. The journal includes current information on the association's activities and reports on technology, conferences, user services, government actions, and reviews of print and electronic resources. Recent articles cover information literacy initiatives, educational technology, and the impact of the USA Patriot legislation. Recommended for all academic and research libraries.

4293. ***Computers in Libraries.*** Formerly (until 1989): *Small Computers in Libraries;* Which incorporated (1986-1988): *Systems Librarian and Automation Review;* (1985-1987): *Bulletin Board Systems;* And (1986-1987): *Public Computing.* [ISSN: 1041-7915] 1981. 10x/yr. USD 98.95 domestic; USD 113 in Canada & Mexico; USD 123 elsewhere. Ed(s): Kathy Dempsey. Information Today, Inc., 143 Old Marlton Pike, Medford, NJ 08055-8750; custserv@infotoday.com; http://www.infotoday.com. Illus., index, adv. Circ: 6000. Vol. ends: Dec. Online: bigchalk; EBSCO Publishing; Florida Center for Library Automation; Gale Group; NewsNet; Northern Light Technology, Inc.; OCLC Online Computer Library Center, Inc.; ProQuest Information & Learning; H.W. Wilson. Reprint: WSH. *Indexed:* B&I, CIJE, CINAHL, CLI, CompLI, EngInd, IBZ, ILP, InfoSAb, LISA, LibLit, MRD, MagInd, MicrocompInd. *Aud.:* Ac, Sa.

This reader-friendly magazine publishes general and practical technical articles on library information technology. Recent issues include discussions of remote patron validation, digital collections, staff training, and virtual reference services. Recommended for academic and special libraries.

4294. ***D T T P.*** Formerly (until 1974): *Documents to the People.* [ISSN: 0091-2085] 1972. q. USD 30 in North America; USD 40 elsewhere. Ed(s): John A Shuler. American Library Association, 50 E Huron St, Chicago, IL 60611-2795; http://www.ala.org. Illus., adv. Circ: 2000. Vol. ends: Dec. Reprint: PQC. *Indexed:* LibLit. *Aud.:* Ac, Sa.

The official publication of ALA's Government Documents Roundtable (GODORT) publishes news of interest to its members and other library and information professionals. This quarterly provides extensive coverage of the roundtable's activities and goals. It considers such issues relevant to the profession as patents, electronic competencies, government activities, and regulatory and legislative issues. Additionally, the publication features technical reports and maps at the local, state, national, and international levels. Essential professional reading for documents librarians.

4295. ***Information Outlook.*** Formerly (until 1997): *Special Libraries.* [ISSN: 1091-0808] 1910. m. USD 125. Ed(s): Leslie Shaver. Special Libraries Association, 1700 18th St, N W, Washington, DC 20009-2514; http://www.sla.org. Illus., index, adv. Circ: 16000. Microform: PQC. Online: bigchalk; Florida Center for Library Automation; Gale Group; Northern Light Technology, Inc.; OCLC Online Computer Library Center, Inc.; ProQuest Information & Learning. Reprint: PQC; PSC. *Indexed:* ABIn, ABM, BAS, BPI, BRI, CBRI, CIJE, CINAHL, CompLI, ConsI, IBZ, InfoSAb, LISA, LibLit, MagInd, MicrocompInd, PAIS, SCI, SSCI. *Aud.:* Ac, Sa.

This monthly journal of the Special Libraries Association reports on issues and trends affecting the field of information management and technology. Feature articles focus on such issues as information architecture, knowledge management, budgeting, copyright, marketing, and innovation. Regular columns include conference updates, discussions of copyright issues, "Communications Outlook" and "Information Trends." Recommended for special libraries.

4296. ***Information Technology and Libraries.*** Formerly (until 1982): *Journal of Library Automation.* [ISSN: 0730-9295] 1968. q. Non-members, USD 50; USD 15 newsstand/cover per issue. Ed(s): Dan Marmion. American Library Association, 50 E Huron St, Chicago, IL 60611-2795; http://www.ala.org. Illus., index, adv. Refereed. Circ: 7000 Controlled. Vol. ends: Mar. Microform: PQC. Online: bigchalk; Florida Center for Library Automation; Gale Group; OCLC Online Computer Library Center, Inc.; ProQuest Information & Learning; H.W. Wilson. Reprint: PQC. *Indexed:* ABIn, ABS&EES, ArtHuCI, CIJE, CINAHL, ChemAb, CompLI, CompR, ConsI, EduInd, IBZ, InfoSAb, LISA, LibLit, MagInd, PAIS, SSCI. *Bk. rev.:* Various number, 300-500 words, signed. *Aud.:* Ac, Sa.

The Library and Information Technology Division of the American Library Association publishes this journal to report on issues affecting its members and other library professionals. The publication addresses issues related to library and information technology, including electronic publishing, digital libraries, bibliographic systems, and universal access. The journal presents software reviews, feature articles, communications, tutorials, and letters to the editor. Recent articles include "Library Systems and Unicode: A Review of the Current State of Development," "An Empirical Analysis of Web Catalog User Experiences," and "E2M: Automatic Generation of MARC-Formatted Metadata by Crawling E-Publications." Recommended for information science and technology professionals.

4297. ***The Journal of Academic Librarianship: articles, features, and book reviews for the academic library professional.*** [ISSN: 0099-1333] 1975. bi-m. EUR 227 (Qualified personnel, EUR 90). Ed(s): David Kohl. Pergamon, The Boulevard, Langford Ln, East Park, Kidlington, OX5 1GB, United Kingdom. Illus., index, adv. Refereed. Circ: 3000. Vol. ends: Nov. Microform: PQC. Online: EBSCO Publishing; ingenta.com; OCLC Online Computer Library Center, Inc.; ScienceDirect; Swets Blackwell; H.W. Wilson. Reprint: PQC. *Indexed:* ABS&EES, AgeL, ArtHuCI, CBRI, CIJE, ConsI, EduInd, IBZ, InfoSAb, LISA, LibLit, SSCI. *Aud.:* Ac, Sa.

This international publication focuses on the practices, trends, and issues affecting college and research libraries. The journal features bibliographic essays and valuable reviews of current professional literature. Recent articles consider the design and evaluation of web sites, engaged library instruction, online fund raising, distance education, and virtual reference services. An important title for academic libraries.

4298. ***Journal of Information Ethics.*** [ISSN: 1061-9321] 1992. s-a. USD 38 domestic; USD 44 foreign; USD 21 newsstand/cover per issue. Ed(s): Robert Hauptman. McFarland & Company, Inc., PO Box 611, Jefferson, NC 28640. Illus., adv. Refereed. *Indexed:* IBZ, InfoSAb, LISA, LibLit, PhilInd, RI-1, SSCI. *Bk. rev.:* 5-7, 800-1,200 words, signed. *Aud.:* Ac, Sa.

This semi-annual publication addresses a broad range of ethical issues relevant to library and information science. Topic coverage includes professional education, censorship, cyberspace, computer security, and information liability approached from philosophical, theoretical, and applied perspectives. Recent articles include "Ethical Concerns Raised by the Use of the Internet," "Moral Conflict for the Film Librarian," and "Ethical Considerations in Citing Scientific Literature and Using Citation Analysis in Evaluation of Research Performance." An important publication for professional and library science collections.

4299. ***Journal of Youth Services in Libraries.*** Formerly (until 1987): *Top of the News.* [ISSN: 0894-2498] 1946. q. USD 40 domestic; USD 50 foreign; USD 12 newsstand/cover. Ed(s): Linda Waddle, Laura Schulte-Cooper. American Library Association, 50 E Huron St, Chicago, IL 60611-2795; http://www.ala.org. Illus., adv. Refereed. Circ: 7000 Paid. Vol. ends: Fall. Microform: PQC. Online: OCLC Online Computer Library Center, Inc.; H.W. Wilson. Reprint: PQC. *Indexed:* BRI, CBRI, CIJE, EduInd, LISA, LibLit, MRD. *Aud.:* Ems, Hs, Ac.

The official journal of two ALA divisions, this publication includes news, columns, bibliographic essays, refereed feature articles, and reviews of professional reading. The articles cover diverse topics and are timely. Typical of ALA divisional journals, this is of high quality and is highly recommended for school and public library professional collections.

4300. ***Law Library Journal.*** [ISSN: 0023-9283] 1908. q. Members, USD 110. Ed(s): Frank Houdek. American Association of Law Libraries, 53 W Jackson Blvd, Ste 940, Chicago, IL 60604; http://bubl.ac.uk/journals/lis/kn/llj/. Illus., index, adv. Refereed. Circ: 5500. Vol. ends: Fall. Microform: PMC. Online: Gale Group; LexisNexis. Reprint: WSH. *Indexed:* ArtHuCI, CJA, CLI, ConsI, ILP, InfoSAb, LISA, LRI, LibLit, SSCI. *Aud.:* Ac, Sa.

As the official journal of the American Associaton of Law Libraries, this quarterly features scholarly articles on law and librarianship. It reports on topics of interest and concern to law librarians, including acquisition, collection development, patron services, and the effects of developing technology on law libraries. Association news and book reviews are included. An essential title for law librarians and legal reference service providers.

4301. ***Libraries & Culture: a journal of library history.*** Former titles: *Journal of Library History, Philosophy and Comparative Librarianship; Journal of Library History. State Library History Bibliography Series.* [ISSN: 0894-8631] 1966. q. USD 77 (Individuals, USD 38). Ed(s): Donald G Davis, Jr. University of Texas Press, Journals Division, 2100 Comal, Austin, TX 78722; journals@uts.cc.utexas.edu; http://www.utexas.edu/utpress/journals/journals.html. Illus., index, adv. Refereed. Circ: 800. Vol. ends: Nov. Microform: PQC. Online: EBSCO Publishing; Florida Center for Library Automation; Gale Group; OCLC Online Computer Library Center, Inc.; Project MUSE; ProQuest Information & Learning; RoweCom Information Quest; Swets Blackwell. Reprint: PQC; PSC. *Indexed:* ABS&EES, AmH&L, BRI, CBRI, ConsI, IBZ, LISA, LibLit, MLA-IB, RI-1, SSCI. *Bk. rev.:* 15-20, 500-1,200 words, signed. *Aud.:* Ac, Sa.

The stated purpose of this journal is to examine the significance of books and libraries in the context of social and cultural history. Recent articles include "The American Library Association in Latin America: American Librarianship as a 'Modern' Model during the Good Neighbor Policy Era," "Returning Jewish Cultural Property: The Handling of Books Looted by the Nazis in the American Zone of Occupation, 1945 to 1952," and "Activism in Library Development: Women's Studies at Rutgers University." The book review section is discerning, critical, and scholarly. A noteworthy interdisciplinary publication.

4302. ***Library Administration and Management.*** Former titles (until 1986): *L A M A Newsletter; L A D Newsletter.* [ISSN: 0888-4463] 1975. q. USD 55 in North America; USD 65 elsewhere; USD 15 newsstand/cover per issue. Ed(s): Robert F Moran, Jr. American Library Association, 50 E Huron St, Chicago, IL 60611-2795; http://www.ala.org. Illus., adv. Circ: 6000. Vol. ends: Winter. Microform: PQC. Online: OCLC Online Computer Library Center, Inc.; H.W. Wilson. Reprint: PQC. *Indexed:* CIJE, InfoSAb, LISA, LibLit. *Aud.:* Ac, Sa.

The official journal of the American Library Association's Library Administration and Management division, this publication is designed to address the daily challenges faced by library administrators and managers. Written by subject experts and practitioners in the library science field, the articles are timely and provide practical advice. Covered topics include the assessment of customer demands, library staff development, job satisfaction, library security, and technology competencies. Highly recommended for professional collections.

4303. ***Library Journal.*** Former titles (until 1976): *L J (Library Journal);* (until 1974): *Library Journal.* [ISSN: 0363-0277] 1876. 20x/yr. USD 134 domestic; USD 155 Canada; USD 210 elsewhere. Ed(s): John Berry. Reed Business Information, 360 Park Ave South, New York, NY 10010; http://www.reedbusiness.com. Illus., index, adv. Sample. Refereed. Circ: 23500. Vol. ends: Dec. Microform: CIS; NBI; RPI; PMC. Online: bigchalk; EBSCO Publishing; Florida Center for Library Automation; Gale Group; LexisNexis; OCLC Online Computer Library Center, Inc.; ProQuest Information & Learning; H.W. Wilson. Reprint: PQC. *Indexed:* ABIn, ABS&EES, AIAP, ASIP, AgeL, ArtHuCI, BAS, BRD, BRI, CBRI, CIJE, CINAHL, ConsI, EduInd, GardL, InfoSAb, LISA, LRI, LibLit, MLA-IB, MRD, MagInd, PAIS, PRA, RI-1, RILM, SSCI. *Aud.:* Ga, Ac, Sa.

Library Journal is the library world's ultimate resource for news and information. Each issue features commentary, technology news, timely articles, and hundreds of evaluative reviews of books, magazines, audio, video, and online products. Recent issues covered such topics as collection development, urban libraries, the automated system marketplace, pay equity, and medical librarianship. A required standard for all libraries.

4304. ***Library Management.*** Incorporates: *Librarian Career Development;* Formerly: *Library Research Occasional Paper.* [ISSN: 0143-5124] 1976. 9x/yr. EUR 11830.91 in Europe; USD 10784 in North America; AUD

13299 in Australasia. Ed(s): Stephen O'Connor. Emerald, 60-62 Toller Ln, Bradford, BD8 9BY, United Kingdom; info@emeraldinsight.com; http://www.emeraldinsight.com/journals/. Refereed. Online: Pub.; EBSCO Publishing; OCLC Online Computer Library Center, Inc.; ProQuest Information & Learning; RoweCom Information Quest; Swets Blackwell. Reprint: PSC; SWZ. *Indexed:* ABIn, InfoSAb, LISA, LibLit. *Aud.:* Ac, Sa.

This journal is dedicated to publishing articles that discuss strategy and innovative developments in library management. With a target audience of managers and academics in the library science field, the publication provides authoritative, international perspectives on the management of information and library services. Topic coverage includes consortia building, leadership, information technology, organizational change, and performance measurement. An essential management tool for library professionals.

4305. ***Library Media Connection: magazine for secondary school library media and technology specialists.*** Formerly: *The Book Report.* [ISSN: 1542-4715] 1982. bi-m. during school yr. USD 49 domestic; USD 67 Canada; USD 71 elsewhere. Ed(s): Carol Simpson. Linworth Publishing, Inc., 480 E. Wilson Bridge Rd., Ste. L, Worthington, OH 43085; linworth@linworthpublishing.com; http://www.linworth.com. Illus., adv. Circ: 20000. Vol. ends: May. Microform: PQC. Reprint: PQC. *Indexed:* BRI, CBRI, CIJE, EduInd, ICM, LibLit, MRD. *Aud.:* Ems, Hs.

This resource provides practical articles, tips, news, and teaching strategies authored by leaders in the library field. The publication offers current information on research, testing, and curriculum planning. Topics explored include bilingual library programming, reading incentives, advocacy, information literacy, technology, and copyright issues. Recommended as a valuable resource for school librarians and library media specialists.

4306. ***Library Mosaics: the magazine for support staff.*** [ISSN: 1054-9676] 1989. bi-m. USD 23 domestic; USD 35 Canada; USD 49 elsewhere. Ed(s): Charles Fox. Yenor, Inc., PO Box 5171, Culver City, CA 90231; rroney@librarymosaics.com; http://www.librarymosaics.com. Illus., adv. Refereed. Circ: 5000 Paid. Vol. ends: Dec. *Indexed:* LISA, LibLit. *Aud.:* Ga, Ac, Sa.

Addressing library, media, and information center support staff, this bimonthly provides articles on special topics, such as reference desk partnering, certification, disaster planning, and equity, as well as practical articles related to support staff roles. Each issue includes news, book and technology reviews, classifieds, support staff profiles, and conference reports from the American Library Association. Recommended for all staff collections.

4307. ***The Library Quarterly.*** [ISSN: 0024-2519] 1931. q. USD 120 print & online eds. (Individuals, USD 40 print & online eds.; Students, USD 30 print & online eds.). Ed(s): Wayne A Wiegand, John C Bertot. University of Chicago Press, Journals Division, PO Box 37005, Chicago, IL 60637; subscriptions@press.uchicago.edu; http://www.journals.uchicago.edu. Illus., index, adv. Refereed. Circ: 1500. Vol. ends: Oct. Microform: MIM; PMC; PQC. Online: EBSCO Publishing; Florida Center for Library Automation; Gale Group; ProQuest Information & Learning. Reprint: ISI; PQC; PSC. *Indexed:* ABS&EES, AgeL, AmH&L, ArtHuCI, BAS, BRD, BRI, CBRI, CIJE, ChemAb, IBZ, InfoSAb, LISA, LibLit, MagInd, PAIS, RI-1, SSCI. *Bk. rev.:* 12-15, 800-1,200 words. *Aud.:* Ac, Sa.

This scholarly journal is committed to the publication of informed research in all aspects of librarianship. Contributors from academicians to librarians cover a broad range of library science topics, including the sociology of knowledge, bibliographic control, cognitive processes and information-seeking behavior, scientific communication, and classification research. Each issue includes critical reviews of books, CD-ROMs, and software. Recommended for academic libraries.

4308. ***Library Resources & Technical Services.*** Formed by the merger of: *Serial Slants; Journal of Cataloging and Classification.* [ISSN: 0024-2527] 1957. q. Non-members, USD 55; USD 15 newsstand/cover per issue. American Library Association, 50 E Huron St, Chicago, IL 60611-2795; http://www.ala.org. Illus., adv. Sample. Refereed. Circ: 6756 Paid and free. Vol. ends: Jan. Microform: PQC. Online: Gale Group; OCLC Online Computer Library Center, Inc.; H.W. Wilson. *Indexed:* ABS&EES, BAS, BRI, CBRI, CIJE, ConsI, InfoSAb, LISA, LibLit, PAIS, SSCI. *Aud.:* Ac, Sa.

As the official publication of the ALA division the Association of Library Collections and Technical Services, this quarterly journal aims to support the scholarly and practical aspects of acquisitions, collection management, serials, preservation, cataloging, and classification. The journal features well-researched articles on technical-service issues and trends. Recommended for library science collections.

4309. ***Medical Reference Services Quarterly.*** [ISSN: 0276-3869] 1982. q. USD 275. Ed(s): M Sandra Wood. Haworth Press, Inc., 10 Alice St, Binghamton, NY 13904-1580; getinfo@haworthpressinc.com; http://www.haworthpressinc.com. Illus., adv. Sample. Refereed. Circ: 721 Paid. Microform: PQC. Reprint: HAW. *Indexed:* BiolAb, CINAHL, ConsI, ExcerpMed, InfoSAb, LISA, LibLit. *Bk. rev.:* 8-12, 500-800 words. *Aud.:* Ac, Sa.

Each quarterly issue of this journal offers articles of current interest and practical value to medical reference and health information providers. Areas of focus include information management education, medical informatics, end-user searching, and the Internet. Past issues have considered hospital library benchmarking, the evaluation of alternative MEDLINE search engines, health information resources, and bibliographic instruction for remote-library users. Recommended professional reading for medical and health science librarians.

4310. ***Reference and User Services Quarterly.*** Formerly (until 1997): *R Q.* [ISSN: 1094-9054] 1960. q. USD 50 domestic; USD 55 in Canada & Mexico; USD 60 elsewhere. Ed(s): Connie Van Fleet, Danny P Wallace. American Library Association, 50 E Huron St, Chicago, IL 60611-2795; http://www.ala.org. Illus., index, adv. Sample. Refereed. Circ: 6000. Vol. ends: Fall. Microform: PQC. Online: EBSCO Publishing; Florida Center for Library Automation; Gale Group; OCLC Online Computer Library Center, Inc.; ProQuest Information & Learning; H.W. Wilson. Reprint: PQC. *Indexed:* AgeL, ArtHuCI, BRI, CBRI, CIJE, ConsI, InfoSAb, LISA, LibLit, MagInd, PAIS, RI-1, SSCI. *Aud.:* Ga, Ac, Sa.

As the official journal of the ALA division Reference and User Services Association, this publication is intended for an audience of reference and adult-service providers in public, academic, and special libraries. Each issue presents informative features on community building, readers' advisory, collection development, and evaluative reviews of databases, reference titles, and professional literature. Recent articles cover public policy, faculty information needs, ready-reference sites, and adult lifelong learning. Highly recommended for all types of libraries.

4311. ***Reference Services Review.*** [ISSN: 0090-7324] 1972. q. EUR 346.91 in Europe; USD 319 in North America; AUD 419 in Australasia. Ed(s): Ilene Rockman. Emerald, 60-62 Toller Ln, Bradford, BD8 9BY, United Kingdom; info@emeraldinsight.com; http://www.emeraldinsight.com/journals/. Illus., index, adv. Sample. Refereed. Circ: 2000. Reprint: PSC. *Indexed:* AgeL, BRI, CBRI, CIJE, ConsI, InfoSAb, LISA, LibLit, RI-1. *Aud.:* Ac, Sa.

This quarterly publication aims to enrich reference knowledge and promote the delivery of effective reference services. To support these goals, the journal explores the full spectrum of reference functions, including models for the delivery of quality service, evaluation of reference sources, and development of learning activities. Articles have covered organizational learning, information resource management, instructional strategy, virtual libraries, and literacy. Recommended for library professional collections.

4312. ***Reforma Newsletter: national association to promote library and information services to Latinos and the Spanish-speaking.*** [ISSN: 0891-8880] 1971. q. USD 35 (Individuals, USD 20). Ed(s): Denice Adkins. Reforma, PO Box 832, Anaheim, CA 92815-0832; denice@webpan.com; http://www.reforma.org. Illus., adv. Circ: 900. Vol. ends: Winter. *Aud.:* Ga, Ac, Sa.

Established in 1971, REFORMA is the National Association to Promote Library and Information Services to Latinos and the Spanish-Speaking. Through its quarterly newsletter, REFORMA keeps its members informed about its current activities, as well as special library services to Hispanics. The newsletter includes chapter news, member profiles, conference highlights, and book reviews. A must-read for individuals and organizations serving Spanish-speaking communities.

4313. *School Library Journal: the magazine of children, young adults & school librarians.* [ISSN: 0362-8930] 1954. m. USD 124 domestic; USD 179 Canada; USD 182 elsewhere. Ed(s): Joe Tessitore. Reed Business Information, 360 Park Ave South, New York, NY 10010; http://www.reedbusiness.com. Illus., index, adv. Sample. Circ: 39500. Vol. ends: Aug. Microform: NBI; PQC. Online: EBSCO Publishing; Florida Center for Library Automation; Gale Group; LexisNexis; OCLC Online Computer Library Center, Inc.; ProQuest Information & Learning; H.W. Wilson. Reprint: PQC. *Indexed:* ASIP, BRD, BRI, CBRI, CIJE, ConsI, EduInd, ICM, LISA, LibLit, MRD, MagInd. *Bk. rev.:* Various number and length. *Aud.:* Sa.

This prominent magazine is directed toward librarians working with young people in public and school libraries. The publication's aim is to provide youth specialists with timely articles, practical information, strategies, and resources. Regular features include columns on book selection and copyright issues, opinion pieces, and reviews of web sites, multimedia, and books. A requisite professional journal for public and school librarians.

4314. *School Library Media Activities Monthly.* [ISSN: 0889-9371] 1984. m. 10/yr. USD 49 domestic; USD 55 foreign. Ed(s): Paula Montgomery, Debra Goodrich. LMS Associates LLC, 17 E Henrietta St, Baltimore, MD 21230; paulam@crinkles.com; http://www.crinkles.com. Illus., adv. Sample. Circ: 14000 Paid. *Indexed:* CIJE, EduInd, LibLit. *Aud.:* Ems, Hs.

This publication supports the practices of K–8 school library specialists by providing inspiring and practical articles that address curriculum and instructional issues. The magazine features useful lesson plans for reference activities and literature appreciation, reviews of books and web sites, and author profiles. Recommended professional journal for school and public librarians.

4315. *School Library Media Research.* Formerly (until 1999): *School Library Media Quarterly Online.* [ISSN: 1523-4320] 1998. 5x/yr. Ed(s): Daniel Callison. American Library Association, 50 E Huron St, Chicago, IL 60611-2795; http://www.ala.org. Illus., adv. Refereed. *Indexed:* CIJE, LibLit. *Aud.:* Ems, Hs.

As the official journal of ALA's American Association of School Librarians division, this publication aims to provide high-quality research articles that are expressly relevant to school library media field. The journal is concerned with instructional theory, teaching methods, and the management and implementation of school library media programs. Topics include the information search process, concept mapping, educational reform, and independent reading. A valuable professional resource for the school library media community.

4316. *Teacher Librarian Journal: the journal for school library professionals.* Formerly (until 1998): *Emergency Librarian.* [ISSN: 1481-1782] 1973. 5x/yr. USD 54. Ed(s): Ken Haycock. Ken Haycock & Associates, Inc., W Broadway, Ste 343, PO Box 101-1001, Vancouver, BC V6H 4E4, Canada; admin@teacherlibrarian.com; http://www.teacherlibrarian.com. Illus., adv. Sample. Refereed. Circ: 10000 Paid. Vol. ends: Jun. Microform: MML; PQC. Online: bigchalk; EBSCO Publishing; Florida Center for Library Automation; Gale Group; LexisNexis; Micromedia ProQuest; OCLC Online Computer Library Center, Inc.; ProQuest Information & Learning; H.W. Wilson. Reprint: PQC. *Indexed:* BRI, CBCARef, CBRI, CEI, CIJE, CPerI, EduInd, ICM, InfoSAb, LISA, LibLit. *Bk. rev.:* Number varies. *Aud.:* Ems, Hs, Ac.

This bimonthly publication is an excellent source of information and resources for library professionals working with children and young adults. Feature articles cover a broad spectrum of topics, including management, information literacy, technology, and instruction collaboration. Reviews evaluate web sites, books, software, and electronic databases. Past issues have discussed student plagiarism, standardization, accelerated reading programs, and electronic portfolios. Highly recommended for school librarians and library media specialists.

U.S. Library of Congress. Information Bulletin. See Free Magazines and House Organs section.

4317. *Young Adult Library Services.* [ISSN: 1541-4302] 2002. s-a. USD 40 domestic; USD 50 foreign. American Library Association, 50 E Huron St, Chicago, IL 60611-2795; http://www.ala.org. Adv. Circ: 3766 Paid and free. *Aud.:* Ems, Hs.

As the official organ of the ALA division Young Adult Library Services Association, this publication is dedicated to providing articles of current research and practice related to youth library services. Journal content explores issues relevant to the profession, such as collection development, leadership, intellectual freedom, and information literacy. The publication reports on the association's activities and offers in-depth reviews of print, nonprint, and online materials. An essential journal for any collection supporting library and information services to youth.

Electronic Journals

4318. *A L A W O N.* [ISSN: 1069-7799] 1992. irreg. American Library Association, Washington Office, 1301 Pennsylvania Ave, N W, Ste 403, Washington, DC 20004; alawash@alawash.org; http://www.ala.org/washoff/publics.html. *Aud.:* Sa.

The American Library Association Washington Office's e-mail publication reports on federal issues affecting the library community, including copyright, funding, intellectual freedom, access to government information, and telecommunications. The e-journal efficiently delivers breaking legislative news.

4319. *A L C T S Newsletter Online.* Supersedes (in Dec. 1998): *A L C T S Newsletter;* Which was formerly (until 1990): *R T S D Newsletter (Resources and Technical Services Division).* [ISSN: 1523-018X] 1976. 4x/yr. Free. Ed(s): Miriam Palm. American Library Association, 50 E Huron St, Chicago, IL 60611-2795; http://www.ala.org. Illus. Online: OCLC Online Computer Library Center, Inc.; H.W. Wilson. Reprint: PQC. *Indexed:* LibLit. *Aud.:* Ac, Sa.

Through its online newsletter, the Association for Library Collections and Technical Services is able to keep its members informed about current issues, association news, and events and developments in the profession. A staple for the technical services community.

4320. *AcqWeb.* 1994. m. Ed(s): Anna Belle Leiserson. Vanderbilt University, Law School, 131 21st Ave South, Nashville, TN 37203-1181; http://acqweb.library.vanderbilt.edu/. *Aud.:* Ac, Sa.

This topnotch web site provides links to a broad range of acquisitions and collection development resources. International in scope, the site features verification tools, vendors and publishers information, links to library associations, and reference resources. A notable site for librarians and other professionals interested in acquisitions and collection development.

4321. *Issues in Science and Technology Librarianship: a quarterly publication of the Science and Technology Section, Association of College and Research Libraries.* [ISSN: 1092-1206] 1991. q. Ed(s): Andrea Duda. Association of College and Research Libraries, Science and Technology Section, 50 E Huron St, Chicago, IL 60611-2795; duda@library.ucsb.edu; http://www.istl.org/. Illus. *Indexed:* InfoSAb, LISA, LibLit. *Aud.:* Ac, Sa.

This online journal focuses on supporting the interests of science and technology librarians. In addition to providing background information and opinions on such varied topics as biotechnology and information literacy, the journal regularly features book reviews, evaluations of Internet resources, database reports, and conference updates. An excellent resource for academic libraries.

■ LINGUISTICS

See also Anthropology; Classical Studies; Education; Literature; Psychology; and Sociology sections.

Margie Ruppel, Reference Librarian, Morris Library, Southern Illinois University, Carbondale, IL 62901; mruppel@lib.siu.edu

Introduction

The field of linguistics presents a significantly diverse palette of journals and magazines. Selections in this chapter range from the general to applied, monolingual to multilingual, regional to international, historical to contemporary, research to pedagogy, empirical to theoretical, to a combination of these types. Applied to the thousands of languages in the world, there is little room to exhaust the field of linguistics.

The far-reaching breadth and depth of linguistics made it difficult to narrow the reviewed journals to the collection in this chapter. Linguistics subfields include morphology, syntax, semantics, dialectology, grammar, pragmatics, phonology, psycholinguistics, sociolinguistics, anthropological linguistics, descriptive linguistics, cognitive linguistics, and language usage. This editor has made a concerted effort to include primarily journals for the core areas of general and theoretical linguistics, rather than for allied areas. Exceptions are well-known publications with a broad readership and major journals for specific languages. In the end, focus was made on the best journals representing general linguistics, theoretical linguistics, various languages, and teaching linguistics and language. As expected, these four foci often overlap.

The general linguistics journals in this chapter were chosen based on personal judgment, in consultation with two resources: *Linguistics: a guide to the reference literature,* by Anna L. DeMiller (Libraries Unlimited, Inc., 2000), and an article from the *Journal of the American Society for Information Science,* titled "Quality judgments of journals as indicators of research performance in the humanities and the social and behavioral sciences," by A.J. Nederhof and R.A. Zwaan (vol. 42, issue 5, pp. 332–340). Both the book and article list core general linguistics journals, with the latter based on opinions of professional linguists. Considered simultaneously, these three things (personal judgment, the book, and the article) led to a recommendation of "core journal" in the entries, with the degree of recommendation ranging from "all academic general linguistics collections" to "only graduate and doctoral general linguistics collections." *Language, Linguistic Inquiry* and *Journal of Linguistics* are examples of core general linguistics journals.

Similar methods were employed to choose the theoretical linguistics journals, with the exception of the Nederhof article. In its place, this editor used a study on core journals for theoretical journals titled "Some aspects of scholarly communication in linguistics: an empirical study" (*Language*, vol. 66, no. 3, pp. 553–557). These considerations produce an overall recommendation of "core journal" in the entries, again varying from "all collections" to "only special or focused collections." Examples of core theoretical linguistics journals include *Natural Language and Linguistic Theory, Linguistic Analysis,* and *The Linguistic Review*. All of the core theoretical linguistics journals are also considered core selections for general linguistics collections.

Journals representing various languages include: *Anthropological Linguistics* (Native American languages), *Australian Journal of Linguistics, Journal of African Languages and Linguistics, Journal of English Linguistics, Journal of French Language Studies, Journal of East Asian Linguistics, Journal of Germanic Linguistics,* and *Journal of Pidgin and Creole Languages*. The journals for teaching linguistics and language arts are: *Applied Linguistics, Linguistics and Education, Modern Language Journal, ELT Journal, Studies in Second Language Acquisition,* and *TESOL Quarterly*.

In order to get a better idea of which linguistics journals are the most useful to researchers, I completed a citation analysis in ISI's (Institute for Scientific Information) Journal Performance Indicators 2001 database. A few of the highest ranked journals (in the 90th percentile for the period of 1980–2001) include *Linguistic Inquiry, Journal of Phonetics, Language, Natural Language & Linguistic Theory,* and *Language in Society*. They are descibed as "highly cited" in the individual reviews, as are those in the 80th- and 70th-percentile brackets. Journals with a lower percentile bracket (60th and below) are described in the entries as "moderately cited," "often cited," or "rarely cited." Many linguistics journals were not in the ISI database.

Because linguistics is a predominantly academic field of study, the majority of titles listed here would appeal to academic and specialized readerships. Librarians looking for a representative academic linguistics journal should consider *Language*. A title such as *Word Ways,* a recreational linguistics journal, would appeal to a more general audience. Although most of the journals in this chapter are considered "core" linguistics journals, libraries with smaller collections will want to limit their selections based on the community they serve. To identify additional linguistics journals, consult The Linguist List (www.linguistlist.org), Linguistic Society of America's list of publications (www.lsadc.org), or *The fifth directory of periodicals: publishing articles on American and English language and literature, criticism and theory, film, American studies, poetry and fiction,* by Richard Barlow (Ohio University Press, 1992).

For more information on the field of linguistics, consult the following associations: International Linguistic Association (www.ilaword.org), Linguistic Society of America (www.lsadc.org), American Dialect Society (www.americandialect.org), International Phonetic Association (www.arts.gla.ac.uk/IPA/ipa.html), Linguistics Association of Great Britain (www.essex.acuk/linguistics/LAGB), International Association of Teachers of English as a Foreign Language (www.iatefl.org), National Federation of Modern Language Teachers Associations (http://polyglot.lss.wisc.edu/mlj/nfmlta.htm), and Teachers of English to Speakers of Other Languages (www.tesol.org).

Basic Periodicals

Ac: *American Speech, Applied Linguistics, International Journal of Lexicography, Journal of English Linguistics, Journal of Linguistics, Journal of Phonetics, Language, Language in Society, Linguistic Analysis, Linguistic Inquiry, The Linguistic Review, Linguistics, Linguistics and Education, Modern Language Journal, Natural Language and Linguistic Theory.*

Basic Abstracts and Indexes

Language Teaching, Linguistics Abstracts, Linguistics and Language Behavior Abstracts, MLA International Bibliography, Social Sciences Citation Index, Sociological Abstracts.

American Journal of Philology. See Classical Studies section.

4322. *American Speech: a quarterly of linguistic usage.* [ISSN: 0003-1283] 1925. q. USD 108 (Individual members, USD 50; USD 27 per issue). Ed(s): Connie C Eble. Duke University Press, 905 W Main St, Ste 18 B, Durham, NC 27701; subscriptions@dukeupress.edu; http://www.dukeupress.edu. Illus., adv. Sample. Refereed. Circ: 1600. Vol. ends: Winter. Microform: PQC. Online: bigchalk; EBSCO Publishing; Gale Group; Ingenta Select; JSTOR (Web-based Journal Archive); Northern Light Technology, Inc.; OCLC Online Computer Library Center, Inc.; Project MUSE; RoweCom Information Quest; Swets Blackwell. Reprint: PSC. *Indexed:* AmH&L, ArtHuCI, BEL&L, CIJE, HumInd, IBZ, L&LBA, LRI, LT&LA, LingAb, MLA-IB, SSCI. *Bk. rev.:* 2-4, 10-20 pages. *Aud.:* Ga, Ac.

This often-cited, core journal for general linguistics covers the "current usage, dialectology, and the history and structure of English in the Western hemisphere." Articles about general linguistic theory that appeal to a wide readership are preferred. *American Speech* is the oldest journal devoted to the speech of North America. "What's in a slur" and "Young American puns: antebellum wordplay and democratic Manhattan" are two recent feature articles. While the easy-to-read articles are generally 20–30 pages in length and total four or five per issue, the book reviews run 15–20 pages in length and only one review is published per issue. Reviews are completely researched and provide commentary in context of other books on the same topic. Particularly noteworthy is the "Among the New Words" section, which features words and phrases new to our lexicon; etymology and examples of usage and meaning are included for each word or phrase. *American Speech* is published by the American Dialect Society (www.americandialect.org). It is recommended for all academic linguistics collections, because of its general nature, orientation to English in the Western hemisphere, and high citation rate. See also: *Journal of Linguistics*.

4323. ***Anthropological Linguistics.*** [ISSN: 0003-5483] 1959. q. USD 120 (Individuals, USD 45). Ed(s): Douglas R Parks. Indiana University, Anthropology Department, Student Services Bldg Rm 130, Bloomington, IN 47405; anthling@indiana.edu; http:/www.indiana.edu/~anthling. Illus., index, adv. Sample. Refereed. Circ: 800 Paid. Vol. ends: Winter. Microform: NRP. Online: Gale Group. Reprint: PSC. *Indexed:* ABS&EES, AICP, AbAn, AnthLit, BAS, BEL&L, HumInd, IBSS, L&LBA, LingAb, MLA-IB, SSCI. *Bk. rev.:* 8-12, 2-4 pages. *Aud.:* Ac.

Published jointly by the Department of Anthropology and the American Indian Research Institute at Indiana University, this journal is a "forum for the full range of scholarly study of the languages and cultures of the peoples of the world, especially the native peoples of the Americas." Articles can be about the cultural, historical, and philological aspects of linguistics, including text and discourse analysis, semantic systems, cultural classifications, prehistory, archival materials, historical documents, and "ethnohistorical papers that draw significantly on linguistic data." Recent articles, generally 20–30 pages long, include "Dynamic embodiment in Assiniboine (Nakota) storytelling" and "Copula clauses in Australian languages: a typological perspective." Book reviews are included in every issue and usually span two or three pages. Recommended for institutions that offer programs in linguistics, anthropology, and Native American studies.

4324. ***Applied Linguistics.*** [ISSN: 0142-6001] 1980. q. GBP 139. Ed(s): Dr. Claire Kramsch, Gabriele Kasper. Oxford University Press, Great Clarendon St, Oxford, OX2 6DP, United Kingdom; jnl.orders@oup.co.uk; http://www3.oup.co.uk/jnls. Illus., adv. Sample. Refereed. Circ: 2225. Vol. ends: Dec. Online: Chadwyck-Healey Incorporated; East View Publications, Inc.; ingenta.com. Reprint: PSC. *Indexed:* ArtHuCI, BrEdI, CIJE, IBZ, L&LBA, LT&LA, LingAb, MLA-IB, SSCI, SWA. *Bk. rev.:* 4-5, 1-3 pages. *Aud.:* Ac.

Published as a joint effort between three associations (the American Association for Applied Linguistics, International Association of Applied Linguistics, and British Association for Applied Linguistics), *Applied Linguistics* seeks to present a principled approach to language education by highlighting the relationship between theoretical and practical areas of linguistics. "Academic Listening: a source of vocabulary acquisition" is the title of a recent article. Readers will be pleased with the four articles per issue, the extensive lists of references, the brief book reviews (average of three per issue), and the list of books received. There is often a forum section for commentary. Because it is heavily cited and bridges the gap between theory and practice, this title is recommended for all institutions where both linguistics and education degrees are granted. See also: *ELT Journal, The Modern Language Review,* and *TESOL Quarterly.*

4325. ***Applied Psycholinguistics: psychological studies of language processes.*** [ISSN: 0142-7164] 1980. q. USD 195 (Individuals, USD 90). Ed(s): Usha Goswami, Martha Crago. Cambridge University Press, The Edinburgh Bldg, Shaftesbury Rd, Cambridge, CB2 2RU, United Kingdom; information@cambridge.org; http://uk.cambridge.org. Illus., index, adv. Sample. Refereed. Vol. ends: Dec. Microform: PQC. Online: EBSCO Publishing; OCLC Online Computer Library Center, Inc.; RoweCom Information Quest; Swets Blackwell. Reprint: SWZ. *Indexed:* AgeL, ArtHuCI, BrEdI, CIJE, L&LBA, LT&LA, LingAb, MLA-IB, PsycholAb, SSCI. *Bk. rev.:* 2-4, 2-4 pages. *Aud.:* Ac, Sa.

Original contributions on psycholinguistic processing comprise the bulk of this journal. Specific topics include development, use, impairment, literacy development, and modalities (spoken, signed, and written), with particular interest on cross-linguistic, cross-learner, and cross-age approaches, language processes, methodological processes, language users, and language learners. Articles, usually seven per issue and 15–20 pages in length, have "clear, applied relevance" to practitioners and researchers in linguistics, psychology, speech and hearing sciences, reading, language teaching, special education, and neurology. Lexical and visual-orthographic processes of Chinese children using ESL in spelling was the focus of a recent article. As this is the main journal for psycholinguistics, evident by its high rate of citations in the literature, it is a definite purchase for academic linguistics collections.

4326. ***Australian Journal of Linguistics.*** [ISSN: 0726-8602] 1981. s-a. GBP 116 (Individuals, GBP 41). Carfax Publishing Ltd., 4 Park Sq, Milton Park, Abingdon, OX14 4RN, United Kingdom; enquiry@tandf.co.uk; http://www.tandf.co.uk/. Adv. Refereed. Circ: 500 Paid. Reprint: PSC. *Indexed:* IBSS, IBZ, L&LBA, LingAb, MLA-IB. *Bk. rev.:* 3, 5-8 pages. *Aud.:* Ac.

Although this journal is the official publication of the Australian Linguistic Society (www.latrobe.edu.au/rclt/als/) and the primary focus is theory-based Australian language and Australian English studies, its overall theme is international linguistics. Articles are commonly based on discourse and corpora as well. Recent articles studied a discourse analysis of the *Yeah-no* marker in Australian English, and Russian verbs that convey a similar meaning but govern different cases. Book reviews range from 1,800 to 2,000 words long, and sometimes appear in the form of lengthy review essays. Recommended for academic libraries that serve Australian linguistic researchers.

4327. ***Canadian Journal of Linguistics.*** [ISSN: 0008-4131] 1954. q. CND 60 (Members, CND 50; Students, CND 18). Ed(s): Anne Rochette. Canadian Linguistic Association, c/o Dept de Linguistique, UQAM, Succ Centre Ville, C P 8888, Montreal, PQ H3C 3P8, Canada; cjlrcl@er.uqam.ca. Illus., index, adv. Sample. Refereed. Circ: 750 Paid. Vol. ends: Dec. Microform: PQC. Reprint: PQC; SWZ. *Indexed:* AbAn, ArtHuCI, BAS, CBCARef, CEI, IBZ, LT&LA, LingAb, MLA-IB, SSCI. *Bk. rev.:* 5-15, 1,000 words. *Aud.:* Ac.

The principal aim of this journal is "to promote the study of linguistics in Canada," especially theoretical linguistics. It accomplishes this goal by publishing articles in English and French, such as "Markedness in right-edge syllabification: parallels across populations" and "The selectional restrictions of French past tenses." There are generally two or three articles and 8–15 book reviews per issue. Articles have a maximum of 8,000 words, while reviews have a maximum of 1,000 words. Books are reviewed only if they relate to the scientific study of language. A list of 15–50 received publications concludes each issue. *Canadian Journal of Linguistics* is cited fairly often in the linguistics literature, which indicates its reputation as a core journal for general and theoretical linguistics. Recommended for general academic linguistics collections.

CLA Journal. See African American section.

4328. ***Cognitive Linguistics: an interdisciplinary journal of cognitive science.*** [ISSN: 0936-5907] 1989. q. EUR 176.60 domestic; EUR 180.20 foreign; EUR 43 newsstand/cover. Ed(s): Arie Verhagen. Mouton de Gruyter, Genthiner Str 13, Berlin, 10785, Germany; mouton@degruyter.de; http://www.degruyter.de. Illus., index, adv. Sample. Refereed. Reprint: PSC; SCH. *Indexed:* ArtHuCI, IBSS, IBZ, L&LBA, MLA-IB. *Bk. rev.:* 0-5, 5-25 pages. *Aud.:* Ac, Sa.

The official purpose of *Cognitive Linguistics* is a "forum for linguistic research of all kinds on the interaction between language and cognition," where cognitive linguistics is the study of language as an instrument for organizing, processing, and conveying information. Specific topics include natural language categorization, linguistic organization, the conceptual interface between syntax and semantics, the relationship between language and thought, and language performance. A recent article in this journal began with an enlightening view on the value of cognitive linguistics: "The indisputable advantage of cognitive linguistics is that it places questions of metaphor and polysemy in the broader perspective of human cognition and conceptual organization." Some of the recent 30-plus-page articles have included "From parts to wholes and back again" and "The semantics of the Spanish subjunctive." Book reviews, not present in every issue, can range from five to 25 pages in length. The Squib section contains short notes on facts, principles, topics for research, problems, puzzles, or commentary. Further information about the International Cognitive Linguistics Association is available at www.cognitivelinguistics.com. The journal's editorial board is composed of prestigious scholars in the field of linguistics. Recommended for most academic general linguistics collections.

4329. ***Diachronica: international journal for historical linguistics.*** [ISSN: 0176-4225] 1980. s-a. EUR 190 combined subscription print & online eds. Ed(s): Joseph C Salmons. John Benjamins Publishing Co., PO Box

36224, Amsterdam, 1020 ME, Netherlands; http://www.benjamins.nl/jbp/index.html. Refereed. Online: ingenta.com; Swets Blackwell. *Indexed:* IBSS, L&LBA, LingAb, MLA-IB. *Bk. rev.:* 4-6, 2-5 pages. *Aud.:* Ac, Sa.

This journal provides a platform for the "presentation and discussion of information concerning all aspects of language change in any and all languages of the globe," especially articles that combine theory and careful analysis of linguistic data. A further description of the journal is a "forum for the exchange and synthesis of information concerning all aspects of historical linguistics and pertaining to all language families." Each issue consists of three to five articles, one review article, four to eight book reviews, and a miscellaneous section containing notes, reports and discussions, and an annotated list of recent publications, all in English, French, or German. A core selection for general linguistics collections. See also *Journal of English Linguistics,* below in this section.

4330. *Dictionaries.* [ISSN: 0197-6745] 1979. a. Members, USD 30. Ed(s): Michael Adams. Dictionary Society of North America, University of Wisconsin-Madison, 6129 Helen C. White Hall, Madison, WI 53706; lvonschn@wisc.edu; http://polyglot.lss.wisc.edu/dsna/index.html. Circ: 500. *Indexed:* L&LBA, MLA-IB. *Bk. rev.:* 5-10, 2-10 pages. *Aud.:* Ac, Sa.

The Dictionary Society of North America's international membership includes "people working on dictionaries, academics who engage in research and writing about dictionaries, dictionary collectors, librarians, booksellers, translators, linguists, publishers, writers, collectors, journalists, and people with an avocational interest in dictionaries." It follows, then, that the society's publication, *Dictionaries,* contains forums and articles on the making, critique, use, collection, and history of dictionaries. In the journal's context, dictionaries are defined as "lists of words or other vocabulary items, with information about their meaning or other linguistic properties." Articles include sketches of lexicographers, descriptions of significant dictionary collections, reviews of dictionaries and books on lexicography, and bibliographies on lexicography. This produces such articles as "Ornamental illustrations in French dictionaries" and "'We didn't realize that lite beer was supposed to suck!': the putative vulgarity of 'X sucks' in American English." Recommended as a supplemental purchase for academic linguistics collections. See also *International Journal of Lexicography,* below in this section.

4331. *E L T Journal: an international journal for teachers of English to speakers of other languages.* Former titles (until 1981): *English Language Teaching Journal;* (until 1973): *English Language Teaching.* [ISSN: 0951-0893] 1946. q. GBP 87. Ed(s): Keith Morrow. Oxford University Press, Great Clarendon St, Oxford, OX2 6DP, United Kingdom; jnl.orders@oup.co.uk; http://www3.oup.co.uk/jnls. Illus., index, adv. Sample. Refereed. Circ: 5400. Vol. ends: Oct. Microform: PQC. Online: Gale Group; ingenta.com; Swets Blackwell. Reprint: PQC; PSC. *Indexed:* BrEdI, CIJE, EduInd, IBZ, L&LBA, LT&LA, MLA-IB. *Bk. rev.:* 2-10, 1-15 pages. *Aud.:* Hs, Ga, Ac.

This unique, practical, and professional journal seeks to "bridge the gap between the everyday practical concerns of ELT professionals and related academic disciplines, such as education, linguistics, psychology, and sociology, that may offer significant insights." It is especially concerned with the principles and practice in which English is taught and learned around the world. Recent articles cover teaching English to young learners, oral skills development, teaching writing, teaching translation, and portfolios. In addition to the brief articles (eight pages each), the following sections appear in each issue: "Readers Respond," "Key Concepts in ELT" (e.g., observation), "Survey Review" (e.g., electronic dictionaries evaluated on ease of use, helpfulness and pronunciation), "Reviews," and "Web sites for the Language Teacher" (e.g., business English resources; Google). *ELT Journal* is published in conjunction with the International Association of Teachers of English as a Foreign Language (www.iatefl.org). It succeeds at meeting the needs of its audience and is recommended for both academic libraries that support teacher education programs and high school libraries. See also: *Applied Linguistics; Linguistics and Education; TESOL Quarterly;* and *The Modern Language Journal.*

4332. *English World-Wide: a journal of varieties of English.* [ISSN: 0172-8865] 1980. s-a. EUR 215 combined subscription print & online eds. Ed(s): Edgar W Schneider. John Benjamins Publishing Co., Klaprozenweg 105, Amsterdam, 1033 NN, Netherlands; subscription@benjamins.nl; http://www.benjamins.com. Illus., adv. Sample. Refereed. Circ: 600. Online: ingenta.com; Swets Blackwell. *Indexed:* BEL&L, IBSS, IBZ, L&LBA, LingAb, MLA-IB, SociolAb. *Bk. rev.:* 3-8, 1-5 pages. *Aud.:* Ac.

This journal is included not because it is a core selection, but because the topic of English dialects and sociolects will be of interest to most linguistic researchers. The journal's primary focus is two-fold: "the 'New Englishes' (including English-oriented pidgins and creoles), e.g., in Africa, Asia, the Pacific region, and the Caribbean, with a strong interest in the social and regional variation of English-speaking countries in Europe, North America, and the southern hemisphere." Articles are empirical, descriptive, or theoretical in nature or a combination of these approaches. Short annotated texts, bibliographies, review essays, and other regular reviews are also published. Whereas the regular reviews are descriptive and do not exceed 1,000 words in length, the review essays are both descriptive and argumentative, and do not exceed 2,000 words. Although this is an optional purchase for general linguistics collections, it is a good background source for linguistics professors and education students who are preparing to teach language arts. See also: *Journal of Pidgin & Creole Languages.*

4333. *Folia Linguistica: acta societatis linguisticae Europaeae.* [ISSN: 0165-4004] 1967. 2x/yr. EUR 192.10 domestic; EUR 195.50 foreign; EUR 94 newsstand/cover. Ed(s): Wolfgang Dressler. Mouton de Gruyter, Genthiner Str 13, Berlin, 10785, Germany; mouton@degruyter.de; http://www.degruyter.de. Illus., index, adv. Sample. Refereed. Reprint: SCH. *Indexed:* ABS&EES, ArtHuCI, BAS, IBSS, IBZ, L&LBA, LT&LA, LingAb, MLA-IB. *Bk. rev.:* 0-1, 1,000 words. *Aud.:* Ac, Sa.

Folia Linguistica's web site states that it "reflects the varied interests of its membership, located primarily but not exclusively in Europe." A look at the Societas Linguistica Europaea's mission gives more clues to the journal's content: "advancement, in European countries and elsewhere, of the scientific study of language in all its respects." Each issue offers research and information on general and comparative linguistics in the form of articles, review articles, and book notices. Occasionally overviews of European research in linguistics are also included. Special issues on current topics are published periodically. Recent special issues have been focused on the history of phonology, and psycholinguistic perspectives on compound processing. New publications are not usually reviewed, but rather summarized and listed in a "publications received" style. Although this is a core journal for general linguistics, it is quite expensive and therefore is a supplemental selection for academic institutions.

4334. *General Linguistics.* [ISSN: 0016-6553] 1955. q. USD 49 (Individuals, USD 25). Ed(s): Robert Yeager. Pegasus Press, University of North Carolina, Asheville, NC 28804; pegpress@interpath.com; http://www.binghampton.edu/. Illus., adv. Sample. Refereed. Circ: 800. Vol. ends: Winter. Microform: PQC. Reprint: PQC. *Indexed:* ABS&EES, AbAn, ArtHuCI, BEL&L, L&LBA, LT&LA, LingAb, MLA-IB, SSCI. *Bk. rev.:* 3-5, 3-10 pages. *Aud.:* Ac.

This journal accepts articles in English, French, or German, on "general theoretical approaches to comparative, historical, and typological data," as well as the allied fields of psycholinguistics and sociolinguistics. A recent article was about Proto-Indo-European glottogenesis. The quality and amount of book reviews are notable, but comprise almost half of each volume. The one to three articles in each volume, however, are thorough and easy to read. Although the journal's title suggests a core selection for academic linguistics collections, its publication schedule should be considered before purchasing. For example, volume 38, which was devoted to African linguistics and literacy, was written in 1998, but not published until 2001. See also *Lingua.*

4335. *International Journal of American Linguistics.* [ISSN: 0020-7071] 1917. q. USD 212 (Individuals, USD 53; Students, USD 38). Ed(s): Keren Rice. University of Chicago Press, Journals Division, PO Box 37005, Chicago, IL 60637; subscriptions@journals.uchicago.edu; http://www.journals.uchicago.edu. Illus., index, adv. Sample. Refereed. Circ: 1300 Paid. Vol. ends: Oct. Microform: PMC; PQC. Online: EBSCO Publishing; Florida Center for Library Automation; Gale Group;

ProQuest Information & Learning. Reprint: ISI; PQC; PSC. *Indexed:* AICP, AbAn, AnthLit, ArtHuCI, CIJE, HAPI, HumInd, IBSS, IBZ, L&LBA, LT&LA, LingAb, MLA-IB, SSCI. *Bk. rev.:* 2-5, 2-4 pages. *Aud.:* Ac, Sa.

This journal examines linguistic data on grammars, historical reconstruction, grammatical fragments and other related "aspects of the native language of the Americas," including description, history, typology, and linguistic theory. The native language of the Americas covers North, Central, and South America, Eskimo-Aleut and "certain creoles and pidgins of the hemisphere." Articles, totaling three or four per issue, may be in any language. Book reviews are generally 1,500–2,000 words long, and fill two to five pages. *International Journal of American Linguistics* is associated with, but not published by, the Society for the Study of the Indigenous Languages of the Americas (http://wings.buffalo.edu/linguistics/ssila/). In the past, it was sponsored by the Linguistic Society of America (1930–1973), the American Anthropological Association (1944–1973), and other associations for various periods. It is moderately cited in the literature, owing to its being a core journal for both general and theoretical linguistics. This journal is a primary selection for academic linguistics collections. See also *Journal of Pidgin & Creole Languages.*

4336. ***International Journal of Corpus Linguistics.*** [ISSN: 1384-6655] 1996. s-a. EUR 180 combined subscription print & online eds. John Benjamins Publishing Co., Klaprozenweg 105, Amsterdam, 1033 NN, Netherlands; subscription@benjamins.nl; http://www.benjamins.com. Illus., index. Sample. Refereed. *Indexed:* IBZ, L&LBA, MLA-IB. *Bk. rev.:* 3-5, 3-15 pages. *Aud.:* Ac, Sa.

Written in English and international in scope, this journal publishes computer-based empirical studies on groups (corpora) of written and spoken texts to provide research in natural language processing (NLP), lexicography, and linguistic description. It is also intended to be a forum where linguists, lexicographers, and language engineers can share expertise, visions, and new resources and tools. Corpus linguistics is important because it develops lexicons to be used in NLP applications and electronic dictionaries. A recent article studies the persuasive language of nonprofit, philanthropic direct mail. Another article is titled, "Lexical Constellations: What Collocates Fail to Tell." At the end of each issue is a supplemental section that contains brief descriptions of recently published research articles and books on similar topics. This journal is a core selection for any collection that supports linguistics programs, because it provides empirical research. See also *International Journal of Lexicography; Dictionaries.*

4337. ***International Journal of Lexicography.*** [ISSN: 0950-3846] 1988. q. GBP 125. Ed(s): Anthony P. Cowie. Oxford University Press, Great Clarendon St, Oxford, OX2 6DP, United Kingdom; jnl.orders@oup.co.uk; http://www3.oup.co.uk/jnls. Illus., adv. Sample. Refereed. Circ: 1000. Vol. ends: Dec. Reprint: PSC. *Indexed:* L&LBA, LingAb, MLA-IB. *Bk. rev.:* 5-8, 1-4 pages. *Aud.:* Ac.

This international and interdisciplinary journal publishes articles on all aspects of lexicography theory and research, specifically dictionaries and other reference works, including design, compilation, and use. All languages are studied, but the focus is on major European languages, "monolingual and bilingual, synchronic and diachronic, pedagogical and encyclopedic." Articles in related fields such as computational linguistics, are also included. *International Journal of Lexicography* routinely features an article on "some practical aspect of dictionary-making and will publish, also on a regular basis, reviews of dictionaries and books." Recent articles include "American freshmen and English dictionaries: 'I had aspersions of becoming an English teacher'" and "Description and prescription in dictionaries of scientific terms." In addition to the two articles, one review article, and five to ten book reviews, the EURALEX (European Association for Lexicography) Newsletter is in each issue. More information about the association can be obtained at www.ims.uni-stuttgart.de/euralex. A core general linguistics selection for most academic libraries. See also *International Journal of Corpus Linguistics; Dictionaries.*

4338. ***International Journal of the Sociology of Language.*** [ISSN: 0165-2516] 1974. 6x/yr. EUR 260 (Individuals, EUR 60; EUR 44 newsstand/cover). Ed(s): Joshua Fishman. Mouton de Gruyter, Genthiner Str 13, Berlin, 10785, Germany; mouton@degruyter.de; http://www.degruyter.de. Illus., adv. Sample. Refereed. Reprint: PSC; SCH. *Indexed:* AnthLit, IBSS, L&LBA, LT&LA, LingAb, MLA-IB, PSA, PsycholAb, SSCI, SociolAb. *Bk. rev.:* 1-3, 3-5 pages. *Aud.:* Ac, Sa.

Nearly all issues of this international, interdisciplinary journal are devoted to specific topics pertaining to the "study of language use in social behavior" in its broadest sense. These special issues ("The Sociolinguistics of Danish" and "Focus on Diaglossia," for examples) rest on the belief that theoretical and empirical approaches complement each other, leading to "language-related knowledge, applications, values, and sensitivities." Each special issue has its own editor. Articles are written primarily in English; sometimes in French, Spanish, and German; and occasionally in Italian. One or two book reviews are in each issue. A core selection for general academic linguistics collections. See also *Language and Society.*

4339. ***International Phonetic Association. Journal.*** Formerly: *Maitre Phonetique.* [ISSN: 0025-1003] 1886. s-a. USD 99 (Individuals, USD 53). Ed(s): Linda Shockey, John K Local. Cambridge University Press, The Edinburgh Bldg, Shaftesbury Rd, Cambridge, CB2 2RU, United Kingdom; information@cambridge.org; http://uk.cambridge.org/journals. Adv. Circ: 900. Microform: PQC. Online: OCLC Online Computer Library Center, Inc. Reprint: PQC; SWZ. *Indexed:* IBSS, L&LBA, LT&LA, LingAb, MLA-IB. *Bk. rev.:* 2-5, 500-2,000 words. *Aud.:* Ac.

A recent article's title, "Some influences on the realization of for and four in American English," illustrates the scope of this journal: theory, description, and use of phonetics and phonology. Contents include articles, correspondence, and reviews on all aspects of phonetics and phonology, encompassing "research papers, discussion, educational materials, examples of phonetic description of particular languages and many other kinds of material relevant to the discipline of phonetics." Approximately ten articles are published in a volume, each 1,000–10,000 words in length. English is the primary language of publication, but French, German, and Russian manuscripts are also published. The International Phonetic Association (www.arts.gla.ac.uk/IPA/ipa.html), established in 1886, is most noted for creating and maintaining the International Phonetic Alphabet, a phonetic standard for all languages. This journal is a core linguistics journal, and an important selection for the study of international phonetics. See also *Journal of Phonetics* (above in this section).

4340. ***Journal of African Languages and Linguistics.*** [ISSN: 0167-6164] 1979. 2x/yr. EUR 120 (Individuals, EUR 28.95; EUR 60 newsstand/cover). Ed(s): Felix K. Ameka, Maarten Mous. Mouton de Gruyter, Genthiner Str 13, Berlin, 10785, Germany; mouton@degruyter.de; http://www.degruyter.de. Illus., adv. Sample. Refereed. Reprint: PSC; SCH; SWZ. *Indexed:* AnthLit, IBSS, L&LBA, MLA-IB. *Bk. rev.:* 2-3, 4-7 pages. *Aud.:* Sa.

All aspects of African language studies are within the purview of this journal, including synchronic and diachronic, and theoretical and empirical. The three or four lengthy research articles, written in both English and French, are generally 15–30 pages in length, while the two or three book reviews of recently published books on African languages and linguistics are typically 1,000 words long. "Grammatical relations and relativization in Lunda" and "Progress in Bantu lexical reconstruction" are the titles of two recent articles. Recommended only for academic institutions where African language programs are offered.

4341. ***Journal of East Asian Linguistics.*** [ISSN: 0925-8558] 1992. q. EUR 366 print or online ed. Ed(s): C T James Huang, Mamoru Salto. Kluwer Academic Publishers, van Godewijckstraat 30, PO Box 17, Dordrecht, 3300 AA, Netherlands. Illus. Sample. Refereed. Vol. ends: Oct. Microform: PQC. Online: EBSCO Publishing; ingenta.com; Kluwer Online; OCLC Online Computer Library Center, Inc.; Ovid Technologies, Inc.; RoweCom Information Quest; Swets Blackwell. Reprint: SWZ. *Indexed:* ArtHuCI, BAS, CIJE, L&LBA, LingAb, MLA-IB, SSCI. *Aud.:* Sa.

Over several years, this journal has expanded its scope to include any language in the East Asian area, in addition to Chinese, Japanese, and Korean. Works of the following nature are especially welcome: theory-based syntax, semantics, pragmatics, phonology, and morphology studies; comparative studies among East Asian languages; comparative studies between an East Asian language and another language; historical development (especially grammatical stages); interdisciplinary works with psycholinguistics, neurolinguistics, and computational linguistics; replies to recent theoretical work; and shorter notes with original observations. Articles include works with a "formal analysis of observed data, or descriptive generalizations calling for an analysis." Recommended for any academic institution that serves Asian linguistics researchers.

4342. *Journal of English Linguistics.* [ISSN: 0075-4242] 1967. q. GBP 241 print & online eds. in Europe, Middle East, Africa & Australasia. Ed(s): Charles F Meyer, Jr. Sage Publications, Inc., 2455 Teller Rd, Thousand Oaks, CA 91320; info@sagepub.com; http://www.sagepub.com. Illus., index, adv. Sample. Refereed. Circ: 600. Vol. ends: Dec. Online: ingenta.com; OCLC Online Computer Library Center, Inc.; RoweCom Information Quest; Swets Blackwell. *Indexed:* AmHI, ArtHuCI, CommAb, IBZ, L&LBA, LingAb, MLA-IB. *Bk. rev.:* 1-4, 4-6 pages. *Aud.:* Sa.

Journal of English Linguistics publishes articles on empirical studies of the modern and historical periods of the English language, in the form of "synchronic and diachronic studies on subjects from Old and Middle English to modern English grammar, corpus linguistics, and dialectology." Articles on topics such as language contact, pidgins/creoles, or stylistics are also published, provided they focus on the English language. Thematic collections of articles (e.g., "Teaching American English") and monographs that present empirical studies are published as a special issue. All articles are 10–25 pages in length and usually total two or three in a regular issue, five to ten in a special issue. Recent articles are titled "Verbal morphology in Cajun vernacular English: a comparison with other varieties of Southern English" and "Teaching 'bad' American English: profanity and other 'bad' words in the liberal arts setting." One to three reviews of books on general and historical linguistics, language variation, sociolinguistics, and dialectology are included in every issue. A basic selection for undergraduate- and graduate-level general linguistics collections. See also *Diachronica.*

4343. *Journal of French Language Studies.* [ISSN: 0959-2695] 1991. 3x/yr. USD 140 (Individuals, USD 58). Ed(s): William J Ashby, Janice Carruthers. Cambridge University Press, The Edinburgh Bldg, Shaftesbury Rd, Cambridge, CB2 2RU, United Kingdom; information@cambridge.org; http://uk.cambridge.org/journals. Illus., adv. Sample. Refereed. Vol. ends: Sep. Online: EBSCO Publishing; OCLC Online Computer Library Center, Inc.; RoweCom Information Quest; Swets Blackwell. Reprint: SWZ. *Indexed:* CIJE, L&LBA, LT&LA, LingAb, MLA-IB. *Bk. rev.:* 10-20, 1-2 pages. *Aud.:* Ac.

This journal publishes, in English and French, both theoretical and descriptive studies on all aspects of French language and linguistics, including phonology, morphology, syntax, lexis, applied linguistics, sociolinguistics, variation, and French language acquisition. "Most work is synchronic in orientation, but historical and comparative items are welcome." Recent articles include "Identifying a French-specific laughter particle" and "The semantic field of Old French *Astele*: the pitfalls of the medieval gloss in lexicography." There are usually five articles (20–30 pages long) and nine book reviews (800 words each) per issue. This publication is useful to academic researchers and other specialists in French linguistics.

4344. *Journal of Germanic Linguistics.* Formerly (until 2000): *American Journal of Germanic Linguistics and Literatures.* [ISSN: 1470-5427] 1989. q. USD 132. Ed(s): Mark L. Louden. Cambridge University Press, information@cambridge.org; http://uk.cambridge.org. Illus., index, adv. Sample. Refereed. Circ: 350. *Indexed:* MLA-IB. *Bk. rev.:* 5, 2-5 pages. *Aud.:* Ac, Sa.

Published by the Society for Germanic Linguistics (http://german.lss.wisc.edu/~sgl), this journal targets a broad range of linguists concerned with "general issues in formal theory, sociolinguistics, and psycholinguistics," specifically phonology, morphology, syntax, semantics, and historical development pertaining to "Germanic languages and dialects from the earliest phases to the present, including English (to 1500) and the extraterritorial varieties." There are two or three articles (20–30 pages long) and about five book reviews (four to six pages long) per issue. Articles are usually written in English, and occasionally in German. Recommended for academic linguistics collections that serve Germanic linguists and students.

4345. *Journal of Linguistics.* [ISSN: 0022-2267] 1965. 3x/yr. USD 155 (Individuals, USD 79). Ed(s): Robert Borsley, Nigel Fabb. Cambridge University Press, The Edinburgh Bldg, Shaftesbury Rd, Cambridge, CB2 2RU, United Kingdom; information@cambridge.org; http://uk.cambridge.org/journals. Illus., index, adv. Sample. Refereed. Vol. ends: Sep. Microform: PQC. Online: EBSCO Publishing; Gale Group; OCLC Online Computer Library Center, Inc.; RoweCom Information Quest; Swets Blackwell. Reprint: SWZ. *Indexed:* AbAn, ArtHuCI, BAS, CIJE, HumInd, IBSS, IBZ, L&LBA, LT&LA, LingAb, MLA-IB, SSCI. *Bk. rev.:* 10-12, 3-6 pages. *Aud.:* Ac.

Although this journal covers all branches of linguistics, it focuses on theoretical linguistics and phonetics. Articles are written in English, but can cover other languages as subjects, and have recently covered misuse of the notion "abduction," and gender as an inflectional category. In addition to the four 15–30 page articles, there is often a lengthy review article, 10–15 shorter reviews (each about five pages), and approximately five "shorter notices" (each one or two pages). It should be noted that the book reviews are solicited. Lastly, there is an extensive list of publications received and a preview of forthcoming articles in the *Journal of Linguistics.* Published for the Linguistics Association of Great Britain (www.essex.ac.uk/linguistics/LAGB/), this journal is often cited in the literature and would make a good selection for basic collections because it covers the broad topic of linguistics. Both association members and nonmembers publish articles. See also *American Speech.*

4346. *Journal of Literary Semantics: an international review.* [ISSN: 0341-7638] 1972. 2x/yr. EUR 93.85 domestic; EUR 96.15 foreign; EUR 45 newsstand/cover. Ed(s): Michael Toolan. Mouton de Gruyter, Genthiner Str 13, Berlin, 10785, Germany; mouton@degruyter.de; http://www.degruyter.de. Illus., adv. Sample. Refereed. Vol. ends: Oct. Reprint: PSC; SCH. *Indexed:* ArtHuCI, IBZ, L&LBA, LT&LA, LingAb, MLA-IB. *Bk. rev.:* 0-3, 4-8 pages. *Aud.:* Ac.

As the title of one recent article illustrates, "Politeness strategies in the discourse of drama: a case study," the mission of this journal is to treat literary texts as a "central, not a peripheral, concern of linguistics." Articles are written in English and also focus on other areas of applied linguistics, specifically, relating the study of literature to other disciplines (psychology, neurophysiology, mathematics, and history). The journal is based at the University of Kent at Canterbury (England) School of European and Modern Language Studies. Recommended for academic collections with corresponding programs. See also *Language and Literature.*

4347. *Journal of Phonetics.* [ISSN: 0095-4470] 1973. q. EUR 523 (Individuals, EUR 145). Ed(s): G. Docherty. Academic Press, Harcourt Pl, 32 Jamestown Rd, London, NW1 7BY, United Kingdom; apsubs@acad.com; http://www.elsevier-international.com/serials/. Adv. Refereed. Reprint: SWZ. *Indexed:* AbAn, ArtHuCI, BEL&L, L&LBA, LT&LA, LingAb, MLA-IB, PsycholAb, SSCI. *Bk. rev.:* 0-3, length varies. *Aud.:* Ac, Sa.

This journal is primarily concerned with reporting experimental work that explains and analyzes phonetic problems in any language. "Theoretical papers are acceptable provided they relate to experimental findings." Topics include speech production, speech acoustics, speech perception, speech synthesis, phonology, psycholinguistics, linguistic analysis, descriptive phonetics, and speech and language acquisition. The target audience is experimental linguists, theoretical linguists, and researchers. In addition to the five to seven ten-page articles per issue, the "Short Notes" section features brief (1,500 words) reports of work in progress. A recent feature article was titled, "Aerodynamic characteristics of trills and phonological patterning." Special thematic issues are published once a year. While *Journal of Phonetics* is a quality publication, it is too specialized and expensive to consider for general academic linguistics collections. See also *International Phonetic Association. Journal* (above in this section).

4348. *Journal of Pidgin and Creole Languages.* [ISSN: 0920-9034] 1986. s-a. EUR 240 combined subscription print & online eds. John Benjamins Publishing Co., Klaprozenweg 105, Amsterdam, 1033 NN, Netherlands; subscription@benjamins.nl; http://www.benjamins.com. Illus. Sample. Refereed. Circ: 650. *Indexed:* ArtHuCI, BEL&L, IBSS, IBZ, L&LBA, LingAb, MLA-IB. *Bk. rev.:* 1-4, 6-10 pages. *Aud.:* Ac, Sa.

This journal represents an "international effort to bring together scholarly treatments of all aspects of pidgin and creole languages," and the deeper goal of applying current research in theory and description of the two languages to "language planning, education and social reform in creole-speaking societies." Articles range from 40 to 50 pages in length, total two or three per issue, and have recently included titles such as "Habitual and Imperfective in Guyanese Creole" and "Restoring pidginization to creole genesis theory." Comprehensive lists of references conclude each article. A few book reviews, three to five pages in length, also comprise each issue. The web site has a glossary of pidgin and creole terms, as well as an index to past issues (www.ling.ohio-state.edu/research/jpcl/). Considering its moderate citation rate and narrow focus, this journal is a core selection for academic institutions where pidgin and creole languages are spoken or studied, but is a supplementary selection elsewhere. See also *English World-Wide*.

4349. ***Journal of Semantics.*** [ISSN: 0167-5133] 1982. q. GBP 136. Ed(s): Peter Bosch. Oxford University Press, Great Clarendon St, Oxford, OX2 6DP, United Kingdom; jnl.orders@oup.co.uk; http://www3.oup.co.uk/jnls. Adv. Refereed. Circ: 750. Reprint: PSC; SWZ. *Indexed:* BEL&L, IBSS, L&LBA, LT&LA, LingAb, MLA-IB, PhilInd. *Bk. rev.:* 0-1, length varies. *Aud.:* Ac, Sa.

Articles in the *Journal of Semantics* accurately reflect the meaning of semantics: analysis and description of the meaning of linguistic expressions, hence the focus on natural language studies. Recent articles have included ones titled "Tense meanings and temporal interpretation" and "The conceptual inactiveness of implicit arguments: evidence from particle verbs and object categorization." Within the realm of semantics, this journal espouses an interdisciplinary integration of philosophical, psychological, and linguistic semantics. To be considered for publication, a manuscript "must report original research relating to questions of comprehension and interpretation of sentences, texts, or discourse in natural language," and contain "empirical relevance, sound theoretic foundation, and formal as well as methodological correctness." A secondary aim is integration with logic, artificial intelligence, and anthropology. Each issue typically contains two or three articles and sometimes a lengthy, critical book review, all in English. A section titled "Notes and Discussions" is often included. A core selection for all academic general linguistics collections.

Journal of Slavic Linguistics. See CIS and Eastern Europe section.

4350. ***Language and Education: an international journal.*** [ISSN: 0950-0782] 1987. q. will be 6/yr from 2003 . GBP 260 & libraries (Individuals, GBP 50 & schools). Ed(s): Viv Edwards. Multilingual Matters Ltd., Frankfurt Lodge, Victoria Rd, Clevedon, BS21 7SJ, United Kingdom; info@multilingual-matters.com; http://www.catchword.co.uk. Illus., index, adv. Sample. Refereed. Online: EBSCO Publishing; Ingenta Select; Swets Blackwell. *Indexed:* BrEdI, CIJE, L&LBA, LT&LA, LingAb. *Bk. rev.:* 1-2, 2-4 pages, signed. *Aud.:* Ac.

Slim at approximately 300 pages per volume, *Language and Education* presents original scholarship on a wide range of issues affecting first- and second-language acquisition. It is published in English and is international in scope, although the majority of research comes from Britain, Australia, and Hong Kong. Articles are bracketed by authors' abstracts and relevant references. An array of pedagogical concerns is addressed, among them language policy, teaching methods, bilingualism, distance learning, and literacy. Articles have included "Decoding as a Cultural Practice and its Effects on the Reading Process of Bilingual Pupils." The price makes it a marginal purchase except for complete collections.

4351. ***Language and Literature.*** [ISSN: 0963-9470] 1992. q. GBP 294 print & online eds. in Europe, Middle East, Africa & Australasia. Ed(s): Katie Wales. Sage Publications Ltd., 6 Bonhill St, London, EC2A 4PU, United Kingdom; info@sagepub.co.uk; http://www.sagepub.co.uk/. Adv. Refereed. Circ: 800. Online: EBSCO Publishing; ingenta.com; OCLC Online Computer Library Center, Inc.; RoweCom Information Quest; Swets Blackwell. *Indexed:* L&LBA, LingAb, MLA-IB. *Bk. rev.:* 1-4, 2-5 pages. *Aud.:* Ac.

While the main focus of this journal is stylistics, its mission states that it publishes the latest research on the "connections between stylistics, critical theory, linguistics, literary criticism and their pedagogical applications." Each issue contains three sections: four or five articles with compendious bibliographies, notes and discussion; and one to four book reviews. "The Italian line in English after Chaucer" and "Revisiting the notion of faithfulness in discourse presentation using a corpus approach" are titles of two recent articles. The "Notes and Discussion" section provides a professional forum for commentary and debate. In addition to the book reviews, a substantial list of books received but not reviewed concludes each issue. Although this is an excellent journal, consider it for selection only if there is extra money in your library's budget. See also *Journal of Literary Semantics*.

4352. ***Language in Society.*** [ISSN: 0047-4045] 1972. 5x/yr. USD 199 (Individuals, USD 79). Ed(s): Jane Hill. Cambridge University Press, The Edinburgh Bldg, Shaftesbury Rd, Cambridge, CB2 2RU, United Kingdom; information@cambridge.org; http://uk.cambridge.org/journals. Illus., adv. Sample. Refereed. Vol. ends: Dec. Microform: PQC. Online: EBSCO Publishing; OCLC Online Computer Library Center, Inc.; RoweCom Information Quest; Swets Blackwell. Reprint: SWZ. *Indexed:* ASSIA, AbAn, AgeL, AnthLit, ArtHuCI, BAS, BEL&L, BRI, BrEdI, CBRI, CIJE, CommAb, HumInd, IBSS, L&LBA, LT&LA, LingAb, MLA-IB, PsycholAb, SSCI, SociolAb. *Bk. rev.:* 10-15, 2-4 pages, signed. *Aud.:* Ac.

A recent article titled "*Well* weird, *right* dodgy, *very* strange, *really* cool: layering and recycling in English intensifiers" contributes to this publication's overall goal: to study speech and language "as aspects of social life." Articles that combine empirical research with general theoretical or methodological interest are preferred. Other recent topics include advances in qualitative analysis, corpora, dense analysis of talk, and "Amen and Hallelujah preaching: discourse functions in African-American sermons." The four or five articles per issue are in English only, and range from 25 to 30 pages in length. Book reviews can be 2,000–2,500 words long. *Language in Society* is a core journal for many reasons: it is heavily cited in the literature; it is known as a core journal for general linguistics; it is the premier journal of sociolinguistics; and it balances empirical findings with theoretical foundations of linguistics. Recommended for any academic collection. See also *International Journal of the Sociology of Language*.

4353. ***Language Variation and Change.*** [ISSN: 0954-3945] 1989. 3x/yr. USD 105 (Individuals, USD 50). Ed(s): Anthony Kroch, David Sankoff. Cambridge University Press, The Edinburgh Bldg, Shaftesbury Rd, Cambridge, CB2 2RU, United Kingdom; information@cambridge.org; http://uk.cambridge.org/journals. Illus., adv. Sample. Refereed. Microform: PQC. Online: EBSCO Publishing; OCLC Online Computer Library Center, Inc.; RoweCom Information Quest. Reprint: SWZ. *Indexed:* AnthLit, CIJE, L&LBA, LT&LA, LingAb, MLA-IB. *Aud.:* Ac.

This journal, written mostly in English but occasionally in French, publishes scientific research on "description and understanding of language variability and change at the levels of the speaker/hearer and the speech community." More specifically, the journal's content focuses on the structure and process of language production, oral or written, from both modern and historical sources. "Writing good Southerne: local and supralocal norms in the Plumpton letter collection" and "*It's not* or *isn't it*? Using large corpora to determine the influences on contraction strategies" are examples of recent feature articles. Book reviews are not published. Considering its price, this journal is an inexpensive supplementary selection for academic general-linguistics collections.

4354. ***Language (Washington).*** [ISSN: 0097-8507] 1925. q. USD 120 (Individuals, USD 65; Students, USD 25). Ed(s): Brian Joseph. Linguistic Society of America, 1325 18th St, N W, Ste 211, Washington, DC 20036-6501; lsa@lsadc.org; http://www.lsadc.org. Illus., adv. Sample. Refereed. Circ: 6200 Paid. Vol. ends: Dec. Online: Gale Group; JSTOR (Web-based Journal Archive); OCLC Online Computer Library Center, Inc.; Project MUSE; RoweCom Information Quest; Swets Blackwell. Reprint: PSC. *Indexed:* ABS&EES, AICP, AnthLit, ArtHuCI, BEL&L, CIJE, HumInd, IBSS, IBZ, L&LBA, LT&LA, LingAb, MLA-IB, PsycholAb, SSCI. *Bk. rev.:* 5-8, 1-4 pages. *Aud.:* Ac.

Language, the journal of the Linguistic Society of America (LSA), is a major scholarly, general linguistics journal that publishes technical articles on problems in linguistic science. It is a perfect example of a scholarly linguistics journal. Recent articles are about forensic linguistics, ordering of affixes, and feature classes in morphology. The four articles in each issue contain meticulous lists of references, and have no maximum length. The eight to ten book reviews (500–1,200 words each) are followed by 40–50 book notices (250 words each) and a list of recent publications (100–200 per issue). At least one author of each submitted article must be a member of the LSA (www.lsadc.org). This journal is unsurprisingly heavily cited in the linguistics literature. Recommended for even the smallest, most general academic linguistics collections.

4355. ***Lingua: international review of general linguistics.*** [ISSN: 0024-3841] 1947. m. EUR 922 (Individuals, EUR 441). Ed(s): J Rooryck. Elsevier BV, North-Holland, Sara Burgerhartstraat 25, Amsterdam, 1055 KV, Netherlands; nlinfo-f@elsevier.nl; http://www.elsevier.nl/homepage/about/us/regional_sites.htt. Illus., index, adv. Sample. Refereed. Circ: 1078. Microform: PQC. Online: ingenta.com; ScienceDirect; Swets Blackwell. Reprint: SWZ. *Indexed:* AbAn, ArtHuCI, BAS, IBZ, L&LBA, LT&LA, LingAb, MLA-IB, SSCI. *Bk. rev.:* 0-3, 5-10 pages. *Aud.:* Ac, Sa.

Lingua focuses on general linguistics problems and successfully targets its intended audience of "any linguist," regardless of specialization. The journal's high citation rate indicates its broad readership. Articles, written mostly in English but sometimes in French and German, about "general theoretical implications" comprise most of the journal's content. Recent articles are titled "Do children produce the melody before the words? A review of developmental intonation research" and "The formal origins of syntactic theory." Feature articles are normally 20–40 pages long. Critical book reviews, usually five to ten pages in length, are not published in every issue. This is hands-down a core selection for both general and theoretical academic linguistics collections. See also *General Linguistics.*

4356. ***Linguistic Analysis.*** [ISSN: 0098-9053] 1975. 2x/yr. USD 134 (Individuals, USD 58). Ed(s): Michael K Brame. Linguistic Analysis, PO Box 2418, Vashon, WA 98070; Info@linguisticanlysis.com. Illus., index, adv. Sample. Refereed. Circ: 1000. Microform: PQC. *Indexed:* ABS&EES, AbAn, ArtHuCI, BAS, CompR, LT&LA, LingAb, MLA-IB, SSCI. *Bk. rev.:* 0-2, 5-15 pages. *Aud.:* Ac, Sa.

Linguistic Analysis, considered a core journal for both general and theoretical linguistics, concentrates on formal phonology, morphology, syntax, and semantics. "A production grammar for Javanese kinship terminology" and "Scrambling in German and Japanese from a minimalist point of view" are the titles of two recent, appealing articles. Articles range from five to 50 pages in length and usually total three per issue. Occasional special, double issues are published, such as the issue on minimalist syntax. Book reviews range from five to 25 pages in length, although only two are published per year. A unique section at the end of each issue, titled "Ungrammatical Notes," provides fun commentary on linguistic topics, such as William Shakespeare's real name. In addition to being a core journal for general and theoretical linguistics alike, *Linguistic Analysis* is also a highly cited journal, and therefore deserves a place in medium and large academic linguistics collections.

4357. ***Linguistic Inquiry.*** [ISSN: 0024-3892] 1970. q. USD 194 (Individuals, USD 60; Students, USD 35). Ed(s): Samuel Jay Keyser. MIT Press, 5 Cambridge Center, Cambridge, MA 02142-1493; journals-orders@mit.edu; http://mitpress.mit.edu. Illus., index, adv. Refereed. Circ: 3200. Vol. ends: Fall. Microform: PQC. Online: EBSCO Publishing; Ingenta Select; OCLC Online Computer Library Center, Inc.; Project MUSE; RoweCom Information Quest; Swets Blackwell. Reprint: ISI; PQC; SCH. *Indexed:* ABS&EES, AbAn, ArtHuCI, BAS, IBSS, L&LBA, LT&LA, LingAb, MLA-IB, SSCI. *Aud.:* Ac.

An article in this journal, "Syllabification in Armenian, Universal Grammar, and the Lexicon," reveals its international nature and its theoretical scope. Its web site says it "keeps readers informed of new theoretical developments based on the latest international discoveries." Articles are in English and range from 20 to 50 pages, each with compendious references. The four articles per issue are authored by some of the world's most well-known linguists. Less extensive research and commentary is published in the "Remarks and Replies" and "Squibs and Discussion" sections. Although it is often considered a core linguistics journal and its articles are heavily cited, this journal is best suited to experts in the field. However, strong consideration should be given for its inclusion in collections, as it is a premier journal for theoretical linguistics research.

4358. ***The Linguistic Review.*** [ISSN: 0167-6318] 1981. 4x/yr. EUR 173.10 domestic; EUR 176.20 foreign; EUR 42 newsstand/cover. Ed(s): Harry van der Hulst. Mouton de Gruyter, Genthiner Str 13, Berlin, 10785, Germany; mouton@degruyter.de; http://www.degruyter.de. Illus., adv. Sample. Refereed. Reprint: SWZ. *Indexed:* ArtHuCI, BAS, BEL&L, IBSS, L&LBA, LT&LA, LingAb, MLA-IB. *Aud.:* Ac.

Syntax, semantics, phonology, and morphology, studied in the context of Generative Grammar, comprise the contents of *The Linguistic Review*. "Critical discussions of theoretical linguistics as a branch of cognitive psychology" and ideas for thematic issues with guest editors are also welcome. Articles, written in English and ending with lengthy lists of references, have recently included the titles, "The distribution of superheavy syllables in standard German" and "Why language acquisition is a snap." The editor recently stated that the journal wishes to increase the number of book reviews, including general reviews and longer review articles. The extensive list of received publications provides an additional benefit. Annual subject and language indexes are published in the journal. Recommended for general academic linguistics collections because it is an often-cited core journal for general and theoretical linguistics.

4359. ***Linguistic Typology.*** [ISSN: 1430-0532] 1997. 3x/yr. EUR 120.10 domestic; EUR 123.15 foreign; EUR 39 newsstand/cover. Ed(s): Frans Plank. Mouton de Gruyter, Genthiner Str 13, Berlin, 10785, Germany; mouton@degruyter.de; http://www.degruyter.de. Adv. Sample. Refereed. Online: EBSCO Publishing; OCLC Online Computer Library Center, Inc. Reprint: PSC; SCH. *Indexed:* IBZ. *Bk. rev.:* 0-8, 3-10 pages. *Aud.:* Ac, Sa.

A recent thematic issue in this journal centered on the degree of complexity in creole grammars. Published in English, by the Association for Linguistic Typology (www.ling.lancs.ac.uk/alt), this international journal contains original research on both the differences and commonalities of all languages, based on core characteristics of sound, grammar, lexicon, and discourse. Other topics include language profiles and family records; basic topical bibliographies; highlights from the history of typology; and literature surveys. Articles range from 20 to 60 pages. *Linguistic Typology* is on the border between a core selection for linguistics collections and a supplementary selection.

4360. ***Linguistics: an interdisciplinary journal of the language sciences.*** [ISSN: 0024-3949] 1963. 6x/yr. EUR 388; EUR 65 newsstand/cover. Ed(s): Wolfgang Klein. Mouton de Gruyter, Genthiner Str 13, Berlin, 10785, Germany; mouton@degruyter.de; http://www.degruyter.de. Illus., adv. Sample. Refereed. Microform: SWZ. Online: EBSCO Publishing; Florida Center for Library Automation; Gale Group; OCLC Online Computer Library Center, Inc.; Swets Blackwell. Reprint: SWZ. *Indexed:* AbAn, ArtHuCI, BAS, HumInd, IBSS, IBZ, L&LBA, LT&LA, LingAb, MLA-IB, PsycholAb, SSCI. *Bk. rev.:* 3-4, 3-7 pages. *Aud.:* Ac.

"Interdisciplinary" is key to this prestigious, moderately cited journal's mission: to serve as an interdisciplinary forum for research in the language sciences, combining the traditional linguistic disciplines of pragmatics, semantics, syntax, morphology, phonology, and first- and second-language acquisition. Articles, which have no length restriction but must be in English, include examples such as "Toward a typology of focus and focus constructions" and "Learning the meaning of verbs: what distinguishes language-impaired from normally developing children." Lists of references are thorough. Occasional issues are thematic, such as the issue on children with Specific Language Impairment across languages. Book reviews are 500–1,000 words long and can cover more than one book. Consider *Linguistics* a core selection for both general and theoretical aspects of graduate linguistics programs.

4361. ***Linguistics and Education: an international research journal.*** [ISSN: 0898-5898] 1988. q. EUR 219 (Individuals, EUR 61). Ed(s): D. Bloome, J. L. Lemke. Pergamon, The Boulevard, Langford Ln, East Park, Kidlington, OX5 1GB, United Kingdom. Illus., adv. Sample. Refereed. Circ: 400. Online: ingenta.com; ScienceDirect; Swets Blackwell. *Indexed:* CIJE, L&LBA, LT&LA, LingAb, MLA-IB. *Bk. rev.:* 0-1, 1,500-6,000 words. *Aud.:* Ac.

The title of a recent article, "Narratives in two languages: assessing performance of bilingual children," conveys this journal's mission: to present research on all topics in linguistics and education, including classroom interaction, language diversity, policy, curriculum, written language learning, language disorders, and the "application of linguistics, sociolinguistics, psycholinguistics, discourse analysis, social semiotics, conversational analysis and ethnomethodology to educational issues." Articles average five per issue and 30–40 pages in length. Occasional special issues are published (e.g., "Narrative analysis in a multicultural society"). Very few book reviews are published (none or one per issue) but are 1,500–6,000 words long. Recommended as a supplementary selection for teacher education collections. See also *ELT Journal, TESOL Quarterly, The Modern Language Journal,* and *Applied Linguistics*.

Linguistics and Philosophy. See Philosophy section.

4362. ***Modern Language Journal: devoted to research and discussion about the learning and teaching of foreign and second languages.*** [ISSN: 0026-7902] 1916. q. USD 102 print & online eds. Blackwell Publishing, Inc., Commerce Place, 350 Main St, Malden, MA 02148; subscrip@blackwellpub.com; http://www.blackwellpublishing.com. Illus., index, adv. Refereed. Circ: 7000. Vol. ends: Dec. Microform: PMC; PQC. Online: EBSCO Publishing; ingenta.com; JSTOR (Web-based Journal Archive); OCLC Online Computer Library Center, Inc.; RoweCom Information Quest; Swets Blackwell; H.W. Wilson. *Indexed:* ABS&EES, ArtHuCI, BEL&L, BRD, BRI, CBRI, CIJE, EduInd, IBZ, L&LBA, LT&LA, MLA-IB, MRD, PsycholAb, SSCI. *Bk. rev.:* 20-30, 1-2 pages. *Aud.:* Hs, Ga, Ac.

As a highly cited, comprehensive scholarly publication, *The Modern Language Journal* (MLJ) is a must-have for every academic library. It publishes articles, research studies, editorials, reports, book reviews, and professional news and announcements relating to modern languages, especially "questions and concerns about the learning and teaching of foreign and second languages." Articles range from 10 to 30 pages in length. A recent article is about evaluating qualitative research in applied linguistics. In addition to excellent articles, there are several other sections in each issue. "News & Notes of the Profession" announces upcoming conferences, calls for papers, requests for proposals, special summer programs, new degree programs, grants received, international research projects, and legislative developments. Another section that increases the value of the journal is titled "In Other Professional Journals." Averaging about ten pages in length, it gives a detailed list of articles published on relevant topics. The "Reviews" section, succinctly organized by subject, contains around 25, 500–2,000-word reviews on books, monographs, software, and other materials that present research results and methods in foreign and second language teaching and learning, intended for use as textbooks and other instructional aids. *MLJ* is published for the National Federation of Modern Language Teachers Associations (http://polyglot.lss.wisc.edu/mlj/nfmlta.htm), whose mission is the "expansion, promotion, and improvement of the teaching of languages, literatures, and cultures throughout the United States." Only 15 to 20 percent of the manuscripts submitted to *MLJ* are accepted. See also *Applied Linguistics, ELT Journal, Linguistics and Education, TESOL Quarterly,* and *Studies in Second Language Acquisition*.

4363. ***Natural Language and Linguistic Theory.*** [ISSN: 0167-806X] 1983. q. EUR 508 print or online ed. Ed(s): Joan Maling. Kluwer Academic Publishers, van Godewijckstraat 30, PO Box 17, Dordrecht, 3300 AA, Netherlands; services@wkap.nl; http://www.wkap.nl. Illus., adv. Sample. Refereed. Vol. ends: Nov. Microform: PQC. Online: EBSCO Publishing; ingenta.com; OCLC Online Computer Library Center, Inc.; Ovid Technologies, Inc.; RoweCom Information Quest; Swets Blackwell. Reprint: SWZ. *Indexed:* AbAn, ArtHuCI, BEL&L, IBZ, L&LBA, LT&LA, LingAb, MLA-IB, SSCI. *Bk. rev.:* 0-1, 5,000 words. *Aud.:* Ac.

Natural Language and Linguistic Theory intends to bring together linguistic phenomena and theoretical research and, in doing so, hopes to make "complex language data accessible to those unfamiliar with the language area being studied," theoretical linguists and graduate students specifically. Articles, all in English, bridge the gap between "descriptive work and work of a highly theoretical, less empirically oriented nature." The theoretical side of the journal's content presents articles on the syntax, semantics, phonology, and lexicon of the natural language, while other examples include quantification, negation, modality, genericity, tense, aspect, anaphora, nominalization, ellipsis, and interrogatives. The journal also welcomes surveys of recent theoretical developments and replies to recent articles. "To be an oblique subject" and "Morphologically conditioned phonological alternations" are the titles of two recent articles. While there are four or five lengthy articles in each issue, there is only one book review per year. This journal is a core selection for both general and theoretical linguistics. Not only is it heavily cited, but it also seeks an audience of researchers, practitioners and students, making it the only linguistics journal to specifically target students in its intended audience.

Scandinavian Studies. See Europe/General section.

Slavic and East European Journal. See CIS and Eastern Europe section.

4364. ***Studies in Language: international journal sponsored by the foundation "Foundations of Language".*** Supersedes: *Foundations of Language.* [ISSN: 0378-4177] 1977. 3x/yr. EUR 370 combined subscription print & online eds. John Benjamins Publishing Co., Klaprozenweg 105, Amsterdam, 1033 NN, Netherlands; subscription@benjamins.nl; http://www.benjamins.com. Illus., adv. Sample. Refereed. Circ: 800. Reprint: SWZ. *Indexed:* AbAn, ArtHuCI, BAS, BEL&L, HumInd, L&LBA, LingAb, MLA-IB, SSCI. *Bk. rev.:* 10-20, 6-8 pages. *Aud.:* Ac, Sa.

Theoretical foundations of language derived from language analysis are at the heart of this highly cited, core journal's content. Issues in contemporary linguistics are discussed in relation to discourse-pragmatic, functional, and typological theories. The emphasis is on "discourse grammar; syntactic, morphological and semantic universals; pragmatics; grammaticalization and grammaticalization theory; and the description of problems in individual languages," as well as historical linguistics. Priority is given to articles containing typological and cross-linguistic perspectives, especially where empirical methodology is used to analyze grammar. Recent contributions include a cross-linguistic typology of demonstratives, and "Systematization and the origin of rules: the case of subject–verb inversion in questions." The usual language of publication is English. In addition to the five articles per issue, there are generally two review articles, four to seven reviews, four book notices, and a long list of publications received. Recommended for general academic linguistics collections.

4365. ***Studies in Second Language Acquisition.*** [ISSN: 0272-2631] 1977. q. USD 153 (Individuals, USD 72). Ed(s): Albert Valdman. Cambridge University Press, The Edinburgh Bldg, Shaftesbury Rd, Cambridge, CB2 2RU, United Kingdom; information@cambridge.org; http://uk.cambridge.org/journals. Illus., adv. Sample. Refereed. Vol. ends: Dec. Microform: PQC. Online: EBSCO Publishing; OCLC Online Computer Library Center, Inc.; RoweCom Information Quest; Swets Blackwell. Reprint: PQC; SWZ. *Indexed:* BAS, CIJE, EduInd, IBZ, L&LBA, LT&LA, MLA-IB. *Bk. rev.:* 5-10, 1-2 pages. *Aud.:* Ac.

Studies in Second Language Acquisition publishes mostly theory-based articles reporting research studies on issues in second and foreign language acquisition of any language. "However, empirical investigations of the interface between second language acquisition and language pedagogy, such as classroom interaction or the effects of instruction" are also published. Recent topics include mapping techniques in vocabulary acquisition, and the compounding parameter in second language acquisition (SLA). The articles have extensive lists of references. The journal's average acceptance rate is 10 to 20 percent. Recommended for most academic linguistics collections. See also *ELT Journal; The Modern Language Journal: Language Learning;* and *TESOL Quarterly.*

4366. ***T E S O L Quarterly: a journal for teachers of English to speakers of other languages and of standard English as a second dialect.*** [ISSN: 0039-8322] 1967. q. USD 285. Ed(s): Sandra McKay. Teachers of English to Speakers of Other Languages, 700 S Washington St, Ste 200, Alexandria, VA 22314; tesol@tesol.edu; http://www.tesol.edu. Illus., adv. Sample. Refereed. Circ: 12000. Vol. ends: Winter. Microform: PQC. Online: Ingenta Select. Reprint: PQC. *Indexed:* CIJE, EduInd, HumInd, IBZ, L&LBA, LT&LA, MLA-IB, SSCI, SSI. *Bk. rev.:* 8-10, 3-5 pages. *Aud.:* Ac.

This exceptional journal is published by Teachers of English to Speakers of Other Languages (TESOL) (www.tesol.org), an international organization that produces professional standards, continuing education, student programs, and enhances communication among specialists who teach English as a second language or standard English as a second dialect. Main topics include the psychology and sociology of language learning and language teaching, curriculum design, testing, evaluation, professional preparation and standards, language planning, instructional methods, materials, and techniques, and research and research methodology. Articles focus on combining theory and practice, thereby producing useful and plausible contributions for a broad readership. Two recent articles contribute to the journal's mission of combining theoretical and practical issues: "Reading in two languages: how attitudes toward home language and beliefs about reading affect the behaviors of underprepared L2 college readers" and "Dueling philosophies: inclusion or separation for Florida's English language learners." Special issues are published once per volume. In addition to the informative articles, readers will be pleased to find brief reports on new research, a forum for commentary, discussions of qualitative and quantitative research issues and teaching issues, and review articles, reviews, and notices on new books. A basic purchase for high school libraries where ESL is of pedagogical concern, and academic institutions supporting teacher education programs. See also *ELT Journal, Modern Language Journal, Applied Linguistics,* and *Studies in Second Language Acquisition.*

Visible Language. See Printing and Graphic Arts section.

■ LITERARY REVIEWS

See also Fiction; Literature; Little Magazines; and News and Opinion sections.

Mary Beth Clack, Research Librarian, Widener Library, Harvard University, Cambridge, MA 02138; mclack@fas.harvard.edu

Laura Farwell Blake, Research Librarian, Widener Library, Harvard University, Cambridge, MA 02138; farwell@fas.harvard.edu

Introduction

The pleasure of compiling and annotating a list of literary reviews is in reading new work from familiar and emerging writers, discovering new explorations in well-known titles, and mappig the the digital world of literary magazines. The range of voices, forms, media, and perspectives is wider than one might suspect in this constellation of titles.

For those journals whose history is long, there are now established web presences. They invite readers to redefine the idea of the literary magazine and even the act of reading.

We have tried to identify electronic journals whose presence on the web is established, because this is a guide for libraries building collections.

The publications here all demand to be read and, in the case of some web publications, to be heard; these short stories, essays, poems, novellas, works of art, and thoughtful prose have the power to provoke, to inspire, to clarify, to create new forms of literary expression and to exemplify the best of the traditional.

Basic Periodicals

Ga, Ac: *The Georgia Review, Hudson Review, The Iowa Review, The Kenyon Review, The North American Review, Ontario Review, The Paris Review, Prairie Schooner, Sewanee Review, TriQuarterly, Virginia Quarterly Review, Web del Sol, The Yale Review.*

Basic Abstracts and Indexes

American Humanities Index, Annual Bibliography of English Language and Literature, Humanities Index, Index of American Periodical Verse, MLA International Bibliography of Books and Articles on the Modern Languages and Literatures.

4367. *Agni.* Formerly (until 1988): *Agni Review.* [ISSN: 1046-218X] 1972. 2x/yr. USD 15 domestic; USD 19 foreign. Ed(s): Askold Melnyczuk. Agni Review, Inc., 236 Bay State Rd, Boston, MA 02215-1403; agni@bu.edu; http://www.bu.edu/. Adv. Circ: 2000. *Indexed:* AmHI, IAPV, MLA-IB. *Aud.:* Ga, Ac.

Agni has featured poetry, short fiction, essays, and reviews since its founding, with an increasing emphasis on international writers. In the past few issues, contemporary German poets were featured, as well as work in translation from Spanish, Armenian, Ukrainian, Swedish, and Russian. Reflecting the salient issues of our times, the most recent issue, (commemorating the 40th anniversary of the review), is devoted to pieces on Amnesty International, nonviolence and literature, and related topics. *Agni* online is hosted by *Web del Sol*, with online issue numbers 1–5 currently available.

4368. *Alaska Quarterly Review.* [ISSN: 0737-268X] 1982. s-a. Individuals, USD 10. Ed(s): Ronald Spatz. University of Alaska at Anchorage, College of Arts and Sciences, 3211 Providence Dr, Anchorage, AK 99508; AYAQR@uaa.alaska.edu; http://www.uaa.alaska.edu/aqr/. Illus. Circ: 2200. Vol. ends: Fall/Winter. Microform: PQC. *Indexed:* AmHI. *Aud.:* Ga, Ac.

Sponsored by the University of Alaska, the review focuses on contemporary art, fiction, short plays, poetry, and literary nonfiction in traditional and experimental styles. Highly acclaimed, the journal conveys a strong sense of the "True North," evidenced on its covers, which feature scenes from both Alaska's natural world and the daily life of its people, and in its content, which emphasizes Alaskan subjects and motifs. A special edition, *Alaska Native Writers, Storytellers and Orators*, appeared in 1999; it highlighted oral traditions and written texts in 20 distinctive native languages. The volume featured selected works (in the original and in translation) and other sources discussing the languages and translation issues. Guided by an editor who is a writer and filmmaker (and who edits *LitSite Alaska*, the statewide literacy web site), the *AQR* web site has well-chosen links to literary review sources. A detailed index to volumes 1–12 also appears.

4369. *Antioch Review.* [ISSN: 0003-5769] 1941. q. USD 72 (Individuals, USD 35; USD 7 newsstand/cover per issue domestic). Ed(s): Robert S Fogarty. Antioch Review, Inc., PO Box 148, Yellow Springs, OH 45387; review@antioch.edu. Illus., index, adv. Circ: 5100. Vol. ends: Fall. Microform: MIM; PMC; PQC. Online: bigchalk; Chadwyck-Healey Incorporated; EBSCO Publishing; Florida Center for Library Automation; Gale Group; Northern Light Technology, Inc.; OCLC Online Computer Library Center, Inc.; ProQuest Information & Learning; H.W. Wilson. Reprint: PQC. *Indexed:* ABS&EES, AgeL, AmHI, ArtHuCI, BAS, BRD, BRI, BiogInd, CBRI, FLI, HumInd, IAPV, IBZ, MLA-IB, MagInd, PAIS, PhilInd, SFSA, SSCI. *Bk. rev.:* 15-30, 300 words. *Aud.:* Ga, Ac.

The *Antioch Review* takes pride in being one of the oldest continuously published literary reviews in the United States, featuring writers "on the up-bounce" of their careers. Its distinguished advisory board (Daniel Bell, Gordon Lish, Mark Strand, and others) marked the magazine's 60th anniversary with a hefty issue, including stories, poetry, and essays (including an erudite essay on the fate of the book by Sven Birkerts). In recent years, the review has increased the amount of space devoted to poetry and reviews and includes an informative "Letter from London." Other theme issues have focused on jazz, new writing, unforgettable characters, and various perspectives on undergraduate life. The web site describes the review's colorful history, noting its penchant for featuring academic writing in a "belles-lettres or journalistic tradition," and contains tables of contents for current and upcoming issues and excerpts of poetry and prose.

4370. *Bellevue Literary Review: a journal of humanity and human experience.* [ISSN: 1537-5048] 2001. s-a. USD 18 (Individuals, USD 12). Ed(s): Danielle Ofri. New York University School of Medicine, 550 First Ave, New York, NY 10016. *Aud.:* Ga,Ac.

Emanating from Bellevue, the oldest public hospital in the United States, and New York University's Department of Medicine, the *Bellevue Literary Review* (*BLR*) calls itself a "journal of humanity and human experience." Fiction, creative nonfiction, poetry, and critical essays are gathered here, with the express aim that contributions "touch upon relationships to the human body, illness, health and healing . . . [and] the creative interpretation of these themes."

Many contributors are health professionals. Currently in its fourth issue (Spring 2003), the review is expanding its range of writing on the human condition. The web site, set against a background of the Bellevue building, contains an interesting history of the hospital, in addition to current-issue and archive links. Readers also find a link to the October 2002 *New York Times* feature article on the unique history of the review, emphasizing its connection with national trends in medical education. It states that medical programs are increasingly using literature to "teach doctors how to write better and clearer case histories and to empathize more with patients." The editor of the *BLR* supports these objectives. Interesting links on the site include, among others, medical journals that have literary columns and/or discuss literature.

4371. ***Boulevard: journal of contemporary writing.*** [ISSN: 0885-9337] 1986. 3x/yr. USD 15; USD 8 newsstand/cover per issue; USD 21 foreign. Ed(s): Richard Burgin. St. Louis University, St. Louis, MO 63108-2103. Illus., adv. Sample. Circ: 4000. *Indexed:* AmHI, IAPV. *Aud.:* Ga, Ac.

This review recently moved to St. Louis University, where the editor continues to feature short fiction, criticism, essays, poetry, and innovative artwork, joined by an illustrious board including Francine Prose, James Tate, and David Mamet. The first issue in the new venue includes pieces by Alice Hoffman, Joyce Carol Oates, and Billy Collins. In addition to general offerings in the above-named categories, *Boulevard* often includes special sections on such topics as "The Other Arts" (for example, interviews about dance with Balanchine, John Cage, and Orson Welles, and essays on film) and the "Separated Families Section," which explores various experiences of separation in particular settings (Native American, Serbo-Croatian, Asian American, Hispanic). The web site is now hosted by editor Richard Burgin (www.richardburgin.com) and displays samples of fiction, essays, poetry, and cover art.

Canadian Fiction. See Fiction: General/Mystery and Detective/General section.

4372. ***Chicago Review.*** [ISSN: 0009-3696] 1946. q. USD 42 (Individuals, USD 18; USD 8 newsstand/cover per issue). Ed(s): Eirik Steinhoff. Chicago Review, 5801 S Kenwood Ave, Chicago, IL 60637-1794; org_crev@orgmail.uchicago.edu. Illus., adv. Refereed. Circ: 2700 Paid. Microform: PQC. Online: bigchalk; Chadwyck-Healey Incorporated; EBSCO Publishing; Florida Center for Library Automation; Gale Group; Northern Light Technology, Inc.; OCLC Online Computer Library Center, Inc.; ProQuest Information & Learning; H.W. Wilson. Reprint: PQC. *Indexed:* ABS&EES, AmHI, ArtHuCI, BAS, HumInd, IAPV, MLA-IB. *Bk. rev.:* 4-9, 2-6 pages signed. *Aud.:* Ga, Ac.

The *Chicago Review* includes fiction, poetry, essays, and a "Notes & Comments" section that brings together interesting bits on trends in poetry and fiction, recent developments in publishing and the art world, and remembrances of notable authors. In keeping with its intent to be an "international journal of writing and cultural exchange," the review features poetry and prose in a wide variety of countries and works not represented in English translations. Special issues are particularly content-rich; recently, they have treated new Polish writing (75 contributors) and "New Writing in German," a 360-page anthology. Both are impressive collections of works by new, "less-exposed writers" as well as well-known authors. Other special issues have centered on French new philosophy and postmodernism. The web edition's archives provide contents capsules for number 16 and following.

4373. ***Colorado Review: a journal of contemporary literature.*** Formerly (until 1965): *Colorado State Review.* [ISSN: 1046-3348] 1955. 3x/yr. USD 34 (Individuals, USD 24). Ed(s): Stephanie G'Schwind, David Milofsky. Colorado State University, English Department, Fort Collins, CO 80523; creview@vines.colostate.edu. Adv. Circ: 1500. *Indexed:* AmHI, IAPV. *Bk. rev.:* Number and length vary. *Aud.:* Ga, Ac, Sa.

Hailing from the Center for Literary Publishing at Colorado State University, the *Colorado Review* began with a commitment to publishing magical realism and translations. Marking its tenth anniversary in 2001, the review has evolved to include new writing and a diverse group of writers, with more fiction and creative nonfiction accompanying poetry, interviews, and book reviews. A recent special issue on Latinos featured a cross-section of current work centering on identity, culture, and history. Aiming to provide a greater literary awareness in Colorado and beyond, its editorial roster includes Jorie Graham, John Ashbery, James Tate, and Forrest Gander.

4374. ***Conjunctions.*** [ISSN: 0278-2324] 1981. s-a. USD 18 domestic; USD 25 foreign. Ed(s): Bradford Morrow. Bard College, Publication Department, PO Box 5000, Annandale On Hudson, NY 12504-5000; http://www.conjunctions.com. Adv. Circ: 7500. *Indexed:* AmHI, IAPV. *Aud.:* Ga, Ac.

Conjunctions has been featuring both new and established writers in its print format for over two decades. Recent theme issues on American poetry and American fiction count Ann Beattie, Julia Alvarez, and Russell Banks among the contributors. In an innovative, "cross-genre" issue, science fiction, fantasy, and horror are included. The skillfully designed electronic version of the journal presents a "living notebook" of innovative fiction, poetry, criticism, drama, art, and interviews. The web site is searchable, and its "Audio Vault" includes such authors as Philip Roth, William Gass, and Italo Calvino reading from their works. The archives hold all past issues with capsule descriptions of contributions and selected full texts. Links to the site include a good variety of literary magazines, bookstores, reviews, publishers, and distributors, as well as a connection to the comprehensive review site *Web del Sol.* The New Postings link previews the 40th anniversary issue.

4375. ***Critical Quarterly.*** [ISSN: 0011-1562] 1959. q. GBP 120 print & online. Ed(s): Colin MacCabe. Blackwell Publishing Ltd., 9600 Garsington Rd, PO Box 805, Oxford, OX4 2DQ, United Kingdom; customerservices@oxon.blackwellpublishing.com; http://www.blackwellpublishing.com/. Illus., adv. Sample. Refereed. Circ: 2200. Vol. ends: Dec. Online: EBSCO Publishing; Gale Group; ingenta.com; OCLC Online Computer Library Center, Inc.; RoweCom Information Quest; Swets Blackwell. Reprint: PSC; SWZ. *Indexed:* ArtHuCI, BEL&L, BRI, BrHumI, CBRI, FLI, HumInd, IBZ, L&LBA, LRI, MLA-IB, RI-1, SSCI, SociolAb. *Aud.:* Ga, Ac.

Originally launched by C. B. Cox and A. E. Dyson to provide a forum for contemporary poetry, fiction, and criticism, *Critical Quarterly* purports to offer a full range of cultural forms, from commentary on the literary canon to debate and discussion of cinema, television, and other aspects of cultural life and studies. The special issue on literary and cultural life in Scotland presented guest writers from the British Isles describing art, football, and alternative media. Recent issues on modernism and women's literary history continue to emphasize the blend of literary criticism, cultural studies, and creative works. Each issue also includes a regular section on current issues in language, education, and politics. A. L. Kennedy, Malcolm Bradbury, A. S. Byatt, Jayne Anne Phillips, and Cornel West have been counted among its illustrious contributors.

4376. ***The Dalhousie Review: a Canadian journal of literature and opinion.*** [ISSN: 0011-5827] 1921. 3x/yr. CND 32.10 (Individuals, CND 22.50). Ed(s): Ronald Huebert. Dalhousie University Press, Ltd., Dalhousie University, Halifax, NS B3H 3J5, Canada; Dalhousie.Review@dal.ca. Illus., index, adv. Refereed. Circ: 800. Vol. ends: Winter. Microform: MML. Online: Gale Group. Reprint: PQC. *Indexed:* ABS&EES, AmH&L, ArtHuCI, BAS, BEL&L, BRI, CBCARef, CBRI, CPerI, GeoRef, HumInd, MLA-IB, PAIS, SSCI. *Bk. rev.:* 2-8, 2-3 pages signed. *Aud.:* Ga, Ac.

An important and established Canadian literary journal, *The Dalhousie Review* regularly presents fiction, poetry, essays, book reviews, and occasional theme issues hosted by guest editors on topics such as Africadian literature and history, Quebec's political culture, and American writing, thinking, and myth-making. The journal sustains a scholarly orientation; pieces on deconstruction, new historicism, and ethical objectivism have appeared. A call for papers for a future issue on medieval culture seeks interpretations of literary, philosophical, historical, musical, and visual texts, in keeping with the esoteric nature of the review and its treatment of a wide range of intellectual interests. In the past few years, the journal has been redesigned, giving it a more contemporary look, including cover motifs that suggest the diverse "windows" of intellectual observation.

4377. ***Denver Quarterly.*** [ISSN: 0011-8869] 1966. q. USD 24 (Individuals, USD 20; USD 6 newsstand/cover per issue). Ed(s): Bin Ramke. University of Denver, Department of English, 495 Sturm Hall, Denver,

CO 80208; bramke@du.edu; http://www.udenver.edu/. Illus., index, adv. Circ: 1500. Vol. ends: Dec. Microform: PQC. Reprint: PQC. *Indexed:* AmHI, IAPV, IBZ, MLA-IB. *Bk. rev.:* 0-3, 3-13 pages, signed. *Aud.:* Ga, Ac.

Housed at the University of Denver, Department of English, the *Denver Quarterly*'s editors publish new and experimental forms of literature. Reflecting the editors' interests, many prose poetry offerings are included. John Ashbery's and Forrest Gander's work is typical of the high-quality content of *DQ*. Reviews and interviews appear along with translations, held in high esteem by the review as an "art form in itself." The web site offers the current issue's table of contents and background information on journal policies.

4378. *DoubleTake.* [ISSN: 1080-7241] 1995. q. USD 32 domestic; USD 42 Canada; USD 47 elsewhere. Ed(s): Randy Testa, Robert Coles. Doubletake Community Service Corp, 55 Davis Sq, Somerville, MA 02144-2908; dtmag@doubletakemagazine.org; http://www.doubletakemagazine.org. Illus., adv. Circ: 45000 Paid. Vol. ends: Fall. *Indexed:* RGPR. *Bk. rev.:* 3-5, 2-3 pages, signed. *Aud.:* Ga, Ac.

DoubleTake radiates energy, containing a mix of fiction, poetry, essays, and photography. The editors describe much of the content as accounts of "what it means to have a life in a particular place and time." Highlighting events of the times, articles have focused on women in prison, with penetrating photographs, narratives, diary entries, and letters describing women's experiences of life in prison. The magazine has devoted more resources to current topics and attracted funding from such notables as Bruce Springsteen and Robert Coles to continue its coverage of same. The web site has been expanded to include more initiatives in the education section (including the participation of Robert Coles and Ken Burns in the Summer Documentary Institute) and an online archive. The "Classroom Companion" section continues to be very useful for secondary-education applications, presenting units of study and creative ways to use *DoubleTake's* articles to enhance high school curricula. Themes include a sense of place, work in America, a sense of identity, and political ideology; the site gives suggestions for activities that develop students' problem solving, creative writing, and visual literacy skills in each of these areas.

4379. *Fence.* [ISSN: 1097-9980] 1998. s-a. USD 20 USD 8 newsstand/cover per issue. Ed(s): Rebecca Wolff. Fence Magazine, Inc., 303 E 8th St, New York, NY 10009. Adv. Circ: 12000. *Aud.:* Ga, Ac.

A newcomer to the literary review category of titles, *Fence*'s stated goal is to publish work by "fence-sitters," or idiosyncratic voices in the literary landscape. Its contents include poetry, fiction, nonfiction, photographs, and original artwork. Presentations from various academic symposia, such as "What's American about Poetry?" and "What's African American about African American Poetry?" have been published in the review. In the symposia sections, such notable writers as Louise Gluck, Jorie Graham, and Geoffrey O'Brien share their thoughts on what is distinctive about American and African American forms and subject matter. Innovative touches characterize the journal, one of which—the regularly featured "Reading List"— includes contributors' commentaries on what they are currently reading or re-reading. The web site features current-issue contents and selected full text.

Fiction. See Fiction: General/Mystery and Detective/General section.

4380. *Field: contemporary poetry and poetics.* [ISSN: 0015-0657] 1969. 2x/yr. USD 14 domestic; USD 18 Canada; USD 21 elsewhere. Ed(s): David Young, David Walker. Oberlin College Press, 10 N Professor St, Oberlin, OH 44074; oc.press@oberlin.edu; http://www.oberlin.edu/~ocpress. Adv. Circ: 1500 Paid. Microform: PQC. *Indexed:* ABS&EES, AmHI, BEL&L, IAPV, MLA-IB. *Bk. rev.:* Number and length vary. *Aud.:* Ac, Sa.

Supported by the Ohio Arts Council, *Field* is dedicated to contemporary poetry and poetics, with fiction, essays, poetry, and book reviews gracing its pages. Special topics have encompassed "Poetry 1999: Three Review Essays" and regular symposia dedicated to a writer's work accompanied by close readings, as in the case of Gwendolyn Brooks. Occasionally, the symposia include notable translations, as for such writers as Rainer Maria Rilke. The web site covers current and back issues, with some excerpts, and a description of the review's poetry prize.

4381. *The Formalist: a journal of metrical poetry.* [ISSN: 1046-7874] 1990. s-a. USD 15 (Individuals, USD 14; USD 7.50 per issue). Ed(s): Mona Baer, William Baer. Formalist Corp., 320 Hunter Dr, Evansville, IN 47711; http://www2.evansville.edu/theformalist/. Vol. ends: Fall/Winter (No. 2). *Bk. rev.:* Number and length vary. *Aud.:* Ac, Sa.

Devoted to metrical poetry, the *Formalist* is an eclectic mix of poems from contemporary writers and from writers of all literary periods and traditions. Its articulated purpose is to "create a forum for formal poetry and to encourage a renewal of interest in traditional poetic craftsmanship" (from Issue 1). Its offerings over the years have included the writings of many illustrious figures, such as X. J. Kennedy, Harold Nemertov, W. D. Snodgrass, Richard Wilbur, and Anthony Hecht. The "Tradition" section includes notable translations and high-quality interviews with writers such as John Hollander presenting thoughts on prosody and the craft of metrical poetry. The review endeavors to publish the works of both academic and new formalists and awards the Howard Nemerov Sonnet Award to honor its first literary advisor and earliest supporter.

4382. *The Georgia Review.* [ISSN: 0016-8386] 1947. q. USD 24 domestic; USD 30 foreign. Ed(s): T R Hummer. University of Georgia, Georgia Review, Athens, GA 30602. Illus., index, adv. Sample. Circ: 5000. Vol. ends: Winter. Microform: PQC. Online: Gale Group. Reprint: PQC. *Indexed:* AmHI, ArtHuCI, BEL&L, BHA, BRI, CBRI, FLI, HumInd, IAPV, MLA-IB. *Bk. rev.:* 4-11, 1-25 pages, signed. *Aud.:* Ga, Ac.

The renowned *Georgia Review* has won several of the Magazine Association of Georgia's GAMMA awards over its 54-year history. An eclectic mix of essays, fiction, drama, poetry, art, and color photography is accompanied by book reviews and book briefs in each issue. Such subjects as writing and fatherhood, American theater 1999–2000, and religion and spirituality have been treated in recent issues. To mark the review's longevity, selected essays from 1947 to 1996 were published in an impressive double issue. Advisory and contributing editors include Henry Louis Gates and Louise Erdrich.

4383. *Gettysburg Review.* [ISSN: 0898-4557] 1988. q. USD 24 domestic; USD 32 foreign. Ed(s): Peter Stitt. Gettysburg College, 300 N Washington St, Gettysburg, PA 17325; http://www.gettysburg.edu/. Illus., index, adv. Circ: 4500 Paid. Vol. ends: Winter. *Indexed:* AmHI, HumInd, IAPV, MLA-IB. *Aud.:* Ga, Ac.

The *Gettysburg Review* is known for its award-winning fiction, poetry, and essays and for capturing numerous design awards for the impact of its graphics and artwork. Among its advisory and contributing editors are Ann Beattie, Rita Dove, Donald Hall, Garrison Keillor, and Richard Wilbur. Pieces first published here are frequently included in annual anthologies, such as the *The Best American Short Stories* and *The Best American Poetry*. An upcoming theme issue will focus on "noir" literature. The web site, the "Gettysburg Review Online," is a monthly update with recent selections and news on authors and awards.

4384. *The Harvard Review.* [ISSN: 1077-2901] 1992. s-a. USD 16 domestic; USD 28 foreign. Ed(s): Christina Thompson. Harvard University, Lamont Library, Cambridge, MA 02138; http://www.hcs.harvard.edu/. Illus., adv. Circ: 3000 Paid. *Indexed:* IAPV, MLA-IB. *Aud.:* Ga, Ac.

Published at Harvard University, *The Harvard Review* changed editors in 2001. Its illustrious editorial board and contributors seek to continue founding editor Stratis Haviaras's goal for the *Review*, that of presenting an "effective discussion of contemporary and world literature." Recent special sections, such as "Writing the Novel," have enlivened this tradition. Poetry, fiction, nonfiction, book reviews, and photos are included in a publication described by contributing associate Seamus Heaney as "readable, various, serious, lively, full of interest." The most recent issue is described by editor Christina Thompson as "roundly international."

4385. ***Hudson Review: a magazine of literature and the arts.*** [ISSN: 0018-702X] 1948. q. USD 34 (Individuals, USD 28; USD 8 newsstand/cover per issue). Ed(s): Paula Deitz. Hudson Review, Inc., 684 Park Ave, New York, NY 10021; hudsonreview@erols.com. Illus., index, adv. Circ: 4500. Vol. ends: Winter. Microform: MIM; PQC. Online: EBSCO Publishing; Gale Group; OCLC Online Computer Library Center, Inc.; ProQuest Information & Learning; H.W. Wilson. Reprint: PQC. *Indexed:* ABS&EES, AmHI, ArtHuCI, BAS, BRI, CBRI, FLI, HumInd, IAPV, IBZ, IDP, MLA-IB, SSI. *Bk. rev.:* 5-7, 2-11 pages, signed. *Aud.:* Ga, Ac.

In addition to essays, memoirs, fiction, poetry, and reviews, *Hudson Review* concentrates on the arts in particular, as well as on literature and culture. As the introductory material in the web site explains, this journal has dealt with the area where "literature bears on the intellectual life of the time and on diverse aspects of American culture." The review's signature "Chronicles" section explores current film, theater, art, music, and dance in depth. To commemorate its 50th-anniversary year, the *Review* highlighted "American Themes" in history, literature, and the arts with regular contributors Joseph Epstein and William H. Pritchard gracing the roster of writers. For its 55th year, an extended issue will be published, along with a historic CD of 20 poets reading work first presented in *Hudson Review*. The web site will feature audio samples of same.

4386. ***The Iowa Review.*** [ISSN: 0021-065X] 1970. 3x/yr. USD 20 (Individuals, USD 18). Ed(s): David Hamilton, Mary Hussman. University of Iowa, Department of English, 308 English - Philosophy Bldg, Iowa City, IA 52242-1492. Illus., index, adv. Circ: 1500. Microform: PQC. Online: Chadwyck-Healey Incorporated; Gale Group. Reprint: PQC. *Indexed:* ABS&EES, ASIP, AmHI, BEL&L, HumInd, IAPV, ILP, MLA-IB. *Bk. rev.:* 2, 2-4 pages, signed. *Aud.:* Ga, Ac.

Sponsored by the esteemed University of Iowa Writing Program and in its 33rd year, the *Review*'s mission has been "nudging along American literature" over the years by presenting new and compelling writers to a larger audience. Its editors aspire to include works that are "local but not provincial," publishing fiction, essays, interviews, poems, and reviews that often depict the Midwestern landscape, but also reflect a global sensibility. With volume 31, the journal began publishing a one-page "Human Rights Index," statistics from the University of Iowa Center for Human Rights. Described by one of its readers as "stately and experimental," the print review is complemented by *Iowa Review Web*, which presents experimental writing and art in *TIR Web*, as well as material from the print journal. The third section of the site, the "91st Meridian," is a "gathering point for veterans and supporters of the University of Iowa's International Writing Program."

4387. ***Jewish Quarterly.*** [ISSN: 0449-010X] 1953. q. GBP 25 in Europe; GBP 35 elsewhere. Ed(s): Matthew Reisz. Jewish Literary Trust Ltd., PO Box 35042, London, NW1 7XH, United Kingdom; http://www.jewishquarterly.org/. Illus., index, adv. Circ: 3000 Controlled. Microform: PQC. Reprint: PQC; SCH. *Indexed:* IJP. *Aud.:* Ga, Ac.

Highly praised in Europe, the *Jewish Quarterly* is less well known in the United States. Fiction, nonfiction, art, and letters from its active readership accompany poetry, interviews, and memoirs in this lively review, which incorporates *Jewish Book News and Reviews*. There is increasing emphasis on the visual arts, literature, and cinema. The section on the Middle East features vigorous debate "without rancor" and political and cultural commentary of interest to a wide audience. Cynthia Ozick, Adrienne Rich, and the late Bruce Chatwin have contributed to its pages. Recent topics include reflections on Jewish writers and culture, multiculturalism, Jewish literature today, emigre artists, refugees, and the rise of anti-Semitism in Great Britain and the rest of Europe.

4388. ***The Kenyon Review: an international journal of literature, culture, and the arts.*** [ISSN: 0163-075X] 1939. 3x/yr. USD 35 (Individuals, USD 25). Ed(s): David H Lynn, Meg Galipoult. Kenyon College, Gambier, OH 43022-9623; http://www.kenyon.edu. Illus., index, adv. Refereed. Circ: 5000 Paid. Online: bigchalk; Chadwyck-Healey Incorporated; EBSCO Publishing; Gale Group; Northern Light Technology, Inc.; OCLC Online Computer Library Center, Inc.; ProQuest Information & Learning; H.W. Wilson. Reprint: PQC. *Indexed:* AIAP, AmHI, ArtHuCI, BRD, BRI, CBRI, HumInd, IAPV, IBZ, MLA-IB. *Bk. rev.:* 1-2, 7-11 pages, signed. *Aud.:* Ga, Ac.

Founded by influential critic and poet John Crowe Ransom, *The Kenyon Review* has had a reputation for high-quality writing and has featured work by Seamus Heaney, Forrest Gander, Alice Hoffman, and Philip Levine. In 1999, it also began presenting "new voices" in the section of the same name. Introduced by a senior writer or critic, these new writers contribute to the array of high-quality poetry, fiction, essays, reviews, interviews, and works in translation that make up each issue of the *Review*. As a result of a recent editorial decision, fewer special or thematically defined issues will be published in the interest of offering more of the best in new writing. Redesign of the print edition a few years ago has been complemented by a web site redesign and expansion. In addition to excerpts from past issues, news items, and literary links, a biweekly feature and selected author interviews appear online.

4389. ***Literary Review.*** Former titles: *Literary Review and Quarto;* (until 1982): *Literary Review.* 1979. 11x/yr. GBP 32 domestic; GBP 39 foreign. Ed(s): Nancy Sladek. The Literary Review and Quarto, Ltd., 44 Lexington St, London, W1R 3LH, United Kingdom; litrev@dircon.co.uk. Illus., adv. Circ: 15000. Vol. ends: Dec. *Bk. rev.:* 4-5. *Aud.:* Ga, Ac.

TLR, as it is known, publishes fiction, poetry, essays on contemporary literature, and reviews from writers around the globe. Examples of topics from past issues include Iranian exiles, North African writers, and Russian women writers. The print journal is substantial in length (over 100 pages). The editors note that "preference is given to essays and reviews on authors who have not received wide coverage in other magazines. We are especially interested in introducing writers from many nations to our readers." Further, "several issues in each volume year are guest-edited and focus on new writing in a specific language or from a specific nation or region." The web site, *TLR Web*, offers selections not found in the print issues, making more available on an ongoing basis to internet readers, while excerpted text from current and past issues is now available on the Web del Sol site. Also available on the web site is the "Writers' Choice Series from TLR," ten writers deemed worthy of more recognition by ten well-known writers.

4390. ***The Literary Review: an international journal of contemporary writing.*** [ISSN: 0024-4589] 1957. q. USD 18 domestic; USD 21 foreign. Ed(s): Rene Steinke. Fairleigh Dickinson University, Literary Review, 285 Madison Ave, Madison, NJ 07940. Refereed. Circ: 2000 Paid and free. Microform: MIM; PQC. Online: bigchalk; Chadwyck-Healey Incorporated; EBSCO Publishing; Florida Center for Library Automation; Gale Group; Northern Light Technology, Inc.; OCLC Online Computer Library Center, Inc.; ProQuest Information & Learning; H.W. Wilson. Reprint: PQC. *Indexed:* ABS&EES, AmHI, ArtHuCI, BRI, HumInd, IAPV, IBZ, MLA-IB. *Bk. rev.:* 4-5. *Aud.:* Ga, Ac.

TLR, as it is known, publishes fiction, poetry, essays on contemporary literature, and reviews from writers around the globe. Examples of topics from past issues include Iranian exiles, North African writers, and Russian women writers. The print journal is substantial in length (over 100 pages). The editors note that "preference is given to essays and reviews on authors who have not received wide coverage in other magazines. We are especially interested in introducing writers from many nations to our readers." Further, "several issues in each volume year are guest-edited and focus on new writing in a specific language or from a specific nation or region." The web site, *TLR Web*, offers selections not found in the print issues, making more available on an ongoing basis to internet readers, while excerpted text from current and past issues is now available on the Web del Sol site. Also available on the web site is the "Writers' Choice Series from TLR," ten writers deemed worthy of more recognition by ten well-known writers.

Manoa. See Little Magazines section.

4391. ***Massachusetts Review: a quarterly of literature, arts and public affairs.*** [ISSN: 0025-4878] 1959. q. USD 30 (Individuals, USD 22). Ed(s): David Lenson, Mary Heath. Massachusetts Review, Inc., South College, University of Massachusetts, Amherst, MA 01003; massrev@external.umass.edu; http://www.massreview.org/. Illus., index, adv. Refereed. Circ: 1500. Microform: PQC. Online: bigchalk; Chadwyck-

Healey Incorporated; EBSCO Publishing; Gale Group; Northern Light Technology, Inc.; OCLC Online Computer Library Center, Inc.; ProQuest Information & Learning; H.W. Wilson. *Indexed:* ABS&EES, AmH&L, AmHI, ArtHuCI, BHA, FLI, HumInd, IAPV, MLA-IB, RI-1, SSI. *Aud.:* Ga, Ac.

Supported by Five Colleges, Inc., the *Massachusetts Review* adds public affairs and social and historical commentary to its literary and arts offerings. Although based in New England, it appeals to a wider audience because of its significant writing on race and culture. Pieces by Julia Alvarez, Stephen Dobyns, Toni Morrison, and Chinua Achebe have appeared in its pages. To mark its 40th anniversary, the *Review* plans special issues on Cuba, Japan, and Egypt. Other theme issues have concentrated on the performing arts, diversity, and a tribute to Allen Ginsburg and American poetry. The stunning covers and "personal witness pieces" also make it remarkable. A companion program, *MR2*, the "audio extension of the journal," is being launched, and radio air dates will be announced on the web site.

4392. ***Michigan Quarterly Review.*** [ISSN: 0026-2420] 1962. q. USD 25 domestic; USD 30 foreign. Ed(s): Laurence Goldstein. University of Michigan, 3574 Rackham Bldg, 915 E Washington St, Ann Arbor, MI 48109-1070; mqr@umich.edu; http://www.umich.edu/~mqr. Illus., index, adv. Refereed. Circ: 1500 Paid. Vol. ends: Fall. Microform: PQC. Online: Chadwyck-Healey Incorporated; Gale Group; OCLC Online Computer Library Center, Inc.; ProQuest Information & Learning; H.W. Wilson. Reprint: PQC. *Indexed:* ABS&EES, AmHI, ArtHuCI, BAS, BEL&L, BHA, BRI, CBRI, FLI, HumInd, IAPV, MLA-IB, PAIS, RI-1, SSCI. *Bk. rev.:* 1-3, 5-16 pages, signed. *Aud.:* Ga, Ac.

Called the University of Michigan's flagship journal, *Michigan Quarterly* has published only special theme issues since 1979. The review's fiction, poetry, prose poetry, book reviews, and criticism are expertly edited and assembled. In a recent issue, Toni Morrison leads off with an article on values in the university. Other notable contributors to the two issues on "Secret Spaces and Childhood" include John Stilgoe, Edmund Wilson, Robert Coles, and Diana Ackerman. A two-part issue, "Jewish in America," calls for personal narratives as well. The forthcoming issue on the 1950s will focus on a range of issues: college life, statism, welfare policy, and masculinity and war, among others. The searchable, browsable web site contains abstracts for contents of the past several issues.

4393. ***Minnesota Review: a journal of committed writing; fiction, poetry, essays, reviews.*** [ISSN: 0026-5667] 1960. s-a. USD 12. Ed(s): Jeffrey Williams. University of Missouri - Columbia, Department of English, 110 Tate Hall, Columbia, MO 65211. Illus., adv. Circ: 1500. Microform: PQC. *Indexed:* AmHI, ArtHuCI, BRI, CBRI, FLI, IAPV, IBZ, MLA-IB, SSCI. *Bk. rev.:* 7, 6-16 pages, signed. *Aud.:* Ga, Ac.

Calling itself a "journal of committed writing," the *Minnesota Review* energetically presents a mix of literature and political commentary. In addition to poetry, fiction, and reviews, much of the content examines issues of interest to academics. Recently, the productive tension between activism and the academy was explored in a collection of articles first written for a conference on the future of graduate education. Sections of interest include "Surveying the Field," with current critical commentary on cutting-edge subjects and a special section highlighting "Fifties Culture." Theme issues of late include those on "Academostars" and an upcoming issue on "Smart Kids," soliciting personal narratives and essays addressing "how 'smart' and/or our textually-oriented selves are constructed." Also sought are pieces on the interaction between class and education from authors who entered English or other humanities fields as adults.

4394. ***The Missouri Review.*** [ISSN: 0191-1961] 1978. 3x/yr. USD 19; USD 7 newsstand/cover per issue. Ed(s): Speer Morgan. University of Missouri at Columbia, 1507 Hillcrest Hall, 3rd Fl -D, Columbia, MO 65211; moreview@showme.missouri.edu; http://www.missourireview.org. Illus., index, adv. Circ: 6500. *Indexed:* AmHI, IAPV, MLA-IB. *Bk. rev.:* 11-18, 1-5 pages, signed. *Aud.:* Ga, Ac.

The Missouri Review features fiction, poetry, essays, interviews, and book reviews; literary criticism is excluded. Theme issues are not determined in advance; rather, they flow from writers' submissions. The editors' creativity is evidenced in two special departments. The "Found Text Feature" presents never-before published works, such as Knopf's selection decisions and famous rejection letters. In the 25th anniversary issue, this section includes production memos and photos from David Selznick. In "History as Literature," seminal primary materials, such as the previously unpublished letters of Neal Cassidy to Jack Kerouac, were included. The web site's redesign provides a reader-friendly sidebar for easy navigation of editorials, features, poetry, fiction, nonfiction, interviews, book reviews, and other content.

4395. ***New Letters: a magazine of writing and art.*** Former titles (until vol.37, 1971): *University Review;* (until vol.30, 1964): *University of Kansas City Review;* (until vol.8, 1942): *University Review.* [ISSN: 0146-4930] 1934. q. USD 20 (Individuals, USD 17). Ed(s): James McKinley. University of Missouri at Kansas City, 5100 Rockhill Rd, Kansas City, MO 64110; mckinley@umkc.edu. Illus., adv. Circ: 1500. *Indexed:* AmHI, ArtHuCI, HumInd, IAPV, MLA-IB. *Aud.:* Ga, Ac.

Affiliated with the University of Missouri at Kansas City, the rubric for *New Letters*, "an international magazine of writing and art: in print and on the air," signals its unique strengths. Artwork figures prominently in the print review, along with poetry, fiction, and essays. The web site features a description of the radio companion to the literary quarterly "New Letters on the Air," which began broadcasting in 1977. Distributed via public radio, the weekly program is devoted to an author's reading from his or her work and an interview with host Angela Elam. Over 800 programs, available on cassette, are listed in the "On the Air" section.

4396. ***New Millennium Writings.*** [ISSN: 1086-7678] 1996. a. USD 12.95. Ed(s): Don Williams. New Messenger Writing and Publishing, PO Box 2463, Knoxville, TN 37901; http://www.writingawards.com. Illus., adv. Sample. Circ: 3300 Controlled. *Aud.:* Ga.

Appealing to a general audience as well as to academics, *New Millennium Writings* considers itself vibrant and adventurous. The introduction in its first issue states: "[I]f it . . . *oscillates*, we will publish it." In addition to poetry, nonfiction, interviews, and artwork, the review has numerous departments, including "Humor," "The Writing Well," "Observations" (usually by editor Williams), "Millennial Moments," and the "Janus File" (containing tributes to well-known authors). Number 11 (vol. 6, no. 1) showcases the "best of the best" interviews and profiles from 1996–2001. The web site has selected links to full texts from the 12 issues published thus far. The pages for describing the contents of each issue have contributors' photos and quoted text from their works in the "Featured Writers" section. Each issue also presents the winners of the *New Millennium* Awards.

4397. ***The New Renaissance: an international magazine of ideas and opinions, emphasizing literature & the arts.*** [ISSN: 0028-6575] 1968. s-a. USD 30 domestic; USD 35 Canada; USD 38 elsewhere. Ed(s): Louise T Reynolds. Friends of the new renaissance, Inc., 26 Heath Rd, 11, Arlington, MA 02474-3645; svanden@spfldcol.edu; http://www.tnrlitmag.net. Illus., index. Circ: 1100 Paid. *Indexed:* AltPI, AmHI, IAPV. *Bk. rev.:* 0-2, 5-7 pages, signed. *Aud.:* Ga, Ac.

Unlike many literary reviews that are published by an academic department or writing program, *the new renaissance* is funded by a grant from the Massachusetts Cultural Council. Its lead articles present ideas and opinions on a range of current-interest topics, such as genetic engineering, childhood immunization, ecology, future studies, and animal rights. Fiction, poetry, essays, and reviews are accompanied by compelling artwork, photos, drawings, and other illustrations. The "Catching Up" department gives updates on prizes, exhibits, editorships, and new publications. Lively exchanges appear in the reader correspondence section.

4398. ***News from the Republic of Letters.*** [ISSN: 1095-1644] 1997. irreg. 3-5/yr. USD 25; USD 32.50 in Canada & Mexico; USD 37.50 elsewhere. Ed(s): Saul Bellow. Republic of Letters, 120 Cushing Ave, Boston, MA 02125; rangoni@bu.edu. Illus. Circ: 1800 Paid. *Bk. rev.:* 1 -2, length varies. *Aud.:* Ga, Ac.

News from the Republic of Letters is an independent review of literature and the arts founded by Nobel Laureate Saul Bellow and current editor Keith Botsford. Tabloid in format for issues 1–11, it offers a challenging and lively collection of essays, poems, reviews, and eloquent, timely "Arias" on major topics of the day. "Among the tasks which the editors consider important is that of bringing attention to important or neglected books" (vol. 1, no. 1, May 1997), including work by gifted writers who are not well known. The current issue is dedicated to W. G. Sebald. The web site contains excerpts from numbers 1–10 and announces that after issue 12 the review will become a biannual issued in paperback.

4399. ***The North American Review.*** [ISSN: 0029-2397] 1815. bi-m. USD 22 domestic; USD 29 Canada; USD 32 elsewhere. North American Review, c/o Robley Wilson, Ed, University of Northern Iowa, Cedar, IA 50614-0516; nar@uni.edu; http://www.uni.edu/. Illus., index, adv. Sample. Refereed. Circ: 4700. Microform: PMC; PQC. Online: bigchalk; Chadwyck-Healey Incorporated; EBSCO Publishing; Florida Center for Library Automation; Gale Group; Northern Light Technology, Inc.; OCLC Online Computer Library Center, Inc.; ProQuest Information & Learning; H.W. Wilson. Reprint: PQC. *Indexed:* AmHI, ArtHuCI, BEL&L, BRI, CBRI, HumInd, IAPV. *Bk. rev.:* 0-1, 3 pages, signed. *Aud.:* Ga, Ac.

Dating from 1815, with a hiatus in the late 1870s, *The North American Review* has long been considered an important literary journal. The *Review*'s history notes that its originally "British flavor" has diminished over the years; it takes pride in having published, among others, Walt Whitman, Henry James, and Joseph Conrad. Recent issues include emerging as well as established writers. Over time, its contents have been expanded to include current affairs and politics as well as literature. The editors aim to take a "broad view of current North American preoccupations—especially the problems of the environment." The journal contains the regular departments "Natural Orders," "Foreign Correspondence," "Kasper," and "Synecdoche." The *Review* has received commendations for its design, illustrations, and award-winning covers. The web site's introductory page lists this celebrated journal's numerous awards, and the online archives house seven web issues.

4400. ***North Dakota Quarterly.*** [ISSN: 0029-277X] 1911. q. USD 30 (Individuals, USD 25). Ed(s): Robert W Lewis. University of North Dakota, PO Box 7209, Grand Forks, ND 58202; ndq@sage.nodak.edu; http://www.und.nodak.edu/org/ndq/. Illus., adv. Refereed. Circ: 600 Paid. *Indexed:* ABS&EES, AmH&L, AmHI, FLI, IAPV, MLA-IB. *Bk. rev.:* 3-8, 2-8 pages, signed. *Aud.:* Ga, Ac.

Emphasis on the Northern Plains characterizes the *North Dakota Quarterly*, and special issues alternate with general-interest issues. Articles and literary pieces (stories, poems, reviews) on such subjects as the language of mountains and American Indian studies have been featured. Many illustrations appeared throughout the American Indian issue, along with articles treating forgotten authors, the revival of Indian languages, and the unique aspects of reservation life. In an upcoming issue, pieces will focus on "Lewis and Clark, 1803–1806, Corps of Discovery." The review also seeks to publish personal essays about "books that mattered," especially on ecological themes. The editor's news notes close each issue.

4401. ***Notre Dame Review.*** [ISSN: 1082-1864] 1995. s-a. USD 20 (Individuals, USD 15; USD 8 newsstand/cover per issue). Ed(s): William O'Rourke, John Matthias. University of Notre Dame, Creative Writing Program, 356 O'Shaughnessy Hall, Notre Dame, IN 46556; english.ndreview.1@nd.edu; http://www.nd.edu/~ndr/review.htm. Illus., adv. Circ: 2000. *Indexed:* AmHI. *Bk. rev.:* 13-18, 50-350 words, signed. *Aud.:* Ga, Ac.

Seeking to provide a "panoramic view" of contemporary American and international writing, the *Notre Dame Review* contains short stories, poetry, reviews, criticism, art, and interviews. The *Review*'s stated goal is to showcase many styles and work that "takes on issues by making the invisible seen." The special web version, "nd[re]view," complements the print journal with special features: interviews, critique and commentary, and sometimes color images and audio related to the authors and artists in the printed review. The print journal and the web site are described as constituting a hybrid print and electronic magazine that "engages readers as a community centered in literary concerns." An online discussion group for readers and authors to exchange views is planned as well.

4402. ***Ontario Review.*** [ISSN: 0316-4055] 1974. s-a. USD 16 domestic; USD 20 foreign. Ed(s): Raymond J Smith. Ontario Review, Inc., 9 Honey Brook Dr, Princeton, NJ 08540; http://www.ontarioreviewpress.com. Illus., index. Sample. Circ: 1200 Paid. Microform: MML. *Indexed:* AmHI, IAPV, MLA-IB. *Aud.:* Ga, Ac.

Though the journal's focus has broadened over time, Raymond Smith and associate editor Joyce Carol Oates established the *Ontario Review* in 1974 to bridge the gap between Canadian and American arts and literatures. Nurturing young writers is one of the editors' main objectives. Handsome and thoughtfully designed, *Ontario Review* includes fiction, poetry, drama, essays, interviews, and photography. Maxine Kumin, Doris Lessing, Reynolds Price, Margaret Atwood, and John Updike have been published here. The web site features the current issue, back issues (tables of contents and full text of selected pieces from issue 44 onward), and a description and excerpts from the forthcoming issue.

Other Voices. See Fiction: General/Mystery and Detective/General section.

Parabola. See General Editorial/General section.

4403. ***The Paris Review: the international literary quarterly.*** [ISSN: 0031-2037] 1953. q. USD 50 (Individuals, USD 40). Ed(s): George A Plimpton. The Paris Review Foundation, Inc., 541 E 72nd St, New York, NY 10021; postmaster@theparisreview.com; http://www.theparisreview.com. Illus., index, adv. Circ: 12000. Microform: PQC. Online: Chadwyck-Healey Incorporated; Gale Group; Northern Light Technology, Inc.; OCLC Online Computer Library Center, Inc.; ProQuest Information & Learning. Reprint: ISI; PQC. *Indexed:* AmHI, ArtHuCI, BEL&L, HumInd, IAPV, MagInd, SSCI, SSI. *Aud.:* Ga, Ac.

This elegant and respected journal had as its founding idea the notion that creative writing, and not literary criticism, should form the center of the review. Since then, it has continued to examine all aspects of the creative process in literature. Each issue is substantial in length and includes fiction, essays, poetry, and, notably, interviews with writers on writing. Jack Kerouac, Philip Roth, and V. S. Naipaul were first published here.

4404. ***Prairie Schooner.*** [ISSN: 0032-6682] 1926. q. USD 26. Ed(s): Hilda Raz. University of Nebraska at Lincoln, 201 Andrews Hall, Lincoln, NE 68588-0334; http://www.unl.edu/schooner/psmain.htm. Index, adv. Circ: 3200. Vol. ends: Winter. Microform: PQC. Online: Chadwyck-Healey Incorporated; Florida Center for Library Automation; Gale Group. Reprint: PQC; PSC. *Indexed:* ABS&EES, AmHI, ArtHuCI, BRI, CBRI, HumInd, IAPV, MLA-IB. *Bk. rev.:* 0-7, 1-8 words, signed. *Aud.:* Ga, Ac.

In 2001, *Prairie Schooner* celebrated its 75th year of publishing poetry, fiction, essays, reviews, and works in translation. It is sponsored by the University of Nebraska–Lincoln, and its distinguished contributors have included Willa Cather, Tennessee Williams, and Raymond Carver. The journal's web site offers excerpts from the current issue and links to tables of contents of past issues. Recent special issues have been devoted to new German literature, poetry, and essays.

4405. ***Salmagundi: a quarterly of the humanities & social sciences.*** [ISSN: 0036-3529] 1965. q. USD 28 (Individuals, USD 20; USD 65 foreign). Ed(s): Robert Boyers, Peggy Boyers. Skidmore College, 815 North Broadway, Saratoga Springs, NY 12866; pboyers@skidmore.edu; http://www.skidmore.edu/. Illus., index, adv. Sample. Refereed. Circ: 4800. Microform: PQC. Online: bigchalk; Chadwyck-Healey Incorporated; Gale Group; Northern Light Technology, Inc.; OCLC Online Computer Library Center, Inc.; ProQuest Information & Learning; H.W. Wilson. Reprint: PQC. *Indexed:* ABS&EES, AmHI, ArtHuCI, BAS, BRI, CBRI, FLI, HumInd, IAPV, L&LBA, MLA-IB, SSCI. *Bk. rev.:* 0-5, 5-23 pages, signed. *Aud.:* Ga, Ac.

Published by Skidmore College, *Salmagundi* is subtitled "a quarterly of the Humanities and Social Sciences," and its scope is, indeed, that expansive. With regular and special columns—including commentary on art, fiction, and international politics, as well as poetry by such writers as Lynn Sharon Schwartz and Louise Gluck, and essays, debates, and interviews—the journal ranges widely through literature and culture. The 35th anniversary issue (Fall 2000/Winter 2001) included over 300 pages of creative and critical works. A forthcoming special issue will consider "Afro-America at the Present Time," with contributors Orlando Paterson, Darryl Pinckney, and others.

4406. *Sewanee Review.* [ISSN: 0037-3052] 1892. q. USD 30 (Individuals, USD 24; USD 8 newsstand/cover). Ed(s): George Core. University of the South, 735 University Ave, Sewanee, TN 37383-1000; rjones@sewanee.edu; http://www.sewanee.edu/sreview/home.html. Illus., index, adv. Circ: 3090 Paid and free. Vol. ends: Oct. Microform: PQC. Online: Chadwyck-Healey Incorporated; EBSCO Publishing; Gale Group. Reprint: PSC. *Indexed:* AmHI, ArtHuCI, BEL&L, BRD, BRI, CBRI, HumInd, IAPV, IBZ, MLA-IB, MagInd, R&TA, RI-1, RILM. *Bk. rev.:* 6-10, 2-6 pages, signed. *Aud.:* Ga, Ac.

The University of the South, in Sewanee, Tennessee, is the home of this venerable journal, begun in 1892. It is a distinguished traditional literary magazine devoted to British and American fiction, poetry, essays, reviews, and criticism. Poets published in its pages include T. S. Eliot, Dylan Thomas, Wallace Stevens, and Howard Nemerov.

4407. *Shenandoah.* [ISSN: 0037-3583] 1950. q. USD 25 (Individuals, USD 22; USD 8 newsstand/cover per issue). Ed(s): Lynn Leech, R T Smith. Washington and Lee University, Shenandoah, Troubadour Theater, 2nd Fl, Lexington, VA 24450-0303. Illus., index, adv. Circ: 1400 Paid. Vol. ends: Winter. Reprint: PQC. *Indexed:* AmHI, ArtHuCI, BRI, CBRI, IAPV, IBZ, MLA-IB. *Bk. rev.:* 0-7, 1-3 pages. *Aud.:* Ga, Ac.

This review was founded in 1950 by Washington and Lee University students and faculty, Tom Wolfe among them. Cover art and graphics are elegant. Short stories and poems accompany interviews, literary essays, brief reviews, and personal essays. Annual prizes are awarded for the best story, poem, and essay published in each volume. A well-established and thoughtful review, with a gentle wit.

Short Story. See Fiction: General/Mystery and Detective/General section.

4408. *South Carolina Review.* [ISSN: 0038-3163] 1968. 2x/yr. Individuals, USD 10. Ed(s): Wayne Chapman. Clemson University, Department of English, 801 Strode Tower, PO Box 340523, Clemson, SC 29634-0523. Illus., adv. Circ: 600. *Indexed:* AmHI, BRI, CBRI, HumInd, IAPV, MLA-IB. *Aud.:* Ga, Ac.

From its home at Clemson University, this review emphasizes Southern and American literature, but its focus is wide, including essays, scholarly criticism, poetry, book reviews, and stories of all sorts. A recent issue includes a delightful in-depth interview with Elmore Leonard. Fall 2001 offered a special issue devoted to essays from the university's seminar on place, an interdisciplinary study of setting.

4409. *The Southern Review.* [ISSN: 0038-4534] 1935. q. USD 50 (Individuals, USD 25). Ed(s): James Olney, Dave Smith. Louisiana State University, 43 Allen Hall, Baton Rouge, LA 70803-5005. Index, adv. Sample. Circ: 3140. Vol. ends: Oct. Microform: PQC; NRP. Online: Chadwyck-Healey Incorporated; EBSCO Publishing; Florida Center for Library Automation; Gale Group; Northern Light Technology, Inc.; OCLC Online Computer Library Center, Inc.; ProQuest Information & Learning; H.W. Wilson. Reprint: PQC; PSC. *Indexed:* AmHI, ArtHuCI, BRI, CBRI, HumInd, IAPV, MLA-IB, RI-1. *Bk. rev.:* 1, 4–6 pages, signed. *Aud.:* Ga, Ac.

Louisiana State University has published this quarterly journal for more than 35 years. Its scope is contemporary literature from the United States and abroad, with an emphasis on Southern history and culture. Poems, short stories, excerpts from novels in progress, reviews, essays, and interviews comprise its contents. The editors note that they emphasize the importance of craftmanship and seriousness of subject matter and eschew sensationalism. Fiction by Richard Bausch and poetry by Wendell Berry, among a wide range of new and established writers, were included in recent issues.

4410. *The Southwest Review.* [ISSN: 0038-4712] 1915. q. USD 30 (Individuals, USD 24). Ed(s): Willard Spiegelman. Southern Methodist University, 307 Fondren Library W, Box 374, Dallas, TX 75275; swr@mail.smu.edu; http://www.smu.edu/~english/. Illus., index, adv. Sample. Circ: 1500 Paid. Vol. ends: Autumn. Microform: PQC. Online: bigchalk; EBSCO Publishing; Florida Center for Library Automation; Gale Group; Northern Light Technology, Inc.; OCLC Online Computer Library Center, Inc.; ProQuest Information & Learning; H.W. Wilson. Reprint: PQC. *Indexed:* AmHI, BEL&L, BRI, CBRI, HumInd, IAPV, IBZ, MLA-IB. *Aud.:* Ga, Ac.

This Texas-based journal of long standing has an esteemed editorial advisory board that includes Joyce Carol Oates, Helen Vendler, and John Hollander. Works of fiction, poetry, and literary and personal essays as well as writing on the arts and culture, travel, and political subjects are published. A recent special issue on human rights in the Americas was guest-edited by Marjorie Agosin. In Fall 2000, the journal undertook initial fundraising for a digitization project, with a goal of making available online all 85 years of the review. The web site (http://southwestreview.org/index.htm) includes some pieces from the print journal.

4411. *Threepenny Review.* [ISSN: 0275-1410] 1980. q. USD 20 domestic; USD 50 foreign. Ed(s): Wendy Lesser. Wendy Lesser, Ed. & Pub., PO Box 9131, Berkeley, CA 94709; http://www.threepennyreview.com. Adv. Circ: 9000 Paid. Microform: PQC. Reprint: PQC. *Indexed:* AltPI, AmHI, BRI, CBRI, IAPV. *Bk. rev.:* 0-7. *Aud.:* Ga, Ac.

The Threepenny Review publishes a lively and varied collection of short fiction; memoirs; reviews of books, film, dance, music, and theater; and essays on such topics as architecture, television, and politics. It is the work of a small staff (two!), aided by consulting editors, including John Berger, Anne Carson, Elizabeth Hardwick, and Gore Vidal. This well-designed journal has beautiful cover art on each issue. The web site includes tables of contents for current and past issues and some digital content. Recently, for example, the spring 2002 issue included a symposium in memory of W. G. Sebald, with contributions from Susan Sontag, Lynne Sharon Schwartz, and Arthur Lubow, among others; it is available on the *review*'s web site. Contributors include Nadine Gordimer, Seamus Heaney, and other writers of note.

4412. *TriQuarterly.* [ISSN: 0041-3097] 1964. 3x/yr. USD 36 (Individuals, USD 24; USD 11.95 newsstand/cover per issue). Ed(s): Susan Hahn. Northwestern University, 633 Clark St, Evanston, IL 60208; http://nupress.nwu.edu/. Illus., index, adv. Sample. Circ: 5000 Paid. Microform: PQC. Online: bigchalk; Chadwyck-Healey Incorporated; EBSCO Publishing; Florida Center for Library Automation; Gale Group; Northern Light Technology, Inc.; OCLC Online Computer Library Center, Inc.; ProQuest Information & Learning; H.W. Wilson. Reprint: PSC. *Indexed:* ABS&EES, AmHI, ArtHuCI, BRI, CBRI, HumInd, IAPV, MLA-IB, SSCI. *Bk. rev.:* 1, lengthy, signed. *Aud.:* Ga, Ac.

This preeminent "international journal of writing, art, and cultural inquiry" has among its contributing editors Rita Dove, John Barth, Robert Pinsky, and Richard Ford. A vibrant publication (too energetic to be called "venerable," despite its long publishing history) with poetry and novellas and novel excerpts alongside short stories and essays, its length (more than 300 pages) allows a full, varied list of contributors.

4413. *Venue.* [ISSN: 1027-0272] 1998. unknown. EUR 117 (Corporations, EUR 182). Ed(s): John Brenkman. Gordon and Breach - Harwood Academic, PO Box 531, Lausanne, 1000, Switzerland. Illus. Sample. *Aud.:* Ga, Ac.

This journal seeks to publish work by writers "dealing with issues that cross boundaries of language and nation." The "Forum" presents literary essays by a diverse group of contributing editors, including K. Anthony Appiah. Its scope is international, covering a wide diversity of cultures, traditions, perspectives, and styles to create a unique literary environment.

4414. *Virginia Quarterly Review: a national journal of literature and discussion.* [ISSN: 0042-675X] 1925. q. USD 22 (Individuals, USD 18). Ed(s): Staige D Blackford. University of Virginia, 1 West Range, PO Box 400223, Charlottesville, VA 22904-4423; jco7e@virginia.edu. Illus., index, adv. Circ: 4200. Vol. ends: Oct. Microform: PMC; PQC. Online: Chadwyck-Healey Incorporated; EBSCO Publishing; Gale Group; Northern Light Technology, Inc.; OCLC Online Computer Library

Center, Inc.; ProQuest Information & Learning; H.W. Wilson. Reprint: PSC. *Indexed:* ABS&EES, AmHI, ArtHuCI, BAS, BHA, BRD, BRI, CBRI, FutSurv, HumInd, IAPV, IBZ, MLA-IB, PAIS, SSCI. *Bk. rev.:* 90-100, 40-2,000 words, signed. *Aud.:* Ga, Ac.

This important journal, in existence for over 75 years, includes work on public affairs, the arts, history, literary essays, fiction, and poetry. The review section is substantial, including in-depth reviews as well as briefer notes on works recently published. Its online presence gives cover art and tables of contents for issues back to 1999, with selected pieces available online at http://www.virginia.edu/vqr.

4415. ***Witness (Farmington Hills).*** [ISSN: 0891-1371] 1987. 2x/yr. USD 22 (Individuals, USD 15). Ed(s): Peter Stine. Oakland Community College, 27055 Orchard Lake Rd, Farmington, MI 48334; http://www.occ.cc.mi.us. Illus., adv. Sample. Refereed. Circ: 1500 Paid. *Indexed:* IAPV. *Aud.:* Ga, Ac.

Witness is a consistently lively and interesting read, containing short stories, poetry, literary essays, memoirs, and photography. It lives, in the words of Stuart Dybek, at "the intersection of ideas and passions." A recent special issue on "Crime in America" includes work from John Balaban, Elmore Leonard, Alyce Miller, Joyce Carol Oates, and Maxine Kumin.

4416. ***The Yale Review.*** [ISSN: 0044-0124] 1911. q. USD 101 print & online eds. Blackwell Publishing, Inc., Commerce Place, 350 Main St, Malden, MA 02148; subscrip@blackwellpub.com; http://www.blackwellpublishing.com. Illus., index, adv. Sample. Circ: 4000. Vol. ends: Oct. Microform: PMC; PQC. Online: EBSCO Publishing; Gale Group; ingenta.com; OCLC Online Computer Library Center, Inc.; RoweCom Information Quest. *Indexed:* ABS&EES, AIAP, ArtHuCI, BAS, BEL&L, BHA, BRD, BRI, CBRI, FLI, HumInd, IAPV, IPSA, MLA-IB, MagInd, PAIS, RGPR. *Bk. rev.:* 4-5, 6-22 pages, signed. *Aud.:* Ga, Ac.

The Yale Review has been published since 1911. Short stories, poetry, personal and literary essays, reviews, and articles discussing history and culture appear here. The journal's long list of major writers includes Robert Penn Warren, Theodore Roethke, Anne Sexton, and, more recently, Richard Wilbur, Anita Brookner, and Cynthia Ozick.

Electronic Journals

4417. ***The Blue Moon Review.*** 1994. irreg. Ed(s): Doug Lawson. The Blue Moon Review, http://thebluemoon.com. *Aud.:* Ga, Ac.

Fiction, poetry, commentary, essays, and creative nonfiction both in text and audio are accompanied by a "Workshop" and "Cafe Blue" in this online journal. The workshop and cafe provide a forum and a discussion list, respectively. The fiction and poetry are a mix in interest, content, and style; much is by very new writers. There are some interesting uses of hypertext within the context of traditional narrative here.

4418. ***The Cortland Review: an online literary magazine.*** [ISSN: 1524-6744] 1997. q. Free. Ed(s): John Spalding. Cortland Review, 527 Third Ave #279, New York, NY 10016; thecortlandreview@mailcity.com; http://www.cortlandreview.com/. *Aud.:* Ga, Ac.

Describing itself as "an online literary magazine in Real Audio," the *Cortland Review* has included recorded poetry and fiction since launching, in issue three, its "Read Along with the Author Series." Occasionally, monthly features also contain audio; an example is the recent "The Poet and the Poem," an exploration of African American roots of rap poetry by German rap poet Bastian Boettcher. Essays and reviews round out each new issue, which is posted quarterly, with monthly updates. The site is well designed and easy to navigate; news and events briefs (with links to stories on other sites) are posted on its entry page, in addition to tables of contents of recent issues. The journal claims an international readership.

4419. ***Evergreen Review.*** [ISSN: 0014-3758] 1998. irreg. Ed(s): Dennis Hathaway. Evergreen Review, 61 Fourth Ave, New York, NY 10003; http://www.evergreenreview.com. Illus. *Bk. rev.:* 1-2, 300-500 words, signed. *Aud.:* Ga, Ac.

This is the digital child of the venerated counterculture journal of the same title founded by Barney Rosset. It is as important a contribution as the print journal was, and it maintains the attitude of its print parent while it uses technology to full effect, featuring photo and textual essays, video articles, and "hyperfiction," as well as traditional fiction, satire, and prose-poetry. A recent issue includes an elegiac and thoughtful photo and text essay (photos by Rosset) remembering Joan Mitchell. The archives include cover art and contents pages for print issues.

4420. ***Exquisite Corpse: a journal of letters and life.*** Formerly (until 1997): *Exquisite Corpse (Print).* 1981. 6x/yr. USD 30; USD 5 newsstand/cover per issue. Exquisite Corpse, c/o Andrei Codrescu, PO Box 25051, Baton Rouge, LA 70894; http://www.corpse.org. Illus. Refereed. Circ: 3500 Paid. *Aud.:* Ga, Ac.

This lively, witty, and interestingly edgy journal is edited by Andrei Codrescu. It has an international scope and feel and publishes multimedia works. Poetry, fiction, reviews, serials, commentary on culture, literature, performance, opinion pieces on public affairs, and online communities (including the "Corpse Cafe") are provided here.

4421. ***Jacket: international poetry and prose magazine.*** [ISSN: 1440-4737] 1997. 3x/yr. Ed(s): John Tranter. Australian Literary Management, 2-A Booth St, Balmain, NSW 2041, Australia. *Aud.:* Ga, Ac, Sa.

Called an "Internet cafe for postmodernists" by *Time* magazine, *jacket* is a free Internet quarterly review of new writing, with poetry, creative prose, interviews, reviews, and informative feature articles. The current number is posted "until it is full," and readers just call up the site periodically—there are no subscriptions per se. Most of the pieces are original, but occasionally material is excerpted from "hard-to-get books or magazines," to increase these publications" readership. Since its inception in 1997, *jacket* has been the winner of the Encyclop?dia Britannica Internet Guide award in 2000 and other awards, featured-site commendations, and other e-site kudos. The editor resides in Sydney, Australia, but he considers the journal an "outer-space thing," with no defining provenance. The web site is "read" by hyperlink, via whatever route the reader wishes to take. An issue contains various clickable green points, or one can search the site by keyword. The dynamic nature of the review is signalled by instructions to click the Refresh button after each selection to ensure currency of the online version. Lively and inventive, *jacket* includes a special hoax issue with extensive bibliography.

4422. ***Web del Sol.*** 1994. m. Ed(s): Mike Neff. Web del Sol, 2915 Fairmont St., Falls Church, VA 22042; http://webdelsol.com. *Aud.:* Ga, Ac.

This is a remarkable publication that could only exist in the digital world. It describes itself as "a literary arts new media complex." It hosts over 25 new and well-established literary publications (some of which are also issued in print), publishes its own online journal, *Del Sol*, and provides reviews, essays, links to arts and literary resources of interest, opportunities to see hypermedia via a "new media portal," and interactive online communities devoted to literature and poetry writing. It further features a section with chapbook pages for writers, including Holly Iglesias, Madison Smartt Bell, and David Ignatow.

■ LITERATURE

See also Africa; African American; China; CIS and Eastern Europe; Classical Studies; Europe; Fiction; Latin American; Lesbian, Gay, Bisexual, and Transgender; Literary Reviews; Little Magazines; Theater; and Women: Feminist and Special Interest sections.

Susan M. Gilroy, Reference Librarian, Lamont Library of the Harvard College Library, Harvard University, Cambridge, MA 02138; sgilroy@fas.harvard.edu

Carrie M. Macfarlane, Instructional Services Librarian for the Harvard College Library, Harvard University, Cambridge, MA 02138; cmmacfar@fas.harvard.edu

Helene Williams, English Bibliographer for the Humanities, Widener Library of the Harvard College Library, Harvard University; helene_williams@harvard.edu

Introduction

The journals in this section publish criticism, analysis, and interpretation of literary works. Many of them explore topics in literary theory and literary history. Increasingly, these journals feature essays informed by interdisciplinary perspectives on literature as well.

Most journals listed here cover literature in the English language, or literature in general. Literature from the U.S. and Great Britain is most generously represented. We have attempted to include all time periods, from Anglo-Saxon to contemporary, and from medieval to postmodern. World literatures in translation have a place among our entries, too. Non-English literatures, however, and the journals that publish in these languages have been excluded from consideration. These areas may be covered in other sections of *Magazines for Libraries*.

The number of literature-related journals continues to grow, and selecting from among them can be a difficult task. Many of the journals listed here are core titles for literature collections, as our annotations indicate. Other titles are major, influential publications in a subfield of literature, and are essential for larger libraries. Substantial electronic journals of literary scholarship still are few in number; we close our chapter with descriptions of several carefully chosen electronic titles.

A major change in this edition is the absence of journals devoted to the work of individual authors, e.g., *Chaucer Review, James Joyce Quarterly, Poe Studies,* and so on. A plethora of these journals exist and it is nearly impossible to provide a representative sample given the space limitations. Selection of author journals to collect may best be based on individual library strengths or an institution's curricular needs. The author journal entries have been replaced by a mix of standard core literature journals that were not reflected in earlier editions, as well as some newer titles with solid critical grounding.

When titles appear in JStor, Project Muse, or Literature Online (LION), three major players in the full-text journal market for literary studies, we have indicated that fact. Dates of coverage vary by title, and are likely to change over time. JStor subscribers should not expect to find the most recent three to five years of publication present in the database.

Basic Periodicals

Ac: *American Literature, Comparative Literature, Contemporary Literature, Essays in Criticism, Modern Fiction Studies, Nineteenth-Century Literature, PMLA, The Review of Contemporary Fiction, Speculum, Studies in English Literature 1500–1900, Victorian Studies, World Literature Today.*

Basic Abstracts and Indexes

American Humanities Index, Annual Bibliography of English Language and Literature, Arts & Humanities Citation Index, Humanities Index, MLA International Bibliography.

4423. *A N Q: A Quarterly Journal of Short Articles, Notes and Reviews.* Supersedes (1962-1986): *American Notes and Queries.* [ISSN: 0895-769X] 1987. q. USD 96 (Individuals, USD 52; USD 24 newsstand/cover per issue). Heldref Publications, 1319 18th St, NW, Washington, DC 20036-1802; subscribe@heldref.org; http://www.heldref.org. Adv. Refereed. Circ: 432. Vol. ends: Fall. Microform: OMN; PQC. Online: bigchalk; Chadwyck-Healey Incorporated; EBSCO Publishing; Florida Center for Library Automation; Gale Group; OCLC Online Computer Library Center, Inc.; ProQuest Information & Learning; H.W. Wilson. Reprint: PSC. *Indexed:* AmHI, ArtHuCI, BRI, CBRI, HumInd, MLA-IB. *Bk. rev.:* 1-7, 2-4 pages, signed. *Aud.:* Ac.

The contents of this publication are true to its title: brief pieces that are not unnecessarily elongated. The notes section averages around 12 articles, two to eight pages each; some are truly notes of just a few paragraphs on a single point, such as "Trimming Shakespeare's Sonnet 18," while others are short scholarly essays on broader topics in English or American literature, such as "Subscribers and Contributors: Vanity Marketing and Subterfuge in *Variety* (Dublin 1795)" or "The Axe in *Sir Gawain and the Green Knight.*" Review essays include evaluations of new editions of standard works, as well as the occasional review of recent book-length bibliographies. Book reviews round out each issue. Full text for issues 10.4 (1997) to the present is available through LION. Recommended for larger literary research collections. (HW)

4424. *A R I E L.* Formerly: *Review of English Literature.* [ISSN: 0004-1327] 1970. q. USD 37 (Individuals, CND 27; Students, CND 15). Ed(s): Pamela J McCallum. University of Calgary, Department of English, SS 1152, 2500 University Dr N W, Calgary, AB T2N 1N4, Canada; http://www.ucalgary.ca/. Illus., index, adv. Refereed. Circ: 900. Vol. ends: Oct. *Indexed:* ArtHuCI, HumInd, IBZ, MLA-IB. *Bk. rev.:* 4-6, 2-3 pages, signed. *Aud.:* Ac.

This quarterly publication devotes itself to the study of International English Literature, Postcolonial Literatures, Commonwealth Literature, New Literatures in English, and World Writing in English. Articles on U.S. and U.K. literature in English are sometimes considered for publication, especially if they explore "intertextual, cultural, historical, or theoretical ties" to new and emerging literatures. Issues typically contain 7–12 articles by international scholars, some original poetry, and book reviews. A recent special issue on "Institutionalizing English Studies: The Post-Colonial/Post-Independence Challenge" included essays on Scottish, Chinese, African, New Zealand literatures, on Third World aesthetics, and on the U.S. beginnings of Commonwealth Studies. Other special topics issues have had such titles as "The Literature of Travel," "Writing the New South Africa," North American Native Writings," and "Small Cultures: The Literature of Micro-States." The *Ariel* homepage links to web sites on similar themes. An important publication for academic libraries and larger public libraries with strong literature collections. (SG)

4425. *American Literary History.* [ISSN: 0896-7148] 1989. q. GBP 108. Ed(s): Gordon Hutner. Oxford University Press, 2001 Evans Rd, Cary, NC 27513; http://www3.oup.co.uk/jnls/. Illus., adv. Refereed. Circ: 1350. Vol. ends: Dec. Online: Chadwyck-Healey Incorporated; EBSCO Publishing; Gale Group; ingenta.com; JSTOR (Web-based Journal Archive); OCLC Online Computer Library Center, Inc.; Project MUSE; RoweCom Information Quest; Swets Blackwell. Reprint: PSC. *Indexed:* AmH&L, ArtHuCI, HumInd, MLA-IB. *Bk. rev.:* 3-5, 8-16 pages, signed. *Aud.:* Ac.

This quarterly describes itself as a forum for "a rich and varied criticism shaping the ways we have come to think about America" and American cultural studies. Edited by Gordon Hutner at the University of Kentucky, *ALH* publishes articles that deal with the idea or development of a national literature from all perspectives: the social, political, and economic aims of American literature; canon formation, periodicity, and genres; gender, ethnic, and Native American issues; reception studies; traditions of American criticism; and interdisciplinary, theoretical, and metacritical approaches to literary inquiry. Articles are scholarly—often quite erudite—and substantial: 20–25 pages (or longer). Typical issues of *ALH* also feature review essays, commentaries, scholarly exchanges, and notes on contributors. Each year, one issue of *ALH* is devoted to a special topic. Recent issues of *ALH* have included essays on such varied topics as Italian-American studies, colonial ethnography, Melville, Updike, the Leo Frank case, and the state of queer studies in American literature. Titles of articles published in *ALH* from 1996 onward can be browsed at the journal's web site, and full-text pdfs from 2002 forward. An e-mail table of contents alerting service is available at no charge. Project Muse subscribers can retrieve the full text of *ALH* articles from volume 12 (2000) forward. Of interest to scholars and students doing advanced or graduate-level research. (SG)

4426. *American Literary Realism, 1870-1910.* [ISSN: 0002-9823] 1967. 3x/yr. USD 35 domestic; USD 45 foreign. Ed(s): Gary Scharnhorst. University of Illinois Press, 1325 S Oak St, Champaign, IL 61820-6903; uipress@uillinois.edu; http://www.press.uillinois.edu. Illus., index, adv. Refereed. Circ: 700. Vol. ends: Spring. *Indexed:* AmH&L, AmHI, ArtHuCI, BEL&L, MLA-IB, SSCI. *Bk. rev.:* 3-7, 1-2 pages, signed. *Aud.:* Ac.

ALR advertises itself as the preeminent journal covering a key transition period in American literature (roughly 1870–1910). It publishes critical essays, scholarly notes, book reviews, documents, and bibliographies on a panorama of great authors from the late nineteenth and early twentieth centuries—Henry James, Edith Wharton, Theodore Dreiser, and Mark Twain among them. Lesser-known figures flourishing at this time are often covered as well. Each issue of *ALR* contains five essays (10–20 pages) and three to seven short (two-page) book reviews. Topics treated in recent numbers include sexuality in *Silas Lapham,* ethnic caricature and literary realism, Kate Chopin's characters, and Stephen Crane's uses of war. A special issue on Willa Cather appeared in Winter 2001. Recent tables of contents can be viewed from the journal's web site. Recommended for all college and university libraries. (SG)

4427. *American Literature: a journal of literary history, criticism, and bibliography.* [ISSN: 0002-9831] 1929. q. USD 193 (Individuals, USD 45). Ed(s): Houston A Baker, Jr. Duke University Press, 905 W Main St, Ste 18 B, Durham, NC 27701; subscriptions@dukeupress.edu; http://www.dukeupress.edu. Illus., index, adv. Refereed. Circ: 4500. Vol. ends: Dec. Microform: MIM; PQC. Online: EBSCO Publishing; Gale Group; Ingenta Select; JSTOR (Web-based Journal Archive); Northern Light Technology, Inc.; OCLC Online Computer Library Center, Inc.; Project MUSE; ProQuest Information & Learning; RoweCom Information Quest; Swets Blackwell. Reprint: ISI; PQC; PSC. *Indexed:* AmH&L, ArtHuCI, BEL&L, BRD, BRI, CBRI, HumInd, IBZ, MLA-IB, RI-1, SSCI. *Bk. rev.:* 25-40, 1-2 pages, signed. *Aud.:* Ac.

Published in cooperation with the Modern Language Association's American Literature Section, *AL* is the premier journal for scholarship in its field. It covers all periods (colonial to contemporary) and all genres from a variety of approaches: historical, critical, bibliographical, and theoretical. A typical issue contains six to eight lengthy scholarly essays (20–30 pages) and a generous selection of book reviews (often totaling 25 or more). In addition, a "Brief Mention" section cites new editions, reprints, collections, and anthologies; an "Announcements" section provides information on upcoming conferences, prizes, grants, and publishing opportunities. Prior to 1991, volumes of *AL* also included bibliographies of newly-published articles on American literature, as well as sections covering "Research in Progress" and "Notes and Queries." One issue a year focuses on a special topic: examples have included "Literature and Science," "Violence, the Body and the South," and "Unsettling Blackness" (a group of essays on the theme of African American cultural productions). Back issues are available on JSTOR; recent issues (from 1999 on) can be accessed on Project Muse. Subscribers can also view recent articles from the journal's web site. An indispensable journal for all academic and larger public libraries. (SG)

4428. *Arizona Quarterly: a journal of American literature, culture and theory.* [ISSN: 0004-1610] 1945. q. USD 16 (Individuals, USD 12; USD 5 newsstand/cover per issue). Ed(s): Edgar A Dryden. University of Arizona, Arizona Board of Regents, 1731 E Second St, Tucson, AZ 85721-0014; azq@u.arizona.edu; http://www.u.arizona.edu. Illus., index, adv. Sample. Refereed. Circ: 800. Vol. ends: Winter. Microform: PQC. Reprint: PSC. *Indexed:* AmH&L, AmHI, MLA-IB. *Aud.:* Ac.

Theoretical, historical, and critical articles on both canonical and non-canonical works of American literature, with a secondary emphasis placed on film. Fiction and poetry are excluded. Each issue contains at least five essays, typically 20–30 pages long, selected for "their solid scholarship, tight argument, contextual awareness" and clarity. The journal's scope is wide-ranging; recent issues have examined topics as diverse as Zane Grey, *Maus,* and the theme of transnationalism in the fiction of U.S. women writers of color. In 1997, a special issue on "The New Western History: An Assessment" received a first-place award from the Council of Editors of Learned Journals; other *AzQ* special issues have been devoted to such topics as humor in contemporary American literature, for example, and Henry James's fiction. Recommended for libraries that support programs in American Studies or American literature. (SG)

4429. *Australian Literary Studies.* [ISSN: 0004-9697] 1963. s-a. AUD 90 (Individuals, AUD 50; AUD 43.80 domestic to individuals & school libraries). Ed(s): Leigh Dale. University of Queensland Press, PO Box 6042, St Lucia, QLD 4067, Australia; uqp@uqp.uq.edu.au; http://www.uqp.uq.edu.au/. Illus., index, adv. Refereed. Circ: 1000. Microform: PQC. Online: EBSCO Publishing; Florida Center for Library Automation; Gale Group; RMIT Publishing. Reprint: PQC. *Indexed:* ArtHuCI, IBZ, MLA-IB, SSCI. *Bk. rev.:* 5, 2-5, signed. *Aud.:* Ac.

Published by the University of Queensland Press, *ALS* aims to provide "informed criticism" and "new perspectives" on Australian literature of all kinds. Issues contain eight to ten articles (10–15 pages in length), signed book reviews, and notes (two to four pages). One noteworthy feature of *ALS* is its annual bibliography, which attempts to list all new books, journal articles, and reviews of Australian writing that have appeared during the previous year. Topics in a single issue of *ALS* can range from the historical (a study of the Melbourne Shakespeare Society) to the critical/interpretive (the poetry of Judith Beveridge) to the theoretical (a discussion of the Australian "canon"). The UQP homepage also links visitors to a growing number of web sites on related topics. Appropriate for research libraries that support Australian studies or comprehensive literature collections. (SG)

4430. *Boundary 2: an international journal of literature and culture.* [ISSN: 0190-3659] 1972. 3x/yr. USD 147 (Individuals, USD 33). Ed(s): Paul A Bove. Duke University Press, 905 W Main St, Ste 18 B, Durham, NC 27701; subscriptions@dukeupress.edu; http://www.dukeupress.edu. Illus., index, adv. Sample. Refereed. Circ: 700. Vol. ends: Fall. Online: EBSCO Publishing; Gale Group; Ingenta Select; JSTOR (Web-based Journal Archive); Northern Light Technology, Inc.; OCLC Online Computer Library Center, Inc.; Project MUSE; ProQuest Information & Learning; RoweCom Information Quest; Swets Blackwell. Reprint: PSC. *Indexed:* ABS&EES, AmHI, AnthLit, ArtHuCI, BHA, FLI, HumInd, IAPV, IBZ, LRI, MLA-IB, SSCI. *Aud.:* Ac.

This scholarly journal, published by Duke University Press, "aims to promote thinking about the demands made on intellectual, political, and cultural life" as a result of "globalization and the most important changes in the world's dominant historical and political narratives." The emphasis is decidedly on the postmodern period and on culture, history, philosophy, and the "human sciences." World literature from earlier periods is also covered, though with somewhat less regularity in recent numbers. Issues usually contain seven to ten critical essays, 20–30 pages long, and notes on contributors. Book reviews and/or books received for review are often also featured, as are interviews with contemporary thinkers, and sometimes, original poetry. Recent articles have treated film history, Edward Said, and Chinese novels of the nineties. Recent special issues have had such titles as "Benjamin Now: Critical Encounters with the Arcades Project" (2003), "The University" (Spring 2000), "Sociology Hesitant: Thinking With W.E.B. DuBois" (Fall 2000), and "Left Conservatism: A Workshop" (Spring 1999). Project Muse subscribers have full-text access to articles from volume 26.3 (Fall 1999) forward. Subscribers can also access full-text pdfs (2000) from the journal's homepage. Highly theoretical, *Boundary 2* is most suitable in larger research collections. (SG)

4431. *The Cambridge Quarterly.* [ISSN: 0008-199X] 1964. q. GBP 110 (Members, USD 203 print & online). Ed(s): David C. Gervais, Geoffrey Wall. Oxford University Press, Great Clarendon St, Oxford, OX2 6DP, United Kingdom; jnl.orders@oup.co.uk; http://www3.oup.co.uk/jnls. Illus., index, adv. Refereed. Circ: 820. Reprint: PSC. *Indexed:* ArtHuCI, BEL&L, BHA, BrHumI, HumInd, MLA-IB. *Bk. rev.:* 3-6, 2-4, signed. *Aud.:* Ac.

This journal devotes itself principally to literary criticism; "its fundamental aim is to take a critical look at accepted views." With some regularity, it also publishes articles on music, cinema, painting, sculpture, and the philosophy of science. Each year, it endows a prize for, and publishes, the best Cambridge University Finals dissertation. *CQ* emphasizes English, American, and continental literatures of all periods, sometimes even from a comparative perspective. Contributors are predominantly (though not exclusively) from British universities. Journal issues typically contain three to four scholarly articles of 15 pages (or more) and three to six signed book reviews. Recent articles have treated such authors as DeLillo, Lorca, Ted Hughes, and James or focused on such topics as "Sargent and the Fate of Portrait Painting," "Historicism and 'Presentism' in Early Modern Studies," and "Derek Walcott's *Omeros* and Dante's *Commedia.*" Recent special issues have been devoted to contemporary poetry, to Racine, and to the art and study of biography (Shakespeare, Hazlitt, Woolf, Barthes, Sartre, and others). At the journal's web site, hosted by Oxford University Press, one can browse tables of contents back to 1996 and view full-text pdfs from 2001 forward. A free e-mail alerting service is also available from the site. *CQ* is an important journal for any academic library that supports British and American literature courses. (SG)

4432. ***Canadian Literature: a quarterly of criticism and review.*** [ISSN: 0008-4360] 1959. q. CND 64.20 (Individuals, CND 48.15). Ed(s): Eva Marie Kroller. University of British Columbia, Buchanan E158, 1866 Main Mall, Vancouver, BC V6T 1Z1, Canada. Illus., adv. Refereed. Circ: 1400. Vol. ends: Winter. Microform: PQC. Online: bigchalk; Chadwyck-Healey Incorporated; OCLC Online Computer Library Center, Inc.; ProQuest Information & Learning. *Indexed:* AmHI, ArtHuCI, BEL&L, BRD, BRI, CBCARef, CBRI, CPerI, HumInd, IAPV, LRI, MLA-IB, SSCI. *Bk. rev.:* 30-40, 1-2 pages, signed. *Aud.:* Ac.

This respected quarterly, which originates at the University of British Columbia, publishes critical and interpretive essays, in both English and French, on all aspects of Canadian writing. Coverage of contemporary Canadian writing is particularly good, and sometimes takes the form of an interview. A typical issue of *Canadian Literature* opens with an editorial essay, followed by five to seven articles of 15–25 pages, an extensive section of brief book reviews (two or three pages apiece), and "Opinions and Notes." Poems by current Canadian writers are interspersed throughout (the journal publishes no fiction, however). Articles treat both established writers (Michael Ondaatje, Margaret Atwood, Alice Munro) and emerging ones. Many issues focus on a particular theme; some recent examples are "Anglo-Francophone Writing," "Asian Canadian Writing," and "First Nations Writing" (devoted to the study of aboriginal authors). The journal's web site is fully searchable and contains extensive information, including tables of contents for all issues back to 1959, some full-text book reviews, and links to web sites for further study of Canadian literature. Appropriate for larger literature collections and for libraries that support Canadian studies. (SG)

4433. ***College Literature.*** [ISSN: 0093-3139] 1974. q. USD 80 (Individuals, USD 40). Ed(s): Kostas Myrsiades. West Chester University, 210 East Rosedale Ave, West Chester, PA 19383; collit@wcupa.edu; http://www.collegeliterature.org. Illus., index, adv. Refereed. Circ: 1000 Paid. Vol. ends: Oct. Online: bigchalk; Chadwyck-Healey Incorporated; EBSCO Publishing; Florida Center for Library Automation; Gale Group; Northern Light Technology, Inc.; OCLC Online Computer Library Center, Inc.; Project MUSE; ProQuest Information & Learning; H.W. Wilson. *Indexed:* ABS&EES, AmHI, ArtHuCI, BEL&L, BRI, CBRI, EduInd, HumInd, L&LBA, MLA-IB, SSCI. *Bk. rev.:* 6-9, 2-5 pages. *Aud.:* Ac.

A triannual journal of scholarly criticism aimed at college and university teachers of literature, *CL* attempts to highlight "innovative ways of studying and teaching new bodies of literature or experiencing old literatures in new ways." Articles emphasize textual analysis, critical theory, comparative or interdisciplinary studies, and pedagogy. Much of the focus is on English, American, and European literatures, although minority, Eastern, Third World, and oral literatures are also represented. Each issue contains at least eight to ten articles of 15–25 pages, several review essays, and individual book reviews. Notes on literary texts are sometimes incorporated, as are commentaries on issues of importance to the teaching of literature (curricular, theoretical, institutional, or the like). Recent numbers have featured articles on George Bataille and Etel Adnan, as well as Edith Wharton and Emily Dickinson. Recent special issues have treated such topics as "Literature and Art," "Diversity and American Poetries," "Teaching Beat Literature," and "Oral Fixations: Cannibalizing Theories, Consuming Hungers" (which included essays on cannibals in Victorian popular fiction and "legal hunger" in Silko). Subscribers to Chadwyck-Healey's Literature Online (LION) database have full-text access back to October 1995. An extremely useful journal for all academic libraries. (SG)

4434. ***Comparative Literature.*** [ISSN: 0010-4124] 1949. q. USD 50 (Individuals, USD 39). Ed(s): George Rowe. University of Oregon, Comparative Literature, 1249 University of Oregon, Eugene, OR 97403-1249; http://www.uoregon.edu. Illus., index. Refereed. Circ: 3000. Vol. ends: Nov. Microform: PQC. Online: bigchalk; Chadwyck-Healey Incorporated; EBSCO Publishing; Gale Group; JSTOR (Web-based Journal Archive); Northern Light Technology, Inc.; OCLC Online Computer Library Center, Inc.; ProQuest Information & Learning; H.W. Wilson. *Indexed:* ABS&EES, ArtHuCI, BAS, BHA, BRI, CBRI, HumInd, IBZ, MLA-IB, RILM. *Bk. rev.:* 2-6, 2-3 pages, signed. *Aud.:* Ac.

CL is the oldest U.S. publication in its field and the official journal of the American Comparative Literature Association (a division of the MLA). It publishes scholarly articles that address important issues of literary history, criticism, or theory from an international perspective. Literatures of all nations and all time periods are covered, so one is as likely to encounter a study of "fictive states" in Africa as an essay comparing the "imperial imagination[s]" of fifth-century Athens and Han China. The journal's major emphasis, however, is clearly on classical, Western European, and American texts. Each issue contains three to four substantial articles (20 or more pages), two to six book reviews, and occasionally, a longer, thematically-organized review of several new publications. The *CL* web site provides tables of contents for forthcoming issues and makes available selected abstracts from issues back to 1999; it also provides a short list of links to related professional organizations, scholarly journals, and comparative literature departments worldwide. Subscribers to Chadwyck-Healey's Literature Online (LION) database have full-text access back to Winter 1989. Appropriate for all academic libraries. (SG)

4435. ***Comparative Literature Studies.*** [ISSN: 0010-4132] 1963. q. USD 55 (Individuals, USD 34.50). Ed(s): Thomas O Beebee. Pennsylvania State University Press, 820 N. University Dr., USB-1, Ste C, University Park, PA 16802-1003; http://www.psupress.org. Illus., index, adv. Sample. Refereed. Circ: 800 Paid. Microform: PQC. Online: EBSCO Publishing; Gale Group; OCLC Online Computer Library Center, Inc.; Project MUSE; RoweCom Information Quest; Swets Blackwell. Reprint: PQC; PSC. *Indexed:* ABS&EES, ArtHuCI, BAS, BEL&L, BRI, CBRI, HumInd, IBZ, MLA-IB, RI-1. *Bk. rev.:* 4-7, 5-7 pages, signed. *Aud.:* Ac.

Published under the auspices of the Department of Comparative Literature at Pennsylvania State University, *CLS* contains comparative articles on literary history, the history of ideas, critical theory, and literary links between authors within and beyond the Western tradition. One issue every two years concerns itself exclusively with East-West literary relationships and is edited in conjunction with the College of International Relations at Nihon University in Japan. The format of a typical issue is three major essays (15 or more pages), and four to seven substantial book reviews (five to seven pages). Special issues may contain 9–12 essays. Recent articles have compared Wallace Stevens and Gustave Flaubert, discussed "intention" in Ogden Nash, and examined murderous mother figures in classical and Renaissance dramas. The most recent special issue included such essays as "Murakami Haruki and Anna Deavere Smith: Truth by Interview," "Understanding Yoshimitsu Yoshihiko's Mysticism," and "The Shaping of Gary Snyder's Ecological Consciousness." Annually since 1999, *CLS* has awarded and published an "A. Owen Aldridge Essay Prize" for outstanding research by a doctoral student in comparative literature. Project Muse subscribers have full-text access to *CLS* from volume 37 (2000) forward. Appropriate for academic, research, and larger public libraries. (SG)

4436. ***Contemporary Literature.*** Formerly: *Wisconsin Studies in Contemporary Literature.* [ISSN: 0010-7484] 1960. q. USD 118 (Individuals, USD 36). Ed(s): Thomas Schaub. University of Wisconsin Press, Journal Division, 1930 Monroe St., 3rd Fl, Madison, WI 53711; journals@uwpress.wisc.edu; http://www.wisc.edu/wisconsinpress/journals. Illus., index, adv. Refereed. Circ: 2100. Vol. ends: Winter. Microform: PQC. Online: bigchalk; EBSCO Publishing; Florida Center for Library Automation; Gale Group; Northern Light Technology, Inc.; OCLC Online Computer Library Center, Inc.; ProQuest Information & Learning; H.W. Wilson. Reprint: PSC. *Indexed:* ABS&EES, AmHI, ArtHuCI, BEL&L, BHA, HumInd, MLA-IB. *Bk. rev.:* 1-4, 10-20 pages, signed. *Aud.:* Ac.

This quarterly journal publishes essays on twentieth-century American, British, and continental literatures in English. While *CL* recognizes a range of critical approaches, articles tend to emphasize the relationships of texts to cultural, historical, or theoretical contexts. One distinguishing feature of this journal is the extended interview with which each issue opens. Recent interview subjects have included both new and established writers, among them William Gass, Harryette Mullen, Kazuo Ishiguro, and Paula Meehan. Four critical essays of 20–30 pages then follow, on topics as diverse as the poetry of Thom Gunn and Geoffrey Hill, Graham Swift's *Waterland,* and ekphrastic technique in the short fiction of Barthelme and Rushdie. Issues usually conclude with a thoughtful, thematically organized review of one or more works of recent scholarship. An important journal for academic and larger public libraries. (SG)

4437. ***Criticism: a quarterly for literature and the arts.*** [ISSN: 0011-1589] 1959. q. USD 73 (Individuals, USD 36). Ed(s): Renata Wassermann. Wayne State University Press, The Leonard N Simons Bldg, 4809 Woodward Ave, Detroit, MI 48201-1309; http://wsupress.wayne.edu/. Illus., index, adv. Refereed. Circ: 1175 Paid. Vol. ends: Fall. Microform: PQC. Online: bigchalk; Chadwyck-Healey Incorporated; Florida Center for Library Automation; Gale Group; Northern Light Technology, Inc.; OCLC Online Computer Library Center, Inc.; Project MUSE; ProQuest Information & Learning; RoweCom Information Quest; Swets Blackwell; H.W. Wilson. Reprint: PQC. *Indexed:* ArtHuCI, BHA, BRI, CBRI, FLI, HumInd, IBZ, MLA-IB, RI-1, SSCI. *Bk. rev.:* 5-8, 2-6 pages, signed. *Aud.:* Ac.

This journal describes itself as a "scholarly publication that examines arts and literatures of all periods and nations, either individually or in their relationships." The majority of contributions focuses on literature, but most issues also contain at least one essay on the visual, performing, or cinematic arts. Most articles are also informed by contemporary critical and cultural theory. The typical issue contains five scholarly essays, 15–40 pages long and five to eight lengthy book reviews. Articles are wide-ranging in subject: a recent issue contains a study of Beckett and poststructuralism, a discussion of Eric Auerbach's *Passio as Passion,* and an examination of Victorian Gothic. Project Muse subscribers have access to recent issues, from 2001 forward; institutions with access to Chadwyck-Healey's Literature Online (LION) database have access to full text back to 1994. Appropriate for larger academic libraries. (SG)

4438. ***Critique (Washington): studies in contemporary fiction.*** [ISSN: 0011-1619] 1958. q. USD 93 (Individuals, USD 48; USD 23.25 per issue). Ed(s): Helen Strang. Heldref Publications, 1319 18th St, NW, Washington, DC 20036-1802; subscribe@heldref.org; http://www.heldref.org. Illus., index, adv. Refereed. Circ: 1000 Paid. Vol. ends: Fall. CD-ROM: ProQuest Information & Learning. Online: bigchalk; Chadwyck-Healey Incorporated; EBSCO Publishing; Florida Center for Library Automation; Gale Group; OCLC Online Computer Library Center, Inc.; ProQuest Information & Learning; H.W. Wilson. Reprint: PSC. *Indexed:* ArtHuCI, BRI, CBRI, HumInd, MLA-IB. *Aud.:* Ac.

This peer-reviewed literary journal devotes itself to essays on contemporary fiction and on the work of emerging writers of significance from any country. It prides itself on a long history of identifying and initiating serious discussions of some the most notable novelists of our times: for example, Bellow and Malamud in the 1950s, Barth and Barthelme in the 1960s, Pynchon and Vonnegut in the 1970s, DeLillo and Garcia Marquez in the 1980s, and Amy Tan and Nurrudin Farah in the 1990s. More recently, the journal has published on such authors as Jeannette Winterson, E.L. Doctorow, Mordechai Richler, Kazuo Ishiguro, and Martin Amis. An issue of *Critique* typically contains eight to ten essays of 10–20 pages. Occasionally, interviews with authors or a small number of book reviews are also included. Recent special issues have been devoted to Robert Coover and to such topics as metafiction and postcolonial writing. Institutions with access to Chadwyck-Healey's Literature Online (LION) database have full-text access back to Winter 1992. Appropriate for all academic libraries. (SG)

4439. ***E L H.*** [ISSN: 0013-8304] 1934. q. USD 140 (Individuals, USD 30). Ed(s): Jonathan Goldberg. Johns Hopkins University Press, Journals Publishing Division, 2715 N Charles St, Baltimore, MD 21218-4363; http://www.press.jhu.edu/. Illus., adv. Refereed. Circ: 1908. Vol. ends: Winter. Microform: PQC. Online: EBSCO Publishing; Florida Center for Library Automation; Gale Group; JSTOR (Web-based Journal Archive); OCLC Online Computer Library Center, Inc.; Project MUSE; ProQuest Information & Learning; RoweCom Information Quest; Swets Blackwell. Reprint: PQC; PSC. *Indexed:* AmH&L, ArtHuCI, BEL&L, HumInd, IBZ, MLA-IB, SSCI. *Aud.:* Ac.

Edited for many years by Ronald Paulson and now by Jonathan Goldberg, *ELH* focuses primarily on major works of English literature from the Renaissance through the Modernist period (and occasionally, beyond). With less regularity, it also publishes scholarly articles on American literature. Known for its high standards, *ELH* does not "seek to sponsor particular methods or aims"; instead, it strives to provide its readers with an "intelligent mix of historical, critical, and theoretical concerns." Each issue of *ELH* contains eight to ten essays, 20–30 pages in length. Book reviews are excluded. Back issues of *ELH* can be accessed online via JSTOR; Project Muse subscribers have full-text access starting with volume 60 (1993). An indispensable journal for all academic and larger public libraries. (SG)

4440. ***E S Q: a journal of the American renaissance.*** Formerly: *Emerson Society Quarterly.* [ISSN: 0093-8297] 1955. q. USD 25 (Individuals, USD 18). Ed(s): Albert von Frank. Washington State University Press, PO Box 645910, Pullman, WA 99164-5910; http://libarts.wsu.edu/. Illus., adv. Refereed. Circ: 625. Vol. ends: No. 4. *Indexed:* AmHI, ArtHuCI, BEL&L, MLA-IB. *Aud.:* Ac.

Founded in 1955 and formerly known as the *Emerson Society Quarterly,* this publication focuses "upon all aspects—literary, religious, philosophical, and historic—of the romantic transcendental tradition emanating from New England." It also encourages criticism of nineteenth-century American writers and texts more generally: through source and influence studies, biographical studies, literary theory, and the history of ideas. Along with Emerson, regular subjects include Thoreau, Melville, Dickinson, Stowe, Poe, and Cooper. Issues typically contain two or three lengthy articles (20–30 pages) and an extended essay that reviews related books on figures and topics in the field, "thereby providing a forum for viewing recent scholarship in broad perspectives." Special issues have focused on the Hawthorne–Melville relationship (volume 46), on Margaret Fuller (volume 44), and on Emerson and Nietzsche (volume 43). An important journal, appropriate for all academic libraries. (SG)

4441. ***Early American Literature.*** Formerly (until 1967): *Early American Literature Newsletter.* [ISSN: 0012-8163] 1966. 3x/yr. USD 40 (Individuals, USD 26). Ed(s): David S Shields. University of North Carolina Press, PO Box 2288, Chapel Hill, NC 27515-2288; uncpress_journals@unc.edu; http://www.uncpress.unc.edu. Illus., index, adv. Refereed. Circ: 800 Paid. Online: bigchalk; Chadwyck-Healey Incorporated; EBSCO Publishing; Florida Center for Library Automation; Gale Group; Northern Light Technology, Inc.; OCLC Online Computer Library Center, Inc.; Project MUSE; ProQuest Information & Learning; RoweCom Information Quest; Swets Blackwell; H.W. Wilson. Reprint: PSC. *Indexed:* AmH&L, AmHI, ArtHuCI, BEL&L, HumInd, MLA-IB, RI-1. *Bk. rev.:* 3, 3-5 pages, signed. *Aud.:* Ac.

This triannual is the flagship journal of the MLA's Division of American Literature to 1800. Its focus is on American literature from its beginnings through the early national period (circa 1830). In addition to studies of English language texts from British America and the U.S., *EAL* publishes articles that treat Native American traditional expressions, colonial Ibero-American literature from North America, colonial American Francophone writings, Dutch colonial, and German American colonial literature. Issues contain five to six scholarly articles (usually 20 or so pages), a review essay or critical forum, and three to four individual book reviews (generally three to five pages). In addition, *EAL* provides notes on all contributors and offers editor's notes and announcements (forthcoming special issues, calls for papers and proposals, etc.). In recent issues, *EAL* has published articles on the Quaker martyr Mary Dwyer, Charles Brockden Brown's "aesthetic sense," Franklin's autobiography, and the popularity of pirate narratives in early nineteenth-century America. Project Muse subscribers have full-text access from 2000 forward; subscribers to Chadwyck-Healey's Literature Online (LION) database can access full text back to 1994. An important journal for libraries that support courses in American literature and culture of this period. (SG)

4442. *Eighteenth-Century Fiction.* [ISSN: 0840-6286] 1988. q. CND 84. Ed(s): David Blewett. University of Toronto Press, Journals Department, 5201 Dufferin St, Toronto, ON M3H 5T8, Canada; journals@utpress.utoronto.ca; http://www.utpjournals.com. Illus. Sample. Refereed. Circ: 800 Paid. *Indexed:* CBCARef, HumInd, LRI, MLA-IB. *Bk. rev.:* 20-25, 1-2 pages, signed. *Aud.:* Ac.

This quarterly journal, produced at McMaster University, publishes articles on "all aspects of imaginative prose" written between 1700 and 1800. It sometimes accepts papers on late seventeenth- and early nineteenth-century works as well, especially if they are discussed in relationship to some aspect of the eighteenth century. Although the languages of publication are English and French, *ECF* encourages articles on the fiction of other languages as well as comparative studies. A typical issue may contain four to five major essays (25–30 pages, some with color images or reproductions), 20 or more short book reviews, and notes on contributors. Sometimes an issue will also include a "Forum" section on a pertinent scholarly or interpretive problem. Recent issues of *ECF* have featured studies of Austen, Defoe, Scott, Sterne, the sentimental novel, historiography, and Fielding's relationship to the deists. Recent special issues of *ECF* have been devoted to topics such as "Reconsidering the Rise of the Novel," "Transformations du genre romanesque au XVIIIe siecle," and "Fiction and Print Culture." The *ECF* web site allows browsing of selected tables of contents back to volume 8 (1999). Appropriate for academic libraries. (SG)

4443. *The Eighteenth-Century Novel.* [ISSN: 1528-3631] 2001. a. USD 94.50. Ed(s): George Justice, Albert J Rivero. A M S Press, Inc., 63 Flushing Ave., # 417, Brooklyn, NY 11205-1005; amserve@earthlink.net. Illus., index. Refereed. *Bk. rev.:* 3-6, 2-3 pages each, signed. *Aud.:* Ac.

A recent offshoot of the series *AMS Studies in the Eighteenth Century,* this annual focuses on novels in English written during the long eighteenth century (i.e., 1660–1815). Contributors are mainly well-established scholars from the U.S. and U.K., but there is increasing representation from European and Asian researchers. Each volume has about 15 articles of 15–20 pages each, as well as three to six thorough book reviews of two to three pages each. This title has not yet been picked up by indexing sources but should have that coverage within the next year or so. The two volumes out thus far include articles ranging from "Clarissa's Cyberspace: The Development of Epistolary Space in Richardson's Clarissa," and "Spies, Pirates, and White Slaves: Encounters with the Algerines in Three Early American Novels," to "Orientalism and Propaganda: The Oriental Tale and Popular Politics in Late-Eighteenth-Century Britain." Each volume has its own index; the tables of contents are also available from the web site. Useful to both novice and experienced researchers. (HW)

4444. *English Language Notes.* [ISSN: 0013-8282] 1963. q. USD 52 (Individuals, USD 28). Ed(s): J Wallace Donald. University of Colorado, English Language Notes, Campus Box 226, Boulder, CO 80309; eln@stripe.colorado.edu; http://www.cusys.edu/. Illus., index, adv. Refereed. Circ: 1100. Vol. ends: Jun. *Indexed:* ArtHuCI, BEL&L, HumInd, IBZ, MLA-IB, RI-1. *Bk. rev.:* 2-3, 2-3 pages, signed. *Aud.:* Ac.

Published under the auspices of the University of Colorado, *ELN* provides a forum for shorter articles on English and American language and literature. Although its scope is broadly conceived, *ELN* tends to emphasize canonical British fiction, poetry, and drama written before the mid-twentieth century. The Middle Ages, Renaissance, and nineteenth century are especially well represented. Issues contain 8–12 scholarly notes of two to ten pages (though some occasionally run longer), two or three individual book reviews or a longer review essay, and a list of "Books received." Articles stress textual interpretation and explication, often on a small portion or the crux of a work, supported by historical, bibliographical, or biographical evidence. A recent number, for example, includes pieces on formulaic expressions of exile in Old English literature, Donne's "The Flea," Edmund Burke's influence on the opening of *Pride and Prejudice,* and two unpublished letters of James Fenimore Cooper. Until the late 1970s, *ELN* also published *The Romantic Movement: A Selective and Critical Bibliography* as an annual supplement to its September issue. A solid journal, *ELN* is recommended for scholars and students at the advanced undergraduate and graduate levels. (SG)

4445. *English Literary Renaissance.* [ISSN: 0013-8312] 1971. 8x/yr. USD 138 print & online eds. Blackwell Publishing Ltd., 9600 Garsington Rd, PO Box 805, Oxford, OX4 2DQ, United Kingdom; customerservices@oxon.blackwellpublishing.com; http://www.blackwellpublishing.com/. Illus., index, adv. Refereed. Circ: 1300. Vol. ends: No. 3. *Indexed:* AmH&L, AmHI, ArtHuCI, BEL&L, MLA-IB, RI-1. *Aud.:* Ac.

Published by the Center for Renaissance Studies at the University of Massachusetts, Amherst, this well-respected journal devotes itself to scholarly study of Tudor and Early Stuart literature (c. 1485–1665). Major figures treated regularly in its pages include Sidney, Shakespeare, Spenser, Donne, and Milton, but *ELR* includes scholarship on lesser-known figures from the period as well. A typical issue may contain five articles, 15–50 pages in length, and a number of illustrations, usually reproductions of contemporary woodcuts and engravings of Renaissance England and Europe. One of the journal's distinctive features is its publication of "rare texts and newly discovered manuscripts of the period." While it does not publish book reviews, *ELR* is known for its frequent inclusion of annotated bibliographies and bibliographical essays on the period, its persons (e.g., Marvell or James I), literary genres (e.g., Elizabethan prose fiction, neo-Latin literature), and special topics. Appropriate for medium-sized and larger academic libraries. (SG)

4446. *English Literature in Transition, 1880-1920.* Formerly (until 1963): *English Fiction in Transition, 1880-1920.* [ISSN: 0013-8339] 1957. q. USD 27 domestic; USD 34 foreign; USD 30 domestic. Robert Langenfeld, Ed. & Pub., Department of English, PO Box 26170, Greensboro, NC 27402-6170. Illus., index, adv. Sample. Refereed. Circ: 900. Vol. ends: No. 4. Microform: PQC. Online: Chadwyck-Healey Incorporated; Florida Center for Library Automation; Gale Group. Reprint: PQC; PSC. *Indexed:* ArtHuCI, BRI, CBRI, HumInd, MLA-IB, SSCI. *Bk. rev.:* 13-14, 3-4 pages, signed. *Aud.:* Ac.

This quarterly journal originates from the University of North Carolina in Greensboro. It covers late Victorian and early twentieth-century British fiction, poetry, and drama, as well as topics of cultural interest. While it regularly publishes book reviews on such major authors as Yeats, Woolf, Conrad, James, Joyce, and Pound, *ELT* accepts critical articles on these writers only when they are linked to discussions of minor figures of the period: Oscar Wilde, e.g., Rudyard Kipling, Walter Pater, H.H. Munro. Typical issues contain four articles (15–25 pages), 13 or 14 book reviews (three to four pages), and on occasion, surveys of research or previously unpublished letters and documents. *ELT* is noteworthy, too, for the annotated bibliographies that issues sometimes include: recent subjects have been E. Nesbit, Ford Madox Ford, W. Somerset Maugham, and "The Economics of Taste: Literary Markets and Literary Value in the Late Nineteenth Century." The journal's web site provides a brief history of the publication and an index of all items that have appeared in *ELT* from 1983 forward. Three earlier indexes (1957–1972, 1973–1982, and 1983–1992) are available in print and can be purchased from the ELT Press. Institutions that subscribe to Chadwyck-Healey's Literature Online (LION) database have access to full-text of articles backs to 1998. Appropriate for medium-sized and larger academic libraries. (SG)

4447. *Essays in Criticism: a quarterly journal of literary criticism.* [ISSN: 0014-0856] 1951. q. GBP 98. Ed(s): Stephen Wall, Dr. Seamus Perry. Oxford University Press, Great Clarendon St, Oxford, OX2 6DP, United Kingdom; jnl.orders@oup.co.uk; http://www3.oup.co.uk/jnls. Illus., index, adv. Refereed. Circ: 1950. Vol. ends: Oct. Microform: MIM; PQC. Online: Florida Center for Library Automation; Gale Group; ingenta.com; Northern Light Technology, Inc.; RoweCom Information Quest; Swets Blackwell. Reprint: PQC; PSC; SWZ. *Indexed:* ArtHuCI, BEL&L, BrHumI, HumInd, IBZ, MLA-IB, RI-1. *Bk. rev.:* 4-5, 5-7 pages, signed. *Aud.:* Ac.

Founded in 1951 by the eminent F.W. Bateson, *E in C* remains one of the most distinguished British journals of literary criticism. It covers canonical English literature of all periods and genres and privileges "originality in interpretation-...allied to the best scholarly standards." Although it has an admitted "Oxford bias," *E in C* is not parochial, and many contributors are affiliated with universities elsewhere. Typically, issues contain three scholarly articles (15–25 pages) and four substantial signed book reviews (five to seven pages). Occasionally, an issue will open with a "Critical Opinion" (recent examples are "Hazlitt's 'Sexual Harassment' " and "Coleridge's Millennial Embarrassments"). In each April number, *E in C* publishes the F.W. Bateson Memorial Lecture, an Oxford address that has been delivered in recent times by notables like Stefan Collini, Frank Kermode, and Paul Muldoon. As part of its 50th anniversary special number, *E in C* produced a cumulative index. Oxford University Press, which publishes *E in C,* offers a free table of contents e-mail alerting service. From the OUP web site, subscribing institutions also have access to pdfs of articles from 1996 forward. An indispensable journal for academic libraries; an excellent choice for larger public libraries. (SG)

4448. ***Exemplaria: a journal of theory in medieval and Renaissance studies.*** [ISSN: 1041-2573] 1989. s-a. USD 45 (Individuals, USD 25; Students, USD 15). Ed(s): R Allen Shoaf. Pegasus Press, Pegasus Press, University of North Carolina - Asheville, Asheville, NC 28804; exempla@nervm.nerdc.ufl.edu; pegpress@interpath.com; http://www.clas.ufl.edu/english/exemplaria; http://www.pegasuspress.org. Illus., adv. Sample. Refereed. Circ: 405. Vol. ends: Autumn. *Indexed:* AmHI, BEL&L, MLA-IB. *Aud.:* Ac.

This journal, which debuted in 1989, has been twice cited by the Council of Editors of Learned Journals: as "Best New Journal" in 1990 and, in 1992, for a special issue, entitled "Reconceiving Chaucer: Literary Theory and Historical Interpretation" (volume 2.1). *Exemplaria* publishes scholarly articles on Anglo-Saxon literature and on English and continental writing of the Middle Ages and Renaissance. Articles cover canonical texts (*Beowulf, Piers Plowman,* and the *Roman de la Rose,* for example), major and minor authors (Christine de Pisan, Chaucer, Malory, Shakespeare, Milton, Donne), and literary genres (the French fabliau, troubadour poetry, Tudor drama, and the like). Approaches may be historical, theoretical, comparative, interdisciplinary, or analytical. Issues usually contain ten articles, 15–40 pages each. Notes on contributors also appear. In addition to special issues on such topics as "Jewish Medieval Studies and Literary Theory" and "Skirting the Texts: Feminism's Re-Readings of Medieval and Renaissance Texts," *Exemplaria* regularly publishes smaller essay "clusters" and symposia within its numbers on topics like "Teaching Chaucer in the Nineties." The *Exemplaria* web site provides tables of contents for all back issues, several recent reprints, and a small list of related web links. A solid journal, appropriate for most academic libraries. (SG)

4449. ***The Explicator.*** [ISSN: 0014-4940] 1942. q. USD 92 (Individuals, USD 48; USD 23 per issue). Ed(s): Paul Haynos. Heldref Publications, 1319 18th St, NW, Washington, DC 20036-1802; subscribe@heldref.org; http://www.heldref.org. Illus., index, adv. Refereed. Circ: 1500. Vol. ends: No. 4. CD-ROM: ProQuest Information & Learning. Online: bigchalk; Chadwyck-Healey Incorporated; EBSCO Publishing; Florida Center for Library Automation; Gale Group; Northern Light Technology, Inc.; OCLC Online Computer Library Center, Inc.; ProQuest Information & Learning; H.W. Wilson. Reprint: PSC. *Indexed:* ArtHuCI, HumInd, IBZ, MLA-IB. *Aud.:* Ac.

One of the few journals entirely devoted to text-based criticism, *The Explicator* publishes short papers (generally no longer than two to four pages) on passages from both prose and poetry. While its emphasis is on the works of English and American literature that are most frequently studied, taught, and anthologized, the journal also accepts interpretive notes on world literatures of all time periods. A single issue may contain 25–30 explications on authors as varied as Horace, Edward Taylor, Conrad, Bessie Head, and Garcia Marquez. No book reviews are included. The journal produces an annual index of article titles for each volume. *The Explicator: A Fifty-Year Index, Volumes 1–50, 1942–1992,* was published separately in 1994. Institutions that subscribe to Chadwyck-Healey's Literature Online (LION) database have access to full text of articles back to Winter 1988. An extremely useful publication for students, scholars, and teachers of literature at the college and university levels. (SG)

4450. ***Journal of Commonwealth Literature.*** [ISSN: 0021-9894] 1965. q. GBP 220 print & online eds. in Europe, Middle East, Africa & Australasia. Ed(s): Geraldine Stoneham, John Thieme. Sage Publications Ltd., 6 Bonhill St, London, EC2A 4PU, United Kingdom; info@sagepub.co.uk; http://www.sagepub.co.uk/. Adv. Sample. Refereed. Circ: 900. *Indexed:* ArtHuCI, BAS, BEL&L, BrHumI, HumInd, MLA-IB. *Bk. rev.:* 20, brief, unsigned. *Aud.:* Ac.

Covering the literature of current and former Commonwealth countries outside of Great Britain, *Journal of Commonwealth Literature* provides two issues a year of scholarly critical articles. The eight to ten articles per issue are 15–20 pages each, with contributors as well as article topics ranging from all over the Commonwealth, from India to Sri Lanka to New Zealand. Recent articles include "Mastering Arachnophobia: The Limits of Self-Reflexivity in African Fiction" and "Imperial Poverty in Robert Tressell's *The Ragged Trousered Philanthropists.*" The third issue each year consists of annotated bibliographies of Commonwealth literature; each country has its own section, beginning with a bibliographic essay of five to seven pages, followed by extensive bibliographies of poetry, fiction, drama, translations, letters, anthologies, criticism (at both book and article level), and studies of individual authors published during the year covered. General bibliographies and research sources are also listed. Available online through Ingenta (2000 to the present), this provides good access to the evolving literary canon of the Commonwealth. (HW)

4451. ***Journal of English and Germanic Philology.*** Former titles: *Journal of English and Germanic Philology; Journal of Germanic Philology.* [ISSN: 0363-6941] 1897. q. USD 90 (Individuals, USD 50). Ed(s): M Kalinke, C Wright. University of Illinois Press, 1325 S Oak St, Champaign, IL 61820-6903; http://www.press.uillinois.edu. Adv. Refereed. Circ: 1200. Microform: MIM; IDC; PMC; PQC. Online: Chadwyck-Healey Incorporated; Florida Center for Library Automation; Gale Group; OCLC Online Computer Library Center, Inc.; ProQuest Information & Learning. Reprint: PQC. *Indexed:* ArtHuCI, BRI, CBRI, HumInd, IBZ, MLA-IB, SSCI. *Bk. rev.:* 20-40, 1-2 pages. *Aud.:* Ac.

This well-established and respected quarterly, founded in 1897, publishes scholarly articles on English, American, German, and Scandinavian literatures and language. The journal's emphasis is on major authors and works from the early Middle Ages through the seventeenth century; with somewhat less frequency, articles on the eighteenth, nineteenth, and early twentieth centuries are also included. Modern and contemporary writing is rarely covered. Most articles take a historical or philological approach and are noted for their erudition. Issues of *JEGP* usually contain four major essays (10–25 pages, on average) and an extensive book review section (often 20 or more, one to two pages each). The October issue always includes an index of *JEGP*'s contents for that year. *JEGP* is indispensable for research collections and recommended for medium and larger academic libraries. (SG)

4452. ***Journal of Modern Literature.*** [ISSN: 0022-281X] 1970. 3x/yr. USD 107; USD 149.80 combined subscription print & online eds. Ed(s): Morton P Levitt. Indiana University Press, 601 N Morton St, Bloomington, IN 47404; journals@indiana.edu. Illus., index, adv. Sample. Refereed. Circ: 1500. Vol. ends: Nov. Microform: PQC. Online: Chadwyck-Healey Incorporated; EBSCO Publishing; Florida Center for Library Automation; Gale Group; OCLC Online Computer Library Center, Inc.; Project MUSE; ProQuest Information & Learning; RoweCom Information Quest; H.W. Wilson. Reprint: PQC; PSC. *Indexed:* ABS&EES, AmHI, ArtHuCI, FLI, HumInd, IBZ, MLA-IB. *Aud.:* Ac.

Advertising itself as "the most important scholarly journal in its field," this quarterly originally emphasized major figures of the Modernist period (1885–1950): James Joyce, Virginia Woolf, D.H. Lawrence, Joseph Conrad, E.M. Forster, Evelyn Waugh, and T.S. Eliot (among others). In recent years, however, *JML* has enlarged its purview beyond English and American authors from that period to encompass all literature written after 1900. Two issues per year contain eight essays (20–30 pages); these are preceded by an "Editor's Introduction" and followed by a section of three or four briefer studies (4–10 pages), called "For the Record." Notes on all contributors are included. Occasionally, *JML* publishes special issues: recent examples are "Joyce and the Joyceans" (1998), "Modern Poetry: from Painting to Politics"(2000), and "Autobiography and Memoir" (forthcoming in 2004). *JML*'s best-known feature may be its annual double issue of recently published research (books, articles, dissertations), many accompanied by brief (250- to 300-word) abstracts. The annual review is arranged under two broad headings: "General Studies" and "Individual Authors." Subcategories of the General Studies section are "Reference and Bibliography," "Literary History," "Themes and Movements," "Regional, National and Ethnic Literatures," "Comparative Studies—Two or More Authors," "Criticism of Modern Literature Generally," "Criticism of Fiction," "Criticism of Poetry," "Criticism of Drama," and "Criticism of Film Literature." The journal's web site provides tables of contents starting with volume 21 (Summer 1997), and a handful of sample articles in full text. Project Muse subscribers have full-text access from volume 22.2 (Winter

1998/1999) on. Institutions that subscribe to Chadwyck-Healey's Literature Online (LION) database also have full-text article access from 1998 forward. An essential journal for all academic and public libraries. (SG)

4453. *M E L U S.* [ISSN: 0163-755X] 1974. q. Institutional members, USD 60; Individual members, USD 50. Ed(s): Katharine T Rodier. Society for the Study of the Multi-Ethnic Literature of the United States, 215 Glenbrook Rd U-4025, Department of English, Storrs, CT 06269-4025; rodier@marshall.edu; http://english.boisestate.edu/melus/index.htm. Illus., index, adv. Refereed. Circ: 1000 Paid. Vol. ends: Winter. Microform: PQC. Online: bigchalk; Chadwyck-Healey Incorporated; EBSCO Publishing; Florida Center for Library Automation; Gale Group; JSTOR (Web-based Journal Archive); OCLC Online Computer Library Center, Inc.; ProQuest Information & Learning; H.W. Wilson. *Indexed:* ABS&EES, AbAn, AmHI, ArtHuCI, HumInd, IBZ, IIBP, MLA-IB. *Bk. rev.:* 5-7, 2-4 pages, signed. *Aud.:* Ac.

This journal publishes articles, interviews, and reviews that represent the multi-ethnic makeup of America. In doing so, it covers a variety of works written by African Americans, Asian and Pacific Americans, ethnically specific European Americans, Latino Americans, and Native Americans. Issues contain about ten articles of 20–30 pages, most of which examine the role of ethnicity in the literature, music, film, and television of the past and present. Most issues center on a particular theme; for example, an article in a recent issue on Native American literature looked at storytelling in the works of Leslie Marmon Silko, and an article in an issue on Jewish American literature examined the stereotype of the Jewish American mother. Credentials of contributors are provided at the end of every issue. Recommended for all academic libraries and large public libraries in urban settings. (CM)

4454. *M L N.* Formerly (until 1962): *Modern Language Notes.* [ISSN: 0026-7910] 1886. 5x/yr. USD 145 (Individuals, USD 43). Ed(s): Rainer Nagele. Johns Hopkins University Press, Journals Publishing Division, 2715 N Charles St, Baltimore, MD 21218-4363; http://www.press.jhu.edu/. Illus., index, adv. Refereed. Circ: 1601. Vol. ends: Dec. Microform: IDC; PMC; PQC. Online: EBSCO Publishing; Florida Center for Library Automation; Gale Group; JSTOR (Web-based Journal Archive); OCLC Online Computer Library Center, Inc.; Project MUSE; RoweCom Information Quest; Swets Blackwell. Reprint: PQC; PSC. *Indexed:* ABS&EES, ArtHuCI, BRI, CBRI, HumInd, IBZ, L&LBA, MLA-IB, SSCI. *Bk. rev.:* 1-13, 2-6 pages, signed. *Aud.:* Ac.

MLN was one of the first journals in the United States to publish criticism of contemporary European literature. It continues to publish scholarly and critical studies in the modern languages as well as works in comparative literature. The first issue of every volume focuses on works in Italian, the second on works in Spanish, the third on works in German, and the fourth on works in French. The fifth issue of every volume covers comparative literature and includes an index to the entire volume. Most articles are written in English, but some are written in Italian, Spanish, German, or French. A typical issue contains seven to ten articles. Articles are often historical and theoretical, and they are generally 20–30 pages long. Book reviews appear in every issue. Project Muse offers a subscription to the electronic version of the journal from volume 108 (1993) onward. JSTOR covers the journal from its origins. This is a major, longstanding literature journal that is recommended for all academic and public libraries. (CM)

4455. *Medium Aevum.* [ISSN: 0025-8385] 1932. s-a. GBP 32 domestic; USD 68 foreign. Ed(s): Jane Taylor, Corinne Saunders. Society for the Study of Mediaeval Languages and Literature, c/o Dr. D.G. Pattison, Hon Treas., Magdalen College, Oxford, OX1 4AU, United Kingdom. Illus., index, adv. Refereed. Circ: 1100. Vol. ends: No. 2. Online: bigchalk; Chadwyck-Healey Incorporated; EBSCO Publishing; Florida Center for Library Automation; Gale Group; Northern Light Technology, Inc.; OCLC Online Computer Library Center, Inc.; ProQuest Information & Learning; H.W. Wilson. *Indexed:* ArtHuCI, BEL&L, BrHumI, HumInd, IBZ, LRI, MLA-IB. *Bk. rev.:* 15-20, 1-2 pages, signed. *Aud.:* Ac.

This journal, published by the Society for the Study of Mediaeval Languages and Literature, supports critical and interpretive research in mediaeval languages and literature. Though the scope of the journal includes all major European languages, its emphasis is on English. Articles are somewhat advanced and are usually accompanied by notes and book reviews. Recent articles have analyzed Anglo-French and Middle English in *Femina Nova,* and representations of the relationship between Abraham and Sarah in old English literature. Issues usually contain five articles of approximately 20 pages, and book reviews are usually no more than two pages long. Subscribers to Chadwyck-Healey's Literature Online (LION) database have full-text access back to 1995. Recommended for academic libraries that support the study of medieval literature and large public libraries with research collections. (CM)

4456. *Modern Fiction Studies.* [ISSN: 0026-7724] 1955. q. USD 107 (Individuals, USD 34). Ed(s): Siobhan Somerville, John N Duvall. Johns Hopkins University Press, Journals Publishing Division, 2715 N Charles St, Baltimore, MD 21218-4363; http://www.press.jhu.edu/. Illus., adv. Refereed. Circ: 2823. Vol. ends: Winter. Microform: PQC. Online: EBSCO Publishing; ProQuest Information & Learning; RoweCom Information Quest; Swets Blackwell. Reprint: PQC; PSC. *Indexed:* ABS&EES, AmHI, ArtHuCI, BHA, BRI, CBRI, HumInd, MLA-IB, SSCI. *Bk. rev.:* 0-40, 1-3 pages, signed. *Aud.:* Ac.

This significant journal publishes articles that analyze prominent works of modern fiction. Most articles employ a historical, interdisciplinary, theoretical, or cultural approach. For example, articles in recent issues looked at the politics behind Virginia Woolf's *Flush;* the use of photography and music in E.L. Doctorow's novel *Ragtime;* and the role of domestic labor in film noir, proletarian literature, and black women's fiction. Each issue contains four to six articles of 20–30 pages, with contributors' credentials provided at the back of the issue. The journal also includes review essays and book reviews. The publication schedule has general issues, which deal with a wide range of texts, alternate with special issues that focus on single topics or specific writers. Project Muse offers a subscription to the electronic version of the journal from volume 40 (1994) forward. This is a major journal in its field, and it is recommended for all academic and public libraries. (CM)

4457. *Modern Language Quarterly: a journal of literary history.* [ISSN: 0026-7929] 1940. q. USD 150 includes online access (Individuals, USD 35 includes online access; USD 38 per issue). Ed(s): Marshall Brown. Duke University Press, 905 W Main St, Ste 18 B, Durham, NC 27701; subscriptions@dukeupress.edu; http://www.dukeupress.edu. Illus., index, adv. Refereed. Circ: 1600. Vol. ends: Dec. Microform: MIM; PMC; PQC. Online: EBSCO Publishing; Florida Center for Library Automation; Gale Group; Ingenta Select; Northern Light Technology, Inc.; OCLC Online Computer Library Center, Inc.; Project MUSE; ProQuest Information & Learning; RoweCom Information Quest; Swets Blackwell. Reprint: PSC. *Indexed:* ABS&EES, ArtHuCI, HumInd, IBZ, MLA-IB, SSCI. *Bk. rev.:* 5-7, 2-4 pages, signed. *Aud.:* Ac.

Since its inception in 1940, *Modern Language Quarterly* has increased its scope from its initial focus on the study of the origins of literature in European languages to its current embrace of all aspects of literary history. It encourages scholarship on literary works from the Middle Ages to the present, including explorations of all aspects of literary change. It particularly welcomes "historicism in relation to feminism, ethnic studies, cultural materialism, discourse analysis, and all other forms of representation and cultural critique." Most issues contain four or five articles. Articles are intellectual but readable and tend to be 20–30 pages in length, with many annotations. Book reviews appear in every issue. Project Muse offers a subscription to the electronic version of the journal from volume 60 (1999) onward. Recommended for medium-sized academic libraries and larger public libraries. (CM)

4458. *Modern Language Review.* [ISSN: 0026-7937] 1905. q. GBP 94. Maney Publishing, Hudson Rd, Leeds, LS9 7DL, United Kingdom; maney@maney.co.uk; http://www.maney.co.uk. Illus. Refereed. Circ: 1800. Vol. ends: Oct. Microform: BHP; PMC. Online: Chadwyck-Healey Incorporated; Gale Group; ingenta.com. *Indexed:* ArtHuCI, BEL&L, BHA, BRI, BrHumI, CBRI, FLI, HumInd, IBZ, MLA-IB, SSCI, SSI. *Bk. rev.:* 90-100, 1-4 pages, signed. *Aud.:* Ac.

This is the flagship journal of the Modern Humanities Research Association in London. It publishes articles and reviews on medieval and modern European literature, with occasional coverage of contemporary authors. The scope of the journal encompasses English, French, Germanic, Hispanic, Italian, Slavonic, and East European languages and literatures. *MLR* also publishes research in linguistics, comparative literature, and critical theory. Articles (in a typical issue, 9–12) are scholarly, yet on the whole, accessible, and are 10–20 pages in length. Approximately one-half of every issue is dedicated to book reviews. Articles about literatures in English that are submitted to the *Modern Language Review* are also considered for publication in the *Yearbook of English Studies,* an annual supplement to the journal. This is one of the oldest journals in its field and it is recommended for all academic libraries and larger public libraries. (CM)

4459. *Modern Philology: a journal devoted to research in medieval and modern literature.* [ISSN: 0026-8232] 1903. q. USD 149 print & online eds. (Individuals, USD 38 print & online eds.; Students, USD 26 print & online eds.). Ed(s): Joshua Scodel, Katie Trumpener. University of Chicago Press, Journals Division, PO Box 37005, Chicago, IL 60637; subscriptions@press.uchicago.edu; http://www.journals.uchicago.edu. Illus., index, adv. Refereed. Circ: 1700 Paid. Vol. ends: May. Microform: IDC; PMC; PQC. Online: EBSCO Publishing; Florida Center for Library Automation; Gale Group; JSTOR (Web-based Journal Archive); ProQuest Information & Learning. Reprint: ISI; PQC; PSC. *Indexed:* ABS&EES, ArtHuCI, BEL&L, BRD, BRI, CBRI, HumInd, IBZ, L&LBA, MLA-IB, RI-1. *Bk. rev.:* 15-30, 2-4 pages, signed. *Aud.:* Ac.

Founded in 1903, *Modern Philology* publishes critical approaches to literary and cultural history, bibliography, and lexicography. The majority of articles focus on works from Britain, the United States, and other English-speaking countries, but articles about literature in French, Spanish, Italian, German, Russian, and other languages are included from time to time. A typical issue contains two or three articles of 20–30 pages, and illustrations are sometimes provided. The style of most articles is approachable, as most authors provide a historical context for their topic. A substantial portion of every issue is devoted to book reviews. The journal's web site offers tables of contents for volumes published in 1996 and later. Recommended for large academic libraries and public libraries with research collections. (CM)

4460. *Mosaic (Winnipeg, 1967): a journal for the interdisciplinary study of literature.* Formerly (until 1978): *Journal for the Comparative Study of Literature and Ideas.* [ISSN: 0027-1276] 1967. q. CND 56.07. Ed(s): Dr. Dawne McCance. University of Manitoba, 208 Tier Bldg, Winnipeg, MB R3T 2N2, Canada; mosaic_journal@umanitoba.ca; http://www.umanitoba.ca/publications/mosaic. Illus., index, adv. Sample. Refereed. Circ: 1000. Vol. ends: Fall. Microform: PQC. Online: Chadwyck-Healey Incorporated; Florida Center for Library Automation; Gale Group; OCLC Online Computer Library Center, Inc.; ProQuest Information & Learning. *Indexed:* AmHI, ArtHuCI, BAS, BEL&L, BHA, CIJE, CPerI, HumInd, MLA-IB, RI-1, RILM. *Aud.:* Ac.

This lively, peer-reviewed journal focuses on the interdisciplinary study of literature. By publishing literary perspectives from a wide variety of disciplines, *Mosaic* attempts to showcase the theoretical, practical, and cultural relevance of postcolonial literary works. Essays are written in either English or French and often cover contemporary topics. Recent articles have discussed globalization, AIDS, and the connection between *The Nutcracker* and the Cold War. Each issue contains six to ten articles of approximately 20 pages, including notes, an abstract, and a paragraph that outlines the author's credentials. Many articles include illustrations. The journal's web site provides tables of contents and abstracts for selected recent volumes. Subscribers to Chadwyck-Healey's Literature Online (LION) database have full-text access back to 1994. Recommended for larger academic libraries that support literature studies. (CM)

4461. *Narrative.* [ISSN: 1063-3685] 1993. 3x/yr. USD 47. Ed(s): James Phelan. Ohio State University Press, 180 Pressey Hall, 1070 Carmack Rd, Columbus, OH 43210-1002; journals@osu.edu; http://www.ohiostatepress.org. Refereed. Circ: 1000 Paid. Microform: PQC. Online: Florida Center for Library Automation; Gale Group; Northern Light Technology, Inc.; OCLC Online Computer Library Center, Inc.; Project MUSE; ProQuest Information & Learning; Swets Blackwell. *Indexed:* AmHI, ArtHuCI, MLA-IB. *Aud.:* Ac.

The official journal of the Society of the Study of Narrative Literature, this triannual publication received the Best New Journal Award by the Council of Editors of Learned Journals when it appeared in 1993. The journal interprets the term broadly; "narrative" is thus a category that includes short fiction, the novel, narrative poetry, history, biography, autobiography, film, and performance art. The journal emphasizes studies of narrative theory, elements, techniques, and forms; the relationships of narrative to other modes of discourse; the power and limits of story; and the influence of narratives upon cultures both past and present. Articles treat British, American, or European subjects, and contributors have included such luminaries as Wayne C. Booth, Robert Scholes, Elaine Showalter, Elizabeth Langland, and Nancy Armstrong. Typical issues contain an editor's column, five or six scholarly essays (10–30 pages), and notes on contributors; an issue may also include a "Dialogue" section of several essays, related by theme or written in response to one another. The contents of the journal is eclectic: in addition to articles on writers like Joyce, Dickens, Kafka, and James, other subjects of study have included the Book of Daniel, Art Spiegelman's *Maus,* and photography as "visual narrative." Recent special issues have focused on "Narratology" (May 2001) and "Narrative and Performance" (May 2000). From the journal's web page, users have access to tables of contents from 1993 onward, links to the Society for the Study of Narrative, conference information, and listservs. Project Muse subscribers have full-text access to all issues from 2002 forward. Recommended for medium-sized and larger academic libraries. (SG)

4462. *New Literary History: a journal of theory and interpretation.* [ISSN: 0028-6087] 1969. q. USD 135 (Individuals, USD 34). Ed(s): Ralph Cohen. Johns Hopkins University Press, Journals Publishing Division, 2715 N Charles St, Baltimore, MD 21218-4363; http://www.press.jhu.edu/. Illus., index, adv. Refereed. Circ: 1688. Vol. ends: Nov. Microform: PQC. Online: EBSCO Publishing; Florida Center for Library Automation; Gale Group; JSTOR (Web-based Journal Archive); OCLC Online Computer Library Center, Inc.; Project MUSE; ProQuest Information & Learning; RoweCom Information Quest; Swets Blackwell. Reprint: PQC; PSC. *Indexed:* ABS&EES, ArtHuCI, BAS, BEL&L, BHA, FLI, HumInd, IBZ, L&LBA, LRI, MLA-IB, PSA, SSCI, SociolAb. *Aud.:* Ac.

Under the continuous editorship of Ralph Cohen at the University of Virginia since the journal's inception in 1969, *New Literary History* focuses on the theory and interpretation of past and present literary works, with an emphasis on articles that delve into literary history, the reading process, and hermeneutics. The journal also publishes articles from other disciplines that help to interpret or define the problems of literary history and literary study. Some articles presume a significant amount of prior knowledge, but explanatory footnotes are usually provided. A typical issue contains 10–15 articles. Articles are generally 15–20 pages long, and author credentials are provided at the end of every issue. Articles that respond to previous essays are shorter in length. Each issue centers on a special topic, and recent issues have covered themes such as "Everyday Life" and "Philosophical and Rhetorical Inquiries." This journal does not publish book reviews. Project Muse offers a subscription to the electronic version of the journal from volume 26 (1995) onward. Recommended for medium and large academic libraries. (CM)

4463. *Nineteenth-Century Literature (Berkeley).* Formerly: *Nineteenth-Century Fiction.* [ISSN: 0891-9356] 1945. q. USD 107 print & online eds. USD 27 newsstand/cover. Ed(s): Joseph Bristow, Tom Wortham. University of California Press, Journals Division, 2000 Center St, Ste 303, Berkeley, CA 94704-1223; journals@ucop.edu; http://www.ucpress.edu/journals. Illus., index, adv. Sample. Refereed. Circ: 2100 Paid. Vol. ends: Mar. Microform: PQC. Online: EBSCO Publishing; Florida Center for Library Automation; Gale Group; Ingenta Select; JSTOR (Web-based Journal Archive); OCLC Online Computer Library Center, Inc. Reprint: PQC. *Indexed:* AmH&L, ArtHuCI, BRI, CBRI, HumInd, IBZ, MLA-IB, RI-1. *Bk. rev.:* 5-10, 2-4 pages, signed. *Aud.:* Ac.

The successor to *Nineteenth-Century Fiction, Nineteenth-Century Literature* publishes essays on the culture of the United States, Britain, the British Empire, and Europe during the nineteenth century. Its topics range from literature and the arts to the history of science and the social sciences. The journal also encourages cross-disciplinary and comparative studies about the popular arts and entertainment of the nineteenth century. Each issue contains four or five articles of approximately 20 pages; many articles are generously annotated. Abstracts of articles appear at the front of every issue and contributors' credentials appear at the back. Full text of the journal (except for the most recent five years) is available through JSTOR. Recommended for medium and large academic libraries as well as public libraries with strong literature collections. (CM)

4464. *Notes and Queries: for readers and writers, collectors and librarians.* [ISSN: 0029-3970] 1849. q. GBP 116. Ed(s): E G Stanley, L G Black. Oxford University Press, Great Clarendon St, Oxford, OX2 6DP, United Kingdom; jnl.orders@oup.co.uk; http://www3.oup.co.uk/jnls. Adv. Refereed. Circ: 1400. Microform: PMC; PQC. Online: Florida Center for Library Automation; Gale Group; ingenta.com; OCLC Online Computer Library Center, Inc.; ProQuest Information & Learning; Swets Blackwell. Reprint: PSC. *Indexed:* AmH&L, ArtHuCI, BEL&L, BHA, BrArAb, BrHumI, HumInd, IBZ, L&LBA, MLA-IB, RILM, SSCI. *Bk. rev.:* 50+, 1-2 pages, signed. *Aud.:* Ac, Sa.

The long-lived *Notes and Queries* is devoted to questions and answers of readers' inquiries in matters of "English language and literature, lexicography, history, and scholarly antiquarianism." Emphasis is on the factual rather than on critical theory and this is a gold mine of little-known facts and connections. Each issue is equally divided between notes and reviews, with 25–45 notes of one to five pages each, and 30–60 signed book reviews of one to two pages each, as well as the occasional reader's reply to previous notes. A lengthy list of books received completes each issue. Recent notes include: "The Middle English Term *Bipen* in Castleford's *Chronicle*" and "A New Allusion by Jonson to Spenser and Essex?" Notes can also be previously unpublished letters or poems. An annual index is published separately. The OUP web site has tables of contents for 1996 to the present, and the full text from 2002 to the present is available free to print subscribers. There is also a link to the *Internet Library of Early Journals* project, which provides page images of issues from 1849 to 1869. A classic must-have journal for literary and interdisciplinary scholars. (HW)

4465. *Novel: A Forum on Fiction.* [ISSN: 0029-5132] 1967. 3x/yr. USD 25 (Individuals, USD 20). Ed(s): Nancy Armstrong. Brown University, Department of Literature, PO Box 1984, Providence, RI 02912; http://www.brown.edu/. Illus., index, adv. Refereed. Circ: 1500. Vol. ends: Spring. Microform: PQC. Online: Chadwyck-Healey Incorporated; EBSCO Publishing; Gale Group; Northern Light Technology, Inc.; OCLC Online Computer Library Center, Inc.; ProQuest Information & Learning; H.W. Wilson. Reprint: PQC. *Indexed:* ABS&EES, ArtHuCI, HumInd, IBZ, MLA-IB. *Bk. rev.:* 5-9, 2-3 pages, signed. *Aud.:* Ac.

This journal looks at the novel in a variety of contexts. Essays usually treat theoretical issues surrounding the novel and attempt to put the novel into its historical and cultural contexts. Most of the literature discussed in the journal was published after 1800 and comes from the United States and Britain, but works from other countries make occasional appearances as well. Recent essays have analyzed the works of authors such as George Eliot and Wilkie Collins, and have introduced themes such as liberal citizenship and consumer culture. A typical issue contains five essays of approximately 20 pages. Author credentials appear at the front of every issue, and a small section of book reviews appears at the back. Subscribers to Chadwyck-Healey's Literature Online (LION) database have full-text access back to 1995. Recommended for all academic libraries and large public libraries with research collections. (CM)

4466. *P M L A.* [ISSN: 0030-8129] 1884. 6x/yr. USD 128 Free to members. Ed(s): Carlos Alonso. Modern Language Association of America, 26 Broadway, 3rd Fl, New York, NY 10004-1789; http://www.mla.org. Illus., index, adv. Sample. Refereed. Circ: 32350 Paid and controlled. Vol. ends: Nov. Microform: PQC. Online: Gale Group; Ingenta Select; JSTOR (Web-based Journal Archive); ProQuest Information & Learning. Reprint: PSC. *Indexed:* ABS&EES, ArtHuCI, BHA, HumInd, IBZ, MLA-IB. *Aud.:* Ac.

PMLA is a significant journal that aims to publish essays that will be of interest to a variety of scholars of language and literature. Its editorial policy states that "the ideal *PMLA* essay exemplifies the best of its kind, whatever the kind." *PMLA* is known for its rigorous editorial standards, and it is one of the most frequently cited journals in its field. The primary focus of this official journal of the Modern Language Association is members of the MLA. Each issue includes announcements of news and events that are relevant to the MLA membership, and all essays are written by MLA members. The journal publishes four issues of essays and one directory issue every year. Essays are scholarly yet accessible and often look at the relationship between language, literature, and culture. Each issue has five to eight articles of 15–20 pages. The first issue of the year usually focuses on a topic; the first issue of 2002 was subtitled "Mobile Citizens, Media States," and the first issue of 2003 was "America: the Idea, the Literature." The directory issue lists the names and addresses of department and program administrators. This journal does not publish book reviews. *PMLA* is a core journal and is recommended for all libraries. (CM)

4467. *Papers on Language and Literature: a journal for scholars and critics of language and literature.* [ISSN: 0031-1294] 1965. q. USD 58 (Individuals, USD 24). Ed(s): Brian Abel Ragen. Southern Illinois University at Edwardsville, Edwardsville, IL 62026; http://www.siue.edu/~pll. Illus., index, adv. Refereed. Circ: 850. Vol. ends: Fall. Microform: PQC. Online: Chadwyck-Healey Incorporated; EBSCO Publishing; Florida Center for Library Automation; Gale Group; OCLC Online Computer Library Center, Inc.; ProQuest Information & Learning; H.W. Wilson. Reprint: PQC. *Indexed:* ABS&EES, ArtHuCI, BEL&L, BHA, HumInd, L&LBA, MLA-IB. *Bk. rev.:* 0-3, 4-6 pages, signed. *Aud.:* Ac.

The scope of this journal is broad, encompassing literary scholarship of all national literatures and historical periods, but the emphasis is usually on Britain and the United States. Essays usually focus on literary history, theory, or interpretation. The journal also publishes book reviews and welcomes the submission of primary sources such as notebooks, letters, and journals (though not many have been printed as of yet). Essays are 20–25 pages in length and attempts are often made to look at well-known authors in new ways. Recent essays have analyzed the ideas of solitude and companionship in the works of Robert Frost, and the moral significance of the revisions that Edith Wharton made to her last chapter of *The Custom of the Country*. The journal's web site includes abstracts of forthcoming articles and links to literature-related web sites. Subscribers to Chadwyck-Healey's Literature Online (LION) database have full-text access back to 1994. Recommended for academic libraries that support research in literature. (CM)

4468. *Philological Quarterly: devoted to scholarly investigation of the classical and modern languages and literatures.* [ISSN: 0031-7977] 1922. q. USD 25 (Individuals, USD 15). Ed(s): William Kupersmith. University of Iowa, 311 English Philosophy Bldg, Iowa, IA 52242-1408; http://www.uiowa.edu/. Illus., adv. Refereed. Circ: 2250. Vol. ends: Fall. Microform: IDC; PMC; PQC. Online: Chadwyck-Healey Incorporated; Florida Center for Library Automation; Gale Group; Northern Light Technology, Inc.; OCLC Online Computer Library Center, Inc.; ProQuest Information & Learning; H.W. Wilson. Reprint: PQC. *Indexed:* ArtHuCI, BRI, CBRI, HumInd, IBZ, L&LBA, MLA-IB. *Bk. rev.:* 0-1, 3-4 pages, signed. *Aud.:* Ac.

Known for its strict editorial standards, this journal publishes scholarly articles, notes, and reviews of literature from classical to modern times. Each issue contains five to six interdisciplinary articles that can vary in length from 15 to 40 pages. Most literary works discussed in the journal are British, but other countries are represented as well. The journal occasionally publishes special issues that focus on a topic or time period; a special issue in 1999 was called "Anthropological Approaches to Old English Literature." Some issues include a small book review section, while others only list "Books Received." Subscribers to Chadwyck-Healey's Literature Online (LION) database have full-text access back to 1997. Recommended for academic libraries that support the advanced study of literature. (CM)

4469. *Religion and Literature.* Formerly: *Notre Dame English Journal.* [ISSN: 0888-3769] 1957. 3x/yr. USD 31 (Individuals, USD 25). Ed(s): James Dougherty, Thomas Werge. University of Notre Dame, Department of English, 356 O'Shaughnessy Hall, Notre Dame, IN 46556; english.randl.1@nd.edu; http://www.nd.edu/~randl. Adv. Refereed. Circ: 500 Paid. *Indexed:* AmHI, ArtHuCI, CPL, MLA-IB, R&TA, RI-1. *Bk. rev.:* 3-5, 5 pages, signed. *Aud.:* Ac.

Formerly titled *The Notre Dame English Journal, Religion and Literature* provides "a forum for discussion of the relations between two crucial human concerns: the religious impulse and the literary forms of any era, place or language." Issues consist of scholarly articles, review essays, and book notices; there are four to five articles per issue, of 20–25 pages each. Recent topics include "John Dryden's *Eleanora* and the Catholic Idea of Humility," and

"Spirit in Motion: Echoes of a Pentecostal Heritage in the Poetry of A.R. Ammons." Solid review essays cover two to three recent publications each, and are quite scholarly; the book notices, on the other hand, cover individual titles published two to three years ago, but at two to three pages each, they are still content-laden and evaluative. One issue annually is devoted to a single theme, such as "Visions of the Other World in Medieval Literature." The web site lists the tables of contents for volumes 5 (1969) to the present. Recommended for larger public and academic libraries. (HW)

4470. ***Restoration: Studies in English Literary Culture, 1660-1700.*** [ISSN: 0162-9905] 1977. s-a. USD 12 domestic; USD 16 foreign. Ed(s): Jack M Armistead. Tennessee Technological University, College of Arts and Sciences, PO Box 5065, Cookeville, TN 38505; GPharris@tntech.edu; http://www2.tntech.edu/cas/Rest.html. Refereed. Circ: 500. *Indexed:* MLA-IB. *Bk. rev.:* 90-120, brief. *Aud.:* Ac.

The focus of *Restoration* is on scholarship that increases the understanding of English literature of the Restoration period: "literary appreciation is enhanced as much by investigating contexts (political, social, philosophical, etc.) as by the study and analysis of literary texts themselves." Issues have four scholarly articles of 15–20 pages each. Some recent examples include "Temporality, Subjectivity, and Neoclassical Translation Theory: Dryden's 'Dedication of the Aeneis'" and "Ovid the Rakehell: The Case of Wycherley." Meeting and project announcements as well as queries are included, as is the occasional letter that discusses previously published articles. Each issue ends with a lengthy annotated list (usually over 100 titles) of current publications—both books and articles—with indexing by subject or individual's name. This list, as well as the articles themselves, reflects the broad grounding of the journal in interdisciplinary scholarship. Recommended for libraries that support upper-level research. (HW)

4471. ***The Review of Contemporary Fiction.*** [ISSN: 0276-0045] 1981. 3x/yr. USD 26 (Individuals, USD 17; USD 8 newsstand/cover per issue). Ed(s): John O'Brien. Center for Book Culture, Inc., 4241 Illinois State University, Normal, IL 61790-4241; contact@dalkeyarchive.com; http://www.dalkeyarchive.com. Illus., index, adv. Refereed. Circ: 2955 Paid and free. Vol. ends: Fall. Microform: PQC. Online: bigchalk; Chadwyck-Healey Incorporated; EBSCO Publishing; Florida Center for Library Automation; Gale Group; Northern Light Technology, Inc.; OCLC Online Computer Library Center, Inc.; ProQuest Information & Learning; H.W. Wilson. *Indexed:* ABS&EES, AmHI, BEL&L, BRI, CBRI, HumInd, IBZ, MLA-IB. *Bk. rev.:* 40-50, 1/2-1 page, signed. *Aud.:* Ac.

This journal takes an all-around look at contemporary fiction, providing literary criticism as well as a forum for new fiction writers who have received critical acclaim. Each issue focuses on a topic, an author, or a group of authors and includes interviews, excerpts from works-in-progress, critical essays, and book reviews. Essays are well informed yet readable and can range in length from 10 to 40 pages, sometimes including illustrations and photographs. Issues contain approximately ten articles plus reviews of new fiction and a list of books received. Recent issues have featured such writers Italo Calvino, Ursule Molinaro, and Louis Zukofsky, and themes such as "Writers on Writing" and "New Japanese Fiction." The journal's web site announces topics of upcoming issues and lists articles published in back issues with links to selected full-text offerings. Subscribers to Chadwyck-Healey's Literature Online (LION) database have full-text access back to 1994. This is a rich and multi-textured journal that should reach a wide audience in both academic and public libraries. (CM)

4472. ***The Review of English Studies: a quarterly journal of English literature and the English language.*** [ISSN: 0034-6551] 1925. 5x/yr. GBP 153. Ed(s): David Bradshaw. Oxford University Press, Great Clarendon St, Oxford, OX2 6DP, United Kingdom; jnl.orders@oup.co.uk; http://www3.oup.co.uk/jnls. Illus., index, adv. Refereed. Circ: 1950. Vol. ends: Nov. Microform: PQC. Online: Chadwyck-Healey Incorporated; Florida Center for Library Automation; Gale Group; ingenta.com; JSTOR (Web-based Journal Archive); Northern Light Technology, Inc.; OCLC Online Computer Library Center, Inc.; ProQuest Information & Learning; RoweCom Information Quest. Reprint: PSC. *Indexed:* ArtHuCI, BEL&L, BRI, BrHumI, CBRI, HumInd, IBZ, L&LBA, MLA-IB. *Bk. rev.:* 25-30, 1-2 pages, signed. *Aud.:* Ac.

Well-respected in its field, *The Review of English Studies* publishes scholarly articles, notes, and reviews of English literature and the English language from its origins to present time. The journal's emphasis is on historical interpretations of literature, but it also publishes "fresh evaluation of writers . . . in the light of newly discovered or existing material." The first half of every issue comprises approximately five 20-page essays, and the last half consists of two-page book reviews. An abstract precedes every article. The journal's web site provides tables of contents for issues dating back to 1996, and abstracts for issues dating back to 1998; it also offers subscribers the full-text content of issues published 2001 and later. Recommended for academic libraries that support advanced studies in literature. (CM)

4473. ***Romanticism: the journal of romantic culture and criticism.*** [ISSN: 1354-991X] 1995. s-a. GBP 65. Ed(s): Drummond Bone, Nicholas Roe. Edinburgh University Press, 22 George Sq, Edinburgh, EH8 9LF, United Kingdom; http://www.eup.ed.ac.uk. Illus., adv. Online: EBSCO Publishing. *Indexed:* MLA-IB. *Bk. rev.:* 10-15, 2-4 pages, signed. *Aud.:* Ac.

This relatively new British journal publishes critical, historical, textual, and bibliographical essays about the literature and culture of the Romantic period. There are six to eight scholarly articles in each issue, and some issues focus on the works of one author. Most articles are approximately 20 pages long. Authors such as Wordsworth, Coleridge, and Byron have appeared frequently in recent issues. Two- to three-page book reviews are printed at the end of every issue. Recommended for academic libraries with strong research collections. (CM)

4474. ***Southern Literary Journal.*** [ISSN: 0038-4291] 1968. s-a. USD 32 (Individuals, USD 22). Ed(s): Fred Hobson, Kimball King. University of North Carolina Press, PO Box 2288, Chapel Hill, NC 27515-2288; uncpress_journals@unc.edu; http://www.uncpress.unc.edu. Illus., index. Refereed. Circ: 650. Microform: PQC. Online: bigchalk; Chadwyck-Healey Incorporated; EBSCO Publishing; Florida Center for Library Automation; Gale Group; Northern Light Technology, Inc.; OCLC Online Computer Library Center, Inc.; Project MUSE; ProQuest Information & Learning; RoweCom Information Quest; Swets Blackwell; H.W. Wilson. Reprint: PQC; PSC. *Indexed:* ArtHuCI, HumInd, MLA-IB, RI-1. *Bk. rev.:* 3-5, 3-4 pages, signed. *Aud.:* Ac.

Southern Literary Journal publishes critical essays that examine the literature and literary history of the American South. Issues contain about eight essays, each about 20 pages in length, and three to five substantial book reviews. Issues frequently include discussions on contemporary women's fiction. Most essays assume prior knowledge, and recent essays have looked at Kate Chopin's first novel *At Fault,* Eudora Welty's short fiction, and representations of ethnicity in the works of various southern writers. Full text of the journal from volume 33 (2000) onward is available through Project Muse. Recommended for academic libraries and public libraries with literature collections. (CM)

4475. ***Speculum: a journal of Medieval studies.*** [ISSN: 0038-7134] 1926. q. Non-members, USD 80. Ed(s): Richard K Emmerson. Medieval Academy of America, 1430 Massachusetts Ave, Cambridge, MA 02138; speculum@medievalacademy.org; http://www.medievalacademy.org/. Illus., index, adv. Refereed. Circ: 6500. Vol. ends: Oct. Microform: MIM; PQC. Online: Gale Group; JSTOR (Web-based Journal Archive). *Indexed:* ABS&EES, ArtHuCI, ArtInd, BEL&L, BHA, BRI, BrArAb, CBRI, HumInd, IBZ, IPB, IndVet, MLA-IB, NumL, RI-1, SSCI, VetBull. *Bk. rev.:* 80-90, 2 pages, signed. *Aud.:* Ac.

Founded in 1926, *Speculum* was the first scholarly journal in North America devoted exclusively to the study of the Middle Ages. It focuses primarily on all aspects of the Middle Ages in Western Europe, but essays on Arabic, Byzantine, Hebrew, and Slavic studies are also included. Recent essays have looked at thirteenth-century female literacy, infanticide in old French literature, and religious views of magic in the late Middle Ages. Approximately four 20- to 30-page essays appear in every issue, along with many brief but rigorous book reviews. Issues also include a "Brief Notices" section in which new books are announced and described. Because of the interdisciplinary nature of the journal, authors consistently provide context for their statements, making the essays accessible to specialists in all areas of study. The journal's web site lists forthcoming articles and provides author indexes to articles published since 1975. Full text of the journal (except for the most recent five years) is available through JSTOR. Noted for the quality of its articles and reviews, this journal is important for academic and public libraries that support the study of medieval literature and culture. (CM)

4476. *Studies in American Fiction.* [ISSN: 0091-8083] 1973. s-a. USD 15 (Individuals, USD 9). Ed(s): Mary Loeffelholz. Northeastern University, Department of English, 406 Holmes Hall, Boston, MA 02115; http://www.northeastern.edu/. Illus., adv. Refereed. Circ: 1300. Vol. ends: Fall. Online: Chadwyck-Healey Incorporated; Florida Center for Library Automation; Gale Group; Northern Light Technology, Inc.; OCLC Online Computer Library Center, Inc.; H.W. Wilson. Reprint: PSC. *Indexed:* AmHI, ArtHuCI, BEL&L, HumInd, MLA-IB. *Bk. rev.:* 1-10, 2 pages, signed. *Aud.:* Ac.

Studies in American Fiction publishes articles, notes, and reviews of the fiction of the United States. Each issue includes five to seven essays of 15–20 pages. Most essays take a historical look at the works of well-known authors such as Ernest Hemingway, Mark Twain, and Kate Chopin. Some essays take a more thematic approach; for example, a recent issue included an essay on abolitionist literature. The journal occasionally publishes short reviews of books about American fiction. Issues sometimes focus on a special topic. Subscribers to Chadwyck-Healey's Literature Online (LION) database have full-text access back to 1998. Recommended for all academic libraries. (CM)

4477. *Studies in English Literature 1500-1900.* [ISSN: 0039-3657] 1961. q. USD 85 (Individuals, USD 29). Ed(s): Logan Browning, Robert L Patten. Johns Hopkins University Press, Journals Publishing Division, 2715 N Charles St, Baltimore, MD 21218-4363; http://www.press.jhu.edu/. Illus., adv. Refereed. Circ: 1742. Microform: PQC. Online: EBSCO Publishing; RoweCom Information Quest; Swets Blackwell. Reprint: PQC; PSC. *Indexed:* AmH&L, ArtHuCI, BiogInd, HumInd, MLA-IB. *Aud.:* Ac.

This journal publishes historical and critical essays on English literature from 1500 to 1900. Each issue has a focus: articles in the winter issue look at the English Renaissance, articles in the spring issue look at Tudor and Stuart Drama, articles in the summer issue are about the Restoration and the eighteenth century, and articles in the autumn issue cover the nineteenth century. Each issue includes approximately ten articles plus an overview of recent studies in the field. Most essays are 20 pages long and are written in an engaging style. Full text of the journal is available from Project Muse, from volume 39 (1999) onward. Subscribers to Chadwyck-Healey's Literature Online (LION) database have full-text access back to 1994. Recommended for medium and large academic libraries as well as public libraries with strong literature collections. (CM)

4478. *Studies in Philology.* [ISSN: 0039-3738] 1903. 4x/yr. USD 40 (Individuals, USD 26). Ed(s): Don Kennedy. University of North Carolina Press, PO Box 2288, Chapel Hill, NC 27515-2288; uncpress_journals@unc.edu; http://www.uncpress.unc.edu. Adv. Refereed. Circ: 1500. Microform: MIM; IDC; PMC; PQC. Online: Chadwyck-Healey Incorporated; EBSCO Publishing; Gale Group; Northern Light Technology, Inc.; OCLC Online Computer Library Center, Inc.; Project MUSE; ProQuest Information & Learning. Reprint: PQC; PSC. *Indexed:* ArtHuCI, BEL&L, HumInd, IBZ, MLA-IB, RI-1. *Aud.:* Ac.

For decades, the focus of this journal was on the Renaissance, and that emphasis still exists, with over half of the articles covering sixteenth- or seventeenth-century English literature. Submission guidelines state that articles must cover pre-1900 English literature, alone or in comparison with Classical, Romance, or Germanic literature. Recent articles include "The Pearl-Maiden's Two Lovers," and "Godly Fear, Sanctification, and Calvinist Theology in the Sermons and 'Holy Sonnets' of John Donne." The web site (http://english.unc.edu/journals/sip.htm) provides general information about the journal, as well as a link to a newly-constructed database that indexes volumes 51–98 (1954–2001), at http://www.unc.edu/student/orgs/cams/SP_Online_Database. In this index, issue contents are listed by volume and author, along with lists of translations, editions, bibliographical issues and articles, and texts and studies issues. Full text from 1994 to the present is available through LION, and as of volume 100 (2003), full text will also be available from Project Muse. Useful for literature research at all levels. (HW)

4479. *Studies in Romanticism.* [ISSN: 0039-3762] 1961. q. USD 60 (Individuals, USD 23). Ed(s): David Wagenknecht. Boston University, Graduate School, 236 Bay State Rd, Boston, MA 02215; http://www.bu.edu/. Illus., index, adv. Refereed. Circ: 1800. Vol. ends: Winter. Microform: PQC. Online: Chadwyck-Healey Incorporated; Florida Center for Library Automation; Gale Group; Northern Light Technology, Inc.; OCLC Online Computer Library Center, Inc.; ProQuest Information & Learning; H.W. Wilson. Reprint: PQC. *Indexed:* ArtHuCI, BEL&L, BHA, HumInd, MLA-IB. *Bk. rev.:* 4-6, 3-4 pages, signed. *Aud.:* Ac.

Studies in Romanticism publishes essays on the literature, arts, and society of the Romantic period in Europe and the United States. Most essays focus on English literature. Each issue contains five to six 20- to 30-page essays as well as several substantial book reviews. The credentials of each contributor are provided at the end of every issue. Essays tend to be somewhat advanced, and recent topics have included the use of secrets in the works of James Hogg; Coleridge's political legacy; and vaccination, Romanticism, and revolution in late eighteenth-century Britain. Recommended for academic libraries and larger public libraries that support advanced research in literature. (CM)

4480. *Studies in Short Fiction.* [ISSN: 0039-3789] 1963. q. USD 22 (Individuals, USD 19). Ed(s): Michael J O'Shea. Newberry College, 2100 College St, Newberry, SC 29108; ssf_ed@newberry.edu; http://www.newberry.edu. Illus., index, adv. Refereed. Circ: 1900 Paid. Vol. ends: Oct. Microform: PQC. Online: bigchalk; Chadwyck-Healey Incorporated; EBSCO Publishing; Florida Center for Library Automation; Gale Group; Northern Light Technology, Inc.; OCLC Online Computer Library Center, Inc.; ProQuest Information & Learning; H.W. Wilson. Reprint: PQC; PSC. *Indexed:* ABS&EES, ArtHuCI, BHA, BRI, CBRI, HAPI, HumInd, MLA-IB. *Bk. rev.:* 5-6, 1-3 pages, signed. *Aud.:* Ac.

The focus of this journal is short fiction, which the journal defines as "short stories, novellas, tales, parables, narrative poems, and oral folk narratives." Its scope is international, but most essays take a critical or interpretive look at relatively well-known American and British fiction since 1800. The journal often exhibits a preference for interdisciplinary approaches. Most issues contain ten essays, notes, and five to six reviews. Recent essays have discussed the works of authors such as Edith Wharton, William Hazlitt, and Ernest Hemingway, and the "Notes" section has included brief source information, textual explication, and unpublished letters. Essays are 15–20 pages in length, and book reviews are short. The journal also publishes an annual index to short fiction in anthologies and a selective annual bibliography of short-story explication. Subscribers to Chadwyck-Healey's Literature Online (LION) database have full-text access back to 1994. This is an important journal for the study of short fiction and is recommended for all academic libraries and larger public libraries. (CM)

4481. *Studies in the Novel.* [ISSN: 0039-3827] 1969. q. USD 35 (Individuals, USD 20). Ed(s): Scott Simkins. University of North Texas, English Department, PO Box 310680, Denton, TX 76203; scotts@unt.edu; http://www.engl.unt.edu. Illus., index. Refereed. Circ: 1700. Vol. ends: No. 4. Microform: PQC. Online: bigchalk; Chadwyck-Healey Incorporated; EBSCO Publishing; Florida Center for Library Automation; Gale Group; Northern Light Technology, Inc.; OCLC Online Computer Library Center, Inc.; ProQuest Information & Learning; H.W. Wilson. Reprint: PQC. *Indexed:* ABS&EES, ArtHuCI, BEL&L, HumInd, MLA-IB. *Bk. rev.:* 5-10, 1-3 pages, signed. *Aud.:* Ac.

This scholarly journal publishes critical and interpretive essays on the novel. Its scope encompasses "novels and novelists of all periods and countries," but many of the works cited are fairly well-known novels from post-1800 Britain and the United States. Recent essays have discussed the works of authors such as Thomas Hardy, M.E. Braddon, and D.H. Lawrence. Issues contain five to six essays, eight to ten reviews of books about novels and novelists, and occasionally, an essay-review. Essays are 20–30 pages in length and often include references to contemporary criticism. The journal's web site provides abstracts of essays and titles of books reviewed in the current issue, an index to the current volume, and a list of all special issues (with a link to a list of the articles in each special issue). Subscribers to Chadwyck-Healey's Literature Online (LION) database have full-text access back to 1994. Recommended for medium and large academic libraries as well as larger public libraries that support the study of literature. (CM)

4482. ***Studies in Twentieth Century Literature.*** [ISSN: 0145-7888] 1976. s-a. USD 30 (Individuals, USD 25). Ed(s): Silvia Sauter, Jordan Stump. Kansas State University, Department of Modern Languages, Eisenhower Hall, Manhattan, KS 66506-1003; silviae@ksu.edu; http://www.ksu.edu/stcl. Illus., index, adv. Refereed. Circ: 500. *Indexed:* ABS&EES, AmHI, ArtHuCI, HumInd, IBZ, MLA-IB. *Bk. rev.:* 7-9, 2-3 pages, signed. *Aud.:* Ac.

This journal publishes theoretical and critical interdisciplinary essays on twentieth-century literature written in French, German, Russian, and Spanish. All articles are written in English. Abstracts of articles are provided at the front of every issue, and some issues include photographs and illustrations. Recent articles have looked at French resistance poetry, and the use of landscape in Anton Chekhov's play *The Cherry Orchard.* Issues contain approximately six articles of 20–30 pages, many with lengthy footnotes, and seven to nine reviews of books from a wide variety of disciplines that "illuminate the literature of the period." Two issues are published each year, at least one of which focuses on a special theme. Recent themes have included French studies at the turn of the millennium and Russian culture of the 1990s. The journal's web site lists tables of contents from volume 1 (1976) onward. Recommended for academic libraries with strong literature collections. (CM)

4483. ***Style (DeKalb).*** [ISSN: 0039-4238] 1967. q. USD 40 (Individuals, USD 28). Ed(s): James M Mellard. Northern Illinois University, Department of English, Dekalb, IL 60115; watson@niu.edu. Adv. Refereed. Circ: 600 Paid. Online: bigchalk; Chadwyck-Healey Incorporated; EBSCO Publishing; Florida Center for Library Automation; Gale Group; OCLC Online Computer Library Center, Inc.; ProQuest Information & Learning; H.W. Wilson. *Indexed:* ABS&EES, ArtHuCI, HumInd, L&LBA, LingAb, MLA-IB. *Bk. rev.:* 0-2, 2-3 pages, signed. *Aud.:* Ac.

Articles in *Style* "address questions of style, stylistics, and poetics, including research and theory in discourse analysis, literary and nonliterary genres, narrative, figuration, metrics, rhetorical analysis, and the pedagogy of style." Additionally, some issues include reviews, interviews, translations, bibliographies (enumerative or annotated), and reports on conferences, web sites, and software. Each issue of *Style* is thematic, with recent topics ranging from "Resources in Stylistics and Literary Analysis" to "The Aesthetics of Robert Penn Warren." The interdisciplinarity of the journal's mission statement is duly reflected in the articles, some examples of which are "Cognitive Mapping in Literary Analysis" and "A Short Bibliographical Guide to the Theory of the Sublime." Issues average ten articles; critical essays run 20 pages or so, while the bibliographies are generally much longer. Each issue contains a call for papers for upcoming issues. *Style* provides breadth not available in all literary journals, and is recommended for upper-division and graduate research. (HW)

4484. ***Texas Studies in Literature and Language.*** [ISSN: 0040-4691] 1959. q. USD 74 (Individuals, USD 32). Ed(s): Tony Hilfer, John Rumrich. University of Texas Press, Journals Division, 2100 Comal, Austin, TX 78722; utpress@uts.cc.utexas.edu; http://www.utexas.edu/utpress/journals/journals.html. Illus., adv. Refereed. Circ: 1000. Vol. ends: Winter. Microform: PQC; NRP. Online: Chadwyck-Healey Incorporated; EBSCO Publishing; Florida Center for Library Automation; Gale Group; OCLC Online Computer Library Center, Inc.; Project MUSE; ProQuest Information & Learning; RoweCom Information Quest; Swets Blackwell. Reprint: PQC; PSC. *Indexed:* ABS&EES, ArtHuCI, BEL&L, BHA, HumInd, IBZ, L&LBA, MLA-IB. *Aud.:* Ac.

Published at the University of Texas at Austin, this journal covers all periods of literary history from the perspective of a variety of disciplines. Most of the works examined are British or American. Each issue has a theme, and an essay at the beginning of the issue introduces the theme and explains how the essays contained relate to it. One recent issue had as its theme "God's Backside" and included an essay on Richard Crashaw's religious poetry; another recent issue looked at "Characters in Narrative and a Discourse of Intoxication" and included essays on the characters in the socially realistic novels of George Eliot, Charles Dickens, and D.H. Lawrence. Most issues have five essays of 20–30 pages. The journal's web site lists tables of contents back to volume 38 (1996). Recommended for academic libraries with strong literature collections and large public libraries with research collections. (CM)

4485. ***Textual Practice: an international journal of radical literary studies.*** [ISSN: 0950-236X] 1987. 3x/yr. GBP 148 (Individuals, GBP 35). Routledge, 11 New Fetter Ln, London, EC4P 4EE, United Kingdom; journals@routldege.com; http://www.routledge.com. Illus., adv. Refereed. Circ: 900. Vol. ends: Winter. Online: EBSCO Publishing; Ingenta Select; RoweCom Information Quest; Swets Blackwell. Reprint: PSC. *Indexed:* ArtHuCI, BrHumI, MLA-IB. *Bk. rev.:* 10-15, 3-6 pages, signed. *Aud.:* Ac.

This scholarly journal describes itself as a "journal of radical literary studies." It publishes essays on modern and postmodern literature from around the world that focuses on "marginal cultures of ethnicity and sexuality." Essays often explore the role of politics and history in these literatures and are approximately 20 pages long. There are six to eight essays in each issue. About one-fourth of every issue comprises book reviews of three to six pages, and longer review essays are occasionally published as well. Abstracts of articles are provided at the end of each issue. The journal's web site includes tables of contents for volume 14 (2000) onward, free 30-day trials of sample online issues, and an order form for a free e-mail contents alerting service. Recommended for large academic libraries that support the advanced study of literature. (CM)

4486. ***Twentieth Century Literature: a scholarly and critical journal.*** [ISSN: 0041-462X] 1955. q. USD 30 (Individuals, USD 25). Ed(s): William McBrien. Hofstra University, 203 Student Center, Hempstead, NY 11550; http://www.hofstra.edu/. Illus., index, adv. Refereed. Circ: 3000. Vol. ends: No. 4. Microform: MIM; PQC. Online: bigchalk; Chadwyck-Healey Incorporated; EBSCO Publishing; Florida Center for Library Automation; Gale Group; JSTOR (Web-based Journal Archive); Northern Light Technology, Inc.; OCLC Online Computer Library Center, Inc.; ProQuest Information & Learning; H.W. Wilson. Reprint: ISI; PQC; PSC. *Indexed:* ArtHuCI, BEL&L, HumInd, IBZ, MLA-IB. *Aud.:* Ac.

Articles in *Twentieth Century Literature* cover all aspects of literature today, including non-English literatures, although British and American fiction are the basis for the majority of essays. Recent articles include a prizewinning essay on Elizabeth Bishop; many comparative articles, such as "Toward a Theory of Rhetoric: Ralph Ellison, Kenneth Burke, and the Problem of Modernism," and thematic essays such as "Ecocritical City: Modernist Reactions to Urban Environments in Miss Lonelyhearts and Paterson." Some issues cover a variety of topics while others are devoted to individual authors, as exemplified by the recent issue on Salman Rushdie, or thematic, such as the upcoming issue on American writers and France. Issues contain between five and seven articles, ranging from 20 to 30 pages. A cumulative index is published every five years. Older issues available through JSTOR. This is a recommended core publication for college and research libraries. (HW)

4487. ***University of Toronto Quarterly: a Canadian journal of the humanities.*** [ISSN: 0042-0247] 1931. q. CND 105 (Individuals, CND 52). Ed(s): Brian Corman. University of Toronto Press, Journals Department, 5201 Dufferin St, Toronto, ON M3H 5T8, Canada; journals@utpress.utoronto.ca; http://www.utpjournals.com. Adv. Circ: 900. Microform: MML; PQC. Online: EBSCO Publishing; Gale Group; LexisNexis; Micromedia ProQuest. *Indexed:* ABS&EES, AmH&L, ArtHuCI, BEL&L, BHA, CBCARef, CIJE, CPerI, HumInd, IBZ, MLA-IB. *Bk. rev.:* In annual review issue, signed. *Aud.:* Ac.

Three of the four issues each year are devoted to critical articles and reviews in the humanities, with an emphasis on English literature. There are anywhere from 4 to 12 articles of 15–25 pages each, covering broad topics such as "The Practice and Theory of Canadian Thematic Criticism: A Reconsideration," or narrow topics such as individual authors (e.g., "Bewildering: The Poetry of Don McKay"). Text is in English and French. The fourth issue each year is the annual bibliography of "Letters in Canada," a selective review of Canadian literature and scholarly works both in English and Canadian French. These extensive bibliographic essays and reviews cover fiction, poetry, drama, translations, and the humanities in general; also included is a master list of books received. This is the most thorough evaluative survey there is of Canadian literature each year. The web site provides tables of contents from 1994 to the present. Recommended for all libraries that support Canadian studies collections or curriculum. (HW)

4488. *Victorian Poetry.* [ISSN: 0042-5206] 1963. q. USD 45 (Individuals, USD 30). Ed(s): Hayden Ward. West Virginia University Press, Victorian Poetry Office, Department of English, PO Box 6296, Morgantown, WV 26506; hattfiel@wvu.edu; http://www.wvu.edu/. Illus., index. Sample. Refereed. Circ: 750 Paid. Vol. ends: Winter. Microform: PQC. Online: EBSCO Publishing; Florida Center for Library Automation; Gale Group; OCLC Online Computer Library Center, Inc.; Project MUSE; RoweCom Information Quest; Swets Blackwell; H.W. Wilson. Reprint: PSC. *Indexed:* ArtHuCI, BHA, HumInd, IBZ, MLA-IB. *Aud.:* Ac.

Victorian Poetry provides articles and notes on British poetry written between 1830 and 1914. The essays cover poets both known—Hopkins, Tennyson, and Hardy—and more obscure but no less deserving—for example, Mathilde Blind, Eliza Keary, and Constance Naden. The fall issue features in-depth, scholarly bibliographical essays on the year's work in Victorian poetry, which cover individual authors and movements (e.g., "Poets of the Nineties," "The Pre-Raphaelites") as well as general materials; the latter essays are especially useful in tracking often-elusive interdisciplinary material. The full text of volume 34:3 (1996) through volume 36 (1998) is available on the web site, and volume 38 (2000) to the present is available via Project Muse. An annual index is published separately. Recommended for larger libraries and those that support Victorian studies curriculum. (HW)

4489. *Victorian Studies: a journal of the humanities, arts and sciences.* [ISSN: 0042-5222] 1957. q. USD 92.50 (Individuals, USD 41). Ed(s): Donald Gray. Indiana University Press, 601 N Morton St, Bloomington, IN 47404; http://www.indiana.edu/~iupress. Illus., adv. Refereed. Circ: 3000. Microform: PQC. Online: EBSCO Publishing; Ingenta Select; RoweCom Information Quest; Swets Blackwell. Reprint: PQC; PSC. *Indexed:* AmH&L, ArtHuCI, BAS, BEL&L, BHA, BRI, CBRI, HumInd, IBZ, LRI, MLA-IB, MathSciNet, SSCI. *Bk. rev.:* 35-45, 2 pages, signed. *Aud.:* Ac.

This high-quality quarterly journal, from Indiana University Press, publishes articles on literature, social and political history, and the histories of education, philosophy, fine arts, economics, law, and science. While the emphasis of the journal is clearly interdisciplinary, the majority of articles concern writers—both major and minor—of the period, sometimes from a comparative perspective. A typical issue has three major scholarly essays (25–35 pages), an extensive book review section (upwards of 35 titles, each averaging two pages), a "Comments & Queries" section, and notes on contributors. Review essays occasionally appear in the journal's pages as well. Recent articles have borne such titles as "An Emigrant and a Gentleman: Imperial Masculinity, British Magazines, and the Colony That Got Away" and "Collaborating in Open Boats: Dickens, Collins, Franklin, and Bligh"; they have also covered such topics as women's biographies, Ruskin and James, Swinburne's aesthetics. The fourth number (Summer issue) of every volume contains an annual bibliography of noteworthy publications relevant to the Victorian period. Project Muse subscribers have access from volume 42.2 (Winter 1999) on. Institutions that subscribe to Chadwyck-Healey's Literature Online have full-text access from volume 37.2 (1994) forward. An indispensable journal, recommended for all academic and larger public libraries. (SG)

4490. *Western American Literature.* [ISSN: 0043-3462] 1966. q. USD 65. Ed(s): Melody Graulich. Western Literature Association, Utah State University, English Department, Logan, UT 84322-3200; wal@cc.usu.edu; http://www.usu.edu/~westlit. Adv. Refereed. Circ: 1200. Microform: PQC. Reprint: ISI; PQC. *Indexed:* AmH&L, AmHI, ArtHuCI, BRI, CBRI, FLI, IBZ, MLA-IB, SSCI. *Bk. rev.:* 8-15, 1-2 pages, signed. *Aud.:* Ac, Sa.

The official publication of the Western Literature Association, *Western American Literature* provides access to some of the less mainstream American literary writings and criticism. Issues have three 20–25 page critical essays and one or two signed essay reviews, along with short book reviews. In special issues, such as "Western Autobiography and Memoir," even the book reviews reflect the theme. Recent articles include "Deadly Kids, Stinking Dogs, and Heroes: The Best Laid Plans in Steinbeck's *Of Mice and Men.*" The essay reviews are scholarly, and use an evaluative approach to several recent works on a single subject, or provide bibliographic information on works and criticism of individual authors. One recent issue included an outstanding "Trends in the Field" bibliographic essay, which looked at the past year of research in Western American literary scholarship. The web site lists the tables of contents for issues from 1995 to the present. Recommended for public or academic libraries that support American literature collections or programs. (HW)

4491. *World Literature Today: a literary quarterly of the University of Oklahoma.* Formerly: *Books Abroad.* [ISSN: 0196-3570] 1927. q. USD 88 (Individuals, USD 40). Ed(s): David Draper Clark. University of Oklahoma, 110 Monnet Hall, Norman, Norman, OK 73019-4033; http://www.ou.edu/worldlit/. Illus., index, adv. Refereed. Circ: 2200. Microform: PQC. Online: bigchalk; Chadwyck-Healey Incorporated; EBSCO Publishing; Florida Center for Library Automation; Gale Group; Northern Light Technology, Inc.; OCLC Online Computer Library Center, Inc.; ProQuest Information & Learning; H.W. Wilson. Reprint: PQC; PSC. *Indexed:* ABS&EES, ArtHuCI, BAS, BEL&L, BRD, BRI, CBRI, HAPI, HumInd, IBZ, MLA-IB, SSCI. *Bk. rev.:* 150-250, 1/2-1 page, signed. *Aud.:* Ac.

World Literature Today is the best in the field in covering literature and criticism of contemporary writing around the globe. Issues have about a dozen articles, including critical essays on adult and children's literature, fiction, poetry, travel essays, interviews with writers, and reviews. Recent features include V.S. Naipaul's 2001 Nobel lecture, with accompanying critical discussion; an interview with Mario Vargas Llosa; and a thematic issue on Japanese writers with essays by Kenzaburo Oe. Brief "best of" essays cover topics such as Brazilian poetry and Canadian fiction. The outstanding review section includes 150–250 English-language reviews of fiction, poetry, drama, and criticism published in more than 60 languages. On the web site users can view the current issue of a recent publication aimed at a more general audience. This online version, *WLT: World Literature Today Magazine,* mirrors much of the print edition, with the major articles, letters, and selected feature reviews. The full-coverage print version is a must for academic and large public libraries. (HW)

Electronic Journals

This subsection lists electronic-only journals of literary criticism; journals that are available both in print and online (usually through JSTOR or Project Muse) are in the previous subsection. Here we have listed substantial and regularly-published electronic-only publications that are based in the United States or other English-speaking countries. The number of stable electronic journals of literary criticism remains small; in fact, one title was eliminated from the previous edition due to its increasingly irregular publication schedule. Those who would like a more comprehensive look at what is available may find *NewJour Electronic Journals & Newsletters* (http://gort.ucsd.edu/newjour/) useful. It is a directory of electronic journals, magazines, and newsletters, and it offers an e-mail alert service for new titles.

4492. *C L C Web: a WWWeb journal.* [ISSN: 1481-4374] 1999. q. Free. Ed(s): Steven Totosy. Purdue University, Department of English, 1530 Stewart Center, PO Box D, West Lafayette, IN 47907-1530; http://clcwebjournal.lib.purdue.edu. Illus. Refereed. Vol. ends: Dec. *Indexed:* MLA-IB. *Bk. rev.:* 3, signed. *Aud.:* Ac.

The *CLCWeb,* published by the Purdue University Press, is a refereed quarterly with articles on comparative literature, cultural studies, and communication studies. It gives special attention to scholarship that combines all three of these areas of study—a field that *CLCWeb* calls "comparative cultural studies." Each issue has 5–15 articles, many of which take a global or cross-disciplinary approach to their topics. Up to three book reviews appear in each issue. Recent articles have looked at Nietzche and war, comparative literature and globalization, and translations of non-English works in Great Britain. (CM)

4493. *Early Modern Literary Studies: a journal of sixteenth- and seventeenth-century English literature.* [ISSN: 1201-2459] 1995. 3x/yr. Free. Ed(s): Dr. Lisa Hopkins. Sheffield Hallam University, Department of English, School of Cultural Studies, c/o Dr. Lisa Hopkins, Ed., Collegiate Crescent Campus, Sheffield, S10 2BP, United Kingdom. Illus. Refereed. Vol. ends: Dec. *Indexed:* BRI, CBCARef, CBRI, MLA-IB. *Bk. rev.:* 8-11, signed. *Aud.:* Ac.

EMLS, edited by Dr. Lisa Hopkins at Sheffield Hallam University, is a rich Internet resource for scholars of early modern English literature. It is a significant electronic journal with a substantial collection of links to other web sites and discussion groups in the field. The electronic journal publishes refereed articles on many aspects of sixteenth- and seventeenth-century English literature, often including topics related to the culture and language of the period. Book reviews and theater reviews appear in every issue, as do responses to previous articles. Recent articles have discussed topics such as realism and desire in the works of Thomas Middleton, the role of the trickster in Jacobean comedy, and identification of Elizabethan pronunciation. (CM)

4494. ***Romanticism on the Net.*** [ISSN: 1467-1255] 1996. q. Ed(s): Michael Eberle-Sinatra. St. Catherine's College, Oxford, OX1 3UJ, United Kingdom; michael.laplace-sinatra@stcatz.ox.ac.uk; http://users.ox.ac.uk/~scat0385/. Refereed. *Indexed:* MLA-IB. *Bk. rev.:* 5-10, signed. *Aud.:* Ac.

Edited by Michael Eberle-Sinatra at the University of Montreal, *Romanticism on the Net* is a quarterly peer-reviewed journal devoted to Romantic studies. Typical issues feature four to eight articles and five to ten book reviews. All contents from previous issues are made available at the site and can be sorted by author or by issue number. Many *RoN* issues are devoted to particular theme and guest-edited; recent examples include "Romanticism and Sexuality" (number 23, August 2001), "Romanticism and Science Fictions" (number 21, February 2001) and "New Texts and Textual Scholarship in British Literature, 1780–1830" (number 19, August 2000). The *RoN* web site also includes information about and from conferences, links to associations of interest to Romanticists, and a select list of other electronic journals in the field. (SG)

Women in Literature and Life Assembly. See Women: Feminist and Special Interest/Electronic Journals section.

■ LITTLE MAGAZINES

See also Alternatives; Literary Reviews; and Literature sections.

Sarah McDaniel, Humanities Librarian, University of California–Berkeley, Berkeley, CA 94720-6000

Introduction

Historically, little magazines have been at the vanguard of literature and the arts, fostering literary movements from Surrealism to the Beats. Today's little magazines are united by their independent spirit and commitment to exposing readers to new ideas, authors, and styles.

Little magazines play an important role in the increasingly centralized publishing world, introducing readers to little-known writers as well as new work by established writers and reflecting a broad spectrum of political, social and aesthetic concerns. Most share a mission of publishing new work in a variety of media, from graphic art and photography to literature, essays, and translations. Many also nurture regional or national communities of writers and artists.

Most little magazines are independent publications affiliated with universities or nonprofit organizations. While independent status allows little magazines to publish non-commercial, experimental material, even established titles often struggle financially. Their format varies widely according to budget and content, from glossy magazines or stately bound journals to stapled chapbooks and slick online publications.

Little magazines were first to publish the work of such literary giants as James Joyce and T.S. Eliot. While it's tough to know which new writers will achieve such stature, little magazines consistently select material that goes on to win prestigious prizes and writers that garner critical acclaim. The commitment of little magazines everywhere is to guarantee readers exposure to new literature, art, and ideas that they would not have encountered in mainstream publications.

Basic Periodicals

Hs: *Five Points, Louisville Review;* Ga: *Doubletake, Five Points, Paris Review, Poetry;* Ac: *Paris Review, Poetry.*

Basic Abstracts and Indexes

American Humanities Index, Index of American Periodical Verse.

4495. ***3rd Bed.*** [ISSN: 1523-6773] s-a. USD 16 (Individuals, USD 14; USD 18 foreign). Ed(s): Vincent Standley. 3rd Bed, 131 Clay St, Central Falls, RI 02863. *Aud.:* Ga, Ac.

An engaging, high-quality, independent publication that features poetry, prose, and artwork from new and lesser-known writers and artists. *3rd Bed* was founded in response to a "lack of openness" to new writers by established literary magazines. The magazine is well-designed and features original artwork and cover art by up-and-coming artists such as Laylah Ali. Recommended for general and academic collections.

Agni. See Literary Reviews section.

Antioch Review. See Literary Reviews section.

The Baffler. See Alternatives/General section.

4496. ***The Baltimore Review.*** [ISSN: 1092-5716] 1996. s-a. USD 14.70; USD 7.95 newsstand/cover per issue. Ed(s): Barbara Westwood Diehl. Baltimore Review, PO Box 410, Riderwood, MD 21139; hdiehl@bcpl.net; http://www.bcpl.net. Illus. Sample. Refereed. *Aud.:* Ga.

Features the short stories and poetry of writers "from the Baltimore area and beyond." Sponsored by the Baltimore Writers' Alliance.

4497. ***Beloit Poetry Journal.*** [ISSN: 0005-8661] 1950. q. USD 23 (Individuals, USD 18). Ed(s): Lee K Sharkey, John Rosenwald. Beloit Poetry Journal Foundation, Inc., 24 Berry Cove Rd., Lamoine, ME 04605-4617; http://www.bpj.org. Refereed. Circ: 770 Paid. *Indexed:* AmHI, ArtHuCI, IAPV. *Aud.:* Hs, Ga, Ac.

Affiliated with Beloit College when it began publication in 1950, *BPJ* declared its editorial and financial independence in 1958. *BPJ* publishes carefully-selected poetry, and was the among the first to publish such poets as Anne Sexton and Gwendolyn Brooks. Occasional "Chapbook Issues"—recently "Poets under 25" and new poets from the People's Republic of China—keep readers up to date. Every issue has reviews of new books by and about poets, intended for librarians as well as the individual reader.

4498. ***Black Warrior Review.*** [ISSN: 0193-6301] 1974. s-a. USD 17 (Individuals, USD 14). Ed(s): Aaron Welborn, Dan Kaplan. Black Warrior Review, PO Box 862936, Tuscaloosa, AL 35486. Adv. Circ: 1800. *Indexed:* AmHI, BRI, CBRI, HumInd, IAPV, MLA-IB. *Aud.:* Ac.

Black Warrior Review publishes contemporary fiction, poetry, and nonfiction from both established and emerging writers. Each issue features a chapbook from a nationally known poet, and often a 6- to 12-page artist portfolio, generally from a Southern artist. Also includes essays, interviews with writers, reviews of small-press fiction, and poetry. A simple, clean design keeps the focus on the writing.

Callaloo. See African American section.

Calyx. See Women: Feminist and Special Interest/Literary and Artistic section.

4499. ***The Chattahoochee Review.*** [ISSN: 0741-9155] 1980. q. USD 16. Ed(s): Lawrence Hetrick. Georgia Perimeter College, 2101 Womack Rd., Dunwoody, GA 30338-4497; http://www.gpc.peachnet.edu/~twadley/cr/index.htm. Index, adv. Circ: 1250. Microform: PQC. *Indexed:* AmHI, IAPV. *Bk. rev.:* 3. *Aud.:* Ga.

The review seeks to "delight, surprise and educate" the educated general public with fiction, poetry, nonfiction, interviews, photography, and graphic art. Selections include both important regional writers and international artists, new and recognized. The presentation is simple and elegant, and each issue contains a section of four-color graphic art reproductions.

Chicago Review. See Literary Reviews section.

4500. ***Clackamas Literary Review.*** [ISSN: 1088-3665] 1997. s-a. USD 10; USD 6 newsstand/cover per issue. Ed(s): Kate Gray, Amanda Coffey. Clackamas Community College, 19600 South Molalla Ave, Oregon City, OR 97045; http://www.clackamas.cc.or.us/clr. Adv. *Indexed:* IAPV, MLA-IB. *Bk. rev.:* 1-2. *Aud.:* Ga, Ac.

CLR promotes the work of emerging writers and established writers of fiction, poetry, and creative nonfiction. Nonfiction selections include essays and occasional interviews. Features a simple design and glossy cover with original artwork.

Conjunctions. See Literary Reviews section.

4501. ***The Cream City Review.*** [ISSN: 0884-3457] 1975. s-a. USD 12; USD 7 newsstand/cover per issue. Ed(s): Karen Auvinen. University of Wisconsin at Milwaukee, English Department, Cream City Review, Box 413, Milwaukee, WI 53201; creamcity@uvm.edu. Adv. Refereed. Circ: 1000 Paid. *Indexed:* AmHI, IAPV. *Bk. rev.:* 1-3. *Aud.:* Ga, Ac.

Cream City Review is operated entirely by students at the University of Wisconsin–Milwaukee. The review takes its name from the cream-colored bricks Milwaukee was once known for. Each thick, semi-annual issue is perfect-bound with a four-color cover, and features a mix of poems, stories, and essays; and visual art by both established and little-known artists are selected. Reviews in each issue address literature, theater, and film.

4502. ***CutBank.*** [ISSN: 0734-9963] 1973. s-a. USD 12. University Of Montana, Department of English, Missoula, MT 59812. Illus., adv. Refereed. Circ: 400. *Indexed:* ASIP, IAPV. *Aud.:* Ga, Ac.

CutBank features art, poetry, and fiction of "high quality and serious intent" by both well-known and previously unpublished artists. Each issue is beautifully illustrated with photographs and other visual art.

DoubleTake. See Literary Reviews section.

4503. ***Ekphrasis.*** [ISSN: 1095-841X] 1997. s-a. USD 12; USD 6 newsstand/cover. Ed(s): Carol Frith, Laverne Frith. Frith Press, PO Box 161236, Sacramento, CA 95816-1236; ekphrasis1@aol.com; http://www.hometown.aol.com/ekphrasis1. *Aud.:* Ga.

A digest-sized, saddle-stapled poetry journal with a clean design. *Ekphrasis* features poems "focused or centered on individual works from any artistic genre." Recent examples include poems on works by Vermeer, Van Gogh, and Miles Davis. *Ekphrasis* does not include reproductions of the source works, as each poem is intended to stand alone as well as to complement the original work.

Fence. See Literary Reviews section.

4504. ***Fiddlehead.*** [ISSN: 0015-0630] 1945. q. CND 24 (Individuals, CND 20). Ed(s): Ross Leckie. University of New Brunswick, Campus House, P.O. Box 4400, Fredericton, NB E3B 5A3, Canada. Circ: 1000. Microform: MML; PQC. Reprint: PSC. *Indexed:* AmHI, ArtHuCI, CPerI. *Bk. rev.:* 6-7. *Aud.:* Ga.

First published in 1945, *Fiddlehead* features short stories, poems, book reviews, and essays, many by Canadian writers. Glossy, full-cover covers feature work of New Brunswick artists.

4505. ***Five Fingers Review.*** [ISSN: 0898-0233] 1984. a. Ed(s): Jaime Robles. Five Fingers Press, PO Box 4, San Leandro, CA 94577-0100; vladstutu@aol.com. Illus. Refereed. Circ: 1500. *Aud.:* Ga, Ac.

Five Fingers Review is "a journal of poetry, prose, fiction and art." Each annual issue has a theme such as "SKIN" or "Gardens in the Urban Jungle." The magazine is committed to supporting experimental forms and new voices, and many of the contributors are from the San Francisco Bay Area.

4506. ***Five Points: a journal of literature and art.*** [ISSN: 1088-8500] 1996. 3x/yr. USD 20; USD 7 per issue. Ed(s): Megan Sexton, David Bottoms. Georgia State University, Department of English, MSC 8R0322, 33 Gilmer Street SE, Unit 8, Atlanta, GA 30303-3088; bburmester@gsu.edu; http://www.gsu.edu/~wwweng. Illus., adv. Sample. Refereed. Circ: 2000. *Indexed:* AmHI, IAPV, MLA-IB. *Aud.:* Hs, Ga, Ac.

An award-winning journal that features poetry, fiction, interviews, and essays by both well-known authors and new literary voices. Recent contributors include Richard Bausch, Philip Levine, and Madison Smartt Bell. *Five Points* seeks to present a convergence of ideas and genres, and includes photography and a sleek graphic design.

4507. ***Geist.*** [ISSN: 1181-6554] 1990. q. CND 32 for 3 yrs. domestic; USD 20 for 3 yrs. foreign; CND 5 newsstand/cover per issue. Ed(s): Stephen Osborne. Geist Foundation, 103 1014 Homer St, Vancouver, BC V6B 2W9, Canada; geist@geist.com; http://www.geist.com. Illus., adv. Circ: 6000 Paid. *Indexed:* CBCARef. *Aud.:* Ga, Ac.

A quarterly "magazine of ideas and culture" that features the best in Canadian fiction, nonfiction, photography, comics, poetry, and "little-known facts of interest." The magazine is published by The Geist Foundation, a nonprofit established in 1990 to bring the work of Canadian writers and artists to public attention, explore the lines between fiction and nonfiction, and present new views of Canada.

4508. ***Image (Seattle): a journal of the arts & religion.*** [ISSN: 1087-3503] 1989. q. USD 36 domestic; USD 46 foreign. Ed(s): Gregory Wolfe. Center for Religious Humanism, 3307 3d Ave W, Seattle, WA 98119-1997; image@imagejournal.org; http://www.imagejournal.org. Adv. Circ: 4000 Paid and controlled. *Indexed:* ChrPI, IAPV, MLA-IB, R&TA, RI-1. *Aud.:* Ga, Ac.

Image is a unique forum for writing and artwork that explores the relationship between art and Judeo-Christian faith through fiction, poetry, painting, sculpture, architecture, film, music, and dance. Issues also include thoughtful essays, interviews, book reviews, and high-quality, four-color reproductions of visual art. Past contributors have included Annie Dillard, Madeline L'Engle, Elie Wiesel, and Bill Viola.

4509. ***Indiana Review.*** Formerly (until 1982): *Indiana Writes.* [ISSN: 0738-386X] 1976. s-a. USD 18 (Individuals, USD 14). Ed(s): Esther Lee, Danit Brown. Indiana Review, Indiana University, Ballantine Hall 465, 1020 E Kirkwood, Bloomington, IN 47405-7103. Illus., adv. Refereed. Circ: 2000. Microform: PQC. *Indexed:* AmHI, IAPV, MLA-IB. *Bk. rev.:* 3-6. *Aud.:* Ga, Ac.

Indiana Review is an award-winning magazine entirely managed and edited by Indiana University graduate students. The nonprofit review is dedicated to showcasing the talents of emerging and established writers "within a wide aesthetic," and has promoted the work of such prestigious writers as Ha Jin, Sherman Alexie, and Raymond Carver. Issues, some themed, include essays, fiction, interviews, poetry, reviews, graphic art, and original cover art.

4510. ***The Journal (Columbus).*** Formerly (until 1987): *Ohio Journal.* [ISSN: 1045-084X] 1972. s-a. USD 14; USD 7 newsstand/cover per issue. Ed(s): Kathy Fagan, Michelle Herman. Ohio State University, Department of English, 421 Denney Hall, 164 W 17th Ave, Columbus, OH 43210. Illus., adv. Circ: 1200 Paid. *Indexed:* IAPV. *Bk. rev.:* 1-2. *Aud.:* Ga, Ac.

The literary journal of The Ohio State University, *The Journal* seeks to identify and encourage emerging writers from Ohio and beyond while also attracting the work of established writers. This journal features short fiction and poetry, as well as excerpts from novels, longer stories, and "daring or wholly original pieces" that cross genres. Each issue also includes book reviews.

Kalliope. See Women: Feminist and Special Interest/Literary and Artistic section.

4511. *Louisville Review.* [ISSN: 0148-3250] 1976. s-a. USD 14. Ed(s): Sena Jeter Naslund. Louisville Review Corporation, Spalding University, 851 S 4th St, Louisville, KY 40203. Circ: 500 Paid and controlled. *Aud.:* Ems, Hs, Ga, Ac.

Since 1976, *TLR* has sought "to import the best writing to local readers, to juxtapose the work of established writers with new writers, and to export the best local writers to a national readership." The *Review* actively promotes the work of new writers, and once published the work of Louise Erdrich when she was still a student. The publication includes a broad selection of poetry and fiction, but also includes drama and a "Children's Corner," which highlights the work of authors grades K–12.

4512. *The Malahat Review.* [ISSN: 0025-1216] 1967. q. CND 30 domestic; CND 40 foreign; CND 10 newsstand/cover per issue. Ed(s): Marlene Cookshaw. Footprint, Victoria, BC, PO Box 1700, Victoria, BC V8W 2Y2, Canada; malahat@uvic.ca; http://web.uvic.ca/malahat. Illus., adv. Refereed. Circ: 1000 Paid. Microform: MML. *Indexed:* ABS&EES, AmHI, ArtHuCI, BAS, BEL&L, CBCARef, CPerI, HumInd, IAPV, MLA-IB. *Bk. rev.:* 5-6. *Aud.:* Ga, Ac.

The Malahat Review presents contemporary, international selections of poetry and fiction. To fulfill a mission of increasing awareness of Canadian writers, each issue features reviews of new publications by Canadian authors.

4513. *Manoa: a Pacific journal of international writing.* [ISSN: 1045-7909] 1988. s-a. USD 40 (Individuals, USD 22). Ed(s): Frank Stewart. University of Hawaii Press, Journals Department, 2840 Kolowalu St, Honolulu, HI 96822-1888; uhpjourn@hawaii.edu; http://www.uhpress.hawaii.edu/. Illus., adv. Sample. Refereed. Circ: 750. Online: EBSCO Publishing; OCLC Online Computer Library Center, Inc.; Project MUSE; RoweCom Information Quest; Swets Blackwell. Reprint: PQC; PSC. *Indexed:* AmHI, IAPV, L&LBA, MLA-IB. *Bk. rev.:* varies; 6-12. *Aud.:* Ga, Ac.

This is a unique literary journal that focuses on writings from the Pacific Rim, including an international selection of fiction, poetry, artwork, and essays of current cultural or literary interest. Each issue has a unique focus and is guest-edited, and features both traditional and contemporary writings. Regular features include original translations of contemporary work from Asian and Pacific nations and book reviews.

4514. *Many Mountains Moving: a literary journal of diverse contemporary voices.* [ISSN: 1080-6474] 1994. s-a. USD 16 domestic; USD 9 newsstand/cover per issue domestic; USD 12 newsstand/cover per issue elsewhere. Ed(s): Naomi Horii. Many Mountains Moving, 420 22nd St, Boulder, CO 80302; http://www.mmminc.org. Illus., adv. Sample. Refereed. Circ: 2500. *Indexed:* AmHI, IAPV. *Aud.:* Ga, Ac.

A "literary journal of diverse contemporary voices" whose mission is to foster appreciation of diverse cultures through literature and art, provide support and recognition for established and emerging writers and artists, and provide a literary space for writers of diverse backgrounds. Each substantial issue (over 300 pages) includes poetry, essays, fiction, and art by both new and acclaimed authors and artists.

4515. *The Marlboro Review.* [ISSN: 1084-452X] 1995. s-a. USD 20 (Individuals, USD 16). Ed(s): Ellen Dudley. The Marlboro Review Inc., PO Box 243, Marlboro, VT 05344; dudley@sover.net; http://www.marlbororeview.com. Illus., adv. Sample. Refereed. Circ: 300. *Bk. rev.:* 3. *Aud.:* Ga, Ac.

The Marlboro Review includes poetry, fiction, interviews, criticism, reviews, translations, and nonfiction. Essays address cultural, scientific, and philosophical issues "from a writer's sensibility."

Meridians. See Women: Feminist and Special Interest/Feminist and Women's Studies section.

Michigan Quarterly Review. See Literary Reviews section.

4516. *New England Review.* Former titles (until 1990): *New England Review and Bread Loaf Quarterly;* (until 1982): *New England Review.* [ISSN: 1053-1297] 1978. q. USD 23 domestic; USD 29 foreign; USD 40 domestic. Middlebury College, Middlebury, VT 05759. Adv. Circ: 3000. Microform: PQC. Online: bigchalk; Chadwyck-Healey Incorporated; Gale Group; Northern Light Technology, Inc.; OCLC Online Computer Library Center, Inc.; ProQuest Information & Learning; H.W. Wilson. Reprint: PQC. *Indexed:* ABS&EES, ArtHuCI, BEL&L, BRI, CBRI, HumInd, IAPV, MLA-IB. *Bk. rev.:* 1. *Aud.:* Ga, Ac.

A literary quarterly "committed to exploration of all forms of contemporary cultural expression in the United States and abroad." Features short fiction, a wide variety of general and literary nonfiction, poetry, essays, book reviews, drama and screenplays, translations, critical reassessments, and interviews. The unusual arrangement—including sections such as "Revaluations," "Cultural History," and "Rediscoveries"—reflects the diversity of the thoughtfully selected material that the journal contains.

New Letters. See Literary Reviews section.

New Millennium Writings. See Literary Reviews section.

4517. *Nimrod: international journal of prose and poetry.* [ISSN: 0029-053X] 1956. s-a. Awards Issue (Fall Publication); Thematic Issue (Spring Publication). USD 25 (Individuals, USD 17.50). Ed(s): Francine Ringold. Nimrod, University of Tulsa, 600 S College Ave, Tulsa, OK 74104-3189. Illus., adv. Refereed. Circ: 4000 Paid. *Indexed:* AmHI, IAPV. *Aud.:* Ga, Ac.

Nimrod seeks to foster discovery of "new, unheralded writers; writers from other lands who become accessible to the English speaking world through translation; established authors who have vigorous new work to present that has not found a home within the establishment." Works include traditional and experimental poetry, prose, and artwork. Each spring issue is themed.

Ontario Review. See Literary Reviews section.

Paris Review. See Literary Reviews section.

4518. *Pleiades: a journal of new writing.* [ISSN: 1063-3391] 1991. s-a. USD 12. Ed(s): Kevin Prufer, Wayne Miller. Pleiades Press, Department of English & Philosophy, Central Missouri State University, Warrensburg, MO 64093. Adv. Circ: 2500. *Indexed:* MLA-IB. *Bk. rev.:* 5-7. *Aud.:* Ga, Ac.

Pleiades is a "journal of new writing" including fiction, poetry, and essays by both new and established writers. Each issue includes several "Introducing" features in which established American writers introduce work by largely unpublished poets and fiction writers. *Pleiades* is known for its reviews of current poetry, fiction, or literary nonfiction, and is committed to reviewing mainly books published by small or university presses. Translations and interviews are also included. Special features have recently included a symposium on "religion and poetry."

4519. *Poetry (Chicago).* [ISSN: 0032-2032] 1912. m. except bimonthly Oct.-Nov. USD 38 (Individuals, USD 35; USD 8.50 newsstand/cover per issue). Ed(s): Joseph Parisi. The Poetry Foundation, 1030 N Clark St., Ste 420, Chicago, IL 60610; http://www.poetrymagazine.org. Adv. Circ: 10000. Vol. ends: Oct/Sep. Microform: PMC; PQC. Online: bigchalk; Chadwyck-Healey Incorporated; EBSCO Publishing; Florida Center for Library Automation; Gale Group; OCLC Online Computer Library Center, Inc.; ProQuest Information & Learning; H.W. Wilson. Reprint: PQC. *Indexed:* ASIP, AmHI, ArtHuCI, BRD, BRI, BiogInd, CBRI, HumInd, IAPV, MagInd. *Bk. rev.:* 2-11. *Aud.:* Ga, Ac.

Since its founding in 1912, *Poetry*'s mission has been "to print the best poetry written today, in whatever style, genre, or approach." The magazine was among the first to publish Carl Sandburg and William Carlos Williams, among other now-classic poets. Independent and not affiliated with any one aesthetic school, *Poetry* is generally regarded as the premier journal of verse, and is recommended for all collections with an interest in poetry. Also includes book reviews and occasional essays.

Prairie Schooner. See Literary Reviews section.

4520. *Prism International: contemporary writing from Canada and around the world.* [ISSN: 0032-8790] 1959. q. CND 28.89 (Individuals, CND 19.26; CND 5 newsstand/cover per issue). Ed(s): Billeh Nickerson. University of British Columbia, Faculty of Arts, Creative Writing Program, E462 1866 Main Mall, Vancouver, BC V6T 1Z1, Canada; prism@interchange.ubc.ca; http://www.arts.ubc.ca/. Adv. Refereed. Circ: 1100 Paid. Microform: MML; PQC. Reprint: PQC. *Indexed:* ABS&EES, AmHI, ArtHuCI, CBCARef. *Aud.:* Ga, Ac.

A quarterly out of Vancouver, British Columbia, *Prism*'s mandate is to publish contemporary writing and translation from Canada and around the world. The magazine features poetry, fiction, drama, and creative nonfiction from both emerging and established writers. Past contributors include Margaret Atwood, Jorge Luis Borges, and Michael Ondaatje.

4521. *River Styx.* [ISSN: 0149-8851] 1975. 3x/yr. Individuals, USD 20; USD 7 newsstand/cover per issue. Ed(s): Richard Newman. Big River Association, 634 N. Grand Blvd. 12, St. Louis, MO 63103-1002. Illus., adv. Circ: 2300. *Indexed:* AmHI, IAPV. *Aud.:* Ga, Ac.

In the early 1970s, a group of St. Louis poets and musicians began reading and jamming together, and issued their first magazine in 1975. Today, *River Styx* is a polished, award-winning journal of poetry, fiction, essays, interviews, and art. First to publish such important writers as Robert Hass, Rita Dove, and Derek Walcott, the magazine continues to feature a mix of new and established writers and artists. At least one issue per year is themed (e.g., "The Monster Issue").

Rocktober. See Music/Popular section.

Room of One's Own. See Women: Feminist and Special Interest/Literary and Artistic section.

4522. *Rosebud: the magazine for people who enjoy good writing.* [ISSN: 1072-1681] 1993. 3x/yr. USD 24 domestic; USD 35 foreign; USD 7.95 newsstand/cover per issue. Ed(s): J Rod Clark. Rosebud, Inc., PO Box 459, Cambridge, WI 53523; jrodclark@smallbytes.net; http://www.itis.com/rosebud. Illus., adv. Sample. Circ: 6000 Paid. *Indexed:* AmHI, IAPV. *Aud.:* Ga.

An entertaining and well-designed "magazine for people who enjoy good writing," *Rosebud* publishes creative prose (fiction and nonfiction), poetry, and visual art. Each issue includes regular features such as a literary crossword puzzle, "URL Sitings," regular columns, and a variety of visual art including comics. There are also occasional "Rosebud Roundtables" on topics such as how the publishing process affects what we read. The magazine strives to include new artists, but each issue also features familiar names such as R. Crumb and Ray Bradbury.

Salamander. See Women: Feminist and Special Interest/Literary and Artistic section.

Small Press Review. See Books and Book Reviews section.

The Southern Review. See Literary Reviews section.

4523. *Stand Magazine.* [ISSN: 0038-9366] 1952. q. GBP 35 (Individuals, GBP 25). Ed(s): John Kinsella, Michael Hulce. Stand Magazine Ltd., c/o School of English, University of Leeds, Leeds, LS2 9JT, United Kingdom; stand@english.novell.leeds.ac.uk. Illus., adv. Circ: 3000 Paid. Vol. ends: Dec. *Indexed:* ArtHuCI, BRI, CBRI, IAPV. *Bk. rev.:* 10. *Aud.:* Ac.

Stand, a quarterly literary magazine established in 1952, was founded in response to our need for accessibility: "what is simple in expression and human in its context; for the chances that the compound will be profound and worth reading are reasonable." Published in England but international in scope, *Stand* features poetry, short fiction, and reviews. Some issues are themed, including a recent double issue on Nobel laureates.

4524. *StoryQuarterly.* [ISSN: 1041-0708] 1975. a. USD 10 per issue. Ed(s): M M Hayes. StoryQuarterly, Inc., PO Box 1416, Northbrook, IL 60065; storyquarterly@yahoo.com; http://www.storyquarterly.com. Illus., adv. Sample. Circ: 2500. *Indexed:* AmHI. *Aud.:* Ga, Ac.

An annual devoted to the short story, *StoryQuarterly* publishes contemporary American and international stories in a full range of styles and forms. *StoryQuarterly* entries have been recognized by both O. Henry Prize Stories and the Pushcart Prize. Past contributors include T. Coraghessan Boyle, J.M. Coetzee, and Alice Hoffman.

4525. *Tin House.* 1999. q. USD 29.90 domestic; USD 45.90 Canada; USD 59.90 elsewhere. Ed(s): Win McCormack. Tin House, PO Box 10500, Portland, OR 97296-0500; tinhouse@pcspublink.com; http://www.tinhouse.com. Illus., adv. *Aud.:* Ga.

Tin House is a slick, attractively-designed literary magazine with offices in Portland, Oregon, and New York. The mission is "to feature the best writers writing about what they are most passionate about, be it in the form of fiction, poetry, or essay, regardless of fashion or timeliness." *Tin House* features both established and little-known authors: each issue features a "New Voices" section. Other unique features include a "Lost and Found" section and lively interviews. Some issues are themed, e.g., "Gimme Shelter" and "Sex."

TriQuarterly. See Literary Reviews section.

4526. *Two Lines: a journal of translation.* [ISSN: 1525-5204] 1995. a. USD 13 domestic; USD 13.50 in Canada & Mexico; USD 15 elsewhere. Ed(s): Olivia E Sears. Two Lines, Box 641978, San Francisco, CA 94164-1978. Illus. Circ: 500. *Aud.:* Ga, Ac.

Two Lines publishes original English translations of international literature, in order to "engage in conversation across languages." Source texts appear across from their translation, either excerpted or in their entirety. Introductions to each piece place the authors within the literary tradition of a country or region. Each annual issue is themed, most recently "Cells" and "Ghosts."

4527. *Two Rivers Review.* [ISSN: 1524-2749] 1998. s-a. USD 12 domestic; USD 20 foreign; USD 6 newsstand/cover per issue. Ed(s): Philip Memmer. Anderie Poetry Press, Box 158, Clinton, NY 13323. Adv. Circ: 350. *Bk. rev.:* 1-2. *Aud.:* Ga.

Two Rivers Review seeks to present readers with "an experience in poetry which is both readable and astounding." Each issue, a simply-designed chapbook of approximately 50 pages, includes work by both well-established and new poets. Selections are favor poems with a "strong sense of craft and purpose."

Virginia Quarterly Review. See Literary Reviews section.

4528. *X C P: Cross-Cultural Poetics.* Former titles (until 1997): *Cross-Cultural Poetics;* (until 1996): *North American Ideophonics.* [ISSN: 1086-9611] 1989. s-a. USD 40 (Individuals, USD 18; USD 10 newsstand/cover per issue). Ed(s): Mark Nowak. College of St. Catherine - Minneapolis, 601 25th Ave S, Minneapolis, MN 55454; manowak@stkate.edu; http://bfn.org/~xcp. Illus. Circ: 750. *Indexed:* BRI, CBRI, IAPV, MLA-IB. *Bk. rev.:* 10-12. *Aud.:* ac.

A mixed-media, cross-cultural literary review that includes art, photography, academic essays and reviews, drama, interviews, short stories, excerpts from longer works, translations, and poetry. Articles and essays tend to the theoretical and academic, and include contributions from well-known academics. The poetry, prose, and art are carefully selected and varied in form and subjects addressed. Each themed issue ends with a substantial section of reviews of both academic and literary works. For academic readers, this is an engaging and informative reading experience.

Zoetrope. See Fiction: General/Mystery and Detective/General section.

4529. ***Zyzzyva: the last word: west coast writers and artists.*** [ISSN: 8756-5633] 1985. 3x/yr. USD 44 domestic; USD 64 foreign. Ed(s): Howard Junker. Zyzzyva, Inc., PO Box 590069, San Francisco, CA 94159-0069; editor@zyzzyva.org; http://www.zyzzyva.org. Illus., index, adv. Sample. Circ: 4000. Vol. ends: Winter. *Indexed:* AmHI, IAPV. *Aud.:* Ac.

Zyzzyva's mandate is to showcase the work of West Coast (currently living in California, Oregon, Washington, Alaska, or Hawaii) writers and artists. Because of its independence, *Zyzzyva* is able to publish a great variety of work, including fiction, poetry, and essays. Each perfect-bound issue opens with a "First Time in Print" feature and contains 30 or more original images.

Electronic Journals

Electronic Little Magazines serve much the same function as their print siblings: they expose readers to a broad spectrum of writing and art. Some electronic Little Magazines exist only online; others act as supplements to print counterparts. The electronic format provides greater flexibility and dissemination: online journals generally require low overhead costs, and they are available, often for free, 24 hours a day to anyone with access to the Internet. Of course, readership is limited to those people with the means of accessing a computer, and it is here that libraries can be expected to fill a highly important role—making equipment available so that magazines such as these can be enjoyed.

4530. ***Archipelago.*** 1996. 4x/yr. Ed(s): Katherine McNamara. Archipelago, PO Box 2485, Charlottsville, VA 22902; editor@archipelago.org; http://archipelago.org. Illus. *Aud.:* Ga, Ac.

A simple, attractive design and clear organization makes *Archipelago* a real pleasure to read online. Each issue includes fiction, poetry, essays, graphic art, and reviews. Translations and interviews are also frequently included. Also available in a download edition and via e-mail subscription.

4531. ***Mudlark: an[e]lectronic journal of poetry & poetics.*** [ISSN: 1081-3500] 1995. irreg. Free. Ed(s): William Slaughter. Mudlark, c/o William Slaughter, Department of English & Foreign Languages, Jacksonville, FL 32224-2645; mudlark@unf.edu; http://www.unf.edu/mudlark/. *Aud.:* Ga, Ac.

An online journal of poetry, *Mudlark*'s motto is "fast load, slow read." The premise is to keep the focus on words rather than design and images. *Mudlark* publishes in three formats: "issues," or electronic chapbooks; "posters," or electronic broadsides; and "flash" poems that address (or feel like) current events.

4532. ***Poetry Daily.*** 1997. d. Ed(s): Diane Boller, Don Selby. Daily Poetry Association, PO Box 1306, Charlottesville, VA 22902-1306; http://www.poems.com. *Aud.:* Ga, Ac.

This online anthology of contemporary poetry brings you a daily poem selected for literary quality and topical or seasonal interest. Also included are biographical information about the poet and the source. The goal is to help readers find poets they like and make it easier for poems to find an audience. Poems are selected from books, magazines, and journals currently in print, and are chosen from the work of poets published in English, both well-known and less established. Past features and daily poems are archived for one year and indexed by poet, title, and date.

4533. ***Poets & Writers Online.*** Poets & Writers, Inc., 72 Spring St, New York, NY 10012; http://www.pw.org. *Aud.:* Hs, Ga, Ac.

This online counterpart to the print publication *Poets & Writers* includes a variety of resources that include a searchable directory of American poets and writers; information on contests, grants, and workshops; online seminars; and advice on topics such as copyright, publishing, and finding a writers conference. The site also includes a popular online forum for writers.

4534. ***The Richmond Review.*** 1995. m. Ed(s): Steven Kelly. The Richmond Review, High Stakes, 21 Great Ormond St, London, WC1N 3JB, United Kingdom; editor@richmondreview.co.uk; http://richmondreview.co.uk. *Bk. rev.:* dozens. *Aud.:* Ga, Ac.

"The UK's first literary magazine to be published exclusively on the World Wide Web." Updated monthly, the site includes poetry, fiction, interviews, book reviews, and feature articles. Updates are also available via e-mail subscription. http://richmondreview.co.uk

4535. ***Zuzu's Petals Quarterly Online.*** Former titles: *Zuzu Petal Annual;* (until 1995): *Zuzu Petal Quarterly.* 1992. q. Zuzu's Petals Literary Resource, Box 4853, Ithaca, NY 14852; info@zuzu.com; http://www.zuzu.com. *Aud.:* Hs, Ga, Ac.

This online-only publication publishes poetry, fiction, essays, articles, and reviews on topics "both literary and experimental." Hypertext fiction and poetry and short multimedia clips are also included. Also links to "Zuzu's Petals Literary Resource," which includes news items, events, and a directory of 10,000 web links for the online creative community.

■ MANAGEMENT, ADMINISTRATION, AND HUMAN RESOURCES

General/Functional Management/Human Resources/Management Education/Operations Research and Management Science/Organizational Behavior and Studies/Strategic Analysis

See also Business; Finance; Labor and Industrial Relations; and Systems sections.

Peggy Tyler, Reference Librarian, Clemson University Libraries, Clemson, SC 29634; ptyler@clemson.edu

Introduction

Management is a broad discipline that studies the processes by which organizations utilize their resources to achieve goals. Management is also an applied practice—the profession of almost 3 million Americans, according to the 2000 census. This huge population of practicing managers and the surrounding academic community of scholars and students studying the field support literally thousands of management newsletters, magazines, and journals. Therefore, this section can only provide a listing of titles that are the core of a management collection, either through the quality of the publications or because of their wide indexing and/or patron demand.

Most of these management journals state that their mission is to present empirical academic research that is scholarly, but still of direct interest and use to those in organizational practice. Even the most theoretical articles usually try to provide a discussion of applications and research implications for working managers. There are also other journals and magazines that provide news and reports of research and trends in the profession—examples of all of these are provided below.

Nearly all of these listed publications are supported by web sites offering a varying level of additional information about the journal and its provider. Many nonprofit and commercial publishers offer sample issues, tables of contents, abstracts, and a selection of articles from recent issues at the journal web site; some provide additional content beyond that available in the print version. Most academic titles provide electronic equivalents to the print journal; these high-quality page images and increased access outside the library have persuaded many librarians to cancel their paper subscriptions. A growing number of journals are bypassing print entirely and are publishing only on the web. Extensive review of all the web-based content for these journals is not possible given the space provided, but web addresses are included whenever available.

Basic Periodicals

Ac: *Academy of Management Journal, Academy of Management Review, Administrative Science Quarterly, California Management Review, HRFocus, Journal of Organizational Behaviour, MIT Sloan Management Review, Personnel Psychology, Training.*

Basic Abstracts and Indexes

ABI/INFORM, Business Periodicals Index, Factiva, Psychological Abstracts.

General

4536. ***Academy of Management Executive: the thinking manager's source.*** Formerly (until 1989): *Academy of Management Executive.* [ISSN: 1079-5545] 1987. q. GBP 101 (Individuals, GBP 44). Ed(s): Dr. Robert C. Ford. Academy of Management, 235 Elm Rd, Box 3020, Briarcliff Manor, NY 10510-3020; http://www.aomonline.org. Illus., adv. Refereed. Circ: 13700. Online: EBSCO Publishing; Gale Group; Northern Light Technology, Inc.; OCLC Online Computer Library Center, Inc.; ProQuest Information & Learning. Reprint: PQC. *Indexed:* ABIn, ABS&EES, AgeL, BPI, SSCI. *Bk. rev.:* Four to eight substantial book reviews. *Aud.:* Ac, Sa.

This is the "practitioner" publication from the Academy of Management, providing business executives with the organizational applications of academic research in management theory. Each issue has a theme such as "Insights from Sports, Disasters, and Innovation" or "How Governments Matter," a "Country Close-up" with two or three interviews and articles about current management practice in a featured country, and a section of interviews with prominent executives. Some of the research summary articles are accompanied by executive commentaries. Recommended for corporate libraries and academic business libraries with comprehensive collections.

4537. ***Academy of Management Journal.*** Formerly (until 1962): *The Journal of the Academy of Management.* [ISSN: 0001-4273] 1958. bi-m. USD 125 domestic; USD 155 foreign. Ed(s): Amme Tsui. Academy of Management, 235 Elm Rd, Box 3020, Briarcliff Manor, NY 10510-3020; academy@pace.edu; http://www.aomonline.org. Illus., index, adv. Refereed. Circ: 11500. Vol. ends: Dec. Microform: PQC. Online: bigchalk; EBSCO Publishing; Gale Group; JSTOR (Web-based Journal Archive); OCLC Online Computer Library Center, Inc.; ProQuest Information & Learning. Reprint: PQC; SCH. *Indexed:* ABIn, AgeL, BAS, BPI, CINAHL, CommAb, ErgAb, PsycholAb, SSCI. *Aud.:* Ac.

AMJ is considered to be the premier experimental research journal for management science. Articles present the results of empirical studies of a wide range of current management practices and theories written by university researchers (primarily in the United States). A strong background in statistical analysis is recommended for readers of the studies' methods and results, but each article concludes with a discussion of how its findings might affect management theory and practice. A must for any academic library supporting a management curriculum.

4538. ***Academy of Management Review.*** [ISSN: 0363-7425] 1976. q. USD 105 in North America; USD 135 elsewhere. Ed(s): Richard J Klimoski. Academy of Management, 235 Elm Rd, Box 3020, Briarcliff Manor, NY 10510-3020; academy@pace.edu; http://www.aomonline.org. Illus., index, adv. Refereed. Circ: 11500. Vol. ends: Oct. Microform: PQC. Online: Gale Group; Northern Light Technology, Inc. Reprint: PQC. *Indexed:* ABIn, AgeL, BPI, IBSS, PsycholAb, SSCI. *Bk. rev.:* 4-5, 1,200 words, signed. *Aud.:* Ac.

Management theory, not professional practice, is the focus of this scholarly journal. Philosophical and analytical essays, critical discussions and debates of new and old theories and methods, and reflective literature reviews are the most common formats for "conceptual articles" aimed at developing new hypotheses for research and broad ideas for managerial practice. Along with four or five book reviews, each issue includes a few pages listing recent business books received by the Academy of Management and a number of book advertisement pages useful for collection development. One of the most heavily cited journals in the discipline, so it is highly recommended for academic libraries.

4539. ***Administrative Science Quarterly.*** [ISSN: 0001-8392] 1956. q. USD 130 (Individuals, USD 65). Ed(s): Donald A Palmer. Cornell University, Johnson Graduate School of Management, 20 Thornwood Drive, Suite 100, Ithaca, NY 14850-1265. Illus., index, adv. Refereed. Circ: 4484 Paid. Vol. ends: Dec. Microform: PQC. Online: bigchalk; The Dialog Corporation; Dow Jones Interactive; EBSCO Publishing; Florida Center for Library Automation; Gale Group; JSTOR (Web-based Journal Archive); Northern Light Technology, Inc.; OCLC Online Computer Library Center, Inc.; ProQuest Information & Learning; H.W. Wilson. *Indexed:* ABCPolSci, ABIn, ATI, ArtHuCI, BAS, BPI, CIJE, CINAHL, CommAb, DSR&OA, HRA, IBSS, IBZ, IPSA, MCR, PAIS, PMA, PRA, PSA, PsycholAb, SFSA, SSCI, SSI, SUSA, SWR&A, SociolAb. *Bk. rev.:* 10-12, 600-1,200 words, signed. *Aud.:* Ac, Sa.

Do not be put off by its 1950s title—this is a very modern (and very influential) organizational studies journal. *ASQ* hides its big brain behind covers with scenic color photographs and off-white pages with unusual margins, layout, and typography. This inviting package contains scholarly articles both experimental and theoretical on topics as wide ranging as how airlines learn from accidents to intercultural interpretations of teamwork. A significant portion of each issue is dedicated to a dozen or more 7-10 paragraph book reviews and a list of publications received. This is a core title for management collections that librarians should pick up and browse on a regular basis.

4540. ***Association Management.*** Formerly: *American Society of Association Executives. Journal.* [ISSN: 0004-5578] 1949. m. USD 50 domestic; USD 55 Canada; USD 60 elsewhere. Ed(s): Keith C Skillman. American Society of Association Executives, 1575 Eye St, N W, Washington, DC 20005-1168; http://www.asaenet.org. Illus., index, adv. Circ: 24000. Vol. ends: Dec. Microform: PQC. Online: EBSCO Publishing; Florida Center for Library Automation; Gale Group; LexisNexis; Northern Light Technology, Inc.; OCLC Online Computer Library Center, Inc.; ProQuest Information & Learning; H.W. Wilson. *Indexed:* ABIn, ATI, AgeL, BPI, LRI, PAIS, PMA. *Aud.:* Sa.

If you run an association, this is the trade publication that comes with your membership in the American Society of Association Executives. This glossy, heavily illustrated monthly magazine is full of how-to's and tips for managing nonprofit organizations. Since it is indexed in most of the basic business abstracts and indexes, demand for articles might be worth the low subscription price, even in libraries where association executives are not commonly found.

4541. ***C M A Management: for strategic business ideas.*** Former titles: *Management for Strategic Business Ideas;* (until 1999): *C M A Magazine;* (until 1995): *C M A. Certified Management Accountant;* (until 1985): *Cost and Management.* [ISSN: 1490-4225] 1926. 10x/yr. USD 43 foreign (Members, CND 29.95; Non-members, CND 48). Ed(s): Rob Colman. Society of Management Accountants of Canada, Mississauga Executive Centre, One Robert Speck Pkwy, Ste 1400, Mississauga, ON L4Z 3M3, Canada; info@cma-canada.org; http://www.cma-canada.org/cmacan/. Illus., index, adv. Circ: 72336. Vol. ends: Dec/Jan. Microform: MML; PQC. Online: EBSCO Publishing; Gale Group; LexisNexis. Reprint: PQC. *Indexed:* ABIn, ATI, CBCARef, CPerI, PMA, SSCI. *Bk. rev.:* 3 book reviews. *Aud.:* Ga, Sa.

A Canadian magazine for management professionals (not just accountants), *CMA Management* provides articles in both English and French about current trends and concerns in management practice. Executives/managers author the feature articles on topics such as e-commerce, entrepreneurship, and biotechnology, supplemented by freelancers, editorial staff, or other society professionals who provide interviews of business executives, "News and Views," and columns. The magazine web site provides access to a large number of full-text pages for each current issue and back issues through 2000. Recommended for Canadian business library collections and academic libraries where there is an interest beyond the free coverage provided online.

4542. ***California Management Review.*** [ISSN: 0008-1256] 1958. q. USD 65 (Individuals, USD 50). Ed(s): David Vogel. University of California at Berkeley, S549 Haas School of Business, Ste 1900, Berkeley, CA 94720-1900; cmr@haas.berkeley.edu; http://haas.berkeley.edu/News/cmr.html. Illus., index, adv. Refereed. Circ: 6500. Vol. ends: Summer. Microform: PQC. Online: Chadwyck-Healey Incorporated; EBSCO Publishing; Northern Light Technology, Inc.; OCLC Online Computer Library Center, Inc.; ProQuest Information & Learning. Reprint: PSC. *Indexed:* ABCPolSci, ABIn, ABS&EES, ATI, BAS, BLI, BPI, CompLI, ExcerpMed, FutSurv, IBSS, IBZ, LogistBibl, PAIS, PMA, RiskAb, SSCI. *Aud.:* Ac, Sa.

A recent redesign reflects *CMR*'s mission of providing scholarly articles that are useful to "both practicing managers and academic researchers." Articles by university faculty and practicing managers have a highly readable style, and two-color printing, clean graphics, pull quotes, and clearly presented tables make current research and review articles accessible to readers of many levels. Each issue clusters articles within two to four major topics such as "Management of Technology," "Internet Strategy," or "Business and Public Policy," with an occasional special issue heavily focused on a forum topic such as "Learning from Hospitals." *CMR*'s web site also offers case studies not published in the journal. Highly recommended for corporate and academic libraries.

4543. ***Corporate Board.*** Formerly (until 1983): *Corporate Director.* [ISSN: 0746-8652] 1980. bi-m. USD 2800 (Individuals, USD 490). Ed(s): Ralph D Ward. Vanguard Publications, Inc., 4440 Hagadorn Rd, Okemos, MI 48864-2414; info@corporateboard.com; http://www.corporateboard.com. Index, adv. Sample. Circ: 4000 Paid. Online: EBSCO Publishing; Florida Center for Library Automation; Gale Group. *Aud.:* Ac, Sa.

This journal is published to provide corporate officers and board members with the latest information on corporate governance. Bimonthly issues typically contain five feature articles about oversight of corporate activities, a review of recent governmental regulations and corporate surveys, an interview with one prominent corporate board member, and extended quotes from speeches and articles written by others. A list of recent corporate board elections results is also included. Expensive and narrowly focused, this journal is only recommended for corporate libraries and universities with executive MBA programs.

4544. ***Director.*** [ISSN: 0012-3242] 1947. m. GBP 39; GBP 54 in Europe; GBP 70 elsewhere. Ed(s): Tom Nash. Director Publications Ltd., 116 Pall Mall, London, SW1Y 5EA, United Kingdom. Illus., adv. Circ: 58441. Microform: PQC. Online: EBSCO Publishing; Gale Group; Northern Light Technology, Inc.; OCLC Online Computer Library Center, Inc.; ProQuest Information & Learning. Reprint: PQC. *Indexed:* ABIn, BPI, PAIS. *Bk. rev.:* 3-4, 100-300 words, signed. *Aud.:* Ac, Sa.

Director is an attractive British monthly magazine that provides insight into the current interests of executive officers in the United Kingdom (the euro, entrepreneurship, cost-cutting, hiring consultants) and profiles of successful and struggling corporations, while also providing its readership with tips on the best fishing vacations and buying an overseas dream home. Each issue includes three or four short book reviews. Recommended for academic libraries with an interest in international business.

4545. ***Directors & Boards.*** [ISSN: 0364-9156] 1976. q. USD 295; USD 325 foreign. Ed(s): James Kristie. Directors & Boards, 1845 Walnut St, 9th Fl, Philadelphia, PA 19103-4709; jkristie@directorsandboards.com; http://www.directorsandboards.com. Illus., index, adv. Circ: 5000. Vol. ends: Summer. Microform: PQC. Online: Factiva; Florida Center for Library Automation; Gale Group; OCLC Online Computer Library Center, Inc. *Indexed:* ABIn, ATI, CLI, LRI, PAIS. *Bk. rev.:* 1-2 signed reviews of about 500 words. *Aud.:* Ac, Sa.

Positioning itself as a journal "written by and for the board elite," this publication still has plenty of useful content for the business student who aspires to corporate governance or simply wants to know what published conversations directors are engaging in. Once each quarter, *Directors & Boards* publishes profiles and interviews with directors, several articles (very applied, about such topics as compensation, liability, performance evaluation, and financial controls), and a number of columns, including a roster of new board directors and a book review or two. Recommended for academic libraries that support business programs.

4546. ***European Management Journal.*** [ISSN: 0263-2373] 1983. bi-m. EUR 617 (Individuals, EUR 125). Ed(s): Paul Stonham. Pergamon, The Boulevard, Langford Ln, East Park, Kidlington, OX5 1GB, United Kingdom. Illus., index, adv. Refereed. Circ: 1000. Vol. ends: Dec. Microform: PQC. Online: Gale Group; ingenta.com; OCLC Online Computer Library Center, Inc.; ScienceDirect; Swets Blackwell. Reprint: PQC; SWZ. *Indexed:* ABIn, BPI, PAIS. *Bk. rev.:* 2-5, 300-800 words. *Aud.:* Ac, Sa.

Scholarly (yet readable) articles on management issues in European Union countries are featured—academic research articles by authors throughout the English-speaking world, case studies, interviews, and "Executive Briefings." This is an exceptionally content-rich source for readers interested in a high level of discourse about European business. Expect two to five substantial reviews in the "Books for Managers" section. The editors are focusing on timely electronic delivery of journal content, even providing uncorrected proofs of articles in press to subscribers. A sample issue is provided online. Highly recommended for academic libraries supporting business students and faculty.

Harvard Business Review. See Business/General section.

4547. ***International Journal of Cross Cultural Management.*** [ISSN: 1470-5958] 2001. 3x/yr. GBP 219 in Europe, Middle East, Africa & Australasia. Ed(s): Terence Jackson, Zeynep Aycan. Sage Publications Ltd., 6 Bonhill St, London, EC2A 4PU, United Kingdom; info@sagepub.co.uk; http://www.sagepub.co.uk/. Refereed. Online: ingenta.com; RoweCom Information Quest; Swets Blackwell. *Indexed:* HRA. *Aud.:* Ac, Sa.

The editorial board of this scholarly journal lists faculty from six continents. The focus of their publication is to contribute to an "understanding of the issues, problems, and practices of managing, working, and organizing across cultures." Its research articles are aimed at students and scholars in international management programs, and include studies on such topics as the adjustment of German workers to living in China, managerial sex-role stereotyping across cultures, and differences in achievement motivation across a selection of manager nationalities. The international focus is reinforced by the inclusion of abstracts in French and Chinese at the end of each article. Recommended for any academic library serving an international business program.

4548. ***Ivey Business Journal: improving the practice of management.*** Former titles (until 1999): *Ivey Business Quarterly;* (until 1997): *Business Quarterly;* (until 1950): *Quarterly Review of Commerce.* [ISSN: 1481-8248] 1933. bi-m. CND 44.94 domestic; CND 48.30 Atlantic; USD 42 United States. Ed(s): Stephen Bernhut. Ivey Management Services, 179 John St, Ste 501, Toronto, ON M5T 1X4, Canada; ibj@ivey.uwo.ca; http://www.ivey.uwo.ca/publications/bq. Illus., adv. Circ: 9123 Paid. Microform: MIM; MML; PQC. Online: The Dialog Corporation; EBSCO Publishing; Florida Center for Library Automation; Gale Group; Micromedia ProQuest; OCLC Online Computer Library Center, Inc.; ProQuest Information & Learning; H.W. Wilson. Reprint: PQC. *Indexed:* ABIn, BPI, CBCARef, CPerI, PAIS, SSCI. *Aud.:* Ac, Sa.

Ivey Business Journal is published by the Richard Ivey School of Business at the University of Western Ontario. Articles are written for business executives and cover popular topics in management such as knowledge management, intellectual property, and employee commitment. Each issue has a case study focusing on a company and an issue. The authors and advertisers are largely Canadian, but the content would be of interest to managers regardless of nationality. Tables of contents and abstracts of articles are available on the web site.

4549. ***Journal of General Management.*** Formed by the merger of (1969-1973): *Journal of Business Finance;* (19??-1973): *Journal of Business Policy.* [ISSN: 0306-3070] 1973. q. GBP 165 includes online access; USD 350 includes online access; GBP 41.25 per issue includes online access. Ed(s): Keith MacMillan. Braybrooke Press Ltd., Remenham House, Remenham Hill, Henley-on-Thames, RG9 3EP, United Kingdom; http://www.braybrooke.co.uk. Illus., index, adv. Circ: 1000. Vol. ends: Summer. Reprint: SWZ. *Indexed:* ABIn, AgeL, ExcerpMed, PAIS, SSCI. *Bk. rev.:* 1 signed, 500 words. *Aud.:* Ac, Sa.

Another British import, this management journal offers five long review or research articles and one book review per issue. Written by academic faculty worldwide, these wide-ranging scholarly articles might be on any subject of interest to its manager audience. Recent topics include mobile phone service, creativity, strategic alliances, and auditing after Enron. The awkward page layout with wide rules along each side margin and cut-and-paste tables detracts from the content. It was recently made available online. Its global focus, wide indexing, and inexpensive price make it a good addition to academic collections.

4550. ***Journal of Management.*** [ISSN: 0149-2063] 1975. bi-m. EUR 344 (Individuals, EUR 134). Ed(s): D. Feldman, K. M. Kacmar. Pergamon, The Boulevard, Langford Ln, East Park, Kidlington, OX5 1GB, United Kingdom. Illus., index, adv. Refereed. Circ: 2000. Vol. ends: No. 6.

Microform: PQC. Online: EBSCO Publishing; Florida Center for Library Automation; Gale Group; ingenta.com; Northern Light Technology, Inc.; OCLC Online Computer Library Center, Inc.; ScienceDirect; Swets Blackwell; H.W. Wilson. *Indexed:* ABIn, BPI, CIJE, PAIS, PMA, PsycholAb, SSCI. *Aud.:* Ac.

The *Journal of Management* is published by the Southern regional division of the Academy of Management. It publishes the same type of articles one would find in the Academy of Management's journal or review—high-quality theoretical and empirical scholarship covering a very broad scope of management science topics. The editors position their journal as a home for "innovative articles based on critical or radical perspectives." There are 5-7 scholarly articles every two months, with at least one issue each year devoted either to a single theme (entrepreneurship, resource-based views of organizations) or to a "Yearly Review of Management," which looks at the current state of research in a wide range of areas. There is a free sample copy online. Recommended for any academic library receiving Academy of Management journals.

4551. *Journal of Management Studies.* [ISSN: 0022-2380] 1964. 8x/yr. GBP 730 print & online eds. Ed(s): Robin Wensley, Karen Legge. Blackwell Publishing Ltd., 9600 Garsington Rd, PO Box 805, Oxford, OX4 2DQ, United Kingdom; customerservices@oxon.blackwellpublishing.com; http://www.blackwellpublishing.com/. Illus., index, adv. Refereed. Circ: 1600. Vol. ends: Nov. Online: EBSCO Publishing; ingenta.com; OCLC Online Computer Library Center, Inc.; RoweCom Information Quest; Swets Blackwell. Reprint: PQC; SWZ. *Indexed:* ABIn, BPI, IBSS, IBZ, IPSA, SSCI. *Bk. rev.:* 5-7, 800-1,000 words (not in every issue). *Aud.:* Ac.

Any of the eight yearly issues of this scholarly journal might have as few as six or as many as thirteen scientific articles on theoretical or highly applied topics in business management. Topics as far-ranging as emotional exhaustion in the workplace, corporate political strategy, delayering management structure, joint ventures and acquisitions, and disciplining professional employees appear in the journal contents. An occasional special issue focuses on a single theme ("Micro-Strategy and Strategizing" or "The Changing Multinational Firm"). The journal has a strong international and cross-cultural focus. Highly recommended for academic libraries serving graduate business schools.

4552. *Journal of Managerial Issues.* [ISSN: 1045-3695] 1989. q. USD 60 (Individuals, USD 45). Ed(s): Charles C Fischer. Pittsburg State University, Department of Economics, Finance & Banking, 1701 South Broadway, Pittsburg, KS 66762-7533; chuck@pittstate.edu; http://www.pittstate.edu/econ/jmi.html. Illus., index. Sample. Refereed. Circ: 1000 Paid. Vol. ends: No. 4. Microform: PQC. Online: bigchalk; EBSCO Publishing; Florida Center for Library Automation; Gale Group; Northern Light Technology, Inc.; OCLC Online Computer Library Center, Inc.; ProQuest Information & Learning. *Indexed:* ABIn, CIJE, CommAb, HRA, IPSA, InfoSAb, PAIS, PRA, PsycholAb, RiskAb. *Aud.:* Ac, Sa.

One of the many academic journals that claim a spot on the bridge providing scholarly research and topical literature reviews to both scholastic and business readership (although the dense statistical nature of most of the articles strongly skew this title to the academic side). Its articles range broadly from finance to human resources to decision-making to CEO pay structures. A manager or student is unlikely to be leafing though its 7-8 quarterly articles, but the large number of indexing and abstracting services that include this title will send many scholars and even practitioners to the shelf to find an article of interest. Recommended for the academic business collection.

Journal of Small Business Management. See Business/Small Business section.

4553. *M I R: Management International Review: journal of international business.* Formerly (until 1990): *Management International Review.* [ISSN: 0938-8249] 1961. q. EUR 142. Ed(s): Klaus Macharzina. Betriebswirtschaftlicher Verlag Dr. Th. Gabler GmbH, Abraham-Lincoln-Str 46, Wiesbaden, 65189, Germany; gabler.service@bertelsmann.de; http://www.gabler.de. Illus., index, adv. Refereed. Circ: 1450 Paid and controlled. Vol. ends: No. 4. Online: Florida Center for Library Automation; Gale Group; Northern Light Technology, Inc.; OCLC Online Computer Library Center, Inc.; ProQuest Information & Learning; H.W. Wilson. Reprint: SWZ. *Indexed:* ABIn, BAS, BPI, ExcerpMed, PAIS, RiskAb, SSCI. *Bk. rev.:* 1-2, 800-2,000 words. *Aud.:* Ac, Sa.

Again, a scholarly research journal that stresses the interaction between theory and practice of management, this time with a decidedly international focus. Its five empirical (and usually statistics-heavy) research articles per issue each provide discussions and models with clear management applications for practice or policy (foreign direct investment, international joint venturing, managerial values across cultures, and so on). There is usually a special theme issue each year (and sometimes two or more) in addition to the quarterly journal, on topics such as "International Management and the Internet—Post-hype." Recommended for all academic libraries with collection interest in international business.

4554. *MIT Sloan Management Review.* Former titles (until 2001): *Sloan Management Review;* (until 1970): *Industrial Management Review.* [ISSN: 1532-9194] 1960. q. USD 148 (Individuals, USD 89). Ed(s): Jane Gebhart. Massachusetts Institute of Technology, 77 Massachusetts Ave, Room E60-100, Cambridge, MA 02139-4307; smr@mit.edu; http://mitsloan.mit.edu/smr. Illus., index, adv. Refereed. Circ: 25000. Vol. ends: Summer. Microform: PQC. Online: EBSCO Publishing; Florida Center for Library Automation; Gale Group; Northern Light Technology, Inc.; OCLC Online Computer Library Center, Inc.; ProQuest Information & Learning; H.W. Wilson. Reprint: PQC; PSC. *Indexed:* ABIn, AgeL, BLI, BPI, CompLI, EngInd, EnvAb, LogistBibl, PAIS, PMA, SSCI. *Bk. rev.:* 6-12, 200-2,000 words. *Aud.:* Ac, Sa.

A scholarly journal that is truly focused on business readers, *MIT Sloan Management Review* is a crisp, readable, four-color illustrated publication that looks and reads enough like a business magazine to keep its research-based contributions from intimidating its audience. Its level is also accessible to undergraduate business students beginning to read research-based business literature. Every issue has a number of single-page "Research Briefs" that provide overviews of recently published or forthcoming studies, 8 to 10 articles primarily reporting studies involving "corporate strategy, leadership, and management of technology and innovation," followed by a couple of short opinion pieces. This is a must-have title for both academic libraries and large public libraries with a substantial business clientele.

4555. *Manage.* [ISSN: 0025-1623] 1925. s-a. USD 5. Ed(s): Douglas E Shaw. National Management Association, 2210 Arbor Blvd, Dayton, OH 45439. Illus., adv. Circ: 54000 Paid and free. Vol. ends: Apr. Microform: PQC. Online: bigchalk; EBSCO Publishing; Florida Center for Library Automation; Gale Group; Northern Light Technology, Inc.; OCLC Online Computer Library Center, Inc.; ProQuest Information & Learning. Reprint: PQC. *Indexed:* ABIn, AgeL. *Aud.:* Sa.

This magazine is published by the National Management Association, a nonprofit leadership development organization. Its articles are short how-to pieces written primarily by management consultants. The full text of recent issues and selected contents from others are available free on the National Management Association's web site. With its easy access, this title is not recommended for library purchase, but a link should be provided on any web guide to management sources.

4556. *Management Decision.* Incorporates: *Journal of Management History; Management in Action; Scientific Business.* [ISSN: 0025-1747] 1963. 10x/yr. EUR 12298.54 in Europe; USD 11329 in North America; AUD 13719 in Australasia. Ed(s): John Peters. Emerald, 60-62 Toller Ln, Bradford, BD8 9BY, United Kingdom; info@emeraldinsight.com; http://www.emeraldinsight.com. Illus. Refereed. Online: Pub.; EBSCO Publishing; Florida Center for Library Automation; Gale Group; OCLC Online Computer Library Center, Inc.; ProQuest Information & Learning; RoweCom Information Quest; Swets Blackwell. Reprint: PSC; SWZ. *Indexed:* ABIn, BPI, BrEdI, PAIS. *Aud.:* Ac, Sa.

Management Decision's publishers list their first audience as consultants (understandable, as they would be able to deduct the $11,000-plus subscription price as a business expense), and corporate and academic libraries as their second. There is much to admire in the nine or ten academically focused and clearly written articles in each of its ten yearly issues that provide "research and reflection" on the context and consequences of business decisions—most focused on strategic choices in the international business arena. Each article includes "Application Questions" at the end to provide readers with immediate relevance of article content to their own business situations. Review articles on management history topics are now also included in each issue. Highly recommended, but only for the most well-funded academic business libraries.

4557. ***Management Today.*** Supersedes: *Manager.* [ISSN: 0025-1925] 1966. m. GBP 40; GBP 2.95 newsstand/cover per issue. Haymarket Business Publications Ltd., 174 Hammersmith Rd, London, W6 7JP, United Kingdom; institute@easynet.co.uk. Illus., index, adv. Circ: 98000. Online: EBSCO Publishing; Florida Center for Library Automation; Gale Group; LexisNexis; Northern Light Technology, Inc.; OCLC Online Computer Library Center, Inc.; ProQuest Information & Learning. *Indexed:* ABIn, BPI, BrEdI, DAAI, ExcerpMed, LRI, MagInd. *Bk. rev.:* 3, 150 words. *Aud.:* Sa.

Subtitled "Not Business as Usual," this glossy U.K. monthly has clearly set out to become the business magazine of choice for young managers on the move up. Written journalistically, often in short bursts of conversational style, there are pages of heavily illustrated short articles heavy on advice for the lower-to-middle rungs of the corporate ladder. The magazine's attractive web site links to selected full-text articles from the current issue along with breaking general and business news in the United Kingdom. Recommended for display among popular reading periodicals in academic business collections—students would benefit from this source of international "infotainment."

4558. ***The McKinsey Quarterly.*** [ISSN: 0047-5394] 1964. q. Free to qualified personnel. McKinsey & Co. Inc., 55 E 52nd St, New York, NY 10022. Illus., index. Circ: 55000. Vol. ends: No. 4. Online: EBSCO Publishing; Florida Center for Library Automation; Gale Group; Northern Light Technology, Inc. *Indexed:* ABIn, BPI, CompLI. *Aud.:* Sa.

McKinsey & Company is a management consulting firm that publishes its "latest thinking on business strategy, finance, and management" in an astoundingly attractive publication—slightly unusual dimensions, unique cover illustrations, and layouts full of color and sophisticated, eye-catching graphics. Articles are written mostly by McKinsey consultants, reporting on recent analyses they have completed on industries and financial trends, interesting reading for both business professionals and business students planning a future as analysts in firms such as McKinsey. Articles (current and back issues) can be read by registering at the journal web site, and the print journal is free to individuals and organizations that McKinsey decides are qualified to receive it (including libraries). Recommended if only for its looks.

4559. ***Nonprofit Management and Leadership.*** [ISSN: 1048-6682] 1990. q. USD 175. Ed(s): Roger A Lohman. Jossey-Bass Inc., Publishers, 989 Market St, San Francisco, CA 94103-1741; jbsubs@jbp.com; http://www.josseybass.com. Illus., index. Refereed. Circ: 1050. Vol. ends: Summer. Online: OCLC Online Computer Library Center, Inc. Reprint: PSC. *Indexed:* ABIn, ASG, BPI, CIJE, HRA, IBSS, JEL, RI-1, SociolAb. *Bk. rev.:* 2-4, 500-2,000 words. *Aud.:* Ac, Sa.

Issues of concern to managers in nonprofit organizations are addressed in this scholarly journal, aimed at both an academic and professional audience (and effectively addressing both). Combining academic research articles (topics often include fundraising, training, governance and leadership) with features such as interviews, case studies, and book reviews, this is a worthwhile journal for those practicing or studying nonprofit administration. Recommended for academic libraries supporting coursework in the subject and special libraries in nonprofit agencies.

Public Administration Review. See Urban Studies section.

4560. ***The Public Manager: the journal for practitioners.*** Formerly (until Spring 1992): *Bureaucrat.* [ISSN: 1061-7639] 1972. q. USD 65 (Individuals, USD 35). Ed(s): Warren Master. Bureaucrat, Inc., 12007 Titian Way, Potomac, MD 20854; tnovo@aol.com; http://www.thepublicmanager.org. Illus., index, adv. Circ: 4000 Paid. Vol. ends: Winter. Online: Florida Center for Library Automation; Gale Group; ProQuest Information & Learning. *Indexed:* ABCPolSci, ABIn, BPI, HRA, IBZ, IPSA, SSCI, SUSA. *Bk. rev.:* 1, 600-800 words. *Aud.:* Ac, Sa.

The Public Manager is produced for government administrators to "write and share ideas about critical public management issues." Quarterly issues include mostly articles about policy and practice in federal agencies, written by government agency analysts or consultants to federal agencies. Some articles would be of interest to regional, state, or local government managers. Articles are very applied, with many case studies and reports of agency practices. Although this journal should be of real interest only to government agency libraries or special libraries in organizations that deal frequently with federal management personnel, its indexing in most major business indexes may create article demand worth its very low price.

4561. ***Public Performance and Management Review.*** Former titles (until 2000): *Public Productivity and Management Review;* (until 1990): *Public Productivity Review.* [ISSN: 1530-9576] 1975. q. USD 310 & Caribbean (Individuals, GBP 66). Ed(s): Marc Holzer. Sage Publications, Inc., 2455 Teller Rd, Thousand Oaks, CA 91320; info@sagepub.com; http://www.sagepub.com. Illus., index, adv. Refereed. Circ: 1450. Vol. ends: Jun. Microform: PQC. Online: EBSCO Publishing; Gale Group; ingenta.com; OCLC Online Computer Library Center, Inc.; ProQuest Information & Learning; RoweCom Information Quest; Swets Blackwell. *Indexed:* ABIn, BPI, CINAHL, PAIS, PMA, SUSA. *Bk. rev.:* Number and length vary. *Aud.:* Ac, Sa.

Managers in the public sector and academics are the intended audience for this scholarly journal that is "dedicated to creative problem solving." Each issue provides 4-5 articles on a single topic in public administration (outsourcing, budgeting, personnel management, training) with a broad international scope. Additional articles report on current research, discuss the application of corporate management techniques to the public sector, or provide a case study that is then commented on by one or more public sector professionals or academic researchers. There are frequently substantial book reviews. Recommended for special libraries in the public sector and academic libraries supporting nonprofit management coursework and research.

4562. ***S A M Advanced Management Journal.*** Former titles (1975-1984): *Advanced Management Journal;* (1969-1974): *S A M Advanced Management Journal.* [ISSN: 0749-7075] 1935. q. USD 49; USD 74 foreign. Ed(s): Moustafa H Abdelsamad. Society for Advancement of Management, Texas A&M University Corpus Christi, College of Business, Corpus Christi, TX 78412; moustafa@falcon.tamucc.edu; http://www.enterprise.tamucc.edu/sam. Illus., index, adv. Refereed. Circ: 5000. Vol. ends: Autumn. Microform: PQC. Online: EBSCO Publishing; Gale Group; OCLC Online Computer Library Center, Inc.; ProQuest Information & Learning; H.W. Wilson. *Indexed:* ABIn, ATI, AgeL, BPI, CompLI, PMA. *Aud.:* Sa.

This slim journal from the Society for Advancement of Management is a quarterly conduit for academics and practicing managers to share research on a very wide range of management topics. The shorter length of articles and less complex language and statistical analysis make this journal a useful title for undergraduates looking for readable primary research; the practical focus of articles makes it useful for managers in the field. Recommended for undergraduate academic collections.

Functional Management

There are hundreds of functional management magazines and journals that provide managers with specific job responsibilities or in specific industries with research reports, news, or overviews of new practices. Among the many topic areas are inventory control, production, product development, supply chain management, information technology, purchasing, research and development, and project management; each of these functions might then have several industry-specific journals within the category (automotive, food and beverage, textile, computing, etc.). The titles mentioned below are a few of the most widely used publications in some of these areas.

4563. ***A P I C S the Performance Advantage: the performance advantage.*** [ISSN: 1056-0017] 1991. m. Non-members, USD 47. Ed(s): David Greenfield. Lionheart Publishing, Inc., 506 Roswell St SE, Ste. 220, Marietta, GA 30060-4101; lpi@lionhrtpub.com; http://lionhrtpub.com; http://www.apics.org/magazine. Illus., index, adv. Circ: 72153. *Indexed:* LogistBibl. *Bk. rev.:* 0-2, signed, one page each. *Aud.:* Sa.

This is one of two publications (also see *Production and Inventory Management Journal* below in this section) by APICS, The Educational Society for Resource Management. This is the APICS member magazine—glossy and full color, with feature articles, case studies, and news on "enterprise management, supply chain management, logistics/warehouse management, and production and inventory management concepts." It is also very much a showcase for manufacturing and service advertisers. Selected full text is available for nonmembers at the association web site. This magazine will be read by practicing supply chain managers and would be of interest to undergraduates considering a career in the field.

4564. ***Industrial Management.*** [ISSN: 0019-8471] 1952. bi-m. USD 39; USD 50 foreign. Ed(s): Jane Gaboury. Institute of Industrial Engineers, 3577 Parkway Ln., Ste. 200, Norcross, GA 30092. Illus. Circ: 3000. Online: EBSCO Publishing; Florida Center for Library Automation; Gale Group; Northern Light Technology, Inc.; OCLC Online Computer Library Center, Inc.; ProQuest Information & Learning; H.W. Wilson. Reprint: PQC. *Indexed:* ABIn, BPI, EngInd, LRI, LogistBibl. *Aud.:* Sa.

This is a practical journal offering professional, prescriptive advice to operating managers and industrial engineers in management positions. There are profiles of successful managers and feature articles on current management issues. The editors encourage submissions "based on experience and actual hands-on operating situations or case studies," such as how to get difficult people to accept change or how to improve white-collar productivity in manufacturing organizations. Recommended for undergraduate reading.

4565. ***International Journal of Logistics Management.*** [ISSN: 0957-4093] 1990. 2x/yr. USD 150 (Individuals, USD 85). Ed(s): Douglas Lambert, Martin Christopher. International Logistics Research Institute, Inc., PO Box 2166, Ponte Vedra Beach, FL 32004-2166; http://www.logisticssupplychain.org. Illus., adv. Refereed. Circ: 2000 Paid. Vol. ends: No. 2. *Indexed:* ABIn, LogistBibl. *Aud.:* Ac, Sa.

This is another journal attempting to provide both scholarly research and practical case histories for academic and professional readers. It succeeds at this with a structured format of 8-10 articles, written primarily by academic researchers, in three categories: a "Special Feature" (an article on a broad topic such as returns management/reverse supply or managing under the threat of terrorism); "Concepts, Theory and Techniques" (3-4 research reports); and "Applications and Implementation" (mostly cases). Coverage is international (authors and articles). Recommended for academic business libraries where international business is of interest.

4566. ***Journal of Product Innovation Management.*** [ISSN: 0737-6782] 1984. bi-m. USD 535 print & online eds. Ed(s): Anthony Di Benedetto, Abbie Griffin. Blackwell Publishing, Inc., Commerce Place, 350 Main St, Malden, MA 02148; subscrip@blackwellpub.com; http://www.blackwellpublishing.com. Illus., index. Sample. Refereed. Circ: 2500. Vol. ends: Nov. Online: EBSCO Publishing; Gale Group; ingenta.com; LexisNexis; ScienceDirect; Swets Blackwell. Reprint: SWZ. *Indexed:* ABIn, C&ISA, CommAb, EngInd, RiskAb, SCI, SSCI. *Bk. rev.:* 3-13, 400-1,700 words. *Aud.:* Ac, Sa.

The Product Development and Management Association intends this journal to cast a wide net into the theoretical and empirical academic research in product design and manufacturing processes and the work of students and professionals in every part of product development process. The journal presents scholarly research articles along with case histories and conceptual reviews from management, applied sciences, and social sciences, with an international and cross-cultural scope. Book reviews and abstracts of articles in other journals are featured in each issue. There is a free sample copy available online. Recommended highly for academic libraries.

4567. ***Journal of Supply Chain Management: a global review of purchasing and supply.*** Former titles (until 1999): *International Journal of Purchasing & Materials Management;* (until 1991): *Journal of Purchasing and Materials Management; Journal of Purchasing.* [ISSN: 1523-2409] 1965. q. USD 59; USD 69 foreign. Ed(s): Alvin Williams. Institute for Supply Management, 2055 E Centennial Circle, Box 22160, Tempe, AZ 85285-2160. Illus., adv. Refereed. Circ: 3000. Vol. ends: Nov (No. 4). Microform: PQC. Online: The Dialog Corporation; Florida Center for Library Automation; Gale Group; OCLC Online Computer Library Center, Inc.; ProQuest Information & Learning; H.W. Wilson. Reprint: SCH. *Indexed:* ABIn, BPI, CompLI, LogistBibl. *Bk. rev.:* Number and length vary. *Aud.:* Ac, Sa.

This is a thin publication with an attractive two-color design and writing style that serves its mission as a provider of information about purchasing, materials, and supply to academics and management professionals. Articles are high quality and written at a level accessible to anyone with an interest in the topic. Five or six articles each quarter analyze the principles and applications of managerial topics in the supply chain (perceptions of supply risk, supplier selection and assessment), a supply management professional from a major company is interviewed (U.S. Postal Service, Waste Management), and a collection of one-paragraph book reviews is offered. Recommended for undergraduate and graduate collections.

4568. ***M I S Quarterly.*** [ISSN: 0276-7783] 1977. q. USD 75 domestic; USD 85 foreign. Ed(s): Jan DeGross, Ron Weber. M I S Research Center, University of Minnesota, Carlson School of Management, Minneapolis, MN 55455. Illus., index, adv. Refereed. Circ: 3000. Vol. ends: Dec. Online: EBSCO Publishing; Florida Center for Library Automation; Gale Group; JSTOR (Web-based Journal Archive); OCLC Online Computer Library Center, Inc.; ProQuest Information & Learning; H.W. Wilson. *Indexed:* ABIn, BPI, CompLI, InfoSAb, SSCI. *Aud.:* Ac, Sa.

Management information systems professionals specialize in the use of information technology to aid managerial decision-making. One would imagine that the publications in this field would be dense and computational, but this journal has a very readable style and layout. Its research articles are theory-based and empirical, but they do discuss applications to professional practice. Along with these longer research articles, there are sections of "Research Notes" and "Issues and Opinions" that provide forums for dialogue about recent articles or current issues in the MIS world. Highly recommended for academic libraries. (Related publications include *MIS Quarterly Executive* [www.misqu.org], the Society for Information Management's publication for practicing managers with a more case-based focus, and *MIS Discovery Research*, a web supplement intended to offer interactive and multimedia versions of MIS research.)

4569. ***Manufacturing and Service Operations Management.*** [ISSN: 1523-4614] 1999. bi-m. USD 153 combined subscription domestic print & online eds.; USD 169 combined subscription foreign print & online eds.; USD 248 combined subscription domestic print & online eds. Ed(s): Garrett van Ryzin. I N F O R M S, 901 Elkridge Landing Rd., Ste. 400, Linthicum, MD 21090-2909; informs@informs.org; http://www.informs.org/pubs/. Illus., adv. Refereed. Circ: 1000 Paid and controlled. Online: EBSCO Publishing; Gale Group; JSTOR (Web-based Journal Archive); ProQuest Information & Learning. *Indexed:* EngInd. *Aud.:* Ac, Sa.

This is a highly technical and applied journal with an interest in any scientific model (mathematical, behavioral, economic, surveys, studies across organizational units) that can be used as a lens through which to view the functional operations of an organization. Recent topics include "Designing a Call Center with Impatient Customers," "Smart Customers in a Promotion Environment," and a study of "component sharing"—using the same version of a part across multiple products. Recommended for graduate academic collections.

4570. ***Production and Inventory Management Journal.*** Former titles (until 1987): *Production and Inventory Management; A P I C S Quarterly Bulletin.* [ISSN: 0897-8336] 1959. q. Members, USD 64; Non-members, USD 80. Ed(s): Susan A Neff. A P I C S - The Educational Society for Resource Management, 5301 Shawnee Rd, Alexandria, VA 22312-2317;

http://www.apics.org. Illus., index. Refereed. Circ: 72000. Vol. ends: No. 4. Online: Florida Center for Library Automation; Gale Group; OCLC Online Computer Library Center, Inc.; ProQuest Information & Learning. Reprint: PQC. *Indexed:* ABIn, AS&TI, ATI, BPI, C&ISA, EngInd. *Aud.:* Sa.

APICS (The Educational Society for Resource Management) is an organization that specializes in professional development and certification in the practice of managing organizational resources. Its research journal also has this educational focus for students and practitioners; articles provide examples from the classroom, from academic research settings, and from the workplace. Models and case studies predominate. Recent articles include "Facilitated Learning Using LGO Projects," "Case Study of Warehouse Layout," and "Scheduling Doctors at a Large Hospital." Recommended for academic libraries.

4571. *Production Planning & Control.* [ISSN: 0953-7287] 1990. 8x/yr. GBP 414. Ed(s): Dr. Stephen J Childe. Taylor & Francis Ltd, 11 New Fetter Ln, London, EC4P 4EE, United Kingdom; info@tandf.co.uk; http://www.tandf.co.uk/journals. Adv. Sample. Refereed. Online: EBSCO Publishing; Ingenta Select; OCLC Online Computer Library Center, Inc.; RoweCom Information Quest; Swets Blackwell. Reprint: PSC. *Indexed:* C&ISA, EngInd, ErgAb. *Bk. rev.:* 1-2, signed. *Aud.:* Ac, Sa.

The field of production planning supports several good publications where academics and managers can share research developments and industry practices. This is yet another of those journals, with a more European focus. Information is provided in a variety of article types—invited keynote papers, research reports, review articles, case studies, field reports, conference notes, and book reviews. Recommended for academic libraries interested in a wider range of journals on this topic.

4572. *Project Management Journal.* Formerly (until 1984): *Project Management Quarterly.* [ISSN: 8756-9728] 1970. q. Membership, USD 119. Ed(s): Parviz F Rad. Project Management Institute, 4 Campus Blvd, Newtown Square, PA 19073; pmihq@pmi.org; http://www.pmi.org. Adv. Refereed. Circ: 85000 Paid. Vol. ends: Dec. *Indexed:* ABIn, BPI, CompLI, RiskAb. *Bk. rev.:* 0-2, 400 words. *Aud.:* Ac, Sa.

The refereed journal of the Project Management Institute (PMI), this publication provides a good balance of research and applied articles of interest to academics and practitioners. There is not a specific industrial focus to its coverage; articles provide a broad view of the topic (for example, "Measure of Software Development Risk," "Evaluation and Selection of Consultants," and "High School Initiative Helps Students View College Planning as Project"). Short news and advice pieces are left to PMI's magazine, *PMNetwork.* Recommended for academic collections.

4573. *Purchasing (Newton): the magazine of total supply chain management.* [ISSN: 0033-4448] 1915. 24x/yr. USD 109.90 domestic (Free to qualified personnel). Ed(s): Doug Smock, Tom Stundza. Reed Business Information, 275 Washington St, Newton, MA 02458; http://www.reedbusiness.com. Illus., index, adv. Circ: 93500 Paid and controlled. Vol. ends: Jun/Dec. Online: EBSCO Publishing; Florida Center for Library Automation; Gale Group; OCLC Online Computer Library Center, Inc.; ProQuest Information & Learning; H.W. Wilson. *Indexed:* ABIn, BPI, C&ISA, EngInd, LRI. *Bk. rev.:* Various number and length. *Aud.:* Ac, Sa.

A glossy, cluttered news magazine for managers throughout the supply chain (with an equally glossy and cluttered web site), *Purchasing* currently focuses its biweekly content on specific industries, currently alternating between a metals edition and an electronics and technology edition. There are short, punchy pieces, many with graphs and tables ranking companies, reporting and forecasting trends, and revealing survey results. Subscribers also receive buyer's guides for chemicals, metals and "e-procurement."

4574. *Quality Management Journal.* [ISSN: 1068-6967] 1993. q. Members, USD 50; Non-members, USD 60. Ed(s): Barbara Flynn. American Society for Quality Control, 611 E Wisconsin Ave, Box 3005, Milwaukee, WI 53201-3005; http://www.asq.org. Illus., adv. Circ: 14000. Vol. ends: Jul (No. 4). *Bk. rev.:* 4-7 500-1000 words. *Aud.:* Ac, Sa.

Quality Management Journal (*QMJ*) is dedicated to the broad and omnipresent topic of the pursuit of quality operations and products, with presentation and discussion of current research on subjects such as "customer defined quality" and several reviews of recent quality management books. The journal's web site is an excellent supplement, providing access to full sample issues plus a selected full-text article from every issue, long abstracts or full texts from the executive briefs of the research articles, and the text of most book reviews. This publication provides a scholarly yet applied view of the topic and is recommended for academic libraries serving management faculty and students.

Quality Progress. See Engineering and Technology/Manufacturing Engineering section.

4575. *R & D Management.* [ISSN: 0033-6807] 1970. q. GBP 530 print & online eds. Ed(s): Alan W Pearson, Jeff Butler. Blackwell Publishing Ltd., 9600 Garsington Rd, PO Box 805, Oxford, OX4 2DQ, United Kingdom; customerservices@oxon.blackwellpublishing.com; http://www.blackwellpublishing.com/. Illus., adv. Refereed. Circ: 1150. Vol. ends: Oct (No. 4). Online: EBSCO Publishing; Gale Group; ingenta.com; OCLC Online Computer Library Center, Inc.; RoweCom Information Quest; Swets Blackwell. Reprint: SWZ. *Indexed:* ABIn, BPI, EngInd, IBZ, PAIS, SSCI. *Bk. rev.:* 2-4, 750-1,000 words. *Aud.:* Ac, Sa.

This journal focuses on the issues managers deal with in organizations or work units developing innovative processes and products, including topics such as "evaluating and introducing disruptive technologies," "effects of creative problem solving training," or "managing virtual R&D teams." There are 7-9 well-written and -edited articles per issue; some issues also have 2-4 book reviews. This publication would be of interest to engineering and design students and faculty as well as management and organizational psychology departments. Highly recommended.

4576. *Research Technology Management: international journal of research management.* Formerly: *Research Management.* [ISSN: 0895-6308] 1958. bi-m. USD 150 (Individuals, USD 65). Ed(s): Michael F Wolff. Industrial Research Institute, 1550 M St, N W, Washington, DC 20005-1712; http://www.iriinc.org. Illus., index. Refereed. Circ: 4200 Paid. Vol. ends: Nov/Dec. Microform: PQC. Online: EBSCO Publishing; Florida Center for Library Automation; Gale Group; Ingenta Select; LexisNexis; OCLC Online Computer Library Center, Inc.; ProQuest Information & Learning; H.W. Wilson. *Indexed:* ABIn, ABS&EES, BPI, EngInd, EnvAb, H&SSA, IUSGP, PAIS, RiskAb, SSCI, WRCInf. *Bk. rev.:* 4-6, 75-300 words. *Aud.:* Ac, Sa.

This publication is typographically cluttered and graphically overstimulated (with a clunky web site to match), but the content has excellent value—lots of well-written, very applied "how to do it in your organization" pieces about a wide range of managerial and technological topics. Issues contain news briefs, an opinion piece, research reports, case studies, and brief reviews of new books and important papers in the field. R&D managers working in high-tech organizations would find a great deal of advice and inspiration. Articles would also be useful and interesting for undergraduates. Recommended for academic libraries.

Risk Management. See Finance/Trade Journals section.

4577. *Supply Chain Management: an international journal.* [ISSN: 1359-8546] 1996. 5x/yr. EUR 1282.16 in Europe; USD 1189 in North America; AUD 1479 in Australasia. Ed(s): Andrew Fearne. Emerald, 60-62 Toller Ln, Bradford, BD8 9BY, United Kingdom; info@emeraldinsight.com; http://www.emeraldinsight.com/journals/. Refereed. Reprint: SWZ. *Indexed:* LogistBibl. *Aud.:* Ac, Sa.

The supply chain is the topic of many functional management journals—what makes this title stand out is its broadly international articles (research applications and case studies are routinely provided beyond North America and Europe) and its high level of scholarship. The journal particularly focuses on the nature of the interactions among the producers of raw materials, manufacturers and retailers. Recent articles include studies of "business-to-business online auctions," "procurement best practice in the food industry," and "the relentless shift to offshore manufacturing." Recommended for graduate-level academic collections.

Supply Chain Management Review. See Transportation section.

Human Resources

Human resources publications tend to concentrate on the applied practice of employee recruitment, selection, training, evaluation, compensation, and development. These titles are very closely related to those in the Organizational Behavior and Studies subsection, but tend to be practitioner journals for managers and executives overseeing HR functions.

Benefits Quarterly. See Labor and Industrial Relations section.

4578. *Compensation and Benefits Review: the journal of total compensation strategies.* Formerly (until 1985): *Compensation Review.* [ISSN: 0886-3687] 1969. bi-m. GBP 247 in Europe, Middle East, Africa & Australasia. Ed(s): Fay Hansen. Sage Publications, Inc., 2455 Teller Rd, Thousand Oaks, CA 91320; info@sagepub.com; http://www.sagepub.com. Illus., index, adv. Circ: 3500. Vol. ends: Nov/Dec. Microform: PQC. Online: The Dialog Corporation; EBSCO Publishing; Gale Group; ingenta.com; LexisNexis; OCLC Online Computer Library Center, Inc.; ProQuest Information & Learning; RoweCom Information Quest; Swets Blackwell; H.W. Wilson. Reprint: SCH. *Indexed:* ABIn, ABS&EES, AgeL, BPI, PAIS, PMA, SSCI. *Bk. rev.:* 1-8, 250-700 words. *Aud.:* Sa.

Although the title might sound like the annual booklet of tables and lists your employer sends you about your retirement and health coverage, this is a professional journal that would be right at home in the strategic management section. Its articles are written by corporate compensation managers who present analyses of pay and benefits for organizational decision makers. The journal is published in the United Kingdom, but it has a U.S. focus; the laws and regulations discussed (Section 529, Fair Labor Standards Act) are for U.S. managers. Not all articles have a legal focus; recent topics include the graying of the workforce, executive compensation, and prescription drug costs. The journal also provides surveys, statistical summaries, and tables to support the content. This is a niche title aimed at practicing HR managers, but it would be a good addition to larger academic collections.

4579. *Compensation and Working Conditions (Print Edition).* Formerly (until 1991): *Current Wage Developments.* [ISSN: 1059-0722] 1956. q. annual index in Dec. issue. USD 18. U.S. Bureau of Labor Statistics, 441 G St, NW, Washington, DC 20212; klein_d@bls.gov; http://www.bls.gov. Illus., index. Vol. ends: Winter. Reprint: CIS; PQC. *Indexed:* AmStI, CJA, PAIS. *Aud.:* Ga, Ac, Sa.

This title has ceased as a print publication. Old and new articles are archived on the U.S. Bureau of Labor Statistics web site at http://www.bls.gov/opub/cwc. It "reports on employee compensation, wages, salaries, benefits, and occupational illnesses" and contains a current statistical section on employer costs for employee compensation, benefits, safety, and health. It also reports on changes related to collective bargaining settlements and unilateral management decisions. Examples of technical notes and tabular data include the employee cost index, national compensation surveys, work stoppages, and injuries and fatalities.

4580. *Employee Responsibilities and Rights Journal.* [ISSN: 0892-7545] 1988. q. USD 373 print or online ed. Ed(s): Gary L Whaley. Kluwer Academic / Plenum Publishers, 233 Spring St Fl 7, New York, NY 10013-1522; http://www.wkap.nl/. Illus., adv. Refereed. Microform: PQC. Online: EBSCO Publishing; ingenta.com; Kluwer Online; OCLC Online Computer Library Center, Inc.; RoweCom Information Quest; Swets Blackwell. Reprint: WSH. *Indexed:* IMFL, IPSA, PAIS, PsycholAb. *Bk. rev.:* 4-6, 2,500-4,000 words. *Aud.:* Ac, Sa.

The title of this publication sounds more like an HR manual than the scholarly journal that it is. Each issue has 4-5 articles written primarily by academic faculty about the legal, ethical, psychological, economic, and social impacts of worker/employer relationships. Article formats very widely from summaries of focus groups, meta-analyses, experimental research, topical reviews, and case studies (among others) and topical coverage is equally broad (implications of Supreme Court decisions on ADA, sleep deprivation research, downsizing, union activity, and bullying are all recent topics). Recommended only for practitioners or graduate HR or organizational psychology collections.

4581. *H R Magazine: strategies and solutions for human resource professionals.* Former titles: *Personnel Administrator;* (until 1954): *Personnel News.* [ISSN: 1047-3149] 1950. m. Non-members, USD 70. Ed(s): Leon Rubis. Society for Human Resource Management, 1800 Duke St, Alexandria, VA 22314-3499; shrm@shrm.org; http://www.shrm.org. Illus., index, adv. Circ: 131000. Vol. ends: Dec. Online: EBSCO Publishing; Florida Center for Library Automation; Gale Group; Human Resources Information Network; OCLC Online Computer Library Center, Inc.; ProQuest Information & Learning; H.W. Wilson. Reprint: PQC. *Indexed:* ABIn, AgeL, BPI, BRI, CBRI, CIJE, LRI, PAIS, PMA, PsycholAb. *Bk. rev.:* 1, 600 words. *Aud.:* Ac, Sa.

The Society for Human Resource Management (SHRM) is the primary organization of HR professionals (and students), and its monthly glossy magazine is the society's traditional voice, especially in libraries (although members may access a number of other electronic publications at the SHRM web site). Each issue has substantial feature articles and at least a dozen shorter columns and regular "departments" covering current HR practices and the larger organizational role of human resources. Every quarter, the magazine includes a pull-out "research supplement" with a review and bibliography on a single topic—human capital as an organizational asset and work/life balance are recent choices. This core HR publication is very widely indexed and will be in demand by undergraduate management students.

4582. *HRfocus: the hands-on tool for human resources professionals.* Formerly (until 1991): *Personnel.* [ISSN: 1059-6038] 1919. m. USD 249 print & online eds. Ed(s): Sue Sandler. Institute of Management & Administration, Inc., 29 W 35th St, 5th Fl, New York, NY 10001-2299; subserve@ioma.com; http://www.ioma.com. Illus., index, adv. Circ: 100000. Vol. ends: Dec. Microform: PQC. Online: EBSCO Publishing; Florida Center for Library Automation; Gale Group; OCLC Online Computer Library Center, Inc.; ProQuest Information & Learning; H.W. Wilson. Reprint: PSC. *Indexed:* ABIn, ATI, BPI, CompLI, ExcerpMed, PMA, PsycholAb, SSCI. *Aud.:* Ga, Sa.

Despite its unassuming appearance as a three-hole-punched newsletter, *HRfocus* is one of the most widely recognized titles in the field. Articles are short, unsigned, and provide legal and regulatory updates, topical advice, and news briefs of recently issued surveys and reports. Every third issue has a four-page "Special Report" insert on a single topic; outsourcing, change management, and workplace violence have been featured recently. This is focused entirely toward HR management professionals, but it should still be purchased by academic libraries.

4583. *Human Resource Management.* [ISSN: 0090-4848] 1962. q. USD 599 domestic; USD 639 in Canada & Mexico; USD 673 elsewhere. Ed(s): Mark Huselid. John Wiley & Sons, Inc., 111 River St, Hoboken, NJ 07030; uscs-wis@wiley.com; http://www.wiley.com. Illus., index, adv. Refereed. Vol. ends: Winter. Microform: PQC. Online: EBSCO Publishing; ScienceDirect; Wiley InterScience. Reprint: PQC; PSC. *Indexed:* ABIn, AgeL, BPI, CINAHL, H&SSA, PAIS, SSCI. *Bk. rev.:* 1, 1,500 words. *Aud.:* Ac, Sa.

This is a scholarly HR journal, with articles ranging from theory-testing in academic settings to field/case studies and experiments to overviews of best practices. Topics cover an enormously wide field of all "people management" issues (including occasional special issues on a single topic such as public section HR or international HR), and articles are written in a style applied enough to be of direct use to practitioners. A few substantial book reviews end each issue, usually on a single theme (leadership, conflict resolution, diversity). Recommended for academic collections.

4584. ***Human Resource Planning.*** [ISSN: 0199-8986] 1978. q. USD 90. Ed(s): Beverly Bachtle Pinzon. Human Resource Planning Society, 317 Madison Ave, Ste 1509, New York, NY 10017; info@hrps.org; http://www.hrps.org. Illus., index, adv. Circ: 3000. Vol. ends: No. 4. Online: EBSCO Publishing; Florida Center for Library Automation; Gale Group; Northern Light Technology, Inc.; OCLC Online Computer Library Center, Inc.; ProQuest Information & Learning; H.W. Wilson. *Indexed:* ABIn, BPI. *Bk. rev.:* 2, 1,000 words. *Aud.:* Ac, Sa.

The Human Resource Planning Society is a nonprofit organization of high-level practitioners who "function as business partners in the application of strategic human resource management practices to their organizations." Their publication therefore focuses on planning and management strategy more than the traditional administrative role of HR. The front half of this slim, well-laid-out journal contains short overviews of the "Current Practices" of HR executives and an editorial piece; the second half has three or four articles, mostly by consultants and researchers on decision-making topics such as outsourcing, organizational learning, or flexible organizational design. Recommended for graduate-level academic collections.

4585. ***Human Systems Management.*** [ISSN: 0167-2533] 1980. q. EUR 358. Ed(s): M Zeleny. I O S Press, Nieuwe Hemweg 6B, Amsterdam, 1013 BG, Netherlands; order@iospress.nl; http://www.iospress.nl. Illus., adv. Refereed. Circ: 400. *Indexed:* ABIn, CompLI, EngInd, IPSA, SSCI. *Bk. rev.:* 1-2, 500-1,000 words. *Aud.:* Ac, Sa.

The topic coverage in this journal is so widely inclusive that it's somewhat difficult to categorize at all. In the sense that its mission is to "understand and shape the organizational and managerial impact of high technology" focusing on the human element in business, it is listed here in the HR journals. This title is indexed in technology and social sciences databases, and covers very current, useful, and interesting issues such as workplace use and business applications of instant messaging, corporate web usability, gender bias and job satisfaction in Eastern Europe, value judgments of wealth and environmental sustainability, and analysis of superior/subordinate e-mail communication. College business and technology collections should include this title.

4586. ***Journal of Compensation & Benefits.*** [ISSN: 0893-780X] 1937. bi-m. USD 170. Ed(s): Diane Roberts. Warren, Gorham and Lamont, 395 Hudson St, 4th Fl, New York, NY 10014; http://www.InsideHR.com. Illus. Vol. ends: May/Jun. *Indexed:* ABIn, ATI, AgeL, BPI. *Aud.:* Ac, Sa.

This is a specialized journal for upper-level human resources professionals, focused on management planning and strategy regarding the provision of benefits and compensation (especially executive compensation). Published by the people who bring you Westlaw and other legal reference works, this publication provides reports on current legal and regulatory activity at state and federal levels and article overviews about major topics such as health care benefits, severance planning, wage analysis, and pension plan financing. The journal's web site provides only subscription information (no tables of contents). Recommended for large academic collections.

4587. ***Journal of Human Resources: education, manpower and welfare economics.*** [ISSN: 0022-166X] 1966. q. USD 150 (Individuals, USD 60). University of Wisconsin Press, Journal Division, 1930 Monroe St., 3rd Fl, Madison, WI 53711; journals@uwpress.wisc.edu; http://www.wisc.edu/wisconsinpress/journals. Illus., index, adv. Refereed. Circ: 2300. Vol. ends: Fall. Microform: MIM; PQC. Online: EBSCO Publishing; Florida Center for Library Automation; Gale Group; JSTOR (Web-based Journal Archive); OCLC Online Computer Library Center, Inc.; ProQuest Information & Learning; H.W. Wilson. Reprint: PQC; PSC. *Indexed:* ABIn, ASG, AgeL, CIJE, CINAHL, EngInd, GeogAbPG, H&SSA, HRA, IBSS, IndMed, JEL, MCR, PAIS, PMA, PRA, PSA, RiskAb, SFSA, SSCI, SSI, SWA, SWR&A, SociolAb, WAE&RSA. *Aud.:* Ac.

The *Journal of Human Resources* now states on its web site in bold, black letters that it "publishes academic papers using the best available empirical methods, principally in the field of economics. It is not a management journal." By redefining its focus as "human capital" rather than the traditionally administrative role of "human resources" it wants to make sure that no one mistakes it as a lightweight "how-to-manage" manual. However, its articles on such topics as decision-making on retaking SATs, economic effects of health events on married couples, worker choices about care of elderly parents, or financial wealth inequality do not remove it from the interest of management scholars. Laden with advanced statistics and mathematical models, this journal is recommended for graduate management (and yes, economics) collections.

4588. ***Journal of Managerial Psychology.*** [ISSN: 0268-3946] 1986. 8x/yr. EUR 9043.91 in Europe; USD 8319 in North America; AUD 10229 in Australasia. Ed(s): Yochanan Altman. Emerald, 60-62 Toller Ln, Bradford, BD8 9BY, United Kingdom; info@emeraldinsight.com; http://www.emeraldinsight.com/journals/. Refereed. Online: Pub.; EBSCO Publishing; Florida Center for Library Automation; Gale Group; OCLC Online Computer Library Center, Inc.; ProQuest Information & Learning; RoweCom Information Quest; Swets Blackwell. Reprint: PSC; SWZ. *Indexed:* ABIn, BrEdI, ErgAb, H&SSA, HRA, RiskAb. *Aud.:* Ac, Sa.

This journal is directed at managers and graduate management students who need to round out a technical education in their areas of expertise with a scholarly overview of issues in managing people. Research and case studies explore theoretical issues in human resources (many with a cross-cultural focus), and provide application to working organizations. Recent article topics include faking of personality questionnaire results and whether codes of ethics produce consistent employee behaviors. There are occasional special issues; the most recent include "Beyond Psychometrics" and "The Management of Expatriates." Recommended for academic business libraries.

4589. ***People Management: magazine for professionals in personnel training and development.*** Formed by the merger of (1982-1995): *Training and Development;* (1969-1992): *Personnel Management;* (1985-1995): *Transition;* Which was formerly: *B A C I E Journal.* [ISSN: 1358-6297] 1995. 25x/yr. GBP 88 domestic; GBP 140 in Europe; GBP 155 elsewhere. Permanent Press, 17 Britton St, London, ECIM STP, United Kingdom; http://www.peoplemanagement.co.uk. Illus., adv. *Indexed:* ABIn, BPI, BrHumI, SWA. *Aud.:* Sa.

This is the U.K. version of the glossy U.S. HR-society magazines. News features, columns and cases are aimed at personnel managers, offering "the information, advice, stimulation and support they need in order to contribute effectively to their organization." Half of each biweekly issue is employment ads ("Appointments"). The current issue is available online in full, along with many other electronic information features. This publication is widely indexed and provides a welcome international alternative to the equivalent U.S. magazines. Larger academic libraries should include it in their management collections.

4590. ***Public Personnel Management.*** Formerly (until 1972): *Personnel Administration and Public Personnel Review;* Which was formed by the merger of (1940-1972): *Public Personnel Review;* (1938-1972): *Personnel Administration.* [ISSN: 0091-0260] 1972. q. USD 50; USD 75 foreign. Ed(s): Karen D Smith. International Personnel Management Association, 1617 Duke St, Alexandria, VA 22314; publications@ipma-hr.org; http://www.ipma-hr.org. Illus., index, adv. Refereed. Circ: 7000. Vol. ends: Winter. Microform: MIM; PQC. Online: bigchalk; EBSCO Publishing; Florida Center for Library Automation; Gale Group; Northern Light Technology, Inc.; OCLC Online Computer Library Center, Inc.; ProQuest Information & Learning; H.W. Wilson. Reprint: PQC. *Indexed:* ABCPolSci, ABIn, ATI, AgeL, BPI, BRI, CBRI, CIJE, CINAHL, CJA, PAIS, PMA, PsycholAb, SSCI. *Aud.:* Ac, Sa.

This is a traditional-looking academic journal whose audience is primarily personnel managers in the public sector. The contents are mostly review articles and cases written by both practitioners and academics, with some empirical studies. There are 9-10 articles each quarter on a very wide range of HR topics; articles do not tend to have a narrow public administration focus, so libraries beyond those with MPA programs may want to consider subscribing to this intelligent (and inexpensive) publication.

4591. ***Supervision: the magazine of industrial relations and operating management.*** Supersedes: *Foreman.* [ISSN: 0039-5854] 1939. m. USD 61 domestic. Ed(s): Nancy Heinzel, Teresa Levinson. National Research Bureau, 320 Valley St, Burlington, IA 52601-5513. Index, adv. Circ: 1500 Paid. Vol. ends: Dec. Microform: PQC. Online: bigchalk; EBSCO

Publishing; Florida Center for Library Automation; Gale Group; Northern Light Technology, Inc.; OCLC Online Computer Library Center, Inc.; ProQuest Information & Learning; H.W. Wilson. Reprint: PQC. *Indexed:* ABIn, AgeL, BPI, ExcerpMed. *Aud.:* Ac, Sa.

Written to a wide audience of practicing managers and supervisors, this magazine presents five or six articles written by management professionals and, in some cases, academicians. The articles contain hands-on solutions to problems faced by supervisors everyday. Examples of recent topics covered include creative supervision, the importance of attitude in becoming a successful manager, and the incorporation of systemic thinking in managerial practice. The magazine's mission is to help supervisors reach goals and objectives and strengthen management skills.

4592. ***T plus D.*** Former titles (until 2001): *Training and Development;* (until 1991): *Training and Development Journal.* [ISSN: 1535-7740] 1945. m. Members, USD 60; Non-members, USD 85. Ed(s): Patricia A Galagan. American Society for Training & Development, 1640 King St, Box 1443, Alexandria, VA 22313; http://www.astd.org. Illus., index, adv. Refereed. Circ: 50000. Vol. ends: Dec. Microform: PQC. Online: EBSCO Publishing; Florida Center for Library Automation; Gale Group; OCLC Online Computer Library Center, Inc.; ProQuest Information & Learning; H.W. Wilson. Reprint: PQC. *Indexed:* ABIn, AgeL, BPI, CIJE, CWI, PMA, PsycholAb, SSCI. *Bk. rev.:* 2-8, 250-1,000 words. *Aud.:* Ac, Sa.

A hipper new name (*T+D* was *Training and Development* before its makeover) and the subtitle "Better Performance through Workplace Learning" reflect this magazine's efforts to remain fresh and relevant after 50 years of publication and to appeal to a new generation of managers. Though still commercial, content does outweigh advertising and illustrations, and articles are long enough to effectively report on and analyze current trends (e-learning, leadership, change management) in some depth. The American Society for Training and Development web site offers additional electronic content to subscribing members. Highly recommended as an undergraduate academic library resource.

4593. ***Training: the magazine covering the human side of business.*** Formerly: *Training in Business and Industry.* [ISSN: 0095-5892] 1964. m. USD 78 domestic; USD 88 Canada; USD 154 elsewhere. Ed(s): Tammy Galvin. V N U Business Publications, 50 S Ninth St, Minneapolis, MN 55402; bmcomm@vnuinc.com; http://www.vnubusinessmedia.com/. Illus., index, adv. Circ: 54385. Vol. ends: Dec. Microform: PQC. Online: EBSCO Publishing; Florida Center for Library Automation; Gale Group; Human Resources Information Network; OCLC Online Computer Library Center, Inc.; ProQuest Information & Learning; H.W. Wilson. Reprint: PQC. *Indexed:* ABIn, AgeL, BPI, CIJE, SFSA. *Bk. rev.:* 1-3, 750 words. *Aud.:* Sa.

There might be more graphics and advertising in this glossy magazine than there is text, but *Training* is a title for HR collections due to its wide circulation in corporate training departments and its inclusion in most basic business indexes; its annual "Top 100" issue ranking "organizations that excel at human capital development" is also influential. There are short, well-written news reports and features about current trends and issues in employee training, discussions of best practices, company profiles and surveys, and short book reviews with a quick, thermometer-like "don't bother, borrow, buy" scale. The magazine's web site provides additional content for subscribers.

4594. ***Workforce (Costa Mesa): H R trends & tools for business results.*** Former titles (until 1997): *Personnel Journal;* (until 1927): *Journal of Personnel Research.* [ISSN: 1092-8332] 1922. m. USD 59 domestic; USD 99 Canada; USD 169 elsewhere. Ed(s): Carroll Lachnit. Crain Communications, Inc., 245 Fischer Ave B-2, Costa Mesa, CA 92626; http://www.crain.com. Illus., index, adv. Circ: 30000 Paid. Vol. ends: Dec. Online: EBSCO Publishing; Florida Center for Library Automation; Gale Group; OCLC Online Computer Library Center, Inc.; ProQuest Information & Learning; H.W. Wilson. Reprint: PQC; PSC. *Indexed:* ABIn, ASG, AgeL, BLI, BPI, BRI, CBRI, CIJE, CompLI, ExcerpMed, PAIS, PMA, PsycholAb, SSCI. *Aud.:* Sa.

Another glossy and graphic HR monthly that is tightly integrated with an equally glossy and graphic web site. Its subtitle, "HR Trends & Tools for Business Results," pretty much describes the outcome-focused content—normative, newsy, focused on new trends, with lots of company and executive profiles and a "Dear Workforce" advice column. Its popular format does not contain bland content, with interesting critical analysis and articles on topics such as the pros and cons of chasing "best companies" lists, the lessons learned from pro baseball, and employee attitude as a selection criterion. Definitely recommended for college collections supporting human resources programs.

Management Education

4595. ***Academy of Management Learning and Education.*** [ISSN: 1537-260X] 2002. 4x/yr. USD 110 (Corporations, USD 150). Academy of Management, 235 Elm Rd, Box 3020, Briarcliff Manor, NY 10510-3020; academy@pace.edu; http://www.aomonline.org. Refereed. Online: EBSCO Publishing. *Aud.:* Ac, Sa.

The newest journal from the Academy of Management, this publication focuses on learning and teaching in both higher education and in corporate training settings. It includes articles in an appealing range of styles—its first issues each included 2-3 scholarly articles (both theoretical and experimental) and essays and interviews on current topics such as "9-11 and Management Education" and "The Darker Side of Power in the Office of the Dean." Rounding out each issue are "Exemplary Contributions," invited articles by distinguished scholars and practitioners, and "Resource Reviews," a section of 4-5 assigned reviews of books and other material (the editors plan to review teaching resources in all media, including videos, computer simulations, and class exercises).

4596. ***Journal of Management Education.*** Former titles (until 1977): *Organizational Behavior Teaching Review; Exchange - The Organizational Behavior Teaching Journal; Teaching Organization Behavior; Teaching of Organization Behavior.* [ISSN: 1052-5629] 1975. bi-m. USD 373 print & online eds. Ed(s): Dale E Fitzgibbons. Sage Publications, Inc., 2455 Teller Rd, Thousand Oaks, CA 91320; info@sagepub.com; http://www.sagepub.com. Illus., adv. Refereed. Circ: 1750. Vol. ends: Nov (No. 4). Reprint: SCH. *Indexed:* HRA, PMA. *Aud.:* Ac.

The *Journal of Management Education* is a forum for educators to share ideas and strategies for teaching management classes, offering specific exercises and assignments along with broader discussions about such issues as gender and cultural stereotyping in the classroom and the benefits and disadvantages of group work. Both theories and applied experiences with teaching tools such as case methods, role-playing, and writing to learn are included, with occasional thematic issues such as teaching about the natural environment and business. Academic libraries at institutions interested developing faculty teaching should subscribe.

4597. ***Management Learning: journal for managerial and organizational learning.*** Incorporates (in 1994): *Management Education and Development.* [ISSN: 1350-5076] 1994. q. GBP 370 print & online eds. in Europe, Middle East, Africa & Australasia. Ed(s): Christopher Grey, Elena Antonacopoulou. Sage Publications Ltd., 6 Bonhill St, London, EC2A 4PU, United Kingdom; info@sagepub.co.uk; http://www.sagepub.co.uk/. Adv. Online: ingenta.com; OCLC Online Computer Library Center, Inc.; ProQuest Information & Learning; RoweCom Information Quest; Swets Blackwell. *Indexed:* ABIn, BrEdI, CIJE, HRA, PsycholAb, SSCI. *Bk. rev.:* 4-6, about 2,000 words. *Aud.:* Ac.

This is an academic journal that is not only about students and teachers in business schools, but also about how learning takes place within organizations. Articles about intergenerational learning among workers and management storytelling are provided alongside those discussing classroom mistrust and the use of critical dialog in MBA programs. Each issue also contains several substantial book reviews. Tables of contents and abstracts are available at the journal web site. Recommended for academic libraries supporting MBA programs and for corporate training libraries.

Operations Research and Management Science

This discipline focuses on using computational models to analyze and improve management decision-making. Academic researchers and practitioners all use a high level of statistical and programming skills to work in this area, so the literature of the field is more often than not mathematically dense.

4598. ***Decision Sciences.*** [ISSN: 0011-7315] 1970. q. USD 255 print & online eds. Ed(s): Ram Naraasimhan. Blackwell Publishing, Inc., Commerce Place, 350 Main St, Malden, MA 02148; subscrip@ blackwellpub.com; http://www.blackwellpublishing.com. Illus., adv. Refereed. Circ: 4000. Vol. ends: Fall. Microform: PQC. Online: ingenta.com; Northern Light Technology, Inc.; ProQuest Information & Learning. *Indexed:* ABIn, ATI, BPI, ExcerpMed, SSCI. *Aud.:* Ac, Sa.

Despite its broad title, this is not a publication on the general science of how people make decisions, but a very applied research journal looking at decision points and processes in business operations and supply chains. Using statistical analyses and computer models, academic researchers address specific problems in service and manufacturing organizations. There are 6-8 articles each quarter, with an occasional special issue (the most recent is "e-Business and Supply Chain Management"). Recommended for academic collections.

4599. ***Interfaces (Linthicum).*** Formerly: *Institute of Management Sciences Bulletin.* [ISSN: 0092-2102] 1971. bi-m. USD 214 print & online eds. (Individuals, USD 164 print & online eds.). Ed(s): Terry P Harrison. I N F O R M S, 901 Elkridge Landing Rd., Ste. 400, Linthicum, MD 21090-2909; informs@informs.org; http://www.informs.org. Illus., index, adv. Sample. Refereed. Circ: 4000 Paid and controlled. Microform: PQC. Online: EBSCO Publishing; JSTOR (Web-based Journal Archive); ProQuest Information & Learning. Reprint: PQC. *Indexed:* ABIn, AS&TI, AgeL, BPI, CompR, ErgAb, ExcerpMed, IBSS, LT&LA, PMA, PsycholAb, SSCI. *Bk. rev.:* 2-4, signed, essay length. *Aud.:* Ac, Sa.

Interfaces is case-based, with 6-8 articles each issue written by managers, consultants, and academics reporting on the results of the implementation of new decision and operations models within a specific industry or organization. Along with these very readable and straightforward application studies, there are usually "Practice Abstracts" (much shorter reports of these same types of projects) and several substantial book reviews, as well as a list of received books that were not reviewed. Highly recommended for all academic business collections.

4600. ***Journal of Operations Management.*** [ISSN: 0272-6963] 1980. bi-m. EUR 436 (Individuals, EUR 57). Ed(s): R. B. Handfield. Elsevier BV, Sara Burgerhartstraat 25, Amsterdam, 1055 KV, Netherlands; nlinfo-f@ elsevier.nl; http://www.elsevier.nl. Illus., index, adv. Sample. Refereed. Circ: 1000. Vol. ends: Nov. Microform: PQC. Online: Gale Group; ingenta.com; ScienceDirect; Swets Blackwell. Reprint: SWZ. *Indexed:* ABIn, C&ISA, EngInd, RiskAb. *Aud.:* Ac, Sa.

Every component in the management of business operations is open for examination in this journal—scheduling, procurement, process and product design, human factors, productivity assessment, purchasing, and many, many more. The one unifying theme for these topics is that they are all examined using the rigorous analytical methods of operations management research. However, even without complete mastery of the computations, students and practitioners will find the theories, concepts, and discussions of each article topic to be understandable. Each journal issue typically contains 5-6 long research articles (15-20 pages). Recommended for academic libraries.

4601. ***Management Science.*** Incorporates: *Management Technology: Monograph of the Institute of Management Science.* [ISSN: 0025-1909] 1954. m. USD 488 print & online eds. (Individuals, USD 185 print & online eds.). Ed(s): Wally Hopp. I N F O R M S, 901 Elkridge Landing Rd., Ste. 400, Linthicum, MD 21090-2909; informs@informs.org; http://www.informs.org. Illus., index, adv. Refereed. Circ: 4000 Paid and controlled. Vol. ends: Dec. Online: EBSCO Publishing; ProQuest Information & Learning. *Indexed:* ABIn, ATI, AgeL, ArtHuCI, BPI, C&ISA, CJA, EngInd, IAA, IBSS, SSCI. *Aud.:* Ac, Sa.

This journal pulls theory-based mathematical models from a diverse range of fields within and beyond the traditional scope of business scholarship—psychology, engineering, economics, accounting, political science—to analyze organizational and operational problems of interest to managers. All business activities are (or could be) addressed by *Management Science* articles; a sample of topics includes pricing of online information products, examination of investor decision-making, inventory control of spare parts, and the effects of replacing members of a team. This is an important journal for academic collections.

4602. ***Managerial and Decision Economics: the international journal of research and progress in management economics.*** [ISSN: 0143-6570] 1980. 8x/yr. USD 1285. John Wiley & Sons Ltd., The Atrium, Southern Gate, Chichester, PO19 8SQ, United Kingdom; customer@wiley.co.uk; http://www.wiley.co.uk. Illus., adv. Refereed. Circ: 700. Microform: PQC. Online: EBSCO Publishing; Gale Group; JSTOR (Web-based Journal Archive); ScienceDirect; Swets Blackwell; Wiley InterScience. Reprint: SWZ. *Indexed:* ABIn, IBSS, JEL, PAIS, RiskAb, ST&MA. *Bk. rev.:* 2-3 about 2,000 words. *Aud.:* Ac, Sa.

This is listed as a management title rather than an economics title because of its applied focus on research "useful for managerial decision-making and management strategy." Economic theory is used to examine an incredibly wide range of organizational topics—for instance, in one issue alone, article topics included economic analyses of the use of student evaluations in universities, the profitability of banks in Shanghai, and demand for game-day attendance in college football. There are frequent special issues focusing on topical areas ("Research Alliances and Collaborations") or particular industries (real estate, casino gambling, sports). Highly recommended for management and economics collections.

4603. ***Omega: international journal of management science.*** [ISSN: 0305-0483] 1973. bi-m. EUR 936. Ed(s): L M Seiford. Pergamon, The Boulevard, Langford Ln, East Park, Kidlington, OX5 1GB, United Kingdom. Illus., index, adv. Refereed. Circ: 1400. Vol. ends: Dec (No. 29). Microform: PQC. Online: Florida Center for Library Automation; Gale Group; ingenta.com; ScienceDirect; Swets Blackwell. *Indexed:* ABIn, ApMecR, CIJE, CJA, EngInd, ExcerpMed, GeogAbPG, IMFL, SSCI. *Aud.:* Ac, Sa.

Omega offers research articles of a highly mathematical nature that review and assess both cutting-edge and traditional management science models and theories, or analyze applications of management techniques in specific settings (manufacturing, service, and educational organizations are all included in its coverage). Longer research articles are supplemented by shorter pieces of review and correspondence. This is a very scholarly journal that is recommended to support graduate management education.

4604. ***Operational Research Society. Journal.*** Formerly (until vol.29, 1978): *Operational Research Quarterly.* [ISSN: 0160-5682] 1950. m. GBP 714 print & online. Ed(s): John Wilson, Terry Williams. Palgrave Macmillan Ltd., Houndmills, Basingstoke, RG21 6XS, United Kingdom; http://www.palgrave.com. Illus., index, adv. Refereed. Vol. ends: Dec. Online: EBSCO Publishing; Gale Group; ingenta.com; JSTOR (Web-based Journal Archive); OCLC Online Computer Library Center, Inc.; RoweCom Information Quest; Swets Blackwell. *Indexed:* ABIn, AgeL, ApMecR, BPI, C&ISA, CJA, EngInd, ExcerpMed, GeoRef, RRTA, RiskAb, SCI, SSCI, ST&MA, WAE&RSA. *Bk. rev.:* 4-6, 300-500 words. *Aud.:* Ac, Sa.

Publishes scholarly articles in the field of operations research. Each issue contains case-oriented papers, theoretical papers (often based on mathematical models), and comments from readers. The journal encourages papers illustrating applications of operations research to real problems. Papers cover a wide range of topics including bus routing, assembly lines, and assigning pupils to schools. A description of the journal, subscription information, and the contents page of the forthcoming issue are available at the publisher's web site.

4605. ***Production and Operations Management.*** [ISSN: 1059-1478] 1992. q. USD 200 (Individuals, USD 70; USD 210 foreign). Ed(s): Kalyan Singhal. Production and Operations Management Society, College of Engineering, Florida International University, Miami, FL 33174; poms@fiu.edu; http://www.poms.org. Illus., adv. Refereed. Circ: 1200 Paid. Vol. ends: Winter. *Indexed:* ABIn. *Aud.:* Ac, Sa.

This is the journal of the Production and Operations Management Society. The operations management research presented in this journal has a decided focus on manufacturing industries. Academics and managers who are interested in the production of physical products (from the management of scheduling and material supply to manufacturing technology to issues of quality and service) are the intended audience for this scholarly journal. There is a healthy mix of applied and theoretical research and reviews of current topics in the field. The society's web site has not updated issue tables of contents since 1998. Recommended for academic collections, particularly those that support graduate business and industrial engineering studies.

Organizational Behavior and Studies

The journals listed here provide more primary scholarly research than the typical titles in the Human Resources subsection. These publications involve theory development and testing, program and test development and evaluation, and systematic problem solving in the personnel and organizational arena of business and industry.

4606. *The International Journal of Organizational Analysis.* [ISSN: 1055-3185] 1993. q. USD 185 (Individuals, USD 80; Students, USD 55). Ed(s): M. Afzalur Rahim. Information Age Publishing, Inc., 80 Mason St., PO Box 4967, Greenwich, CT 06830; order@infoagepub.com; http://www.infoagepub.com. Illus., index, adv. Sample. Refereed. Vol. ends: Oct. *Indexed:* ABIn, IBSS, RiskAb, SociolAb. *Bk. rev.:* 0-2, 750-1,000 words. *Aud.:* Ac, Sa.

The 3-4 scholarly articles in each quarterly issue of this publication are indexed in most of the important management/social science databases and cover many original topics of interest to students and researchers in organizational studies. Recent articles study comparisons of entrepreneurs and managers, the willingness of CEOs to delegate, and the role of self-fulfilling prophecy in organizational decline. There are also a variety of case studies, teaching simulations and exercises, and book reviews throughout the year. The journal has no web presence to speak of. Recommended for academic collections.

4607. *Journal of Applied Behavioral Science.* [ISSN: 0021-8863] 1965. q. USD 493 print & online eds. Ed(s): Clayton Alderfer. Sage Publications, Inc., 2455 Teller Rd, Thousand Oaks, CA 91320; info@sagepub.com; http://www.sagepub.com. Illus., index, adv. Refereed. Circ: 2800. Vol. ends: Nov. *Indexed:* ABCPolSci, ABIn, ABS&EES, AgeL, ErgAb, HRA, IPSA, PSA, PsycholAb, SFSA, SSCI, SSI, SWA, SWR&A, SociolAb. *Aud.:* Ac, Sa.

This is the journal of the nonprofit NTL Institute, providing research papers, case studies, review articles/essays, and biographical sketches focused on interpersonal relationships and how people and organizations manage and adapt to change. The scholarly articles are peer reviewed and provide empirical research on topics such as gender and race in the workplace, organizational learning, and interorganizational collaboration. Recommended for larger academic collections.

4608. *Journal of Organizational Behaviour.* Formerly (until 1988): *Journal of Occupational Behaviour.* [ISSN: 0894-3796] 1979. 8x/yr. USD 1495. Ed(s): Denise M Rousseau. John Wiley & Sons Ltd., The Atrium, Southern Gate, Chichester, PO19 8SQ, United Kingdom; customer@wiley.co.uk; http://www.wiley.co.uk. Illus., adv. Refereed. Microform: PQC. Online: EBSCO Publishing; Gale Group; JSTOR (Web-based Journal Archive); ScienceDirect; Swets Blackwell; Wiley InterScience. Reprint: ISI; PQC; SWZ. *Indexed:* ABIn, ASSIA, AgeL, CJA, CommAb, ErgAb, HRA, IBZ, PRA, PsycholAb, RiskAb, SFSA, SSCI, SWA. *Bk. rev.:* Occasional. *Aud.:* Ac, Sa.

Articles in this journal report scholarly research and theory testing in all facets of managing humans in organizations. The coverage listed in their "aims and scope" says it all: "motivation, work performance, equal opportunities at work, job design, career processes, occupational stress, quality of work life, job satisfaction, personnel selection, training, organizational change, research methodology in occupational/organizational behavior, employment, job analysis, behavioral aspects of industrial relations, managerial behavior, organizational structure and climate, leadership and power." The research studies are accompanied by opinion pieces, a new "Incubator" section for the presentation of new theory exploration or research attempts, and occasional book reviews. This is another core title in management psychology and should be held by any academic library supporting the discipline.

4609. *Journal of Organizational Excellence.* Incorporates (19??-2003): *Competitive Intelligence Review;* Which was formerly (until 1990): *Competitive Intelligencer;* Formerly (until 2000): *National Productivity Review.* [ISSN: 1531-1864] 1981. q. USD 465 in North America; USD 489 elsewhere; USD 512 combined subscription in North America for print and online eds. Ed(s): Jo-Ann Wasserman. John Wiley & Sons, Inc., 111 River St, Hoboken, NJ 07030; uscs-wis@wiley.com; http://www.wiley.com. Illus., adv. Vol. ends: Fall. Microform: PQC. Online: Gale Group; Northern Light Technology, Inc.; OCLC Online Computer Library Center, Inc.; ProQuest Information & Learning; ScienceDirect; Wiley InterScience. Reprint: PQC; PSC. *Indexed:* ABIn, BPI, PAIS. *Bk. rev.:* 8-10 300-500 words. *Aud.:* Ac, Sa.

The buzzword-y title should tip you off that this journal is aimed at executives and consultants looking for tools and strategies to most effectively manage their "human capital" for organizational success. The publication very effectively carries out its applied mission—its descriptive/prescriptive articles provide overviews and corporate case studies about topics such as post-9/11 workplace values, using time as an employee benefit, and performance benefits of worker understanding of company pay processes. There are also book reviews and short surveys of current articles written in the field. Recommended for academic business collections.

4610. *Organization: the interdisciplinary journal of organization, theory and society.* [ISSN: 1350-5084] 1994. bi-m. GBP 490 in Europe, Middle East, Africa & Australasia. Ed(s): Gibson Burrell, Marta Calas. Sage Publications Ltd., 6 Bonhill St, London, EC2A 4PU, United Kingdom; info@sagepub.co.uk; http://www.sagepub.co.uk/. Adv. Refereed. Circ: 1100. Online: EBSCO Publishing; ingenta.com; OCLC Online Computer Library Center, Inc.; RoweCom Information Quest; Swets Blackwell. *Indexed:* CommAb, HRA, IBSS, IPSA, PSA, SSCI, SWA, SociolAb. *Aud.:* Ac, Sa.

The articles in this publication tend to be very reflective (even philosophical) analyses of management theory and current organizational thought—the editors speak of the journal's "ethos," not its mission or scope. This atypical approach toward writing about organizational theory and behavior provides students with a broader way of thinking about their research topics. Examples of recent article themes include spirituality in organizations, ethics involving research subjects, effects of media coverage of mergers and acquisitions, and multiple analyses of the implications of the failure of Enron. Recommended for larger academic collections.

4611. *Organization Science.* [ISSN: 1047-7039] 1990. q. USD 221 (Individuals, USD 188). Ed(s): Claudia Bird Schoonhoven. I N F O R M S, 901 Elkridge Landing Rd., Ste. 400, Linthicum, MD 21090-2909; informs@informs.org; http://www.informs.org. Illus., adv. Refereed. Circ: 1900. Vol. ends: Nov/Dec. Online: EBSCO Publishing; JSTOR (Web-based Journal Archive); ProQuest Information & Learning. *Indexed:* ABIn, IBSS, PsycholAb, SSCI. *Aud.:* Ac.

As implied by the title, this scholarly journal falls among those using empirical studies (and the occasional case history) to look at organizational functions. Authors from throughout the social sciences and management provide 5-7 long articles in each issue primarily examining work systems, with a strong focus on learning and information and communication processes. Special issues over the last few years include "Knowledge, Knowing, and Organizations," "Trust in an Organizational Context," and "Communication Processes for Virtual Organizations." Recommended for academic collections—its interdisciplinary nature does not limit it to business libraries.

4612. *Organization Studies.* [ISSN: 0170-8406] 9x/m. GBP 490 print & online eds. in Europe, Middle East, Africa & Australasia. Ed(s): David C Wilson, Hari Tsoukas. Sage Publications Ltd., 6 Bonhill St, London, EC2A 4PU, United Kingdom; info@sagepub.co.uk; http://www.sagepub.co.uk/. Illus., adv. Refereed. Circ: 1900 Paid and controlled. Vol. ends: No. 6. Online: EBSCO Publishing; Florida Center for Library Automation; Gale Group; ingenta.com; Northern Light

Technology, Inc.; OCLC Online Computer Library Center, Inc.; ProQuest Information & Learning; Swets Blackwell. Reprint: PSC; SCH. *Indexed:* ABIn, BAS, CINAHL, IBSS, IPSA, PSA, PsycholAb, RiskAb, SSCI, SociolAb. *Bk. rev.:* 3-10, 150-900 words. *Aud.:* Ac, Sa.

This journal is an excellent model of what we say scholarly publications are supposed to do—provide educated conversation among scholars in the discipline. One of the most international titles in this field, *Organization Studies* publishes primary research articles, shorter "Research Notes" providing preliminary findings or research ideas not fully formed into a study, and a section called "Essais," which gives authors a forum for debating theories and methods. There are also a number of long book reviews and shorter "Book Notes" in each issue. Coverage is especially strong in the study of cultural similarities and differences. Highly recommended for libraries supporting graduate programs in applied social sciences.

4613. ***Organizational Dynamics.*** [ISSN: 0090-2616] 1972. q. EUR 149 (Individuals, EUR 154). Ed(s): Fred Luthans. Pergamon, The Boulevard, Langford Ln, East Park, Kidlington, OX5 1GB, United Kingdom. Illus., index. Circ: 4000. Vol. ends: Spring. Microform: PQC. Online: EBSCO Publishing; Florida Center for Library Automation; Gale Group; ingenta.com; Northern Light Technology, Inc.; OCLC Online Computer Library Center, Inc.; RoweCom Information Quest; ScienceDirect; Swets Blackwell; H.W. Wilson. *Indexed:* ABIn, AgeL, BPI, PMA, PsycholAb, SSCI. *Bk. rev.:* 2-6, 700-900 words. *Aud.:* Ac, Sa.

The journal is relatively thin compared to many others in the category, but a typical issue has seven substantial scholarly articles—recent topics include effects of technology on HR, improving conversations within organizations, management of processes such as leadership and mentoring in a virtual environment, and work-life balance. It presents empirical research mixed with case studies, theoretical overviews, and interviews. Professional managers are the primary audience, and the articles provided are appropriately balanced among inquiry, overviews, and applications. Highly recommended for undergraduate and graduate collections.

4614. ***Organizational Research Methods.*** [ISSN: 1094-4281] 1998. q. GBP 413 print & online eds. in Europe, Middle East, Africa & Australasia. Ed(s): Larry Williams. Sage Publications, Inc., 2455 Teller Rd, Thousand Oaks, CA 91320; info@sagepub.com; http://www.sagepub.com. *Indexed:* HRA, IBZ, RiskAb, SociolAb. *Bk. rev.:* Number and length vary. *Aud.:* Ac, Sa.

This Academy of Management publication assumes an understanding of management/organizational psychology research methods at a doctoral level, so it is recommended only for libraries with doctoral programs or a substantial research faculty in these fields. Each issue's 4-5 articles compare existing quantitative and qualitative methods and research designs currently used by organizational researchers, discuss the development of new methods, or introduce tests and measures from other disciplines to the management field. The journal also includes essays and reviews on methods, point/counterpoint debates, measurement evaluations, a "teacher's corner," and book and computer software reviews.

4615. ***Personnel Psychology.*** [ISSN: 0031-5826] 1948. q. USD 70 domestic; USD 79.50 foreign. Ed(s): John R Hollenbeck. Personnel Psychology, Inc., 520 Ordway Ave, Bowling Green, OH 43402-2756; ppsych@personnelpsychology.com. Illus., index, adv. Sample. Refereed. Circ: 2800. Vol. ends: Winter. Microform: PQC. Online: EBSCO Publishing; Florida Center for Library Automation; Gale Group; Northern Light Technology, Inc.; OCLC Online Computer Library Center, Inc.; ProQuest Information & Learning; H.W. Wilson. *Indexed:* ABIn, AgeL, BPI, BRI, CBRI, CIJE, CommAb, PMA, PsycholAb, RiskAb, SSCI. *Bk. rev.:* 15-20, 1,000-1,500 words. *Aud.:* Ac, Sa.

Personnel Psychology is a core scholarly journal in this field; every academic library whose schools offer management and applied psychology classes should subscribe. It is empirical, with each issue offering six or seven studies examining variables in workplace selection, performance, and evaluation. Recent topics include validation of 360-degree feedback systems, use of biodata, and development of a measure for core self-evaluation. After the research articles, there is a "Scientist-Practitioner Forum" piece focused on addressing a problem or issue facing personnel practitioners (such as putting personnel surveys on the web or use of a specific job-analysis model). The journal is one of the best library collection development tools in this discipline—each issue also has a book review section in the back where 15-20 books receive substantial reviews, followed by a list of unreviewed material received by their editorial office.

Strategic Analysis

These journals cover a specific managerial process involving both industry research and the study of changes in organizational strategies for competitive advantage.

4616. ***Business Strategy and the Environment.*** Incorporates: *Greening of Industry Newsletter.* [ISSN: 0964-4733] 1992. bi-m. USD 845. John Wiley & Sons Ltd., The Atrium, Southern Gate, Chichester, PO19 8SQ, United Kingdom; customer@wiley.co.uk; http://www.wiley.co.uk. Illus., adv. Refereed. Vol. ends: Dec. *Indexed:* EnvAb, PollutAb. *Bk. rev.:* Signed, number and length vary. *Aud.:* Ac, Sa.

This scholarly journal is concerned with both the business environment and the earth's environment—the focus of the technical research articles and shorter research reports called "BSE Briefings" is on how organizations can make better strategic decisions about the environmental impacts and regulations surrounding their businesses. There are occasional special issues (most about aspects of sustainability), and issues often have book reviews and lists of books and publications received. Recommended for academic business and environmental collections.

4617. ***Business Strategy Review.*** [ISSN: 0955-6419] 1990. q. GBP 140 print & online eds. Ed(s): Paul Willman, Patrick Barwise. Blackwell Publishing Ltd., 9600 Garsington Rd, PO Box 805, Oxford, OX4 2DQ, United Kingdom; jnlinfo@blackwellpublishers.co.uk; http://www.blackwellpublishing.com/. Circ: 1200. Online: EBSCO Publishing; Florida Center for Library Automation; Gale Group; ingenta.com; OCLC Online Computer Library Center, Inc.; RoweCom Information Quest; Swets Blackwell. Reprint: PSC. *Indexed:* ABIn. *Bk. rev.:* Several books on a theme are reviewed together in a signed article. *Aud.:* Ac, Sa.

Business Strategy Review (*BSR*) is sponsored by the London Business School, and it offers a global view on current business decision-making. There are articles reporting academic research (on topics such as "transformational outsourcing" or business-to-business e-commerce) and consultant pieces on executive coaching, corporate blogs, or how to work with Americans. All the pieces are written in a very accessible style. Issues also include case studies, company histories, interviews, and often a set of book reviews around a single theme. Highly recommended.

4618. ***Journal of Business Strategy.*** Incorporates (1975-1995): *Small Business Reports;* Incorporates (1989-1994): *Journal of European Business;* Which incorporated (1990-1991): *Journal of Pricing Management.* [ISSN: 0275-6668] 1980. bi-m. EUR 205.54 in Europe; USD 199 in North America; AUD 339 in Australasia. Ed(s): Paul Wood, Nanci Healy. Emerald, 60-62 Toller Ln, Bradford, BD8 9BY, United Kingdom; info@emeraldinsight.com; http://www.emeraldinsight.com/journals/. Illus. Vol. ends: Dec. Microform: PQC. Online: EBSCO Publishing; Factiva; Florida Center for Library Automation; Gale Group; LexisNexis; Northern Light Technology, Inc.; OCLC Online Computer Library Center, Inc.; ProQuest Information & Learning. Reprint: PQC; SCH. *Indexed:* ABIn, ABS&EES, BPI, LRI, LogistBibl, PAIS, SUSA. *Bk. rev.:* 5-7 mid-length. *Aud.:* Ac, Sa.

The glossy-covered magazine version of this journal has now passed into the hands of Emerald, which plans a makeover to bring the look in line with its other management publications (see *Strategy & Leadership* below in this section). The content continues to be short (3-4 page) descriptive/prescriptive pieces that direct advice and analysis at managers in all phases of business operations. The earlier version of the magazine was a welcome information source for undergraduate papers and presentations—the new version will probably be similarly useful.

4619. *Long Range Planning.* [ISSN: 0024-6301] 1968. bi-m. EUR 1203 (Individuals, EUR 177). Ed(s): C. Baden-Fuller. Pergamon, The Boulevard, Langford Ln, East Park, Kidlington, OX5 1GB, United Kingdom. Illus., index, adv. Refereed. Circ: 4700. Vol. ends: Dec. Microform: MIM; PQC. Online: ingenta.com; ScienceDirect; Swets Blackwell. *Indexed:* ABIn, AIAP, AgeL, BPI, EngInd, EnvAb, ExcerpMed, FutSurv, PAIS, SSCI, SUSA. *Bk. rev.:* 4-7, 400-2,000 words. *Aud.:* Ac, Sa.

The focus here is on management goal setting and planning, with topics such as risk management, emerging markets, and supply forecasting. Executive summaries are provided for the several scholarly research articles in each issue, and there are usually 3-4 longer book reviews followed by several pages of very short abstracts of books on business strategy. This title is quite expensive; recommend purchase only if demand from its inclusion in most business/management indexes calls for a subscription in your library.

4620. *Strategic Change.* Formerly (until 1996): *Journal of Strategic Change.* [ISSN: 1086-1718] 1992. 8x/yr. USD 595. Ed(s): David E Hussey. John Wiley & Sons Ltd., The Atrium, Southern Gate, Chichester, PO19 8SQ, United Kingdom; customer@wiley.co.uk; http://www.wiley.co.uk. Illus., adv. Refereed. Circ: 450. Vol. ends: Nov/Dec. Microform: PQC. Online: EBSCO Publishing; ScienceDirect; Wiley InterScience. Reprint: SWZ. *Bk. rev.:* 3, 300-400 words. *Aud.:* Ac, Sa.

A thin journal with 4-5 articles in each of its eight yearly issues, *Strategic Change* offers a scholarly, yet applied, view of the management of change in corporations and their operating environment. The article coverage is very well selected, with topical research articles (outsourcing, technological innovation, the impact of change on workers) and case studies with an international orientation (airlines, ambulance services, London taxicabs, pub franchises). This is an important topic handled very well, and the journal is recommended for academic business collections.

4621. *Strategic Management Journal.* [ISSN: 0143-2095] 1979. 13x/yr. USD 1425. Ed(s): Dan Schendel. John Wiley & Sons Ltd., The Atrium, Southern Gate, Chichester, PO19 8SQ, United Kingdom; customer@wiley.co.uk; http://www.wiley.co.uk. Illus., index, adv. Refereed. Circ: 4000. Vol. ends: Dec. Microform: PQC. Online: EBSCO Publishing; Wiley InterScience. Reprint: ISI; PQC; PSC; SWZ. *Indexed:* ABIn, ArtHuCI, BAS, BPI, EngInd, IBSS, SSCI. *Aud.:* Ac, Sa.

Skimming the articles of several issues of this journal is like following an ongoing high-level discussion among academics and practitioners in strategic management. There are presentations of scholarly research and shorter "research notes" hitting the highlights of other studies, interspersed with some commentary and editorial opinion. The topics, though treated in a very scholarly manner, are usually practical in nature ("increasing firm value through detection and prevention of white-collar crime" or "proactive environmental strategies". Recommended for academic collections supporting graduate business programs.

4622. *Strategy + Business.* [ISSN: 1083-706X] 1995. q. USD 38 domestic; USD 48 foreign; USD 12.95 newsstand/cover per issue domestic. Ed(s): Randall Rothenberg. Booz, Allen & Hamilton, Inc., 101 Park Ave, New York, NY 10178. Adv. Circ: 105870 Paid and controlled. *Indexed:* C&ISA, LogistBibl. *Aud.:* Ga, Sa.

This striking-looking magazine (and its equally well-designed web site) provides information about trends and innovations in strategic management. The heavily illustrated contents include reports of academic research studies, interviews with top managers, case studies and personal narratives, news articles, and many essays/reviews about business books. The publisher is Booz Allen Hamilton, a major management consulting firm, but contributors come from throughout the business and scholarly world. Although aimed at executives, the topic coverage would be of interest to business students or investors. Free registration at the magazine's web site provides access to the text or pdf files of most of the magazine pages published since 1995; print subscriptions are also available.

4623. *Strategy & Leadership.* Incorporates (1996-2001): *The Antidote;* Formerly (until 1996): *Planning Review;* Which superseded (in 1985): *Managerial Planning;* Which was formerly: *Budgeting.* [ISSN: 1087-8572] 1972. bi-m. EUR 868.91 in Europe; USD 449 in North America; AUD 1299 in Australasia. Ed(s): Robert Randall. Emerald, 60-62 Toller Ln, Bradford, BD8 9BY, United Kingdom; info@emeraldinsight.com; http://www.emeraldinsight.com. Illus., adv. Refereed. Vol. ends: Nov/Dec. Reprint: PSC. *Indexed:* ABIn, ATI, BPI, CompLI, PAIS. *Bk. rev.:* Number and length vary. *Aud.:* Ac, Sa.

This very attractive, modern, and streamlined journal publishes most of its six yearly issues on a single theme—"using scenarios for decision-making," "corporate social responsibility," "mergers and acquisitions," or "new territory for leadership." The 5-6 "feature articles" on each theme are written by management consultants who discuss specific areas of strategy development and application or describe case studies, supplemented by "Guru Interviews," book reviews, and conference reports. At the end of each issue are "Quick Takes" listing the "key points and action steps" from each of the feature articles. The web version of this journal is also very appealing and user-friendly. Readable and widely indexed, this title is recommended for academic libraries.

Electronic Journals

4624. *Journal of Competitive Intelligence and Management.* 2003. q. Society of Competitive Intelligence Professionals, 1700 Diagonal Rd, Ste 600, Alexandria, VA 22314; info@scip.org; http://www.scip.org. Refereed. *Aud.:* Ac, Sa.

The Society of Competitive Intelligence Professionals (SCIP) has ceased *Competitive Intelligence Review* and turned to a web-only journal. New in 2003, *Journal of Competitive Intelligence and Management* plans to include "all aspects of CI and related management fields" and "to further the development of CI and to encourage greater understanding of the management of competition." Only one issue was available for viewing, but its content appears to be scholarly and readable. SCIP is an important source for competitive intelligence information, so the future progress of this web journal is worth keeping an eye on.

4625. *Management.* [ISSN: 1286-4692] 1998. irreg. Free. Ed(s): Bernard Forges, Martin Evans. D M S P Research Center, Paris-Dauphine University, Paris, 75775 Cedex 16, France; management@dauphine.fr; http://www.dmsp.dauphine.fr/MANAGEMENT/ . Refereed. *Bk. rev.:* Number and length vary. *Aud.:* Ac, Sa.

This e-journal of peer-reviewed research articles on "management research, strategy, and organizational theory" encourages diversity—in the broad range of research methods and topics used by its authors, and in the truly international scope of its coverage. Its advisory and editorial boards consist of research faculty worldwide and articles are published in the authors' own languages (most are in English). The site also includes book reviews and an open forum for debate. Updating is irregular—articles are published as soon as they are accepted—but the journal occasionally puts together a special issue on a single topic, so far including organizational downsizing, careers and new science, and "Deconstructing Las Vegas." Recommended for academic libraries.

4626. *Public Administration and Management: an interactive journal.* [ISSN: 1087-0091] 1996. s-a. Free. Ed(s): Jack Rabin, Robert Munzenrider. Public Administration and Management, 2103 Fairway Ln, Harrisburg, PA 17112; JXR11@spaef.com; http://www.pamij.com. Illus. Refereed. *Aud.:* Ac, Sa.

This peer-reviewed journal first appeared on the web in 1996, and has now provided almost two dozen issues written by scholars and public service managers. There are frequent single-topic "symposia" (personal integrity, organizational development in health care) and volumes with articles on a variety of topics; recent topics include the management of e-mail, allocating human organs, and applying spiritual wisdom. The web site has an outdated and distracting design, but the articles themselves are worthwhile. Academic libraries are recommended to provide a link to this site in their electronic journals listings.

■ MARINE SCIENCE AND TECHNOLOGY

Judith B. Barnett, Professor/Catalog Librarian, University of Rhode Island Library, Kingston, RI 02881

Introduction

Seventy percent of the earth's surface is covered by the oceans. Scientists working in the fields of biology, chemistry, geology, and physics endeavor to understand all facets of the influence of the oceans on human life. Research on such topics as the role of the marine environment in the development of hurricanes, global warming and sea level change, greenhouse gases, changes in the abundance of fish species, and newly discovered hydrothermal vent animals is reported in the journal articles in this section. With the application of increasingly sophisticated technology such as remote sensing, the borders between the marine disciplines are dissolving and huge data banks are being created for exchange among scientists working in such fields as seabed mapping, marine gravity, seafloor sediments, and ocean optics.

Most of the journals in this subject area are highly specialized and are geared to academic collections serving scientists and researchers. Several commercial publishers produce the majority of the estimated 350 English-language titles in the field. Most of the titles are available both in print and by online subscription and their rapidly escalating costs have made it impossible for even the most comprehensive marine science collections to include all of them. The titles included here are the relatively more general ones and represent only a fraction of the journals in the field. Articles in general science periodicals, such as *Scientific American* and *Discover*, report developments in the field to the adult layperson or high school student.

Bibliographic access is provided in print and online formats by general abstracting and indexing services such as *Chemical Abstracts* and *Biological Abstracts*, as well as by specialized sources such as *Aquatic Sciences and Fisheries Abstracts, Oceanographic Literature Review*, and *Oceanic Abstracts. Applied Science and Technology Index, General Science Index*, and *Readers' Guide* provide indexing of the popular titles, including those in the areas of marine affairs and ocean management.

Basic Periodicals

Hs, Ga: *California Wild, Explorations, 41 Degrees N., Underwater Naturalist;* Ac: *Deep-Sea Research, Parts 1 and 2, Journal of Marine Research, Journal of Physical Oceanography, Limnology and Oceanography, Marine Biology, Marine Chemistry, Marine Ecology–Progress Series, Marine Geology, Oceanography.*

Basic Abstracts and Indexes

Aquatic Sciences and Fisheries Abstracts, Oceanographic Literature Review, Oceanic Abstracts

4627. ***41 Degrees N.*** 2000. 3x/yr. Free Rhode Island residents. Ed(s): Malia Schwartz. University of Rhode Island, Sea Grant College Program, Bay Campus, Narragansett, RI 02882; http://seagrant.gso.uri.edu. *Aud.:* Hs, Ga, Ac, Sa.

Articles on marine science, biology, agriculture, water quality, watershed management and habitat restoration in Rhode Island, New England, and beyond are geared to the educated layperson. Recent articles cover eelgrass, coastal zone management, oysters in Rhode Island salt ponds, and fishing vessel accidents. Enhanced with many photos and diagrams, it includes notices of meetings and publications of interest to the public. Suitable for public and high school libraries, its treatment of environmental issues extends beyond Rhode Island.

American Fisheries Society. Transactions. See Fish, Fisheries, and Aquaculture section.

4628. ***Aquatic Botany: an international scientific journal dealing with applied and fundamental research on submerged, floating and emergent plants in marine and freshwater ecosystems.*** [ISSN: 0304-3770] 1975. m. EUR 1099. Ed(s): Dr. G Bowes, Jan Vermaat. Elsevier BV, Sara Burgerhartstraat 25, Amsterdam, 1055 KV, Netherlands; nlinfo-f@elsevier.nl; http://www.elsevier.nl. Illus., index, adv. Refereed. Vol. ends: No. 4. Microform: PQC. Online: ingenta.com; ScienceDirect; Swets Blackwell. Reprint: SWZ. *Indexed:* ApEcolAb, BiolAb, CAPS, ChemAb, EnvAb, ExcerpMed, ForAb, GeoRef, GeogAbPG, HortAb, OceAb, RRTA, S&F, SCI, SWRA, ZooRec. *Bk. rev.:* 1-2, 1,000-3,000 words, signed. *Aud.:* Ac.

Of wider scope than *Botanica Marina,* this international journal deals with applied and fundamental research on submerged, floating, and emerging plants in marine and freshwater ecosystems. Thermal pollution, the effects of herbicides and all aspects of plant production and decomposition are within its scope. Each issue carries about four articles and two short communications on the structure, functions, dynamics, and classification of aquatic plant ecosystems. Recent papers cover the use of sediment fertilization for seagrass restoration, use of a radio-tracer technique to study decomposition dynamics of a bloom forming macroalga, and the impact of agriculture and mining activities on wetlands.

4629. ***Aquatic Conservation: marine and freshwater ecosystems.*** [ISSN: 1052-7613] 1991. bi-m. USD 830. John Wiley & Sons Ltd., The Atrium, Southern Gate, Chichester, PO19 8SQ, United Kingdom; customer@wiley.co.uk; http://www.wiley.co.uk. Illus., adv. Refereed. Circ: 500. Vol. ends: No. 4. Microform: PQC. Online: EBSCO Publishing; ScienceDirect; Swets Blackwell; Wiley InterScience. Reprint: SWZ. *Indexed:* ApEcolAb, BiolAb, GeogAbPG, OceAb, PollutAb, SWRA, WRCInf, ZooRec. *Bk. rev.:* 3, 500-1,000 words. *Aud.:* Ac, Sa.

Original papers, short communications, and review articles cover all aspects of the conservation of aquatic biological resources. Freshwater, brackish, and marine habitats are within the scope of this journal, which publishes practical studies in conservation as well as theoretical considerations of underlying principles. It aims to serve scientists, policymakers, and nature conservation organizations. Recent articles treat floodplains of a southern alpine river, trophic modeling of a harvested benthic ecosystem, and the effects of protection measures on Mediterranean fish.

4630. ***Aquatic Ecology: a multidisciplinary journal relating to processes and structures at different organizational levels.*** Former titles (until 1997): *Netherlands Journal of Aquatic Ecology;* (until 1992): *Hydrobiological Bulletin;* (until 1973): *Hydrobiologische Vereniging. Mededelingen.* [ISSN: 1386-2588] 1975. q. EUR 311 print or online ed. Ed(s): Ramesh D Gulati. Kluwer Academic Publishers, van Godewijckstraat 30, PO Box 17, Dordrecht, 3300 AA, Netherlands. Adv. Refereed. Online: EBSCO Publishing; ingenta.com; Kluwer Online; OCLC Online Computer Library Center, Inc.; Ovid Technologies, Inc.; RoweCom Information Quest; Swets Blackwell. *Indexed:* ApEcolAb, BiolAb, ChemAb, ExcerpMed, GeogAbPG, OceAb, PollutAb, SWRA, ZooRec. *Bk. rev.:* 2-3, 1,000 words, signed. *Aud.:* Ac, Sa.

This journal serves as a forum for freshwater and marine ecologists to address and evaluate ecological issues. Original papers relate to the ecology of fresh, brackish, estuarine, and marine environments and include both fundamental and applied research in field and laboratory. Environmental factors in aquatic ecosystems and food web studies are of particular interest. Recent articles treat nitrogen fixation associated with seagrasses, patterns of prey selectivity in a copepod species, the effects of nutrient concentrations on a North Carolina phytoplankton community, and Nile tilapia blood chemistry under the impact of water pollution.

4631. ***Aquatic Geochemistry.*** [ISSN: 1380-6165] 1995. q. USD 374 print or online ed. Ed(s): John W Morse. Kluwer Academic Publishers, van Godewijckstraat 30, PO Box 17, Dordrecht, 3300 AA, Netherlands; services@wkap.nl; http://www.wkap.nl. Illus. Refereed. Vol. ends: No. 4. Online: EBSCO Publishing; ingenta.com; Kluwer Online; OCLC Online Computer Library Center, Inc.; Ovid Technologies, Inc.; RoweCom Information Quest; Swets Blackwell. Reprint: SWZ. *Indexed:* ChemAb, ForAb, GeoRef, GeogAbPG, M&GPA, OceAb, PollutAb, S&F, SWRA. *Aud.:* Ac.

Theoretical, experimental, and modeling studies relative to the geochemistry of natural waters and their interaction with rocks and minerals appear in this international journal. A typical issue of four or five articles focuses on such subjects as beryllium geochemistry in a Czech Republic catchment, geochemistry of an ice-covered lake in the Canadian Arctic, and pyritization of iron in Gulf of Mexico sediments.

4632. ***Aquatic Living Resources: international journal devoted to aquatic resources.*** Incorporates: *Revue des Travaux de l'Institut des Peches Maritimes;* Formerly (until 1987): *Aquatic Living; I F R E M E R. Revue des Travaux.* [ISSN: 0990-7440] 1928. bi-m. EUR 304. Ed(s): Brigitte Milcendeau. Elsevier France, Editions Scientifiques et Medicales, 23 Rue Linois, Paris, 75724, France; academic@elsevier.fr; http://www.elsevier.fr. Illus. Refereed. Circ: 950. Online: ingenta.com; ScienceDirect; Swets Blackwell. *Indexed:* BiolAb, HortAb, IndVet, OceAb, RRTA, S&F, SWRA, VetBull, WAE&RSA, ZooRec. *Aud.:* Ac, Sa.

Original papers, review articles, and notes deal with the production and exploitation of the living resources of marine and freshwater environments. Studies in biology and ecology treat living resources as environmental indicators. Recent articles focus on pelagic fisheries in Scotland, biotic and abiotic factors in the growth of Baltic Sea sprat, and selection of new candidates for finfish aquaculture. A recent special issue is devoted to catfish biology and culture.

4633. ***Aquatic Mammals.*** [ISSN: 0167-5427] 1972. 3x/yr. USD 95. Ed(s): Jeanette Thomas. Western Illinois University Regional Center, 3561 60th St, Moline, IL 61265. Illus. Refereed. Circ: 300. Vol. ends: No. 3. *Indexed:* BiolAb, DSR&OA, IndVet, OceAb, VetBull, ZooRec. *Bk. rev.:* 1, 1,000 words. *Aud.:* Ac, Sa.

Similar in scope to *Marine Mammal Science*, this journal covers all aspects of the care, conservation, medicine, and science of aquatic animals. Recent issues of ten research articles cover beluga whale visual abilities, marine dolphin whistles in a Brazilian bay, and interaction of two whale species in Hawaii and Marquesas Islands cetaceans.

4634. ***Atlantic Geology.*** Former titles (until 1990): *Maritime Sediments and Atlantic Geology;* (until 1982): *Maritime Sediments.* [ISSN: 0843-5561] 1965. 3x/yr. CND 60 (Individuals, CND 35; Members, CND 30). Ed(s): Sandra M Barr. Atlantic Geoscience Society, Department of Geology, Acadia University, PO Box 116, Wolfville, NS B0P 1X0, Canada; sandra.barr@acadiau.ca. Illus., index, adv. Refereed. Circ: 350. Vol. ends: No. 3. *Indexed:* BiolAb, DSR&OA, GeoRef, GeogAbPG, OceAb, PetrolAb, ZooRec. *Aud.:* Ac.

Original research papers, notes, and discussions treat all aspects of the geology of Atlantic Canada and adjacent areas. Articles in English or French focus on such subjects as geophysical imaging of a shallow aquifer, coastal change in Nova Scotia, Late Quaternary sea-level variations in the North Atlantic, and marine palynology records from Atlantic Canada.

Atmosphere-Ocean. See Atmospheric Sciences section.

4635. ***Botanica Marina.*** [ISSN: 0006-8055] 1957. bi-m. EUR 1006.20 (Individuals, EUR 160.80; Individual members, EUR 156.20). Ed(s): G T Boalch. Walter de Gruyter GmbH & Co. KG, Genthiner Str. 13, Berlin, 10785, Germany; bot.mar.editorial@degruyter.de; http://www.degruyter.com/journals/bm. Illus., index, adv. Sample. Refereed. Circ: 450 Paid. Online: EBSCO Publishing; OCLC Online Computer Library Center, Inc.; Swets Blackwell. Reprint: PSC; SCH. *Indexed:* BiolAb, CAPS, ChemAb, DSR&OA, ForAb, HortAb, OceAb, SCI, SWRA, ZooRec. *Aud.:* Ac.

Original contributions, short communications, and reviews cover all aspects of marine botany, including marine microbiology and marine mycology. A typical issue of 10 to 12 articles covers such subjects as the effects of ionic aluminum on an invasive seaweed, a nontoxic dinoflagellate from the Gulf of California, volatile compounds from some Black Sea brown algae, and taxonomic notes on marine algae from Malaysia.

4636. ***Bulletin of Marine Science.*** Formerly: *Bulletin of Marine Science of the Gulf and Caribbean.* [ISSN: 0007-4977] 1951. bi-m. USD 225 (Individuals, USD 85; Students, USD 45). Ed(s): Samuel C Snedaker. Rosenstiel School of Marine and Atmospheric Science, 4600 Rickenbacker Causeway, Miami, FL 33149-1098; bms@rsmas.miami.edu; http://www.rsmas.miami.edu/bms/. Refereed. Circ: 1000 Paid. Reprint: SWZ. *Indexed:* AnBeAb, ApEcolAb, B&AI, BiolAb, ChemAb, DSR&OA, EnvAb, ExcerpMed, ForAb, GeoRef, GeogAbPG, IndVet, M&GPA, OceAb, PetrolAb, PollutAb, RRTA, S&F, SCI, SWRA, VetBull, WAE&RSA, ZooRec. *Bk. rev.:* 3, 300 words, signed. *Aud.:* Ac, Sa.

Research papers deal with the tropical and subtropical waters of the world's oceans. Marine biology, biological oceanography, fisheries, marine affairs, applied marine physics, marine geology and geophysics, meteorology and physical oceanography are within its scope. Special sections of each issue are devoted to new taxa and coral reefs. Occasional special issues such as one on cephalopod biomass and production are published. Recent articles cover grouper reproduction, the impact of incidental kills by gill nets on Brazilian dolphins, and biological invasions in aquatic systems.

4637. ***Cahiers de Biologie Marine.*** [ISSN: 0007-9723] 1960. q. EUR 226.89 domestic; EUR 222.22 foreign. Ed(s): Claude Jouin Toulmond. Station Biologique de Roscoff, Place Georges Teissier, BP 74, Roscoff, Cedex 29682, France; jouin@sb-roscoff.fr; http://www.sb-roscoff.fr/cbmintro_eng.html. Illus., adv. Refereed. Circ: 400. *Indexed:* BiolAb, ChemAb, DSR&OA, GeoRef, GeogAbPG, HortAb, PollutAb, S&F, SCI, SWRA, WAE&RSA, ZooRec. *Aud.:* Ac, Sa.

Articles in English or French on all aspects of biology of marine organisms and of biological oceanography are published in this international journal. A typical issue of eight articles may also include reviews on current topics and selected papers from international symposia or workshops. Recent papers describe a new species of carnivorous deep-sea sponge, comparative morphology of the feeding apparatus in a polychaete, experimental nutrition in a coral, and zooplankton distribution in two lagoons in the northern Adriatic Sea.

4638. ***California Wild: natural sciences for thinking animals.*** Formerly (until 1997): *Pacific Discovery.* [ISSN: 1094-365X] 1948. q. USD 12.95 domestic; USD 22 foreign. Ed(s): Keith Howell. California Academy of Sciences, Golden Gate Park, San Francisco, CA 94118; calwild@calacademy.org; http://www.calacademy.org/calwild. Illus., adv. Circ: 30000. Microform: PQC. *Indexed:* BiolAb, BiolDig, DSR&OA, GeoRef, ZooRec. *Bk. rev.:* 4, 300 words, signed. *Aud.:* Hs, Ga.

Beautifully illustrated articles written for the informed layperson cover all aspects of the natural history of the West Coast. Among the many devoted to marine subjects are those reporting on sea turtles, kelp islands, an alien alga, and coho salmon. This is an excellent publication for general collections on either coast.

Canadian Journal of Fisheries and Aquatic Sciences. See Fish, Fisheries, and Aquaculture section.

4639. ***Continental Shelf Research.*** [ISSN: 0278-4343] 1982. 19x/yr. EUR 1792 (Qualified personnel, EUR 226). Ed(s): Michael B Collins, Richard W Sternberg. Pergamon, The Boulevard, Langford Ln, East Park, Kidlington, OX5 1GB, United Kingdom. Refereed. Vol. ends: No. 21. Microform: PQC. Online: ingenta.com; ScienceDirect; Swets Blackwell. *Indexed:* DSA, DSR&OA, GeoRef, GeogAbPG, IndVet, M&GPA, OceAb, PollutAb, S&F, SCI, SWRA, VetBull, WRCInf. *Aud.:* Ac, Sa.

Articles by physical, chemical, and biological oceanographers, marine sedimentologists, geologists and geochemists, marine biologists and ecologists, emphasize interdisciplinary research in the field of continental shelf research. Occasional special issues report on the results of large international projects or specific subjects. Sections are devoted to notes, instrumentation, and methods. Recent papers focus on surface circulation in the southwest Atlantic, current meter monitoring of the Norwegian Atlantic slope, salinity and temperature variations in large Baltic Sea gulfs, and a primary production model for the East China Sea.

4640. ***Coral Reefs.*** Formerly: *International Society for Reef Studies. Journal.* [ISSN: 0722-4028] 1982. 4x/yr. EUR 480 domestic; EUR 489.90 foreign. Ed(s): T Hughes, R E Dodge. Springer-Verlag, Tiergartenstr 17, Heidelberg, 69121, Germany. Adv. Refereed.

Microform: PQC. Online: EBSCO Publishing; RoweCom Information Quest; ScienceDirect; Springer LINK; Swets Blackwell. Reprint: ISI. *Indexed:* BiolAb, DSR&OA, GeoRef, GeogAbPG, OceAb, PollutAb, SCI, SWRA, ZooRec. *Aud.:* Ac, Sa.

Reflecting the importance of experimentation, modeling, quantification, and applied science in reef studies, this journal includes about five articles in each issue as well as shorter notes, review articles, and reports. Studies cover community ecology of reef organisms, biogeochemical cycles, reef response to stress, and paleoceanography of coral reefs and islands. Reproductive ecology of a deep-sea coral in the northwest Atlantic, luminescent lines in Great Barrier Reef corals, and long-term dynamics of coral reefs in St. John, U.S. Virgin Islands, are examples of recent articles.

4641. *Deep-Sea Research. Part 1: Oceanographic Research Papers.* Supersedes in part (until 1993): *Deep-Sea Research. Part A: Oceanographic Research Papers;* Which had former titles (until 1979): *Deep-Sea Research (New York, 1977);* (until 1977): *Deep-Sea Research and Oceanographic Abstracts;* (until 1961): *Deep-Sea Research (New York, 1953).* [ISSN: 0967-0637] 1953. 38x/yr. EUR 3909 (Qualified personnel, EUR 265). Ed(s): M Bacon. Pergamon, The Boulevard, Langford Ln, East Park, Kidlington, OX5 1GB, United Kingdom. Illus., index, adv. Refereed. Vol. ends: No. 10. Microform: PQC. Online: Gale Group; ingenta.com; ScienceDirect; Swets Blackwell. *Indexed:* BiolAb, ChemAb, DSR&OA, EngInd, ExcerpMed, GeoRef, GeogAbPG, M&GPA, OceAb, PetrolAb, SCI, SWRA, ZooRec. *Aud.:* Ac, Sa.

With emphasis on an interdisciplinary approach, this authoritative journal covers a wide range of oceanographic studies including those of the sea floor and the ocean-atmosphere boundary layer. The solution of instrumental and laboratory problems are also within its scope. Recent articles cover eastern Mediterranean benthic protozoan communities, bioluminescence flow visualization in the ocean, surface layer temperature inversion in the Bay of Bengal, and convection and restratification in the Labrador Sea.

4642. *Deep-Sea Research. Part 2: Topical Studies in Oceanography.* Supersedes in part (in 1993): *Deep-Sea Research. Part A, Oceanographic Research Papers;* Which was formerly (until 1978): *Deep-Sea Research (New York, 1977);* (until 1976): *Deep-Sea Research and Oceanographic Abstracts;* (until 1961): *Deep-Sea Research (New York, 1953).* [ISSN: 0967-0645] 1993. 26x/yr. EUR 2818 (Qualified personnel, EUR 156). Ed(s): John Milliman. Pergamon, The Boulevard, Langford Ln, East Park, Kidlington, OX5 1GB, United Kingdom. Refereed. Microform: PQC. Online: ingenta.com; ScienceDirect; Swets Blackwell. *Indexed:* ChemAb, EngInd, GeoRef, GeogAbPG, M&GPA, OceAb, S&F, SCI, ZooRec. *Aud.:* Ac, Sa.

Issues are devoted to the results of large-scale international and interdisciplinary projects. Many have CD-ROM appendixes dealing with nontext materials such as numerical data, images, and video. Recent issues treat oceanography and marine biology of the East China Sea and physical oceanography of the southern African region. Along with *Deep Sea Research. Part 1*, it is essential for marine science collections.

Dynamics of Atmospheres and Oceans. See Atmospheric Sciences section.

4643. *Estuaries: a journal of research on any aspect of natural science and management applied to estuaries.* Formerly: *Chesapeake Science.* [ISSN: 0160-8347] 1978. bi-m. USD 360 in North America; USD 375 elsewhere. Ed(s): Stephen T Threlkeld. Estuarine Research Federation, 2018 Daffodil, PO Box 510, Port Republic, MD 20676; stt@estuaries-olemiss.edu; http://erf.org/journal.html. Illus., index, adv. Refereed. Circ: 1800. Vol. ends: No. 4. Microform: MIM; PMC; PQC. Reprint: PQC. *Indexed:* ApEcolAb, BiolAb, ChemAb, DSR&OA, ExcerpMed, ForAb, GeoRef, GeogAbPG, M&GPA, OceAb, PollutAb, S&F, SCI, SWRA, WRCInf, ZooRec. *Bk. rev.:* 2, 500 words. *Aud.:* Ac, Sa.

A wide range of coastal environments such as estuaries, lagoons, wetlands, tidal rivers, watersheds, and near-shore coastal waters are the focus of original research papers, reviews, and comments. Its scope has been broadened from North American studies to now include any aspect of research worldwide on physical, chemical, geological, or biological systems. Tidal vertical migrations in a salt marsh snail, harmful algal blooms in Chesapeake Bay, and GIS mapping of Barnegat Bay, New Jersey, seagrasses are the subjects of recent studies. Freshwater inflow is the subject of a recent special issue. Suitable for collections serving oceanographers and marine biologists.

4644. *Estuarine, Coastal and Shelf Science.* Formerly (until 1982): *Estuarine and Coastal Marine Science.* [ISSN: 0272-7714] 1973. 16x/yr. EUR 2445. Ed(s): D. S. McLusky, S. D. Sulkin. Academic Press, Harcourt Pl, 32 Jamestown Rd, London, NW1 7BY, United Kingdom; apsubs@acad.com; http://www.elsevier-international.com/serials/. Illus., index, adv. Refereed. Vol. ends: No. 6. Online: EBSCO Publishing; ingenta.com; OCLC Online Computer Library Center, Inc.; RoweCom Information Quest; ScienceDirect; Swets Blackwell. Reprint: SWZ. *Indexed:* BiolAb, ChemAb, DSR&OA, EnvAb, ExcerpMed, FPA, ForAb, GeoRef, GeogAbPG, M&GPA, OceAb, PetrolAb, PollutAb, RRTA, S&F, SCI, SWRA, WAE&RSA, WRCInf, ZooRec. *Aud.:* Ac, Sa.

This international, multidisciplinary journal publishes articles devoted to the analysis of biological, chemical, and physical phenomena in waters from the continental shelf to the upper limits of the tidal zone. Its scope comprises zoology, botany, geology, sedimentology, physical oceanography, numerical models, and chemical processes. Recent articles treat colored dissolved organic matter in Narragansett Bay, Rhode Island, and its effect on phytoplankton, suspended particles and aggregates in the Baltic Sea, changes in brackish water eelgrass due to coastal eutrophication, and residual flow in a Bangladesh estuary. Both *Estuaries* and *Estuarine, Coastal and Shelf Science* are important to marine collections because of concern with deteriorating environmental conditions and increased coastal urban populations.

4645. *Explorations (La Jolla): global discoveries for tomorrow's world.* Incorporates (in 1994): *Scripps Institution of Oceanography. Annual Report;* Which was formerly (until 1984): *Scripps Institution of Oceanography (Year);* (until 1978): *S I O Scripps Institution of Oceanography;* (until 1976): *Scripps Institution of Oceanography. Annual Report;* (until 1972): *S I O: A Report on the Work and Programs of Scripps Institution of Oceanography.* [ISSN: 1075-2560] 1994. q. Ed(s): Nan P Criqui. Scripps Institution of Oceanography, Technical Publications Office, University of California at San Diego, 9500 Gilman Dr, La Jolla, CA 92093-0233; techpubs@sio.uscd.edu. Illus. Circ: 18000. *Indexed:* GeoRef. *Aud.:* Hs, Ga, Ac, Sa.

Ongoing research and scientific activities of the Scripps Institution of Oceanography, La Jolla, are featured in this magazine aimed at the public, alumni, the scientific community, and friends of the institution. Reports cover the broad range of scientific investigations carried on by Scripps scientists in such areas as infrasound, biomimicry in marine animals, Gulf of California marine reserves, and drugs from the sea. The winter issue features a videocassette and program guide. For the educated layperson as well as interested students who may be considering a career in oceanography.

Fisheries. See Fish, Fisheries, and Aquaculture section.

Fishery Bulletin. See Fish, Fisheries, and Aquaculture section.

4646. *Global and Planetary Change.* [ISSN: 0921-8181] 1988. 20x/yr. EUR 1311 (Qualified personnel, EUR 199). Ed(s): S. Cloetingh, C. Covey. Elsevier BV, Sara Burgerhartstraat 25, Amsterdam, 1055 KV, Netherlands; nlinfo-f@elsevier.nl; http://www.elsevier.nl. Illus., index, adv. Refereed. Vol. ends: No. 6. Microform: PQC. Online: ingenta.com; ScienceDirect; Swets Blackwell. *Indexed:* EnvAb, ForAb, GeoRef, GeogAbPG, M&GPA, OceAb, PollutAb, S&F, SCI, SSCI, SWRA, WAE&RSA, ZooRec. *Aud.:* Ac.

Focusing on the record of change in earth history and the analysis and prediction of recent and future changes, the journal publishes research articles on changes in the chemical composition of the oceans and atmosphere, climate change, sea level variations, and global geophysics, tectonics, ecology, and biogeography. Recent articles cover sub-ice volcanoes and ancient oceans, subglacial lakes in Iceland, east Asian winter monsoon variations during the past million years, and late Quaternary palaeoenvironmental changes in southwestern Australia. Recent special issues cover the global carbon cycle, sea level fluctuations in the Mediterranean, and clastic sedimentology of climate changes.

4647. *Global Atmosphere and Ocean System.* Former titles (until 1995): *Atmosphere - Ocean System;* (until 1993): *Ocean - Air Interactions.* [ISSN: 1023-6732] 1986. q. GBP 516 (Individuals, GBP 88; Corporations, GBP 854). Taylor & Francis Ltd, 11 New Fetter Ln, London, EC4P 4EE, United Kingdom; http://www.tandf.co.uk/journals. Illus. Refereed. Reprint: PSC. *Indexed:* M&GPA, OceAb, PollutAb, SWRA. *Bk. rev.:* 3, 1,000 words, signed. *Aud.:* Ac.

The editors aim for a "forum for exciting research and stimulating new ideas related to understanding the atmosphere-ocean system and climate change." Both theoretical and experimental articles reflect the interdisciplinary nature of the field, which comprises atmospheric chemistry, marine biology, and geological topics related to climate change. Recent articles treat wind and wave data analysis for the Aegean Sea, the role of wind direction on internal waves on the Iberian Shelf, and the impact of the North Atlantic oscillation on European temperature. Articles on innovative developments in remote-sensing devices from earth-based or satellite instruments may also be included; a recent special issue is devoted to the POSEIDON operational oceanographic system.

4648. *Global Biogeochemical Cycles: an international journal of global change.* [ISSN: 0886-6236] 1987. q. USD 528. Ed(s): A F Spilhaus. American Geophysical Union, 2000 Florida Ave, N W, Washington, DC 20009-1277; http://www.agu.org. Illus., adv. Refereed. Vol. ends: No. 4. Microform: Pub.; AIP. *Indexed:* Agr, ChemAb, FPA, ForAb, GeoRef, GeogAbPG, HortAb, M&GPA, OceAb, PollutAb, S&F, SCI, SWRA, WAE&RSA. *Aud.:* Ac.

Broad areas of global change involving the geosphere and biosphere are within the scope of this journal. Marine, hydrologic, atmospheric, extraterrestrial, geologic, biologic, and human causes of and response to environmental change on time scales of millions of years are within its purview. Methyl bromide cycling in a North Atlantic ocean warm-core eddy, the atmospheric methanol budget and ocean implication, fluvial sediment flux to the Arctic ocean, and upper ocean carbon fluxes in the Atlantic ocean have been covered in recent issues, which contain about 25 articles each.

4649. *Harmful Algae.* [ISSN: 1568-9883] 2002. q. EUR 260 (Individuals, EUR 62). Ed(s): Dr. Sandra E. Shumway, Theodore Smayda. Elsevier BV, Sara Burgerhartstraat 25, Amsterdam, 1055 KV, Netherlands; nlinfo-f@elsevier.nl; http://www.elsevier.nl. *Indexed:* BiolAb, OceAb. *Aud.:* Ac.

This journal publishes original research articles and reviews that aim "to provide a forum to promote knowledge of harmful microalgae, including cyanobacteria, as well as monitoring, management and control of these organisms." Humans have associated red tide with fish kills for millennia; increasing eutrophication by human activities has caused an increase in these incidents. About 100 species of microalgae produce specific toxins that can cause the death of livestock drinking from affected fresh water bodies, or of fish and shellfish in the sea, or of humans who consume them. Recent articles focus on toxin production in migrating dinoflagellates, the association of blue green algal toxins in surface drinking water and liver cancer in Florida, the role of harmful algae and eutrophication in a Kuwait Bay fish kill, and effects of winds, tides, and river runoff on algal blooms in Hiroshima Bay.

4650. *I C E S Journal of Marine Science.* Former titles (until 1991): *Conseil International pour l'Exploration de la Mer. Journal;* (until 1968): *Conseil Permanent International pour l'Exploration de la Mer. Journal.* [ISSN: 1054-3139] 1926. 8x/yr. EUR 848 (Individuals, EUR 245). Ed(s): Niels Daan. Academic Press, Harcourt Pl, 32 Jamestown Rd, London, NW1 7BY, United Kingdom; apsubs@acad.com; http://www.elsevier-international.com/serials/. Adv. Refereed. Circ: 1000. Online: EBSCO Publishing; ingenta.com; OCLC Online Computer Library Center, Inc.; RoweCom Information Quest; ScienceDirect; Swets Blackwell. Reprint: SWZ. *Indexed:* BiolAb, ChemAb, DSR&OA, EnvAb, GeoRef, GeogAbPG, IndVet, OceAb, PollutAb, RRTA, S&F, SCI, SWRA, VetBull, WAE&RSA, ZooRec. *Aud.:* Ac, Sa.

Covering a broad spectrum of ocean management and conservation issues comprising oceanography, marine habitats, and living resources, the scope of this journal has been expanded to include economic, social, and public administration studies of general interest to marine scientists. Proceedings of symposia sponsored by ICES (International Council for the Exploration of the Sea) are an integral part of the journal. Recent papers cover distribution fields for aquatic ecosystem components, estimation and compensation models for the shadowing effect in dense fish aggregations, population fecundity in Barents Sea capelin, and consistency in the correlation of school parameters across years and stocks.

4651. *I E E E Journal of Oceanic Engineering.* [ISSN: 0364-9059] 1976. q. USD 235 in North America; USD 270 elsewhere. Ed(s): William M Carey. Institute of Electrical and Electronics Engineers, Inc., 445 Hoes Ln, Piscataway, NJ 08854-1331; subscription-service@ieee.org; http://www.ieee.org. Illus., index, adv. Refereed. Vol. ends: No. 4. Online: EBSCO Publishing; I E E E. *Indexed:* AS&TI, C&ISA, DSR&OA, EngInd, GeoRef, H&SSA, IAA, M&GPA, OceAb, PetrolAb, SCI. *Aud.:* Ac, Sa.

All applications of electrical and electronic engineering pertaining to all bodies of water are within the scope of this journal. The design and testing of water-oriented systems as well as their scientific, technical, and industrial uses are included. Recent special issues are devoted to underwater image and videoprocessing, open ocean aquaculture engineering, and engineering advances in exploring the Asian marginal seas.

4652. *Journal of Coastal Conservation.* [ISSN: 1400-0350] 1995. 2x/yr. SEK 400; EUR 48; USD 42. Ed(s): F van der Meulen, R Paskoff. Opulus Press AB, Gamla Vaegen 40, Grangaerde, 77013, Sweden. Adv. Refereed. Online: Swets Blackwell. *Indexed:* BiolAb, ForAb, GeogAbPG, RRTA, S&F, WAE&RSA. *Aud.:* Ac, Sa.

Publishing research articles on the management of the coastal zone, this journal focuses on the European region. It covers both natural and human sciences such as geomorphology, physical geography, hydrology, soil science, animal and plant ecology, recreation studies, urban ecology, and coastal engineering and planning as they relate to coastal patterns and processes. Recent articles cover the evaluation of the coastal environment for marine birds, salt-marsh communities of the north Norfolk coast, using GIS for sighting artificial reefs, and water quality management of southern England harbors.

4653. *Journal of Coastal Research: an international forum for the littoral sciences.* [ISSN: 0749-0208] 1985. q. USD 145. Ed(s): Charles W Finkl, Jr. Coastal Education & Research Foundation, Inc., PO Box 210187, Royal Palm Beach, FL 33421-0187; cfinkl@gate.net. Illus., index, adv. Refereed. Circ: 1500. Vol. ends: No. 4. *Indexed:* AS&TI, BiolAb, C&ISA, DSR&OA, ExcerpMed, ForAb, GeoRef, GeogAbPG, M&GPA, OceAb, PollutAb, RRTA, S&F, SCI, SSCI, SWRA, WAE&RSA, ZooRec. *Bk. rev.:* 2, 1,000 words, signed. *Aud.:* Ac, Sa.

All aspects of coastal research are within the broad scope of this interdisciplinary journal. Concerned with broad environmental issues such as water supply, beach erosion, and coastal zone management, the journal aims to promote communication between specialists in different disciplines. Recent articles in a typical 20-article issue treat a numerical model of wave propagation on mild slopes, coastal management in Northern Ireland, Middle Holocene sea level and evolution of the Gulf of Mexico coast, and wetland loss by erosion in a Spanish marsh. Review articles, book and symposia reviews, communications, and news are also published.

4654. *Journal of Experimental Marine Biology and Ecology.* [ISSN: 0022-0981] 1967. 28x/yr. EUR 3816. Ed(s): Dr. Sandra E. Shumway, Dr. T. Underwood. Elsevier BV, Sara Burgerhartstraat 25, Amsterdam, 1055 KV, Netherlands; nlinfo-f@elsevier.nl; http://www.elsevier.nl. Illus., index, adv. Refereed. Vol. ends: No. 2. Microform: PQC. Online: EBSCO Publishing; ingenta.com; ScienceDirect; Swets Blackwell. Reprint: ISI; SWZ. *Indexed:* ApEcolAb, B&AI, BiolAb, CAPS, ChemAb, DSR&OA, EnvAb, ExcerpMed, ForAb, GeoRef, HortAb, IndVet, OceAb, PollutAb, S&F, SCI, SSCI, SWRA, VetBull, ZooRec. *Bk. rev.:* 1, 1,000 words, signed. *Aud.:* Ac.

Focusing on experimental work from field and laboratory, this journal covers the biochemistry, physiology, behavior, and genetics of marine plants and animals in relation to their ecology. Studies of littoral, inshore, offshore and deep-sea ecosystems and papers describing new techniques, methods, and apparatus are published. More specialized than *Marine Biology*, it has recently published articles on the effects of vegetation among three species of fiddler crabs, Antarctic krill diet, the effects of dietary zinc on shell biomineralization in an abalone, and differential accumulation of cadmium in a sea anemone. Suitable for research collections in biology and biological oceanography.

4655. *Journal of Marine Research.* [ISSN: 0022-2402] 1937. bi-m. USD 140 (Individuals, USD 60). Ed(s): George Veronis. Sears Foundation for Marine Research, Kline Geology Laboratory, Yale University, New Haven, CT 06520-8109. Illus., index. Refereed. Circ: 1000. Vol. ends: No. 6. Microform: PMC; PQC. Online: Gale Group; Ingenta Select. *Indexed:* ApMecR, B&AI, BiolAb, ChemAb, DSR&OA, ExcerpMed, GSI, GeoRef, GeogAbPG, M&GPA, OceAb, PetrolAb, PollutAb, SCI, SWRA, ZooRec. *Aud.:* Ac, Sa.

With a focus on interdisciplinary research, this journal publishes theoretical or descriptive articles primarily in physical oceanography. Tidal motion enhancement around islands, tracing Amazon River water into the Caribbean Sea, the dispersion of pairs of internal inertial gravity waves, and the transport and digestive alteration of diatoms in mudflat sediments are the subjects of recent papers in an average issue of five articles. The high quality and reasonable price of this journal make it suitable for all marine science collections.

4656. *Journal of Marine Systems.* [ISSN: 0924-7963] 1990. 28x/yr. EUR 1950. Ed(s): J Nihoul, W J Wiseman. Elsevier BV, Sara Burgerhartstraat 25, Amsterdam, 1055 KV, Netherlands; nlinfo-f@elsevier.nl; http://www.elsevier.nl. Illus., adv. Refereed. Vol. ends: No. 4. Microform: PQC. Online: ingenta.com; ScienceDirect; Swets Blackwell. *Indexed:* EngInd, EnvAb, GeoRef, GeogAbPG, M&GPA, OceAb, PollutAb, S&F, SCI, SWRA, ZooRec. *Aud.:* Ac.

Serving as a "medium of exchange for those engaged in marine research where there exists an interplay between geology, chemistry, biology and physics," this journal publishes research papers and reviews on all aspects of marine science. Papers that extend beyond the limit of a single discipline and that "follow the rationale of system analysis" are emphasized. The age of radioactive tracers, generation of cyclonic eddies in a Baltic Sea basin following dense water inflows, uptake of atmospheric carbon dioxide in the Barents Sea, and stable isotopic compositions of overwintering copepods in arctic and subarctic waters are the subjects of recent articles. The physics and biology of ocean fronts, exchange processes at the ocean margins, and ventilation of Black Sea anoxic waters are the subjects of recent special issues.

4657. *Journal of Physical Oceanography.* [ISSN: 0022-3670] 1971. m. USD 445 (Members, USD 60). Ed(s): Peter Muller. American Meteorological Society, 45 Beacon St, Boston, MA 02108; amsinfo@ametsoc.org. Illus., index, adv. Refereed. Circ: 1397. Vol. ends: No. 12. Online: EBSCO Publishing; Northern Light Technology, Inc. *Indexed:* ApMecR, BiolAb, CCMJ, ChemAb, DSR&OA, EngInd, GeoRef, GeogAbPG, IAA, M&GPA, MathSciNet, OceAb, PetrolAb, SCI, SWRA. *Aud.:* Ac, Sa.

Research papers on the physics of the ocean and the processes operating at its boundaries are published in this international journal. Observational, theoretical, and modeling studies relating to interactions of the ocean with other components of the earth system, as well as studies involving lakes or laboratory tanks focused on understanding the ocean are included. Recent papers cover circulation in the Irish Sea, warm-core eddies studied by laboratory experiments and numerical modeling, bifurcation of the North Equatorial Current in the Pacific, and a model study of internal tides in a coastal frontal zone. The Labrador Sea deep convection experiment is the subject of a recent special issue.

4658. *Journal of Plankton Research.* [ISSN: 0142-7873] 1979. m. GBP 449. Ed(s): D H Cushing. Oxford University Press, Great Clarendon St, Oxford, OX2 6DP, United Kingdom; jnl.orders@oup.co.uk; http://www3.oup.co.uk/jnls. Illus., index, adv. Refereed. Circ: 850. Vol. ends: No. 3. Online: EBSCO Publishing; HighWire Press; ingenta.com; OCLC Online Computer Library Center, Inc.; Ovid Technologies, Inc.; RoweCom Information Quest; Swets Blackwell. Reprint: PSC; SWZ. *Indexed:* AnBeAb, ApEcolAb, ArtHuCI, BiolAb, CAPS, ChemAb, DSR&OA, FPA, ForAb, GeoRef, IndVet, OceAb, PollutAb, S&F, SCI, SWRA, ZooRec. *Bk. rev.:* 1, 500 words, signed. *Aud.:* Ac, Sa.

Papers dealing with both zooplankton and phytoplankton in marine, freshwater, and brackish environments are within the scope of this journal. The ecology, physiology, distribution, life histories, and taxonomy of planktonic organisms are some of the subjects covered in a typical issue of seven articles and several short communications. Recent research papers cover phytoplankton blooms and fish recruitment rate, modeling the population dynamics of a toxic dinoflagellate in Hiroshima Bay, Japan, and assessment of oxidative stress in a planktonic diatom in response to UVA and UVB radiation.

4659. *Journal of Sea Research.* Formerly (until vol.35, 1996): *Netherlands Journal of Sea Research.* [ISSN: 1385-1101] 1961. 8x/yr. EUR 494 (Qualified personnel, EUR 114). Ed(s): C. J.M. Philippart, G. C. Cadee. Elsevier BV, Sara Burgerhartstraat 25, Amsterdam, 1055 KV, Netherlands; nlinfo-f@elsevier.nl; http://www.elsevier.nl. Refereed. Circ: 600. Online: ingenta.com; ScienceDirect; Swets Blackwell. *Indexed:* BiolAb, ChemAb, DSR&OA, EnvAb, ExcerpMed, GeoRef, GeogAbPG, M&GPA, OceAb, SCI, ZooRec. *Aud.:* Ac, Sa.

Articles on all types of marine and estuarine systems, benthic as well as pelagic, that contribute to the understanding of marine ecosystems, are within the scope of this journal. Emphasizing fundamental research, the fields of marine biology, marine geology, marine chemistry, and physical oceanography are included. Recent papers cover bivalve recruitment in the Wadden Sea after a severe winter, marine dinoflagellate survival strategies, time variation of floc properties in a settling column and Irish Sea whiting variability and growth.

4660. *Limnology and Oceanography.* [ISSN: 0024-3590] 1956. 8x/yr. USD 350. American Society of Limnology and Oceanography, Inc., 1444 Eye St. NW #200, Washington, DC 20005; business@aslo.org; http://www.aslo.org. Illus., index. Refereed. Circ: 5300 Paid. Vol. ends: No. 8. *Indexed:* AnBeAb, ApEcolAb, B&AI, BiolAb, ChemAb, EnvAb, ExcerpMed, GSI, GeoRef, GeogAbPG, IndVet, M&GPA, OceAb, PollutAb, S&F, SCI, SWRA, WRCInf, ZooRec. *Bk. rev.:* 2, 750 words, signed. *Aud.:* Ac, Sa.

Aiming to promote understanding of aquatic ecosystems, the journal publishes original articles about all aspects of limnology and oceanography. Emphasis is on the empirical, rather than the theoretical or methodological approach. Issues of this essential journal include about 25 full-length articles, as well as shorter notes, announcements, and news of the society that represents all aquatic disciplines. Recent studies cover carbon acquisition of bloom-forming marine phytoplankton, meristematic oxygen variability in eelgrass, trophic relationships among Southern Ocean copepods and krill, and complex interactions of climatic and ecological controls on macroalgal recruitment. Occasional special issues cover the comparative ecology of freshwater and marine ecosystems and light in shallow waters.

4661. *Limnology and Oceanography: Methods.* [ISSN: 1541-5856] 2003. m. USD 378. American Society of Limnology and Oceanography, Inc., 5400 Bosque Blvd, Ste 680, Waco, TX 76710-4446; business@aslo.org; http://www.aslo.org. *Aud.:* Ac, Sa.

Intended as a rapid publication supplement to the journal *Limnology and Oceanography*, this online journal publishes methodological papers. They may cover "new measurement equipment, techniques for analyzing observations or samples, methods for. . . interpreting information" and analyses of metadata. Papers are peer reviewed. Comments on papers, as well as suggestions about details of a particular method, are also included.

4662. *Marine and Freshwater Research.* Formerly (until 1995): *Australian Journal of Marine and Freshwater Research.* [ISSN: 1323-1650] 1950. 8x/yr. AUD 730 for print & online eds. (Individuals, AUD 150 for print & online eds.). Ed(s): Ann Grant. C S I R O Publishing, 150 Oxford St, Collingwood, VIC 3066, Australia; publishing@csiro.au; http://www.publish.csiro.au/. Illus., index, adv. Refereed. Circ: 700. Vol. ends: No. 8. Microform: PQC. Online: EBSCO Publishing; Ingenta

Select; OCLC Online Computer Library Center, Inc.; Swets Blackwell. *Indexed:* AnBeAb, ApEcolAb, BiolAb, C&ISA, ChemAb, DSR&OA, EnvAb, ExcerpMed, FS&TA, ForAb, GeoRef, GeogAbPG, HortAb, IndVet, M&GPA, OceAb, PollutAb, RRTA, S&F, SCI, SWRA, VetBull, WAE&RSA, ZooRec. *Aud.:* Ac, Sa.

This journal publishes original contributions and review articles in marine, estuarine, or freshwater research in both the Northern and Southern hemispheres. Its scope includes physical oceanography, marine chemistry, and marine and estuarine biology and limnology, as well as multidisciplinary papers such as those in biogeochemistry. Recent papers cover predation by southern sea lions on artisanal fishing catches in Uruguay, temporal persistence of benthic invertebrate communities in southeastern Australian streams, folic acid in Adriatic Sea coastal waters and magnesium, calcium and strontium in waters of the southern Tasman Sea. Occasional special issues cover lobster biology and management and the management of Australia's southeast fishery.

4663. ***Marine Biological Association of the United Kingdom. Journal.*** [ISSN: 0025-3154] 1887. bi-m. USD 570. Ed(s): P E Gibbs, R. Seed. Cambridge University Press, The Edinburgh Bldg, Shaftesbury Rd, Cambridge, CB2 2RU, United Kingdom; information@cambridge.org; http://uk.cambridge.org/journals. Illus., index, adv. Refereed. Vol. ends: No. 4. Microform: BHP; PQC. Online: EBSCO Publishing; OCLC Online Computer Library Center, Inc.; RoweCom Information Quest; Swets Blackwell. Reprint: SWZ. *Indexed:* B&AI, BiolAb, ChemAb, DSR&OA, ForAb, GeoRef, IndVet, PollutAb, S&F, SCI, VetBull, WRCInf, ZooRec. *Aud.:* Ac, Sa.

Original research articles, reviews, and short communications cover all aspects of marine biology and oceanography such as ecological surveys and population studies of oceanic, coastal and shore communities, physiology and experimental biology, taxonomy, and morphology and life history of marine animals and plants. Papers are also published on developing techniques for the sampling, recording, capture, and observation of marine organisms, and chemical analyses of sea water. Recent studies treat organotin compounds in two English estuaries, population dynamics of a sponge-dwelling isopod, molluscs on subtidal cliffs, and squid reproduction in the eastern Mediterranean.

4664. ***Marine Biology: international journal on life in oceans and coastal waters.*** [ISSN: 0025-3162] 1967. m. EUR 3970 domestic; EUR 4018.20 foreign; EUR 397 newsstand/cover per issue. Ed(s): O Kinne. Springer-Verlag, Tiergartenstr 17, Heidelberg, 69121, Germany. Illus., adv. Sample. Refereed. Vol. ends: No. 4. Microform: PQC. Online: EBSCO Publishing; Gale Group; RoweCom Information Quest; ScienceDirect; Springer LINK; Swets Blackwell. Reprint: ISI. *Indexed:* AnBeAb, ApEcolAb, B&AI, BiolAb, CAPS, ChemAb, DSA, DSR&OA, EnvAb, ExcerpMed, FS&TA, ForAb, HortAb, IndVet, OceAb, S&F, SCI, SWRA, VetBull, ZooRec. *Aud.:* Ac, Sa.

Original contributions on plankton, experimental biology, molecular biology (including biochemistry, physiology, and behavior), biosystem research, evolution, and theoretical biology related to the marine environment appear in this journal. Articles on apparatus and techniques employed in marine biological research, underwater exploration and experimentation are also within its scope. Recent papers cover penguin ingestion, breathing and vocalization; diatoms of the microphytobenthic community, impacts of trawling on meiofauna assemblages, and gonad morphology and colony composition in a coral-dwelling damselfish.

4665. ***Marine Biotechnology.*** Formed by the merger of (1992-1998): *Molecular Marine Biology and Biotechnology;* (1993-1998): *Journal of Marine Biotechnology.* [ISSN: 1436-2228] 1998. bi-m. USD 514; USD 101.90 per issue. Ed(s): T Chen, Y Le Gai. Springer-Verlag, Journals, 175 Fifth Ave., New York, NY 10010-7703; journals@springer-ny.com; http://www.springer-ny.com. Illus., adv. Refereed. Vol. ends: No. 4. Online: EBSCO Publishing; RoweCom Information Quest; ScienceDirect; Springer LINK; Swets Blackwell. *Indexed:* BioEngAb, BiolAb, ChemAb, DSA, ForAb, HortAb, IndMed, IndVet, OceAb, PollutAb, S&F, SCI, VetBull, ZooRec. *Aud.:* Ac, Sa.

Serving as the official journal of the European Society for Marine Biotechnology, Japanese Society of Marine Biotechnology and Pan American Marine Biotechnology Association, this journal publishes articles describing the molecular biology, genetics, cell biology, and biochemistry of any aquatic prokaryote or eukaryote. Papers on biotechnological applications and marine natural products that address fundamental questions or demonstrate novel technical developments also appear. Important applications of marine biotechnology include marine-based industrial materials, energy production of marine microorganisms, useful natural products from the sea, and biofouling and corrosion of marine infrastructures. Appropriate for specialized collections.

4666. ***Marine Chemistry: an international journal for studies of all chemical aspects of the marine environment.*** [ISSN: 0304-4203] 1972. 20x/yr. EUR 1820 (Qualified personnel, EUR 294). Ed(s): Frank J Millero. Elsevier BV, Sara Burgerhartstraat 25, Amsterdam, 1055 KV, Netherlands; nlinfo-f@elsevier.nl; http://www.elsevier.nl. Illus., adv. Refereed. Vol. ends: No. 4. Microform: PQC. Online: ingenta.com; ScienceDirect; Swets Blackwell. *Indexed:* BiolAb, ChemAb, DSR&OA, ExcerpMed, GeoRef, GeogAbPG, M&GPA, OceAb, PetrolAb, PollutAb, SCI, SWRA, WRCInf. *Aud.:* Ac, Sa.

Original studies and reviews focus on "chemistry in the marine environment, with emphasis on the dynamic approach." All aspects of the field from chemical processes to theoretical and experimental work are covered. Recent papers in a typical five to ten article issue treat chemical speciation of iron in northeast Atlantic Ocean surface waters, germanium cycling in New Zealand waters, instrumental determination of organic carbon in marine sediments, and reference materials for oceanic carbon dioxide analysis. Special issues on large deltas and their impact on coastal zones and thermodynamics and kinetics in natural waters have recently appeared. An important title for marine science research collections.

4667. ***Marine Ecology - Progress Series.*** [ISSN: 0171-8630] 1979. 20x/yr. EUR 3521 domestic; EUR 3592 Sat. foreign. Ed(s): O Kinne. Inter-Research, Nordbuente 23, Oldendorf, 21385, Germany; marita@int-res.com; http://www.int-res.com. Illus., index, adv. Refereed. Circ: 1000. Vol. ends: No. 3. *Indexed:* ApEcolAb, BiolAb, ChemAb, DSA, ForAb, GeoRef, GeogAbPG, HortAb, IndVet, PollutAb, S&F, SCI, SWRA, VetBull, ZooRec. *Aud.:* Ac, Sa.

This publication "serves as a worldwide forum for all aspects of marine ecology, fundamental and applied." Research articles, reviews, and notes cover the fields of microbiology, botany, zoology, ecosystem research, biological oceanography, ecological aspects of fisheries and aquaculture, pollution, environmental protection, conservation, and resource management. Ammonium uptake by seagrass communities, seasonal variations in the dynamics of microbial plankton communities in the Gulf of Trieste, Trans-Tasman Sea larval transport, and source of Aegean Sea harbor porpoises are the subjects of recent papers. An essential title for marine science collections.

4668. ***Marine Environmental Research.*** Incorporates (in 1991): *Oil and Chemical Pollution;* Which was formerly (until 1982): *Journal of Oil and Petrochemical Pollution.* [ISSN: 0141-1136] 1978. 10x/yr. EUR 1305. Ed(s): Dr. John Widdows, Dr. R. Spies. Elsevier Ltd., The Boulevard, Langford Ln, Oxford, OX5 1GB, United Kingdom. Illus., index, adv. Refereed. Vol. ends: No. 5. Microform: PQC. Online: ingenta.com; ScienceDirect; Swets Blackwell. *Indexed:* BiolAb, ChemAb, DSA, DSR&OA, EngInd, EnvAb, ExcerpMed, FPA, FS&TA, ForAb, GeoRef, IndMed, IndVet, OceAb, PetrolAb, PollutAb, S&F, SCI, SWRA, VetBull, WAE&RSA, WRCInf, ZooRec. *Aud.:* Ac, Sa.

Original research papers on "chemical, physical, and biological interactions in the oceans and coastal waters" are published in this international journal, which seeks to serve as "a forum for new information on biology, chemistry and toxicology and syntheses that advance understanding of marine environmental processes." Both anthropogenic and natural causes of changes in marine ecosystems involving biochemical, physiological, and ecological consequences of contaminants to marine organisms and ecosystems are included. Recent articles in a typical five-article issue treat tolerance of marine mussels to chlorination, the input of atmospheric lead to marine sediments in a southeast Pacific coastal area, heavy metal contamination and mining impact on a Greenland fjord, and the impact of oil-derived products on echinoderm behavior and biochemistry.

Marine Fisheries Review. See Fish, Fisheries, and Aquaculture section.

4669. ***Marine Geodesy: an international journal of ocean surveys, mapping and sensing.*** [ISSN: 0149-0419] 1977. q. USD 367 (Individuals, USD 168). Ed(s): Dr. Narendra Saxena. Taylor & Francis Inc, 325 Chestnut St, Suite 800, Philadelphia, PA 19016; info@taylorandfrancis.com; http://www.taylorandfrancis.com/. Illus. Refereed. Vol. ends: No. 4. Online: EBSCO Publishing; Ingenta Select; OCLC Online Computer Library Center, Inc.; RoweCom Information Quest; Swets Blackwell. Reprint: PSC. *Indexed:* DSR&OA, EnvAb, GeoRef, GeogAbPG, M&GPA, OceAb, SSCI. *Bk. rev.:* 3, 500 words. *Aud.:* Ac, Sa.

Covering such topics as topography and mapping, satellite altimetry, bathymetry, positioning, geoid determination, acoustics and space instrumentation, this journal aims "to stimulate progress in ocean surveys, mapping and remote sensing by promoting problem-oriented research in the marine environment." Technical notes and news are also included in a typical issue of four articles. Recent articles focus on the effect of sea level variability on the estimation of mean sea surface gradients, spatial variation of sea level trend along the Bangladesh Coast, gravity, mean sea surface and bathymetry models comparison in the Canary Islands, and absolute calibration of TOPEX/POSEIDON altimeters.

4670. ***Marine Geology: international journal of marine geology, geochemistry and geophysics.*** [ISSN: 0025-3227] 1964. 44x/yr. EUR 3016 (Qualified personnel, EUR 184). Ed(s): John T Wells, Herve Chamley. Elsevier BV, Sara Burgerhartstraat 25, Amsterdam, 1055 KV, Netherlands; nlinfo-f@elsevier.nl; http://www.elsevier.nl. Illus., index, adv. Refereed. Vol. ends: No. 4. Microform: PQC. Online: ingenta.com; ScienceDirect; Swets Blackwell. Reprint: SWZ. *Indexed:* ChemAb, DSR&OA, EngInd, GeoRef, GeogAbPG, M&GPA, OceAb, PetrolAb, PollutAb, SCI. *Aud.:* Ac, Sa.

Research and review articles and short papers cover developments in the fields of marine geology, geochemistry, and geophysics. Shelf-to-canyon sediment-transport processes on the continental margin off California, assymetric sedimentation on young ocean floor at the East Pacific Rise, problems with biogenic silica measurement in marginal seas, and the relationship of glacial iceberg surges in the North Atlantic to climatic warming are the subjects of recent articles.

4671. ***Marine Geophysical Researches: an international journal for the study of the earth beneath the sea.*** [ISSN: 0025-3235] 1970. bi-m. EUR 511 print or online ed. Ed(s): J C Sibuet, Kathleen Crane. Kluwer Academic Publishers, van Godewijckstraat 30, PO Box 17, Dordrecht, 3300 AA, Netherlands; services@wkap.nl; http://www.wkap.nl. Illus., adv. Refereed. Microform: PQC. Online: EBSCO Publishing; ingenta.com; Kluwer Online; OCLC Online Computer Library Center, Inc.; Ovid Technologies, Inc.; RoweCom Information Quest; Swets Blackwell. Reprint: SWZ. *Indexed:* ChemAb, DSR&OA, EngInd, GeoRef, M&GPA, OceAb, PetrolAb, SCI. *Aud.:* Ac, Sa.

A more specialized title than *Marine Geology*, this journal focuses on "description and analysis of structures that can be investigated with geophysical methods only, and the study of the physical processes that led to the origin of these structures." New techniques for seafloor imaging are also within its scope. Recent papers treat lithospheric structure below the eastern Arabian Sea based on gravity and seismic data, seismic expressions of deep-shelf depositional and erosional morphologies in the North Sea, small-scale lacustrine drifts in Lake Baikal, and Cenozoic contourite drift development in the northern Norwegian Sea.

4672. ***Marine Georesources and Geotechnology.*** Formed by the merger of (1975-1993): *Marine Geotechnology;* (1977-1993): *Marine Mining.* [ISSN: 1064-119X] 1993. q. USD 324 (Individuals, USD 172). Ed(s): Ronald Chaney, Michael Cruickshank. Taylor & Francis Inc, 325 Chestnut St, Suite 800, Philadelphia, PA 19016; info@taylorandfrancis.com; http://www.taylorandfrancis.com/. Illus., index, adv. Refereed. Circ: 260. Vol. ends: No. 4. Microform: PQC. Online: EBSCO Publishing; Ingenta Select; OCLC Online Computer Library Center, Inc.; RoweCom Information Quest; Swets Blackwell. Reprint: PQC; PSC. *Indexed:* AS&TI, BiolAb, C&ISA, ChemAb, DSR&OA, EngInd, EnvAb, GeoRef, GeogAbPG, MinerAb, OceAb, PetrolAb, SCI, SWRA. *Aud.:* Ac, Sa.

Research in seafloor sediment and rocks is reported in papers contributed by oceanographers, ocean engineers, geophysicists, and geologists in universities, government, and industry. Areas covered include marine minerals exploration and recovery, anchoring and mooring systems, bottom installations and coastal engineering structures. Recent articles treat properties of marine clays in East Asia, observations of the sediment-water interface in marine and fresh water environments, a Mexican beach environment as a potential source of placer minerals, and erosion and deposition rates in the Bay of Bengal coast. For collections serving ocean engineers and geological oceanographers.

4673. ***Marine Log.*** Former titles (until 1987): *Marine Engineering - Log;* (until 1979): *Marine Engineering - Log International;* (until 1977): *Marine Engineering - Log;* (until 1956): *Marine Engineering;* (until 1953): *Marine Engineering Shipping and Review;* (until 1935): *Marine Engineering & Shipping Age;* (until 1921): *Marine Engineering;* (until 1920): *International Marine Engineering;* (until 1906): *Marine Engineering.* [ISSN: 0897-0491] 1878. m. USD 35 domestic; USD 60 foreign. Ed(s): Nicholas Blenkey. Simmons - Boardman Publishing Corp., 345 Hudson St, 12th floor, New York, NY 10014-4502; http://www.marinelog.com/. Illus., adv. Circ: 26323 Paid and controlled. Vol. ends: Dec. Microform: PQC. *Indexed:* AS&TI, EngInd, EnvAb, ExcerpMed. *Aud.:* Sa.

This trade journal is dedicated "to providing marine industry professionals with the information they need to enable them to design, build and operate vessels, rigs and offshore structures, profitably, safely, legally and in an environmentally responsible manner." It carries national and international news relating to marine and maritime issues, equipment, software, and personnel, as well as numerous classified ads. Offshore security, funding for ferries, high-speed catamarans, and distinctive ships from Korea are topics of recent articles that cover a wide spectrum of military and commercial maritime activity. An annual U.S. marine directory is also issued.

4674. ***Marine Mammal Science.*** [ISSN: 0824-0469] 1985. q. USD 110 in North America; USD 120 elsewhere. Society for Marine Mammalogy, c/o Allen Press, Inc, Box 1897, Lawrence, KS 66044-8897; sfmm@allenpress.com; http://pegasus.cc.ucf.edu/~smm/. Illus., adv. Refereed. *Indexed:* AnBeAb, ApEcolAb, BiolAb, DSA, DSR&OA, GeoRef, IndVet, OceAb, RRTA, SCI, VetBull, ZooRec. *Bk. rev.:* 3, 2,000 words. *Aud.:* Ac, Sa.

Original research articles, reviews, notes, letters, and invited opinion papers present "significant new findings on marine mammals resulting from original research on their form and function, evolution, systematics, physiology, biochemistry, behavior, population biology, life history, genetics, ecology and conservation." The thermal function of phocid seal fur, reducing dolphin mortality with acoustic warning devices attached to fishing nets, a biopsy system for small cetaceans, and diets of beaked whales in the Sea of Okhotsk are the subjects of recent articles. Approximately fifteen articles, frequently by National Marine Fisheries Service scientists, appear in each issue.

4675. ***Marine Policy: the international journal of ocean affairs.*** [ISSN: 0308-597X] 1977. bi-m. EUR 788. Ed(s): E D Brown. Pergamon, The Boulevard, Langford Ln, East Park, Kidlington, OX5 1GB, United Kingdom. Illus., index, adv. Refereed. Vol. ends: No. 6. Microform: PQC. Online: ingenta.com; ScienceDirect; Swets Blackwell. *Indexed:* DSR&OA, EnvAb, ExcerpMed, FutSurv, GeoRef, GeogAbPG, IBSS, OceAb, PAIS, SSCI, WAE&RSA. *Aud.:* Ac, Sa.

Articles aimed at providing researchers, analysts, and policy makers with legal, political, social, and economic analysis are written by international lawyers, political scientists, marine economists, and marine resource managers. Subjects covered include international, regional, and national marine policies; institutional arrangements for the management and regulation of marine activities such as fisheries and shipping; conflict resolution; marine pollution and environment; conservation and use of marine resources. Recent articles cover civil liability for oil pollution damage, fishery management in Trinidad and Tobago, renewable energy from the ocean, and economic benefit of the Steller sea lion protection program. Suitable for political science, marine affairs, and marine science collections.

4676. ***Marine Pollution Bulletin: the international journal for marine environmentalists, scientists, engineers, administrators, politicians and lawyers.*** [ISSN: 0025-326X] 1970. s-m. EUR 1027 (Qualified personnel, EUR 204). Ed(s): Charles Sheppard, J Pearce. Pergamon, The Boulevard, Langford Ln, East Park, Kidlington, OX5 1GB, United Kingdom. Illus., index, adv. Refereed. Circ: 2000. Vol. ends: No. 12. Microform: PQC. Online: ingenta.com; ScienceDirect; Swets Blackwell. *Indexed:* ApEcolAb, BiolAb, ChemAb, DSA, DSR&OA, EngInd, EnvAb, ExcerpMed, FPA, FS&TA, ForAb, GeoRef, GeogAbPG, HortAb, IndMed, IndVet, M&GPA, OceAb, PetrolAb, PollutAb, RRTA, S&F, SCI, SSCI, SWRA, VetBull, WAE&RSA, WRCInf, ZooRec. *Bk. rev.:* 2, 500 words. *Aud.:* Ac, Sa.

This journal is concerned with the rational use of maritime and marine resources in estuaries, seas and oceans, as well as documenting marine pollution and introducing new forms of measurement and analysis. Research reports, reviews, news articles, opinion pieces, and conference reports appear along with information on new products. Monthly issues make up one volume per year, and the second volume includes special issues on such topics as marine pollution and ecotoxicology, marine environmental modeling and contaminants in the Arctic. Valuable for both marine affairs and marine science collections.

4677. ***Marine Technology Society Journal: the international, interdisciplinary society devoted to ocean and marine engineering, science and policy.*** Incorporates: *Ocean Soundings.* [ISSN: 0025-3324] 1963. q. USD 120 domestic; USD 135 foreign. Ed(s): Gregory Stone. Marine Technology Society, Inc., 5565 Sterrett Place, 108, Columbia, MD 21044; mtspubs@aol.com; http://www.mtsociety.org. Illus., index, adv. Refereed. Circ: 3200. Vol. ends: No. 4. Online: Northern Light Technology, Inc.; OCLC Online Computer Library Center, Inc.; ProQuest Information & Learning; H.W. Wilson. *Indexed:* AS&TI, B&AI, BiolAb, ChemAb, DSR&OA, EngInd, EnvAb, ExcerpMed, GeoRef, GeogAbPG, M&GPA, OceAb, PetrolAb, SCI, SSCI, SWRA, ZooRec. *Bk. rev.:* 1-3, 500 words. *Aud.:* Ac, Sa.

The areas of marine technology, marine resources, ocean and coastal engineering, and marine policy and education are the focus of this journal. Papers range from technical articles to marine management studies. Recent issues are devoted to renewable ocean energy, marine archaeology, the U.S. National Marine Sanctuary Program, and the U.S. Commission on Ocean Policy. Another useful title for science and technology as well as for marine affairs collections.

4678. ***Maritime Policy and Management: an international journal of shipping and port research.*** Formerly: *Maritime Studies and Management.* [ISSN: 0308-8839] 1973. q. GBP 467 (Individuals, GBP 228). Ed(s): James McConville. Taylor & Francis Ltd, 11 New Fetter Ln, London, EC4P 4EE, United Kingdom; info@tandf.co.uk; http://www.tandf.co.uk/journals. Illus., index, adv. Vol. ends: No. 4. Online: EBSCO Publishing; Ingenta Select; OCLC Online Computer Library Center, Inc.; RoweCom Information Quest; Swets Blackwell. Reprint: PSC. *Indexed:* C&ISA, DSR&OA, GeogAbPG, JEL, OceAb, PollutAb. *Bk. rev.:* 1-4, 400-600 words. *Aud.:* Ac, Sa.

Appropriate for collections covering the business, economic, sociolegal, and management aspects of maritime affairs, this journal is aimed at policymakers and managers throughout the fields of shipping and ports. Both theoretical and practical articles concern port and shipping management, the effects of national and international legislation on maritime trade, and changing economic conditions and their effects on shipping. Performance and traffic at Indian ports, third party ship management, Chinese container terminals, and the UK tonnage tax are the subjects of recent articles. Conference notices, book reviews, and news items also appear.

4679. ***National Wetlands Newsletter.*** [ISSN: 0164-0712] 1979. bi-m. USD 40. Ed(s): Teresa Opheim. Environmental Law Institute, 1616 P St, S W, Ste 200, Washington, DC 20036. Illus., index. Circ: 1000. Vol. ends: No. 6. *Indexed:* EnvAb, PAIS. *Bk. rev.:* 2, 200 words. *Aud.:* Ga, Sa.

Information and analysis on issues and trends in the law, science, and management of wetlands, floodplains, and coastal water resources is aimed at government officials, policy makers, and scientists. The latest news articles, press releases, updates on federal and state court decisions, and conference notices are available via the online version. Listings of recently published wetland books, reports, videos, and electronic materials are provided. Recommended for general as well as specialized collections as a valuable information resource for the informed citizen-activist.

4680. ***Ocean & Coastal Management: international journal dedicated to the study of all aspects of ocean and coastal management.*** Former titles (until 1992): *Ocean and Shoreline Management;* (until 1988): *Ocean Management.* [ISSN: 0964-5691] 1973. m. EUR 1241. Ed(s): B Cicin-Sain, R W Knecht. Pergamon, The Boulevard, Langford Ln, East Park, Kidlington, OX5 1GB, United Kingdom. Illus., adv. Refereed. Vol. ends: No. 44. Microform: PQC. Online: ingenta.com; ScienceDirect; Swets Blackwell. Reprint: SWZ. *Indexed:* BiolAb, DSR&OA, EngInd, EnvAb, ExcerpMed, GeoRef, GeogAbPG, IPSA, M&GPA, OceAb, PAIS, PollutAb, SSCI, SWRA, WAE&RSA. *Bk. rev.:* 1-2, 300-600 words. *Aud.:* Ac, Sa.

All aspects of ocean and coastal management at local, regional, national, and international levels are covered in this international, interdisciplinary journal. In comparison to *Marine Policy*, there is more emphasis on coastal management. Articles link the natural and physical sciences, policy analysis, and law to planning and management issues. Topics include analytical approaches to management, interactions among various ocean and coastal uses, resolution of multiple-use conflicts, alternative regimes, and institutional arrangements for integrated management of ocean and coastal areas. Recent articles cover tropical seascape ecosystem interactions, substitutions and restorations; bycatch mitigation tools; sustainability of wilderness sea kayaking in the Bay of Fundy; and management of large marine ecosystems. Changing technologies and patterns of use, and the governance of oceans and coasts are the topics of recent special issues. Suitable for academic and social science collections.

4681. ***Ocean Challenge.*** Supersedes (in 1990): *Challenger Society. Newsletter;* Which superseded (in 1975): *Challenger Society. Proceedings.* [ISSN: 0959-0161] 1990. 3x/yr. GBP 80; USD 152. Ed(s): Angela Colling. Parjon Information Services, Parjon Information Services, Haywards Heath, RH16 2YX, United Kingdom; http://www.soc.soton.ac.uk/others/csms/ochal/chall.htm. Adv. Circ: 600. *Aud.:* Hs, Ga, Ac, Sa.

The Challenger Society for Marine Science aims "to encourage a wider interest in the study of the seas and to raise awareness of the need for the proper management of the marine environment." Its members comprise both professionals in the field and educated laypeople. Its journal carries a broad range of articles such as historical accounts of the scientific results of the nineteenth-century survey ship *HMS Challenger* and Indian Ocean phenomena. Oceanographic news, book reviews, comment pieces, conference listings, and letters are also included. Emphasis is on the United Kingdom and Europe.

4682. ***Ocean Engineering: an international journal of research and development.*** [ISSN: 0029-8018] 1968. 18x/yr. EUR 2116 (Qualified personnel, EUR 233). Ed(s): Michael E McCormick, Rameswar Bhattacharyya. Pergamon, The Boulevard, Langford Ln, East Park, Kidlington, OX5 1GB, United Kingdom. Illus., index, adv. Refereed. Circ: 1200. Vol. ends: No. 28. Microform: PQC. Online: East View Publications, Inc.; ingenta.com; ScienceDirect; Swets Blackwell. *Indexed:* AS&TI, ApMecR, C&ISA, ChemAb, DSR&OA, EngInd, ExcerpMed, GeoRef, H&SSA, OceAb, PetrolAb, SCI, SWRA. *Aud.:* Ac, Sa.

Research papers and review articles cover exploration and use of the oceans for scientific knowledge, increased food production, and increased exploitation of mineral, oil, and gas resources. Articles focus on an environment that presents engineering problems as difficult as those encountered in space exploration. The design and construction of ships and structures, submarine soil mechanics, coastal engineering, hydrodynamics, ocean energy, aquacultural engineering, underwater acoustics, and instrumentation are within the scope of the journal. Recent papers treat coupled tide-wave-surge processes in the Yellow Sea, submerged breakwater performance, anchor deployment for deep water floating offshore equipment, and the estimation of forces exerted on cylindrical piles. Issues also included a calendar of meetings, news, and notices.

4683. ***Oceanography: serving ocean science and its applications.*** [ISSN: 1042-8275] 1988. q. USD 100; USD 115 in Canada & Mexico; USD 125 elsewhere. Ed(s): Larry Atkinson. Oceanography Society, 5912 Lemay Rd, Rockville, MD 20851-2326; anne@ccpo.odu.edu; http://tos.org/. Illus., adv. Refereed. Circ: 2000 Paid. Vol. ends: No. 4. *Indexed:* GeoRef, M&GPA, OceAb, ZooRec. *Bk. rev.:* 2, 1,000 words, signed. *Aud.:* Ga, Ac, Sa.

This journal "exists to promote and chronicle all aspects of ocean science and its applications." Brief articles, critical essays, reviews dealing with topics of interest to the ocean-science community, news, and meeting reports are included. One of the few general interest technical publications in a field of specialization, it also publishes special issues on such topics as progress reports on major international oceanographic programs.

4684. ***Oceanus: reports on research at the Woods Hole Oceanographic Institution.*** Incorporates in 1994: *Woods Hole Oceanographic Institution. Reports on Research.* [ISSN: 0029-8182] 1952. s-a. USD 15 domestic; USD 18 Canada; USD 25 elsewhere. Ed(s): Laurence Lippsett. Woods Hole Oceanographic Institution, Mail Stop 5, Woods Hole, MA 02543-1050; http://www.whoi.edu/oceanus. Illus., index, adv. Refereed. Circ: 6000. Vol. ends: No. 2. Microform: PQC. Online: Florida Center for Library Automation; Gale Group; Northern Light Technology, Inc.; OCLC Online Computer Library Center, Inc.; ProQuest Information & Learning; H.W. Wilson. Reprint: PQC. *Indexed:* AS&TI, B&AI, BiolAb, BiolDig, ChemAb, DSR&OA, EnvAb, ExcerpMed, FutSurv, GSI, GeoRef, M&GPA, OceAb, PollutAb, SCI, SSCI, ZooRec. *Aud.:* Hs, Ga, Ac, Sa.

Although it temporarily suspended publication at the end of 2000, this title is included because it may have resumed publication by press time. One of the few titles aimed at the educated layperson, it covers marine policy as well as science in articles written by scientists at Woods Hole Oceanographic Institution. Appropriate for both public libraries and academic institutions, it has an attractive format with numerous illustrations.

4685. ***Offshore (Tulsa).*** Incorporates: *Oilman.* [ISSN: 0030-0608] 1954. m. USD 75 domestic; USD 99 foreign; USD 6.50 per issue domestic. Ed(s): William Furlow. PennWell Corp., 1421 S Sheridan Rd, Tulsa, OK 74112; Headquarters@PennWell.com; http://www.pennwell.com. Illus., adv. Circ: 40000 Controlled. Vol. ends: No. 12. Microform: PQC. Online: EBSCO Publishing; Florida Center for Library Automation; Gale Group; LexisNexis; OCLC Online Computer Library Center, Inc. Reprint: PQC. *Indexed:* AS&TI, BrTechI, C&ISA, DSR&OA, GeoRef, PetrolAb. *Aud.:* Sa.

Focusing on the oil and gas industry in its worldwide offshore operations, this trade journal covers seismic services, exploration, drilling, production, pipelining, transportation, marine and underwater engineering and communications, naval architecture design and construction, diving services, marine support facilities, and applied research in oceanography and meteorology. Useful for business as well as technology collections.

4686. ***Ophelia: international journal of marine biology.*** [ISSN: 0078-5326] 1964. 2x/yr. DKK 1730. Ed(s): T. Fenchel. Apollo Books, Kirkeby Sand 19, Stenstrup, 5771, Denmark; apollobooks@vip.cybercity.dk; http://www.apollobooks.com. Illus., index, adv. Refereed. Circ: 600. Vol. ends: No. 3. *Indexed:* BiolAb, ChemAb, DSR&OA, GeoRef, IndVet, OceAb, PollutAb, SCI, VetBull, ZooRec. *Aud.:* Ac, Sa.

Focusing primarily on marine life in Scandinavian waters, this journal occasionally publishes supplements on specific topics in marine biology and ecology. Recent articles cover blue mussels in a Danish fjord, plankton dynamics in a Norwegian fjord, and a Baltic Sea amphipod. Reasonably priced and attractively printed, it is a useful title for academic marine biology collections.

4687. ***Progress in Oceanography.*** [ISSN: 0079-6611] 1963. 16x/yr. EUR 2139 (Qualified personnel, EUR 156). Ed(s): Charles B. Miller, Detlef R. Quadfasel. Pergamon, The Boulevard, Langford Ln, East Park, Kidlington, OX5 1GB, United Kingdom. Illus., index, adv. Refereed. Vol. ends: No. 4. Microform: PQC. Online: ingenta.com; ScienceDirect; Swets Blackwell. *Indexed:* ApMecR, BiolAb, ChemAb, DSR&OA, EngInd, GeoRef, GeogAbPG, M&GPA, OceAb, PollutAb, SCI, SWRA, ZooRec. *Aud.:* Ac, Sa.

This journal publishes "the longer, more comprehensive papers that most oceanographers feel are necessary, on occasion, to do justice to their work." Contributions are reviews or treatises on a developing oceanographic subject and represent all areas of the field. Observations on the 1997-98 El Nino along the western coast of North America, physical and biological conditions and processes in the northeast Pacific Ocean, and benthic processes and dynamics at the northwest Iberian margin are the subjects of recent special issues.

4688. ***Sarsia: North Atlantic marine science.*** [ISSN: 0036-4827] 1961. bi-m. GBP 121 (Individuals, GBP 33). Taylor & Francis A S, Cort Adelersgt. 17, Solli, PO Box 2562, Oslo, 0202, Norway; journals@tandf.no. Illus., index. Refereed. Circ: 750. Vol. ends: No. 4. Reprint: PSC. *Indexed:* BiolAb, ChemAb, DSR&OA, ExcerpMed, GeoRef, OceAb, SCI, ZooRec. *Aud.:* Ac, Sa.

This international journal serves as a forum for research on all aspects of oceanography and marine biology, with particular emphasis on the North Atlantic, Nordic, and Arctic environments. Papers on new instruments and methods, short communications, reviews, symposium proceedings, and special issues reporting the results of research programs are also included. Recent articles treat southern Norway heterozoan carbonates, pelagic cod and haddock juveniles on the Faroe plateau, the food of Norwegian spring-spawning herring in relation to the annual cycle of zooplankton, and marine gastrotrich fauna in Corsica.

4689. ***Sea Technology: for design engineering and application of equipment and services for the marine and defense environment.*** Formerly: *Undersea Technology.* [ISSN: 0093-3651] 1960. m. USD 40 domestic; USD 50 foreign; USD 4.50 newsstand/cover. Ed(s): Michele B. Umansky. Compass Publications, Inc. (Arlington), 1501 Wilson Blv, Ste 1001, Arlington, VA 22209. Illus., index, adv. Circ: 21500. Vol. ends: No. 12. Microform: PQC. Online: Northern Light Technology, Inc.; ProQuest Information & Learning. Reprint: PQC. *Indexed:* AS&TI, ApMecR, BiolAb, BiolDig, C&ISA, DSR&OA, EngInd, ExcerpMed, GeoRef, GeogAbPG, H&SSA, M&GPA, OceAb, PetrolAb, PollutAb, SWRA. *Aud.:* Sa.

Developments in ocean mining, ocean engineering, environmental monitoring, marine resources, naval affairs, and ocean business are reported in this trade publication. Its focus is marine technology, diving ships and structures, antisubmarine warfare, product development, offshore resources, research vessel activity, and marine electronics. Appropriate for business as well as marine science and ocean engineering collections, it has recently published articles on instrumentation, a coastal mooring system, a universal handling winch, and aptodes to measure oxygen in the aquatic environment. An annual buyers guide directory is issued.

4690. ***Underwater Naturalist.*** [ISSN: 0041-6606] 1962. irreg. 2-3/yr. USD 30 (Individuals, USD 25). Ed(s): D W Bennett. American Littoral Society, Sandy Hook, Highlands, NJ 07732; http://www.bullit.org/als.htm. Illus., index, adv. Circ: 9000. Vol. ends: No. 4. Microform: PQC. Reprint: PQC. *Indexed:* BRI, BiolAb, BiolDig, CBRI, SWRA, ZooRec. *Bk. rev.:* 3, 500 words. *Aud.:* Hs, Ga, Sa.

The environmental conservation, protection, and educational objectives of the American Littoral Society are the focus of this journal. Articles aimed at the educated layperson treat topics related to coasts, oceans, estuaries, freshwater rivers, and lakes. A report of the member-conducted fish-tagging program and short field notes reporting on natural history observations in various coastal areas appear regularly. A recent special issue is devoted to Delaware's coast.

Electronic Journals

Earth Interactions. See Atmospheric Sciences/Electronic Journals section.

4691. *HydroWire.* 1998. d. University of South Florida, Ocean Modeling and Prediction Laboratory, linae@kelvin.marine.usf.edu; http://www.hydrowire.org/. *Aud.:* Ac, Sa.

Sponsored by the American Geophysical Union Ocean Sciences Section, American Society of Limnology and Oceanography, Estuarine Research Federation, and The Oceanography Society, this online newsletter serves as a communication link for the aquatic sciences community. Intended as an up-to-date source of news and communication.

4692. *Marine Models Electronic Record.* irreg. Ed(s): William D Cohen. Marine Biological Laboratory, 7 MBL St, Woods Hole, MA 02543-1015; cschachi@mbl.edu; http://www.mbl.edu/. Refereed. *Aud.:* Ac, Sa.

A peer-reviewed electronic journal and database on aquatic organisms, this publication is intended to be of special value to biomedical research. Papers cover the collection and husbandry of marine model organisms, the preparation of their cells or tissues, and research techniques and experimental protocols specifically applicable to these systems. Associated with *The Biological Bulletin*, it provides an outlet for results obtained at the Marine Biological Laboratory of the Woods Hole Oceanographic Institution and at similar facilities throughout the world.

4693. *Ocean Modelling (OMOD).* [ISSN: 1463-5011] Elsevier Inc., 360 Park Ave. S, New York, NY 10010-1710; usinfo-f@elsevier.com; http://www.elsevier.com. *Aud.:* Ac, Sa.

Aimed at marine scientists, marine technologists, ocean and coastal engineers, data managers and computer scientists, this journal covers ocean-atmosphere interaction based on direct observation, or through analytical, numerical, or laboratory models. Eddy mass transport for the Southern Ocean, data-model-error compatibility, anisotropic horizontal viscosity for ocean models, and the nested structure of Arctic thermohaline intrusions are the subjects of recent articles.

■ MATHEMATICS

Research Journals

J. Parker Ladwig, Mathematics Library, University of Notre Dame, 009 Hayes-Healy Center, Notre Dame, IN 46556-5641; 574-631-3617; FAX: 574-631-9660; ladwig.1@nd.edu

Introduction

Mathematics is a word that can invoke a sense of dread, mystery, or logicial precision. It is one of the world's oldest intellectual pursuits and continues to fascinate its devotees even today. Mathematics is loved for a variety of reasons: its simple, but beautiful formulas, its problems with definite answers, its proofs that have been a model of philosophical demonstration, or its discipline of abstraction. Unfortunately, it is also a subject that builds upon itself so carefully that most advanced mathematics is inaccessible to those who have not spent years in its study.

The library has been called the mathematician's laboratory, and thus the task of libraries should be to foster a budding interest and then to support that interest once it has started to blossom. As a result, this section has been divided into two parts: magazines other than research journals, and research journals. The section of other magazines draws attention to those titles that can foster a reader's interest. They should be considered by every library. Research journals are those of interest to academic settings where research is pursued in mathematics, not just its instruction. Some of the largest public libraries might also find this section of interest. Research journals could be further divided in several ways: those published by universities, professional associations, or learned societies; those that focus mainly on either pure or applied mathematics; those that are still independently published; or those that are distinguished by their age. Five are strongly recommended, in order of importance: *Annals of Mathematics, Publications Mathematiques, Journal of the American Mathematical Society* (see *Notices*), *SIAM Journal on Applied Mathematics* (see *SIAM Review*), and *Acta Mathematica.* There is not a separate section for electronic journals because most mathematics journals are available electronically, generally full text, but at least with tables of contents. The web pages should be consulted for the most up-to-date information (although not necessarily the most complete).

In crafting this list, several factors have been considered: whether the title has been a consistent part of *Magazines for Libraries* over the years, whether the articles are mainly in English, the title's reputation among mathematicians and librarians, its subscription price and price per page, its citation pattern as calculated by ISI's impact factor, its publisher, and finally its ability to fill a niche unfilled by other titles. Several venerable, but pricey, research journals have been added since the last edition. They may not be the best value, but librarians should be aware of them. Also, several research journals with a more narrow specialization have been removed (e.g., *Mathematics of Computation*) because an attempt has been made to concentrate on those titles with the broadest scope. The reviews below contain quotes from the magazine, mention the presence of book reviews, and provide recommendations. Finally, librarians and mathematicians especially interested in libraries should be aware of the professional association for academic mathematics librarians: the Physics-Astronomy-Mathematics (PAM) Division of the Special Libraries Association. PAM's home page is http://www.sla.org/division/dpam, and PAM members are always eager to help.

Basic Periodicals

Ems: *Mathematics Teaching in the Middle School* (see *Mathematics Teacher*), *Teaching Children Mathematics;* Hs: *Mathematics Magazine* (see *American Mathematical Monthly*), *Mathematics Teacher;* Ga: *Journal of Recreational Mathematics, The Mathematical Intelligencer, Mathematics Magazine* (see *American Mathematical Monthly*); Ac: *American Mathematical Monthly; Bulletin of the American Mathematical Society, Notices; SIAM Review.*

Basic Abstracts and Indexes

MathSciNet.

4694. *American Mathematical Monthly.* [ISSN: 0002-9890] 1894. 10x/yr. USD 177. Ed(s): Bruce Palka. Mathematical Association of America, 1529 18th St, N W, Washington, DC 20036; http://www.maa.org. Illus., index, adv. Refereed. Circ: 18000. Vol. ends: No. 10. Microform: PQC. Online: Gale Group; JSTOR (Web-based Journal Archive); Northern Light Technology, Inc.; OCLC Online Computer Library Center, Inc.; ProQuest Information & Learning. Reprint: PQC. *Indexed:* BiolAb, CCMJ, CIJE, EngInd, GSI, MathSciNet, SCI. *Bk. rev.:* 1-4, 1,200-2,000 words, signed. *Aud.:* Hs, Ga, Ac, Sa.

The *American Mathematical Monthly* is a distinguished publication of the Mathematical Association of America (MAA; http://www.maa.org). The MAA was founded in 1915 and is the "largest professional society that focuses on undergraduate mathematics education." The *Monthly*'s articles "inform, stimulate, challenge, enlighten, and even entertain. . . . They may be expositions of old or new results, historical or biographical essays, speculations or definitive treatments, broad developments, or explorations of a single application. Novelty and generality are far less important than clarity of exposition and broad appeal." The *Monthly* is divided into four sections: "Articles," "Notes" (e.g., "The Right-Hand Derivative of an Integral"), "Problems and Solutions," and "Reviews." Other sections are occasionally added, for example, "Editor's Endnotes." There are a few lengthy, signed book reviews and sometimes a section called "Telegraphic Reviews." These are short and "designed to alert readers ... to new books appropriate to mathematics teaching and research." The *Monthly* is a basic resource for academic libraries and may be of interest to some high schools and general and special adults. The MAA publishes four other magazines:

Focus [ISSN: 0731-2040] 1981. 9/yr. Membership only. Tables of contents online at http://www.maa.org/pubs/focus.html. Mathematical Assoc. of America, 1529 Eighteenth St., N.W., Washington, DC 20036. The newsletter of the MAA. Contains information about "MAA activities, news about mathematics and the mathematical community, and articles about interesting ideas in mathematics, mathematics education, and related areas." There are no book reviews. It may be of interest to high schools, academic libraries, and some general and special adults.

Math Horizons [ISSN: 1072-4117] 1993. 4/yr. $45. Tables of contents online at http://www.mathcs.carleton.edu/math_horizons/. Mathematical Assoc. of America, 1529 Eighteenth St., N.W., Washington, DC 20036. "A [glossy] magazine for students interested in mathematics that aims to expand their intellectual and career horizons." There are no book reviews. It is recommended for academic libraries and may also be suitable for high schools and general and special adults.

Mathematics Magazine [ISSN: 0025-507X] 1926. 5/yr. $131. Tables of contents available online at http://www.maa.org/pubs/mathmag.html. Mathematical Assoc. of America, 1529 Eighteenth St., N.W., Washington, DC 20036. "Aims to provide lively and appealing mathematical expositions ... accessible to undergraduates." It is divided into five sections: "Articles," "Notes" (e.g., "Using Tangent Lines to Define Means"), "Problems," "Reviews," and "News and Letters." There are several medium-length, unsigned book reviews in each issue. It is a basic resource for general adults and academic libraries and may be suitable for some high schools and special adults.

The College Mathematics Journal [ISSN: 0746-8342] 1970. 5/yr. $85. Tables of contents are available online at http://www.maa.org/pubs/cmj.html. Mathematical Assoc. of America, 1529 Eighteenth St., N.W., Washington, DC 20036. Provides "articles that ... enrich undergraduate instruction and enhance classroom learning." The articles cover a mix of mathematics education and pure, applied, and recreational mathematics (cf. *Journal for Research in Mathematics Education* under *Mathematics Teacher*). There are 15–20 short- to medium-length, signed book reviews. It is recommended for academic libraries and may be suitable for some high schools and general and special adults.

Annals of Probability. See Statistics section.

Annals of Statistics. See Statistics section.

Applied Statistics. See *Royal Statistical Society. Journal. Series C. Applied Statistics* in the Statistics section.

Chance. See Statistics section.

JASA. See Statistics section.

4695. *Journal of Recreational Mathematics.* [ISSN: 0022-412X] 1968. q. USD 165 (Individuals, USD 35.95). Ed(s): Charles Ashbacher, Colin RJ Singleton. Baywood Publishing Co., Inc., 26 Austin Ave, Amityville, NY 11701; info@baywood.com; http://www.baywood.com. Illus. Sample. Refereed. Vol. ends: No. 4. *Indexed:* GSI. *Bk. rev.:* 3-6, 300-600 words, signed. *Aud.:* Hs, Ga, Ac.

The *Journal of Recreational Mathematics* is intended to fulfill the need of those who desire a periodical uniquely devoted to the lighter side of mathematics. No special mathematical training is required. You will find such things as number curiosities and tricks, paper-folding creations, chess and checker brain-teasers, articles about mathematics and mathematicians, and discussion of some higher mathematics and their applications to everyday life and to puzzle-solving. It includes some occasional word games and cryptography, a lot to do with magic squares, map-coloring, geometric dissections, games with a mathematical flavor, and many other topics generally included in the fields of puzzles and recreational mathematics. Its nontextbook approach will clarify in a recreational form many of the abstract concepts wrestled with in formal classroom situations. There are several medium-length, signed book reviews in each issue. This is a basic resource for general adults, and may be suitable for high schools, academic libraries, and special adults.

Journal of Symbolic Logic. See Philosophy section.

4696. *Mathematical Gazette.* [ISSN: 0025-5572] 1894. 3x/yr. GBP 55 domestic; GBP 59 foreign. Ed(s): Gerry Leversha. Mathematical Association, 259 London Rd, Leicester, LE2 3BE, United Kingdom; office@m-a.org.uk; http://www.m-a.org.uk. Illus., index, adv. Circ: 3000. Vol. ends: No. 3. Reprint: PQC. *Bk. rev.:* 25-35, 600-1,500 words, signed; 10-15, 100-300 words, signed. *Aud.:* Hs, Ac, Sa.

The *Mathematical Gazette* is now over a century old. It is the chief publication (among seven) of the United Kingdom's Mathematical Association (http://www.m-a.org.uk/), founded in 1871 to improve education in mathematics. In addition to its expository articles, the *Gazette* contains regular sections for letters, problems, and extensive medium-length and short, signed book reviews. The focus is on the teaching and learning of mathematics for audiences 15–20 years old. Recommended for high schools, academic libraries, and special adults who want to know about those interested in mathematics who live outside of the United States.

4697. *The Mathematical Intelligencer.* [ISSN: 0343-6993] 1978. q. USD 72. Ed(s): Chandler Davis. Springer-Verlag, Journals, 175 Fifth Ave., New York, NY 10010-7703; journals@springer-ny.com; http://www.springer-ny.com. Illus., index, adv. Refereed. Vol. ends: No. 4. Microform: PQC. Online: EBSCO Publishing; Gale Group; Springer LINK. Reprint: ISI; SWZ. *Indexed:* CCMJ, GSI, MathSciNet, SCI, SSCI. *Bk. rev.:* 2-5, 1,000-2,000 words, signed. *Aud.:* Hs, Ga, Ac, Sa.

The Mathematical Intelligencer is what mathematicians read for enjoyment. It "publishes articles about mathematics, about mathematicians, and about the history and culture of mathematics. Articles ... inform and entertain a broad audience of mathematicians, including many mathematicians who are not specialists in the subject of the article. Articles might discuss a current fad or a past trend, theorems or people, history or philosophy, applications or theory." Articles are written in a casual style, often with humor or controversy, and there are a number of pictures and graphics. There are a few medium-length to long, signed book reviews. It is recommended as a basic resource for almost every type of library, and if you can only afford one magazine, this is the one that best captures the spirit of mathematics.

4698. *Mathematics Teacher.* [ISSN: 0025-5769] 1908. 9x/yr. USD 95 (Individuals, USD 65; Students, USD 40.50). National Council of Teachers of Mathematics, 1906 Association Dr, Reston, VA 20191-9988; nctm@nctm.org; http://www.nctm.org. Illus., adv. Refereed. Circ: 50000 Paid. Microform: PQC. Online: EBSCO Publishing; Gale Group; Northern Light Technology, Inc.; OCLC Online Computer Library Center, Inc.; ProQuest Information & Learning; H.W. Wilson. Reprint: PQC. *Indexed:* BRI, BioInd, CBRI, CIJE, ECER, EduInd, MRD. *Bk. rev.:* 5-8, 100-300 words, signed. *Aud.:* Ems, Hs, Ac, Sa.

Mathematics Teacher is the oldest journal published by the National Council of Teachers of Mathematics (NCTM). In fact, the NCTM was founded in 1920, 12 years after the first issue. The NCTM is the world's largest organization for teaching mathematics and includes members from the United States and Canada. Its mission is "to provide the vision and leadership necessary to ensure a mathematics education of the highest quality for all students." It is well known for its *Principles and Standards for School Mathematics*, and those selecting NCTM journals should be aware that the NCTM was involved in what came to be known as the "Math Wars." Some professional mathematicians still view the NCTM with suspicion. *Mathematics Teacher* is "devoted to improving mathematics instruction in grade 8 through two-year and teacher-education colleges." "It offers activities, lesson ideas, teaching strategies, and problems through in-depth articles, departments, and features, . . . [and includes] great resources for secondary teachers, preservice teachers, and teacher educators." Each issue has several short, signed book reviews. It is a basic magazine recommended for high schools and may be suitable for academic libraries and some middle schools. The NCTM's other magazines include:

Teaching Children Mathematics (formerly *Arithmetic Teacher*) [ISSN: 1073-5836] 1954. 9/yr. Can be included with $68 NCTM membership. Online at http://my.nctm.org/eresources/journal_home.asp?journal_id=4. National Council of Teachers of Mathematics, 1906 Association Dr., Reston, VA 20191-9988. An official journal of the NCTM, it is "a forum for the exchange of ideas and a source of activities and pedagogical strategies for mathematics education pre-K–6. It presents new developments in curriculum, instruction, learning, and teacher education; interprets the results of research; and in general provides information on any aspect of the broad spectrum of mathematics education appropriate for preservice and in-service teachers." It also includes several short to medium-length, signed book reviews per issue. It is a basic magazine for elementary schools.

Mathematics Teaching in the Middle School (formerly *Arithmetic Teacher*) [ISSN: 1072-0839] 1954. 9/yr. Can be included with $68 NCTM membership. Online at http://my.nctm.org/eresources/journal_home.asp?journal_id=3. National Council of Teachers of Mathematics, 1906 Association Dr., Reston, VA 20191-9988. An official journal of the NCTM, it is "intended as a resource for middle school students, teachers, and teacher educators. The focus of the journal is on intuitive, exploratory investigations that use informal reasoning to help students develop a strong conceptual basis that leads to greater mathematical abstraction." It includes several short to medium-length, signed book reviews per issue. It is a basic magazine for middle schools.

Journal for Research in Mathematics Education [ISSN: 0021-8251] 199. 5/yr. $90 with NCTM membership. Online at http://my.nctm.org/eresources/journal_home.asp?journal_id=1. National Council of Teachers of Mathematics, 1906 Association Dr., Reston, VA 20191-9988. An official journal of the NCTM, it is "devoted to the interests of teachers of mathematics and mathematics education at all levels—preschool through adult. It is a forum for disciplined inquiry into the teaching and learning of mathematics." It includes articles, brief reports, and commentaries on research, and a few lengthy, signed book reviews (cf. *College Mathematics Journal* and *American Mathematical Monthly*). Recommended for academic libraries and may be of interest to high schools and special adults.

ON-Math, the Online Journal of School Mathematics [ISSN: not available—electronic only] 2002. 4/yr. Membership only. Online at http://my.nctm.org/eresources/journal_home.asp?journal_id=6. National Council of Teachers of Mathematics, 1906 Association Dr., Reston, VA 20191-9988. It is "a peer-reviewed journal developed and designed exclusively for the electronic medium in which it is published." Its mission is "to serve as a resource for all those involved in school mathematics. It presents a broad range of ideas for teaching and learning mathematics at any level, from early childhood to young adult. The journal will capitalize on the unique opportunities afforded by electronic media." There are no book reviews. Although this magazine is new, it promises to be a good vehicle for bringing together interest in mathematics education at all levels. Recommended for elementary, middle, and high schools and for some academic libraries and special adults.

4699. *Pi Mu Epsilon Journal.* [ISSN: 0031-952X] 1949. s-a. USD 20 for 2 yrs. domestic; USD 25 for 2 yrs. foreign. Ed(s): Brigitte Servatius. Pi Mu Epsilon, Inc, c/o Michelle Schultz, Dept of Mathematical Sciences, Las Vegas, NV 89154-4020; http://www.pme-math.org. Illus., adv. Refereed. Circ: 3500 Paid. Microform: PQC. Reprint: PQC. *Aud.:* Hs, Ac, Sa.

The *Pi Mu Epsilon Journal* (*PME*) is the official publication of the Pi Mu Epsilon National Honorary Mathematics Society (http://www.pme-math.org). PME was founded in 1914 at Syracuse University and currently has over 300 chapters at colleges and universities throughout the United States. "In its quest to promote mathematics, Pi Mu Epsilon sponsors a journal devoted to topics in mathematics accessible to undergraduate students." In addition to its articles, many written by undergraduates, there are sections for problems and puzzles, but no book reviews. Of the undergraduate journals, it tends to focus the most on pure mathematics. Recommended for academic libraries, special adults, and perhaps some high schools.

4700. *U M A P Journal.* [ISSN: 0197-3622] 1980. q. USD 165, Libraries, USD 140 (Individuals, USD 69). Ed(s): P J Campbell. Consortium for Mathematics and Its Applications, 57 Bedford St, Ste 210, Lexington, MA 02420-4428. Illus., index, adv. Circ: 1500. Vol. ends: No. 4. *Indexed:* EduInd. *Bk. rev.:* 3-10, 250-1,500 words. *Aud.:* Hs, Ga, Ac, Sa.

The *UMAP Journal* is published by the Consortium for Mathematics and Its Applications (COMAP; http://www.comap.com/). COMAP was founded in 1980 and is a nonprofit organization whose mission is to improve mathematics education for students of all ages. It "works with teachers, students, and business people to create learning environments where mathematics is used to investigate and model real issues in our world." Some of its partners include the National Science Foundation, the Mathematical Association of America, the National Council of Teachers of Mathematics, and the Society for Industrial and Applied Mathematics. COMAP also publishes magazines of interest to elementary and high schools. *UMAP* "blends contemporary teaching modules with commentaries and articles to create a boldly different periodical. Each issue puts several real-world problems under a mathematical lens, and demonstrates how real people are using mathematics in their jobs and lives." It includes medium-length, signed book reviews. Of the undergraduate journals listed in this section, *UMAP* is the one most focused on applied mathematics. It is recommended for academic libraries and may be suitable for high schools and general and special adults.

Research Journals

4701. *Acta Mathematica.* [ISSN: 0001-5962] 1882. q. 2 vols/yr. GBP 190 in Europe; USD 275 elsewhere. Ed(s): Uffe Haagerup. Institut Mittag-Leffler, Auravaegen 17, Djursholm, 18260, Sweden. Illus., index. Refereed. Vol. ends: No. 2. Reprint: SWZ. *Indexed:* CCMJ, MathSciNet, SCI. *Aud.:* Ac, Sa.

Acta Mathematica is an official journal of the Royal Swedish Academy of Sciences. The academy was founded in 1739 and was "modelled on the pattern of the Royal Society of London." *Acta Mathematica* is sometimes referred to as *Acta Mathematica-Djursholm,* after its city of publication, to distinguish it from other journals of the same title. It contains research papers in all fields of mathematics. Most of the papers are in English, but some are in French or German. Although more than 600 pages are published annually, there are only about 10 to 15 articles. These tend to be papers that are highly cited and of lasting importance. There are no book reviews, but the journal recently became available online (www.kva.se/KVA_Root/index_eng.asp). It is strongly recommended for academic libraries and special adults.

4702. *American Journal of Mathematics.* [ISSN: 0002-9327] 1878. bi-m. USD 285 (Individuals, USD 89). Ed(s): Bernard Shiffman. Johns Hopkins University Press, Journals Publishing Division, 2715 N Charles St, Baltimore, MD 21218-4363; http://www.press.jhu.edu/. Illus., index, adv. Refereed. Circ: 1322. Vol. ends: No. 6. Microform: PMC; PQC. Online: EBSCO Publishing; Florida Center for Library Automation; Gale Group; JSTOR (Web-based Journal Archive); OCLC Online Computer Library Center, Inc.; Project MUSE; RoweCom Information Quest; Swets Blackwell. Reprint: PQC; PSC. *Indexed:* CCMJ, MathSciNet, SCI, SSCI. *Aud.:* Ac, Sa.

The *American Journal of Mathematics*, published by Johns Hopkins University Press, is "the oldest mathematics journal in the Western Hemisphere in continuous publication ... and ranks as one of the most respected and celebrated journals in the field." The journal "does not specialize, but instead publishes articles of broad appeal covering the major areas of contemporary mathematics." Each year, there are 40–50 articles, totaling about 1,400 pages. There are no book reviews. It is recommended for academic libraries and special adults.

4703. *American Mathematical Society. Notices.* [ISSN: 0002-9920] 1954. 11x/yr. Institutional members, USD 306; Individual members, USD 228; Non-members, USD 382. Ed(s): Anthony W Knapp. American Mathematical Society, 201 Charles St, Providence, RI 02904-2294; cust-serv@ams.org; http://www.ams.org/notices. Illus., index, adv. Sample. Refereed. Circ: 30000 Paid and free. Vol. ends: No. 10. Microform: PQC. Online: EBSCO Publishing. Reprint: PQC. *Indexed:* CCMJ, CompR, MathSciNet. *Bk. rev.:* 1-2, 4,000-6,000 words signed. *Aud.:* Ac, Sa.

Notices is the capstone publication of the American Mathematical Society (AMS; http://www.ams.org) and is a basic resource for academic libraries. It is also strongly recommended for special adults, general adults, and perhaps even some high schools. The AMS was founded in 1888 to "further the interests of mathematical research and scholarship" and is one of the most important mathematical societies in the world. *Notices* contains articles that "address mathematics, mathematical news and developments, issues affecting the profession, mathematics education at any level, the AMS and its activities, and other such topics of interest to *Notices* readers." The articles are not written for experts, so this magazine is comparable to the *Mathematical Intelligencer* in both type and importance. There are one or two lengthy, signed book reviews in each issue. The AMS publishes and distributes a number of journals. Those with the broadest focus have been included below, but also see http://www.ams.org/journals/ for more information.

Abstracts. [ISSN: 0192-5857] 1894. 4/yr. $90. American Mathematical Society, 201 Charles St., Providence, RI 02904-2294. The abstracts published are "those submitted by authors who intend to present them at AMS meetings or who wish to announce research results." They are sorted by the 2000 Mathematics Subject Classification, listed on the back of each issue, which unfortunately does not correspond with either the Dewey or Library of Congress classifications. There are about 600 pages published per year, with 5–6 abstracts per page. Further information may be found at http://www.ams.org/bookstore-getitem/item=ABS/. Recommended for academic libraries and special adults.

Bulletin. New Series. [ISSN: 0273-0979] 1894. 11/yr. $286. Online at http://www.ams.org/bull. American Mathematical Society, 201 Charles St., Providence, RI 02904-2294. The journal contains articles of two types: "papers that present a clear and insightful exposition of significant aspects of contemporary mathematical research . . . ; and brief, timely reports on important mathematical developments." It also contains 4–8 long, signed book reviews per issue (3,000–5,000 words). This is a basic resource for academic libraries and special adults and should be considered for general adults.

Electronic Research Announcements. [ISSN: 1079-6762]. Free online at http://www.ams.org/era. American Mathematical Society, 201 Charles St., Providence, RI 02904-2294. "This electronic-only journal publishes research announcements (up to about ten journal pages) of significant advances in all branches of mathematics. A research announcement should be designed to communicate its contents to a broad mathematical audience and should meet high standards for clarity as well as mathematical content." There are 12–15 articles per year, but no book reviews. Recommended for academic libraries and special adults.

Journal. [ISSN: 0894-0347] 1988. 4/yr. $197. Online at http://www.ams.org/jams. American Mathematical Society, 201 Charles St., Providence, RI 02904-2294. It is "devoted to research articles of the highest quality in all areas of pure and applied mathematics"—the AMS's most significant research articles. There are 25–30 articles per year, totaling about 1,000 pages, but no book reviews. Strongly recommended for academic libraries and special adults.

Memoirs. [ISSN: 0065-9266] 1950. 6 mailings/yr. $444. A list of volumes is online at http://www.ams.org/bookstore/memoseries. American Mathematical Society, 201 Charles St., Providence, RI 02904-2294. This can be subscribed to like a journal, but it is more like a monographic series. Though there are six mailings per year, each mailing contains more than one volume. "Memoirs is a series devoted to the publication of research in all areas of pure and applied mathematics. Manuscripts accepted for publication are similar to those published in *Transactions*. . . . Each issue contains either a single monograph or a group of related papers." There are about 30 articles published per year, totaling about 3,000 pages, and no book reviews. Because it is comparable to *Transactions*, it contains important research, but not as important as that found in the *Journal*. Recommended for academic libraries and special adults.

Proceedings. [ISSN: 0002-9939] 1950. 12/yr. $727. Online at http://www.ams.org/proc. American Mathematical Society, 201 Charles St., Providence, RI 02904-2294. It is "devoted to shorter research articles (not to exceed ten printed pages) in all areas of pure and applied mathematics. Very short notes not to exceed two printed pages are also accepted and appear under the heading 'Shorter Notes.' Items deemed suitable include an elegant new proof of an important and well-known theorem, an illuminating example or counterexample, or a new viewpoint on familiar results." The papers are divided into seven sections: A. Algebra, Number Theory, and Combinatorics; B. Analyis; C. Applied Mathematics; D. Geometry; E. Logic and Foundations; F. Statistics and Probability; and G. Topology. Longer papers may be found in *Transactions*. There are around 500 articles published per year in some 4,000 pages, with no book reviews. Recommended for academic libraries and special adults.

Transactions. [ISSN: 0002-9947] 1900. 12/yr. $1,192. Online at http://www.ams.org/tran. American Mathematical Society, 201 Charles St., Providence, RI 02904-2294. Like the *Proceedings*, it is "devoted to research articles in all areas of pure and applied mathematics," but papers are longer than ten pages. There are roughly 250–300 articles per year in more than 5,000 pages. There are no book reviews. Recommended for academic libraries and special adults.

4704. *Annals of Mathematics.* Formerly (until 1884): *The Analyst.* [ISSN: 0003-486X] 1874. bi-m. USD 250 (Individuals, USD 68). Johns Hopkins University Press, Journals Publishing Division, 2715 N Charles St, Baltimore, MD 21218-4363; http://www.press.jhu.edu/. Illus., index. Refereed. Circ: 1585. Vol. ends: No. 3. Microform: PMC; PQC. Online: JSTOR (Web-based Journal Archive). Reprint: PQC. *Indexed:* CCMJ, MathSciNet, SCI. *Aud.:* Ga, Ac, Sa.

The *Annals of Mathematics* is one of the most highly respected journals of mathematics. It is an inexpensive, university journal published with the cooperation of Princeton University and the Institute for Advanced Study (IAS; http://www.ias.edu/). The IAS was founded in 1930 and "over the past seventy-two years ... has been home to some of the most highly regarded thinkers of the twentieth century," including Albert Einstein and Andrew Wiles. *Annals* publishes articles in all areas of mathematics research. It recently became available through Project Euclid (http://www.projecteuclid.org), a Scholarly Publishing and Academic Resources Coalition (SPARC) Scientific Communities Partner. There are 35–45 articles published per year, totaling about 1,600 pages. There are no book reviews. It is strongly recommended for academic libraries and special adults and may be suitable for some general adults.

4705. *Cambridge Philosophical Society. Mathematical Proceedings.* Formerly: *Cambridge Philosophical Society. Proceedings. Mathematical and Physical Sciences.* [ISSN: 0305-0041] 1843. bi-m. USD 570. Ed(s): C B Thomas. Cambridge University Press, The Edinburgh Bldg, Shaftesbury Rd, Cambridge, CB2 2RU, United Kingdom; information@cambridge.org; http://uk.cambridge.org/journals. Illus., index, adv. Refereed. Vol. ends: No. 3. Microform: PMC; PQC. Online: EBSCO Publishing; OCLC Online Computer Library Center, Inc.; RoweCom Information Quest; Swets Blackwell. *Indexed:* ApMecR, CCMJ, ChemAb, DSR&OA, EngInd, GeoRef, MathSciNet, SCI. *Aud.:* Ac, Sa.

Cambridge Philosophical Society. Mathematical Proceedings is an important university journal published by Cambridge University Press (cf. *Annals of Mathematics* and *American Journal of Mathematics*). Begun in the mid-nineteenth century, it "covers the whole range of pure and applied mathematics, theoretical physics and statistics." There are 70–80 articles published each year in about 600 pages. There are no book reviews. This journal is recommended for academic libraries and special adults.

4706. *Canadian Journal of Mathematics.* [ISSN: 0008-414X] 1945. bi-m. Members, CND 120 for print or online ed.; Non-members, CND 240 for print or online ed. Ed(s): Henri Darmon, Niky Kamran. Canadian Mathematical Society, 577 King Edward, Ste 109, PO Box 450, Ottawa, ON K1N 6N5, Canada; memberships@cms.math.ca; http://www.cms.math.ca. Illus., adv. Refereed. Circ: 1400. Vol. ends: No. 6. Microform: PQC. Online: EBSCO Publishing. *Indexed:* CCMJ, MathSciNet, SCI, ST&MA. *Aud.:* Ac, Sa.

The *Canadian Journal of Mathematics* (*CJM*) is an official publication of the Canadian Mathematical Society (http://www.cms.math.ca/). The society was founded in 1945 as the Canadian Mathematical Congress, and "the founding members hoped that this congress [would] be the beginning of important mathematical development in Canada." Longer articles are included in the *CJM*, and shorter articles are published in the *Canadian Mathematical Bulletin* (not listed here). To be included, "papers must treat new mathematical research, be well written, and be of interest to a reasonable segment of the mathematical community." Papers are generally in English, but may also be in French. There are 40–50 articles per year for a total of about 1,400 pages. It is recommended for academic libraries and special adults.

4707. *Duke Mathematical Journal.* [ISSN: 0012-7094] 1935. 15x/yr. USD 1529 includes online access (Individuals, USD 800 includes online access). Ed(s): Jonathan Wahl. Duke University Press, 905 W Main St, Ste 18 B, Durham, NC 27701; subscriptions@dukeupress.edu; http://www.dukeupress.edu. Illus., index, adv. Refereed. Circ: 950. Vol. ends: No. 3. Microform: MIM; PQC; NRP. Reprint: ISI; PQC; PSC. *Indexed:* CCMJ, MathSciNet, SCI. *Aud.:* Ac, Sa.

The *Duke Mathematical Journal* (*DMJ*) is one of the more important of the university journals (cf. *Annals of Mathematics* and *American Journal of Mathematics*). Unfortunately, it is also one of the journals most like the largest commercial publishers in terms of its price, nearly $1,400 per year. In 1991, it began to publish *International Mathematics Research Notices* separately (*IMRN* is now published by Hindawi Publishing Corp.). *DMJ* focuses on pure mathematics and publishes 90–100 articles per year in about 2,500 pages. There are no book reviews. Recommended for academic libraries and special adults.

4708. *Historia Mathematica: international journal of the history of mathematics.* [ISSN: 0315-0860] 1974. q. EUR 351 (Individuals, EUR 112). Ed(s): U. Bottazzini, C. Fraser. Academic Press, 525 B St, Ste 1900, San Diego, CA 92101-4495; apsubs@acad.com; http://www.academicpress.com. Illus., adv. Refereed. Online: EBSCO Publishing; ingenta.com; OCLC Online Computer Library Center, Inc.; RoweCom Information Quest; ScienceDirect; Swets Blackwell. *Indexed:* ArtHuCI, CCMJ, IBZ, MathSciNet, SSCI. *Bk. rev.:* 1-2, 1,000-1,500 words, signed; 1-2, 500-600 words, signed; 18-22 pages of 50- to 100-word abstracts. *Aud.:* Ga, Ac, Sa.

Historia Mathematica is the most important journal covering the history and sometimes the philosophy of mathematics. It is the official publication of the International Commission for the History of Mathematics (http://www.math.uu.nl/ichm/). It "publishes historical scholarship on mathematics and its development in all cultures and time periods," and while most of the articles are in English, some are in French or German. It includes, besides research articles, one or two lengthy, signed book reviews and many pages of abstracts of recent publications. These reviews and abstracts try to cover everything published about the history of mathematics. Each year, there are about 15 research articles in the 500 pages published. Recommended for academic libraries and special adults and may be suitable for some general adults.

4709. *I M A Journal of Applied Mathematics.* Supersedes in part (in 1981): *Institute of Mathematics and Its Applications. Journal.* [ISSN: 0272-4960] 1981. bi-m. GBP 390. Ed(s): David J. Needham, Alan R. Champneys. Oxford University Press, Great Clarendon St, Oxford, OX2 6DP, United Kingdom; jnl.orders@oup.co.uk; http://www3.oup.co.uk/jnls. Illus., adv. Sample. Refereed. Circ: 750. Vol. ends: No. 6. Online: EBSCO Publishing; ingenta.com; OCLC Online Computer Library Center, Inc.; RoweCom Information Quest; Swets Blackwell. Reprint: PSC. *Indexed:* ApMecR, C&ISA, CCMJ, ChemAb, EngInd, ExcerpMed, GeoRef, IAA, MathSciNet, SCI. *Aud.:* Ac, Sa.

The *IMA Journal of Applied Mathematics* is published for the Institute of Mathematics and Its Applications (http://www.ima.org.uk/). The institute was founded in the United Kingdom in 1964 and is "the professional and learned society for qualified and practising mathematicians. Its mission is to promote mathematics in industry, business, the public sector, education and research." Oxford University Press publishes five other journals on its behalf, including the *IMA Journal of Numerical Analysis* (not listed here). It aims to publish "in all areas of the application of mathematics. It also seeks to publish papers on new developments of existing mathematical methods. . . . Longer papers that survey recent progress in topical fields of mathematics and its applications are also published." It publishes about 30 articles per year in 600 pages. There are no book reviews. This journal is recommended for academic libraries and special adults.

4710. *Indiana University Mathematics Journal.* Former titles (until 1970): *Journal of Mathematics and Mechanics;* (until 1956): *Journal of Rational Mechanics and Mathematics.* [ISSN: 0022-2518] 1952. 6x/yr. USD 285 includes CD-ROM (Individuals, USD 100 includes CD-ROM). Ed(s): Hari Bercovi. Indiana University, Department of Mathematics, Rawles Hall 115, Bloomington, IN 47405-7106; sadam@indiana.edu; http://www.iumj.indiana.edu. Illus., index. Refereed. Circ: 675 Paid. Vol. ends: No. 4. *Indexed:* CCMJ, EngInd, IAA, MathSciNet, SCI. *Aud.:* Ac, Sa.

The *Indiana University Mathematics Journal* is an important university journal (cf. *Annals of Mathematics* and *American Journal of Mathematics*). It focuses on "significant research articles in both pure and applied mathematics" even though its former title suggests a more applied emphasis. Each year, there are about 40–50 articles in about 2,000 pages. Its web site is confusing, but some articles are available in full text. There are no book reviews. Recommended for academic libraries and special adults.

4711. *Institut des Hautes Etudes Scientifiques, Paris. Publications Mathematiques.* [ISSN: 0073-8301] 1959. s-a. EUR 298 domestic; EUR 305.50 foreign; EUR 179 newsstand/cover per issue. Ed(s): E Ghys. Springer-Verlag, Tiergartenstr 17, Heidelberg, 69121, Germany. Illus., adv. Sample. Refereed. *Indexed:* CCMJ, MathSciNet. *Aud.:* Ga, Ac, Sa.

Publications Mathematiques de L'IHES is one the most important European mathematics journals. Many articles are published in English, the rest in French or German. It is sponsored by the Institut des Hautes Etudes Scientifiques in France, which is "an institute of advanced research in mathematics and theoretical physics with an interest in epistemology and the history of science." The IHES was founded in 1958 and is the European counterpart of the Institute for Advanced Studies (cf. *Annals of Mathematics*). *Publications Mathematiques* is, simply stated, "an international journal publishing papers of highest scientific level." There are about ten articles per year totaling about 500 pages. Back volumes are available electronically from http://www.numdam.org/en/, a program instituted on behalf of the French National Center for Scientific Research (CNRS), which "addresses the retro-digitization of mathematics documents published in France." Strongly recommended for academic libraries and special adults; it may be of interest to some general adults.

4712. *Inventiones Mathematicae.* [ISSN: 0020-9910] 1966. m. EUR 2470 domestic; EUR 2518.20 foreign; EUR 247 newsstand/cover per issue. Ed(s): J.-M Bismut, G Faltings. Springer-Verlag, Tiergartenstr 17, Heidelberg, 69121, Germany. Illus., adv. Sample. Refereed. Vol. ends: No. 3. Microform: PQC. Online: EBSCO Publishing; RoweCom Information Quest; ScienceDirect; Springer LINK; Swets Blackwell. Reprint: ISI. *Indexed:* CCMJ, MathSciNet, SCI. *Aud.:* Ac, Sa.

Inventiones Mathematicae was founded in 1966 by Springer-Verlag and has become one of the most prestigious journals for pure mathematics. Its purpose is modestly stated: "to bring out new contributions to mathematics." Some of the articles are in German or French. It publishes about 75–80 articles per year in 2,100 pages. Though it is the most expensive journal in this section, Springer has only increased the price from $2,755 in 1996 to $2,909 in 2003, an increase of roughly 1% per year. There are no book reviews. Strongly recommended for academic libraries and special adults.

4713. *Journal fuer die Reine und Angewandte Mathematik.* [ISSN: 0075-4102] 1826. m. EUR 2266.40 domestic; EUR 2283.80 foreign; EUR 196 newsstand/cover. Walter de Gruyter GmbH & Co. KG, Genthiner Str. 13, Berlin, 10785, Germany; wdg-info@degruyter.de; http://www.degruyter.de. Adv. Refereed. Circ: 800 Paid and controlled. Microform: PMC; PQC. Online: EBSCO Publishing; OCLC Online Computer Library Center, Inc.; Swets Blackwell. Reprint: PQC; SCH. *Indexed:* CCMJ, MathSciNet, SCI. *Aud.:* Ac, Sa.

The *Journal fur die reine und angewandte Mathematik* is a distinguished European journal, the oldest mathematics journal still in publication. It was founded in 1826 by August Leopold Crelle and has come to be known as *Crelle's Journal*. Many articles are in English, the remainder in German or French. As its name indicates, it publishes significant articles in both pure and applied mathematics. There are about 90–100 articles per year in some 3,000 pages. Because of its price, it is probably not the best value for many libraries, but it still worth considering for academic libraries and special adults.

4714. *London Mathematical Society. Proceedings.* [ISSN: 0024-6115] 1865. bi-m. USD 870 print & online eds. Ed(s): Karin Erdmann, Bryan J Birch. Cambridge University Press, The Edinburgh Bldg, Shaftesbury Rd, Cambridge, CB2 2RU, United Kingdom; information@cambridge.org; http://uk.cambridge.org. Illus., index, adv. Refereed. Circ: 1400. Vol. ends: No. 3. Microform: PMC; PQC. Online: EBSCO Publishing; OCLC Online Computer Library Center, Inc.; RoweCom Information Quest; Swets Blackwell. *Indexed:* ApMecR, CCMJ, MathSciNet, SCI, ST&MA. *Aud.:* Ac, Sa.

The *Proceedings, Third Series* is the flagship publication of the London Mathematical Society (LMS; http://www.lms.ac.uk) and is recommended for academic libraries and special adults. The LMS was founded in 1865 and is the major British learned society for mathematics. It also publishes other journals, two of which are listed below. These three magazines cover a broad spectrum of advanced mathematics, including some applied areas.

Bulletin of the London Mathematical Society [ISSN: 0024-6093] 1969. 6/yr. $351. Online at http://uk.cambridge.org/journals/blm. Cambridge Univ. Press, 40 W. 20th St., New York, NY 10011-4211. Contains shorter articles and 4–8 signed book reviews of 800 to 1,500 words, overview articles, short research papers, obituaries, and other matters of interest to members. Recommended for academic libraries and special adults.

Journal of the London Mathematical Society [ISSN: 0024-6107] 1926. 6/yr. $766. Online at http://uk.cambridge.org/journals/jlm. Cambridge Univ. Press, 40 W. 20th St., New York, NY 10011-4211. In its second series, it contains medium-length articles but no book reviews. Recommended for academic libraries and special adults.

4715. *Pacific Journal of Mathematics.* [ISSN: 0030-8730] 1951. m. 10/yr. USD 340 (Individuals, USD 170). Ed(s): V S Varadarajan. University of California at Berkeley, Department of Mathematics, 970 Evans Hall, Berkeley, CA 94720-3840; http://math.berkeley.edu. Illus., index, adv. Refereed. Circ: 200. Vol. ends: No. 10. Reprint: PSC. *Indexed:* CCMJ, MathSciNet, SCI. *Aud.:* Ac, Sa.

The *Pacific Journal of Mathematics* is the least important of the university journals listed in this section (cf. *Annals of Mathematics* and *American Journal of Mathematics*), but it is still worth mentioning. It is published by the University of California–Berkeley and supported by a number of West Coast universities. The focus is primarily on pure mathematics, and there are about 110–120 articles published each year in about 2,500 pages. Its web site is unpretentious, but some articles are available in full text, and there is an electronic index to previous issues. There are no book reviews. Recommended for academic libraries and special adults.

4716. *Quarterly Journal of Mathematics.* Formerly (until 1930): *Messenger of Mathematics.* [ISSN: 0033-5606] 1949. q. GBP 204. Ed(s): B F Steer, W B Stewart. Oxford University Press, Great Clarendon St, Oxford, OX2 6DP, United Kingdom; jnl.orders@oup.co.uk; http://www3.oup.co.uk/jnls. Illus., index, adv. Refereed. Circ: 825. Vol. ends: No. 4. Microform: PQC. Online: EBSCO Publishing; ingenta.com; RoweCom Information Quest; Swets Blackwell. Reprint: PSC. *Indexed:* CCMJ, MathSciNet, SCI, ST&MA. *Aud.:* Ac, Sa.

The *Quarterly Journal of Mathematics* is an important journal published by the Oxford University Press (cf. *Annals of Mathematics* and *American Journal of Mathematics*). It "publishes original contributions to pure mathematics. Areas such as algebra, differential geometry, and global analysis receive particular emphasis. However, the journal avoids specialization." There are about 35–40 articles published each year in roughly 500 pages. There are no book reviews. Recommended for academic libraries and special adults.

4717. *Quarterly of Applied Mathematics.* [ISSN: 0033-569X] 1943. q. USD 120. Ed(s): Walter F Freiberger. Brown University, Division of Applied Mathematics, 182 George St, Providence, RI 02940; http://www.brown.edu/. Illus., adv. Refereed. Circ: 1600. Vol. ends: No. 4. Microform: PQC. Reprint: PQC. *Indexed:* AS&TI, ApMecR, BiolAb, CCMJ, ChemAb, EngInd, IAA, MathSciNet, PetrolAb, SCI. *Bk. rev.:* 9-18, 50-200 words, unsigned. *Aud.:* Ac, Sa.

The *Quarterly of Applied Mathematics* is an important university journal published by Brown University (cf. *Annals of Mathematics* and *American Journal of Mathematics*). It "prints original papers in applied mathematics which have an intimate connection with applications. . . . The editors welcome particularly contributions which will be of interest both to mathematicians and to scientists and engineers." There are about 35–40 articles published each year in roughly 800–900 pages and a number of short, unsigned book reviews interspersed throughout each issue. Recommended for academic libraries and special adults.

4718. *S I A M Review.* [ISSN: 0036-1445] 1959. q. USD 282. Ed(s): Margaret H Wright. Society for Industrial and Applied Mathematics, 3600 University City Science Center, Philadelphia, PA 19104-2688; http://www.epubs.siam.org. Illus., index, adv. Refereed. Circ: 10223. Vol. ends: No. 4. Online: Gale Group; JSTOR (Web-based Journal Archive); RoweCom Information Quest; Swets Blackwell. *Indexed:* AS&TI, ApMecR, BRI, C&ISA, CBRI, CompR, DSR&OA, EngInd, SCI, SSCI, ST&MA. *Bk. rev.:* 10-25, 300-1,500 words, signed. *Aud.:* Ac, Sa, Ga.

SIAM Review is an official publication of the Society for Industrial and Applied Mathematics (SIAM; http://www.siam.org). SIAM was founded in the 1950s, and its goal is "to ensure the strongest interactions between mathematics and other scientific and technological communities." Each issue has five sections: "Survey and Review," "Problems and Techniques," "SIGEST," "Education," and "Book Reviews." The "[Survey and Review section] features papers with a deliberately integrative and up-to-date perspective on a major topic in applied or computational mathematics or scientific computing." "[Problems and Techniques] contains focused, specialized papers . . . informing readers about interesting problems, techniques and tools." "[SIGEST includes] digested versions of selected papers from SIAM's [other] journals." "Education" contains articles for students, not faculty, that might be interesting enough to include in courses, but are not typically in textbooks. The "Book Review" section contains a featured review or two and a number of other medium-length, signed reviews. It is a basic resource for academic libraries and should also be considered for special adults and some general adults (i.e., large public libraries). In addition to the *SIAM Review* and the *SIAM Journal on Applied Mathematics*, listed below, SIAM publishes 11 other journals (see http://epubs.siam.org/). Many of these are the most important journals in their fields. They have not been included here because of their specialized nature. I strongly recommend that research libraries consider one of SIAM's six packages.

SIAM Journal on Applied Mathematics [ISSN: 0036-1399] 1970. 6/yr. $450. Online at http://epubs.siam.org/sam-bin/dbq/toclist/SIAP. Society for Industrial and Applied Mathematics, 3600 University Science Center, Philadelphia, PA 19104-2688. This is the original SIAM journal, and it is available on JSTOR. It "publishes research articles that treat scientific problems using methods that are of mathematical interest. Appropriate subject areas include the physical, engineering, financial, and life sciences." It includes 80–120 articles in 2,200 pages. There are no book reviews. Strongly recommended for academic libraries and special adults.

4719. *Studies in Applied Mathematics (Malden).* Formerly (until 1968): *Journal of Mathematics and Physics.* [ISSN: 0022-2526] 1922. 8x/yr. USD 853 print & online eds. Blackwell Publishing, Inc., Commerce Place, 350 Main St, Malden, MA 02148; subscrip@blackwellpub.com; http://www.blackwellpublishing.com. Illus., adv. Refereed. Vol. ends: No. 3. Microform: PQC. Online: EBSCO Publishing; ingenta.com; OCLC Online Computer Library Center, Inc.; RoweCom Information Quest; Swets Blackwell. *Indexed:* AS&TI, ApMecR, CCMJ, DSR&OA, EngInd, MathSciNet, SCI. *Aud.:* Ac, Sa.

Studies in Applied Mathematics is an important university journal published for the Massachusetts Institute of Technology (cf. *Annals of Mathematics* and *American Journal of Mathematics*). It "reports research results involving the core concepts of applied mathematics research . . . The domain . . . is the interplay between mathematics and applied disciplines." There are about 30–35 articles published each year in roughly 800–900 pages. There are no book reviews. Recommended for academic libraries and special adults.

■ MEDIA AND AV

See also Communications; Education; Films; and Television, Video, and Radio sections.

Xiaochang Yu, Systems Librarian, VCU Libraries, Virginia Commonwealth University, Richmond, VA 23284-2033; FAX: 804-828-0151; xyu@vcu.edu

Introduction

The magazines listed in this section will appeal to the interests of several audiences. About half are research-oriented journals whose primary audiences are professors and researchers in instructional technology. Many essays in these journals discuss theoretical and methodological issues related to educational and communication technology. Others are popular magazines intended mainly for media specialists and other practitioners in schools, colleges, and business and industry sectors. Many articles in these popular magazines offer hands-on experiences of applying technology to media services and provide critical evaluations of new technology and products. Most of the titles in this section have some web presence.

Like many other fields, audiovisual and media technology have become increasingly computer-integrated. Computer-assisted animation, multimedia presentation, web video technology, etc., are widely discussed topics in the field these days. Therefore, readers may also consult computer-related sections in this book as well as sections referred to in cross-references in this section.

Basic Periodicals

Educational Technology Research and Development, Innovations in Education and Teaching International, International Journal of Instructional Media, Presentations, TechTrends.

Basic Abstracts and Indexes

Current Index to Journals in Education, Education Index, ERIC.

4720. ***A V Guide: the learning media newsletter.*** Former titles: *A V Guide Newsletter; Educational Screen and Audio Visual Guide.* [ISSN: 0091-360X] 1922. m. USD 15 domestic; USD 18 foreign; USD 2 newsstand/cover per issue. Ed(s): Natalie Ferguson. Educational Screen, Inc., 380 E Northwest Hwy, Des Plaines, IL 60016-2282; nferguson@sgcmail.com. Illus., index, adv. Sample. Circ: 1000 Paid. Vol. ends: Dec. Microform: PQC. Reprint: PQC. *Indexed:* EduInd. *Aud.:* Ems, Hs, Ac.

This monthly newsletter provides timely information on audiovisual products, such as videos, DVDs, instructional equipment, and educational software. Distributor information is included for each introduced product. One of the weaknesses of this publication is the lack of critical evaluation of products covered. However, the newsletter still provides an inexpensive way of keeping informed of new products and services available to media practitioners and teachers.

4721. ***A V Video & Multimedia Producer: production and presentation technology.*** Formed by the merger of (1995-1996): *Multimedia Producer;* (1984-1996): *A V Video;* Which incorporated (in 1990): *Video Management;* Which was formerly: *Video Manager;* (until 1984): *Video User;* (until 1980): *V U Marketplace;* A V Video was formerly (until 1984): *Audio Visual Directions;* (until 1980): *Audio Visual Product News.* [ISSN: 1090-7459] 1996. m. USD 53 United States (Free to qualified personnel). Ed(s): Beth Marchant. Knowledge Industry Publications, Inc., 2700 Westchester Ave, Ste 107, Purchase, NY 10577; http://www.kipinet.com. Illus., adv. Circ: 101420 Paid and controlled. Vol. ends: Dec. Online: Gale Group. *Indexed:* CompLI. *Aud.:* Ac, Sa.

In late 1996, *AV Video & Multimedia Producer* were combined into *AV Video and Multimedia Producer.* The combination reflects the fact that audiovisual services and multimedia services have become increasingly integrated. Since November 2000, the magazine has focused more on the producer side of multimedia products. The publication continues to feature significant changes in audiovisual and multimedia production and presentation technology. Each issue has two major parts: feature articles and departments. Feature articles offer in-depth coverage of new technologies and stories of applying technology in media services. Departments provide easily located information on a variety of interesting topics. In its "Test Patterns" section, for instance, hands-on reviews of new technology and products are offered. The publication includes extensive advertising and a valuable advertisers' index.

4722. ***British Journal of Educational Technology.*** Formerly: *Journal of Eductional Technology.* [ISSN: 0007-1013] 1970. q. GBP 293 print & online eds. Ed(s): Nick Rushby. Blackwell Publishing Ltd., 9600 Garsington Rd, PO Box 805, Oxford, OX4 2DQ, United Kingdom; customerservices@oxon.blackwellpublishing.com; http://www.blackwellpublishing.com/. Illus., index, adv. Refereed. Circ: 1200. Vol. ends: Sep. Microform: PQC. Online: EBSCO Publishing; ingenta.com; OCLC Online Computer Library Center, Inc.; RoweCom Information Quest; Swets Blackwell; H.W. Wilson. Reprint: PQC; SWZ. *Indexed:* BrEdI, CIJE, EduInd, EngInd, ErgAb, L&LBA, SSCI. *Bk. rev.:* 10, 150-500 words. *Aud.:* Ac.

This scholarly journal addresses theory, development, and applications of technologies in education, training, and communications with such specific topics as computer-assisted instruction, information technology for people with special needs, and the design and production of educational materials. Each issue contains articles, colloquium reports, and reviews. Articles are refereed and tend to be analytical and research-oriented. Colloquium reports have a conversational style and may include sections such as short think-pieces, reactions to previous contributions, and so forth. The journal includes more book reviews than any other magazine covered in this section.

Educational and Training Technology International. See *Innovations in Education and Training International.*

4723. ***Educational Media International.*** Former titles (until 1997): *E M I - Educational Media International;* (until 1986): *Educational Media International;* (until 1971): *Audio-Visual Media.* 1961. q. GBP 195 (Individuals, GBP 50). Ed(s): Prof. John Hedberg. Routledge, 11 New Fetter Ln, London, EC4P 4EE, United Kingdom. Illus., adv. Refereed. Circ: 500. Microform: PQC. Online: EBSCO Publishing; Ingenta Select; RoweCom Information Quest; Swets Blackwell. Reprint: PQC; PSC. *Indexed:* BrEdI, CIJE, CommAb, EduInd, ExcerpMed. *Bk. rev.:* 2-3, 500 words. *Aud.:* Ac.

This journal focuses on innovations in educational technology. A typical issue begins with an editorial that summarizes 7 to 12 short articles included in the issue. Each article begins with abstracts in three languages: English, French, and Dutch. Articles are easy to read. Some of them are basically empirical studies reporting practices in specific regions or countries. Because *Educational Media International* is the official journal of the International Council for Educational Media, whose membership list consists of 27 countries, both its authors and audience are worldwide. Also covered are association activities. The journal provides a valuable forum for the exchange of ideas and experiences among media professionals in different countries.

Educational Technology. See Education/Specific Subjects and Teaching Methods: Technology section.

Educational Technology Research and Development. See Education/Specific Subjects and Teaching Methods: Technology section.

4724. ***Innovations in Education and Teaching International.*** Former titles: *Innovations in Education and Training International;* (until 1995): *Educational and Training Technology International;* (until 1989): *Programmed Learning and Educational Technology; Programmed Learning.* [ISSN: 1470-3297] 1964. q. GBP 176 (Individuals, GBP 47). Ed(s): Gina Wisker, Philip Barker. Routledge, 11 New Fetter Ln, London, EC4P 4EE, United Kingdom. Illus., adv. Refereed. Circ: 1200. Vol. ends: Nov. Microform: PQC. Online: EBSCO Publishing; Ingenta Select; OCLC Online Computer Library Center, Inc.; RoweCom Information Quest; Swets Blackwell. Reprint: PQC; PSC. *Indexed:* AgeL, BrEdI, CIJE, IBZ, SSCI. *Bk. rev.:* 2-4, 750-1,000 words. *Aud.:* Ac.

The scope of this publication, which covers various topics in education and training, is much broader than most other journals listed in this section. Many articles are focused on instructional technology, but this quarterly publication of the Staff and Educational Development Association also covers such topics as the self-evident nature of teaching and motivation theories. It includes such topics as integrating web technologies into education and training, online professional development for academic staff, and technology-enabled distance learning. Publications include papers, case studies, and opinions. Papers are well researched and case studies are focused. The contributors are educators from all over the world. This journal takes a more theoretical approach than *Educational Media International,* another publication from Routledge (above in this section). Recommended for academic libraries.

4725. *Instructional Science: an international journal of learning and cognition.* [ISSN: 0020-4277] 1971. bi-m. EUR 502 print or online ed. Ed(s): Peter Goodyear, Patricia A Alexander. Kluwer Academic Publishers, van Godewijckstraat 30, PO Box 17, Dordrecht, 3300 AA, Netherlands. Illus., index, adv. Sample. Refereed. Vol. ends: Nov. Microform: PQC. Online: EBSCO Publishing; ingenta.com; Kluwer Online; OCLC Online Computer Library Center, Inc.; Ovid Technologies, Inc.; RoweCom Information Quest; Swets Blackwell. Reprint: SWZ. *Indexed:* BrEdI, CIJE, CommAb, CompR, EduInd, HEA, IBSS, IBZ, L&LBA, PsycholAb, SSCI. *Bk. rev.:* 2-3, length varies. *Aud.:* Ac.

A typical issue of this scholarly journal consists of two to four in-depth articles. Although many articles deal with instructional technology, the journal covers a wide range of disciplines in education. The focus is on promoting a deeper understanding of the nature and theory of the teaching and learning process. As such, the approach is highly academic. Recent topics include educational use of communication technologies, networked learning, and artificial intelligence in education. Articles are written by experts worldwide, and many articles require some background knowledge.

4726. *International Journal of Instructional Media.* [ISSN: 0092-1815] 1973. q. USD 165 domestic; USD 175 foreign. Ed(s): Phillip J Sleeman. Westwood Press, Inc., 116 E 16th St, New York, NY 10003-2112. Illus., index. Refereed. Circ: 500. Vol. ends: No. 4. *Indexed:* CIJE, EduInd, IBZ. *Bk. rev.:* 2-3, 2-21 pages. *Aud.:* Ac.

This journal contains original articles concerning rising issues in instructional media in particular and educational technology in general. Areas of research include computer technology, telecommunications, distance-teaching technology, instructional media and technology, interactive video, software applications, and instructional-media management. Articles are well researched, and most of them take conceptual approaches to the process of applying instructional technology to teaching and learning. Both advantages and disadvantages of various applications of educational techniques are discussed. Recommended for academic libraries.

4727. *Journal of Educational Technology Systems.* Formerly: *Journal of Educational Instrumentation.* [ISSN: 0047-2395] 1972. q. USD 237. Ed(s): Thomas T Liao, David C Miller. Baywood Publishing Co., Inc., 26 Austin Ave, Amityville, NY 11701; info@baywood.com; http://www.baywood.com. Illus., index, adv. Sample. Refereed. *Indexed:* C&ISA, CIJE, CompLI, EduInd, EngInd, IBZ, InfoSAb, L&LBA, MicrocompInd, RiskAb. *Aud.:* Ac.

Journal of Educational Technology Systems is the official publication of the Society for Applied Learning Technology. It "deals with systems in which technology and education interface and is designed to inform educators who are interested in making optimum use of technology." Most of the articles are focused on education-related computer technology and its impacts on teaching and learning. Each issue starts with an editorial overview that summarizes all the articles in the issue. Articles are generally research-oriented and accompanied by abstracts. Most of the pieces are by college professors. An index to each volume is contained in the last issue. It is an established, peer-reviewed publication and belongs in libraries that offer resources on educational technology.

4728. *Media & Methods: educational products, technologies & programs for schools & universities.* Formerly: *Teachers Guide to Media and Methods.* [ISSN: 0025-6897] 1964. 5x/yr. USD 33.50; USD 51.50 foreign. Ed(s): Christine Weiser. American Society of Educators, 1429 Walnut St, Philadelphia, PA 19102; michelesok@aol.com; http://www.media-methods.com. Illus., index, adv. Circ: 42000. Vol. ends: May/Jun. Microform: PQC. Online: EBSCO Publishing; OCLC Online Computer Library Center, Inc.; H.W. Wilson. *Indexed:* CIJE, ConsI, EduInd, InfoSAb, MRD, MicrocompInd, RGPR. *Bk. rev.:* 4-5, 150-200 words. *Aud.:* Ems, Hs, Ac.

Each issue has feature articles and departments. Articles are easy to read and provide hands-on experiences to meet the practical needs of media specialists and school librarians. Because media and school library services have become increasingly computer dependent, it is not surprising that many articles deal with computer-related technologies. Readers will also find valuable information on selection and evaluation of various media products, including laptops, digital cameras, DVD players, multimedia projectors, multimedia TV, and visual presenters.

4729. *Presentations: technology and techniques for effective communication.* Former titles (until 1993): *Presentation Products;* (until 1992): *Presentation Products Magazine.* [ISSN: 1072-7531] 1988. m. USD 69 domestic (Free to qualified personnel). Ed(s): Tad Simons. V N U Business Publications, 50 S Ninth St, Minneapolis, MN 55402; bmcomm@vnuinc.com; http://www.vnubusinessmedia.com/. Illus., adv. Circ: 70000 Controlled. Vol. ends: Dec. Microform: PQC. Online: EBSCO Publishing; Northern Light Technology, Inc.; OCLC Online Computer Library Center, Inc.; ProQuest Information & Learning. *Indexed:* ABIn, CompLI, InfoSAb, MicrocompInd. *Aud.:* Ac, Sa.

This illustrated publication contains updated information on presentation products, which range from overhead projectors to multimedia notebooks to web-graphics creation tools. Articles are most valuable for audiovisual and media professionals seeking advice and tips about selecting and using new presentation equipment. Among the useful special features is the annual "Buyers Guide to Presentation Products," which appears in the December issue. Recommended for libraries in institutions with strong media departments.

4730. *Public Broadcasting Report: the authoritative news service for public broadcasting and allied fields.* Incorporates (1967-1997): *E T V Newsletter (Educational Television).* [ISSN: 0193-3663] 1978. bi-w. USD 464; USD 487 foreign. Ed(s): Patrick Ross. Warren Publishing Inc., 2115 Ward Ct, N W, Washington, DC 20037; http://www.idpa.org/ndpawarr.html. Illus., index. Sample. Vol. ends: Dec. Online: Gale Group; LexisNexis; NewsNet; Northern Light Technology, Inc. *Aud.:* Sa.

Public Broadcasting Report covers a broader range of areas than its predecessor, *ETV Newsletter.* This newsletter provides timely news on happenings in the public-broadcasting business, which includes PBS, NPR, CPB, ETV, and ITV. Many of the reports can be called inside stories, for example, reports on government policy issues in public broadcasting. Coverage also includes educational training programs, awards, grants, and personnel issues. The publication has earned its reputation of providing authoritative news on public broadcasting. However, the price for this biweekly newsletter may intimidate some potential subscribers.

School Library Media Research. See Library and Information Science section.

4731. *TechTrends: for leaders in education and training.* Former titles (until 1985): *Instructional Innovator; Audiovisual Instruction with Instructional Resources; Audiovisual Instruction.* [ISSN: 8756-3894] 1956. bi-m. USD 55 domestic; USD 63 foreign. Ed(s): Carol Koetke. Association for Educational Communication and Technology (A E C T), 1800 N Stonelake Dr., Ste 2, Bloomington, IN 47404; aect@aect.org. Illus., index, adv. Refereed. Circ: 6400 Paid and free. Vol. ends: Nov. Reprint: PQC. *Indexed:* CIJE, EduInd, InfoSAb, MRD, MicrocompInd. *Aud.:* Ems, Hs, Ac.

This peer-reviewed magazine is the official publication of the Association for Educational Communications and Technology. It provides school media specialists and other educators a forum for exchanging personal experiences of applying technology in education and training. Emphasis is on new and practical ideas and first-hand experience. Articles have a conversational style and are easy to follow. Regular columns and departments are of popular interest, including "Web & Wild," "MegaBits," "New Products," and "E-Learning by Design." Recommended.

T.H.E. Journal. See Free Magazines and House Organs section.

Electronic Journals

4732. *Interactive Multimedia Electronic Journal of Computer - Enhanced Learning.* [ISSN: 1525-9102] 1999. irreg. Ed(s): Jennifer J Burg, Anne Boyle. Wake Forest University, 1834 Wake Forest Rd, Winston Salem, NC 27106; imej@wfu.edu; http://imej.wfu.edu/. Refereed. *Aud.:* Ac.

This peer-reviewed online journal aims at promoting computer-enhanced learning in higher education. Also important to its goals is advocating electronic publication in the academic world. It is well organized with exciting multimedia features and a sophisticated search engine. All back issues are searchable.

4733. *M C Journal: the journal of academic media librarianship.* [ISSN: 1069-6792] 1993. irreg. Free. Ed(s): Lori Widzinski. State University of New York at Buffalo, c/o Lori Widzinski, Ed, Health Sciences Library, Media Resources Center, Abbott Hall, Buffalo, NY 14214-3002; widz@buffalo.edu; http://wings.buffalo.edu/publications/mcjrnl/. Illus. Refereed. *Indexed:* LISA, LibLit. *Aud.:* Ac.

This peer-reviewed publication is by and for academic media librarians and specialists. A typical issue contains two to four articles of varying length. Most articles address practical issues facing media services in academic libraries, and some of them are mainly descriptions of new projects. All the back issues, since 1993, are searchable. *MC* offers a valuable forum for the exchange of ideas and experiences among academic librarians and specialists.

4734. *Media History Monographs.* 1997. q. Free. Ed(s): David Copeland, Patrick S Washburn. Ohio University, E. W. Scripps School of Journalism, Athens, OH 45701; http://www.scripps.ohiou.edu. Refereed. *Indexed:* AmH&L. *Aud.:* Ac.

Too long for most journals, but too short for most books. Faced with this dilemma, the editors of the monographs have decided to publish such scholarship in journal form online. The subject is journalism and mass communications, primarily concerning history with some attention to ongoing activities. (BK)

■ MEDICINE AND HEALTH

Consumer Health/Family Planning/Health Care Delivery/Health Industry/Health Professions/Medical Problems/Medicine—Professional/Medicine and Society/Public Health

Susan R. Poorbaugh (SRP), AHEC Librarian, Greenblatt Library, Medical College of Georgia, Augusta, GA 30912-4400; spoorbau@mail.mcg.edu (Medicine and Health section; Consumer Health; Family Planning)

Linda E. Bunyan (LEB), Manager, Medical Library/Bookstore, Summa Health System, 55 N. Arch St., Suite 3-G, Akron, OH 44304; bunyanL@summa-health.org (Medical Problems)

Marilee M. Creelan (MMC), Head, Collection Services, Greenblatt Library, Medical College of Georgia, Augusta, GA 30912-4400; mcreelan@mail.mcg.edu (Health Care Delivery; Health Industry; Medical Problems; Medicine and Society; Electronic Journals)

Wendy Hess (WH), Systems Librarian, Summa Health System, 55 N. Arch St., Akron, OH 44304; HessW@summa-health.org (Health Professions)

Douglas Joubert, Digital Information Librarian, Greenblatt Library, Medical College of Georgia, Augusta, GA 30912-4400; djoubert@mail.mcg.edu (Medicine—Professional)

Jane K. Olsgaard (JKO), Science Bibliographer, Thomas Cooper Library, University of South Carolina, Columbia, SC 29208; olsgaardjane@sc.edu (Public Health)

Karen Rosati, Head, Serials, School of Medicine Library, University of South Carolina, Columbia, SC 29208; krosati@med.sc.edu (Medical Problems)

Introduction

The scope of this section features the more popular journals that satisfy the needs of both the health professional and the general public. The field of medical and health-related journals continues to grow as electronic-only journals join print/full text combinations. Health topics are the number one search subject on the Internet. A 2001 survey showed that 70 percent of Internet searches are for a health topic, including diseases and conditions, health-care delivery policies, home health care, and recent legislative health policies.

The majority of the titles represented in this section are available in an electronic format, whether it is full text of featured articles, abstracts only, table of contents, or a searchable index of past issues. Most journals offer online, full-text access to subscribers of the print issue. Some of the consumer health newsletters online differ slightly from the print issue, with the electronic version allowing updates to easily occur. A caveat to relying exclusively on electronic format: full-text access, archive copies, and easy access are at the will of the publishers and may change without warning as more and more publishers merge.

Currently, more than 1,000 titles indexed by *Index Medicus* and *Cumulated Index to Nursing and Allied Health Literature,* and formerly by *Hospital Library Index* and *Consumer Health & Nutrition Index,* are available on web platforms from such vendors as Ovid Technologies, EBSCO, MDConsult, National Library of Medicine databases, and ScienceDirect. With the exception of NLM, for-profit vendors tend to package and then market a specific group of titles, making it difficult for librarians to choose titles that best suit the needs of their collections. The librarians may be forced to purchase unused titles from the vendor package for the want of a few required titles.

In addition to using this volume as a guide, librarians may turn to less-commercial sources, such as the National Library of Medicine's *Locator Plus* and *PubMed* (which searches over 11 million MEDLINE citations starting in the 1960s) and then linking to participating online journals.

Library vendors and commercial publishing houses continue to develop and market new collection-development plans and departments to assist libraries in selection. Libraries are also referred to the Brandon-Hill lists for small libraries and for allied health collections, published biennially in the *Bulletin of the Medical Library Association.* As well, the Brandon-Hill list for nursing collections is published biennially in *Nursing Outlook.* The National Library of Medicine includes both lists on its web site. (SRP)

Basic Periodicals

CONSUMER HEALTH. Hs: *FDA Consumer, Harvard Health Letter, Health;* Ga: *FDA Consumer, Harvard Health Letter, Health, Mayo Clinic Health Letter, Prevention, Tufts University Health & Nutrition Letter.*

FAMILY PLANNING. Hs: *Johns Hopkins University. Population Information Program. Population Reports. English Edition;* Ga: *The Compleat Mother;* Ac: *Birth, Educator's Update, Journal of Midwifery and Women's Health;* Sa: *Journal of Obstetric, Gynecologic, and Neonatal Nursing.*

HEALTH CARE DELIVERY. Ga: *Caring;* Ac: *Medical Care Research and Review;* Sa: *Journal of Health Care for the Poor and Underserved.*

HEALTH INDUSTRY. Ga: *Health Forum, Modern Healthcare;* Ac: *Health Care Management Review, Healthcare Financial Management, Inquiry;* Sa: *The Joint Commission Journal on Quality and Safety, Journal of Healthcare Management, Journal of Nursing Administration.*

HEALTH PROFESSIONS. Hs: *Imprint;* Ga: *Nursing Outlook;* Ac: *Nursing Education Perspectives, Nursing Outlook;* Sa: *The Health Care Manager, Nursing Management.*

MEDICAL PROBLEMS. Ga: *Arthritis Today, CA, Diabetes Self-Management;* Ac: *CA.*

MEDICINE—PROFESSIONAL. Ga: *Nursing [year], RN;* Ac: *American Journal of Nursing, JAMA, New England Journal of Medicine;* Sa: *Postgraduate Medicine.*

MEDICINE AND SOCIETY. Ga: *Hastings Center Report;* Ac: *Hastings Center Report;* Sa: *Journal of Law, Medicine & Ethics.*

PUBLIC HEALTH. Hs: *Public Health Reports;* Ga: *American Journal of Public Health, Public Health Reports;* Sa: *Family and Community Health, Morbidity and Mortality Weekly Report.*

Basic Abstracts and Indexes

Cumulative Index to Nursing and Allied Health Literature, Index Medicus.

Consumer Health

The consumer health subsection contains magazines and newsletters written for the public or general consumers of health information. The majority of items listed here have a broad subject content that addresses general wellness, exercise, diet, and other consumer health interests. Some specialty items appear, and virtually all continuing consumer health periodicals appear online in some form today. (SRP)

4735. *Child Health Alert.* [ISSN: 1064-4849] 1983. 10x/yr. USD 29 domestic; USD 34 in Canada & Mexico. Ed(s): Allen A Mitchell. Child Health Alert, PO Box 610228, Newton, MA 02461. Illus., index. Sample. Vol. ends: Jun. Online: bigchalk; EBSCO Publishing; Gale Group; Northern Light Technology, Inc.; OCLC Online Computer Library Center, Inc.; ProQuest Information & Learning. *Aud.:* Ga, Sa.

In keeping with its mission, *Child Health Alert,* an independent newsletter, evaluates the latest developments regarding the health and safety of children, helpfully interpreting current health information in reader-friendly format. The newsletters include information about medications, product recalls, safety hints, and general child health-care tips. Articles are authored by a team of professional doctors and educational specialists. The web site is complementary to the printed issues. A search engine is available to search back issues. Examples of recent articles include: "What are the risks of herbal therapies for children?," "Should Parents Buy Antibacterial Products?," and "Beware of the Kiss of the Peanut Eater." Free full text for the issues of the past five years is available at http://www.childhealthalert.com/index.html. This newsletter is a good source for public libraries, medical libraries with a consumer health focus, and school libraries that serve a child care interest. (SRP)

4736. *Consumer Reports on Health.* Formerly: *Consumer Reports Health Letter.* [ISSN: 1058-0832] 1989. m. USD 24 domestic; USD 30 foreign. Ed(s): Ronni Sandroff. Consumers Union of the United States, Inc., 101 Truman Ave, Yonkers, NY 10703-1057. Illus., index. Sample. Circ: 360000. Vol. ends: Dec. Online: EBSCO Publishing; Gale Group; LexisNexis; OCLC Online Computer Library Center, Inc. *Indexed:* BiolDig, CINAHL. *Aud.:* Ga.

Consumer Reports on Health provides current information regarding health care and health products for the entire family. Content in the articles is from the top medical researchers and both national and international health care authorities. Each issue is dedicated to a specific topic. Regular columns include "News," "Office Visits," and "Letters." Some full text is available at http://www.consumerreports.org/main/home.jsp. Subscribers had a choice of either a print or an electronic version of this newsletter, delivered through Newstand, Inc. Relying on Consumers Union's unbiased reputation, this newsletter is recommended for a public or consumer health library. (SRP)

4737. *Environmental Nutrition: the newsletter of food, nutrition and health.* Formerly: *Environmental Nutrition Newsletter.* [ISSN: 0893-4452] 1977. m. USD 30. Ed(s): Susan Male Smith. Environmental Nutrition, Inc., 52 Riverside Dr, Ste 15A, New York, NY 10024-6599. Illus. Sample. Circ: 85000. Online: EBSCO Publishing; Florida Center for Library Automation; Gale Group; Northern Light Technology, Inc. *Indexed:* Agr. *Aud.:* Ga.

Recently awarded the Editorial Excellence Award from the Newsletter's Publishers Foundation, this newsletter prides itself on its independence (no sponsors, no advertisements) in delivering reader-friendly, bottom-line guidance on food and nutrition. Topics from cancer to cautions on food safety to herbal remedies and miracle supplements are covered. Nutrition comparison charts help the consumer shop for best buys among brand-name foods. A feature story from each issue is available on the web site (http://www.environmentalnutrition.com/index.htm). Back issues from 1996 are included on the web page along with a searchable index for subscribers. (SRP)

4738. *F D A Consumer.* Formerly: *F D A Papers.* [ISSN: 0362-1332] 1967. bi-m. USD 14. Ed(s): Dori Stehlin. U.S. Food and Drug Administration, Office of Public Affairs, 5600 Fishers Ln, Rockville, MD 20857. Illus., index. Sample. Circ: 28000 Paid. Vol. ends: Dec. Microform: PQC. Online: bigchalk; The Dialog Corporation; EBSCO Publishing; Florida Center for Library Automation; Gale Group; OCLC Online Computer Library Center, Inc.; ProQuest Information & Learning; H.W. Wilson. Reprint: PQC. *Indexed:* AgeL, Agr, BiolDig, ConsI, DSA, ExcerpMed, FS&TA, GSI, IUSGP, IndVet, LRI, MagInd, PAIS, RGPR, VetBull, WAE&RSA. *Aud.:* Hs, Ga, Ac.

The official magazine of the Food and Drug Administration, *FDA Consumer* provides new and comprehensive information on getting and staying healthy. It also offers information about current FDA activities regarding regulatory products such as food, drugs, animal drugs and food, cosmetics, and medical devices. The audience intended is the public consumer, health professionals, and educators. Some articles are full text on the FDA web page (http://www.fda.gov/fdac/). The print subscription and the online version differ. More updates can be found on the online version.

A searchable subject index for issues from 1985 to June 1999 is available on the web site. Articles in *FDA Consumer* may be republished without permission. Departments include "Letters," "Updates," "Observations," "FDA Gov.," "Summaries of Court Actions," "Investigator's Reports," and "The Last Word." This publication is recommended for consumer health libraries and public and school libraries. (SRP)

4739. *A Friend Indeed: for women in the prime of life.* [ISSN: 0824-1961] 1984. bi-m. CND 30; CND 40 foreign. Ed(s): Janine O'Leary Cobb. A Friend Indeed Publications Inc., 3575 Blvd Saint Laurent, Ste 708, Montreal, PQ H2X 2T7, Canada. Illus., index. Sample. Circ: 6000 Paid. Vol. ends: Feb. *Indexed:* CINAHL, CWI. *Aud.:* Ga.

A Friend Indeed provides information and support to women in menopause and midlife. It provides up-to-date information on topics such as the pros and cons of hormone therapy, diabetes at midlife, hysterectomy, menopausal migraines, vitamins and complementary therapies, heart disease in women, osteoporosis, breast cancer, and weight and body image. *AFI* has provided women with unbiased information about menopause since 1984. As a nonprofit organization it exists solely through the support of our subscriber base. Authors are researchers affiliated with these fields. Articles are well-researched yet written with the consumer in mind. Articles from current and past issues include: "Natural Hormones: Are They a Safe Alternative?," "Challenges of Change: Midlife, Menopause and Disability," and "The Menopause Wars: HRT in the Spotlight." Regular columns include "Book Reviews," letters for readers called "The Exchange," and "Hot Flashes," and most recent health issues that are highlighted by the editor. Though the audience for this newsletter is limited to women during their midlife, it would still be a great addition to a public or consumer health library. (SRP)

4740. *Harvard Health Letter: a publication for the general readership, designed to provide accurate and timely health information.* Formerly: *Harvard Medical School Health Letter.* [ISSN: 1052-1577] 1975. m. USD 28 domestic; USD 40 Canada; USD 47 elsewhere. Ed(s): Dr. Thomas H Lee, Peter Wehrein. Harvard Health Publications Group, 164 Longwood Ave, Boston, MA 02115. Illus., index. Sample. Refereed. Circ: 300000 Paid. Vol. ends: Oct. Online: EBSCO Publishing; Factiva; Florida Center for Library Automation; Gale Group; Northern Light Technology, Inc.; OCLC Online Computer Library Center, Inc. *Indexed:* BiolDig, CINAHL, ConsI, MagInd, RGPR, SportS. *Aud.:* Hs, Ga, Ac.

Harvard Health Letter was the first consumer health newsletter published by a major medical institution. Since 1975, the newsletter has "led the way in patient advocacy, encouraging readers to take greater responsibility for the management of their own and their family's health, and in their dealings with medical professionals." Updated monthly, this newsletter offers reader-friendly information on a variety of topics, including Alzheimer's disease, cancer, heart disease, weight management, and health care delivery issues. Examples of some recent articles include "Is the Atkins Diet on to Something?," "A New Wave of Treatment," and "Prescription Drug Cards." Additional online resources and a searchable index are available to subscribers. (SRP)

4741. *Harvard Heart Letter.* [ISSN: 1051-5313] 1990. m. USD 28 domestic; USD 40 Canada; USD 47 elsewhere. Ed(s): Dr. Thomas H Lee, Nancy Ferrari. Harvard Health Publications Group, 164 Longwood Ave, Boston, MA 02115. Illus. Sample. Circ: 150000. Vol. ends: Aug. Online: EBSCO Publishing; Factiva; Florida Center for Library Automation; Gale Group; Northern Light Technology, Inc.; OCLC Online Computer Library Center, Inc. *Indexed:* BiolDig. *Aud.:* Ga.

This newsletter focuses on cardiac health care, offering expert advice and authoritative information to readers who may already suffer from heart disease or are concerned about their risk. Regular departments include "Ask a Doctor" and "Special Health Topics," relating to cardiac disease. Titles from recent articles include "Avoid an Aspirin Roadblock," "Fish Oil Supplements," and "Put Your Heart in to Prevention." Though the scope of this newsletter is limited to cardiac care, it is recommended for a public or consumer health library. The current issue is provided free at http://www.health.harvard.edu/newsletters/hrttext.shtml. Additional resources and a back-issue search are available to subscribers. (SRP)

4742. *The Harvard Mental Health Letter.* Formerly (until 1990): *Harvard Medical School Mental Health Letter.* [ISSN: 1057-5022] 1984. m. USD 72 domestic; USD 80 Canada; USD 87 elsewhere. Ed(s): Michael Craig Miller. Harvard Health Publications Group, 10 Shattuck St., 6th fl., Boston, MA 02115; hhp@hms.harvard.edu. Illus. Sample. Circ: 75000 Paid. Vol. ends: Jun. Online: EBSCO Publishing; Factiva; Florida Center for Library Automation; Gale Group; Northern Light Technology, Inc.; OCLC Online Computer Library Center, Inc. *Indexed:* BiolDig, CINAHL, ConsI. *Aud.:* Hs, Ga, Ac.

For over 20 years, this newsletter has delivered information, current thinking, and debate on mental health issues to both the health professional and the layman. Contents include a review of professional literature and articles authored by experts in their fields of mental health issues, with references cited. Recent topics include autism, new treatments for cocaine addiction, and panic disorder. Regular columns include "In Brief" and "Special Health Reports." Information provided in this newsletter is useful to both the consumer and the mental health professional and can be accessed at http://www.health.harvard.edu/aboutmental.shtml. Additional online resources, including additions to back issues, are available to subscribers. (SRP)

4743. *Health.* Formed by the merger of (1990-1992): *In Health;* (1969-1991): *Health (New York);* Which was formerly (1969-1981): *Family Health;* Which incorporated (1950-1976): *Today's Health.* [ISSN: 1059-938X] 1992. 10x/yr. USD 15.97 domestic; USD 23.97 foreign; USD 2.99 newsstand/cover per issue. Ed(s): Barbara Paulsen. Time Health Media Inc., 2100 Lakeshore Dr., Birmingham, AL 35209-6721. Illus., adv. Sample. Circ: 1407660 Paid. Vol. ends: Nov/Dec. Microform: PQC. Online: EBSCO Publishing; Gale Group. Reprint: PQC. *Indexed:* AgeL, BiolAb, BiolDig, CINAHL, CPerI, ConsI, GSI, GeoRef, H&SSA, MagInd, PEI, RGPR, SportS. *Aud.:* Hs, Ga.

Supported by the Women's Health Symposium and with well over one million readers, *Health* provides comprehensive, reader-friendly articles translated from professional health literature. The web site (http://www.health.com/) complements the printed issue. Some full-text articles are linked from the web site, as are other features such as signing up for newsletters, e-diets, and exercise programs. Recent articles in the printed issues include "Foods that Fight Fibroids," "Walk Your Way to a Better Body," and "Diseases of the Mind." (SRP)

4744. *HealthFacts.* [ISSN: 0738-811X] 1976. m. USD 25 domestic; USD 29 in Canada & Mexico; USD 36 in Europe. Ed(s): Maryann Napoli. Center for Medical Consumers, 130 Macdougal St., New York, NY 10012-5030. Illus., index. Sample. Circ: 12000. Vol. ends: Dec. Online: bigchalk; EBSCO Publishing; Florida Center for Library Automation; Gale Group; Northern Light Technology, Inc.; OCLC Online Computer Library Center, Inc.; ProQuest Information & Learning. *Indexed:* CINAHL, MagInd. *Aud.:* Ga.

This newsletter, from the Center for Medical Consumers, a nonprofit advocacy organization, offers a wide variety of medical and health care issues from a consumer perspective. In addition to articles on medical procedures, appropriate treatment, and non-medical alternatives, features include information about misleading drug ads, public access to information about doctor and hospital performance, and medical decisions made by managed care organizations. Excerpts of articles are included on the web page (http://www.medicalconsumers.org/pages/newsletter.html) along with an article index. Titles of recent articles include "Medical Errors," "Are Women the Next Customer for Viagra?," and "Duct Tape as a Wart Remover." Because articles are reported without bias, *HealthFacts* should be included in a consumer health collection. (SRP)

4745. *Johns Hopkins Medical Letter Health after 50.* [ISSN: 1042-1882] 1989. m. USD 28. Ed(s): Patrice Benneward. Rebus Inc., 632 Broadway, 11th Fl, New York, NY 10012; health_after_50@enews.com. Illus. Sample. Circ: 475000 Paid. Vol. ends: Feb. *Indexed:* CINAHL. *Aud.:* Ga.

Published specifically for health consumers over the age of 50, this eight-page newsletter offers "unparalleled commentary and insights on the latest news and developments in modern health care." Edited by well-known experts, the articles dispel myths and report on medical facts backed up by solid research and evidence-based medicine. A wide range of topics are covered, from prostate cancer treatments to spirituality and healing. Each month a featured article is available full-text on the web site. Regular columns include "House Calls," when consumers write to an expert for advice. The web site (http://www.hopkinsafter50.com/index.html) features an index from 1997 to the present and an archive from the past two years. Though this newsletter is targeted to a specific age group, any reader can benefit from the articles. Highly recommended for a public or consumer health library. (SRP)

4746. *Mayo Clinic Health Letter: reliable information for a healthier life.* [ISSN: 0741-6245] 1983. 12x/yr. USD 27 domestic; USD 34 in Canada & Mexico; USD 42 elsewhere. Ed(s): Aleta Capelle. Mayo Medical Ventures, 200 First St, S W, Centerplace S, Rochester, MN 55905; http://www.mayoclinic.com/. Illus., index. Circ: 7920000. Vol. ends: Dec. *Indexed:* BiolDig, CINAHL, ConsI, MagInd, RGPR. *Aud.:* Hs, Ga.

This eight-page newsletter offers reliable, accurate, and practical information on current health and medical news. Articles reflect the expertise of over 1,000 Mayo Clinic physicians, covering topics from walking for weight loss, to new medical treatments. Each issue focuses on a specific health topic with in-depth essays. Color illustrations add value for readers, and an alphabetized, year-end index lists covered topics. The consumer health web site from the Mayo Clinic (http://www.mayoclinic.com/home) complements the newsletter. (SRP)

4747. *Nutrition Forum.* Former titles (until 1997): *Nutrition and Health Forum;* (until 1996): *Nutrition Forum.* [ISSN: 1093-4545] 1984. bi-m. USD 50 (Individuals, USD 35). Ed(s): Lewis Vaughn. Prometheus Books Inc., 59 John Glenn Dr., Amherst, NY 14228; http://www.quackwatch.com/04consumereducation/nf.html. Illus., index, adv. Sample. Circ: 2000. Vol. ends: Nov/Dec. Online: bigchalk; EBSCO Publishing; Gale Group; Northern Light Technology, Inc.; ProQuest Information & Learning. *Indexed:* ConsI. *Bk. rev.:* Various number and length; includes ratings. *Aud.:* Ga.

This bimonthly newsletter offers information on basic nutrition and nutrition fads, fallacies, and quackery. Connected with the consumer health watchdog Quackwatch (http://www.quackwatch.com/index.html), *Nutrition Forum* features timely, authoritative analyses of dubious nutrition claims, products, and practitioners. Also provides reliable information from respected, and researched, nutritionists and physicians. A regular department reviews and rates books on a three-point scale. Very good newsletter on nutrition for a consumer health library that offers the consumer a means to compare nutrition trends. (SRP)

4748. ***People's Medical Society Newsletter.*** [ISSN: 0736-4873] 1983. bi-m. Membership, USD 24. Ed(s): Karla Morales. People's Medical Society, P.O. Box 868, Allentown, PA 18105-0868; info@peoplesmed.org; http://www.peoplesmed.org. Illus., index. Sample. Circ: 65000. Vol. ends: Dec. Online: EBSCO Publishing; Gale Group; Northern Light Technology, Inc.; ProQuest Information & Learning. *Indexed:* CINAHL. *Bk. rev.:* 1-2. *Aud.:* Ga.

Published by the People's Medical Society, a leading advocacy group, this newsletter adheres to the group's mission by making available "previously unavailable information into the hands of ordinary people so that they can make informed decisions about their own health care." Topics covered include diabetes, alternative medicine, hospital bill error, and high blood pressure, among others. The web site has a searchable index for members to use for back issues of this newsletter and others published by this society (http://www.peoplesmed.org/index.html). The web site offers links to all viewers to some full-text articles from other society newsletters. (SRP)

4749. ***Prevention: the magazine for better health.*** [ISSN: 0032-8006] 1950. m. USD 21.97 domestic; CND 32 Canada; USD 42.97 elsewhere. Ed(s): Rosemary Ellis. Rodale, 33 E Minor St, Emmaus, PA 18098; info@rodale.com; http://www.rodale.com. Illus., index, adv. Sample. Circ: 3100000. Vol. ends: Dec. Microform: PQC. Online: bigchalk; EBSCO Publishing; Florida Center for Library Automation; Gale Group; OCLC Online Computer Library Center, Inc.; ProQuest Information & Learning; H.W. Wilson. Reprint: PQC. *Indexed:* CPerI, GSI, MagInd, RGPR. *Aud.:* Hs, Ga.

Since 1950, *Prevention* has informed over 12 million readers on new developments in nutrition, fitness, weight control, food preparation, alternative medicine, and body care, motivating them to take care of their health. Regular departments include "Your Health," "Natural Healing," "Fitness," "Healthy Living," and "Food and Nutrition." The web site (http://www.prevention.com/) supplements the printed issues, offering a sample of full-text, feature articles for all viewers and password-protected information for subscribers. The reputation of Rodale Press and the popularity of this journal make it a must for a public, high school, or consumer health library. (SRP)

Shape. See Women section.

4750. ***Tufts University Health & Nutrition Letter.*** Formerly (until 1997): *Tufts University Diet and Nutrition Letter.* [ISSN: 1526-0143] 1983. m. USD 28 domestic; USD 33 foreign. Ed(s): Dr. Stanley N Gershoff. W H White Publications, 50 Broadway, 15th Fl, New York, NY 10004-1607; tuftshnltr@aol.com. Illus. Sample. Circ: 200000. Microform: PQC. Online: EBSCO Publishing; Florida Center for Library Automation; Gale Group; OCLC Online Computer Library Center, Inc.; ProQuest Information & Learning. *Indexed:* Agr, BiolDig, CINAHL, ConsI, MagInd. *Aud.:* Hs, Ga.

Tufts University Health & Nutrition Letter offers the latest, scientific-based information on topics such as choosing food wisely, controlling weight, preventing disease, and staying fit. The editorial staff and the Tufts University School of Nutrition Science and Policy, an acknowledged leader in the field, pride themselves on fully researching all the topics in this newsletter. Easy-to-read articles contain topics such as cereals' nurtitional level, fish oil supplements, and how what you eat affects your memory. This web site (http://www.healthletter.tufts.edu/index.html) offers sample articles, a table of contents of past issues from October 2000, and an annual index starting in 1996. This is an excellent newsletter for those in the general public who are interested in nutrition. (SRP)

4751. ***University of California, Berkeley. Wellness Letter: the newsletter of nutrition, fitness, and stress management.*** [ISSN: 0748-9234] 1984. m. USD 28 domestic; CND 36 Canada; USD 39 elsewhere. Ed(s): Dale A Ogar. Health Letter Associates, PO Box 412, New York, NY 10012-0007; http://www.wellnessletter.com/. Illus. Sample. Circ: 500000 Paid. Vol. ends: Sep. Online: Florida Center for Library Automation; Gale Group; OCLC Online Computer Library Center, Inc. *Indexed:* BiolDig, CINAHL, ConsI, MagInd. *Aud.:* Hs, Ga.

From the School of Public Health at the University of California, Berkeley, this newsletter draws upon the expertise of the School of Public Health, other researchers at Berkeley, and top researchers worldwide, simplifying and evaluating the research for the consumer. As the title indicates, the main focus is the prevention of illness rather than treatments. Titles of recent articles include "Oral Electrification: Has the Moment Arrived?," "Breezing Through Exercise," and "Growth Industry: Seeking the Fountain of Youth." The web site features one full-text article from the current issue, brief summaries of other articles, and the "Ask the Experts" column. A searchable index from 1997 is offered in addition to special features for subscribers. The reputation of UC–Berkeley, easy-to-understand articles, and a user-friendly web site make this newsletter a must for high school and public libraries. (SRP)

4752. ***Vibrant Life: abundant living for you and your family.*** Former titles: *Your Life and Health; Life and Health.* [ISSN: 0749-3509] 1904. bi-m. USD 16.95. Ed(s): Larry Becker. Review and Herald Publishing Association, 55 W Oak Ridge Dr, Hagerstown, MD 21740; http://www.rhpa.org. Illus., index, adv. Sample. Circ: 50000. Vol. ends: Nov/Dec. Online: bigchalk; Gale Group; Northern Light Technology, Inc.; OCLC Online Computer Library Center, Inc.; ProQuest Information & Learning. Reprint: PQC. *Indexed:* CINAHL. *Aud.:* Ga.

Vibrant Life is a health and fitness publication for men and women ages 30 to 50. It offers easy-to-read articles that promote the physical, mental, and spiritual aspects of a healthier lifestyle from a practical, Christian perspective. Topics covered include the latest breakthroughs in medicine, health, nutrition, and exercise; personal interviews with leading personalities on health topics; there is also seasonal, health-related material. In addition to feature articles, regular departments include "Recipes," "Herb Watch," and "Kids Body Shop." The web site offers subscriber information, a searchable index for "Herb Watch," and recipes from past issues, a preview of the next issue, and opportunities to join recipes groups. This colorful, easy-to-read publication is recommended for a public library. (SRP)

Family Planning

This subset focuses on population issues, birth control, maternal care, women and infant health, midwifery, and natural childbirth. See also Family and Marriage, Population Studies, and Women sections. (SRP)

4753. ***A W H O N N Lifelines: promoting the health of women and newborns.*** [ISSN: 1091-5923] 1997. bi-m. USD 116. Ed(s): Anne Katz. Sage Publications, Inc., 2455 Teller Rd, Thousand Oaks, CA 91320; info@sagepub.com; http://www.sagepub.com. Illus., index, adv. Sample. Refereed. Circ: 20200 Paid. Vol. ends: Dec. CD-ROM: Ovid Technologies, Inc. Online: HighWire Press. *Indexed:* CINAHL. *Aud.:* Ac, Sa.

Winner of the 2002 Silver Excel Award for Scholarly Journals from the National Association of Publications, this is a publication from the Association of Women's Health, Obstetric and Neonatal Nurses. *AWHONN Lifelines* is read by more than 23,000 health-care professionals whose main focus is health care for women and infants, including nutrition, gynecology, and maternal/neonatal nursing issues. Print subscribers also receive an online, full-text version. Authors and readers of this publication are mainly practicing nurses. The format is concise and easy to read. Recent article titles include "When the Bough Breaks: Effects of Divorce on Infants," "Pregnant with Cystic Fibrosis," and "Culturally Competent Care." (SRP)

4754. ***Birth: issues in perinatal care.*** Formerly (until 1981): *Birth and the Family Journal.* [ISSN: 0730-7659] 1973. q. USD 296 except Canada & Mexico, for print & online eds. Ed(s): Diony Young. Blackwell Publishing, Inc., Commerce Place, 350 Main St, Malden, MA 02148; subscrip@blackwellpub.com; http://www.blackwellpublishing.com. Illus., index, adv. Sample. Refereed. Circ: 3500. Vol. ends: Dec. Microform: PQC. Online: ingenta.com; Munksgaard & Blackwell Science's Synergy; Ovid Technologies, Inc.; RoweCom Information Quest; Swets Blackwell. Reprint: ISI; PQC. *Indexed:* ASSIA, CINAHL, DSA, ExcerpMed, IndMed, PsycholAb, SSCI. *Bk. rev.:* 2-3. *Aud.:* Ac, Sa.

For academic and special libraries, *Birth* is a multidisciplinary journal that addresses current issues and practices in the care of childbearing women, infants, and families. The intended audience for *Birth* is professionals in maternal and neonatal health. Readers also include caesarean educators, adoption/relinquish counselors, natural family counselors, and infertility educators. Columns, News, Media Reviews, Editorials, Calendar, and Letters are regular features. Editorially independent articles reflect current topics such as "Swedish Women's Interest in Home Birth and In-Hospital Birth Center Care," "Healthy Steps for Teen Parents," and "U.S. Trends in Obstetric Procedures, 1990–2000." Full text is online for print subscribers. (SRP)

4755. ***The Compleat Mother: the magazine of pregnancy, birth and breastfeeding.*** [ISSN: 0829-8564] 1985. q. Ed(s): Jody McLaughlin. Compleat Mother, 720 Fourth Ave, N W, Box 209, Minot, ND 58702. Illus., index, adv. Sample. Circ: 20000. Vol. ends: Winter. *Aud.:* Ga.

This journal is for the general public and would be a great addition to a consumer health collection. The main focus of this journal is to promote natural childbirth, extended breastfeeding, and a neighbor-friendly approach to childbearing, humor included. The online issue features full-text articles. The web site links to feature articles from similar periodicals. A monthly e-mail update is offered to subscribers. Articles in the *Compleat Mother* are submitted by readers and include "The Persistence of Fathers" and "Antenatal Testing—The Truth Be Told." There are also reprints of summaries of articles from more scholarly publications, newswire articles from Reuters Health (e.g., "Diet, Exercise Help Breastfeeding Moms Lose Weight"), and government press releases. (SRP)

4756. ***Johns Hopkins University. Population Information Program. Population Reports. English Edition.*** Formerly: *George Washington University. Population Information Program. Population Reports.* [ISSN: 0887-0241] 1973. 4x/yr. Free to qualified personnel. Ed(s): Bryant Robey. Johns Hopkins University, Population Information Program, 111 Market Pl, Baltimore, MD 21202-4012; PopRepts@welchlink.welch.jhu.edu; http://www.juccp.org. Illus. Sample. Circ: 81000. Vol. ends: Dec. Online: EBSCO Publishing. *Aud.:* Hs, Ga, Ac, Sa.

Published quarterly, *Population Reports* is distributed to more than 154,000 addresses, with 86 percent of the issues going to developing countries. It is published in English, French, Portuguese, and Spanish, with some issues in Arabic, Russian, and Turkish and available online in Spanish and French. Each issue is assigned to one of 11 different series, with comprehensive and up-to-date review of research and programming. The journal is available online at http://www.jhuccp.org/pr/. A sample of articles include: "Helping Women Use the Pill," "Closing the Condom Gap," and "The Urban Poor." A credit and bibliography section offers information about author credentials and additional resources. Articles are easy to understand yet well-referenced, making this publication suitable for public, consumer health, special, and academic libraries. (SRP)

4757. ***Journal of Midwifery and Women's Health.*** Former titles (1973-1999): *Journal of Nurse - Midwifery; American College of Nurse - Midwives. Bulletin;* (until 1969): *American College of Nurse - Midwifery. Bulletin.* [ISSN: 1526-9523] 1955. bi-m. USD 302 (Individuals, USD 128; Students, USD 82). Ed(s): T. King. Elsevier Inc., 360 Park Ave. S, New York, NY 10010-1710; usinfo-f@elsevier.com; http://www.elsevier.com. Illus., index, adv. Sample. Refereed. Vol. ends: Nov/Dec. Microform: PQC. Online: ingenta.com; ScienceDirect. *Indexed:* AgeL, CINAHL, ExcerpMed, IndMed, SSCI. *Bk. rev.:* 8, 300-400 words. *Aud.:* Ac, Sa.

An official publication of the American College of Nurse-Midwives, this international journal focuses on current knowledge in the fields of nurse-midwifery, parent-child health, obstetrics, gynecology, family planning, and primary care. The literature correlates with the attitudes, policies, and positions of the organization. Scholarly articles are written by nurses, nurse-midwives, and physicians. Recent article titles include "New directions in midwifery education: The Master's of Science in Midwifery Degrees," "Bridging Midwifery Borders," and "Quality Management Activities in the Obstetric Triage Setting." For a brief time, full-text access is available to all as a promotion by Elsevier. Departments include media reviews, journal reviews, editorials, a classified section, and a recently added international section. This journal is suggested for academic and special libraries. (SRP)

4758. ***Journal of Obstetric, Gynecologic, and Neonatal Nursing.*** Incorporates (1990-1993): *A W H O N N's Clinical Issues in Perinatal and Women's Health Nursing;* Which was formerly (until 1992): *N A A C O G's Clinical Issues Perinatal and Women's Health Nursing;* Former titles (until 1985): *J O G N Nursing; Nurses Association of the American College of Obstetricians and Gynecologists. Bulletin News; Nurses Association of A.C.O.G. Bulletin.* [ISSN: 0884-2175] 1972. bi-m. USD 596 print & online eds. Ed(s): Lillian Biller, Karen B Haller. Sage Science Press, 2455 Teller Rd, Thousand Oaks, CA 91320; sagescience@sagepub.com; http://www.sagesciencepress.com. Illus., adv. Refereed. Circ: 24042. Vol. ends: Nov/Dec. CD-ROM: Ovid Technologies, Inc. Microform: PQC. Online: HighWire Press; ingenta.com; OCLC Online Computer Library Center, Inc.; Ovid Technologies, Inc.; ProQuest Information & Learning; RoweCom Information Quest; Swets Blackwell. *Indexed:* CINAHL, IndMed. *Bk. rev.:* 2-4, 400-600 words. *Aud.:* Ac, Sa.

This peer-reviewed journal from the Association of Women's Health, Obstetric and Neonatal Nurses (AWHONN) addresses the health care needs of childbearing families, newborns, and women's health. The official journal of AWHONN is intended for nurses, nursing students, and the other care professionals with interests in women and infant health. The research-oriented focus is on trends in health care delivery systems, advance nursing practices, and clinical scholarship. Full text is online for subscribers. Recent articles include "Publication Ethics: Copyright and Self-Plagiarism," "Homeopathy and Women's Health Care Age," "Herbal Therapy Use by Perimenopausal Women," and "Posttraumatic Stress Symptoms in Mothers of Premature Infants." Sections include "Editorials," "Guest Columnist," "Principles and Practice," "Clinical Studies," and "Clinical Issues." This journal is best suited to academic libraries with nursing programs and hospital libraries that serve nurses and researchers. (SRP)

4759. ***M C N: American Journal of Maternal Child Nursing.*** [ISSN: 0361-929X] 1976. bi-m. USD 109 (Individuals, USD 39; USD 13 per issue). Ed(s): Margaret Comerford Freda. Lippincott Williams & Wilkins, 530 Walnut St, Philadelphia, PA 19106-3621; http://www.lww.com. Illus., index, adv. Sample. Circ: 22000. Vol. ends: Nov/Dec. CD-ROM: Ovid Technologies, Inc. Microform: PQC. Online: Ovid Technologies, Inc. Reprint: PQC. *Indexed:* AgeL, CINAHL, IMFL, IndMed. *Aud.:* Ac, Sa.

This peer-reviewed journal keeps to its mission of providing timely, relevant information to very experienced and/or advanced-practice nurse practicing in perinatal, neonatal, midwifery, and pediatric specialties. To meet this mission, *MCN* publishes "clinically relevant practice and research articles" authored by nurse professionals that lead readers to evidence-based practice. Examples of recent articles include "School Violence: An Insider View," "Postpartum Beliefs and Practices Among Non-Western Cultures," and "Caring for the Infertile Woman." Ongoing columns include "Editorials," "Second Opinion," "The New Networking," "Focus of the Law," "Letters," and "Toward Evidence-Based Practice." Some issues include articles with a CE opportunity. This journal is a must for academic and special libraries that serve the nursing and midwifery professions. Online access through Ovid. (SRP)

4760. ***Midwifery Today with International Midwife.*** Former titles (until 199?): *Midwifery Today and Childbirth Education with International Midwife;* Formed by the merger of (1987-1996): *Midwifery Today;* (1995-1996): *International Midwife.* 1987. q. USD 50 domestic; USD 60 in Canada & Mexico; USD 75 elsewhere. Ed(s): Jan Tritten, Alice Evans. Midwifery Today with International Midwife, PO Box 2672, Eugene, OR 97402. Illus., index, adv. Sample. Circ: 2500. *Indexed:* CINAHL, CWI, FemPer, GendWatch. *Bk. rev.:* 4, 150 words. *Aud.:* Ga, Ac, Sa.

This journal is written for midwives, nurses, childbirth educators, birth practitioners, and others who support the midwifery model of childbirth. According to its web site, *Midwifery Today* is "committed to promoting safe, healthy and happy outcomes for mothers and babies" and is based on the belief that the midwifery model of "non-interventive, preventive care should be the standard of care throughout the world." Included in the journal are "International Midwife" and a 12-page newsletter, "The Birthkit." Articles are scholarly and concise, yet the publication aims for a balance of "softer personal and/or philosophical articles, including birth-related art, poetry and humor." Each issue has a theme, such as "Interventions."

Articles from a select issue include "Elective Cesarean: A Betrayal of Trust," "The Art of Questioning," and from International Midwife, "Midwifing for Midwives: Protecting the Sacred Circle." Departments include "Media Reviews," "Poetry," "News," "Journal Abstracts," and "Networking." The web site is user-friendly. This publication is recommended for consumer health libraries and any library with midwives and child birth professionals as patrons. (SRP)

4761. *Perspectives on Sexual and Reproductive Health.* Formerly (until 2002): *Family Planning Perspectives.* [ISSN: 1538-6341] 1969. bi-m. USD 52 (Individuals, USD 42). Ed(s): Patricia Donovan. Alan Guttmacher Institute, 120 Wall St, 21st Fl, New York, NY 10005; http://www.guttmacher.org. Illus., index, adv. Refereed. Circ: 5000 Paid and free. Vol. ends: Nov/Dec. Microform: CIS; PQC. Online: EBSCO Publishing; Gale Group; Northern Light Technology, Inc.; ProQuest Information & Learning. Reprint: PQC. *Indexed:* AbAn, BiolAb, BiolDig, CINAHL, CWI, EnvAb, ExcerpMed, HRA, IMFL, IndMed, PAIS, PsycholAb, SFSA, SSCI, SWA, SWR&A. *Aud.:* Various number and length.

Perspectives on Sexual and Reproductive Health, formerly titled *Family Planning Perspectives,* remains focused on the most compelling reproductive health issues in our society. Findings from the Guttmacher Institute as well as research from other distinguished social scientists are featured. The articles are scholarly and academic-based, with an intended audience of family planning professionals, policymakers, and program providers. Articles deal with contraceptive issues, trends and determinants, abortion, legal issues, and maternal and child health. Some full-text articles are available on the web site. (SRP)

Population Reports. See *Johns Hopkins University. Population Information Program. Population Reports. English Edition.*

4762. *Special Delivery.* [ISSN: 1083-5008] 1977. q. USD 20 domestic; USD 23 in Canada & Mexico; USD 25 elsewhere. Ed(s): Annmarie Kalmar. Association of Labor Assistants & Childbirth Educators, PO Box 390436, Cambridge, MA 02139; alacehq@aol.com; http://www.alace.org. Illus., adv. Sample. Circ: 2000 Paid. Vol. ends: Winter. Online: Gale Group; Northern Light Technology, Inc.; OCLC Online Computer Library Center, Inc.; SoftLine Information. *Indexed:* GendWatch. *Bk. rev.:* Number varies, 150 words, signed. *Aud.:* Ga, Sa.

This quarterly journal from the Association of Labor Assistants and Childbirth Educators (ALACE) is intended for midwives, childbirth educators, and other health professionals engaged in childbirth issues. Topics of up-to-date articles include pregnancy and birth, controversies in care, midwifery, women's health issues, and parenting. Continuing education and a calendar of upcoming ALACE events are also included. Articles are authored by ALACE directors and officers, midwives, and childbirth professionals. Though this journal is intended for ALACE membership, it is recommended for special libraries that serve childbirth educators. (SRP)

4763. *Studies in Family Planning.* Incorporates: *Current Publications in Family Planning.* [ISSN: 0039-3665] 1963. q. USD 105 print & online. Blackwell Publishing, Inc., Commerce Place, 350 Main St, Malden, MA 02148; subscrip@blackwellpub.com; http://www.blackwellpublishing.com. Illus., index. Refereed. Circ: 6000 Paid and free. Vol. ends: Dec. Microform: PQC; NRP. Online: Florida Center for Library Automation; Gale Group; JSTOR (Web-based Journal Archive); LexisNexis; Northern Light Technology, Inc.; OCLC Online Computer Library Center, Inc. Reprint: PQC. *Indexed:* ABS&EES, ASSIA, ArtHuCI, BAS, BiolAb, CINAHL, CWI, DSA, EIP, EnvAb, ExcerpMed, GeogAbPG, IBSS, IBZ, IMFL, IndMed, PAIS, PRA, RRTA, SFSA, SSCI, SWA, SociolAb, WAE&RSA. *Bk. rev.:* 3-4. *Aud.:* Ac, Sa.

A peer-reviewed international journal, *Studies in Family Planning* is concerned with "all aspects of reproductive health, fertility regulation, and family planning programs in both developing and developed countries." Authors and readers are researchers who focus on family planning, program directors, and other health professionals interested in contraceptive issues. Articles are scholarly and with a scope that includes the politics of reproduction, reproduction and religion, social issues, and reproductive rights. Recent article titles include "Contraceptive Use Before and After Marriage in Shanghai," "Pregnancy Termination among South African Adolescents," and "Maternal Mortality in India: An Update." Sections include "Data Section" (demographic and survey results), "Book Review," and "Other Notable Publications." The journal is available for download at http://www.popcouncil.org/sfp/default.asp for subscribers only; abstracts, author index, cumulative index, subject, and geographic index are available to others. (SRP)

Health Care Delivery

The journals covered in this subsection concern health care utilization by and delivery systems for special populations. Subject focus includes long-term care, home health services, hospices, nursing homes, and health care utilization and delivery to the aged and the poor. See also Death and Dying section. (MMC)

4764. *Caring (Washington).* Supersedes: *Home Health Review.* [ISSN: 0738-467X] 1982. m. USD 45. Ed(s): Margaret J Cushman. National Association for Home Care, 228 Seventh St, S E, Washington, DC 20003-4306. Illus., index, adv. Sample. Circ: 5927. Vol. ends: Dec. *Indexed:* ASG, AgeL, CINAHL. *Aud.:* Ac, Sa.

Caring offers informative and in-depth articles written by experts in the home care and hospice fields. The journal aims to address the critical issues and needs of Americans "on the fringes of life." Current issues, technology, and trends in home care and hospice services are regular features. In *Caring,* professionals in home care and hospice services deliver quality articles about home health care and hospice that are incisive and useful to both clinicians and family. Recent editions have covered research on the role of informal caregivers, the meaning of the growth in health care technology, and enhancing communications with multicultural patient populations. *Caring* provides accessible, pertinent, and affordable information to home health care professionals, consumers, and their families. (MMC)

4765. *Journal of Aging Studies.* [ISSN: 0890-4065] 1987. q. EUR 313 (Individuals, EUR 127). Ed(s): Dr. J. F. Gubrium. Pergamon, The Boulevard, Langford Ln, East Park, Kidlington, OX5 1GB, United Kingdom. Refereed. Microform: PQC. Online: EBSCO Publishing; Florida Center for Library Automation; Gale Group; ingenta.com; OCLC Online Computer Library Center, Inc.; ScienceDirect; Swets Blackwell; H.W. Wilson. *Indexed:* ASG, AgeL, IMFL, PAIS, SSCI, SSI, SociolAb. *Aud.:* Ga, Ac, Sa.

The *Journal of Aging Studies* aims to provide scholarly information and new interpretations of the aging experience in a multidisciplinary framework that includes the behavioral sciences, social sciences, and the humanities. This journal provides important and pertinent articles related to the psychological and sociological aspects of aging and geriatric care. Recent issues have highlighted topics such as personal narratives and storytelling in later life, loss and views of the self in Alzheimer's disease, and mother-daughter conflict and feminist gerontology. The *Journal of Aging Studies* is an appropriate title for academic, large public, and health-sciences libraries. (MMC)

4766. *Journal of Health Care for the Poor and Underserved.* [ISSN: 1049-2089] 1990. q. USD 315 & Caribbean. Ed(s): Virginia Brennan. Sage Publications, Inc., 2455 Teller Rd, Thousand Oaks, CA 91320; info@sagepub.com; http://www.sagepub.com. Illus., index, adv. Sample. Refereed. Circ: 2000. Vol. ends: Nov. Microform: PQC. Online: Chadwyck-Healey Incorporated; ingenta.com; OCLC Online Computer Library Center, Inc.; ProQuest Information & Learning. *Indexed:* ASSIA, AgeL, CINAHL, CJA, H&SSA, HRA, IIBP, IndMed, PRA, PsycholAb, RiskAb, SFSA, SSCI, SUSA, SWR&A, SociolAb. *Bk. rev.:* Number varies, 500-1,500 words. *Aud.:* Ac, Sa.

This journal focuses exclusively on contemporary health care issues of low-income and other medically underserved communities in the U.S. It is a scholarly, peer-reviewed publication with articles written by professionals in the field. Regular features include original papers and research reports, guest editorials, literature reviews, critical summaries, and noteworthy program evaluations. Recent articles have discussed racial disparities in the incidence of lung cancer, utilization of health services by underserved Mexican American women, and utilization of health services by the homeless. This title will be useful for urban libraries and academic urban studies collections. (MMC)

4767. ***Medical Care Research and Review.*** Former titles (until Mar. 1995): *Medical Care Review; Public Health Economics and Medical Care Abstracts.* [ISSN: 1077-5587] 1944. q. GBP 277 print & online eds. in Europe, Middle East, Africa & Australasia. Ed(s): Thomas Rice, Jeffrey Alexander. Sage Publications, Inc., 2455 Teller Rd, Thousand Oaks, CA 91320; info@sagepub.com; http://www.sagepub.com. Illus., adv. Sample. Refereed. Circ: 1300. Vol. ends: Dec. Microform: PQC. Online: ingenta.com; OCLC Online Computer Library Center, Inc.; ProQuest Information & Learning; RoweCom Information Quest; Swets Blackwell. Reprint: PQC. *Indexed:* ASG, ASSIA, AgeL, CINAHL, ExcerpMed, HRA, IndMed, MCR, PAIS, SSCI. *Bk. rev.:* 2-3, 200-300 words. *Aud.:* Ac, Sa.

Each issue of this journal provides the latest information on empirical research and data trends in the health services field. Using evaluation of previous data, and review-type articles that offer synthesized empirical and theoretical research, *Medical Care Research and Review* offers timely information on topics such as managed care plans, racial and ethnic disparities in medical services, health care and politics, informed consent, competition/regulation, and health care financing. This is a valuable selection for libraries with collections geared toward research-oriented business, health-care, administrative, and policy-making professionals. (MMC)

4768. ***National Medical Association. Journal.*** [ISSN: 0027-9684] 1908. m. USD 129 (Individuals, USD 156; USD 13 newsstand/cover per issue domestic). Ed(s): A. Paul Kelly. National Medical Association, 1012 Tenth St, NW, Washington, DC 20001; ktaylor@nmanet.org; http://www.nmanet.org. Illus., index, adv. Sample. Refereed. Circ: 36000 Controlled. Vol. ends: Dec. Online: bigchalk; ProQuest Information & Learning. *Indexed:* AgeL, BiolAb, CJA, ChemAb, DSA, ExcerpMed, H&SSA, IndMed, MCR, PsycholAb. *Aud.:* Ac, Sa.

The National Medical Association (NMA) is a nonprofit professional organization devoted to presenting health care issues as they relate to African American and other underserved populations. The journal carries peer-reviewed, scholarly articles that focus on health care and related issues of urban and minority populations from clinicians and researchers in various practice and research settings. Recent issues treat such topics as hypertension and treatment compliance among African Americans, the quality of diabetic care and patient satisfaction, and managing chronic renal insufficiency. The journal includes well-documented clinical research, communications, editorials, and NMA news briefs. (MMC)

Health Industry

This subsection contains periodicals that focus on the business aspects of health care: administration, management, finance, marketing, regulation, and general industry news. (MMC)

4769. ***Dental Economics.*** Formerly: *Oral Hygiene.* [ISSN: 0011-8583] 1911. m. USD 90 domestic; USD 124 in Canada & Mexico; USD 173 elsewhere. Ed(s): Joseph Blaes. PennWell Corp., 1421 S Sheridan Rd, Tulsa, OK 74112; Headquarters@PennWell.com; http://www.pennwell.com. Illus., index, adv. Sample. Circ: 100000 Controlled. Vol. ends: Dec. Online: Northern Light Technology, Inc.; ProQuest Information & Learning. *Indexed:* ATI. *Aud.:* Ac, Sa.

Circulated free to practicing dentists, *Dental Economics* offers practical office management tips and personal-finance ideas that are applicable to many other health care professionals in private practice. Information on new products and training videos will be of special interest to practicing dentists and students. Authors are business consultants and dentists. Recent articles deal with managed care plans, full-mouth dentistry, digital radiology radiology and photography, and group practice planning. Lots of advertising, product profiles, and continuing-education and tax information make the journal useful to professional readers. Indexing is available to other users in the online versions of *Hospital Literature Index.* (MMC)

4770. ***Frontiers of Health Services Management.*** [ISSN: 0748-8157] 1984. q. USD 85 domestic; USD 95 foreign; USD 23 newsstand/cover. Ed(s): Leonard Friedman. Health Administration Press, One North Franklin St, Ste 1700, Chicago, IL 60606-3491; ache@ache.org; http://www.ache.org/hap.cfm. Illus. Sample. Circ: 2500. Vol. ends: Summer. Microform: PQC. Online: EBSCO Publishing; Northern Light Technology, Inc.; OCLC Online Computer Library Center, Inc.; ProQuest Information & Learning. Reprint: PQC. *Indexed:* ABIn, AgeL, ExcerpMed. *Aud.:* Ac, Sa.

Frontiers of Health Services Management is a publication of the American College of Healthcare Executives. Each of the quarterly issues addresses a current management topic. The lengthy investigations of new trends make it a good complement to some of the more news-oriented magazines. Recent issues give thorough discussions of investing wisely in information technology, addressing the nursing shortage, leadership and spirituality, and managing executive error. The main article, commentaries, and author replies are written by administrators, consultants, and physicians. Each issue has an editorial, and the commentaries are introduced by the editor. The journal is most appropriate for schools of hospital administration, academic medical-center libraries, and planning-oriented libraries. (MMC)

4771. ***Health Care Management Review.*** [ISSN: 0361-6274] 1976. q. USD 199 (Individuals, USD 79). Lippincott Williams & Wilkins, 16522 Hunters Green Pkwy., Hagerstown, MD 21740; http://www.lww.com. Illus., adv. Sample. Refereed. Vol. ends: Fall. Microform: PQC. Online: bigchalk; EBSCO Publishing; Florida Center for Library Automation; Gale Group; OCLC Online Computer Library Center, Inc.; Ovid Technologies, Inc.; ProQuest Information & Learning. Reprint: PQC. *Indexed:* ABIn, AgeL, BPI, CINAHL, ExcerpMed, H&SSA, IndMed, MCR, SSCI. *Bk. rev.:* Various number and length. *Aud.:* Ac, Sa.

Each issue of *Health Care Management Review* carries eight to ten somewhat scholarly articles on a variety of topics for health administrators and for administrative nurses and physicians. Authors are consultants, administrators, and college professors, with a few RNs, MSNs, and physicians. The primary objective of the journal is to provide health care administrators, researchers, and management practitioners with "theoretical frameworks and principles...[of] health services management." Recent major topics treated include models of patient satisfaction, communication issues and mergers, organizational learning and telemedicine, and virtual health-care organizations. The journal is made more interesting by the inclusion of thought-provoking editorials, guest editorials, and commentaries. There are lengthy, useful references accompanying all articles. Recommended for schools of business and hospital administration and large hospital libraries. (MMC)

4772. ***Health Forum.*** Former titles: *Hospitals and Health Networks;* (until 1993): *Hospitals.* 1936. m. USD 80 domestic; USD 150 foreign; USD 9 newsstand/cover per issue. Ed(s): Mary Grayson. American Hospital Publishing, Inc., 1 N Franklin St, 27th Fl, Chicago, IL 60606-3421; http://www.aha.org. Illus., index, adv. Sample. Circ: 100000. Vol. ends: Dec. Reprint: PQC. *Indexed:* ABIn, ATI, AgeL, BPI, CINAHL, ChemAb, ExcerpMed, IndMed, LRI, MCR, SCI, SSCI. *Aud.:* Ga, Ac, Sa.

Health Forum, the official journal of the American Hospital Association (AHA), is distributed to the top management of American hospitals. It is the journal most asked for by administrators in hospital libraries; and it is oriented to public policy and reflects the opinions and interests of hospital chief executive officers. The "resources" at the web site are password-protected. The format is that of a modern newsmagazine, with a sometimes lengthy cover story, feature articles, and many columns and short news stories. Writers are usually AHA staff or the magazine's journalists. Typical recent articles discuss how hospitals can make the genomic revolution practical, new trends in nurse call centers, methodology in putting quality theory into practice, and issues of allergic reactions to scented products among staff and patients. This journal is a must for colleges and large public libraries. (MMC)

4773. ***Health Progress.*** Formerly (until 1984): *Hospital Progress.* [ISSN: 0882-1577] 1920. bi-m. USD 50 domestic; USD 60 foreign. Ed(s): Carrie Stetz. Catholic Health Association of the United States, 4455 Woodson Rd., St. Louis, MO 63134-3797; http://www.chausa.org. Illus., index, adv. Sample. Circ: 12000. Vol. ends: Dec. Microform: PQC. Online: Northern Light Technology, Inc.; ProQuest Information & Learning. Reprint: PQC. *Indexed:* ASG, AgeL, CINAHL, CPL, ExcerpMed, IndMed, MCR, SWR&A. *Bk. rev.:* 2, 500-1,000 words. *Aud.:* Ga, Ac, Sa.

This publication of the Catholic Health Association of the United States brings a concern with ethics, values, and priority-setting to health care management. The authors report practical research results in arenas where human concerns or quality issues face technological and financial challenges. Special columns such as "Reflections" and "Communication Strategies" bring the personal insights of administrators and practitioners to difficult issues of genetics research, access to the system, and justice in the managed-care era. Each issue includes several articles that apply a value or vision to aspects of health care, such as community involvement, ethics committees, or indigent care. There are many educational opportunites listed. See the web site (http://chausa.org) as well for resources and services. This journal is a well-indexed value for community planners and students. (MMC)

4774. *Healthcare Financial Management.* Former titles (until 1982): *Hospital Financial Management;* (until 1968): *Hospital Accounting.* [ISSN: 0735-0732] 1946. m. USD 102 domestic; USD 170 foreign. Ed(s): Marilyn Ferdinand. Healthcare Financial Management Association, 2 Westbrook Corporate Center, Ste 700, Westchester, IL 60154-5700; http://www.hfma.org/. Illus., index, adv. Sample. Circ: 34000 Paid and controlled. Vol. ends: Dec. Microform: PQC. Online: The Dialog Corporation; EBSCO Publishing; Florida Center for Library Automation; Gale Group; Northern Light Technology, Inc.; OCLC Online Computer Library Center, Inc.; ProQuest Information & Learning; H.W. Wilson. Reprint: PQC. *Indexed:* ABIn, ATI, AgeL, B&I, BPI, CINAHL, ExcerpMed, LRI. *Bk. rev.:* 4, 1,000 words. *Aud.:* Ac, Sa.

Because this journal is the official publication of the Healthcare Financial Management Association, it contains national news of the field and association news as well as articles on a broad range of topics related to this subject. Most authors are managers or executives of firms specializing in health care financial consulting. There are four or five lengthy articles each month. Three main-focus areas of integrated systems, managed care, and group practice management carry briefer treatments. Typical articles from recent issues discuss the bribery law, designing an effective chargemaster, and accounting methods for cash flow. A dozen regular departments include career development, health care regulations, and mergers and acquisitions. Special reports discuss integrated delivery systems, managed care, and group practice management. The current issue (only) can be found full-text at http://www.hfma.org/publications/magazine.html publications.html, as can an index of recent years. The library that can afford only one journal in this area should buy this one. A necessary purchase for business schools and hospital libraries. (MMC)

4775. *Inquiry (Rochester): the journal of health care organization, provision and financing.* [ISSN: 0046-9580] 1963. q. USD 75 (Individuals, USD 60; USD 75 elsewhere). Ed(s): Ronny Frishman, Katherine Swartz. Blue Cross and Blue Shield of the Rochester Area, PO Box 25399, Rochester, NY 14625; http://www.inquiryjournal.org. Illus., index, adv. Refereed. Circ: 2500. Vol. ends: Winter. Microform: PQC. Online: Gale Group; OCLC Online Computer Library Center, Inc.; ProQuest Information & Learning. Reprint: PQC. *Indexed:* ABIn, AgeL, BPI, CINAHL, ExcerpMed, HRA, IndMed, JEL, MCR, PAIS, SCI, SSCI, SSI. *Bk. rev.:* 3-6, length varies. *Aud.:* Ac, Sa.

Inquiry is an established health-care financing journal and a good buy for the price. An average of eight scholarly and substantive articles per issue are written by analysts and professors of public health, economics, or health care administration. Typical recent topics include medical assistance needs of welfare leavers, how ownership affects hospital efficiency, the changing view of hospital capacity standards, and effects of alcohol benefits in employee health plans. Articles are accompanied by lengthy notes, bibliographies, and numerous graphs and charts. Books reviewed are the more important public policy works. Libraries that cater to health administrators, practitioners, interns, and students should carry this journal. (MMC)

4776. *The Joint Commission Journal on Quality and Safety.* Former titles (until 2003): *The Joint Commission Journal on Quality Improvement;* (until 1993): *Q R B - Quality Review Bulletin.* 1974. m. USD 195 domestic; USD 220 in Canada & Mexico; USD 235 elsewhere. Ed(s): Steve Berman. Joint Commission Resources, Inc., 1 Renaissance Blvd., Oakbrook Terrace, IL 60181; http://www.jcrinc.com. Illus., index, adv. Sample. Refereed. Circ: 7955. Vol. ends: Dec. *Indexed:* AgeL, CINAHL, ExcerpMed, IndMed, MCR, SSCI, SWR&A. *Aud.:* Ac, Sa.

The Joint Commission on Accreditation of Healthcare Organizations, the major accrediting agency for health care organizations in the United States, publishes this title "to serve as a forum for practical approaches to improving quality and value in health care." This is the premier journal in the field. The authors are quality-assurance administrators, consultants, physicians, and nurses. Each issue carries several well-documented articles that present quality-assurance/improvement research and case studies. Recent topics include improving medication safety through self-assessment, planning patient-centered care, and improving compliance with guidelines for care of acute myocardial infarction. The value of this bulletin is enhanced by a section of abstracts culled from various medical journals. All libraries with a health administration emphasis will want to carry this journal. (MMC)

4777. *Journal of Health Care Finance.* Formerly: *Topics in Health Care Financing.* [ISSN: 1078-6767] 1974. q. USD 199. Ed(s): James J Unland. Aspen Publishers, Inc., 1185 Avenue of the Americas, New York, NY 10036; customer.service@aspenpubl.com; http://www.aspenpublishers.com. Illus., adv. Sample. Vol. ends: Summer. Microform: PQC. Online: bigchalk; EBSCO Publishing; Florida Center for Library Automation; Gale Group; OCLC Online Computer Library Center, Inc.; Ovid Technologies, Inc.; ProQuest Information & Learning. *Indexed:* ABIn, AgeL, BPI, CINAHL, ExcerpMed, IndMed, LRI, MCR. *Aud.:* Ac, Sa.

The quarterly *Journal of Health Care Finance* presents one theme in each issue for an audience of hospital finance staff and health care planners. Top consultants, business professors, and corporate financial planners explore health care finance topics in depth, with substantive articles supported by useful bibliographies. A recent article discusses the use of microcomputers to improve capital decisions. The articles are well written and practical. For medical and business school libraries and larger hospital libraries. (MMC)

4778. *Journal of Healthcare Management.* Former titles: *Hospital and Health Services Administration; Hospital Administration.* [ISSN: 1096-9012] 1956. bi-m. USD 85 domestic; USD 95 foreign; USD 23 newsstand/cover. Ed(s): Kyle Grazier. Health Administration Press, One North Franklin St, Ste 1700, Chicago, IL 60606-3491; ache@ache.org; http://www.ache.org/hap.cfm. Illus. Sample. Refereed. Circ: 28000. Microform: PQC. Online: EBSCO Publishing; Florida Center for Library Automation; Gale Group; OCLC Online Computer Library Center, Inc.; Ovid Technologies, Inc.; ProQuest Information & Learning. Reprint: PQC. *Indexed:* ABIn, ATI, AgeL, CINAHL, ExcerpMed, LRI, MCR, SSCI. *Bk. rev.:* 8, 250-400 words. *Aud.:* Ac, Sa.

This journal features lengthy research articles by health care administrators, financial planners, and educators on public policy in the health arena. There is a strong emphasis on decision making, financial management, organizational structure and policies, nursing management, and policy strategies. Recent issues discuss the ability to accurately predict hospital failures, hospital community benefits other than charity care, patient satisfaction in the emergency room, and adding value to patient satisfaction surveys. (MMC)

4779. *The Journal of Nursing Administration.* [ISSN: 0002-0443] 1971. 11x/yr. USD 297 (Individuals, USD 97; USD 18 per issue). Ed(s): Suzanne P Smith. Lippincott Williams & Wilkins, 530 Walnut St, Philadelphia, PA 19106-3621; custserv@lww.com; http://www.lww.com. Illus., index, adv. Sample. Refereed. Circ: 11397. Vol. ends: Dec. CD-ROM: Ovid Technologies, Inc. Microform: PQC. Online: Ovid Technologies, Inc. *Indexed:* AgeL, CIJE, CINAHL, ExcerpMed, IndMed, SSCI. *Bk. rev.:* Occasional. *Aud.:* Ac, Sa.

Published by Lippincott Williams & Wilkins (www.lww.com), this journal covers a variety of administrative topics and carries news of people and trends in the field. The authors are practitioners who address subjects for fellow administrators, educators, and students. Some issues carry a substantial signed book review. A recurring theme is the development of new nurse administrators. Special departments discuss legal issues, evidence-based practice, and specific management cases. Recent issues treat such topics as the effect of LPN reductions on RN patient load, the nursing shortage, telephone nursing advice services, and culture commitments and the merger situation. Although geared to top nurse administrators, this title is a must for nursing-school collections. (MMC)

4780. ***Laboratory Medicine.*** Formerly (until 1970): *Bulletin of Pathology;* Incorporates: *Technical Improvement Service Bulletin.* [ISSN: 0007-5027] 1965. m. USD 75 (Individuals, USD 60; USD 11 per issue domestic). Ed(s): Paul Philipsher. American Society for Clinical Pathology, 2100 W Harrison St, Chicago, IL 60612; info@ascp.org; http://www.ascp.org. Illus., adv. Refereed. Circ: 160567. Vol. ends: Dec. Microform: PQC. *Indexed:* CINAHL, ChemAb, ExcerpMed, IndVet, SSCI. *Aud.:* Ac, Sa.

This publication of the American Society of Clinical Pathologists carries six to eight articles that deal with a variety of technological, procedural, and professional issues. Recent articles have covered diagnostic tests for acute respiratory syndrome (SARS), laboratory preparedness for bioterrorism, and spotting emerging pathogens. Technically challenging, this magazine is highly interesting, even to general readers, especially those desiring knowledge of medical inquiry into contagious diseases. An inexpensive and authoritative publication, *Laboratory Medicine* should be purchased for academic medical center libraries and special collections that serve laboratory professionals. (MMC)

4781. ***M G M A Connexion.*** Former titles: *Medical Group Management Journal;* (until 1987): *Medical Group Management.* 1953. 10x/yr. USD 175 (Individuals, USD 95). Ed(s): Brenda Hull. Medical Group Management Association, 104 Inverness Terrace E, Englewood, CO 80112; beh@mgma.com; http://www.mgma.com. Illus., index, adv. Sample. Circ: 32000. Vol. ends: Nov/Dec. Microform: PQC. *Indexed:* ExcerpMed, MCR. *Bk. rev.:* 1-3, length varies. *Aud.:* Ac, Sa.

The official journal of the Medical Group Management Association, this magazine provides organizational news as well as administrative and financial information for members and the academic and business community. Authors are administrators, accountants, academicians, and the occasional physician. The focus of the content is socioeconomic concerns and business strategies for medical-group practices. Recent articles discuss the economics of centralized billing, referrals, and profitable faculty practice plans. The book reviews are quite good and should be useful to libraries. Appropriate for medical and business schools and large hospital library collections. (MMC)

4782. ***Medical Economics.*** [ISSN: 0025-7206] 1923. s-m. USD 109 domestic; USD 175 foreign; USD 10 newsstand/cover per issue. Ed(s): Jeff Forster. Medical Economics Company, 5 Paragon Dr, Montvale, NJ 07645-1742. Illus., adv. Circ: 154515. Vol. ends: Dec. Microform: RPI; PQC. Online: The Dialog Corporation; Florida Center for Library Automation; Gale Group; Northern Light Technology, Inc.; OCLC Online Computer Library Center, Inc. *Indexed:* ABIn, ATI, AgeL, BPI, CINAHL, LRI, MCR, PAIS. *Aud.:* Ac, Sa.

Complimentary copies of *Medical Economics* are received by many practicing physicians. The magazine deals with practice management, socioeconomic realities of private practice, and personal-finance issues. Articles are written by journal staff, consultants, and physicians describing personal office practice experiences. Recurring themes for physicians in practice are dealing with problem patients, avoiding malpractice suits, and personal finances. Recent articles discuss managing care in the home, reporting problem physicians, inventions and the patent process, and mutual funds. Recent issues of the journal are available to the public at http://www.memag.com/, which also contains various other medical news and wellness information. Medical school and hospital libraries should collect this indexed title. It is also a useful magazine for businesses that serve a physician clientele. (MMC)

4783. ***Modern Healthcare (Year): the newsmagazine for administrators and managers in hospitals, and other healthcare institutions.*** Incorporates: *Modern Healthcare (Long-Term Care); Modern Healthcare (Short-Term Care); Modern Hospital; Modern Nursing Home.* [ISSN: 0160-7480] 1974. w. USD 145 domestic; USD 236 Canada; USD 199 elsewhere. Ed(s): David Burda. Crain Communications, Inc., 360 N Michigan Ave, Chicago, IL 60601-3806; http://www.crain.com. Illus., index, adv. Sample. Circ: 79371 Controlled. Vol. ends: Dec. Online: EBSCO Publishing; Factiva; Florida Center for Library Automation; Gale Group; LexisNexis; OCLC Online Computer Library Center, Inc.; ProQuest Information & Learning; H.W. Wilson. *Indexed:* ABIn, AIAP, API, ATI, AgeL, B&I, BPI, CINAHL, ExcerpMed, IndMed, LRI. *Aud.:* Ga, Ac, Sa.

This is the weekly newsmagazine of the health care community. *Modern Healthcare* covers news stories of health care institutions and their administrators. It focuses not just on Washington, D.C., but on success stories and failures all over the United States. A dozen feature articles may make up the "Week in Healthcare," and there are regular departments on regional news, systems, technology, and finance. Stories cover news of new limits on residents' hours, increased federal scrutiny of joint ventures, the cost of cardiac care, and the increasing role of physician CEOs. Well-illustrated, and carrying cartoons and humor, it has the style of a lively American newsweekly. Everyone who wants to be informed on the business of health care reads it, and students use it for reports. For university, hospital, and public libraries. (MMC)

4784. ***Nursing Administration Quarterly.*** [ISSN: 0363-9568] 1976. q. USD 199 (Individuals, USD 79). Lippincott Williams & Wilkins, 16522 Hunters Green Pkwy., Hagerstown, MD 21740; http://www.lww.com. Illus., adv. Vol. ends: Summer. Microform: PQC. Online: bigchalk; EBSCO Publishing; Florida Center for Library Automation; Gale Group; OCLC Online Computer Library Center, Inc.; Ovid Technologies, Inc.; ProQuest Information & Learning. Reprint: PQC. *Indexed:* AgeL, CINAHL. *Bk. rev.:* 2-3, 500-1,000 words, signed. *Aud.:* Ac, Sa.

This quarterly research journal of nursing administration is geared to academic researchers, clinicians, and students. Each issue carries eight to ten substantial articles on such themes as the future of nurse executives in changing delivery systems and the health care revolution. There are guest editorials, lengthy book reviews, and a section on nursing informatics. All libraries that cater to nursing students should carry this journal. The articles are practical and well-researched, with numerous references. The broader coverage of The *Journal of Nursing Administration* (see above in this section) makes this a second choice for smaller hospital libraries. (MMC)

4785. ***Nursing Economics: the journal for health care leaders.*** [ISSN: 0746-1739] 1983. bi-m. USD 70 (Individuals, USD 54). Ed(s): Kenneth J Thomas, Connie R Curran. Jannetti Publications, Inc., East Holly Ave, Box 56, Pitman, NJ 08071-0056; NEJRNL@ajj.com; http://www.ajj.com/. Illus., index. Sample. Refereed. Vol. ends: Nov. Online: bigchalk; EBSCO Publishing; Florida Center for Library Automation; Gale Group; Northern Light Technology, Inc.; OCLC Online Computer Library Center, Inc.; ProQuest Information & Learning. *Indexed:* AgeL, CINAHL, SSCI. *Aud.:* Ac, Sa.

Nursing Economics is a sound and practical title for nursing administration collections. Most of the authors are nursing consultants, university faculty, or top administrators and educators. Recent issues covered include minimum staffing ratios, the aging nurse workforce, and shift work as a cause of the nursing shortage. This is a particularly attractive journal, with numerous high-quality illustrations and tables. All major articles carry references and suggestions for further reading. The "Perspectives in Ambulatory Care" department keeps nurses up to date on cutting-edge research on ambulatory care. *Nursing Economics* belongs in academic and hospital collections. (MMC)

Health Professions

This subsection includes a sampling of the very large literature aimed at specific health professions. Many of these journals are published by professional organizations for their memberships. These are some of the major titles in nursing and the allied health professions that are of interest to students, practitioners, and the lay public. (MMC)

4786. ***The Health Care Manager.*** Former titles: *Health Care Supervisor; Health Care Supervisors Journal.* [ISSN: 1525-5794] 1982. q. USD 199 (Individuals, USD 79). Lippincott Williams & Wilkins, 16522 Hunters Green Pkwy., Hagerstown, MD 21740; http://www.lww.com. Illus., adv.

Refereed. Vol. ends: Jun. Online: EBSCO Publishing; Florida Center for Library Automation; Gale Group; OCLC Online Computer Library Center, Inc.; Ovid Technologies, Inc.; ProQuest Information & Learning. *Indexed:* ABIn, CINAHL. *Aud.:* Ac, Sa.

The title of *Health Care Supervisor* was changed to *The Health Care Manager* beginning with volume 18, issue one, in September 1999. *The Health Care Manager* provides practical management information for managers in institutional health-care settings. It addresses managerial issues that include purchasing technology, managing in downsized organizations, labor relations strategies, and handling performance problems. In addition to clear, well-written articles, it also offers a helpful column called "Case in Health Care Management" to show possible solutions to a hypothetical management crisis. Intended for practicing managers, this journal will also be useful teaching tool. Recommended for academic and hospital libraries. (MMC)

4787. ***Home Healthcare Nurse.*** Incorporates (1979-1983): *Nephrology Nurse.* [ISSN: 0884-741X] 1983. 12x/yr. USD 198.95 (Individuals, USD 49.95; USD 8 per issue). Ed(s): Carolyn J Humphrey. Lippincott Williams & Wilkins, 530 Walnut St, Philadelphia, PA 19106-3621; http://www.lww.com. Illus., adv. Sample. Refereed. Circ: 8791. Reprint: PQC. *Indexed:* AgeL, CINAHL. *Aud.:* Sa.

Home Healthcare Nurse is "a peer-reviewed journal addressing the educational information needs of practicing home care nurses while stimulating creative and productive approaches to the changing healthcare environment." The journal has an attractive, modern news journal format with excellent illustrations. Each issue has eight to ten feature articles, each three to five pages in length. Some articles are well referenced. Recent issues provide help for dealing with the CLIA Survey, information on patients with communications disorders, and multiple articles on needed nutrition topics. Authors are academic nursing faculty and public policy leaders in the nursing profession. Highly recommended for hospital libraries and academic nursing library collections. (MMC)

4788. ***Imprint (New York).*** Formerly: *N S N A Newsletter.* [ISSN: 0019-3062] 1968. 5x/yr. USD 15. Ed(s): Caroline Jaffe. National Student Nurses' Association, 555 W 57 St, New York, NY 10019. Illus., index, adv. Sample. Circ: 34000. Vol. ends: Dec/Jan. *Indexed:* BHA, CINAHL. *Aud.:* Hs, Ac.

Imprint is the official publication of the National Student Nurses Association. Geared toward nursing students, this journal provides information on the activities of the NSNA, articles on nursing topics, and scholarship information. The current table of contents and selected articles from the issues of February/March 1997 to present are available online at http://www.nsna.org/pubs/index.html. Recent subjects include transitioning from student to the workplace, army nursing and leadership skills, and the value of mentoring. This informative and inexpensive publication deserves a place in academic and hospital libraries that serve institutions with nursing education programs. (WH)

4789. ***International Nursing Review.*** [ISSN: 0020-8132] 1926. q. GBP 75 print & online eds. Blackwell Publishing Ltd., 9600 Garsington Rd, Oxford, OX4 2ZG, United Kingdom; customerservices@oxon.blackwellpublishing.com; http://www.blackwellpublishing.com. Illus., adv. Sample. Refereed. Circ: 3500. Vol. ends: Nov/Dec. Microform: PQC. Online: EBSCO Publishing; ingenta.com; Munksgaard & Blackwell Science's Synergy; OCLC Online Computer Library Center, Inc.; Ovid Technologies, Inc.; RoweCom Information Quest; Swets Blackwell. Reprint: PQC. *Indexed:* ASSIA, CINAHL, IndMed. *Bk. rev.:* Various number and length. *Aud.:* Ac, Sa.

International Nursing Review is the official publication of the International Council of Nurses. It addresses a variety of nursing issues, such as ethics, primary health care, credentialing, and continuing education. Topics discussed in recent articles include new nurse graduates' understanding of competence, home-based care of the terminally ill in Botswana, the nursing education system in the People's Republic of China, and evaluating the beta version of the International Classification for Nursing Practice. The international perspective and range of current and historical subjects covered make this journal an essential part of any nursing collection. Recommended for all larger hospital and academic libraries that serve nurses and nursing students. The web site is http://www.icn.ch/fr_INRsubscribe.htm and includes table of contents and selected sections from current and past issues available as pdf files. Subscription information and guidelines for authors are also listed. (WH)

4790. ***Nursing Education Perspectives.*** Former titles: *Nursing and Health Care Perspectives; N and H C Perspectives on Community;* (until 1995): *Nursing and Health Care;* Which superseded (in 1980): *N L N News.* [ISSN: 1536-5026] 1952. bi-m. USD 65 (Individuals, USD 40). Ed(s): Leslie Block. National League for Nursing, 61 Broadway, New York, NY 10006-2701; nlnweb@nln.org; http://www.nln.org. Illus., adv. Sample. Refereed. Circ: 9000 Paid. CD-ROM: Ovid Technologies, Inc. Reprint: PQC. *Indexed:* AgeL, CIJE, CINAHL, MCR, SSCI. *Bk. rev.:* 0-7, length varies. *Aud.:* Ac, Sa.

This National League of Nursing publication focuses on the connection between nursing and the community, sharing information, and affecting health outcomes. There is also strong emphasis on nursing education, due in part to the fact that nursing education programs are accredited by the NLN. Article topics featured recently include workforce development in nursing, community partnership, and why women and men choose nursing as a career. Strongly recommended for all libraries that serve institutions with nursing education programs. (WH)

4791. ***Nursing Management.*** Formerly (until 1981): *Supervisor Nurse.* [ISSN: 0744-6314] 1970. m. USD 139 (Individuals, USD 39.95; USD 7 newsstand/cover per issue). Ed(s): Melissa A. Fitzpatrick. Lippincott Williams & Wilkins, 351 W Camden St, Baltimore, MD 21201; http://www.lww.com. Illus., adv. Sample. Circ: 98789 Controlled. Vol. ends: Dec. Microform: PQC. Online: bigchalk; EBSCO Publishing; Gale Group; Northern Light Technology, Inc.; OCLC Online Computer Library Center, Inc.; Ovid Technologies, Inc.; ProQuest Information & Learning. Reprint: PQC. *Indexed:* ABIn, AgeL, CINAHL. *Bk. rev.:* 0-2, length varies. *Aud.:* Ac, Sa.

Although this publication is directed mainly at nurses in management positions, it contains articles that may be of interest to nurses on all levels. Continuing education opportunities for a fee are offered through both the print version of the journal and online at http://www.nursingmanagement.com/. The web site also includes current and past tables of contents and selected full-text articles back to 1999. Recent articles discussed using barcodes at the bedside to prevent medication errors, nursing identity and merger opportunities, and management of burn injuries. In addition to the articles, there is a section devoted to JCAHO questions and another section addressing legal issues in nursing. This is a must-have for academic and special libraries with nursing collections. (WH)

4792. ***Nursing Outlook.*** [ISSN: 0029-6554] 1953. bi-m. USD 113 (Individuals, USD 59; Students, USD 29). Ed(s): Dr. Carole A Anderson. Mosby, Inc., 11830 Westline Industrial Dr, St Louis, MO 63146-3318; http://www.us.elsevierhealth.com. Illus., index, adv. Sample. Refereed. Circ: 5852. Vol. ends: Nov/Dec. Microform: PQC. Online: EBSCO Publishing; RoweCom Information Quest; ScienceDirect. Reprint: PQC. *Indexed:* AgeL, CIJE, CINAHL, ECER, IndMed, MCR, PsycholAb, SSCI, SSI, SWR&A. *Bk. rev.:* Various number and length. *Aud.:* Ac, Sa.

The official publication of the American Academy of Nursing, *Nursing Outlook* features articles written by nurses, physicians, and other health care experts. Issues include four to five articles, along with commentary, editorials, meetings information, and news from the American Academy of Nursing. Subjects of articles include distance education, population health, evidence-based medicine, and nursing education. *Nursing Outlook* is also known for publishing the *Brandon/Hill Selected List of Nursing Books and Journals* (for health sciences collections). Tables of contents and abstracts are available at http://www.us.elsevierhealth.com/, as well as selected article, full-text for a fee. Recommended for libraries of all sizes with nursing collections. (WH)

Medical Problems

The Internet is now one of the most popular resources for health information; most of these print journals offer full or partial access on the web. Since these titles are devoted to consumer/patient education about specific diseases, they will be useful to public and hospital libraries that meet the demand for consumer health information. These titles are low cost and many are free. Patients/caregivers will appreciate referrals to these authoritative and reliable print and online resources. (MMC)

4793. *AIDS Treatment News.* [ISSN: 1052-4207] 1986. 18x/yr. USD 325 (Individuals, USD 140). Ed(s): John S James. A T N Publications, 1233 Locust St., # 5, Philadelphia, PA 19107-5400; http://www.aidsnews.org. Illus., index, adv. Sample. Circ: 1500 Paid. Online: Factiva; Gale Group; OCLC Online Computer Library Center, Inc. *Aud.:* Ga, Ac, Sa.

This eight-page newsletter states as its purpose the reporting of experimental and standard treatments available to persons with AIDS or those who are HIV-positive. The newsletter options and combinations of treatments found helpful by AIDS and HIV-positive patients without supporting any specific treatment. News reports are culled from medical journals, conference reports, and interviews. News briefs include announcements of conferences, clinical trials, contacts, Internet resources, etc. This newsletter is found in free full text, back to 1986. A great resource for the public, this responsible, thoughtful newsletter is recommended for libraries that serve AIDS populations. (KR)

4794. *Arthritis Today: the magazine for help and hope.* Formerly (until 1987): *National Arthritis News.* [ISSN: 0890-1120] 1980. bi-m. USD 12.95; USD 4.95 newsstand/cover. Ed(s): Beth Blaney, Cindy McDaniel. Arthritis Foundation, 1330 W Peach Tree St, Atlanta, GA 30309; atmail@arthritis.org; http://www.arthritis.org. Illus., adv. Sample. Circ: 650000 Paid. Vol. ends: Nov/Dec. Online: Florida Center for Library Automation; Gale Group; OCLC Online Computer Library Center, Inc. *Aud.:* Ga, Sa.

Arthritis Today is a glossy, colorful, professional-looking magazine produced by the Arthritis Foundation for arthritis patients and for those with arthritis-related conditions such as fibromyalgia and lupus. Features include personal profiles, drug therapies (both conventional and alternative), exercise regimens, and topics such as meditation and pain-free computer use. Regular departments include "Research Spotlight," "Life Style" (daily living tips), and "On Call," a question-and-answer column by a panel of medical experts. The current monthly issue is online at arthritis.org. Public and consumer health libraries will find this useful. (KR)

4795. *C A: a cancer journal for clinicians.* [ISSN: 0007-9235] 1950. bi-m. USD 41 (Individuals, USD 95). Ed(s): Suzanne Cassidy, Harmon J Eyre. Lippincott Williams & Wilkins, 530 Walnut St, Philadelphia, PA 19106-3621; custserv@lww.com; http://www.lww.com. Illus., index, adv. Sample. Refereed. Circ: 150000 Controlled. Vol. ends: Nov/Dec. Microform: PQC. Online: EBSCO Publishing; Florida Center for Library Automation; Gale Group; HighWire Press; OCLC Online Computer Library Center, Inc. Reprint: PQC. *Indexed:* BiolAb, CINAHL, ExcerpMed, IndMed, SCI. *Aud.:* Hs, Ga, Ac, Sa.

Published by the American Cancer Society. The audience of *CA* is primary care physicians, and its purpose is providing current information on all aspects of cancer diagnosis, treatment, and prevention. The web site http://CAonline.AmCancer.Soc.org offers free access to full text of all content in a searchable format. The annual January–February issue on cancer statistics includes U.S. figures and some international statistics. The authoritative articles are written by researchers and physicians. Illustrations include tables and graphs that summarize data concisely. Print subscriptions are free to clinicians and other health professionals; by e-mail, issues are offered via journal@cancer.org. Institutions must license directly with the publisher. Highly recommended for public, academic, and special libraries. (MMC)

4796. *Coping with Cancer.* Formerly: *Coping.* [ISSN: 1544-5488] 1986. bi-m. USD 19 domestic; USD 25 foreign. Ed(s): Kay Thomas. Media America, PO Box 682268, Franklin, TN 37068-2268. Illus., adv. Sample. Circ: 80000 Paid and controlled. Vol. ends: Dec. *Aud.:* Ga, Sa.

This glossy, 60-page magazine ranges from practical advice on coping with cancer to the inspirational stories of survivors. Recent articles address spiritual distress, workplace issues for cancer survivors, and treatment side effects. Clinical articles are peer-reviewed. The "Survivor-to-Survivor Bulletin Board" enables patients to locate others with similar diagnoses for correspondence and support. The ads alone are invaluable for helping patients find products useful for their comfort. Compare this with *In Touch,* below. (LEB)

4797. *Diabetes Care.* [ISSN: 0149-5992] 1978. m. USD 600 in USA & Mexico (Individuals, USD 300 in USA & Mexico). Ed(s): Mayer B Davidson, Aime M Ballard. American Diabetes Association, 1701 N. Beauregard St., Alexandria, VA 22311-1717; customerservice@diabetes.org; http://www.diabetes.org. Illus., adv. Refereed. Circ: 13500 Paid. CD-ROM: Ovid Technologies, Inc. Microform: PQC. Online: bigchalk; EBSCO Publishing; Factiva; Florida Center for Library Automation; Gale Group; HighWire Press; Northern Light Technology, Inc.; OCLC Online Computer Library Center, Inc.; Ovid Technologies, Inc.; ProQuest Information & Learning. Reprint: PQC. *Indexed:* Agr, CINAHL, ChemAb, DSA, ExcerpMed, HortAb, IndMed, RRTA, SCI, SSCI. *Aud.:* Ga, Ac, Sa.

A highly respected and authoritative journal, *Diabetes Care* is directed to specialized health care personnel and is very research-oriented, but it will certainly be of interest to the portion of the educated lay public familiar with diabetes and its terminology. All issues previous to the current year are available free in full-text/pdf back to January 1978 at http://care.diabetesjournals.org/. (MMC)

4798. *Diabetes Forecast: the healthy living magazine for 50 years.* Formerly: *A.D.A. Forecast.* [ISSN: 0095-8301] 1948. m. Membership, USD 28. Ed(s): Andrew Keegan. American Diabetes Association, 1701 N. Beauregard St., Alexandria, VA 22311-1717; customerservice@diabetes.org; http://www.diabetes.org. Illus., adv. Sample. Circ: 400000. Vol. ends: Dec. Online: bigchalk; EBSCO Publishing; Florida Center for Library Automation; Gale Group; Northern Light Technology, Inc.; OCLC Online Computer Library Center, Inc.; ProQuest Information & Learning. *Indexed:* Agr, CINAHL. *Aud.:* Hs, Ga, Ac, Sa.

Diabetes Forecast is a 100-plus-page glossy publication of the American Diabetes Association (Membership, Michael A. Pfeifer, Amer. Diabetes Assn., 1701 Beauregard St., Alexandria, VA 22311), presenting tips for day-to-day coping with diabetes. Regularly appearing departments include the "Recipe Cards," "Making Friends" (pen pals), "Diabetes Advocate" (health legislation and issues affecting diabetes), "Reflections" (personal narratives), and "Shopper's Guide." "Kid's Corner" appears four times yearly with puzzles, games, stories, and jokes. Advertisements must meet strict guidelines for inclusion. The table of contents of the latest issue is available online, with the full text of selected articles from current and back issues. A recent issue covered ten tips for foot care, dealing with diabetes in college, and the placebo response. A real bargain and recommended for public and consumer health libraries. (MMC)

4799. *Diabetes Self-Management.* [ISSN: 0741-6253] 1983. bi-m. USD 18; USD 4 newsstand/cover per issue. Ed(s): James Hazlett. R.A. Rapaport Publishing, Inc., 150 W 22nd St, New York, NY 10011; staff@diabetes-self-mgmt.com; http://www.diabetes-self-mgmt.com. Illus., adv. Sample. Circ: 470000 Paid. Vol. ends: Nov/Dec. *Indexed:* CINAHL. *Aud.:* Hs, Ga, Sa.

Diabetes Self-Management focuses on those activities that diabetics can manage for themselves such as cooking, shopping, and exercise. Recent articles have covered herbal therapies in diabetic management, treating impotence, and treating gastric symptoms of diabetes. The web site (http://www.diabetes-self-mgmt.com/) is most attractive and includes the table of contents from the latest issue and full text of a couple of feature articles, selected articles from back issues, and additional information that does not appear in the journal. This low-cost and practical journal should be in all libraries with print consumer health collections. Refer web users to the site. (KR)

4800. *Epilepsy U S A.* Formerly (until 1991): *National Spokesman.* [ISSN: 1060-9369] 1972. 8x/yr. USD 25. Ed(s): Karina Barrentine. Epilepsy Foundation of America, 4351 Garden City Dr., Ste. 406, Landover, MD 20785; postmaster@efa.org; http://www.efa.org. Illus. Sample. Circ: 23000. Vol. ends: Dec. *Aud.:* Ga, Sa.

Epilepsy USA now appears in a glossy 22-page magazine format, in full color. The issues feature articles by patients and family members. Recent articles included dating and epilepsy, and appropriate sports for those with epilepsy. Regular columns are "Epilepsy Answer Place," "Letter Exchange" (pen pals), and "Capitol Comments" (health legislation). The "Marketplace" column reviews books, audios, and videos of interest to patients and families. The articles are full-text at the web site (http://www.epilepsyfoundation.org) where anyone can sign up for regular e-mail newsletter service for free. The services offered on the web are more robust than the little magazine has been. Print may no longer be necessary except for "pamphlet" use in special situations. (MMC)

4801. *Foundation Focus.* [ISSN: 0897-6759] 1977. 3x/yr. Members, USD 25. Crohn's & Colitis Foundation of America, Inc., 386 Park Ave S, New York, NY 10016-7374; info@ccfa.org. Adv. Circ: 65000. *Aud.:* Sa.

This 22-page magazine addresses the whole range of digestive diseases: inflammatory bowel disease, ulcerative colitis, Crohn's, etc. Recent articles have addressed insurance issues, research news, and the fear of surgery. The column "Mutual Help Network" serves to help patients locate people with conditions similar to their own for support and correspondence. The above web site has a "Medical Central" section with the latest information on these diseases. This publication would be especially useful for consumer health libraries. The web site is especially robust. (LEB)

4802. *Grapevine: the international monthly journal of Alcoholics Anonymous.* [ISSN: 0362-2584] 1944. m. USD 15 domestic; USD 23 foreign. Ed(s): Ames Sweet. Alcoholics Anonymous Grapevine, Inc., PO Box 1980, New York, NY 10163-1980; gveditorial@aagrapevine.org; http://www.aagrapevine/@org. *Aud.:* Sa.

This 60-plus page booklet describes itself as the international journal of Alcoholics Anonymous. The goal is to express the "individual way of working the program." Most articles are personal accounts from individuals in various stages of AA's 12-step program. Other features include cartoons, letters, a calendar of events, and word puzzles. An index of articles appears in the December issue. A Spanish version, *La Vina,* is available from the web site. For another approach, see *The Journal of Rational Recovery* below. (KR)

4803. *In Touch (Melville): cancer prevention and treatment: the good health guide.* [ISSN: 1522-7510] 1999. bi-m. USD 19.50 domestic; USD 25.50 Canada; USD 34.50 elsewhere. Ed(s): Randi Londer Gould, Dr. Steve Rosen. P R R, Inc., 48 S Service Rd, Melville, NY 11747-2335; intouch@cancernetwork.com; http://www.cancernetwork.com. Adv. Circ: 80000 Paid and controlled. *Aud.:* Ga, Sa.

In Touch is a glossy 72-page magazine that began publishing in 1999, offering celebrity covers and profiles. Articles include reports on clinical trials, trends in medical research, and the pros and cons of controversial treatments. Recent issues have also addressed music therapy, meditation, and care for caregivers. The web site above offers only the table of contents for the latest issue, but serves as an information source for virtually every type of cancer and treatment. Compared with *Coping with Cancer* above, this is a less personal, flashier production. With 1,268,000 new cases of cancer per year, there is plenty of room for both. Back issues are available for free at http://www.intouchlive.com. (LEB)

4804. *Journal of Rational Recovery.* [ISSN: 1065-2019] 1988. bi-m. USD 32 domestic; USD 50 foreign; USD 11 base vol(s). per issue). Rational Recovery Systems, Inc., Box 800, Lotus, CA 95651; http://www.rational.org/. *Aud.:* Ga, Ac, Sa.

Jack and Lois Trimpey founded an alternative to Alcoholics Anonymous; this is their publication. Each issue includes several letters from those supporting and opposing *Rational Recovery;* and the editor, Jack, develops and explains his philosophy via responses to those letters. In blunt language, both editors emphasize individual moral responsibility within a non-theistic framework, while opposing the disease view of addiction. The site http://www.rational.org/recovery features live and recorded "talk show" discussion by J. Trimpey. This is an important resource for libraries that desire to offer alternative points of view. (LEB)

4805. *Lupus News.* [ISSN: 0732-0280] 1979. q. USD 25 domestic; USD 35 foreign. Ed(s): Jenny Allan. Lupus Foundation of America, Inc., 1300 Piccard Dr, Ste 200, Rockville, MD 20850; lupusnews@aol.com; http://www.lupus.org. Illus. Sample. Refereed. Circ: 55000. *Aud.:* Ga, Sa.

This colorful 24-page newsletter serves as the official newsletter of the Lupus Foundation of America. Chapter news, personal profiles, and current research studies are reported. The magazine comes with paid membership and is not available online, but further information about the diseases is available at http://www.lupus.org. A question-and-answer column with answers by physicians appears in each issue. This is a worthwhile addition to any consumer health collection. (LEB)

4806. *Mamm: women, cancer and community.* 1997. 10x/yr. USD 14.95 domestic; USD 24.95 foreign. Ed(s): Gwen Darien. MAMM LLC, 41 E 11th St, 11th Fl, New York, NY 10003; elsieh@mamm.com. Adv. *Indexed:* CINAHL, FemPer. *Bk. rev.:* 1-2, 250 words. *Aud.:* Ga, Sa.

MAMM is a glossy 64-page magazine that primarily targets breast cancer patients, while occasionally addressing ovarian cancer. Articles cover a wide range of topics, such as dealing with hair loss, depression, how friends can help cancer patients, and discrimination at work. Scattered throughout the issues are pointers to additional information via web sites, phone numbers, addresses, books, etc. The organizational web site (http://www.mamm.com) provides additional information about the journal and cancer organizations in general. This is a must for any women's health collection. (LEB)

4807. *Ostomy Quarterly.* [ISSN: 0030-6517] 1963. q. USD 25 domestic; USD 30 Canada; USD 40 elsewhere. Ed(s): Thomas Kimball. United Ostomy Association, Inc., 19772 MacArthur Blvd, Ste 200, Irvine, CA 92612-2405. Illus., index, adv. Sample. Refereed. Circ: 29000. Vol. ends: Fall. *Aud.:* Ga, Ac, Sa.

Articles in this quarterly cover the care and management of ostomies, written by health care professionals and experienced osteomates. Personal accounts of living with a stoma, diet advice, and the physical, mental, and emotional effects of ostomies are also offered. There are occasional book and audiovisual reviews. Several personal profiles of osteomates appear in each issue, as well as news of association activities and conferences, in addition to Q&A columns. Advertisers offer an array of appliances, clothing, and related products used by osteomates. See the journal web site at http://www.uoa.org/publications_oq.htm. Recommended for public libraries as well as consumer health collections. (KR)

4808. *Quest (Tucson).* Former titles (until 1994): *M D A Reports;* (until 1992): *M D A Newsmagazine; M D A News - Muscular Dystrophy Association; Muscular Dystrophy News.* [ISSN: 1087-1578] 1950. bi-m. USD 14 domestic; USD 22 foreign. Ed(s): Carol Sowell. Muscular Dystrophy Association, Inc., 3300 E Sunrise Dr, Tucson, AZ 85718-3208; http://www.mdausa.org. Illus., adv. Sample. Circ: 115000 Paid and controlled. Vol. ends: Fall. *Bk. rev.:* 1-2, 150 words. *Aud.:* Ga, Sa.

Covering muscular dystrophy and 40 neuromuscular diseases, this glossy 70-page magazine features articles on sleep problems, vitamin supplements, vision problems, and massage therapy. The "Resources" column reviews products useful to those with disabilities, including occasional books and videos. As a publication of the Muscular Dystrophy Association, *Quest* highlights its activities. Advertisements offer products to assist mobility and independence. The above web site includes the feature articles from the current issue, as well as from several recent issues (approximately a year). *Quest* is free to all patients with neuromuscular diseases, and its low cost makes it an attractive addition to consumer health collections. (LEB)

Medicine—Professional

Health care personnel will find titles in this subsection both germane and practical. Information in these periodicals should supplement professional practice and facilitate scholarly research. Physicians, nurses, and allied health professionals will find these journals useful. Experts in the prescribed areas discuss various aspects of pathologic processes, preventive medicine, public health, and health maintenance. Many journal articles provide continuing-education opportunities. (DJJ)

4809. *AIDS Patient Care and S T Ds.* Formerly (until 1996): *AIDS Patient Care.* [ISSN: 1087-2914] 1987. m. USD 378 (Individuals, USD 194). Ed(s): Jeffrey Laurence. Mary Ann Liebert, Inc. Publishers, 2 Madison Ave, Ste 210, Larchmont, NY 10538-9957; info@liebertpub.com; http://www.liebertpub.com. Illus., adv. Sample. Refereed. Vol. ends: Dec. Online: EBSCO Publishing; Gale Group; Ingenta Select; OCLC Online Computer Library Center, Inc.; Ovid Technologies, Inc.; RoweCom Information Quest; Swets Blackwell. Reprint: PSC. *Indexed:* CINAHL, ExcerpMed, H&SSA, RiskAb, SSCI. *Aud.:* Ga, Ac, Sa.

This international, peer-reviewed journal contains a wealth of material on all aspects of AIDS, HIV, and AIDS-related topics. Each monthly issue includes eight to ten short articles that include extensive illustrations, graphics, charts, and bibliographic references. *AIDS Patient Care and STDs* will meet the needs of doctors, nurses, and allied health workers who work with populations affected by and infected with HIV. The journal includes title articles, an editorial section, and updates called "Antiviral Briefs" and "Drug Developments and STD News." *AIDS Patient Care and STDs* is well researched and the editorial board is worldwide. Diagnosis, patient care, and treatment are all covered in detail; side issues that involve education, prevention, and epidemiology are also considered. This journal is a very complete and thorough source of information to anyone who desires the latest information on all aspects of AIDS. (DJJ)

4810. *American Dental Association. Journal.* [ISSN: 0002-8177] 1913. m. USD 121 (Individuals, USD 100; USD 12 newsstand/cover per issue domestic). Ed(s): Dr. Lawrence Meskin. American Dental Association, 211 E Chicago Ave, Chicago, IL 60611; jada@ada.org; http://www.ada.org. Illus., index, adv. Refereed. Circ: 150000 Paid. Vol. ends: Dec. Microform: PQC. Online: Gale Group; ingenta.com. Reprint: PQC. *Indexed:* AbAn, BiolAb, CINAHL, ChemAb, GSI, IndMed, MCR, SCI, SSCI. *Aud.:* Ac, Sa.

A monthly journal, *JADA* is considered the nation's foremost dental journal. Sponsored by the American Dental Association (http://www.ada.org), each issue contains peer-reviewed articles that cover all the latest aspects of dentistry. Dentists and others would find the reviews, clinical reports, dental research, and editorials extremely useful. A continuing education program with related articles in each issue is also offered. Items covered include the following broad categories: "Cosmetic and Restorative Care," "Research," "Clinical Practice," "Continuing Education," and "Informatics and Technology." Additionally, there are sections on "Views," "Letters to the Editor," and "News." Illustrations are in color, articles are referenced, and a dental calendar of events is presented. Especially for dentists and any researchers or consumers seeking dental information. (DJJ)

4811. *American Family Physician.* Formerly (until 1970): *G P.* [ISSN: 0002-838X] 1950. 24x/yr. USD 144 (Individuals, USD 108). Ed(s): Jay Siwek. American Academy of Family Physicians, 11400 Tomahawk Creek Pkwy, Leawood, KS 66211-2672; afpedit@aafp.org; http://www.aafp.org. Illus., index, adv. Sample. Refereed. Circ: 179315 Paid and controlled. Vol. ends: Dec. Microform: PMC; PQC. Online: bigchalk; EBSCO Publishing; Florida Center for Library Automation; Gale Group; LexisNexis; MD Consult; Northern Light Technology, Inc.; OCLC Online Computer Library Center, Inc.; ProQuest Information & Learning; H.W. Wilson. Reprint: PQC. *Indexed:* AgeL, CINAHL, ChemAb, DSA, ExcerpMed, GSI, H&SSA, HortAb, IndMed, IndVet, LRI, MCR, PEI, RRTA, RiskAb, SCI, SSCI. *Aud.:* Ga, Ac, Sa.

The purpose of this peer-reviewed journal is to provide medical information and continuing education to physicians. The six to eight major articles in each issue cover a wide variety of topics that include diagnosis, treatment, clinical studies, and statistics. Referenced articles include graphs, charts, and illustrations. Evidence-based guidelines are used and doctors in the field write all articles. This journal presents a balanced account of treatment pros and cons, along with handouts of patient information and CME credits. A newsletter at the beginning of each issue gives information pertinent to physicians. There are also sections on "Clinical Briefs," "Photo Quiz," a "CME Calendar," and the journal summary section "POEMs and Tips from Other Journals." Excellent color illustrations accompany many of the articles. Materials here would be of special value to physicians, but could be useful to all health care personnel. Full text of recent years is available at http://www.aafp.org/afp. (DJJ)

4812. *American Journal of Health Behavior.* Formerly (until 1996): *Health Values.* [ISSN: 1087-3244] 1977. bi-m. USD 167 (Individuals, USD 90). Ed(s): Elbert D Glover. P N G Publications, PO Box 4593, Star City, WV 26504-4593; pglover@wvu.edu; http://www.ajhb.org. Illus., index, adv. Refereed. Circ: 2000 Paid. Microform: PQC. Online: EBSCO Publishing; ProQuest Information & Learning. *Indexed:* ASSIA, AgeL, CIJE, CINAHL, CJA, PEI, PsycholAb, RiskAb, SFSA, SSCI, SociolAb. *Aud.:* Ac, Sa.

American Journal of Health Behavior is the official publication of the American Academy of Health Behavior. The journal's objectives are to provide comprehensive coverage of the various aspects of health-related behaviors. By examining issues such as diet, smoking, and exercise and how these issues affect health, articles seek to reinforce a holistic approach to disease prevention. This journal is in its third decade and is international in scope. Nurses, allied health personnel, and consumers will find the general topics both useful and informative. (DJJ)

4813. *American Journal of Nursing.* [ISSN: 0002-936X] 1900. m. USD 129 (Individuals, USD 39; USD 7 per issue). Ed(s): Diana J Mason. Lippincott Williams & Wilkins, 345 Hudson St, 16th Fl, New York, NY 10014-4502; custserv@lww.com; http://www.lww.com. Illus., index, adv. Sample. Circ: 347781. Vol. ends: Dec. CD-ROM: Ovid Technologies, Inc. Microform: PMC; PQC. Online: Gale Group; OCLC Online Computer Library Center, Inc.; Ovid Technologies, Inc. Reprint: PQC. *Indexed:* ASG, ASSIA, AgeL, BRI, CBRI, CINAHL, ChemAb, ECER, GSI, H&SSA, IMFL, IndMed, MCR, PAIS, PsycholAb, SCI, SSCI, SSI, SWA, SWR&A. *Bk. rev.:* Various number and length. *Aud.:* Ga, Ac, Sa.

AJN is one of the nursing profession's foremost publications and is the official journal of the American Nurses' Association. *American Journal of Nursing* is peer-reviewed, well written, and easy to comprehend. Articles include a complete bibliography as well as color illustrations that complement the individual articles. *AJN* includes the opportunity for continuing education credits, with a number of articles. Wide varieties of topics are included, such as "Drug Watch," "Practice Errors," "Pain Control," "Emerging Infections," and "Clinical Quick Takes." *AJN* covers all aspects of nursing practice. Articles are practical and demonstrate hands-on experience. Some full text is available at http://www.nursingworld.org/. *AJN* is one of the essential journals to have in any collection due to its relevance and comprehensive coverage for nurse practitioners. (DJJ)

4814. *American Medical Women's Association. Journal.* Formerly: *Woman Physician.* [ISSN: 0098-8421] 1946. q. USD 135 (Individuals, USD 70). Ed(s): Wendy Chavkin. American Medical Women's Association, Inc., 801 N Fairfax Dr, Ste 400, Alexandria, VA 22314; info@amwa-doc.org; http://www.amwa-doc.org. Illus., index, adv. Sample. Refereed. Circ: 10000 Paid. Microform: PQC. Reprint: PQC. *Indexed:* BiolAb, H&SSA, IndMed, RiskAb, SWA. *Bk. rev.:* Various number and length. *Aud.:* Ac, Sa.

JAMWA provides commentary on women's health issues and provides important updates on care, diagnosis, and treatment. Female physicians are the primary audience of this peer-reviewed journal. Doctors, social workers, and allied health professionals provide well-based content focused on the medical concerns of women in society. Topics include alcohol use during pregnancy, cancer screening, tobacco control in women and girls, and informed consent for research. Articles include graphs, charts, and complete bibliographies. There are also editorials, book reviews, and a federal report section on different relevant topics. *JAMWA* (the web site is http://www.jamwa.org) would be useful and valuable to all professional women in health care. (DJJ)

4815. *Canadian Nurse.* Formed by the merger of: *Infirmiere Canadienne; Canadian Nurse.* 1905. 10x/yr. CND 36 domestic; USD 50 United States; CND 60 elsewhere. Ed(s): Judith Haines. Canadian Nurses Association, 50 Driveway, Ottawa, ON K2P 1E2, Canada; pubss@cna-nurses.ca; http://www.cna-nurses.ca. Illus., index, adv. Sample. Circ: 112000. Vol. ends: Nov. Microform: PMC; PQC. Reprint: PQC. *Indexed:* AgeL, CBCARef, CINAHL, CPerI. *Aud.:* Ga, Ac, Sa.

This is the Canadian counterpart to *AJN: American Journal of Nursing* and it discusses all aspects of nursing in Canada. The four or five major articles per issue cover many timely and useful topics such as nursing education, nursing leadership, staffing, and respite care. Articles are easy to understand, have excellent illustrations, and include bibliographic references. Separate sections on "First Person," "Nurses to Know," and nursing news appear in each issue. As well, the journal includes an "Access Section," which is the Canadian Nurses Association information section. *Canadian Nurse* would be a valuable resource for nurses, allied health personnel, students, and consumers. (DJJ)

Health Care for Women International. See Women: Feminist and Special Interest/Feminist and Women's Studies section.

4816. ***Inside M S.*** Incorporating (in 1983): *Focus on Research; M S Messenger; National Multiple Sclerosis Society. Annual Report; Patient Service News.* [ISSN: 0739-9774] 1983. q. Free to membership. Ed(s): Martha King. National Multiple Sclerosis Society, 733 Third Ave, New York, NY 10017-3288; editor@nmss.org; http://www.nationalmssociety.org. Illus., adv. Circ: 680000. Online: EBSCO Publishing; Florida Center for Library Automation; Gale Group; OCLC Online Computer Library Center, Inc.; ProQuest Information & Learning. *Bk. rev.:* 2-3, 250 words. *Aud.:* Sa.

Inside MS is a full-color, large-print magazine for people afflicted by multiple sclerosis and their families. MS patients and health care professionals contribute content, which includes sections on society news, fundraising, and public policy. In addition, this publication includes book and audio reviews of interest to MS patients. The magazine is available online at http://www.nationalmssociety.org/InsideMS.asp. (DJJ)

4817. ***J A M A: The Journal of the American Medical Association.*** Former titles (until 1960): *American Medical Association. Journal;* (until 1883): *American Medical Association. Transactions.* [ISSN: 0098-7484] 1848. w. 48/yr. USD 365 print & online eds. Ed(s): Dr. Richard Glass, Dr. Phil Fontanarosa. American Medical Association, 515 N State St, Chicago, IL 60610-0946; amaa@ama-assn.org; http://www.ama-assn.org. Illus., index, adv. Sample. Refereed. Circ: 332337 Paid. Vol. ends: Jun/Dec. CD-ROM: Ovid Technologies, Inc. Microform: PMC; PQC. Online: The Dialog Corporation; EBSCO Publishing; Florida Center for Library Automation; Gale Group; OCLC Online Computer Library Center, Inc.; Ovid Technologies, Inc.; ProQuest Information & Learning. Reprint: PQC. *Indexed:* ABS&EES, AbAn, AgeL, BiolAb, BiolDig, CINAHL, CJA, DSA, EnvAb, ExcerpMed, FS&TA, GSI, H&SSA, HortAb, IndMed, IndVet, LRI, MLA-IB, MagInd, PEI, PRA, RRTA, S&F, SCI, SUSA, VetBull, WAE&RSA. *Bk. rev.:* Various number and length. *Aud.:* Ac, Sa.

Produced by the American Medical Association, *JAMA* is one of the premier, peer-reviewed journals in medicine. International in scope, *JAMA* articles are the ones frequently cited by the news media. This journal lists as its objectives the promotion of medicine and the betterment of patient health through outstanding articles, physician education, and "Original Contributions," "Clinician's Corner," "Special Communication," and "News and Analysis" are featured sections. *JAMA* also includes information on medical meetings, book reviews, reader service, and physician licensure. Each issue has an attractive work of art on the cover and includes a "Patient Page" for handouts plus CME articles for doctors. Highly recommended for physicians and other allied health professionals. (DJJ)

4818. ***Journal of Practical Nursing.*** [ISSN: 0022-3867] 1951. q. USD 15; USD 25 foreign. Ed(s): Helen Larsen. National Association for Practical Nurse Education and Service, Inc., 1400 Spring St, Ste 330, Silver Spring, MD 20910. Illus., index, adv. Sample. Refereed. Circ: 13000. Vol. ends: Dec. Microform: PQC. Reprint: PQC. *Indexed:* AgeL, CINAHL. *Aud.:* Ga, Ac, Sa.

LPNs are the focus of materials and articles in the *Journal of Practical Nursing.* Content focuses on legal, political, and psychosocial aspects of practical nursing. Other topics include preceptorship, cultural sensitivity, and the value of prayer. Many materials have to do with choosing nursing as a career, nursing schools that provide LPN education, professional activities, and continuing education updates. Journal includes well-written articles, which include references. This journal would be of most value to nurses and nursing students who want to stay current on topics in their field. (DJJ)

4819. ***The Lancet (North American Edition).*** [ISSN: 0099-5355] 1966. w. USD 676 (Individuals, USD 151). Ed(s): Dr. Richard Horton. The Lancet Publishing Group, 84 Theobald's Rd, London, WC1X 8RR, United Kingdom; http://www.thelancet.com. Illus., index, adv. Sample. Refereed. Circ: 18000. Vol. ends: Jun/Dec. Microform: PQC. Online: bigchalk; EBSCO Publishing; Florida Center for Library Automation; Gale Group; LexisNexis; OCLC Online Computer Library Center, Inc.; ProQuest Information & Learning. *Indexed:* AgeL, BiolAb, CINAHL, DSA, GSI, H&SSA, IndVet, LRI, MagInd, RiskAb, WRCInf. *Bk. rev.:* Various number and length. *Aud.:* Ga, Ac, Sa.

This international British publication with its excellent articles and worldwide scope contains informative articles that are frequently mentioned by the news media. Each weekly issue contains up-to-date medical news, research information, and current commentary that medical professionals would find useful. All materials are peer-reviewed and cover diagnosis, therapy, etiology, and other important developments in the treatment of disease. Many of the illustrations are in color. There is an extensive "Correspondence" section, which includes legal, ethical, and moral questions in regard to medicine. There is also a section called the "Dissecting Room," where everything from art and history to science and humor is discussed. *The Lancet* (http://www.thelancet.com) would be of particular interest to doctors and allied health personnel because of its well-earned reputation as a leader in publishing research results and technical information. (DJJ)

4820. ***Medical Clinics of North America.*** Formerly: *Medical Clinics.* [ISSN: 0025-7125] 1916. bi-m. USD 223 (Individuals, USD 135; Students, USD 68). W.B. Saunders Co., Independence Sq W, Ste 300, the Curtis Center, Philadelphia, PA 19106-3399; elspcs@elsevier.com; http://www.us.elsevierhealth.com/. Illus., index. Sample. Refereed. Vol. ends: Nov. Microform: PMC; PQC. Online: MD Consult. Reprint: ISI; PQC. *Indexed:* AgeL, BiolAb, CINAHL, ChemAb, DSA, ExcerpMed, IndMed, RRTA, SCI, SSCI. *Aud.:* Ac, Sa.

Each volume of this hardbound, bimonthly series takes all aspects of one particular disease, such as travel medicine, liver ailments, obesity, chronic pain, or pancreatic disease, and discusses it thoroughly. Areas examined include diagnosis, etiology, treatment, diet, epidemiology, genetics, and clinical features. Medical experts in the relevant special field write the dozen articles in each volume. The journal includes illustrations, maps, charts, graphs, and a complete bibliography. The publisher's web site is http://www.wbsaunders.com. This journal would be extremely useful for physicians who are interested in finding very specific information about a particular topic, as opposed to materials for the average consumer. (DJJ)

4821. ***Medical Letter on Drugs and Therapeutics (English Edition): on drugs and therapeutics.*** [ISSN: 0025-732X] 1959. fortn. USD 55. Ed(s): Dr. Mark Abramowicz. Medical Letter, Inc., 1000 Main St, New Rochelle, NY 10801; custserv@medicalletter.org; http://www.medicalletter.org. Illus., index. Sample. Refereed. Circ: 150000. Vol. ends: Dec. Online: EBSCO Publishing; Gale Group. *Indexed:* CINAHL, ExcerpMed, IndMed. *Aud.:* Ac, Sa.

This peer-reviewed newsletter deals with drugs and drug use, and each bi-weekly issue features two or three different products. The journal provides clinical trials, adverse effects, absorption and dissolution, dosage, cost, and pharmacology information for each featured drug. Additionally, new products are compared in cost and effect to those that are already on the market. Referenced articles include a summary paragraph, which provides a total drug summary. This publication is brief, relevant, and to the point; it comes with a CME self-examination program attached. *The Medical Letter* (http://www.medletter.com) is an excellent critical source for up-to-date drug information and would be of particular value to physicians looking for unbiased information on new pharmaceuticals. (DJJ)

4822. ***New England Journal of Medicine.*** [ISSN: 0028-4793] 1812. w. USD 439 (Individuals, USD 139). Ed(s): Dr. Jeffrey M Drazen. Massachusetts Medical Society, 860 Winter St, Waltham, MA 02451-1411; http://www.massmed.org/. Illus., index, adv. Sample. Circ: 231126 Paid. Vol. ends: Jun/Dec. CD-ROM: Ovid Technologies, Inc. Microform: PMC; PQC. Online: EBSCO Publishing; Gale Group; HighWire Press; Ovid Technologies, Inc.; RoweCom Information Quest.

Indexed: ASG, AbAn, AgeL, BiolAb, BiolDig, CINAHL, CJA, ChemAb, DSA, DSR&OA, EnvAb, ExcerpMed, FS&TA, FutSurv, GSI, H&SSA, HortAb, IndMed, IndVet, LRI, MCR, MagInd, PsycholAb, RRTA, RiskAb, S&F, SCI, SSCI, SWR&A, VetBull, WAE&RSA. *Bk. rev.:* Various number and length. *Aud.:* Ac, Sa.

The New England Journal of Medicine, the official publication of the Massachusetts Medical Society, is a peer-reviewed journal of original research, clinical cases, and review articles. Illustrations are frequently in color, and issues include original research, reviews, editorials, case records of the Massachusetts General Hospital, and correspondence. Recent medical books also reviewed as well as a list of conferences and educational programs. Experts in the field of medicine contribute articles that cover all aspects of diseases including diagnosis, treatment, controversies, and new developments. All articles include extensive abstracts and references. *The New England Journal of Medicine* is essential for physicians and valuable to anyone looking for medical information. (DJJ)

4823. *The Nurse Practitioner: the American journal of primary health care.* [ISSN: 0361-1817] 1975. m. USD 149 (Individuals, USD 49; USD 9 per issue). Ed(s): Linda J Pearson. Lippincott Williams & Wilkins, 351 W Camden St, Baltimore, MD 21201; http://www.lww.com. Illus., index, adv. Sample. Refereed. Circ: 24653. Vol. ends: Dec. Microform: PQC. Online: bigchalk; EBSCO Publishing; Gale Group; Northern Light Technology, Inc.; OCLC Online Computer Library Center, Inc.; Ovid Technologies, Inc.; ProQuest Information & Learning. Reprint: PQC. *Indexed:* AgeL, CINAHL, IndMed. *Aud.:* Ac, Sa.

The purpose and mission of this peer-reviewed journal is to provide professional information to, and meet the needs of, nurse practitioners. Regular departments include "Short Communication" and "Literature Reviews." "Literature Reviews" focuses on the major fields of practice: oncology, cardiovascular care, pediatric/adolescent care, preventive care, respiratory care, women's health care, and urology. Articles are complete with abstracts and references. A section of "Product News" discusses new products on the market. Nurses and other allied health professionals interested in clinical information will find this well-researched journal to be of value. (DJJ)

4824. *Nursing (Year): the voice and vision of nursing.* [ISSN: 0360-4039] 1971. m. USD 99 (Individuals, USD 34; USD 6 newsstand/cover per issue). Ed(s): Cheryl L Mee. Lippincott Williams & Wilkins, 351 W Camden St, Baltimore, MD 21201; http://www.lww.com. Illus., index, adv. Sample. Circ: 300424 Paid. Vol. ends: Dec. Microform: PQC. Online: EBSCO Publishing; Gale Group; OCLC Online Computer Library Center, Inc.; ProQuest Information & Learning. *Indexed:* AgeL, CINAHL, GSI, IndMed. *Bk. rev.:* Various number and length, some signed. *Aud.:* Ga, Ac, Sa.

This well illustrated, peer-reviewed nursing journal provides nurses with "accurate, current, and relevant information and services to excel in clinical and professional roles." *Nursing* is an excellent how-to publication for patient care; the seven or eight articles in each issue discuss and give detailed information about patient care procedures. Nursing also provides opportunities for CEU credits. There are separate columns for "Drug Challenge," "Medication Errors," "Advice, p.r.n.," "InfoBytes," and "Career Focus." *Nursing* covers all aspects of the field of nursing. Nurses, allied health care personnel, and the consumer will find this publication of value. (DJJ)

4825. *The Physician and Sportsmedicine: a peer reviewed journal of medical aspects of sports, exercise and fitness.* [ISSN: 0091-3847] 1973. m. Ed(s): Dr. Gordon O Matheson. McGraw-Hill Companies, Inc., 4530 W 77th St Ste 350, Minneapolis, MN 55435; http://www.mcgraw-hill.com/. Illus., index, adv. Refereed. Circ: 114100. Vol. ends: Dec. Microform: PQC. Online: The Dialog Corporation; Dow Jones Interactive; EBSCO Publishing; Gale Group; LexisNexis; NewsNet; ProQuest Information & Learning. Reprint: PQC. *Indexed:* AgeL, CIJE, CINAHL, ExcerpMed, GSI, H&SSA, LRI, PEI, SSCI, SportS. *Aud.:* Hs, Ga, Ac, Sa.

The Physician and Sportsmedicine is a peer-reviewed journal that focuses on all aspects of sports and sports-related activities. Articles are illustrated and topics include obesity, diet, seizures, exercise, osteoporosis, and how a more active, healthy lifestyle can help to overcome many of these problems. Illustrations are in color and most articles include charts, graphs, and diagrams. The journal has a continuing education program attached to certain articles. There is a section of "Pearls" with helpful hints in diagnosis of sports-medicine-related problems, besides the "News Briefs" and "Research to Practice" materials. *The Physician and Sportsmedicine* would be extremely useful to physicians called upon to treat sports-related injuries and anyone else who has an interest in the field. (DJJ)

4826. *Postgraduate Medicine: the journal of applied medicine for physicians providing primary care.* [ISSN: 0032-5481] 1947. m. USD 54 domestic; USD 56 in Canada & Mexico; USD 130 elsewhere. Ed(s): Peter Setness. McGraw-Hill Companies, Inc., 4530 W 77th St Ste 350, Minneapolis, MN 55435; http://www.mcgraw-hill.com/. Illus., index, adv. Sample. Refereed. Circ: 130000. Vol. ends: Jun/Dec. Microform: PMC; PQC. Online: Dow Jones Interactive; EBSCO Publishing; Factiva; Gale Group; LexisNexis; NewsNet; Northern Light Technology, Inc.; ProQuest Information & Learning. Reprint: PQC. *Indexed:* AgeL, BiolAb, CINAHL, ChemAb, ExcerpMed, IndMed, IndVet, RRTA, SCI, SSCI, VetBull, WAE&RSA. *Aud.:* Ga, Ac, Sa.

Postgraduate Medicine focuses on the primary care physician; its mission is to aid in the etiology, diagnosis, and treatment of relatively common illness. Major articles deal with common conditions such as migraine headache, stroke, influenza, and diabetes. Articles include color illustrations and graphs and charts. Each issue includes "Clinical Updates," which focuses on a specific clinical syndrome, and a section on "Continuing Education." The journal would be useful for primary care physicians, allied health professionals, and medical students. It may also serve as a source of consumer health information. (DJJ)

4827. *R N.* [ISSN: 0033-7021] 1937. m. USD 35 domestic; USD 50 foreign; USD 10 newsstand/cover per issue. Ed(s): Marianne Dekker Mattera. Medical Economics Company, 5 Paragon Dr, Montvale, NJ 07645-1742; http://www.rnweb.com. Illus., index, adv. Sample. Circ: 250000. Vol. ends: Dec. CD-ROM: Ovid Technologies, Inc. Microform: RPI; PQC. Online: EBSCO Publishing; Florida Center for Library Automation; Gale Group; OCLC Online Computer Library Center, Inc.; Ovid Technologies, Inc.; ProQuest Information & Learning; H.W. Wilson. *Indexed:* AgeL, CINAHL, GSI, LRI, MagInd. *Aud.:* Ga, Ac, Sa.

RN (http://www.rnweb.com) is a refereed journal containing topical articles that are characterized by thorough and sound research. Contributors present material in a clear and concise manner, which facilitates understanding. Certain articles have CE credits attached to them, and a home study program is available. Regular columns in each issue, which include down-to-earth, practical information, are "Clinical Highlights," "Ethics in Action," "Legally speaking," and "Drug Update." There is a conference planner that lists upcoming events. Full text of the journal is available to subscribers. This attractive publication is of value to all nurses, allied health professionals, and consumers. (DJJ)

4828. *Surgical Clinics of North America.* [ISSN: 0039-6109] 1912. bi-m. USD 273 (Individuals, USD 183; Students, USD 92). W.B. Saunders Co., Independence Sq W, Ste 300, the Curtis Center, Philadelphia, PA 19106-3399; http://www.us.elsevierhealth.com/product.jsp?isbn=1055937x. Illus., index, adv. Refereed. Microform: PQC. Online: MD Consult. Reprint: ISI; PQC. *Indexed:* BiolAb, CINAHL, ChemAb, ExcerpMed, IndMed, SCI. *Aud.:* Ac, Sa.

Published by Saunders (http://www.wbsaunders.com), each volume of this hard-bound, bimonthly series takes one surgical topic and covers all aspects in detail. Different surgical experts discuss each topic and surgical procedures are analyzed in detail. In addition, themes focus on diagnosis, clinical presentation, medical management, indications for surgery, surgical technique, treatment of complications, and therapeutic issues. Recent topics include thoracic surgery, wound healing, breast cancer, and anorectal cancer. Comprehension is facilitated by illustrations, charts, graphs, and black-and-white photographs. *Surgical Clinics* is an excellent resource for the specialist or for any physician who wishes to delve more deeply into a particular topic. (DJJ)

Women's Health Issues. See Women: Feminist and Special Interest/Feminist and Women's Studies section.

Medicine and Society

Titles included in this subsection deal with health care issues important in public life, debate, and policy-making, with significant coverage of ethical, cultural, and legal issues of health care in society. The selected titles will be of value to clinicians, policymakers, scholars, and to the general public. (MMC)

4829. ***Cambridge Quarterly of Healthcare Ethics: the international journal for healthcare ethics and ethics committees.*** [ISSN: 0963-1801] 1992. q. USD 156 (Individuals, USD 72). Ed(s): Thomasine Kushner, Steve Heilig. Cambridge University Press, The Edinburgh Bldg, Shaftesbury Rd, Cambridge, CB2 2RU, United Kingdom; information@cambridge.org; http://uk.cambridge.org/journals. Illus., adv. Sample. Refereed. Vol. ends: Fall. Online: EBSCO Publishing; OCLC Online Computer Library Center, Inc.; RoweCom Information Quest. *Indexed:* ASSIA, AgeL, CINAHL, IndMed, PhilInd, SSCI. *Aud.:* Ga, Ac, Sa.

One of the most important tiles in the field, the *Cambridge Quarterly* is a scholarly journal designed to meet the needs of health care decision-makers and institutional bioethics committees. The journal responds specifically to the diverse needs of ethics committees members. Recent articles cover bioethics and defense, family-centered decision-making, and virtue and mentoring in the development of professionalism. Regular features include responses and dialogue, substantive book reviews, and noteworthy abstracts of important articles from other journals. The *Cambridge Quarterly* is highly recommended for academic health sciences libraries, large public libraries, and large hospital libraries. (MMC)

4830. ***Hastings Center Report.*** Formerly: *Hastings Center Studies.* [ISSN: 0093-0334] 1971. bi-m. USD 100 & libraries (Individuals, USD 76; Students, USD 50 & seniors). Ed(s): Gregory Kaebnick. Hastings Center, Rte 9D, Garrison, NY 10524; mail@thehastingscenter.org; http://www.thehastingscenter.org/. Illus., index. Sample. Refereed. Circ: 8500. Vol. ends: Nov/Dec. Reprint: PQC. *Indexed:* ABS&EES, AgeL, ArtHuCI, BRI, BiolAb, CBRI, CINAHL, FutSurv, GSI, IMFL, IndMed, LRI, MCR, PAIS, PhilInd, RI-1, SSCI, SSI, SWR&A, SociolAb. *Bk. rev.:* 2-3. *Aud.:* Ga, Ac, Sa.

The *Hastings Center Report* is both a scholarly journal and accessible to both health practitioners and the general public. One of the best titles in the field, articles are often illustrated with striking photographs. The coverage is of all medical ethics topics and especially the most controversial of the day. Regular features and columns include case studies, book reviews, a Capital report, a law report, and essays. A recent issue addressed the inadvertent effects of germline research, congenital syndromes and family decisions, and judicial dismantling of the Americans with Disabilities Act. This title belongs in the medical, nursing, and ethics collections of all university and public libraries. (MMC)

4831. ***The Journal of Clinical Ethics.*** [ISSN: 1046-7890] 1990. q. USD 130 (Individuals, USD 67). Ed(s): Dr. Edmund G Howe. The Journal of Clinical Ethics, Inc., University Publishing Group, 138 W Washington St, Hagerstown, MD 21740. Illus., index. Sample. Refereed. Vol. ends: Winter. *Indexed:* AgeL, ArtHuCI, CINAHL, IndMed, PhilInd, SSCI, SociolAb. *Bk. rev.:* 2, length varies. *Aud.:* Ac, Sa.

The *Journal of Clinical Ethics* is a practical guide to touch clinical decision-making on behalf of patients. It offers a scholarly, peer-reviewed and balanced guide to ethics practiced in day-to-day clinical situations. There are several current case reports in each issue, as well as reviews, research, and letters. Recent issues have covered helping patients to find meaning; legal trends in bioethics; and mediation and the medical advisory panel model. This is an excellent source for the various administrators, health care providers, attorneys, and religious authorities involved in daily health-care decisions. (MMC)

4832. ***Journal of Health Politics, Policy and Law.*** [ISSN: 0361-6878] 1976. bi-m. USD 275 includes online access (Individuals, USD 60 includes online access; USD 46 per issue). Ed(s): Mark Schlesinger. Duke University Press, 905 W Main St, Ste 18 B, Durham, NC 27701; subscriptions@dukeupress.edu; http://www.dukeupress.edu. Illus., adv. Sample. Refereed. Circ: 2100. Vol. ends: Dec. Microform: WSH; PMC; PQC. Online: EBSCO Publishing; Gale Group; Ingenta Select; OCLC Online Computer Library Center, Inc.; Project MUSE; ProQuest Information & Learning; RoweCom Information Quest; Swets Blackwell. Reprint: PSC; WSH. *Indexed:* ABIn, ASG, AgeL, BiolAb, CINAHL, CLI, ExcerpMed, FutSurv, H&SSA, HRA, IBSS, ILP, IPSA, IndMed, JEL, LRI, MCR, PAIS, PRA, PSA, SSCI, SociolAb. *Bk. rev.:* 2-5 essays. *Aud.:* Ac, Sa.

The *Journal of Health Politics, Policy, and Law* is a scholarly title that fully covers topics of politics, policies, and legislation in health care. Recent articles have addressed such topics as older Americans and health insurance reform, interest groups and drug programs, and challenging power in the pharmaceutical industry. This journal is notable for the lengthy and thorough book reviews it carries. It is useful to both clinicians and libraries. Although specialized, the title is recommended for all health-care organization collections. (MMC)

4833. ***The Journal of Law, Medicine & Ethics.*** Formerly: *Law, Medicine and Health Care;* Formed by the merger of: *Medicolegal News; Nursing Law and Ethics.* [ISSN: 1073-1105] 1973. q. USD 195 (Individuals, USD 105). Ed(s): Dr. Kathleen M Boozang. American Society of Law, Medicine & Ethics, 765 Commonwealth Ave, Ste 1634, Boston, MA 02215; mvasko@aslme.org; orders@allenpress.com; http://www.allenpress.com. Illus., adv. Sample. Refereed. Circ: 5000. Vol. ends: Winter. Microform: WSH; PQC. Online: EBSCO Publishing; Florida Center for Library Automation; Gale Group; OCLC Online Computer Library Center, Inc.; ProQuest Information & Learning; West Group; H.W. Wilson. Reprint: WSH. *Indexed:* AgeL, CINAHL, CJA, CLI, H&SSA, ILP, LRI, PAIS, PsycholAb, RI-1, RiskAb, SCI, SSCI. *Bk. rev.:* 1-4, essay length. *Aud.:* Ga, Ac, Sa.

This title and the *American Journal of Law & Medicine* are included with membership in the American Society of Law, Medicine & Ethics. This peer-reviewed journal offers heavily referenced articles written by professionals in the field. Physicians, lawyers, and those involved in academia contribute balanced, well-written, and information-rich articles on medico-legal/ethical issues for the medical professional as well as for the general public. Recent issues have treated issues of treatment for pain in a full-issue symposium, genetic discrimination, and unionization of health care workers. An excellent choice for both academic and public libraries. (MMC)

4834. ***Journal of Medical Ethics.*** [ISSN: 0306-6800] 1975. bi-m. GBP 178 (Individuals, GBP 112 print & online eds.). Ed(s): Julian Savalescu. B M J Publishing Group, B M A House, Tavistock Sq, London, WC1H 9JR, United Kingdom; info.norththames@bma.org.uk; http://www.bmjjournals.com/. Illus., index. Refereed. Vol. ends: Dec. Online: bigchalk; EBSCO Publishing; Florida Center for Library Automation; Gale Group; HighWire Press; Northern Light Technology, Inc.; OCLC Online Computer Library Center, Inc.; Ovid Technologies, Inc.; ProQuest Information & Learning; RoweCom Information Quest; Swets Blackwell. *Indexed:* AgeL, ArtHuCI, BiolAb, CINAHL, CJA, ExcerpMed, H&SSA, IndMed, PSA, PhilInd, RI-1, RiskAb, SCI, SSCI, SSI, SociolAb. *Bk. rev.:* 5-10, 300-1,000 words. *Aud.:* Ga, Ac, Sa.

The *Journal of Medical Ethics* is a scholarly, well-referenced publication and tackles up-to-date and controversial topics in medical ethics on an international level. Recent articles include topics such as informed consent, ethics and gene therapy, ethical requirements/reporting in clinical trials, and human rights and medicine. Regular features include case studies, book reviews, correspondence, and news and notes. This intellectual publication is valuable and accessible to both clinicians and public audiences. This title is an important asset for any well-developed ethics collection. (SRW)

4835. ***The Journal of Medicine and Philosophy: a forum for bioethics and philosophy of medicine.*** [ISSN: 0360-5310] 1976. bi-m. EUR 322 print & online eds. (Individuals, EUR 59). Ed(s): H Tristram Englehardt, Jr. Swets & Zeitlinger BV, PO Box 800, Lisse, 2160 SZ, Netherlands; orders@swets.nl; http://www.swets.nl. Illus., index, adv. Refereed. Vol. ends: No. 6. Microform: PQC. Online: EBSCO Publishing; Gale Group; OCLC Online Computer Library Center, Inc.; RoweCom Information Quest; Swets Blackwell. Reprint: SWZ. *Indexed:* AgeL, ArtHuCI, BiolAb, ExcerpMed, HumInd, IBSS, IBZ, IndMed, PhilInd, RI-1, SSCI. *Bk. rev.:* 0- 2, essay length. *Aud.:* Ac, Sa.

The Journal of Medicine and Philosophy is an international, interdisciplinary publication that delivers broad coverage of shared themes in bioethical and philosophical issues. It is scholarly but accessible to students and others interested in these topics. Recent articles treat the subjects of cloning and identity, co-joined twins and ethical issues, organ donation, and concepts of sacrifice. This journal also provides generous bibliographies that contain many foreign-language titles. This somewhat expensive title should be considered for libraries with a need for comprehensive coverage and a global viewpoint. (MMC)

4836. ***The Milbank Quarterly: a journal of public health and health care policy.*** Former titles (until 1985): *Health and Society;* (until 1973): *Milbank Memorial Fund Quarterly;* (until 1934): *Milbank Memorial Fund Quarterly Bulletin.* [ISSN: 0887-378X] 1923. q. USD 142 print & online eds. Ed(s): Bradford H Gray. Blackwell Publishing, Inc., Commerce Place, 350 Main St, Malden, MA 02148; subscrip@blackwellpub.com; http://www.blackwellpublishing.com. Illus., index, adv. Sample. Refereed. Circ: 3000. Vol. ends: Dec (No. 4). Microform: PQC. Online: EBSCO Publishing; Gale Group; ingenta.com; Northern Light Technology, Inc.; OCLC Online Computer Library Center, Inc.; Ovid Technologies, Inc.; RoweCom Information Quest; Swets Blackwell. *Indexed:* ASG, ASSIA, AgeL, ArtHuCI, BAS, BPI, BiolAb, ChemAb, FutSurv, HRA, IBSS, IndMed, MCR, PAIS, PsycholAb, SCI, SFSA, SSCI, SSI, SWR&A, SociolAb. *Aud.:* Ac, Sa.

Published for more than 70 years, The *Milbank Quarterly* examines the implications of health policy and explores "the social origins of health in our society" by carrying lengthy and well-documented articles that feature peer-reviewed original research, policy review and analysis, and commentary from professionals in the field. Authors include clinicians, senior administrators, and academics. Recent issues have covered barriers to the expression of dissatisfaction with health care, patents and cancer therapeutics innovations, and the role of employee benefits in healthcare. This journal belongs in university collections and in strong ethics collections. (MMC)

4837. ***Psychosomatics: the journal of consultation and liaison psychiatry.*** [ISSN: 0033-3182] 1960. bi-m. USD 338 print & online eds. (Individuals, USD 151 print & online eds.; Students, USD 67 print & online eds.). Ed(s): Dr. Thomas Wise. American Psychiatric Publishing, Inc., 1000 Wilson Blvd, Ste 1825, Arlington, VA 22209; appi@psych.org; http://www.psychiatryonline.org. Illus., index. Sample. Refereed. Circ: 2500. Vol. ends: Nov/Dec. Microform: PQC. Online: EBSCO Publishing; HighWire Press; Northern Light Technology, Inc.; ProQuest Information & Learning; RoweCom Information Quest. Reprint: PQC. *Indexed:* AgeL, BiolAb, CINAHL, ChemAb, ExcerpMed, IndMed, PsycholAb, SCI, SSCI, SWR&A. *Bk. rev.:* 2-4, length varies. *Aud.:* Ga, Ac, Sa.

Psychosomatics is a peer-reviewed publication that provides coverage of shared themes in the psychosocial, psychiatric, and medical areas of study. Research articles are thoroughly reviewed and offer numerous, useful, and attractive tables/charts. Full text is available for print subscribers and a table of contents for nonsubscribers is available at http://psy.psychiatryonline.org/. Recent articles address the mounting body of medical misinformation on the Internet, cortisol response of patients with chronic fatigue syndrome, and a delirium rating scale for children and teens. Regular features include editorials, special articles, original research reports, drug interaction updates, lengthy book reviews, and letters. Useful for practitioners in many specialties, this title is recommended for both academic medical and hospital libraries. (MMC)

Public Health

The Public Health subsection addresses the physical, mental, and environmental health of communities and populations at risk. Prevention through health education and promotion is emphasized. (JKO)

4838. ***American Journal of Health Promotion.*** [ISSN: 0890-1171] 1986. bi-m. USD 129.95 (Individuals, USD 99.95). American Journal of Health Promotion, PO Box 15847, N. Hollywood, CA 91615-1584; http://www.healthpromotionjournal.com. Illus., adv. Refereed. Circ: 4567. Vol. ends: No. 6. *Indexed:* ABIn, ASIP, ASSIA, AgeL, CIJE, CINAHL, ExcerpMed, H&SSA, HRA, PEI, PsycholAb, SFSA, SSCI. *Aud.:* Ac, Sa.

This professional journal concentrates on research articles in health promotion, although the articles will appeal to a wide range of health care providers. Some articles are followed by the section "So What?," which provides implications of the article for practitioners and researchers who are interested in the subject area. Exercise, nutrition, smoking, worksite health, weight loss, and health promotion to special target groups are topics covered. The *Art of Health Promotion* newsletter, which combines the best of the science and the practice of health promotion, has been bound with the journal. Regular sections include abstracts that relate to health promotion published in other journals. A new study is critiqued and added to the journal's DataBase chart. (JKO)

4839. ***American Journal of Public Health.*** Supersedes in part (in 1971): *American Journal of Public Health and the Nation's Health;* Which was formed by the 1927 merger of: *American Journal of Public Health; Nation's Health.* [ISSN: 0090-0036] 1911. m. USD 200 (Individuals, USD 165). Ed(s): Dr. Michael Ibrahim. American Public Health Association, 800 I St, NW, Washington, DC 20001; http://www.apha.org. Illus., index, adv. Sample. Refereed. Circ: 35000. Vol. ends: Dec. CD-ROM: Ovid Technologies, Inc. Microform: PMC; PQC. Online: bigchalk; EBSCO Publishing; Gale Group; HighWire Press; Northern Light Technology, Inc.; OCLC Online Computer Library Center, Inc.; Ovid Technologies, Inc.; ProQuest Information & Learning; H.W. Wilson. *Indexed:* ABIn, ABS&EES, ASG, ASSIA, AbAn, AgeL, ArtHuCI, BiolAb, BiolDig, CIJE, CINAHL, CJA, ChemAb, DSA, DSR&OA, EnvAb, ExcerpMed, FPA, FS&TA, ForAb, GSI, H&SSA, HRA, IndMed, IndVet, MCR, PEI, PollutAb, PsycholAb, RRTA, RiskAb, S&F, SCI, SFSA, SSCI, SSI, SWA, SWR&A, SWRA, VetBull, WAE&RSA. *Bk. rev.:* 3, various length. *Aud.:* Ga, Ac, Sa.

This is the official journal for the American Public Health Association. Articles cover the many facets of public health, and they are original research and peer-reviewed. This journal is probably the first source most people would use for information on this subject. Each issue features a theme of current interest. Recent examples are climate change, immigration and health, HIV/AIDS, smoking, environmental and occupational health, aging and health, and health risks and mortality. In addition to book reviews, there is a listing of electronic resources of interest. Complete tables of contents and selected abstracts for the journal from July 1997 to the present are available on the web. Starting with August 2001, the journal became available online in full text. A search engine is available for searching articles from January 1995 to the present. The citation and abstract can be viewed free online with the ability to purchase a text copy of the article. (JKO)

4840. ***Canadian Journal of Public Health.*** [ISSN: 0008-4263] 1910. bi-m. CND 94.76 domestic; USD 114 United States; USD 147 elsewhere. Ed(s): Gerald Dafoe. Canadian Public Health Association, 1565 Carling Ave, Ste 400, Ottawa, ON K1Z 8R1, Canada; http://www.cpha.ca. Illus., index, adv. Sample. Refereed. Circ: 3000. Vol. ends: Nov/Dec (No. 6). Microform: PMC; PQC. Online: bigchalk; Micromedia ProQuest; Northern Light Technology, Inc.; ProQuest Information & Learning. Reprint: PQC. *Indexed:* AbAn, AgeL, BiolAb, BiolDig, CBCARef, CINAHL, ChemAb, DSA, ExcerpMed, FS&TA, H&SSA, IndMed, IndVet, MCR, PEI, PollutAb, RRTA, RiskAb, S&F, SSCI, SportS, VetBull, WAE&RSA. *Bk. rev.:* 0-2. *Aud.:* Ac, Sa.

This journal, from the Canadian Public Health Association, focuses on well-researched articles to meet the needs of public health workers involved in a wide variety of health care projects and topics. Sample topics include heart disease, cancer prevention, tobacco knowledge and use, childhood immunizations, and risk behaviors. Abstracts are in French and English; so are some of the feature articles. Online citations are available from January/February 1996 (Volume 87) and abstracts are linked for all articles, starting with 2002 issues (Volume 93). Scope and coverage are similar to that of the *American Journal of Public Health* (see above in this subsection). (JKO)

4841. ***Family and Community Health: the journal of health promotion and maintenance.*** [ISSN: 0160-6379] 1978. q. USD 199 (Individuals, USD 79). Lippincott Williams & Wilkins, 16522 Hunters Green Pkwy., Hagerstown, MD 21740; http://www.lww.com. Illus. Sample. Circ: 1900 Paid. Vol. ends: Jan. Microform: PQC. Online: bigchalk; EBSCO

Publishing; Florida Center for Library Automation; Gale Group; OCLC Online Computer Library Center, Inc.; Ovid Technologies, Inc.; ProQuest Information & Learning. Reprint: PQC. *Indexed:* AgeL, CINAHL, CJA, H&SSA, IMFL, PEI, PsycholAb, RiskAb, SSCI, SociolAb. *Bk. rev.:* 5, 300-600 words. *Aud.:* Ac, Sa.

Family and Community Health publishes four issues, each focusing on a specific topic. The articles provide practical information from health care practitioners who are committed to holistic health. Emphasis is on the teaching of ways to prevent illness through nutrition, exercise, and health appraisals. More recent themes include "Women's Health," "Violence in the Family," and "Cancer Prevention and Control." This is a good journal in which to find descriptions of creative programs in family and community health promotion. (JKO)

4842. ***Health Education & Behavior.*** Formerly (until vol.24, 1997): *Health Education Quarterly;* Which superseded (in 1980): *Health Education Monographs.* [ISSN: 1090-1981] 1957. bi-m. USD 738. Ed(s): Mark Zimmerman. Sage Publications, Inc., 2455 Teller Rd, Thousand Oaks, CA 91320; info@sagepub.com; http://www.sagepub.com. Illus., index, adv. Refereed. Circ: 2200. Vol. ends: Nov/Dec. Microform: PQC. Online: ingenta.com; OCLC Online Computer Library Center, Inc.; ProQuest Information & Learning; Swets Blackwell. Reprint: PQC. *Indexed:* AgeL, CIJE, CINAHL, CJA, CommAb, EduInd, ExcerpMed, H&SSA, HRA, IndMed, PEI, PsycholAb, SFSA, SSCI, SWR&A. *Bk. rev.:* 0-2, 1,200 words. *Aud.:* Ac, Sa.

As the official publication of the Society for Public Health Education, this journal strives to publish authoritative and practical information on health issues for a broad range of health professionals. Emphasis is on understanding factors associated with people's behavior and how these affect their health. Each journal issue carries seven or eight articles dealing with research or theoretical issues, often with a separate discussion of implications for practitioners. The shorter format of "Practice Notes" serves to keep readers informed about new and exemplary strategies for health education from around the world. Some articles carry CHES continuing education credits. From the web site (http://www.sph.umich.edu/hbhe/heb), detailed information is available about the journal, and most article abstracts are available from October 1997. (JKO)

4843. ***Journal of Health Education.*** Formerly: *School Health Review.* [ISSN: 1055-6699] 1970. bi-m. USD 120 USD 20 newsstand/cover per issue. American Alliance for Health, Physical Education, Recreation, and Dance, 1900 Association Dr, Reston, VA 20191-1599; info@aahperd.org; http://www.aahperd.org. Adv. Refereed. Circ: 11500. Microform: PQC. Reprint: ISI; PQC. *Indexed:* AgeL, Agr, CIJE, CINAHL, ECER, EduInd, H&SSA, MRD, PEI, SportS. *Bk. rev.:* 2-3, signed. *Aud.:* Hs, Ga, Ac, Sa.

The *American Journal of Health Education* has a broad scope for providing research, teaching, and health promotion articles for the four areas of interest to the American Alliance for Health, Physical Education, Recreation, and Dance, and related fields. The articles are directed toward the health educator who is working with people from elementary through college and community levels. A brief reports section focuses on practical "how-to" aspects of health education. Each issue has articles that can be used for CEU self-study credit. Abstracts are available online for one year at http://www.aahperd.org/aahperd/AJHE-abstracts.html. (JKO)

Morbidity and Mortality Weekly Report. See Government Periodicals—Federal section.

4844. ***Public Health Reports: the public health journal that you want to read.*** Former titles (until 1973): *Health Services Report;* (until 1972): *H S M H A Health Reports;* (until 1970): *Public health reports.* [ISSN: 0033-3549] 1878. bi-m. GBP 86. Oxford University Press, 2001 Evans Rd, Cary, NC 27513; http://www3.oup.co.uk/jnls/. Illus., index, adv. Sample. Refereed. Circ: 8000. Vol. ends: Nov/Dec. Microform: CIS; PMC; PQC. Online: EBSCO Publishing; Gale Group; HighWire Press; ingenta.com; Northern Light Technology, Inc.; RoweCom Information Quest; Swets Blackwell. Reprint: CIS; PQC; PSC. *Indexed:* ABS&EES, AgeL, Agr, AmStI, CINAHL, CJA, ChemAb, DSA, EngInd, ExcerpMed, GSI, H&SSA, IUSGP, IndMed, IndVet, MagInd, PAIS, PEI, RRTA, S&F, SCI, SSCI, SSI, SWR&A, SWRA, VetBull, WAE&RSA. *Bk. rev.:* 2, signed. *Aud.:* Hs, Ga, Ac, Sa.

The format provides four to eight research articles that describe important scientific, programmatic or technological developments for public health. Each issue contains editorials, letters, news and notes, original research articles, and international reports. Lots of black-and-white photos and graphs support the easy reading of these articles. Supplemental issues focus on one topic. A searchable "Tables of Content and Abstracts" archive is available online for subscribers, and a free e-mail alerting service for searching information in the "Table of Contents" allows readers to be notified when a new *Public Health Reports* goes online. The web site is http://phr.oupjournals.org. (JKO)

Women & Health. See Women: Feminist and Special Interest/Feminist and Women's Studies section.

Electronic Journals

4845. ***Advance for Medical Laboratory Professionals.*** Formerly (until 199?): *Advance for Medical Technologists.* [ISSN: 1088-5676] 1989. bi-w. Ed(s): Lisa Brzezicki. Merion Publications, Inc., 2900 Horizon Dr, PO Box 61556, King of Prussia, PA 19406; advance@merion.com; http://www.advanceweb.com. Illus., adv. Circ: 63900. Vol. ends: Dec. *Aud.:* Ac, Sa.

The periodical, primarily aimed at professionals in the allied health sciences, is free to members in about a dozen professional societies. The journal is now provided completely online, with an opportunity to register to receive the printed newsletter. There does not appear to be an archive. Each issue contains a feature article that deals with laboratory systems concerns, both scientific and organizational. Each issue has up to three feature articles, such as "Pathophysiology of Nutritionally Impaired States," "A New Marker for Schizophrenia??," and so on. Other departments handle aspects of organizational affairs, such as conferences, licensure issues, and employment trends. *Advance* is always in the forefront of medical technology developments. (MMC)

4846. ***B E T A.*** [ISSN: 1058-708X] 1989. q. Ed(s): Leslie Hanna, Liz Highleyman. San Francisco AIDS Foundation, PO Box 426182, San Francisco, CA 94142-6182; beta@sfaf.org; http://www.sfaf.org/beta.html. *Aud.:* Sa.

This quarterly online publication "covers developments in AIDS treatment research." Past issues can be browsed by date of publication or by date. Topics covered on a regular basis include "Research Notes," "Women & HIV/AIDS," "Drug Watch," "Alternative/Complementary Treatments," "Nutrition/Food Safety," "Side Effects of Treatment," etc. Almost all of the information is duplicated in Spanish. *BETA* is also available in print [1058-708X] and published on a quarterly basis and distributed free of charge to subscribers. This publication offers comprehensive coverage of all aspects of treatment and research. The fact that it is free only adds to the impressive value of this site. Highly recommended. (LEB)

4847. ***Bulletin of the History of Medicine.*** [ISSN: 1086-3176] 1933. Johns Hopkins University Press, Journals Publishing Division, http://www.press.jhu.edu/. Illus., index. Sample. Vol. ends: Winter. *Bk. rev.:* Various number and length. *Aud.:* Ga, Ac.

The *Bulletin* is the official publication of the American Association for the History of Medicine, in collaboration with the Johns Hopkins Institute of the History of Medicine. The journal is a top offering in the field of the history of medicine, and is available in full text as part of Project Muse (http://muse.jhu.edu). Nonsubscribers may see only an extensive table of contents. The journal explores concepts of clinical care, health, responses to disease, and healing in various world cultures and eras. Recent articles treat dental pathology in ancient Mesopotamia, nineteenth-century public health laws in Great Britain, and the effect of medical knowledge on theological debate in the thirteenth century. Of interest to scholars and history buffs, the *Bulletin* carries in-depth book reviews, many illustrations, and well-documented articles. (MMC)

4848. ***Dairy Council Digest: an interpretive review of recent nutrition research.*** [ISSN: 0011-5568] 1929. bi-m. Free. National Dairy Council, O'Hare International Center, 10255 W. Higgins Rd., Ste. 900, Rosemont, IL 60018-5616; http://www.nationaldairycouncil.org. Illus. Sample. Circ: 25000. Vol. ends: Dec. Microform: PQC. Online: Northern Light Technology, Inc.; ProQuest Information & Learning. *Indexed:* DSA. *Aud.:* Ga, Ac, Sa.

In January 1999, this publication became available only online. Each issue covers a single topic, with extensive references. Examples from recent issues are "The Role of Dairy Foods and Activity for Grooming Children," "A New Look at Dietary Patterns and Hypertension," "Health-Enhancing Properties of Dairy Ingredients," and "Health Benefits of Dairy Foods for Minorities." Although targeted at nutrition professionals, this excellent online journal contains content of interest to consumers. (MMC)

4849. ***Educator's Update.*** [ISSN: 1092-2687] 1996. bi-m. USD 24. Ed(s): Gloria A Roberts. Planned Parenthood Federation of America, Inc., 810 Seventh Ave, New York, NY 10019; http://www.plannedparenthood.org/library/PPFA-LIBRARY/EdUpIndex.htm. Illus. Sample. Circ: 150. *Aud.:* Ga, Ac, Sa.

Full text is online beginning with the October 1999 issue. Bibliographic information is divided into sections: "Books," "Articles," "Videos," "Web Sites," "Conferences," and "Planned Parenthood Affiliate Training." A new section, "Evaluation Corner," offers advice and tips about planning and conducting evaluation of sexuality education and prevention programs for pregnancy, STIs, and HIV. Articles are authored by Planned Parenthood directors and family planning health professionals. This journal is a great resource for family planning centers, high school libraries, and special libraries that have educational programs. (SRP)

4850. ***Essential Drugs Monitor.*** [ISSN: 1015-0919] 1986. s-a. Free. Ed(s): R. Laing. World Health Organization, Department of Essential Drugs & Medicines Policy, Geneva, 1211, Switzerland; darec@who.ch; http://www.who.int/medicines. Circ: 200000. *Indexed:* CINAHL. *Aud.:* Ga, Ac.

An objective view of drug use and control worldwide, this is published by the World Health Organization in English, French, Spanish, and Russian. It is more than simply a bulletin on the problem of drugs, although this is a major sector. The data are objective and range from such things as public education and therapeutic guides to drug management. The publisher points out that the publication "contains regular features on national drug policies, rational drug use, supply, operational research and public education, together with reviews of relevant publications." The latter feature is of particular value to libraries. (BK)

4851. ***Family Medical Practice On-Line: the international journal of family medical practice and primary care.*** [ISSN: 1360-0176] 1995. m. Free. Ed(s): Dr. Thomas F Heston. Priory Lodge Education Ltd., 2 Cornflower Way, Moreton, CH46 1SV, United Kingdom; solutions@priory.com; http://www.priory.com/. Illus. Refereed. Circ: 30000 Controlled. *Aud.:* Ga, Sa.

While this medical journal is primarily for English doctors, most of the data will be of value to those in America as well as to laypeople with an understanding and appreciation of medical terminology. The articles—some technical, others within the grasp of an interested reader—cover major issues in modern medicine from diagnoses to handling patients. There are excellent notes on current research. See, too, the book reviews as well as reviews of software, videos, films, etc. Note well: This is one of the few free medical journals on the web. True, it acts as a publicity arm for the publisher, but this has nothing to do with the impressive editorial content. (BK)

4852. ***Health Transition Review.*** [ISSN: 1036-4005] 1991. s-a. Free. Ed(s): Alan G Hill. Health Transition Review, c/o Harvard School of Public Health, Dept of Population & International Health, Boston, MA 02115; http://www-nceph.anu.edu.au/htc/html/htr.htm. Circ: 2000. *Indexed:* AICP, IBSS, ST&MA. *Aud.:* Ga.

Although published in Australia, this semi-popular health magazine will interest any layperson anywhere. Common health problems are discussed, as are findings of recent research. Most of it is free of jargon. Particular focus is on what the editors term the "social cultural and behavioral determinants of health," e.g., diet, smoking, noise, etc. (BK)

4853. ***HeartWeb.*** 1995. irreg. Ed(s): Seymour Furman. Amadeus Multimedia Technologies, Ltd., 3 Roland Rd, Irvington, NY 10533; http://www.heartweb.org/. *Aud.:* Sa.

A "peer-reviewed cardiology journal," this "takes advantage of the power of multimedia presentations to allow the user to search the Web and to find links to pertinent other publications." The "official site" of the Association of Physician Assistants in Cardiovascular Surgery, this is unusual in that it is scholarly and free. While it is prepared for doctors, at least some of its material can be read by interested laypersons. (BK)

4854. ***Homeopathy Online.*** 1996. bi-m. Ed(s): Chris Kurz. Homeopathy Mailing List, enos@wolfenet.com; http://www.lyghtforce.com/homeopathyonline/. *Aud.:* Ga, Sa.

Recent issues of this objective homeopathy journal have featured such topics as "A Homeopathic Expedition into the Amazon Rainforest," the botanical family *Umbelliferae,* and an article on the history of British homeopathy. There are regular features on homeopathic education, letters to the editor, "a bulletin board for the homeopathic community," and similar aids. An excellent choice. (MMC)

NLM Newsline. See Free Magazines and House Organs section.

4855. ***Priorities for Health.*** Former titles (until 1999): *Priorities for Long Life and Good Health;* (until 1979): *A C S H News and Views.* [ISSN: 1522-645X] 1979. q. USD 25. Ed(s): Jack Rasso. American Council on Science and Health, 1995 Broadway, 2nd Fl, New York, NY 10023-5560; http://www.prioritiesforhealth.com/. Adv. Circ: 7000. *Indexed:* AgeL, CINAHL. *Aud.:* Ga.

This journal is published by "a consumer education consortium concerned with issues related to food, nutrition, chemicals, pharmaceuticals, lifestyles, the environment, and health." Each issue contains several articles on topics such as multiple chemical sensitivity, electroconvulsive therapy, electrolysis, and wheat-bran fiber. Although still available in print, this publication is now considered "primarily an on-line periodical." The web version, however, provides information that is not in the print version, such as updates to articles and links to articles in back issues. This publication provides an opinionated but informative angle on consumer health information. (DAA)

4856. ***Your Health Daily.*** 1997. d. New York Times Company, 100 Ave. of the Americas, New York, NY 10013; http://www.yourhealthdaily.com/. *Aud.:* Ga.

Health news for the general reader, this is prepared by a medical news service. What makes it original is that it is published in *The New York Times* and several other daily newspapers. The mark of reliability is evident in the stories, which cover matters of interest to the layperson. These may run from popular explanations of Viagra to what, if anything, can be done about the common cold and being overweight. As an expanded version of *The New York Times'* health page, this is an excellent source of information for the public. Highly recommended. (BK)

4857. ***Your Life - Your Choice.*** [ISSN: 1488-0253] 1997. s-m. Free. Ed(s): Brigitte Synesael. Your Life - Your Choice, 188 Gammage St, London, ON N5Y 2B3, Canada; yourlife@life-choices.com; http://www.life-choices.com. Adv. Circ: 3000. *Aud.:* Ga.

What are the best choices for alternative medical aids? In this newsletter, the editor offers numerous short articles and tips to answer that question. Professionals are frequent contributors. The flag flying over the items is "Your health is your responsibility." Specific health questions, at least of a nontechnical type, are answered via e-mail. Note: This journal is underwritten, in part, by herbal and related advertisers. (BK)

■ MEN

Charles A. Skewis, Head, Collection & Resource Services, Georgia Southern University, Statesboro, GA 30460-8074; cskewis@gasou.edu

Thomas L. Kilpatrick, Professor Emeritus, Southern Illinois University Libraries, Carbondale, IL 62901-6632; tkilpatr@lib.siu.edu

Introduction

Only in the last 20 years have men's magazines come out from under the counter at the local newsstand. In fact, the term *men's magazines* still carries a negative connotation to some people, conjuring up images of nude models, off-color jokes, and unsavory stories packaged in glossy covers and plastic wrap. Those publications stll exist, but an increasing number of high-quality journals focusing on the interests of the male reader are currently available, including such titles as *Details, FHM, Men's Journal,* and *Gear.* In addition to magazines of a general nature, several niche magazines seem to be doing well, among them *New Man,* which focuses on the Christian male; and *At-Home Dad* and *Full-Time Dads,* which appeal to thousands of concerned fathers. The one niche publication that helped launch and legitimize the men's magazine movement is the health and bodybuilding journal. *Men's Health* has been the acknowledged leader in this area since 1986, but a number of other titles exist, including *Exercise for Men Only* and *Men's Fitness,* and these should not be ignored. Interest in research concerning men's issues is on the increase, and the number of research journals is growing gradually. Among the best are *The Aging Male, Journal of Men's Studies,* and *Men and Masculinities.* Two new titles, *Fathering* and *International Journal of Men's Health,* should also be noted. Finally, the Internet is becoming a factor in men's publishing, as most major journals now have an online presence, and some of the small publishers have converted to web-only publication and distribution. Unfortunately, indexing services and libraries have lagged behind publishers and vendors in recognizing the quality and the demand for these publications, so indexing sources, and indeed the journals themselves, are not always easy to find. Librarians can do their male patrons a favor by examining the list of available journals and placing subscriptions for a number of appropriate titles.

Basic Periodicals

Ga: *Details, FHM, GQ, Men's Health, Men's Journal;* Sa: *The Aging Male, International Journal of Men's Health, Journal of Men's Studies, Men and Masculinities.*

4858. ***The Aging Male.*** [ISSN: 1368-5538] 1998. q. GBP 145 (Individuals, GBP 85). Ed(s): Bruno Lunenfeld. Parthenon Publishing Group, Richmond House, White Cross, South Road, Lancaster, LA1 4XQ, United Kingdom; mail@parthpub.com; http://www.parthpub.com/. Illus., adv. Sample. Refereed. Circ: 1200 Paid. Vol. ends: No. 4. Online: Ingenta Select; OCLC Online Computer Library Center, Inc.; Swets Blackwell. *Indexed:* ExcerpMed. *Bk. rev.:* 12-15, 200 words. *Aud.:* Ac.

The official journal of the International Society for the Study of the Aging Male, this title fills an obvious void in the academic and professional literature concerning manhood and masculinity. Peer-reviewed research articles examine the aging process, health care, disease, treatment, pharmacology, and other topics relating to the aging male. A review of related literature appears in each issue. This title reflects the growing interest in research on the aging of society, which can only gain in importance as life expectancy rises. An essential purchase for every medical and research library.

4859. ***American Cowboy.*** Former titles: *American Cowboy Magazine;* (until 1979): *Hoof and Horn.* [ISSN: 1079-3690] 1931. bi-m. USD 16.95; USD 26.95 in Canada & Mexico; USD 31.95 elsewhere. Ed(s): Jesse Mullins. American Cowboy, L.L.C., PO Box 820, Buffalo, WY 82834; http://www.americancowboy.com/. Illus., adv. Sample. Circ: 85000 Paid. Vol. ends: No. 6. *Bk. rev.:* 5, 200 words, signed. *Aud.:* Ga.

American Cowboy hit the newsstands in 1994 and has created a comfortable niche for itself, particularly in the American West. "Cowboying is more than an occupation," says editor Jesse Mullins. "It's a state of mind. More than that, it's a set of values, a standard and a way to live and believe." That pretty well sums up the creed of *American Cowboy.* With good editorial leadership, it has become a slick combination of text and pictures that celebrates the cowboy and immortalizes the West, past and present. Cattle ranching, gunfighters of the Old West, and the rodeo circuit are typical of the topics that appear in these pages. Other interesting features include columns on food, travel, fashion, cowboy memorabilia, Western poetry, horsemanship, and festivals. *American Cowboy* is a smooth and colorful magazine that men will enjoy when they can get it away from the womenfolk.

4860. ***Arena (London): the grown-up magazine for men.*** [ISSN: 0955-0046] 1986. m. GBP 23; GBP 3.20 newsstand/cover per issue. Ed(s): Greg Williams. Emap Metro Ltd, 2nd Fl, Block A, Exmouth House, Pine St, London, EC1R 0JL, United Kingdom; philbembridge@theface.co.uk. Illus., adv. *Indexed:* DAAI. *Bk. rev.:* 6, 200 words, signed. *Aud.:* Ga.

Arena is a sophisticated general-interest magazine with a strong male orientation similar to *Esquire,* its American counterpart. Work, leisure, politics, travel, fashion, biography, sports, and other topics of interest to the culture-conscious male are treated in grand style. *Arena* is highly recommended for the library that seeks reading material with an international bent for the sophisticated male. *Arena Homme Plus,* a biannual by the same publisher, will also be enjoyed by men interested in cutting-edge trends in fashion.

4861. ***At-Home Dad: promoting the home-based father.*** [ISSN: 1081-5767] 1994. q. USD 15. Ed(s): Peter Baylies. At-Home Dad, 61 Brightwood Ave, North Andover, MA 01845; athomedad@aol.com; http://www.athomedad.com. Illus., adv. Circ: 1000. Online: OCLC Online Computer Library Center, Inc.; SoftLine Information. *Indexed:* GendWatch. *Aud.:* Ga, Sa.

At-Home Dad is an appealing mix of fun, facts, suggestions, and inspiration for men who are primary caregivers for their children. Articles cover every facet of parenting and child rearing from swimming lessons to dealing with "down" times when the children are away from home. Columns offer advice on raising children and sources of information and help in meeting the challenge. The "At-Home Dad Network," a section that appears in each issue of the newsletter, provides news of the Dad-to-Dad support group. *At-Home Dad* is an excellent selection for a specialized library clientele.

4862. ***Bikini.*** [ISSN: 1073-7936] 1993. m. USD 18.95 domestic; USD 40 Canada; USD 75 elsewhere. Ed(s): Marvin Scott Jarrett. RayGun Media, Inc., 2812 Santa Monica Blvd, Ste 204, Santa Monica, CA 90404; bikini@raygun.com; http://www.raygun.com. Illus., adv. *Aud.:* Ga, Sa.

Pop culture runs rampant in this colorful magazine, which is sure to appeal to the collegiate man. Filled with the latest word on action, film, cars, celebrities, rock music, and other "in" topics, *Bikini* is a textual and visual collage with the hippest of articles interspersed with exotic images and bold photography. *Bikini* has matured since its inception, but the guys still love it—and women do, too.

4863. ***Details.*** [ISSN: 0740-4921] 1982. 10x/yr. USD 7.97 domestic; USD 27 Canada; USD 31 elsewhere. Fairchild Publications, Inc., 7 W 34th St, New York, NY 10001-8191. Illus., adv. Sample. Circ: 476290 Paid. Vol. ends: No. 12. *Indexed:* ASIP. *Aud.:* Ga, Ac.

A trendy magazine directed at style-conscious young men in their twenties and thirties, *Details* is outspoken, outrageous, and very readable. Fashion, grooming, style, sex, politics, adventure, and popular culture are highlighted in a slick, attractive, and browsable format that is designed to compete with *GQ* for readership. Public and college libraries will find it very popular.

4864. ***Everyman.*** Formerly (until 1992): *Men's Magazine.* [ISSN: 1199-1461] 1992. bi-m. USD 20. Ed(s): David Shackleton. Everyman, PO Box 4617, Ottawa, ON K1S 5H8, Canada. Online: OCLC Online Computer Library Center, Inc.; SoftLine Information. *Bk. rev.:* 3, 400 words, signed. *Aud.:* Ga, Sa.

Everyman is the official magazine of the Canadian men's movement. Its focus is "men's growth toward wholeness and balancing the gender debate," according to editor and publisher David Shackleton. Themes for each issue—love and relationships, aging and death, custody and access, violence, equality, boys, fatherhood, and rights and responsibilities—are indicative of the range of topics addressed by the publication, which features articles, poetry, letters, news, a calendar of events, and reviews. A useful feature is a four-page spread called "Resources for Men," which lists social-service organizations throughout Canada. *Everyman* is an attractive, thought-provoking journal for the man who takes manhood seriously.

4865. *Exercise for Men Only.* [ISSN: 0882-4657] 1985. bi-m. USD 35.15; USD 40.95 foreign; USD 4.95 newsstand/cover per issue foreign. Ed(s): Cheh N Low. Chelo Publishing Inc., 350 Fifth Ave, Ste 3323, New York, NY 10118. Illus. Vol. ends: No. 6. *Aud.:* Ga.

Sitting on the newsstand, this title blends in perfectly with dozens of other muscle and bodybuilding magazines. The difference becomes apparent, however, as soon as you open it. Certainly, flexed pectorals are in evidence, but this is more than a showcase for the expanded male body. Illustrated articles concerning bodybuilding are interspersed with feature articles that concern nutrition, sports medicine, health, beach fashions, psychology, and grooming to create a very readable magazine. Public librarians who need bodybuilding materials and want the most for their money will do well to look here.

4866. *F H M.* Formerly (until 1992): *For Him Magazine.* [ISSN: 0966-0933] 1985. m. GBP 29.97 United Kingdom; GBP 56 rest of Europe; GBP 79 United States. Ed(s): Ed Needham. Emap Metro Ltd., Mappin House, 4 Winsley St, London, W1W 8HF, United Kingdom. Illus., adv. Sample. Circ: 81104 Paid. *Indexed:* DAAI. *Aud.:* Ga.

This classy publication for men, which originated in England in 1985, has now gone international. However, it continues to focus on cutting-edge topics, and the latest in fashion, entertainment, lifestyles, jobs, celebrities, sports, fast cars, and adventure for the sophisticated young man. Equally intriguing is the format, which integrates a wealth of information, opinion, and pointed satire into neat capsules, lavishly illustrated with eye-catching photographs. Pricey, but a popular title with the 20-to-40 age group, *FHM* is now affordable for most libraries. A quarterly fashion supplement titled *FHM Connections* may also prove interesting.

4867. *Fathering Magazine: the online magazine for men with families.* [ISSN: 1091-5516] 1995. m. Free. Ed(s): Alexander Sheldon. Fathering Enterprises, Inc., PO Box 231891, Houston, TX 77223; sheldon@fathermag.com; http://www.fathermag.com/. Illus., adv. Circ: 1000000. *Aud.:* Ac, Sa.

A scholarly, peer-reviewed journal intended for teachers, students, and practitioners, *Fathering* includes research and practice-based articles on all aspects of fatherhood and the male in the role of parent. Issues covered include parenting, father/child relationships, divorce, stepfathers, child custody, and more. A companion title for *Journal of Men's Studies,* published by the same company, *Fathering* is a title that every academic and research library should own.

4868. *Full-Time Dads: because parenting isn't a hobby!* [ISSN: 1055-2367] 1993. bi-m. USD 18. Ed(s): James McLoughlin. Full-Time Dads, 193 Shelley Ave, Elizabeth, NJ 07208-1061. Illus., adv. Circ: 375 Paid. *Bk. rev.:* 200-500 words, signed. *Aud.:* Ga.

The goal of *Full-Time Dads* is to enhance and promote the role of fathers in the family and society. To that end, this publication offers a wide range of articles and features that cover family relationships, stay-at-home fathers, single parenting, divorce, health, and a wealth of other topics. Need a quick and easy recipe that will appeal to kids? Try *Full-Time Dads.* Need legal assistance, vacation suggestions, or parenting tips? You got it: *Full-Time Dads.* Librarians should definitely consider this title for their male clientele. Back issues are available online.

4869. *G Q: gentlemen's quarterly for men.* [ISSN: 0016-6979] 1957. m. USD 15 domestic; USD 37 Canada; USD 38 elsewhere. Ed(s): Arthur Cooper. Conde Nast Publications Inc., 4 Times Square, 5th Fl, New York, NY 10036; gqmag@aol.com; http://www.gq.com. Illus., adv. Circ: 757558 Paid. Vol. ends: Winter. Microform: PQC. Online: Gale Group. Reprint: PQC. *Indexed:* ASIP, DAAI, MagInd, RGPR. *Aud.:* Hs, Ga, Ac.

The leading fashion magazine for the American male, *GQ* is the first stop for the man-on-the-go with an interest in looking good and being seen in the right places. Quality writing, amply illustrated with eye-catching photography, appeals to the "in crowd." Feature articles emphasize clothing, travel, and dining, with frequent glimpses into the private lives of the current trendsetters. The young, style-conscious male will find useful the regular columns on grooming, finance, fashion, and music and will enjoy the occasional fiction that finds its way into *GQ.* Librarians will find it a favorite among young men for browsing and in-depth reading.

4870. *Gear.* [ISSN: 1099-6494] 1998. m. USD 17.95; USD 3.50 newsstand/cover per issue domestic; CND 4.50 newsstand/cover per issue Canada. Ed(s): Aaron Hicklin, Bob Guccione. Guccione Media LLC, 450 W 15th St Ste 504, New York, NY 10011; gearmag@earthlink.net. Illus., adv. Sample. *Bk. rev.:* 4, 200 words. *Aud.:* Ga.

Broad vision, a progressive editorial board, and an enviable staff of writers and photographers produce an impressive magazine that has proven to be right on target with aware males in the 21-to-50 age group. Everything male is fair game for *Gear,* from politics, religion, and business to fashion, health, sex, sports, entertainment, music, and literature—all served up with humor, forthrightness, and eye appeal that are certain to attract readers. Libraries will want to consider *Gear* along with *Esquire* and *Details* for their male browsers.

4871. *Harvard Men's Health Watch.* [ISSN: 1089-1102] 1996. m. USD 24 domestic; USD 40 Canada; USD 47 elsewhere. Harvard Health Publications Group, 164 Longwood Ave, Boston, MA 02115. Online: EBSCO Publishing; Florida Center for Library Automation; Gale Group. *Aud.:* Ga, Sa.

Harvard Men's Health Watch synthesizes current reseach on men's health issues into brief but meaty articles that can be readily understood by the layman. Diet, heart disease, baldness, sexual dysfunction, prostate cancer, diabetes, and Alzheimer's disease are only a few topics that are treated. A no-nonsense format gives the reader answers to health questions and provides background and current information suitable for consultation with a primary physician. This title will be popular in public and medical libraries, and even the doctor's office.

4872. *International Journal of Men's Health.* [ISSN: 1532-6306] 2002. 3x/yr. USD 150 (Individuals, USD 50; USD 15 per issue). Men's Studies Press, PO Box 32, Harriman, TN 37748-0032; http://www.mensstudies.com. Index, adv. Sample. Refereed. *Aud.:* Ga, Sa.

Articles on all aspects of men's health can be found within the covers of this journal. The primary audience is educators, students, researchers, and professionals in the fields of medicine, health sciences, behavioral and social sciences, and public health. Every academic and research library should subscribe to this important research journal.

Journal of African American Men. See African American section.

4873. *Journal of Men's Studies: a scholarly journal about men and masculinities.* [ISSN: 1060-8265] 1992. 3x/yr. USD 150 (Individuals, USD 50). Ed(s): James A Doyle. Men's Studies Press, PO Box 32, Harriman, TN 37748-0032; http://www.mensstudies.com. Illus., adv. Sample. Refereed. Circ: 390 Paid. Vol. ends: May. *Indexed:* GendWatch, HumInd, SFSA, SSI. *Bk. rev.:* 4, 800 words. *Aud.:* Ac, Sa.

This journal concerning men and masculinity helps fill a void in the areas of psychosocial and sexual scholarship. The academic and professional communities constitute the target audience for this essential journal, which offers high-quality, peer-reviewed research that touches on a variety of disciplines, including anthropology, history, literature, psychology, and sociology. The *Journal of Men's Studies* is a first-rate tool to aid in defining modern man in a volatile, ever-changing culture. Every academic and research library should subscribe to this title.

4874. *Journeymen.* [ISSN: 1061-8538] 1991. q. USD 18; USD 24 Canada. Ed(s): Paul S Boynton. Journeymen, 513 Chester Turnpike, Candia, NH 03034. Illus., adv. *Bk. rev.:* 1, 2,000 words signed. *Aud.:* Ga.

A small but intriguing magazine, *Journeymen* is described as a "participatory networking publication intended to help men make connections with each other." Within its covers the reader will find addressed such issues as father–son relationships, men's health, marriage, divorce, friendship, language and gender, and intimacy. Literary forms include, but are not limited to, poetry, essays, interviews, and book reviews. *Journeymen* is a sensitive and sensible alternative to the mainstream sex- and fashion-laden publications that permeate the men's magazine market.

4875. *Just for Black Men: for strong, positive caring brothers.* [ISSN: 1090-0365] 1996. bi-m. USD 18 domestic; USD 24 Canada; USD 27 elsewhere. Ed(s): Kate Feguson. Black Men Publications, 46 Violet Ave, Poughkeepsie, NY 12601. Illus., adv. *Bk. rev.:* 3, 200 words. *Aud.:* Ga.

Just for Black Men is one of only a handful of magazines for the young and style-conscious black male. Designed to appeal to the 20-to-40 age group, it is heavily into lifestyle, health and fitness, and sports, with secondary emphasis on the latest in men's fashion, business and financial advice, travel, and Black celebrities. *Just for Black Men* oozes sensuality, but does it with class. Photos of Black supermodels stand side-by-side with articles on fatherhood, self-esteem, and health. This is an excellent title for libraries that need materials to appeal to the style-conscious man of color.

4876. *The Liberator (Forest Lake): male call.* Formerly: *Legal Beagle.* [ISSN: 1040-3760] 1968. m. USD 24 in North America; USD 48 elsewhere. Ed(s): Richard F Doyle. Men's Defense Association, 17854 Lyons St, Forest Lake, MN 55025; rdoyle@mensdefense.org; http://www.mensdefense.org/. Illus., adv. Sample. Circ: 2000 Controlled. Vol. ends: Dec. *Bk. rev.:* 28 pages, signed. *Aud.:* Sa.

Pro-male in every respect, *The Liberator* represents a small but growing group of activist men who are dedicated to preserving the rights of males, particularly in such areas as divorce court, child custody, and visitation rights. The editors espouse a traditional view of the family and family values, and of men and masculinity, and they present their views in a straightforward manner with little regard for current trends or political correctness. Topics include domestic relations, feminist trends and legislation, child-abuse cases, the masculine ethic, and parental rights. Some readers will find this journal to be exactly what they want, and others will take offense at its bluntness and conservative views—but rest assured that *The Liberator* will be read.

4877. *Maxim: for men.* [ISSN: 1092-9789] 1997. m. USD 14.97 domestic; USD 24.97 Canada; USD 34.97 elsewhere. Ed(s): Keith Blanchard. Dennis Maxim, Inc., 1040 Ave of the Americas, 23rd Fl, New York, NY 10018; editors@maximmag.com. Illus., adv. Sample. Circ: 2500000 Paid. Vol. ends: Dec. *Aud.:* Ga.

Maxim appears regularly on newsstands throughout the United States, and has gradually found its way onto a few library periodical racks. It is a slick, good-looking magazine that will attract male readers. Its provocative cover does the trick, but there's as much meat as cheesecake within. Health, holidays, sports, technology, investing, fashion, and sex are all grist for the *Maxim* mill. A fascination for the slightly offbeat is also apparent. Inquisitive librarians and readers may check out the title through its online full-text web site.

4878. *Men and Masculinities.* [ISSN: 1097-184X] 1998. q. GBP 275 print & online eds. in Europe, Middle East, Africa & Australasia. Ed(s): Michael S Kimmel. Sage Publications, Inc., 2455 Teller Rd, Thousand Oaks, CA 91320; info@sagepub.com; http://www.sagepub.com. Illus. Sample. Refereed. Vol. ends: Apr (No. 4). *Indexed:* HRA, IBSS, PSA, RRTA, SFSA, SWA, SociolAb. *Bk. rev.:* 6, 1,500 words, signed. *Aud.:* Ac, Sa.

Men and Masculinities is an important title in the area of research in men's studies. All topics are considered, including psychology, psychiatry, education, social and family relations, work, and sexuality. With a focus on research and an emphasis on quality, its editors insist that all articles pass the test of blind peer-review before publication. An editorial board made up of scholars from throughout the world ensures a broad base of scholarship and provides a forum for American and international researchers. Research and academic libraries throughout the world should subscribe.

4879. *Men's Fitness: when performance counts.* Formerly (until 1987): *Joe Weider's Sports Fitness.* [ISSN: 0893-4460] 1985. m. USD 14.97 domestic; USD 29.97 foreign; USD 3.99. Ed(s): Peter Sikowitz. Weider Publications, 21100 Erwin St, Woodland Hills, CA 91367; http://www.mensfitness.com. Illus., adv. Sample. Circ: 550000 Paid. Vol. ends: No. 12. Online: America Online, Inc.; EBSCO Publishing; Gale Group; OCLC Online Computer Library Center, Inc. *Indexed:* MagInd, PEI. *Aud.:* Hs, Ga, Ac.

The man who wants to be healthy can't do better than *Men's Fitness,* a magazine dedicated to helping men live fit, healthy, and active lives and have fun while they're doing it. Regular topics include not only fitness (gym workouts, participatory activities, thrill sports, team sports, etc.) but also nutrition, health, sports medicine, psychology, sexuality, men's issues, and travel. The well-rounded man will want *Men's Fitness;* the well-meaning librarian will want to provide it for him. This title is also published in Spanish [ISSN: 1532-457X].

4880. *Men's Health (United States Edition): tons of useful stuff.* [ISSN: 1054-4836] 1986. 10x/yr. USD 24.94 domestic; CND 39.50 Canada; USD 24.10 elsewhere. Ed(s): David Zinczenko, Peter Moore. Rodale, 33 E Minor St, Emmaus, PA 18098; info@rodale.com; http://www.rodale.com. Illus., adv. Circ: 1625000 Paid. Vol. ends: Dec (No. 10). Online: bigchalk; EBSCO Publishing; Gale Group; OCLC Online Computer Library Center, Inc.; ProQuest Information & Learning; H.W. Wilson. *Indexed:* CINAHL, MagInd, RGPR. *Aud.:* Hs, Ga, Ac.

Men's Health is riding high on the current health-and-fitness trend in the United States, and well it should, for it is the best of a growing number of health publications that target the men's market. A variety of entertaining and well-written articles on such topics as aging, survival in an urban environment, stress, workouts, sexuality, and selecting sports equipment are interspersed with regular columns on travel, nutrition, father–son relationships, and news. Many of the items are based on research, although they have been popularized for the casual reader. High school, public, and academic librarians will find this title popular wherever the guys congregate.

4881. *Men's Journal.* [ISSN: 1063-4657] 1992. m. USD 9.97 domestic; USD 25.97 foreign. Ed(s): Robert Wallace. Wenner Media, Inc., 1290 Ave of Americas, New York, NY 10104; mjsubs@aol.com. Illus., adv. Circ: 566943. *Indexed:* ASIP. *Bk. rev.:* 4, 200 words, signed. *Aud.:* Hs, Ga.

A publication for the active male, *Men's Journal* consists of about equal parts sports, action, and travel reading, with a hint of the good life for savor. Known for its exquisite photography and exceptional writing, it is aimed at the active man who wants to get the most out of life. An article about American heroes may stand side-by-side with one about climbing Mt. Everest and a word portrait of author William Vollmann's best friend, along with columns on the latest innovations in digital and other equipment, sports, fashion trends, health, grooming, sex, cars, books, and music. Librarians who browse this title will be won over.

4882. *Men's Voices.* Former titles (until Sep. 1997): *M.E.N. Magazine; Seattle M.E.N. Newsletter.* [ISSN: 1520-247X] 1981. q. USD 20. Ed(s): Bert H Hoff. White Rock Alternative, 7552 31st Ave, N E, Seattle, WA 98115; berthoff@wln.com; http://www.vix.com/menmag/. Illus., adv. Sample. Circ: 1000. *Bk. rev.:* 6, 200 words, signed. *Aud.:* Ga, Sa.

A local publication that has gone national, *Men's Voices* has become a publishing leader in men's rights and the male experience since its introduction in 1981. Unlike some of its counterparts, *Men's Voices* acknowledges pro-feminist opinions and issues and attempts to treat male/female points-of-view in an unbiased, truthful, and politically correct manner. Articles, poetry, book reviews, and interviews with such leaders of the men's movement as Michael Meade and Robert Bly make this an important title for the library that seeks to provide access to diverse opinions. Check out the web version.

4883. *Menz Magazine.* [ISSN: 1202-7472] 1994. q. CND 15; CND 19.50 foreign. Ed(s): Clayton Anderson. Better One Media, 300 Leo Parizeau, Ste 1901, Montreal, PQ H2W 2N1, Canada; editor@menz.com; http://www.menz.com. Adv. Circ: 50000. *Indexed:* CBCARef. *Bk. rev.:* 2, 200-500 words. *Aud.:* Ga.

Canada's premier magazine for men, *Menz Magazine* is a good-looking, general publication for the average male, focusing on finance, health, fitness, adventure, food, and the Canadian lifestyle. Reviews of new technology, entertainment, cars, and fashion trends round out the journal. Beautiful women are in evidence, but not to the same degree as in American counterparts. Librarians should definitely give this title consideration for its slightly different take on modern man.

4884. ***New Man: the magazine about becoming men of integrity.*** [ISSN: 1077-3959] 1994. bi-m. USD 19.95; USD 3.95 newsstand/cover per issue. Ed(s): Robert Andrescik. Strang Communications Co., 600 Rinehart Rd, Lake Mary, FL 32746. Illus., adv. Circ: 225000. *Indexed:* ChrPI. *Bk. rev.:* 4, 200 words, signed. *Aud.:* Ga.

New Man is not just your typical men's magazine; it is a magazine for the *Christian* male. Topics are far-ranging, from parenting, personal growth, and mental health to finances, software, and automobiles—all approached from a religious perspective. *New Man* is a good-looking alternative for the man who is more interested in personal development, family life, and spiritual growth than in just looking good.

Penthouse. See Sexuality section.

Playboy. See Sexuality section.

4885. ***Razor: more than just a way of life.*** 2000. bi-m. USD 12.97 domestic; USD 21.97 Canada; USD 47.97 elsewhere. Ed(s): Craig Vasiloff. Razor Magazine LLC, 8601 N Scottsdale Rd, Ste 330, Scottsdale, AZ 85253. Adv. *Aud.:* Ga.

Razor's mission is to provide cutting-edge information for men on the go, especially in the areas of entertainment, music, fashion, and health. A beautiful magazine for the 20- to 40-year-old male, *Razor* focuses on up-and-coming young actors and musicians, new trends in automobiles, the best sporting venues, gadgets, men's fashion, and much more. Articles and columns will inspire, shock, titillate, and inform, and the eye-catching layout and photography add visual impact to the word. Librarians should consider *Razor* along with *GQ, FHM,* and *Menz Magazine.*

4886. ***Sex & Health.*** Former titles (until 1997): *Men's Confidential Newsletter;* (until 1993): *Men's Health Newsletter.* [ISSN: 1097-4717] 1985. m. USD 48. Ed(s): Michael Lafavore. Rodale, 33 E Minor St, Emmaus, PA 18098; http://www.rodale.com. Illus., adv. Circ: 110000 Paid. *Aud.:* Ga.

A newsletter that focuses on medical advice for men, *Sex & Health* addresses health, aging, stress, nutrition, and hygiene, but it places particular emphasis on sexual issues. Most of the articles are brief, very readable, and based on research. Two columns, "Better Sex" and "Ask Sex & Health," address sexual problems with candor and insight. Back issues are available online at http://sexandhealth.com.

4887. ***Stuff: for men.*** [ISSN: 1524-2838] 1998. m. USD 9.97 domestic; USD 19.97 Canada; USD 29.97 elsewhere. Ed(s): Sky Shineman. Dennis Publishing, Inc., 1040 Ave of the Americas, 23rd Fl, New York, NY 10018. Illus., adv. *Bk. rev.:* 2, 200 words. *Aud.:* Ga.

Men's toys, and tools too, are the focus of this upscale consumer shopper's guide produced by the publishers of *Maxim.* The latest in audio, video, online, office, and home technologies are reviewed in detail, along with hiking boots, motorcycles, radar detectors, sporting dogs, and anything else that might appeal to the active male ego. There are articles, too, such as "The 25 Greatest Cars of All Time." The newest films, books, videos, and CDs are reviewed. *Stuff* will intrigue the male population with its cutting-edge information, slick presentations, and beautiful models.

4888. ***Subject Magazine.*** [ISSN: 1472-2879] 2001. 3x/yr. GBP 5.95. Ed(s): Ross Cottingham. Stable Publications Ltd., PO Box 31959, London, W2 5YA, United Kingdom; info@subject-magazine.com; http://www.subject-magazine.com. *Bk. rev.:* 8, 200 words, signed. *Aud.:* Ga.

A men's magazine without skin? It's been done before, but not very often, and that's just one of the reasons that this new title focusing on the male reader is such a pleasant surprise. *Subject Magazine* is a publication of considerable substance, with interesting news bites; meaty articles on current topics; biographical sketches of rising stars in the entertainment, business, and science fields; and critical reviews of the newest book, film, television, and music offerings. Articles such as an unofficial tour of London pubs and a search for a good pint add a bit of levity and local color, while a healthy serving of information on entertainment trend-setters insures a wide readership. The articles are beautifully packaged with superb photography, colorful backgrounds, and eye-catching layouts. Somewhat reminiscent of *Men's Journal, Subject Magazine* offers a broader scope with a British flavor.

4889. ***Today's Father.*** [ISSN: 1081-1540] 1993. q. USD 15; USD 2.50 newsstand/cover per issue. Ed(s): Brock E Griffin. National Center for Fathering, 10200 W 75th St, Ste 267, Shawnee Mission, KS 66204. Adv. Circ: 50000. *Bk. rev.:* 5-10, 50 words. *Aud.:* Ga.

Described as a magazine "for men who want to be better dads," *Today's Father* is a slick, full-color publication chock-full of information on all phases of parenting. Articles, surveys, interviews, cartoons and comic strips, news, and book recommendations make up the bulk of this enhanced newsletter, which is sponsored by the National Center for Fathering.

4890. ***Transitions (Minneapolis).*** [ISSN: 0886-862X] 1981. bi-m. Membership, USD 30. Ed(s): Jim Lovestar. National Coalition of Free Men, PO Box 582023, Minneapolis, MN 55458; ncfm@ncfm.org; http://www.ncfm.org. Illus., adv. Sample. Online: ProQuest Information & Learning. *Indexed:* GendWatch. *Bk. rev.:* 1, 500 words, signed. *Aud.:* Ga, Sa.

"*Transitions* is intended as an educational forum for new ideas and articulation of men's issues," according to its mission statement. The official newsletter of the National Coalition of Free Men, *Transitions* mirrors the goal of the organization, which is to achieve true equity between the sexes. However, because of activist positions among many feminist groups, this journal appears to be at odds with the women's movement. Domestic violence against men, divorce, child custody, and male-bashing are frequently dealt with in *Transitions,* as are the changing roles of women and their impact on men. Obviously a publication with an agenda, this journal nevertheless presents well-documented arguments against gender biases by authorities in the area of men's studies and asks thought-provoking questions of leaders and legislators who have pushed the feminist agenda at all costs. Every library that promotes activist women's issues should subscribe to *Transitions* in order to provide perspective.

Electronic Journals

4891. ***Adventure Time Magazine.*** 1996. m. Ed(s): Gary Winterhalter. Adventure Time Magazine, http://www.adventuretime.com. *Aud.:* Ga.

Here the focus is on activities that challenge strength, endurance, and intelligence. Even if the reader doesn't want to drive a dog team across the frozen tundra or kayak down a dangerous river, men will enjoy the opportunity to read about someone else's adventures in doing those things. Well written, although biased toward difficult sports.

4892. ***DadMag.com.*** irreg. DADMAG.com, LLC, 1333 N Kingsbury, Ste 100, Chicago, IL 60622; InfoCenter@Dadmag.com; http://www.dadmag.com/. *Bk. rev.:* 10, 200 words. *Aud.:* Ga, Sa.

An online journal that celebrates fatherhood, *Dadmag.com* looks at topics from single fatherhood to rearing teens. Feature articles, editorials, reviews, and reader opinion are all included. The enterprising librarian may want to bookmark this site. The quality of the articles is good, and the price is certainly right.

4893. ***Menstuff: the national men's resource.*** Former titles: *Menstuff (Print);* (until 1993): *National Men's Resource Calendar.* 1985. q. Free. Ed(s): Gordon Clay. National Men's Resource Center, PO Box 800, San Anselmo, CA 94979-0800; menstuff@menstuff.org; http://www.menstuff.org. Illus. *Bk. rev.:* Up to 20, 100 words. *Aud.:* Ga, Sa.

Menstuff is the official organ of the National Men's Resource Center, an association founded to support awareness of men's issues and help to end men's isolation. Current news and articles concerning issues such as divorce and child custody, families, abuse, sexuality, violence, and health appear regularly, as do book reviews on as many as 20 books per issue. A calendar of events, lists of men's service organizations, and other sources of information and assistance for men are regular features. This site is essential for the research directory alone. Every library should have this web site bookmarked or hot-linked for quick and easy access.

4894. ***SharpMan.com: the ultimate guide to men's living.*** 1998. w. Ed(s): Y M Reiss. SharpMan Media LLC, 11718 Barrington Ct., No. 702, Los Angeles, CA 90049; http://www.sharpman.com. Circ: 60000. *Aud.:* Ga.

An online lifestyle journal for young men, *SharpMan* emphasizes dating, toys, work, grooming, travel, and health for young men of high school age through age 30. Articles are short, interesting, matter-of-fact, and to the point, and they cover a wide range of topics that young men will find useful in their daily lives. High school librarians especially may want to bookmark this site for future reference.

■ MIDDLE EAST

Donald Altschiller, History Bibliographer, Mugar Memorial Library, Boston University, Boston, MA 02215

Introduction

The term "Middle East" often connotes to many Americans a few immediate associations: the Arab-Israeli conflict, oil, and most recently, the American war against militant Islam and the Iraqi regime. Yet our knowledge of this area, once known as the "cradle of civilization"—the birthplace of three world religions, our system of writing, and agriculture—suffers from several misconceptions about its ethnic and religious diversity. The region is inhabited not only by Arab Muslims and Israeli Jews but by many others: non-Arab Muslims (Kurds, Turks, Iranians), Jews from Arab countries (Morocco, Egypt, Syria, Yemen), and a wide range of Christians (Assyrians, Melkites, Armenians, Maronites, Eastern Orthodox and Roman Catholics). To better understand the historical background and the religious and ethnic complexity of the region, one needs to go beyond the popular press and look at the eclectic range of journals focusing on the Middle East. This section is a major revision of the 11th edition and greatly enlarges the topical range of publications. Although some journals covered in earlier editions have been omitted, I hope the inclusion of lesser-known periodicals will alert librarians to important Middle East topics and geographical areas too often ignored.

Current Contents of Periodicals on the Middle East is an outstanding source for recent articles appearing in a wide variety of both general and specialized journals. (See entry on the *MERIA Journal*, http://meria.idc.ac.il/currentcontents/currentcontents.html.)

Basic Periodicals

International Journal of Middle East Studies, Middle East Journal, Middle East Quarterly, Middle Eastern Studies.

Basic Abstracts and Indexes

Historical Abstracts, Index Islamicus, Index to Jewish Periodicals, Middle East: Abstracts and Index, PAIS International in Print.

4895. ***Arab Studies Journal.*** [ISSN: 1083-4753] 1993. 2x/yr. USD 25 (Individuals, USD 15). Ed(s): Bassam S.A. Haddad. Georgetown University, Center for Contemporary Arab Studies, ICC 485, Washington, DC 20057. *Indexed:* IBSS. *Bk. rev.:* 10-15. *Aud.:* Ac.

Published by graduate students affiliated with the Georgetown University Center for Contemporary Arab Studies and the New York University Hagop Kevorkian Center for Near Eastern Studies, this journal includes multidisciplinary articles on Arab and Middle East Studies. It has presented special issues on Islamic Law and Society, Language and Culture, and Middle East Exceptionalism.

4896. ***Assyrian Star.*** [ISSN: 0004-6051] 1951. bi-m. USD 20. Assyrian-American National Federation, c/o Jatrum Zaia, Box 192, Turlock, CA 95380. Illus., adv. Circ: 1500 Controlled. *Bk. rev.:* Notices and short reviews. *Aud.:* Ga, Ac.

Aimed at the Assyrian diaspora in the United States, this 50-year-old publication contains an eclectic range of articles on Assyrian culture and history (including the only Assyrian on the *Titanic*!) plus announcements and news about community activities in the United States and profiles of notable Assyrian-Americans. The journal also publishes articles on present-day Assyrian communities and individuals living in Iraq, Iran, and elsewhere. Published in both English and Assyrian, it has featured special issues on music, political parties and organizations, and the Assyrian language and calligraphy.

4897. ***Azure: ideas for the Jewish nation.*** [ISSN: 0793-6664] 1996. s-a. USD 26 for 2 yrs. domestic; USD 40 for 2 yrs. foreign; USD 8 newsstand/cover. Ed(s): Daniel Polisar. Shalem Center, 22A Hatzfira St., Jerusalem, Israel; shalem@shalem.org.il; http://www.shalem.org.il/azure.htm. Adv. Refereed. *Indexed:* IJP. *Bk. rev.:* 2-3. *Aud.:* Ga, Ac.

Published by a political institute in Israel, this journal contains articles offering politically conservative perspectives on Jewish nationalism and Israeli history and culture. Critical of some left-wing writings by Israeli historians, this journal provides an important counterbalance to the prevailing historiography in some Israel-oriented journals. A recent article (summer 2002) by Yehoshua Porath, the eminent historian of Palestinian nationalism, debunks many myths by Israeli historical revisionists about the War of Independence.

4898. ***The Cyprus Review: a journal of social, economic and political issues.*** [ISSN: 1015-2881] 1989. s-a. USD 60 (Individuals, USD 40). Ed(s): Nicos Peristianis. Intercollege - Research and Development Center, PO Box 4005, Nicosia, 1700, Cyprus; antoniad@intercol.edu. Adv. Circ: 150. Online: Data-Star; The Dialog Corporation. *Indexed:* IBSS, IPSA, JEL, LingAb, PAIS, PRA, PSA, SociolAb. *Aud.:* Ac.

This semi-annual English-language journal publishes articles on a wide range of social science issues pertaining to Cyprus, including anthropology, economics, history, international relations, and political science, among other topics.

4899. ***Digest of Middle East Studies.*** [ISSN: 1060-4367] 1992. s-a. USD 50. Ed(s): Mohammed Aman. University of Wisconsin at Milwaukee, Milwaukee School of Library and Information Science, PO Box 413, Milwaukee, WI 53201; barajas@slis.wwu.edu. Refereed. Circ: 500. *Indexed:* BRD, ENW. *Bk. rev.:* Various number and length. *Aud.:* Ac.

This journal mostly reviews books, journals, films, and other media devoted to a wide variety of Middle Eastern topics including Islam, the Arab countries, Israel, Iran, Afghanistan, Pakistan, and Turkey. In addition, *DOMES* publishes a few essays in every issue. A compact and nicely designed publication, it informs librarians and library users about many materials not cited or reviewed elsewhere.

4900. ***International Journal of Middle East Studies.*** [ISSN: 0020-7438] 1970. q. plus two bulletins. USD 215; USD 245 combined subscription print & online eds. Ed(s): Juan Cole. Cambridge University Press, The Edinburgh Bldg, Shaftesbury Rd, Cambridge, CB2 2RU, United Kingdom; information@cambridge.org; http://uk.cambridge.org/journals. Illus., adv. Refereed. Vol. ends: Spring. Microform: PQC. Online: Gale Group; JSTOR (Web-based Journal Archive). Reprint: PQC; SWZ. *Indexed:* ABCPolSci, AICP, AbAn, AmH&L, ArtHuCI, CommAb, IBSS, IPSA, L&LBA, MLA-IB, PAIS, PRA, PSA, RRTA, SSCI, SSI, SociolAb, WAE&RSA. *Bk. rev.:* Various number and length. *Aud.:* Ac.

Published under the auspices of the Middle East Studies Association of North America, this quarterly journal publishes articles and book reviews on the Arab world, Israel, Iran, Afghanistan, Turkey, the Caucasus, and Muslim South Asia from the seventh century to the present time. The articles are multidisciplinary, covering history, political science, international relations, economics, anthropology, sociology, and related humanities disciplines including literature, religion, and philosophy. The articles and the extensive book review section are aimed primarily at scholars and academic specialists.

4901. ***Israel Studies.*** [ISSN: 1084-9513] 1996. 3x/yr. USD 85; USD 119 combined subscription print & online eds. Ed(s): Dr. S. Ilan Troen. Indiana University Press, 601 N Morton St, Bloomington, IN 47404; journals@indiana.edu. Adv. Refereed. Circ: 500. Online: EBSCO Publishing; Florida Center for Library Automation; Gale Group; OCLC Online Computer Library Center, Inc.; Project MUSE; ProQuest Information & Learning; RoweCom Information Quest; SoftLine Information; Swets Blackwell; H.W. Wilson. Reprint: PSC. *Indexed:* AmH&L, IJP, IPSA, PRA, SSI. *Aud.:* Ac.

Edited by a distinguished historian, this journal publishes an eclectic range of articles on Israeli history, politics and culture. Especially noteworthy is the inclusion of primary source documents. Nicely designed, this journal also includes photographs and illustrations.

4902. ***The Jerusalem Report.*** [ISSN: 0792-6049] 1990. bi-w. ILS 240 domestic; USD 69 in US & Canada; USD 79.97 elsewhere. Ed(s): David Horovitz. Jerusalem Report, PO Box 1805, Jerusalem, 91017, Israel. Illus., adv. Online: LexisNexis. *Indexed:* IJP. *Aud.:* Ga.

Although this news magazine mainly covers Israel and the Jewish diaspora, it also provides excellent coverage of the wider Middle East. The magazine has earned much respect throughout the region for its critical and hard-hitting articles on Israel and also the Arab world. An excellent publication for both public and academic libraries.

4903. ***Journal of Iranian Research and Analysis.*** Formerly: *C I R A Bulletin.* [ISSN: 1525-9307] 1995. s-a. USD 30. Ed(s): Hamid Zangeneh. Center for Iranian Research and Analysis, 275 Mount Carmel Ave, Hamden, CT 06518-1949; mahmood.monshipour@quinnipiac.edu; http://faculty.quinnipiac.edu/libarts/monshipouri/cira/. *Bk. rev.:* 5. *Aud.:* Ac.

Published by a research institute at Quinnipiac University in Hamden, Connecticut, this specialized journal attempts to "promote free exchange of ideas on Iran and the Middle East." Written by Iranian and non-Iranian scholars, the journal contains both long and short essays, commentaries, and a book review section.

4904. ***The Journal of Israeli History: studies in Zionism and statehood.*** Formerly (until Spring 1993): *Studies in Zionism;* Which superseded (in 1982): *Zionism: Studies in the History of the Zionist Movement and of the Jews in Palestine - Ha-Tsiyonut.* [ISSN: 1353-1042] 1980. s-a. GBP 142 print & online eds. Ed(s): Derek J Penslar, Anita Shapira. Frank Cass Publishers, Crown House, 47 Chase Side, Southgate, London, N14 5BP, United Kingdom; jnlsubs@frankcass.com; http://www.frankcass.com/jnls/. Illus., adv. Sample. Refereed. Vol. ends: Fall. *Indexed:* AmH&L, IBSS, IBZ, IJP, R&TA, RI-1. *Bk. rev.:* Numerous, length varies. *Aud.:* Ac, Sa.

Published earlier under different titles, this fine historical journal has expanded its coverage from the pre-state period and the study of Zionism to multidisciplinary study of the State of Israel, the Israeli-Palestinian conflict and Israel's relation with the Jewish diaspora. One special issue (vol. 20, no. 2/3) contains outstanding essays on both left-wing and right-wing Israeli historical revisionists. Edited by two major scholars, this journal provides an important forum for current research on the history and culture of the Jewish state.

4905. ***Journal of Muslim Minority Affairs.*** Formerly: *Institute of Muslim Minority Affairs. Journal.* [ISSN: 1360-2004] 1979. s-a. GBP 145 (Individuals, GBP 47). Ed(s): Saleha S Mahmood. Carfax Publishing Ltd., 4 Park Sq, Milton Park, Abingdon, OX14 4RN, United Kingdom; enquiry@tandf.co.uk; http://www.tandf.co.uk/. Adv. Online: bigchalk; EBSCO Publishing; Ingenta Select; Northern Light Technology, Inc.; OCLC Online Computer Library Center, Inc.; ProQuest Information & Learning; RoweCom Information Quest. Reprint: PSC. *Indexed:* AmH&L, BAS, IBSS, IBZ, PAIS, PSA, RI-1, SociolAb. *Aud.:* Ac, Sa.

This semi-annual journal is the only periodical devoted to the discussion of Muslim communities in non-Muslim societies. Although Muslims are the largest religious group in the Middle East, this journal has also explored the interactions between Maronite Christians and Muslims in Lebanon and Christian identity in the Jordanian Arab culture. In addition, it has covered the situation of Middle East Muslims in Europe, including Kurdish activism on the Continent and Moroccan youth literature in the Netherlands.

4906. ***Journal of Near Eastern Studies.*** Former titles (until 1941): *American Journal of Semitic Languages and Literatures;* (until 1895): *Hebraica.* [ISSN: 0022-2968] 1884. q. USD 174 print & online eds. (Individuals, USD 50 print & online eds.; Students, USD 31 print & online eds.). Ed(s): Robert D Biggs. University of Chicago Press, Journals Division, PO Box 37005, Chicago, IL 60637; subscriptions@press.uchicago.edu; http://www.journals.uchicago.edu. Illus., index, adv. Refereed. Circ: 2100 Paid. Vol. ends: Oct. Microform: MIM; PMC; PQC. Online: The Dialog Corporation; EBSCO Publishing; Florida Center for Library Automation; Gale Group; JSTOR (Web-based Journal Archive); ProQuest Information & Learning. Reprint: ISI; PQC; PSC; SCH. *Indexed:* A&ATA, AbAn, AnthLit, ArtHuCI, BAS, BHA, HumInd, IBSS, IBZ, L&LBA, MLA-IB, NTA, OTA, PRA, R&TA, RI-1, SSCI. *Aud.:* Ac.

While the other journals in this section mostly cover the modern Middle East, this century-old academic periodical is devoted exclusively to ancient and medieval cultures of the region. The articles are written by scholars and cover archaeology, history, linguistics, religion, law, science, the Hebrew Bible, and Islamic Studies. An eminent journal for larger academic libraries.

4907. ***Journal of Palestine Studies: a quarterly on Palestinian affairs and the Arab-Israeli conflict.*** [ISSN: 0377-919X] 1971. q. USD 125 print & online eds. USD 35 newsstand/cover. Ed(s): Hisham Sharabi, Philip Mattar. University of California Press, Journals Division, 2000 Center St, Ste 303, Berkeley, CA 94704-1223; journals@ucop.edu; http://www.ucpress.edu/journals. Illus., index, adv. Refereed. Circ: 3250 Paid. Vol. ends: Summer. Microform: PQC. Online: Ingenta Select; Northern Light Technology, Inc. Reprint: PQC. *Indexed:* ABCPolSci, AltPI, AmH&L, ArtHuCI, IBSS, IBZ, IPSA, PAIS, PSA, SSCI, SociolAb. *Aud.:* Ac, Sa.

Published by the Washington, D.C.–based Institute of Palestine Studies, this journal is the pre-eminent English-language academic publication devoted to Palestinian Arab history and the Arab-Israeli conflict. Although it publishes some partisan articles on this long-festering conflict, the journal also includes objective reference material not usually accessible elsewhere. In addition, the "Bibliography of Periodical Literature" contains very useful citations.

Journal of South Asian and Middle Eastern Studies. See Asia and the Pacific/South Asia section.

4908. ***Mediterranean Quarterly: a journal of global issues.*** [ISSN: 1047-4552] 1989. q. USD 56 includes online access (Individuals, USD 28 includes online access; USD 14 per issue). Ed(s): Raymond C Ewing, Nikolaos A Stavrou. Duke University Press, 905 W Main St, Ste 18 B, Durham, NC 27701; subscriptions@dukeupress.edu; http://www.dukeupress.edu. Adv. Refereed. Circ: 650. Online: EBSCO Publishing; Ingenta Select; OCLC Online Computer Library Center, Inc.; Project MUSE; RoweCom Information Quest; Swets Blackwell. Reprint: PSC. *Indexed:* ABS&EES, IBSS, IPSA, PAIS, PRA, PSA. *Bk. rev.:* Number and length vary. *Aud.:* Ac.

Although covering an area much broader than the region usually termed the Middle East, this journal publishes many pertinent articles, such as "The Death of the Oslo Accords: Israeli Security Options in the Post-Arafat Era," "Policy toward Algeria after a Decade of Isolation," and "Sudan: Living in Terror." The authors include diplomats, legislators, and scholars, and they provide both analytical and prescriptive viewpoints. Also includes a book review section.

4909. ***Middle East Insight.*** [ISSN: 0731-9371] 1980. bi-m. USD 98 (Individuals, USD 48). Ed(s): George A Nader. International Insight, Inc., 1156 15th St NW #500, Washington, DC 20005-1718; editors@mideastinsight.org; http://www.mideastinsight.org. Illus., adv. Circ: 5000. *Indexed:* IJP, PAIS. *Aud.:* Ga.

Printed on coated paper with color photographs, this journal can honestly boast about "providing the widest possible range of views." The bimonthly publishes eclectic essays on the Arab-Israeli conflict, America's relations with the Arab world, and the militarization of the Middle East, among many other topics.

4910. ***Middle East Journal.*** [ISSN: 0026-3141] 1947. q. USD 48 (Individuals, USD 36). Ed(s): Michael Dunn. Middle East Institute, 1761 N St, N W, Washington, DC 20036; http://www.mideasti.org/. Illus., adv. Refereed. Circ: 4500. Vol. ends: Fall. Microform: PQC. Online: Chadwyck-Healey Incorporated; Florida Center for Library Automation; Gale Group; Northern Light Technology, Inc.; OCLC Online Computer Library Center, Inc.; ProQuest Information & Learning. Reprint: PQC. *Indexed:* ABCPolSci, ABS&EES, AICP, AmH&L, ArtHuCI, BAS, BRD, BRI, CBRI, HumInd, IBSS, IPSA, PAIS, PRA, PSA, RI-1, RRTA, RiskAb, SSCI, SSI, SociolAb. *Bk. rev.:* Various number and length. *Aud.:* Ga, Ac.

Published by one of the oldest Middle East institutes not affiliated with a university, this journal covers the history, politics, and economy of nations from North Africa to Pakistan, the newly emerging nations of Central Asia, and the Caucasus. Written by scholars, the journal publishes accessible articles that may interest fellow academics and also serious lay readers. The book review section called "Recent Publications" should alert acquisition librarians to many publications not generally cited elsewhere.

4911. ***Middle East Quarterly.*** [ISSN: 1073-9467] 1994. q. USD 57.50 (Individuals, USD 40; Students, USD 27). Middle East Forum, 1500 Walnut St, Ste 1050, Philadelphia, PA 19103-4624; mideastq@aol.com. Illus., adv. Refereed. Circ: 2100 Paid. Online: EBSCO Publishing; Florida Center for Library Automation; Gale Group; Ingenta Select; LexisNexis. Reprint: PSC. *Indexed:* BRI, CBRI, IBSS, IJP, IPSA, IndIslam, PAIS, PSA, SociolAb. *Aud.:* Ga, Ac.

Several years before the 9/11 terrorist attacks, this journal—probably alone among all Middle East publications—published articles warning about the imminent dangers posed by Islamic extremists and Osama bin Laden. An article in *MEQ* predicted that terrorists would hijack airplanes and crash them into skyscrapers. Unapologetically asserting its goal to "define and promote American interests in the Middle East," this journal has published pathbreaking essays on the United States and the Arab world, the Arab-Israeli and other regional conflicts, and the rise of terrorism.

4912. ***Middle East Report.*** Former titles (until 1988): *M E R I P Middle East Report;* (until 1986): *M E R I P Reports;* Which incorporates (1970-1973): *Pakistan Forum.* [ISSN: 0899-2851] 1971. q. USD 70 domestic; USD 92 in Canada & Mexico; USD 84 elsewhere. Middle East Research & Information Project, 1500 Massachusetts Ave NW, Suite 119, Washington, DC 20005. Illus., index, adv. Refereed. Circ: 6200. Microform: PQC. Online: EBSCO Publishing; ingenta.com; JSTOR (Web-based Journal Archive); OCLC Online Computer Library Center, Inc.; RoweCom Information Quest; Swets Blackwell. *Indexed:* AltPI, GeogAbPG, IBSS, IPSA, IndIslam, PAIS, PSA, SWA. *Aud.:* Ga, Ac, Sa.

Originally published as a six-page mimeographed newsletter in 1971, *Middle East Report* has become the leading left-oriented publication offering critical analysis of American foreign and economic policy in this region. The journal is thematic: Some issues are devoted to individual countries, including Turkey, Lebanon, and Iran, among others. Topical issues have also covered migration, labor, gender and sexuality, political Islam, and urbanization. *Middle East Report* has devoted particular attention to the Arab-Israeli conflict and, most recently, the war in Iraq.

4913. ***Middle East Studies Association Bulletin.*** [ISSN: 0026-3184] 1967. 2x/yr. Membership, USD 90. Ed(s): Ann M Lesch. Middle East Studies Association of North America, Inc., University of Arizona, 1643 E Helen St, Tucson, AZ 85721; mesana@u.arizona.edu. Illus., index, adv. Circ: 2200 Paid. Vol. ends: Dec. *Indexed:* ABS&EES, AICP, AmH&L, BHA, IBSS, IBZ, IPSA, PSA, RI-1. *Bk. rev.:* Various number and length. *Aud.:* Ac.

Although this journal publishes primarily book reviews, each issue contains a few essays on diverse Middle East topics. In addition, the *Bulletin* occasionally publishes lists of recent doctoral degree recipients, lists of conference programs, and some reviews of audiovisual materials. The web site provides access to selected articles.

4914. ***Middle Eastern Studies.*** [ISSN: 0026-3206] 1964. bi-m. GBP 350 print & online eds. Ed(s): Sylvia Kedourie. Frank Cass Publishers, Crown House, 47 Chase Side, Southgate, London, N14 5BP, United Kingdom; jnlsubs@frankcass.com; http://www.frankcass.com/jnls/. Illus., adv. Sample. Refereed. Microform: PQC. Online: bigchalk; EBSCO Publishing; Florida Center for Library Automation; Gale Group; Ingenta Select; Northern Light Technology, Inc.; OCLC Online Computer Library Center, Inc.; ProQuest Information & Learning. *Indexed:* ABCPolSci, AbAn, AmH&L, ArtHuCI, BrHumI, GeogAbPG, IBSS, IBZ, IPSA, PSA, SSCI, SSI, SociolAb. *Aud.:* Ac, Sa.

Founded by the late scholar Elie Kedourie and now edited by his wife Sylvia Kedourie, this journal publishes articles on the history of the modern Middle East. A demanding scholar, Prof. Kedourie established a possibly unique policy among academic journals: no biographical notes on contributors. "I want articles to be judged on their merit and not with reference to the author's background." This 40-year-old publication still maintains its scholarly integrity and is one of the major academic journals covering the Middle East.

4915. ***Nineveh.*** [ISSN: 0749-5919] 1978. 3x/yr. USD 20 domestic; USD 25 Canada; USD 30 elsewhere. Ed(s): Robert Karoukian. Assyrian Foundation of America, PO Box 2660, Berkeley, CA 94702; sargonmichael@yahoo.com; http://www.assyrianfoundation.org. *Bk. rev.:* 5-10. *Aud.:* Ga, Ac, Sa.

This unusual publication features articles on Assyrians, the indigenous people of Iraq, southwest Turkey, and parts of Syria and Iran. Despite persecution, this community remarkably has been able to maintain its distinct culture, literature, and language. The magazine publishes a veritable smorgasbord of items on this ancient Christian group: memoirs of immigrants, organizational news, excerpts from scholarly journals, book reviews, discussion of artifacts and archaeology, sport news, poetry, and recipes. The journal has published excerpts of documents captured during the 1991 Gulf War discussing Iraqi persecution of Assyrians. This illustrated journal is published in English and Assyrian.

4916. ***Palestine - Israel Journal of Politics, Economics and Culture.*** [ISSN: 0793-1395] 1994. q. USD 60 (Individuals, USD 50). Ed(s): Ziad Abu Zayyad, Daniel Bar-Tal. Palestine - Israel Journal of Politics, Economics and Culture, 4 El Hariri St., Jerusalem, , Israel; pij@palnet.com; http://www.pij.org. Index, adv. Sample. Refereed. *Indexed:* AltPI, IBSS, IJP, PAIS. *Aud.:* Hs, Ga, Ac, Sa.

Edited and written by Israeli Jews and Palestinian Arabs, this unique English-language journal provides varying perspectives on the contentious issues of their conflict, mostly from a leftist perspective. The journal has an admirable aim: "to promote rapprochement and better understanding between peoples, and it strives to discuss all issues without prejudice and without taboos."

4917. ***Perceptions: journal of international affairs.*** [ISSN: 1300-8641] q. Ministry of Foreign Affairs, Center for Strategic Research, Kircicegi Sok 8-3, Ankara, 06700, Turkey. *Indexed:* PAIS. *Aud.:* Ac,Sa.

Although Turkey is the largest country in the Middle East, its foreign policy receives surprisingly less mainstream media coverage than its neighbors. Published by a "consultative body of the Turkish Ministry of Foreign Affairs with the responsibility of bringing to the attention of decision makers independent, unbiased views," this journal offers foreign policy perspectives from both Turkish and other diplomats in addition to Turkish academics.

4918. ***Al- Raida.*** [ISSN: 0259-9953] 1976. q. USD 25 domestic; USD 30 foreign. Ed(s): Dr. Samira Aghacy. Beirut University College, Institute for Women's Studies in the Arab World, PO Box 13 5053, Beirut, , Lebanon; al-raida@lau.edu.lb. Illus., adv. Circ: 700. *Indexed:* CWI, SWA. *Aud.:* Ac, Sa.

The Arab Human Development Report (United Nations Development Programme, 2002) reported the serious plight of women throughout the Arab world. This feminist journal publishes articles on all aspects of women's lives in this region, providing coverage of topics seldom, if ever, discussed in other publications: battered women, women and the environment, incarcerated Arab women, and also women's sexuality. Although many articles focus on Lebanon, this journal also publishes essays about Arab women in many countries.

4919. *Turkish Studies.* [ISSN: 1468-3849] 2000. 3x/yr. GBP 120 print & online eds. Ed(s): Barry Rubin. Frank Cass Publishers, Crown House, 47 Chase Side, Southgate, London, N14 5BP, United Kingdom; jnlsubs@frankcass.com; http://www.frankcass.com/jnls/. Adv. Sample. Refereed. Vol. ends: Fall. *Indexed:* AmH&L, PSA. *Bk. rev.:* Various number and length. *Aud.:* Ac.

Edited by the prolific scholar Barry Rubin, this important journal publishes a wide range of articles by scholars from Turkey, Israel, Europe, and elsewhere. It has published special issues on political parties in Turkey and on Turkey-European Union relations. It also contains an excellent book review section.

4920. *Turkish Studies Association Bulletin.* [ISSN: 0275-6048] 1976. s-a. USD 50 (Individuals, USD 30). Turkish Studies Association, c/o Douglas Howard, Ed, Calvin College, Grand Rapids, MI 49546. Adv. Circ: 500. *Bk. rev.:* Various number and length. *Aud.:* Ac.

Published by the nonprofit, nonpolitical Turkish Studies Association founded in 1971, this journal includes short research articles, reports of meetings and conferences, book reviews, and notices from members.

Electronic Journals

4921. *M E R I A Journal.* 1997. q. Free. Ed(s): Barry Rubin. Global Research in International Affairs, Interdisciplinary Center, Herzliya, Israel; gloria@idc.ac.il; http://gloria.idc.ac.il. Refereed. Circ: 10065 Controlled. *Aud.:* Ga, Ac, Sa.

MERIA is an outstanding gateway to important web sites on the Middle East. In addition, it provides access to the *MERIA Journal*, an electronic publication that reaches a reported 18,000 readers including leading policy makers and academics. The site contains "MERIA News," a monthly item with short articles and announcements and the invaluable "Current Contents of Periodicals on the Middle East." Especially useful are the "MERIA Research Guides," offering bibliographies and web resources compiled by country experts. *MERIA* attracted international attention before the Iraq war in 2003 when the British media reported that an official British government publication used material from the site without citing the source. *MERIA* is a major resource for both scholars and general readers.

4922. *Middle East Media Research Institute.* 1998. d. Middle East Media Research Institute, PO Box 27837, Washington, DC 20038-7837. *Aud.:* Ga, Ac, Sa.

Following the 9/11 attacks, many Americans have engaged in much public self-criticism about their lack of knowledge of the Arab and Muslim world. This web site is an essential source for acquiring a deeper understanding and knowledge of current Middle East affairs and viewpoints. The MEMRI site provides translations of the Arabic-, Farsi-, and Hebrew-language media. The topics covered are remarkably broad: the United States and the Middle East, inter-Arab relations, Arab-Israeli conflict, jihad and terrorism, and reform in the Arab and Muslim world. The translations are often unique, providing an opportunity to read the same material that is published and widely disseminated throughout the region. The translations are verbatim, and the editors offer no commentary. Some Middle East scholars have called this the most invaluable source for current information on the Middle East.

■ MILITARY

John R. Vallely, Catalog Librarian, Standish Library, Siena College, Loudonville, NY 12211; vallely@siena.edu

Introduction

Given recent world events, magazines and monographs that treat military issues will undoubtedly continue to prosper for the forseeable future. Librarians need to note the distinction between the two types of publishing that are generally grouped under the heading "military." The first category is a journal that discusses contemporary military and security affairs and weapons. These journals are considered as "national security" in scope. The second type, "military history," rarely devotes space to current events, but instead concentrate on wars, battles, campaigns, arms, and personalities from the military past. An apt example of the former is *Parameters*, while the appropriately titled *Journal of Military History* is an example of the latter. Librarians should also note that the term "military" usually includes topics devoted to air and sea warfare as well as fighting done on land.

Basic Periodicals

Hs: *Airman, All Hands, Marines, Soldiers*; Ga: *Air Force Magazine, Armed Forces Journal, Army, Aviation History, Defense Monitor, Leatherneck, Military History, MHQ*; Ac: *AirForces Monthly, Airpower, Armed Forces and Society, Armed Forces Journal, Civil Wars, Defense Monitor, Jane's Defence Weekly, Jane's Navy International, Journal of Military History, The Journal of Slavic Military Studies, The Journal of Strategic Studies, Military Review, Naval War College Review, Parameters, RUSI Journal.*

Basic Abstracts and Indexes

Air University Library Index to Military Periodicals.

4923. *The Air and Space Power Journal.* Former titles (until 2002): *The Aerospace Power Journal;* (until 1999): *Airpower Journal;* (until 1987): *Air University Review.* 1947. q. USD 24 domestic; USD 30 foreign. Ed(s): Lt.Col. Anthony Cain. U.S. Air Force, Air University, Maxwell Air Force Base, 401 Chennault Cir, Montgomery, AL 36112-6428; apj@maxwell.af.mil; http://www.airpower.maxwell.af.mil. Illus., index. Sample. Refereed. Circ: 20000 Controlled. Vol. ends: Winter. Microform: PQC. Online: Northern Light Technology, Inc. *Indexed:* ABS&EES, AUNI, BAS, EngInd, IBZ, IUSGP, PAIS, PRA. *Bk. rev.:* Number varies, 200–500 words. *Aud.:* Ac.

The U.S. Air Force's Air University, located at Maxwell Air Force Base, is the center for advanced study of airpower, air and space warfare, and the role of an air force in overall national security within the American defense community. Its publication, *The Air and Space Power Journal*, offers serving officers the opportunity to contribute scholarly essays that contribute to the ongoing doctrinal and organizational debates. The articles cover questions of unit structure, training and managing personnel, critiques of tactical and strategic policies, and other topics relevant to the Air Force and its future. Given the importance of airpower to American security planning for the twenty-first century, *The Air and Space Power Journal* should be considered for academic libraries. Public libraries located in military communities should also subscribe.

4924. *Air Force Magazine: the force behind the force.* Formerly: *Air Force and Space Digest.* [ISSN: 0730-6784] 1942. m. USD 30. Ed(s): Robert S Dudney. Air Force Association, 1501 Lee Hwy, Arlington, VA 22209-1198; http://www.afa.org. Illus., adv. Circ: 200000 Paid. Vol. ends: Dec. *Indexed:* ABS&EES, AUNI, C&ISA, EngInd, IAA, PRA. *Bk. rev.:* 5, 150–200 words. *Aud.:* Ga, Ac.

Students, scholars, and aviation buffs interested in charting changes and trends in U.S. Air Force doctrine and institutional planning will find *Air Force Magazine* a useful, indeed critical, resource. Sponsored by the Air Force Association, it typically carries articles on policy that are written by officers charged with developing such positions or who served in command situations where such positions were part of their daily assignment. The journal is also extremely useful for tracking Air Force unit tables of organization and force structure, gathering data on high ranking officer assignments, and a great deal of other internal Air Force matters. The May issue, "Air Force in Facts and Figures" is a treasure trove of useful information. Interested readers may also check the Air Force Association's web site for related stories. Academic libraries should consider this journal. Public libraries will find it accessible to many readers.

Air Force Times. See under *Army Times.*

4925. *Air International.* Formerly: *Air Enthusiast.* [ISSN: 0306-5634] 1971. m. GBP 40.80 domestic; USD 73.60 United States; GBP 3.40 newsstand/cover per issue. Ed(s): Malcolm English. Key Publishing Ltd., PO Box 100, Stamford, PE9 1XQ, United Kingdom; http://www.keypublishing.com. Illus., index, adv. Circ: 16014. *Indexed:* C&ISA, IAA. *Aud.:* Ga.

Intended for those military aviation readers in the general public who possess a relatively keen awareness of high-tech weapons systems and modern warplane technology, *Air International* features detailed analyses of contemporary military airplanes, airpower doctrine, information on advances in weaponry and avionics, and plans and trends in the world's air forces. Industry news and brief aircraft and technology updates add to the data presented in the more in-depth essays. Heavily illustrated and bursting with facts and data, it should find an audience in public libraries with patrons interested in aviation.

4926. *AirForces Monthly: the world's leading military aviation magazine.* [ISSN: 0955-7091] 1988. m. GBP 40.80 domestic; USD 75.75 foreign; GBP 3.40 newsstand/cover per issue. Ed(s): Alan Warnes. Key Publishing Ltd., PO Box 100, Stamford, PE9 1XQ, United Kingdom; ann.saundry@keypublishing.com; http://www.keypublishing.com. Illus., adv. Circ: 25787. *Aud.:* Ga, Ac.

At first glance, *AirForces Monthly* appears to be yet another example of the slick, glossy, profusely illustrated aviation journals competing for dollars from a public with an insatiable appetite for the latest news on advanced combat aircraft. A closer examination reveals a resource that combines high-quality content and data to go along with the attractive format. Each issue contains six to eight articles on diverse, current military aviation subjects (e.g., the Pakistani Air Force Academy, Sweden's air force, the Royal Air Force's transport fleet) that provide an accurate and timely introduction to the topic in a style relatively free of extraneous technical jargon. The main articles are accompanied by brief but detailed updates and news items on international air forces and related defense subjects. Intelligently written and beautifully laid out, *AirForces Monthly* should find audiences in both academic and public libraries.

Airman. See under *Marines.*

4927. *Airpower: the story of combat aviation.* [ISSN: 1067-1048] 1971. bi-m. USD 25; USD 31 foreign. Ed(s): Joseph V Mizrahi. Sentry Books, Inc., 10718 White Oak Ave, Box 3324, Granada Hills, CA 91344. Illus., adv. Circ: 80000. *Aud.:* Ga.

An aviation history magazine with emphasis on military aircraft and history, *Airpower* and its mirror image, *Wings*, is one of those rare publications where the captions that accompany the dozens of illustrations and line drawings may contain more useful information than the articles themselves. Each issue will customarily have two illustration-rich essays centering on a detailed examination of a specific military aircraft or an overview of aerial operations in a particular theater of operations/battle/campaign. Samples from issues are discussions of two late World War II Japanese aircraft and early U.S. Air Force jet fighters. Each issue also contains ordering information on a large number of earlier issues. A veteran of the long and intense competition in aviation journals, *Airpower* will continue to occupy a front rank. Public libraries could add *Airpower* or *Wings*.

All Hands. See under *Marines.*

4928. *Armed Forces and Society: an interdisciplinary journal on military institutions, civil-military relations, arms control and peacekeeping, and conflict management.* [ISSN: 0095-327X] 1972. q. USD 220 (Individuals, USD 76). Ed(s): Patricia M Shields. Transaction Publishers, 35 Berrue Circle, Rutgers University, Piscataway, NJ 08854-8042; trans@transactionpub.com; http://www.transactionpub.com. Illus., index, adv. Refereed. Circ: 600. Vol. ends: Summer. Microform: PQC. Online: EBSCO Publishing; Florida Center for Library Automation; Gale Group; Ingenta Select; OCLC Online Computer Library Center, Inc.; ProQuest Information & Learning. Reprint: PSC. *Indexed:* ABCPolSci, ABS&EES, AUNI, AgeL, AmH&L, BAS, BRI, CBRI, EngInd, IBSS, IBZ, IPSA, PAIS, PRA, PSA, PsycholAb, RI-1, SSCI, SSI, SociolAb. *Bk. rev.:* 5–10, 300–500 words. *Aud.:* Ac.

The interplay between social forces and the military forces they represent and safeguard continues to grow in interest among academics. While the general public tends to concentrate on battle and war studies, scholarly attention is increasingly drawn towards military sociology. *Armed Forces and Society* is, as the title suggests, an exception to this general rule. A publication of the prestigious Inter-University Seminar on Armed Forces and Society of Northwestern University, it is the single most reputable journal in the military sociology field. The essays are especially rewarding for students interested in the role of women in international armed forces, the condition of ethnic peoples in uniform, and the relationships of soldiers within military units. The five to seven articles are all accompanied by bibliographic citations and are written by specialists in the field. An essential resource for academic libraries.

4929. *Armed Forces Journal.* Former titles (until Feb. 2003): *Armed Forces Journal International;* (until 1973): *Armed Forces Journal.* 1863. m. USD 60 in US & Canada; USD 145 elsewhere. Ed(s): John G Roos. Army Times Publishing Co., 6883 Commercial Dr, Springfield, VA 22159; afji@afji.com; http://www.afji.com. Illus., adv. Sample. Circ: 40000 Controlled and free. Vol. ends: Dec. Microform: PQC. Online: EBSCO Publishing; Gale Group. Reprint: PQC. *Indexed:* ABS&EES, AUNI, EngInd. *Aud.:* Ga, Ac.

This is a very reliable, often authoritative periodical resource for timely information and analysis on the status of the U.S. armed forces, the state of Defense Department short and long range planning, congressional relations with the Pentagon, the defense industry and the weapons systems it produces, and detailed discussions of the American defense budget and the key players who control it. Indeed, the ongoing critique of budget issues separates *Armed Forces Journal International* from most other magazines that treat national security topics. The editorial staff and writers have an intimate knowledge of current defense issues and a refreshing awareness of how these issues play out inside the Beltway. The critical, at times controversial stories that result have earned it a place in the front ranks in military publishing. The articles are not overly long, but the writers do assume a substantial amount of knowledge on the part of the reader. Special updates on particular U.S. services or on specific foreign states' present security capabilities are included with updates on weapon systems, procurement, industry overviews, and discussions of Capitol Hill personalities and committee oversight. A most valuable tool for its independent and critical view of the contemporary American defense establishment and the world in which it operates. Suitable for public as well as college and university libraries.

4930. *Army.* [ISSN: 0004-2455] 1950. m. Non-members, USD 33; USD 3 newsstand/cover per issue. Ed(s): Mary Blake French. Association of the U.S. Army, 2425 Wilson Blvd, Arlington, VA 22201-3326; armymag@ausa.org; http://www.ausa.org. Illus., adv. Circ: 85000 Paid. Vol. ends: Dec. *Indexed:* ABS&EES, AUNI. *Bk. rev.:* 2–3, 500 words. *Aud.:* Ga, Ac.

Army provides informative and generally well-written essays on the current status of the U.S. Army as well as articles on planning for future force structure and weapons systems. Published by soldiers with extensive experience and intended for active duty officers and individuals from the civilian sector interested in the environment in which the Army must operate, it offers examples of the critical evaluation of military doctrine and the pressures that provide the undercurrent for revising the relevant Army training and operational procedures and practices. It is sponsored by the Association of the U.S. Army, and the authors' views reflect those of the officer corps in general. Smaller updates on recent Army and Army-related news items and overviews of pending legislation are included. For academic libraries and selected public libraries.

4931. *Army Times.* [ISSN: 0004-2595] 1940. w. USD 52. Ed(s): Tobias Naegele. Army Times Publishing Co., 6883 Commercial Dr, Springfield, VA 22159; http://www.armytimes.com. Illus., adv. Circ: 316954 Paid. Microform: PQC. Reprint: PQC. *Indexed:* AUNI. *Aud.:* Ga, Ac.

The four U.S. military weekly newspapers (*Army Times, Air Force Times, Marine Times,* and *Navy Times*) are comparable in type, format, and appeal. All are tabloids and are aimed at active duty, reserve, and retired personnel from the nation's uniformed services. The serviceman and woman and their dependents are kept informed in a timely fashion of those "quality of life" matters that are critical to their personal, professional, and social lives within such large and impersonal bureaucracies. Topics like pay, health benefits and options, housing and housing allowances, promotion, and food are interspersed with reports on uniforms, training, unit structure, weapons systems, the defense budget, and public policy related to the military. Any library located near a base or serving military personnel and their families should carry the relevant publication.

Similar in scope are the three younger siblings of *Army Times* (same publisher and address), noted below.

Air Force Times [ISSN: 0002-2403] 1947. w. USD 52. Lance Bacon. www.armytimes.com. Illus., adv. Circ: 90000. Microform: UMI.

Navy Times [ISSN: 0028-1697] 1951. w. USD 52. Alex Neill. www.armytimes.com. Illus., adv. Circ: 90000. Microform: UMI.

Marine Corps Times 1940. w. USD 52. Rob Colenso, Jr. Illus., adv.

4932. *Aviation History.* Former titles: *Aviation; Aviation Heritage.* [ISSN: 1076-8858] 1990. bi-m. USD 17.95 domestic; USD 23.95 Canada; USD 3.99 newsstand/cover per issue. Ed(s): Carl Von Wodtke, Arthur H Sanfelici. PRIMEDIA Special Interest Publications, History Group, 741 Miller Dr, S E, D2, Leesburg, VA 20175; brentd@cowles.com; http://www.thehistorynet.com. Illus., adv. Circ: 73365 Paid. *Aud.:* Ga.

A popular magazine aimed squarely at the military and aircraft enthusiast, *Aviation History* concentrates on action-intensive articles presented in a heavily illustrated format. Sample topics from recent issues include a B-24 bombing raid on Magdeburg in World War II, early U.S. Marine jet fighters, and Slovakia's leading fighter ace of the Second World War. Shorter pieces on significant pilots, planes, and aircraft designers and aviation personalities combine with a number of advertisements to complete each issue. For public and high school libraries.

4933. *Civil Wars.* [ISSN: 1369-8249] 1998. q. GBP 197 print & online eds. Ed(s): David Keithly, Caroline Kennedy-Pipe. Frank Cass Publishers, Crown House, 47 Chase Side, Southgate, London, N14 5BP, United Kingdom; jnlsubs@frankcass.com; http://www.frankcass.com/jnls/. Illus., index, adv. Sample. Refereed. Vol. ends: Winter. *Indexed:* AmH&L, IPSA, PSA. *Aud.:* Ac.

Civil wars, ethnic conflicts, and intrastate racial and religious tensions are a continuing problem for nation states in the developing world as well as in those regions where one expects to find more stable governments. *Civil Wars* attempts to offer a forum for scholars and qualified observers to not only report on the civil strife in specific regions and countries but to present the forces behind the fighting and offer solutions acceptable as alternatives to the violence. The coverage is international, and the journal offers readers the opportunity to keep abreast of unrest and internal conflict in parts of the world not normally followed in such detail in traditional news outlets. While other popular and scholarly periodicals may carry articles and updates on thses events, *Civil Wars* provides a balanced and reasonably comprehensive format in a single journal. As peacekeeping initiatives become more common for the United States, the United Nations, NATO, and other bodies, *Civil Wars* will garner a larger audience. For academic libraries.

4934. *Defense Monitor.* [ISSN: 0195-6450] 1972. 10x/yr. USD 45. Ed(s): Col. Daniel Smith. Center for Defense Information, 1779 Massachusetts Ave, N W, Washington, DC 20036-2109; cdi@igc.apc.org; jmason@cdi.org; http://www.cdi.org. Illus. Circ: 35000. Vol. ends: Dec. *Indexed:* AUNI, PRA. *Aud.:* Ga, Ac.

Readers seeking intelligent and reasoned alternative arguments to White House and Defense Department military policy and short- and long-range planning on national security initiatives will find a home with *Defense Monitor.* The editor and writers are highly informed observers of internal Washington, indeed many are retired officers, and they are competent to critically evaluate policy decisions and weapons procurement efforts with other specialists. The analyses and dissection of the Defense Department's annual budget is far superior to that found in most other periodicals and is clearly the journal's strength. As reasoned and informed a critique of contemporary military and security policy as one can find, *Defense Monitor* belongs in all academic libraries. Public libraries should give this journal serious consideration.

4935. *Jane's Defence Weekly.* Formerly (until 1984): *Jane's Defence Review.* [ISSN: 0265-3818] 1980. w. GBP 220 domestic; GBP 230 in Europe; USD 350 in the Americas. Ed(s): Carol Reed. Jane's Information Group, Sentinel House, 163 Brighton Rd, Coulsdon, CR5 2YH, United Kingdom; info@janes.co.uk; http://www.janes.com. Illus., adv. Online: Factiva; Gale Group. *Indexed:* AUNI, C&ISA. *Aud.:* Ga, Ac, Sa.

Jane's Defence Weekly is one of the better known of the Jane's Information Group's national security and military technology publications. The articles, while usually brief, are uniformly well researched, accurate, and topical. Illustrations and charts complement and expand upon the text. The articles cover all aspects of the contemporary scene: naval, ground, air, space, intelligence, and the technology and weapon systems that are relevant to them. While authoritative and highly respected, it is most assuredly not for the uninitiated. The defense and technical jargon can be difficult even for the specialist to grapple with. An essential resource for college and university libraries and for those public libraries with a clientele interested in current military topics and high-technology military issues.

4936. *Jane's Navy International.* Formerly (until 1995): *Navy International;* Which incorporated (in 1986): *Combat Craft;* Which was formerly: *Navy.* [ISSN: 1358-3719] 1895. 10x/yr. GBP 120 domestic; GBP 125 in Europe; USD 185 in the Americas. Ed(s): P Howard. Jane's Information Group, Sentinel House, 163 Brighton Rd, Coulsdon, CR5 2YH, United Kingdom; info@janes.co.uk; http://www.janes.com. Illus., adv. Circ: 2500. Online: Gale Group. *Aud.:* Ac, Ga.

Jane's and navies are two terms that frequently merge into one when speaking with naval officers and civilians who are interested in naval policy. Begun in the latter part of the nineteenth century by an Englishman who was long attracted to warships, Jane's is now a mini-industry of naval and defense publishing. As the name suggests, *Jane's Navy International* is a journal specializing in in-depth treatment of contemporary navies, warships and warship design, naval policies of all nations with maritime interests, and general discussions of the political security matters that drive naval strategy. Illustrations and charts add immeasurably to the reader's ability to follow the reporting. An excellent source for academic and public libraries specializing in the topic.

4937. *Joint Force Quarterly.* [ISSN: 1070-0692] 1993. q. USD 22 domestic. Ed(s): Lt.Col. James J Caralano. National Defense University, NDU-NSS-JFQ, 300 Fifth Ave (Bldg 62, Rm 212), Washington, DC 20319-5066; jfq1@ndu.edu; http://www.dtic.mil/doctrine/jel/jfq_pubs/index.htm. Illus., index. Sample. Circ: 36622. Online: EBSCO Publishing; Florida Center for Library Automation; Gale Group; ProQuest Information & Learning. *Indexed:* AUNI, PAIS. *Bk. rev.:* 4, 500 words. *Aud.:* Ac.

Joint operations is one of the most significant trends shaping American military thought and posture in the post–Cold War environment. It implies restructuring forces to include shared command and responsibilities on the part of all the nation's armed forces. *Joint Force Quarterly* is published by the National Defense University and may be taken as the "official" voice for joint operations within the American military establishment. Each of the eight or more articles per issue address the problems inherent in such a radical departure from traditional practices while simultaneously offering the latest doctrinal philosophy in addressing these problems. While the concept of military operations being conducted by unified command staffs may seem esoteric to some, it is a vital part of contemporary U.S. military policy. A journal that debates and highlights these issues should be in academic libraries and public libraries that serve a military population.

4938. *Journal of Military History.* Formerly (until vol.52): *Military Affairs.* [ISSN: 0899-3718] 1937. q. USD 75; USD 105 combined subscription. Ed(s): Larry Bland, Bruce Vandervort. Society for Military History, George C Marshall Library, Virginia Military Institute, Lexington, VA 24450-1600; http://www.smh-hq.org/. Illus., index, adv. Sample. Refereed. Circ: 3300 Paid. Vol. ends: Oct. Microform: PQC. Online: bigchalk; Chadwyck-Healey Incorporated; Gale Group; JSTOR (Web-based Journal Archive); Northern Light Technology, Inc.; OCLC Online Computer Library Center, Inc.; ProQuest Information & Learning. Reprint: PSC. *Indexed:* ABS&EES, AUNI, AmH&L, ArtHuCI, BAS, BRI, CBRI, HumInd, IBZ, SSCI. *Bk. rev.:* Number varies, 200-300 words. *Aud.:* Ga, Ac.

The most respected of the scholarly journals in the military history field, *Journal of Military History* is published by the Society for Military History, the most prestigious of the many and varied historical associations concerned with the study of the military past. Each issue typically contains three or more historical essays buttressed by the required number of bibliographic citations and featuring writing styles that easily stand the test of comparison with leading scholarly journals from other academic disciplines. Topics are not limited to the American military experience and are capable of being read and understood by nonscholars. The book review section is extensive, as is the section listing new periodical literature of interest to military historians. Members of the Society for Military History receive a subscription as part of their membership. A necessary addition to all college and university libraries. Public libraries may wish to consider it as a supplement to popular military periodicals.

4939. *The Journal of Slavic Military Studies.* Formerly (until 1993): *Journal of Soviet Military Studies.* [ISSN: 1351-8046] 1988. q. GBP 263 print & online eds. Ed(s): David Glantz, Christopher Donnelly. Frank Cass Publishers, Crown House, 47 Chase Side, Southgate, London, N14 5BP, United Kingdom; jnlsubs@frankcass.com; http://www.frankcass.com/jnls/. Illus., adv. Sample. Refereed. *Indexed:* AUNI, AmH&L, IBSS, IBZ, IPSA, PSA. *Bk. rev.:* Various number and length. *Aud.:* Ac.

Interest in Russian and Eastern European political and military policy and history has certainly lost the attention of many since the fall of the Soviet Union. Scholarship in the field has benefited from the opening of archives and the ability of former soldiers and academics within those societies to perform their research without being restrained by closed research facilities or official obstruction. The former *Journal of Soviet Military Studies* continues to publish scholarly essays on the diverse national security issues within the former Soviet bloc. Libraries and educators should remain aware of the volatile nature in the regions covered and retain quality journals that explore defense and political issues in Russia and in its neighboring states. A well-received, scholarly journal whose articles discuss the uncertain world in which these societies now find themselves, *Journal of Slavic Military Studies* will assuredly deserve to remain in academic libraries that support Russian Studies and current international affairs.

4940. *The Journal of Strategic Studies.* [ISSN: 0140-2390] 1978. q. GBP 268 print & online eds. Ed(s): John Gooch. Frank Cass Publishers, Crown House, 47 Chase Side, Southgate, London, N14 5BP, United Kingdom; jnlsubs@frankcass.com; http://www.frankcass.com/jnls/. Illus., index, adv. Sample. Refereed. Microform: PQC. Online: EBSCO Publishing; Ingenta Select. *Indexed:* AmH&L, ArtHuCI, BAS, BrHumI, EngInd, IBSS, IPSA, PSA, PsycholAb, SSCI, SociolAb. *Bk. rev.:* 11–12, 500 words. *Aud.:* Ac.

The Journal of Strategic Studies concentrates on national security, military policy, and international relations from the twentieth century to today's headlines. An important scholarly contributor for historians, political scientists, military historians, and economists, the journal's essays will certainly be difficult for the reader who is not well versed in the issues or time periods under discussion. The student of such debates, and even the well-informed generalist, will benefit from the comprehensive coverage and in-depth information provided. The book review section ensures the reader will be kept reasonably current with new monograph literature in the discipline. For university and college libraries.

4941. *Leatherneck: magazine of the Marines.* [ISSN: 0023-981X] 1917. m. USD 29 domestic; USD 3.50 newsstand/cover. Ed(s): Walter G Ford. Marine Corps Association, Bldg. 715, MCB, PO Box 1775, Quantico, VA 22134. Illus., index, adv. Sample. Circ: 91981. Vol. ends: Dec. Microform: PQC. Online: bigchalk; Northern Light Technology, Inc.; ProQuest Information & Learning. Reprint: PQC. *Bk. rev.:* 5, 200 words. *Aud.:* Hs, Ga.

Named after the Revolutionary War nickname of the United States Marines, *Leatherneck* is published by the Marine Corps Association and stands as an unabashed and unapologetic defender of Marine Corps history and traditions. The historical articles cover selected campaigns, battles, and personalities from the Marine Corps' long and colorful past. The writing is not critical but concentrates on describing the courage and sacrifice that lay at the foundation of this elite branch of service. Updates on the contemporary Marine Corps, brief book reviews of new works on Marine Corps history and related topics, and obituaries of recently deceased officers and enlisted personnel supplement the regular essays. While the battle studies and biographies can be enjoyed by all readers, the journal will undoubtedly be of most interest to those with a Marine Corps connection. Public libraries should consider this magazine.

4942. *M H Q: the quarterly journal of military history.* [ISSN: 1040-5992] 1988. q. USD 39.95 domestic; USD 49.95 Canada; USD 59.95 elsewhere. Primedia Enthusiast Group, 741 Miller Dr, SE, Ste D-2, Leesburg, VA 20175; http://www.primedia.com. Illus., index, adv. Circ: 30000 Paid. Vol. ends: Summer. *Indexed:* AmH&L, RGPR. *Bk. rev.:* 2-4, 200-300 words. *Aud.:* Hs, Ga, Ac.

Popular history journals are routinely condemned by academics as being sophomoric in their approach to the topic. Although this is certainly true in many cases, *MHQ* stands out among its peers for featuring well-written and well-researched articles written by military historians of some note. While the essays do not include bibliographic citations, they nonetheless conform to many of the standards imposed on scholarly writing. Each richly illustrated issue has as many as eight main articles to go along with regular sections on military terminology, military art, weapons and their influence on tactics, and strategic discussions. The featured articles are some eight pages in length and include a short biography of the author. Sample essays from recent magazines are the personal narrative of a Union artilleryman at the Battle of Antietam, General Brusilov's offensive in 1916, Socrates as a warrior, the U.S. 15th Air Force in World War II, and British cavalryman George Goring and his exploits in the English Civil War. Public and high school libraries should have no trouble finding readers for this quality popular journal. Academic libraries will also find that students appreciate having it as an alternative to the more scholarly publications available on library shelves.

4943. *Marine Corps Gazette: the professional magazine for United States Marines.* [ISSN: 0025-3170] 1916. m. USD 23 domestic; USD 39 foreign; USD 3.50 newsstand/cover per issue foreign. Ed(s): Col John E Greenwood. Marine Corps Association, Bldg. 715, MCB, PO Box 1775, Quantico, VA 22134; http://www.mca-marines.org. Illus., index, adv. Sample. Circ: 31675. Vol. ends: Dec. Microform: PQC. Online: Gale Group; Northern Light Technology, Inc.; OCLC Online Computer Library Center, Inc.; ProQuest Information & Learning. Reprint: PQC. *Indexed:* AUNI, BRI, CBRI, PAIS. *Bk. rev.:* 6, 300–750 words. *Aud.:* Ga, Ac.

In common with similar journals from the other services (*Air Force Magazine*, *Army*, and *Proceedings*), *Marine Corps Gazette* publishes essays on the current state of and projected or anticipated long-range changes in America's elite offensive force. The articles offer critical suggestions for the Marine Corps mission as interpreted by serving officers and civilian specialists. A valuable tool for research on the unique role the Marine Corps plays within the Navy and in American military policy. For public libraries serving a military population.

Marine Corps Times. See under *Army Times*.

4944. ***Marines.*** [ISSN: 1056-9073] 1983. m. USD 16. Ed(s): Fred Carr, Jr. U.S. Marine Corps, Division of Public Affairs, Media Branch, HQMC, 2 Navy Annex, Washington, DC 20380-1775; http://www.usmc.mil/marines/default.htm. Illus. Sample. Vol. ends: Dec. Online: EBSCO Publishing; Florida Center for Library Automation; Gale Group. *Aud.:* Hs, Ga.

Marines, *Airman*, *All Hands*, and *Soldiers* are the service magazines published by the Marine Corps, Air Force, Navy, and Army for enlisted personnel and potential volunteers. *Marines*, in common with the others, is an attractive and heavily illustrated window into the world of the young man or woman new to service life. Articles cover military society, pay, benefits, housing, and all those other topics associated with beginning a new career in the armed forces. Public libraries and high school libraries should subscribe. Note that the armed services web sites carry some of the articles.

The other similar publications are:

Airman: magazine of America's Air Force [ISSN: 0002-2756] 1957. m. $24. Jerry R. Stringer. Air Force News Agency. Air Force News Agency, AFNEWS/IIOA, 203 Norton St., Kelly AFB, TX 78241-6105. Subs. to: Supt. of Docs., U.S. Govt. Printing Office, P.O. Box 371954, Pittsburgh, PA 15250-7954; http://www.af.mil/news/airman. Illus. Sample. Circ: 600,000. Vol. ends: Dec. *Aud:* Hs, Ga.

All Hands [ISSN: 0002-5577] 1922. m. $22. Marie G. Johnston. Naval Media Center, Publg. Div., Naval Station Anacostia, Bldg. 168, 2701 S. Capitol St. S.W., Washington, DC 20402. Subs. to: Supt. of Docs., U.S. Govt. Printing Office, Washington, DC 20402; http://www.chinfo.navy.mil/navalib/allhands/ah-top.html. Illus. Sample. Circ: 87,000; Vol. ends: Dec. Microform: UMI. *Aud:* Hs, Ga.

Soldiers: the official U.S. Army magazine [ISSN: 0093-8440] 1946. m. $24. Keith F. Jordan. U.S. Dept. of the Army. Subs. to: Supt. of Docs., U.S. Govt. Printing Office, P.O. Box 371954, Pittsburgh, PA 15250-7954; http://www.redstone.army.mil/soldiers/index.html. Illus. Sample. Circ: 250,000. Vol. ends: Dec. Microform: UMI. *Aud:* Hs, Ga.

4945. ***Military History.*** [ISSN: 0889-7328] 1984. 6x/yr. USD 23.95 domestic; USD 29.95 Canada; USD 47.95 elsewhere. Ed(s): Jon Guttman. PRIMEDIA Special Interest Publications, History Group, 741 Miller Dr, S E, D2, Leesburg, VA 20175; jong@cowles.com; http://www.thehistorynet.com. Adv. Circ: 113330 Paid. *Indexed:* AUNI. *Aud.:* Ga.

A lavishly illustrated magazine aimed at the general public, *Military History* offers a refreshingly diverse series of articles on the military past. These topics range from ancient warfare (a time period usually ignored by other popular military history–oriented periodicals) to the present day. Also included are pieces on famous generals and admirals, as well as essays on relatively unknown military leaders from the past. A particular weapon and the role it played in its time may also be found in every issue. Interviews with veterans of twentieth-century battles and campaigns are enlightening, highly informative, and add a personal touch. For public libraries.

4946. ***Military Review (English Edition): the professional journal of the United States Army.*** [ISSN: 0026-4148] 1922. bi-m. USD 30 domestic; USD 37.50 foreign. Ed(s): Lt.Col. G L Humphries, Lt.Col. Jonathan Smidt. U.S. Army Command and General Staff College, 290 Grant Ave, Bldg 77, Leavenworth, KS 66027-1254. Illus., index. Sample. Circ: 27000 Paid and controlled. Vol. ends: Dec. Microform: PQC. Online: bigchalk; EBSCO Publishing; Northern Light Technology, Inc.; OCLC Online Computer Library Center, Inc.; ProQuest Information & Learning. *Indexed:* ABS&EES, AUNI, AmH&L, BAS, IBZ, IPSA, IUSGP, PAIS, RiskAb. *Bk. rev.:* 6–11, 200–300 words. *Aud.:* Ac.

Far from being a bastion of blind resistance to change, the American military establishment has always engaged in constant evaluation and unending critical assessment of their institution's practices and traditions. The U.S. Command and General Staff College's *Military Review* is one of the oldest and most respected service voices. Founded "to provide a forum for the open exchange of ideas on military affairs," it features articles that probe accepted policies and suggest redefinitions of current Army beliefs and practices. Samples articles from recent issues include "US Army decisionmaking: past, present and future," "Tactically responsive firepower," and "US and British approaches to force protection." The articles may be beyond the reach of those new to the discussion, but they will certainly be appreciated by specialists in both academic and military communities. For academic libraries.

4947. ***National Defense: NDIA's business and technology journal.*** Formerly: *Ordnance;* Incorporates: *American Defense Preparedness Association. Annual Directory; Defense Manager;* Which was formerly: *A F M A Bulletin.* [ISSN: 0092-1491] 1920. 10x/yr. USD 35; USD 40 foreign. Ed(s): Sandra Erwin. National Defense Industrial Association, 2111 Wilson Blvd, Ste 400, Arlington, VA 22201-3001; http://www.ndia.org. Illus., adv. Circ: 35000. Vol. ends: May/Jun. Online: Gale Group; Northern Light Technology, Inc.; OCLC Online Computer Library Center, Inc.; ProQuest Information & Learning. Reprint: PQC. *Indexed:* AUNI, ChemAb, EngInd. *Aud.:* Ga, Ac.

The leading and most authoritative and informative voice for the "military-industrial complex," *National Defense* is the official publication of the National Defense Industrial Association. The articles serve to update industry, military, and civilian readers on changes within the procurement marketplace and the nature of current and proposed weapons research and development. The publication is, of course, an advocate for the industries it represents, and the articles reflect that point of view. A useful resource for academic libraries that support teaching in national security and business topics.

4948. ***National Guard.*** Formerly (until 1979): *National Guardsman.* [ISSN: 0163-3945] 1947. m. Non-members, USD 25. Ed(s): Pamela Kane. National Guard Association of the United States, One Massachusetts Ave, N W, Washington, DC 20001; http://www.ngaus.org. Illus., adv. Circ: 70000. Vol. ends: Dec. Microform: PQC. Online: Northern Light Technology, Inc.; ProQuest Information & Learning. Reprint: PQC. *Indexed:* AUNI. *Aud.:* Ga, Ac.

The National Guard has played a central, if frequently forgotten, part in American wars and in American military policy and civilian-military relations. That central role has been increasingly threatened in recent years, and the National Guard's relations with the active forces are the source of continuing debate. *National Guard* offers Guard officers and civilian supporters the opportunity to defend their place in the Defense Department and to educate the public on National Guard combat history. The journal also updates readers on military benefits, unit changes, and personnel news. Public libraries should consider this.

4949. ***Naval History.*** [ISSN: 1042-1920] 1987. bi-m. Members, USD 18; Non-members, USD 20. Ed(s): Fred Schultz, Julianne Olver. U S Naval Institute, 291 Wood Rd, Annapolis, MD 21402; http://www.usni.org. Illus., adv. Circ: 35000. *Indexed:* AmH&L. *Aud.:* Ac., Ga.

The U.S. Naval Institute enjoys a solid reputation for the journal *Proceedings* and for its military/naval book publishing. *Naval History* is directed more toward the general public. A typical issue featured a discussion on Pearl Harbor movies, the U.S.S. Utah during the Pearl Harbor attack, and British Admiral Horatio Nelson at the Battle of Copenhagen during the Napoleonic Wars. Each article included photographs and illustrations of the warships and naval personalities involved. Sailors, and many in the general public, will enjoy the descriptions of sea battles and sailors at risk on the high seas. Few should have difficulty coping with the naval terminology and limited use of technical data. While academic libraries with extensive holdings in naval history may consider this, public library patrons will benefit the most.

4950. ***Naval War College Review.*** [ISSN: 0028-1484] 1948. q. Free to qualified personnel. Ed(s): Catherine Kelleher. U.S. Naval War College, 686 Cushing Rd, Code 32, Newport, RI 02841-1207; press@nwc.navy.mil; http://www.nwc.navy.mil/press. Illus., index. Sample. Circ: 9500 Controlled. Vol. ends: Autumn. Microform: BHP; MIM; PQC. Online: bigchalk; EBSCO Publishing; Gale Group; Northern Light Technology, Inc.; OCLC Online Computer Library Center, Inc.; ProQuest Information & Learning. Reprint: PQC. *Indexed:* ABS&EES, AUNI, AmH&L, BAS, BRI, CBRI, IBZ, IPSA, IUSGP, PRA, PSA. *Bk. rev.:* 20–25, 300–500 words. *Aud.:* Ac.

Founded in 1948 as "a forum for discussion of public policy matters of interest to the maritime services," *Naval War College Review* is published by the U.S. Navy's Naval War College, an advanced school for the training of selected officers from the Navy and other U.S. services as well as selected foreign military personnel and U.S. and international civilian specialists. The journal has always included a mix of critical and scholarly essays on contemporary maritime and national security topics as well as pieces on naval history. The current advisory panel that oversees *Naval War College Review* includes some of the most respected and significant naval historians and military history scholars in the United States, and the consistently high quality of the writing and research in each issue reflects this oversight. In addition to the six to eight articles, each issue contains a book review section written by current students at the school. These reviews tend to be somewhat uneven in quality, but they are fairly comprehensive in scope. There is no other academic journal devoted to naval history and maritime policy that offers the quality, depth, and breadth of the *Review*. It is the most important such journal in the marketplace. Interested libraries should note that it is available free of charge to any library the publishers deem appropriate. A phone call and letter to the publisher are necessary to determine qualifications.

Navy Times. See under *Army Times*.

4951. *Parameters (Carlisle).* [ISSN: 0031-1723] 1971. q. USD 26 domestic; USD 36.40 foreign. Ed(s): Col. Robert Taylor. U.S. Army War College, Attn: Parameters, 122 Forbes Ave, Carlisle, PA 17013-5238. Illus., index. Sample. Refereed. Circ: 13500. Vol. ends: Winter. Microform: PQC. Online: EBSCO Publishing; Florida Center for Library Automation; Gale Group; OCLC Online Computer Library Center, Inc.; ProQuest Information & Learning. *Indexed:* ABCPolSci, AUNI, BRD, BRI, CBRI, IBZ, IUSGP, PAIS, PSA, RGPR. *Bk. rev.:* 4–13, 500–1,000 words. *Aud.:* Ac.

The U.S. Army War College in Carlisle, Pennsylvania, is the forum where the Army's senior officers and selected members from the civilian community debate public policy and military strategy issues relating to contemporary American national security. *Parameters* is the college's journal, and it includes essays growing out of these discussions. Most issues center around a specific topic, and the papers will represent the thought of some of the Army's most advanced minds. As such, *Parameters* is a necessary tool for any student interested in these ongoing conversations on military policy and for any college and university preparing graduates in international affairs. For academic libraries.

4952. *R U S I Journal.* Formerly: *Royal United Service Institution. Journal.* [ISSN: 0307-1847] 1858. bi-m. GBP 58; USD 95. Ed(s): Miss I Bleken. Royal United Services Institute for Defence Studies, Whitehall, London, SW1A 2ET, United Kingdom; defence@rusids.demon.co.uk; http://www.rusi.org. Illus., adv. Circ: 4000. Vol. ends: Dec. Microform: PQC. Reprint: PQC. *Indexed:* AUNI, EngInd, IBZ, PAIS. *Bk. rev.:* Number varies, 200–300 words. *Aud.:* Ac.

The study of military affairs and military history has long been a staple of book and magazine publishing within the United Kingdom. The Royal United Services Institute's journal is a solid and authoritative introduction to British views and opinions on the modern military and on contemporary national security questions. The analyses may be difficult to comprehend for those new to the subject matter, but the more advanced and sophisticated reader will derive enormous benefit from exposure to points of view not normally encountered in American defense journals. The book review section provides the American student with critiques of monographs that may not be discussed in American journals for some time to come. For college and university periodical collections.

4953. *Sea Power.* Formerly: *Navy - the Magazine of Sea Power.* [ISSN: 0199-1337] 1958. m. Individuals, USD 25; Military, USD 15. Ed(s): James D Hessman. Navy League of the United States, 2300 Wilson Blvd, Arlington, VA 22201-3308; mail@navyleague.org; http://www.navyleague.org. Illus., adv. Circ: 74000. Vol. ends: Dec. Microform: PQC. Online: EBSCO Publishing; Gale Group; Northern Light Technology, Inc.; OCLC Online Computer Library Center, Inc.; ProQuest Information & Learning. *Indexed:* ABS&EES, AUNI. *Aud.:* Ga, Ac.

Sea Power is the official publication of the Navy League of the United States. The articles are uniformly supportive of the goals and missions of the Navy and Marine Corps. A very useful and accurate tool for data and detailed overviews of present and planned warships, weapons systems, maritime technology, and the military and civilian research and development policies that support them. The special January issue, *Almanac of Sea Power*, is a comprehensive resource for the status of American naval and maritime power. For academic and selected public libraries.

Soldiers. See under *Marines*.

4954. *Strategic Review.* [ISSN: 0091-6846] 1973. q. Ed(s): Andrew J. Bacevich. Boston University, Center for International Relations, 154 Bay State Rd, Boston, MA 02215; bacevich@bu.edu; http://www.bu.edu/ir/cir.html. Illus. Refereed. Circ: 2000. Vol. ends: Fall. *Indexed:* ABCPolSci, ABS&EES, AUNI, BAS, IPSA, PAIS, PRA, SSI. *Bk. rev.:* 1–2, 1,000–5,000 words. *Aud.:* Ac.

Scholarly journals dealing with contemporary decision-making and policy review are of incalculable importance in academic libraries that support strong international relations and defense policy programs. *Strategic Review*, published by the U.S. Strategic Institute, stands as the leading American voice in such journals. The essays are written by academic and military specialists in the field and are intended for an audience that is comfortable with both the technical nature and overlapping dimensions of the debate over national policies. The directors of the U.S. Strategic Institute voted to dissolve the organization as of June 2001. The last issue was published in spring 2001. The journal will be published by the Center for International Relations of Boston University beginning in summer 2002. If this does come to pass, university and college libraries should examine it. Public libraries with a sophisticated reading public may wish to consider the revamped journal as well.

4955. *U S Naval Institute. Proceedings.* [ISSN: 0041-798X] 1874. m. Membership, USD 37. Ed(s): Fred H Rainbow. U S Naval Institute, 291 Wood Rd, Annapolis, MD 21402; http://www.usni.org. Illus., index, adv. Circ: 75000 Paid. Vol. ends: Dec. Microform: PQC. Online: EBSCO Publishing; Gale Group; OCLC Online Computer Library Center, Inc.; ProQuest Information & Learning. Reprint: PQC. *Indexed:* ABS&EES, AUNI, BAS, ChemAb, DSR&OA, GeoRef, PAIS. *Bk. rev.:* 3, 500–1,000 words. *Aud.:* Ga, Ac.

The United States Naval Institute is a private society composed principally of active and retired U.S. Navy and Marine Corps officers interested in serving as advocates on naval policy and as protectors of the nation's maritime heritage. As such, it is a major publisher of military history monographs, and it publishes two journals concerned with maritime affairs, *Naval History* and *Proceedings*. *Proceedings* has a long publishing history (since 1874) behind it and should be considered a solid resource for researching contemporary naval policy and events. While a majority of the articles are written to defend a particular point of view or to urge acceptance of a new weapons system or naval strategy, the argumentative nature of these essays serves to highlight the sometimes acrimonious doctrinal debates that have always played a prominent role in shaping military decision-making. The articles thus serve as a window into current naval thinking and, as such, are invaluable for the student of modern naval affairs. One significant change from previous years has been the scaling back of the reporting on international navies. These reviews served as a very useful introduction to the state of Cold War naval forces. These overviews have been revised to reflect the vast changes in fleet sizes across the globe. *Proceedings* remains a leading journal for students of contemporary security policy. Highly recommended for academic libraries.

4956. *Vietnam.* [ISSN: 1046-2902] 1988. bi-m. USD 23.95 domestic; USD 47.95 foreign; USD 3.99 newsstand/cover per issue. Ed(s): David Zabecki. PRIMEDIA Special Interest Publications, History Group, 741 Miller Dr, S E, D2, Leesburg, VA 20175; sbailey@cowles.com; http://www.thehistorynet.com. Illus., adv. Sample. Circ: 60000 Paid. Vol. ends: Apr. *Bk. rev.:* 2, 800–1,000 words. *Aud.:* Ga.

After a difficult and sputtering start, monographs on the Vietnam War are enjoying widespread popularity and acceptance. The periodical literature devoted to the conflict continues to lag behind, however. The single most impressive popular journal that covers the conflict is *Vietnam*. Similar to *World War II* in style and format, *Vietnam* concentrates on the military side of the war, but there are occasional articles on the political and societal aspects of the conflict. The interviews with U.S. veterans and the descriptions of the difficulties faced by

Americans in combat are responsible for its large following among veterans and among those whose family members served during the period. Brief articles on weaponry, military units, and personalities are integrated with the longer battle study pieces. Public and school libraries should consider this. Academic libraries that are comfortable with including popular journals in their history holdings will find this a useful addition.

4957. ***Wings (Granada Hills).*** [ISSN: 1067-0637] 1971. bi-m. USD 25; USD 31 foreign. Ed(s): Joseph V Mizrahi. Sentry Books, Inc., 10718 White Oak Ave, Box 3324, Granada Hills, CA 91344. Illus., adv. Circ: 60000. *Aud.:* Ga.

As with its counterpart, *Airpower*, *Wings* is a profusely illustrated aviation history magazine. The two or three articles per issue are always accompanied by a large number of relevant photographs with captions that supplement the material. Special topical issues (e.g., World War I fighter planes, the German air force in World War II, comparison of Japanese and American aircraft in the Pacific fighting) are published periodically and are always well received by readers. Each issue includes information on ordering past numbers. *Wings* enjoys a loyal following and will remain popular with military aviation and aircraft history enthusiasts. Public libraries may want to consider *Wings* or *Airpower*.

4958. ***World War II.*** [ISSN: 0898-4204] 1986. 7x/yr. USD 17.95 domestic; USD 23.95 Canada; USD 3.99 newsstand/cover per issue. Ed(s): Mike Haskew. PRIMEDIA Special Interest Publications, History Group, 741 Miller Dr, S E, D2, Leesburg, VA 20175; merideep@cowles.com; http://www.thehistorynet.com. Adv. Circ: 180676 Paid. *Aud.:* Ga.

The Second World War continues to hold the attention of historians and the general public alike. This longstanding fascination with the war and the political and military leaders who directed it shows no signs of abating in the near future. Libraries with small or weak holdings in World War II will likely find their patrons voting with their feet as they go elsewhere to satisfy their curiosity about this most significant of twentieth-century wars. Public libraries in particular will find willing readers for *World War II*. It features battle studies, campaign analyses, interviews with veterans from both sides, discussions of armaments and their importance, essays on military and political personalities, and short book reviews in a beautifully illustrated format. The editors devote roughly equal time to both the European and Asian theaters of operation and to the combat on air, sea, and land with articles that are unusually comprehensive and uniformly well written.

■ MILITARY GAMES

General/House Organs/Other, Overseas Wargaming Periodicals

Joseph Straw, Associate Professor of Library Administration, University of Illinois at Urbana-Champaign, Reference Library, 1408 W. Gregory Drive, Urbana, IL 61801; jstraw@uiuc.edu

Introduction

Wargames and simulations of strategy have a very long history. Perhaps one of the earliest strategy games played for entertainment was Wei-Hai, developed in Ancient China. Wei-Hai, also called Go, involved controlling territory with the avaliable game pieces. The predecessor of chess, Chaturanga was played in India at the beginning of the seventh century. Chaturanga had strong military overtones with game pieces that represented solidiers making formal moves across a board that looked very much like a modern chessboard. The use of gaming in actual warfare, either to teach tactics or to create simulation modules for operational strategy, lagged behind its use as an instrument of fun and diversion. Up until nearly the end of the eighteenth century, warfare remained highly formalized with political and adminstrative skills valued as much as a good battle plan. It was only later that the need for wargaming by military professionals would be recognized as an essential element of planning.

Wargaming as we know it today is of more recent origin. In 1824 the Prussian lieutenant George Heinrich Rudolf Johann von Reisswitz introduced a game called "Instructions for the Representation of Tactical Maneuvers under the Guise of a Wargame" to his army superiors. This German Kriegspiel (wargame) used topographical maps and calculation formulas based on practical experience to resolve simulated combat. The Kriegspiel quickly caught on in the Prussian Army and soon spread across Europe.

The years following the introduction of Reisswitz's Kriegspiel demonstrated the need to train military professionals using gaming or simulation models. The new face of warfare in the industrial nineteenth century posed whole new challenges to military planners. Communication and transportation changes such as the telegraph and railroads allowed larger armies to be mobilized and positioned with much greater speed. The complexities of waging war in this new industrial system required considerable thought and planning before the armies took the field. Coordinating the huge military matrix with a nation's industrial infrastructure required the services of a "general staff" that could "game out" the various options that would be faced in wartime. Wargaming became an important element in training the general staff and in formulating a nation's war plan. By the beginning of the twentieth century, all industrial nations had wargaming as a part of their military planning, a practice that remains until this day.

The spread of wargaming among military professionals was mirrored by its popularity in the general public. In 1913, H.G. Wells released his classic game "Little Wars," which used toy soldiers and artillery that shot rounds to knock down the opposing pieces. The marriage of military miniatures with wargames was the basic gaming system for the first half of the twentieth century, and still remains popular today. Charles Roberts developed a game called "Tactics" in 1953, which was the first entirely paper wargame. The game had a board and cardboard counters that represented military units of different strengths and capabilities. A mathematical formula was used to calculate the results of simulated encounters. This game was immensely popular and spawned hundreds of other board simulation games. The basic design of "Tactics" has influenced the look of all the board wargames that have followed.

Board wargames remained the bread and butter of the gaming hobby until the emergence of PC-based gaming systems in the early 1980s. PC gaming software and the Internet have added a powerful dimension to the wargame. The computional advantages are obvious, operational speed can be generated, multiple players can participate more easily, and virtual reality can simulate the actual combat. These features often make these gaming systems the first choices for people coming into the hobby.

While military miniatures, board games, and computer systems remain staples of military gaming, the last decades have seen a growing number of people acting out simulations and military combat. The popularity of activities like paintball and laser tag clearly put people into simulated tactical situations. A vast number of people are taking up the hobby of historical reenacting, and finding satisfaction in getting a real sense of what it might be like to be a soldier in a different era. These hobbies are adding an interesting dimension to the mix of things that make up military gaming today.

Over the years many publications have served as avenues of communication for military and gaming enthusiasts. Unfortunately, many of these publications do not come from mainstream presses and are not covered by indexing and abstracting services. Despite the popularity of military games in general, the gaming community is intensely local and often writes for a very small group of gamers with a similar interest. Many publications are not around for long, and sometimes the only reliable ones come from the vendors that produce the games.

Libraries have an interest in serving this group of potential users. Many libraries have purchased actual wargames, but because of the pieces and size of many gaming systems, this can prove to be tricky and problematic. Generally, libraries should know if a gaming club exists in the local community and start their gaming collections with a newsletter put out by that group. Future acquisitions might best be aided by the gamers themselves, who would best know their own needs and the need of the gaming community in general.

Basic Periodicals

Hs, Ga: *The Courier, Fire & Movement, Miniature Wargames, Strategy & Tactics, Vae Victis (in French).*

General

This section contains publications that cover wargaming in a general sense. They may cover any level of play or type of gaming system. Some are produced by publishers, manufacturers, or vendors, but they must also provide articles about the gaming products of other companies.

4959. ***Action Pursuit Games.*** [ISSN: 0893-9489] 1987. m. USD 33. Ed(s): Jessica Sparks. C F W Enterprises, Inc., 4201 W Van Owen Pl, Burbank, CA 91505; http://www.cfwenterprises.com. Illus., adv. Circ: 80000. *Aud.:* Hs, Ga.

The leading magazine for the game and sport of paintball. This activity rapidly gained popularity in the the early to mid-1990s. The popularity has somewhat leveled off in recent years, but a large group of core people keeps the hobby active and vital. This magazine contains feature articles that focus on game strategies, safety, and equipment. Extensive advertisements also point people to places where paintball-related products can be purchased. Users consulting the advertising should probably be aware that most of the products are somewhat on the "high end" and may not be suited to people getting started in the hobby. This publication would be good for public libraries in communities that have paintball enthusiasts.

4960. ***Battlefleet.*** 1966. q. GBP 13.50. Ed(s): Stuart Barnes. Naval Wargames Society, c/o Stuart Barnes, 5 Clifton Pl, Ilfrancombe, EX 349jj, United Kingdom. *Aud.:* Hs, Ga.

Battlefleet is the quarterly journal of the Naval Wargames Society based in Great Britain. The journal covers a wide range of articles on any aspect of naval wargaming. This publication also contains reviews of gaming systems and updates on naval modelling. *Battlefleet* would be a good addition to a public library that has a active community of military gamers.

4961. ***C3i.*** 1992. q. USD 22. G M T Games, Box 1308, Hanford, CA 93232. *Aud.:* Hs, Ga.

This magazine is designed for players of GMT board games. GMT makes a number of historical wargames that span a number of different periods. The articles consist of gaming tips, game pieces, and general military history. This publication would well serve a public library with an active military gaming group.

4962. ***Camp Chase Gazette: where the Civil War comes alive.*** [ISSN: 1055-2790] 1972. 10x/yr. USD 28. Ed(s): Nicky Hughes. Camp Chase Publishing Company, Inc., PO Box 707, Marietta, OH 45750; http://www.campchase.com. Adv. Sample. Circ: 4200 Paid. *Aud.:* Hs, Ga.

Camp Chase Gazette is the only nationally distributed magazine that deals with the popular hobby of Civil War reenacting. The articles report on topics of interest for reenactors, and they give a national calendar of events for activities that are happening around the country. A subscription to this publication would most benefit public libraries that cater to a known group of Civil War reenactors.

4963. ***The Citizens' Companion: the voice of civilian reenacting.*** [ISSN: 1075-9344] 1993. q. USD 24 domestic; USD 30 foreign. Ed(s): Susan Lyons Hughes. Camp Chase Publishing Company, Inc., PO Box 707, Marietta, OH 45750; campchase@aol.com; http://www.campchase.com. Adv. Sample. Circ: 1200 Paid. *Aud.:* Hs, Ga.

This interesting magazine for civilian reenactors is a supporting piece for the *Camp Chase Gazette.* It has articles about the role of civilians in the Civil War and pieces about period attire and dress. This would be a good selection for a public library that caters to an active group of Civil War reenactors.

4964. ***Command Magazine: military history, strategy & analysis.*** [ISSN: 1059-5651] 1989. bi-m. USD 19.95; USD 42.95 foreign. Ed(s): Ty Bomba. X T R Corp., PO Box 4017, San Luis Obispo, CA 93403; perello@aol.com. Illus., index, adv. *Aud.:* Hs, Ga.

Still one of the better magazines for this hobby. *Command* combines military history with discussions on general wargaming. Excellent, lavishly illustrated, and well researched military history articles grace the pages of this publication. Many of the military history articles are substantial contributions to their fields. This magazine would be a strong addition for public libraries with an interest in wargaming or general military history.

4965. ***Competitive Edge.*** irreg. USD 14 for 2 issues plus games. Ed(s): Jon Compton. One Small Step, 613 N Morada Ave, West Covina, CA 91790. *Aud.:* Hs, Ga.

A small periodical with general information about wargaming and military miniatures. The content is highly specialized and designed for the experienced gamer. This could be a purchase for a public library that serves a known gaming community.

4966. ***The Courier (Brockton): North America's foremost miniature wargaming magazine.*** [ISSN: 1062-8371] 1979. q. USD 19 domestic; USD 28 foreign; USD 5.95 newsstand/cover per issue. Ed(s): Richard L. Bryant. Courier Publishing Co. (Brockton), PO Box 1878, Brockton, MA 02403-1878; mgluteus@aol.com; http://www.thecouriermagazine.com. Illus., adv. Circ: 15000 Paid. *Aud.:* Hs, Ga.

This magazine is the principle publication for minatures wargamers. In recent decades, miniature wargaming has become a more specialized branch of this hobby. *The Courier* contains articles about new game rules, and general advice about painting and acquiring military miniatures. Military miniatures remains one of the most skillful and creative branches of military hobbying. This publication would serve well in a public library with an active gaming community.

4967. ***Critical Hit.*** q. Ed(s): Trevor Holman. Critical Hit, P.O. Drawer 79, Croton Falls, NY 10519. Illus. *Aud.:* Hs, Ga.

This magazine supports the players of "Critical Hit" wargames. This vendor is best known for its popular game called "Squad Leader" and other games based on World War II historical scenarios. This publication has articles on new games, as well as tips for playing games from the current product line. Most of the the articles are for hardcore gamers, and public libraries might want to consider getting this publication at the request of wargaming patrons.

4968. ***Fire & Movement: the forum of conflict simulation.*** [ISSN: 0147-0051] 1976. q. USD 22 domestic; USD 26 Canada; USD 28 elsewhere. Ed(s): David McElhanon. Decision Games, PO Box 21598, Bakersfield, CA 93390; decsion@iwvisp.com; http://www.decisiongames.com. Illus., index, adv. Circ: 2000. *Aud.:* Hs, Ga.

Published by Decision Games, this magazine reviews a wide variety of historical board and online games. This publication has detailed reviews of new wargames, and includes advice on playing and purchasing gaming systems. Published for the general gaming audience, public libraries should purchase this publication for active wargamers.

4969. ***Games, Games, Games.*** [ISSN: 1357-1508] 1986. 10x/yr. GBP 26 domestic; GBP 29 in Europe; GBP 35 United States. Ed(s): Paul Evans. S F C Press (Small Furry Creatures), 17 Crendon St, High Wycombe, HP 136LJ, United Kingdom; http://www.sfcp.co.uk. Illus., adv. *Aud.:* Hs, Ga.

This British publication claims to cover the whole gaming industry, but it spends most of its time covering wargames. The magazine includes reviews and playing tips for all kinds of board and online wargames. This publication has excellent coverage of the wargaming community in Europe. Public libraries with users that have a general interest in gaming would most benefit from this magazine.

4970. ***Line of Departure.*** q. USD 15. Line of Departure, 3835 Richmond Ave, Ste 192, Staten Island, NY 10312. *Aud.:* Hs, Ga.

Line of Departure contains reviews and playing advice for a wide selection of wargames. This publication is geared to the experienced gamer, and libraries might want to get it at the request of hardcore wargamers.

4971. ***Miniature Wargames.*** [ISSN: 0266-3228] 1983. m. GBP 37 domestic; GBP 42 foreign; GBP 3.20 newsstand/cover per issue domestic. Ed(s): Iain Dickie. Pireme Publishing Ltd., Wessex House, St Leonards Rd, Bournemouth, BH8 8QS, United Kingdom. Illus., index, adv. Circ: 10000 Paid. *Aud.:* Hs, Ga.

A very respected publication that covers miniature wargaming in the United Kingdom. *Miniature Wargames* is packed with colorful illustrations and modelling advice for collectors of military miniatures. The articles cover all historical periods, and naval modelling is also covered in detail. This magazine has something for anyone who might be interested in miniatures, and it would be of value to libraries that serve users with a general interest in military modelling.

4972. *Moves.* Former titles (until 1990): *Wargamer;* (until 1987): *Moves.* [ISSN: 1073-5151] 1972. q. USD 22 domestic; USD 26 Canada; USD 28 elsewhere. Decision Games, PO Box 21598, Bakersfield, CA 93390; decsion@iwvisp.com. Illus., adv. Circ: 2600. *Aud.:* Hs, Ga.

This magazine focuses on the strategic board game products produced by Decision Games. It includes reviews of new games and support for players using the current products. Some of the articles contain commentaries on active games. This publication might best find a home in public library collections that support users with avid gaming interests.

4973. *Panzerschreck.* irreg. Minden Games, 9573 W Vogel Ave, Peoria, AZ 85345; minden2@hotmail.com; http://www.homestead.com/minden_games/. *Aud.:* Hs, Ga, Ac.

Panzerschreck is an unusual publication with no formal subscription. Each issue must be requested separately. This is a publication for the solitaire gamer, and each issue includes a complete game. The game inserts come with rules, maps, counters, and other assorted game parts. The parts and inserts would create a lot of problems for libraries trying to collect all of the issues. Most libraries would be best served collecting single issues at the request of gamers in the community.

4974. *Paper Wars.* Formerly (until 1993): *Wargame Collector's Journal.* 1991. bi-m. USD 29.95 domestic; USD 48 in Europe; USD 54 elsewhere. Ed(s): John Burtt. Omega Games, PO Box 2191, Valrico, FL 33595; omegagames@aol.com; http://paperwarsmag.tripod.com/. Illus., adv. *Aud.:* Hs, Ga.

Paper Wars is a good reviewing source for wargames from a variety of different companies, and includes reviews of books in military history. This publication might enhance a public library collection that serves users with an interest in wargaming or general military history.

4975. *Perfidious Albion.* 1976. triennial. Ed(s): Charles Vasey. Perfidious Albion, 75 Richmond Park Rd, London, SW14 8JY, United Kingdom. *Aud.:* Ga.

This publication provides some clever reviews of a wide variety of board and online wargaming systems. The articles have a strong bent toward the gaming community in the United Kingdom, but a lot of American gaming products are also examined. This could be a good source of wargame reviews for collections that serve active gaming communities.

4976. *Simulacrum: a quarterly journal of board wargame collecting & accumulating.* 1999. q. CND 21 domestic; USD 21 United States; USD 25 elsewhere. Ed(s): John Kula. Simulacrum, c/o John Kula, 2 Lekwammen Dr, Victoria, BC V9A 7M2, Canada; kula@telus.net . *Aud.:* Hs, Ga.

One of the leading peridicals for collectors of board wargames. The articles are loaded with information on past wargames and tips about finding and collecting the games. This publication would be of interest to public libraries that have users interested in collecting games and toys.

Simulation & Gaming. See Sociology and Social Work/General section.

4977. *Strategist.* m. USD 15. Ed(s): Tim Watson, Vickie Watson. Strategy Gaming Society, 87-6 Park Ave, Worcester, MA 01605; phillies@wpi.edu; http://pages.about.com/strategygames. *Bk. rev.:* Occasionally. *Aud.:* Hs, Ga.

This publication is the monthly newsletter of the Strategy Gaming Society (SGS). The newsletter contains articles about new games, gaming reviews, scenarios, and information about new Internet resources. The articles are of interest to wargamers at all levels.

4978. *Strategy and Tactics: the magazine of conflict simulation.* Former titles (until 1988): *Strategy and Tactics Magazine;* (until 1982): *Strategy and Tactics.* [ISSN: 1040-886X] 1967. bi-m. USD 99 domestic; USD 109 Canada; USD 129 elsewhere. Ed(s): Joseph Miranda. Decision Games, PO Box 21598, Bakersfield, CA 93390; http://www.decisiongames.com. Illus., index, adv. Circ: 10000. *Aud.:* Hs, Ga.

This is one of the most respected publications for wargaming and general military history. *Strategy & Tactics* contains articles from all periods of military history. This magazine also includes articles about possible future conflicts and alternative history scenarios. Reviews of gaming products and advice about wargaming are included; the subjects of feature articles are extensively covered. The content is well researched, and articles are often excellent contributions to the overall field of military history. For any public library with an interest in gaming, this would be a good addition to the collection. The articles on military history may even be of value to some academic collections.

4979. *Tournaments Illuminated.* [ISSN: 0732-6645] 1967. q. Members, USD 35. Ed(s): Nancy Beattie. Society for Creative Anachronism, PO Box 360789, Milpitas, CA 95036-0789. Illus., adv. Circ: 22000. *Aud.:* Hs, Ga, Ac.

This is the official publication of the Society for Creative Anachronisms. This is one of the largest groups dedicated to medieval reenacting. One of the largest areas of interest is the medieval soldier, and the pages are loaded with articles about the armor and weapons of the medieval period. A good selection for public libraries with users interested in historical reenacting. The Society of Creative Anachronisms is active on many colleges campuses, and academic libraries might also benefit from having this publication.

4980. *Vae Victis.* [ISSN: 0242-312X] 1974. bi-m. FRF 200. Ed(s): Frederic Bey. Histoire et Collection, 5 avenue de la Republique, Paris, 75541, France; fredbey@club-internet.fr; http://www.vaevictis.com. Circ: 15000. *Aud.:* Hs, Ga, Ac.

This French-language publication is one of the better sources for the wargaming and military history scene in Europe. Excellent articles and reviews appear on a broad range of wargaming topics, and well-researched articles are also offered on general military history. This publication would be useful for public and academic libraries with strong French-language collections.

4981. *Valkyrie.* [ISSN: 1355-2767] 1994. m. GBP 3 newsstand/cover per issue. Ed(s): Dave Renton. Partizan Press, 816-818 London Rd, Leigh-on-sea, Southend, SS9 3NH, United Kingdom; partizan@compuserve.com. Illus. Circ: 12000. *Aud.:* Hs, Ga.

Perhaps the leading publication for players of role-playing and fantasy games. Many of these games have strong elements of strategy built in, even if they may not be centered on historical or current reality. Public libraries that cater to a group of role-playing and fantasy gamers might want to purchase this publication.

4982. *Wargames Illustrated.* [ISSN: 0957-6444] 1987. m. GBP 32 domestic; GBP 34 foreign; GBP 2.75 newsstand/cover per issue. Ed(s): Duncan Macfarlane. Stratagem Publications Ltd., 18 Lovers Ln, Newark, NG24 1HZ, United Kingdom; illustrated@wargames.co.uk; http://www.wargames.co.uk. Illus., adv. *Aud.:* Hs, Ga.

An interesting British publication that has excellent articles about board and miniature wargaming products. Some of the miniatures features are very well done, with eye-catching illustrations. A possible purchase for public libraries with wargaming users.

House Organs

These publications are concerned with the products of their own company. These are usually geared to players of one game or to a family of games. Readers would need to be familar with the ins and out of a vendor's gaming system to benefit from these publications.

4983. *Alnavco Log.* Formerly: *Alnavco Distributors: the Report.* 1966. 3x/yr. Free. Ed(s): Pete Paschall. Alnavco, Box 9, Belle Haven, VA 23306. Illus. Circ: 2000. *Aud.:* Hs, Ga.

This publication is a newsletter for one of the largest distributors of military miniatures. *Alnavco* specializes in naval models, but it also has a large armored-vehicle product line. The newsletter contains articles on general modelling, painting, and the use of miniatures in wargaming. This newsletter would be a good addition to public libraries that have collections of modelling literature.

4984. *The Art of War.* irreg. Clash of Arms Games, Byrne Bldg., No. 205, Lincoln & Morgan Sts., Phoenixville, PA 19460. Illus. *Aud.:* Hs, Ga.

The Art of War is a magazine published to support the users of Clash of Arms (COA) gaming systems. Clash of Arms makes a number of elaborate wargames that mainly deal with World War II historical scenarios. The magazine contains articles about military history, tactical gaming situations, and rules updates for COA games. This publication would work best in a public library with a visible local military gaming community.

4985. *The Boardgamer.* 1995. q. USD 13. Ed(s): Bruce Monnin. The Boardgamer, 177 S Lincoln St, Minster, OH 45865-1240. *Aud.:* Hs, Ga.

This magazine is designed to support players of Avalon Hill boardgames. It also provides a review and commentary of games played at the World Boardgaming Championships. *The Boardgamer* would best be acquired by public libraries that have an active gaming community.

4986. *The Europa Magazine.* irreg. G R D Games, 10832 Metcalf Rd., Emmett, MI 48022-1508. *Aud.:* Hs, Ga.

This publication supports the players of GRD board games. These games are very intense, map-driven historical scenarios that are centered on World War II themes. The games are almost like "general staff" modules with very high standards of play. Mostly high-level wargamers would use the material in this publication, and public libraries should only purchase at the request of very serious gamers.

4987. *Tac News.* 1987. bi-m. Free. G H Q, 28100 Woodside Rd, Shorewood, MN 55331; customerservice@ghqmodels.com; http://www.ghqmodels.com/. *Aud.:* Hs, Ga.

This interesting newsletter covers military modelling and wargaming with miniatures. The newsletter also contains general military history articles that mostly deal with World War II topics. Public libraries with users interested in military modelling would most benefit from this publication.

4988. *Wargamers Information.* 1975. s-a. USD 3 for 12 issues. Ed(s): Rick Loomis. Flying Buffalo Inc., PO Box 1467, Scottsdale, AZ 85252; http://www.flyingbuffalo.com. Circ: 500. *Aud.:* Hs, Ga.

A publication for players of Flying Buffalo games. This magazine reviews new games and suggests playing tips for the current line of products. This vendor makes many card-based and board wargaming products. Designed for a hardcore gaming audience, this publication could best be used in a public library that serves an active group of gamers.

Other, Overseas Wargaming Periodicals

Alea. Ludopress, Avda. Primavera 71, 08290-Cerdanyola del Valles, Barcelona, Spain. Includes games.

Battles and Leaders. [ISSN: 0155-7807] St. Mary's, N.S.W., Australia.

Casus Belli. One rue du Colonel Pierre Avia, 75015 Paris, France.

Hexagones. Les Compagnies d'Ordonnance, 15, rue est Vandervelde, 6040 Jumet, Belgium.

Der Musketier. U. Blennemann, Rosental 76, 4320 Hattigen, Germany.

The Private. 122A Central Road, Worcester Park, Surrey KT4 8HT, England.

Sabre. [ISSN: 0157-0048] Melbourne, Victoria, Australia.

Six Angles. Masuhiro Yamasaki. 408, I-22-10 Iragawa, Sayama City, Sayama 350-13, Japan. Includes games.

Electronic Journals

The numbers of electronic magazines, journals, and newsletters for this hobby are legion. Most have very short lives and are very difficult to track down. Knowing the individual title or URL is often make-or-break in finding a particular publication. An excellent place to start is the *Grognard* site at http://grognard.com. This is an outstanding gateway to the online world of military gaming. Information and links are available to multiple gaming simulations, reviews, and actual games. This site has one of the deepest collections of links to online wargaming periodicals. The *Wargamers Ring* at http://www.marinergames.com/webring/wargamer.htm is also an excellent gateway to online wargaming information, with 500 affiliated sites currently making up the ring. Sites like these are really the places to go for someone who is coming into the hobby through the Internet.

■ MODEL MAKING AND COLLECTING

Static Models/Model Railroads/Live Steam/Model Airplanes and Rockets/Model Automobiles/Model Ships/Military Miniatures/Miniature Figures/Construction Sets/Dollhouse Miniatures/Toy Collecting

Frederick A. Schlipf, Executive Director, The Urbana Free Library, 201 S. Race St., Urbana, IL 61801; Adjunct Associate Professor, Graduate School of Library and Information Science, University of Illinois, Urbana, IL 61801; fschlipf@uiuc.edu; FAX: 217-367-4061

Introduction

The magazines in this section are concerned with building, operating, and collecting models of railroads, airplanes, automobiles, ships, military hardware, and other types of machinery; of buildings and furniture; and of soldiers and other figures.

There are millions of adults and young adults in the United States who are serious model builders, operators, and collectors—in addition to perhaps an equally large number of armchair hobbyists who enjoy reading and daydreaming about model building and collecting but never actually get around to doing much about it. Taken together, the two groups form a substantial part of the population, and libraries need to serve both groups.

In several subdivisions of model making, there are three kinds of people—builders, operators, and collectors—and in many cases they do not read the same magazines. Most builders are craftspeople who like to construct models, operators prefer to spend their time actually doing something with models, and collectors are interested in old toys or in outstanding examples of modern craftsmanship. Although these three types of activities frequently overlap, in many cases one magazine will not meet the needs of all types of people.

Hobby magazine publishers range from large professional firms with five or more hobby magazines to one- or two-person labors of love, staffed by enthusiasts with second jobs. The largest U.S. hobby magazine publisher is Kalmbach, which publishes six model-building and -collecting magazines. Other major magazine publishers include Air Age and Carstens in the United States, and Nexus, Peco, and Traplet in Great Britain.

Hobby magazines come and go, as a comparison of this section with the same one in the previous edition of *Magazines for Libraries* demonstrates. Publishers try out new titles and occasionally abandon them. Publishers sometimes find that costs are outrunning income and give it all up. When editors (who are often owners) retire, sometimes no one is left to take up the reins. Unfortunately, some excellent special-interest magazines are among the deceased. Since the previous edition of *Magazines for Libraries*, for example, such excellent model building and collecting magazines as *Model Ship Builder, Plastic Figure & Playset Collector*, and *Spielzeug Antik Revue* have ceased publication.

In addition to subscription sales, bookstore sales, and newsstand sales, model-building and -collecting magazines are widely sold in hobby shops, comic book shops, and other specialized outlets. Some magazines sell the majority of their press runs in specialty shops at retail rather than by subscription.

MODEL MAKING AND COLLECTING

Most model magazines have somewhat similar contents. Among the most commonly encountered articles and features are those concerned with the following:

1. How-to-do-it information. Articles in this area form the bulk of the editorial contents of many hobby magazines. These articles range from explanations of specific techniques to step-by-step directions for completing particular models or assembling individual kits. Frequently articles on specific models are also designed to illustrate methods of solving general model-building problems.

2. Prototype information. To a modeler, a "prototype" is the original object upon which a model is based. Modelers interested in building prototypically accurate models spend a great deal of time hunting for reliable, detailed information on the structural details, inscriptions, and colors of specific prototypes.

3. Product reviews. Because most model builders make extensive use of commercial products, reviews form an important part of most magazines. Frequently they are careful and evaluative, but some publishers are accused of glossing over weaknesses to avoid offending the manufacturers who provide most of their advertising revenue, and in a few magazines, product reviews are essentially filler.

4. Reviews of books and videos about the hobby and about prototype equipment. These are particularly useful to libraries for acquisitions purposes because they discuss large numbers of items that the more general reviewing media may regard as too specialized to cover or may subject to less-informed scrutiny.

5. Photographs of outstanding models, hobby events, and interesting prototypes.

6. Plans and drawings for model making. These are an important part of many model-making magazines, and the quality varies enormously from magazine to magazine. Top-quality plans and photographs are of great importance but expensive to produce, and this is one area in which the poorer magazines are weak. Some plans, particularly those for flying model aircraft, model ships, and large-scale model trains are too large to print in magazines. A couple of publishers insert folded plans in their magazines, but other magazines print plans in reduced sizes and offer full-sized copies for an extra fee.

7. Articles on manufacturers. These are found in most model magazines. Often they are based on factory visits.

8. Studies of collectible models. These may be concerned with models on a particular theme (such as *Star Wars* toys) or by a specific maker. Some articles of this type include collectors' prices.

9. Advertising. Advertising is important to model makers because it is usually informational rather than simple hype. Many hobbyists read magazines for the ads as well as for the editorial content. Advertising in hobby magazines is of three general types: (*a*) *Manufacturers' advertisements.* In model magazines, these serve in large part to make modelers aware of new products, although some promote such long-term products as paint, adhesives, etc. (*b*) *Mail-order retailers' advertisements.* Like computer magazines, some model-building and -collecting magazines have massive ads listing hundreds of items. The offerings of a single retailer may run to pages of minuscule type. (*c*) *Classified advertisements.* In the past, classified ads in some magazines grew to become virtually international exchange points for hobbyists, and a few magazines consisted of little else. But this function has been drastically reduced by the growth of the Internet.

The intent of this section is to list the most important magazines in each of the model-making and -collecting hobbies. The titles listed include not only the dominant ones in each hobby but also some excellent, specialized titles that cover specific areas that the major magazines tend to gloss over or ignore. Other good sources of information on model magazines include advertisements in the magazines and the staff members of large hobby shops.

Several magazines are published for the members of hobby associations, and many of these are available for subscription by nonmembers. Some of these magazines are primarily house organs and are excluded from this list, but others contain a great deal of solid information, and some provide the only serious coverage of their fields.

Because *Magazines for Libraries* is aimed at North American libraries and readers, relatively few non–English language magazines are reviewed in this section. Those that appear below either include important information not included in American magazines or are in areas where no strong American magazine exists.

A very large number of model-making and -collecting magazines is published in Great Britain. Because of the common language, they lend themselves to export. Many British titles serve primarily to supplement American magazines, but a few are vital to American hobbyists. Central among these are *Constructor Quarterly, Model Auto Review, The Model Engineer*, and *Radio Control Jet International.*

In an attempt to improve overseas sales, in recent years many British model magazines have added "international" to their titles. Sometimes this is justified, but sometimes not. Look for coverage of U.S. prototypes or advertisements from U.S. firms.

Libraries that subscribe to model magazines will notice a few specific problems:

1. Libraries tend to buy the same half-dozen magazines and ignore the rest. Given the fact that there is frequently one dominant magazine in an area, this practice is understandable, but the result is extremely limited collection depth both regionally and nationally. Because their interloan requests typically go unfilled, many serious hobbyists have given up on libraries. Two possible solutions exist: First, some of the major national hobby associations maintain research libraries that may be willing to provide copies of articles. And second, hobbies represent a fertile field for modestly priced cooperative collection development projects.

2. Model-making magazines are poorly indexed. Few are covered by standard indexing or abstracting services. Many model-making magazines have their own annual indexes, but few provide cumulative indexes. And virtually all indexes to model magazines have vocabulary control problems.

3. Modelers like to page through long runs of old magazines. This is a very reasonable activity, reflecting the difficulty in indexing modeling material, the necessarily serendipitous nature of much hobby information-finding, and the function of hobby advertising as informative rather than persuasive. Unfortunately for modelers, searching magazines in this way is not approved by interlibrary loan librarians.

4. Oversewn binding is a poor practice. This is due to the great importance of measured drawings in many model magazines. Drawings in bound magazines cannot be made to lie truly flat for copying, and drawings that are bled across center spreads are completely ruined by oversewing. Librarians who are serious about serving model builders should consider using either pamphlet boxes or rod binders for storage of titles that feature measured drawings.

5. Few model-making magazines are available in microform, but most publishers have extensive stocks of back issues available for sale.

6. Model magazines do not appear with the long-term regularity that serials librarians adore. Many magazines change frequency, some skip issues, and others change their titles or absorb other magazines. Many are numbered sequentially from their first issues, rather than in annual volumes, and some are paginated sequentially from their first issues. Some issues have no dates at all. To help librarians determine whether their collections are complete, notes on title and frequency changes are included in the listings for several magazines.

For readers, coping with model magazines is more a matter of acquiring technical knowledge of the hobby than of acquiring higher education, and this means that the traditional reader-level designations used in *Magazines for Libraries* are of limited utility in this section. Virtually all the model-making magazines listed here should be accessible to any high school student who has the appropriate hobby background and technical vocabulary, just as they may pose problems for adults who are only starting out.

None of the magazines reviewed below is concerned exclusively with prototype information, although most devote space to the subject. Most modelers, however, are eager to read about what they model, especially to locate modeling information. From a modeler's point of view, the most useful magazines and books are specialized, with detailed information, drawings, and color schemes. Promotional or "bargain" books that claim to cover the world of trains, aircraft, or tanks in one volume are as useless to modelers as they are to other enthusiasts in those areas.

The world of model hobbies changes all the time, and this is reflected in the model hobby magazines. For example, many modelers continue to shift away from difficult construction projects. Although the model-building world is still full of crafts people, more and more operating equipment is sold ready to run or in bolt-together kits, leaving owners free to get on with the business of putting models through their paces or arranging complex dioramas. Better and better die making leaves many builders of scale models challenged more by high-quality painting than by assembly. The growing availability of microcircuitry and space-age construction materials has influenced operating models greatly. Today, programmable radio controls, digital sound effects, and such enhancements as model aircraft flight recorders are everywhere. And the number of model and toy collectors continues to increase.

Basic Periodicals

For an extremely small collection: Ems, Hs, Ga: *FineScale Modeler, Model Airplane News,* and *Model Railroader.* For a somewhat larger collection: Ems, Hs, Ga: *Amazing Figure Modeler, Classic Toy Trains, Dollhouse Miniatures, FineScale Modeler, Flying Models, Garden Railways, Historical Miniature, Model Airplane News, Model Railroader, Quiet Flyer, Radio Control Boat Modeler, Radio Control Car Action, Railroad Model Craftsman, Scale Auto, Seaways' Ships in Scale,* and *Sport Rocketry.*

Static Models

Static models are nonworking models—primarily plastic models of ships, airplanes, automobiles, military equipment, soldiers and other figures, and dioramas. They are grouped here for discussion because a number of magazines cover models in more than one of these areas. This coverage makes sense because the same companies make kits in most of these areas, the kits all involve similar modeling techniques, and people interested in building static models often build a wide variety of plastic kits.

Static model building is a tremendously popular hobby. Mass-produced plastic-model kits are sold by the millions, and the numbers of adults and children who buy and build them are huge. In addition to mass-produced kits is a huge variety of more specialized products, including low-volume production kits made of cast resin or vacuum-molded plastic sheet, detail parts for the upgrading or conversion of mass-produced kits, model figures in cast metal and resin, more difficult wood and metal kits, etc.

Reflecting the growing specialization of hobby publishing, no mainstream U.S. magazine is devoted to the entire spectrum of static models, and the ones listed in this section are all foreign. Among these, three of the most useful to American modelers are *Hobby Japan,* because of the many model kits that originate in Japan, *Allt om Hobby,* which covers the entire Scandinavian modeling scene, and *Scale Models International,* which covers plastic modeling from a British perspective.

Rather than subscribing to one of the static-model magazines, many American libraries should first consider some of the specialized magazines covering specific types of static models. Among the best of these are *Scale Aviation Modeller International* (in the Model Airplanes and Rockets subsection); *Model Cars* and *Scale Auto* (in the Model Automobiles subsection); *Model Shipwright* and *Seaways' Ships in Scale* (in the Model Ships subsection); *FineScale Modeler, Historical Miniature, Military Miniatures in Review,* and *Military Modelling* (in the Military Miniatures subsection); *Amazing Figure Modeler, KitBuilders Magazine, Modeler's Resource,* and *Prehistoric Times* (in the Miniature Figures subsection); and *Dollhouse Miniatures* (in the Dollhouse Miniatures subsection).

4989. *Allt om Hobby.* [ISSN: 0002-6190] 1966. 8x/yr. SEK 360; USD 44. Ed(s): Freddy Stenbom. Allt om Hobby AB, PO Box 90133, Stockholm, 12021, Sweden; freddy.stenbom@hobby.se; http://www.hobby.se. Illus., adv. Circ: 30000. *Bk. rev.:* Various number and length. *Aud.:* Hs, Ga, Sa.

Allt om Hobby is Scandinavia's leading model magazine, aimed particularly at readers in Norway, Sweden, Denmark, and Finland. It covers a wide range of model-making and operating activities, with particular emphasis on operating models—trains, airplanes, and cars. For anyone interested in hobbies in Scandinavia, or in models of Scandinavian prototypes, this is an attractive and respected publication. In Swedish only. *Allt om Hobby* also publishes a line of books on electronics for model railroaders; many of these are available in English translation through their American importer, Maerklin Inc., and are not equalled by American publications.

4990. *Hobby Japan.* 1969. m. Hobby Japan Co., 5-26-5 Sendagaya, Shibuya-ku, Tokyo, Japan. Illus. *Aud.:* Hs, Ga.

Hobby Japan is Japan's leading model magazine, and at between 300 and 400 pages per issue, it is probably the thickest model magazine in the world. Like other magazines devoted to static models, *Hobby Japan* covers model cars, airplanes, and military. It devotes the most attention, however, to model figure kits, ranging from robots and Godzillas to the heroines of Japanese "manga" comics and animated films. Most Japanese hobby magazines are impossible for Americans to figure out, but *Hobby Japan*'s article titles—and occasional captions—are in English, and that helps a great deal. Japanese model magazines are of interest to American modelers because of the huge range of model kits manufactured in Japan. Although it's possible to deduce modeling techniques by studying the photographs in the articles, most Americans who read *Hobby Japan* probably do so to keep up with new kit production and to learn proper color schemes. *Hobby Japan* also publishes *Hobby Japan Extra,* an oversized quarterly magazine with issues devoted to specific topics. Subscriptions to *Hobby Japan* are not available in the United States, but some retail stores have copies brought in by air at a cost of about $20 an issue.

4991. *Scale Models International.* Incorporates: *Scale Auto Modeller;* Formerly (until Aug.1983): *Scale Models;* Incorporates: *P A M News International; Model.* [ISSN: 0269-834X] 1969. m. USD 72. S A M Publications, Media House, 21 Kingsway, Bedford, MK42 9BJ, United Kingdom; mail@sampublications.com; http://www.sampublications.com. Illus., adv. *Bk. rev.:* Brief. *Aud.:* Hs, Ga.

Scale Models International is one of the few English-language magazines that covers the traditional range of static model kits, including automobiles, trucks, planes, ships, military armor, science fiction, and figures. It is published in the UK by SAM publications, which also publishes *Scale Aviation Modeller* and *Model Aircraft Monthly* (see the subsection on Model Airplanes and Rockets). Contents include listings of new kits and aftermarket detail parts, detailed articles on assembling and improving new kits, brief prototype information, and reports and schedules of UK model shows. All illustrations are in color.

Scale Models International was founded in 1969 as *Scale Models* and added "international" to its name in 1983. In 2001, it was acquired by SAM Publications, which merged the magazine with its own three-year-old *Scale Auto Modeller.* The last issue of *Scale Auto Modeller* was published in November 2001.

Model Railroads

Model railroading is one of the most popular of all model-making hobbies. Its leading magazines have circulations equalled only by flying-model magazines. Memberships in its two major U.S. organizations—the National Model Railroad Association and the Train Collectors Association—total about 50,000.

Mechanical toy trains running on tracks were developed in the 1880s, and exact scale models—as opposed to toys—emerged during the period between the world wars.

At times, scale modelers have been fiercely independent of those who use toy trains, but in recent years most of the high-quality toys have become far more realistic, and the division between scale models and toy trains is much less pronounced today than it was 30 years ago.

Model railroading involves a wider variety of activities than do most model hobby areas. Modelers build locomotives and cars, build miniature buildings, construct elaborate operating layouts involving all sorts of electronic controls, hold complex operating sessions simulating real railroads in action, and collect scale models and old toys. The most impressive model railroad layouts are operating historical dioramas of amazing complexity and technical sophistication.

The primary internal division within the field of scale model railroading is on the basis of scale—the ratio in size between the model and the real world. A modeler in most other hobby areas can easily work in a variety of scales because models can be displayed and operated individually, but a train layout is an integrated whole, and all equipment needs to match in scale and operate on the same gauge (width) of track. A scale modeler therefore tends to pick one scale and stick with it for years. (Collectors, however, tend to leave their trains standing idle on shelves and are less constrained by scale.) The most common gauges, in order of increasing size, are N, H0, 0, and G, with H0 by far the most popular.

The contents of model railroad magazines reflect the wide variety of hobby activities. Typical articles cover construction projects; outstanding layouts and models; track plans, with emphasis on potential for operation; electronic projects; construction and painting methods; prototype equipment and buildings, usually illustrated with photographs and plans; antique toy trains; and new products. Most model railroad magazines try to cover the relevant topics and gauges with a balanced assortment of articles rather than with many monthly columns.

More excellent magazines are published on model railroads than on any other model-building or -collecting hobby. The ones listed below are the best of their types, but there are many others, and even those libraries that subscribe to all the magazines here have not exhausted the worthwhile magazines in the field.

The dominant American general model railroad magazine is *Model Railroader,* followed by *Railroad Model Craftsman.* Both have long histories in the hobby. Among the more specialized magazines, the most impressive are probably *Garden Railways, Mainline Modeler,* and *Narrow Gauge and Short Line Gazette,* but there are many other excellent magazines. Those reviewed here include *Finescale Railroader, Model Railroading,* and *Railmodel Journal.*

Toy train collectors are primarily interested in mass-produced toys rather than handcrafted scale models, and they try to collect them in the original condition in which they left the factory. The leading publications on toy train collecting are *Train Collectors Quarterly* and *Classic Toy Trains.* Both are excellent.

Model railroad magazines published in the United States do not pay a great deal of attention to foreign railroads. Because many Americans are extremely interested in foreign trains—in part because of the wide availability of high-quality European models in this country—libraries should seriously consider subscribing to one or more foreign model railroad magazines. The six annotated here—*Railway Modeller* and *Continental Modeller* from England; *Eisenbahn Magazin, LGB Telegram, Maerklin Magazin,* and *MIBA-Miniaturbahnen* from Germany; and *Loco Revue* from France—are among the very best.

Because the major magazines tend to concentrate on H0 trains, several specialty magazines are published for modelers interested in less popular scales. Three good examples of these are reviewed here: *N-Scale, S Gaugian,* and *0 Gauge Railroading.*

One area of model railroading is covered in the Live Steam subsection. This is the hobby of constructing working steam locomotives. Building live steam engines is a complex undertaking calling for a high degree of skill in metalworking, and the hobby has more in common with building other types of working miniature machines than it does with building model electric trains.

Prototype information is extremely important to any modeler who is attempting to re-create the equipment and atmosphere of an actual railroad. This information is available in a variety of magazines and books. The most useful publications from the model builder's point of view are those that provide extremely specialized technical information rather than pretty pictures of trains. Among the best magazines are those published by railroad historical societies and devoted to the history and equipment of individual railroads. *Mainline Modeler* lists about 60 of these societies each month, including addresses and subscription rates, and librarians should check to see whether high-quality publications are available on the railroads that serve or once served their individual areas.

4992. *Classic Toy Trains.* [ISSN: 0895-0997] 1987. 9x/yr. USD 39.95; USD 5.50 newsstand/cover per issue. Ed(s): Neil Besougloff. Kalmbach Publishing Co., PO Box 1612, Waukesha, WI 53187-1612; webmaster@kalmbach.com; http://wwwclasstrain.com. Illus., adv. Sample. Circ: 63438 Paid. Vol. ends: Dec. *Bk. rev.:* 0-5, 200-300 words. *Aud.:* Hs, Ga.

Classic Toy Trains is a successful and important magazine covering toy trains both as collectors' items and as operating toys. It features articles on the history of toy trains and the people who manufactured them, layout construction, collectors and their collections, repair and maintenance of old toys, new products, and forthcoming swap meets for collectors. It also contains a very substantial amount of advertising, although the growth of Internet sales has diminished the number of exchange ads for old equipment. Most of the articles are on the two dominant American toy train firms, Lionel and American Flyer, but the magazine covers other historic companies, plus such modern manufacturers of three-rail trains as K-Line, MTH, and Williams. The magazine is unusually attractive, with a handsome layout, a large number of fine color illustrations, and literate and entertaining writing. Compared with the *Train Collectors Quarterly,* the other important American publications on toy trains, *Classic Toy Trains* is less scholarly and focuses more on new products.

For serials librarians, here are the frequency changes for *CTT*: one-shot test issue (1987); quarterly (1988–1989, with only two issues in 1988); bimonthly (1990–1995, with seven issues in 1995); eight issues per year (1996–1998), and nine issues per year (1999–date). The nine issues appear monthly, with the exception of April, June, and August.

4993. *Continental Modeller.* [ISSN: 0955-1298] 1979. m. GBP 28.80 domestic; GBP 40.80 foreign; GBP 2.40 newsstand/cover per issue. Ed(s): Andrew Burnham. Peco Publications and Publicity Ltd., Beer, Seaton, EX12 3NA, United Kingdom; http://www.peco-uk.com. Illus., index, adv. Sample. Vol. ends: Dec. *Bk. rev.:* 3-10, 50-300 words. *Aud.:* Hs, Ga.

Aimed at British model railroaders interested in equipment from throughout the world, *Continental Modeller* covers not only Western European equipment but also railroads in the former Soviet bloc, Africa, Australia, and Asia, with emphasis on the United States, Western Europe, and the former British Empire. It is published by Peco, a British manufacturer of model railroad equipment. Peco also publishes *Railway Modeller* (see below in this section), which is Britain's leading model railroad magazine. *Continental Modeller* is similar to that publication in format, with solid articles and mostly color illustrations. For libraries that want coverage of European equipment in English, or articles with photographs and measured drawings of equipment from odd corners of the world, *Continental Modeller* is a good choice.

4994. *Eisenbahn Modellbahn Magazin.* [ISSN: 0342-1902] 1963. m. EUR 67.80 domestic; EUR 73.80 foreign; EUR 6.15 newsstand/cover. Ed(s): Hans-Joachim Gilbert. Alba Publikation Alf Teloeken GmbH & Co. KG, Willstaetterstr 9, Duesseldorf, 40549, Germany; braun@alba-verlag.de; http://www.alba-publikation.de. Illus., index, adv. Circ: 39000 Controlled. Vol. ends: Dec. *Bk. rev.:* 0-15, 75-300 words. *Aud.:* Ga.

Eisenbahn Modellbahn Magazin ("railroad and model railroad magazine") is the official publication of the national association of German rail fans and model railroaders (BDEF, Bundesverband Deutscher Eisenbahn-Freunde, e.v.) and of the association of German museum and tourist railroads (VDMT, Verband Deutscher Museums- und Touristikbahnen, e.v.). It is divided roughly in half into articles on prototype railroads and on model trains. The prototype news notes, photographs, drawings, and maps are excellent; although they concentrate on Germany, they include all of Europe. The model railroad section, like those of other continental magazines, places relatively little emphasis on construction from scratch and more emphasis on commercial, ready-to-run equipment and on layout construction. The magazine has excellent product reviews, extensive classified ads, lots of color illustrations, and strong opinions. It also provides brief coverage of antique toy train collecting. All in all, it is probably the most useful and attractive general model railroad magazine published in Europe. In German only.

4995. *Finescale Railroader.* Formerly (until 1995): *Outdoor Railroader.* [ISSN: 1090-3518] 1991. q. USD 26 domestic; USD 39 foreign. Ed(s): Russ Reinberg. Westlake Publishing Co., 1574 Kerryglen St, Westlake Village, CA 91361; finescalerr@msn.com; http://www.finescalerr.com/. *Aud.:* Hs, Ga.

The primary focus of *Finescale Railroader* is extremely accurate and detailed scale models in larger scales, mostly between 1:20 and 1:48. The special appeal of these models is the extensive amount of scale detail that large scales make possible. The magazine is aimed at scale modelers who like large-scale model trains but find that the emphasis on outdoor operation in *Garden Railways* is not what they want. The contents of *Finescale Railroader* are typical of many model railroad magazines, including articles on layouts, new products, construction projects, contest results, etc. *Finescale Railroader* was known as *Outdoor Railroader* from 1991 through 1997, when the name and volume numbering changed and the emphasis switched to indoor models.

4996. *Garden Railways.* [ISSN: 0747-0622] 1984. bi-m. USD 27.95 domestic; USD 34 foreign; USD 5.50 newsstand/cover per issue. Ed(s): Marc Horovitz. Kalmbach Publishing Co., PO Box 1612, Waukesha, WI 53187-1612; mhorovitz@gardenrailways.com; http://www.gardenrailways.com. Illus., adv. Sample. Circ: 35843 Paid. Vol. ends: Nov/Dec. *Aud.:* Hs, Ga.

The last 30 years have seen a tremendous growth in garden railroads, and *Garden Railways* is the leading American magazine devoted specifically to the subject. It is a very high-quality publication, with well-written and attractively illustrated articles. Most of the articles are concerned with the specific problems of outdoor train layouts, including earthworks, roadbed, track, electrical systems, and other civil engineering issues. Other articles cover individual model railroads, new products and the companies that make them, and structures and scenic details. (*Garden Railways* is probably the only U.S. train magazine with a regular gardening column.) Although *Garden Railways* is an especially important acquisition for libraries in areas where gentle climates make outdoor railroading easy, people build garden railways in every part of the country. Each issue includes a folded set of large-scale plans (including construction suggestions) bound into the center of the magazine—a great service, but perhaps not the easiest thing for libraries to deal with. *Garden Railways* was acquired by Kalmbach in 1996, but its editor is the same and its contents remain relatively unchanged.

4997. ***L G B Telegram.*** [ISSN: 1056-893X] q. USD 24 in North America; DEM 38 elsewhere. Ed(s): Frances Kehlbeck Civello. Buffington Associates, PO Box 332, Hershey, PA 17033; Stationmaster@LGBTelegram.com; http://www.lgbtelegram.com/. *Aud.:* Hs, Ga.

Lehmann, one of Germany's great old toy firms, helped revolutionize the model railroad hobby in 1968 when it introduced a new line of large-size toy trains, reversing a decades-long move toward increasingly small models. LGB ("Lehmann Gross Bahn," or "Lehmann Large Train" in English) trains have a wide following in America, where they are frequently used for outdoor layouts. *LGB Telegram* is an official English-language publication of the German manufacturer, which also publishes *LGB Telegramm* in German, and it is clearly a company publication, with strong stress on LGB products, maintenance, conversions, and layouts, plus information on the actual narrow-gauge mountain railroads on which most LGB models are based. The magazine is attractively printed on heavy stock, with all color illustrations. Compared with *Maerklin Magazin* (see below, in this subsection) *LGB Telegram* has far less editorial content, but it may be a good choice for libraries in areas (such as California) where outdoor railroads using LGB equipment are especially popular.

4998. ***Loco Revue: la passion du train miniature.*** [ISSN: 0024-5739] 1937. m. except Aug. FRF 298; FRF 340 foreign. Ed(s): Christian Fournereau. Editions Loco-Revue, 12 rue de Sablan, Le Sablen, BP 104, Auray, Cedex 56401, France; locorevue@locorevue.com; http://www.locorevue.com. Illus., index, adv. Sample. Circ: 18079. Vol. ends: Dec. *Bk. rev.:* 1-6, 50-300 words. *Aud.:* Hs, Ga.

Loco Revue is the leading French model railroad magazine. It includes French-language articles on construction techniques, special projects, events in the world of model trains, new products, and prototype railroads. It is also one of the most beautiful of all model-making magazines, illustrated almost completely in color, including large numbers of photographs of layouts with extensive scenic detail based on the French countryside. The high-quality photographs and extensive concentration on French railroad equipment, structures, and scenery—as well as information on the products of the more obscure French model railroad companies—will make it valuable to any modeler interested in French equipment.

4999. ***M I B A - Die Eisenbahn im Modell.*** Former titles (until 1996): *M I B A Miniaturbahnen; Miniaturbahnen.* [ISSN: 1430-886X] 1948. m. EUR 78 domestic; EUR 88 foreign; EUR 6.50 newsstand/cover. Ed(s): Thomas Hilge. M I B A Verlag GmbH, Senefelderstr 11, Nuernberg, 90409, Germany; http://www.miba.de. Illus., index, adv. Circ: 40000. Vol. ends: Dec. *Bk. rev.:* 0-8, 50-350 words. *Aud.:* Hs, Ga.

MIBA-Miniaturbahnen is Germany's senior model railroad magazine, dating back to the days after World War II when Germany's infrastructure was still in ruins and most model trains were earmarked for export. Unlike *Eisenbahn Modellbahn Magazin,* it is devoted almost exclusively to model trains, with relatively few articles on the prototype. *MIBA-Miniaturbahnen* is heavily illustrated in color. It is a particularly good source of information on new developments in the model railroad industry in Europe, with major coverage each spring of the new products displayed at the Nuremberg Fair. For any library that wants extensive pictorial coverage of the European model train industry and of handsome German model train layouts, this is an excellent choice. Annual subscriptions include a thirteenth issue on the Nuremberg Fair. In German only. MIBA also publishes the quarterly *MIBA Spezial,* with each issue providing in-depth coverage of a single topic.

5000. ***Maerklin-Magazin: Zeitschrift fuer grosse und kleine Modell-Eisenbahner.*** [ISSN: 0024-9688] 1965. 6x/yr. EUR 4.80 newsstand/cover. Ed(s): Michael Echterbecker. Modellbahnen-Welt Verlags GmbH, Postfach 940, Goeppingen, 73009, Germany. Illus., index, adv. Sample. Circ: 80000. *Bk. rev.:* 2-4, 150-250 words. *Aud.:* Hs, Ga.

In years past, many of the great toy train firms sponsored magazines for the children and adults who used their products. These magazines were similar to other model railroad magazines, but the main emphasis was on building layouts using the company's trains. Of all these magazines, *Maerklin Magazin* is the most important current example. Maerklin is the oldest—and in dollar sales the largest—model railroad company in the world. Large numbers of people construct Maerklin layouts and collect old Maerklin trains. The contents of *Maerklin Magazin* are generally typical of European model railroad magazines, with lots of articles on prototype railroads, model-building projects, electronic projects, layout construction, and events for railroad enthusiasts. The magazine pays a great deal of attention to new Maerklin products, which is understandable given the corporate sponsorship, but it also provides a great deal of information on noncompetitive products of other manufacturers (such as model buildings and scenery) for use in layout construction. The magazine is handsomely designed and printed in full color. For the many Americans who like German railroads or Maerklin trains, this is an excellent acquisition. In German only.

5001. ***Mainline Modeler.*** [ISSN: 0199-5421] 1980. m. USD 42 domestic; USD 49 Canada; USD 125 elsewhere. Ed(s): Robert L Hundman. Mainline Modeler, 13110 Beverly Park Rd, Mukilteo, WA 98275; http://www.mainlinemodeler.com/. Illus., adv. Sample. Circ: 14000. Vol. ends: Dec. *Bk. rev.:* 0-10, 50-250 words. *Aud.:* Ga, Sa.

Mainline Modeler is an outstanding publication, one of the best of the more specialized model railroad magazines. Unlike such general magazines as *Model Railroader,* its scope is limited to material on prototype locomotives, railroad cars, and railroad structures and to methods of building particularly accurate models of them. The magazine is a particularly strong source of information on constructing accurate models of historic freight cars. About two-thirds of the articles consist of careful historical studies of equipment with detailed instructions for scratch-building or for modifying existing commercial kits to produce highly accurate models. The rest of the articles consist of prototype information, with the detailed photographs and drawings modelers need to build accurate models, but with no information on how to build actual models. The drawings and photographs are of very high quality and are reproduced clearly on excellent paper. Among the magazine's useful features are the monthly listing of the names and addresses of about 60 railroad historical societies and the "Scuttlebutt" column of model railroad industry news and forecasts.

5002. ***Model Railroader.*** [ISSN: 0026-7341] 1934. m. USD 39.95 domestic; USD 50 foreign; USD 4.95 newsstand/cover per issue. Ed(s): Terry Thompson. Kalmbach Publishing Co., PO Box 1612, Waukesha, WI 53187-1612; http://www.modelrailroader.com. Illus., index, adv. Sample. Circ: 177679 Paid. Vol. ends: Dec. Microform: PQC. Online: bigchalk; EBSCO Publishing; Gale Group; Northern Light Technology, Inc.; OCLC Online Computer Library Center, Inc.; ProQuest Information & Learning; H.W. Wilson. *Indexed:* BRI, CBRI, ConsI, IHTDI, MagInd, RGPR. *Bk. rev.:* 0-8, 100-400 words. *Aud.:* Hs, Ga.

Model Railroader is the dominant magazine in model railroading, a first-rate publication with a circulation double that of any other model railroad magazine and perhaps the highest circulation of any model-making magazine in the world. It covers virtually the entire spectrum of scale model railroad activities, including the construction of trains and buildings, layout design and construction, wiring, prototype information, contests, meetings, and outstanding models and layouts. It also includes extensive schedules of forthcoming events. The magazine's production standards are high. Photographs are crisp and finely printed, all (except historic black-and-white images) in color. Most articles are illustrated with excellent original artwork, and editing and composition are consistently professional. For the library subscribing to only one model railroad magazine, *Model Railroader* is clearly the choice. The problem is that so many libraries subscribe only to *Model Railroader* that access to other fine publications on model trains is far too limited.

5003. ***Model Railroading.*** [ISSN: 0199-1914] 1979. 12x/yr. USD 39.95 domestic; USD 48 foreign. Ed(s): Randall Lee. Highlands Station Inc., 2600 S Parker Rd, Ste 1-211, Aurora, CO 80014; randylee@modelrailroadingmag.com; http://www.modelrailroadingmag.com. Illus., index, adv. Sample. Circ: 14751. Vol. ends: Dec. *Aud.:* Hs, Ga.

This attractively produced publication emphasizes building scale models of modern railroads. It is concerned more with constructing accurate models rather than laying track or operating layouts. Among the magazine's specialties, with articles in every issue, are diesel locomotives, modern freight cars, and intermodal freight facilities. It also covers software and electronics for use with model railroads. The current owners of *Model Railroading,* who purchased the magazine in mid-1996, have strong backgrounds in the hobby, and the result is a colorful and interesting publication, well written and professionally produced. The ten issues per year include bimonthly issues in January/February and March/April.

5004. ***N-Scale.*** [ISSN: 1045-5140] 1989. bi-m. USD 28. Ed(s): Robert L Hundman. Mainline Modeler, 13110 Beverly Park Rd, Mukilteo, WA 98275. Illus., adv. Sample. Vol. ends: Nov/Dec. *Aud.:* Ga.

N-Scale, like *0 Gauge Railroading* and *S Gaugian* (see below in this subsection), is designed to serve those who find too much concentration on H0 in the core magazines, such as *Model Railroader* (see above in this subsection). N-scale trains are the smallest popular model trains, about half the size of H0-scale trains. Because so much N-scale landscape can be fitted into a small space, N-scale trains make it more possible to re-create sweeping scenery in miniature, and modelers concentrate more on layout development than on detailed construction of individual pieces of rolling stock. N-gauge enthusiasts have also developed national standards for modular layouts, and modelers frequently set up temporary layouts consisting of sections owned by many individual hobbyists and brought to a central location. *N-Scale* has excellent articles, crisp printing, and high-quality paper. Compared with *Mainline Modeler* (above in this section), which is published by the same company, *N-Scale* is a more general-purpose magazine and places more emphasis on new products and modeling techniques.

5005. ***Narrow Gauge and Short Line Gazette.*** [ISSN: 0148-2122] 1975. bi-m. USD 28 domestic; USD 38 foreign. Ed(s): Robert W Brown. Benchmark Publications, Ltd., PO Box 26, Los Altos, CA 94023. Illus., adv. Sample. Circ: 16000. Vol. ends: Jan/Feb. *Bk. rev.:* 4-8, 100-400 words. *Aud.:* Ga.

Narrow Gauge and Short Line Gazette specializes in material on the backwoods railroads of North America, particularly the small two- and three-foot-gauge mining and logging lines that lent such distinctive charm to transportation in the mountains. For years modelers have found the diminutive narrow-gauge equipment a fascinating challenge. Some of the finest scratch-building is done in this area, and the influence of narrow gaugers on the hobby has been much greater than their numbers would suggest. The *Gazette* is the most important publication in this popular specialty area. It concentrates on detailed prototype information and accurate model building and is a physically handsome magazine, with a clean, elegant layout and with fine photographs and good drawings carefully reproduced on high-quality paper. Libraries that already subscribe to a basic scale model railroad publication should consider the *Narrow Gauge and Short Line Gazette,* particularly if they are located in areas that once had narrow-gauge railroads.

5006. ***O Gauge Railroading.*** Formerly: *O Scale Railroading.* [ISSN: 1062-1482] 1969. 7x/yr. USD 29.95 domestic; USD 39.40 in Canada & Mexico; USD 43.95 elsewhere. Ed(s): Fred M Dole. O G R Publishing, Inc., 33 Sheridan Rd, Poland, OH 44514; http://www.ogauger.com. Illus., adv. Circ: 31000 Paid. *Bk. rev.:* 0-3, 250-1,000 words. *Aud.:* Hs, Ga.

High rail trains are the modern descendants of Lionel trains. They run on 0 gauge three-rail toy train track, but in many ways are nearly scale models. *0 Gauge Railroading* has the largest circulation of any magazine devoted to a single model railroad gauge. It provides extensive coverage of both high rail trains (which are collected and operated by vast numbers of people) and scale-0 trains (which are the hobby of a very small fraternity). Unlike the toy-train-collecting magazines, *0 Gauge Railroading* concentrates on actually building layouts and operating trains. And unlike the scale model magazines, it places relatively little emphasis on building from scratch. Articles include evaluative reviews of new equipment, layout construction, troubleshooting equipment, technical information on maintenance and repair, etc. *0 Gauge Railroading* is well written and edited, with articles by actual toy-train operators. It features large numbers of color photographs of equipment and layouts.

5007. ***Railmodel Journal: modeling from the prototype.*** [ISSN: 1043-5441] 1989. m. USD 48 domestic; USD 60 foreign; USD 5.95 newsstand/cover per issue. Ed(s): Robert Schleicher. Golden Bell Press Inc., 2403 Champa St, Denver, CO 80205; http://www.goldenbellpress.com. Illus., index, adv. Vol. ends: May. *Bk. rev.:* Occasional. *Aud.:* Hs, Ga.

Railmodel Journal is an excellent specialized publication edited by one of the most experienced writers in the field. Much of the magazine is devoted to methods of upgrading kits and of using commercial components to create accurate scale models. Its special areas of concentration are accurate freight car and diesel locomotive modeling, and creating models of the kinds of intermodal facilities and trackside industries that keep freight cars busy. Concentration is almost completely on H0 scale. *Railmodel Journal* has an unusual number of articles with detailed, step-by-step instruction photos. It is well edited and attractively printed on coated stock.

5008. ***Railroad Model Craftsman.*** [ISSN: 0033-877X] 1933. m. USD 34.95 domestic; USD 45 foreign; USD 4.50 newsstand/cover per issue. Ed(s): William Schaumburg. Carstens Publications, Inc., PO Box 700, Newton, NJ 07860-0777; http://www.rrmodelcraftsman.com. Illus., index, adv. Sample. Circ: 95000. Vol. ends: May. *Bk. rev.:* book and video reviews: 1-5, 500-2000 words. *Aud.:* Hs, Ga.

Railroad Model Craftsman is *Model Railroader*'s major competitor and an excellent magazine. Like *Model Railroader,* it covers virtually all aspects of model railroading, including construction of model locomotives, railroad cars, and trackside buildings; design, construction, and wiring of layouts; prototype detail; outstanding models and layouts; product, book, and video reviews; and conventions, contests, and other hobby activities. Comparing the two journals is difficult because both magazines are trying to reach the same audience and are looking for the same kind of material. *Craftsman*'s how-to-do-it articles are sometimes a little more down-to-earth and detailed, and therefore suited to the skills of ordinary modelers; some of its articles are longer and more detailed; and it devotes less space to electronics—but these are minor differences. *Model Railroader* is one of the world's major model magazines. *Railroad Model Craftsman* stands very strongly in second place among U.S. general-purpose model railroad magazines. Libraries of any size need both.

5009. ***Railway Modeller: for every British railway enthusiast.*** [ISSN: 0033-8931] 1949. m. GBP 28.80 domestic; GBP 40.80 foreign; GBP 2.40 newsstand/cover per issue. Ed(s): John Brewer. Peco Publications and Publicity Ltd., Beer, Seaton, EX12 3NA, United Kingdom; http://www.peco-uk.com. Illus., index, adv. Sample. Circ: 44827. Vol. ends: Dec. *Bk. rev.:* 0-5, 100-500 words. *Aud.:* Hs, Ga.

Railway Modeller is Great Britain's leading model railroad magazine, and together with its sister publication, *Continental Modeller* (see above in this subsection), it dominates the field. Like *Model Railroader* (above) in the United States, *Railway Modeller* covers a general range of model railroad subjects, but it places relatively less emphasis on operation and electrical systems and more on finished layouts. In large part, this reflects the British tradition of model railroading, which tends to be one of elegant, uncluttered layouts with careful attention to accurate historical detail and large numbers of scratch-built structures. Because of its emphasis on British rolling stock and scenery and its many attractive photographs, it overlaps U.S. publications very little. In addition to a wide range of articles, it includes extensive advertising, particularly for British hobby shops, and calendars of meetings, exhibitions, and swap meets. *Railway Modeller* is a good choice for a library that wants a magazine on British model railroading, but it is necessary to remember that more Americans use Continental equipment than British equipment because the majority of outstanding manufacturers of European-prototype ready-to-run equipment are in Germany.

5010. ***S Gaugian.*** [ISSN: 0273-6241] 1962. bi-m. USD 32 domestic; USD 39 foreign. Ed(s): Donald J Heimburger. Heimburger House Publishing Co., 7236 W Madison St, Forest Park, IL 60130; http://www.heimburgerhouse.com/sgaugian. Illus., adv. Sample. Circ: 5000 Paid. Vol. ends: Nov/Dec. *Bk. rev.:* 3-12, 100-800 words. *Aud.:* Hs, Ga.

S-gauge trains are built to a scale of 1:64 and run on 7/8-inch gauge track, about halfway between H0 and 0 gauges. S gauge was originally developed by the American Flyer Company under A.C. Gilbert's ownership at the end of World War II. Although regular Flyer production ended in 1966, enthusiasm for the gauge continues among collectors and operators of old American Flyer equipment, as well as among hobbyists who work with scale model S-gauge equipment and with reissues from Lionel, which purchased the American Flyer trademark and tooling. *S Gaugian* concentrates on those aspects of model railroads that are peculiar to S gauge, covering both scale and tinplate (American Flyer) topics. Issues typically include news of new S-gauge products, S-gauge construction projects, layout pictures, articles on collecting and repairing American Flyer trains, and so on. For those with an interest in S gauge, this is the most important magazine. Since 1984, Heimburger House has also published the semi-annual *Sn3 Modeler* for people who build 1:64 scale models of narrow-gauge equipment.

5011. ***Train Collectors Quarterly.*** [ISSN: 0041-0829] 1955. q. USD 14. Ed(s): Bruce D Manson, Jr. Train Collectors Association, Willow Street, Box 619, Lancaster, PA 17584; http://www.traincollectors.org/. Illus., index. Sample. Circ: 32000 Controlled. Vol. ends: Oct. *Bk. rev.:* Occasional. *Aud.:* Hs, Ga.

Train Collectors Quarterly is the official journal of the Train Collectors Association, the largest of the U.S. toy-train collectors associations. Most of the articles are detailed studies of the history, current operations, and products of various companies like Lionel, American Flyer, Ives, Marx, Carlisle & Finch, Maerklin, etc. The magazine places primary emphasis on American firms, but information on a huge variety of manufacturers is included. Other articles cover association activities and the layouts and collections of various members. Train collectors are capable of exceptionally scholarly research, and some articles are impressively detailed. The fact that the editor can draw on the collective knowledge of some 30,000 experts means that the articles tend to be unusually authoritative. The main competition for the *Quarterly* is Kalmbach's *Classic Toy Trains.* Generally speaking, the *Train Collectors Quarterly* is the more scholarly of the two; it speaks with great authority and it carries no advertising. *Classic Toy Trains* is a more commercial magazine, with shorter and more popularly oriented articles, better graphics and photography, and extensive advertising. Both are excellent publications.

Live Steam

Modelers interested in live steam build and operate steam-powered equipment in miniature. In many respects, "live steamers" have a lot in common with people who build and operate flying model airplanes; both are working with the real thing in small size rather than with scale miniatures that—although they may bear a closer external resemblance to the prototype—are completely different mechanically.

Most live-steam models are substantial. The majority of live-steam model railroads, for example, are designed to haul full-sized adults, even if some of the smaller locomotives are scarcely larger than shoe boxes.

Constructing most live-steam models requires a great deal of technical skill. Although ready-to-run models and bolt-together kits are available—primarily for smaller models—most live-steam projects require a substantial amount of machine shop work.

Modelers interested in live-steam models build a variety of types of equipment. The greatest number of modelers build model railroad equipment. Others build stationary steam engines (of the type that once powered factories), small steam-powered launches (generally reminiscent of the *African Queen*), and traction engines (the sort of equipment that once powered old threshing machines).

The two most important magazines concerned with live steam are the U.S. monthly *Live Steam* and the British biweekly *Model Engineer.* A U.S. library selecting just one will probably pick *Live Steam* because of the American technical terms and the addresses of U.S. suppliers. *Model Engineer,* however, offers many special advantages, including a wider range of projects, and it has the special distinction of being the world's oldest model-building magazine.

Even though other magazines deal with model trains and ships, the highly technical nature of live-steam modeling means that material that appears in live-steam magazines is not duplicated in other sources.

One special characteristic of live-steam publications is the tendency of projects to be covered in articles that may continue for two years or more, with a new segment appearing in every issue. For this reason, modelers will want access to considerable runs of these magazines when certain projects interest them.

There are vastly fewer modelers in this area than in such extremely popular areas as model railroads, flying models, and static models because working with live-steam equipment is both difficult and expensive. But the hobby has many followers, and libraries in large communities should have at least one magazine on the subject.

5012. ***Live Steam.*** Formerly: *Live Steam Magazine.* [ISSN: 0364-5177] 1966. bi-m. USD 37.95 domestic; USD 46.95 Canada; USD 44.95 elsewhere. Ed(s): Clover Mckinley. Village Press, Inc., 2779 Aero Park Dr, Traverse City, MI 49686; http://www.villagepress.com/livesteam. Illus., index, adv. Sample. Circ: 12300 Paid. Vol. ends: Dec. *Bk. rev.:* Occasional. *Aud.:* Sa.

Live Steam is the major U.S. magazine in its subject area. It includes articles on the construction of a variety of live-steam equipment, with primary emphasis placed on steam locomotives, marine engines, and stationary steam engines. It also includes articles on construction techniques, specific types of fittings, toolmaking, the activities of associations and hobbyists (including schedules of forthcoming meetings), and occasionally prototype equipment. Most of the information is of a highly specialized, technical nature. Most articles are illustrated with a large number of excellent technical drawings. In recent years, *Live Steam* has widened its scope and broadened its contents. It is well edited and illustrated, primarily in color. U.S. libraries that can afford only one magazine on live steam will find this the best choice.

5013. ***Model Engineer.*** [ISSN: 0026-7325] 1898. 26x/yr. GBP 58 domestic; GBP 73 in Europe; GBP 74.50 elsewhere. Ed(s): Neil Read, Mike Chrisp. Nexus Special Interests, Carrington Business Park, Manchester Rd, Urmston, M31 4YR, United Kingdom; info@nexusmedia.com; http://www.hhc.co.uk/. Illus., index, adv. Sample. Circ: 50000. Vol. ends: Jun/Dec. *Bk. rev.:* 0-2, 200-300 words. *Aud.:* Sa.

Model Engineer is the oldest model-building magazine in the world. In many respects, it is very similar to the U.S. publication *Live Steam* (see above in this subsection), for its primary emphasis is on working miniature steam locomotives, stationary steam engines, and traction engines. Its scope, however, is somewhat wider, for it includes more historical prototype information, more book reviews, and much more extensive coverage of model contests, which are far more prevalent in Great Britain than in the United States. It also includes articles on constructing models that are not steam-powered, including hot-air engines, clocks, railroad accessories, tools, and so on; and it takes a more active interest in the history of technology and in the historical preservation of machinery. U.S. users will find *Model Engineer* particularly useful because of the information it provides on British sources of supplies and equipment. However, they may have occasional trouble coping with some of the British technical vocabulary.

In 1997, the publisher, Nexus, converted some of its magazines to what it called a "lunar" schedule. Semimonthly magazines changed to biweeklies, with 26 rather than 24 issues a year; monthly magazines were published once every four weeks, with 13 rather than 12 annual issues; and so on.

Model Airplanes and Rockets

People interested in model airplanes and rockets fall into three very distinct groups. The first includes people who build and operate flying models, usually by radio control (the "r/c" that appears in some titles); they form a large and important group, most closely allied with people who operate r/c model automobiles and racing boats. An allied area is model rockets; although these share at least air space with flying models, they have completely different organizations and publications.

The second group consists of the builders of static (nonoperating) scale models of airplanes and spacecraft; their hobby has virtually nothing to do with flying models, but it has much in common with building nonoperating scale automobiles, boats, and military armor.

The third group includes collectors of factory built miniature aircraft, particularly small diecast metal planes.

These divisions in the hobby are reflected in publishing patterns, for no major magazine covers more than one type of model airplanes.

No major U.S. magazine is devoted exclusively to building static aircraft models. Good coverage of military aircraft is provided in *FineScale Modeler* (see the Military Miniatures subsection). Greater concentration on model planes is provided in the British publication *Scale Aviation Modeller International,* while *Model Aircraft Monthly* provides extensive prototype information with suggestions for suitable kits. Spacecraft and other science fiction models receive some coverage in *The Modeler's Resource* (see the subsection on Miniature Figures).

Material on collecting small diecast airplanes is found in *Model Auto Review* (see the subsection on Model Automobiles) and *Lee's Toy Review* (see the subsection on Miniature Figures).

Model flying ranks with model railroading and static-model building as one of the three most popular of all model-building hobbies, and the purchase of magazines in this area is therefore of particular importance.

Most of the people who build and operate flying models are interested primarily in small-scale aircraft and rockets that fly well rather than in detailed scale models, and their frequent concentration on operation rather than on strictly prototypical appearance makes this hobby—along with operating model automobiles and racing boats—somewhat different from the other model-making hobbies. In many ways, the r/c airplane, ship, and auto hobbies are as much sports as they are model making.

Because the various r/c hobbies differ from other model hobbies, the publishing patterns in the r/c hobbies differ as well. These differences are most clearly visible in the magazines' heavy use of monthly columns, in their construction articles, and in their physical layout.

Model airplane flying includes a large number of special-interest areas, each with adherents who want to find something of interest in each issue of a magazine, and some publishers have responded by filling the magazines with more or less regular monthly columns in the various specialty areas. Although this may be necessary to hold the readership, it can give the magazines a choppy flavor and lead to a lot of "filler" material when columnists can't think of anything to say.

Construction articles in flying-model airplane magazines normally do not include plans, although they may illustrate the plans in miniature. Model airplane builders work from full-size plans, and only the very smallest of these can fit on the pages of a magazine. To back up their construction articles, therefore, many of the magazines listed here offer full-size plans for sale at prices ranging from about $3 for small models to more than $30 for large models with six- or seven-foot wingspans. The majority of plans are run off in low volume on blueprint equipment and can be obtained on demand years after traditionally printed plans would be out of print.

Other components of flying-model airplane magazines include product reviews, which are often extremely thorough, articles on contests and meetings, articles on construction methods, and a large number of advertisements for the amazing range of high-tech equipment available in the field. For the most part, the magazines have little or no prototype information and very few book reviews.

Flying-model-airplane magazines, along with r/c boat and car magazines, don't look like other modeling magazines. Because the emphasis of the hobby is more on operation than on the construction of highly detailed scale models, there is less need for the fine photography sought by magazines in other model-building areas. Many of the photographs, therefore, are small snapshots of hobbyists or of equipment in operation. To enliven their covers, some r/c magazines still feature pretty girls in bikinis holding model airplanes (although with changing times, many are now ostensibly flying the planes), while others have adopted exuberantly colorful and image-laden layouts reminiscent of the covers of hot rod magazines.

The best general U.S. flying-model airplane magazines are probably *Flying Models, Model Airplane News, Model Aviation,* and *R/C Modeler.* All four are excellent and popular publications. Although there is a lot of duplication among them, no library of any size should try to get by with just one.

In the late 1990s, two new areas of model aviation emerged. One is silent flight, including gliders and electrically powered aircraft. The important U.S. magazine is *Quiet Flyer.* The second new area is miniature radio-controlled aircraft, which were made possible by the miniaturization of electric control components. There are two speciality titles in this area, *Backyard Flyer* and *Radio Control Microflight.*

In the past, flying-model airplane magazines sometimes covered r/c model boats and cars, but they ceased to do so as specialized magazines appeared in those areas.

Model rocketry is a hobby fairly well divorced from other model flying activities, but it is tremendously popular, especially with schoolchildren and youth groups, because it is exciting and inexpensive. Because of the number of young people involved in the hobby, organizational leaders estimate the number of participants may be in the millions. Annual sales of model rocketry equipment are probably around $40 million. Model rocketry is ignored by the model aircraft magazines, but the field is covered by three specialty publications: *Extreme Rocketry, High Power Rocketry,* and *Sport Rocketry.*

In addition to the U.S. magazines mentioned above, there are some excellent British, European, and Japanese magazines on model flying. For the most part, however, foreign publications of general scope are less likely to include important material missing from U.S. publications in this field than they are in, for example, model railroading, where the emphasis on different prototypes matters more. Some excellent British specialty magazines, however, have worked to fill international niches by covering material that is often omitted from U.S. publications. These include two magazines reviewed here—*Radio Control Jet International* and *Model Helicopter World.* The third British flying model magazine reviewed here is *Silent Flight,* which covers some of the same material as *Quiet Flyer.*

5014. *Backyard Flyer.* [ISSN: 1542-2135] 2001. bi-m. USD 19.95 domestic; USD 29.95 Canada; USD 34.95 elsewhere. Ed(s): Jon Chappell. Air Age Publishing, 100 E Ridge Rd., Ridgefield, CT 06877-4606; http://www.airage.com. Illus., adv. *Aud.:* Hs, Ga.

Backyard Flyer is a new magazine from Air Age, which publishes a variety of model-making magazines. The magazine reflects the rapid growth of radio control miniature aircraft, which was made possible in the late 1990s by the continuing development of electric propulsion for model aircraft plus miniature radio control components. The result is model airplanes whose small size and silent flight make operating in backyards, schoolyards, parks, and gymnasiums possible, and whose light weight eliminates the need for special liability insurance. The popularity of radio control miniature aircraft is reflected in the magazine's rapid progress from quarterly to bimonthly publication in 2003. *Backyard Flyer* is designed to appeal to new hobbyists, including children, and features the lively graphics typical of Air Age publications. For specialists, Air Age also publishes *Radio Control Microflight* (see below in this subsection).

5015. *Extreme Rocketry.* 2000. 9x/yr. USD 39.95 domestic; USD 59.95 Canada. Ed(s): Brent McNeely. RocketeerMedia, 3020 Bryant Ave, Las Vegas, NV 89102. Adv. *Aud.:* Ga, Sa.

Extreme Rocketry covers much the same topics as *High Power Rocketry,* with emphasis on large model rockets that blast their way miles into the air. It includes product reviews, how-to-do-it articles, interviews with hobbyists and manufacturers, histories of the hobby, calendars of forthcoming "launches,"—and recently, articles on complications resulting from Homeland Security. The magazine includes particularly extensive coverage of the rocket launches themselves, with many color pictures of modelers and their rockets. After publishing five bimonthly issues in 2000, *Extreme Rocketry* converted to nine issues per year in 2001.

5016. *Flying Models: the model builder's how-to-do-it magazine.* [ISSN: 0015-4849] 1927. m. USD 34.95 domestic; USD 45 Canada. Ed(s): Frank Fanelli. Carstens Publications, Inc., PO Box 700, Newton, NJ 07860-0777. Illus., adv. Sample. Circ: 35000. Vol. ends: Dec. *Aud.:* Hs, Ga.

Flying Models is the oldest of all U.S. flying-model magazines and one of the oldest model-making magazines in the world. It is not as thick as some of the other flying-model magazines, but it has more editorial material each month than some of them do. Although it is an up-to-date publication, *Flying Models,* like *Model Aviation* (see below in this section), still devotes space to traditional free-flight and control line models (which the strictly r/c magazines tend to ignore), as well as to new trends, such as microscale and ducted fans. Contents include the usual columns (including columns on new developments in the hobby), construction articles, product reviews, and meeting reports, but there is a substantial number of more-general articles as well, including something each month for novice hobbyists. Like some other magazines in its field, *Flying Models* maintains a plan service for full-size drawings of projects that have appeared as articles. Years ago, *Flying Models* included material on r/c model boats, but it no longer does so, and libraries that need material in that area should subscribe to *Radio Control Boat Modeler.*

5017. *High Power Rocketry.* [ISSN: 1070-5244] 1968. 9x/yr. USD 46. Ed(s): Bruce E Kelly. H P R Publishing, Box 970009, Orem, UT 84097-0009. Illus. Circ: 9000. *Aud.:* Hs, Ga.

Under its earlier names, *High Power Rocketry* was the official journal of the Tripoli Rocketry Association, which is devoted to large model rockets that can blast their way literally miles into the air. The magazine separated from the association in 1993, but it is still published as a service to its members. Like the National Association of Rocketry, which publishes *Sport Rocketry* (see below in this section), the Tripoli Rocketry Association is particularly concerned with issues of safety, liability insurance, and legal clearance for launches. (The association is called "Tripoli" because one of its founders helped finance the club by selling some gold coins his father acquired in Tripoli during World War II.) *High Power Rocketry*'s articles are primarily concerned with reports on launches and with detailed information on model rocket technology, which can be very high-tech indeed, but also on full-sized missiles. The magazine is well edited and printed, with many illustrations in color.

5018. *Model Aircraft Monthly.* [ISSN: 1475-3405] 2001. m. GBP 33 domestic; GBP 38 in Europe; GBP 43 elsewhere. Ed(s): Richard Franks. S A M Publications, Media House, 21 Kingsway, Bedford, MK42 9BJ, United Kingdom; mail@sampublications.com; http://www.sampublications.com. Adv. Circ: 25000 Paid. *Aud.:* Hs, Ga, Sa.

Model Aircraft Monthly is intended to provide the detailed prototype information that modelers need to create exact scale models. The magazine is published by SAM publications, which also publishes *Scale Aviation Modeller* and *Scale Models International.* Each issue includes articles on a variety of aircraft, primarily military, with historical notes and large numbers of photographs. Many of the photos are of the odd details that modelers need to know but are often not visible in regular photographs, such as the insides of wheel wells or cockpits. Other material includes fold-out scale drawings and artwork depicting various aircraft paint schemes. Articles often include information on suitable kits, but the magazine leaves detailed how-to-do-it information to other publications. One useful feature is a monthly list of about 200 model and aircraft web sites. *Model Aircraft Monthly* is well illustrated—in color where the original photographs were in color.

5019. *Model Airplane News.* [ISSN: 0026-7295] 1929. m. USD 29.95 domestic; USD 44.95 Canada; USD 54.95 elsewhere. Ed(s): Tom Atwood. Air Age Publishing, 100 E Ridge Rd., Ridgefield, CT 06877-4606; http://www.airage.com. Illus., adv. Sample. Circ: 90000 Paid. Vol. ends: Dec. Microform: PQC. Online: bigchalk; EBSCO Publishing; Gale Group; Northern Light Technology, Inc.; ProQuest Information & Learning. *Indexed:* ConsI, MagInd. *Aud.:* Hs, Ga.

Model Airplane News is the second oldest U.S. flying-model magazine and one of the most popular. Much of the editorial content consists of articles on construction, flying techniques, new products, flying meets, and competitions, as well as regular monthly features on various specialties. It places particular emphasis on new commercial products, with both announcements and detailed test reviews. Its special theme issues on such topics as model helicopters are impressive, as are its annual buyers' guides. Until a few years ago, *Model Airplane News* included coverage of free-flight and control line models, but now it concentrates almost exclusively on radio control. It also includes a substantial amount of material on ready-to-fly equipment. Like other Air Age publications, it has graphics that are much more elaborate and bright than those of the more traditional model magazines. Of the general magazines on radio control model airplanes, *Model Airplane News* will be the first choice for many libraries. Air Age also publishes *Radio Control Car Action, Radio Control Nitro, Radio Control Microflight, Backyard Flyer,* and *Radio Control Boat Modeler.*

5020. *Model Aviation.* [ISSN: 0744-5059] 1975. m. USD 12, Libraries, USD 16 (Individuals, USD 24). Ed(s): Sheila Ames Webb. Academy of Model Aeronautics, 5161 E Memorial Dr, Muncie, IN 47302; http://www.modelaircraft.org/Intro.htm. Illus., index, adv. Circ: 170000. Vol. ends: Dec. *Indexed:* IHTDI. *Bk. rev.:* occasional. *Aud.:* Hs, Ga, Sa.

Model Aviation is the official organ of the Academy of Model Aeronautics (AMA), probably the largest association of model builders in the world. Compared with other flying-model magazines, *Model Aviation* tends to be straightforward and businesslike and even more structured, with about 15 monthly columns and departments providing virtually complete coverage of all the specialized areas of flying models. It also includes construction articles, monthly reports from national and regional officers, organizational business, and a calendar of forthcoming "sanctioned" events that can run up to 15 pages of fine print. It provides extensive coverage of contests and competitions, which is appropriate for an organization that establishes rules for and sponsors contests in more than 100 categories. Although *Model Aviation* is clearly an organizational publication, it has a large amount of solid, general material and is very highly regarded in the field. Like some other flying-model magazines, it also offers a plans service. The AMA has a number of affiliated special-interest groups, some with their own publications. *Model Aviation*'s school and public library subscription prices are particularly attractive.

5021. *Model Helicopter World.* [ISSN: 0953-7880] 1988. m. GBP 34 domestic; GBP 44 in Europe; GBP 54 elsewhere. Ed(s): Jon Tanner. Traplet Publications Ltd, Traplet House, Severn Dr, Upton-upon-Severn, WR8 0JL, United Kingdom; mhw@traplet.co.uk; http://www.traplet.com. Illus., index, adv. *Aud.:* Hs, Ga.

Model Helicopter World is dedicated to one of the most specialized and difficult areas of model flying, one where the slightest operator error or mechanical failure can mean an expensive disaster. Articles deal with equipment, flying techniques, maintenance and repairs, new products, aerobatics, competitive flight patterns, fine-tuning equipment, contest results, forthcoming events, etc., including new electrically powered helicopters. Like the many other Traplet hobby magazines, *Model Helicopter World* is attractively printed, in full color. It is the major English-language publication in its specialty area.

5022. *Quiet Flyer Magazine.* Former titles: *S & E Modeler Magazine; Sailplane and Electric Modeler.* 1995. m. USD 36 in North America; USD 52 elsewhere; USD 6.50 newsstand/cover per issue. Ed(s): Wil Byers. Kiona Publishing Inc., 3448 Eastlake Dr., PO Box 4250, W. Richland, WA 99353; wilbyers@earthlink.net; http://www.quietflyer.com. Illus., adv. Circ: 30000 Controlled. Vol. ends: Dec. *Aud.:* Hs, Ga, Sa.

Quiet Flyer Magazine specializes in radio control gliders and electric model aircraft. Traditionally, virtually all flying models were noisy things, with internal combustion engines that frequently failed to endear their owners to people nearby, particularly as suburban sprawl encroached on traditional model aircraft flying fields. In the 1990s, therefore, the emergence of silent flight was a particularly important development. *Quiet Flyer Magazine* is the only U.S. silent flight magazine and an unusually excellent publication, with demanding product reviews, in-depth construction and design articles by experts, and a great deal of extremely useful and interesting technical information (reflecting the editor's background as a consulting engineer). Special interests include such recent breakthroughs as electric ducted fans and electric helicopters.

For serials librarians, the magazine was published bimonthly through 2000. It converted to nine issues a year in 2001, to ten issues annually in 2002, and to monthly in 2003. Originally titled *S & E Modeler* (as in "sailplane and electric"), its name was changed to the much more accessible *Quiet Flyer* in October 2002.

5023. *R/C Modeler.* [ISSN: 0033-6866] 1963. m. USD 28 domestic; USD 38 foreign; USD 3.99 newsstand/cover per issue. R - C Modeler, 144 W Sierra Madre Blvd, Sierra Madre, CA 91024; rcmcorp@aol.com; http://www.rcmmagazine.com. Illus., index, adv. Sample. Vol. ends: Dec. *Bk. rev.:* 3-8, 100-150 words. *Aud.:* Hs, Ga.

RC Modeler is one of the most popular of all model airplane magazines. In the past it was substantially thicker than the other flying-model magazines because of the huge volume of advertising it carried, including multipage sales lists from mail order houses. This advertising made *RC Modeler* the standard hobby source for commercial information, and some modelers referred to it as "the catalog." Today, with the growth of web-based sales, the magazine is less massive. The editorial contents of *RC Modeler* are fairly typical. About eight or nine columns or standard features appear each month; the rest of the magazine consists primarily of excellent construction articles, in-depth product reviews, reports on events, and so on. *RC Modeler* also maintains an unusually impressive plans service, with some 1,000 different plans available.

5024. *Radio Control Jet International.* [ISSN: 0968-3291] 1993. bi-m. GBP 16 domestic; GBP 21 in Europe; USD 38 United States. Ed(s): Simon Delaney. Traplet Publications Ltd, Traplet House, Severn Dr, Upton-upon-Severn, WR8 0JL, United Kingdom; rcji@traplet.com; http://www.traplet.com. Illus., index, adv. *Aud.:* Hs, Ga.

Radio Control Jet International is a British publication on an interesting, extremely high-speed specialty area that has traditionally received very little attention in U.S. magazines. *Radio Control Jet International* covers such unusual subjects as turboprops and ducted fans, and it includes both combat and passenger jets. (Small electrically powered ducted fans have appeared in recent years and are covered in regular model flying magazines, but they aren't in the same potent league as real jets, which routinely travel at an actual 200 miles per hour.) Articles concentrate on how-to-do-it information, activities among those who build and fly model jets, new products, schedules of forthcoming meets, and so on. Like other Traplet publications, it tends to feature long, detailed articles on how to assemble specific kits.

Of all the many British magazines with "international" appended to their titles, this one is the most genuinely international, with reports on activities and advertisements from all over the world. Many articles cover model-jet activities in the United States, and probably more U.S. firms advertise in *Radio Control Jet International* than in any other non–U.S.-based model-building magazine.

5025. *Radio Control Microflight.* [ISSN: 1527-2214] 1999. m. USD 29.95 domestic; CND 44.95 Canada. Air Age Publishing, 100 E Ridge Rd., Ridgefield, CT 06877-4606; http://www.airage.com. *Aud.:* Ga, Sa.

Radio Control Microflight is Air Age's specialist alternative to its more popular *Backyard Flyer* magazine. Both deal with the new generation of small, electrically powered aircraft models that lend themselves to safe operation in parks, gymnasiums, and school yards. *Radio Control Microflight* appears to have a unique format among current model making magazines; it consists of a monthly 16-page newsletter, accompanied by controlled access to a large web site. The publishers have taken advantage of the flexibility of the database format by including plans and video clips to download.

5026. *Scale Aviation Modeller International.* [ISSN: 1356-0530] 1995. m. GBP 76 domestic; GBP 41 in Europe; GBP 46 elsewhere. Ed(s): Richard Franks. S A M Publications, Media House, 21 Kingsway, Bedford, MK42 9BJ, United Kingdom; mail@sampublications.com; http://www.sampublications.com. Illus. Circ: 40000. *Bk. rev.:* about 8 per issue, 100-500 words. *Aud.:* Hs, Ga, Sa.

Scale Aviation Modeller International is an attractive magazine devoted to static models of aircraft. Its articles include reviews of kits (often with pictures of all parts, as well as of the finished models), customizing accessories, and decals; how-to-do-it information on constructing specific kits or on converting kits to other prototypes; pictures of contest-winning models; schedules of U.K. model shows; and excellent prototype coverage, with the kinds of drawings, detail photographs, and color renditions of paint schemes and markings that modelers need to create accurate models. With the exception of historic black-and-white photographs, all illustrations are in color. *Scale Aviation Modeller International* is well edited and cleanly printed on good-quality paper. Unlike a few other British model magazines, which appear to have added "international" to their titles merely to improve U.S. sales, this is a publication with genuinely international scope. No U.S. magazine is devoted exclusively to static models of aircraft, and none includes the models of nonmilitary aircraft found in *Scale Aviation Modeller.*

SAM publications also publishes *Scale Models International* (see the Static Models subsection) and *Model Aircraft Monthly.* The latter contains prototype detail of great use to modelers, but no actual model-making information.

5027. *Silent Flight.* [ISSN: 0963-2808] 7x/yr. GBP 21 domestic; GBP 25.27 in Europe; USD 46 United States. Nexus Special Interests, Carrington Business Park, Manchester Rd, Urmston, M31 4YR, United Kingdom; info@nexusmedia.com; http://www.hhc.co.uk/. Illus., adv. *Aud.:* Hs, Ga.

Silent Flight is concerned specifically with model gliders and electric-powered models, the same general area that is covered by the U.S. publication *Quiet Flyer.* Gliders can be launched by tow line or just tossed into the air from hilltops. This is a specialized area, because the vast majority of flying model aircraft are powered by miniature internal-combustion engines, many of which sound very much like a noisy insect trapped in your ear. Contents include construction articles, product reviews, and many reports on flying events.

5028. *Sport Rocketry.* Formerly: *American Spacemodeling.* [ISSN: 1076-2701] 1958. 6x/yr. USD 47 domestic; USD 56 foreign. Ed(s): Thomas Beach. National Association of Rocketry, 1311 Edgewood Dr, Altoona, WI 54720. Illus., adv. Circ: 7500 Paid. Vol. ends: Dec. *Aud.:* Hs, Ga.

Sport Rocketry is the official publication of the National Association of Rocketry and a fine magazine in its own right, with well-written articles and all-color illustrations. Articles include product reviews and testing, reports on meets and competitions, how-to-do-it information, plans, information on operational safety, and lists of scheduled events. Subscribing to *Sport Rocketry* is a good idea for two reasons. First, although model rocketry is a tremendously popular hobby, especially with young people, it is ignored by model airplane magazines. Second, the National Association of Rocketry has led the way in making model rocketry an extremely safe hobby, and the information in *Sport Rocketry* is therefore particularly valuable. *Sport Rocketry* is concerned primarily with small rockets that climb to 500 to 1,500 feet; for those interested in large model rockets that climb to two or three miles, the suitable magazines are *High Power Rocketry* and *Extreme Rocketry* (above in this subsection).

Model Automobiles

Hobbyists interested in model automobiles work in five fairly specific areas: building static models, building and operating radio-controlled models, collecting die-cast toys and custom-built models, collecting antique toy cars, and slot racing.

The hobby of static model car building has a great deal in common with other kinds of static model construction. Hobbyists who build nonworking models are interested in information on new kits, kit customizing, kit bashing (combining parts from two or more kits), and occasionally building from scratch. Magazine articles tend to center on specific projects, model construction and painting techniques, new kits, and finished models and contests. Builders of static model cars are particularly interested in the sexy end of the spectrum—sports cars, racing cars, muscle cars, and dragsters, as well as such custom conversions as street rods, lowriders, and funny cars. Libraries needing a magazine devoted entirely to static model cars will want to purchase *Scale Auto* and consider *Model Cars.*

Radio-controlled (r/c) model cars have boomed in popularity in the last 15 or 20 years. They have much in common technically with radio-controlled model airplanes, including impressive technical sophistication, as well as frequent pictures of pretty girls displaying new models in the hobby magazines. Most r/c cars are built to 1/8, 1/10, or 1/12 scale, although huge 1/5-scale cars are growing in popularity. R/c cars vary in appearance from customized sedans to Indy cars to the kind of pickups with immense wheels one sometimes sees in small towns on Saturday nights. All are designed for extreme performance—hard-road racing, drag racing, carpet racing, off-road racing, sled pulling, etc.—and as in the case of r/c model airplanes, the r/c model car hobby is half model building and half sport. Most cars are built from fairly simple bolt-together kits, and the articles in magazines tend to center on racing events, product reviews, customized body work, and kit modification, especially using various aftermarket parts to improve performance. The primary U.S. magazine in the area of radio-controlled model cars is *Radio Control Car Action.* Other US publications include *R/C Car, Radio Control Nitro,* and *Xtreme R/C Cars.* Among a number of useful British publications is *Radio Race Car International.*

Hobbyists who collect die-cast and custom-built model cars collect old toy cars; modern, factory-built cars; or custom-built models. Die-cast cars include the small toy metal vehicles made by such companies as Tootsietoy, Matchbox, Corgi, Dinky, and so on, as well as elegant and expensive modern models made for collectors. Today, a four-inch metal model automobile from an artisan maker can cost $100 or more. By far the most popular scale is 1:43—substantially smaller than the 1:25 common in the area of static car models—but production ranges from about 1:18 to 1:87. A serious collector may own thousands of cars. Some coverage on cars of this type is provided by *Scale Auto* and *Model Cars,* but the specialist magazine is *Model Auto Review,* which is essential reading for any really serious collector. Three U.S. collector publications specialize in toy vehicles—*Toy Cars & Models, Toy Farmer,* and *Toy Trucker & Contractor.*

Antique toy cars and trucks made of cast iron or sheet steel in the United States, France, Germany, and other countries are avidly sought by toy collectors. *Antique Toy World* and *Toy Shop* (see the subsection Toy Collecting) provide extensive coverage of this area of collecting, as well as coverage of collecting old die-cast toy cars and trucks.

Three U.S. collector publications specialize in toy vehicles—*Toy Cars & Models, Toy Farmer,* and *Toy Trucker & Contractor.*

Slot car racing is a hobby that boomed in the 1960s. During their hectic heyday, slot cars briefly threatened to destroy sales of popularly priced model trains. But interest in slot cars declined in the 1970s and 1980s. Now the hobby has rebounded, but as a more high-tech adult hobby rather than a discount store standard. Slot cars are electrically powered models that operate on layouts similar to model train layouts. The name comes from the guidance system, which uses a pin on the bottom of the car running in a slot in the roadbed. Some people operate small-scale slot cars (about 1:64 of full size) on home layouts, but serious racing takes place with larger-scale (about 1:24) cars on commercial race tracks. The record for traversing a standard twisty 155-foot course is 1.61 seconds—a scale speed of over mach 2! Slot cars receive little coverage outside of the hobby's specialty publications, such as *Scale Auto Racing News.*

5029. ***Model Auto Review.*** [ISSN: 0267-2715] 1982. 10x/yr. GBP 39 domestic; GBP 48 in Europe; GBP 57 elsewhere. Ed(s): Rod Ward. Malvern House Publications, PO Box SM2, Leeds, LS25 5XA, United Kingdom; http://www.zeteo.com. Illus., adv. Sample. Circ: 4000 Paid. *Bk. rev.:* 0-2, 100-200 words. *Aud.:* Hs, Ga.

Model Auto Review is generally regarded as the best and most authoritative magazine specializing in diecast and custom-built model cars. Although it covers the usual range of topics in static model cars, the majority of its attention is devoted to diecast models as collectible objects, with special concentration on the work of small firms of artisans. As a result of this approach, *Model Auto Review* has become a journal of record for the hobby, and pages are numbered sequentially from the first issue for ease of reference. The articles approach the subject in a variety of ways. Many deal with new production, with the history of the various toy companies, or with models by specific modern makers. Others center on various prototypes, such as Volkswagen Beetles, Rileys, or even Batmobiles. In recent years, coverage has been expanded to cover collectible diecast model airplanes. The editorial contents are literate, fun to read, and (most importantly in collector areas of this type) uninfluenced by advertising. The magazine is neatly printed, but compact, with 300–500 very small photographs (about half in color) in each issue.

5030. ***Model Cars.*** Formerly (until 1998): *Plastic Fanatic.* [ISSN: 1527-4608] 1985. 9x/yr. USD 29 domestic; USD 39 foreign. Ed(s): Gregg Hutchings. Golden Bell Press Inc., 2403 Champa St, Denver, CO 80205; http://www.goldenbellpress.com. Illus. *Bk. rev.:* occasional. *Aud.:* Hs, Ga, Sa.

Model Cars magazine is devoted to static scale models of road vehicles. Scales covered range from 1:87 to 1:8, but the vast majority of the magazine is devoted to 1:24 and 1:25 scales—the most popular scales for static car models. Typical issues include reviews of new kits, conversion parts, and supplies; plus how-to-do-it articles (including impressive information on dioramas and super detailing); extensive coverage of contests; and articles on outstanding modelers and their work. Many how-to-do-it articles are extremely clearly illustrated with step-by-step photographs. The magazine is heavily illustrated, mostly in color.

5031. ***R/C Car.*** [ISSN: 1097-0711] m. USD 4.50 newsstand/cover domestic; CND 5.50 newsstand/cover Canada; USD 31.98 Canada. Daisy - Hi-Torque Publishing Co., Inc., 25233 Anza Dr, Valencia, CA 91355. *Aud.:* Hs, Ga, Sa.

R/C Car is a popular model racing car magazine by a company that specializes in car magazines. In addition to *R/C Car,* Daisy/Hi-Torque publishes seven off-road "real" car and bicycle magazines, such as *Motocross Action* and *Dirt Bike.* Articles in *R/C Car* focus on racing products and technology, with lots of emphasis on both internal combustion and electric power, evaluative reviews of new products, tests of commercial equipment, information on mofications and tuning, and reports on events, competitions and results, and individual racers and their accomplishments. The magazine's articles are well written, and its format is typical of radio control auto magazines, which tend to resemble hot rod magazines. *R/C Car* has bright, busy covers and colorful layouts, including attractive original artwork.

5032. ***Radio Control Car Action.*** [ISSN: 0886-1609] 1985. m. USD 27.95 domestic; USD 49.95 foreign; USD 4.99 newsstand/cover domestic. Ed(s): Jon Chappell. Air Age Publishing, 100 E Ridge Rd., Ridgefield, CT 06877-4606; http://www.airage.com. Illus., adv. Sample. Circ: 93000. Vol. ends: Dec. *Aud.:* Hs, Ga.

Radio Control Car Action is a colorful publication with extremely lively graphics. It is the most important publication in its field and one of the most physically massive of all model hobby magazines. *Radio Control Car Action* is published by Air Age, which also publishes *Radio Control Nitro, Radio Control Boat Modeler, Model Airplane News, Backyard Flyer,* and *Radio Control Microflight.* The fact that radio-controlled electric- and gasoline-powered cars are a high-tech hobby is reflected in the magazine's editorial contents and advertising. Most of the articles are concerned with evaluating commercially available kits and parts and using them to gain maximum performance advantage, as well as with modifying equipment, troubleshooting, racing techniques, and major racing events. Coverage includes both electric- and gas- ("nitro") powered cars. Each issue includes a tremendous range of advertisements for cars and parts for aftermarket modifications.

5033. ***Radio Control Nitro.*** [ISSN: 1529-8361] 2000. 8x/yr. USD 19.95 domestic; USD 29.95 Canada; USD 34.95 elsewhere. Ed(s): Tom Atwood. Air Age Publishing, 100 E Ridge Rd., Ridgefield, CT 06877-4606; http://www.airage.com. *Bk. rev.:* Occasional. *Aud.:* Hs, Ga, Sa.

Radio Control Nitro is published by Air Age, which also publishes *Radio Control Car Action, Model Airplane News, Radio Control Microflight,* and *Backyard Flyer. Radio Control Nitro* is devoted entirely to fuel- (as opposed to electric-) powered cars. The "nitro" in the title is nitromethane, an additive to model racing car fuel. Gas-powered model racing cars can deliver impressive speeds, with the fastest clocked at over 100 real miles per hour—somewhere over a scale Mach 1. The magazine is typical of Air Age publications, with bright and busy graphics and a youthful feel. Like many other hobby magazines, *Radio Control Nitro* has changed frequency of publication, increasing during its brief life from quarterly to bimonthly to the current eight issues a year.

5034. ***Radio Race Car International.*** [ISSN: 0268-3334] 1985. m. GBP 33 domestic; GBP 40 in Europe; USD 59 United States. Ed(s): Chris Deakin. Traplet Publications Ltd, Traplet House, Severn Dr, Upton-upon-Severn, WR8 0JL, United Kingdom; rrci@traplet.com; http://www.traplet.com. Illus., adv. Sample. Vol. ends: Dec. *Aud.:* Hs, Ga.

Radio Race Car International is the oldest magazine published by Traplet, which produces a total of twelve magazines—eight model-building magazines plus four craft magazines. It covers much the same ground as *Radio Control Car Action,* and other U.S. r/c car magazines, but it provides a British and continental perspective. It also covers U.S. events, but in much less detail than American magazines do. Typical articles cover new products, product reviews with construction suggestions, tips for tuning and adjusting, driving techniques, and race results Although *Radio Race Car International* is not a first choice for U.S. libraries, it is an attractive and useful second magazine on the subject.

5035. ***Scale Auto.*** Formerly: *Scale Auto Enthusiast.* 1979. bi-m. USD 24.95 domestic; USD 33 foreign; USD 4.45 newsstand/cover per issue. Ed(s): Mark Thompson. Kalmbach Publishing Co., PO Box 1612, Waukesha, WI 53187-1612; http://www.kalmbach.com. Illus., adv. Sample. Circ: 30820 Paid. Vol. ends: Apr. *Aud.:* Hs, Ga.

Scale Auto (formerly *Scale Auto Enthusiast*) is the leading American publication devoted to static models of automobiles. Most of its articles are concerned with scale modeling. They include kit reviews, plus articles on kit construction, superdetailing, modification, and painting. Construction articles often feature useful step-by-step photos. The magazine concentrates on injection-molded styrene kits, but articles and reviews also deal with low-volume production kits in metal and resin and with aftermarket detailing and conversion parts. Other articles deal with prototype information, general construction methods, new products, contest results, and other outstanding models. Monthly columns cover new kits in plastic and resin, model trucks, and coming events. The magazine is printed all in color, and the quality of photographs, editing, drawings, and layout is generally high. *Scale Auto* was published bimonthly through the end of 1998, converted to eight issues a year starting in 1999, and returned to bimonthly with the August 2003 issue.

5036. ***Scale Auto Racing News.*** [ISSN: 1522-4635] 1979. m. USD 29.95 domestic; USD 40 in Canada & Mexico; USD 70 in Australia & New Zealand Japan & Pacific Rim. Ed(s): John Ford. Ford Publishing, 2634 Robert Rd, Aransas Pass, TX 78336; johnford@slotmail.org; http://www.scaleautoracing.com. Illus., adv. Sample. Circ: 5000. Vol. ends: Dec. *Aud.:* Hs, Ga.

Scale Auto Racing News covers all standard types of slot car equipment, ranging from larger cars built to scales of 1:24 and 1:32 to smaller H0-gauge cars, which are often somewhat larger than the 1:87 scale the name implies. Slot cars boomed beginning in the 1960s, when every toy department and discount store had endless stacks of H0 slot racing sets, and hobby shops all over the country installed race tracks for larger-scale cars. The hobby suffered disastrous declines in the 1970s and 1980s, but in recent years it has regained popularity. Although slot car racing will probably never be what it was in its heyday, today there are active racing groups and tracks in most major urban areas. *Scale Auto Racing News* devotes virtually all of its attention to reports on racing activities, and a high percentage of the illustrations are utilitarian photographs of people holding trophies or model cars. In recent years, the magazine has upgraded from newsprint to coated stock, with a corresponding improvement in appearance.

5037. ***Toy Cars and Models.*** Formerly (until 2000): *Toy Cars & Vehicles;* Which incorporated: *Model Car Journal.* [ISSN: 1533-6913] 1974. m. USD 29.98; USD 5.50 per issue. Ed(s): Merry Dudley. Krause Publications, Inc., 700 E State St, Iola, WI 54990-0001; info@krause.com; http://www.krause.com. Illus., adv. Circ: 18921 Paid and free. *Aud.:* Hs, Ga.

Toy Cars and Models is a collector-oriented magazine from Krause, which also publishes the tabloids *Toy Shop* and *Antique Trader.* Typical articles cover plastic kits and slot cars (both from the viewpoint of the collector rather than the builder or operator), die-cast models, collector prices, toy company histories, industry news, show calendars, book reviews, collectors' prices, and nostalgia for old toys. The magazine concentrates in particular on "Hot Wheels," which are widely collected in the U.S.

Toy Cars and Models has changed owners, formats, and titles in recent years. In March 1998, Krause purchased *Model Car Journal* and converted it to a tabloid to match its other magazines. In the fall of 1999, the title was changed to *Toy Cars and Vehicles,* and the tabloid format was abandoned in favor of a standard magazine format. Finally, in the fall of 2000, the title was again changed, this time to the current *Toy Cars and Models.*

5038. ***Toy Farmer.*** [ISSN: 0894-5055] 1978. m. USD 23.95 domestic; USD 31.95 foreign; USD 3.95 newsstand/cover per issue domestic. Ed(s): Cathy Scheibe. Toy Farmer Ltd., 7496 106th Ave, S E, La Moure, ND 58458-9404. Illus., adv. Circ: 28000. *Bk. rev.:* Occasional. *Aud.:* Hs, Ga, Sa.

Toy Farmer is published for collectors of farm miniatures, particularly models of farm machinery and implements. Farm toy collecting is a specialized hobby rather poorly covered in more general publications. Like other toy collector magazines, *Toy Farmer* includes articles on toy manufacturers and their histories, new production, individual collectors and their collections, restoration of old toys and other how-to information, scheduled swap meets, reports on shows, auction results, and a substantial amount of specialized advertising. In recent years, the magazine's primarily black-and-white illustrations have been upgraded to all color. Collecting farm toys is an extremely popular hobby, especially in the Midwest, and libraries in that area in particular should seriously consider subscribing to this magazine. The publisher of *Toy Farmer* also publishes *Toy Trucker & Contractor* (see below).

5039. ***Toy Trucker and Contractor.*** [ISSN: 1051-2187] 1983. m. USD 23.95 domestic; USD 31.95 elsewhere; USD 3.95 newsstand/cover per issue domestic. Ed(s): Cathy Scheibe. Toy Farmer Ltd., 7496 106th Ave, S E, La Moure, ND 58458-9404. Illus., adv. Circ: 6300. *Aud.:* Hs, Ga.

Toy Trucker & Contractor is a companion publication to *Toy Farmer* (reviewed above in this subsection), which it strongly resembles. It is aimed at collectors of small-scale and larger toy dump trucks, semis, wreckers, logging equipment, fire engines, cranes, dozers, loaders, graders, scrapers, concrete mixers, and so on—the huge variety of fascinating industrial vehicles seen in America. Articles cover individual manufacturers, the history of toy production, new items, collectors and their collections, show schedules and reports, and auction results. The magazine also has extensive specialized advertising. In the last couple of years, the magazine has converted from primarily black-and-white illustrations to full color.

5040. ***Xtreme R C Cars.*** [ISSN: 1535-9646] 1995. m. USD 19.99. Ed(s): Mike Velez. Think Omnimedia LLC, 5171 Edison Ave, Ste C, Chino, CA 91710. Illus. Circ: 19000. *Aud.:* Hs, Ga.

Xtreme R/C Cars is a fairly new magazine in this very popular hobby area, but it has quickly grown to substantial size and impressive editorial contents. Its primary focus is on competitive racing using nitro-and electric-powered cars. In comparison with other r/c car magazines, it devotes a great deal of space to how-to-do-it information, including not only converting and reworking models but also racing techniques. Other articles include evaluative reviews of new products and reports on racing events. Like other r/c car magazines, the format of *R/C Cars* is more reminiscent of a hot rod magazine than of a model magazine, with bright covers, colorful interior layouts, and pretty girls.

Model Ships

Hobbyists interested in model ships work in a variety of areas, including plastic ship models, wooden kit and scratch-built models, radio-controlled power boats, and antique toy boats.

Plastic ship model kits come in a large variety of types, from Mediterranean galleys to the most modern military equipment. Emphasis among the manufacturers is primarily on models of powered ships, particularly the ships of twentieth-century navies. Because plastic kits must sell in huge numbers to justify the investment in die sinking, the concentration on steamships is understandable, for sailing ships are so complex to build that they are hard to sell in sufficient quantities. In addition, plastic is not the best material for masts, spars, and sails. Some coverage at a basic level is provided by magazines such as *FineScale Modeler,* which covers static military models of all types and has occasional articles on model ships, and general static model magazines like *Scale Models International.*

Building wooden ship models is an ancient and complex craft. Outstanding ship models are museum pieces, and building even ordinary models is an amazingly involved undertaking. The best models literally reproduce the originals plank by plank. Two of the magazines annotated here devote a great deal of attention to wooden ship models. *Seaways' Ships in Scale* covers both scratch building and wooden kit assembly, while *Model Shipwright* is concerned exclusively with scratch building. *Marine Modelling International* is a more general publication with coverage that extends beyond wooden ship models

Paying attention to kit assembly is important. Wooden ship kits are frequently crude affairs, with unclear or incomplete or ill-considered instructions, unsatisfactory fittings (small metal parts), misshapen hulls, and erroneous rigging diagrams. This means that building a wooden ship kit can have much more in common with scratch building than one might wish, and detailed articles on building specific kits can be extremely useful. As an illustration of the problems with wooden ship kits, people in the trade estimate that a high percentage of the total kits sold are purchased by inexperienced builders who underestimate their difficulty and never complete them.

Most libraries interested in providing a magazine on wooden ship models will probably start with *Seaways' Ships in Scale,* which is only remaining U.S. specialty magazine in its area, and consider *Model Shipwright.*

Radio-controlled (r/c) power boats can be either stately scale models cruising at dignified speeds or high-powered racers whizzing noisily around like drops of water on a hot skillet. The important U.S. magazine covering r/c racing boats is *Radio Control Boat Modeler,* which is published by Air Age. R/c scale boats are covered in *Model Yachting, Marine Modelling International, Model Shipwright,* and *Seaway's Ships in Scale.*

Antique toy boats are scarce and are collected by relatively few people. There is no magazine dedicated to the subject. The best coverage occurs very occasionally in toy collectors' magazines that focus on an upscale market, such as *Antique Toy World.*

Because building a model ship can be so complex, articles on scratch-building model ships or assembling complex kits tend to run on and on in many installments, sometimes for more than a year. The best articles are sometimes published as books after the series is complete. This publishing pattern is much like that in the area of live-steam modeling.

Because of their large size, full-scale plans for scale model ships are hard to publish in magazines, so publishers frequently sell plans on the side or refer the reader to sources of plans.

Scale model shipbuilding is also a scholarly undertaking. Articles tend to be laden with historical and mechanical detail and the wonderfully obscure technical vocabulary that only an ancient craft like shipbuilding can develop. Although there is little in the ship magazines that is overwhelmingly arcane, words like *gudgeon, sponson, cathead, binding strake, tampion,* and *royal futtock* may intimidate the uninitiated. Buy a nautical dictionary.

5041. *Marine Modelling International.* Formerly: *Marine Modelling.* 1985. m. GBP 24.95 domestic; GBP 34.95 in Europe; USD 49 United States. Ed(s): Chris Jackson. Traplet Publications Ltd, Traplet House, Severn Dr, Upton-upon-Severn, WR8 0JL, United Kingdom; mm@traplet.com; http://www.traplet.com. Illus., adv. *Bk. rev.:* Occasional. *Aud.:* Hs, Ga.

Marine Modelling International is a British publication from Traplet, which publishes a total of eight model-making magazines. In general, *Marine Modelling*'s central emphasis is on operating scale model (as opposed to high-speed racing) r/c ships and sailing yachts, but it also includes static models. It also emphasizes models of modern steel ships rather than wooden sailing ships. It frequently includes articles on steam-powered models and on prototype ships, and it provides schedules of hobby shows and model yacht regattas in every issue. Like some other model ship magazines, *Marine Modelling International* offers a plans service, with large-scale plans available on special order.

5042. *Model Shipwright.* [ISSN: 0264-2220] 1972. q. GBP 26.50 domestic; USD 52.50 United States; CND 78.50 Canada. Chrysalis Books, 9 Blenheim Court, Brewery Rd, London, N7 9NT, United Kingdom; modelshipwright@chrysalisbooks.co.uk; http://www.conwaymaritime.com. Illus., index, adv. Sample. Circ: 3500. *Bk. rev.:* 3-5, 250-850 words. *Aud.:* Sa.

Model Shipwright is a British publication concerned with scratch-building models of historical ships, and it is obviously aimed at expert builders. It is the most elegantly produced of the model ship magazines, and the models that appear in its pages are frequently of superb quality. Prototypes covered run the gamut from ancient to contemporary. Articles cover both static and powered models. Most articles are concerned with specific construction projects, but others describe and illustrate outstanding models, prototype ships, and model-building techniques. The magazine has extremely good drawings, high-quality photographs, excellent typography, and sewn signatures. Each issue includes a full-scale plan, folded and inserted loose in the magazine; plans for other ships are provided in miniature, with sources for full-size versions usually noted. *Model Shipwright*'s publisher specializes in books on model ships and on the history of ships and shipbuilding.

5043. *Model Yachting.* q. American Model Yachting Association, c/o Membership Secretary Michelle Dannenhoffer, 558 Oxford Ave, Melbourne, FL 32935; mdannenhof@msn.com; http://www.amya.org. *Aud.:* Ga, Sa.

Model yacht racing is an ancient and elegant hobby. It began in the United States in the 1870s, with models launched from rowboats in open bodies of water, then graduated to artifical ponds in the 1930s. The hobby really began in the 1970s, however, with the introduction of radio-controlled models, and this spurred the founding of the American Model Yachting Association (AMYA). R/c sailboats can be extremely large, with some schooners up to 6 or 8 feet long. Like owners of full-sized sailboats, members of the AMYA compete at "regattas" in a wide variety of classes. *Model Yachting* includes articles on new products, how-to-do-it information, reports on events, and columns—much in the style of *Model Aviation*—on the various classes of boats. The magazine is cleanly printed in black and white, with color covers.

5044. *Radio Control Boat Modeler.* Formerly (until 1988): *American Boat Modeler.* [ISSN: 1043-8009] 1986. bi-m. USD 19.95 domestic; USD 29.95 Canada; USD 34.95 elsewhere. Ed(s): Debra Cleghorn. Air Age Publishing, 100 E Ridge Rd., Ridgefield, CT 06877-4606; http://www.airage.com. Illus., adv. Sample. Circ: 20700. Vol. ends: Nov. *Aud.:* Hs, Ga.

Radio Control Boat Modeler is published by Air Age, which also produces *Model Airplane News, Radio Control Car Action, Radio Control Nitro,* and *Backyard Flyer.* All of these magazines are similar in appearance, with extremely bright, professional graphics and layout, and with strong editorial concentration on commercial products and their use. *Radio Control Boat Modeler*'s major emphasis is on high-speed racing boats, the kind that compete in North American Model Boat Association and International Model Power Boat Association races. However, it also pays some attention to r/c sailing yachts (which are radio controlled but dependent on sails for power) and to powered scale models of nonracing boats. Articles include product reviews (frequently extremely detailed), detailed information on kit assembly, modifying and tuning equipment, technical hints, reports on racing events, schedules of upcoming races, and general how-to information.

5045. *Seaways' Ships in Scale.* Formerly (until 1992): *Seaways.* [ISSN: 1065-8904] 1990. bi-m. USD 26.95 domestic; USD 29.95 in Canada & Mexico; USD 38 elsewhere. Ed(s): Jim Raines. Seaways Publishing, Inc., 2271 Constitution Dr, San Jose, CA 95124-1204; seaways@seaways.com; http://www.seaways.com. Illus., index, adv. Circ: 6000 Paid. Vol. ends: Nov/Dec. *Bk. rev.:* 1, 200-500 words. *Aud.:* Hs, Ga, Sa.

When *Seaways' Ships in Scale* began publication, it contained a fairly even mixture of material on prototype ships and on building ship models, but it now deals primarily with model building. Articles include both general descriptions of projects and detailed how-to articles that may be continued for several issues. The magazine covers a wide range of topics, including both wood and steel ships as well as r/c models. Most issues include book reviews and reference material particularly helpful to newcomers to such a challenging hobby. Unlike most model-building magazines, *Seaways' Ships in Scale* frequently includes the mailing addresses of its authors. It is well edited, adequately illustrated, and printed on high-quality stock. Seaways' web site contains indexes to model shipbuilding materials. When *Model Shipbuilder* ceased publication, *Seaways' Ships in Scale* was left as the only U.S. specialized title in the field of static ship models.

Military Miniatures

Hobbyists interested in military miniatures fall into two basic groups: scale modelers and toy collectors. The scale modelers construct and paint models and dioramas of soldiers and military equipment, while the toy collectors are interested in mass-produced models of such famous toy soldier firms as Mignot, Heyde, Hausser, Lineol, and Britains, Ltd.

Scale modelers who build static (nonworking) models of military armor and vehicles have a lot in common with modelers who build other types of static models, and the publications they read reflect this similarity. They work primarily with plastic kits, frequently carrying out extensive modifications and switching parts from kit to kit to reproduce specific prototypes.

MODEL MAKING AND COLLECTING

The most popular American magazine dealing with scale military models is *FineScale Modeler,* which provides some coverage of other types of static models as well. Excellent articles also appear in the British specialist publications *Military Modelling* and *Military in Scale.* Specialized coverage of military armor and vehicle models is provided by *Military Miniatures in Review.*

Making miniature soldiers is more a matter of extremely elaborate painting than it is of complex construction techniques. Modelers in this area work from metal or plastic kits and devote endless hours to careful painting of the tremendous amount of detail present in some military regalia. Many people who paint miniature figures also construct elaborate dioramas, or scenes with figures posed in appropriate surroundings.

Techniques suitable to painting miniature soldiers and building military dioramas are also suitable to nonmilitary figure painting and diorama building, and there can be considerable overlap between the fields of military miniatures and nonmilitary figures. Some people interested in nonmilitary model figures read the military-miniatures magazines for information on modeling and painting techniques, and people who build military figures may read some of the magazines listed in the Miniature Figures subsection.

One American magazine, *Historical Miniature,* is devoted specifically to miniature soldiers and provides excellent coverage of the field.

The senior publication on military miniatures is the British magazine *Military Modelling,* which is particularly useful for information on British and continental military costumes. Other useful overseas publications include *Figurines* from France and *Military in Scale* from Britain.

Toy soldier collecting as a serious hobby has developed since the late 1930s. However, the mass production of toy soldiers dates back to the mid-eighteenth century. Until fairly recent times the industry was centered in Germany, France, England, and to some extent the United States. Although toy soldiers are much less popular with children today than they were a generation or two ago, a large number of small firms produce collectors' miniatures in the style of old toy soldiers.

The leading toy soldier collectors' magazine is *Old Toy Soldier,* which is the authority on its subject. A British publication, *Toy Soldier and Model Figure,* provides colorful coverage of current production of collectible toy soldiers.

5046. *Figurines.* [ISSN: 1259-0312] bi-m. FRF 220 domestic; FRF 240 foreign. Ed(s): Dominique Breffort. Histoire & Collections, 5 ave. de la Republique, Paris, 75541, France; figurines@histecoll.com; http://www.histofig.com/figurines. Illus. *Aud.:* Hs, Ga.

Figurines is a very attractive French publication devoted primarily to model soldiers. It includes extensive coverage of new products, how-to-do-it and hobby show information, profiles on contest-winning models, and kit reviews. It also includes prototype information on military uniforms, primarily French. *Figurines* has unusually excellent photographs and artwork, all printed in color on heavy, coated stock. These should be useful to all modelers, but particularly to those with a special interest in warfare on the Continent. In French only.

5047. *FineScale Modeler.* [ISSN: 0277-979X] 1981. 10x/yr. USD 39.95 domestic; USD 50 foreign; USD 4.95 newsstand/cover per issue. Ed(s): Mark Thompson. Kalmbach Publishing Co., PO Box 1612, Waukesha, WI 53187-1612; http://www.kalmbach.com. Illus., index. Sample. Circ: 63047 Paid. Vol. ends: Dec. *Indexed:* IHTDI. *Bk. rev.:* 3-30, 50-150 words. *Aud.:* Hs, Ga.

FineScale Modeler is the most popular American magazine concerned with military models and with the general construction of static models. At least three-quarters of its content is concerned with plastic models of military aircraft, ships, armor, vehicles, and figures. Other models very occasionally covered include automobiles and other road vehicles, civilian aircraft, ships, science fiction, and dioramas. Most of the articles cover construction, combining specific projects with pointers on model-building techniques. Most plastic modelers do a great deal of kit modifying ("customizing") and combining ("kit bashing") to arrive at models of specific prototypes or of equipment for which no kits are available, and many of the construction articles in *FineScale Modeler* are concerned with this type of work. Other articles cover specific modeling techniques, new products, and prototype information. This title is typical of Kalmbach publications. Its extremely professional production—literate editing, excellent photographs, and consistently fine drawings by Kalmbach's staff—is indicative of the quality that a large and successful hobby publisher can achieve. Considering the tremendous popularity of building military models from plastic kits, only small libraries should be without *FineScale Modeler.* For serials librarians, *FineScale Modeler* published three issues in 1985, five in 1986, six in 1987, five in 1988, seven in 1989, eight per year in 1990 through 1994, nine in 1995, and ten per year starting in 1996.

5048. *Historical Miniature.* [ISSN: 1097-3230] 1996. bi-m. USD 42 domestic; USD 53 in Canada & Mexico; USD 66 in Europe. Ed(s): Steven Weakley. R & K Productions, 31316 Via Colinas, Unit 105, Westlake Village, CA 91362; http://www.mmhq.com/~hmm. Illus. Circ: 4000. *Bk. rev.:* Occasional. *Aud.:* Hs, Ga.

Historical Miniature is devoted specifically to scale models of people, primarily soldiers, but also occasionally civilians and pop culture figures. Articles cover a wide range of topics, including painting techniques, constructing and modifying figures, critical reviews of kits, lists of new items available, model shows (with many handsome color photographs of contest-winning models), famous modelers and their work, companies that produce models, coming events, and book reviews. Because much of the art of military miniatures lies in outstanding painting techniques, good coverage of the hobby requires high-quality photography. *Historical Miniature* excels in this respect, with a large number of excellent photographs in every issue, all in color. The magazine is informative, well edited, and attractively printed on high-quality paper.

5049. *Military in Scale.* Formerly (until 1992): *In Scale.* [ISSN: 0967-7062] 1991. m. GBP 24.95 United Kingdom; GBP 34.95 in the European Union; USD 49 United States. Ed(s): Spencer Pollard. Traplet Publications Ltd, Traplet House, Severn Dr, Upton-upon-Severn, WR8 0JL, United Kingdom; mis@traplet.com; http://www.traplet.com. Illus., adv. *Bk. rev.:* 3-8, 100-250 words. *Aud.:* Hs, Ga.

Military in Scale is published in England by Traplet, which also publishes seven other model-building magazines. Although it covers model soldiers to some extent, it concentrates heavily on prototype information and on static models of equipment—aircraft, tanks, field pieces, road vehicles, and dioramas. It is illustrated entirely in color. The majority of its articles consist of detailed, critical instructions on how to assemble and improve upon commercial kits and how to convert them to other prototypes. Because the vast majority of modelers work from kits rather than from scratch, this approach is very useful. The magazine also includes extensive calendars of forthcoming model shows in the United Kingdom and Ireland.

5050. *Military Miniatures in Review.* q. USD 35 domestic; USD 45 Canada; USD 53 Mexico. Ed(s): Pat Stansell. Ampersand Publishing Co., 235 N E 6th Ave, Ste G, Delray Beach, FL 33483; mmir35701@aol.com. Illus. Circ: 9000. *Bk. rev.:* 100-200 words. *Aud.:* Hs, Ga, Sa.

Military Miniatures in Review is devoted almost entirely to the construction of historically accurate models of military vehicles and armor. Most of the articles show how to construct and modify kits. These articles usually include evaluations of kit quality; information on how to overcome assembly problems; instructions for adding extra detail, improving existing detail, and making modifications; painting methods; reference photos of appropriate prototypes; and citations to sources of additional prototype information. Briefer coverage is devoted to information on new kits, after market conversion and detail parts, model figures, and books. *Military Miniatures in Review* features large numbers of unusually excellent photographs (about half in color), clear writing, clean typography, high-quality paper, and consistently entertaining turns of phrase.

5051. *Military Modelling.* [ISSN: 0026-4083] 1971. 15x/yr. GBP 45 domestic; GBP 56.50 in Europe; USD 82.50 United States. Ed(s): Ken Jones. Nexus Special Interests, Carrington Business Park, Manchester Rd, Urmston, M31 4YR, United Kingdom; info@nexusmedia.com; http://www.hhc.co.uk/. Illus., adv. Sample. Circ: 60000. Vol. ends: Dec. *Bk. rev.:* 5-10, 100-300 words. *Aud.:* Hs, Ga.

The British *Military Modelling* is the senior magazine concerned with scale models of soldiers and military equipment, and it has an international reputation. This publication covers the entire field, but it places particular emphasis on prototype information on historic military uniforms, with excellent color paintings and extremely detailed text. It also includes articles on military history, military armor and vehicles, outstanding figures and dioramas by hobbyists, model techniques, new commercial products, and hobby shows, contests, and other activities. Although the emphasis is on British uniforms, coverage is worldwide. *Military Modelling* is well written and printed, with excellent color and black-and-white photographs. In 1997 *Military Modelling* converted from 12 issues a year to 13 four-weekly issues plus six special issues, for a total of 19 issues a year, and in 1999 it converted to a total of 15 issues a year.

5052. *Old Toy Soldier.* Formerly (until 1990): *Old Toy Soldier Newsletter.* [ISSN: 1064-4164] 1976. q. USD 25 domestic; USD 35 Canada; USD 56 elsewhere. Ed(s): Norman Joplin. O T S N, Inc., PO Box 13324, Pittsburgh, PA 15243-0324; raytoys@aol.com; http://www.oldtoysoldier.com. Illus., index, adv. Sample. Circ: 1900 Paid. *Bk. rev.:* 1-2, 400-500 words. *Aud.:* Hs, Ga.

Old Toy Soldier is an attractively produced magazine concerned with collecting what were originally low-cost, mass-produced toys rather than expensive scale models. Articles include detailed examinations of various aspects of the history and production of the major toy firms in Europe and America, plus reports on shows and auctions, reports on new model soldiers, book reviews, and calendars of forthcoming events. The magazine also includes a wide variety of advertisements for old soldiers or modern products made in a similar style. Issues are substantial, running to anything from 90 to 140 pages. *Old Toy Soldier* is nicely printed, the photographs are serviceable (and black and white), and the quality of writing is generally excellent. For the old toy soldier collector, this is the most important publication.

After 25 years of publishing *Old Toy Soldier,* Jo and Steve Sommers created a final five-year index and then sold their publication to Ray Haradin, an antique toy dealer, who transferred publication to Pittsburgh at the end of 2001. The most noticeable changes have been vastly expanded coverage of shows where collectors meet to buy and sell toy soldiers, and perhaps fewer historical articles.

Miniature Figures

Hobbyists interested in miniature figures include both scale modelers and toy collectors. The scale modelers construct and paint models and dioramas, while the toy collectors are interested in mass-produced models, preferably in factory-new condition. Although the subject interests of figure modelers and collectors vary widely, they tend to be particularly interested in two major areas. The first of these is military figures, and the second is popular-culture figures, ranging from monsters to science fiction heroes to exotic pinups.

Although making and collecting miniature figures is still a small hobby compared to model railroading or model aircraft building, it has developed an avid following over the last 20 years and is not covered by nonspecialized magazines. The growth of the model figure hobby has occurred primarily in the area of popular culture rather than toy soldiers. The attendance patterns at hobby shows suggest that this trend may continue in the future, because the people who attend the pop-culture-figure meetings are usually younger than those at the military miniature meetings.

One source of the rapid growth of miniature-figure hobbies is the growth of the "garage kit" business. Garage kits are produced in small numbers by small firms with low-tech equipment. Most garage kits are made in casting resin. Garage kits are available in many areas of model building, including both complete kits and aftermarket modification parts for standard plastic kits, but they are especially popular for model figures. Because the labor in garage kits is tied up more in individual kit production than in die making, a producer can make money selling only 100-200 kits, instead of the tens or hundreds of thousands required to make money with traditional injection-molded plastic kits. Small production runs lead to garage kits that quickly go out of production, which makes access to current magazines especially important to garage kit builders.

Modelers who construct miniature figures and dioramas will find the articles on painting model soldiers in *Historical Miniature* and *Military Modelling* (see the subsection on Military Miniatures) useful for information on techniques. However, for those not interested in miniature soldiers, the military publications offer few advertisements and no product reviews.

One reason the nonspecialist magazines may have shied away from covering nonmilitary scale model figures is the tendency of figure modelers to concentrate on science fiction and horror figures and, to a lesser degree, pinups. Hobby magazines have traditionally been rather prudish, probably because many young people are interested in models, and publishers have worried about possible repercussions from including "adult" material in their magazines.

The most important three American magazines that concentrate specifically on constructing miniature figures, particularly garage kits and other popular culture figures, are *Amazing Figure Modeler, Kitbuilders Magazine,* and *The Modeler's Resource.* They have a great deal of important material found in no other place.

The most difficult aspect of model figure construction is painting. All the model figure magazines mentioned above include articles on painting, but art magazines are another source of information.

Collectors of toy figures are for the most part involved in a different hobby. The production of injection-molded plastic figures began in the 1950s. Compared with the metal figures they nearly dislodged from the toy market, many plastic figures featured vastly superior molded detail, but they were usually sold unpainted, although traditional makers of toy soldiers also produced hand-painted plastic figures at higher prices. Many plastic figures were sold individually or by the bagful in dime stores, but others came in large boxed sets (so-called "playsets"), often with colorfully lithographed steel buildings. Other figures were given away as premiums. Production in many areas continues today, and America's stores are full of everything from *Star Wars* characters to the endless mesomorphs representing professional wrestlers and others of that ilk.

Collecting mass-produced plastic figures—both individual figures and play sets—has become an increasingly popular hobby in the last dozen years. The military figures among these are covered to some extent in such general toy soldier magazines as *Old Toy Soldier* (see the Military Miniatures subsection), while the toy figures are covered to some degree in such toy collector publications as *Toy Shop* (see the Toy Collecting subsection). However, there are two excellent specialist publications: *Lee's Toy Review* and *Tomart's Action Figure Digest.* A third widely respected publication, *Plastic Figure & Playset Collector,* ceased publication with the February 2002 issue due to the editor's health.

Prehistoric Times is the only major model figure magazine devoted to a specific, narrow subject category—in this case dinosaurs. As with other model figure magazines, for those interested in this area there is no substitute.

5053. *Amazing Figure Modeler.* 1994. q. USD 28 domestic; USD 40 Canada; USD 50 elsewhere. Ed(s): Terry Webb. Amazing Publications & Communications, Box 30885, Columbus, OH 43230. *Bk. rev.:* Occasional. *Aud.:* Hs, Ga.

Amazing Figure Modeler is concerned almost exclusively with garage kits. The editor formerly wrote the garage kit portions of *Model and Toy Collector*; published *The Garage,* a garage kit current-awareness newsletter; and wrote three books on garage kits. Each issue of the magazine includes about 18 articles on new kits, individual sculptors, kit construction, garage kit shows, and so on, with particularly useful information on painting techniques. Among its most interesting regular features are its comparative reviews of kits of the same subject from different sculptors. *Amazing Figure Modeler* is well written and edited and is the best of the garage kit magazines, with authoritative and entertaining contents, high-quality photographs (many in color) on heavy, coated stock, and dramatic cover art.

5054. *Kitbuilders Magazine.* Formerly: *Kit Builders and Glue Sniffers.* 1990. q. USD 27; USD 6.50 newsstand/cover per issue. Ed(s): Larry Burbridge. Kitbuilders, Inc., PO Box 38876, Sacramento, CA 95838. Circ: 8000. *Bk. rev.:* Occasional. *Aud.:* Hs, Ga.

Kitbuilders Magazine concentrates primarily on garage kits and other model figures. Contents include reports on shows, photos and articles on model-building projects, how-to articles, and announcements of new kits. The new publishers plan to convert the magazine from its traditional black-and-white photography to full color and to maintain its strong pop culture orientation. *Kitbuilders* has deep roots in the garage kit hobby. It was founded by Gordy Dutt in 1990 as *Kitbuilders and Glue Sniffers.* In 1994, Dutt changed the magazine's name to *Kitbuilders,* taking active steps to move it from something of an in-group publication to one of wider general interest. In 1999, Dutt sold the publication to Larry Burbridge, a Chicago-area hobbyist and show organizer, who in turn sold it to Dan and Barbara Jorgensen in 2003.

5055. ***Lee's Toy Review.*** Formerly (until 2001): *Action Figure News & Toy Review.* [ISSN: 1545-0651] 1990. m. USD 43.95 domestic; USD 61.95 Canada; USD 128.95 elsewhere. Ed(s): Leonard J Lee, III. Lee Publications, PO Box 322, Monroe, CT 06468. Illus., adv. Circ: 15000. *Bk. rev.:* Occasional. *Aud.:* Hs, Ga.

The main focus of the attractive, well-edited *Lee's Toy Review* is collecting licensed figures made for children and for collectors, although in the past few years the magazine has begun expanding into such areas as Hot Wheels, diecast airplanes, transformers, and mass-produced military toys. Reflecting its change in scope, the magazine's name changed from *Action Figure News & Toy Review* to *Lee's Toy Review* with the August 2001 issue.

The licensed figures in *Lee's Toy Review* include everything from G.I. Joe and Ninja Turtles to figures from *Star Wars, Ghostbusters,* and *Reservoir Dogs.* Articles focus not only on the figures themselves but also on manufacturers, licensing news, designers, packaging, etc. One distinctive feature of the magazine is the multi-page price guides that appear in every issue, with coverage varying from month to month. The magazine also includes calendars of forthcoming collectors' shows.

5056. ***Modeler's Resource.*** 1994. q. USD 16 domestic; USD 30 in Canada & Mexico; USD 37 in Europe & S America. Ed(s): Fred DeRuvo. Modeler's Resource, 4120 Douglas Blvd #306-372, Granite Bay, CA 95746-5936; modres@surewest.net; http://www.modelersresource.com/. *Bk. rev.:* Occasional book and video reviews. *Aud.:* Hs, Ga.

The Modeler's Resource is an excellent magazine devoted primarily to figure models, with a few sci-fi vehicles now and then. From fairly simple beginnings in the mid-1990s, it has developed into a colorful and professional production. Each issue includes about a dozen articles and columns on sculpting methods, assembling and painting new kits, new products, prepainted miniatures, scratch building, solving kit problems, contest-winning models, product evaluations, interviews with artists, show schedules, and so on. In 2000, *The Modeler's Resource* (perhaps as a result of being picked up by a national distributor) eliminated semi-nude pinups—a long-term staple of model figure magazines—from its pages. The magazine is well edited, fun to read, and full of useful information. It's attractively printed—much of it in color—on coated stock. *The Modeler's Resource* was originally published quarterly. It converted to bimonthly after about three years, then returned to quarterly starting with the October 2003 issue (no. 54).

5057. ***Prehistoric Times.*** 1993. bi-m. USD 36 domestic; USD 45 in Latin America and Europe; USD 55 newsstand/cover per issue in Asia. Ed(s): Michael Fredericks. Prehistoric Times, 145 Bayline Cir, Folsom, CA 95630-8077; pretimes@aol.com. Adv. Circ: 10000. *Aud.:* Hs, Ga, Sa.

Prehistoric Times is for people who like dinosaurs. The primary focus of the magazine is on dinosaur models and how to build them, but it also includes information on new scientific discoveries, dinosaur art and how to create it, the history of dinosaurs in popular culture, dinosaur kits, and collectible dinosaur toys—as well as material on other prehistoric animals. The range of available dinosaur kits is impressive, including both large- and small-scale replicas of living dinosaurs, plus models of dinosaur skeletons. *Prehistoric Times* is simply but cleanly produced, with about two-thirds of the contents in black and white on good-quality uncoated stock, and about one-third in color on coated stock. Dinosaur model making may seem like an extraordinarily obscure hobby, but it's amazing how many people—including hundreds of thousands of children—are fascinated by the animals.

Construction Sets

Many children—particularly in the pre-digital age—grew up spending endless hours creating elaborate structures and machines with a wide variety of construction sets. Many of the brands—such as Lincoln Logs, Tinkertoy, and Lego—are household names.

A few types of construction sets have been sufficiently complex to emerge as adult hobbies as well as toys. Preeminent among these are the stone architectural block sets and the metal construction sets that emerged in the late Nineteenth and early Twentieth centuries.

Anchor Blocks are synthetic stone blocks designed to create architectural models. Unlike other architectural blocks, they have no alignment pins, but are held together by weight and friction. Originally designed by Froebel, the inventor of the kindergarten, they were first developed by the Lilienthal brothers (better known as aviation pioneers), then purchased and expanded into an extremely sophisticated toy and hobby by F.A. Richter, a wealthy manufacturer, who made his "Anker Steinbaukasten" one of the world's most popular toys, with the largest sets including thousands of blocks and weighing hundreds of pounds. A few other firms also manufactured small sets of stone building blocks, but Richter dominated the market. Today, Anchor Blocks may be the oldest manufactured toy in the world, with the products of the modern factory intermixing easily with those of 1880.

Although there were Nineteenth century precursors, the first commercially successful metal construction set was Meccano, invented by Frank Hornby in England in 1901. Its major competitor was Erector, developed in the United States by A.C. Gilbert in 1913, but there were as many as 500 similar products. The basic principle of most metal construction sets is perforated metal strips, held together by nuts and bolts, and supplemented by suitable axles, wheels, and cover plates. Although all of these products were designed as toys, the largest sets were extremely complex, with an impressive variety of special parts. Spare parts were sold individually to adults undertaking elaborate projects, both models and special-purpose laboratory equipment. Metal construction sets play a far less important role in the toy market today than they did in years past, but about a dozen lines are still in production.

The major magazines published on Anchor Blocks and metal construction sets are all aimed at adult hobbyists who are interested in construction designs, assembly methods, and the history of construction sets and the companies that made them. The important publication on Anchor Blocks is the *Mededelingenblad,* published in the Netherlands by the Club van Anker-vrienden (Club of Anchor Enthusiasts). Magazines on Meccano include the British publications *Constructor Quarterly* and *The International Meccanoman.* Coverage of Erector is much less extensive, but there are club newsletters (not reviewed here) such as *The Southern California Meccano & Erector Club Newsletter* (contact through http://www.erector.webnexus.com), *The A.C. Gilbert Heritage Society Newsletter* (http://www.acghs.org), and the *Canadian Modeling Association for Meccano and Allied Systems* (www.memeshadow.net/cmamas/).

Information on a wide variety of manufacturers appears in the British publication *Other Systems Newsletter.*

In general, all publications on construction sets are aimed at international audiences.

The only magazines that provide any useful coverage of construction sets are specialized ones of the type listed here. Libraries interested in providing coverage will want to begin with *Constructor Quarterly* and the *Mededelingenblad.*

5058. ***Constructor Quarterly.*** 1988. q. GBP 50 domestic; GBP 52 in Europe; GBP 56 in US & Canada. Ed(s): Robin Johnson. R J Publications, 17 Ryegate Rd, Crosspool, Sheffield, S10 5FA, United Kingdom; robin.johnson@ars.aon.co.uk. *Aud.:* Sa.

Constructor Quarterly is devoted to building models with Meccano, the British grandfather of metal construction sets. Most articles feature original designs for models of such fascinatingly varied equipment as cars, trucks, cranes, clocks, mechanical games, railroads, bridges, steam shovels, factory machines, carnival rides, military armor, ships, automata, and even architecture—all the work of individual enthusiasts. In addition, there are occasional articles on the history of Meccano and schedules of forthcoming events in the United Kingdom.

Constructor Quarterly is the successor to the *Sheffield Meccano Guild Newsletter* and the closest heir to the old *Meccano Magazine,* published for many years by the original company, which also made Hornby trains and Dinky toys.

Constructor Quarterly is excellently written and one of the most physically handsome of all model making and collecting magazines, published to art book standards on heavy coated stock, with crisp and professional color photographs that show technical detail with unusual clarity.

RJ Publications also publishes books on the construction of massive Meccano models, such as *Eric Taylor's Giant Lorry-Mounted Crane.*

5059. *The International Meccanoman.* 1988. 3x/yr. GBP 14. Ed(s): Paul J Joachim. International Society of Meccanomen, c/o Adrian Williams,Treas., Bell House, 72A Old High St, Oxford, OX3 HW, United Kingdom; corvus@tinyworld.co.uk. Illus. Sample. Circ: 650 Paid. *Bk. rev.:* Occasional. *Aud.:* Sa.

The International Meccanoman is the journal of the International Society of Meccanomen, which is intended by its members to be a successor to Frank Hornby's *Meccano Guild.* Articles cover new mechanical designs and construction details, new models, club activities and contests, the history of Meccano, individual enthusiasms, and so on. Some of the projects can be amazingly sophisticated, including, for example, differential analyzers (mechanical analog computers). Although the focus is clearly on Meccano, the magazine also includes information on Meccano licensees and competitors worldwide. The magazine is cleanly printed in black and white. The subscription price to *International Meccanoman* is the cost of annual membership in the society, which is currently available only to individuals.

5060. *Mededelingenblad.* [ISSN: 1383-1992] 1979. q. Membership, EUR 40.85. Ed(s): Jan van der Werff. Club van Anker-vrienden, c/o Hans Cornelissen, Rembrandstraat 64, Nijmegen, NL-6521 MG, Netherlands; http://www.ankerstein.org. Circ: 250. *Bk. rev.:* Occasional. *Aud.:* Sa.

The Club van Anker-vrienden (Club of Anchor Enthusiasts) is centered in the Netherlands but has members worldwide. Like some scholarly journals, the *Mededelingenblad* is published in the language of each author, with articles in Dutch, German, and English (U.S. subscriptions include translations of the non-English portions of the magazine). Articles feature the history of Anchor Blocks, new designs and plans, descriptions and photographs of new projects by Anchor enthusiasts, construction methods, the history of the company and of the Richter family, club activities, and auction results. Despite its limited circulation, the magazine provides color illustrations by including high-quality color photocopies to be cut apart and tipped in by the subscriber. The *Mededelingenblad* is a club publication, but club activities form only a small part of the magazine, and it will be of interest to anyone who likes architectural model making. Subscribers to the magazine may purchase a complete set of nearly 25 years of back issues on six CDs from the club's American agent for only twelve dollars!

5061. *Other Systems Newsletter.* s-a. GBP 3 domestic; GBP 3.50 in Europe; GBP 4 elsewhere. Ed(s): Tony Knowles. Other Systems Newsletter, c/o Tony Knowles, 7 Potters Way, Laverstock, Salisbury, SP1 1PY, United Kingdom. *Bk. rev.:* Occasional. *Aud.:* Sa.

Other Systems Newsletter provides detailed historical information on the wide variety of metal construction sets made by manufacturers other than Meccano in England and Erector in the United States. Each issue contains about 30 pages of detailed articles and news notes, accompanied by many clear reproductions of packaging, individual parts, and construction diagrams. Starting in April 2003, in order to permit binding in either portrait or landscape format, *Other Systems Newsletter* began to be published as loose sheets printed on one side only. At the same time, it converted to color printing.

Dollhouse Miniatures

Although children have played with dollhouses for generations, the emergence of dollhouse miniatures as a widespread adult hobby has occurred only during the last 25 or 30 years, making it one of the newest of the model-making hobbies.

Hobbyists in this area build and collect miniatures of furniture and other domestic objects. Usually they incorporate them in model scenes, either room boxes, which consist of single-room dioramas, or entire model buildings.

Many hobbyists in this area are essentially collectors of elegant miniatures made by modern craftspeople. Hundreds of these makers advertise in the dollhouse magazines and attend the national and regional shows, where the finest models tend to change hands. The best dollhouse miniatures are expensive; a high-quality chair can cost $50 or more, and some miniatures actually cost as much as the original objects on which they are based. Balancing this, the worst of the mass-produced dollhouse miniatures sold in hobby and craft shops can be disappointingly crude.

Other hobbyists collect antique dollhouses and their furniture. Many of these are items of tremendous charm—and high prices.

In addition to collectors, there are many hobbyists who build their own models from kits or from scratch.

Dollhouse miniatures are larger than most other models; most are built to a scale of 1:12, but some smaller ones are built to a scale of 1:24, about the same scale as that used for large model soldiers and the very largest of mass-produced model trains, and even 1:48, the size of 0 gauge model trains and larger scale model aircraft. Compared with other areas of model building, there are relatively fewer kits on the market, especially the kind of inexpensive plastic kits that in other areas of static model building provide an entry point for beginners and a source of materials for "kit-bashing" by the more experienced. Although sales of dollhouse miniatures are not sufficient to justify the creation of injection molds, in other areas of model building there is extensive low volume production in casting resin and low melting point metal alloys.

Currently available American magazines in this area include *Dollhouse Miniatures* and *Miniature Collector. Dollhouse Miniatures* covers the wider range of topics. *Miniature Collector* devotes space to both new miniatures and to antique dollhouses, but it contains little information on building miniatures. The British magazine *International Dolls House News* offers the advantage of a British and European perspective in English.

5062. *Dollhouse Miniatures.* Former titles (until 1997): *Nutshell News; Miniatures Catalog.* [ISSN: 1094-1916] 1978. m. USD 39.95; USD 4.95 newsstand/cover per issue. Ed(s): Melanie Buellesbach. Kalmbach Publishing Co., PO Box 1612, Waukesha, WI 53187-1612; http://www.kalmbach.com. Illus., index, adv. Sample. Circ: 30201 Paid. Vol. ends: Dec. *Indexed:* IHTDI. *Bk. rev.:* 2-3, 100-300 words. *Aud.:* Hs, Ga.

Dollhouse Miniatures is the leading general magazine in its field. It emphasizes the work of both professional miniaturists and individual hobbyists. The typical issue contains columns on new miniatures, new kits, collectible miniatures, and forthcoming shows and exhibits, plus about 12 to 14 articles more or less evenly divided between the work of professional miniature makers and collections of individual hobbyists on one hand and construction projects on the other. *Dollhouse Miniatures* is well edited with a sprightly writing style and excellent photographs. A large number of ads for commercial miniaturists and miniature shops is included. One interesting feature of the magazine is the inclusion of addresses for many contributors; this is understandable in the case of commercial miniaturists, who are seeking customers, but unusual in the case of how-to articles. The professional production quality is typical of Kalmbach publications.

5063. *International Dolls House News.* [ISSN: 1354-2281] 1971. bi-m. GBP 22.50 domestic; GBP 30 in Europe; USD 45 United States. Ed(s): Esther Forder, Nick Forder. Ashdown Publishing Ltd., Avalon Ct, Star Rd, Partridge Green, RH13 8RY, United Kingdom; esther.forder@btinternet.com. Illus., adv. Vol. ends: Dec. *Bk. rev.:* Various number and length. *Aud.:* Hs, Ga.

International Dolls House News includes detailed studies of individual modern dollhouses, reports on collectors' shows, articles on antique doll houses and furnishings, and information on architectural detail. The magazine has some coverage of do-it-yourself projects, but it is primarily concerned with new and old collectibles, including antique toys. The magazine is handsomely printed on heavy, coated stock, with many color photos, and it is probably the most important of the British dollhouse magazines.

5064. *Miniature Collector.* [ISSN: 0199-9184] 1976. m. USD 37.95 domestic; USD 49.95 foreign. Ed(s): Barbara J Aardema. Scott Publications, 30595 Eight Mile, Livonia, MI 48152-1798; contactus@scottpublications.com; http://www.scottpublications.com. Illus., adv. Circ: 38000 Paid. Vol. ends: Apr. *Aud.:* Hs, Ga.

This attractive magazine concentrates on collecting dollhouses, dollhouse furnishings, and appropriately sized dolls. It includes articles on artisans and their work, individual dollhouses and their furnishings, private collections of miniatures, museums and special exhibits, club activities, special projects, and miniatures characteristic of various eras. But it also covers antique dollhouses and miniatures, restoration of antique dollhouses and dollhouse furniture, and auctions. And it has a few do-it-yourself projects. The magazine is well written and very handsomely illustrated with excellent color photos of outstanding miniatures.

Nutshell News. See *Dollhouse Miniatures.*

Toy Collecting

Hobbyists collect a wide variety of old toys, and many of these relate directly to the types of models covered in this section. Among the most popular toys collected are trains; soldiers; die-cast cars; sheet steel vehicles of all sorts; cast iron toys, particularly banks and vehicles; construction sets, such as Erector and various types of blocks; boats; airplanes; mechanical figures, including all sorts of animated models of people, animals, cartoon characters, robots, etc.; teddy bears; and dolls, dollhouses, and dollhouse miniatures.

In the area of toy collecting—as in model making in general—it is hard to estimate how many people are actively involved. Collectors sometimes appear more numerous than they really are because their constant buying and selling leads them to dominate Internet auction sites, just as their classified advertising packed some magazines a few years ago. On the basis of national association memberships, magazine subscriptions, and other data, it's reasonable to guess that there are as many as 500,000 extremely serious toy collectors in the United States.

Sorting out toy-collecting publications is made more difficult by the fact that many people who call themselves toy collectors usually exclude two major areas—toy train collecting and doll collecting—where enthusiasts tend to have their own groups. "Toy collecting" in the narrow sense of the term, therefore, tends to center on airplanes, road vehicles, figures other than dolls, robots, banks, lithographed toys, pop culture miscellany, and various sorts of automata.

It's also possible to divide toy collectors by the eras of toys they collect. The "elite" among collectors is probably the group that collects the scarce, high-priced toys made before World War I, when all toy production involved a great amount of hand labor and the products of the great European toy makers were elegant and expensive. Others collect toys from the period between the World Wars, when toys were still made of traditional materials (metal, wood, and paper). In recent years, however, the huge growth in toy collecting appears to be in the area of post-World War II toys, including everything from "baby boom" toys to toys still in production, many of which are heavily merchandised to collectors. There's also a great deal of personal nostalgia involved in toy collecting, and the emphasis on more-recent toys on the part of collectors may be due in large part to the passage of time, in addition to lower prices and greater availability.

The popularity of toy collecting as a hobby is reflected in the number of magazines in the area, both the general magazines listed here and the specialty magazines that appear in other subsections.

The general toy-collecting magazines published in the United States place primary stress on advertising. Because toy collectors spend a lot of their time buying and selling, advertising—along with information on forthcoming swap meets and auctions—is always important to them. Advertisements include not only buy-and-sell ads for old toys but also ads for new "collectible" toys made to appeal to collectors of older toys. Of the two magazines reviewed here, *Antique Toy World* is the best place to keep track of what's happening at the elite end of the toy-collecting market, while *Toy Shop* provides more general coverage.

Spielzeug Antik Revue, a German publication that included far better historical detail and better illustrations, unfortunately ceased publication at the end of 2002.

In addition to the general toy-collecting magazines there are a substantial number of specialized publications that include articles and advertisements for toy collectors. Among the specialized magazines listed in this section that concentrate most heavily on collecting antique toys are *Classic Toy Trains* and *Train Collectors Quarterly* (in the Model Railroads subsection); *Model Auto Review, Toy Cars & Models, Toy Farmer,* and *Toy Trucker & Contractor* (in the Model Automobiles subsection); *Old Toy Soldier* and *Toy Soldier and Model Figure* (in the Military Miniatures subsection); *Action Figure News & Toy Review* (in the Miniature Figures subsection); *Miniature Collector* (in the Dollhouse Miniatures subsection); and *Mededelingenblad* and *Other Systems Newsletter* (in the Construction Sets subsection). In addition, many other magazines include occasional articles on collecting antique toys.

5065. *Antique Toy World.* [ISSN: 0742-0420] 1971. m. USD 39.95 domestic; USD 80 Canada; USD 90 elsewhere. Ed(s): Dale Kelley. Antique Toy World, PO Box 34509, Chicago, IL 60634. Illus., adv. Sample. Vol. ends: Dec. *Bk. rev.:* 0-12, 100-500 words. *Aud.:* Hs, Ga, Sa.

Antique Toy World is aimed primarily at collectors of mechanical toys. Although a few articles are intended to be scholarly, the vast majority are very informal. They concentrate on collectors and their collections, toy museums, toy shows (swap meets) and auctions, toys with various themes, famous toy companies, and general nostalgia for old toys. Each issue also includes a list of about 200 forthcoming events for toy collectors, primarily toy shows, where thousands of collectors meet to buy and sell. Advertisements make up the bulk of the magazine, and they are a useful source of information on buyers, sellers, and prices. The scope of *Antique Toy World* is international, with many advertisements, lists of events, and reports of toy sales from England and the continent. The magazine is most useful as a source of solid information on forthcoming events, prices realized at auctions and sales and asked by toy dealers, current enthusiasms among toy collectors, books in the field, and the names and addresses of toy museums, dealers, and collectors.

5066. *Toy Shop.* Incorporates: *Toy Trader;* (in 1999?): *Toy Collector and Price Guide;* Which was formed by the merger of (1990-1993): *Toy Collector Magazine;* (1992-1993): *Toys & Prices.* [ISSN: 0898-5650] 1988. bi-w. USD 33.98 domestic; USD 80.98 foreign. Ed(s): Sharon Korbeck. Krause Publications, Inc., 700 E State St, Iola, WI 54990-0001; info@krause.com; http://www.krause.com. Illus., adv. Circ: 20423 Paid and free. Vol. ends: Dec. *Bk. rev.:* 5-10, 75-150 words. *Aud.:* Hs, Ga, Sa.

Toy Shop is a tabloid publication reminiscent of other collectors' publications, such as *The Antique Trader, Coin World,* and *Linn's Stamp News.* In its early years, *Toy Shop* consisted entirely of advertisements, but in 1996 Krause Publications merged it with *Toy Collector and Price Guide,* a monthly magazine that combined articles on various kinds of toys with lists of current collector values. In 1999, Krause acquired *Toy Trader,* a publication similar to *Toy Shop,* and also merged it with *Toy Shop.* Articles and advertisements in *Toy Shop* concentrate on toys that originally sold at popular prices, including action figures, Barbie dolls, diecast cars, games, and the general run of licensed toys. The magazine also includes very extensive listings of forthcoming toy swap shows and occasional price guides. This is a substantial publication, running to about 75 pages every two weeks.

Krause also publishes *Toy Cars & Models* (see the subsection on model automobiles) and *Antique Trader,* in addition to a wide range of collector guides and hobby how-to-do-it books.

Electronic Journals

Today, most magazines in the area of model making and collecting have their own web sites. By and large, these exist to promote purchase of the magazines. The best ones are updated frequently and list the contents of current and prior issues.

In addition, there is at least one paid electronic journal, *Radio Control Microflight* (see the subsection on Model Airplanes and Rockets), which is provided as part of a journal subscription and features very solid contents.

There are also a number of free electronic journals and hobby web sites. While some are excellent, many are disappointingly unprofessional. They are erratically updated, are often virtually unedited, have very limited contents, and come and go frequently.

As in other areas of commerce, the range of manufacturers' model hobby web sites is immense, but none has solved the problem of painful slowness when compared with simply paging through a printed catalog or scanning the advertisements in a magazine.

■ MUSIC

General/Popular

See also Music Reviews section.

Esther Gillie, Digital Services Coordinator of the Music Library, University of Illinois Urbana Champaign, 1114 Nevada St., Urbana, IL 61801; gillie@uiuc.edu (General subsection)

Ralph Montilio, Serial and Stacks Assistant of the Hilles Library, Harvard University, 59 Shepard St., Cambridge, MA 01238; montilio@fas.harvard.edu (General subsection)

Constance A. Mayer, Public Services Librarian, Eda Kuhn Loeb Music Library of the Harvard College Library, Harvard University, Cambridge, MA 02138; mayer@fas.harvard.edu (Popular subsection)

Introduction

The general music section lists titles of scholarly periodicals published mainly in the United States and Europe. Journals concerning performance areas such as instrumental, vocal, and choral music; genres such as opera and chamber music; disciplines such as musicology, music theory, music education, and ethnomusicology; areas of interest such as particular eras or music technology are included. Journals that focus on a single composer or instrument (with the exception of keyboard instruments) are not included.

Titles in the popular music section represent the broad range of topics currently of interest to both academics and general audiences and include scholarly journals devoted to the study of popular music; magazines devoted to jazz, blues, rock, folk, and country; and magazines centering on instruments, instrumental technique, and electronic gear.

Basic Periodicals

GENERAL. Hs: *American Music Teacher, Choral Journal, Instrumentalist, Music Educators Journal;* Ga: *American Music, The Musical Quarterly, Opera News;* Ac: *Journal of Music Theory, Journal of Research in Music Education, American Musicological Society. Journal.*

POPULAR. Hs, Ga, Ac: *Rolling Stone.* Select others as needed.

Basic Abstracts and Indexes

International Index to Music Periodicals, Music Index, RILM Abstracts of Music Literature.

General

5067. ***Acta Musicologica.*** [ISSN: 0001-6241] 1928. 2x/yr. Members, DEM 135. Ed(s): Rudolf Flotzinger. Baerenreiter Verlag, Heinrich-Schuetz-Allee 35, Kassel, 34131, Germany; order@baerenreiter.com; http://www.baerenreiter.com. Illus., index, adv. Refereed. Vol. ends: Dec. *Indexed:* ArtHuCI, IBZ, IIMP, MusicInd, RILM. *Aud.:* Ac, Sa.

Scholarly contributors worldwide present research on various musics from musicological and ethnomusicological perspectives in this journal published by the International Musicological Society. A wide variety of eras, composers, research methodologies, and issues are presented, as well as tributes to eminent musicologists and information on upcoming conferences. Articles appear in numerous languages including English, French, German, Italian, and Spanish. Of interest particularly to musicologists, it is recommended for academic music libraries.

5068. ***American Music.*** [ISSN: 0734-4392] 1983. q. USD 50 (Individuals, USD 40). Ed(s): David Nicholls. University of Illinois Press, 1325 S Oak St, Champaign, IL 61820-6903; http://www.press.uillinois.edu. Illus., adv. Sample. Refereed. Circ: 1650 Paid. Vol. ends: Winter. Microform: PQC. Online: Chadwyck-Healey Incorporated; Florida Center for Library Automation; Gale Group; Northern Light Technology, Inc.; OCLC Online Computer Library Center, Inc.; ProQuest Information & Learning. *Indexed:* ABS&EES, ArtHuCI, BRI, CBRI, HumInd, IIMP, MusicInd, RILM. *Bk. rev.:* 10-12, 1,000 words, signed. *Aud.:* Ga, Ac, Sa.

Published in cooperation with the Society for American Music, this journal is devoted to all aspects of music in America. Articles on American composers, performers, publishers, institutions, events, and the American music industry are presented. Musical genres include jazz, folk, dance, theater, blues, popular, and classical. Book and record reviews, bibliographies, and discographies are included. Tables of contents are available online at the publisher's web site. Of interest to performers and scholars, this publication is recommended for academic and public libraries.

5069. ***American Music Teacher: the official journal of music teachers national association.*** [ISSN: 0003-0112] 1951. bi-m. Non-members, USD 30. Ed(s): Marcie G Lindsey. Music Teachers National Association, Inc., Carew Tower, 441 Vine St, Ste 505, Cincinnati, OH 45202-2814; www.mtna.org. Illus., adv. Circ: 25000. Vol. ends: Jun/Jul. Microform: PQC; MUE. Online: Chadwyck-Healey Incorporated; Florida Center for Library Automation; Gale Group; Northern Light Technology, Inc.; OCLC Online Computer Library Center, Inc.; ProQuest Information & Learning; H.W. Wilson. Reprint: PQC. *Indexed:* BRI, CBRI, EduInd, IBZ, IIMP, MusicInd. *Bk. rev.:* 5-7, 500 words, signed. *Aud.:* Ac, Sa.

The purpose of *American Music Teacher*, the official publication of the Music Teachers National Association (MTNA), is to provide articles, reviews, and regular columns that inform, educate, and challenge music teachers and foster excellence in the music teaching profession. Issues include articles and columns that reflect the interests of the broad spectrum of teachers served by MTNA; announcements of national, state and local news; opportunities for professional enrichment and opportunities for students; and discussions of issues and trends in the music field. Of interest to private and collegiate music teachers, it is recommended for academic and large public libraries.

5070. ***American Musicological Society. Journal.*** Formerly: *American Musicological Society. Bulletin.* [ISSN: 0003-0139] 1948. q. USD 95 print & online eds. USD 34 newsstand/cover. University of California Press, Journals Division, 2000 Center St, Ste 303, Berkeley, CA 94704-1223; journals@ucop.edu; http://www.ucpress.edu/journals. Illus., index, adv. Refereed. Circ: 4800. *Indexed:* ArtHuCI, BAS, BHA, HumInd, IBZ, IIMP, MLA-IB, MusicInd, RI-1, RILM. *Bk. rev.:* 3-5, 3,000 words, signed. *Aud.:* Ac, Sa.

The *Journal of the American Musicological Society* publishes refereed articles in various fields of musicology including history, theory, criticism, analysis, aesthetics, and ethnomusicology. Many articles deal with the history of Western art music. A typical issue includes three extensive articles (many approaching 50 pages in length), signed book reviews, and a list of publications received that includes books and scholarly editions of music. Abstracts are located at the end of articles. The last issue of each volume contains an index to the volume. The journal's web site contains tables of contents with abstracts from 1970 to the present. Recommended for academic libraries.

5071. ***Cambridge Opera Journal.*** [ISSN: 0954-5867] 1989. 3x/yr. USD 112 (Individuals, USD 55). Ed(s): Mary Hunter. Cambridge University Press, The Edinburgh Bldg, Shaftesbury Rd, Cambridge, CB2 2RU, United Kingdom; information@cambridge.org; http://uk.cambridge.org/journals. Illus., adv. Refereed. Vol. ends: Nov. Reprint: SWZ. *Indexed:* BrHumI, IIMP, IIPA, MusicInd, RILM. *Bk. rev.:* 1-2, 6-10 pages, signed. *Aud.:* Ac, Sa.

Known for its reputable scholarship, the *Cambridge Opera Journal* contains material on all aspects of the European canon, as well as American opera and musical theater, non-Western music theater, and operas written since 1945. Articles provide information on topics such as form, style, composers, eras, staging, gender studies, literature, ballet, history, and other related topics. Issues include illustrations, music examples, and reviews of recent publications of importance in the field. Of interest to performers and scholars, it is recommended for academic and large public libraries.

5072. *Chamber Music.* Former titles (until 1986): *Chamber Music Magazine;* (until 1983): *American Ensemble.* [ISSN: 1071-1791] 1978. bi-m. USD 28. Ed(s): Karissa Krenz. Chamber Music America, 305 Seventh Ave, 5th Fl, New York, NY 10001-6008. Adv. Circ: 13000. *Indexed:* IIMP, MusicInd. *Bk. rev.:* 2-3, 500-1,000 words, signed. *Aud.:* Ac, Sa.

Chamber Music is the official publication of Chamber Music America, an organization committed to promoting artistic excellence and economic stability within the profession and to ensuring that chamber music is a vital part of American life. Complete with color photos, articles feature interviews with various chamber ensembles; information on conferences, workshops, and festivals; strategies for economic planning; and guidance regarding technological concerns. Styles discussed range from classical to jazz to popular music. The table of contents is available online. Of interest to performers, educators, students, and chamber music aficionados, it is recommended for academic and large public libraries.

5073. *Choir & Organ.* [ISSN: 0968-7262] 1993. bi-m. GBP 19.25 United Kingdom & Ireland; USD 34.95 in US & Canada; GBP 29.95 elsewhere. Ed(s): Matthew Power. Orpheus Publications Ltd., 3 Waterhouse Sq, 138-142 Holborn, London, EC1N 2NY, United Kingdom. Adv. Circ: 8000 Paid. Online: EBSCO Publishing. *Indexed:* BrHumI, IIMP, MusicInd, RILM. *Aud.:* Ac, Sa.

Choir & Organ is a classical music magazine for organists and musicians, choir and choral directors, singers, organ builders, and lovers of choral and organ music. Articles provide insights into the careers of leading organists and choral conductors, examine important instruments, and provide comprehensive news and reviews of new publications, recordings, and events. Many color photos of organs are included in each issue. Recommended for academic and public libraries.

5074. *Choral Journal.* [ISSN: 0009-5028] 1959. m. Aug.-May. USD 35. Ed(s): Carroll Gonzo. American Choral Directors Association, PO Box 6310, Lawton, OK 73506-0310; chojo@sirinet.net; http://www.choralnet.org/. Illus., index, adv. Refereed. Circ: 18000 Paid. Vol. ends: May. Microform: PQC. Reprint: PQC. *Indexed:* IIMP, MusicInd, RILM. *Bk. rev.:* 3-5, 200-500 words, signed. *Aud.:* Hs, Ac, Sa.

The American Choral Directors Association publishes The *Choral Journal* to provide its members with practical and scholarly information about choral music and its performance. Articles and columns cover topics such as rehearsal techniques, composers, history, form and style of choral music, interviews with eminent conductors and composers, performance practice, vocal pedagogy, and educational techniques and philosophies. Issues include association news, convention information (January issue), and reviews of recordings, music, and books. Recommended for academic, public, and high school libraries.

5075. *Clavier: a magazine for pianists and organists.* [ISSN: 0009-854X] 1962. 10x/yr. USD 19. Ed(s): Judy Nelson. The Instrumentalist Co., 200 Northfield Rd, Northfield, IL 60093-3390. Illus., index, adv. Circ: 16000. Vol. ends: Dec. *Indexed:* ABS&EES, ArtHuCI, EduInd, IIMP, MusicInd, RILM, SSCI. *Aud.:* Hs, Ac, Sa.

Clavier is published for piano teachers and students and offers practical information and innovative ideas for educators, students, and performers. Articles are written by veteran teachers and performers who share their experience in working with all levels of students. Leading educators discuss new ideas and advice for piano teachers including teaching and repertoire suggestions. Issues include interviews and profiles of teachers and artists, articles on the business side of teaching, new music reviews, competition information, and ideas for rekindling the interest and enthusiasm of students. Recommended for academic, public, and high school libraries.

5076. *Computer Music Journal.* [ISSN: 0148-9267] 1977. q. USD 195 print & online eds. (Individuals, USD 77 print & online eds.; USD 14 newsstand/cover per issue). Ed(s): Douglas Keislar. MIT Press, 5 Cambridge Center, Cambridge, MA 02142-1493; journals-orders@mit.edu; http://mitpress.mit.edu. Illus., adv. Refereed. Circ: 4000. Vol. ends: Winter. Microform: PQC. Online: EBSCO Publishing; Florida Center for Library Automation; Gale Group; Ingenta Select; OCLC Online Computer Library Center, Inc.; Project MUSE; RoweCom Information Quest; Swets Blackwell. Reprint: PQC. *Indexed:* ArtHuCI, C&ISA, CompLI, CompR, EngInd, IBZ, IIMP, InfoSAb, LISA, MusicInd, RILM, SCI. *Bk. rev.:* 2-3, 1,500 words, signed. *Aud.:* Ac, Sa.

The quarterly *Computer Music Journal* is a print publication with an annual music DVD. Issues present information on the skills, technologies, and future of digital sound and all musical applications of computers. Generally included are four feature articles, announcements of contests, conferences, symposia, and numerous reviews of events, publications, multimedia, recordings, and products. It is also available online through Project Muse. Intended for musicians, composers, scientists, engineers, and computer enthusiasts interested in contemporary and electronic music, as well as anyone exploring computer-generated sound, it is recommended for academic libraries.

5077. *Conductors Guild. Journal.* [ISSN: 0734-1032] 1980. s-a. USD 30 domestic; USD 45 elsewhere. Ed(s): Jacques Voois. Conductors Guild, Inc., 6219 N Sheridan Rd, Chicago, IL 60660-1729; conguild@aol.com. Illus., adv. Circ: 1800. Vol. ends: Summer/Fall. *Indexed:* RILM. *Bk. rev.:* 5-8, 1,000-1,500 words, signed. *Aud.:* Hs, Ac, Sa.

The goal of this journal is to advance the art and practice of conducting by publishing articles that will serve conductors needs and interests. The scope of articles ranges from world-famous orchestras to community orchestras; topics include the history of conducting and its practitioners, particular aspects of orchestral works (e.g., metronome markings in Beethoven symphonies), and guides to the performance of specific pieces (e.g., a guide to performing Bruckner's E-minor symphony). Also included in some issues are transcripts of sessions from Conductors' Guild conferences and seminars, and errata in musical scores. A typical issue will contain five to seven articles and several substantive book reviews. Recommended for academic, large public, and large high school libraries.

5078. *Contemporary Music Review.* [ISSN: 0749-4467] 1984. q. GBP 269 (Individuals, GBP 55; Corporations, GBP 448). Ed(s): Peter Nelson. Taylor & Francis Ltd, 11 New Fetter Ln, London, EC4P 4EE, United Kingdom; http://www.tandf.co.uk/journals. Refereed. Online: EBSCO Publishing; Gale Group. Reprint: PSC. *Indexed:* HumInd, IIMP, MusicInd. *Bk. rev.:* Various number and length. *Aud.:* Ga, Ac.

Contemporary Music Review publishes articles and interviews on contemporary composition in all its aspects, techniques, aesthetics, technology, relationships to other disciplines, and its relationship to performers. Each issue has a specific topic or theme, e.g., "Performers on Performance," and consists of ten interviews with musicians talking about their art and how they interact with the music they perform. Some issues may focus on a composer, e.g., Luigi Nono. Articles are often understandable to readers with a nonprofessional interest in music. Each issue contains four to ten articles of 10–30 pages each. Articles begin with abstracts and a list of keywords and often contain a discography. Some articles provide notes and references, and some issues offer indexes. Book reviews appear only occasionally. Recommended for academic and large public libraries.

5079. *Council for Research in Music Education. Bulletin.* [ISSN: 0010-9894] 1963. q. USD 30 (Individuals, USD 20; Students, USD 12). Ed(s): Gregory Denardo. University of Illinois at Urbana-Champaign, School of Music, 1114 W Nevada, Urbana, IL 61801; denardo@uiuc.edu; http://www.music.uiuc.edu/Division/Mus_Ed.html. Illus., index. Refereed. Circ: 2000. Microform: PQC. Reprint: PQC. *Indexed:* ArtHuCI, CIJE, EduInd, MusicInd, PsycholAb, RILM, SSCI. *Bk. rev.:* 1-3, 750-1,000 words, signed. *Aud.:* Ac, Sa.

Published as a service to music education for all ages, this official bulletin of the Council for Research in Music Education (CRME) intends to encourage researchers and to serve as a disseminator of information concerning existing research. Article topics include teaching methodologies, repertoire lists, assessments, motivation, music perception, etc. Issues include critiques of doctoral dissertations in the field of music education, book reviews, reports of original research, and reports from seminars and conferences sponsored by other organizations such as the International Society for Music Education. Of particular interest to music teachers, the *Bulletin of the Council for Research in Music Education* is recommended for academic and large public libraries.

5080. ***Current Musicology.*** [ISSN: 0011-3735] 1965. 2x/yr. USD 36 (Individuals, USD 16; Students, USD 13). Ed(s): Mark Burford. Columbia University, Department of Music, 614 Dodge Hall, Mail Code 1812, New York, NY 10027-7004; current-musicology@columbia.edu; http://www.columbia.edu/~ds193/cm.html. Illus., index, adv. Circ: 1500 Paid. Microform: PQC. Online: bigchalk; Chadwyck-Healey Incorporated; Gale Group; OCLC Online Computer Library Center, Inc.; ProQuest Information & Learning. Reprint: PQC. *Indexed:* ABS&EES, ArtHuCI, HumInd, IIMP, MusicInd, RILM. *Bk. rev.:* 3-4, 8-10 pages, signed. *Aud.:* Ac, Sa.

Published by the Department of Music at Columbia University, *Current Musicology* serves as an international forum for scholarly music research, seeking to reflect the forefront of thought in historical musicology, ethnomusicology, and music theory, as well as music cognition, philosophy of music, and interdisciplinary studies. Special sections are devoted to specific topics such as teaching music survey courses, music theory, computer music, and composers. Reviews of collections, in-depth discussions of recent publications, and book reviews are included in each issue. Recommended for academic libraries.

5081. ***Early Music.*** [ISSN: 0306-1078] 1973. q. GBP 117. Ed(s): Tess Knighton. Oxford University Press, Great Clarendon St, Oxford, OX2 6DP, United Kingdom; jnl.orders@oup.co.uk; http://www3.oup.co.uk/jnls. Illus., index, adv. Refereed. Circ: 3500. Vol. ends: Nov. Microform: PQC. Online: Chadwyck-Healey Incorporated; Florida Center for Library Automation; Gale Group; Northern Light Technology, Inc.; OCLC Online Computer Library Center, Inc.; ProQuest Information & Learning. Reprint: PQC; PSC. *Indexed:* AmH&L, ArtHuCI, BHA, BrHumI, HumInd, IIMP, MusicInd, RILM. *Bk. rev.:* 2-4, 750-1,000 words, signed. *Aud.:* Ac, Sa.

Early Music presents information about earlier musical repertoires. Articles, written by scholars and performers of international reputation, discuss issues such as period instruments, performance practice, notation, iconography, and historical contexts. Some issues are dedicated to a particular theme to mark the anniversary of a composer or to explore otherwise uncharted territory such as the music of the New World or the early musical traditions of non-Western cultures. Numerous book, music, and recording reviews, and announcements of festivals and workshops are included in each issue. Also available online. Of interest to anyone studying early music and how it is being interpreted today, it is recommended for academic libraries.

5082. ***Early Music History: studies in medieval and early modern music.*** [ISSN: 0261-1279] 1982. a. USD 115 (Individuals, USD 68). Ed(s): Iain Fenlon. Cambridge University Press, The Edinburgh Bldg, Shaftesbury Rd, Cambridge, CB2 2RU, United Kingdom; information@cambridge.org; http://uk.cambridge.org. Illus., adv. Microform: PQC. Online: OCLC Online Computer Library Center, Inc.; Swets Blackwell. *Indexed:* ArtHuCI, IIMP, RILM. *Bk. rev.:* 2, 2,500 words, signed. *Aud.:* Ac, Sa.

Early Music History is devoted to the study of music from the early Middle Ages to the end of the seventeenth century. Published annually, it focuses on the music of Britain, America, and Europe, emphasizing interdisciplinary research and new methodological ideas. Topics include manuscript studies, textual criticism, iconography, studies of the relationship between words and music, and the relationship between music and society. Several book reviews are included in each issue. Recommended for academic libraries.

5083. ***Ethnomusicology.*** [ISSN: 0014-1836] 1953. 3x/yr. USD 75 (Individuals, USD 60; Students, USD 30). Ed(s): Peter Manuel. University of Illinois Press, 1325 S Oak St, Champaign, IL 61820-6903; http://www.press.uillinois.edu. Illus., index, adv. Refereed. Circ: 2000. Vol. ends: Fall. Microform: PQC. Online: bigchalk; Chadwyck-Healey Incorporated; Gale Group; Northern Light Technology, Inc.; OCLC Online Computer Library Center, Inc.; ProQuest Information & Learning. Reprint: PQC. *Indexed:* ABS&EES, AICP, AbAn, AnthLit, ArtHuCI, BAS, HumInd, IBSS, IBZ, IIMP, MLA-IB, MusicInd, RILM, SSCI. *Bk. rev.:* 6-8, 500-1,000 words, signed. *Aud.:* Ac, Sa.

This journal is published by the Society for Ethnomusicology, which was founded to promote the research, study, and performance of music in all historical periods and cultural contexts. Concepts discussed are multidisciplinary and worldwide in scope, and are aimed at a diverse audience of musicians, musicologists, folklorists, popular culture scholars, and cultural anthropologists. Recent article topics include Cambodian classical music and jazz rhythm. There are reviews of books, recordings, and visual media. The table of contents is also available online. Recommended for academic and large public libraries.

5084. ***Fontes Artis Musicae.*** [ISSN: 0015-6191] 1953. q. USD 60 (Individuals, USD 38). Ed(s): John Wagstaff. International Association of Music Libraries, Archives and Documentation Centres (U.S.), 8551 Research Way, Ste 180, Middleton, WI 53562; http://www.areditions.com/. Illus., index, adv. Refereed. Circ: 2200 Paid. Vol. ends: Dec. *Indexed:* ArtHuCI, IIMP, LISA, LibLit, MusicInd, RILM, SSCI. *Bk. rev.:* 4-6, 500-750 words, signed. *Aud.:* Ac, Sa.

Fontes Artis Musicae is published by the International Association of Music Libraries, Archives and Documentation Centres (IAML). Issues include reports from IAML committees, working groups, branches, and officers; memorials; reviews of music resources; and announcements of upcoming events. Articles are in French, English, and German. It is also available online. Of interest mainly to music librarians, archivists, bibliographers, and musicologists, it is recommended for academic libraries.

5085. ***Instrumentalist: a magazine for school and college band and orchestra directors, professional instrumentalists, teacher-training specialists in instrumental music education and instrumental teachers.*** [ISSN: 0020-4331] 1946. m. USD 22. Ed(s): Elizabeth Dallman. The Instrumentalist Co., 200 Northfield Rd, Northfield, IL 60093-3390. Illus., index, adv. Circ: 18000. Vol. ends: Jul. *Indexed:* EduInd, IIMP, MusicInd, RILM. *Aud.:* Hs, Ga, Ac, Sa.

Instrumentalist is a commercial publication targeting high school and academic band and orchestra directors. The articles, written by experienced directors and performers, cover topics such as rehearsal techniques, conducting tips, programming ideas, instrument clinics, master classes, repertoire analyses, and interviews with composers, performers, conductors, and teachers. Monthly new music reviews, numerous color photos, job guides, summer camp directories, and announcements of upcoming festivals are included. Of interest to school band and orchestra directors, it is recommended for academic, large public, and high school libraries.

5086. ***International Journal of Music Education.*** Formerly (until 1983): *Australian Journal of Music Education.* [ISSN: 0255-7614] 1967. s-a. USD 40. Ed(s): Jack Dobbs, Anthony Kemp. International Society for Music Education, PO Box 909, Nedlands, W.A. , Australia; isme@iinet.net.au; http://www.isme.org. Illus., adv. Refereed. Circ: 2000. Microform: PQC; NRP. Reprint: PQC. *Indexed:* IIMP, MusicInd, RILM. *Aud.:* Ac, Sa.

This journal is published by the International Society for Music Education. Articles concern the teaching and learning of music, particularly targeting international audiences and issues. Topics such as culture, heritage, innovations in music education, preservation, popular music, aesthetics, philosophy, and other concerns are discussed. While the articles are printed in English, abstracts in French, German, and Spanish are included. Of interest to teachers of all levels of students, it is recommended for academic libraries.

5087. ***International Musician.*** [ISSN: 0020-8051] 1901. m. USD 25 domestic; USD 30 Canada; USD 35 elsewhere. Ed(s): Antoinette Follett, Tom Lee. American Federation of Musicians of the United States and Canada, 1501 Broadway, New York, NY 10036; http://www.mediamanager.com/slist/intulmuscian.html. Illus., adv. Circ: 110000 Paid. Vol. ends: Jun. Microform: PQC. Reprint: PQC. *Indexed:* IIMP, MusicInd. *Aud.:* Ga, Ac, Sa.

International Musician is received by all members of the American Federation of Musicians and is an essential source of union information and communication. Covering all genres of music, this publication reports on happenings and changes in the music business. Articles describe and comment on trends in the music industry, the benefits of union membership, and the accomplishments of the union; provide advice on planning and programs for the future; give legal information; and advertise services for musicians. Each issue contains a cover story on a successful musician or group; reports on union news and accomplishments; offers health advice and resources for self-improvement; and presents short articles on member anniversaries and achievements, including a section focusing on marketability and tips for success, plus editorials. Each issue also has classified advertising with categories for auditions, items for sale, items wanted, and lost or stolen instruments. Recommended for public and academic libraries.

5088. ***Journal of Music Theory.*** [ISSN: 0022-2909] 1957. s-a. USD 32 (Individuals, USD 24; Students, USD 20). Ed(s): Ramon Satuenpra. Yale University, School of Music, PO Box 208310, New Haven, CT 06520; http://www.yale.edu/. Illus., index, adv. Refereed. Circ: 1700. Vol. ends: Fall. Microform: MIM; PQC. Reprint: PQC. *Indexed:* ArtHuCI, IIMP, MusicInd, RILM, SSCI. *Bk. rev.:* 2-3, 3-6 pages, signed. *Aud.:* Ac.

This journal publishes scholarly articles on historical and contemporary theoretical and technical considerations involved in music composition. Examples of recent article titles are "A Cognitive Theory of Musical Meaning," and "Counterpoint and Analysis in Fourteenth-Century Song." Each issue contains at least two book reviews of three to six pages each. The second number of each volume contains an index to the volume. The journal's web site provides access to an author index from 1982 to 1997, and the tables of contents of current and past issues. Recommended for academic libraries.

5089. ***Journal of Music Therapy.*** [ISSN: 0022-2917] 1964. q. USD 125 domestic; USD 135 foreign. Ed(s): Jayne Standley. American Music Therapy Association, 8455 Colesville Rd, Ste 1000, Silver Spring, MD 20910-3392; subscribe@musictherapy.org; http://www.musictherapy.org. Illus., index. Refereed. Circ: 6000. Vol. ends: Winter. Microform: PQC. Online: OCLC Online Computer Library Center, Inc.; ProQuest Information & Learning; H.W. Wilson. Reprint: PQC. *Indexed:* AgeL, ArtHuCI, ECER, EduInd, IIMP, IndMed, MusicInd, PsycholAb, RILM, SSCI. *Aud.:* Ac, Sa.

This journal, published by the American Music Therapy Association, presents scholarly articles for music therapists, psychologists, psychiatrists, and others in related fields. Articles document both theoretical and experimental studies into the effects music can have on physiological, emotional and mental states, e.g., relaxation, attention, and memory. Aspects of music therapy education and problems of students in the field are also considered. Each issue contains three to five articles with abstracts and references. Recent article titles include "Music Therapy Assessment for Severely Emotionally Disturbed Children: A Pilot Study," and "Experiences and Concerns of Students during Music Therapy Practica." An index appears in the last issue of each volume. Recommended for academic libraries.

5090. ***Journal of Musicology: a quarterly review of music history, criticism, analysis, and performance practice.*** [ISSN: 0277-9269] 1982. q. USD 132 print & online eds. USD 34 newsstand/cover. Ed(s): John Nadas. University of California Press, Journals Division, 2000 Center St, Ste 303, Berkeley, CA 94704-1223; journals@ucop.edu; http://www.ucpress.edu/journals. Illus., adv. Refereed. Circ: 1300 Paid. Vol. ends: Fall. Microform: PQC. Online: EBSCO Publishing; Florida Center for Library Automation; Gale Group; Ingenta Select; Northern Light Technology, Inc.; OCLC Online Computer Library Center, Inc. *Indexed:* ABS&EES, ArtHuCI, HumInd, IBZ, IIMP, MusicInd, RILM, SSCI. *Aud.:* Ac, Sa.

The *Journal of Musicology* publishes scholarly articles on music history, criticism and analysis, performance practice, and archival research. Readers are primarily scholars, performers, and college teachers. Each issue contains four to five articles with abstracts appearing at the end of articles. Tables of contents back to 1995 are available at the publisher's web site. The journal's web site (www.journalofmusicology.org) has links to issues and abstracts back to the summer of 2001. Recommended for academic and large public libraries.

5091. ***Journal of Research in Music Education.*** [ISSN: 0022-4294] 1953. q. Membership. Ed(s): Cornelia Yarbrough. The National Association for Music Education (M E N C), 1806 Robert Fulton Dr, Reston, VA 20191-4348; http://www.menc.org. Illus. Refereed. Circ: 3300. Vol. ends: Winter. Microform: PQC. Online: Chadwyck-Healey Incorporated; EBSCO Publishing; Florida Center for Library Automation; Gale Group; OCLC Online Computer Library Center, Inc.; ProQuest Information & Learning; H.W. Wilson. Reprint: PQC. *Indexed:* ArtHuCI, CIJE, EduInd, IIMP, MusicInd, PsycholAb, RILM, SSCI. *Aud.:* Ac, Sa.

This journal publishes the results of historical, philosophical, descriptive, and experimental research in music education. Articles are critiqued by an editorial committee of scholars and are intended to increase the knowledge of researchers as well as music teachers in all settings. Each issue contains approximately six articles written by professional educators and announcements that often include calls for papers. Issues begin with a short "Focus" section written by the editor that gives an overview of that issue's contents with additional comments on topics or contributors. Examples of recent articles include "Self-Evaluation Tendencies of Junior High Instrumentalists" and "Perception and Cognition in Music: Musically Trained and Untrained Adults Compared to Sixth-Grade and Eighth-Grade Children." Recommended for academic, high school, and large public libraries.

5092. ***Journal of Singing: the official journal of the National Association of Teachers of Singing.*** Former titles (until Sep. 1995): *N A T S Journal;* (until May 1985): *N A T S Bulletin.* [ISSN: 1086-7732] 1944. 5x/yr. Individuals, USD 35. Ed(s): Richard Sjoerdsma. National Association of Teachers of Singing, Inc., 4745 Sutton Park Court, Ste 201, Jacksonville, FL 32224; info@nats.org; http://www.nats.org. Illus., index, adv. Refereed. Circ: 7000 Paid. Microform: PQC. Reprint: PQC. *Indexed:* IIMP, MusicInd, RILM. *Bk. rev.:* 1-2, 300-500 words, signed. *Aud.:* Ac, Sa.

The National Association of Teachers of Singing publishes this journal for students and teachers of singing in all countries. Articles present information on topics such as repertoire, vocal techniques, standards, care of the voice, teaching methodologies, and singing as physical therapy. Issues include announcements of upcoming events, conferences, and workshops; reviews of books, music, and recordings; and organizational information. Of interest to singers, vocal coaches, and choral conductors, it is recommended for academic and large public libraries.

5093. ***Leonardo Music Journal.*** [ISSN: 0961-1215] 1991. a. USD 60 (Individuals, USD 30). Ed(s): Nicolas Collins, Roger F Malina. MIT Press, 5 Cambridge Center, Cambridge, MA 02142-1493; journals-orders@mit.edu; http://mitpress.mit.edu. Refereed. *Indexed:* ABM, ArtHuCI, HumInd, IBZ, RILM. *Aud.:* Ac, Sa.

Leonardo Music Journal features peer-reviewed articles written by artists and scientists about the interaction of science and music. Subject areas investigate how new technologies interact with the composition and presentation of music, how science is affecting the understanding of music, and how sound is combined with other media to form new art forms. The journal's audience includes musicians, composers, sound artists, scientists, theoreticians, and instrument makers. Each annual issue contains approximately ten articles and comes with a CD that contains musical examples related to that issue's topic. The journal's web site contains selected articles, contents and abstracts of current and previous issues, and contents and sound files of previous CDs. Recommended for academic libraries.

5094. ***Medical Problems of Performing Artists.*** [ISSN: 0885-1158] 1986. q. USD 76 (Individuals, USD 56; USD 20 newsstand/cover per issue). Ed(s): Alice Brand Fonbrener. Hanley & Belfus, Inc., 210 S 13th St, Philadelphia, PA 19107; http://www.elsevierhealth.com. Illus., index, adv. Refereed. Circ: 1000. *Indexed:* ArtHuCI, BiolAb, ExcerpMed, IDP, IIMP, IIPA, MusicInd, SSCI. *Bk. rev.:* 1, 250 words, signed. *Aud.:* Ac, Sa.

This journal publishes reviewed articles that focus on the origin, diagnosis, and treatment of medical problems encountered by performing artists. These include muscular and neurological disorders, anxieties, stress, voice and hearing disorders, repetitive stress injuries, substance abuse, etc. As the official journal of the Performing Arts Medicine Association, this journal acts as a forum for medical and academic professionals to communicate their research findings and practices. Each issue contains approximately six articles with abstracts and abstracts of relevant articles in other journals, with occasional book reviews. Recommended for academic and large public libraries.

5095. ***Music and Letters.*** [ISSN: 0027-4224] 1920. q. GBP 106. Ed(s): N Fortune, L J Brooks. Oxford University Press, Great Clarendon St, Oxford, OX2 6DP, United Kingdom; jnl.orders@oup.co.uk; http://www3.oup.co.uk/jnls. Illus., index, adv. Refereed. Circ: 1500. Vol. ends: Nov. Microform: PQC. Online: Florida Center for Library Automation; Gale Group; ingenta.com; OCLC Online Computer Library Center, Inc.; ProQuest Information & Learning; Swets Blackwell. Reprint: PSC; SWZ. *Indexed:* AmH&L, ArtHuCI, HumInd, IBZ, IIMP, MLA-IB, MusicInd, RILM, SSCI. *Bk. rev.:* 25, 500-1,000 words, signed. *Aud.:* Ac, Sa.

Music and Letters publishes articles on historical, analytical and critical musicology, covering all musical periods. Subjects of articles are derived mostly from letters, documents, reminiscences, and other written records. Some recent examples are documents of memories of Beethoven by his contemporaries, the examination of and inferences drawn from a contract between Mozart and a publisher, and the influence of French poetic rhythm on Verdi's operas. A typical issue contains approximately three articles, eight to ten music reviews, and many book reviews. The journal's web site contains full texts of articles from 2002 forward, and tables of contents of issues back to 1996. Recommended for academic libraries.

5096. ***Music Educators Journal.*** [ISSN: 0027-4321] 1914. 5x/yr. Membership. Ed(s): Francis S Ponyck. The National Association for Music Education (M E N C), 1806 Robert Fulton Dr, Reston, VA 20191-4348; http://www.menc.org. Illus., index, adv. Refereed. Circ: 67000. Vol. ends: May. Microform: PQC. Online: Chadwyck-Healey Incorporated; EBSCO Publishing; Gale Group; OCLC Online Computer Library Center, Inc.; ProQuest Information & Learning; H.W. Wilson. Reprint: PQC; PSC. *Indexed:* AgeL, ArtHuCI, BAS, BRI, CBRI, CIJE, ECER, EduInd, IBZ, IIMP, MusicInd, RILM. *Bk. rev.:* 8, 150-200 words, signed. *Aud.:* Ems, Hs, Ga, Ac, Sa.

As the official magazine of the Music Educators National Conference (MENC), this journal focuses on the approaches and methods used for teaching music in schools, colleges, community orchestras, and other education environments. Sample article topics include a report on the interaction of music teachers and music therapists in helping children, one teacher's method for teaching blues and jazz improvisation to teenagers, and advice on vocal exercises to help elementary school children learn and enjoy singing. Each issue contains five to six articles, approximately eight short book reviews, and video reviews. "Samplings" provides abstracts of articles published in other MENC journals. Recommended for all libraries and music teachers.

5097. ***Music Library Association. Notes.*** [ISSN: 0027-4380] 1942. q. USD 80 (Individuals, USD 70). Ed(s): Linda Solow Blotner. Music Library Association, 8551 Research Way, Suite 180, Middleton, WI 53562; mla@areditions.com; http://www.musiclibraryassoc.org. Illus., index, adv. Refereed. Circ: 2900. Vol. ends: Jun. Microform: PQC. Online: Chadwyck-Healey Incorporated; EBSCO Publishing; Florida Center for Library Automation; Gale Group; OCLC Online Computer Library Center, Inc.; Project MUSE; RoweCom Information Quest; Swets Blackwell; H.W. Wilson. *Indexed:* ArtHuCI, BRD, BRI, CBRI, HumInd, IDP, IIMP, LISA, LibLit, LingAb, MusicInd, RILM. *Bk. rev.:* 40-50, 250-500 words, signed. *Aud.:* Ac, Sa.

Notes, the quarterly journal of the Music Library Association, publishes articles on contemporary and historical issues in music librarianship, music bibliography, and music publishing. Each issue contains two to four articles, but the main body of the journal is an extensive section of signed book reviews with subheadings for popular music, ethnomusicology, composers, reference books, instruments, and music reviews. Issues also contain a long list of books recently published, a few sound recording, digital media, and software reviews, music publishers catalogs, and new periodicals. Highly recommended for all music librarians and bibliographers.

5098. ***Music Perception.*** [ISSN: 0730-7829] 1983. q. USD 218 print & online eds. USD 55 newsstand/cover. Ed(s): Robert Gjerdingen. University of California Press, Journals Division, 2000 Center St, Ste 303, Berkeley, CA 94704-1223; journals@ucop.edu; http://www.ucpress.edu/journals. Illus., index, adv. Refereed. Circ: 700 Paid. Vol. ends: Summer. Microform: PQC. Online: EBSCO Publishing; Florida Center for Library Automation; Gale Group; Ingenta Select; OCLC Online Computer Library Center, Inc. *Indexed:* ArtHuCI, IIMP, L&LBA, MusicInd, PsycholAb, RILM, SSCI. *Bk. rev.:* 2, 2,000-3,500 words, signed. *Aud.:* Ac, Sa.

Music Perception publishes articles on research into musical experience and interpretation. Papers are written by scientists and musicians with critical, methodological, theoretical, and empirical perspectives into how music is heard and perceived. Topics include the disciplines of psychology, psychophysics, linguistics, neurology, artificial intelligence, acoustics, and music theory. Examples of articles are "Listener's Perception of English Cathedral Girl and Boy Choristers," and "Effects of Musical Tempo and Mode on Arousal, Mood, and Spatial Abilities." Each issue contains four to five articles 15–25 pages in length, two to four book reviews, and announcements of future conferences and meetings. For subscribers, the web site provides tables of contents, abstracts, and full texts of articles from 2001 forward. Recommended for academic libraries.

5099. ***Music Theory Spectrum.*** [ISSN: 0195-6167] 1979. s-a. USD 97 print & online eds. USD 50 newsstand/cover. Ed(s): Daniel Harrison. University of California Press, Journals Division, 2000 Center St, Ste 303, Berkeley, CA 94704-1223; journals@ucop.edu; http://www.ucpress.edu/journals. Adv. Refereed. Circ: 1300. *Indexed:* ArtHuCI, IBZ, IIMP, MusicInd, RILM. *Bk. rev.:* 5-6. *Aud.:* Ac.

The official print journal of the Society for Music Theory, this publication documents and analyzes various areas of interest in the discipline. Some issues contain diverse articles on theory and music composition; other issues focus around a particular topic or theory, e.g., "Klumpenhower Networks." Issues generally contain four articles 10–35 pages each, and five to six extensive book reviews. Some issues also contain announcements for new books and sections for reader response. Subscriptions are included with membership in the society. The web site contains access to tables of contents with abstracts back to 1997. Recommended for academic libraries.

5100. ***Musical America International Directory of the Performing Arts.*** Formerly (until 1968): *Musical America Annual Directory Issue.* [ISSN: 0735-7788] 1960. a. USD 105. Commonwealth Business Media, Inc., 400 Windsor Corporate Ctr., 50 Millstone Rd., Ste. 200, East Windsor, NJ 08520-1415. Illus., index, adv. Circ: 15000 Paid and controlled. *Aud.:* Hs, Ga, Ac.

Musical America International Directory of the Performing Arts provides a broad range of over 14,000 listings of arts organizations worldwide. The directory contains a categorical and alphabetical index of the more than 10,000 advertisers that appear in this annual publication. It also contains articles on the "Musician of the Year" in the categories of ensemble, composer, conductor, instrumentalist, and vocalist, and reports of artists' managers on their artists and achievements of the past year. Directory listings are divided into United States and Canada, and International listings, with each of these categories subdivided into orchestras, opera companies, choral groups, dance companies, festivals, music schools and departments, record companies, magazines, and radio stations. The directory's web site contains three main sections on industry news, directory articles, and listings. Directory articles, press releases, and a calendar of events are available to all; industry news, listings (e.g., orchestras, competitions, schools), and reviews of performances are for subscribers only. Recommended for all collections that serve musicians and music users.

5101. ***The Musical Quarterly.*** [ISSN: 0027-4631] 1915. q. GBP 96. Ed(s): Leon Botstein. Oxford University Press, Great Clarendon St, Oxford, OX2 6DP, United Kingdom; jnl.orders@oup.co.uk; http://www3.oup.co.uk/jnls. Illus., index, adv. Refereed. Circ: 2300. Vol. ends: Winter. Microform: PMC; PQC. Online: Gale Group; ingenta.com; Project MUSE. Reprint: PSC. *Indexed:* ABS&EES, ArtHuCI, BRD, BRI, CBRI, HumInd, IBZ, IIMP, MLA-IB, MagInd, MusicInd, RGPR, RILM. *Aud.:* Ga, Ac.

The Musical Quarterly publishes peer-reviewed articles that focus on connections between music and contemporary culture (including society and politics), current philosophies of music history and analysis, and the relations between the history of music and the history of art and literature. Each issue contains sections on "American Musics," "Music and Culture," and "Institutions,

Technology, and Economics." There are approximately seven to nine articles with notes. The last issue of each volume contains a subject and author index to the volume. The web site contains the table of contents of issues from 1996 forward. Recommended for public and academic libraries.

5102. *Nineteenth-Century Music.* [ISSN: 0148-2076] 1977. triennial. USD 130 print & online eds. USD 45 newsstand/cover. Ed(s): James Hepokoski, Lawrence Kramer. University of California Press, Journals Division, 2000 Center St, Ste 303, Berkeley, CA 94704-1223; journals@ucop.edu; http://www.ucpress.edu/journals. Illus., index, adv. Refereed. Circ: 1300 Paid. Vol. ends: Spring. Online: EBSCO Publishing; Florida Center for Library Automation; Gale Group; Ingenta Select; OCLC Online Computer Library Center, Inc. Reprint: PQC. *Indexed:* ABS&EES, AmH&L, ArtHuCI, HumInd, IIMP, MusicInd, RILM. *Bk. rev.:* 1, 4,000 words, signed. *Aud.:* Ac, Sa.

Nineteenth Century Music includes research about all types of music written in the time period between ca. 1780 and 1920 and covers a broad spectrum of research issues in musicology, analysis, criticism, theory, and interdisciplinary studies. Typical articles in this refereed journal cover topics such as composition, performance, social and cultural context, hermeneutics, gender studies, and historiography. Included are in-depth reviews of books and performances. Also available online. Recommended for academic libraries.

5103. *Opera News.* [ISSN: 0030-3607] 1936. m. USD 30 domestic; USD 45 foreign; USD 3.95 newsstand/cover per issue. Ed(s): F Paul Driscoll, Rudolph S Rauch. Metropolitan Opera Guild, Inc., 70 Lincoln Center Plaza, New York, NY 10023; http://www.metguild.org/. Illus., index, adv. Circ: 100000 Paid. Vol. ends: Jul/Jun. Microform: PQC. Online: bigchalk; Chadwyck-Healey Incorporated; EBSCO Publishing; Florida Center for Library Automation; Gale Group; Northern Light Technology, Inc.; OCLC Online Computer Library Center, Inc.; ProQuest Information & Learning; H.W. Wilson. Reprint: PQC. *Indexed:* ABS&EES, ArtHuCI, BRI, BiogInd, CBRI, HumInd, IIMP, IIPA, MagInd, MusicInd, RGPR, RILM. *Bk. rev.:* 1-3, 500 words, signed. *Aud.:* Ga, Ac.

Published by the Metropolitan Opera Guild, *Opera News* provides fans with the latest news and information on the Metropolitan Opera company and opera around the world. Each glossy issue contains approximately seven articles that provide history and analysis of selected works, and profiles of artists and composers. A section of the magazine offers information on upcoming Metropolitan Opera broadcasts with lists of cast members, synopses of plots, and references to further information on each opera. Also included in each issue is the latest opera and opera-related news, concert reviews arranged by cities, CD and video reviews, and a few book reviews. A two-page "Dateline" section lists upcoming performances worldwide. Subscribers have access to a web archive that contains all issues from 1991 up to the present, searchable by keywords, names, and phrases. Recommended for public and academic libraries.

5104. *Opera Quarterly.* [ISSN: 0736-0053] 1983. q. GBP 118. Ed(s): E Glasgow, Joe L Law. Oxford University Press, Great Clarendon St, Oxford, OX2 6DP, United Kingdom; jnl.orders@oup.co.uk; http://www3.oup.co.uk/jnls. Illus., adv. Refereed. Circ: 4100. Vol. ends: Fall. Online: Chadwyck-Healey Incorporated; Gale Group; ingenta.com; OCLC Online Computer Library Center, Inc.; Project MUSE; ProQuest Information & Learning; Swets Blackwell. Reprint: PSC. *Indexed:* ABS&EES, AmH&L, ArtHuCI, HumInd, IBZ, IIMP, IIPA, MusicInd, RILM. *Bk. rev.:* 4-5, 1,000-1,500 words, signed. *Aud.:* Ga, Ac.

The *Opera Quarterly* publishes articles on opera history, studies, and analyses of works, along with interviews and remembrances. The summer issue commemorates a special composer, singer, or topic (recently, tenor Alfredo Kraus; and Berlioz and French grand opera). Each issue contains approximately six articles (often with illustrations), four or five book reviews, approximately nine CD reviews, and two or three video reviews. Also listed are books and CDs received. Subscribers have access to the web site with full texts of articles from 2002 forward. Recommended for large public and academic libraries.

5105. *The Orff Echo.* [ISSN: 0095-2613] 1968. 4x/yr. USD 36 (Individuals, USD 60). Ed(s): Caprice Lawless. American Orff-Schulwerk Association, 3105 Lincoln Blvd, Cleveland, OH 44118-2035; bxfn94b@prodigy.com. Adv. Refereed. Circ: 5100. *Indexed:* MusicInd. *Aud.:* Ems, Hs, Ga, Ac, Sa.

This is the official publication of the American Orff-Schulwerk Association, an organization dedicated to the creative teaching approach developed by Carl Orff and Gunild Keetman. Their mission is to demonstrate and promote the value of the Orff Schulwerk ideals of music and movement, to support professional development opportunitites, and to align applications of the approach with the changing needs of American society. Articles cover such topics as the lifelong learner, building musical skills, music as therapy, musical process, and the inner voice of music. Issues include book, recording, and video reviews, study listings, teaching tips, and information on recent research. Of interest to music teachers of all levels, it is recommended for elementary, high school, academic, and public libraries.

5106. *Perspectives of New Music.* [ISSN: 0031-6016] 1962. s-a. USD 110 (Individuals, USD 40; Students, USD 30). Ed(s): Benjamin Boretz, John Rahn. Perspectives of New Music, Inc., University of Washington, Music, Box 353450, Seattle, WA 98195-3450; pnm@u.washington.edu; http://www.perspectiveofnewmusic.org/. Illus., index, adv. Refereed. Circ: 1350 Paid. Vol. ends: Summer. Microform: PQC. Online: bigchalk; Chadwyck-Healey Incorporated; EBSCO Publishing; Factiva; Florida Center for Library Automation; Gale Group; Northern Light Technology, Inc.; OCLC Online Computer Library Center, Inc.; ProQuest Information & Learning; H.W. Wilson. Reprint: PQC. *Indexed:* ABS&EES, ArtHuCI, HumInd, IBZ, IIMP, MusicInd, RILM. *Aud.:* Ac, Sa.

Perspectives of New Music publishes articles on people and developments in contemporary music. Articles contain speculative research, analyses, technical concerns, sociological, philosophical, and cultural studies, and interviews and reviews. Occasional issues contain articles in honor of an important musician. Readership mainly consists of composers, performers, scholars, and others interested in contemporary music. Issues generally contain approximately nine articles with musical diagrams and notation. Recommended for academic libraries.

5107. *Philosophy of Music Education Review.* [ISSN: 1063-5734] 1993. s-a. USD 50 (Individuals, USD 25). Ed(s): Estelle R. Jorgensen. Indiana University Press, 601 N Morton St, Bloomington, IN 47404; journals@indiana.edu; http://iupjournals.org. Refereed. *Indexed:* EduInd, IIMP, MusicInd, PhilInd, RILM. *Bk. rev.:* 1, 500-1,000 words. *Aud.:* Ac, Sa.

Philosophy of Music Education Review publishes philosophical research in music education presented by scholars, artists, and teachers worldwide. Articles address such topics as the marginalization of the arts, ethics, teacher preparation, the nature and scope of education, current teaching practices, reform initiatives, teaching native musics, multiculturalism, and philosophies of music education. Issues include a column for responses to previously published articles, and a detailed book review. Of interest to music educators and music scholars, it is recommended for academic libraries. Also available online through Project Muse.

5108. *Psychology of Music.* [ISSN: 0305-7356] 1973. q. GBP 173 print & online eds. in Europe, Middle East, Africa & Australasia. Sage Publications Ltd., 6 Bonhill St, London, EC2A 4PU, United Kingdom; info@sagepub.co.uk; http://www.sagepub.co.uk/. Illus., index. Refereed. Circ: 700. Online: Chadwyck-Healey Incorporated; ingenta.com. *Indexed:* BrEdI, IIMP, MusicInd, PsycholAb, RILM. *Bk. rev.:* 2, 1,000 words, signed. *Aud.:* Ac, Sa.

The aim of the Society for Research in Psychology of Music and Music Education is to provide an international forum for researchers in the fields of psychology of music and music education to encourage the exchange of ideas and to disseminate research findings. To that end, they publish *Psychology of Music* as a platform to address such topics as the interaction of music and social behavior in various venues, gender issues, cognitive processes, group dynamics, and emotions, perceptions, and development as affected by music. Issues include book reviews. Also available electronically. Of interest to performers, teachers, and scholars, it is recommended for academic libraries.

5109. ***Psychomusicology: a journal of research in music cognition.*** [ISSN: 0275-3987] 1981. s-a. USD 27 domestic; USD 33 foreign. Ed(s): Randall G Pembrook. Florida State University, Center for Music Research, 214 KMU, Tallahassee, FL 32306-1180. Refereed. Circ: 300. *Indexed:* EduInd, IIMP, MusicInd, PsycholAb, RILM. *Aud.:* Ac, Sa.

Psychomusicology presents research concerning all aspects of music cognition (music performance, pitch and scale recognition, tonality, rhythm, melody, composition, improvisation, musical development, music emotions, neurology of music, etc.). Issues include reports of experimental research, reviews of extended research works, theoretical papers that are based on experimental research, and brief reports of research in progress, replications, commentaries on trends in psychomusicology, and brief notes on research methodology and instrumentation. Of interest to teachers, performers, and scholars, it is recommended for academic libraries.

5110. ***The Strad: a monthly journal for professionals and amateurs of all stringed instruments played with the bow.*** [ISSN: 0039-2049] 1890. m. GBP 49.95 United Kingdom & Ireland; USD 79.50 in US & Canada; GBP 63 elsewhere. Ed(s): Naomi Sadler. Orpheus Publications Ltd., 3 Waterhouse Sq, 138-142 Holborn, London, EC1N 2NY, United Kingdom. Illus., adv. Sample. Circ: 17000 Paid. Microform: PQC; WMP. Online: EBSCO Publishing. Reprint: PQC. *Indexed:* ArtHuCI, BrHumI, IBZ, IIMP, MusicInd. *Bk. rev.:* 3-5, length varies. *Aud.:* Ac, Sa.

The Strad focuses on all people and things related to the most popular string instruments (violin, viola, cello). Topics of articles include profiles of orchestras, ensembles, performers and luthiers, profiles of teachers and explication of their methods, instruction on playing technique, a focus on special instruments, etc. Each issue contains approximately 12 articles, three to five book reviews, approximately 25 short reviews of CDs, and 10-15 short reviews of concerts. The magazine's web site contains a "Strings Business Directory" that has links to schools, groups, and organizations for playing, teaching, and instrument making. Links are also provided for job searching, concerts, and selected radio stations worldwide. With a free membership, the site also provides access to archived articles. Recommended for public and academic libraries.

5111. ***Strings: the magazine for players and makers of bowed instruments.*** [ISSN: 0888-3106] 1986. 8x/yr. USD 36 domestic; USD 51 Canada; USD 66 elsewhere. Ed(s): Dan Warrick. String Letter Publishing, PO Box 767, San Anselmo, CA 94979-0767; strings1@aol.com; http://stringsmagazine.com/. Adv. Circ: 16700. *Indexed:* IIMP, MusicInd. *Aud.:* Ac, Sa.

Strings is a commercial magazine devoted to all aspects of stringed instruments played with a bow, such as violin, viola, violoncello, and double bass. Articles feature topics such as instrument care and repair, repertoire, performance issues, interviews with players and composers, information about various violin makers, and materials used in creating stringed instruments. Issues include news of string events, a concert calendar, interviews with notable string players, information on contests and workshops, and reviews of recordings, books, and music. Special issues include a summer study guide and a music school directory. Also available electronically. Of interest to string players, teachers, and stringed instrument makers and repair persons, it is recommended for academic and public libraries.

5112. ***Tempo (London, 1939): a quarterly review of modern music.*** [ISSN: 0040-2982] 1939. q. USD 59 (Individuals, USD 32). Ed(s): Calum MacDonald. Cambridge University Press, The Edinburgh Bldg, Shaftesbury Rd, Cambridge, CB2 2RU, United Kingdom; information@cambridge.org; http://uk.cambridge.org. Illus., adv. *Indexed:* ArtHuCI, BrHumI, MusicInd, RILM. *Bk. rev.:* 2-4, 1,500 words, signed. *Aud.:* Ac, Sa.

Tempo publishes articles on twentieth- and twenty-first-century classical music that include profiles of composers and musicians, interviews, aesthetic studies, and historical and analytical studies of composers' works. Articles are international in scope. Each issue generally contains five or six articles, book and CD reviews, and reviews of world premieres. A "News" section lists premieres of new compositions, new books received, and appointments. Recommended for academic libraries.

Women and Music. See Women: Feminist and Special Interest/Feminist and Women's Studies section.

5113. ***The World of Music.*** [ISSN: 0043-8774] 1958. 3x/yr. EUR 47 domestic; EUR 50 foreign. Ed(s): Max Peter Baumann. V W B - Verlag fuer Wissenschaft und Bildung, Zossener Str 55, Berlin, 10961, Germany; 100615.1565@compuserve.com; http://www.vwb-verlag.com. Illus., adv. Circ: 1200. Reprint: SWZ. *Indexed:* ArtHuCI, BAS, IBSS, IIMP, MLA-IB, MusicInd, RILM, SSCI. *Bk. rev.:* 5, 750-1,000 words, signed. *Aud.:* Ac, Sa.

The World of Music publishes the latest ethnomusicological studies of the world's musical traditions and music-related arts. Each issue focuses on a specific topic or geographic region, e.g., "Indigenous Popular Music in North America" and "Body and Ritual in Buddhist Musical Culture." Issues contain six to eight articles, with an equal number of book and CD reviews. Articles vary in length from 5 to 20 pages and often include notes and bibliographies. Issues include photographs and musical examples. The journal's web site (www.uni-bamberg.de/~ba2fm3/wom.htm) includes a list of titles, tables of contents, and abstracts from 1997 to the present. Recommended for academic libraries.

Popular

5114. ***Alternative Press.*** [ISSN: 1065-1667] 1969. m. USD 12 domestic; USD 36 in Canada & Mexico; USD 60 elsewhere. Ed(s): Jason Pettigrew, David Segal. Alternative Press Magazine, Inc., 6516 Detroit Ave, Ste 5, Cleveland, OH 44102-3057; publisher@altpress.com. Illus., adv. *Indexed:* IIMP. *Aud.:* Ga.

Since its beginnings in 1985, *Alternative Press* has been an important source of information about cutting-edge music in the areas of alternative, indie, ska, electronic, dub, industrial, punk, techno, underground, ambient, and experimental rock. In addition to feature articles and interviews with indie bands, it includes columns about new technology, book reviews, celebrity profiles, fashion spreads, and film reviews. An extensive recording review section includes many titles not covered by mainstream popular magazines.

5115. ***The Beat (Los Angeles): reggae, African, Caribbean, world music.*** Formerly: *Reggae and African Beat.* [ISSN: 1063-5319] 1982. bi-m. USD 20 domestic; USD 25 in Canada & Mexico; USD 40 elsewhere. Ed(s): C.C. Smith. Bongo Productions, PO Box 65856, Los Angeles, CA 90065; getthebeat@aol.com. Illus., adv. Circ: 25000 Paid. *Aud.:* Ga.

A primary source for information about reggae, African, Caribbean, and related world musics. Issues contain feature articles, reviews, interviews, discographies, and cultural information.

5116. ***Billboard (New York): the international newsweekly of music, video, and home entertainment.*** [ISSN: 0006-2510] 1894. w. 51/yr. USD 299 in US & Canada; USD 330 in Europe; USD 555 in Australia & New Zealand. Ed(s): Keith Girard. V N U Business Publications, 770 Broadway, New York, NY 10003; bmcomm@vnuinc.com; http://www.vnubusinessmedia.com/. Illus., adv. Circ: 40000 Paid. Microform: BHP; PQC; NRP. Online: America Online, Inc.; The Dialog Corporation; EBSCO Publishing; Florida Center for Library Automation; Gale Group; OCLC Online Computer Library Center, Inc.; ProQuest Information & Learning; H.W. Wilson. Reprint: PQC. *Indexed:* ArtHuCI, B&I, BPI, CBRI, CommAb, HumInd, IIMP, IIPA, LRI, MusicInd, RILM, SFSA, SSCI. *Aud.:* Ga.

A leading music industry research and information source, this publication reports on entertainment trends, technological developments, media formats, legal concerns, marketing, live performances, national and regional music scenes, and performing artists. The charts, compiled from a national sample of retail store sales reports, list bestselling titles in a variety of categories including mainstream pop, modern rock, jazz, country, rap, rhythm and blues, Latin, dance, classical, and world music. Reviews tend to focus on announcing and promoting new releases. Special spinoff publications include the following annuals: *Billboard History of Rock 'n' Roll* (CD-ROM), *Billboard's International Buyer's Guide of the Music-Record-Tape Industry, Billboard's International Talent and Touring Directory*, and *Billboard's Year-End Awards Issues.* Available online.

5117. *Black Beat.* Formerly (until 1983): *Soul Teen.* [ISSN: 0745-8649] 1974. m. USD 21.95 United States; USD 27.95 Canada; USD 29.95 rest of world. Sterling - Macfadden Partnership, 233 Park Ave S, 6th Fl, New York, NY 10003. Illus., adv. *Aud.:* Ga.

Targeted to African American teenagers, this title purports to offer the latest in urban music news. Issues contain feature stories liberally interspersed with glossy, full-page photos as well as departments covering the Los Angeles and New York music scenes, fan correspondence, news notes, concise artist profiles, up-and-coming acts, stage productions, recording reviews, editorials on social topics, and current books of potential interest to the readership.

5118. *Bluegrass Unlimited.* [ISSN: 0006-5137] 1966. m. USD 24 domestic; USD 34 Canada; USD 36 elsewhere. Ed(s): Sharon K. Watts, Peter V Kuykendall. Bluegrass Unlimited Inc., PO Box 771, Warrenton, VA 20188-0771; info@bluegrassmusic.com. Illus., adv. Circ: 23957 Paid. *Indexed:* IIMP, MLA-IB, MusicInd, RILM. *Aud.:* Ga.

Created in 1966, *Bluegrass Unlimited* is dedicated to furthering bluegrass, acoustic, and old-time country music. Well-written features enhanced by visually stimulating layouts cover a broad range of relevant topics from historical and current personalities to stylistic analysis. Columns include "Reviews" (CDs, books, and videos), "National Bluegrass Survey" (top songs and albums), "New Releases," and "Personal Appearance Calendar."

5119. *Circus: america's rock magazine.* Former titles (until 1979): *Circus Weekly;* (until 1978): *Circus.* [ISSN: 0009-7365] 1969. m. USD 24 domestic; USD 36 foreign; USD 4.25 newsstand/cover per issue. Ed(s): Gerald Rothberg. Circus Enterprises Corp., 6 W 18th St, New York, NY 10011. Illus., adv. Circ: 307092 Paid and controlled. *Aud.:* Ga.

Aimed at teen readers, this heavily illustrated magazine contains news, pictures, interviews with favorite artists and bands, and many full-page color photos of the stars. The emphasis is on mainstream hard rock, with artists like Korn, Limp Bizkit, Marilyn Manson, and Nirvana featured.

5120. *Contemporary Christian Music.* Former titles (until 1986): *Contemporary Christian;* (until 1983): *Contemporary Christian Music.* [ISSN: 1049-3379] 1978. m. USD 19.95 domestic; USD 27.95 Canada; USD 33.95 elsewhere. Ed(s): John W Styll. C C M Communications, 104 Woodmont Blvd, 3rd fl, Nashville, TN 37205. Illus., adv. Circ: 80000. *Indexed:* ChrPI, IIMP. *Bk. rev.:* Various number and length. *Aud.:* Ga.

Seeking "to promote spiritual growth by using contemporary Christian music as a window into issues of life and faith," this publication effectively supplements more mainstream pop music magazines with its coverage of the Christian Contemporary genre. Feature articles include spotlights on individual artists and groups, concert reviews, and commentary on Christian music in general. Each issue includes book and CD reviews.

5121. *D J Times: the international magazine for the professional mobile & club DJ.* [ISSN: 1045-9693] 1988. m. USD 30 domestic; USD 40 in Canada & Mexico; USD 55 elsewhere. Ed(s): Jim Tremayne. Testa Communications, Inc., 25 Willowdale Ave, Port Washington, NY 11050; djtimes@testa.com; http://www.djtimes.com. Illus., adv. *Indexed:* IIMP. *Aud.:* Ga, Sa.

A primary source of information about products, technologies, and news relevant to the professional DJ, this publication will also prove interesting to serious fans of modern dance music. Feature articles focus on both people and technology. Special departments include "Mobile of the Month," "Taking Care of Business," "Gear," "Marketplace" (classified advertising), "Sounding Off" (a column guested by audio pros), "Feedback" (industry professionals answering reader questions), and "Club Spotlight." Current recordings in a variety of styles including house, techno, R&B, hip-hop, freestyle, trip-hop, experimental, drum-n-bass, and pop are reviewed in the "Grooves" section. The table of contents and selected full text is available online at the publisher's web site.

5122. *Down Beat: jazz, blues, and beyond.* [ISSN: 0012-5768] 1934. m. USD 29.95 domestic; USD 43.45 elsewhere; USD 3.50 newsstand/cover per issue. Ed(s): Jason Koransky. Maher Publications, 102 N Haven Rd, Elmhurst, IL 60126; jasonk@downbeatjazz.com; http://www.downbeat.com. Illus., adv. Circ: 98441. Microform: PQC. Online: bigchalk; Chadwyck-Healey Incorporated; Florida Center for Library Automation; Gale Group; OCLC Online Computer Library Center, Inc.; ProQuest Information & Learning. Reprint: PQC. *Indexed:* ArtHuCI, CBRI, IIBP, IIMP, MagInd, MusicInd, RGPR, RILM. *Bk. rev.:* 25-35, 500-1,000 words. *Aud.:* Ga.

An essential publication devoted to jazz, blues, and other forms of improvised music, *Down Beat* features interviews and biographies of artists, news, CD reviews (25 to 35 per issue), performance and product reviews, and reports on new talent.

5123. *Goldmine: the record collector's marketplace.* Former titles (until 1985): *Record Collectors Goldmine; Goldmine.* [ISSN: 1055-2685] 1974. bi-w. USD 39.95; USD 24.95 for 6 mos.; USD 3.95 newsstand/cover per issue. Ed(s): Greg Loescher. Krause Publications, Inc., 700 E State St, Iola, WI 54990-0001; info@krause.com; http://www.krause.com. Illus., adv. Circ: 30189 Paid and free. Microform: PQC. Online: Chadwyck-Healey Incorporated. *Indexed:* IIMP, MusicInd. *Aud.:* Ga.

For almost 30 years, *Goldmine* has been the world's largest marketplace for collectible records, CDs, and music memorabilia covering rock, blues, country, folk, and jazz. Although it's particularly useful for the lengthy ad section devoted to the purchase and sale of vintage recordings and notices of upcoming collector conventions, it also contains extensive, well-written feature articles, discographies, and recording reviews.

5124. *Guitar One: the magazine you can play.* Former titles (until 1995): *Guitar Magazine; Guitar for the Practicing Musician.* [ISSN: 1089-6406] 1983. m. USD 19.95 domestic; USD 34.95 Canada; USD 4.99 newsstand/cover per issue. Ed(s): Troy Nelson. Cherry Lane Magazines, Inc., 6 E. 32nd St., 11th Fl., New York, NY 10016; GuitarOne@cherrylane.com; http://www.cherrylane.com. Illus., adv. Circ: 140000. *Aud.:* Ga.

Marketed to serious guitarists, this publication features instructional playing tips, note-for-note song transcriptions, and interviews with leading artists who explain their music and the gear they need to create it. It also includes music news for a variety of styles from hard rock and heavy metal to jazz, blues, and pop. There are extensive product reviews that cover instruments and equipment for all budgets, but no recordings reviews.

5125. *Guitar Player: for professional and amateur guitarists.* [ISSN: 0017-5463] 1967. m. USD 24 domestic; USD 39 foreign; USD 4.50 newsstand/cover per issue. Ed(s): Emily Fasten, Bill Evans. United Entertainment Media, Inc., 2800 Campus Dr, San Mateo, CA 94403; info@musicplayer.com; http://www.musicplayer.com. Illus., adv. Circ: 135003. Reprint: PQC. *Indexed:* IIMP, LRI, MagInd, MusicInd. *Aud.:* Ga.

Aimed at both professional and amateur guitar players and focusing on blues-rock, jazz, and heavy metal, this magazine includes lessons for guitar players, interviews with leading guitarists, song transcriptions, and product reviews.

5126. *Guitar World.* [ISSN: 1045-6295] 1980. m. USD 23.94 domestic; USD 59.91 foreign; USD 4.95 newsstand/cover per issue domestic. Harris Publications, Inc., 1115 Broadway, 8th Fl, New York, NY 10010-2803; GWedit@aol.com; http://www.guitarworld.com. Illus., adv. Circ: 191486 Paid. *Indexed:* MusicInd. *Aud.:* Ga.

Particularly useful for the beginning guitar student or casual fan, this magazine covers a broad range of musical styles including rock, heavy metal, blues, and acoustic. Each issue includes profiles of notable pop guitarists, complete song transcriptions that range from classic rock to newer popular songs, instructional lessons written by noted guitar celebrities, questions and answers regarding technical problems, equipment and recordings reviews, and the "Collector's Choice" column, which describes famous memorabilia.

5127. ***Jazz Education Journal.*** Former titles (until 2001): *Jazz Educators Journal; National Association of Jazz Educators. Newsletter; N A J E Educator.* [ISSN: 1540-2886] 1968. bi-m. USD 36 domestic; USD 46 foreign. Ed(s): Antonio Garcia. International Association of Jazz Educators, PO Box 724, Manhattan, KS 66505-0724; info@iaje.org. Illus., adv. Refereed. Circ: 7500. *Indexed:* IIBP, IIMP, MusicInd, RILM. *Aud.:* Ac.

Sponsored by the International Association of Jazz Educators (IAJE), this journal is a prime source for news and information in the field of jazz education. Issues include feature articles on top jazz artists, reviews, transcriptions, and industry news with a pedagogical focus. Most of the content, contributed by educators in the field, documents curricular innovations, teaching methodologies, and school group performances. Selected full-text access is available at the IAJE web site.

5128. ***The Jazz Report: voice of the artist.*** [ISSN: 0843-3151] 1987. q. USD 3.95 per issue. Ed(s): Greg Sutherland. King Sutherland Productions, 14 London St, Toronto, ON M6G 1M9, Canada; jazzmag@pathcom.com. Illus., adv. *Aud.:* Ga. Ac.

Geared toward academics, collectors, and musicians, but accessible to the lay reader, this publication features artist profiles and interviews, essays on a variety of topics, news reports, CD reviews, and product reports related to jazz and blues. Selected full-text access is available at the publisher's web site.

5129. ***Jazziz.*** [ISSN: 0741-5885] 1983. m. USD 69.95; USD 2.95 newsstand/cover per issue. Ed(s): Larry Blumenfeld. Jazziz Magazine, Inc., 3620 N W 43rd St Ste D, Gainesville, FL 32606; jazziz@sprintmail.com; http://www.jazziz.com. Illus., adv. Circ: 150000. *Indexed:* IIMP, RILM. *Aud.:* Ga.

This innovative and stylish publication seeks to introduce its audience to new music and new ideas about the jazz genre. Monthly issues include feature articles on a variety of topics, profiles of jazz personalities, news and events, reviews, and an accompanying compact disc that frequently includes new or unusual music. Table of contents and selected full-text access is available at the publisher's web site.

5130. ***JazzTimes: America's jazz magazine.*** Supersedes: *Radio Free Jazz.* [ISSN: 0272-572X] 1972. 10x/yr. USD 23.95 domestic; USD 35.95 Canada; USD 59.95 elsewhere. Ed(s): Mike Joyce. Jazz Times Inc., 8737 Colesvlle Rd, 5th FL, Silver Spring, MD 20910-3921; advertising@jazztimes.com; http://www.jazztimes.com. Illus., adv. Circ: 88417. Microform: PQC. Reprint: PQC. *Indexed:* IIBP, IIMP, MusicInd. *Aud.:* Ga.

JazzTimes provides comprehensive and in-depth coverage of the contemporary international jazz scene including progressive blues and fusion. Each issue contains profiles of emerging and established stars plus over 100 reviews of the latest CDs, books, videos, audio and video equipment, and performances. Directories of jazz clubs, education programs, record labels, and music festivals are useful as reference guides.

5131. ***Journal of Country Music.*** Formerly: *Country Music Foundation News Letter.* [ISSN: 0092-0517] 1970. 3x/yr. USD 18 domestic; USD 23 foreign. Ed(s): Jeremy Tepper. Country Music Foundation, Inc., 222 5th Ave., S, Nashville, TN 37203-4206. Illus., adv. Circ: 4000. *Indexed:* ArtHuCI, IIMP, MLA-IB, MusicInd, RILM. *Bk. rev.:* Various number and length. *Aud.:* Ac.

This authoritative source, a publication of the Country Music Foundation, features biographical articles, interviews with performers, and book and recording reviews. Folklorists and musicologists contribute overview essays on the historical development of specific musical styles.

5132. ***Keyboard: the world's leading music technology magazine.*** Formerly (until 1981): *Contemporary Keyboard.* [ISSN: 0730-0158] 1975. m. USD 25.95 domestic; USD 40.95 foreign. Ed(s): Greg Rule. United Entertainment Media, Inc., 2800 Campus Dr, San Mateo, CA 94403; http://www.musicplayer.com. Illus., adv. Circ: 66000. Microform: PQC. Online: Chadwyck-Healey Incorporated; EBSCO Publishing; Gale Group; ProQuest Information & Learning. Reprint: PQC. *Indexed:* IIMP, MusicInd, RILM. *Aud.:* Ga.

Although *Keyboard* covers both acoustic and electronic performance in a wide variety of musical styles, it is probably most useful for its extensive coverage of newer technologies in music performance and recording. Among the regular features are equipment and software reviews, new product announcements, information on recording techniques, master classes with leading performers, artist interviews, business and marketing advice, and recording reviews. Selected full-text access is available at the publisher's web site.

5133. ***Living Blues: the magazine of the African American blues tradition.*** [ISSN: 0024-5232] 1970. bi-m. USD 21; USD 27 Canada; USD 33 elsewhere. Ed(s): Scott Barretta. University of Mississippi, Center for the Study of Southern Culture, Barnard Observatory, PO Box 1848, University, MS 38677-9836; LivingBlues@LivingBluesOnline.com; http://www.LivingBluesOnline.com. Illus., adv. Circ: 25000. Microform: PQC. *Indexed:* IIBP, IIMP, MLA-IB, MusicInd, RILM. *Aud.:* Ac.

Living Blues provides a scholarly forum for the written and photographic documentation of the historical and contemporary blues genre. Biographical profiles and interviews with major blues figures and lesser-known traditional artists in their cultural context form the core of the journal, but current blues news, festival listings, radio charts, recording reviews, and recent acquisitions of the Center for the Study of Southern Culture are also included. Table of contents and selected full-text access is available at the publisher's web site.

Maximum Rock'n'roll. See Zines section.

5134. ***Metal Edge: hard rock's #1 magazine.*** Former titles: *T V Picture Life, Metal Edge;* (until 1984): *T V Picture Life.* [ISSN: 1068-2872] 1957. m. USD 29.95 domestic; USD 35.95 Canada; USD 37.95 elsewhere. Sterling - Macfadden Partnership, 233 Park Ave S, 6th Fl, New York, NY 10003; info@sterlingmacfadden.com. Illus., adv. Circ: 65000 Paid. *Aud.:* Ga.

Designed for the youthful reader, *Metal Edge* covers hard rock, heavy metal, and the personalities involved in its production. Regular features include performer biographies and interviews, current news about heavy metal groups, tour and concert schedules, and CD reviews. A directory of contact information for various heavy metal bands and fan clubs and an abundance of color photos add to the magazine's value.

5135. ***New Musical Express.*** Incorporates (1926-2000): *Melody Maker.* [ISSN: 0028-6362] 1952. w. GBP 78.60 domestic; USD 104 United States; GBP 80 in Europe. Ed(s): Ben Knowles. I P C ignite! Ltd., King's Reach Tower, Stamford St, London, SE1 9LS, United Kingdom; http://www.ipcmedia.com/. Illus., adv. Circ: 90763. Microform: RPI. *Aud.:* Ga.

This weekly rock music magazine is one of the better sources for information about the British pop music scene. Using a tabloid format, it presents music news and gossip, interviews with stars, an abundance of international concert reviews, and charts listing the top indie, rock, rhythm and blues, and dance albums and singles for the United Kingdom.

5136. ***Popular Music.*** [ISSN: 0261-1430] 1982. 3x/yr. USD 148 (Individuals, USD 60). Ed(s): Keith Negus. Cambridge University Press, The Edinburgh Bldg, Shaftesbury Rd, Cambridge, CB2 2RU, United Kingdom; information@cambridge.org; http://uk.cambridge.org/journals. Illus., adv. Microform: PQC. Online: Gale Group; OCLC Online Computer Library Center, Inc.; Swets Blackwell. Reprint: SWZ. *Indexed:* HumInd, MusicInd, RILM. *Bk. rev.:* Various number and length. *Aud.:* Ac.

One of the more important sources for the scholarly study of popular music, this journal is international and multidisciplinary in scope. It covers such diverse disciplines as anthropology, musicology, sociology, literature, ethnomusicology, gender studies, and any others that can be shown to have relevance to the subject. Each issue contains substantive scholarly articles, shorter topical pieces, and a large book review section. A feature that will be particularly useful for library collection managers is "Booklist," an annual annotated list in the October issue of popular music titles from around the world. Available online.

5137. ***Popular Music & Society.*** [ISSN: 0300-7766] 1972. q. USD 135 (Individuals, USD 50). Routledge, 4 Park Sq, Milton Park, Abingdon, OX14 4RN, United Kingdom; http://www.routledge/journal/journals.html. Illus., index, adv. Circ: 1000. Microform: PQC; NRP. Online: bigchalk; Chadwyck-Healey Incorporated; EBSCO Publishing; Florida Center for Library Automation; Gale Group; Northern Light Technology, Inc.; OCLC Online Computer Library Center, Inc.; ProQuest Information & Learning; H.W. Wilson. Reprint: PQC; PSC. *Indexed:* ArtHuCI, BRI, CBRI, CommAb, HumInd, IBZ, IIMP, MRD, MusicInd, PRA, RILM, SFSA, SSCI. *Bk. rev.:* Various number and length. *Aud.:* Ac.

This journal offers a scholarly approach to the study of popular music and its interaction with the culture. Research articles employing a variety of methodologies, including interviews and profiles, historical surveys, content analyses, and various quantitative methods explore rock, country, jazz, blues, and other popular music styles. The book review section is a particularly useful and authoritative evaluation tool. Available online.

5138. ***Rapport: the modern guide to books, music & more.*** Formerly (until 1991): *West Coast Review of Books.* [ISSN: 1061-6861] 1974. bi-m. USD 19.95. Ed(s): David Dreis. Rapport Publishing Co., Inc., 5265 Fountain Ave, Upper Terrace 6, Los Angeles, CA 90029. Illus., adv. Circ: 50000. *Indexed:* BRI, CBRI. *Bk. rev.:* Various number and length. *Aud.:* Ga.

This unique publication contains in-depth, rated reviews of the latest books and compact discs as well as articles and interviews with writers and musicians. There is a tendency to emphasize jazz, but other styles are represented as well.

Rockrgrl. See Zines section.

5139. ***Roctober.*** 1992. 3x/yr. USD 10 domestic; USD 15 in Canada & Mexico; USD 20 elsewhere. Ed(s): Jake A Austen. Roctober, 1507 E 53rd St, 617, Chicago, IL 60615. Illus., adv. Circ: 3500. *Bk. rev.:* 10, 200 words. *Aud.:* Ga. Ac.

An eclectic music journal that covers obscure genres and musicians. It includes in-depth features, interviews with musicians, extensive critical discographies, and bizarre music-themed comics. Tables of contents and selected full-text access is available at the publisher's web site.

5140. ***Rolling Stone.*** [ISSN: 0035-791X] 1967. bi-w. USD 11.97 domestic; USD 38 Canada; USD 65 elsewhere. Ed(s): Eric Needham. Wenner Media, Inc., 1290 Ave of Americas, New York, NY 10104; rollingstone@echonyc.com; http://www.rollingstone.com/. Illus., adv. Circ: 1250000 Paid. CD-ROM: ProQuest Information & Learning. Microform: PQC. Online: America Online, Inc.; EBSCO Publishing; Florida Center for Library Automation; Gale Group; Northern Light Technology, Inc.; OCLC Online Computer Library Center, Inc.; ProQuest Information & Learning. *Indexed:* BRI, CBCARef, CBRI, CPerI, FLI, IIMP, IIPA, MRD, MagInd, MusicInd, RGPR, RI-1. *Bk. rev.:* Various number and length. *Aud.:* Ga.

For over 35 years, *Rolling Stone* has been a primary source for the latest news about American popular culture, music, celebrities, and politics. High-quality journalism, as well as authoritative recording, book, and film reviews add to its value.

5141. ***Sing Out!: the folksong magazine.*** [ISSN: 0037-5624] 1950. q. USD 25 United States; USD 30 Canada; USD 43 elsewhere. Ed(s): Mark D Moss. Sing Out Corporation, PO Box 5460, Bethlehem, PA 18015-0460. Illus., adv. Circ: 12000 Paid and free. Microform: PQC. Reprint: PQC. *Indexed:* ASIP, AltPI, IIMP, MLA-IB, MagInd, MusicInd, RILM. *Bk. rev.:* Various number and length. *Aud.:* Ga.

Sing Out seeks to preserve the cultural diversity and heritage of all traditional and contemporary folk musics and to encourage making folk music a part of everyday life. In support of that goal, each issue contains complete lead sheets for at least 20 traditional and contemporary folk songs as well as feature articles and interviews, instrumental teach-ins, abundant recording and book reviews, and folk festival and camp listings. Regular columns cover the folk process, songwriting, storytelling, and children's music. Tables of contents and midi files of songs are available at the publisher's web site.

Slug & Lettuce. See Zines section.

5142. ***The Source (New York, 1988): the magazine of hip-hop music, culture & politics.*** [ISSN: 1063-2085] 1988. m. USD 19.95 domestic; USD 40.95 Canada; USD 69.95 elsewhere. Ed(s): Carlito Rodriguez. Source Publications, 215 Park Ave S, 11 Fl, New York, NY 10003-1603. Illus., adv. Circ: 370700 Paid. *Indexed:* IIBP, IIMP, IIPA. *Aud.:* Ga.

The Source covers all aspects of hip-hop, including interviews with rappers, profiles of groups, concert and recording reviews, and descriptive analyses of the cultural and political environments where the music thrives and continues to evolve.

5143. ***Spin.*** [ISSN: 0886-3032] 1985. m. USD 9.95 domestic; USD 14.05 Canada; USD 40.05 elsewhere. Ed(s): Sia Michel. Vibe - Spin Ventures, 215 Lexington Ave, 6th Fl, New York, NY 10016; spinonline@aol.com. Illus., adv. Circ: 550000 Paid. Microform: PQC. *Indexed:* ASIP, IIPA. *Aud.:* Ga.

This glitzy, ad-intensive magazine is aimed at teens and young adults who are interested in contemporary rock and the culture surrounding it. Monthly issues contain reviews and brief articles on film, fashion, art, politics, and music, including ska, pop, rhythm-and-blues, hip-hop, and rap.

Vibe. See African American section.

Electronic Journals

5144. ***Amazing Sounds: the alternative music e-magazine.*** 1996. irreg. Amazing Sounds, http://www.amazings.com/ingles.html. *Aud.:* Hs, Ga, Ac.

An illustrated online zine that contains well-written news articles, biographies, interviews, album reviews, and links to online resources covering alternative genres such as electronic music, ambient, new instrumental music, world music, electroacoustic, and New Age.

5145. ***Ethnomusicology Online.*** [ISSN: 1092-7336] 1995. a. Ed(s): Karl Signell. Ethnomusicology Online, University of Maryland, Music Dept., Baltimore, MD 21228; signell@umbc.edu; http://umbc.edu/eol. Refereed. *Indexed:* MLA-IB. *Bk. rev.:* Various number and length. *Aud.:* Ac, Sa.

This annual e-journal provides information on ethnomusicology resources worldwide. Issues can include reviews of books, journals, articles, recordings, visual media, dissertations, software, and web sites, complete with graphics and audio examples. Memorials and obituaries are occasionally listed, and there is a list of links to other online resources relevant to ethnomusicology such as institutions, publications, books, teachers, and other world music sites. A table of contents to each issue provides easy access, and the index to multimedia reviews is searchable by author, by geographic area, and by map location. Of interest to performers, musicologists, ethnomusicologists, and students, it is recommended for academic and public libraries.

5146. ***Eunomios.*** s-a. Ed(s): Paolo Rosato, Fulvio Delli Pizzi. Eunomios, staff@eunomios.org; http://www.eunomios.org/. *Aud.:* Ac, Sa.

Eunomios is an open online journal devoted to the theory, analysis, and semiotics of music. It hosts user-contributed papers, and publication on the web site occurs almost immediately, without editing or peer review. A forum for discussion and debating issues related to the articles published is an interesting feature. There is a very useful list of links to electronic journals, institutes, and other resources. Recommended for academic libraries.

5147. ***Journal of Seventeenth - Century Music.*** [ISSN: 1089-747X] 1995. irreg. Ed(s): Bruce Gustafson. Society for Seventeenth - Century Music, 337 W James St, Lancaster, PA 17603. Illus. Refereed. *Bk. rev.:* Various number and length. *Aud.:* Ac, Sa.

This is the official journal of the Society for Seventeenth-Century Music. Issues generally include a lengthy article; reviews of newly published books, editions of music, and compact discs; and a note from the editor or responses from readers. Articles and reviews often contain links to notes and references and sometimes to digital illustrations or sound files. Authors of articles are encouraged to include additional reference material, appendixes, texts of archival documents, etc. All articles are refereed. Subjects of articles and reviews are the musical cultures of the seventeenth century examined from historical perspectives, theory, aesthetics, performance, dance, and theater. Recommended for academic libraries.

5148. ***MandoZine.*** 1996. bi-m. Ed(s): John Baxter. MandoZine, http://www.mandozine.com. *Aud.:* Hs, Ga.

This is a publication devoted entirely to the mandolin of yesteryear, which apparently continues to hold its own among both young and old. There are lessons for the beginner as well as helpful aids for the expert strummer. In fact, most of the material seems to be directed to the person who is just starting out on the mandolin. For those who simply want to listen, there are reviews, notes, and comments on the music produced by mandolin players. (BK)

5149. ***Music Technology Buyer's Guide.*** a. USD 6.95 newsstand/cover per issue. United Entertainment Media, Inc., 2800 Campus Dr, San Mateo, CA 94403; info@musicplayer.com; http://www.musicplayer.com. *Aud.:* Hs, Ga.

Focusing primarily on the topic of jazz guitar, this freely available online magazine contains feature articles, guitar lessons employing audio examples, and an extensive list of links to related web sites.

5150. ***Music Theory Online.*** [ISSN: 1067-3040] 1993. bi-m. Free. Ed(s): Timothy J Koozin. Society for Music Theory, Indiana University School of Music, 1201 E 3rd St, Bloomington, IN 47405; mto-editor@societymusictheory.org; http://societymusictheory.org/mto. Illus., adv. Refereed. *Indexed:* RILM. *Bk. rev.:* 1. *Aud.:* Ac, Sa.

Music Theory Online is the electronic journal of the Society for Music Theory, whose primary goal is to promote the study and teaching of music theory by providing resources for the publication of research, and to support and encourage people interested in the field. The online publication supplements *Music Theory Spectrum* (below), the society's print journal. Each online issue features one or two peer-reviewed research articles, a book review, new dissertations, announcements of conferences, calls for papers, job listings in music theory, and commentary. Articles include abstracts, references, and keywords. Issues vary in number from four to six per year. Searches can be performed by author, volume, dissertation, or keyword. Recommended for academic libraries.

■ MUSIC REVIEWS

Erica L. Coe, Assistant Professor, Reference & Digital Initiatives Librarian, Roesch Library, University of Dayton, 300 College Park, Dayton, OH 45469-1360; erica.coe@notes.udayton.edu

Introduction

There are many magazines that include music or audio equipment reviews, but this section is devoted to those magazines that concentrate primarily on such reviews. Because of this criterion, there are more magazines that focus on classical music and jazz than other genres. Magazines for popular genres such as rock and pop tend to focus on the culture, lifestyle, and fashion surrounding the music, rather than reviews. Please refer to the Music section to find magazines for a wider array of genres.

As always, advances in technology affect the music industry. Two new music formats have gained in popularity recently: SACD (Super Audio CD) and DVD-A (DVD-Audio). Developed by Sony and Philips, SACD uses Direct Stream Digital (DSD) recording technology to reproduce the original sound more accurately, allowing for a more natural, high-quality sound. SACDs can be played on existing CD players, but the sound quality will be closer to that of a normal CD. DVD-A, developed by Panasonic and based on the video format (DVD video), also provides a more accurate sound quality, with additional room for liner notes, album cover artwork, music videos, artist commentary, and Internet links. DVD-As can be played on most DVD video players, but not on CD players at the present time. A few of the magazines in this section include reviews of the music recorded on the new formats and the audio equipment being developed to support the formats. For more reviews, go to the *High Fidelity Review* web site (http://www.highfidelityreview.com).

The previous edition included a subsection for *The Schwann Record Guides.* These reference resources have been removed because the company was bought in 2001 by Alliance Entertainment Corporation (AEG), who owns the All Media Group (AMG). AMG publishes the *All-Music Guide* electronic journal that is reviewed in this section. In addition, AMG publishes reference books on rock, jazz, blues, country, electronica, and soul. More information is provided in the "Products" section of the AMG web site (http://www.allmediaguide.com).

The Electronic Journals subsection is for magazines that do not have a print equivalent. The magazines listed here represent stable sites with a publisher and/or editor, a staff of reviewers, and feature articles, interviews, or essays. There are, of course, numerous web sites that provide music reviews. One noteworthy site is *Classical CD Review: a site for the serious record collector* (http://classicalcdreview.com) with reviews by well-established reviewers. To find additional web sites, consult online directories such as Google (http://directory.google.com) and Yahoo! (http://dir.yahoo.com). Google includes two relevant sections under "Music: Magazines and E-zines" (http://directory.google.com/Top/Arts/Music/Magazines_and_E-zines) and "Music: Reviews" (http://directory.google.com/Top/Arts/Music/Reviews). Yahoo! also includes sections under "Music for Reviews" (http://dir.yahoo.com/Entertainment/Music/Reviews) and for "News and Media," which includes magazines (http://dir.yahoo.com/Entertainment/Music/News_and_Media/Magazines).

All of the print magazines also have online versions, many with archives of full-text music reviews and, in some cases, full-text articles. Details of the online version are given under the print version. Librarians are encouraged to visit the web sites to determine if a subscription to the magazine is needed.

Basic Periodicals

Hs: *All-Music Guide;* Ga: *Absolute Sound, All-Music Guide, American Record Guide, BBC Music Magazine, Gramophone, Sensible Sound, Stereophile;* Ac: *All-Music Guide, BBC Music Magazine, American Record Guide, Fanfare, Gramophone, Stereophile.*

Basic Abstracts and Indexes

Music Article Guide, Music Index, RILM Abstracts of Music Literature.

5151. ***The Absolute Sound: the high end journal of audio & music.*** [ISSN: 0097-1138] 1973. 6x/yr. USD 36 domestic; USD 39 Canada; USD 65 elsewhere. Ed(s): Harry Pearson. Absolute Multimedia Inc., 8121 Bee Caves Rd., Ste. 100, Austin, TX 78746-4938; info@avguide.com; http://www.theabsolutesound.com. Illus., index, adv. Sample. Circ: 33000. Vol. ends: Dec/Jan. Microform: PQC. *Aud.:* Ac, Sa.

The Absolute Sound explores music from production to reproduction. Covering both music recordings and audio equipment, this magazine has it all for the discriminating music lover. The audio reviews cover high-end products that range from affordable to pricey. A separate column covers analog products. Reviews cover physical attributes, performance quality, and comparisons to similar products. The testing process and recordings used are also discussed. A sidebar highlights specifications, manufacturer information, and a list of associated equipment when appropriate. The music review section is divided by genre and covers classical, jazz, and popular. A new section, "Absolute Audiophilia," covers "recordings of exceptional sonic merit in all musical genres, with special emphasis given over to audiophile-label releases." The "New Formats" section covers releases in SACD (Super Audio CD) and DVD-A (DVD-Audio). Reviews focus on the music and performance with recording and production quality mentioned at the end. The online version contains a table of contents, selected articles, and subscription information. For access to product and music reviews, the user is connected to AVguide.com, which includes all reviews from *The Absolute Sound* and its sister publication *The Perfect Vision: High Performance Home Theater.* Music reviews are provided in full and linked to Amazon-

.com for buying information. Unfortunately, product reviews only provide specifications and manufacturer information at no cost. Full product reviews are available for download at $3.00 each. Highly recommended for public and academic libraries.

5152. *American Record Guide: classical recordings and music in concert.* Formerly: *American Music Lover.* [ISSN: 0003-0716] 1935. bi-m. USD 42 (Individuals, USD 35; USD 7.69 newsstand/cover per issue). Ed(s): Donald R Vroon. Record Guide Productions, 4412 Braddock St, Cincinnati, OH 45204; rightstar@aol.com. Illus., index, adv. Sample. Circ: 8000 Paid and free. Vol. ends: Dec. Online: bigchalk; Chadwyck-Healey Incorporated; EBSCO Publishing; Gale Group; Northern Light Technology, Inc.; OCLC Online Computer Library Center, Inc.; ProQuest Information & Learning. Reprint: PQC. *Indexed:* ASIP, BRI, CBRI, IIMP, MagInd, MusicInd, RGPR. *Bk. rev.:* Various number and length. *Aud.:* Ga, Ac.

The *American Record Guide* includes over 500 classical music reviews in each issue. The bulk of the reviews are arranged by composer in the "Guide to Records" section. The smaller "Collections" section is arranged by genre. Reviews, ranging from 250 to 500 words, usually evaluate the music and performance with less emphasis on recording quality. Often the music reviewed is placed in the context of the composer's other work or the performer's repertoire. Each issue contains an "Overview" article that provides an extensive review of recordings by one composer. The magazine also includes book, video, and live-performance reviews, as well as articles on current events in the classical music world. An annual index appears in the January/February issue. The web site gives basic information including purpose and subscription rates. Full text of this magazine is available in the *EBSCOhost Academic Search* database from July 1993 to present. The Find Articles web site (www.findarticles.com) contains full-text articles from *ARG* from March 2001 to September 2002. The large number of reviews makes this an excellent magazine for public and academic libraries.

5153. *B B C Music Magazine: the complete monthly guide to classical music.* [ISSN: 0966-7180] 1992. m. GBP 45 domestic; GBP 79 in Europe; GBP 89 elsewhere. B B C Worldwide Ltd., Woodlands, 80 Wood Ln, London, W12 0TT, United Kingdom; bbcworldwide@bbc.co.uk; http://www.bbcworldwide.com. Illus., index, adv. Circ: 68104. Vol. ends: Aug. *Indexed:* IIMP, IIPA, RILM. *Bk. rev.:* Various number and length. *Aud.:* Ga, Ac.

BBC Music Magazine, "the world's best-selling classical music magazine," includes at least 150 reviewed and rated music recordings per issue. Reviews are categorized by genre and average 200-300 words. The focus is on classical music, but brief sections for jazz and world music are included. Typical entries cover personal impressions of the performance and the background of the work. The performance is often compared with other recordings of the piece, with a benchmark version cited. Both performance and sound quality are rated on a one- to five-star system. Book and DVD reviews are also included. An index of reviews for each issue is listed in the back. In addition to the monthly feature articles, news, and interviews, a CD of a full-length work or works accompanies each issue. A listening guide for the CD includes a description of each track. The online version of the magazine includes the top five reviews for the current month, the "Editor's Picks" for past months, and subscription information. With readable, intelligent reviews, *BBC Music Magazine* is recommended for general and academic libraries.

5154. *Dirty Linen: folk & world music.* [ISSN: 1047-4315] 1988. bi-m. USD 22 domestic; USD 30 Canada; USD 40 elsewhere. Ed(s): Paul Hartman. Dirty Linen, Ltd., PO Box 66600, Baltimore, MD 21239-6600; editor@dirtylinen.com; http://www.dirtylinen.com. Illus., adv. Circ: 20000. Vol. ends: Jun/Jul. Online: Chadwyck-Healey Incorporated. *Indexed:* IIMP. *Bk. rev.:* Various number and length. *Aud.:* Hs, Ga, Ac.

Dirty Linen celebrates folk, roots, traditional, blues, bluegrass, and world music. There are approximately 150 music reviews per issue. The two main review sections are "Recordings" with 300- to 500-word reviews and "Linen Shorts" with 100- to 150-word reviews. Other sections are devoted to compilations, small-label world-music releases, and children's music. Each issue also includes news, performer and songwriter profiles, and articles, interviews, concert reviews, tour schedules, and book and video reviews. Record-company addresses for albums reviewed in the issue are also included, with a full list of companies on the web site. The online version includes subscription information, a table of contents, and excerpts from the current issue. The "Gig Guide," a list of tour dates, can be searched by artist, state/province, or event/festival. This highly readable magazine is recommended for all libraries serving users interested in folk and world music.

5155. *Fanfare (Tenafly): the magazine for serious record collectors.* [ISSN: 0148-9364] 1977. bi-m. USD 36 domestic; USD 51 foreign; USD 6 newsstand/cover per issue. Ed(s): Joel Flegler. Fanfare, Inc., 273 Woodland St, Tenafly, NJ 07670. Illus., adv. Sample. Circ: 20000. Vol. ends: Jul/Aug. Online: Chadwyck-Healey Incorporated. *Indexed:* BRI, CBRI, IIMP, MusicInd, RILM. *Bk. rev.:* Various number and length. *Aud.:* Ga, Ac.

Since its inception, *Fanfare* was intended to provide informative reviews without being "stuffy and academic," and this is still the case. Reviews are written in an easy-to-read, descriptive, and informal style. Each issue includes over 300 reviews of classical recordings and collections, with reviews ranging from 400 to 500 words. Some reviews focus on the performance and comparisons with other recordings, while others focus more on the background of the composer or piece. If mention is made of the engineering quality, it is only a sentence or two. The magazine also includes interviews with performers and composers, label profiles, industry articles, a jazz column, and book reviews. Annual indexes for recent volumes are available for $12 each. The new web site includes samples of current reviews, a list of current reviews, and subscription information. With numerous and lengthy reviews, this magazine is highly recommended for public and academic libraries.

5156. *Gramophone: your guide to the best in recorded classical music.* [ISSN: 0017-310X] 1923. 13x/yr. GBP 46 domestic; GBP 61 in Europe; GBP 86 to Middle East, S. America, Africa & India. Ed(s): James Jolly. Gramophone Publications Ltd., 38-42 Hampton Rd, Teddington, TW11 0JE, United Kingdom; info@gramophone.co.uk; http://www.gramophone.co.uk. Illus., index, adv. Sample. Circ: 53000 Paid. Vol. ends: May. *Indexed:* IIMP, MusicInd. *Aud.:* Ga, Ac.

Gramophone goes beyond the ordinary classical music magazine by offering audio reviews in addition to music reviews. The music review section has around 150-200 reviews per issue and is divided by genre. The focus is on the music and performance, and in some instances even the record company is evaluated. Little to no mention is given to sound and recording quality. A review index is included in each issue. The audio reviews detail the equipment and its performance with prices given in British pounds. Regular columns include profiles of and interviews with performers and composers. An index is published annually, covering 12 months running from June to May, and it includes features, composers, and artists. The best feature of the online version of the magazine is the "GramoFile" database that includes over 30,000 classical CD, DVD, LP, and cassette reviews from the magazine back to 1983, with hundreds more being added each month. Access is free, but users are required to register in order to search. Some reviews from "GramoFile" are available without registration via the monthly "Editor's Choice Top 10 Recordings" and the "Recommended Recordings" based on the *Classical Good CD Guide.* One drawback of the database is the lack of direct links to CD purchasing information at online media stores, however the "Shop" link connects to a British online media store. The online version also includes selected news, feature articles, interviews, obituaries, details of *Gramophone* publications, a section devoted to their annual awards, and free access to the *Grove Concise Dictionary of Music.* Two additional sections, "Concert Listings" and "Industry Labels & Distributors," focus on the United Kingdom. Highly recommended for public and academic libraries.

5157. *Hi-Fi News: pure audio excellence.* Formerly (until 2000): *Hi-Fi News and Record Review;* Which was formed by the merger of (1956-1971): *Hi-Fi News;* (1970-1971): *Record Review.* [ISSN: 1472-2569] 1971. m. GBP 39 domestic; GBP 51.40 in Europe; GBP 69 elsewhere. Ed(s): Steve Harris. I P C Country & Leisure Media Ltd., King's Reach Tower, Stamford St, London, SE1 9LS, United Kingdom; http://www.ipcmedia.com. Illus., index, adv. Sample. Circ: 21196. Vol. ends: Dec. Microform: PQC. *Indexed:* BrTechI. *Aud.:* Ga, Ac.

Hi-Fi News, like *Absolute Sound,* covers both "Hardware" and "Software" for discriminating audiophiles. The "Hardware" section reviews the physical attributes and performance quality of high-end audio equipment, including comparisons to similar products. Most reviews include a sidebar that highlights the technology and key features of the product. Like *The Sensible Sound* and *Stereophile,* the "Lab Test" reviews also include graphs charting various performance specifications. There are more pictures of the products than in other audio magazines, with the additional photos highlighting features mentioned in the review. Another U.K.-based publication, *Hi-Fi News* lists prices in British pounds and gives the British supplier telephone number. The "Software" section includes music reviews divided by genre and covers classical, jazz, and rock. The "Audiophile" section reviews DVD-A and SACD recordings. Reviews can focus on the performance, comparisons with other recordings, sound quality, or the background of the composer or piece. Performance and sound quality are rated at the end of each review. The online version includes the current issue?s table of contents, a preview of the next issue, subscription information, and a link to an online vendor. Also included is an audio product review index dating back to 1998. Highly recommended for public and academic libraries.

JazzTimes. See Music/Popular section.

5158. *Sensible Sound: helping audiophiles and music lovers to spend less and get more.* [ISSN: 0199-4654] 1977. bi-m. USD 29 domestic; USD 49 Mexico, C. America & S. America; USD 59 in Europe. Ed(s): Karl A Nehring. Sensible Sound, 403 Darwin Dr., Snyder, NY 14226; advertising@sensiblesound.com. Illus., adv. Sample. Circ: 16850 Paid and free. Vol. ends: Winter. *Aud.:* Ga, Ac.

The goal of *Sensible Sound* is to provide readers with reviews of audio equipment that they can actually afford to buy. Lengthy, in-depth reviews cover the physical attributes, set-up procedure, performance quality, and comparisons to similar products. The testing process and recordings used are also discussed. Some reviews also include graphs charting various performance specifications. The music review section includes 30-40 reviews covering mainly classical music. Unlike *Absolute Sound* and *Hi-Fi News,* the music reviews seldom mention sound quality. The web site provides subscription and advertising information. A unique pay-per-question "Advice" section provides a questionnaire for readers to ask for individual advice about components and systems. Highly recommended for public and academic libraries serving budget-minded audiophiles.

Sound & Vision. See Television, Video, and Radio section.

Splendid. See Zines/Electronic Journals section.

5159. *Stereophile.* [ISSN: 0585-2544] 1962. m. USD 12.97 domestic; USD 25.97 Canada; USD 27.97 elsewhere. Ed(s): John Atkinson. Primedia Consumer Media & Magazine Group, 200 Madison Ave, New York, NY 10016; http://www.primedia.com. Illus., index, adv. Circ: 80000 Paid. Vol. ends: Dec. *Aud.:* Ga, Ac.

Stereophile reviews both high-end audio equipment and music. Feature articles might cover audio equipment, a performer interview, or an electronics show. The equipment reports cover the physical attributes, performance quality, and comparisons to similar products. The testing process and recordings used are also discussed. Some reviews also include graphs charting various performance specifications. Sidebars give manufacturer information, price, specifications, measurements, and associated equipment when applicable. Follow-up articles take a new look at a product previously reviewed. The CD reviews feature a recording of the month, with other reviews listed by genre—classical, rock/pop, and jazz. The music and performance are the main focus, with some reviews mentioning sound quality. Various columns cover analog products, industry news, letters, and other issues about equipment and music. The December issue includes the "Products of the Year." The online version offers subscription information, a table of contents and selected articles from the current issue, and classifieds. The web site also gives numerous points of access to past issues. The "Archives/Reviews" section provides selected reviews and articles grouped by type of product or subject, including music reviews. A searchable index of columns and features from September 1962 to December 1997 provides volume, issue, and page numbers. Past issues dating back to 2000 include tables of contents and selected articles. A catalog of music recordings allows users to order titles from *Stereophile.* Links to reviews are provided when available. The extensive coverage of both audio equipment and music makes this a must-have for libraries serving both neophyte and serious audiophiles.

Electronic Journals

5160. *All About Jazz.* irreg. Ed(s): Nils Jacobson, Chris Slawecki. All About Jazz, 761 Sproul Road, #211, Springfield, PA 19064; http://www.allaboutjazz.com/. Adv. *Bk. rev.:* Various number and length. *Aud.:* Hs, Ga, Ac, Sa.

All About Jazz covers the past, present, and future of jazz from an international perspective. The extensive "Reviews" section covers CDs, books, box sets/compilations, CD-ROMS, DVD and video, concerts and festivals, new releases, live recordings, vinyl albums, and recommendations. The CDs subsection is divided by time frame (daily, monthly, and archive) and by genre (big band, blues, funk, fusion, and Latin). The archive includes reviews dating back to 1997 and can be browsed or searched. The recommendations subsection includes editor's picks for the previous year, "Building a Jazz Library," and other recommended reviews. The "Global Jazz" section includes recording reviews divided by major U.S. cities and other continents. Reviews are easy to read, and focus on the music, performance, and sometimes the background of the work. A link is generally provided to the label's web site. Contents also include discussion forums, interviews, profiles, and columns, as well as directories of jazz musicians, venues, radio stations, and record labels. Recommended for both neophytes and serious jazz aficionados.

5161. *All-Music Guide.* 1994. m. All-Music Guide, http://www.allmusic.com. *Aud.:* Ems, Hs, Ga, Ac, Sa.

This eclectic site covers rock, country, jazz, new age, world, folk, bluegrass, rap, reggae, easy listening, blues, gospel/ccm, and vocal. Classical music is linked to a separate site, AMG Classical (http://www.allclassical.com). After choosing a category, users can choose a decade or select from a list of the main styles of the genre. Various tabs at the top of the page also take the user to other sections. The "Styles" section includes a complete list of the various styles for the chosen genre. "Music Maps" and "Essays" trace the roots of various genres and styles and list the major artists. The "Key Artists" section includes biographical information, related artists, music maps, discography, other albums the artist and songs appear on, song highlights, and a bibliography. The "Key Albums" section includes album information, a link to Barnes & Noble, an album review, song tracks (some with individual reviews), related albums, credits, and a list of album releases. There is even a "Library View" link that gives bibliographic information in the MARC format. The "New Releases" section provides album information, song tracks, and credits, but generally not a review. Users can also search the site by artist, album, song, style, or label. The classical site can be searched by composer/performer, work title/keyword, or album title. It can be browsed by composer, period, or genre. A music glossary and a list of the best of the previous year are also helpful. Highly recommended for all music lovers.

5162. *C D Hotlist.* 1999. m. Ed(s): Rick Anderson. CD Hotlist, Electronic Resources/Serials Coordinator, The University Libraries, University of Reno, Reno, NV 89557; rickand@unr.edu; http://www2.library.unr.edu/anderson/cdhl/index.htm. *Aud.:* Ga, Ac.

CD Hotlist is a monthly recommendation service that provides a list of only those items the editors think are beneficial for libraries. Reviews are divided by genre, focusing on classical and jazz, with additional sections for world/ethnic, country/folk, and rock/pop. Entries include the recording information, period, release type (new, reissue, compilation, box set, etc.), and list price from Amazon.com. Links are provided to the labels web site. A brief review describes the best qualities of the album and includes a recommendation as to the type of library that would benefit from the recording. Lists are available back to 2000. Highly recommended for all libraries purchasing music.

5163. *Classics Today: your online guide to classical music.* 1999. d. Ed(s): David Vernier, David Hurwitz. Classics Today, dvernier@classicstoday.com; http://www.classicstoday.com. *Aud.:* Hs, Ga, Ac, Sa.

Updated daily, the reviews in *Classics Today* cover the latest releases. A minimum of five new reviews are added each day, with older reviews being moved to the "30-Day Review Summary." Reviews are well written and often cite a reference recording for comparison. The reviews also include a one-to-ten scale rating of performance and sound quality. Recordings receiving a "ten" for both will be listed in the monthly "10/10 Reviews." There are three search forms for reviews. The basic search includes an entry box for work title/album title and drop-down menus for genre, composer, label, and ratings. The artist search has drop-down menus for ensemble/orchestra, conductor, and soloist. The advanced search includes all of the criteria from the basic and artist search forms. There are three feature articles added each month, and one is always the "Disc of the Month." The other two articles may include editorials, interviews, commentary, or comparative discographies. Recommended for both neophytes and classical aficionados.

5164. ***In Music We Trust.*** 1997. m. Ed(s): Alex Steininger. In Music We Trust, Inc., 15213 SE Bevington Ave, Portland, OR 97267. Adv. Circ: 25000. *Aud.:* Hs, Ga, Ac, Sa.

Started in 1997 as "a vehicle in which to help expose talented artists to a larger audience," *In Music We Trust* has broadened into a label, a national publicity company, and a zine. The zine covers rock/pop, punk/hardcore, metal/hard Rock, country/bluegrass, electronic/gothic, rap/r&b, and ska/swing/jazz. Each month, over 100 reviews are added, with most reviews covering rock/pop. Reviews vary in length, but all are well written and provide an overall impression of the album. Links are provided to the artist's and label's web sites when available. The zine also includes feature articles, interviews, show reviews, and DVD reviews. Every issue back to 1997 is archived. This easy-to-navigate site is recommended for anyone looking for music that might not be reviewed elsewhere.

5165. ***jazzreview.com.*** d. Ed(s): Samira Elkouh. JazzReview.com, 10033 W. Ruby Ave., Milwaukee, WI 53225; morrice@jazzreview.com. *Bk. rev.:* Number and length vary. *Aud.:* Hs, Ga, Ac, Sa.

This jazzy web site is appealing to the eye and the ear. Front and center is the "Jazz Review Corner" that includes a CD review database, concert reviews, jazz viewpoints, book reviews, and guest CD reviews. Like *Classics Today,* the review database is updated daily and covers the latest releases. The database includes over 3,000 reviews that can be sorted by artist, year, or style. Styles range from traditional and straight-ahead/classic to contemporary and fusion. Blues and world music are also included. Insightful, well-written reviews focus on the music and performance, and sometimes mention the background of the artist or work. Links are included to web sites of the record label or artist. *jazzreview.com* also has artist interviews, biographies, jazz photography, news, a discussion room, and a listening room. This easy-to-use web site is recommended for all libraries serving jazz lovers.

5166. ***SoundStage.*** 1995. m. Free. Ed(s): Marc Mickelson. Schneider Publishing, 390 Rideau St, Box 20068, Ottawa, ON K1N 9N5, Canada; feedback@soundstage.com; http://www.sstage.com. *Aud.:* Hs, Ga.

SoundStage focuses on music and high-end audio. Audio reviews cover physical attributes, performance quality, comparisons to similar products, the testing process, and recordings used. Most reviews include a sidebar with a very helpful summary highlighting sound, features, use, and value. Associated equipment is also listed in a sidebar when applicable. The product information includes price, warranty, and full manufacturer information giving the mailing address, e-mail (when available), and web site. The site includes only reviews for the current month, but there is a link to AudioVideoReviews.com, which features the archived equipment reviews for *SoundStage, Home Theater & Sound, GoodSound!,* onhifi.com, onhometheater.com, and MastersOnAudio.com—all part of the SoundStage Network. Music reviews cover pop/rock/rap/alternative, folk/country/gospel, progressive/world, jazz/blues, classical, and remasters/reissues. There are a few reviews covering the SACD and DVD-A formats. Music is rated on musical performance, recording quality, and overall enjoyment. Reviews are available back to 1997 by genre in the archive and in the listings of the year's best. Recommended for all libraries serving audiophiles.

■ NATIVE AMERICANS

Suzanne L. Wones, John F. Kennedy School of Government Library, 79 JFK Street, Cambridge, MA 02138; suzanne_wones@harvard.edu

Introduction

Periodicals in this section are written by, for, or about Native Americans and Canadians; often all three qualifications apply. Newspapers like the *Navajo Times, the Confederated Umatilla Journal*, and *The Eastern Door* cover tribal and local news and events. *Indian Country Today* and the *Native American Times* cover Native news from all over the country. Academic journals tend to be interdisciplinary in nature and cover Native history, literature, culture, and language. Consumer magazines examine Native art, crafts, education, news, and events. All of these titles work to ensure that Native American perspectives, issues, and concerns neglected in the mainstream press are reported on, analyzed, and published.

The cessation of *Native Monthly Reader* has left a gap in material available for Native American youth. The Circle Corporation has attempted to help fill this gap by putting out a new publication, *New Voices: News and Arts from a Native Youth Perspective*, which comes out three times a year. Written by and for Native American youth, this is a welcome addition to the field. Tribal newspapers are appropriate for local high schools, and several other publications include sections specifically aimed at children or teens. *American Indian* has "Coyote's Place," a two-page section of articles and activities for kids, and *News from Native California* includes articles by and for young people. Another good selection for high school libraries is *Native Peoples,* which provides a study guide and covers topics likely to be of interest to high school students.

Native American periodicals publishing only in an electronic format remain scarce. After a yearlong hiatus, the electronic journal *Native Realities* returned to publishing on the web. However, technical difficulties in transferring old releases to the new format of the site continue to frustrate visitors. While solely electronic publications are rare, most of the periodicals reviewed in this section now have web sites. The content and sophistication of these sites vary greatly, as does the amount of content they include. The major newspapers usually have full-text articles from the current issue online, and many of them include at least some articles from past issues as well. *Ethnic Newswatch* also provides online access to a number of Native periodicals, and *Project Muse* has several of the academic titles in their database.

Basic Periodicals

Hs: *The Circle, Native Peoples, New Voices, Winds of Change;* Ga: *The Circle, Indian Country Today, Native Americas, Native Peoples;* Ac: *American Indian Culture and Research Journal, American Indian Quarterly, Canadian Journal of Native Studies, Studies in American Indian Literatures, Tribal College, Wicazo Sa Review.*

Basic Abstracts and Indexes

Abstracts in Anthropology, Alternative Press Index, America: History and Life, Anthropological Literature, Current Index to Journals in Education, Historical Abstracts, Ethnic NewsWatch.

5167. ***American Indian.*** [ISSN: 1528-0640] 2000. q. Free to members. National Museum of the American Indian, 4220 Silver Hill Rd, Suitland, MD 20746; http://www.nmai.si.edu/. *Aud.:* Hs, Ga.

American Indian is the quarterly magazine of the Smithsonian's National Museum of the American Indian (NMAI). It is an attractive, glossy publication with many striking illustrations. The staff, editorial board, and editorial committee are composed overwhelmingly of Native Americans. Each issue contains three or four feature articles, museum news, description of collections and exhibits, a calendar of museum events, and a guest essay. Also included are a two-page children's section, "Coyote's Place," and "Did You Know?," a short education piece designed to "highlight a little-known but important fact about Native history and accomplishment." Recent feature articles cover the NMAI inaugural Pow Wow on the National Mall, showcase four contemporary artists, and introduce the Aboriginal Peoples Television Network. This engaging magazine is a good choice for public libraries, as well as academic libraries supporting either Native Studies or museum studies programs.

American Indian and Alaska Native Mental Health Research. See under Electronic Journals, this section.

5168. *American Indian Art Magazine.* Formerly (until 1977): *American Indian Art.* [ISSN: 0192-9968] 1975. q. USD 20 domestic; USD 24 foreign. Ed(s): Tobi Taylor. American Indian Art, Inc., 7314 E Osborn Dr, Scottsdale, AZ 85251. Illus., index, adv. Refereed. Circ: 25000. Vol. ends: Nov. *Indexed:* ABM, AICP, AbAn, AmH&L, AnthLit, ArtInd. *Bk. rev.:* 1-4, 500-1,500 words. *Aud.:* Ac, Sa.

This high-quality publication has many lovely photographs to illustrate the articles. Its primary audience is collectors of Native American art and it features a large number of ads, primarily for art galleries. Featured articles cover all types of Indian art, from contemporary visual artists and dance performances to in-depth analyses of traditional cultural motifs and artifacts. Issues also include coverage of recent art auctions and a calendar of gallery exhibits. A regular column, "Legal Briefs," covers recent cases dealing with issues in collecting American Indian art. Examples of recent articles include a review of an exhibit of Native American art at the Peabody Essex Museum, an analysis of nine paintings by Naiche of the Chiricahuas, and a discussion of glasswork by Native artists. This is an excellent choice for art collectors, museums, and academic libraries that support fine-arts departments.

5169. *American Indian Culture and Research Journal.* Formerly: *American Indian Culture Center. Journal.* [ISSN: 0161-6463] 1971. q. USD 60 (Individuals, USD 25). Ed(s): Duane Champagne. University of California at Los Angeles, American Indian Studies Center, 3220 Campbell Hall, PO Box 951548, Los Angeles, CA 90095-1548; aisc@ucla.edu. Illus., adv. Refereed. Circ: 1900. Online: Gale Group; OCLC Online Computer Library Center, Inc.; H.W. Wilson. Reprint: PQC. *Indexed:* AICP, AbAn, AgeL, AmH&L, AmHI, AnthLit, ArtHuCI, BRI, CBRI, CIJE, CJA, HumInd, IBZ, L&LBA, MLA-IB, PSA, SSCI, SSI, SociolAb. *Bk. rev.:* 20, 2-4 pages. *Aud.:* Ac, Sa.

This is an interdisciplinary academic journal spanning disciplines such as literature, history, and sociology. Issues typically contain six or seven articles, a commentary section, eight or nine poems by Native poets, and as many as 20 book reviews. Feature articles in recent issues have discussed the conflict between cultural traditions and economic development, owls in stories and images of the Ojibwa and Midweiwin tribes, and the correlation between violence and AIDS among Native American women. The "Commentary" section is devoted to recent events and issues affecting American Indians. The web site is strictly informational, but it does include an searchable index for the journal. This title is essential for any collection supporting American Indian or Native American Studies.

5170. *American Indian Law Review.* [ISSN: 0094-002X] 1973. s-a. USD 20. Ed(s): Michelle A Carr. University of Oklahoma, College of Law, 300 Timberdell Rd, Norman, OK 73019; http://www.law.ou.edu/lawrevs/ailr. Adv. Circ: 700. Microform: WSH; PMC. Online: Gale Group; LexisNexis; West Group. Reprint: WSH. *Indexed:* CLI, ILP, LRI. *Bk. rev.:* infrequent, 250 words. *Aud.:* Ac, Sa.

This formal law review contains articles on current or past legal matters in the United States or Canada. Recent topics include taxation of nonmember Indians in Indian Country, reparations and justice for American Indians, and the interactions of state and tribal courts in Wisconsin. The "Notes" and "Recent Developments" sections provide brief updates on Indian legal issues. Special features often include expository essays on recent developments regarding particular issues, such as a recent report of the National Gambling Impact Study Commission. The journal's web site provides extensive indexing to the entire journal through various access points: tribe, subject, legislation, treaties, and statutes. A cumulative print index can be purchased from the publisher as well. No full texts are available on the web site, but there is access through LexisNexis and Westlaw, and reprints are available, as well as subscription and contributor information. This journal is essential for all law school libraries, most academic libraries supporting Native American Studies programs, and others interested in this complex area of U.S. law and daily Native American life.

5171. *American Indian Quarterly.* [ISSN: 0095-182X] 1974. q. USD 75 (Individuals, USD 30; USD 18 newsstand/cover per issue). Ed(s): Devon A Mihesuah. University of Nebraska Press, 233 N 8th St, Lincoln, NE 68588-0255; pressmail@unl.edu. Illus., index, adv. Refereed. Microform: PQC. Online: bigchalk; EBSCO Publishing; Factiva; Florida Center for Library Automation; Gale Group; LexisNexis; Northern Light Technology, Inc.; OCLC Online Computer Library Center, Inc.; Project MUSE; ProQuest Information & Learning; RoweCom Information Quest; SoftLine Information; Swets Blackwell; H.W. Wilson. Reprint: PSC. *Indexed:* AICP, AbAn, AmH&L, AnthLit, BRI, CBRI, CIJE, HumInd, IBZ, L&LBA, LRI, MLA-IB, RI-1, SociolAb. *Bk. rev.:* 6-30, 400-800 words. *Aud.:* Ac, Sa.

This is a peer-reviewed interdisciplinary journal. It includes original poetry, interviews, and book reviews in addition to analytical academic articles. Disciplines covered include anthropology, history, literature, and religion. Recent topics discussed have been the American Indian integration of baseball, postmodernism and American Indian identity in the work of James Welch, and the origin of Miccosukee Tribal sovereignty. An essential purchase for academic libraries.

5172. *American Indian Report.* [ISSN: 0894-4040] 1985. m. USD 49.95 domestic; USD 64.95 Canada; USD 100 elsewhere. Ed(s): Marguerite Carroll. Falmouth Institute, Inc., 3702 Pender Dr, Ste 300, Fairfax, VA 22030-6066; http://www.falmouthinstitute.com. Adv. Sample. Circ: 8000 Paid. *Aud.:* Hs, Ga.

This is a glossy monthly news magazine. Each issue covers news and events affecting Native Americans today. In addition to the feature articles, each issue contains several regular sections titled "Spotlight," "Fedwatch," "Eye on Enterprise," "Business Report," "Tribal News," "Webwatch," and "Perspectives." "Fedwatch" summarizes legislation and court decisions that impact American Indians. "Webwatch" highlights a web site each month of interest to Native American communities. Feature articles cover issues regarding health, the environment, education, trends within tribes, and other topics. An excellent layout and thorough coverage of issues make this title a recommended purchase for libraries supporting Native American populations and Native American Studies programs.

5173. *Canadian Journal of Native Education.* Formerly: *Indian-Ed.* [ISSN: 0710-1481] 1973. q. Individuals, CND 26.75. University of Alberta, Educational Policy Studies, 7 104 Education Centre North, Edmonton, AB T6G 2G5, Canada; naomi@phys.ualberta.ca. Illus., adv. Sample. Refereed. Circ: 700 Paid. Vol. ends: Dec (No. 2). Microform: MML. Online: bigchalk; Micromedia ProQuest; Northern Light Technology, Inc.; ProQuest Information & Learning. *Indexed:* CEI, CIJE, L&LBA. *Bk. rev.:* 10, 750-1,250 words. *Aud.:* Ac, Sa.

This academic journal is a Canadian counterpart to the *Journal of American Indian Education.* The focus is on Canadian Native education but the journal welcomes submissions on the education of indigenous peoples worldwide. Recent issues include articles on practices and principles for researching with native peoples, decolonizing education in Canadian universities, and a case study examining deafness from a cultural perspective. The spring/summer issue is a theme issue, such as the recent "Exemplary Indigenous Education," in which authors shared experiences on the subject. Contributors include education students as well as professors and scholars. A noteworthy feature is the inclusion of "teaching stories and essays," a "forum for the voices of those who have important knowledge about Native education through reflecting on their own practice, philosophy, or world view." Honoring the traditional First Nations philosophy of education, an "elder advisor" is part of the editorial board. An excellent resource for tribal college libraries and academic libraries supporting schools of education.

5174. *Canadian Journal of Native Studies.* [ISSN: 0715-3244] 1981. s-a. CND 51 (Individuals, CND 30). Ed(s): Samuel Corrigan, Don McCaskill. Brandon University, Native Studies Dept., Brandon, MB R7A 6A9, Canada. Illus., index. Refereed. Vol. ends: No. 2. Microform: MML. *Indexed:* AICP, AmH&L, AnthLit, CBCARef, CPerI, RI-1. *Bk. rev.:* 15-20, 1,000-2,000 words. *Aud.:* Ac, Sa.

This refereed interdisciplinary journal is the official publication of the Canadian Indian/Native Studies Association. Emphasis is on Canadian issues, although some discussion of Native issues and events in the United States is included. There are book reviews of primarily Canadian titles. Abstracts are provided in both English and French. Recent scholarship examines social welfare and the

First Nations of North America, the political history of indigenous peoples of Russia, and unanticipated challenges in providing Native education. Full texts of articles from 1981 to 1996 are available on the web site. This is an important title for libraries supporting Native Studies programs.

5175. ***Cherokee Observer: the only independent Cherokee newspaper.*** [ISSN: 1077-0968] 1993. m. USD 20 domestic; USD 41.50 foreign. Ed(s): Franklin McLain, Sr. Cherokee Observer Inc., P.O.Box 487, Blackwell, OK 74631-0487; cwyob@accesscc.com; http://www.cherokeeobserver.org. Illus., adv. Sample. Circ: 3000 Paid. Vol. ends: Dec (No. 12). *Indexed:* ENW. *Aud.:* Ga.

The descriptive subtitle for this unique publication is "the only independent Cherokee newspaper." Focus is on Cherokee Nation politics, preservation of the Cherokee language and culture, and international indigenous rights. A web site provides links to current articles, information about Cherokee National laws and issues, contact information for tribal officials, and resources for learning the Cherokee language. The *Cherokee Observer* is important for libraries with a strong local interest in Cherokee culture and politics.

5176. ***The Circle: Native American news and arts.*** [ISSN: 1067-5639] 1979. m. USD 20 domestic; USD 40 foreign. Ed(s): Catherine Whipple. The Circle, 3355 36th Avenue S, Minneapolis, MN 55406. Adv. *Bk. rev.:* 3-4, length varies. *Aud.:* Hs, Ga.

The Circle is a newspaper from Minnesota focusing primarily on Native news from that state, but also covering some stories from around the country. It has a strong colloquial voice, especially from the columnists who are forthright and frequently funny in their writings. Each issue features community and arts calendars and the "Native City Arts" section focusing on Native artists. Their youth section has broken out and is now available as a separate publication titled "New Voices: News and Arts from a Native Youth Perspective." *The Circle* has a strong web site that is easy to use, attractive, and has full texts of issues back to 1996. This title is a good choice for Great Lakes area libraries, especially public and school libraries.

5177. ***Confederated Umatilla Journal.*** 1995. m. USD 12. Ed(s): Wil Phinney. Confederated Tribes of the Umatilla Indian Reservations, PO Box 638, Pendleton, OR 07801; info@ctuir.com; http://www.umatilla.nsn.us. Adv. Circ: 6800 Paid and controlled. *Aud.:* Hs, Ga, Sa.

This monthly newspaper for the Confederated Umatilla Tribes of the Umatilla Indian Reservation in Oregon has won awards for excellence from the Native American Journalists Association for the past three years. Covering news and events for Umatilla Tribes, articles are well written and laid out. School news and sports are also covered. Environmental news and health news and issues are regular features. This thorough newspaper is recommended for public and school libraries in the Northwest and for academic libraries supporting Native American Studies programs.

5178. ***The Eastern Door: Kanien'keha:ka Na'kon:ke Rontehnhohanonhnha.*** [ISSN: 1193-8374] 1992. w. CND 62; USD 68 United States; CND 118 elsewhere. Ed(s): Kenneth Deer. Kahnawake Mohawk Territory Newspaper, PO Box 1170, Kahnawake, PQ J0L 1B0, Canada; easterndoor@axess.com; http://www.easterndoor.com. Illus., adv. Sample. Circ: 2200 Paid. Vol. ends: Jan. *Bk. rev.:* 1-2, 500 words. *Aud.:* Hs, Ga.

The Eastern Door is a local newspaper for the Kahnawake Mohawk Territory in Quebec. Published weekly, it covers local news, police reports, letters to the editor, community events, obituaries, birthday announcements, memorials, and reprints of news items from other Native papers in the United States and Canada. A special section promotes Mohawk culture with individual profiles, coverage of tribal events, and translations of articles from English to the Mohawk language. Recent article topics include the status of a construction project for a new business complex, the financial crisis facing local medical transportation, and the relocation and expansion of a local multimedia development business. The web site provides archives with some full text back to 1992 and more complete coverage from 1999 to the present.

5179. ***European Review of Native American Studies.*** [ISSN: 0238-1486] 1987. s-a. EUR 20.45; USD 29. Ed(s): Christian Feest. European Review of Native American Studies, c/o Christian Feest, Ed., Fasanenweg 4 A, Altenstadt, 63674, Germany; cff.ssk@t-online.de. Illus., adv. Sample. Refereed. Circ: 600. Vol. ends: No. 2. *Indexed:* AICP, AmH&L, AnthLit, IBZ, MLA-IB. *Bk. rev.:* 3-6, 400-1,200 words. *Aud.:* Ac, Sa.

This academic journal provides an interesting perspective as it primarily functions as a venue for European scholars to publish on Native American Studies. Interdisciplinary in nature, articles range in scope covering topics in the fields of religion, art, history, and literature. Issues include book reviews, obituaries, and coverage of international conferences and workshops. Academic libraries that support Native American Studies programs will want to include this title in their holdings.

5180. ***Indian Country Today.*** Formerly (until 1992): *Lakota Times.* [ISSN: 1066-5501] 1981. w. USD 48 domestic; USD 83 in Canada & Mexico; USD 227 elsewhere. Ed(s): Kerri Lis, Tim Johnson. Indian Country Today, 3059 Seneca Turnpike, Canastota, NY 13032; editor@indiancountry.com. Illus., adv. Sample. Circ: 22000. *Indexed:* B&I, ENW. *Aud.:* Hs, Ga, Ac.

Indian Country Today continues to be the major national Native weekly newspaper in the United States. It regularly carries sections titled "News from the Nations," "Trade & Commerce," and "Lifeways." "Lifeways" covers Native arts and culture. This publication also carries most traditional newspaper items such as classified ads, obituaries and personals, editorials, letters to the editor, and cartoons. Articles cover news from all states and tribes and other topics of national interest. This well-respected newspaper is an excellent title for all public and academic libraries. The web site provides an attractive online version of the paper and full texts of selected articles from the past two years.

5181. ***Inuit Art Quarterly.*** [ISSN: 0831-6708] 1986. q. CND 26.75 domestic; USD 25 United States; CND 39 elsewhere. Ed(s): Marybelle Mitchell. Inuit Art Foundation, 2081 Merivale Rd, Nepean, ON K2G 1G9, Canada; http://www.inuitart.org. Illus., index, adv. Circ: 1923 Paid. Vol. ends: Winter. *Indexed:* ABM, AICP, AbAn, ArtInd, CBCARef, IBZ. *Bk. rev.:* 1-2, 500-1,000 words. *Aud.:* Ga, Ac, Sa.

Published by the Inuit Art Foundation (IAF), *Inuit Art Quarterly* focuses on contemporary art, issues, and artists of Canada's Inuit people. Feature articles discuss various styles of Inuit art and spotlight specific artists and their work. Each issue also includes curatorial notes, a calendar of exhibits and shows, book reviews, and an "In Memoriam" column. There are many lovely photographs and illustrations. An index to past volumes is available from the Inuit Art Foundation. The IAF web site has ordering information, but no excerpts from the magazine. Recommended for collectors and for regional and art libraries with an interest in this area.

5182. ***Inuktitut.*** [ISSN: 0020-9872] 1959. 3x/yr. CND 37.80 domestic; CND 60 foreign. Ed(s): Sydney Sackett. Inuit Tapirisat of Canada, 170 Laurier Ave W, Ste 510, Ottawa, ON K1P 5V5, Canada; itc@tapirisat.ca; http://www.tapirisat.ca. Illus. Circ: 6600. Microform: MML; PQC. Online: LexisNexis; Micromedia ProQuest. *Indexed:* AICP, CBCARef, CPerI. *Bk. rev.:* Occasional, 500 words. *Aud.:* Ga, Sa.

Inuktitut is a large, beautiful quarterly for the Canadian Inuit population. It is a cultural and educational magazine dedicated to promoting use of the Inuktitut language, and it is published in Inuktitut, English, and French, with each page neatly divided so that the languages lie side by side in columns. Typical content includes articles on the arts, language, and culture of the Inuit, stories from tribal elders, a youth section, and book reviews. A recent issue focuses on Inuit political history and includes a piece by Canada's first Inuk MP, an interview with William Tagoona, and an article by a former political activist on "Life After Leadership." The publisher's web site is visually striking and has a great deal of information about the culture, history, and current state of Inuit people in Canada. Past issues are available on the site in pdf format.

5183. ***Journal of American Indian Education.*** [ISSN: 0021-8731] 1961. 3x/yr. USD 45 (Individuals, USD 20). Ed(s): Octaviana Trujillo. Arizona State University, Center for Indian Education, College of Education, Box 871311, Tempe, AZ 85287-1311; http://seamonkey.ed.asu.edu/~gene/cie/

journal.html. Illus., index. Refereed. Circ: 1000. Vol. ends: Spring (No. 3). Microform: PQC; NRP. Online: OCLC Online Computer Library Center, Inc.; H.W. Wilson. Reprint: PQC. *Indexed:* AbAn, CIJE, EduInd, HEA, L&LBA, SociolAb. *Aud.:* Ac, Sa.

This scholarly journal publishes papers specifically related to the education of American Indians and Alaska Natives. It favors articles on applied research, but more analytical articles are also included. The emphasis is on research initiated, conducted, and interpreted by Native educators and scholars. Recently, contributors have explored the classroom motivation of Native students in college, standards-based education in rural Alaska, and the results of a campus ethnoviolence survey at a university with a large number of American Indians students. A simple web site provides full texts of volumes from 1961 to 1997, subscription information, and the ability for contributors to submit manuscripts electronically. Small (only two or three articles in each issue), but of excellent quality, this title is essential for college libraries with education departments and collections.

5184. *Journal of Chickasaw History and Culture.* Formerly (until 2003): *Journal of Chickasaw History.* 1995. q. Membership, USD 20. Ed(s): Matthew DeSpain. Chickasaw Historical Society, PO Box 1548, Ada, OK 74820; rwg@oklahoma.net. Illus. Refereed. Circ: 600. *Aud.:* Ga, Ac.

This compact scholarly journal from The Chickasaw Historical Society is dedicated to Chickasaw history and culture. Emphasis is on oral history, archeology, anthropology, and ethnohistory. About a third of each issue is reserved for "Nation News," obituaries, genealogy, and news from the society. A recent two part series provided articles on each of the Chickasaw Nation governors from 1856 to 1988. The web site features summaries of all the issues, but not any full texts of articles. This is a good addition for public and college libraries in Chickasaw territories and for Native Studies departments.

5185. *Mazina'igan: a chronicle of the Lake Superior Ojibwe.* 1984. q. Free. Ed(s): Sue Erickson. Great Lakes Indian Fish & Wildlife Commission, 100 Maple St., Odanah, WI 54861. Illus. Sample. Circ: 13500. *Aud.:* Hs, Ga, Sa.

Published by the Great Lakes Indian Fish and Wildlife Commission, the focus of this newspaper is on water and land use in the Great Lakes region. The newspaper also covers local tribal news, events, and sports. A regularly featured children's section promotes the Ojibwe culture and language. Recent issues carry stories on new off-reservation hunting rights on Oak Island, a nonprofit organization devoted to countering defamation of Indian people, and updates on relations between local tribes and the U.S. Forest Service. The no-frills web site contains full texts of articles back to spring 1999. This valuable–and free–periodical belongs in all Midwest libraries.

5186. *Native American Times.* Formerly (until 2001): *Oklahoma Indian Times.* [ISSN: 1542-4928] 1995. 2x/m. USD 20. Oklahoma Indian Times Inc., Box 692050, Tulsa, OK 74169; http://www.okit.com/. Illus. Circ: 36000. *Bk. rev.:* Occasional. *Aud.:* Hs, Ga.

Native American Times is now publishing twice a month as it continues to provide solid news coverage of national Native American news. Oklahoma news is highlighted, but stories from across the United States make up the majority of articles. Monthly sections in addition to news are: "Indian Gaming," "Health," "Arts & Entertainment," "Education," and "Editorial." Recent stories cover conflict between the Kiowa tribe and the BIA, opposition to the use of "Redskins" as a high school mascot in Oklahoma, the destruction of aboriginal pictographs in Oregon, and a gift of 1.2 million dollars from the Cherokee Nation to public schools. A web site provides full texts of issues from 2000 to the present. News articles from 1999 are also available. A good choice for all Oklahoma libraries, for those serving Native American communities, and for those supporting Native American Studies programs.

5187. *Native Americas: hemispheric journal of indigenous issues.* Former titles (until 1992): *Akwe Kon Journal; Northeast Indian Quarterly; Indian Times.* [ISSN: 1092-3527] 1984. q. USD 39 (Individuals, USD 24). First Nations Development Institute, 11917 Main St, Fredericksburg, VA 22408; info@firstnations.org; http://www.firstnations.org. Illus., adv. Circ: 8500. Vol. ends: Winter (No. 4). *Indexed:* AICP, AltPI, CIJE, ENW. *Bk. rev.:* 1-4, 1,000-2,000 words. *Aud.:* Ga, Ac.

Native Americas is a remarkable journal that provides in-depth articles, analyses, and discussions on a wide range of social, economic, and philosophical Native issues from both North and South America. Native writers predominate. In 2002 publishing of *Native Americas* moved from Cornell University to the First Nations Development Institute in Fredericksburg, Virginia. The shift in publishing has not compromised the quality of this publication. Recent articles examine cultural survival among urban Indians, problems with the federal tribal recognition process, and impact of gaming on tribes. Regular columns include "Indigenous Rights Watch," "Hemispheric Digest" (news items), and "The Public Eye," which is a series of opinion pieces on topical issues. Regular book review essays usually cover two or three similar titles. The vibrant web site offers solid background to the journal. Columns and selected full texts of articles from the current issue are available, as are tables of contents for back issues. This award-winning, thoughtful journal is recommended for all libraries.

5188. *Native Peoples: arts and lifeways.* Incorporates: *Native Artists.* [ISSN: 0895-7606] 1987. bi-m. USD 19.95 domestic; USD 28 Canada; USD 56 elsewhere. Ed(s): Dan Gibson. Media Concepts Group, Inc., 5333 N Seventh St, Ste C 224, Phoenix, AZ 85014. Illus., index, adv. Circ: 105000 Paid. Vol. ends: Summer (No. 4). *Indexed:* ArtInd, BRI, CBRI, CIJE. *Bk. rev.:* 2-3, 650-850 words. *Aud.:* Hs, Ga.

Native Peoples is an award-winning publication that is well designed and very appealing. It is an excellent magazine for the general public and is found on many newsstands. With a focus on contemporary Native American arts and culture, it features articles on Native artists, musicians, food, crafts, and events. Native news and accomplishments by Native individuals are regularly covered, and book, video, and museum reviews frequently appear as well. All the features are well written and beautifully illustrated. Examples of recent article topics include Native Americans involved in scientific and technical fields, Native textile arts, and a guide to the Native art galleries in Scottsdale, Arizona. A calendar of Native events and exhibits nationwide is included in the winter and summer issues. *Native Peoples* also provides a study guide for each issue to facilitate using the magazine in classrooms, which is available free in print or on their web site. *Native Peoples* is affiliated with a number of museums and organizations, including the Smithsonian's National Museum of the American Indian, the Heard Museum, and the Institute of American Indian Arts Museum. The web site has tables of contents for all issues with online ordering possible for past articles. Each of the sections from the print magazine has an online counterpart. This magazine is highly recommended for all libraries.

5189. *Navajo Times.* Former titles (until 1987): *Navajo Times Today;* (until 1984): *Navajo Times.* 1957. w. USD 55; USD 110 foreign. Ed(s): Duane A. Beyal. Navajo Times Company, PO Box 310, Window Rock, AZ 86515. Adv. Circ: 17200 Paid. Microform: LIB. *Aud.:* Ga, Sa.

The *Navajo Times* is the official community newspaper for the Navajo Nation. It covers reservation news, politics, and events, as well as national issues affecting Navajoland. It also features editorials, advertisements, a sports section, education notes, military notes, and community notes. A special arts section appears periodically. The web site is well designed and makes available full texts of articles from the current issue, but not from previous ones. This is an important paper from the country's largest Indian tribe and is recommended for regional and local libraries, as well as collections supporting Native American Studies programs.

5190. *New Voices (Minneapolis): news and arts from a Native youth perspective.* 2002. 3x/yr. USD 15. Ed(s): Jenn Torres. The Circle, 3355 36th Avenue S, Minneapolis, MN 55406; info@thecirclenews.org; http://www.thecirclenews.org/. Circ: 6000 Paid and controlled. *Bk. rev.:* 1-2, 500 words. *Aud.:* Ems, Hs.

New Voices is a fresh new publication from the publisher that produces *The Circle: Native American News and Arts.* Each issue is about 15 pages long. Articles are written by and for Native American youth. Articles range from music, art, book and film reviews, to in-depth pieces on Native American leaders, traditions, and history. Page-length opinion pieces from contributors and shorter letters to the editor let the voices of Native American youth be heard loud and clear. Lighter fare is included in an advice column from teens for teens, horoscopes, quizzes, fake personal ads, and the like. This is an excellent resource for school libraries and public libraries serving Native American communities.

5191. ***News from Native California: an inside view of the California Indian world.*** [ISSN: 1040-5437] 1987. q. USD 19 domestic; USD 27 foreign. Ed(s): Margaret Dubin. Clapperstick Institute, PO Box 9145, Berkeley, CA 94709; nnc@heydaybooks.com; http://www.heydaybooks.com/news. Illus., index, adv. Circ: 4500 Paid. Vol. ends: No. 4. *Indexed:* AICP, AltPI. *Bk. rev.:* 1, 500-1,200 words. *Aud.:* Hs, Ga, Sa.

This appealing magazine covers a wide range of topics touching on Native life in California. These include politics, the arts, language, history, personal narrative, book and video reviews, poems, legislation, and more. The focus is on individuals, their accomplishments, lifestyles, and even obituaries. *News From Native California* allows for a diverse group of voices to be heard, even including articles by younger Native Americans. A recently added section, "Vitamin A(yyy)," addresses health, nutrition, and fitness issues. Also included in each issue is a calendar of upcoming events. The web site includes tables of contents for issues and some limited full-text articles. It also has a calendar of events and a useful collection of links. *News from Native California* is recommended for California libraries and other libraries with a strong interest in California and/or Native Americans.

Oklahoma Indian Times. See *Native American Times.*

5192. ***Studies in American Indian Literatures.*** [ISSN: 0730-3238] 1977. q. USD 35 (Individuals, USD 25). Ed(s): Malea Powell. Studies in American Indian Literatures, Department of English, California State University at San Bernardino, San Bernardino, CA 92407. Illus., adv. Refereed. Circ: 350. Vol. ends: Winter. *Indexed:* AICP, CIJE, MLA-IB. *Bk. rev.:* 10, 1,000-2,400 words. *Aud.:* Ac, Sa.

SAIL covers all types of Native American literatures from traditional stories to contemporary novels, plays, essays, and poetry. Recent issues feature articles on the dialogic nature of American Indian resistance, an interview with Joseph Buchac, and a literary essay on Greg Sarris's *Grand Avenue*. Contributors are drawn largely from Native and non-Native professors, scholars, and graduate students in the English literature field. Each issue contains an index of the major tribal nations mentioned within. The web site has full texts of articles from Series 1 (1977–1987). Full texts of articles from Series 2 (1989 to the present) are online if the publisher has been able to get copyright permission from the authors. Quite a number are now available and more will be added as permissions are obtained. The site also includes very helpful issue and author indexes for both series. The only journal focusing exclusively on Native North American literatures, *SAIL* is a solid choice for libraries supporting programs in literature and Native American Studies.

5193. ***Tribal College: journal of American Indian higher education.*** [ISSN: 1052-5505] 1989. q. USD 30 (Individuals, USD 22). Ed(s): Marjane Ambler. American Indian Higher Education Consortium, PO Box 720, Mancos, CO 81328; info@tribalcollegejournal.org. Illus., index, adv. Sample. Vol. ends: Summer (No. 4). *Indexed:* CIJE, ENW, EduInd, HEA. *Bk. rev.:* 2, 300 words. *Aud.:* Ga, Ac, Sa.

This unique magazine is both for and about the 31 Indian-controlled tribal colleges in the United States and Canada. Articles address the challenges faced by these schools as well as their news, achievements, and resources. General issues of Native education are also discussed. Examples of recent features include an article on how a tribal college is helping tribes benefit from the tourism generated by the bicentennial of Lewis and Clark's expedition, ways tribal colleges make tribal history come alive on campus, and the problems and politics faced by today's tribal college presidents. Regular departments feature profiles of tribal colleges, news on recent activities at various schools, book reviews, a "Land Grant Department," and pieces by college students and administrators. An especially noteworthy feature for librarians is the "Resource Guide," regular bibliographic essays of both print and electronic resources on topics featured in that issue. The web site provides scanned cover images, tables of contents, and a few selected articles. *Tribal College Journal* is an essential publication for all academic libraries, especially those with schools of education.

5194. ***Whispering Wind: American Indian: past & present.*** [ISSN: 0300-6565] 1967. bi-m. USD 21 domestic; USD 36 foreign. Jack Heriard, Ed. & Pub., PO Box 1390, Folsom, LA 70437-1390; whiswind@i-55.com; http://www.writtenheritage.com/. Illus., index, adv. Sample. Refereed. Circ: 24000. Vol. ends: No. 6. *Indexed:* AICP, ENW. *Bk. rev.:* 4-6, 300-500 words. *Aud.:* Hs, Sa.

Whispering Wind states that its goal is "to help preserve the art and craftsmanship of Native American material culture." It has been devoted to the re-creation of traditional Native American crafts and dance regalia and as such has been popular for years among Boy Scouts and hobbyists seeking to make their own dance outfits. While the perspective and orientation is clearly that of outsiders to Native cultures, it is deeply respectful and shows admiration for traditional Native arts and crafts. One piece in a recent issue is by a Native American writer who discusses Kiowa battle dress in the context of her family history. Educational articles include historical essays and cultural pieces discussing designs and dance traditions. The "Learning Corner" feature gives clear, step-by-step instructions, accompanied by drawings or photographs, for the creation of items such as jingle dress cones and feather decoration wraps. Powwow protocol, traditions, regalia, and music make up another large part of this magazine. Book and music reviews are regular features. Articles may discuss museum collections or Native American cultural institutions. A calendar of upcoming Indian and non-Indian powwows is included, as are classified advertisements for craft suppliers, a very useful resource for those making dance outfits. The web site includes powwow dates, a collection of resource links, and contact and subscription information. A summary of issues is available online, but there are no full texts of articles. This title will be of interest for public libraries in general, especially those with active scouting organizations in the area or those serving urban Native American populations.

5195. ***Wicazo Sa Review: a journal of Native American studies.*** [ISSN: 0749-6427] 1985. s-a. USD 50 (Individuals, USD 20). Ed(s): Elizabeth Cook-Lynn. University of Minnesota Press, 111 Third Ave S, Ste 290, Minneapolis, MN 55401-2520; ump@tc.umn.edu. Illus., adv. Sample. Refereed. Circ: 400. Vol. ends: No. 2. *Indexed:* AmH&L, CIJE, MLA-IB. *Bk. rev.:* 1-2, 800 words. *Aud.:* Ac.

This excellent interdisciplinary journal is one of the core titles in Native American Studies, along with the venerable *American Indian Quarterly* and *American Indian Culture and Research Journal* (both above in this section). Issues contain articles, interviews, and essays that provide "inquiries into the Indian past and its relationship to the vital present." The journal's interdisciplinary nature means that the scholarship includes literary, historical, legal, cultural, sociological, and religious issues. There is a recent two-part special issue on "Sovereignty and Governance." Most of the authors are Native academics or professors, often those teaching in Native American Studies programs. This is an essential title for all academic libraries.

5196. ***Winds of Change: American Indian education & opportunity.*** [ISSN: 0888-8612] 1986. q. Non-members, USD 24. Ed(s): James R Weidlein. A I S E S Publishing, 4450 Arapahoe Ave Ste 100, Boulder, CO 80303-9102; woc@indra.com; http://www.aises.uthscsa.edu. Illus., index, adv. Sample. Circ: 60000 Paid. Vol. ends: Fall. *Indexed:* CIJE. *Bk. rev.:* 2-10, 250-600 words. *Aud.:* Hs, Ac, Sa.

Winds of Change is a well-designed, full-color magazine that focuses on career and educational advancement for Native Americans. Published by the American Indian Science and Engineering Society (AISES), it seeks to encourage and support Native students interested in higher education and careers in the sciences. Articles focus on a wide range of educational and workplace subjects. Recent topics include a discussion of tribal autonomy, diabetes among Native Americans, using traditional knowledge in a scientific setting, and encouraging students to pursue health and education professions. A superb resource for supporting Natives in higher education, *WOC* is very practical and publishes an annual "Guide to Internships, Co-ops, and Minority School Programs" and an annual college guide for high school students. Regular departments include guest editorials, "News from AISES," and a resume service, which invites Native subscribers to complete a resume form and return it; *WOC* will then forward the resumes with a cover letter to the advertisers the reader is interested in working for. A conference issue is also published annually. The web site provides cover images and tables of contents for issues from 1997 to the present. The site features full texts of a few selected articles and some tips for applying to colleges. *WOC* offers a unique perspective on education for academic libraries with teacher education programs. It is essential for high school guidance counselors and college placement offices serving Native students. A highly useful journal for any library serving high school, college, and general adult Native populations.

Windspeaker. See Canada section.

Electronic Journals

5197. *American Indian and Alaska Native Mental Health Research.* Former titles (until 1986): *White Cloud Journal of American Indian Mental Health;* (until 1982): *White Cloud Journal of American Indian - Alaska Native Mental Health.* [ISSN: 0893-5394] 1978. 3x/yr. USD 35; USD 44 foreign. National Center for American Indian Mental Health Research, University of Colorado Health Sciences Center, Department of Psychiatry, PO Box 6508, Aurora, CO 80045-0508; billie.greene@uchsc.edu ; http://www.uchsc.edu/ai/ncaianmhr. Illus., index, adv. Refereed. Circ: 1000. *Indexed:* AnthLit, CIJE, CJA, IndMed, PsycholAb, SSCI, SWR&A. *Aud.:* Ac, Sa.

This is a refereed scientific journal available only in an electronic format. It is available free on the web and is published in pdf format. The web site also provides full tables of contents for back issues, but they are not searchable. Print copies of back issues are available for a fee. The journal carries empirical research, program evaluations, case studies, unpublished dissertations, and other articles in the behavioral, social, and health sciences that relate to the mental health status of American Indians and Alaska Natives. This is a key source for information on mental health issues (including addiction, children's issues and school performance, and abuse) not available elsewhere. Recent topics of discussion include a therapeutic meditation technique for use with Native American adolescents and partnerships between vocational rehabilitation and substance abuse programs. This title is recommended for psychology, social work, education, and Native Studies collections.

5198. *Native Realities.* 2001. irreg. Wordcraft Circle of Native Writers and Storytellers, 1744 Del Cielo Dr, NW Albuquerque, NM 87105-1044; nativerealities@comcast.net; http://www.wordcraftcircle.org/. *Aud.:* Ga, Ac.

Now in its third year, *Native Realities* continues to present original literature from Native writers in an electronic format. The journal comes from the Wordcraft Circle, a national organization whose vision is to "ensure that the voices of Native writers and storytellers–past, present, and future–are heard throughout the world." Quarterly issues support this vision by publishing original poems, stories, plays, and even excerpts from published novels. Although *Native Realities* is a valuable source for learning about and enjoying Native American literature, it has had an uneven publishing history.

Slate. See General Editorial-Internet section.

■ NEWS AND OPINION

See also Alternatives; General Editorial; and Newspapers sections.

Kara L. Robinson, Information Services Librarian, Libraries and Media Services, Kent State University, Kent, OH 44242; krobinso@kent.edu

Introduction

The events of September 11 and after served to demonstrate both the advantages and disadvantages of weekly and monthly news periodicals. Unlike their electronic and newspaper counterparts, these publications lack immediacy. This time lag can make it difficult for potential readers to accept that there is anything more to the story than what they've already seen and heard. However, this supposed negative is in fact the print titles' chief advantage, since they have the time to develop a story, to separate truth from rumor, and report in greater detail without having to worry about filling many hours of airtime or inches of newspaper column space. In these days of "instant" news, there is still a place and purpose for the titles in this section.

In this edition, several long-time titles from previous editions have been deleted. This decision was reached based on the low number of libraries that currently carry these titles. In these times of tightening library budgets, such titles are luxuries, particularly in cases where content from these publications is available on the web. Omitted are: *Against the Current,* which is available as part of Alt-PressWatch; *Black Flag,* available on the web at http://flag.blackened.net/blackflag; *Democratic Left,* on the web at http://www.dsausa.org/dl/index.html; *Socialist,* the current issue on the web at http://www.sp-usa.org/socialist/index.html; and *The Harris Poll. Ripon Forum* has also been omitted because it does not appear to be currently published—none of the holding libraries have an issue newer than spring 2002 and its companion web site has not been updated since 2000.

With the above listed omissions, the remaining titles should be considered valuable, if not necessary, for any balanced collection. Many represent viewpoints not easily acquired from other publications. Many points on the ideological spectrum are covered, with several titles on each "edge." On the left side of the ideological spectrum are *Dissent* and *Monthly Review,* among others. The mainstream, ideologically middle-of-the-road publications are *Newsweek, Time,* and *U.S. News & World Report.* Representation of conservative or right-wing viewpoints includes *The American Spectator, Human Events,* and *National Review.*

The second part of this section has a small list of web-based or electronic-only news sources, including the major news web sites like cnn.com. Some of the more entertaining sites are not included since they don't fall into this section's working definition of "news and opinion." Among those excluded are the *Sources Ejournal* (http://www.dso.com), since it is really aimed at those deeply into conspiracy theories; the *Drudge Report* (http://www.drudgereport.com), which is largely gossip with the small redeeming feature of offering links to multiple news sites; and *The Smoking Gun* (http://www.thesmokinggun.com), which posts files from government, law enforcement, and the courts that the site's managers claim are exclusive to them.

Basic Periodicals

Hs: *New Perspectives Quarterly, Newsweek, Time;* Ga, Ac: *The Nation, National Review, New Perspectives Quarterly, The New Republic, Newsweek, Time, U.S. News & World Report.*

Basic Abstracts and Indexes

Alternative Press Index, PAIS International, Periodical Abstracts, Readers' Guide to Periodical Literature.

5199. *American Enterprise: politics, business and culture.* Formerly (until 1990): *Public Opinion (Washington).* [ISSN: 1047-3572] 1978. bi-m. Individuals, USD 29; Corporations, USD 56. Ed(s): Karl Zinsmesiter. American Enterprise Institute for Public Policy Research, c/o Pat Ford, 1150 17th St N W, Washington, DC 20036. Illus., adv. Circ: 15000. Vol. ends: Nov/Dec. Microform: NBI. Online: EBSCO Publishing; Florida Center for Library Automation; Gale Group; Northern Light Technology, Inc.; OCLC Online Computer Library Center, Inc.; ProQuest Information & Learning; H.W. Wilson. *Indexed:* ABCPolSci, ABS&EES, AgeL, IPSA, JEL, LRI, MagInd, PAIS, SSI. *Bk. rev.:* 5, length varies, signed. *Aud.:* Ga, Ac.

The *American Enterprise* claims to be a different kind of conservative publication, and it is. A typical issue examines one topic in depth, along with recurring features such as a digest that summarizes current research from universities, think tanks, and investigative publications. The magazine bases its arguments on "irrefutable research, not armchair opinions." This claim is backed up by the inclusion of the "Opinion Pulse" section that concludes each issue. This section, which is composed of the results of recent surveys conducted by such pollsters as Gallup, Louis Harris, and CBS, provides a valuable, nonpartisan insight into the attitudes of the American public.

The print publication's companion web site includes tables of contents for all issues back to 1995. The majority of articles from 1996 to the previous year are available. Few full-text articles from the current year are available. The web site does not include the "Opinion Pulse" section of the print magazine. One notable feature of the web version is the "Hot Flash" column, described as "breaking news and commentary." The column is archived back to November 1999. A section called "TAE Classic" offers "newly relevant past articles." The site also includes search capability and covers of the magazine back to January/February 1995. *TAE* should be considered a worthwhile addition, particularly for academic libraries.

5200. *The American Spectator.* Former titles (until 1976): *Alternative; an American Spectator; Alternative.* [ISSN: 0148-8414] 1967. bi-m. USD 39 domestic; USD 42 foreign; USD 3.95 newsstand/cover per issue. Ed(s): Spencer Reiss. The American Spectator, 1611 N Kent St, Ste 901, Arlington, VA 22209; editor@spectator.org; http://www.spectator.org. Illus., index, adv. Sample. Circ: 139000 Paid. Vol. ends: Dec. Microform: BHP; PQC. Online: EBSCO Publishing; Florida Center for Library Automation; Gale Group; LexisNexis; Northern Light Technology, Inc.; OCLC Online Computer Library Center, Inc.; ProQuest Information & Learning; H.W. Wilson. Reprint: ISI. *Indexed:* ABS&EES, ASIP, BRI, BiogInd, CBRI, MagInd, PAIS, RGPR, SUSA. *Bk. rev.:* 6, 1,500 words, signed. *Aud.:* Ga, Ac.

The American Spectator "tries to look where the mainstream media don't, whether for reasons of politics or habit." The articles are sharp, pungent, and definitely demonstrate a libertarian-conservative bias, not unexpected from a publication that has included the Children's Defense Fund on its list of enemies. Features include "Ben Stein's Diary" and "The Continuing Crisis," short news entries from around the world. This title remains a valuable one for libraries seeking to balance their collections.

The magazine's companion web site, called *The American Prowler* includes a "coming attractions" version of the current print issue and one or two full-text articles. A very limited archive going back to the September/October 2002 issue is available; again, only a handful of each issue's articles is available. The site offers daily features and columns, including such gems as "Enemy of the Week," "Political Hay," and "The Daily Grind."

Business Week. See Business/General section.

5201. *Commentary: journal of significant thought and opinion on contemporary issues.* [ISSN: 0010-2601] 1945. m. USD 45 domestic; USD 56 foreign. Ed(s): Neal Kozodoy. American Jewish Committee, 165 E 56th St, New York, NY 10022; http://www.commentarymagazine.com. Index, adv. Sample. Refereed. Circ: 26000. Vol. ends: Jun/Dec. Online: bigchalk; Chadwyck-Healey Incorporated; EBSCO Publishing; Florida Center for Library Automation; Gale Group; Northern Light Technology, Inc.; OCLC Online Computer Library Center, Inc.; ProQuest Information & Learning; H.W. Wilson. Reprint: PQC. *Indexed:* ABCPolSci, ABS&EES, ArtHuCI, BAS, BEL&L, BHA, BRD, BRI, CBRI, FLI, FutSurv, HumInd, IBSS, IJP, IPSA, LRI, MLA-IB, MRD, MagInd, PAIS, PRA, RGPR, RI-1, SSCI, SSI. *Bk. rev.:* 5, 1,500-2,000 words, signed. *Aud.:* Ga, Ac.

Commentary is one of a number of periodicals that present discussion of Jewish concerns in the United States and abroad. Unlike most of those publications, however, it presents a moderate rather than a liberal perspective. It publishes lengthy articles of general interest and often includes examples of current Jewish fiction. Because it has a unique position as the voice of moderate Jewish thought, it should be considered by libraries carrying any of the more liberal Jewish publications and by libraries seeking to add moderate voices to their holdings.

The companion web site offers the table of contents of the current issue and free searching of the complete archive of *Commentary* back to 1945. Selected current articles are available for free; all others are available for a fee. Many articles offer a choice of pdf or html format. The "Letters" section, "famous the world over" according to the editors, is available in full text for the current issue of the magazine.

Commonweal. See Religion section.

5202. *The Contemporary Review.* Incorporates: *Fortnightly.* [ISSN: 0010-7565] 1866. m. GBP 47 domestic; GBP 44 in Europe; GBP 48 elsewhere. Ed(s): Richard Mullen. Contemporary Review Co. Ltd., 12 Campbell Ct, Bramley, Basingstoke, RG26 5EA, United Kingdom. Illus., index, adv. Sample. Circ: 680000. Vol. ends: Jun/Dec. Microform: PMC; PQC. Online: Chadwyck-Healey Incorporated; EBSCO Publishing; Florida Center for Library Automation; Gale Group; Northern Light Technology, Inc.; OCLC Online Computer Library Center, Inc.; ProQuest Information & Learning; H.W. Wilson. *Indexed:* BAS, BRI, CBRI, FLI, HumInd, MLA-IB, RI-1. *Bk. rev.:* Various number and length, signed. *Aud.:* Ga, Ac.

The Contemporary Review is one of England's oldest intellectual political journals. The journal is "editorially independent," which allows for a variety of articles from both commissioned and freelance "writers from around the world with first-hand knowledge of their subjects." Global coverage includes the arts, travel, and religion, as well as political and social topics of the day. Each issue includes an average of 50 reviews of varying lengths. The well-researched articles are detailed but still comprehensible to the average reader. An interesting quirk of this title is that each issue is exactly 64 pages long. The objective of the journal is "to approach contemporary questions with more objectivity and depth than is frequently possible in daily and weekly publications." It certainly achieves its goal.

The accompanying web site continues to only provide information about the publication. It is helpful if you are an author seeking submission information, but if you are seeking archived articles, you won't find them here.

5203. *Current (Washington, 1960).* [ISSN: 0011-3131] 1960. m. except Mar.-Apr., Jul.-Aug. combined. USD 84 (Individuals, USD 41; USD 8.40 per issue). Ed(s): Joyce Horn. Heldref Publications, 1319 18th St, NW, Washington, DC 20036-1802; subscribe@heldref.org; http://www.heldref.org. Illus., index, adv. Refereed. Circ: 1400 Paid. Vol. ends: Jan. CD-ROM: ProQuest Information & Learning. Online: Gale Group. Reprint: PSC. *Indexed:* ABS&EES, ArtHuCI, HRA, IBZ, LRI, MagInd, RGPR, SSCI. *Aud.:* Hs, Ga, Ac.

"*Current* is a reprint magazine, not limited by ideological bent, nor by any preconceived subject matter; articles are selected for originality and relevancy to America today." The articles reprinted do represent a number of different ideologies and sources, but there is very little explanation given as to why those particular articles were selected to be reprinted. Also, little or no background information is given about the authors and their view on the issues discussed. This title could be useful in fostering class discussion, more so if the articles employed were opposing viewpoints on the same topic. The value of this title is limited by these drawbacks, and in these times of shrinking serials budgets, this publication may be one that libraries will regard as a luxury.

5204. *Dissent (New York).* [ISSN: 0012-3846] 1954. q. USD 34 (Individuals, USD 22). Ed(s): Mitchell Cohen, Michael Walzer. Foundation for the Study of Independent Social Ideas, Inc., 310 Riverside Dr, Ste 1201, New York, NY 10025; advertise@dissentmagazine.org; http://www.dissentmagazine.org. Illus., index, adv. Sample. Circ: 10000 Paid. Vol. ends: Fall (No. 4). Microform: PQC. Online: EBSCO Publishing; Gale Group; OCLC Online Computer Library Center, Inc.; ProQuest Information & Learning; SoftLine Information; H.W. Wilson. Reprint: PSC. *Indexed:* ABCPolSci, AltPI, BAS, BRI, CBRI, FLI, FutSurv, IPSA, LRI, PAIS, PSA, SSCI, SSI, SWR&A, SociolAb. *Bk. rev.:* 5, 2,000 words, signed. *Aud.:* Ga, Ac.

"A magazine of the left, *Dissent* is also a magazine of independent minds. A magazine of strong opinions, *Dissent* is also a magazine that welcomes the clash of strong opinions." This statement indicates the ideals for which *Dissent* strives, and for the most part these ideals are reached. The articles are structured to allow readers to draw their own conclusions. Opposing views are welcome and seem to make the argument for social democracy that much clearer. Most serials collections will benefit from the addition of this title.

The revamped web site offers an archive of selected full-text articles back to 1999. A search function is available, as is a complete index to the whole publishing run of the title back to 1954. This index gives complete citation information and, in the case of review items, gives the title and author of the reviewed work. The site also offers an online salon for discussion of *Dissent* articles.

The Economist. See Economics section.

Foreign Affairs. See Political Science/International Relations section.

5205. *The Gallup Poll Tuesday Briefing.* Former titles (until 2002): *Gallup Poll Monthly;* (until Dec. 1989): *Gallup Report; Gallup Opinion Index; Gallup Political Index.* [ISSN: 1542-8885] 1965. m. USD 149. Ed(s): Frank Newport. Gallup Organization, 901 F St., NW, Washington, DC 20004-1417; http://www.gallup.com. Illus., index, adv. Circ: 1300. Vol. ends: Dec. Online: Gale Group. *Indexed:* PAIS, RI-1. *Aud.:* Ac.

This is a monthly overview of the major polls conducted by the Gallup organization. This title contains valuable and current information for any library needing data on American attitudes and opinions. However, unless each issue is checked, a reader may have difficulty determining what topic is covered where.

The Gallup web site offers much the same poll data as the print source. However, the web site is text-heavy, which makes it a bit tricky to use. There is a simple keyword search, but it is not in an obvious place on the page. Although much of the content is freely accessible, the site now offers some content as subscription only; this includes Gallup's "Tuesday Briefings," which are the most current poll results. Libraries that do not have the budget to purchase the print version should feel confident in offering the online version to their patrons.

The Guardian. See Newspapers/General section.

5206. *Human Events: the national conservative weekly.* [ISSN: 0018-7194] 1944. w. USD 49.95. Ed(s): Thomas S Winter. Eagle Publishing, Inc., One Massachusetts Ave, N W, Washington, DC 20001; http://www.phillips.com. Illus., index, adv. Sample. Circ: 70000 Paid. Vol. ends: Dec. Microform: BHP; PQC; NRP. Online: Chadwyck-Healey Incorporated; EBSCO Publishing; Northern Light Technology, Inc.; ProQuest Information & Learning. Reprint: PQC. *Indexed:* BRI, CBRI. *Bk. rev.:* Various number and length, signed. *Aud.:* Ga, Ac.

Human Events "has not only defended conservative principles, but helped define them for the rest of the movement." Reporting from Washington puts this title in the heart of the action. Features like "Inside Washington," "Capital Briefs," and "Across America" keep readers up to date with political and legislative news both nationally and locally. Although its reporting of news is objective, its analysis is strongly partisan, with the "Hillary Watch" feature serving as ample evidence of its conservative viewpoint. Among regular contributors to this title is Ann Coulter, the publication's legal correspondent and well-known conservative author. This title does include media reviews, and it should be noted that each review includes an acceptability rating. *Human Events* should be considered an important contribution to the literature of the American Right.

The companion web site offers selected articles from the current issue, and table of contents information for the other articles in that issue. The site also has links to articles and commentary from other sources, a selection of "Special Reports." The archives go back to September 2000; as with the current issue, only selected articles are available full-text. There is a also a search option.

5207. *In These Times.* [ISSN: 0160-5992] 1976. bi-w. Individuals, USD 24.95. Ed(s): James Weinstein. Institute for Public Affairs, 2040 N Milwaukee Ave, 2nd Fl, Chicago, IL 60647-4002; itt@inthesetimes.com. Illus., adv. Circ: 20000. Vol. ends: Nov. Microform: PQC. Online: LexisNexis. Reprint: PQC. *Indexed:* AltPI, PAIS, PRA. *Bk. rev.:* Various number and length. *Aud.:* Ga, Ac.

In These Times "features award-winning investigative reporting about corporate malfeasance and government wrongdoing, insightful analysis of national and international affairs, and sharp cultural criticism about events and ideas that matter." The emphasis is on U.S. news and issues, although international topics are also covered. Some of the more entertaining features include the "Dear Mr. Vonnegut" column and the "Appall-o-meter." *In These Times* has been the recipient of several Project Censored (www.projectcensored.org) awards over the years for "covering news ignored by the mainstream media."

The web site offers articles from the current issue in their entirety, and also an online comment option. Current archived issues can be either browsed or searched. Older articles are searchable, but there is no indication of the date range of the archive.

5208. *Interview (New York).* Formerly (until 1989): *Andy Warhol's Interview.* [ISSN: 0149-8932] 1969. m. USD 14.97 domestic; USD 37.50 Canada; USD 45 elsewhere. Ed(s): Ingrid Sischy. Brant Publications, Inc., 575 Broadway, 5th Fl, New York, NY 10012. Illus., adv. Circ: 155803 Paid. Vol. ends: Dec (No. 12). Microform: PQC. Online: EBSCO Publishing; Gale Group. Reprint: PQC. *Indexed:* ASIP, FLI, IIFP, MRD, MagInd, RGPR. *Bk. rev.:* Various number and length. *Aud.:* Ga, Ac.

More akin to a fashion magazine than a news publication, *Interview* serves as a roadmap to American popular culture. The articles, interviews, and reviews tend to be short and punchy. The magazine is heavily illustrated, sometimes making it difficult to differentiate between the content and the advertisements. Libraries serving patrons with an interest in American popular culture should make an effort to acquire this title. For all others, this is a strictly optional title.

Le Monde Diplomatique. See Europe section.

5209. *Monthly Review: an independent socialist magazine.* [ISSN: 0027-0520] 1949. m. Jul.-Aug. comb. USD 48 (Individuals, USD 29). Ed(s): Robert W McChesney, John Bellamy Foster. Monthly Review Foundation, 122 W 27th St, 10th fl, New York, NY 10001; mrmag@monthlyreview.org; http://www.monthlyreview.org/. Illus., index, adv. Refereed. Circ: 6000 Paid. Vol. ends: Dec. Microform: PQC. Online: bigchalk; EBSCO Publishing; Florida Center for Library Automation; Gale Group; Northern Light Technology, Inc.; OCLC Online Computer Library Center, Inc.; ProQuest Information & Learning; H.W. Wilson. Reprint: PQC. *Indexed:* ABS&EES, AltPI, AmH&L, BAS, IBZ, MagInd, PAIS, PRA, PSA, RGPR, RRTA, SSCI, SSI, SociolAb, WAE&RSA. *Bk. rev.:* Various number and length, signed. *Aud.:* Ga, Ac.

This is a serious and respected magazine, one that seeks to "speak (sic) to workers and labor organizers no less than to academics, and against class exploitation, no less than against racial and sexual oppression." This goal leads to a publication that is more scholarly discourse than news periodical. Each issue contains four to six lengthy well-written articles, often from noteworthy contributors. Occasionally, there will be a single topical focus, as in a recent and rather unusual issue on "Cultures of the U.S. Left." Libraries seeking to expand their collections would do well to consider this title.

The web site offers the full text of each issue back to February 2001. Selected older full-text articles and "Notes from the Editors" are also available. The web site offers simple keyword searching.

Mother Jones. See General Editorial/General section.

5210. *The Nation.* [ISSN: 0027-8378] 1865. w. except the second week in Jan.; bi-w. in July & Aug. USD 52 domestic; USD 70 foreign; USD 2.75 newsstand/cover per issue. Ed(s): Katrina Vanden Heuvel. The Nation Company, L.P., 33 Irving Pl, 8th Fl, New York, NY 10003; info@thenation.com; http://www.thenation.com. Illus., index, adv. Sample. Circ: 97213. Vol. ends: Jun/Dec. CD-ROM: ProQuest Information & Learning. Microform: PMC; PQC. Online: bigchalk; EBSCO Publishing; Factiva; Florida Center for Library Automation; Gale Group; LexisNexis; Northern Light Technology, Inc.; OCLC Online Computer Library Center, Inc.; ProQuest Information & Learning; H.W. Wilson. Reprint: PQC. *Indexed:* ABS&EES, AgeL, AltPI, ArtHuCI, BRD, BRI, CBRI, FLI, FutSurv, IAPV, LRI, MRD, MagInd, PAIS, PRA, RGPR, SSCI. *Bk. rev.:* 4, 1,000 words, signed. *Aud.:* Ga, Ac.

Proud of being "a wholly owned subsidiary of our own conscience" rather than a publication from a media conglomerate, *The Nation* is one of the most openly left-wing publications in existence. That does not mean that it will not criticize where criticism may be due, including its partisans and fellow left-leaning publications, though naturally its best shots tend to be aimed at its ideological opposites. The writing is crisp and concise, a joy to read. The multiple short editorials at the beginning of each issue cover a wide range of topics, from the recent developments in cloning to the status of the publishing industry. One enjoyable feature for individual subscribers, which may be a bit of a problem for libraries, is the crossword puzzle included in each issue. *The Nation* is a valuable resource for any library.

Its companion web site offers a portion of the articles from the current issue; many of these full-text articles also have links for background and related information. The site also features web-only articles and blogs. Selected articles from 1999 to the present are freely accessible. There is a fully searchable historical archive of *The Nation* with all the articles ever published available. Contact the publisher for further information.

National Journal. See Political Science/Comparative and American Politics section.

5211. *National Review: a journal of fact and opinion.* [ISSN: 0028-0038] 1955. bi-w. USD 59 domestic; USD 80.50 foreign; USD 3.95 newsstand/cover per issue. Ed(s): Rich Lowry. National Review, Inc., 215 Lexington Ave, New York, NY 10016; nronline@nationalreview.com; http://www.nationalreview.com/. Illus., index, adv. Circ: 15664 Paid. Vol. ends: No. 25. CD-ROM: ProQuest Information & Learning. Microform: NBI; PQC. Online: bigchalk; The Dialog Corporation; EBSCO Publishing; Florida Center for Library Automation; Gale Group; LexisNexis; Northern Light Technology, Inc.; OCLC Online Computer Library Center, Inc.; ProQuest Information & Learning; H.W. Wilson. Reprint: PQC. *Indexed:* ABS&EES, AgeL, BAS, BRD, BRI, CBRI, FLI, FutSurv, LRI, MRD, MagInd, RGPR, RI-1. *Bk. rev.:* 4, 1,000 words, signed. *Aud.:* Ga, Ac.

National Review remains happily conservative, although it will occasionally strike at its own, as in David Frum's recent article about "Unpatriotic Conservatives." That kind of rare surprise aside, *National Review* maintains the verve and sting that have long been its hallmarks and continues to take the left to task in numerous articles. In addition to pointedly right-wing editorials, each issue features a number of short articles on items of current interest, a longer feature article, and reviews of the arts. There are also numerous political cartoons scattered throughout. This title should be considered a necessity in academic and public libraries.

The companion web site *National Review Online* is more of a stand-alone operation with excellent content and unique features, such as "Word of the Day" and "The Corner," a combination of a news highlights service and quick commentary site. From the print publication, the web site merely offers abstracts to the articles in the current issue.

5212. *The New American (Appleton).* Formed by the merger of (1958-1985): *American Opinion;* (1965-1985): *Review of the News.* [ISSN: 0885-6540] 1985. bi-w. USD 39; USD 2.95 newsstand/cover per issue domestic; USD 3.95 newsstand/cover per issue Canada. Ed(s): Gary Benoit. American Opinion Publishing Inc., PO Box 8040, Appleton, WI 54912. Illus. Sample. Circ: 50000 Paid. Vol. ends: Dec. Microform: PQC. Online: Gale Group; ProQuest Information & Learning. Reprint: PQC. *Bk. rev.:* Various number and length, signed. *Aud.:* Ga, Ac.

The New American presents a mixture of news and commentary from a decidedly right-wing, fundamentalist Christian perspective, not unexpected from a title published by a subsidiary of the John Birch Society. A goal of this publication is to expose the behind-the-scenes forces shaping American politics and culture. This apparently includes taking on those who would appear to be on the same side, such as Fox News and the Bush administration. This title should be considered for libraries that need to balance out their collection with more right-wing resources.

The companion web site features selected articles and the table of contents from the current issue. Special online "departments" include "The Right Answers" and "Worth Repeating." Available full text of back issues is limited, but you can purchase back issues of the print title or a CD-ROM that includes full text of issues from 1985 to 2001. The site has search capabilities and a subject index to articles available online.

New Criterion. See Art/General section.

5213. *The New Leader: a bi-monthly of news and opinion.* [ISSN: 0028-6044] 1927. bi-m. USD 42. Ed(s): Myron Kolatch. American Labor Conference on International Affairs, Inc., 275 Seventh Ave, New York, NY 10001. Illus., index, adv. Sample. Circ: 25000. Vol. ends: Dec. Microform: PQC; NRP. Online: bigchalk; The Dialog Corporation; EBSCO Publishing; Florida Center for Library Automation; Gale Group; Northern Light Technology, Inc.; OCLC Online Computer Library Center, Inc.; ProQuest Information & Learning; H.W. Wilson. Reprint: PQC. *Indexed:* ABS&EES, BEL&L, BRD, BRI, CBRI, FLI, LRI, MRD, MagInd, PAIS, RGPR. *Bk. rev.:* 3-4, 1,200-1,500 words, signed. *Aud.:* Ga, Ac.

Now in its eightieth year of publication, *New Leader* has outlasted many short-lived publications like *George.* Although featuring respected voices such as National Public Radio's Daniel Schorr, the news and opinion sections take a back seat to the detailed and always entertaining literature and culture sections. The bimonthly publication schedule plays a role in making *New Leader*'s news and opinion pages less than timely. Still, it is a strong publication, but not one of primary importance for most libraries.

5214. *New Perspectives Quarterly.* Formerly (until 1988): *Center for the Study of Democratic Institutions. Center Magazine.* [ISSN: 0893-7850] 1967. 4x/yr. USD 277 print & online eds. Ed(s): Nathan Gardels. Blackwell Publishing, Inc., Commerce Place, 350 Main St, Malden, MA 02148; subscrip@blackwellpub.com; http://www.blackwellpublishing.com. Illus., adv. Sample. Refereed. Circ: 15000. Vol. ends: No. 5. Microform: PQC. Online: bigchalk; EBSCO Publishing; Gale Group; ingenta.com; Northern Light Technology, Inc.; OCLC Online Computer Library Center, Inc.; RoweCom Information Quest; Swets Blackwell; H.W. Wilson. *Indexed:* ABS&EES, BAS, IBZ, MagInd, PAIS, RGPR, SSI. *Bk. rev.:* Various number and length. *Aud.:* Hs, Ga, Ac.

NPQ, as this journal is familiarly known, publishes in each issue a selection of articles relating to a central theme. They are are drawn from numerous viewpoints and present many sides of the same issue. These diverse points of view, often from internationally recognizable figures such as Jimmy Carter, are an excellent basis for informed classroom discussion. In addition to themed sections, typically three per issue of varying lengths, *NPQ* also contains shorter articles on world news, culture, literature, and philosophy. Occasionally, it also includes a question-and-answer interview with a notable person. This stimulating and enlightening periodical would be a worthwhile purchase for any library.

There is now a companion web site at http://www.digitalnpq.org. Full-text articles from the current print issue and a limited selection of older articles are available. The "Global Viewpoint" column is also found on the web site.

5215. *The New Republic: a journal of politics and the arts.* [ISSN: 0028-6583] 1914. w. 48/yr., in 2 vols. USD 79.97 domestic; USD 99.97 Canada; USD 119.97 foreign. Ed(s): Peter Beinart. New Republic, 1331 H St NW, Ste 700, Washington, DC 20005-4737; tnr@aol.com; http://www.thenewrepublic.com. Illus., index, adv. Circ: 95260 Paid. Vol. ends: Jun/Dec. CD-ROM: ProQuest Information & Learning. Microform: NBI; PMC; PQC. Online: The Dialog Corporation; EBSCO Publishing; Florida Center for Library Automation; Gale Group; LexisNexis; Northern Light Technology, Inc.; OCLC Online Computer Library Center, Inc.; ProQuest Information & Learning; H.W. Wilson. Reprint: PQC. *Indexed:* ABIn, AgeL, ArtHuCI, BAS, BEL&L, BRD, BRI, BiogInd, CBRI, CPerI, EnvAb, FLI, FutSurv, IAPV, LRI, MRD, MagInd, PRA, RGPR, RI-1, SSCI. *Bk. rev.:* Various number and length. *Aud.:* Ga, Ac.

The New Republic has had found its niche as an inside-the-Beltway publication and is in a position to "cover issues before they hit the mainstream." The articles are readable and to the point. Although some might deplore the lack of partisan fervor in this publication, its evenhanded coverage of the issues confronting the United States has gained it "the loyalty of influential readers on all points of the political spectrum." Its neutrality of opinion should be considered a positive attribute by libraries seeking a balanced collection.

The companion web site offers a mix of articles on politics and the arts. Abstracts of selected articles from the current print issue are available; the complete article is available to subscribers of the print version for free or with a subscription to *The New Republic Digital.* Letters to the editor from both the print and online versions are accessible without charge. One of the more interesting attributes of the site is the "Media Kit" section, which offers the demographics of both its online users and print subscribers.

5216. *New Statesman.* Formerly (until 1996): *New Statesman & Society;* Which was formed by the 1988 merger of: *New Statesman;* (1962-1988): *New Society.* [ISSN: 1364-7431] 1988. w. GBP 136 (Individuals, GBP 62). Ed(s): Peter Wilby. New Statesman Ltd., 7th Fl Victoria Station House, 191 Victoria St, London, SW1E 5NE, United Kingdom; sbrasher@newstatesman.co.uk; http://www.newstatesman.co.uk. Illus., index, adv. Circ: 21000. Vol. ends: Jun/Dec. Microform: PMC; PQC.

Online: bigchalk; EBSCO Publishing; Florida Center for Library Automation; Gale Group; Northern Light Technology, Inc.; OCLC Online Computer Library Center, Inc.; ProQuest Information & Learning; H.W. Wilson. *Indexed:* BRD, BRI, BrHumI, CBRI, FLI, LRI, MRD, MagInd, MusicInd, SSCI, SSI, SWA. *Bk. rev.:* 8, 750 words, signed. *Aud.:* Ga, Ac.

Proclaiming itself "Britain's premier current affairs magazine," *New Statesman* continues to be an interesting and lively read. The publication is split approximately 60/40 in favor of news and politics, with the focus, naturally, on those issues of greatest interest in the United Kingdom. The "back half" has columns on food, drink, the Internet, and the media. As a source of British news and thought, this title is a worthwhile selection for larger public libraries and academic libraries. Libraries that carry *The Spectator* should subscribe to this title as well.

The accompanying web site offers some freely accessible content. Most of the material on the site is available for a fee, including archived articles back to 1995. Subscribers to the print version have free access to current content; it appears that archival content is fee-based for all.

5217. ***Newsweek.*** [ISSN: 0028-9604] 1933. w. USD 42.66 United States; MXP 995 Mexico. Ed(s): Richard M. Smith, Dorothy Kalins. Newsweek, Inc., 251 W 57th St, New York, NY 10019-1894; customer.care@newsweek.com. Illus., index, adv. Circ: 3100000. Vol. ends: Jun. Microform: NBI; PMC; PQC. Online: bigchalk; EBSCO Publishing; Factiva; Florida Center for Library Automation; Gale Group; LexisNexis; ProQuest Information & Learning; H.W. Wilson. Reprint: PQC. *Indexed:* ABIn, AgeL, BHA, BLI, BRD, BRI, BiogInd, BiolDig, CBCARef, CBRI, CINAHL, CPerI, EnvAb, FLI, FutSurv, IDP, IIPA, LRI, MRD, MagInd, MusicInd, RGPR. *Bk. rev.:* 2-5, 500-1,300 words, signed. *Aud.:* Hs, Ga, Ac.

Newsweek is one of the three major newsweeklies to which nearly every library, public or academic, typically subscribes. For readers, the choice between *Newsweek, Time,* and *U.S. News & World Report* is largely one of personal preference. These three publications are similar in format and content (frequently all three will have the same topic as their cover story). Which *Newsweek* features are unique? The "Perspectives" page, full of humorous quotes and editorial cartoons that trigger smiles and thought, is one of a kind. Another unique feature is "Conventional Wisdom," which looks at trends or topics in the news and gives them a thumbs up or down. All in all, *Newsweek* remains an excellent publication from cover to cover, and it should be considered a standard source by all libraries.

The *Newsweek* web site is now a partnership venture with MSNBC.com, which means the content from that site is available as well. The content of the current issue is online in full-text; older issues are archived. "The Newsweek Archives contain most of the stories from the domestic edition since January 1993, most stories from the international editions since January 1999, and all Web Exclusives since June 2000." Searching the archives is free, but retrieving the full texts online is a for-fee proposition.

5218. ***People.*** Formerly: *People (New York).* [ISSN: 0093-7673] 1974. w. USD 113.88. Ed(s): Martha Nelson. Time, Inc, Time & Life Bldg, Rockefeller Center, 1271 Ave of the Americas, New York, NY 10020-1393; http://www.people.com/. Illus., adv. Circ: 3250000 Paid. Vol. ends: Jun/Dec. Microform: PQC. Online: America Online, Inc.; bigchalk; EBSCO Publishing; Factiva; Florida Center for Library Automation; Gale Group; LexisNexis; MediaStream, Inc.; OCLC Online Computer Library Center, Inc.; ProQuest Information & Learning; H.W. Wilson. *Indexed:* BRI, CBRI, CPerI, MagInd, RGPR. *Bk. rev.:* 5-7, 150-250 words. *Aud.:* Ga.

Although included in this section, *People* just barely qualifies as a news publication. It offers news of the entertainment world as well as occasional stories about "real" folks. It is a entertaining read, light and fun. Libraries looking to add to their leisure collection should definitely have this title.

The companion web site is jam packed and a bit difficult to navigate. The open access resources on the site are limited to the table of contents of the most current issue and links to web sites offering additional information related to *People* magazine stories. The rest of the content of the web site is subscriber-only; AOL users and subscribers to the magazine have access; individuals who buy copies at the newsstand can gain temporary access.

5219. ***The Progressive (Madison).*** [ISSN: 0033-0736] 1909. m. USD 50 (Individuals, USD 32; USD 58 foreign). Ed(s): Matthew Rothschild. The Progressive, Inc., 409 E Main St, Madison, WI 53703; circ@progressive.org; http://www.progressive.org. Illus., index, adv. Sample. Circ: 30000 Paid. Microform: PQC. Online: bigchalk; EBSCO Publishing; Florida Center for Library Automation; Gale Group; OCLC Online Computer Library Center, Inc.; ProQuest Information & Learning; H.W. Wilson. Reprint: PQC. *Indexed:* ABS&EES, AgeL, AltPI, BAS, BRI, CBRI, FutSurv, LRI, MRD, MagInd, PAIS, PRA, RGPR. *Bk. rev.:* 2, 1,200 words, signed. *Aud.:* Ga, Ac.

The Progressive strives to be a "journalistic voice for peace and social justice at home and abroad." The emphasis is on investigative reporting and the analysis of and commentary on political, economic, and social issues, as well as on culture and the arts. The articles and columns often mix humor with their insights. The statement "not afraid to take a stand, and not afraid to have a little fun" fits this publication. It is an excellent resource for those wanting to dig a little deeper into a topic.

The companion web site offers "This Just In: *The Progressive* Editor's online commentaries," an archive of online articles from 1998 to the present, and a selection of "notable" articles from the print version.

5220. ***The Public Interest.*** [ISSN: 0033-3557] 1965. q. Individuals, USD 25. Ed(s): Adam Wolfson. The National Interest, Inc., 1112 16th St, N W, Ste 530, Washington, DC 20036. Illus., adv. Sample. Refereed. Circ: 6000. Vol. ends: Summer. Microform: PQC. Online: Chadwyck-Healey Incorporated; EBSCO Publishing; Florida Center for Library Automation; Gale Group; Northern Light Technology, Inc.; OCLC Online Computer Library Center, Inc.; ProQuest Information & Learning; H.W. Wilson. *Indexed:* ABCPolSci, ABIn, AIAP, AgeL, AmH&L, ArtHuCI, BAS, BPI, BRI, CBRI, CIJE, CJA, EIP, FutSurv, IBSS, IPSA, LRI, MCR, PAIS, PMA, PRA, PSA, RGPR, RI-1, SFSA, SSCI, SSI, SUSA, SWR&A, SociolAb. *Bk. rev.:* Various number and length, signed. *Aud.:* Ga, Ac.

The founding mission of *The Public Interest* can be summed up as "making a difference." The magazine meets this goal by offering serious and lengthy pieces by scholars and researchers, the type of articles that inform without indoctrinating. Among the issues it focuses on are domestic policy, particularly education, welfare, housing, poverty, politics, and culture. This is the type of resource college students writing papers should be using to support their arguments. The articles typically provide answers and provoke new questions. This title should be strongly considered for all institutions supporting undergraduate studies.

The web site features a sampling of articles from the most recent two issues and a listing of what can be found in the print version. The archive goes back to fall 1999. Each archived issue includes a table of contents and the full texts of three selected articles. The site offers no search capability.

5221. ***Public Opinion Quarterly: journal of the American Association for Public Opinion Research.*** [ISSN: 0033-362X] 1937. q. GBP 86. Ed(s): Katherine Jackson, Peter V Miller. Oxford University Press, Great Clarendon St, Oxford, OX2 6DP, United Kingdom; jnl.orders@oup.co.uk; http://www3.oup.co.uk/jnls. Illus., index, adv. Refereed. Vol. ends: Winter. Microform: CIS; PQC. Online: EBSCO Publishing; Florida Center for Library Automation; Gale Group; JSTOR (Web-based Journal Archive); ProQuest Information & Learning. Reprint: PQC; PSC. *Indexed:* ABCPolSci, ABIn, ABS&EES, ATI, AgeL, AmH&L, BAS, BRI, CBRI, CJA, CommAb, IBSS, IPSA, MagInd, PAIS, PRA, PSA, PsycholAb, SSCI, SSI, SociolAb. *Bk. rev.:* Various number and length. *Aud.:* Ac, Sa.

"*Public Opinion Quarterly* is hospitable to all points of view, provided only that they help to illuminate problems of public opinion and communication." Most of this title is devoted to scholarly articles analyzing trends and problems in public opinion research. These articles can provide valuable information on methodologies employed, but they may be too scholarly and detailed for the general reader. The section that is most accessible is "Trends," which includes an overview of a topic and the data from several different polls relating to that topic. Only libraries supporting researchers in public opinion studies, communication studies, and similar areas must have this title; other libraries can survive without it.

The web site now offers subscribers access to complete issues back to winter 1996; the site has a list of institutions currently registered to access the electronic edition. Older issues are available as part of a subscription to JSTOR (www.jstor.org). It is now possible to search the available issues back to winter 1996, and to search titles and authors of back issues available from JSTOR. A most important aspect of the web site is the "Notice to Contributors," which lists the manuscript submission requirements for this publication. The site also has a listing of the journal's editorial board, subscription information, and information about getting permission for reprints.

Reason. See Civil Liberties/Political-Economic Rights section.

5222. *The Responsive Community: rights and responsibilities.* [ISSN: 1053-0754] 1991. q. USD 70 (Individuals, USD 27). Ed(s): Amitai Etzioni. The George Washington University, The Institute for Communitarian Policy Studies, 2130 H St, N W, Ste 703, Washington, DC 20052; comnet@gwu.edu; http://www.gwu.edu/~ccps. Illus., adv. Sample. Circ: 2000 Paid and free. Vol. ends: No. 4. *Indexed:* PAIS, PSA, SSCI, SociolAb. *Bk. rev.:* Various number and length. *Aud.:* Ga, Ac.

Responsive Community explores the relationships between individual rights and community responsibilities through the investigation of relevant social, ethical, philosophical, and moral issues. "This new responsive communitarian philosophy articulates a middle way between the politics of radical individualism and excessive statism." In voicing this philosophy, *Responsive Community* takes on any and all individuals and groups that oppose it. This title features an impressive range of contributors, from Senator John McCain to David Blunkett, Home Secretary of the United Kingdom, to Scott Simon, host of National Public Radio's "Weekend Edition." Included in each issue are "The Community's Pulse," brief survey results on various issues, and "Libertarians, Authoritarians, Communtarians," which presents brief commentaries reflecting each of these perspectives. This quarterly expresses a unique viewpoint. Libraries should strongly consider adding it to their collections.

The web site offers tables of contents for the complete run of issues from 1990 to the present. A very small number of the articles from the most recent issues are available in full-text. The site also links to the Communtarian Network web site.

Social Policy. See Sociology and Social Work/General section.

5223. *The Spectator.* [ISSN: 0038-6952] 1828. w. GBP 105 domestic; GBP 127 in Europe; GBP 131 Canada. Ed(s): Boris Johnson. The Spectator (1828) Ltd., 56 Doughty St, London, WC1N 2LL, United Kingdom; editor@spectator.co.uk; http://www.spectator.co.uk. Illus., index, adv. Circ: 46400. Microform: PMC; PQC. Online: bigchalk; Florida Center for Library Automation; Gale Group; Northern Light Technology, Inc.; OCLC Online Computer Library Center, Inc.; ProQuest Information & Learning. Reprint: PQC. *Indexed:* ABS&EES, BRI, CBRI. *Bk. rev.:* Various number and length, signed. *Aud.:* Ga, Ac.

The Spectator claims that "there is no party line to which our writers are bound—originality of thought and elegance of expression are the sole editorial constraints." It is a slightly more conservative counterpart to *New Statesman.* This title covers British news and culture with writing is crisp, sharp, and full of British wit and expression. As with *New Statesman,* this publication is split between news and culture. Numerous editorial cartoons are a notable feature of each issue, some universally understandable, some definitely British. As with the major U.S. newsweeklies, the choice between *The Spectator* and *New Statesman* is definitely a matter of personal and political preference. Libraries that have one of these titles should definitely have the other as well.

The web site offers selected articles and features from the print version. Complete full-text archives arranged by issue go back to September 2000. The archives do include the wonderful editorial cartoons, which are located by a link in the listing for each issue.

5224. *Tikkun Magazine: a bi-monthly Jewish critique of politics, culture and society.* [ISSN: 0887-9982] 1986. bi-m. USD 29 domestic; USD 39 in Canada & Mexico; USD 43 elsewhere. Ed(s): Michael Lerner. Institute for Labor & Mental Health, 2107 Van Ness Ave, Ste 302, San Francisco, CA 94109-2571; magazine@tikkun.org; http://www.tikkun.org. Illus., adv. Sample. Circ: 40000. Vol. ends: Nov/Dec. Online: EBSCO Publishing; Florida Center for Library Automation; Gale Group; LexisNexis; OCLC Online Computer Library Center, Inc.; ProQuest Information & Learning; SoftLine Information; H.W. Wilson. *Indexed:* ABS&EES, AltPI, BRI, CBRI, HumInd, IJP, MagInd, RI-1. *Bk. rev.:* Various number and length. *Aud.:* Ga, Ac.

Tikkun exists "as the liberal alternative to the voices of Jewish conservatism and spiritual deadness in the Jewish world and as the spiritual alternative to the voices of materialism and selfishness in Western society." The resulting publication is a stimulating compilation of articles, poetry, fiction, and discussion of contemporary Jewish concerns. Unafraid of controversy, the magazine often take stands that are unusual within the Jewish community, as on the issue of Palestinian rights. One of the most noteworthy characteristics of this title is the point-counterpoint nature of some articles. The spirituality of this publication is clear in its tone and its special features, such as the special supplements for religious holidays. *Tikkun* should be considered for most collections because it represents a unique voice for Jewish concerns.

The web site offers selections from the current issue and a searchable archive of articles for which it holds copyright back to September-October 1998 (because of the copyright issue, the poetry selections are typically not available online). Additional back issues are planned. The supplements to the print version are also available in pdf format. The "Media Critique" section allows members of the "*Tikkun* Community" the opportunity to add their voice to critiques regarding "misleading" stories from other media sources.

5225. *Time.* [ISSN: 0040-781X] 1923. w. USD 24.95 domestic; USD 3.95 newsstand/cover per issue. Time, Inc, Time & Life Bldg, Rockefeller Center, 1271 Ave of the Americas, New York, NY 10020-1393; http://www.time.com/time/. Illus., index, adv. Circ: 4122699 Paid. Vol. ends: Jun. CD-ROM: ProQuest Information & Learning. Microform: PQC. Online: bigchalk; Dow Jones Interactive; EBSCO Publishing; Factiva; Florida Center for Library Automation; Gale Group; LexisNexis; MediaStream, Inc.; OCLC Online Computer Library Center, Inc.; ProQuest Information & Learning; H.W. Wilson. *Indexed:* ABIn, AgeL, BEL&L, BLI, BRD, BRI, BiogInd, BiolDig, CBRI, CINAHL, CPerI, EnvAb, FLI, FutSurv, IDP, IIPA, LRI, MRD, MagInd, RGPR, RI-1. *Bk. rev.:* Various number and length, signed. *Aud.:* Hs, Ga, Ac.

Selecting among the three major U.S. newsweeklies is largely a matter of personal preference. *Time* continues to tweak its appearance, and occasionally one wonders where the news in this newsmagazine went. Special features, such as its recent anniversary issue that featured "80 Days that Changed the World," add value and interest. The "Your Time" section at the back of the magazine includes often useful and enlightening information on health, family, technology, and money. *Time* remains a publication to which all libraries should subscribe.

The *Time* web site provides searchable archives of the U.S. edition back to 1985, as well as *Time Asia*, *Time Europe*, and the spinoff publication *On.* Searching is free, but articles older than two weeks are only available for a fee. In addition to a flat per-article fee, Time.com offers a 24-hour pass and a 30-day pass. There is an archive of the magazine's covers. Frequently searched topics are collected in a "Hot Topics" section to aid research. There is also a selection of "Newsfiles" that are "single-topic collections of content on issues, events and people that are most often searched for on Time.com." Both "Hot Topics" and "Newsfiles" contain a mix of free and premium content.

5226. *U S A Today (Valley Stream).* Former titles (until 1978): *Intellect; School and Society.* [ISSN: 0161-7389] 1915. m. USD 29 domestic; USD 35 Canada; USD 9.50 newsstand/cover per issue. Ed(s): Robert Rothenberg. S A E Inc., 99 W Hawthorne Ave, Ste 518, Valley Stream, NY 11580-6101. Illus., index, adv. Circ: 257000. Microform: PMC; PQC. Online: The Dialog Corporation; EBSCO Publishing; Florida Center for Library Automation; Gale Group; MediaStream, Inc.; OCLC Online Computer Library Center, Inc.; ProQuest Information & Learning; H.W. Wilson. Reprint: PQC. *Indexed:* ABS&EES, BRI, BiolDig, CBRI, CIJE, EduInd, FLI, HEA, LRI, MagInd, NewsAb, RGPR, SSCI, WSA. *Bk. rev.:* 2-4, 200-750 words, signed. *Aud.:* Ga, Ac.

A very different type of publication than the Gannett newspaper of the same name, *U.S.A. Today* is a monthly newsmagazine with a format similar to *Time* or *Newsweek.* Even with an editorial board largely comprised of faculty members and researchers, the content of *U.S.A. Today* is not that different from its more mainstream counterparts in that it publishes a mixture of information on many different topics. Although this cornucopia of subject matter can seem overwhelming at first, many useful and entertaining facts can be gleaned once the reader learns how to proceed. A broad spectrum of contributors results in an evenhanded examination of the issues. Because it is a monthly, its strength lies in its analysis of events rather than in providing breaking news. In addition to its regular issues, *U.S.A. Today* publishes special newsletters on various subjects.

5227. *U S News & World Report.* [ISSN: 0041-5537] 1933. w. USD 24.97 domestic; USD 51.64 Canada; USD 3 newsstand/cover per issue. Ed(s): Stephen G Smith. U S News & World Report Inc., 1050 Thomas Jefferson St, NW, Washington, DC 20007; letters@usnews.com; http://www.usnews.com. Illus., adv. Circ: 2195668 Paid. Vol. ends: Jun. Online: bigchalk; The Dialog Corporation; EBSCO Publishing; Factiva; Florida Center for Library Automation; Gale Group; LexisNexis; OCLC Online Computer Library Center, Inc.; ProQuest Information & Learning; H.W. Wilson. *Indexed:* AgeL, CBCARef, CINAHL, CPerI, EnvAb, FutSurv, GeoRef, LRI, MagInd, PAIS, RGPR, RI-1. *Aud.:* Hs, Ga, Ac.

Although *U.S. News & World Report* has the smallest circulation of the three major newsweeklies, it tends to be more highly regarded than the other two. Considered to be more objective and reliable than *Time* or *Newsweek, U.S. News* is also regarded as being slightly more conservative. This perception is not wholly inaccurate, but the editors do believe in calling them as they see them, sometimes resulting in unexpected opinions. *U.S. News* is written more for the person interested in serious reporting and thoughtful discussion; unlike the other two, the question of what happened to the news is never asked about this title. The "Washington Whispers" column provides an amusing and often insightful glimpse behind the scenes in the nation's capital. The positive attributes of this publication make it an excellent choice for all libraries.

The web site offers archives back to 1992. Searching is free, but there is a fee for any article older than two weeks. The very popular college rankings are available on this site as well, however the full version is now premium content (a teaser version is available for free).

5228. *Us Weekly.* Formerly (until 2000): *Us.* [ISSN: 1529-7497] 1977. w. USD 65 domestic; USD 75 Canada; USD 99 elsewhere. Ed(s): Jack Wright. Us Weekly L L C, 1290 Ave of the Americas, New York, NY 10104-0298; letters@usmagazine.com. Illus., adv. Circ: 800000 Paid. Microform: PQC. Online: ProQuest Information & Learning. *Indexed:* ASIP. *Aud.:* Ga.

Similar to *People, Us Weekly* also focuses on news of the entertainment world. Where *People* seems to be a bit breezy, *Us Weekly* takes its role as entertainment reporter more seriously. Articles on "real" people or current issues outside of the entertainment world will not be found here. This is not to say that this is a dry or boring read; no publication with a regular feature called "Fashion Police" could be. A good title for leisure reading or popular culture collections.

There is a companion web site for information about the magazine. One useful feature of the site is the ability to search through the back issues of the magazine (back to February 1999). However, the content of those issues is not available online.

5229. *The Washington Monthly.* [ISSN: 0043-0633] 1969. 10x/yr. USD 29.95 domestic; USD 39.95 foreign. Ed(s): Paul Glastris. Washington Monthly LLC, 733 15th St, Washington, DC 2005; editors@washingtonmonthly.com; http://www.washingtonmonthly.com. Illus., adv. Sample. Circ: 33000. Vol. ends: Feb. Microform: PQC. Online: The Dialog Corporation; EBSCO Publishing; Florida Center for Library Automation; Gale Group; Northern Light Technology, Inc.; OCLC Online Computer Library Center, Inc.; ProQuest Information & Learning; H.W. Wilson. *Indexed:* AgeL, BRI, CBRI, FutSurv, IPSA, LRI, MagInd, PAIS, RGPR, RI-1, SSI. *Bk. rev.:* Various number and length, signed. *Aud.:* Ga, Ac.

"*The Monthly,*" as its devotees call it, is "journalism that isn't afraid to shake some sense into the system." This remains a wonderful, witty, and fearless publication that will take on "sacred cows" on both sides without indulging in "tired partisan debate." Articles are well written, entertaining, and supported by logic that critics often find difficult to refute. The sly, irreverent tone is a large part of this publication's attraction; one might not agree with the viewpoint, but it is fun to read. This is a journal that deserves a home in every library.

The Washington Monthly Online provides frequently updated news and opinion from the editors, regular columns like "Tilting at Windmills," selected articles from the current issue, and a features archive with selected articles from past issues.

5230. *The Weekly Standard.* [ISSN: 1083-3013] 1995. 48x/yr. USD 78 domestic; USD 114 foreign; USD 3.95 newsstand/cover per issue. Ed(s): William Kristol. News America Incorporated, 1211 Ave. of the Americas, New York, NY 10036. Illus., adv. Circ: 60000. Vol. ends: Sep. Online: LexisNexis; ProQuest Information & Learning. *Indexed:* PAIS, RGPR. *Bk. rev.:* Various number and length, signed. *Aud.:* Ga, Ac.

A conservative publication, *The Weekly Standard* invites you to "join the vast right-wing conspiracy" by subscribing. The typical issue covers politics and government but ventures into other areas as well. Its "Parody" section is not to be missed; anyone or anything from *The New York Times* to the "Today" show to French military history are ripe to be skewered. As a weekly, this would be a good choice for collections that do not have *Human Events* and wish to supplement *National Review.*

The freely available portion of the web site is called "Daily Events." Much of the content is available only to subscribers. Subscribers to the print version also get access to the complete contents of the site.

World Policy Journal. See Political Science/International Relations section.

5231. *Z Magazine.* Formerly: *Zeta Magazine.* [ISSN: 1056-5507] 1988. m. USD 40 (Individuals, USD 30). Ed(s): Lydia Sargent, Eric Sargent. ZCommunications, 18 Millfield St, Woods Hole, MA 02543; lydia.sargent@zmag.org; http://www.zmag.org. Illus. Sample. Circ: 26000. Vol. ends: Dec. *Indexed:* AltPI, PAIS. *Bk. rev.:* Various number and length. *Aud.:* Ga, Ac.

Z Magazine is "dedicated to resisting injustice, defending against repression, and creating liberty. It sees the racial, gender, class, and political dimensions of personal life as fundamental to understanding and improving contemporary circumstances; and it aims to assist activist efforts for a better future." Lofty goals for a magazine, but ones definitely reflected in its content and character. Authors often use humor to make their points, and the publication typically features several pointed political cartoons. *Z Magazine* offers a number of standing subsections in its "Commentary" section, including "Conservative Watch," "Reproductive Rights," and "Gay and Lesbian Notes." On the whole, this should be a welcome addition to any library's collection.

The *Z Magazine* web site offers the full texts of issues back to January 1997. The archive can be searched by author or topic.

Electronic Journals

These electronic resources provide news, but they are not set up as "serials." They are updated frequently throughout the day, often have video and sound clips, and tend not to be archived.

CNN Interactive. CNN Network. www.cnn.com.

FoxNews. Fox News Network. www.foxnews.com.

MSNBC. NBC Network and Microsoft Corporation. www.msnbc.com/news.

NPR News Now. National Public Radio. www.npr.org/news.

5232. *ForeignWire.com.* Incorporates: *Tower Magazine.* 1996. w. Ed(s): Harvey Morris. ForeignWire.com, 5 Admirals Court, London, SE1 2LJ, United Kingdom. *Aud.:* Hs, Ga, Ac.

This web site offers English-language news and analysis from around the world. Features include top stories, additional daily headlines from countries and regions, and in-depth analysis of selected issues. A service offering update by e-mail is available. There is an extremely limited archive, arranged by country; none of the included articles is more recent than 2001. Although more of a newspaper site, this is still a good tool for locating news stories that might not otherwise be easily accessible.

Slate. See General Editorial-Internet section.

■ NEWSPAPERS

General/Newspaper Indexes/Web-based Newspapers/Commercial Web News Systems

See also newspapers in other sections (CIS, Europe, etc.) and check the index for specific titles not included here.

Jim Ronningen, Associate Librarian, Social Sciences, 218 Doe Library, University of California, Berkeley, CA 94720-6000; jronning@ library.berkeley.edu; FAX 510-642-6830

Introduction

For those of us with the newspaper habit, the nagging question has been "How much longer?"—that is, how much longer can we leaf through sheets of paper in the morning instead of having to go online. The good news is that, at least for major newspapers that dominate their markets, there are no compelling reasons to stop printing in the foreseeable future, though papers with smaller subscriber bases continue to be in danger of failing or getting swallowed up. The bad news for print addicts is that, although the basic news content will appear in both print and web editions of a newspaper, a lot of interesting new initiatives from editorial staffs (that includes all of the reporters and other writers, not just editors) appear only on the web sites. It's important to know what your library users may be missing by sticking to print only; more on that in the section titled "Web-Based Newspapers."

Depending upon which financial quarter you look at, there's certainly recent evidence of profitability for the major chains; however, the general financial picture for newspaper publishing over the past few years reflects the nation's dismal economy. The symptoms of recession were exacerbated by the chilling effects of the Iraq War on advertising expenditures. For newspapers, advertising is a much more important source of revenue than subscriptions or single-copy purchases. A *Financial Times* article of April 8, 2003 describes the trend in lower-than-expected earnings for newspaper and other media companies due to drops in ad space sold. And to make matters worse, the cost of newsprint was likely to go up significantly after years of price cuts gave publishers a breather. Analyst reports were predicting a 5–6 percent newsprint price increase in spring 2003 (Merrill Lynch "FlashNote," January 24, 2003).

Of course, bigger players are generally better able to absorb these hits. Depending upon how leery you are of corporate consolidation, the concentration of power at the top may be better or worse than you'd feared: There are hundreds of publishers competing in the newspaper industry, but the top 20 firms, led by Gannett, Knight-Ridder, and the Tribune, account for nearly one-fifth of the total circulation ("Freedonia Focus on Newspaper Publishing," The Freedonia Group of industry analysts, November 2002). According to the same report, there are approximately 1,400 daily, 900 Sunday, and more than 7,500 weekly papers published in the United States. Some dailies don't produce a weekend or Sunday edition, while some join forces with competitors to produce combined Sunday editions. This and other economizing strategies, such as increased content sharing with other papers owned by the same corporate parent, are attractive to the CFO but often result in less choice for the reading public.

Knowing about the corporate practices of the publishers of the papers you choose for your library is important. Cost-cutting measures like downsizing will naturally affect the quality of the reporting. For example, if you're in an area where a small chain of suburban papers is a primary source for print news, are they cutting staff and forcing each reporter to cover multiple beats in a more superficial way? Is more space being given to general news derived from wire service stories? Then the primary value of these papers, the local focus, has been diminished. Also, learn if you can how much influence the corporate parent may have over the editorial slant or even the content of the stories. Publishers can deny it until they're blue in the face, but pressure from the ownership is a concern consistently voiced in academic journalism reviews, in watchdog projects like the *Censored* annuals of underreported stories, and by the journalists themselves.

The simple need to sell more papers can steer an editorial policy toward removing anything the least bit challenging or potentially controversial. It's undeniable that a quick, upbeat, and pared-down presentation of the news has become popular and influential—those are characteristics of the nation's best-selling newspaper, Gannett's *USA Today*. It's precisely those aspects that prevent me from recommending *USA Today* for libraries (though I know it may be needed to meet patron demand). It does feature longer stories than in its earlier, graphics-festooned years, but compared to in-depth reporting that addresses complexity, it's the paper equivalent of broadcast soundbites, a safe source for "news lite," which gets national distribution in front of hotel room doors but doesn't go very far toward helping your patrons become truly well-informed. It's better to subscribe to one or more of the nationally distributed titles known for quality and thoroughness, like *The New York Times*, and, of course, collect papers with good coverage of your state and community.

Do keep in mind those papers that can give a voice to people who may not have an outlet in the mainstream press. For instance, urban areas often have "street sheets" published on behalf of the destitute, who write from personal experience about issues like the avoidance of shelters by the homeless or how they're treated by the police. Papers targeted toward particular racial or ethnic groups, neighborhoods, and interest cohorts such as senior citizens or organized labor should be collected if your library serves them. (This chapter only reviews general-interest titles and can't begin to cover focused-readership newspapers.) Communities with sizable populations of younger adults often have "alternative" weeklies that, though they tend to shoot from the hip, sometimes investigate things that the local daily might avoid. The subject of younger readers brings us back to the issue of paper versus online: Readership demographic studies done by MORI Research for the Newspaper Association of America show a clear decrease in newspaper use by people under 35 and a sharp increase in web-based news use. This age gap may factor in to your decision-making about balancing the newspapers and online access you provide to your library patrons.

Basic Newspapers

All libraries: Every local newspaper, including those that may provide news and viewpoints that may not be reflected in the mass-circulation dailies; state and regional newspapers for their broader scope; at least one national newspaper of quality that offers comprehensive, in-depth reporting on national and international events; and foreign newspapers, if possible, because they can broaden horizons and have the eye-opening effect of revealing how often mainstream newspapers in the United States share a homogenous point of view.

Basic Abstracts and Indexes

Depending upon your library's budget and focus, the possibilities here are numerous. Collecting title-specific indexes for the newspaper titles you subscribe to is an obvious choice; they may be available in print, on CD-ROM, or online. This may be unnecessary if you have access to an aggregator that indexes your titles and may provide article content as well.

General

5233. ***Atlanta Journal - Constitution.*** Formed by the merger of (1868-2001): *Atlanta Journal;* (1868-2001): *Constitution (Atlanta).* 2001. d. USD 13.99 per month in city; USD 16.99 per month out of city. Ed(s): Julia Wallace. Cox Enterprises, 72 Marietta St N W, Atlanta, GA 30303. *Aud.:* Ga.

On November 5, 2001, the merger of *Constitution* and *Journal*, begun in 1950, entered its final phase: Combined editorial staffs began producing the seven-day-per-week, mornings-only newspaper that has become the major regional newspaper for the South. (Afternoon delivery was phased out over several months.) In open letters to the community, a pledge was made to make every attempt to preserve the diversity that was perceived as an advantage of having separate editorial staffs, with some changes promised, such as expanded editorial pages. That expansion happened, excellent coverage of local and regional news continues, and in recent years there has been a decrease in reliance upon wire services for national and international stories.

5234. *The Baltimore Sun.* 1837. d. USD 294.60. Tribune Publishing Company, 373 1/2 W 19th St, Ste A, Houston, TX 77008. Circ: 465513. *Bk. rev.:* Various number and length. *Aud.:* Ga.

The 167-year-old *Sun* has received lots of goodwill from newspaper aficionados nationwide, but of course goodwill doesn't pay the bills and more people in the area are abandoning print or buying the *Washington Post*, which covers the D.C.–Baltimore metropolis and adds the strength of its political coverage and stronger national and international resources. As circulation has declined, staff has been reduced since 2000, when the paper became part of the *Tribune* chain. In 2002, a cable television executive lacking a journalism background took over as publisher, which raised some eyebrows among the paper's devotees. A bright spot was the announcement of a 2003 Pulitzer in beat reporting to Diana K. Sugg for her work on health and medical issues. While its tradition of fine reporting is kept alive by reporters such as Sugg, the *Sun* has come under criticism for not hitting as hard as it used to in coverage of state and local politics.

5235. *The Boston Globe.* [ISSN: 0743-1791] 1872. d. USD 540. Ed(s): Matthew V. Storin. New York Times Company, 135 Morrissey Blvd., Boston, MA 02107; http://www.boston.com/globe/. Circ: 705727. *Aud.:* Ga.

Some newspapers that are important to their regions may still lose readers who go elsewhere for national and international news. The *Globe*, however, successfully offers the full spectrum of coverage, keeping the promise implied in its slogan "Your world, unfolding daily." As well as having bureaus around New England and in New York and Washington, D.C., it has foreign bureaus in Asia, Europe, Russia, Latin America, Canada, and the Middle East. When it became a part of the *New York Times* family in 1993, resources in coverage outside New England increased. Today, its stature as a Boston institution is reinforced by the development of the *Globe* web site and its parent site, Boston.com, which reflect and augment the paper's content in a well-integrated, logical way; foster reader involvement; and include prominent links to information about *Globe* operations. The paper shows no signs of becoming an afterthought to the digital edition—this appears to be a mutually beneficial relationship. The *Globe* was the recipient of the 2003 Pulitzer for public service in recognition of articles on the scandal of sexual abuse by priests in the Catholic Church.

5236. *Chicago Tribune.* [ISSN: 1085-6706] 1963. d. USD 372.52. Ed(s): James O'Shea, Anne Marie Lipinski. Tribune Company, 435 N Michigan Ave, Chicago, IL 60611; ctc-editor@tribune.com. Adv. Circ: 584097. *Bk. rev.:* Various number and length. *Aud.:* Ga.

The *Tribune* is the farthest-reaching source for Midwest regional news and the largest-circulation paper in Chicago itself. (The *Chicago Sun-Times* doesn't lag that far behind, however, and Chicagoans are lucky to have a choice between the *Tribune* and the more populist voice of the *Sun-Times*.) The paper is the flagship of the Tribune Company, a large empire with holdings in a variety of media. It has the resources for staff coverage of national and international events and has a long history of awards, from Pulitzers to more-local press association kudos. For libraries in the Chicagoland area, a subscription is a no-brainer, but the diversity and complexity of the region would demand inclusion of other titles reflecting racial, ethnic, neighborhood, labor, and other interests.

5237. *The Christian Science Monitor.* [ISSN: 0882-7729] 1908. 5x/w. USD 25. Ed(s): John Selover. The Christian Science Publishing Society, One Norway St, Boston, MA 02115-3122; http://www.csmonitor.com. Illus., adv. Circ: 71924 Paid. Microform: PQC. Online: bigchalk; The Dialog Corporation; EBSCO Publishing; Factiva; Gale Group; LexisNexis; Newsbank, Inc.; Northern Light Technology, Inc.; OCLC Online Computer Library Center, Inc.; ProQuest Information & Learning. *Indexed:* ATI, BRD, BRI, CBRI, LRI, MusicInd, NewsAb, NumL. *Aud.:* Ga.

Imagine that you're going to publish a newspaper. You're under no obligation to stretch your resources thin by trying to report on every noteworthy current event, resulting in coverage that's broad but shallow. Instead, you can choose your subjects and examine them in depth. This is what *The Christian Science Monitor* (*CSM*) has done very well for almost a century. In coverage of the war in Iraq, for example, so many aspects of the fall of the Hussein regime were analyzed that most other papers seemed blinkered in comparison (especially those that ventured no further than passing on progress reports given at military press briefings). It's not entirely theme-oriented, of course, and features regular sections, such as business, that one would expect to find in a daily newspaper. Those sections also carry out the mission of exploring further than most other papers do. Libraries with small budgets that can afford only one newspaper to bring national and international scope to their readers could look to the very economical *CSM*.

5238. *Financial Times (North American Edition).* [ISSN: 0884-6782] 1985. d. Mon.-Sat. USD 298 domestic; CND 498 Canada. The Financial Times Inc., 1330 Ave of the Americas, New York, NY 10019; http://www.ft.com. Illus., adv. Circ: 107973. CD-ROM: Chadwyck-Healey Incorporated. Microform: RPI. Online: Factiva; Gale Group; LexisNexis; OCLC Online Computer Library Center, Inc. *Indexed:* B&I, ChemAb. *Aud.:* Ga.

For some readers who are looking for a tighter focus on business news than is found in the more all-encompassing *Wall Street Journal*, the *Financial Times* may be preferred. It is what it claims to be, a "world business newspaper," with a global network of around 500 journalists and a well-established presence in the money capitals of the world. The first section of this pink-newsprint title is a mix of business and general news, with op/ed pages and a little space for the arts, but beyond that the emphasis is on finance, markets, industries, and companies. Noteworthy are the special reports, over 200 yearly, giving lengthier analysis of selected topics. A typical example is "World Steel Industry" in April 2003, describing manufacturing in major steel-producing countries, regional issues, mergers, and market conditions.

5239. *The Globe and Mail.* Formed by the 1936 merger of: *Globe (Toronto); Mail and Empire;* Which was formerly (until 1929): *Daily Mail and Empire;* Which was formed by the 1895 merger of: *Empire; Toronto Daily Mail;* Which was formerly (1872-1880): *Mail (Toronto).* [ISSN: 0319-0714] 1844. d. Mon.-Sat. CND 257.40. Ed(s): Richard Addis. Globe and Mail Publishing, 444 Front St W, Toronto, ON M5V 2S9, Canada; http://www.globeandmail.com. Illus., adv. Circ: 381783 Paid. Microform: NRP. Online: Factiva; Gale Group. *Indexed:* B&I, BRI, CBCARef, CBRI, CPerI. *Bk. rev.:* Various number and length. *Aud.:* Ga.

The Globe and Mail, owned by the media conglomerate Bell Globemedia, is a nationally distributed newspaper with the largest circulation in Canada. This results in the macro view that one would expect, having the wherewithal for good provincial, national, and international reportage, but sometimes leaves one wanting supplemental news sources about Toronto itself. Politics and business coverage are particularly thorough, including the "Report on Business" magazine. The opinion section is more substantial than the usual two pages. Its role as a nation's newspaper would be strengthened by a better interrelationship with its web site, which should become increasingly important as the percentage of readers turning to the web grows larger.

5240. *The Guardian.* Formerly (until 1959): *Manchester Guardian.* [ISSN: 0261-3077] 1821. d. Mon.-Sat. GBP 488 in British Isles surface mail; GBP 640 elsewhere surface mail; GBP 732 in Europe incl. Ireland (Airmail)). Ed(s): Alan Rusbridger. Guardian Newspapers Ltd., 164 Deansgate, Guardian Newspapers Ltd, Manchester, M60 2RR, United Kingdom; http://www.guardian.co.uk. Illus., adv. Circ: 378516. CD-ROM: Chadwyck-Healey Incorporated. Microform: PQC. Online: LexisNexis; ProQuest Information & Learning. Reprint: PQC. *Indexed:* BAS, BrHumI, NewsAb. *Bk. rev.:* Various number and length. *Aud.:* Ga.

The Guardian is that rare breed of reputable, general-interest newspaper that isn't afraid to present news in a raw, direct way. For example, all of the major newspapers reported on the crisis in medical care for civilian casualties of the Iraq War, but *The Guardian* ran many clear pictures of the human beings affected, including one of Ali Ismaeel Abbas, the boy who lost his family and both arms in a missile attack. (The picture became symbolic and famous worldwide, but it got little exposure in the United States.) Many papers play along with an entertainer's publicist's restrictions; but in a *Guardian* piece about parental control, we have Charlotte Church, voice of an angel but teenager anyway, sporting her T-shirt reading "My Barbie is a crack whore." (Her mom made her stop wearing it in public.) For your library, you may need to choose papers with more of a propriety filter in their editorial policy, but it's an eye-opener to compare this with some newspapers that carefully sidestep the blunt truth. Not to be confused with those notoriously trashy British tabloids, this is an award-winning newspaper with high standards and good coverage of the United Kingdom, Europe, the rest of the world, and local issues, often done through longer feature stories. Nationally distributed, it's sometimes depicted as the younger Briton's choice over the more staid *Times*, but I think that's an unfair characterization.

5241. *The Los Angeles Times.* [ISSN: 0458-3035] 1886. d. USD 546. Ed(s): Michael Parks. Times Mirror Company, Times Mirror Square, Los Angeles, CA 90053; letters@news.latimes.com. Circ: 991480. *Bk. rev.:* Various number and length. *Aud.:* Ga.

Knowing that a paper is locally owned can make a huge difference for the careful reader. For the *Los Angeles Times*, when the powerful Chandler family owned it, one had a much better sense of how it shaped and reflected the character of Los Angeles. Like it or not, it was a very "establishment" organ with deep roots and vast influence. Since the Tribune chain bought it in 2000, it has joined that category of papers that seem like they could come from just about any major American city. Fourteen special community sections were axed, with the promise of continued coverage of major regional issues. Stories with larger scope are well represented, as expected, and excellent work by the reporting staff continues. 2003 Pulitzers were awarded for national reporting (Alan Miller and Kevin Sack) and feature writing (Sonia Nazario). Arts and entertainment coverage is quite extensive, but the economic importance of the entertainment industry in Southern California has usually meant that *The Times* avoids rocking that particular boat.

5242. *The Miami Herald.* [ISSN: 0898-865X] 1910. d. USD 312. Ed(s): Doug Clifton. Knight-Ridder Inc., One Herald Plaza, Miami, FL 33132-1693. Circ: 418242. Online: EBSCO Publishing; Factiva; LexisNexis; Newsbank, Inc.; ProQuest Information & Learning. *Aud.:* Ga.

Three factors seem to be behind the shrinkage of *The Miami Herald* in recent years: economics, technology, and demographics. In response to dropping circulation, the paper has implemented budget cuts and reduced pages (though not in general news), it's paid a lot of attention to building its web sites in reaction to the gradual shift away from print, and of course it has a growing Spanish-speaking constituency. In the last case, the shrinkage is accompanied by expansion into a sister newspaper, the *Nuevo Herald.* The Spanish-language paper is not a translation of the English one, but a very different animal with its own staff and editorial choices. (Mike Clary, in the May/June 2000 *Columbia Journalism Review*, asks rhetorically, "Would you create another newspaper to compete with your own?" but goes on to describe how they're serving two distinct audiences.)

Currently, the Miami Herald Publishing Company produces *The Miami Herald, The Herald* (for Broward County), *El Nuevo Herald*, and the *Miami Herald International Edition*, which is distributed in 14 countries in Latin America and the Caribbean. Newspaper fans follow *The Miami Herald* as the principal print news source from a very interesting spot, where North American, Caribbean, and Latin American cultures come together. Making it even more interesting is humorist Dave Barry, who has been at the *Herald* since 1983.

5243. *The New York Times.* [ISSN: 0362-4331] 1851. d. USD 374.40; USD 0.75 newsstand/cover per issue. Ed(s): Bill Keller, Gail Collins. New York Times Company, 229 W 43rd St, New York, NY 10036; http://www.nytimes.com. Illus., adv. Circ: 1100000. CD-ROM: ProQuest Information & Learning. Microform: PQC. Online: bigchalk; The Dialog Corporation; Factiva; Gale Group; LexisNexis; ProQuest Information & Learning. *Indexed:* B&I, BHA, BPI, BRD, BRI, BiolDig, CBRI, CWI, ChemAb, EnvAb, FutSurv, GSI, IIMP, IIPA, LRI, MRD, MagInd, MusicInd, NewsAb, RGPR, RI-1, RILM. *Bk. rev.:* Various number and length. *Aud.:* Ga.

With national distribution in multiple editions, *The New York Times* is the single best newspaper in the United States for comprehensive daily coverage of national and international events. The depth is unmatched: Rarely does one finish reading an article with any relevant questions left unanswered. It often includes the full text of such documents as major political speeches. Wallowing in the Sunday *Times* (while eating bagels!) is a ritual for many who want to immerse themselves in analysis of current events, arts reviews, and lifestyle subjects. Major awards are a regular occurrence, and in 2003 a Pulitzer for investigative reporting was given to Clifford J. Levy. My only gripe—and this is certainly not *The Times*'s fault—is that, for some people, displaying it has become such a signifier of "intellectual correctness" that it makes me wonder if they're curious enough to read any other news sources. For libraries, inclusion is an obvious choice, supplemented of course by more-local newspapers and others with a narrower focus.

5244. *San Francisco Chronicle.* 1865. d. San Francisco Chronicle, 901 Mission St., San Francisco, CA 94103; http://www.sfgate.com. Circ: 539563 Paid. *Aud.:* Ga.

The *San Francisco Chronicle* successfully surveys the very diverse, sometimes fractious San Francisco Bay Area and extends its coverage via local editions throughout Northern California. It has reporters covering city, regional, state, and national affairs, with some foreign assignments, and of course it draws upon outside news sources as well. After years of being regarded as rather flaky and lightweight, today it has built a good reputation for accuracy and a serious effort to be responsive to the many communities and interest groups that proliferate like the microclimates in the Bay Area. Through editorial choices and graphic design, it projects a strong sense of where it comes from, avoiding the bland, placeless front-page look of so many large metropolitan dailies. It reflects the liberal politics and relatively high level of tolerance that the area is famous for; a feature on a home renovation, for example, treats the fact that the owners are a same-sex couple as a nonissue. Subject matter getting special attention includes the regional high-tech industry, for which the *Chronicle* gets stiff competition in the *San Jose Mercury News*.

5245. *Seattle Times.* [ISSN: 0745-9696] 1896. d. USD 156; USD 0.25 newsstand/cover; USD 1.50 newsstand/cover Sun. The Seattle Times Company, 1120 John St, Seattle, WA 98109; opinion@seattletimes.com. Adv. *Aud.:* Ga.

As of this writing, Seattle is blessed with two good dailies, but a legal battle began in spring 2003 over their joint operating agreement. Of the two, the *Seattle Times* has more-extensive resources than the *Post-Intelligencer*, having actually increased staff in recent years (which is an element in the dispute). It tends to have more-complete local and regional coverage, making it the most important print news source in the Pacific Northwest, but pulls in most national and international content from outside news services. There are frequent, thorough features about the computer industry, as should be the case in the Kingdom of Microsoft, and good coverage of other regionally important enterprises, such as fisheries and aircraft manufacturing. It deserves mention that their competitor, the *P-I*, can now boast a multiple Pulitzer-winning editorial cartoonist in David Horsey (his first was received in 1999 and another came in 2003).

5246. *T L S: the Times literary supplement.* Formerly (until 1969): *Times Literary Supplement.* [ISSN: 0307-661X] 1902. w. GBP 69; GBP 2.20 newsstand/cover per issue; GBP 80 in Europe. Ed(s): Peter Stothard. T S L Education Ltd., Admiral House, 66-68 E Smithfield, London, E1 1BX, United Kingdom; webmaster@the-tls.co.uk; http://www.tsleducation.co.uk. Illus., index, adv. Circ: 34000. Vol. ends: Dec. Microform: RPI. *Indexed:* ArtHuCI, BHA, BNI, BRD, BRI, CBRI, HumInd, LRI, MLA-IB, RI-1, RILM, SSCI. *Bk. rev.:* Various number and length. *Aud.:* Ga, Ac.

The *Times Literary Supplement* (*TLS*) is truly a remarkable publication. Since 1902, the *TLS* has covered the English-speaking publishing world and elevated the literary review into a genre in its own right. Known for lengthy, in-depth reviews that sometimes resemble small literary studies, the *TLS* is famous for its notable contributors, ranging from T. S. Eliot and Virginia Woolf to Italo Calvino, Gore Vidal, Seamus Heaney, and George Steiner, among others. While focusing on literature, the *TLS* covers any subject influencing the current intellectual debate, including translations, as well as the current theater, opera, and film. The web site is clean, without frills or too many ads, and it provides full texts of selected articles. The site includes subject access and an online newsletter. Subscribers receive access to the complete edition. Indispensable.

5247. *The Times.* Formerly (until 1788): *Daily Universal Register.* [ISSN: 0140-0460] 1785. d. Mon.-Sat. GBP 78 domestic; GBP 0.35 newsstand/cover per issue. Times Newspapers Ltd., 1 Pennington St, London, E98 1ST, United Kingdom; http://www.thetimes.co.uk/. Illus., index, adv. Circ: 619682. CD-ROM: Chadwyck-Healey Incorporated. Microform: RPI. Online: bigchalk; Factiva; Gale Group. Reprint: PSC. *Indexed:* BNI, BrHumI, BrTechI, GeoRef, LRI. *Aud.:* Ga, Ac.

The Sunday Times. [ISSN: 0956-1382] 1822. w. GBP 78; GBP 1.10 newsstand/cover per issue. http://www.sunday-times.co.uk. Illus., adv. Circ: 1309594. CD-ROM: Chadwyck-Healey Incorporated. Microform: RPI. Online: Gale Group. *Indexed:* BNI, BrHumI, BrTechI, DAAI. *Aud:* Ga.

The Times—or *The London Times* as it is sometimes referred to—is arguably the world's most famous newspaper. Published uninterruptedly since 1785, *The Times* is the most authoritative source for British political, legal, business, cultural, and social news. *The Sunday Times* is equally well known for its in-depth, award-winning news coverage and commentary, as well as its literary section. The web site is user-friendly and well organized, though extensive, and numerous sections are reserved to subscribers only. The archive provides access to back issues to 1985 and is available for a fee. The complete archive of *The Times* (1785–1985) is currently being made available digitally from another publisher, specializing in subscriptions to institutions. Highly recommended for all libraries covering international news; indispensable for research libraries and large public libraries.

5248. *Wall Street Journal (Eastern Edition).* Supersedes (in 1959): *Wall Street Journal.* [ISSN: 0099-9660] 1889. d. Mon.-Fri. USD 189; USD 1 newsstand/cover per issue. Ed(s): Paul E. Steiger, Robert L Bartley. Dow Jones & Co., Inc., 200 Liberty St, New York, NY 10281; http://www.wsj.com. Illus., adv. Circ: 1857050 Paid. Microform: PQC. Online: Dow Jones Interactive; Factiva; Gale Group; ProQuest Information & Learning. Reprint: PQC. *Indexed:* B&I, BLI, BPI, BRI, CBRI, ChemAb, FutSurv, GardL, LogistBibl, MCR, MusicInd, NewsAb, PAIS, RI-1. *Aud.:* Ga.

The expansion of The *Wall Street Journal*'s scope from finance to general news is linked to its growth into a national, mass-circulation newspaper. It's clear that there was a market for it; the *WSJ* is the second-best-selling newspaper in the United States, after *USA Today*. The financial data and reportage are still there, of course, but they share space with national and international events well dissected and fit into a pro-business news package. The stories are consistently well researched and expertly written; as with The *New York Times*, the writers and editors seem to anticipate readers' questions very well and answer them completely. A subscription will be a necessity for any library with patrons who follow the markets, especially the older generation, which isn't used to going online for the latest news and numbers. And it should be noted that part of its appeal is the aura of success it imparts: Just by holding a copy of The *Wall Street Journal*, young strivers can feel like they're on their way, even if they're unemployed.

5249. *The Washington Post.* [ISSN: 0190-8286] 1877. d. USD 748.80. Ed(s): Leonard Downie, Jr. Washington Post Co., 1150 15th St, N W, Washington, DC 20071. Circ: 709578. *Bk. rev.:* Various number and length. *Aud.:* Ga.

The Washington Post is the preeminent newspaper for analysis of federal politics; post-Watergate, the national spotlight on it has never wavered. It's known for aggressive investigative reporting, as well as for being a part of the very power structure it reports on, in the sense that there have been close "inside the Beltway" relationships that outsiders were not privy to. Its opinion pages are, unsurprisingly, very influential. Not a national newspaper in the sense of expanding its focus with nationwide distribution in mind, it still has great coverage of issues around the country as well as those at a national and international level, and it has by no means neglected its coverage of the D.C. region. In 2003, a Pulitzer was awarded to the staff for explanatory reporting, for a series of articles on corporate scandals in the United States.

Newspaper Indexes

The early twenty-first century showed a clear shift away from print and CD-ROM indexing toward online products, many of which index and provide content in one package. At this writing, we're still in that transitional period. This section has shrunk since the previous edition, and more emphasis is placed on the indexing featured in commercial web news systems.

ProQuest Information and Learning, which was Bell & Howell in a former life, owns University Microfilms International (UMI), still the largest publisher of indexes (and microfilm) for individual mainstream newspaper titles. Their monopoly in this area means that it's unnecessary and boring to list title by title their indexes for our recommended newspapers (the rare non-UMI exceptions have been noted). Look at the UMI web site (http://www.umi.com/) and contact them for information. In addition to those major titles which are not indexed by UMI, I've included indexes which cover multiple titles. Some notable changes: British Newspaper Index ceased in 2000 and Canadian Index ceased in 2001; they are succeeded by web-based products which offer indexing and some full text. Keep in mind that some newspapers' own web sites offer searchable archives of their articles, with recent ones free and older ones available for a small fee.

5250. *Financial Times Index (Monthly).* [ISSN: 0265-4237] 1981. m. Primary Source Microfilm, High Holborn House, 50/51 Bedford Row, London, WC1R 4LR, United Kingdom; psmcs@gale.com; http://www.galegroup.com/psm/. Online: The Dialog Corporation. *Aud.:* Ga.

Provides monthly print indexing with annual hardbound cumulative volumes. Access points include personal, country, company, and survey entries. The print index for this title continues, but the CD-ROM that included indexing, *British Newspaper Index,* ceased in 2000. See "Commercial Web News Systems."

5251. *National Newspaper Index.* [ISSN: 0273-3676] 1979. m. USD 3200. Gale Group, 27500 Drake Rd, Farmington Hills, MI 48331-3535; galeord@gale.com; http://www.gale.com. Illus. *Aud.:* Ga.

This online database contains front-to-back indexing of *The Christian Science Monitor*, *The New York Times*, and *Wall Street Journal*. Sources also include *PR Newswire, Japan Economic Newswire, Reuters Financial Report, New York Times Book Review* and *New York Times Magazine*. Selective indexing is provided for *The Washington Post* and *The Los Angeles Times*.

5252. *Newspaper Abstracts.* 1989. d. ProQuest Information & Learning, 300 N Zeeb Rd., PO Box 1346, Ann Arbor, MI 48106-1346. *Indexed:* NewsAb. *Aud.:* Ga.

This online database provides cover-to-cover indexing of news articles and features from more than 30 major newspapers, including *The New York Times, Atlanta Constitution* (with selected articles from the *Atlanta Journal*), *Boston Globe, Chicago Tribune, Christian Science Monitor, USA Today, Los Angeles Times, Wall Street Journal,* and *Washington Post.* Coverage dates begin with 1986. Updated daily. The CD-ROM product has changed: It now covers five top U.S. publications and is called *Newspaper Abstracts Major Papers*.

5253. *Times Index.* Formerly (until 1973): *Index to the Times.* [ISSN: 0260-0668] 1906. m. plus a. cumulation. USD 1054.70. Primary Source Microfilm, High Holborn House, 50/51 Bedford Row, London, WC1R 4LR, United Kingdom; psmcs@gale.com; http://www.galegroup.com/psm/. Illus. Circ: 1000. Microform: Pub. *Aud.:* Ga.

Provides citations to and abstracts of all articles in the London *Times* and *Sunday Times,* as well as the *Times Education Supplement, Times Higher Education Supplement,* and *Times Literary Supplement.* Updated monthly. The print index continues, but the *British Newspaper Index,* which indexed it on CD-ROM, ceased in 2000. See "Commercial Web News Systems."

Web-based Newspapers

Web sites hosted by newspaper publishers became common by 2000, and most offered the same sets of features. Organization by categories similar to those in a print edition, searchability, archives, and links to related stories are the bare minimum shared by all. This section will review a handful of the best, those which have some special quality, and it won't venture into the much, much larger and varied category of web sites which offer news. Even the concept of "web-based newspapers" is something that's getting a little fuzzy around the edges, and may become irrelevant in the near future.

Many studies show a demographic shift away from newspaper readership and toward web-based news sources which may or may not be related to a newspaper. A Newspaper Association of America telephone survey conducted in 2002 graphs out as a steady upward ramp for frequency of newspaper use correlated to age. Comments from those who've reached maturity during the web era (heard today by those of us who serve college-age library users) consistently reflect their incredulity that anyone could be entirely satisfied with a tree-killer that gets updated only once a day. So, the importance of having the imprimatur of a print newspaper stamped on the web site may decrease over time, and broadcast-based news from a network like CNN or even Internet service-provider news can look just as legitimate to younger users. They're also accustomed to looking for different qualities in a web news source than newspaper users do. The web-based news they value offers vastly improved timeliness, new ways to be entertaining, and easy linkage to things they can use in their lives—from a movie review it's just a few clicks to buy tickets; from an article on an international relief organization it's easy to jump to more information from the group's own site. There doesn't need to be a parent newspaper to do this.

On the production side of the equation, it has to be recognized that most news content for mass consumption is created by media conglomerates which have multiple outlets for their product, and paper is not high on their list. A trusted, historically strong newspaper brand wouldn't be cast aside lightly, but that important brand recognition can be incorporated into related web media. Marketing to newspaper readers was never an exact science, but marketing to web users may be—exact measurements can be taken of when they're visiting a site and what they're clicking on within it, so methods like programming for "dayparts" can be used to accurately direct types of content according to different conditions and times of day (MORI Research, January 2003). Also, years have gone by since there were any new gimmicks to sell more newspapers, but new web functions are regularly being adopted by news sites to draw readers in. A recent example from msnbc.com was a chance to test your ability to screen airport luggage by examining actual x-ray images of suitcases scrolling on a "conveyor" across the screen. The graphic proof that it's hard to spot weapons this way was an instructive addition to the site's reports on airport security and how important the (often underpaid) staff have become.

Of course there isn't a brick wall between newspaper readers and web site users; as long as both media are available, many people will use both. The best web sites from newspaper publishers stand alone as complete news sources but also provide related information about the print title, and may offer image files of the front page of that day's paper or a downloadable digital version of the whole paper for a fee. The core content is usually presented centrally on the screen, and the more developed sites will offer digital sidebars which augment the reporting, such as photo galleries, sound or video clips and links to related articles and resources. Using these sites is a real-life lesson in the concept of media convergence, as we see how any digital information can be shaped and reshaped for an effective presentation. Of course, the ability to alter news in digital format is a threat that's been much discussed, which brings us back to the notion that paper may die but a trusted news brand should hold its value.

Finding newspaper web sites is usually as easy as typing the name of the newspaper into the box of a good search site like Google. The web version may go by a different name, but there's enough linkage to the newspaper name that the site will be found. And of course ISPs and web portals offer pages (which they hope will be your homepage) that have links to commonly sought resources such as news.

5254. *The Boston Globe Online.* New York Times Company, 135 Morrissey Blvd., Boston, MA 02107; http://www.boston.com/globe/. *Aud.:* Ga.

Boston.com is a great example of a well-planned interrelationship between a print newspaper and a web site. Various ways of getting to the newspaper's content are presented, and the possibilities of web technology are fully exploited to overcome the limitations of print. The links to the newspaper are very complete: We get access to the web version of the paper, pdf files of the printed front page, a low-graphics version, a headlines e-mail service, and a link for subscribers to the electronic edition (a digital version of the print edition available for downloading). Web functions include several ways of searching the content; access to articles in different configurations, including simple alphabetical arrangement; free subscription to e-mail newsletters that go beyond the headlines to employment, travel, business, personals, and the Sunday *Globe*'s Ideas section; and a "Globe Services" area including newspaper history, organization, awards, and contact information, as well as marketing information for advertisers. Contrary to the notion of paper as static and the web as dynamic, this site also groups together long-term links to collected articles about events of continuing interest, so users can return to the same place for updates. Archives are freely searchable, but the full text of articles must be purchased for a small fee.

5255. *The Christian Science Monitor.* Ed(s): Karla Vallance. The Christian Science Publishing Society, One Norway St, Boston, MA 02115-3122; http://www.csmonitor.com. *Bk. rev.:* Various number and length. *Aud.:* Ga.

The things that make the print *Christian Science Monitor* (*CSM*) so good are present in the web site, too: It encourages you to take an in-depth look at selected current events and keeps the reputation for fairness and writing that respects a reader's intelligence. The scope (as described in "The Monitor Difference," one of several explanatory pieces about the publication) is truly global. The impression of quiet, reasonable discourse is furthered by the muted design of the site, which makes others seem like they're shouting. Ad space is limited. The current print edition's content is presented in its entirety, and archived articles from the previous five days are free. A schedule of modest fees applies to articles that appeared before that. The emphasis on longer features is balanced by frequent, brief updates compiled from wire services. Some may think of the *CSM* as a "quaint old lady" who wouldn't know about the latest technology, but that's belied by the many digital versions and by-products offered here, including an XML section with links to articles formatted for easy digestion by personal aggregator software.

5256. *FT.com.* d. The Financial Times Inc., Castle House, 37-45 Paul St, London, EC2A 4LS, United Kingdom; http://www.ft.com. *Aud.:* Ga.

FT.com is free, and the *Wall Street Journal Interactive Edition* is not—that, for those interested in money, may be the simple deciding factor in a choice between the two. Pop-up ads come with the territory. Subscribing to an expanded *FT* is possible, and necessary for a small percentage of the content; industry and company surveys and data are also part of the subscription package. As with the print *Financial Times*, *FT.com* is focused on business and the events that affect it, but is broad in geographic scope, with impressive worldwide resources reflecting multiple global perspectives, the British one being most prominent. In newspaper terms, it would be like reading *The Economist* (which has a habit of referring to itself as a newspaper but is covered in our economics chapter) if that fine weekly became a daily. Of course, in web terms daily and weekly lose their grip and what matters is whether the news arrives on your screen in a timely fashion. Global coverage demands 24/7 vigilance, and *FT.com* has it. Site design is both clean and busy at the same time, with data boxes and ads squeezed in just a few steps short of clutter. Research tools such as analyst reports from sources like Multex Investor Research are accessible, with basic profiles free but anything more detailed requiring payment.

5257. *The Guardian Internet Edition.* Guardian Newspapers Ltd., http://www.guardian.co.uk/guardian/. *Aud.:* Ga.

Here's a fine example of how a news publisher today addresses the past, present, and future: The *Guardian Internet Edition* has most of the stories that appear in the *Guardian* newspaper, uses present web technology to expand upon that, and points readers to the broader *Guardian Unlimited* site, which shows every indication that this is where the whole operation is eventually headed. The *Unlimited* brings together all of the resources from the publishing group, including the *Guardian Weekly* and the Sunday *Observer*, and its organization and look don't have any echoes of print—it's like the latest evolutionary stage of a creature that has completely adapted to a new environment. In anticipation of users exploring these interrelationships, there are prominent links to elements of the main sites (*Internet Edition, Weekly, Unlimited, Observer*) with clear textual explanations. The *Internet Edition* makes it easy to learn the organization of the paper, such as which sections appear on which days, and of course it offers such standard features as a searchable archive of articles that appeared online (retrievable free). Much appreciated is the uniform design throughout this family of web pages, clear and easy to read with lots of white space separating elements. There seems to be a graphic design equivalent to a local zoning ordinance here—even the ads share the overall look, which in my opinion makes them more attractive and effective.

5258. ***The Mercury News.*** d. San Jose Mercury News, 750 Ridder Park Drive, San Jose, CA 95190; http://www0.mercurycenter.com/. *Aud.:* Ga.

This web site was one of the first newspaper sites to really exploit the electronic technology, which is appropriate as *The Mercury News* is the major daily in Silicon Valley. The functions that once made it cutting-edge are now common to all newspaper web sites, but it's still noteworthy for a couple of reasons: It shows a responsiveness to the needs of local communities by including Spanish and Vietnamese publications (*Nuevo Mundo* and *Viet Mercury*), which is food for thought about how wWeb technology can facilitate multiple versions for adapting to future social diversification. The tech economy web site, *Silicon-Valley.com*, is a good model of a site specifically for a readership that is very likely to look online exclusively. The parent site is a node in Knight-Ridder's RealCities national network of "leading media properties" (the terminology today being as all-inclusive as possible given the multiplicity of media now and to come), and a handy map leads the reader to other wWeb-based news sources in the chain.

Commercial Web News Systems

The following list of vendors offering online full-text news databases attempts to be a representative sample. It does not include mega-packages in which news content is only a small percentage of the total. The market is changing rapidly; it seems that any company which previously sold print indexes, CD-ROMs or film has a new online option which features at least some text content. Databases are being sold and folded in to other products, and smaller companies are getting snapped up by larger ones or entering into partnerships (try exploring the combined resources of ProQuest/UMI/Chadwick-Healey to get an impression of the complexity). Change is also to be expected in the products' look and functionality—sometimes the interfaces are even tweaked to implement the suggestions of the librarians who use them. It's certainly all worthwhile, though, because these databases give library users access to sources which were previously available to only the most determined and mobile scholars. To offer added value to their text archives some sources include timely news feeds from newswires, but that kind of enhancement has become less valuable as excellent, free news sources have become established on the web.

Accessible Archives. Accessible Archives Inc., 697 Sugartown Rd., Malvern, PA 19355. http://www.accessible.com. Provides full-text primary source materials from eighteenth- and nineteenth-century newspapers and magazines, through databases such as *The Pennsylvania Gazette 1728-1800, The Civil War: A Newspaper Perspective, African American Newspapers: The 19th Century.* and *Godey's Lady Book.*

Alt-Press Watch. ProQuest, 300 North Zeeb Rd., PO Box 1346, Ann Arbor, MI 48106-1346. www.il.proquest.com. The description of this database calls its sources "the alternative and independent press" which may still leave one wondering. Scanning the title list, a mix of newspapers and magazines, is the best method for getting it. Some examples: *The Advocate*, *Auto-Free Times*, *Creative Loafing* (in four Southern cities), *Industrial Worker*, *Miami New Times*, *SF Weekly*, *Youth Today*.

Canadian Business & Current Affairs (CBCA). ProQuest Information and Learning, 300 North Zeeb Rd., PO Box 1346, Ann Arbor, MI 48106-1346. www.il.proquest.com. Full text for over 300 serials, indexing for over 700, *CBCA* covers *The Globe and Mail* and other major Canadian papers. The successor to *Canadian Index.* A related ProQuest product, *Paper of Record*, is an online historic newspaper archive for Canada, with some source material dating back as far as 1752.

Custom Newspapers. Infotrac/Gale/Thomson, 27500 Drake Rd., Farmington Hills, MI 48331. http://www.gale.com. This product replaces *British Newspaper Index* and goes well beyond it. Titles can be chosen from an extensive list of British and American papers. The earliest start date, which applies to many entries on the *Custom Newspapers* source list, is January 1996. Allows setting up a customized source list and search parameters, letting users create their own electronic edition.

Ethnic NewsWatch. ProQuest Information and Learning, 300 North Zeeb Road, PO Box 1346, Ann Arbor, MI 48106-1346. www.il.proquest.com. *Ethnic NewsWatch* is a full-text database of over 200 newspapers and magazines "of the ethnic, minority and native press," in English and Spanish. The search interface is available in Spanish as well as English. Sources range from small to relatively large circulation pubs, with titles like the *New York Amsterdam News*, the *Navajo Times*, the *Armenian Reporter*, *El Sol de Texas* and *AsianWeek*.

Factiva. Dow Jones Reuters Business Interactive Ltd., 105 Madison Ave., 10th floor, New York, NY 10016. http://www.factiva.com. Succeeds *Dow Jones Interactive*. Factiva is a large full-text database with a focus on business research, drawing upon newspapers, newswires, trade journals, newsletters, magazines and transcripts. A simple company name search can yield a very complete picture of relevant recent events.

FACTS.com. Facts on File News Services, 512 Seventh Ave., 22nd floor, New York, NY 10018. http://www.facts.com/online-fdc.htm. This five-part reference suite includes the *Facts on File World News Digest*, which features reworked news source material. The format is useful in environments where prepackaged topic searches are appropriate; not the place to go for large databases of verbatim news articles. Other files in the suite are almanacs, selected current issues, or science oriented.

Global NewsBank. NewsBank Inc., 5020 Tamiami Trail North, Suite 110, Naples, FL 34103. http://www.newsbank.com. Global NewsBank is an online information system which offers grouped, topic-oriented links which are helpful for the less-experienced researcher. The worldwide resources include transcribed broadcasts. Excellent for students researching the varying perspectives on international issues.

Historical Newspapers. ProQuest, 300 North Zeeb Road, PO Box 1346, Ann Arbor, MI 48106-1346. http://www.proquestcompany.com. Historical Newspapers Online contains four major historical resources: *Palmer's Index to the Times* covering the period from 1790 to 1905 in *The Times*; *The Official Index to the Times* which takes the coverage forward from 1906 to 1980; *The Historical Index to the New York Times* which covers *The New York Times* from 1851-September 1922; *Palmer's Full Text Online 1785-1870*, providing access to the full-text articles referenced in *Palmer's Index to the Times.*

LEXIS-NEXIS Academic Universe. Reed Elsevier plc, 25 Victoria St., London SW1H 0EX, UK. http://www.lexis-nexis.com. LexisNexis Academic Universe is the simplified, user-friendly package derived from the huge Lexis-Nexis database of news text. Full text from almost all major US newspapers is here, with the notable exception being *Wall Street Journal*'s abstracts only. The database provides news, financial, medical, and legal text from newspapers, broadcasts, wire services, government documents and other categories. Images and graphics are not included. Of (probably long-term) interest is the March 2003 addition of translated transcripts from *Al-Jazeera.* International resources in Dutch, French, German, Italian, Portuguese, and Spanish are also included.

NewsBank Full-Text Newspapers; NewsBank Libraries can customize a subscription to create a list of local titles. The community-level information can be a valuable resource for public libraries, and is often under the radar screen of other aggregators with a more macro level of coverage.

Newspaper Source. EBSCO Publishing, 10 Estes St., Ipswich, MA 01938. http://www.epnet.com. The patchwork quilt of full-text, indexing and abstracting in this online source (which is also available on CD-ROM) can be valuable but pay close attention to coverage details. *The Christian Science Monitor* is here cover-to-cover back to January 1995, but with other titles there's partial coverage with too many exceptions to list.

World News Connection. National Technical Information Service, U.S. Department of Commerce, Springfield, VA 22161. http://wnc.fedworld.gov/description.html. Distributed by the National Technical Information Service, U.S. Department of Commerce, WNC provides web access to full-text, English translations of current non-U.S. media sources beginning in 1996. A derivative of intelligence-gathering efforts begun over 60 years ago, there are sources here you won't find transcribed in other full-text databases, such as local radio broadcasts of government statements. This is the online continuation of the *FBIS* and *JPRS* index and content microform systems.

■ NUMISMATICS

David Van de Streek, Library Director, York Campus, Penn State University, Lee R. Glatfelter Library, 1031 Edgecomb Ave., York, PA 17403; SDV1@PSU.EDU

Introduction

Numismatics includes both collecting and studying coins, paper money, tokens, medals, and associated areas. Of these, the most popular without question is coin collecting, which in recent years has grown significantly, primarily as a result of the ten-year-long state quarters program. It is estmated that within the United States, several million people are actively involved in some fashion with numismatics, while many more million have a peripheral interest.

Despite this wide interest, only a handful of numismatic periodicals have a broad enough content base to attract and maintain a solid readership level. While there are certainly many more publications in this field, most are limited by scope or readership potential, limiting their usefulness to libraries. Of the periodicals listed in this section, six (*CoinWorld, Coinage, Coins, Numismatist, Numismatic News, World Coin News*) have broad enough coverage that they can be thought of as general numismatic resources, even though a high proportion of their material is specifically about coins. Each contains enough about paper money, tokens, and some of the very specialized areas of numismatics, that these will be useful to a wide audience of collectors and specialists.

With the exception of *Paper Money,* periodicals in this field are liberally filled with dealer advertising and price lists, which should not be taken as a sign that these are lacking in quality. To most readers this is not a distraction, with many regularly refering to and relying on these ads and listings either to make purchases or to help them approximate the value of their own collections.

Librarians looking for one representative numismatic periodical should strongly consider *Coin World.* This weekly has long been well respected within the field, and its place as the highest circulating numismatic publication certainly indicates its wide acceptance and authority within numismatics.

Basic Periodicals

Hs: *Coins;* Ga: *Coin World, Coinage, Coins, Numismatist;* Ac: *Numismatist.*

Basic Abstracts and Indexes

Numismatic Literature.

5259. ***Bank Note Reporter: complete monthly guide for paper money collectors.*** [ISSN: 0164-0828] 1973. m. USD 35; USD 19.99 for 6 mos.; USD 3.50 newsstand/cover per issue. Ed(s): Dave Harper. Krause Publications, Inc., 700 E State St, Iola, WI 54990-0001; info@krause.com; http://www.krause.com. Illus., adv. Sample. Circ: 8420 Paid and free. Vol. ends: Dec. *Indexed:* NumL. *Bk. rev.:* Occasional, 200-400 words. *Aud.:* Ga, Sa.

This is a tabloid-sized newspaper that broadly covers the collecting of paper money and other forms of financial paper, such as checks, stock certificates, and military payment coupons. With a predominant focus on U.S. currency, this is mainly a source of current information about the hobby and the collector's market, but it includes feature material as well. Feature articles are typically about a specific piece of currency or a group of related currencies, and usually provide historical overviews of monetary events and other significant events relating to that currency. A standard feature is a price guide that represents approximate retail prices for most U.S. paper money issues. The web site has one full-text article from the most recent issue plus selected other articles available only to subscribers or registrants with Krause Publications. This is the most complete source available for paper money collectors.

5260. ***Coin Prices: complete guide to U.S. coin values.*** [ISSN: 0010-0412] 1967. bi-m. USD 18.98 domestic; USD 29.98 foreign; USD 4.25 newsstand/cover per issue foreign. Ed(s): Bob Van Ryzin. Krause Publications, Inc., 700 E State St, Iola, WI 54990-0001; info@krause.com; http://www.krause.com. Illus., adv. Sample. Circ: 58757 Paid and free. Microform: MIM; PMC; PQC. *Aud.:* Hs, Ga.

Virtually the entire contents of this magazine is a price guide for all regularly issued United States coins, dating from 1792 to the present. Prices reflect an average retail value, approximating what a buyer would pay to acquire a coin. Each listed coin has a range of prices that correspond with various quality grades for that coin, spanning heavily circulated to uncirculated. Specific issues of the magazine also have an additional section on prices for more specialized areas of the numismatic market, such as paper money, and Colonial coins (those used before the United States minted its own money). Coin values frequently change, making this bimonthly publication a more timely resource than annual price guides. The magazine is printed entirely on newsprint, lessening its production quality, but its useful content has been a staple for collectors for decades, and should continue to be so.

5261. ***Coin World: world's #1 publication for coin collectors.*** Formerly: *Numismatic Scrapbook.* [ISSN: 0010-0447] 1960. w. USD 36.95; USD 2 newsstand/cover per issue. Ed(s): Beth Deisher. Amos Press Inc., PO Box 150, Sidney, OH 45365; cweditor@amospress.com. Illus., adv. Sample. Circ: 87000. Vol. ends: Dec. Microform: PQC. Reprint: PQC. *Indexed:* NumL. *Bk. rev.:* 1-3, 200-400 words. *Aud.:* Hs, Ga.

This has the highest readership of any numismatic publication, and is probably the most widely respected. A weekly, tabloid-sized newspaper, it covers a broad range of numismatic interests and events, mixing current news items with feature material. Both regular articles and contributed features are typically written by specialists in that field, many of whom are acknowledged experts, and most of whom are highly regarded within numismatics. Coverage extends to virtually all areas of numismatics, and includes numerous items that are important for collectors in enhancing their knowledge and collecting skills. This is one of the better sources for monitoring current coin-market conditions, featuring a monthly pull-out section that lists approximate retail prices throughout the scale of grading quality for every regularly issued U.S. coin. The web site has selected articles in full text from the most current issue, as well as a keyword searchable archive of full-text articles for the most recent three years (subscribers have access to an electronic version of each new issue plus an archive). This is an informative, instructional, and comprehensive publication, with quality features and departments, and it should be a primary resource for most libraries.

5262. ***Coinage.*** [ISSN: 0010-0455] 1964. m. USD 24; USD 3.99 newsstand/cover per issue. Ed(s): Ed Reiter. Miller Magazines, Inc, 4880 Market St, Ventura, CA 93003-2888; http://www.millermags.com. Illus., adv. Sample. Circ: 150000 Paid. Vol. ends: Dec. Microform: PQC. *Indexed:* NumL. *Aud.:* Ga.

This is a good general-interest magazine that covers a wide variety of numismatic topics. Feature articles most often focus on currently significant numismatic events, but also include historically based material and useful informational items about collecting in general. An interesting regular feature is "Coin Capsule," which highlights the coinage or significant numismatic events of a random year, along with the perspective of that year's noteworthy historical, political, and cultural events. The magazine has good writing, is generally well produced, and features excellent close-up color photography of coins and paper money. None of the magazine's material is available at the web site. Because its general content and broad coverage can appeal to both beginning and experienced collectors, this should be considered as part of a basic collection.

5263. ***Coins.*** [ISSN: 0010-0471] 1955. m. USD 25.98; USD 3.95 newsstand/cover per issue. Ed(s): Bob Van Ryzin. Krause Publications, Inc., 700 E State St, Iola, WI 54990-0001; info@krause.com; http://www.krause.com. Illus., adv. Sample. Circ: 56579 Paid and free. Vol. ends: Dec. Microform: PMC; PQC. *Indexed:* NumL. *Bk. rev.:* Occasional, 600-800 words. *Aud.:* Hs, Ga.

This general-interest magazine is one of the standards in the field, and it covers most areas of numismatics. It differs from other numismatic publications in that each issue is typically focused on a specific theme, such as silver dollars, with four to six lengthy feature articles devoted to that topic. The magazine is then rounded out with additional features, news items, and regularly appearing columns. Its material is generally oriented towards those collectors with modest budgets and similarly modest collecting expertise. A price guide to retail coin values is a regular feature, but it is less comprehensive than those in other sources, listing only the most frequently traded U.S. coins. A distracting part of the magazine is that its latter two-thirds is printed on newsprint-quality paper with black-and-white graphics. The web site has one full-text article from the most recent issue, plus selected other articles available only to subscribers or registrants with Krause Publications. This magazine can be used either as part of a basic collection or as a complement to one.

5264. ***Numismatic News: the complete information source for coin collectors.*** [ISSN: 0029-604X] 1952. w. USD 32 domestic; USD 147.98 foreign. Ed(s): Dave Harper. Krause Publications, Inc., 700 E State St, Iola, WI 54990-0001; info@krause.com; http://www.krause.com. Illus., adv. Sample. Circ: 33200 Paid and free. Vol. ends: Dec. Microform: PMC; PQC. *Indexed:* NumL. *Bk. rev.:* Occasional, 100-300 words. *Aud.:* Hs, Ga.

A tabloid-sized newsweekly, this is primarily a source of current news that touches on most areas of numismatics. Much of its coverage concerns events that generally affect conditions within the coin market, such as auctions and coin show activities. Some of its regular columns and occasional articles feature lesser known and less popular areas of collecting, such as tokens, and these can be good introductions to those fields. There is a monthly pull-out supplement, a price guide listing approximate retail prices for all but a few U.S. coins in their respective grading levels of quality. The web site has one full-text article from the most recent issue, plus selected other articles available only to subscribers or registrants with Krause Publications.

5265. ***Numismatist: for collectors of coins, medals, tokens and paper money.*** Incorporates (1987-1994): *First Strike;* (1951-1981): *A N A Club Bulletin.* [ISSN: 0029-6090] 1888. m. Non-members, USD 33; USD 5 newsstand/cover per issue. Ed(s): Barbara J Gregory. American Numismatic Association, 818 N Cascade Ave, Colorado Springs, CO 80903-3279; http://www.money.org. Illus., index, adv. Sample. Circ: 27500 Controlled. Vol. ends: Dec. *Indexed:* ABS&EES, BHA, NumL. *Bk. rev.:* 3-5, 50-100 words. *Aud.:* Ga, Ac.

This is the membership publication of the American Numismatic Association, which is the premiere collecting and leadership society in American numismatics. The longest continuously published magazine in the field, this is a wide-ranging resource that combines news and information with comprehensive feature material. Both regular articles and feature material are well written and frequently scholarly, with many contributed by some the most knowledgeable and respected names in numismatics. One of the purposes of the magazine has always been to serve as an educational forum for collectors, and as such, much of its content is interesting and informative, touching on almost any aspect of numismatics. The web site has a table of contents for the most recent twelve issues, along with one or two full-text articles. An archive includes a handful of noteworthy full-text articles. This is a very inclusive publication that offers something for almost every collector, and it should be a part of almost any basic collection.

5266. ***Paper Money: official bimonthly publication of The Society of Paper Money Collectors.*** [ISSN: 0031-1162] 1962. bi-m. USD 30 membership. Ed(s): Fred Reed. Society of Paper Money Collectors, Inc., PO Box 117060, Carrollton, TX 75011. Illus., adv. Sample. Circ: 2500. Vol. ends: Nov/Dec. *Indexed:* NumL. *Bk. rev.:* 1, 250 words. *Aud.:* Ga, Sa.

This is the membership journal of the Society of Paper Money Collectors, and its content embraces both the collecting and the study of all forms of paper money and any related form of fiscal paper. Feature articles are primarily historical treatments of specific issues of money, and these frequently include information on specific banks as well as individuals associated with that money. Some issues of the magazine are theme oriented, with all feature material focusing on specific currency, such as fractional money. Articles are contributed by society members, many of whom are acknowledged authorities. Although this is a thin journal, it is well produced and generally scholarly. The web site has a contents list for the current issue that includes a one-sentence summary of each article, but there is no full-text material available. This is a specialty publication that should appeal to paper money collectors who appreciate historical content and context.

5267. ***World Coin News.*** [ISSN: 0145-9090] 1973. m. USD 27.98 domestic; USD 49.98 foreign; USD 3.50 per issue. Ed(s): Dave Harper. Krause Publications, Inc., 700 E State St, Iola, WI 54990-0001; info@krause.com; http://www.krause.com. Illus., adv. Sample. Circ: 9491 Paid and free. Vol. ends: Dec. Microform: PMC. *Indexed:* NumL. *Aud.:* Ga.

This is the only comprehensive numismatic publication that deals exclusively with international coinage. A tabloid-sized newspaper, it mixes current news articles with usually lengthy feature articles on coins, tokens, medals, and occasionally paper money. Features are informative and well written, frequently including the historical context of selected coins or numismatic events. Some of its material is also useful in helping collectors develop or refine their collecting knowledge and skills. The web site has one full-text article from the most recent issue plus selected other articles available only to subscribers or registrants with Krause Publications. Collecting world coinage is not nearly as popular as collecting U.S. coinage, limiting the potential audience for this publication, but it is still a useful periodical and can supplement core numismatic titles.

Electronic Journals

5268. ***CoinFacts.com.*** 1999. irreg. CoinFacts.com, Inc., PO Box 900, La Jolla, CA 92038-0900; ron@coinfacts.com; http://www.coinfacts.com/. *Aud.:* Hs, Ga.

Although this site is light on textual content, it is a very good source of reference information on specific U.S. coins. At its heart are magnified color images of every coin design in U.S. coinage history, along with mintage statistics and additional information for each year that the specific design was used. Each of those years links to an electronic price guide that provides an approximate retail price for that coin in its various levels of grading quality. Another interesting feature of the site is its "Cool Coins Tour," which showcases both rare and common coins by providing close-up images and textual information about those coins. The site does have full-text current news articles and press releases on numismatics, as well as a one-year archive of those articles. This is a very useful and convenient site for coin identification, pricing, and reference information.

5269. ***CoinLink.com.*** 1995. irreg. CoinLink, PO Box 916909, Longwood, FL 32791-6909. *Aud.:* Ga.

This is a very good source of current information both on collecting and on the numismatic market. Focusing primarily on the major areas of numismatics plus the precious metals market, this has a 30-day archive of full-text news articles and opinion pieces culled from newswires and numismatic publications. Of particular value for collectors is the section "The Collector's Corner," which has a six-month archive of full-text articles, plus links to club listings, message boards, and price guides listing approximate retail pricing for both coins and paper money. A planned addition to this section is a coin encyclopedia. Additional site links go to numerous numismatic dealers and product suppliers. This is a very comprehensive and useful site for almost anyone having an interest in numismatics.

■ OCCUPATIONS AND CAREERS

See also Education; and Labor and Industrial Relations sections.

Jan A. Maas, Division Chief, Education & Job Information Center, Brooklyn Public Library, Grand Army Plaza, Brooklyn, NY 11238; j.maas@brooklynpubliclibrary.org

Introduction

With the economy still stalling and unemployment rates holding steady in many parts of the country, job-hunters often turn to the library for helpful resources. The Occupations and Careers section presents a mix of standard magazines, available for your patrons in paper format, and electronic journals and job-hunting sites, available anywhere via the World Wide Web.

The list of standard magazines includes journals that feature practical information for job-seekers: career profiles, resume-writing tips, interview coaching, and, of course, employment advertisements. Also on the list are research journals for counselors and human resources personnel, as well as periodicals that emphasize data and statistical analysis or report on theoretical and practical approaches to counseling and employee development.

More and more, however, information for job-hunters is migrating to the web and taking on the characteristics of Internet job-hunting sites, offering job search engines and a place to post a resume.

In all, the Occupations and Careers section offers a broad array of magazines, hybrids, and electronic journals that serve differing publics: from the high school student, average job-seeker, or midlife career-changer, to the employment counselor, policy researcher, or person with a disability or special need.

Basic Periodicals

Hs: *Career Opportunities News, Career World, Occupational Outlook Quarterly;* Ga: *Affirmative Action Register, Career Opportunities News, National Ad Search, Occupational Outlook Quarterly;* Ac: *Career Opportunities News, Career Planning and Adult Development Journal, Journal of Career Development, National Ad Search, Occupational Outlook Quarterly;* Sa: *Careers and the Disabled, Journal of Employment Counseling, Journal of Volunteer Administration.*

Basic Abstracts and Indexes

Current Index to Journals in Education.

5270. ***Affirmative Action Register: the E E O recruitment publication.*** [ISSN: 0146-2113] 1974. m. Individuals, USD 15; Free to qualified personnel. Joyce R. Green, Ed. & Pub., 8356 Olive Blvd., St. Louis, MO 63132; aareeo@concentric.net; http://www.aar-eeo.com. Illus., adv. Sample. Circ: 60000 Controlled. Vol. ends: Feb/Aug. *Aud.:* Ga, Ac.

This publication is a copious collection of job ads for qualified minorities, women, veterans, and the disabled. Most ads are large, covering a quarter-page or more, and include complete job description, qualifications, and instructions for submission of resumes. Although most advertisers are colleges and universities seeking faculty or administrators, some government and social agencies also submit ads. An index lists the advertising institutions by name. The online version lists positions by category. An important resource for any library serving job-seekers.

5271. ***ArtSearch: the national employment service bulletin for the performing arts.*** [ISSN: 0730-9023] 1981. s-m. 23/yr. USD 75 in US & Canada; USD 125 elsewhere. Ed(s): Carol Van Keuren. Theatre Communications Group, Inc., 520 Eighth Ave 24th Fl, New York, NY 10018; tcg@tcg.org; http://www.tcg.org. Adv. Sample. Circ: 6200. *Aud.:* Ga, Ac.

ArtSearch is a popular job placement bulletin for the performing arts, including arts administration. Each edition contains about 300 advertisements. Administrative positions are listed for executive managers as well as artistic directors. Other jobs are listed for the fields of production and design, career development, and education. An online version of *ArtSearch* is also available by subscription.

Black Collegian. See College and Alumni section.

Black Enterprise. See African American section.

Career Development for Exceptional Individuals. See Disabilities section.

5272. ***The Career Development Quarterly.*** Formerly (until 1986): *Vocational Guidance Quarterly.* [ISSN: 0889-4019] 1952. q. USD 80 (Individuals, USD 45). Ed(s): Spencer Niles. American Counseling Association, 5999 Stevenson Ave, Alexandria, VA 22304-3300; http://www.counseling.org. Illus., index, adv. Sample. Refereed. Circ: 5900. Vol. ends: Jun. Reprint: PQC. *Indexed:* ABS&EES, AgeL, CIJE, EduInd, HEA, PsycholAb, SSCI, SWA, SWR&A. *Aud.:* Ac, Sa.

This professional and scholarly journal publishes research on the theory and practice of all aspects of career development, including counseling, occupational resources, labor market dynamics, and career education. This research seeks to address career development issues among a broad range of populations, including women, minorities, the aging, and youth at risk. As a result, it usually features case studies that present problems and practical solutions, along with more theoretical studies. A year-end review summarizes career and counseling research from other publications.

5273. ***Career Opportunities News.*** [ISSN: 0739-5043] 1983. 6x/yr. USD 75. Ferguson Publishing Co., c/o Facts On File, Inc., 132 W 31st St, 17th Fl, New York, NY 10001; CustServ@factsonfile.com; http://www.fergpubco.com/. Index. Vol. ends: May/Jun. *Bk. rev.:* 1-8, 75 words. *Aud.:* Hs, Ga, Ac.

This bimonthly surveys trends in the professions, government employment, and the general U.S. labor market. It offers well-documented facts and figures gleaned from reports by government agencies, private associations, and academic foundations, presented in short, easy-to-read articles. There are special columns for women and minorities. This journal is a valuable tool for career counselors, college students, and job seekers at all levels and deserves a place in college and public library collections.

5274. ***Career Planning and Adult Development Journal.*** [ISSN: 0736-1920] 1982. q. Membership, USD 59 includes Career Planning and Adult Development Network. Ed(s): Steven E Beasley. Career Planning and Adult Development Network, 4965 Sierra Rd, San Jose, CA 95132; info@careertrainer.com; http://www.careernetwork.com. Illus., adv. Sample. Circ: 1000. Vol. ends: Winter (No. 4). *Indexed:* CIJE. *Bk. rev.:* 40-50, 350 words. *Aud.:* Sa.

This quarterly is published primarily for professionals in the human resources field, career counselors, and others concerned with helping adults make career choices and transitions. Guest editors often build each issue around a specific topic, and the result is a series of well-researched, highly readable articles that combine theoretical material with practical advice. Recent issues have dealt with such topics as career development in Spanish-speaking nations and adult assessment instruments. Occasionally, an entire issue is devoted to book reviews of works in the field. Membership in the sponsoring organization also includes a subscription to *Career Planning and Adult Development Network Newsletter,* an announcement of international conferences and workshops.

5275. ***Career World.*** Formed by the 1981 merger of: *Career World 1; Career World 2;* Which was formerly (until 1977): *Career World;* Incorporates: *Real World.* [ISSN: 0744-1002] 1972. 6x/yr. USD 33.95. Ed(s): Charles Piddock. Weekly Reader Corp., 200 First Stamford Pl, PO Box 120023, Stamford, CT 06912-0023; http://www.weeklyreader.com. Illus., index. Sample. Circ: 114365 Paid. Vol. ends: May. Microform: PQC. Online: bigchalk; EBSCO Publishing; Florida Center for Library Automation; Gale Group; Northern Light Technology, Inc.; OCLC Online Computer Library Center, Inc.; ProQuest Information & Learning; H.W. Wilson. *Indexed:* ICM, RGPR. *Aud.:* Ems, Hs.

This magazine is especially useful for students in grades 7 to 12 as they begin to explore career paths and educational options, and for teachers as they guide them toward the future. Each issue is filled with articles on career trends (including salary scales) and practical tips for job hunting or starting one's own business. Students can also read about colleges and scholarships, vocational training, and job interview skills. The overall approach of this clearly written, brightly illustrated publication is geared to realistic expectations and the hard work involved in making one's life a success. Teachers get a special edition that includes lesson plans and discussion aids. Highly recommended for school or public libraries.

Careers & Colleges. See Teenagers section.

5276. *Careers & the Disabled.* Formerly: *Careers and the Handicapped.* [ISSN: 1056-277X] 1986. 5x/yr. USD 12. Ed(s): James Schneider. Equal Opportunity Publications, Inc., 445 Broad Hollow Rd, Ste 425, Melville, NY 11747; info@eop.com; http://www.eop.com. Illus., adv. Sample. Circ: 11674. *Bk. rev.:* 3-5, 150 words. *Aud.:* Ac, Sa.

People living with disabilities—in sight, hearing, or motor activity, for instance—will value this magazine for its excellent coverage of issues that concern the disabled and the employment opportunities available to them. In addition to giving general job-hunting advice on resume writing and interviewing, this publication focuses on careers and occupational fields suitable for the disabled. Many articles take the form of personality profiles of people with disabilities who are achieving their career goals. Others report on legal issues such as the Americans with Disabilities Act (ADA) or on steps that can be taken to improve accessibility in various environments. A unique feature is a page in Braille featuring information for the blind. Also included is a career directory acknowledging companies that are committed to recruiting entry-level and professional people with disabilities. This magazine deserves a place in any library that serves a significant number of people with disabilities.

The Chronicle of Higher Education. See Education/Higher Education section.

Entrepreneur. See Business/Small Business section.

5277. *Equal Opportunity.* Formerly: *Equal Opportunity: The Minority Student Magazine.* 1969. 3x/yr. USD 13. Ed(s): James Schneider. Equal Opportunity Publications, Inc., 445 Broad Hollow Rd, Ste 425, Melville, NY 11747; info@eop.com; http://www.eop.com. Illus., adv. Sample. Circ: 15000. Vol. ends: Spring. *Bk. rev.:* 3-6, 100-150 words. *Aud.:* Ga, Ac.

Subtitled "the career magazine for minority graduates," this publication focuses on the needs of African Americans, Hispanics, Asians, and Native Americans. Articles emphasize careers with potential for minorities or tell the stories of people who have achieved success in industry, government, or the professions. Other articles present general tips on interviewing, job hunting, or getting along in the corporate environment. Although this advice is addressed to members of minority groups, it would be equally useful to anyone trying to find a job. Also included is an affirmative-action career directory, listing companies that are committed to recruiting "members of minority groups who are entry-level graduates and professionals." The list gives the addresses of human resources departments and, in some cases, the names of contacts within companies or organizations. Highly recommended for libraries that serve minority populations.

5278. *Federal Career Opportunities.* [ISSN: 0279-2230] 1974. bi-w. USD 175; USD 19.97 per month online. Ed(s): Judelle A McArdle. Federal Research Service, Inc., 7360 Mcwhorter Pl., Ste. 201, Annandale, VA 22003-5633; http://www.fedjobs.com. Illus., adv. Vol. ends: Dec. *Aud.:* Hs, Ga, Ac.

Anyone interested in a job with the federal government should make a habit of reviewing biweekly issues of this publication because it lists thousands of government jobs—in the United States and around the world. *Federal Career Opportunities* (*FCO*) is basically a list, and is not graphically designed to be anything else, but careful study will reveal that everything a job hunter needs is here: position titles, series and grade numbers, announcement numbers, closing dates, and application addresses. The publisher, a private company not affiliated with any government agency, also produces a fee-based electronic version of government job listings through its web site. This is updated every weekday. Highly recommended for college libraries and job information centers of public libraries.

5279. *Federal Jobs Digest.* [ISSN: 0739-1684] 1977. bi-w. USD 112.50 (Individuals, USD 125). Ed(s): Peter E Ognibene. Federal Jobs Digest, 220 White Plains Rd, Tarrytown, NY 10591. Illus., adv. Circ: 3500 Paid. *Aud.:* Ga.

This biweekly newspaper lists more than 13,000 current federal job openings throughout the nation and overseas. It also features articles on trends in federal hiring needs and detailed advice on how to apply for a federal job. At the web site listed above, registered users may view jobs and post a resume; some fees may be involved.

Hispanic Times Magazine. See Latino Studies section.

5280. *Journal of Career Development.* Formerly (until 1984): *Journal of Career Education.* [ISSN: 0894-8453] 1972. q. USD 508 print or online ed. Ed(s): Norman C Gysbers. Kluwer Academic / Plenum Publishers, 233 Spring St Fl 7, New York, NY 10013-1522; http://www.wkap.nl/. Illus., index, adv. Sample. Refereed. Vol. ends: Summer (No. 4). Microform: PQC. Online: EBSCO Publishing; ingenta.com; Kluwer Online; OCLC Online Computer Library Center, Inc.; Ovid Technologies, Inc.; Swets Blackwell. Reprint: PQC. *Indexed:* ABS&EES, BusEdI, CIJE, EduInd, HEA, HRA, PsycholAb, SSCI, SWR&A. *Aud.:* Ac, Sa.

Scholarly articles in this quarterly present research in the theory and practice of the field of career education and development, with a focus on how research can influence practice. The populations studied are diverse: adults and adolescents, people with special needs, the gifted, minorities, and families. Counselors and clinicians, as well as social scientists and policymakers, will find rich material in this periodical. This is highly suitable for academic and specialized libraries. Contents are available online at the publisher's web site.

5281. *Journal of Employment Counseling.* [ISSN: 0022-0787] 1965. q. Free to members; Non-members, USD 40. Ed(s): Norman E Amundson. American Counseling Association, 5999 Stevenson Ave, Alexandria, VA 22304-3300; http://www.counseling.org. Illus., index, adv. Sample. Refereed. Circ: 1500. Vol. ends: Dec. Microform: PQC. Online: bigchalk; EBSCO Publishing; Florida Center for Library Automation; Gale Group; Northern Light Technology, Inc.; OCLC Online Computer Library Center, Inc.; ProQuest Information & Learning; H.W. Wilson. Reprint: PQC; PSC. *Indexed:* ASSIA, AgeL, CIJE, EduInd, HEA, PsycholAb, SFSA, SSCI, SWR&A. *Aud.:* Ac, Sa.

Addressed to professional employment counselors, this quarterly presents scholarly research that seeks to illuminate the practice and theory of the field. Well-documented articles report on such topics as psychological stress, older women workers, and the role of paraprofessionals in the employment counseling field. The emphasis is on theory that might make a practical difference in a professional counseling situation. This is a periodical of high interest and value to those in the field, deserving a place in an academic or professional library.

5282. *Journal of Volunteer Administration.* Supersedes (in 1982): *Volunteer Administration.* [ISSN: 0733-6535] 1968. q. USD 45 domestic; USD 55 in Canada & Mexico; USD 60 elsewhere. Ed(s): Mary Merrill. Association for Volunteer Administration, PO Box 32092, Richmond, VA 23294-2092; avaintl@mindspring.com. Illus., index, adv. Sample. Refereed. Circ: 2500 Paid. Vol. ends: Fall. *Indexed:* AgeL, CIJE, PAIS. *Aud.:* Ac, Sa.

This quarterly is a forum for those involved in volunteer administration, a subject that essentially covers anything related to volunteers themselves, volunteer programs, or volunteer management. Articles follow a scholarly style, analyzing data and reporting on research on the theory and practice of volunteerism, including the history and philosophy of the field. Occasional articles present training designs and other practical measures to increase the effectiveness of volunteers. The magazine deserves a place in any academic library that serves students of education and other social sciences, and could be useful to administrators of social agencies that are dependent on volunteer help.

5283. *Kennedy's Career Strategist: a monthly guide to career planning success and job satisfaction.* [ISSN: 0891-2572] 1986. 10x/yr. USD 65. Ed(s): Marilyn Moats Kennedy. Career Strategies, 1150 Wilmette Ave, Wilmette, IL 60091; mmkcareer@aol.com; http://www.espan.com/docs/moats.html. Illus., index. Sample. Circ: 2000. Vol. ends: Dec. *Bk. rev.:* 1-2, 150 words. *Aud.:* Ga.

This monthly guide, written in an easy, no-nonsense style, offers advice to middle managers and other professionals on how to get and keep a job, and how to move on graciously when the time comes. The newsletter features short, punchy articles on everything from advice on interviewing to handling job stress. Included also is a section of news briefs. Of major interest to active job seekers and career counselors.

Monthly Labor Review. See *U.S. Bureau of Labor Statistics. Monthly Labor Review* in the Labor and Industrial Relations section.

5284. *N A C E Journal: the international magazine of placement and recruitment.* Former titles: *Journal of Career Planning & Employment;* (until 1995): *Journal of College Placement.* [ISSN: 1542-2046] 1940. 4x/yr. Free to members; Non-members, USD 72. Ed(s): Jerry Bohovich. National Association of Colleges and Employers, 62 Highland Ave, Bethlehem, PA 18017-9085; info@naceweb.org; http://www.naceweb.org. Illus., index, adv. Sample. Circ: 4200. Vol. ends: May. Microform: PQC. Online: bigchalk; Gale Group; OCLC Online Computer Library Center, Inc. Reprint: PQC. *Indexed:* ATI, BRI, CBRI, CIJE, EduInd, HEA, PAIS, PMA. *Bk. rev.:* 10-12, 100-250 words. *Aud.:* Ac.

This quarterly, the journal for placement officers, employment counselors, and other members of the National Association of Colleges and Employers, focuses on major trends in the human relations field. Regular features include Legal Q&A and Resources Reviews. Articles cover such topics as diversity, internships, campus recruitment, and changing employment markets. It also features news about people in the field, industries and individual companies, conferences and awards, and upcoming career fairs and other events.

5285. *National Ad Search.* Former titles: *Ad Search. The Weekly National Want Ad Digest; Ad Search. The National Want Ad Newspaper.* [ISSN: 0744-7140] 1968. 50x/yr. USD 250 domestic; USD 312 Canada; USD 280 for 6 mos. elsewhere. Ed(s): Doris M Morey. National Ad Search, Inc., PO Box 2083, Milwaukee, WI 53201-2083; nas@execpc.com; http://www.nationaladsearch.com. Adv. *Aud.:* Ga.

This weekly publishes more than 2,500 job ads culled from more than 65 major U.S. newspapers. Fields covered include finance, communications, education, engineering, medicine, and law. It also includes ad agency listings and a resume exchange for subscribers. Internet users may sign up at the web site for a free trial, but they must subscribe for full service.

5286. *Occupational Outlook Quarterly.* [ISSN: 0199-4786] 1957. q. Sep.-June. USD 9.50. U.S. Bureau of Labor Statistics, 2 Massachusetts Ave, N E, Washington, DC 20212; http://stats.bls.gov/emppub4.htm. Illus., index. Sample. Circ: 15000. Vol. ends: Winter. Microform: CIS; NBI; PQC. Online: bigchalk; EBSCO Publishing; Florida Center for Library Automation; Gale Group; Northern Light Technology, Inc.; OCLC Online Computer Library Center, Inc.; ProQuest Information & Learning; H.W. Wilson. Reprint: CIS. *Indexed:* ABIn, ASG, AgeL, AmStI, BPI, CIJE, EduInd, IUSGP, MagInd, PAIS, RGPR. *Aud.:* Hs, Ga, Ac.

At least one major article in each issue focuses on a particular career while other pieces cover various aspects of the labor market or highlight jobs with a strong potential for growth. This publication always contains a wealth of data, including projections about the future of the labor force, industry, and a large variety of occupations. The magazine's attractive graphics and easy-to-read style have made it a favorite among high school and college students researching careers. It may be of equal value to midlife career changers who are assessing new employment opportunities. Highly recommended for school, academic, and public libraries.

Success. See General Editorial/General section.

Techniques. See Education/Specific Subjects and Teaching Methods: Techniques section.

Training. See Management, Administration, and Human Resources/ Human Resources section.

Vocational Guidance Quarterly. See *Career Development Quarterly.*

Volunteer Administration. See *Journal of Volunteer Administration.*

Work and Occupations. See Sociology and Social Work/General section.

Working Mother. See Women section.

Electronic Journals

5287. *America's Job Bank.* irreg. America's Job Bank, http://www.ajb.dni.us/. *Aud.:* Ga.

This site was established as a partnership between the U.S. Department of Labor and some 1,800 state employment service offices. Searchers can look for jobs by occupational categories or keyword, or by military code or job number, and then pick a state or ZIP code to narrow their search. Almost two million job openings are included. Users who need a complete personal search may register for the free Career Assistant, which allows them to post a resume and receive responses from employers. The site is now part of CareerOneStop and offers entry to America's Career Information Net and America's Service Locator.

5288. *Career Journal.* irreg. Dow Jones & Co., Inc., 200 Liberty St, New York, NY 10281; http://www.wsj.com. *Aud.:* Ga.

This web site has taken over the functions of the popular *National Employment Business Weekly,* formerly published by *The Wall Street Journal* and now ceased. It features current articles from *The Wall Street Journal* that relate to careers and employment opportunities. A vast array of columns is available at the click of a mouse: from salary and hiring information to job hunting advice, to tips on managing a career. Seachers can look for jobs via keyword search or location. Although the ads are aimed at a business audience, the features are worthwhile for anyone trying to navigate today's job-hunting waters.

5289. *JobWeb.* irreg. National Association of Colleges and Employers, 62 Highland Ave, Bethlehem, PA 18017-9085. *Aud.:* Ga, Ac.

Maintained by the National Association of Colleges and Employers, *JobWeb* is an electronic gateway to career planning and employment information. While primarily designed as a connection between employers and recent college graduates, it is also valuable for any college-educated member of the public. Sections of the site include Online Career Fair (with information about many employers), Resumes & Interviews, Articles Library, and Salary Information.

5290. *Monster.com.* irreg. Monster Network, http://www.monster.com/. *Aud.:* Ga.

More than a site for posting resumes, *Monster.com* also includes listings for U.S. and international job openings. It provides a free search service called "My Monster," which takes one's resume and ideal job specifications and searches continually for matching employment ads on the Internet.

5291. *The New Social Worker: the magazine for social work students and recent graduates.* [ISSN: 1073-7871] 1994. q. USD 15 domestic; USD 21 Canada; USD 27 elsewhere. Ed(s): Linda Grobman. White Hat Communications, PO Box 5390, Harrisburg, PA 17110-0390; linda.grobman@paonline.com; http://www.socialworker.com/. Adv. *Indexed:* SWR&A. *Aud.:* Sa.

Social workers and students can talk over what is going on in terms of jobs available, working problems, legislation, and other subjects, in the "social worker career chat room" on this site. It also includes an online social work education directory and a link to a graduate school directory. A winner for anyone in this field or contemplating such work.

5292. *The Riley Guide.* irreg. The Riley Guide, webmaster@ rileyguide.com; http://www.rileyguide.com/. *Aud.:* Ga.

A pioneering job-hunting Internet site, *The Riley Guide* is still the first place to turn for accurate, ad-free employment information on the web. It maintains numerous links to job-information sites, career-planning services, and research resources. The site also includes sections on general recruiters and job banks in most areas of the country and around the world, and highlights career resources for women, minorities, and other groups.

One can search for jobs in scores of fields, including agriculture, government, health care, legal services, the natural sciences, nonprofits, and many more. Also included are links to resume-writing and interviewing guides. The site is enhanced by an alphabetical index. Maintained by Margaret F. (Riley) Dikel, a former librarian, it has been cited for excellence by *Yahoo! Internet World* and by Richard Bolles, author of *What Color Is Your Parachute? The Internet Guide*.

■ OFFICE MANAGEMENT

See also Business; and Management, Administration, and Personnel sections.

Susan M. Moore, Catalog Librarian and Bibliographer, Rod Library, University of Northern Iowa, 1227 W. 27th St., Cedar Falls, IA 50613-3675; Susan.Moore@uni.edu

Introduction

The following journals have as their focus the office environment and are of importance to office employees and managers. Topics covered range from the broad (new technology, sick-building syndrome, intranet applications) to the narrow (specific software applications, voice mail, ergonomics). Most of the journals are geared to the office management professional who is increasingly being asked to expand his or her knowledge in areas formerly the province of systems engineers. Broader business topics such as employee management, productivity enhancement, and total quality management are occasionally included.

Basic Periodicals

Ga, Ac, Sa: *Office Solutions.*

Basic Abstracts and Indexes

ABI/INFORM, Business Education Index, Business Index, Business Periodicals Index.

5293. *I S Analyzer Case Studies.* Former titles (until 1994): *I S Analyzer;* (until Sep.1987): *E D P Analyzer.* [ISSN: 1080-1146] 1963. m. USD 365 domestic; USD 345 foreign. Ed(s): Joanne Cummings. 400 Group, 990 Washington St., Ste. 308, Dedham, MA 02026-6700; http://www.the400group.com. Illus., index. Vol. ends: Dec. Microform: PQC. Online: Gale Group. Reprint: PQC. *Indexed:* ABIn, AS&TI, BPI, CompLI. *Aud.:* Ac, Sa.

This journal provides concise articles of advice and analysis for the information systems professional. Each issue is essentially one article with a commentary and executive summary at the end. The journal often includes case studies. Topics covered include continuous quality improvement programs, data center automation, information technology infrastructure, and cooperative systems.

5294. *Information Technology and People.* Former titles (until vol.6, no.1, 1992): *Technology and People; Office - Technology and People.* [ISSN: 0959-3845] 1982. q. EUR 2793.79 in Europe; USD 2539 in North America; AUD 3199 in Australasia. Ed(s): Eleanor H Wynn. Emerald, 60-62 Toller Ln, Bradford, BD8 9BY, United Kingdom; info@emeraldinsight.com; http://www.emeraldinsight.com/journals/. Illus., adv. Refereed. Vol. ends: Dec. Reprint: PSC. *Indexed:* ABIn, CompLI, InfoSAb, LISA, MicrocompInd. *Aud.:* Ga, Ac, Sa.

Providing an international perspective on the use of technology in the workplace, this publication takes an interdisciplinary approach to its social and organizational aspects. Articles concern the study of the theoretical effect technology has on the social processes in an organization, as well as how various organizations have implemented new technology.

5295. *Office Solutions: the magazine for office professionals.* Formerly (until 2000): *Office Systems (Year);* Incorporates: *Managing Office Technology;* Which was formerly (until June 1993): *Modern Office Technology;* (1956-1983): *Modern Office Procedures.* [ISSN: 1529-1804] 1984. m. USD 36. Ed(s): Lisa Bouchey. Quality Publishing Inc., 252 N. Main St., Ste. 200, Mt. Airy, NC 27030; osod@os-od.com; http://www.os-od.com. Illus., adv. Circ: 100225 Paid and controlled. Vol. ends: Dec. Microform: PQC. Online: Florida Center for Library Automation; Gale Group; ProQuest Information & Learning. *Indexed:* ABIn, BPI, CompLI, ConsI, MagInd. *Bk. rev.:* Number and length vary. *Aud.:* Ga, Ac, Sa.

This publication is geared toward those working in the office management field and covers the wide variety of issues facing office managers and office workers today. Topics include privacy issues, telecommuting, workplace styles, and the impact of technology on office work. Also included are product reviews, product announcements, and book reviews. Recommended.

5296. *OfficePro.* Formerly (until 1997): *Secretary.* [ISSN: 1096-5807] 1942. 9x/yr. USD 25. Ed(s): Angela Hickman Brady. Stratton Publishing and Marketing Inc., 5501 Backlick Rd, Ste 240, Springfield, VA 22206. Illus., adv. Circ: 37000 Paid. Vol. ends: Dec. Reprint: PQC. *Indexed:* BusEdI, CIJE. *Bk. rev.:* 5, 225 words. *Aud.:* Hs, Ga, Ac.

This magazine contains articles of particular interest to the office manager or secretary, as well as other office workers. Topics covered include personal-information management software, events planning, handling international guests, and career guidance. A regular feature, "Word Watching," provides guidance in word usage with common errors and correct examples. Recommended.

■ PALEONTOLOGY

See also Biological Sciences; and Earth Sciences sections.

Kebede Gessesse, Head, Biological and Environmental Sciences Library, Duke University, Durham, North Carolina 27708; kebg@duke.edu; FAX: 919-681-7606

Introduction

Paleontology is the study of the forms of life existing in prehistoric or geologic times. By studying the fossils in progressively older rocks, the paleontologist attempts to establish an account of how all the animals and plants that make up the modern biosphere evolved from their earliest beginnings. The field of paleontology has a broad scope, encompassing the study of both fossil animals and fossil plants. As knowledge in this specialized field has advanced, many subdivisions have formed. For instance, the study of fossil plants is known as paleobotany. The study of small fossils for which a microscope is often needed is known as micropaleontology. When referring to the more interpretative "biological" aspects of the science, the term *paleobiology* is used. And while paleozoology would suggest the study of fossil animals, the preferred term is *vertebrate paleontology.* Stratigraphy is another subfield that is interlinked with the discipline of paleontology. It refers to the study of the strata and the total environment of the earth through its succession. Clearly, it is important that paleontologists be knowledgeable about both geology and biology.

An independent section for serial publications in paleontology began with the ninth edition of this book. This entire section is dedicated to the broader heading of paleontology, which includes an assortment of publications in general paleontology, paleobiology, stratigraphy, paleobotany, paleoclimatology, and micropaleontology. With the addition of two more titles in the eleventh edition, the paleontology section contains 26 entries.

The publications described under this section are not intended to constitute a comprehensive list of research resources, and selections are mostly restricted to English-language periodicals. However, most of the journals included in the section are appropriate for academic and specialized collections; only a few general or popular titles are suitable for secondary schools or public libraries. Because of the relatively high subscription prices of these journals, most libraries will have to choose titles carefully.

Basic Periodicals

Ac: *Journal of Paleontology; Lethaia; Palaeogeography, Palaeoclimatology, Palaeocology;* Sa: *Historical Biology, Journal of Foraminiferal Research, Micropaleontology, Review of Paleobotany and Palynology.*

Basic Abstracts and Indexes

Bibliography and Index of Geology, Bibliography and Index of Micropaleontology, Zentralblatt fuer Geologie und Palaeontologie.

5297. ***Acta Palaeontologica Polonica.*** [ISSN: 0567-7920] 1956. q. USD 90 (Individuals, USD 75). Ed(s): Zofia Kielan-Jaworowska. Polska Akademia Nauk, Instytut Paleobiologii, ul Twarda 51-55, Warsaw, 00-818, Poland. Illus., adv. Refereed. Circ: 500. *Indexed:* BiolAb, DSR&OA, GeoRef, PetrolAb, VetBull, ZooRec. *Bk. rev.:* 0-1; 500-1,200 words. *Aud.:* Ac, Sa.

Acta Palaeontologica Polonica is a quarterly journal published by the Institute of Paleobiology of the Polish Academy of Sciences. It is general in scope, covering all areas of paleontology. *Acta Palaeontologica Polonica* emerged in 1956 from the Acta Geologica Polonica, which first appeared in 1950. Initially, papers in Polish, French, and occasionally Russian had been accepted along with those in English. But for the last 20 years English is the exclusive language of the journal, accompanied by brief summaries in Polish. This is one of the most highly respected journals in the field of paleontology. Appropriate for comprehensive academic collections.

5298. ***Alcheringa.*** [ISSN: 0311-5518] 1975. s-a. AUD 132 (Individuals, AUD 82.50). Ed(s): Glen Brock, Anthony J Wright. Geological Society of Australia Inc., Ste 706, 301 George St, Sydney, NSW 2000, Australia; misha@gsa.org.au; http://www.gsa.org.au. Illus. Refereed. Circ: 600. Vol. ends: No. 4. *Indexed:* GeoRef, PetrolAb, SCI, ZooRec. *Aud.:* Ac, Sa.

Published by the Association of Australasian Palaeontologists of the Geological Society of Australia, this journal covers all aspects of paleontology and its ramifications for the earth and biological sciences, including taxonomy, biostratigraphy, micropaleontology, paleobotany, paleobiology, paleoecology, biogeography, biogeochemistry, and the study of trace fossils. It publishes review articles from time to time. Occasionally, a single number may be devoted to several articles on a single topic. This is a high-quality scholarly journal with an emphasis on well-executed and informative line drawings, photographs, and other illustrations. "Alcheringa" is a popularized English version of an aboriginal expression that is interpreted to mean "in the beginning" or "from all eternity." Two volumes are published in one. Five to eight papers appear per issue, most of them 15–25 pages long. Recommended for comprehensive college and university collections.

5299. ***American Paleontologist: a newsmagazine of earth sciences.*** [ISSN: 1066-8772] 1992. q. Membership, USD 30. Ed(s): Warren D Allmon. Paleontological Research Institution, 1259 Trumansburg Rd, Ithaca, NY 14850-1398; http://www.englib.cornell.edu/pri/. Illus., adv. *Indexed:* GeoRef, ZooRec. *Aud.:* Ga, Sa.

American Paleontologist is an official publication of the Paleontological Research Institution (PRI). Established in 1992, this publication is relatively new. It is primarily a newsletter for the professional paleontologist with a number of short, two- to four-page articles on significant happenings in paleontology and related fields, including the broader scope of earth sciences. Each issue contains "Calendars" of forthcoming meetings for the current and following years. Issues do not exceed ten pages and are distributed in folio paper format. The information value to paleontologists makes this title worthy of consideration for the general paleontology collection.

Boreas: an international jouranl of quaternary research See Earth Sciences section.

5300. ***Bulletins of American Paleontology.*** [ISSN: 0007-5779] 1895. 2x/yr. USD 160 domestic; USD 165 foreign. Ed(s): Warren D Allmon. Paleontological Research Institution, 1259 Trumansburg Rd, Ithaca, NY 14850-1398; http://www.englib.cornell.edu/pri/. Illus., adv. Refereed. Reprint: PSC. *Indexed:* BiolAb, GeoRef, PetrolAb, ZooRec. *Aud.:* Ac, Sa.

Begun in 1895, *Bulletins of American Paleontology* is the oldest paleontological journal published in the Western Hemisphere. Published by the Paleontological Research Institution (PRI), a prominent organization actively engaged in the promotion and development of paleontological study, it publishes peer-reviewed monographic works in any area of paleontology, especially descriptive systematics requiring high-quality photographic illustrations. *BAP* usually comprises two or more separate monographs in two volumes each year. It is an important journal serving paleontological researchers as an outlet for their significant, longer articles and monographs (i.e., more than 200 pages), for which high-quality photographic illustrations and the large quarto format are required. Useful for colleges with paleontology teaching and research programs; also appropriate for comprehensive collections.

5301. ***Fossils and Strata: a monograph series in palaeontology and biostratigraphy.*** [ISSN: 0300-9491] 1972. irreg. Ed(s): Hans Joergen Hansen. Taylor & Francis A S, Cort Adelersgt. 17, Solli, PO Box 2562, Oslo, 0202, Norway. Illus., adv. Sample. Online: EBSCO Publishing. Reprint: PSC. *Indexed:* BiolAb, GeoRef, SWRA, ZooRec. *Aud.:* Ac, Sa.

Fossils and Strata is an international series of monographs and memoirs in paleontology and stratigraphy, published through cooperation among the Scandinavian countries. This journal forms part of the same structured publishing program as the journals *Lethaia* and *Boreas.* These two journals are fully international and accept papers in their respective sectors of science without national preferences. *Fossils and Strata,* however, contains more-comprehensive systematic and regional monographs emanating primarily from Sweden, Norway, Finland, Denmark, and Germany. Although articles in German and French may be accepted, the use of English is strongly preferred. In spite of the regional scope and composition of the editorial staff, this journal provides a nucleus of research results that is of general interest in international paleontology and stratigraphy. Appropriate for academic collections where indicated by faculty research interests.

5302. ***Geobios: paleontology, stratigraphy, paleoecology.*** [ISSN: 0016-6995] 1968. bi-m. EUR 149 (Individuals, EUR 91). Ed(s): Patrick Racheboeuf. Elsevier BV, Sara Burgerhartstraat 25, Amsterdam, 1055 KV, Netherlands; nlinfo-f@elsevier.nl; http://www.elsevier.nl. Illus., index, adv. Refereed. Circ: 850. Vol. ends: Dec (No. 6). *Indexed:* BiolAb, GeoRef, GeogAbPG, PetrolAb, SCI, SSCI. *Bk. rev.:* 0-5, 1,500-2,000 words. *Aud.:* Ac, Sa.

Geobios publishes original research articles of international rank on paleontology, stratigraphy, and paleoecology. The related subjects of paleobotany and paleogeography are within its scope. In accordance with editorial policy, articles do not exceed 30 printed pages, including text, figures, tables, and references. To accommodate longer contributions, the new "Supplements" series has been introduced. It is similar in content to *Geobios: an international journal of life sciences on earth,* but in scope, the latter has more emphasis on the biological sciences. Since 1992, *Geobios* publishes original papers in French, English, Spanish, and German. Despite its French editorial orientation, this journal maintains an international scope in contributions, editors, and topics. Recommended for the academic collection and research libraries.

5303. ***Historical Biology: an international journal of paleobiology.*** [ISSN: 0891-2963] 1988. q. GBP 427 (Individuals, GBP 87). Ed(s): R D K Thomas. Taylor & Francis Ltd, 11 New Fetter Ln, London, EC4P 4EE, United Kingdom; http://www.tandf.co.uk/journals. Illus. Refereed. Vol. ends: No. 4. Online: RoweCom Information Quest; Swets Blackwell. Reprint: PSC. *Indexed:* GeoRef, ZooRec. *Bk. rev.:* Number and length vary. *Aud.:* Ac, Sa.

This journal covers developments in the sciences concerned with the history of life through geological time and the biology of past organisms. It encourages a diversity of approaches in this field and emphasizes modern and controversial topics. *Historical Biology* is broad in scope. It includes paleobiology, paleontology, paleobiogeography, evolutionary processes and patterns, molecular paleontology, extinction, phenomena, and aspects of geology, geochemistry, and geophysics that have a direct bearing on paleontological questions. Because of its diverse coverage, the title is highly recommended as a basic paleontological journal for college and university collections.

5304. ***Journal of Foraminiferal Research.*** Supersedes: *Cushman Foundation for Foraminiferal Research. Contributions.* [ISSN: 0096-1191] 1971. q. USD 90 (Members, USD 40). Ed(s): Ronald E Martin. Cushman Foundation for Foraminiferal Research, MRC 121 NMNH, Smithsonian Institution, Washington, DC 20560; http://cushforams.niu.edu. Illus., index, adv. Sample. Refereed. Circ: 800. Vol. ends: No. 4. *Indexed:* BiolAb, DSR&OA, GeoRef, PetrolAb, SCI, SWRA, ZooRec. *Aud.:* Ac, Sa.

The *Journal of Foraminiferal Research* is the official publication of the Cushman Foundation for Foraminiferal Research, Department of Paleobiology, National Museum of Natural History, Smithsonian Institution. This publication contains contributions from the Cushman Laboratory for Foraminiferal Research first published between 1925 and 1950 and from the Cushman Foundation for Foraminiferal Research published between 1950 and 1970. *JFR* publishes original papers of international interest dealing with the foraminifera and allied groups of organisms. Papers that deal with foraminifera as part of stratigraphic or ecologic studies as well as review articles are also included. This is a highly respected scholarly journal. Appropriate for specialized or comprehensive academic collections.

5305. ***Journal of Paleolimnology.*** [ISSN: 0921-2728] 8x/yr. EUR 1108 print or online ed. Ed(s): John P Smol, William M Last. Kluwer Academic Publishers, van Godewijckstraat 30, PO Box 17, Dordrecht, 3300 AA, Netherlands. Illus., index, adv. Sample. Refereed. Microform: PQC. Online: EBSCO Publishing; ingenta.com; Kluwer Online; OCLC Online Computer Library Center, Inc.; Ovid Technologies, Inc.; RoweCom Information Quest. Reprint: SWZ. *Indexed:* BiolAb, ChemAb, GeoRef, GeogAbPG, M&GPA, PollutAb, SCI, SWRA, ZooRec. *Aud.:* Ac, Sa.

This journal is multidisciplinary in nature; it publishes papers that are concerned with all aspects of the reconstructions and interpretations of lake histories, including paleoenvironmental studies of rivers and woodlands, and research contributions from biological, chemical, and geological perspectives. Both applied and theoretical papers are encouraged. In addition, the *Journal of Paleolimnology* is a major repository for papers dealing with climatic change as well as other pressing topics, such as global environmental change, lake acidification, long-term monitoring, and other aspects of lake ontogeny. Taxonomic and methodological papers are also acceptable, provided they are of relatively broad interest. New equipment designs are frequently featured. In addition to original data and ideas, the *Journal of Paleolimnology* publishes review articles, commentaries, and program announcements. A relevant book review section is also featured. This title should be given preference for core collections.

5306. ***Journal of Paleontology.*** [ISSN: 0022-3360] 1927. bi-m. USD 116. Ed(s): Brian J Witzke, Ann F Budd. Paleontological Society, PO Box 1897, Lawrence, KS 66044-8897; http://www.paleosoc.org/. Illus., index, adv. Refereed. Circ: 3500. Vol. ends: Nov (No. 6). Microform: PQC. Online: bigchalk; BioOne; Gale Group; Northern Light Technology, Inc.; OCLC Online Computer Library Center, Inc.; ProQuest Information & Learning. *Indexed:* AbAn, B&AI, BiolAb, DSR&OA, GeoRef, OceAb, PetrolAb, SCI, SSCI, ZooRec. *Bk. rev.:* 4, 500 words. *Aud.:* Ac, Sa.

A must for the core collection, the *Journal of Paleontology* publishes original articles and notes on the systematics of fossil organisms and the implications of systematics to all aspects of paleobiology and stratigraphic paleontology. It contains both research papers and field reports covering former living organisms from the recent past back to the earliest fossils known. Emphasis is given to taxonomic paleontology and its implications, including those aspects of paleobiology and stratigraphic paleontology. It also includes brief articles in its "Paleontological Notes" section, as well as updates on taxonomy, discussions of earlier papers, and news of the society. Both terrestrial and marine environments are within the scope of the journal. Each issue contains 14 to 20 articles. In spite of an entirely American editorial board, this journal has a slightly more international focus than *Palaeontology* (respectively reviewed in this section). It will be of high value not only in paleontology but in biological sciences collections as well.

5307. ***Journal of Palynology.*** Formerly (until 1972): *Palynological Bulletin.* [ISSN: 0022-3379] 1966. s-a. INR 700; USD 60. Ed(s): A R Kulkarnj Bir Bahadur. Today and Tomorrow's Printers & Publishers, 24 B-5 Desh Bandhu Gupta Rd., Karol Bagh, New Delhi, 110 005, India. Illus., index, adv. Circ: 400. *Indexed:* BiolAb, ChemAb, ForAb, GeoRef, HortAb. *Aud.:* Ac, Sa.

Covers all aspects of pollen spore studies, from algae to angiosperms, from present-day plants to fossils. Due to its regional scope, this specialized journal should be considered an important addition to a research-oriented botanical collection.

5308. ***Journal of Vertebrate Paleontology.*** [ISSN: 0272-4634] 1981. q. USD 250 domestic; USD 270 foreign. Ed(s): Mark V H Wilson. Society of Vertebrate Paleontology, 60 Revere Drive, Suite 500, Northbrook, IL 60062; svp@vertpaleo.org; http://www.vertpaleo.org. Illus., index, adv. Refereed. Vol. ends: Dec (No. 4). *Indexed:* BiolAb, GeoRef, SCI, ZooRec. *Bk. rev.:* 0-4, 1,000-2,000 words. *Aud.:* Ac, Sa.

This journal publishes original contributions on all aspects of paleontology, including vertebrate origins, evolution, functional morphology, taxonomy, biostratigraphy, and paleoecology. Only papers in English are accepted for publication. Quality and significance of research are the criteria for acceptance of articles. Issues generally contain 10 to 12 articles, eight to ten pages in length. There are three categories of articles: rapid communications (contributions of immediate interest to the scientific community); regular articles, not exceeding 50 double-spaced pages; and short manuscripts published as "Notes." This is one of the leading journals in the field. An important research tool in paleontological studies.

5309. ***Lethaia: an international journal of palaeontology and stratigraphy.*** [ISSN: 0024-1164] 1968. q. GBP 144. Ed(s): Svend Stouge. Taylor & Francis A S, Cort Adelersgt. 17, Solli, PO Box 2562, Oslo, 0202, Norway; journals@tandf.no; http://www.tandf.co.uk. Illus., index, adv. Refereed. Circ: 1000. Vol. ends: No. 4. Microform: PQC. Online: EBSCO Publishing; Ingenta Select; OCLC Online Computer Library Center, Inc.; RoweCom Information Quest; Swets Blackwell. Reprint: ISI; PSC. *Indexed:* AbAn, BiolAb, DSR&OA, GeoRef, PetrolAb, SCI, ZooRec. *Bk. rev.:* 1, 700 words. *Aud.:* Ac, Sa.

Cosponsored by the National Councils for Scientific Research in Denmark, Finland, Norway, and Sweden, this is the official journal of the International Palaeontological Association. It publishes articles of international interest in the fields of paleontology and stratigraphy. The articles concentrate on the development of new ideas and methods and descriptions of new features of wide significance rather than routine descriptions. Paleobiology and ecostratigraphy are the core topics of the journal. Occasionally, an issue includes discussions of previously published papers, short notes on current paleontological research, and literature reviews. It is recommended highly for comprehensive paleontological collections.

5310. ***Marine Micropaleontology.*** [ISSN: 0377-8398] 1976. 16x/yr. EUR 1150. Ed(s): J Lipps, A. Mackensen. Elsevier BV, Sara Burgerhartstraat 25, Amsterdam, 1055 KV, Netherlands; nlinfo-f@elsevier.nl; http://www.elsevier.nl. Illus. Sample. Refereed. Vol. ends: Nov (No. 4). Microform: PQC. Online: EBSCO Publishing; ingenta.com; ScienceDirect; Swets Blackwell. Reprint: SWZ. *Indexed:* BiolAb, DSR&OA, EngInd, GeoRef, GeogAbPG, OceAb, PetrolAb, SCI, ZooRec. *Bk. rev.:* 0-1, 3,000 words. *Aud.:* Ac, Sa.

Marine Micropaleontology is an international journal publishing results of research in all fields of marine micropaleontology of the ocean basins and continents, ranging from paleoceanography, evolution, ecology and paleoecology, biology and paleobiology, biochronology, paleoclimatology, taphonomy, to the systematic relationships of higher taxa. It is highly relevant in academic and research institutions where teaching and research programs in paleontology are offered. The international orientation of this journal is reflected in its papers and editorial board. Papers published in *Marine Micropaleontology* are highly cited. This publication fills a gap in library collections and is a first choice for any academic library with a teaching program in paleontology and/or marine sciences.

5311. *Micropaleontology.* [ISSN: 0026-2803] 1954. q. USD 360 (Individuals, USD 180). Ed(s): John A Van Couvering. American Museum of Natural History, Central Park West at 79th St, New York, NY 10024-5192; http://www.micropress.org. Illus. Refereed. Circ: 900. Vol. ends: No. 4. Microform: MIM; PQC. Online: BioOne; OCLC Online Computer Library Center, Inc. Reprint: PQC. *Indexed:* BiolAb, ChemAb, DSR&OA, GeoRef, GeogAbPG, OceAb, PetrolAb, SCI, ZooRec. *Bk. rev.:* 0-1, 200-1,000 words. *Aud.:* Ac, Sa.

Micropaleontology is an international peer-reviewed journal. It is a specialized publication that publishes original research papers on the morphology and paleobiology of fossilized microorganisms, as well as on their use in dating and correlating sedimentary strata. The field of micropaleontology is an important tool in the study of sedimentary rocks and is widely used by the petroleum industry. Each volume includes a supplemental issue that accommodates papers longer than the 30- to 40-page articles normally published. This is the only paleontology journal devoted to the study of fossilized microorganisms.

5312. *Palaeogeography, Palaeoclimatology, Palaeoecology: an international journal for the geo-sciences.* [ISSN: 0031-0182] 1965. 52x/yr. EUR 3193 (Qualified personnel, EUR 283). Ed(s): F Surlyk, D. J. Bottjer. Elsevier BV, Sara Burgerhartstraat 25, Amsterdam, 1055 KV, Netherlands; nlinfo-f@elsevier.nl; http://www.elsevier.nl. Illus., index, adv. Sample. Refereed. Microform: PQC. Online: ingenta.com; ScienceDirect; Swets Blackwell. Reprint: ISI; SWZ. *Indexed:* AbAn, ApEcolAb, BiolAb, BrArAb, ChemAb, DSR&OA, EngInd, EnvAb, ForAb, GeoRef, GeogAbPG, M&GPA, OceAb, PetrolAb, S&F, SCI, SSCI, SWRA, ZooRec. *Bk. rev.:* 3-5, 1,500-2,000 words. *Aud.:* Ga, Ac, Sa.

This is an interdisciplinary journal that publishes original research drawing upon paleontology and other disciplines to understand ancient and recent earth environments. It is an international medium for the publication of multidisciplinary original studies and reviews in the fields of paleoenvironmental geology. Occasional special issues are devoted to one topic, such as oxygen and carbon isotopes in foraminifera, plate tectonics and biogeography in the southwestern Pacific Ocean, or the Euroamerican coal province. By cutting across the traditional boundaries of established sciences, it provides an interdisciplinary forum where problems of general interest can be discussed. Subject coverage is similar to that in *Lethaia* (above in this section), which is less expensive. It is supplemented by *Global and Planetary Change* (ISSN: 0921-8181. m. $917). Extremely expensive, but indispensable to highly specialized collections serving researchers in the geosciences.

5313. *Palaeontographical Society. Monographs (London).* Formerly: *Monographs of the Palaeontological Society.* [ISSN: 0269-3445] 1848. a. GBP 90 (Individuals, GBP 33). Ed(s): M Williams, A W A Rushton. Palaeontographical Society, Department of Paleontology, Natural History Museum, Cromwell Rd, London, SW7 5BD, United Kingdom. Illus., index. Refereed. Circ: 368. *Indexed:* BiolAb, GeoRef, ZooRec. *Aud.:* Ac, Ga.

The Palaentographical Society issues an annual volume of serially numbered publications. These may be either a single complete monograph or part of a continuing monograph. Recommended for college and university libraries.

5314. *Palaeontology.* [ISSN: 0031-0239] 1957. bi-m. GBP 360 print & online eds. Ed(s): D.J. Batten, Dr. J. Clack. Blackwell Publishing Ltd., 9600 Garsington Rd, PO Box 805, Oxford, OX4 2DQ, United Kingdom; customerservices@oxon.blackwellpublishing.com; http://www.blackwellpublishing.com/. Illus., index. Refereed. Circ: 2000. Vol. ends: No. 6. Reprint: SWZ. *Indexed:* BiolAb, DSR&OA, GeoRef, OceAb, PetrolAb, SCI, ZooRec. *Aud.:* Ga, Ac, Sa.

Published by the Palaeontological Association in London, *Palaeontology* presents research papers and reviews covering the fields of paleontology and paleobiology. The journal consists solely of research articles, except for a yearly report of the association. Each issue consists of 10 to 12 research articles. Papers are published on all aspects of paleontology, including paleozoology, paleobotany, paleoecology, micropaleontology, paleobiogeography, and stratigraphy. A high standard of illustration is a feature of the journal. The association also publishes *Special Papers in Palaeontology* as a supplement. Although this is considered a primary research journal, many of the articles have a practical or applied flavor. Because of its broad scope and importance to the literature of paleontology and its allied disciplines, this journal is strongly recommended for college and university libraries.

5315. *Palaios.* [ISSN: 0883-1351] 1986. bi-m. USD 175. Ed(s): Christopher G Maples. S E P M, 1741 E. 71st St., Tulsa, OK 74136-5108; orders@allanepress.com; http://www.sepm.org. Illus., index, adv. Refereed. Circ: 1300. Vol. ends: No. 6. *Indexed:* BiolAb, DSR&OA, EngInd, GeoRef, GeogAbPG, M&GPA, PetrolAb, SCI, ZooRec. *Bk. rev.:* 0-2, 300-800 words. *Aud.:* Ga, Ac, Sa.

This journal publishes research articles that focus on the impact of life on Earth history as recorded in the paleontological and sedimentological records. *Palaios* serves to disseminate information to an international spectrum of geologists interested in a broad range of such topics as biogeochemistry, ichnology, sedimentology, stratigraphy, paleoecology, paleoclimatology, and paleoceanography. Each issue features several comprehensive articles as well as numerous short papers, book reviews, relevant news, and announcements. Because of its interdisciplinary approach, this journal is recommended for college or university libraries that do not require specialized and comprehensive coverage afforded by other paleontological journals.

5316. *Paleobiology.* [ISSN: 0094-8373] 1975. q. USD 90. Ed(s): John M Pandolfi, William M DiMichele. Paleontological Society, PO Box 1897, Lawrence, KS 66044-8897; ps@allenpress.com. Illus., index, adv. Refereed. Circ: 2400. Vol. ends: Fall (No. 4). Microform: PQC. Online: BioOne; JSTOR (Web-based Journal Archive); OCLC Online Computer Library Center, Inc.; ProQuest Information & Learning. Reprint: PQC. *Indexed:* AbAn, ApEcolAb, BiolAb, BrArAb, DSR&OA, FPA, ForAb, GeoRef, PetrolAb, S&F, SCI, ZooRec. *Bk. rev.:* 1, 1,500-2,000 words. *Aud.:* Ac, Sa.

Published by the Paleontological Society, this primary journal presents contributions dealing with all biological aspects of the history of life. Emphasis is on biological or paleobiological processes and patterns, including macroevolution, speciation, extinction, functional morphology, molecular paleontology, phylogeny, and paleoecology. Occasionally, an issue includes the "Current Research" section, which presents short overviews of research in progress and a discussion of earlier papers. Each issue has 10 to 14 articles, as well as book reviews. This journal and *Journal of Paleontology* (above in this section), also published by the society, are reasonably priced and of high quality. *Paleobiology* is recommended for academic collections where paleontology is offered as a research program.

5317. *Paleoceanography.* [ISSN: 0883-8305] 1986. bi-m. USD 395. Ed(s): Larry Peterson, Michael Arthur. American Geophysical Union, 2000 Florida Ave, N W, Washington, DC 20009-1277; http://www.agu.org. Illus., index. Sample. Refereed. Vol. ends: Dec (No. 6). Microform: Pub.; AIP. *Indexed:* EngInd, GeoRef, GeogAbPG, M&GPA, OceAb, PetrolAb, SCI, ZooRec. *Aud.:* Ac, Sa.

Ranked #2 of 117 titles in Geosciences and Interdisciplinary in the 2000 *Journal Citation Reports, Paleoceanography* is the core title for paleontology and earth sciences research. It focuses on original contributions dealing with the marine sedimentary record from the present ocean basins and margins and from exposures of ancient marine sediments on the continents. The scope of this journal is global as well as regional, and covers all eras (Precambrian to the Quaternary). Recommended for inclusion in current subscription holdings at institutions where graduate programs in geology and marine science are offered.

5318. *Paleontological Journal.* [ISSN: 0031-0301] 1959. bi-m. USD 3580 in North America; USD 4126 elsewhere. Ed(s): Alexi Y Rozanov. M A I K Nauka - Interperiodica, Profsoyuznaya ul 90, Moscow, 117997,

Russian Federation; compmg@maik.ru; http://www.maik.rssi.ru. Illus., adv. Refereed. Circ: 425. Vol. ends: Dec (No. 6). Microform: PQC. Reprint: PSC. *Indexed:* GeoRef. *Bk. rev.:* 0-1, 1,500-3,000 words. *Aud.:* Ga, Ac, Sa.

Paleontological Journal (Paleontoloicheskii Zhurnal) is the principal Russian periodical in paleontology. Though focused on paleontology, this publication includes articles on historical geology and archaeology of interest to a wider audience worldwide. Publishing both original studies and comprehensive reviews, the journal aims to stimulate wide interdisciplinary cooperation and understanding among workers in the fields of paleobotany and palynology. Included in its scope are application of the disciplines to plant systematics, historical geology, archaeology, and allergy research and treatment. It also publishes studies on evolution of organisms, ecosystems, and biosphere, and provides invaluable information on biostratigraphy with an emphasis on Eastern Europe and Asia. Appropriate for general and academic collections.

5319. *Palynology.* Supersedes (in 1977): *Geoscience and Man;* Incorporates (1970-1976): *American Association of Stratigraphic Palynologists. Proceedings of the Annual Meeting.* [ISSN: 0191-6122] 1975. a. USD 70 (Individuals, USD 45). Ed(s): Owen Davis. American Association of Stratigraphic Palynologists Foundation, c/o Vaughn M Bryant, Jr, Palynology Laboratory, Texas A & M Univ, College Station, TX 77843-4352; vbryant@tamu.edu; http://www.palynology.org. Illus., index. Circ: 980 Paid. *Indexed:* AnthLit, BiolAb, GeoRef, PetrolAb, ZooRec. *Aud.:* Ac, Sa.

Palynology is published annually by the American Association of Stratigraphic Palynologists Foundation for distribution to members of the association and other interested persons. Scientific collection, scientific study, and scientific research data relating to palynology are the prime focus of this specialized journal. Despite its North American focus, this journal's scope is similar to that of the *Paleontological Journal* (above). Important for both geological and biological collections.

5320. *Quaternary Science Reviews: international multidisciplinary review and research journal.* [ISSN: 0277-3791] 1982. 24x/yr. EUR 1541 (Qualified personnel, EUR 220). Ed(s): Jim Rose, P. U. Clark. Pergamon, The Boulevard, Langford Ln, East Park, Kidlington, OX5 1GB, United Kingdom. Refereed. Microform: PQC. Online: ingenta.com; ScienceDirect; Swets Blackwell. *Indexed:* AbAn, AnthLit, BrArAb, CAPS, ChemAb, EngInd, GeoRef, GeogAbPG, M&GPA, NumL, OceAb, SCI, SWRA, ZooRec. *Bk. rev.:* Number and length vary. *Aud.:* Ac, Sa.

Quaternary Science Reviews covers all aspects of Quaternary science and includes geology, geomorphology, geography, archaeology, soil science, paleobotany, paleontology, paleoclimatology, and the full range of applicable dating methods. *QSR* also publishes papers with new data, especially those containing a review function or those which can be so adapted for a wider perspective, for example, as in methods of dating. *QSR* keeps readers abreast of the wider issues relating to new developments in the field. It also includes occasional issues devoted to Quaternary geochronology, with the aim of providing Quaternary geologists and archaeologists with a reference source discussing progress and problems of dating techniques applicable to the Quaternary. The scope of this publication is focused on review papers, systematic studies, and progress reports, as well as occasional conference proceedings. (KG)

5321. *Review of Palaeobotany and Palynology: an international journal.* [ISSN: 0034-6667] 1967. 20x/yr. EUR 1880 (Qualified personnel, EUR 139). Ed(s): H. Kerp, H Visscher. Elsevier BV, Sara Burgerhartstraat 25, Amsterdam, 1055 KV, Netherlands; nlinfo-f@elsevier.nl; http://www.elsevier.nl. Illus., index, adv. Refereed. Microform: PQC. Online: ingenta.com; ScienceDirect; Swets Blackwell. Reprint: SWZ. *Indexed:* AbAn, BiolAb, CAPS, DSR&OA, FPA, ForAb, GeoRef, GeogAbPG, HortAb, PetrolAb, S&F, SCI, ZooRec. *Aud.:* Ac, Sa.

The *Review of Paleobotany and Palynology* is an international journal for research in all fields of paleobotany and palynology, and dealing with groups of organisms that range from marine palynomorphs to higher land plants. Publishing both original studies and comprehensive reviews, it aims to stimulate wide interdisciplinary cooperation and understanding among working scientists in these fields. The scope includes, but is not limited to, systematics, evolution, paleobiology, historical geology, biostratigraphy, biochronology, paleogeography, and archaeology. The journal especially encourages the publication of articles in which paleobotany and palynology are applied for solving fundamental geological and biological problems. This journal is costly, but solid and suitable for the large collection with a specialized interest in paleobotany.

5322. *University of Kansas. Paleontological Contributions. New Series.* Formed by the 1992 merger of: *University of Kansas. Paleontological Contributions. Articles; University of Kansas. Paleontological Contributions. Papers; University of Kansas. Paleontological Contributions. Monographs.* [ISSN: 1046-8390] 1947. irreg. Ed(s): Roger L Kaesler. University of Kansas, Paleontological Institute, 121 Lindley Hall, Lawrence, KS 66045; kaesler@ukans.edu; http://www.geo.ukansas.edu/newsite/research/labs/paleo.html. Illus. Refereed. Circ: 700. *Indexed:* BiolAb, GeoRef, ZooRec. *Aud.:* Ga, Ac, Sa.

This is a serial publication intended primarily to publish research results in paleontology done by workers at the University of Kansas or with close ties to the university, based on Kansas materials, or related to scientific projects sponsored by the university. It is a refereed serial publication. The new *Contributions* series consolidates into one format the three series—*Monographs, Articles,* and *Papers*—that used to be published independently. Each number varies in page count. These publications are distributed as exchanges to scientific institutions and libraries throughout the world and on standing order. Although the publication may hardly be a first choice for research libraries, most general collections will find it valuable. Also belongs in comprehensive university collections.

Electronic Journals

5323. *Palaeontologia Electronica.* [ISSN: 1094-8074] 1998. s-a. Ed(s): Norman MacLeod. Texas A & M University, Department of Oceanography, College Station, TX 77843-3146; http://palaeo-electronica.org/index.htm. Refereed. *Indexed:* GeoRef, ZooRec. *Aud.:* Ac, Sa.

Palaeontologia Electronica is the first electronic journal ever published in paleontology. Published simultaneously on the web (http://palaeo-electronica.org) and on CD-ROM (ISSN: 1532-3056), it is an internationally sponsored, peer-reviewed general paleontological journal of the widest possible scope. Contributions from members of the professional paleontological and biological communities are encouraged and are given prior consideration for inclusion in *Palaeontologia Electronica.* Unlike traditional print-based journals, *Palaeontologia Electronica* is highly graphical in both format and content. Each volume of the journal is available free of charge on the web for one publishing year. An important source for addition to collections in geology and biological sciences.

■ PARAPSYCHOLOGY

Christianne L. Casper, Faculty Librarian, Broward Community College, South Campus Library, 7200 Pines Blvd., Pembroke Pines, FL 33024; a012724t@bcfreenet.seflin.lib.fl.us

Introduction

There have been accounts of paranormal experiences throughout history and across all cultures. These events are described as unusual experiences that appear to be unexplainable through known scientific principles. Parapsychology is the study of such paranormal phenomena. There are those who study parapsychology with total belief that they will prove the existence of paranormal phenomena, while others are completely skeptical, working aggressively to explain such phenomena in known scientific terms. Then there are those who fall in the middle, who are open to all possibilities but believe that the burden of proof lies with those who make paranormal claims. Popular interest in parapsychology has steadily increased, and this has produced a growing number of journals to inform and promote parapsychological research.

Two of the oldest and most prominent journals published are from the American Society for Psychical Research and the Society for Psychical Research (British). They are both core journals for any parapsychological collection. The *Journal of Parapsychology* and the *Journal of Religion and Psychical Research* provide a professional forum for psychical research. There are other journals that simply seek to provide information on paranormal and strange phenomena. These include the *Fortean Times* (British) and *Nexus Magazine* (Australian). Then there are those journals that take on the role of skepticism, investigating paranormal claims in order to separate scientfic findings from media sensationalism. These would include *Skeptical Inquirer* and *Skeptic*. The journals reviewed here provide a wide range of information on parapsychology and paranormal studies.

Basic Periodicals

Ga, Ac: *American Society for Psychical Research. Journal, Journal of Parapsychology, Journal of Religion & Psychical Research, Skeptic, Skeptical Inquirer;* Sa: *American Society for Psychical Research. Journal, Journal of Parapsychology, Journal of Religion and Psychical Research, Skeptical Inquirer, Society for Psychical Research. Journal.*

Basic Abstracts and Indexes

Exceptional Human Experience.

5324. ***American Society for Psychical Research. Journal.*** [ISSN: 0003-1070] 1907. q. USD 80 (Individuals, USD 45; Students, USD 25). Ed(s): Rhea A White. American Society for Psychical Research, Inc., 5 W 73rd St, New York, NY 10023. Illus., index. Sample. Refereed. Circ: 2000. Vol. ends: Oct. Microform: PQC. Reprint: PQC. *Indexed:* PsycholAb, SSCI, SSI. *Bk. rev.:* 3-4. *Aud.:* Ac, Sa.

The American Society for Psychical Research was founded in 1885 and is the oldest psychic research organization in the United States. Its journal is known for its informative, scholarly coverage of topics including, but not limited to, ESP, precognition, psychokinesis, and psychic healing. The journal includes scholarly reports, research, and field studies focusing on firsthand reports of paranormal phenomena. Issues average about four articles, with tables/graphs, footnotes, and references. Some issues include a correspondence column and a book review section. The society's web site includes sample articles.

5325. ***Fortean Times: the journal of strange phenomena.*** [ISSN: 0308-5899] 1973. m. GBP 30; GBP 37.50 in Europe; GBP 45 elsewhere. Ed(s): Robert J M Rickard, Paul Sieveking. John Brown Citrus Publishing, The New Boathouse, 136-142, Bramley Rd, London, W10 6SR, United Kingdom; ft@johnbrown.co.uk; http://www.forteantimes.com. Illus., adv. Circ: 60193 Paid. *Bk. rev.:* 7-9. *Aud.:* Ga, Ac, Sa.

Fortean Times was founded to continue the investigative research of Charles Fort (1874–1932), one of the first UFOlogists and a skeptical investigator of the bizarre and unusual. This publication provides news, reviews, research on strange phenomena, psychic experiences, prodigies, and portents from around the world. While the publication maintains a humorous air, its goal is to provide thought-provoking, educational information. The articles provide resources that usually include recommended readings, surfings, and/or notes. In addition to articles, each issue includes book reviews, "Strange Days," and "Forum." The online edition includes the table of contents for the current issue, brief book reviews, an article archive, breaking news, a gallery, and exclusive features.

5326. ***Journal of Parapsychology: a scientific quarterly dealing with extrasensory perception, the psychokinetic effect and related topics.*** [ISSN: 0022-3387] 1937. q. Individuals, USD 40; Students, USD 25. Ed(s): John Palmer. Parapsychology Press, 402 N Buchanan Blvd, Durham, NC 27701-1728; journal@rhine.org; http://www.rhine.org. Illus., index, adv. Sample. Refereed. Circ: 1000 Paid. Vol. ends: Dec. Microform: PQC. Online: EBSCO Publishing; Florida Center for Library Automation; Gale Group; Northern Light Technology, Inc.; OCLC Online Computer Library Center, Inc.; ProQuest Information & Learning; H.W. Wilson. Reprint: ISI; PQC. *Indexed:* BRI, BiolAb, CBRI, ExcerpMed, IBZ, PsycholAb, SSCI, SSI. *Bk. rev.:* 3-5. *Aud.:* Ac, Sa.

The *Journal of Parapsychology,* founded by J. B. Rhine, was one of the first scholarly parapsychology journals published. Its primary focus is to provide a professional forum for original research reports on experimental parapsychology. In addition to the technical experimental reports, the journal includes surveys of literature, book reviews, and correspondence. An important section provided in most issues is "Parapsychological Abstracts," half-page abstracts of significant articles published in related journals. Abstracts from recent issues are available online at www.rhine.org.

5327. ***Journal of Religion & Psychical Research: a scholarly quarterly dealing with religion, psychical research, and related topics.*** [ISSN: 0731-2148] 1979. q. USD 20 domestic; USD 30 Canada; USD 38 foreign. Ed(s): Dr. Donald R Morse. Academy of Religion and Psychical Research, PO Box 614, Bloomfield, CT 06002-0614. Index. Sample. Circ: 200. Vol. ends: Oct. *Indexed:* RI-1. *Bk. rev.:* 3-5. *Aud.:* Ac, Sa.

The *Journal of Religion and Psychical Research* was established to provide a forum among clergy, academics, and researchers concerning religion, philosophy, and psychical research. There are about five articles in each issue, some with references. In addition, there are research proposals, abstracts of completed research, views and comments, book reviews, and correspondence. Recommended for religion or parapsychology collections.

5328. ***Nexus Magazine (Australian Edition).*** [ISSN: 1039-0170] 1987. bi-m. AUD 29 domestic; AUD 45 per issue in SE Asia; AUD 55 per issue South Africa. Ed(s): Duncan M Roads. Nexus Magazine Pty Ltd., PO Box 30, Mapleton, QLD 4560, Australia; editor@nexusmagazine.com; http://www.nexusmagazine.com/. Illus., adv. Circ: 45000 Paid. Vol. ends: Nov/Dec (No. 6). *Bk. rev.:* 10-14. *Aud.:* Ga.

Nexus Magazine is an international periodical that looks at global issues and science news dealing with controversial phenomena and the unexplained. Each issue includes "Global News," "Science News," "The Twilight Zone," and five to seven articles. In addition, there is a large selection of book reviews as well as video and music reviews. The online version includes the table of contents for the current issue and previously published articles. There is a catalogue of books and materials published by Nexus, a chatroom, and a list of web sites of interest.

5329. ***Skeptic.*** [ISSN: 1063-9330] 1992. q. Membership, USD 30. Ed(s): Michael Shermer. Millenium Press, 2761 N Marengo Ave, Box 338, Altadena, CA 91001; arcie@netcom.com; http://www.skeptic.com/. Illus., index, adv. Sample. Refereed. Circ: 10000 Paid. Vol. ends: Nov. Online: EBSCO Publishing; Florida Center for Library Automation; Gale Group; Northern Light Technology, Inc.; OCLC Online Computer Library Center, Inc.; ProQuest Information & Learning; H.W. Wilson. *Indexed:* ASIP, BRI, CBRI, GSI, RI-1. *Bk. rev.:* 5-7. *Aud.:* Ga, Ac.

Skeptic promotes scientific and critical thinking while examining information on a variety of topics, including pseudoscience, pseudohistory, the paranormal, magic, superstition, fringe claims, and revolutionary science. The features included in every issue are "Articles," "News," "Forum," "Book Reviews," and "Junior Skeptic." Some issues of *Skeptic* also include movie and audio reviews. The online version provides the table of contents for the current issue, archives, book reviews, and "Junior Skeptic."

5330. ***Skeptical Inquirer: the magazine for science and reason.*** Formerly (until 1977): *Zetetic.* [ISSN: 0194-6730] 1976. bi-m. USD 32.50. Ed(s): Ken Frazier. Committee for the Scientific Investigation of Claims of the Paranormal, PO Box 703, Buffalo, NY 14226-0703; http://www.csicop.org. Illus., index. Circ: 50000. Online: Florida Center for Library Automation; Gale Group; Northern Light Technology, Inc.; OCLC Online Computer Library Center, Inc.; ProQuest Information & Learning. *Indexed:* GeoRef, MagInd, RGPR, RI-1. *Bk. rev.:* 2-4. *Aud.:* Ga, Ac, Sa.

Skeptical Inquirer focuses on what the scientific community knows about claims of the paranormal, as opposed to media sensationalism. The journal encourages scientific research and evidence when investigating paranormal phenomena. Standard features include "News and Comment," "Notes of a Fringe Watcher," "Forum," "Articles of Note," "New Books," and "Letters to the Editor." In addition to parapsychology, topics investigated include UFOs, alternative therapy, psychic claims, astrology, skepticism in general, and other paranormal experiences. The online version includes an index of articles, special features, and online articles.

5331. ***Society for Psychical Research. Journal.*** [ISSN: 0037-9751] 1884. q. GBP 20; USD 36. Ed(s): Zofia Weaver. Society for Psychical Research, 49 Marloes Rd, London, W8 6LA, United Kingdom. Illus., index, adv. Sample. Vol. ends: Oct. *Indexed:* IBZ, PsycholAb. *Bk. rev.:* Occasional. *Aud.:* Sa.

The journal of the Society for Psychical Research is one of the oldest parapsychological publications. It aims to objectively examine paranormal experiences and reports that appear to be otherwise inexplicable. The journal publishes field and case studies, experimental reports, book reviews, and historical and theoretical papers. All papers are strictly peer reviewed. There are approximately five articles per issue, complete with tables, graphs, and references. Correspondence is also included. The Society for Psychical Research is in the process of making all their journals available online.

Steamshovel Press. See Zines section.

Electronic Journals

5332. ***The Anomalist (Online Edition).*** Formerly (until 2002): *The Anomalist (Print Edition).* 1994. s-a. Free. Ed(s): Patrick Huyghe. The Anomalist, PO Box 577, Jefferson Valley, NY 10535. *Aud.:* Ga.

The Anomalist explores the unexplained mysteries of science, nature, and history. In the fall of 2002, *The Anomalist* combined its print and web editions to create one online journal. This journal includes news from around the world that is updated daily, as well as original articles, commentaries, and book reviews. In addition, there are the "High Strangeness Reports," the "A Files," and "Quotable Fort" (quotations from Charles Fort). Article archives are also available.

■ PARENTING

Caroline M. Kent, Head of Research Services, Widener Library, Harvard University, Cambridge, MA 02138

Introduction

Are there publications that can actually help a new (or even experienced) parent?! Certainly there is a market for such publications, particularly in an era when many parenting individuals are separated from the older generations of their families—generations that carry parenting wisdom and experience. It is also arguable that parenting is now more complicated in this era of dual-career families, single and divorced parents, and alternative families of all sorts. Even those families practicing a more traditional family form with a stay-at-home mom may find the lack of neighborhoods and extended family daunting. The modern reality is that there aren't too many parents who don't feel that they need all the help they can get!

Parenting magazines really fall neatly into two categories: magazines that are general enough to contain articles of interest to a wide range of families; and magazines containing articles interesting to particular parents, such as adoptive or single parents. It should also be acknowledged that there are many national parenting web sites that do not easily fall into the category of e-zines. There is content on these sites that is serial in nature, but a substantial portion of the site may actually be guided (or unguided) message boarding. Because of the nature of these sites, they are not included in this list. However, libraries wishing to create robust resource link pages must consider them. One large and impressive example of sources in this category is ParentSoup (www.parentsoup.com).

There aren't many journals in this section that would hold appeal to most college and university libraries. The exception to that would be any school that has active child development or family therapeutic program.

In addition to the titles listed here, there are a large number of excellent local parenting magazines (such as *Boston Parents' Paper* and *Black Parenting Today: Information and Resources for Greater Philadelphia Families*). Public libraries should identify such publications for their areas and include them in current collections.

Basic Periodicals

Ga: *American Baby, Baby Talk, Child, FamilyFun, Parent & Child, Parenting, Parents*

Basic Abstracts and Indexes

Education Index, ERIC, Exceptional Child Education Resources, Psychological Abstracts, Reader's Guide to Periodical Literature

5333. ***American Baby: for expectant and new parents.*** Formerly: *Mothers-to-Be - American Baby.* [ISSN: 0044-7544] 1938. m. USD 23.94 domestic; USD 39.94 Canada. Meredith Corp., 125 Park Ave, 19th Fl, New York, NY 10017; http://www.meredith.com. Illus., adv. Sample. Circ: 2000000. *Indexed:* CINAHL, MagInd. *Aud.:* Ga.

There aren't too many American families with young children who don't read or at least receive issues of this magazine. Expectant parents can get it free for several months. It is the oldest and most reliable of the commercial baby-parenting magazines, containing a wide range of short, easy-to-read articles on baby and parent health issues, developmental discussions, baby care, and family issues. In addition to the huge number of advertisements for baby-related products, it also contains discussion and reviews of new products. There are advice columns covering everything from behavior to health and nutrition. The magazine also has a healthy and well-maintained web site that is updated frequently. All public libraries should should invest in this.

5334. ***And Baby.*** 2001. bi-m. USD 29.95 for 2 yrs.; USD 4.99 newsstand/cover per issue; USD 6.99 newsstand/cover per issue Canada. Ed(s): Deanne Mussolf-Crouch. Out of the Box Publishing, 55 Washington St, Ste 812, Brooklyn, NY 11201; deannemc@aol.com. Adv. *Bk. rev.:* 2-4. *Aud.:* Ga.

This new journal contains features on gay, lesbian, bisexual, and transgender parenting. Articles look at issues such as legislative matters, discrimination, fashion, and psychology. Recent articles include "Where's the Mom?," "Rosie O'Donnell: Mother," and "Surviving the Bible Belt." Its format is slicker and more commercial than other publications of its kind, and there are often wonderful photographic images included. Any public library addressing the concerns of a gay or lesbian population should purchase this title.

5335. ***Baby Talk.*** Former titles (until 2000): *Parenting's Baby Talk;* (until 199?): *Baby Talk Magazine;* (until 1977): *New Baby Talk;* (until 1976): *Baby Talk.* [ISSN: 1529-5389] 1935. 10x/yr. USD 19.95; USD 1.95 newsstand/cover per issue. Ed(s): Susan Kane. Time Publishing Ventures, 1325 Ave of the Americas, 27th Fl, New York, NY 10019; http://www.parenting.com. Illus., adv. Sample. Circ: 1800000. Vol. ends: Nov. *Indexed:* RGPR. *Bk. rev.:* 2.3. *Aud.:* Ga.

Baby Talk, one of the oldest continuing parenting magazines, is targeted to the needs of expectant mothers and parents of newborns. For these readers, it is even free for the asking. Packed with short, informative articles on baby care, health, developmental concerns, family issues, and product discussions, it also has regular columns, many of them based on readers' questions (such as "Wit and Wisdom" and "Ask Dr. Mom"). Every public library should consider this publication.

5336. ***Brain, Child: the magazine for thinking mothers.*** [ISSN: 1528-5170] q. USD 18 domestic; USD 26 foreign; USD 5 newsstand/cover. Ed(s): Stephanie Wilkinson, Jennifer Niesslein. Brain, Child, PO Box 714, Lexington, VA 24450; publisher@brainchildmag.com. Adv. Vol. ends: Winter. *Bk. rev.:* 2-4. *Aud.:* Ga, Ac.

How can we resist a journal that says in its mission statement that "motherhood is worthy of literature"? Or that this "isn't your typical magazine. We couldn't cupcake-decorate our way out of a paper bag." This journal is totally irresistible! Each issue contains a mix of intriguing essays, feature articles, humor, fiction, and art—some of which has some powerful names attached, such as Barbara Kingsolver, Mary Gordon, and Alice Hoffman (all mothers themselves). This isn't a how-to magazine; rather, it is a why-do-we-do-it-at-all magazine. Recent essays include "Why I Hate Dr. Sears," "The Bad Mother Did It," and "Should You Argue in Front of the Kids?" Funny, thought-provoking, and full of terrific reads, this magazine should be considered by any college library with a writing program and any public library with the right constituency.

5337. ***Child: the essential guide for parents.*** Formerly (until 1986): *For Today's Children.* [ISSN: 0894-7988] 1986. 10x/yr. USD 12.97; USD 3.50 newsstand/cover per issue. Ed(s): Kate Kelly Smith. Gruner + Jahr U.S.A. Publishing, 375 Lexington Ave, New York, NY 10017-5514; corpcomm@gjusa.com; http://www.gjusa.com. Illus. Circ: 1020000 Paid. Vol. ends: Dec/Jan. *Bk. rev.:* 8, 75 words. *Aud.:* Ga.

Child is certainly more upscale than many parenting magazines, which work to target a very broad constituency. It could be regarded as the most Martha Stewart-esque of parenting publications: Its format is large and its design less jam-packed and busy, which allows for more sustained reading. It lacks the choppy "mom-has-only-five-minutes-for-reading" quality that many other magazines have. That being said, the actual subject matter is identical. Titles of recent articles include "20-Page Family Travel Guide," "Kidstyle Coast to Coast," and "The Truth Behind the Autism Epidemic." The articles are thoughtful and somewhat more in-depth that other parenting journals. Although our houses may be less neat, our children less clean, and our shopping limited to outlet malls, we still find this magazine a pleasure to read. Any public library with a parenting population should consider purchasing it.

Child & Family Behavior Therapy. See Family and Marriage section.

5338. ***Christian Parenting Today.*** Formerly: *Christian Parenting.* [ISSN: 1065-7215] 1988. q. USD 17.95; USD 3.95 newsstand/cover per issue. Ed(s): Carla Barnhill. Christianity Today International, 465 Gundersen Dr, Carol Stream, IL 60188. Adv. Circ: 81000. Online: Gale Group. *Indexed:* ChrPI. *Bk. rev.:* 2-3 25 words. *Aud.:* Ga, Sa.

There are many magazines that claim to be the single Christian "voice" with advice for parents. *Christian Parenting Today* has the broadest, most inclusive viewpoint. It includes not only specific features on spiritual issues but also more generalized articles on parenting issues—as seen through a Christian ethical lens. It also has a well-developed web site (www.christianparenting.net) that contains web-specific features and message boarding. For public libraries serving active Christian populations; church libraries should also consider its purchase.

5339. ***Exceptional Parent: the magazine for families and professionals.*** [ISSN: 0046-9157] 1971. m. USD 36 domestic; USD 47 Canada. Ed(s): Rick Rader. Exceptional Parent, 65 State Rt 4, River Edge, NJ 07661-1949; epmag12@aol.com; http://families.com. Illus., index. Sample. Circ: 65000 Paid. Vol. ends: Dec. Microform: PQC. Online: bigchalk; Gale Group; Northern Light Technology, Inc.; OCLC Online Computer Library Center, Inc.; ProQuest Information & Learning; H.W. Wilson. Reprint: PQC. *Indexed:* CIJE, CINAHL, ECER, EduInd, IMFL, IndMed, PsycholAb. *Bk. rev.:* 3-4, 50 words. *Aud.:* Ga, Sa.

This fascinating magazine contains both advice on parenting exceptional children and information on being an alternatively abled parent. Recent feature articles include "Ray Kurzwiel; Q & A on Technology," "Financing Your Mobility Needs," and "Airline Travel for Children with Special Needs." The magazine is packed with product information and reviews, health information, discussions of educational issues, and book reviews, in addition to the feature articles. It is also well indexed. All public libraries and any college or university with an education program should consider its purchase.

5340. ***FamilyFun.*** [ISSN: 1056-6333] 1991. 10x/yr. USD 10 domestic; USD 22 Canada; USD 30 elsewhere. Ed(s): Barbara Findlen, Ann Halloch. Family Fun, Inc., 244 Main St, Northampton, MA 01060; FAFcustserv@cdsfulfillment.com. Illus., adv. Circ: 1175000 Paid. *Bk. rev.:* 5-6, 75-100 words. *Aud.:* Ga.

Well, okay, so it's Disney, or a branch of Disney, that publishes this magazine. But if there's one thing that the Disney magicians are good at conjuring up, it's fun, right? The format is nice, with great photographs of kids and their families—all having fun! There are craft activities, rainy-day-fun ideas, traveling-with-the-kids ideas, and party ideas of all kinds, as well as reviews of toys and games, books, and videos. This is actually a wonderful magazine, jam-packed with ideas for even the most creative of parents. It is really the only magazine that has children's activities as its total focus; therefore, it is an invaluable addition to any parenting magazine collection. Any public library not located in a retirement home should purchase this. Very highly recommended.

Fathering Magazine. See Men section.

Full-Time Dads See Men section.

5341. ***Gay Parent.*** [ISSN: 1545-6714] 1998. bi-m. USD 20 domestic; USD 30 foreign. Ed(s): Angeline Acain. Gay Parent, Box 750852, Forest Hills, NY 11375-0852; http://www.gayparentmag.com. *Bk. rev.:* 1, 150 words, signed. *Aud.:* Ga.

Gay Parent is one of the more thoughtful parenting magazines in print. It assumes that its readership is interested in substantive book reviews, extensive interviews, and legislative information. It periodically publishes lists of gay-friendly private schools and camps, and articles on adoption and foster care. Subscribers may elect to get the full text of the magazine online for a reduced subscription rate. This magazine will be well placed in any public library with a parent population interested in diverse family structures.

5342. ***Gifted Child Today Magazine: the nation's leading resource for nurturing talented children.*** Former titles (until 1993): *Gifted Child Today; G C T (Gifted, Creative, Talented Children).* [ISSN: 1076-2175] 1978. q. USD 29.95 domestic; USD 39.95 foreign. Ed(s): Susan Johnsen. Prufrock Press, PO Box 8813, Waco, TX 76714-8813; http://www.prufrock.com. Illus., adv. Sample. Circ: 20000. Reprint: PQC. *Indexed:* CIJE, ECER, EduInd. *Bk. rev.:* 3-5, 100 words. *Aud.:* Ga, Sa.

This magazine is intended to support both teachers and parents of gifted children. It is full of articles not only on the educational theory of the teaching of the gifted but also ideas for both curriculum development and learning plans for home. Recent articles include "Internet Investigations—Solving Mysteries on the Information Superhighway," "Lessons Learned from Terrorism," and "Why Teachers Need To Be Readers." Recommended for school libraries, academic libraries supporting education programs, and large public libraries.

Hip Mama: the parenting zine. See Zines section.

5343. ***The Jewish Parent Connection.*** [ISSN: 1071-8826] 8x/yr. USD 10. Ed(s): Joyce Lempel. Torah Umesorah - National Society for Hebrew Day Schools (Manhattan), Parent Enrichment Program, 160 Broadway, 4th Fl, New York, NY 10038. Adv. Sample. Circ: 22600. *Indexed:* IJP. *Aud.:* Ga.

Although it might appear to be geared toward Hebrew day school issues, this newsletter actually covers a broad range of topics. Some specifically relate to parenting in the Jewish faith, but others cover more generalized topics such as homework. Although the newsletter is small in format, the articles are thoughtful and interesting. Recommended for public libraries serving relevant populations, and for colleges and universities training teachers for Hebrew day schools.

Mothering. See Family and Marriage section.

5344. ***Parent & Child: the learning link between home & school.*** [ISSN: 1070-0552] 1993. 6x/yr. USD 8. Ed(s): Pam Abrams. Scholastic Inc., 555 Broadway, New York, NY 10012-0399; http://www.scholastic.com. Adv. Circ: 1200000 Paid. *Bk. rev.:* 3-4, 25 words. *Aud.:* Ga, Sa.

Parent & Child has an interesting life, both as a printed magazine that covers learning issues from birth to about six years, and as part of Scholastic's larger web presence, which not only includes this magazine's content, but also takes the reader further through middle school. Not surprisingly, Scholastic has collected an advisory board for the magazine that includes several national early childhood experts. The articles are short and informative and are intended to bridge a child's preschool learning experience with its learning life at home. The magazine presents learning and health issues, behavioral and developmental information, and lots of activites for parents to use at home. All public libraries should consider this magazine; also, learning resource centers at schools training early childhood staff should purchase it.

5345. ***Parenting.*** [ISSN: 0890-247X] 1987. m. 10/yr. USD 12; USD 3.50 newsstand/cover. Ed(s): Janet Chan. Time Publishing Ventures, 1325 Ave of the Americas, 27th Fl, New York, NY 10019; http://www.parenting.com. Illus., adv. Circ: 1300000 Paid and controlled. Online: bigchalk; EBSCO Publishing; Gale Group; OCLC Online Computer Library Center, Inc.; ProQuest Information & Learning; H.W. Wilson. Reprint: PSC. *Indexed:* MagInd, RGPR. *Bk. rev.:* 4-6, 40-50 words. *Aud.:* Ga.

Parenting is jam-packed with information for parents, particularly new parents. Like many parenting publications, its articles diminish in number and usefulness as the child becomes older (perhaps this is based on the assumption that only new parents need help!). There are many columns and departments, such as "Your Health" and "Reviews," as well as quizzes, recipes, feature articles, and product reviews—all packaged in short, quick-read columns, certainly a necessary length for new parents. The ads alone make this magazine extremely useful. The associated web site has related, complementary information, also packaged neatly and effectively. This useful and reliable magazine is highly recommended for any public library serving families.

Parenting's Baby Talk. See *Baby Talk.*

5346. ***Parents: on rearing children from crib to college.*** Former titles (until 1993): *Parents' Magazine;* (until 1985): *Parents;* (until 1978): *Parents' Magazine;* (until 1977): *Parents' Magazine and Better Homemaking; Parents' Magazine and Better Family Living;* Incorporates (1976-1981): *Parents Home;* Which incorporated (in Apr. 1981): *Handy Andy Magazine.* [ISSN: 1083-6373] 1926. m. USD 15.98 domestic; USD 3.50 newsstand/cover per issue. Ed(s): Sally Lee. Gruner + Jahr U.S.A. Publishing, 375 Lexington Ave, New York, NY 10017-5514; http://www.parents.com. Illus. Circ: 2200000 Paid and controlled. CD-ROM: ProQuest Information & Learning. Online: Gale Group; OCLC Online Computer Library Center, Inc.; ProQuest Information & Learning; H.W. Wilson. *Indexed:* BRI, BiogInd, CBRI, CINAHL, ConsI, EduInd, IHTDI, MagInd, RGPR. *Bk. rev.:* 4-5, 50 words. *Aud.:* Ga.

Parents has in many ways become the industry standard for parenting magazines. Like many others, its focus tends to be on early childhood development and health topics rather than on issues associated with older children. There are many regular columns covering child development and health, maternal and parental health—often focused on readers' questions. Current columns include "What's It Really Like?," "Work & Family," and "Good Manners." Feature articles include many short pieces on family life, home style, fun time, and health and safety, to name just a few departments. Recent article titles include "The 15 Foods Moms Should Eat Every Week," "Are You Overprotective?," and "Best Bargain Vacations." Highly recommended for any public library addressing the needs of families.

5347. ***Pediatrics for Parents: the newsletter for anyone who cares for a child.*** [ISSN: 0730-6725] 1980. m. USD 20 domestic; USD 23 Canada; USD 26 elsewhere. Ed(s): Dr. Richard J Sagall. Pediatrics for Parents, Inc., 747 S Third St, Unit 3, Philadelphia, PA 19147-3324; pediatricsforparents@pobox.com; http://www.moms-refuge.com/. Sample. Circ: 1000 Paid. Microform: PQC. Online: bigchalk; EBSCO Publishing; Gale Group; Northern Light Technology, Inc.; OCLC Online Computer Library Center, Inc.; ProQuest Information & Learning. *Aud.:* Ga.

This is similar to many other health newsletters now widely available, although it is the only one specifically targeted to children's health issues. It has a loose-leaf format (and libraries should be prepared for the storage and retention issues associated with that). Articles are clear and highly informative. Recent articles include "Fructose Intolerance," "SIDS & Race," and "Immunizing College-Bound Students." Although some of these topics are periodically covered in more general parenting titles, *Pediatrics for Parents* contains much information otherwise unavailable to lay people. The online version of the newsletter allows subscribers to access pdf versions of articles significantly before the print version is mailed out. Any public library serving parents should consider purchasing this title.

Single Mother: a support group in your hands. See Singles section.

Stepfamilies. See *Your Stepfamily: embrace the journey.*

Topics in Early Childhood Special Education. See Disbilities section.

5348. ***Twins: the magazine for parents of multiples.*** [ISSN: 0890-3077] 1984. bi-m. USD 25.95 domestic; USD 31.95 Canada; USD 35.95 elsewhere. Ed(s): Susan Alt. Business Word, Inc., 11211 E Arapahoe Rd, Ste 101, Centennial, CO 80112-3851; http://www.businessword.com. Illus. Sample. Circ: 50000 Paid and controlled. Vol. ends: Nov/Dec. *Bk. rev.:* 2-3,50 words. *Aud.:* Ga.

Oh, my. Double the joy—and double the trials of parenthood! Although there probably isn't a parent of twins (or triplets) that would have it any other way, there's no question that there are particular issues, both logistical and psychological, of handling the children of multiple birth. With fertility technologies increasing in use and sophistication, twinning (and beyond!) is much more common than it once was, so a cheerful, helpful magazine like *Twins* is welcome. It contains product reviews, feature articles, developmental discussions, and more. Recent features include "Am I an I or a We?," "Car Seat Guide," and "Twins Reunited with Birth Parents." Articles are thoughtful, often highly personal discussions of issues and successes. Recommended for public libraries.

Working Mother See Women section.

5349. ***Your Stepfamily: embrace the journey.*** Former titles (until Aug.2002): *S A A Families;* (until 2000): *Stepfamilies;* (until 1989): *Stepfamily Bulletin.* [ISSN: 1545-2492] 1980. bi-m. USD 21 domestic; USD 33 foreign. Y S F, Llc., 2615 Three Oaks Rd., Ste 1B, Cary, IL 60013. Illus. Circ: 1200. Vol. ends: Winter. Microform: PQC. Reprint: PQC. *Bk. rev.:* 2-3, 50 words. *Aud.:* Ga,Sa.

It is perhaps a sign of our times that, in 20 years, this publication has gone from being a simple newsletter to becoming a full-fledged, glossy publication. This is the official journal of the Stepfamily Association of America. Each issue has interesting regular columns such as "Your Ex," "Your Boundaries," and "Your Stepfamily of the Month." Several feature articles are also included. Recent article titles include "Invest in Your Stepteen Portfolio," "He Said She Said," and "Create a Family Whereever You Go." Public libraries should consider this, as should any special or academic library associated with a family therapeutic program.

Electronic Journals

5350. ***Family Matters!*** 1999. m. Free. Ed(s): Laura Ramirez. Kokopellis Treasures, 5231 Rosehill Crt, Reno, NV 89502-7785; soulful@aol.com. Circ: 5573. *Bk. rev.:* 2-4. *Aud.:* Ga.

Family Matters! is a very thoughtful and vital online magazine. The brainchild of psychologist Laura Ramirez, it focuses on the psychology of parenting and ethics and values in families. Recent articles include "Tips for Raising Biracial Children," "Children's Book Reviews: Books That Teach Your Child about Life," "The Vitality of Boys," and "In Praise of the Black Sheep." Any public library serving families should consider linking to this site.

5351. ***The Informed Parent: the weekly internet magazine of the 21st century.*** m. Ed(s): John H Samson. Intermag Productions, 23546 Coyote Springs Dr, Diamond Bar, CA 91765; http://www.informedparent.com. *Aud.:* Ga.

The Informed Parent is published by the Pediatric Medical Center of Long Beach, California. Articles are written by staff and other experts in the fields of education, social work, and psychology. Titles of recent features include "Directives for the Autistic Child," "Resistant Staph—A New Plague?" and

"CT- Scan Versus MRI." The articles are well written and informative, and a loosely indexed online archive is maintained. Further, the site offers a list of both children's and adult books on health topics that is linked to Amazon.com. This is a clear, well-developed site that all public libraries serving families should consider.

5352. *Main Street Mom.* w. Ed(s): Mia Cronan. Word Results, Co., PO Box 851, Scott Depot, WV 25560; subscribeme@mainstreetmom.com; http://www.mainstreetmom.com/. *Bk. rev.:* Various number and length. *Aud.:* Ga.

In years past, it was assumed by publishers that the readers of such magazines as *Good Housekeeping* and *Redbook* were women who were keeping house and being stay-at-home moms. Not so anymore. But women who do choose to stay at home and parent often find themselves alone, without the traditional neighborhood and family supports that they once had. This online publication is intended to fill this gap. It contains a wide range of feature articles, some on parenting but also on cooking, crafts, and family issues. Recent article titles include "Household Behavioral Modification," "Courtesy Doesn't Stop with Saying 'I Do'," and "The Importance of the Family Dinner." One interesting feature that goes beyond formal articles is the hosted message board offering help on an ever-changing and wide variety of topics. And these online discussions are attended by an international group of moms: While I was on for five minutes, there were women from Tupelo, Mississippi; New York City; Melbourne, Australia; Ontario; and Tasmania engaged in active discussion—a truly global neighborhood! Any public library serving a large population of stay-at-home parents should consider linking to this resource.

5353. *Parent News (Champaign).* [ISSN: 1093-0442] 1995. bi-m. Ed(s): Anne Robertson. E R I C Clearinghouse on Elementary and Early Childhood Education, University of Illinois at Urbana, 51 Gerty Dr, Champaign, IL 61820-7469; http://www.npin.org/pnews.html. *Bk. rev.:* 2-3, 50 words. *Aud.:* Ga, Ac.

This resource is published by the National Parent Information Network, which is part of ERIC. It clearly states its mission as providing "access to research-based information about the process of parenting, and about family involvement in education." In addition to feature articles, there are resource lists, conference calendars, links to relevant web sites, and book reviews. Titles of recent feature articles include "Making Homework Work," "Media Literacy in School and at Home," and "Single Parenting and Children's Academic Achievement." All public libraries serving families should link to this free resource, as should colleges and universities with education programs.

■ PEACE

Suhasini L. Kumar, Reference Librarian, Carlson Library, University of Toledo, 2801 W. Bancroft St., Toledo, OH 43606; Skumar@utnet.utoledo.edu

Introduction

We live in a deeply troubled world, where peaceful coexistence is constantly being threatened by terrorism, increase in biological and chemical weapons of mass destruction, recurring disputes between states and ethnic groups, racist violence, poverty, and violations of human rights. Wordsworth might well have alluded to the world we live in today when he lamented "much it grieved my heart to think what man has made of man." Although the world presents a dismal picture with what appears to be insurmountable deterrents to peace, many of these problems can be resolved by cultivating a sense of responsibility for all mankind, and by consciously working toward creating an environment of peace.

There are several organizations, societies, and associations that are committed to peace and that strive relentlessly to eliminate war and establish peace. They consider it to be of vital importance to teach people the basic tenets of peaceful coexistence, and to inculcate in them a strong desire for a culture of peace. They publish books, journals, and newsletters in order to keep people informed about every aspect of peace and explore every event and incident that might threaten to explode into a dispute, and provide in-depth analysis of various conditions and offer possible solutions to these controversial situations.

Peace associations like the Canadian Peace Research and Education Association, the International Peace Research Association, and the Peace Science Society (International) usually publish scholarly journals with well-researched articles that include statistical information and empirical tests with results. Journals such as the *Journal of Peace Research, The Journal of Conflict Resolution,* and *Conflict Management and Peace Science* are some of the journals that fall into this category. There are also newsletters and grassroots publications that ardently support peace and provide news and articles that would be of interest to people from every stratum of society and encourage readers to voice their opinions freely. *Peace Action* and *Peace Magazine* are examples of this type of publication.

There has been a remarkable increase in the number of peace journals available on the Internet, and many publishers are also trying to offer access to archival information. There are several journals and newsletters that are available both in print and online. Although a subscription is usually required for Internet access to these publications, some of them, such as the newsletter *Peace Watch,* are free.

The periodicals selected for this section represent a broad array of journals, magazines, and newsletters that are committed to the pursuit of peace. The authors and editors of these publications are international contributors who are passionately involved with peace efforts. These publications have proven to be a valuable source of information to academicians, researchers, peace activists, and other advocates of peace.

Basic Periodicals

Hs: *Arms Control Today, Fellowship, Peace Review;* Ac: *Arms Control Today, Bulletin of the Atomic Scientists, Conflict Management and Peace Science, Journal of Conflict Resolution, Journal of Peace Research, Peace & Change, Peace Review.*

Basic Abstracts and Indexes

Alternative Press Index, Peace Research Abstracts Journal.

5354. *Action Report.* Former titles: *Peace Action;* (until 1993): *SANE - Freeze News;* (until 1990): *SANE World - Freeze Focus.* 1961. 4x/yr. USD 28. Ed(s): Gordon Clark. Peace Action, 1819 H St, N W, Ste 420, Washington, DC 20006-3603; paprog@igc.apc.org; http://www.webcom.com/peaceact/. Illus. Circ: 38000. Vol. ends: Winter. Microform: PQC. Reprint: PQC. *Aud.:* Ga.

The newsletter *Action Report,* which was formerly known as *Peace Action* and *Sane/Freeze News,* is a quarterly publication of Peace Action, one of the largest grassroots peace and justice organizations, and reports on its activities. Striving toward achieving a peaceful society where the threat of nuclear or conventional war no longer exists, it reports on issues relating to peace and nonviolence. Published for the supporters of Peace Action and Peace Action Education Fund, the newsletter encourages readers to act on vital issues concerning peace. This newsletter can be a source of inspiration to peace activists and educators alike.

5355. *Arms Control Today.* [ISSN: 0196-125X] 1971. 10x/yr. USD 60 (Individuals, USD 50; Students, USD 25). Ed(s): Miles A Pomper. Arms Control Association, 1726 M St, N W, Ste 201, Washington, DC 20036-4504; aca@armscontrl.org; http://www.armscontrol.org. Illus., index, adv. Sample. Circ: 3000. Vol. ends: Dec. Microform: PQC. Online: bigchalk; EBSCO Publishing; Florida Center for Library Automation; Gale Group; Northern Light Technology, Inc.; OCLC Online Computer Library Center, Inc.; ProQuest Information & Learning. *Indexed:* PAIS. *Bk. rev.:* 1, 800-1,200 words. *Aud.:* Ac.

The Arms Control Association, through its magazine *Arms Control Today,* provides policy makers, the press, and interested public with authoritative information, analysis, and commentary on arms control proposals, treaties, negotiations and agreements, and related national security issues. It emphasizes arms control and is dedicated to promoting a better understanding of topics that concern arms control. The magazine offers comprehensive data and intelligence on national security issues. Although the magazine emphasizes arms control, peace is what it strives for, because arms control eventually leads to peace and stability. Each issue begins with a "Focus" essay, which highlights an important issue related to arms control. Interviews with important decision makers in the arms control arena are well documented. There are several feature articles. In a recent article titled "How Will the Iraq War Change Global Nonproliferation Strategies?," the author examines how leading policy makers in the administration would like the nonproliferation regimes to change and tries to outline key questions one must answer to forge a new strategy. The "News and Negotiations" section has articles such as "IAEA 'Taken Aback' By Speed of Iran's Nuclear Program" and "Talks Focus on Coping with Bombs When the Shooting Stops." A bibliography with citations to current literature on topics relevant to the subject being discussed is found in each issue. Each issue ends with news briefs. An excellent resource for academic libraries and research centers.

5356. ***Bulletin of the Atomic Scientists: the magazine of global security news and analysis.*** Formerly (until 1946): *Bulletin of the Atomic Scientists of Chicago.* [ISSN: 0096-3402] 1945. bi-m. USD 28 domestic; USD 30 in Canada & Mexico; USD 35 elsewhere. Ed(s): Bret Lortie, Linda Rothstein. Educational Foundation for Nuclear Science, 6042 S Kimbark Ave, Chicago, IL 60637; schwartz@thebulletin.org. Illus., index, adv. Refereed. Circ: 9000. CD-ROM: ProQuest Information & Learning. Microform: MIM; NBI; PQC. Online: bigchalk; EBSCO Publishing; Florida Center for Library Automation; Gale Group; Northern Light Technology, Inc.; OCLC Online Computer Library Center, Inc.; ProQuest Information & Learning; H.W. Wilson. Reprint: PQC. *Indexed:* ABCPolSci, ABS&EES, AltPI, BAS, BRD, BRI, BiogInd, BiolAb, BiolDig, CBRI, CIJE, ChemAb, EngInd, EnvAb, ExcerpMed, FutSurv, GSI, GeoRef, H&SSA, MRD, MagInd, PAIS, PRA, RGPR, RI-1, SCI, SSCI. *Bk. rev.:* Various number and length. *Aud.:* Ga, Ac, Sa.

Founded in 1945 by two atomic scientists, Eugene Rabinowitch and Hyman Goldsmith, this journal has become a vehicle for promoting the demise of nuclear weapons worldwide. It is published by the Educational Foundation for Nuclear Science (EFNS), whose mission is to educate citizens about global security issues, especially the continuing dangers posed by nuclear and other weapons of mass destruction. Feature articles cover such topics as the international weapons trade, analysis of the causes of world conflict, prescriptions for survival, and nuclear weapon statistics. It provides the general public, policy makers, scientists, and journalists with nontechnical, scientifically sound, policy-relevant information about nuclear weapons and other global security issues. Available online.

5357. ***Conflict Management and Peace Science.*** Formerly (until 1981): *Journal of Peace Science.* [ISSN: 0738-8942] 1974. biennial. USD 30 per vol. Ed(s): Glen Palmer. Peace Science Society (International), Pennsylvania State University, Department of Political Science, University Park, PA 16802-6200; http://pss.la.psu.edu. Illus. Refereed. Circ: 1000. Vol. ends: No. 2. Reprint: SCH. *Indexed:* ABCPolSci, JEL, PAIS, PRA, SSCI. *Bk. rev.:* 1, 1,200 words. *Aud.:* Ac.

Committed to the scientific study of conflict and conflict analysis, *Conflict Management and Peace Science* is published by the Peace Science Society (International) at Pennsylvania State University. This society's main objective is to encourage the exchange of ideas and promote studies on peace analysis using scientific methods. Scholars and an international group of experts who specialize in diverse fields contribute articles to this journal. A recent issue includes articles such as "The Political Future of Afganistan and its Implications for U.S. Policy" and "The Power of Place and the Future of Spatial Analysis in the Study of Conflict." Research articles provide empirical results based on statistical tests. Each issue includes five or six articles, each preceded by an abstract. A list of references provides the researcher with further readings. Primarily written for a scholarly clientele, the journal will be useful in academic and research libraries.

5358. ***Fellowship.*** Formerly (until 1935): *The World Tomorrow.* [ISSN: 0014-9810] 1918. bi-m. USD 25 domestic; USD 35 foreign. Ed(s): Richard L Deats. Fellowship of Reconciliation, 521 N Broadway, Box 271, Nyack, NY 10960; http://www.forusa.org. Illus., index, adv. Sample. Refereed. Circ: 9000 Paid. Vol. ends: Nov/Dec. Microform: PQC. Online: ProQuest Information & Learning; SoftLine Information. Reprint: PQC. *Indexed:* AltPI, MRD, PAIS, PRA, RI-1. *Bk. rev.:* 6, 350 words. *Aud.:* Hs, Ga, Ac.

Fellowship is an important multifaith, multicultural magazine committed to justice and peace. It is published by the organization Fellowship of Reconciliation (FOR) and is one of the longest-running peace journals in the United States. Published since 1935, it follows its predecessor, *The World Tomorrow,* which began in 1918. Committed to active nonviolence as a way of life, *Fellowship* serves FOR's mission and strives for an ideal world of peace.

A recent article provides "Six Arguments for Everybody Against the Invasion of Iraq." There are also debates on peace and justice. *Fellowship* provides interesting reading with feature articles, interviews, poems, and news briefs. Philosophical and reflective, *Fellowship* is concerned with conflict resolution through the united effort of all peoples. A very useful resource for public and academic libraries.

5359. ***International Journal on World Peace.*** [ISSN: 0742-3640] 1984. q. USD 30 (Individuals, USD 20; Students, USD 10). Ed(s): Gordon L Anderson. Professors World Peace Academy, 2285 University Ave., W. Ste. 200, St. Paul, MN 55114-1635; ijwp@pwpa.org; http://www.pwpa.org. Illus., index, adv. Sample. Refereed. Circ: 10000. Vol. ends: Dec. Microform: PQC. Online: bigchalk; EBSCO Publishing; Florida Center for Library Automation; Gale Group; Northern Light Technology, Inc.; OCLC Online Computer Library Center, Inc.; ProQuest Information & Learning. *Indexed:* IBZ, IPSA, PAIS, PRA, PSA, PsycholAb, SSCI, SWR&A, SociolAb. *Bk. rev.:* 6, 150-1,100 words. *Aud.:* Ga, Ac.

International Journal on World Peace is a scholarly publication devoted to peace and cuts across all disciplines, politics, and philosophies. It is published by the Professors World Peace Academy, and its editorial board consists of scholars from several countries ranging from Australia and the United States to Norway and India. Recent issues have articles on "Attaining Peace in Divided Societies: Five Principles of Emerging Doctrine" and "Making Globalization Work for the Have Nots." The authors include a diverse group of international scholars. A news section and book reviews follow feature articles. The journal should provide interesting reading to patrons in both public and academic libraries.

5360. ***International Peacekeeping.*** [ISSN: 1353-3312] 1994. q. GBP 219 print & online eds. Ed(s): Michael Pugh. Frank Cass Publishers, Crown House, 47 Chase Side, Southgate, London, N14 5BP, United Kingdom; jnlsubs@frankcass.com; http://www.frankcass.com/jnls/. Illus., adv. Sample. Refereed. Vol. ends: Winter. *Indexed:* AmH&L, IBSS, IPSA, PSA, SociolAb. *Bk. rev.:* 4-6. *Aud.:* Ac.

International Peacekeeping essentially examines the theory and practice of peacekeeping. It propagates the theory that peacekeeping is primarily a political act. This refereed journal analyzes peacekeeping concepts and operations and provides in-depth research on peace and conflict resolution. The journal provides debates and articles on sanction enforcements; international policing; and the relationship between peacekeepers, state authorities, rival factions, civilians, and governmental organizations. There is an interesting section devoted to eyewitness accounts and a "Digest of Operations" section. This is an important resource for academic and research institutions that foster peace studies.

5361. ***International Security.*** [ISSN: 0162-2889] 1976. q. USD 144 (Individuals, USD 45; Students, USD 26). Ed(s): Steven E Miller. MIT Press, 5 Cambridge Center, Cambridge, MA 02142-1493; journals-orders@mit.edu; http://mitpress.mit.edu. Illus., index, adv. Refereed. Circ: 5530. Vol. ends: Winter. Microform: PQC. Online: EBSCO Publishing; Florida Center for Library Automation; Gale Group; Ingenta Select; JSTOR (Web-based Journal Archive); LexisNexis; OCLC Online Computer Library Center, Inc.; Project MUSE; RoweCom Information Quest; Swets Blackwell; H.W. Wilson. Reprint: PQC; PSC. *Indexed:* ABCPolSci, ABS&EES, AUNI, ArtHuCI, BAS, FutSurv, IBSS, IBZ, IPSA, PAIS, PRA, PSA, RiskAb, SSCI, SSI. *Aud.:* Ac.

International Security is mainly concerned with international peacekeeping. It is published by the Belfer Center for Science and International Affairs at Harvard University. Scholarly, well-researched articles analyze all aspects of international security and are contributed by experts in the theory and practice of peacekeeping. The publication is committed to "timely analysis" of security issues. It provides information on new developments in the areas of causes and prevention of war; ethnic conflict and peacekeeping; post–Cold War security problems; European, Asian, and regional security; nuclear forces and strategy; arms control and weapons proliferation; and post-Soviet security issues and diplomatic and military history. The "Editor's Note" provides an introduction to essays in the journal. This is a valuable resource for academic and research libraries that promote peace and international studies.

5362. *Journal of Conflict Resolution: research on war and peace between and within nations.* Formerly: *Conflict Resolution.* [ISSN: 0022-0027] 1957. bi-m. GBP 448 print & online eds. in Europe, Middle East, Africa & Australasia. Ed(s): Bruce M Russett. Sage Publications, Inc., 2455 Teller Rd, Thousand Oaks, CA 91320; info@sagepub.com; http://www.sagepub.com. Illus., index, adv. Refereed. Circ: 2200. Vol. ends: Dec. Microform: PQC. Online: Pub.; EBSCO Publishing; Florida Center for Library Automation; Gale Group; ingenta.com; JSTOR (Web-based Journal Archive); OCLC Online Computer Library Center, Inc.; ProQuest Information & Learning; RoweCom Information Quest; Swets Blackwell. Reprint: PQC. *Indexed:* ABCPolSci, ABS&EES, BAS, CIJE, CJA, CommAb, IBSS, IPSA, JEL, PAIS, PRA, PSA, PsycholAb, RiskAb, SSCI, SSI, SWR&A, SociolAb. *Aud.:* Ac.

The *Journal of Conflict Resolution* is a scholarly journal that focuses on international conflict. It has articles and research reports on intergroup conflicts within and between nations and promotes a better understanding of war and peace. This is the official publication of the Peace Science Society (International). The editorial board members belong to universities and colleges from all over the world. This scholarly journal is mainly directed toward academicians and researchers and is described as "an inter-disciplinary journal of social scientific theory and research on human conflict." The journal usually contains six to eight articles that focus on solid measurable facts and carefully reasoned arguments. *JCR* provides you with the latest ideas, approaches, and processes in conflict resolution. It offers theoretical and empirical results that intend to provide a better understanding of military strategy and war. Detailed research projects provide statistics, tables, charts, graphs, and results of case studies. Articles include abstracts and references. An excellent resource for academic libraries that focus on peace studies.

5363. *Journal of Peace Research: an interdisciplinary and international quarterly of scholarly work in peace research.* [ISSN: 0022-3433] 1964. bi-m. GBP 480 print & online eds. in Europe, Middle East, Africa & Australasia. Ed(s): Nils Petter Gleditsch. Sage Publications Ltd., 6 Bonhill St, London, EC2A 4PU, United Kingdom; info@sagepub.co.uk; http://www.sagepub.co.uk/. Illus., index, adv. Refereed. Circ: 1550. Vol. ends: Nov. Microform: PQC. Online: Gale Group; ingenta.com; JSTOR (Web-based Journal Archive); OCLC Online Computer Library Center, Inc.; RoweCom Information Quest; Sage Publications, Inc.; Swets Blackwell. *Indexed:* ABCPolSci, AmH&L, ArtHuCI, BRI, BrHumI, CBRI, CommAb, FutSurv, HRA, IBSS, IBZ, IPSA, JEL, PAIS, PRA, PSA, RiskAb, SFSA, SSCI, SSI, SUSA, SWA, SWR&A, SociolAb. *Bk. rev.:* 15-20, 150-450 words. *Aud.:* Ga, Ac.

Journal of Peace Research is published by the International Peace Research Association (IPRA). Edited at the Peace Research Institute, it is supported by the Nordic Publishing Board in Social Sciences (NOPS). It is an interdisciplinary, international quarterly and provides empirical, theoretical, and timely articles on global security and peace. It addresses the causes of violence, methods of conflict resolution, and ways of sustaining peace. Authors from over 50 countries have published in this journal. Each issue of *Journal of Peace Research* includes an extensive review section that presents and evaluates leading books in the field of peace research. This journal keeps the reader abreast of the latest developments in the area of peace studies and will be appreciated in academic libraries and peace research centers.

5364. *Nonviolent Activist.* Formerly (until 1984): *W R L News.* [ISSN: 8755-7428] 1945. bi-m. USD 25 (Non-members, USD 15). Ed(s): Judith Mahoney Pasternak. War Resisters League, 339 Lafayette St, New York, NY 10012-2782; wrl@igc.org; http://www.nonviolence.org/wrl. Illus., index, adv. Sample. Circ: 10000. Vol. ends: Nov/Dec. Microform: PQC. *Indexed:* AltPI. *Bk. rev.:* 1-3, 300-500 words. *Aud.:* Ga, Ac.

The *Nonviolent Activist,* a notable grassroots publication, is the official magazine of one of the most important American peace organizations, the War Resisters League (WRL). The WRL affirms that all war is a crime against humanity and is determined not to support any kind of war, international or civil, and strives nonviolently for the removal of all causes of war. The *Nonviolent Activist* reflects the ideals of the WRL. It carries articles related to peace and social justice issues. There are sections for book reviews, letters, activists' news, and War Resisters League news. A very good resource for peace activists and researchers interested in world peace.

Nuclear Resister. See Zines section.

5365. *Peace & Change: a journal of peace research.* [ISSN: 0149-0508] 1972. q. USD 329 print & online eds. Blackwell Publishing, Inc., Commerce Place, 350 Main St, Malden, MA 02148; subscrip@blackwellpub.com; http://www.blackwellpublishing.com. Illus., index, adv. Refereed. Circ: 1300. Vol. ends: Oct. Online: EBSCO Publishing; ingenta.com; OCLC Online Computer Library Center, Inc.; RoweCom Information Quest; Swets Blackwell. *Indexed:* ABS&EES, IPSA, PAIS, PRA, PSA, RiskAb, SUSA. *Bk. rev.:* 3-4, essay length. *Aud.:* Ga, Ac.

This scholarly journal publishes analytical and deductive articles on peace and conflict resolution. It addresses a wide variety of topics concerning nonviolence, peace movements and activists, conflict resolution, race and gender issues, cross-cultural studies, international conflict, and post–Cold War concerns. The journal attempts to transcend national, disciplinary, and other arbitrary boundaries while trying to link peace research, education, and activism. Each issue has four to five feature articles, a review essay, book reviews, and a notes section with short biographical information about each author. This journal would be useful in an academic library or research center.

5366. *Peace and Conflict: journal of peace psychology.* [ISSN: 1078-1919] 1995. q. USD 295. Ed(s): Richard Wagner. Lawrence Erlbaum Associates, Inc., 10 Industrial Ave, Mahwah, NJ 07430-2262; journals@erlbaum.com; http://www.erlbaum.com/. Illus., index, adv. Refereed. Vol. ends: Dec. Reprint: PSC. *Indexed:* IBSS, IPSA, PAIS, PRA, PSA, RiskAb, SociolAb. *Bk. rev.:* 4, 500-600 words. *Aud.:* Ac.

Peace and Conflict: Journal of Peace Psychology is published by the American Psychological Association's Division of Peace Psychology. The journal strives to support the ideals of the division and helps advance psychological knowledge that would build "peace in the world at large and within nations, communities, and families." The journal tries to apply information gathered from various areas in the field of psychology to solving issues relating to peace. It advocates equity, social justice, and protection of the environment, which it considers to be the hallmark of world order and peace. The journal publishes clinical, research-oriented articles; historical work; policy analysis; case studies; essays; interviews; and book reviews. This would be a fine addition to peace research centers and academic libraries.

5367. *Peace Magazine.* [ISSN: 0826-9521] 1985. bi-m. CND 17.50 domestic; CND 20 foreign. Ed(s): Metta Spencer. Canadian Disarmament Information Service (CANDIS), Peace Magazine, PO Box 248, Toronto, ON M5S 2S7, Canada. Illus., index, adv. Sample. Circ: 2666 Paid. Vol. ends: Nov/Dec. Microform: MML. Online: bigchalk; Gale Group; Micromedia ProQuest. *Indexed:* ABS&EES, AltPI, CBCARef, CPerI, PRA. *Bk. rev.:* 3-4, 250-600 words. *Aud.:* Hs, Ga, Ac.

The Peace Magazine is a peace quarterly that consists of articles, news stories, book and film reviews, letters, and a calendar of events focusing on peace issues. It is published by the Canadian Disarmament Information Service (CANDIS), a group of people dedicated to educating the public on every aspect of peace. Articles deal with subjects related to the terrible effects that wars have on people, their minds, and the minds of their children. They address human rights abuses, inequity, corrupt governance, and intolerance of diversity. Articles are written by activists, journalists, and scholars. This illustrated 32-page magazine includes an eight-page section produced in collaboration with Science for Peace. In a current article about Israel and Palestine, authors discuss the prolonged conflict in the Middle East and possible ways of resolving it and bringing security, democracy, and stability to this area. The "Our Readers Write" section encourages readers to voice their opinions on issues that concern them; readers also offer their comments on articles from previous issues. There is a book review section and a news section, "Newsworthy," which highlights peace issues. A good resource for public, high school, and academic libraries.

5368. ***Peace Research: the Canadian journal of peace studies.*** [ISSN: 0008-4697] 1969. 2x/yr. CND 73 (Individuals, CND 36). Ed(s): Dr. M V Naidu. M.V. Naidu, Ed. & Pub., c/o Brandon University, 270 18th St, Brandon, MB R7A 6A9, Canada; naidu@brandonu.ca. Illus., index, adv. Refereed. Circ: 1000. Vol. ends: Nov. Microform: MML. *Indexed:* ABS&EES, CBCARef, CPerI, PRA, SFSA. *Bk. rev.:* 1-2, 500-1,000 words. *Aud.:* Ga, Ac.

This journal focuses on studies in peace education, peace research, and peace movements. Deeply committed to the eradication of violence, armament, and war, it advocates nonviolence, disarmament, and peaceful settlement of disputes. Articles address human rights issues relating to equality, liberty, justice, economic development, environmental protection, cultural advancement, feminism, and humanism. A recent journal has articles about "Bush Administration's Nuclear Weapon Policy," "Pedagogies of Hope: Peace Education for the Transformation of the Culture of Violence and War," and "Humanitarian Response to the Use of Weapons of Mass Destruction." Published under the auspices of the Canadian Peace Research and Education Association (CPREA), the journal concludes with the CPREA newsletter. Academicians and researchers from all over the world contribute articles. Academic libraries and peace research centers will find this journal a useful resource.

5369. ***Peace Research Reviews.*** [ISSN: 0553-4283] 1967. irreg. approx. 3/yr. CND 72 for 2 yrs. Ed(s): Hanna Newcombe. Peace Research Institute-Dundas, 25 Dundana Ave, Dundas, ON L9H 4E5, Canada; info@prid.on.ca; http://www.prid.on.ca. Illus., adv. Circ: 400. Vol. ends: No. 6. *Indexed:* ABCPolSci. *Aud.:* Ac.

This learned journal from the Peace Research Institute, Dundas, provides in-depth scholarly articles on topics related to peace. *Peace Research Reviews* is dedicated to the study of peace, with each volume exclusively devoted to one major theme. A recent issue focuses on "Politics, Economics, and Ethics." The journal has a bibliography and a brief biography of each author. The editor, Hanna Newcombe, is also the editor of *Peace Research Abstracts Journal. Peace Research Reviews* could be a valuable addition to any research collection concerned with peace studies.

5370. ***Peace Review: the international quarterly of world peace.*** [ISSN: 1040-2659] 1989. q. GBP 254 (Individuals, GBP 55). Ed(s): Robert Elias. Carfax Publishing Ltd., 4 Park Sq, Milton Park, Abingdon, OX14 4RN, United Kingdom; enquiry@tandf.co.uk; http://www.tandf.co.uk/. Illus., index, adv. Sample. Refereed. Circ: 500. Vol. ends: Dec. Reprint: PSC. *Indexed:* AltPI, CJA, IBZ, IPSA, PAIS, PRA, PSA, SociolAb. *Bk. rev.:* 2-3, 1,000-1,500 words. *Aud.:* Ga, Ac.

Peace Review is a multidisciplinary, transnational journal that focuses on research and analysis and is directed toward important issues and controversies that hinder the maintenance of peace. The journal publishes articles related to peace research and may include human rights issues, conflict resolution, protection of the environment, and anything else concerned with peace. The journal's aim is to present the results of this research in short, informative essays. Each issue generally relates to a particular theme; sometimes essays relating to other topics are also published in the same issue. Contributors include journalists, political scientists, teachers, activists, theologians, and peace enthusiasts. Articles such as "The U.S. Role in the Collapse of the Peace Process" and "Women and Peace Dialogue in the Middle East" grace a current issue. Apart from articles and other features, there is a separate section on recommended books and videos.

Peace Watch. See Government Periodicals—Federal section.

5371. ***Security Dialogue.*** Formerly (until 1992): *Bulletin of Peace Proposals.* [ISSN: 0967-0106] 1970. q. GBP 299 print & online eds. in Europe, Middle East, Africa & Australasia. Ed(s): Pavel Baev, Anthony McDermott. Sage Publications Ltd., 6 Bonhill St, London, EC2A 4PU, United Kingdom; info@sagepub.co.uk; http://www.sagepub.co.uk/. Illus., index, adv. Vol. ends: Dec. Microform: PQC. Online: EBSCO Publishing; ingenta.com; OCLC Online Computer Library Center, Inc.; RoweCom Information Quest; Sage Publications, Inc.; Swets Blackwell. *Indexed:* BAS, IBSS, IBZ, IPSA, PAIS, PRA, PSA, RiskAb, SSCI, SociolAb. *Aud.:* Ac.

Security Dialogue provides the most current information on global peace and security. It offers new ideas on important issues concerning peace and security. It intends to provoke thought and reflection through "interregional dialogue" on issues concerning international security. A current issue focuses on the politics of the South China Sea; articles such as "The South China Sea: ASEAN's Security Concerns about China" and "China, the U.S.A. and the South China Sea Conflicts" are found in this special issue. The journal provides expert coverage on topics such as the role of the United Nations, conflict prevention, mediation, sovereignty, and intervention. This journal could prove to be a very useful resource in academic or research libraries that specialize in peace research.

■ PETS

See also Animal Welfare; Birds; Horses; Sports; and Veterinary Science sections.

Holly Hedden, Public Services Manager, Bowling Green Public Library, Bowling Green, KY 42101; hollyh@bgpl.org

Introduction

There are relatively few magazines devoted specifically to pets. Many of them are dedicated to a particular species, such as *Dog World* and *Bird Talk,* while others limit themselves to the concerns of an individual breed, for example *German Shepherd Dog Review* and *National Birman Fanciers News.* When trying to identify titles by breed, national breed organizations will be a good starting place. The *Encyclopedia of Associations* is a good reference tool for locating contact information for such groups.

The basic pet-related magazine titles provide reliable information about health care, feeding, grooming, raising, behavior, and generally enjoying life with pets, as well as content that is enlightening and entertaining. A recent trend seems to be pet culture magazines that highlight animal-themed art of all kinds, describe activities that pets and people can share, and report on the changing place of animals in human society. Articles about pet health, behavior, and care may also be found in general publications such as *Good Housekeeping* and *Southern Living.* Readers should note the qualifications of authors in these general publications as well as in titles devoted to pets. Inaccurate information is sometimes provided about topics of great current interest.

Online serials in this area continue to be volatile and of wildly varying quality. Most contain little original content and are either infrequently updated or do not provide information about their update schedule or the dates of items previously posted.

Most of the print magazines reviewed here also have a presence on the Internet. These accompanying sites range from those providing a glimpse of the tables of contents of previous issues and subscription information to those with full-text features, message boards, directories, events calendars, and extensive advertising.

Basic Periodicals

Hs: *Cat Fancy, Dog Fancy;* Ga: *A.F.A. Watchbird, Aquarium Fish Magazine, Cat Fancy, Dog Fancy, Dog World, Tropical Fish Hobbyist;* Ac: *Anthrozoos.*

5372. ***A F A Watchbird: the official publication of the American Federation of Aviculture.*** [ISSN: 0199-543X] 1974. q. Members, USD 30. Ed(s): Dale Thompson. American Federation of Aviculture, PO Box 7312, Kansas City, MO 64116-0012; http://www.afa.birds.org/afa. Illus., adv. Circ: 5000. Vol. ends: Nov/Dec. *Aud.:* Hs, Ga, Ac.

The mission of the American Federation of Aviculture (AFA) is to promote aviculture. *AFA Watchbird* carries articles about birds in aviaries (both private and public), birds in the wild, and news of the AFA and its conventions. Articles are written by veterinarians, avian biologists, and aviculturists. They cover breeding, feeding, housing, raising, bird behavior, and health concerns. The AFA web site provides access to an online store, AFA news and history, a representative table of contents, and featured articles from past issues of the *Watchbird.*

5373. ***A K C Gazette: the official journal for the sport of purebred dogs.*** Formerly (until 1995): *Pure-Bred Dogs, American Kennel Gazette.* [ISSN: 1086-0940] 1889. m. USD 29.93 domestic; USD 39.93 Canada; USD 44.93 elsewhere. American Kennel Club, Inc., 262 Madison Ave, New York, NY 10016; http://www.akc.org. Illus., index, adv. Circ: 57575. Vol. ends: Dec. Microform: PQC. Reprint: PQC. *Aud.:* Ga, Sa.

This official publication of the American Kennel Club (AKC) is an excellent source of information about the club and its business. It reflects the aim of the AKC to maintain and preserve the integrity of a purebred registry and to promote the sport of purebred dogs through appropriate events. Though it is primarily of interest to those who show, breed, groom, or train purebred dogs, articles covering health, behavior, and training will be of interest to a more general audience. Writers for the magazine include veterinarians, trainers, animal behaviorists, and AKC judges. Each issue profiles a particular breed in-depth and also includes breed columns containing numerous brief pieces on issues of concern for individual breeds. The AKC web site provides the table of contents of a recent issue of the *Gazette* and a wealth of information on such topics as choosing a dog, safety tips, health and nutrition, the "Kids' Corner" (a newsletter about responsible dog ownership), legislative alerts, AKC news and products, breed standards, breeder and rescue contacts, and more.

5374. ***Animal Wellness Magazine.*** Formerly (until 2000): *Animal.* 2000. 6x/yr. USD 19.95; CND 24.95. Ed(s): Dana Cox. Animal Group, Inc., 419 George St. North, Peterborough, ON K9H 3R4, Canada. *Aud.:* Hs, Ga.

The focus of this magazine is on the well-being of companion animals (mainly cats and dogs) and reflects a concern for seeking alternatives to Western medicine. Typical features might address holistic skin care, aromatherapy, healing massage, or purchasing pet health insurance. Non–health-related items such as celebrity interviews and reports on wildlife conservation groups are also included. Regular columns feature new product and service information, a health Q&A, and book reviews. *Animal Wellness* is a slim but attractive publication with good writing quality. The web site is not a significant supplementary resource at this time, providing excerpts from some current feature articles and columns, the current table of contents, and a search feature for holistic veterinarians.

5375. ***Animals.*** Formerly: *Our Dumb Animals.* [ISSN: 0030-6835] 1868. bi-m. USD 19.94. Ed(s): Joni Praded. Massachusetts Society for the Prevention of Cruelty to Animals, 350 S Huntington Ave, Boston, MA 02130; animals@enews.com; http://www.americast.com; http://www.mspca.org/. Illus., adv. Circ: 92000. Vol. ends: Nov/Dec. Microform: PQC. Online: EBSCO Publishing; Gale Group; Northern Light Technology, Inc. Reprint: PQC. *Indexed:* BiolDig. *Bk. rev.:* 2, 250-450 words. *Aud.:* Hs, Ga.

Animals, the award-winning magazine of the Massachusetts Society for the Prevention of Cruelty to Animals/American Humane Education Society (MSPCA/AHES), contains well-written pieces about companion animals and animals in the wild. Topics covered include animal conservation, behavior, and research, human/animal interaction, and environmental concerns. Regular features of the publication are brief news items, a companion-animal health question-and-answer column, a profile of an individual who works with or for animals, book reviews, and highlights of wildlife-viewing vacation spots. This is a good choice for school or public libraries. *Animals* will only be issued twice in 2003, but the editors anticipate a quick return to their regular publication schedule. There is no web site specifically corresponding to the magazine, but the MSPCA site contains a wealth of information about the organization and issues such as pet care, animal adoption, animal-related legislation, and living harmoniously with wildlife.

5376. ***Animals Exotic and Small.*** [ISSN: 1526-7857] 1988. bi-m. USD 25 domestic; USD 45 foreign. Ed(s): Debbie Hosley. Animals Exotic and Small, 1320 Mountain Ave, Norco, CA 92860-2852; acs@animalsexoticandsmall.com; http://www.animalsexoticandsmall.com. Index. Circ: 7500. *Aud.:* Ga, Sa.

This magazine is printed on sturdy newsprint and is illustrated with black-and-white photos and other graphics. *Animals Exotic and Small* focuses on providing information for owners of unusual or exotic pets, such as buffalos, skunks, hedgehogs, sugar gliders, venomous snakes, monkeys, and California variegated mutant sheep, although some more common pets such as rabbits and birds are also included. Articles address health and medical issues, legislative topics, breeding, raising, housing, feeding, and behavior. The majority of these are written by owners or breeders citing their personal experiences, and writing quality varies. The publication also includes book and video reviews and classified ads. This is a good resource for otherwise potentially difficult-to-find information. Extensive advertising will help owners of unusual pets locate hard-to-find merchandise. On the web site, subscribers can access the contents of recent issues. All visitors may view classified ads, use the message board, and access a list of categorized links. The calendar of events is now found exclusively on the web site, and can be a bit difficult to use.

5377. ***Anthrozoos: a multidisciplinary journal on the interactions of people and animals.*** [ISSN: 0892-7936] 1987. q. USD 55 (Individuals, USD 40). Ed(s): A L Podberscek. Delta Society, 289 Perimeter Rd E, Renton, WA 98055-1329; http://www.dumedia.com/delta.html. Illus., index, adv. Refereed. Circ: 1200. Vol. ends: No. 4. *Indexed:* AgeL, Agr, ArtHuCI, EnvAb, FoVS&M, IndVet, PsycholAb, RRTA, SCI, SSCI, VetBull. *Bk. rev.:* 1-3, 300-750 words. *Aud.:* Ac.

This refereed journal of the International Society for Anthrozoology is produced in cooperation with the Humane Society of the United States and the International Association of Human-Animal Interaction Organizations and published by Purdue University Press. The bulk of the journal consists of "Reviews and Research Reports" describing studies of various aspects of human-animal interaction and their findings. Recent topics include pet cats' responses to human handling and cooperative fishing interactions between aboriginal Australians and dolphins. Thoughtful commentaries, substantive book reviews, meeting announcements, and abstracts are also notable features of *Anthrozoos.* While this publication is primarily of interest to scholars and students, it will appeal to anyone concerned about human–animal interrelationships. Its multidisciplinary nature makes it readable for the layperson (jargon is discouraged).

5378. ***Aquarium Fish Magazine: fishkeeping - the art and the science.*** [ISSN: 0899-045X] 1988. m. USD 24.97 domestic; USD 35.47 Canada; USD 40.97 elsewhere. Ed(s): Russ Case. Fancy Publications, Inc., PO Box 57900, Los Angeles, CA 90057; http://www.animalnetwork.com. Illus., adv. Circ: 47000. Vol. ends: Dec. *Bk. rev.:* 1, 2,000-3,000 words. *Aud.:* Hs, Ga.

Aquarium Fish Magazine is an excellent resource for keepers of saltwater or freshwater aquariums or ponds. Contributors are well-qualified, experienced hobbyists or professionals and the writing is of high quality. An attractive layout and abundance of good color photo illustrations add to the appeal. Features and departments address individual species information (feeding, habits, requirements), aquarium and pond maintenance (lighting, filtration, equipment), plants, health, and problem solving. Numerous regular question-and-answer columns either give succinct, informative answers to numerous inquiries or use one or two questions as the jumping-off point for a detailed response. There is a special question-and-answer section just for kids. Examples of recent topics include setting up a saltwater aquarium, good and bad wrasses for reefs, and dealing with aggressive fish. The web site of *Aquarium Fish Magazine* provides access to the table of contents of the current issue, species profiles, a calendar of events, links to related sites, and a searchable library of information. Visitors also have the opportunity to participate in online forums.

5379. ***The Bark: the modern dog culture.*** [ISSN: 1535-1734] 1997. q. USD 15. Ed(s): Claudia Kawczynska. The Bark, 2810 8th St, Berkeley, CA 94710; editor@thebark.com; http://www.thebark.com. Adv. Circ: 75000 Paid and controlled. *Aud.:* Ga.

The Bark touts itself as "the modern dog culture magazine." It differs in emphasis from the other canine titles reviewed here, presenting book and film reviews, visual art, photo essays, poetry, book excerpts, short fiction, and brief news items (this may be the only dog magazine to announce that the Egyptian Museum in Cairo is seeking adopters for its mummified pet collection). It also offers information about canine behavior, health, and care, and about places and ways to travel with your pets. The advertising (dog-friendly spas, canine dog care, pet portraits) reveals the primary audience to be those who can and do pamper their pets. This is an attractive publication with good-quality writing, emphasizing ways to get more involved in your dog's life (or to get your dog more involved in your life). Its irreverant motto is "Dog is my co-pilot." *The Bark*'s web site consists of four components: an "E-zine" with a selection of feature articles, news briefs, poetry, prose, art, and commentary; "Community," with links to canine organizations, a list of events, and dog advocacy information; a "Shop" where one can purchase a subscription or *Bark* products, or link to web sites of the magazine's advertisers; and the "Archives," which are under development.

5380. ***Bird Talk: dedicated to better care of pet birds.*** Formerly (until 198?): *International Bird Talk;* Incorporates (1978-1995): *Bird World;* (1928-1950): *American Canary Magazine.* [ISSN: 0891-771X] 1982. m. USD 27.97 domestic; USD 3.99 newsstand/cover per issue domestic; USD 5.99 newsstand/cover per issue foreign. Ed(s): Laura Doering, Melissa Kauffman. Fancy Publications, Inc., 3 Burroughs, Irvine, CA 92618-2804; birdtalk@fancypubs.com. Illus., index, adv. Circ: 140000 Paid. Vol. ends: Dec. *Bk. rev.:* 1-3, 200-300 words. *Aud.:* Hs, Ga.

This publication provides informative feature articles on such topics as avian diet, introducing birds to other household pets, keeping birds healthy, bird rescue, photographing birds, and other subjects of interest to bird owners, including profiles of individual bird species. The magazine is attractive and well written, with contributors including veterinarians that specialize in avian care, avian behaviorists, aviculturists, and experienced bird owners. Regular departments include sections devoted to finches and canaries and to lories and softbills, a show calendar, a directory of advertisements from bird breeders, and an avian buyer's guide (classified ads for clubs, products, and services for birds). The scope of topics covered makes this an excellent choice for library collections. The web site describes the feature articles of the current issue and provides search access to selected features from past issues in the "Library" section. Additional resources available online include species profiles, a browsable reference library, question-and-answer departments, and an online "community" that visitors can join.

5381. ***Cat Fancy: cat care for the responsible owner.*** Supersedes (in 1986): *International Cat Fancy.* [ISSN: 0892-6514] 1965. m. USD 25.97 domestic; USD 36.47 Canada; USD 41.97 elsewhere. Ed(s): Amanda Luke. Fancy Publications, Inc., 3 Burroughs, Irvine, CA 92618-2804; catfancy@fancypubs.com; http://www.animalnetwork.com. Illus., index, adv. Circ: 276000 Paid. Vol. ends: Dec. *Bk. rev.:* 1-2, 150-450 words. *Aud.:* Hs, Ga, Ac.

This publication will be the first choice for the average cat owner. It is an attractive magazine with many color photos, and provides features with practical advice and basic information on health concerns, grooming, and feeding. A different breed profile in each issue provides a good overview. Responsible cat ownership is emphasized. Each issue also includes a breeder directory, highlights of cat-related products, "Kids for Cats" pages with contributions by and for kids, and a show calendar. Features are well written and contain enough information to be useful, but generally not so much as to overwhelm. This publication is recommended for public libraries, large academic libraries, and veterinarians' waiting rooms. *Cat Fancy* has an extensive web site, as do the other titles by Fancy Publications. Visitors to the site can access information on cat care, health, nutrition, behavior and more in the "Resources" section; view current issue content descriptions; read weekly online features; participate in online forums; and view upcoming events, breeder information, classifieds, an index of recent years' issues, and weekly breed profiles.

5382. ***Dog Fancy.*** Former titles (until 1986): *International Dog Fancy; Dog Fancy.* [ISSN: 0892-6522] 1970. m. USD 25.97 domestic; USD 36.47 Canada; USD 41.97 elsewhere. Ed(s): Steven Biller. Fancy Publications, Inc., 3 Burroughs, Irvine, CA 92618-2804; dogfancy@fancypubs.com; http://www.animalnetwork.com. Illus., index, adv. Circ: 286182 Paid. *Bk. rev.:* 1-4, 100-350 words. *Aud.:* Hs, Ga.

Dog Fancy is an attractive publication that provides informational and entertaining items. It covers topics that include health, travel, training, behavior, selection, and breed information for dog owners and potential dog owners. The coverage of topics is less in-depth than that of *Dog World* or *Dogs in Canada,* and it is geared more toward the average pet owner and less toward the breeder or competitor. Each issue contains a lot of variety; resources include a breeder directory, highlighted dog accessories, and news items, as well as breed profiles, classifieds, human-interest stories, and a section for "junior fanciers." This title is recommended for high school and public libraries and veterinarians' waiting rooms. As with other Fancy Publications, the web site of this magazine is worth visiting. It includes weekly features, brief breed profiles and breeder information, online forums, classifieds, a calendar of events, a "Resources" section with tips on practical topics from behavior and training to nutrition, an index to articles from recent years' issues, current issue content descriptions, and links to animal organizations' web sites.

5383. ***Dog World: the authority on dog care.*** [ISSN: 0012-4893] 1916. m. USD 19.95 domestic; USD 30.69 Canada; USD 31.62 elsewhere. Fancy Publications, Inc., 3 Burroughs, Irvine, CA 92618-2804; editor@animalnetwork.com; http://www.animalnetwork.com. Illus., index, adv. Circ: 65000 Paid. Vol. ends: Dec. Microform: PQC. Online: EBSCO Publishing; OCLC Online Computer Library Center, Inc. *Aud.:* Ga, Sa.

Dog World is a good source for in-depth articles on health, behavior, and breed profiles. Dog owners, breeders, and trainers will find information on raising, caring for, training, and traveling with dogs. The articles are written by qualified experts whose credentials are prominently displayed. Upcoming dog shows and other events are listed, and there is an extensive section of breeder's advertisements. Readers will also find book reviews and information on new products. The broad range of topics in each issue ensures that most readers will find something of interest. Visitors to *Dog World Online* will find the current issue's table of contents, profiles of many dog breeds, an article index, breeders' classifieds, a searchable events and show calendar, and a Resources section with categorized articles on topics such as nutrition, health, and behavior.

5384. ***Dogs in Canada.*** Incorporates (1975-1976): *Dogs Annual;* Which was formerly (until 1974): *Kennel Directory.* [ISSN: 0012-4915] 1889. m. CND 41.73 domestic; CND 57 United States; CND 92 elsewhere. Apex Publishing Ltd., 89 Skyway Ave, Ste 200, Etobicoke, ON M9W 6R4, Canada; info@dogsincanada.com; http://www.dogsincanada.com. Illus., adv. Circ: 25374. *Indexed:* CBCARef. *Bk. rev.:* 1-2, 300-600 words. *Aud.:* Ga, Sa.

Dogs in Canada is a publication for members of the Canadian Kennel Club and has particular appeal for dog fanciers, although some items will be of interest to the average dog owner. Articles on health issues, dog shows, grooming, behavior, and breed-specific topics are written by veterinarians, judges, behaviorists, and other qualified professionals. "Breedlines" (breed-specific issues and information), club news, and other items of interest that pertain to specific breeds are submitted by national breed clubs and readers. Show news and reprints of old *Kennel & Bench* articles are also featured. Each issue includes a directory of clubs and a listing of upcoming unofficial events. The *Dogs Annual* special issue is a good source for general information on selecting a dog, finding a breeder, feeding, grooming, and generally enjoying life with a dog. It also includes several directories including rescue clubs and an extensive list of breeders. The web site provides a selection of recent articles, breeder listings and advertisements, breed information including a brief history and general characteristics, a directory of rescue clubs, and some information on cat breeds.

5385. ***Freshwater and Marine Aquarium: the magazine dedicated to the tropical fish enthusiast.*** [ISSN: 0160-4317] 1978. m. USD 22. R - C Modeler, 144 W Sierra Madre Blvd, Sierra Madre, CA 91024; http://www.rcmmagazine.com. Illus., adv. Circ: 34000. Vol. ends: Dec. *Indexed:* ZooRec. *Bk. rev.:* 1-2, 600-900 words. *Aud.:* Ga, Sa.

Freshwater and Marine Aquarium includes information about specific freshwater and marine fish, aquarium concerns such as maintenance and health topics, descriptions of Internet sites, and Q&A columns. Additional features may include book and product reviews and articles that describe aquariums open to the public. Authors often suggest sources for further reading. The variety of topics and of depth of coverage makes this title appropriate for the relatively casual aquarist as well as the more devoted. Online contents at the *Freshwater and Marine Aquarium* web site include links to associations' web sites, an organization spotlight, a list of upcoming events with links, the table of contents of the current magazine, and books available for purchase. Additional content is accessible by magazine subscribers.

5386. *Modern Dog.* [ISSN: 1703-812X] 2002. q. CND 14.83 domestic; USD 20 United States; USD 34 elsewhere. Modern Dog, 1941 Whyte Ave, Vancouver, BC V6J 1B4 , Canada; connie@moderndog.ca. Adv. *Aud.:* Ga.

Touted as "the lifestyle magazine for urban dogs and their companions," *Modern Dog* is a leisure magazine for affluent city dog owners, a hybrid of fashion magazine and pet publication. In addition to a breed profile, each issue includes "Ask the Expert" columns, fashion photography, recipes (some for people, some for dogs), and a canine horoscope. You may also find features on travel, apartment hunting, canine behavior, or dog-themed art. Advertising ranges from pet accessories to rental cars to upscale hotels that welcome four-legged guests. This is a glossy publication penned by staff writers and other qualified professionals. It has a decided Canadian bent, but most of the content will also be relevant to readers in the U.S. The web site for *Modern Dog* is limited to subscription information and resources to help dog owners obtain canine-friendly housing. This magazine is recommended for larger public libraries.

5387. *Our Animals.* [ISSN: 0030-6789] 1906. q. USD 25 donation. Ed(s): Paul M Glassner. San Francisco Society for the Prevention of Cruelty to Animals, 2500 16th St, San Francisco, CA 94103. Illus., adv. Circ: 50000. Vol. ends: No. 4. *Aud.:* Hs, Ga.

Our Animals is a publication of the San Francisco Society for the Prevention of Cruelty to Animals (SF/SPCA). This inspiring journal is filled with stories and photos of companion animals who are or have been in need of help and of volunteers and adopters. It also carries stories about the special programs of the SF/SPCA, including its Hearing Dog Program. The SF/SPCA is a model organization for sheltering, rehabilitating, training, and adopting out companion animals, and it is the home of the celebrated Maddie Pet Adoption Center. *Our Animals* is of interest to shelter or humane society workers, volunteers, and anyone interested in issues facing homeless, abused, or neglected animals. The positive tone and upbeat feature articles of this publication also make it appealing and appropriate for children. The table of contents of the current issue and a selection of stories from recent issues are available at the SF/SPCA web site, along with a wealth of information about the organization, its programs and services, and caring for companion animals.

Pure-Bred Dogs/American Kennel Gazette. See *AKC Gazette.*

5388. *Rare Breeds Journal.* Incorporates in part: *The Jumping Pouch.* [ISSN: 1048-986X] 1987. bi-m. USD 25 domestic; USD 35 in Canada & Mexico; USD 50 elsewhere. Ed(s): Maureen Neidhardt. Rare Breeds Journal, PO Box 66, Crawford, NE 69339; rarebreed@bbc.net; http://www.ckcusa.com/webads/exotics/rarebre.htm. Illus., adv. Sample. Circ: 3000 Paid. Vol. ends: Jan/Feb. *Bk. rev.:* 10-12, 50-100 words. *Aud.:* Sa.

This publication is not strictly pet-oriented, but it also includes items relating to alternative livestock and wildlife. *Rare Breeds Journal* will be a useful addition to the collection in areas where people are raising, breeding, or selling camels, llamas, chinchillas, wallabies, kangaroos, baby doll sheep, or other exotic animals not covered in most other pet or livestock journals. It provides a forum for the exchange of information about the health, breeding, keeping, feeding, raising, and marketing of these animals. Additional resources include news of various exotic-breeds associations; a breeders directory; a listing of organizations, registries, and clubs; and advertisements. The publication is mostly in black and white. It is written by owners and breeders relating their personal experiences; consequently the writing quality varies. The web site provides access to lists of breeders and associations. *Rare Breeds Journal* is recommended for a specialized audience.

5389. *Tropical Fish Hobbyist.* [ISSN: 0041-3259] 1952. m. USD 40; USD 51 in Canada & Mexico; USD 60 elsewhere. Ed(s): Glen S Axelrod. T.F.H. Publications, Inc., One T F H Plaza, Third and Union Aves, Neptune, NJ 07753; editor@tfh.com; http://www.tfh.com. Illus., index, adv. Circ: 60000. Vol. ends: Aug. *Indexed:* ZooRec. *Bk. rev.:* 1, 200-300 words. *Aud.:* Ga, Ac, Sa.

Tropical Fish Hobbyist is a very attractive publication with lots of color photos. It will appeal to serious aquarium enthusiasts and anyone ready to expand beyond a minimal-maintenance aquarium set-up. It covers topics of interest to freshwater and saltwater aquarists, including keeping, feeding, breeding, lighting, health, and characteristics of specific species. Some items concerning aquarium plants, invertebrates, and reptiles and amphibians may also be found. The annual index in the January issue will help readers locate these. *TFH* includes a balance of practical advice and more general information, and several Q&A sections. It also contains a lot of advertisements and a calendar of events and list of society and club meetings and other announcements. *TFH* claims to be "the world's most widely read aquarium monthly."

Electronic Journals

Ark Online. See Animal Welfare/Electronic Journals section.

5390. *Rainbowfish On-Line.* [ISSN: 1328-4541] 1996. irreg. Ed(s): Adrian Tappin. Rainbowfish On-Line, 5 Atlanta St, Manly, QLD 4179, Australia; atappin@ecn.net.au; http://pandora.nla.gov.au/tep/10348. *Aud.:* Sa.

This online magazine contains a wealth of information for the rainbowfish enthusiast concerning the care and keeping of rainbowfish in captivity; there is also information about the natural habitat of these fish. This is an attractive publication generously supplemented with illustrative maps, photos, tables, and graphs. Photos, descriptions, and general introductions to the various rainbowfish species are provided, along with references for further exploration.

■ PHILATELY

Joe Bourneuf, Head of Reference Services, Widener Library, Harvard University, Cambridge, MA 02138

Introduction

"A feller isn't thinkin' mean
Collectin' stamps;
His tho'ts are mostly good and clean
Collectin' stamps;
He doesn't knock his fellow men
Or harbor any grudges then;
A feller's at his finest when
He's collectin' stamps."

—Silas Weatherby (*New York Times,* Jan. 31, 1937, p. 112)

Collecting stamps, or more formally, philately, is among the most popular hobbies in the world. The British royal family has, over several generations, amassed one of the world's finest collections, but a beginner can buy an album and packet of stamps for a few dollars at a local hobby shop.

The world's first postage stamp, the famous British "Penny Black," was issued May 6, 1840. Collecting stamps gained such a numerous and devoted following within just a few years that it was ridiculed as a crazy fad in the popular press of the time. The first philatelic magazine appeared in 1862. There were over 800 such journals in the early part of the twentieth century; today there are perhaps 340.

Advanced collectors often specialize in a particular country, others focus on a theme, for example, only stamps celebrating medicine or those with pictures of fish or obelisks. Others are devoted to the rare stamps with errors, such as the famous 100 accidentally printed showing an upside down biplane, issued in 1918 and now valued at $100,000. Although there are stamp magazines covering almost every collecting specialty, they are not reviewed here because their audience is relatively limited. The following titles are selected for their broad, general appeal and, to a lesser extent, for their coverage of the United States, Canada, and Great Britain, as these stamps have generally proved of greatest interest to American library users.

Basic Periodicals

Ems: *Philatelic Observer;* Hs: *Scott Stamp Monthly, Stamp Collector;* Ga: *American Philatelist, Linn's Stamp News, Scott Stamp Monthly;* Ac: *American Philatelic Congress. Congress Book, American Philatelist, Philatelic Literature Review.*

5391. ***American Philatelic Congress. Congress Book.*** Formerly (until 1956): *Original Papers on Philatelic Themes Presented by Invitation.* [ISSN: 0271-390X] 1935. a. Members, USD 17.50; Non-members, USD 20. Ed(s): Barbara Mueller. American Philatelic Congress, c/o Russell V Skavaril, 222 E Torrence Rd, Columbus, OH 43214-3834. Illus., index. Circ: 1000. *Aud.:* Ac, Sa.

This annual should be in any library supporting philatelic interests. Each volume contains original scholarly papers presented by invitation of the American Philatelic Congress (APC). Each lengthy, thoroughly researched paper is well illustrated with photographs and includes a bibliography. The volume also includes a description of the competitive awards given by the APC to recognize contributions to philatelic knowledge, a listing of current winners, and references to a variety of other APC activities.

5392. ***American Philatelist.*** [ISSN: 0003-0473] 1887. m. USD 40 domestic; USD 43 in Canada & Mexico; USD 50 elsewhere. Ed(s): Barb Boal. American Philatelic Society, Inc., PO Box 8000, State College, PA 16803; http://www.philately.com/philately/aps.htm. Illus., index. Sample. Circ: 50000 Paid. Vol. ends: Dec. *Indexed:* A&ATA, ABS&EES, BRI, CBRI. *Bk. rev.:* 7, 50-300 words. *Aud.:* Ga, Ac.

American Philatelist is the official publication of the American Philatelic Society (APS), the leading philatelic organization in the United States. Despite the title, this magazine is worldwide in scope and covers all aspects of stamp collecting. Articles are general or historical in nature and supplemented with color illustrations of stamps and postal documents. Monthly columns include a detailed description of the most recent stamps issued by the U.S. government, a guide to stamp shows and stamp bourses, and the "Glassine Surfer," with tips and links on surfing the Internet to find information on stamp collecting. The links can be accessed online via the APS web site. This journal also offers news to its members of society activities and classified ads. An annual author and subject index is published in the December issue. This high-quality journal is essential for all general collections. *American Philatelist* is also available online. The web version lists the table of contents of the featured articles from September 1995 to date, but no links are provided to the text of the articles. However, links are provided for the monthly column "Glassine Surfer," instructions for authors, advertising information, and an electronic guide to stamp shows and stamp exchanges.

5393. ***Canadian Philatelist.*** [ISSN: 0045-5253] 1950. bi-m. Members, CND 25; Non-members, CND 30. Ed(s): Tony Shaman. Philaprint Ltd., First Canadian Pl, PO Box 100, Toronto, ON M5X 1B2, Canada. Illus., index, adv. Circ: 3000 Controlled. Vol. ends: Nov/Dec. Microform: MML. *Bk. rev.:* 7-10, 350 words. *Aud.:* Ga, Ac.

The official publication of the Royal Philatelic Society of Canada, the leading philatelic organization in the country, *Canadian Philatelist* presents articles in English and French primarily on the stamps and postal history of Canada. It covers older and current areas of interest to collectors of Canadian stamps. Regular columns include an auction and events calendar, news from the Canada Post, vignettes of early British North American postal history, letters to the editor, and a listing of Canadian stamps recently issued. Each magazine issue also contains society news, reports, and a listing of chapter meetings.

5394. ***Gibbons Stamp Monthly.*** Formerly (until 1977): *Stamp Monthly.* [ISSN: 0954-8084] 1890. m. GBP 31.20 domestic; GBP 52 in Europe; GBP 67 elsewhere. Ed(s): Hugh Jefferies. Stanley Gibbons Publications Ltd., 5 Parkside, Christchurch Rd, Ringwood, BH24 3SH, United Kingdom; info@stanleygibbons.co.uk; http://www.stanleygibbons.com. Illus., index, adv. Sample. Circ: 25000 Paid. Vol. ends: May. *Bk. rev.:* 5-10, 50-100 words. *Aud.:* Ga.

This glossy British magazine offers articles and news of interest to collectors of stamps and other postal materials issued in the United Kingdom and the Commonwealth. It enjoys a wide circulation, especially within the British Isles, due to its readable, popular articles. There are also more erudite pieces intended for the serious collector. Regular features include catalog price updates, first-day covers, varieties, auctions, fairs, and competitions. Each issue also contains the most recent new-issue supplement to the *Stanley Gibbons Stamp Catalogue,* the most popular stamp catalog published in Great Britain.

5395. ***Global Stamp News.*** [ISSN: 1060-0361] 1990. m. USD 8.95. Ed(s): Jan Brandewie. Brandewie Inc., 110 N Ohio Ave, Box 97, Sidney, OH 45365. Illus., adv. Sample. Circ: 36000 Controlled. *Bk. rev.:* 1-4, 100-900 words. *Aud.:* Hs, Ga.

Advertisers cover most of the expenses of publishing this tabloid, making it one of the best values in stamp publishing. *Global Stamp News* is an informative publication with more than 60 pages in each monthly issue. Numerous advertisements are interspersed with short articles, many of which are submitted by readers. These informative articles represent a wide variety of worldwide collecting interests and evidence a shared fascination with stamps. Regular features include a Canada corner, Judaica philately, "hands-on" history, a philatelic quiz, and announcements of stamp shows.

5396. ***Linn's Stamp News.*** Formerly: *Linn's Weekly Stamp News.* [ISSN: 0161-6234] 1928. w. USD 39.90; USD 2 newsstand/cover per issue. Ed(s): Michael Schreiber, Michael Laurence. Amos Press Inc., 911 Vandemark Rd, Box 482, Sidney, OH 45365; http://www.linns.com. Illus., adv. Sample. Circ: 55000 Paid. Vol. ends: Dec. Microform: PQC. *Bk. rev.:* 1-5, 50-400 words. *Aud.:* Ga.

This tabloid is the world's highest circulation weekly philatelic newspaper. Articles cover all aspects of stamp collecting worldwide, with a special emphasis on the United States and Canada. *Linn's* has a particular appeal for those collectors and stamp dealers who actively buy and sell stamps, as it strives to provide accurate and timely information on the stamp market. An extensive classified section, regular columns and news articles on stamp market tips and trends, and numerous advertisements form the basis of a stamp marketplace for the buying, selling, and exchanging of all varieties of philatelic materials. News and information are provided on stamp societies, stamp events, show awards, auction calendars, new worldwide issues, the U.S. stamp program, postmarks, forgeries, cachets, and covers. *Linn's Stamp News* is also available online (www.linns.com). This dynamic web site is keyword searchable and includes links to several of the feature articles in the current weekly issue, current information on the price performance of U.S. stamps, a stamp show calendar searchable by month or by state, and weekly updates on the U.S., U.N., and Canadian stamp programs. There is a reference section (with hyperlinks) that includes a glossary of philatelic terms, listings of the world's postal administrations and postal history societies, and a tutorial of stamp collecting basics. Linns.com has also developed the first Internet search engine designed just for stamp collectors (www.stampsites.com), which focuses solely on philatelic web sites.

5397. ***Philatelic Literature Review.*** [ISSN: 0270-1707] 1942. q. USD 30 (Individuals, USD 15). Ed(s): William L Welch, Jr. American Philatelic Research Library, PO Box 8000, State College, PA 16803; wlwelch@stamps.org; http://www.stamps.org/TheLibrary/lib_AbouttheAPRL.htm. Illus., index, adv. Sample. Circ: 2750. Vol. ends: Dec. *Indexed:* BRI, CBRI. *Bk. rev.:* 10-20, 100-750 words. *Aud.:* Ac, Sa.

Philatelic Literature Review is published by the American Philatelic Research Library, the largest public philatelic library in the United States. The value of this periodical as a reference tool is threefold: knowledgeable, in-depth book reviews written by specialists in the field; biographical and research articles on the history of philately; and original, comprehensive indexes and bibliographies on all aspects of stamp collecting. Each issue also features market information, news from the American Philatelic Research Library, a directory of dealers, and a philatelic literature clearinghouse where members list philatelic literature for sale or wanted for purchase. This is essential for any collection supporting research in the field.

5398. ***Philatelic Observer.*** [ISSN: 0273-5598] 1963. bi-m. USD 9. Ed(s): Jennifer Arnold. Junior Philatelists of America, Inc., PO Box 2625, Albany, OR 97321-0643. Illus., adv. Sample. Circ: 1000. Vol. ends: Nov/Dec. *Bk. rev.:* Occasional. *Aud.:* Ems, Hs.

Philatelic Observer is published by the Junior Philatelists of America (JPA), a stamp society run by and for stamp collectors age 18 and under, providing news and information for collectors in this age group. Helpful advice is given for beginning stamp collectors. Of special interest to children are the puzzles, quizzes, contests, educational projects, and free stamp materials offered in each issue. Readers are given details on how to form a stamp club, find a pen pal, and participate in JPA activities. Regular features include a stamp show calendar, mail auctions, and classified advertisements. Recommended for public libraries.

5399. ***Postal History Journal.*** [ISSN: 0032-5341] 1957. 3x/yr. USD 30; USD 35 in Canada & Mexico; USD 40 elsewhere. Ed(s): Robert Dalton Harris, Diane F DeBlois. Postal History Society, Inc., c/o Kalman V. Illyefalvi, Sec.-Treas., 8207 Daren Ct., Pikesville, MD 21208-2211. Illus., index, adv. Circ: 600 Controlled. Vol. ends: Oct. Microform: PQC. Reprint: PQC. *Bk. rev.:* 2-5, 100-400 words. *Aud.:* Ac, Sa.

This journal is renowned for its scholarly, well-researched articles and commentaries on all aspects of postal history worldwide. Annotated bibliographies of American and foreign postal-history articles published in other journals can be found in each issue, as well as news and information for members of the Postal History Society. *Postal History Journal* won the 1992 Diane D. Boehret Award given by the American Philatelic Congress and the Gold for philatelic literature periodicals at the August 1999 Stampshow held in Cleveland, Ohio. Recommended for all comprehensive collections.

5400. ***Scott Stamp Monthly.*** Supersedes in part (until 1982): *Scott's Monthly Stamp Journal;* Which was formerly: *Scott's Monthly Journal.* [ISSN: 0737-0741] 1920. m. USD 17.95 United States; USD 25.95 Canada; USD 40.95 elsewhere. Ed(s): Michael Baadke. Scott Publishing Company, 911 Vandemark Rd, PO Box 828, Sidney, OH 45365; http://www.scottonline.com. Illus., index, adv. Sample. Circ: 28000 Paid. Vol. ends: Dec. *Bk. rev.:* 1-3, length varies. *Aud.:* Hs, Ga.

This tabloid is issued by the publisher of the annual *Scott Standard Postage Stamp Catalogue,* the philatelist's bible. An update to the *Catalogue,* giving revised valuations as they occur, is a key part of each issue. Each issue also provides general-interest articles on stamps worldwide, with color illustrations, appealing to philatelists of all ages. Monthly columns provide articles that re-create popular historical subjects through stamps, give tips for working with stamps, and discuss postal errors and postal history. Each issue also features a full-color comic ("Amazing Stamp Stories"), puzzles, an auction calendar, and a listing by date of issue of the most recent stamps issued by the United States, Canada, and the United Nations. The "Free for All" column tells how subscribers can get a free stamp or souvenir sheet each month. This magazine is recommended for all public libraries.

5401. ***Stamp Collector.*** Incorporates (1936-2000): *Stamp Wholesaler;* Formerly: *Western Stamp Collector.* [ISSN: 0277-3899] 1931. bi-w. USD 32.98 domestic; USD 71.98 foreign; USD 2.25 per issue. Ed(s): Wayne Youngblood. Krause Publications, Inc., 700 E State St, Iola, WI 54990-0001; http://www.krause.com. Illus., adv. Sample. Circ: 15221 Paid and free. Vol. ends: Dec (No. 26). *Bk. rev.:* Occasional. *Aud.:* Hs, Ga.

This colorful tabloid is filled with articles that discuss international developments in the stamp market and provide information to help the reader make buying and selling decisions. Feature articles are rarely more than one page in length, but they provide timely news coverage designed for both beginning and experienced collectors. Each issue contains an extensive show calendar (both large and small stamp shows are covered) and auction guide, a large classified section, how-to articles, collecting tips, and information on new U.S. and foreign issues. Although it is similar in format and content to its larger competitor, *Linn's Stamp News,* it is worth noting that *Stamp Collector* is the only U.S. stamp news publication to post circulation growth in the past few years.

5402. ***Stamp Magazine.*** [ISSN: 0307-6679] 1934. m. GBP 28.80 domestic; GBP 41.63 in Europe; GBP 62.60 elsewhere. Ed(s): Steve Fairclough. I P C Country & Leisure Media Ltd., Focus House, Dingwall Ave, Croydon, CR9 2TA, United Kingdom; http://www.ipcmedia.com. Illus., adv. Vol. ends: Dec. *Bk. rev.:* 0-5, 50-150 words. *Aud.:* Ac, Ga.

The emphasis of this magazine is clearly first on Great Britain, and secondly on the Commonwealth, but the rest of the world is hardly neglected. Each issue contains a variety of news pieces, as well as substantial articles running several pages, that appeal both to the general and specialized collector. Other regular features include auction news, a calendar of upcoming British stamp fairs and international stamp exhibitions, and, of particular importance, an exhaustive listing of new-stamp issues from every country with a cross-reference index to popular themes from among these. It is printed on high-quality paper, permitting excellent color illustrations. *Stamp Magazine* is naturally most popular with collectors of British stamps, but is of sufficient general interest to be considered for larger public libraries.

5403. ***Topical Time.*** [ISSN: 0040-9332] 1949. bi-m. Non-members, USD 30. Ed(s): George E Griffenhagen. American Topical Association, Inc., PO Box 50820, Albuquerque, NM 87181-0820; atastamps@juno.com; http://home.prcn.org/~pould/ata/. Illus., index, adv. Circ: 5000. Vol. ends: Nov/Dec. *Bk. rev.:* 5-10, 100-500 words. *Aud.:* Ga, Sa.

Many collect stamps focused on a subject or theme rather than on a nation or philatelic formats such as first-day covers. *Topical Time* is the only English-language philatelic magazine solely devoted to the interests of topical stamp collectors. Each issue contains several articles on specific topics or themes being collected. For example, a recent issue carries a piece on stamps depicting the iris flower and another on stamps honoring the invention of the telephone. A regular feature is the index to topical periodical articles that have appeared in other stamp magazines. As the official publication of the American Topical Association, it offers society news, including a monthly update on the activities of study groups focusing on a particular topic. Members are encouraged to join one or more groups, and to submit articles to *Topical Time.*

Electronic Journals

In the last two years, the number of philatelic web sites has grown exponentially, but most are vendor sites or auction sites, which are not appropriate for review because they are not electronic journals, magazines, or newletters. There are web sites affiliated with three of the recommended print philatelic magazines (see *American Philatelist, Linn's Stamp News,* and *Scott Stamp Monthly,* above in this section). But there is only one true electronic philatelic journal: *Stamps. Net: the Internet magazine for stamp collectors.* Of special note should be the search engine designed just for stamp collectors, StampSites.com (http://www.stampsites.com), which gathers over 20,000 worldwide stamp-related web sites each month into one search engine. The default search is by keyword, but an advanced options search can be performed using Boolean operators, proximity searching, and truncation.

5404. ***Stamps.Net: the Internet magazine for stamp collectors.*** 1998. irreg. Ed(s): Randy L Neil. U S I D, Inc, 6175 NW 153rd St, 201, Miami Lakes, FL 33014; http://www.stamps.net. *Aud.:* Hs, Ga.

Stamps.Net is the sole general-interest stamp e-journal without a print counterpart. It provides up-to-the-minute philatelic news via one featured story, updated on a weekly basis, and an archive of previous articles, plus stamp news from general sources as well as other philatelic magazines. These news stories often reach the web site before they reach the philatelic weeklies, and feature colorful illustrations and graphics. *Stamps.Net* also issues stamp theft bulletins and provides links to philatelic societies, clubs, and stamp show web sites. A link is also provided to *StampFinder,* a global stamp exchange web site offering one-stop shopping for more than 800,000 stamps from numerous dealers, plus links to dealer web sites, and voluminous classified advertisements.

■ PHILOSOPHY

R. Scott Harnsberger, Associate Professor, Newton Gresham Library, Sam Houston State University, Huntsville, TX 77341-2179; lib_rsh@shsu.edu; FAX: 936-294-3780

Introduction

An important and often overlooked aspect of philosophy periodicals is their potential to support research in a broad range of scholarly inquiry. Articles published in the journals listed in this section address problems and issues in fields as diverse as art, education, law, linguistics, literature, politics, psychology, religion, science, and sociology, to name a few.

Philosophy journals have become increasingly specialized since the 1950s. Most major subdivisions of the field, as well as many prominent philosophers, have publications devoted to them. Several journals have been founded in recent years with the goal of promoting a dialogue either between Anglo-American and continental European philosophers or philosophers working within the European community itself.

In the aftermath of the events of September 11 and the invasion of Iraq, articles that analyze and explicate philosophical issues surrounding war, terrorism and political violence, human rights, national reconciliation, restorative justice, pacifism, etc., will likely assume an increasingly important role in public policy debates.

Although a number of philosophy periodicals are being published in an electronic-only format, the lack of indexing is preventing them from making significant impact on the field.

Basic Periodicals

Ac: *Ethics, Journal of Philosophy, Mind, Nous, Philosophical Studies, Philosophy and Public Affairs, Philosophy of Science;* Sa: *Journal of Symbolic Logic.*

Basic Abstracts and Indexes

Arts and Humanities Citation Index, Humanities Index, The Philosopher's Index, Repertoire Bibliographique de la Philosophie.

5405. *American Philosophical Quarterly.* [ISSN: 0003-0481] 1964. q. USD 220 (Individuals, USD 50). Ed(s): Dale Jacquette. North American Philosophical Publications, Inc., 1151 Freeport Road, 154, Fox Chapel, PA 15238. Illus., index. Sample. Refereed. Circ: 1800. *Indexed:* ArtHuCI, HumInd, IBSS, IBZ, IPB, PhilInd, RILM, SSCI. *Aud.:* Ac.

This is an excellent general philosophy journal that publishes technical, critical essays on specific problems, arguments, and issues in the areas of metaphysics, epistemology, philosophy of mind, ethics, philosophy of language, and action theory. The "Recent Work" series appears occasionally and provides an overview of scholarly work on selected philosophers or philosophical topics.

5406. *Analysis.* [ISSN: 0003-2638] 1933. q. GBP 36 print & online eds. Ed(s): Michael Clark. Blackwell Publishing Ltd., 9600 Garsington Rd, PO Box 805, Oxford, OX4 2DQ, United Kingdom; jnlinfo@blackwellpublishers.co.uk; http://www.blackwellpublishers.co.uk/. Illus., index, adv. Refereed. Circ: 1350. Vol. ends: No. 4. Online: EBSCO Publishing; ingenta.com; OCLC Online Computer Library Center, Inc.; RoweCom Information Quest; Swets Blackwell. Reprint: PQC; SWZ. *Indexed:* ArtHuCI, CCMJ, IBSS, IPB, L&LBA, MathSciNet, PhilInd. *Aud.:* Ac.

Analysis publishes relatively short articles that either advance or critique precisely defined arguments or positions in contemporary analytic philosophy, chiefly in the areas of metaphysics, philosophical logic, philosophy of language, philosophy of mind, epistemology, and ethics.

5407. *Ancient Philosophy.* [ISSN: 0740-2007] 1980. s-a. USD 70 (Individuals, USD 32). Ed(s): Ronald Polansky. Mathesis Publications, Inc., Department of Philosophy, Duquesne University, Pittsburgh, PA 15282. Illus., adv. Refereed. Circ: 750. Vol. ends: No. 2. Reprint: PSC. *Indexed:* HumInd, IPB, PhilInd, RI-1. *Bk. rev.:* 15-20, 1,000-2,000 words, signed. *Aud.:* Ac.

The articles in this journal are principally on Plato and Aristotle, although others deal with their contemporaries, the Presocratics, the Neoplatonists, and medieval commentators on Aristotle. Each issue averages eight to ten articles (all of which are extensively footnoted and accompanied by bibliographies) and two to four discussion papers. This journal is a good supplement to *Phronesis* (below in this section) for larger academic collections where ancient philosophy is emphasized.

5408. *Archiv fuer Geschichte der Philosophie.* [ISSN: 0003-9101] 1976. 3x/yr. EUR 143.85 domestic; EUR 146.15 foreign; EUR 50 newsstand/cover. Ed(s): Dorothea Frede, Wolfgang Bartuschat. Walter de Gruyter GmbH & Co. KG, Genthiner Str. 13, Berlin, 10785, Germany; wdg-info@degruyter.de; http://www.degruyter.de. Illus., index, adv. Refereed. Circ: 750 Paid. Vol. ends: No. 3. Reprint: SCH. *Indexed:* ArtHuCI, IBZ, IPB, MLA-IB, PhilInd. *Bk. rev.:* 5-10, 500-1,000 words. *Aud.:* Ac.

This journal features a broad base of international scholarship on the history of philosophy, with articles in both English and German. The articles address specific problems and issues in the writings of the major philosophers from antiquity to the early twentieth century.

5409. *Aristotelian Society. Proceedings. Supplementary Volume.* [ISSN: 0309-7013] 1887. a. GBP 64 print & online eds. Ed(s): Anthony Price. Blackwell Publishing Ltd., 9600 Garsington Rd, PO Box 805, Oxford, OX4 2DQ, United Kingdom; jnlinfo@blackwellpublishers.co.uk; http://www.blackwellpublishing.com/. Illus. Sample. Refereed. Online: EBSCO Publishing; ingenta.com; OCLC Online Computer Library Center, Inc.; RoweCom Information Quest; Swets Blackwell. Reprint: SWZ. *Indexed:* PhilInd. *Aud.:* Ac.

The Aristotelian Society is one of the oldest and most distinguished organizations for Anglo-American philosophers. The annual proceedings, published in June as a supplementary volume to the quarterly journal, contain papers read at the annual joint sessions of the Aristotelian Society and the Mind Association, leading off with the presidential address. This publication invariably represents exemplary standards of scholarship, and it is highly recommended for all collections.

Asian Philosophy. See Asia and the Pacific/General section.

5410. *Australasian Journal of Philosophy.* [ISSN: 0004-8402] 1923. q. GBP 64. Ed(s): Maurice Goldsmith. Oxford University Press, Great Clarendon St, Oxford, OX2 6DP, United Kingdom; jnl.orders@oup.co.uk; http://www3.oup.co.uk/jnls. Illus., index, adv. Sample. Refereed. Circ: 1225 Paid. Vol. ends: No. 4. Microform: MIM. Online: Chadwyck-Healey Incorporated; EBSCO Publishing; ingenta.com; RoweCom Information Quest; Swets Blackwell. *Indexed:* ArtHuCI, BrHumI, IPB, PhilInd, SSCI. *Bk. rev.:* 5-10, 750-1,000 words, signed. *Aud.:* Ac.

This journal is the official publication of the Australasian Association of Philosophy and therefore will be of special interest to philosophers from that region. Many of the contributors are Australian, although others are from North America and Europe. A majority of the articles deal with contemporary issues in metaphysics, epistemology, philosophy of science, and ethics. Short critiques of arguments that have appeared in recently published articles and books—as well as replies—are gathered in the "Discussions" section. One book is singled out and given an extended review in each issue under "Critical Notice." This is a good general publication for larger collections.

5411. *Bibliographie de la Philosophie.* [ISSN: 0006-1352] 1937. q. USD 135. Ed(s): Jean Pierre Cotten. International Institute of Philosophy, 8 rue Jean Calvin, Paris, 75005, France. Index, adv. Circ: 1100. Vol. ends: No. 4. *Aud.:* Ac.

This classified bibliography is published by the International Institute of Philosophy with the aid of UNESCO, the French National Centre for Scientific Research, and the Centre of Documentation and Philosophical Bibliography of the University of Franche Comte. Each issue contains brief descriptive summaries (averaging 100–250 words) of approximately 450 philosophy books published worldwide. The abstracts are authored by scholars representing "national centers" in more than 50 countries and are generally written in English, French, German, Italian, and Spanish. The fourth number of each volume contains an author/title index. Although not a source for critical evaluations, this is a good companion to *Philosophical Books* (below in this section) for collection development purposes.

Bioethics. See Civil Liberties/Bioethics: Reproductive Rights, Right-to-Life, and Right-to-Die section.

5412. *British Journal for the History of Philosophy.* [ISSN: 0960-8788] 1993. 3x/yr. GBP 203 (Individuals, GBP 93). Ed(s): G A J Rogers. Routledge, 11 New Fetter Ln, London, EC4P 4EE, United Kingdom; info@routledge.co.uk; http://www.routledge.com. Illus., index, adv. Sample. Refereed. Circ: 400. Vol. ends: No. 3. *Indexed:* AmH&L, BrHumI, IPB, PhilInd. *Bk. rev.:* 10-15, 750-1,000 words, signed. *Aud.:* Ac.

This publication, sponsored by the British Society for the History of Philosophy, emphasizes the context—intellectual, political, and social—in which philosophical texts were created. Articles are also published on historical topics in the natural and social sciences and theology when they bear on philosophical problems. The focus is mainly on European philosophy, especially British, during the period from the Renaissance to the 1940s.

5413. *The British Journal for the Philosophy of Science.* [ISSN: 0007-0882] 1950. q. GBP 79. Ed(s): Peter Clark. Oxford University Press, Great Clarendon St, Oxford, OX2 6DP, United Kingdom; jnl.orders@oup.co.uk; http://www3.oup.co.uk/jnls. Illus., index, adv. Sample. Refereed. Circ: 1700. Vol. ends: No. 4. Online: Chadwyck-Healey Incorporated; EBSCO Publishing; Florida Center for Library Automation; Gale Group; ingenta.com; JSTOR (Web-based Journal Archive); Northern Light Technology, Inc.; OCLC Online Computer Library Center, Inc.; ProQuest Information & Learning; RoweCom Information Quest; Swets Blackwell. Reprint: PSC. *Indexed:* ArtHuCI, CCMJ, HumInd, IBZ, IPB, MathSciNet, PhilInd, PsycholAb, SCI, SSCI. *Bk. rev.:* 8-12, 1,000-3,000 words, signed. *Aud.:* Ac.

As the official publication of the British Society for the Philosophy of Science, this journal features articles, symposia, discussion papers, and literature surveys on the logic, methods, and philosophy of science, in addition to conceptual issues in various scientific disciplines (including the social sciences) and the philosophy of mathematics. In fact, its scope is very similar to its American counterpart, *Philosophy of Science*, although the British title has perhaps more historically oriented discussions. This is a polished, professional, core collection journal.

5414. *British Journal of Aesthetics.* [ISSN: 0007-0904] 1960. q. GBP 106. Ed(s): Peter Lamarque. Oxford University Press, Great Clarendon St, Oxford, OX2 6DP, United Kingdom; jnl.orders@oup.co.uk; http://www3.oup.co.uk/jnls. Illus., index, adv. Sample. Refereed. Circ: 1800. Vol. ends: No. 4. Microform: PQC. Online: Chadwyck-Healey Incorporated; EBSCO Publishing; Florida Center for Library Automation; Gale Group; ingenta.com; Northern Light Technology, Inc.; OCLC Online Computer Library Center, Inc.; ProQuest Information & Learning; RoweCom Information Quest; Swets Blackwell. Reprint: PQC; PSC. *Indexed:* ABCT, ABM, ArtHuCI, ArtInd, BEL&L, BHA, BrHumI, CommAb, FLI, HumInd, IBZ, IDP, IPB, MLA-IB, MusicInd, PhilInd, SSCI. *Bk. rev.:* 8-12, 250-1,000 words. *Aud.:* Ac.

The British Society of Aesthetics, which sponsors this journal, is an international organization committed to promoting the study, research, and discussion of the fine arts and related types of experience from a philosophical, psychological, sociological, scientific, historical, critical, and educational standpoint. The journal publishes articles analyzing the traditional philosophical issues in the field, in addition to examining the aesthetic theories of such individuals as Plato, Kant, Hutcheson, Nietzsche, Wittgenstein, Derrida, and Goodman. Areas receiving attention include architecture, drama, literature, the fine arts, the performing arts, and photography.

5415. *Canadian Journal of Philosophy.* [ISSN: 0045-5091] 1971. q. CND 50 (Individuals, CND 25; Students, CND 15). Ed(s): Michael Stingl. University of Calgary Press, University of Calgary, Faculty of Education ETD 722, 2500 University Dr N W, Calgary, AB T2N 1N4, Canada; wgee@ucalgary.ca; http://www.ucalgary.ca/ucpress. Illus., index, adv. Refereed. Circ: 1100. Vol. ends: No. 4. Microform: MML. Online: Gale Group. *Indexed:* ArtHuCI, CBCARef, CPerI, HumInd, IBSS, IBZ, IPB, LRI, MLA-IB, MathSciNet, PhilInd, RI-1, SSCI. *Bk. rev.:* 2-5, 2,500-5,000 words. *Aud.:* Ac.

As one might expect, many of the contributors to Canada's leading philosophy journal are associated with Canadian universities, although numerous authors are from outside the country (principally the United States, Great Britain, France, and Australia). The strengths of the journal lie in ethics, social and political philosophy, epistemology, and the history of philosophy. Articles appear in French now and then, but the majority are in English. Excellent thematic supplementary volumes are published annually, and they are free to individual subscribers.

Criminal Justice Ethics. See Criminology and Law Enforcement section.

5416. *Dialogue (Waterloo): Canadian philosophical review - revue canadienne de philosophie.* [ISSN: 0012-2173] 1962. q. CND 95 domestic; USD 95 elsewhere. Ed(s): Eric Dayton, Claude Panaccio. Wilfrid Laurier University Press, 75 University Ave W, Waterloo, ON N2L 3C5, Canada; press@wlu.ca; http://www.wlupress.wlu.ca. Illus., adv. Refereed. Circ: 1200 Paid. *Indexed:* ArtHuCI, BRI, CBRI, CCMJ, HumInd, IPB, L&LBA, LRI, MLA-IB, MathSciNet, PhilInd, RI-1, SSCI. *Bk. rev.:* 15-20, 500-2,500 words. *Aud.:* Ac.

As the official journal of the Canadian Philosophical Association, *Dialogue* publishes articles and critical notices on all branches of philosophy from a variety of perspectives in both French and English. Many of the authors are associated with Canadian universities, and the editors especially want to promote a dialogue between Anglophone and Francophone philosophers in Canada.

5417. *Diogenes.* [ISSN: 0392-1921] 1952. q. GBP 210 in Europe, Middle East, Africa & Australasia. Ed(s): Paola Costa, Roger Caillos. Sage Publications, Inc., 2455 Teller Rd, Thousand Oaks, CA 91320; info@sagepub.com; http://www.sagepub.com. Illus., index, adv. Refereed. Circ: 600 Controlled. Vol. ends: No. 4. Online: EBSCO Publishing; Florida Center for Library Automation; Gale Group; ingenta.com; OCLC Online Computer Library Center, Inc.; RoweCom Information Quest; Swets Blackwell; H.W. Wilson. *Indexed:* ABS&EES, ArtHuCI, HumInd, IPB, L&LBA, MLA-IB, PSA, PhilInd, SociolAb. *Aud.:* Ga, Ac.

Diogenes is published under the auspices of the International Council for Philosophy and Humanistic Studies with the support of UNESCO. The articles are authored by a diverse range of international scholars who discuss cultural issues from a broadly defined philosophical perspective in such areas as anthropology, economics, education, history, literature, drama, and sociology.

Economics and Philosophy. See Economics section.

Environmental Ethics. See Environment and Conservation section.

5418. *Erkenntnis: an international journal of analytic philosophy.* [ISSN: 0165-0106] 1930. bi-m. EUR 699 print or online ed. Ed(s): Wilhelm K Essler, Wolfgang Spohn. Kluwer Academic Publishers, van Godewijckstraat 30, PO Box 17, Dordrecht, 3300 AA, Netherlands. Illus., index, adv. Sample. Refereed. Vol. ends: No. 3. Microform: PQC. Online: EBSCO Publishing; ingenta.com; Kluwer Online; OCLC Online Computer Library Center, Inc.; Ovid Technologies, Inc.; RoweCom Information Quest; Swets Blackwell. Reprint: SWZ. *Indexed:* ArtHuCI, BHA, CCMJ, IPB, L&LBA, MathSciNet, PhilInd. *Bk. rev.:* 2-6, 1,000-2,000 words. *Aud.:* Ac.

Erkenntnis publishes highly technical articles either analyzing current systematic issues or presenting original research in epistemology, philosophical logic, philosophy of mathematics, philosophy of science, ontology and metaphysics, philosophy of mind, and practical philosophy (e.g., philosophy of action, philosophy of law, and ethics). Articles sometimes appear in German, but the majority are in English. An advanced journal for graduate-level collections.

5419. *Ethical Theory and Moral Practice: an international forum.* [ISSN: 1386-2820] 1998. 5x/yr. EUR 318 print or online ed. Ed(s): F R Heeger, A W Musschenga. Kluwer Academic Publishers, van Godewijckstraat 30, PO Box 17, Dordrecht, 3300 AA, Netherlands. Illus. Sample. Refereed. Online: EBSCO Publishing; ingenta.com; Kluwer Online; OCLC Online Computer Library Center, Inc.; Ovid Technologies, Inc.; RoweCom Information Quest; Swets Blackwell. *Indexed:* IBSS, IPB, PhilInd. *Aud.:* Ac, Sa.

This journal features articles from a wide variety of philosophical perspectives, including lesser-known European traditions that have been neglected in the mainstream philosophy publications. An attempt is also being made to foster interdisciplinary cooperation between ethics and the empirical disciplines—including medicine, economics, sociology, and law—with the aim of breaking down the barriers between practical and theoretical ethics. The editors also invite contributions that address the relationship between moral beliefs and views of life. Articles are generally in English, with some in French or German. A specialized publication for collections with comprehensive holdings in ethics.

5420. *Ethics: an international journal of social, political, and legal philosophy.* Formerly (until 1938): *International Journal of Ethics.* [ISSN: 0014-1704] 1890. q. USD 167 (Individuals, USD 40; Students, USD 29). Ed(s): John Deigh. University of Chicago Press, Journals Division, PO Box 37005, Chicago, IL 60637; subscriptions@press.uchicago.edu; http://www.journals.uchicago.edu. Illus., adv. Refereed. Circ: 3200 Paid. Vol. ends: Jul. Microform: MIM; PMC; PQC. Online: EBSCO Publishing; Florida Center for Library Automation; Gale Group; JSTOR (Web-based Journal Archive); ProQuest Information & Learning. Reprint: ISI; PQC; PSC; SCH; WSH. *Indexed:* ABCPolSci, AgeL, ArtHuCI, BRD, BRI, CBRI, CLI, CommAb, HumInd, IBSS, IBZ, IPB, IPSA, LRI, MLA-IB, PRA, PSA, PhilInd, RI-1, SSCI, SSI, SociolAb. *Bk. rev.:* 35-45, 250-7,500 words, signed. *Aud.:* Ac.

Ethics is a leading journal in the fields of social and political philosophy and ethics. It serves as a forum for the discussion of both traditional and contemporary utilitarian and deontological normative theories, as well as a wide range of meta-ethical topics. In addition to moral philosophy, *Ethics* is also important for philosophy of law, public policy issues, religious ethics, normative economics, international law, and social and rational choice theory. Symposia centered around themes, theories, or recently published books are often featured. The numerous book reviews range from lengthy review essays to brief "Book Notes." Highly recommended for all collections.

5421. *Ethics & Behavior.* [ISSN: 1050-8422] 1991. q. USD 405. Ed(s): Gerald P Koocher. Lawrence Erlbaum Associates, Inc., 10 Industrial Ave, Mahwah, NJ 07430-2262; journals@erlbaum.com; http://www.erlbaum.com/. Illus., adv. Sample. Refereed. Vol. ends: No. 4. Reprint: PSC. *Indexed:* ASSIA, PAIS, PhilInd, PsycholAb, RiskAb, SSCI. *Bk. rev.:* 1-3, 500-750 words. *Aud.:* Ac.

Articles in this journal address issues in ethical and social responsibility in human behavior, ethical dilemmas or professional misconduct in health and human services delivery, moral aspects of conducting research on human and animal subjects, fraud in scientific research, and public-policy issues involving ethical problems (e.g., environmental ethics). Special thematic issues appear occasionally (e.g., "Control Groups in Psychosocial Intervention Research"). Although aimed principally at an audience of clinical practitioners in psychology, psychiatry, psychotherapy, and counseling, *Ethics and Behavior* would provide excellent support for courses in applied ethics.

5422. *European Journal of Philosophy.* [ISSN: 0966-8373] 1993. 3x/yr. GBP 219 print & online eds. Ed(s): Robert Stern. Blackwell Publishing Ltd., 9600 Garsington Rd, PO Box 805, Oxford, OX4 2DQ, United Kingdom; customerservices@oxon.blackwellpublishing.com; http://www.blackwellpublishing.com/. Illus., index. Sample. Refereed. Vol. ends: No. 3. Online: EBSCO Publishing; ingenta.com; OCLC Online Computer Library Center, Inc.; RoweCom Information Quest. *Indexed:* ArtHuCI, IBSS, IPB, L&LBA, PhilInd, SociolAb. *Bk. rev.:* 5-7, 750-5,000 words. *Aud.:* Ac.

This journal was founded with the goal of serving as a forum for the exchange of ideas among philosophers working within the various European schools of thought, who tended to be culturally isolated before the political upheavals of the 1990s. Contributions, however, are welcome from both sides of the Atlantic. For collections emphasizing European traditions of philosophy broadly conceived, both historical and contemporary.

5423. *Faith and Philosophy.* [ISSN: 0739-7046] 1984. q. USD 55 (Individuals, USD 40). Ed(s): William Hasker. Society of Christian Philosophers, Department of Philosophy, Asbury College, Wilmore, KY 40390-1198; fpjournl@aol.com; www.faithandphilosophy.com. Illus., index, adv. Refereed. Circ: 1500. Microform: PQC. *Indexed:* ChrPI, IPB, PhilInd, R&TA, RI-1. *Bk. rev.:* 2-7, 750-1,000 words. *Aud.:* Ac.

Articles in *Faith and Philosophy* address philosophical issues from a Christian perspective, discuss philosophical questions arising within the Christian faith, and critically analyze the philosophical foundations of Christianity. The journal attracts contributions from leading philosophers of religion, including William Alston, D.Z. Phillips, Alvin Plantiga, and Richard Swinburne. The October issue of each volume is devoted to a single theme (e.g., "Wittgensteinianism and Religion"). In light of its high-quality scholarship and modest price, this journal should find a place in college libraries supporting courses in religious studies.

5424. *History and Philosophy of Logic.* [ISSN: 0144-5340] 1980. q. GBP 273 (Individuals, GBP 137). Ed(s): Peter Simons. Taylor & Francis Ltd, 11 New Fetter Ln, London, EC4P 4EE, United Kingdom; info@tandf.co.uk; http://www.tandf.co.uk/journals. Illus., adv. Sample. Refereed. Vol. ends: No. 4. Online: EBSCO Publishing; Ingenta Select; OCLC Online Computer Library Center, Inc.; RoweCom Information Quest; Swets Blackwell. Reprint: PSC. *Indexed:* ArtHuCI, CCMJ, IPB, MathSciNet, PhilInd, SSCI. *Bk. rev.:* 4-6, 250-4,000 words. *Aud.:* Ac.

The emphasis of this journal is on the general history and philosophy of logic, excluding work on very recent topics and specialized studies in philosophical logic. The scope is ancient to modern, East to West, with articles appearing in English, French, or German. The authors explore the existential and ontological aspects of logic, in addition to analyzing the relationship between classical and nonclassical logic and the application of logic in other fields, such as mathematics, economics, science, and linguistics. This journal is also a good source for discussions of the logical writings of such major historical figures as Aristotle, Descartes, Leibniz, Frege, Russell, and Quine.

5425. *History of Philosophy Quarterly.* [ISSN: 0740-0675] 1984. q. USD 175 (Individuals, USD 40). Ed(s): Nicholas Rescher. North American Philosophical Publications, Inc., 1151 Freeport Road, 154, Fox Chapel, PA 15238; journals@uillinois.edu; http://www.press.uillinois.edu. Illus., index. Sample. Refereed. Circ: 500. Vol. ends: No. 4. *Indexed:* IBZ, IPB, PhilInd, RI-1. *Aud.:* Ac.

Critical discussions of the work of major philosophers from Plato to Wittgenstein, with an emphasis on the value of historical studies for contemporary issues, make this a good supplement to the *Journal of the History of Philosophy,* which should be the first choice for most academic libraries.

5426. *Human Studies: a journal for philosophy and the social sciences.* [ISSN: 0163-8548] 1978. q. EUR 379 print or online ed. Ed(s): George Psathas. Kluwer Academic Publishers, van Godewijckstraat 30, PO Box 17, Dordrecht, 3300 AA, Netherlands. Illus., index, adv. Sample. Refereed. Circ: 500. Vol. ends: No. 4. Microform: PQC. Online: EBSCO Publishing; ingenta.com; Kluwer Online; OCLC Online Computer Library Center, Inc.; Ovid Technologies, Inc.; RoweCom Information Quest; Swets Blackwell. Reprint: ISI; SWZ. *Indexed:* ABS&EES, IBSS, IMFL, IPB, L&LBA, LingAb, MLA-IB, PSA, PhilInd, SSCI, SWA, SociolAb. *Bk. rev.:* 1-3, 1,000-3,000 words. *Aud.:* Ac.

This publication, which serves as the official journal of the Society for Phenomenology and the Human Sciences, publishes empirical, methodological, philosophical, and theoretical investigations—particularly those embracing a broadly defined phenomenological perspective—on topics in the social sciences, including psychology, sociology, anthropology, history, geography, linguistics, semiotics, ethnomethodology, and political science. For collections with strong holdings in the social sciences.

5427. *Hume Studies.* [ISSN: 0319-7336] 1975. s-a. USD 40 (Individuals, USD 35). Ed(s): Elizabeth S Radcliffe, Kenneth P Winkler. Hume Society, c/o Mikael M. Karlsson, Department of Philosophy, University of Iceland, Reykjavik, 101, Iceland; secretary@humesociety.org; http://www.humesociety.org. Illus., adv. Refereed. Circ: 800 Paid. Vol. ends: No. 2. Microform: MML. Reprint: PSC. *Indexed:* IBZ, IPB, PhilInd, RI-1. *Aud.:* Ac.

The eighteenth-century Scottish philosopher David Hume has exerted a tremendous influence on contemporary philosophy. This journal, published by the Hume Society, features historical and systematic research on all facets of Hume's philosophy: metaphysics, epistemology, philosophy of mind, ethics, political philosophy, and philosophy of religion. Articles are usually in English, with some in French, German, or Italian.

5428. *Husserl Studies.* [ISSN: 0167-9848] 1984. 3x/yr. EUR 275 print or online ed. Ed(s): William R McKenna. Kluwer Academic Publishers, van Godewijckstraat 30, PO Box 17, Dordrecht, 3300 AA, Netherlands. Illus., index, adv. Sample. Refereed. Vol. ends: No. 3. Microform: PQC. Online: EBSCO Publishing; ingenta.com; Kluwer Online; OCLC Online Computer Library Center, Inc.; Ovid Technologies, Inc.; RoweCom Information Quest; Swets Blackwell. Reprint: SWZ. *Indexed:* ArtHuCI, IPB, PhilInd, RI-1, SSCI. *Bk. rev.:* 1-3, 1,500-3,000 words. *Aud.:* Ac.

The German philosopher Edmund Husserl (1859–1938) is the central figure in the phenomenological movement. This journal serves as a forum for historical, systematic, interpretive, and comparative studies on Husserl and phenomenology in general. Although the editor encourages intercultural and interdisciplinary submissions, most authors concentrate on narrowly defined problems of exegesis or analysis drawn from Husserl's writings. The journal also publishes important texts from Husserl's *Nachlass* and an ongoing international Husserl bibliography. The articles are in English and German.

Hypatia. See Women: Feminist and Special Interest/Feminist and Women's Studies section.

5429. *Idealistic Studies: an interdisciplinary journal of philosophy.* [ISSN: 0046-8541] 1971. 3x/yr. USD 52 (Individuals, USD 32). Ed(s): Gary Overvold. Philosophy Documentation Center, PO Box 7147, Charlottesville, VA 22906-7147. Illus., index, adv. Refereed. Circ: 600. Vol. ends: No. 3. Reprint: PSC. *Indexed:* ArtHuCI, IPB, PhilInd, RI-1, SSCI. *Aud.:* Ac.

Critical studies on idealistic themes, in addition to historical and contemporary statements of idealistic argumentation, are the main focus of this journal. Philosophical movements related to idealism are also covered, including phenomenology, neo-Kantianism, historicism, hermeneutics, life philosophy, existentialism, and pragmatism. It is an especially good source for the critical analysis of idealism in the philosophy of Berkeley, Hegel, Fichte, Schelling, Bradley, McTaggart, and others.

5430. *Inquiry: an interdisciplinary journal of philosophy.* [ISSN: 0020-174X] 1958. q. GBP 118 (Individuals, GBP 42). Routledge, 11 New Fetter Ln, London, EC4P 4EE, United Kingdom; info@routledge.co.uk; http://www.routledge.co.uk. Illus., index, adv. Refereed. Circ: 1200. Vol. ends: No. 4. Microform: PQC. Online: EBSCO Publishing; Gale Group; Ingenta Select; OCLC Online Computer Library Center, Inc.; RoweCom Information Quest; Swets Blackwell. Reprint: ISI; PSC. *Indexed:* ArtHuCI, BAS, BPI, HumInd, IBSS, IBZ, IPB, IPSA, L&LBA, MCR, MLA-IB, PSA, PhilInd, RI-1, SSCI, SWR&A. *Bk. rev.:* 1-3, 1,500-3,000 words. *Aud.:* Ac.

Articles in this English-language Norwegian journal address both practical and theoretical problems, and the authors attempt to explicate the basic assumptions at work in the issues under discussion. Most articles deal with metaphysics, epistemology, philosophy of mind, ethics, social and political philosophy, and Continental philosophy. Contributions in areas such as environmental ethics often contain discussions on the cutting edge of the profession. The book reviews take the form of lengthy symposia or review essays. This is an important journal for all collections.

International Journal for Philosophy of Religion. See Religion section.

5431. *International Journal of Philosophical Studies.* [ISSN: 0967-2559] 1993. q. GBP 230 (Individuals, GBP 65). Ed(s): Dermot Moran. Routledge, 11 New Fetter Ln, London, EC4P 4EE, United Kingdom. Illus., adv. Sample. Refereed. Vol. ends: No. 4. Online: EBSCO Publishing; Ingenta Select; OCLC Online Computer Library Center, Inc.; RoweCom Information Quest; Swets Blackwell. Reprint: PSC. *Indexed:* ArtHuCI, CPL, IBSS, IPB, PhilInd. *Bk. rev.:* 10-15, 250-2,500 words. *Aud.:* Ac.

By featuring contributors like Noam Chomsky, Donald Davidson, David Pears, and John Searle, this relaunched journal has assumed a place as an important international philosophy publication. The editor wants to promote a mutual comprehension and dialogue between the "analytic" and "Continental" styles of philosophy and to combine discussions of contemporary problems with articles on the history of philosophy that shed light on the current debate. The three book review sections range from lengthy "Critical Notices" to "Books Briefly Noted."

5432. *International Philosophical Quarterly.* [ISSN: 0019-0365] 1961. q. USD 55 (Individuals, USD 32). Ed(s): Joseph W Koterski. Philosophy Documentation Center, PO Box 7147, Charlottesville, VA 22906-7147. Illus., index, adv. Refereed. Circ: 1400 Paid. Vol. ends: No. 4. Microform: PQC. Online: Gale Group; OCLC Online Computer Library Center, Inc.; H.W. Wilson. Reprint: PQC; PSC. *Indexed:* ABS&EES, ArtHuCI, BAS, BEL&L, BRI, CBRI, CPL, HumInd, IPB, LRI, PhilInd, RI-1, SSCI. *Bk. rev.:* 10-15, 500-1,000 words. *Aud.:* Ac.

As a joint collaboration of Fordham University and the Facultes Universitaires Notre-Dame de la Paix (Namur, Belgium), this journal serves as an international forum for the exchange of philosophical ideas between the United States and Europe and between East and West through the publication of creative, critical, and historical articles in the intercultural tradition of theistic, spiritualist, and personalist humanism.

Journal of Chinese Philosophy. See China section.

5433. *The Journal of Ethics: an international philosophical review.* [ISSN: 1382-4554] 1997. q. EUR 333 print or online ed. Ed(s): J Angelo Corlett. Kluwer Academic Publishers, van Godewijckstraat 30, PO Box 17, Dordrecht, 3300 AA, Netherlands. Illus. Sample. Refereed. Vol. ends: No. 4. Online: EBSCO Publishing; ingenta.com; Kluwer Online; OCLC Online Computer Library Center, Inc.; RoweCom Information Quest; Swets Blackwell. *Indexed:* CINAHL, IPB, PhilInd. *Aud.:* Ac.

This journal features articles on contemporary issues in ethics, political philosophy, and public affairs, including infrequently discussed topics like interracial coalitions and secessionist movements. Contributors occasionally focus on the ethical works of major historical figures such as Hume and Mill. Selected studies are also published on bioethics and jurisprudence.

5434. *Journal of Indian Philosophy.* [ISSN: 0022-1791] 1970. bi-m. EUR 549 print or online ed. Ed(s): Phyllis Granoff. Kluwer Academic Publishers, van Godewijckstraat 30, PO Box 17, Dordrecht, 3300 AA, Netherlands. Illus., index, adv. Sample. Refereed. Microform: PQC. Online: EBSCO Publishing; ingenta.com; Kluwer Online; OCLC Online Computer Library Center, Inc.; Ovid Technologies, Inc.; RoweCom Information Quest; Swets Blackwell. Reprint: SWZ. *Indexed:* ArtHuCI, BAS, IBSS, IPB, MLA-IB, PhilInd, RI-1. *Aud.:* Ac, Sa.

The specialized studies in this journal presuppose a thorough familiarity with the philosophical systems embodied in the religious traditions of the Indian subcontinent and Tibet, particularly Hinduism, Buddhism, and Jainism. The authors critically analyze and explicate both traditional and contemporary arguments and issues in metaphysics, epistemology, philosophical logic, philosophy of language, philosophy of religion, and ethics.

Journal of Medicine and Philosophy. See Medicine and Health/Medicine and Society section.

5435. *Journal of Philosophical Logic.* [ISSN: 0022-3611] 1972. bi-m. EUR 540 print or online ed. Ed(s): Rohit Parikh, Albert Visser. Kluwer Academic Publishers, van Godewijckstraat 30, PO Box 17, Dordrecht, 3300 AA, Netherlands. Illus., index, adv. Sample. Refereed. Vol. ends: No. 6. Microform: PQC. Online: EBSCO Publishing; ingenta.com; Kluwer Online; OCLC Online Computer Library Center, Inc.; Ovid Technologies, Inc.; RoweCom Information Quest; Swets Blackwell. Reprint: SWZ. *Indexed:* ArtHuCI, CCMJ, IBZ, IPB, L&LBA, MLA-IB, MathSciNet, PhilInd, SSCI. *Aud.:* Ac, Sa.

Published under the auspices of the Association for Symbolic Logic, this journal features articles on the entire spectrum of philosophical logic (e.g., inductive logic, modal logic, deontic logic, tense logic, free logic, many-valued logics, relevance logics, and the logic of questions, commands, preferences, and conditions); issues in ontology and epistemology that utilize formal logic (e.g., abstract entities, propositional attitudes, and truth conditions); and philosophical issues involving logical theory in philosophy of language, philosophy of mathematics, and philosophy of science. For graduate-level collections.

5436. *Journal of Philosophy.* Formerly (until 1921): *The Journal of Philosophy, Psychology and Scientific Methods.* [ISSN: 0022-362X] 1904. m. USD 75 (Individuals, USD 35; Students, USD 20). Ed(s): Michael Kelly. Journal of Philosophy, Inc., 709 Philosophy Hall, Columbia University, New York, NY 10027. Illus., index, adv. Refereed. Circ: 4500. Vol. ends: No. 12. Microform: PMC. Online: Gale Group; JSTOR (Web-based Journal Archive). *Indexed:* ArtHuCI, BEL&L, BHA, BRD, BRI, CBRI, CCMJ, DSR&OA, HumInd, IBSS, IPB, LRI, MLA-IB, MathSciNet, PhilInd, RI-1, SSCI. *Bk. rev.:* 1-2, 1,000-3,000 words. *Aud.:* Ac.

Each isssue of this distinguished journal contains two or three articles, generally on topics of interest to the professional academic philosophy community in the United States. The subjects discussed usually fall into the areas of metaphysics, epistemology, philosophy of mind, philosophy of language, philosophical logic, social and political philosophy, ethics, action theory, and esthetics. A core collection journal.

Journal of Philosophy of Education. See Education/Comparative Education and International section.

5437. *Journal of Speculative Philosophy: a quarterly journal of history, criticism, and imagination.* [ISSN: 0891-625X] 1987. q. USD 52 (Individuals, USD 34). Ed(s): Vincent M Colapietro, John J Stuhr. Pennsylvania State University Press, 820 N. University Dr., USB-1, Ste C, University Park, PA 16802-1003; pspjournals@psu.edu; http://www.psupress.org. Illus., index, adv. Sample. Refereed. Circ: 300. Vol. ends: No. 4. Microform: PQC. Online: EBSCO Publishing; OCLC Online Computer Library Center, Inc.; Project MUSE; RoweCom Information Quest; Swets Blackwell. Reprint: PQC; PSC. *Indexed:* IBZ, IPB, PhilInd. *Bk. rev.:* 1-2, 750-1,250 words. *Aud.:* Ac.

This journal revives the nineteenth-century publication of the same title, the first in the United States devoted primarily to philosophy and the one in which Peirce, James, Dewey, and other notables published some of their early essays. The emphasis here is on systematic and interpretive essays dealing with basic philosophical questions. The stated goal of the editors is to promote a constructive interaction between Continental and American philosophy, rather than to publish scholarly articles about philosophical movements or historical figures. In addition, the journal occasionally publishes articles on art, literature, and religion that are not strictly or narrowly philosophical in their orientation.

5438. *Journal of Symbolic Logic.* [ISSN: 0022-4812] 1936. q. Institutional members, USD 575; Individual members, USD 70; Students, USD 35 membership. Association for Symbolic Logic, 124 Raymond Ave, Vassar College, PO Box 742, Poughkeepsie, NY 12604; asl@vassar.edu; http://www.aslonline.org. Illus., index. Refereed. Circ: 2500. Vol. ends: No. 4. Microform: PMC; PQC. Online: Gale Group; JSTOR (Web-based Journal Archive). *Indexed:* CCMJ, HumInd, IPB, MathSciNet, PhilInd, SCI, SSCI. *Bk. rev.:* 10-15, 1,000-2,000 words. *Aud.:* Ac, Sa.

This journal, sponsored by the Association for Symbolic Logic, is aimed at an audience of professional logicians and mathematicians. It publishes highly technical articles on all formal aspects of symbolic and mathematical logic. In addition, subscribers also receive *The Bulletin of Symbolic Logic,* a quarterly publication that features both broad expository and survey articles of a general nature as well as announcements of new ideas and results in all areas of logic. This is a core collection title for graduate-level collections.

Journal of the History of Ideas. See Cultural-Social Studies section.

5439. *Journal of the History of Philosophy.* [ISSN: 0022-5053] 1963. q. USD 86 (Individuals, USD 28). Ed(s): Gerald A. Press. Johns Hopkins University Press, Journals Publishing Division, 2715 N Charles St, Baltimore, MD 21218-4363; http://www.press.jhu.edu/. Illus., index, adv. Refereed. Circ: 1300. Vol. ends: No. 4. Microform: PQC. Online: bigchalk; Chadwyck-Healey Incorporated; Gale Group; Northern Light Technology, Inc.; OCLC Online Computer Library Center, Inc.; Project MUSE; ProQuest Information & Learning. Reprint: PQC; PSC. *Indexed:* AmH&L, ArtHuCI, BEL&L, HumInd, IBSS, IBZ, IPB, PRA, PhilInd, RI-1, SSCI. *Bk. rev.:* 15-20, 750-1,000 words. *Aud.:* Ac.

This leading journal for the history of Western philosophy generally deals with the works of the major philosophers, although studies are also published on other figures, including Islamic philosophers (e.g., al-Ghazali and Averroes), lesser-known medieval and Renaissance philosophers (e.g., Desgabets, Gersonides, and Henry of Ghent) and scientists (e.g., Boyle and Newton). Articles sometimes appear in foreign languages, but the majority are in English.

Journal of the Philosophy of Sport. See Sports/Physical Education, Coaching, and Sports Sciences section.

5440. *The Journal of Value Inquiry.* [ISSN: 0022-5363] 1967. q. EUR 456 print or online ed. Ed(s): Thomas Magnell. Kluwer Academic Publishers, van Godewijckstraat 30, PO Box 17, Dordrecht, 3300 AA, Netherlands. Illus., index, adv. Sample. Refereed. Vol. ends: Oct/Dec. Microform: PQC. Online: EBSCO Publishing; ingenta.com; Kluwer Online; OCLC Online Computer Library Center, Inc.; Ovid Technologies, Inc.; RoweCom Information Quest; Swets Blackwell. Reprint: SWZ. *Indexed:* ArtHuCI, IPB, PhilInd, RI-1, SSCI. *Bk. rev.:* 3-5, 1,000-2,000 words. *Aud.:* Ac.

This important journal covers the entire spectrum of axiology. One will find articles on the nature, justification, and epistemic status of values, as well as studies exploring values in a broad range of contexts, including aesthetics, ethics, law, politics, science, society, and technology.

5441. *Kant Studien: philosophische Zeitschrift der Kant-Gesellschaft.* [ISSN: 0022-8877] 1896. 4x/yr. EUR 125.10 domestic; EUR 128.20 foreign; EUR 35 newsstand/cover. Ed(s): Gerhard Funke, Manfred Baum. Walter de Gruyter GmbH & Co. KG, Genthiner Str. 13, Berlin, 10785, Germany; wdg-info@degruyter.de; http://www.degruyter.de. Illus., index, adv. Refereed. Circ: 1200 Paid and controlled. Vol. ends: No. 4. Reprint: SCH. *Indexed:* ArtHuCI, BHA, IBZ, IPB, MLA-IB, PhilInd. *Bk. rev.:* 4-6, 750-1,500 words. *Aud.:* Ac.

The principal focus of this publication of the Kant-Gesellschaft is Immanuel Kant, who is arguably the most important philosopher of the modern period. Authors also discuss other philosophers and mathematicians from time to time, such as Descartes, Leibniz, Hume, Hegel, and Frege. A very useful bibliography on all aspects of Kantian studies is featured in the fourth issue of each volume. The articles are in English, French, or German.

5442. ***Law and Philosophy: an international journal for jurisprudence and legal philosophy.*** [ISSN: 0167-5249] 1982. bi-m. EUR 511 print or online ed. Ed(s): Heidi M Hurd, Michael S Moore. Kluwer Academic Publishers, van Godewijckstraat 30, PO Box 17, Dordrecht, 3300 AA, Netherlands. Illus., index, adv. Sample. Refereed. Microform: WSH; PQC. Online: EBSCO Publishing; Gale Group; ingenta.com; Kluwer Online; OCLC Online Computer Library Center, Inc.; RoweCom Information Quest; Swets Blackwell. Reprint: SWZ; WSH. *Indexed:* ArtHuCI, CLI, IBSS, IBZ, ILP, IPB, LRI, PSA, PhilInd, SSCI, SociolAb. *Bk. rev.:* Occasional, 750-1,500 words. *Aud.:* Ac.

Law professors with an interest in philosophical issues in their discipline will find *Law and Philosophy* to be a valuable title. The journal publishes articles authored by philosophers and legal theorists on contemporary issues in areas as justice, rights, liberty, punishment, moral and criminal responsibility, legal ethics, legal positivism, and legal reasoning and interpretation. A good choice for philosophy, law, and criminology collections.

5443. ***Linguistics and Philosophy: a journal of natural language syntax, semantics, logic, pragmatics, and processing.*** [ISSN: 0165-0157] 1977. bi-m. EUR 549 print or online ed. Ed(s): Manfred Krifka. Kluwer Academic Publishers, van Godewijckstraat 30, PO Box 17, Dordrecht, 3300 AA, Netherlands; services@wkap.nl; http://www.wkap.nl. Illus., index, adv. Sample. Refereed. Vol. ends: No. 6. Microform: PQC. Online: EBSCO Publishing; ingenta.com; Kluwer Online; OCLC Online Computer Library Center, Inc.; RoweCom Information Quest; Swets Blackwell. Reprint: SWZ. *Indexed:* ArtHuCI, IBSS, IBZ, IPB, L&LBA, LT&LA, LingAb, MLA-IB, PhilInd, SSCI. *Aud.:* Ac.

This journal publishes specialized studies in all traditional areas of philosophy of language and linguistics in addition to dealing with such topics as artificial intelligence and language, systems of logic with strong connections to natural language, philosophical problems raised by linguistics as a science, and linguistics as it has relevance to other disciplines, including psychology and sociology.

5444. ***Logique et Analyse.*** Formerly (until 1958): *Centre National Belge de Recherches de Logique. Bulletin Interieur.* [ISSN: 0024-5836] 1954. 4x/yr. BEF 1100 domestic; BEF 1200 foreign. Nationaal Centrum voor Navorsingen in de Logica, c/o Jean-Paul van Bendegem, Vrije Universiteit Brussel, Faculteit Letteren en Wijsbegeer, Sectie Wijsbegeerte, Brussels, 1050, Belgium; jpvbende@vub.ac.be. Illus., index. Refereed. Circ: 1000. Vol. ends: Dec. *Indexed:* CCMJ, IBZ, IPB, MathSciNet, PhilInd. *Aud.:* Ac, Sa.

This quarterly publication of the Centre National de Recherches de Logique/Nationaal Centrum voor Navorsingen in de Logica presents highly technical articles in English, French, German, and Dutch on a wide range of topics in philosophical and symbolic logic, philosophy of language, and philosophy of mathematics. Tends to be late in publication. For graduate-level collections.

Medieval Philosophy and Theology. See Religion section.

5445. ***Metaphilosophy.*** [ISSN: 0026-1068] 1970. 5x/yr. GBP 240 print & online eds. Ed(s): Armen T. Marsoobian. Blackwell Publishing Ltd., 9600 Garsington Rd, PO Box 805, Oxford, OX4 2DQ, United Kingdom; customerservices@oxon.blackwellpublishing.com; http://www.blackwellpublishing.com/. Illus., adv. Refereed. Circ: 650. Vol. ends: No. 4. Online: EBSCO Publishing; ingenta.com; OCLC Online Computer Library Center, Inc.; RoweCom Information Quest; Swets Blackwell. Reprint: SWZ. *Indexed:* ArtHuCI, IBZ, IPB, L&LBA, PRA, PSA, PhilInd. *Bk. rev.:* 2-6, 1,000-4,000 words. *Aud.:* Ac.

The editor of *Metaphilosophy* invites articles that emphasize the foundation, scope, function, and direction of philosophy; the justification of philosophical methods and arguments; the relationships and connections between different schools or fields of philosophy; aspects of philosophical systems; presuppositions of philosophical schools; the relationship of philosophy to other disciplines; and the relevance of philosophy to social and political action. *Metaphilosophy* has frequently been at the forefront of publishing on new trends in the discipline, such as antifoundationalism, philosophy for children, feminist philosophy, applied philosophy, and the use of computers in philosophy. Recent special issues have been devoted to "Global Justice" and "The Philosopher as Public Intellectual."

5446. ***Mind: a quarterly review of philosophy.*** [ISSN: 0026-4423] 1876. q. GBP 80. Ed(s): Michael G F Martin, Paul Noordhof. Oxford University Press, Great Clarendon St, Oxford, OX2 6DP, United Kingdom; jnl.orders@oup.co.uk; http://www3.oup.co.uk/jnls. Illus., index, adv. Refereed. Circ: 3250. Vol. ends: No. 4. Microform: PMC; PQC. Online: EBSCO Publishing; Gale Group; ingenta.com; Northern Light Technology, Inc.; RoweCom Information Quest; Swets Blackwell. Reprint: PSC. *Indexed:* ArtHuCI, CCMJ, HumInd, IBSS, IBZ, IPB, L&LBA, LRI, MLA-IB, MathSciNet, PhilInd, SSCI. *Bk. rev.:* 30-40, 1,000-1,500 words. *Aud.:* Ac.

Mind has long been a preeminent British philosophy journal, particularly during the period when it published many classic articles under the editorships of G. K. Stout, G. E. Moore, and Gilbert Ryle. This journal is especially strong in epistemology, metaphysics, philosophy of language, philosophical logic, and philosophy of mind.

5447. ***Monist: an international quarterly of general philosophical inquiry.*** [ISSN: 0026-9662] 1890. q. USD 50 (Individuals, USD 30). Ed(s): Barry Smith. Hegeler Institute, c/o Sherwood J.B. Sugden, 315 Fifth St, Peru, IL 61354; philomon1@netscape.net. Illus., index, adv. Refereed. Circ: 1300 Paid. Vol. ends: No. 4. Online: EBSCO Publishing; Florida Center for Library Automation; Gale Group; OCLC Online Computer Library Center, Inc.; H.W. Wilson. Reprint: PSC. *Indexed:* ArtHuCI, HumInd, IBZ, IPB, PSA, PhilInd, RI-1, SSCI. *Aud.:* Ac.

Each issue of The *Monist* averages ten articles centered on a single topic selected by the editorial board and coordinated by an advisory editor. These topics range from the traditional (e.g., "Evil") to the contemporary (e.g., "Cognitive Theories of Mental Illness"). Its broad scope, high-quality scholarship, and reasonable cost combine to make The *Monist* a very attractive publication.

5448. ***New Nietzsche Studies.*** [ISSN: 1091-0239] 1996. a. Membership, USD 40. Ed(s): David B Allison, Babette E Babich. Nietzsche Society, Department of Philosophy, Fordham University, New York, NY 10023; Babich@Fordham.Edu; http://www.fordham.edu/gsas/phil/new_nietzsche_society.html. *Indexed:* IPB. *Bk. rev.:* 8-12, 500-1,000 words, signed. *Aud.:* Ac.

Scholarship on the German existentialist Friedrich Nietzsche has accelerated considerably in the past decade. This journal serves as forum for critical discussions of all facets of Nietzsche's philosophy and related themes by contributors from both Europe and North America. Issues are often centered around topics (e.g., "Nietzsche and the Death of God(s)"). In addition, selected texts from both Nietzsche and his contemporaries are published when they are deemed to be important for ongoing research.

5449. ***Notre Dame Journal of Formal Logic.*** [ISSN: 0029-4527] 1960. q. USD 45 (Individuals, USD 25). Ed(s): Michael Detlefsen, Peter Cholak. University of Notre Dame, Notre Dame, IN 46556. Illus., index, adv. Refereed. Circ: 825. Vol. ends: No. 4. *Indexed:* CCMJ, IPB, MathSciNet, PhilInd. *Bk. rev.:* Occasional, 500-2,500 words. *Aud.:* Ac, Sa.

This journal will be of interest to specialists working in all areas of philosophical and mathematical logic, including the philosophy, history, and foundations of logic and mathematics. There is more of an emphasis here on philosophy of language and formal semantics for natural languages than one finds in *The Journal of Symbolic Logic*. A recent special two-part issue was devoted to "Logicism and the Paradoxes: A Reappraisal." Tends to be late in publication. For graduate-level collections.

5450. ***Nous.*** [ISSN: 0029-4624] 1967. bi-m. USD 433 print & online eds. Ed(s): Jaegwon Kim, Ernest Sosa. Blackwell Publishing, Inc., Commerce Place, 350 Main St, Malden, MA 02148; subscrip@blackwellpub.com; http://www.blackwellpublishing.com. Illus., index, adv. Sample. Refereed. Circ: 1200. Vol. ends: No. 4. Microform: PQC. Online: EBSCO Publishing; ingenta.com; JSTOR (Web-based Journal Archive); OCLC Online Computer Library Center, Inc.; RoweCom Information Quest; Swets Blackwell. *Indexed:* ArtHuCI, CCMJ, IBZ, IPB, L&LBA, MathSciNet, PhilInd, RI-1. *Bk. rev.:* 2-3, 2,000-4,000 words. *Aud.:* Ac.

Nous features articles on a wide range of subjects, chiefly in the fields of metaphysics, epistemology, philosophical logic, philosophy of religion, ethics, and the history of philosophy. Subscribers also receive two annual supplementary publications, *Philosophical Perspectives* and *Philosophical Issues.* The lengthy book reviews take the form of "Critical Studies." This high-quality journal belongs in all but the smallest collections.

5451. ***Oxford Studies in Ancient Philosophy.*** [ISSN: 0265-7651] 1983. a. USD 78 per vol. Ed(s): David Sedley. Oxford University Press, Great Clarendon St, Oxford, OX2 6DP, United Kingdom; enquiry@oup.co.uk; http://www.oup.co.uk/. Illus. Refereed. *Indexed:* IPB. *Aud.:* Ac.

This annual publication features scholarly articles on all facets of ancient philosophy authored by leading philosophers and classicists on an international level. Although most of the essays have the writings of Plato and Aristotle as their focus, the reader will also find studies of the Presocratics, the Pyrrhonists, the Stoics, and other thinkers of antiquity as well. Rather than simply being expository, the authors concentrate on exegesis and critical analysis of primary texts. One will often encounter untransliterated Greek, although there is an effort to keep this at a minimum except in extended passages. Each volume contains an *index locorum.*

5452. ***Pacific Philosophical Quarterly.*** Formerly (until vol.61, Jan. 1980): *Personalist.* [ISSN: 0279-0750] 1920. q. GBP 115 print & online eds. Ed(s): Janet Levin, Sharon A Lloyd. Blackwell Publishing Ltd., 9600 Garsington Rd, PO Box 805, Oxford, OX4 2DQ, United Kingdom; jnlinfo@blackwellpublishers.co.uk; http://www.blackwellpublishing.com/. Illus., index, adv. Refereed. Circ: 850. Vol. ends: No. 4. Microform: PQC. Online: EBSCO Publishing; Gale Group; ingenta.com; OCLC Online Computer Library Center, Inc.; RoweCom Information Quest; Swets Blackwell. Reprint: PQC; PSC. *Indexed:* ArtHuCI, BEL&L, HumInd, IPB, L&LBA, MLA-IB, PSA, PhilInd, SSCI. *Aud.:* Ac.

Despite its regional title, this journal has an international editorial board. Each issue contains four to seven articles dealing chiefly with metaphysics, epistemology, philosophy of science, philosophical logic, ethics, and the history of philosophy. Special thematic issues are published occasionally.

5453. ***Philosophical Books.*** [ISSN: 0031-8051] 1960. q. GBP 181 print & online eds. Ed(s): Anthony Ellis. Blackwell Publishing Ltd., 9600 Garsington Rd, PO Box 805, Oxford, OX4 2DQ, United Kingdom; jnlinfo@blackwellpublishers.co.uk; http://www.blackwellpublishing.com/. Illus., index, adv. Refereed. Circ: 850. Vol. ends: No. 4. Online: EBSCO Publishing; ingenta.com; OCLC Online Computer Library Center, Inc.; RoweCom Information Quest; Swets Blackwell. Reprint: SWZ. *Indexed:* ArtHuCI, IPB, L&LBA, PhilInd. *Bk. rev.:* Various number and length. *Aud.:* Ac.

Philosophical Books offers reviews of newly published English-language books and serials in the field and is therefore a valuable collection development tool. One book is singled out for a more lengthy lead review in each issue under the heading "Critical Notice." The other reviews are arranged by the following subject categories: new journals, history of philosophy, general philosophy, logic, metaphysics, epistemology, philosophy of language, philosophy of mind, ethics, political philosophy, social philosophy, aesthetics, and philosophy of religion. Surveys of recent work in specific subject areas are also published.

5454. ***Philosophical Forum.*** [ISSN: 0031-806X] 1942. q. USD 204 print & online eds. Blackwell Publishing, Inc., Commerce Place, 350 Main St, Malden, MA 02148; subscrip@blackwellpub.com; http://www.blackwellpublishing.com. Illus., index, adv. Refereed. Circ: 460 Paid. Vol. ends: No. 4. Online: EBSCO Publishing; ingenta.com; OCLC Online Computer Library Center, Inc.; RoweCom Information Quest; Swets Blackwell; H.W. Wilson. *Indexed:* ArtHuCI, HumInd, IBZ, IPB, IPSA, PSA, PhilInd, RI-1, SSCI. *Aud.:* Ac.

The editor of *Philosophical Forum* encourages diverse approaches and viewpoints, whether critical or constructive, speculative or analytic, systematic or historical. Recent special issues present new translations of historical philosophical essays and philosophical poetry. The journal should be consulted by those seeking new themes or trends in contemporary philosophy outside the analytic mainstream in such areas as ethics, social and political philosophy, aesthetics, feminist philosophy, and Continental philosophy.

5455. ***Philosophical Investigations.*** [ISSN: 0190-0536] 1978. q. GBP 192 print & online eds. Ed(s): D Z Phillips. Blackwell Publishing Ltd., 9600 Garsington Rd, PO Box 805, Oxford, OX4 2DQ, United Kingdom; jnlinfo@blackwellpublishers.co.uk; http://www.blackwellpublishing.com/. Illus., index, adv. Refereed. Circ: 650. Vol. ends: No. 4. Online: EBSCO Publishing; ingenta.com; OCLC Online Computer Library Center, Inc.; RoweCom Information Quest; Swets Blackwell. Reprint: SWZ. *Indexed:* ArtHuCI, IPB, L&LBA, PhilInd, RI-1. *Bk. rev.:* 2-6, 1,000-5,000 words. *Aud.:* Ac.

Scholars interested in the work of the influential twentieth-century philosopher Ludwig Wittgenstein will find this to be a valuable title. In addition to presenting critical studies on Wittgenstein, the journal also features selections from Wittgenstein's unpublished writings and lectures (based on the lecture notes of his students). Although Wittgenstein is the principal focus of *Philosophical Investigations,* articles are also published on a wide range of topics in contemporary analytical philosophy, particularly those of the kind addressed in the writings of British ordinary-language philosophers like J. L. Austin and Gilbert Ryle.

5456. ***The Philosophical Quarterly.*** [ISSN: 0031-8094] 1950. q. GBP 127 print & online eds. Ed(s): Stephen Read. Blackwell Publishing Ltd., 9600 Garsington Rd, PO Box 805, Oxford, OX4 2DQ, United Kingdom; jnlinfo@blackwellpublishers.co.uk; http://www.blackwellpublishing.com/. Illus., index, adv. Refereed. Circ: 1600. Microform: PQC. Online: EBSCO Publishing; Gale Group; ingenta.com; JSTOR (Web-based Journal Archive); OCLC Online Computer Library Center, Inc.; RoweCom Information Quest; Swets Blackwell. Reprint: PQC; SWZ. *Indexed:* ArtHuCI, CCMJ, HumInd, IBSS, IPB, LRI, MLA-IB, MathSciNet, PhilInd, SSCI. *Bk. rev.:* 10-15, 500-3,000 words. *Aud.:* Ac.

Sponsored by the Scots Philosophical Club and the University of Saint Andrews, this is one of the better-quality analytic philosophy journals published in the United Kingdom. The predominant subjects treated are epistemology, metaphysics, philosophical logic, philosophy of language, and ethics.

5457. ***Philosophical Review.*** [ISSN: 0031-8108] 1892. q. USD 60 (Individuals, USD 36; Students, USD 22). Ed(s): Harold Hodes, Richard W Miller. Cornell University, Sage School of Philosophy, 327 Goldin Smith Hall, Ithaca, NY 14853-3201; phil-review@cornell.edu; http://www.arts.cornell.edu/philrev. Illus., index, adv. Refereed. Circ: 3265 Paid. Vol. ends: No. 4. Microform: MIM; PMC; PQC. Online: Gale Group. Reprint: PQC. *Indexed:* ArtHuCI, BAS, BRI, CBRI, DSR&OA, HumInd, IBZ, IPB, L&LBA, LRI, MLA-IB, PhilInd, SSCI. *Bk. rev.:* 15-20, 1,000-2,500 words. *Aud.:* Ac.

The *Philosophical Review* is one of the oldest continuously published philosophy periodicals in the United States and has featured the writings of many distinguished philosophers, particularly during the postwar era. Each issue contains three or four articles critically analyzing issues in all major areas of the field, with an emphasis on metaphysics, epistemology, philosophy of mind, and ethics. The journal is also known for the excellence of its scholarship in the history of philosophy.

5458. ***Philosophical Studies: an international journal for philosophy in the analytic tradition.*** [ISSN: 0031-8116] 1950. 15x/yr. EUR 1322 print or online ed. Ed(s): Keith Lehrer, Stewart Cohen. Kluwer Academic Publishers, van Godewijckstraat 30, PO Box 17, Dordrecht, 3300 AA, Netherlands; services@wkap.nl; http://www.wkap.nl. Illus., index, adv. Sample. Refereed. Vol. ends: No. 3. Microform: PQC. Online: EBSCO

Publishing; ingenta.com; Kluwer Online; OCLC Online Computer Library Center, Inc.; Ovid Technologies, Inc.; RoweCom Information Quest; Swets Blackwell. Reprint: SWZ. *Indexed:* ArtHuCI, BHA, CCMJ, CPL, IBZ, IPB, IPSA, L&LBA, MLA-IB, MathSciNet, PSA, PhilInd, RI-1, SSCI. *Aud.:* Ac.

Founded by Herbert Feigl and Wilfrid Sellars, *Philosophical Studies* has established itself as one of the foremost journals for analytical philosophy. The focus is on contemporary issues, as well as traditional problems explored from new perspectives, particularly in the fields of metaphysics, epistemology, philosophy of mind, philosophical logic, philosophy of science, action theory, and ethics. Authors generally advance tightly argued, original theses, although others contribute historically oriented discussions. In addition to covering issues devoted to papers presented at regional meetings of the American Philosophical Association, the journal also publishes several thematic issues each year coordinated by guest editors. Despite its high cost, this is a core collection journal.

5459. *Philosophical Topics.* Formerly: *Southwestern Journal of Philosophy.* [ISSN: 0276-2080] 1970. 2x/yr. USD 32.50 (Individuals, USD 20). Ed(s): Christopher Hill. University of Arkansas Press, 201 Ozark Ave, Fayetteville, AR 72701; http://www.uapress.com. Illus., adv. Refereed. Circ: 750. Vol. ends: No. 2. Reprint: ISI. *Indexed:* ArtHuCI, IPB, PhilInd, SSCI. *Aud.:* Ac.

Philosophical Topics has evolved from a regional journal into a publication featuring exclusively invited papers, many of which are authored by leading scholars on an international level. Each issue averages ten articles centered around a major historical period, broad area of philosophy, or prominent philosopher.

5460. *Philosophy.* [ISSN: 0031-8191] 1925. q. plus two supplements. USD 270. Ed(s): Anthony O'Hear. Cambridge University Press, The Edinburgh Bldg, Shaftesbury Rd, Cambridge, CB2 2RU, United Kingdom; information@cambridge.org; http://uk.cambridge.org/journals. Illus., index, adv. Refereed. Vol. ends: No. 4. Microform: PQC. Online: EBSCO Publishing; Gale Group; OCLC Online Computer Library Center, Inc.; RoweCom Information Quest; Swets Blackwell. *Indexed:* ArtHuCI, BAS, DSR&OA, HumInd, IPB, LRI, MathSciNet, PRA, PhilInd, PsycholAb, RI-1, SSCI. *Bk. rev.:* 5-7, 1,000-2,500 words. *Aud.:* Ac.

As the official journal of the Royal Institute of Philosophy (RIP), this journal has a decidedly British bent, and most authors are from the United Kingdom. All branches of philosophy are discussed in its pages, and no emphasis is placed on any particular school or method. Even the nonspecialist will find the articles accessible because, as the editor admonishes, "Contributors are expected to avoid all needless technicality." The Royal Institute of Philosophy Lecture Series, previously published separately and invariably representing the highest standards of scholarship, is now published as *RIP Supplements* and included in the price for institutional subscribers.

5461. *Philosophy and Literature.* [ISSN: 0190-0013] 1976. s-a. USD 80 (Individuals, USD 29). Ed(s): Denis Dutton, Garry Hagberg. Johns Hopkins University Press, Journals Publishing Division, 2715 N Charles St, Baltimore, MD 21218-4363; http://www.press.jhu.edu/. Illus., index, adv. Sample. Refereed. Circ: 979. Vol. ends: No. 2. Online: EBSCO Publishing; OCLC Online Computer Library Center, Inc.; Project MUSE; RoweCom Information Quest; Swets Blackwell. Reprint: PSC. *Indexed:* ABS&EES, AmHI, ArtHuCI, BEL&L, BRI, CBRI, IPB, L&LBA, MLA-IB, PhilInd, SSCI. *Bk. rev.:* 10-15, 750-2,000 words. *Aud.:* Ac.

This interdisciplinary journal, sponsored by Bard College, publishes philosophical interpretations of literature (American, British, and Continental), literary investigations of classic works of philosophy, articles on the aesthetics of literature, philosophy of language as it pertains to literature, and the literary theory of criticism. Special thematic issues (e.g., "Symposium on Ken Burns's *Jazz*") are published occasionally. Recommended for both literature and philosophy collections.

5462. *Philosophy and Phenomenological Research.* [ISSN: 0031-8205] 1940. bi-m. USD 150 (Individuals, USD 39). Ed(s): Ernest Sosa. International Phenomenological Society, Brown University, Box 1947, Providence, RI 02912; ppr@brown.edu; http://www.brown.edu/Departments/Philosophy/ppr.html. Illus., index, adv. Refereed. Microform: PQC. Online: Ingenta Select; JSTOR (Web-based Journal Archive). Reprint: PSC. *Indexed:* ABS&EES, ArtHuCI, HumInd, IBZ, IPB, MLA-IB, PhilInd, PsycholAb, RI-1, SSCI. *Bk. rev.:* 6-8, 750-1,500 words. *Aud.:* Ac.

Philosophy and Phenomenological Research is in the upper echelon of analytic philosophy journals. Although it serves as the official organ of the International Phenomenological Society, one will find articles on a broad range of subjects, with an emphasis on metaphysics, epistemology, philosophy of mind, ethics, and issues in the history of philosophy when they have relevance to contemporary problems. Discussion papers, symposia (often focusing on recent books), and supplementary volumes are also published.

5463. *Philosophy and Public Affairs.* [ISSN: 0048-3915] 1971. q. USD 115 print & online. Blackwell Publishing, Inc., Commerce Place, 350 Main St, Malden, MA 02148; subscrip@blackwellpub.com; http://www.blackwellpublishing.com. Illus., index, adv. Sample. Refereed. Circ: 2037. Microform: PQC. Online: Gale Group; JSTOR (Web-based Journal Archive); OCLC Online Computer Library Center, Inc.; Project MUSE; ProQuest Information & Learning; Swets Blackwell. Reprint: PQC; WSH. *Indexed:* ABCPolSci, AgeL, ArtHuCI, CJA, FutSurv, HumInd, IBSS, IPB, IPSA, LRI, PRA, PSA, PhilInd, RI-1, SSCI, SociolAb. *Aud.:* Ac.

Philosophy and Public Affairs is an important journal for the critical examination of contemporary ethical, political, social, legal, and public-policy issues. Some authors focus on explicating broad concepts, such as autonomy, justice, political obligation, and punishment, whereas others deal with specific sociopolitical issues like abortion, affirmative action, disarmament, and pornography. One will also find historically oriented discussions of ethical and political theorists (e.g., Locke, Rousseau, Hegel, and Mill). This title is an excellent choice for philosophy, law, and political science collections.

5464. *Philosophy and Rhetoric.* [ISSN: 0031-8213] 1968. q. USD 55 (Individuals, USD 34). Ed(s): Stephen H Browne. Pennsylvania State University Press, 820 N. University Dr., USB-1, Ste C, University Park, PA 16802-1003; pspjournals@psu.edu; http://www.psupress.org. Illus., index, adv. Refereed. Circ: 576 Paid. Microform: PQC. Online: EBSCO Publishing; OCLC Online Computer Library Center, Inc.; Project MUSE; RoweCom Information Quest; Swets Blackwell. Reprint: PQC; PSC. *Indexed:* ArtHuCI, IBZ, IJCS, IPB, MLA-IB, PhilInd, RI-1, SSCI. *Bk. rev.:* 2-4, 500-1,000 words. *Aud.:* Ac.

This journal is a good source for studies of theoretical issues concerning the relationship between philosophy and rhetoric (including the relationship between formal and informal logic and rhetoric); philosophical aspects of argumentation and argumentation within the discipline of philosophy itself; the nature of rhetoric of historical figures and during historical periods; rhetoric and human culture and thought; and psychological and sociological aspects of rhetoric. Recommended for philosophy, English, and speech communication collections.

5465. *Philosophy & Social Criticism: an international, inter-disciplinary journal.* Formerly: *Cultural Hermeneutics.* [ISSN: 0191-4537] 1973. 7x/yr. GBP 552 print & online eds. in Europe, Middle East, Africa & Australasia. Ed(s): David Rasmussen. Sage Publications Ltd., 6 Bonhill St, London, EC2A 4PU, United Kingdom; info@sagepub.co.uk; http://www.sagepub.co.uk/. Illus., index, adv. Sample. Refereed. Circ: 1000. Vol. ends: No. 6. *Indexed:* ABS&EES, AltPI, BHA, IBSS, IPB, IPSA, PSA, PhilInd, RI-1, SSCI, SociolAb. *Aud.:* Ac.

This wide-ranging interdisciplinary journal serves as a forum for the discussion of political philosophy, social theory, ethics, hermeneutics, literary theory, aesthetics, feminism, modernism and postmodernism, neostructuralism and deconstruction, universalism and communitarianism, and so forth. Those interested in the work of modern Continental philosophers—Adorno, Arendt, Derrida, Habermas, Foucault, Ricouer, and others—will find this publication to be a valuable resource.

5466. ***Philosophy East and West: a quarterly of comparative philosophy.*** [ISSN: 0031-8221] 1951. q. USD 50 (Individuals, USD 35). Ed(s): Roger T Ames. University of Hawaii Press, Journals Department, 2840 Kolowalu St, Honolulu, HI 96822-1888; uhpjourn@hawaii.edu; http://www.uhpress.hawaii.edu/. Illus., index, adv. Sample. Refereed. Circ: 1200. Vol. ends: No. 4. Microform: PQC. Online: bigchalk; Chadwyck-Healey Incorporated; EBSCO Publishing; Florida Center for Library Automation; Gale Group; OCLC Online Computer Library Center, Inc.; OhioLINK; Project MUSE; ProQuest Information & Learning; RoweCom Information Quest; Swets Blackwell; H.W. Wilson. Reprint: ISI; PQC; PSC. *Indexed:* ArtHuCI, BAS, HumInd, IBSS, IBZ, IPB, L&LBA, LRI, MLA-IB, PhilInd, R&TA, RI-1, SSCI. *Bk. rev.:* 2-5, 500-5,000 words. *Aud.:* Ac.

Philosophy East and West publishes specialized studies on Asian philosophy and comparative intercultural articles on the philosophical traditions of East and West, particularly those exhibiting the relevance of philosophy for the art, literature, science, and social practice of Asian civilizations. Special issues are occasionally published on such themes as "The Philosophy of Jainism" and "Nondualism, Liberation, and Language." The general scope of this publication is much broader than that of the *Journal of Indian Philosophy.* It is a good choice for both philosophy and Asian Studies collections.

5467. ***Philosophy Now: a magazine of ideas.*** [ISSN: 0961-5970] 1991. 6x/yr. GBP 24 (Individuals, GBP 12.75; GBP 2.80 newsstand/cover per issue United Kingdom). Ed(s): Anja Steinbauer. Philosophy Now, 25 Blandfield Rd, London, SW12 8BQ, United Kingdom; rick.lewis@philosophynow.demon.org.uk. Illus., adv. Circ: 9500 Paid. *Indexed:* BrHumI. *Bk. rev.:* 3-4, 750-1,500 words. *Aud.:* Ga.

This magazine, which receives a wide distribution through bookstores and newsstands in Great Britain, is aimed at making philosophy accessible to the educated layperson. The editors solicit articles that discuss any philosophical topic of general interest so long as they are written in a "lively, readable, and nontechnical style," preferably without footnotes or jargon. The articles are generally accompanied by illustrations, such as photographs, cartoons, or caricatures. Each issue includes at least one interview with a practicing philosopher. *Philosophy Now* would be a good choice for public libraries where magazines like *The Humanist* and *Skeptical Inquirer* are popular.

5468. ***Philosophy of Science: official journal of the Philosophy of Science Association.*** [ISSN: 0031-8248] 1934. 5x/yr. USD 165 (Individuals, USD 18; Students, USD 25). Ed(s): Noretta Koertge. University of Chicago Press, Journals Division, PO Box 37005, Chicago, IL 60637; subscriptions@press.uchicago.edu; http://www.journals.uchicago.edu. Illus., index, adv. Refereed. Circ: 2200. Vol. ends: Dec. Microform: PMC; PQC. Online: EBSCO Publishing; Florida Center for Library Automation; Gale Group; JSTOR (Web-based Journal Archive); ProQuest Information & Learning. *Indexed:* ArtHuCI, BiolAb, CCMJ, DSR&OA, HumInd, IBZ, IPB, MathSciNet, PhilInd, PsycholAb, RI-1, SCI, SSCI. *Bk. rev.:* 2-4, 1,500-2,000 words. *Aud.:* Ac.

This important journal publishes articles dealing with fundamental issues in the philosophy of science, including the logic of deductive, nomological, and statistical explanations; the nature of scientific laws and theories; observation; evidence; confirmation; induction; probability; and causality. In addition, contributors analyze philosophical issues arising within the context of the physical sciences (e.g., space, time, and quantum mechanics); the biological sciences (e.g., evolution, reductionism, and teleology); the cognitive sciences (e.g., artificial intelligence and connectionism); the social sciences (e.g., decision theory); and mathematics. Supplementary issues are published containing the contributed and symposia papers presented at the biennial meetings of the Philosophy of Science Association. This is an essential journal for all academic libraries.

5469. ***Philosophy of the Social Sciences.*** [ISSN: 0048-3931] 1971. q. GBP 261 print & online eds. in Europe, Middle East, Africa & Australasia. Ed(s): Ian C Jarvie. Sage Publications, Inc., 2455 Teller Rd, Thousand Oaks, CA 91320; info@sagepub.com; http://www.sagepub.com. Illus., index, adv. Sample. Refereed. Circ: 1300. Vol. ends: No. 4. Online: EBSCO Publishing; Gale Group; ingenta.com; RoweCom Information Quest; Swets Blackwell. Reprint: PQC. *Indexed:* ArtHuCI, CBCARef, CPerI, IBSS, IPB, IPSA, PSA, PhilInd, SSCI, SSI, SociolAb. *Bk. rev.:* 1-2, 750-7,500 words. *Aud.:* Ac.

This interdisciplinary journal publishes articles, discussions, symposia, review essays, and literature surveys on philosophical issues arising within the entire spectrum of the social and behavioral sciences. The editors strive to promote debate between different—and often conflicting—schools of thought. The journal also publishes the papers presented at the annual St. Louis Roundtable on Philosophy of the Social Sciences. This is a valuable title for philosophers as well as social scientists, particularly economists, linguists, political scientists, psychologists, and sociologists.

5470. ***Philosophy, Psychiatry & Psychology.*** [ISSN: 1071-6076] 1994. q. USD 158 (Individuals, USD 85). Ed(s): K W M Fulford, John Sadler. Johns Hopkins University Press, Journals Publishing Division, 2715 N Charles St, Baltimore, MD 21218-4363; http://www.press.jhu.edu/. Illus., adv. Sample. Refereed. Circ: 592. Vol. ends: No. 4. Online: EBSCO Publishing; RoweCom Information Quest; Swets Blackwell. Reprint: PSC. *Indexed:* PhilInd, PsycholAb. *Bk. rev.:* Occasional, 5,000-7,000 words. *Aud.:* Ac.

This journal is sponsored by the Association for the Advancement of Philosophy and Psychiatry, the Royal Institute of Philosophy, and the Royal College of Psychiatrists Philosophy Group. The articles address a broad range of philosophical issues relevant to psychiatry and abnormal psychology, in addition to dealing with topics in clinical theory and methodology that have a bearing on philosophical problems in such areas as metaphysics, epistemology, and ethics. The contributors represent many disciplines, including general medicine, law, neuroscience, social science, anthropology, nursing, and theology. Recent thematic issues deal with such issues as Aristotle's functionalism, feminism, and schizophrenia.

5471. ***Philosophy Today.*** [ISSN: 0031-8256] 1957. q. USD 36 domestic; USD 43 foreign. Ed(s): David Pellauer. DePaul University, Department of Philosophy, Byrne Hall, 2219 N. Kenmore Avenue, Chicago, IL 60614; phltoday@condor.depaul.edu. Illus., index, adv. Refereed. Circ: 1180. Vol. ends: No. 4. Microform: PQC. Online: Chadwyck-Healey Incorporated; Gale Group; Northern Light Technology, Inc.; OCLC Online Computer Library Center, Inc.; ProQuest Information & Learning. Reprint: PQC. *Indexed:* ArtHuCI, CPL, HumInd, IPB, PhilInd. *Aud.:* Ac.

Articles in *Philosophy Today* focus primarily on phenomenology and existentialism and address the interests of scholars and teachers within the Christian tradition. Philosophers discussed in recent issues include Kierkegaard, Nietzsche, Habermas, Marcuse, and Derrida. A supplementary issue is also published each year that contains selected papers from the annual meeting of the Society for Phenomenology and Existential Philosophy. Recommended for libraries needing this type of perspective.

5472. ***Phronesis: a journal for ancient philosophy.*** [ISSN: 0031-8868] 1956. q. EUR 158 print & online eds. (Individuals, EUR 99 print & online eds.). Ed(s): K Algra, C Rowe. Brill Academic Publishers, Inc., PO Box 9000, Leiden, 2300 PA, Netherlands; cs@brill.nl; http://www.brill.nl. Illus., index, adv. Refereed. Circ: 1100. Vol. ends: No. 4. Reprint: SWZ. *Indexed:* ArtHuCI, IBZ, IPB, PhilInd. *Bk. rev.:* 1-2, 1,000-2,000 words. *Aud.:* Ac.

Phronesis is the leading journal devoted exclusively to all aspects of ancient Greek and Roman thought, including logic, metaphysics, epistemology, ethics, political philosophy, philosophy of science, psychology, and medicine. A majority of the contributors undertake a critical textual analysis of the works of Plato and Aristotle, particularly those involving new or neglected issues, although others adopt a broader historical approach. Occasional articles deal with early Stoicism or the later Hellenistic period. The articles may be in English, French, German, or Italian.

5473. ***Ratio.*** [ISSN: 0034-0006] 1957. q. GBP 251 print & online eds. Ed(s): John G Cottingham. Blackwell Publishing Ltd., 9600 Garsington Rd, PO Box 805, Oxford, OX4 2DQ, United Kingdom; jnlinfo@blackwellpublishers.co.uk; http://www.blackwellpublishing.com/. Illus., adv. Refereed. Circ: 700. Vol. ends: No. 4. Online: EBSCO Publishing; ingenta.com; OCLC Online Computer Library Center, Inc.; RoweCom Information Quest; Swets Blackwell. Reprint: SWZ. *Indexed:* ArtHuCI, IPB, L&LBA, PSA, PhilInd, SSCI. *Bk. rev.:* 1-2, 1,000-2,500 words. *Aud.:* Ac.

Ratio publishes articles analyzing contemporary issues in metaphysics, epistemology, philosophical logic, and ethics. One aim of the journal is to encourage a dialogue between philosophers writing in English and those who work principally in German. The December issue features papers presented at the annual philosophy conference held at the University of Reading (England). Themes in recent years have included "Meaning and Representation" and "Philosophy of Body."

5474. ***The Review of Metaphysics: a philosophical quarterly.*** [ISSN: 0034-6632] 1947. q. USD 55 (Individuals, USD 35; Students, USD 20). Ed(s): Jude P Dougherty. Philosophy Education Society, Inc., Catholic University of America, Washington, DC 20064; mail@reviewofmetaphysics.com; http://www.reviewofmetaphysics.org. Illus., index, adv. Refereed. Circ: 1691 Paid. Vol. ends: No. 4. Microform: PQC. Online: Florida Center for Library Automation; Gale Group; Northern Light Technology, Inc.; OCLC Online Computer Library Center, Inc.; ProQuest Information & Learning; H.W. Wilson. *Indexed:* ABS&EES, ArtHuCI, BHA, BRI, CBRI, HumInd, IBZ, IPB, LRI, PhilInd, RI-1, SSCI. *Bk. rev.:* 30-35, 500-1,000 words. *Aud.:* Ac.

The editor of *The Review of Metaphysics* solicits "definitive contributions to philosophical knowledge" and "persistent, resolute inquiries into root questions, regardless of the writer's affiliation." The majority of articles center on issues in metaphysics, philosophy of mind, phenomenology and existentialism, ethics, and the history of philosophy. Each issue includes abstracts of articles in current philosophy periodicals, generally written by the authors. The September issue contains a list of doctoral dissertations awarded by North American universities during the previous academic year.

5475. ***Revue de Metaphysique et de Morale.*** [ISSN: 0035-1571] 1893. q. EUR 55 domestic; EUR 70 foreign. Ed(s): Jean-Francois Marquet. Presses Universitaires de France, Departement des Revues, 6 av. Reille, Paris, 75685 Cedex 14, France; revues@puf.com. Illus., adv. Refereed. Circ: 1700. Vol. ends: No. 4. Microform: IDC. Reprint: SCH. *Indexed:* ArtHuCI, IPB, MLA-IB, PhilInd, RI-1. *Bk. rev.:* 5-7, 250-1,500 words. *Aud.:* Ac.

This leading French journal was established by Xavier Leon, who also founded the Societe Francaise de Philosophie in 1901. Thematic issues are published on a wide spectrum of philosophical topics. Occasionally, one will also find French-language translations of writings by German philosophers such as Nietzsche, Brentano, and Husserl. Contributions come from both sides of the Atlantic, with the majority of articles in French.

5476. ***Revue Internationale de Philosophie.*** [ISSN: 0048-8143] 1938. q. BEF 2000. Universa - Wetteren, Rue Hoender 24, Wetteren, 9230, Belgium. Illus., adv. Refereed. Vol. ends: No. 4. Microform: IDC. Reprint: ISI; SCH. *Indexed:* ArtHuCI, IBZ, IPB, MLA-IB, PhilInd. *Bk. rev.:* 1-5, 500-2,500 words. *Aud.:* Ac.

Each issue of this Belgian journal averages six to eight articles in English, French, German, or Italian, centering on a particular movement, philosopher, or problem. The fact that the contributors are frequently acknowledged authorities on their subjects—for example, Terence Irwin on Aristotle, Daniel Hausman on economic theory, Richard Rorty on pragmatism, and Michael Ruse on philosophy of biology—makes this an important publication.

5477. ***Revue Philosophique.*** Formerly: *Revue Philosophique de la France et de l'Etranger.* 1876. q. EUR 65 domestic; EUR 77 foreign. Ed(s): Yvon Bres. Presses Universitaires de France, Departement des Revues, 6 av. Reille, Paris, 75685 Cedex 14, France; revues@puf.com. Illus., index. Refereed. Vol. ends: No. 4. Reprint: PSC. *Indexed:* ArtHuCI, IBZ, IPB, IPSA, PhilInd, SSCI. *Bk. rev.:* 30-40, 250-2,500 words. *Aud.:* Ac.

This French-language journal publishes thematic issues on philosophical topics and individual philosophers. It is a particularly good source for scholarly studies of French philosophers such as Descartes, Malebranche, Pascal, Rousseau, Comte, and Sartre.

5478. ***Revue Philosophique de Louvain.*** Former titles (until 1946): *Revue Neo-Scolastique de Philosophie;* (until 1910): *Revue Neo-Scolastique.* [ISSN: 0035-3841] 1894. q. EUR 63. Ed(s): T Lucas, M Ghins. Peeters, Bondgenotenlaan 153, Leuven, 3000, Belgium. Illus., index, adv. Refereed. Circ: 1400. Vol. ends: Nov. *Indexed:* ArtHuCI, BHA, CPL, IBZ, IPB, MLA-IB, PhilInd, SSCI. *Bk. rev.:* 20-25, 250-1,000 words. *Aud.:* Ac.

This French-language journal, founded by Cardinal Mercier, is significant for its scholarship in the history of philosophy, with a focus on the major French and German philosophers. One will also find studies on lesser-known figures such as Marc Richir, Gustav Siewerth, and Emmanuel Tourpe. The "Chroniques" section in each issue provides detailed news concerning the philosophy profession. Recommended for larger collections.

5479. ***Social Epistemology: a journal of knowledge, culture and policy.*** [ISSN: 0269-1728] 1987. q. GBP 251 (Individuals, GBP 121). Ed(s): Joan Leach. Routledge, 11 New Fetter Ln, London, EC4P 4EE, United Kingdom; info@routledge.co.uk; http://www.routledge.co.uk. Illus., index, adv. Sample. Refereed. Circ: 171. Vol. ends: No. 4. Online: EBSCO Publishing; Ingenta Select; OCLC Online Computer Library Center, Inc.; RoweCom Information Quest; Swets Blackwell. Reprint: PSC. *Indexed:* IPB, PSA, PhilInd, SociolAb. *Bk. rev.:* 5-7, 750-2,000 words. *Aud.:* Ac.

Articles in this journal, authored by scholars from a variety of disciplines, present empirical research regarding the production, assessment, and validation of knowledge as well as explore the normative ramifications of such research. These discussions are generally the product of several contributors and take the form of critical symposia, open peer commentary reviews, dialectical debates, applications, provocations, reviews and responses, and so forth. This type of approach tends to lead to a thorough exploration of the topic at hand from a number of divergent viewpoints. The journal is now collaborating with the Society for Social Studies of Science (4S) and the European Association for the Study of Science and Technology (EASST). This title is a good choice for both philosophy and social science collections.

5480. ***Social Philosophy and Policy.*** [ISSN: 0265-0525] 1983. s-a. USD 124 (Individuals, USD 48). Ed(s): Ellen Frankel Paul, Fred D. Miller. Cambridge University Press, The Edinburgh Bldg, Shaftesbury Rd, Cambridge, CB2 2RU, United Kingdom; information@cambridge.org; http://uk.cambridge.org/journals. Illus., adv. Refereed. Circ: 1000. Vol. ends: No. 2. Reprint: SWZ. *Indexed:* ABS&EES, ASSIA, ArtHuCI, IBSS, IPB, IPSA, PSA, PhilInd, RI-1, SSCI, SociolAb. *Aud.:* Ac.

Each issue of this interdisciplinary journal is devoted to a single theme involving contemporary debates on social, political, economic, legal, and public policy issues. The editors aim for a diversity of viewpoints, and the contributors represent many disciplines, including philosophy, law, economics, sociology, and political science. Recent issues focus on such topics as "Bioethics" and "Autonomy." The general orientation of this journal is similar to that of *Philosophy and Public Affairs.*

5481. ***The Southern Journal of Philosophy.*** [ISSN: 0038-4283] 1963. 4x/yr. USD 36 (Individuals, USD 24; Students, USD 12). Ed(s): Nancy D Simco. University of Memphis, Department of Philosophy, Clement Hall 327, Memphis, TN 38152; lsadler@memphis.edu; http://cas.memphis.edu/philosophy/. Illus., adv. Refereed. Circ: 1400 Paid. Vol. ends: No. 4. Microform: PQC. Reprint: PQC; PSC. *Indexed:* ArtHuCI, IPB, PhilInd, RI-1, SSCI. *Aud.:* Ac.

Although this is a solid general philosophy periodical, the supplementary volumes—available separately but included in the subscription—are especially noteworthy. They contain the featured papers presented at the annual Spindel Conference held at the University of Memphis. This series, taken as a whole, has resulted in an impressive body of scholarship.

5482. ***Studia Logica: an international journal for symbolic logic.*** [ISSN: 0039-3215] 1953. 9x/yr. EUR 929 print or online ed. Ed(s): Ryszard Wojcicki. Kluwer Academic Publishers, van Godewijckstraat 30, PO Box 17, Dordrecht, 3300 AA, Netherlands; services@wkap.nl; http://www.wkap.nl. Illus., index. Sample. Refereed. Vol. ends: No. 3. Microform: PQC. Online: EBSCO Publishing; ingenta.com; Kluwer Online; OCLC Online Computer Library Center, Inc.; Ovid Technologies, Inc.; RoweCom Information Quest; Swets Blackwell. Reprint: SWZ. *Indexed:* BiolAb, CCMJ, EngInd, IPB, MLA-IB, MathSciNet, PhilInd. *Bk. rev.:* 5-7, 500-1,000 words. *Aud.:* Ac, Sa.

Sponsored by the Institute of Philosophy and Sociology, Polish Academy of Sciences, this English-language journal publishes articles on technical issues in symbolic and philosophical logic. The focus is primarily on the semantics, methodology, and applications of logical systems, particularly when new and important technical results appear. A recent special issue is devoted to partiality and modality. Recommended for graduate-level collections.

Studies in History and Philosophy of Modern Physics. See *Studies in History and Philosophy of Science Part B: Studies in History and Philosophy of Modern Physics* in the Physics section.

5483. ***Studies in History and Philosophy of Science Part A.*** [ISSN: 0039-3681] 1970. q. EUR 426 (Qualified personnel, EUR 54). Ed(s): Nicholas Jardine, Marina Frasca-Spada. Pergamon, The Boulevard, Langford Ln, East Park, Kidlington, OX5 1GB, United Kingdom. Illus., index, adv. Sample. Refereed. Circ: 1100. Microform: PQC. Online: Gale Group; ingenta.com; ScienceDirect; Swets Blackwell. *Indexed:* AmH&L, ArtHuCI, BiolAb, CCMJ, GeoRef, HumInd, IBSS, IPB, MathSciNet, PhilInd, SCI, SSCI, SociolAb. *Bk. rev.:* 1-7, 1,500-2,500 words. *Aud.:* Ac.

This journal publishes historical, methodological, philosophical, and sociological investigations into problems and issues in the sciences, with the exception of modern physics, which is covered in the companion publication *Studies in History and Philosophy of Modern Physics.* Some authors focus on the work of individual philosophers and scientists (e.g., Galileo, Leibniz, Paley, Comte, Popper, and Kuhn), while others address philosophical themes in the history of science (e.g., "The Importance of Mathematical Conceptualisation"). Recommended for collections emphasizing the history of science.

5484. ***Synthese: an international journal for epistemology, methodology and philosophy of science.*** [ISSN: 0039-7857] 1936. 15x/yr. EUR 1652 print or online ed. Ed(s): John Symons, Jaakko Hintikka. Kluwer Academic Publishers, van Godewijckstraat 30, PO Box 17, Dordrecht, 3300 AA, Netherlands; services@wkap.nl; http://www.wkap.nl. Illus., index, adv. Sample. Refereed. Vol. ends: No. 3. Microform: PQC. Online: EBSCO Publishing; ingenta.com; Kluwer Online; OCLC Online Computer Library Center, Inc.; Ovid Technologies, Inc.; RoweCom Information Quest; Swets Blackwell. Reprint: SWZ. *Indexed:* ArtHuCI, IBZ, IPB, L&LBA, MLA-IB, MathSciNet, PhilInd, SCI, SSCI. *Bk. rev.:* 1-2, 5,000-7,500 words. *Aud.:* Ac.

Articles in *Synthese* bring formal methods of philosophical analysis to bear on issues in the history and philosophy of science, epistemology, mathematical and philosophical logic, philosophy of language, and philosophy of mathematics. Contributors include not only philosophers but also mathematicians, scientists, and economists writing on the philosophical aspects or formal methodological problems in their respective disciplines. Although *Synthese* is a highly technical and very costly journal, it is nevertheless recommended for graduate-level collections.

5485. ***Telos: a quarterly journal of critical thoughts.*** [ISSN: 0090-6514] 1968. q. USD 95 (Individuals, USD 45). Ed(s): Paul Piccone. Telos Press Ltd., 431 E 12th St, New York, NY 10009; telospress@aol.com. Illus., adv. Circ: 3000. Vol. ends: No. 4. Microform: PQC. Reprint: PQC. *Indexed:* ABS&EES, AltPI, IBSS, IPB, IPSA, PSA, PhilInd, RI-1, SociolAb. *Bk. rev.:* 5-7, 1,000-5,000 words. *Aud.:* Ga, Ac.

Telos emphasizes discussions of current social and political issues, particularly as they pertain to the United States, the Commonwealth of Independent States, and Eastern Europe; Continental philosophy, with a focus on deconstruction (De Man and Derrida); the Frankfurt school (Adorno, Habermas, and Marcuse) and Foucault; and topics involving contemporary academia, culture, and religion. Philosophers, as well as political scientists and educated laypersons, will find much of interest in this provocative publication.

5486. ***Theory and Decision: an international journal for multidisciplinary advances in decision sciences.*** [ISSN: 0040-5833] 1970. 8x/yr. EUR 792 print or online ed. Ed(s): Bertrand Munier. Kluwer Academic Publishers, van Godewijckstraat 30, PO Box 17, Dordrecht, 3300 AA, Netherlands; services@wkap.nl; http://www.wkap.nl. Illus., index, adv. Sample. Refereed. Vol. ends: No. 4. Microform: PQC. Online: EBSCO Publishing; ingenta.com; Kluwer Online; OCLC Online Computer Library Center, Inc.; RoweCom Information Quest; Swets Blackwell. Reprint: SWZ. *Indexed:* ArtHuCI, C&ISA, CommAb, EngInd, IBSS, IBZ, IPB, IPSA, JEL, MathSciNet, PSA, PhilInd, PsycholAb, RiskAb, SSCI, SociolAb. *Aud.:* Ac.

This interdisciplinary journal publishes highly technical articles on mathematical and computer science models; preference and uncertainty modeling; multicriteria decision making; social choice, negotiation, and group decision; game theory, gaming, and conflict analysis; rationality, cognitive processes, and interactive decision making; and methodology and philosophy of the social sciences. The journal attracts contributors on an international level from many fields, including philosophy, economics, management, statistics, operations research, finance, mathematics, psychology, and sociology. Recommended for graduate-level collections.

5487. ***Utilitas.*** Formed by the 1988 merger of: *Bentham Newsletter; Mill Newsletter.* [ISSN: 0953-8208] 1978. 3x/yr. USD 176 (Individuals, USD 50). Ed(s): Roger Crisp. Cambridge University Press, The Edinburgh Bldg, Shaftesbury Rd, Cambridge, CB2 2RU, United Kingdom; information@cambridge.org; http://uk.cambridge.org. Illus., adv. Sample. Refereed. Circ: 900. Vol. ends: No. 2. Online: EBSCO Publishing. *Indexed:* AmHI, IBSS, IPB, PhilInd. *Bk. rev.:* 4-6, 500-2,500 words. *Aud.:* Ac.

This journal, which is supported by the International Society for Utilitarian Studies, is a more polished publication than either of the newsletters that were its predecessors. The scope goes beyond utilitarianism's two greatest proponents (Jeremy Bentham and John Stuart Mill) and encompasses all aspects of utilitarian thought—its historical development, including its opponents, and contemporary utilitarian themes in ethics, politics, economics, jurisprudence, literature, and public policy. This is an important publication for collections emphasizing ethics (both historical and contemporary), political philosophy, and intellectual history.

5488. ***Zeitschrift fuer Philosophische Forschung.*** [ISSN: 0044-3301] 1947. q. EUR 98 (Students, EUR 49). Ed(s): Otfried Hoeffe, Christof Rapp. Vittorio Klostermann, Frauenlobstr 22, Frankfurt Am Main, 60487, Germany; verlag@klostermann.de; http://www.klostermann.de. Illus., index, adv. Refereed. Circ: 1200. Vol. ends: No. 4. *Indexed:* ArtHuCI, BAS, BHA, IBZ, IPB, PhilInd, SSCI. *Bk. rev.:* 6-12, 1,000-2,500 words. *Aud.:* Ac.

This leading German philosophy journal is a good source for historically oriented discussions, particularly on ancient philosophy and German philosophy (with Kant, Hegel, and Heidegger receiving much attention). Some articles are in English, but the majority are in German.

Electronic Journals

5489. ***Contretemps.*** [ISSN: 1443-7619] 2000. irreg. Ed(s): John Dalton. University of Sydney, Department of General Philosophy, Rm s411 Main Quad A14, Sydney, NSW 2006, Australia. *Bk. rev.:* Various number and length. *Aud.:* Ac.

Contributors to this Australian journal bring the perpective of Continental philosophy to bear on a diverse range of issues in aesthetics, cultural and literary studies, critical theory, ethics, and politics, in addition to exploring aspects of the work of such European philosophers as Adorno, Deleuze, Derrida, Heidegger, Kierkegaard, and Merleau-Ponty.

5490. ***Electronic Journal of Analytic Philosophy.*** [ISSN: 1071-5800] 1993. a. Free. Ed(s): Istvan Berkeley. The University of Louisiana at Lafayette, Edith Garland Dupre Library, Philosophy, The University of Louisiana at Lafayette, P.O. Drawer 43770, Lafayette, LA 70504-3770. Illus. Refereed. *Aud.:* Ac.

This was the first philosophy journal to be published in an electronic-only format. Each thematic issue is coordinated by a guest editor. Recent contributors have been exploring topics in cognitive science, epistemology, and philosophy of mind, with a recent issue devoted to a reappraisal of the philosophy of Gilbert Ryle.

5491. ***Essays in Philosophy.*** [ISSN: 1526-0569] s-a. Ed(s): Michael F Goodman. Humboldt State University, Department of Philosophy, c/o Michael F Goodman, Ed, Arcata, CA 95521. Refereed. *Bk. rev.:* Various number and length. *Aud.:* Ac.

This journal publishes thematic issues coordinated by guest editors, which have featured essays on topics in epistemology, ethics, feminism and gender studies, political and social philosophy, and the work of individual philosophers including Wittgenstein and Rawls.

5492. ***The Journal of Philosophy, Science & Law.*** 2001. bi-m. The Journal of Philosophy, Science and Law, c/o Jason Borenstein, Ed, PO Box 4089, Atlanta, GA 30302; editor@psljournal.com; http://www.psljournal.com/. *Bk. rev.:* Various number and length. *Aud.:* Ac.

Articles in this journal, which is sponsored by the Georgia Institute of Technology School of Public Policy and the University of Miami Ethics Programs, deal with moral and legal aspects of scientific evidence, research in science and technology, teaching ethical and legal guidelines within the scientific disciplines, bioethics, and related topics. Its scope is somewhat similar to that of *Jurimetrics.* News items and editorials are also published.

5493. ***Philosophers' Imprint.*** [ISSN: 1533-628X] 2001. q. Ed(s): Stephen Darwall. University of Michigan, Library, 435 S State St, An Arbor, MI 48109-1009. Refereed. *Aud.:* Ac.

This journal was founded by members of the philosophy faculty at the University of Michigan with the goal of countering the prevailing notions that electronic publishing is not prestigious and electronic literature is not authoritative. Many articles published to date have focused on issues in metaphysics and philosophical logic. Interested readers who wish to be notified when new articles are posted may subscribe to an electronic mailing list.

5494. ***Sorites: electronic quarterly of analytical philosophy.*** [ISSN: 1135-1349] 1995. q. Ed(s): Lorenzo Pena, Guillermo Hurtado. Spanish Institute for Advanced Studies, Center for Analytic Philosophy, Pinar 25, Madrid, 28006, Spain; http://www.ifs.csic.es/sorites/. *Indexed:* MathSciNet. *Aud.:* Ac.

Although this English-language electronic journal is headquartered in Spain, it has an international board of editorial advisors. The contributors endeavor to bring the methods and tools of contemporary analytic philosophy—including conceptual clarity, formal rigor, and careful argumentation—to bear on a wide range of subjects in theoretical and applied philosophy. Many of the articles published to date have concentrated on issues in metaphysics and philosophical logic.

PHOTOGRAPHY

Michael J. Hemment, Research Librarian and Coordinator or E-Texts in the Humanities, Harvard College Library, Widener Library, Harvard University, Cambridge, MA 02138; hemment@fas.harvard.edu

Introduction

Ansel Adams once said, "You don't take a photograph, you make it." With the increasing digitization of photography in recent years, this adage could not be truer. Affordable image editing software has brought "digital darkrooms" to the masses, home photo printers are producing impressive results, and the latest cameras feature megapixels, memory cards, and photo stitching aids. To keep up with these innovations, a number of new magazines have sprouted that focus exclusively on digital photography. Most traditional photo magazines are adapting themselves to the "digital revolution" by balancing the latest "imaging" tools and techniques with film-based photography. Others remain true to what they call the "pure art" of wet process photography. Scholarly journals on photographic art have been slow to include digital images, but this will likely change as the quality gap between film and digital images continues to close.

Basic Periodicals

Hs: *Photographer's Forum, Popular Photography & Imaging;* Ga: *Afterimage, American Photo, Aperture, Petersen's Photographic, Popular Photography & Imaging;* Ac: *Afterimage, Aperture, Exposure, Petersen's Photographic, Photo Techniques, Photographer's Forum, Popular Photography & Imaging.*

Basic Abstracts and Indexes

Imaging Abstracts.

5495. ***Afterimage: the journal of media arts and cultural criticism in the social and decision sciences.*** [ISSN: 0300-7472] 1972. bi-m. USD 40 (Individuals, USD 30). Ed(s): Karen Vanmeenen. Visual Studies Workshop, 31 Prince St, Rochester, NY 14607; afterimg@servtech.com. Illus., index. Sample. Circ: 10000. Vol. ends: May/Jun. Microform: PQC. Online: bigchalk; EBSCO Publishing; Florida Center for Library Automation; Gale Group; Northern Light Technology, Inc.; OCLC Online Computer Library Center, Inc.; ProQuest Information & Learning; H.W. Wilson. Reprint: PQC. *Indexed:* ABM, ArtInd, BHA, BRI, CBRI, FLI, IIFP, MRD. *Bk. rev.:* 3-5, 1,500 words. *Aud.:* Hs, Ga, Ac.

Afterimage features the work of emerging artists, covers developments in cultural theory, and presents scholarly essays. It contains lists of films, video, photography, and alternative publishing, as well as interviews with artistic and critical figures. Interdisciplinary and scholarly in nature, this nonprofit publication is well suited to academic libraries.

5496. ***American Photo.*** Formerly (until 1990): *American Photographer.* [ISSN: 1046-8986] 1978. bi-m. USD 12.95 domestic; USD 20.95 foreign; USD 4.99 newsstand/cover per issue. Ed(s): David Schonauer. Hachette Filipacchi Media U.S., Inc., 1633 Broadway, 41st Fl, New York, NY 10019; http://www.hfmus.com. Illus., adv. Sample. Circ: 255971 Paid. Vol. ends: Nov/Dec. Microform: NBI. Online: Gale Group. *Indexed:* ASIP, ArtInd, MagInd. *Bk. rev.:* Occasional, length varies. *Aud.:* Ga.

With a focus on creative photography and photographers, this popular magazine profiles the personalities behind the lens and their contributions to art, history, fashion, journalism, and advertising. Features include reviews of exhibitions and books, picture portfolios, reader photos, and stories on working professionals. Equipment reviews can be helpful but are generally less in-depth than those found in peer publications. As in most popular photo magazines, there is a substantial amount of ad content in the back matter.

5497. ***Aperture.*** [ISSN: 0003-6420] 1952. q. USD 40. Ed(s): Melissa Harris. Aperture Foundation, Inc., 20 E 23rd St, New York, NY 10010. Illus., adv. Circ: 17000. Microform: PQC. Online: Gale Group; OCLC Online Computer Library Center, Inc.; H.W. Wilson. Reprint: PQC. *Indexed:* ABM, ABS&EES, ArtHuCI, ArtInd, BHA, HumInd. *Aud.:* Hs, Ga, Ac.

Aperture magazine has been described by leading professionals as "the most serious and the most valuable periodical in the photographic world." Showcasing a wide variety of photographic art from some of the world's most renowned photographers, this is a journal where the gallery-like images—highly selected and of exceptional quality—are the main focus. Even the paper, printing, and binding materials are top-notch. For all of these reasons, back issues are highly sought after. This is an essential title for academic institutions, while other libraries may also want to enrich their collection with this fine journal.

5498. ***B & W Magazine: for collectors of fine photography.*** [ISSN: 1522-4805] 1999. bi-m. USD 29.50 domestic; USD 49.50 in Canada & Mexico; USD 69.50 elsewhere. B & W Magazine, PO Box 700, Arroyo Grande, CA 93421. Adv. Circ: 20000 Paid. *Aud.:* Ga, Ac, Sa.

Global in perspective, each issue of *B & W* highlights the best in contemporary black-and-white photography, fashion, design, and popular culture. Other features include innovations in photographic technique, information on the market scene, photographer spotlights, and book reviews. The quality of the paper and printing is truly excellent. Suitable for academic libraries, museums, and large public collections.

5499. ***Blind Spot.*** [ISSN: 1068-1647] 1993. s-a. USD 25 domestic; USD 33 Canada; USD 45 elsewhere. Ed(s): Kim Zorn Caputo. Blind Spot, Inc., 210 11th Ave, 10th Fl, New York, NY 10001; editors@blindspot.com. Illus., adv. *Indexed:* ArtInd. *Aud.:* Ga, Ac.

Contains unconventional, new, and never-before-published photography. *Blind Spot* strikes a happy balance between showcasing emerging artists and established talent. Well-written articles complement the superb photographs. Artists interested in the craft of photography and current trends will enjoy this journal. Those interested in the latest equipment and technologies should look elsewhere. Here, again, it's all about the images. This title will be of special interest to public and academic libraries serving fine arts researchers.

5500. ***Camerawork: a journal of photographic arts.*** Formerly: *S F Camerawork Quarterly.* [ISSN: 1087-8122] 1984. s-a. USD 40 domestic; USD 35 foreign. Ed(s): Marnie Gillett. S F Camerawork, 1246 Folsom St, San Francisco, CA 94103; http://www.sfcamerawork.org. Adv. Circ: 2500. Reprint: PSC. *Indexed:* ABM, ArtInd. *Bk. rev.:* 8, 150 words. *Aud.:* Ga, Ac.

Dedicated to communicating about contemporary photography and related media through a series of educational and artistic programs, this theme-based journal, published by the nonprofit San Francisco Camerawork, features articles on contemporary culture and art, book reviews, exhibitions, and artists. Recent issues have included themes such as: "A Search for the Male Form," "Reimagining the West: A New History," and "Cocktail Hour: Examining New Imagery in the AIDS Era." Scholarly in tone, this is a good choice for academic and fine arts libraries.

5501. ***Digital Photographer.*** [ISSN: 1532-6012] 1998. bi-m. USD 9.95 domestic; USD 15.95 foreign; USD 4.99 newsstand/cover per issue. Miller Magazines, Inc, 4880 Market St, Ventura, CA 93003-2888; http://www.millermags.com. Adv. *Aud.:* Hs, Ga, Ac, Sa.

Digital Photographer, the best-selling digital photo magazine, is geared toward the beginner or amateur enthusiast. Regularly featured articles include what to look for when buying a digital camera, how to edit captured images on a home computer, creating web-ready images, how to select a "photo-quality" printer, the importance of resolution and storage, and more. Every issue contains consumer guides and equipment tests accompanied by fact sheets for potential buyers. Librarians will find that issues of this magazine will quickly become as dog-eared as those of *Popular Photography.* Suitable for public and some academic libraries.

DoubleTake. See Literary Reviews section.

5502. ***eDigitalPhoto.com.*** [ISSN: 1529-2177] 2000. bi-m. USD 19.95 domestic; USD 32.95 Canada; USD 34.95 foreign. Ed(s): Joe Farace. Primedia Enthusiast Group, 5211 South Washington Ave, Titusville, FL 32780; http://www.primedia.com. Adv. *Aud.:* Hs, Ga, Ac, Sa.

A magazine and a web site, this journal covers the digital imaging beat and reports on the latest gear, techniques, and hardware. The emphasis here is on web resources and "digital darkroom" techniques, but equipment reviews are also included. It includes very little on individual photographers, the profession, or photography as art. A good companion to *Digital Photographer.* Recommended for public and selected academic libraries.

5503. ***Exploring Digital Photography.*** Formerly (until 2002): *Digital Photo Pro.* [ISSN: 1542-2151] 2001. m. USD 107 domestic; USD 127 foreign. Ed(s): Craig Watkins, Stephen Dow. Element K Journals, 2165 Brighton-Henrietta Townline Rd, Ste 3, Rochester, NY 14623; http://www.elementkjournals.com. *Aud.:* Hs, Ga, Ac.

Exploring Digital Photography teaches readers how to compose professional-looking shots, make the transition to an all-digital environment, preserve images by making smart archiving decisions, and much more. This is a refreshing new magazine with an emphasis on digital technique over equipment. Photoshop neophytes and other imaging software users will also find many useful articles here. Recommended for public and academic libraries.

5504. ***Exposure (Oxford).*** [ISSN: 0098-8863] 1963. biennial. Membership, USD 35; USD 15 per issue. Ed(s): Joel Eisinger. Society for Photographic Education, 110 Art Bldg., Miami University, Oxford, OH 45056; socphotoed@aol.com; http://spenational.org. Illus., adv. Refereed. Circ: 1700. *Indexed:* ABM, ArtInd, BHA. *Aud.:* Hs, Ga, Ac.

For more than 30 years, *Exposure* has brought its readers a lively mix of scholarly insight, historical perspectives, critical dialogue, educational issues, and reviews of contemporary photographic publications. Published by the Society for Photographic Education, a nonprofit organization based at Miami University, *Exposure* is "devoted to the analysis and understanding of photography" and welcomes outside submissions. A recommended title for academic collections.

5505. ***History of Photography.*** [ISSN: 0308-7298] 1976. q. GBP 203 (Individuals, GBP 107). Ed(s): Graham Smith. Taylor & Francis Ltd, 11 New Fetter Ln, London, EC4P 4EE, United Kingdom; info@tandf.co.uk; http://www.tandf.co.uk/journals. Illus., adv. Sample. Refereed. Vol. ends: Winter. Online: EBSCO Publishing. Reprint: PSC. *Indexed:* ABCT, ABM, AIAP, ArtHuCI, ArtInd, BAS, BHA, SSCI. *Aud.:* Ac.

Scholarly in content and tone, this journal examines the history and early development of photography. Articles discuss the earliest uses of photography in exploration, science and war, and lives of notable practitioners and inventors; the influence of photography on painting and sculpture; the history of photojournalism; and the preservation and restoration of old photographs. This is strictly for academic libraries and special collections.

5506. ***News Photographer: dedicated to the service and advancement of news photography.*** Formerly (until 1974): *National Press Photographer.* [ISSN: 0199-2422] 1946. m. USD 38 domestic; USD 45.50 Canada; USD 60 elsewhere. Ed(s): Donald Winslow. National Press Photographers Association, Inc., 3200 Croasdaile Dr, Ste 306, Durham, NC 27705; http://www.nppa.org. Illus., adv. Sample. Circ: 11500 Paid and free. Vol. ends: Dec. Microform: PQC. Online: bigchalk; EBSCO Publishing; Florida Center for Library Automation; Gale Group; Northern Light Technology, Inc.; OCLC Online Computer Library Center, Inc.; ProQuest Information & Learning. *Bk. rev.:* 3-4, 150 words. *Aud.:* Hs, Ga, Ac.

Widely regarded as THE professional journal for photojournalists, *News Photographer* contains articles, interviews, profiles, history, and news relating to still and television news photography. The application of new imaging technologies to journalism has been a hot topic recently. Recommended for academic collections, selected corporate libraries, and public institutions supporting journalistic research.

5507. ***Outdoor Photographer: scenic - travel - wildlife - sports.*** [ISSN: 0890-5304] 1985. 10x/yr. USD 19.94; USD 4.99 newsstand/cover per issue. Ed(s): Rob Sheppard. Werner Publishing Corporation, 12121 Wilshire Blvd 1200, Los Angeles, CA 90025-1176; editors@outdoorphotographer.com; http://www.outdoorphotographer.com. Illus., adv. Sample. Circ: 215000 Paid. Vol. ends: Dec. *Aud.:* Ga.

Preparing yourself and your gear for Arctic cold or rain forest heat and humidity? Begin with this essential how-to and where-to magazine for the outdoor photographer. *Outdoor Photographer* provides timely articles on travel destinations and favorite places recommended by pros and readers, and seasonal specials on where to find the best outdoor photo opportunities. Geared to all levels, this magazine also includes articles on lighting, exposure, and filter, as well as photo equipment reviews and film recommendations for particular environments. Recommended for public and academic libraries.

5508. ***P C Photo.*** [ISSN: 1094-1673] unknown. USD 11.97 domestic; USD 21.97 foreign; USD 3.99 newsstand/cover per issue. Ed(s): Rob Sheppard. Werner Publishing Corporation, 12121 Wilshire Blvd 1200, Los Angeles, CA 90025-1176; pcphotomag@neodata.com. Adv. *Indexed:* MicrocompInd. *Aud.:* Hs, Ga, Ac.

Whether you are interested in "digital darkrooms" or the latest digital cameras, this magazine covers the latest technologies, trends, and methods. Articles are filled with advice and tips aimed at beginners and amateurs who are interested in improving their digital photography. Advanced Photoshop users and digital photography veterans will find most articles a bit too basic. *PC Photo* also includes reviews of new cameras, scanners, software, and other photography-related devices. Especially well-suited to public libraries.

5509. ***Petersen's Photographic.*** Former titles (until 1979): *Petersen's PhotoGraphic Magazine; Photographic Quarterly.* [ISSN: 0199-4913] 1972. m. USD 9.97 domestic. Ed(s): Ron Leach. Primedia Consumer Media & Magazine Group, 200 Madison Ave, New York, NY 10016; http://www.primedia.com. Illus., index, adv. Sample. Circ: 204537 Paid. Microform: PQC. Online: The Dialog Corporation; Florida Center for Library Automation; Gale Group; OCLC Online Computer Library Center, Inc.; ProQuest Information & Learning; H.W. Wilson. *Indexed:* BRI, CBRI, ConsI, IHTDI, MagInd, RGPR. *Aud.:* Hs, Ga, Ac.

Like *Popular Photography,* this magazine emphasizes equipment reviews and how-to articles for beginning and amateur photographers. It also contains timely information on workshops, schools, contests, books, seminars, and photo travel. Public libraries subscribe to this publication because it addresses a general audience.

5510. ***Photo District News.*** [ISSN: 1045-8158] 1980. m. USD 55 domestic; USD 68 Canada; USD 88 elsewhere. Ed(s): Holly Hughes. V N U Business Publications, 770 Broadway, New York, NY 10003; bmcomm@vnuinc.com; http://www.vnubusinessmedia.com/. Circ: 23000 Paid. Online: EBSCO Publishing; Florida Center for Library Automation; Gale Group; ProQuest Information & Learning. *Aud.:* Hs, Ga, Ac.

Considered by many to be the best general photography trade magazine, *Photo District News* features the work of up-and-coming photographers as well as interviews key players in the advertising and design communities. It gives a wide view of the industry, with useful advice to help commercial photographers manage their businesses better. *Photo District News* contains national and local information including the areas of copyright and tax laws, business trends, sources, and suppliers.

5511. ***Photo Techniques.*** Former titles (until vol.17, no.1, 1996): *Darkroom and Creative Camera Techniques; Darkroom Techniques.* [ISSN: 1083-9054] 1979. bi-m. USD 22.95 domestic; USD 4.95 newsstand/cover per issue; USD 32.95 foreign. Ed(s): Michael Johnston. Preston Publications, Inc., 6600 W. Touhy Ave., Niles, IL 60714-0312; http://www.phototechmag.com. Illus., adv. Sample. Circ: 32500. Vol. ends: Nov/Dec. *Indexed:* IHTDI, PhotoAb. *Aud.:* Ga, Ac.

Photo Techniques is written for the photographer who has a passion for advanced imaging techniques. It features diverse articles on location shooting, lighting, equipment applications, Adobe Photoshop step-by-step, darkroom secrets, portraiture, product evaluations, alternative processes, portfolio illustrating techniques, and more. In addition, there are guides to cameras, films, paper, scanners, darkroom supplies, and useful accessories. Readers will not find page after page of glossy images here, but rather technical articles by professionals in the field. Recommended for both public and academic library collections.

5512. ***Photographer's Forum: magazine for the emerging professional.*** Formerly: *Student Forum.* [ISSN: 0194-5467] 1978. q. USD 15. Ed(s): Glen R Serbin. Serbin Communications, Inc., 511 Olive St, Santa Barbara, CA 93101; http://www.serbin.com. Illus., adv. Sample. Circ: 15000. Vol. ends: Aug. *Indexed:* ABM. *Bk. rev.:* Various number and length. *Aud.:* Hs, Ac.

Established in 1977, *Photographer's Forum* magazine is intended for the emerging professional photographer. Features include interviews with master photographers, feature articles on commercial and fine art photography, book reviews, a portfolio section, and information on workshops. Aspiring professional photographers of all ages would benefit from this excellent publication. Recommended for public, secondary school, and academic libraries.

5513. ***Photovision: art & technique.*** 2000. bi-m. USD 24.95; USD 4.95 newsstand/cover per issue. Ed(s): Thomas Harrop. H.A.S.T. Publishing, Inc., 233 Sweetgrass Overlook, Crestone, CO 81131. Adv. *Bk. rev.:* Various number and length. *Aud.:* Ac, Sa.

Resisting the digital bandwagon, *Photovision* is a magazine dedicated to the "pure craft" of photography, meaning traditional wet process photography. It serves as a forum where photographers can discuss and appreciate pure photographic art and craft. All of the images in this journal are created without the aid of digital technology, and that's the way they like it! Professional artists and traditionalists will embrace this approach. Appropriate for both public and academic libraries.

5514. ***Popular Photography & Imaging.*** Former titles (until 2003): *Popular Photography;* (until 1955): *Photography;* Incorporates (1937-1989): *Modern Photography;* Which was formerly (until 1949): *Minicam Photography.* [ISSN: 1542-0337] 1937. m. USD 11.97 domestic; USD 19.97 foreign. Ed(s): Jason Schneider. Hachette Filipacchi Media U.S., Inc., 1633 Broadway, 41st Fl, New York, NY 10019. Illus., index, adv. Sample. Circ: 454741 Paid. Vol. ends: Dec. Microform: NBI; PQC. Online: America Online, Inc.; The Dialog Corporation; Gale Group. Reprint: PQC. *Indexed:* A&ATA, BRI, CBRI, ChemAb, ConsI, FLI, IHTDI, MagInd, RGPR. *Bk. rev.:* Various number and length. *Aud.:* Hs, Ga, Ac.

The undisputed king of the consumer photo magazines, *Popular Photography & Imaging* focuses primarily on 35mm and digital photography, catering to beginning and amateur photo enthusiasts. It features in-depth equipment reviews, incisive but often repetitive instructional articles, film tests, reader photos and questions, and coverage of the latest digital imaging technologies. This magazine is perennially useful for familiarizing oneself with the latest technology and basic photographic techniques. Public libraries will want to start here when building their photography journal collection. A must-have for academic libraries as well.

5515. ***Shutterbug.*** Formerly: *Shutterbug Ads.* [ISSN: 0895-321X] 1971. m. USD 17.95 domestic; USD 30.95 Canada; USD 32.95 elsewhere. Primedia Enthusiast Group, 5211 South Washington Ave, Titusville, FL 32780; http://www.primedia.com. Illus., adv. Circ: 140000. *Indexed:* IHTDI. *Aud.:* Ga, Ac.

Shutterbug is a popular magazine for amateur and professional photographers. It distinguishes itself by covering many types of photography and equipment beyond 35mm—everything from subminiature to super-large format to digital. Traditional wet darkroom how-tos are also featured. If you are looking for product reviews and tests, *Popular Photography* has the most, but this title is generally limited to 35mm and digital equipment. *Shutterbug* sometimes reviews large- or medium-format cameras and lenses as well. Other sections include classic collectibles, interviews with professional photographers, and a question-and-answer column. *Shutterbug* features ads for used, vintage, and collectible equipment. Recommended for public and academic libraries.

Electronic Journals

5516. ***Apogee Photo.*** 1996. m. Ed(s): Susan Harris. Apogee Photo, Inc., PO Box 730, Conifer, CO 80433; info@apogeephoto.com; http://www.apogeephoto.com/. *Aud.:* Ga.

This online magazine is host to one of the largest numbers of photo workshops and tour programs on the web. Geared to novice shutterbugs as well as serious amateurs, it includes reference to a wide variety of books, videos, and print publications. Recognized photographers, including Bob Hitchman, John Sexton, and John Gerlach, regularly contribute articles. This is a winner of numerous web site awards, and librarians of all types should know about this journal and recommend it to their patrons.

5517. *ePHOTOzine.* 2001. irreg. Ed(s): Peter Bargh. ePHOTOzine, mail@ephotozine.com. Adv. *Aud.:* Hs, Ga, Ac.

With a goal of bringing serious photographers of all levels together to share photo tips, ideas, and techniques, this web site is filled with equipment reviews, how-to guides, contests, book and magazine reviews, guides to stock libraries, and much more. A little busy in its design, it nonetheless contains a wealth of resources, particularly on digital imaging. Library patrons of all types interested in photography will benefit from this site.

5518. *Kodak e-Magazine: the online photography magazine.* 2000. m. Eastman Kodak Co., 343 State St, Rochester, NY 14650; http://www.kodak.com. *Aud.:* Ems, Hs, Ga, Ac, Sa.

Kodak's *e-Magazine* has a superb array of resources for photo enthusiasts. Each issue contains feature articles on artists, photo exhibits, book reviews, tips for making better pictures, conversations with photographers, and links to other Kodak projects, like the Digital Learning Center. This is a site that libraries of all types should keep bookmarked.

5519. *PhotoResource Magazine.* [ISSN: 1099-7636] 1996. w. s-m. Free. Ed(s): William Johnson. Botatography, Inc., 918 W 14th St, Portales, NM 88130-6740; info@photoresource.com; http://www.photoresource.com. *Aud.:* Ga.

This site offers very current information, including calendars of events, web links, reviews, online learning, professional opportunities, and software—there's even a very useful glossary. Hobbyists and professionals should all know about this trove of free information. A great resource.

■ PHYSICS

David A. Tyckoson, Director of Public Services, Henry Madden Library, California State University, Fresno, CA 93740

Introduction

Physics is one of the most basic of all of the sciences, concerning itself with the fundamental questions of the nature and function of the universe. Physicists often regard their discipline as the hardest of the hard sciences—the one on which all other fields of science are built. In its basic form, physics is the study of matter, motion, space, time, energy, and the forces that link them all together. What we now call physics was once known as "natural philosophy," the eighteenth-century name for the empirical study of the external world. As physics has matured and evolved as a discipline, it has become highly specialized, developing a number of subdisciplines that could almost be treated as separate sciences in and of themselves. Areas such as acoustics, optics, gravitation, electromagnetism, mechanics, plasmas, particles, waves, quantum mechanics, astrophysics, nanotechnology, and the solid state are prime examples of this specialization. Researchers typically work within the confines of one of these subdisciplines and have little understanding of the details of the others.

Physics journals mirror the specialization of research in the field. Over time, physics journals have been subdivided into parts and sections or have split off into entirely new titles dealing with ever more focused topics. For example, the most significant journal in the field, *Physical Review*, was published as a single journal until 1969, but it is now distributed as eight distinct titles, two of which are available only electronically. In addition to proliferating by sectionalizing, physics journals are also growing tremendously in size. A single section of the *Physical Review* can contain tens of thousands of pages in one calendar year. There is more physics research being published today than at any time throughout history.

Because of the high degree of specialization in physics, a researcher in one subdiscipline has great difficulty reading and understanding the literature of another area. Physics journals reflect this specialization and are written for researchers, not a general audience. These journals serve primarily as archives of the progress of physics research, recording for history the results of experimental and theoretical findings. It requires a strong understanding of mathematics to be able to read most physics research reports. Anyone with less than a graduate-level education in mathematics will probably be lost reading most of these titles. Even those journals that are written for a wider audience contain a fair amount of mathematics, requiring the reader to wade through integrals and differential equations to fully comprehend the concepts being discussed.

As a result of the high degree of specialization within the field and its reliance upon higher-level mathematics, very few researchers actually read the papers published in physics journals. In some cases, there may be only a dozen scientists worldwide who can truly understand the results of a given research project—and most of them probably are aware of the findings long before the paper is published in a physics journal. The journal serves primarily to document their progress and to establish precedent in scientific discovery.

For many years, the premier journals in the field have been published by the major professional associations. The American Institute of Physics and the Institute of Physics in the United Kingdom are the two preeminent organizations in the field, and they publish the two most significant journals: the *Physical Review* and the *Journal of Physics*, respectively. As association publications, the costs of these publications are somewhat lower than those of commercial journals (although prices are still in the thousands of dollars per year per section for both of these titles). These two organizations alone publish over half of all the titles on this list. National societies in other nations, such as Japan and Canada, publish similar journals. European professional physics organizations have combined their efforts to produce the *European Physical Journal*. Despite the fact that many of these journals are published overseas, English has become the dominant language in the field of physics, and virtually every published article is written in English. As commercial publishers have merged over the past two decades, the publication of physics research journals has become concentrated in just a few publishing houses. Elsevier, Academic Press, and Taylor and Francis predominate in the commercial physics journal market.

Because of this extreme volume and specialization, the prices of physics journals are higher than those in almost any other discipline. The least expensive journal costs well over $100 per year, and it is common for subscriptions to cost over $1,000 per year. Subscriptions to some physics journals are upward of $10,000 per year (note that all journals in that price range have been automatically excluded from being recommended in *Magazines for Libraries*). The only certainty with physics journals is that the volume of research and the price of the publications will continue to increase.

Fortunately, electronic communications have changed the way that physics information is exchanged. In addition to the electronic equivalents of print publications, several peer-reviewed electronic physics journals are currently being published. The first such journal was the *New Journal of Physics*, a project of the Institute of Physics and its German equivalent. The *European Physical Journal* (*EPJ*) followed suit by creating the electronic *EPJ Direct*, and the American Institute of Physics started *Physical Review Special Topics*. Each of these journals publishes original research results, and each is distributed on the web without restriction or cost to the user.

Another pricing model for physics journals that is currently being tested is the pay-per-article concept. The *Virtual Journals in Science and Technology* project of the American Institute of Physics uses this scheme. These journals, which cover five different specializations in the field of physics, do not publish original research papers. Instead, they bring together articles on these emerging fields from a wide range of parent journals. Libraries that subscribe to those journals are able to get the articles free. Articles from nonsubscribed journals are available for purchase on an individual basis. Regardless of which pricing mechanism becomes dominant, it is clear that electronic delivery of physics information is the way of the future.

Rather than rely on journals for scholarly communication, physicists have long relied upon preprints, which are essentially drafts of articles that are released prior to publication. For example, the Stanford Linear Accelerator Center indexes and provides electronic access to over 500,000 preprints of articles on high energy physics. These preprints are freely available and include the full text of articles from many of the journals included in this section, as well as many other journals, technical reports, conference papers, and theses. Services such as this have already replaced journals as a means of communicating research results and in the future may replace journals as publication media as well.

Only libraries that support physics research programs should consider purchasing the majority of the titles on this list. Even then, the extremely high costs require librarians to be judicious in their choices. In many cases, it may be more cost effective to order individual articles as requested by readers rather than to subscribe to specific journals. *Physics Today, Physics World,* and the *Industrial Physicist* are the only print physics journals that a public library should even consider buying. Most general readers will get their physics news from general-science magazines rather than from these more specialized titles. Fortunately, the free physics news services on the web—*Physical Review Focus* and *Physics News Preview*—will allow many libraries to offer their patrons access to interesting physics information written for a general audience at little or no cost. The future of the printed physics journal is very much in doubt. As more and more such information becomes available on the web, researchers and students are getting most of their information in that format. If low-cost electronic journals prevail, libraries will be able to continue to build research collections in physics and the rest of the sciences. If journal costs continue to rise, more and more libraries will be unable to provide even basic physics research collections. Fortunately, those libraries that do not support physics research need only to subscribe to one or two of these titles.

Basic Periodicals

Hs: *American Journal of Physics, Physics Education, Physics Teacher, Physics Today;* Ga: *Industrial Physicist, Optics and Photonics News, Physical Review Focus, Physics Today, Physics World;* Ac: *American Journal of Physics, Applied Physics Letters, Industrial Physicist, Journal of Applied Physics, Journal of Physics, Physical Review, Physical Review Letters, Physics Letters, Physics Today.*

Basic Abstracts and Indexes

Physics Abstracts.

5520. ***Acoustical Society of America. Journal.*** [ISSN: 0001-4966] 1929. m. USD 1325 print & online eds. Ed(s): Allan D Pierce. Acoustical Society of America, 2 Huntington Quadrangle, Ste. 1NO1, Mellville, NY 11747-4502. Illus., index, adv. Refereed. Circ: 7800 Paid. Vol. ends: Jun/Dec. Microform: AIP. Online: EBSCO Publishing; RoweCom Information Quest; Swets Blackwell. *Indexed:* AS&TI, AgeL, ApMecR, BiolAb, CPI, ChemAb, DSR&OA, EngInd, EnvAb, ErgAb, ExcerpMed, GeoRef, GeogAbPG, IAA, IndMed, L&LBA, LingAb, M&GPA, MLA-IB, OceAb, PetrolAb, PsycholAb, SCI, SSCI, ZooRec. *Aud.:* Ac, Sa.

As the primary official publication of the Acoustical Society of America, this journal is the premier outlet for the publication of research in the areas of sound waves, sound transmission, and acoustical phenomena. Topics include linear and nonlinear acoustics, aeroacoustics, atmospheric sound, underwater sound, ultrasonics, quantum acoustics, transduction, structural acoustics, vibration, noise control, instrumentation, physiological acoustics, psychological acoustics, speech, communications systems, and bioacoustics. Theoretical, experimental, and applied results are all included, along with comments on previously published articles and letters to the editor. Updates on patents, standards, and news of the association are also provided. A unique feature of this journal is its "Tutorial Review" section, which serves as a means of teaching members about new findings in the field. In order to keep members aware of other research in the field, the journal also publishes a bibliography of world literature on acoustics. Downloaded from the INSPEC, Medline, and NTIS databases, *References to Contemporary Papers on Acoustics* is issued as a service to researchers in the field. The *Acoustics Research Letters Online* serves as an electronic letters section of this journal. As the most comprehensive journal in the world on this branch of physics, the *Journal of the Acoustical Society of America* belongs in every physics collection.

5521. ***Advances in Physics.*** [ISSN: 0001-8732] 1952. 8x/yr. GBP 1772. Ed(s): David Sherrington. Taylor & Francis Ltd, 11 New Fetter Ln, London, EC4P 4EE, United Kingdom; info@tandf.co.uk. Illus., adv. Sample. Refereed. Circ: 1200. Vol. ends: Nov/Dec. Online: EBSCO Publishing; Ingenta Select; OCLC Online Computer Library Center, Inc.; RoweCom Information Quest; Swets Blackwell. Reprint: PSC. *Indexed:* C&ISA, ChemAb, EngInd, GeoRef, IndMed, SCI. *Aud.:* Ac, Sa.

Advances in Physics has narrowed its scope to publish state-of-the-art reviews solely in the area of condensed-matter physics. These reviews present the current state of human knowledge within this highly specialized subfield of physics and serve as benchmarks in our knowledge of the physical universe. Because of the comprehensiveness of the research, most papers in this journal are very long, often over 100 pages each. Many issues consist of a single article that essentially serves as a monograph on the topic under consideration. One of the key features of each article is its bibliography, which lists all the important past research on the topic under consideration. A new section has been added that publishes shorter but provocative articles written by leaders in the field. These articles, called "Perspectives," are intended to be controversial and to promote debate. *Annals of Physics, Contemporary Physics,* and *Reports on Progress in Physics* (all below in this section) also publish review articles, but these journals are all aimed at the nonspecialist. *Advances in Physics* is written for the specialized researcher or student of condensed matter and will only be of marginal value to the nonspecialist or to scientists working in other disciplines.

5522. ***American Journal of Physics.*** Formerly (until 1940): *American Physics Teacher.* [ISSN: 0002-9505] 1933. m. USD 480 combined subscription domestic print & online eds.; USD 500 combined subscription in Canada, Mexico, Central and South America and Caribbean for print and online eds.; USD 533 combined subscription in Europe, Asia, Middle East, Africa and Oceania for print & online eds. Ed(s): Jan Tobochnik. American Association of Physics Teachers, Communications Dept., One Physics Ellipse, College Park, MD 20740-3845; aapt-pubs@aapt.org; http://www.aapt.org. Illus., index, adv. Sample. Refereed. Circ: 7000. Vol. ends: Dec. Microform: AIP. Online: EBSCO Publishing; Gale Group; RoweCom Information Quest; Swets Blackwell. *Indexed:* AS&TI, ArtHuCI, CCMJ, CIJE, CPI, ChemAb, DSR&OA, EngInd, GSI, MathSciNet, SCI, SSCI. *Bk. rev.:* various number and length. *Aud.:* Hs, Ac, Ga.

While most physics journals serve solely as archives of original research results, the *American Journal of Physics* exists to help teachers do a better job of teaching about physics. As the official journal of the American Association of Physics Teachers, this title is devoted to the instructional and cultural aspects of the physical sciences. Rather than concentrating on new research results, this journal focuses on methods of teaching physics to students at the college level. It consists of articles on applying educational theories to physics teaching, using innovative methodologies to demonstrate physical properties, using demonstrations and experiments to convey physics principles, and introducing new apparatus and equipment. Papers on the historical, philosophical, and cultural nature of physics are also included. The journal contains—in addition to full papers—letters, notes, book reviews, and editorials. A highly useful section for teachers is "Questions and Answers," in which problems are presented in one issue and readers are invited to send in solutions to be published in future issues. Taking advantage of new technology while keeping publication costs down, color images that accompany articles are published on the web site. While high copyright fees are charged by most physics journals, in this journal readers are encouraged to copy the articles and ideas and use them in the classroom. Subscribers also receive *Physics Education Research*, an irregular supplement to the *American Journal of Physics*, which provides a publication outlet for research results on the scientific investigation of teaching and learning in physics. All libraries supporting college physics courses should subscribe to this title.

5523. ***Annalen der Physik.*** [ISSN: 0003-3804] 1790. m. EUR 614. Ed(s): U Eckern. Wiley - V C H Verlag GmbH, Boschstrasse 12, Weinheim, 69469, Germany; subservice@wiley-vch.de; http://www.wiley-vch.de. Illus., index, adv. Sample. Refereed. *Indexed:* CCMJ, ChemAb, EngInd, GeoRef, MathSciNet, SCI. *Aud.:* Ac, Sa.

As the oldest continuously published German physics journal, *Annalen der Physik* occupies a historic place in the physics literature. The journal publishes original papers in the areas of experimental, theoretical, applied, and mathematical physics, and related areas. Throughout its long history, it has published some of the most important papers in the field, including Einstein's original papers on relativity. Unlike many other long-standing journals, this title continues to cover the entire field of physics rather than specializing in a particular subdiscipline. In addition to original research papers, the journal also includes review articles, conference proceedings, and even some selected dissertations. Even though it is a German journal, the vast majority of papers are published in English. Although it has been surpassed in prestige by several other prominent physics journals, such as *Journal of Physics* and the *Physical Review* (see below), *Annalen der Physik* is still an important component of any comprehensive physics collection.

5524. ***Annals of Physics.*** [ISSN: 0003-4916] 1957. 12x/yr. USD 5462 (Individuals, EUR 1992). Ed(s): Frank Wilczek. Academic Press, 525 B St, Ste 1900, San Diego, CA 92101-4495; apsubs@acad.com; http://www.academicpress.com. Illus., index, adv. Sample. Refereed. Online: EBSCO Publishing; ingenta.com; OCLC Online Computer Library Center, Inc.; RoweCom Information Quest; ScienceDirect; Swets Blackwell. *Indexed:* CCMJ, ChemAb, DSR&OA, EngInd, IAA, MathSciNet, SCI. *Aud.:* Ac, Sa.

Unlike most physics research journals, which publish brief reports of original research aimed at the specialist in the field, *Annals of Physics* provides a medium for the publication of original research of wider significance that is of interest to the broader scientific community. Although it is impossible for every paper to be readily understood by every reader, the goal of *Annals of Physics* is to provide sufficient background information and explanation that a reader who has worked in the field within the past several years will be able to follow the arguments and understand the conclusions. The editors emphasize clarity and intelligibility in their selection of articles, and they see this title as serving the needs of readers who are interested in following developments throughout the wide array of subspecializations that comprise the field of physics. The journal publishes papers on any physics topic, including theory, methodology, and applications. Because of the need for extensive background material, the articles in this journal are very long, often more than 50 pages. *Contemporary Physics, Reports on Progress in Physics,* and *Reviews of Modern Physics* (all below in this section) all serve the same general purpose as *Annals of Physics,* and each is useful for a college-level physics collection.

5525. ***Applied Optics.*** [ISSN: 0003-6935] 1962. 3x/m. USD 2437 domestic; USD 2554 in Canada, Mexico, Central and South America & Caribbean; USD 2713 in Europe, Asia, Middle East, Africa & Oceania. Ed(s): Glenn Boreman. Optical Society of America, Inc., 2010 Massachusetts Ave, N W, Washington, DC 20036-1023; info@osa.org; http://www.osa.org. Illus., index, adv. Refereed. Circ: 4000. Microform: AIP. *Indexed:* AS&TI, BPI, BioEngAb, C&ISA, ChemAb, DSR&OA, EngInd, ExcerpMed, GeoRef, GeogAbPG, M&GPA, OceAb, PhotoAb, SCI, SSCI, SWRA. *Aud.:* Ac, Sa.

Along with the *Journal of the Optical Society of America* and *Optics Letters* (see below), *Applied Optics* is one of the official journals of the Optical Society of America. While the other two titles publish reports of original research, this journal concentrates on the applications of optical principles and methods. It is published in three sections, each representing one division of the society. Monthly issues rotate subject coverage through the sections, with each part appearing four times per year. The first section covers information processing, including optical communications, data storage, optical computing, pattern recognition, and signal processing. The second section covers optical technology and biomedical optics, including instrumentation, microscopy, fiber optic sensors, interferometry, and biomedical optics. The third section focuses on lasers, photonics, and environmental optics, covering such topics as remote sensing, atmospheric optics, lasers, and scattering. In addition to full-length papers, the journal provides a calendar of events of interest to members and occasional notes on equipment and methodologies. This is one of the core journals in the field of optics, and it belongs in any physics or engineering research collection.

5526. ***Applied Physics. A: Materials Science & Processing.*** Former titles: *Applied Physics A: Solids and Surfaces;* Supersedes in part (in 1981): *Applied Physics;* Which superseded: *Zeitschrift fuer Angewandte Physik.* [ISSN: 0947-8396] 1973. 14x/yr. EUR 2640 domestic; EUR 2688.20 foreign; EUR 227 newsstand/cover per issue. Ed(s): M Stuke. Springer-Verlag, Tiergartenstr 17, Heidelberg, 69121, Germany. Illus., adv. Refereed. Microform: PQC. Online: EBSCO Publishing; RoweCom Information Quest; ScienceDirect; Springer LINK; Swets Blackwell. Reprint: ISI. *Indexed:* ChemAb, EngInd, IAA, PhotoAb, SCI. *Aud.:* Ac, Sa.

Applied Physics is a monthly journal for the rapid publication of experimental and theoretical investigations in applied research. It is issued in two sections. *Part A* primarily covers the condensed state, including nanostructured materials and their applications. It publishes full-length articles and short, rapid communications. Many of the issues are devoted to a papers on a single topic, often presenting the proceedings of relevant conferences or Festschriften. This journal is published in cooperation with the German Physical Society and was originally published under its German title, *Zeitschrift fuer Angewandte Physik.* Much of the research reported in this title is still conducted in German universities and research centers. However, following the movement toward English as the international language of science, all of the papers accepted are published in English.

Part B (0721-7269) covers lasers and optics, including laser physics, linear and nonlinear optics, ultrafast phenomena, photonic devices, optical and laser materials, quantum optics, laser spectroscopy of atoms, molecules and clusters, and the use of laser radiation in chemistry and biochemistry. Both parts of this journal participate in the Springer *Online First* publication scheme, where articles appear online before the paper issue is distributed. For libraries seeking a comprehensive physics collection, this journal will serve as a European complement to the *Journal of Applied Physics* (below).

5527. ***Applied Physics Letters.*** [ISSN: 0003-6951] 1962. w. USD 2450 print and online eds. Ed(s): Nghi Q Lam. American Institute of Physics, 2 Huntington Quadrangle, Ste 1NO1, Melville, NY 11747-4502; info@aip.org; http://www.aip.org. Illus., index, adv. Refereed. Microform: Pub. Online: EBSCO Publishing; RoweCom Information Quest; Swets Blackwell. *Indexed:* AS&TI, CPI, ChemAb, EngInd, GeoRef, PhotoAb, SCI. *Aud.:* Ac, Sa.

This title serves as the letters section of the *Journal of Applied Physics* (below in this section). As such, it provides for the rapid dissemination of key data and physical insights, including new experimental and theoretical findings on the applications of physics to all branches of science, engineering, and technology. This journal emphasizes developments in rapidly evolving fields, such as nanotechnology, semiconductor lasers, magnetic devices, and applied biophysics. Because all of the papers accepted are letters, they are extremely brief, with none longer than two printed pages. In addition to original research results, each issue also includes comments on previously published material. This can result in lively debate over the accuracy and interpretation of experimental results. Along with the accompanying *Journal of Applied Physics,* this title is the most heavily cited journal in the field. It is one of the core journals for physics and belongs in any physics research collection.

Biophysical Journal. See Biological Sciences/Biochemistry and Biophysics section.

5528. ***Canadian Journal of Physics.*** [ISSN: 0008-4204] 1929. m. CND 420 (Individuals, CND 128). Ed(s): Gordon Drake. N R C Research Press, Building M 55, Ottawa, ON K1A 0R6, Canada; http://www.nrc.ca/cisti/journals/. Illus., index, adv. Refereed. Circ: 777. Vol. ends: Dec. Microform: MML; PMC; PQC. Online: CISTI; EBSCO Publishing; ingenta.com; RoweCom Information Quest; Swets Blackwell. Reprint: PQC. *Indexed:* AS&TI, BiolAb, C&ISA, CBCARef, ChemAb, DSA, DSR&OA, EngInd, GeoRef, IAA, PetrolAb, PhotoAb, SCI, SSCI. *Aud.:* Ac, Sa.

As an official publication of the National Research Council of Canada, the *Canadian Journal of Physics* is the premier physics publication emanating from that nation. It covers all branches of physics, including mathematical physics, particle physics, nuclear physics, atomic and molecular physics, electromagnetism, optics, gases, fluid dynamics, plasmas, condensed matter, and space physics. Most of the articles are published in English, although French-language articles are also accepted. The majority of articles are full research reports, although shorter rapid communications and research notes are also accepted. The journal also publishes review articles and tutorials that bring together and explain previously published research results. Some issues consist entirely of proceedings of physics conferences. Although this journal is an official publication of the Canadian government, it is not restricted to Canadian authors, and it attracts research reports from around the world. For papers that have extensive data or mathematical analysis that are too long to include in a published article, the National Research Council maintains a depository to which subscribers have access. This is the major Canadian journal in physics and should be part of any comprehensive physics research collection.

5529. ***Communications in Mathematical Physics.*** [ISSN: 0010-3616] 1965. 27x/yr. EUR 3990 domestic; EUR 4088.10 foreign; EUR 178 newsstand/cover per issue. Ed(s): A Jaffe. Springer-Verlag, Tiergartenstr 17, Heidelberg, 69121, Germany. Illus., index, adv. Sample. Refereed. Microform: PQC. Online: EBSCO Publishing; RoweCom Information Quest; ScienceDirect; Springer LINK; Swets Blackwell. Reprint: ISI. *Indexed:* CCMJ, MathSciNet, SCI. *Aud.:* Ac, Sa.

The field of physics relies heavily on high-level mathematics as a tool for developing new theories and in explaining experimental results. Whether attempting to explain the nature of fundamental particles, exploring the heavens, or defining the motion of an apple, physicists always attempt to explain natural phenomena as mathematical functions. *Communications in Mathematical Physics* was developed in order to present physicists with a source for learning new mathematical techniques and presenting new research findings. It also attempts to generate among mathematicians an increased awareness and appreciation for the current problems in physics. All branches of physics are covered, although particular emphasis is placed on statistical physics, quantum theory, dynamical systems, atomic physics, relativity, and disordered systems. The common thread among all of the papers is the strong mathematical approach to the problem. This journal complements the *Journal of Mathematical Physics* (see below) and belongs in comprehensive physics collections.

5530. ***Computer Physics Communications: an international journal and program library for computational physics and computer programs in physics.*** [ISSN: 0010-4655] 1969. 29x/yr. EUR 4966 (Individuals, EUR 1655). Elsevier BV, North-Holland, Sara Burgerhartstraat 25, Amsterdam, 1055 KV, Netherlands; nlinfo-f@elsevier.nl; http://www.elsevier.nl/homepage/about/us/regional_sites.htt. Illus., index, adv. Sample. Refereed. Online: ingenta.com; ScienceDirect. Reprint: SWZ. *Indexed:* C&ISA, CCMJ, ChemAb, CompR, EngInd, GeoRef, MathSciNet, SCI. *Aud.:* Ac, Sa.

Computer Physics Communications is an international interdisciplinary journal dealing with the applications of computing to physics and physical chemistry. The journal publishes articles on research that use computational techniques to solve physical problems, as well as papers that discuss computational analysis and methods. In addition, subscribers have access to a web site containing a program library of actual computer software that may be used for these purposes. This arrangement eliminates many of the problems of publishing actual program code. Most of the older programs in the library were written in FORTRAN for mainframe systems, while newer entries tend to be PC-based and run under Windows, UNIX, or Linux. Some are available in other scientific programming languages, including Maple and Mathematica. With the program library, researchers are able to duplicate or modify experiments that would be otherwise difficult to conduct. Each issue of the journal is evenly divided between articles and program descriptions. This journal is unique in providing not only original research articles, but also the research tools used in compiling the information.

5531. ***Contemporary Physics.*** [ISSN: 0010-7514] 1959. bi-m. GBP 436 (Individuals, GBP 140). Ed(s): P L Knight. Taylor & Francis Ltd, 11 New Fetter Ln, London, EC4P 4EE, United Kingdom; info@tandf.co.uk; http://www.tandf.co.uk/journals. Illus., index, adv. Refereed. Vol. ends: Nov/Dec. Microform: MIM; PMC. Online: EBSCO Publishing; Gale Group; Ingenta Select; OCLC Online Computer Library Center, Inc.; RoweCom Information Quest; Swets Blackwell. Reprint: PSC. *Indexed:* ChemAb, EngInd, ExcerpMed, GSI, GeoRef, IAA, PhotoAb, SCI. *Aud.:* Ac, Sa.

Contemporary Physics is a review journal, similar to *Advances in Physics* (see above), *Physics Reports,* and *Reports on Progress in Physics* (see below). Whereas the other journals are written primarily for physicists, the audience of *Contemporary Physics* is the general scientist. Articles appearing in this journal have more background material and are more accessible to a wide audience, although a strong scientific background is still required. The journal attempts to explain the essential physical concepts of each topic and to relate those concepts to more familiar aspects of physics. Because of this emphasis, students and scientists in other scientific disciplines can use this journal to learn about important developments in the field of physics. In addition to the review articles, the journal publishes numerous reviews of physics books that are of interest to a wider audience. *Contemporary Physics* is the most readable of all of the physics review journals and belongs in any college physics collection.

5532. ***Critical Reviews in Solid State & Materials Sciences.*** Former titles: *C R C Critical Reviews in Solid State and Materials Sciences; C R C Critical Reviews in Solid State Sciences.* [ISSN: 1040-8436] 1970. q. USD 575 (Individuals, USD 110 print & online eds.). Ed(s): Paul Holloway. C R C Press, Llc, 2000 Corporate Blvd, N W, Boca Raton, FL 33431-9868; journals@crcpress.com; http://www.crcpress.com. Illus., index. Refereed. Circ: 570. *Indexed:* BiolAb, C&ISA, ChemAb, EngInd, SCI. *Aud.:* Ac, Sa.

Like all journals in the "Critical Reviews" series, this journal publishes only invited papers on topics related to materials science and the solid state. Subjects covered are highly specialized subfields of physics, including molecular physics, crystals, films, defects, microelectronics, and alloys. Each issue usually contains a single article, often hundreds of pages in length, that provides a comprehensive survey of the topic being discussed. These state-of-the-art reviews serve as benchmarks in the progress of solid-state physics and materials research. Each article contains an extensive bibliography of other research in the field. Although other journals also publish review articles, *Critical Reviews in Solid State & Materials Sciences* is unique in that it evaluates as well as compiles. Authors of papers in this journal are expected to give their expert opinions on the value of previously published research results, guiding the reader to those that will have the greatest relevance and impact. This title is essential for any collection supporting research in materials science or the solid state. Libraries should also consider other titles in CRC Press's *Critical Reviews* series if those titles support the research interests of the library.

5533. ***Cryogenics: the international journal of low temperature engineering & research.*** [ISSN: 0011-2275] 1960. m. EUR 1939. Ed(s): S W Van Sciver, L. Bottura. Pergamon, The Boulevard, Langford Ln, East Park, Kidlington, OX5 1GB, United Kingdom. Illus., index, adv. Sample. Refereed. Vol. ends: Dec (No. 41). Microform: PQC. Online: ingenta.com; ScienceDirect; Swets Blackwell. *Indexed:* AS&TI, ApMecR, BioEngAb, BiolAb, BrTechI, C&ISA, CEA, ChemAb, EngInd, SCI. *Bk. rev.:* various number and length. *Aud.:* Ac, Sa.

Cryogenics is the world's leading journal focusing on all aspects of cryoengineering and cryogenics. Papers published in *Cryogenics* cover a wide variety of subjects in low-temperature engineering and research. Topics covered include low-temperature engineering, measurement science, superconductors, properties of materials, heat transfer, low-temperature electronics, and low-temperature physics. The majority of the publication consists of full-length research papers, although some shorter research notes and technical notes are also included. Conference reports and review articles are published on an occasional basis, in addition to book reviews, news features, and a calendar of events relevant to the field. As the premier journal for low-temperature studies, this journal belongs in any physics or engineering collection supporting research in this field.

5534. ***European Journal of Physics.*** [ISSN: 0143-0807] 1980. bi-m. USD 790 print & online. Ed(s): A I M Rae. Institute of Physics Publishing, Dirac House, Temple Back, Bristol, BS1 6BE, United Kingdom; custserv@iop.org; http://www.iop.org/. Illus., index, adv. Sample.

Refereed. Vol. ends: Nov. Microform: AIP. Online: EBSCO Publishing; ingenta.com; RoweCom Information Quest; ScienceDirect; Swets Blackwell. *Indexed:* CCMJ, ChemAb, EngInd, MathSciNet. *Aud.:* Ga, Ac, Sa.

As "the European voice of physics teachers in university-level education," The *European Journal of Physics* publishes articles of relevance to physics students and faculty. It contains articles on such topics as reflections on the fundamentals of physics education; pedagogical studies on specific topics within physics and physics teaching; educational policies in physics and their implementation; cultural, historical, social, and technological implications of physics; and the interrelationships between physics and other disciplines. Because the papers are intended to aid in the teaching of the subject rather than to present original research results, the editors encourage authors to avoid high-level mathematics, thus making the papers more accessible to a general audience. Articles are accepted in English, French, and German, with English predominating. Full papers and letters are accepted, along with comments on previously published works. Occasional special issues follow specific themes. This title is the European equivalent of the *American Journal of Physics* (above) and is a useful supplement to a college or university physics collection.

5535. *European Physical Journal A. Hadrons and Nuclei.* Incorporates in part (1903-2000): *Anales de Fisica;* (1855-1999): *Societa Italiana di Fisica. Nuovo Cimento A;* Which was formerly (until 1971): *Nuovo Cimento A;* Former titles (until 1997): *Zeitschrift fuer Physik A. Hadrons and Nuclei;* (until 1991): *Zeitschrift fuer Physik. Section A. Atomic Nuclei;* (until 1986): *Zeitschrift fuer Physik. Section A: Atoms and Nuclei; Zeitschrift fuer Physik.* [ISSN: 1434-6001] 1920. m. EUR 2268 domestic; EUR 2316.20 foreign; EUR 227 newsstand/cover per issue. Ed(s): T Walcher, R A Ricci. Springer-Verlag, Tiergartenstr 17, Heidelberg, 69121, Germany. Illus., adv. Refereed. Microform: PMC; PQC. Online: EBSCO Publishing; RoweCom Information Quest; Springer LINK; Swets Blackwell. Reprint: ISI. *Indexed:* ChemAb, SCI. *Aud.:* Ac, Sa.

In 1998, the German, French, and Italian Physical Societies decided to merge their journals into a single publication. The *European Physical Journal* in all six of its parts is the result of that merger. The Spanish and Portuguese physics journals are now also included in this new title, giving even greater credibility to The *European Journal of Physics* as a voice for physics researchers on the continent. *Part A* of this new endeavor directly replaces the *Zeitschrift fuer Physik A* and *Il Nuovo Cimento A*. It covers the specialized subfield of high-energy physics relating to hadrons and nuclei, including nuclear structure, nuclear reactions, heavy-ion physics, weak interactions, and related interdisiplinary topics. Both full-length research papers and short research notes are included. Although this is a European journal, all of the articles are in English. All five sections of The *European Physical Journal* are supplemented by an online, peer-reviewed electronic journal titled *EPJdirect*. The *European Physical Journal* is now the premier physics journal published on the continent, and it belongs in all physics research collections.

5536. *European Physical Journal B. Condensed Matter.* Incorporates in part (1903-2000): *Anales de Fisica;* Formed by the merger of (1991-1998): *Journal de Physique I;* (1980-1998): *Zeitschrift fuer Physik B: Condensed Matter;* Which was formerly (until 1975): *Zeitschrift fuer Physik B (Condensed Matter and Quanta);* (1963-1973): *Physik der Kondensierten Materie - Physique de la Matiere Condensee - Physics of Condensed Matter;* Supersedes in part (1982-1999): *Societa Italiana di Fisica. Nuovo Cimento D;* Which incorporated in part (1855-1965): *Nuovo Cimento; Miscellanee de Chimica, Fisica e Storia Naturale;* Which superseded in part (in 1843): *Giornale Toscano di Scienze Mediche Fisiche e Naturali;* (until 1840): *Nuovo Giornale dei Letterati;* Which superseded (in 1822): *Accademia Italiana di Scienze Lettere ed Arti. Giornale Scientifico e Letterario;* (until 1809): *Giornale Pisano di Letteratura, Scienze ed Arti;* (until 1807): *Giornale Pisano dei Letterati;* (1802-1806): *Nuovo Giornale dei Letterati;* Which superseded (1771-1796): *Giornale dei Letterati.* [ISSN: 1434-6028] 1998. s-m. EUR 3336 domestic; EUR 3432.60 foreign; EUR 167 newsstand/cover per issue. Ed(s): S Grossman, A Paoletti. Springer-Verlag, Tiergartenstr 17, Heidelberg, 69121, Germany. Illus., index, adv. Refereed. Microform: PMC; PQC. Online: EBSCO Publishing; RoweCom Information Quest; Springer LINK; Swets Blackwell. Reprint: ISI. *Indexed:* CCMJ, ChemAb, EngInd, GeoRef, MathSciNet, SCI. *Aud.:* Ac, Sa.

As a part of the project to reorganize journals published by the various European nations, The *European Physical Journal* was created. *Part B* takes the place of five former titles: *Il Nuovo Cimento D, Journal de Physique I & II, Zeitschrift fuer Physik B, Anales de Fisica,* and *Portugaliae Physica*. This title concentrates on solid-state physics and covers such topics as solid- and condensed-state physics, quantum solids and liquids, mesoscopic physics, surfaces and interfaces, nonlinear physics, and statistical physics. Although the main focus is on the solid state, this section also contains articles on statistical physics and interdisciplinary topics. The majority of the articles are full-length research reports, although some rapid notes of important findings are also published. All of the articles are published in English. In order to speed publication, this section participates in a new electronic service called *Online First*. With this service, subscribers are allowed to read articles online prior to publication of the print edition. Like all other sections of The *European Physical Journal,* this title participates in the electronic publication program called *EPJdirect*. With the combined coverage of five former journals, this title has become one of the major sources in the field. It belongs in comprehensive physics collections.

5537. *European Physical Journal C. Particles and Fields.* Incorporates in part (1903-2000): *Anales de Fisica;* (1855-1999): *Societa Italiana di Fisica. Nuovo Cimento A;* Which was formerly (until 1971): *Nuovo Cimento A;* Former titles (until 1997): *Zeitschrift fuer Physik C: Particles and Fields; Zeitschrift fuer Physik. Section C: Particles and Fields.* [ISSN: 1434-6044] 1979. 24x/yr. EUR 5250 domestic; EUR 5346.30 foreign; EUR 263 newsstand/cover per issue. Ed(s): D Haidt, D Bartels. Springer-Verlag, Tiergartenstr 17, Heidelberg, 69121, Germany. Illus., index, adv. Sample. Refereed. Microform: PMC; PQC. Online: EBSCO Publishing; RoweCom Information Quest; Springer LINK; Swets Blackwell. Reprint: ISI. *Indexed:* CCMJ, ChemAb, MathSciNet, SCI. *Aud.:* Ac, Sa.

As another section of the reorganized physics journals published in Europe, *Section C* of The *European Physical Journal* covers high-energy physics, including both theoretical and experimental research. The journal specializes in reporting research results from the world's leading laboratories, including CERN, Fermilab, and KEK. Topics covered include scattering, high-energy reactions, electroweak interactions, quantum chromodynamics, astroparticle physics, and quantum field theory. This section of the journal is the continuation of *Il Nuovo Cimento A* and *Zeitshcrift fuer Physik C.* Both full-length articles and rapid notes are included. Occasional issues contain the proceedings of relevant conferences. Although this is a European journal, all of the articles are published in Engligh. This section also participates in the *EPJdirect* and *Online First* electronic-publishing projects. This is the premier journal for European research in particle physics, and it belongs in comprehensive physics collections.

5538. *European Physical Journal D. Atoms, Molecules, Clusters and Optical Physics.* Incorporates in part (1903-2000): *Anales de Fisica;* Formed by the merger of (1991-1998): *Journal de Physique II;* (1986-1998): *Zeitschrift fuer Physik D;* Supersedes in part (1982-1999): *Societa Italiana di Fisica. Nuovo Cimento D;* Which incorporated in part (1855-1965): *Nuovo Cimento;* Which superseded (1843-1847): *Cimento; Miscellanee de Chimica, Fisica e Storia Naturale;* Which superseded in part (in 1843): *Giornale Toscano di Scienze Mediche Fisiche e Naturali;* (until 1840): *Nuovo Giornale dei Letterati;* Which superseded (in 1822): *Accademia Italiana di Scienze Lettere ed Arti. Giornale Scientifico e Letterario;* (until 1809): *Giornale Pisano di Letteratura, Scienze ed Arti;* (until 1807): *Giornale Pisano dei Letterati;* (1802-1806): *Nuovo Giornale dei Letterati;* Which superseded (1771-1796): *Giornale dei Letterati.* [ISSN: 1434-6060] 1998. 15x/yr. EUR 1752 domestic; EUR 1812.30 foreign; EUR 141 newsstand/cover per issue. Ed(s): G Grynberg, I V Hertel. Springer-Verlag, Tiergartenstr 17, Heidelberg, 69121, Germany. Illus., index, adv. Refereed. Circ: 700. Online: EBSCO Publishing; RoweCom Information Quest; Springer LINK; Swets Blackwell. *Indexed:* CCMJ, ChemAb, GeoRef, MathSciNet, SCI. *Aud.:* Ac, Sa.

The fourth section of The *European Physical Journal* is devoted to atomic, molecular, cluster, and optical physics. This journal was formed through the combination of three similar journals: *Il Nuovo Cimento D, Journal de Physique,* and *Zeitschrift fuer Physik D.* Topics in this section include atomic and molecular structure, spectroscopy, collisions, chaos theory, cluster dynamics, and quantum optics. Both full-length research reports and brief communications are included. All of the papers are published in English even though they represent the results of European research. This section also participates in the *Online First* and *EPJdirect* electronic-publishing processes. Recommended for comprehensive physics collections.

5539. ***European Physical Journal E. Soft Matter Physics.*** Formed by the merger of part of (1903-2000): *Anales de Fisica;* part of (1998-2000): *European Physical Journal. B. Condensed Matter Physics; Journal de Physique.II; Zeitschrift fuer Physik. B, Condensed Matter; Nuovo Cimento della Societa Italiana di Fisica. Sections A and D.* [ISSN: 1292-8941] 2000. 12x/yr. EUR 1524 domestic; EUR 1572.20 foreign; EUR 153 newsstand/cover per issue. Ed(s): A M Donald, J F Joanny. Springer-Verlag, Haber Str 7, Heidelberg, 69126, Germany. Adv. Sample. Refereed. *Indexed:* EngInd, SCI. *Aud.:* Ac, Sa.

The final section of The *European Physical Journal* covers all of the areas that are left out of Parts A–D. Section E is the successor to *Il Nuovo Cimento D, Journal de Physique,* and *Zeitschrift fuer Physik B.* It includes a mixture of papers on biological sciences, materials science, liquid crystals, supermolecules, surfaces, and interfaces. Like each of the other sections of this journal, all of the articles are published in English. Most articles are full research papers, but some short communications are also included. Like the other sections of *European Physical Journal,* section E also participates in *EPJdirect,* the online rapid-communication service of the European Physical Society. It also is involved with the *Online First* service, where subscribers can obtain online copies of papers prior to print publication. This journal is recommended only for comprehensive physics collections.

5540. ***Foundations of Physics: an international journal devoted to the conceptual and fundamental theories of modern physics, biophysics, and cosmology.*** [ISSN: 0015-9018] 1970. m. USD 1804 print or online ed. Ed(s): Alwyn van der Merwe. Kluwer Academic / Plenum Publishers, 233 Spring St Fl 7, New York, NY 10013-1522; http://www.wkap.nl/. Illus., index, adv. Refereed. Vol. ends: Dec. Microform: PQC. Online: EBSCO Publishing; ingenta.com; Kluwer Online; OCLC Online Computer Library Center, Inc.; Ovid Technologies, Inc.; RoweCom Information Quest; Swets Blackwell. *Indexed:* CCMJ, EngInd, MathSciNet, SCI. *Bk. rev.:* various number and length. *Aud.:* Ac, Sa.

One of the major objectives of modern physics research is to develop a single unified theory that can explain all physical properties, effects, and interactions. Ever since Einstein proposed that researchers work toward a single theory of the universe, various scientists have approached this problem from a number of angles. *Foundations of Physics* serves as an outlet for the publication of research in this specific area of the field of physics. Much of the material covers cosmology, quantum mechanics, wave theory, gravitation, general relativity, and gauge theory. Articles tend to be speculative in nature and often question existing theoretical concepts. This journal is somewhat unusual in the field of physics in that it stresses theory rather than experimental results. Only full-length papers are accepted. Letters are published in a sister journal, *Foundations of Physics Letters.* Because of its focus on one of the single most important questions in physics today, this title is a useful addition to comprehensive collections in theoretical physics.

5541. ***General Relativity and Gravitation.*** [ISSN: 0001-7701] 1970. m. USD 1499 print or online ed. Ed(s): Hans-Juergen Schmidt. Kluwer Academic / Plenum Publishers, 233 Spring St Fl 7, New York, NY 10013-1522; http://www.wkap.nl/. Illus., index, adv. Refereed. Vol. ends: Dec. Microform: PQC. Online: EBSCO Publishing; ingenta.com; Kluwer Online; OCLC Online Computer Library Center, Inc.; RoweCom Information Quest; Swets Blackwell. *Indexed:* CCMJ, EngInd, IAA, MathSciNet, SCI. *Bk. rev.:* various number and length. *Aud.:* Ac, Sa.

Einstein spent much of his professional life working on the theories of gravity and relativity. This journal was developed to continue that research. Although it primarily publishes research papers on the theoretical and experimental aspects of these two areas, it also includes letters, review articles, book reviews, conference programs, and news items. Most of the articles are of a highly theoretical nature, which is inherent to the subject matter. As the official publication of the International Committee on General Relativity and Gravitation, this journal serves as the premier source for research on and discussion of the two topics in its title. It was founded by some of the most prominent researchers in twentieth-century physics, and it maintains those high standards today. *General Relativity and Gravitation* is an important title in any comprehensive collection on theoretical physics.

5542. ***The Industrial Physicist.*** [ISSN: 1082-1848] 1995. bi-m. USD 159 domestic; USD 189 elsewhere. Ed(s): Kenneth J McNaughton. American Institute of Physics, 2 Huntington Quadrangle, Ste 1NO1, Melville, NY 11747-4502; http://www.aip.org/journal_catalog/. Illus., index, adv. Refereed. Circ: 60000. Vol. ends: Dec. Microform: Pub. Online: EBSCO Publishing. *Indexed:* C&ISA, CPI, ChemAb, EngInd, MicrocompInd. *Bk. rev.:* various number and length. *Aud.:* Ga, Ac, Sa.

The audience of most physics journals has traditionally consisted of researchers, teachers, and students. While these groups are all very important in the development of the field of physics, most practicing physicists actually work for companies involved with research and development. In order to meet the needs of this large segment of the physics community, the American Institute of Physics created a new publication for this specific audience: *The Industrial Physicist.* This journal publishes information directly relevant to physicists in the workplace, including news, equipment trends, new products, international marketing, career advancement, workplace relations, and salary surveys. Articles published cover the entire range of the discipline of physics, including semiconductors, optics, robotics, computing, superconductivity, and electronics. Articles included in this journal do not report results of original research, but provide reviews and news of advances in the industry. The glossy format and high readability will interest engineers and scientists working in a wide range of disciplines, as well as physics students. The journal is also available online at http://www.tipmagazine.com. Some articles in the web version use multimedia applications to enhance their value. With its low price, wide interest, and quality production, this title is recommended for all physics and engineering collections.

5543. ***International Journal of Theoretical Physics.*** [ISSN: 0020-7748] 1968. m. USD 1617 print or online ed. Ed(s): David Finkelstein. Kluwer Academic / Plenum Publishers, 233 Spring St Fl 7, New York, NY 10013-1522; http://www.wkap.nl/. Illus., index, adv. Sample. Refereed. Vol. ends: Dec. Microform: PQC. Online: EBSCO Publishing; ingenta.com; Kluwer Online; OCLC Online Computer Library Center, Inc.; Ovid Technologies, Inc.; RoweCom Information Quest; Swets Blackwell. *Indexed:* ArtHuCI, CCMJ, ChemAb, EngInd, MathSciNet, SCI. *Aud.:* Ac, Sa.

One of the major goals of modern physics is to develop a grand unification theory that links all known physical forces. Dedicated to the unification of the latest physics research, The *International Journal of Theoretical Physics* seeks to map the direction of future research arising from new analytical methods, including the latest progress in the use of computers, and to complement traditional physics research by providing fresh inquiry into quantum measurement theory, relativistic field theory, and other similarly fundamental areas. It covers such topics as quantum theory, space-time structure, and quantum communication, cosmology, gravity, space-time, and topology. Only full-length research papers are accepted. Occasional special issues contain the proceedings of conferences related to unification theory. *Foundations of Physics* (see above) serves a similar objective and contains very similar material. With the continuing search for a grand unification theory, both of these journals will remain important for comprehensive physics collections.

5544. ***J E T P Letters.*** [ISSN: 0021-3640] 1965. s-m. USD 2145 print and online eds. Ed(s): Vsevolod F Gantmakher. M A I K Nauka - Interperiodica, Profsoyuznaya ul 90, Moscow, 117997, Russian Federation; compmg@maik.ru; http://www.maik.rssi.ru. Illus., index. Refereed. Online: EBSCO Publishing; RoweCom Information Quest; Swets Blackwell. *Indexed:* ApMecR, CPI, ChemAb, CompLI, EngInd, IAA, SCI. *Aud.:* Ac, Sa.

JETP Letters is the English-language version of the important Russian-language *Pis'ma v Zhurnal Eksperimental'noi i Teoreticheskoi Fiziki.* It is the letters section of The *Journal of Experimental and Theoretical Physics* (see below). It publishes short research papers in all areas of physics, including gravitation, field theory, elementary particles and nuclei, plasma, nonlinear phenomena, condensed matter, superconductivity, superfluidity, lasers, and surfaces. This title is the Russian equivalent of *Physics Letters* and *Physical Review Letters* (see below). *JETP Letters* serves as an indicator of the current state of physics research in Russia and the former Soviet Union. It remains one of the most cited physics journals in the world and belongs in any comprehensive physics collection.

5545. *Japanese Journal of Applied Physics.* [ISSN: 0021-4922] 1962. m. Part 1; s-m. , Part 2. Ed(s): Atsushi Koma, Yoshinobu Aoyagi. Institute of Pure and Applied Physics, Toyokaiji Bldg, no.12, 6-9-6 Shinbashi, Minato-ku, Tokyo, 105-0004, Japan; subscription@ipap.jp; http://www.ipap.jp. Illus., index. Refereed. Circ: 3900. Online: J-Stage. Reprint: PQC. *Indexed:* A&ATA, C&ISA, CerAb, ChemAb, EngInd, GeoRef, IAA, PhotoAb, SCI. *Aud.:* Ac, Sa.

As one of the world powers in the development and application of new technology, Japan is the source of much significant research in physics, technology, and related fields. The *Japanese Journal of Applied Physics* is the primary publication outlet for Japanese research in these subject areas. Subjects covered include semiconductors, superconductors, magnetism, optics, condensed matter, surfaces, films, nuclear science, chemical physics, and instrumentation. The journal is issued in two sections. Part 1 includes full research papers, short notes, and review articles. Occasional issues present the proceedings of conferences of interest to readers. Part 2 is reserved for letters and is published more frequently in order to provide rapid distribution of this information. Although the journal is Japanese, all of the articles are published in English. Articles published since 1993 are now available at no charge on the Internet. Readers and institutions must register with the journal, but no subscription fee is required. Tables of contents and abstracts are in html format, with the full text available in pdf. As one of the major journals covering Japanese research, this title is essential to provide balanced coverage of worldwide physics research.

5546. *Journal of Applied Physics.* [ISSN: 0021-8979] 1931. s-m. USD 3700 print and online eds. Ed(s): Steve J Rothman, James P Viccaro. American Institute of Physics, 2 Huntington Quadrangle, Ste 1NO1, Melville, NY 11747-4502; http://www.aip.org/journal_catalog/. Illus., index, adv. Refereed. Microform: Pub. Online: EBSCO Publishing; Gale Group; RoweCom Information Quest; Swets Blackwell. *Indexed:* AS&TI, ApMecR, CPI, ChemAb, DSR&OA, EngInd, GeoRef, IAA, PetrolAb, PhotoAb, SCI. *Aud.:* Ac, Sa.

The *Journal of Applied Physics* is a primary journal for the publication of significant new research results in the application of physics to modern technology. As opposed to most other physics journals, which concentrate on theoretical or experimental advances, this journal specializes in the application of physical concepts to industrial processes and to other scientific disciplines. Its articles emphasize the understanding of the physics underlying modern technology, but distinguish from technology on the one side and pure physics on the other. Topics include semiconductors, superconductors, metals, alloys, amorphous materials, lasers, optics, electronic devices, magnetic materials, and surfaces and films. The common thread is that the articles describe the uses and applications of a physical concept rather than its theoretical foundations. Full papers and brief communications are included in each issue. Letters are contained in the sister publication *Applied Physics Letters* (see above) and review articles are published in *Applied Physics Reviews* (see above). These three titles comprise the premier journal collection for publication of research on applied physics. As such, they belong in any physics research collection.

5547. *Journal of Chemical Physics.* [ISSN: 0021-9606] 1931. w. USD 5270 print and online eds. Ed(s): J C Light, Donald Levy. American Institute of Physics, 2 Huntington Quadrangle, Ste 1NO1, Melville, NY 11747-4502; http://www.aip.org/journal_catalog/. Illus., index. Refereed. Microform: Pub. Online: EBSCO Publishing; RoweCom Information Quest; Swets Blackwell. *Indexed:* ApMecR, BiolAb, CEA, CPI, ChemAb, EngInd, GeoRef, IAA, PetrolAb, SCI. *Aud.:* Ac, Sa.

The purpose of The *Journal of Chemical Physics* is to bridge the gap between the journals in physics and those in chemistry by publishing quantitative research based on physical principles and techniques as applied to chemical systems. As the boundary between these two disciplines continues to narrow, there is an increasing number of researchers working on issues related to both fields of study. Topics typically covered include spectroscopy, molecular interactions, scattering, photochemistry, quantum chemistry, molecular structure, statistical mechanics, thermodynamics, polymers, and surfaces. Most of this journal consists of full-length research reports, although brief communications, letters, and notes are also published. As the leading journal to focus on the crossover between physics and chemistry, this title belongs in any research collection devoted to either of these two fields.

5548. *Journal of Computational Physics.* [ISSN: 0021-9991] 1966. 18x/yr. EUR 5603 (Individuals, EUR 516). Ed(s): G. Tryggvason. Academic Press, 525 B St, Ste 1900, San Diego, CA 92101-4495; apsubs@acad.com; http://www.academicpress.com. Illus., index, adv. Refereed. Online: EBSCO Publishing; ingenta.com; OCLC Online Computer Library Center, Inc.; RoweCom Information Quest; ScienceDirect; Swets Blackwell. *Indexed:* ApMecR, CCMJ, ChemAb, EngInd, ExcerpMed, GeoRef, IAA, MathSciNet, SCI. *Aud.:* Ac, Sa.

The mission of The *Journal of Computational Physics* is to publish material that will assist in the accurate solution of scientific problems by numerical analysis and computational methods. Most of the papers deal with the development and application of algorithms for the solution of physical problems. The papers do not contain new research findings, but provide scientists with the methodology for conducting and refining the research process using mathematical processes. Papers dealing solely with hardware or software are excluded; each article must discuss the applications of computing to a physical or mathematical problem. Papers that cross disciplinary boundaries are encouraged. Full-length research reports, short notes, and letters to the editor are all accepted. This journal supplements other physics research titles and belongs in comprehensive collections.

5549. *Journal of Experimental and Theoretical Physics.* Formerly: *Soviet Physics - J E T P.* [ISSN: 1063-7761] 1955. m. USD 4254 print and online eds. Ed(s): A F Andreev. M A I K Nauka - Interperiodica, Profsoyuznaya ul 90, Moscow, 117997, Russian Federation; compmg@maik.ru; http://www.maik.rssi.ru. Illus., index. Refereed. Vol. ends: Jun/Dec. Microform: AIP. Online: EBSCO Publishing; RoweCom Information Quest. *Indexed:* ApMecR, CCMJ, CPI, ChemAb, EngInd, MathSciNet, SCI. *Aud.:* Ac, Sa.

The *Journal of Experimental and Theoretical Physics* is an English translation of the Russian-language *Zhurnal Eksperimental'noi i Teoreticheskoi Fiziki,* the most prominent of all Russian physics journals. During the Soviet era, Russian physicists were among the world's leaders in physics research, and this journal served as the primary publication outlet for their findings. Although Russian influence has declined somewhat since 1990, this journal is still an important source for Russian research. Although it is a Russian journal, it accepts papers from researchers anywhere around the world. The journal is published simultaneously in both English and Russian. Only full-length research papers are included. Letters and short communications appear in the sister publication *JETP Letters* (see above). Topics typically covered include nuclear physics, atomic physics, plasmas, and materials science. This journal remains one of the primary Russian physics research journals, and it belongs in any comprehensive physics collection.

5550. *Journal of Magnetism and Magnetic Materials.* [ISSN: 0304-8853] 1976. 45x/yr. EUR 6661. Ed(s): A. J. Freeman, S. D. Bader. Elsevier BV, North-Holland, Sara Burgerhartstraat 25, Amsterdam, 1055 KV, Netherlands; nlinfo-f@elsevier.nl; http://www.elsevier.nl. Illus., index, adv. Sample. Refereed. Circ: 800. Microform: PQC. Online: EBSCO Publishing; ingenta.com; ScienceDirect; Swets Blackwell. Reprint: SWZ. *Indexed:* C&ISA, ChemAb, EngInd, GeoRef, SCI. *Aud.:* Ac, Sa.

As one of the basic forces of physics, magnetism is a property that has been widely studied. The *Journal of Magnetism and Magnetic Materials* provides an important forum for the disclosure and discussion of original contributions covering the whole spectrum of topics, from basic magnetism to the technology and applications of magnetic materials and magnetic recording. Theoretical, experimental, and applied-research papers are all included, and a special section of the journal is devoted to papers on the use of magnetic materials for information storage and retrieval. The journal also publishes letters to the editor, short communications, and occasional review articles. Some issues contain the proceedings of conferences relating to magnetism or magnetic materials. This title is also part of the *Condensed Matter Web*, an Internet collection that brings together articles on condensed matter from a number of different journals. This journal belongs in any library supporting research in this field.

5551. ***Journal of Mathematical Physics.*** [ISSN: 0022-2488] 1960. m. USD 2380 print and online eds. Ed(s): R G Newton. American Institute of Physics, 2 Huntington Quadrangle, Ste 1NO1, Melville, NY 11747-4502; http://www.aip.org/journal_catalog/. Illus., index. Refereed. Vol. ends: Dec. Microform: Pub.; PMC. Online: EBSCO Publishing; RoweCom Information Quest; Swets Blackwell. *Indexed:* CCMJ, CPI, ChemAb, EngInd, IAA, MathSciNet, SCI. *Aud.:* Ac, Sa.

Much of modern physics relies heavily on higher-level mathematics, so much so that some theories are proven entirely with mathematical techniques. The purpose of this journal is to provide a place for the publication of articles dealing with mathematical physics. It covers the applications of mathematics to specific problems in physics, the development of mathematical techniques and research methods, and the application of mathematics to physical theories. Topics include quantum mechanics, classical mechanics, particles and fields, relativity, gravitation, and dynamical systems. An annual special issue provides in-depth analysis of one specific aspect of mathematical physics. The editors request that the mathematics be presented in such a way as to be understandable by a wide audience within the physics community. Even so, most of the articles will require a graduate-level understanding of mathematics and physics in order to completely comprehend the material. This title is an important addition to any graduate physics collection.

5552. ***Journal of Physics A: Mathematical and General.*** Former titles: *Journal of Physics A: Mathematical, Nuclear and General; Journal of Physics; Physical Society. Proceedings.* [ISSN: 0305-4470] 1968. w. USD 6340 print & online. Ed(s): E Corrigan. Institute of Physics Publishing, Dirac House, Temple Back, Bristol, BS1 6BE, United Kingdom; custserv@iop.org; http://www.iop.org/. Illus., index. Sample. Refereed. Microform: AIP. Online: EBSCO Publishing; ingenta.com; RoweCom Information Quest; Swets Blackwell. *Indexed:* ApMecR, CCMJ, ChemAb, DSR&OA, EngInd, GeoRef, IAA, MathSciNet, SCI, ST&MA. *Aud.:* Ac, Sa.

As the British counterpart to The *Physical Review* (see below), The *Journal of Physics* is one of the two most prominent physics titles in the world. It is also one of the most heavily cited sources in the field and is used and respected by researchers worldwide. Like The *Physical Review,* this journal is issued in many parts that cover different subdisciplines of physics. *Part A* covers mathematical and general physics, including statistical physics, chaotic and complex systems, numerical methods, classical and quantum mechanics, and field theory. As such, it is primarily concerned with the fundamental mathematical and computational methods underpinning modern physics. The journal uses a classification system to place articles on similar topics in the same section. Both full-length research papers and letters to the editor are included, along with short corrections to previously published material. Occasional special issues are devoted to specific topics. This title belongs in every physics research collection.

5553. ***The Journal of Physics and Chemistry of Solids: an international journal.*** [ISSN: 0022-3697] 1956. m. EUR 4276 (Qualified personnel, EUR 78). Ed(s): Y Fujii, A Bansil. Pergamon, The Boulevard, Langford Ln, East Park, Kidlington, OX5 1GB, United Kingdom. Illus., index, adv. Refereed. Circ: 2300. Vol. ends: Dec. Microform: MIM; PQC. Online: ingenta.com; ScienceDirect; Swets Blackwell. *Indexed:* ApMecR, C&ISA, ChemAb, EngInd, GeoRef, SCI, SSCI. *Aud.:* Ac, Sa.

The Journal of Physics and Chemistry of Solids is a medium for publication of research in condensed matter and materials science. Emphasis is placed on experimental and theoretical work that contributes to a basic understanding of and new insight into the properties and behavior of condensed matter. General areas of interest are the electronic, spectroscopic, and structural properties of solids; and the statistical mechanics and thermodynamics of condensed systems, including perfect and defect lattices, surfaces, interfaces, thin films and multilayers, amorphous materials and nanostructures, and layered and low dimensional structures. Typical articles include the preparation and structural characterization of novel and advanced materials, especially in relation to the measurement and interpretation of their electrical, magnetic, optical, thermal, and mechanical properties, phase transitions, electronic structure, and defect properties, and the application of appropriate experimental and theoretical techniques in these studies. Submissions are encouraged in all the above areas, but especially those that emphasize fundamental aspects of materials science. From time to time, special Issues of the journal containing invited articles devoted to topical or rapidly developing fields are published. Only full-length articles are accepted, with letters published in the related *Solid State Communications* (see below). Occasional issues present conference proceedings or review articles within the overall scope of the journal. For comprehensive physics research collections.

5554. ***Journal of Physics B: Atomic, Molecular and Optical Physics.*** Former titles: *Journal of Physics B: Atomic and Molecular Physics; Physical Society. Proceedings.* [ISSN: 0953-4075] 1968. s-m. USD 4425 print & online. Ed(s): K Burnett. Institute of Physics Publishing, Dirac House, Temple Back, Bristol, BS1 6BE, United Kingdom; custserv@iop.org; http://www.iop.org/. Illus., index. Sample. Refereed. Microform: AIP. Online: EBSCO Publishing; ingenta.com; RoweCom Information Quest; ScienceDirect; Swets Blackwell. *Indexed:* ApMecR, C&ISA, ChemAb, EngInd, IAA, SCI. *Aud.:* Ac, Sa.

As part of the *Journal of Physics* collection of titles, this is one of the most prominent physics journals published worldwide. This section covers atomic, molecular, and optical physics, including such topics as atoms, ions, molecules, and clusters; their interaction with particles and fields; spectroscopy; quantum optics; nonlinear optics; laser physics; and those aspects of astrophysics that deal with elementary, ionic, or molecular properties or processes. This journal is similar in coverage and scope to *Part B* of the *Physical Review* (see below). In addition to publishing full-length research reports, the journal also publishes letters to the editor and occasional review articles. The editors have recently tightened the requirements for letters, with the implication that fewer letters are expected to be published, but those that are accepted will be of high quality. Occasional special issues are devoted to a single topic or present the proceedings of a relevant conference. This is one of the most respected journals in the field, and it belongs in every physics research collection.

5555. ***Journal of Physics: Condensed Matter.*** Formed by the 1989 merger of: *Journal of Physics F: Metal Physics; Journal of Physics C: Solid State Physics;* Which was formerly: *Physical Society. Proceedings.* [ISSN: 0953-8984] 1968. w. 50/yr. USD 8335 print & online. Ed(s): A M Stoneham. Institute of Physics Publishing, Dirac House, Temple Back, Bristol, BS1 6BE, United Kingdom; custserv@iop.org; http://www.iop.org/. Illus., index. Sample. Refereed. Circ: 1123. Microform: AIP. Online: EBSCO Publishing; ingenta.com; RoweCom Information Quest; ScienceDirect; Swets Blackwell. *Indexed:* ApMecR, C&ISA, ChemAb, EngInd, GeoRef, SCI. *Aud.:* Ac, Sa.

Another journal in the important *Journal of Physics* collection, this section is devoted to articles on experimental and theoretical studies of the structural, thermal, mechanical, electrical, magnetic, optical, and surface properties of condensed matter. Specific topics include crystalline and amorphous metals, semiconductors and insulators, glasses, liquids, liquid crystals, plastic crystals, polymers, and superfluids. This journal was formed by the merger of *Sections C* and *F* of the *Journal of Physics.* It maintains separate sections within the publication for articles on surface science and research on liquids and soft matter, along with different editorial boards for these two topics. Full research papers, review articles, and letters to the editor are all included. Occasional issues present the proceedings of a conference in the field. As part of the *Journal of Physics,* this title belongs in all physics research collections.

5556. ***Journal of Physics D: Applied Physics.*** Formerly (until 1967): *British Journal of Applied Physics.* [ISSN: 0022-3727] 1950. s-m. USD 2900 pirnt & online. Ed(s): A I Ferguson. Institute of Physics Publishing, Dirac House, Temple Back, Bristol, BS1 6BE, United Kingdom; custserv@iop.org; http://www.iop.org/. Illus., index, adv. Sample.

Refereed. Circ: 1217. Microform: AIP. Online: EBSCO Publishing; ingenta.com; RoweCom Information Quest; ScienceDirect; Swets Blackwell. *Indexed:* AS&TI, BiolAb, C&ISA, ChemAb, DSR&OA, EngInd, GeoRef, PhotoAb, SCI. *Aud.:* Ac, Sa.

The *Journal of Physics D* is concerned with all aspects of applied-physics research. The editors have intentionally left the scope as broad as possible in order to attract papers on a wide range of topics, including microelectronic properties and applications, superconductors, solid-state devices, optical phenomena, laser physics, plasma physics, properties of condensed matter, thin films, and applied magnetism. In addition to publishing articles on applications of physics to other fields, the journal also publishes theoretical, computational, and experimental studies. The editors are particularly interested in publishing articles on novel effects and new materials. Full-length research papers, letters to the editor, review articles, and short communications are all included. This title is the British equivalent of the *Journal of Applied Physics* (see above) and is an essential component of all physics research collections.

5557. *Journal of Physics G: Nuclear and Particle Physics.* Formerly: *Journal of Physics G: Nuclear Physics.* [ISSN: 0954-3899] 1975. m. USD 2815 print & online. Ed(s): H Stocker. Institute of Physics Publishing, Dirac House, Temple Back, Bristol, BS1 6BE, United Kingdom; custserv@iop.org; http://www.iop.org/. Illus., index. Sample. Refereed. Circ: 745. Vol. ends: Dec. Microform: AIP. Online: EBSCO Publishing; ingenta.com; RoweCom Information Quest; ScienceDirect; Swets Blackwell. *Indexed:* ChemAb, GeoRef, SCI. *Aud.:* Ac, Sa.

As the final section of the *Journal of Physics* collection, *Part G* covers nuclear and particle physics. Within this broad framework, the journal focuses on the physics of elementary particles and fields, intermediate-energy physics, nuclear physics, particle astrophysics, cosmic rays, gamma ray and neutrino astronomy, and dark matter. In addition to theoretical and experimental papers, the journal also publishes articles on experimental techniques, methods for data analysis, and instrumentation. Full-length research papers, letters to the editor, review articles, and brief notes are all included. Some issues contain the proceedings of conferences in the fields covered by the journal. This journal is the British equivalent of *Physical Review Sections C* and *D* (see below), and it belongs in any physics research collection.

5558. *Journal of Plasma Physics.* [ISSN: 0022-3778] 1967. 10x/yr. USD 876 (Individuals, USD 355). Ed(s): R A Cairns. Cambridge University Press, The Edinburgh Bldg, Shaftesbury Rd, Cambridge, CB2 2RU, United Kingdom; information@cambridge.org; http://uk.cambridge.org/journals. Illus., index, adv. Refereed. Vol. ends: May/Nov. Microform: PQC. Online: EBSCO Publishing; OCLC Online Computer Library Center, Inc.; RoweCom Information Quest; Swets Blackwell. Reprint: SWZ. *Indexed:* ApMecR, ChemAb, EngInd, IAA, SCI. *Aud.:* Ac, Sa.

Plasma physics is a branch of physics that has applications in a wide variety of fields, including astrophysics, fluids, and nuclear physics. This specialized journal publishes original-research reports on plasma science in all of these areas. Basic topics include the fundamental physics of plasmas, ionization, kinetic theory, particle orbits, stochastic dynamics, wave propagation, solitons, stability, shock waves, transport, heating, and diagnostics. Applications include fusion, laboratory plasmas and communications devices, laser plasmas, technological plasmas, space physics, and astrophysics. Both theoretical and experimental results are presented, along with applications of plasma science in other fields. This journal belongs in specialized and comprehensive physics collections.

5559. *Measurement Science and Technology.* Former titles (until 1990): *Journal of Physics E: Scientific Instruments; Journal of Scientific Instruments.* [ISSN: 0957-0233] 1968. m. USD 1630 print & online. Ed(s): P Hauptmann. Institute of Physics Publishing, Dirac House, Temple Back, Bristol, BS1 6BE, United Kingdom; custserv@iop.org; http://www.iop.org/. Illus., index, adv. Sample. Refereed. Vol. ends: Dec. Microform: AIP. Online: EBSCO Publishing; ingenta.com; RoweCom Information Quest; ScienceDirect; Swets Blackwell. *Indexed:* AS&TI, ApMecR, BiolAb, BrTechI, C&ISA, CEA, ChemAb, DSR&OA, EngInd, ExcerpMed, GeoRef, GeogAbPG, HortAb, IAA, IndVet, PhotoAb, S&F, SCI. *Aud.:* Ac, Sa.

Experimental research in physics relies a great deal on specialized equipment and precise instrumentation. This journal is devoted to the study of measurement, including theory, applications, and practice. It covers instrumentation in physics, chemistry, biology, environmental science, and engineering. Topics of interest include sensing and sensor technology, signal processing, metrology, measurement techniques using electromagnetic radiation, acoustics and ultrasonics, spectroscopy, nuclear measurements, imaging techniques, tomography, holography, and microscopy. Full-length research papers, rapid communications, review articles, design notes, and conference reports are all included. This title is part of the *Journal of Physics* collection and is the British equivalent of the *Review of Scientific Instruments* (see below). It belongs in any physics research collection.

5560. *Molecular Physics: an international journal in the field of chemical physics.* [ISSN: 0026-8976] 1958. s-m. GBP 3048 (Individuals, GBP 513). Taylor & Francis Ltd, 11 New Fetter Ln, London, EC4P 4EE, United Kingdom; info@tandf.co.uk; http://www.tandf.co.uk/journals. Illus., index, adv. Refereed. Online: EBSCO Publishing; Ingenta Select; OCLC Online Computer Library Center, Inc.; RoweCom Information Quest; Swets Blackwell. Reprint: PSC. *Indexed:* ChemAb, EngInd, IAA, SCI, SSCI. *Aud.:* Ac, Sa.

Molecular Physics publishes reports of an experimental and theoretical nature on the structure and properties of atomic and molecular physics. The journal considers all aspects of the physics and biophysics of molecules, particularly the structure and dynamics of individual molecules and molecular assemblies. It also publishes papers on fundamental reaction kinetics and the structure and reactivity of molecules adsorbed on surfaces and at interfaces. Four types of articles are accepted: "Papers" are full-length articles that report completed research; "Preliminary Communications" describe aspects of current research whose immediate publication has a strong benefit to the physics community; "Research Notes" provide brief comments on continuing research; and "Invited Articles" provide state-of-the-art reviews of selected topics. For comprehensive physics or chemistry collections.

5561. *Nanotechnology.* [ISSN: 0957-4484] 1990. bi-m. USD 770 print & online (Individuals, USD 385 print only). Ed(s): M Welland, Dr. Nina Couzin. Institute of Physics Publishing, Dirac House, Temple Back, Bristol, BS1 6BE, United Kingdom; custserv@iop.org; http://www.iop.org/. Adv. Refereed. Circ: 400. Online: EBSCO Publishing; ingenta.com; RoweCom Information Quest; ScienceDirect; Swets Blackwell. *Indexed:* BioEngAb, C&ISA, ChemAb, EngInd, SCI. *Aud.:* Ac, Sa.

Nanotechnology is the study of phenomena in extremely small dimensions, usually on the order of the size of a hydrogen atom. Nanotechnology has applications in many industries, including computing, automotive design and control, plastics, telecommunications, and materials science. From its inception a decade or so ago, it has become a dominant field for physics research. *Nanotechnology* is the official publication of the Institute of Physics dedicated to this area of research, publishing original research results in the field. Occasional articles evaluating the state of the nanotechnology industry, tutorials, editorials, and letters to the editor are also included. Some issues present the proceedings of conferences in the field. A related web site, nanotechweb.org, provides links to news, conferences, employment opportunities, and key papers on nanotechnology from other scientific journals. As the premier journal covering this new branch of physics, this title belongs in every collection supporting research in the field.

5562. *Optical Society of America. Journal A: Optics, Image Science, and Vision.* Formerly (until 1993): *Optical Society of America. Journal A, Optics and Image Science;* Which superseded in part (in 1983): *Optical Society of America. Journal.* [ISSN: 1084-7529] 1917. m. USD 1371 domestic; USD 1411 in Canada, Mexico, Central and South America & Caribbean ; USD 1465 in Europe, Asia, Middle East, Africa & Oceania. Ed(s): Barbara Williams, James R Fienup. Optical Society of America, Inc., 2010 Massachusetts Ave, N W, Washington, DC 20036-1023; info@osa.org; http://www.osa.org. Illus., index, adv. Refereed. Circ: 2800

Paid. Vol. ends: Dec. Online: EBSCO Publishing. *Indexed:* AS&TI, ApMecR, BiolAb, C&ISA, CCMJ, CPI, ChemAb, DSR&OA, EngInd, ErgAb, GeoRef, IAA, IndMed, MathSciNet, PsycholAb, SCI, SSCI. *Aud.:* Ac, Sa.

As one-half of the official journal of the Optical Society of America, this title is the premier publication outlet for research in the field of optics. *Part A* presents results of a general or basic nature relating to classical optics, image science, and vision. Topics include vision and color, imaging systems, image processing, wave propagation, diffraction, scattering, coherence, polarization, optical systems, atmospheric or ocean optics, optical devices, fiber optics, holography, and lithography. Both full-length papers and brief communications are accepted. Letters to the editor are published in a sister journal, *Optics Letters* (see below). Along with the *Journal of the Optical Society of America B* (below), this title forms the core of the optics literature and belongs in all physics collections.

5563. ***Optical Society of America. Journal B: Optical Physics.*** Supersedes in part (in 1983): *Optical Society of America. Journal.* [ISSN: 0740-3224] 1917. m. USD 1371 domestic; USD 1405 in Canada, Mexico, Central and South America & Caribbean; USD 1457 in Europe, Asia, Middle East, Africa & Oceania. Ed(s): Barbara Williams, G I Stegeman. Optical Society of America, Inc., 2010 Massachusetts Ave, N W, Washington, DC 20036-1023; info@osa.org; http://www.osa.org. Illus., index, adv. Refereed. Circ: 2300 Paid. Microform: AIP. *Indexed:* AS&TI, ApMecR, BiolAb, C&ISA, CCMJ, CPI, ChemAb, DSR&OA, EngInd, GeoRef, MathSciNet, PhotoAb, PsycholAb, SCI. *Aud.:* Ac, Sa.

As the second half of the official journal of the Optical Society of America, this title comprises part of the core literature in the field of optics. *Part B* emphasizes laser spectroscopy and modern quantum optics, but it also covers nonlinear optics, fiber optics, and photorefractive materials, effects, and devices. Like its sister section, *Journal of the Optical Society of America Part A,* it publishes full-length research reports, brief communications, and occasional review articles. Letters are published in the related *Optics Letters* (see below). As major journals in one of the most prominent branches of physics, *Parts A* and *B* belong in all physics collections.

5564. ***Optics & Photonics News.*** Formerly (until 1990): *Optics News.* [ISSN: 1047-6938] 1975. m. USD 99 combined subscription domestic print & online eds.; USD 114 combined subscription in Canada, Mexico, Central and South America & Caribbean for print & online eds.; USD 124 combined subscription in Europe, Asia, Middle East, Africa & Oceania for print & online eds. Ed(s): Lisa Rosenthal. Optical Society of America, Inc., 2010 Massachusetts Ave, N W, Washington, DC 20036-1023; info@osa.org; http://www.osa.org. Illus., index, adv. Circ: 22000. Vol. ends: Dec. *Indexed:* EngInd. *Bk. rev.:* various number and length. *Aud.:* Ga, Ac, Sa.

This journal serves as the official newsletter for the Optical Society of America. It provides its members with the usual news of the organization, reviews of new products, calendars of meetings and events, and employment opportunities. In addition, it contains interesting feature articles dealing with current topics in the field of optics. These articles are written for the nonspecialist and are accessible to a wide readership. Most feature articles avoid high-level mathematics and are accompanied by quality color photographs. Although physics is by nature a rather dry field of study and not known for its entertainment value, this is one of the few physics journals to contain a regular humor section. With its low price, glossy format, general readability, and wide range of interest, it is a good title for any science or physics collection.

5565. ***Optics Communications: a journal devoted to the rapid publication of contributions in the field of optics and interaction of light with matter.*** [ISSN: 0030-4018] 1969. 84x/yr. EUR 5369 (Qualified personnel, EUR 950). Ed(s): F Abeles, S. Kawata. Elsevier BV, North-Holland, Sara Burgerhartstraat 25, Amsterdam, 1055 KV, Netherlands; nlinfo-f@elsevier.nl; http://www.elsevier.nl. Illus., index, adv. Refereed. Vol. ends: No. 187 - No. 200. Microform: PQC. Online: EBSCO Publishing; ingenta.com; ScienceDirect; Swets Blackwell. Reprint: SWZ. *Indexed:* C&ISA, ChemAb, EngInd, GeoRef, IAA, PhotoAb, SCI. *Aud.:* Ac, Sa.

Optics Communications publishes short reports and full-length articles in the field of optics and on optical applications in other branches of physics. Topics include propagation, diffraction, and scattering; optical information processing; image analysis; optical communications; optical phenomena in atomic, molecular, and nuclear physics; optics of condensed matter; lasers; quantum optics; and nonlinear optics. Emerging areas of optical science and technology such as free-electron lasers, synchrotron radiation sources and applications, x-ray optics, and neural networks are also included. Articles primarily of a mathematical or computational nature are not accepted for publication. Most articles published in this journal are brief reports of new findings, although some longer articles also appear. This title plays a similar role as *Optics Letters* (see below) for reporting new developments in the field. It also supplements the major optics journals, such as *Applied Optics* and *Journal of the Optical Society of America* (see above) and is recommended only for comprehensive optics collections.

5566. ***Optics Letters.*** [ISSN: 0146-9592] 1977. s-m. USD 1401. Ed(s): Barbara Williams, Anthony M Johnson. Optical Society of America, Inc., 2010 Massachusetts Ave, N W, Washington, DC 20036-1023; info@osa.org; http://www.osa.org. Illus., index. Refereed. Circ: 3100 Paid. Vol. ends: Jan/Dec. Microform: AIP. Online: EBSCO Publishing. *Indexed:* AS&TI, C&ISA, CPI, ChemAb, EngInd, ExcerpMed, IAA, PhotoAb, SCI. *Aud.:* Ac, Sa.

Optics Letters serves as the letters-to-the-editor section for both *Applied Optics* and the *Journal of the Optical Society of America* (see above). It presents short papers on recent research results in optical science, including atmospheric optics, quantum electronics, Fourier optics, integrated optics, and fiber optics. Criteria used in determining acceptability of contributions include newsworthiness to a substantial part of the optics community and the effect of rapid publication on the research of others. This is a core journal in the field of optics, and it belongs in any collection supporting research in this field.

5567. ***Philosophical Magazine A: Physics of Condensed Matter, Structure, Defects and Mechanical Properties.*** Formerly (until 1995): *Philosophical Magazine A: Physics of Condensed Matter, Defects and Mechanical Properties;* Which superseded in part (in 1978): *Philosophical Magazine.* [ISSN: 1364-2804] 1798. 18x/yr. GBP 2642 for both Philosophical Magazines A & B. Ed(s): Lindsay Greer. Taylor & Francis Ltd, 11 New Fetter Ln, London, EC4P 4EE, United Kingdom; info@tandf.co.uk; http://www.tandf.co.uk/journals. Illus., index, adv. Refereed. Vol. ends: Jun/Dec. *Indexed:* ApMecR, ChemAb, DSR&OA, EngInd, GeoRef, SCI. *Aud.:* Ac, Sa.

With a 200-plus-year publication history, *Philosophical Magazine* is one of the world's oldest journals devoted to the field of physics. Its name derives from an earlier era, when physics was known as "natural philosophy." As with most physics journals, this publication has become more specialized over time, and it now focuses solely on condensed-matter physics. *Part A* covers structure, defects, and mechanical properties. *Part B (ISSN: 1364-2812)* focuses on statistical mechanics and electronic, optical, and magnetic properties. Only full-length research papers are published. Letters to the editor are included in a related journal, *Philosophical Magazine Letters. Philosophical Magazine* continues to be an important journal in the field of physics and belongs in any collection covering condensed matter.

5568. ***Physical Review A (Atomic, Molecular and Optical Physics).*** Formerly (until 1989): *Physical Review A (General Physics);* Which superseded in part (in 1970): *Physical Review.* [ISSN: 1050-2947] 1893. m. USD 2065 combined subscription domestic print and online eds.; USD 2155 combined subscription in Canada, Mexico, Central and South America and Caribbean for print and online eds.; USD 2220 combined subscription in Europe, Asia, Middle East, Africa and Oceania for print and online eds. Ed(s): B Crasemann. American Physical Society, One Physics Ellipse, College Park, MD 20740-3843; http://www.aps.org. Illus., index. Refereed. Vol. ends: Jun/Dec. Microform: AIP; BHP. Online: EBSCO Publishing; Swets Blackwell. *Indexed:* ApMecR, CCMJ, CPI, ChemAb, EngInd, GeoRef, IAA, MathSciNet, SCI. *Aud.:* Ac, Sa.

The *Physical Review* collection of journals is simply the most prestigious set of physics journals published anywhere in the world. Along with its British counterpart, the *Journal of Physics* collection (see above), the various components of the *Physical Review* comprise the core research journal literature of the field. Like many other journals in the sciences, the *Physical Review* has been divided into a number of sections that cover specific branches and subdisciplines of physics. *Section A* covers the broad areas of atomic, molecular, and optical physics. Specific topics include fundamental theoretical concepts, atomic and molecular structure, collisions and interactions, interactions with solids and surfaces, clusters, matter waves, quantum information, electromagnetic field effects, and quantum optics. Full-length articles, brief reports, comments, and short rapid communications are accepted, with letters being published in the related *Physical Review Letters* (see below). Like all of the sections of the *Physical Review,* the number of articles and pages published is tremendous, often reaching 1,500 pages in a single issue. However, even with thousands of articles published each year, the refereeing process is very selective, resulting in the rejection of over half of all articles submitted. The large number of papers published has forced the editors to stop numbering the pages consecutively. They use a paper/page system instead. A new feature for all sections of the *Physical Review* as of January 2003 is the incorporation of color images. Color images are not included in the print edition, but are included in the web version of appropriate papers. As one section of the most important journal in the field, this title belongs in every physics research collection.

5569. *Physical Review B: Condensed Matter and Materials Physics.* Former titles (until 1998): *Physical Review B (Condensed Matter);* (until Jul. 1978): *Physical Review B (Solid State);* Which superseded in part (in 1970): *Physical Review.* [ISSN: 1098-0121] 1893. 48x/yr. USD 5740 combined subscription domestic print and online eds.; USD 6030 combined subscription in Canada, Mexico, Central and South America and Caribbean for print and online eds. ; USD 6300 combined subscription in Europe, Asia, Middle East, Africa and Oceania for print & online eds. Ed(s): P D Adams. American Physical Society, One Physics Ellipse, College Park, MD 20740-3843; http://www.aps.org. Illus., index. Refereed. Microform: AIP. Online: EBSCO Publishing; Swets Blackwell. *Indexed:* ApMecR, CPI, ChemAb, EngInd, GeoRef, IAA, PhotoAb, SCI. *Aud.:* Ac, Sa.

The second section of the *Physical Review* is devoted to condensed matter and materials science. Topics include semiconductors, surface physics, structure and mechanical properties of materials, disordered systems, dynamics and lattice effects, magnetism, superfluidity, and superconductivity. Because of the extremely large number of papers published, the journal has been further divided, with the first issue of each month covering structure, phase transitions, magnetism, and superconductivity and the second issue covering electronic structure, semiconductors, surfaces, and low dimensions. Full-length papers predominate, but short, rapid communications are also accepted. Letters to the editor are published in the related *Physical Review Letters* (see below). Like all sections of the *Physical Review*, this section is not for the casual reader. It publishes more than 40,000 pages each year of primary research results of a highly technical nature. In order to facilitate publication with such a large number of papers, the editors have ceased numbering the pages consecutively and use a paper numbering system instead. Along with the *Journal of Physics: Condensed Matter* (see above), *Part B* of the *Physical Review* presents the most important research in the field. Like all of the sections of the *Physical Review,* it belongs in every physics research collection.

5570. *Physical Review C (Nuclear Physics).* Supersedes in part (1893-1969): *Physical Review.* [ISSN: 0556-2813] 1970. m. USD 1585 combined subscription domestic print and online eds.; USD 1650 combined subscription in Canada, Mexico, Central and South America and Caribbean for print and online eds. ; USD 1685 combined subscription in Europe, Asia, Middle East, Africa and Oceania for print & online eds. Ed(s): S M Austin. American Physical Society, One Physics Ellipse, College Park, MD 20740-3843; http://www.aps.org. Illus., index. Refereed. Vol. ends: Jun/Dec. Microform: AIP; BHP. Online: EBSCO Publishing; Swets Blackwell. *Indexed:* ApMecR, CPI, ChemAb, EngInd, SCI. *Aud.:* Ac, Sa.

Part C of the *Physical Review* covers nuclear physics, including nuclear structure, nucleon-nucleon interactions, nuclear reactions, relativistic nuclear collisions, hadronic physics and quantum chromodynamics, the electroweak interaction, and nuclear astrophysics. Both full-length research papers and brief reports are included, along with comments on previously published research. Letters to the editor are published in the separate *Physical Review Letters* (see below). Like all of the parts of the *Physical Review*, this section is the most prestigious journal published in its branch of physics. Although this journal does not contain as many articles as other parts of the *Physical Review*, it has also adopted the article/page numbering system instead of consecutive page numbers. Along with the *Journal of Physics G* (see above), this title represents the core literature of nuclear physics and belongs in any physics research collection.

5571. *Physical Review D (Particles, Fields, Gravitation and Cosmology).* Supersedes in part (1893-1969): *Physical Review.* [ISSN: 0556-2821] 1970. 24x/yr. USD 3230 combined subscription domestic print & online eds.; USD 3390 combined subscription in Canada, Mexico, Central and South America and Caribbean for print and online eds.; USD 3500 combined subscription in Europe, Asia, Middle East, Africa and Oceania for print & online eds. . Ed(s): L Brown. American Physical Society, One Physics Ellipse, College Park, MD 20740-3843; http://www.aps.org. Illus., index. Refereed. Microform: AIP; BHP. Online: EBSCO Publishing; Swets Blackwell. *Indexed:* ApMecR, CCMJ, CPI, ChemAb, EngInd, IAA, MathSciNet, SCI. *Aud.:* Ac, Sa.

This section of the *Physical Review* covers particles, fields, gravitation, and cosmology. The first issue of each month is devoted to particles and fields, while the second issue covers those two topics plus gravitation and cosmology. Specific topics typically include cosmic rays, collisions, particle decay, electroweak interactions, quantum chromodynamics, particle beams, general relativity, supergravity, astrophysics, field theory, gauge theory, and the grand unification theory. Both full-length research reports and short, rapid communications are accepted, with the former predominating. Occasional review articles also appear on an irregular basis. Letters appear in the related *Physical Review Letters* (see below). Like the other sections of the *Physical Review,* the number of articles published each year is tremendous, filling tens of thousands of pages. As with the other sections of the *Physical Review*, the edtiros have abandoned sequential page numbering in favor of an article/page system. Along with all the other parts of the journal, *Part D* is the premier journal in the world covering its branch of physics and belongs in every physics research library.

5572. *Physical Review E (Statistical, Nonlinear, and Soft Matter Physics).* [ISSN: 1063-651X] 1993. m. USD 2130 combined subscription domestic print and online eds.; USD 2370 combined subscription in Canada, Mexico, Central and South America, Caribbean, Europe, Asia, Middle East, Africa and Oceania for print & online eds. Ed(s): I Oppenheimer. American Physical Society, One Physics Ellipse, College Park, MD 20740-3843; http://www.aps.org. Illus., index. Refereed. Vol. ends: Jun/Dec. Microform: AIP; PQC. Online: EBSCO Publishing; Swets Blackwell. *Indexed:* CCMJ, CPI, ChemAb, EngInd, IndMed, MathSciNet, SCI, SSCI. *Aud.:* Ac, Sa.

The final section of the *Physical Review* covers statistical, nonlinear, and soft-matter physics. This section of the journal has become so large that it is published in two parts with sixteen subsections. A single monthly issue may run into several thousand pages. Topics include statistical methods, fluids, granular materials, liquid crystals, complex fluids, biological physics, chaos theory, plasmas, physics of beams, classical physics, and computational physics. Full articles, brief research reports, and rapid communications of important findings are all accepted, along with comments on previously published material. Letters are published in the related *Physical Review Letters* (see below). As with all other sections of the *Physical Review,* the editors reject over half of all papers submitted. The journal no longer uses page numbering, but rather an article/page numbering system. *Part E* , as one part of the most prestigious physics journal in the world, belongs in any physics research collection.

5573. *Physical Review Letters.* [ISSN: 0031-9007] 1958. w. USD 2810 combined subscription domestic print and online eds.; USD 2945 combined subscription in Canada, Mexico, Central and South America and Caribbean for print and online eds.; USD 3025 combined subscription in Europe, Asia, Middle East, Africa and Oceania for print & online eds. Ed(s): Martin Blume. American Physical Society, One Physics

Ellipse, College Park, MD 20740-3843; http://www.aps.org. Illus., index. Refereed. Microform: AIP. Online: EBSCO Publishing; Swets Blackwell. *Indexed:* ApMecR, CCMJ, CPI, ChemAb, EngInd, GeoRef, IAA, IndMed, MathSciNet, PhotoAb, SCI. *Aud.:* Ac, Sa.

This title is the letters-to-the-editor section for all parts of the *Physical Review* (see above). It publishes brief reports of important discoveries in any branch of physics, including general physics; gravitation and astrophysics; elementary particles and fields; nuclear physics; atomic, molecular, and optical physics; plasmas and beam physics; condensed matter; and interdisciplinary topics. Like its parent journal, *Physical Review Letters* is one of the most respected and most cited journals in all of physics. It was one of the very first letters-only journals and was established in order to speed publication of important research results. Many other journals have since copied this format. It maintains the high editorial standards of the *Physical Review.* Even though hundreds of pages are published each week, the editors reject over half of all papers submitted. *Physical Review Letters* is the single most prestigious journal of its kind and belongs in every research collection.

5574. *Physical Society of Japan. Journal.* Formerly: *Physico-Mathematical Society of Japan. Proceedings.* [ISSN: 0031-9015] 1946. m. JPY 75000 combined subscription for print & online eds. Ed(s): M Matsushita. Institute of Pure and Applied Physics, Toyokaiji Bldg, no.12, 6-9-6 Shinbashi, Minato-ku, Tokyo, 105-0004, Japan; subscription@ipap.jp; http://www.ipap.jp. Illus., index. Refereed. Circ: 2600. Vol. ends: Dec. Online: J-Stage. *Indexed:* ApMecR, CCMJ, ChemAb, EngInd, GeoRef, IAA, MathSciNet, PhotoAb, SCI. *Aud.:* Ac, Sa.

This title is the official journal of the Physical Society of Japan. As such, it publishes some of the most significant physics research conducted in Japan and throughout the rest of Asia. All of the subdisciplines of physics are covered, including classical physics, fluids and plasmas, particles and fields, and atomic physics. However, the journal publishes more papers in the area of condensed matter than in all others combined and seems to be moving toward a specialization in this area. Although the journal is published in Japan, all of the articles are written in English, making them accessible to the wider scientific community. Full-length scientific papers, research notes, and letters to the editor are all included. The journal is now also available online at no charge, although readers must register with the society. The online version contains all articles published since 1985, providing an extensive backfile. All letters, articles, and research notes are available in pdf format. Taking full advantage of the electronic environment, citations in bibliographies are linked to the complete article when they cite this title and its sister publication, the *Japanese Journal of Applied Physics.* This title is the Japanese equivalent of the other national journals included here, and it belongs in comprehensive physics research collections.

5575. *Physics Education.* [ISSN: 0031-9120] 1966. bi-m. USD 395 print & online. Ed(s): K Parker. Institute of Physics Publishing, Dirac House, Temple Back, Bristol, BS1 6BE, United Kingdom; custserv@iop.org; http://www.iop.org/. Illus., index, adv. Sample. Refereed. Vol. ends: Nov. Microform: AIP. Online: EBSCO Publishing; ingenta.com; RoweCom Information Quest; ScienceDirect; Swets Blackwell. *Indexed:* BrEdI, CIJE, ChemAb, MRD, SWA. *Bk. rev.:* Various number and length. *Aud.:* Hs, Ga, Ac.

Physics Education is a British publication that seeks to inform and stimulate high school and beginning undergraduate college students. As such, it is one of the few physics journals that is understandable to a general audience. The editors seek to provide teachers with a forum for discussing ideas and methods for teaching physics, assessment techniques, updates on research in the field, and strategies for classroom management. Articles are written for the nonspecialist and avoid much of the higher-level mathematics inherent in most physics publications. The goals of the journal are to cover the wide range of topics included in the field of physics, to enhance the standards and quality of teaching, to make physics more attractive to students and teachers, to keep teachers up to date on new developments in the field, and to provide a forum for the sharing of ideas about teaching physics. Each issue contains articles on new developments in physics, ideas for teaching physical concepts, profiles of prominent scientists, reviews of resources that can be used by physics teachers, news from the field, and even a little humor. The electronic version is supplemented by multimedia content, such as worksheets, spreadsheets, programs, and video clips. This journal is the British equivalent of *The Physics Teacher* (see below). For those libraries seeking to add a general-physics journal to their collections, this is an excellent choice.

5576. *Physics Letters. Section A: General, Atomic and Solid State Physics.* Supersedes in part (in 1967): *Physics Letters.* [ISSN: 0375-9601] 1962. 84x/yr. EUR 4379. Ed(s): V M Agranovich, A R Bishop. Elsevier BV, North-Holland, Sara Burgerhartstraat 25, Amsterdam, 1055 KV, Netherlands; nlinfo-f@elsevier.nl; http://www.elsevier.nl/homepage/about/us/regional_sites.htt. Illus., index. Sample. Refereed. Vol. ends: No. 278 - No. 291. Microform: PQC. Online: EBSCO Publishing; ingenta.com; ScienceDirect; Swets Blackwell. *Indexed:* CCMJ, ChemAb, DSR&OA, EngInd, GeoRef, MathSciNet, SCI. *Aud.:* Ac, Sa.

Physics Letters is a publication outlet for rapid communication of significant, original, and timely research results. Articles tend to be very brief, with longer review articles printed in the related journal *Physics Reports* (see below). *Section A* of the journal is the general-physics portion, covering all branches of physics except nuclear and particle physics. Topics usually included are general physics, statistical physics, nonlinear science, nanoscience, molecular physics, condensed matter, plasmas, and fluids. Articles are accepted for publication based upon the originality of the research, desirability for speedy publication, and the clarity of the presentation. This journal publishes an incredible number of articles, producing around 12,000 pages in a single year. Along with the *Physical Review Letters* (see above), it is one of the most cited and most prominent letters journals in the field. The publisher provides a free e-mail table of contents service for anyone interested in what is being published in this journal. It belongs in any physics research collection.

5577. *Physics Letters. Section B: Nuclear, Elementary Particle and High-Energy Physics.* Supersedes in part (in 1967): *Physics Letters.* [ISSN: 0370-2693] 1962. 108x/yr. EUR 8835 (Qualified personnel, EUR 4336). Ed(s): L. Alvarez-Gaume, J. P. Blazoit. Elsevier BV, North-Holland, Sara Burgerhartstraat 25, Amsterdam, 1055 KV, Netherlands; nlinfo-f@elsevier.nl; http://www.elsevier.nl/homepage/about/us/regional_sites.htt. Illus., index. Sample. Refereed. Vol. ends: No. 497 - No. 523. Microform: PQC. Online: EBSCO Publishing; ingenta.com; ScienceDirect; Swets Blackwell. *Indexed:* CCMJ, ChemAb, DSR&OA, EngInd, MathSciNet, SCI. *Aud.:* Ac, Sa.

Physics Letters B is the complement to *Physics Letters A* (see above). It covers the two areas excluded from part A: nuclear and particle physics. Because of the specialized nature of the field, different editors cover papers in experimental, theoretical, and high-energy nuclear physics. Despite its more limited subject scope, this section is the larger of the two parts, reflecting the vast amount of research published in nuclear and particle physics. In some years, over 50,000 pages are printed in a single calendar year. Papers published in this section are the results of research conducted at laboratories around the world, reflecting the international aspect of high-energy physics. Like most physics research journals, each article must be the result of original research and must not have appeared in print before. This journal is frequently used to determine precedent in scientific discoveries in its fields of interest. Both sections of *Physics Letters* should be a part of any serious physics research collection.

5578. *Physics of Fluids.* Formerly: *Physics of Fluids A: Fluid Dynamics;* Which superseded in part (in 1989): *Physics of Fluids.* [ISSN: 1070-6631] 1958. m. USD 2165 print & online eds. Ed(s): Andreas Acrivos, John Kim. American Institute of Physics, 2 Huntington Quadrangle, Ste 1NO1, Melville, NY 11747-4502; http://www.aip.org/journal_catalog/. Illus., index. Refereed. Vol. ends: Dec. Microform: Pub. Online: EBSCO Publishing; RoweCom Information Quest; Swets Blackwell. *Indexed:* ApMecR, CCMJ, CPI, ChemAb, EngInd, GeoRef, GeogAbPG, M&GPA, MathSciNet, SCI. *Aud.:* Ac, Sa.

This journal is the official publication of the Division of Fluid Dynamics of the American Physical Society. It is devoted to the publication of original research in the field of gases, liquids, and complex or multiphase fluids. Specific areas covered include kinetic theory, fluid dynamics, wave phenomena, hypersonic physics, hydrodynamics, compressible fluids, boundary layers, conduction, and chaotic phenomena. Material on plasmas and plasma physics is published in the related *Physics of Plasmas* (see below), which can be purchased in combination with this title at a reduced rate. Full papers, brief reports, and letters are all accepted. A related web site (http://ojps.aip.org/phf/gallery) provides images from the annual Gallery of Fluid Motion exhibition held at the meeting of the American Physical Society. Comments on previously published papers are also included, sometimes leading to interesting scientific debate. This is the primary journal for research in fluids and belongs in any comprehensive physics collection.

5579. *Physics of Plasmas.* Formerly: *Physics of Fluids B: Plasma Physics;* Which superseded in part (in 1989): *Physics of Fluids.* [ISSN: 1070-664X] 1958. m. USD 2505 print and online eds. Ed(s): R C Davidson. American Institute of Physics, 2 Huntington Quadrangle, Ste 1NO1, Melville, NY 11747-4502; http://www.aip.org/journal_catalog/. Illus., index. Refereed. Vol. ends: Dec. Microform: Pub. Online: EBSCO Publishing; RoweCom Information Quest; Swets Blackwell. *Indexed:* CCMJ, CPI, ChemAb, EngInd, MathSciNet, SCI. *Aud.:* Ac, Sa.

Physics of Plasmas is devoted to original contributions to and reviews of the physics of plasmas, including magnetofluid mechanics, kinetic theory, and statistical mechanics of fully and partially ionized gases. Formerly published with *Physics of Fluids,* the two journals were separated in 1994. Specific topics covered by this journal include equilibria, waves, particle beams, nonlinear behavior, lasers, radiation, astrophysics, plasma chemistry, physics of dense plasmas, and containment techniques. Full-length articles, brief reports, and letters to the editor are all included. This journal is one of the standard sources of information in this branch of physics, and it belongs in any collection supporting research in this area.

5580. *Physics Reports: a review section of Physics Letters.* Incorporates (1983-1991): *Computer Physics Reports;* (1972-1975): *Case Studies in Atomic Physics.* [ISSN: 0370-1573] 1971. 102x/yr. EUR 5004. Ed(s): J V Allaby, D D Awschalom. Elsevier BV, North-Holland, Sara Burgerhartstraat 25, Amsterdam, 1055 KV, Netherlands; nlinfo-f@elsevier.nl; http://www.elsevier.nl/homepage/about/us/regional_sites.htt. Illus., index. Sample. Refereed. Vol. ends: No. 338 - No. 353. Microform: PQC. Online: EBSCO Publishing; ingenta.com; ScienceDirect; Swets Blackwell. *Indexed:* CCMJ, ChemAb, EngInd, GeoRef, IAA, MathSciNet, SCI. *Aud.:* Ac, Sa.

In contrast to its sister publications, *Physics Letters A and B* (see above), which publish brief papers presenting new research findings, *Physics Reports* publishes lengthy articles designed to provide state-of-the-art reviews that benchmark research in various fields. Each issue contains a single article, which is usually somewhat longer than a literature review but shorter than a monograph. The reviews are specialist in nature but contain enough background and introductory material to be understandable to physicists who are working in other subdisciplines. In addition to identifying significant developments and trends, the extensive literature reviews serve as indexes to the topic being discussed. Subjects can be from any field of physics, and the editorial board consists of specialists in a variety of fields who are able to judge the quality and accuracy of the manuscripts. This title is similar in scope to *Contemporary Physics* (see above) and *Reports on Progress in Physics* (below), although *Physics Reports* is written at the highest level of the three. Any of the three would be useful additions to a college physics collection.

5581. *The Physics Teacher.* [ISSN: 0031-921X] 1963. 9x/yr. USD 290 domestic; USD 310; USD 343. Ed(s): Karl Mamola. American Association of Physics Teachers, c/o Jane Chambers, Journal Coordinator, One Physics Ellipse, College Park, MD 20740-3845; aapt-pubs@aapt.org; http://www.aapt.org. Illus., index, adv. Refereed. Circ: 11000 Paid. Vol. ends: Dec. Microform: AIP. Reprint: PQC. *Indexed:* CIJE, CPI, ChemAb, EduInd, GSI, MRD. *Bk. rev.:* Various number and length. *Aud.:* Hs, Ga, Ac.

The Physics Teacher is dedicated to the strengthening of physics teaching at the introductory level. As such, it is the primary journal of interest to high school physics teachers. Articles are written for the nonspecialist and present physics principles without the higher-level mathematics that usually accompanies such reports. Articles cover topics of interest to students and to the general public, often focusing on the applications of physical principles to everyday life. In addition to full articles, the journal also publishes frequent symposia that provide teachers with new ideas and teaching methods, notes on interesting applications and phenomena, information on equipment and apparatus for teaching physics, editorials, web sites, and book reviews. Every month, the journal publishes several problems for readers to solve and follows this up in the next issue with solutions and the names of the first five people to answer correctly. Beginning in 2003, library subscribers also have access to the online edition of this journal at http://www.aapt.org/tpt. This journal is similar to its British equivalent, *Physics Education* (see above). *The Physics Teacher* is a very readable journal and one of the few that is approachable by both the specialist and nonscientist. Although it is primarily aimed at high school teachers, it is one of the few physics journals that should be considered for general library collections.

5582. *Physics Today.* [ISSN: 0031-9228] 1948. m. USD 250. Ed(s): Steve Benka. American Institute of Physics, 2 Huntington Quadrangle, Ste 1NO1, Melville, NY 11747-4502; http://www.aip.org/journal_catalog/. Illus., index, adv. Sample. Refereed. Circ: 121872 Controlled. Vol. ends: Dec. Microform: Pub. Online: EBSCO Publishing; Gale Group. *Indexed:* A&ATA, AS&TI, ApMecR, ArtHuCI, BRI, BrTechI, CBRI, CIJE, CPI, ChemAb, DSR&OA, EngInd, ExcerpMed, GSI, GeoRef, IAA, LRI, M&GPA, MagInd, MathSciNet, RGPR, SCI, SSCI. *Aud.:* Hs, Ga, Ac.

Physics Today is unique in that it is the only true general-interest physics journal currently being published. This is reflected in its circulation, which is much higher than that of any other physics journal. *Physics Today* serves as a news source for anyone interested in the field of physics, including scientists, teachers, students, and the general public. The wide appeal of this journal is evidenced by the fact that it is the only physics journal to be indexed in the *Readers' Guide to Periodical Literature.* Articles are written specifically for the nonspecialist and present advanced physical concepts without burdening the reader with advanced mathematics. With color photographs, well-written prose, and timely and engaging subject matter, this is the only physics journal that consistently could be considered for newsstand distribution. In addition to the articles, each issue provides news of recent discoveries, conference updates, editorials, book reviews, new-product announcements, obituaries, positions available, and political updates. As the official newsletter of the American Institute of Physics, it also serves as a source for association news and events. *Physics Today* is essential for any college or university library and should be considered by public and school libraries as well. Unless a library supports a physics research program, this title is the only physics journal that should even be considered for purchase.

5583. *Physics World.* Formerly (until 1988): *Physics Bulletin;* Incorporates: *Physics in Technology.* [ISSN: 0953-8585] 1950. m. USD 330 in USA, Canada & Mexico Free to members IOP. Ed(s): P Rodgers. Institute of Physics Publishing, Dirac House, Temple Back, Bristol, BS1 6BE, United Kingdom; custserv@iop.org; http://www.iop.org/. Illus., index, adv. Refereed. Vol. ends: Dec. Microform: AIP. Online: EBSCO Publishing. *Indexed:* C&ISA, CerAb, ChemAb, EngInd, ExcerpMed, GeoRef, SSCI. *Bk. rev.:* various number and length. *Aud.:* Hs, Ga, Ac.

This journal is the British equivalent of *Physics Today* (see above). As such, it attempts to present physics news and information to a general audience of scientists and the public. It is the newsletter of the British Institute of Physics and provides members with the same type of information and services that *Physics Today* does for members of the American Institute of Physics. Each issue contains feature articles, product reviews, job ads, editorials, letters, humor, and association news. Like its American counterpart, the journal's articles are written for the nonscientist and may be appreciated by general adult readers. *Physics World* is one of the few physics journals published for a general audience and is an excellent choice for addition to any college or general library collection.

5584. *Reports on Progress in Physics.* [ISSN: 0034-4885] 1934. m. USD 2225 print & online. Ed(s): C J Humphrey. Institute of Physics Publishing, Dirac House, Temple Back, Bristol, BS1 6BE, United Kingdom; custserv@iop.org; http://www.iop.org/. Illus., index. Sample. Refereed. Vol. ends: Dec. Microform: AIP. Online: EBSCO Publishing; ingenta.com; RoweCom Information Quest; ScienceDirect; Swets Blackwell. *Indexed:* A&ATA, ApMecR, CCMJ, ChemAb, DSR&OA, GeoRef, GeogAbPG, IAA, MathSciNet, SCI. *Aud.:* Ac, Sa.

Reports on Progress in Physics publishes review articles in all subdisciplines of physics. Articles combine a critical evaluation of the field with a reliable and accessible introduction to the topic, making the articles accessible to a wider scientific community. As with all review journals, articles tend to be long, often over 100 pages. Topics include particles and fields, nuclear physics, condensed matter, biophysics, astrophysics, surface science, plasma physics, and lasers. All of the articles are invited by the editors from distinguished researchers in the field. This journal is similar in scope to *Contemporary Physics* and *Physics Reports* (see above). College libraries should subscribe to at least one of these titles, and research libraries will probably wish to get all three.

5585. *Review of Scientific Instruments.* Former titles (until 1929): *Journal of the Optical Society of America and Review of Scientific Instruments;* (until 1921): *Journal of the Optical Society of America.* [ISSN: 0034-6748] 1917. m. USD 1690 print and online eds. Ed(s): Albert T Macrander. American Institute of Physics, 2 Huntington Quadrangle, Ste 1NO1, Melville, NY 11747-4502; http://www.aip.org/journal_catalog/. Illus., index, adv. Refereed. Vol. ends: Dec. Microform: Pub. Online: EBSCO Publishing; RoweCom Information Quest; Swets Blackwell. *Indexed:* AS&TI, ApMecR, BiolAb, CPI, ChemAb, DSR&OA, EngInd, ExcerpMed, GeoRef, IAA, PhotoAb, PsycholAb, SCI. *Aud.:* Ac, Sa.

Modern physics research relies heavily on sophisticated instrumentation to make measurements, conduct experiments, analyze data, and test current theories. *Review of Scientific Instruments* is a specialized journal whose role is to evaluate equipment, apparatus, experimental techniques, and mathematical analysis of results. This journal publishes original research articles and literature reviews on instruments in physics, chemistry, and the life sciences. The editors interpret the concept of instrumentation very widely and include all of the tools used by the modern scientist. In addition to full articles, it also provides notes on new instruments and materials, letters to the editor, and occasional conference proceedings from relevant meetings. Because of its focus on instrumentation, many manufacturers also advertise their products in this journal. This title is similar in scope to the British *Measurement Science and Technology* (see above). North American libraries that serve scientific researchers will want to subscribe to *Review of Scientific Instruments*, and comprehensive physics and scientific research libraries will probably need both titles.

5586. *Reviews of Modern Physics.* [ISSN: 0034-6861] 1929. q. USD 505 combined subscription domestic print and online eds.; USD 515 combined subscription in Canada, Mexico, Central and South America and Caribbean for print and online eds.; USD 535 combined subscription in Europe, Asia, Middle East, Africa and Oceania for print & online eds. Ed(s): Martin Blume, George Bertsch. American Physical Society, One Physics Ellipse, College Park, MD 20740-3843; bertsch@phys.washington.edu; http://rmp.aps.org. Illus., index. Refereed. Microform: AIP; MIM. Online: EBSCO Publishing; Swets Blackwell. *Indexed:* AS&TI, ApMecR, BiolAb, CCMJ, CPI, ChemAb, DSR&OA, EngInd, ExcerpMed, GSI, GeoRef, IAA, IndMed, MathSciNet, SCI. *Aud.:* Ac, Sa.

Reviews of Modern Physics enhances communication among physicists by publishing comprehensive scholarly reviews and tutorials on significant topics in modern physics. Like *Contemporary Physics, Physics Reports,* and *Reports on Progress in Physics* (see above), the articles do not contain results of original research but collect and synthesize existing research on topics of current interest. Research from any branch or subdiscipline of physics is included, although articles from newly developing fields are given preference. In addition to lengthy review articles, some shorter colloquia articles are also included. This title is especially useful for helping physics teachers and graduate students keep abreast of recent developments. To enhance this role, the journal also accepts occasional tutorial articles aimed primarily at students or those new to the field. *Reviews of Modern Physics* is the most cited of all physics review journals and belongs in most physics research collections.

5587. *Solid State Communications.* [ISSN: 0038-1098] 1963. 48x/yr. EUR 3852 (Qualified personnel, EUR 442). Ed(s): Manuel Cardona. Pergamon, The Boulevard, Langford Ln, East Park, Kidlington, OX5 1GB, United Kingdom. Illus., index, adv. Sample. Refereed. Circ: 2000. Microform: MIM; PQC. Online: EBSCO Publishing; ingenta.com; ScienceDirect; Swets Blackwell. *Indexed:* ApMecR, C&ISA, ChemAb, EngInd, GeoRef, SCI. *Aud.:* Ac, Sa.

This journal serves as the letters section of the *Journal of Physics and Chemistry of Solids* (see above). It publishes short papers on important new research developments in condensed-matter science, including material on the basic physics of materials and devices, microstructures, superconductors, and nanostructures. The emphasis is on brevity, with papers usually under four pages in length. A coherent quantitative treatment emphasizing new physics is expected rather than a simple accumulation of experimental data. Papers published may be experimental or theoretical in nature. On occasion, the editors publish a longer research paper on a topic of broad interest in solid-state physics. These papers contain not only new research results, but also background information on the field. Like its parent title, *Solid State Communications* belongs in graduate research physics collections.

5588. *Studies in History and Philosophy of Science Part B: Studies in History and Philosophy of Modern Physics.* [ISSN: 1355-2198] 1995. q. EUR 431 (Qualified personnel, EUR 54). Ed(s): J Butterfield. Pergamon, The Boulevard, Langford Ln, East Park, Kidlington, OX5 1GB, United Kingdom. Illus., index. Sample. Refereed. Vol. ends: Dec. Microform: PQC. Online: ingenta.com; ScienceDirect; Swets Blackwell. *Indexed:* AmH&L, ArtHuCI, CCMJ, IBSS, IPB, MathSciNet, PhilInd. *Aud.:* Ac, Sa.

As scientists make new discoveries and develop new theories, they also change the ways in which we understand and approach our world. Advances in physics—such as quantum theory, field theory, and relativity—have given us new tools for measuring the universe. One result of these dramatic changes has been a rise in the study of the history of science, with particular emphasis on the history of modern physics. This journal has been developed specifically to research in this area. The primary focus is on physics from the mid/late-nineteenth century to the present, the period of emergence of the kind of theoretical physics that came to dominate the exact sciences in the twentieth century. Two sister journals in the "Studies in History and Philosophy of Science" series examine science in general (*Part A*) and the biological and medical sciences (*Part C*). In each section, original articles and review essays are published. Because the focus is on the history of ideas, many of the articles are understandable by a wider audience. This journal belongs in any collection dealing with the history of science.

Electronic Journals

5589. *I N S P E C (Institute of Electrical Engineering).* [ISSN: 1529-7853] 2000. unknown. USD 150. Ed(s): Robert Apfel. American Institute of Physics, 2 Huntington Quadrangle, Ste 1NO1, Melville, NY 11747-4502; publish@aip.org; http://ojps.aip.org. *Aud.:* Ac, Sa.

Acoustics Research Letters Online (*ARLO*) is the electronic letters companion to the *Journal of the Acoustical Society of America.* It covers the entire range of the discipline of acoustics, including linear and nonlinear acoustics; aeroacoustics; underwater sound; architectural acoustics; ultrasonics; speech, music, and noise; the physiology and psychology of hearing; and biomedical acoustics. Like all letters journals, articles tend to be short. However, because this journal is published on the web, it allows for the use of multimedia applications and graphic images. Articles are archived on CD-ROM along with the contents of the *Journal of the Acoustical Society of America.* This journal is one of the core titles in the field and belongs in any library supporting research in acoustics.

5590. *European Physical Journal Direct.* [ISSN: 1435-3725] 1998. m. Free. Springer-Verlag, Tiergartenstr 17, Heidelberg, 69121, Germany. Refereed. *Aud.:* Ac, Sa.

EPJ Direct is an electronic supplement to the *European Physical Journal.* Articles in *EPJ Direct* cover all subdisciplines of physics and are grouped into collections based on the five sections of its parent journal. As an electronic journal, this title has several advantages over its print companions. It allows for rapid publication of research results, it can publish articles of any page length, and it can incorporate multimedia presentations into the articles. Best of all, the publisher is providing this journal at no charge and with no restrictions.

Unfortunately, the number of articles actually published in this title is very small when compared to its print version. For example, *Section B, Condensed Matter,* has published a total of five articles in five years. Despite the low numbers of articles, the concept of *EPJ Direct* is one that should be applauded. Because it is available electronically at no cost, it should be a part of any physics research collection.

5591. ***New Journal of Physics.*** [ISSN: 1367-2630] 1998. a. Free. Ed(s): Alex Bradshaw, Jorge Pullin. Institute of Physics Publishing, Dirac House, Temple Back, Bristol, BS1 6BE, United Kingdom; custserv@iop.org; http://www.iop.org/. Illus. Refereed. *Indexed:* MathSciNet. *Aud.:* Ac, Sa.

The *New Journal of Physics* is an electronic-only publication produced cooperatively by the British and German Institutes of Physics. The scope of the journal is the entire range of the field of physics, including experimental, theoretical, and applied research. By publishing only in electronic format, the journal allows for rapid distribution of articles of any length. All of the articles are subject to the standard peer review process, but they are not limited by the space and distribution considerations of the print format. Unique among all physics research journals (and rare among scientific journals in any discipline), the *New Journal of Physics* is available to readers at no cost. The journal is funded by article charges paid by the authors, which is similar to the page charges of print journals. Although the number of articles published each year is fairly small, the editors of this journal want to make it the leading journal in the field by publishing articles of outstanding quality. Many of the articles are "Focus" articles, which are lengthy reviews or tutorials on specific topics in physics. Because of the ideal pricing model and the ease of electronic access, this journal should be available in all college libraries.

5592. ***Optics Express.*** [ISSN: 1094-4087] 1997. 26x/yr. Free. Ed(s): Joseph Eberly. Optical Society of America, Inc., 2010 Massachusetts Ave, N W, Washington, DC 20036-1023; info@osa.org; http://www.opticsexpress.com. Refereed. *Aud.:* Ac, Sa.

Optics Express publishes original, peer-reviewed articles that report new developments of interest to the optics community in all fields of optical science and technology. All subfields of optics are covered, including theory, experimentation, and application. The journal is available free through the web, with back issues available for purchase on CD-ROM. In addition, all of the articles are archived in the society's Optics Infobase, which provides web access for subscribers to articles published in any Optical Society of America journal. True to its name, *Optics Express* provides rapid publication, with an average of 47 days from submission to publication. It also allows authors to publish an unlimited number of color images. Many of the articles contain multimedia content that enhances the understanding of the physical concepts discussed. Because it is available to all researchers electronically at no charge, this journal belongs in all physics collections.

5593. ***Physical Review Focus.*** [ISSN: 1539-0748] 1998. m. Ed(s): David Ehrenstein. American Physical Society, One Physics Ellipse, College Park, MD 20740-3843; http://focus.aps.org. *Aud.:* Ga, Ac, Sa.

Issued in electronic format only, *Physical Review Focus* is intended to provide wider distribution for research published in the print *Physical Review* and *Physical Review Letters.* Articles published in this electronic journal are summaries of key research published in other sections of the *Physical Review,* but rewritten for a more general audience. They still require a strong understanding of basic physics and are intended to promote communication between the different subdisciplines of the field. Links are provided to the electronic originals, so that subscribers can obtain the full text of the original paper if desired. *Physical Review Focus* also links to the electronic *Physics News Update* and *Physics News Preview*. Because there is no access charge and the articles are written for a wider audience, this is a good general-physics source that libraries may wish to provide.

5594. ***Physical Review Special Topics - Accelerators and Beams.*** [ISSN: 1098-4402] 1998. q. American Physical Society, One Physics Ellipse, College Park, MD 20740-3843; http://www.aps.org/prstab/. Refereed. *Indexed:* CPI. *Aud.:* Ac,Sa.

Physical Review Special Topics: Accelerators and Beams is the first all-electronic section of the prestigious *Physical Review.* It covers the full range of accelerator science and technology; subsystem and component technologies; beam dynamics; applications of accelerators; and design, operation, and improvement of accelerators used in science and industry. All papers are required to contain significant, new research findings. Because of its electronic nature, there is no limit to the number of pages or illustrations that can be included in any given article. All of the articles are provided in pdf or zip formats. Another important feature of the electronic nature of this publication is that most articles are freely available, without restriction, to any reader. In addition to the original research articles, the journal links to relevant papers published in other sections of the *Physical Review* and the *Physical Review Letters.* This title is recommended for any library supporting specialized research in this area.

5595. ***Physics News Update: the American Institute of Physics bulletin news.*** w. American Institute of Physics, 2 Huntington Quadrangle, Ste 1NO1, Melville, NY 11747-4502; info@aip.org; http://www.aip.org. *Aud.:* Hs, Ga, Ac, Sa.

Physics News Update is a digest of physics news compiled from journals, newspapers, magazines, conferences, and other sources. Issued only in electronic format, it is designed to present the results of physics research to a wide audience. Readers are able to access the journal on the web or through a weekly e-mail alert service. Each issue contains several interesting articles on new developments in the field, a selection of "Physics News Graphics," which are high-quality images demonstrating physical concepts, and links to other physics news web sites. Archives are available on the web back to 1990. This title is available at no charge and is a good example of how the web can be used to promote research in a specific field of study. The material in this electronic journal is written so that it will reach a wide range of readers, from students to specialists. This electronic journal should be a part of any physics collection.

5596. ***Virtual Journal of Applications of Superconductivity.*** s-m. Ed(s): John R Clem. American Institute of Physics, 1 Physics Ellipse, College Park, MD 20740-3843; aipinfo@aip.org; http://www.aip.org. *Aud.:* Ac, Sa.

As one of several titles in the "Virtual Journals" series produced by the American Institute of Physics, this title is very different from other scientific research journals. Like all of the titles in the series, it focuses on a specialized, developing area within the discipline of physics. The journal does not accept original research papers, but reproduces articles that have already been published in a number of other physics and related journals. The title is completely electronic and has no print equivalent. Access to the full text of the articles is based upon subscriptions to the original source journals. If a library subscribes to a journal used as a source for the *Virtual Journal*, the article is freely available to the reader. If a library does not subscribe to the source journal, that article is available on a pay-per-article basis. Costs range from $15 to $25 per article. In addition to the articles, the journal provides a wide variety of web links to authoritative sites about superconductivity. These sites range from tutorials for the beginner to advanced research information. This journal is part of an experiment by the American Institute of Physics. Four similar journals covering the areas of biological physics research, nanoscience technology, quantum information, and ultrafast science are also available in the "Virtual Journals in Science and Technology" series. This journal should be available in any library supporting research in superconductivity.

5597. ***Virtual Journal of Biological Physics Research: a monthly multijournal compilation of the latest research on biological physics.*** 2000. m. Ed(s): Robert H Austin. American Physical Society, One Physics Ellipse, College Park, MD 20740-3843. Index, adv. Refereed. *Aud.:* Ac, Sa.

As one of five virtual electronic journals published by the American Institute of Physics, the *Virtual Journal of Biological Physics Research* covers biological applications of physical concepts. Topics covered include membrane biophysics, biological networks, molecular interactions, cellular and multicellular phenomena, instrumentaion, and molecular dynamics. This journal does not publish original research, but it reprints articles published in its many source journals. Articles are available online to subscribers of those source journals.

Nonsubscribers may purchase individual articles, which are usually priced at $15-$25. The benefit of this title is that it brings together material that may be found in a wide variety of other journals. It belongs in specialized physics or biology collections.

5598. *Virtual Journal of Nanoscale Science & Technology: a weekly multijournal compilation of the latest research on nanoscale systems.* 2000. w. Ed(s): David Awschalom. American Physical Society, One Physics Ellipse, College Park, MD 20740-3843; http://www.vjnano.org/nano/?jsessionid=2294321011825203149. Adv. Refereed. *Aud.:* Ac, Sa.

Nanoscale science is essentially the study of solid-state physics at the quantum level. This has become an important subfield of physics, with many new developments in both theory and application. Because results of research in this field are published in a wide range of sources, the American Institute of Physics began the *Virtual Journal of Nanoscale Science and Technology* to pull this information together. In several ways, this journal is very different from other scientific research journals. First of all, it does not accept original papers for publication but reproduces papers that have already been published in a number of other source journals. Second, the journal is only available on the web and has no print equivalent. Finally, access to the articles is based upon subscriptions to the original source journals. If a library subscribes to a journal used as a source for the *Virtual Journal*, the article is freely available. If a library does not subscribe to the source journal, that article is available on a pay-per-article basis. Costs range from $15 to $25 per article. This journal is part of an experiment by the American Institute of Physics. Three similar journals covering the areas of biological physics research, quantum information, superconductivity, and ultrafast science are also available in the "Virtual Journals in Science and Technology" series. The journal should be available in any library supporting research in nanotechnology.

5599. *Virtual Journal of Quantum Information: a multijournal compilation of research in quantum computing, cryptography, and communication.* 2001. m. Ed(s): David DiVincenzo. American Physical Society, One Physics Ellipse, College Park, MD 20740-3843. *Aud.:* Ac, Sa.

The *Virtual Journal of Quantum Information* is a specialized journal covering quantum computing and information. It is one of five experimental virtual journals published by the American Institute of Physics. Rather than publishing the results of original research, these journals bring together previously published material from a wide variety of source journals. Article are available to subscribers of the source journals or may be purchased on an individual basis at a cost of $15-$25 each. This journal belongs in specialized physics and computing collections.

5600. *Virtual Journal of Ultrafast Science.* 2002. m. Free. Ed(s): Philip H Bucksbaum. American Institute of Physics, 1 Physics Ellipse, College Park, MD 20740-3843; http://www.aip.org. Vol. ends: Dec. *Aud.:* Ac, Sa.

Ultrafast science deals with physical phenomena that occur in the range of one-trillionth of a second (one picosecond) to one-quadrillionth of a second (one femtosecond), or even less. This new electronic journal covers all applications and research into such phenomena. Areas covered include measurement techniques, atomic and molecular physics, condensed-matter physics, photonics, and applications in chemistry and biophysics. As one of five virtual journals published by the American Institute of Physics, the *Virtual Journal of Ultrafast Science* brings together articles published in a wide range of source journals. Articles are available free online to subscribers of the source journals and are available for a fee (approximately $15-$25) for nonsubscribers.

■ POLITICAL SCIENCE

General and Political Theory/Comparative and American Politics/International Relations

Nancy J. Becker, Assistant Professor, Division of Library & Information Science, St. John's University, 8000 Utopia Pkwy., Jamaica, NY 11439; 718-990-1452; beckern@stjohns.edu

Cheryl LaGuardia, Head of Instructional Services for the Harvard College Library, Harvard University, Cambridge, MA 02138; claguard@fas.harvard.edu

Introduction

The increasingly interdisciplinary nature of the social sciences and the humanities, including political science, added to recent and ongoing world events, have extended the potential audience for the titles in this section well beyond political science professionals. Because *Magazines for Libraries* has several other sections that include hundreds of journal titles closely aligned with the discipline of political science, the focus of this section is to avoid overlap with other sections, including Africa, Asia, CIS and Eastern Europe, Civil Liberties, Europe, Middle East, News and Opinion, and Peace.

Many journals here are well established, several having been published for over a century. Many are also scholarly research publications with contributors consisting mainly of faculty members from various U.S. and foreign institutions. So the majority of political science materials listed here will continue to be of greatest interest to academic libraries and the central hubs of larger metropolitan public libraries. However, the attempt has also been made to identify titles with wider appeal that are accessible to a broader audience. These are so noted.

This section is divided into three subsections: General and Political Theory, Comparative and American Politics, and International Relations, with a short subsection of electronic journals. These divisions represent the way political science has been subdivided for years and how this section was organized in previous editions.

Included journals represent mainstream, conservative, liberal, and socialist perspectives, a mix that provides both librarians and users a choice of philosophies and ideas to use in their investigation and evaluation of politics, public affairs, public policy, and foreign policy issues of the day. An attempt has also been made to identify journals offering viewpoints of areas beyond the United States. This is especially important given current topics promising to engage the interest of political scientists, for example, the continuing conflict in Iraq, the shifting political situation in Liberia, and ongoing concerns about terrorism worldwide.

Basic Periodicals

Hs: *Congressional Digest, Current History, International Affairs, National Journal;* Ga: *Brookings Review, Congressional Digest, CQ Weekly, Current History, Foreign Affairs, Foreign Policy, National Journal, SAIS Review, World Affairs;* Ac: *American Journal of Political Science, American Political Science Review, American Politics Research, American Academy of Political and Social Science. Annals, The Cato Journal, Comparative Politics, CQ Weekly, Foreign Affairs, Foreign Policy, International Organization, International Studies Quarterly, Journal of Politics, Journal of Theoretical Politics, Latin American Politics & Society, Orbis, Policy Studies Journal, Political Science Quarterly, Polity, Presidential Studies Quarterly, Publius, World Policy Journal, World Politics.*

Basic Abstracts and Indexes

ABC Political Science, America: History and Life, International Political Science Abstracts, PAIS International in Print, Political Science Abstracts, Social Sciences Citation Index, Social Science Index.

General and Political Theory

5601. ***American Academy of Political and Social Science. Annals.*** [ISSN: 0002-7162] 1891. bi-m. USD 490. Ed(s): Alan W Heston. Sage Publications, Inc., 2455 Teller Rd, Thousand Oaks, CA 91320; info@sagepub.com; http://www.sagepub.com. Illus., adv. Refereed. Circ: 4800. Vol. ends: Nov. Microform: IDC; PMC; NRP. Online: Pub.; Florida Center for Library Automation; Gale Group; ingenta.com; LexisNexis; OCLC Online Computer Library Center, Inc.; ProQuest Information & Learning. Reprint: PSC. *Indexed:* ABCPolSci, ABS&EES, AgeL, AmH&L, BAS, BEL&L, BRD, BRI, BrArAb, CBRI, CJA, CommAb, CompR, FutSurv, HEA, HRA, IBSS, IPSA, JEL, LRI, MagInd, PAIS, PRA, PSA, RGPR, RI-1, SFSA, SSCI, SSI, SUSA, SociolAb. *Bk. rev.:* 15-25, 500-800 words. *Aud.:* Ga, Ac, Sa.

Continuously published since 1889, this frequently cited and widely indexed journal uses a single-theme format to provide an in-depth and well-balanced exploration of contemporary social and political science topics. Each issue is guest edited by an expert who then invites interdisciplinary contributions from scholars, researchers, and policy makers. Professionals seeking to keep abreast of current issues in the field, as well as students needing a comprehensive review of a significant topic, will find this approach particularly useful. Issues also include an index, a book review section, and, usually in the November issue, the papers presented at the academy's annual meeting, along with questions and answers. Accessible to a broad audience, this classic source of social and political science information belongs in every academic library and, when the cost is not prohibitive, in the collections of other libraries as well.

5602. ***American Journal of Political Science.*** Formerly: *Midwest Journal of Political Science.* [ISSN: 0092-5853] 1950. q. USD 255 print & online eds. Ed(s): Kim Quaile Hill, Jan Leighley. Blackwell Publishing, Inc., Commerce Place, 350 Main St, Malden, MA 02148; subscrip@blackwellpub.com; http://www.blackwellpublishing.com. Illus., adv. Refereed. Circ: 4200. Vol. ends: No. 4. Microform: PQC; NRP. Online: EBSCO Publishing; Gale Group; ingenta.com; JSTOR (Web-based Journal Archive); OCLC Online Computer Library Center, Inc.; ProQuest Information & Learning. Reprint: SCH. *Indexed:* ABCPolSci, ABS&EES, AmH&L, ArtHuCI, BAS, CJA, IBSS, IBZ, IPSA, LRI, PAIS, PRA, PSA, RiskAb, SSCI, SSI, SUSA, SWA, SociolAb. *Aud.:* Ac.

This highly regarded and widely read political science journal claims to be open to all members of the profession and all areas of the discipline. Although *AJPS* covers American politics, public policy, international relations, comparative politics, and political theory, approximately 50 percent of the submitted manuscripts focus on American political behavior and institutions. Each issue includes essays and research reports as well as a "Workshop" section devoted to methodological discussions. The research reports are well documented and replete with statistical analyses, reflecting the scholarly audience targeted by this journal.

Anarchy. See Zines section.

5603. ***Asian Journal of Political Science.*** [ISSN: 0218-5377] 1993. s-a. EUR 97 (Individuals, EUR 60). Ed(s): Leo Suryadinata, Shamsul Haque. Times Media Academic Publishing, 1 New Industrial Rd, Times Centre, Singapore, 536196, Singapore; tap@tpl.com.sq; http://www.timesone.com.sg/tap. Illus., adv. Refereed. Circ: 250. Vol. ends: No. 2. *Indexed:* BAS, IBSS, IBZ, IPSA, PAIS, PSA, SociolAb. *Bk. rev.:* 5-10, 1,250 words. *Aud.:* Ac.

Sponsored by the Department of Political Science of the National University of Singapore, this refereed journal publishes articles on political theory, comparative politics, international relations, and public administration. As the title suggests, the journal concentrates on issues related to or relevant for Asia. The table of contents provides brief abstracts of the approximately seven articles per issue, and the book review section includes five to ten reviews and a list of books and monographs received. With its scholarly orientation and its Asian focus, this journal is most appropriate for academic libraries supporting Asian Studies programs.

Australian Journal of Politics and History. See Asia and the Pacific/Australia and the Pacific section.

Bayou La Rose. See Zines section.

5604. ***British Journal of Political Science.*** [ISSN: 0007-1234] 1971. q. USD 239 (Individuals, USD 67). Ed(s): David Sanders, Albert Weale. Cambridge University Press, The Edinburgh Bldg, Shaftesbury Rd, Cambridge, CB2 2RU, United Kingdom; information@cambridge.org; http://uk.cambridge.org/journals. Illus., index, adv. Refereed. Vol. ends: Oct. Microform: PQC. Online: EBSCO Publishing; Florida Center for Library Automation; Gale Group; JSTOR (Web-based Journal Archive); OCLC Online Computer Library Center, Inc.; RoweCom Information Quest; Swets Blackwell. Reprint: SWZ. *Indexed:* ABCPolSci, AmH&L, BAS, HRA, IBSS, IPSA, PAIS, PRA, PSA, RRTA, SSCI, SSI, SWA, SociolAb, WAE&RSA. *Aud.:* Ac.

Highly regarded within the field, *British Journal of Political Science* asserts that "works addressed to problems of general significance to students of politics will be published whatever the period(s) or place(s) drawn upon for evidence." Each issue typically includes five or so research reports, one review article, and several notes and comments. Although the range of topics and the affiliations of the authors reflect the journal's international orientation, most of the articles focus on Western Europe and the United States. Articles have included "Exploring uncharted territory: the Irish presidential election 1997," "The past in the present: a cleavage theory of party response to European integration," and "Senate elections in the United States, 1920–1994." The journal is recommended mainly for academic libraries.

5605. ***Brookings Review.*** Formerly: *Brookings Bulletin.* [ISSN: 0745-1253] 1962. q. USD 17.95 domestic; USD 24.95 foreign. Ed(s): Brenda Szittya. Brookings Institution Press, 1775 Massachusetts Ave, NW, Washington, DC 20036-2188. Illus., adv. Circ: 20000. Vol. ends: No. 4. Microform: PQC. Online: EBSCO Publishing; Florida Center for Library Automation; Gale Group; Northern Light Technology, Inc.; OCLC Online Computer Library Center, Inc.; ProQuest Information & Learning; H.W. Wilson. Reprint: PQC. *Indexed:* ABIn, ABS&EES, AgeL, HRA, IBSS, IPSA, PAIS, PRA, PSA, RGPR, SFSA. *Aud.:* Hs,Ga, Sa.

The Brookings Institution is a major Washington-based think tank that aims to serve as a "bridge between scholarship and public policy." The work of this nonprofit research organization includes economic, foreign policy, and governmental studies. Its publication, *Brookings Review*, "is designed to make Brookings research and public policy proposals accessible to a wide audience." Each issue focuses on a single current or emerging topic with background articles, as well as discussions of public policy implications and related legislation and regulatory pronouncements. For example, issues have focused on the state of the presidential appointment process and welfare reform. An excellent choice for many libraries.

5606. ***Canadian Journal of Political Science.*** Supersedes in part (in 1967): *Canadian Journal of Economics and Political Science;* Which was formerly (1928-1934): *Contributions to Canada Economics.* [ISSN: 0008-4239] 1968. q. CND 65 CND 21 per issue domestic. Ed(s): Sandra Burt, Andrew Cooper. Wilfrid Laurier University Press, 75 University Ave W, Waterloo, ON N2L 3C5, Canada; press@wlu.ca; http://www.wlupress.wlu.ca. Illus., index, adv. Refereed. Circ: 1580 Paid. Vol. ends: No. 4. Microform: MML. Online: Gale Group; Ingenta Select. *Indexed:* ABCPolSci, ABS&EES, AmH&L, ArtHuCI, BAS, CBCARef, CPerI, CommAb, IBSS, IBZ, IPSA, LRI, PAIS, PRA, PSA, RiskAb, SSCI, SSI, SociolAb. *Bk. rev.:* 35, 650-700 words. *Aud.:* Ac, Sa.

This official publication of the Canadian Political Science Association publishes scholarly and research articles in all areas of political science. The primary emphasis is on Canadian politics and the contributors are Canadian academics. Some articles are written in French, but the majority are in English, and an abstract in French and English accompanies each article. The journal also publishes reviews of books written by both Canadian and non-Canadian authors, as well as comments and replies to articles.

Conservatively Incorrect. See Zines/Electronic Journals section.

5607. *Constellations: an international journal of critical and democratic theory.* Formerly (until 1994): *Praxis International.* [ISSN: 1351-0487] 1981. q. GBP 313 print & online eds. Ed(s): Andrew Arato, Nancy Fraser. Blackwell Publishing Ltd., 9600 Garsington Rd, PO Box 805, Oxford, OX4 2DQ, United Kingdom; customerservices@oxon.blackwellpublishing.com; http://www.blackwellpublishing.com/. Illus., adv. Refereed. Vol. ends: No. 4. Microform: PQC. Online: EBSCO Publishing; ingenta.com; OCLC Online Computer Library Center, Inc.; RoweCom Information Quest; Swets Blackwell. Reprint: PQC; SWZ. *Indexed:* AltPI, IBSS, IPB, IPSA, PSA, PhilInd, SociolAb. *Bk. rev.:* 2-5, 2,000-3,000 words. *Aud.:* Ac, Sa.

Constellations "examines the creative ferment of critical social and political thought with the goal of setting the international agenda for radical philosophy and social criticism for the future." Contributors are international scholars. Although occasional thematic issues are published, the typical issue includes six or so articles as well as book reviews. Articles have included "The Democratic Problem of the White Citizen" and "Classifying Acts: State Speech, Race, and Democracy." Appropriate for graduate students and specialists.

Gender and Development. See Women: Feminist and Special Interest/Feminist and Women's Studies section.

5608. *History of Political Thought.* [ISSN: 0143-781X] 1980. q. GBP 73 print & online (Individuals, GBP 38 print & online). Ed(s): Janet Coleman, Iain Hampshire-Monk. Imprint Academic, PO Box 200, Exeter, EXS 5YX, United Kingdom; sandra@imprint.co.uk; http://www.imprint.co.uk. Illus., index, adv. Refereed. Circ: 750 Paid. Vol. ends: No. 4. Online: ingenta.com; OCLC Online Computer Library Center, Inc.; Swets Blackwell. *Indexed:* ABCPolSci, AmH&L, ArtHuCI, IBSS, IPB, IPSA, PSA, PhilInd, SSCI, SociolAb. *Bk. rev.:* 2-7, 625 words. *Aud.:* Ac.

This journal focuses exclusively on "the historical study of political ideas and associated methodological problems." It publishes refereed articles on political theorists and philosophers (e.g., Plato, Hobbes, Marx, and Rousseau) and on political thought during a particular era (e.g., Ancient Greece, Middle Ages, Renaissance, and Reformation). Contributors include academics from various disciplines (e.g., philosophy, English, history, and political science). A typical issue includes six or seven very scholarly articles, a review article, and five book reviews. Highly recommended for academic libraries supporting programs in political science.

5609. *International Political Science Review.* [ISSN: 0192-5121] 1980. q. GBP 195 print & online eds. in Europe, Middle East, Africa & Australasia. Ed(s): Nazli Choucri, Jean Laponce. Sage Publications Ltd., 6 Bonhill St, London, EC2A 4PU, United Kingdom; info@sagepub.co.uk; http://www.sagepub.co.uk/. Illus., index, adv. Refereed. Circ: 2200. Vol. ends: No. 4. Microform: WSH; PMC; PQC. Online: EBSCO Publishing; Gale Group; ingenta.com; OCLC Online Computer Library Center, Inc.; RoweCom Information Quest; Sage Publications, Inc.; Swets Blackwell. Reprint: WSH. *Indexed:* ABCPolSci, ArtHuCI, BAS, IBSS, IPSA, PRA, PSA, SSCI, SSI, SociolAb. *Aud.:* Ac.

This is the official publication of the International Political Science Association. Most issues are devoted to a single topic, e.g., "Management of Social Transformation." The themes and editors for forthcoming issues are listed in the back of the current issue. Although some articles are in French with English abstracts, the majority are in English, accompanied by an abstract in French. The editors and their international advisory board seek articles on important and controversial disciplinary issues, as well as those that explore new methodologies and areas of inquiry. Recommended for academic libraries seeking to present diverse viewpoints on international political science issues.

5610. *Journal of Politics.* [ISSN: 0022-3816] 1939. q. USD 153 print & online eds. Blackwell Publishing, Inc., Commerce Place, 350 Main St, Malden, MA 02148; subscrip@blackwellpub.com; http://www.blackwellpublishing.com. Illus., index, adv. Refereed. Circ: 4000. Vol. ends: Nov. Microform: PQC. Online: Gale Group; ingenta.com; RoweCom Information Quest; Swets Blackwell. *Indexed:* ABCPolSci, ABS&EES, AgeL, AmH&L, ArtHuCI, BAS, BRI, CBRI, CommAb, IBSS, IPSA, LRI, PAIS, PRA, PSA, SSCI, SSI, SWA, SociolAb. *Bk. rev.:* 25, 700-800 words. *Aud.:* Ac.

This highly regarded title is the oldest regional political science journal in the United States. Described as a general journal of political science, *The Journal of Politics* publishes scholarly research and analytical pieces in American politics, comparative and international politics, and political theory. A "Research Notes" section provides a forum for methodology discussions, including responses and counterresponses to critiques of data analyses published in earlier articles. A typical issue also includes a substantial collection of book reviews and occasionally review essays of several books on a similar theme. These reviews are useful as a selection tool for the political science bibliographer.

5611. *Journal of Theoretical Politics.* [ISSN: 0951-6298] 1989. q. GBP 363 combined subscription print & online eds. in UK, Europe, Middle East, Africa & Australasia; USD 599 combined subscription elsewhere print & online eds. Ed(s): Keith Dowding, Jan-Erik Lane. Sage Publications Ltd., 6 Bonhill St, London, EC2A 4PU, United Kingdom; info@sagepub.co.uk; http://www.sagepub.co.uk/. Illus., index, adv. Sample. Refereed. Circ: 800. Vol. ends: No. 4. Online: EBSCO Publishing; ingenta.com; OCLC Online Computer Library Center, Inc.; RoweCom Information Quest; Sage Publications, Inc.; Swets Blackwell. *Indexed:* ABCPolSci, CJA, IBSS, IBZ, IPSA, PRA, SSCI. *Aud.:* Ac.

This well-respected international journal focuses exclusively on the theoretical aspects of political science research. Targeting a wide audience while espousing a broad scope, the journal publishes articles for social scientists "which evaluate the relative merits of competing theories to explain empirical phenomena, and original syntheses of recent theoretical developments in diverse fields." A typical issue includes four or five well-documented research reports or theoretical discussions and several research notes. The latter serve as a forum for questioning and clarifying earlier reports. Recommended for upper-level academic libraries.

Meridians. See Women: Feminist and Special Interest/Feminist and Women's Studies section.

5612. *New Political Science: a journal of politics & culture.* [ISSN: 0739-3148] 1979. q. GBP 169 (Individuals, GBP 50). Ed(s): George Katsiaficas. Carfax Publishing Ltd., 4 Park Sq, Milton Park, Abingdon, OX14 4RN, United Kingdom; enquiry@tandf.co.uk; http://www.tandf.co.uk/. Illus., index, adv. Refereed. Circ: 300 Paid. Vol. ends: No. 4. Online: EBSCO Publishing; Ingenta Select; RoweCom Information Quest; Swets Blackwell. Reprint: PSC. *Indexed:* ABS&EES, AltPI, IBZ, IPSA, PAIS, PSA, SociolAb. *Bk. rev.:* 5, 1,000-1,250 words. *Aud.:* Ac, Sa.

This official publication of the Caucus for a New Political Science (CNPS), a section of the American Political Science Association, strives "to make the study of politics relevant to the struggle for a better world." Committed to progressive social change, *New Political Science* targets both general and specialized audiences and holds that political and cultural development are inextricably intertwined. Each issue typically includes five or so articles, a commentary piece, and a review section. The latter includes thematic reviews, review essays, and book reviews, as well as a selected list of books submitted for review. Many issues also focus on a single topic, e.g., "Sudan: Identity, diversity and religion." Although it is not widely indexed, this international left-wing journal is often provocative, and it provides a publishing outlet for a diverse group of American academics.

5613. *P S: Political Science & Politics.* Incorporates (1974-1990): *Political Science Teacher;* Formerly (until 1988): *P S (Washington, DC);* Which supersedes in part (in 1968): *American Political Science Review.* [ISSN: 1049-0965] 1968. q. USD 475 combined subscription print & online eds. Ed(s): Robert Hauck. Cambridge University Press, information@cambridge.org; http://uk.cambridge.org. Illus., index, adv. Refereed. Circ: 16000. Vol. ends: No. 4. Microform: PQC. Online: bigchalk; Florida

Center for Library Automation; Gale Group; JSTOR (Web-based Journal Archive); OCLC Online Computer Library Center, Inc.; ProQuest Information & Learning; H.W. Wilson. Reprint: PQC. *Indexed:* ABCPolSci, ABS&EES, AgeL, ArtHuCI, CIJE, IBSS, IPSA, PAIS, PSA, SSCI, SSI, SWR&A. *Aud.:* Ac, Sa.

PS departs from traditional academic journals in both format and content. Looking like a thick magazine, *PS* publishes both scholarly articles and pieces more typically associated with trade publications. The audience for this journal includes political scientists seeking information outside their specific areas of expertise and teaching faculty. News from the American Political Science Association is reported in each issue, as well as sections on "Features," "The Teacher," and "The Profession." Symposium and e-symposium issues are also published. A good choice for academic libraries and political science departments.

5614. ***The Political Quarterly.*** [ISSN: 0032-3179] 1930. q. GBP 135 print & online eds. Ed(s): Tony Wright, Andrew Gamble. Blackwell Publishing Ltd., 9600 Garsington Rd, PO Box 805, Oxford, OX4 2DQ, United Kingdom; jnlinfo@blackwellpublishers.co.uk; http://www.blackwellpublishing.com/. Illus., index, adv. Refereed. Vol. ends: No. 5. Microform: RPI; PMC. Online: EBSCO Publishing; Gale Group; ingenta.com; OCLC Online Computer Library Center, Inc.; RoweCom Information Quest; Swets Blackwell. Reprint: SWZ. *Indexed:* ABCPolSci, AIAP, AgeL, ArtHuCI, BAS, BrHumI, CommAb, HumInd, IBSS, IBZ, IPSA, IndVet, PAIS, PSA, SSCI, SSI, SociolAb, WAE&RSA. *Bk. rev.:* 10, 800-1,000 words. *Aud.:* Ga, Ac, Sa.

This British publication focuses primarily on British and European public policy "from a centre left perspective." Although the articles are serious and thought provoking, they are neither pedantic nor jargon-laden. Most contributors are British, and a typical issue includes nine or so articles, "Reports and Surveys," and book reviews. A special topical issue is published annually. Recommended for academic libraries.

5615. ***Political Research Quarterly.*** Formerly (until 1993): *Western Political Quarterly.* [ISSN: 1065-9129] 1948. q. USD 50 (Individuals, USD 30; Students, USD 11). Ed(s): Lyn Ragsdall, Bill Dixon. University of Utah, Political Science Department, 260 S Central Campus Dr Rm 252, Salt Lake City, UT 84112-9153; lynda.roberts@poli-sci.utah.edu. Illus., index, adv. Sample. Refereed. Circ: 2300 Paid. Vol. ends: No. 4. Online: bigchalk; Gale Group; JSTOR (Web-based Journal Archive); Northern Light Technology, Inc.; OCLC Online Computer Library Center, Inc.; ProQuest Information & Learning; H.W. Wilson. *Indexed:* ABCPolSci, ABS&EES, AmH&L, BAS, BRI, CBRI, IBSS, IBZ, IPSA, LRI, MLA-IB, PAIS, PRA, PSA, SSCI, SSI, SUSA, SociolAb. *Aud.:* Ac, Sa.

The official journal of the Western Political Science Association. Often quite readable and interesting, this title publishes both original research and field essays. The reported research often includes complex quantitative analysis as well as model-building discussions. The field essays, however, may be of interest to an audience beyond academe, as each essay summarizes and integrates current knowledge in a specific research area, e.g., "Regulatory policy-making in the American states: A review of theories and evidence." A bibliography of recent field essays is available on the *Political Research Quarterly* web site. Recommended for academic libraries.

5616. ***Political Studies.*** [ISSN: 0032-3217] 1953. 5x/yr. GBP 371 print & online eds. Ed(s): Jane Tinkler, Patrick Dunleavy. Blackwell Publishing Ltd., 9600 Garsington Rd, PO Box 805, Oxford, OX4 2DQ, United Kingdom; jnlinfo@blackwellpublishers.co.uk; http://www.blackwellpublishing.com/. Illus., index, adv. Refereed. Vol. ends: No. 5. Microform: PQC. Online: EBSCO Publishing; Gale Group; ingenta.com; OCLC Online Computer Library Center, Inc.; RoweCom Information Quest; Swets Blackwell. Reprint: PSC. *Indexed:* ABCPolSci, AmH&L, ArtHuCI, BAS, BrHumI, CJA, IBSS, IPSA, PAIS, PRA, PSA, RI-1, SSCI, SSI, SWA, SociolAb. *Bk. rev.:* 75, length varies. *Aud.:* Ac.

This official journal of Britain's Political Studies Association publishes "new and significant work in all fields of political science, without restriction on themes, approaches or geographical focus." Most contributors are British, and a typical issue includes several articles that focus primarily on Europe and the United Kingdom. "Debates" provides a forum for comments and rejoinders related to previously published articles as well as lively discussions of current issues. The extensive book review section is well organized by area and subdivision, making it an excellent selection tool. For those libraries seeking the British perspective, this journal is an excellent choice.

5617. ***Political Theory: an international journal of political philosophy.*** [ISSN: 0090-5917] 1973. bi-m. GBP 421 print & online eds. in Europe, Middle East, Africa & Australasia. Ed(s): Stephen K White. Sage Publications, Inc., 2455 Teller Rd, Thousand Oaks, CA 91320; info@sagepub.com; http://www.sagepub.com. Illus., index, adv. Refereed. Circ: 2200. Vol. ends: No. 6. Microform: PQC. Online: EBSCO Publishing; Gale Group; ingenta.com; RoweCom Information Quest; Swets Blackwell. Reprint: PQC; PSC. *Indexed:* ABCPolSci, ABS&EES, ArtHuCI, IBSS, IPB, IPSA, PAIS, PRA, PSA, PhilInd, SSCI, SSI, SUSA, SociolAb. *Bk. rev.:* 5-7, 1,750 words. *Aud.:* Ac.

This highly regarded scholarly journal discusses current and historical political theories and covers philosophers like Aristotle, Marx, Foucault, Hobbes, Locke, and Heidegger. Justice, feminism, liberalism, communism, utilitarianism, political order, enlightenment, and modernism are also covered. Each issue includes several feature articles, a critical exchange, and review essays. Some issues also include a special symposia section, e.g., "Imaging Americans." For academic libraries only.

5618. ***Polity.*** [ISSN: 0032-3497] 1968. q. USD 50 (Individuals, USD 30; Students, USD 17). Ed(s): Nicholas Xenos. Publications Inc., 426 Thompson Hall, University of Massachusetts, Box 752, Amherst, MA 01003; polity@polsci.umass.edu. Illus., index, adv. Refereed. Circ: 1300 Paid. Vol. ends: No. 4. Microform: PQC. Online: Florida Center for Library Automation; Gale Group. *Indexed:* ABCPolSci, ABS&EES, AgeL, AmH&L, ArtHuCI, BAS, FutSurv, HRA, IPSA, PAIS, PRA, PSA, SSCI, SSI, SUSA. *Aud.:* Ac.

This is the official journal of the Northeastern Political Science Association. Covering a wide range of topics, *Polity* publishes articles, review essays, research notes, and occasionally a forum on a special topic. Recent issues focus on "Liberalism and Community" and "City Beautiful." Although scholarly research reports are published here, other, more accessible topical discussions are also included. As a general political science journal, *Polity* is an excellent choice for most libraries.

The Public Eye. See Women: Feminist and Special Interest/Feminist and Women's Studies section.

5619. ***The Review of Politics.*** [ISSN: 0034-6705] 1939. q. USD 52 (Individuals, USD 25). Ed(s): Walter Nicgorski. University of Notre Dame, Review of Politics, PO Box B, Notre Dame, IN 46556-0762; rop.editor.1@nd.edu; http://www.nd.edu/~rop/. Illus., index, adv. Sample. Refereed. Circ: 1700. Vol. ends: No. 4. Microform: PMC; PQC. Online: Chadwyck-Healey Incorporated; EBSCO Publishing; Florida Center for Library Automation; Gale Group; Northern Light Technology, Inc.; OCLC Online Computer Library Center, Inc.; ProQuest Information & Learning; H.W. Wilson. Reprint: PQC; PSC. *Indexed:* ABCPolSci, ABS&EES, AmH&L, BAS, BRI, CBRI, CPL, IBSS, IBZ, IPSA, LRI, PAIS, PRA, PSA, SSCI, SSI. *Aud.:* Ac.

The Review of Politics claims to "emphasize the philosophical and historical approach to politics." Past contributors have included Hannah Arendt, John Kenneth Galbraith, Edward Shils, and Jacques Maritain. Most current contributors are American or Canadian scholars who approach the issues from a Judeo-Christian perspective. Articles have included "Religion and Politics the American Way: The Exemplary William Dean Howells" and "Liberal Impediments to Liberal Education: The Assent to Locke." Book reviews are also published.

Turning the Tide. See Zines section.

Women & Politics. See Women: Feminist and Special Interest/Feminist and Women's Studies section.

Comparative and American Politics

5620. ***Alternatives: global, local, political.*** [ISSN: 0304-3754] 1974. 5x/yr. USD 108 (Individuals, USD 49). Ed(s): R B J Walker, D L Sheth. Lynne Rienner Publishers, 1800 30th St, Ste 314, Boulder, CO 80301-1026; http://www.rienner.com. Illus., adv. Sample. Refereed. Circ: 800 Paid. Vol. ends: No. 5. Microform: WSH; PQC. Online: EBSCO Publishing; Florida Center for Library Automation; Gale Group. Reprint: WSH. *Indexed:* ABCPolSci, AltPI, ArtInd, BiogInd, CBCARef, CLI, EnvAb, FutSurv, IBSS, IBZ, ILP, IPSA, MagInd, PAIS, PRA, PSA, RGPR, SSCI, SociolAb. *Aud.:* Ac.

Published in association with the Center for the Study of Developing Societies (India), the ICU Peace Research Institute (Japan), the World Order Models Project, and the Center for Global Change and Governance, Rutgers University–Newark, each issue includes four or five articles that focus on some aspect of world policy. Articles have included "Security in the South China Sea," "Frontier Politics: Sex, Gender, and the Deconstruction of the Public Sphere," and "The Politics of Legitimacy in International Relations: A Critical Examination of NATO's Intervention in Kosovo." Some volumes are special topical issues and guest edited, e.g., "Poetic World Politics." A good choice for academic libraries seeking to include alternative viewpoints.

5621. ***American Political Science Review.*** Incorporated (1904-1914): *American Political Science Association. Proceedings.* [ISSN: 0003-0554] 1906. q. USD 475 print & online eds. Ed(s): Lee Sigelman. Cambridge University Press, The Edinburgh Bldg, Shaftesbury Rd, Cambridge, CB2 2RU, United Kingdom; information@cambridge.org; http://uk.cambridge.org. Illus., index, adv. Sample. Refereed. Circ: 15000. Vol. ends: No. 4. Microform: MIM; PMC; PQC. Online: Florida Center for Library Automation; Gale Group; JSTOR (Web-based Journal Archive); OCLC Online Computer Library Center, Inc.; ProQuest Information & Learning; H.W. Wilson. *Indexed:* ABCPolSci, ABS&EES, AgeL, AmH&L, ArtHuCI, BAS, BEL&L, BRD, BRI, BiogInd, CBRI, CIJE, CommAb, FutSurv, IBSS, IPSA, JEL, PAIS, PSA, RGPR, SSCI, SSI, SWR&A. *Bk. rev.:* 70-80, 600-700 words. *Aud.:* Ac, Sa.

As the official publication of the American Political Science Association, *APSR* claims to be "the leading journal of political science research." Covering all subfields of political science, each issue of the journal typically includes scholarly articles, a forum section, and extensive book reviews. The articles, which are uniformly well researched and documented, provide an excellent overview of the field's literature and research as well as of the current concerns of political scientists. The book reviews are categorized by subfield: political theory, American politics, comparative politics, and international relations. The breadth and depth of these reviews makes *APSR* an indispensable tool for political science selectors.

5622. ***American Politics Research.*** Formerly (until 2000): *American Politics Quarterly.* [ISSN: 1532-673X] 1973. bi-m. GBP 413 in Europe, Middle East, Africa & Australasia . Ed(s): Tom Holbrook. Sage Publications, Inc., 2455 Teller Rd, Thousand Oaks, CA 91320; info@sagepub.com; http://www.sagepub.com. Illus., index, adv. Refereed. Circ: 1250. Vol. ends: No. 4. Reprint: PSC. *Indexed:* ABCPolSci, AgeL, AmH&L, CJA, CommAb, IPSA, PAIS, PRA, PSA, RiskAb, SSCI, SSI, SUSA, SWA, SociolAb. *Aud.:* Ac.

American Politics Research, formerly *American Politics Quarterly*, "promotes research in all areas of US political behaviour—including urban, state and national policies, as well as pressing social problems requiring political solutions." Recently published studies, which often include complex data analysis and theoretical model-building, have examined political parties, political and legislative behavior, public policy and opinion, and the courts and the legal process. Representative articles include "Policy Balancing Models and the Split-Ticket Voter, 1972–1996" and "Survey Bias on the Front Porch: Are All Subjects Interviewed Equally?" Occasionally, the journal publishes thematic issues, e.g., forecasting success in presidential elections. Recommended for upper-division and graduate level libraries.

5623. ***C Q Weekly.*** Formerly (until vol.56, no.15, 1998): *Congressional Quarterly Weekly Report.* [ISSN: 1521-5997] 1945. w. 48/yr. USD 1696. Ed(s): Susan Benkelman. Congressional Quarterly Inc., 1414 22nd St, N W, Washington, DC 20037; http://www.cq.com. Illus., index, adv. Sample. Circ: 11000. Vol. ends: No. 52. Microform: MIM; PQC. Online: EBSCO Publishing; Gale Group. Reprint: PQC. *Indexed:* ABS&EES, BLI, LRI, MagInd, PAIS, SSI. *Aud.:* Hs, Ac, Sa.

With its reputation for comprehensive and nonpartisan reporting, *CQ Weekly* provides premier coverage of all aspects of Congress, its personalities, its relations with the executive branch, the status of House and Senate bills and resolutions, hearings, the political parties and their leadership, etc. This title is also an excellent source for inside information that is frequently omitted in daily newspapers. Full or partial texts of significant presidential or other speeches are occasionally included, as well as congressional votes on major bills, confirmation hearings, and other roll calls. Although expensive, this weekly publication belongs in every large U.S. public and academic library. Students in particular will find this title useful for identifying term paper and/or speech topics.

5624. ***The Cato Journal: an interdisciplinary journal of public policy analysis.*** [ISSN: 0273-3072] 1981. 3x/yr. USD 50 (Individuals, USD 24). Ed(s): James A Dorn. Cato Institute, 1000 Massachusetts Ave, N W, Washington, DC 20077-0172; http://www.cato.org. Illus., adv. Refereed. Circ: 3200. Vol. ends: No. 3. Online: EBSCO Publishing; Florida Center for Library Automation; Gale Group; Northern Light Technology, Inc.; ProQuest Information & Learning. Reprint: WSH. *Indexed:* ABCPolSci, ABIn, ABS&EES, AgeL, AmH&L, BAS, CLI, EnvAb, IBSS, ILP, IPSA, JEL, PAIS, PRA, PSA, SSCI, SUSA. *Bk. rev.:* 4-6, 800-1,000 words. *Aud.:* Ac, Sa.

The Cato Institute is a Washington-based public policy research foundation that espouses a libertarian/market-liberalism philosophy. Committed to the "principles of limited government, individual liberty, and peace," the institute supports examinations of myriad issues, including Social Security, monetary and natural resources policies, and military spending. Articles published by *The Cato Journal* are often based on papers from the institute's major policy conferences. The target audience is the intelligent layman, and the aim is to achieve greater public involvement in policy questions and debates.

5625. ***Commonwealth and Comparative Politics.*** Former titles (until 1997): *The Journal of Commonwealth & Comparative Politics; Journal of Commonwealth Political Studies.* [ISSN: 1466-2043] 1961. 3x/yr. GBP 197 print & online eds. Ed(s): Roger Charlton, Vicky Randall. Frank Cass Publishers, Crown House, 47 Chase Side, Southgate, London, N14 5BP, United Kingdom; jnlsubs@frankcass.com; http://www.frankcass.com/jnls/. Illus., index, adv. Refereed. Vol. ends: No. 3. Microform: PQC. Online: EBSCO Publishing; Gale Group; Ingenta Select. *Indexed:* ABCPolSci, AmH&L, BAS, BrHumI, GeogAbPG, IBSS, IPSA, PAIS, PSA, RRTA, SSCI, SociolAb, WAE&RSA. *Bk. rev.:* 15-30, 1,000 words. *Aud.:* Ac, Sa.

This publication focuses on the "politics of Commonwealth countries related explicitly to issues of general significance for students of comparative politics." A typical issue includes four scholarly articles, a review symposium on a forthcoming book, and book reviews. Articles have included "Democratic Consolidation and Government Changeover in the Irish Free State" and "Ethnic Conflict in Malaysia Revisited." Tables of contents, with article abstracts, are available on the journal web site.

5626. ***Comparative Political Studies.*** [ISSN: 0010-4140] 1968. 10x/yr. GBP 482 in Europe, Middle East, Africa & Australasia. Ed(s): James A Caporaso. Sage Publications, Inc., 2455 Teller Rd, Thousand Oaks, CA 91320; info@sagepub.com; http://www.sagepub.com. Illus., index, adv. Refereed. Circ: 1650. Vol. ends: No. 6. Microform: PQC. Online: Pub.; Chadwyck-Healey Incorporated; Florida Center for Library Automation; Gale Group; ingenta.com; OCLC Online Computer Library Center, Inc.; ProQuest Information & Learning; RoweCom Information Quest; Swets Blackwell. *Indexed:* ABCPolSci, ABS&EES, ArtHuCI, BAS, CommAb, IBSS, IPSA, PAIS, PRA, PSA, RRTA, SSCI, SSI, SWA, SociolAb, WAE&RSA. *Bk. rev.:* 2-4, 1,500 words. *Aud.:* Ac, Sa.

One of the premier titles in comparative politics, this interdisciplinary journal serves as an international forum for discussions of comparative methodology, theory, and research. A typical issue includes four well-documented articles and two lengthy book reviews. Topics range "from democracy in the Third World to civil-military relations in the Middle East, from electoral systems and party politics in Eastern Europe to economic performance in Latin America, from comparisons of political asylum in North America and western Europe to national conflicts in Asian countries." Recommended for academic libraries.

5627. ***Comparative Politics.*** [ISSN: 0010-4159] 1968. q. USD 60 (Individuals, USD 30). Ed(s): Kenneth P Erickson, I L Markovitz. City University of New York, Political Science Program, 365 Fifth Ave, New York, NY 10016-4309. Illus., Refereed. Circ: 2000. Vol. ends: No. 4. Microform: MIM; PQC. Online: Gale Group; JSTOR (Web-based Journal Archive). Reprint: PQC. *Indexed:* ABCPolSci, ABS&EES, AgeL, AmH&L, ArtHuCI, BAS, IBSS, IPSA, PAIS, PRA, PSA, RRTA, SSCI, SSI, SociolAb, WAE&RSA. *Bk. rev.:* 2-4, 4,000 words. *Aud.:* Ac, Sa.

This premier journal in comparative politics is sponsored, edited, and published by the Ph.D. program in political science of the City University of New York. "Devoted to the comparative analysis of political institutions and behavior," the journal publishes articles by faculty and doctoral candidates in political science. Each issue typically contains five articles with abstracts, as well as an in-depth review piece. The titles and authors of forthcoming articles are listed in the back of each issue. Articles have included "Democratization in Germany," "Cultural Values and Political Trust: A Comparison of the People's Republic of China and Taiwan," and "Assessing the Consequences of Electoral Democracy: Subnational Legislative Changes in Mexico." This standard title is recommended for academic libraries.

5628. ***Congress & the Presidency: a journal of capital studies.*** Former titles (until 1981): *Congressional Studies;* (until 1978): *Capitol Studies.* [ISSN: 0734-3469] 1972. s-a. USD 27 (Individuals, USD 17; Students, USD 14). Ed(s): Susan Webb Hammond, Charles E Walcott. American University, Center for Congressional and Presidential Studies, 4400 Massachusetts Ave, N W, Washington, DC 20016-8022; candp@american.edu; http://www.american.edu/ccps. Illus., adv. Refereed. Circ: 650. Vol. ends: No. 2. *Indexed:* ABCPolSci, AIAP, AmH&L, CommAb, IPSA, PAIS, SSCI. *Bk. rev.:* 6-8, 800-1,000 words. *Aud.:* Ac, Sa.

This interdisciplinary journal of history and political science focuses on the presidency, the Congress, and the relationship between these two institutions. National policy making is also examined, and most authors are American academics. A typical issue includes four articles, a review essay, and book reviews of varying lengths. Recommended for academic libraries.

5629. ***Congressional Digest: the pro & con monthly.*** [ISSN: 0010-5899] 1921. m. except June/July & Aug./Sep. USD 59 domestic; USD 66.25 in Canada & Mexico; USD 67.50 elsewhere. Ed(s): Sarah Orrick. Congressional Digest Corp., 3231 P St, N W, Washington, DC 20007; http://www.congressionaldigest.com. Illus., index. Vol. ends: Dec. Online: Gale Group. *Indexed:* LRI, MagInd, PAIS, RGPR, SSI. *Aud.:* Hs, Ga, Ac, Sa.

This journal provides in-depth coverage of the pros and cons of public-policy issues. Using a single-theme format, each issue includes a series of background articles on the topic, followed by a "Pro & Con" section that serves as a forum for various viewpoints on that topic. The overall result is a well-balanced treatment of currently important and often controversial issues. *Congressional Digest* will appeal to a wide audience, including laypersons seeking greater understanding of current events and students writing research papers. Debate teams will find this title particularly useful: the National Forensic League's "National Policy Debate Topic" is the focus of an entire issue each year. Recommended for all libraries.

Critical Review. See Cultural-Social Studies section.

5630. ***Electoral Studies.*** [ISSN: 0261-3794] 1982. q. EUR 671 (Individuals, EUR 182). Ed(s): Dr. Harold D Clarke, Geoffrey Evans. Pergamon, The Boulevard, Langford Ln, East Park, Kidlington, OX5 1GB, United Kingdom. Illus., index, adv. Refereed. Vol. ends: No. 4. Microform: PQC. Online: ingenta.com; ScienceDirect; Swets Blackwell. *Indexed:* ABCPolSci, IBSS, IPSA, PAIS, PSA, SSCI. *Aud.:* Ac, Sa.

This refereed journal analyzes electoral systems and voter behavior and reports election results from around the world. Typically, each issue includes five or six highly theoretical or research-oriented articles as well as "Notes on Recent Elections" and "Cycle of Elections." The latter section charts national elections in countries with populations over one million and includes an index to the *Electoral Studies* issue in which each country's results were last reported. The journal also contains the section "Electoral Inquiry," which examines methodological issues related to the study of the electoral process.

5631. ***Environmental Politics.*** [ISSN: 0964-4016] 1992. q. GBP 241 print & online eds. Ed(s): Christopher Roots, Andrew Dobson. Frank Cass Publishers, Crown House, 47 Chase Side, Southgate, London, N14 5BP, United Kingdom; jnlsubs@frankcass.com; http://www.frankcass.com/jnls/. Illus., index, adv. Sample. Refereed. Vol. ends: Winter. Microform: PQC. Online: EBSCO Publishing; Gale Group; Ingenta Select. *Indexed:* EnvAb, IBSS, IPSA, PSA, SSI, SWA, SociolAb, WAE&RSA, ZooRec. *Bk. rev.:* 20-25, 150-500 words. *Aud.:* Ac, Sa.

This scholarly journal is devoted to "the study of environmental politics, with a primary, though not exclusive, focus on industrialised countries." The refereed articles explore environmental movements and parties; international, national, and local public policy implementation; commentary on new ideas and theories; and increasingly important international environmental issues. Although this journal is highly specialized and therefore not appropriate for many libraries, the book reviews provide good coverage of environmental publications. Recommended for academic libraries serving strong environmental programs.

5632. ***European Journal of Political Research.*** [ISSN: 0304-4130] 1973. 8x/yr. USD 669 print & online eds. Blackwell Publishing Ltd., 9600 Garsington Rd, PO Box 805, Oxford, OX4 2DQ, United Kingdom; customerservices@oxon.blackwellpublishing.com; http://www.blackwellpublishing.com/. Illus., index, adv. Refereed. Microform: PQC. Online: EBSCO Publishing; ingenta.com; Kluwer Online; OCLC Online Computer Library Center, Inc.; Ovid Technologies, Inc.; RoweCom Information Quest; ScienceDirect; Swets Blackwell. Reprint: SWZ. *Indexed:* ABCPolSci, CommAb, IBSS, IPSA, PSA, RiskAb, SSCI, SWA, SociolAb, WAE&RSA. *Aud.:* Ac, Sa.

As the official publication of the European Consortium for Political Research, this well-regarded, English-language journal includes both original work and translations of important articles from other sources. The journal focuses primarily on Europe, publishing articles that are often theoretical or comparative in nature. Political parties and electoral behavior are frequent topics. Articles have included "Globalization, government spending and taxation in the OECD" and "Partisan responses to Europe: Comparing Finnish and Swedish political parties." Most appropriate for large academic libraries.

Governing. See Government Periodicals—State and Local/General section.

5633. ***Government and Opposition: an international journal of comparative politics.*** [ISSN: 0017-257X] 1965. q. USD 174 print & online eds. Ed(s): M Moran. Blackwell Publishing Ltd., 9600 Garsington Rd, PO Box 805, Oxford, OX4 2DQ, United Kingdom; customerservices@oxon.blackwellpublishing.com; http://www.blackwellpublishing.com/. Illus., index, adv. Refereed. Circ: 1500 Paid. Vol. ends: No. 4. Reprint: PSC. *Indexed:* ABCPolSci, ArtHuCI, BAS, BrHumI, IBSS, IPSA, PAIS, PSA, SSCI, SSI, SociolAb. *Bk. rev.:* 8-12, 1,000-1,500 words. *Aud.:* Ac, Sa.

This well-respected journal publishes commissioned papers and refereed articles on single-country cases and the analysis of comparative data. Targeting a broad audience, *Government and Opposition* is less theoretical and more accessible than some of its counterparts. Typically, each issue includes five or six articles, several lengthy book reviews, and an occasional review article. Topics covered have included elections in Spain and Romania, American civic disengagement, and the European Union. Recommended for academic libraries.

5634. ***The Independent Review: a journal of political economy.*** [ISSN: 1086-1653] 1996. q. USD 83.95 (Individuals, USD 28.95; USD 7.50 newsstand/cover per issue). Ed(s): David J Theroux, Robert Higgs. Independent Institute, 100 Swan Way, Oakland, CA 94621-1428; review@independent.org. Illus., index, adv. Refereed. Circ: 4000 Paid. Vol. ends: No. 4. *Indexed:* BRI, CBRI, CommAb, IPSA, JEL, PAIS, PRA, PSA, RiskAb. *Bk. rev.:* 6-8, 1,500 words. *Aud.:* Ac.

Published under the auspices of the Independent Institute, this journal of political economy reflects the conservative bent of that think tank, and many articles espouse a classic tradition of limited government and free markets. The journal targets a broad audience, and, although there are reports of empirical economic research, most articles are accessible to both the generalist and lay reader. Contributors include policy experts and scholars from various disciplines, and most articles focus on the political economic implications of U.S. public policy. A typical issue includes seven to nine articles and five or six lengthy book reviews. Recommended for academic libraries seeking balance in the ideological perspectives of the collection.

5635. ***International Journal of Public Opinion Research.*** [ISSN: 0954-2892] 1989. q. GBP 170. Ed(s): Wolfgang Donsbach, Robert M. Worcester. Oxford University Press, Great Clarendon St, Oxford, OX2 6DP, United Kingdom; jnl.orders@oup.co.uk; http://www3.oup.co.uk/jnls. Illus., adv. Refereed. Circ: 1000. Vol. ends: No. 4. Reprint: PSC. *Indexed:* ArtHuCI, CommAb, IBSS, IPSA, PAIS, PRA, PSA, SSCI, SociolAb. *Bk. rev.:* 1-3, 750 words. *Aud.:* Ac, Sa.

Sponsored by the World Association for Public Opinion Research, this refereed journal provides a multidisciplinary and international forum for discussions of public-opinion theory and research. Methodologies, particularly public-opinion surveys and polling, are well covered. The journal also publishes articles on public opinion as a psychosocial dynamic that shapes individual and group behaviors and attitudes. The review section includes recent books and articles of interest that have been published in peer-reviewed journals. A highly specialized journal recommended for academic libraries supporting graduate programs in the social sciences.

5636. ***Journal of Democracy.*** [ISSN: 1045-5736] 1990. q. USD 105 domestic; USD 112 in Canada & Mexico; USD 116 elsewhere. Ed(s): Larry Diamond, Marc F Plattner. Johns Hopkins University Press, Journals Publishing Division, 2715 N Charles St, Baltimore, MD 21218-4363; jlorder@jhupress.jhu.edu; http://www.press.jhu.edu/. Illus., index, adv. Refereed. Circ: 3709. Vol. ends: No. 4. Online: EBSCO Publishing; Gale Group; OCLC Online Computer Library Center, Inc.; Project MUSE; RoweCom Information Quest; Swets Blackwell. Reprint: PSC; SWZ. *Indexed:* ABCPolSci, ABS&EES, IBSS, IBZ, IPSA, PAIS, PSA, SSCI, SSI, SociolAb. *Bk. rev.:* 2-3, 1,500-1,750 words. *Aud.:* Ac, Sa.

With its exclusive focus on democracy, this journal serves as an international forum for discussions of democratic theory and practice across the globe, "including political institutions, parties and elections, civil society, ethnic conflict, economic reform, public opinion, the role of the media, and constitutionalism." Intended as a resource for both general readers and scholars, this very readable journal publishes analytical and scholarly essays, field reports, book reviews, news updates, election results, and excerpts from important speeches. Contributors include academics, government officials, and leaders of democratic movements. Recommended for academic libraries supporting political science programs.

5637. ***Legislative Studies Quarterly.*** [ISSN: 0362-9805] 1976. q. USD 110 (Individuals, USD 40). Ed(s): Michelle L Wiegand. University of Iowa, Comparative Legislative Research Center, 334 Schaeffer Hall, Iowa City, IA 52242-1409; http://www.uiowa.edu. Illus., index, adv. Refereed. Circ: 1000. Vol. ends: No. 4. Microform: PQC. Online: JSTOR (Web-based Journal Archive). Reprint: PQC; WSH. *Indexed:* ABCPolSci, ABS&EES, IBSS, IBZ, IPSA, PRA, PSA, SSCI, SociolAb. *Aud.:* Ac, Sa.

This international journal publishes research on representative assemblies, including "scholarly work on parliaments and legislatures, their relations to other political institutions, their functions in the political system, and the activities of their members both within the institution and outside." There are no editorial limits on settings and time periods covered, but the research approaches must be "consistent with the normal canons of scholarship." A comparative legislative research section was introduced five years ago to emphasize the international scope of the journal. However, despite this new direction, the majority of articles continue to focus on American legislative bodies, and most authors are American academics.

5638. ***The National Interest.*** [ISSN: 0884-9382] 1985. q. USD 31 (Individuals, USD 26; USD 7 newsstand/cover per issue). Ed(s): Adam Garfinkle. The National Interest, Inc., 1615 L St NW, Ste 1230, Washington, DC 20036. Illus., adv. Circ: 15000 Paid. Vol. ends: Winter. Microform: PQC. Online: EBSCO Publishing; Florida Center for Library Automation; Gale Group; LexisNexis; Northern Light Technology, Inc.; OCLC Online Computer Library Center, Inc.; ProQuest Information & Learning; H.W. Wilson. *Indexed:* ABS&EES, AmH&L, IBSS, IPSA, PAIS, PSA, SSI, SociolAb. *Bk. rev.:* 5, 1,500 words. *Aud.:* Ga, Sa.

While retaining its commitment to stimulating discussions of American foreign policy and world politics, *The National Interest* has undergone a number of editorial changes. Despite these changes, however, the overall approach of the journal remains the same: It views international affairs "as a human activity in which many strands—political power, history, culture, economics, religion, science and military force—all intertwine." Targeting a broad audience, the contributors include academics, policy specialists, and highly placed officials of the current and past Republican administrations. With its strong conservative and libertarian leanings, this title would be an excellent choice to balance the liberal publications in the collection.

5639. ***National Journal: the weekly on politics and government.*** Incorporates: *National Issues Outlook;* Former titles: *National Journal Reports; National Journal.* [ISSN: 0360-4217] 1969. w. USD 1499. Ed(s): Michael Kelly, Charles Green. National Journal Group, Inc., 1501 M St, N W, Ste 300, Washington, DC 20005; orders@nationaljournal.com; http://www.nationaljournal.com. Illus., index, adv. Circ: 8400. Vol. ends: No. 52. Microform: PQC. Online: bigchalk; EBSCO Publishing; Factiva; Florida Center for Library Automation; Gale Group; LexisNexis; OCLC Online Computer Library Center, Inc.; ProQuest Information & Learning. *Indexed:* ABS&EES, AgeL, BAS, BLI, EnvAb, LRI, MCR, PAIS. *Aud.:* Hs, Ga, Ac.

This conservative weekly provides "authoritative, nonpartisan coverage and analysis of key political and policy developments." Articles are staff-written and typically cover the presidency, Congress, health and welfare, economics, lobbying, foreign affairs, and the media. Extensively illustrated and engagingly written, *National Journal* appeals to and is accessible by a broad audience. A good choice for many libraries, but the magazine's high cost may deter smaller libraries and others with shrinking journals budgets.

5640. ***New Politics: a journal of socialist thought.*** [ISSN: 0028-6494] 1961. s-a. USD 20 domestic; USD 24 foreign; USD 6 newsstand/cover per issue. Ed(s): Julius Jacobson, Phyllis Jacobson. New Politics Associates, Inc., 328 Clinton St, Brooklyn, NY 11231; newpol@igc.apc.org; http://www.wilpaterson.edu/wpcpages/icip/newpol/. Illus., index, adv. Circ: 3500 Paid. Vol. ends: No. 4. Microform: PQC. Online: ProQuest Information & Learning; SoftLine Information. Reprint: PQC. *Indexed:* ABS&EES, AltPI, HRA, IBSS, IPSA, PAIS, PRA, PSA, SUSA, SociolAb. *Bk. rev.:* 1-10, 1,500-2,000 words. *Aud.:* Ac, Sa.

This well-established radical journal provides a forum for the independent socialist left. Squarely aligned with the poor and working class, labor unions, feminism, and affirmative action, the journal covers labor and social movements with an emphasis on cultural and intellectual history. Each 200-page, semi-annual issue includes a theme-based symposium, numerous commentary articles, and book and film reviews.

5641. ***Parliamentary Affairs: devoted to all aspects of parliamentary democracy.*** [ISSN: 0031-2290] 1947. q. GBP 160. Ed(s): F. Ridley. Oxford University Press, Great Clarendon St, Oxford, OX2 6DP, United Kingdom; jnl.orders@oup.co.uk; http://www3.oup.co.uk/jnls. Illus., index, adv. Refereed. Circ: 1550. Vol. ends: No. 4. Microform: PQC. Online: EBSCO Publishing; Florida Center for Library Automation; Gale Group; HighWire Press; ingenta.com; Northern Light Technology, Inc.;

OCLC Online Computer Library Center, Inc.; ProQuest Information & Learning; RoweCom Information Quest; Swets Blackwell. Reprint: PSC. *Indexed:* ABCPolSci, ArtHuCI, BrHumI, IBSS, IBZ, IPSA, PAIS, PSA, SSCI, SSI, SociolAb. *Bk. rev.:* 3, 1,500 words. *Aud.:* Ac, Sa.

Published by the Hansard Society for Parliamentary Government, this journal covers "all the aspects of government and politics directly or indirectly connected with Parliament and parliamentary systems in Britain and throughout the world." The emphasis is on articles useful to a broad audience rather than scholarly research reports directed at specialists. The book section includes reviews organized by topic and, in spring, an annotated bibliography of government publications for the previous parliamentary session. Occasionally, theme issues are published.

5642. *Policy Studies Journal.* [ISSN: 0190-292X] 1972. q. USD 530 print & online eds. Ed(s): Mack Shelley. Blackwell Publishing, Inc., Commerce Place, 350 Main St, Malden, MA 02148; subscrip@blackwellpub.com; http://www.blackwellpub.com. Illus., index, adv. Refereed. Circ: 2400. Vol. ends: No. 4. Online: bigchalk; Chadwyck-Healey Incorporated; EBSCO Publishing; Florida Center for Library Automation; Gale Group; ingenta.com; Northern Light Technology, Inc.; OCLC Online Computer Library Center, Inc.; ProQuest Information & Learning; H.W. Wilson. Reprint: PQC. *Indexed:* ABCPolSci, ABS&EES, ASG, AgeL, AmH&L, ArtHuCI, BRI, CBRI, CJA, EnvAb, FutSurv, GeogAbPG, HRA, IPSA, InfoSAb, LRI, PAIS, PRA, PSA, SSCI, SSI, SUSA, SWA, SociolAb. *Bk. rev.:* 25, 125-1,000 words. *Aud.:* Ac, Sa.

This scholarly journal focuses on public policy issues at all levels of government. Welcoming a comparative approach to the study of these topics, a typical issue includes three or four articles, review essays, notes and announcements, and a "Symposium" section. The latter examines a single topic, e.g., "Uncertainty and Environmental Policy" and "The Changing Face(s) of Ireland." Submissions to *Policy Studies Journal* are refereed, with a reported manuscript acceptance rate of nine percent. Subscribers also receive *Policy Studies Review.*

5643. *Political Communication: an international journal.* Formerly (until 1992): *Political Communication and Persuasion.* [ISSN: 1058-4609] 1980. q. USD 324 (Individuals, USD 135). Ed(s): David L Swanson. Taylor & Francis Inc, 325 Chestnut St, Suite 800, Philadelphia, PA 19016; info@taylorandfrancis.com; http://www.taylorandfrancis.com/. Illus., adv. Refereed. Vol. ends: No. 4. Online: EBSCO Publishing; Gale Group; Ingenta Select; OCLC Online Computer Library Center, Inc.; RoweCom Information Quest; Swets Blackwell. Reprint: PSC. *Indexed:* ABCPolSci, ArtHuCI, CJA, CommAb, IBSS, IPSA, PAIS, PRA, PSA, SSCI, SSI, SociolAb. *Aud.:* Ac, Sa.

This interdisciplinary journal focuses on a broad range of topics related to the international study of politics and communication. Research reports and some highly theoretical articles are published, while regular "Symposium" issues investigate key topics in depth. Most contributors are academics or doctoral students, and both the new and established media are well covered, e.g., "Connecting and disconnecting with civic life: Patterns of Internet use and the production of social capital." Highly recommended for all academic libraries supporting political science and/or communication programs.

5644. *Politics and Society.* [ISSN: 0032-3292] 1970. q. GBP 344 print & online eds. in Europe, Middle East, Africa & Australasia. Ed(s): Mary Ann Twist. Sage Publications, Inc., 2455 Teller Rd, Thousand Oaks, CA 91320; info@sagepub.com; http://www.sagepub.com. Illus., index, adv. Refereed. Circ: 1400. Vol. ends: No. 4. Microform: PQC. Online: Pub.; EBSCO Publishing; Florida Center for Library Automation; Gale Group; ingenta.com; OCLC Online Computer Library Center, Inc.; ProQuest Information & Learning; RoweCom Information Quest; Swets Blackwell. Reprint: SCH. *Indexed:* ABCPolSci, ABS&EES, ASSIA, AltPI, AmH&L, ArtHuCI, BAS, HRA, IBSS, IPSA, PRA, PSA, RiskAb, SSCI, SSI, SociolAb. *Aud.:* Ac, Sa.

This well-respected scholarly journal provides an alternative viewpoint on political theory and in the social sciences. It publishes theoretical and philosophical articles and empirical research from "Marxist, post-Marxist and other radical perspectives." Topics covered include "the theory of state, class analysis, politics of gender, methodological individualism and rational choice, and the future of capitalism and socialism." Occasional theme issues are also published, e.g., "Deliberative Democracy." Appropriate for academic libraries and some public libraries.

5645. *Presidential Studies Quarterly.* Formerly: *Center for the Study of the Presidency. Center House Bulletin.* [ISSN: 0360-4918] 1972. q. USD 255 print & online. Ed(s): Susan A Mathews, Georg C Edwards, III. Blackwell Publishing, Inc., Commerce Place, 350 Main St, Malden, MA 02148; subscrip@blackwellpub.com; http://www.blackwellpublishing.com. Illus., index, adv. Refereed. Circ: 6000. Vol. ends: No. 4. Microform: PQC. Online: bigchalk; Florida Center for Library Automation; Gale Group; ingenta.com; Northern Light Technology, Inc.; OCLC Online Computer Library Center, Inc.; ProQuest Information & Learning; Sage Publications, Inc.; Swets Blackwell; H.W. Wilson. Reprint: PQC. *Indexed:* ABCPolSci, ABS&EES, AmH&L, BRI, CBRI, CommAb, HRA, IBSS, IPSA, PAIS, PRA, PSA, RI-1, SFSA, SSI, SUSA. *Bk. rev.:* 6-10, 800-1,200 words. *Aud.:* Ac, Sa.

This official publication of the Center for the Study of the Presidency focuses exclusively on the U.S. presidency. All living ex–U.S. presidents have honorary positions on the center's board of trustees. The journal publishes "articles and book reviews on presidents, the operations of the White House, presidential decision making, presidential relations with Congress, the courts, the bureaucracy, the public, and the press, and on the president's involvement in public policy issues in both domestic and international arenas." In addition, several sections have been added to each issue in recent years, including The Polls, The Law, The Contemporary Presidency, and Source Material. The premier scholarly journal on the presidency, *PSQ* also appeals to a more general audience because of the topic and the accessibility of the writing.

5646. *Publius: the journal of federalism.* [ISSN: 0048-5950] 1971. q. USD 42 (Individuals, USD 32). Ed(s): John Kincaid. Meyner Center for the Study of State and Local Government, 002 Kirby Hall of Civil Rights, Lafayette College, Easton, PA 18042-1785. Illus., index, adv. Refereed. Circ: 1200 Paid. Vol. ends: No. 4. Microform: PQC. Online: bigchalk; Factiva; Florida Center for Library Automation; Gale Group; Northern Light Technology, Inc.; OCLC Online Computer Library Center, Inc.; ProQuest Information & Learning; H.W. Wilson. Reprint: PQC. *Indexed:* ABCPolSci, ABS&EES, AmH&L, ArtHuCI, IBSS, IBZ, IPSA, PAIS, PRA, PSA, SSCI, SSI, SUSA, SociolAb. *Bk. rev.:* 3-6, 1,000-1,500 words. *Aud.:* Ac, Sa.

Assuming the pen name used by Alexander Hamilton, John Jay, and James Madison, *Publius* is "devoted to the increase and diffusion of knowledge about federalism and intergovernmental relations." The journal covers the principles, institutions, and processes of federalism through its theoretical and analytical articles and empirical research reports and book reviews. Many of the articles focus on the United States; however, there is also coverage of other parts of the world, particularly Australia, Canada, and the European Union. The title is widely indexed and appropriate for academic libraries.

5647. *Scandinavian Political Studies: a journal for the Nordic Political Science Association.* Supersedes (1968-1977): *Scandinavian Political Studies Yearbook.* [ISSN: 0080-6757] 1966. q. USD 214 print & online eds. Ed(s): Sverker Gustavsson, Barry Holmstrom. Blackwell Publishing Ltd., 9600 Garsington Rd, PO Box 805, Oxford, OX4 2DQ, United Kingdom; jnlinfo@blackwellpublishers.co.uk; http://www.blackwellpublishing.com/. Illus., index, adv. Refereed. Circ: 600. Vol. ends: No. 4. Microform: PQC. Online: EBSCO Publishing; Ingenta Select; ingenta.com; OCLC Online Computer Library Center, Inc.; RoweCom Information Quest; Swets Blackwell. *Indexed:* ABCPolSci, AmH&L, IBSS, IPSA, PSA, RiskAb, SSCI, SWA, SociolAb. *Bk. rev.:* 1-3, 1,250 words. *Aud.:* Ac, Sa.

As the only English-language political science journal published in Scandinavia, this journal covers "policy and electoral issues affecting the Scandinavian countries, and sets those issues in European and global context." The majority of articles are very scholarly and heavily footnoted pieces contributed by Scandinavian authors. Some recent topics include school choice policies and various aspects of the political party system. Occasionally, there is also coverage of Europe outside Scandinavia.

5648. ***Science & Society: a journal of marxist thought and analysis.*** [ISSN: 0036-8237] 1936. q. USD 170 (Individuals, USD 33). Ed(s): David Laibman. Guilford Publications, Inc., 72 Spring St, 4th Fl, New York, NY 10012; info@guilford.com; http://www.guilford.com. Illus., index, adv. Refereed. Circ: 2500. Vol. ends: No. 4. Microform: MIM; PQC; NRP. Online: Gale Group; Ingenta Select; Northern Light Technology, Inc.; OCLC Online Computer Library Center, Inc.; ProQuest Information & Learning; RoweCom Information Quest; Swets Blackwell. Reprint: ISI; PQC. *Indexed:* ABCPolSci, ABS&EES, ASSIA, AltPI, AmH&L, ArtHuCI, BRI, CBRI, IBSS, IPSA, JEL, MLA-IB, PAIS, PSA, RI-1, SSCI, SSI, SociolAb. *Bk. rev.:* 4-15, 500-1,000 words. *Aud.:* Ac, Sa.

Science and Society publishes well-documented articles on "political economy and the economic analysis of contemporary societies" through the lens of the Marxist tradition. Both general and theme issues are published, and the journal also includes book reviews and articles on "social and political theory, history, labor, ethnic and women's studies, aesthetics, literature and the arts." Appropriate for academic libraries.

5649. ***Third World Quarterly: journal of emerging areas.*** [ISSN: 0143-6597] 1979. bi-m. GBP 397 (Individuals, GBP 85). Ed(s): Shahid Qadir. Carfax Publishing Ltd., 4 Park Sq, Milton Park, Abingdon, OX14 4RN, United Kingdom; enquiry@tandf.co.uk; http://www.tandf.co.uk/. Illus., index, adv. Refereed. Circ: 6000. Vol. ends: No. 6. Online: bigchalk; EBSCO Publishing; Gale Group; Ingenta Select; Northern Light Technology, Inc.; OCLC Online Computer Library Center, Inc.; ProQuest Information & Learning; RoweCom Information Quest; Swets Blackwell. Reprint: PSC. *Indexed:* AltPI, AmH&L, BAS, BrHumI, DSR&OA, ForAb, GeogAbPG, IBSS, IBZ, IPSA, PAIS, PSA, RRTA, S&F, SSCI, SSI, SWA, SociolAb, WAE&RSA. *Bk. rev.:* 1-3, 1,500 words. *Aud.:* Ga, Ac, Sa.

This influential journal focuses on the emerging Third World, publishing both "provocative and exploratory articles." *Third World Quarterly* covers crucial issues of global concern from an interdisciplinary perspective and bridges "the academic terrains of the various contemporary area studies—African, Asian, Latin American and Middle Eastern." Most contributors are American or British Commonwealth academics or postgraduate students, but all contributions are refereed by regional experts. The comprehensive book review section is enhanced by the "WorldViews Resource Guide" published in each issue. This is a superb but expensive publication.

5650. ***West European Politics.*** [ISSN: 0140-2382] 1978. 5x/yr. GBP 337 print & online eds. Ed(s): Gordon Smith, Klaus H Goetz. Frank Cass Publishers, Crown House, 47 Chase Side, Southgate, London, N14 5BP, United Kingdom; jnlsubs@frankcass.com; http://www.frankcass.com/jnls/. Illus., index, adv. Sample. Refereed. Vol. ends: No. 4. Microform: PQC. Online: EBSCO Publishing; Florida Center for Library Automation; Gale Group; Ingenta Select; Northern Light Technology, Inc. *Indexed:* ABCPolSci, AmH&L, BrHumI, GeogAbPG, HRA, IBSS, IBZ, IPSA, PAIS, PRA, PSA, SSCI, SSI, SWA, SociolAb, WAE&RSA. *Bk. rev.:* 15, 800 words. *Aud.:* Ac, Sa.

This journal covers the major political and social issues and developments in western European countries, including the European Union. A typical issue includes about eight articles, a debate section, and book reviews. Although contributors and the editorial advisory board include American and European scholars, the majority of articles are written by Europeans with an almost exclusively European focus. Coverage of the role of the United States in European politics is surprisingly limited. Although many of the articles are scholarly treatises, the target audience for this journal is both practitioners and academics.

International Relations

5651. ***Asian Perspective: quarterly journal of regional & international affairs.*** [ISSN: 0258-9184] 1977. q. KRW 60000 domestic; USD 60 foreign. Ed(s): Melvin Gurtov. Kyungnam University, Institute for Far Eastern Studies, 28-42 Samchung dong, Chongro-gu, Seoul, 110230, Korea, Republic of; ifes@kyungnam.ac.kr. Illus., adv. Refereed. Circ: 2300. Vol. ends: No. 3. *Indexed:* BAS, EIP, IBSS, IPSA, PAIS, PSA, SociolAb. *Aud.:* Ac, Sa.

Published by the Institute for Far Eastern Studies and Portland State University, this journal focuses "on the social sciences with a particular emphasis on world/comparative politics and Asia's regional affairs." Although there are contributions from doctoral students, most articles are authored by international academics. Every third issue of the journal is devoted to Asia Pacific Economic Cooperation (APEC) topics, and the thematic emphasis of every fourth issue is determined by a guest editor.

5652. ***Australian Journal of International Affairs.*** Formerly: *Australian Outlook.* [ISSN: 1035-7718] 1947. 3x/yr. GBP 145 (Individuals, GBP 60). Ed(s): S Lawson. Carfax Publishing Ltd., 4 Park Sq, Milton Park, Abingdon, OX14 4RN, United Kingdom; enquiry@tandf.co.uk; http://www.tandf.co.uk/. Illus., index, adv. Refereed. Circ: 2600. Vol. ends: No. 3. Online: bigchalk; EBSCO Publishing; Ingenta Select; Northern Light Technology, Inc.; OCLC Online Computer Library Center, Inc.; ProQuest Information & Learning; RMIT Publishing; RoweCom Information Quest; Swets Blackwell. Reprint: PQC; PSC. *Indexed:* ABCPolSci, AmH&L, ArtHuCI, BAS, BrHumI, IBSS, IBZ, IPSA, PAIS, PSA, SSCI, SociolAb. *Bk. rev.:* 16–18, 600 words. *Aud.:* Ga, Ac, Sa.

This journal of the Australian Institute of International Affairs aims to "publish high quality scholarly research on international political, social, economic and legal issues, especially (but not exclusively) within the Asia-Pacific region." Each issue includes traditional scholarly articles and commissioned commentaries on international and foreign policy. In addition to book reviews and review articles, *AJIA* also publishes an annual review of Australian foreign policy. Although many contributors are Australian, there is significant international representation among the authors. Articles have included "Cambodia and Southeast Asia" and "Australia and America: Renewal and Reinvention."

5653. ***Brown Journal of World Affairs.*** Formerly (until 1994): *Brown Journal of Foreign Affairs.* [ISSN: 1080-0786] 1994. s-a. USD 16; USD 7.95 newsstand/cover per issue. Ed(s): James Dreier, David Estlund. Brown University, PO Box 1930, Providence, RI 02912. Adv. Online: EBSCO Publishing. *Indexed:* PAIS. *Aud.:* Ac.

The focus of this semi-annual journal is "contemporary issues in international politics and economics." A typical issue includes six to ten articles on each of two main topics as well as several essays. For example, one issue examines "The Caspian Question and Global Economic Government." The forward to each issue is an editorial essay that provides an excellent introduction. Contributors include well-known public figures like Madeleine Albright, Boutros Boutros-Ghali, Jimmy Carter, Mikhail Gorbachev, and Shimon Peres. Each issue also has an author index to previously published articles. Appropriate for academic libraries.

5654. ***Cooperation and Conflict: Nordic journal of international studies.*** [ISSN: 0010-8367] 1965. q. GBP 232 in Europe, Middle East, Africa & Australasia. Ed(s): Iver B Neumann. Sage Publications Ltd., 6 Bonhill St, London, EC2A 4PU, United Kingdom; info@sagepub.co.uk; http://www.sagepub.co.uk/. Illus., adv. Refereed. Circ: 900. Vol. ends: No. 4. Microform: PQC. Online: ingenta.com; OCLC Online Computer Library Center, Inc.; RoweCom Information Quest; Sage Publications, Inc.; Swets Blackwell. Reprint: ISI; SCH. *Indexed:* ABCPolSci, HRA, IBSS, IBZ, IPSA, PAIS, PRA, PSA, SociolAb. *Bk. rev.:* 1-2, 500-1,000 words. *Aud.:* Ac, Sa.

This official journal of the Nordic International Studies Association is the only English-language journal devoted to international relations from a Scandinavian perspective. The theoretical articles and empirical research reports focus on "foreign policy, the Nordic countries in world affairs, international relations as process, European cooperation and conflict, the role of big and small powers in the new global context, and the role of the Baltic states in Europe." The editorial board and article authors include Nordic scholars and international Nordic specialists. Essential reading for scholars interested in international relations and northern Europe.

5655. ***Current History: a journal of contemporary world affairs.*** [ISSN: 0011-3530] 1914. m. 9/yr. USD 34 domestic; USD 43.75 foreign. Ed(s): William W Finan, Jr. Current History, Inc., 4225 Main St, Philadelphia, PA 19127; editorial@currenthistory.com; http://www.currenthistory.com. Illus., index, adv. Sample. Refereed. Circ: 20000 Paid. Vol. ends: Dec. Microform: NBI; PQC. Online: Chadwyck-Healey Incorporated; EBSCO Publishing; Gale Group; OCLC Online Computer Library Center, Inc.; ProQuest Information & Learning. *Indexed:* ABCPolSci, ABS&EES, ArtHuCI, BAS, BRI, CBCARef, CBRI, CPerI, HumInd, IBSS, LRI, MagInd, PAIS, PRA, RGPR, RRTA, SSCI, WAE&RSA. *Bk. rev.:* 1 or 2, 400-600 words. *Aud.:* Hs, Ga, Ac.

This privately owned journal has been covering world affairs since its founding in 1914 by the *New York Times*. Typically, each issue examines one country or region in depth; however, occasionally an issue will focus solely on a policy concern. Appealing to a broad audience, issues include six or seven articles, one or two book reviews, and, on the back cover, a map of the targeted country or region. There is also an excellent "Month in Review" section that provides an international chronology of events, organized by country. The *Current History* web site provides a schedule of the thematic emphasis of forthcoming issues. Recommended as an excellent and inexpensive selection for public and academic libraries.

East European Politics & Societies. See CIS and Eastern Europe section.

5656. ***European Journal of International Relations.*** [ISSN: 1354-0661] 1995. q. GBP 332 in Europe, Middle East, Africa & Australasia. Ed(s): Friederich V Kratochwil. Sage Publications Ltd., 6 Bonhill St, London, EC2A 4PU, United Kingdom; info@sagepub.co.uk; http://www.sagepub.co.uk/. Illus., index, adv. Refereed. Vol. ends: No. 4. *Indexed:* IPSA, PRA, PSA, SSCI, SociolAb. *Aud.:* Ac, Sa.

This interdisciplinary journal has emerged as one of the most important sources for international relations scholarship. Dedicated to stimulating and disseminating cutting-edge theoretical and empirical research, the journal publishes well-documented articles on foreign policy analysis and international political economy, law, and organizations. Although the journal "pays special attention to Europe and its sub-regions," it does not support a particular disciplinary school or approach, nor is it limited by its emphasis on a particular methodology. Recommended for academic libraries.

5657. ***Fletcher Forum of World Affairs.*** Formerly (until 1988): *Fletcher Forum.* [ISSN: 1046-1868] 1977. s-a. USD 25 (Individuals, USD 18). Ed(s): Brian Jackson. Fletcher School of Law and Diplomacy, Tufts University, Medford, MA 02155; forum@tufts.edu; http://www.tufts.edu/fletcher/forum.html. Illus., adv. Refereed. Circ: 1600. Vol. ends: No. 2. Microform: WSH. Online: Gale Group; LexisNexis; West Group. Reprint: WSH. *Indexed:* ABCPolSci, ABS&EES, BAS, CLI, IPSA, LRI, PAIS, PRA. *Bk. rev.:* 5, 1,250 words. *Aud.:* Ac, Sa.

This publication of the Fletcher School of Law and Diplomacy at Tufts University "features articles on international law, politics, economics, technology, and diplomacy." Some articles are relatively short (about 10–15 pages); however, lengthier and more thoroughly documented articles are published in the "Issues & Policy" section, providing substantial historical context for major policy issues. Authors include academics, United Nations and other international agency heads, members of the current or previous U.S. administrations, doctoral candidates, and members of the Fletcher School of Law and Diplomacy. Articles have included "Peace in Afghanistan" and "Technology and Globalization." A good choice for academic libraries.

5658. ***Foreign Affairs.*** [ISSN: 0015-7120] 1922. bi-m. USD 44 domestic; USD 54 Canada; USD 79 elsewhere. Ed(s): James F Hoge, Jr. Council on Foreign Relations, Inc., 58 E 68th St, New York, NY 10021; foraff@cfr.org; http://foreignaffairs.org/. Illus., adv. Refereed. Circ: 110000. Vol. ends: No. 6. CD-ROM: ProQuest Information & Learning. Microform: WSH; PMC; PQC. Online: bigchalk; Chadwyck-Healey Incorporated; EBSCO Publishing; Factiva; Florida Center for Library Automation; Gale Group; LexisNexis; Northern Light Technology, Inc.; OCLC Online Computer Library Center, Inc.; ProQuest Information & Learning; H.W. Wilson. Reprint: PSC; WSH. *Indexed:* ABCPolSci, ABIn, ABS&EES, AgeL, AmH&L, BAS, BRI, CBRI, CPerI, DSR&OA, FutSurv, IBSS, IBZ, IPSA, JEL, MagInd, PAIS, PRA, PSA, RGPR, RI-1, SSCI, SSI. *Bk. rev.:* 4-6, 125-1,850 words. *Aud.:* Ga, Ac, Sa.

This is arguably the most important foreign affairs journal in the world. Published by the Council on Foreign Relations and read by decision-makers around the world, *Foreign Affairs* has been at the forefront of global policy analysis since 1922. Contributors include prominent academics, well-known political and governmental figures, and respected journalists. The articles are well-written, thought-provoking pieces that provide authoritative analyses, and their influence is felt around the world. The journal is also an excellent source for reviews of the most important books on international affairs. Highly recommended as the foreign affairs journal of choice for all types of libraries.

5659. ***Foreign Policy (Washington): the magazine of global politics, economics and ideas.*** [ISSN: 0015-7228] 1970. bi-m. USD 19.95 domestic; USD 27.95 in Canada & Mexico; USD 32.95 elsewhere. Ed(s): Moises Naim. Carnegie Endowment for International Peace, 1779 Massachusetts Ave, N W, Washington, DC 20036-2103; http://ceip.org/. Illus., index, adv. Refereed. Circ: 25000. Microform: PQC. Online: bigchalk; EBSCO Publishing; Florida Center for Library Automation; Gale Group; OCLC Online Computer Library Center, Inc.; ProQuest Information & Learning; H.W. Wilson. Reprint: PQC; WSH. *Indexed:* ABCPolSci, ABIn, ABS&EES, ASIP, AmH&L, CLI, DSR&OA, FutSurv, IBSS, ILP, IPSA, LRI, MagInd, PAIS, PRA, PSA, RGPR, RRTA, SSCI, SSI, WAE&RSA. *Bk. rev.:* 3-5, 1,500-2,500 words. *Aud.:* Ga, Ac, Sa.

Similar to *Foreign Affairs* in coverage, this journal differentiates itself by aiming to become "an indispensable reference" for the specialist while also engaging and entertaining the general reader. Most articles are analytical essays or opinion pieces written in a jargon-free style, and many include helpful charts and sidebars. The journal has introduced a number of new sections over the past few years, including "Think Again" ("the equivalent of a guerilla attack on conventional wisdom"); the "FP Interview"; and "Want to Know More?" (a guide to additional information on topics discussed in the articles). Additional features include reviews of foreign-language books, highlights from specialty journals, and a review of useful web sites. These added features and the accessibility of the articles make *Foreign Policy* a good choice for most libraries.

5660. ***Global Governance: a review of multilateralism and international organizations.*** [ISSN: 1075-2846] 1995. q. USD 108 (Individuals, USD 49). Ed(s): W Andy Knight, S Neil MacFarlane. Lynne Rienner Publishers, 1800 30th St, Ste 314, Boulder, CO 80301-1026; http://www.rienner.com. Illus., index, adv. Sample. Refereed. Circ: 1500 Paid. Vol. ends: No. 4. Microform: WSH. Online: EBSCO Publishing; Factiva; Florida Center for Library Automation; Gale Group; ProQuest Information & Learning. Reprint: WSH. *Indexed:* CJA, IBSS, IPSA, PAIS, PRA, PSA, SSCI, SociolAb, WAE&RSA. *Aud.:* Ac, Sa.

A project of the Academic Council on the United Nations System, this refereed journal examines "the impact of international institutions and multilateral processes on economic development; peace and security; human rights; and preservation of the environment." Contributors include scholars, practitioners, and prominent governmental figures. Reflecting various multidisciplinary and multicultural perspectives, a typical issue includes "Global Insights," followed by four articles. Topics addressed have included corruption and global governance and multilateral financial institutions.

5661. ***Global Society: journal of interdisciplinary relations.*** Formerly (until 1996): *Paradigms.* [ISSN: 1360-0826] 1986. q. GBP 280 (Individuals, GBP 53). Ed(s): Jarrod Wiener. Carfax Publishing Ltd., 4 Park Sq, Milton Park, Abingdon, OX14 4RN, United Kingdom; enquiry@tandf.co.uk; http://www.tandf.co.uk/. Illus., index, adv. Refereed. Vol. ends: No. 4. Online: EBSCO Publishing; Ingenta Select; Northern Light Technology, Inc.; OCLC Online Computer Library Center, Inc.; RoweCom Information Quest; Swets Blackwell. Reprint: PSC. *Indexed:* BrHumI, IBSS, IBZ, IPSA, PAIS, PSA, SociolAb. *Aud.:* Ac, Sa.

This scholarly journal assumes a multidisciplinary perspective as it examines the internationalization of social interaction. Most issues include five or six research-quality articles, but occasionally the journal also publishes review articles and "Replies" by prominent authors to previously published work. This very specialized journal is appropriate for academic libraries supporting graduate programs in political science and related fields.

5662. *International Affairs (London, 1944).* Former titles (until 1943): *International Affairs Review Supplement;* (until 1939): *International Affairs (London, 1931);* (until 1930): *Royal Institute of International Affairs. Journal.* [ISSN: 0020-5850] 1922. 5x/yr. USD 305 print & online eds. Ed(s): Caroline Soper. Blackwell Publishing Ltd., 9600 Garsington Rd, PO Box 805, Oxford, OX4 2DQ, United Kingdom; customerservices@oxon.blackwellpublishing.com; http://www.blackwellpublishing.com/. Illus., index, adv. Refereed. Vol. ends: No. 4. Microform: PMC. Online: EBSCO Publishing; Gale Group; ingenta.com; JSTOR (Web-based Journal Archive); OCLC Online Computer Library Center, Inc.; RoweCom Information Quest; Swets Blackwell. Reprint: PSC. *Indexed:* ABCPolSci, AmH&L, ArtHuCI, BAS, BrHumI, IBSS, IPSA, PAIS, PRA, PSA, RRTA, SSCI, SSI, WAE&RSA. *Bk. rev.:* 80-120, 500-700 words. *Aud.:* Hs, Ac, Sa.

A publication of the Royal Institute of International Affairs, this journal targets a broad audience of specialists, generalists, and laypersons. Most of the well-written and accessible articles are commissioned pieces that examine current issues in European and international affairs. Each issue focuses on a particular topic (e.g., the climate change debate) and includes seven or eight articles followed by an extensive book review section. There are as many as 100 reviews in each issue, and they are well organized by subareas within the field. Widely considered the premier source for book reviews in international affairs, this journal is an excellent choice for academic and larger public libraries.

5663. *International Organization.* [ISSN: 0020-8183] 1947. q. USD 136 (Individuals, USD 43). Ed(s): Lisa Martin, Thomas Risse. Cambridge University Press, The Edinburgh Bldg, Shaftesbury Rd, Cambridge, CB2 2RU, United Kingdom; information@cambridge.org; http://uk.cambridge.org. Illus., adv. Refereed. Circ: 3000 Paid. Vol. ends: No. 4. Microform: PQC. Online: EBSCO Publishing; Ingenta Select; RoweCom Information Quest; Swets Blackwell. Reprint: PQC; PSC. *Indexed:* ABIn, ABS&EES, AmH&L, BAS, CLI, CommAb, DSR&OA, FutSurv, IBSS, IBZ, IPSA, JEL, LRI, PAIS, PSA, RRTA, SSCI, SSI, SociolAb, WAE&RSA. *Bk. rev.:* 0-3, 2,500-3,000 words. *Aud.:* Ac, Sa.

The scope of this scholarly journal is international affairs in the broadest sense. Sponsored by the World Peace Foundation, the journal covers "trade policies and the GATT, environmental disputes and agreements, European integration, alliance patterns and war, bargaining and conflict resolution, economic development and adjustment, and international capital movements." Most articles are lengthy, theoretically based, and authored by academics and doctoral students. Review essays are also published. This is a key publication for all academic libraries.

5664. *International Studies Quarterly: journal of the International Studies Association.* Formerly (until 1966): *Background; Background on World Politics.* [ISSN: 0020-8833] 1957. q. USD 753 print & online eds. Blackwell Publishing, Inc., Commerce Place, 350 Main St, Malden, MA 02148; subscrip@blackwellpub.com; http://www.blackwellpublishing.com. Illus., index, adv. Refereed. Circ: 4400. Vol. ends: No. 4. Microform: PQC. Online: EBSCO Publishing; Gale Group; ingenta.com; JSTOR (Web-based Journal Archive); OCLC Online Computer Library Center, Inc.; RoweCom Information Quest; Swets Blackwell. *Indexed:* ABCPolSci, ABS&EES, ArtHuCI, BAS, BrHumI, DSR&OA, HRA, IBSS, IPSA, PAIS, PRA, PSA, RiskAb, SSCI, SSI, SUSA, SWA, SociolAb. *Aud.:* Ac, Sa.

This scholarly journal focuses on disciplinary and interdisciplinary questions related to international studies. Most contributors are American academics and doctoral students, and many articles are highly theoretical reports of empirical and normative research. Authors are required to make data accessible to allow for replication and cumulation of research results. The editors also invite "high-quality manuscripts in comparative politics, environmental politics, gender and identity studies, interdisciplinary studies and those more generally in the nonpositivist tradition." Highly recommended for academic libraries.

5665. *Journal of Common Market Studies.* [ISSN: 0021-9886] 1962. q. plus Annual Review. GBP 413 print & online eds. Ed(s): John Peterson, Iain Begg. Blackwell Publishing Ltd., 9600 Garsington Rd, PO Box 805, Oxford, OX4 2DQ, United Kingdom; customerservices@oxon.blackwellpublishing.com; http://www.blackwellpublishers.ac.uk. Illus., index, adv. Refereed. Circ: 1400. Vol. ends: No. 4. Microform: WSH. Online: EBSCO Publishing; ingenta.com; OCLC Online Computer Library Center, Inc.; RoweCom Information Quest; Swets Blackwell. Reprint: PQC; WSH. *Indexed:* ABCPolSci, ABIn, BAS, BPI, BrHumI, CLI, IBSS, IBZ, ILP, IPSA, JEL, PAIS, PSA, RRTA, S&F, SSCI, SSI, WAE&RSA. *Bk. rev.:* 8-15, 500 words. *Aud.:* Ac, Sa.

Journal of Common Market Studies focuses exclusively on European integration, publishing theoretical and empirical articles that address related issues from a political science and/or economics perspective. The journal's stated aim is "to provide an information source which can be used as a reference tool for teaching and research." Most of the editorial board and most contributors are European scholars. Each fall, an annual review is published that includes a chronology and guide to key developments in European Union policies and affairs. Recommended for academic libraries and other libraries supporting businesses with operations in the European Union.

The Journal of Communist Studies and Transition Politics. See CIS and Eastern Europe section.

5666. *Latin American Politics and Society.* Former titles (until 2001): *Journal of Interamerican Studies and World Affairs;* (until 1970): *Journal of Inter-American Studies.* [ISSN: 1531-426X] 1959. q. USD 108 (Individuals, USD 49). Ed(s): William C Smith. University of Miami, Miami, FL 33124-3010; JISWA@sis.miami.edu. Illus., index, adv. Refereed. Circ: 1000 Paid. Vol. ends: No. 4. Microform: PQC. Online: bigchalk; EBSCO Publishing; Florida Center for Library Automation; Gale Group; OCLC Online Computer Library Center, Inc.; ProQuest Information & Learning; H.W. Wilson. Reprint: PQC. *Indexed:* ABCPolSci, ABS&EES, AmH&L, BAS, GeogAbPG, HAPI, HumInd, IBSS, IPSA, JEL, PAIS, PRA, PSA, RiskAb, SSCI, SSI. *Bk. rev.:* 1-15, 750 words. *Aud.:* Ac, Sa.

This interdisicplinary journal publishes original research, scholarly analyses, and opinion essays, the latter in its new "Policy Issues" section, as well as articles focused on research methodology. Topics include "democratization and political institutions; social change and civil society; civil-military relations; the political economy of market reforms; environmental politics; and regional integration and interamerican relations in a globalizing world." Both researchers and practitioners will find this journal a useful resource for deepening their understanding of the ongoing social and political transformations occurring in Latin America.

5667. *New Left Review.* [ISSN: 0028-6060] 1960. bi-m. GBP 90 includes online access (Individuals, GBP 30 includes online access; Students, GBP 20 includes online access). Ed(s): Susan Watkins, Perry Anderson. New Left Review Ltd., 6 Meard St, London, W1F 0EG, United Kingdom; mail@newleftreview.org; http://www.newleftreview.org. Illus., adv. Refereed. Circ: 8000. Vol. ends: Nov/Dec. Online: Gale Group. *Indexed:* AltPI, ArtHuCI, BAS, BrHumI, IBSS, IPSA, PAIS, SSCI, SSI, SWA, WAE&RSA. *Aud.:* Ac, Sa.

For over 40 years, this leftist magazine has published articles on social theory and political analysis as well as cultural commentaries. Reflective of its egalitarian perspective, *New Left Review* is strongly pro-labor/working-class in its orientation, but it is not merely a vehicle for left-wing polemics. Rather, each issue typically includes well-researched and well-written thematic articles and several review articles. Highly recommended for all academic and large public libraries.

5668. ***Orbis (Kidlington): a journal of world affairs.*** [ISSN: 0030-4387] 1957. q. EUR 313 (Individuals, EUR 95). Ed(s): David Eisenhower. Pergamon, The Boulevard, Langford Ln, East Park, Kidlington, OX5 1GB, United Kingdom; nlinfo-f@elsevier.nl; http://www.elsevier.nl. Illus., index, adv. Refereed. Circ: 3500. Vol. ends: No. 45. Microform: PQC; NRP. Online: EBSCO Publishing; Florida Center for Library Automation; Gale Group; ingenta.com; Northern Light Technology, Inc.; OCLC Online Computer Library Center, Inc.; ScienceDirect; Swets Blackwell; H.W. Wilson. Reprint: PSC. *Indexed:* ABCPolSci, ABS&EES, FutSurv, IBSS, IPSA, PAIS, PRA, PSA, SSI, SociolAb. *Bk. rev.:* 10-25, 250-500 words. *Aud.:* Ac, Sa.

Orbis, a publication of the Foreign Policy Research Institute, provides "articulate, expert, but lively debates on the quest for post–cold war strategies and wise American policy toward Russia, Europe, the Pacific Rim, and the developing world." Each issue is either entirely or largely focused on a specific topic. Review essays, illustrations, and maps are also included.

5669. ***Policy Sciences: an international journal devoted to the improvement of policy making.*** [ISSN: 0032-2687] 1970. q. EUR 475 print or online ed. Ed(s): John D Montgomery. Kluwer Academic Publishers, van Godewijckstraat 30, PO Box 17, Dordrecht, 3300 AA, Netherlands; services@wkap.nl; http://www.wkap.nl. Illus., index, adv. Refereed. Vol. ends: No. 4. Microform: PQC. Online: EBSCO Publishing; Gale Group; ingenta.com; Kluwer Online; OCLC Online Computer Library Center, Inc.; Ovid Technologies, Inc.; RoweCom Information Quest; Swets Blackwell. Reprint: SWZ. *Indexed:* ABCPolSci, ABIn, AgeL, ArtHuCI, CommAb, EIP, FutSurv, GeogAbPG, HRA, IBSS, IPSA, InfoSAb, JEL, MCR, PAIS, PRA, PSA, RiskAb, SSCI, SUSA, SociolAb. *Aud.:* Ac, Sa.

This very scholarly journal examines national and international policy issues from an interdisciplinary perspective. Most articles are well-documented conceptual or theoretical pieces, although occasionally research reports are also published. The number of articles in each issue ranges from as few as five to as many as twelve. Articles have included "Varieties of issue incompleteness and coordination: An example from ecosystem management" and "Interdependency, beliefs, and coalition behavior: A contribution to the advocacy coalition framework." Recommended for libraries supporting graduate programs in political science or public affairs.

5670. ***Political Science Quarterly: the journal of public and international affairs.*** [ISSN: 0032-3195] 1886. q. USD 249 (Individuals, USD 42). Ed(s): Demetrios Caraley. Academy of Political Science, 475 Riverside Dr, Ste 1274, New York, NY 10115-1274. Illus., index, adv. Refereed. Circ: 8000 Paid. Vol. ends: No. 4. Microform: PMC; PQC. Online: bigchalk; EBSCO Publishing; Florida Center for Library Automation; Gale Group; Ingenta Select; JSTOR (Web-based Journal Archive); Northern Light Technology, Inc.; OCLC Online Computer Library Center, Inc.; ProQuest Information & Learning; H.W. Wilson. Reprint: PQC; PSC. *Indexed:* ABCPolSci, ABS&EES, AbAn, AgeL, AmH&L, ArtHuCI, BAS, BRD, BRI, CBRI, FutSurv, IBSS, IBZ, IPSA, LRI, PAIS, PRA, PSA, RRTA, SSCI, SSI, SUSA, SWR&A, SociolAb, WAE&RSA. *Bk. rev.:* 25-30, 250-500 words. *Aud.:* Ac, Sa.

One of the most venerable journals in the field, *Political Science Quarterly* has been continuously published since 1886. Its target audience includes both scholars and the general reader. Each issue includes five or six articles on government, politics, and policy. Written by leading scholars, these pieces often include a historical perpsective in the discussion. Traditionally, each presidential election is followed by an early analysis of the election in the spring issue. The book review section is extensive, often including as many as 35 reviews supplemented by a list of reference books and other publications of interest. These reviews create an indispensable resource for political science selectors. Highly recommended.

5671. ***Review of International Studies.*** [ISSN: 0260-2105] 1974. q. plus one supplement . USD 218 (Individuals, USD 69). Ed(s): Theo Farrell, Bice Maiguashca. Cambridge University Press, The Edinburgh Bldg, Shaftesbury Rd, Cambridge, CB2 2RU, United Kingdom; information@cambridge.org; http://uk.cambridge.org/journals. Illus., index, adv. Refereed. Vol. ends: No. 4. Online: EBSCO Publishing; OCLC Online Computer Library Center, Inc.; RoweCom Information Quest; Swets Blackwell. *Indexed:* ABCPolSci, AmH&L, BrHumI, IBSS, IPSA, JEL, PAIS, PRA, PSA, RiskAb, SSCI, SociolAb. *Aud.:* Ac, Sa.

The "flagship journal of the British International Studies Association," this title publishes research reports, review and teaching articles, and occasionally interviews with prominent members of the field. A special thematic issue is published annually, and the forum section provides an arena for debates and rejoinders. A good choice for libraries seeking to extend their coverage of international relations beyond the North American perspective.

5672. ***S A I S Review: a journal of international affairs.*** [ISSN: 0036-0775] 1956. 2x/yr. USD 75 (Individuals, USD 26). Ed(s): Dune Lawrence, Christi Siver. Johns Hopkins University Press, Journals Publishing Division, 2715 N Charles St, Baltimore, MD 21218-4363; http://www.press.jhu.edu/. Illus., index, adv. Refereed. Circ: 553. Vol. ends: No. 2. Online: EBSCO Publishing; Gale Group; OCLC Online Computer Library Center, Inc.; Project MUSE; RoweCom Information Quest; Swets Blackwell; H.W. Wilson. Reprint: PSC. *Indexed:* ABCPolSci, ABS&EES, BAS, ForAb, IBSS, IPSA, PAIS, PSA, SSCI, SSI. *Bk. rev.:* 8, 1,500 words. *Aud.:* Ga, Ac, Sa.

Often straddling "the boundary between scholarly inquiry and practical experience," *SAIS Review* seeks "to bring a fresh and policy-relevant perspective to global political, economic, and security issues." The typical issue of *SAIS* includes articles on contemporary issues printed in a large font. Every issue also includes a section devoted to reviews of books and films. Special issues have focused on migration, religion and global affairs, and Europe and Asia. Contributors include prominent government officials and policy analysts as well as scholars and journalists. Highly recommended for academic and large public libraries.

5673. ***Washington Quarterly.*** Formerly: *Washington Review of Strategic and International Studies.* [ISSN: 0163-660X] 1978. q. USD 152 print & online eds. (Individuals, USD 44 print & online eds.; Students, USD 28 print & online eds.). Ed(s): Alexander T J Lennon. MIT Press, 5 Cambridge Center, Cambridge, MA 02142-1493; journals-orders@mit.edu; http://mitpress.mit.edu. Illus., adv. Refereed. Circ: 3500. Vol. ends: No. 4. Microform: PQC. Online: EBSCO Publishing; Florida Center for Library Automation; Gale Group; Ingenta Select; LexisNexis; OCLC Online Computer Library Center, Inc.; Project MUSE; RoweCom Information Quest; H.W. Wilson. Reprint: PQC; PSC. *Indexed:* ABCPolSci, ABS&EES, AgeL, ArtHuCI, BAS, CJA, FutSurv, IBSS, IPSA, PAIS, PSA, SSCI, SSI. *Aud.:* Ga, Sa.

This publication of the Center for Strategic and International Studies "focuses on policy and the way in which analysis of international events must be translated into policy choices and actions." It covers international security; political-military problems; trade, finance, and economics; and the process and challenge of foreign policy. Accessible to the nonspecialist, the articles are well written and reflective of diverse viewpoints. Contributors include academics, research analysts, journalists, and doctoral students from the United States and abroad. An excellent title for libraries seeking to provide a source of intelligent discourse on international events and public policy.

5674. ***World Affairs (Washington).*** [ISSN: 0043-8200] 1837. q. USD 95 (Individuals, USD 52). Ed(s): Joyce Horn. Heldref Publications, 1319 18th St, NW, Washington, DC 20036-1802; subscribe@heldref.org; http://www.heldref.org. Illus., index, adv. Refereed. Circ: 600. Vol. ends: Summer. Microform: PQC. Online: bigchalk; EBSCO Publishing; Florida Center for Library Automation; Gale Group; OCLC Online Computer Library Center, Inc.; ProQuest Information & Learning; SoftLine Information; H.W. Wilson. Reprint: PSC. *Indexed:* ABCPolSci, ABS&EES, ArtHuCI, BAS, BRI, IBZ, IPSA, PAIS, PSA, SSCI, SSI. *Aud.:* Ga, Ac.

This publication of the American Peace Society is one of the oldest journals on international relations. Intending to provide "multiple perspectives on contemporary issues in international relations," *World Affairs* has a long history of publishing insightful analyses of difficult foreign policy issues. Articles have considered global arms control, negotiations with North Korea, and Israeli political violence. Contributions are made by international academics and military and governmental professionals. A typical issue includes several relatively short articles as well as interviews and commentaries. The audience for *World Affairs* includes the specialist and the informed layperson.

5675. *World Policy Journal.* [ISSN: 0740-2775] 1983. q. USD 37 (Individuals, USD 30; USD 7.95 newsstand/cover per issue). Ed(s): Linda Wrigley, Karl Meyer. World Policy Institute, 66 Fifth Ave, 9th Fl, New York, NY 10011; wpj@newschool.edu; http://worldpolicy.org/. Illus., index, adv. Refereed. Circ: 5000. Vol. ends: No. 4. Microform: PQC. Online: bigchalk; EBSCO Publishing; Florida Center for Library Automation; Gale Group; Northern Light Technology, Inc.; OCLC Online Computer Library Center, Inc.; ProQuest Information & Learning; SoftLine Information; H.W. Wilson. *Indexed:* ABCPolSci, ABS&EES, AltPI, AmH&L, ArtHuCI, BAS, FutSurv, IPSA, PAIS, PRA, PSA, SSCI, SSI, SociolAb. *Bk. rev.:* 1-2, 1,500 words. *Aud.:* Ga, Ac, Sa.

World Policy Journal is a well-respected, moderately left-of-center/progressive journal of international affairs. Traditionally, this title concentrated on core policy articles that emphasized international economic affairs and civil society. However, the journal has undergone some changes and expansion of its scope. Seeking to help shape "a new American foreign policy," the journal now offers "reflective essays on realism and idealism in American foreign policy, historical reconsideration, profiles, book review articles, reportage and international cultural coverage." Contributors are often prominent individuals, including Daniel Bell, Tina Rosenberg, and Robert McNamara. This is an excellent and reasonably priced journal that will appeal to a broad audience.

5676. *World Politics (Baltimore): a quarterly journal of international relations.* [ISSN: 0043-8871] 1948. q. USD 113 (Individuals, USD 32). Ed(s): Harold James. Johns Hopkins University Press, Journals Publishing Division, 2715 N Charles St, Baltimore, MD 21218-4363; http://www.press.jhu.edu/. Illus., index, adv. Refereed. Circ: 3368. Vol. ends: No. 4. Microform: PQC. Online: EBSCO Publishing; Gale Group; RoweCom Information Quest; Swets Blackwell. Reprint: PQC; PSC; SCH. *Indexed:* ABCPolSci, ABS&EES, AmH&L, BRD, BRI, CBRI, FutSurv, GeogAbPG, IBSS, IBZ, IPSA, MagInd, PAIS, PSA, RI-1, RRTA, RiskAb, SSCI, SSI, SociolAb, WAE&RSA. *Bk. rev.:* 5-8, 2,000 words. *Aud.:* Ac, Sa.

Produced under the editorial sponsorship of Princeton University's Center of International Studies, *World Politics* is arguably the premier international relations journal. It publishes in-depth research and theoretical articles, review articles, and notes. Topics covered include international relations, comparative politics, political theory, and foreign policy modernization. Articles have included "Fiscal Decentralization: A Political Theory with Latin American Cases" and "Eugenic Ideas, Political Interests, and Policy Variance: Immigration and Sterilization Policy in Britain and the U.S." Highly recommended.

Electronic Journals

5677. *Jouvert: a journal of postcolonial studies.* [ISSN: 1098-6944] 1997. 3x/yr. Free. Ed(s): Steven Luyendyk, Deborah Wyrick. North Carolina State University, College of the Humanities and Social Sciences, Box 8105, Department of English, Raleigh, NC 27695-8105; http://social.chass.ncsu.edu/jouvert/. Refereed. *Indexed:* MLA-IB. *Aud.:* Ac.

Jourvert is a refereed and multidisciplinary electronic journal that publishes "fully argued and fully researched scholarly work that opens new perspectives" on postcolonial studies. In addition to postcolonial theory and politics, the journal covers literature, history, and the arts, and it actively "solicits interviews, substantial creative work with a postcolonial theme, book reviews, and reader commentary." Some recent articles include "Humpty Dumpty and the Despotism of Fact: A Critique of Stephen Howe's Ireland and Empire," "Transcultural Writing: Ahdaf Soueif's Aisha as a Case Study," and "Adventures in Imperial Anthropography (A Nineteenth-Century Pastiche)." Appropriate for libraries supporting graduate programs in political science.

5678. *N A T O Integrated Data Service.* 1992. irreg. N A T O Integrated Data Service, NATO Headquarters, Brussels, 1110, Belgium; natodoc@hq.nato.int; http://www.nato.int/structur/nids/nids.htm. *Aud.:* Sa.

NATO Integrated Data Service (NIDS) "facilitates computer access to NATO press releases, communiques and official statements, speeches, printed reference books and other documentation" through daily bulletins. NIDS also provides access to materials distributed by NATO civilian and military agencies and publishes the *NATO Review*. The latter provides informative analyses of NATO issues and is available in English and numerous other languages. NIDS information is accessible through the NATO web site or available via e-mail distribution. An excellent electronic resource for those needing to keep abreast of NATO activities.

■ POPULATION STUDIES

Meghan Dolan, Data Reference Librarian, Numeric Data Services, Harvard College Library, Harvard University, Cambridge, MA 02138

Introduction

The literature of population studies is as diverse as the fields and approaches that comprise it as a discipline. Population studies is a confluence of many areas, including anthropology, psychology, sociology, economics, political science, and history. The convergence of theoretical perspectives, as well as quantitative and qualitative research methods, allows researchers to explore issues such as socioeconomic change, migration, fertility, mortality, development, and epidemiology, and to place these issues in a broader, more global context. The "cross-pollination" of research projects in parallel fields allows researchers to gain fresh insights and perspectives on their own work, which benefits the application of this research on international policymaking in areas such as economic planning and development.

Basic Periodicals

Ga: *American Demographics, Population Bulletin;* Ac: *Demography, European Journal of Population, Population and Development Review, Population Research and Policy Review.*

5679. *American Demographics: consumer trends for business leaders.* Incorporates (1994-1998): *Marketing Tools.* [ISSN: 0163-4089] 1979. m. USD 58. Ed(s): John McManus. Media Central, 470 Park Ave. S., 8th Fl., New York, NY 10016; adedit@inside.com; http://www.mediacentral.com. Illus., adv. Circ: 35000. Vol. ends: No. 12. Microform: PQC. Online: bigchalk; Dow Jones Interactive; EBSCO Publishing; Florida Center for Library Automation; Gale Group; LexisNexis; OCLC Online Computer Library Center, Inc.; ProQuest Information & Learning; H.W. Wilson. *Indexed:* ABIn, ASG, AgeL, B&I, BPI, EnvAb, FutSurv, MagInd, PAIS, SSI. *Aud.:* Ga.

American Demographics researches the consumer population; the marketing and media industries are its main audience. The magazine focuses on spending behavior related to the consumer's age, education, geography, income, and lifestyle. It "provides detailed insights into spending, growth, and demographics in key consumer market segments." Recent articles deal with focus groups, the effect of wireless communication, religious identity and mobility, consumer confidence surveys, and culture and shopping habits. The articles are supported with data collected by educational institutions, government agencies, and private companies. A very dynamic and interesting publication.

5680. *Canadian Studies in Population.* [ISSN: 0380-1489] 1974. s-a. USD 42 (Individuals, USD 24; Students, USD 12). Ed(s): Wayne W McVey, Jr. University of Alberta, Department of Sociology, 5-21 Tory Building, Edmonton, AB T6G 2H4, Canada. Illus. Circ: 350. Vol. ends: No. 2. *Indexed:* CBCARef, PAIS, SociolAb. *Bk. rev.:* 2, 500-700 words. *Aud.:* Ac.

Canadian Studies in Population has traditionally focused on issues relating to Canadian immigration, but recent issues show that the focus has shifted to include manuscripts that are more international in scope. A recent issue is subtitled "Special Issue on Migration and Globalization." Other recent issues publish articles covering the Republic of Iran, Ghana, the United States, South Africa, and China. Article topics include human capital flows, fertility, mortality, and the effects of globalization on different populations within Canada. Abstracts are typically in both English and French, and most articles are in English. An online index arranged by volume is available on the publisher's web site: http://www.canpopsoc.org/publications/journal.html. The index includes most articles published in the journal since its inception in 1974, and gives author name, title, and abstract.

Continuity and Change. See History section.

5681. *Demography.* [ISSN: 0070-3370] 1964. q. USD 85. Population Association of America, 8630 Fenton St, Ste 722, Silver Spring, MD 20910-3812; info@popassoc.org; http://www.popassoc.org; http://www.jstor.org/journals/0070330.html. Illus., adv. Refereed. Circ: 4000. Vol. ends: No. 4. Online: bigchalk; Gale Group; JSTOR (Web-based Journal Archive); Northern Light Technology, Inc.; OCLC Online Computer Library Center, Inc.; Project MUSE; ProQuest Information & Learning; RoweCom Information Quest; Swets Blackwell; H.W. Wilson. *Indexed:* ABIn, ABS&EES, ASSIA, AbAn, AgeL, BAS, CJA, EnvAb, GeogAbPG, IBSS, IMFL, IndMed, JEL, PAIS, PollutAb, SSCI, SSI, SociolAb. *Aud.:* Ac.

Demography is an "esoteric, inclusive and multidisciplinary" peer-reviewed journal with an international scope. Disciplines include the social sciences, public health, statistics, geography, history, and business. The language is clear and the topics are quite interesting. Manuscripts are mainly textual in format; some articles include tables, models, graphs, and maps. Recent articles include such topics as family planning and fertility, cohabitation, child care costs, disease rates and declines, AIDS and the elderly, and family dynamics. Authors of published manuscripts are required to make their data sets available to others at a reasonable cost for three years after publication.

5682. *Diaspora: a journal of transnational studies.* [ISSN: 1044-2057] 1991. 3x/yr. CND 63 (Individuals, CND 31). Ed(s): Khachig Tololyan. University of Toronto Press, Journals Department, 5201 Dufferin St, Toronto, ON M3H 5T8, Canada; journals@utpress.utoronto.ca; http://www.utpjournals.com. Illus., adv. Refereed. Circ: 500. Vol. ends: Winter. Online: EBSCO Publishing. *Indexed:* ABS&EES, BAS, PSA, SociolAb. *Aud.:* Ac, Sa.

Diaspora is an international, multidisciplinary, refereed journal that publishes articles related to "past, existing or emerging" communities. Authors of recent articles are researchers in the fields of literature, anthropology, history, psychology, political science, and sociology. The concepts and language of the articles are truly academic, touching on topics such as transnational migration, the relationship between Jewish Americans and Israel, Portuguese migrants in (West) Germany, and the return migration of Japanese Brazilians to Japan.

5683. *European Journal of Population.* Formerly (until 1983): *European Demographic Information Bulletin.* [ISSN: 0168-6577] 1970. q. EUR 376 print or online ed. Ed(s): France Mesle, Evert van Imhoff. Kluwer Academic Publishers, van Godewijckstraat 30, PO Box 17, Dordrecht, 3300 AA, Netherlands. Illus., adv. Refereed. Circ: 400. Vol. ends: No. 4. Online: EBSCO Publishing; ingenta.com; Kluwer Online; OCLC Online Computer Library Center, Inc.; Ovid Technologies, Inc.; RoweCom Information Quest; Swets Blackwell. Reprint: SWZ. *Indexed:* ASSIA, AgeL, ArtHuCI, IBSS, PAIS, SFSA, SSCI, SWA, SociolAb. *Bk. rev.:* 3, 1,000-1,200 words. *Aud.:* Ac.

European Journal of Population publishes articles that cover population trends in European, non-European, and developing countries. It is multidisciplinary in scope, with authors from the fields of sociology, anthropology, geography, political science, and history. Recent topics include alcohol-related mortality in Europe, childbirth in Sub-Saharan Africa, fertility transition in India, and fertility decline in Russia. The publication is aimed toward an academic audience, which is evident in the use of language and definition of concepts.

5684. *Immigrants & Minorities.* [ISSN: 0261-9288] 1982. 3x/yr. GBP 186 print & online eds. Ed(s): Colin Holmes, David Mayall. Frank Cass Publishers, Crown House, 47 Chase Side, Southgate, London, N14 5BP, United Kingdom; jnlsubs@frankcass.com; http://www.frankcass.com/jnls/. Illus., adv. Sample. Refereed. Microform: PQC. *Indexed:* ASSIA, AmH&L, BAS, BrHumI, HRA, IBSS, IBZ, IPSA, PSA, SWA, SociolAb. *Bk. rev.:* 10-20, 500-700 words. *Aud.:* Ac.

Immigrants and Minorities is an international, refereed, scholarly journal. There are typically four articles and 10 to 20 book reviews per issue. Authors are mainly academics from the fields of history, political science, sociology, and European Studies. Recent articles focus on Irish immigration to Britain, Indo-Guyanese migration, and social inclusion and the Polish community at Bradford. The final issue of each volume contains an index of all works published throughout the year.

Journal of Family History. See Family and Marriage section.

5685. *Journal of Population Economics.* [ISSN: 0933-1433] 1988. q. EUR 449 domestic; EUR 459.90 foreign; EUR 135 newsstand/cover per issue. Ed(s): K F Zimmermann. Springer-Verlag, Tiergartenstr 17, Heidelberg, 69121, Germany. Illus., adv. Sample. Refereed. Online: EBSCO Publishing; RoweCom Information Quest; ScienceDirect; Springer LINK; Swets Blackwell. *Indexed:* AgeL, GeogAbPG, IBSS, JEL, SSCI. *Aud.:* Ac.

Journal of Population Economics is international in scope, with articles focusing on the relationship between economics and population trends. Each issue presents three or four specific topics. The most recent topics include welfare, social security, and migration. There are two to four manuscripts published per topic, and each includes an abstract and a list of keywords. Charts, graphs, and models are often included.

Migration World. See Ethnic Studies section.

5686. *Population and Development Review.* [ISSN: 0098-7921] 1975. q. USD 105 print & online. Ed(s): Paul Demeny. Blackwell Publishing, Inc., Commerce Place, 350 Main St, Malden, MA 02148; subscrip@blackwellpub.com; http://www.blackwellpublishing.com. Illus. Refereed. Circ: 5000. Vol. ends: No. 4. Microform: PQC. Online: Florida Center for Library Automation; Gale Group; JSTOR (Web-based Journal Archive); OCLC Online Computer Library Center, Inc. Reprint: PQC. *Indexed:* ABCPolSci, ABS&EES, ASSIA, AgeL, AmH&L, AnthLit, BAS, CWI, EIP, EnvAb, GeogAbPG, IBSS, IMFL, JEL, PAIS, PRA, PSA, RRTA, SFSA, SSCI, SSI, SUSA, SWA, SociolAb, WAE&RSA. *Bk. rev.:* 6, 700 words. *Aud.:* Ac.

Population and Development Review is an international multidisciplinary journal. Authors are typically academicians and researchers from universities, nonprofit foundations, and nongovernmental organizations. The manuscripts are in English, with abstracts provided in English, Spanish, and French. The December issue provides an index to all articles published throughout the year. Each issue contains the following sections: "Articles," "Notes and Commentary," "Data and Perspectives," "Archives," "Book Reviews," and Documents. Topics in recent issues focus on fertility, reproduction, and family planning.

5687. *Population and Environment.* Former titles (until vol.4, 1981): *Journal of Population; Population (New York).* [ISSN: 0199-0039] 1978. bi-m. EUR 658 print or online ed. Ed(s): Kevin MacDonald. Kluwer Academic / Plenum Publishers, 233 Spring St Fl 7, New York, NY 10013-1522; http://www.wkap.nl/. Illus., adv. Refereed. Microform: PQC. Online: Gale Group; ingenta.com; Kluwer Online; OCLC Online Computer Library Center, Inc.; Ovid Technologies, Inc.; RoweCom Information Quest; Swets Blackwell. Reprint: ISI; PQC. *Indexed:* AgeL, BiolAb, CIJE, EnvAb, ExcerpMed, HEA, IBSS, IBZ, PAIS, PRA, PSA, PollutAb, PsycholAb, SSCI, SUSA, SWR&A, SociolAb. *Bk. rev.:* 1, 900 words. *Aud.:* Ac.

Population and Environment focuses on issues that impact the relationship between demography and the environment. This journal is geared toward an academic audience, but the language used and arguments presented will be accessible to anyone with an interest in population trends and their effect on the environment. Each issue includes a two- to four-page book review. Authors of recently published works are from the fields of geography, biology, and public affairs.

5688. ***Population Bulletin.*** [ISSN: 0032-468X] 1945. q. USD 49; USD 7 newsstand/cover per issue. Ed(s): Mary Kent. Population Reference Bureau, Inc., 1875 Connecticut Ave, N W, Ste 520, Washington, DC 20009; popref@prb.org; http://www.prb.org. Illus. Circ: 5000 Paid. Online: Gale Group; OCLC Online Computer Library Center, Inc.; ProQuest Information & Learning. *Indexed:* ABS&EES, ASSIA, AgeL, BAS, BiolAb, EIP, EnvAb, FutSurv, JEL, PAIS, RI-1, SCI, SSCI, SSI. *Aud.:* Ga.

Population Bulletin is published by the Population Reference Bureau. Its intended audience includes "policymakers, educators, the media and concerned citizens working in the public interest." The bulletin's scope is international, with each issue focusing on a specific topic. Articles are enhanced with interesting tables, photographs, maps, and diagrams. Each issue focuses on a specific topic. Recent topics include poverty in America, the HIV/AIDS pandemic, and the factors that drive U.S. population growth. The bulletin is available free online at www.prb.org.

5689. ***Population Research and Policy Review.*** [ISSN: 0167-5923] 1980. bi-m. EUR 495 print or online ed. Ed(s): Elwood Carlson. Kluwer Academic Publishers, van Godewijckstraat 30, PO Box 17, Dordrecht, 3300 AA, Netherlands; services@wkap.nl; http://www.wkap.nl. Illus. Refereed. Microform: PQC. Online: EBSCO Publishing; ingenta.com; Kluwer Online; OCLC Online Computer Library Center, Inc.; RoweCom Information Quest; Swets Blackwell. Reprint: SWZ. *Indexed:* AgeL, ArtHuCI, CIJE, CJA, GeogAbPG, IBSS, IMFL, IPSA, JEL, PAIS, PRA, PSA, SSCI, SUSA, SWA, SWR&A, SociolAb. *Bk. rev.:* 3, 400-500 words. *Aud.:* Ac.

Population Research and Policy Review is the official publication of the Southern Demographic Association. The journal focuses on international issues, with recent articles about Cote d'Ivoire, Bangladesh, Egypt, Ethiopia, Uganda, and North Carolina. The publication states that issues will "include demographic, economic, social, political and health research papers." Each published article is preceded by an abstract and a list of keywords. There are typically three articles published in each issue.

5690. ***Population Studies: a journal of demography.*** [ISSN: 0032-4728] 1947. 3x/yr. GBP 112 (Individuals, GBP 85). Ed(s): John Simons. Routledge, 11 New Fetter Ln, London, EC4P 4EE, United Kingdom; info@routledge.co.uk; http://www.routledge.co.uk. Illus., adv. Refereed. Circ: 1500 Paid. Online: Gale Group; Ingenta Select. Reprint: PQC; PSC. *Indexed:* ABIn, AICP, ASSIA, AmH&L, ArtHuCI, BAS, BiolAb, EnvAb, ExcerpMed, GeogAbPG, IBSS, IBZ, PAIS, PSA, RRTA, SSCI, SociolAb, WAE&RSA. *Bk. rev.:* 6-8, 500 words. *Aud.:* Ac.

Population Studies is an international, multidisciplinary scholarly journal that publishes manuscripts of interest to "demographers, sociologists, economists, anthropologists, social statisticians, geographers, historians, epidemiologists, health scientists, and policy analysts." Recent articles cover migration in Mexico, infant and child mortality in Holland, and living arrangements in Indonesia, Singapore, and Taiwan. Data tables, graphs, and charts are often included within the text. There are book reviews in each issue.

5691. ***Population Trends.*** [ISSN: 0307-4463] 1975. q. GBP 70. Stationery Office, 51 Nine Elms Ln, London, SW8 5DA, United Kingdom; book.orders@theso.co.uk; http://www.national-publishing.co.uk. Illus. Circ: 1700. *Indexed:* IndMed, PAIS. *Aud.:* Ac.

Population Trends is published by the Office for National Statistics and is the principal source of articles on population and demographic trends in the United Kingdom. There are between three and five articles per issue. Recent topics include the decline of intergenerational care of older people, changes in economic and social roles, one parent families, and estimates of trends in births by birth order. Most articles include charts, graphs, or maps. Each issue also includes data tables that range in topic from vital statistics and components of population change to international migration and marriage and divorce statistics. The journal is available online for viewing and downloading in pdf format. The data tables are sometimes a bit tricky to print.

■ PRINTING AND GRAPHIC ARTS

Donna B. Smith, Assistant Head of Technical Services, W. Frank Steely Library, Northern Kentucky University, Highland Heights, KY 41099

Wendy Wood, Head of Cataloging, W. Frank Steely Library, Northern Kentucky University, Highland Heights, KY 41099

Introduction

Communicating the message visually is the job of the graphic designer and the printer. Designers and printers are working with more innovation and persuasion to inform, entertain, and impress visually inundated and discriminating audiences. Clients look to these groups for marketing, technical, and high-impact graphic support. Competition is becoming stiffer as computers allow individuals with no formal training in graphic arts or printing to enter the field. Successful professionals in the future will need to be much more active in the marketing of their skills.

Recent years have witnessed major changes in the graphic arts and printing industries, including the rise of desktop publishing, the Internet boom, and digital technology. Designers and printers make use of new technology to create images that are more visually active than ever before. The computer empowers them to create images that once would have been prohibitive in both time and expense. Printers are beginning to focus more on communications and technology. They are using new digital technologies to add value to their services and moving into products and services not traditionally associated with printing. It is transforming into an imaging business that feeds a variety of media, only one of which is print. But reports of print's demise are greatly exaggerated. Although the Internet seems to be where the action is, it still has inherent typographic limitations and does not allow as much freedom to experiment with composition and typography as does print.

As in most industries today, graphic artists and printers must remain current with the latest technology and marketing innovations. Therefore, the majority of publications recommended here are trade publications that provide necessary and timely information to practitioners, managers, suppliers, and anyone else interested in visual communications. They may cover the entire graphic communications industry or target specific segments, such as gravure printers, calligraphers, or screen printers. Most magazines provide practical how-to information, and many profile artists, design studios, and printing firms. Some provide a showcase of leading designs in the industry by sponsoring competitions and displaying the winners in special issues. The trade publications also address the business side of the industry: legal concerns, environmental regulations, economic trends, marketing and sales, and management issues. Scholarly publications focus on the history of printing and new research in the field. Such publications are closely tied to bibliography, the study of the book. Strictly electronic publications are not prevalent in this field as yet. Although some publications are available online, these versions complement or coexist with the print issues.

Basic Periodicals

Ga: *Communication Arts, Print, Step Inside Design;* Ac: *American Printer, Communication Arts, Graphis, Print, Printing History, Visible Language;* Sa: *Communication Arts, Graphis, Print, Printing News, The Seybold Report.*

Basic Abstracts and Indexes

Press.

5692. ***American Printer: the graphic arts managers magazine.*** Former titles (until 1982): *American Printer and Lithographer;* (until 1979): *Inland Printer - American Lithographer.* [ISSN: 0744-6616] 1883. m. USD 73 domestic (Free to qualified personnel). Ed(s): Mayu Mishina. Primedia Business Magazines & Media, Inc., 29 N Wacker Dr, Chicago, IL 60606; inquiries@primediabusiness.com; http://www.primediabusiness.com. Illus., adv. Sample. Circ: 85779 Controlled. Vol. ends: Mar/Sep. Microform: PQC. Online: bigchalk;

EBSCO Publishing; Factiva; Florida Center for Library Automation; Gale Group; LexisNexis; Northern Light Technology, Inc.; OCLC Online Computer Library Center, Inc.; ProQuest Information & Learning; H.W. Wilson. *Indexed:* ABIn, AS&TI, BPI, ChemAb, PhotoAb. *Aud.:* Ac, Sa.

Essentially directed toward the print shop manager, this trade publication provides practical information on current issues in the printing industry. It focuses attention on the use of new equipment and technology, an important feature for today's printers. It offers seven or eight feature articles discussing such topics as management, marketing, production, purchasing, sales, and technology. Regular columns highlight industry news, new equipment and electronic tools, and classifieds. An annual feature is the "Top 50 Fastest Growing Printers" competition.

5693. *British Printer: leading technical journal of the printing industry.* [ISSN: 0007-1684] 1888. m. GBP 55. Ed(s): Jane Ellis. C M P Information Ltd., Riverbank House, Angel Ln, Tonbridge, TN9 1SE, United Kingdom; enquiries@cmpinformation.com. Illus., index, adv. Sample. Circ: 14014. Vol. ends: Dec. *Indexed:* B&I, BrTechI, EngInd. *Aud.:* Ac, Sa.

This trade publication is England's leading industry magazine. It is written for the main buyer of products or services. Each issue offers 10 to 12 feature articles discussing all areas of printing, prepress, and in-plant operations. Regular columns include industry news, new products, and classifieds. This title's major focus is on the production and quality of printing, with less attention paid to the business side. Of special interest are profiles of printing businesses and software reviews.

5694. *Communication Arts.* [ISSN: 0010-3519] 1959. 8x/yr. USD 53; USD 70 Canada; USD 110 elsewhere. Ed(s): Patrick S Coyne. Coyne & Blanchard, Inc., PO Box 10300, Palo Alto, CA 94303-0000; ca@commarts.com; http://www.commarts.com. Illus., adv. Circ: 73443 Paid. Vol. ends: Dec. *Indexed:* ABM, ArtInd, DAAI. *Bk. rev.:* 2, 500-600 words, signed. *Aud.:* Ga, Ac, Sa.

Communication Arts is a high-quality trade publication for commercial artists. Special issues serve as juried showcases for leading work in advertising, design, illustration, interactive design, and photography. Regular issues offer seven or eight feature articles that may profile design studios and artists or highlight special advertising and design projects. Regular columns address design issues, legal affairs, coming events, new graphic art materials, new books, and technology. Articles tend to pay special attention to the use of computers in design and production work. This title is an important addition to any graphic arts collection.

5695. *Flexo.* Formerly (until 1984): *Flexographic Technical Journal.* [ISSN: 1051-7324] 1976. m. USD 55 domestic; USD 92 foreign. Ed(s): Michael Derosa. Foundation of Flexographic Technical Association, 900 Marconi Ave, Ronkonkoma, NY 11779-7212; rmoran@vax.fta-ffta.org; http://www.fta-ffta.org. Illus., adv. Sample. Circ: 19000. Vol. ends: Dec. *Indexed:* EngInd. *Aud.:* Ac, Sa.

FLEXO is the official journal of the Foundation of Flexographic Technical Association, which is devoted to advancing flexographic technology. This relief printing process is especially popular in the packaging and newspaper industries. Although mainly a trade publication directed toward managers and technicians, *FLEXO*'s audience includes anyone who is interested in learning more about the technical aspects of flexography. Articles include such topics as designing packaging, comparing flexo presses, and examining printing techniques. The articles are written by practitioners, so they are informative and practical. Some issues include tutorials for beginners in flexographic technology. Articles provide useful, detailed illustrations demonstrating flexographic printing. An annual feature is the association's market perspective and prospectus report, which examines the previous year's industry results and predicts market trends for the next year. Regular columns highlight new products, events, and association news.

5696. *G A T F World.* Formed by the merger of (1971-1989): *E C B Newsletter;* (1947-1989): *Graphic Arts Abstracts;* (1970-1989): *G A T F Environmental Control Report;* (1970-1989): *G A T F (Year).* [ISSN: 1048-0293] 1989. bi-m. USD 75 domestic; USD 100 foreign. Ed(s): Frances M Wieloch. Graphic Arts Technical Foundation, 200 Deer Run Rd, Sewickley, PA 15143-2600; http://www.gaft.org. Illus., adv. Sample. Circ: 24000. Vol. ends: Nov/Dec. *Indexed:* GAA. *Bk. rev.:* 6-10, 200 words. *Aud.:* Ac, Sa.

This is the magazine of the Graphic Arts Technical Foundation, a member-supported organization that promotes scientific, technical, and educational advancements in the graphic communication industries. Generally covering prepress and press, each issue offers five or six in-depth articles on current trends, such as digital imaging. The articles are useful for the practitioner, as they generally address new technologies and products. One section focuses on foundation news, conference reports, and training workshops. Regular departments relay information about industry news, resources, and environmental issues. Two special supplements are published annually, "The GATF Technology Forecast" and a comprehensive report of GATF's "Tech Alert" conference.

5697. *Graphic Arts Monthly: the magazine of the printing industry.* Formerly: *Graphic Arts Monthly and the Printing Industry.* [ISSN: 1047-9325] 1929. m. USD 142.99 domestic (Free to qualified personnel). Reed Business Information, 360 Park Ave South, New York, NY 10010; http://www.reedbusiness.com. Illus., index, adv. Circ: 75000 Controlled. Vol. ends: Dec. Microform: CIS. Online: The Dialog Corporation; EBSCO Publishing; Florida Center for Library Automation; Gale Group; Northern Light Technology, Inc.; OCLC Online Computer Library Center, Inc.; ProQuest Information & Learning; H.W. Wilson. *Indexed:* ABIn, BPI, ChemAb, PhotoAb. *Aud.:* Ga, Ac, Sa.

This trade publication is directed at managers and practitioners in the printing and graphic arts fields. It provides coverage of business news and new technological developments in the industry. It features methods that save time and money in production operations. Each issue contains five or six main articles, ranging from comparisons of prepress machines to colorful exhibits of design projects. Marketing, legal issues, industry news, cost estimating, and paper and ink handling are covered in regular columns. This title is a good general source of industry information and is recommended for any graphic arts collection.

5698. *Graphis: international journal of visual communication.* [ISSN: 0017-3452] 1944. bi-m. USD 90. Ed(s): Jamie Reynolds. Graphis Inc, 307 Fifth Ave, 10th Fl, New York, NY 10016. Illus., adv. Circ: 23000. Vol. ends: Nov/Dec. *Indexed:* ABM, ArtHuCI, ArtInd, BHA, DAAI, FLI. *Bk. rev.:* 3, 200-300 words, signed. *Aud.:* Ac, Sa.

Graphis, which is published in English, German, and French, is international in scope. This high-quality glossy publication provides seven or eight feature articles, many of which display the work of architects, designers, illustrators, photographers, and graphic artists. The contributors, drawn from the graphic arts field, impart practical information about design, graphics, and illustration. Columns in every issue include global reports of industry news, book reviews, exhibitions, and product information. This title is a good addition to a graphic arts or a fine arts collection.

5699. *Gravure.* Former titles (until 1986): *Gravure Bulletin; Gravure Technical Association Bulletin.* [ISSN: 0894-4946] 1950. bi-m. USD 65. Ed(s): Laura Wayland Smith Hatch. Gravure Association of America, Inc., 1200A Scottsville Rd, Rochester, NY 14624-5703; lwshatch@gaa.org; http://www.gaa.org. Illus., adv. Sample. Circ: 2375 Paid. *Indexed:* EngInd. *Aud.:* Ac, Sa.

This is the trade publication of the Gravure Association of America, which promotes the advancement of the gravure printing industry. This title's main focus is on the technological developments in this high-quality, expensive process. Feature articles examine such topics as new products and materials, environmental concerns, training programs, and automation development. The business side of the industry is covered as well, with timely information on industry news and personnel moves, an events calendar, marketing advice, and association news.

5700. ***High Volume Printing.*** [ISSN: 0737-1020] 1982. bi-m. USD 75. Ed(s): Ray Roth. Innes Publishing Company, PO Box 7280, Libertyville, IL 60048-7280. Illus., adv. Sample. Circ: 38720. Vol. ends: Dec. Microform: PQC. Online: ProQuest Information & Learning. *Indexed:* EngInd. *Aud.:* Ac, Sa.

This "large-plant management magazine" is directed mainly at print managers and covers operations from prepress to postpress. Its audience consists of printers, trade binderies, and color trade houses with more than 20 employees. As a trade publication, this title provides the latest industry news and trends. Subjects include management issues, industry trends, economic forecasts, the book industry, regulatory issues, technology, and equipment. Also included are useful case studies depicting how a particular company handled a production problem. Regular departments focus on the usual trade news, personnel, and events.

5701. ***How: design ideas at work.*** [ISSN: 0886-0483] 1985. bi-m. USD 49 domestic; USD 71 foreign; USD 9.95 newsstand/cover domestic. Ed(s): Bryn Mooth. F & W Publications, Inc., 1507 Dana Ave, Cincinnati, OH 45207; http://www.fwpublications.com. Illus., adv. Sample. Circ: 35006. Vol. ends: Dec. *Indexed:* ABM, DAAI, IHTDI. *Aud.:* Ac, Sa.

This is an instructional trade magazine that addresses the ideas and techniques graphic design professionals use to create their work. Directed toward practitioners and design firm managers, it provides hands-on advice on making a design studio more profitable, more professional, and more high-profile in the industry. Special issues focus on international design, typography, and interactive design, and there is a business annual. Feature articles may include reports on new trends in materials and technology, buyer's guides to scanners, comparisons of soy-based inks, or advice on insurance needs. Regular columns discuss legal issues, profile design firms, report on trade shows and conferences, review electronic tools, and provide general industry news.

5702. ***In-Plant Printer: the in-plant management magazine.*** Former titles: *In-Plant Printer Including Corporate Imaging;* (until 1993): *In-Plant Printer and Electronic Publisher;* (until 1986): *In-Plant Printer; In-Plant Offset Printer.* [ISSN: 1071-832X] 1961. bi-m. USD 75 domestic; USD 95 foreign. Ed(s): Sharon Spielman. Innes Publishing Company, PO Box 7280, Libertyville, IL 60048-7280. Illus., adv. Circ: 30526. Microform: PQC. Online: OCLC Online Computer Library Center, Inc.; ProQuest Information & Learning. Reprint: PQC. *Indexed:* ABIn, EngInd. *Aud.:* Sa.

In-plant printing operations include the printing departments in corporations, government agencies, and institutions. This journal targets the special needs of the graphic artists, desktop publishers, and electronic prepress specialists that work in these shops. Particular emphasis is placed on the latest digital technologies and on the management skills needed to make those technologies work effectively.

5703. ***Ink Maker: for manufacturers of printing inks and related graphic arts specialty colors.*** Formerly (until 198?): *American Inkmaker.* 1922. m. USD 66. Ed(s): Linda M Casatelli. Cygnus Business Media, Inc., 445 Broad Hollow Rd, Melville, NY 11747-3601; http://www.cygnuspub.com. Illus., index, adv. Circ: 5000 Paid. Vol. ends: Dec. *Indexed:* B&I, ChemAb. *Bk. rev.:* Various number and length. *Aud.:* Sa.

This international trade publication targets manufacturers of printing inks and related graphic arts specialty colors. It highlights raw materials and equipment, reports on printing processes and markets, and provides a global perspective on industry issues. Articles cover topics ranging from workflow issues to the pigment industry. Monthly interviews with printers provide information on their clients' needs. Calendars of industry conferences and shows are provided.

5704. ***Instant & Small Commercial Printer.*** Formerly: *Instant Printer.* [ISSN: 1044-3746] 1982. 12x/yr. USD 85. Ed(s): Anne Marie Mohan. Innes Publishing Company, PO Box 7280, Libertyville, IL 60048-7280. Adv. Circ: 50953. Microform: PQC. Online: ProQuest Information & Learning. *Indexed:* EngInd. *Aud.:* Sa.

This journal targets the quick printers, the small commercial shops with fewer than 20 employees, and all franchises. It publishes how-to articles and case histories on printing and photocopy reproduction. Management stories are aimed at helping the entrepreneurial audience with everyday problems and examining new areas for growth.

Letter Arts Review. See Craft/Calligraphy section.

5705. ***PackagePrinting: for printers and converters of labels, flexible packaging and folding cartons.*** Former titles (until 1999): *Package Printing & Converting;* (until 1987): *Package Printing;* (until Mar. 1978): *Package Printing and Diecutting;* Which was formed by the merger of: *Diemaking, Diecutting and Converting; Gravure; Flexography Printing and Converting.* [ISSN: 1536-1039] 1974. m. USD 59 domestic; USD 79 Canada; USD 104 elsewhere. Ed(s): Susan Friedman. North American Publishing Company, 401 N Broad St, 5th Fl, Philadelphia, PA 19108-1074; http://www.napco.com. Illus., index, adv. Circ: 24250 Controlled. Vol. ends: Dec. Microform: PQC. Reprint: PQC. *Indexed:* ABIn, B&I, EngInd. *Aud.:* Sa.

This trade publication targets the industry of container and package design and production. Diemaking/diecutting, tags, labels, and tape, as well as flexible packaging, folding cartons, and corrugated containers—all this industry's focus—are the journal's subjects. Articles included each month discuss innovations in the equipment needed to manufacture these containers and labels. Inks and printing techniques, suppliers, and management issues are also discussed.

5706. ***Print: America's graphic design magazine.*** Incorporates (in 1976): *Packaging Design.* [ISSN: 0032-8510] 1940. bi-m. USD 57 domestic; USD 72 Canada; USD 98 elsewhere. Ed(s): Joyce Rutler Kaye. Krause Publications, Inc., 700 E State St, Iola, WI 54990-0001; info@krause.com; http://www.krause.com. Illus., index, adv. Circ: 56788. Vol. ends: No. 6. Microform: PQC. Online: EBSCO Publishing; Florida Center for Library Automation; Gale Group; Northern Light Technology, Inc.; OCLC Online Computer Library Center, Inc.; ProQuest Information & Learning; H.W. Wilson. Reprint: PQC. *Indexed:* ABM, ABS&EES, ArtInd, DAAI, FLI. *Aud.:* Ga, Ac, Sa.

The purpose of this high-quality glossy journal is to provide thorough and wide-ranging coverage of the graphic design field. Directed mainly at practitioners, it provides in-depth articles on pertinent topics. Half of the six issues published each year are devoted to juried showcases of leading work in graphic design. The annual "Regional Design" issue organizes artists' work by geographic region. Highly aware of the development of digital technology, *Print* has a "Digital Design and Illustration" issue that explores the effects of computers on design. This title is an important addition to any graphic design collection.

5707. ***Printing Historical Society. Journal.*** [ISSN: 0079-5321] 1965. a. GBP 30 (Individuals, GBP 25). Ed(s): Philip Wickens. Printing Historical Society, St Bride Institute, Fleet St, Bride Ln, London, EC4Y 8EE, United Kingdom. Circ: 650. *Bk. rev.:* 6-9, 200-300 words, signed. *Aud.:* Ac, Sa.

All aspects of printing history and the preservation of equipment and printed materials are examined. Contributors include practitioners and researchers in the printing field. Three to four articles are featured and are scholarly in nature. Shorter articles and book reviews appear in the society's *Bulletin,* which appears as part of the journal. Historically important typefaces that have been revived are also reviewed. The *Bulletin* features society news and a list of antiquarian book catalogs. Both publications are free to society members.

5708. ***Printing History.*** [ISSN: 0192-9275] 1979. s-a. USD 50 (Individuals, USD 40). Ed(s): David Pankow. American Printing History Association, PO Box 4519, New York, NY 10163; http://www.printinghistory.org. Illus., adv. Sample. Refereed. Vol. ends: No. 2. *Indexed:* AmH&L, LibLit, MLA-IB. *Bk. rev.:* 3, 500-600 words, signed. *Aud.:* Ga, Ac.

This scholarly publication offers five or six research articles on topics that may range from profiles of leaders in the field to fifteenth-century papermaking. Its main focus is on American printing history, but its actual range is much broader and includes international developments that influenced the industry. Contributors are researchers in the field. This journal is only available through membership in the association. It is a useful addition to any printing history collection.

5709. ***Printing Impressions.*** Incorporates: *Printing Management.* [ISSN: 0032-860X] 1958. m. USD 90; USD 110 Canada; USD 135 elsewhere. Ed(s): Mark T Michelson. North American Publishing Company, 401 N Broad St, 5th Fl, Philadelphia, PA 19108-1074; http://www.napco.com. Illus., adv. Sample. Circ: 94046. Microform: PQC. Online: Gale Group; Northern Light Technology, Inc.; OCLC Online Computer Library Center, Inc.; ProQuest Information & Learning. Reprint: PQC. *Indexed:* ABIn, B&I, EngInd. *Aud.:* Ac, Sa.

This trade publication offers commercial printers, graphic artists, and newspaper publishers up-to-date information in the areas of printing, marketing, finance, and technology. Each issue includes profiles of successful businesses, how-to reports on recent technological advances, management advice, and a calendar of events. New products are reviewed. News about important people in the printing industry is a prominent feature.

5710. ***Printing News.*** Former titles: *Printing News - East;* (until Oct. 1989): *Printing News.* 1928. w. 51/yr. USD 24.95; USD 30.95 in Canada & Mexico; USD 134.95 elsewhere. Ed(s): Patrick Henry. Cygnus Business Media, Inc., 445 Broad Hollow Rd, Melville, NY 11747-3601. Illus., adv. Sample. Circ: 9000. Online: Gale Group. *Indexed:* EngInd. *Aud.:* Sa.

This is the weekly newspaper for printing industry professionals in New York, New Jersey, Connecticut, and Pennsylvania. Each issue includes feature articles, industry and product news, and a calendar of events. Two special issues cover the Graphic Communications exhibit held annually in Philadelphia and the Graph Expo held annually in New York City. This is an important resource for printing and graphics professionals in the Eastern states.

5711. ***Professional Printer.*** Incorporates: *Printing Technology.* [ISSN: 0308-4205] 1957. bi-m. Non-members, GBP 24. Ed(s): Nessan Cleary. Institute of Printing, The Mews, Hill House, Clanricarde Rd, Tunbridge Wells, TN1 1PJ, United Kingdom; http://wwww.globalprint.com/uk/iop. Illus., index, adv. Sample. Refereed. Circ: 1700. Vol. ends: Dec. Microform: PQC. Reprint: PQC. *Indexed:* BrTechI, EngInd, LISA. *Aud.:* Ac, Sa.

This publication of the Institute of Printing, based in London, provides coverage of the institute's activities and issues as well as innovations in printing technology occurring all over the United Kingdom. Membership news and conferences of the institute are announced. Each issue also includes scholarly, scientific articles on the printing process, new techniques, or evaluations of new technology. Many articles are written by professors and include bibliographical references, charts, and graphs. *Professional Printer* offers well-researched information to its readers.

5712. ***Pulp & Paper.*** Former titles (until 1947): *Pulp & Paper Industry;* (until 1945): *Pacific Pulp & Paper Industry.* [ISSN: 0033-4081] 1927. m. s-m. Nov. USD 135; USD 165 in Canada & Mexico; USD 185 elsewhere. Paperloop, 55 Hawthorne, Ste 600, San Francisco, CA 94105; info@paperloop.com ; http://www.pponline.com/. Illus., adv. Sample. Circ: 41900 Controlled. Vol. ends: Dec. Microform: CIS; PQC. Online: EBSCO Publishing; Florida Center for Library Automation; Gale Group; OCLC Online Computer Library Center, Inc.; ProQuest Information & Learning. Reprint: PQC. *Indexed:* ABIn, AS&TI, Agr, B&I, BPI, ChemAb, ExcerpMed, FPA, ForAb. *Aud.:* Ac, Sa.

The definitive journal of the paper industry, this monthly publication provides information about all aspects of paper production. New technological developments, better productivity and efficiency, and cost savings are only a few of the topics covered. Each issue includes financial information about the international paper market and worldwide timber supplies. Upcoming conferences and their programs are outlined. This is required reading for paper industry professionals.

5713. ***Quaerendo: a quarterly journal from the Low Countries devoted to manuscripts and printed books.*** [ISSN: 0014-9527] 1971. 4x/yr. EUR 174 print & online eds. (Individuals, EUR 99 print & online eds.). Ed(s): Croiset van Uchelen. Brill Academic Publishers, Inc., PO Box 9000, Leiden, 2300 PA, Netherlands; cs@brill.nl; http://www.brill.nl. Illus., index, adv. Sample. Refereed. Circ: 750. Vol. ends: No. 4. *Indexed:* AmH&L, BEL&L, BHA, IBZ. *Bk. rev.:* Various number and length. *Aud.:* Ac.

Devoted to the history of printing, this journal presents scholarly articles in English, French, and German. Important manuscripts, collections, and recent discoveries are highlighted. Book reviews and information about upcoming exhibits and conferences are provided. *Quaerendo* is delightful reading for anyone who loves books.

5714. ***Screen Printing.*** [ISSN: 0036-9594] 1953. m. plus a. Buyers' Guide. USD 42 domestic; USD 62 Canada; USD 65 elsewhere. Ed(s): Tom Frecska. S T Publications Inc., 407 Gilbert Ave, Cincinnati, OH 45202; sduccill@stpubs.com; http://www.screenweb.com. Illus., index, adv. Sample. Circ: 19751. Vol. ends: Dec. *Indexed:* A&ATA, EngInd, PhotoAb. *Aud.:* Ac, Sa.

This journal reflects its artistic focus by providing readers with clear instructions for a polished end-product. Included also is technical information about screen-printing systems, care and maintenance of screen-printing equipment, and industry trends. New products are also highlighted. *Screen Printing* is the foremost journal in the screen-printing industry.

5715. ***The Seybold Report (Analyzing Publishing Technologies).*** Formerly: *Seybold Report on Publishing Systems;* Which incorporates (1986-2001): *Seybold Report on Internet Publishing;* Which was formerly (until 1996): *Seybold Report on Desktop Publishing;* (until 1982): *Seybold Report; Editing Technology.* [ISSN: 1533-9211] 1971. s-m. USD 595 domestic; USD 595 Canada; USD 640 elsewhere. Ed(s): Peter E Dyson. Seybold Publications, 528 E Baltimore Ave, Box 644, Media, PA 19063. Illus., index. Sample. Online: EBSCO Publishing; Gale Group; Northern Light Technology, Inc. *Indexed:* EngInd. *Aud.:* Ac, Sa.

This international journal is very clearly organized so that the publishing professional can see at a glance the important issues and developments in the electronic prepress industry. Information about new technologies and capabilities is combined with financial reports and discussions about legal implications. Overviews of conference proceedings are provided. This is essential reading for anyone in the publishing industry or anyone selecting a publishing system.

5716. ***Solutions!: the official publication of TAPPI and PIMA.*** Former titles (until 2001): *T A P P I Journal;* (until 1982): *T A P P I;* (until 1949): *Technical Association Papers.* 1920. m. Membership. Ed(s): Donald G Meadows. Technical Association of the Pulp and Paper Industry, Technology Park Atlanta, Box 105113, Atlanta, GA 30348; dmeadows@tappi.org; http://www.tappi.org. Illus., index, adv. Sample. Refereed. Circ: 38000. Vol. ends: Dec. Microform: MIM; PMC. *Indexed:* A&ATA, AS&TI, Agr, BiolAb, C&ISA, CEA, ChemAb, EngInd, EnvAb, ExcerpMed, FPA, ForAb, GeogAbPG, HortAb, PhotoAb, S&F, SCI, SSCI, WAE&RSA. *Aud.:* Ac, Sa.

A very comprehensive journal of the paper industry, *Solutions!* combines journalistic articles with peer-reviewed papers. Every aspect of paper production is discussed, including finances and industry trends. Its readership is largely members of the Technical Association of the Pulp and Paper Industry, so each issue includes information about the association and its conferences.

5717. ***Step Inside Design: the world of design from the inside out.*** Formerly (until 2002): *Step-by-Step Graphics.* [ISSN: 1540-2436] 1985. bi-m. USD 42 domestic; USD 73.83 foreign; USD 7.95 newsstand/cover per issue. Ed(s): Emily Potts. Dynamic Graphics, Inc., 6000 N Forest Park Dr, Peoria, IL 61614-3592. Illus., index, adv. Sample. Circ: 46000. Vol. ends: Nov/Dec. *Indexed:* DAAI. *Aud.:* Ga, Ac.

This colorful, eye-catching magazine offers graphic artists insight and advice about their chosen field. Articles include specific, detailed instructions about currently popular techniques. Advice about how to sell oneself and one's work is also a frequent feature. Practical business and career tips contained in each issue make this publication a must-read for visual communicators.

5718. ***Trace (New York): A I G A journal of graphic design.*** Former titles (until Jan. 2001): *A I G A Journal of Graphic Design;* (1965-1982): *American Institute of Graphic Arts. Journal;* (1947-1953): *A I G A Journal.* 1947. 3x/yr. Non-members, USD 14. Ed(s): Andrea Codrington. American Institute of Graphic Arts, 164 Fifth Ave, New York, NY 10010-5900; http://www.aiga.org. Illus., adv. Circ: 9000. Vol. ends: No. 3. *Indexed:* ABM, AIAP, ArtInd, DAAI. *Aud.:* Ac, Sa.

The American Institute of Graphic Arts's reconceived journal addresses the practice of graphic design and how it relates to changing trends in culture. One unique aspect of this journal is that it is designed by a different studio every year. The influence of cultural, business, and technological environments on graphic design is examined.

5719. ***U & l c.*** [ISSN: 0362-6245] 1974. q. Ed(s): John D Berry. International Typeface Corp., 200 Ballardvale St, Wilmington, MA 01887-1069; info@itcfonts.com; http://www.itcfonts.com. Illus., adv. Sample. Circ: 70000. Vol. ends: No. 4. Microform: PQC. *Indexed:* ArtInd, DAAI. *Aud.:* Ga, Ac.

This typographic journal remains true to its focus, with frequent articles on type and visual experimentation with typefaces. It also branches out into other areas by profiling filmmakers, printers, and pioneers of electronic publishing, for example. Its unique layout makes distinguishing between advertisements and feature articles a challenge.

5720. ***Visible Language: the triannual concerned with all that is involved in our being literate.*** Formerly (until 1970): *Journal of Typographic Research.* [ISSN: 0022-2224] 1967. 3x/yr. USD 65 (Individuals, USD 35). Ed(s): Sharon H Poggenpohl. Illinois Institute of Technology, Institute of Design, 350 N La Salle St, Chicago, IL 60610; poggenpohl@id.iit.edu; http://www.id.iit.edu/visiblelanguage. Illus., index, adv. Circ: 1600. Vol. ends: Sep. Microform: PQC. Online: ProQuest Information & Learning; H.W. Wilson. *Indexed:* ABCT, ABM, ArtHuCI, ArtInd, BAS, BHA, BRD, CIJE, ErgAb, GAA, InfoSAb, L&LBA, MLA-IB, PsycholAb, SSCI. *Aud.:* Ac.

This scholarly journal is concerned with written language (as opposed to verbal language) and its impact on humanity and civilization. Literacy is a frequent topic, but there are also many others, including typography, the effect of computer technology on the written word, and semantics. Many issues are devoted to a specific topic. *Visible Language* is important reading for language scholars and researchers.

■ PSYCHOLOGY

Paul Fehrmann, Reference Librarian, Information Services, Libraries and Media Services, Kent State University, Kent, OH 44242

Introduction

Psychology is a discipline that studies human functioning, development, and behavior. Psychology is also a profession, with representatives in a variety of settings who provide services based on studies of human functioning, development, and behavior. Thus, in addition to research and study leading to knowledge in psychology, there are also services provided by psychologists in a variety of settings, such as rehabilitation, medicine, community mental health, law, government, education, and industry.

With respect to professional communication, psychology continues to rely primarily on "traditional journals" for sharing and promoting the development of its ever-growing body of knowledge; and this section covers those. However, although most of the resources discussed in this section are "paper" journals, an increasing number of these journals have equivalent content available on the Internet; electronic versions of the issues are available for many, and I try to indicate where this is the case. Additionally, a small list at the end of this section gives information on a number of "electronic journals" in psychology that are available exclusively on the Internet. The electronic journals vary in content, of course, but also in manner of access and appearance; and the attempt here has also been to select resources for demonstrated continuity and potential for use by students, researchers, and professionals, as well as including a number that might serve a general reader.

With respect to special topics, during the 1990s—the "Decade of the Brain"—increased attention was given to basic and applied work from "cognitive" perspectives in psychology, although behavioral and psychodynamic approaches continued with important contributions to theory and clinical work; and each of these three key areas continues to find coverage in titles listed below. Other selections also represent areas of recent increased emphasis, such as the applied area of health psychology and the basic-research area of neuroscience. Moreover, special agendas, such as the current "Decade of Behavior" (initiated by the American Psychological Association and supported by many others), drive some research activities with their emphasis on improving health, safety, education, prosperity, and democracy, and so increased publication might be expected in these areas.

Many titles identified here have an intended international audience and regularly contain contributions from a worldwide community of scholars; however, selections included here are primarily English-based. Comprehensive or specialized selectors will wish to consider non-English publications.

Items included here will also be found most useful by those involved in higher education, research, or clinical settings; and a significant number of selections are those that are basic for libraries in such settings. At the same time, a number of titles (including several electronic journals) have been identified as potentially useful for wider, general audiences.

As noted above, many subdomains of research and service provision are found in psychology, and this diversity is reflected in the large group of titles related to psychology in resources such as *Ulrich's Periodicals Directory.* There one finds titles that focus on study and/or service related to specific areas, e.g., ethnic issues and concerns, sports, schizophrenia, or eating disorders. Others are selective, with their focus on certain schools of theory, clinical assessment, or intervention. Although most of these narrower topical areas are given some coverage in one or more of the titles here, other resources should be consulted for additional titles that focus on specialized topics. Readers will also want to examine other sections of this edition of *Magazines for Libraries*, as quite a few additional titles treating topics related to psychological research and/or service will be found in sections such as African American; Aging; Asian American; Disabilities; Education; Ethnic Studies; Family and Marriage; Lesbian, Gay, Bisexual, and Transgender; Linguistics; Medicine and Health; Parapsychology; Parenting; Philosophy; Political Science; Population Studies; Religion; Sociology; Sports; and Women.

Furthermore, among others, two additional resources can be useful for journal information. The first is the American Psychological Association's *Journals in Psychology,* a resource that lists over 300 journals. A second impressive resource (covering over 2,000 titles) is that supervised by Dr. Armin Gunther (Augsburg), covering English-, German-, French-, Dutch-, and Spanish-language journals in psychology. It can be found on the Internet at http://www.psycline.org.

Because psychology is necessarily wide-ranging in subject matter, editors typically describe a journal's subject or general topic areas. The annotations here include this general information, as well as examples of specific topics recently covered. In addition, editors often indicate the *kind of articles* that readers can expect. For example, readers commonly find that articles are empirical, theoretical, experimental, review, or case studies. As a guide then, these article types are discussed below.

If an article reports *empirical research,* this usually means that it will include data. Data are recorded, observation-based information. These data, gathered by an author, are discussed and referred to as the basis for conclusions. All empirical-research articles are also influenced or guided by theory. In contrast, although *theoretical articles* do not have to include data, they do involve discussion of such things as concepts, implications, conceptual relations, explanatory frameworks, reasoning for conclusions, and criticisms.

A third type of article reports on *experimental research.* Although experimental approaches are numerous in psychology, experimental-research articles usually involve reports on designed interventions of an author that aim to do something to subjects being studied (humans, animals, or computer simulations). Reactions to or effects of such interventions are watched and data are gathered to answer the author's research questions. Experimental studies are usually empirical (including computer simulations), although not all empirical study is experimental. For example, researchers making "naturalistic" observations in natural settings can gather data, and so are doing empirical work, though "interventions" are not used on subjects observed. Experimental-research articles can also include explicit statements of implications for theory.

Reviews are a fourth type of article. These usually involve evaluation of published articles that focus on a certain topic. As such, reviews provide very useful overviews for a reader wishing to "know what's been done" in an area. Such articles can include criticism, comparison, evaluation, integration, or summation, and one kind of review, called meta-analysis, is a special quantitative kind of review that has been very significant for psychology.

Finally, a fifth kind of article, presenting a *case study*, usually reports on work or experience with individual instances of psychological phenomena related to a journal's chosen subject area. These reports can draw on numerous information resources related to the individual case being considered.

Again, journals in psychology vary in their emphasis on the different kinds of articles; and so in each of the journal annotations that follow, I have tried to indicate the type(s) of articles readers might typically expect to find, as well as listing examples of specific topics recently covered.

Basic Periodicals

Hs, Ga: *Psychology Today;* Ac: *American Psychologist, Annual Review of Psychology, Archives of General Psychiatry, Contemporary Psychology, Psychological Bulletin, Psychological Review.*

Basic Abstracts and Indexes

Biological Abstracts, Current Contents, ERIC, Index Medicus, PsycINFO, Social Sciences Index.

5721. ***A P S Observer.*** [ISSN: 1050-4672] 1988. m. USD 75. Ed(s): Brian Weaver. American Psychological Society, 1010 Vermont Ave, NW, Ste 1100, Washington, DC 20005-4907; http://www.psychologicalscience.org. Illus., adv. Circ: 15030. *Aud.:* Ga, Ac.

The American Psychological Society, with close to 14,000 members, is dedicated to advancing "scientific psychology and its representation as a science on the national level." This inexpensive monthly publication provides news of and for the society, news on grants and other federal activities relevant to psychology, a section by and for graduate students in psychology, and news about jobs in psychology. In addition, selected articles from recent issues are available on the Internet, along with employment listings. This is another title, similar to the *APA Monitor,* that all libraries supporting programs in psychology should consider.

5722. ***Acta Psychologica: international journal of psychonomics.*** [ISSN: 0001-6918] 1941. 9x/yr. EUR 838 (Individuals, EUR 328). Ed(s): J. Wagemans, P. Koele. Elsevier BV, North-Holland, Sara Burgerhartstraat 25, Amsterdam, 1055 KV, Netherlands; nlinfo-f@elsevier.nl. Illus., index, adv. Sample. Refereed. Microform: PQC. Online: ingenta.com; ScienceDirect; Swets Blackwell. *Indexed:* AgeL, BiolAb, CommAb, ErgAb, IndMed, L&LBA, PsycholAb, SSCI, SWA. *Bk. rev.:* 0-3, 1,000-2,500 words. *Aud.:* Ac, Sa.

This international journal focuses on human experimental psychology. Article emphasis is on "empirical studies and evaluative review articles that increase the theoretical understanding of human capabilities," although "papers concerned with social processes, development, psychopathology, neuroscience or computational modelling are also welcome" if they have "direct importance to experimental psychologists." The journal also publishes book reviews and a list of books received. Recent issues have looked at topics such as the effects of acute bouts of exercise on cognition, hemispheric differences in stop task performance, decision making under internal uncertainty, the influence of irrelevant stimulus changes on stimulus and response repetition effect, recognition thresholds for plane-rotated pictures of familiar objects, prehension in young children with Down syndrome, and states of awareness across multiple memory tasks. Recent special issues also looked at judgment and decision-making issues and at functional neuroanatomy of the mind. Internet access to a table of contents and to an index has also been available. Libraries supporting programs in experimental psychology will want this title.

5723. ***Aggressive Behavior: a multidisciplinary journal devoted to the experimental and observational analysis of conflict in humans and animals.*** [ISSN: 0096-140X] 1975. bi-m. USD 1695 United States; USD 1755 in Canada & Mexico; USD 1806 elsewhere. Ed(s): Ronald Baenninger. John Wiley & Sons, Inc., 111 River St, Hoboken, NJ 07030; uscs-wis@wiley.com; http://www.wiley.com. Illus., index, adv. Refereed. Circ: 550. Vol. ends: No. 6. Microform: PQC. Online: EBSCO Publishing; Gale Group; Wiley InterScience. Reprint: ISI; PSC. *Indexed:* AgeL, AnBeAb, BiolAb, CJA, ChemAb, CommAb, ExcerpMed, IndVet, PEI, PRA, PsycholAb, RRTA, RiskAb, SCI, SSCI, VetBull, ZooRec. *Bk. rev.:* 0-3, 800-1,000 words. *Aud.:* Ac, Sa.

As the official journal of the International Society for Research on Aggression, this title provides articles on "overt or implied conflict behavior." Articles can be empirical, theoretical, or review, and readers can expect coverage of factors that underlie or influence aggression or that explore the consequences (physiological and/or behavioral) of being subject to aggression. Contributions come from those working in such fields as animal behavior, anthropology, ethnology, psychiatry, psychobiology, psychology, and sociology. The journal's *Guide to the Literature on Aggressive Behavior* is Internet-accessible, along with a table of contents for the journal. Averaging seven articles, recent issues have looked at teasing, rejection, and violence (case studies of school shootings), strain-specific aggressive behavior of male mice submitted to different husbandry procedures, sex differences in genetic and environmental effects on aggression, survey results and characteristics that predict assault and injury to personnel working in mental health facilities, if beliefs about aggression predict physical aggression to partners, executive cognitive functioning and aggression, enhancing children's responsibility to take action against bullying, SCL-90-R profiles in a sample of severely violent psychiatric inpatients, and the correlations between aggression, impulsiveness, social problem-solving, and alcohol use. Special issues also looked at abstracts from the 14th World Meeting of the International Society for Research on Aggression and at bullying in the schools. Other more general journals look at aggression to some extent, but researchers or students of violent behavior will appreciate this as one of the more focused titles in their libraries.

5724. ***American Academy of Child and Adolescent Psychiatry. Journal.*** Formerly: *American Academy of Child Psychiatry. Journal.* [ISSN: 0890-8567] 1962. m. USD 253 print & online eds. (Individuals, USD 144 print & online eds.; USD 26 per issue). Ed(s): Dr. Mina K. Dulcan. Lippincott Williams & Wilkins, 351 W Camden St, Baltimore, MD 21201; http://www.lww.com. Illus., adv. Refereed. Circ: 10175. Vol. ends: Nov/Dec. CD-ROM: Ovid Technologies, Inc. Microform: Pub. Online: Florida Center for Library Automation; Gale Group; MD Consult; OCLC Online Computer Library Center, Inc.; Ovid Technologies, Inc.; Swets Blackwell; H.W. Wilson. *Indexed:* BiolAb, CJA, EduInd, ExcerpMed, IMFL, IndMed, PsycholAb, SCI, SSCI, SSI, SWR&A. *Aud.:* Ac, Sa.

The purpose of this title, as the academy's official journal, is to advance theory, research, and clinical practice pertaining to child or adolescent psychiatry. Articles are written by those working within various frameworks, including genetic, epidemiological, neurobiological, cognitive, behavioral, and psychodynamic. Diagnostic-reliability and -validity studies are published, as are efficacy studies looking at psychotherapeutic or psychopharmacological treatment. There are about 15 articles in each issue. Recent issues examine a recalling of childhood psychopathology (more than 10 years later); paroxetine versus clomipramine in adolescents with severe major depression; suicidal behavior and violence in male adolescents; psychological comorbidity and stress reactivity in children and adolescents with recurrent abdominal pain and anxiety disorders; monozygotic twins discordant for ADHD; and brain maturation and subtypes of conduct disorder. Tables of contents and article abstracts are available at http://www.jaacap.com. Those involved with child and adolescent research and study will want this title.

5725. ***American Journal of Clinical Hypnosis.*** [ISSN: 0002-9157] 1958. q. USD 125 (Individuals, USD 62.50). Ed(s): Claire Frederick, MD. American Society of Clinical Hypnosis, 140 N Bloomingdale Rd, Bloomingdale, IL 60108; info@asch.net; http://www.asch.net. Illus., adv.

Sample. Refereed. Circ: 3000. Vol. ends: Apr. Reprint: PQC. *Indexed:* AgeL, ArtHuCI, BiolAb, ExcerpMed, IndMed, PsycholAb, SSCI. *Bk. rev.:* 3, 500-1,000 words. *Aud.:* Ac, Sa.

The articles in this journal, which often report case studies, are typically written by practitioners or researchers. With an average of six main articles, recent issues have looked at conversational assessment of hypnotic ability to promote hypnotic responsiveness, development of the Hypnotic State Assessment Questionnaire, operationalizing trance using a psychophenomenological approach, defining hypnosis as a trance vs. cooperation, acupuncture and clinical hypnosis for facial and head and neck pain, EEG P300 event-related markers of hypnosis, the use of a skill-based activity in therapeutic induction, treating symptoms and risk factors of major depression, and a response set theory of hypnosis (expectancy and physiology). Article abstracts are available at the web site, and a related title is the *International Journal of Clinical and Experimental Hypnosis* (see below in this section). Along with practitioners who use hypnosis, libraries should consider both titles if they are supporting research or study in clinical work related to mental health. Medical libraries will also benefit from access.

5726. ***American Journal of Community Psychology.*** [ISSN: 0091-0562] 1973. 8x/yr. USD 880 print or online ed. Ed(s): W S Davidson. Kluwer Academic / Plenum Publishers, 233 Spring St Fl 7, New York, NY 10013-1522; http://www.wkap.nl/. Illus., index, adv. Sample. Refereed. Vol. ends: Dec. Microform: PQC. Online: EBSCO Publishing; Florida Center for Library Automation; Gale Group; ingenta.com; Kluwer Online; Northern Light Technology, Inc.; OCLC Online Computer Library Center, Inc.; Ovid Technologies, Inc.; ProQuest Information & Learning; RoweCom Information Quest; Swets Blackwell. *Indexed:* ASSIA, AgeL, CINAHL, CJA, ECER, ExcerpMed, H&SSA, IBZ, IMFL, IndMed, PRA, PsycholAb, RiskAb, SFSA, SSCI, SSI, SUSA, SWR&A, SociolAb. *Aud.:* Ac, Sa.

This journal publishes "quantitative and qualitative research on community psychological interventions," and the focus can be on the individual, the group, the neighborhood, the community, or society. Recent issues have covered adolescents' relationships with their "very important" nonparental adults, social contexts (transcending their power and their fragility), effectiveness of mentoring programs for youth, implications of evidence-based practice for community health, battered women's coping strategies and psychological distress, and a conceptual framework for promotion of social change. Tables of contents and abstracts are available online, as well as fee-based access to full texts. Those who will find this title useful include professionals working with communities or societal concerns. Other social psychology journals cover some of these issues, but all academic libraries supporting undergraduate and graduate programs in sociology, social work, and psychology should consider this title.

5727. ***American Journal of Forensic Psychology: interfacing issues of psychology and law.*** [ISSN: 0733-1290] 1983. q. USD 85 in US & Canada; USD 110 elsewhere. Ed(s): Debbie Miller. American College of Forensic Psychiatry, PO Box 5870, Balboa Island, CA 92662; psychlaw@sover.net; http://www.forensicpsychiatry.cc/. Refereed. Circ: 500. Vol. ends: No. 4. Microform: WSH; PMC. Reprint: WSH. *Indexed:* CJA, ExcerpMed, PsycholAb. *Bk. rev.:* 3, 800 words. *Aud.:* Ac, Sa.

This publication of the American College of Forensic Psychology provides articles (about four per issue) addressing issues at the interface of psychology and the law, with the primary focus being forensic skills and issues related to litigation of civil and criminal cases pertaining to mental disorders and mental disability. Recent issues include looks at such topics as motivational interviewing and preparing people for change, a step-by-step guide to writing and defending an expert report, linking juror predudgment and pretrial publicity knowledge, the science of happiness (unlocking the mysteries of mood), suggestibility and confessions, and issues in conducting child sex abuse evaluations. Libraries will want to have this title if they support those who provide or who are studying to provide psychological services in legal settings. *Law and Human Behavior* and *Psychology, Public Policy, and Law* (see below) are related titles.

5728. ***American Journal of Orthopsychiatry.*** [ISSN: 0002-9432] 1930. q. USD 140 (Individuals, USD 82; Members, USD 73). Ed(s): Carlos E. Sluzki. American Psychological Association, 750 First St, NE, Washington, DC 20002-4242; http://www.apa.org/. Illus., index, adv. Refereed. Circ: 13000. Vol. ends: Oct. Microform: PQC. Online: EBSCO Publishing; Gale Group; OCLC Online Computer Library Center, Inc.; ProQuest Information & Learning; ScienceDirect. Reprint: PQC. *Indexed:* ASSIA, AgeL, BRD, BiolAb, CINAHL, CJA, ChemAb, ECER, EduInd, ExcerpMed, H&SSA, IBSS, IMFL, IndMed, PsycholAb, RiskAb, SCI, SFSA, SSCI, SSI, SWA, SWR&A, SociolAb. *Aud.:* Ac, Sa.

The broad aim of this journal is to "inform public policy, professional practice, and knowledge production relating to mental health and human development, from a multidisciplinary and interprofessional perspective." Articles may be theoretical, research, clinical, or policy-oriented. Recent articles address such topics as complex adoption and assisted reproductive technology, group practices to empower low-income minority women coping with chemical dependency, the role of personal contact with HIV-infected people, homicidality in schizophrenia, stress and uplifts during times of political tension (Jews and Arabs in Israel), the social grid of community medication management, and an investigation of racial partiality in child welfare assessments of attachment. Internet access to recent tables of contents and abstracts is available. Should be considered for collections that support public mental health policy study or research; academic or clinical mental health programs can also benefit.

5729. ***American Journal of Psychiatry.*** Formerly (until vol.78, 1921): *American Journal of Insanity.* [ISSN: 0002-953X] 1844. m. USD 399 print & online eds. (Individuals, USD 229 print & online eds.; Individual members, USD 157 print & online eds.). Ed(s): Dr. Nancy C Andreasen. American Psychiatric Publishing, Inc., 1000 Wilson Blvd, Ste 1825, Arlington, VA 22209; appi@psych.org; http://www.appi.org. Illus., index, adv. Refereed. Circ: 44000. Vol. ends: Dec. CD-ROM: Ovid Technologies, Inc. Microform: PMC; PQC. Online: bigchalk; EBSCO Publishing; Gale Group; HighWire Press; LexisNexis; Northern Light Technology, Inc.; OCLC Online Computer Library Center, Inc.; Ovid Technologies, Inc.; ProQuest Information & Learning. *Indexed:* ASSIA, AbAn, AgeL, ArtHuCI, BAS, BRI, BiolAb, CBRI, CINAHL, CJA, ChemAb, DSA, ExcerpMed, H&SSA, IBZ, IndMed, L&LBA, MCR, PEI, PsycholAb, RI-1, RiskAb, SCI, SSCI, SSI, SWR&A. *Bk. rev.:* 10-15, 250-1,000 words. *Aud.:* Ac, Sa.

This core journal in psychiatry includes articles that focus on developments in biological psychiatry as well as on treatment innovations and forensic, ethical, economic, and social topics. The reader typically will find a special overview article on a topic of general interest to psychiatry, regular articles that report original work in psychiatric medicine and clinical research, and shorter reports of preliminary studies, replications, or "negative studies of important topics." With approximately 15 regular articles and 6 brief reports, recent issues have looked at the influence of gender on ADHD in children referred to a psychiatric clinic, gender differences in panic disorder (findings from the national comorbidity survey), relation of medial temporal lobe volumes to age and memory function in nondemented adults with Down syndrome, efficacy of sertraline in the long-term treatment of obsessive-compulsive disorder, diagnostic efficiency of borderline personality disorder criteria in hospitalized adolescents, and Internet support groups for depression (a one-year prospective cohort study). As the official journal of the American Psychiatric Association, it includes association news, as well as the previous month's table of contents from the *British Journal of Psychiatry.* Tables of contents, abstracts, and keyword searches of recent articles are also available on the Internet. Libraries supporting graduate programs in clinical psychology, counseling psychology, and psychiatry should provide access to this title.

5730. ***American Journal of Psychology.*** [ISSN: 0002-9556] 1887. q. USD 140 (Individuals, USD 65). Ed(s): Donelson E Dulany. University of Illinois Press, 1325 S Oak St, Champaign, IL 61820-6903; uipress@uillinois.edu; http://www.press.uillinois.edu. Illus., index, adv. Sample. Refereed. Circ: 2200 Paid. Vol. ends: Winter. Microform: MIM; PMC; PQC. Online: Chadwyck-Healey Incorporated; Florida Center for Library Automation; Gale Group; Northern Light Technology, Inc.; OCLC Online Computer Library Center, Inc.; ProQuest Information & Learning.

Reprint: PQC; PSC. *Indexed:* ASSIA, AbAn, AgeL, ArtHuCI, BRI, BiolAb, CBRI, ChemAb, CommAb, ErgAb, GSI, IBZ, IndMed, L&LBA, PsycholAb, SSCI, SSI. *Bk. rev.:* 4-6, 450-3,000 words. *Aud.:* Ac, Sa.

This journal—founded by the American Psychological Association's first president, G. Stanley Hall—aims to address issues in "the basic science of the mind," including "reports of original research in experimental psychology, theoretical presentations, combined theoretical and experimental analyses, historical commentaries, obituaries of prominent psychologists, and in-depth reviews of significant books." Each issue contains about five articles, and recent topics include chronometric analysis of the storage of alphabetic information in human memory, effect of deprivation level on the magnitude of positive induction in discriminative straight-alley performance, the robustness of medical expertise, configural biases and reversible figures, disambiguating conscious and unconscious influences, the limits of involuntary word processing, and satisficing in hypothesis generation. Issues also typically include thorough book reviews. Internet access to tables of contents (since 1990 at this writing) and abstracts (from 1998) is available, as well as an index to book reviews (from the late 1980s). Libraries that support programs in psychology should own this title.

5731. *American Psychoanalytic Association. Journal.* [ISSN: 0003-0651] 1953. q. USD 295 (Individuals, USD 135; USD 37.50 per issue in US & Canada). Ed(s): Arnold D Richards. Analytic Press, Inc., 101 West St, Hillsdale, NJ 07642; TAP@analyticpress.com; http://www.analyticpress.com. Illus., index, adv. Refereed. Circ: 6500. Vol. ends: No. 4. Reprint: PSC. *Indexed:* ASSIA, AgeL, BHA, BiolAb, ExcerpMed, IBZ, IndMed, PsycholAb, SSCI. *Bk. rev.:* 12-20, 800-2,500 words. *Aud.:* Ac, Sa.

Articles in this official journal of the American Psychoanalytic Association are contributed primarily by professionals working in settings that provide instruction or clinical services based on psychoanalysis. Each issue has an average of eight articles. In recent issues, topics include the fate of the dream in contemporary psychoanalysis; the analyst's desire and the problem of narcissistic resistances; analysis and psychotherapy by telephone: 20 years of clinical experience; the holding function of theory; silent thoughts, spoken wishes: when candidate experience of the supervisor converges with patient fantasies; and slow magic: psychoanalysis and "the disenchantment of the world." Association news is also included. Abstracts of recent articles are available on the Internet, and there is an online keyword tool for searching a bibliography of psychoanalytic journal articles, books, and book reviews.

5732. *American Psychologist.* [ISSN: 0003-066X] 1946. m. USD 491 (Members, USD 12; Non-members, USD 206). Ed(s): Dr. Ed Diener, Norman B Anderson. American Psychological Association, 750 First St, NE, Washington, DC 20002-4242; journals@apa.org; http://www.apa.org/. Illus., adv. Sample. Refereed. Circ: 102000. Vol. ends: Dec. Microform: PMC; PQC. Online: EBSCO Publishing; Gale Group; OCLC Online Computer Library Center, Inc.; Ovid Technologies, Inc.; ProQuest Information & Learning; ScienceDirect. Reprint: PSC. *Indexed:* ABS&EES, ASSIA, AgeL, ArtHuCI, BiolAb, CIJE, CJA, ChemAb, CommAb, FutSurv, H&SSA, IBSS, IBZ, IndMed, LRI, MLA-IB, PRA, PsycholAb, RI-1, SFSA, SSCI, SSI, SWA, SWR&A. *Aud.:* Ga, Ac, Sa.

The *American Psychologist* is the official journal of the American Psychological Association (APA). In addition to publishing news of and for the APA, the journal includes "articles covering current issues in psychology, the science and practice of psychology, and psychology's contribution to public policy." The goal is to include articles written in a "style that is accessible to and of interest to all psychologists, regardless of area of specialization." Topics recently examined include psychological data and policy debates regarding affirmative action, the implications for practicing psychology in the era of managed care, media ratings for violence and sex and their implications for policymakers and parents, research ethics for mental health science involving ethnic minority children and youths, the psychology of globalization, and genetic testing and psychology: new roles and responsibilities. An annual section lists the APA-accredited graduate programs in psychology. Recent tables of contents and abstracts and select key articles are available on the Internet. All libraries supporting study and research in psychology should include this title. Other libraries may also wish to have it as a general resource for keeping abreast of developments in psychology.

5733. *Annual Review of Psychology.* [ISSN: 0066-4308] 1950. a. USD 155 (Individuals, USD 65). Ed(s): Samuel Gubins, Susan T Fiske. Annual Reviews, 4139 El Camino Way, Palo Alto, CA 94303-0139; service@annualreviews.org; http://www.annualreviews.org. Illus., index, adv. Sample. Refereed. CD-ROM: Ovid Technologies, Inc. Microform: PQC. Online: EBSCO Publishing; Florida Center for Library Automation; Gale Group; HighWire Press; Northern Light Technology, Inc.; OCLC Online Computer Library Center, Inc.; Ovid Technologies, Inc.; ProQuest Information & Learning; Swets Blackwell; H.W. Wilson. Reprint: PSC. *Indexed:* AgeL, BAS, BiolAb, CJA, ChemAb, ExcerpMed, IBSS, IBZ, IndMed, L&LBA, MRD, PsycholAb, SCI, SSCI, SSI. *Aud.:* Ga, Ac, Sa.

This annual continues as a standard resource for high-quality, in-depth overviews of developments in psychology, written by professionals in psychology. Beginning with a chapter written by a distinguished psychologist, issues regularly cover developments in such areas as social psychology, psychopathology, developmental psychology, and cognitive psychology. A chapter looking at psychology in a particular country (recently, Canada) is also occasionally included for international awareness. Recent overviews look at such topics as episodic memory: from mind to brain; human aggression, emotions, morbidity, and mortality: new perspectives from psychoneuroimmunology; motivational beliefs, values, and goals; cultural influences on personality; causes of eating disorders; conceptual issues in the development, persistence, and treatment of sleep disorder (insomnia) in adults; and socioeconomic status and child development. Users will appreciate both the content and the extensive current bibliographies. Each volume contains both subject and author indexes, as well as chapter/title indexes for preceding volumes. Abstracts of current chapters and tables of contents of recent issues are also available on the Internet, as are full-text articles. All academic libraries can benefit from this title, and all libraries supporting programs in psychology should own it. Other libraries might also consider this among a number of titles that can make overviews of psychology accessible for an educated lay audience.

5734. *Anxiety, Stress and Coping.* Formerly: *Anxiety Research.* [ISSN: 1061-5806] 1988. q. GBP 454 (Individuals, GBP 117; Corporations, GBP 740). Ed(s): Reinhard Pekrun, Krys Kaniasty. Brunner - Routledge (UK), 27 Church Rd, Hove, BN3 2FA, United Kingdom; information@brunner-routledge.co.uk; http://www.brunner-routledge.co.uk. Illus. Refereed. Online: EBSCO Publishing; OCLC Online Computer Library Center, Inc.; Swets Blackwell. Reprint: PSC. *Indexed:* H&SSA, PsycholAb, SSCI, SWA. *Aud.:* Ac.

This international journal provides a forum for the study of anxiety, stress, and coping. Such related topics as the antecedents and consequences of stress and emoting are also covered. The articles include research reports, theoretical papers, and "interpretative literature reviews or meta-analyses." Case studies and clinical, therapeutic, or educational articles that further theory and research may also be considered. With an average of six articles, recent issues have covered such topics as evaluation of a pathoplastic relationship between anxiety sensitivity and panic disorder, roles of leisure in coping with stress among university students, children's reactions to a war situation as a function of age and sex, benefits and interindividual differences in children's responses to extended and intensified relaxation training, stress resistance resources and coping in pregnancy, effects of physical exercise on resources evaluation, and body self-concept and well-being among older adults. Tables of contents and abstracts are available online. Libraries supporting research and study with this focus should have this title, as well as the *Journal of Anxiety Disorders* (see below). Academic settings or training programs leading to relevant clinical service based on medical or behavioral sciences will also benefit.

The APA Monitor. See *Monitor on Psychology.*

5735. *Applied Psychological Measurement.* [ISSN: 0146-6216] 1976. bi-m. GBP 344 in Europe, Middle East, Africa & Australasia. Ed(s): David J Weiss, Mark Reckase. Sage Publications, Inc., 2455 Teller Rd, Thousand Oaks, CA 91320; info@sagepub.com; http://www.sagepub.com. Illus., index, adv. Sample. Refereed. Circ: 975 Paid. Vol. ends: Dec.

Microform: PQC. Online: ingenta.com; OCLC Online Computer Library Center, Inc.; ProQuest Information & Learning; RoweCom Information Quest; Swets Blackwell. Reprint: PSC. *Indexed:* BiolAb, CIJE, IBZ, MathSciNet, PsycholAb, SSCI. *Bk. rev.:* 1-2, 500-1,000 words. *Aud.:* Ac, Sa.

The aim of this journal is to publish empirical research, and its domain is "the application of techniques of psychological measurement to substantive problems in all areas of psychology and related disciplines." Here the reader will find articles reporting empirical research and methodological developments; brief reports of exploratory, small-sample, or replication studies; computer program reviews of commercially available software packages used in applied measurement; book reviews; and announcements of statistical and measurement meetings, symposia, and workshops. Topics recently covered include estimating the parameters of a structural model for the latent traits in Rasch's model for speed tests, Bayesian method for the detection of item preknowledge in computerized adaptive testing, implementing content constraints in alpha-stratified adaptive testing using a shadow trust approach, a comparison of item-fit statistics for the three-parameter logistic model, sample size requirements for comparing two alpha coefficients, determining the significance of correlations corrected for unreliability and range restriction, and the precision of gain scores under an item response theory perspective: a comparison of asymptotic and exact conditional inference about change. Regular readers should have advanced understanding of statistics, although articles that are purely statistical usually are not found here. Researchers and students will appreciate access to this title if they need to consult current work in the general categories noted above. Those in graduate training that includes psychological measurement in clinical settings may also want this title, because it potentially supports understanding the interpretation of measurement. Those looking for articles on actual use of assessment techniques in clinical settings should consult such titles as *Psychological Assessment,* the *Journal of Applied Behavioral Analysis,* or the *Journal of Personality Assessment* (see below).

5736. ***Applied Psychophysiology and Biofeedback.*** Formerly (until 1997): *Biofeedback and Self Regulation.* [ISSN: 1090-0586] 1975. q. USD 562 print or online ed. Ed(s): Carol Bischoff, Frank Andrasik. Kluwer Academic / Plenum Publishers, 233 Spring St Fl 7, New York, NY 10013-1522; http://www.wkap.nl/. Illus., index, adv. Refereed. Vol. ends: Dec. Microform: PQC. Online: EBSCO Publishing; ingenta.com; Kluwer Online; OCLC Online Computer Library Center, Inc.; Ovid Technologies, Inc.; RoweCom Information Quest; Swets Blackwell. *Indexed:* AgeL, BiolAb, ExcerpMed, IndMed, PsycholAb, SSCI. *Aud.:* Ac, Sa.

Research and clinical experience provide a significant body of techniques and tools pertaining to self-regulation of physiological processes, and this interdisciplinary title serves as a key resource for the study of the interrelationships of physiological systems, cognition, social and environmental parameters, and health. Contributions draw from psychology, psychiatry, psychosomatic and physical medicine, and cybernetics, and they can be theoretical, experimental, or clinical research papers. Priority has been given to original research contributing to theory, practice, or evaluation of applied psychophysiology and biofeedback. Reviews, position papers, and case studies can also be found, as well as abstracts of the annual association meeting presentations. Recent issues examine such topics as changes in physiological arousal to gambling cues among participants in motivationally enhanced cognitive-behavior therapy for pathological gambling, EEG signature and phenomenology of alpha/theta neurofeedback training versus mock feedback, a task force report on methodology and empirically supported treatments, a template for developing guidelines for the evaluation of the clinical efficacy of psychophysiological interventions, the role of spirituality in health care, and neurofeedback treatment for ADHD in children: a comparison with methylphenidate. Recent tables of contents are available online. Along with psychologists, researchers, and clinical practitioners, those who can benefit from this title include nurses, physicians, psychiatrists, physical therapists, dentists, and rehabilitation professionals.

5737. ***Archives of General Psychiatry.*** [ISSN: 0003-990X] 1959. m. USD 365. Ed(s): Jack D Barchas. American Medical Association, 515 N State St, Chicago, IL 60610-0946; amaa@ama-assn.org; http://www.ama-assn.org. Illus., index. Refereed. Circ: 38500. Vol. ends: Dec. CD-ROM: Ovid Technologies, Inc. Microform: PQC. Online: The Dialog Corporation; EBSCO Publishing; Florida Center for Library Automation; Gale Group; OCLC Online Computer Library Center, Inc.; Ovid Technologies, Inc.; ProQuest Information & Learning. *Indexed:* AgeL, BiolAb, CJA, ChemAb, ExcerpMed, IMFL, IndMed, PsycholAb, SCI, SSCI. *Aud.:* Ac, Sa.

This journal of the American Medical Association seeks "to inform and to educate its readers as well as to stimulate debate and further exploration into the nature, causes, treatment and public health importance of mental illness." Averaging ten original articles, recent issues have included material on cognitive therapy for relapse prevention for bipolar affective disorder, lifetime history of depression and carotid atherosclerosis in middle-aged women, induced panic attacks shift (aminobutyric acid type a receptor modulatory neuroactive steroid composition in patients with panic disorder), family study of affective spectrum disorder, predictors of mortality in eating disorders, screening for serious mental illness in the general population, severity, chronicity, and timing of maternal depression and risk for adolescent offspring diagnoses in a community sample, and posttraumatic stress disorder and the incidence of nicotine, alcohol, and other drug disorders in persons who have experienced trauma. Tables of contents and abstracts are available at the journal's Internet site, as is fee-based full text. In addition to clinicians, students and researchers pursuing work in psychiatry should have access to this title. It should also be considered for collections supporting graduate work in clinical and counseling psychology.

5738. ***Archives of Sexual Behavior: an interdisciplinary research journal.*** [ISSN: 0004-0002] 1971. bi-m. USD 876 print or online ed. Ed(s): Kenneth J Zucker. Kluwer Academic / Plenum Publishers, 233 Spring St Fl 7, New York, NY 10013-1522; http://www.wkap.nl/. Illus. Sample. Refereed. Vol. ends: Dec. Online: EBSCO Publishing; Florida Center for Library Automation; Gale Group; ingenta.com; Kluwer Online; OCLC Online Computer Library Center, Inc.; Ovid Technologies, Inc.; ProQuest Information & Learning; RoweCom Information Quest; Swets Blackwell. *Indexed:* AbAn, AgeL, ArtHuCI, BiolAb, CJA, ChemAb, ExcerpMed, H&SSA, HEA, IMFL, IndMed, IndVet, PsycholAb, RI-1, RiskAb, SFSA, SSCI, SSI, SWA, SociolAb, VetBull. *Bk. rev.:* 3-6, 1,000 words. *Aud.:* Ac, Sa.

The aim of this journal is to promote understanding of human sexual behavior. Material published is for professionals, and relevant submissions are accepted from a variety of academic disciplines. With an average of six articles, recent issues include an exploration of emotional response to erotic stimulation in men with premature ejaculation: effects of treatment with clomipramine; psychological outcomes and gender-related development in complete androgen insensitivity syndrome; handedness, sexual orientation, and gender-related personality traits in men and women; an evolutionary perspective of sex-typed toy preferences: pink, blue, and the brain; the relation between mood and sexuality in heterosexual men; the relation between mood and sexuality in gay men; and masculinity, femininity, and transsexualism. Tables of contents and abstracts are available online. Those who can benefit from this journal include those who are pursuing research in sexuality or who are studying for relevant clinical services in medicine, psychology, or rehabilitation.

5739. ***Behavior Modification.*** [ISSN: 0145-4455] 1977. bi-m. GBP 430 in Europe, Middle East, Africa & Australasia. Ed(s): Michel Hersen, Alan S Bellack. Sage Publications, Inc., 2455 Teller Rd, Thousand Oaks, CA 91320; http://www.sagepub.com. Illus., index, adv. Refereed. Circ: 1500. Vol. ends: Oct. *Indexed:* AgeL, CIJE, ECER, EduInd, ExcerpMed, HRA, IndMed, PsycholAb, SFSA, SSCI, SSI, SUSA, SociolAb. *Bk. rev.:* 0-1, 400 words. *Aud.:* Ac, Sa.

This journal covers assessment and behavior modification approaches to problems in psychiatric, clinical, education, and rehabilitation settings and includes papers covering measurement and modification of behavior in normal populations, presentations of single-case experimental research and group-comparison design studies, reviews and theoretical discussions, treatment manuals, and program descriptions. With an average of six articles, recent issues look at modifying behavioral variability in moderately depressed students, observational assessment of toy preferences among young children with disabilities in inclusive settings, long-term effects of a brief-distraction intervention on children's laboratory pain reactivity, a comparison of contingent and noncontingent interspersal of preferred academic tasks, HIV sexual risk reduction interventions for youth: a review and methodological critique of randomized controlled trials, and maintenance of health behavior change in preventive cardiology: internalization and self-regulation of new behaviors. Recommended for clinical settings and for all academic libraries supporting programs that include practical studies in the promotion of behavioral change. Useful companion journals for those in clinical behavioral services are *Behavior Therapy, Behaviour Research and Therapy, Cognitive Therapy and Research,* and the *Journal of Applied Behavioral Analysis* (see below).

5740. ***Behavior Research Methods, Instruments, and Computers: a journal of the Psychonomic Society.*** Formerly (until 1984): *Behavior Research Methods and Instrumentation.* [ISSN: 0743-3808] 1968. q. USD 183 (Individuals, USD 79). Ed(s): Jonathan Vaughn. Psychonomic Society, Inc., 1710 Fortview Rd, Austin, TX 78704; jbellquist@psychonomic.org; http://www.psychonomic.org. Illus., index, adv. Refereed. Circ: 1150. Vol. ends: Dec. Microform: PQC; NRP. Online: Ingenta Select; Swets Blackwell. Reprint: PQC. *Indexed:* AnBeAb, BiolAb, ErgAb, IndMed, L&LBA, PsycholAb, SSCI, ZooRec. *Bk. rev.:* 0-1, 400 words. *Aud.:* Ac.

To support experimental psychology, this journal of the Psychonomic Society includes articles that focus on methods, techniques, instrumentation, and computer applications in research in experimental psychology. With 10–15 articles per issue, recent topics include number-of-translation norms for Dutch–English translation pairs; PatPho: a phonological pattern generator for neural networks; a novel rotometer based on a RISC microcontroller; immediate and delayed memory tasks: a computerized behavioral measure of memory, attention, and impulsivity; "active" and "passive" learning of three-dimensional object structure within an immersive virtual-reality environment; MouseTrace: a better mousetrap for catching decision processes; and a comparison of four computer-based telephone interviewing methods: getting answers to sensitive questions. Internet access to tables of contents of current issues is available. Academic libraries supporting coursework in experimental psychology should consider this title.

5741. ***Behavior Therapy.*** [ISSN: 0005-7894] 1970. 4x/yr. USD 150 (Individuals, USD 75; USD 163 in Canada & Mexico). Ed(s): David A. F. Haaga. Association for Advancement of Behavior Therapy, 305 Seventh Ave, Ste 16A, New York, NY 10001; publication@aabt.org; http://www.aabt.org. Illus., index, adv. Sample. Refereed. Circ: 3500. Vol. ends: Fall. *Indexed:* AgeL, BiolAb, CJA, ECER, ExcerpMed, PsycholAb, SSCI, SSI, SWA. *Aud.:* Ac, Sa.

This journal, published by the Association for the Advancement of Behavior Therapy, covers the application of behavioral and cognitive behavioral science to clinical problems. Empirical research is emphasized, although methodological, theoretical, and evaluative review articles and selected case and replication studies are included. Along with special series, recent issues, averaging ten articles, examine assessing clinical significance: application to the Beck Depression Inventory, self-criticism in generalized social phobia and response to cognitive-behavioral treatment, predictors of response to problem-solving treatment of depression in primary care, the role of emotion in the psychological functioning of adult survivors of childhood sexual abuse, treatment of panic disorder via the Internet: a randomized trial of a self-help program, and kernels of truth or distorted perceptions: self and observer ratings of social anxiety and performance. Clinicians, students, and researchers involved with the application of cognitive and behavioral science to treatment issues will find this title very useful. Recent tables of contents and abstracts are available on the Internet. Other titles for similar clinical purposes include *Behavior Modification* (see above), *Behaviour Research and Therapy,* and the closely related *Journal of Applied Behavioral Analysis* (see below).

5742. ***Behavioral and Brain Sciences: an international journal of current research and theory with open peer commentary.*** [ISSN: 0140-525X] 1978. bi-m. USD 490 (Individuals, USD 168). Ed(s): Barbara L Finlay, Jeffrey A Gray. Cambridge University Press, The Edinburgh Bldg, Shaftesbury Rd, Cambridge, CB2 2RU, United Kingdom; information@cambridge.org; http://uk.cambridge.org/journals. Illus., index, adv. Sample. Refereed. Vol. ends: Dec. Microform: PQC. Online: EBSCO Publishing; Gale Group; OCLC Online Computer Library Center, Inc.; RoweCom Information Quest; Swets Blackwell. Reprint: SWZ. *Indexed:* AnBeAb, ArtHuCI, BiolAb, ExcerpMed, IBSS, IBZ, IndMed, L&LBA, PsycholAb, SCI, SSCI, SociolAb. *Bk. rev.:* 0-30, 500-2,000 words. *Aud.:* Ac, Sa.

Each issue of this journal provides three or four lead articles presenting work in psychology, neuroscience, behavioral biology, or cognitive science. Lead articles can present empirical research with broad scope and implications, theoretical work systematizing a body of research, or novel interpretations. Critiques or syntheses of existing empirical or theoretical work are also welcome. The responses of 15–30 professional commentators are also published along with each lead article, as are responses of the main author to this "internationally based open peer commentary." Moreover, additional interaction between lead author and peers can appear over a period of years, always with citation of the originally published dialogue. Recent articles examine such topics as the relationship between object manipulation and language development in Broca's area: a connectionist simulation of Greenfield's hypothesis, two visual systems and two theories of perception: an attempt to reconcile the constructivist and ecological approaches, the ultimate and proximate bases of empathy, a precis of how children learn the meaning of words, robots as good models of biological behavior, a sensorimotor account of vision and visual consciousness, and the Theory of Event Coding (TEC): a framework for perception and action planning. Internet access to recent tables of contents is available, along with full-text preprints of forthcoming articles. Academic libraries supporting relevant undergraduate and graduate programs should have this highly regarded title, as should libraries at institutions pursuing research in behavioral science.

5743. ***Behavioral Neuroscience.*** Supersedes in part (in 1983): *Journal of Comparative and Physiological Psychology.* [ISSN: 0735-7044] 1947. bi-m. USD 563 (Members, USD 121; Non-members, USD 213). Ed(s): Dr. John F. Disterhoft. American Psychological Association, 750 First St, NE, Washington, DC 20002-4242; journals@apa.org; http://www.apa.org/. Illus., index, adv. Sample. Refereed. Circ: 1700. Vol. ends: Jan. Microform: PMC; PQC. Online: EBSCO Publishing; Gale Group; OCLC Online Computer Library Center, Inc.; Ovid Technologies, Inc.; ProQuest Information & Learning; ScienceDirect. Reprint: PSC. *Indexed:* AbAn, Agr, AnBeAb, B&AI, BiolAb, ChemAb, DSA, ExcerpMed, IndMed, PsycholAb, SCI, SSCI, SSI, ZooRec. *Aud.:* Ac, Sa.

The primary aim of this title is to publish current original research on the biological bases of behavior. Either single- or multiple-experiment studies can be found, as well as review articles and theoretical work. Reports of research from a wide range of biological sciences are appropriate, as long as the work is clearly relevant to understanding behavior. Similarly, studies from a variety of behavioral sciences are welcome so long as they are clearly related to biological processes. With each issue containing about 20 regular articles, recent topics include asgenetic variations in CCK-sub-2 receptor in PVG hooded and Sprague-Dawley rats and its mRNA expression on cat exposure, the interaction of fraternal birth order and body size in male sexual orientation, failure to produce conditioning with low-dose trimethylthiazoline or cat feces as unconditioned stimuli, additive wake-promoting actions of medial basal forebrain noradrenergic alpha1- and beta-receptor stimulation, effects of D-cycloserine on extinction of conditioned freezing, impact of nicotine withdrawal on novelty reward and related behaviors, and cooperation between memory systems: acetylcholine release in the amygdala correlates positively with performance on a hippocampus-dependent task. Access to recent tables of contents and abstracts is available online. The *Journal of Cognitive Neuroscience* and *Psychophysiology* (below) are two other journals that relate behavioral concepts/observations to physiological/biological processes. Libraries supporting advanced studies at the intersection of biology and the behavioral sciences will want to consider providing access to all three journals.

5744. ***Behaviour Research and Therapy: an international multi-disciplinary journal.*** Incorporates (1978-1995): *Advances in Behaviour Research and Therapy;* (1979-1992): *Behavioral Assessment.* [ISSN: 0005-7967] 1963. m. EUR 1358 (Qualified personnel, EUR 310). Ed(s): G.Terrence Wilson. Pergamon, The Boulevard, Langford Ln, East Park, Kidlington, OX5 1GB, United Kingdom. Illus., index, adv.

Refereed. Circ: 4300. Vol. ends: No. 12. Microform: MIM; PQC. Online: Gale Group; ingenta.com; ScienceDirect; Swets Blackwell. *Indexed:* AgeL, BiolAb, CINAHL, ExcerpMed, HEA, IndMed, MLA-IB, PsycholAb, SSCI, SSI, SWR&A. *Aud.:* Ac, Sa.

A major goal in psychology has been to change maladaptive or dysfunctional behavior, and one key approach has been to use intervention research based on psychological learning theory. This journal seeks to cover this area, with special attention to cognitive behavioral approaches, and to do so in a way relevant to those in psychiatry, clinical psychology, and behavioural medicine or medical psychology, as well as in education and social work. Topics recently covered include a comparison of metacognitions in patients with hallucinations, delusions, panic disorder, and non-patient controls; behavioral activity associated with onset in chronic tic and habit disorder; pain anxiety among chronic-pain patients; relationship of shyness to social phobia and other psychiatric disorders; a prospective study on the effects of negative information on childhood fear; hoarding behaviors in a large college sample; psychophysiologic effects of applied tension on the emotional fainting response to blood and injury; and spontaneous decay of covert compulsive urges. Tables of contents and abstracts are online, as is fee-based full text. For behavior interventions, related titles include *Behavior Modification* and *Behavior Therapy* (above) and the *Journal of Applied Behavior Analysis* (below). Libraries will want this title to support clinical service or coursework related to behavioral assessment and intervention in clinical settings.

Biofeedback and Self-Regulation. See *Applied Psychophysiology and Biofeedback.*

5745. *British Journal of Psychiatry.* Former titles (until 1962): *Journal of Mental Science;* (until 1856): *Asylum Journal of Psychiatry.* [ISSN: 0007-1250] 1853. m. GBP 226 (Individuals, GBP 188). Ed(s): Greg Wilkinson. Royal College of Psychiatrists, 17 Belgrave Sq, London, SW1X 8PG, United Kingdom; rcpsych@rcpsych.ac.uk ; http://bjp.rcpsych.org/. Illus., index, adv. Sample. Refereed. Circ: 13000. Vol. ends: No. 6. CD-ROM: Ovid Technologies, Inc. Online: EBSCO Publishing; HighWire Press; Ovid Technologies, Inc. *Indexed:* ASSIA, AgeL, BiolAb, CINAHL, CJA, ChemAb, ExcerpMed, H&SSA, IMFL, IndMed, PsycholAb, SCI, SSCI, SWA. *Bk. rev.:* 6-20, 300 words. *Aud.:* Ac, Sa.

Published monthly by the Royal College of Psychiatrists, this title covers all branches of psychiatry, especially clinical aspects, and most contributors are psychiatrists. Reviews, theoretical work, and empirical research are provided, as well as comments on important articles published elsewhere, a comprehensive book review section, and a correspondence column. Recent issues, averaging 15 regular articles and 6 brief reports, look at such areas as olanzepine-induced tardive dyskinesia, adjunctive fluvoxamine with clozapine, neuroticism and depression, racial discrimination as a cause of mental illness, discrimination and delusional ideation, medical outcomes of pregnancy in women with psychotic disorders and their infants in the first year after birth, retention in psychiatry, decision-making and euthanasia, risks of combination neuroleptic treatment, and influence of cohort effects on patterns of suicide in England and Wales, 1950–1999. A series of supplements, sent free to subscribers, provide additional in-depth coverage of selected areas. One of these, for example, looks at the ramifications of personality disorder in clinical pracatice. Internet access to tables of contents and abstracts is also available. Libraries supporting training or research in psychiatry or clinical psychology will want to have this title.

5746. *British Journal of Psychology.* [ISSN: 0007-1269] 1904. q. GBP 215 (Individuals, GBP 53). Ed(s): Geoffrey Underwood. The British Psychological Society, St Andrews House, 48 Princess Rd E, Leicester, LE1 7DR, United Kingdom; mail@bps.org.uk; http://www.bps.org.uk/publications/journals.cfm. Illus., index, adv. Sample. Refereed. Circ: 2800. Vol. ends: Nov. Microform: PQC. Online: bigchalk; EBSCO Publishing; Florida Center for Library Automation; Gale Group; Ingenta Select; Northern Light Technology, Inc.; OCLC Online Computer Library Center, Inc.; ProQuest Information & Learning; Swets Blackwell; H.W. Wilson. Reprint: ISI; SWZ. *Indexed:* ASSIA, AgeL, ArtHuCI, BiolAb, BrEdI, CIJE, CJA, CommAb, ErgAb, H&SSA, IBSS, IBZ, IMFL, IndMed, L&LBA, LRI, MLA-IB, PsycholAb, SSCI, SSI, SociolAb. *Bk. rev.:* 0-5, 500-1,000 words. *Aud.:* Ac, Sa.

This key journal of the British Psychological Society seeks to provide articles dealing with topics of interest to researchers from more than one specialty; that address topics or issues at the interface between different specialties or sections of psychology; that take different or contrasting methodological or theoretical approaches to a single topic; that deal with novel areas, theories, or methodologies; that offer integrative reviews, particularly where the review offers new analysis (e.g., meta-analysis), new theory, or new implications for practice; that deal with the history of psychology; or that offer interdisciplinary work where the contribution from, or to, psychological theory or practice is clear. With an average of nine articles, recent issues cover such topics as visuospatial abilities of chess players, sex differences in general knowledge, semantic memory and reasoning ability, cultural factors and causal beliefs (rational and magical thinking in Britain and Mexico), conditional reasoning and the Tower of Hanoi: the role of spatial and verbal working memory, a mass participation experiment into the possible existence of extrasensory perception, performance on theory of mind tasks declining in old age, and the role of masculinity and distinctiveness in judgments of human male facial attractiveness. A recent special issue focuses on cognition. Libraries supporting psychology programs will want to consider this title.

5747. *Canadian Psychology.* Former titles: *Canadian Psychological Review; Canadian Psychologist.* [ISSN: 0708-5591] 1959. q. CND 95 (Individuals, CND 55). Ed(s): Thomas Hadjistavropoulos. Canadian Psychological Association, 151 Slater St, Ste 205, Ottawa, ON K1P 5H3, Canada; http://www.cpa.ca. Illus., index, adv. Refereed. Circ: 5000. Microform: MML. Online: EBSCO Publishing; Micromedia ProQuest; OCLC Online Computer Library Center, Inc.; Ovid Technologies, Inc.; ProQuest Information & Learning; ScienceDirect. *Indexed:* ASSIA, AgeL, ArtHuCI, BiolAb, CBCARef, CPerI, PsycholAb, SSCI, SociolAb. *Aud.:* Ac.

This publication of the Canadian Psychological Association seeks to provide "generalist articles in areas of theory, research, and practice that are potentially of interest to a broad cross-section of psychologists." Articles can have theoretical, research, or practice-related emphasis. Central articles published in English are summarized in French and vice versa. With an average of four articles in its regular section and an equal number focusing on professional issues, recent issues look at such topics as cost effectiveness and medical cost-offset considerations in psychological service provision, integrating neural networks into decision-making and motivational theory: rethinking VIE theory, the once and future Hebb synapse, preferred strategies for learning ethics in the practice of a discipline, the relative importance of the ethical principles adopted by the American Psychological Association, and music cognition and the cognitive psychology of film structure. A recent special issue looks at qualitative research: history, theory, and practice. Tables of contents and abstracts are available on the association's Internet site. Academic libraries with programs in psychology should consider providing access to this title.

5748. *Clinical Psychology: science and practice.* [ISSN: 0969-5893] 1994. q. USD 330. Ed(s): David H Barlow. Oxford University Press, 2001 Evans Rd, Cary, NC 27513; http://www3.oup.co.uk/jnls/. Illus., index, adv. Refereed. Circ: 6000. Vol. ends: Dec. Online: EBSCO Publishing; HighWire Press; ingenta.com; Ovid Technologies, Inc.; RoweCom Information Quest; Swets Blackwell. Reprint: PSC. *Indexed:* AgeL, ExcerpMed, SSCI. *Bk. rev.:* 1, 1,200-2,000 words. *Aud.:* Ac, Sa.

This publication of the Society of Clinical Psychology (Division 12) of the American Psychological Association covers the science and practice of clinical psychology. Articles include "scholarly topical reviews of research, theory, and application to diverse areas of the field, including assessment, intervention, service delivery, and professional issues." With an average of ten articles, recent issues include looks at providing interdisciplinary geriatric team care, anger treatment for adults: a meta-analytic review, cognitive case formulation—science or science fiction, panic disorder and smoking, methods for disseminating research products and increasing evidence-based practice, prescription privileges for psychologists, and child sexual abuse and sexual revictimization. One special issue has a series of articles on "mindfulness" interventions and training. Recent tables of contents and abstracts of current articles are available on the Internet. Libraries supporting clinical psychology programs should have this title.

5749. ***Clinical Psychology Review.*** [ISSN: 0272-7358] 1981. 8x/yr. EUR 1007 (Individuals, EUR 219). Ed(s): Dr. Alan S Bellack, Michel Hersen. Pergamon, The Boulevard, Langford Ln, East Park, Kidlington, OX5 1GB, United Kingdom. Illus., adv. Sample. Refereed. Vol. ends: No. 8. Microform: PQC. Online: ingenta.com; ScienceDirect; Swets Blackwell. *Indexed:* AgeL, CJA, ExcerpMed, IndMed, PsycholAb, SSCI. *Bk. rev.:* 0-4, 300 words. *Aud.:* Ac, Sa.

This journal provides substantive reviews covering issues in clinical psychology in order to help clinical psychologists keep up-to-date on relevant issues outside their immediate areas of expertise. Areas covered include psychopathology, psychotherapy, behavior therapy, behavioral medicine, community mental health, assessment, and child development. Psychophysiology, learning therapy, and social psychology are included if they have a clear relationship to research or practice in clinical psychology. Although integrative literature reviews and summary reports of innovative, ongoing clinical-research programs may also occasionally be published, reports on individual research studies are not appropriate. With an average of five articles, recent issues cover such topics as assessment of mood in adults who have severe or profound mental retardation, spanking children: the controversies, findings and new directions, a review of the role of illness models in severe mental illness, review and treatment implications of neuropsychology of obsessive-compulsive disorder, the dimensional view of personality disorders: a review of the taxometric evidence, and psychiatric comorbidity in anorexia and bulimia nervosa: nature, prevalence, and causal relationships. Internet access to tables of contents and abstracts is available. Libraries supporting clinical or counseling psychology programs and those working in related clinical settings will also find it useful. All academic libraries supporting programs that involve preparation for clinical work in the behavioral sciences can benefit from this title.

5750. ***Cognition: international journal of cognitive psychology.*** [ISSN: 0010-0277] 1972. m. EUR 1225 (Qualified personnel, EUR 210). Ed(s): Jacques Mehler. Elsevier BV, Sara Burgerhartstraat 25, Amsterdam, 1055 KV, Netherlands; nlinfo-f@elsevier.nl; http://www.elsevier.nl. Illus., index, adv. Sample. Refereed. Vol. ends: Dec. Microform: PQC. Online: ingenta.com; ScienceDirect; Swets Blackwell. Reprint: SWZ. *Indexed:* ArtHuCI, BiolAb, CIJE, EngInd, ExcerpMed, IBSS, IndMed, L&LBA, LT&LA, LingAb, MLA-IB, PhilInd, PsycholAb, SCI, SSCI. *Aud.:* Ac.

An international community of authors contributes to this publication, which focuses on the study of the mind. Both theoretical and empirical papers are included, and any aspect of cognition is appropriate. Submissions are accepted from researchers in linguistics, computer science, neuroscience, mathematics, ethology, philosophy, and psychology. Less-frequent discussion of neurological or brain processes is included here, compared to such journals as *Cognitive Neuropsychology* (below) or *Behavioral Neuroscience* (above). With three to six articles, recent issues look at such topics as spontaneous number discrimination of multi-format auditory stimuli in cotton-top tamarins, surprises as low probabilities (or high contrasts), smilarity as transformation, constraining the comprehension of pronominal expressions in Chinese, and direct causation in the linguistic coding and individuation of causal events. Recent tables of contents, abstracts, and brief articles are available on the Internet. A related title is *Cognitive Science* (below), and both journals are desirable for libraries supporting advanced study in cognition.

5751. ***Cognitive Development.*** [ISSN: 0885-2014] 1986. q. EUR 281 (Individuals, EUR 114). Ed(s): Peter Bryant. Elsevier Ltd., The Boulevard, Langford Ln, Oxford, OX5 1GB, United Kingdom. Illus., index, adv. Refereed. Circ: 500. Vol. ends: No. 4. Reprint: ISI. *Indexed:* CIJE, PsycholAb, SSCI. *Bk. rev.:* 1, 3,000 words. *Aud.:* Ac, Sa.

Cognitive development, the obvious focus of this title, includes areas of perception, memory, and language, as well as concepts, thinking, problem-solving, intelligence, acquisition of knowledge, and social cognition, with articles that are empirical or theoretical in emphasis. An average of five articles in recent issues look at such topics as cultural and experiential differences in the development of folk-biological induction, artificial life and Piaget, a constructivist approach to understanding the development of reasoning about rights and authority within cultural contexts, what conservation anticipation reveals about cognitive change, children's solutions of logical versus empirical problems, and inferring the goals of a nonhuman agent. Tables of contents and abstracts are available on the Internet. This title focuses more on children and cognition than other titles in the cognitive field. Libraries supporting study and research in child development, as well as those pursuing related work in education or psychology, will want this journal.

5752. ***Cognitive Neuropsychology.*** [ISSN: 0264-3294] 1984. 8x/yr. GBP 625 (Individuals, GBP 202). Ed(s): Alfonso Caramazza. Psychology Press, 27 Church Rd, Hove, BN3 2FA, United Kingdom; http://www.psypress.co.uk/. Illus., index. Sample. Refereed. Circ: 1000. Online: EBSCO Publishing; Ingenta Select; OCLC Online Computer Library Center, Inc.; RoweCom Information Quest; Swets Blackwell. Reprint: PSC. *Indexed:* ASSIA, AgeL, ArtHuCI, BiolAb, ExcerpMed, L&LBA, MLA-IB, PsycholAb, SSCI. *Bk. rev.:* 0-1, 1,500 words. *Aud.:* Ac, Sa.

This title looks at cognitive processes from a neuropsychological perspective. All stages of development are appropriate, including both abnormal and normal processes, and contributors are from an international community of scholars. The publication aims to publish "full-length and short empirical reports as well as theoretical articles and occasional reviews that advance our understanding of human cognition and its neural substrate." Recent issues, with an average of four articles, look at evidence for detrimental effects of word-level information in alexia, rigid and nonrigid objects in canonical and noncanonical views: hemisphere-specific effects on object identification, implicit location encoding via stored representations of familiar objects: neuropsychological evidence, normal and impaired spelling in a connectionist dual-route architecture, an influence of syntactic and semantic variables on word form retrieval, an evaluation of statistical procedures for comparing an individual's performance with that of a group of controls, and transient binding by time: neuropsychological evidence from anti-extinction. Tables of contents and abstracts for recent issues can be found online. Other titles in this section that address psychology and neurological functioning include *Developmental Neuropsychology, Behavioral Neuroscience,* and the broader *Behavioral and Brain Sciences.* This highly cited title will be useful for those pursuing advanced study and research in cognition, neuropsychology, clinical psychology, and psychiatry.

5753. ***Cognitive Psychology.*** [ISSN: 0010-0285] 1970. 8x/yr. EUR 780 (Individuals, EUR 401; Students, EUR 198). Ed(s): Dr. G. D. Logan. Academic Press, 525 B St, Ste 1900, San Diego, CA 92101-4495; apsubs@acad.com; http://www.academicpress.com. Illus., adv. Refereed. Online: EBSCO Publishing; Gale Group; ingenta.com; OCLC Online Computer Library Center, Inc.; RoweCom Information Quest; ScienceDirect. Reprint: SWZ. *Indexed:* CIJE, CommAb, EduInd, ErgAb, IBZ, IndMed, L&LBA, MLA-IB, PsycholAb, SSCI, SSI. *Aud.:* Ac.

This title covers human memory, language processing, perception, problem-solving, and thinking. The focus is on "original empirical, theoretical, and tutorial papers, methodological articles, and critical reviews," and it seeks to provide "extensive articles that have a major impact on cognitive theory and/or provide new theoretical advances." With two to three lengthy articles (typically more than 30 pages each), recent issues cover such topics as challenging the widespread assumption that connectionism and distributed representations go hand-in-hand, representational shifts during category learning, a cognitive complexity metric applied to cognitive development, forgetting curves' implications for connectionist models, task switching: a PDP model, systems of spatial reference in human memory, and the role of retrieval structures in memorizing music. Internet access is available to recent tables of contents and article abstracts. Libraries supporting programs in cognitive science or cognitive psychology will want this title, as well as two other titles in this section: *Cognition* and *Cognitive Science.*

5754. ***Cognitive Science: a multidisciplinary journal of artificial intelligence, linguistics, neuroscience, philosophy and psychology.*** [ISSN: 0364-0213] 1977. bi-m. EUR 343 (Individuals, EUR 138). Ed(s): Robert L Goldstone. Elsevier Ltd., The Boulevard, Langford Ln, Oxford, OX5

1GB, United Kingdom. Illus., index, adv. Refereed. Circ: 2400. Vol. ends: Oct/Dec. Reprint: ISI. *Indexed:* AbAn, CIJE, ErgAb, ExcerpMed, IBSS, L&LBA, MLA-IB, PsycholAb, SSCI. *Aud.:* Ac, Sa.

As the official journal of the Cognitive Science Society, this interdisciplinary resource aims to be a leading journal for "developments on the study of minds and other intelligent systems." There are four types of articles: regular articles (about 30 pages), extended articles (for particularly noteworthy research requiring greater treatment, about 45 pages), brief articles (about 10 pages), and letters to the editor. Recent issues, averaging four articles, look at such topics as integrating analogical mapping and general problem solving: the path-mapping theory; perception as informally encapsulated (the theory-ladenness of perception); cognitive templates for religious concepts: cross-cultural evidence for recall of counter-intuitive representations; structural systematicity in distributed, statically bound visual representations; gesture offers insight into problem-solving in adults and children; and an action selection mechanism for "conscious" software agents. This is a significant title for libraries supporting programs in cognitive science, cognitive psychology, or neuropsychology.

5755. ***Cognitive Therapy and Research.*** [ISSN: 0147-5916] 1977. bi-m. USD 812 for print or online ed. Ed(s): Rick E Ingram. Kluwer Academic / Plenum Publishers, 233 Spring St Fl 7, New York, NY 10013-1522; http://www.wkap.nl/. Illus., index, adv. Sample. Refereed. Vol. ends: Dec. Microform: PQC. Online: EBSCO Publishing; ingenta.com; Kluwer Online; OCLC Online Computer Library Center, Inc.; RoweCom Information Quest; Swets Blackwell. *Indexed:* AgeL, BiolAb, ExcerpMed, IMFL, PsycholAb, SSCI. *Aud.:* Ac, Sa.

This journal serves as an interdisciplinary forum for presenting research and theory on "the role of cognitive processes in human adaptation and adjustment." Contributions include experimental, theoretical, methodological, review, and technical articles. Case studies and briefer reports are also included. Recent issues, which have averaged six articles, include looks at such topics as exploring the intensity paradox in emotional Stroop interference; cognitive vulnerability to hopelessness depression; social anxiety dimensions, neuroticism, and the contours of positive psychological functioning; cognitive development and worry in normal children; relationship satisfaction and hindsight memory biases in couples' reports of relationship events; trait and self-presentational dimensions of perfectionism among women with anorexia nervosa; and factor structure of the Relationship Belief Inventory. Recent tables of contents and abstracts of upcoming articles are available on the Internet. Clinicians from a number of disciplines, as well as students and researchers in clinical or counseling psychology, will be helped by having this journal available in their libraries.

5756. ***Consulting Psychology Journal: practice and research.*** Former titles (until 1992): *American Psychological Association. Division of Consulting Psychology. Journal; American Psychological Association. Division of Consulting Psychology. Bulletin.* [ISSN: 1065-9293] 1992. q. USD 140 (Members, USD 35; Non-members, USD 65). Ed(s): Richard Diedrich. American Psychological Association, 750 First St, NE, Washington, DC 20002-4242; journals@apa.org; http://www.apa.org/. Illus., adv. Refereed. Circ: 1100. Vol. ends: No. 4. Reprint: PSC. *Indexed:* PsycholAb. *Aud.:* Ac, Sa.

A publication of the Division of Consulting Psychology (Division 13) of the American Psychological Association. Contents include theoretical articles, original research, in-depth reviews of the research literature in specific areas of consultation practice, case studies, and division news. Recent issues cover the relationship between the constructs of leadership as operationalized through the Leadership Personality Survey (LPS), followership as operationalized by the Power of Followership Survey, the marathon encounter group: vision and reality, creating caring organizations, gaining and sustaining organizational support through a sociotechnical intervention, the prevalence of corporate transitions and their impact on both the corporation and individuals, and facilitating intervention adherence in executive coaching: a model and methods. Additionally, one special issue examines the topic of leadership development, while another looks at training and education in organizational consulting psychology. Access to tables of contents and abstracts for current articles are available on the Internet. Those who are involved in the study or practice of consulting will appreciate having this title.

5757. ***Contemporary Psychology: A P A Review of Books: a journal of reviews.*** Formerly: *Contemporary Psychology.* 1956. bi-m. USD 355 (Members, USD 53; Non-members, USD 134). Ed(s): Robert J Sternberg. American Psychological Association, 750 First St, NE, Washington, DC 20002-4242; journals@apa.org; http://www.apa.org/. Illus., index, adv. Refereed. Circ: 2900. *Indexed:* ArtHuCI, BRI, BiolAb, CBRI, SSCI. *Bk. rev.:* 50-60, 100-1,500 words. *Aud.:* Ga, Ac, Sa.

Many journals in psychology provide reviews of books in a given topical subarea of psychology. However, this title continues as the key resource for reviews of books (as well as films, audiotapes, and other media) from virtually all areas of psychology. Material reviewed is intended to present a cross-section of psychological literature suitable for a broad readership of scholars in psychology. Recent books reviewed include *The Mind Doesn't Work That Way: The Scope and Limits of Computational Psychology; History and Theories of Psychology: A Critical Perspective; Methods of Theoretical Psychology; Contemporary Issues in Modeling Psychopathology; Children With Traumatic Brain Injury: A Parent's Guide; Race and Morality: How Good Intentions Undermine Social Justice and Perpetuate Inequality* and *Talk of Love: How Culture Matters.* Its "Point/Counterpoint" discussion of previously published reviews provides an ongoing assessment of reviews and materials reviewed. Moreover, tables of contents from recent issues are available on the Internet. All academic libraries supporting psychology should have this title. Public libraries might also consider it for those who wish to monitor developments in psychology.

5758. ***The Counseling Psychologist.*** [ISSN: 0011-0000] 1973. bi-m. USD 495. Ed(s): Robert T Carter. Sage Publications, Inc., 2455 Teller Rd, Thousand Oaks, CA 91320; info@sagepub.com; http://www.sagepub.com. Illus., adv. Refereed. Circ: 5400. Vol. ends: Oct. Microform: PQC. Online: Florida Center for Library Automation; Gale Group; ingenta.com; OCLC Online Computer Library Center, Inc.; ProQuest Information & Learning; Swets Blackwell. Reprint: PQC. *Indexed:* ABS&EES, ASSIA, AgeL, CIJE, CJA, EduInd, H&SSA, HEA, HRA, IMFL, PsycholAb, SFSA, SSCI, SSI. *Aud.:* Ac, Sa.

As the official publication of the APA's Division of Counseling Psychology, this journal focuses on the theory, research, and practice of counseling psychology. Each issue includes a major article or set of articles on a given theme, along with additional "Response" articles. Frequent professional, scientific, international, and special-populations forums present position papers, survey reports, and illustrations of innovative techniques for those involved in counseling psychology. Recent issues include coverage of the integrated problem-solving model of crisis intervention; understanding mid-career development; lesbian, gay, and bisexual theory building and research; technologically enriched and boundaryless lives; and the integration of career psychology. A recent special issue looks at current directions in Chicana/Chicano psychology. Another major, related title is the *Journal of Counseling Psychology* (see below).

5759. ***Current Directions in Psychological Science.*** [ISSN: 0963-7214] 1992. bi-m. USD 1384 print & online eds. Ed(s): Alan E Kazdin. Blackwell Publishing, Inc., Commerce Place, 350 Main St, Malden, MA 02148; subscrip@blackwellpub.com; http://www.blackwellpublishing.com. Illus., adv. Refereed. Vol. ends: Dec. *Indexed:* AgeL, ErgAb, PsycholAb, SSCI. *Aud.:* Ac, Sa.

This publication of the American Psychological Society seeks to provide a "window onto important trends and controversies in psychology." Its review articles (about six per issue, of 2,000–2,500 words each) cover the entire spectrum of scientific psychology and its applications. Although the articles are written by experts, they are designed to be accessible to general readers and those outside the research subspecialties covered. Recent coverage looks at math anxiety: personal, educational, and cognitive consequences, the field of adolescent romantic relationships, enhancing the cognitive vitality of older adults, sources of bias in memory for emotions, social comparison: why, with whom, and with what effect, the volutionary psychology of facial attractiveness, the confidence of eyewitnesses in their identifications from lineups, and the development of judgment and decision making during childhood and adolescence. Internet access to recent tables of contents is available. All academic libraries and some larger public libraries will have patrons who will appreciate this readable coverage of psychology.

5760. ***Developmental Psychology.*** [ISSN: 0012-1649] 1969. bi-m. USD 472 (Members, USD 93; Non-members, USD 186). Ed(s): Dr. James L. Dannemiller. American Psychological Association, 750 First St, NE, Washington, DC 20002-4242; journals@apa.org; http://www.apa.org/. Illus., adv. Refereed. Circ: 5000. Vol. ends: Dec. Microform: PQC. Online: EBSCO Publishing; Gale Group; OCLC Online Computer Library Center, Inc.; Ovid Technologies, Inc.; ProQuest Information & Learning; ScienceDirect. Reprint: PQC; PSC. *Indexed:* ASSIA, AgeL, ArtHuCI, BiolAb, CIJE, CJA, CommAb, EduInd, IBZ, IndMed, MLA-IB, PsycholAb, SFSA, SSCI, SSI, SWA, SWR&A. *Aud.:* Ac, Sa.

All stages of human development are the domain of this journal, although articles examining other species are appropriate if they have important implications for human development. Any variable that affects human psychological development may be considered; and while empirical work is emphasized, scholarly reviews, theoretical articles, and social-policy papers are also accepted. Special consideration is given to field research, cross-cultural studies, gender and ethnicity, and other socially important topics. Recent issues (with 10 to 15 articles) look at such topics as longitudinal analysis of flexibility and reorganization in early adolescence: a dynamic systems study of family interactions; race and the workforce: occupational status, aspirations, and stereotyping among African American children; patterns of knowledge in children's addition; the effect of experience on children's use of video-presented information; adolescents' reasoning about exclusion from social groups; children with lesbian parents: a community study; classroom discourse as a predictor of changes in children's beliefs about their academic capabilities; and assessing secure base behavior in adulthood: development of a measure, links to adult attachment representations, and relations to couples' communication and reports of relationships. A recent special looks at violent children. Internet access to recent tables of contents and article abstracts is available. Academic libraries supporting research and study related to normal human development should have this title.

5761. ***Developmental Review: perspectives in behavior and cognition.*** [ISSN: 0273-2297] 1981. q. EUR 421 (Individuals, EUR 174; Students, EUR 102). Ed(s): C J Brainerd. Academic Press, 525 B St, Ste 1900, San Diego, CA 92101-4495; apsubs@acad.com; http://www.academicpress.com. Illus., index, adv. Sample. Refereed. Vol. ends: Dec. Online: EBSCO Publishing; ingenta.com; OCLC Online Computer Library Center, Inc.; RoweCom Information Quest; ScienceDirect; Swets Blackwell. Reprint: SWZ. *Indexed:* AgeL, BiolAb, CIJE, IBZ, L&LBA, PsycholAb, SSCI. *Aud.:* Ac.

Conceptual issues in developmental psychology are the focus of this international interdisciplinary journal, and its subject matter is drawn from such fields as biology, sociology, education, and pediatrics, as well as psychology. Work submitted may be applied or basic, and populations studied may be from any species or age range so long as discussion and implications are pertinent to understanding psychological development. Historical, method-and-design, or social-policy analyses are all appropriate article types for submission, as are theoretical statements, reviews of literature, programmatic research summaries, integrated collections of papers on a single theme, and empirical findings that are "provocative" and particularly relevant to developmental theory. With an average of five articles, recent issues cover such topics as parenting and psychosocial development of IVF children; behavior genetics of aggression in children; dyadic synchrony: its structure and function in children's development; the development of real-world knowledge and reasoning in real-world contexts; emic perspectives on risk in African childhood; proximal and distal influences on development: the model of developmental adaptation; and memory processes underlying misinformation effects in child witnesses. A recent special issue covers forensic developmental psychology. Abstracts and tables of contents are available at the Internet site. Academic libraries supporting research and study in psychological development should have this title.

5762. ***Educational Psychologist.*** [ISSN: 0046-1520] 1963. q. USD 385. Ed(s): Philip H Winne, Lyn Corno. Lawrence Erlbaum Associates, Inc., 10 Industrial Ave, Mahwah, NJ 07430-2262; journals@erlbaum.com; http://www.erlbaum.com/. Illus., adv. Refereed. Circ: 3700. Vol. ends: Fall. Microform: PQC. Online: EBSCO Publishing; Ingenta Select; OCLC Online Computer Library Center, Inc.; RoweCom Information Quest; Swets Blackwell. Reprint: PQC; PSC. *Indexed:* EduInd, PsycholAb, SSCI. *Aud.:* Ac, Sa.

The goal of this journal is to cover issues, problems, and research in the field of educational psychology. Readers will find scholarly essays, reviews, critiques, and contributions of a theoretical nature. Articles that primarily report empirical studies, as typically found with methods and results, will not likely be included. With an average of seven articles, recent issues cover such topics as cognitive load measurement techniques with regard to their contribution to cognitive load theory; the expertise reversal effect; the claimed role of emotional intelligence (EI) in the educational and school context; achievement goal theory and affect: an asymmetrical bidirectional model; qualitative approaches to investigating self-regulated learning; why schools should teach for wisdom; parental involvement in student homework; emotions and self-regulation during test taking; and sociocultural and constructivist theories of learning: ontology, not just epistemology. Additionally, one special issue examines the schooling of ethnic minority children and youth. Those involved with psychology related to educational settings will be especially interested in this title. A related publication that includes more-empirical research is the *Journal of Educational Psychology* (not listed here).

5763. ***Environment and Behavior.*** [ISSN: 0013-9165] 1969. bi-m. GBP 423 in Europe, Middle East, Africa & Australasia. Ed(s): Robert B Bechtel. Sage Publications, Inc., 2455 Teller Rd, Thousand Oaks, CA 91320; info@sagepub.com; http://www.sagepub.com. Illus., index, adv. Sample. Refereed. Circ: 1500. Vol. ends: Nov. Microform: PQC. Online: Chadwyck-Healey Incorporated; Florida Center for Library Automation; Gale Group; ingenta.com; OCLC Online Computer Library Center, Inc.; ProQuest Information & Learning; RoweCom Information Quest; Swets Blackwell. Reprint: PQC. *Indexed:* ABS&EES, AIAP, ASSIA, AgeL, ArtHuCI, CIJE, CJA, EnvAb, ExcerpMed, GeoRef, HRA, IBSS, IBZ, MagInd, PRA, PSA, PsycholAb, SFSA, SSCI, SSI, SUSA, SWA, SWRA, SociolAb. *Bk. rev.:* 2, 600 words. *Aud.:* Ac, Sa.

In this journal, published in cooperation with the Environmental Design Research Association, readers will find articles pertaining to "the influence of the physical environment on human behavior." The behavior studied can be that of individuals, groups, or institutions, and both experimental and theoretical work is included. Containing an average of five articles, recent issues cover such topics as trust and social representations of the management of threatened and endangered species; incentives, morality, or habit: predicting students' car use for university routes; the role of permanent student artwork in students' sense of ownership in an elementary school; building walls of brick and breaching walls of separation; and the significance and impact of Ervin H. Zube's contributions to environment-behavior studies. A recent special issue looks at environmental cognition, space, and action. Useful for those who study the interaction of humans with their environment.

5764. ***European Psychologist.*** Formerly (until 1995): *German Journal of Psychology.* [ISSN: 1016-9040] 1977. q. USD 99 (Individuals, USD 49; Members, USD 39). Ed(s): Kurt Pawlik. Hogrefe & Huber Publishers, 44 Brattle St., 4th Fl., Cambridge, MA 02138; http://www.hhpub.com/journals. Illus., adv. Sample. Refereed. Vol. ends: Feb. Online: EBSCO Publishing; OCLC Online Computer Library Center, Inc.; Ovid Technologies, Inc.; ProQuest Information & Learning; ScienceDirect. *Indexed:* ASSIA, GJP, IBZ, L&LBA. *Aud.:* Ac.

This title's goal is to serve as "the English language voice of psychology in Europe, [providing a] general platform for communication and cooperation among psychologists throughout Europe and worldwide." It is published in cooperation with the European Federation of Professional Psychology Associations and supported by other psychology organizations in Europe. Its scope is all specializations in psychology, and it includes original articles "written for a non-specialist, general readership in psychology," as well as reviews of a broader field or topical context, reports, commentaries, news, and book and journal reviews. Contributions have come from, for example, Germany, Israel, Sweden, Austria, England, Spain, Finland, Italy, and the Netherlands. Recent issues examine life after heart transplantation; a cross-cultural investigation of social support and burnout; the role of the immune system in psychology and neuroscience; the longitudinal impact of perceived self-regulatory efficacy and parental communication on violent conduct; coping with school-related and family stresses in healthy and clinically referred adolescents; the role of gender and culture in romantic attraction; and the construction and the construct validation of an extensive test battery for use in the selection process in business and business education. One special issue looks at the contribution of genetics to psychology; and one addtional set of articles looks at psychology doctoral studies programs in Belgium, France, Germany, Italy, Spain, Sweden, Switzerland, the United Kingdom, and the United States. Recent content listings and article abstracts are available on the Internet. Libraries may wish to provide this title as one means of access to psychological research and practice in Europe.

Feminism & Psychology. See Women: Feminist and Special Interest/ Feminist and Women's Studies section.

5765. *Health Psychology.* [ISSN: 0278-6133] 1982. bi-m. USD 259 (Members, USD 53; Non-members, USD 84). Ed(s): Dr. Arthur A Stone. American Psychological Association, 750 First St, NE, Washington, DC 20002-4242; journals@apa.org; http://www.apa.org/. Illus., adv. Refereed. Circ: 7700. Vol. ends: Dec (No. 6). Reprint: PSC. *Indexed:* ASSIA, AbAn, AgeL, ExcerpMed, FS&TA, IndMed, PsycholAb, SSCI, SSI, SWR&A. *Bk. rev.:* 0-1, 1,500 words. *Aud.:* Ac, Sa.

This journal provides articles on the relationship between behaviors and both physical health and illness. Empirical-research reports are the primary type of work published, and integrative work pertinent to a broad spectrum of reader backgrounds is especially welcome. Areas covered include assessment or diagnostic issues, as well as intervention or treatment approaches, and research can be at the individual, group, multicenter, or community level. With an average of ten articles, recent issues cover psychological adjustment among African American breast cancer patients; memory in pediatric patients undergoing conscious sedation for aversive medical procedures; predicting adolescent eating and activity behaviors: the role of social norms and personal agency; the validity of various theoretical assumptions about cognitive and behavioral change following a communication recommending condom use; psychological factors associated with fruit and vegetable intake and with biomarkers in adults from a low-income neighborhood; correlates of unhealthy weight-control behaviors among adolescents: implications for prevention programs; psychological impact of colorectal cancer screening; and inhibitory effects of drinker and nondrinker prototypes on adolescent alcohol consumption. Contributors to this title are primarily psychologists, although both psychiatrists and psychologists contribute to *Psychosomatic Medicine* (see below). Programs in behavioral medicine and those studying psychology and health will benefit from both journals. Other related titles include *Psychology and Health* and the *Journal of Pediatric Psychology* (below).

5766. *Hispanic Journal of Behavioral Sciences.* [ISSN: 0739-9863] 1979. q. GBP 319 in Europe, Middle East, Africa & Australasia. Ed(s): Dr. Amado M Padilla. Sage Publications, Inc., 2455 Teller Rd, Thousand Oaks, CA 91320; info@sagepub.com; http://www.sagepub.com. Illus., adv. Refereed. Circ: 1200. Vol. ends: Nov. Microform: PQC. Online: Florida Center for Library Automation; Gale Group; ingenta.com; OCLC Online Computer Library Center, Inc.; ProQuest Information & Learning; RoweCom Information Quest; Swets Blackwell. Reprint: PQC. *Indexed:* ASG, AgeL, CIJE, CJA, HAPI, HEA, IMFL, L&LBA, PsycholAb, SFSA, SSCI, SSI, SociolAb. *Bk. rev.:* 0-1, 400-800 words. *Aud.:* Ac.

This English-language journal seeks to publish both empirical and conceptual articles, multiple–case study reports, critical reviews of the literature, reports of new instruments, and scholarly notes that are of theoretical interest or deal with methodological issues related to Hispanic populations. Recent issues cover such topics as Latino cultural differences in maternal assessments of attention deficit/hyperactivity symptoms in children; whether gender differences in income exist for self-employed Hispanics residing in California (data from the 1990 U.S. decennial census); Latinos in the United States in 2000; change processes in family therapy with Hispanic adolescents; effects of Latino acculturation and ethnic identity on mental health outcomes; ethnopsychological method and the psychological assessment of Mexican Americans; the role of educational background, activity, and past experiences in Mexican-descent families' science conversations; Hispanic density and economic achievement in American metropolitan regions; and the the instructional behaviors and beliefs of Mexican American mothers with their preschool-age children. In addition, one recent issue looks at "Conversations within Mexican-Descent Families: Diverse Contexts for Language Socialization and Learning." Academic libraries supporting psychological study of and for Hispanic populations will want this title.

5767. *History of Psychology.* [ISSN: 1093-4510] 1998. q. USD 125 (Members, USD 37; Non-members, USD 43). Ed(s): Michael M Sokal. American Psychological Association, 750 First St, NE, Washington, DC 20002-4242; journals@apa.org; http://www.apa.org/. Illus., adv. Refereed. Circ: 860. Vol. ends: Jan. Online: EBSCO Publishing; OCLC Online Computer Library Center, Inc.; Ovid Technologies, Inc.; ProQuest Information & Learning; ScienceDirect. Reprint: PSC. *Indexed:* AmH&L. *Aud.:* Ga, Ac.

As indicated in the title, this journal's focus is on "all aspects of psychology's past and of its interrelationship with the many contexts within which it has emerged and has been practiced." The journal also includes coverage of such areas as historical psychology (the history of consciousness and behavior); psychohistory; theory in psychology as it pertains to history, historiography, biography, and autobiography; and the teaching of the history of psychology. With an average of three main articles (15–30 pages), recent issues look at British female academics' comparative-psychology research niche in the early twentieth century; Wundt, Voelkerpsychologie, and experimental social psychology, late nineteenth-century neurology, and the emergence of psychoanalysis; pioneers of comparative psychology in America, 1843–1890: Lewis H. Morgan, John Bascom, and Joseph LeConte; orientalism in Euro-American and Indian psychology: historical representations of "natives" in colonial and postcolonial context; and not "giving psychology away": the MMPI and public controversy over testing in the 1960s. The journal regularly includes commentary and a section on graduate study opportunities, and access to tables of contents and abstracts are available at the Internet site. This is a good selection for academic libraries seeking to support the topical areas described above, and public libraries may also wish to consider this title. A related title is *Journal of the History of the Behavior Sciences* (see below).

5768. *International Journal of Clinical and Experimental Hypnosis.* Formerly (until 1958): *Journal of Clinical and Experimental Hypnosis.* [ISSN: 0020-7144] 1953. q. EUR 419 (Individuals, EUR 91). Ed(s): Arreed Barabasz. Swets & Zeitlinger BV, PO Box 800, Lisse, 2160 SZ, Netherlands; orders@swets.nl; http://www.swets.nl. Illus., adv. Refereed. Circ: 2500. Vol. ends: Oct. Microform: PQC. Online: ProQuest Information & Learning. Reprint: PQC. *Indexed:* BiolAb, ExcerpMed, IndMed, PsycholAb, SCI, SSCI, SWR&A. *Bk. rev.:* 3, 400-600 words. *Aud.:* Ac, Sa.

For over 47 years, this journal has provided information about hypnosis for students, researchers, and practitioners in the areas of medicine, psychiatry, psychology, and health care. Clinical and experimental studies, theoretical discussion, and historical and cultural material are included, and one section looks at problems in clinical practice. Among numerous topical areas are multiple-personality disorder, self-hypnosis, forensic uses, and relief of pain. An average of six articles in recent issues look at such topics as the "Big Five" and hypnotic suggestibility; autonomic reactivity to cognitive and emotional stress of low-, medium-, and high-hypnotizable healthy subjects; hypnotic responsivity from a developmental perspective: nsights from young children; suggestibility and negative priming: two replication studies; hypnosis for the control of HIV/AIDS-related pain; and how practitioners and others can make scientifically viable contributions to clinical-outcome research using the single-case time-series design. A recent issue looks at Mesmer, Franklin, and the Royal Commission. A related title covering hypnosis is the *American Journal of Clinical Hypnosis* (above). Tables of contents and abstracts are available at the the Society for Clinical and Experimental Hypnosis Internet site. Students, researchers, and clinicians studying or using hypnosis will find access to both titles very helpful.

5769. *International Journal of Eating Disorders.* [ISSN: 0276-3478] 1981. 8x/yr. USD 1450 domestic; USD 1530 in Canada & Mexico; USD 1598 elsewhere. Ed(s): Dr. Michael Strober. John Wiley & Sons, Inc., 111 River St, Hoboken, NJ 07030; uscs-wis@wiley.com;

http://www.wiley.com. Adv. Refereed. Circ: 1200. Reprint: PSC. *Indexed:* AbAn, AgeL, Agr, BiolAb, CINAHL, DSA, ExcerpMed, FS&TA, H&SSA, IndMed, PEI, PsycholAb, RRTA, RiskAb, SSCI, SSI, SWA. *Aud.:* Ac, Sa.

This journal is an official publication of the Academy of Eating Disorders and is included with membership to the organization. Types of articles include basic research, clinical, theoretical, and case studies. Content covers "a variety of aspects of anorexia nervosa, bulimia, obesity and other atypical patterns of eating behavior and body weight regulation in clinical and normal populations," with attention to "psychological, biological, psychodynamic, socio-cultural, epidemiologic, or therapeutic correlates" of such eating phenomena. With an average of 11 articles, recent issues look at such topics as olanzapine treatment of anorexia nervosa; perfectionism in anorexia nervosa; comparison of assessments of children's eating-disordered behaviors by interview and questionnaire; ethnicity and differential access to care for eating disorder symptoms; internalization of ideal body shapes in 9–12-year-old girls; cognitive performance deficits in dieters; eating disorders co-occurance with personality disorders; and brain dopamine associated with eating behaviors in humans. Internet access to tables of contents and abstracts are provided by the publisher.

5770. ***International Journal of Group Psychotherapy.*** [ISSN: 0020-7284] 1951. q. USD 285 (Individuals, USD 85). Ed(s): Les R Greene. Guilford Publications, Inc., 72 Spring St, 4th Fl, New York, NY 10012; info@guilford.com; http://www.guilford.com. Illus., adv. Sample. Refereed. Circ: 5400. Vol. ends: Oct. Reprint: ISI; PQC. *Indexed:* ASSIA, AgeL, BiolAb, CJA, ExcerpMed, IndMed, PsycholAb, SSCI, SSI, SWR&A, SociolAb. *Bk. rev.:* 5, 750 words. *Aud.:* Ac, Sa.

As the official journal of the American Group Psychotherapy Association, this title provides a means for researchers and practitioners to monitor developments in group psychotherapy. Any aspect of theory, research, practice, or teaching related to group psychotherapy may be covered. With an average of five articles, recent issues cover such topics as group therapeutic approaches for people with eating problems; a systematic program to enhance clinician group skills in an in-patient psychiatric hospital; group counseling to enhance adolescents' close friendships; interpersonal predictors of group therapy outcome for complicated grief; change during and after long-term analytic group psychotherapy; and the functions of acting-out within analytic group psychotherapy and its transformation into dreams. Although other titles provide some coverage of group therapy, this focused journal can benefit all libraries supporting clinical counseling or therapy.

5771. ***The International Journal of Psychoanalysis.*** Incorporates (in 1992): *International Review of Psycho-Analysis.* [ISSN: 0020-7578] 1920. bi-m. GBP 219 print & online (Individuals, GBP 141 print & online; Students, GBP 55 print & online). Ed(s): Martin S O'Neill, Paul Williams. Institute of Psychoanalysis, 112a Shirland Rd, London, W9 2EQ, United Kingdom. Illus., index, adv. Refereed. Circ: 6700. Vol. ends: Dec. Online: EBSCO Publishing; Ingenta Select; Swets Blackwell. *Indexed:* AgeL, ArtHuCI, BiolAb, ExcerpMed, IBSS, IBZ, IndMed, PsycholAb, SSCI. *Bk. rev.:* 8-10, 750-3,000 words. *Aud.:* Ac, Sa.

This journal, originated by Sigmund Freud and Ernest Jones, continues to provide articles within the psychoanalytic tradition. Areas covered include "Methodology, Psychoanalytic Theory and Technique, The History of Psychoanalysis, Clinical Contributions, Research and Life-Cycle Development, Education and Professional Issues, Psychoanalytic Psychotherapy, and Interdisciplinary Studies." Published in English, French, German, and Spanish, it also includes the *Bulletin of the International Psychoanalytic Association,* sharing news of association and related activities worldwide. Containing an average of 11 articles, recent issues cover such topics as reassessment of psychoanalytic education; reader and story, viewer and film: on transference and interpretation; psychoanalytic figures as transference objects; the relationship between psychoanalysis and schizophrenia; the phenomenon of not being able to dream (as opposed to not being able to remember one's dreams); a brief history of illusion: Milner, Winnicott, and Rycroft; cognitive neuroscience and psychoanalysis working together on memory; understanding the contribution of psychoanalysis to ethics through examining the work of certain philosophers, especially Kant; the distinction between implicit (nonconscious) and explicit (conscious) knowledge made by cognitive scientists applied to the psychoanalytic idea of repressed contents; and the rape of Medusa in the temple of Athena: aspects of triangulation in the girl. Tables of contents and abstracts are available on the Internet, as is a journal search engine. Those with interest in psychoanalysis would benefit from access to this title. Libraries supporting advanced work in psychology should also consider it.

5772. ***Journal of Abnormal Child Psychology.*** [ISSN: 0091-0627] 1973. bi-m. USD 812 print or online ed. Ed(s): Susan B Campbell. Kluwer Academic / Plenum Publishers, 233 Spring St Fl 7, New York, NY 10013-1522; http://www.wkap.nl/. Illus., adv. Refereed. Vol. ends: Dec. Microform: PQC. Online: bigchalk; EBSCO Publishing; Florida Center for Library Automation; Gale Group; ingenta.com; Kluwer Online; Northern Light Technology, Inc.; OCLC Online Computer Library Center, Inc.; Ovid Technologies, Inc.; ProQuest Information & Learning; RoweCom Information Quest; Swets Blackwell. *Indexed:* ASSIA, BiolAb, CIJE, CJA, ECER, ExcerpMed, IBZ, IMFL, IndMed, PsycholAb, SSCI, SSI. *Aud.:* Ac, Sa.

This title is for those concerned with child and adolescent psychopathology. Etiology, assessment, epidemiology, and pharmacological intervention are areas included, and, within these areas, neurotic and organic disorders, delinquency, psychosomatic conditions, and disorders of behavior in mental retardation are examined. Original empirical and correlational research has been the emphasis, and recent issues cover such topics as family expressiveness and parental emotion coaching and children's emotion regulation and aggression; reactive aggression in boys with disruptive-behavior disorders; patterns of friendship among girls with and without attention-deficit/hyperactivity disorder; neurocognitive performance of 5- and 6-year-old children who meet criteria for attention deficit/hyperactivity disorder at 18-months follow-up; and early parent–child relations and family functioning of preschool boys with pervasive hyperactivity. One special issue looks at child and family characteristics as predictors and outcomes in the Multimodal Treatment Study of ADHD, while another special section looks at a methodology for identifying specific psychological deficits. Libraries supporting clinical work or study and research related to abnormal behavior in childhood and adolescence will want this publication. Related titles include the *Journal of Child Psychology and Psychiatry and Allied Disciplines* and the *Journal of Clinical Child Psychology* (below).

5773. ***Journal of Abnormal Psychology.*** Supersedes in part (in 1965): *Journal of Abnormal and Social Psychology.* [ISSN: 0021-843X] 1906. q. USD 277 (Members, USD 56; Non-members, USD 114). Ed(s): Dr. Timothy B Baker. American Psychological Association, 750 First St, NE, Washington, DC 20002-4242; journals@apa.org; http://www.apa.org/. Illus., adv. Refereed. Circ: 6700. Vol. ends: Jan. Microform: PMC; PQC. Online: EBSCO Publishing; Gale Group; OCLC Online Computer Library Center, Inc.; Ovid Technologies, Inc.; ProQuest Information & Learning; ScienceDirect. Reprint: PQC; PSC. *Indexed:* ASSIA, AgeL, BiolAb, BiolDig, CJA, ECER, ExcerpMed, IndMed, MLA-IB, PsycholAb, SFSA, SSCI, SSI, SWA, SWR&A. *Aud.:* Ac, Sa.

This journal of the American Psychological Association (APA) publishes articles on basic research and theory in the etiology of abnormal behavior. General topics include psychopathology; normal processes in abnormal individuals; pathological or atypical features in the behavior of normal persons; experimental studies, with human or animal subjects, related to pathological or abnormal emotions or behavior; sociocultural effects on pathological processes; and tests of hypotheses from psychological theories that relate to abnormal behavior. The emphasis is on adding to knowledge and understanding of abnormal behavior, in either its etiology, description, or change. For articles dealing with the diagnosis or treatment of abnormal behavior, the related APA *Journal of Consulting and Clinical Psychology* (below) should be consulted. Containing 15–20 articles, recent issues cover such topics as interpretation revealed in the blink of an eye: depressive bias in the resolution of ambiguity; drinking to cope and alcohol use and abuse in unipolar depression; neuropsychology, genetic liability, and psychotic symptoms in those at high risk of schizophrenia; the differential functions of imagery and verbal thought in insomnia; implicit and explicit attitudes toward high-fat foods in obesity; memory distortion in people reporting abduction by aliens; working memory for visual features and conjunctions in schizophrenia; construct validity of depressive personality disorder; confirmatory factor analyses of posttraumatic stress symptoms in deployed and nondeployed veterans of the Gulf War; and implicit and explicit alcohol-related cognitions in heavy and light drinkers. Tables of contents and abstracts of current articles are available on the Internet. Libraries supporting research and study of abnormal behavior should have this basic title.

5774. *Journal of Anxiety Disorders.* [ISSN: 0887-6185] 1987. bi-m. EUR 558 (Individuals, EUR 127). Ed(s): Michel Hersen. Pergamon, The Boulevard, Langford Ln, East Park, Kidlington, OX5 1GB, United Kingdom. Illus. Refereed. Circ: 1500. Microform: PQC. Online: ingenta.com; ScienceDirect; Swets Blackwell. *Indexed:* AgeL, BiolAb, ExcerpMed, H&SSA, IndMed, PsycholAb, RiskAb, SSCI. *Aud.:* Ac, Sa.

This international, interdisciplinary journal provides coverage of aspects of anxiety disorders found in any age group, including assessment, diagnosis, and classification; psychosocial and psychopharmacological treatment; and genetics, epidemiology, and prevention. Theoretical and review articles are included "if they contribute substantially to current knowledge in the field." Sections are also provided for clinical reports (single-case experimental designs and "preliminary but innovative case series") and book reviews. Recent issues look at cognitive-behavioral treatment of food neophobia in adults; long-term course of panic disorder: an 11-year follow-up; metacognitive differences in obsessive-compulsive disorder; examining the impact of sudden and violent deaths; screening for social anxiety disorder in the clinical setting using the Liebowitz Social Anxiety Scale; worry and heart rate variables: autonomic rigidity under challenge; priming panic interpretations in children of patients with panic disorder; superstitiousness and perceived anxiety control as predictors of psychological distress; obsessions and compulsions and intolerance for uncertainty in a nonclinical sample; and symptom presentations of older-adult crime victims. Recent tables of contents as well as abstracts are available on the Internet. Those who train for or provide clinical services for anxiety-related problems will benefit from this title, along with *Anxiety, Stress, and Coping* (above).

5775. *Journal of Applied Behavior Analysis.* [ISSN: 0021-8855] 1968. q. USD 75 (Individuals, USD 28; Students, USD 14). Ed(s): Wayne Fisher. Society for the Experimental Analysis of Behavior, Inc. (Lawrence), c/o Department of Human Development, University of Kansas, Lawrence, KS 66045. Illus., adv. Refereed. Circ: 4000 Paid. Online: Gale Group; OCLC Online Computer Library Center, Inc.; H.W. Wilson. *Indexed:* ABIn, AgeL, BiolAb, CIJE, CommAb, ECER, IndMed, PsycholAb, SSCI, SSI. *Aud.:* Ac, Sa.

This highly regarded title provides "original publication of reports of experimental research involving applications of the experimental analysis of behavior to problems of social importance." Technical articles relevant to such research and discussion of issues related to behavioral applications are also included. Moreover, an interesting recent addition involves publication of "student questions" to facilitate use of this journal's content as an instructional tool with relevant university coursework. With an average of 12 articles and briefer reports, recent issues examine such topics as the status of knowledge for using punishment: implications for treating behavior disorders; feedback and its effectiveness in a computer-aided personalized system of instruction; evaluating the function of applied behavior analysis: a bibliometric analysis; shaping exhale durations for breath CO detection for men with mild mental retardation; reinforcing efficacy of food on performance during pre- and postmeal sessions; the effects of noncontingently available alternatives stimuli on functional analysis outcomes; sensitivity of children's behavior to probability reward: effects of a decreasing-ratio lottery system on math performance; and assessment of mand selection for functional communication training packages. In addition to selected full-text articles from recent issues available on the Internet site, search software provides full-text searches of a database containing more than 5,000 abstracts that have accompanied articles in this journal since 1968. The use of behavioral analysis and intervention techniques has been very fruitful in psychology, and professionals, students, or researchers who wish to monitor current practice and new developments should have access to this title.

5776. *Journal of Applied Psychology.* [ISSN: 0021-9010] 1917. bi-m. USD 431 (Members, USD 80; Non-members, USD 164). Ed(s): Sheldon Zedeck. American Psychological Association, 750 First St, NE, Washington, DC 20002-4242; journals@apa.org; http://www.apa.org/. Illus., adv. Refereed. Circ: 5100. Vol. ends: Jan. Microform: PMC; PQC. Online: EBSCO Publishing; Gale Group; OCLC Online Computer Library Center, Inc.; Ovid Technologies, Inc.; ProQuest Information & Learning; ScienceDirect. Reprint: PQC; PSC. *Indexed:* ABIn, ASSIA, AgeL, BiolAb, CINAHL, CJA, CommAb, EduInd, ErgAb, ExcerpMed, IAA, IBSS, IBZ, IndMed, PsycholAb, SSCI, SSI, SWA. *Aud.:* Ac, Sa.

This journal of the American Psychological Association is devoted to original research that contributes to understanding any aspect of any field of applied psychology, with the exception of clinical psychology and applied experimental or human factors. Articles primarily involve quantitative research and will be of interest to psychologists doing research or working in a variety of settings, including universities, industry, government, urban affairs, police and correctional systems, health and educational institutions, transportation and defense systems, labor unions, and consumer affairs. Topical areas include personnel selection, performance measurement, training, work motivation, job attitudes, eyewitness accuracy, leadership, drug and alcohol abuse, career development, the conflict between job and family demands, work behavior, work stress, organizational design and interventions, technology, polygraph use, the utility of organizational interventions, consumer buying behavior, and cross-cultural differences in work behavior and attitudes. With an average of 12 articles, recent issues examine customer service providers' attitudes relating to customer service and customer satisfaction in the customer–server exchange; the relationship of emotional exhaustion to work attitudes, job performance, and organizational citizenship behaviors; the validity of psychophysiological detection of information with the Guilty Knowledge Test: a meta-analytic review; online bargaining and interpersonal trust; using theory to evaluate personality and job performance relations: a socioanalytic perspective; negative self-efficacy and goal effects revisited; working 61 plus hours a week: why managers do it; and latent constructs of proximal and distal motivation predicting performance under maximum test conditions. Internet access to recent tables of contents, article abstracts, and select articles is available.

5777. *Journal of Child Psychology & Psychiatry & Allied Disciplines.* [ISSN: 0021-9630] 1960. 8x/yr. USD 481 print & online eds. Ed(s): Francesca Happe, Jim Stevenson. Blackwell Publishing Ltd., 9600 Garsington Rd, PO Box 805, Oxford, OX4 2DQ, United Kingdom; customerservices@oxon.blackwellpublishing.com; http://www.blackwellpublishing.com/. Illus., index, adv. Refereed. Circ: 4700. Vol. ends: Nov. Microform: PQC. Online: EBSCO Publishing; Gale Group; ingenta.com; Munksgaard & Blackwell Science's Synergy; OCLC Online Computer Library Center, Inc.; Ovid Technologies, Inc.; RoweCom Information Quest; Swets Blackwell. Reprint: PQC. *Indexed:* ASSIA, AgeL, BiolAb, BrEdI, CIJE, CINAHL, CJA, ECER, EduInd, ExcerpMed, H&SSA, IndMed, L&LBA, PsycholAb, SSCI, SSI, SociolAb. *Bk. rev.:* 2-12, 350-2,000 words. *Aud.:* Ac, Sa.

This journal publishes reports concerned with developmental psychopathology and developmental disorders in childhood and adolescence. Readers will find empirical research, case studies, review articles, and reports of clinical work. The first issue of the journal each year identifies current and future research trends. With an average of eight articles, including several in the "Debate and Argument" section, recent issues examine such topics as autism and a deficit in broadening the spread of visual attention; the pitch of maternal voice: a comparison of mothers suffering from depressed mood and nondepressed mothers reading books to their infants; parental mental health and children's adjustment: the quality of marital interaction and parenting as mediating factors; reliability of the ICD-10 classification of adverse familial and environmental factors; joint attention training for children with autism using behavior modification procedures; children's color choices for completing drawings of affectively characterized topics; and empathy and response to distress in children with Down syndrome. Tables of contents and abstracts for recent articles are available online. Libraries supporting behavioral-science training or research dealing with clinical work with children and adolescents will wish to have this title, along with the *Journal of Abnormal Child Psychology* (above) and *Journal of Clinical Child Psychology* (below).

5778. *Journal of Clinical Child and Adolescent Psychology.* Formerly (until 2001): *Journal of Clinical Child Psychology.* [ISSN: 1537-4416] 1972. q. USD 445. Ed(s): Wendy K Silverman. Lawrence Erlbaum Associates, Inc., 10 Industrial Ave, Mahwah, NJ 07430-2262; journals@

erlbaum.com; http://www.erlbaum.com/. Illus., index, adv. Refereed. Circ: 1700. Vol. ends: Dec. Online: EBSCO Publishing; Gale Group; Ingenta Select; RoweCom Information Quest; Swets Blackwell. Reprint: PQC; PSC. *Indexed:* ASSIA, CJA, ECER, H&SSA, IMFL, IndMed, PEI, PsycholAb, RiskAb, SSCI, SSI. *Bk. rev.:* 0-2, 100-200 words. *Aud.:* Ac, Sa.

This is the official journal of the American Psychological Association's Clinical Child Psychology Division. Articles cover theory, assessment, intervention, program development, and training. Original research, reviews, material related to training and professional practice, and papers on child advocacy are all part of its offerings. Averaging ten articles, recent issues look at these topics: an overview of the major contributions of 11 recent scholarly books on ADHD; predictors of continued suicidal behavior in adolescents following a suicide attempt; the relations among perceived racism and externalizing symptoms, internalizing symptoms, hopelessness, and self-concept in African American boys; religiousness and depressive symptoms among adolescents; the impact of a program aimed at reducing reoffending among juveniles transferred to adult court; background on three widely used epidemiological measures of effect: the risk ratio, the odds ratio, and the population attributable fraction; social skills training in children with ADHD; suppressed attention to rejection, ridicule, and failure cues in youth; and measuring cognitive vulnerability to depression in adolescence: reliability, validity, and gender differences. A recent special issue looks at the topic of information-processing factors in child and adolescent psychopathology. Libraries will want this title if they support research and study in clinical psychology, especially if the focus is on children. Agencies providing clinical service will also find access useful. Related titles are the *Journal of Abnormal Child Psychology,* the *Journal of Child Psychology and Psychiatry and Allied Disciplines* (both above in this section), and the *Journal of Pediatric Psychology* (below in this section).

5779. *Journal of Clinical Psychiatry.* Formerly (until 1978): *Diseases of the Nervous System.* [ISSN: 0160-6689] 1940. bi-m. USD 120 print only (Individuals, USD 89 print & online eds). Ed(s): Dr. Alan J Gelenberg, John S Shelton. Physicians Postgraduate Press, Inc., PO Box 752870, Memphis, TN 38175-2870; http://www.psychiatrist.com. Illus., index, adv. Sample. Refereed. Circ: 33000. Vol. ends: Dec. Microform: PQC. Online: Northern Light Technology, Inc. Reprint: PQC. *Indexed:* AgeL, BRI, BiolAb, CBRI, CIJE, CINAHL, ChemAb, DSA, ExcerpMed, H&SSA, HortAb, IMFL, IndMed, PsycholAb, RiskAb, SCI, SSCI. *Bk. rev.:* 4, 50-500 words. *Aud.:* Ac, Sa.

All aspects of psychiatry are covered here. With an average of eight articles, recent issues cover such topics as a double-blind, placebo-controlled trial of the safety and efficacy of selegiline transdermal system without dietary restrictions in patients with major depressive disorder; lamotrigine in patients with bipolar disorder and cocaine dependence; integrated family and individual therapy for bipolar disorder; results of the National Depressive and Manic-Depressive Association 2000 survey of individuals with bipolar disorder; a randomized placebo-controlled trial of risperidone for the treatment of aggression, agitation, and psychosis of dementia; sexual changes after stroke; and gender differences in pathological gambling. One special issue examines chronic major depression, and one recent issue looks at the role of GABA in neuropsychiatric disorders. Internet access to recent tables of contents is available. Students, researchers, and practitioners in clinical psychology and psychiatry will appreciate access to this relatively inexpensive title.

5780. *Journal of Cognitive Neuroscience.* [ISSN: 0898-929X] 1989. 8x/yr. USD 450 for print & electronic eds. (Individuals, USD 98 for print & electronic eds.; Students, USD 62 for print & electronic eds.). Ed(s): Michael S Gazzaniga. MIT Press, 5 Cambridge Center, Cambridge, MA 02142-1493; journals-orders@mit.edu; http://mitpress.mit.edu. Illus. Refereed. Circ: 1200. Online: EBSCO Publishing; Florida Center for Library Automation; Gale Group; HighWire Press; Ingenta Select; OCLC Online Computer Library Center, Inc.; RoweCom Information Quest; Swets Blackwell. Reprint: PQC. *Indexed:* EngInd, ExcerpMed, IndMed, L&LBA, PsycholAb, SCI, SSCI. *Aud.:* Ac.

Serving an international audience as the official publication of the Cognitive Neuroscience Institute, this title seeks to provide a "single forum for research on the biological bases of mental events." Empirical, theoretical, and research papers are published, and contributions address both psychological and mental functioning as well as underlying related brain events, neurophysiology, or neuroanatomy. Each issue has about seven articles plus occasional interviews. Recent issues examine neuroimaging studies of word and pseudoword reading: consistencies, inconsistencies, and limitations; lateralization of prefrontal activity during episodic memory retrieval: evidence for the production-monitoring hypothesis; category-specific representations of social and nonsocial knowledge in the human prefrontal cortex; enhanced pitch sensitivity in individuals with autism: a signal detection analysis; motion perception in autism; dissociating hippocampal versus basal ganglia contributions to learning and transfer; form-from-motion: MEG evidence for time course and processing sequence; and long-latency ERPs and recognition of facial identity. Internet access to tables of contents for past and forthcoming issues are available online. Researchers and those pursuing advanced studies in neuropsychology or neuroscience will benefit from access to this title. Related journals include *Behavioral Neuroscience* and *Cognitive Neuropsychology* (above).

5781. *Journal of Comparative Psychology.* Supersedes in part (in 1983): *Journal of Comparative and Physiological Psychology.* [ISSN: 0735-7036] 1947. q. USD 166 (Members, USD 33; Non-members, USD 66). Ed(s): Meredith J West. American Psychological Association, 750 First St, NE, Washington, DC 20002-4242; journals@apa.org; http://www.apa.org/. Illus., index, adv. Refereed. Circ: 1400. Vol. ends: Feb. Microform: PQC. Online: EBSCO Publishing; Gale Group; OCLC Online Computer Library Center, Inc.; Ovid Technologies, Inc.; ProQuest Information & Learning; ScienceDirect. Reprint: PQC; PSC. *Indexed:* AbAn, B&AI, BiolAb, ChemAb, IndMed, PsycholAb, SCI, SSCI, SSI, ZooRec. *Aud.:* Ac.

This publication is a forum for original empirical and theoretical research—a comparative perspective—on the behavior, cognition, perception, and social relationships of diverse species. Studies can be descriptive or experimental and can be conducted in the field or in captivity. Research on humans can be found, although articles most commonly focus on other species. With approximately 12 articles, recent issues cover the following: using visual reinforcement to establish stimulus control of responding of Siamese fighting fish (*Betta splendens*); preference for novel flavors in adult Norway Rats (*Rattus norvegicus*); extinction of conditioned sexual responses in male Japanese quail (*Coturnix japonica*): role of species-typical cues; withholding information in semifree-ranging Tonkean macaques (*Macaca tonkeana*); strategy planning in cats (*Felis catus*) in a progressive elimination task; ontogeny of social behavior in the megapode Australian brush-turkey (*Alectura lathami*); and delayed alternation in honeybees (*Apis mellifera*). Internet access to tables of contents and abstracts of recent articles is available. Libraries supporting experimental-psychology programs will want this title, as will libraries that support other research in animal behavior.

5782. *Journal of Consulting and Clinical Psychology.* Formerly (until 1967): *Journal of Consulting Psychology.* [ISSN: 0022-006X] 1937. bi-m. USD 474 (Members, USD 98; Non-members, USD 197). Ed(s): Lizette Peterson-Homer. American Psychological Association, 750 First St, NE, Washington, DC 20002-4242; journals@apa.org; http://www.apa.org/. Illus., index, adv. Refereed. Circ: 7800. Vol. ends: Jan. Microform: PMC; PQC. Online: EBSCO Publishing; Gale Group; OCLC Online Computer Library Center, Inc.; Ovid Technologies, Inc.; ProQuest Information & Learning; ScienceDirect. Reprint: PQC; PSC. *Indexed:* ASSIA, AgeL, BiolAb, CIJE, CJA, CommAb, ECER, ExcerpMed, IndMed, PRA, PsycholAb, SFSA, SSCI, SSI, SWR&A. *Aud.:* Ac, Sa.

This journal continues as a central resource for those involved with research or study in clinical psychology. It covers the diagnosis or treatment of abnormal behavior but does not cover the etiology or descriptive pathology of abnormal behavior. The latter are more appropriately found in the APA's *Journal of Abnormal Psychology* (above). There are typically over 20 articles, and recent topics include PTSD treatment and five-year remission among patients with substance use and posttraumatic stress disorders; effectiveness of cognitive therapy for depression in a community mental health center; the relationship between aggressive attributional style and violence by psychiatric patients; the prevalence and impact of large, sudden improvements during adolescent therapy for depression: a comparison across cognitive-behavioral, family, and supportive therapy; syndromal structure of psychopathology in children of

Thailand and the United States; screening for disruptive-behavior syndromes in children: the application of latent class analyses and implications for prevention programs; and cognitive-behavioral treatment of late-life generalized anxiety disorder. In addition, occasionally, selected topics are covered in special sections with a collection of related articles. Internet access to tables of contents and abstracts of recent articles is available. All libraries supporting research and study in clinical psychology must have this title, and it is desirable for libraries supporting other programs that study abnormal human behavior. Professional settings will benefit as well.

5783. ***Journal of Counseling Psychology.*** [ISSN: 0022-0167] 1954. q. USD 182 (Members, USD 39; Non-members, USD 78). Ed(s): Dr. Jo-Ida Hansen. American Psychological Association, 750 First St, NE, Washington, DC 20002-4242; journals@apa.org; http://www.apa.org/. Illus., index, adv. Refereed. Circ: 8900. Vol. ends: Dec. Microform: PQC. Online: EBSCO Publishing; OCLC Online Computer Library Center, Inc.; Ovid Technologies, Inc.; ProQuest Information & Learning; ScienceDirect. Reprint: PQC; PSC. *Indexed:* ABIn, ASSIA, AgeL, BRI, CBRI, CIJE, CJA, EduInd, ExcerpMed, HEA, PsycholAb, SFSA, SSCI, SSI, SWA, SWR&A. *Aud.:* Ac, Sa.

In this journal, readers will find articles on counseling in colleges and universities; in private and public counseling agencies; and in business, school, religious, and military settings. Special attention is given to empirical studies on the evaluation and application of counseling programs and to theoretical articles. The selection and training of counselors, the development of counseling materials and methods, and applications of counseling to special populations and problem areas are other areas covered. With an average of 12 articles, recent issues examine development and validation of the Counselor Activity Self-Efficacy Scales; the Religious Commitment Inventory–10: development, refinement, and validation of a brief scale for research and counseling; effects of a method of self-supervision for counselor trainees; the use of early identification of treatment and problem-solving strategies in routine practice; symptom improvement and length of treatment in ethnically similar and dissimilar client-therapist pairings; parental attachment, self-esteem, and antisocial behaviors among African American, European American, and Mexican American adolescents; and psychological separation, attachment security, vocational self-concept crystallization, and career indecision: a structural equation analysis. Internet access to tables of contents and abstracts of recent articles is available. Practitioners, undergraduate and graduate students, and researchers in counseling will benefit from access to this title. A related title is *Counseling Psychologist* (above).

5784. ***Journal of Cross-Cultural Psychology.*** [ISSN: 0022-0221] 1970. bi-m. USD 548 & Caribbean. Ed(s): Fons Van de Vijver. Sage Publications, Inc., 2455 Teller Rd, Thousand Oaks, CA 91320; info@sagepub.com; http://www.sagepub.com. Illus., index, adv. Refereed. Circ: 2000. Microform: PQC. Online: EBSCO Publishing; Florida Center for Library Automation; Gale Group; ingenta.com; OCLC Online Computer Library Center, Inc.; ProQuest Information & Learning; RoweCom Information Quest; Swets Blackwell. Reprint: PQC; PSC. *Indexed:* ABS&EES, ASSIA, AbAn, AgeL, ArtHuCI, BAS, CIJE, CommAb, HRA, IBZ, L&LBA, PRA, PsycholAb, SFSA, SSCI, SSI, SWA, SociolAb. *Bk. rev.:* 0-5, 300-500 words. *Aud.:* Ac, Sa.

This journal—published for the Center for Cross-Cultural Research, Department of Psychology, Western Washington University, in affiliation with the International Association for Cross-Cultural Psychology—contains exclusively cross-cultural research reports. Its emphasis is on empirical research, studying variables influenced by culture, with subjects from at least two different cultural groups. The concern is with individual differences and variation across cultures rather than with societal variation, e.g., sociology. Research exclusively on members of ethnic minorities within one country must be replicable among or across clearly distinguishable culture groups. Contributions are accepted from disciplines other than psychology. With an average of eight articles, recent issues cover social support provision and cultural values in Indonesia and Britain; the structure and personality correlates of affect in Mexico: evidence of cross-cultural comparability using the Spanish language; comparing typological structures across cultures by multigroup latent class analysis; a comparison of depressive symptoms in African Americans and Caucasian Americans; cultural similarities and a distance perspective on cross-cultural differences in emotion recognition; the relationship between individualism-collectivism, face, and feedback and learning processes in Hong Kong, Singapore, and the United States; and regrets of action and inaction across cultures. All libraries with programs that focus on the study of cultures should have this title.

5785. ***Journal of Experimental Child Psychology.*** [ISSN: 0022-0965] 1964. m. EUR 1402 (Individuals, EUR 656; Students, EUR 341). Ed(s): Dr. Robert V. Kail. Academic Press, 525 B St, Ste 1900, San Diego, CA 92101-4495; apsubs@acad.com; http://www.academicpress.com. Illus., index, adv. Refereed. Vol. ends: Dec. Online: EBSCO Publishing; Gale Group; ingenta.com; OCLC Online Computer Library Center, Inc.; RoweCom Information Quest; ScienceDirect; Swets Blackwell. *Indexed:* BiolAb, CIJE, EduInd, IBZ, IndMed, MLA-IB, PsycholAb, SCI, SSCI, SSI. *Aud.:* Ac, Sa.

Articles in this title generally focus on psychology of the normal child. As its title suggests, empirical research reports predominate; theoretical work, critical reviews, and brief notes on methodology or apparatus are also found. With an average of six articles, recent issues look at genetic and environmental influences on individual differences in printed-word recognition; infants' learning, memory, and generalization of learning for bimodal events; memory and suggestibility in maltreated children: age, stress arousal, dissociation, and psychopathology; solving spatial tasks with unaligned layouts: the difficulty of dealing with conflicting information; the effects of minority status in the classroom on children's intergroup attitudes; and children's strategies in computational estimation. Tables of contents are available via e-mail from the publisher. Those who study or research normal-child psychology will want this title, along with *Developmental Psychology, Developmental Review* (both above), and the *Journal of Youth and Adolescence* (below).

5786. ***Journal of Experimental Psychology: Animal Behavior Processes.*** Supersedes in part (in 1975): *Journal of Experimental Psychology.* [ISSN: 0097-7403] 1916. q. USD 196 (Members, USD 41; Non-members, USD 86). Ed(s): Mark E Bouton. American Psychological Association, 750 First St, NE, Washington, DC 20002-4242; journals@apa.org; http://www.apa.org/. Illus., index, adv. Refereed. Circ: 2000. Vol. ends: Dec. Microform: PQC. Online: EBSCO Publishing; Gale Group; OCLC Online Computer Library Center, Inc.; Ovid Technologies, Inc.; ProQuest Information & Learning; ScienceDirect. Reprint: PQC; PSC. *Indexed:* BiolAb, DSA, IBZ, IndMed, IndVet, PsycholAb, SCI, SSCI, SSI, ZooRec. *Aud.:* Ac, Sa.

Psychology relies in a fundamental way on scientific research. This publication of the American Psychological Association (APA) and the four listed immediately below should be considered as five key titles in any complete basic collection supporting research and study in experimental psychology. First, the *Journal of Experimental Psychology: Applied* provides articles that "bridge practically oriented problems and psychological theory." The goal of the *Journal of Experimental Psychology: Animal Behavior Processes* publishes theoretical and experimental studies of animal behavior processes. The aim of *Journal of Experimental Psychology: General* is to furnish scholarly articles of interest to the "entire community of experimental psychologists." The *Journal of Experimental Psychology: Human Perception and Performance* focuses on "perception, formulation and control of action, and related cognitive processes." The *Journal of Experimental Psychology: Learning, Memory, and Cognition* provides articles on "basic processes of cognition, learning, memory, imagery, concept formulation, problem solving, decision making, thinking, reading and language processing." For each of these titles, Internet access is available for current tables of contents and article abstracts. Libraries supporting study of research in experimental psychology should have this set, if possible, or individually relevant titles if library users are involved in a segment of experimental psychology related to one of the titles. Contact and pricing information for individual titles in this set are available at the APA's Internet site (www.apa.org).

5787. ***Journal of Experimental Social Psychology.*** [ISSN: 0022-1031] 1965. bi-m. EUR 869 (Individuals, EUR 316; Students, EUR 132). Ed(s): B Park. Academic Press, 525 B St, Ste 1900, San Diego, CA 92101-4495; apsubs@acad.com; http://www.academicpress.com. Illus., adv. Refereed. Vol. ends: Nov. Online: EBSCO Publishing; Gale Group; ingenta.com; OCLC Online Computer Library Center, Inc.; RoweCom Information Quest; ScienceDirect; Swets Blackwell. *Indexed:* ArtHuCI, BiolAb, CJA, CommAb, IBSS, IBZ, LRI, PsycholAb, RI-1, SSCI, SSI. *Aud.:* Ac.

Social phenomena are examined here, with coverage on social motivation, social cognition, attitude and belief processes, and group processes. Although "experimental and conceptually based research" is emphasized, especially as it advances theory in social psychology, theoretical analyses, literature reviews, and methodological reports are also published. Averaging five articles, recent issues examine effects of situational power on automatic racial prejudice; preferred changes in power differences: effects of social comparison in equal and unequal power relations; inferring the importance of arguments: order effects and conversational rules; the impact of stereotypic associations on category-based and individuating impression formation; cognitive stimulation and interference in groups: exposure effects in an idea generation task; the role of perceived negativity in the moderation of African Americans' implicit and explicit racial attitudes; priming against your will: how accessible alternatives affect goal pursuit; and accuracy and bias in stereotypes about the social and political attitudes of women and men. Access to tables of contents is also available via e-mail from the publisher. Libraries will want this title if they support research and study pertaining to the understanding of the social factors listed above. The related *Journal of Social Psychology* (below) also should be considered.

5788. *Journal of Humanistic Psychology.* [ISSN: 0022-1678] 1961. q. GBP 332 print & online eds. in Europe, Middle East, Africa & Australasia. Ed(s): Thomas C Greening. Sage Publications, Inc., 2455 Teller Rd, Thousand Oaks, CA 91320; info@sagepub.com; http://www.sagepub.com. Illus., index, adv. Refereed. Circ: 3000. Vol. ends: Fall. Microform: PQC. Online: Florida Center for Library Automation; Gale Group; ingenta.com; OCLC Online Computer Library Center, Inc.; ProQuest Information & Learning; RoweCom Information Quest; Swets Blackwell. Reprint: PQC. *Indexed:* ABS&EES, ASSIA, AgeL, ArtHuCI, CIJE, CommAb, HRA, IMFL, PsycholAb, RI-1, SSCI, SSI. *Aud.:* Ac, Sa.

This journal, founded by Abraham Maslow and Anthony Sutich, is the official publication of the Association for Humanistic Psychology. Readers will find experiential reports, theoretical work, personal essays, and analyses and research based on humanistic approaches. With seven to ten articles in each issue, recent issues include such topics as the impermanence of being: toward a psychology of uncertainty; curtailing the use of restraint in psychiatric settings; people are more important than pills in recovery from mental disorder; informed consent and the psychiatric drugging of children; a tribute to Frank Barron; what eminent people have said about the meaning of life; and relational healing: to be understood and to understand. Libraries that want to provide reading with a humanistic-psychology perspective should consider this title.

5789. *Journal of Mathematical Psychology.* [ISSN: 0022-2496] 1964. bi-m. EUR 1191 (Individuals, EUR 564; Students, EUR 192). Ed(s): Richard Schweikert. Academic Press, 525 B St, Ste 1900, San Diego, CA 92101-4495; apsubs@acad.com; http://www.academicpress.com. Illus., index, adv. Refereed. Vol. ends: Dec. Online: EBSCO Publishing; ingenta.com; OCLC Online Computer Library Center, Inc.; RoweCom Information Quest; ScienceDirect; Swets Blackwell. *Indexed:* BiolAb, CCMJ, IBZ, MathSciNet, PsycholAb, SSCI. *Bk. rev.:* 1-5, 100-3,000 words. *Aud.:* Ac.

This publication aims to cover all areas of mathematical psychology. Fundamental measurement and mathematical models receive ongoing attention, and such areas have included those using connectionist, other neural network, and/or information-processing concepts. Theoretical or empirical works from a wide spectrum of disciplines are equally welcome. Recent issues include such topics as skill set analysis in knowledge structures; techniques for oblique factor rotation of two or more loading matrices to a mixture of simple structure and optimal agreement; a tandem random walk model of the SAT paradigm: response times and accumulation of evidence; a meaningful justification for the representational theory of measurement; using students' statistical thinking to inform instruction; and aspiration-based and reciprocity-based rules in learning dynamics for symmetric normal-form games. Access to tables of contents is available via e-mail from the publisher. This title will benefit researchers and students in psychology who require access to quantitative studies and work using models of behavior. *Psychometrika* (below) is another useful journal for discussion and research on quantitiative models and psychology.

5790. *The Journal of Mind and Behavior.* [ISSN: 0271-0137] 1980. q. USD 120 (Individuals, USD 46; Students, USD 32). Ed(s): Dr. Raymond C. Russ. Institute of Mind & Behavior, PO Box 522, New York, NY 10014; http://kramer.ume.maine.edu/~jmb/. Illus., index, adv. Sample. Refereed. Circ: 1191 Controlled. *Indexed:* ExcerpMed, L&LBA, PhilInd, PsycholAb, SSCI, SWR&A, SociolAb. *Bk. rev.:* 0-4, 300-2,000 words. *Aud.:* Ac.

Since its inception, the focus of this title has been on issues that arise from considering the multiple interrelationships possible between mind and behavior. The journal publishes scholarly articles written for and by an interdisciplinary audience, and although all scholarly approaches are welcome, theoretical discussion dominates. Recent issues, averaging nine articles, look at such topics as perceptual experience and its contents; the experiential presence of objects to perceptual consciousness: Wilfrid Sellars, sense impressions, and perceptual takings; eliminativist undercurrents in the new wave model of psychoneural reduction; a critical review of twin and adoption studies of criminality and antisocial behavior; and structural causation and psychological explanation. One issue gives special attention to "Choice and chance in the formation of society: behavior and cognition in social theory." Internet access to tables of contents and abstracts of all articles published since 1980 are available. Libraries wishing to emphasize theoretical discussion in psychology may wish to include this title.

5791. *Journal of Occupational and Organizational Psychology.* Former titles: *Journal of Occupational Psychology; Occupational Psychology.* [ISSN: 0963-1798] 1922. q. GBP 145 & libraries (Individuals, GBP 36). Ed(s): John Arnold. The British Psychological Society, St Andrews House, 48 Princess Rd E, Leicester, LE1 7DR, United Kingdom; mail@bps.org.uk; http://www.bps.org.uk/publications/journals.cfm. Illus., index, adv. Sample. Refereed. Circ: 3100. Vol. ends: Dec. Online: EBSCO Publishing; Florida Center for Library Automation; Gale Group; Ingenta Select; OCLC Online Computer Library Center, Inc.; ProQuest Information & Learning; Swets Blackwell. Reprint: ISI; SWZ. *Indexed:* ABIn, ASSIA, AgeL, BiolAb, BrEdI, ErgAb, H&SSA, IBSS, IBZ, IndMed, PsycholAb, SSCI, SWA, SociolAb. *Bk. rev.:* 3, 500-1,000 words. *Aud.:* Ac, Sa.

This publication of the British Psychological Association seeks to promote the understanding of people and organizations at work. Articles on industrial, organizational, engineering, vocational, and personnel psychology are accepted, as are those involving behavioral studies in ergonomics and industrial relations. Included are empirical studies, critical surveys, theoretical studies, methodology papers, and assessments of the application of psychology to work settings. There are six to nine articles per isssue. Recent issues cover such topics as a critical re-examination and analysis of cognitive ability tests using the Thorndike model of fairness; the measurement of organizational justice in organizational change programs; perceived job insecurity among dual-earner couples; development of the sales locus of control scale; the influence of motives and goal orientation on feedback seeking; using a single-item approach to measure facet job satisfaction; performance disparities between whites and ethnic minorities (real differences or assessment bias); personality similarity effects (relational and perceived) on peer and supervisor ratings and the role of familiarity and liking; and gender, context, and leadership styles. Libraries will want this title if they support research and study related to occupational psychology.

5792. *Journal of Pediatric Psychology.* Formerly: *Pediatric Psychology.* [ISSN: 0146-8693] 1976. 8x/yr. GBP 296. Ed(s): Ronald T Brown. Oxford University Press, Great Clarendon St, Oxford, OX2 6DP, United Kingdom; jnl.orders@oup.co.uk; http://www3.oup.co.uk/jnls. Illus., index. Sample. Refereed. Circ: 2000. Microform: PQC. Online: EBSCO Publishing; HighWire Press; ingenta.com; OCLC Online Computer Library Center, Inc.; Ovid Technologies, Inc.; RoweCom Information

Quest; Swets Blackwell. Reprint: PSC. *Indexed:* BiolAb, CINAHL, ExcerpMed, IMFL, IndMed, PollutAb, PsycholAb, RiskAb, SFSA, SSCI, SWR&A. *Bk. rev.:* 5-8, 150-3,000 words. *Aud.:* Ac, Sa.

As the official journal of the Society of Pediatric Psychology (Division 54, American Psychological Association), this interdisciplinary title covers the relation between the psychological and physical well-being of children and adolescents and their families. Some of the general areas include psychological and developmental factors contributing to the etiology, course, treatment, and outcome of pediatric conditions; the promotion of health and health-related behaviors; the prevention of injury and illness among children and youth; and issues related to the training of pediatric psychologists. Analytical reviews of research, brief scientific reports, and scholarly case studies from authors in psychology and related disciplines are all found here. Recent topics include interactions between children with juvenile rheumatoid arthritis; blood glucose estimations in adolescents with Type 1 diabetes: predictors of accuracy and error; stress and adaptation in mothers of children with cerebral palsy; the Hemophilia Growth and Development Study: caregiver report of youth and family adjustment to HIV disease and immunologic compromise; living with childhood cancer: a practical guide to help families cope; preparing psychologists to link systems of care in managing and preventing children's health problems; a prospective study of the relationship over time of behavior problems, intellectual functioning, and family functioning in children with sickle cell disease: a report from the Cooperative Study of Sickle Cell Disease; pain reactivity and somatization in kindergarten-age children; and psychological adjustment of children and adolescents with chronic arthritis: a meta-analytic review. Tables of contents and abstracts are available at the publisher's web site. Psychologists and others working with children in medical or other clinical settings will benefit from this title, as will those pursuing research or study related to clinical services to children.

5793. *Journal of Personality.* Formerly (until 1945): *Character and Personality.* [ISSN: 0022-3506] 1932. bi-m. USD 628 print & online eds. Blackwell Publishing, Inc., Commerce Place, 350 Main St, Malden, MA 02148; subscrip@blackwellpub.com; http://www.blackwellpublishing.com. Illus., index, adv. Sample. Refereed. Circ: 2000. Vol. ends: Dec. Online: EBSCO Publishing; Gale Group; ingenta.com; OCLC Online Computer Library Center, Inc.; RoweCom Information Quest; Swets Blackwell. *Indexed:* ASSIA, AgeL, ArtHuCI, BiolAb, CommAb, EduInd, IBSS, IBZ, IndMed, PsycholAb, SFSA, SSCI, SSI, SWA. *Aud.:* Ac, Sa.

The general aim of this journal is to emphasize "scientific investigations in the field of personality." Emphasis is "particularly on personality and behavior dynamics, personality development, and individual differences in the cognitive, affective, and interpersonal domains." There are five to ten articles per issue. Coverage has looked at personality judgments in adolescents' families: the perceiver, the target, their relationship, and the family; witnessing interpersonal psychological aggression in childhood: implications for daily conflict in adult intimate relationships; personality and close relationships: embedding people in important social contexts; delay of gratification: impulsive choices and problem behaviors in early and late adolescence; life satisfaction as a momentary judgment and a stable personality characteristic: the use of chronically accessible and stable source; the role of personality in task and relationship conflict; and personality profiles and the prediction of categorical personality disorders. In addition, one special issue looks at psychology and the study of religion. Tables of contents and abstracts are available online from publisher. Academic libraries supporting study and research in personality should consider this title.

5794. *Journal of Personality and Social Psychology.* Supersedes in part (in 1965): *Journal of Abnormal and Social Psychology.* [ISSN: 0022-3514] 1925. m. USD 999 (Members, USD 181; Non-members, USD 364). Ed(s): Dr. Ed Diener, Dr. Chester A. Insko. American Psychological Association, 750 First St, NE, Washington, DC 20002-4242; journals@apa.org; http://www.apa.org/. Illus., index, adv. Refereed. Circ: 5100. Vol. ends: Dec. Microform: PQC. Online: EBSCO Publishing; Gale Group; OCLC Online Computer Library Center, Inc.; Ovid Technologies, Inc.; ProQuest Information & Learning; ScienceDirect. Reprint: PQC; PSC. *Indexed:* ABS&EES, AgeL, ArtHuCI, BAS, BiolAb, CIJE, CJA, CommAb, HEA, IBSS, IBZ, IPSA, IndMed, L&LBA, MLA-IB, PsycholAb, RI-1, SFSA, SSCI, SSI, SUSA, SWA, SWR&A, SociolAb, SportS. *Aud.:* Ac, Sa.

This major journal of the American Psychological Association covers all areas of personality and social psychology, with an emphasis on empirical reports and articles organized into such sections as "Attitudes and Social Cognition," "Interpersonal Relations and Group Processes," and "Personality and Individual Differences." Recent coverage includes looks at measuring self-enhancement independent of ability; inspiration as a psychological construct; a psychometric analysis of students' daily social environments and natural conversations; personalities of politicians and voters: unique and synergistic relationships; cardiovascular correlates of emotional expression and suppression: content and gender context; the effect of evidence of literal immortality on self-esteem striving in response to mortality salience; resource loss, resource gain, and emotional outcomes among inner-city women; and quantifying construct validity. Internet access to recent tables of contents and article abstracts is available. Libraries supporting programs in behavioral sciences will want this title, and also the *Journal of Personality* (above), especially when users are concerned with basic research in personality.

5795. *Journal of Personality Assessment.* Former titles (until 1970): *Journal of Projective Techniques and Personality Assessment;* (until 1962): *Journal of Projective Techniques;* (until 1949): *Rorschach Research Exchange and Journal of Projective Techniques;* (until 1946): *Rorschach Research Exchange.* [ISSN: 0022-3891] 1936. bi-m. in 2 vols. USD 430. Ed(s): Gregory Meyer. Lawrence Erlbaum Associates, Inc., 10 Industrial Ave, Mahwah, NJ 07430-2262; journals@erlbaum.com; http://www.erlbaum.com/. Illus., index, adv. Sample. Refereed. Circ: 2700. Vol. ends: Winter. Microform: PQC. Online: EBSCO Publishing; Ingenta Select; OCLC Online Computer Library Center, Inc.; RoweCom Information Quest; Swets Blackwell. Reprint: PQC; PSC. *Indexed:* ASSIA, AgeL, BiolAb, ECER, ExcerpMed, H&SSA, IndMed, PsycholAb, RiskAb, SSCI. *Aud.:* Ac, Sa.

Other listings in this section describe titles that focus on theories of personality. This title, as the official publication of the Society for Personality Assessment, covers assessment issues. Its focus is on the development and utilization of assessment methods, including the use of "psychological test or interview data to measure or describe personality processes or their behavioral implications." Empirical, theoretical, and pedagogical articles are accepted. Both normal and abnormal personalities (all ages) are covered. Recent issues, averaging 15 articles, look at psychological measures as predictors of military training performance; measuring epistemic curiosity and its diversive and specific components; construct validity of the Relationship Profile Test; Beck Depression Inventory-II items associated with self-reported symptoms of ADHD in adult psychiatric outpatients; the use of the Ego Impairment Index across the schizophrenia spectrum; Rorschach measures of aggressive drive derivatives: a college student sample; construct validity of the Life Orientation Test; and the Infrequency-Posttraumatic Stress Disorder Scale for the MMPI-2: development and initial validation with veterans presenting with combat-related PTSD. In addition to researchers and students taking advanced courses in assessment, those who will find this material useful include professionals in clinical, counseling, forensic, community, cross-cultural, education, and health psychology settings.

5796. *Journal of School Psychology.* [ISSN: 0022-4405] 1963. bi-m. EUR 335 (Individuals, EUR 69; Students, EUR 27). Ed(s): Robert Pianta. Pergamon, The Boulevard, Langford Ln, East Park, Kidlington, OX5 1GB, United Kingdom. Illus., index, adv. Refereed. Circ: 2000. Vol. ends: Dec. Microform: PQC. Online: ingenta.com; ScienceDirect; Swets Blackwell. Reprint: ISI; PQC. *Indexed:* CIJE, ECER, EduInd, L&LBA, PsycholAb, SSCI. *Aud.:* Ac, Sa.

Articles in this journal report on research and practice related to school psychology as both a "scientific and an applied specialty." Averaging seven articles each, recent issues look at such topics as keeping adolescents safe from harm: management strategies of African American families in a high-risk community; defining autism: professional best practices and published case law; the relation of children's concerns about punishment to their aggression; pediatric topics in the school psychology literature: publications since 1981;

raising healthy children through enhancing social development in elementary school; and ethnic differences in grade trajectories during the transition to junior high. A special issue looks at school psychology from a public-health perspective. Abstracts and tables of contents are available on the publisher's web site. Along with such titles as *School Psychology Review* (below), this title is desirable for libraries that support programs in school psychology and related courses in education.

5797. *The Journal of Social Psychology.* [ISSN: 0022-4545] 1929. bi-m. USD 181 domestic; USD 197 foreign; USD 30.25 per issue. Ed(s): Jean Carlick. Heldref Publications, 1319 18th St, NW, Washington, DC 20036-1802; subscribe@heldref.org; http://www.heldref.org. Illus., adv. Sample. Refereed. Circ: 1600. Microform: PQC. Online: bigchalk; Chadwyck-Healey Incorporated; EBSCO Publishing; Florida Center for Library Automation; Gale Group; LexisNexis; Northern Light Technology, Inc.; OCLC Online Computer Library Center, Inc.; ProQuest Information & Learning; H.W. Wilson. Reprint: PSC; SWZ. *Indexed:* ASSIA, AgeL, ArtHuCI, BAS, BiolAb, CIJE, CJA, CWI, CommAb, ECER, ExcerpMed, HEA, HRA, IBSS, IPSA, IndMed, L&LBA, LRI, PRA, PSA, PsycholAb, SSCI, SSI, SUSA, SWA, SWR&A, SociolAb. *Aud.:* Ac, Sa.

This title seeks to support integrative work across the social sciences by publishing experimental, empirical, and field studies of groups, cultural effects, cross-national problems, language, and ethnicity. Additionally, sections on "Notes—Current Problems and Resolutions," "Cross-Cultural Notes," and "Replications and Refinements" are designed to promote improvements in previously established generalizations. Recent issues, with 13 to 15 articles, examine such topics as applying a social identity paradigm to examine the relationship between men's self-esteem and their attitudes toward men and women; sociocultural influences on body image and body changes among adolescent boys and girls; perception of the minority's collective identity and voting behavior: the case of the Palestinians in Israel; dogmatic behavior among students: testing a new measure of dogmatism; conflict resolution and peer mediation in middle schools: extending the process and outcome knowledge base; value domains of Turkish adults and university students; and general versus specific victim blaming. Those needing access to a broad spectrum of professional research in social psychology will want this title. Related titles include the *Journal of Cross-Cultural Psychology* and the *Journal of Experimental Social Psychology* (both above) and *Personality and Social Psychology Bulletin* (below).

5798. *Journal of the History of the Behavioral Sciences.* [ISSN: 0022-5061] 1965. q. USD 320 domestic; USD 348 foreign; USD 352 combined subscription domestic for print and online eds. Ed(s): Raymond E Fancher. John Wiley & Sons, Inc., 111 River St, Hoboken, NJ 07030; uscs-wis@wiley.com; http://www3.interscience.wiley.com/journalfinder.html. Illus., index, adv. Refereed. Circ: 800. Vol. ends: Oct. Microform: PQC. Online: EBSCO Publishing; ScienceDirect; Swets Blackwell; Wiley InterScience. Reprint: PQC; PSC. *Indexed:* ABS&EES, AbAn, AmH&L, ArtHuCI, IBSS, IndMed, PsycholAb, SSCI. *Bk. rev.:* 3-5, 500-1,800 words. *Aud.:* Ac, Sa.

This peer-reviewed, international journal is devoted to the "scientific, technical, institutional, and cultural history of the social and behavioral sciences." Research articles and book reviews are published as well as news and notes that "cover the development of the core disciplines of psychology, anthropology, sociology, psychiatry and psychoanalysis, economics, linguistics, communications, political science, and the neurosciences." Papers and book reviews from related fields may also be found, including contributions from the history of science and medicine, historical theory, and historiography. Recent article topics include the disappearance of classical conditioning before Pavlov; origins of the cognitive (r)evolution; negotiating illness: doctors, patients, and families in the nineteenth century; the intellectual origins of the McCulloch-Pitts neural networks; the introduction of the psychology of religion to the Netherlands; the original conception of the social dimensions of cognition, emotion, and behavior held by early American social psychologists; adaptive will: the evolution of ADD; and brave new worlds: trophallaxis and the origin of society in the early twentieth century. Internet access is available for current tables of contents and for abstracts of current articles. Along with its value for librarians, this journal certainly can be useful to students and researchers in history as well as to those in the behavioral sciences. A related title is *History of Psychology* (above).

5799. *Journal of Vocational Behavior.* [ISSN: 0001-8791] 1971. bi-m. EUR 1051 (Individuals, EUR 510; Students, EUR 259). Ed(s): Mark L Savickas. Academic Press, 525 B St, Ste 1900, San Diego, CA 92101-4495; apsubs@acad.com; http://www.academicpress.com. Illus., index, adv. Refereed. Vol. ends: Dec. Online: EBSCO Publishing; ingenta.com; OCLC Online Computer Library Center, Inc.; RoweCom Information Quest; ScienceDirect; Swets Blackwell. *Indexed:* AgeL, CIJE, CINAHL, HEA, PSA, PsycholAb, SSCI, SWA, SociolAb. *Aud.:* Ac, Sa.

The focus of this journal is on career choice, career implementation, and vocational adjustment and adaptation. Theoretical, empirical, and methodological work are all accepted, and developments in instrumentation and research methodology and evaluations of programs or interventions also are included. Articles about the effective functioning of organizations, as opposed to that of individuals, are usually found elsewhere—for example, in the *Journal of Occupational and Organizational Psychology* (above). With an average of ten articles, recent issues look at the moderating effect of exchange ideology on the relation between perceptions of organizational politics and manager-rated retention; college seniors' concerns about career-marriage conflict; L. Gottfredson's revised theory of circumscription and compromise; the relation of self-efficacy and interest (a meta-analysis); dispositional and motivational variables related to the propensity to mentor others and to the provision of career and psychosocial mentoring; the development and psychometric evaluation of 17 scales measuring confidence or self-efficacy with respect to basic domains of vocational activity among undergraduate students and adults; and variations in human capital investment activity by age. Also, a recent special issue looks at innovating career development using advances in life course and life-span theory. Internet access to tables of contents and article abstracts is available. Libraries supporting study, research, and/or professional work with career choice and development issues will want this title.

5800. *Journal of Youth and Adolescence: a multidisciplinary research publication.* [ISSN: 0047-2891] 1972. bi-m. USD 766 print or online ed. Ed(s): Daniel Offer. Kluwer Academic / Plenum Publishers, 233 Spring St Fl 7, New York, NY 10013-1522; http://www.wkap.nl/. Illus., adv. Refereed. Vol. ends: Dec. Microform: PQC. Online: bigchalk; EBSCO Publishing; Florida Center for Library Automation; Gale Group; ingenta.com; Kluwer Online; OCLC Online Computer Library Center, Inc.; Ovid Technologies, Inc.; ProQuest Information & Learning; RoweCom Information Quest; Swets Blackwell. *Indexed:* ASSIA, AgeL, CIJE, CJA, CommAb, EduInd, ExcerpMed, HEA, IBZ, IMFL, PsycholAb, SFSA, SSCI, SSI, SUSA, SWA, SociolAb. *Aud.:* Ac, Sa.

This journal aims to be multidisciplinary, drawing upon and serving the work of those in a variety of fields, including psychology, psychiatry, sociology, biology, and education, among others. Articles are experimental/data-based, theoretical, reviews, or "clinical reports of relevance to research." With an average of seven articles, recent issues look at interpersonal correlates of peer victimization among young adolescents; longitudinal relations among depression, stress, and coping in high-risk youth; the importance of family and school domains in adolescent deviance: African American and Caucasian youth; happy adolescents: the link between subjective well-being, internal resources, and parental factors; the positive psychology of interested adolescents; a short-term longitudinal study of pubertal change, gender, and psychological well-being of Mexican early adolescents; psychosocial correlates of intimacy achievement among adolescent fathers-to-be; the role of peer influence across adolescent risk behaviors; and impact of acculturation and gender on identity process and outcome. Those pursuing research, clinical work, or studies related to adolescents will appreciate access to this basic resource.

5801. *Law and Human Behavior.* [ISSN: 0147-7307] 1977. bi-m. USD 754 print or online ed. Ed(s): Richard Wiener. Kluwer Academic / Plenum Publishers, 233 Spring St Fl 7, New York, NY 10013-1522; http://www.wkap.nl/. Illus., adv. Refereed. Vol. ends: Dec. Microform: PQC. Online: EBSCO Publishing; Gale Group; ingenta.com; Kluwer

Online; OCLC Online Computer Library Center, Inc.; RoweCom Information Quest; Swets Blackwell. Reprint: WSH. *Indexed:* AgeL, BiolAb, CJA, CLI, ExcerpMed, ILP, IMFL, IndMed, LRI, PSA, PsycholAb, RiskAb, SSCI, SociolAb. *Aud.:* Ac, Sa.

As the official journal of the American Psychology–Law Society of the American Psychological Association (Division 41), this title provides a forum for articles focusing on relationships between human behavior and the law, our legal system, and the legal process. Original research, reviews of past research, and theoretical studies from professionals in criminal justice, law, psychology, sociology, psychiatry, political science, education, communication, and other areas germane to the field all may be found. An adversary forum is offered for debate on relevant topics. Recent issues cover such topics as jurors' perceptions of adolescent sexual-assault victims who have intellectual disabilities; the differences between defendants predicted restorable and not restorable to competency; taking responsibility for an act not committed: the influence of age and suggestibility; the relationship between competency to stand trial, competency to waive interrogation rights, and psychopathology; suspects, lies, and videotape: an analysis of authentic high-stakes liar; and rethinking the probative value of evidence: base rates, intuitive profiling, and the "postdiction" of behavior. A recent special issue also looks at the role of psychology in civil litigation. The division's web site is at the main APA site. Libraries supporting law programs or research in law should consider this title. Those involved with forensic psychology should also have access to this title and the *American Journal of Forensic Psychology* (above).

5802. ***Media Psychology.*** [ISSN: 1521-3269] 1999. q. USD 255. Ed(s): Jennings Bryant, David Roskos-Ewoldsen. Lawrence Erlbaum Associates, Inc., 10 Industrial Ave, Mahwah, NJ 07430-2262; journals@erlbaum.com; http://www.erlbaum.com/. Adv. Refereed. Reprint: PSC. *Indexed:* ArtHuCI, SSCI. *Aud.:* Ac, Sa.

Communication media are increasingly part of our lives, and this relatively new interdisciplinary journal aims to provide "theoretically oriented empirical research . . . at the intersection of psychology and media communication . . . [looking at] media uses, processes, and effects . . . [for those] who are interested in the psychological antecedents and consequences of communicating via mass media (television), telecommunications media (computer networks), and personal media (multimedia)." With an average of three lengthy articles (20 pages) and an equally long "theoretical integrative essay," recent issues look at such topics as world wide wait: exploring physiological and behavioral effects of download speed; parasocial interaction: a review of the literature and a model for future research; the connection between the motivations for reading women's beauty and fashion magazines and the presence of anorexic cognitions; moral judgment as a predictor of enjoyment of crime drama; the influence of affective state on the Internet; the impact of televised songs on children's and young adults' memory of educational content; the effects of exposure to television programming that contains both violent actions and macho portrayals of male characters on subsequent self-reports of aggression and hostility; film analysis and psychophysiology: effects of moments of impact and protagonists; and the effects of reading very violent versus mildly violent comic books on the interpretation of ambiguous provocation situations. Libraries supporting studies in communication, and those that support studies and research in psychology and media, should consider this title.

5803. ***Monitor on Psychology.*** Formerly: *A P A Monitor;* Incorporates: *American Psychological Association. Employment Bulletin.* [ISSN: 1529-4978] 1970. m. 11/yr. USD 80 (Non-members, USD 46). Ed(s): Sara Martin. American Psychological Association, 750 First St, NE, Washington, DC 20002-4242; journals@apa.org; http://www.apa.org/. Illus., adv. Sample. Circ: 116000. Microform: PQC. *Aud.:* Ga, Ac, Sa.

This monthly newspaper of the American Psychological Association continues to provide timely coverage of developments in psychology. In addition to news covering all areas of association matters and psychology job listings, the *Monitor* includes reports and material emanating from the association's Science, Education, Practice, and Public Interest Directorates, which can be understood by and useful to those who are not professionals in psychology. Recent short articles in the "In Brief" section look at such topics as rates of psychotropic drug use for children and adolescents; babies reacting to emotions on television; both halves of brain processing emotional speech; hostility as best predictor of heart disease in men; nothing good about working in a cubicle; hormone therapy reducing memory among Alzheimer's patients; and how religion influences people's ability to cope. Although the publication is not indexed, full text of selected articles from current issues are available on the Internet. All libraries that support behavioral-science research, study, or practice should have this title. The publication might also very well serve as a method of monitoring and providing insight into psychology for the general public.

5804. ***Neuropsychology.*** [ISSN: 0894-4105] 1987. q. USD 171 (Members, USD 49; Non-members, USD 99). Ed(s): Dr. James T Becker. American Psychological Association, 750 First St, NE, Washington, DC 20002-4242; journals@apa.org; http://www.apa.org/. Illus., adv. Refereed. Circ: 4500. Vol. ends: Dec. Reprint: PSC. *Indexed:* AgeL, ExcerpMed, IndMed, L&LBA, PsycholAb, SSCI. *Aud.:* Ac, Sa.

This title aims to foster basic research, to integrate basic and applied findings, and to promote improved practice in the field of neuropsychology. Articles include original empirical research in the field, as well as scholarly reviews and theoretical work promoting research on the relation between the brain and cognitive, emotional, and behavioral functions. The focus for articles may be on neuropsychological functions in both normal and disordered states and across the life span. Applied clinical research is also found. Recent issues, with approximately 18 articles in each, examine such topics as inhibitory control following perinatal brain injury; category learning deficits in Parkinson's disease; semantic and letter fluency in Spanish-English bilinguals; mental-rotation deficits following damage to the right basal ganglia; gender differences in learning and memory after pediatric traumatic brain injury; enhanced negative priming in Parkinson's disease; commonalities and differences in the working memory components underlying letter and category fluency tasks: a dual-task investigation; and the role of the anterior commissure in callosal agenesis. Tables of contents and abstracts are available online for recent issues, as well as full text of selected recent articles. Other related titles in this section include *Behavioral Neuroscience,* and the broader *Behavioral and Brain Sciences* (both above). Advanced students and researchers in the field of neuropsychology and those involved in related area studies will benefit from access to this title.

5805. ***Neuropsychology, Development and Cognition. Section A: Journal of Clinical and Experimental Neuropsychology.*** Supersedes (in 1994): *Journal of Clinical and Experimental Neuropsychology;* Which was formerly: *Journal of Clinical Neuropsychology.* [ISSN: 1380-3395] 1979. 8x/yr. EUR 1015 print & online eds. (Individuals, EUR 439). Ed(s): Wilfred G van Gorp, Daniel Tranel. Swets & Zeitlinger BV, PO Box 800, Lisse, 2160 SZ, Netherlands; orders@swets.nl; http://www.swets.nl. Illus., index, adv. Sample. Refereed. Online: EBSCO Publishing; RoweCom Information Quest; Swets Blackwell. Reprint: SWZ. *Indexed:* AgeL, BiolAb, ECER, ExcerpMed, IndMed, L&LBA, PsycholAb, SCI, SSCI. *Bk. rev.:* 0-3, 1,500 words. *Aud.:* Ac, Sa.

This international journal publishes research on the neuropsychological consequences of brain disease, disorder, and dysfunction. It also seeks to promote the integration of theories, methods, and research findings in clinical and experimental neuropsychology. The primary emphasis is on empirical research, although theoretical and methodological papers, critical reviews of content areas, and theoretically relevant case studies are also welcome. With an average of 14 articles, recent issues examine such topics as subjective and objective assessment methods of mental imagery control: construct validation of self-report measures; assigned versus self-set goals and their impact on the performance of brain-damaged patients; inhibition of expected movements in Tourette's syndrome; RT and non-RT methodology for semantic priming research with Alzheimer's patients; interpreting reaction time measures in between-group comparisons; training of working memory in children with ADHD; behavioral characterization of mild cognitive impairment; redefining the factor structure of the Wechsler Memory Scale-III: confirmatory factor analysis with cross-validation; and remembering and knowing in a patient with amnesic syndrome. Potential readers include "psychologists working directly in neuropsychology, clinical psychologists with interests in neuropsychology, psychiatrists, neurologists, and pediatricians, as well as those in speech pathology." Access to this journal's tables of contents and abstracts of recent articles is available on the Internet. A related title is *Cognitive Neuropsychology* (above).

5806. ***Organizational Behavior and Human Decision Processes: a journal of fundamental research and theory in applied psychology.*** Formerly (until 1985): *Organizational Behavior and Human Performance.* [ISSN: 0749-5978] 1966. bi-m. EUR 1787 (Individuals, EUR 836; Students, EUR 395). Ed(s): J. R. Edwards. Academic Press, 525 B St, Ste 1900, San Diego, CA 92101-4495; apsubs@acad.com; http://www.academicpress.com. Illus., index, adv. Refereed. Online: EBSCO Publishing; Gale Group; ingenta.com; OCLC Online Computer Library Center, Inc.; RoweCom Information Quest; ScienceDirect; Swets Blackwell. *Indexed:* ABIn, AgeL, BPI, CINAHL, CommAb, IBSS, IBZ, LRI, PsycholAb, RI-1, SSCI. *Aud.:* Ac, Sa.

This journal provides articles that describe "fundamental research in organizational behavior, organizational psychology, and human cognition, judgment, and decision making." Articles can be empirical, theoretical, literature reviews, and on methodological developments. Broad topical areas include perception, cognition, judgment, attitudes, emotion, well-being, motivation, choice, and performance. Recent specific article topics look at selection of strategies for narrowing choice options; duplex decomposition and general segregation of lotteries of a gain and a loss; types of inconsistency in health-state utility judgments; poetic justice or petty jealousy (the esthetics of revenge); sabotage in the workplace: the role of organizational injustice; the distortion of criteria after decision making; challenge versus threat effects on the goal-performance relationship; and gender composition, situational strength, and team decision-making accuracy. Online access is available to the current table of contents and to abstracts of current articles. Clearly, libraries will want to consider this publication if they support research and study in psychology as it relates to organizations and group processes. Related titles include the *Journal of Occupational and Organizational Psychology* and the *Journal of Experimental Social Psychology* (both above).

5807. ***Perceptual and Motor Skills.*** [ISSN: 0031-5125] 1949. bi-m. USD 370. Ed(s): S A Isbell, Bruce Ammons. Dr. C.H. Ammons, Ed. & Pub., PO Box 9229, Missoula, MT 59807. Illus., index. Sample. Refereed. Circ: 2000. *Indexed:* AbAn, AgeL, ArtHuCI, BiolAb, CIJE, CINAHL, CommAb, ECER, ErgAb, ExcerpMed, HEA, IBZ, IndMed, L&LBA, MLA-IB, PEI, PsycholAb, RILM, SCI, SSCI, SSI, SWA, SportS. *Bk. rev.:* 2-6, 120 words. *Aud.:* Ac, Sa.

In order to "encourage scientific originality and creativity," this historically basic journal provides approximately 50–60 brief articles per issue covering a wide range of topics related to perception or motor skills. Material can be experimental or theoretical. Recent issues look at such topics as confirmatory factor analysis of the Group Environment Questionnaire with co-acting sports; effects of self-assessment on retention in rule-based learning; intrusive effects of implicitly processed information on explicit memory; color and number preferences of patients with psychiatric disorders in eastern Turkey; effects of pyridoxine on dreaming; courtship communication and perception; attitudes of undergraduate majors in elementary education toward mathematics through a hands-on manipulative approach; sex differences in susceptibility to the Poggendorff illusion; and apparent distance in actual, three-dimensional video-recorded, and virtual reality. Libraries supporting research or study in psychology will want this good general resource.

5808. ***Personality and Social Psychology Bulletin.*** Formerly: *American Psychological Association. Division of Personality and Social Psychology. Proceedings.* [ISSN: 0146-1672] 1975. m. USD 1009 print & online eds. Ed(s): Frederick Rhodewalt. Sage Publications, Inc., 2455 Teller Rd, Thousand Oaks, CA 91320; info@sagepub.com; http://www.sagepub.com. Illus., adv. Circ: 4200. Microform: PQC. Online: Florida Center for Library Automation; Gale Group; ingenta.com; OCLC Online Computer Library Center, Inc.; ProQuest Information & Learning; RoweCom Information Quest; Swets Blackwell. Reprint: PQC. *Indexed:* ASSIA, AgeL, CIJE, CommAb, IBZ, IMFL, PSA, PsycholAb, SFSA, SSCI, SSI, SUSA, SWA, SociolAb. *Aud.:* Ac, Sa.

This official journal of the Society for Personality and Social Psychology publishes empirical, theoretical, and review articles, with all areas of personality and social psychology included. Recent issues, averaging ten articles, offer material on the role of conflict over emotional expression for subjective and interpersonal functioning; mood as information in making attributions to discrimination; tactical differences in coping with rejection sensitivity; counterfactual thinking and self-motives; whether racial category labels and lay beliefs about human traits have a combined effect on people's perception of, and memory for, racially ambiguous faces; sex differences in judgments of physical attractiveness; narcissism, social rejection, and aggression; the excluded player in coalition formation; how both degree of identification and the individual's position within the group influence aspects of group loyalty; the relationship between a ruminative-responses style and the reluctance to initiate instrumental behavior; the role of television viewing in eliciting subjective self-awareness and positive self-feelings; and the vulnerability of values to attack (inoculation of values and value-relevant attitudes). Related titles are the *Journal of Experimental Social Psychology* and the *Journal of Social Psychology* (both above). Libraries that support research and instruction in social phenomena will want this resource.

5809. ***Political Psychology.*** [ISSN: 0162-895X] 1979. bi-m. USD 728 print & online eds. Ed(s): Eugene Borgida. Blackwell Publishing, Inc., Commerce Place, 350 Main St, Malden, MA 02148; subscrip@blackwellpub.com; http://www.blackwellpublishing.com. Illus., adv. Refereed. Microform: PQC. Online: EBSCO Publishing; ingenta.com; OCLC Online Computer Library Center, Inc.; RoweCom Information Quest. *Indexed:* ABS&EES, ASSIA, ArtHuCI, IBSS, IPSA, PRA, PSA, PsycholAb, RiskAb, SSCI, SociolAb. *Bk. rev.:* 0-3, 500 words. *Aud.:* Ac, Sa.

This journal's focus is the interrelationships between psychology and political processes. In this journal of the International Society of Political Psychology, case studies, theoretical work, and empirical research can be found. With an average of eight main articles, recent issues examine such topics as the impact of individual and interpersonal factors on perceived news media bias; the theory of authoritarianism; efficacy, employment, and disability; September 11 and the origins of strategic surprise; right-wing authoritarianism; party identification and attitudes toward feminism in student evaluations of the Clinton-Lewinsky story; citizens' ambivalence about abortion; and sources of civic orientation among American youth: trust, religious valuation, and attributions of responsibility. Because this journal draws from work pursued in many areas—such as philosophy, history, political science, psychology, anthropology, international relations, and economics—it could be useful for those in a variety of disciplines.

5810. ***Professional Psychology: Research and Practice.*** Formerly (until 1982): *Professional Psychology.* [ISSN: 0735-7028] 1969. bi-m. USD 249 (Members, USD 49; Non-members, USD 99). Ed(s): Dr. Mary Beth Kenkel. American Psychological Association, 750 First St, NE, Washington, DC 20002-4242; journals@apa.org; http://www.apa.org/. Illus., index, adv. Refereed. Circ: 7800. Vol. ends: Jan. Microform: PQC. Online: EBSCO Publishing; Gale Group; OCLC Online Computer Library Center, Inc.; Ovid Technologies, Inc.; ProQuest Information & Learning; ScienceDirect. Reprint: PQC; PSC. *Indexed:* AgeL, CJA, PsycholAb, RI-1, SFSA, SSCI, SSI. *Aud.:* Ac, Sa.

This APA publication publishes articles on the applications of psychology. Data-based, theoretical, and review articles can be found, and contributions with assessment, treatment, or practice implications are encouraged. Articles also address the scientific foundations of professional psychology. In addition to work focusing on specific applications, articles include public-policy papers; presentations on current developments in defined areas of psychology (e.g., psychology of women, clinical neuropsychology, forensic psychology, and health psychology); standards; and information about graduate and continuing education. With an average of ten articles plus four brief reports, recent issues examine such topics as considerations in addressing cultural differences in psychotherapy; basic and advanced competence in collaborating with clergy; the role of psychologists in psychiatric settings over the past century; managed mental health care (a client's perspective); clinical web pages; the impact of September 11 on psychologists; psychologists reflect on their sexual relationships with clients, supervisees, and students (occurrence, impact, rationales, and collegial intervention); changes in counseling-center client problems across 13 years; the prevalence of depressive symptoms and clinical depression in ethnic minorities (and if current health service utilization is congruent with needs and the effectiveness of treatments); the impact of sign language interpreter and therapist moods on deaf recipient mood; and 15 effective play-therapy techniques. Tables of contents and abstracts of articles in recent issues are available online. All libraries supporting programs aimed at training for applied or clinical work in psychology should have this title. Professional psychologists will also want access, as might libraries that support other human-services fields. A related title is the *Journal of Applied Psychology* (above).

5811. *Psychological Assessment.* [ISSN: 1040-3590] 1989. q. USD 237 (Members, USD 49; Non-members, USD 99). Ed(s): Stephen N Haynes. American Psychological Association, 750 First St, NE, Washington, DC 20002-4242; journals@apa.org; http://www.apa.org/. Illus., adv. Refereed. Circ: 5700. Vol. ends: Feb. Reprint: PSC. *Indexed:* AgeL, CIJE, ErgAb, ExcerpMed, IndMed, PsycholAb, SSCI, SSI. *Aud.:* Ac, Sa.

The focus here is clinical psychological assessment and evaluation. Presentations on the development, validation, or evaluation of assessment techniques will be found, and empirical research is stressed. The types of responses/behaviors assessed can vary (e.g., cognitive or motor responses), as can the approach used (e.g., inventories, interviews, direct observation, physiological measurement, and CAI). Recent issues, averaging 11 main articles and two briefer reports, examine the validity of the Impact of Events Scale (IES) and the Posttraumatic Stress Disorder (PTSD) Symptom Scale, Self-Report version (PSS-SR); the construct validity of the Eating Disorder Inventory; the clinical validity of the Chinese Personality Assessment Inventory; the applicability of traditional and revised models of psychopathy to the Psychopathy Checklist; the development of a revised version of the Obsessive-Compulsive Inventory; construct validity of a measure of acculturative stress in African Americans; psychopathy screening of incarcerated juveniles; and measuring stress resilience and coping in vulnerable youth. Also, a recent special section looks at cognitive science and psychological assessment. Internet access to recent contents listings and article abstracts is available. Libraries supporting service, research, or study related to assessment of psychological functioning should have this title. An important related title is *Journal of Applied Behavior Analysis* (above).

5812. *Psychological Bulletin.* [ISSN: 0033-2909] 1904. bi-m. USD 398 (Members, USD 81; Non-members, USD 164). Ed(s): Harris M Cooper. American Psychological Association, 750 First St, NE, Washington, DC 20002-4242; journals@apa.org; http://www.apa.org/. Illus., index, adv. Refereed. Circ: 5800. Vol. ends: Dec. Microform: PMC; PQC. Online: EBSCO Publishing; Gale Group; OCLC Online Computer Library Center, Inc.; Ovid Technologies, Inc.; ProQuest Information & Learning; ScienceDirect. Reprint: PQC; PSC. *Indexed:* ABIn, ASSIA, AgeL, ArtHuCI, BiolAb, CIJE, CJA, ErgAb, IBSS, IBZ, IndMed, MLA-IB, PsycholAb, SCI, SSCI, SSI, SWA, SWR&A. *Aud.:* Ac, Sa.

This publication reviews substantive developments in scientific psychology. Reviews are evaluative and integrative, and readers can find articles that summarize and present developments within a particular research area in psychology or that present a "bridge between related specialized fields within psychology or between psychology and related fields." Articles dealing with contemporary social issues are also welcome. Methodological articles should be submitted to the journal *Psychological Methods,* and original theoretical articles should be submitted to *Psychological Review* (both below). Recent issues, averaging seven main articles, include such topics as a meta-analysis of sex differences in smiling; a review and critique of category systems for classifying ways of coping; sensitivity and attachment interventions in early childhood; the association between socioeconomic status and physical health (the role of negative emotions); logic and human reasoning: an assessment of the deduction paradigm; acute stress disorder: a synthesis and critique; the effects of praise on children's intrinsic motivation; and genetic and environmental influences on antisocial behavior. Access to recent contents listings and article abstracts is available on the web. All libraries providing service to programs in psychology should have this title.

5813. *Psychological Inquiry: an international journal of peer commentary and review.* [ISSN: 1047-840X] 1990. q. USD 490. Ed(s): Ralph Erber, Leonard L Martin. Lawrence Erlbaum Associates, Inc., 10 Industrial Ave, Mahwah, NJ 07430-2262; journals@erlbaum.com; http://www.erlbaum.com/. Illus., adv. Refereed. Vol. ends: No. 4. Reprint: PSC. *Indexed:* PsycholAb, SSCI, SociolAb. *Aud.:* Ac, Sa.

This journal seeks to provide theoretical and issue-oriented articles in the areas of personality, social, developmental, health, and clinical psychology. Each issue of this international forum provides a seminar-like exposure to a given topic, with lead articles of about 20 pages, about ten short "Commentary" responses, and a closing response by the original author. Target articles are usually not empirical or applied. This format corresponds to that of *Behavioral and Brain Sciences* (above), and both of these high-quality titles present themselves as international journals of peer commentary. Recent issues look at such topics as hope, religion, and psychology; evolutionary psychology; and affective influences on interpersonal behavior. This title should be in all libraries that support studies in psychology, especially where it is felt that readers can benefit from monitoring in-depth coverage of single topics.

5814. *Psychological Medicine.* [ISSN: 0033-2917] 1970. 8x/yr. USD 528 (Individuals, USD 242). Ed(s): Eugene Paykel, Kenneth Kendler. Cambridge University Press, The Edinburgh Bldg, Shaftesbury Rd, Cambridge, CB2 2RU, United Kingdom; information@cambridge.org; http://uk.cambridge.org/journals. Illus., adv. Refereed. Vol. ends: Nov. CD-ROM: Ovid Technologies, Inc. Microform: PQC. Online: EBSCO Publishing; OCLC Online Computer Library Center, Inc.; Ovid Technologies, Inc.; RoweCom Information Quest; Swets Blackwell. Reprint: SWZ. *Indexed:* ASSIA, AgeL, ArtHuCI, CINAHL, CJA, ChemAb, DSA, ExcerpMed, H&SSA, IBZ, IMFL, IndMed, PsycholAb, RRTA, SCI, SSCI. *Bk. rev.:* 0-2, 500. *Aud.:* Ac, Sa.

This journal continues to provide original research in clinical psychiatry or in the basic sciences related to clinical psychiatry. Empirical, theoretical, and research review papers are all included. Professionals in biological fields of study typically associated with medicine and those in psychological and social sciences whose work relates to medicine will find this title useful. Recent issues include such topics as general practitioners' attitudes to patients who have learning disabilities; increased serum albumin, gamma globulin, immunoglobulin IgG, and IgG2 and IgG4 in autism; the episode length in bipolar depression and the relationship between antidepressant therapy and episode length; spouse similarity for antisocial behavior in the general population; searching for a Gulf War Syndrome using cluster analysis; remembering or knowing: electrophysiological evidence for an episodic memory deficit in schizophrenia; prenatal life and post-natal psychopathology: evidence for negative gene–birth weight interaction; and personality disorders and depression. Access to recent tables of contents and article abstracts are available online. Libraries supporting research or higher-level studies related to psychology and medicine will want this title.

5815. *Psychological Methods.* [ISSN: 1082-989X] 1996. q. USD 171 (Members, USD 36; Non-members, USD 65). Ed(s): Dr. Stephen G West. American Psychological Association, 750 First St, NE, Washington, DC 20002-4242; journals@apa.org; http://www.apa.org/. Illus., index, adv. Refereed. Circ: 5100. Vol. ends: Feb. Online: EBSCO Publishing; OCLC Online Computer Library Center, Inc.; Ovid Technologies, Inc.; ProQuest Information & Learning; ScienceDirect. Reprint: PSC. *Indexed:* ErgAb, IndMed, SSCI. *Aud.:* Ac.

This journal supports the development and dissemination of methods for collecting, analyzing, understanding, and interpreting psychological data. Articles are theoretical, quantitative, empirical, or methodological. Additionally, reviews of important methodological issues, tutorials, articles illustrating innovative applications of new procedures to psychological problems, articles on the teaching of quantitative methods, and reviews of statistical software are also included. If broad enough, empirical and theoretical articles on specific tests or test construction may be found; they may also be more appropriate for *Psychological Assessment* (above). Recent issues, averaging six articles, cover such topics as mediation in experimental and nonexperimental studies; when fit indices and residuals are incompatible; the Path Analysis controversy: a new statistical approach to strong appraisal of verisimilitude; confidence intervals, hypothesis testing, and sample size requirements; the role of qualitative research in psychological journals; field experiments in the social sciences; and three-way component analysis. Recent tables of contents and article abstracts are available on the Internet. Libraries concerned with research in psychology should have this title.

5816. ***Psychological Reports.*** [ISSN: 0033-2941] 1955. bi-m. 2 vols./yr. USD 370. Ed(s): Bruce Ammons, Douglas Ammons. Dr. C.H. Ammons, Ed. & Pub., PO Box 9229, Missoula, MT 59807. Illus. Sample. Refereed. Circ: 1800. *Indexed:* ABS&EES, AgeL, ArtHuCI, BiolAb, CINAHL, CJA, CommAb, ErgAb, ExcerpMed, HEA, IBZ, IMFL, IndMed, LRI, PsycholAb, RI-1, SCI, SFSA, SSCI, SSI, SWA. *Bk. rev.:* 3, 50-250 words. *Aud.:* Ac, Sa.

This publication has served general psychology for more than 40 years and continues to provide approximately 70 articles per issue covering a wide variety of topics. Experimental, theoretical, and speculative work can be found. Recent issues examine essentialist thinking about depression: evidence for polarized beliefs; sibling effects, environment influences, and school dropout; castration anxiety and phobias; correlations of sense of humor and sleep disturbance ascribed to worry; comparison of two exercise programs on general well-being of college students; cult suicide and physician-assisted suicide; responses to lost letters about a 2000 general-election amendment to abolish prohibition of interracial marriages in Alabama; meta-analysis of relations of stress propensity with subjective stress and strain; what proportion of heterosexuals is ex-homosexual; intrinsic religiosity and aggression in a sample of intercollegiate athletes; and individual personality characteristics related to suggestibility. All libraries supporting programs in psychology should have this title.

5817. ***Psychological Review.*** [ISSN: 0033-295X] 1894. q. USD 308 (Members, USD 60; Non-members, USD 138). Ed(s): Keith Rayner. American Psychological Association, 750 First St, NE, Washington, DC 20002-4242; journals@apa.org; http://www.apa.org/. Illus., index, adv. Refereed. Circ: 5100. Vol. ends: Dec. Microform: PMC; PQC. Online: EBSCO Publishing; Gale Group; OCLC Online Computer Library Center, Inc.; Ovid Technologies, Inc.; ProQuest Information & Learning; ScienceDirect. Reprint: PSC. *Indexed:* AgeL, BiolAb, CIJE, ErgAb, IBSS, IBZ, IndMed, MLA-IB, PsycholAb, RiskAb, SCI, SSCI, SSI, SWA, SWR&A, SociolAb. *Aud.:* Ac, Sa.

Presentations of "important theoretical contributions to any area of scientific psychology" are the submissions sought by this publication of the American Psychological Association. Emphasis is on work that advances theory, but other work critiquing theory or exhibiting the relative superiority of one over another theoretical explanatory approach can also be appropriate. Literature reviews, presentations of methodology or design problems, and empirical research reports are less likely to be accepted. With an average of seven offerings in the main-article section and three in the "Theoretical Notes" section, recent issues look at such topics as symbolic-connectionist theory of relational inference and generalization; how power influences behavior; theoretical status of latent variables; core affect and the psychological construction of emotion; a discussion of the elusive nature of the concept of randomness; and a probabilistic and context-sensitive model of choice behavior. All academic libraries supporting study in psychology should have this long-standing, basic resource for psychology.

5818. ***Psychological Science.*** [ISSN: 0956-7976] 1990. m. USD 1384 print & online eds. Ed(s): James E Cutting. Blackwell Publishing Ltd., 9600 Garsington Rd, PO Box 805, Oxford, OX4 2DQ, United Kingdom; customerservices@oxon.blackwellpublishing.com; http://www.blackwellpublishing.com/. Illus., adv. Sample. Refereed. Online: East View Publications, Inc.; EBSCO Publishing; Gale Group; ingenta.com; OCLC Online Computer Library Center, Inc.; RoweCom Information Quest. *Indexed:* AgeL, ArtHuCI, ErgAb, HEA, IndMed, L&LBA, PRA, PsycholAb, SSCI, SSI, SWR&A, SociolAb. *Aud.:* Ac, Sa.

This journal of the American Psychological Society is offered as a resource covering psychological research, theory, or application from all fields of psychology. Preference is for articles having general theoretical significance or broad interest across specialties in psychology and related fields. Formats include general articles on problems, issues, and developments, broadly significant research articles, and briefer research reports. Recent articles look at why illusory causation occurs; children's use of landmark; a quasi-signal detection analysis of daily interactions between close relationship partners; the role of effort in perceiving distance; fitness effects on the cognitive function of older adults (a meta-analytic study); models of consistency; and the effects of fear and anger on perceived risks of terrorism. Furthermore, an important supplement to *Psychological Science, Psychological Science in the Public Interest* is a journal published three times annually that explores important topics of public interest in areas where psychological science may have the potential to inform and improve public policy. Topics covered in the supplement have included class size and student achievement; the scientific status of projective techniques; and a look at psychological science improving diagnostic decisions. Internet access to recent tables of contents and abstracts are available for *Psychological Science*. Libraries supporting programs in psychology should have this title. This readable scientific journal can also benefit all academic libraries.

5819. ***Psychology & Health: an international journal.*** [ISSN: 0887-0446] 1987. bi-m. GBP 583 (Individuals, GBP 87). Ed(s): Paul Norman. Brunner - Routledge (UK), 11 New Fetter Ln, London, EC4P 4EE, United Kingdom; www.tandf.co.uk/journals. Illus., adv. Sample. Refereed. Vol. ends: No. 6. Online: EBSCO Publishing; OCLC Online Computer Library Center, Inc. Reprint: PSC. *Indexed:* AgeL, CINAHL, PsycholAb, SSCI, SWA. *Bk. rev.:* 0-3, 300. *Aud.:* Ac, Sa.

The aim of this journal is to promote "the study and application of psychological approaches to health and illness." General areas of coverage include "psychological aspects of physical illness, treatment processes and recovery: psychosocial factors in the etiology of physical illnesses; health attitudes and behavior, including prevention; the individual-health care system interface, particularly communication and psychologically based interventions." Readers will find original research (including experimental studies), reviews, and short reports. Theoretical work and "new psychological approaches and interventions in health-related fields" can also be included. Recent issues cover such topics as components of hostility and verbal communication of emotion; relaxation training in children; expectations influencing recovery from oral surgery; a disposition toward seeing the world as comprehensible, manageable, and meaningful linked to greater stress resistance and better health; cognitive and social contextual approaches to understanding the practice of safer sex; alexithymia and cardiovascular risk in older adults: psychosocial, psychophysiological, and biomedical correlates; the optimistic bias: a meta-analytic review; adaptive tasks in multiple sclerosis; and task and scheduling self-efficacy as predictors of exercise behavior. Libraries with sections on behavioral medicine should consider this title. Related journals include *Health Psychology* and *Journal of Pediatric Psychology* (both above), and *Psychosomatic Medicine* (below).

5820. ***Psychology of Women Quarterly.*** [ISSN: 0361-6843] 1976. q. USD 243 print & online eds. Ed(s): Jacquelyn White. Blackwell Publishing, Inc., Commerce Place, 350 Main St, Malden, MA 02148; subscrip@blackwellpub.com; http://www.blackwellpublishing.com. Illus., index, adv. Refereed. Vol. ends: Dec. Microform: PQC. Online: EBSCO Publishing; Gale Group; ingenta.com; Ovid Technologies, Inc.; RoweCom Information Quest; Swets Blackwell. Reprint: SWZ. *Indexed:* ABS&EES, ASSIA, AbAn, AgeL, CIJE, CJA, FemPer, H&SSA, HEA, HRA, IBSS, IMFL, PsycholAb, RiskAb, SFSA, SSCI, SSI, SUSA, SWA, SWR&A, SociolAb, WSA, WSI. *Bk. rev.:* 4-10, 500-1,000 words. *Aud.:* Ga, Ac, Sa.

This journal provides "empirical research, critical reviews, theoretical articles, brief reports and invited book reviews related to the psychology of women and gender." Topics include sex-related comparisons, psychobiological factors, sexuality, social and cognitive processes, life-span role development and change, career activities, harassment and violence issues, psychological distress and well-being, and therapeutic processes. With an average of seven articles, recent issues examine the effects of group consciousness on African American women's attributions to prejudice; perceptions of sexual intent: the impact of condom possession (gender differences); the relationship between gender, hostile sexism, benevolent sexism, and reactions to a seemingly innocuous genre of sexist humor; the ways in which African American women use religion/spirituality to cope and to construct meaning in times of adversity; anger after childbirth: an overlooked reaction to postpartum stressor; factorial and construct validity of the Body Parts Satisfaction Scale–Revised: an examination of minority and nonminority women; what women should be, shouldn't be, are allowed to be, and don't have to be (contents of prescriptive gender stereotypes); the subculture of street-level sex work (including the social environment, drug use and abuse, and violence); trait judgments of stay-at-home and employed parents (social role and/or shifting standards); and sex differences and the self: classic themes, feminist variations, and postmodern challenges. Internet access to recent tables of contents and article abstracts is available. Libraries supporting programs in psychology and women's studies programs should consider this title.

5821. *Psychology, Public Policy, and Law.* [ISSN: 1076-8971] 1995. q. USD 158 (Members, USD 33; Non-members, USD 66). Ed(s): Dr. Jane Goodman-Delahunty. American Psychological Association, 750 First St, NE, Washington, DC 20002-4242; journals@apa.org; http://www.apa.org/. Illus., adv. Sample. Refereed. Circ: 2300. Vol. ends: Dec. Reprint: PSC. *Indexed:* CJA, SSCI. *Aud.:* Ga, Ac, Sa.

This journal focuses on the "links between psychology as a science and public policy and law." Its articles are meant to critically evaluate the contributions and potential contributions of psychology to public policy and legal issues, and to assess the desirability of different public policy and legal alternatives in light of the scientific knowledge base in psychology. They are also meant to articulate research needs that address public policy and legal issues for which there is currently insufficient theoretical and empirical knowledge, or to publish the results of large-scale empirical work that addresses such concerns, and to examine public policy and legal issues relating to the conduct of psychology and related disciplines. Recent issues include such topics as the personality paradox in offender profiling: a theoretical review of the processes involved in deriving background characteristics from crime scene actions; compelled mental health examinations, liability decisions, and damage awards in sexual harrassment cases; making law modern (a contextual model of justice); actuarial versus clinical assessments of dangerousness; an investigation of prejudice against black defendants in the American courtroom; and jury decision making: 45 years of empirical research on deliberating groups. Access to tables of contents and abstracts is available at the publisher's web site. Libraries will want this title if they serve scholars or professionals in the fields of law, psychology, or public policy. A related title is *Law and Human Behavior* (above).

5822. *Psychology Today.* [ISSN: 0033-3107] 1967. bi-m. USD 18 domestic; USD 26 Canada; USD 30 elsewhere. Ed(s): Kaja Perina. Sussex Publishers Inc., 49 E 21st St, 11th Fl, New York, NY 10010. Illus., index, adv. Circ: 350000. CD-ROM: ProQuest Information & Learning. Microform: NBI. Online: bigchalk; The Dialog Corporation; EBSCO Publishing; Florida Center for Library Automation; Gale Group; Northern Light Technology, Inc.; OCLC Online Computer Library Center, Inc.; ProQuest Information & Learning; H.W. Wilson. *Indexed:* ABIn, AgeL, BRD, BRI, BiolDig, CBCARef, CBRI, CJA, CPerI, ECER, ExcerpMed, FLI, FutSurv, LRI, MagInd, MusicInd, PRA, RGPR, RI-1, SSCI, SSI, SportS. *Aud.:* Hs, Ga, Ac.

This title continues to provide a widely appreciated forum for popular psychology, providing brief articles that are readable and interesting. It has regular sections covering relationships, the brain, work, health, nutrition, parenting, and education. Recent issues cover Susan Sarandon and activisim, the emptiness/depression of successful CEOs, telepathy, and sex surrogates. Other short sections offer culture and media reviews, "Q & A with Our Therapist," and looks at historic moments in psychology. Most public libraries will want this title, and academic libraries may, too.

5823. *Psychometrika: a journal devoted to the development of psychology as a quantitative rational science.* [ISSN: 0033-3123] 1936. q. USD 100. Ed(s): Ulf Bockenholt. Psychometric Society, c/o Ontario Institute for Studies in Education, 252 Bloor St W, Toronto, ON M5S 1V6, Canada; http://www.psychometrika.org. Illus., index, adv. Refereed. Circ: 2200. Vol. ends: Dec. Microform: PQC. Reprint: PQC. *Indexed:* BiolAb, CCMJ, CIJE, CommAb, ErgAb, IBZ, MathSciNet, PsycholAb, SSCI, ST&MA. *Bk. rev.:* 2-3, 350-1,200 words. *Aud.:* Ac, Sa.

Psychometrika covers development of quantitative models of psychological phenomena, quantitative methodology in the behavioral sciences, and the use of such methodology. Articles can be empirical only if "they involve new or particularly interesting use of quantitative techniques." Averaging ten articles each, recent issues present such topics as hypergeometric family and item overlap rates in computerized adaptive testing; an MCMC-method for models with continuous latent responses; transforming three-way arrays to maximal simplicity; tests of homogeneity of means and covariance matrices for multivariate incomplete data; psychometrics (from practice to theory and back): 15 years of nonparametric multidimensional IRT, DIF/test equity, and skills diagnostic assessment; nonparametric goodness-of-fit tests for the Rasch model; pairwise comparisons of trimmed means for two or more groups; and what we can learn from the path equations: identifiability, constraints, equivalence. Internet access to recent content listings is available. Libraries supporting advanced use of mathematics for psychological theory and research will want this title. A related title is the *Journal of Mathematical Psychology* (above).

5824. *Psychonomic Bulletin & Review.* Formerly (until 1994): *Psychonomic Society. Bulletin.* [ISSN: 1069-9384] 1973. bi-m. USD 164 (Individuals, USD 70). Ed(s): David A Balota. Psychonomic Society, Inc., 1710 Fortview Rd, Austin, TX 78704; jbellquist@psychonomic.org; http://www.psychonomic.org. Illus., index, adv. Refereed. Circ: 2200. Vol. ends: Dec. Microform: PQC; NRP. Online: Ingenta Select; Swets Blackwell. Reprint: PQC. *Indexed:* AgeL, BiolAb, ErgAb, HEA, IBZ, IMFL, IndMed, L&LBA, MLA-IB, PsycholAb, SSCI. *Aud.:* Ac.

This journal of the Psychonomic Society provides broad coverage of topics in all areas of experimental psychology. Although the journal is primarily dedicated to publication of theory and review articles, brief reports of experimental work may be found. General areas of coverage include animal learning and behavior, sensation and perception, cognitive psychology and development, psycholinguistics, memory, psychobiology and cognitive neuroscience, educational psychology, and social cognition. Averaging about 14–20 articles, recent issues examine such topics as when wrong predictions provide more support than right ones; the role of perceptual object representations in the control of eye movements and attention; volatile visual representations: failing to detect changes in recently processed information; rats learning the spatial pattern in which hidden caches of food are located; using false photographs to create false childhood memories; comparing techniques for estimating automatic retrieval: effects of retention interval; consolidation theory and retrograde amnesia in humans; and the influence of the lexicon on speech read word recognition. Internet access is available for tables of contents of current and forthcoming issues. This title should be available for undergraduate and graduate students and researchers in psychology.

5825. *Psychophysiology: an international journal.* Formerly: *Psychophysiology Newsletter.* [ISSN: 0048-5772] 1964. 7x/yr. GBP 334 print & online eds. Blackwell Publishing, Inc., Commerce Place, 350 Main St, Malden, MA 02148; subscrip@blackwellpub.com; http://www.blackwellpublishing.com. Illus., index, adv. Refereed. Circ: 2100. Vol. ends: Nov. Microform: PQC. Online: EBSCO Publishing; ingenta.com; OCLC Online Computer Library Center, Inc.; RoweCom Information Quest; Swets Blackwell. Reprint: PQC. *Indexed:* AgeL, BiolAb, ErgAb, ExcerpMed, IBZ, IndMed, L&LBA, PsycholAb, SCI, SSCI. *Bk. rev.:* Number and length vary. *Aud.:* Ac, Sa.

This journal of the Society for Psychophysiological Research supports advances in psychophysiological research. Intended to examine and explore the relation between physiological and psychological aspects of brain and behavior, articles can be theoretical, evaluative reviews of literature or empirical or methodological. Sections include a "Special Reports/Fast Track" section (featuring brief, current papers of special interest), book reviews, meeting announcements, and fellowship opportunities. Averaging 12 articles each, recent issues include looks at electrophysiological insights into language processing in schizophrenia; affective modulation of eyeblink startle with reward and threat; stability of children's and adolescents' hemodynamic responses to psychological challenge: a three-year longitudinal study of a multiethnic cohort of boys and girls; competitiveness and hemodynamic reactions to competition; stress and selective attention: the interplay of mood, cortisol levels, and emotional information; the heritability of error rate on the antisaccade task among female twin youths; and the influence of control and physical effort on cardiovascular reactivity to a video game task. Internet access to recent tables of contents, abstracts, and full-text options are available at the publisher's web site. Researchers or advanced students in psychology, psychiatry, or related fields will appreciate access to this title if they are pursuing studies of physiological activity related to psychological factors.

5826. ***Psychosomatic Medicine.*** [ISSN: 0033-3174] 1938. bi-m. USD 544 (Individuals, USD 276; USD 99 per issue). Ed(s): Dr. David S. Sheps. Lippincott Williams & Wilkins, 351 W Camden St, Baltimore, MD 21201; http://www.lww.com. Illus., adv. Refereed. Circ: 2245. Vol. ends: Dec. CD-ROM: Ovid Technologies, Inc. Microform: Pub.; RPI. Online: HighWire Press; Ovid Technologies, Inc. Reprint: PSC. *Indexed:* AgeL, BiolAb, ChemAb, ExcerpMed, H&SSA, IndMed, PsycholAb, RiskAb, SCI, SSCI. *Bk. rev.:* 4, 900-1,500 words. *Aud.:* Ac, Sa.

This title, as the American Psychosomatic Society's official journal, publishes articles that promote understanding of the relation between biological, psychological, social, and behavioral factors and human health and disease. Recent topics include the association between alexithymia in adulthood and social situation of the child's family at the time of the child's birth; a test of an interpersonal model of hypochondriasis; the relationship of stress and coping skills; the potential mediating role of presleep arousal to sleep patterns in good sleepers and insomnia sufferers; the association between the menses and suicide attempts; whether depressive symptoms increase the risk for the onset of coronary disease; cytokines in depression and heart failure; single-photon emission computerized tomography and neurocognitive function in patients with chronic fatigue syndrome; the effects of anger expression on incidence of cardiovascular disease; psychosocial treatments for multiple unexplained physical symptoms; and the changing face of pain: evolution of pain research in psychosomatic medicine. Prior to the society's annual convention, this title includes abstracts of presentations to be given at the convention. Tables of contents, article abstracts, and a subject/author index to recent volumes are available on the society's web site. Libraries supporting study and research or clinical service in behavioral medicine should have this title, along with *Psychological Medicine* and *Psychology and Health* (both above).

Psychotherapy Networker. See Family and Marriage section.

5827. ***Rehabilitation Psychology.*** Formerly (until 1971): *Psychological Aspects of Disability.* [ISSN: 0090-5550] 1954. q. USD 140 (Members, USD 35; Non-members, USD 48). Ed(s): Bruce M Caplan. American Psychological Association, 750 First St, NE, Washington, DC 20002-4242; journals@apa.org; http://www.apa.org/. Illus., adv. Refereed. Circ: 1700 Paid. Vol. ends: Jan. Reprint: PSC. *Indexed:* AgeL, CINAHL, ExcerpMed, IMFL, PsycholAb, SSCI. *Bk. rev.:* 0-3, 400-600 words. *Aud.:* Ac, Sa.

As the official journal of the American Psychological Association's Division of Rehabilitation Psychology, this publication aims to promote the understanding of important psychological problems in rehabilitation and the capacity to offer effective assistance in ameliorating those problems. As noted in the journal's description, rehabilitation psychologists "consider the entire network of biological, psychological, social, environmental, and political factors that affect the functioning of persons with disabilities or chronic illness." Articles found in this publication can be "experimental investigations, survey research, evaluations of specific interventions, outcome studies, historical perspectives, relevant public policy issues, conceptual/theoretical formulations with implications for clinical practice, reviews of empirical research, detailed case studies, and professional issues." With an average of five articles each, recent issues include such topics as making decisions about the design and conduct of stress and coping research; psychological distress in workers with traumatic upper- or lower-limb amputations following industrial injuries; how purpose in life influences adjustment after spinal cord injury; activity limitation and depression: perspectives of older African American women and their close companions; cognitive screening in geriatric rehabilitation; consumer participation in disability research: the golden rule as a guide for ethical practice; the relationship of ambivalent coping to depression symptoms and adjustment; benefits of assistance dogs; gender differences in nutritional risk for rural adults with disability; a critical review of studies on the impact of telecommunication-based interventions for persons with chronic disabilities; and the relationship of coping style and illness uncertainty to psychological distress in individuals with Parkinson's disease and their primary caregivers. Tables of contents for recent issues are available on the web; abstracts for most the recent issue are online. Professionals from a variety of clinical and academic settings contribute to research in rehabilitation or are involved in rehabilitation services (e.g., sociology, medicine, public policy); and libraries supporting work in all these settings can benefit those they serve with access to this title.

5828. ***School Psychology Quarterly.*** Formerly: *Professional School Psychology.* [ISSN: 1045-3830] 1960. q. USD 215 (Individuals, USD 60). Ed(s): Rik Carl D'Amato. Guilford Publications, Inc., 72 Spring St, 4th Fl, New York, NY 10012; info@guilford.com; http://www.guilford.com. Illus., adv. Refereed. Circ: 2700. Vol. ends: Winter. Reprint: PQC. *Indexed:* CIJE, L&LBA, PsycholAb, SSCI. *Bk. rev.:* 0-1, 600 words. *Aud.:* Ac, Sa.

As the official journal of APA's Division of School Psychology, this journal promotes the scientific understanding of research, theory, and practice as related to school psychology. With an average of eight articles each, recent issues examine a qualitative study of the beliefs and practices of school psychologists and teachers; the relationships among perceived social support and academic, behavioral, and social indicators (for 1,711 students in grades 3 through 12); treatment of selective mutism: a best-evidence synthesis; school-based psychosocial interventions for childhood depression: acceptability of treatments among school psychologists; the influence of attachment on school completion; the scientific evidence on the effectiveness of early childhood educational programs; and a Delphi study designed to identify essential cross-cultural competencies for school psychologists. One recent special issue also covers evidence-based interventions in school psychology. Libraries serving programs in school psychology will want to provide this title, along with the *Journal of School Psychology* (above) and *School Psychology Review* (below).

5829. ***School Psychology Review.*** Formerly (until 1979): *School Psychology Digest.* [ISSN: 0279-6015] 1972. q. USD 80 (Individuals, USD 50). Ed(s): Susan M Sheridan. National Association of School Psychologists, 4340 East West Hwy, Ste 402, Bethesda, MD 20814-4411; nasp8455@aol.com; http://www.nasponline.org/publications/sprindex.html. Illus., adv. Refereed. Circ: 19000 Paid. Vol. ends: No. 4. Microform: PQC. Online: EBSCO Publishing; Florida Center for Library Automation; Gale Group; Northern Light Technology, Inc.; OCLC Online Computer Library Center, Inc.; ProQuest Information & Learning; H.W. Wilson. Reprint: PQC. *Indexed:* CIJE, EduInd, PsycholAb, SSCI. *Aud.:* Ac, Sa.

This title continues to serve as key forum for school psychology. As the official journal of the National Association of School Psychologists, it seeks to provide original research, reviews of theoretical and applied topics, case studies, and coverage of intervention techniques of interest to psychologists who work in educational settings. Averaging ten articles each, recent issues include such topics as a comparison of retention rates using traditional, drill sandwich, and incremental rehearsal flash card methods; the extent to which curriculum-based measurement survey-level mathematics assessment varies as a function of type of survey-level assessment used; an analysis of the Brief Assessment Model for academic problems; and classroom behaviors that enable academic learning. A special miniseries looks at issues in data-based decision making in special education. In addition, one recent special issue also looks at interventions for social-emotional needs of children, while another special issue looks at demographics and roles in school psychology. Internet access to tables of contents and summaries of recent articles are available on the web. Libraries supporting programs in school psychology should have this title, and they should also consider the *Journal of School Psychology* and *School Psychology Quarterly* (both above). Those pursuing research or study for service in educational settings will also benefit from access.

5830. ***Sexual Abuse: a journal of research and treatment.*** Formerly (until 1995): *Annals of Sex Research.* [ISSN: 1079-0632] 1988. q. EUR 350 print or online ed. Ed(s): Judith V. Becker. Kluwer Academic / Plenum Publishers, 233 Spring St Fl 7, New York, NY 10013-1522; http://www.wkap.nl/. Illus., adv. Refereed. Online: EBSCO Publishing; ingenta.com; Kluwer Online; OCLC Online Computer Library Center, Inc.; RoweCom Information Quest; Swets Blackwell. *Indexed:* CJA, IndMed, PsycholAb, SociolAb. *Aud.:* Ac, Sa.

Sexual Abuse is the official journal of the Association for the Treatment of Sexual Abusers. It specializes in publishing "the latest original research and scholarly reviews on both clinical and theoretical aspects of sexual abuse, thoroughly investigating its causes, consequences, and treatment strategies." Its target audience is "those working in both clinical and academic environments, including psychologists, psychiatrists, social workers, and therapists/counselors, as well as corrections officers and allied professionals in children's services." Recent issues look at such topics as predicting psychological distress in sex offender therapists; implications for treatment of sexual offenders of the Ward and Hudson model of relapse, the Colorado Sex Offender Risk Scale; young female sex offenders: assessment and treatment issues; perceptions of child sexual abuse: victim and perpetrator characteristics; treatment efficacy (and lay versus legal opinions of abuse); victim empathy, social self-esteem, and psychopathy in rapists; what makes sex offenders confess; the components of false memory defense used by convicted and self-confessed child molesters and their advocates to negate their criminal behavior; and the necessity of including siblings in the treatment of victims of child sexual abuse. Tables of contents and abstracts for recent issues are available on the publisher's web site, along with a sample issue and a keyword search of the journal.

5831. ***Teaching of Psychology.*** [ISSN: 0098-6283] 1974. q. USD 295. Ed(s): Randolph A Smith. Lawrence Erlbaum Associates, Inc., 10 Industrial Ave, Mahwah, NJ 07430-2262; journals@erlbaum.com; http://www.erlbaum.com/. Illus., adv. Sample. Refereed. Circ: 3200. Vol. ends: Dec. Microform: PQC. Online: EBSCO Publishing; Ingenta Select; OCLC Online Computer Library Center, Inc.; RoweCom Information Quest; Swets Blackwell. Reprint: PQC; PSC. *Indexed:* ABS&EES, AgeL, CIJE, EduInd, PsycholAb, SSCI. *Bk. rev.:* 0-3, 1,500 words. *Aud.:* Ac.

As the official journal of APA's Division on the Teaching of Psychology, this title serves all those who teach psychology, from secondary school to graduate study and continuing-education settings, with the goal of improving the teaching and learning of psychology. Material can include empirical research on teaching and learning, essays on teaching or innovative course descriptions, curriculum designs, bibliographic material, demonstrations and laboratory projects, and reviews. With an average of 12 articles each, recent issues look at implementing and evaluating a writing course for psychology majors; a web-based interactive tutorial used to present hypothesis-testing concepts; an argument for a laboratory in introductory psychology; a peer-advising course for undergraduate psychology majors; an exercise using small-group discussion and individual problem-based learning to teach critical thinking about the Internet; a case for teaching about loss as part of a psychology curriculum; and an active learning activity to allow students to experience stereotyping and consider the social stigma often directed toward gays and lesbians. Libraries supporting those who teach (or study to teach) psychology will want to provide access to this unique title.

Women & Therapy. See Women: Feminist and Special Interest/Feminist and Women's Studies section.

Electronic Journals

5832. ***The Behavior Analyst Today: a context for science with a commitment for change.*** [ISSN: 1539-4352] 1999. q. Ed(s): Joseph D. Cautilli. The Behavior Analyst Today, 401 S. Quince, Ste. 2R, Philadelphia, PA 19147. Adv. Refereed. *Aud.:* Ac, Sa.

Seeking to serve the scientific community, this publication emphasizes "functionalism and behavioral approaches to verbal behavior." Areas of focus include "clinical behavior analysis, behavior models of child development, community based behavioral analytic interventions, and behavioral philosophy." Readers can expect to find "original research, reviews of subdisciplines, theoretical and conceptual work, applied research, program descriptions, research in organizations and the community, clinical work, and curriculum developments." Issues contain 6–16 articles, available in pdf format, 115–120 pages long. A recent issue contains coverage of these topics: building constructive prison environments, the molar view of behavior and its usefulness in behavior analysis, the clinical significance of the outcome questionnaire, the role of reinforcement schedules in behavior pharmacology, traditional behavioral couple therapy and integrative behavioral couple therapy, sexual-conditioning studies, and inconspicuous sources of behavioral control. An online index to the volumes, listing contents of issues, has been available at the Internet site. Professionals and students in clinical work will find useful material here.

5833. ***Behavioral Parenting Abstracts.*** 2002. q. Ed(s): Timothy Vollmer. Cambridge Center for Behavioral Studies, 336 Baker Ave., Concord, MA 01742-2107; http://www.behavior.org. *Aud.:* Ga, Ac, Sa.

This newsletter is "primarily designed for behavior analysts and other professionals working with children and families." The goals are to cover "issues that involve parents and families in general, with an emphasis on behavioral approaches," and to assist researchers and practitioners in their efforts to monitor work in the field. Each issue covers a different topic, with abstracts of reviewed literature and an article (articles do not necessarily exactly mirror reviewed topics). Available as pdf's (20–26 pages), the first issue covered parent training, with an article on "Training Parents Reported for or at Risk of Child Abuse and Neglect to Identify and Treat Their Children's Illnesses." The second issue looked at home-based academic interventions. This looks like a good resource to consult for students and clinicians who work with children and families.

5834. ***Current Research in Social Psychology.*** [ISSN: 1088-7423] 1995. irreg. Free. Ed(s): Lisa Troyer. University of Iowa, Department of Sociology, Center for the Study of Group Processes, Iowa City, IA 52242-1401; http://www.uiowa.edu/~grpproc/crisp/crisp.html. Illus. Refereed. *Indexed:* SociolAb. *Aud.:* Ac.

This peer-reviewed journal covering all aspects of social psychology is indexed in "Sociological Abstracts." Readers will find, along with typical research reports, specialized technical pieces, descriptions of methodological improvements, and even reports of studies that failed to produce conclusive results. Another goal has been to publish brief reports of quick studies or narrow technical developments. Recent issues examine anxiety-induced response perseverance and stereotyping change; couple variability in marital aggrandizement: idealization and satisfaction within enduring relationships; the multifaceted nature of prejudice: psychophysiological responses to ingroup and outgroup ethnic stimuli; Machiavellianism, belief in a just world, and the tendency to worship celebrities; alternative factor models of the Expagg Scale: a re-evaluation using confirmatory factor analysis; and evaluation strategies, self esteem, and athletic performance. Researchers and students in social psychology should consider this among the scholarly sources they monitor and read.

5835. ***Dynamical Psychology: an international, interdisciplinary journal of complex mental processes.*** Formerly (until 1995): *PsychoScience.* 1993. irreg. Ed(s): Ben Goertzel. Dynamical Psychology, c/o InteliGenesis Corp, Ben Goertzel, New York, NY 10011; ben@goertzel.org; http://goertzel.org/dynapsyc/dynacon.html. Refereed. *Bk. rev.:* Various number and length. *Aud.:* Ac.

This journal provides a forum for examining "the patterns by which psychological processes unfold through time, and the emergent, persistent structures which arise as a consequence of this unfolding." It is a continuation of the paper journal *PsychoScience,* which existed from 1993 to 1995; the contents of the paper issues of *PsychoScience* are available online, too, along with the new *DynaPsych* material. Perspectives of contributors may vary, ranging from cognitive, behavioral, nonlinear-science, or physics-oriented to sociological, phenomenological, or transpersonal. Types of contributions include research articles presenting experimental data, computational experiments, mathematical analyses, or clearly formulated theoretical ideas; informal essays presenting more-personal, wide-ranging views on aspects of the mental process; survey articles presenting summaries of past contributions or synthesizing ideas and results from different paradigms; brief commentaries pertaining to the contents of research articles, essays, survey articles, or other commentaries; and book reviews. Recent topics include understanding the evolution of categorization: an interdisciplinary approach; motion control and consciousness; the dynamics of affective liquids; and fractal dynamics of the psyche. Those studying consciousness from any of a variety of perspectives may find that access to these offerings provides interesting reading.

5836. ***Evolutionary Psychology: an international journal of evolutionary approaches to psychology and behavior.*** [ISSN: 1474-7049] irreg. Ed(s): Ian Pitchford. Ian Pitchford, Ed.& Pub., Creighton University School of Medicine, Department of Psychiatry, Omaha, NE 68131. Refereed. *Bk. rev.:* Various number and length. *Aud.:* Ac, Sa.

The goal of this new publication is "to foster communication between experimental and theoretical work, on the one hand, and historical, conceptual, and interdisciplinary writings across the whole range of the biological and human sciences, on the other." One recent article looks at "The maternal dominance hypothesis: questioning Trivers and Willard." Book reviews are lengthy; one recent review looks at "Cycles of Contingency: Developmental Systems and Evolution." A recent guest editorial topic provides "Confessions of a Closet Sociobiologist: Personal Perspectives on the Darwinian Movement in Psychology." Contributions are available in both html and pdf formats. Another high-quality resource that may be good to monitor for students and researchers in related fields.

5837. ***German Journal of Psychiatry.*** [ISSN: 1433-1055] 1998. irreg. Ed(s): Borwin Bandelow. University of Goettingen, Department of Psychiatry, Von-Siebold-Str 5, Goettingen, 37075, Germany; bbandel@gwdg.de; http://www.gwdg.de/~bbandel. Refereed. *Aud.:* Ac, Sa.

This English-language professional journal is very easy to use and is very readable, with high-quality formatting. Recent issues include articles on striato-cerebellar abnormalities in never-treated schizophrenia: evidence for neurodevelopmental etiopathogenesis; the brain and chronic pain; aripiprazole, a "dopamine-serotonin system stabilizer" in the treatment of psychosis; camp approach: an effective, alternate in-patient treatment setting for substance dependence (a report from India); treatment of intravenous buprenorphine dependence: a randomized open clinical trial; personality assessment in morbid obesity; and quality assurance of the community placement of institutional residents. Articles have typically been displayed in pdf format. Should be considered as a journal to monitor by those in psychiatry, as well clinical psychology and psychiatric nursing.

5838. ***Gestalt!*** [ISSN: 1091-1766] 1997. irreg. Gestalt Global Corporation, http://www.g-g.org/gestalt-global/index.html. *Aud.:* Ac, Sa.

This journal provides "full-text articles, interviews, and information about Gestalt therapy, theory, practice, and practitioners." Recent issues include these topics: a commentary on Cartesian and post-Cartesian trends in relational psychoanalysis; contemporary challenges in the application of Perls's five-layer theory; straddling the boundary between Gestalt therapy and psychodrama; and love, admiration, or safety: a system of Gestalt diagnosis of borderline, narcissistic, and schizoid adaptations that focuses on what is figure for the client. One recent issue looks at the value of defining useful terms associated with the discipline of Gestalt therapy, including discussion of Gestalt constructs (from "Awareness" to "Structured Ground"). Useful for students, faculty, or professionals who are studying or involved with clinical work in psychology.

5839. ***The Human Nature Review.*** [ISSN: 1476-1084] irreg. Ed(s): Ian Pitchford, Robert M Young. Ian Pitchford, Ed.& Pub., Creighton University School of Medicine, Department of Psychiatry, Omaha, NE 68131. *Bk. rev.:* Various number and length. *Aud.:* Ga, Ac, Sa.

The possible subject areas for this interdisciplinary resource include anthropology, archeology, artificial intelligence, behaviour genetics, cognitive science, developmental psychology, economics, ethology, evolutionary biology, evolutionary psychology, genetics, law, linguistics, neuropsychology, neuroscience, paleoanthropology, philosophy, politics, primatology, psychiatry, psychology, psychotherapy, sociology, sociobiology (and debates about them); history, philosophy and social studies in the human sciences; Darwinian scholarship; hermeneutics; biography and autobiography; psychoanalytic and psychodynamic approaches, and more. Contributions to this Internet portal are added frequently; there is a "Daily News" section, in addition to an archives section and reviews of disciplines and issues. A significant role does seem to be book reviews, making this a source similar to *Contemporary Psychology* (above). Users can access material in html or pdf format. Dates of reviews are given, and contact information for reviewers is also provided. A very good option for those who wish to monitor interdisciplinary work on "human nature."

5840. ***International Bulletin of Political Psychology.*** [ISSN: 1094-6039] 1996. w. . Free. Ed(s): Richard W Bloom. Embry-Riddle Aeronautical University, Humanities and Social Science Department, 3200 Willow Creek Rd, Prescott, AZ 86301; http://coas.pr.erau.edu/index.html. *Aud.:* Ga, Ac, Sa.

This weekly publication's goal is to provide content that will "sensitize social scientists, public officials, mass media representatives, informed citizenry, and social activists to the psychology of politics and the politics of psychology." In addition to articles from the publisher (unsigned), reprints from other sources ("IBPP Research Associates") are periodically included, as well as other relevant announcements (e.g., books, conferences, and other events). Recent articles in the publication's "Trend" section look at such topics as the life and death of Saddam and Osama and where's the person in personality—the personality of politicians. One article in the "Article" section examines what's wrong with the Rorschach, while another special article looks at commentaries on a world at war: SARS, weapons of mass destruction, preemption, the United Nations, international respect and confidence, and truth. A keyword-in-title-or-full-text search engine is available for archives of 1,200 articles. Archived articles can be accessed in html or pdf format. An interesting source for monitoring issues in political psychology.

5841. ***Journal of Articles in Support of the Null Hypothesis.*** [ISSN: 1539-8714] 2002. q. Ed(s): Stephen Reysen. Reysen Group, 911 Mission St, Santa Cruz, CA 95060. Refereed. *Aud.:* Ac, Sa.

This journal publishes "original experimental studies in all areas of psychology where the null hypothesis is supported." The emphasis is on empirical reports with "sound methods, and sufficient power." Special preference can be given "if the empirical question is approached from several directions." Theoretical articles may be accepted. An important goal is "reducing the file drawer problem, and reducing the bias in psychological literature. Without such a resource, researchers could be wasting their time examining empirical questions that have already been examined." Received/acceptance dates are given on the professionally formatted (html) articles. And with two articles per issue, initial issues have looked at these topics: birth category effects on the Gordon Personal Profile variables; mediators of HIV risk among African American men; a brief cognitive-behavioral intervention for HIV prevention among injection drug users and cocaine smokers not in treatment; multiple targets of organizational identification: the role of identification congruency; whether fetal malnourishment puts infants at risk of caregiver neglect because their faces are unappealing; interpreting null results: improving presentation and conclusions with confidence intervals; and the generality of behavioral confirmation to gender role stereotypes. Students, researchers, and professionals should all periodically monitor this resource.

5842. ***Methods of Psychological Research.*** [ISSN: 1432-8534] 1996. irreg. Ed(s): Jurgen Rost. German Psychology Society, Institute for Science Education, University of Kiel, Kiel, 24098, Germany; rost@ipn.uni-kiel.de; http://www.mpr-online.de/. *Aud.:* Ac, Sa.

This journal is the official organ of the Methods Section of the German Psychology Society. Methodology articles are provided on issues in decision theory, evaluation research, classification theory, mathematical models, measurement theory, exploratory data analysis, test theory, statistics, research design, and the theory of science. Contributions are published in German, English, or both, and recent articles (available in pdf format) include these: the role of expectations in investigating multitrait-multimethod matrices by Procrustes rotation; time dependence of growth parameters in latent growth curve models with time-invariant covariates; a method for the analysis of hierarchical dependencies between items of a questionnaire; a goodness-of-fit measure for the Mokken double monotonicity model that takes into account the size of deviations; the odds favor antitypes: a comparison of tests for the identification of configural types and antitypes; and implicit concept mapping: a computerized tool for knowledge assessment in undergraduate psychology. Researchers and students in advanced-psychology programs should have access to the rigorous articles contained here.

5843. ***Prevention & Treatment.*** [ISSN: 1522-3736] 1998. irreg. Ed(s): Dr. Martin E. P. Seligman. American Psychological Association, 211 E 70th St, New York, NY 10021; http://www.apa.org/. Adv. Refereed. *Aud.:* Ac, Sa.

This refereed publication of the APA seeks to cover empirical and theoretical research on prevention. Included are articles on the outcome of psychotherapy and social and environmental interventions, biologically oriented therapy, and the combination of such interventions. Moreover, readers may find integrative reviews of literature relevant to "therapy, prevention, and the underlying personality processes as they relate to interventions." An important intention is to also include peer-reviewed commentaries and the authors' replies. Still another goal is to publish, with peer commentary, an electronic reprint of current articles they consider to be very important in all of psychological science. One recent example of the latter is the paper "On the Social Psychology of the Psychological Experiment: With Particular Reference to Demand Characteristics and their Implications" by Martin T. Orne of Harvard; an introductory article and nine commentaries accompany this offering. A contemporary article (with an introduction and nine commentaries) looked at "The Emperor's New Drugs: An Analysis of Antidepressant Medication Data Submitted to the U.S. Food and Drug Administration." Articles are provided and formatted very nicely in html. All who are involved in clinical work, study, and/or research in therapy should consider this resource.

5844. *PsyArt: an online journal for the psychological study of the arts.* [ISSN: 1088-5870] 1997. irreg. Free. Ed(s): Norman Holland. University of Florida, Institute of Psychological Study of the Arts (IPSA), Gainesville, FL 32601; http://www.clas.ufl.edu/ipsa/intro.htm. *Indexed:* MLA-IB. *Aud.:* Ac, Sa.

This journal provides a focus for work on "psychological studies of the arts: literature, film, visual arts, or music." Articles are provided in html making access easy using browser software. Recent articles cover Rudyard Kipling's loss of Ayah; the processes of ego dissolution and recuperation in Wordsworth's poem "I Wandered Lonely as a Cloud"; R. D. Laing and the work of Alasdair Gray; incorporative identifications of mourning and melancholia: a textual causerie; and coping with Holocaust trauma in Zipi Reibenbach's *Choice and Destiny*. This source offers good scholarly selections that students of the arts might consider.

5845. *Psyche (Greenville, Online Edition): an interdisciplinary journal of research on consciousness.* [ISSN: 1039-723X] 1994. irreg. Free. Ed(s): Patrick Wilken. Association for the Scientific Study of Consciousness, Caltech, Div of Biology, 139-74, Pasadena, CA 91125; http://psyche.cs.monash.edu.au/. Refereed. *Bk. rev.:* Number varies; lengthy. *Aud.:* Ac, Sa.

As an official journal of the Association for the Scientific Study of Consciousness, this publication is dedicated to the interdisciplinary exploration of the nature of consciousness and its relation to the brain. It publishes material relevant to that exploration from the perspectives afforded by the disciplines of cognitive science, philosophy, psychology, neuroscience, artificial intelligence, and anthropology. Interdisciplinary discussions are particularly encouraged. Research articles report original research; survey articles report the state of the art in some area(s); discussion notes critique previous research; and tutorials introduce a subject area relevant to the study of consciousness to nonspecialists. Contributions come from an international community, and important features are reviews of books and symposia (critical dialogue/exchanges between academics/professionals from a variety of disciplines). Recent offerings include a review of Margaret Livingstone's *Vision and Art: The Biology of Seeing*; numerous commentaries on Barry Dainton's book *Stream of Consciousness: Unity and Continuity in Conscious Experience*; a review of Joseph Levine's *Purple Haze*; an article examining three dominant positions in the philosophy of mind on the nature and distribution of consciousness; an article on the decoupling of "explicit" and "implicit" processing in neuropsychological disorders; and an article on the reliability of visual filling-in at the blind spot and how it is influenced by the distribution of spatial attention in and around the blind spot. Subscriptions to the plain ASCII version of *Psyche* are available also. This is a valuable resource to monitor for those studying consciousness and its relation to the brain.

5846. *Psychiatry On-Line.* [ISSN: 1359-7620] 1994. m. Free. Ed(s): Dr. Ben Green. Priory Lodge Education Ltd., 2 Cornflower Way, Moreton, CH46 1SV, United Kingdom; solutions@priory.com; http://www.priory.com/. Refereed. Circ: 60000 Controlled. *Aud.:* Ac, Sa.

This peer-reviewed journal with a significant international editorial board is one of several offered to the medical community by the publisher. The articles are primarily for professionals. Browsing for articles is easy, though organization by topical areas could be helpful, and dates of publication are found on most articles. Recent issues look at such topics as smoking in patients with mental disorders: observations in a developing country; the prediction of response to lithium in affective disorders; child custody access evaluation: cultural perspectives; mindfulness in mental health; and clozapine-induced cardiomyopathy. Worth monitoring if one is training in clinical psychology or psychiatry or providing service in either area.

5847. *Psychology in Spain.* [ISSN: 1137-9685] 1998. a. USD 25 (Individuals, USD 15). Ed(s): Jose Ramon Fernandez Hermida. Colegio Oficial de Psicologos. Espana, Secretaria Estatal, Claudio Coello, 46, 2o Dcha., Madrid, 28001, Spain; psyspain@correo.cop.es; http://www.cop.es/publicaciones/psyspain/. *Aud.:* Ac, Sa.

This peer-reviewed publication is "published annually by the Colegio Oficial de Psicologos (COP–Spanish Psychological Association). Its purpose is to disseminate in the English language the best Spanish psychology published in COP journals. Each issue of *Psychology in Spain* will look for balance among the different professional and scientific fields in Spanish psychology, in an effort to offer a wide range of the best work, thought and research being produced in each field. Selection is carried out by a qualified editorial board made up of several of the most prestigious specialists in Spanish academic and professional psychology." Browsing for articles is straightforward, involving looking through a table of contents for selected annual issues. A search engine is also available to find archived material. Articles are displayed in an attractive html format, with links to pdf versions, and with possibilities for posting responses to the articles. Recent issues cover these topics: body shape and eating disorders in a sample of students in the Basque country: a pilot study; metaevaluation of a total quality management evaluation system; coping strategies in psychotics: conceptualization and research results; teamwork in different communication contexts: a longitudinal study; family intervention program in schizophrenia: two-year follow-up of the Andalusia study; anticipatory anxiety in women recalled for further mammogram breast cancer screening; body-image disturbance in eating disorders: a meta-analysis; and quality-of-life parameters in terminal oncological patients in a home care unit. Another good choice for those who wish to monitor international research in psychology.

5848. *Psycoloquy (Online): a refereed journal of peer commentary in psychology, neuroscience and cognitive science.* Formerly: *Psycoloquy (Print).* 1990. irreg. Free. Ed(s): Stevan Harnad. Psycoloquy, c/o Cognitive Sciences Centre, Dept. of Electronics & Computer Science,, Univ. of Southampton, Zepler Bldg, Highfield, SO17 1BJ, United Kingdom; psyc@pucc.princeton.edu; http://www.cogsci.soton.ac.uk/~harnad/psyc.html. Illus., index. Refereed. *Bk. rev.:* Number and length vary. *Aud.:* Ac, Sa.

As the first scholarly electronic publication in psychology, *Psycoloquy* has served the academic community well. Since 1990, this refereed, international, interdisciplinary journal has published target articles and peer commentary in all areas of psychology and in cognitive science, neuroscience, behavioral biology, artificial intelligence, robotics/vision, linguistics, and philosophy. This publication is supported by the American Psychological Association, and target articles include looks at these topics: behavioral knowledge and structural complexity in McCulloch-Pitts Systems; whether connectionist models are theories of cognition; and whether AI is the right method for cognitive science. Recent book reviews with attending commentaries look at *Principles of Cognition, Language and Action: Essays on the Foundations of a Science of Psychology*; and *Psychological Concepts and Biological Psychiatry: A Philosophical Analysis.* Material at the web site is found through browsing by topic, volume, or year or by keyword search. For those interested in quality dialogue in psychology, this clearly is a title to include.

5849. *Self-Help and Psychology Magazine.* 1994. d. Free. Marlene Maheu, Ed. & Pub., 106 Thorn St, San Diego, CA 92103; drm@cybertowers.com; http://cybertowers.com/selfhelp. Adv. Circ: 184000. *Aud.:* Ga.

This attractive resource aims to be "an educational publication written by mental health professionals" (and graduate students) "for the discussion of general psychology as applied to our everyday lives." It is very easy to find material related to a variety of interests. Along with other sections and articles, topical areas include addictions; aging; careers and work; chronic illness; death, grief, and suicide; depression and anxiety; dreams and dreaming; eating disorders; gay/lesbian/bisexual/transgender; humor, health, and spirituality; Internet psychology and cyber-affairs; marriage and divorce; men; parenting; personal growth; psychotherapy; relationships; sexuality; sports and performance; trauma and violence; weight loss/control; and women. Browsing is easy, like flipping through a magazine, and for the most part dates of articles are given. Those wanting access to a general self-help resource may wish to bookmark access to this friendly publication.

■ REAL ESTATE

See also Architecture; Building and Construction; and Home sections.

Harrison Dekker, Coordinator of Data Services, Doe/Moffitt Libraries, Univeristy of California at Berkeley, 212 Doe Library, Berkeley, CA 94720-6000

Introduction

The field of real estate and its literature are constantly adapting to change. Variable economic factors like interest rates and business cycles are partially responsible, as are a variety of demographic influences. But perhaps technological innovation has effected the most change. Technology impacts the ways that properties are produced, managed, and bought. With respect to finance, information technology has reduced much of the "guesswork" that was once involved in key areas such as the appraisal of property values and the assessment of risk associated with lending. Most real estate decision-makers now have at their disposal advanced analytical models and the data and computing power necessary to apply them. Given these factors and the key role real estate plays in the economy, it's easy to see why the incentive is high for publishers to keep their readers informed with the latest information.

The periodicals covered in this section will appeal most to readers with the following interests: First are the hands-on professionals involved in activities like sales, marketing, and management of property. Second are individuals involved in the financial aspects of real estate like appraisal, investing, and lending. A third group to whom these publications will be of interest are trade association professionals who fulfill a variety of roles such as training and developing standards and improved practices in the field. Fourth are public officials engaged in such activities as planning, zoning, and taxation. Last but not least are the educators, researchers, and students in the academic fields of business, finance, and economics. Accordingly, these periodicals are most appropriate for college libraries, corporate and governmental special libraries, and large public libraries.

Basic Periodicals

Ac, Sa: *Real Estate Economics, Real Estate Review, Realtor Magazine.*

Basic Abstracts and Indexes

ABI/Inform, Business Index, Business Periodicals Index, PAIS International in Print.

5850. *Appraisal Journal.* [ISSN: 0003-7087] 1932. q. USD 100 (Non-members, USD 48; Students, USD 30). Ed(s): Margo J Wright. Appraisal Institute, 550 W. Van Buren St., # 1000, Chicago, IL 60607-3805; http://www.appraisalinstitute.org. Illus., index. Circ: 21000 Paid. Vol. ends: Oct. Microform: PQC. Online: EBSCO Publishing; Florida Center for Library Automation; Gale Group; Northern Light Technology, Inc.; OCLC Online Computer Library Center, Inc.; ProQuest Information & Learning; H.W. Wilson. Reprint: PQC; PSC. *Indexed:* ABIn, ATI, BPI, PAIS, RiskAb. *Bk. rev.:* 1-3, 500-700 words. *Aud.:* Ac, Sa.

Articles in the *Appraisal Journal* are "carefully selected to ensure that key considerations in valuation assignments are presented thoroughly and pragmatically." As such, the journal will be of particular interest to practicing real estate appraisers. Articles might also be of interest to students of economics or statistics in search of examples of practical applications in their areas of study. While most articles describe specific techniques of the appraisal trade, recent issues explore broader topics in real estate such as ethics and taxation. The typical issue contains eight to ten articles of about ten pages each, each preceded by a 75- to 100-word abstract. The bulk of the articles are written by practitioners with a smattering of academic authors. Tables of contents are available on the Appraisal Institute's web site, www.appraisalinstitute.org.

5851. *Assessment Journal.* Formed by the 1994 merger of: *Assessment and Valuation Legal Reporter; I A A O Update;* Which was formerly (until 1987): *International Association of Assessing Officers. News Bulletin; Property Tax Journal;* Which was formerly (until 1982): *Assessors Journal; Assessment Digest; International Assessor; I A A O Newsletter; Assessors News Letter - A N L.* [ISSN: 1073-8568] 1994. bi-m. Non-members, USD 200. Ed(s): Christine Zibas. International Association of Assessing Officers, 130 E Randolph, Ste 850, Chicago, IL 60601. Illus., index, adv. Sample. Circ: 8450. Vol. ends: Nov/Dec. Microform: PQC. Online: EBSCO Publishing; Northern Light Technology, Inc.; OCLC Online Computer Library Center, Inc.; ProQuest Information & Learning. Reprint: PQC. *Indexed:* ABIn, ATI, PAIS, SUSA. *Aud.:* Ac, Sa.

Targeted to appraisal and property taxation professionals, the *Assessment Journal* strives to provide "useful articles about innovative and technological developments in appraisal techniques, methods, and programs, as well as information and articles from around the world that capture the progress of this ever-changing industry." To accommodate the changing needs and interests of the appraisal profession, the journal has recently revamped its content, particularly with respect to coverage of such leading-edge technology as geographic information systems (GIS), automated valuation models (AVM), and computer-assisted mass appraisal systems (CAMA). Also, as part of the content makeover, the "Legal Reporter" and member news sections are no longer included; these are now published in a newly created trade magazine called *Fair & Equitable.* Full text of both publications is available online to members of the International Association of Assessing Officers or by subscription.

5852. *Building Operating Management: the national magazine for commercial and institutional buildings construction, renovation, facility mangement.* Formerly: *Building Maintenance and Modernization.* [ISSN: 0007-3490] 1954. m. Free to qualified personnel. Ed(s): Ed Sullivan. Trade Press Publishing Corp., 2100 W Florist Ave, PO Box 694, Milwaukee, WI 53209; http://www.tradepress.com. Illus., index, adv. Circ: 70000. Vol. ends: Dec. Microform: PQC. Reprint: PQC. *Indexed:* CIJE. *Aud.:* Ac, Sa.

Building Operating Management is a glossy trade publication targeted to the "executives who own or manage high-rise office buildings, college campuses, school districts, hospitals, medical clinics, retail chains, hotels and government buildings." The articles tend to be concisely written and focus on the myriad of issues related to the management of such facilities—from structural, technological, and energy-related issues to security and managerial practices. Contributors are mostly staff and freelance writers, plus the occasional industry expert. Content includes a significant amount of advertising pertinent to the industry. The free web site (www.facilitiesnet.com/bom) contains full text of most issues from June 2000 forward.

5853. *Global Real Estate News: the voice of the international real estate industry.* Former titles: *Appraisal Review and Mortgage Underwriting Journal; Appraisal Review Journal.* 1978. bi-m. USD 65. Ed(s): Robert Johnson. International Real Estate Institute, 1224 N Nokomis N E, Alexandria, MN 56308-5072. Adv. Circ: 10000. *Aud.:* Ac, Sa.

This newspaper is published by the International Real Estate Institute, a professional association for property managers, investors, and other individuals "affected by international real estate issues and concerns." Each issue contains numerous short articles focusing on specific real estate topics in primarily western European countries. Many articles feature trade statistics that might be difficult to track down from other sources. Other potentially elusive items can be found, such as a directory of foreign real estate associations. Though the publication will be of most interest to professionals, the statistical content and trend summaries could prove useful to students of business. The association has a web site, but it currently offers access only to issues from 2001.

5854. *Journal of Property Management: the official publication of the Institute of Real Estate Management.* Incorporates: *Operating Techniques and Products Bulletin.* [ISSN: 0022-3905] 1934. bi-m. USD 43.95 domestic; USD 54.95 Canada; USD 87.90 elsewhere. Ed(s): Nancy Pekala. Institute of Real Estate Management, 430 N Michigan Ave, Chicago, IL 60611; custserv@irem.org; http://www.irem.org. Illus., index, adv. Sample. Vol. ends: Nov/Dec. Online: EBSCO Publishing; Florida

Center for Library Automation; Gale Group; Northern Light Technology, Inc.; OCLC Online Computer Library Center, Inc.; ProQuest Information & Learning; H.W. Wilson. *Indexed:* ABIn, ATI, BPI, IBZ, PAIS, SUSA. *Aud.:* Ac, Sa.

Articles in the *Journal of Property Management* are written for managers, owners, investors, and other real estate professionals involved in the management of apartments, condominiums, office buildings, shopping centers, and industrial properties. The intent is to serve as a forum where new trends can be discussed and ideas shared. Recent issues discuss such timely topics as the impact of the Internet on the rental market (50 percent of renters now use it shop for a rental) and the demographic trends that are having a favorable impact on rental housing. Practical topics are covered (e.g., how to cope with graffiti), as are relevant tax, law, finance, and technology issues. The journal's web site provides the full text of selected articles from the current issue only.

5855. ***Journal of Real Estate Finance and Economics.*** [ISSN: 0895-5638] 1988. 8x/yr. USD 782 print or online ed. Ed(s): James B Kau, Steven Grenadier. Kluwer Academic Publishers, 101 Philip Dr, Assinippi Park, Norwell, MA 02061; kluwer@wkap.com; http://www.wkap.nl. Illus., adv. Sample. Refereed. Microform: PQC. Online: EBSCO Publishing; ingenta.com; Kluwer Online; OCLC Online Computer Library Center, Inc.; RoweCom Information Quest; Swets Blackwell. Reprint: PQC; SWZ. *Indexed:* IBSS, JEL, SSCI, SUSA. *Aud.:* Ac, Sa.

The *Journal of Real Estate Finance and Economics* is intended as a forum for researchers to publish theoretical works and the results of empirical research on real estate and related topics. Articles will be of greatest interest to scholars at or beyond the graduate level in such fields as finance, accounting, urban economics, and public policy. It is assumed that readers have a firm grasp of the jargon and quantitative techniques used in scholarly writing in finance and economics. Each article includes an abstract, subject keywords, and identifies the institutional affiliation of the author(s).

5856. ***Journal of Real Estate Literature.*** [ISSN: 0927-7544] 1993. s-a. NLG 375. Ed(s): Karl L Gunterman. American Real Estate Society, c/o James R Webb, Cleveland State University, Dept of Finance, Cleveland, OH 44114; http://www.aresnet.org. Illus., index. Sample. Refereed. Circ: 1500. Microform: PQC. Online: EBSCO Publishing; ingenta.com; Kluwer Online; Northern Light Technology, Inc.; RoweCom Information Quest; Swets Blackwell. Reprint: SWZ. *Indexed:* ABIn, IBSS, JEL, PollutAb, SUSA. *Bk. rev.:* 1-2, 1,000-1,500 words, signed. *Aud.:* Ac, Sa.

The *Journal of Real Estate Literature* is intended "to provide a source of information to encourage academic research and teaching in the field of real estate." Each issue contains one or more 10- to 20-page articles in each of the following sections: Review Articles, International Articles, and Real Estate Information Technology. Also included are reviews of books, doctoral dissertations, and working papers. A particularly noteworthy feature is a current contents section that features title listings by journal, subject, and author indexes. The journal's web site provides an archive of article abstracts from past issues, searchable by title, author, year, or keyword.

5857. ***The Journal of Real Estate Portfolio Management.*** [ISSN: 1083-5547] 1995. q. USD 105 academic, Libraries, USD 325 (Individuals, USD 95). Ed(s): Willard McIntosh, Marc A Louargand. American Real Estate Society, c/o James R Webb, Cleveland State University, Dept of Finance, Cleveland, OH 44114. Illus., adv. Refereed. Circ: 1300 Paid. Online: EBSCO Publishing; Northern Light Technology, Inc.; OCLC Online Computer Library Center, Inc.; ProQuest Information & Learning. *Indexed:* ABIn, IBSS, JEL. *Aud.:* Ac, Sa.

This journal publishes research on "all aspects of real estate investment and portfolio management." The work of both corporate and academic writers is represented. Although some articles rely heavily on the mathematical equations and proofs typical of scholarly work in finance, the journal maintains a policy that "articles must be understandable by the average institutional real estate investor." The full text of all articles published from 1995 forward can be downloaded from the journal's web site, http://business.fullerton.edu/jrepm.

5858. ***Journal of Real Estate Research.*** [ISSN: 0896-5803] 1986. bi-m. USD 475, Libraries, USD 360 (Individuals, USD 105 academic). Ed(s): Ko Wang. American Real Estate Society, c/o James R Webb, Cleveland State University, Dept of Finance, Cleveland, OH 44114; http://business.fullerton.edu/journal/. Adv. Refereed. Circ: 1200. *Indexed:* ABIn, AIAP, IBSS, JEL, SUSA. *Aud.:* Ac,Sa.

This journal publishes academic research in real estate with the theoretical and quantitative approach typical of economic and finance literature. What sets the journal apart from others in the field is an editorial policy to accept only manuscripts with a business decision making theme. The intended audience is, therefore, not merely an academic one, although the sophisticated and technical nature of the articles seems to assume graduate-level training. The journal states that "the business decision maker in areas such as development, finance, management, market analysis, marketing, and valuation" may find the research useful. Complementing the printed publication is a web site containing the full text of all past articles.

5859. ***National Real Estate Investor.*** [ISSN: 0027-9994] 1958. m. plus a. Directory. USD 85; USD 145 foreign. Primedia Business Magazines & Media, Inc. (Atlanta), 6151 Powers Ferry Rd, N W, Atlanta, GA 30339-2941; inquiries@primediabusiness.com; http://www.primediabusiness.com/. Illus., index, adv. Circ: 33708. Vol. ends: Dec. Microform: PQC. Online: bigchalk; EBSCO Publishing; Factiva; Florida Center for Library Automation; Gale Group; LexisNexis; OCLC Online Computer Library Center, Inc.; ProQuest Information & Learning; H.W. Wilson. Reprint: PQC. *Indexed:* ABIn, AIAP, BPI, CINAHL, LRI, PAIS. *Aud.:* Ac, Sa.

National Real Estate Investor is a trade journal targeted to "professionals involved in construction, development, finance/investment, property management, corporate real estate and real estate services." Each issue presents several feature articles covering a wide range of commercial real estate topics. Also included are sections on trends and strategies and regular columns such as "Financing Today," "Washington Wire," and "Money and Real Estate." Associated with the journal is a web site that allows browsing of articles back to 1995 and offers supplemental features like "Best of the Best" rankings.

5860. ***Real Estate Economics: journal of the American Real Estate and Urban Economics Association.*** Former titles (until 1995): *American Real Estate and Urban Economics Association. Journal;* (until 1992): *A R E U A Journal;* (until 1977): *American Real Estate and Urban Economics Association. Journal.* [ISSN: 1080-8620] 1973. q. USD 295 print & online eds. Blackwell Publishing, Inc., Commerce Place, 350 Main St, Malden, MA 02148; subscrip@blackwellpub.com; http://www.blackwellpublishing.com. Illus., index. Refereed. Circ: 1500. Vol. ends: Winter. Microform: PQC. Online: ingenta.com; Northern Light Technology, Inc.; ProQuest Information & Learning; Swets Blackwell. Reprint: PQC. *Indexed:* ABIn, AgeL, BPI, IBZ, JEL, RiskAb, SSCI. *Aud.:* Ac, Sa.

In publication since 1973, *Real Estate Economics* is "the oldest academic journal concentrating on the real estate industry." As typical with scholarly economic writing, readers without graduate-level training may find the material too technical. This is not to say, however, that a nonacademic audience will find nothing of interest. Industry professionals with the appropriate quantitative skills who wish to become familiar with the latest tools for analyzing real estate decision-making will find relevant content. A typical issue features six or so articles of 20 to 30 pages in length. Noteworthy is the journal's new web site that allows search and retrieval of articles published since the first volume.

5861. ***Real Estate Issues.*** [ISSN: 0146-0595] 1976. q. Individuals, USD 48; USD 15 newsstand/cover per issue. Ed(s): Richard Marchitelli. The Counselors of Real Estate, 430 N Michigan Ave, Chicago, IL 60611; cre@interaccess.com; http://www.cre.org. Illus., index, adv. Refereed. Circ: 2000. Vol. ends: Winter. Microform: PQC. Online: EBSCO Publishing; Florida Center for Library Automation; Gale Group; Northern Light Technology, Inc.; OCLC Online Computer Library Center, Inc.; ProQuest Information & Learning. *Indexed:* ABIn, AIAP. *Aud.:* Ac, Sa.

Real Estate Issues is published for commercial real estate professionals. Its coverage of issues both practical and theoretical, however, provides relevant content for a much broader audience. The publishers suggest that in addition to those working directly in the commercial real estate field, potential readers might include "academics, planners, architects, developers, economists, government personnel, lawyers, and accountants." For the most part, the authors are certified Counselors of Real Estate, meaning that they are members of the professional association responsible for publication of the journal. This gives it a bit of an "insider" feel but does not seem to detract in any significant way from the content. Worth noting is the journal's web site (http://www.cre.org/newsandmarketinfo/rei_abs.cfm), which provides article abstracts from issues dating back to 1980.

5862. *Real Estate Law Journal.* [ISSN: 0048-6868] 1972. q. USD 141.50; USD 219.45 foreign. R I A Group, 395 Hudson St, New York, NY 10014. Microform: PQC. Online: Gale Group. Reprint: PQC; WSH. *Indexed:* ABIn, BLI, CLI, ILP, LRI, PAIS, SSCI. *Aud.:* Ac, Sa.

This journal covers a broad range of issues pertaining to areas where legal matters and real estate issues intersect. In addition to regular columns covering court decisions, tax issues, environmental matters, and a "Digest of Selected Articles," each issue presents two or three feature articles. Although a fair number are written by real estate attorneys, articles by tax specialists, financial experts, and public officials are also presented. Subject matter will be of particular interest to real estate and legal professionals, but the layperson with a basic knowledge of legal terminology may also find some useful material. A recent issue, for instance, features accessible articles on broker liability and seller disclosures, both of which might be of interest to the average home buyer or seller.

5863. *Real Estate Review.* [ISSN: 0034-0790] 1971. q. USD 200. Ed(s): Arthur Margon. West Group, 610 Opperman Dr, Eagan, MN 55123-1396. Illus., index, adv. Vol. ends: Winter. Microform: PQC. Online: EBSCO Publishing; Gale Group. Reprint: PQC; WSH. *Indexed:* ABIn, ATI, AgeL, BLI, BPI, CLI, ILP, LRI, PAIS, SSCI. *Aud.:* Ac, Sa.

Real Estate Review provides "authoritative guidance and on-target strategies dealing with the modern real estate market." It publishes pieces by both practitioners and academics and manages to maintain a focused, how-to approach to current real estate issues. A typical issue features six or seven articles usually under ten pages in length. Particular attention seems to be paid to page layout in this publication. Text, tables, and charts all seem designed to promote readability. Overall, the journal does a very good job of providing up-to-date information derived from both academic research and the practical experience of real estate professionals.

5864. *Realtor Magazine.* Formerly (until 1997): *Today's Realtor;* Which was formed by the merger of (1968-1996): *Real Estate Today;* (1980-1996): *Realtor News.* [ISSN: 1522-0842] 1996. m. Non-members, USD 54. Ed(s): Stacey Moncrieff. National Association of Realtors (Chicago), 430 N Michigan Ave, Chicago, IL 60611; infocentral@realtors.org; http://www.realtormag.com. Illus., adv. Sample. Circ: 750000. Microform: PQC. Online: Gale Group. Reprint: PQC. *Indexed:* AgeL, BPI, LRI, MagInd. *Aud.:* Ac, Sa.

Realtor Magazine is a glossy and visually appealing trade publication. Subtitled "The Business Tool for Real Estate Professionals," it contains practical information for Realtors and real estate agents. A particular emphasis is placed on advice pertaining to the residential market, e.g., how to deal with difficult customers, how to effectively arrange furniture in a sale home, etc. In addition, there's a regular "Front Lines" section that focuses on relevant news, trends, analysis, and noteworthy people in the industry. Other regular features are a buying guide and law, ethics, and technology columns. Worth mentioning is the Realtor.org web site that provides information to supplement the print articles.

■ RELIGION

Rev. Loring A. Prest, Electronic Resources Librarian, Louis L. Manderino Library, California University of Pennsylvania, California, PA 15419; prest@cup.edu

Introduction

Few topics produce the depth of response as the mention of "religion." For some, religion is the salvation of humanity. For others, it is the source of humanity's woes. Just mentioning the subject can produce an emotional reaction ranging from conviction to consternation. Yet, religion is one of the oldest subjects in human history and one of the most pervasive. From the earliest civilizations until today, it has played a role in every culture. A well-rounded education, therefore, must include the study of religion.

The study of religion is complicated by several factors, however, beginning with its inherent subjectivity. Religion involves one's personal beliefs, often regarding very ultimate issues and metaphysical claims. These beliefs cannot be subjected to the type of validation used in many of the "hard sciences." By its very nature, the study of a religion will be handled differently by those who are "inside" and those who are "outside" looking in. Each perspective offers advantages and disadvantages. Outsiders, free from a personal connection, may be in a position to make more objective assessments regarding the religion. Insiders, however, often understand the fine distinctions that exist within a religion and its various traditions that are lost on the outsider.

This subjectivity has collection development implications. Libraries need to include a range of religious publications so that their patrons can hear from both sides. Given the ecumenical spirit of our times, many of the titles in this section try to provide balanced, multiple views. And yet, even assuming an ecumenical spirit is somewhat of a position in itself—and one not universally shared. There are titles in this section that require their authors to adopt a particular theological stance. Naturally, people who share this stance will find these titles desirable. Those who find this editorial policy too limiting, however, should not ignore these publications. For those on the outside looking in, they can be the best means to gaining a sharper understanding of this particular theological position.

Another factor that makes religion such a challenging subject is that it is interconnected with a wide range of other disciplines. Many humanities subjects are represented as adjunct disciplines in the titles of journals in this section: history, literature, philosophy, psychology, sociology, medicine, and science. One cannot properly study many of these topics without considering the role of religion. Libraries supporting these humanities disciplines should include some of these titles—even when there is no specific religious studies program. Can one study European history without considering ecclesiastical history? Or sociology without taking into account the impact of religion? Religion as a subject is both self-contained and connected to many others.

In light of the previous comments, it should be clear that preparing a selective list of religious publications from the many available is a daunting task. Omission from this section should be interpreted carefully. The scope of *Magazines for Libraries* limits inclusion to English-language journals. As a consequence, several very scholarly and highly respected publications are not included in this section. It is also impossible to include publications from every Christian denomination, although some denominational publications are included, due to their wider appeal and utility to those beyond that particular tradition. Although Christianity receives more coverage than the other religions due to its historic role in Western culture and hence publishing, Judaism, Islam, Buddhism, and Hinduism are also represented at the scholarly and popular level. Many of the titles in this section are geared toward academic libraries, but there are suggestions for public libraries as well. Since it is assumed that seminary libraries would be interested in just about all of the titles in this section, it seemed unnecessary to mention them in the recommendations.

The web offers wonderful access to descriptions of many of these journals—and sometimes even their contents. Often this will include tables of contents, abstracts, searchable indexes, and even the full text of articles and issues. Web sites offering significant (and free) information to the visitor are noted in the annotations, along with a description of what was available at the time of this writing. Those seeking additional, or more current, information are encouraged to visit the journal web sites.

Basic Periodicals

Ga: *America, B R, Christian Century, The Humanist, The Other Side;* Ac: *America, American Academy of Religion. Journal, B R, Church History, The Humanist, Journal of Biblical Literature, Journal of Ecclesiastical History, The Journal of Religion, Journal of Theological Studies, Judaism, Muslim World, Religious Studies Review.*

Basic Abstracts and Indexes

Catholic Periodical and Literature Index, New Testament Abstracts, Old Testament Abstracts, Religion Index One: Periodicals, Religious and Theological Abstracts.

5865. *America.* [ISSN: 0002-7049] 1909. w. bi-w., Jul. & Aug. USD 43 domestic; USD 65 foreign. Ed(s): Thomas J Reese. America Press Inc., 106 W 56th St, New York, NY 10019; america@americapress.org; http://www.americapress.org. Illus., index, adv. Sample. Circ: 41000 Paid. Vol. ends: Jun/Dec. CD-ROM: ProQuest Information & Learning. Microform: PQC. Online: bigchalk; EBSCO Publishing; Florida Center for Library Automation; Gale Group; Northern Light Technology, Inc.; OCLC Online Computer Library Center, Inc.; ProQuest Information & Learning; H.W. Wilson. *Indexed:* ABS&EES, BAS, BRD, BRI, BiogInd, CBRI, CPL, FLI, LRI, MRD, MagInd, NTA, OTA, RGPR. *Bk. rev.:* 2-3, 1,000-1,300 words, signed. *Aud.:* Ga, Ac.

This weekly covers religious, political, ethical, and social issues from the Jesuit Catholic perspective. It is intended "for the thinking Catholic and those who want to know what Catholics are thinking." Articles are written for both the layperson and the religious professional. In addition to timely discussions of current events, issues include literary items, reviews of the arts and literature, and commentary on lectionary texts. Recent articles include "A Campaign to Divide the Church in the Holy Land," "Justice in Executive Compensation," and "Substance Abuse: The Feminine Mystique." The web site (www.americamagazine.org) offers free access to book reviews (2000 on), editorials (1998 on), and selected full-text articles (1998 on). There is a searchable index for articles from 1988 on that provides free abstracts and option to purchase full text. Like *The Christian Century,* which represents the Protestant viewpoint (see below, this section), this journal is a basic title that is recommended for both public and academic libraries.

5866. *American Academy of Religion. Journal.* Formerly (until 1967): *Journal of Bible and Religion.* [ISSN: 0002-7189] 1933. q. USD 135. Ed(s): Glenn Yocum. Oxford University Press, 2001 Evans Rd, Cary, NC 27513; http://www3.oup.co.uk/jnls/. Illus., index, adv. Refereed. Circ: 9000 Paid. Vol. ends: Winter. Microform: PQC. Online: EBSCO Publishing; Gale Group; ingenta.com; OCLC Online Computer Library Center, Inc. Reprint: PSC. *Indexed:* AmH&L, ArtHuCI, BAS, BRD, BRI, CBRI, HumInd, IBZ, LRI, MLA-IB, NTA, OTA, PSA, R&TA, RI-1, SSCI, SociolAb. *Bk. rev.:* 15-20, 900-2,000 words, signed. *Aud.:* Ac.

This is the publication of the respected scholarly association The American Academy of Religion. Authors are well-known scholars, and the articles are very substantive. The concept of religion is approached from a fairly broad perspective. Islam, Judaism, Christianity, and other world religions are examined using insights from a variety of disciplines, including ethics, psychology, and sociology. Some recent articles reveal the kind of coverage provided: "Singing the Glory of Asceticism: Devotion of Asceticism in Jainism," "Reenchanting Nature: Modern Western Shamanism and Nineteenth-Century Thought," "Byzantium, Orthodoxy, and Democracy," and "A Post-Kantian Perspective on Recent Debates about Mystical Experience." In addition to scholarly articles, issues include a number of well-developed book reviews. This is a basic title for academic institutions with religious studies programs.

5867. *American Baptist Quarterly: a Baptist journal of history, theology and ministry.* Former titles (until vol.25, 1982): *Foundations;* (until 1958): *Chronicle.* [ISSN: 0745-3698] 1938. q. USD 35, Libraries, USD 27 USD 21 domestic. Ed(s): Robert Johnson. American Baptist Historical Society, PO Box 851, Valley Forge, PA 19482. Illus., index, adv. Sample. Refereed. Circ: 1200. Vol. ends: Dec. Microform: PQC. Reprint: PQC. *Indexed:* AmH&L, R&TA, RI-1. *Bk. rev.:* 0-1, 500-1,400 words, signed. *Aud.:* Ga, Ac, Sa.

The historic contributions that Baptists (and other "free churches") have made to American culture are often underappreciated. *ABQ* provides valuable access to this "free church" perspective on historical, theological, biblical, religious, and social issues. As an American Baptist publication, much of the material is drawn from authors within that tradition, but not exclusively. Recent articles include "Believing in America: Faith and Politics in Early National Virginia," "The Social Ministries of American Baptist Churches and Clergy," and "Denominationalism, Centralization, and Baptist Principles: Observations by a Somewhat Perplexed Baptist." Baptist churches cover a broad theological spectrum, with the American Baptist Churches in the USA representing a more moderate and progressive position. Combining this title with *Baptist History and Heritage* (published by the more conservative Southern Baptist Convention; see below, this section) would provide balanced coverage of the Baptist perspective in the United States. Recommended for large public and academic libraries.

5868. *American Journal of Theology & Philosophy.* [ISSN: 0194-3448] 1980. 3x/yr. USD 36 (Individuals, USD 21). Ed(s): Jennifer G. Jesse, J Wesley Robbins. Highlands Institute for American Religious and Philosophical Thought, P. O. Box 2009, Highlands, NC 28741; http://www.iusb.edu/~wrobbins/ajtp/EditorialPolicy.html. Adv. Refereed. Circ: 450. *Indexed:* PhilInd, R&TA, RI-1. *Bk. rev.:* 0-1, 150-500, signed. *Aud.:* Ac, Sa.

The disciplines of theology and philosophy are often closely related. This journal seeks to investigate this intersection by publishing "articles on American theology and its dialogue with philosophy," especially philosophy utilizing the American philosophical tradition. Although rooted in American thought, international contributions are not ignored. The four to five articles per issue are well documented and intended for an academic audience. Recent titles include "Utopia, Dystopia: The Pragmatic Value of Visions," "Modernisms in Theology: Interpreting American Liberal Theology, 1805-1955," "From Ecological Trinitarianism to Life-centered Technology," and "My Passage from Panentheism to Pantheism." Philosophers and theologians interested in coverage from the American perspective will appreciate this journal. Recommended for academic libraries.

5869. *Anglican Theological Review.* [ISSN: 0003-3286] 1918. q. USD 40 (Individuals, USD 32). Ed(s): Charles Hefling. Anglican Theological Review, Inc., 600 Haven St, Evanston, IL 60201. Illus., index, adv. Sample. Refereed. Circ: 1700 Paid. Vol. ends: No. 4. Microform: PQC. Online: EBSCO Publishing; Northern Light Technology, Inc.; ProQuest Information & Learning. Reprint: PQC. *Indexed:* IBZ, NTA, OTA, R&TA, RI-1. *Bk. rev.:* 25-30, 600-1,400 words, signed. *Aud.:* Ac, Sa.

Although an "independent" publication, the *ATR* is supported by Episcopal and Anglican seminaries in the United States and Canada and seeks to encourage and develop theological reflection in the Anglican tradition. Issues are typically thematic and often reflect Anglican concerns (e.g., "Hooker after 400 Years" and "Law and Community"), although authors come from a variety of traditions. The journal explores the relationships that exist between various areas of study: theology, history of religions, philosophy, language studies, human sciences, and the arts. Issues include articles (sometimes with response articles), poetry, reflection pieces, art reviews, review articles, and book reviews. Recent articles include "The Ordering of Community: New Testament Perspectives," "From Monarch to Bishop: Covenant, Torah, and Community Formation in the Old Testament and the Anglican Communion," and "From Heresy to Sex, Experience to Principle: The Emerging Theology of Title IV." Recommended for academic libraries with an interest in theological studies.

5870. *B R.* Formerly (until 2003): *Bible Review.* 1985. bi-m. USD 24 domestic; USD 30 foreign. Ed(s): Molly Dewsnap, Hershel Shanks. Biblical Archaeology Society, 4710 41st St, N W, Washington, DC 20016. Illus., index. Sample. Circ: 50000 Paid. Vol. ends: Dec. Online: ProQuest Information & Learning. *Indexed:* AbAn, HumInd, IJP, NTA, OTA, R&TA, RI-1. *Bk. rev.:* 2-3, 1,000 words, signed. *Aud.:* Ga, Ac.

This valuable publication bridges the gap between scholars and general readers in the field of biblical studies. Articles are written for general readers by well-known scholars (e.g., Paula Fredriksen, John Dominic Crossan, Stephen J. Patterson, Ben Witherington III). Inclusive of Protestant, Catholic, and Jewish traditions, *BR* reflects a nondenominational, modern, and scholarly approach to biblical texts and theology. Although not written for experts, the letters to the editor reflect a readership that includes laity, clergy, and not a few professors. Like its sister publication, *Biblical Archaeology Review, BR* is printed on glossy paper and each issue is beautifully illustrated with color photographs and artwork. Recent articles include "Unlikely Heroes: Women as Israel," "Jews and Christians: Seeing the Prophets Differently," "Moses: From Vigilante to Lawgiver," and "How December 25 Became Christmas." Selected current articles are available online at www.bib-arch.org/bswb_BR/indexBR.html. The combination of quality authors, informative articles, beautiful presentation, and appeal to a wide range of readers makes *BR* an excellent and highly recommended basic title for public and academic libraries.

5871. ***Baptist History and Heritage.*** [ISSN: 0005-5719] 1965. 3x/yr. Membership, USD 30; Students, USD 20; Senior citizens, USD 25. Ed(s): Pamela R Durso. Baptist History & Heritage Society, PO Box 728, Brentwood, TN 37027-0728; cdeweese@tnbaptist.org; http://www.baptisthistory.org. Illus., index. Sample. Refereed. Circ: 1000 Paid. Vol. ends: Oct. *Indexed:* AmH&L, ChrPI, IBZ, R&TA, RI-1. *Bk. rev.:* 3, 250-300 words, signed. *Aud.:* Ga, Ac.

This journal presents the perspective of the largest Baptist association (and second-largest religious body) in the United States, the Southern Baptist Convention. Each slim issue addresses a particular theme, such as "Baptists and Judaism," "Global Baptists," or "Baptists and the Social Gospel." The narrow focus of this publication limits its appeal, but it provides a useful resource for understanding the Southern Baptist perspective. Sample articles from somewhat recent issues are available at www.baptisthistory.org/bhh.htm. Public libraries serving populations with an interest in Baptist studies and undergraduate libraries supporting courses in Baptist thought and history will find this a useful addition.

The Beltane Papers. See Women: Feminist and Special Interest/Special Interest section.

5872. ***The Bible Today: a periodical promoting understanding and appreciation of scripture for life & ministry.*** [ISSN: 0006-0836] 1962. bi-m. USD 39 (Individuals, USD 28; USD 5 newsstand/cover per issue). Ed(s): Rev. Donald Senior. Liturgical Press, St John's Abbey, Collegeville, MN 56321-7500; http://www.litpress.org/mag/bt.html. Illus., index, adv. Sample. Circ: 6900. Vol. ends: Nov. Microform: PQC. Reprint: PQC. *Indexed:* CPL, NTA, OTA. *Bk. rev.:* 35-40, 50-200 words, signed. *Aud.:* Ga, Ac.

Written for nonexperts by experts, *The Bible Today* seeks to show how modern biblical scholarship can give direction to one's life and ministry. The first section of each issue is thematic, focusing on a particular subject or book of the Bible (e.g., "Biblical Prayer," "Second Isaiah"). Other sections include "Translating Biblical Texts" (a look at various translations over time), "Puzzling Passages" (examination of curious portions of the Bible), "Window into the Biblical World" (a look at daily life in biblical times), announcements, and book reviews (divided into two sections: Old and New Testaments). Readers are generally involved in ministry as either clergy or laity. Although a large part of the readership is Catholic, writers represent a wide variety of traditions. Given the diversity and notable credentials of the journal's authors, along with its practical spiritual emphasis, this publication will appeal to laypeople from many traditions. This would be a good choice for public libraries.

Biblical Archaeology Review. See Archaeology section.

The B'nai B'rith I J M. See Fraternal, Club, and Service Organizations section.

5873. ***Buddhist - Christian Studies.*** [ISSN: 0882-0945] 1981. a. USD 30; USD 42 combined subscription print & online eds. Ed(s): Terry C Muck, Rita Gross. University of Hawaii Press, Journals Department, 2840 Kolowalu St, Honolulu, HI 96822-1888; uhpjourn@hawaii.edu; http://www.uhpress.hawaii.edu/. Illus., adv. Sample. Refereed. Circ: 750. Online: EBSCO Publishing; Florida Center for Library Automation; Gale Group; OCLC Online Computer Library Center, Inc.; Project MUSE; ProQuest Information & Learning; RoweCom Information Quest; Swets Blackwell. Reprint: PQC; PSC. *Indexed:* R&TA, RI-1. *Bk. rev.:* 10-15, 800-1000, signed. *Aud.:* Ac, Sa.

This interesting journal reflects the dialogue taking place between Buddhists and Christians. Articles are written by respected authors from both religions, typically involve a "statement and response" or interview format, and usually address particular themes, such as "Buddhist And Christian Views of Economics," "Buddhist Responses to Christian Spiritual Practice," and "Christian Responses to Buddhist Spiritual Practice." Issues also contain essays, editorials, and conference reports. Listening in on the conversation between Buddhist and Christian adherents is valuable and enlightening. The tables of contents for all volumes are available online at www.uhpress.hawaii.edu/journals/bcs. Highly recommended for academic libraries that include Buddhist and/or comparative-religion studies.

5874. ***C C A R Journal: a reform Jewish quarterly.*** Former titles (until Summer 1991): *Journal of Reform Judaism; C C A R Journal.* [ISSN: 1058-8760] 1953. q. USD 24. Ed(s): Rabbi Rifat Sonsino. C C A R Press, 355 Lexington Ave, 18th Fl, New York, NY 10017-6603. Illus., adv. Circ: 2400. Vol. ends: Spring. Microform: PQC. Reprint: PQC. *Indexed:* IJP, R&TA, RI-1. *Bk. rev.:* 3-4, 800-1,200 words, signed. *Aud.:* Ga, Ac, Sa.

This journal "seeks to explore ideas and issues of Judaism and Jewish life, primarily—but not exclusively—from a Reform Jewish perspective." The Central Conference of American Rabbis (CCAR) is the organized rabbinate of Reform Judaism, which represents a progressive branch of Judaism open to change and pluralism. Articles may represent a symposium ("Human Sexuality"), a response to an issue from the CCAR Responsa Committee ("Compulsory Immunization"), or deal with various topics ("The Postmodern Mood in the Synagogue," "The Progressive Zionism of Louis Brandeis and Stephen Wise"). Issues also include poetry, editorials, and book reviews. The articles are interesting without being too technical for a general reader. This publication helps to clarify the differing perspectives within Judaism, which may be especially important to those outside of Judaism who are unaware of the diversity within it. The tables of contents and a very limited number of articles from 1996 on are available at the journal's web site (www.ccarnet.org/journal). Recommended for academic and large public libraries.

5875. ***Catholic Biblical Quarterly.*** [ISSN: 0008-7912] 1939. q. USD 25. Ed(s): Alfred Cody. Catholic Biblical Association of America, Catholic University of America, Washington, DC 20064. Illus., index, adv. Sample. Refereed. Circ: 4230. Vol. ends: Oct. Online: EBSCO Publishing; Gale Group; Northern Light Technology, Inc.; OCLC Online Computer Library Center, Inc.; ProQuest Information & Learning; H.W. Wilson. *Indexed:* ArtHuCI, CPL, HumInd, IBZ, NTA, OTA, R&TA, RI-1, SSCI. *Bk. rev.:* 60-65, 400-1,100 words, signed. *Aud.:* Ac, Sa.

Although labeled "Catholic," this journal is much broader—both in authors and readers—and is one of the premier resources for biblical studies. Articles focus on the biblical texts of the Old and New Testaments, are written by major scholars, and are extremely well documented and scholarly. Article topics range from broader concepts ("Prophecy as Divination," "Jesus as Messiah in the Gospel of Luke: Discerning a Pattern of Correction") to examinations of small passages in great detail ("From Remnant to Seed of Hope for Israel: Romans 9:27-29," "The Prophetic Dimension of the Divine Name: On Exodus 3:14a and Its Context"). The advanced nature of the articles makes them less appealing to a general reader. For critical research, however, they are extremely useful. The book review section, which comprises about half of each issue, is valuable for those interested in following trends in biblical studies. A standard in seminary libraries, both Catholic and Protestant, *CBQ* is highly recommended for any academic library supporting religious studies programs.

5876. ***The Christian Century.*** [ISSN: 0009-5281] 1886. bi-w. USD 49. Ed(s): John Buchanan. Christian Century, 104 S Michigan Ave, Ste 700, Chicago, IL 60603; main@christiancentury.org; http://www.christiancentury.org. Illus., index, adv. Circ: 30000 Paid and free. Vol. ends: Dec. CD-ROM: ProQuest Information & Learning. Microform: NBI; PQC. Online: EBSCO Publishing; Florida Center for Library Automation; Gale Group; Northern Light Technology, Inc.; OCLC Online Computer Library Center, Inc.; ProQuest Information & Learning; H.W. Wilson. *Indexed:* ABS&EES, BAS, BRD, BRI, CBRI, FLI, IAPV, IBZ, LRI, MRD, MagInd, NTA, PRA, R&TA, RGPR, RI-1. *Bk. rev.:* 1-3, 1,000-3,000 words, signed. *Aud.:* Ga.

The Christian Century is a weekly journal of opinion and news from the moderate to liberal Protestant perspective, a format similar to *America* in the Catholic tradition (see above, this section). Writers are drawn from both Protestant and non-Protestant circles and include well-known and new theologians, historians, and church leaders. *The Christian Century* believes that "Christians must articulate their faith in a way that is socially meaningful and intellectually compelling." As a result, articles cover a wide range of topics relating to religious, cultural, political, and global issues. Literary and poetic items, such as film and book reviews, are also included. Most of the current issue is available online at www.christiancentury.org. Read by both laypeople and professionals (especially clergy), this is a basic publication that should be in most public and academic libraries.

5877. ***Christianity and Literature.*** Formerly: *Conference on Christianity and Literature. Newsletter.* [ISSN: 0148-3331] 1951. q. USD 35 (Individuals, USD 25; Students, USD 20). Ed(s): Robert Snyder. Conference on Christianity and Literature, State University of West Georgia, Carrollton, GA 30118-2200; rsnyder@westga.edu. Illus., adv. Sample. Refereed. Circ: 1100 Paid. Vol. ends: Summer (No. 4). *Indexed:* ABS&EES, ArtHuCI, BEL&L, ChrPI, HumInd, MLA-IB, R&TA, RI-1. *Bk. rev.:* 9-12, 1,200-2,500 words, signed. *Aud.:* Ga, Ac, Sa.

Christianity and Literature "is devoted to the scholarly exploration of how literature engages Christian thought, experience, and practice." Sponsored by the national Conference on Christianity and Literature, the journal does not presuppose any particular theological orientation, yet it "respects an orthodox understanding of Christianity as a historically defined faith." Articles range from 4,000 to 9,000 words each, while examining broad topics ("What Is Reading For?") and specific subjects ("Mentors and Proteges: Spiritual Evolution in Georges Bernanos' *Under Satan's Sun* and *The Diary of a Country Priest*"). Issues also include poetry and announcements. Recommended for academic libraries.

5878. ***Christianity Today.*** Incorporates (1997-200?): *Christianity Online.* [ISSN: 0009-5753] 1956. m. USD 24.95 domestic; USD 27.95 foreign. Ed(s): David Neff. Christianity Today International, 465 Gundersen Dr, Carol Stream, IL 60188. Illus., index, adv. Circ: 153000. Vol. ends: Dec. Microform: PQC. Online: bigchalk; EBSCO Publishing; Florida Center for Library Automation; Gale Group; Northern Light Technology, Inc.; OCLC Online Computer Library Center, Inc.; ProQuest Information & Learning; H.W. Wilson. *Indexed:* ABS&EES, BAS, BRD, BRI, BiogInd, CBRI, CPerI, ChrPI, LRI, MagInd, NTA, OTA, PRA, R&TA, RGPR, RI-1. *Bk. rev.:* 5-6, 600-1,000 words, signed. *Aud.:* Ga.

Started as an evangelical counterpart to the mainline *The Christian Century, CT* maintains its expressed commitment to the evangelical perspective. This glossy, well-illustrated magazine covers theology, biblical studies, and contemporary politics and social issues. Although *CT* shares some similarities with *The Other Side* (see below, this section) and *Sojourners,* it is more conservative and more doctrinal than these publications. Recent articles include "Apocalypse Again—and Again," "The Bush Doctrine," and "A Shrink Gets Stretched: Why Psychologist Larry Crabb Believes Spiritual Direction Should Replace Therapy." Although access to the current issue is limited, the full texts of many articles back to 1999 are available at www.christianitytoday.com/ctmag. As a leading voice for evangelicalism in the United States, this is an important magazine for public and academic library collections.

5879. ***Church History: studies in Christianity and culture.*** [ISSN: 0009-6407] 1932. q. USD 75 domestic; USD 100 foreign. Ed(s): Grant Wacker. American Society of Church History, PO Box 8517, Red Bank, NJ 07701-8517; aschnoff@aol.com. Illus., index, adv. Refereed. Circ: 3400. Vol. ends: Dec. Online: bigchalk; Chadwyck-Healey Incorporated; EBSCO Publishing; Florida Center for Library Automation; Gale Group; Northern Light Technology, Inc.; OCLC Online Computer Library Center, Inc.; ProQuest Information & Learning; H.W. Wilson. *Indexed:* ABS&EES, AmH&L, ArtHuCI, BEL&L, BHA, BRI, CBRI, ChrPI, HumInd, IBZ, OTA, R&TA, RI-1, SSCI. *Bk. rev.:* 30-50, 250-1,200 words, signed. *Aud.:* Ac, Sa.

This journal from the American Society of Church History is a valuable resource for researching church history. Issues typically include five or six well-documented articles that are between 6,000 and 11,000 words long (excluding endnotes). Contributions are to be "grounded in original research, inform specialists, interest historians of Christianity in general, and defend a clear thesis." Coverage includes all areas of the history of Christianity, including non-Western expressions. Recent articles include "Historical Fact And Exegetical Fiction in The Carolingian Vita S. Sualonis," "Simon Magus, Nicolas of Antioch, and Muhammad," and "Pilgrims and Progress: How Magazines Made Thanksgiving." The large number of book reviews, along with lengthy review essays, which take up half of each issue, will benefit scholars and librarians seeking to keep abreast of recent literature in the field. The tables of contents and abstracts are available for issues since 1998 at www.churchhistory.org/Journal. The web site also offers author and article title keyword searching of all issues since the first volume. Because so much of Western history is intertwined with church history, both history and religion departments will find this journal useful. Recommended as a basic title for all academic libraries.

5880. ***Commonweal.*** [ISSN: 0010-3330] 1924. bi-w. USD 44 domestic; CND 49 Canada; USD 54 elsewhere. Ed(s): Paul Baumann, Patrick Jordan. Commonweal Foundation, 475 Riverside Dr, Rm 405, New York, NY 10115; commonweal@msn.com; http://www.commonwealmagazine.org. Illus., adv. Circ: 18000 Paid. CD-ROM: ProQuest Information & Learning. Microform: MIM; PMC; PQC. Online: bigchalk; Chadwyck-Healey Incorporated; EBSCO Publishing; Florida Center for Library Automation; Gale Group; Northern Light Technology, Inc.; OCLC Online Computer Library Center, Inc.; ProQuest Information & Learning; H.W. Wilson. Reprint: PQC. *Indexed:* ABS&EES, BAS, BEL&L, BRD, BRI, CBRI, CPL, FLI, IAPV, LRI, MLA-IB, MRD, MagInd, NTA, OTA, RGPR, RI-1. *Bk. rev.:* 3-4, 900-1,900 words, signed. *Aud.:* Ga.

Like *America* (see above, this section), *Commonweal* presents a Catholic perspective on current events. They differ in that *Commonweal* takes a more aggressive stance. Opinions are clearly stated on a wide variety of matters including religion, politics, public affairs, literature, the arts, and social and cultural issues. The magazine used to claim to present a "slightly liberal Catholic perspective." In response to the question of stance, the current reply is: "Liberal? Conservative? Depends on the issue & the writer." Recent articles include "The Language of Redemption: The Catholic Poets Adam Zagajewski, Marie Ponsot, and Lawrence Joseph," "History Lite: Goldhagen, the Holocaust, and the Truth," "We Hold These Truths: The Mission of a Catholic Law School," and "Catholics and the Liberal Tradition: Still Compatible." Although published by Catholic laypeople, other views are often represented. Table of contents and selected archived articles since 1997 are available online at www.commonwealmagazine.org. This is a useful publication that is accessible to most readers. Recommended for public and undergraduate libraries.

5881. ***Concilium: international review of theology.*** [ISSN: 0010-5236] 1965. 5x/yr. GBP 48 (Individuals, GBP 29). S C M Press, 9-17 St Albans Pl, London, N1 0NX, United Kingdom; scmpress@btinternet.com. Illus., adv. Sample. Refereed. Circ: 1000. Vol. ends: Dec. *Indexed:* NTA. *Aud.:* Ac.

For global theological discussion within a post–Vatican II Catholic perspective, this is a noteworthy publication. Although Catholic in origin, contributors include important scholars drawn from other traditions and religions and from all parts of the globe. Issues are completely thematic, utilize varying editors, and include about a dozen 6- to 15-page articles that are well researched. Although authors represent many nationalities, articles are in English, often via translation. Recent issues deal with "Rethinking Martyrdom," "The Discourse of Human Dignity," and "Learning from Other Faiths." The tables of contents for issues as far back as 1965 (with some exceptions) are available online at www.concilium.org/english.htm. Recommended for academic libraries with collection interests in theology.

5882. ***Cross Currents (New York).*** Former titles (until 1990): *Religion and Intellectual Life;* (until 1983): *N I C M Journal for Jews and Christians in Higher Education.* [ISSN: 0011-1953] 1950. q. USD 50 (Individuals, USD 30; USD 10 newsstand/cover). Ed(s): Kenneth Arnold. Association for Religion and Intellectual Life, 475 Riverside Dr, Ste 1945, New York, NY 10115; cph@crosscurrents.org; http://www.aril.org. Illus., index, adv. Sample. Refereed. Circ: 5000. Vol. ends: Winter. Online: bigchalk; EBSCO Publishing; Florida Center for Library Automation; Gale Group; OCLC Online Computer Library Center, Inc.; ProQuest Information & Learning; H.W. Wilson. Reprint: PSC. *Indexed:* ABS&EES, BAS, BHA, CPL, HumInd, MLA-IB, R&TA, RI-1. *Bk. rev.:* 6-8, 400-2,000 words, signed. *Aud.:* Ac, Sa.

Cross Currents gives voice to the Association for Religion and Intellectual Life, which believes that religion and intellectual life are not antithetical, so long as religion can be viewed in new and inclusive ways. Authors come from a variety of traditions and faiths. Articles are well documented and intellectually stimulating. Recent examples include "Post-Modernism and Its Secrets: Religion Without Religion," "American Muslims and a Meaningful Human Rights Discourse in the Aftermath of September 11, 2001," and "Why Is the City So Important for Christian Theology?." Issues also include poetry, review essays, and book reviews. Selected current and archived articles since 1996 are available online at www.crosscurrents.org. Given its commitment to "connecting the wisdom of the heart and the life of the mind," *Cross Currents* will appeal to intellectuals seeking to remain connected to religion. Highly recommended for academic libraries; larger public libraries may also want to consider it.

5883. ***Eastern Buddhist.*** [ISSN: 0012-8708] 1965. s-a. JPY 3000; USD 25; USD 30 foreign. Eastern Buddhist Society, Otani University, Koyama-cho, Kyoto-shi, 603-8152, Japan; scholars@emory.edu. Illus., adv. Refereed. Circ: 1200. Vol. ends: Autumn. *Indexed:* ArtHuCI, BAS, HumInd, IBSS, MLA-IB, RI-1. *Bk. rev.:* 2-4, 1,500-2,000 words, signed. *Aud.:* Ac, Sa.

Finding scholarly and critical journals that deal with Eastern Buddhism (Mahayana Buddhism) that are accessible to English readers is not particularly easy. In addition to fulfilling that assignment, this publication does so at a cost that is very reasonable. Substantial articles that are refereed and well researched provide an open and critical study of all aspects of Eastern Buddhism ("The Cardinal Virtues of the Bodhisattva in Dogen's Shobogenzo Zuimonki," "Protect the Dharma, Protect the Country: Buddhist War Responsibility and Social Ethics"). Authors represent current scholars from both the East and West, with all articles in English. Table of contents for all issues (including the original series, 1921–1958) is available online at www.otani.ac.jp/EBS/journal.html. Highly recommended for academic institutions seeking to support research in Buddhism.

5884. ***Ecumenical Review.*** Formerly (until 1948): *Christendom.* [ISSN: 0013-0796] 1935. q. CHF 47.50 domestic; USD 35 foreign. Ed(s): Raiser Konrad. World Council of Churches, 150 route de Ferney, PO Box 2100, Geneva, 1211, Switzerland; http://www.wcc-coe.org/. Illus., index, adv. Circ: 3500. Microform: PQC. Online: EBSCO Publishing; Florida Center for Library Automation; Gale Group; Northern Light Technology, Inc.; OCLC Online Computer Library Center, Inc.; ProQuest Information & Learning. Reprint: PQC. *Indexed:* ArtHuCI, BRI, CBRI, HumInd, IBZ, IMFL, NTA, OTA, PRA, R&TA, RI-1, SSCI. *Bk. rev.:* 3-5, 800-1,000 words, signed. *Aud.:* Ac, Sa.

As the official quarterly of the World Council of Churches (WCC), this is an important resource for studying the ecumenical movement. Scholarly, well-written articles examine ecumenical issues in general and the work of the WCC in particular. Issues are topical, covering a range of subjects from "religious freedom and proselytism to work in a sustainable society, from the place of the Roman Catholic Church in the search for Christian unity to the tensions that arise when the church faces questions of human sexuality." The journal offers other features that are useful for research and collection development, such as reports and speeches from WCC assemblies and committees. The section "Significant Ecumenical Journals" provides access to the tables of contents for a number of related journals. Although general collections will find this journal too specialized, academic libraries supporting ecumenical research will find it essential.

5885. ***Evangelical Quarterly: an international review of Bible and theology.*** [ISSN: 0014-3367] 1929. q. USD 70.40 (Individuals, USD 45.80). Ed(s): I Howard Marshall. The Paternoster Press, Kingstown Broadway, PO Box 300, Carlisle, CA3 0QS, United Kingdom; 100526.3434@compuserve.com. Illus., index, adv. Circ: 1100. Microform: PQC. Reprint: PQC. *Indexed:* ChrPI, IBZ, NTA, OTA, R&TA, RI-1. *Bk. rev.:* 8-20, 800-1,600, signed. *Aud.:* Ac.

This publication presents evangelical Christianity, primarily from the British perspective. As stated in the subtitle, coverage includes both biblical and theological topics. Recent titles include "The Hermeneutical Framework of Social-Scientific Criticism: How Much Can Evangelicals Get Involved?," "Gog and Magog: the History of a Symbol," and "Jesus and the Food Laws: A Reassessment of Mark 7:19b." Abstracts are included at the end of each article. Book reviews occupy about a quarter of each issue. In addition to assisting with collection development, the reviewers' comments provide insights into contemporary evangelical thinking. This is a quality publication, edited by a well-known scholar, representing an important perspective on biblical and theological studies. Recommended for academic libraries.

5886. ***Evangelical Theological Society. Journal.*** Formerly (until 1968): *E T S Bulletin.* [ISSN: 0360-8808] 1958. q. USD 30. Ed(s): Andreas Kostenberger. Evangelical Theological Society, c/o James Borland, Sec Treas, 200 Russell Woods Dr, Lynchburg, VA 24502-3574; http://www.etsjets.org. Illus., index, adv. Refereed. Circ: 4300. Vol. ends: Dec. Microform: PQC. Online: ProQuest Information & Learning. Reprint: PQC. *Indexed:* ChrPI, NTA, OTA, R&TA, RI-1. *Bk. rev.:* 16-20, 600-2,000 words, signed. *Aud.:* Ac, Sa.

This journal is a scholarly forum for those who adhere to an "evangelical" theology (which includes the inerrancy of the Bible and trinitarian theology). Committed to fostering "conservative biblical scholarship," it only publishes articles representative of this viewpoint. Within these parameters, however, it offers well-researched articles that reflect some of the best scholarship within evangelical circles on biblical and theological subjects. Recent titles include "Is Our Reading the Bible the Same as the Original Audience's Hearing It? A Case Study in the Gospel of Mark," "Public Theology and Prophecy Data: Factual Evidence that Counts for the Biblical World View," and "Why Scientists Must Believe in God: Divine Attributes of Scientific Law." Issues include book reviews and occasional reports and news items from the society. A valuable forum for those who share the evangelical perspective, this journal is also useful for those outside of evangelicalism who are seeking to understand it. A staple at evangelical institutions, this title should be considered by libraries seeking a well-balanced collection in theology and biblical studies.

Feminist Theology. See Women: Feminist and Special Interest/Feminist and Women's Studies section.

5887. ***Harvard Theological Review.*** [ISSN: 0017-8160] 1908. q. USD 88 (Individuals, USD 44). Ed(s): Francois Bovon. Cambridge University Press, The Edinburgh Bldg, Shaftesbury Rd, Cambridge, CB2 2RU, United Kingdom; information@cambridge.org; http://uk.cambridge.org/journals. Illus., index, adv. Sample. Refereed. Circ: 1500 Paid. Vol. ends: Oct. Online: Florida Center for Library Automation; Gale Group; Northern Light Technology, Inc.; OCLC Online Computer Library Center, Inc.; Swets Blackwell; H.W. Wilson. Reprint: PSC. *Indexed:* ArtHuCI, BHA, HumInd, IBZ, MLA-IB, NTA, OTA, R&TA, RI-1, SSCI. *Aud.:* Ac.

Harvard is a name associated with academic scholarship and excellence. The *Harvard Theological Review* is a worthy bearer of this name. Articles are very well written, fairly lengthy (15–25 pages), and reveal the high level of research and documentation one would expect. Commensurate with this scholarship, articles tend to be narrow in scope, e.g., "Does God Lie to His Prophets? The Story of Micaiah ben Imlah As a Test Case," "Witchcraft and the Sense-of-the-Impossible in Early Modern Spain: Some Reflections Based on the Literature of

Superstition (ca. 1500-1800)," and "The Philosophical Foundations of Soloveitchik's Critique of Interfaith Dialogue." Coverage "embraces the history and philosophy of religious thought in all traditions and periods—including Hebrew Bible, New Testament, Christianity, Jewish studies, theology, ethics, archaeology, and comparative religious studies." In addition to articles and shorter "Notes and Observations," an annual section provides summaries of doctoral dissertations accepted in Harvard's Th.D. and Ph.D. programs. Not for the casual reader, this journal is intended for specialists and scholars. It is, therefore, highly recommended for academic and research libraries.

5888. ***History of Religions.*** [ISSN: 0018-2710] 1961. q. USD 153 (Individuals, USD 44; Students, USD 29). Ed(s): Gary L Ebersole. University of Chicago Press, Journals Division, PO Box 37005, Chicago, IL 60637; subscriptions@press.uchicago.edu; http://www.journals.uchicago.edu. Illus., index, adv. Sample. Refereed. Circ: 1500 Paid. Vol. ends: May. Microform: PMC. Online: EBSCO Publishing; Florida Center for Library Automation; Gale Group; ProQuest Information & Learning. Reprint: ISI; PQC; PSC. *Indexed:* AICP, AbAn, AmH&L, AnthLit, ArtHuCI, BAS, HumInd, IBSS, IBZ, LRI, MLA-IB, NTA, OTA, R&TA, RI-1, SSCI. *Bk. rev.:* 0-15, 400-1,800 words, signed. *Aud.:* Ac.

This is an advanced journal interested in "the study of religious phenomena from prehistory to modern times, both within particular traditions and across cultural boundaries." Interdisciplinary in nature, authors from around the world draw upon philosophy, theology, sociology, psychology, and history in their analysis of religion. Coverage extends to all world religions: modern, ancient, and prehistoric. Recent articles include "Rules of Purity and Confessional Boundaries: Maliki Debates about the Pollution of the Christian," "Divining an Author: The Idea of Authorship in an Indian Religious Tradition," and "Buddhist Rain-making in Early Japan: The Dragon Kind and the Ritual Careers of Esoteric Monks." Tables of contents since 1996 may be viewed at www.journals.uchicago.edu/HR. Highly recommended for academic libraries.

5889. ***Horizons: the journal of the college theology society.*** [ISSN: 0360-9669] 1974. s-a. USD 40 (Individuals, USD 16). College Theology Society, c/o Walter Conn, Ed., 800 Lancaster Ave., Villanova, PA 19085-1699. Illus., adv. Refereed. Circ: 1410 Paid. Microform: PQC. Online: EBSCO Publishing; OCLC Online Computer Library Center, Inc. Reprint: PQC. *Indexed:* ArtHuCI, CPL, NTA, OTA, R&TA, RI-1, SSCI. *Bk. rev.:* 25-30, 400-1,600 words, signed. *Aud.:* Ac.

The College Theology Society is a professional society of college and university professors. Although originally and still predominately Roman Catholic, the society is "increasingly ecumenical in its membership and concerns." The society seeks both to develop the academic discipline of religion and to promote its effective instruction. *Horizons* is intended to help fulfill these objectives by exploring "developments in Catholic theology, the total Christian tradition, human religious experience, and the concerns of creative teaching in the college and university environment." Written for both the student and the scholar, articles deal with the content of religious studies ("Continuity Amidst Disruption: The Spirit and Apostolic Succession at the Reformation," "Dominus Iesus and Asian Theologies") and discussion of creative teaching ideas ("Theology in a Catholic University: Newman's Significance for Today"). Editorial essays, occasional reports from the society, a review symposium (multiple reviews of the same book), and book reviews fill out the issue. *Horizons* is recommended for academic libraries.

5890. ***The Humanist: a magazine of critical inquiry and social concern.*** [ISSN: 0018-7399] 1941. bi-m. Individuals, USD 24.95. Ed(s): Fred Edwords. American Humanist Association, PO Box 1188, Buffalo, NY 14226-7188; thehumanist@juno.com; http://www.humanist.net. Illus., adv. Sample. Refereed. Circ: 15000. Vol. ends: Dec. Microform: PQC. Online: EBSCO Publishing; Florida Center for Library Automation; Gale Group; Northern Light Technology, Inc.; OCLC Online Computer Library Center, Inc.; ProQuest Information & Learning; H.W. Wilson. *Indexed:* BRI, CBRI, CIJE, ECER, FLI, FutSurv, HRA, HumInd, IBZ, LRI, MRD, MagInd, PAIS, PhilInd, RGPR, RI-1, SSCI. *Bk. rev.:* 0-3, 600-1,200 words, signed. *Aud.:* Ga, Ac.

In contrast to many of the other journals in this section, *The Humanist* takes a nontheistic, secular, and naturalistic approach to its coverage. So why is it included among religious titles? The reason is that "humanism serves, for many humanists, some of the psychological and social functions of a religion, but without belief in deities, transcendental entities, miracles, life after death, and the supernatural" (www.americanhumanist.org). Furthermore, many religiously liberal people agree with humanism's rejection of the supernatural, without going as far as the humanist commitment to naturalism ("the conviction that the universe or nature is all that exists or is real"). Religion, in its more progressive forms, and humanism are not as antithetical as they may at first appear. One of the fellows of the Jesus Seminar authored an article in *The Humanist* on "The Psychology of Biblicism." Religious topics are frequently discussed from the humanist perspective ("Religion and the Quest for a Sustainable World"), making this a valuable addition to library collections. Articles usually focus on social issues, such as the environment, civil liberties, human rights, and international relations. Philosophical, scientific, and other contemporary concerns are also discussed. The magazine's web site (www.thehumanist.org) includes tables of contents and brief summaries of issues from 1995 to the present. This is a basic title that deserves a place in public and academic libraries.

5891. ***International Journal for Philosophy of Religion.*** [ISSN: 0020-7047] 1970. bi-m. EUR 441 print or online ed. Ed(s): Eugene Thomas Long, Frank R Harrison, III. Kluwer Academic Publishers, van Godewijckstraat 30, PO Box 17, Dordrecht, 3300 AA, Netherlands. Illus., index, adv. Refereed. Vol. ends: Jun/Dec. Microform: PQC. Online: EBSCO Publishing; Gale Group; ingenta.com; Kluwer Online; OCLC Online Computer Library Center, Inc.; Ovid Technologies, Inc.; RoweCom Information Quest; Swets Blackwell. Reprint: SWZ. *Indexed:* ArtHuCI, HumInd, IBSS, PhilInd, R&TA, RI-1. *Bk. rev.:* 0-4, 600-1,000 words, signed. *Aud.:* Ac.

The philosophical study of religion is an important aspect of many religious studies programs. This journal "provides a medium for the exposition, development, and criticism of important philosophical insights and theories relevant to religion in any of its varied forms," and it is intended for a "wide range of thoughtful readers, especially teachers and students of philosophy, philosophical theology, and religious thought." According to the masthead, the journal focuses on the philosophical study of religion but is not committed to any particular philosophical or religious position within that framework. Although an international journal, all of the articles are in English. Articles are scholarly without being too lengthy. Recent examples include "Divine Omniscience and Knowledge *de Se*," "The Logic and Language of Nirvana: a Contemporary Interpretation," and "Moral Evil: the Comparative Response." Issues may also include symposia, discussions, reviews, notes, and news. A free sample issue, along with tables of contents since 1997, may be found at www.kluweronline.com/issn/0020-7047. Recommended for academic libraries. (Compare with *Religious Studies* below, this section.)

5892. ***The International Journal for the Psychology of Religion.*** [ISSN: 1050-8619] 1991. q. USD 340. Ed(s): Raymond F Paloutzian. Lawrence Erlbaum Associates, Inc., 10 Industrial Ave, Mahwah, NJ 07430-2262; journals@erlbaum.com; http://www.erlbaum.com/. Illus., adv. Sample. Refereed. Vol. ends: No. 4. Reprint: PSC. *Indexed:* ASSIA, PsycholAb, R&TA, RI-1. *Bk. rev.:* 1-2, 500-1,500 words, signed. *Aud.:* Ac, Sa.

Religion intersects a number of disciplines, including psychology. Researchers who are interested in the nexus of religion and psychology will find this journal to be a valuable resource. The stated audience includes "psychologists, theologians, philosophers, religious leaders, neuroscientists, and social scientists." The journal is "devoted to psychological studies of religious processes and phenomena in all religious traditions," and "provides a means for sustained discussion of psychologically relevant issues that can be examined empirically and concern religion in the most general sense." Articles are scientific, use statistical analysis, and are fairly extensive in length. They cover a variety of topics, including "social psychology of religion, religious development, conversion, religious experience, religion and social attitudes and behavior, religion and mental health, and psychoanalytic and other theoretical interpretations of religion." Recent articles include "The Effect of Religious-Spiritual Coping on Positive Attitudes of Adult Muslim Refugees From Kosovo and Bosnia," "Why Do Religious Fundamentalists Tend to be Prejudiced?," and

"Negatively Reinforcing Personal Extrinsic Motivations: Religious Orientation, Inner Awareness, and Mental Health in Iran and the United States." Issues also contain perspective papers, review essays, and a limited number of book reviews. As an international journal, authors are drawn from around the world, although all articles are in English. The journal's web site (www.catchword.com/erlbaum/10508619) offers tables of contents since 2000, plus an online sample issue. Recommended for academic libraries.

5893. *International Journal of Hindu Studies.* [ISSN: 1022-4556] 1997. 3x/yr. USD 150 (Individuals, USD 60; Students, USD 30). Ed(s): Sushil Mittal. World Heritage Press, 1270 St Jean, St Hyacinthe, PQ J2S 8M2, Canada. Illus., index, adv. Sample. Refereed. Circ: 150. Vol. ends: Dec. *Indexed:* BAS. *Bk. rev.:* 30-35, 500-900 words, signed. *Aud.:* Ac, Sa.

This important, relatively new journal fills a significant niche by providing an accessible, English-language, scholarly journal covering Hinduism. Scholars from around the world contribute articles incorporating comparative or theoretical studies arising from the disciplines of the social sciences and humanities vis-a-vis Hinduism. Although the scope of Hindu coverage is intentionally broad and vague, the journal is "less concerned with the intrinsic forms of Hinduism and its history." Instead, it focuses on "Hinduism's adaptations to a wide range of historical circumstances and ecological, economic, and political possibilities and . . . on the Hindu forms that work 'on the ground' in particular places and times to generate special kinds of social, cultural, and psychological order and problems." In other words, the journal seeks to go beyond simply describing "*what* Hinduism is" by answering the question "*why* is Hinduism the way it is?" Typical articles include "The Indo-European Prehistory of Yoga," "Macrocosm, Mesocosm, and Microcosm: The Persistent Nature of 'Hindu' Beliefs and Symbolic Forms," and "The Many Lives of Dandin: The Kavyadarsa in Sanskrit and Tamil." The large number of book reviews will assist those interested in keeping abreast of Hindu scholarship. Academic libraries supporting religious studies programs should seriously consider adding this title to their collection.

5894. *International Review of Mission.* [ISSN: 0020-8582] 1911. q. CHF 47.50; USD 35. Ed(s): Christopher Duraisingh. World Council of Churches, 150 route de Ferney, PO Box 2100, Geneva, 1211, Switzerland. Illus., index, adv. Circ: 3500. Vol. ends: Oct. Microform: PQC. Online: EBSCO Publishing; Florida Center for Library Automation; Gale Group; Northern Light Technology, Inc.; OCLC Online Computer Library Center, Inc.; ProQuest Information & Learning. Reprint: PQC; PSC. *Indexed:* AICP, BAS, ChrPI, HumInd, R&TA, RI-1. *Bk. rev.:* 0-5, 200-1,000 words, signed. *Aud.:* Ac, Sa.

From its very beginning, Christianity has been mission oriented. For many Christians, the understanding of that mission has changed and developed as churches have adjusted to a more pluralistic world. As a result, the concept of "mission" has evolved into something more modern. This journal, which represents the voice of the Conference on World Mission and Evangelism of the World Council of Churches (the primary global organization promoting ecumenism and interreligious dialogue), offers well-researched papers seeking to examine and facilitate this evolution. Issues contain articles, editorials, and "documentation" (statements and reports from various bodies and conferences). Recent articles include "From Management to Vision: Issues for the British Churches Negotiating Decline and Change," "Latin American Pentecostalisms and Western Postmodernism: Reflections on a Complex Relationship," and "The Context of Christian Witness in the 21st Century." The "Bibliography on Mission Studies," included in each issue, provides a guide to books, articles, and other publications. It is divided into subject areas and is occasionally briefly annotated. Thanks to the efforts of the Centre for the Study of Christianity in the Non-Western World (University of Edinburgh), a cumulative, searchable list of all of these bibliographies from 1912 to the present is available online at webdb.ucs.ed.ac.uk/divinity/cmb. This is a standard journal at seminaries and is highly recommended for academic libraries supporting religious studies programs.

5895. *Interpretation (Richmond): a journal of Bible and theology.* [ISSN: 0020-9643] 1947. q. USD 30 (Individuals, USD 23; USD 6 newsstand/cover per issue). Ed(s): William P Brown. Union Theological Seminary, 3401 Brook Rd, Richmond, VA 23227; email@interpretation.org; http://www.interpretation.org. Illus., adv. Refereed. Circ: 7000 Paid. Vol. ends: Oct. Microform: PQC. Online: EBSCO Publishing; Florida Center for Library Automation; Gale Group; OCLC Online Computer Library Center, Inc.; ProQuest Information & Learning; H.W. Wilson. Reprint: PQC. *Indexed:* ArtHuCI, BRI, CBRI, ChrPI, HumInd, IBZ, NTA, OTA, R&TA, RI-1, SSI. *Bk. rev.:* 3-4 major, 800-1,200 words; 25-30 minor, 200-450 words, signed. *Aud.:* Ga, Ac.

Widely read by professionals in the church and in academic circles, this is a very useful and accessible journal. Articles tend to be brief but are fully documented. Issues are thematic and cover both theological and biblical studies, such as "Biblical Faith and History," "Teaching the Bible Today," "Parables," and "Scripture and Theology." Writers include scholars from a variety of traditions. Each issue includes a feature known as "Between Text and Sermon," which presents a short exposition of four passages corresponding to the upcoming readings in the Common Lectionary. Clergy find this a particularly useful feature, even though four readings every quarter is somewhat limited. The book reviews are interesting and well done. Seminary libraries have included this in their collections for years and should continue to do so. The current table of contents and the full texts of book reviews since 2001 are available at www.interpretation.org/index.htm. Although useful to scholars, the level of writing is not beyond the educated individual. Unlike a number of academic journals on religion, the connection of biblical studies and theology to the church is apparent in this publication. Recommended for public and academic libraries.

5896. *Japanese Journal of Religious Studies.* Formerly (until 1974): *Contemporary Religions in Japan.* [ISSN: 0304-1042] 1960. s-a. JPY 5000 (Individuals, JPY 3500; Students, JPY 3000). Ed(s): Robert Kisala. Nanzan University, 18 Yamazato-cho, Showa-ku, Nagoya-shi, 466-8673, Japan; http://www.nanzan-u.ac.jp/. Illus., index, adv. Refereed. Circ: 600. Vol. ends: Fall. Online: EBSCO Publishing; OCLC Online Computer Library Center, Inc. Reprint: PQC. *Indexed:* ArtHuCI, BAS, IBSS, IBZ, R&TA, RI-1. *Bk. rev.:* 0-15, 1,000-3,000 words, signed. *Aud.:* Ac, Sa.

When a collection of journals is limited to those available in English, a bias toward European and American coverage naturally develops. This journal helps to counter this trend by providing a distinctively different perspective. The *Japanese Journal of Religious Studies* is published by the Nanzan Institute for Religion and Culture, which is committed to "the interdisciplinary study of the relations between religion and culture with particular reference to the Far East, and more specifically Japan, [and] the promotion of mutual understanding among Christianity and other religions." Drawing especially (but not exclusively) on Japanese authors, this journal presents English-language articles (with abstracts) and book reviews. Recent articles include "Did Dogen Go to China? Problematizing Dogen's Relation to Ju-ching and Chinese Ch'an," "Grave Changes: Scattering Ashes in Contemporary Japan," and "Ethnicity, Sagehood and the Politics of Literacy in Asuka Japan." For those with the ability to read them, Japanese characters appear in the text following Romanized transliterations. In addition to the tables of contents from the first issue in 1974 to the present, full-text articles from 1986 to 1988 (html format) and 1993 to the present (pdf format) are available online at www.nanzan-u.ac.jp/SHUBUNKEN/publications/jjrs. This is a valuable and affordable publication that will improve the range of perspectives within a religious studies collection. Highly recommended for academic libraries.

5897. *Journal for the Scientific Study of Religion.* [ISSN: 0021-8294] 1961. q. USD 100 print & online eds. Ed(s): Ted Jelen. Blackwell Publishing, Inc., Commerce Place, 350 Main St, Malden, MA 02148; subscrip@blackwellpub.com; http://www.blackwellpublishing.com. Illus., index, adv. Refereed. Circ: 3500. Vol. ends: Dec. Microform: PQC. Online: EBSCO Publishing; Gale Group; ingenta.com; OCLC Online Computer Library Center, Inc.; RoweCom Information Quest; Swets Blackwell; H.W. Wilson. Reprint: PQC. *Indexed:* ABS&EES, AbAn, ArtHuCI, BAS, CJA, HumInd, IBSS, IBZ, IJP, LRI, MLA-IB, OTA, PRA, PSA, PsycholAb, R&TA, RI-1, SSCI, SociolAb. *Bk. rev.:* 4-8, 600-1,500 words, signed. *Aud.:* Ac.

While *Zygon* (see below, this section) explores the dialogue between science and religion, this journal, from the Society for the Scientific Study of Religion, uses scientific methods to examine religious institutions and experiences. Sociological, psychological, anthropological, and both quantitative and qualitative methods are employed in the investigation of religion. Many articles often reflect this scientific orientation through a technical research format, while others are written more like essays. Researchers interested in statistical data regarding religion will find the articles very interesting. Although not always necessary, in the more technical pieces a background in statistics will be helpful. Recent articles include "Linked Lives, Faith, and Behavior: Intergenerational Religious Influence on Adolescent Delinquency," "Race Differences in Congregational Social Service Activity," and "Secularization and Aging in Britain: Does Family Formation Cause Greater Religiosity?" The journal's web site (www.blackwellpublishing.com/journal.asp?ref=0021-8294) provides tables of contents and abstracts since 2000, and a sample issue. This publication provides an important social sciences perspective on religion, as evidenced by the large number of indexes covering it. Highly recommended for academic libraries.

5898. *Journal for the Study of the New Testament.* [ISSN: 0142-064X] 1978. q. GBP 100 (Individuals, GBP 35; Students, GBP 26.50). Ed(s): David G Horrell. Sheffield Academic Press Ltd, Mansion House, 19 Kingfield Rd, Sheffield, S11 9AS, United Kingdom; jjoyce@continuumbooks.com; http://www.continuumjournals.com/. Illus., index, adv. Refereed. Vol. ends: Jun. *Indexed:* NTA, R&TA, RI-1. *Bk. rev.:* 2-7, 300-400 words, signed. *Aud.:* Ac.

Anyone involved in studying biblical texts will benefit from access to this journal (and its twin covering the Old Testament—see the next entry). It clearly focuses on the exegesis of the New Testament, "including innovative work from historical perspectives, studies using social-scientific and literary theory or developing theological, cultural and contextual approaches." Articles will appeal to "scholars, teachers in the field of New Testament, postgraduate students and advanced undergraduates." Recent articles include "The Historic Present in Matthew's Gospel: A Survey and Analysis Focused on Matthew 13.44," "Parable Metonymy and Luke's Kerygmatic Framing," "The Origin of Paul's Doctrine of the Two Adams in 1 Corinthians 15.45-49," and "John's Gospel: A Two-Level Drama?" Articles are original, well documented, and moderate in length. The editorial board includes several significant names in biblical studies. Like its twin, *JSOT*, this journal is highly recommended for academic libraries supporting biblical studies research.

5899. *Journal for the Study of the Old Testament.* [ISSN: 0309-0892] 1976. q. GBP 125 (Individuals, GBP 40; Students, GBP 30). Ed(s): John Jarick, Keith Whitelam. Sheffield Academic Press Ltd, Mansion House, 19 Kingfield Rd, Sheffield, S11 9AS, United Kingdom; jjoyce@continuumbooks.com; http://www.continuumjournals.com/. Illus. Refereed. Vol. ends: No. 5. *Indexed:* NTA, OTA, R&TA, RI-1. *Bk. rev.:* 500 are included in the special annual issue, 100-700 words, signed. *Aud.:* Ac.

Like its sibling publication covering the New Testament (see above entry), this journal is a standard resource for students of the Old Testament (OT). Since it focuses on OT exegesis, articles are closely related to the biblical text. This may include exegetical analysis of particular passages or discussions of textual transmission and history. Archaeology may be a suitable subject if it promotes the understanding of a biblical passage. *JSOT* presents quality articles that are well documented and useful for research. Recent titles include "Narrative Obscurity of Samson's hdyx in Judges 14.14 and 18," "Pharaoh's Daughter, Solomon's Palace, and the Temple: Another Look at the Structure of 1 Kings 1–11," and "Darius in Place of Cyrus: The First Edition of Deutero-Isaiah (Isaiah 40.1–52.12) in 521 BCE." Since 1998, the annual publication of "Book List for The Society for Old Testament Study" has been one of the annual issues of *JSOT.* This special issue contains almost 500 book reviews 100-700 words in length. Like *Journal for the Study of the New Testament*, *JSOT* is edited by significant scholars and is highly recommended for academic libraries where there is an interest in Old Testament studies.

5900. *Journal of Biblical Literature.* [ISSN: 0021-9231] 1881. q. USD 100 (Members, USD 35; Non-members, USD 75). Ed(s): Gail R O'Day. Society of Biblical Literature, P.O. Box 2243, Williston, VT 05495-2243; sblexec@sbl-site.org; http://www.sbl-site.org. Illus., index, adv. Refereed. Circ: 5000 Paid and free. Vol. ends: Winter. Microform: PMC; PQC. Online: bigchalk; Chadwyck-Healey Incorporated; EBSCO Publishing; Gale Group; Northern Light Technology, Inc.; OCLC Online Computer Library Center, Inc.; ProQuest Information & Learning; H.W. Wilson. Reprint: PQC. *Indexed:* ArtHuCI, BRI, CBRI, HumInd, IBZ, IJP, NTA, OTA, R&TA, RI-1, SSCI. *Bk. rev.:* 20-25, 900-1,500 words, signed. *Aud.:* Ac.

From the distinguished Society of Biblical Literature, this is a premier journal in the area of biblical studies. World-renowned scholars present original research dealing with the text of the Jewish and Christian scriptures. Many articles are very narrow in scope, limiting themselves to the examination of Hebrew and Greek words or phrases. Because the articles are intended for other scholars, familiarity with the original languages is expected of the reader. The emphasis on *biblical* studies is evident in this sampling of titles: "Jewish Laws on Illicit Marriage, the Defilement of Offspring, and the Holiness of the Temple: a New Halakic Interpretation of 1 Corinthians 7:14," "The Circumscription of the King: Deuteronomy 17:16-17 in Its Ancient Social Context," and "What's in a Name? Neo-Assyrian Designations for the Northern Kingdom and their Implications for Israelite History and Biblical Interpretation." In addition to the six to ten major articles, there are also "Critical Notes" offering short responses to other published works and previous articles. The extensive number of book reviews (often written by noted scholars) provide a guide to current literature, including non-English titles. Book reviews published since 1998 are available online at www.bookreviews.org (along with additional reviews). This is an indispensable, basic journal for any academic collection interested in biblical studies.

5901. *Journal of Church and State.* [ISSN: 0021-969X] 1959. q. USD 39 (Individuals, USD 25). Ed(s): Derek H Davis. Baylor University, J M Dawson Institute of Church-State Studies, PO Box 97308, Waco, TX 76798-7308; http://www.baylor.edu/Church_State/. Index, adv. Sample. Refereed. Circ: 1700. Vol. ends: Fall. Microform: WSH; PMC; PQC. Online: bigchalk; EBSCO Publishing; Florida Center for Library Automation; Gale Group; OCLC Online Computer Library Center, Inc.; ProQuest Information & Learning; H.W. Wilson. Reprint: WSH. *Indexed:* ABS&EES, AmH&L, ArtHuCI, BAS, BRI, CBRI, CLI, ChrPI, HumInd, IBSS, IBZ, LRI, PAIS, PSA, R&TA, RI-1, SociolAb. *Bk. rev.:* 35-40, 300-800 words, signed. *Aud.:* Ac, Sa.

The relationship between church and state has been a vexing issue throughout most of church history. This journal is for those interested in this relationship. Each issue includes six or more scholarly, documented articles dealing with "constitutional, historical, philosophical, theological, and sociological studies on religion and the body politic in various countries and cultures of the world." Although the United States receives significant attention, coverage includes situations—and authors—from around the world. Important ecclesiastical documents, government legislation, and court decisions are occasionally included. Recent articles include "Revealing Liberalism in Early America: Rethinking Religious Liberty and Liberal Values," "Lessons for Today? The Church-State Relationship in Twentieth-Century Christian Ecumenical Thought," and "Adopting ~In God We Trust' As the U.S. National Motto." A very useful feature is the international "Notes on Church-State Affairs," which lists recent events regarding church–state relationships by country. The United States section receives special attention and is subdivided by topics, such as abortion, courts, denominational matters, education, politics, and the like. Another tool for researchers is a section listing recent doctoral dissertations dealing with church–state concerns. The full text of the "Notes on Church-State Affairs," the editorials, and the tables of contents from the past two volumes is available on the journal's web site (www3.baylor.edu/Church_State/journal_of_church_&_state.htm). Since the relationship between church and state is relevant to several disciplines beyond religion (e.g., political science), academic libraries are strongly urged to consider including this interesting journal in their collection.

5902. *Journal of Early Christian Studies.* Supersedes (in 1993): *Second Century;* Incorporates (1972-1993): *Patristics.* [ISSN: 1067-6341] 1981. q. USD 111 domestic; USD 119.20 in Canada & Mexico; USD 122 elsewhere. Ed(s): Elizabeth A Clark, J Patout Burns. Johns Hopkins University Press, Journals Publishing Division, 2715 N Charles St, Baltimore, MD 21218-4363; http://www.press.jhu.edu/. Illus., adv. Sample. Refereed. Circ: 1444. Vol. ends: Winter. Online: EBSCO

Publishing; RoweCom Information Quest; Swets Blackwell. Reprint: PSC. *Indexed:* ArtHuCI, IBZ, MLA-IB, NTA, R&TA, RI-1, SSCI, SociolAb. *Bk. rev.:* 10-20, 400-1,000 words, signed. *Aud.:* Ac.

This journal limits its coverage to the first 600 years (100-700 CE) of the history and theology of the Christian church. (For more extensive coverage, see *Journal of Ecclesiastical History* below, this section.) The focus on the early church, along with the fact that it is produced by the North American Patristics Society, makes this an important journal for researchers interested in patristic studies. Articles present original scholarly work, are appropriately documented, and begin with an abstract. Examples of recent titles include "Augustine and the Making of Marriage in Roman North Africa," "Infected Sheep and Diseased Cattle, or the Pure and Holy Flock: Cyprian's Pastoral Care of Virgins," "Race and Universalism in Early Christianity," and "Plagiarism and Lay Patronage of Ascetic Scholarship: Jerome, Ambrose and Rufinus." Tables of contents (including subject headings for the articles) and abstracts for issues since 1996 can be found at muse.jhu.edu/journals/journal_of_early_christian_studies. This is an indispensable title for academic libraries supporting research in patristics.

5903. ***Journal of Ecclesiastical History.*** [ISSN: 0022-0469] 1953. q. USD 248 (Individuals, USD 99). Ed(s): Diarmaid MacCulloch, Martin Brett. Cambridge University Press, The Edinburgh Bldg, Shaftesbury Rd, Cambridge, CB2 2RU, United Kingdom; information@cambridge.org; http://uk.cambridge.org/journals. Illus., adv. Sample. Refereed. Circ: 1250. Vol. ends: Oct. Microform: PQC. Online: EBSCO Publishing; Florida Center for Library Automation; Gale Group; OCLC Online Computer Library Center, Inc.; RoweCom Information Quest; Swets Blackwell. *Indexed:* AmH&L, ArtHuCI, BHA, BrArAb, HumInd, NTA, NumL, R&TA, RI-1, SSCI. *Bk. rev.:* 60-75, 300-700 words, signed. *Aud.:* Ac.

This is one of the major publications in religious studies. Each issue contains about five substantial, scholarly articles covering "all aspects of the history of the Christian Church . . . both as an institution and in its relations with other religions and society at large." Recent articles include "Scripture, Style and Persuasion in Seventeenth-Century English Theories of Preaching," "Church and Society in Aberdeen and Glasgow, c. 1800–c. 2000," and "University Cultural Wars: Rival Protestant Pieties in Early Twentieth-Century Princeton." About a third of each issue is devoted to book reviews, providing a significant overview of current literature. Researchers and those involved in collection development will find this feature to be extremely useful. Since any study of European or American history inevitably involves ecclesiastical history, this journal will benefit both history and religious studies programs. This is a solid, useful journal of the highest caliber that belongs in every academic library.

5904. ***Journal of Ecumenical Studies.*** [ISSN: 0022-0558] 1964. q. USD 40 domestic; USD 45 foreign. Ed(s): Nancy Krody, Leonard Swidler. Journal of Ecumenical Studies, Temple University (022-38), 1114 W Berks St, Rm 511, Philadelphia, PA 19122-6090. Illus., index, adv. Sample. Refereed. Circ: 1300 Paid. Vol. ends: Fall. Microform: WSH; PMC. Online: EBSCO Publishing; Florida Center for Library Automation; Gale Group; OCLC Online Computer Library Center, Inc.; H.W. Wilson. Reprint: WSH. *Indexed:* ABS&EES, AmH&L, ArtHuCI, BAS, CLI, CPL, HumInd, IBZ, IJP, ILP, NTA, OTA, R&TA, RI-1, SSCI. *Bk. rev.:* 10-15, 350-700 words, signed. *Aud.:* Ac, Sa.

This ecumenical journal is concerned with issues of interreligious and interideological dialogue. Each issue includes six to eight well-documented articles covering theology, liturgy, and ecumenical issues within Christianity and between Christianity and other world religions. Typical articles include "Religionless Christianity and Vulnerable Discipleship: The Interfaith Promise of Bonhoeffer's Theology," "Presbyterians Pioneer the Vatican II Sunday Lectionary: Three Worship Models Converge," and "The Word of God: What Can Christians Learn from Muslim Attitudes toward the Qur'an?" Like many journals, *JES* provides coverage of recent monographic literature through its book reviews. An unusual feature, however, is the guide to recent *journal* literature relevant to ecumenical studies from around the world. This "Ecumenical Resources" section categorizes articles by country and then by publication (foreign-language titles also include an English translation). "Ecumenical Events" provides a succinct summary of recent conferences, dialogues, etc., that are important to the ecumenical movement. Publication has become irregular in recent years (there was a year and a half delay in finishing the 2001 volume), but the editor intends to return to a normal schedule soon. Hopefully this will occur, since this is a very useful journal, and it is highly recommended for academic libraries interested in ecumenical studies.

Journal of Feminist Studies in Religion. See Women: Feminist and Special Interest/Feminist and Women's Studies section.

5905. ***Journal of Jewish Studies.*** [ISSN: 0022-2097] 1948. s-a. GBP 56 (Individuals, GBP 32). Ed(s): Geza Vermes, Tessa Rajak. Oxford Centre for Hebrew and Jewish Studies, Yarnton Manor, Yarnton, OX1 1PY, United Kingdom. Illus., adv. Refereed. Circ: 1000. Vol. ends: Oct. Microform: PQC. Reprint: PSC. *Indexed:* ArtHuCI, BrHumI, IBSS, IJP, NTA, OTA, R&TA, RI-1. *Bk. rev.:* 25-30, 400-3,000 words, signed. *Aud.:* Ac, Sa.

This interdisciplinary journal is one of the important forums for the scholarly investigation of Jewish history, literature, and religion. Each issue contains about ten substantive articles plus a large number of book reviews (approximately one-third of the issue). Recent titles include "Rabbinic Traditions about Roman Persecutions of the Jews: A Reconsideration," "Abraham's Oracular Tree (T. Abr. 3:1-4)," and "Comments on Textual Details: Relationships between Masorah and Midrash." Scholars from a number of disciplines that are interested in Judaism (e.g., history, religion, biblical studies) will find this a valuable addition to the library's collection. Highly recommended for academic libraries.

5906. ***Journal of Presbyterian History.*** Former titles (until 1996): *American Presbyterians: Journal of Presbyterian History;* (until 1984): *Journal of Presbyterian History;* (until 1961): *Presbyterian Historical Society Journal.* [ISSN: 1521-9216] 1901. q. USD 70 (Individuals, USD 50). Ed(s): Tricia Manning. Presbyterian Historical Society, 425 Lombard St, Philadelphia, PA 19147; tmanning@history.pcusa.org; http://www.history.pcusa.org/. Illus., index. Sample. Refereed. Circ: 900. Vol. ends: Winter. *Indexed:* AmH&L, ArtHuCI, BAS, BEL&L, R&TA, RI-1, SSCI. *Bk. rev.:* 5-10, 400-600 words, signed. *Aud.:* Ac, Sa.

Anyone with a specific interest in the history of the American Presbyterian and Reformed traditions should consider this journal. It is designed to "inform, nurture, and promote among its readers an understanding and appreciation of religious history in its cultural setting (specifically Presbyterian and Reformed history), [and] educate readers as to the importance of preserving that history." Articles are well written and will appeal to both the general reader and the specialist. Recent examples include "Of Missionaries, Multiculturalism, and Mainstream Malaise: Reflections on the 'Presbyterian Predicament,'" "Shattered and Divided: Itinerancy, Ecclesiology, and Revivalism in the Presbyterian Awakening," and "Miami University 1809–2002: From Presbyterian Enterprise to Public Institution." Issues often include the text of important documents. Two older full-text sample issues and the table of contents for all issues since 1999 are available online at history.pcusa.org/pubs/journal. Like other denominational journals, the appeal of the *Journal of Presbyterian History* will be somewhat limited, and may be too specific for many general collections. Seminary libraries of various traditions should include it, however, as well as academic libraries with an interest in Presbyterian history.

5907. ***Journal of Psychology and Theology: an evangelical forum for the integration of psychology and theology.*** [ISSN: 0091-6471] 1973. q. USD 40 domestic; USD 52 foreign. Ed(s): Patricia L Pike. Biola University, Rosemead School of Psychology, 13800 Biola Ave, La Mirada, CA 90639-0001. Illus., adv. Refereed. Circ: 1700. Vol. ends: Winter. Microform: PQC. Online: bigchalk; The Dialog Corporation; EBSCO Publishing; Florida Center for Library Automation; Gale Group; ProQuest Information & Learning. Reprint: PQC. *Indexed:* AgeL, ArtHuCI, ChrPI, IBZ, IMFL, OTA, PsycholAb, R&TA, RI-1, SSCI. *Bk. rev.:* 4-6, 750-1,000 words, signed. *Aud.:* Ac.

The relationship between psychology and theology can be viewed from several perspectives, depending on which discipline is given priority. Although this journal seeks to promote the integration of these two disciplines, theology sets the boundaries for drawing conclusions. Consistent with its subtitle, the editorial policy states that "all articles should be consistent with an evangelical [theological] position." Psychological conclusions that are counter to this theology are not accepted. Although some issues were occasionally thematic in the past, the last six issues have all been thematic, perhaps reflecting a shift in policy. Some of these topics include "Psychotherapy and Spiritual Direction," "Human Sexuality," and "Evolutionary Psychology." Articles often include charts, graphs, and tables. Recent articles include "Integrating Spiritual Direction Functions in the Practice of Psychotherapy," "Sexual Script Theory: An Integrative Exploration of the Possibilities and Limits of Sexual Self-Definition," and "Intelligent Design Psychology and Evolutionary Psychology on Consciousness: Turning Water Into Wine." Issues also include a "Journal File," a review of articles appearing in other journals, and book reviews. An index of all articles, with abstracts, from the first volume on is available at the journal's web site (www.biola.edu/jpt). Those who advocate an evangelical approach to psychology will definitely want this journal in their collections. Its usefulness, however, is not limited to those who agree with its editorial position. Those who reject its basic presupposition could still find it to be a useful resource—both for its statistics and for its insights into understanding the evangelical perspective on this area of study. Recommended for academic libraries.

5908. *The Journal of Religion.* Former titles: *American Journal of Theology;* (until 1921): *Biblical World;* (until 1892): *The Old and New Testament Student;* (until 1889): *Old Testament Student;* (until 1883): *Hebrew Student.* [ISSN: 0022-4189] 1882. q. USD 128 print & online eds. (Individuals, USD 33 print & online eds.; Students, USD 26 print & online eds.). Ed(s): Kathryn E Tanner, Catherine Brekus. University of Chicago Press, Journals Division, PO Box 37005, Chicago, IL 60637; subscriptions@press.uchicago.edu; http://www.journals.uchicago.edu. Illus., index, adv. Refereed. Circ: 2200. Vol. ends: Oct. Microform: MIM; PMC; PQC. Online: EBSCO Publishing; Florida Center for Library Automation; Gale Group; ProQuest Information & Learning. Reprint: ISI; PQC; PSC. *Indexed:* ArtHuCI, BAS, BEL&L, BRD, BRI, CBRI, HumInd, IPB, MLA-IB, NTA, OTA, R&TA, RI-1, SSCI, SociolAb. *Bk. rev.:* 50-60, 750-1,500 words, signed. *Aud.:* Ac.

Published by the highly regarded Divinity School at the University of Chicago, this journal "promotes critical and systematic inquiry into the meaning and import of religion," embracing "all areas of theology (biblical, historical, ethical, constructive) as well as other types of religious studies (literary, social, psychological, philosophical)." Each issue has four or five lengthy articles written by scholars for scholars, reflecting an appropriate level of research and depth. Authors are not bound to any particular ideological orientation. Recent titles include "The Suffering of Isis/Io and Paul's Portrait of Christ Crucified (Gal. 3:1): Frescoes in Pompeian and Roman Houses and in the Temple of Isis in Pompeii," "Woman as God, God as Woman: Mysticism, Negative Theology, and Luce Irigary," and "Communicative Bodies and Economies of Grace: The Role of Sacrifice in the Christian Understanding of the Body." In addition to the substantial articles, about half of each issue is devoted to book reviews, making this a valuable resource for both scholars and bibliographers. The tables of contents (including the list of book reviews) from 1996 on is available at www.journals.uchicago.edu/JR. This is a leading publication in the area of religion and is recommended as a basic title for academic libraries.

5909. *Journal of Religion and Health.* [ISSN: 0022-4197] 1961. q. USD 557 print or online ed. Ed(s): Barry Ulanov. Kluwer Academic / Plenum Publishers, 233 Spring St Fl 7, New York, NY 10013-1522; http://www.wkap.nl/. Illus., index, adv. Refereed. Vol. ends: Winter. Microform: PQC. Online: EBSCO Publishing; ingenta.com; Kluwer Online; OCLC Online Computer Library Center, Inc.; RoweCom Information Quest; Swets Blackwell. Reprint: ISI; PQC. *Indexed:* AgeL, ArtHuCI, ExcerpMed, IJP, PsycholAb, R&TA, RI-1, SSCI. *Bk. rev.:* 15-20, 300-800 words, signed. *Aud.:* Ga, Ac.

The title of this journal conveys its central philosophy that religion and health are connected, and that human physical, emotional, and spiritual well-being are indivisible. Articles examine the relevance of religious studies to "current medical and psychological research" at "both a theoretical and practical level." Contributions are accepted from writers of all religious, medical, and psychological viewpoints. Articles frequently include statistical data and are prefaced with an abstract. Recent articles include "Ritual in Western Medicine and Its Role in Placebo Healing," "Discerning the Behavior of the Suicide Bomber: The Role of Vengeance," and "The Relationship Between Religion, Spirituality, Psychological Adjustment, and Quality of Life among People with Multiple Sclerosis." Tables of contents and abstracts since 1997, along with a sample full-text issue, are available at www.kluweronline.com/issn/0022-4197/contents. Written on a level accessible to the general reader, this journal will also appeal to specialists. Recommended for academic, medical, and large public libraries.

5910. *Journal of Religious Ethics.* [ISSN: 0384-9694] 1973. 3x/yr. USD 118 print & online eds. Blackwell Publishing, Inc., Commerce Place, 350 Main St, Malden, MA 02148; subscrip@blackwellpub.com; http://www.blackwellpublishing.com. Illus., adv. Sample. Refereed. Circ: 1200. Vol. ends: Fall. Microform: PQC. Online: EBSCO Publishing; Gale Group; ingenta.com; OCLC Online Computer Library Center, Inc.; RoweCom Information Quest; Swets Blackwell. *Indexed:* ABS&EES, ArtHuCI, HumInd, LRI, OTA, PRA, PhilInd, R&TA, RI-1, SSCI. *Bk. rev.:* 1-2 review essays, 25 pages each, signed. *Aud.:* Ac, Sa.

Ethics has always been one of the central topics in the field of religious studies. Those interested in religious ethics will find this journal to be a valuable resource. Although an independent publication, it is sponsored by four significant institutions (Florida State University, Emory University, Indiana University, University of Tennessee at Knoxville). Journal articles are focused on three primary concerns: "studies in comparative religious ethics, considerations of foundational conceptual and methodological issues, and historical studies of influential figures and texts." Articles must be original works, range from 20 to 30 pages in length, and are often thematically related within an issue. As part of its mission to promote dialogue, some issues include an essay-response(s)-reply format. In lieu of the normal book review section, there are typically one or two very lengthy (20-30 pages) book review essays, covering several books. Tables of contents and abstracts for issues from 1999 to the present can be found on the publisher's web site (www.blackwellpublishing.com/journal.asp?ref=0384-9694). This is an important journal for religious studies collections and for people working in related fields such as philosophy, history, literary studies, and social sciences. Highly recommended for academic libraries.

5911. *Journal of Theological Studies.* [ISSN: 0022-5185] 1899. s-a. GBP 161. Ed(s): M D Hooker, Graham Gould. Oxford University Press, Great Clarendon St, Oxford, OX2 6DP, United Kingdom; jnl.orders@oup.co.uk; http://www3.oup.co.uk/jnls. Illus., index, adv. Sample. Refereed. Circ: 1500. Vol. ends: Oct. Microform: PQC. Online: Florida Center for Library Automation; Gale Group; ingenta.com; Northern Light Technology, Inc.; OCLC Online Computer Library Center, Inc.; ProQuest Information & Learning; Swets Blackwell. Reprint: PSC. *Indexed:* ArtHuCI, BHA, BrHumI, HumInd, IBZ, MLA-IB, NTA, OTA, R&TA, RI-1. *Bk. rev.:* 180-200, 400-2,500 words, signed. *Aud.:* Ac, Sa.

This noteworthy journal comes from one of the world's outstanding universities (Oxford). It contains substantial articles written by significant scholars and is indexed in a wide range of sources. *JTS* covers the whole range of theological studies, including Christian theology, biblical study of both the Old and New Testaments, church history, philosophy of religion, and ethics. "Ancient and modern texts, inscriptions, and documents that have not before appeared in type are also reproduced." Issues typically contain about six scholarly articles. Recent articles include "How Early Is the Doctrine of *Creatio ex Nihilo*?," "The Eighteen Benedictions and the *Minim* before 70 CE," "The Last Days of Vandal Africa: An Arian Commentary on Job and its Historical Context," and "The Proposed Aramaic Background to Mark 9:11." Book reviews make up as much as three-quarters of each issue. These range from modest to lengthy and are written by reputable authors. Researchers and librarians seeking to keep abreast of the literature in the field will find this to be a tremendous asset. The journal's web site (www.oup.co.uk/theolj) offers tables of contents from 1996 on. This is highly recommended as a basic title for any academic library supporting religious studies research.

5912. *Judaism: a quarterly journal of Jewish life and thought.* [ISSN: 0022-5762] 1952. q. USD 35 (Individuals, USD 20). Ed(s): Murray Baumgarten. American Jewish Congress, Stephen Wise Congress House, 15 E 84th St, New York, NY 10028. Illus., index, adv. Refereed. Circ: 6000. Vol. ends: Oct. Microform: PQC. Online: bigchalk; EBSCO Publishing; Florida Center for Library Automation; Gale Group; OCLC

Online Computer Library Center, Inc.; ProQuest Information & Learning; H.W. Wilson. Reprint: PQC. *Indexed:* ABS&EES, ArtHuCI, HumInd, IBZ, IJP, MLA-IB, NTA, OTA, R&TA, RI-1, SSCI. *Bk. rev.:* 2-5, 3,000-6,000 words, signed. *Aud.:* Ga, Ac.

This journal "is dedicated to the creative discussion and exposition of the religious, moral, and philosophical concepts of Judaism and their relevance to the problems of modern society." The broad range of coverage leads to an interesting mixture of articles. A recent issue includes "The Question of Middle Eastern Studies," " Images at Work Versus Words at Play: Michelangelo's Art and the Artistry of the Hebrew Bible," and "Amen and Amen: Blessings of a Heretic (Like Me)." The articles are rather scholarly, although they may also appeal to some general readers. Like Christian publications that assume a familiarity with Christianity, a knowledge of Judaism is helpful when reading this journal. Tables of contents of issues since 1994 may be viewed online at humwww.ucsc.edu/judaism/judaism.html. This is an important resource that provides wide coverage of Judaism. Compare with *Modern Judaism* (below, this section). Recommended for large public libraries and as a basic title for academic libraries.

Lilith. See Women: Feminist and Special Interest/Special Interest section.

5913. *Literature and Theology: an international journal of religion, theory and culture.* [ISSN: 0269-1205] 1987. q. GBP 119. Ed(s): David Jasper, G Ward. Oxford University Press, Great Clarendon St, Oxford, OX2 6DP, United Kingdom; jnl.orders@oup.co.uk; http://www3.oup.co.uk/jnls. Illus., adv. Sample. Refereed. Circ: 800. Vol. ends: Dec. Reprint: PSC. *Indexed:* BrHumI, IBZ, MLA-IB, NTA, R&TA, RI-1. *Bk. rev.:* 5-10, 400-1,000 words, signed. *Aud.:* Ac, Sa.

Covering another of the many intersections between religion and other disciplines, this journal studies the relationship of literature and religion. It is "a forum for interdisciplinary dialogue, inviting both close textual analysis and broader theoretical speculation as ways of exploring how religion is embedded within culture." Produced by Oxford University Press and closely associated with the Society for Literature and Religion, this is a very high quality publication. Although "international" in scope, many of the authors appear to be European or North American, and articles often focus on Western cultural and religious traditions. Each issue contains about six articles (usually less than 6,000 words each), plus book reviews and a short "Notices and Reports" section. Recent articles include "The Narratee as Confessor in Margaret Laurence's *The Fire-Dwellers*," "Typology and Theology in Northrop Frye's Biblical Hermeneutic," and "Images of Religion in South Pacific Fiction: An Interpretation of *Pouliuli.*" Tables of contents and abstracts since 1996 can be found online at www.oup.co.uk/litthe. Due to its high quality and interdisciplinary appeal, this title is highly recommended for academic libraries.

5914. *Medieval Philosophy and Theology.* [ISSN: 1057-0608] 1991. s-a. USD 85 (Individuals, USD 40). Ed(s): Scott MacDonald. Cambridge University Press, The Edinburgh Bldg, Shaftesbury Rd, Cambridge, CB2 2RU, United Kingdom; information@cambridge.org; http://uk.cambridge.org/journals. Illus., adv. Refereed. *Indexed:* IPB. *Aud.:* Ac.

Picking up chronologically at about the time when the *Journal of Early Christian Studies* (see above, this section) leaves off, *Medieval Philosophy and Theology* covers the era from the patristic period through the neoscholasticism of the seventeenth century. Within this time period, it provides interdisciplinary, original research covering "all areas of medieval philosophy, including logic and natural science, and . . . medieval theology, including Christian, Jewish and Islamic." Published by Cambridge University Press and edited by scholars from a number of European and North American countries, this is a first-rate journal that will appeal to a wide range of scholars in philosophy, theology, and history. Recent articles include "Al-Ghazali on Possibility and the Critique of Causality," "Maimonides' Demonstrations: Principles and Practice," and "Aquinas's Abstractionism." There is no regular book review section, although the journal "occasionally publishes review articles and article-length critical discussions of important books in the field." This is a valuable addition for medieval studies and is highly recommended for academic libraries.

5915. *Mennonite Quarterly Review.* [ISSN: 0025-9373] 1927. q. USD 30. Ed(s): John D Roth. Goshen College, 1700 S Main St, Goshen, IN 46526; pr@goshen.edu; http://www.goshen.edu. Illus., index, adv. Sample. Refereed. Circ: 1000. Vol. ends: Oct. *Indexed:* ABS&EES, AmH&L, ChrPI, IBZ, PRA, R&TA, RI-1. *Bk. rev.:* 7-12, 100-600 words, signed. *Aud.:* Ac, Sa.

The Anabaptist-Mennonite tradition has been an important part of church history, yet is often overlooked. This scholarly journal provides a valuable remedy for this situation by focusing on the Amish, Hutterian Brethren, Anabaptists, Radical Reformation, and related history and religious thought. Articles are scholarly but not beyond the level of an educated reader. Recent titles include "Thinking Theologically about War against Iraq," "Amish Tourism: 'Visiting Shipshewana Is Better than Going to the Mall,'" "Worldly Preachers and True Shepherds: Anticlericalism and Pastoral Identity among Anabaptists of the Lower Rhine," and "Key Decisions in the Lives of the Old Order Amish: Joining the Church and Migrating to Another Settlement." The book reviews provide access to unique materials that may not be covered in other periodical literature. The journal's web site (www.goshen.edu/mqr) offers selected full-text articles from current and recent issues (1997 on), plus a searchable index of articles from all volumes. Recommended for academic libraries.

5916. *Methodist History.* [ISSN: 0026-1238] 1962. q. USD 20 domestic; USD 22 foreign; USD 30 for 2 yrs. domestic. Ed(s): Charles Yrigoyen, Jr. United Methodist Church, General Commission on Archives & History, PO Box 127, Madison, NJ 07940. Illus., adv. Refereed. Circ: 1000. Vol. ends: Jul. Microform: PQC. *Indexed:* AmH&L, BAS, PRA, R&TA, RI-1. *Bk. rev.:* 1-5, 50-500 words, signed. *Aud.:* Ac, Sa.

Like *Baptist History and Heritage* and *Journal of Presbyterian History* (both above, in this section), *Methodist History* provides specific denominational coverage. An official publication of The United Methodist Church, it is the primary journal for the history of Methodism. Coverage includes Methodist history in the United States, Europe, and around the world. Issues contain both articles (less than 5,000 words) and notes on historical sources and documents. The well-written articles are useful for researchers and laypersons alike, including titles such as "Sarah Perrin (1721-1787): Early Methodist Exhorter," "When Did Methodism Begin? Who Cares? Questions That Will Not Go Away," and "John Wesley's Reading: Evidence in the Book Collection at Wesley's House, London." Although coverage is probably too narrow for general collections, libraries with a special interest in either American (generally) or Methodist (specifically) church history should consider this journal.

5917. *Modern Judaism.* [ISSN: 0276-1114] 1981. 3x/yr. GBP 91. Ed(s): Dr. Steven T Katz. Oxford University Press, Great Clarendon St, Oxford, OX2 6DP, United Kingdom; jnl.orders@oup.co.uk; http://www3.oup.co.uk/jnls. Illus., index, adv. Refereed. Circ: 540. Online: EBSCO Publishing; Gale Group; ingenta.com; RoweCom Information Quest; Swets Blackwell. Reprint: PSC. *Indexed:* ABS&EES, AmH&L, ArtHuCI, BHA, HumInd, IBZ, IJP, R&TA, RI-1. *Bk. rev.:* 1-3, 2,000-3,000 words. *Aud.:* Ac, Sa.

This journal "provides a distinctive, interdisciplinary forum for discussion of the modern Jewish experience. Articles focus on topics pertinent to the understanding of Jewish life today and the forces that have shaped that experience," such as the rise of modern anti-Semitism, the Holocaust, the Zionist movement, and the establishment of the state of Israel. Articles focus on sociological, rather than biblical or ritual, issues. Recent articles reveal this perspective: "~We're Not Jews': Imagining Jewish History and Jewish Bodies in Contemporary Multicultural Literature," "Agonism in Faith: Buber's Eternal Thou after the Holocaust," and "The Role of the Roman Catholic Church in the Formation of Modern Anti-Semitism: *La Civilta Cattolica,* 1850-1879." Tables of contents and abstracts since 2000 can be found online at www.oup.co.uk/modjud. A comparison of *Modern Judaism* and *Judaism* (see above, this section) reveals that although they both share an interest in the sociological issues of Judaism, *Judaism* covers a larger span of history and appears to include more specifically religious topics. Both titles, therefore, meet specific needs and are important scholarly resources for information on Judaism. Like *Judaism, Modern Judaism* is recommended for large public and academic libraries.

5918. *Muslim World: a journal devoted to the study of Islam and Christian-Muslim relationships past and present.* Formerly (until 1948): *Moslem World.* [ISSN: 0027-4909] 1911. q. USD 153 print & online eds. Ed(s): Jane Smith, Ibrahim Abu Rabi. Blackwell Publishing, Inc., Commerce Place, 350 Main St, Malden, MA 02148; subscrip@blackwellpub.com; http://www.blackwellpublishing.com. Illus., index, adv. Sample. Refereed. Circ: 1200 Paid. Vol. ends: Oct. Microform: PQC. Online: EBSCO Publishing; Gale Group; ingenta.com; Northern Light Technology, Inc.; OCLC Online Computer Library Center, Inc.; ProQuest Information & Learning; H.W. Wilson. Reprint: PQC; PSC. *Indexed:* ABS&EES, AmH&L, ArtHuCI, BAS, HumInd, IPSA, MLA-IB, R&TA, RI-1. *Bk. rev.:* 2-3, 500-2,000 words, signed. *Aud.:* Ac, Sa.

The dialog between Islam and Christianity is a very important issue, making this a very important journal. Since its inception, the goal of this publication has been to interpret Islam to Christians—a priority made clear in the subtitle: "A journal devoted to the study of Islam and Christian-Muslim relations in past and present." Articles are written by both Muslims and Christians and deal with issues from around the world. Recent titles include "Reordering Islamic Orthodoxy: Muhammad ibn 'Abdul Wahhab," "Modernist Islam in Southeast Asia: A New Examination," and "Trouble Wherever They Went: American Missionaries in Anatolia and Ottoman Syria in the Nineteenth Century." Arabic words are transliterated into the Latin alphabet, a useful feature for those not familiar with Arabic. Given the importance of Islam as a world religion and the role of this publication in presenting its dialogue with Christianity, *The Muslim World* is recommended as a basic title for academic libraries.

5919. *National Catholic Reporter.* [ISSN: 0027-8939] 1964. w. USD 39.95 domestic; USD 61.95 foreign. Ed(s): Michael Farrell. National Catholic Reporter Publishing Company, Inc., 115 E Armour Blvd, PO Box 419493, Kansas City, MO 64141; http://www.natcath.org. Illus., adv. Sample. Circ: 48000. Microform: PQC. Online: bigchalk; Florida Center for Library Automation; Gale Group; Northern Light Technology, Inc.; OCLC Online Computer Library Center, Inc.; ProQuest Information & Learning. Reprint: PQC. *Indexed:* ASIP, CPL, LRI, MagInd. *Bk. rev.:* 1-2, 700-1,000 words, signed. *Aud.:* Ga, Ac.

Although more a newspaper in format than a magazine (part of what distinguishes it from *America* and *Commonweal,* above in this section), the usefulness of the *National Catholic Reporter* to libraries should not be overlooked. It is a major forum for popular American Roman Catholic discussion of news and religious, social, and moral issues. Although Roman Catholic in orientation, *NCR* is inspired by the Second Vatican Council and "an ecumenical spirit." The orientation of *NCR* reflects the mission of the publishing organization: "It emphasizes solidarity with the oppressed and respect for all. It understands that peace, justice and integrity of environment are not only goals but also avenues of life." Managed by laypeople and offering an independent viewpoint, *NCR* is committed to covering both the successes and the failings of the Catholic church. As a weekly, stories are very relevant and related to current events, and may include statistics and surveys. Features include book and movie reviews, as well as "listings for retreats, renewal programs and educational opportunities." *NCR* often publishes the full texts of official Roman Catholic Church pronouncements (in English). Although Catholic in orientation, writers are drawn from other faiths as well. Selected full-text articles from current and recent issues are available online at www.natcath.org. The site also offers a searchable index that retrieves a large amount of full-text material as far back as 1996. As both a readable and useful resource, *NCR* is recommended for public and academic libraries.

5920. *New Oxford Review.* Formerly (until Feb. 1977): *American Church News.* [ISSN: 0149-4244] 1940. m. 11/yr. USD 19. Ed(s): Dale Vree. New Oxford Review, Inc., 1069 Kains Ave, Berkeley, CA 94706. Illus., adv. Circ: 14728 Paid. Vol. ends: Dec. Microform: PQC. Online: Northern Light Technology, Inc.; ProQuest Information & Learning. Reprint: PQC. *Indexed:* CPL, RI-1. *Bk. rev.:* 1 major, 1,500 words; 6-7 minor, 300-400 words, signed. *Aud.:* Ga, Ac.

Reflecting what the editors consider an "orthodox Catholic" view, the *NOR* offers monthly commentary on social, theological, and ecclesiastical issues. Not shy about controversy, articles challenge current views and often advocate what might be considered more traditional (what the editors consider "orthodox") positions. This perspective is revealed in these recent articles: "Christian/Jewish Marriages: Recipes for Disaster," "The Neo-Pagans Are Giving Ancient Paganism a Bad Name," and "A Purely Secular Argument against Abortion." Writers are usually Catholic, but not always. Since *NOR* provides a distinctly different perspective on the Catholic church than either *America* or *Commonweal,* it is recommended for public and academic libraries.

5921. *The Other Side: strength for the journey.* Formerly: *Freedom Now.* [ISSN: 0145-7675] 1965. bi-m. USD 24 domestic; USD 33 foreign. Ed(s): Douglas Davidson, Dee Dee Risher. The Other Side, Inc., PO BOX 3000, Denville, NJ 07834-9494; subs@theotherside.org; http://www.theotherside.org. Illus., adv. Circ: 12000 Paid. Microform: PQC. Online: Florida Center for Library Automation; Gale Group. *Indexed:* AltPI, BRI, CBRI, ChrPI, MRD, R&TA, RI-1. *Aud.:* Ga.

This attractive publication, including abundant illustrations printed on glossy paper, provides an alternative, more liberal, perspective on the Christian faith. *The Other Side* advocates "a healing Christian vision that's biblical and compassionate, appreciative of the creative arts, and committed to the intimate intertwining of personal spirituality and social transformation." This mission is accomplished through challenging articles that examine issues of peace, faith, and justice from a clearly Christian, but not sectarian or fundamentalist, perspective. Writers reflect the editorial commitment to ecumenism and diversity of thought, and include noted authors (Walter Brueggemann, Virginia Ramey Mollenkott, Dorothee Soelle, Walter Wink). The conservative Christian perspective is represented in a number of publications (see *Christianity Today* above, this section). *The Other Side* provides an important balance to a library's collection by offering an alternative "Christian" view from a more liberal perspective. This is important, because it will dispel the notion that Christianity is monolithic. Tables of contents and selected full-text articles from 1997 on are available online at www.theotherside.org. Recommended as a basic title for public and undergraduate academic libraries.

The Public Eye. See Women: Feminist and Special Interest/Feminist and Women's Studies section.

5922. *Religion: the established journal of the history, structure and theory of religion and religions.* [ISSN: 0048-721X] 1970. q. EUR 297 (Individuals, EUR 90). Ed(s): Robert Segal, I Strenski. Academic Press, Harcourt Pl, 32 Jamestown Rd, London, NW1 7BY, United Kingdom; apsubs@acad.com; http://www.elsevier-international.com/serials/. Illus., adv. Sample. Refereed. Circ: 600. Vol. ends: Oct. Online: EBSCO Publishing; Gale Group; ingenta.com; OCLC Online Computer Library Center, Inc.; RoweCom Information Quest; ScienceDirect; Swets Blackwell. Reprint: SWZ. *Indexed:* ArtHuCI, BAS, HumInd, IBSS, NTA, OTA, RI-1, SSCI. *Bk. rev.:* 7-10, 1,000-1,700 words, signed. *Aud.:* Ac, Sa.

This journal provides a forum for interdisciplinary and cross-cultural research in religious studies, drawing on the disciplines of anthropology, history, political theory, economics, psychology, and sociology. As an international journal, coverage extends to all of the major world religions, and includes a wide range of authors. Articles are scholarly and include abstracts. Recent titles include "Recent trends in Sri Lankan Buddhism," "Technophilia and Nature Religion: the Growth of a Paradox," and "Tradition, Authority and the Native American Graves Protection and Repatriation Act." Tables of contents and abstracts since 1993, along with a full-text sample issue, are available at www.elsevier.com/locate/issn/0048-721X. Given the academic nature and the scope of the articles, this journal will appeal to a limited audience of specialists within academia. Although not for every library, it is recommended for institutions supporting interdisciplinary and cross-cultural research in religious studies.

5923. *Religion and American Culture: a journal of interpretation.* [ISSN: 1052-1151] 1991. s-a. USD 82 print & online eds. USD 42 newsstand/cover. Ed(s): Thomas Davis. University of California Press, Journals Division, 2000 Center St, Ste 303, Berkeley, CA 94704-1223; journals@ucop.edu; http://www.ucpress.edu/journals. Illus., adv. Refereed. Circ: 766. Vol. ends: Summer. Online: EBSCO Publishing; Florida Center for Library Automation; Gale Group; Ingenta Select; OCLC Online Computer Library Center, Inc. *Indexed:* AmH&L, ArtHuCI, ChrPI, HumInd, PRA, R&TA, RI-1. *Aud.:* Ac, Sa.

This journal seeks to examine and interpret the important relationship between religion and American culture (past and present), and is published for the Center for the Study of Religion and American Culture. Authors employ a variety of methodological approaches and theoretical perspectives. Issues usually begin with a "Forum" section, in which several scholars are asked to address a particular topic of current relevance to religion and American culture, such as "Teaching the Introductory Course in American Religion" or "The Future of the Study of Religion and U.S. Culture." Three to five lengthy articles (20 to 40 pages) investigate the relationship between religion and American culture. Recent titles include "Islamizing the Black Body: Ritual and Power in Elijah Muhammad's Nation of Islam," "Women and Christian Practice in a Mahican Village," and "Replacing Memory: Latter-Day Saint Use of Historical Monuments and Narrative in the Early Twentieth Century." Issues occasionally include lengthy review essays. Because of its interdisciplinary nature and broad range of topics, this journal will appeal to a variety of scholars and general readers as well. Useful at a number of levels, this is recommended for public and academic libraries.

5924. ***Religious Studies: an international journal for the philosophy of religion and theology.*** [ISSN: 0034-4125] 1965. q. USD 212 (Individuals, USD 89). Ed(s): P A Byrne. Cambridge University Press, The Edinburgh Bldg, Shaftesbury Rd, Cambridge, CB2 2RU, United Kingdom; information@cambridge.org; http://uk.cambridge.org/journals. Illus., index, adv. Sample. Refereed. Circ: 1220. Vol. ends: Dec. Microform: PQC. Online: East View Publications, Inc.; EBSCO Publishing; Florida Center for Library Automation; Gale Group; OCLC Online Computer Library Center, Inc.; RoweCom Information Quest; Swets Blackwell. Reprint: SWZ. *Indexed:* ArtHuCI, BAS, BRI, BrHumI, CBRI, HumInd, IJP, IPB, NTA, PhilInd, R&TA, RI-1, SSCI. *Bk. rev.:* 2 major, 1,200-2,000 words; 3-5 minor, 300-400 words; signed. *Aud.:* Ac, Sa.

This international scholarly resource is primarily concerned with the philosophy of religion. Although mostly British in orientation, authors also come from continental Europe, the United States, and—to a lesser extent—the rest of the world. Articles reflect a philosophical approach and often involve the use of formal logic. Recent titles include "Descartes on the Immutability of Divine Will," "Religion and the Pursuit of Truth," and "Eternally Incorrigible: The Continuing-Sin Response to the Proportionality Problem of Hell." Abstracts are included at the beginning of each article. The philosophy of religion is an important area of religious studies, and this journal is one of the important resources in this area (compare with *International Journal for Philosophy of Religion* above, this section). Highly recommended for academic libraries.

5925. ***Religious Studies Review: a quarterly review of publications in the field of religion and related disciplines.*** [ISSN: 0319-485X] 1975. q. USD 55 (Individuals, USD 40; Students, USD 25). Council of Societies for the Study of Religion, CSSR Executive Office, Valparaiso University, Valparaiso, IN 46383-6493; cssr@valpo.edu; http://www.cssr.org. Illus., index, adv. Sample. Refereed. Circ: 3500. Vol. ends: Oct. Online: EBSCO Publishing; OCLC Online Computer Library Center, Inc. *Indexed:* BRI, CBRI, NTA, OTA, PRA, R&TA, RI-1. *Bk. rev.:* over 1,000 annually, see annotation, signed. *Aud.:* Ac, Sa.

Published by the Council of Societies for the Study of Religion, a federation of eleven associations, *Religious Studies Review* provides "a quarterly review of publications in the field of religion and related disciplines." Each issue is devoted to reviewing current literature. "Articles" are actually lengthy and detailed bibliographic essays, such as "The Invigoration of Kierkegaardian Ethics," "The Tao of the West and the Emerging Discipline of Daoist Studies," and "Beyond the Daily Dose of Hatred: Religion and the Study of White Separatism." In addition to the review essays, the "Notes on Recent Publications" provides short descriptions of a large number of new titles, categorized under a controlled list of topic headings. The full list of headings appears in each issue, even when the heading is empty. Covering over 1,000 titles annually, this is an invaluable tool for collection developers and anyone interested in keeping up with recent literature in the field. Any academic library supporting religious studies should consider this an indispensable, basic title.

5926. ***Review and Expositor.*** Formerly: *Baptist Review and Expositor.* [ISSN: 0034-6373] 1904. q. USD 24; USD 30 foreign. Ed(s): E Glenn Hinson. Review & Expositor, Inc., PO Box 6681, Louisville, KY 40206-0681. Illus., index, adv. Circ: 2000. Vol. ends: Fall. Microform: PQC. Reprint: PQC. *Indexed:* NTA, OTA, R&TA, RI-1. *Bk. rev.:* 30-50, 300-700 words, signed. *Aud.:* Ga, Sa.

This theological journal is "dedicated to free and open inquiry of issues related to the Church's mission in the contemporary world." While "Baptist in its heritage," *Review and Expositor* seeks to be "ecumenical in its outlook, and global in its vision," balancing "scholarly analysis with practical application." Issues are thematic, e.g., "The Book of Job," "The Preaching Ministry in a Movie Culture," and "Sexuality and the Church." Issues contain articles dealing with the theme as well as expository articles covering biblical passages. Although scholarly, the counterbalancing practicality results in articles that are of interest to both scholars and general readers. The book reviews are arranged topically under the headings "Biblical Studies," "Historical-Theological Studies," and "Ministry Studies." This is a useful journal for those seeking to understand the Baptist tradition, both from within and without. Recommended for academic and large public libraries.

SageWoman. See Women: Feminist and Special Interest/Special Interest section.

5927. ***Scottish Journal of Theology.*** [ISSN: 0036-9306] 1948. q. USD 112 (Individuals, USD 50). Ed(s): Bryan Spinks, Ian Torrance. Cambridge University Press, The Edinburgh Bldg, Shaftesbury Rd, Cambridge, CB2 2RU, United Kingdom; information@cambridge.org; http://uk.cambridge.org/journals. Illus., index, adv. Sample. Refereed. Circ: 1800. Vol. ends: No. 4. Reprint: PSC. *Indexed:* ArtHuCI, HumInd, IBZ, NTA, OTA, R&TA, RI-1. *Bk. rev.:* 10-15, 500-1,000 words, signed. *Aud.:* Ac, Sa.

This international journal covers systematic, historical, and biblical theology in the Christian tradition. It provides "an ecumenical forum for debate, and engages in extensive reviewing of theological and biblical literature." Articles are 5,000 to 8,000 words in length and are written by leading scholars from a variety of traditions and world locations. Recent titles include "Luke and the Trinity: an Essay in Ecclesial Biblical Theology," "A Tradition of Civility: the Natural Law as a Tradition of Moral Inquiry," and "Last Things First: Karl Barth's Theological Exegesis of 1 Corinthians in *The Resurrection of the Dead.*" Issues also include "an article-length review of a recent book, with a reply from the author," as well as a large number of book reviews. This is an important periodical for theological research within the Christian tradition, and is highly recommended for academic libraries supporting this discipline.

5928. ***Sociology of Religion: a quarterly review.*** Former titles (until vol.54, 1993): *Sociological Analysis;* (until 1964): *American Catholic Sociological Review.* [ISSN: 1069-4404] 1940. q. USD 60. Ed(s): Nancy Nason-Clark. Association for the Sociology of Religion, 3520 Wiltshire Dr, Holiday, FL 34691-1239; swatos@microd.com; http://www.sociologyofreligion.com. Illus., index, adv. Refereed. Circ: 1595. Vol. ends: Winter. Microform: PQC. Online: bigchalk; EBSCO Publishing; Florida Center for Library Automation; Gale Group; Northern Light Technology, Inc.; OCLC Online Computer Library Center, Inc.; ProQuest Information & Learning; H.W. Wilson. Reprint: PQC. *Indexed:* ABS&EES, ASSIA, ArtHuCI, CPL, HEA, IBSS, IPSA, PSA, R&TA, RI-1, SSCI, SSI, SWA, SociolAb. *Bk. rev.:* 10-12, 600-1,000 words, signed. *Aud.:* Ac.

This journal, a voice for the Association for the Sociology of Religion, specifically examines the intersection of sociological and religious studies. Articles cover "theoretical and empirical issues" and provide a "a forum for scholarship in the classic tradition of comparative, historical and theoretical work." The interdisciplinary approach of this publication leads to very interesting articles (about five to seven in each issue) that are well written and carefully documented. Recent articles include "Dimensions of Social Stratification and Anomie as Factors of Religious Affiliation in El Salvador," "How Monochromatic is Church Membership? Racial-Ethnic Diversity in Religious Community," and "Mapping American Adolescent Subjective Religiosity and Attitudes of Alienation Toward Religion: A Research Report." This journal is uniquely dedicated to research into the sociology of religion, making it appealing to a range of researchers. It is highly recommended for academic libraries.

Sojourners. See Alternatives section.

5929. ***Studies in World Christianity: the Edinburgh review of theology and religion.*** [ISSN: 1354-9901] 1995. s-a. GBP 67. Edinburgh University Press, 22 George Sq, Edinburgh, EH8 9LF, United Kingdom; http://www.eup.ed.ac.uk. Illus., adv. Sample. Vol. ends: No. 2. Online: EBSCO Publishing. *Indexed:* R&TA. *Bk. rev.:* 15-20, 250-1,200 words, signed. *Aud.:* Ac.

In an era of rising periodical prices, it is difficult just to maintain current subscriptions. Adding new ones is a real challenge. This relatively new title, however, deserves consideration as an addition to many collections. A criticism of many English-language journals dealing with Christianity is that they are too preoccupied with Western and European expressions of it. As this faith has spread around the globe, indigenous cultures have shaped Christianity into new forms and raised issues that go beyond Western philosophical preoccupations. *SWC* seeks to meet "the need for a truly intercultural, interdisciplinary journal" that can serve as a forum for discussing these global developments in theology, biblical studies, church history, morality, and religious studies. Although it comes from Edinburgh University Press, the authors represent a wide range of nationalities. Discussions of world religions are part of the cross-cultural conversation, but the focus is on world (non-Western) Christianity. Recent articles include "Muhammad: Prophet of Liberation—a Christian Perspective from Political Theology," "Alternative and Complementary Theologies: The Case of Cosmic Energy with Special Reference to Chi," and "Spirit Mediums in Zimbabwe: Religious Experience in and on Behalf of the Community." The global perspective of this journal fills an important niche in journal coverage of Christianity. Unfortunately, the journal has fallen behind in its publication schedule (although it is still listed as active in *Ulrich's*). Assuming that it returns to a normal schedule, academic libraries are strongly encouraged to add this title to their collections.

5930. ***Theological Studies.*** [ISSN: 0040-5639] 1940. q. USD 32 (Individuals, USD 24). Ed(s): Michael A Fahey. Theological Studies, Inc., c/o Michael A. Fahey, Marquette University, P. O. Box 1881, Milwaukee, WI 53201-1881; michael.fahey@marquette.edu. Illus., index, adv. Sample. Refereed. Circ: 4619 Paid. Vol. ends: Dec. Microform: PQC. Online: bigchalk; Chadwyck-Healey Incorporated; EBSCO Publishing; Florida Center for Library Automation; Gale Group; Northern Light Technology, Inc.; OCLC Online Computer Library Center, Inc.; ProQuest Information & Learning; H.W. Wilson. *Indexed:* ArtHuCI, BHA, BRI, CBRI, CPL, HumInd, IBZ, NTA, OTA, R&TA, RI-1, SSCI. *Bk. rev.:* 25-30 major, 700-800 words; 20-25 minor, 250-400 words; signed. *Aud.:* Ac, Sa.

This major theological publication reflects the Roman Catholic perspective of the Jesuits. Articles offer original, scholarly research on theological issues either relating to, or viewed from, the Jesuit viewpoint. Recent examples include "Revisiting the Franciscan Doctrine of Christ," "Sacrifice Unveiled or Sacrifice Revisited: Trinitarian and Liturgical Perspectives," and "Marriage: Developments in Catholic Theology and Ethics." Scholars and bibliographers will benefit from the extensive book review coverage of recent literature relevant to theological studies. This is a very useful (and quite reasonably priced) resource for those interested in Catholic theology, including both Catholics and non-Catholics. Recommended for academic libraries.

5931. ***Theology Digest.*** [ISSN: 0040-5728] 1953. q. USD 15; USD 17 foreign. Ed(s): Bernhard Asen. Theology Digest, Inc., 3634 Lindell Blvd., St. Louis, MO 63108-3395; thdigest@slu.edu. Illus., index, adv. Circ: 3019 Paid. Microform: PQC. *Indexed:* CPL, OTA, R&TA. *Bk. rev.:* 250-275, 75-125 words, signed. *Aud.:* Ac, Sa.

The increasing costs of periodicals often forces the unfortunate cancellation of titles. Libraries that subscribe to *TD* should look elsewhere to save money. This very inexpensive publication offers substantial value—especially to libraries with minimal theological holdings. *TD* is the *Readers' Digest* of theological literature—but with more substance. *TD* provides condensations of articles from more than 400 journals dealing with theology, biblical studies, ethics, liturgy, ecumenism, and ministry. These sources range from major journals to "African and Asian journals not readily accessible to the global theological community." All digests are in English despite a variety of source languages. Those concerned with the quality of condensations should note that every digest is approved by the author of the original article prior to publication. Although a digest is not a substitute for the original article, this publication provides cost-effective access to a wide range of literature. Materials discovered in digest form can be obtained in their complete form via interlibrary loan. The "Book Survey" section covers "all important religious books published or distributed in the United States." Although the comments are brief and descriptive rather than evaluative, this is still a very useful feature. For very minimal cost, *TD* provides excellent coverage of current religious thought in journals and monographs. Libraries that already subscribe to a large number of religious titles may find *TD* less necessary, but it is highly recommended for public and academic libraries with more limited religious collections.

5932. ***Theology Today.*** [ISSN: 0040-5736] 1944. q. USD 28 domestic (Students, USD 19.95). Ed(s): Patrick D Miller. Theology Today, PO Box 821, Princeton, NJ 08542-0803. Illus., index, adv. Sample. Refereed. Circ: 14000 Paid. Vol. ends: Jan. Microform: MIM; PQC. Online: Gale Group; Northern Light Technology, Inc.; OCLC Online Computer Library Center, Inc.; ProQuest Information & Learning; H.W. Wilson. Reprint: PQC. *Indexed:* ArtHuCI, BHA, BRI, CBRI, HumInd, IBZ, LRI, NTA, OTA, PRA, R&TA, RI-1, SSCI. *Bk. rev.:* 15-30, 200-1,500 words, signed. *Aud.:* Ga, Ac.

As the title implies, this journal discusses theological issues that are relevant for today's world. Although published by Princeton Theological Seminary, it seeks to be an "ecumenical" journal and boasts an impressive editorial board. The five or six articles per issue are engaging and scholarly, but they try to avoid technical language in order to remain accessible to the general reader. Recent titles include "Christological Transformation in *The Mirror of Souls*, by Marguerite Porete," "Catherine of Siena, Justly Doctor of the Church?," and "Changing The Rules: Just War Theory in the Twenty-first Century." Poetry and a useful collection of book reviews round out each issue. In the spirit of "open access," the journal's web site (theologytoday.ptsem.edu) provides free access to the full texts of articles, features, and book reviews from 1958 to 1996. This date range has expanded in recent years, so perhaps it will continue to grow. Material from 1997 on is not available, except for the table of contents and abstracts from the current issue. This journal is particularly useful to anyone interested in keeping abreast of current trends in theological discourse. It is highly recommended for academic libraries and may be appropriate for larger public libraries.

5933. ***Tricycle: the Buddhist review.*** [ISSN: 1055-484X] 1991. q. USD 24 domestic; USD 29 elsewhere; USD 7.50 newsstand/cover per issue domestic. Ed(s): James Shaheen, Helen Tworkov. Buddhist Ray, Inc., 92 Vandam St, 3rd Fl, New York, NY 10013; tricycle@well.com; http://www.tricycle.com. Illus., adv. Circ: 55000 Paid. Vol. ends: Summer. *Indexed:* BRI, CBRI, IAPV, RI-1. *Bk. rev.:* 4-6, 400-1,000 words, signed. *Aud.:* Ga.

This interesting magazine serves the general reader who is interested in American Buddhism. "Unaffiliated with any one Buddhist school or sect, *Tricycle* is a wide-open forum for exploring contemporary and historic Buddhist activity and its impact on mainstream culture." Reflecting the interaction between Buddhism and American culture, "*Tricycle* values tradition, orthodoxy, and critical thinking" while also honoring "diversity, political awareness, and sexuality." The eye-catching full-color cover encourages one to look inside. The photographs and artwork are black and white but still effectively illustrate the material. Issues include interviews and profiles, analysis of contemporary issues, discussions about the meaning and practice of Buddhism, artwork, fictional pieces, and reviews of books and films. Articles are fewer than 3,000 words in length. Libraries that offer popular magazines from the Christian perspective should include this publication as an appropriate counterpart representing Buddhist views. Recommended for public and undergraduate academic libraries.

5934. ***Weavings: a journal of the Christian spiritual life.*** [ISSN: 0890-6491] 1986. bi-m. USD 24 in North America; USD 27.50 elsewhere. Ed(s): John S Mogabgab. The Upper Room, 1908 Grand Ave, PO Box 340004, Nashville, TN 37203-0004; http://www.upperroom.org. Illus. Circ: 40000 Paid. Vol. ends: Nov/Dec. *Indexed:* ChrPI, RI-1. *Bk. rev.:* 1-2, 600-900 words, signed. *Aud.:* Ga.

In the midst of so many academic journals examining religion from all angles and in minute detail, it is easy to overlook the fact that religion is—for its practitioners—about finding and living a spiritual life. This is a journal for practitioners within the Christian tradition. Although published by The United Methodist Church, authors represent a variety of traditions. *Weavings* "provides a forum in which our life in the world and the spiritual resources of the Christian heritage encounter and illuminate one another." The title reflects the journal's mission to explore "the many ways God's life and human lives are being woven together in the world." Each issue explores a particular theme ("Behold the Beauty of the Lord," "Practicing the Presence of God") through articles, meditations, poetry, fiction, and artwork. Articles run from 1,250 to 2,500 words and are intended to appeal to both professionals and laypeople. Representing a practical approach to applied religion, this journal would be appreciated by many readers. Recommended for public libraries.

5935. ***Worship: concerned with the issues of liturgical renewal.*** [ISSN: 0043-941X] 1926. bi-m. USD 38 (Individuals, USD 28; USD 5 newsstand/cover per issue). Ed(s): Kevin Seasoltz. Liturgical Press, St John's Abbey, Collegeville, MN 56321-7500; http://www.sja.osb.org/worship/. Illus., index, adv. Sample. Refereed. Circ: 4400. Vol. ends: Nov. Microform: PQC. Reprint: PQC. *Indexed:* CPL, NTA, OTA, R&TA, RI-1. *Bk. rev.:* 1-10, 500-1,200 words, signed. *Aud.:* Ac, Sa.

As the etymology of "liturgy" implies, worship is the work of the people, including the rituals that express the beliefs of the faithful. *Worship* is an ecumenical journal that examines liturgical theology and practice. Like a number of journals in this section, it is interdisciplinary, examining the relationship between Christianity and culture. Specifically, "it seeks to reflect on the role that the various theological disciplines, as well as the arts and social sciences, play in shaping Christian worship and the lives of worshipping Christians in the world." Although initially Roman Catholic in orientation, since 1967 the journal has intentionally appointed Protestant and Eastern Christian liturgical scholars to its editorial board in an effort to be more ecumenical. Currently, the board includes Lutherans and Methodists as well as Roman Catholics. Regardless of one's tradition, however, this publication will appeal more to those interested in "high church" rather than "low church" liturgical forms. Each issue is just under 100 pages long and contains several substantial and well-documented articles, plus book reviews and occasionally music reviews (hymnals, songbooks, choir pieces, etc.). Recent articles include "Holy Ground: Biblical and Liturgical Reorientation in the World," "Liturgy and (Post)Modernity: A Narrative Response to Guardini's Challenge," and "Forum: Eucharist as the Intersection between Memory and Forgetfulness." The tables of contents from 1999 to the present are available online at www.saintjohnsabbey.org/worship. This is a very useful publication for research in the area of worship, making it an obvious choice for seminary libraries. Academic libraries interested in liturgical studies should also receive it.

5936. ***Zygon: journal of religion and science.*** [ISSN: 0591-2385] 1966. q. USD 155 print & online eds. Blackwell Publishing, Inc., Commerce Place, 350 Main St, Malden, MA 02148; subscrip@blackwellpub.com; http://www.blackwellpublishing.com. Illus., index, adv. Sample. Refereed. Circ: 2400. Vol. ends: Dec. Microform: PQC. Online: EBSCO Publishing; Gale Group; ingenta.com; OCLC Online Computer Library Center, Inc.; RoweCom Information Quest; Swets Blackwell. *Indexed:* ArtHuCI, BRI, CBRI, HumInd, IPB, NTA, OTA, PhilInd, PsycholAb, R&TA, RI-1, SSCI, SociolAb. *Bk. rev.:* 0-5, 1,300-3,000 words, signed. *Aud.:* Ac.

The title of this journal derives from the Greek word "zygon," meaning "yoke." This reflects its philosophy that religion and science should be yoked in a mutual effort to provide knowledge and understanding. In the premodern world, religion and science were interconnected in the construction of worldviews. With the rise of the scientific method, however, religion and science have become disconnected, and in some cases foes. *Zygon* seeks to challenge this separation by keeping "united what may often become disconnected: values with knowledge, goodness with truth, religion with science." The mission of the journal is to bring "together the best thinking of the day from the physical, biological, and social sciences with ideas from philosophy, theology, and religious studies." Authors are as likely to come from the realm of science as from religion. Do not view this as a so-called "creation science" publication. Evolution and other modern scientific concepts are not challenged; instead, they are viewed as concepts to be integrated into religious discussion. Articles are scholarly and documented, but not beyond an educated reader. Recent examples include "Randomness, Contingency, and Faith: Is There a Science of Subjectivity?," "Varieties of Religious Naturalism," "Kantian Ethics: After Darwin," and "Some Hindu Insights on a Global Ethic in the Context of Diseases and Epidemics." Articles critical of *Zygon's* viewpoint are included if they "contribute to a constructive dialogue between scientific knowledge and concerns about fundamental meaning and values." The well-developed book reviews vary from none to six per issue, with one review per issue being typical. Tables of contents and abstracts from 1997 to the present, along with a free sample issue, are available at www.blackwellpublishing.com/journal.asp?ref=0591-2385. Given the continued separation (tension?) that often exists between religion and science in academic circles, academic libraries are strongly encouraged to include this interesting title.

■ ROBOTICS

Sharon L. Siegler, Engineering Librarian, Lehigh University Information Resources, Fairchild/Martindale Library, 8A Packer Ave., Bethlehem, PA 18015; sls7@lehigh.edu; FAX: 610-758-6524

Introduction

As the robotics field has matured, it has shrunk; figuratively, that is. Much new work in robotics involves nanotechnology; there is now the *Journal of Micromechatronics*, a merger of robotics, mechatronics, and nanotechnology. A delicious irony is found at the IEEEXplore web site, which politely but directly states "No Robots Please"; they mean that intelligent agent harvesters are prohibited, but it is a curious statement to find at the same site that hosts two of the top-ranked robotics journals. Although there is still plenty of research on robots used in large-scale production such as the automotive industry, finer-scale work such as clinical laboratory applications is also prevalent. The scholarly titles remain and have even been augmented, but much of the trade literature is subsumed within the standard magazines of the relative industries such as industrial engineering or materials manufacturing. A number of good titles, some of which are targeted for the consumer, are not included because they are in Japanese. The extreme range in prices, with some good scholarly titles available for less than $200 and others nearly ten times that, continues; price increases have also been large. One saving grace is that many of the journals augment work in other fields, so that academic and corporate libraries can often find "two for one" selections serving both robotics and another engineering or business activity.

Basic Periodicals

Hs: *Real Robots* Ga: *IEEE Robotics and Automation Magazine* Ac: *Autonomous Robots, IEEE Transactions on Robotics and Automation, International Journal of Robotics Research, Robotica, Robotics and Autonomous Systems.*

Basic Abstracts and Indexes

Applied Science and Technology Index, Engineering Index, INSPEC.

5937. ***A I Magazine.*** [ISSN: 0738-4602] 1980. q. USD 190 (Individuals, USD 95). Ed(s): David Leake. A A A I Press, 445 Burgess Dr, Menlo Park, CA 94025; info@aaai.org; http://www.aaai.org. Illus., index, adv. Refereed. Circ: 6000 Paid. Vol. ends: Dec. Online: Florida Center for Library Automation; Gale Group; OCLC Online Computer Library Center, Inc.; ProQuest Information & Learning; H.W. Wilson. *Indexed:* AS&TI, CompLI, EngInd, InfoSAb, LISA, MicrocompInd, SCI. *Bk. rev.:* 2, 2,000-4,000 words. *Aud.:* Ac, Sa.

As the official journal of the American Association for Artificial Intelligence, this publication is a cross between a magazine and a research journal. Each issue contains about a half-dozen articles as well as reports, events, society news, and spirited book reviews. The articles are not so dense as to be purely theoretical and can be read by students/practitioners outside the field, but they are research papers. Papers average ten pages, are well illustrated, and include good bibliographies. Authors are both academic and industrial researchers. Although "artificial intelligence" is not "robotics," each issue has at least one robotics article, and many of the remainder discuss solutions to logistics, reasoning, and data-gathering problems that can be readily applied to robotics. While hardly a frivolous publication, there is still room for a sense of humor and competition, with annual features on Robot Rescue, the Robot Challenge, the Mobile Robot Competition, and the world RoboCup soccer championship. The web site provides free tables of contents from volume one forward, with abstracts for most articles.

5938. ***Advanced Robotics.*** [ISSN: 0169-1864] 1986. 10x/yr. EUR 903 combined subscription print & online eds.; USD 1129 combined subscription print & online eds. Ed(s): K Kosuge. V S P, PO Box 346, Zeist, 3700 AH, Netherlands; vsppub@compuserve.com; http://www.vsppub.com. Illus., adv. Sample. Refereed. Vol. ends: No. 8. Online: EBSCO Publishing; Ingenta Select. *Indexed:* ApMecR, C&ISA, EngInd. *Aud.:* Ac, Sa.

Truly an international effort, this is the official journal of the Robotics Society of Japan, published by a small Dutch firm and featuring articles by Russians, Germans, Arabs, Japanese, and others. Most articles are research papers, but issues may include short communications, topical reviews, reports, and meeting notes. Recent article topics include lip-synchronized robot speech, a flexible spine for a humanistic robot, and robot teams involved in cooperative tasks. The treatment is theoretical with a practical emphasis. Mounted on Ingenta Select, articles may be searched in full text, individual articles have a "related articles" option, and links to references are added continuously as electronic versions of the linked articles become available. Although not inexpensive (the price has doubled since it was last reviewed), this title deserves greater notice in academic libraries.

5939. ***Applied Artificial Intelligence: an international journal.*** [ISSN: 0883-9514] 1987. 10x/yr. GBP 560 (Individuals, GBP 252). Ed(s): Robert Trappl. Taylor & Francis Inc, 325 Chestnut St, Suite 800, Philadelphia, PA 19016; info@taylorandfrancis.com; http://www.taylorandfrancis.com/. Illus. Sample. Refereed. Vol. ends: No. 8. Microform: PQC. Online: EBSCO Publishing; Ingenta Select; OCLC Online Computer Library Center, Inc.; RoweCom Information Quest; Swets Blackwell. Reprint: PSC. *Indexed:* C&ISA, CompLI, EngInd, ErgAb, SSCI. *Aud.:* Ac.

Although this is an "artificial intelligence" title, a good deal of the application portion is robotics research. The usual point of view is the robot as intelligent agent, as evinced by a recent issue on engineering agent systems. Much of the rest of the issues involves computer intelligence or modeling intelligence using computers. The latest trend seems to be "knowledge discovery." Articles can be lengthy, often running to 20 or more pages. The web site includes free e-mailed tables of contents. The paper subscription for institutions includes online access through the publisher and several document suppliers.

5940. ***Assembly Automation.*** [ISSN: 0144-5154] 1980. q. EUR 5534.29 in Europe; USD 5119 in North America; AUD 6349 in Australasia. Ed(s): Clive Loughlin. Emerald, 60-62 Toller Ln, Bradford, BD8 9BY, United Kingdom; info@emeraldinsight.com; http://www.emeraldinsight.com. Illus. Refereed. Online: Pub.; EBSCO Publishing; OCLC Online Computer Library Center, Inc.; ProQuest Information & Learning; RoweCom Information Quest; Swets Blackwell. Reprint: PSC. *Indexed:* ABIn, BrTechI. *Bk. rev.:* 3, 500 words. *Aud.:* Ac, Sa.

Part of a suite of robotics-related titles published by MCB, *Assembly Automation* features automation in flexible manufacturing processes, some of which involve robots. Application areas include electrical products, clothing, and pharmaceuticals. Each issue is composed of short research articles, illustrated new-product reviews of a page or less, company news, "mini-features" describing practical solutions or techniques, media reviews (books, software), patent abstracts, the "Internet Page" (one-paragraph reviews of useful web sites), and editorial commentary. The research articles may be authored by academics, practicing engineers, or journal staff. Recent issues include articles on bin-picking methods, automatic adhesive bonding, and tool selection. The electronic version utilizes the same access points and features as its sister publication, *Industrial Robot.* This is a very expensive title in the field, to be considered only by industry libraries and those academic institutions with large consulting efforts in manufacturing and robotics.

5941. ***Autonomous Robots.*** [ISSN: 0929-5593] 1994. bi-m. USD 668 print or online ed. Ed(s): George A Bekey. Kluwer Academic Publishers, 101 Philip Dr, Assinippi Park, Norwell, MA 02061. Refereed. Online: EBSCO Publishing; ingenta.com; Kluwer Online; OCLC Online Computer Library Center, Inc.; Ovid Technologies, Inc.; RoweCom Information Quest; Swets Blackwell. Reprint: SWZ. *Indexed:* ApMecR, CompLI, EngInd, SCI. *Aud.:* Ac, Sa.

As the title indicates, this journal specializes in papers on robots that are self-sufficient, which is defined as capable of performing in real-world environments. These robots acquire data through sensors, process it, perform their tasks, and are often mobile (legged, tracked, even finned). Each issue is comprised of a half-dozen lengthy articles of 15 or more pages, often illustrated with black-and-white photographs of the robots *in situ*, plus data, graphs, formulae, and numerous references. The authorship is international, from academia and industrial-research laboratories and often with collaboration from both. A recent issue features "space robots," i.e., robots designed for space and planetary exploration. There are several articles on the "Mars Rover," discussion of teleorobotics (those familiar arms on the International Space Station), and even one on a "robonaut." This title is highly ranked in the ISI journal impact factors for robotics. Modestly priced for a scholarly technical journal, it is warmly recommended for academic and industrial collections.

Control Engineering Practice. See Computer Science and Automation/ Computer Science section.

5942. ***I E E E - A S M E Transactions on Mechatronics.*** [ISSN: 1083-4435] 1996. q. USD 565 in North America; USD 600 elsewhere. Ed(s): Masayoshi Tomizuka. Institute of Electrical and Electronics Engineers, Inc., 445 Hoes Ln, Piscataway, NJ 08854-1331; subscription-service@ieee.org; http://www.ieee.org. Illus., index. Refereed. Vol. ends: No. 4. Online: EBSCO Publishing; I E E E; Swets Blackwell. *Indexed:* C&ISA, EngInd, H&SSA, SCI. *Aud.:* Ac, Sa.

"Mechatronics" is defined by the *Transactions* as "the synergetic integration of mechanical engineering with electronic and intelligent computer control in design and manufacture of industrial products and processes." In other words, the field covers a lot of territory, and this title is actually the joint effort of several IEEE societies and ASME divisions. As in the other *IEEE Transactions* (and the *ASME Journals*), papers are highly mathematical, well referenced, and illustrated with tables and flowcharts rather than with glossies of mobile robots. Mechatronics is still a hot research area; there is also the *Journal of Microelectromechanical Systems*, another ASME and IEEE cosponsored title.

5943. ***I E E E Robotics and Automation Magazine.*** [ISSN: 1070-9932] 1994. q. USD 270 in North America; USD 305 elsewhere. Ed(s): Kimon P Valavanis. Institute of Electrical and Electronics Engineers, Inc., 445 Hoes Ln, Piscataway, NJ 08854-1331; subscription-service@ieee.org; http://www.ieee.org. Illus., index, adv. Refereed. Vol. ends: No. 4. Online: EBSCO Publishing; I E E E. *Indexed:* AS&TI, EngInd. *Aud.:* Ga, Ac, Sa.

This magazine of the IEEE Robotics and Automation Society publishes the more practical material not suitable for its *Transactions.* Not really a glossy magazine, it is still attractive, with color covers, many features, a nice presentation, and relatively short, well-illustrated articles. Each issue presents the substantive material first, then wraps up with society business, calls for papers, industry news, and the like. The magazine's own web site includes tables of contents, with abstracts, plus author and subject indexes for all volumes through 2000. Often there are synopses of the research published in the IEEEXplore version, including color illustrations, video clips, and slide presentations that cannot yet be presented at IEEEXplore. The latter site features high-quality, pdf versions of the articles, plus links to cited references. The content level is quite approachable by undergraduates and lay readers, making this a suitable selection for a large public or small academic library as well as those with active robotics research.

5944. ***I E E E Transactions on Robotics and Automation.*** Formerly (until 1988): *I E E E Journal of Robotics and Automation.* [ISSN: 1042-296X] 1985. bi-m. USD 545 in North America; USD 580 elsewhere. Ed(s): Richard A Volz. Institute of Electrical and Electronics Engineers, Inc.,

445 Hoes Ln, Piscataway, NJ 08854-1331; subscription-service@ieee.org; http://www.ieee.org. Illus., index. Refereed. Vol. ends: No. 6. Online: EBSCO Publishing; Gale Group; I E E E; Swets Blackwell. *Indexed:* AS&TI, C&ISA, EngInd, SCI, SSCI. *Bk. rev.:* 1, 2,000 words. *Aud.:* Ac, Sa.

The top-ranked (ISI Impact Factor) journal in the field, this section of the *IEEE Transactions* publishes papers by the international research community. The emphasis is on mechanical operation (such as grasping or manipulation), sensors, recognition, and mobility, with some attention to large-scale use problems. A typical issue has several lengthy papers, a few short articles, announcements, and the occasional book review. Often, a special topic will be developed over several papers. The lag time from submission to publication has considerably shortened in recent years. The new "articles which cite this one" in the IEEEXplore service promises to be a very useful addition. This is a core title for a robotics collection and is useful in any electrical or mechanical engineering program. The IEEE publishes several *Transactions* and magazines that cover robotics in varying degrees. One of them, the *IEEE Transactions on Automatic Control* (not reviewed here) is a high-impact journal that should be consulted for specific problems in the control of robotic parts.

5945. *Industrial Robot: an international journal.* Incorporates: *Service Robot.* [ISSN: 0143-991X] 1973. bi-m. EUR 6958.91 in Europe; USD 6479 in North America; AUD 7709 in Australasia. Ed(s): Clive Loughlin. Emerald, 60-62 Toller Ln, Bradford, BD8 9BY, United Kingdom; info@emeraldinsight.com; http://www.emeraldinsight.com/journals/. Illus., adv. Refereed. Reprint: PSC. *Indexed:* ABIn, AS&TI, ApMecR, BrTechI, C&ISA, EngInd, SCI. *Bk. rev.:* 3, 500 words. *Aud.:* Sa.

Industrial Robot is the oldest magazine in English devoted to robotics. Although robotic applications in any area may be included, the principal interest is in large-scale industries, such as automobiles, construction, shipbuilding, plastics, and the military. Each issue is composed of short research articles, illustrated new-product reviews of a page or less, company news, "mini-features" describing practical solutions or techniques, media reviews (books, software), patent abstracts, the "Internet Page," with one-paragraph reviews of useful web sites, plus editorial commentary. The research articles may be authored by academics, practicing engineers, or journal staff. The electronic version includes a link to the Internet Research Register for Advanced Automation, a searchable list of current research maintained by MCB, under the direction of an editorial board. Electronic access is through the Emerald Library (MCB's consolidated web service). All editorial matter can be displayed in html or Adobe Acrobat pdf formats; sometimes RealPage (Ingenta Select viewer) is also available. Book reviews include links to Internet bookstores. A free tables-of-contents alerting service is available to registered users. References within articles are linked to full text as provided by Ingenta Select; there appears to be no CrossRef or direct linking to publisher sites. This is a very expensive title in the field, to be considered only by industry libraries and those academic institutions with large consulting efforts in robotics.

5946. *Institution of Mechanical Engineers. Proceedings. Part I: Journal of Systems and Control Engineering.* [ISSN: 0959-6518] 1992. bi-m. USD 824 in the Americas; GBP 514 elsewhere. Ed(s): C R Burrows. Professional Engineering Publishing, Northgate Ave, Bury St Edmunds, IP32 6BW, United Kingdom; orders@pepublishing.com; http://www.pepublishing.com. Illus. Sample. Refereed. Circ: 800 Paid. Online: EBSCO Publishing; Ingenta Select; OCLC Online Computer Library Center, Inc.; RoweCom Information Quest; Swets Blackwell. *Indexed:* AS&TI, ApMecR, BrTechI, C&ISA. *Bk. rev.:* 1, 1,000 words. *Aud.:* Ac.

This journal covers all aspects of mechanical control, including robots, manipulators, actuators, and mechatronics. The point of view is generally modeling, simulation, design, mathematics, and computation. Although the occasional article features a complete robot entity (such as a one-legged hopping robot), papers are more likely to discuss parts of a robot: a manipulator, a sensor, a navigational device. Publication is quite speedy, often within six months of receipt of the manuscript. The title is often referenced by other robotics-related journals, perhaps because of the theory behind the parts, and it will be a good support publication for a comprehensive robotics collection.

5947. *International Journal of Flexible Manufacturing Systems: design, analysis and operation of manufacturing and assembly systems.* [ISSN: 0920-6299] 1988. q. USD 411 print or online ed. Ed(s): Kathryn E Stecke. Kluwer Academic Publishers, 101 Philip Dr, Assinippi Park, Norwell, MA 02061. Illus., index. Sample. Refereed. Vol. ends: No. 4. Microform: PQC. Online: EBSCO Publishing; ingenta.com; Kluwer Online; OCLC Online Computer Library Center, Inc.; Ovid Technologies, Inc.; RoweCom Information Quest; Swets Blackwell. Reprint: PQC; SWZ. *Indexed:* ABIn, EngInd. *Aud.:* Ac, Sa.

Flexible manufacturing often involves robots in the process. This journal discusses the procedural aspects (scheduling, modeling, sequencing) of their use, not the actual designs of the robots or automata involved. This point is well documented in an article on holonic machining equipment. "Holins" are autonomous agents, cooperating in self-organizing systems. Articles are quite lengthy and well referenced; authors are usually academics but occasionally are practitioners. There is more emphasis on management techniques than on the technology per se. The web site includes the usual tables of contents and author instructions; the improved article search interface includes date fields, a "match references" form, and cross-journal searching. This is a good title for academic institutions with strong programs in industrial engineering and manufacturing technology as well as robotics, and for industrial concerns with highly automated production processes.

5948. *International Journal of Robotics and Automation.* [ISSN: 0826-8185] 1986. q. USD 230. Ed(s): R Colbaugh. ACTA Press, 4500-16th Ave NW, Ste 80, Calgary, AB T3B 0M6, Canada; comments@actapress.com; http://www.actapress.com. Adv. *Indexed:* ApMecR, C&ISA, EngInd. *Aud.:* Ac.

Although this journal has been publishing since 1986, it has only recently caught the attention of the larger world. Published by a small specialty press, it features succinct, ten-page articles by an international range of academic authors. About half of the articles deal with the functions of robots (as opposed to robots as a whole) and are especially concerned with manipulation, spatial recognition, and wireless activity. The other half feature programming issues. Most issues are arranged around a theme, such as "Compliance and Compliant Mechanisms" or "Web-based Robotics and Automation." Almost every issue has a list of upcoming conferences. The publisher's web site is minimal, but tables of contents beginning with 2000 are included with the journal's basic description information. Although issues are slim, so is the price; this title is attractive to college as well as university and corporate libraries.

5949. *International Journal of Robotics Research.* [ISSN: 0278-3649] 1982. m. GBP 789 in Europe, Middle East, Africa & Australasia. Ed(s): John M Hollerbach. Sage Publications Ltd., 6 Bonhill St, London, EC2A 4PU, United Kingdom; info@sagepub.co.uk; http://www.sagepub.co.uk/. Illus., index. Sample. Refereed. Circ: 1340. Vol. ends: Dec. Microform: PQC. Online: ingenta.com; OCLC Online Computer Library Center, Inc.; ProQuest Information & Learning; RoweCom Information Quest; Swets Blackwell. Reprint: PQC. *Indexed:* AS&TI, ApMecR, BrTechI, C&ISA, CompLI, CompR, EngInd, ErgAb, IAA, SCI, ZooRec. *Aud.:* Ac, Sa.

Billing itself as the first scholarly publication in robotics, it is second-most-cited journal in the field. The articles are relatively lengthy (averaging 20 pages each), and the treatment is highly mathematical. Although there is some attention paid to larger systems, most papers consider specific aspects of robot function, such as light-sensing, flexing of manipulators, force sensing, or motion variables. Experimentation is almost always on laboratory-scale equipment, although the intent is application to actual production environments. There is no indication of the submission/publication date lag, but most recent articles reference papers within a year of publication, and the "Communications" articles appear to be within six months. In the March 2001 issue, the "multimedia editors" announced plans to include multimedia appendixes (datasets, code, models, and simulations), available at the journal's web site. Two years later, there was no indication that this has been implemented, neither at the publisher's site nor Ingenta Select. Ingenta does indicate a "cited references" feature, but it was not functioning at the time of this evaluation. This is an excellent title with good value for the money for any institution engaged in robotics research.

5950. ***J A L A.*** [ISSN: 1535-5535] 1997. USD 240 (Individuals, USD 180). Ed(s): Robin A Felder. Association for Laboratory Automation, Health Science Center, University of Virginia, Box 572, Charlottesville, VA 22908. *Indexed:* ExcerpMed. *Aud.:* Ac, Sa.

The laboratories featured in the journal are clinical testing facilities. With much of their work involving sterile environments and/or possibly dangerous substances, robots have come to be standard equipment. Almost every issue has at least one article on specialized robotic systems as used in the laboratory environment. This is a glossy magazine for the practitioner with three- to four-page color illustrated articles, usually with minimal references, but authored by experts in the field and peer reviewed. Issues since 1999 are available free via Ingenta Select, but this was under review as of spring 2003. Although for the specialized collection, its cross-disciplinary nature may be a plus for some organizations.

5951. ***J S M E International Journal. Series C, Mechanical Systems, Machine Elements and Manufacturing.*** Former titles (until 1997): *J S M E International Journal. Series C: Dynamics, Control, Robotics, Design and Manufacturing;* (until 1993): *J S M E International Journal. Series 3: Vibration, Control Engineering, Engineering for Industry;* Supersedes in part (in 1988): *J S M E International Journal;* Which was formerly (until 1986): *J S M E Bulletin.* [ISSN: 1344-7653] 1958. q. Members, USD 68; Non-members, USD 125. Japan Society of Mechanical Engineers, Shinanomachi-Rengakan Bldg, 35 Shinano-Machi, Tokyo, 160-0016, Japan; http://www.jsme.or.jp/english/indene.htm. Illus., index. Refereed. Vol. ends: No. 4. *Indexed:* ApMecR, BioEngAb, C&ISA, ChemAb, EngInd, H&SSA, SCI. *Aud.:* Ac, Sa.

The *Journal* of the Japanese Society of Mechanical Engineers (JSME) is divided into three parts: *Series A. Mechanics and Materials Engineering, Series B. Fluids and Thermal Engineering,* and *Series C,* which includes robotics. *Series C* could just as easily be titled "Mechatronics" because that is the new shorthand for robotics, control, and manufacturing design. Almost all of the authors are Japanese or Chinese; many of the papers are translations from the JSME's Japanese-language *Transactions.* Publication costs are partly supported by the Japanese Ministry of Education and by page charges, so that the cost of all three sections of the *Journal* is very inexpensive, even for nonmembers. Papers are highly theoretical and quite specialized, but they seek to solve/resolve actual problems. Citations are just as likely to be to American or European publications as to Japanese, so that the reader has glimpses into both worlds. The publication lag for original papers averages 18 months, but the revision process also includes updating literature references. A nicely priced addition to an academic robotics collection and suitable for industrial research organizations.

5952. ***Journal of Dynamic Systems, Measurement and Control.*** [ISSN: 0022-0434] 1971. q. Members, USD 50 print & online eds.; Non-members, USD 300 print & online eds. Ed(s): A Galip Ulsoy. A S M E International, Three Park Ave, New York, NY 10016-5990; infocentral@asme.org; http://www.asme.org. Illus., index, adv. Refereed. Circ: 2500. Vol. ends: Dec. Microform: PQC. Online: EBSCO Publishing; Gale Group; Swets Blackwell. Reprint: PQC. *Indexed:* AS&TI, ApMecR, C&ISA, CEA, EngInd, ExcerpMed, SCI. *Aud.:* Ac, Sa.

To those outside the field, the *Journal of Dynamic Systems, Measurement and Control* may seem an unlikely title for a top robotics publication. The clues are "control" and "dynamic," because these play a large part in the design and use of robots. Recent articles discuss biped walking robots, teleorobotics, and friction coefficients in robot tasks. As a research journal, it is heavy on mathematics, usually illustrated with tables and graphs but with an occasional photograph, and has extensive references. With the advent of electronic paper submission, the lag time to publication has decreased by several months. The journal is mounted via the AIP system, providing not only alternative display formats (pdf, html, and PostScript), but interlinking of references and searching via SPIN. An excellent interdisciplinary title.

5953. ***Journal of Intelligent and Robotic Systems: theory and applications.*** Incorporates (in 1994): *Mechatronic Systems Engineering.* [ISSN: 0921-0296] 1988. m. EUR 1136 print or online ed. Ed(s): Spyros G Tzafestas. Kluwer Academic Publishers, van Godewijckstraat 30, PO Box 17, Dordrecht, 3300 AA, Netherlands. Illus., index. Sample. Refereed. Vol. ends: No. 4. Microform: PQC. Online: EBSCO Publishing; ingenta.com; Kluwer Online; OCLC Online Computer Library Center, Inc.; Ovid Technologies, Inc.; RoweCom Information Quest; Swets Blackwell. Reprint: SWZ. *Indexed:* ApMecR, C&ISA, EngInd, ErgAb, PsycholAb, SSCI. *Aud.:* Ac.

Taking a largely theoretical approach to robotics, this journal publishes five or six lengthy papers per issue. Most involve modeling of either robot components or the tasks that they perform. Some are mathematical discussions of techniques or systems that may be adapted to or incorporated in specific types of robots or in the overall systems governing them. Recent work features concrete floor finishing robots, path planning for biped robots, and modeling the "pyscho-physical" state of robots. Authorship is international, with most researchers from academia, but there is a fair percentage of industrial collaboration. This journal appears to be an attempt to blend theoretical artificial intelligence with robotics, itself a highly practical field, and it may be too specialized for all but the most complete academic program.

5954. ***Journal of Micromechatronics.*** [ISSN: 1389-2258] 1999. q. EUR 195 combined subscription print & online eds.; USD 244 combined subscription print & online eds. Ed(s): Paolo Dario, Ronald Fearing. V S P, PO Box 346, Zeist, 3700 AH, Netherlands; vsppub@compuserve.com; http://www.vsppub.com. Refereed. Online: EBSCO Publishing; Ingenta Select; Swets Blackwell. *Aud.:* Ac.

A merger of robotics, mechatronics, and nanotechnology, this fledgling journal is peppered with intriguing articles about small-scale robots. Covering both theory and application, the journal is interested in high-precision micro-components for electronics, biomedical, and consumer markets. Sample articles include "Wing Transmission for a Micromechanical Flying Insect," and "Alice the Sugar-Cube Robot," but not all titles are this fanciful; most are similar to "Low-Power Silicon Articulated Microrobots." Authors are from internationally recognized organizations and papers average more than ten pages in length. The online edition is mounted through Ingenta Select, which has only two of the four available issues as of this writing. This new title in an evolving field deserves a close look by libraries that have robotics and nanotechnology interests.

5955. ***Journal of Robotic Systems.*** [ISSN: 0741-2223] 1984. m. USD 2275 domestic; USD 2395 in Canada & Mexico; USD 2497 elsewhere. Ed(s): Gerardo Beni, Susan Hackwood. John Wiley & Sons, Inc., 111 River St, Hoboken, NJ 07030; uscs-wis@wiley.com; http://www.wiley.com. Illus., index, adv. Sample. Refereed. Circ: 750. Vol. ends: Dec. Microform: PQC. Online: EBSCO Publishing; ScienceDirect; Wiley InterScience. Reprint: PSC. *Indexed:* AS&TI, ApMecR, C&ISA, EngInd, IAA, SCI. *Aud.:* Ac, Sa.

Featuring research articles, the *Journal of Robotic Systems* is at once practical and theoretical—practical because the robots involved are either working models or production floor systems; theoretical because the treatments involve designs or systems that can be used as models or applied in other environments, rather than specific techniques for a specific application. Almost every article features an actual robot rather than a theoretical concept. Illustrations are usually graphs, computer models, and flowcharts. The editors have largely achieved rapid-communication publication, with an average lag time of nine months between submission and publication of an article. There are occasional thematic issues and new-product information, the latter describing highly specialized equipment. The Wiley web site offers pdf versions (with bookmarks), cross-reference linking, and searching within the Wiley system. Although a quality journal, this is one of the most expensive publications in the robotics area (and issues are slim).

5956. ***Mechanism and Machine Theory.*** Formerly: *Journal of Mechanisms.* [ISSN: 0094-114X] 1966. m. EUR 2296 (Qualified personnel, EUR 87). Ed(s): Terry E Shoup, A Kecskemethy. Pergamon, The Boulevard, Langford Ln, East Park, Kidlington, OX5 1GB, United Kingdom. Illus., index, adv. Sample. Refereed. Circ: 1000. Vol. ends: No. 8. Microform: PQC. Online: ingenta.com; ScienceDirect; Swets Blackwell. *Indexed:* ApMecR, C&ISA, CCMJ, EngInd, MathSciNet, SCI. *Bk. rev.:* 1, 2,000 words. *Aud.:* Ac.

The emphasis here is on theory, with most papers making extensive use of mathematical symbols rather than engineering diagrams. However, the topics generally concern practical applications, such as robot joints, manipulators, and kinematics. This is the official journal of the International Federation for the Theory of Machines and Mechanisms, and the authors reflect the international membership. An occasional non-English paper appears. The publication lag is often two years. Electronic access is through Science Direct, with excellent searching, display, and linking options. For the academic library with a strong engineering mechanics/manufacturing program.

5957. ***Mechatronics: the science of intelligent machines.*** [ISSN: 0957-4158] 1991. 10x/yr. EUR 994 (Qualified personnel, EUR 77). Ed(s): I. C. Ume, R W Daniel. Pergamon, The Boulevard, Langford Ln, East Park, Kidlington, OX5 1GB, United Kingdom. Illus., index. Sample. Refereed. Vol. ends: No. 8. Microform: PQC. Online: ingenta.com; ScienceDirect; Swets Blackwell. *Indexed:* ApMecR, C&ISA, SCI. *Aud.:* Ac, Sa.

A relatively new title in this emergent hybrid field, *Mechatronics* is chiefly interested in papers on the design of machines and systems that include some level of computer-based intelligence. Articles are fairly lengthy, averaging 20 pages or more. The major application thrust is specific robotic parts, as opposed to a multifunction and/or mobile robot. Examples of this are such phrases as "two-axis arm motion" and "five-bar finger with redundant activators." Once or twice a year, an issue is thematic, such as "Miniature Actuators." The latter reflects the trend in robotics to miniaturization, not to say nanotechnology. Compare this title with the *IEEE/ASME Transactions on Mechatronics*, which is both cheaper and has a higher ISI impact factor.

5958. ***Real Robots.*** [ISSN: 1474-1512] fortn. Eaglemoss Publications Ltd., 5 Cromwell Rd, London, SW7 2HR, United Kingdom; http://www.eaglemoss.co.uk. *Aud.:* Hs.

This is an unusual product, a combination magazine and do-it-yourself kit. Aimed at the hobbyist, each issue has several articles, but it also includes parts to build whatever the latest project is. The articles are full-color glossies, more like sound bytes (image bytes?) than articles, but highly entertaining. Unlike the usual magazine, it's not only possible but encouraged to start with the first issue, so that the subscriber can acquire all of the previous kits. Libraries, however, will probably want the "magazine without components" subscription, offered at BP 1.50 per issue. The hardest part may be convincing your serials vendor that you are serious. Encouraged for the public library, it might catch the fancy of some colleges, especially those who participate in robot competitions.

5959. ***Robotica.*** [ISSN: 0263-5747] 1983. bi-m. USD 495 (Individuals, USD 170). Ed(s): J Rose. Cambridge University Press, The Edinburgh Bldg, Shaftesbury Rd, Cambridge, CB2 2RU, United Kingdom; information@cambridge.org; http://uk.cambridge.org/journals. Illus., index, adv. Sample. Refereed. Circ: 650. Vol. ends: No. 6. Online: EBSCO Publishing; OCLC Online Computer Library Center, Inc.; RoweCom Information Quest; Swets Blackwell. Reprint: SWZ. *Indexed:* BRI, BrTechI, C&ISA, CBRI, EngInd, ErgAb, IAA. *Bk. rev.:* 2, 500-1,500 words. *Aud.:* Ac, Sa.

One of the earliest professional journals on robotics, *Robotica* has remained focused on its mission over the years. It is hard to find an article in any issue that does not have "robot" somewhere in the title (although nowadays it may be part of a word, such as "microrobots"). Although papers are research-level quality, there is always attention to working mechanisms rather than just theoretical modeling. Following the usual academic formula, papers are well illustrated and heavily referenced. Many issues are thematic, in whole or in part, expanding on such topics as languages and robot software or microactuators. Aside from some of the best book reviews in the field, the occasional "Reports & Surveys" section provides a real synthesis of what is happening now in the field and what actually did happen to some of those great ideas of the past. This is an excellent journal, useful in both industry and academia and inexpensive enough for college libraries.

5960. ***Robotics and Autonomous Systems.*** Formerly (until 1988): *Robotics.* [ISSN: 0921-8890] 1985. 16x/yr. EUR 1411. Ed(s): T. Arai, R. Dillmann. Elsevier BV, North-Holland, Sara Burgerhartstraat 25, Amsterdam, 1055 KV, Netherlands; nlinfo-f@elsevier.nl; http://www.elsevier.nl/homepage/about/us/regional_sites.htt. Illus., index, adv. Sample. Refereed. Circ: 1200. Vol. ends: No. 4. Online: EBSCO Publishing; Gale Group; ingenta.com; ScienceDirect; Swets Blackwell. Reprint: SWZ. *Indexed:* ApMecR, C&ISA, CompLI, EngInd. *Aud.:* Ac, Sa.

This journal is affiliated with the Intelligent Autonomous Systems Society. The title should be compared with the publication *Robotics and Computer-Integrated Manufacturing*, published by Elsevier under the Pergamon imprint. Both are research journals featuring quality scholarly papers. They are not competitors, though, but two aspects of the same field: large-scale and/or whole machines versus specific aspects of parts of machines. *Robotics and Autonomous Systems* will publish titles such as "Geometric Constraint Identification and Mapping for Mobile Robots," while *Robotics and Computer-Integrated Manufacturing* will print "Improved Robotic Deburring." A calendar of robotics meetings and events is included in each issue.

5961. ***Robotics and Computer - Integrated Manufacturing: an international journal.*** Incorporates (1988-1998): *Computer Integrated Manufacturing Systems;* Which incorporated (1988-1991): *Advanced Manufacturing Engineering.* [ISSN: 0736-5845] 1984. bi-m. EUR 981. Ed(s): A Sharon. Pergamon, The Boulevard, Langford Ln, East Park, Kidlington, OX5 1GB, United Kingdom; http://www.elsevier.nl. Illus., index, adv. Sample. Refereed. Circ: 2500. Vol. ends: No. 6. Microform: PQC. Online: ingenta.com; ScienceDirect; Swets Blackwell. *Indexed:* AS&TI, C&ISA, CompLI, EngInd, ErgAb. *Aud.:* Ac.

This is a research journal with a mission: dissemination of proven research (either in the laboratory or on the shop floor) of manufacturing technologies and systems. This includes robotics, flexible automation, mechatronics, and rapid-response (or agile) manufacturing. Almost every author is associated with an engineering department of a large university, with research usually funded by a government agency, so that laboratory work predominates. Illustrations are largely flowcharts, line drawings, and screen images, and articles are well referenced and current. Another Elsevier title, *Computer Integrated Manufacturing Systems,* has been absorbed by this publication. As a result, each issue is divided into two sections: "Manufacturing" and "Product and Process Development." This title can do double duty, covering mechanical and industrial engineering topics as well as robotics.

■ SAFETY

See also Medicine and Health section.

Elna L. Saxton, Head, Periodicals & Microforms Department, University of Cincinnati Libraries, P.O. Box 210033, Cincinnati, OH 45221-0033; Elna.Saxton@uc.edu

Introduction

The world has changed in recent years with a national dialogue on safety at work and home. The need for accurate and up-to-date health and safety information has never been more important. Terrorism and other intentional acts of violence are included in safety management and planning for risk reduction. At the same time, increasing reliance on information technologies has heightened competition and the pace of work, causing workers and supervisors to quickly adapt. Lengthy planning periods are a luxury; the emphasis is instead on innovative safety solutions and incorporating safety into the business culture from orientation through to ongoing assessments and inspections. Improving safety leads to improved control of costs and liabilities, and improved working conditions for employees leads to improved productivity.

These periodicals share a common objective: to disseminate research results, promote ongoing investigation of safety topics, and advance the discussion of safety. While these titles focus on general and cross-disciplinary safety themes, other important periodicals are available that are more subject-specific, e.g., *Journal of Agricultural Safety and Health, Journal of Fire Sciences, Journal of Traffic Safety Education*, and *Structural Safety.* In addition to periodicals, there are many informative newsletters, loose-leaf services, and directories that focus on safety. Although few exclusively electronic publications are available in this subject area, many of the entries for print publications have an electronic counterpart that includes contents data, selected articles, or full-text article access. Trade publications usually have an online archive with no charge for accessing articles.

Basic Periodicals

Hs, Ga: *Job Safety and Health Quarterly, Safety and Health;* Ac, Sa: *Accident Analysis & Prevention, Journal of Safety Research, Safety Science.*

Basic Abstracts and Indexes

Health and Safety Science Abstracts.

5962. ***A I H A Journal: journal for the science of occupational and environmental health and safety.*** Former titles (until 2002): *A I H A J;* (until 2000): *American Industrial Hygiene Association Journal;* (until 1957): *American Industrial Hygiene Association Quarterly;* (until 1946): *Industrial Hygiene.* [ISSN: 1542-8117] 1940. bi-m. USD 185. Ed(s): Dr. Howard J. Cohen. American Industrial Hygiene Association, 2700 Prosperity Ave, Ste 250, Fairfax, VA 22031-4307; infonet@aiha.org; http://www.aiha.org. Illus., index, adv. Refereed. Circ: 12200 Paid. Vol. ends: Dec. Online: EBSCO Publishing. *Indexed:* ABIn, AS&TI, BiolAb, C&ISA, CerAb, ChemAb, DSA, EnvAb, ErgAb, ExcerpMed, FPA, ForAb, H&SSA, IBZ, IndMed, IndVet, PollutAb, S&F, SCI, SSCI, VetBull. *Aud.:* Ac, Sa.

The American Industrial Hygiene Association (AIHA) is dedicated to recognizing, evaluating, and controlling potential occupational health hazards in the workplace or community. This journal is for the health and safety specialist, offering reports on technical and experimental studies and articles on applied research. Recent developments are presented in occupational and environmental topics ranging from protective equipment and indoor air quality to ergonomics and emergency response. Also included are a listing of consultants, AIHA membership information, new products, product indexes, and Proficiency Analytical Testing (PAT) program reports. The PAT program provides quality control reference samples to laboratories in 17 countries, with the goal of assisting the laboratory in improving performance. Indexes are available online at www.aiha.org.

5963. ***Accident Analysis & Prevention.*** [ISSN: 0001-4575] 1969. bi-m. EUR 1225 (Qualified personnel, EUR 304). Ed(s): Frank A Haight. Pergamon, The Boulevard, Langford Ln, East Park, Kidlington, OX5 1GB, United Kingdom. Illus., index, adv. Sample. Refereed. Vol. ends: Oct. Microform: PQC. Online: ingenta.com; ScienceDirect; Swets Blackwell. *Indexed:* AgeL, BiolAb, C&ISA, CJA, EngInd, ErgAb, ExcerpMed, H&SSA, IndMed, PEI, PsycholAb, SSCI. *Aud.:* Ac, Sa.

Sponsored by the International Association for Accident and Traffic Medicine and the International Research Committee on Biokinetics of Impacts, this periodical is devoted to accidental injury and damage, both pre-injury and immediate post-injury. Coverage includes transportation, industrial, domestic, and recreational injury factors, but the majority of the reports are traffic related. Topics from a recent issue include a study on the impact of hands-free communication while driving, interurban road safety, and guardrail funding. Case studies, commentary, and research papers are all accepted for publication. An index is included in the last issue of each volume. Regional planners, research scientists, civil engineers, trauma physicians, psychologists, and public health planners are the target audience. Table of contents data are available on the publisher's web site.

5964. ***American Journal of Industrial Medicine.*** [ISSN: 0271-3586] 1980. m. USD 3525 United States; USD 3645 in Canada & Mexico; USD 3747 elsewhere. Ed(s): P J Landrigan. John Wiley & Sons, Inc., 111 River St, Hoboken, NJ 07030; uscs-wis@wiley.com; http://www.wiley.com. Illus., index, adv. Refereed. Circ: 1150. Vol. ends: Jun/Dec. Microform: PQC. Online: EBSCO Publishing; ScienceDirect; Wiley InterScience. *Indexed:* BiolAb, C&ISA, CJA, ChemAb, DSA, ErgAb, ExcerpMed, FPA, ForAb, H&SSA, IndMed, IndVet, PollutAb, RRTA, RiskAb, S&F, SCI, SSCI, WAE&RSA. *Aud.:* Ac, Sa.

Subscribers to this title receive access to substantive reports of original research, review articles, case studies, and analyses of policy. Each issue contains from 10 to 20 highly rigorous and technical studies. Specific topics include occupational and environmental disease, pesticides, cancer, occupational and environmental epidemiology, disease surveillance, ergonomics, dust diseases, lead poisoning, neurotoxicology, and endocrine disruptors. Letters of comment and criticism are accepted for publication and provide further discussion of the research. This journal is useful for any scholarly occupational safety and environmental health collection.

American Journal of Public Health. See Medicine and Health/Public Health section.

5965. ***Annals of Occupational Hygiene.*** [ISSN: 0003-4878] 1958. 8x/yr. GBP 590. Ed(s): Trevor Ogden, Stephen Rappaport. Oxford University Press, Great Clarendon St, Oxford, OX2 6DP, United Kingdom; jnl.orders@oup.co.uk; http://www3.oup.co.uk/jnls. Illus., index, adv. Sample. Refereed. Circ: 1700. Vol. ends: Dec. Microform: PQC. Online: HighWire Press; ingenta.com; Ovid Technologies, Inc.; ScienceDirect; Swets Blackwell. *Indexed:* BiolAb, BiolDig, C&ISA, CerAb, ChemAb, EngInd, ErgAb, ExcerpMed, H&SSA, IndMed, IndVet, PollutAb, SCI, SSCI. *Bk. rev.:* 1, 730 words, signed. *Aud.:* Ac, Sa.

This official journal of the British Occupational Hygiene Society (www.bohs.org) aims to promote a healthy working environment by publishing research and reports on health hazards and risks that arise in the course of employment. It includes papers on basic mechanisms, on human aspects and technology, and on environmental risks to humans when these are work-related. The research reports are of interest to scientists, engineers, and medical professionals concerned with the recognition, quantification, management, and control of work-related health hazards.

5966. ***Applied Ergonomics: human factors in technology and society.*** [ISSN: 0003-6870] 1969. bi-m. EUR 841 (Qualified personnel, EUR 204). Ed(s): John R. Wilson, K C Parsons. Pergamon, The Boulevard, Langford Ln, East Park, Kidlington, OX5 1GB, United Kingdom. Illus., index, adv. Sample. Refereed. Vol. ends: Dec. Microform: PQC. Online: Gale Group; ingenta.com; ScienceDirect; Swets Blackwell. *Indexed:* AgeL, BiolAb, EngInd, ErgAb, ExcerpMed, H&SSA, IndMed, PEI, PsycholAb, SCI, SSCI. *Aud.:* Ac, Sa.

This is "the journal of people's relationships with equipment, environments, and work systems." Reports cover the practical applications of ergonomic design and research. A broad focus makes this periodical useful both to specialists and to all those interested in ergonomic factors at work or play. Areas covered include applications in the office, industry, consumer products, information technology, and military design. Occasional issues focus on specific topics; a recent issue presents specialized coverage of corporate initiatives in ergonomics. "PatentsALERT" includes abstracts of recently issued patents in the United States and patent applications filed from more than 90 countries. Table of contents data is available from ContentsDirect at www.elsevier.nl/locate/ContentsDirect.

5967. ***Applied Occupational & Environmental Hygiene.*** Formerly (until vol.5, no.1, 1990): *Applied Industrial Hygiene.* [ISSN: 1047-322X] 1986. m. USD 427 (Individuals, USD 227). Ed(s): J Thomas Pierce. Taylor & Francis Inc, 325 Chestnut St, Suite 800, Philadelphia, PA 19016; info@taylorandfrancis.com; http://www.taylorandfrancis.com/. Illus., index, adv. Sample. Refereed. Circ: 5000 Paid. Vol. ends: Dec. Online: EBSCO Publishing; Ingenta Select; OCLC Online Computer Library Center, Inc.; RoweCom Information Quest; Swets Blackwell. Reprint: PSC. *Indexed:* C&ISA, ChemAb, EnvAb, ErgAb, ExcerpMed, H&SSA, IndMed, PollutAb. *Bk. rev.:* 1, 525 words, signed. *Aud.:* Ac, Sa.

Published for the American Conference of Governmental Industrial Hygienists, this title provides original studies and reports on general industrial hygiene, engineering control, occupational and environmental epidemiology, occupational and environmental medicine, ergonomics and human factors, applied toxicology, and applied environmental chemistry. The reports and articles are readable, useful, and focused on situations encountered in work life. An extensive review board includes representatives from government, academia, and industry. Useful departments include case studies, hazard controls, discussion of online resources, continuing education, book reviews, and new products. A table of contents service is available at www.tandf.co.uk/journals.

5968. ***Disaster Prevention and Management.*** Incorporates: *Disaster Management.* [ISSN: 0965-3562] 1992. 5x/yr. EUR 5566.91 in Europe; USD 5099 in North America; AUD 7739 in Australasia. Ed(s): Dr. H C Wilson. Emerald, 60-62 Toller Ln, Bradford, BD8 9BY, United Kingdom; info@emeraldinsight.com; http://www.emeraldinsight.com/journals/. Refereed. Online: Pub.; EBSCO Publishing; OCLC Online Computer Library Center, Inc.; ProQuest Information & Learning; RoweCom Information Quest; Swets Blackwell. Reprint: PSC; SWZ. *Indexed:* GeogAbPG, H&SSA, RRTA, RiskAb, SWRA. *Aud.:* Ac, Sa.

This periodical specializes in the field of disaster prevention and management, publishing reports relating to disaster emergency and crisis management. Following the terrorist attacks of September 11, civil protection and defense systems worldwide have received much scrutiny. Academics, practitioners, and policy makers will benefit from the examination of hazard mitigation and research on disaster-related risks. A table of contents alerting service is available at the publisher's web site.

Environmental Health Perspectives. See Government Periodicals—Federal section.

5969. ***Ergonomics: an international journal of research and practice in human factors and ergonomics.*** [ISSN: 0014-0139] 1957. 15x/yr. GBP 1498 (Individuals, GBP 735). Ed(s): Rob Stammers. Taylor & Francis Ltd, 11 New Fetter Ln, London, EC4P 4EE, United Kingdom; info@tandf.co.uk; http://www.tandf.co.uk/journals. Illus., index, adv. Sample. Refereed. Vol. ends: Dec. Microform: NRP. Online: EBSCO Publishing; Gale Group; Ingenta Select; OCLC Online Computer Library Center, Inc.; RoweCom Information Quest; Swets Blackwell. Reprint: PSC. *Indexed:* AS&TI, AbAn, AgeL, ApMecR, BAS, BioEngAb, BiolAb, C&ISA, CINAHL, ChemAb, CompLI, EngInd, ErgAb, ExcerpMed, H&SSA, IAA, IBZ, IndMed, PAIS, PsycholAb, SCI, SSCI. *Bk. rev.:* 3, 616 words, signed. *Aud.:* Ac, Sa.

This journal is the official publication of the Ergonomics Society and the International Ergonomics Association. Research reports are published on the psychological, physiological, anatomical, and engineering design aspects of employment and leisure activities. Research from developing countries is also included. Tables and charts are used effectively. Recent topics include spinal loads during lifting, physiologic response to mattress firmness, and evaluating shift scheduling. A regular news section, "Ergonomics International," is published in conjunction with the International Ergonomics Association. Table of contents data is available from www.tandf.com/journals.

Family Safety & Health. See Family and Marriage section.

FDA Consumer. See Medicine and Health/Consumer Health section.

5970. ***Injury Prevention.*** [ISSN: 1353-8047] 1995. q. GBP 172 (Individuals, GBP 85 print & online eds.). Ed(s): I B Pless. B M J Publishing Group, B M A House, Tavistock Sq, London, WC1H 9JR, United Kingdom; info.norththames@bma.org.uk; http://www.bmjpg.com/. Illus., index, adv. Sample. Refereed. Vol. ends: Dec. Microform: PQC. Online: EBSCO Publishing; Florida Center for Library Automation; Gale Group; HighWire Press; RoweCom Information Quest; Swets Blackwell. Reprint: PQC. *Indexed:* CINAHL, H&SSA, IndMed, PEI. *Bk. rev.:* 2, 857 words, signed. *Aud.:* Ac, Sa.

International and interdisciplinary in scope, this publication seeks to inform readers about injury prevention and control for all age groups. Injuries represent a major health and safety concern. Decreasing injury through research and improved prevention techniques is the primary activity of safety professionals. For libraries with safety or community health collections, the articles and special reports collected by the editors will raise critical issues and fulfill research needs. Issues contain editorials, op/ed pieces, research letters, items on methodology, and research reports.

5971. ***International Journal of Occupational and Environmental Health.*** [ISSN: 1077-3525] 1995. q. USD 106 (Individuals, USD 86; USD 25 newsstand/cover per issue). Hanley & Belfus, Inc., 210 S 13th St, Philadelphia, PA 19107; http://www.elsevierhealth.com. Illus., index, adv. Refereed. Circ: 1000. *Indexed:* CINAHL, ErgAb, ExcerpMed, IndMed. *Aud.:* Ga, Ac, Sa.

International and diverse in scope, this title offers in-depth research reports on the relationship between human health and the environment. Included are editorials and letters to the editor, as well as brief reports, research articles, and conference reports. Libraries will find this a valuable addition for a socioenvironmental perspective. Excellent coverage is given to the occupational and environmental concerns of developing countries.

5972. ***Job Safety and Health Quarterly.*** [ISSN: 1057-5820] 1989. q. USD 17. Ed(s): Kerri Lawrence. U.S. Occupational Safety and Health Administration, Office of Public Affairs, Rm N3647, 200 Constitution Ave, N W, Washington, DC 20210; http://www.osha-slc.gov/html/jshq-index.html. Illus., index. Vol. ends: Summer. *Indexed:* BPI. *Aud.:* Ga, Ac, Sa.

Published by the Occupational Safety and Health Administration (OSHA), this magazine has regular columns that provide current information on meetings, regulatory issues, small business perspectives, and education opportunities. In a recent issue, OSHA's role in national emergency response for hazardous materials is reviewed. Regulations expected to be under development or review by the agency during a specified period are briefly listed. Full-text access to this magazine is available on the OSHA web site. Libraries will find this title useful as a nontechnical source of safety-regulation news and general information.

5973. ***Journal of Safety Research.*** [ISSN: 0022-4375] 1982. 5x/yr. EUR 715. Ed(s): Thomas Planek, Mei-Li Lin. Pergamon, The Boulevard, Langford Ln, East Park, Kidlington, OX5 1GB, United Kingdom. Illus., index, adv. Sample. Refereed. Vol. ends: Winter. Microform: PQC. Online: Gale Group; ingenta.com; ScienceDirect; Swets Blackwell. *Indexed:* AgeL, BiolAb, EngInd, ErgAb, H&SSA, PsycholAb, RiskAb, SSCI, SUSA. *Aud.:* Ac, Sa.

The *Journal of Safety Research* is an international publication of the National Safety Council, a nongovernmental, nonprofit, public service association. The stated goal is to apply accident research, analysis, and theory to management of injury, illness, and property loss due to accidents. Reports of analytical research are published in all areas of safety including traffic, industry, farm, home, school, and public health. An abstract section provides citations and summaries of research reported in other publications, separated into broad topical areas such as traffic, industry, and public health. It provides excellent quality as well as quantity of information within a broad scope of safety research. An annual author/title index, which does not index the abstract section, is included in the final issue of each volume. Table of contents data is available from the Contents-Direct service at http://contentsdirect.elsevier.com

5974. ***Occupational Hazards: magazine of health & environment.*** [ISSN: 0029-7909] 1938. m. USD 50 domestic; USD 70 Canada; USD 100 elsewhere. Ed(s): Stephen Minter. Penton Media, Inc., 1300 E 9th St, Cleveland, OH 44114-1503; information@penton.com; http://www.penton.com. Illus., index, adv. Sample. Circ: 60000 Controlled. Vol. ends: Dec. Microform: PQC. Online: bigchalk; EBSCO Publishing; Florida Center for Library Automation; Gale Group; Northern Light Technology, Inc.; OCLC Online Computer Library Center, Inc.; ProQuest Information & Learning; H.W. Wilson. Reprint: PQC. *Indexed:* ABIn, BPI, ChemAb, H&SSA, LRI, PMA. *Aud.:* Ga, Ac, Sa.

Coverage includes legislative, regulatory, and scientific developments; how-to articles; and services and products. Safety professionals use this publication to stay up-to-date on OSHA, NIOSH, and EPA compliance requirements and to improve their safety and industrial hygiene programs. Recent issues include such topics as allergies, asbestos, and ergonomics and hearing loss. The publisher offers a searchable article archive, buyers' guide, training topics, news, and events calendar at www.occupationalhazards.com. This trade publication is a worthy addition to collections used by practitioners.

5975. ***Occupational Health & Safety.*** Former titles (until 1976): *The International Journal of Occupational Health & Safety;* (until 1974): *International Industrial Medicine and Surgery;* (until 1969): *The International Journal of Industrial Medicine & Surgery;* (until 1967): *Industrial Medicine and Surgery;* (until 1949): *Industrial Medicine and Surgery Trauma;* (until 1949): *Industrial Medicine.* [ISSN: 0362-4064] 1932. m. USD 99 United States; USD 109 Canada; USD 119 elsewhere. Ed(s): Jerry Laws. Stevens Publishing Corp., 5151 Beltline Rd, 10th fl, Dallas, TX 75240; http://www.stevenspublishing.com/. Illus., index, adv. Sample. Circ: 93000 Paid and free. Vol. ends: Dec. Microform: PQC. Online: bigchalk; Northern Light Technology, Inc.; OCLC Online Computer Library Center, Inc.; ProQuest Information & Learning. Reprint: PQC. *Indexed:* ABIn, AgeL, BPI, BiolAb, CINAHL, ChemAb, ErgAb, H&SSA, IndMed, PAIS, RiskAb. *Aud.:* Hs, Ga, Ac, Sa.

This journal includes solid reporting on workplace safety trends and research along with articles on management and training issues. Coverage of specific safety issues will assist the practitioner. Recent topics include fire protection, dermal protection, mold testing, the aging workforce, and safety goggles. Editorials provide an interesting discussion of hot topics. Information on new products and publications and on developing technologies for safety skills and training make this trade magazine invaluable for practitioners.

5976. ***Professional Safety.*** Formerly (until 1974): *American Society of Safety Engineers. Journal.* [ISSN: 0099-0027] 1956. m. Members, USD 17.50; Non-members, USD 60. Ed(s): Sue Trebswether. American Society of Safety Engineers, 1800 E Oakton St, Des Plaines, IL 60018-2187; http://www.asse.org. Illus., index, adv. Sample. Refereed. Circ: 30000 Paid. Vol. ends: Dec. Online: EBSCO Publishing; Northern Light Technology, Inc.; OCLC Online Computer Library Center, Inc.; ProQuest Information & Learning; H.W. Wilson. Reprint: PQC. *Indexed:* ABIn, AS&TI, AgeL, EngInd, ErgAb, H&SSA. *Bk. rev.:* 2, 150-250 words, signed. *Aud.:* Hs, Ga, Ac, Sa.

Perusing this readable and colorful magazine on a monthly basis will keep the practitioner up-to-date and introduce the generalist to a variety of safety concerns. Published by the American Society of Safety Engineers for the professional safety specialist, this periodical highlights developments in the research and technology of accident prevention. Workplace safety, personal safety, trends, program management, and legal issues are covered in an easy-to-read format that will appeal to all safety enthusiasts. "Research Briefs" provides abstracts of research reported in other publications. Other regular features include a calendar of events and letters to the editor.

5977. ***Safety and Health: the international safety, health and environmental magazine.*** Former titles (until 1986): *National Safety and Health News;* (until May 1985): *National Safety News.* [ISSN: 0891-1797] 1919. m. Members, USD 45; Non-members, USD 58.50. Ed(s): John Dyslin. National Safety Council, 1121 Spring Lake Dr, Itasca, IL 60143; http://www.nsc.org. Illus., index, adv. Sample. Circ: 50000 Controlled. Microform: PQC. Online: Gale Group. Reprint: PQC. *Indexed:* AgeL, BPI, ChemAb, H&SSA, LRI, PEI. *Bk. rev.:* 1, 500 words, signed. *Aud.:* Hs, Ga.

The National Safety Council partners with various entities to develop training and conduct safety research. For an inexpensive membership rate the National Safety Council (a nongovernmental, not-for-profit, public service organization) offers members the benefit of this substantive publication and several others at a reduced subscription rate. *Safety and Health* seeks to reduce workplace injuries by providing educational, practical, and innovative information about workplace safety to workers, safety professionals, and industry leaders. Use of graphics and photos enhance the articles. This trade publication describes problems and proposes solutions in accessible terms. Recommended for all basic-level safety collections.

5978. ***Safety Science.*** Formerly (until 1992): *Journal of Occupational Accidents.* [ISSN: 0925-7535] 1977. 10x/yr. EUR 908. Ed(s): A R Hale. Elsevier BV, Sara Burgerhartstraat 25, Amsterdam, 1055 KV, Netherlands; nlinfo-f@elsevier.nl; http://www.elsevier.nl. Illus., index, adv. Sample. Refereed. Microform: PQC. Online: ingenta.com; ScienceDirect; Swets Blackwell. *Indexed:* BiolAb, C&ISA, EngInd, ErgAb, ExcerpMed, H&SSA, PAIS, SSCI. *Aud.:* Ac, Sa.

This title provides international coverage and a multidisciplinary approach to safety issues. Research reports not only discuss hazards at work, but also analyze leisure, home, and transportation accidents. Each issue contains from four to eight research reports. The journal focuses primarily on original research papers, but also accepts review papers and case studies for publication. Charts, tables, and graphs capably present the data. These rigorous studies provide data for safety engineers and inspectors, industrial engineers, research scientists, and ergonomists.

5979. ***Work and Stress.*** [ISSN: 0267-8373] 1987. q. GBP 207 (Individuals, GBP 103). Ed(s): Tom Cox. Taylor & Francis Ltd, 11 New Fetter Ln, London, EC4P 4EE, United Kingdom; info@tandf.co.uk; http://www.tandf.co.uk/journals. Adv. Refereed. Online: EBSCO Publishing; Ingenta Select; OCLC Online Computer Library Center, Inc.; RoweCom Information Quest; Swets Blackwell. Reprint: PSC. *Indexed:* ASSIA, AgeL, CINAHL, CJA, ErgAb, ExcerpMed, H&SSA, PsycholAb, SSCI, SociolAb. *Aud.:* Ac, Sa.

Stress has a wide-ranging impact on all aspects of life, including safety at work and home. This international and multidisciplinary periodical publishes empirical reports, reviews, case studies, and theoretical papers on stress-related issues such as burnout, corporate culture, shift work, work-family conflict, and information technology. A recent special issue focuses on musculoskeletal disorders, psychosocial factors, and computer work. Researchers, policy makers, labor union personnel, and managers will find the discussion of individual, social, organizational, and societal issues useful as they seek to design work systems that maximize productivity and well-being while minimizing negative outcomes.

■ SCIENCE AND TECHNOLOGY

Amy L. Paster, Head, Life Sciences Library, 408 Paterno Library, Pennsylvania State University, University Park, PA 16802; alp4@psu.edu; FAX: 814-863-9684

Introduction

What exactly is "science"? According to Webster's Collegiate Dictionary science can be described as "knowledge covering general truths or the operation of general laws especially as obtained and tested through scientific method: such knowledge concerned with the physical world and its phenomena." Technology is just as difficult to define. Webster's describes technology as applied science or "a scientific method of achieving a practical purpose." Now, what is a science and technology magazine? For the purpose of this section, a science and technology magazine is one that focuses on the broad interdisciplinary nature of science. For specific fields of science, see the appropriate individual section, such as Engineering and Technology, Atmospheric Sciences, or Mathematics. The titles in this section encompass a number of different perspectives including technology, electronics, sociology, philosophy, and the history of science. The titles are also written on different levels ranging from trade magazines to academic journals. The audiences also range from the general public to researchers, and from students to teachers.

Electronic publishing continues to affect science journal publishing. The advantages of the Internet are the quick delivery of information and the interactive capabilities. A click of the mouse can link users to related articles on the subject and lengthy bibliographies, or users can immediately send their comments and suggestions to the author. Although most of the journals in this section do have web sites with free access, in some cases that access is limited to the table of contents and article abstracts. In those cases the full information is usually available for a fee. There are a number of ways to access full-text science and research titles online. Most of these are aggregators like SPARC, HighWire Press, Wiley InterScience, or Elsevier ScienceDirect, which are all subscription services. The fees for these services vary depending on the size of the library customer base, and sometimes the print subscriptions are tied into the electronic.

The journal annotations in this section often include the URL of the journal or publisher web site and, in some cases, what a user can find at that site.

This list of science and technology magazines covers a range of publications that merit consideration by librarians. It is by no means a complete list of all science and technology titles. Libraries should also remember to check with their state academy of science and with local organizations for appropriate publications.

Basic Periodicals

Ems: *Current Science, Science and Children* (see also titles in Children section); Hs: *Discover, Science News, Scientific American;* Ga: *Discover, Popular Science, Science, Science News, Scientific American;* Ac: *American Scientist, Discover, Nature, New Scientist, Science, Science News, ScienceDaily, Scientific American, Technology Review.*

Basic Abstracts and Indexes

Applied Science and Technology Index, General Science Index.

5980. ***American Scientist: published in the interest of scientific research.*** [ISSN: 0003-0996] 1913. bi-m. USD 65 (Individuals, USD 28; USD 4.75 newsstand/cover per issue domestic). Ed(s): Rosalind Reid. Sigma XI, Scientific Research Society, PO Box 13975, 99, Alexander, NC 27709; editors@amsci.org. Illus., index, adv. Circ: 95000. Vol. ends: Dec. Microform: PMC; PQC. Online: bigchalk; EBSCO Publishing; Florida Center for Library Automation; Gale Group; Northern Light Technology, Inc.; OCLC Online Computer Library Center, Inc.; ProQuest Information & Learning; H.W. Wilson. Reprint: ISI; PQC. *Indexed:* AS&TI, AbAn, AnBeAb, AnthLit, ApEcolAb, BHA, BRI, BiogInd, BiolAb, BiolDig, BrArAb, CBRI, ChemAb, CompR, DSR&OA, EngInd, EnvAb, ExcerpMed, FutSurv, GSI, GardL, GeoRef, GeogAbPG, IndMed, IndVet, InfoSAb, L&LBA, M&GPA, NumL, PsycholAb, SCI, SSCI, SWRA, ZooRec. *Bk. rev.:* 10-15, 100-500 words, signed. *Aud.:* Ga, Ac.

American Scientist reports on a broad range of science topics. All articles are written by scholars who are well known in their individual fields of expertise. Recent articles topics include cosmology, saving reefs, and how the retina works. Academic libraries should find the extensive book review section especially useful for collection development. The web site gives the full text of some of the articles, abstracts of the rest, and a list of all books reviewed in that issue. This periodical belongs in all four-year college and university libraries.

5981. ***British Journal for the History of Science.*** Formerly (until 1962): *British Society for the History of Science. Bulletin.* [ISSN: 0007-0874] 1962. q. USD 180. Ed(s): Crosbie Smith. Cambridge University Press, The Edinburgh Bldg, Shaftesbury Rd, Cambridge, CB2 2RU, United Kingdom; information@cambridge.org; http://uk.cambridge.org/journals. Illus., adv. Refereed. Circ: 1450. Vol. ends: Dec. Microform: PQC. Online: EBSCO Publishing; Gale Group; OCLC Online Computer Library Center, Inc.; ProQuest Information & Learning; RoweCom Information Quest; Swets Blackwell. Reprint: PQC; PSC. *Indexed:* AmH&L, ArtHuCI, CCMJ, ChemAb, GeoRef, HumInd, IBZ, MathSciNet, SCI, SSCI, ZooRec. *Bk. rev.:* 15-20, 1,000-2,500 words, signed. *Aud.:* Ac, Sa.

A thoughtful and comprehensive journal with an interdisciplinary approach that relates to history, economics, and general culture. Articles are scholarly and deal with current topics as well as historical. The journal also has an extensive book review section. Recommended for libraries with serious collections in science, humanities, and the history of science.

5982. ***The Bulletin of Science, Technology & Society.*** [ISSN: 0270-4676] 1981. bi-m. GBP 413 in Europe, Middle East, Africa & Australasia . Ed(s): Bill Vanderburg. Sage Publications, Inc., 2455 Teller Rd, Thousand Oaks, CA 91320; info@sagepub.com; http://www.sagepub.com. Illus., index. Refereed. Circ: 350 Paid. Vol. ends: No. 6. Microform: MIM; PQC. Online: ingenta.com; OCLC Online Computer Library Center, Inc.; RoweCom Information Quest; Swets Blackwell. *Indexed:* ArtHuCI, CIJE, CommAb, EngInd, HRA, PRA, PSA, SSCI, SociolAb. *Bk. rev.:* 10-15, 75-100. *Aud.:* Ac, Sa.

This is a refereed journal "dedicated to the advancement of our understanding of the roles of science and technology in our world and to the use of this understanding in the application of science and technology to ensure that human values and aspirations are satisfied and that the life-supporting capacities of the biosphere are not diminished." Subjects include the place of science and technology in societies; technology, science, and public policy; technology assessment; the impact of technology on human values and religious insights; and the public understanding of technology and science. The journal also contains news items regarding public and scholarly events in the area of STS, book notes, and news of professional activities. This title is for university science collections and special libraries that have a strong emphasis on technology and society.

Current Science. See Classroom Magazines/Science section.

5983. ***Discover: the world of science.*** [ISSN: 0274-7529] 1980. m. USD 29.95 domestic; USD 39.95 Canada; USD 44.95 elsewhere. Ed(s): Stephen Petranck. Disney Publishing Worldwide Inc., 114 Fifth Ave, New York, NY 10011-5690; letters@discover.com; http://www.discover.com. Illus., adv. Circ: 1088269. Vol. ends: Dec. Microform: PQC. Online: The Dialog Corporation; EBSCO Publishing; Florida Center for Library Automation; Gale Group; MediaStream, Inc.; Northern Light Technology, Inc.; OCLC Online Computer Library Center, Inc.; ProQuest Information & Learning; H.W. Wilson. Reprint: PQC. *Indexed:* ASIP, AgeL, BiolDig, CBCARef, CPerI, CompLI, DSR&OA, EnvAb, GSI, GeoRef, IAA, MagInd, RGPR. *Bk. rev.:* 2-3, 100-150 words, signed. *Aud.:* Ems, Hs, Ga, Ac.

Discover remains one of the best general science periodicals for all levels of readership. The articles are timely and easy to read. Each issue contains a cover story and several feature stories on topics ranging from emotions and the brain to squid sensitivity. There is also a mind-boggler puzzle in each issue that is educational and entertaining. Reviews include not only books but also museums and the occasional movie or toy. There is also a section that includes books, journals, and web sites that provide additional information on topics featured in that issue. This all-purpose publication belongs in all libraries from the most general to the most specialized. The web site includes the full texts of several of the magazine's longer articles.

5984. ***Endeavour: a review of the progress of science and technology in the service of mankind.*** [ISSN: 0160-9327] 1942. q. EUR 431 (Individuals, EUR 92). Ed(s): E Henry Nicholls. Elsevier Ltd., Trends Journals, 68 Hills Rd, Cambridge, CB2 1LA, United Kingdom; http://www.elsevier.nl. Illus., index, adv. Sample. Refereed. Circ: 10000. Microform: MIM; PQC. Online: Gale Group; ingenta.com; ScienceDirect; Swets Blackwell. *Indexed:* A&ATA, ApMecR, BHA, BiolAb, BrTechI, C&ISA, CCMJ, ChemAb, DSR&OA, EngInd, ExcerpMed, GSI, GeoRef, HortAb, IndMed, M&GPA, MathSciNet, PsycholAb, SCI, WAE&RSA, ZooRec. *Bk. rev.:* 15-20, 300-500, words, signed. *Aud.:* Ga, Ac.

Articles cover a wide range of topics and are alternately technical and popular in style, with numerous illustrations. Recent articles include one on soil bacteriology and a story about the first woman to circumnavigate the globe. Book reviews are numerous, well written, and reflect the publication's extremely varied coverage, which includes the history of science, technology, and medicine. For academic libraries.

Gender, Technology & Development. See Women: Feminist and Special Interest/Feminist and Women's Studies section.

5985. ***Isis: international review devoted to the history of science and its cultural influences.*** [ISSN: 0021-1753] 1912. q. USD 271 (Individuals, USD 67; Students, USD 29). Ed(s): Margaret W. Rossiter. University of Chicago Press, Journals Division, PO Box 37005, Chicago, IL 60637; subscriptions@press.uchicago.edu; http://www.journals.uchicago.edu. Illus., index, adv. Refereed. Circ: 4200. Vol. ends: Dec. Microform: PMC; PQC; NRP. Online: EBSCO Publishing; Florida Center for Library Automation; Gale Group; JSTOR (Web-based Journal Archive); ProQuest

Information & Learning. Reprint: ISI; PQC; SCH. *Indexed:* ABS&EES, AltPI, AmH&L, ArtHuCI, BRI, BiolAb, CBRI, CCMJ, ChemAb, DSR&OA, EngInd, GSI, GeoRef, HumInd, IBZ, IPB, IndMed, MathSciNet, PSA, RI-1, SCI, SSCI, SociolAb. *Bk. rev.:* 70, 500-1,000 words, signed. *Aud.:* Ac, Sa.

This journal is the official publication of the History of Science Society. The society seeks to foster interest in the history of science and its social and cultural relations, to provide a forum for discussion, and to promote scholarly research in the history of science. Each issue is comprised of two or three lengthy articles, one or two shorter pieces, and more than 70 signed book reviews. Recent article topics include rethinking big science and the 50th anniversary of the discovery of the double helix. A separate critical bibliography of nearly 300 pages is issued annually as part of the subscription. Indispensable to academic libraries interested in the subject area.

5986. ***Issues in Science and Technology.*** [ISSN: 0748-5492] 1984. q. USD 92 (Individuals, USD 46; USD 11.50 newsstand/cover). Ed(s): Kevin Finneran, Bill Hendrickson. Issues in Science and Technology, PO Box 830688, Richardson, TX 75083-0688. Illus., index, adv. Sample. Refereed. Circ: 12500 Paid. Vol. ends: Summer (No. 4). Microform: PQC. Online: bigchalk; EBSCO Publishing; Florida Center for Library Automation; Gale Group; OCLC Online Computer Library Center, Inc.; ProQuest Information & Learning; H.W. Wilson. *Indexed:* ASIP, AbAn, AgeL, BiolDig, CIJE, CompLI, EngInd, EnvAb, FutSurv, GSI, GeoRef, LRI, M&GPA, MCR, MagInd, PAIS, PollutAb, RGPR, RI-1, SCI, SSCI, SWRA. *Bk. rev.:* 3-4, 500 words, signed. *Aud.:* Hs, Ga, Ac, Sa.

This title is published to inform public opinion and to raise the quality of private and public decision-making by providing a forum for discussion and debate. Typical subjects include standardized testing of students, invasive aquatic species, and transportation safety. Letters to the editor and book reviews add dimension to the discussions. The writing is nontechnical and aimed at the interested layperson. For all college science collections.

5987. ***Journal of College Science Teaching.*** [ISSN: 0047-231X] 1971. 7x/yr. Membership, USD 77. Ed(s): Claudia Link, Lester G Paldy. National Science Teachers Association, 1840 Wilson Blvd, Arlington, VA 22201; http://www.nsta.org/. Illus., index, adv. Refereed. Circ: 5200 Paid and free. Vol. ends: May. Microform: PQC. Online: Gale Group; ProQuest Information & Learning. Reprint: PQC. *Indexed:* BiolAb, CIJE, ChemAb, EduInd, GeoRef, MRD. *Bk. rev.:* 1-3, 500 words, signed. *Aud.:* Hs, Ac.

Aimed at both teachers and college science majors, *Journal of College Science Teaching* is a no-nonsense publication written in an accessible style but designed for serious readers. This is the journal of the National Science Teachers Association. Feature articles are on such timely topics as evaluating active learning and environmental literacy for all students. This is an excellent publication for colleges that offer courses in science education. The journal web site offers online extensions for feature articles.

5988. ***Journal of Research in Science Teaching: the official journal of the National Association for Resarch in Science Teaching.*** [ISSN: 0022-4308] 1963. 10x/yr. USD 965 domestic; USD 1065 in Canada & Mexico; USD 1150 elsewhere. Ed(s): William C Kyle. John Wiley & Sons, Inc., 111 River St, Hoboken, NJ 07030; uscs-wis@wiley.com; http://www.wiley.com. Illus., adv. Sample. Refereed. Circ: 2850. Vol. ends: Dec. Microform: PQC. Online: EBSCO Publishing; ScienceDirect; Wiley InterScience. Reprint: PQC; PSC. *Indexed:* CIJE, EduInd, EngInd, PsycholAb, SSCI, SWA. *Aud.:* Ac.

This official journal of the National Association for Research in Science Teaching publishes "research articles related to the philosophy, historical perspective, teaching strategies, curriculum development and other topics related to science education." Articles are scholarly and directed toward toward high school and college level teachers. Recent article titles include "Predictors of Well-Structured and Ill-Structured Problem Solving in an Astronomy Simulation" and "From Nationwide Standardized Testing to School-Based Alternative Embedded Assessment in Israel: Students' Performance in the Matriculation 2000 Project." This is an important journal, but one whose audience is likely to be limited to faculty in schools of education and their graduate students. Price is also a factor, at $900 per year for print or $945 for a combination print and online. Available online through Wiley Interscience http://interscience.wiley.com.

5989. ***Journal of Scientific Exploration.*** [ISSN: 0892-3310] 1987. q. USD 125 (Individuals, USD 65). Ed(s): Dr. Bernhard Haisch. Society for Scientific Exploration, Department of Astronomy, P. O. Box 3818, Charlottesville, VA 22903-0818; http://www.scientificexploration.org. Illus., index. Sample. Refereed. Circ: 3000. Vol. ends: No. 4. Online: EBSCO Publishing; Ingenta Select. *Indexed:* EngInd, IBZ, M&GPA. *Bk. rev.:* 5, 1,000 words, signed. *Aud.:* Ac, Sa.

The only scholarly publication devoted to "all areas of anomalies research" in all scientific disciplines. Topics covered range from parapsychology and dreaming to wave-particle duality. This journal features research articles, letters to the editor, and book reviews. Electronic subscriptions began with Volume 12. Pricing is modest for this format. There is no additional charge to institutions for the access to the electronic format. Recommended for university libraries and research institutions.

5990. ***The National Academies In Focus.*** Formerly (until 2001): *National Research Council. NewsReport.* [ISSN: 1534-8334] 1951. 4x/yr. USD 10 domestic; USD 12 foreign. Ed(s): Valerie Chase. National Academy of Sciences, 2101 Constitution Ave., NW, Washington, DC 20418; http://www.nas.edu. Illus. Refereed. Circ: 17000. Microform: PQC. Online: ProQuest Information & Learning. Reprint: PQC. *Indexed:* GeoRef. *Aud.:* Hs, Ga, Ac.

This magazine features the activities of the United States National Academies, which serve as independent advisers to the federal government on scientific and technical questions of national importance. The National Academies of Science and its sister institutions—the National Research Council, the National Academy of Engineering, and the Institute of Medicine—collectively are called the National Academies. The articles are well within the understanding of high school students and the general public. Features include short articles on education and research; engineering and technology; health, safety, and technology issues; and environment and resources. There is also a listing of new projects undertaken by the units of the National Academies and a listing of new books available from the National Academy Press. This title is available full-text online and has a simple search function. Recommended for academic, high school, and public libraries.

5991. ***Natural History.*** Incorporates: *Nature Magazine.* [ISSN: 0028-0712] 1900. 10x/yr. USD 30 domestic; USD 40 foreign; USD 3.95 newsstand/cover per issue. Ed(s): Ellen Goldensohn. American Museum of Natural History, Central Park West at 79th St, New York, NY 10024-5192; nhmag@amnh.org. Illus., index, adv. Refereed. Circ: 300000. Vol. ends: Dec. CD-ROM: ProQuest Information & Learning. Microform: PQC. Online: bigchalk; The Dialog Corporation; EBSCO Publishing; Florida Center for Library Automation; Gale Group; Northern Light Technology, Inc.; OCLC Online Computer Library Center, Inc.; ProQuest Information & Learning; H.W. Wilson. *Indexed:* ABS&EES, AICP, AbAn, AgeL, AnthLit, BRD, BRI, BiolAb, BiolDig, CBRI, DSR&OA, EnvAb, GSI, GardL, GeoRef, MagInd, PRA, RGPR, RI-1, SCI, SSCI, ZooRec. *Bk. rev.:* 2-3, 500-750 words, signed. *Aud.:* Hs, Ga, Ac.

This is the magazine of the American Museum of Natural History, an institution dedicated to understanding and preserving biological and cultural diversity. The articles reflect this broad scope and cover topics including astronomy, earth sciences, and microscopic forms of life. This very readable magazine has a number of features, including brief news items, feature stories, editorials, and a listing of the events at the museum. The only drawback is the number of distracting advertisements, which are usually placed in the middle of an article. All in all, this periodical takes a popular approach to specialized subjects. Public and academic libraries will want to subscribe to this very reasonably priced title. Table of contents and selected stories are available at www.naturalhistory.com.

5992. ***Nature: international weekly journal of science.*** Incorporates (1971-1973): *Nature. Physical Science;* (1971-1973): *Nature. New Biology.* [ISSN: 0028-0836] 1869. w. GBP 112 in Europe; USD 159 United States; USD 170 Canada. Nature Publishing Group, The

MacMillan Building, 4 Crinan St, London, N1 9XW, United Kingdom; http://www.nature.com/. Illus., index, adv. Refereed. Circ: 60185. Vol. ends: Dec. CD-ROM: Ovid Technologies, Inc. Microform: PMC; PQC. Online: EBSCO Publishing; Ovid Technologies, Inc.; Swets Blackwell. *Indexed:* A&ATA, AICP, Agr, AnBeAb, AnthLit, ApEcolAb, ApMecR, ArtHuCI, B&AI, BAS, BRI, BiolAb, BiolDig, BrArAb, BrEdI, BrTechI, C&ISA, CBRI, ChemAb, DSA, DSR&OA, EngInd, EnvAb, ExcerpMed, FPA, FS&TA, FoVS&M, ForAb, FutSurv, GSI, GeoRef, GeogAbPG, HortAb, IAA, IndMed, IndVet, LingAb, M&GPA, MathSciNet, MinerAb, NumL, OceAb, PRA, PetrolAb, PollutAb, PsycholAb, S&F, SCI, SSCI, SWRA, VetBull, WAE&RSA, WRCInf, ZooRec. *Bk. rev.:* 3-5 500-1,000 words, signed. *Aud.:* Ac, Sa.

Nature is an international journal covering all areas of science. It contains review articles, original research, reports, commentaries on the latest happenings in the sciences, editorials, and "News and Views," a department that critically examines new scientific research and findings. Other useful features include book and product reviews, letters, and a comprehensive classified job listing. This authoritative journal belongs in every academic and special library; large public libraries should also include it in their collections. The table of contents and selected sections are vailable online at http://nature.com/nature. Full-text online is available for an additional charge.

5993. ***New Scientist: the global science and technology weekly.*** Formerly (until 1971): *New Scientist and Science Journal;* Which was formed by the merger of: *New Scientist;* (1965-1971): *Science Journal.* [ISSN: 0262-4079] 1956. w. GBP 117.30 domestic; USD 140 United States; CND 215 Canada. Ed(s): Jeremy Webb. Reed Business Information Ltd., 151 Wardour St, London, W1F 8WE, United Kingdom; http://www.reedinfo.co.uk/. Illus., index. Refereed. Circ: 100923. Vol. ends: Dec. Online: EBSCO Publishing; Florida Center for Library Automation; Gale Group; LexisNexis; MediaStream, Inc.; ProQuest Information & Learning; H.W. Wilson. *Indexed:* A&ATA, AS&TI, AbAn, AnBeAb, ApEcolAb, ApMecR, ArtHuCI, BAS, BRD, BRI, BiolAb, BiolDig, BrArAb, BrHumI, BrTechI, CBRI, CEA, CPerI, ChemAb, DSA, DSR&OA, EngInd, EnvAb, FS&TA, ForAb, FutSurv, GSI, GeoRef, H&SSA, HortAb, IAA, IBZ, IndVet, LISA, M&GPA, NumL, PRA, PollutAb, RRTA, S&F, SCI, SWA, SWRA, WAE&RSA, WRCInf, ZooRec. *Bk. rev.:* 5, 500 words, signed. *Aud.:* Hs, Ga, Ac.

According to the masthead, this title is "the world's leading science and technology weekly." *New Scientist* is the British counterpart to *Science* (below in this section) and complements it. There are feature articles on a wide variety of topics such as cold fusion, gulf war syndrome, and tracking war crimes. In addition, there are news briefs, editorials, opinion pieces, and a question-and-answer section called "The Last Word." Also of interest are the career and postgraduate positions listings. This title should be considered essential for all libraries.

5994. ***Popular Science: the what's new magazine.*** Formerly: *Popular Science Monthly.* [ISSN: 0161-7370] 1872. m. USD 19.95 domestic; USD 49.95 foreign. Ed(s): Scott Mowbray. Time4 Media, Inc., 2 Park Ave, New York, NY 10016; http://www.popsci.com. Illus., index, adv. Circ: 1550000 Paid. CD-ROM: ProQuest Information & Learning. Microform: NBI; PMC; PQC. Online: bigchalk; The Dialog Corporation; EBSCO Publishing; Gale Group; Northern Light Technology, Inc.; OCLC Online Computer Library Center, Inc.; ProQuest Information & Learning. Reprint: PQC. *Indexed:* CBCARef, CPerI, ConsI, EnvAb, GSI, GeoRef, IAA, ICM, IHTDI, MagInd, RGPR. *Aud.:* Ems, Hs, Ac.

Another longstanding title in the field, *Popular Science* has been around for more than 125 years. According to the cover it is the world's largest science and technology magazine. Areas covered include aviation and space, science and technology, computers and software, automotive and home technology, medicine and health, and electronics. It is presented in an easy-to-read, heavily illustrated format. Table of contents and selected articles are available online at www.popsci.com. *Popular Science* belongs in academic, high school, and public libraries.

5995. ***R & D Magazine: the voice of the research & development community.*** Former titles (until Jul. 1995): *Research & Development;* (until 1984): *Industrial Research and Development;* Which was formed by the merger of (1959-1978): *Industrial Research;* (1950-1978): *Research - Development;* Which was formerly (until 1960): *Industrial Laboratories.* 1978. 12x/yr. USD 107.99 domestic; USD 142.50 Canada; USD 136.50 Mexico. Ed(s): Tim Studt. Reed Business Information, 2000 Clearwater Dr, Oak Brook, IL 60523; http://www.reedbusiness.com. Illus., index, adv. Refereed. Circ: 100095 Controlled. Vol. ends: Dec. Microform: CIS. Online: The Dialog Corporation; Gale Group. *Indexed:* ABIn, BPI, ChemAb, EngInd, ExcerpMed, IAA, LRI, MagInd, SCI, SSCI. *Aud.:* Ac, Sa.

This title concentrates on technological trends and products. Subject coverage is very broad and includes automation and robotics and laboratory architecture and design. Each issue includes new products and job listings. One issue each year is a product source catalog. The journal also gives awards each year to the most creative scientists. Essential for business and technical libraries, and for any college that offers technologically related programs.

5996. ***Research in Science & Technological Education.*** [ISSN: 0263-5143] 1983. s-a. GBP 374 (Individuals, GBP 89). Ed(s): Chris Brown. Carfax Publishing Ltd., 4 Park Sq, Milton Park, Abingdon, OX14 4RN, United Kingdom; enquiry@tandf.co.uk; http://www.tandf.co.uk/. Illus., adv. Refereed. Online: EBSCO Publishing; Ingenta Select; Northern Light Technology, Inc.; OCLC Online Computer Library Center, Inc.; ProQuest Information & Learning; RoweCom Information Quest; Swets Blackwell. Reprint: PSC. *Indexed:* BrEdI, CIJE, EngInd, PsycholAb, SWA. *Aud.:* Ac,Sa.

Research in Science and Technological Education publishes original research from throughout the world dealing with science education and technological education. The articles are refereed and subject areas include psychological, sociological, economic, and organizational aspects of science and technological education. The main aim of the journal is to allow specialists working in these areas the opportunity of publishing their findings for the benefit of institutions, teachers, and students. Recommended for university libraries.

5997. ***School Science and Mathematics: journal for all science and mathematics teachers.*** [ISSN: 0036-6803] 1901. 8x/yr. USD 70 (Individuals, USD 40). Ed(s): Lawrence B Flick, Norman Lederman. School Science and Mathematics Association, Weniger Hall 237, Oregon State University, Corvallis, OR 97331-6508; pratt@bloomu.edu; http://osu.orst.edu/pubs/ssm. Illus., index, adv. Sample. Refereed. Circ: 3000 Paid. Vol. ends: May. Microform: PMC; PQC. Online: EBSCO Publishing; Florida Center for Library Automation; Gale Group; OCLC Online Computer Library Center, Inc.; ProQuest Information & Learning; H.W. Wilson. Reprint: PQC. *Indexed:* CIJE, ChemAb, EduInd, ExcerpMed. *Aud.:* Ac.

Published by the School Science and Mathematics Association and designed for instructors, this journal emphasizes practical teaching methods supported by the latest research studies. Regular features include in-depth research articles, mathematical problems and solutions, and association news. Recently published articles discuss students' understanding of the particulate nature of matter and nontraditional college students and the role of collaborative learning. This title is recommended for high schools and colleges where math and science education are emphasized.

5998. ***Science.*** Formerly (until 1957): *The Scientific Monthly.* [ISSN: 0036-8075] 1880. w. Ed(s): Don Kennedy. American Association for the Advancement of Science, 1200 New York Ave, N W, Washington, DC 20005; membership@aaas.org; http://www.scienceonline.org. Illus., index, adv. Sample. Refereed. Circ: 155000. Vol. ends: Dec. CD-ROM: Ovid Technologies, Inc. Microform: PMC; PQC. Online: bigchalk; The Dialog Corporation; EBSCO Publishing; Florida Center for Library Automation; Gale Group; HighWire Press; JSTOR (Web-based Journal Archive); OCLC Online Computer Library Center, Inc.; Ovid Technologies, Inc.; ProQuest Information & Learning; RoweCom Information Quest. Reprint: PQC. *Indexed:* A&ATA, AS&TI, AbAn, AgeL, Agr, AnBeAb, AnthLit, ApEcolAb, ArtHuCI, B&AI, BHA, BRD, BRI, BiolAb, BiolDig, BrArAb, C&ISA, CBRI, CCMJ, CIJE, CJA, ChemAb, CompR, DSA, EnvAb, ExcerpMed, FPA, FS&TA, FoVS&M, ForAb,

FutSurv, GSI, GeoRef, GeogAbPG, HortAb, IAA, IndMed, IndVet, InfoSAb, LRI, M&GPA, MCR, MLA-IB, MagInd, MathSciNet, NumL, OceAb, PRA, PetrolAb, PollutAb, PsycholAb, RGPR, RRTA, S&F, SCI, SWRA, VetBull, WAE&RSA, ZooRec. *Bk. rev.:* 2-3, 2,500 words, signed. *Aud.:* Ga, Ac, Sa.

This journal promotes itself as "a forum for the presentation and discussion of important issues related to the advancement of science, including the presentation of minority or conflicting points of view rather than by publishing only material on which a consensus has been reached." Each issue has brief stories on news that occurred that week, numerous research articles, book reviews, interesting new web sites, an editorial, job postings, an essay, and letters to the editor. All areas of science are covered in the research articles. Also available is *Science's Next Wave,* a weekly online publication that covers scientific training, career development, and the science job market. This is one of the core science and technology titles and belongs in all libraries.

Science and Children. See Classroom Magazines/Teacher and Professional section.

5999. *Science & Technology Review.* Formerly (until July 1995): *Energy and Technology Review.* [ISSN: 1092-3055] 1975. m. Free. Ed(s): Sam Hunter. University of California, Lawrence Livermore National Laboratory, 7000 East Ave, PO Box 808, Livermore, CA 94551-0808; hunter6@llnl.gov; http://www.llnl.gov/str/. Illus. Circ: 27000. Vol. ends: No. 10. *Aud.:* Hs, Ga.

An easy-to-read report on activities at one of the world's leading scientific centers, the Livermore National Laboratory (LNL). There are excellent articles on all aspects of science and technology from energy and the environment to general scientific problems. This title is also available full-text online at the journal's web site. Each issue includes two or three feature articles, research highlights, news of the LNL, and recent patents and awards. Recommended for college and university libraries that support science programs and public libraries.

6000. *Science Books & Films: your guide to science resources for all ages.* Formerly (until 1975): *A A A S Science Books.* [ISSN: 0098-342X] 1965. bi-m. USD 45. Ed(s): Maria Sosa. American Association for the Advancement of Science, 1200 New York Ave, N W, Washington, DC 20005. Illus., index, adv. Circ: 4500. Vol. ends: Dec. Microform: PQC. Reprint: PQC. *Indexed:* BRD, BRI, CBRI, MRD. *Bk. rev.:* 85-100, 200 words, signed. *Aud.:* Ems, Hs, Ga.

If you are responsible for recommending or purchasing science materials, this is the title for you. *SB&F* provides critical reviews of the scientific accuracy and presentation of print, audiovisual, and electronic resources intended for use in science, technology, and mathematics education. The reviews are written by scientists in academia and industry, teachers, librarians, and media specialists. In addition to the reviews, there is normally a featured bibliography on a science topic of interest. Sections include adult, young adult, and children's books. There are also seperate sections for AV materials, software, and science on TV. A handy index is also included in each issue. This title is a key selection tool for any public or academic librarian or media specialist. Available online at http://SBFonline.com to paid subscribers.

6001. *Science Education.* [ISSN: 0036-8326] 1916. bi-m. USD 875 domestic; USD 935 in Canada & Mexico; USD 986 elsewhere. Ed(s): Nancy Brickhouse. John Wiley & Sons, Inc., 111 River St, Hoboken, NJ 07030; uscs-wis@wiley.com; http://www.wiley.com. Illus., adv. Refereed. Circ: 2050. Vol. ends: Nov. Microform: PQC. Online: EBSCO Publishing; Gale Group; Swets Blackwell; Wiley InterScience. Reprint: PQC; PSC. *Indexed:* ArtHuCI, BAS, CIJE, EduInd, PsycholAb, SSCI. *Bk. rev.:* Various number and length. *Aud.:* Hs, Ac.

Publishes original articles on the latest issues and trends occurring internationally in science curriculum, instruction, learning, policy, and preparation of science teachers with the aim of advancing our knowledge of science education theory and practice. There are also a number of special sections covering issues and trends, science learning in everyday life, and book reviews. Available online from Wiley InterScience. For colleges that have graduate science education programs and can afford it at over $100 per issue.

Science News. See Classroom Magazines/Science section.

6002. *Science Progress: a review journal of current scientific advance.* [ISSN: 0036-8504] 1894. q. GBP 195. Science Reviews Ltd., PO Box 314, St Albans, AL1 4ZG, United Kingdom; http://www.scilet.com. Illus., index, adv. Refereed. Circ: 900. Online: Florida Center for Library Automation; Gale Group. Reprint: ISI. *Indexed:* BiolAb, ChemAb, EngInd, GeoRef, GeogAbPG, IndMed, IndVet, SCI, VetBull. *Aud.:* Ac.

Science Progress gives as its objective "to excite people's interest in areas of science, technology, and medicine with which they are not familiar." Each article is fairly lengthy, which is why there are only four or five per issue. The format is very clean and easy to read. Topics cover everything from the origin of life to the gastrointestinal diseases of Napoleon in Saint Helena. This title is recommended for academic libraries that serve advanced students.

Science Scope. See Classroom Magazines/Teacher and Professional section.

6003. *Science, Technology & Human Values.* Supersedes (in 1988): *Sciencie and Technology Studies;* Which was formerly (until 1986): *4S Review;* (until 1983): *4S. Society for Social Studies of Science;* (until 1976): *SSSS. Newsletter of the Society for Social Studies of Science.* [ISSN: 0162-2439] 1972. q. GBP 276 print & online eds. in Europe, Middle East, Africa & Australasia. Ed(s): Ulrike Felt. Sage Publications, Inc., 2455 Teller Rd, Thousand Oaks, CA 91320; info@sagepub.com; http://www.sagepub.com. Illus., adv. Refereed. Circ: 1900. Online: EBSCO Publishing; Florida Center for Library Automation; Gale Group; ingenta.com; JSTOR (Web-based Journal Archive); OCLC Online Computer Library Center, Inc.; ProQuest Information & Learning; RoweCom Information Quest; Swets Blackwell. *Indexed:* ArtHuCI, CIJE, CommAb, EnvAb, IPSA, PAIS, PRA, PSA, PhilInd, RI-1, SSCI, SociolAb. *Bk. rev.:* 2, 1,000 words, signed. *Aud.:* Ac, Sa.

This is the official journal of the Society for Social Studies of Science and exists to "facilitate communications across conventional boundaries that separate the disciplines and across national boundaries that separate scholars." The research in this journal deals with the development and dynamics of science and technology, including their involvement in politics, society, and culture. Whether this publication is better suited to the scientific or social studies collection of a library is an open question, but it certainly belongs in one or the other.

6004. *Scientific American.* [ISSN: 0036-8733] 1845. m. USD 34.97 domestic; USD 49 Canada; USD 55 elsewhere. Ed(s): John Rennie. Scientific American, Inc., 415 Madison Ave, New York, NY 10017-1111; comments@sciam.com. Illus., index, adv. Refereed. Circ: 681122 Paid. Vol. ends: Dec. Microform: PMC; PQC; NRP. Online: bigchalk; EBSCO Publishing; Florida Center for Library Automation; Gale Group; OCLC Online Computer Library Center, Inc.; ProQuest Information & Learning. *Indexed:* ABIn, ABS&EES, AS&TI, AbAn, AgeL, Agr, AnthLit, ApMecR, ArtHuCI, B&AI, BAS, BHA, BRD, BRI, BiolAb, BiolDig, BrArAb, BrTechI, CBCARef, CBRI, CIJE, CINAHL, CPerI, ChemAb, CompLI, DSA, DSR&OA, EngInd, EnvAb, ExcerpMed, FPA, FS&TA, ForAb, FutSurv, GSI, GardL, GeoRef, GeogAbPG, IAA, IHTDI, IPSA, IndMed, IndVet, InfoSAb, M&GPA, MCR, MagInd, MathSciNet, NumL, PAIS, PEI, PRA, PollutAb, RGPR, RRTA, S&F, SCI, SSCI, SUSA, SWRA, WAE&RSA, WRCInf, ZooRec. *Bk. rev.:* 3, 1,000 words, signed. *Aud.:* Hs, Ga, Ac, Sa.

Scientific American has been published for more than 150 years and for good reason. It is a highly respected, informative magazine. There are numerous features covering science and the citizen, technology and business, and even mathematical recreation. One interesting feature is "50, 100 and 150 Years Ago," which contains short snippets from earlier issues of the journal. The journal updated its image recently and did away with the "Amateur Scientist" column but added several new ones, including one that describes science-oriented destinations for travelers. There are numerous color illustrations that add to the interest of the stories. All high school, academic, and special libraries should have this journal. Public libraries will also want it because of its reputation, indexing, and comprehensive coverage of science and technology at a reasonable price.

6005. ***The Scientist: the newspaper for the life sciences professional.*** [ISSN: 0890-3670] 1986. s-m. USD 72 (Individuals, USD 36; Students, USD 24). Ed(s): Richard Gallagher. The Scientist, Inc., 3600 Market St, Ste 450, Philadelphia, PA 19104-2645; info@the-scientist.com; http://www.the-scientist.com. Illus., adv. Refereed. Circ: 53000 Controlled. Online: EBSCO Publishing; Florida Center for Library Automation; Gale Group; ProQuest Information & Learning. *Indexed:* BiolDig, EnvAb, GeoRef, SCI, SSCI. *Aud.:* Ac.

This title reports on and analyzes the issues and events that impact the world of life scientists. Articles cover a variety of topics such as stem cell research, asthma and genetics, and natural solutions to pollution. There are opinion pieces, specific news items for professional scientists, laboratory technology reports, and personal and professional opportunities. Product information and job postings round out this handy publication. Necessary for any library that has scientists involved in day-to-day research.

6006. ***Social Studies of Science: an international review of research in the social dimensions of science and technology.*** Formerly (until 1975): *Science Studies.* [ISSN: 0306-3127] 1971. bi-m. GBP 490 print & online eds. in Europe, Middle East, Africa & Australasia. Ed(s): Michael J Lynch. Sage Publications Ltd., 6 Bonhill St, London, EC2A 4PU, United Kingdom; info@sagepub.co.uk; http://www.sagepub.co.uk/. Illus., index, adv. Refereed. Circ: 1200. Vol. ends: Dec. Reprint: PSC. *Indexed:* AmH&L, ArtHuCI, CIJE, DSR&OA, EngInd, ExcerpMed, GeoRef, HRA, IBSS, IBZ, IPB, IPSA, SCI, SSCI, SWA. *Bk. rev.:* 1-3, lengthy, signed. *Aud.:* Ac.

This periodical provides lengthy and scholarly articles on the social dimensions of science and technology. Articles have discussed Stephen Jay Gould as a historian of science, and scientific authority and liberal democracy in the Oppenheimer case. All scientific fields are covered, including the philosophy and history of science. This journal is meant for scholars, since the casual reader may have difficulty with some of the more technical topics. The book review section offers very lengthy reviews and comparisons that are useful to collection development librarians.

6007. ***Technology and Culture.*** [ISSN: 0040-165X] 1960. q. USD 130 (Individuals, USD 40). Ed(s): John Staudenmaier. Johns Hopkins University Press, Journals Publishing Division, 2715 N Charles St, Baltimore, MD 21218-4363; http://www.press.jhu.edu/. Illus., index, adv. Refereed. Circ: 2912. Vol. ends: Oct (No. 4). Microform: PQC; NRP. Online: EBSCO Publishing; Gale Group; ProQuest Information & Learning; RoweCom Information Quest; Swets Blackwell. Reprint: ISI; PQC; PSC. *Indexed:* A&ATA, ABS&EES, AS&TI, AmH&L, ArtHuCI, BAS, BHA, BRI, BrArAb, CBRI, ExcerpMed, IBSS, IBZ, NumL, RI-1, RRTA, SSCI, SSI, SociolAb, WAE&RSA. *Bk. rev.:* 30-40, 500-1,000 words, signed. *Aud.:* Ac, Sa.

Technology and Culture investigates the interaction of technology with its social and cultural environment. Every year one issue consists of a bibliography of current publications in the history of technology, which comprises more than 2,500 citations. A very useful feature of this title is the extensive book review section, which is often more than 50 pages long. In addition to the reviews, there are usually four or five scholarly articles. Occasionally, there will also be exhibit reviews from various U.S. and international museums. Highly recommended for all history of science and technology collections and large engineering collections.

6008. ***Technology Review: MITs national magazine of technology & innovation.*** Former titles (until 1998): *MIT's Technology Review;* (until 1997): *Technology Review.* [ISSN: 1099-274X] 1899. 10x/yr. USD 30 domestic; USD 40 Canada; USD 60 elsewhere. Ed(s): Robert Buderi. Massachusetts Institute of Technology, One Main St, 7th Fl, Cambridge, MA 02142; trcomments@mit.edu; http://www.mit.edu/org/t/techreview/www/tr. Illus., index, adv. Circ: 300000. Vol. ends: Nov/Dec. Microform: PQC. Online: bigchalk; The Dialog Corporation; EBSCO Publishing; Florida Center for Library Automation; Gale Group; Northern Light Technology, Inc.; OCLC Online Computer Library Center, Inc.; ProQuest Information & Learning; H.W. Wilson. Reprint: PQC. *Indexed:* ABIn, ABS&EES, AS&TI, ASG, BPI, BRI, BiolAb, BiolDig, C&ISA, CBRI, CPerI, ChemAb, CompLI, EngInd, EnvAb, ExcerpMed, FutSurv, GSI, GeoRef, IAA, InfoSAb, LRI, MagInd, MicrocompInd, PAIS, PRA, RGPR, RiskAb, SCI, SSCI, SUSA. *Bk. rev.:* 2-3, 500-800 words, signed. *Aud.:* Hs, Ga, Ac, Sa.

Technology Review is aimed at "not only the cognoscente but the general public." New developments are covered extensively, with practical and industrial applications emphasized. Feature stories are interesting and varied. There are occasional special theme issues concentrating on one specific topic. Regular departments write about market developments and innovations from every area of technology. This publication belongs in junior college and college libraries as well as in public libraries with substantial science collections.

Electronic Journals

InterJournal. See Engineering and Technology/Electronic Journals section.

6009. ***Natural SCIENCE.*** [ISSN: 1206-940X] 1997. w. Heron Publishing, 202-3994 Shelbourne St, Victoria, BC V8N 3E2, Canada; http://naturalscience.com/ns/nshome.html. *Aud.:* Hs, Ga.

Scientists who wish to reach laypeople of all ages use this magazine to explain their findings—and their hunches—in their fields and related areas. This is not a magazine in the technical sense but more of an aggregated site of science information. In addition to articles, there are numerous links to news sites, other free magazines, and specific subject sites. For instance, there is a link to the Discovery Channel and NASA SciNews. The articles are only a very small part of this title, and it is probably more useful for its multitude of links. It warrants a look by interested adults and, certainly, high school students.

6010. ***Network Science.*** [ISSN: 1092-7360] m. Network Science Corporation, 412 Carolina Blvd, Isle Of Palms, SC 29451; http://www.netsci.org. *Aud.:* Ac, Sa.

This title is presented by about half a dozen corporate sponsors ranging from pharmaceutical to computer companies. Network Science Corporation is a nonprofit organization and was founded "to assist in science education by supporting the development of science and technology, by facilitating the timely exchange of information as a means of enhancing professional development, and by fostering public awareness of advances in the therapeutic management of diseases." *NetSci* is a combination of scientific focus articles and general resources for scientists within the pharmaceutical and biotechnology industries. Recommended for research libraries.

6011. ***Science Beat.*** 1999. m. Ed(s): Jeffrey Kahn. Ernest Orlando Lawrence Berkeley National Laboratory, Public Information Department, 1 Cyclotron Rd MS-65, Berkeley, CA 94720; http://www.lbl.gov. *Aud.:* Hs, Ga,Ac,Sa.

Science Beat can be described as scientific news for those who want to know but don't speak the language. The information online here has been translated and interpreted by science writers. Links to additional information are usually included. Recent articles include a short piece about the springtail insect and a longer story about the "Drake's plate" hoax.

6012. ***Science Now.*** 3x/school-academic yr. SIRS Inc, PO Box 2348, Boca Raton, FL 33427; http://www.sirs.com/corporate/newsletters/snow/snowtoc.htm. *Aud.:* Hs, Sa.

This is jointly published by the Walter Orr Roberts Institute at the University Cooperation for Atmospheric Research and SIRS, Inc. (Social Issues Resources Series). Therefore, this publication deals heavily with the atmospheric sciences. Directed at high school teachers in search of new ideas for science teaching, this site offers practical guides to weather-related projects and talks. Each issue covers one topic; examples of previous subjects covered are early Antarctic exploration, lightning, and the societal impacts of hurricanes. A fine source of lesson plans for high schools and more-advanced middle school students.

6013. ***ScienceDaily.*** 1995. d. Ed(s): Dan Hogan. Science Daily, 41 Jo Mar Dr, Sandy Hook, CT 06482; http://www.sciencedaily.com. *Aud.:* Hs, Ga, Ac, Sa.

ScienceDaily is "a free online magazine covering science, technology, and medicine." The articles are news releases submitted by universities and research organizations from around the world. A contact name and a link to the organization's web site are always given. In addition, *ScienceDaily* offers access to other science-related sites and a chance to buy science books online. It is possible to search by specific topic. Ad-free access is available for a small fee ($10 for six months). Appropriate for all libraries.

■ SERIALS

See also Journalism and Writing; Library Periodicals; and Newspapers sections.

M. Dina Giambi, Assistant Director for Library Technical Services, University of Delaware Library, Newark, DE 19717-5267; dinag@udel.edu; FAX: 302-831-1046

Introduction

All segments of the serials arena are facing turbulent and unsettling times. A downturn in the U.S. economy has resulted in unprecedented budget reductions in all types and sizes of libraries, which has exacerbated the struggle to maintain existing print and electronic journal collections as an ever-growing number of electronic resources continue to appear. Libraries must also deal with electronic-serial prices that are just as readily susceptible to increases as print subscriptions. Consolidation is occurring as publishers, serial vendors, and integrated library system vendors are being acquired by other companies. In some cases, the company making the acquisition is a different type of organization from the company that it is buying. The traditional duties and responsibilities of serials staff have grown to include the negotiation of complex license agreements and the constant monitoring of web resources to verify that access is maintained.

The library science journals in this section plus *Folio* offer libraries, publishers, and the various types of vendors an extensive body of practical and theoretical literature. *Serials Librarian* and *Serials Review* serve their audiences most effectively. *Victorian Periodicals Review* concentrates on the study of nineteenth-century periodicals. *U.S. Government Subscriptions*, noted here, and *U.S. Government Periodicals Index*, listed in the Abstracts and Indexes section, and its online counterpart, *Government Periodicals Universe*, provide support for documents work.

Directories such as *Ulrich's Periodicals Directory* and those published by serial vendors are excluded as are Internet resources such as *SERIALST.*

Basic Periodicals

Ac, Sa: *The Serials Librarian, Serials Review.*

Basic Abstracts and Indexes

U.S. Government Periodicals Index.

Bulletin of Bibliography. See Bibliography section.

DTTP. See Library and Information Science section.

6014. ***Folio: the new dynamics of magazine publishing.*** Incorporates (in 1993): *Folio's Publishing News;* Which was formerly (until 1988): *Publishing News.* [ISSN: 0046-4333] 1972. m. USD 96 domestic; USD 116 in Canada & Mexico; USD 199 elsewhere. Primedia Business Magazines & Media, Inc., 261 Madison Ave, 9th Fl, New York, NY 10016; inquiries@primediabusiness.com; http://www.primediabusiness.com. Illus., adv. Sample. Circ: 10383. Microform: PQC. Online: The Dialog Corporation; EBSCO Publishing; Florida Center for Library Automation; Gale Group; OCLC Online Computer Library Center, Inc.; ProQuest Information & Learning; H.W. Wilson. Reprint: PQC. *Indexed:* ABIn, BPI, LRI, PAIS. *Aud.:* Sa.

This trade publication has a new subtitle, "the new dynamics of magazine publishing," and a new editor, as it continues to serve as "a guide to better mag-making" in an industry that is constantly evolving to "remain profitable in a challenging media environment." A broad and diverse mix of articles are included in each issue on topics such as advertising, circulation, copyright, digital publishing, fulfillment, the Internet, and marketing. Recent articles have included "Crisis at the Mills: The Ripple Effect of Painful Paper Cuts" and "Rethinking a Great American Magazine [*Playboy*]." Standard features include columns on new magazines, web site launches, industry people, and an extensive yellow pages section with a directory of magazine suppliers and professional services, publishers' representatives, and a classified section. Annual offerings include a circulation salary survey and editorial excellence awards. Full text is available online. *Folio* is definitely recommended to anyone with an interest in the magazine publishing industry. See http://www.foliomag.com for additional information.

6015. ***Serials: the journal for the serials community.*** [ISSN: 0953-0460] 1988. 3x/yr. Membership, GBP 78.38. Ed(s): Hazel Woodward, Helen Henderson. United Kingdom Serials Group, c/o Alison Whitehorn, Business Manager, Hilltop, Heath End, Newbury, RG20 0AP, United Kingdom; uksg.admin@dial.pipex.com; http://www.uksg.org. Illus., index, adv. Sample. Vol. ends: No. 3. *Indexed:* InfoSAb, LISA. *Bk. rev.:* 3-4, 500 words, signed. *Aud.:* Ac, Sa.

Although this publication continues to be a benefit of membership in the United Kingdom Serials Group(UKSG), its scope has been expanded by making subscriptions available to nonmembers. The focus of the UKSG is "to encourage the exchange and promotion of ideas on printed and electronic serials and the process of scholarly communication." Content is broadly based with articles such as "The Impact of Disintermediation and the New Economy on STM Electronic Information Systems," "Planning the Digital Library: A Virtual Impossibility?," and "The National Electronic Library Programme: The Backbone of the Information Supply in the Electronic Research Environment in Finland." Some articles are based on presentations given at the UKSG annual conferences and seminars. Regular columns provide information on the UKSG, people in the news, and new products and services as well as book and serial reviews. Full text is available online. Institutions with an interest in serials management or publishing, particularly on an international level, should consider this title. See http://www.ingentaselect.com/titles/09530460.htm for more information.

6016. ***The Serials Librarian: the international journal of theory, research & practice on serial, continuing, and integrating print & electronic resources.*** [ISSN: 0361-526X] 1976. 4x/yr. USD 275. Ed(s): Jim Cole. Haworth Press, Inc., 10 Alice St, Binghamton, NY 13904-1580; getinfo@haworthpressinc.com; http://www.haworthpressinc.com. Illus., adv. Sample. Refereed. Circ: 869 Paid. Vol. ends: No. 4. Microform: PQC. Reprint: HAW; WSH. *Indexed:* ABS&EES, CINAHL, ChemAb, ConsI, ExcerpMed, IBZ, InfoSAb, LISA, LibLit, SSCI. *Bk. rev.:* 6, 500 words, signed. *Aud.:* Ac, Sa.

Extensive coverage is provided by this title for all aspects of serials librarianship. This is evidenced by articles such as "Forging the Future for Archival Concerns and Resource Sharing," "The Pricing Implications of Site and Consortia Licensing into the Next Millennium," and "Do We Catalog or Not? How Research Libraries Provide Bibliographic Access to Electronic Journals in Aggregated Databases." An ongoing series of articles written by various authors analyze the "Journals of the Century" in diverse subject areas ranging from the American religious experience to agriculture and veterinary medicine. The "Serials Report" column provides news of the serials field related to libraries, librarians, vendors of all types, publishers, etc. Reviews of both American and foreign publications are included. Full text is available online. Given the scope of the subjects presented, this journal is essential for academic, many special libraries, and some large public libraries. Serious consideration should be given to selection of this title, which should also be compared to *Serials Review.* See http://haworthpress.com/store/product.asp?sku=J123 for additional information.

6017. ***Serials Review.*** [ISSN: 0098-7913] 1975. q. EUR 244 (Individuals, EUR 90). Ed(s): Connie Foster. Elsevier Ltd., The Boulevard, Langford Ln, Oxford, OX5 1GB, United Kingdom. Illus., index, adv. Sample. Refereed. Vol. ends: No. 4. *Indexed:* BRI, CBRI, ConsI, InfoSAb, LISA, LibLit, PAIS, PRA. *Bk. rev.:* 6, 1,000 words, signed. *Aud.:* Ac, Sa.

This peer-reviewed journal serves as a "source of continuing education and information for serials, acquisitions and collection development librarians as well as individuals in the commercial sector of the serials industry." Comprehensive in its approach, issues offer articles in numerous subject areas such as "Mergers and Acquisitions in the Library Marketplace: Opportunity or Threat?," "Title-Level Analytics for Journal Aggregators," and "Pricing Electronic Information: A Snapshot of New Serials Pricing Models." A number of columns appear on a regular basis, such as "Electronic Journal Forum," "Serials Spoken Here: Reports on Conferences, Institutes, and Seminars," and "Bits and Bytes: Serials Systems Insights," which describes experiences with the serials check-in component of various integrated library systems. Reviews of books are presented in "Tools of the Serials Trade," and "Serials Review Index" offers lists of serial publications that are reviewed in nearly 140 journals covering many subjects. Full text is available online. The wide spectrum of topics encompassed by this journal make it a basic to be examined for selection by academic and special libraries as well as some large public libraries along with *Serials Librarian.* See http://www.elsevier.nl/locate/issn/00987913 for more information.

U.S. Government Periodicals Index. See Abstracts and Indexes section.

6018. ***U.S. Government Subscriptions.*** Formerly: *Government Periodicals and Subscription Services.* q. Free. U.S. Government Printing Office, Superintendent of Documents, PO Box 371954, Pittsburgh, PA 15250-7954; gpoaccess@gpo.gov; http://www.access.gpo.gov. *Aud.:* Ac, Sa.

Guidelines for the purchase of periodicals and subscription services of U.S. government agencies are presented in this informative resource. Detailed ordering options, methods of payment, address, and telephone numbers are given. Subscription services are identified clearly as are those titles that have had a subscription price change since the previous edition. Entries for each title include frequency, U.S. and foreign prices, SUDOCS class number, a description of the title's coverage and its intended audience, and back issue availability. Agency and subject indexes are provided. Each new edition includes lists of discontinued and new subscriptions as well as title changes. Although free copies of the catalog continue to appear in paper format, the most recent issue is also available through the GPO web site at http://bookstore.gpo.gov/subscriptions.

6019. ***Victorian Periodicals Review.*** Formerly: *Victorian Periodicals Newsletter.* [ISSN: 0709-4698] 1968. q. CND 57 (Individuals, CND 40; Students, CND 33). Ed(s): William H Scheuerle. University of Toronto Press, Journals Department, 5201 Dufferin St, Toronto, ON M3H 5T8, Canada; journals@utpress.utoronto.ca; http://www.utpjournals.com. Illus., index, adv. Sample. Refereed. Circ: 650. Vol. ends: No. 4. Reprint: PQC. *Indexed:* AmH&L, AmHI, BEL&L, CBCARef, IBZ, MLA-IB. *Bk. rev.:* Various number and length, signed. *Aud.:* Ac.

Published quarterly, this unique title focuses solely "on the editorial and publishing history of Victorian periodicals. Its emphasis is on the importance of periodicals for an understanding of the history and culture of Victorian Britain, Ireland, and the Empire." Edited by the Research Society for Victorian Periodicals, an individual subscription includes membership in the society. Issues include articles covering such diverse subjects as "Constructing the Victorian Artist: National Identity, the Political Economy of Art and Biographical Mania in the Periodical Press" and "The Ideology of Domesticity: The Regulation of the Household Economy in Victorian Women's Magazines." Special issues are devoted to topics such as "Cornhill Magazine." In addition to articles, a comprehensive survey of the field is offered by presenting a book review section that varies in length and a bibliography of articles related to journals from 1800 to 1914 that appears periodically. Highly recommended for any library collection with strengths in nineteenth-century studies. See http://utpjournals.com/jour.ihtml?lp=vpr/vpr.html for more information.

SEXUALITY

Sex Positive

See also Men; and Zines sections.

Daniel C. Tsang, Politics Bibliographer, 380 Main Library, University of California, P.O. Box 19557, Irvine, CA 92623; dtsang@uci.edu; 949-824-4978; FAX: 949-824-2700

Andrea Plaid, Graduate School of Library and Information Science (GSLIS) Graduate, Simmons College, Boston, MA 02115; magdalenemasks@hotmail.com (Sex Positive subsection)

Introduction

Sex, although widely practiced, still appears to be a taboo topic for library shelves. The more scholarly collections may contain such titles as *Journal of Homosexuality*, the *Journal of Sex Research*, or *Archives of Sexual Behavior*, but for titles that veer beyond academia into more-explicit depictions of the phenomenon, their absence from libraries is quite glaring.

Sexually explicit periodicals, often termed "adult magazines," proliferate in American society; even the corner drugstore may stock a few. Thousands of new videos are released each year, as *AVN*, or *Adult Video News*, the bible of the porn industry, ably documents. Mass marketed all over the United States (in some states more discreetly than in others), porn publishers and editors proclaim themselves to be advocates of sexual liberation and free speech. They may shock some people, since much of the output appears to arouse and stimulate only certain areas of the body; only a few publications attempt to reach the mind. The proliferation of erotic videos has also spawned a related publishing trend: what a *New York Times* essayist called meta-porn, or porn-on-porn, with review publications that attempt to document, critique, or promote that scene. The prolific migration of erotic content to the electronic world has made such imagery and text almost ubiquitous and unavoidable, making any web surfer a potential instant critic.

The proliferation of independently produced, noncommercial zines with some erotic content brings a new dimension to the sex scene. There is perhaps more attempt at analysis, deconstruction, and intellectual stimulation in these publications. Like their profit-making and market-oriented contemporaries, these zines also may shock the sexually inhibited.

Taken together, these publications reflect contemporary popular culture and society's obsession with matters sexual. Libraries can ill afford to ignore these publications, even if acquiring even one of them may challenge the hardiest librarian to see how far he or she is willing to uphold the Library Bill of Rights.

The recent downturn in the economy has, ironically, resulted in those losing jobs in dot-coms finding they can still make a living in the thriving erotic entertainment world. If libraries are to better serve their communities, we might consider doing more than letting just the corner drug store, liquor store, or adult bookstore satisfy the public's demand for erotica. Some titles have managed to penetrate library walls, as evidenced by the few cataloged under the subject heading Erotic Literature—Periodicals. Other more scholarly titles have also managed to enter the hallowed halls of academia. In this supposedly liberated era, patrons are unlikely to heed the advice that used to be found in many card catalogs: "For Sex, see Librarian." They want to find it themselves and for themselves. With even the U.S. Supreme Court endorsing formerly taboo sexual behavior, libraries have no excuse not to collect this material. (DT)

Basic Periodicals

Ga: *Adam Film World Directory of Adult Films, Adam Gay Video Directory, Adult Video News, The Guide, Libido, OG, On Our Backs, Penthouse, Playboy;* Ac: *Adam Film World Directory of Adult Film, Adam Gay Video Directory, Adult Video News, Annual Review of Sex Research, The Guide, Journal of Homosexuality, Journal of Sex Research, Journal of the History of Sexuality, Libido, OG, On Our Backs, Penthouse, Playboy, Sexualities, Sexuality and Culture, Spectator;* Sa: *Prometheus, SHE.*

Basic Abstracts and Indexes

Gay and Lesbian Abstracts.

6020. ***Adam Film World Guide Directory of Adult Film.*** Former titles: *Adam Film World Guide Directory; Adam Film World Guide.* [ISSN: 0743-6335] 1984. a. USD 10.95 domestic; USD 12.95 foreign. Ed(s): Jared Rutter. Knight Publishing Corporation, 8060 Melrose Ave, Los Angeles, CA 90046; http://www.adultplayground.com/. Illus., adv. *Aud.:* Ga, Ac.

Like its gay counterpart *Adam Gay Video Directory*, this annual directory of the heterosexual adult-film industry is profusely illustrated with photos of porn stars, more female than male, who are profiled in a "Performers" section. Over 100 new DVDs are reviewed in each issue, as well as hundreds of other videos, plus short synopses of some 700 older videos. The reviews of new videos are arranged alphabetically by title, each with a plot synopsis, overall rating (up to five stars), and a descriptive "erotic rating" (e.g., "volcanic"). Sexual themes are noted, along with cast, credits, and current manufacturer. Amateur and fetish videos are also reviewed. A special section reviews Internet erotica sites, complete with URLs. Most useful are the retail and manufacturer source directories. An essential purchase for the serious student of this genre. (DT)

6021. ***Adam Gay Video Directory.*** a. USD 13.80 domestic; USD 16.95 foreign. Ed(s): Doug Lawrence. Knight Publishing Corporation, 8060 Melrose Ave, Los Angeles, CA 90046; http://www.adultplayground.com/. Illus., adv. *Aud.:* Ga, Ac.

This perfect-bound annual directory is still the best guide to the gay adult-video industry. Similiar to its straight-market counterpart, *Adam Film World Directory of Adult Films*, this publication is profusely illustrated with color photos of hundreds of adult-film stars, many sporting erections. Categories include performers, directors, "in memoriam," reviews, previews, awards, a themes index, mail order/internet sources, a distributors index, and a retail stores index. More than 200 current major male porn stars are featured, with their videographies. Several hundred of the current videos and DVDs are critically reviewed and rated, with explicit illustrations; cast members are listed as well. An additional 350 other films or videos from the 1970s to today are also listed, with synopses included. Most useful are the various indexes, including sources for obtaining the videos. An indispensable source for the serious student of this genre. (DT)

6022. ***Adam Gay Video Erotica.*** 1996. s-a. USD 13 newsstand/cover per issue domestic; USD 15 newsstand/cover per issue foreign. Ed(s): Doug Lawrence. Knight Publishing Corporation, 8060 Melrose Ave, Los Angeles, CA 90046. *Aud.:* Sa.

This adult magazine serves as a historical record highlighting films of particular porn stars or interviews with selected adult erotic entertainment performers. The focus here is on folks who star in gay porn (who may or may not identify as gay). We learn about their sexual proclivities and the films they have starred in during their adult industry career. Each issue is profusely illustrated with explicit color photos; one issue has 400 such photos, for each of the gay porn stars profiled. A helpful list of manufacturers of the videos referenced in each issue is included. Only for dedicated collectors of this genre. (DT)

6023. ***Adult Video News: the adult entertainment monthly.*** [ISSN: 0883-7090] 1982. m. USD 78 domestic; USD 198 foreign. Ed(s): Mike Ramone. A V N Publications Inc., 9414 Eton Ave, Chatsworth, CA 91311; http://www.avn.com. Illus., adv. Sample. Circ: 45000 Paid. *Aud.:* Ga, Ac.

The flagship publication of the adult-video industry—which rakes in several billion dollars per year—*AVN*, or *Adult Video News*, founded with $900 by several college students, is today the bible of the porn industry; it is what *Billboard* is to the music industry. With 9,000 or more hard-core videos entering the commercial market each year, *AVN* manages to highlight the most marketable. There are feature articles on specific new films and videos and legal advice to porn retailers as well as a "Religious Right Watch," but the bulk of the perfect-bound magazine is devoted to capsule reviews of new erotic films, videos, and DVDs, as well as reviews of hardware, e.g., vibrators or latex pants. While largely heterosexual in its approach, gay and bisexual videos are also reviewed. The magazine is profusely illustrated with explicit color photos and ads from the industry. *AVN Online*, the spinoff web journal, contains enough material that consumers will find useful and at times even enlightening. There are also daily and weekly e-mail updates available. In the paper edition, many of the news items deal with confrontations with state and church, but the meat is in the technical know-how for adult web developers. There may even be a feature on PHP, the computer scripting language, or book reviews on cascading style sheets or Internet firewalls. A serious essay might address zoning laws; a less serious one might feature Asian beauties as the "niche market." You will also find in a "Test Data" section, reviews of new electronics and software. A "Browser Box" may even contain sample Java script. A "Links" section provides URLs of relevant web sites. Aimed at retailers, it is nonetheless highly recommended for the serious collector. The web version is archived back to 1998 with more selected content for the earlier issues. (DT)

6024. ***The American Sex Scene: Guide to Bordellos.*** m. USD 49.95. Ed(s): Michael Phoenix. Qlimax, 313 N York Rd, Hatboro, PA 19040. *Aud.:* Ga, Ac.

Billing itself as the "definitive reference for commercial sex," this magazine with a glossy cover and newsprint inside does include information on numerous sex establishments, such as massage parlors and escort services. Selected cities or states are featured in each issue; twice a year, an annual guide to sex is serialized. There is also a classified section that claims to be "second to none!" There are quite a lot of personal ads. It has even reprinted from the web a question-and-answer column written by the head of the Electronic Frontier Foundation on prostitution and the Internet and another on police harassment of prostitutes in San Francisco. One issue offers an analysis of that city's task force proposals on prostitution. In addition, readers write in to report their sex-seeking experiences across the United States. A necessary addition to serious collections. (DT)

6025. ***Annual Review of Sex Research.*** [ISSN: 1053-2528] 1990. a. USD 92 (Individuals, USD 56). Ed(s): Julia C Heiman. Society for the Scientific Study of Sexuality, PO Box 416, Allentown, PA 18105; thesociety@inetmail.att.net; http://www.sexscience.org. Illus. Circ: 500. *Indexed:* ASSIA, AbAn, BiolAb, CJA, IBZ, IMFL, IndMed, PsycholAb, SFSA, SSI, SWA, SWR&A. *Aud.:* Ac,Sa.

This scholarly journal from a sexualities research society covers an eclectic range of sex research issues in each annual issue. It attempts to "synthesize recent theoretical and research advances in specific topic areas." Recent areas covered include intersexuality and penile erection. Its coverage is technical and specialized, even medical, in contrast to the society's main, more accessible *Journal of Sex Research*. Included are literature reviews of a particular research field, such as "sexual victimization." Mainly of interest to the serious sex researcher or graduate student specializing in the field. Editors vary from issue to issue. (DT)

6026. ***Bad Attitude: a lesbian sex magazine.*** [ISSN: 0896-9531] 1984. s-a. USD 35 domestic; USD 60 foreign. Ed(s): Jasmine Sterling. Bad Attitude, Inc., PO Box 390 110, Cambridge, MA 02139; http://www.lifestyle.com/lesbian. Illus., adv. Circ: 5000. *Bk. rev.:* 2, 500-1,000 words. *Aud.:* Ga, Ac.

This magazine celebrates the female body and is called *Bad Attitude* "because that's what women who take their sexuality into their own hands (so to speak) are told they have." Rebelling against societal strictures on sex, this glossy features photographers and their often explict work and lesbian fiction (illustrated). In recent years, it has veered toward making its sado-masochistic focus more central; on the web, it calls itself the "ultimate lesbian S&M magazine." A beautifully laid-out magazine that is definitely worth adding to your erotica collection. (DT)

6027. ***The Erotic Review.*** 1996. m. GBP 25; GBP 3.50 newsstand/cover per issue; USD 6.95 newsstand/cover per issue. The Erotic Review, 44 Lexington St, London, W1R 3LH , United Kingdom. Illus., adv. Circ: 30000. *Bk. rev.:* 4; 200-750 words. *Aud.:* Ga, Ac, Sa.

This literary erotica magazine from the United Kingdom includes novel excerpts, fiction, book reviews, video reviews, and an advice column ("Dear Antonia: Nookie dilemma? Have it solved..."). One issue even includes an excerpt from the novel *Gordon* by Edith Templeton, a publication that had previously been banned. The stories included are high quality and generally have a heterosexual focus. Issues may have a theme, e.g., "Sexual Healing: The Doctors and Nurses Issue," focusing on stories involving the health profession. Its regular interview section has included even a subject who was a teenage male hustler. Book reviews cover alternative press titles rarely reviewed elsewhere, for example, a book on transgender erotica. The illustrations are artistic and include both art and photography, without the blatant images of other erotica publications. They do include drawings of erect penises. Advertisements tout chemicals, sex toys, and videos. Selected articles appear on its web site. Highly recommended for more forward-looking collections. (DT)

6028. ***Fetish.*** [ISSN: 1098-3341] 1997. q. USD 29.70. Ed(s): Alan Terrance, Abby Ehmann. Hawke International Publications, PO Box 77750, San Francisco, CA 94107; terrance@fetishmag.org; http://www.fetishmag.com. *Aud.:* Ga, Ac.

It bills itself as an adult publication, but *Fetish* is unlike other adult magazines. Instead of in-your-face explicit photos, the ones here depict what you might encounter on your evening saunter to a nearby nightclub, especially if you live in a lively, urban enclave with diverse sexualities. The magazine celebrates contemporary fetishism by exploring, visually and with text, sex toys, adornments, fashion, and the club-scene subculture. A regular "Newsbites" section shows what you're missing (it includes reports on new books, such as "Deviant Desires"). There is also coverage of the club scene in "Fetish Nation." New web sites and new videos are reviewed. Well-drawn cartoons and striking photography add to the value of this magazine. While it is primarily heterosexually focused (the photos and artwork seem to depict females almost exclusively), it does not ignore developments in the gay scene. This magazine well documents the popular club scene and what is considered sexually appealing in that culture. It currently seems to be in hiatus and but has placed selected back issue content on its web site. (DT)

6029. ***FirstHand Magazine: experiences for loving men.*** [ISSN: 0744-6349] 1980. m. USD 45. Ed(s): Don Dooley. FirstHand Ltd., PO Box 1314, Teaneck, NJ 07666; firsthand3@aol.com. Illus., adv. Circ: 60000. *Bk. rev.:* 3, 250 words. *Aud.:* Ga, Ac.

Reader-written erotica for the homosexual male is the focus of this publication, which has spawned many imposters as well as its own spinoffs. The reader won't know if the stories are true, but the chance that people may have actually experienced what they write about makes the stories much more stimulating. Not limited to fiction, the booklet-size magazine also contains reviews of adult videos, mainstream films and books, a regular "Survival Kit" section that includes columnists giving advice on the law, health (formerly called "AIDS Watch"), sex ("Sex Acts"), and relationships. Fiction contributors have included such established gay writers as Michael Bronski, Harold Fairbanks, Steve Warren, and John St. James. Thus, the quality here of the writing is better than its many imitators. Explicit drawings are included. Recommended for gay studies collections. (DT)

The Guide. See Lesbian, Gay, Bisexual, and Transgender section.

Journal of Homosexuality. See Lesbian, Gay, Bisexual, and Transgender section.

Journal of Sex Research. See Sociology and Social Work/General section.

Journal of the History of Sexuality. See History section.

Loving More Magazine. See Zines section.

6030. ***O G: Oriental Guys: presenting a positive image of Asian men.*** [ISSN: 0818-6065] 1987. q. USD 22.50 per issue. Ed(s): Ian Withers. O G Magazine, 1164 Bishop St, Ste 124 293, Honolulu, HI 96813; http://www.ogusa.com. Illus., adv. Circ: 12000. *Aud.:* Ga, Ac.

An oversized perfect-bound publication, this artbook-like periodical does more than feature color photos of nude Asian males. In *Oriental Guys*, the photography is excellent; the models are apparently ordinary males discovered nude in various locales in Asia. But if the erotica is what draws most readers, especially "rice queens" (those attracted to Asians), the more intellectually inquisitive will find interesting articles about gay activism in Asia, much of it ignored by the mainstream gay community in its own publications. There are also interviews with important figures in the gay Asian diasporic community. It has recently been coming out more irregularly, but it remains a highly recommended addition. (DT)

6031. ***On Our Backs: the best of lesbian sex.*** [ISSN: 0890-2224] 1984. bi-m. USD 34.95; USD 5.95 newsstand/cover per issue; CND 6.95 newsstand/cover per issue Canada. Ed(s): Erin Findlay. Blush Entertainment, HAF Enterprises, PO Box 500, Missouri City, TX 7759-9904. Illus., adv. Circ: 15000. Vol. ends: No. 6. *Bk. rev.:* 6-10, 100 words. *Aud.:* Ga, Ac.

For more than a decade, *On Our Backs* has challenged the feminist movement to put the "sex" back into the struggle. Unabashedly sexual, this magazine (now a sister publication of the more mainstream *girlfriends*) is profusely illustrated with erotic photos of females (such as those by noted photographer Tee Corrine), but it's also chock-full of advice columns (e.g., "Should I Scrump My Coworker's Girlfriend?" by celebrity Nina Hartley), such features as the regular *On Our Backs* interview (e.g., with the "vivacious Candida Royalle"), and book excerpts, such as one from *The Survivor's Guide to Sex.* Fiction includes stories such as "Filipina Butch" and "At the Almador Motel." There is also a book review section that features the latest finds, and a video review section. In all, a welcome alternative to the commercial products, one that celebrates lesbian sexuality in its various and explicit permutations. Highly recommended. (DT)

6032. ***Penthouse: the magazine of sex, politics and protest.*** [ISSN: 0090-2020] 1969. m. USD 29.95 domestic; USD 57.95 foreign; USD 7.99 newsstand/cover. Ed(s): Peter Bloch, Bob Guccione. General Media Communications, Inc., 11 Penn Plaza, 12th Fl, New York, NY 10001. Illus., adv. Circ: 980106. *Indexed:* ASIP, LRI, RI-1. *Aud.:* Ga, Ac.

Its new subtitle tells it all: No longer just a clone of *Playboy* as the "international magazine for men" (its former subtitle), this long-standing heterosexual erotica magazine stands out as a strong proponent of sexual freedom and free speech. It is decidedly on the side of those who fight state repression. In addition to explicit photography (both female and male), the magazine offers strong investigative reportage and analysis of national and international issues by the likes of Joe Conason, Alan Dershowitz, and Nat Hentoff. For more than two decades, until his death in 2001, journalist Tad Szulc's writings graced its pages. Some may dislike how women are depicted in its fiction, news clips, or full-page color layouts, but one cannot dismiss its outstanding contribution by alerting readers to the latest threats to our liberties, such as an article on "Whose Homeland Security?" Regular departments include "Online Humor," "Technomania," "Politics in the Miltary," "Men's Health & Fitness," and "Ribald Rimes." For the thinking person's collection. (DT)

6033. ***Playboy: entertainment for men.*** [ISSN: 0032-1478] 1953. m. USD 29.97 domestic; USD 47.05 Canada; USD 45 elsewhere. Ed(s): James Kamisky, Hugh Hefner. Playboy Enterprises, Inc., 680 N Lake Shore Dr, Chicago, IL 60611; http://www.playboy.com. Illus., adv. Sample. Circ: 3150000 Paid. Vol. ends: No. 12. Microform: BHP; PQC. Online: Gale Group. Reprint: PQC. *Indexed:* ASIP, BEL&L, FLI, LRI, MRD, MagInd. *Bk. rev.:* 6-9, 200 words, signed. *Aud.:* Ga, Ac.

America's best-selling men's magazine for over half-century, *Playboy* continues to publish high quality fiction, nonfiction and its well-regarded "Playboy Interview" with notable subjects. The "Playmate of the Month" centerfold is still offered. Readers definitely have to wade through pages of color nudes (mainly of women) but if the pictures don't interest a reader, the text offerings are definitely the "meat" of the magazine. Now it also highlights "DVD of the month" and includes what's available online on its web site. A new addition is a regular "20Q" column, where politicians or other notables are asked 20 questions; it's a shorter and more concise version of the "Playboy Interview." Reviews cover films, music, games, DVDs, and books. Sexual liberation may be commonplace in many regions, and its message of "entertainment for men" may sound dated and sexist, but the audience is still there for this magazine. (DT)

6034. ***Prometheus.*** 1973. q. Non-members, USD 35. Ed(s): M Tod. TES Association, PO Box 2783, New York, NY 10163; prometheus@tes.org; http://www.tes.org/prometheus/prometheus.html. Adv. *Bk. rev.:* 5-6, 250-500 words. *Aud.:* Ga, Ac, Sa.

Founded as the publication of the established sado-masochistic organization The Eulenspiegel Society, *Prometheus* now serves as the membership magazine for the TES Association, the society's not-for-profit parent. TES notes: "What separates us from typical BDSM magazines is that we like to appeal to the intellect with our many articles as well as display beautiful pictures and drawings. With our mixed genre, this is a magazine that appeals to both men and women." BD means bondage and discipline; SM means sadomasochism. This magazine's approximately 100 pages offer news about leather pride and advice to new initiates into the subculture. A helpful glossary of terms guides you through the personal ads. Photos portray naked males and females in various types of bondage and discipline situations. Contents include fiction, articles on safety, and personal essays. For collections that want to cover the broad range of sexualities. (DT)

6035. ***Sex Education.*** [ISSN: 1468-1811] 2001. 3x/yr. GBP 115 (Individuals, GBP 39). Ed(s): Michael Reiss. Carfax Publishing Ltd., 4 Park Sq, Milton Park, Abingdon, OX14 4RN, United Kingdom; enquiry@tandf.co.uk; http://www.tandf.co.uk/. Reprint: PSC. *Indexed:* BrEdI, SociolAb. *Aud.:* Ac, Sa.

Focusing on sexual education (or lack of) within schools and the family as well as society, this journal's scope is not limited to the United States or Europe. An article in an early issue covered, for example, sex education about AIDS in selected countries in Asia and the Pacific. It delineated the heterosexual bias in some of the government-sponsored programs. Other articles have addressed the difficulties in teaching sex education to boys, or the limits of abstinence-only sex education. Its editorial board includes members from around the globe. It notes that it "does not assume that sex education takes place only in educational institutions and the family. Contributions are therefore welcomed which, for example, analyse the impacts of media and other vehicles of culture on sexual behaviour and attitudes." The journal is accessible: "Medical and epidemiological papers (e.g., of trends in the incidences of sexually transmitted infections) will not be accepted unless their educational implications are discussed adequately." Highly recommended for coverage often ignored or politicized. (DT)

Sexual Abuse. See Psychology section.

6036. ***Sexual Addiction & Compulsivity: the journal of treatment and prevention.*** [ISSN: 1072-0162] 1994. q. USD 188 (Individuals, USD 84). Ed(s): Patrick J Carnes. Brunner - Routledge (US), 325 Chestnut St, Ste 800, Philadelphia, PA 19106; postmaster@bmpub.com. Circ: 1000. Online: EBSCO Publishing; Ingenta Select; OCLC Online Computer Library Center, Inc.; Swets Blackwell. Reprint: PSC. *Indexed:* CJA, ExcerpMed. *Aud.:* Ac, Sa.

This journal of the National Council on Sexual Addiction and Compulsivity focuses on all aspects of sexual addiction, described as a "growth phenomenon." Article topics include addiction among lesbians, seropositive men who have sex with men, ephebophiles, and priests. It offers continuing education material for professionals. Articles may also provide guidance to working sex therapists on guidelines for relating to clients. (DT)

Sexual and Relationship Therapy. See Family and Marriage section.

6037. ***Sexualities: studies in culture and society.*** [ISSN: 1363-4607] 1998. q. GBP 291 print & online eds. in Europe, Middle East, Africa & Australasia. Ed(s): Ken Plummer. Sage Publications Ltd., 6 Bonhill St, London, EC2A 4PU, United Kingdom; info@sagepub.co.uk; http://www.sagepub.co.uk/. Illus., index, adv. Sample. Refereed. Circ: 1200. Vol. ends: Nov. *Indexed:* IBZ, SWA, SociolAb. *Bk. rev.:* 3-11, length varies, signed. *Aud.:* Ac.

Sexualities was developed to address emerging research about "the changing nature of the social organization of human sexual experience in the late modern world." Interdisciplinary and international in scope, it provides scholarly articles, interviews, and commentary that are analytical and ethnographic. Feminist, gender, and gay and lesbian studies are included in its scope. Topics include the impact of new technologies on sexualities, queer theory, methodologies of sex research, sex work, and the stratification of sexualities by class, race, gender, and age. Tables of contents, plus abstracts, are available on the publisher's web site, along with a sample issue and a free e-mail contents alert service. (BJG)

6038. ***Sexuality and Culture.*** [ISSN: 1095-5143] 1997. q. USD 60; USD 192. Ed(s): Barry M Dank. Transaction Publishers, 35 Berrue Circle, Rutgers University, Piscataway, NJ 08854-8042; trans@transactionpub.com; http://www.transactionpub.com. Adv. Circ: 300. *Indexed:* SociolAb. *Aud.:* Ga, Ac.

Originally an annual, this journal emerged out of concern about "sexual correctness" (or political correctness involving sexualities), especially in face of sexual harassment policies in academia. It now covers a broader range of issues, perhaps no less controversial. Recent issues critically explore affirmative action and child sexual abuse research. Its editorial board includes some of the big names in sex research even as it takes on a daunting task of critiquing established norms. Look here for analysis of contemporary sexual politics and culture that is often missing from more mainstream journals. (DT)

Sexuality and Disability. See Disabilities section.

6039. ***SHE.*** irreg. Ed(s): Cameron Scholes. Draculina Publishing, PO Box 587, Glen Carbon, IL 62034. *Aud.:* Ga, Ac, Sa.

This magazine primarily focuses on female stars in Asian cinema, especially Japanese but also Hong Kong films, and in several special issues has focused on "pink" films from the region. There are interviews with legendary porn filmmakers or female porn stars, as well as prodigious lists and reviews of Asian erotic cinema. Japanese "sinema" is the focus of one issue. A special section reviews U.S. videos, not necessarily erotic. The writing is often provocative, revealing perhaps a strong attraction to Asian women. Sure to be an eye-opener for anyone interested in getting further into Asian sinema. (DT)

SIECUS Report. See Civil Liberties/Bioethics: Reproductive Rights, Right to Life, and Right-to-Die section.

6040. ***Spectator (Berkeley): California's original adult newsmagazine.*** [ISSN: 0894-9751] w. USD 39. Ed(s): Layne Winklebleck. Bold Type, Inc., PO Box 1984, Berkeley, CA 94701-1984; Layne@spectator.net; http://www.spectator.net. Illus., adv. *Aud.:* Ga, Ac.

More than just a contact magazine for the "sexually active adult," this tabloid has intelligent analyses of matters sexual by such writers as Carol Queen, David Steinberg, and the former Pat Califia—now Patrick Califia-Rice (who once wrote a weekly "Topping the News" column). Carol Queen has been writing about the union struggle of sex workers in San Francisco. This magazine deserves wider readership than just the person seeking a date. While it contains calendar listings for the San Francisco Bay area, the publication cannot be dismissed as "local" or even just statewide in its scope. The centerfold might contain multiple photos of a female model posing nude, or it might just be the continuation of a well-illustrated article on kinky sex. The magazine has now also migrated to the web, and its online version is available free at www.spectatormag.com, with an archive by contributor or photographer, topic, or date. It also has archived reviews, features, and interviews. This web site should be linked in many progressive library collections. (DT)

Sex Positive

The sex-positive movement arose in the 1990s from, among other things, the "sex wars" in feminist circles during the 1980s: Feminist critiques about pornography became arguments about any and all depictions and expressions of female (and male) sexuality in popular culture and private life. Some of the movement's influences include (1) the blossoming pro-sex Third Wave feminist movement; (2) the lesbian/gay/bisexual/transgender/queer-questioning (LGBTQ) movement, which continues to fight for the acceptance of nonheterosexual identities; (3) the continuing AIDS epidemic, which made people reconsider and reeducate themselves about their their sexual practices; (4) the increasing erotica monograph market in mainstream publishing, which Daniel Tsang alludes to in his introduction to this Sexuality section; and (5) the coalescing of those who enjoy historically frowned-upon activities like bondage and discipline, dominance and submission, and sadomasochism (known collectively as BDSM), and polyamory—due in part to the Internet's rising popularity. According to Google's archives, the first appearance of "sex-positive" was on Usenet in 1990. In 1991, Robert Francoeur's *Descriptive Dictionary and Atlas of Sexology* had an entry for the term—probably the first time in a printed reference source.

Borrowing from sex-positive activist Hanne Blank's definition for the word in her article for the fall 2002 issue of *Bitch: Feminist Response to Pop Culture*, a sex-positive magazine is an online and/or print periodical which has, as its philosophy, the sex depicted moving beyond the "radical acceptance of consensual [and] pleasurable adult sexuality" and into working "to improve people's access to an empowering and inclusive culture of sexuality." At its best, the magazine challenges—among other issues—racist and classist imagery typically associated with sexually explicit magazines, regardless of the genders/sex (male, female, transgender, intersex) and sexualities (straight, gay/lesbian, bisexual, polyamory) involved.

Since I agree with Mr. Tsang's critique about libraries' current handling of sexually explicit magazines, zines, and e-zines, and because Mr. Tsang covers some of the best sex-positive print magazines (*On Our Backs*) and electronic magazines (*Scarlet Letters*), I will not repeat his words or work. I will concentrate on other online magazines, mainly because they reflect many of the sex-positive communities' electronic constituencies that continue to find support online.

6041. *Dimensions Magazine.* [ISSN: 1057-7386] 1988. q. USD 30 domestic; USD 36 Canada; USD 60 elsewhere. Ed(s): Conrad Blickenstorfer. Shardco, Inc., PO Box 640, Folsom, CA 95763-0640; http://www.dimensionsmagazine.com. *Aud.:* Ga.

This is the online counterpart of a long-running magazine. It views itself as "*Playboy* for those who prefer the fat figure, only *Dimensions* is geared not only to men but also to women who love to see their own body type featured in a national magazine." The publication moves beyond the erotic to include articles on health and activism. It is inclusive in showing women of color. (AP)

6042. *Erotica Readers and Writers Association.* 1998. m. Free. Erotica Readers Association, . *Bk. rev.:* Number and length vary. *Aud.:* Ga.

"Dedicated to readers and writers of erotica since 1996, [this magazine is intended for] an international community of women and men interested in the provocative world of erotica." The publication features not only erotic fiction but also music and book reviews. It includes erotica written by and about people of color, white LGBTQ, and white full-figured women, and a section dedicated to the craft of erotic writing. Highly recommended. (AP)

6043. *Good Vibes Magazine.* 1997. m. Free. Ed(s): Violet Blue. Good Vibrations, 1210 Valencia St, San Francisco, CA 94110. *Aud.:* Ga.

Published by Good Vibrations, the renowned sex shop and one of the major forces in the sex-positive movement. One of the best-written and most inclusive electronic sex-positive magazines. Regular contributors include sex-positive activists Carol Queen, Hanne Blank, and Patrick (Pat) Calfia. Very highly recommended. (AP)

6044. *Nerve (Online edition): literate smut.* 1997. m. Free. Ed(s): Genevieve Field. Nerve.com, 520 Broadway, 6th Floor, New York, NY 10012; info@nervemag.com; http://www.nerve.com. Illus., adv. *Bk. rev.:* yes. *Aud.:* Ga.

Created because sex "is a subject in need of a fearless, intelligent forum for both genders. We believe that women (men too, but especially women) have waited long enough for a smart, honest magazine on sex." The web site boasts 1.67 million visitors per month and 465,095 registered users. The few images of people of color tend to fall into "noble savage" cliches (strong black woman, black people in whiteface, hot latinos, china-doll/dragon-lady dichotomies). The magazine includes virtually no images of zaftig people and does take a tokenism approach to LGBTQ and disability. Overall, however, it is an intelligent, literate, and fun publication. Recommended. (AP)

6045. *The Position.* 2000. w. Free. Ed(s): Christian Ettinger, Robert T Francoeur. The Position, L.L.C., 233 5th Ave, Ste 2A, New York, NY 10016. Adv. *Bk. rev.:* Various number and length. *Aud.:* Ga.

This publication chronicles sex in New York City, the United States, and the world. It does not publish erotica but uses journalistic-style reporting instead of a literary approach. It connects sexual expression to larger First Amendment issues. Although it is inclusive of sexual identities and practices, it tends to pander to some racial stereotypes, like the ubiquitous black prostitute. Recommended for its factual approach. (AP)

6046. *Shades Beyond Gray.* 1996. irreg. Free. Ed(s): Sossity O Chiricuzio. Shades Beyond Gray, soc@shadesbeyondgray.com; http://www.shadesbeyondgray.com/. *Aud.:* Ga.

"Made for, by, and about consenting adult freaks who consider respect, fun, and negotiation to be integral to a happy, healthy sexual experience." The journal tends toward some amateurish erotica and tokenism, but that is balanced by its prose, especially the articles written by sex-positive activist Susie Bright. Lighthearted in spirit and fun to read. Recommended. (AP)

6047. *Venus or Vixen: read some smut!* 1996. a. Free. Ed(s): Cara Bruce, Lisa Montanarelli. Venus or Vixen, 815 Washington St, Box No. 3, Oakland, CA 94607; staff@venusorvixen.com; http://www.venusorvixon.com. *Bk. rev.:* Number and length varies. *Aud.:* Ga.

This "pansexual, pro-sexual erotic web zine . . . offers the finest in erotic fiction, sex-related feature articles, book, web and toy reviews, and erotic artwork." It is published by anthology editor and author Cara Bruce, who edited *Best Bisexual Women's Erotica* and *Viscera: An Anthology of Bizarre Erotica*. Although there are precious few images and stories about sexually disenfranchised people, the ones presented are humanizing depictions. Highly recommended. (AP)

Electronic Journals

6048. *Clean Sheets.* 1998. w. Ed(s): Susannah Indigo. Clean Sheets, http://www.cleansheets.com/. *Aud.:* Ga, Ac.

Founded by a "small group of writers who dreamed of an online erotic magazine that didn't take itself too seriously, but still did its best to be fresh, clear and exciting," it sees itself as "Good Vibrations [the sex-toy store] meets Salon.com." It seeks to foster a dialog on sexuality. Each Wednesday, this online zine updates various sections. Sections include articles, exotica, fiction, poetry, and reviews. Art work is featured in an archived gallery. Contributors include David Steinberg. It even pays for fiction and poetry. An online archive—free to all browsers—preserves all contributions. Overall, a well-designed site that serves up a pleasant experience. Highly recommended. (DT)

6049. *Libido: the journal of sex and sensibility.* [ISSN: 0899-8272] 1988. q. Ed(s): Marianna Beck, Jack Hafferkamp. Libido, PO Box 146721, Chicago, IL 61614; rune@mcs.com; http://www.sensualsource.com. Illus., adv. Sample. Circ: 10000. *Indexed:* AltPI. *Bk. rev.:* 6, 500-3,000 words. *Aud.:* Ga, Ac.

This well-designed journal has now migrated to the web, continuing to offer some of the best writing on sexual politics and erotica. The editors explain: "Printing is very expensive for a small erotic magazine. We can reach more people with more exciting content by publishing on the web." It describes itself as "a journal about sex that's geared to turn on your mind and your body. It's a web site (formerly a magazine) for women and men who read and think." It is an online journal that is "sex-positive, gender-equal, and all embracing in terms of sexual orientation." It also claims to be "both intellectually demanding as well as stimulating." There is poetry, reader-written fiction, and, most notably, highly artistic photography, some from its annual photography contest. More recently, it seems to be adding only fiction to its web site, and there is a fiction archive online. Vintage erotica now appear in an online gallery and art museum, and there is also a book review archive. A free monthly e-newsletter is available. Back issues of the print version (47 issues; 1988 through 2000) have been made available via its web site. A highly recommended title for adding to the library online catalog. (DT)

6050. *Nifty Erotic Stories Archive.* 1992. Nifty Archive Alliance, PMB 159, 333 Mamaroneck Ave, White Plains, NY 10605; nifty@gaycafe.com; http://www.nifty.org/nifty. *Aud.:* Ga, Ac, Sa.

This online archive of alternative-sexuality erotica covers fiction involving male–male, female–female, bisexuals, bestiality, intergenerational, interracial, and other sexual combinations. It specifically excludes heterosexual stories, but it provides links to many other sites. Within each category included, there are even further subcategories, e.g., under "gay," there are urination, high school, and adult–youth fiction, among many others. The site includes material from presses no longer publishing, e.g., Acolyte Press. There is also a list of rejected stories, a list of removed stories (because of copyright, for instance), and submissions of stories (http://www.nifty.org/nifty/submission.html). Although the site is free, donations are sought to maintain it. This site warns that it contains sexually explicit text and is for adults. It is an indispensable source for raw, uncensored erotica. (DT)

6051. ***Sauce Box: the e-zine of of literary erotica.*** q. Ed(s): Guillermo Bosch. Sauce Box, GuillermoBosch@guillermobosch.com; http://www.guillermobosch.com/. *Aud.:* Ga.

This journal, once subtitled "the e-zine of literary erotica," has been consistently published each quarter since spring, 1996. Its entire archive is online (some in pdf format, mostly in html for easier loading). The journal now contains an editor's commentary in each issue. Not your typical erotic journal, this one addresses political issues such as war, and includes poetry set in the Vietnam War, or as the contributing poet wrote, the "American War," as the Vietnamese call it. Heterosexual in focus, the stories are often continued in a subsequent issue. One of the best e-zines of this genre. (DT)

6052. ***Scarlet Letters: a journal of femmerotica.*** 1997. 4x/yr. Ed(s): Heather Corinna. Scarlet Letters, PO Box 300105, Minneapolis, MN 55403-5105; http://scarletletters.com/. Adv. *Aud.:* Ga.

Like its sister web sites *Scarleteen* (sex education for teens: www.scarleteen-.com) and *Femmerotica* (www.femmerotica.com), this e-zine is owned and operated completely by women. These sites together draw, at 75 percent, "one of the highest percentages of female readers of any sexual site online." Its avowed mission is "to produce quality material addressing numerous aspects of sexuality with a woman's taste and sensibility, which include all genders, age groups and orientations." The zine includes fiction, editorials, interviews, columns, an interactive community, and a sex advice section, "Sexuality One on One," that aims to provide "accurate" sexuality information and advice. There is also erotic art and photography. For less than $5 a month, a complete online archive for back issues is available, with proceeds benefiting *Scarleteen*, its sex-education clearinghouse. Highly recommended. (DT)

Sexing the Political. See Women: Feminist and Special Interest/ Electronic Journals section.

■ SINGLES

Sarah J. Hammill, Reference Librarian, Biscayne Bay Campus Library, Florida International University, 3000 NE 151st Street, North Miami, FL 33181; hammills@fiu.edu; Fax: 305-940-6865

Introduction

According to the 2000 U.S. Census, over 93 million Americans are unmarried adults. The Census defines *unmarried* as never married, widowed, or divorced. Single adults constitute approximately 44 percent of the adult population in this country. The number of unmarried households continues to rise. In 1970, there were approximately 53 million unmarried Americans. In the last 30 years the number of single people has increased by approximately 75 percent. As a result, the networking inplications for unmarried America are enormous.

There are numerous ways to meet single people: frequenting nightclubs, attending singles events, responding to singles ads in local newspapers, or registering for one of the many online dating services are just a few of those ways. Popular literature claims that some of the best places to meet other singles are at the laundromat, the library, or the grocery store. Granted, these are all tried-and-true ways to meet single people. However, are the people one meets at these places healthy in mind, body, and spirit? The publications below are geared to individuals who want advice on meeting other singles and insights on how to live healthfully, think positively, and enjoy life, whether alone or with the love of one's life.

The numerous publications for singles come in a variety of formats, both electronically and in print: newsletters, glossy magazines, tabloids, and newspapers. Some focus on a specific region of the country, and others focus on specific interests and activities. Many are based on Christian theology, while the main purpose of others is personal ads. All intend to provide a forum for singles to meet others, learn about the rights of singles, and offer self-improvement. Most of the publications below can be classified into three categories: spiritual, outdoor and nature, and regional. Overall, most of the publications are produced by independent agencies or a single person. As a result of rising publishing costs, the titles come and go. The bibliography below lists the publications that I was able to review.

Basic Periodicals

Most titles have a regional, Christian, or subject-specific focus.

6053. ***Active Single's Life.*** 1973. m. USD 20. Ed(s): Walt Briem. Voice Publishing, PO Box 98080, Des Moines, WA 98198-0080; activslife@aol.com; http://www.nwasl.com. Adv. Circ: 10000. *Bk. rev.:* Number and length vary. *Aud.:* Ga.

This newspaper focuses on single adults in the Northwest. It offers self-help articles, personal ads, and features on well-known singles in the area. Regular departments include "Singles Events," "Singles Resources," "Singles Bites," "Singles Q&A," and "Book Reviews."

6054. ***Christian Single: the magazine for successful single living.*** [ISSN: 0191-4294] 1979. m. USD 19.95. LifeWay Press, 127 Ninth Ave N, Nashville, TN 37234-0140. Illus., adv. Sample. Vol. ends: Mar. *Bk. rev.:* 3, 250 words. *Aud.:* Ga.

The mission statement of *Christian Single* says it "is the magazine for successful single living, providing practical answers to the real-life needs of today's single adults, challenging them to intensify their faith and impact their community." This is a glossy publication with colorful photos and enlightening articles. Regular features include letters to the editor, articles about prominent single adults (athletes, musicians, actors, etc.), "Direct Line," a question-and-answer section, and book and video reviews. The magazine is free of advertising. It is a member of the Evangelical Press Association and the Gospel Music Association. Recommended for public and church libraries.

6055. ***CountrySingles.com.*** Formerly (until 2001): *Solo R F D (Rural Free Delivery) (Print).* m. Country Singles, PO Box 2139, Sioux Falls, SD 57101; publisher@countrysingles.com; http//www.countrysingles.com. Adv. *Aud.:* Ga.

A monthly newspaper, *Countrysingles.com* is primarily for Illinois, Missouri, Iowa, Minnesota, South Dakota, and Wisconsin residents. However, it contains interesting tidbits for singles everywhere. It offers short articles with such trivia as what people in this country call soft drink and how Viagra needs romance for success. In addition, it contains singles ads for 18-wheelers and a calendar of events. A fun, easy-to-read newspaper.

6056. ***Family Bible Study: Single Adult Learner Guide.*** Former titles (until 2000): *A Single Pursuit: Bible Studies for Single Adults; Life and Work Pursuits: Bible Studies for Single Adults; Single Adult Bible Study;* (until 1982): *Collegiate Bible Study.* [ISSN: 1526-5854] q. USD 11.35. LifeWay Christian Resources, 1 Lifeway Plaza, Nashville, TN 37234; customerservice@lifeway.com; http://www.lifeway.com. Circ: 210000. *Aud.:* Ga.

Part of the Family Bible study curriculum series, *Single Adult Learner Guide* is a quarterly publication that contains lesson plans for Christian singles. Each issue is broken down into monthly themes with weekly lesson plans. In addition, there are scripture readings for each day of the week.

6057. ***Jacob's Well.*** 1982. q. Membership, USD 35. Ed(s): Irene Varley. North American Conference of Separated and Divorced Catholics, PO Box 360, Richland, OR 97870; nacsdc@oneworld.com; http://www.nacsdc.org. Adv. Circ: 3000. *Bk. rev.:* 2. *Aud.:* Ga.

The official publication of the North American Conference of Separated and Divorced Catholics (NACSDC), *Jacob's Well* focuses on helping church members who are suffering from separation and divorce. Readers are encouraged to experience reconciliation and healing, and to start a new life in the church through articles, stories, and regular columns. In addition, there are articles and essays for remarried Catholics. It contains book reviews and conference information. The small amount of advertising is on books and videos for separated and divorced Catholics.

NACSDC also publishes a monthly newsletter, *Professional Newsletter.* Both publications are recommended for church libraries.

6058. ***One2One Magazine: making real connections.*** 2002. bi-m. USD 29.99; USD 4.95 newsstand/cover per issue. Ed(s): Ken Hatlestad. One2One Magazine, 9903 Santa Monica Blvd, Ste 175, Beverly Hills, CA 90212; editor@one2onemag.com; http://www.one2onemag.com. Adv. *Aud.:* Ga.

A glossy magazine with a strong emphasis on dating tips, fashion, and image. It contains a question-and-answer section with John Gray, author of *Men Are from Mars, Women Are from Venus.*

6059. ***Outdoor Singles Network.*** 1989. q. Membership, USD 75 print & online eds.; USD 55 per issue. Ed(s): Kathleen Menke. O S N - U, PO Box 781, Haines, AK 99827-0781; osn@kcd.com; http://www.kcd.com/ci/osn. Adv. *Aud.:* Ga.

A quarterly newsletter for singles between the ages of 19 and 90 who love the outdoors. It primarily features personal ads for people looking for pen-pals, new friends, trip companions, soulmates, etc. Online and paper subscriptions are available.

6060. ***Possibilities for Romantic Eligibles Magazine.*** Formerly: *Trellis Singles Magazine.* 1975. q. USD 9. Ed(s): Debby Gosse. Possibilities for Romantic Eligibles Magazine, 205 Mark Twain Ave, San Rafael, CA 94903. Adv. Circ: 43000. *Aud.:* Ga.

This quarterly publication based in Northern California has short articles on being single, how to find a date, and what to do and not do on a first date. It includes a party and events calendar, and contains many advertisements for singles events, online dating, and matchmaking services.

6061. ***Single Mother: a support group in your hands.*** [ISSN: 1074-0775] 1991. bi-m. USD 19 membership included. Ed(s): Andrea Engber. National Organization of Single Mothers, Inc., PO Box 68, Midland, NC 28107; solomom@bellsouth.net. Illus. Sample. Circ: 4000 Paid. Online: Northern Light Technology, Inc.; OCLC Online Computer Library Center, Inc.; SoftLine Information. *Indexed:* GendWatch. *Bk. rev.:* 1, 450 words. *Aud.:* Ga.

A bimonthly newsletter created by Andrea Engber, founder of the National Organization of Single Mothers. *SingleMother* is dedicated to helping single mothers meet the challenges of daily life. It includes powerful quotes about single motherhood as well as helpful articles for single moms. Recommended for public libraries.

6062. ***Single Scene - Arizona.*** Formerly: *Single Scene.* 1972. 6x/yr. USD 9.50. Ed(s): Janet L Jacobsen. Single Scene - Arizona, PO Box 10159, Scottsdale, AZ 85271; singles@primenet.com; http://www.primenet.com/~singles. Adv. Circ: 5000. *Aud.:* Ga.

Single Scene regularly deals with news, information, and personals for Arizona's heterosexual singles. It has a calendar of events, "National Singles News Briefs," "Local Singles News Briefs," a directory of over 60 singles groups, personal ads, and articles dealing with the single life.

6063. ***Singles Network: of New York's Capital region.*** Former titles: *Singles Outreach Services Newsletter; S O S Newsletter.* 1983. m. Membership, USD 30. Ed(s): Gregg Kim. Singles Outreach Services, 435 New Karner Rd, PO Box 12511, Albany, NY 12212; http://www.singlesoutreach.org/. Adv. Circ: 5500. *Aud.:* Ga.

Singles Network is a monthly newsletter packed full of calendar events for singles. It includes diverse and interesting activities such as white-water river rafting, swing dancing lessons, and quilt making. The scope is limited to the Albany, New York, region, and any single in the area can find something to do using this newsletter.

6064. ***Singles Network Newsletter.*** [ISSN: 1524-797X] 1996. m. USD 5 USD 24 domestic. Ed(s): Bonnie Stephens. Singles Network Newsletter, PO Box 13, Springfield, VA 22150; john100@erols.com; bonnietexas@mindspring.com. Adv. Circ: 250 Paid and controlled. *Aud.:* Ga.

Contains helpful and interesting articles on various topics including accepting yourself, tips to tell if you are really in love, and how to take control of your life. There are positive expressions, poems, and quotations throughout this really enjoyable newsletter.

6065. ***Singles Scene - Spirit & Life.*** Formerly: *Singles Scene (Allardt).* 1981. m. USD 29.95. Ed(s): Sandra Turner. Sandra S. Turner, Ed. & Pub., PO Box 310, Allardt, TN 38504; spiritlif@aol.com; http://members.aol.com/spiritlif/homepage.html. Adv. Circ: 5500. *Bk. rev.:* Occasional. *Aud.:* Ga.

This monthly spiritual publication offers an advice column, stories of successful relationships, and personal ads. The "Singles Gallery" includes selected photos of individuals searching for their soul mate.

6066. ***Singles' Serendipity.*** 1985. bi-m. USD 12. Ed(s): Judy Lanier. Singles' Serendipity, PO Box 8117, Jacksonville, FL 32239-0117. Adv. Circ: 55000. *Aud.:* Ga.

Established in 1985, this magazine has over 95,000 readers. It includes personal ads from both men and women, and there is a special Spanish-language section. These personal ads, mostly from Floridians, are the primary purpose of the magazine. It also includes a few articles. The publication is a member of the Singles Press Association.

6067. ***Strategic Adult Ministries Journal.*** Formerly: *Single Adult Ministries Journal.* 1982. 6x/yr. USD 24. Ed(s): Terry Fisher. David C. Cook Publishing Co., 4050 Lee Vance View, Colorado Springs, CO 80918; hoodood@aol.com; http://www.cookministries.com. Adv. Circ: 5000. *Indexed:* ChrPI. *Bk. rev.:* Number varies, 300 words. *Aud.:* Ga.

Strategic Adult Ministry Journal, a transdenominational publication of Cook Communications Ministries, is dedicated to providing practical help, ideas, and encouragement for those involved in front-line ministries with singles and young adults. Each issue is based on a central theme such as building community, single parenting, or facing change. Issues include articles, statistics, and book reviews. Recommended for church libraries.

6068. ***Unmarried America: news for unmarried workers, consumers, taxpayers and voters.*** 1999. q. Members, USD 10. Ed(s): Tom Coleman. American Association for Single People, PO Box 11030, Glendale, CA 91205; mail@unmarriedamerica.org; http://www.singlesrights.com. *Bk. rev.:* Number and length vary. *Aud.:* Ga.

The mission of *Unmarried America* is fulfilled by conducting research and providing information and advice to members, elected officials, corporate policy makers, and the media. It is a publication of the American Association for Single People. It contains well-written articles on the rights of singles, research on singles, and accomplishments by singles. It is available in print and electronically.

■ SOCIOLOGY AND SOCIAL WORK

General/Social Work and Social Welfare

See also Aging; Criminology and Law Enforcement; Cultural-Social Studies; Ethnic Interests; Family and Marriage; Law; and Population Studies sections.

Sherry DeDecker, Head, Government Information Center, and Social Sciences Librarian, Davidson Library, University of California, Santa Barbara, CA 93106-9010

Introduction

The field of sociology draws from diverse subject matter. Because of the nature of cross-disciplinary study, librarians should also consult journals from the subject areas listed above.

In addition to journals in the basic periodicals list below, the full list includes the major journals representing the diversity of this field. For methods of quantitative and qualitative research, consult such journals as *Quality and Quantity, Evaluation Review, Journal of Mathematical Sociology, SMR: Sociological Methods and Research,* and some new titles: *Qualitative Social Work* and *Indicators.* Several journals are targeted to a specific audience, such as *International Journal of the Sociology of Law, JPMS: Journal of Political and Military Sociology, Journal of Leisure Research, Journal of Sex Research,* and *Journal of Rural Studies.* Some journals cover specific social issues, such as *Child Abuse and Neglect* and *Deviant Behavior.* There are several journals published by professional associations, such as *American Sociological Review, Sociology,* and *Social Work.*

A comprehensive library collection would include journals with an international focus: *International Sociology, International Social Work,* and a new title, *Global Social Policy,* are especially competent in this area. Any well-rounded collection will include journals reflecting research in foreign countries; for example, *Sociological Research, Acta Sociologica, British Journal of Sociology, Cahiers Internationaux de Sociologie, Canadian Review of Sociology, Chinese Sociology and Anthropology,* and two newcomers: *European Societies* and *Journal of European Social Policy.* Publications targeting professionals in the field are *Administration in Social Work, American Sociologist, Social Work Education, Teaching Sociology,* and *Contemporary Sociology.*

To maintain a focus on technology and its effects, librarians will want to look at such journals as *Technology in Society* and *Social Science Computer Review.*

Most of the journals constitute the core of undergraduate and graduate study in sociology or social work. Also included are some titles appropriate for public libraries, school libraries, and libraries serving social services professionals.

Basic Periodicals

GENERAL. Ga: *Journal of Social Issues, Policy & Practice, Social Forces, Social Policy, Social Problems, Society;* Ac: *American Journal of Sociology, American Sociological Review, British Journal of Sociology, Current Sociology, International Sociology, Journal of Social Issues, Sex Roles, Social Forces, Social Policy, Social Problems, Social Psychology Quarterly, Social Research, Society, Sociological Review, Sociology, Sociology of Education.*

SOCIAL WORK AND SOCIAL WELFARE; Ga: *Child Welfare, Children & Schools, Policy & Practice;* Ac: *British Journal of Social Work, Child Welfare, Children and Schools, Children and Youth Services Review, Clinical Social Work Journal, Families in Society, Health & Social Work, International Social Work, Policy & Practice, Research on Social Work Practice, Social Service Review, Social Work, Social Work with Groups.*

Basic Abstracts and Indexes

ASSIA: Applied Social Sciences Index and Abstracts, Social Sciences Citation Index, Social Sciences Index and Social Sciences Abstracts, Social Services Abstracts, Social Work Abstracts, Sociological Abstracts.

General

6069. ***Acta Sociologica.*** [ISSN: 0001-6993] 1955. q. GBP 165 in Europe, Middle East, Africa & Australasia. Ed(s): Hera Hallbera Bjornsdottir, Runar Vilhjalmsson. Sage Publications Ltd., 6 Bonhill St, London, EC2A 4PU, United Kingdom; info@sagepub.co.uk; http://www.sagepub.co.uk/. Illus., index, adv. Sample. Refereed. Circ: 3200. Microform: PQC; SWZ. Online: EBSCO Publishing; Gale Group; Ingenta Select; ingenta.com; OCLC Online Computer Library Center, Inc.; RoweCom Information Quest; Sage Publications, Inc.; Swets Blackwell. Reprint: ISI; SWZ. *Indexed:* ABCPolSci, AbAn, CJA, HRA, IBSS, IPSA, L&LBA, PAIS, PSA, SFSA, SSCI, SSI, SUSA, SWA, SociolAb. *Bk. rev.:* 4-6, signed. *Aud.:* Ac.

Published in English by the Scandinavian Sociological Association, this journal provides international research in all substantive areas of sociology, with the majority of the research involving Scandinavian countries. The journal contains at least one review essay as well as an extensive book review section, and frequently a comment section. Recommended for academic libraries with graduate programs in sociology.

Amerasia Journal. See Asian American section.

6070. ***American Journal of Sociology.*** [ISSN: 0002-9602] 1895. bi-m. USD 296 (Individuals, USD 13.20; Individual members, USD 44). Ed(s): William L Parish. University of Chicago Press, Journals Division, PO Box 37005, Chicago, IL 60637; subscriptions@journals.uchicago.edu; http://www.journals.uchicago.edu. Illus., index, adv. Sample. Refereed. Circ: 5000. Vol. ends: May. Microform: PQC. Online: EBSCO Publishing; Florida Center for Library Automation; Gale Group; JSTOR (Web-based Journal Archive); ProQuest Information & Learning. Reprint: ISI; PQC; PSC; SCH. *Indexed:* ABCPolSci, ABS&EES, AICP, ASG, ASSIA, AbAn, AgeL, AmH&L, ArtHuCI, BAS, BRD, BRI, CBRI, CIJE, CJA, CommAb, IBSS, IBZ, IMFL, IPSA, PAIS, PRA, PSA, PsycholAb, RI-1, RRTA, SFSA, SSCI, SSI, SUSA, SWA, SWR&A, SociolAb, WAE&RSA. *Bk. rev.:* 20-40, signed. *Aud.:* Ga, Ac, Sa.

Published by the University of Chicago since 1895, this journal is one of the major research sources in the field of sociology. Research methodology used for subjects is well documented and comprehensive; topics cover a broad spectrum of theoretical and empirical sociological research. There is an extensive book review section. Strongly recommended for academic libraries with a curriculum in sociology and for special and public libraries with social services clientele.

6071. ***American Sociological Review.*** [ISSN: 0003-1224] 1936. bi-m. USD 160 (Members, USD 35; Non-members, USD 80). Ed(s): Charles Camic, Franklin D Wilson. American Sociological Association, 1307 New York Ave, N W, Ste 700, Washington, DC 20005-4701; publications@asanet.org; http://www.asanet.org. Illus., index, adv. Refereed. Circ: 11500. Vol. ends: Dec. Microform: MIM; PQC. Online: Gale Group; Ingenta Select; JSTOR (Web-based Journal Archive); OCLC Online Computer Library Center, Inc.; ProQuest Information & Learning. Reprint: PQC. *Indexed:* ABCPolSci, ABS&EES, ASSIA, AbAn, AgeL, AmH&L, ArtHuCI, BAS, BEL&L, CBRI, CIJE, CJA, CommAb, DSR&OA, HRA, IBSS, IBZ, IPSA, PAIS, PRA, PSA, PsycholAb, RI-1, RRTA, SFSA, SSCI, SSI, SUSA, SWA, SWR&A, SociolAb, WAE&RSA. *Aud.:* Ga, Ac.

The official publication of the American Sociological Association, *ASR* provides comprehensive coverage of theoretical and empirical research in all fields of sociology. The diverse contributions focus on a multitude of topics, including research from countries other than the United States. Strongly recommended for all academic libraries with programs in sociology and for research-oriented public libraries.

6072. ***The American Sociologist.*** [ISSN: 0003-1232] 1969. q. USD 208 (Individuals, USD 64). Ed(s): Lawrence Nichols. Transaction Publishers, 35 Berrue Circle, Rutgers University, Piscataway, NJ 08854-8042; trans@transactionpub.com; http://www.transactionpub.com. Illus., adv.

Sample. Refereed. Circ: 500. Vol. ends: Winter. Microform: PQC. Online: EBSCO Publishing; Florida Center for Library Automation; Gale Group; Ingenta Select. Reprint: PQC; PSC; SWZ. *Indexed:* AgeL, CIJE, CJA, IBSS, IBZ, IPSA, PAIS, PSA, SSCI, SSI, SWA, SociolAb. *Bk. rev.:* 1-2, length varies. *Aud.:* Ac.

This journal publishes research that examines "new trends in the profession and focuses on how sociologists shape and influence social policy and the intellectual issues of the age." Topics include various schools of thought, historical analyses of the profession, and the state of sociology as a discipline. Some issues are thematic; recent issues focus on Canadian sociology, the history of sociology, and the sociology of law. Recommended for academic libraries with graduate programs in sociology.

Armed Forces and Society. See Military section.

6073. *British Journal of Sociology.* [ISSN: 0007-1315] 1950. q. USD 320 print & online. Blackwell Publishing Ltd., 9600 Garsington Rd, PO Box 805, Oxford, OX4 2DQ, United Kingdom; customerservices@oxon.blackwellpublishing.com; http://www.blackwellpublishing.com/. Illus., index, adv. Sample. Refereed. Circ: 2700. Vol. ends: Dec. Microform: WMP. Online: EBSCO Publishing; Gale Group; Ingenta Select; JSTOR (Web-based Journal Archive); OCLC Online Computer Library Center, Inc.; RoweCom Information Quest; Swets Blackwell. Reprint: PSC. *Indexed:* ABIn, AICP, ASSIA, AbAn, AgeL, ArtHuCI, BAS, CIJE, CJA, CommAb, IBSS, IBZ, IPSA, IndMed, PAIS, PSA, RI-1, SSCI, SSI, SWA, SociolAb. *Bk. rev.:* 10-20, signed. *Aud.:* Ac.

Published by the London School of Economics and Political Science, this is one of the more prestigious sociology journals. Articles cover research and philosophical discussions of issues relating to the social sciences with a focus on politics and economics. Topics include discussion of economic and sociological ideologies and theories, gender issues, and employment and labor issues. A recent thematic issue contains articles on the topic of workplace studies. Research tends to be focused on Western countries, especially Great Britain. Sociologists as well as librarians will appreciate the extensive book review section. Recommended for academic libraries with graduate programs in the social sciences.

6074. *Cahiers Internationaux de Sociologie.* [ISSN: 0008-0276] 1946. s-a. Individuals, EUR 46. Ed(s): G Balandier. Presses Universitaires de France, Departement des Revues, 6 av. Reille, Paris, 75685 Cedex 14, France; revues@puf.com; http://puf.ornis.fr. Illus., index. Refereed. Circ: 3500. Vol. ends: Dec. Reprint: SCH. *Indexed:* BAS, IBSS, IPB, IPSA, PAIS, PSA, SSCI, SociolAb. *Bk. rev.:* 3-10, signed. *Aud.:* Ac.

Articles in this journal are published in French, but abstracts are in English as well. Coverage is on a variety of philosophical issues related to the field of sociology, both historical and current. Issues tend to be thematic; recent topics have been new methods of communication, and analyses of the various areas of sociology. Recommended for academic libraries with doctoral programs in sociology.

6075. *Canadian Journal of Sociology.* [ISSN: 0318-6431] 1975. q. CND 98.13 (Individuals, CND 53.74). Ed(s): Nico Stehr. University of Toronto Press, Journals Department, 5201 Dufferin St, Toronto, ON M3H 5T8, Canada; journals@utpress.utoronto.ca; http://www.utpjournals.com. Illus., index, adv. Sample. Refereed. Circ: 850 Paid. Vol. ends: Fall. Microform: MML. Online: EBSCO Publishing; Florida Center for Library Automation; Gale Group; LexisNexis; Micromedia ProQuest. Reprint: PSC. *Indexed:* ABS&EES, ASSIA, AgeL, AmH&L, ArtHuCI, CBCARef, CJA, CPerI, CommAb, IBSS, IMFL, PSA, SSCI, SWA, SociolAb. *Bk. rev.:* 8-10, signed. *Aud.:* Ac.

Published with a grant from the Social Sciences and Humanities Research Council of Canada and with support from the Department of Sociology, University of Alberta, this journal gathers research relating primarily to social services and policies in Canada, although some articles cover general sociological and economic topics. Volumes are divided into articles, commentary sections, review essays, and book reviews. Abstracts are in French and English; some articles are in French. Recommended for academic libraries supporting advanced programs in sociology and Canadian Studies.

6076. *The Canadian Review of Sociology and Anthropology.* [ISSN: 0008-4948] 1964. q. Institutional members, CND 120. Canadian Sociology and Anthropology Association, Concordia University, 1455 bd de Maisonneuve Ouest, Rm SB323, Montreal, PQ H3G 1M8, Canada; csaa@vax2.concordia.ca; http://alcor.concordia.ca./~csaa1/. Illus., adv. Refereed. Circ: 1400. Vol. ends: Nov. Microform: MIM; PQC; NRP. Online: bigchalk; EBSCO Publishing; Florida Center for Library Automation; Gale Group; OCLC Online Computer Library Center, Inc.; ProQuest Information & Learning; H.W. Wilson. Reprint: PSC. *Indexed:* ABS&EES, AICP, AbAn, AgeL, AmH&L, AnthLit, ArtHuCI, CBCARef, CJA, CPerI, CommAb, IBSS, IBZ, IPSA, PSA, PsycholAb, RI-1, RRTA, SSCI, SSI, SWA, SociolAb, WAE&RSA. *Bk. rev.:* 6-12, signed. *Aud.:* Ac.

Published by the Canadian Sociology and Anthropology Association with a grant from the Social Sciences and Humanities Research Council of Canada, this journal covers research in both fields. Abstracts are in English and French; articles are published in either language. Coverage is given to topics of historical and current interest. There are occasional special issues; recently, one on the academy in the twenty-first century. Although other countries are included, most of the research is focused on Canadian agencies, policies, and programs. Recommended for academic libraries with sociology and anthropology curricula.

6077. *Child Abuse & Neglect.* Formerly: *International Journal on Child Abuse and Neglect.* [ISSN: 0145-2134] 1977. m. EUR 1341 (Qualified personnel, EUR 186). Ed(s): Dr. John M. Leventhal, M. Roth. Pergamon, The Boulevard, Langford Ln, East Park, Kidlington, OX5 1GB, United Kingdom. Illus., adv. Sample. Refereed. Circ: 1500. Vol. ends: No. 12. Microform: PQC. Online: Gale Group; ingenta.com; ScienceDirect; Swets Blackwell. *Indexed:* ASSIA, BrEdI, CIJE, CJA, ECER, EduInd, ExcerpMed, H&SSA, IBSS, IBZ, IUSGP, IndMed, PsycholAb, RiskAb, SSCI, SSI, SWR&A, SociolAb. *Aud.:* Ac, Sa.

This is the official publication of the International Society for Prevention of Child Abuse and Neglect. Most articles are in English, and many contain French and Spanish abstracts. International coverage includes topics dealing with psychology, psychiatry, social work, medicine, nursing, law, law enforcement, legislation, education, anthropology, and advocacy. Recommended for academic and special libraries supporting programs in social work, child psychology, criminal justice, law, medicine, or social services.

6078. *Child and Youth Care Forum: an independent journal of day and residential child and youth care practice.* Former titles (until 1990): *Child and Youth Care Quarterly;* (until 1987): *Child Care Quarterly.* [ISSN: 1053-1890] 1971. bi-m. USD 576 for print or online ed. Ed(s): Jerome Beker, Doug Magnuson. Kluwer Academic / Plenum Publishers, 233 Spring St Fl 7, New York, NY 10013-1522; http://www.wkap.nl/. Illus., index, adv. Sample. Refereed. Vol. ends: Dec. Microform: PQC. Online: EBSCO Publishing; ingenta.com; Kluwer Online; OCLC Online Computer Library Center, Inc.; Ovid Technologies, Inc.; RoweCom Information Quest; Swets Blackwell. Reprint: ISI; PQC. *Indexed:* ASSIA, CIJE, ECER, EduInd, IMFL, PsycholAb, SFSA, SSCI, SUSA, SWR&A. *Aud.:* Ac, Sa.

This journal is directed at improving child care services by providing "a channel of communication and debate including material on practice, selection and training, theory and research, and professional issues." It is aimed at professionals in child and youth care settings as well as instructors. Articles are a mixture of empirical and observational research and shared practical experiences. Recommended for public and special libraries serving child care professionals and academic libraries with social services or education curricula.

6079. *Child Maltreatment.* [ISSN: 1077-5595] 1996. q. GBP 301 in Europe, Middle East, Africa & Australasia. Ed(s): Mark Chaffin. Sage Publications, Inc., 2455 Teller Rd, Thousand Oaks, CA 91320; info@sagepub.com; http://www.sagepub.com. Illus., index, adv. Sample. Refereed. Circ: 4000 Paid. Vol. ends: Nov. *Indexed:* ASSIA, CINAHL, CJA, H&SSA, IBZ, IndMed, RiskAb, SFSA, SociolAb. *Aud.:* Ac.

This is the official publication of the American Professional Society on the Abuse of Children. It publishes research on all aspects of child maltreatment, including causes, prevention, and intervention. There are occasional special sections dedicated to specific topics, such as legal options with sex offenders, medical practice standards, and parent training and abuse prevention. The journal contains an annual index. Recommended for academic libraries with child psychology or social work programs.

6080. *Children and Youth Services Review: an international multidisciplinary review of the welfare of young people.* [ISSN: 0190-7409] 1979. m. EUR 954 (Qualified personnel, EUR 158). Ed(s): Dr. Duncan Lindsey. Pergamon, The Boulevard, Langford Ln, East Park, Kidlington, OX5 1GB, United Kingdom. Illus., index. Sample. Refereed. Circ: 1200. Vol. ends: Dec. Microform: PQC. Online: Gale Group; ingenta.com; ScienceDirect; Swets Blackwell. *Indexed:* ASG, ASSIA, CIJE, CJA, ECER, ExcerpMed, PsycholAb, SFSA, SSCI, SSI, SWR&A, SociolAb. *Bk. rev.:* 2-4, signed. *Aud.:* Ac, Sa.

The goal of this prominent social services journal is "to provide a forum for the critical analysis and assessment of social service programs designed to serve young people throughout the world." There are numerous special issues; recent topics include welfare reform and its impact on families, research and evaluation of family preservation services, and child welfare demonstration projects. Strongly recommended for academic libraries supporting social work, child psychology, or social services programs, and for special libraries with social services clientele.

6081. *Children's Legal Rights Journal.* [ISSN: 0278-7210] 1979. q. Members, USD 48; Non-members, USD 63. Ed(s): Kristie Cary. William S. Hein & Company, Incorporated, 1285 Main St, Buffalo, NY 14209-1987; mail@wshein.com; http://www.wshein.com. Illus. Sample. Refereed. Circ: 400. Vol. ends: Fall. Microform: Pub. Online: Gale Group. Reprint: WSH. *Indexed:* AgeL, CIJE, CLI, ECER, ILP, LRI. *Bk. rev.:* 1-2, signed. *Aud.:* Ac, Sa.

Published in conjunction with the the American Bar Association Center on Children and the Law, National Association of Counsel for Children, and Loyola University Chicago School of Law, this journal covers topics for professionals involved in working with children. Each issue contains legislative and court updates and a "Spotlight On" section highlighting a program or organization that has successfully dealt with a problem involving children; recently coverage is on the "Amber Plan," also known as the "Amber Alert," the system to recover children soon after their abduction. Some issues are topical; recent coverage is on the issue of education and children's rights. Highly recommended for law libraries and academic libraries with law or social services programs.

6082. *Chinese Sociology and Anthropology.* [ISSN: 0009-4625] 1968. q. USD 825 (Individuals, USD 140). Ed(s): Gregory Guldin, Zhou Daming. M.E. Sharpe, Inc., 80 Business Park Dr, Armonk, NY 10504; custserv@mesharpe.com; http://www.mesharpe.com. Illus., index, adv. Refereed. Vol. ends: Summer. Reprint: PSC. *Indexed:* BAS, IBSS, SSCI, SSI, SWA. *Aud.:* Ac.

This journal contains unabridged translations of articles from Chinese sources, primarily scholarly journals or articles published in book form. It provides a window into policies and events in China. Issues are thematic and compiled by guest editors; recent topics have included eldercare issues in contemporary China, and explorations of Chinese anthropology. Many articles represent first- and secondhand accounts of incidents, while others report on historical events. Recommended for academic libraries with programs in sociology and anthropology.

6083. *Comparative Sociology.* Formerly (until 2001): *International Journal of Comparative Sociology.* [ISSN: 1569-1322] 1960. q. EUR 215 print & online eds. (Individuals, EUR 105 print & online eds.). Ed(s): Masamichi Sasaki. Brill Academic Publishers, Inc., PO Box 9000, Leiden, 2300 PA, Netherlands; cs@brill.nl; http://www.brill.nl. Illus., adv. Refereed. Vol. ends: Nov. Microform: SWZ. Online: EBSCO Publishing; Gale Group; Ingenta Select; Northern Light Technology, Inc.; OCLC Online Computer Library Center, Inc. Reprint: SWZ. *Indexed:* ABCPolSci, AICP, ASSIA, AgeL, ArtHuCI, BAS, CJA, IBSS, IBZ, IPSA, PSA, RI-1, SSCI, SSI, SWA, SociolAb. *Bk. rev.:* 4-6, signed. *Aud.:* AC.

This international journal publishes studies of different cultures on a comparative basis. Sample topics include race, religion, and caste; transition to capitalism in Russia and China; and historical roots of immigration and integration. There are some special issues; recently, on human values and social change. Because of the diverse nature of the content, this is highly recommended for academic libraries supporting sociology, anthropology, or political science progams.

6084. *Contemporary Sociology.* [ISSN: 0094-3061] 1972. bi-m. USD 160 (Individuals, USD 80; Members, USD 35). Ed(s): JoAnn Miller, Robert Perrucci. American Sociological Association, 1307 New York Ave, N W, Ste 700, Washington, DC 20005-4701; http://www.umass.edu/sociol/consoc/consoc.html. Illus., index, adv. Refereed. Circ: 7200. Vol. ends: Nov. Microform: PQC. Online: Gale Group; Ingenta Select; JSTOR (Web-based Journal Archive); OCLC Online Computer Library Center, Inc.; ProQuest Information & Learning. Reprint: PQC. *Indexed:* ABS&EES, ArtHuCI, BRD, BRI, CBRI, IBSS, IBZ, PSA, RI-1, SSCI, SSI, SociolAb. *Bk. rev.:* 50-60, signed. *Aud.:* Ac.

This journal contains a collection of in-depth reviews of books on sociology, social welfare, and social policy issues. The journal is divided into a symposia section on a particular theme, several review essays, and a collection of signed reviews in a variety of subject areas. Recent themes are books on German feminist politics, and utopian visions. A commentary section includes responses from readers or authors. The November issue contains an index for materials reviewed throughout the year. Reviewers are selected from various universities and research institutions; unsolicited reviews are not accepted. A valuable addition to the collection of academic libraries.

6085. *Critical Horizons: journal of social and critical theory.* [ISSN: 1440-9917] 2000. a. EUR 85 print & online eds. (Individuals, EUR 33 print & online eds.). Ed(s): John Rundell. Brill Academic Publishers, Inc., PO Box 9000, Leiden, 2300 PA, Netherlands; cs@brill.nl; http://www.brill.nl. Adv. Sample. Refereed. *Indexed:* PSA, SociolAb. *Aud.:* Ac.

This journal aims to explore the human condition of critical thought by "actively promoting debate across established boundaries and beyond established traditions." Articles are a mixture of philosophical and sociological conceptual explorations, with some issues centering around a common theme. Recent issues contain articles based on such themes as the concept of modernity and civilization, and conceptualization of the "other" from philosophical, critical, and postcolonial theories. Recommended for academic libraries with graduate programs in sociology and philosophy.

6086. *Critical Sociology.* Formerly: *Insurgent Sociologist.* [ISSN: 0896-9205] 1969. 3x/yr. EUR 109 print & online eds. (Individuals, EUR 43 print & online eds.). Ed(s): David Fasenfest. Brill Academic Publishers, Inc., 112 Water St, Ste 400, Boston, MA 02109; cs@brillusa.com; http://www..brill.nl/ejournals/ejournals.html. Illus., adv. Refereed. Circ: 850. Microform: PQC. Online: EBSCO Publishing; Ingenta Select; OCLC Online Computer Library Center, Inc.; Swets Blackwell. *Indexed:* AltPI, BAS, CJA, IBSS, PSA, SWA, SociolAb. *Bk. rev.:* 4-6, signed. *Aud.:* Ac.

This journal publishes articles with a critical perspective on the capitalist system. The intent is to provide nontraditional treatments of traditional themes: "It has published work mainly within the broadest boundaries of the Marxist tradition, although it has also been home to post-modern, feminist, and other radical arguments." There are occasional thematic issues, recently covering critical race and ethnic studies. Provision of alternative points of view makes this a recommended title for academic libraries supporting sociology and political science curricula.

6087. *Current Sociology.* [ISSN: 0011-3921] 1952. bi-m. GBP 390 in Europe, Middle East, Africa & Australasia. Ed(s): Dennis Smith. Sage Publications Ltd., 6 Bonhill St, London, EC2A 4PU, United Kingdom; info@sagepub.co.uk; http://www.sagepub.co.uk/. Illus., adv. Sample. Refereed. Circ: 2000. Vol. ends: Oct. *Indexed:* ASSIA, HRA, IBSS, IBZ, IPSA, PAIS, PSA, PsycholAb, RiskAb, SSCI, SSI, SociolAb, SportS, WAE&RSA. *Bk. rev.:* Number and length vary. *Aud.:* Ac.

A publication of the International Sociological Association, this journal focuses on theoretical research on current topics of interest to the international community of sociologists. Abstracts are published in English, French, and Spanish. Beginning in 2003, book reviews were added, and two monograph issues per year are published. With an international editorial board and broad contributions from the sociological community, this journal makes a significant contribution to the field of sociological theory. Recommended for academic libraries with programs in sociology.

6088. ***Deviant Behavior.*** [ISSN: 0163-9625] 1979. bi-m. USD 405 (Individuals, USD 159). Ed(s): Craig J Forsyth. Taylor & Francis Inc, 325 Chestnut St, Suite 800, Philadelphia, PA 19016; info@taylorandfrancis.com; http://www.taylorandfrancis.com/. Illus., adv. Sample. Refereed. Circ: 300. Microform: PQC. Online: EBSCO Publishing; Ingenta Select; OCLC Online Computer Library Center, Inc.; RoweCom Information Quest; Swets Blackwell. Reprint: PQC; PSC. *Indexed:* AbAn, ArtHuCI, BiolAb, CJA, PRA, PsycholAb, RiskAb, SFSA, SSCI, SUSA, SociolAb. *Bk. rev.:* 1-2, signed. *Aud.:* Ac, Sa.

This international journal covers the area of deviance through its publication of refereed theoretical, descriptive, methodological, and applied papers. Recent topics include exploration of the relationship between adolescent drinking and violence, religiosity and perceptions of crime seriousness, and playful deviance as an urban leisure activity. This journal has a broad appeal to sociologists, criminologists, psychologists, and social workers, among others. Its in-depth and varied subject coverage makes it a valuable addition to all academic libraries and to special libraries serving social services clientele.

6089. ***Economy and Society.*** [ISSN: 0308-5147] 1972. q. GBP 197 (Individuals, GBP 60). Ed(s): Nikolas Rose. Routledge, 11 New Fetter Ln, London, EC4P 4EE, United Kingdom; info@routledge.co.uk; http://www.routledge.co.uk. Illus., index, adv. Sample. Refereed. Circ: 1300. Vol. ends: Nov. Microform: PQC. Online: EBSCO Publishing; Gale Group; Ingenta Select; OCLC Online Computer Library Center, Inc.; RoweCom Information Quest; Swets Blackwell. Reprint: PQC; PSC. *Indexed:* AltPI, ArtHuCI, BAS, CJA, IBSS, IBZ, IPSA, JEL, PSA, RI-1, SSCI, SSI, SWA, SociolAb. *Bk. rev.:* 1-2, signed. *Aud.:* Ac.

This publication covers questions "ranging from economic governance to developments in the life sciences and beyond, and publishes major new work on current issues confronting progressive politics throughout Europe and North America, Australasia and the Pacific Rim." There are occasional thematic issues, recently covering such topics as contemporary feminism's concern with the political, and the technological economy. There are one or two extensive review articles at the end of most issues. Recommended for academic libraries with graduate programs in sociology, economics, or political science.

Ethnic and Racial Studies. See Ethnic Studies section.

6090. ***European Journal of Social Theory.*** [ISSN: 1368-4310] 1998. q. GBP 336 in Europe, Middle East, Africa & Australasia. Ed(s): Gerard Delanty. Sage Publications Ltd., 6 Bonhill St, London, EC2A 4PU, United Kingdom; info@sagepub.co.uk; http://www.sagepub.co.uk/. Illus., index, adv. Sample. Refereed. Vol. ends: Nov. *Indexed:* IBSS, IBZ, IPSA, PSA, SociolAb. *Bk. rev.:* 2-4, signed. *Aud.:* Ac.

This journal provides a worldwide forum for contemporary social thought by reflecting the commonalities in European social theory. Its transnational and multidisciplinary approach is supported by an international editorial board. Issues include a viewpoints section inviting debate on covered topics. Some issues are thematic; recent coverage has been on a variety of topics surrounding development of an E.U. cultural identity. Recommended for academic libraries with graduate programs in sociological, political science, and international studies.

6091. ***European Journal of Sociology.*** [ISSN: 0003-9756] 1960. 3x/yr. USD 158 (Individuals, USD 59). Ed(s): Jon Elster, Christopher Hann. Cambridge University Press, The Edinburgh Bldg, Shaftesbury Rd, Cambridge, CB2 2RU, United Kingdom; information@cambridge.org; http://uk.cambridge.org/journals. Illus., index, adv. Refereed. Vol. ends: Nov. Microform: PQC. Reprint: SWZ. *Indexed:* ASSIA, ArtHuCI, BAS, IBSS, IBZ, IPSA, PAIS, PSA, RI-1, SSCI, SSI, SociolAb, WAE&RSA. *Aud.:* Ac.

This journal provides broad international coverage of sociology topics, with articles published in French, English, or German. Special emphasis is given to the processes of change in Eastern Europe, as well as to the various expressions of ethnicity and nationalism. Some issues are thematic, recently covering mysticism and ascetism, and priorities of social justice. Recommended for academic libraries with doctoral programs in the social sciences.

6092. ***European Societies.*** [ISSN: 1461-6696] 1999. q. GBP 212 (Individuals, GBP 83). Ed(s): Thomas P Boje. Routledge, 11 New Fetter Ln, London, EC4P 4EE, United Kingdom. Adv. Refereed. Online: EBSCO Publishing; Ingenta Select; RoweCom Information Quest; Swets Blackwell. Reprint: PSC. *Indexed:* PSA, SociolAb. *Bk. rev.:* 4-6, signed. *Aud.:* Ac.

Published by the European Sociological Association, this journal publishes research on Europe rather than research by Europeans. The journal aims to cover "social theory and analysis on three levels: the European level itself, comparative research on Europe, and Europe in international perspective." The intended audience is sociologists, economists, political scientists, and social policy analysts. Sample recent articles cover the sociology of the euro, economic sociology in France, a comparison of class in the new democracies in Europe with Western democracies, and the Russian labor market. Recommended for academic libraries with programs in sociology.

6093. ***European Sociological Review.*** [ISSN: 0266-7215] 1985. 5x/yr. GBP 190. Ed(s): Hans-Peter Blossfeld. Oxford University Press, Great Clarendon St, Oxford, OX2 6DP, United Kingdom; jnl.orders@oup.co.uk; http://www3.oup.co.uk/jnls. Illus., adv. Sample. Refereed. Circ: 750. Vol. ends: Dec. Online: Chadwyck-Healey Incorporated; EBSCO Publishing; HighWire Press; ingenta.com; JSTOR (Web-based Journal Archive); OCLC Online Computer Library Center, Inc.; RoweCom Information Quest; Swets Blackwell. Reprint: PSC. *Indexed:* ASSIA, CJA, IBSS, IPSA, PSA, SSCI, SWA, SociolAb. *Bk. rev.:* 5-7, signed. *Aud.:* Ac.

Published in association with the European Consortium for Sociological Research, this journal covers international research studies in all fields of sociology, with major emphasis on western European countries. Recent articles cover intermarriage between Turks and Kurds in contemporary Turkey, job mobility and earnings growth based on data from Sweden, and inequalities of education in Germany. Recommended for academic libraries with graduate programs in sociology.

6094. ***Evaluation: international journal of theory, research and practice.*** [ISSN: 1356-3890] 1995. q. GBP 280 in Europe, Middle East, Africa & Australasia. Ed(s): Elliot Stern. Sage Publications Ltd., 6 Bonhill St, London, EC2A 4PU, United Kingdom; info@sagepub.co.uk; http://www.sagepub.co.uk/. Illus., index, adv. Sample. Refereed. Vol. ends: Oct. *Indexed:* ASSIA, CJA, HRA, IBSS, PRA, PSA, SociolAb. *Bk. rev.:* 1-2, signed. *Aud.:* Ac.

Published on behalf of the Tavistock Institute, this journal "encourages dialogue between different evaluation traditions such as program evaluation, technology assessment, auditing, value-added studies, policy evaluation and quality assessment." Research has a broad scope, covering evaluation of such areas as regional development policies, social and education programs, health technologies, and international development projects, as well as teaching evaluation. Abstracts in French are included. Regular features are a section on visits to the world of practice and news from the community. Recommended for academic libraries with graduate programs in sociology or economics.

6095. ***Evaluation Review: a journal of applied social research.*** Formerly (until vol.4, Feb. 1980): *Evaluation Quarterly.* [ISSN: 0193-841X] 1977. bi-m. GBP 406 in Europe, Middle East, Africa & Australasia. Ed(s): Richard A Berk. Sage Publications, Inc., 2455 Teller Rd, Thousand Oaks, CA 91320; info@sagepub.com; http://www.sagepub.com. Illus., index, adv. Sample. Refereed. Circ: 1600. Vol. ends: Dec. Microform: PQC.

Online: Gale Group; ingenta.com; OCLC Online Computer Library Center, Inc.; ProQuest Information & Learning; RoweCom Information Quest; Swets Blackwell. *Indexed:* AgeL, CIJE, CJA, CLI, HRA, IBSS, LRI, PAIS, PsycholAb, SFSA, SSCI, SSI, SWR&A, SociolAb, WAE&RSA. *Aud.:* Ac, Sa.

This journal publishes discussion of methodological and state-of-the-art developments relating to applied evaluation. Recent topics include the assessment of effects of school-based intervention on unscheduled transfers of elementary school children, characteristics of parents in an adolescent lifestyle choice study, and examining the impact of external influences on police use of deadly force over time. Of interest to sociologists, policy makers, and political scientists, it is recommended for academic libraries with graduate programs in these fields.

6096. ***Global Social Policy: an interdisciplinary journal of public policy and social development.*** [ISSN: 1468-0181] 2001. 3x/yr. GBP 219 in Europe, Middle East, Africa & Australasia. Ed(s): Bob Deacon. Sage Publications Ltd., 6 Bonhill St, London, EC2A 4PU, United Kingdom; info@sagepub.co.uk; http://www.sagepub.co.uk/. Refereed. Online: ingenta.com; RoweCom Information Quest; Swets Blackwell. *Indexed:* PSA, SociolAb. *Bk. rev.:* 6-8, signed. *Aud.:* Ac.

This new interdisciplinary journal "analyzes the contribution of a range of international actors to global social policy discourse and practice and encourages discussion of the implications for social welfare of the dynamics of the global economy." Each issue contains a social policy forum: In the first issue, individuals from a range of international organizations and social movements responded to the question of the most important global governance reforms that would lead to securing greater global justice. Articles have been written on economic and social ideas within the United Nations, social policy in Chile, pension reform in China, and social welfare in Lebanon. Due to its broad coverage, this journal is highly recommended for all academic libraries.

6097. ***Group & Organization Management: an international journal.*** Formerly (until Mar. 1992): *Group and Organization Studies.* [ISSN: 1059-6011] 1976. bi-m. GBP 427 in Europe, Middle East, Africa & Australasia. Ed(s): Alison M Konrad. Sage Publications, Inc., 2455 Teller Rd, Thousand Oaks, CA 91320; info@sagepub.com; http://www.sagepub.com. Illus., index, adv. Sample. Refereed. Circ: 1300. Vol. ends: Dec. Microform: PQC. Online: EBSCO Publishing; Florida Center for Library Automation; Gale Group; ingenta.com; OCLC Online Computer Library Center, Inc.; ProQuest Information & Learning; RoweCom Information Quest; Swets Blackwell. Reprint: PQC. *Indexed:* ABIn, CIJE, CINAHL, CommAb, ErgAb, HRA, IMFL, PsycholAb, SFSA, SSCI, SWA. *Aud.:* Ac, Sa.

Published in cooperation with the Eastern Academy of Management, this journal focuses on research and evaluation of human resources management and group studies. Some issues are thematic; recently, defining the domain of workplace-diversity scholarship, with articles on applying innovation strategy in racially diverse workforces, gender demography and organization performance, and user needs assessment to resolve controversies in diversity training design. Recommended for academic libraries, special libraries serving management clientele, and public libraries with a strong business collection.

6098. ***Group Processes & Intergroup Relations.*** [ISSN: 1368-4302] 1998. q. GBP 284 in Europe, Middle East, Africa & Australasia. Ed(s): Dominic Abrams, Michael Hogg. Sage Publications Ltd., 6 Bonhill St, London, EC2A 4PU, United Kingdom; info@sagepub.co.uk; http://www.sagepub.co.uk/. Adv. Refereed. Circ: 900. *Indexed:* SociolAb. *Aud.:* Ac.

This publication will be of interest to social psychologists as well as sociologists; its focus is research on group and intergroup relations. There are occasional thematic issues; recently covering intergroup contact, with articles on ethnic prejudice, fostering meaningful racial engagement through intergroup dialogues, and a longitudinal study on the effects of ingroup and outgroup friendships on ethnic attitudes in college. Recommended for academic libraries with sociology and psychology programs.

6099. ***Human Relations: towards the integration of the social sciences.*** [ISSN: 0018-7267] 1947. m. GBP 702 in Europe, Middle East, Africa & Australasia. Ed(s): Paul Willman. Sage Publications Ltd., 6 Bonhill St, London, EC2A 4PU, United Kingdom; info@sagepub.co.uk; http://www.sagepub.co.uk/. Illus., index, adv. Sample. Refereed. Circ: 2000. Vol. ends: Dec. Microform: PQC. Online: EBSCO Publishing; Gale Group; ingenta.com; Kluwer Online; Northern Light Technology, Inc.; OCLC Online Computer Library Center, Inc.; Ovid Technologies, Inc.; ProQuest Information & Learning; RoweCom Information Quest; Swets Blackwell. *Indexed:* ABIn, AICP, ASSIA, AbAn, AgeL, ArtHuCI, BPI, CINAHL, CJA, CommAb, ErgAb, HRA, IBSS, IMFL, PAIS, PRA, PSA, PsycholAb, SSCI, SSI, SWA, SociolAb. *Bk. rev.:* 1-2, signed. *Aud.:* Ac.

This international journal provides an interdisciplinary forum for research on issues crossing the entire range of the social sciences, with a strong management focus. Sample topics include organization and management theory, ethical choice in managerial work, and the role of privatization in shaping characteristics of managers. Sponsored by the Tavistock Institute of London, this journal is recommended for academic libraries with social sciences and business collections.

6100. ***Indicators (Armonk): the journal of social health.*** [ISSN: 1535-7449] 2002. q. USD 220 includes online access (Individuals, USD 50). Ed(s): Jeffrey Madrick. M.E. Sharpe, Inc., 80 Business Park Dr, Armonk, NY 10504; mesinfo@usa.net; http://www.mesharpe.com. Reprint: PSC. *Aud.:* Ac.

This new journal is dedicated to "developing and analyzing a comprehensive set of measures of the well-being of the United States and other countries, in order to help develop policies that can improve the true standard of living for all." Articles cover topics such as sustainability and quality-of-life indicators, polling indicators about civil liberties in time of war, the challenge of measuring earnings mobility, and infant mortality rates. Articles cover current as well as historical indexes. Highly recommended for all academic libraries.

International Journal of Comparative Sociology. See *Comparative Sociology.*

6101. ***International Journal of Contemporary Sociology: a discussion journal of contemporary ideas and research.*** Formerly: *Indian Sociological Bulletin.* [ISSN: 0019-6398] 1963. s-a. USD 60 (Individuals, USD 35; Students, USD 25). Ed(s): Raj P Mohan. Joensuu University Press, c/o Professor M'hammed Sabour, Dept of Sociology, PL 111, Joensuu, 80101, Finland; mhammed.sabour@joensuu.fi; http://www.joensuu.fi. Illus., adv. Refereed. Circ: 200 Paid. Vol. ends: Oct. Microform: PQC. Reprint: PQC. *Indexed:* ASSIA, CJA, IBZ, IPSA, PSA, SSCI, SociolAb. *Bk. rev.:* 2-4, signed. *Aud.:* Ac.

This journal provides a forum for the international exchange of ideas from researchers in all areas of sociology. Theoretical as well as practical applications of the principles of sociology are covered; the international focus makes this a particularly useful source. Recent articles cover topics in China, Rwanda, Nigeria, Afghanistan, and Iran, as well as several European countries. Some issues are thematic; recent coverage is of genocide and society. Recommended for academic libraries with graduate programs in sociology.

6102. ***International Journal of Sociology.*** Formerly (until 1971): *Eastern European Studies in Sociology and Anthropology.* [ISSN: 0020-7659] 1971. q. USD 198 (Individuals, USD 140). Ed(s): Tadeusz Krauze, Jr. M.E. Sharpe, Inc., 80 Business Park Dr, Armonk, NY 10504; custserv@mesharpe.com; http://www.mesharpe.com. Illus., adv. Sample. Refereed. Vol. ends: Dec. Reprint: PSC. *Indexed:* ASSIA, AnthLit, BAS, IPSA, PAIS, PSA, RiskAb, SSI, SWA, SociolAb. *Aud.:* Ac.

This international journal publishes translations of sociological research from non–English-speaking societies around the world. Most issues are thematic; recent issues cover psychosocial aspects of radical systemic change in Poland, and union disruption in the United States, Canada, and the United States, with statistics available for many countries. Recommended for academic libraries with graduate programs in sociology and political science.

6103. *International Journal of the Sociology of Law.* Formerly (until vol.7, 1979): *International Journal of Criminology and Penology.* [ISSN: 0194-6595] 1972. q. EUR 345 (Individuals, EUR 90). Ed(s): S Savage, J Carrier. Academic Press, Harcourt Pl, 32 Jamestown Rd, London, NW1 7BY, United Kingdom; apsubs@acad.com; http://www.elsevier-international.com/serials/. Illus., index, adv. Sample. Refereed. Online: EBSCO Publishing; Gale Group; ingenta.com; OCLC Online Computer Library Center, Inc.; RoweCom Information Quest; ScienceDirect; Swets Blackwell. Reprint: SWZ. *Indexed:* ASSIA, CJA, CJPI, CLI, IBSS, ILP, LRI, PSA, PsycholAb, RiskAb, SSCI, SSI, SociolAb. *Bk. rev.:* 4-7, signed. *Aud.:* Ac, Sa.

This journal publishes research on all areas of sociolegal study, including antidiscrimination law, police powers, criminal law, international law, legal reform, the prosecution process, sentencing, and immigration law. There are research articles as well as contributions from practitioners in the legal process and law enforcement fields. The opportunity to compare legal processes between countries will be of interest to academic libraries with doctoral programs in sociology, political science, and law.

6104. *International Sociology.* [ISSN: 0268-5809] 1986. q. GBP 247 print & online eds. in Europe, Middle East, Africa & Australasia. Ed(s): Said Amir Arjomand. Sage Publications Ltd., 6 Bonhill St, London, EC2A 4PU, United Kingdom; info@sagepub.co.uk; http://www.sagepub.co.uk/. Illus., index, adv. Sample. Refereed. Circ: 3900. Vol. ends: Dec. Online: ingenta.com; OCLC Online Computer Library Center, Inc.; RoweCom Information Quest; Sage Publications, Inc.; Swets Blackwell. Reprint: PSC. *Indexed:* ABS&EES, ASSIA, BAS, CJA, HRA, IBSS, IBZ, IPSA, PAIS, PSA, RiskAb, SCI, SFSA, SSCI, SociolAb. *Bk. rev.:* 2-4, signed. *Aud.:* Ac.

This journal of the International Sociological Association includes studies in the areas of social organization, societal change, and comparative sociology. Articles are published in English; the back of each issue contains abstracts in French and Spanish. One of the four annual issues is focused on a significant theme in international sociology such as, recently, on national sociological associations. Recommended for academic libraries with graduate programs in sociology.

6105. *Journal of Classical Sociology.* [ISSN: 1468-795X] 2001. 3x/yr. GBP 219 print & online eds. in Europe, Middle East, Africa & Australasia. Ed(s): Bryan Turner, John O'Neill. Sage Publications Ltd., 6 Bonhill St, London, EC2A 4PU, United Kingdom; info@sagepub.co.uk; http://www.sagepub.co.uk/. Adv. Refereed. Online: ingenta.com; OCLC Online Computer Library Center, Inc.; Swets Blackwell. *Indexed:* SociolAb. *Aud.:* Ac.

This new journal focuses on international contributions to the study of classical sociology. It "elucidates the origins of sociology and also demonstrates how the classical tradition renews the sociological imagination in the present day." Recent articles have been written on the works of J.K. Galbraith, Max Weber, Pierre Bourdieu, and Emile Durkheim. Recommended for academic libraries with programs in sociology.

Journal of Comparative Family Studies. See Family and Marriage section.

Journal of Divorce & Remarriage. See Family and Marriage section.

6106. *Journal of European Social Policy.* [ISSN: 0958-9287] 1991. q. GBP 309 print & online eds. in Europe, Middle East, Africa & Australasia. Ed(s): Graham Room. Sage Publications Ltd., 6 Bonhill St, London, EC2A 4PU, United Kingdom; info@sagepub.co.uk; http://www.sagepub.co.uk/. Adv. Refereed. Circ: 400. *Indexed:* ASSIA, AgeL, GeogAbPG, HRA, IBSS, PRA, PSA, SFSA, SSCI, SWA, SociolAb. *Bk. rev.:* 4-6, signed. *Aud.:* Ac.

This journal publishes analysis of European social policy issues, including aging, benefits, family policy, gender, health care, international organizations, migration, poverty, professional mobility, unemployment, and the voluntary sector. In addition to articles, there are debates, a European briefing section, and a digest section covering the latest European legislation and research. Recommended for academic libraries with programs in sociology.

Journal of Family Issues. See Family and Marriage section.

6107. *Journal of Health and Social Behavior.* Formerly (until 1967): *Journal of Health and Human Behavior.* [ISSN: 0022-1465] 1960. q. USD 140 non-members (Individuals, USD 70 non-members; Members, USD 30). Ed(s): Michael Hughes. American Sociological Association, 1307 New York Ave, N W, Ste 700, Washington, DC 20005-4701; publications@asanet.org; http://www.asanet.org. Illus., index, adv. Refereed. Circ: 3500 Paid. Vol. ends: Dec. Microform: MIM; PQC. Online: Gale Group; Ingenta Select; JSTOR (Web-based Journal Archive); OCLC Online Computer Library Center, Inc.; ProQuest Information & Learning. Reprint: PQC. *Indexed:* ASSIA, AbAn, AgeL, BiolAb, CJA, ExcerpMed, IBZ, IndMed, PEI, PsycholAb, RiskAb, SSCI, SSI, SWR&A, SociolAb. *Aud.:* Ac, Sa.

This publication of the American Sociological Association applies sociological concepts to the fields of health, illness, and medicine, favoring articles that build on the knowledge of medical sociology. There are occasional special issues, recently on selecting outcomes for the sociology of mental health. Recommended for academic libraries with programs in sociology and the health sciences, and for medical libraries.

6108. *Journal of Health & Social Policy.* [ISSN: 0897-7186] 1989. q. USD 425 domestic; USD 573.75 domestic; USD 616.25 domestic. Ed(s): Marvin D Feit. Haworth Press, Inc., 10 Alice St, Binghamton, NY 13904-1580; getinfo@haworthpressinc.com; http://www.haworthpressinc.com. Illus., adv. Sample. Refereed. Circ: 172 Paid. Microform: PQC. Reprint: HAW. *Indexed:* ASG, AbAn, ExcerpMed, H&SSA, IBZ, IMFL, IPSA, PAIS, PEI, PSA, PsycholAb, RRTA, RiskAb, SUSA, SWR&A, SociolAb, WAE&RSA. *Bk. rev.:* 1-2, signed. *Aud.:* Ac, Sa.

Articles in this journal focus on a variety of health care issues for social service practitioners. Some issues are thematic and can be purchased separately, a recent issue titled "Evaluation Research in Child Welfare." Coverage is international; recent articles cover on malaria control programs in the Third World and sexual harassment in Turkey. Recommended for academic libraries with graduate programs in social work or the health professions and special libraries serving social services clientele.

6109. *Journal of Historical Sociology.* [ISSN: 0952-1909] 1988. q. GBP 257 print & online eds. Blackwell Publishing Ltd., 9600 Garsington Rd, PO Box 805, Oxford, OX4 2DQ, United Kingdom; customerservices@oxon.blackwellpublishing.com; http://www.blackwellpublishing.com/. Refereed. Online: EBSCO Publishing; Gale Group; ingenta.com; OCLC Online Computer Library Center, Inc.; RoweCom Information Quest; Swets Blackwell. Reprint: PQC; SWZ. *Indexed:* AICP, AmH&L, ArtHuCI, BrHumI, CJA, IBSS, PSA, SSCI, SWA, SociolAb. *Aud.:* Ac.

Edited by an international panel of historians, anthropologists, geographers, and sociologists, this journal provides interdisciplinary coverage of a broad spectrum of social sciences topics. As well as refereed articles, the journal presents review essays and commentary in its "Issues and Agendas" section. Recent topics include a history of urban space and politico-economic systems; recent approaches to the history of voluntary welfare; race and political formations of English Chesapeake colonies; and the social, political, and cultural dynamics of the English state. Recommended for academic libraries with programs in sociology.

Journal of Homosexuality. See Lesbian, Gay, Bisexual, and Transgender section.

Journal of Human Resources. See Management, Administration, and Human Resources/Human Resources section.

6110. ***Journal of Leisure Research.*** [ISSN: 0022-2216] 1968. q. USD 60 (Members, USD 25; Non-members, UZS 40). Ed(s): David Scott. National Recreation and Park Association, 22377 Belmont Ridge Rd, Ashburn, VA 20148-4501. Illus., index, adv. Refereed. Microform: PQC. Online: bigchalk; EBSCO Publishing; Florida Center for Library Automation; Gale Group; Northern Light Technology, Inc.; OCLC Online Computer Library Center, Inc.; ProQuest Information & Learning; H.W. Wilson. Reprint: PQC; PSC. *Indexed:* ASSIA, AgeL, CIJE, CJA, CommAb, ForAb, H&SSA, IBSS, IMFL, MagInd, PEI, PollutAb, PsycholAb, RRTA, RiskAb, S&F, SSCI, SSI, SportS, WAE&RSA. *Aud.:* Ac.

This journal is published by the National Recreation and Park Association in cooperation with Texas A&M University. Focus is on original investigations contributing knowledge directly to the field of leisure studies. Sample topics include research on women and leisure, emotion and stress in leisure sport activities, and work-leisure relations. Recommended for academic libraries with programs in sociology or physical education.

Journal of Marriage and Family. See Family and Marriage section.

6111. ***Journal of Mathematical Sociology.*** [ISSN: 0022-250X] 1971. q. GBP 781 (Individuals, GBP 277). Ed(s): Patrick Doreian. Taylor & Francis Ltd, 11 New Fetter Ln, London, EC4P 4EE, United Kingdom; http://www.tandf.co.uk/. Illus., index, adv. Sample. Refereed. Online: EBSCO Publishing; OCLC Online Computer Library Center, Inc. Reprint: PSC. *Indexed:* CJA, IBSS, PsycholAb, SSCI, SociolAb. *Aud.:* Ac.

This journal publishes articles in all areas of mathematical sociology as well as those of joint interest to sociologists and other social and behavioral scientists. Articles deal primarily with "the use of mathematical models in social science, the logic of measurement, computers and computer programming, applied mathematics, statistics, or quantitative methodology." Recent articles cover interpersonal influence and attitude change toward conformity in small groups, a Boolean model of role discrimination, and historical evolution and mathematical models. Recommended for academic libraries with doctoral programs in sociology.

6112. ***The Journal of Peasant Studies.*** [ISSN: 0306-6150] 1973. q. GBP 252 print & online eds. Ed(s): Tom Brass. Frank Cass Publishers, Crown House, 47 Chase Side, Southgate, London, N14 5BP, United Kingdom; jnlsubs@frankcass.com; http://www.frankcass.com/jnls/. Illus., index, adv. Sample. Refereed. Microform: PQC. Online: Ingenta Select. *Indexed:* AICP, AbAn, AmH&L, AnthLit, ArtHuCI, BAS, BrHumI, DSA, FPA, ForAb, GeogAbPG, IBSS, IBZ, IPSA, PAIS, PSA, RRTA, S&F, SSCI, SWA, SociolAb, WAE&RSA. *Bk. rev.:* 1-2, signed. *Aud.:* Ac.

This journal publishes research on the political economy of agrarian change. In a section titled "Peasants Speak," various peasant movements are explored. There are occasional thematic issues, recently on Latin American peasants. Recommended for academic libraries with graduate or doctoral programs in sociology, anthropology, history, or political science.

6113. ***Journal of Political and Military Sociology: an international interdisciplinary and semi-annual publication.*** [ISSN: 0047-2697] 1973. s-a. USD 44 (Individuals, USD 30; Students, USD 20). Ed(s): George A Kourvetaris. J P M S, c/o Dept. of Sociology, Northern Illinois University, Dekalb, IL 60115; tkogak1@coin.cso.niu.edu; http://www.JPMS.niu.edu. Illus., index, adv. Sample. Refereed. Circ: 2000. Microform: PQC. Online: EBSCO Publishing; OCLC Online Computer Library Center, Inc.; ProQuest Information & Learning. Reprint: PQC; SCH. *Indexed:* ABCPolSci, ABS&EES, AUNI, AmH&L, BAS, CJA, HRA, IPSA, PAIS, PRA, PSA, RI-1, SSCI, SociolAb. *Bk. rev.:* 8-10, signed. *Aud.:* Ac.

This journal publishes research in the area of political and military sociology. "Politics" and "military" are broadly defined as "strategic institutions and power structures that command major economic and non-economic societal resources." Some issues are thematic, with guest editors. Recent article topics include the Armenian genocide in official Turkish records, an exploration of the political role of intellectuals in Western societies, and linkages between sociometric modernization and national political development. Recommended for academic libraries supporting graduate programs in sociology, political science, or military science.

6114. ***Journal of Rural Studies.*** [ISSN: 0743-0167] 1985. q. EUR 585. Ed(s): Paul Cloke. Pergamon, The Boulevard, Langford Ln, East Park, Kidlington, OX5 1GB, United Kingdom. Illus., index, adv. Sample. Refereed. Vol. ends: Oct. Microform: PQC. Online: Gale Group; ingenta.com; ScienceDirect; Swets Blackwell. *Indexed:* AgeL, ArtHuCI, CIJE, CJA, DSA, EnvAb, FPA, ForAb, GeogAbPG, HortAb, IBSS, IndVet, PAIS, PSA, RRTA, RiskAb, S&F, SSCI, SSI, SWA, SociolAb, VetBull, WAE&RSA. *Bk. rev.:* 10-15, signed. *Aud.:* Ac.

This journal publishes research relating to such rural issues as society, demography, housing, employment, transport, services, land use, recreation, agriculture, and conservation. International and interdisciplinary in scope, the journal gives particular emphasis to planning policy and management issues. Topics include economic hardship, religion, and mental health during the Midwestern farm crisis; digital development in rural areas; and unemployment and employability in remote rural labor markets. Recommended for academic libraries with doctoral programs in sociology.

6115. ***Journal of Sex Research.*** [ISSN: 0022-4499] 1965. q. USD 158 (Individuals, USD 99). Ed(s): John D DeLamater. Society for the Scientific Study of Sexuality, PO Box 416, Allentown, PA 18105; http://www.sexscience.org. Illus., adv. Refereed. Circ: 1750. Vol. ends: Nov. Microform: PQC. Online: EBSCO Publishing; Florida Center for Library Automation; Gale Group; Northern Light Technology, Inc.; OCLC Online Computer Library Center, Inc.; ProQuest Information & Learning; H.W. Wilson. Reprint: PQC; SWZ. *Indexed:* ASSIA, AbAn, AgeL, ArtHuCI, BAS, CJA, CommAb, ExcerpMed, IBZ, IMFL, PsycholAb, SFSA, SSCI, SSI, SWA, SWR&A, SociolAb. *Bk. rev.:* 4-6, signed. *Aud.:* Ac.

A publication of the Society for the Scientific Study of Sexuality, this journal is designed to "stimulate research and to promote an interdisciplinary understanding of the diverse topics in contemporary sexual science." It has an extensive editorial advisory board. Some issues are thematic; a recent focus is a review of the literature on promoting sexual health and responsible sexual behavior. Recommended for academic libraries with social sciences programs, especially those supporting research in human sexuality.

6116. ***Journal of Social Issues.*** [ISSN: 0022-4537] 1944. q. USD 449 print & online eds. Ed(s): Irene Hanson Frieze. Blackwell Publishing, Inc., Commerce Place, 350 Main St, Malden, MA 02148; subscrip@blackwellpub.com; http://www.blackwellpublishing.com. Illus., adv. Sample. Refereed. Vol. ends: Winter. Microform: PMC; PQC. Online: EBSCO Publishing; Florida Center for Library Automation; Gale Group; ingenta.com; OCLC Online Computer Library Center, Inc.; RoweCom Information Quest; Swets Blackwell. *Indexed:* ABCPolSci, ASSIA, AbAn, AgeL, BAS, CIJE, CJA, CommAb, GeogAbPG, IBSS, IMFL, IPSA, LRI, PAIS, PRA, PSA, PsycholAb, RI-1, RiskAb, SFSA, SSCI, SSI, SUSA, SWA, SWR&A, SociolAb. *Aud.:* Ga, Ac.

This interdisciplinary journal is published for the Society for the Psychological Study of Social Issues, a division of the American Psychological Association. It "brings behavioral and social science theory, empirical evidence, and practice to bear on human problems." Volumes are thematic; recent issues cover international perspectives on the well-being of older adults, and theoretial approaches and educational initiatives for community involvement. Unsolicited manuscripts are not accepted. A subscription includes the online journal *Analyses of Social Issues and Public Policy*. With its broad subject coverage, this journal is highly recommended for all academic libraries and larger public libraries.

New Statesman. See News and Opinion section.

6117. ***Nonprofit and Voluntary Sector Quarterly.*** [ISSN: 0899-7640] 1971. q. USD 330 print & online eds. Ed(s): Steven Rathgeb Smith. Sage Publications, Inc., 2455 Teller Rd, Thousand Oaks, CA 91320;

info@sagepub.com; http://www.sagepub.com. Illus., index. Sample. Refereed. Circ: 800. Vol. ends: Dec. Microform: PQC. Online: EBSCO Publishing; ingenta.com; OCLC Online Computer Library Center, Inc.; ProQuest Information & Learning; RoweCom Information Quest; Swets Blackwell. Reprint: PQC. *Indexed:* ASG, ASSIA, HRA, IBZ, IPSA, PRA, PSA, RiskAb, SSCI, SUSA, SociolAb. *Bk. rev.:* 4-6, signed. *Aud.:* Ga, Ac.

A publication of the Association for Research on Nonprofit Organizations and Voluntary Action (ARNOVA), this journal focuses on voluntarism, citizen participation, philanthropy, civil society, and nonprofit organizations. A recent special issue features articles presented at the ARNOVA annual conference. There are special sections with research notes and commentary. Recommended for academic libraries with sociology or social work programs and for larger public libraries.

Public Welfare. See *Policy & Practice of Public Human Services* in the Social Work and Social Welfare subsection.

6118. *Qualitative Sociology.* [ISSN: 0162-0436] 1978. q. EUR 692 print or online ed. Ed(s): Robert Zussman. Kluwer Academic / Plenum Publishers, 233 Spring St Fl 7, New York, NY 10013-1522; http://www.wkap.nl/. Illus., index, adv. Sample. Refereed. Microform: PQC. Online: EBSCO Publishing; ingenta.com; Kluwer Online; OCLC Online Computer Library Center, Inc.; Ovid Technologies, Inc.; RoweCom Information Quest; Swets Blackwell. Reprint: PQC. *Indexed:* AbAn, CJA, IBZ, IMFL, PSA, PsycholAb, SWA, SWR&A, SociolAb. *Bk. rev.:* 6-8, signed. *Aud.:* Ac.

This journal is a collection of research on qualitative interpretation and analysis of social life. Some issues are thematic; a recent issue deals with the topic of sexual involvement in social research. Other recent articles cover the backlash against affirmative action; and gender, power, and identity among Evangelical and Muslim women in the United States. Recommended for academic libraries with sociology programs.

6119. *Quality and Quantity: international journal of methodology.* [ISSN: 0033-5177] 1967. 6x/yr. EUR 659 print or online ed. Ed(s): Vittorio Capecchi. Kluwer Academic Publishers, van Godewijckstraat 30, PO Box 17, Dordrecht, 3300 AA, Netherlands; services@wkap.nl; http://www.wkap.nl. Illus. Sample. Refereed. Microform: PQC. Online: EBSCO Publishing; ingenta.com; Kluwer Online; OCLC Online Computer Library Center, Inc.; Ovid Technologies, Inc.; RoweCom Information Quest; Swets Blackwell. Reprint: SWZ. *Indexed:* ArtHuCI, IndMed, PSA, SSCI, ST&MA, SociolAb. *Aud.:* Ac.

This international journal provides a forum for research correlating the fields of mathematics and statistics with the social sciences, particularly sociology, economics, and social psychology. Methodology for scientific results in the social sciences is explored in such areas as causal analysis, models of classification, graph theory applications, and mathematical models of sociological behavior. Topics cover such issues as the constant comparative method in the analysis of qualitative interviews, measuring motives for media exposure, and estimating the size of the homeless population in Budapest, Hungary. Recommended for academic libraries with curricula supporting graduate and doctoral studies in sociology and related social sciences disciplines.

6120. *Rural Sociology: devoted to scientific study of rural and community life.* [ISSN: 0036-0112] 1936. q. USD 107. Ed(s): Gary Green. Rural Sociological Society, 211 Mumford Hall, University of Missouri, Columbia, MO 65211-6200; ruralsoc@missouri.edu; http://www.ruralsociology.org. Illus., index, adv. Refereed. Circ: 3000 Controlled. Vol. ends: Winter. Microform: PQC. Online: EBSCO Publishing; Gale Group; Northern Light Technology, Inc.; ProQuest Information & Learning. *Indexed:* ABS&EES, ASSIA, AbAn, AgeL, Agr, AmH&L, ArtHuCI, B&AI, CIJE, CJA, DSA, FPA, ForAb, GeogAbPG, IBSS, IBZ, IMFL, IPSA, PAIS, PSA, PsycholAb, RI-1, RRTA, RiskAb, S&F, SCI, SSCI, SSI, SUSA, SWA, SWR&A, SociolAb, WAE&RSA. *Bk. rev.:* 4-6, signed. *Aud.:* Ac.

The official journal of the Rural Sociological Society focuses on development of rural sociology through research, teaching, and extension work. Some issues center around a theme; recently, spatial inequality and diversity. Other recent articles cover the role of local development organizations in rural America, and factors influencing farmers' expectations to sell agricultural land for nonagricultural uses. Recommended for academic libraries with graduate programs in sociology and agriculture.

6121. *Sex Roles.* [ISSN: 0360-0025] 1975. s-m. EUR 1070 print or online ed. Ed(s): John C Chrisler. Kluwer Academic / Plenum Publishers, 233 Spring St Fl 7, New York, NY 10013-1522; http://www.wkap.nl/. Illus., index, adv. Sample. Refereed. Vol. ends: Jul/Dec. Microform: PQC. Online: EBSCO Publishing; Florida Center for Library Automation; Gale Group; ingenta.com; Kluwer Online; OCLC Online Computer Library Center, Inc.; Ovid Technologies, Inc.; ProQuest Information & Learning; RoweCom Information Quest; Swets Blackwell. *Indexed:* ABS&EES, ASSIA, AbAn, AgeL, AnthLit, ArtHuCI, CIJE, CJA, CommAb, ExcerpMed, FemPer, HEA, IMFL, L&LBA, PSA, PsycholAb, SFSA, SSCI, SSI, SWA, SWR&A, SociolAb, WSA. *Bk. rev.:* 2-4, signed. *Aud.:* Ac.

This is a heavily used journal in academic libraries. Authors contribute empirical studies and theoretical articles relating to gender-role socialization, perceptions, and attitudes. Studies have explored gender-role development, sexist discrimination, gender stereotyping, and gender differences in work and family roles. There is a "Brief Reports" section that focuses on research studies. Highly recommended for academic libraries.

Sexualities. See Sexuality section.

6122. *Simulation & Gaming: an international journal of theory, design and research.* Formerly (until 1990): *Simulation and Games.* [ISSN: 1046-8781] 1970. q. GBP 355 print & online eds. in Europe, Middle East, Africa & Australasia. Ed(s): David Crookall. Sage Publications, Inc., 2455 Teller Rd, Thousand Oaks, CA 91320; info@sagepub.com; http://www.sagepub.com. Illus., index, adv. Sample. Refereed. Circ: 1800 Paid. Vol. ends: Dec. Microform: PQC. Online: EBSCO Publishing; Gale Group; ingenta.com; Northern Light Technology, Inc.; RoweCom Information Quest; Swets Blackwell. Reprint: PQC. *Indexed:* ABCPolSci, ABS&EES, AgeL, BRI, CIJE, CommAb, CompR, HRA, IBSS, IPSA, LRI, MRD, PAIS, PRA, PSA, PsycholAb, RiskAb, SSCI, SSI, SociolAb. *Aud.:* Ac.

This is the official journal of the Association for Business Simulation and Experiential Learning, the International Simulation and Gaming Association, the Japan Association of Simulation and Gaming, the North American Simulation and Gaming Association, and the Society for Intercultural Education, Training, and Research in the United States. An international forum is provided for discussion of issues, applications, and research related to man, man–machine, and machine simulations of social processes. Theoretical papers cover simulations in research and teaching, empirical studies, and technical papers on gaming techniques. There are special issues devoted to a particular theme; a recent topic is Internet-mediated simulation and gaming. There is a special section on reports and communications and a review section for simulation games. The "News and Notes" section provides conference and other information on the five associations. Recommended for academic libraries with graduate programs in sociology.

6123. *Social Compass: international review of sociology of religion.* [ISSN: 0037-7686] 1953. q. GBP 215 print & online eds. in Europe, Middle East, Africa & Australasia. Ed(s): Albert Bastenier. Sage Publications Ltd., 6 Bonhill St, London, EC2A 4PU, United Kingdom; info@sagepub.co.uk; http://www.sagepub.co.uk/. Illus., index, adv. Sample. Refereed. Vol. ends: Dec. *Indexed:* ASSIA, ArtHuCI, BAS, CommAb, IBSS, IBZ, IPSA, PSA, R&TA, RI-1, SSCI, SociolAb. *Bk. rev.:* 1-2, signed. *Aud.:* Ac.

The journal of the International Federation of Institutes for Social and Socio-Religious Research is published in French and English, with abstracts in the second language. The authors write on aspects of religion as they relate to the field of sociology. Issues are thematic, focusing on key issues in current research on religion in society. Recent topics include religious restoration in eastern Europe, and paradigms for interpreting religion today. The journal includes the *Proceedings of the International Society for the Sociology of Religion.* Recommended for academic libraries with programs in religious studies relating to sociology.

6124. ***Social Forces.*** Formerly (until 1925): *The Journal of Social Forces.* [ISSN: 0037-7732] 1922. q. USD 73 (Individuals, USD 44). Ed(s): Richard L Simpson. University of North Carolina Press, PO Box 2288, Chapel Hill, NC 27515-2288; uncpress_journals@unc.edu. Illus., index, adv. Refereed. Circ: 4140 Paid and controlled. Vol. ends: Jun. Microform: MIM; PMC; PQC. Online: bigchalk; Chadwyck-Healey Incorporated; EBSCO Publishing; Florida Center for Library Automation; Gale Group; JSTOR (Web-based Journal Archive); Northern Light Technology, Inc.; OCLC Online Computer Library Center, Inc.; Project MUSE; ProQuest Information & Learning; RoweCom Information Quest; Swets Blackwell; H.W. Wilson. Reprint: PSC. *Indexed:* ABCPolSci, ABS&EES, ASSIA, AbAn, AgeL, AmH&L, ArtHuCI, BAS, BRI, CBRI, CIJE, CJA, CommAb, GeogAbPG, H&SSA, HRA, IBSS, IBZ, IMFL, IPSA, PAIS, PRA, PSA, PsycholAb, RI-1, RRTA, RiskAb, SFSA, SSCI, SSI, SUSA, SWA, SWR&A, SociolAb. *Bk. rev.:* 25-30, signed. *Aud.:* Ga, Ac.

This highly regarded journal, published in association with the Southern Sociological Society, contains research on all aspects of the social sciences, particularly on the relationship between outside systems and the individual. Recent topics cover such diverse areas as racial threat and social control, globalization in international trade, lethal assaults against the police, and U.S. migration experience and fertility. There is an extensive book review section. This is one of the more influential journals in sociology. Highly recommended for all academic libraries and for larger public libraries.

6125. ***Social Indicators Research: an international and interdisciplinary journal for quality-of-life measurement.*** [ISSN: 0303-8300] 1974. 15x/yr. EUR 1350 print or online ed. Ed(s): Alex C Michalos. Kluwer Academic Publishers, van Godewijckstraat 30, PO Box 17, Dordrecht, 3300 AA, Netherlands; services@wkap.nl; http://www.wkap.nl. Illus., index, adv. Sample. Refereed. Vol. ends: Dec. Microform: PQC. Online: EBSCO Publishing; Gale Group; ingenta.com; Kluwer Online; OCLC Online Computer Library Center, Inc.; Ovid Technologies, Inc.; RoweCom Information Quest; Swets Blackwell. Reprint: SWZ. *Indexed:* ASSIA, AgeL, BAS, CJA, CommAb, ForAb, FutSurv, GeogAbPG, IBSS, IBZ, IMFL, IndMed, PAIS, PSA, PhilInd, PsycholAb, RRTA, RiskAb, S&F, SSCI, SUSA, SWA, SWR&A, SociolAb, WAE&RSA. *Bk. rev.:* 2-3, signed. *Aud.:* Ac.

With an international editorial board, this journal publishes research on problems relating to measurement of all aspects of the quality of life. Recent topics include a study of the influence of Ecstasy use on the coping strategies of loneliness in young adults, measurement of the household as an economic unit in Arctic aboriginal communities, and demographic trends in Korea and their social implications. Recommended for academic libraries with graduate programs in political and social sciences.

6126. ***Social Networks: an international journal of structural analysis.*** [ISSN: 0378-8733] 1979. q. EUR 359. Ed(s): Linton C Freeman, Ronald L Breiger. Elsevier BV, North-Holland, Sara Burgerhartstraat 25, Amsterdam, 1055 KV, Netherlands; nlinfo-f@elsevier.nl; http://www.elsevier.nl/homepage/about/us/regional_sites.htt. Illus., index, adv. Sample. Refereed. Microform: PQC. Online: ingenta.com; ScienceDirect; Swets Blackwell. Reprint: SWZ. *Indexed:* AICP, AgeL, AnthLit, CJA, HRA, IBSS, PsycholAb, SCI, SSCI, SUSA, SociolAb. *Aud.:* Ac.

This interdisciplinary journal is published in association with the International Network for Social Network Analysis. It provides a "common forum for representatives of anthropology, sociology, history, social psychology, political science, human geography, biology, economics, communications science and other disciplines who share an interest in the study of the structure of human relations and associations that may be expressed in network form." Recent topics include interviewer effects in measuring network size, ego-centered networks and the ripple effect, and detecting measurement bias in respondent reports of personal networks. Recommended for academic libraries with graduate programs in the social sciences.

6127. ***Social Policy.*** [ISSN: 0037-7783] 1970. q. USD 185 (Individuals, USD 45). Ed(s): Michael J Miller. Organize Training Center - Social Policy, PO Box 1297, Pacifica, CA 94044; sclplcy@aol.com; http://www.socialpolicy.org. Illus., adv. Circ: 4000 Paid. Vol. ends: Winter. CD-ROM: H.W. Wilson. Microform: PQC. Online: EBSCO Publishing; Florida Center for Library Automation; Gale Group; Northern Light Technology, Inc.; OCLC Online Computer Library Center, Inc.; ProQuest Information & Learning; H.W. Wilson. Reprint: PQC. *Indexed:* ABCPolSci, ASSIA, AgeL, AltPI, CIJE, FLI, FutSurv, IBSS, IPSA, MCR, PAIS, PRA, PSA, SSCI, SSI, SUSA, SWR&A, SociolAb. *Bk. rev.:* 1-3, signed. *Aud.:* Hs, Ga, Ac.

This magazine "offers a progressive alternative to liberalism, and coverage of the movements that work 'beneath the radar' of the national media." Most articles take the form of discussion, reports, or opinion forums. Issues center on a wide variety of social service topics; recently, on community organizing, with a focus on organizing immigrants and refugees. Another issue presents articles on engaged Buddhism. Because of the readability of this journal and the value of alternative opinions, it is recommended for high school, public, and academic libraries.

6128. ***Social Policy and Administration.*** Formerly: *Social and Economic Administration.* [ISSN: 0144-5596] 1967. 7x/yr. GBP 408 print & online eds. Ed(s): John Baldock, Catherine Jones Finer. Blackwell Publishing Ltd., 9600 Garsington Rd, PO Box 805, Oxford, OX4 2DQ, United Kingdom; customerservices@oxon.blackwellpublishing.com; http://www.blackwellpublishing.com/. Illus., index, adv. Sample. Refereed. Circ: 900. Vol. ends: Dec. Online: EBSCO Publishing; ingenta.com; OCLC Online Computer Library Center, Inc.; RoweCom Information Quest; Swets Blackwell. Reprint: SWZ. *Indexed:* ASSIA, AgeL, CJA, IBSS, MCR, PAIS, PSA, RRTA, SSCI, SWA, SociolAb, WAE&RSA. *Bk. rev.:* 4-7, signed. *Aud.:* Ac.

This journal provides an international forum for discussion of social policy issues and their effects on social services. It seeks to engender debate about topical and controversial issues. Some issues are thematic; a recent one focuses on countries of the eastern Mediterranean, with articles on Turkey and the European Union, social policy in Greece, and Islam, social traditions and family planning. Other issues have focused on welfare reform, long-term care, and health care in various countries. Recommended for academic libraries with graduate programs in the social sciences.

6129. ***Social Problems.*** [ISSN: 0037-7791] 1953. q. USD 129 print & online eds. USD 35 newsstand/cover. Ed(s): James A Holstein. University of California Press, Journals Division, 2000 Center St, Ste 303, Berkeley, CA 94704-1223; journals@ucop.edu; http://www.ucpress.edu/journals. Illus., index, adv. Sample. Refereed. Circ: 3600 Paid. Microform: PQC. Online: EBSCO Publishing; Florida Center for Library Automation; Gale Group; Ingenta Select; Northern Light Technology, Inc.; OCLC Online Computer Library Center, Inc. Reprint: PQC. *Indexed:* ABS&EES, ASSIA, AgeL, AmH&L, ArtHuCI, BAS, CIJE, CJA, CommAb, ExcerpMed, FutSurv, IBSS, IBZ, IPSA, LRI, PAIS, PSA, PsycholAb, RI-1, RiskAb, SSCI, SSI, SWA, SWR&A, SociolAb. *Aud.:* Ga, Ac.

This official journal of the Society for the Study of Social Problems is one of the standards in any sociology department. Many issues are thematic; recent articles have been published on the topics of race, gender, and wages; economics and women's lives; and social and cultural capital. Subjects are explored in depth, usually through empirical research, and references are often extensive. Highly recommended for all academic libraries and larger public libraries.

6130. ***Social Psychology Quarterly.*** Former titles (until 1978): *Social Psychology;* (until 1977): *Sociometry.* [ISSN: 0190-2725] 1937. q. USD 140 (Individuals, USD 70; Members, USD 30). Ed(s): Cecelia Ridgeway. American Sociological Association, 1307 New York Ave, N W, Ste 700, Washington, DC 20005-4701; publications@asanet.org; http://www.lemoyne.edu. Illus., adv. Refereed. Circ: 3000. Vol. ends:

Dec. Microform: MIM; PQC. Online: Ingenta Select; JSTOR (Web-based Journal Archive); OCLC Online Computer Library Center, Inc.; ProQuest Information & Learning. Reprint: PQC. *Indexed:* ABS&EES, ASSIA, AgeL, CJA, IMFL, IPSA, L&LBA, MLA-IB, PSA, PsycholAb, RiskAb, SSCI, SSI, SWA, SociolAb. *Aud.:* Ac.

This publication of the American Sociological Association publishes theoretical and empirical studies exploring the link between the individual and society. Interdisciplinary in scope, it divides issues into the categories of articles and research notes. Recent articles explore the relationship between perceived discrimination and depression, successful adaptation in the later years, and an analysis of presidential candidates' nonverbal vocal communication. Recommended for academic libraries with programs in sociology.

6131. ***Social Research: an international quarterly of the social science.*** [ISSN: 0037-783X] 1934. q. USD 85 (Individuals, USD 30). Ed(s): Arien Mack. New School University, 65 Fifth Ave, Rm 344, New York, NY 10003. Illus., adv. Refereed. Circ: 3000. Vol. ends: Dec. Microform: PMC; PQC. Online: bigchalk; Chadwyck-Healey Incorporated; EBSCO Publishing; Florida Center for Library Automation; Gale Group; OCLC Online Computer Library Center, Inc.; ProQuest Information & Learning; H.W. Wilson. Reprint: PQC; PSC. *Indexed:* ABCPolSci, ABS&EES, ASSIA, AgeL, AmH&L, ArtHuCI, BAS, BHA, BRI, CBRI, CommAb, IBSS, IBZ, IPB, IPSA, LRI, MLA-IB, PAIS, PRA, PSA, SSCI, SSI, SociolAb. *Aud.:* Ac.

This journal is published by the Graduate Faculty of Political and Social Science of the New School for Social Research, founded in 1933 as a university-in-exile for scholars escaping European totalitarianism. It provides a forum for theoretical discussion on a variety of social science topics, with submissions from authors from many countries. There is a strong political tone to many of the entries. Issues usually focus on a broad subject area: Recent topics include the status of women in developing countries; and the U.S. record regarding international justice, war crimes, and terrorism. Recommended for academic libraries with programs in sociology and political science.

6132. ***Social Science Computer Review.*** Formed by the merger of: *Social Science Microcomputer Review; Computers and the Social Sciences;* Formerly (until 1984): *Political Science Micro Review.* [ISSN: 0894-4393] 1983. q. GBP 327 in Europe, Middle East, Africa & Australasia. Ed(s): G David Garson. Sage Publications, Inc., 2455 Teller Rd, Thousand Oaks, CA 91320; info@sagepub.com; http://www.sagepub.com. Illus., index, adv. Sample. Refereed. Circ: 700 Paid. Vol. ends: Nov. Online: EBSCO Publishing; ingenta.com; RoweCom Information Quest; Swets Blackwell. *Indexed:* ASSIA, ArtHuCI, BRI, C&ISA, CBRI, CompLI, IBZ, InfoSAb, LISA, MicrocompInd, PSA, PsycholAb, SSCI, SWR&A, SociolAb. *Bk. rev.:* 2-4, signed. *Aud.:* Ac.

This journal covers social science instructional and research applications of computing, as well as social science research on societal impacts of information. Some issues are thematic; recently, state-of-the-art computer-based methods have been explored, and articles on e-government have been published in another issue. In addition to book reviews, there are software reviews and a "News and Notes" section with listings of online sites, services, and products. Recommended for academic libraries with graduate programs in the social sciences.

Social Science Research. See Cultural-Social Studies section.

Social Work in Education. See *Children & Schools* in the Social Work and Social Welfare subsection.

6133. ***Society: social science & modern society.*** Formerly (until 1972): *Trans-Action: Social Science and Modern Society.* [ISSN: 0147-2011] 1963. bi-m. USD 216 (Individuals, USD 60; Students, USD 42). Ed(s): Jonathan Imber. Transaction Publishers, 35 Berrue Circle, Rutgers University, Piscataway, NJ 08854-8042; trans@transactionpub.com; http://www.transactionpub.com. Illus., index, adv. Sample. Refereed. Circ: 4000. Vol. ends: Oct. Microform: PQC. Online: EBSCO Publishing; Florida Center for Library Automation; Gale Group; Ingenta Select; Northern Light Technology, Inc.; OCLC Online Computer Library Center, Inc.; ProQuest Information & Learning. Reprint: PQC; PSC. *Indexed:* ABCPolSci, AgeL, BAS, BRD, BRI, CBRI, CIJE, CJA, CommAb, FLI, FutSurv, IBSS, IPSA, LRI, MCR, MagInd, PAIS, PRA, PSA, RGPR, RI-1, SSCI, SUSA, SWR&A, SociolAb. *Bk. rev.:* 4-6, signed. *Aud.:* Hs, Ga, Ac.

This journal publishes articles and research on a variety of topics, with emphasis on subjects of current interest. Discussion articles are arranged under thematic headings of culture and society, social science and public policy, and society abroad. Each issue has a symposium; recent topics include faith-based initiatives; and disciplines, professions, and breakouts. Many articles are discussions of opinion by respected sociologists and are at a level understandable by high school students. Recommended for high school, public, and academic libraries.

6134. ***Sociological Forum: official journal of the Eastern Sociological Society.*** [ISSN: 0884-8971] 1986. q. EUR 446 print or online ed. Ed(s): Robert Max Jackson. Kluwer Academic / Plenum Publishers, 233 Spring St Fl 7, New York, NY 10013-1522; kluwer@wkap.com; http://www.wkap.nl/. Illus., index, adv. Sample. Refereed. Microform: PQC. Online: ingenta.com; JSTOR (Web-based Journal Archive); Kluwer Online; OCLC Online Computer Library Center, Inc.; Ovid Technologies, Inc.; RoweCom Information Quest; Swets Blackwell. *Indexed:* AgeL, ArtHuCI, HRA, IBSS, IMFL, PRA, PsycholAb, SFSA, SSCI, SociolAb. *Bk. rev.:* 2-3, signed. *Aud.:* Ac.

This journal publishes research on sociological and organizational change as well as articles that relate sociology to other disciplines. Emphasis is on innovative articles developing topics or areas in new ways or directions. There are occasional special issues; race and ethnicity is a recent topic of one; another issue takes a look at the part that gender plays in sociological analyses. Recommended for academic libraries with programs in sociology.

6135. ***Sociological Inquiry.*** [ISSN: 0038-0245] 1930. q. USD 120 print & online eds. Blackwell Publishing, Inc., Commerce Place, 350 Main St, Malden, MA 02148; subscrip@blackwellpub.com; http://www.blackwellpublishing.com. Illus., index, adv. Refereed. Circ: 3000. Microform: PQC. Online: Gale Group; ingenta.com; Swets Blackwell. Reprint: PQC; SCH. *Indexed:* ABCPolSci, ASSIA, AbAn, AgeL, AmH&L, ArtHuCI, CJA, CommAb, IMFL, IPSA, PRA, PSA, RI-1, SSCI, SSI, SWA, SociolAb. *Bk. rev.:* 2-4, signed. *Aud.:* Ac.

Sponsored by Alpha Kappa Delta, the International Sociology Honor Society, this journal publishes research on all aspects of sociology. There are occasional special issues, a recent one publishing articles on "Justice for Self, Group, and Nation." An upcoming feature is the publishing of "state of the discipline" articles aimed at graduate and undergraduate students. Recommended for all academic libraries with sociology programs.

6136. ***Sociological Methods & Research.*** [ISSN: 0049-1241] 1972. q. GBP 339 print & online eds. in Europe, Middle East, Africa & Australasia. Ed(s): Christopher Winship. Sage Publications, Inc., 2455 Teller Rd, Thousand Oaks, CA 91320; info@sagepub.com; http://www.sagepub.com. Illus., index, adv. Sample. Refereed. Circ: 1550. Vol. ends: May. Microform: PQC. Online: EBSCO Publishing; ingenta.com; RoweCom Information Quest; Swets Blackwell. Reprint: PQC. *Indexed:* ASSIA, BAS, CJA, CommAb, IBSS, IMFL, MathSciNet, PAIS, SSCI, SWR&A, SociolAb. *Aud.:* Ac.

This journal focuses on qualitative and quantitative research methodology in the social sciences. A variety of perspectives are represented, including sociology, psychology, anthropology, political science, and education, among others. A recent special issue of qualitative research on the front lines of controversy published articles on lessons from a case study of rampage school-shootings, and extended case method as a tool for multilevel analysis of school violence. Recommended for academic libraries with graduate programs in the social sciences.

6137. ***Sociological Perspectives.*** Formerly (until 1982): *Pacific Sociological Review.* [ISSN: 0731-1214] 1958. q. USD 235 print & online eds. USD 60 newsstand/cover. Ed(s): Peter Nardi. University of California Press,

Journals Division, 2000 Center St, Ste 303, Berkeley, CA 94704-1223; journals@ucop.edu; http://www.ucpress.edu/journals. Illus., index, adv. Sample. Refereed. Circ: 2300. Vol. ends: Sep. Microform: PQC. Online: EBSCO Publishing; Florida Center for Library Automation; Gale Group; Ingenta Select; Northern Light Technology, Inc.; OCLC Online Computer Library Center, Inc. Reprint: PQC. *Indexed:* ABCPolSci, AbAn, AgeL, ArtHuCI, BAS, CJA, IBSS, IMFL, IPSA, PSA, PsycholAb, SSCI, SSI, SUSA, SWA, SWR&A, SociolAb. *Aud.:* Ac.

This is the official journal of the Pacific Sociological Association. Abstracts are available in English, Chinese, Japanese, and Spanish. Research focuses on social processes related to economic, political, anthropological, and historical issues. There are occasional special issues, a recent one on gender and sports. Recommended for academic libraries with programs in sociology.

6138. ***Sociological Quarterly.*** Formerly: *Midwest Sociologist.* [ISSN: 0038-0253] 1960. q. USD 238 print & online eds. USD 60 newsstand/cover. Ed(s): Kevin Leicht. University of California Press, Journals Division, 2000 Center St, Ste 303, Berkeley, CA 94704-1223; journals@ucop.edu; http://www.ucpress.edu/journals. Illus., index, adv. Sample. Refereed. Circ: 2590 Paid. Vol. ends: Nov. Microform: WSH. Online: EBSCO Publishing; Florida Center for Library Automation; Gale Group; Ingenta Select; OCLC Online Computer Library Center, Inc. Reprint: PQC; WSH. *Indexed:* ABCPolSci, ABS&EES, AbAn, AgeL, AmH&L, ArtHuCI, BAS, CJA, CommAb, IBSS, IMFL, IPSA, PAIS, PRA, PSA, PsycholAb, RI-1, SSCI, SSI, SWA, SWR&A, SociolAb. *Aud.:* Ac.

Published for the Midwest Sociological Society, this journal covers all topics related to the field of sociology, especially topics of current interest. Articles are arranged under themes, designed to reach a broad audience: Recent coverage has been given to consequences of racial segregation and economic change; uses of social movement framing; and technology, surveillance, and gender. Recommended for academic libraries with programs in the social sciences.

Sociological Research. See CIS and Eastern Europe section.

6139. ***The Sociological Review.*** [ISSN: 0038-0261] 1908. q. GBP 200 print & online eds. Ed(s): Rosemary Deem, Mike Savage. Blackwell Publishing Ltd., 9600 Garsington Rd, PO Box 805, Oxford, OX4 2DQ, United Kingdom; customerservices@oxon.blackwellpublishing.com; http://www.blackwellpublishing.com/. Illus., adv. Sample. Refereed. Circ: 2000. Vol. ends: Nov. Microform: PQC. Online: EBSCO Publishing; Gale Group; ingenta.com; OCLC Online Computer Library Center, Inc.; RoweCom Information Quest; Swets Blackwell. Reprint: PQC; PSC; SWZ. *Indexed:* AICP, ASSIA, AgeL, BRI, CBRI, IBSS, IMFL, IPSA, PSA, PsycholAb, SSCI, SSI, SWA, SociolAb. *Bk. rev.:* 10-12, signed. *Aud.:* Ac.

This is the longest established sociological journal in Great Britain, publishing theoretical research and empirical studies in the fields of sociology, social anthropology, and related subjects, such as cultural and women's studies, social policy, and industrial relations. Much of the research centers on Britain and Europe. There is an extensive book review section, as well as a monograph series published once or twice a year. Highly recommended for academic libraries with graduate programs in sociology.

6140. ***Sociological Spectrum: official journal of the Mid-South Sociological Association.*** Formed by the merger of: *Sociological Symposium; Sociological Forum.* [ISSN: 0273-2173] 1980. q. USD 318 (Individuals, USD 139). Ed(s): DeAnn K Gauthier. Taylor & Francis Inc, 325 Chestnut St, Suite 800, Philadelphia, PA 19016; info@taylorandfrancis.com; http://www.taylorandfrancis.com/. Illus., index, adv. Sample. Refereed. Circ: 600. Vol. ends: Oct/Dec. Online: EBSCO Publishing; Ingenta Select; OCLC Online Computer Library Center, Inc.; RoweCom Information Quest; Swets Blackwell. Reprint: PQC; PSC. *Indexed:* AgeL, CJA, IBSS, IMFL, PRA, PSA, SSCI, SUSA, SociolAb. *Aud.:* Ac.

The official journal of the Mid-South Sociological Association, this publication covers research in the fields of sociology, social psychology, anthropology, and political science. There are occasional special issues, with recent focus on immigrants in the new South. Recommended for academic libraries with sociology programs.

6141. ***Sociological Theory.*** [ISSN: 0735-2751] 4x/yr. USD 161 print & online eds. Ed(s): Jonathan H. Turner. Blackwell Publishing, Inc., Commerce Place, 350 Main St, Malden, MA 02148; subscrip@blackwellpub.com; http://www.blackwellpublishing.com. Adv. Refereed. Circ: 2300. *Indexed:* ASSIA, IBSS, SSCI, SociolAb. *Aud.:* Ac.

A publication of the American Sociological Association, this journal provides an international, interdisciplinary forum for investigation of all types of sociological theory. Issues often include a commentary and debate section. Recent articles cover religious nationalism, globalization theories, theory of movement repression, and changing forms of inequality. Highly recommended for academic libraries with graduate programs in sociology.

6142. ***Sociology: a journal of the British Sociological Association.*** [ISSN: 0038-0385] 1967. 5x/yr. GBP 220 print & online eds. in Europe, Middle East, Africa & Australasia. Ed(s): Tony Spybey, Maggie O'Neill. Sage Publications Ltd., 6 Bonhill St, London, EC2A 4PU, United Kingdom; info@sagepub.co.uk; http://www.sagepub.co.uk/. Illus., index, adv. Sample. Refereed. Circ: 3700. Vol. ends: Nov. Microform: PQC. Online: EBSCO Publishing; Florida Center for Library Automation; Gale Group; ingenta.com; Northern Light Technology, Inc.; OCLC Online Computer Library Center, Inc.; ProQuest Information & Learning; RoweCom Information Quest; Sage Publications, Inc.; Swets Blackwell. Reprint: PQC. *Indexed:* ABIn, ASSIA, BAS, CJA, CommAb, IBSS, IBZ, IPSA, PSA, RRTA, SSCI, SSI, SWA, SociolAb, WAE&RSA. *Bk. rev.:* 20-25, signed. *Aud.:* Ac.

This prestigious journal makes a substantial contribution to the field of sociology with its extensive research publications. Articles are theoretical and empirical studies, with the major focus on Great Britain and the rest of Europe. The editorial board is primarily British, with an international advisory board. Frequently, issues are arranged around themes, such as the recent articles on global refugees. There are often sections with research notes and comments. The book review section is extensive, with an occasional review symposium. Highly recommended for academic libraries with programs in sociology.

6143. ***Sociology of Education: a journal of research in socialization and social structure.*** Formerly (until 1963): *Journal of Educational Sociology.* [ISSN: 0038-0407] 1927. q. USD 140 (Individuals, USD 70; Members, USD 30). Ed(s): Karl L Alexander. American Sociological Association, 1307 New York Ave, N W, Ste 700, Washington, DC 20005-4701; publications@asanet.org; http://www.asanet.org. Illus., adv. Refereed. Circ: 2800. Vol. ends: Oct. Microform: PMC; PQC. Online: Gale Group; Ingenta Select; JSTOR (Web-based Journal Archive); OCLC Online Computer Library Center, Inc.; ProQuest Information & Learning. Reprint: PQC; PSC. *Indexed:* ASSIA, AgeL, CIJE, EduInd, HEA, IBZ, PAIS, PsycholAb, SSCI, SSI, SWA, SociolAb. *Aud.:* Ac.

This publication of the American Sociological Association provides a forum for research that examines how social institutions and individuals within those institutions affect educational processes and social development. Recent topics include unequal spending within school districts, perceived quality and methodology in graduate department ratings, and the influence of gender and personal relationships on science and technology involvement. Recommended for academic libraries with programs in sociology and education.

6144. ***Sociology of Health and Illness: a journal of medical sociology.*** Incorporates (in 1999): *Sociology of Health and Illness Monograph Series.* [ISSN: 0141-9889] 1979. 6x/yr. GBP 315 print & online eds. Ed(s): Robert Dingwall, Veronica James. Blackwell Publishing Ltd., 9600 Garsington Rd, PO Box 805, Oxford, OX4 2DQ, United Kingdom; jnlinfo@blackwellpublishers.co.uk; http://www.blackwellpublishing.com/. Illus., index, adv. Sample. Refereed. Circ: 950. Vol. ends: Nov. Online: EBSCO Publishing; Gale Group; ingenta.com; OCLC Online Computer Library Center, Inc.; RoweCom Information Quest; Swets Blackwell. Reprint: PSC. *Indexed:* ASSIA, AgeL, ArtHuCI, CINAHL, ExcerpMed, IBSS, MCR, PSA, PsycholAb, SSCI, SSI, SWA, SociolAb. *Bk. rev.:* 8-12, signed. *Aud.:* Ac.

This international journal publishes empirical and qualitative research on all aspects of health, illness, and medicine. There is an annual special issue, with articles surrounding a theme, recently, the interconnection between criminology and medical sociology, and a sociological perspective on rationing. Recommended for academic libraries with sociology, medical, or social work programs.

Sociology of Religion. See Religion section.

6145. ***Teaching Sociology.*** [ISSN: 0092-055X] 1973. q. USD 140 (Individuals, USD 70; Members, USD 30). Ed(s): Helen A Moore. American Sociological Association, 1307 New York Ave, N W, Ste 700, Washington, DC 20005-4701; publications@asanet.org; http://www.lemoyne.edu. Illus., adv. Refereed. Circ: 2300. Vol. ends: Oct. *Indexed:* ASSIA, AgeL, ArtHuCI, CIJE, EduInd, IBZ, SSCI, SWA, SociolAb. *Bk. rev.:* 10-12, signed. *Aud.:* Ac.

This publication of the American Sociological Association contains articles, notes, and reviews designed to aid teachers of sociology. The journal includes research articles, practical approaches, and interviews, as well as book, film, video, and software reviews. Highly recommended for academic libraries with graduate and doctoral programs in sociology.

6146. ***Technology in Society: an international journal.*** Announced as: *Sociotechnology.* [ISSN: 0160-791X] 1979. q. EUR 876 (Individuals, EUR 208). Ed(s): George Bugliarello, A George Schillinger. Pergamon, The Boulevard, Langford Ln, East Park, Kidlington, OX5 1GB, United Kingdom. Illus., index, adv. Sample. Refereed. Circ: 2000. Vol. ends: No. 23. Microform: PQC. Online: ingenta.com; ScienceDirect; Swets Blackwell. *Indexed:* ABS&EES, ArtHuCI, BAS, CommAb, EngInd, EnvAb, ExcerpMed, FutSurv, GeogAbPG, InfoSAb, PSA, PsycholAb, SSCI, SociolAb. *Aud.:* Ac.

This international journal publishes research on the economic, political, and cultural dynamics relating to the role of technology within society, as well as the social forces that shape technological decisions. Recent articles cover the digital divide, the global telecommunications industry, technology policy initiatives in countries, and the interdependency of progress and technology. Recommended for libraries with graduate programs in the social sciences.

Theory and Decision. See Philosophy section.

6147. ***Theory and Society: renewal and critique in social theory.*** [ISSN: 0304-2421] 1974. bi-m. EUR 503 print or online ed. Ed(s): Janet Gouldner. Kluwer Academic Publishers, van Godewijckstraat 30, PO Box 17, Dordrecht, 3300 AA, Netherlands; services@wkap.nl; http://www.wkap.nl. Illus., index, adv. Sample. Refereed. Vol. ends: Nov. Microform: PQC. Online: EBSCO Publishing; ingenta.com; JSTOR (Web-based Journal Archive); Kluwer Online; OCLC Online Computer Library Center, Inc.; RoweCom Information Quest; Swets Blackwell. Reprint: SWZ. *Indexed:* ASSIA, ArtHuCI, BAS, CommAb, IBSS, IPSA, PAIS, PSA, SSCI, SociolAb. *Bk. rev.:* 2-4, signed. *Aud.:* Ac.

This journal provides a forum for theoretical essays that analyze social processes. The subject matter is broad, covering current as well as historical topics. Issues have covered national identity, social capital, migration, social movements, and the sociology of ideas. Recommended for academic libraries with graduate programs in sociology.

6148. ***Theory, Culture & Society: explorations in critical social science.*** [ISSN: 0263-2764] 1982. bi-m. GBP 435 print & online eds. in Europe, Middle East, Africa & Australasia. Ed(s): Mike Featherstone. Sage Publications Ltd., 6 Bonhill St, London, EC2A 4PU, United Kingdom; info@sagepub.co.uk; http://www.sagepub.co.uk/. Illus., index, adv. Sample. Refereed. Vol. ends: Nov. Reprint: PSC. *Indexed:* AICP, ASSIA, AltPI, CommAb, FLI, HRA, IBSS, IBZ, IPSA, PRA, PSA, PhilInd, SSCI, SUSA, SociolAb. *Bk. rev.:* 1-2, signed. *Aud.:* Ac.

This journal provides an international forum for discussion of theoretical and philosophical issues related to the relationship between humans and society in a cultural context. "The journal features papers by and about modern social and cultural theorists such as Foucault, Bourdieu, Baudrillard, Goffman, Bell, Parsons, Elias, Gadamer, Luhmann, Habermas and Giddens." Some issues are thematic; a recent special issue topic is sociality/materiality, with articles on the status of the object in social science. Recommended for academic libraries with graduate programs in sociology.

Violence Against Women. See Women: Feminist and Special Interest/ Feminist and Women's Studies section.

6149. ***Work and Occupations: an international sociological journal.*** Formerly (until 1982): *Sociology of Work and Occupations.* [ISSN: 0730-8884] 1974. q. GBP 344 print & online eds. in Europe, Middle East, Africa & Australasia. Ed(s): Daniel B Cornfield. Sage Publications, Inc., 2455 Teller Rd, Thousand Oaks, CA 91320; info@sagepub.com; http://www.sagepub.com. Illus., index, adv. Sample. Refereed. Circ: 1250. Vol. ends: Nov. Microform: PQC. Online: Pub.; bigchalk; EBSCO Publishing; Florida Center for Library Automation; Gale Group; ingenta.com; OCLC Online Computer Library Center, Inc.; ProQuest Information & Learning; RoweCom Information Quest; Swets Blackwell. Reprint: PQC. *Indexed:* ABIn, ASG, ASSIA, AgeL, BPI, BRI, CIJE, CJA, ErgAb, H&SSA, HRA, IBSS, IMFL, PRA, PsycholAb, SFSA, SSCI, SUSA, SWA, SociolAb. *Bk. rev.:* 4-6, signed. *Aud.:* Ac.

Explores issues relating to sociological analysis of work and occupations, both with current topics and in historical context. Recent topics include the glass ceiling, the relationship of intelligence and education to job satisfaction, worker cooperatives, and the relationship between long work hours and psychological distress. There are occasional special issues, a recent one focusing on the implications of changing patterns of time use for the sociology of work. Recommended for academic libraries with graduate programs in sociology, economics, or business.

6150. ***Youth & Society.*** [ISSN: 0044-118X] 1969. q. GBP 319 print & online eds. in Europe, Middle East, Africa & Australasia. Ed(s): Kathryn G Herr. Sage Publications, Inc., 2455 Teller Rd, Thousand Oaks, CA 91320; info@sagepub.com; http://www.sagepub.com. Illus., index, adv. Refereed. Circ: 1250. Vol. ends: Jun. Microform: PQC. Online: Pub.; Chadwyck-Healey Incorporated; EBSCO Publishing; Florida Center for Library Automation; Gale Group; ingenta.com; OCLC Online Computer Library Center, Inc.; ProQuest Information & Learning; RoweCom Information Quest; Swets Blackwell. *Indexed:* ABS&EES, ASSIA, CIJE, CJA, CommAb, H&SSA, HEA, IPSA, PSA, PsycholAb, RiskAb, SFSA, SSCI, SSI, SUSA, SWA, SWR&A, SociolAb. *Aud.:* Ac, Sa.

This interdisciplinary publication focuses on child and youth socialization, with emphasis on adolescents and young adults. Sample topics include explorations of various theories of youth development, aggression among adolescents, adolescent suicidal behavior, and the impact of exposure of youth to sexual material on the Internet. The wide range of topics makes this a useful publication for undergraduate students researching social issues; psychology, social work, or education majors; and practitioners. Highly recommended for academic libraries.

Social Work and Social Welfare

6151. ***Administration in Social Work: the quarterly journal of human services management.*** [ISSN: 0364-3107] 1977. q. USD 500 domestic; USD 675 Canada; USD 725 elsewhere. Ed(s): Leon Ginsberg. Haworth Press, Inc., 10 Alice St, Binghamton, NY 13904-1580; getinfo@haworthpressinc.com; http://www.haworthpress.com. Illus., adv. Sample. Refereed. Circ: 972 Paid. Vol. ends: Winter. Microform: PQC. Reprint: HAW. *Indexed:* ABIn, ASSIA, AbAn, AgeL, CINAHL, HRA, IBZ, IMFL, PRA, PsycholAb, SFSA, SSCI, SSI, SWR&A, SociolAb. *Bk. rev.:* 2-4, signed. *Aud.:* Ac, Sa.

This official journal of the National Network for Social Work Managers contains a collection of research on current administration and management issues in social and human services. Policy, legal and financing issues, and innovative techniques and technologies are covered. A twice yearly feature entitled "Management Currents" provides topical updates. Recommended for academic and special libraries supporting sociology, social work, and human services management programs.

6152. *The British Journal of Social Work.* [ISSN: 0045-3102] 1971. 8x/yr. GBP 295. Ed(s): Mark Drakeford, Ian Butler. Oxford University Press, Great Clarendon St, Oxford, OX2 6DP, United Kingdom; jnl.orders@oup.co.uk; http://www3.oup.co.uk/jnls. Illus., adv. Refereed. Circ: 1550. Microform: PQC. Online: Chadwyck-Healey Incorporated; EBSCO Publishing; Gale Group; HighWire Press; ingenta.com; OCLC Online Computer Library Center, Inc.; RoweCom Information Quest; Swets Blackwell. Reprint: PSC. *Indexed:* ASG, ASSIA, AgeL, CJA, HRA, IBSS, IBZ, PRA, PsycholAb, SFSA, SSCI, SUSA, SWA, SWR&A, SociolAb. *Bk. rev.:* 10-15, signed. *Aud.:* Ac.

This is the official journal of the British Association of Social Workers and the leading academic social work journal in Great Britain. Articles cover contemporary developments in social work, policies in Britain affecting social work programs, and some cross-cultural and cross-national studies. There are occasional special issues—recently covering social work and social justice, and social work and new labor. There is a substantial book review section, and often critical commentaries and research notes. Highly recommended for academic libraries with sociology and social work programs.

6153. *Child and Adolescent Social Work Journal.* Supersedes (in 1982): *Family and Child Mental Health Journal;* Which was formerly (until 1980): *Issues in Child Mental Health;* (until vol.5, 1977): *Psychosocial Process.* [ISSN: 0738-0151] 1970. bi-m. USD 576 for print or online ed. Ed(s): Thomas K Kenemore. Kluwer Academic / Plenum Publishers, 233 Spring St Fl 7, New York, NY 10013-1522; http://www.wkap.nl/. Illus., adv. Sample. Refereed. Online: EBSCO Publishing; Gale Group; ingenta.com; Kluwer Online; OCLC Online Computer Library Center, Inc.; Ovid Technologies, Inc.; RoweCom Information Quest; Swets Blackwell. *Indexed:* ASSIA, IMFL, PsycholAb, RiskAb, SSI, SWA, SWR&A, SociolAb. *Bk. rev.:* 1-3, signed. *Aud.:* Ac, Sa.

This journal publishes original research on clinical social work practice with children, adolescents, and their families. Clinicians and other service providers share their experience and knowledge with their colleagues. Program evaluation, analysis of risk behaviors, and empirical studies of specific populations are just some of the areas of coverage. Recommended for academic libraries supporting social work programs, as well as for libraries serving social services professionals.

6154. *Child & Family Social Work.* [ISSN: 1356-7500] 1996. q. GBP 260 for print & online eds. Ed(s): Nina Biehal. Blackwell Publishing Ltd., 9600 Garsington Rd, Oxford, OX4 2ZG, United Kingdom; customerservices@oxon.blackwellpublishing.com; http://www.blackwellpublishing.com. Adv. Circ: 425. *Indexed:* CINAHL, SWR&A, SociolAb. *Bk. rev.:* 6-8, signed. *Aud.:* Ac, Sa.

This journal publishes articles on research, theory, policy, and practice in the field of social work with children and their families. Aimed at researchers, practitioners, policy makers, and managers, coverage is broad, on such social service issues as foster children, runaways, caregivers, family support, and child protection. There is a "Policy Digest" section that publishes brief contributions on policy debates in various countries or short policy articles. There are occasional special issues; upcoming topics are social work responses to asylum-seeking children, and monitoring outcomes for children. Recommended for academic libraries with programs in social work and other libraries serving social services clientele.

6155. *Child Welfare: journal of policy, practice and program.* Formerly: *Child Welfare League of America. Bulletin.* [ISSN: 0009-4021] 1920. bi-m. USD 134 (Individuals, USD 99; Students, USD 75). Ed(s): Gary R Anderson, Julie Gwin. Child Welfare League of America, Inc., 440 First St, N W, 3rd Fl, Washington, DC 20001-2085. Illus., index, adv. Sample. Refereed. Circ: 12000. Vol. ends: Nov/Dec. Microform: PQC. Online: bigchalk; EBSCO Publishing; Northern Light Technology, Inc.; OCLC Online Computer Library Center, Inc.; ProQuest Information & Learning. Reprint: PQC; PSC. *Indexed:* ABS&EES, ASSIA, CIJE, CINAHL, CJA, ECER, EduInd, H&SSA, HRA, IBSS, IndMed, PAIS, PsycholAb, RI-1, RiskAb, SFSA, SSCI, SSI, SWR&A, SociolAb. *Aud.:* Ga, Ac, Sa.

Published by the Child Welfare League of America, this journal covers research as well as practical aspects of the health, educational, and psychological needs of children. Articles cover such diverse topics as foster parents, gender identity, and working with child abuse victims. Some issues are thematic; recent coverage is given to the crisis in rural child welfare. Authors are social services practitioners as well as researchers. Highly recommended for academic, public, and special libraries with social services clientele.

6156. *Children & Schools: a journal of social work practice.* Formerly (until 2000): *Social Work in Education.* [ISSN: 1532-8759] 1978. q. USD 45 domestic to NASW members (Non-members, USD 75). Ed(s): Paula Delo, Wilma Peebles-Wilkins. N A S W Press, 750 First St, N E, Ste 700, Washington, DC 20002-4241; orders@allenpress.com; http://www.naswpress.org. Illus., index, adv. Refereed. Circ: 3700 Paid. Vol. ends: Oct. Microform: PQC. Online: EBSCO Publishing; ProQuest Information & Learning. Reprint: PQC. *Indexed:* ASSIA, AbAn, AgeL, BrEdI, CIJE, CINAHL, ECER, EduInd, IMFL, PsycholAb, SWR&A, SociolAb. *Aud.:* Ac, Sa.

The focus of this journal, published by the National Association of Social Workers, is on professional materials relevant to social work services in education, from early-intervention programs through adult education. The journal addresses "school social workers, other pupil personnel professionals, educational institutions, family agencies, child and family health and mental health agencies, the juvenile justice system, and others concerned about education." Two special issues planned are on evidence-based practice, and school readiness and early childhood education. Recommended for elementary and high school libraries with a professional collection and for academic libraries supporting education or social work programs.

6157. *Clinical Social Work Journal.* [ISSN: 0091-1674] 1973. q. USD 589 for print or online ed. Ed(s): Carolyn Saari. Kluwer Academic / Plenum Publishers, 233 Spring St Fl 7, New York, NY 10013-1522; http://www.wkap.nl/. Illus., adv. Sample. Refereed. Vol. ends: Winter. Microform: PQC. Online: EBSCO Publishing; Gale Group; ingenta.com; Kluwer Online; Northern Light Technology, Inc.; OCLC Online Computer Library Center, Inc.; Ovid Technologies, Inc.; ProQuest Information & Learning; RoweCom Information Quest; Swets Blackwell. Reprint: ISI; PQC. *Indexed:* ASSIA, AgeL, HRA, IMFL, PRA, PsycholAb, SFSA, SSCI, SSI, SWR&A, SociolAb. *Bk. rev.:* 1-2, signed. *Aud.:* Ac, Sa.

Sponsored by the Clinical Social Work Federation, this journal is devoted exclusively to clinical social work practice and theory. Topics covered are theories of development and psychopathology, research pertinent to clinical education, patient profiles, and therapist interventions. Some issues center around a theme; recently, the topic of loss in a variety of circumstances has been explored. Recommended for academic libraries supporting social work programs and for libraries serving social services professionals.

6158. *European Journal of Social Work: the forum for the social work professional.* [ISSN: 1369-1457] 1998. 3x/yr. GBP 164 (Individuals, GBP 33). Ed(s): Walter Lorenz, Dr. Hans-Uwe Otto. Taylor & Francis Ltd, 11 New Fetter Ln, London, EC4P 4EE, United Kingdom; http://www.tandf.co.uk/journals. Illus., adv. Sample. Refereed. Circ: 550. Vol. ends: Nov. Online: EBSCO Publishing; OCLC Online Computer Library Center, Inc.; RoweCom Information Quest; Swets Blackwell. Reprint: PSC. *Indexed:* PAIS, SociolAb. *Bk. rev.:* 8-10, signed. *Aud.:* Ac.

This journal publishes theoretical debates, empirical research, accounts of practice, and topical essays on the social professions. Although it has an international editorial board, its major focus is on European countries. Recent articles have covered such topics as social work education in Great Britain, homelessness in Germany, single mothers in Venice, and social work in New Zealand. Each issue contains article summaries in French, German, and Spanish. There is a bulletin section with developments in other countries, upcoming conferences, and relevant resources. Recommended for academic libraries with graduate programs in sociology and social work.

6159. *Families in Society: the journal of contemporary human services.* Formerly (until Jan. 1990): *Social Casework.* [ISSN: 1044-3894] 1920. q. USD 143 (Individuals, USD 60). Ed(s): William Powell. Families International, Inc., 11700 West Lake Park Dr, Milwaukee, WI 53224. Illus., adv. Refereed. Circ: 2400 Paid. Vol. ends: Dec. Microform: PQC. Online: bigchalk; Florida Center for Library Automation; Gale Group;

OCLC Online Computer Library Center, Inc.; ProQuest Information & Learning; H.W. Wilson. Reprint: PQC; PSC. *Indexed:* ASG, ASSIA, AgeL, ArtHuCI, BRI, CBRI, CJA, ECER, HRA, IMFL, PSA, PsycholAb, RI-1, RiskAb, SFSA, SSCI, SSI, SWA, SWR&A, SociolAb. *Bk. rev.:* 2-4, signed. *Aud.:* Ac, Sa.

Published for the Alliance for Children and Families and the oldest social work journal in North America, this is a standard title in any library's social work collection. Articles are written for social work professionals, covering theory, practice, and public-policy issues relating to the field of family counseling and treatment. Articles are arranged under broad themes; recently, social justice, challenges to social service delivery, abuse interventions, ethics, and agency issues. Highly recommended for all academic libraries with social work and sociology programs, as well as for medical libraries and libraries serving social services professionals.

Family Process. See Family and Marriage section.

Family Relations. See Family and Marriage section.

6160. *Health & Social Work.* [ISSN: 0360-7283] 1976. q. USD 105 (Members, USD 45; Non-members, USD 80). Ed(s): Colleen M Galambos. N A S W Press, 750 First St, N E, Ste 700, Washington, DC 20002-4241; press@naswdc.org; http://www.naswpress.org. Illus., index, adv. Refereed. Circ: 6500. Vol. ends: Nov. Microform: PQC. Online: bigchalk; Chadwyck-Healey Incorporated; EBSCO Publishing; Florida Center for Library Automation; Gale Group; Northern Light Technology, Inc.; OCLC Online Computer Library Center, Inc.; ProQuest Information & Learning. Reprint: PQC. *Indexed:* ASG, ASSIA, AbAn, AgeL, BiolAb, CIJE, CINAHL, CJA, ECER, ExcerpMed, H&SSA, HRA, IBSS, IMFL, IndMed, PsycholAb, RiskAb, SSCI, SSI, SWR&A, SociolAb. *Bk. rev.:* 5-6, signed. *Aud.:* Ac, Sa.

Published by the National Association of Social Workers, this journal provides research on issues relevant to social workers in all health fields. The journal includes opinion papers, practice forums, and reports on current legislative and political issues that have implications for social work practice in health settings. Recent issues include articles focusing on new challenges and opportunities in the field, and the fit between health and mental health services and a variety of cultural groups. Recommended for academic libraries with a social work or nursing curriculum and for medical libraries.

6161. *International Social Work.* [ISSN: 0020-8728] 1958. q. GBP 289 print & online eds. in Europe, Middle East, Africa & Australasia. Ed(s): Francis J Turner. Sage Publications Ltd., 6 Bonhill St, London, EC2A 4PU, United Kingdom; info@sagepub.co.uk; http://www.sagepub.co.uk/. Illus., index, adv. Sample. Refereed. Circ: 950. Vol. ends: Oct. Microform: PQC. Online: EBSCO Publishing; Gale Group; ingenta.com; RoweCom Information Quest; Swets Blackwell. Reprint: PQC. *Indexed:* ASSIA, HRA, IBZ, PRA, PsycholAb, RRTA, SSCI, SSI, SUSA, SWR&A, SociolAb. *Bk. rev.:* 8-10, signed. *Aud.:* Ac, Sa.

This is the official journal of the International Association of Schools of Social Work, the International Council on Social Welfare, and the International Foundation of Social Workers. Its major focus is on "international themes in the delivery of services, the functions of social work professionals, and the education of social workers." Articles are especially targeted to social work policy and practice; examples include discriminatory attitudes towards individuals with mental health or intellectual disabilities, social work values, field education in developing countries, and teaching abroad. Abstracts are in English, French, Spanish, Chinese, and Arabic. Recommended for academic libraries with social work programs and libraries serving social work professionals.

Journal of Analytic Social Work. See *Psychoanalytic Social Work.*

Journal of Gerontological Social Work. See Aging section.

Journal of Marital and Family Therapy. See Family and Marriage section.

6162. *Journal of Social Work.* [ISSN: 1468-0173] 2001. 3x/yr. GBP 219 print & online eds. in Europe, Middle East, Africa & Australasia. Ed(s): Steven M Shardlow. Sage Publications Ltd., 6 Bonhill St, London, EC2A 4PU, United Kingdom; info@sagepub.co.uk; http://www.sagepub.co.uk/. Adv. Refereed. Online: ingenta.com; RoweCom Information Quest; Swets Blackwell. *Indexed:* HRA. *Bk. rev.:* 8-10, signed. *Aud.:* Ac.

This new international journal "encourages the publication and development of key aspects of social work, while also publishing material at the interface of the human service professions." Recent articles cover the politics of systems theory, public law protection of vulnerable adults, the impact of policy changes on human service nonprofit agencies, and violence in social care. In addition to an extensive book review section, there are occasional software reviews. Recommended for academic libraries with social work programs.

6163. *Journal of Sociology and Social Welfare.* [ISSN: 0191-5096] 1973. q. USD 65 (Individuals, USD 35; Students, USD 25). Ed(s): Frederick MacDonald. Western Michigan University, School of Social Work, c/o Frederick MacDonald, Mg Ed, 1903 W Michigan Ave, Kalamazoo, MI 49008-5034; macdonald@wmich.edu. Illus., index, adv. Refereed. Circ: 650. Vol. ends: Dec. Microform: PQC. Online: EBSCO Publishing; Florida Center for Library Automation; Gale Group; OCLC Online Computer Library Center, Inc.; H.W. Wilson. Reprint: PQC. *Indexed:* AgeL, CJA, PsycholAb, SSCI, SSI, SWR&A, SociolAb. *Bk. rev.:* 5-7, signed. *Aud.:* Ac, Sa.

This journal publishes "a broad range of articles which analyze social welfare institutions, policies, or problems from a social scientific perspective or otherwise attempt to bridge the gap between social science theory and social work practice." At least one issue a year is thematic, such as a recent one on temporary assistance for needy families. Recent articles include research on various types of welfare states, exploratory research in public social service agencies, and a cultural analysis of media representations, contested spaces, and sympathy for the homeless. Recommended for academic libraries with sociology and social work programs.

6164. *Policy & Practice of Public Human Services.* Formerly (until Winter 1998): *Public Welfare.* [ISSN: 1520-801X] 1943. q. USD 75 domestic; USD 95 foreign. Ed(s): Amy Tucci. American Public Human Services Association, c/o Publication Services, 810 First St, N E, Ste 500, Washington, DC 20002-4267; sbarnes@aphsa.org; http://www.aphsa.org. Illus., index, adv. Circ: 4000. Vol. ends: Fall. Microform: PQC. Online: EBSCO Publishing; Florida Center for Library Automation; Gale Group; Northern Light Technology, Inc.; OCLC Online Computer Library Center, Inc.; ProQuest Information & Learning; H.W. Wilson. Reprint: ISI; PQC; PSC. *Indexed:* AgeL, CJA, MCR, PAIS, SSCI, SSI, SWR&A, SociolAb. *Aud.:* Hs, Ga, Ac, Sa.

This publication of the American Public Human Services Association publishes articles on current health and human services issues in a highly readable style that will be understandable by a large audience. Social policy issues, reports of significant works of human service practitioners, social work theory and legislation, and various ideological points of view are represented. Special sections include "View from the Nation's Capital," "Dispatches from the States," a section abstracting recent books, and a listing of upcoming conferences and events. Recommended for high school, public, and academic libraries.

6165. *Psychoanalytic Social Work.* Former titles (until 1999): *Journal of Analytic Social Work;* (until 1992): *Journal of Independent Social Work.* [ISSN: 1522-8878] 1987. s-a. USD 300 domestic; USD 405 Canada; USD 435 elsewhere. Ed(s): Jerrold R Brandell. Haworth Press, Inc., 10 Alice St, Binghamton, NY 13904-1580; getinfo@haworthpressinc.com; http://www.haworthpressinc.com. Illus., adv. Sample. Refereed. Circ: 164 Paid. Vol. ends: Winter. Reprint: HAW. *Indexed:* ASSIA, AbAn, CIJE, CJA, HRA, IBZ, IMFL, PsycholAb, SFSA, SWA, SWR&A, SociolAb. *Bk. rev.:* 2-4, signed. *Aud.:* Ac, Sa.

This journal focuses on clinical, theoretical, research, and applied psychoanalysis issues surrounding psychoanalytic social work. Articles include case studies, reviews of the literature, work with special populations, innovative techniques, and major psychoanalytic themes. Recommended for academic libraries with social work programs and medical libraries serving social work professionals.

6166. ***Qualitative Social Work: research and practice.*** [ISSN: 1473-3250] 2002. q. USD 446 print & online eds. (Individuals, USD 63 print & online eds.). Ed(s): Roy Ruckdeschel, Ian Shaw. Sage Publications Ltd., 6 Bonhill St, London, EC2A 4PU, United Kingdom; info@sagepub.co.uk; http://www.sagepub.co.uk/. *Bk. rev.:* 1-2, signed. *Aud.:* Ac.

This new journal provides a forum for qualitative research and evaluation and approaches to social work practice. Broad topics include the role of critical perspectives within social work, development of practitioner research, interpretive and narrative approaches to research and practice, and the linking of various disciplines through the evolving interest in cultural studies. In addition to research articles, there are articles on practice and teaching and technical applications. There are occasional thematic issues, such as one focusing on critical social work. Recommended for academic libraries supporting social work programs.

6167. ***Research on Social Work Practice.*** [ISSN: 1049-7315] 1990. bi-m. GBP 344 print & online eds. in Europe, Middle East, Africa & Australasia. Ed(s): Bruce A Thyer. Sage Publications, Inc., 2455 Teller Rd, Thousand Oaks, CA 91320; info@sagepub.com; http://www.sagepub.com. Illus., index, adv. Sample. Refereed. Circ: 1200. Vol. ends: Nov. *Indexed:* ASG, ASSIA, AgeL, CIJE, CJA, HRA, PRA, PsycholAb, SFSA, SSCI, SSI, SUSA, SWR&A, SociolAb. *Bk. rev.:* 2-4, signed. *Aud.:* Ac.

Sponsored by the Society for Social Work and Research, this highly regarded journal focuses on evaluation research and methods of assessment in social work practice. Regular features include outcome studies, new methods of assessment, and invited essays. There are in-depth special issues covering topics such as research on social work practice in Chinese communities and in Ireland, and technology and social work. Highly recommended for academic libraries supporting a social work curriculum.

6168. ***Social Service Review.*** [ISSN: 0037-7961] 1927. q. USD 146 (Individuals, USD 42; Students, USD 28). Ed(s): Michael R Sosin. University of Chicago Press, Journals Division, PO Box 37005, Chicago, IL 60637; subscriptions@press.uchicago.edu; http://www.journals.uchicago.edu. Illus., index, adv. Sample. Refereed. Circ: 1700 Paid. Vol. ends: Dec. Microform: MIM; PMC; PQC. Online: EBSCO Publishing; Florida Center for Library Automation; Gale Group; ProQuest Information & Learning. Reprint: ISI; PQC; PSC. *Indexed:* ASG, ASSIA, AgeL, AmH&L, BRI, CBRI, CJA, ExcerpMed, IBSS, IMFL, IPSA, LRI, MCR, PAIS, PSA, RI-1, SFSA, SSCI, SSI, SUSA, SWR&A, SociolAb. *Bk. rev.:* 5-7, signed. *Aud.:* Ga, Ac.

Sponsored and edited by the faculty of the School of Social Service Administration of the University of Chicago, this journal covers comprehensive international research on topics related to social policy, social treatment, social change, and social work education, both historical and current. Issues covered include child welfare, health care, social welfare policy, homelessness, clinical practice, and juvenile delinquency. Social services in other countries are covered as well. Book reviews are extensive. Highly recommended for academic libraries with programs in sociology or social work and for larger public libraries.

6169. ***Social Work.*** [ISSN: 0037-8046] 1956. q. USD 105 Free to members; (Non-members, USD 80). Ed(s): Jeanne C Marsh. National Association of Social Workers, 750 First St, N E, Ste 700, Washington, DC 20002; press@naswdc.org; http://www.naswpress.org/publications/news/news.html. Illus., index, adv. Refereed. Circ: 165000 Paid. Vol. ends: Nov. Microform: PQC. Online: EBSCO Publishing; Florida Center for Library Automation; Gale Group; Northern Light Technology, Inc.; OCLC Online Computer Library Center, Inc.; ProQuest Information & Learning. Reprint: PQC. *Indexed:* ASSIA, AbAn, AgeL, ArtHuCI, BRI, CBRI, CIJE, CINAHL, CJA, ECER, ExcerpMed, HRA, IndMed, LRI, PAIS, PRA, PsycholAb, SFSA, SSCI, SSI, SWA, SWR&A, SociolAb. *Bk. rev.:* 1-2, signed. *Aud.:* Ac, Sa.

This publication of the National Association of Social Workers is a standard for library social work collections. Research focuses on empirical studies, case studies, and analyses of programs, issues, and public policies affecting social work practice. Some issues are thematic; one recent focus is on social work roles and ethics. There are three special columns: "Points and Viewpoints," "Practice Update," and "Commentary." Highly recommended for academic libraries with sociology and social work programs, and for libraries serving social service professionals.

6170. ***Social Work Education.*** [ISSN: 0261-5479] 1980. bi-m. GBP 309 (Individuals, GBP 78). Ed(s): Michael Preston Shoot. Carfax Publishing Ltd., 4 Park Sq, Milton Park, Abingdon, OX14 4RN, United Kingdom; enquiry@tandf.co.uk; http://www.tandf.co.uk/. Circ: 800. Online: EBSCO Publishing; Ingenta Select; RoweCom Information Quest; Swets Blackwell. Reprint: PSC. *Indexed:* ASSIA, BrEdI, IBSS, IBZ, SWA, SWR&A, SociolAb. *Aud.:* Ac, Sa.

This journal publishes articles concerned with the theory and practice of social care and social work education at all levels and in many countries. Recent articles have been on mature students in social work education, European teaching experiences, the role of tutoring, innovations, and action research. Recommended for libraries supporting schools of social work.

6171. ***Social Work in Health Care: the journal of health care work.*** [ISSN: 0098-1389] 1975. q. 2 vols./yr. USD 300 domestic; USD 405 Canada; USD 435 elsewhere. Ed(s): Gary Rosenburg. Haworth Press, Inc., 10 Alice St, Binghamton, NY 13904-1580; getinfo@haworthpressinc.com; http://www.haworthpressinc.com. Illus., adv. Sample. Refereed. Circ: 1858 Paid. Microform: PQC. Reprint: HAW. *Indexed:* ASG, ASSIA, AgeL, BiolAb, CINAHL, ExcerpMed, HRA, IBZ, IMFL, IndMed, MCR, PRA, PsycholAb, SFSA, SSCI, SWA, SWR&A, SociolAb. *Bk. rev.:* 1-2, signed. *Aud.:* Ac, Sa.

This journal of the Society for Social Work Leadership in Health Care publishes research for social workers on all aspects of health care, including clinical practice, education, and health policy. Articles are written by medical social workers as well as researchers. There are special issues that can be purchased separately; recently, on use of clinical data-mining in practice-based research of social work in hospital settings. Recommended for academic libraries supporting social work programs and for libraries serving professionals in the field of medical social work.

6172. ***Social Work Research.*** Supersedes in part (in 1994): *Social Work Research and Abstracts;* Which was formerly (until 1977): *Abstracts for Social Workers.* [ISSN: 1070-5309] 1977. q. USD 105 (Members, USD 45; Non-members, USD 75). Ed(s): Enola K Proctor. N A S W Press, 750 First St, N E, Ste 700, Washington, DC 20002-4241; orders@allenpress.com; http://www.naswpress.org. Illus., index, adv. Refereed. Circ: 3000 Paid. Vol. ends: Dec. Microform: PQC. Online: EBSCO Publishing; Florida Center for Library Automation; Gale Group; Northern Light Technology, Inc.; ProQuest Information & Learning. *Indexed:* ASG, ASSIA, AbAn, AgeL, CIJE, CINAHL, CJA, HRA, PsycholAb, SFSA, SSCI, SSI, SWR&A, SociolAb. *Aud.:* Ac, Sa.

This National Association of Social Workers journal publishes research in the areas of social work and social welfare. Recent studies published have been on how welfare recipients become independent, therapeutic process for psychiatric emergency room clients, and an in-depth study of welfare interaction among states. A research methodology section evaluates research design instruments. Highly recommended for academic libraries supporting social work programs or graduate programs in sociology, and for libraries serving social work professionals.

6173. ***Social Work with Groups: a journal of community and clinical practice.*** [ISSN: 0160-9513] 1978. q. USD 480 domestic; USD 648 Canada; USD 696 elsewhere. Ed(s): Roselle Kurland, Andrew Malekoff. Haworth Press, Inc., 10 Alice St, Binghamton, NY 13904-1580; getinfo@haworthpressinc.com; http://www.haworthpressinc.com. Illus., adv. Sample. Refereed. Circ: 1012 Paid. Microform: PQC. Online: Gale Group. *Indexed:* ASG, ASSIA, AgeL, CJA, HRA, IBZ, IMFL, PsycholAb, SSCI, SSI, SWA, SWR&A, SociolAb. *Bk. rev.:* 5-7, signed. *Aud.:* Ac, Sa.

This journal addresses the issue of group work in social work and social services agencies. The latest developments in research and practice are addressed, with articles covering such topics as family group conferencing, social work in community centers, and personal experiences of group workers. Includes book and video reviews. Recommended for academic libraries with social work programs and libraries serving social services professionals.

Suicide and Life-Threatening Behavior. See Death and Dying section.

Electronic Journals

6174. ***Sociological Research Online: an electronic journal.*** [ISSN: 1360-7804] 1996. q. GBP 110 (Free to individuals). Ed(s): Nicola Green, Amanda Coffey. Sage Publications Ltd., 6 Bonhill St, London, EC2A 4PU, United Kingdom; info@sagepub.co.uk; http://www.sagepub.co.uk/. Illus., adv. Refereed. *Indexed:* IBSS, PAIS, SSCI, SociolAb. *Bk. rev.:* 12-14, signed. *Aud.:* Ac.

This online-only journal is published through a consortium that includes the Universities of Surrey and Stirling, the British Sociological Association, and Sage Publications. It publishes theoretical and empirical studies in sociology and issues that engage in current political and cultural debates. In addition to the journal articles, there are two special sections: a collection of academic "think pieces" from a sociological perspective related to a theme from current events, such as the events of September 11, and a thematic collection created from articles, reviews, and research resouces published in earlier issues. Recommended for academic libraries with sociology and social work programs.

■ SPIRITUALITY AND WELL-BEING

Jerilyn Marshall, Head of Reference & Instructional Services, Rod Library, University of Northern Iowa, Cedar Falls, IA 50613
jerilyn.marshall@uni.edu

Introduction

Seeking a spiritual existence and attaining a feeling of well-being through the search have become parts of the daily lives of millions of people in recent years. While some seek to adhere to a traditional religious discipline, others practice in nontraditional religions. Still others attest to no particular religious belief, but weave parts of several beliefs into a personally meaningful spiritual system. This section includes magazines that reflect the variety of spiritual paths that a person can follow in order to attain personal transformation and a sense of well-being. There are several well-established popular magazines in this section, along with some others that are newer, more esoteric, or more specialized. The magazines all have one thing in common: A spiritual focus underlies most or all of their articles. They are all meant to appeal to an audience of those who are spiritually oriented or who are interested in transforming themselves through attainment of a higher consciousness. The magazines in this section are not primarily focused on the rules and doctrines of particular religions, even if they are written for practitioners of a religion.

This section of *Magazines for Libraries* was initially titled "New Age," and it has kept that name since 1992, through five editions (7th to 11th). The very first time it appeared it featured not only spiritual periodicals but also those that advocated unified peaceful action in order to affect both the local and general environments. From edition to edition the content and focus changed slightly, until in the 11th edition the goal was to include only spiritually oriented magazines. Every introduction in the last five editions has stated that personal spiritual transformation is a basic quality of the New Age movement, and personal transformation is still an essential goal of the periodicals listed in the current edition. By 2003, the term "New Age" had become a bit out of date, although its principles have not. The quest for spirituality and personal transformation is ongoing and as strong as ever. The title of this section has been changed to "Spirituality and Well-Being" in order to more accurately reflect the nature of the magazines that had been listed here for the past several editions. The change in title and focus did lead to the elimination of one magazine that was listed here in the last edition. *Alternative Medicine* no longer seemed to belong here, because recent issues do not indicate any spiritual focus at all. This edition also sees the reinstatement of *Yoga Journal* and *Body & Soul* (formerly titled *New Age*), which were previously excluded due to the large amounts of advertising they carry. A few periodicals included in the last edition were omitted due to the inability to obtain a sample issue. These include *Light of Consciousness, Personal Transformation,* and *Yoga International.*

The magazines in this section are not widely indexed. *Alternative Press Index* covers a couple of them, and *ReVision* is included in EBSCO's online products (1990-) and also in Expanded Academic ASAP (1997-).

Basic Periodicals

Ga: *Body & Soul.*

6175. ***Body & Soul: balanced living in a busy world.*** Former titles: *New Age;* (until 1998): *New Age Journal;* (until 1983): *New Age Magazine; New Age Journal.* [ISSN: 1539-0004] 1974. bi-m. plus a. special issue. USD 12 domestic; USD 4.95 domestic; USD 5.99 Canada. Ed(s): Jennifer Cook. New Age Publishing, Inc., 42 Pleasant St, Watertown, MA 02172. Illus., adv. Sample. Circ: 200000 Paid. Vol. ends: Nov/Dec. Microform: PQC. *Indexed:* AgeL, AltPI, BRI, CBRI. *Aud.:* Ga.

One of the most widely distributed magazines focusing on spirituality and well-being is *Body & Soul.* Its publisher's mission is "to inspire and empower people in their quest for a healthier and more spiritually fulfilling life." The articles are written for a general audience. The magazine aims to provide information on nurturing the spiritual health and well-being of the body and mind. Nutrition, meditation, yoga, and a healthy lifestyle are all prominently featured in recent issues. There are also interviews and features on individuals, written in a journalistic style. The magazine does not advocate any one belief system, and the articles are not religious in nature. They guide the reader to the spiritual experience through everyday life and through self-discovery and community activity. Advertising takes up a little over half of each issue. The articles are useful and very readable. Despite the large amount of advertising, *Body & Soul* is a popular and useful magazine that will be most interesting to patrons of public libraries.

6176. ***Circle Magazine: celebrating nature, spirit & magic.*** Formerly: *Circle Network News.* 1980. 4x/yr. USD 19 domestic; USD 25 in Canada & Mexico; USD 34 in Europe. Ed(s): Dennis Carpenter, Selena Fox. Circle Sanctuary, PO Box 219, Mt. Horeb, WI 53572; circle@mhtc.net. Illus., adv. *Aud.:* Ga.

Circle Magazine "provides news, rituals, and other information pertaining to Wiccan traditions, Shamanism, Goddess Spirituality, Ecofeminism, Animism, and other forms of contemporary Paganism." It includes first-person narratives, how-to articles, artwork, and creative writing. Articles on topics such as "Herbcraft," "Family Focus," "Nature Communication," and "Leader Skills" are regularly featured. The annual theme of the 2003 issues was "Celebrating the Seasons of Life"; the spring issue celebrates "Birth & Childhood"; the summer issue, "Youth"; the fall issue, "Adulthood"; and the winter issue, "Elderhood." Original artwork and photographs are in black and white, with the magazine cover in color. Regular features highlight goddesses and deities of nature. A regular news column discusses legal cases and issues related to the rights of those who follow pagan religions. There are many ads as well as a classified section. The main audience for the magazine will be those who are interested in nature spirituality in all of its many forms. It is published by Circle Sanctuary, "a nonprofit international Nature Spirituality resource center and a legally recognized Shamanic Wiccan church," located on a 200-acre nature preserve in Mt. Horeb, Wisconsin.

6177. ***Emergence (Sedona).*** [ISSN: 1040-8975] 1989. q. USD 43 domestic; USD 56 Canada; USD 62 elsewhere. Light Technology Publishing, PO Box 3540, Flagstaff, AZ 86003; sedonajo@sedonajo.com ; http://www.sedonajo.com/. *Bk. rev.:* Number and length varies. *Aud.:* Ga.

Readers of this journal draw inspiration from its many articles on spiritual topics. The focus is on channeling, defined by the *American Heritage Dictionary* as "the act or practice of serving as a medium through which a spirit guide purportedly communicates with living persons." The majority of the pieces in this magazine are written by people who are channeling ethereal beings with names such as Mother Gaia, Quan Yin, and Nademus. The articles are generally positive in nature, and there are several predictive articles in each issue, some based on astrology and numerology. Regular columns cover such topics as dream interpretation, advice for the lovelorn, and herbalism and the "mineral kingdom." There is even a column called "The Movie Mystic" that reviews recently released feature films from a spiritual point of view. This publication will be of great interest to those interested in a nontraditional, explorational view of spirituality. Each issue features book and music reviews. The web site (http://www.sedonajournal.com/sje) includes excerpts from issues dating back to 1999.

6178. *Entheos: the journal of psychedelic spirituality.* 2001. s-a. USD 50 (Individuals, USD 28). Ed(s): Mark Hoffman. Entheomedia, HC71, Box 34, Taos, NM 87571; entheos70@aol.com; http://www.entheomedia.com/. Illus. Refereed. *Aud.:* Ac.

Entheos is a unique journal that publishes scholarly articles highlighting the role of entheogens in human spirituality. Entheogens are also known as hallucinogens or psychedelics. Recognizing that this topic is not covered in most of mainstream scholarship, the publisher hopes to provide accurate, relevant, and current research to those who are interested. Many of the articles explore the historical and anthropological aspects of the subject of entheogens. Articles interpreting works of art are also featured. Titles of articles in a recent issue include "The Mushroom Gods of Ancient India," "The Entheogenic Eucharist of Mithras," and "Two Paintings of J.W.M. Turner." The journal is targeted towards academic specialists in a variety of subject areas, but the articles are also understandable to nonspecialists. Spirituality or religion is mentioned in all of the articles. Each article is illustrated and includes footnotes. There are additional illustrations and other material on the journal's web site (http://www.entheomedia.com). The journal is printed on demand in limited numbers, and is available by subscription. It is most suited to academic libraries.

6179. *Mandala: Buddhist News Magazine.* Incorporates: *Mandala Newsletter.* [ISSN: 1075-4113] 1987. 4x/yr. USD 22 domestic; USD 28 foreign; USD 6.95 per issue. Ed(s): Helen Chang. Foundation for the Preservation of the Mahayana Tradition, 125B La Posta Rd, Taos, NM 87571. Adv. Circ: 8000. *Aud.:* Ga.

Mandala is published by the nonprofit Foundation for the Preservation of Mahayana Tradition. According to *Encyclopaedia Britannica,* Mahayana Buddhism developed in the first century A.D. "as a more liberal and innovative interpretation of the Buddha's teachings" than was available through the more traditional Theravada Buddhism. This form of Buddhism has many adherents in eastern Asia and in countries of the Western world. *Mandala* aims to inspire inner spiritual awakening and deep understanding among individuals and groups. The articles are written from a Buddhist perspective but are still of general interest. Many of them feature practical applications of and thoughtful treatments of Buddhist principles. Regular columns feature such topics as relationships and health. The magazine is printed in color on glossy paper. It includes some advertising for religious and spiritual products and services. Its web site (http://www.mandalamagazine.org) includes tables of contents for issues dating back to 1995. This magazine would be appropriate for both public and academic libraries.

6180. *Mountain Record.* [ISSN: 0896-8942] 1981. q. USD 20; USD 27.50 foreign. Ed(s): Konrad Ryushin Marchaj. Dharma Communications, Inc., S. Plank Rd., Box 197MR, Mt. Tremper, NY 12457; mreditor@dharma.net; http://www.dharma.net/mr/journal.shtml. Adv. Circ: 5000 Paid. *Bk. rev.:* Various number and length. *Aud.:* Ga, Sa.

Published at the Zen Mountain Monastery in Mt. Tremper, New York, *Mountain Record* examines "the heart of Zen training, and the challenges encountered in meditation practice and in actualization of wisdom in the world." The primary audience for this magazine is the spiritual practitioner of the Zen tradition. It does include articles that would be easily understandable by a general audience; however, many of the articles seem to require at least a moderate knowledge of Zen and its principles. A few of the articles are not focused towards Zen history and practice. For example, one issue features an excerpt from Maya Lin's book *Boundaries* describing her experience in designing the Vietnam Veterans Memorial. Black-and-white illustrations are scattered throughout each issue. *Mountain Record* won the 2002 Utne Independent Press Award for "Spiritual Coverage." This somewhat specialized magazine would be useful in libraries carrying a wide variety of spiritual and religious periodicals.

6181. *PanGaia: creating an earth wise spirituality.* Formerly (until 1997): *Green Man.* [ISSN: 1096-0996] 1993. q. USD 18; USD 23; USD 5.95 newsstand/cover per issue. Ed(s): Anne Newkirk Niven. Blessed Bee, Inc., PO Box 641, Point Arena, CA 95468; info@blessedbee.com; http://www.blessedbee.com. Adv. Circ: 5500 Paid. *Indexed:* AltPI. *Bk. rev.:* Various number and length. *Aud.:* Ga.

Pangaia, a Pagan spiritual magazine, is decidedly more lighthearted than most other periodicals with a spiritual focus. Each issue is organized around a theme. Examples of recent themes include "Myth and Legend," and "Wisdom of the East." Many of the articles are personal narratives or other creative writing that is in line with the issue's theme. For example, an issue on "Cat Magic" includes a story on the symbolism associated with various wild cats. Each issue also features a book review column, an advice column, and a gardening column. Black-and-white illustrations and photographs are peppered throughout; the covers are in color. *Pangaia* would be welcome in public libraries with a clientele interested in Paganism. Its web site (http://www.pangaia.com) offers basic information on the Pagan and Gaian religions.

6182. *ReVision: A Journal of Consciousness and Transformation.* Formerly: *Revision.* 1978. q. USD 74 (Individuals, USD 41; USD 18.50 per issue). Ed(s): Rachel Zuses. Heldref Publications, 1319 18th St, NW, Washington, DC 20036-1802; subscribe@heldref.org; http://www.heldref.org. Illus., index, adv. Sample. Refereed. Circ: 650. Vol. ends: No. 4. Microform: PQC. Online: Gale Group; ProQuest Information & Learning. Reprint: PSC. *Indexed:* AltPI, PsycholAb, RI-1. *Aud.:* Ac.

ReVision is a bit different from the other periodicals listed in this section. It belongs here because it emphasizes "transformative dimensions of current and traditional thought and practice." It isn't overtly spiritual; however, many of its articles touch on spiritual, religious, and philosophical topics. Most articles are written in the first person and are scholarly yet readable. Almost all include footnotes and citations to other sources, and the editorial board consists primarily of faculty members of universities and other institutions in the United States and the United Kingdom. Each issue is organized around a theme. Recent themes include "Indigenous Language Revitalization" and "Fierce Goddesses, Great Mothers, and Yoginis: The Archaeomythology of Devotion." The journal contains almost no advertising. It would be most appropriate in academic and larger public libraries.

SageWoman. See Women: Feminist and Special Interest/Special Interest section.

6183. *Shambhala Sun: buddhism culture meditation life.* Formerly (until Apr. 1992): *Vajradhatu Sun.* [ISSN: 1190-7886] 1978. bi-m. CND 36 domestic; USD 24 United States; USD 36 elsewhere. Ed(s): Melvin McLeod. Shambhala Sun, 1585 Barrington St, Ste 300, Halifax, NS B3J 1Z8, Canada; magazine@shambhalasun.com; http://www.shambhalasun.com. Illus., adv. Circ: 35000 Paid. *Indexed:* CBCARef, RI-1. *Bk. rev.:* Number and length vary. *Aud.:* Ga.

This attractively designed magazine is published by an organization founded by the Buddhist teacher Chogyam Trungpa Rinpoche. The subtitle "Buddhism, Culture, Meditation, Life" indicates the publication's broad scope. Many of the articles start out explaining a Buddhist concept and then proceed to illustrate how to apply the concept in daily life. There are also interviews with well-known Buddhist practitioners. The writing style is simple and direct, and the layout is inviting. Each issue includes regular columns on subjects such as cooking, health, yoga, and environmental design. There is usually one lengthy book review as well as several brief ones. Although each issue is peppered with advertising, all ads are for products to enhance the spiritual practices of meditation, yoga, etc. The magazine's web site (http://www.shambhalasun.com) includes excerpts from issues as far back as January 1995.

■ SPORTS

General/Physical Education, Coaching, and Sports Sciences/Specific Sports

See also Boats and Boating; Environment and Conservation; Fishing; Hiking, Climbing, and Outdoor Recreation; and Hunting and Guns sections.

Betsy Park, Head, Reference Department, The University of Memphis Libraries, Memphis, TN 38152; ehpark@memphis.edu

Harriet Alexander, former Reference Librarian, Reference Department, The University of Memphis Libraries

Introduction

Sports play an important role in the lives of many Americans. We spend money on equipment, apparel, instruction, travel, and supporting our favorite teams and players. We participate in organized and individual sports, dedicating much of our leisure time to bowling, water-skiing, football, or golf. We enjoy sports as spectators and fans, watching and cheering for our favorite amateur and professional teams and athletes on television or on the field. This interest in sports has spawned a large number of magazines, newspapers, and academic journals. These publications can be classified as those for the participant, for the spectator or fan, or for the scholar, researcher, or clinician. In general, magazines for the participant contain instructional articles, information on nutrition, injury prevention, physical and mental preparation, travel, equipment, clothing, and personalities. A golfer can learn to overcome the first-tee jitters, a recreational scuba diver can investigate the latest in wetsuits, and a young football player can learn to attack the line of scrimmage. Magazines and newspapers for spectators and fans can provide hours of entertainment with information about favorite teams and players. In addition to feature articles, interviews, statistics, charts, and competitions, these publications often include quizzes and crossword puzzles. If you want to know how your baseball team is doing or what your favorite football player eats for breakfast, there is a magazine for you. Academic and scholarly journals present research and information to further knowledge and inform scholars, students, clinicians, and practitioners in the field. Many of these report research in sports medicine, on the art and science of human movement, and on the behavioral aspects, business, economics, history, philosophy, psychology, and sociology of sports. There is even one academic journal devoted to the literature of sport.

Since the last edition of *Magazines for Libraries*, there have been changes in publications selected. Some have ceased publication, while others are threatened with extinction; some publications have merged and some have migrated to strictly online versions. A few new magazines have been launched. The increased web presence of sports publications is notable. Almost every magazine and journal now has some presence on the web with interactive features and updated news not available in the print format. Many magazines use an e-mail alerting service to inform readers of new issues and developments. Another development of note is the growth of the aggregator databases such as those produced by the Gale Group, EBSCO, ProQuest, and others. These vendors provide access to articles in electronic journals through their various databases. Libraries and individual users may no longer subscribe to a particular magazine, but access it instead through one of the aggregator databases.

There is an abundance of choices for sports reading. It is impossible to review every publication, but an attempt has been made to locate representative magazines from a wide variety of sports. It is hoped that the periodical selection below, which includes general, physical education, coaching, sports sciences, and a number of specific sports, will help individuals and libraries in deciding which to purchase and read.

Basic Periodicals

GENERAL. All levels: *E S P N The Magazine, The Sporting News, Sports Illustrated.*

PHYSICAL EDUCATION, COACHING, AND SPORTS SCIENCES. Ems: *Journal of Teaching in Physical Education, Teaching Elementary Physical Education;* Hs: *Coach and Athletic Director, Journal of Physical Education, Recreation and Dance;* Ac: *Adapted Physical Activity Quarterly, American Journal of Sports Medicine, Journal of Applied Biomechanics, Journal of Physical Education, Recreation and Dance, Journal of Teaching in Physical Education, Quest, Research Quarterly for Exercise and Sport.*

SPECIFIC SPORTS. All levels: *Baseball America, Basketball Digest, Bicycling, Football Digest, Golf Magazine, Hockey News, International Figure Skating, Runner's World, Ski, Soccer America, Tennis, VolleyballUSA.*

Basic Abstracts and Indexes

Physical Education Index, SPORTDiscus.

General

6184. ***E S P N The Magazine.*** [ISSN: 1097-1998] 1998. bi-w. USD 26 domestic; CND 45 Canada. Disney Publishing Worldwide Inc., 114 Fifth Ave, New York, NY 10011-5690. Illus., adv. Sample. Circ: 850000. *Aud.:* Hs, Ga, Ac.

Published since 1998, *ESPN The Magazine* is an oversized (12-inch x 10-inch), general-interest sports magazine. Each biweekly issue contains over 100 pages, with lots of photographs and advertisements. Regular departments include a commentary by "The Sports Guy," an informal "chat room," double-page spreads of various sporting events, and "The Jump" (brief reports of big sports stories, statistics, and a question and answer section). Several columns are written by ESPN SportsCenter personalities. Feature articles touch on a variety of sports and players. The writing style is informal, sometimes humorous. The print magazine is supplemented by its electronic version at http://espn.go.com/magazine. This newsmagazine will be popular with readers at public and academic libraries.

6185. ***Juco Review.*** [ISSN: 0047-2956] 1948. 9x/yr. USD 30 domestic; USD 50 foreign. Ed(s): George E Killian. National Junior College Athletic Association, PO Box 7305, Colorado Springs, CO 80933-7305; gkillian@njcaa.org; http://www.njcaa.org. Illus., adv. Sample. Circ: 3000. Microform: PQC. Reprint: PQC. *Indexed:* PEI, SportS. *Aud.:* Ac.

Juco Review, the official magazine of the National Junior College Athletic Association, is published monthly September through May. The focus of the association is to "promote and foster junior college athletics on intersectional and national levels so that results will be consistent with the total educational program of its members." The publication contains association news, coaching strategies and techniques, statistics, highlights of national championships, and other information. Each month a particular college is featured. One of the issues examined contains a "post 9/11 checklist" with information for international students. Issues run approximately 20–25 pages. Appropriate for two-year colleges with intersectional programs.

6186. ***The Sporting News.*** [ISSN: 0038-805X] 1886. 60x/yr. USD 78 domestic; USD 124.80 Canada; USD 3.99 newsstand/cover. Ed(s): John Rawlings. Vulcan Print Media, 10176 Corporate Square Dr., Ste. 200, St. Louis, MO 63132-2924; http://sportingnews.com/. Illus., adv. Circ: 515000 Paid. Vol. ends: Dec. Microform: BHP; PQC; NRP. Online: EBSCO Publishing; Gale Group; LexisNexis; Northern Light Technology, Inc.; OCLC Online Computer Library Center, Inc.; ProQuest Information & Learning. Reprint: PQC. *Indexed:* ASIP, MagInd, SportS. *Aud.:* Ga.

Since 1886, *The Sporting News*, which bills itself as "the first newsweekly in sports," has been reporting the news of sports. Each 60-page issue contains numerous photographs and current information on professional baseball, football, basketball, hockey, and stock car racing, as well as collegiate basketball and football. Articles provide in-depth coverage of teams and players, plus statistics, strategies, and scouting reports. Readers can submit short questions and receive responses in a column called "M@il Bonding." Daily news, links to *The Sporting News* radio, and fantasy baseball (plus fantasy football soon) can be found at the web site, www.sportingnews.com. Sports fans will find this publication of interest at public libraries.

6187. ***Sports Illustrated.*** [ISSN: 0038-822X] 1954. w. USD 45 domestic; USD 50.66 Canada; USD 3.50 newsstand/cover. Ed(s): Norman Pearlstine, Terry McDonnell. Time Inc., Sports Illustrated Group, Sports Illustrated Bldg, 135 W 50th St, 4th Fl., New York, NY 10020-1393; http://sportsillustrated.cnn.com/si_online/. Illus., index, adv. Circ: 3150000 Paid. Microform: PQC. Online: bigchalk; CompuServe Inc.; The Dialog Corporation; EBSCO Publishing; Factiva; Florida Center for Library Automation; Gale Group; LexisNexis; MediaStream, Inc.; OCLC Online Computer Library Center, Inc.; ProQuest Information & Learning; H.W. Wilson. *Indexed:* BRI, BiogInd, CBCARef, CBRI, CPerI, MagInd, PEI, RGPR, SportS. *Aud.:* Ems, Hs, Ga, Ac.

A staple of sports journals, *Sports Illustrated* is the most widely read and respected sport magazine. Since 1954, this award-winning publication has covered all types of popular sports, players, teams, and society. Issues are filled with excellent photography and well-written articles. Each 70- to 80-page issue contains letters to the editor, one or two longer feature articles, several shorter articles, analysis, commentary and predictions, and insights. Selected articles are available free at the web site, sportsillustrated.cnn.com. Recommended for public, school, and academic libraries.

Sports Illustrated for Kids. See Children section.

6188. ***Tuff Stuff.*** [ISSN: 1041-4258] 1983. m. USD 29.95 domestic; USD 61.95 foreign. Ed(s): Rocky Landsverk. Krause Publications, Inc., 700 E State St, Iola, WI 54990-0001; info@krause.com; http://www.krause.com. Adv. Circ: 199606 Paid and free. *Aud.:* Ga.

Fans who collect sports and entertainment cards, collectibles, memorabilia, and autographed items will read *Tuff Stuff*, which bills itself as "the #1 guide to sports cards and collectibles." In addition to extensive price guides, the publication contains news and trading information and a few in-depth articles on players, entertainers, or the collectibles industry. Each issue contains over 200 pages. Selected full text from the magazine is available for free at www.collect.com, with additional full text for subscribers. Suitable for public libraries.

Physical Education, Coaching, and Sports Sciences

Adapted Physical Activity Quarterly. See Disabilities section.

6189. ***Aethlon: the journal of sport literature.*** Formerly (until 1988): *Arete.* [ISSN: 1048-3756] 1983. s-a. USD 50 (Individual members, USD 40). Ed(s): Don Johnson. Sports Literature Association, East Tennessee State University, Box 70270, Johnson City, TN 37614; sla@etsu.edu. Illus., adv. Refereed. Circ: 650 Paid. *Indexed:* BRI, CBRI, MLA-IB, PEI. *Bk. rev.:* 20, 500 to 2,000 words. *Aud.:* Ac.

Published by the Sports Literature Association, *Aethlon* "is a scholarly journal designed to celebrate the marriage of serious, interpretive literature with the world of play, games, and sport." The journal publishes poetry, fiction, nonfiction, drama, critical articles, and book reviews. Issues run approximately 200 pages, with approximately twenty manuscripts interspersed with poems. Contributions, both serious and humorous, are enjoyable to read. English professors, novelists, short story writers, poets, and dramatists all write for this journal. This is particularly suitable for academic libraries, but public libraries may also find it a worthy addition.

6190. ***American Journal of Sports Medicine.*** Formerly (until 1976): *Journal of Sports Medicine.* [ISSN: 0363-5465] 1972. 8x/yr. USD 368. Ed(s): Ann E Donaldson, Dr. Robert E Leach. Sage Publications, Inc., 2455 Teller Rd, Thousand Oaks, CA 91320; info@sagepub.com; http://www.sagepub.com. Illus., index, adv. Refereed. Circ: 10754 Paid. Vol. ends: Nov/Dec. Microform: PQC. Online: bigchalk; EBSCO Publishing; Florida Center for Library Automation; Gale Group; HighWire Press; MD Consult; Northern Light Technology, Inc.; OCLC Online Computer Library Center, Inc.; ProQuest Information & Learning. *Indexed:* AbAn, BiolAb, CINAHL, EduInd, ExcerpMed, GSI, H&SSA, IndMed, PEI, SCI, SportS. *Aud.:* Ac, Sa.

The official publication of the American Orthopaedic Society for Sports Medicine, *The American Journal of Sports Medicine* is a bimonthly peer-reviewed publication focusing on research and case studies related to a variety of sports injuries, their treatment, rehabilitation, and frequency of occurrence. While the print journal has been available since 1972, the online version contains an archive going back to 1998 for subscribing members and is available as an added benefit only to print subscribers. The part of the online site open to nonsubscribers includes contents for future issues and contents indexing and abstracts for issues dating from 1976. This title is appropriate for academic and medical libraries.

6191. ***Athletic Business.*** Formerly (until 1984): *Athletic Purchasing and Facilities.* [ISSN: 0747-315X] 1977. m. USD 55 domestic. Ed(s): Andrew Cohen. Athletic Business Publications, Inc., 4130 Lien Rd, Madison, WI 53704-3602; editors@athleticbusiness.com. Illus., index, adv. Circ: 42301 Controlled. *Indexed:* SportS. *Aud.:* Ac, Sa.

Published since 1977, the monthly *Athletic Business* is a trade journal covering the business end of sports and athletics, including such areas as equipment, corporate wellness programs, facility planning, marketing, management, and design. It is distributed free to qualified professionals, who run the gamut from facility owners to YMCAs, YWCAs, JCCs, sports and health clubs, and correctional facilities (not libraries). Feature articles are supplemented by columns on sports law, college programs, high school programs, recreation industry, profit-making hints, and a huge amount of advertising of equipment, facility floor coverings, and ceilings. Special issues include a "Buyers Guide" published in February and an "Architectural Showcase" published in June. Since professionals, including high school and university athletic coaches, can qualify for a free subscription to this magazine, it is suggested that only academic libraries with strong business programs will want to purchase a subscription.

6192. ***Athletic Therapy Today.*** [ISSN: 1078-7895] 1996. bi-m. USD 156 (Individuals, USD 39). Ed(s): Gary B. Wilkerson. Human Kinetics Publishers, Inc., PO Box 5076, Champaign, IL 61825-5076; orders@hkusa.com; http://www.humankinetics.com. Illus., index, adv. Refereed. Circ: 2099 Paid. Reprint: PSC. *Indexed:* CINAHL, ExcerpMed, H&SSA, PEI. *Bk. rev.:* 3, 100 words. *Aud.:* Ac, Sa.

Athletic Therapy Today is a peer-reviewed but not a research-oriented journal. This bimonthly has been published since 1996 as a professional journal focused on providing practical application and advice to sports medicine specialists. Individual issues consist of approximately 60 pages, containing about six articles, most of which focus on a specific theme. Issues also contain columns on clinical evaluation and testing, case reviews, injury management, disabilities, conditioning, nutrition notes, book reviews and news information, and several others of professional interest. Articles are relatively brief and written conversationally. Suitable for medical and academic libraries.

6193. ***Athletics Administration: official publication of the National Association of Collegiate Directors of Athletics.*** [ISSN: 0044-9873] 1966. bi-m. Non-members, USD 15. Ed(s): Laurie Garrison. Host Communications, Inc., 546 E Main St, Lexington, KY 40508; info@hostcommunications.com; http://www.hostcommunications.com. Illus., index, adv. Sample. Circ: 6500. *Indexed:* SportS. *Bk. rev.:* 1-2, 150 words. *Aud.:* Ac, Sa.

Athletics Administration is the official publication of the National Association of Collegiate Directors of Athletics. It is primarily an informative professional journal, containing practical articles of interest to college coaches. Issues of approximately 40 pages include short articles on such topics as "Championship Travel," "NACDA Directors' Cup Presentations," and "Resume Verification." These articles are supplemented by buying guides and columns on association news, news from related associations, literature reviews, and a calendar of upcoming events. This bimonthly is appropriate for academic libraries.

6194. ***British Journal of Sports Medicine.*** Incorporates: *British Association of Sport and Medicine. Bulletin.* [ISSN: 0306-3674] 1968. q. GBP 221 (Individuals, GBP 100 print & online eds.). Ed(s): Janet O'Flaherty, Paul McCrory. B M J Publishing Group, B M A House, Tavistock Sq, London, WC1H 9JR, United Kingdom; info.norththames@bma.org.uk; http://www.bmjjournals.com/. Illus., adv. Refereed. Vol. ends: Dec.

Microform: PQC. Online: EBSCO Publishing; Florida Center for Library Automation; Gale Group; HighWire Press; Ovid Technologies, Inc.; ProQuest Information & Learning; RoweCom Information Quest; SilverPlatter Information, Incorporated; Swets Blackwell. *Indexed:* CINAHL, CJA, ErgAb, ExcerpMed, H&SSA, IndMed, PEI, RRTA, SCI, SSCI, SportS. *Bk. rev.:* Number and length vary. *Aud.:* Ac, Sa.

One of the most well-known and well-regarded journals in the field of sports medicine is the official journal of the British Association of Sport and Medicine, the *British Journal of Sports Medicine*. Published since 1968, each issue of this bimonthly publication runs about 80 to 100 pages. The approximately 20 articles per issue are divided into sections: editorials, leaders, reviews (of research), original articles, case studies, and the postscript that contains news, a calendar, and book reviews. The coverage includes "all aspects of sports medicine, the management of sports injury, exercise physiology, sports psychology, physiotherapy and the epidemiology of exercise and health." The web site at http://bjsm.bmjjournals.com offers online access to the journal since 2000. A highly recommended title for academic libraries with programs in health sciences.

6195. *Canadian Journal of Applied Physiology.* Former titles (until 1992): *Canadian Journal of Sport Sciences; Canadian Journal of Applied Sport Science.* [ISSN: 1066-7814] 1976. bi-m. USD 221 (Individuals, USD 59). Ed(s): Terry Graham. Human Kinetics Publishers, Inc., PO Box 5076, Champaign, IL 61825-5076; http://www.humankinetics.com. Illus., index, adv. Refereed. Circ: 974 Paid and free. Vol. ends: Dec. Microform: MML. Online: EBSCO Publishing. *Indexed:* BiolAb, CBCARef, CINAHL, ChemAb, ErgAb, ExcerpMed, H&SSA, IBZ, IndMed, PEI, PsycholAb, SCI, SSCI, SportS. *Bk. rev.:* 2, 350 words. *Aud.:* Ac, Sa.

The bimonthly *Canadian Journal of Applied Physiology* began publication in 1984 as a resource for "exercise physiologists, fitness researchers, and health care professionals as well as other basic and applied physiological scientists." Each issue is approximately 150 pages and contains sections labeled research contributions, technical notes, rapid communication, invited review, and/or book review. Articles are written in English or French by geographically diverse and multidisciplinary authors from universities and research institutes worldwide. The publication's subtitle, *Physical Activity, Health, and Fitness*, gives the general tenor of subject matter included in this peer-reviewed journal. Technical language from the biological sciences is used throughout, making this journal primarily of interest to academic libraries with related programs.

6196. *Clinical Journal of Sport Medicine.* Former titles (until 1990): *Canadian Academy of Sport Medicine Review; Canadian Academy of Sport Medicine Newsletter.* [ISSN: 1050-642X] 1975. q. USD 399 (Individuals, USD 224; Qualified personnel, USD 104). Ed(s): Willem Meeuwisse. Lippincott Williams & Wilkins, 530 Walnut St, Philadelphia, PA 19106-3621; http://www.lww.com. Illus., adv. Refereed. Circ: 2170 Paid. Vol. ends: Oct. Online: Ovid Technologies, Inc.; Swets Blackwell. Reprint: PQC. *Indexed:* ExcerpMed, H&SSA, IndMed, PEI, SCI, SportS. *Aud.:* Ac, Sa.

The *Clinical Journal of Sport Medicine* is an international refereed journal for clinicians interested in sport medicine. It publishes research, reviews, and case reports on "diagnostics, therapeutics, and rehabilitation in healthy and physically challenged individuals of all ages and levels of sport and exercise participation." The editorial board consists of physicians and PhDs from Australia, Canada, South Africa, the United Kingdom, and the United States. Typical article topics include concussions among university football and soccer players, wrist pain in young gymnasts, exercise in children with type 2 diabetes, and the effectiveness of worksite physical activity programs. An interesting feature is the "Sport Medicine Journal Club" that provides an in-depth summary with conclusions and often commentary of recent literature in the field. From 2001 to date, the journal is available online for subscribers at www.cjsportmed-.com. This publication is appropriate for medical and academic libraries.

6197. *Coach and Athletic Director.* Former titles (until 1995): *Scholastic Coach and Athletic Director;* (until 1994): *Scholastic Coach;* Incorporates (1921-198?): *Athletic Journal.* [ISSN: 1087-2000] 1931. 10x/yr. USD 14.98 domestic; USD 41.95 foreign. Ed(s): Herman L Masin. Scholastic Inc., 555 Broadway, New York, NY 10012-0399; http://www.scholastic.com. Illus., index, adv. Circ: 50692. Microform: PQC. Online: Gale Group. Reprint: PSC. *Indexed:* EduInd, PEI, SportS. *Bk. rev.:* Various number and length. *Aud.:* Hs, Ga, Ac.

Published monthly during the school year with an additional combined summer issue in May/June since 1931, this is a professional magazine aimed at high school and college-level athletic coaches. News, information and advice on sports (including baseball, basketball, football, softball, soccer), strength training, and administrative activities are provided in an entertaining style using nontechnical language. Issues include book and equipment reviews and a special annual issue (February) with a buyer's guide to facilities and equipment. Online subscriptions are available at www.coachadguide.com. This title is appropriate for high school and academic libraries.

6198. *International Journal of Sport Nutrition & Exercise Metabolism.* Formerly (until Mar.2000): *International Journal of Sport Nutrition.* [ISSN: 1526-484X] 1991. bi-m. USD 221 (Individuals, USD 59). Ed(s): Emily M. Haymes, Ronald J. Maughan. Human Kinetics Publishers, Inc., PO Box 5076, Champaign, IL 61825-5076; orders@hkusa.com; http://www.humankinetics.com. Illus., index, adv. Sample. Refereed. Circ: 1228 Paid. Vol. ends: Dec. Reprint: PSC. *Indexed:* Agr, CINAHL, ChemAb, DSA, ExcerpMed, GSI, HortAb, IBZ, IndMed, PEI, RRTA, SportS. *Bk. rev.:* Number and length vary. *Aud.:* Ac, Sa.

Published by Human Kinetics, this is a highly technical peer-reviewed journal focused on a specific topic that draws upon the fields of biochemistry, physiology, psychological medicine, and sport and exercise sciences. Scholarly research articles are the focus of the journal. Issues also include articles on practical applications, book and media reviews, and editorials. In 2000, the words *and Exercise Metabolism* were added to the title to reflect the overlap of the scientific disciplines of exercise biochemistry and sport nutrition. This publication is appropriate to academic and medical libraries supporting programs in sport medicine and sport sciences.

6199. *International Journal of Sports Medicine.* [ISSN: 0172-4622] 1980. 8x/yr. EUR 387.80; EUR 58 newsstand/cover. Ed(s): Maria Hopman, W M Sherman. Georg Thieme Verlag, Ruedigerstr 14, Stuttgart, 70469, Germany; kunden.service@thieme.de; http://www.thieme.de. Illus., adv. Refereed. Circ: 1500 Paid and controlled. *Indexed:* BiolAb, ChemAb, DSA, ExcerpMed, H&SSA, IndMed, PEI, RRTA, SCI, SSCI, SportS. *Bk. rev.:* 1, 500-750 words. *Aud.:* Ac, Sa.

Published since 1980, the *International Journal of Sports Medicine* publishes eight issues per year. Its approximately 80- to 100-page issues contain sections on physiology and biochemistry, training and testing, nutrition, clinical sciences, behavioral sciences, orthopedics and biomechanics, and immunology. Its oversize issues contain English-language research articles that are highly technical and largely originate outside the United States. The journal publishes letters to the editor, short articles on recent work that merits rapid dissemination, review articles, and original research. Typical article titles include "Adipose Tissue and Muscle Metabolism during Exercise," "Neuromuscular Adaptations after Eccentric Training," "Erythropoiesis and Living High–Training Low," and "Electrical Stimulation after Knee Surgery." This journal is ranked 13th among the sport sciences with an impact factor of 1.309 in the 2001 ISI Journal Citation Reports. Appropriate to medical and academic libraries.

6200. *The International Journal of the History of Sport.* Formerly: *British Journal of Sports History.* [ISSN: 0952-3367] 1984. 5x/yr. GBP 293 print & online eds. Ed(s): J A Mangan. Frank Cass Publishers, Crown House, 47 Chase Side, Southgate, London, N14 5BP, United Kingdom; jnlsubs@frankcass.com; http://www.frankcass.com/jnls/. Illus., index, adv. Sample. Refereed. Microform: PQC. Online: Ingenta Select. *Indexed:* AmH&L, BrHumI, IBSS, IBZ, PEI, RRTA, SportS. *Bk. rev.:* 15-20, 800 words. *Aud.:* Ac.

Anthropologists, sociologists, historians, and others interested in the "historical study of sport in its political, cultural, social, educational, economic, spiritual and aesthetic dimensions" will enjoy *The International Journal of the History of Sport.* Each issue contains 200 or more pages with 8 to 20 articles and extensive book reviews. There is an interesting variety of subjects covered, including the origins of golf, images of sport and gender in *Punch*, the ancient Olympic games and the Salt Lake City scandals, and soccer in South Asia. As its name implies, articles are written by an international multidisciplinary group of scholars. Issues of the journal from 2001 on are available online to subscribers. This peer-reviewed journal is most appropriate to academic libraries.

6201. *International Review for the Sociology of Sport.* Formerly (until 1983): *International Review of Sport Sociology.* [ISSN: 1012-6902] 1966. q. GBP 286 print & online eds. in Europe, Middle East, Africa & Australasia. Ed(s): Alan Tomlinson. Sage Publications Ltd., 6 Bonhill St, London, EC2A 4PU, United Kingdom; info@sagepub.co.uk; http://www.sagepub.co.uk/. Illus., adv. Refereed. Circ: 1000. Vol. ends: Dec. Online: ingenta.com; OCLC Online Computer Library Center, Inc.; RoweCom Information Quest; Sage Publications, Inc.; Swets Blackwell. Reprint: SCH. *Indexed:* BAS, IBZ, PEI, RRTA, S&F, SociolAb, SportS. *Bk. rev.:* 2-3, 200 words. *Aud.:* Ac.

Published by Sage Publications since 1966, the *International Review for the Sociology of Sport* is the official publication of the International Sociology of Sport Association. This academic quarterly is a refereed journal that contains worldwide research in English that is not limited to sociology but also includes related fields such as anthropology, cultural and women's studies, history, geography, semiotics, political economy, and interdisciplinary research. Book and audiovisual reviews are included, as well as abstracts in several languages. Appropriate for academic libraries.

6202. *International Sports Journal.* [ISSN: 1094-0480] 1997. s-a. USD 14. Ed(s): Thomas Katsaros. University of New Haven Foundation, 300 Orange Ave, West Haven, CT 06516; mharvey@charger.newhaven.edu. Online: EBSCO Publishing; ProQuest Information & Learning. *Indexed:* PEI. *Aud.:* Ac.

This peer-reviewed quarterly that began publication in 1997 purports to include "empirical and theoretical articles that can be applied or be pertinent to current sports issues and practices or contribute to academic research in the international sports community." Each issue contains about 15 English-language articles, most of which are written by academics despite the invitation to members of the general sports community to submit articles. Written for the sports professional, much of the issue examined appears to include hard-core research, frequently using statistical analysis and jargon specific to particular sports. Recommended for academic institutions only.

Journal of Aging and Physical Activity. See Aging section.

6203. *Journal of Applied Biomechanics.* Formerly (until 1992): *International Journal of Sport Biomechanics.* [ISSN: 1065-8483] 1985. q. USD 184 (Individuals, USD 49). Ed(s): Thomas S. Buchanan. Human Kinetics Publishers, Inc., PO Box 5076, Champaign, IL 61825-5076; orders@hkusa.com; http://www.humankinetics.com. Illus., index, adv. Refereed. Circ: 1088 Paid. Reprint: PSC. *Indexed:* AS&TI, CINAHL, EngInd, ErgAb, ExcerpMed, IBZ, PEI, SSCI, SportS. *Aud.:* Ac, Sa.

An official journal of the International Society of Biomechanics, this is a technical journal. Articles accepted for publication in this peer-reviewed quarterly include original research, technical notes that may report changes in instruments or methods, research reviews, digests of workshop proceedings, and brief communications of important results/concepts. Topics of concern relate not only to exercise and sport, but also modeling, clinical biomechanics, gait and posture, and relations between the muscles and the skeleton or nervous system. This journal is appropriate for academic and medical libraries.

Journal of Applied Physiology. See Biological Sciences/Physiology section.

6204. *Journal of Athletic Training.* Former titles (until 1992): *Athletic Training; National Athletic Trainers Association. Journal.* [ISSN: 1062-6050] 1956. q. USD 32; USD 40 foreign. Ed(s): Leslie Neistadt, David Perrin. National Athletic Trainers Association, Inc., 2952 N Stemmons Fwy, Dallas, TX 75247; http://www.nata.org/. Illus., index, adv. Refereed. Circ: 29000 Paid and controlled. Vol. ends: Oct/Dec. Microform: PQC. Online: bigchalk; Northern Light Technology, Inc.; ProQuest Information & Learning. Reprint: PQC. *Indexed:* BiolAb, CIJE, CINAHL, ExcerpMed, PEI, SportS. *Bk. rev.:* 4, 350 words. *Aud.:* Ac, Sa.

A product of the National Athletic Trainers' Association, the *Journal of Athletic Training* is a quarterly peer-reviewed journal whose mission is "to enhance communication among professionals interested in the quality of healthcare for the physically active through education and research in prevention, evaluation, management, and rehabilitation of injuries." Theme-related issues are frequent; two recent ones focus on ankle instability and athletic training education. The oversized issues (approximately 8.5" x 11") contain about 120–150 pages and are subdivided into sections including Original Research, Clinical Practice, and Case Reports. Articles are supplemented by editorials, letters, and announcements. A suggested acquisition for academic institutions with sport sciences and physical education training programs.

6205. *Journal of Orthopaedic and Sports Physical Therapy.* [ISSN: 0190-6011] 1971. m. USD 215. Ed(s): Richard P Difabio. Sports Physical Therapy Section, 201 S Capitol Ave, Ste 505, Indianapolis, IN 46225-1058; http://www.spts.org. Illus., index, adv. Refereed. Circ: 19255 Paid. Microform: WWS. *Indexed:* CINAHL, ExcerpMed, H&SSA, IndMed, PEI, SportS. *Bk. rev.:* 4, 300 words. *Aud.:* Ac, Sa.

This is the official publication of the Orthopaedic and Sports Physical Therapy Sections of the American Physical Therapy Association. The peer-reviewed journal, of interest to clinicians, faculty, and students, publishes research reports, literature reviews, case studies, "resident's case problems," letters to the editor, and clinical and invited commentaries. Manuscripts address "scientific, clinical, or professional issues relevant to physical therapy." Each monthly issue contains four to six articles (although a few have as many as ten), with numerous black-and-white photographs, figures and tables, abstracts from the literature of the field, and book and product reviews. Issues from 2002 forward are available to subscribers online at the journal web site, http://jospt.org. This purchase is suitable for medical and academic libraries.

6206. *Journal of Physical Education, Recreation and Dance.* Former titles (until May 1981): *Journal of Physical Education and Recreation;* (until 1975): *Journal of Health, Physical Education, Recreation.* [ISSN: 0730-3084] 1896. m. 9/yr. USD 125 institutions and libraries; Free to members; (Non-members, USD 65). Ed(s): Michael T Shoemaker. American Alliance for Health, Physical Education, Recreation, and Dance, 1900 Association Dr, Reston, VA 20191-1599; info@aahperd.org; http://www.aahperd.org. Illus., index, adv. Refereed. Circ: 20000 Paid. Vol. ends: Dec. Microform: PMC; PQC. Online: bigchalk; Florida Center for Library Automation; Gale Group; OCLC Online Computer Library Center, Inc.; ProQuest Information & Learning. Reprint: ISI; PQC. *Indexed:* CIJE, EduInd, IDP, IIPA, MRD, PEI, RRTA, SportS, WAE&RSA. *Aud.:* Hs, Ga, Ac.

This is the primary professional publication for teachers of physical education. Published nine times a year by the American Alliance for Health, Physical Education, Recreation and Dance, it has been in continuous publication since 1896. The editor selects a wide variety of articles containing research reports and teaching practice, and each issue includes a list of new books, a calendar of conferences, workshops, news, letters, and law reviews. School and academic libraries are the most appropriate subscribers.

6207. *Journal of Sport and Exercise Psychology.* Formerly: *Journal of Sport Psychology.* [ISSN: 0895-2779] 1979. q. USD 184 (Individuals, USD 49). Ed(s): Robert Eklund. Human Kinetics Publishers, Inc., PO Box 5076, Champaign, IL 61825-5076; orders@hkusa.com; http://www.humankinetics.com. Illus., index, adv. Sample. Refereed. Circ: 1299 Paid. Vol. ends: Dec. Reprint: PSC. *Indexed:* BiolAb, EduInd, ErgAb, H&SSA, IBZ, PEI, PsycholAb, RRTA, RiskAb, SSCI, SSI, SportS. *Bk. rev.:* 1, 800-1,000 words. *Aud.:* Ac.

As the official publication of the North American Society for the Psychology of Sport and Physical Activity since 1979, this journal explores the relationship between human behavior and sports and/or exercise. Appropriate fields of concern include social, clinical, developmental, and experimental psychology; psychobiology; and personality. Issues are divided into sections containing sport psychology and exercise psychology. Each issue contains abstracts of recent publications in the field, book reviews, technical articles, and occasionally position papers. This refereed journal is most suitable for academic libraries.

6208. *Journal of Sport and Social Issues.* [ISSN: 0193-7235] 1977. q. GBP 237 print & online eds. in Europe, Middle East, Africa & Australasia. Ed(s): Cheryl Cole. Sage Publications, Inc., 2455 Teller Rd, Thousand Oaks, CA 91320; info@sagepub.com; http://www.sagepub.com. Illus., index, adv. Refereed. Circ: 550. Vol. ends: Nov. *Indexed:* ABS&EES, AltPI, H&SSA, HEA, PAIS, PEI, RRTA, RiskAb, SFSA, SportS. *Bk. rev.:* Occasional. *Aud.:* Ac.

This quarterly journal acts as a forum for research and thought-provoking essays on the interrelationship between sports and sociology, economics, history, psychology, political science, anthropology; and media, gender, and ethnic studies. Each issue is divided into three sections with different functions: focus (theme-based research articles), trends (research and notes on developing and traditional topics), and views (essays and reviews). This refereed journal is most suitable for academic libraries.

6209. *Journal of Sport Behavior.* [ISSN: 0162-7341] 1978. q. USD 30; USD 55 foreign. Ed(s): Elise Labbe-Coldsmith, M Cay Welsh. University of South Alabama, Department of Psychology, Life Sciences Building, Room 320, Mobile, AL 36688-0002; elabbe@usamail.usouthal.edu. Illus., index. Refereed. Circ: 450. CD-ROM: ProQuest Information & Learning. Microform: PQC. Online: bigchalk; EBSCO Publishing; Florida Center for Library Automation; Gale Group; Northern Light Technology, Inc.; OCLC Online Computer Library Center, Inc.; ProQuest Information & Learning. *Indexed:* PEI, PsycholAb, RRTA, RiskAb, SportS, WAE&RSA. *Bk. rev.:* Occasional. *Aud.:* Ac.

This is a peer-reviewed journal publishing empirical, investigative, and theoretical articles on behavior in sports and games. Articles generally run 15 to 20 pages and contain lengthy bibliographies. Topics addressed may be quite diverse. One issue contains articles on self-esteem and coping, success and failure in university athletes, effects of exercise, and sports marketing to black consumers. Suitable for academic libraries.

6210. *Journal of Sport History.* [ISSN: 0094-1700] 1974. 3x/yr. USD 70 (Individuals, USD 50). North American Society for Sport History, c/o Ronald A Smith, Box 1026, Lemont, PA 16851-1026; ras14@psu.edu; http://www.nassh.org. Illus., adv. Refereed. Circ: 1000. Vol. ends: Fall. *Indexed:* ABS&EES, AgeL, AmH&L, ArtHuCI, PEI, SSCI, SportS. *Bk. rev.:* 10-20, 800-1,000 words. *Aud.:* Ac.

Published three times a year by the North American Society for Sport History, the *Journal of Sport History* fosters research in sports history, the content ranging in period from the late nineteenth century to the 1990s and in subject matter from theory (deconstructionism) to regional, national, and international events. Scholarly articles are supplemented by an extensive book review section and occasional museum exhibit and media reviews. This peer-reviewed journal is appropriate for academic libraries.

6211. *Journal of Sport Management.* [ISSN: 0888-4773] 1987. q. USD 184 (Individuals, USD 49). Ed(s): Julia Glahn, Laurence Chalip. Human Kinetics Publishers, Inc., PO Box 5076, Champaign, IL 61825-5076; orders@hkusa.com; http://www.humankinetics.com. Adv. Refereed. Circ: 1126 Paid. Reprint: PSC. *Indexed:* IBZ, PEI, RRTA, RiskAb, SSCI, SportS. *Bk. rev.:* Number and length vary. *Aud.:* Ac, Sa.

This is the official journal of the North American Society for Sport Management. It publishes articles on the theoretical and applied aspects of management to sport, exercise, dance, and play. Typical contents include 3 or 4 longer research and review articles, with shorter research notes and/or position papers. Manuscripts are peer reviewed and written by university faculty. Regular features include book reviews, abstracts of relevant journal articles, and a list of upcoming conferences. Each issue is approximately 85 pages long. This publication is of interest to professionals, researchers, and students of sports management. Recommended for academic libraries with management programs related to sport, exercise, dance, or play.

6212. *Journal of Sport Rehabilitation.* [ISSN: 1056-6716] 1992. q. USD 184 (Individuals, USD 49). Ed(s): Christopher Ingersoll. Human Kinetics Publishers, Inc., PO Box 5076, Champaign, IL 61825-5076; orders@hkusa.com; http://www.humankinetics.com. Illus., index, adv. Refereed. Circ: 566 Paid. Vol. ends: Nov. Reprint: PSC. *Indexed:* CINAHL, ExcerpMed, H&SSA, IBZ, PEI. *Bk. rev.:* 1-2, 250-350 words. *Aud.:* Ac, Sa.

This peer-reviewed quarterly includes original research reports, case studies, reviews of research, and commentary appropriate to the field of sport rehabilitation, particularly as it involves evaluation and treatment of injuries, both physical and psychological. Each issue consists of approximately 80 pages containing about 5 to 7 articles. According to the mission statement, the journal "is intended to provide an international, multidisciplinary forum to serve the needs of all members of the sports medicine team, including athletic trainers/therapists, sport physical therapists/physiotherapists, sports medicine physicians, and other involved professionals." Published since 1992, this journal eschews technical language and is appropriate to both medical and academic libraries that provide support to rehabilitation and physical education programs.

6213. *Journal of Sports Economics.* [ISSN: 1527-0025] 2000. q. USD 316. Ed(s): Leo H Kahane, Todd L Idson. Sage Publications, Inc., 2455 Teller Rd, Thousand Oaks, CA 91320; info@sagepub.com; http://www.sagepub.com. Refereed. Online: EBSCO Publishing; ingenta.com; OCLC Online Computer Library Center, Inc.; RoweCom Information Quest; Swets Blackwell. *Indexed:* PEI, RRTA. *Bk. rev.:* 3-4, 250-500 words. *Aud.:* Ac.

Theoretical, applied, and empirical research are included in the *Journal of Sports Economics*, a refereed quarterly journal of the International Association of Sports Economists. Published since 2000, the journal focuses on areas of concern such as collective bargaining and wage determination and other labor- and finance-related topics. The English-language articles are not limited to the United States, but have included Italian, Japanese, and British submissions. Economic formulas and technical language make this primarily an academic journal for universities with strong economics programs.

6214. *The Journal of Sports Medicine and Physical Fitness.* [ISSN: 0022-4707] 1961. q. USD 198 (Individuals, ITL 120000). Ed(s): A Del Monte, F La Cava. Edizioni Minerva Medica, Corso Bramante 83-85, Turin, 10126, Italy; journals.dept@minervamedica.it; http://www.minervamedica.it. Illus., index, adv. Refereed. Circ: 5000 Paid. Microform: SWZ. Online: ProQuest Information & Learning. Reprint: SWZ. *Indexed:* CINAHL, ChemAb, ExcerpMed, IndMed, PEI, RRTA, SSCI, SportS. *Aud.:* Ac, Sa.

The Italian-based *Journal of Sports Medicine and Physical Fitness* is a peer-reviewed English-language journal that covers a broad span of topics including applied physiology, preventive medicine, sports medicine and traumatology, and sports psychology. Although original research is the primary venue, the journal also accepts technical notes, case reports, and special articles on the history of sports medicine, teaching methodology, and economic and legislative reports. This quarterly is appropriate largely for academic and medical libraries.

6215. *Journal of Sports Sciences.* [ISSN: 0264-0414] 1983. m. GBP 835. Ed(s): Alan Nevill. Taylor & Francis Ltd, 4 Park Sq, Milton Park, Abingdon, OX14 4RN, United Kingdom; info@tandf.co.uk; http://www.tandf.co.uk/. Illus., adv. Sample. Refereed. Online: EBSCO Publishing; Florida Center for Library Automation; Gale Group; Ingenta Select; OCLC Online Computer Library Center, Inc.; RoweCom Information Quest; Swets Blackwell. Reprint: PSC. *Indexed:* ApMecR, BiolAb, ErgAb, ExcerpMed, H&SSA, IBZ, IndMed, PEI, RRTA, S&F, SportS. *Bk. rev.:* Various number and length. *Aud.:* Ac, Sa.

The British-based *Journal of Sports Sciences* is a refereed journal of international scope. Interest in the "human sciences" as applied to sport and exercise extends the subject matter of this journal to include biomechanics, sport psychology, medicine, and physiotherapy. English-language articles are contributed by British, Australian, French, and other international scientists. Original research is supplemented by brief editorials and announcements. Technical language makes this quarterly appropriate to academic and medical libraries.

6216. ***Journal of Strength and Conditioning Research.*** Formerly: *Journal of Applied Sports Research.* [ISSN: 1064-8011] 1987. q. USD 105 print & online eds. Ed(s): William J Kraemer. National Strength and Conditioning Association, P. O. Box 9908, Colorado Springs, CO 80932-0908; nsca@nsca-lift.org; http://www.nsca-lift.org. Illus., index, adv. Refereed. Circ: 16780 Paid. Vol. ends: Dec. *Indexed:* CINAHL, IBZ, PEI, SSCI, SportS. *Aud.:* Ac, Sa.

The official journal of the National Strength and Conditioning Association, this peer-reviewed quarterly publishes articles "to advance the knowledge about strength and conditioning through research." Focus is on the provision of research articles that provide practical recommendations for the practitioner, thus bridging the gap between pure research and its exercise in the field. The research articles are written in English by an international group of scholars. Issues are approximately 200 pages long and typically contain 25 or more original research articles. The journal also publishes brief reviews of the literature by scientific experts and symposia related to the journal's mission. This is an appropriate purchase for medical and academic libraries.

6217. ***Journal of Teaching in Physical Education.*** [ISSN: 0273-5024] 1981. q. USD 184 (Individuals, USD 49). Ed(s): Bonnie Tjeerdsma Blankenship, Deborah Tannehill. Human Kinetics Publishers, Inc., PO Box 5076, Champaign, IL 61825-5076; orders@hkusa.com; http://www.humankinetics.com. Illus., index, adv. Sample. Refereed. Circ: 1183 Paid. Vol. ends: Jul. Reprint: PSC. *Indexed:* CIJE, EduInd, IBZ, PEI, PsycholAb, RRTA, SSCI, SportS. *Aud.:* Ems, Hs, Ac.

This quarterly journal is concerned with research of issues involved in the teaching of physical education, including methodology, curriculum, and teacher education. Subject matter is not limited to schools and universities but also covers the community and the sports profession. Each issue contains six or seven articles of approximately 15–20 pages in length. As a peer-reviewed journal, it focuses on research rather than practice, uses the more technical language of social science/education research methodology, and is more appropriate for academic libraries than school or public libraries.

6218. ***Journal of the Philosophy of Sport.*** [ISSN: 0094-8705] 1974. s-a. USD 146 (Individuals, USD 39). Ed(s): Nicholas Dixon. Human Kinetics Publishers, Inc., PO Box 5076, Champaign, IL 61825-5076; http://www.humankinetics.com. Illus., adv. Refereed. Circ: 590. Reprint: PSC. *Indexed:* CBCARef, PEI, PhilInd, RRTA, SSCI, SportS. *Bk. rev.:* 3-4, essay length. *Aud.:* Ac.

This peer-reviewed journal from the International Association for the Philosophy of Sport publishes longer research and theoretical articles, shorter essays, and book reviews of current or classical works relevant to the philosophy of sport. Topics as diverse as the pleasure of popular dance, the morality of boxing, competitive sports and war, and gender equity in sports are treated. Each issue contains three or four longer articles and two or three shorter essays and book reviews, all written by academics. The journal was published annually until 2001 and semi-annually since then. This is an interesting journal suitable for academic libraries.

6219. ***Medicine and Science in Sports and Exercise.*** Formerly: *Medicine and Science in Sports.* [ISSN: 0195-9131] 1969. m. USD 505 (Individuals, USD 296; USD 49 per issue). Ed(s): Kenneth O. Wilson. Lippincott Williams & Wilkins, 351 W Camden St, Baltimore, MD 21201. Illus., index, adv. Refereed. Circ: 13148. Vol. ends: Dec. Microform: Pub.; PQC. Online: Gale Group; OCLC Online Computer Library Center, Inc.; Ovid Technologies, Inc.; Swets Blackwell; H.W. Wilson. *Indexed:* AbAn, AgeL, BiolAb, CINAHL, ChemAb, EduInd, ExcerpMed, GSI, H&SSA, IAA, IndMed, PEI, PsycholAb, RRTA, SCI, SSCI, SportS, VetBull, WSA. *Bk. rev.:* 2-5, 200 words. *Aud.:* Ac, Sa.

The official publication of the American College of Medicine, *Medicine and Science in Sports and Exercise* has been published since 1969. Taking a multidisciplinary approach, this monthly is a forum for exercise physiologists, physical therapists, physiatrists, sports physicians, and athletic trainers. Original research, clinical investigations, and research reviews are included within its pages. The oversize (approximately 8.5"x 11") issues contain approximately 24–26 articles and are divided into sections. The Clinical Sciences section includes both clinical and clinically relevant investigations. The Basic Sciences section includes original investigations and epidemiology. The Applied Sciences section is subdivided into articles relating to biodynamics, psychobiology and behavioral sciences, and physical fitness and performance. Book reviews are included in the Special Communications at the end. As one of the most prestigious and cited journals in the field of sports medicine, this peer-reviewed journal is most appropriate for academic and medical libraries.

6220. ***Motor Control.*** [ISSN: 1087-1640] 1997. q. USD 224 (Individuals, USD 56). Ed(s): Mark L Latash. Human Kinetics Publishers, Inc., PO Box 5076, Champaign, IL 61825-5076; orders@hkusa.com; http://www.humankinetics.com. Illus., adv. Refereed. Circ: 242. Reprint: PSC. *Indexed:* ErgAb, IBZ, IndMed, PEI. *Bk. rev.:* Number and length vary. *Aud.:* Ac, Sa.

This official journal of the International Society of Motor Control is a peer-reviewed quarterly providing "a multidisciplinary, international forum for the exchange of scientific information on the control of human movement across the lifespan, including issues related to motor disorders." Editors and authors are academicians from an international list of academic and research institutions and a wide variety of disciplines including biomechanics, kinesiology, neurophysiology, neuroscience, psychology, physiology, and rehabilitation. Each issue contains approximately 100 pages and five to ten articles. In addition to research papers, the journal occasionally publishes reprints of classical articles, review articles, book reviews, commentaries, and quick communications. Suitable for medical and academic libraries.

6221. ***The N C A A News.*** Incorporates: *Football Statistics Rankings.* [ISSN: 0027-6170] 1964. fortn. Members, USD 12; Non-members, USD 24; Students, USD 15. National Collegiate Athletic Association, 700 W Washington Ave, Box 6222, Indianapolis, IN 46206-6222. Illus., adv. Circ: 20000. *Indexed:* SportS. *Aud.:* Hs, Ac.

As the official publication of the National Collegiate Athletic Association, this newspaper provides news, statistics, and commentary for all NCAA teams. A regular column highlights the major activities within the association, such as TV basketball ratings and attendance at women's volleyball games. The free online version at www.ncaa.org contains employment listings and other links.

Palaestra. See Disabilities section.

6222. ***Pediatric Exercise Science.*** [ISSN: 0899-8493] 1989. q. USD 195 (Individuals, USD 52). Ed(s): Dr. Thomas Rowland. Human Kinetics Publishers, Inc., PO Box 5076, Champaign, IL 61825-5076; orders@hkusa.com; http://www.humankinetics.com. Illus., adv. Refereed. Circ: 594 Paid and free. Vol. ends: Nov. Reprint: PSC. *Indexed:* CINAHL, ExcerpMed, IBZ, PEI, RiskAb, SSCI, SportS. *Bk. rev.:* Occasional. *Aud.:* Ac, Sa.

Pediatric Exercise Science is the official publication of the North American Society of Pediatric Exercise Medicine and the European Group of Pediatric Work Physiology. Published since 1989, this peer-reviewed quarterly focuses on physical activity in childhood, its therapeutic role in chronic disease, its importance in the maintenance of health, and children's response to physical exercise. The research articles are written in English by an international group of clinicians and academic researchers. Issues are approximately 100–150 pages in length, each containing 6 to 9 review or original research articles and editor's notes and digests of recent research. This journal is most appropriate for medical and academic libraries.

The Physician and Sportsmedicine. See Medicine and Health/Medicine—Professional section.

6223. ***Quest (Champaign).*** [ISSN: 0033-6297] 1963. q. USD 184 (Individuals, USD 49). Ed(s): John M Dunn. Human Kinetics Publishers, Inc., PO Box 5076, Champaign, IL 61825-5076; orders@hkusa.com; http://www.humankinetics.com. Illus., adv. Sample. Refereed. Circ: 1330 Paid and free. Vol. ends: Nov. Microform: PQC. Online: EBSCO Publishing. Reprint: PSC. *Indexed:* CIJE, EduInd, IBZ, PEI, RRTA, SSCI, SportS. *Bk. rev.:* Number and length vary. *Aud.:* Ac.

Quest is the official publication of National Association for Physical Education in Higher Education. Since 1963, this quarterly, peer-reviewed journal "examines not only critical issues facing physical educators, but also research developments in the sport sciences and other subdisciplines of human movement." The periodical also publishes commemorative lectures from invited presentations, appropriate conference papers, and book reviews. As far back as 1995, one issue per year has included the conference papers of the American Academy of Kinesiology and Physical Education. The theme of the conference for 2003 was "Preparing Future Faculty." Articles vary in length from approximately 10 to 20 pages, and issues may include as few as five or as many as ten articles. Appropriate for colleges or universities with strong physical education programs.

6224. *Research Quarterly for Exercise and Sport.* Formerly (until 1980): *American Alliance for Health, Physical Education and Recreation. Research Quarterly.* [ISSN: 0270-1367] 1930. q. USD 175 (Individuals, USD 60; USD 42 per issue). Ed(s): Stephen Silverman. American Alliance for Health, Physical Education, Recreation, and Dance, 1900 Association Dr, Reston, VA 20191-1599; info@aahperd.org; http://www.aahperd.org. Illus., index, adv. Refereed. Circ: 7000. Vol. ends: Dec. Microform: PMC; PQC. Online: bigchalk; Florida Center for Library Automation; Gale Group; OCLC Online Computer Library Center, Inc.; ProQuest Information & Learning. Reprint: ISI; PQC; PSC. *Indexed:* AgeL, ArtHuCI, BiolAb, CIJE, EduInd, ErgAb, ExcerpMed, IBZ, IndMed, PEI, PsycholAb, RRTA, SSCI, SportS. *Aud.:* Ac.

This journal of the American Alliance for Health, Physical Education, Recreation and Dance (AAHPERD) has been published since 1930. Its mission is to "publish refereed research articles on the art and science of human movement, which contribute to the knowledge and development of theory, either as new information, substantiation or contraction of previous findings, or application of new or improved techniques." *RQES*, an oversize journal measuring approximately 8.5 inches x 11 inches, adds more than 50 articles a year to the literature of this field. Issues are divided into Articles and Research Notes sections; the former is further subdivided into fields such as Biomechanics, Growth and Motor Development, Measurement and Evaluation, Motor Control and Learning, Pedagogy, Physiology and Psychology, so readers can quickly focus on topics of concern to them. An annual supplement includes abstracts of research consortium papers from the AAHPERD national convention. Recommended for academic libraries.

Shape. See Women section.

6225. *Sociology of Sport Journal.* [ISSN: 0741-1235] 1984. q. USD 184 (Individuals, USD 49). Ed(s): Nancy Theberge. Human Kinetics Publishers, Inc., PO Box 5076, Champaign, IL 61825-5076; orders@hkusa.com; http://www.humankinetics.com. Illus., index, adv. Refereed. Circ: 1119 Paid. Vol. ends: Dec. Reprint: PSC. *Indexed:* AgeL, ArtHuCI, CBCARef, CIJE, IBZ, PEI, RRTA, RiskAb, SSCI, SSI, SociolAb, SportS. *Bk. rev.:* 1, 750 words. *Aud.:* Ac.

Designed "to stimulate and communicate research, critical thought, and theory development on sociology of sport issues," this is a publication of the North American Society for the Sociology of Sport. Issues of this peer-reviewed quarterly generally contain four articles with original research and book reviews. Bibliographies, research notes, and short papers on curriculum issues may also be included. Abstracts in English and French precede the English-language articles. The readership includes sport sociologists, sport psychologists, and coaches. This is an appropriate addition for academic libraries.

6226. *Sport History Review.* Former titles (until 1995): *Canadian Journal of History of Sport;* (until Dec. 1981): *Canadian Journal of History of Sport and Physical Education.* [ISSN: 1087-1659] 1970. s-a. USD 168 (Individuals, USD 42). Ed(s): Don Morrow. Human Kinetics Publishers, Inc., PO Box 5076, Champaign, IL 61825-5076; orders@hkusa.com; http://www.humankinetics.com. Illus., adv. Sample. Refereed. Circ: 259 Paid. Vol. ends: Nov. Reprint: PSC. *Indexed:* ABS&EES, AmH&L, PEI, RRTA, SportS. *Bk. rev.:* 6, 750 words. *Aud.:* Ac.

This Canadian journal contains "articles whose method of analysis or application and appeal is more universally or fundamentally relevant to an international readership." Both English- and French-language articles are accepted. Two issues are published each year containing usually three or four articles (although occasionally as many as six) and a book review section with several reviews. A recent issue contains the following articles: "Brutality in Football and the Creation of the NCAA: A Codified Moral Compass in Progressive America," "Passive Participation: The Selling of Spectacle and the Construction of Maple Leaf Gardens, 1931," and "L'education physique en France sous la Quatrieme Republique (1945–1959)." This journal is most appropriate to academic libraries in institutions with a strong focus on history and/or the international aspect of sport.

6227. *Sport Marketing Quarterly: for professionals in the business of marketing sport.* [ISSN: 1061-6934] 1992. q. USD 143 (Individuals, USD 43; Students, USD 36). Ed(s): Brian Crow. Fitness Information Technology Inc., Box 4425, University Ave, Morgantown, WV 26504-4425; fit@fitinfotech.com; http://www.fitinfotech.com. Illus., index, adv. Sample. Refereed. Online: EBSCO Publishing. Reprint: PSC. *Indexed:* PEI. *Bk. rev.:* Number and length vary. *Aud.:* Ac, Sa.

The peer-reviewed *Sport Marketing Quarterly* provides information and research for both professionals and academic researchers. Beginning publication in 1992, it provides archival copies of its issues online at www.fitinfotech.com at $4.50 per article downloaded. Current-year copies are available only in print. Issues consist of approximately 50 pages that contain four or five research articles and departments that include an interview or profile, a case study, an article on a legal issue, and book reviews. Typical articles are "Sport Spectator Consumption Behavior," "Corporate Sales Activities and the Retention of Sponsors in the National Basketball Association (NBA)," "Olympic Games Host City Marketing: An Exploration of Expectations and Outcomes," and "An Analysis of Online Marketing in the Sport Industry: User Activity, Communication Objectives, and Perceived Benefits." The journal is an appropriate selection for academic libraries with a strong marketing/sports bias.

6228. *The Sport Psychologist.* [ISSN: 0888-4781] 1987. q. USD 184 (Individuals, USD 49). Ed(s): Vikky Krane. Human Kinetics Publishers, Inc., PO Box 5076, Champaign, IL 61825-5076; orders@hkusa.com; http://www.humankinetics.com. Illus., adv. Refereed. Circ: 1250 Paid. Vol. ends: Dec. Reprint: PSC. *Indexed:* IBZ, PEI, PsycholAb, RRTA, SSCI, SportS. *Bk. rev.:* 2, 100-500 words. *Aud.:* Ac, Sa.

Issues of this journal are divided into sections including applied research, professional practice, book and media reviews, and a bulletin board. This refereed quarterly for the clinician and academic has been in publication since 1987. Its mission is to be "a forum to stimulate and disseminate knowledge that focuses on the application and practice of sport psychology." A special emphasis of the journal is on the delivery of psychological services to practitioners such as athletes and coaches. Issues are between 100 and 140 pages in length, containing about four or five English-language articles written almost exclusively by an international community of academic participants. Typical articles from a recent issue include "Contextual Influences on Moral Functioning of College Basketball Players," "Enhancing Performance and Skill Acquisition in Novice Basketball Players with Instructional Self-Talk," "Integrating Web Pages and E-mail into Sport Psychology Consultations," and "Evaluating the Effectiveness of Applied Sport Psychology Practice: Making the Case for a Case Study Approach." Suitable for academic collections emphasizing sports and/or psychology.

6229. *Strategies (Reston): a journal for physical and sport educators.* [ISSN: 0892-4562] 1987. bi-m. USD 80 (Individuals, USD 40; USD 14 newsstand/cover per issue). Ed(s): Dora Schield, Judith C Young. American Alliance for Health, Physical Education, Recreation, and Dance, 1900 Association Dr, Reston, VA 20191-1599; info@aahperd.org; http://www.aahperd.org. Illus., adv. Refereed. Circ: 7500 Paid. *Indexed:* CIJE, EduInd, PEI. *Aud.:* Ems, Hs, Ac.

A publication of the American Alliance for Health, Physical Education, Recreation and Dance, *Strategies* is a peer-reviewed magazine published six times a year for physical education teachers and coaches at all levels. Not a research-oriented journal, it seeks articles that "identify a problem and offer concrete, step-by-step solutions or describe ~best practices' for typical coach/teacher activities or responsibilities." The 30- to 35-page issues contain approximately 10 to 12 articles each. Articles are written conversationally in nontechnical language making this professional magazine appropriate for large public and school libraries as well as academic libraries.

6230. *Strength and Conditioning Journal.* Former titles (until 1999): *Strength and Conditioning;* (until 1994): *N S C A Journal;* (until 1992): *National Strength and Conditioning Journal;* (until 1981): *National Strength Coaches Association Journal.* [ISSN: 1524-1602] 1979. bi-m. USD 105 print & online eds. Ed(s): Jeff Chandler. Allen Press Inc., PO Box 1897, Lawrence, KS 66044; http://www.allenpress.com/. Illus., index, adv. Refereed. Circ: 23000 Paid. *Indexed:* CINAHL, IBZ, PEI, SportS. *Bk. rev.:* 3, 100-250 words. *Aud.:* Ac, Sa.

This, the professional journal of the National Strength and Conditioning Association, publishes peer-reviewed articles reporting practical information from research studies and/or knowledge gained by experienced professionals on "resistance training, sports medicine and science, and issues facing the strength and conditioning professional." Each bimonthly issue contains approximately five feature articles and nine columns. Columns vary with each issue but may include "Bridging the Gap" (between research and practice), "Exercise Techniques," "Research Digest," "College Coaches Corner," "High School Corner," "Nutrition Notes," and the like. The publication's audience includes strength coaches, personal trainers, physical therapists, athletic trainers, and other strength and conditioning professionals. An electronic version is available at www.nsca-lift.org. Recommended for academic libraries.

6231. *Teaching Elementary Physical Education.* [ISSN: 1045-4853] 1990. bi-m. USD 136 (Individuals, USD 34). Ed(s): Rohn Koester, Peter Werner. Human Kinetics Publishers, Inc., PO Box 5076, Champaign, IL 61825-5076; orders@hkusa.com; http://www.humankinetics.com. Illus., adv. Refereed. Circ: 4008 Paid. Vol. ends: Nov. Online: EBSCO Publishing. Reprint: PSC. *Indexed:* IBZ, PEI. *Bk. rev.:* 4-5, 250 words. *Aud.:* Ems, Ac.

Focused on the needs of K-8 physical education teachers, *Teaching Elementary Physical Education* provides information on a wide variety of topics, including "developmentally appropriate activities, assessment, integration, implementing NASPE's national standards, dance, gymnastics, and games, curriculum development, self-esteem and responsibility, inclusion of all students," etc. Individual issues of this bimonthly professional journal are approximately 30–40 pages and may contain as many as seven or as few as two articles. Issues also include columns on curriculum, how to put research into practice, developmental skills, lifestyle, and bookmarks to appropriate web sites. Elementary and middle-school libraries and academic libraries serving higher education institutions training physical educators may wish to subscribe to this publication.

6232. *Women in Sport and Physical Activity Journal.* [ISSN: 1063-6161] 1992. s-a. Members, USD 18; Non-members, USD 20. Ed(s): Lynda Ransdell. Women of Diversity Productions, 5790 N Park St, Las Vegas, NV 89129; dvrsty@aol.com. Illus. Vol. ends: Fall. *Indexed:* CWI, FemPer, GendWatch, H&SSA, PEI, RiskAb. *Bk. rev.:* 4, lengthy. *Aud.:* Ac, Sa.

Women in Sport and Physical Activity Journal, published since 1992, is affiliated with both the National Association for Girls and Women in Sport and the International Association of Physical Education and Sports for Girls and Women and is a product of a grant from the Women's Sport Foundation. The journal focuses on peer-reviewed research articles about women's involvement in and/or perspectives on sport and physical activity. Issues include these sections: Original Investigations, Commentary, and Book and Video Reviews. Approximately 200 pages in length, each issue contains about eight articles. Its low price makes it a valuable acquisition for all academic libraries.

Specific Sports

6233. *Amateur Wrestling News.* [ISSN: 0569-1796] 1955. 12x/yr. USD 33. Ed(s): Ron Good. Amateur Wrestling News, PO Box 54679, Oklahoma City, OK 73154. Illus., adv. Circ: 10000. *Indexed:* SportS. *Aud.:* Hs, Ga.

Amateur Wrestling News bills itself as the "oldest publication devoted to all phases of amateur wrestling" and covers high school, collegiate, and Olympic wrestling, including women's, freestyle, and Greco-Roman. Issues regularly contain interviews with coaches and profiles of players, teams, and competitions. The magazine publishes complete rankings and reporting of high school state meets and all the various collegiate association championships. The web site at http://www.amateurwrestlingnews.com contains links to high school and college teams and to wrestling camps. This publication is suitable for high school and academic libraries.

6234. *American Fencing.* [ISSN: 0002-8436] 1949. q. Non-members, USD 16. Ed(s): Meg Galipault. United States Fencing Association, Inc., One Olympic Plaza, Colorado Springs, CO 80909-5774; http://www.usfencing.org. Illus., adv. Circ: 12000. Microform: PQC. *Indexed:* SportS. *Aud.:* Hs, Ga, Ac.

American Fencing, the official journal of the United States Fencing Association (USFA), reports the news, people, tournaments, rankings, rules, training, techniques, and equipment of the sport of fencing. The publication features articles and essays about fencing and issues surrounding the sport. The association's web site at http://www.usfencing.org contains additional information about competitions, USFA news, coaching, and more. A good resource for high school and academic libraries with fencing programs.

6235. *American Hockey Magazine.* Former titles: *American Hockey and Arena; United States Hockey and Arena Biz; Hockey and Arena Biz; U S Hockey Biz.* [ISSN: 8756-3789] 1973. 10x/yr. Ed(s): Harry Thompson. T P G Sports, Inc., 6160 Summit Dr, Ste 375, Minneapolis, MN 55430; info@tpgsports.com; http://www.tpgsports.com. Illus., adv. Circ: 425000. *Indexed:* SportS. *Aud.:* Hs, Ga, Ac.

Players, coaches, parents, and fans of amateur ice and inline hockey will find the *American Hockey Magazine* of interest. This magazine, the official publication of USA Hockey and USA Hockey InLine, publishes profiles, rules, strategies, tips, instructional articles, and articles on league and tournament play. The February issue contains an annual camp directory. Each 60-page issue is filled with photographs and columns on coaching, refereeing, regional news, and personalities. A "Hats Off" column highlights USA Hockey and USA Hockey InLine members, from juniors through adults, for their outstanding contributions and accomplishments. The association's web site at http://usahockey.com features hockey news, terminology, safety, tournaments and events, championships, and information on rink management. With the increasing interest in hockey, this publication will be popular in public, high school, and academic libraries.

6236. *Baseball America.* Formerly (until 1982): *All-America Baseball News.* [ISSN: 0745-5372] 1981. 26x/yr. USD 51.95; USD 3.25 newsstand/cover per issue; USD 4.50 newsstand/cover per issue Canada. Baseball America, Inc., 201 W Main St, Ste 201, Durham, NC 27701; letters@baseballamerica.com; http://www.baseballamerica.com. Illus., adv. Circ: 70000. *Aud.:* Ga, Ac.

This newsprint magazine provides comprehensive coverage for all major, minor, and collegiate Division I teams, as well as some international and the best high school teams and players. Articles highlight teams, players, coaches, statistics, averages, and leagues. The magazine publishes an annual review of baseball books, weekly ratings of college teams, and season previews. The print publication is updated by the magazine's web site, which contains current information on teams and players, statistics, and news. Recommended for public, high school, and academic libraries.

6237. *Baseball Digest.* [ISSN: 0005-609X] 1941. m. USD 29.95 domestic; USD 40 foreign; USD 5.99 newsstand/cover per issue. Ed(s): John Kuenster. Century Publishing Co., 990 Grove St, Evanston, IL 60201-4370; bb@centurysports.net; http://www.centurysports.net. Illus., adv. Circ: 150000. Vol. ends: Dec. Microform: PQC. Reprint: PQC. *Indexed:* CPL, PEI, SportS. *Aud.:* Hs, Ga.

Published since 1941 and calling itself the "oldest baseball magazine," *Baseball Digest* features articles, interviews, statistics, charts, and rosters of major league baseball. Departments include letters, quizzes, crossword puzzles, deaths, and a rules corner. The current issue's table of contents is available at the publisher's web site, http://www.centurysports.net/baseball. This monthly newsprint publication is suitable for high school and public libraries.

6238. ***Basketball Digest.*** [ISSN: 0098-5988] 1973. 8x/yr. USD 29.95 domestic; USD 40 foreign; USD 4.99 newsstand/cover per issue. Ed(s): William Wagner. Century Publishing Co., 990 Grove St, Evanston, IL 60201-4370; cs@centurysports.net; http://www.centurysports.net. Illus., adv. Circ: 105837 Paid. Vol. ends: Jan. Microform: PQC. Reprint: PQC. *Indexed:* PEI. *Aud.:* Hs, Ga.

Like other Century publications of the same ilk, *Basketball Digest* is a cheaply produced publication of newsprint in a small *TV Guide* size package. Published a venerable 30 years, it is the oldest-produced basketball-focused magazine available today. Feature articles cover teams, tournaments, and players both male and female for college and national associations. Extras follow the proven Century publication formula of editorials, letters, quizzes, and statistics. Published eight months of the year, it may be an appropriate acquistion for school and public libraries in towns in which basketball is a favored sport.

6239. ***Bicycling.*** Formerly: *American Cycling Magazine;* Which incorporated (in 1981): *American Cyclist.* [ISSN: 0006-2073] 1962. m. 11/yr. USD 14.94 domestic; CND 24.97 Canada; USD 37.97 elsewhere. Ed(s): Stephen Madden, William Strickland. Rodale, 33 E Minor St, Emmaus, PA 18098; info@rodale.com; http://www.rodale.com. Illus., adv. Circ: 400000 Paid. Microform: NBI; PQC. Online: bigchalk; EBSCO Publishing; Florida Center for Library Automation; Gale Group; OCLC Online Computer Library Center, Inc.; ProQuest Information & Learning; H.W. Wilson. Reprint: PQC. *Indexed:* ASIP, ConsI, IHTDI, MagInd, PEI, RGPR, SportS. *Aud.:* Hs, Ga, Ac.

This is a glossy magazine for the serious bicyclist. Articles on cycling competitions, vacation and pleasure rides, upcoming events, equipment maintenance and repair, product reviews, clothing, training tips, and fitness are included on a regular basis. Cover stories feature best buys, extensive interviews, suggested rides, and other information of interest to cyclists. *Mountain Bike* magazine is now a supplement to *Bicycling* and included in the subscription price. Suitable for public libraries.

6240. ***Black Belt: world's leading magazine of self-defense.*** [ISSN: 0277-3066] 1962. m. USD 32 domestic; USD 38 foreign; USD 4.99 newsstand/cover per issue. Ed(s): Robert Young. Black Belt Communications, Inc., 24715 Rockefeller Ave, Valencia, CA 91355. Illus., adv. Circ: 100000. Vol. ends: Dec. *Aud.:* Hs, Ga, Ac.

The monthly *Black Belt*, sometimes described as the "standard" or "definitive" martial arts magazine, covers all the numerous martial arts (more than fifteen). Published since 1962, *Black Belt* focuses on self-defense. Articles concentrate on various types of arts, their philosophy and principles, spiritual and historical aspects of the sport, and techniques. Columns repeated in each 150-page issue include a news digest, guest editorials from celebrity martial artists, nutrition, exercise, sports medicine, gear, film coverage, a directory of martial arts schools, and more. The online site at www.blackbeltmag.com, not a replacement for the print magazine, contains news, the directory and tips for beginners, and online shopping for books and other items, including back issues of the magazine. The journal is appropriate for any library collection.

6241. ***Bowling Digest.*** [ISSN: 8750-3603] 1983. bi-m. USD 29.95 domestic; USD 40 foreign; USD 5.99 newsstand/cover per issue. Ed(s): Brett Ballentine. Century Publishing Co., 990 Grove St, Evanston, IL 60201-4370; cs@centurysports.net; http://www.centurysports.net. Illus., adv. Circ: 95035 Paid. Vol. ends: Dec. *Indexed:* PEI, SportS. *Aud.:* Hs, Ga.

Bowling is the sport of millions and *Bowling Digest* covers the amateur and professional field, with in-depth coverage of the PBA, PWBA, ABC, WIBC, and international competition. A substantial portion of each issue is devoted to instruction with articles by Pro Bowlers Association champions Parker Bohn III and Bill Spigner, Pro Women's Bowling Association champion Kim Adler, and Team USA coach John Jowdy. The April issue features an annual bowling ball buyer's guide, while the December issue includes a gift guide. This publication would appeal to readers in high school and public libraries.

6242. ***Collegiate Baseball: the voice of amateur baseball.*** [ISSN: 0530-9751] 1957. m. 14/yr. USD 25; USD 43 for 2 yrs. Ed(s): Lovis Pavlovich, Jr. Collegiate Baseball Newspaper Inc., c/o Lou Pavlovich, Jr, Ed, Box 50566, Tucson, AZ 85703; cbn@baseballnews.com; http://www.baseballnews.com. Illus., adv. Circ: 7000. Vol. ends: Oct. Microform: PQC. *Aud.:* Hs, Ac.

Published twice a month during the season (January through May) and in June, July, September, and October, *Collegiate Baseball* provides up-to-date content for anyone interested in amateur high school or college baseball. The newspaper contains editorials, letters to the editor, news, rules and regulations, tips for training and game improvement, spotlights on outstanding players, and statistics and standings for all college divisions and high school teams. Well-known players and coaches write many of the columns. Generally, college and high school pre-season information appears in the January issue; the April issue has a special high school feature; a preview of the College World Series appears in June; the All American issue is published in July; September contains a roundup of summer baseball; and a buying guide for baseball-related products appears in October. An appropriate purchase for high school and academic libraries with baseball programs.

6243. ***Football Digest.*** [ISSN: 0015-6760] 1971. 10x/yr. USD 29.95 domestic; USD 40 foreign; USD 5.99 newsstand/cover per issue. Ed(s): Jim O'Connor. Century Publishing Co., 990 Grove St, Evanston, IL 60201-4370; cs@centurysports.net; http://www.centurysports.net. Illus., adv. Circ: 233636 Paid. Vol. ends: Aug. Microform: PQC. Reprint: PQC. *Indexed:* PEI, SportS. *Aud.:* Hs, Ga.

Century publishes *Football Digest* ten months out of the year. Both college and professional football are covered in this publication that profiles and interviews players and coaches, lists team-by-team statistics, and annually awards players, teams, and coaches with its highest accolades. Editorials, letters, brief columns on school teams, and historical commentary round out the 80-page issues. Football fans will like it because it does more than just rehash games, providing projections for the coming year, informed opinions on topics, and behind-the-scenes information. Lack of indexing makes this a current-year-only purchase for public libraries. The web site for the publisher contains archival pronouncements of Football Digest's Players of the Year, Defensive Players of the Year, Coaches of the Year, and Rookies of the Year.

6244. ***Golf Digest.*** [ISSN: 0017-176X] 1950. m. USD 14.97 domestic; CND 27.58 Canada; USD 43.94 elsewhere. Ed(s): Steve Binder. The Golf Digest Companies, 20 Westport Rd, Wilton, CT 06897. Illus., adv. Circ: 1557814 Paid. Microform: PQC. Online: EBSCO Publishing; Florida Center for Library Automation; Gale Group. *Indexed:* ConsI, PEI, SportS. *Aud.:* Hs, Ga, Ac.

Golf Digest belies its name. Each issue of this monthly numbers over 200 pages. Often referred to as "The Golfer's Bible," the magazine almost overloads its readers with advice. Readers often report dramatic changes in their handicaps—and point to the magazine as a form of cheap golf lessons. Detailed articles are written by and about famous professional golfers, and photographs break down their swings for comparative purposes. Occasional features focus on golf history, golf courses, country clubs, and interviews with major players. Advertising focuses on golf equipment, automobiles (no doubt, to get to the courses), and travel to golfing paradises. A subscription to this magazine will delight all duffers frequenting public and academic libraries

6245. ***Golf Magazine.*** Former titles (until 1991): *Golf (New York);* (until 1986): *Golf Magazine.* [ISSN: 1056-5493] 1959. m. USD 19.95 domestic; USD 29.95 Canada; USD 49.95 elsewhere. Ed(s): James Frank. Time4 Media, Inc., 2 Park Ave, New York, NY 10016; http://www.golfonline.com. Illus., adv. Circ: 1400000 Paid. Microform: PQC. Online: EBSCO Publishing; Gale Group; ProQuest Information & Learning. Reprint: PQC. *Indexed:* ASIP, ConsI, MagInd, PEI, RGPR, SportS. *Aud.:* Hs, Ga, Ac.

Since 1959, *Golf Magazine* has published articles on golf equipment, rules, instruction, golf courses, golf vacation and travel, interviews with golfers, and golfing events. A regular column, "Private Lessons," provides one- to two-page instructions for game improvement for everyone from the beginner to the senior to the experienced golfer. Although similar to *Golf Digest*, the two publications complement one another. A suitable purchase for public and academic libraries.

6246. *Hockey Digest.* [ISSN: 0046-7693] 1972. 8x/yr. USD 29.95 domestic; USD 40 foreign; USD 4.99 newsstand/cover per issue. Ed(s): William Wagner. Century Publishing Co., 990 Grove St, Evanston, IL 60201-4370; cs@centurysports.net; http://www.centurysports.net. Illus., adv. Circ: 94190. Vol. ends: Jul. Microform: PQC. Reprint: PQC. *Indexed:* PEI, SportS. *Aud.:* Hs, Ga.

The fourth major-league sport in North America, hockey, has its loyal fans, and *Hockey Digest* is one of the two top-competing magazines devoting coverage to the National Hockey League, the professional wing of the sport. The size of the magazine is similar to *TV Guide*. It contains low-quality black-and-white pictures on newsprint. Articles cover teams, historical and financial articles on the NHL, interviews with hockey personalities, coverage of minor leagues, comparisons of players, and ratings of managers and players. Editorials, letters, a "Quick Quiz," and statistics round out each 90-page issue. School and public libraries in northernmost states and in cities with hockey teams may want to subscribe to this inexpensive publication.

6247. *Hockey News: the international hockey weekly.* [ISSN: 0018-3016] 1947. 42x/yr. CND 53.45 domestic; USD 49.95 United States; GBP 156.95 in Europe. Transcontinental Media, Inc., 25 Sheppard Ave West, Ste 100, Toronto, ON M2N 6S7, Canada; info@transcontinental.ca; http://www.transcontinental-gtc.com. Illus., adv. Circ: 110000. Microform: MML. *Indexed:* CPerI, SportS. *Aud.:* Ga.

Hockey News, published weekly during the hockey season and on alternate weeks during the off-season, focuses on North American hockey. The magazine, printed on newsprint, is richly illustrated. Typical contents include editorials, opinion pieces, letters to the editor, news in brief, player profiles and interviews, statistics, and specials on rookies, goalies, or other topics. Each team in the National Hockey League receives in-depth coverage in every issue. Less detail is provided for teams in the minor pro, junior, and collegiate leagues. The magazine's web site at www.thehockeynews.com allows fans to sign up for daily updates. This title is appropriate for public libraries.

6248. *International Figure Skating.* [ISSN: 1070-9568] 1993. bi-m. USD 19 domestic; USD 28 Canada; USD 39 elsewhere. Ed(s): Lois Elfman. Ashton International Media, Inc., 44 Front St, Ste 280, Worcester, MA 01608; ifsmag@aol.com; http://www.ifsmagazine.com. Illus., adv. Circ: 30000. *Aud.:* Hs, Ga.

International Figure Skating reports the news, business, and personalities of figure skating, with coverage of recent U.S. and international competitions. The cover story in each issue profiles popular skaters. This is not a magazine with advice on training or becoming a figure skater, but one about the business of figure skating. It is a glossy magazine with numerous photographs and will appeal to skaters and would-be skaters alike. The magazine's web site at www.ifsmagazine.com provides access to selected stories. The site also has a section with online snapshots of photo shoots from the magazine. The magazine is appropriate for high school and public libraries.

6249. *International Gymnast.* Former titles (until 1986): *International Gymnast Magazine;* (until 1982): *International Gymnast;* (until 1981): *International Gymnast Magazine;* (until 1979): *International Gymnast;* (until 1975): *Gymnast;* Incorporates: *Gymnastics World;* (1966-1971): *Mademoiselle Gymnast; Modern Gymnast.* [ISSN: 0891-6616] 1972. 10x/yr. USD 30 domestic; USD 35.31 Canada; USD 50 elsewhere. Ed(s): Dwight Normile, Nadia Comaneci. Paul Ziert & Associates, Inc., PO Box 721020, Norman, OK 73070-4788; orders@intlgymnast.com. Illus., adv. Circ: 20000 Paid. Online: OCLC Online Computer Library Center, Inc.; ProQuest Information & Learning. Reprint: PQC. *Indexed:* SportS. *Aud.:* Hs, Ga.

As befits a sport whose fans relate to particular personalities, *International Gymnast* focuses on the individuals who compete in the field. The ten yearly issues are approximately 40 pages in length and contain primarily biographical profiles and coverage of international events and teams. Articles are lavishly illustrated and supplemented by columns containing letters, new products, a calendar, a brief fictional series, and a kids' page—the last pointing to a large segment of the magazine's readership/interest group. The past 25 years have seen a resurgence of interest in this sport. This magazine is appropriate for schools with gymnastic teams and for public libraries.

6250. *Journal of Asian Martial Arts.* [ISSN: 1057-8358] 1992. q. USD 75 (Individuals, USD 32; USD 9.75 newsstand/cover per issue domestic). Ed(s): Michael A DeMarco. Journal of Asian Martial Arts, 821 W 24th St, Erie, PA 16502; info@goviamedia.com; http://www.goviamedia.com. Illus., index, adv. Sample. Refereed. Circ: 12000 Paid and controlled. *Indexed:* PEI. *Bk. rev.:* 3, 750-1,200 words. *Aud.:* Ga, Ac.

This quarterly publishes articles of interest to the serious student of the martial arts. Each issue contains approximately 120 pages and is divided into three sections. "Academic Articles" report scholarly research from disciplines as diverse as cultural anthropology, comparative religion, psychology, film theory, and the like. There are normally two articles in this section, each running approximately 25 pages in length. "General Articles" are somewhat shorter but still substantial interviews (with master practitioners and scholars) or reports on a genre or technique. "Media Reviews" contain reviews of books and audiovisuals on the martial arts. For example, one issue presents articles on the arts in Okinawa, Japan, China, and Mongolia; on styles such as aikido, taijiquan, wrestling, and karate; and on body mechanics, self-defense, and injury treatment. Articles are illustrated with drawings and photographs. Suitable for large public and academic libraries.

6251. *Journal of Swimming Research.* [ISSN: 0747-5993] 1984. a. USD 15 domestic; USD 25 in Canada & Mexico; USD 35 elsewhere. Ed(s): J M Stager. American Swimming Coaches Association, 2101 N Andrews Ave, 107, Fort Lauderdale, FL 33311; http://www.swimmingcoach.org. Adv. Refereed. Circ: 5000 Paid. *Indexed:* PEI, SportS. *Aud.:* Ac, Sa.

The peer-reviewed *Journal of Swimming Research* (JSR) is the official publication of the American Swimming Coaches Association in cooperation with the United States Swimming's Sport Medicine Committee. The audience for this journal is students, academics, and coaches. The journal describes itself as a "researcher-to-coach publication" and as such publishes reports on research and reviews of the science of swimming that have practical applications. Each approximately 50-page issue contains four or five articles. An extensive bibliography of swimming research is published annually. The journal is free with membership in the American Swimming Coaches Association. This publication is appropriate for academic libraries at institutions with a strong swimming program.

6252. *Kickoff (New York).* [ISSN: 1542-2038] 2003. q. USD 12.95 domestic; USD 28 elsewhere; USD 3.99 newsstand/cover domestic. Ed(s): Mitchell Lavnick. Lifestyle Ventures, LLC, 250 W 57th St, Ste 420, New York, NY 10107. Adv. *Aud.:* Ems, Hs, Ga.

Published since 2003, *Kickoff* is a glossy magazine geared toward young football players. Sponsored by Pop Warner, a nonprofit organization for youth (ages 5 to 16) football and cheerleading, the magazine contains articles on strategy, drills, plays, training, nutrition, advice from professional players, and collecting. Young players will appreciate the cartoons, games, and contests in each issue. An appropriate selection for elementary, high school, and public libraries in areas where organized youth football is popular.

6253. *Pro Football Weekly.* [ISSN: 0032-9053] 1968. 32x/yr. USD 49.95 for 16 issues; USD 79.95 for 32 issues. Ed(s): Sue Nemitz. Primedia Enthusiast Group, 302 Saunders Rd, Ste 100, Riverwoods, IL 60015; http://www.primedia.com. Illus., adv. Circ: 125262. *Aud.:* Ga.

This newspaper publishes news of professional football, including team rosters and schedules, player profiles, fantasy football, arena football, NFL Europe, player transactions, and opinion pieces. Noted sports columnists write many of the feature columns. This publication will attract any true football fan. The newspaper is supplemented by an online site at www.profootballweekly.com. The publication is suitable for public libraries.

6254. *Rodale's Scuba Diving: the magazine divers trust.* Incorporates (1987-1992): *Fisheye View Scuba Magazine.* [ISSN: 1060-9563] 1992. 11x/yr. USD 21.98 domestic; CND 32.98 Canada; USD 39.98 elsewhere. Ed(s): Buck Butler. Rodale, 33 E Minor St, Emmaus, PA 18098; info@rodale.com; http://www.rodale.com. Illus., adv. Circ: 185000. *Aud.:* Ga.

Scuba Diving publishes articles covering all aspects of scuba diving, equipment, techniques, training, fitness, and travel. The training section is extensive and covers everything from how to reboard a small boat, to the dangers of drinking and diving, to attaining better buoyancy, to advanced diving techniques. This is a glossy magazine with almost as much advertising as text and will interest the diving enthusiast and professional. Suitable for public and academic libraries in areas of the country where scuba diving is popular.

6255. *Runner's World.* Incorporates (1978-1987): *Runner;* Former titles (until 1987): *Rodale's Runner's World;* (until 1985): *Runner's World; Distance Running News.* [ISSN: 0897-1706] 1966. m. USD 24.50 domestic; CND 31.50 Canada; USD 50 elsewhere. Ed(s): Amby Burfoot, David Willey. Rodale, 33 E Minor St, Emmaus, PA 18098; rwdcustserv@cdsfulfillment.com; http://www.rodale.com. Illus., index, adv. Circ: 520000. Microform: PQC. Online: bigchalk; EBSCO Publishing; Florida Center for Library Automation; Gale Group; Northern Light Technology, Inc.; OCLC Online Computer Library Center, Inc.; H.W. Wilson. Reprint: PQC. *Indexed:* ConsI, MagInd, PEI, RGPR, SportS. *Aud.:* Ga, Ac.

Serious and recreational runners will enjoy *Runner's World.* Of the two issues examined, one features longer informative articles on training, while the other contains articles on nutrition, endurance, workouts, and training. Columns and departments include rave runs (beautiful places to run), letters, nutrition, injury prevention and training advice, product reviews, vacation tips, and racing reports. The magazine's web site at www.runnersworld.com contains selected articles and links to relevant sites. A useful purchase for academic and public libraries.

6256. *Running & FitNews.* Former titles (until 1984): *Running and Fitness; Jogger.* [ISSN: 0898-5162] 1983. m. USD 40 (Members, USD 25). American Running Association, 4405 East West Hwy, Ste 405, Bethesda, MD 20814; run@americanrunning.org; http://www.americanrunning.org. Illus., index. Circ: 15000 Paid. Online: EBSCO Publishing; Gale Group. *Indexed:* CINAHL, SportS. *Aud.:* Ga, Ac.

This well-regarded newsletter of the American Running Association provides nutrition, training, health, and sport medicine information for the running enthusiast. The eight pages published every month briefly deal with topics such as marathons, injuries, general health, fitness, races, and nutritional suggestions for the runner. Articles are written by the editor and reviewed by an editorial board that consists of clinicians and academics. Lack of indexing and security problems may prove a hindrance for its inclusion in smaller libraries.

6257. *Running Times: the runner's best resource.* [ISSN: 0147-2968] 1977. 10x/yr. USD 23 domestic; USD 35 Canada; USD 55 elsewhere. Ed(s): Jonathan Beverly. Fitness Publishing Inc., 213 Danbury Rd, Wilton, CT 06897-4006. Illus., adv. Circ: 76494. *Indexed:* SportS. *Aud.:* Ga, Ac.

Only serious competitive runners with experience need apply as subscribers to this magazine that would be likely to overwhelm the beginning or weekend runner. Running vacations, running while pregnant and running strollers (as in baby's), the Chicago marathon, and foreign-born American runners are some of the topics covered in recent issues. The ten issues published each year also include columns by an exercise physiologist and on sports medicine, training, tips, equipment, racing news, calendars, a high school page, and a section of classified ads. For libraries catering to competitive athletes.

6258. *Ski: the magazine of the ski life.* Incorporates: *Ski Life.* [ISSN: 0037-6159] 1936. 8x/yr. USD 13.94 domestic; USD 20.94 Canada; USD 21.94 elsewhere. Ed(s): Kendall Hamilton. Time4 Media, Inc., 929 Pearl St, Ste 200, Boulder, CO 80302; http://www.time4.com. Illus., adv. Circ: 426403 Paid. Microform: PQC. Online: EBSCO Publishing; Gale Group; OCLC Online Computer Library Center, Inc.; ProQuest Information & Learning. Reprint: PQC. *Indexed:* ConsI, PEI, SportS. *Aud.:* Ga, Ac.

With its beautiful photography, tips on ski travel, vacations, resorts, and towns, *Ski* will attract the recreational skier. The 150-page issues regularly include instruction, tips for injury prevention, training, and lifestyle articles. Annually, the magazine publishes reviews of resorts and a buyer's guide. The magazine's web site contains selected articles, a buyer's guide, snow reports, a calendar of events, a discussion forum, and more. Suitable for public libraries.

6259. *Skiing Magazine.* [ISSN: 0037-6264] 1948. 7x/yr. USD 12.95 domestic; CND 14.97 Canada; USD 16.97 elsewhere. Ed(s): Perkins Miller. Time4 Media, Inc., 929 Pearl St, Ste 200, Boulder, CO 80302; mailbox@skinet.com. Illus., adv. Circ: 400730 Paid. Microform: PQC. Online: EBSCO Publishing; Gale Group; OCLC Online Computer Library Center, Inc.; ProQuest Information & Learning. *Indexed:* ConsI, MagInd, PEI, RGPR, SportS. *Bk. rev.:* Occasional. *Aud.:* Ga, Ac.

The 150–170 pages of each issue of *Skiing Magazine* are fairly evenly divided between space devoted to articles and that devoted to advertising as is appropriate for a sports magazine focused more on travel and the geography of the sport than on practical means for improving one's technique or becoming a professional skier. Because skiing is seasonal, articles on more general aspects of outdoor life are also included. Published since 1936, this magazine comes out seven times a year. Lavish photographs of mountain scenery make one long for winter, snow, and mountains. Sometimes dubbed a "rich man's magazine," it is an appropriate acquisition for libraries in mountain states where skiing is popular.

6260. *Soccer America.* Formerly: *Soccer West.* [ISSN: 0163-4070] 1971. w. 50/yr. USD 79 domestic; USD 119 Canada; USD 189 elsewhere. Ed(s): Paul Kennedy. Berling Communications, Inc., 1235 10th St, Berkeley, CA 94710; http://www.socceramerica.com. Illus., adv. Circ: 32750 Paid. Microform: PQC. Reprint: PQC. *Indexed:* SportS. *Bk. rev.:* 1, 800 words. *Aud.:* Ga.

This weekly magazine provides news, statistics, scores, reports, and analysis of U.S. and international soccer, including the MLS, WUSA, and collegiate teams. Players are highlighted in informative articles. A recent addition is the Youth Digest section, which covers competitive youth soccer. A monthly tournament calendar provides a comprehensive listing of soccer tournaments in the United States and abroad. The publication's web site at www.socceramerica.com provides access to selected articles and links of interest to the soccer fan. Recommended for public, high school, and academic libraries.

6261. *Soccer Digest.* [ISSN: 0149-2365] 1978. bi-m. USD 29.95 domestic; USD 40 foreign; USD 4.99 newsstand/cover per issue. Ed(s): William Wagner. Century Publishing Co., 990 Grove St, Evanston, IL 60201-4370; cs@centurysports.net; http://www.centurysports.net. Illus., adv. Circ: 36122 Paid. Vol. ends: Nov. Microform: PQC. Reprint: PQC. *Indexed:* PEI. *Aud.:* Hs, Ga, Ac.

Published bimonthly, *Soccer Digest* provides comprehensive coverage of soccer, including U.S., European, and South American clubs and all major international competitions. This small magazine (7.5 inches x 5.5 inches) includes feature articles with interviews and profiles of players, leagues, teams, and competitions. League schedules and a soccer quiz are a regular part of the magazine. Since this publication does not have an index, libraries will want to keep current issues (one year) only. A suggested purchase for high school and public libraries.

6262. *Soccer Journal.* [ISSN: 0560-3617] 1941. 8x/yr. USD 60 in US & Canada; USD 80 in Europe; USD 90 in Asia. Ed(s): Tim Schum. National Soccer Coaches Association of America, West Gymnasium, Binghamton University, Binghamton, NY 13902-6000; tschum@binghamton.edu; http://www.nscaa.com. Illus., adv. Circ: 16000 Paid. *Indexed:* PEI, SportS. *Aud.:* Hs, Ac.

As the official publication of the National Soccer Coaches Association of America, *Soccer Journal* focuses on information for the soccer coach. Each issue contains articles on instruction, tactics, techniques, discipline, safety, training, diet, and conditioning for the game. Diagrams of soccer games, news from the field, and columns by the association president and executive director are regular features. It is interesting to note that the Member Benefits column in the three issues examined contains information for coaches on relocating and selling their homes. A useful addition for school and academic libraries with soccer programs.

Sports 'n Spokes. See Disabilities section.

6263. *Swimming World and Junior Swimmer.* Former titles: *Junior Swimmer - Swimming World; Swimming World.* [ISSN: 0039-7431] 1960. m. USD 29.95 domestic; USD 40.95 foreign. Ed(s): Phillip Whitten, Bob Ingram. Sports Publications, Inc., 228 Nevada St, El Segundo, CA 90245; editorial@swiminfo.com; http://www.swiminfo.com. Illus., adv. Circ: 33143 Paid. Vol. ends: Dec. Online: bigchalk; EBSCO Publishing; ProQuest Information & Learning. Reprint: PQC. *Indexed:* PEI, SportS. *Aud.:* Hs, Ga, Ac.

The audience for this publication is the competitive swimmer (particularly the swimmer who aspires to the Olympics), his/her parents, coaches, and officials. A monthly since 1960, *Swimming World and Junior Swimmer* publishes information about local, national, and international competitions, articles by and about Olympic swimmers, and articles on technique, training, diet, and mental preparation. The junior swimmer section contains articles that seek to motivate and inspire this age group to compete. The February issue contains an annual listing of summer swim camps. Suitable for high school, public, and academic libraries in areas where competitive swimming is popular.

6264. *Tennis.* [ISSN: 0040-3423] 1965. 10x/yr. USD 18 domestic; USD 29.96 newsstand/cover per issue Canada; USD 34 newsstand/cover per issue elsewhere. Ed(s): Mark Woodruff. Miller Publishing Group, Miller Sports Group, Tennis, 810 7th Ave, Frnt 4, New York, NY 10019-5818; http://www.tennis.com. Illus., index, adv. Circ: 700000. Microform: PQC. Online: EBSCO Publishing; Gale Group; H.W. Wilson. *Indexed:* ConsI, MagInd, PEI, RGPR, SportS. *Aud.:* Hs, Ga, Ac.

Produced both for the novice and the advanced tennis enthusiast, *Tennis* is a slick magazine with numerous excellent photographs. Tennis instruction is supplemented with profiles of the professional players, coverage of major tournaments, equipment and gear reviews, and information on nutrition, health, and fitness geared to the tennis player. Published since 1965, *Tennis* is the most popular magazine in the sport—first-time members of the U.S. Tennis Association receive a subscription free with membership. Almost all of the approximately 100-page issues are devoted to content other than advertising, which is unusual among the more popular single-sport magazines. The magazine is appropriate to school, public, and academic libraries.

6265. *Track & Field News.* [ISSN: 0041-0284] 1948. m. USD 43.95 domestic; USD 64 in Canada & Mexico; USD 54 foreign. Ed(s): Garry Hill. Track & Field News, 2570 El Camino Real, 606, Mountain View, CA 94040; biz@trackandfieldnews.com. Illus., adv. Circ: 26000 Paid. Microform: PQC. *Indexed:* SportS. *Aud.:* Hs, Ga, Ac.

The oldest magazine in this sport, *Track and Field News* has been in continuous publication since 1948. Although it purports to cover high school programs, emphasis is on collegiate and international athletes and events (such as the Olympics and world championships). Feature articles are brief and are supplemented by schedules of competitions, record lists, editorials, statistics, letters, and brief biographical notes. This consumer product is a probable inclusion in the collections of large public libraries and high schools and academic institutions with a major emphasis on track and field events.

6266. *Track Coach.* Former titles (until 1995): *Track Technique: Official Technical Publication;* (until 1981): *Track Technique.* [ISSN: 1085-8792] 1960. q. USD 20 domestic; USD 24 foreign. Ed(s): Russ Ebbets. Track & Field News, 2570 El Camino Real, 606, Mountain View, CA 94040; biz@trackandfieldnews.com; http://www.trackandfieldnews.com. Illus. Circ: 3000 Paid. Microform: PQC. *Indexed:* SportS. *Aud.:* Hs, Ac.

Track Coach, formerly titled *Track Technique*, is designated by USA Track and Field as its "official technical publication." Each issue is approximately 30 pages long and contains about five practical articles that speak to teaching methods, techniques for track athletes, improvement of athletic performance, and the biomechanics of movement. A World Roundup of brief notes and letters to the editor are supplemental. University coaches are the most frequent writers. Recommended for high school and academic libraries with track and field programs.

6267. *Triathlete.* Formed by the merger of (1984-1986): *Tri-Athlete;* (1983-1986): *Triathlon.* [ISSN: 0898-3410] 1986. m. USD 21.95 domestic; USD 26.95 Canada; USD 28.95 elsewhere. Ed(s): Christina Gandolfo. Triathlon Group North America, 2037 San Elijo Ave, Cardiff, CA 92007-0550. Illus., adv. Circ: 105000. *Indexed:* SportS. *Aud.:* Ga, Ac.

Triathlete is one of two major monthly magazines focusing on triathlon competition. Published by the Triathlon Group of North America since 1986, the one hundred or so pages of each issue follow a regular format that includes columns and departments such as editorial, letters, and news. The columns section includes the feature column by Scott Tinley that subscribers often allude to as a major asset to the magazine, and articles on fitness, speed, equipment and gear reviews (usually bikes and shoes), and new techniques, tests, and other developments that affect triathletes. Since the triathlon is an amateur, but strenuously competitive, sport, its appeal is not as broad as that of golf or tennis. Some of the more exhaustive public and academic sports collections may find this an appropriate addition.

6268. *U S A Today Sports Weekly.* 2002. w. USD 34.95; USD 19.50 for 6 mos. U S A Today, 7950 Jones Branch Dr, McLean, VA 22108-0605. Adv. *Aud.:* Ga.

This newspaper publishes news articles, schedules, scores, and statistics on baseball and football. *USA Today Sports Weekly* is a combination of *USA Today Baseball Weekly* and *USA Today Football Weekly*. Both sections feature professional and collegiate teams and players, scouting reports, trades, training, and league reports. The baseball section has a column devoted to fantasy baseball. This would be a popular addition to public libraries.

6269. *VeloNews: the journal of competitive cycling.* Former titles (until 1974): *Cyclenews;* (until 1972): *Northeast Bicycle News.* [ISSN: 0161-1798] 1972. 20x/yr. USD 49.97 domestic; CND 96 Canada; USD 109 per issue elsewhere. Ed(s): Kip Mikler. Inside Communications, 1830 N 55th St, Boulder, CO 80301-2703; velonews@7dogs.com; http://www.velonews.com. Illus., adv. Circ: 49000. Microform: PQC. *Indexed:* SportS. *Aud.:* Ga, Ac.

Since 1972, the tabloid *VeloNews* has reported competitive bicycling news, including profiles of cyclists and teams; reports of major races in the United States and Europe; articles on training, health and nutrition, injury prevention, products and equipment; and news articles (such as one on drug testing). Each issue publishes a calendar of races in the United States and Canada. The print publication is supplemented by a web site, www.velonews.com, which contains information on current races, technical and training information, and news items. This site also has a number of links to other sites of interest to cycling enthusiasts. Appropriate for public libraries in areas where competitive cycling is popular.

6270. *Volleyball.* [ISSN: 1058-4668] 1990. m. USD 19.97 domestic; USD 28 Canada; USD 39 elsewhere. Ashton International Media, Inc., 44 Front St, Ste 280, Worcester, MA 01608. Illus., adv. Circ: 61184 Paid. *Indexed:* PEI. *Aud.:* Ga, Ac.

All facets of volleyball—indoor, beach, juniors, and college—are covered in this magazine. Articles are typically short, with many graphics and photographs. Features include interviews with players or coaches, event coverage, international volleyball, equipment and accessories, instruction, fitness, and nutrition. Issues usually run about 60 pages. The magazine's web site at www.volleyballmag.com includes at least one article to stimulate interest, plus a listing of some of the departments in the current issue. The site also includes selected reprints of articles on instruction and fitness and nutrition. Recommended for public libraries and academic libraries at institutions with volleyball programs.

6271. *VolleyballUSA.* Former titles (until 1992): *Inside U S A Volleyball; Volleyball U S A.* 1972. q. USD 10; USD 20 foreign. U S A Volleyball, 715 S Circle Dr, Colorado Springs, CO 80910-2368; volleyballusa@usav.org; http://www.usavolleyball.org. Illus., adv. Sample. Circ: 85000. *Bk. rev.:* 2, 250 words. *Aud.:* Hs, Ga.

The official publication of the United States Volleyball Association, *Volleyball USA* provides current information on volleyball in the United States, including indoor and beach volleyball, and national, junior, collegiate, and disabled teams. In addition to association activities, this glossy publication contains tournament and competition news as well as shorter articles on players, nutrition, weight training, and psychology. Public and high school libraries in areas where volleyball is a popular sport will find this a useful addition.

6272. *WakeBoarding.* [ISSN: 1079-0136] 1993. 9x/yr. USD 19.97 domestic; USD 28.97 per issue Canada; USD 37.97 per issue elsewhere. Ed(s): Tom Smith. World Publications LLC, 460 N Orlando Ave, Ste 200, Winter Park, FL 32789; info@worldpub.net; http://www.worldpub.net. Illus., adv. Circ: 45823 Paid. *Aud.:* Ga.

Since 1993, *WakeBoarding* has chronicled the relatively new sport of wakeboarding, which is described as a combination of waterskiing and snowboarding. Each 150- to 200-page issue features news, information and product releases, equipment reviews, profiles of wakeboarders, coverage of amateur and professional events, and instruction (for the advanced wakeboarder), along with lots of photographs and advertisements. The online version is at www.wakeboardingmag.com. Since wakeboarding is a growing water sport, public libraries in areas where it is popular should consider adding this to their collection.

6273. *The Water Skier.* [ISSN: 0049-7002] 1951. 9x/yr. USD 25 domestic; USD 30 foreign. Ed(s): Scott Atkinson. U S A Water Ski, 1251 Holy Cow Rd, Polk City, FL 33868-8200; memberservices@usawaterski.org; http://usawaterski.org/. Illus., index, adv. Sample. Circ: 28000 Controlled. *Indexed:* ConsI, MagInd, SportS. *Aud.:* Ga, Ac.

As the official publication of USA Water Ski, *The Water Skier* publishes articles of interest to the athletes and enthusiasts of competitive water skiing (including traditional, show, wakeboard, collegiate, kneeboard, barefoot, racing, and disabled). Each 50-page issue is filled with instructional articles, reports from tournaments, athlete and team profiles, water skiing safety, and listings of ski camps and schools. Issues contain lots of action-packed photographs. A link to the magazine and selected articles is available from the association's web page at www.usaski.org. Recommended for public and academic libraries.

6274. *Women's Basketball.* [ISSN: 1524-9204] 1999. q. USD 19.97 domestic; USD 28 Canada; USD 39 elsewhere. Ed(s): Gabrielle Hanna. Ashton International Media, Inc., 44 Front St, Ste 280, Worcester, MA 01608; wbinfo@aol.com; http://www.wbmagazine.com. Adv. *Aud.:* Hs, Ga.

Women and basketball fans alike will enjoy *Women's Basketball.* Published since 1999, "the first magazine devoted to the sport of women's basketball" covers the game at the high school, collegiate, and professional levels. Each issue of about 35 pages is filled with photographs and informative articles. Typical contents include a cover story (usually an in-depth profile of an athlete); feature articles on topics such as recruiting, high school coaches, college transfers, and the like; profiles of players and coaches; and, during the season, competitions. Articles on basketball news, training, strategy, athletic gear, and high school and amateur basketball round out each issue. The magazine's web site allows readers access to parts of feature articles to entice them to subscribe. An appropriate addition for high school and public libraries.

6275. *Wrestling U S A (Missoula).* Formerly: *Scholastic Wrestling News.* [ISSN: 0199-6258] 1964. m. USD 31 domestic; USD 41 foreign. Ed(s): Lanny Bryant. Wrestling U.S.A. Magazine, 109 Apple House Ln, Missoula, MT 59802-3324; wrestling@montana.com; http://www.wrestlingusa.com. Illus., adv. Sample. Circ: 14000. *Aud.:* Hs, Ac.

Wrestling USA publishes articles about youth, high school, and collegiate wrestling. Regular features include news, weight training, sports medicine, events and tournaments, and high school and collegiate teams. The journal's web site at www.wrestlingusa.com provides access to the tables of contents of issues from 2001 to the present and links to employment opportunities and other sites of interest to those involved with high school and collegiate wrestling. Appropriate for high school and academic libraries with wrestling programs.

Electronic Journals

6276. *Clinical Kinesiology (Online Edition).* Former titles (until 2002): *Clinical Kinesiology (Print Edition);* (until 1987): *American Corrective Therapy Journal;* (until 1967): *Association for Physical and Mental Rehabilitation. Journal.* 1947. q. USD 50 (Individuals, USD 35). American Kinesiotherapy Association, c/o Clinical Kinesiology, San Diego State University, San Diego, CA 92182-7251; geri@tkp.com. Illus., index, adv. Refereed. Circ: 1064. Microform: PQC. *Indexed:* BiolAb, CINAHL, ExcerpMed, IndMed, PEI, PsycholAb, SportS. *Aud.:* Ac, Sa.

The official journal of the American Kinesiotherapy Association, *Clinical Kinesiology* publishes theoretical and research manuscripts on the treatment of disease, injury, or deformity through therapeutic exercise and education. In 2003 this publication began publishing only as an online journal. The inaugural online issue contains two articles, one on yoga and flexibility and the other on the validation of a mobility obstacle course. Articles can be viewed as a web page or a pdf file. Suitable for academic libraries at institutions with physical education, sports medicine, and/or physical therapy programs.

6277. *The Club Tread Report.* 1995. m. Ed(s): Robert Braun. Braun's Bicycle & Fitness, 27 Scott St, Kitchener, ON N2H 2P8, Canada; club-tread-report@bltg.com; http://www.bltg.com/ctreport/. *Aud.:* Hs, Ga.

Club Tread Report, a free electronic newsletter, contains news and information about cycling, including technical tips, product reviews, cycling club news, and classified advertisements. Approximately ten issues are published per year. Past issues are available at the web site. Readers can access this newsletter at http://www.bltg.com/ctreport or register to receive it by e-mail.

6278. *Coaching Science Abstracts.* 1995. bi-m. Free. Ed(s): Brent S Rushall. Sports Science Associates, 4225 Orchad Dr, Spring Valley, CA 919977; brushall@mail.sdsu.edu; http://www-rohan.sdsu.edu/dept/coachsci/index.htm. *Aud.:* Hs, Ac, Sa.

Since 1995, Brent S. Rushall, Department of Exercise and Nutritional Studies, San Diego State University, has published the free online abstracting journal *Coaching Science Abstracts* to assist coaches, exercise science students, and those interested in applied sport science in locating recent research. Older articles are abstracted if the professor believes they contain current and useful information. Recent issues also contain personal communications, e-mails, and notes about the topic. Articles are chosen by Dr. Rushall's students and from his own personal research. *Coaching Science Abstracts* is published six times per year. Issues are typically thematic and scheduled to be updated every three years. Abstracts contain a citation, a brief description of the methodology and results, and an "Implications" section that interprets the study. Each issue contains a short introduction followed by anywhere from 25 to 100 abstracts. Dr. Rushall may also include his own commentary on the topic as part of the issue. Suitable for high school and academic libraries.

6279. *N A I A News Weekly Edition.* Former titles (until 1998): *N A I A News (Print Monthly Edition); N A I A News and Coach.* 1950. w. USD 30. Ed(s): Dave Webster. National Association of Intercollegiate Athletics, P.O. Box 472200, Tulsa, OK 74147-2200; http://www.naia.org/weeklyed.html. Circ: 8000. Microform: PQC. Reprint: PQC. *Indexed:* SportS. *Aud.:* Ac.

NAIA News Weekly Edition, the official publication of the National Association of Intercollegiate Athletics, is a free online newsletter. The publication reports association news and publishes articles about players, coaches, teams, and championships. Daily archives for the past year are available at the web site. It is best to access this electronic newsletter through the NAIA web site, which provides access to additional information of interest to those interested in intercollegiate athletics. Suitable for academic libraries.

6280. *Sportscience.* Formerly (until 1998): *Sportscience News.* [ISSN: 1174-9210] 1997. irreg. Ed(s): Will Hopkins. Internet Society for Sport Science, http://www.sportsci.org. Refereed. *Indexed:* PEI. *Aud.:* Hs, Ga, Ac.

The Internet Society for Sport Science group (primarily composed of academics in sports and exercise science), under the leadership of Professor Will Hopkins, has produced an interesting and useful electronic journal that publishes research resources, topical information (conference reports, opinion pieces), and some original research. Articles undergo a blind peer-review process. A recent issue includes the annual report of impact factors of journals in sports sciences and an opinion and reaction piece. Earlier issues contain more content. For example, a previous issue contains two opinion pieces and commentary, an article on the effects of a vegetarian diet on performance in strength sports, and a piece on the effects of training in the heat on cycling performance at normal temperatures. The editorial in this same earlier issue questioned whether *Sportscience* could continue to be published, citing lack of contributors and constraints on the editor's time. Readers should watch and hope that this e-journal survives.

■ STATISTICS

Katherine M. Weir, Business Librarian, 8900 Milner Library, Illinois State University, Normal, IL 61790-8900; kay@exchange1.mlb.ilstu.edu; FAX: 309-438-3676

Introduction

Statistics are as old as such human records as censuses and records of ownership. Descriptive statistics date from the Middle Ages, but it was only in the nineteenth century that statistical theory and methods began to evolve. Much of the theory of statistics was developed in the twentieth century. Originally, the term "statistics" was applied to the collection and analysis of data about the political state, such as tax, trade, and demographic information and vital statistics. Over time, usage has expanded to include the collection and analysis of data about human and natural phenomena of all kinds upon which to base decisions in the face of uncertainty. For ease of discussion, the field is often divided into descriptive and analytical statistics, or statistical theory and statistical method. In addition, there are specialties based on techniques, e.g., computational statistics and stochastic modeling, or on disciplines, e.g., biometrics and econometrics. Statistical publishing reflects these divisions, with journals concentrating on theoretical statistics, applied statistics, or applications in specific disciplines.

Statistics is based on the mathematics of probability, and most statistical publications include a great deal of mathematical notation. As noted in the annotations, some journals place mathematical derivations and proofs in an appendix, in order to make the text more accessible to the nonstatistician. Figures and tables are common in statistical publications and have not been noted in the entries. Because illustrations of other types are rare, they have been noted.

There are few statistics publications of interest to the general public; most periodicals in the field are research journals with a limited audience even among academicians and specialists. Perhaps the most accessible journal to the general adult reader is *Chance*, a publication of the American Statistical Association (ASA). *JASA*, also a publication of the ASA, is designed for the widest audience: professionals in virtually all fields, from actuaries to sociologists. All but the largest public libraries may wish to limit their collecting to these two journals. School libraries may find *Teaching Statistics* (all grades) or the *American Statistician* (high school) useful. At the college level, the electronic *Journal of Statistics Education* is an excellent source of practical information and creative ideas for the teaching of probability and statistics.

Journals on the basic list, plus a few specialized journals selected to meet the curricular and faculty needs of a particular library, will suffice for many college libraries. Colleges and universities supporting statistics programs will find many of the titles listed to be valuable additions to their collections.

Basic Periodicals

Ga: *Chance;* Ac: *Advances in Applied Probability, Annals of Applied Probability, Annals of Probability, Annals of Statistics, Computational Statistics, JASA, Royal Statistical Society. Journal. Series C. Applied Statistics.*

Basic Abstracts and Indexes

Mathematical Reviews, Statistical Theory & Method Abstracts.

6281. ***Advances in Applied Probability.*** [ISSN: 0001-8678] 1969. q. GBP 145.50 (Individuals, GBP 48.50). Ed(s): C C Heyde. Applied Probability Trust, School of Mathematics, University of Sheffield, Sheffield, S3 7RH, United Kingdom; s.c.boyles@sheffield.ac.uk; http://www.appliedprobability.org. Illus., index, adv. Refereed. Circ: 1100. Vol. ends: Dec. *Indexed:* ABIn, BiolAb, CCMJ, EngInd, GeoRef, MathSciNet, RiskAb, SCI, SSCI, ST&MA. *Aud.:* Ac, Sa.

Each issue contains a general applied probability section and a stochastic geometry and statistical applications section. Accepted for publication are review articles, longer research papers in applied probability, expository articles on areas of mathematics of interest to probabilists, articles on scientific topics for which probability models can be developed, conference papers not elsewhere published, and letters to the editor. The editor in chief and 24 of 30 editors are shared with the companion publication, *Journal of Applied Probability,* in which shorter research papers are published. However, the editors may publish accepted papers in either journal, based on available space. Each issue contains 10 to 12 articles of 10 to 30 pages. Most articles are in English, but articles in French are also accepted for publication. This title is similar in coverage to *Annals of Applied Probability.* Colleges and universities with statistics programs should subscribe to either or both of these publications.

6282. ***American Statistician.*** [ISSN: 0003-1305] 1947. q. USD 75 (Individuals, USD 15; Students, USD 15). American Statistical Association, 1429 Duke St, Alexandria, VA 22314-3415; http://www.amstat.org/. Illus., adv. Vol. ends: Nov. Microform: MIM; PMC; PQC; NRP. Online: EBSCO Publishing; Ingenta Select; Northern Light Technology, Inc. Reprint: SWZ. *Indexed:* ABIn, CCMJ, ChemAb, DSR&OA, GeoRef, MathSciNet, PAIS, SCI, SSCI, SSI, ST&MA. *Bk. rev.:* 4-5, 800-1,200 words. *Aud.:* Ac.

Intended for use by teachers and practicing statisticians, each issue contains approximately 15 articles in four departments. Most articles are four to six pages long, but a few are as short as three pages or as long as nine pages. More than half of the articles are published as "General." Most articles feature topics for classroom discussion or demonstration or for useful applications for practitioners. The "Teacher's Corner" contains four to six articles for teachers of college mathematics or applied-statistics courses. Course content and pedagogy are equally stressed. The "Statistical Practice" department features articles of interest to a broad audience of practitioners, such as brief descriptions of new developments and innovative applications of known methodologies. "Statistical Computing and Graphics" includes articles on developments in statistical computing and reviews of software. Includes reviews of undergraduate textbooks and other teaching materials.

6283. ***Annals of Applied Probability.*** [ISSN: 1050-5164] 1991. q. USD 130. Ed(s): Asmussen Soeren. Institute of Mathematical Statistics, 9650 Rockville Pike, Ste L2310, Bethesda, MD 20814-3998; staff@imstat.org; http://www.imstat.org. Illus., index, adv. Refereed. Circ: 2500 Paid. Vol. ends: Nov. *Indexed:* CCMJ, MathSciNet, SCI, ST&MA. *Aud.:* Ac, Sa.

This journal publishes applications-oriented research articles. Theoretical articles are published by the Institute of Mathematical Statistics (IMS) in its *Annals of Probability.* The 8 to 12 articles in each issue vary from 15 to 40 pages each, and issues average 200–300 pages each. The IMS has nearly 100 corporate and institutional members, including many research universities. Membership and authorship are international. Most colleges and universities with programs in statistics should acquire this title and/or *Advances in Applied Probability.*

6284. ***Annals of Probability.*** [ISSN: 0091-1798] 1973. q. USD 200. Ed(s): Thomas Kurtz. Institute of Mathematical Statistics, 9650 Rockville Pike, Ste L2310, Bethesda, MD 20814-3998; staff@imstat.org; http://www.imstat.org. Illus., index, adv. Refereed. Circ: 2700 Paid. Vol. ends: Oct. Microform: PQC. Online: JSTOR (Web-based Journal Archive). *Indexed:* CCMJ, MathSciNet, SCI, SSCI, ST&MA. *Aud.:* Ac, Sa.

The *Annals of Probability* publishes contributions to the theory of probability, expository papers, and surveys of areas in vigorous development. Each issue contains 20 to 25 research articles averaging 15 to 40 pages. As a result, issues contain 300 to 500 pages. The Institute of Mathematical Statistics (IMS) has nearly 100 corporate and institutional members, including many research universities. Membership and authorship are international. Most colleges and universities should acquire this title. The IMS also publishes the *Annals of Applied Probability.*

6285. *Annals of Statistics.* Supersedes in part: *Annals of Mathematical Statistics.* [ISSN: 0090-5364] 1973. bi-m. USD 220. Ed(s): John I. Marden, Jon A. Wellner. Institute of Mathematical Statistics, 9650 Rockville Pike, Ste L2310, Bethesda, MD 20814-3998; staff@imstat.org; http://www.imstat.org. Illus., index, adv. Refereed. Circ: 4300 Paid. Vol. ends: Dec. Microform: PQC. *Indexed:* CCMJ, MathSciNet, SCI, SSCI, ST&MA. *Aud.:* Ac, Sa.

The editors seek to position this journal at the forefront of mathematical statistical research. They encourage submission of articles advancing the underlying concepts and theories of statistical science. In addition, articles concerning the role of statistics in interdisciplinary investigations of major contemporary social and scientific problems are sought, as are articles describing developments in computational methodology. Issues average 300 to 500 pages, and each contains 20 to 30 articles. Recommended for most college and university libraries.

6286. *Australian & New Zealand Journal of Statistics.* Formed by the merger of (1959-1998): *Australian Journal of Statistics;* (1966-1998): *New Zealand Statistician.* [ISSN: 1369-1473] 1998. q. GBP 94 print & online eds. Ed(s): Chris J Lloyd, Rob J Hyndman. Blackwell Publishing Asia, 550 Swanston St, Carlton South, VIC 3053, Australia; subs@blackwellpublishingasia.com; http://www.blackwellpublishing.com/. Illus., index, adv. Sample. Refereed. Circ: 1369. Vol. ends: Dec. Microform: PQC. Online: EBSCO Publishing; ingenta.com; OCLC Online Computer Library Center, Inc.; RoweCom Information Quest; Swets Blackwell. Reprint: SWZ. *Indexed:* CCMJ, IBSS, MathSciNet, PAIS, SSCI, ST&MA. *Bk. rev.:* 3-6, 300-1,000 words. *Aud.:* Ac, Sa.

Each issue of this official journal of the Statistical Society of Australia contains six to ten articles. The editors seek a balance between theoretical and applied articles, and especially encourage submission of articles concerning new applications of established methods, newly developed methods, and case studies of interesting applications. However, most articles published are theoretical articles in the fields of mathematical statistics, probability, and econometrics. Authorship is international.

6287. *Bernoulli: a journal of mathematical statistics and probability.* [ISSN: 1350-7265] 1995. bi-m. Non-members, EUR 250. Ed(s): William van Zwel, Sara de Geer. International Statistical Institute, Princes Beatrixlaan 428, PO Box 950, Voorburg, 2270 AZ, Netherlands; isi@cbs.nl; http://www.cbs.nl/isi. Refereed. Circ: 1500 Paid. Online: EBSCO Publishing; ingenta.com; OCLC Online Computer Library Center, Inc.; RoweCom Information Quest; Swets Blackwell. *Indexed:* CCMJ, MathSciNet, SCI, ST&MA. *Aud.:* Ac, Sa.

The official publication of the Bernoulli Society accepts original research contributions providing background, derivation, and discussion of the results, as well as review articles and scholarly historical reviews for all aspects of statistics and probability. Each issue contains between 8 and 13 articles.

6288. *Biometrics.* Formerly (until 1947): *Biometrics Bulletin.* [ISSN: 0006-341X] 1945. q. USD 200 print & online eds. Ed(s): Marie Davidian, Tony Pettitt. Blackwell Publishing Ltd., 9600 Garsington Rd, Oxford, OX4 2ZG, United Kingdom; customerservices@oxon.blackwellpublishing.com; http://www.blackwellpublishing.com. Illus., index, adv. Refereed. Circ: 8000. Vol. ends: Dec. Microform: BHP; PMC; PQC. Online: ingenta.com; JSTOR (Web-based Journal Archive); ProQuest Information & Learning. *Indexed:* AS&TI, AbAn, ApMecR, B&AI, BioEngAb, BiolAb, CCMJ, ChemAb, DSA, DSR&OA, EngInd, ExcerpMed, FPA, FS&TA, ForAb, HortAb, IndMed, IndVet, MathSciNet, RRTA, S&F, SCI, SSCI, ST&MA, VetBull, WRCInf, ZooRec. *Bk. rev.:* 10-20, 600-1,000 words. *Aud.:* Ac, Sa.

The primary goals of this journal are to promote the use of statistical methods in the biological sciences and encourage sharing of ideas between experimental biologists and those concerned with analysis and statistical methodology. To make methodology papers accessible to experimental biologists, they are required to describe biological applications and use real data with the inclusion of intermediate steps in examples. Extensive mathematical derivations are placed in appendixes. Papers on biological subjects report conclusions reached by mathematical or statistical analysis, illustrate the use of less well known analytical techniques, or apply standard techniques in a new field. A typical issue contains as many as 40 articles of 3–12 pages each.

6289. *Biometrika.* [ISSN: 0006-3444] 1901. q. GBP 92. Ed(s): D. M. Titterington. Oxford University Press, Great Clarendon St, Oxford, OX2 6DP, United Kingdom; jnl.orders@oup.co.uk; http://www3.oup.co.uk/jnls. Illus., index. Refereed. Circ: 3700. Vol. ends: Dec. Microform: PMC; PQC. Online: EBSCO Publishing; ingenta.com; JSTOR (Web-based Journal Archive); RoweCom Information Quest; Swets Blackwell. Reprint: PQC; PSC. *Indexed:* AS&TI, B&AI, BiolAb, CCMJ, ChemAb, DSA, ExcerpMed, HortAb, MathSciNet, SCI, SSCI, ST&MA, ZooRec. *Aud.:* Ac, Sa.

Widely indexed and well established, *Biometrika* accepts articles covering a wide range of topics. The emphasis is on original theoretical contributions with potential or direct value in applications. Each issue includes 15 to 20 articles of 10–20 pages each and two or three short miscellaneous notes. A majority of the articles are by British and American authors.

6290. *Canadian Journal of Statistics.* [ISSN: 0319-5724] 1973. q. CND 150 domestic; USD 110 domestic; CND 160 United States. Ed(s): Richard A Lockhart. Statistical Society of Canada, 1485 Laperriere St, Ottawa, Ontario K1Z 7S8, ON K1Z 7S8, Canada; admin@ssc.ca; http://www.ssc.ca. Illus., index, adv. Refereed. Circ: 1350 Paid. Vol. ends: Dec. *Indexed:* CCMJ, IBSS, MathSciNet, PAIS, ST&MA. *Aud.:* Ac, Sa.

This Canadian equivalent of the American Statistical Association journal is international in scope, but more than half of the articles it publishes are written by Canadians. Although articles may be written in either English or French, most are in English. Abstracts are printed in both English and French. The journal publishes original work in the theory and applications of statistics, including survey papers and articles of theoretical, applied, or pedagogical interest. Most issues contain 10 or 11 articles of 10–12 pages each.

6291. *Chance (New York, 1988): a magazine of the American Statistical Association.* [ISSN: 0933-2480] 1988. q. USD 79. Ed(s): H S Stern, Dalene Stengl. Springer-Verlag, Journals, 175 Fifth Ave., New York, NY 10010-7703; journals@springer-ny.com; http://www.springer-ny.com. Illus., index, adv. Refereed. Vol. ends: No. 4. Microform: PQC. Online: Springer LINK. Reprint: SWZ. *Indexed:* CCMJ, CompLI, MathSciNet, PollutAb. *Aud.:* Hs, Ga.

Articles are aimed at informed lay readers interested in data analysis and those who use statistical methods in their work. The style is popular rather than scholarly, and additional readings are suggested for those seeking a better understanding of the topic. Each issue contains five to seven articles of five to seven pages each. Subject matter ranges from statistical methods and technical issues to public-policy concerns, sports, and other general-interest topics. One of the few statistical magazines of interest to the general adult reader.

6292. *Communications in Statistics: Simulation and Computation.* Supersedes in part (with vol.5, 1976): *Communications in Statistics.* [ISSN: 0361-0918] 1972. q. USD 1310. Ed(s): N Balakrishnan. Marcel Dekker Inc., 270 Madison Ave, New York, NY 10016-0602; http://www.dekker.com. Illus., index, adv. Refereed. Circ: 725. Vol. ends: Nov. Reprint: SWZ. *Indexed:* CCMJ, EngInd, MathSciNet, SCI, SSCI, ST&MA. *Aud.:* Ac, Sa.

The three *Communications in Statistics* journals are designed as vehicles for the rapid dissemination of new ideas in their respective areas of statistics. This journal focuses on the interaction of statistics and computer science. Articles may present tables of and algorithms for statistical functions and numerical solutions to problems by the use of simulation or special functions. Each issue contains 12 to 14 articles. Suitable for collections emphasizing computational statistics.

6293. ***Communications in Statistics: Theory and Methods.*** Superseded in part (with vol.5, 1976): *Communications in Statistics.* [ISSN: 0361-0926] 1970. m. USD 2995. Ed(s): N Balakrishnan. Marcel Dekker Inc., 270 Madison Ave, New York, NY 10016-0602; http://www.dekker.com. Illus., index, adv. Refereed. Circ: 800. Vol. ends: Dec. Reprint: SWZ. *Indexed:* CCMJ, EngInd, GeoRef, MathSciNet, SCI, ST&MA. *Aud.:* Ac, Sa.

Of the three *Communications in Statistics* journals, *Theory and Methods* is broadest in scope. The journal has a strong mathematical orientation to the application of statistical methods to practical problems. It publishes survey articles and discussions of practical statistical problems, whether or not the authors have solutions to present. Articles focus on new applications of statistical methods to problems in government and industry. Each monthly issue contains 15 to 18 articles varying in length from 8 to 30 pages each. Based on their content and cost, the three *Communications in Statistics* journals are suitable for college and university libraries with extensive statistics collections.

6294. ***Computational Statistics.*** Formerly: *C S Q - Computational Statistics Quarterly.* [ISSN: 0943-4062] 1982. q. EUR 330 domestic; EUR 341 foreign; EUR 99 newsstand/cover per issue. Ed(s): W Haerdle, J Newton. Physica-Verlag GmbH und Co., Postfach 105280, Heidelberg, 69042, Germany; physica@springer.de. Illus. Refereed. Vol. ends: No. 4. Microform: PQC. Online: EBSCO Publishing; RoweCom Information Quest; Springer LINK. *Indexed:* CCMJ, EngInd, MathSciNet, ST&MA. *Bk. rev.:* 1, 700-800 words. *Aud.:* Ac, Sa.

Computational Statistics publishes applications and methodological research focusing on the contribution to and influence of computing and statistics upon each other. The intended audience includes computer scientists, mathematicians, and statisticians. Topics covered include biometrics, econometrics, data analysis, graphics, simulation, algorithms, knowledge-based systems, and Bayesian computing. Issues contain six to eight articles of approximately 20 pages each and usually a software and/or book review. Although published in Germany, the text is in English. Recommended for libraries supporting statistics programs.

6295. ***Computational Statistics and Data Analysis.*** Incorporates (1975-1991): *Statistical Software Newsletter.* [ISSN: 0167-9473] 1983. m. EUR 1637. Ed(s): S P Azen, Erricos Kontoghiorghes. Elsevier BV, North-Holland, Sara Burgerhartstraat 25, Amsterdam, 1055 KV, Netherlands; nlinfo-f@elsevier.nl; http://www.elsevier.nl. Illus., index, adv. Sample. Refereed. Circ: 1000. Vol. ends: No. 35 - No. 37. Microform: PQC. Online: EBSCO Publishing; ingenta.com; ScienceDirect; Swets Blackwell. Reprint: SWZ. *Indexed:* CCMJ, EngInd, GeoRef, GeogAbPG, MathSciNet, SSCI, ST&MA. *Bk. rev.:* 2-3, 120-300 words. *Aud.:* Ac, Sa.

This official journal of the International Association of Statistical Computing is dedicated to the dissemination of methodological research and applications. Each issue contains approximately eight refereed articles in three sections: "Computational Statistics," "Statistical Methodology for Data Analysis," and "Special Applications." The "Statistical Software Newsletter" forms a fourth section. The intended audience includes statisticians, computer center professionals, and scientific and social researchers at a postgraduate level. Due to its expense, it is only suitable for comprehensive or specialized collections.

6296. ***Institute of Statistical Mathematics. Annals.*** [ISSN: 0020-3157] 1949. q. EUR 775. Ed(s): R Shimizu. Kluwer Academic Publishers, van Godewijckstraat 30, PO Box 17, Dordrecht, 3300 AA, Netherlands; services@wkap.nl; http://www.wkap.nl. Refereed. Circ: 1500. Microform: PQC. Online: EBSCO Publishing; ingenta.com; Kluwer Online; OCLC Online Computer Library Center, Inc.; Ovid Technologies, Inc.; RoweCom Information Quest; Swets Blackwell. *Indexed:* BAS, CCMJ, CompLI, EngInd, GeoRef, IBSS, MathSciNet, SCI, ST&MA. *Aud.:* Ac, Sa.

This Japanese journal provides an international forum for the communication of developments in theoretical and applied statistics. It especially welcomes papers that will lead to significant improvements in the practice of statistics. Each issue contains 10 to 15 lengthy articles. Recommended for comprehensive statistics collections.

6297. ***International Statistical Review.*** Formerly (until 1972): *International Statistical Institute Review.* [ISSN: 0306-7734] 1933. 3x/yr. Non-members, EUR 68. Ed(s): Asta M Manninen, Elja Arjas. International Statistical Institute, Princes Beatrixlaan 428, PO Box 950, Voorburg, 2270 AZ, Netherlands; isi@cbs.nl; http://www.cbs.nl/isi. Illus., index, adv. Refereed. Circ: 2000. Reprint: SWZ. *Indexed:* GeoRef, IndVet, SCI, SSCI, ST&MA, VetBull. *Aud.:* Ac, Sa.

This journal accepts expository and review articles of interest to a wide readership. Topics may include statistical theory, methodology, applications, education, computing, graphics, data analysis, the history of statistics, official statistics, demography, and survey statistics. The editors seek to create a forum for discussion of issues involving the statistics profession as a whole.

6298. ***J A S A.*** Former titles (until 1922): *American Statistical Association. Quarterly Publications;* (until 1912): *American Statistical Association. Publications.* [ISSN: 0162-1459] 1888. q. Members, USD 39; Non-members, USD 310; Students, USD 10. American Statistical Association, 1429 Duke St, Alexandria, VA 22314-3415; asainfo@amstat.org; http://www.amstat.org/. Illus., index, adv. Refereed. Circ: 12000. Vol. ends: Dec. Microform: PMC; PQC; NRP. Online: EBSCO Publishing; Florida Center for Library Automation; Gale Group; Ingenta Select; JSTOR (Web-based Journal Archive); ProQuest Information & Learning. Reprint: PQC; SWZ. *Indexed:* ABIn, BPI, BiolAb, CCMJ, CJA, CompR, ExcerpMed, HortAb, IBSS, JEL, LRI, MathSciNet, PsycholAb, SCI, SSCI, ST&MA. *Bk. rev.:* 10-20, 500-1,000 words. *Aud.:* Ac, Sa.

The membership rolls of the American Statistical Association include professionals from fields as disparate as biology, economics, government, and sociology. This diverse audience is reflected in the wide range of topics presented in *JASA* and the many indexes and abstracts that index the journal. Most articles are ten pages or less, and as many as 45 appear in each issue. Although brief, each article is substantive as befits the "flagship publication" of the association. Articles are separated into two categories: "Applications and Case Studies" and "Theory and Methods." Given the wide-ranging and inclusive scope of this publication, it is recommended for all research collections.

6299. ***Journal of Applied Probability.*** [ISSN: 0021-9002] 1964. q. GBP 145.50 (Individuals, GBP 48.50). Ed(s): C C Heyde. Applied Probability Trust, School of Mathematics, University of Sheffield, Sheffield, S3 7RH, United Kingdom; s.c.boyles@sheffield.ac.uk; http://www.appliedprobability.org. Illus., index, adv. Refereed. Circ: 1500. Vol. ends: Dec. *Indexed:* ABIn, BiolAb, CCMJ, EngInd, MathSciNet, RiskAb, SCI, SSCI, ST&MA. *Aud.:* Ac, Sa.

This international journal is published by the Applied Probability Trust in association with the London Mathematical Society. It publishes research papers of 20 pages or less and short notes on applications of probability theory to the biological, physical, social, and technological sciences. It shares its editorial board with its companion publication, *Advances in Applied Probability.* Based on available space, the editors may publish accepted articles in either journal. Most articles are in English, but articles in French are also published. Recommended for colleges and universities with programs in statistics.

6300. ***Journal of Applied Statistics.*** Formerly (until 1984): *Bulletin in Applied Statistics.* [ISSN: 0266-4763] 1975. 10x/yr. GBP 838 (Individuals, GBP 227). Ed(s): Gopal K Kanji. Routledge, 11 New Fetter Ln, London, EC4P 4EE, United Kingdom; http://www.routledge.com. Adv. Refereed. Online: bigchalk; EBSCO Publishing; Ingenta Select; Northern Light Technology, Inc.; OCLC Online Computer Library Center, Inc.; ProQuest Information & Learning; RoweCom Information Quest; Swets Blackwell. Reprint: PSC. *Indexed:* CCMJ, EngInd, GeogAbPG, JEL, MathSciNet, ST&MA. *Bk. rev.:* Occasional. *Aud.:* Ac, Sa.

Accepts articles on the design and application of statistical methods to research problems in all disciplines. Each issue contains an average of 10 to 12 articles. The journal publishes occasional combined and/or thematic issues. Brief responses or discussion comments accompany some articles. Some issues include book reviews.

Journal of Business and Economic Statistics. See Business section.

6301. *Journal of Computational and Graphical Statistics.* [ISSN: 1061-8600] 1992. q. Members, USD 55; Non-members, USD 90. American Statistical Association, 1429 Duke St, Alexandria, VA 22314-3415; asainfo@amstat.org; http://www.amstat.org/. Refereed. *Indexed:* CCMJ, MathSciNet, ST&MA. *Aud.:* Ac, Sa.

A joint publication of the American Statistical Association, the Institute of Mathematical Statistics, and the Interface Foundation of North America, the journal publishes original contributions in the fields of computational statistics and data visualization, including theory, applications, review articles, and software reviews and comparisons. Authors may submit additional material for posting on the web site to extend or complement an article. Each issue contains about 12 articles or a discussion article with several responses and three or more ordinary articles.

6302. *Metrika: international journal for theoretical and applied statistics.* [ISSN: 0026-1335] 1953. bi-m. EUR 399 domestic; EUR 415.40 foreign; EUR 80 newsstand/cover per issue. Ed(s): U Gather, F Pukelsheim. Physica-Verlag GmbH und Co., Postfach 105280, Heidelberg, 69042, Germany; physica@springer.de. Illus., index, adv. Refereed. Circ: 1000. Vol. ends: No. 3. Microform: PQC. Online: EBSCO Publishing; RoweCom Information Quest; ScienceDirect; Springer LINK; Swets Blackwell. Reprint: SWZ. *Indexed:* CCMJ, JEL, MathSciNet, ST&MA. *Bk. rev.:* 2-4, 1,000-1,400 words. *Aud.:* Ac, Sa.

Metrika is an international research journal for theoretical and applied statistics. It publishes papers in mathematical statistics and statistical methods, especially those presenting new developments in theoretical statistics. Importance is attached to applicability of the proposed statistical methods and results. Although published in Germany, the text is in English. Authorship is international, but at least half of the authors are German. Issues average six articles of 6–20 pages each, with a few articles as long as 30 pages.

Oxford Bulletin of Economics and Statistics. See Economics section.

Psychometrika. See Psychology section.

The Review of Economics and Statistics. See Economics section.

6303. *Royal Statistical Society. Journal. Series A: Statistics in Society.* Former titles (until 1988): *Royal Statistical Society. Journal. Series A: General;* (until 1948): *Royal Statistical Society. Journal;* (until 1887): *Statistical Society. Journal.* [ISSN: 0964-1998] 1838. q. GBP 195 print & online eds. Ed(s): C D Payne, N G Best. Blackwell Publishing Ltd., 9600 Garsington Rd, PO Box 805, Oxford, OX4 2DQ, United Kingdom; customerservices@oxon.blackwellpublishing.com; http://www.blackwellpublishing.com/. Illus., adv. Sample. Refereed. Circ: 5700. Microform: BHP. Online: EBSCO Publishing; ingenta.com; JSTOR (Web-based Journal Archive); OCLC Online Computer Library Center, Inc.; RoweCom Information Quest; Swets Blackwell. Reprint: PSC. *Indexed:* ApMecR, CCMJ, CJA, DSR&OA, IBSS, IPSA, IndVet, JEL, MathSciNet, PAIS, PSA, RRTA, SCI, SSCI, ST&MA, SociolAb, WAE&RSA. *Aud.:* Ac, Sa.

This journal focuses on applications of statistics to public policy and social issues, including health, education, religious, legal, and demographic topics. Papers with mathematical expositions must also include a narrative explanation of the argument to make them accessible to professionals in many disciplines. The journal seeks thorough analyses of applications with substantial statistical content. It also publishes methodological papers that contain illustrative applications involving appropriate data. Beginning with 1999, data sets associated with papers can be obtained at http://www.blackwellpublishers.co.uk/rss/. The society also publishes three other journals: *Royal Statistical Society. Journal. Series B: Statistical Methodology; Royal Statistical Society. Journal. Series C: Applied Statistics;* and *The Statistician* (*Royal Statistical Society. Journal. Series D*).

6304. *Royal Statistical Society. Journal. Series B: Statistical Methodology.* Formerly (until 1997): *Royal Statistical Society. Journal. Series B: Methodological.* [ISSN: 1369-7412] 1934. q. GBP 130 print & online eds. Ed(s): A C Davidson, D Firth. Blackwell Publishing Ltd., 9600 Garsington Rd, PO Box 805, Oxford, OX4 2DQ, United Kingdom; customerservices@oxon.blackwellpublishing.com; http://www.blackwellpublishers.co.uk/Scripts/. Illus., index, adv. Sample. Refereed. Circ: 4500. Vol. ends: No. 4. Reprint: PSC. *Indexed:* ApMecR, CCMJ, HortAb, IBSS, IPSA, MathSciNet, SCI, SSCI, ST&MA. *Aud.:* Ac, Sa.

As the methodological and theoretical publication of the Royal Statistical Society, this journal publishes articles that contribute to the understanding of statistics. Articles focus on the logical and philosophical basis of statistical theory, new methods of collecting or analyzing data, comparisons or new applications of existing methods, the development and analysis of stochastic models, and discussion of new methodologies in statistical computation and simulation. Beginning with 1998, data sets associated with papers can be obtained online at http://www.blackwellpublishers.co.uk/rss/. The society also publishes three other journals: *Royal Statistical Society. Journal. Series A: Statistics in Society*; *Royal Statistical Society. Journal. Series C: Applied Statistics*; and *The Statistician* (*Royal Statistical Society. Journal. Series D*).

6305. *Royal Statistical Society. Journal. Series C: Applied Statistics.* [ISSN: 0035-9254] 1952. q. GBP 130 print & online eds. Ed(s): G. Molenberghs, A W Bowman. Blackwell Publishing Ltd., 9600 Garsington Rd, PO Box 805, Oxford, OX4 2DQ, United Kingdom; customerservices@oxon.blackwellpublishing.com; http://www.maths.ntu.ac.nk/rss/journals.html. Illus., index, adv. Sample. Refereed. Circ: 5400. Vol. ends: No. 4. *Indexed:* BrArAb, CCMJ, EngInd, GeoRef, IBSS, IPSA, MathSciNet, SCI, SSCI, ST&MA. *Aud.:* Ac, Sa.

Aimed at practicing statisticians, this publication of the Royal Statistical Society presents articles stressing the practical application of the methods discussed. Topics covered include design issues arising from practical problems, applications of statistical computing, and methodological developments arising from the solution of practical problems. The editors especially encourage submission of articles describing interdisciplinary work. Detailed algebraic development is avoided. Beginning with 1998, data sets associated with papers can be obtained online at http://www.blackwellpublishers.co.uk/rss/. The journal is suitable for most college and university libraries. The society also publishes three other journals: *Royal Statistical Society. Journal. Series A: Statistics in Society; Royal Statistical Society. Journal. Series B: Statistical Methodology;* and *The Statistician* (*Royal Statistical Society. Journal. Series D*).

6306. *Sankhya. Series A: Indian journal of statistics.* [ISSN: 0581-572X] 1933. q. USD 75. Scientific Publishers, 5-A New Pali Rd., Near Hotel Taj Hari Mahal, PO Box 91, Jodhpur, 342 003, India; info@scientificpub.com; http://www.scientificpub.com. Illus., index, adv. Circ: 1500. Vol. ends: Oct. Microform: PMC. *Indexed:* BiolAb, CCMJ, ChemAb, MathSciNet, PAIS, SSCI, ST&MA. *Bk. rev.:* 3-5, 200-450 words. *Aud.:* Ac, Sa.

Sankhya is published in two series. Series A focuses on probability and mathematical statistics. Most articles are primarily mathematical presentations, with little discussion. The 10 to 12 articles in each issue range from 10 to 25 pages in length. Authorship is international, with a large number of contributors from Asian countries.

6307. *Sankhya. Series B: Indian journal of statistics.* [ISSN: 0581-5738] 1933. q. USD 75. Scientific Publishers, 5-A New Pali Rd., Near Hotel Taj Hari Mahal, PO Box 91, Jodhpur, 342 003, India; info@scientificpub.com; http://www.scientificpub.com. Illus., index, adv. Circ: 1400. Vol. ends: Dec. Microform: PMC. *Indexed:* BiolAb, CCMJ, ChemAb, MathSciNet, PAIS, SSCI, ST&MA. *Bk. rev.:* 3-5, 400-600 words. *Aud.:* Ac, Sa.

Sankhya is published in two series. Series B accepts papers of broad interest in applied statistics and quantitative economics. The focus is on analysis of original data, new applications of established and newer methodologies, and the development of new techniques for immediate application. Each issue contains 10 to 12 articles and several book reviews. Authorship is international.

6308. ***Scandinavian Journal of Statistics: theory and applications.*** [ISSN: 0303-6898] 1974. q. GBP 144 print & online eds. Ed(s): Lennart Bondesson. Blackwell Publishing Ltd., 9600 Garsington Rd, PO Box 805, Oxford, OX4 2DQ, United Kingdom; jnlinfo@blackwellpublishers.co.uk; http://www.blackwellpublishing.com/. Illus., index, adv. Sample. Refereed. Circ: 700. Vol. ends: Dec. Online: EBSCO Publishing; ingenta.com; OCLC Online Computer Library Center, Inc.; RoweCom Information Quest; Swets Blackwell. Reprint: SWZ. *Indexed:* CCMJ, MathSciNet, SCI, ST&MA. *Aud.:* Ac, Sa.

Published jointly by the Danish Society for Theoretical Statistics, the Finnish Statistical Society, the Norwegian Statistical Society, and the Swedish Statistical Association, this is an international journal with worldwide authorship. The journal publishes research in both theoretical and applied statistics as well as statistically motivated papers concerning relevant aspects of other fields. Articles range from 8 to 30 pages in length, with mathematical derivations and proofs presented as appendixes.

6309. ***Statistica Sinica.*** [ISSN: 1017-0405] 1991. q. TWD 3000 (Individuals, USD 50). Ed(s): J L Wang. Academia Sinica, Institute of Statistical Science, 128, Sec 2 Yen-chiu-Yuan Rd, Taipei, 115, Taiwan, Republic of China; http://www.stat.sinica.edu.tw/. Refereed. *Indexed:* CCMJ, MathSciNet, SCI, ST&MA. *Aud.:* Ac, Sa.

Cosponsored by the International Chinese Statistical Association and the Institute of Statistical Science, Academia Sinica of Taiwan, this journal publishes articles on all aspects of statistics and probability, including theory, methods, and applications. Some issues have a theme; others are general in coverage. Authorship is international. Suitable for most college and university libraries.

6310. ***Statistical Science: a review journal.*** [ISSN: 0883-4237] 1986. q. USD 110. Ed(s): Leon Gleser. Institute of Mathematical Statistics, 9650 Rockville Pike, Ste L2310, Bethesda, MD 20814-3998; staff@imstat.org; http://www.imstat.org. Illus., index, adv. Refereed. Vol. ends: Nov. Microform: PQC. *Indexed:* CCMJ, EngInd, MathSciNet, SCI, SSCI, ST&MA. *Aud.:* Ac, Sa.

Statistical Science is a companion publication to the Institute of Mathematical Statistics' *Annals of Applied Probability, Annals of Probability,* and *Annals of Statistics.* Each issue includes an extensive interview with a distinguished statistician and three or four review or survey articles, some with comments. The goal of the journal is to present a broad range of contemporary statistical thought at a technical level accessible to practitioners, teachers, researchers, and students of statistics and probability.

6311. ***The Statistician.*** [ISSN: 0039-0526] 1950. q. GBP 114 print & online eds. Ed(s): G M Clarke, L C Wolstenholme. Blackwell Publishing Ltd., 9600 Garsington Rd, PO Box 805, Oxford, OX4 2DQ, United Kingdom; jnlinfo@blackwellpublishers.co.uk; http://www.blackwellpublishers.co.uk/. Illus., index, adv. Sample. Refereed. Vol. ends: No. 4. Microform: PQC. Online: EBSCO Publishing; ingenta.com; JSTOR (Web-based Journal Archive); OCLC Online Computer Library Center, Inc.; RoweCom Information Quest; Swets Blackwell. Reprint: PSC. *Indexed:* ExcerpMed, GeoRef, IBSS, MathSciNet, PAIS, RiskAb, SCI, SSCI, ST&MA. *Bk. rev.:* 12-20, 400-900 words. *Aud.:* Ac, Sa.

The Statistician publishes articles concerning applications of statistics to administrative and research problems from applied science, business, and government. The journal seeks to promote the proper application of statistical methods and to provide an international forum of exchange among statisticians and users of statistical techniques in a wide range of disciplines. In addition to publishing the papers presented at the annual Conference on Applied Statistics in Ireland, the journal presents original articles, reviews, case studies, and book reviews. The society also publishes three other journals: *Royal Statistical Society. Journal. Series A: Statistics in Society; Royal Statistical Society. Journal. Series B: Statistical Methodology; and Royal Statistical Society. Journal. Series C: Applied Statistics* (all reviewed in this section).

6312. ***Stochastic Models.*** Formerly (until 2000): *Communications in Statistics. Stochastic Models.* [ISSN: 1532-6349] 1985. q. USD 1310. Ed(s): Peter Taylor. Marcel Dekker Inc., 270 Madison Ave, New York, NY 10016-0602; http://www.dekker.com. Illus., index, adv. Refereed. Circ: 600. Vol. ends: Nov. Microform: RPI. Online: EBSCO Publishing; OCLC Online Computer Library Center, Inc.; RoweCom Information Quest. Reprint: SWZ. *Indexed:* CCMJ, EngInd, MathSciNet, ST&MA. *Aud.:* Ac, Sa.

This journal offers an interdisciplinary approach to the application of probability theory, with articles presenting methodologies ranging from the analytic and algorithmic to the experimental. Articles describe the practical applications of stochastic models to phenomena in the natural sciences, technology, and operations research. Each issue contains 8–10 articles of 10–30 pages each. One of three *Communications in Statistics* journals, *Stochastic Models* is also an affiliated publication of the Institute for Operations Research and the Management Sciences. Suitable for specialized and comprehensive collections.

6313. ***Teaching Statistics: an international journal for teachers of pupils aged up to 19.*** [ISSN: 0141-982X] 1979. 3x/yr. GBP 37 print & online eds. Ed(s): G W Goodall. Blackwell Publishing Ltd., 9600 Garsington Rd, PO Box 805, Oxford, OX4 2DQ, United Kingdom; customerservices@oxon.blackwellpublishing.com; http://www.blackwellpublishing.com/. Illus., index, adv. Refereed. Circ: 1050 Paid. Vol. ends: Sep. Online: EBSCO Publishing; ingenta.com; OCLC Online Computer Library Center, Inc.; RoweCom Information Quest; Swets Blackwell. *Indexed:* BrEdI, CIJE. *Bk. rev.:* 1-2, 500-600 words. *Aud.:* Ac.

Teaching Statistics intends to inform, entertain, and encourage teachers of statistics and those who employ statistics in their teaching of other disciplines at all levels, from elementary grades through college. Articles stress classroom teaching and the proper use of statistics and statistical concepts in teaching. Each issue contains nine or ten articles in some or all of the following categories: "Classroom Notes," "Computing Corner," "Curriculum Matters," "Data Bank," "Practical Activities," "Project Parade," "Net Benefits," "Historical Perspective," "Research Report," "Standard Errors," "Apparatus Reviews," "Book Reviews," and "News & Notes." Although most articles are by British or Commonwealth authors, the topics are of interest to teachers elsewhere.

6314. ***Technometrics: a journal of statistics for the physical, chemical and engineering sciences.*** [ISSN: 0040-1706] 1959. q. USD 60. Ed(s): Karen Kafadar. American Statistical Association, 1429 Duke St, Alexandria, VA 22314-3415; http://www.amstat.org/. Illus., index, adv. Refereed. Circ: 5200. Vol. ends: Nov. Microform: PQC. Online: EBSCO Publishing; Ingenta Select; Northern Light Technology, Inc. Reprint: PQC. *Indexed:* AS&TI, BiolAb, C&ISA, EngInd, GeoRef, MathSciNet, PsycholAb, SCI, SSCI, ST&MA. *Bk. rev.:* 30-40, 300-1,600 words. *Aud.:* Ac, Sa.

The purpose of this joint publication of the American Society for Quality Control and the American Statistical Association is to foster the use and development of statistical methods in the sciences. Articles accepted for publication describe new statistical techniques or new applications of established techniques, provide detailed explanations of specific statistical methods, or discuss the problems of applying statistical methods to problems in the sciences. Each issue contains six or seven articles and over 30 book reviews. Occasionally, a paper presented at a conference is published, along with the discussion and author's reply from that meeting.

6315. ***Theory of Probability and Its Applications.*** [ISSN: 0040-585X] 1956. q. USD 618 (Individual members, USD 100). Ed(s): Yu V Proklorov, Natasha Brunswick. Society for Industrial and Applied Mathematics, 3600 University City Science Center, Philadelphia, PA 19104-2688; siam@siam.org; http://www.epubs.siam.org. Illus., adv. Refereed. Circ: 1172. Vol. ends: Dec. *Indexed:* ApMecR, CompR, SCI, ST&MA. *Aud.:* Ac, Sa.

Theory of Probability and Its Applications is a translation of the Russian journal *Teoriya Veroyatnostei i ee Primeneniya,* edited by Yu. V. Prokhorov. Each English-language issue is published approximately one year after the original Russian-language issue. The journal accepts papers on all aspects of theory and applications of probability, statistics, and stochastic processes. Issues typically contain eight articles and eight to ten shorter "Communications." Articles are highly mathematical, with brief introductions and very little discussion. Because these contributions are not available elsewhere in translation, this is a valuable source. Recommended for highly specialized and research collections.

Electronic Journals

6316. ***Electronic Communications in Probability.*** [ISSN: 1083-589X] 1996. a. Ed(s): W S Kendall. Institute of Mathematical Statistics, 9650 Rockville Pike, Ste L2310, Bethesda, MD 20814-3998; ejpecp@math.washington.edu; http://math.washington.edu/~ejpecp/. *Indexed:* CCMJ, MathSciNet. *Aud.:* Ac, Sa.

Electronic Communications in Probability accepts short submissions on all aspects of probability. Longer submissions are posted on the companion *Electronic Journal of Probability.* Subscriptions are not necessary; subscribers receive tables of contents only by e-mail. All text is available only at the web site. A new volume is begun each January, and entries are posted as they are accepted throughout the year. Volumes contain from 5 to 14 entries. Users choose the viewing format for each entry, usually from among pdf, PostScript, and DVI formats.

6317. ***Electronic Journal of Probability.*** 1996. a. Free. Ed(s): Richard Bass. Institute of Mathematical Statistics, 9650 Rockville Pike, Ste L2310, Bethesda, MD 20814-3998; ejpecp@math.washington.edu; http://www.math.washington.edu/~ejpecp/. Illus., index. Refereed. Vol. ends: Dec. *Indexed:* CCMJ, MathSciNet. *Aud.:* Ac, Sa.

The *Electronic Journal of Probability* accepts submissions on all aspects of probability. Longer submissions are posted on the *Journal* and brief entries are posted on the companion publication *Electronic Communications in Probability.* Subscriptions are not necessary; subscribers receive tables of contents only by e-mail. All text is available only at the web site. A new volume is begun each January, and papers are posted as they are accepted throughout the year. Volumes of the *Journal* contain from 8 to 19 papers. Users choose the viewing format for each article, usually from among pdf, PostScript, and DVI formats.

6318. ***InterStat.*** 1995. irreg. Free. InterStat, rgkrut@hdvt.edu; http://interstat.stat.vt.edu/interstat. Refereed. *Aud.:* Ac, Sa.

InterStat accepts submissions on all aspects of statistics, including research articles, discussions of new methodologies and techniques, teaching methods, and philosophical articles. Authors submit papers to the editor most closely associated with the content of the article from a board of 55 with a wide range of interests and expertise. There is no uniform style imposed: The editor is the sole judge of readability and hence acceptability for each paper. Individual authors retain copyright for their works. Articles are posted in pdf and PostScript formats as they are accepted. Viewers may locate articles by month and year or by means of a keyword, title, or author search. From 4 to 16 articles are published each year.

6319. ***Journal of Statistical Software.*** 1996. irreg. Ed(s): Jan de Leeuw. University of California at Los Angeles, Department of Statistics, 405 Hilgard Ave, Box 951361, Los Angeles, CA 90095-1361; deleeuw@stat.ucla.edu; http://www.stat.ucla.edu/journals/jss/. Refereed. *Aud.:* Ac, Sa.

The *Journal of Statistical Software* publishes a wide range of submissions concerning software in the field of statistics, including descriptions of software, manuals and users guides, software code, data sets, and reviews or comparisons of software. The submissions are not limited in length and may include brief articles or manuals of 1,000 pages or more. Each submission constitutes an issue within the year's volume; the number of issues per year is not restricted and varies from four to nine. Authors retain the copyright, but downloading and printing by users is expected. A note of warning: Although most issues are divided into several files, there is no indication of the size of each file and some files are very large.

6320. ***Journal of Statistics Education.*** [ISSN: 1069-1898] 1993. 3x/yr. Ed(s): Thomas H Short. American Statistical Association, 1429 Duke St, Alexandria, VA 22314-3415; http://www.amstat.org/publications/jse/. Refereed. *Aud.:* Ems, Hs, Ac.

The *Journal of Statistics Education* (*JSE*) is a refereed electronic journal on the teaching of statistics at all levels, from elementary to postgraduate and workplace education. Typical issues contain approximately five articles, a "Teaching Bits" section, and perhaps a "Datasets and Stories" section. Topics for articles include teaching techniques, comparisons of methods, statistical literacy, literature reviews, and sample projects or assignments. The associated JSE Information Service includes information for teachers and archives of EDSTAT-L, a statistics education discussion list.

■ TEENAGERS

See also Children; Comic Books; Men; and Women sections.

Philip C. Howze, Social Sciences Librarian, Library Affairs, Morris Library 6632, Southern Illinois University Carbondale, Carbondale, IL 62901-6632; phowze@lib.siu.edu; FAX: 618-453-3440

Introduction

Teenagers will visit their local libraries more often when the word gets out that some of their favorite magazines are available! That said, magazines for young people can be quite a mixed bag because they seek to appeal to numerous niches within the 13- to 19-year-old cohort. Teens may be attracted to a particular magazine for any number of reasons, ranging from comics to advice columns to horoscopes that appear on a monthly basis. And of course, there are the pictures of teen celebrities! The bottom line, however, is that publishers of magazines for teenagers know that, as a group, they have a nice chunk of purchasing power, and that attracts vendors to buy ad space. According to Jody Foote (*MFL,* 10th ed., p. 1353), most magazines for teenagers can be divided into four broad categories: (1) club-oriented magazines (sponsored by clubs and organizations whose members are teenagers); (2) literary magazines (dedicated to publishing works by or about teenagers); (3) fashion/beauty magazines (beauty tips, advice on clothing, accessories, relationship columns, horoscopes, etc.—the predominant category of teen magazines); and (4) fan magazines (glossy pinups, interviews with teen celebrities). New to the teen scene is a growing number of electronic journals, most fitting into the above broad categories.

When selecting magazines for teenagers, a balanced approach is advised. After the teen reader flips though the glossy pages of his or her magazine of choice (usually fashion/beauty or fan magazines), it is not uncommon to discover that the periodical has not held his or her interest for very long. While this section does not include sports, hobby, or special-interest magazines, it is still advised to subscribe to a varied group of teen publications.

Basic Periodicals

Hs: *Seventeen, Teen, Teen People.*

Basic Abstracts and Indexes

Access, Magazine Index Plus/ASAP, Readers' Guide to Periodical Literature.

6321. ***All About You.*** [ISSN: 1090-3712] 1984. q. USD 2.95 newsstand/ cover per issue. Ed(s): Jane Fort. Primedia Consumer Media & Magazine Group, 200 Madison Ave, New York, NY 10016; http://www.primedia.com. Illus., adv. Sample. Circ: 325000 Paid. Online: Gale Group. *Aud.:* Ems, Hs.

This magazine is geared to young people in their early teens. There are regular departments that include movie reviews and fashion and beauty tips. Additional features found in just about all teen magazines are included in every issue, such as fitness, relationships, and horoscopes.

6322. ***Campus Life.*** [ISSN: 0008-2538] 1942. 9x/yr. USD 19.95. Ed(s): Chris Lutes. Christianity Today International, 465 Gundersen Dr, Carol Stream, IL 60188. Illus., adv. Sample. Circ: 100000 Paid. Microform: PQC. Online: EBSCO Publishing; Gale Group. Reprint: PQC. *Indexed:* ChrPI. *Aud.:* Hs.

This popular teen magazine is published by Christianity Today. There are regular departments including feature articles, humor, and advice. Feature articles are, at least, not offensive, and at best, vehicles for learning, growth, and self-awareness. Sample topics include sex, relationships, faith and values, and true-life stories. Lots of interesting reading and well laid out with plenty of photos. Recommended for public libraries.

6323. ***Careers & Colleges.*** Formerly: *Careers.* [ISSN: 1065-9935] 1981. q. USD 15 per academic year; USD 3.95 newsstand/cover per issue domestic. Ed(s): Don Rauf. Chalkboard Communications, L L C, 107 Maple Pl, Keyport, NJ 07735; ccmagazine@aol.com; http://www.careersandcolleges.com. Illus., adv. Sample. Circ: 35000 Paid. *Aud.:* Hs.

This colorful magazine is quite different from what one usually expects from a typical teen publication. Its contents are devoted to making the transition from high school to college life. In this self-billed "ultimate survival guide to life after high school," the reader will find such topics as campus life, making the grade, surviving the everyday stuff, fiscal fitness, and life after high school SATs. A fun-to-read magazine filled with practical advice and interesting web sites.

6324. ***Cicada (Peru).*** [ISSN: 1097-4008] 1998. bi-m. USD 35.97; USD 7.95 newsstand/cover per issue. Ed(s): Marianne Carus. Cricket Magazine Group, 315 Fifth St, PO Box 300, Peru, IL 61354; http://www.cricketmag.com. Illus. Circ: 14000 Paid. *Aud.:* Ems, Hs.

Cicada is a literary magazine for teenagers and young adults. There are too few literary magazines devoted to young people, and it is good to see that this one is generous in the number of writings published. Fiction and poetry are the venues in which authors treat personal or philosophical concerns. Sample titles of short works include "The Way Back," "Sonnet: Ode to a Bitter Tomato," and "When I Didn't Have Eyebrows." The writing, given the intended age group, is very good. Young writers with a flair for poetry or prose are encouraged to read the guidelines for submission of work. Highly recommended for public libraries.

6325. ***The Foxfire Magazine.*** Formerly (until 1992): *Foxfire.* [ISSN: 1084-5321] 1967. s-a. USD 12.95 domestic; USD 24.95 foreign. Ed(s): Angie Cheek. Foxfire Fund, Inc., M 2837, Hwy 441 South, PO Box 541, Mountain City, GA 30562; foxfire@foxfire.org. Illus., adv. Sample. Circ: 12000. Microform: PQC. Reprint: PQC. *Indexed:* ASIP, MLA-IB, RILM. *Aud.:* Ems, Hs.

This is a literary magazine dedicated to the preservation of Appalachian folklore. Written and published by Rabun County (Georgia) High School students, this magazine combines storytelling, oral histories, reminiscences, artifacts, and photographs to capture the essence of Appalachia. It has regular departments including news, history, pictures, articles, and discussion. The writing is just fabulous, in a folksy way. That this quality of folklore is put together by teenagers makes it all the more appealing. Highly recommended for public libraries and college libraries.

6326. ***Girl.*** [ISSN: 1530-9118] 1998. q. USD 11.95 domestic; USD 27 foreign; USD 2.95 newsstand/cover per issue domestic. Ed(s): Cara Kagan. Lewit & LeWinter, Inc., 200 Central Park S., Apt. 26B, New York, NY 10019-1448. Illus. *Aud.:* Ems, Hs.

This magazine is mostly devoted to fashion for teenage girls. It is different from many other teen magazines in that it does not contain wall-to-wall layouts of Twiggy-esque models; in fact, the editors use models of various sizes to emphasize the message that "beauty is in being," regardless of one's size or shape. Readers are encouraged to provide feedback on the quality of the magazine as well as on what to include in future issues. Look for the regular departments (fashion, makeup, entertainment, etc.) in this interesting publication.

6327. ***High School Writer (senior high edition).*** Former titles: *High School Writer of the Midwest;* (until 1988): *High School Writer of Minnesota.* [ISSN: 1048-3373] 1985. m. Sep.-May. USD 59.95 for 25 copies. Ed(s): Barbara Eiesland. Writer Publications, PO Box 718, Grand Rapids, MN 55744. Illus. Sample. Circ: 38000 Paid. *Aud.:* Hs.

This magazine is for high school students in language arts classes. Schools subscribing to the magazine may have their students submit works of fiction, nonfiction, and poetry for publication, and prizes are awarded for excellent writing. Highly recommended for writing classes at the senior high school level to give young authors a venue to showcase their work. There is also a separate edition for junior high school students.

6328. ***Jump: for girls who dare to be real.*** [ISSN: 1092-6984] 1997. 8x/yr. USD 15.90 United States; CND 26.72 Canada; USD 27.47 newsstand/cover per issue elsewhere. Gruner + Jahr U.S.A. Publishing, 375 Lexington Ave, New York, NY 10017-5514. Illus., adv. Sample. Circ: 400000. *Aud.:* Ems, Hs.

This magazine appears to be devoted primarily to matters related to health and fitness for teenage girls. This is another teen publication that is sensitive to the message it sends by the models it includes, and it chooses among people of various shapes and sizes. Articles deal with health topics more than glitz or celebrity interviews. Recommended for public libraries.

New Moon. See Children section.

6329. ***Quill & Scroll.*** [ISSN: 0033-6505] 1926. 4x/yr. USD 13. Ed(s): Richard P Johns. Quill and Scroll Society, School of Journalism and Mass Communication, Univ of Iowa, Iowa City, IA 52242; http://www.uiowa.edu/~quill-sc/. Illus., adv. Sample. Circ: 12800 Paid. Microform: PQC. Reprint: PQC. *Indexed:* CIJE. *Bk. rev.:* 7-11, 100-300 words. *Aud.:* Ems, Hs.

This magazine is the publication of the Quill & Scroll Society, the International Honorary Society for High School Journalists, housed at the University of Iowa's prestigious School of Journalism. High school journalists, as well as instructors and advisors, contribute articles related to high school productions such as newspapers, yearbooks, reporting, and constitutional issues. Also included are book reviews and announcements of workshops and institutes. Very informative, with very good writing on useful issues related to journalism at the high school level. Recommended for school, public, and academic libraries.

6330. ***Seventeen.*** [ISSN: 0037-301X] 1944. m. USD 12 domestic; USD 22 Canada; USD 24 elsewhere. Ed(s): Atoosa Rubenstein. Hearst Magazines, 1440 Broadway, 13th Fl, New York, NY 10018; HearstMagazines@hearst.com; http://www.hearstcorp.com/magazines/. Illus., adv. Sample. Circ: 2350000 Paid. CD-ROM: ProQuest Information & Learning. Microform: NBI; PQC. Online: Gale Group. Reprint: PQC. *Indexed:* CBCARef, CPerI, MRD, MagInd, RGPR. *Aud.:* Hs.

This is clearly the most popular teen magazine published today. While it enjoys a wide readership, it primarily appeals to teenage females. This publication has led the field of teen magazines for years by not straying from the classic formula for success that it invented. The formula includes regular features and departments that girls look forward to: celebrity interviews, fashion exposes, and that "clean, girl-next-door" look that makes models covet a prestigious appearance on the cover. Regular departments include "My Seventeen," beauty, fashion, love and sex, "Reality Check," school and college, and horoscopes. Highly recommended for both public and academic libraries.

6331. ***Streams.*** 1986. a. USD 10. Ed(s): Richard Spiegel. Ten Penny Players, Inc., 393 St Pauls Ave, Staten Island, NY 10304-2127; http://tenpennyplayers.org. Circ: 6000. *Aud.:* Hs.

This publication is a multi-volume anthology of "expressive writings" by teenagers in New York City. Poetry, fiction, and nonfiction are accepted from the "typical, disabled and gifted" attending high school classes in such "diverse locations as hospitals, jails, shelters and hotels." Published since 1987, this magazine has showcased the work of many talented but disadvantaged young people. The essence of their creativity is rooted in the ability to make their circumstances speak and achieve texture. Excellent for creative writing classes. Highly recommended for school and public libraries.

6332. ***Teen.*** [ISSN: 0040-2001] 1957. m. USD 9.97 domestic; USD 22.97 Canada; USD 24.97 elsewhere. Ed(s): Tommi Tilden. Primedia Consumer Media & Magazine Group, 200 Madison Ave, New York, NY 10016; information@primedia.com; http://www.primedia.com. Illus., adv. Sample. Circ: 2000000 Paid. Microform: PQC. Online: The Dialog Corporation; Gale Group. *Indexed:* ASIP, MagInd, RGPR. *Aud.:* Ems, Hs.

This magazine tries to be reader-centered but ends up following the teen magazine formula anyway. Its focus is on teenage girls. Regular departments include "All about You," "411," "Star Stuff," and "Stylin'." There are polls and quizzes as well as poetry and real-life stories. It is fun, colorful, everything a teenage girl would want from this kind of publication.

6333. ***Teen Beat.*** [ISSN: 1056-0513] 1976. m. USD 29.95; USD 3.99 newsstand/cover per issue. Ed(s): Karen Williams. Primedia Youth Entertainment Group, 470 Park Ave S, 8th Fl, New York, NY 10016; http://www.primediainc.com. Illus., adv. Circ: 150000. *Aud.:* Ems.

This monthly entertainment magazine is published primarily for girls in their early teen years. It is glossy and colorful. There are pinups, centerfolds, and posters of musicians and stars who appeal to this group. *Teen Beat* is also a formula magazine, with regular columns on fashion and beauty, Q&A, celebrity interviews, celebrity advice, horoscope, personal facts about the stars, and much more. It is professionally laid out and will definitely appeal to a young readership.

6334. ***Teen People.*** [ISSN: 1096-2832] 1998. 10x/yr. USD 10 domestic; USD 16.95 Canada; USD 2.99 newsstand/cover per issue. Ed(s): Susan Pocharski, Christina Ferrari. Time, Inc, Time & Life Bldg, Rockefeller Center, 1271 Ave of the Americas, New York, NY 10020-1393; editor@peoplemag.com; http://www.time.com/time/. Illus., adv. Sample. Circ: 1450000. Online: EBSCO Publishing; Gale Group; OCLC Online Computer Library Center, Inc.; ProQuest Information & Learning; H.W. Wilson. *Indexed:* ICM. *Aud.:* Ems, Hs.

From the publisher of *People* and geared to the teen market, this first-rate publication includes feature articles about the lives of stars and "regular" people as well, all dealing with real-life issues. "Up close and personal" in style, this is a well-designed magazine with regular departments according to the formula: celebrity profiles, style (makeup, clothing), games, gossip, personal advice, chat, and contests. It will definitely be popular among teen readers. Recommended for public libraries.

6335. ***Teen Star Zine: the casting call newsletter for young performers.*** 1993. m. USD 10. Gina Young, Ed. & Pub., 5863 Chevy Chase Pkwy, Box 22, Washington, DC 20015; ggy200@is7.nyu.edu. Illus., adv. Circ: 200. *Aud.:* Ems, Hs.

For the young person who wants to know where auditions are being held in just about any of the performing arts, this publication provides that information—particularly for those living in the environs of Washington, D.C., Maryland, and Virginia. More a newsletter than a magazine, short articles are published on how to get established in show business and on how to put together a portfolio. It is a kind of trade paper for teens who dance, act, sing, or model. Available to subscribers only.

6336. ***Teen Times.*** [ISSN: 0735-6986] 1945. q. Non-members, USD 7. Ed(s): Beth Carpenter. Family Career and Community Leaders of America, 1910 Association Dr, Reston, VA 20191; http://www.fhahero.org. Illus., adv. Sample. Circ: 230000. *Aud.:* Ems, Hs.

This magazine is the voice of Family, Career, and Community Leaders of America (FCCLA) a "national career and technical student organization for young men and women in family and consumer sciences education in public and private school through grade 12." FCCLA replaces what was formerly known as Future Homemakers of America, and it attempts to address those traits that will make young people leaders in whatever they try to accomplish. There are FCCLA chapters around the country, and this magazine includes a schedule of national events, fund-raising ideas, and articles dealing with important national issues. Available to subscribers only.

6337. ***Xpress.*** Former titles: *Y A B A Framework (Young American Bowling Alliance);* (until 1990): *Y A B A World; Junior Bowler.* 1964. 6x/yr. USD 10. Ed(s): Tracy Kucavich. Young American Bowling Alliance, 5301 S 76th St, Greendale, WI 53129; http://wingnut.foxnet.net/users/bowling/yaba.html. Adv. Circ: 25000 Controlled. *Indexed:* SportS. *Aud.:* Ems, Hs.

This magazine is published by the Young American Bowling Alliance and is oriented to its members who want to learn more about the sport. Laid out like a sports magazine for teens, it includes professional rankings and profiles of professional and young champion bowlers, awards and prizes won by young bowlers, information on scholarships, and a listing of bowling-related events taking place across the country. Information on changes to bowling rules and regulations is also included.

6338. ***Y M.*** Former titles (until 1986): *Young Miss Magazine;* (until 1985): *Young Miss;* (until 1966): *Calling All Girls.* [ISSN: 0888-5842] 1953. m. USD 12; USD 29.97 Canada; USD 3.50 newsstand/cover per issue. Gruner + Jahr U.S.A. Publishing, 375 Lexington Ave, New York, NY 10017-5514; http://www.gjusa.com. Illus., adv. Sample. Circ: 2221937 Paid. Microform: PQC. *Indexed:* ICM. *Aud.:* Hs.

This magazine follows the classic formula, if there is one, for appealing to early teenage girls. Regular short features are included on such topics as beauty, boys, stars, and style. In addition, there are the usual fun departments, including "Cool Thought," a horoscope, a diary, a quiz, and "Say Anything." The glossy, entertaining format, coupled with the presentation of a variety of topics and showcased personalities, makes this an interesting read.

6339. ***Y O! Youth Outlook.*** [ISSN: 1526-243X] 1991. m. Individuals, USD 15; Students, USD 12. Ed(s): Kevin Weston. Pacific News Service, 275 9th St, San Francisco, CA 94103; http://www.pacificnews.org. Illus., adv. Circ: 25000. *Aud.:* Hs.

This newspaper is published both in print and web formats and is written to appeal to the tastes of young people on the West Coast, the San Francisco Bay Area in particular. While it is not clear that it provides what the intended audience wants, there are short stories, music, videos, cartoons, poetry, and pieces on social activism. In addition, the web site, which is updated three times a week, provides archives, "e-graffiti," and chat. Tributes to fallen classmates in high school shootings, as well as gangs in schools, are commonly reported news events. This is a forum for young people to reflect and express themselves—whether or not someone is listening.

6340. ***Your Prom.*** [ISSN: 1067-005X] 1990. a. USD 3.99 newsstand/cover per issue. Primedia Consumer Media & Magazine Group, 200 Madison Ave, New York, NY 10016; information@primedia.com; http://www.primedia.com. Illus., adv. Sample. Circ: 800000. *Aud.:* Hs.

This magazine is published annually for young people who are making plans to attend that most important event of a high school career, the prom. It is basically a nationwide advertisement fair for retail and rental stores and for prom dresses and everything to accessorize them. Filler articles are included to round out the thematic nature of the magazine on such topics as skin care, beauty, and after-prom parties. The premier magazine for prom goers.

Electronic Journals

6341. ***Cyberteens.*** 1996. m. Able Minds, 1750-1 30th St, Ste 170, Boulder, CO 80301; info@ableminds.com; http://www.cyberteens.com. Adv. *Aud.:* Hs.

This interactive e-zine is for young people who like their magazines on the web. Regular sections include fun and games, shop the net, cool links, creativity, news and views, and work and school. In addition to the well-written sections, there are surveys and interviews with celebrities. It could use more photographs. It is geared toward older teens and will appeal more to girls than boys.

6342. ***FreshAngles.*** irreg. Ed(s): Kristen Boswell. FreshAngles, http://www.freshangles.com/. *Aud.:* Hs.

This e-zine is published by the students of Bergen County (New Jersey) High School. It is as interesting and concentrated as the students whose hands it is in during a given period. Regular sections are "Realtime News," "TheZone Sports," "Diversionz," "Xpressions Gallery," "Teen Fashion," "My World," and "Guidance." Two other noteworthy features are a picture archive for homework or fun called "Ditto" and a search engine for teens called "Teenlinx."

6343. ***Just for Girls.*** 1996. m. Girl Scouts of the U.S.A., 420 Fifth Ave, New York, NY 10018-2798; misc@girlscouts.org; http://www.girlscouts.org. *Bk. rev.:* Number and length vary. *Aud.:* Hs.

This is the official magazine of the Girl Scouts of America. There are regular departments (articles, pictures, poems, stories, book reviews, etc.) as well as scouting news and announcements of meetings and other events. There are always a number of interesting pieces in this magazine, and it is recommended as a good read for any teenage girl.

6344. ***Spank! Youth Culture Online.*** 1995. m. Ed(s): Robin Thompson. Ububik New Media Research, #505, 300 Meredith Rd NE, Calgary, AB T2E 7A8, Canada; http://www.spankmag.com. *Indexed:* CBCARef. *Aud.:* Hs.

This magazine could be considered a textbook for Introduction to the Avant Garde 101. Its snappy, provocative articles combine with the regular departments to form a sweet and sour blend likely to appeal to quick-witted, intellectual youth. If longevity is a mark of success, then this magazine is just that, with seven years running (and any web site that has been up for seven years is a success). Regular departments include body and health, dating and relationships, fashion, sexuality, stress, and other teen stuff. Examples of article topics include cafeteria food, "how I learned to cuss," and prostitution at sixteen. Self-described as "youth culture defined by youth," this magazine is sometimes safe and teenagerish, at other times refreshingly daring. Recommended for public libraries.

■ TELEVISION, VIDEO, AND RADIO

See also Electronics; Films; and Media and AV sections.

Emily A. Hicks, Head of Bibliographic Management & Assistant Professor, Roesch Library, University of Dayton, 300 College Park, Dayton, OH 45469-1360; Emily.Hicks@notes.udayton.edu

Introduction

The world of television, video, and radio continues to expand as new technologies are introduced. It is difficult to pick up a magazine about the television industry without seeing the words digital cable, interactive TV, or on-demand TV. The radio industry is exploring digital radio signals, satellite radio, and Internet radio broadcasting. Digital video production is becoming more and more popular as equipment, software, and technologies become more affordable. Several publications have broadened their scope to accommodate readers' interests as the development and refinement of these technologies helps to blur the lines between these three industries.

The field of home entertainment has expanded far beyond the TV, VCR, and stereo system. Today's consumer seeks information about home theater systems, complete with high-performance sound, flat-screen TV, and HDTV. Home entertainment magazines are full of reviews covering an ever-increasing array of products. The DVD market continues to grow as well, and many established magazines have expanded to include this wildly popular video format. Still other magazines have been created solely for the DVD audience.

The Internet is an important tool for accessing and evaluating the resources reviewed here. Many of the print publications have companion web sites that can be explored before a subscription is placed. Although some sites can only be fully accessed by subscribers, evaluators should be able to determine the focus of a particular publication through its corresponding web site. Several of the sites also offer free electronic newsletters and electronic forums on a variety of topics. The world of television, video, and radio continues to evolve and thrive by incorporating new technologies into the old, thus guaranteeing the public's continued interest.

Basic Periodicals

Ems: *Popular Communications;* Ga: *Popular Communications, Satellite Orbit, Sound & Vision, Widescreen Review;* Ac: *Broadcasting & Cable, Current, Digital Video Magazine, InterMedia, Journal of Broadcasting and Electronic Media, Radio Ink, SMPTE Motion Imaging Journal* Sa: *Monitoring Times.*

Basic Abstracts and Indexes

Film Literature Index, UnCover.

Adbusters: journal of the mental environment. See Alternatives section.

Afterimage. See Photography section.

6345. ***Broadcasting & Cable.*** Former titles (until 1993): *Broadcasting (Washington);* (until 1957): *Broadcasting Telecasting;* (until 1948): *Broadcasting - The News Magazine of the Fifth Estate;* Incorporated (in 1961): *Television;* (in 1953): *Telecast;* (in 1933): *Broadcast Reporter; Broadcast Advertising.* [ISSN: 1068-6827] 1931. w. 51/yr. USD 179 combined subscription domestic print & online eds.; USD 239 combined subscription Canada print & online eds.; USD 350 combined subscription elsewhere print & online eds. Ed(s): Harry Jessell. Reed Business Information, 2 Rector St., # 26L, New York, NY 10006-1819; http://www.reedbusiness.com. Illus., adv. Sample. Circ: 36000 Controlled. Vol. ends: Dec. Microform: CIS; PQC. Online: The Dialog Corporation; EBSCO Publishing; Florida Center for Library Automation; Gale Group; LexisNexis; Northern Light Technology, Inc.; OCLC Online Computer Library Center, Inc.; ProQuest Information & Learning; H.W. Wilson. Reprint: PQC. *Indexed:* ABIn, BPI, BiogInd, IIPA, LRI, PAIS. *Aud.:* Ac, Sa.

This weekly industry publication covers a wide range of topics from broadcast and cable television to radio, satellite, and interactive multimedia. *Broadcasting & Cable* contains short, informative feature articles, programming information, Nielsen ratings, and the latest news, including FCC regulations and station sales. Regular columns titled "Fates & Fortunes" and "Facetime" report job changes, obituaries, and recent activities of industry people. Each issue also includes a classified section. Corporate libraries in the communications industry, academic libraries with communications or business departments, and public libraries with a well-developed business section will find this publication useful.

6346. ***C Q: the radio amateurs' journal.*** Incorporates: *C Q: V H F Ham Radio Above 50 MHZ.* [ISSN: 0007-893X] 1945. m. USD 15 domestic; USD 37 in Canada & Mexico; USD 38 elsewhere. Ed(s): Rich M Moseson. C Q Communications, Inc., 25 Newbridge Rd, Hicksville, NY 11801-2805. Illus., adv. Sample. Circ: 113309. Vol. ends: Dec. *Indexed:* IHTDI. *Aud.:* Ac, Sa.

CQ contains detailed how-to articles, product reviews, and feature articles on a broad range of topics, including "How the Internet Can Save Your Repeater" and "The Use of Pringles Containers to Enhance Network Security." A recent issue highlights the relationship between ham radio and the space program in the wake of the Columbia shuttle tragedy. *CQ* also includes the latest government regulation news and information on upcoming conventions, contests, and awards. This publication will appeal to all ham radio enthusiasts and is suitable for the libraries that serve them. The company recently began publishing *CQ VHF,* a quarterly for people interested in VHF ham radio above 50 MHz. This publication had been merged into *CQ: amateur radio,* but due to popular demand it has been brought back as a separate magazine.

6347. ***Camcorder & ComputerVideo.*** Former titles: *Camcorder;* (until 1989): *Camcorder Report;* (until 1988): *Super Television;* (until 1987): *Home Satellite TV.* [ISSN: 1091-0441] 1985. m. USD 23; USD 2.95 newsstand/cover per issue. Ed(s): Bob Wolenik, James L Miller. Miller Magazines, Inc, 4880 Market St, Ventura, CA 93003-2888. Adv. Circ: 115000. Online: Gale Group. *Aud.:* Hs, Ga, Sa.

This publication will appeal to all levels of video enthusiasts. *Camcorder & ComputerVideo* covers the latest trends in video photography and desktop video production through product reviews, expert advice, and how-to articles. Sample articles include "Re-Edit Your DVDs," "Ticks, Hums, Hiss and Pops," "C.S.I. Videos," and "Make Video, Not War." Recommended for public and school libraries.

6348. ***Current (Washington, 1980): The Public Telecommunications Newspaper.*** Former titles: *N A E B Letter; National Association of Educational Broadcasters Newsletter.* [ISSN: 0739-991X] 1980. bi-w. USD 60; USD 115 Canada; USD 135 elsewhere. Ed(s): Steve Behrens. Current Publishing Committee, 1612 K St, N W, Ste 704, Washington, DC 20006; current@ix.netcom.com; http://www.current.org. Illus., adv. Sample. Circ: 6100 Paid. Vol. ends: No. 23. *Indexed:* RGPR. *Aud.:* Ac, Sa.

Current is a biweekly newspaper about public broadcasting. It covers a wide range of topics, including history of public broadcasting, technological advances, and people in the field of public broadcasting. *Current Online* provides news briefs, employment opportunities, calendar of events, database of key historical documents of public broadcasting, and an archive of feature articles. Recommended for any library serving a population interested in the public broadcasting system.

6349. ***D V D Etc.*** [ISSN: 1543-6144] 2002. 10x/yr. USD 19.95 domestic; USD 35.95 Canada; USD 39.95 elsewhere. Avodah Publishing, LLC, terence@dvdetc.com. Adv. *Aud.:* Ga, Sa.

Fans of digital home video entertainment will find plenty to like about *DVD Etc.* With regular columns such as "DVDs MIA (Missing In Action)," which compiles the movies and TV shows that readers want to see released on DVD; "Etcetera," which reports the latest DVD news; and "Surf's Up," which highlights the magazine's web site pick of the month; the magazine has something for everyone. Sample features include "Restoration Techniques: Classic Film to DVD" and "Director's Cut: Joss Whedon, Director of Buffy the Vampire Slayer, Angel, and Firefly." Reviews of DVDs and many related products are included. The magazine, links to the online store, and DVD-related forums are also available online at www.dvdetc.com. Discussions on the "Home Theater Forum" are reprinted in a regular column called "The Monthly Post." Recommended for all public and school libraries.

6350. ***D V D Guide.*** 2000. q. USD 19.95; USD 5.95 newsstand/cover per issue. N V I Publishing Group, 10 Forest Ave., Paramus, NJ 07652-5214. Adv. *Aud.:* Hs, Ga.

DVD Guide is a comprehensive listing of recently released movies, special-interest programs, and music videos. The listings include domestic and foreign titles from major studios as well as independent filmmakers. Titles are grouped under headings such as "New Releases," "Coming Soon," and "Editorial Picks." The guide also features special listings such as "DVD Gifts for the Season," "Rock Concerts Live on DVD," and "AFI Top 100 Films on DVD." The *Complete DVD Guide CD-ROM* allows the user to search by title, actor, director, genre, and more. Users can also use the CD-ROM to build a database of the DVD titles they own. Recommended for all public and school libraries.

6351. ***Digital Video Magazine.*** Formerly (until Jun. 1994): *Desktop Video World.* [ISSN: 1075-251X] 1993. m. USD 29.97; USD 44.97 Canada; USD 42.97 Mexico. Ed(s): Dominic Milano. C M P Media LLC, 600 Harrison St, San Francisco, CA 94107. Illus., adv. Circ: 40000. Vol. ends: Dec. Online: Factiva; Florida Center for Library Automation; Gale Group. *Indexed:* MicrocompInd. *Aud.:* Ac, Sa.

Digital Video Magazine provides news, tutorials, case studies, and product reviews to digital industry professionals. Additional information and discussion forums can be found on its companion web site (http://www.dv.com). Sample articles include "Editors as Storytellers: How to Find the Story While Editing Your Footage" and "Training Spaces: The Making of a Pier 1 Training Video Series." Recommended for industry and academic libraries as well as public libraries serving interested groups.

6352. ***FMedia!: the FM radio newsletter.*** [ISSN: 0890-6718] 1987. m. USD 75. Ed(s): Bruce F Elving. F M Atlas Publishing, PO Box 336, Esko, MN 55733-0336; FmAtlas@aol.com; http://users.aol.com/fmatlas/. Illus. Sample. Circ: 300 Paid and controlled. Vol. ends: No. 11. *Aud.:* Ac, Sa.

This newsletter provides monthly updates to the *FM Atlas,* which records format, licensing, and operating changes in the FM radio industry. *FMedia!* also includes news about emerging technologies such as digital audio broadcasting and low power FM. This publication is similar to *M Street Journal* in content, but with a more independent feel. Suitable for public and academic libraries with an interest in FM radio broadcasting.

6353. ***Home Theater.*** Former titles: *CurtCo's Home Theater; CurtCo's Home Theater Technology.* [ISSN: 1096-3065] 1994. m. USD 12.97 domestic. Ed(s): Adrienne Maxwell, Maureen Jenson. Primedia Consumer Media & Magazine Group, 200 Madison Ave, New York, NY 10016; http://www.primedia.com. Adv. *Indexed:* FLI. *Aud.:* Ga.

Home Theater contains industry news, DVD and CD reviews, and extensive product reviews. Although primarily geared toward the high-end consumer home theater market, the publication does include some more moderately priced components. In addition to covering home theater equipment, *Home Theater* also provides advice on home theater environments from the best lighting techniques to the most effective noise reduction. This glossy publication is best suited for medium to large public libraries.

Independent Film & Video Monthly. See Films section.

6354. ***InterMedia.*** Formerly: *I B I Newsletter.* [ISSN: 0309-118X] 1973. bi-m. GBP 70. Ed(s): Annelise Berendt, Rex Winsbury. International Institute of Communications (IIC), Tavistock House., S., Tavistock St, London, WC2E 7PH, United Kingdom. Illus., adv. Sample. Circ: 1500. Vol. ends: No. 6. Microform: PQC. Online: ProQuest Information & Learning. Reprint: PQC. *Indexed:* ABIn, CommAb, FutSurv, IIFP, PAIS. *Aud.:* Ac, Sa.

InterMedia, published by the International Institute of Communications, covers emerging policy issues in the broadcasting and telecommunications industries and features contributions from professionals in a variety of fields, including law, academia, and journalism. Sample articles include "Wireless Local Area Networks and the European 3G Tragedy," "All Change: Environmental Journalism Meets Development," and "Broadband in South Korea: A Model for Broadband Success?" This journal's international scope and well-written content make it a good choice for academic libraries, especially those serving large numbers of communications students.

6355. ***Journal of Broadcasting and Electronic Media.*** Formerly (until 1985): *Journal of Broadcasting.* [ISSN: 0883-8151] 1956. q. USD 86.50 in US & Canada; USD 102 elsewhere. Ed(s): Thomas Lindlof. Broadcast Education Association, 1771 N St, N W, Washington, DC 20036; lindlof@uky.edu; http://www.beaweb.org. Refereed. Circ: 2200. Microform: WSH; PMC; PQC. Online: EBSCO Publishing; Florida Center for Library Automation; Gale Group; OCLC Online Computer Library Center, Inc.; ProQuest Information & Learning. Reprint: PQC; WSH. *Indexed:* AgeL, ArtHuCI, CIJE, CJA, CLI, CommAb, HumInd, IIFP, IJCS, ILP, LRI, PAIS, PsycholAb, RI-1, SFSA, SSCI, SSI, SWA. *Aud.:* Ac.

The *Journal of Broadcasting and Electronic Media* is a scholarly publication devoted to the study and advancement of the communication industry from a broad range of viewpoints, including historical, technological, cultural, and social. Sample articles include "Gatekeeping International News: An Attitudinal Profile of U.S. Television Journalists," "Interactivity in Television: Use and Impact of an Interactive Program Guide," and "Is Online Buying Out of Control?: Electronic Commerce and Consumer Self-Regulation." This publication is strongly recommended for academic libraries.

Journal of Popular Film and Television. See Films section.

6356. ***M Street Daily.*** 2002. d. M Street Corporation, 81 Main St, Ste 2, Littleton, NH 03561. *Aud.:* Ac, Sa.

M Street Publications purchased *Inside Radio* in August 2002 and merged it with their daily newsletter, *M Street Daily.* The new publication continues to deliver radio news, industry trends, and related research five days a week to subscribers via e-mail and fax. Each issue also includes Arbitrends and stock reports as well as employment opportunities. Recommended for libraries that serve industry professionals or a large population of communications students. A good alternative is *M Street Journal,* which provides much of the same information on a weekly basis.

6357. ***The M Street Journal: radio's journal of record.*** [ISSN: 1052-7109] 1984. bi-w. USD 139. Ed(s): Tom Taylor. M Street Corporation, 81 Main St, Ste 2, Littleton, NH 03561; streaming@insideradio.com; http://www.mstreet.net. Illus., adv. Sample. Vol. ends: Dec. *Aud.:* Ac, Sa.

M Street Journal is printed biweekly with weekly online updates and provides subscribers with a majority of the news released in its daily companion publication. Compilations of all call letter and format changes as well as changes in station owners and facilities from the daily edition are included in the weekly edition. FCC regulations and other industry news items are summarized as well. *M Street Journal* is recommended for most libraries, except for those where the timeliness of the daily edition would be more appropriate.

6358. ***Media, Culture & Society.*** [ISSN: 0163-4437] 1979. bi-m. GBP 495 print & online eds. in Europe, Middle East, Africa & Australasia. Ed(s): John R Corner, Colin Sparks. Sage Publications Ltd., 6 Bonhill St, London, EC2A 4PU, United Kingdom; info@sagepub.co.uk; http://www.sagepub.co.uk/. Illus., adv. Refereed. Online: EBSCO Publishing; Gale Group; ingenta.com; OCLC Online Computer Library Center, Inc.; ProQuest Information & Learning; RoweCom Information Quest; Sage Publications, Inc.; Swets Blackwell. Reprint: PSC. *Indexed:* ASSIA, AnthLit, ArtHuCI, CommAb, DAAI, FLI, HRA, IBSS, IBZ, IIFP, IPSA, PRA, PSA, SSCI, SSI, SociolAb. *Bk. rev.:* Number and length vary. *Aud.:* Ac.

This interdisciplinary, scholarly journal provides an international forum for research and discussion exploring how media and related technologies affect our lives. Sample articles include "Digital Interactivity in Public Memory Institutions: The Uses of New Technologies in Holocaust Museums," "The MIT Media Lab: Techno Dream Factory or Alienation as a Way of Life?," "Virtual Togetherness: An Everyday-Life Experience," and "Doing IT for the Kids: Re-examining Children, Computers, and the 'Information Society.'" Commentaries and book reviews are also included. Strongly recommended for academic libraries.

6359. ***Monitoring Times.*** [ISSN: 0889-5341] 1982. m. USD 24.95; USD 4.25 newsstand/cover per issue. Ed(s): Rachel Baughn. Grove Enterprises, Inc., PO Box 98, 7540 Hwy 64 W, Brasstown, NC 28902-0098; mteditor@grove-ent.com; http://www.grove-ent.com/hmpgmt.html. Illus., adv. Sample. Circ: 28000 Paid. Vol. ends: Dec. *Indexed:* ASIP. *Aud.:* Hs, Ga, Ac, Sa.

Monitoring Times provides extensive listings of radio and scanner communications, including shortwave, satellite, and ham radio. It includes international broadcasting program schedules, information about pirate and clandestine stations, expert listening tips, industry news, interviews, new-product tests, and frequency listings for specialty groups such as the military and air traffic control. Sample articles include "Radio in Germany: From Spark-Gap to Digital Shortwave" and "Digital Radio Mondiale—HiFi for AM Radio." Suitable for most public and academic libraries.

6360. ***Multichannel News.*** Incorporates (2000-2001): *Broadband Week.* [ISSN: 0276-8593] 1980. 51x/yr. USD 139 domestic; USD 209 foreign. Ed(s): Kent Gibbons. Reed Business Information, 2 Rector St., # 26L, New York, NY 10006-1819; http://www.reedbusiness.com. Adv. Circ: 22000. Microform: FCM. Online: EBSCO Publishing; Florida Center for Library Automation; Gale Group; LexisNexis; Northern Light Technology, Inc.; OCLC Online Computer Library Center, Inc.; ProQuest Information & Learning. *Indexed:* B&I. *Aud.:* Ac, Sa.

This weekly publication for the cable TV and telecommuncations industries covers news, programming, advertising, marketing, technology, and government regulations. Technological changes in the telecom and cable broadcast markets are covered in a special section called "Broadband Week." *Multichannel News Online* (www.multichannel.com) provides daily news updates, early previews of the print edition, archives, and links to related industry sites to subscribers. Strongly recommended for industry libraries and academic libraries that have an emphasis on broadcasting and the television industry.

6361. ***The Perfect Vision: high performance home theater.*** [ISSN: 0895-4143] 1986. bi-m. USD 19.95 domestic; USD 27.95 Canada; USD 50 elsewhere. Ed(s): Robert Harley. Absolute Multimedia Inc., 8121 Bee Caves Rd., Ste. 100, Austin, TX 78746-4938; info@avguide.com. Illus., adv. Circ: 20000. Vol. ends: Nov/Dec. *Aud.:* Ac, Sa.

The Perfect Vision is a consumer publication with an emphasis on technical information. The in-depth product reviews and feature articles will appeal to video and audio lovers. Regular columns such as "Coming Attractions," "Real-World Home Theater," and "HDTV Insider" showcase the latest trends in home entertainment. Reviews of newly released DVDs are also included. *The Perfect Vision* is suitable for medium to large public libraries.

6362. ***Popular Communications.*** Incorporates: *Scan Magazine.* [ISSN: 0733-3315] 1982. m. USD 28.95 domestic; USD 35.95 in Canada & Mexico; USD 45.95 elsewhere. Ed(s): Harold Ort. C Q Communications, Inc., 25 Newbridge Rd, Hicksville, NY 11801-2805; cq@cq-amateur-radio.com; http://www.cq-amateur-radio.com. Illus., adv. Sample. Circ: 92238. Vol. ends: No. 12. Reprint: PSC. *Indexed:* ABS&EES, IHTDI. *Bk. rev.:* 4, 300-450 words. *Aud.:* Hs, Ga, Sa.

Popular Communications provides information about radio and scanner communications through feature articles and regular columns such as "Homeland Security," "The Wireless Connection," "Broadcast Technology," "Ham Discoveries," "World Band Tuning Tips," "Plane Sense," and "Loose Connection." The publication provides a good overview of the receiving end of the broadcasting world and includes listings for world, national, regional, local, and pirate radio stations. Suitable for high school and public libraries.

Public Broadcasting Report. See Media and AV section.

6363. ***QST: devoted entirely to amateur radio.*** [ISSN: 0033-4812] 1915. m. Membership. Ed(s): Mark Wilson. American Radio Relay League, Inc., 225 Main St, Newington, CT 06111; rdstraw.arrl.org; http://www.arrl.org. Illus., adv. Sample. Circ: 170000. Vol. ends: Dec. Microform: PQC. Online: Northern Light Technology, Inc.; OCLC Online Computer Library Center, Inc.; ProQuest Information & Learning; H.W. Wilson. Reprint: PQC. *Indexed:* AS&TI, ConsI. *Bk. rev.:* 1, 825 words. *Aud.:* Ac, Sa.

Published by the American Radio Relay League, this high-quality monthly magazine contains news and features for the amateur radio operator. *QST* includes product reviews, how-to articles, and practical advice. Each issue features a variety of regular columns, such as "Amateur Radio World," which reports the latest information about international radio legislation. Other topics include space communications, digital advances, and historical information. Subscribers have access to the online archives and other amateur radio resources. Strongly recommended for school libraries that support related curricula as well as public libraries serving amateur radio enthusiasts.

6364. ***Radio Ink.*** [ISSN: 1064-587X] 1986. fortn. USD 167 domestic; USD 225 foreign. Ed(s): Eric Rhoads, Ed Ryan. Streamline Publishing, Inc., 224 Datura St, Ste 701, West Palm Beach, FL 33401; radiolink@aol.com. Illus., adv. Sample. Circ: 9000. Vol. ends: No. 26. *Aud.:* Ac, Sa.

Radio Ink is a comprehensive industry publication for radio broadcasting professionals. Each issue, along with the related electronic newsletter, covers a broad range of topics from sales and marketing to programming. Feature articles highlight industry trends and radio broadcasting professionals. Recommended for industry libraries, academic libraries with communications departments, and medium to large public libraries.

6365. ***S M P T E Motion Imaging Journal.*** Formerly: *S M P T E Journal.* 1916. m. USD 130. Society of Motion Picture and Television Engineers, 595 W Hartsdale Ave, White Plains, NY 10607-1824. Illus., adv. Circ: 10000. Microform: PMC; PQC. Reprint: PQC. *Indexed:* AS&TI, ApMecR, C&ISA, ChemAb, EngInd, ExcerpMed, FLI, PhotoAb, SCI. *Aud.:* Ac, Sa.

The Society of Motion Picture and Television Engineers publishes this journal for its members. The publication's name was changed to *SMPTE Motion Imaging Journal* in October 2002. This scholarly journal contains research and papers on the latest technical and scientific advances in motion imaging, including archiving, digital technology, and image quality. *SMPTE Motion Imaging Journal* also contains society and industry news. Industry professionals as well as communications students will find this publication useful. Recommended for academic libraries with communications departments and industry libraries.

6366. ***Satellite Direct: the magazine of direct-broadcast satellite communications.*** Formerly (until 1987): *Satellite Dealer.* [ISSN: 0892-3329] 1983. m. USD 34.95 domestic; USD 76.95 in HI, AK, PR & US Possessions; USD 81.95 Canada. Ed(s): Candace Korchinski. Vogel Communications Inc., 701 5th Ave, 36th Fl, Seattle, WA 98104. Illus., adv. Circ: 300000. Vol. ends: Dec. *Aud.:* Hs, Ga.

Satellite Direct is the program guide to the DirecTV digital satellite system. Daily channel lineups, local listings, and special sections for movies, sporting events, and children's programming are included. Feature articles and regular columns spotlight upcoming shows, entertainment news, and the latest trends in TV technology. Daily updates and programming changes for both *Satellite Direct* and *Satellite Orbit* can be found on the *Dishing It Out* page accessible via a link from each magazine's web site. Recommended only for libraries with an adequate DirecTV viewing audience.

6367. ***Satellite Orbit: complete national TV programming guide.*** Supersedes (in 1985): *Satguide.* [ISSN: 0732-7668] 1982. m. USD 45.95 domestic; USD 79.95 in Hawaii, Arkansas, Puerto Rico & US possessions; USD 84.95 Canada. Ed(s): Candace Korchinski. Vogel Communications Inc., 701 5th Ave, 36th Fl, Seattle, WA 98104. Illus., adv. Circ: 214953. Vol. ends: Dec. *Aud.:* Ems, Hs, Ga.

Satellite Orbit provides national satellite TV programming, complete with channel lineups, daily guides, programming-plus stations, sports, special events, pay-per-view, and movies. It also includes a satellite locator section with satellite radio listings and a separate channel lineup for Dish Network customers. Upcoming shows, celebrity news, and the latest technology trends are featured. Daily updates and programming changes for both *Satellite Orbit* and *Satellite Direct* can be found on the *Dishing It Out* page accessible via a link from each magazine's web site. Recommended for any public or school library.

6368. ***Smart T V & Sound: interactive T V & D V D - MP3 - Internet audio & video - satellite tv.*** Formerly (until 2001): *Smart T V.* [ISSN: 1545-0244] 1997. 2x/yr. USD 14.97 domestic; USD 24.97 Canada; USD 39.97 elsewhere. Ed(s): Stephen Muratore. York Publishing, PO Box 4591, Chico, CA 95927. Illus., adv. Circ: 50000. Vol. ends: Fall (No. 2). *Aud.:* Hs, Ga.

Smart TV & Sound is an accessible publication for the average electronics consumer interested in the latest technologies and products for home entertainment. It includes product reviews and regular columns such as "Noise: The Latest News in Interactive Technology," "New Gear," "Audio In," and "Smart Discs." Sample articles include "The Changing Look of TV: Walled Gardens and TV Portals" and "Interactive TV In the 21st Century." Recommended for school and public libraries interested in expanding general-interest or entertainment holdings.

6369. ***Sound & Vision: home theater - audio - video - multimedia - movies - music.*** Formerly (until 2003): *Stereo Review's Sound and Vision;* Which was formed by the merger of (1960-1999): *Stereo Review;* Which was formerly (until 1968): *HiFi Stereo Review;* Which incorporated (1959-1989): *High Fidelity;* (1978-1999): *Video Magazine;* Which was formerly (until 1987): *Video (New York).* [ISSN: 1537-5838] 1999. 10x/yr. USD 12 domestic; USD 22 foreign; USD 4.50 newsstand/cover. Ed(s): Bob Ankosko, Brian Fenton. Hachette Filipacchi Media U.S., Inc., 1633 Broadway, New York, NY 10019; http://www.hfmus.com. Illus., index, adv. Circ: 400000 Paid. Vol. ends: Dec. Microform: NBI; PQC. Online: America Online, Inc.; The Dialog Corporation; Gale Group. *Indexed:* BRI, CBRI, ConsI, IIMP, MagInd, MusicInd, RGPR, RILM. *Aud.:* Hs, Ga, Sa.

Sound & Vision is a consumer publication with broad appeal. It provides detailed reviews of a wide range of products, including DVD players, plasma TVs, LCD video projectors, home theater speaker systems, and universal remotes. Regular features and articles highlight the newest trends in entertainment technology. Sample articles include "The Sounds of Silence," "Making the HDTV Connection," and "Digital Radio Comes Down to Earth." Recommended for public, high school, and academic libraries.

TV Guide. See General Editorial/General section.

6370. ***Video Systems: the magazine for video professionals.*** [ISSN: 0361-0942] 1975. m. USD 70 domestic; USD 90 foreign. Ed(s): Michael Goldman. Primedia Business Magazines & Media, Inc., 9800 Metcalf Ave., Overland Park, KS 66212; inquiries@primediabusiness.com; http://www.primediabusiness.com. Illus., adv. Sample. Circ: 50006. Vol. ends: No. 12. Microform: PQC. Online: bigchalk; Factiva; Gale Group; LexisNexis; OCLC Online Computer Library Center, Inc.; ProQuest Information & Learning; H.W. Wilson. Reprint: PQC. *Aud.:* Ac, Sa.

Video Systems presents articles, news, and product reviews revolving around four key concepts of video technology—shoot, edit, display, and integrate. This well-rounded industry publication presents articles on a variety of topics, including the use of video in military training and the role of video in corporate communications and business training programs. The web site offers several related electronic newsletters in addition to expanded information about many of the features in the printed edition. Recommended for industry and academic libraries.

6371. ***Video Watchdog: the perfectionist's guide to fantastic video.*** [ISSN: 1070-9991] 1990. m. USD 48 domestic; USD 66 foreign; USD 6.50 newsstand/cover per issue. Ed(s): Tim Lucas. Video Watchdog, PO Box 5283, Cincinnati, OH 45205-0283; videowd@aol.com; http://www.cinemaweb.com/videowd. Illus. *Indexed:* IIFP. *Bk. rev.:* Number and length vary. *Aud.:* Hs, Ga.

Video Watchdog provides critical reviews of the latest home video and DVD releases in the sci-fi, horror, B-movie, and underground genres. Recent feature articles include "Portals to a Shadowed Past: 4 Silent Horror Classics Revisited" and "A Phildickian Look at Minority Report." A column called "Audio Watchdog" presents reviews of film and TV soundtracks, while related book reviews are presented in a column called "Biblio Watchdog." Recommended for public, high school, and academic libraries.

6372. ***Videography.*** [ISSN: 0363-1001] 1976. m. USD 72 domestic (Free to qualified personnel). Ed(s): Mark J Foley. United Entertainment Media, Inc., Entertainment Technology Group, 460 Park Ave South, 9th Fl, New York, NY 10016. Illus., adv. Sample. Circ: 41000. Vol. ends: Dec. Online: Gale Group; Northern Light Technology, Inc.; ProQuest Information & Learning. *Indexed:* FLI, MRD. *Aud.:* Sa.

Videography is a glossy industry publication covering all aspects of video making from production, postproduction, and audio to graphics, special effects, and streaming. Feature articles and product reviews are geared toward the video professional and assume a working knowledge of the industry. Employment opportunities and classified ads are also included. Recommended for academic libraries and larger public libraries with specialized collections.

6373. *Videomaker: camcorders - editing - computer video - audio & video production.* [ISSN: 0889-4973] 1986. m. USD 22.50 domestic; USD 32.50 Canada; USD 47.50 elsewhere. Ed(s): Stephen Muratore, Matthew York. York Publishing, PO Box 4591, Chico, CA 95927. Illus., index, adv. Sample. Circ: 80000. Vol. ends: Dec. Online: Gale Group. *Indexed:* CompLI, IHTDI. *Aud.:* Hs, Ac, Sa.

This publication is geared toward the beginner and semiprofessional with easy-to-understand feature articles and regular columns providing practical, how-to advice. Sample articles include "10 Ways to Steady Your Shooting," "Framing Good Shots," and "Six Ways to Soup Up Your Computer for Video Editing." Reviews of low- to mid-priced equipment are included in the "Test Bench" column. *Videomaker* is recommended for public and school libraries.

6374. *Widescreen Review: the essential home theatre resource.* 1993. m. USD 40 domestic; USD 50 in Canada & Mexico; USD 90 elsewhere. Ed(s): Gary Reber. W S R Publishing, 27645 Commerce Center Dr., Temecula, CA 92590; wsrgary@widescreenreview.com; http://www.widescreenreview.com. Illus., adv. Circ: 48000. *Aud.:* Ga, Sa.

Widescreen Review is a consumer publication for the home theater enthusiast. Feature articles and regular columns present a wide range of home theater-related topics such as "HD-DVD Prospects" and "DVD Blues." Also included are in-depth equipment reviews, critical reviews of DVDs, a DVD discography, and a DVD/D-VHS release schedule. Recommended for all public and school libraries.

Electronic Journals

6375. *Broadcast Archive.* irreg. Free. Ed(s): Barry Mishkind. Broadcast Archive, 2033 S. Augusta Pl., Tuscon, AZ 85710; barry@broadcast.net; http://www.oldradio.com. *Aud.:* Hs, Ga, Sa.

Barry Mishkind, "The Eclectic Engineer," has collected an impressive amount of material on pioneer and currently broadcasting radio stations at this free site called *The Broadcast Archive.* While it emphasizes professional radio broadcasting, it also includes information about early amateur broadcasting. The site documents stories of early radio stations and the people who built them as well as links to related software and databases. Sample pages include "Jurassic Radio," "War Stories," and "Top Ten List of Excuses for Ignoring FCC Rules." Recommended for anyone interested in the history of radio broadcasting.

6376. *C N N. com.* 1995. d. C N N, 1 CNN Center, Atlanta, GA 30303; cnn@cnn.com; http://cnn.com. *Aud.:* Hs, Ga, Ac.

This easy-to-use site features online news and information that is continuously updated as well as a schedule of CNN-TV's programming. The home page features "Top Stories" and provides links to a variety of other sections from technology and sports to entertainment and travel. *CNN.com* also produces an online international version. Recommended as a good general online news source.

6377. *OnVideo: guide to home video releases.* [ISSN: 1094-3676] 1995. d. Ed(s): Harley W Lond. OnVideo, PO Box 17377, Beverly Hills, CA 90209; onvideo@cyberpod.com; http://www.onvideo.org. Adv. *Aud.:* Ga.

OnVideo provides a list of videos and DVDs coming to video stores each week. The site includes brief reviews listing story lines, directors, actors, MPAA ratings, year of theatrical release, running times, and release dates. The site also includes related links, widescreen release information, and a tutorial on searching for videos. Useful for anyone who wants up-to-date information on the latest video and DVD releases.

6378. *P B S Previews.* 1995. w. Public Broadcasting Service, 1320 Braddock Pl, Alexandria, VA 22314; http://www.pbs.org. *Aud.:* Ga.

PBS Previews lists the current programming available on the Public Broadcasting System, including background information and educational tips for many of the programs. The interested user can check local listings as well as sign up for the weekly newsletter.

■ THEATER

Caroline M. Kent, Head of Research Services, Widener Library, Harvard University, Cambridge, MA 02138; cmkent@fas.harvard.edu; FAX: 617-495-0403

Elizabeth McKeigue, Research Librarian, Widener Library, Harvard University, Cambridge, MA 02138; mckeigue@fas.harvard.edu; FAX: 617-496-9802

Introduction

As varied as the topics of study in drama/theater is the range of journals that are available. Consumer and current performance titles (e.g., *American Theater, Variety,* and *Theatre Record*) are well known and can boast high circulation numbers. A wide variety of academic titles cover historical issues, some dramaturgy, and some comparative drama (e.g., *Asian Theatre Journal, New Theatre Quarterly,* and *Modern Drama*). Journals focused on playwriting and some that reproduce current play scripts (e.g., *The Dramatist, Avant-Scene Theatre*) are also of great importance to any theater collection. Not as prolific are journals that are predominantly focused on technical issues (e.g., *Entertainment Design*). Most academic libraries will want a selection of titles covering a range of issues. Others will want to decide if their users need current performance information, literary studies, community theater support, or something more specialized.

There continues to be a dearth of quality electronic-only journals that focus on theater. E-journals fall into two areas: academic journals and zines. Academic journals, such as *PAJ*, are supported online by academic presses and are also available in print. These are likely to maintain good interfaces and archives and to support continued and stable use. Less stable, but equally interesting for information on current theater productions, are the fresh new zines appearing online such as the *Off-Off Broadway Review*. The production and archiving of these materials are less predictable, but, because they are usually free, libraries should consider pointing to them. There is also a wealth of local e-journals with rich content on local theatrical productions that are not specifically included here. The journals listed here are limited to those focused on international, London, or New York theater.

A final note: As with all journal selection focusing on contemporary and avant-garde art, a library must be careful that it is choosing materials that not only will be useful for library users but, in addition, will be acceptable to the library's social/political environment. Many of the modern performance journals have fascinating but extreme content. Requesting sample issues freely should help avoid an unhappy reaction or, at the very least, prepare you for a possible reaction.

Basic Periodicals

Hs: *American Theatre, Dramatics, Entertainment Design, New Theatre Quarterly, Theater;* Ga: *American Theatre, Entertainment Design, Modern Drama, New Theatre Quarterly, Stage Directions, Theater, Variety;* Ac: *American Theatre, Canadian Theatre Review, Comparative Drama, Entertainment Design, Journal of Dramatic Theory and Criticism, Modern Drama, New Theatre Quarterly, Nineteenth Century Theatre, PAJ, TDR, Theater, Theatre Journal.*

Basic Abstracts and Indexes

Academic Index, Humanities Index, MLA International Bibliography.

6379. *American Drama.* [ISSN: 1061-0057] 1991. s-a. USD 25 (Individuals, USD 15). Ed(s): Yashdip Bains, Norma Jenckes. American Drama Institute, c/o English Department ML69, University of Cincinnati, Cincinnati, OH 45221-0069; american.drama@uc.edu; http://www.uc.edu/www/amdrama. Illus., index. Sample. Refereed. Vol. ends: Spring. Online: Gale Group; H.W. Wilson. *Indexed:* HumInd, IIPA, MLA-IB. *Bk. rev.:* Occasional. *Aud.:* Ac.

This quintessential journal on the American theater—Edward Albee is on the Advisory Board—contains studies of drama from all time periods, although the primary focus is the twentieth century to the present. Recent issues contain critical articles on the works of William Saroyan, William Inge, and David

Mamet. Also included are biographical studies, like a recent article on the working relationship between Eugene O'Neill and Susan Glaspell. Occasional interviews are included. Some issues may have general themes, such as Broadway musicals. Its web version contains abstracts of some articles only, and not all issues are available; but this will be very useful for any library considering this title. College and university libraries with serious drama departments or comparative literature programs should consider purchasing this journal.

6380. ***American Theatre: the monthly forum for news, features and opinion.*** [ISSN: 8750-3255] 1984. 10x/yr. USD 35 domestic; USD 50 foreign. Ed(s): Jim O'Quinn. Theatre Communications Group, Inc., 355 Lexington Ave, New York, NY 10017; tcg@tcg.org; http://www.tcg.org. Illus., adv. Sample. Circ: 24400. Vol. ends: Dec. Microform: PQC. Online: bigchalk; EBSCO Publishing; Florida Center for Library Automation; Gale Group; Northern Light Technology, Inc.; OCLC Online Computer Library Center, Inc.; ProQuest Information & Learning. *Indexed:* ASIP, BRI, CBRI, HumInd, IIPA, RI-1. *Bk. rev.:* Various number, 400-1,200 words. *Aud.:* Ga, Ac.

This magazine is the only American publication that offers such a broad overview of the current trends in the nonprofit American theater scene. A recent issue includes a special section with an article by veteran producer Zelda Fichandler commenting on the health of artistry in contemporary theater. Each issue contains three or four articles, sometimes the complete text of a new short play. Of particular interest are columns such as "Critic's Notebook," "Global Spotlight," and "This [Month] on Stage," which lists theatrical schedules from around the country—although far from complete, it certainly gives an overview of many productions around the nation. A substantial portion of the magazine's content is online at the publisher's web site (www.tcg.org), although articles are archived for only two years. Thus, it would be an invaluable addition to any college or university library, as well as any large public library addressing the needs of serious theatergoers.

6381. ***Asian Theatre Journal.*** Supersedes: *Asian Theatre Reports.* [ISSN: 0742-5457] 1984. s-a. USD 55 (Individuals, USD 28). Ed(s): Samuel L Leiter. University of Hawaii Press, Journals Department, 2840 Kolowalu St, Honolulu, HI 96822-1888; uhpjourn@hawaii.edu; http://www.uhpress.hawaii.edu/. Illus., adv. Sample. Refereed. Circ: 500. Vol. ends: Fall. Online: Gale Group; Northern Light Technology, Inc.; RoweCom Information Quest; Swets Blackwell. Reprint: PQC; PSC. *Indexed:* ArtHuCI, BAS, IBZ, IDP, IIPA, MLA-IB. *Bk. rev.:* 4-6, 1,000-1,500 words. *Aud.:* Ac.

The wonderfully rich worlds of Asian theater traditions are closed off to many Americans because of language issues. *Asian Theatre Journal,* therefore, published in English by the University of Hawaii Press, is an excellent source for American theater historians and practitioners. This journal focuses on both traditional and modern styles of performance. Each issue contains several articles, which may be descriptive of a particular tradition (such as Asian puppetry), the history of a play or characters, or textual analysis. The report section may contain reports of conferences, theater festivals, or an interview with a luminary on a particular topic. Finally, there is a book review section. The journal is elegantly illustrated with both color and black-and-white photographs. An online version of this journal is currently available through subscription from Project Muse. Academic research libraries with either a serious drama department or an East Asian literature department should consider this publication.

6382. ***Avant Scene Theatre.*** [ISSN: 0045-1169] 1949. 24x/yr. EUR 150 domestic; EUR 179 foreign. Editions de l' Avant Scene, 6 rue Git-le-Coeur, Paris, 75006, France; astheatre@aol.com. Illus., adv. Sample. *Indexed:* ArtHuCI, IBZ. *Aud.:* Ac.

This journal offers a full play script by a major contemporary author, such as Fremond or Besse, in each issue. It also publishes notes on other new plays, interviews, and reviews. Handsomely illustrated with production photographs, cartoons, and drawings, it should be considered for purchase by university libraries or any smaller academic setting with a serious program in contemporary French literature.

6383. ***Bandwagon: the journal of the Circus Historical Society.*** [ISSN: 0005-4968] 1956. bi-m. USD 27 domestic; USD 32 foreign. Ed(s): Fred D Pfening, Jr. Circus Historical Society, 1075 W Fifth Ave, Columbus, OH 43212. Illus., adv. Sample. Circ: 1400. Vol. ends: Nov/Dec. *Indexed:* IIPA. *Aud.:* Ac.

Clearly not every library addressing the needs of a theatrical or drama audience should purchase a magazine entirely devoted to the circus; however, this magazine is the only source for much of the knowledge and information it contains. *Bandwagon* presents six to ten articles with historical information, varying in length from 1 to 15 pages. These articles are often the reminiscences of former or current circus owners as well as performers, such as Gunther Gebel-Williams, Lucio Cristiani, and Clyde Beatty. The pages are well illustrated from a variety of archival sources. It also periodically includes reviews of books, particular performances, and the circus season. The journal has some serious flaws. For example, it is not indexed in commercial services, and the articles sometimes lack scholarly attribution. Libraries with a serious theater history collection or that service the needs of a broad performing arts audience should consider purchasing it. For many college and university libraries, other academic titles that periodically address circus issues from a social or historical point of view may suffice.

6384. ***Canadian Theatre Review.*** [ISSN: 0315-0836] 1974. q. CND 85 (Individuals, USD 35; CND 10.50 newsstand/cover per issue). University of Toronto Press, Journals Department, 5201 Dufferin St, Toronto, ON M3H 5T8, Canada; journals@utpress.utoronto.ca; http://www.utpjournals.com. Illus., index, adv. Sample. Circ: 800. Microform: MML. Online: EBSCO Publishing; Gale Group; LexisNexis. *Indexed:* ArtHuCI, BAS, CPerI, HumInd, IIPA, MLA-IB. *Bk. rev.:* 2-4, 800-1,200 words. *Aud.:* Ac.

This journal is the major magazine of record for Canadian theater. It focuses mainly on contemporary and often avant-garde theater productions. Each issue is organized around a theme, e.g., "Youth. Theatre. Politics." Included in each issue are at least one complete playscript related to the issue theme, articles, and reviews. It contains six to ten articles related to the theme, a new play script, an opinion/forum section ("Carte Blanche"), and performance and book reviews. The journal is well illustrated with production photographs. This interesting journal would be well placed in an academic collection that maintains a collection focus on contemporary theater and drama.

6385. ***Comparative Drama.*** [ISSN: 0010-4078] 1967. q. USD 32 domestic; USD 35 foreign. Ed(s): Luis Gamez. Western Michigan University, Dept. of English, Kalamazoo, MI 49008-5092. Illus., index. Sample. Refereed. Circ: 900 Paid. Vol. ends: Winter. Microform: PQC. Online: bigchalk; Florida Center for Library Automation; Gale Group; OCLC Online Computer Library Center, Inc.; ProQuest Information & Learning; H.W. Wilson. Reprint: PQC. *Indexed:* ABS&EES, ArtHuCI, BAS, BRI, CBRI, HumInd, IIPA, MLA-IB. *Bk. rev.:* 6-8, 500-1,500 words. *Aud.:* Ac.

This journal looks at drama and theater from a strictly literary point of view. It is academic in nature and gives equal treatment to the various genres of drama (ancient, medieval, renaissance, and modern). Recent topics include a comparative analysis of Michel de Montaigne's *Essais* and *King Lear*, textual analysis, and a study on the thematic relationship between a twentieth-century Russian-Jewish play, *The Dybbuk*, and the Noh plays of Japan in the fourteenth century. Sometimes an entire issue will be centered on a single theme, such as "Tragedy's Insights." Its coverage is broad in terms of time period and geography. An important scholarly journal for college or university library collections.

6386. ***Dramatics: the magazine for students and teachers of theatre.*** Formerly: *Dramatics-Dramatic Curtain.* [ISSN: 0012-5989] 1929. 9x/yr. USD 18; USD 28 foreign. Ed(s): Don Corathers. Educational Theatre Association, 2343 Auburn Ave, Cincinnati, Cincinnati, OH 45219-2815; dcorathers@etassoc.org; http://www.etassoc.org/. Illus., index, adv. Sample. Circ: 39000 Paid. Vol. ends: Dec. Microform: PQC. Reprint: PQC. *Indexed:* IIPA. *Aud.:* Hs, Ac.

This is one of the few publications that are specifically directed at the interests of the collegiate drama student. Published by the Educational Theatre Association, the articles are not scholarly in nature, but rather provide practical articles on acting, directing, and design that will be of use to drama students and educators. Its content ranges from technique articles and columns, e.g., "The Actor's Toolbox," to the full text of short plays. In addition, there is a great deal of information on internships, summer employment, collegiate and institute dramatic programs, and auditions. Colleges and universities that support a drama program should consider this publication. Also, high school libraries might consider its purchase.

6387. *The Dramatist.* Formerly: *Dramatists Guild Quarterly.* 1964. bi-m. USD 25. Ed(s): Greg Bossler. Dramatists Guild, Inc., 1501 Broadway, Ste 701, New York, NY 10036; http://www.dramaguild.com. Illus., adv. Sample. Circ: 8200. Vol. ends: Winter. *Indexed:* IIPA. *Aud.:* Ac, Sa.

The Dramatists Guild is the single most important professional society for serious playwrights, dramatists, and lyricists. Its organ journal, *The Dramatist*, is therefore an important publication. It usually contains eight to ten articles; these articles may contain discussions of some aspect of playwriting, interviews with well-known playwrights, the political and social opinions of playwrights as they affect their writings, or discussions of theatrical companies. There is also a "Dramatists Diary," which lists plays in production around the country, newly published plays and recordings, and recently published books by guild members. This magazine would have great value for any library addressing the needs of a serious playwriting program.

Dramatists Guild Quarterly. See *The Dramatist.*

6388. *Entertainment Design: the art and technology of show business.* Supersedes (in 1999): *T C I - Theatre Crafts International;* Which was formed by the merger of (1967-1992): *Theatre Crafts; Theatre Crafts International;* Which incorporated: *Cue International;* Which was formerly: *Cue Technical Theatre Review.* [ISSN: 1520-5150] 1992. 11x/yr. USD 29.99. Ed(s): David Johnson. Primedia Business Magazines & Media, Inc., 9800 Metcalf Ave., Overland Park, KS 66212; http://www.primediabusiness.com. Illus., adv. Sample. Circ: 25000 Paid. Microform: PQC. Online: bigchalk; EBSCO Publishing; Florida Center for Library Automation; Gale Group; LexisNexis; OCLC Online Computer Library Center, Inc.; ProQuest Information & Learning; H.W. Wilson. *Indexed:* ArtHuCI, ArtInd, BRI, CBRI, DAAI, EduInd, FLI, IIPA, LRI, MagInd, RGPR. *Bk. rev.:* 4-6, 400-600 words. *Aud.:* Ac, Sa.

This magazine's focus is the art and technology of the entertainment business. It includes news columns, business information, special reports, and articles on the design of particular productions (both theatrical and some film). It is handsomely and extensively illustrated with production and product photographs. It contains product information in its articles, in its reports of trade shows, and in the advertisements. *Entertainment Design* has a large, tabloid format that the library purchaser should be aware of. Its web version contains much of the print, but the format is less than appealing, despite its availability back to 1999. It also lacks some of the illustrative materials available in the print version. The print publication would be an excellent addition to any library with theatrical production collections.

6389. *Figura: zeitschrift fuer theater und spiel mit figuren.* Formerly (until 1992): *Puppenspiel und Puppenspieler.* [ISSN: 1021-3244] 1960. 4x/yr. CHF 36 domestic; CHF 40 foreign. Ed(s): Elke Krafka. U N I M A Suisse, Postfach 2328, Winterthur, 8401, Switzerland. Illus., adv. Sample. Circ: 1150. *Indexed:* BHA. *Bk. rev.:* 2-5, 200-400 words. *Aud.:* Ac, Sa.

Puppetry has never held the same level of fascination for Americans as it has for Germans, Austrians, and the Swiss—that is, until the advent of Jim Henson! This little journal contains broad international coverage of the puppetry "scene." It includes performance reviews, festival announcements, and general news and notes. In addition, it is well illustrated and often contains technical articles that are well diagrammed and therefore language-independent. The text is usually in German and French. Academic libraries addressing the concerns of a serious theater department should consider its purchase. In addition, special libraries in performance art centers that support a technical audience should consider its purchase.

6390. *Journal of American Drama and Theatre.* [ISSN: 1044-937X] 1989. 3x/yr. USD 12 domestic; USD 18 foreign. Ed(s): Daniel Gerould, Vera Mowry Roberts. Martin E. Segal Theatre Center, The Graduate School and University Center, The City University of New York, New York, NY 10016-4309; mestc@gc.cuny.edu; http://web.gc.edu.mestc. Illus., adv. Refereed. Circ: 3400 Paid. Vol. ends: Fall. *Indexed:* IIPA. *Aud.:* Ac, Sa.

This fascinating journal focuses on research on American playwrights, plays, and the American contemporary theater scene in general. Each issue contains six to eight articles. Recent articles have been interdisciplinary in nature. In particular, they examine theater from an anthropological or sociological point of view. For example, recent titles include "When the ~A' Word Is Never Spoken: Fear of Intimacy and AIDS in Lanford Wilson's *Burn This*" and "Haunting the Social Unconscious: Naomi Wallace's *In the Heart of America.*" Best suited for large academic collections or special libraries addressing the needs of a serious theater community.

6391. *Journal of Dramatic Theory and Criticism.* [ISSN: 0888-3203] 1986. s-a. USD 25 (Individuals, USD 15; Students, USD 10). Ed(s): John Gronbeck Tedesco. Journal of Dramatic Theory and Criticism, Hall Center for the Humanities, 211 Watkins Home, Lawrence, KS 66045-2967. Illus., adv. Sample. Refereed. Circ: 426 Paid. Vol. ends: Spring. *Indexed:* ABS&EES, IIPA, MLA-IB. *Bk. rev.:* 8-12, 800-1,500 words. *Aud.:* Ac.

This journal is primarily focused on dramatic theory and issues as they are expressed in production, and this makes its orientation unusual. In particular, its focus is on "new theories and methodologies pertinent to performance and performance texts and performance criticism which attempts to yield new insights into theatrical works." The six to ten scholarly articles are substantive and international in coverage. Recent articles include textual analysis, such as "The Biblical Subtext in Beckett's *Waiting for Godot*" and commentary on theater as performance, such as "The Body as Fluid Dramaturgy: Live Art, Corporeality, and Perception." The journal also includes very long, detailed international performance reviews and excellent book reviews. Academic libraries with a serious and active theater department should consider purchasing this journal.

6392. *Latin American Theatre Review: a journal devoted to the theatre and drama of Spanish & Portuguese America.* [ISSN: 0023-8813] 1967. s-a. USD 40 (Individuals, USD 20). Ed(s): George W Woodyard. Center of Latin American Studies, 107 Lippincott Hall, University of Kansas, Lawrence, KS 66045; latamst@ukans.edu; http://www.ukans.edu/~latamst. Illus., index, adv. Sample. Refereed. Circ: 1200. *Indexed:* ArtHuCI, HAPI, IIPA, MLA-IB. *Bk. rev.:* 15-25, 500-1,000 words. *Aud.:* Ac.

This is a unique source. Each issue contains 12–20 articles on festivals, theater scenes, and historical issues of the Spanish- and Portuguese-language theater worlds in the Americas. It also includes a broad range of reviews that cover performances, plays, books, and conferences. The text of the articles may be in English, Spanish, or Portuguese. Each issue also has an excellent source bibliography. Any academic library with a theater history collection or Hispanic literature collection should consider the purchase of this title.

6393. *Modern Drama.* [ISSN: 0026-7694] 1958. q. CND 45. Ed(s): Ric Knowles. University of Toronto Press, Journals Department, 5201 Dufferin St, Toronto, ON M3H 5T8, Canada; journals@utpress.utoronto.ca; http://www.utpjournals.com. Illus., index, adv. Sample. Refereed. Circ: 2000. Vol. ends: Winter. Microform: MML. Online: bigchalk; EBSCO Publishing; Florida Center for Library Automation; Gale Group; OCLC Online Computer Library Center, Inc.; ProQuest Information & Learning. *Indexed:* ABS&EES, ArtHuCI, CBCARef, CPerI, FLI, HumInd, IBZ, IIPA, MLA-IB, RI-1. *Bk. rev.:* 8-12, 500-1,000 words. *Aud.:* Ac.

This journal looks at contemporary drama from an academic point of view. The articles are scholarly and substantive, but they do not lack in liveliness and interest. Recent topics include commentary and analysis on the works of modern playwrights like Caryl Churchill, August Wilson, John Guare, and Tony Kushner. Although far from the leading edge of modern performance theory, the eight to ten articles often contain analyses of very current materials. An article written by Elin Diamond recently won the Association for Theatre in Higher

Education Essay Prize for outstanding critical article for her essay "Modern Drama/Modernity's Drama." There are also extensive and interesting book reviews in each issue and an annual bibliography in the Summer issue. This journal would be well placed in any academic library collection supporting contemporary drama and literature programs.

6394. ***New Theatre Quarterly.*** Formerly (until 1985): *Theatre Quarterly.* [ISSN: 0266-464X] 1971. q. USD 110 (Individuals, USD 50). Ed(s): Clive Barker, Simon Trussler. Cambridge University Press, The Edinburgh Bldg, Shaftesbury Rd, Cambridge, CB2 2RU, United Kingdom; information@cambridge.org; http://uk.cambridge.org/journals. Illus., adv. Sample. Vol. ends: Nov. Microform: PQC. Online: Gale Group. Reprint: SWZ. *Indexed:* AmH&L, ArtHuCI, HumInd, IIPA, MLA-IB. *Bk. rev.:* 15-20, 200-400 words. *Aud.:* Ac.

NTQ is a serious publication covering issues of modern performance and dramaturgy. It claims also to provide a forum "where prevailing dramatic assumptions can be subjected to vigorous critical questioning." Its prose style is not stodgy, however; rather, it is interesting and eye-catching and therefore more widely approachable than that of some academic journals. *NTQ* usually contains eight to ten scholarly articles that are international in coverage. Some recent titles include "Simple Pleasures: The Ten-Minute Play, Overnight Theatre, and the Decline of the Art of Storytelling" and "Performance, Embodiment, Voice: The Theatre/Dance Cross-Overs of Dodin, Bausch, and Forsythe." Its book reviews are less substantive than those of other academic journals, but they could be useful for either selection or personal purposes. This publication is recommended for academic libraries and special libraries addressing modern performance issues.

New York Shakespeare Society Bulletin. See *Shakespeare Bulletin: a journal of performance, criticism, and scholarship.*

6395. ***Nineteenth Century Theatre.*** Formerly (until 1987): *Nineteenth Century Theatre Research;* Incorporates (1976-1979): *N C T R Newsletter.* [ISSN: 0893-3766] 1973. s-a. GBP 17 (Individuals, GBP 11). Ed(s): Jacky Bratton. University of London, Department of Drama, Theatre and Media Arts, Royal Holloway, Egham, TW20 0EX, United Kingdom. Illus., adv. Sample. Circ: 400. Microform: PQC. Reprint: PQC. *Indexed:* AmH&L, AmHI, ArtHuCI, IIPA, MLA-IB. *Bk. rev.:* 4-5, 1,500-3,000 words. *Aud.:* Ac.

This publication is so unassuming in format and appearance that it is easy to overlook. However, it is a well-edited little journal that contains interesting materials not available elsewhere, and it is well covered in indexing services. Each issue contains two or three feature articles covering nineteenth-century performance issues in the United States, Western Europe, and Russia. Its articles are not limited to theater; all performance forms may be covered. It contains a notes section that may list information on databases or other resources. Its book reviews are substantial and informative. Any academic library collection covering nineteenth-century literature or intellectual history would be well served by including this journal.

6396. ***P A J.*** Formerly (until 1998): *Performing Arts Journal.* [ISSN: 1520-281X] 1976. 3x/yr. USD 68 (Individuals, USD 26). Ed(s): Bonnie Marranca, Gautam Dasgupta. Johns Hopkins University Press, Journals Publishing Division, 2715 N Charles St, Baltimore, MD 21218-4363; jlorder@jhupress.jhu.edu; http://www.press.jhu.edu/. Illus., adv. Sample. Refereed. Circ: 1130. Vol. ends: Sep. *Indexed:* ABM, ABS&EES, AmHI, ArtHuCI, BRI, CBRI, FLI, HumInd, IIPA, MLA-IB. *Bk. rev.:* Occasional. *Aud.:* Ac, Sa.

This journal covers contemporary international performance: dance, theater, and performance art. Each issue contains eight to ten articles, performance reviews, and opinion pieces. Topics of some recent articles are the development of directing as a profession and art as spiritual practice. Sometimes an issue may have a theme. The journal often contains reviews of new works in theater, dance, film, and opera, and occasionally book reviews. Its illustrations are extensive and fascinating. Recommended for academic or special academic libraries where contemporary and avant-garde performance artistry is important. *PAJ* is currently available online (ISSN: 1520-281X) as part of Johns Hopkins' Project Muse. As with most Project Muse titles, the text is easily accessed and read. Academic institutions may have subscriptions to individual titles.

6397. ***Performance Research: a journal of performing arts.*** [ISSN: 1352-8165] 1996. q. GBP 217 (Individuals, GBP 56). Ed(s): Richard Gough. Routledge, 11 New Fetter Ln, London, EC4P 4EE, United Kingdom; journals@routldege.com; http://www.routledge.com/routledge/journal/journals.html. Illus. Sample. Refereed. Reprint: PSC. *Indexed:* ABM, ArtHuCI, BrHumI, IIPA. *Bk. rev.:* Occasional. *Aud.:* Ac, Sa.

This journal contains articles that look at performance from an interdisciplinary, sometimes historic, perspective. Each issue centers on a particular theme, such as "On Memory" and "Departures [travel]." Current article titles include "Anatomizing a Postcolonial Tragedy: Ken Saro-Wiwa and the Ogonis" and "Baudrillard and the Ambiguities of Radical Illusion." The content can be fascinating and sometimes extreme in nature, but it is a fair representation of the far edge of avant-garde performance art. It also contains occasional book reviews. Academic and special collections that support serious, contemporary theatrical research should own this title.

6398. ***Playbill: the national magazine of the theatre.*** [ISSN: 0032-146X] 1884. m. USD 24 domestic; USD 31 foreign; USD 2.50 newsstand/cover per issue. Ed(s): Judy Samelson. Playbill Inc., 525 7th Ave., Rm. 1801, New York, NY 10018-4918; http://www.playbill.com. Illus., adv. Sample. Circ: 2785000. *Indexed:* IIPA. *Aud.:* Ga.

This is the consumer-style magazine that is distributed free to theatergoers in many theaters. The theater edition and the newsstand edition both contain information for many plays, general articles on the theater, backstage topics, fashion, and food ads, but only the theater edition contains the program inserts. It is a little presumptuous to call it a "national" magazine, but it certainly contains information of general interest. Libraries with populations of theatergoers should consider this publication (although access to the online version might suffice for many), as should serious theater history library collections.

6399. ***Plays: the drama magazine for young people.*** [ISSN: 0032-1540] 1941. m. Oct-May; except Jan.-Feb. combined. USD 30 domestic; USD 38 Canada; USD 50 elsewhere. Ed(s): Sylvia K Burack. Plays Magazine, P.O. Box 600160, Newton, MA 02460. Illus., index, adv. Sample. Circ: 15000 Paid. Vol. ends: Dec. Microform: PQC. Online: bigchalk; EBSCO Publishing; Florida Center for Library Automation; Gale Group; Northern Light Technology, Inc.; ProQuest Information & Learning. Reprint: PQC. *Indexed:* BiogInd, CPerI, ICM, MagInd. *Bk. rev.:* 10-15, 50-100 words. *Aud.:* Ems, Hs, Ga.

The venerable magazine *Plays* has provided many of us with early dramatic experience. Each issue contains between 9 and 12 short plays, with subjects ranging from historic to holidays, to skits and comedies, to a dramatized classic (e.g., *The Mummy*). The plays are arranged by general grade level (Junior and Senior High, Middle and Lower Grade), and each contains production notes that include casting and staging suggestions. The plays do not hold up to some of the great classic plays available for the young, but they provide invaluable practice and filler titles. The book review section contains a rather odd mix of titles with very sketchy annotations. With new editorship, some of these flaws may be eliminated. The plays are not copyright-free, but any current subscriber may produce copies for the cast and produce the play royalty-free. This magazine should be included in the library of any school with a drama program or club. It should also be included in public library children's collections.

6400. ***Research in Drama Education.*** [ISSN: 1356-9783] 1996. s-a. GBP 141 (Individuals, GBP 55). Ed(s): John Somers. Carfax Publishing Ltd., 4 Park Sq, Milton Park, Abingdon, OX14 4RN, United Kingdom; enquiry@tandf.co.uk; http://www.tandf.co.uk/. Illus., adv. Vol. ends: Aug. Online: EBSCO Publishing; Ingenta Select; Northern Light Technology, Inc.; OCLC Online Computer Library Center, Inc.; ProQuest Information & Learning; RoweCom Information Quest; Swets Blackwell. Reprint: PSC. *Indexed:* BrEdI, MLA-IB. *Bk. rev.:* 4-6, 800-1,500 words. *Aud.:* Ac.

This interesting journal is devoted entirely to the various uses of drama and theater in education, youth and children's theaters, drama education, and research in community theater. It is primarily directed at youth or high school level teachers of drama, but would be a valuable resource for drama students intending to teach. Each issue contains six to ten articles. Issues also include book reviews and, frequently, abstracts of dissertations. Recent titles include "Training Teachers' Behaviour," "Curricula in Question: Directing Textbooks and Shifting Paradigms," and "Quantifiable Evidence, Reading Pedagogy, and Puppets." Any academic library with a drama/theater department or an education department should consider purchasing this publication.

6401. ***Restoration & Eighteenth Century Theatre Research.*** [ISSN: 0034-5822] 1962. s-a. USD 15. Ed(s): Jessica Munns. Restoration & Eighteenth Century Theatre Research, English Dept, University of Denver, Sturm Hull, Denver, CO 80208; http://www.du.edu/english/pamplet.htm. Illus. Refereed. *Indexed:* AmH&L, IIPA, MLA-IB. *Bk. rev.:* 1-2, 1,000 words. *Aud.:* Ac.

This small academic journal's mission is to publish articles on Restoration drama. Each issue includes four to six articles covering the plays, playwrights, and performers of that era. It is a highly specialized journal. Given the popularity of that era for both study and performance, it should be considered by any academic library with a strong English literature program.

6402. ***Revue d'Histoire du Theatre.*** Formerly (until 1996): *Revue de la Societe d'Histoire du Theatre.* [ISSN: 1291-2530] 1948. q. EUR 57 domestic; EUR 60 in Europe; EUR 63 elsewhere. Societe d'Histoire du Theatre, BnF - 58 rue de Richelieu, Paris, 75084 Cedex 02, France; info@sht.asso.fr; http://www.sht.asso.fr. Illus., index, adv. Sample. Refereed. Reprint: SWZ. *Indexed:* AmH&L, ArtHuCI, BHA, IBZ, IIPA, MLA-IB, RILM, SSCI. *Bk. rev.:* 4-8, 500-1,500 words. *Aud.:* Ac.

This is the main publication of the Societe d'Histoire du Theatre in France. Each issue contains four to six scholarly articles on the history of theater and the analysis of drama. The focus is predominantly on French theater, but articles do appear on the drama of other Western European countries. This publication would be best placed in serious theater history collections and university libraries.

6403. ***Shakespeare Bulletin: a journal of performance, criticism, and scholarship.*** Incorporates (1976-1992): *Shakespeare on Film Newsletter;* Formerly: *New York Shakespeare Society Bulletin.* [ISSN: 0748-2558] 1982. q. USD 20. Ed(s): James P Lusardi, June Schlueter. Lafayette College, 17 Watson Hall, Easton, PA 18042; lusardij@lafayette.edu; http://www.ampere.scale.uiuc.edu/shapespeare/56/. Illus., adv. Refereed. Circ: 1000 Paid. Vol. ends: Nov. *Indexed:* BEL&L, IIPA, MLA-IB. *Bk. rev.:* 5-10, 600-1,000 words. *Aud.:* Ac, Sa.

The *Bulletin* attempts to capture information on all Shakespearean performances, both live and on film, throughout the United States. It also contains some information on English-speaking productions from Canada, Great Britain, and other parts of the world. Each issue includes two to four serious articles on Shakespeare, from textual analysis to theater design. There are extensive performance, film, and book reviews. Recent reviews have included the Folger Theatre's production of *Macbeth* and the Pennsylvania Shakespeare Company's production of *A Midsummer Night's Dream.* Any academic library with a serious English literature collection should consider purchasing this journal. In addition, any library addressing the needs of theater companies that routinely perform Shakespearean drama should purchase it.

Shakespeare on Film Newsletter. See *Shakespeare Bulletin: a journal of performance, criticism, and scholarship.*

6404. ***Show Music: the musical theatre magazine.*** [ISSN: 8755-9560] 1981. q. USD 23 domestic; USD 35 foreign. Ed(s): Max O Preeo. Goodspeed Opera House, PO Box 466, East Haddam, CT 06423-0466; subscriptions@showmusic.org; http://www.goodspeed.org. Adv. Circ: 5200 Paid. *Aud.:* Ga, Sa.

This interesting magazine is published by the Goodspeed Opera House. However, its coverage is not limited to the Goodspeed's productions. Each issue contains three to five feature articles, interviews, and production reviews of musical theater throughout the United States, with a small amount of coverage devoted to other English-language productions worldwide. It is a form of performance that is generally ignored by the more "serious" publications, but one that deserves more attention given its continued popularity. Any public library serving a theatergoing population or any performance or music library should consider purchasing this title.

6405. ***Slavic and East European Performance.*** Formerly (until 1991): *Soviet and East European Performance.* [ISSN: 1069-2800] 1981. 3x/yr. USD 10 domestic; USD 20 foreign. Ed(s): Marvin Carlson. Martin E. Segal Theatre Center, The Graduate School and University Center, The City University of New York, New York, NY 10016-4309; mestc@gc.cuny.edu; http://web.gc.edu.mestc. *Aud.:* Ac.

It is hard to talk about modern political theater and performance art without discussing the theater traditions found in Eastern European nations and countries formerly in the Soviet Union. The deep theatric traditions of these countries, however, are often unavailable to American researchers and drama students because of language barriers. This wonderful journal, completely in English, gives us that necessary access. Each issue contains performance reviews, production information, and articles on both current and historic topics. A recent issue includes articles on the Sarajevo International Theatre Festival, an interview with Alexander Popov of the Moscow Art Theatre, and a review of the St. Petersburg theatrical season. At its low cost, this journal would be well placed in any academic or special library serving the needs of theater communities interested in political or dissident performance.

6406. ***Stage Directions.*** [ISSN: 1047-1901] 1988. 10x/yr. USD 26. Ed(s): Julie Davis. Lifestyle Ventures, LLC, 250 W 57th St, Ste 420, New York, NY 10107. Illus., adv. Sample. Circ: 20000 Paid. *Bk. rev.:* 2-3, 400 words. *Aud.:* Ga, Ac.

This is the only U.S. publication that tries to address the specific needs of "regional, academic, and community" theaters, although the best audience would probably be community and small academic theater groups. Each issue has six to ten articles on such practical subjects as cost-saving ideas, dramatic effects and techniques, and computer control issues. There is also supplier information, articles describing particular theaters and their companies, columns on computers and networked resources, book reviews, and technical issues. Its online version does not give the user access to the entire publication. Rather, it includes the table of contents for each issue published since 1988 and links to selected articles online. Since the journal is not carried by the major indexing services, this would be a good site to get a preview of the journal and a way to get access to the contents of previous issues. This magazine would be a useful resource for any public library with an active community theater or any college library with an active drama department.

6407. ***Studies in Theatre and Performance.*** [ISSN: 1468-2761] 2000. 3x/yr. GBP 90 (Individuals, GBP 30). Ed(s): Lesley Wade-Soule, Jane Milling. Intellect Ltd., PO Box 862, Bristol, BS99 1DE, United Kingdom; http://www.intellectbooks.com. Refereed. *Bk. rev.:* 6-8, 600-800 words. *Aud.:* Ac.

This title was transformed from a working paper series into a tri-annual journal in 2000. While the focus is primarily on British and European productions, it is an impressive new entry into the field of performance studies and important for American collections. Recent articles include "Theatrical Truth: the Dialogue between Audience and Performance" and "Revisiting Brecht: Preparing *Galileo* for Production." The intent of the journal is a practical one: to share methods and the results of practical research. Any academic library with a serious theater and/or performance art program should consider its purchase.

6408. ***T D & T: Theatre Design & Technology.*** Formerly: *Theatre Design and Technology.* [ISSN: 1052-6765] 1965. q. Membership, USD 48. Ed(s): David Rodger. U S Institute for Theatre Technology, Inc., 6443 Ridings Rd, Syracuse, NY 13206-1111. Illus., adv. Sample. Circ: 4200. Vol. ends: Sep. Microform: PQC. Online: Chadwyck-Healey Incorporated; OCLC Online Computer Library Center, Inc.; H.W. Wilson. Reprint: PQC. *Indexed:* ABS&EES, AIAP, API, ArtInd, DAAI, IDP, IIPA. *Bk. rev.:* 3-5, 200-600 words. *Aud.:* Ac, Sa.

This excellent publication is directed at professional theater and production designers. It contains articles on theater design, production design, and particular production or technical issues. It also often profiles particular designers or architects. There are columns with product reviews, book reviews, and a listing of the contents of international design journals. In addition to special collections, this journal would be well placed in any academic library with theatrical production or architectural programs.

6409. *T D R: the journal of performance studies.* Former titles (until 1988): *Drama Review;* (until 1968): *T D R;* (until 1967): *Tulane Drama Review;* (until 1957): *Carleton Drama Review.* [ISSN: 1054-2043] 1955. q. USD 136 print & online eds. (Individuals, USD 40 print & online eds.; Students, USD 22 print & online eds.). Ed(s): Richard Schechner. MIT Press, 5 Cambridge Center, Cambridge, MA 02142-1493; journals-orders@mit.edu; http://mitpress.mit.edu. Illus., index, adv. Sample. Circ: 5000. Vol. ends: Winter. Microform: PQC. Online: EBSCO Publishing; Florida Center for Library Automation; Gale Group; Ingenta Select; OCLC Online Computer Library Center, Inc.; Project MUSE; RoweCom Information Quest; H.W. Wilson. Reprint: PQC. *Indexed:* ABS&EES, AmHI, ArtHuCI, BAS, BRI, CBRI, HumInd, IDP, IIPA, MLA-IB, MagInd. *Bk. rev.:* 6-10, 400-2,000 words. *Aud.:* Ac.

This is an extremely important American performance publication published by MIT Press for the Tisch School at New York University, now available either in print or online by subscription. Each issue contains 10–20 articles, often organized around a central theme. The coverage of the articles is broad, both in terms of topic and of country of origin. Recent issues contain articles titled "Where Are the Muslim Feminist Voices?: A Question Asked in September 2001," "Ecoactivist Performance: The Environment as Partner in Protest?," and "Pilgrimage as a Pedagogical Practice in Contemporary Taiwanese Theatre." There are extensive reviews and descriptions of contemporary and often avant-garde performances with photographic illustrations, and some readers will find the topics overly politicized and socially shocking. That being said, however, this is still a serious journal. The journal's book reviews are substantial and thought-provoking. Like the rest of the journal, they both challenge and inform. From 1999 on, this journal is available through Project Muse. This title should be included in any university collection and in any library addressing the needs of contemporary performance artists.

6410. *Theater Heute.* [ISSN: 0040-5507] 1960. m. EUR 124 domestic (Students, EUR 85). Ed(s): Michael Merschmeier. Friedrich Berlin Verlagsgesellschaft mbH, Reinhardtstr 29, Berlin, 10117, Germany; verlag@friedrichberlin.de; http://www.friedrichberlin.de. Illus., adv. Sample. Circ: 20000 Controlled. *Indexed:* ArtHuCI, IBZ, IIPA. *Aud.:* Ac, Sa.

This popular German magazine covers contemporary theater issues in that country. It is beautifully illustrated, with photographs that are so striking they almost make the journal's purchase worthwhile simply on their account! The articles are well written, although popular in style. There are news notes, information on German theater personalities, and usually a full play script. Any academic library collection supporting interest either in world theater or in modern German drama or literature should consider its purchase.

6411. *Theater (New Haven).* Formerly (until vol.8, no.2 & 3, 1976): *Yale - Theatre.* [ISSN: 0161-0775] 1968. 3x/yr. USD 88 includes online access (Individuals, USD 30 includes online access). Ed(s): Erika Munk. Duke University Press, 905 W Main St, Ste 18 B, Durham, NC 27701; subscriptions@dukeupress.edu; http://www.dukeupress.edu. Illus., index, adv. Sample. Circ: 1100. Microform: PQC. Online: EBSCO Publishing; Ingenta Select; OCLC Online Computer Library Center, Inc.; Project MUSE; RoweCom Information Quest; Swets Blackwell. Reprint: PSC. *Indexed:* ArtHuCI, FLI, HumInd, IIPA, MLA-IB. *Bk. rev.:* 2-3, 600-1,800 words. *Aud.:* Ac.

Theater is the publication of the venerable, sometimes controversial, but always interesting Yale School of Drama. (Duke University Press is now publishing this journal for the Yale School of Drama.) *Theater*'s articles very much reflect the social politics of contemporary theater thinkers, artistic directors, and writers. Recent titles include "Tony Kushner's *Homebody/Kabul*: Staging History in a Post-colonial World" and "The Death (and Life) of American Theater Criticism: Advice to the Young Critic." The political perspective is both fascinating and controversial. Each issue contains four to six articles, usually organized around a theme. The editors try to include at least one new "pathbreaking" play per issue, and some issues contain several. The articles are often illustrated with what are sometimes breathtaking production photographs. *Theater* is an invaluable part of any serious academic theater journal collection. It is also recommended for academic libraries and special libraries addressing themselves to modern performance issues.

Theatre Crafts. See *Entertainment Design.*

Theatre History in Canada/Histoire du Theatre au Canada. See *Theatre Research in Canada.*

6412. *Theatre Journal (Baltimore).* Formerly (until 1979): *Educational Theatre Journal.* [ISSN: 0192-2882] 1949. q. USD 108 (Individuals, USD 35). Ed(s): David Roman, Harry J Elam, Jr. Johns Hopkins University Press, Journals Publishing Division, 2715 N Charles St, Baltimore, MD 21218-4363; http://www.press.jhu.edu/. Illus., adv. Sample. Refereed. Circ: 3327. Vol. ends: Dec. Microform: PQC. Online: EBSCO Publishing; Florida Center for Library Automation; Gale Group; OCLC Online Computer Library Center, Inc.; Project MUSE; ProQuest Information & Learning; RoweCom Information Quest; Swets Blackwell. Reprint: PQC; PSC. *Indexed:* AIAP, ArtHuCI, BAS, BRI, CBRI, CIJE, EduInd, HumInd, IIPA, MLA-IB. *Bk. rev.:* 8-12, 1,000-1,800 words. *Aud.:* Ac.

This is predominantly an academic journal, but the breadth of its articles and reviews would make it a staple in any public library collection addressing the needs of serious theatergoers/students. Each issue contains approximately six articles, a performance review section, and book reviews. The articles are substantial and refereed. They may cover topics from a social or historical point of view, or they may analyze text. Occasionally, the articles will be organized around a central theme. The performance review section contains analytical reviews of, for the most part, American theater productions (although some foreign productions do appear). Regional theaters and repertory company productions are well covered. *Theatre Journal* is currently available online as part of Johns Hopkins' Project Muse. As with most Project Muse titles, the text is easily accessed and read. Academic institutions may have subscriptions to individual titles.

6413. *Theatre Notebook: journal of the history and technique of the British theatre.* [ISSN: 0040-5523] 1946. 3x/yr. GBP 17; USD 34. Ed(s): Russell Jackson. Society for Theatre Research, c/o The Theatre Museum, 1E Tavistock St, London, WC2E 7PA, United Kingdom; http://www.unl.ac.uk/str. Illus., index, adv. Sample. Refereed. Circ: 1200. Vol. ends: Oct. *Indexed:* ArtHuCI, BHA, BrHumI, HumInd, IBZ, IIPA, MLA-IB. *Bk. rev.:* 4-8, 400-1,000 words. *Aud.:* Ac.

This journal, produced by the Society for Theatre Research, contains five to eight articles covering such topics as the history of particular productions, theater companies, actors, and theater/costume/playbill design. Its content is both lively and scholarly. It also includes a "Notes and Queries" section, obituaries, and book reviews. All university libraries, as well as smaller academic libraries supporting a drama history program, should consider this journal's purchase.

Theatre Quarterly. See *New Theatre Quarterly.*

6414. *Theatre Record.* Formerly (until 1991): *London Theatre Record.* [ISSN: 0962-1792] 1981. bi-w. GBP 120 domestic; GBP 150 rest of world; USD 300 rest of world. Ed(s): Ian Herbert. Theatre Record, 305 Whitton Dene, Isleworth, TW7 7NE, United Kingdom; editor@theatrerecord.demon.co.uk; http://www.theatrerecord.demon.co.uk. Illus., index, adv. Sample. *Indexed:* IIPA. *Aud.:* Ga, Ac.

Theatre Record reprints reviews of existing London theater productions and produces lists of upcoming productions. Like the *National Theatre Critics' Reviews* (above in this section), it makes for fascinating casual or serious reading for people interested in theater productions. Academic or public libraries with a serious theatergoing population might consider this journal's purchase, although its cost will probably limit it to only the largest library collections.

6415. *Theatre Research in Canada.* Formerly (until vol.13): *Theatre History in Canada.* [ISSN: 1196-1198] 1980. s-a. CND 32 (Individuals, CND 25; Students, CND 22). Ed(s): Bruce Barton. University of Toronto, Graduate Centre for Study of Drama, 214 College St, Toronto, ON M5T 2Z9, Canada; trican@chass.utoronto.ca. Illus. Refereed. Circ: 490. Microform: MML. *Indexed:* ArtHuCI, CBCARef, CPerI, IIPA, MLA-IB. *Bk. rev.:* 3-5, 1,000-1,500 words. *Aud.:* Ac.

Although the focus is on Canadian theater history, several of the four to six articles in each issue are on the theater traditions of other countries. The content of this journal is very interesting, and there seems to be a greater interdisciplinary and intellectual historical inclination than can be found in some other journals. The text is bilingual, and a substantial portion of the journal is in French. It also contains book reviews in both French and English. Any college or university with a serious theater history program should consider this title for purchase.

6416. *Theatre Research International.* Formerly: *Theatre Research.* [ISSN: 0307-8833] 1958. 3x/yr. USD 152 (Individuals, USD 45). Ed(s): Brian Singleton, Christopher Balme. Cambridge University Press, The Edinburgh Bldg, Shaftesbury Rd, Cambridge, CB2 2RU, United Kingdom; information@cambridge.org; http://uk.cambridge.org/journals. Illus., index, adv. Sample. Refereed. Circ: 1200. Microform: PQC. Online: Florida Center for Library Automation; Gale Group; Northern Light Technology, Inc.; OCLC Online Computer Library Center, Inc.; ProQuest Information & Learning; RoweCom Information Quest; Swets Blackwell. *Indexed:* AmH&L, ArtHuCI, BrHumI, HumInd, IBZ, IDP, IIPA, MLA-IB. *Bk. rev.:* 10-14, 600-1,000 words. *Aud.:* Ac.

Each issue contains four to seven articles covering the dramaturgy of a particular country and technical and historical studies of plays and performances. The journal is very international and broad in its coverage, although an issue may focus on a single country or region, such as "Theatre in Australia and New Zealand." Its book reviews are excellent and substantive. The cost of this journal will probably make its purchase prohibitive to all but university research collections.

6417. *Theatre Survey.* [ISSN: 0040-5574] 1956. s-a. USD 85. Ed(s): Rosemarie K Bank. Cambridge University Press, The Edinburgh Bldg, Shaftesbury Rd, Cambridge, CB2 2RU, United Kingdom; information@cambridge.org; http://uk.cambridge.org/journals. Illus., adv. Sample. Refereed. Circ: 860. Vol. ends: Nov. Microform: PQC. Online: bigchalk; Gale Group; Northern Light Technology, Inc.; OCLC Online Computer Library Center, Inc.; ProQuest Information & Learning; H.W. Wilson. *Indexed:* ABS&EES, AmH&L, ArtHuCI, HumInd, IDP, IIPA, MLA-IB, SSCI. *Bk. rev.:* 10-12, 1,000-1,400 words. *Aud.:* Ac.

This is a relatively small, but very interesting, journal. It is the organ of the American Society for Theatre Research, and as such, it contains scholarly performance studies. Recent changes in editorial policy have resulted in the inclusion of a broader number of geographic and subject areas. The four to six articles in each issue are not limited to drama but also include a variety of theatrical media, such as pageants and vaudeville. Each issue contains 10–12 substantive book reviews. In addition, there is often a very unusual and informative "Sources" section, which contains information about exhibits of theatrical materials, reports of theater archives, and notices of other interesting resources. University libraries and specialized theatrical collections should consider the purchase of this title.

6418. *Theatre Topics.* [ISSN: 1054-8378] 1991. 2x/yr. USD 58 (Individuals, USD 29). Ed(s): Stacy Wolf. Johns Hopkins University Press, Journals Publishing Division, 2715 N Charles St, Baltimore, MD 21218-4363; http://www.press.jhu.edu/. Illus., adv. Sample. Refereed. Circ: 2016. Vol. ends: Sep. Online: EBSCO Publishing; RoweCom Information Quest; Swets Blackwell. Reprint: PSC. *Indexed:* AmHI, BEL&L, EduInd, IIPA, MLA-IB. *Aud.:* Ac.

This journal is published by the Johns Hopkins University Press "in cooperation with the Association for Theatre in Higher Education." It contains about six articles in the areas of dramaturgy, performance, and theater pedagogy. *Theatre Topics* is directed more at the theater practitioner than the Johns Hopkins *Theatre Journal.* As a result, its articles are more practical and less historical and analytic in nature. The style and content are rigorous, however, and articles often contain references to further readings and resources. In all, it is an impressive publication. It would be useful in particular to university and collegiate drama teachers, directors, and students and, more generally, to thoughtful theatrical personnel everywhere. *Theatre Topics* is currently available online as part of Johns Hopkins' Project Muse. As with most Project Muse titles, the text is easily accessed and read. Academic institutions may have subscriptions to individual titles.

6419. *TheatreForum: international theatre journal.* [ISSN: 1060-5320] 1992. s-a. USD 35 (Individuals, USD 20; USD 7.50 newsstand/cover per issue). Ed(s): Jim Carmody, Theodore Shank. University of California at San Diego, Theatre Department, 9500 Gilman Dr, La Jolla, CA 92093-0344; theatreforum@ucsd.edu. Illus., adv. Sample. Circ: 1500 Paid and controlled. *Indexed:* IIPA, MLA-IB. *Aud.:* Ac.

This interesting, relatively new journal contains articles on international contemporary theater issues. Its international coverage is quite broad. Interestingly, its U.S. coverage has a distinct bias toward West Coast productions; this nicely balances it against other U.S. journals that are biased toward the New York theater scene. It also contains new play scripts, descriptions of companies, and occasional interviews. Two recent articles are titled "Songs from the Between: Wishhounds Theatre's Blue Sky Transmission, a Tibetan Book of the Dead" and "Between Longing and Despair: The Plays of Theresia Walser." This fascinating publication should be considered for any academic theater collection, particularly those of the western half of the United States.

6420. *Variety: the international entertainment weekly.* [ISSN: 0042-2738] 1905. 50x/yr. USD 259 domestic; USD 279 in Canada & Mexico; USD 359 in Europe. Ed(s): Peter Bart. Reed Business Information, 5700 Wilshire Blvd, Ste 120, Los Angeles, CA 90036; http://www.reedbusiness.com. Illus., adv. Sample. Circ: 35000. Microform: BHP; NRP. Online: EBSCO Publishing; Florida Center for Library Automation; Gale Group; LexisNexis; OCLC Online Computer Library Center, Inc.; ProQuest Information & Learning; H.W. Wilson. *Indexed:* BPI, FLI, IIFP, IIPA, LRI, MRD, MagInd, MusicInd. *Aud.:* Ga.

Known best by laypeople for its legendary language ("Celebs & films Czech in to Karlovy Vary " or "ABC shuffle strives for promo mojo "), *Variety* is, in show biz, the unofficial official journal. It contains extensive information on the business of entertainment, columns full of juicy insider tidbits, and reviews galore of films, TV, and theater. While its primary focus is on film and television, it does include some information on the business side of theater production. *Variety* is also available full-text online, free to print subscribers. Any large public library and any academic library should consider its purchase.

6421. *Western European Stages.* [ISSN: 1050-1991] 1989. 3x/yr. USD 15 domestic; USD 20 foreign. Ed(s): Marvin Carlson. Martin E. Segal Theatre Center, The Graduate School and University Center, The City University of New York, New York, NY 10016-4309; mestc@gc.cuny.edu; http://web.gc.edu.mestc. Illus., index. Sample. *Aud.:* Ac, Sa.

This wonderful and unique publication is a record of contemporary Western European theatrical performances. It is an apt substitute for a country-by-country collection of performance record publications, something that only the largest of academic libraries can support. It also contains interviews and articles on the theater scenes of particular countries or cities. Given its price and coverage, any academic or special library with an active performance community should consider its purchase.

Electronic Journals

6422. *AisleSay: the Internet magazine of stage reviews and opinion.* 1995. w. Ed(s): David Spencer. TheatreNet Enterprizes, 41 07 42nd St, Ste 4B, Long Island City, NY 11014; aislesay@aislesay.com; http://www.aislesay.com. *Bk. rev.:* 1-2, 400-800 words. *Aud.:* Ga.

This wonderful little publication includes reviews of theater productions from the United States. There is also some limited coverage of productions in Canada and Australia. The reviews are most similar to those found in newspapers or popular journals; they are concise, interesting, and timely. Most reviews are submitted during the first week of a play's run. Reviews are archived on secondary pages organized by city or country. *AisleSay* also contains reviews of performance-related recordings; these are concise and well done. The book review section is the least effective, not so much because of what the reviewers say about the books, but because the number of reviews is relatively small. The site also contains a group of "Special Features," a group of articles, conference reports, and interviews. These make fascinating reading, but unfortunately they are not dated. Any public library of substantial size should point to this site. Any academic library with a theatergoing constituency should also consider it.

6423. *CurtainUp: the Internet magazine of theater news, reviews and features.* 1997. 3x/w. Ed(s): Elyse Sommer. CurtainUp, PO Box 751133, Forest Hills, NY 11375; esommer@pipeline.com; http://www.curtainup.com. *Aud.:* Ga, Ac, Sa.

This is a wonderful source for reviews and information about current (and near-past) theatrical productions. Its richest areas are in the New York and Berkshires productions, reflecting the main editor's location. But there are several well-known contributing editors, so regular reports for productions in Toronto, London, and Washington, D.C., also appear. The site's organization is very navigable and user-friendly. There is also a subscription service through which individual readers will be notified of changes to the site. Any public or academic library with a theatergoing clientele should include this on its list of web sites.

6424. *London Theatre News.* [ISSN: 1064-0312] 1988. 10x/yr. USD 51 domestic; USD 70 foreign. Ed(s): Roger B Harris. London Theatre News, 12 E 86th St, New York, NY 10028. Adv. Circ: 2100 Paid. *Aud.:* Ga, Ac.

This well-maintained web site is an excellent place for quick lookups of London productions. Its editor, Darren Dalglish, both provides selections of reviews from other well-known sources and writes many reviews himself. There are many newsworthy bits about the London theater scene in general, as well as ticket sources, London maps, tours and walks, etc. While the material is not in-depth, it is an excellent and simple starting place for anyone looking for London theatrical performance information.

6425. *O O B R: The Off-Off-Broadway Review.* unknown. Free. Ed(s): John Chatterton. O O B R, c/o Judd Hollander, 341 W 24th St Ste 20F, New York, NY 10011; listings@oobr.com; http://www.oobr.com. *Aud.:* Ga, Sa.

This interesting e-journal collects both listing information and reviews for productions done off, far off, and out of(!) the mainstream theaters of New York. The site is a good one, in terms of both design and content. In keeping with more up-to-date design, it has few graphics, no frames, and loads easily and quickly—a relief after many of the image- and frame-heavy sites so common now. New York's centrality and importance to the American theater world will make this site of interest to any library with a serious theatergoing constituency.

6426. *Playbill On-Line.* 1994. d. Playbill Inc., 525 7th Ave., Rm. 1801, New York, NY 10018-4918; http://www.playbill.com. Adv. *Aud.:* Ga.

Anyone who has been in an American commercial theater is familiar with the *Playbill* program, which gives the cast, the number of acts, intermissions, and background on the play. In addition, it is chock-full of advertisements, usually of a local nature. The coverage in the web site is not dramatically different—except that it is all in one place, and therefore a very useful tool for planning for visits to NYC. There is some non–New York coverage, including a little international, but that coverage is spotty, and only the New York coverage can be depended on for completeness. There are also feature articles, gossip, a chat room, casting calls, and links to purchase tickets. A must for New York theatergoers, particularly for the up-to-date schedules.

■ TRANSPORTATION

See also Aeronautics and Space Science; Automobiles and Motorcycles; Marine Science and Technology; Safety; and Travel and Tourism sections.

Mary Kathleen Geary, Public Services Librarian, Transportation Library, Northwestern University Library, 1970 Sheridan Rd., Evanston, IL 60208-2300; m-geary@northwestern.edu

Introduction

Transportation is a vast topic encompassing many disciplines: science and technology, government regulation, sociology, economics, political science, demography, construction, environmentalism, geography, business, finance, and human resources. All of these major topics can be further subdivided by a variety of transportation modes: air transport, motor vehicles and drivers, railroading, trucking, logistics, pipelines, urban transport, water transport, and intermodal transport. The journals in this section have been selected for their ability to address one or more transportation topics or modalities; they represent expertise, professionalism, and the highest journalistic standards in the field.

Basic Periodicals

Ga: *Transportation Quarterly;* Ac: *Journal of Transport Economics and Policy, Journal of Transportation Engineering, Transportation Journal, Transportation Quarterly,* Transportation Research (various publications).

Basic Abstracts and Indexes

Engineering Index, Transport, TRISonline, TRANweb Compendex.

Accident Analysis & Prevention. See Safety section.

6427. *Air Cargo World: international trends and analysis.* Former titles (until 1982): *Air Cargo Magazine;* (until 1976): *Cargo Airlift; Air Transportation.* [ISSN: 0745-5100] 1910. m. USD 58 domestic; USD 78 foreign. Air Cargo World, 980 Canton St., # 1-D, Roswell, GA 30075-7207. Illus., index, adv. Circ: 21080 Controlled. Vol. ends: Dec. Microform: PQC. Online: Florida Center for Library Automation; Gale Group; Northern Light Technology, Inc.; OCLC Online Computer Library Center, Inc.; ProQuest Information & Learning; H.W. Wilson. Reprint: PQC. *Indexed:* LogistBibl. *Bk. rev.:* Occasional. *Aud.:* Sa.

This trade journal provides coverage of cargo services, carriers, facilities, equipment, and industry trends throughout the world. Regular features include articles, columns surveying news from regions around the world, updates on people in the industry, at-a-glance industry statistical indicators, and upcoming events. Annually, special directories are published for cargo carriers, express delivery companies, cargo aircraft, and freight forwarders. The web site contains these directories as well as the full text of selected articles at http://aircargoworld.com.

Air Transport World. See Aeronautics and Space Science section.

6428. *Airfinance Journal.* [ISSN: 0143-2257] 1980. 11x/yr. GBP 525 combined subscription domestic includes online access; EUR 852 combined subscription in Europe includes online access; USD 795 combined subscription elsewhere includes online access. Ed(s): Doug Cameron. Euromoney Institutional Investor plc., Nestor House, Playhouse Yard, London, EC4V 5EX, United Kingdom; http://www.euromoney.com. Adv. Circ: 2920 Paid. Online: Florida Center for Library Automation; Gale Group; OCLC Online Computer Library Center, Inc.; ProQuest Information & Learning; H.W. Wilson. *Indexed:* ABIn, B&I, BPI. *Aud.:* Sa.

This trade journal is geared toward both the practitioner and the researcher in the area of air transportation. It includes feature articles, industry news, and important industry statistical tables; its coverage is international. A password is required to access the journal electronicaly at http://www.airfinancejournal.com/contents/publications/afj. Appropriate for large, general collections and special collections

6429. ***Airline Business: the voice of airline managements.*** [ISSN: 0268-7615] 1985. m. GBP 80; USD 130; EUR 130. Ed(s): Kevin O'Toole, Colin Baker. Reed Business Information Ltd., Quadrant House, The Quadrant, Brighton Rd, Sutton, SM2 5AS, United Kingdom; http://www.reedbusiness.co.uk/. Illus., adv. Circ: 31000. Vol. ends: Dec. Online: Data-Star; EBSCO Publishing; Factiva; Florida Center for Library Automation; Gale Group; LexisNexis; OCLC Online Computer Library Center, Inc.; ProQuest Information & Learning; Reuters Business Briefing; H.W. Wilson. *Indexed:* B&I, C&ISA. *Aud.:* Sa.

This trade journal provides worldwide coverage of business affairs in all aspects of the airline industry. Topics include developments in regions of the world as well as in specific countries, analysis of policy changes, people who impact the industry, and financing issues. Regular features include commentary, news digests, events calendars, and new appointments. Annual features include the "Airline Business 100" and "Airports Review." The primary audience is airline managers. The web site offers brief synopses of feature articles and can be accessed at http://www.airlinebusiness.com with a password. Appropriate for special collections.

6430. ***Airline Monitor: a review of trends in the airline and commercial jet aircraft industries.*** USD 950; USD 1150 combined subscription print & online eds. Ed(s): Edmund S Greanslet. E S G Aviation Services, 636 Third St South, Jacksonville Beach, FL 32250; theairlinemonitor@mac.com; http://www.airlinemonitor.com. *Aud.:* Ac, Sa.

Published by ESG Aviation Services, this periodical is a unique and thorough source of statistical and financial information on the domestic air transportation industry, including forecasting. It is geared toward the professional and the researcher. Each issue includes an executive summary followed by tables of data current within a month. A password is required to access the periodical's online version at http://www.airlinemonitor.com. Appropriate for academic or special libraries.

6431. ***Airliners: the world's airline magazine.*** [ISSN: 0896-6575] 1988. bi-m. USD 24.95 domestic; USD 35.95 newsstand/cover per issue foreign; USD 5.50 newsstand/cover per issue domestic. Ed(s): Jon Proctor. World Transport Press, 1200 NW 72nd Ave, Miami, FL 33126. Illus., adv. Circ: 45000 Paid. Vol. ends: Nov/Dec. *Bk. rev.:* 4–8, 200–400 words, signed. *Aud.:* Ga.

Targeting the commercial airline enthusiast, this publication offers detailed coverage of international, national, and local airlines, including industry news and events, local special-interest stories, book reviews, and some statistical information. Airplane modeling and collecting are occasionally featured. It includes color photography and elaborate layouts. The journal can be accessed at http://www.airlinersonline.com, password required. Appropriate for general collections

6432. ***Airlines International.*** [ISSN: 1360-6387] 1995. bi-m. Members, GBP 90; Non-members, GBP 120. Ed(s): Russell Stevens. Insight Media Ltd., 26-30 London Rd, Twickenham, TW1 3RR, United Kingdom; email@insightgrp.co.uk. Illus., adv. Circ: 10000 Controlled. Vol. ends: Nov/Dec. *Aud.:* Sa.

This journal covers the international commercial airline industry, emphasizing airline management, economics, current industry events, and some statistical information. Published for International Aviation Transport Association (IATA) members, it is aimed at specialists and includes an IATA calendar of events, an "Inside IATA" section, and an archived feature-article index. Appropriate for special collections.

6433. ***Airport Magazine.*** [ISSN: 1048-2091] 1989. bi-m. USD 35 domestic; USD 50 foreign. American Association of Airport Executives, 601 Madison St, Ste 400, Alexandria, VA 22314; ellen.horton@airportnet.org; http://www.airportnet.org. Illus., index, adv. Circ: 7000. Vol. ends: Nov/Dec. *Aud.:* Sa.

This publication of the American Association of Airport Executives is for specialists, addressing airport management, legislation, technology, research reports, economics, and current industry events. It features airport traffic and on-time statistics as well as requests for proposals. The electronic version of this journal can be accessed at http://www.airportnet.org/depts/publications/amhmpg.htm. Appropriate for special collections.

6434. ***Airport World.*** [ISSN: 1360-4341] 1996. bi-m. Members, USD 150; Non-members, USD 200. Ed(s): Charles Tyler. Insight Media Ltd., 26-30 London Rd, Twickenham, TW1 3RR, United Kingdom. Illus., adv. Circ: 8000. *Aud.:* Sa.

Published for the Airports Council International, this journal addresses global airport issues. Geared to the practitioner, it covers industry news and events, technology, safety, automation, the environment, legislation, regulation, airport planning and maintenance, management, and finance. Each issue includes feature articles, a calendar of events, airport traffic data and other statistics, project briefs, a section highlighting a specific airport, and a global airport news section. The annotated tables of contents for current and past issues can be accessed at http://www.insightgrp.co.uk/aw.html. Appropriate for special collections.

6435. ***Airports International Magazine.*** Former titles (until 1971): *Airports International Directory; Airports International.* 1968. 9x/yr. USD 175; USD 19 newsstand/cover per issue. Ed(s): Tom Allett. Key Publishing Ltd., PO Box 100, Stamford, PE9 1XQ, United Kingdom; ann.saundry@keypublishing.com; http://www.keypublishing.com. Adv. Sample. Circ: 13962. Online: Gale Group. *Indexed:* B&I. *Aud.:* Ga, Sa.

This publication is international in coverage. Although geared to the specialist, it will have some appeal to the enthusiast. It addresses current airport trends, news and events, economics, and technology, and it features local and human interest stories. Abstracts of current feature articles are available at http://www.airportsinternational.co.uk. A large, inclusive general collection may be interested in this title; otherwise, it is appropriate for special collections.

6436. ***American Shipper: ports, transportation and industry.*** Former titles (until 1991): *American Shipper Magazine;* (until 1976): *Florida Journal of Commerce - American Shipper;* (until 1974): *Florida Journal of Commerce.* [ISSN: 1074-8350] 1959. m. USD 120 in North America; USD 240 elsewhere. Ed(s): David A Howard. Howard Publications, 300 W Adams St, Ste 600, Jacksonville, FL 32201. Illus., adv. Circ: 13000. Vol. ends: Dec. Microform: PQC. Online: Gale Group; Northern Light Technology, Inc. Reprint: PQC. *Indexed:* BPI, H&SSA, LogistBibl, OceAb, PAIS, PollutAb, SWRA. *Aud.:* Sa.

This trade journal targets the practitioner. It is international in coverage, with an emphasis on domestic logistics. Each issue addresses six subjects of interest: logistics, forwarding, integrated transport, ocean transport, land transport, and ports. There are also sections on shippers' case law and corporate appointments. A password is required to access the online version of this journal at http://www.americanshipper.com. Appropriate for special libraries.

Aviation Week and Space Technology. See Aeronautics and Space Science section.

6437. ***Aviation Week's Business and Commercial Aviation.*** Formerly (until 2000): *Business and Commercial Aviation.* [ISSN: 1538-7267] 1958. m. USD 52 domestic; USD 58 in Canada & Mexico; USD 79 elsewhere. McGraw-Hill Companies, Inc., 1221 Ave of the Americas, New York, NY 10020; http://www.mcgraw-hill.com/. Illus., adv. Circ: 52000. Microform: PQC. Online: The Dialog Corporation; Gale Group. *Indexed:* AS&TI, EngInd, LRI. *Aud.:* Sa.

This trade journal targets the practitioner and addresses the commercial aviation industry with a decided emphasis on business flying. Its coverage is international. Each issue includes industry news and events, feature articles, statistics, commentary, product reviews, classifieds, a resale marketplace, and a section devoted to the causes of accidents. Selected feature articles can be accessed at http://www.aviationnow.com/avnow/news/channel_bca.jsp?view=top. Appropriate for special libraries.

6438. ***Better Roads.*** [ISSN: 0006-0208] 1931. m. USD 95 foreign (Free to qualified personnel). James Informational Media, Inc., 2720 S. River Rd., Ste. 126, Des Plaines, IL 60018; kirk@jiminc.com; http://www.jiminc.com. Illus., adv. Circ: Controlled. Vol. ends: Dec. *Indexed:* C&ISA, EngInd, EnvAb. *Bk. rev.:* Number and length vary. *Aud.:* Sa.

Published by James Informational Media for specialists in the fields of road construction, maintenance, and repair, this journal includes industry news, government contract information, book and video reviews, product ratings and reviews, a calendar of industry events, and a forum for letters and professional comment, along with technically rich feature articles. The December issue contains a pull-out calendar of industry events for the entire year. Archived articles can be accessed at http://www.betterroads.com. Appropriate for engineering and transportation collections.

6439. ***Bridge Design & Engineering: the definitive publication for bridge professionals worldwide.*** [ISSN: 1359-7493] 1995. q. GBP 200; USD 330. Ed(s): Helena Russell. Hemming Group Ltd., 32 Vauxhall Bridge Rd, London, SW1V 2SS, United Kingdom; http://www.hemming-group.co.uk/page.asp?partID=1. Illus., adv. Circ: 6000 Controlled. *Bk. rev.:* 2–4, 150–250 words. *Aud.:* Ac, Sa.

This journal targets the practitioner. It is international in coverage and addresses bridge aesthetics, design, construction, and management It includes industry news, product information, a calendar of events, and listings of conferences and competitions. The online version can be accessed at http://www.bridgeweb.com, but a subscription is required for full content. Appropriate for special libraries.

6440. ***Bus Ride.*** [ISSN: 0192-8902] 1965. 10x/yr. USD 35 domestic; USD 39 Canada; USD 44 elsewhere. Ed(s): Karen Crabtree, Bruce Sankey. Friendship Publications, Inc, 1550 E Missouri Ave, Ste 100, Phoenix, AZ 85014-2455. Illus., adv. Circ: 13500. Vol. ends: Dec. *Aud.:* Sa.

This journal addresses the passenger bus industries of the United States and Canada and is meant for bus and transit specialists. It includes current industry news and events, legislative and regulatory information, product reviews, feature articles, and a report on the European passenger bus industry. The current issue of the journal's online version can be accessed at http://www.bridgeweb.com. Appropriate for special collections.

6441. ***Cargo Systems.*** Former titles (until 1994): *Cargo Systems International.* [ISSN: 1362-766X] 1973. m. GBP 175 in UK; GBP 230 in Europe; USD 368 in North America. Ed(s): Julian Pryke. Informa Group PLC, 69-77 Paul St, London, EC2A 4LQ, United Kingdom; http://www.cargosystems.net. Illus., adv. Circ: 7500. Vol. ends: Dec. *Indexed:* EngInd, ExcerpMed. *Aud.:* Sa.

Worldwide coverage of containerized and noncontainerized cargo-handling systems is the focus of this magazine. The news and feature sections concentrate on shipping and port issues, economic factors, industry progress and updates, intermodal issues, safety, and new products and equipment. The magazine issues frequent supplements on special topics like terminal operations, reefer systems, and privatization. Special reports issued by this journal can be accessed at http://www.informamaritime.com/lpp802. Appropriate for special libraries.

6442. ***Commercial Carrier Journal for Professional Fleet Managers.*** Former titles (until 1998): *Chilton's Commercial Carrier Journal for Professional Fleet Managers;* (until 1990): *Commercial Carrier Journal for Professional Fleet Managers;* (until 1989): *Chilton's C C J;* (until 1984): *Chilton's Commercial Carrier Journal;* (until 1982): *Chilton's C C J;* (until 1977): *Commercial Car Journal.* [ISSN: 1099-4173] 1911. m. USD 48 domestic; USD 78 Canada; USD 86 elsewhere. Randall Publishing Company, 3200 Rice Mine Road, N E, Tuscaloosa, AL 35406; http://www.randallpub.com. Illus., index, adv. Circ: 87000 Controlled. Vol. ends: Dec. Microform: CIS; PQC. Online: EBSCO Publishing; Gale Group; OCLC Online Computer Library Center, Inc. Reprint: PQC. *Indexed:* B&I, PAIS. *Aud.:* Sa.

As one of the important trade journals in the truck fleet management industry, this publication contains articles on operations, equipment maintenance, management, regulation, and safety. Regular features include road tests of vehicles, industry news, events and editorials, and a classified section. Annually, the magazine reports on the "Top 100" U.S. truck lines and provides a range of buyer's guides on truck equipment, fleet products and services, and information technology. The current month, archived cover stories, and the Top 100 list can be accessed at http://www.etrucker.com/default.asp?magid=3. Appropriate for special libraries

6443. ***Community Transportation Reporter: the magazine of community transit industry.*** Formerly (until Jun. 1987): *Rural Transportation Reporter.* [ISSN: 0895-4437] 1984. 9x/yr. USD 35. Ed(s): Barbara Rasin Price. Community Transportation Association of America, 1341 G St. NW, Ste 600, Washington, DC 20005. Illus., index, adv. Circ: 10000 Controlled. Vol. ends: Nov/Dec. *Bk. rev.:* Number and length vary. *Aud.:* Ga,Sa.

Published by the Community Transportation Association of America, this journal addresses all forms of community transportation, bus, rail, and paratransit. Geared toward the specialist, it would be of use to interested community members. It includes current industry news and events, legislation and regulatory matters, available resources, and feature articles. A substantial annual book review section is published in the July/August issue. The current issue and backlog can be accessed at http://www.ctaa.org/ct. Appropriate for large, inclusive general collections and special collections.

Commuter World. See *Regional Airline World.*

6444. ***Containerisation International.*** [ISSN: 0010-7379] 1967. m. GBP 115 in UK; GBP 160 in Europe; USD 343 in North America. Ed(s): Jane Degerlund. Informa Publishing, 69-77 Paul St, London, EC2A 4IQ, United Kingdom. Illus., adv. Circ: 11000. Vol. ends: Dec. Reprint: PQC. *Aud.:* Ac, Sa.

This publication covers worldwide business, management, and policy issues for a variety of transportation modes, but with an emphasis on shipping and ports. The feature articles cover specific carriers; analysis of some aspect of the industry; issues for carriers, shippers, and terminals; regional coverage; and regulatory analysis. Each issue contains updates on business, the world fleet, charters, shippers, and news on intermodal transport, terminals, information technology, and statistics on key industry indicators. The web site offers late-breaking news at http://www.ci-online.co.uk. Appropriate for special collections.

Distribution. See *Logistics Management.*

6445. ***Fairplay: the international shipping weekly.*** Former titles (until 1989): *Fairplay International Shipping Weekly; Fairplay International Shipping Journal.* [ISSN: 0960-6165] 1883. w. GBP 280 in Europe; USD 465 United States; GBP 360 elsewhere. Ed(s): John Prime. Fairplay Publications Ltd., PO Box 96, Coulsdon, CR5 2TE, United Kingdom; http://www.fairplay.co.uk. Illus., adv. Circ: 4379 Paid. Vol. ends: Apr/Dec. *Bk. rev.:* Number and length vary. *Aud.:* Sa.

This journal is devoted to the international shipping industry and covers industry news and events including shipbuilding and port news, legislation, regulation, safety, labor and management issues, liner operations, ship sales, and cargo information. Feature articles tend to be brief news flashes, except for the cover story. In addition to international coverage, each issue highlights the shipping industry within a specific nation or region. Alternate issues include book reviews. The section on the shipping market includes graphs, tables, and statistics. The online version of the journal can be accessed at http://www.fairplay.co.uk. Appropriate for a large business collection or a transportation collection.

6446. ***Fleet Owner.*** Formerly: *Fleet Owner: Big Fleet Edition;* Superseded in part: *Fleet Owner.* [ISSN: 1070-194X] 1928. m. USD 45 domestic; USD 60 Canada; USD 80 elsewhere. Ed(s): Jim Mele. Primedia Business Magazines & Media, Inc., 11 River Bend Dr S, Box 4949, Stamford, CT 06907-0949; inquiries@primediabusiness.com; http://www.primediabusiness.com. Illus., adv. Circ: 103014 Controlled. Vol. ends: Dec. Microform: PQC. Online: Gale Group. Reprint: PQC. *Indexed:* ABIn, BPI, ChemAb, EngInd. *Aud.:* Sa.

This journal targets the specialist and addresses the public and private sectors of truck fleet management. Coverage includes fleet management industry news and events, equipment, management, information technology, legislation, safety, and product analysis. It devotes significant attention to e-commerce and web resources. The defunct journal *Business Trucking* has arranged for occasional column space in *Fleet Owner.* The online version of this journal can be accessed at http://fleetowner.com/ar/fleet_car_story/index.htm. Appropriate for special collections.

Flight International. See Aeronautics and Space Science section.

6447. ***Great Lakes Seaway Log: the international transportation magazine of midcontinent North America.*** Former titles: *Great Lakes Seaway Review; Seaway Review;* Which incorporates (1968-1977): *Limnos.* 1972. bi-w. USD 32 domestic; USD 42 Canada. Ed(s): David L Knight. Harbor House Publishers, Inc., 221 Water St, Boyne City, MI 49712-1244; harbor@harborhouse.com. Illus., adv. Circ: 1200 Paid and controlled. Vol. ends: Apr/Jun. Microform: PQC. *Indexed:* GeoRef. *Aud.:* Ga,Sa.

Addresses commercial shipping and the maritime industries throughout the Great Lakes and St. Lawrence Seaway areas. Coverage includes shipping industry news and events, legislation and regulation, technology, naval architecture and engineering, ports, import/export, fleet data, and feature articles. Each issue highlights a specific port. The "Shipyard Report" section is a unique feature: Broken down by marine repair or shipbuilding company, it supplies the name of the vessel, owner, nature of work being done, and anticipated date of completion. An index to past issues can be accessed at http://www.greatlakes-seawayreview.com. Appropriate for a large general collection interested in the Great Lakes or a special collection.

6448. ***Heavy Duty Trucking: the business magazine of trucking.*** [ISSN: 0017-9434] 1968. m. USD 65 domestic; USD 130 foreign. Ed(s): Bill Tracy, Andrew Ryder. Newport Communications (Irvine), 38 Executive Pk, Ste 300, Irvine, CA 92614; aryder@truckinginfo.com; http://www.truckinginfo.com. Illus., adv. Circ: 100500 Controlled. Vol. ends: Dec. *Aud.:* Sa.

This journal is published by the Newport Communications Group expressly for fleet owners operating trucks within classes seven and eight (26,000 pounds gross vehicle weight). It covers the heavy trucking fleet industry, including industry news and events, legislation, safety, technology, and equipment. Statistics, including tables and graphs, are provided on diesel fuel costs, by state; truck sales by manufacturer; and trucking trends. Buyer's guides, offered several times annually, are a significant supplement to the journal. Now available online at http://www.heavydutytrucking.com/library.asp. Appropriate for special collections

6449. ***I E E E Transactions on Intelligent Transportation Systems.*** [ISSN: 1524-9050] 2000. q. USD 370 in North America; USD 405 elsewhere. Ed(s): Chelsea C White, III. Institute of Electrical and Electronics Engineers, Inc., 445 Hoes Ln, Piscataway, NJ 08854-1331; subscription-service@ieee.org; http://www.ieee.org. Refereed. *Aud.:* Ac, Sa.

This scholarly publication focuses on the application of information technology to systems across all modes of transportation. Some of the topics it considers include (but are not limited to) communications, sensors, man–machine interfaces, decision systems, controls, simulation, reliability, and standards. Frequently, issues of the journal focus on a specific subject. The online version of this journal can be accessed at http://ieeexplore.ieee.org/Xplore/DynWel.jsp. Appropriate for special collections.

6450. ***I T E Journal.*** Former titles: *Transportation Engineering;* (1933-1977): *Traffic Engineering.* [ISSN: 0162-8178] 1930. m. USD 60 in North America; USD 80 elsewhere. Ed(s): Linda S Streaker. Institute of Transportation Engineers, 1099 14th St., NW, Ste 300 West, Washington, DC 20005-3438; lstreaker@ite.org; http://www.ite.org/. Illus., adv. Refereed. Circ: 15000 Paid and controlled. Vol. ends: Dec. Microform: PQC. Online: OCLC Online Computer Library Center, Inc.; ProQuest Information & Learning; H.W. Wilson. Reprint: PQC. *Indexed:* ABIn, AS&TI, C&ISA, EngInd, EnvAb, ExcerpMed, PAIS, PetrolAb, SSCI, SUSA. *Bk. rev.:* Occasional, up to 250 words. *Aud.:* Ac, Sa.

Written by and for transportation engineers and planners, this refereed journal thoroughly covers the field of surface transportation. It focuses largely on North America, particularly the United States, but occasionally includes features from other parts of the world. Regular features include news on people, projects, places, and research as well as resources available; a calendar of events and meetings; and positions available. The web site offers a searchable index back to 1950 and, for members, full-text articles back to 1970 at http://www.ite.org/itejournal/index.asp. Appropriate for special collections.

6451. ***I T S International: advanced technology for traffic management and urban mobility.*** Formerly: *I T S - Intelligent Transport Systems.* [ISSN: 1463-6344] 1995. 6x/yr. GBP 100; USD 165. Ed(s): David Crawford. Route One Publishing Ltd., Horizon House, Azalea Dr, Swanley, BR8 8JR, United Kingdom; subs@routeonepub.com; http://www.routeonepub.com. Illus., adv. Sample. Circ: 21421. *Aud.:* Sa.

This journal addresses the specialist in the international intelligent transportation systems (ITS) industry. Its coverage includes ITS industry news and events, technology, product analysis and review, and feature articles on highlighted ITS issues, such as telematics, tolling systems, or multi-modal systems Each issue includes a focus on the ITS industry within a specific geographic area, a current-events section, and a listing of appointments and promotions within the field. Feature articles from the annual buyer's guide as well as the full texts of opinion articles can be found online at http://www.itsinternational.com/mag/index.htm. Appropriate for engineering and transportation collections.

6452. ***Inbound Logistics: for today's business logistics managers.*** Former titles (until July 1985): *Inbound Traffic Guide; Thomas Register's Inbound Traffic Guide.* [ISSN: 0888-8493] 1981. 12x/yr. Ed(s): Felecia J Stratton. Thomas Publishing Company, Five Penn Plaza, New York, NY 10001. Illus., adv. Circ: 52000. Vol. ends: Dec. *Indexed:* LogistBibl. *Aud.:* Sa.

Geared to the specialist, this journal addresses the international logistics industry. Coverage includes logistics industry news and events, technology, business management, personnel management, legislation, and feature articles; a strong emphasis is placed on e-commerce and information technology. Special sections address logistics in the Americas, the Pacific community, and the European Community. A voluminous supplementary, "Logistics Planner," is published in January. Each issue includes a calendar of logistics industry events and a section devoted to evaluating logistics-oriented web sites. The online version can be accessed at http://www.inboundlogistics.com/magazine/index.shtml. Appropriate for special collections.

Interavia. See Aeronautics and Space Science section.

6453. ***Intermodal Business.*** Formerly: *Intermodal Week.* 1996. w. Energy Argus, Inc., 129 Washington St, Ste 400, Hoboken, NJ 07030; info@energyargus.com; http://www.energyargus.com. *Aud.:* Sa.

This biweekly publication addresses the international intermodal transportation industry, with an emphasis on containerization. It is geared to the practitioner. Coverage includes industry news and events, legislation, technology, intermodal projects, and statistics. Each issue includes an in-depth interview with an industry representative, news articles, news analysis, and conference notices. Archived articles can be accessed at http://www.energyargus.com. Appropriate for special libraries.

6454. ***International Journal of Automotive Technology and Management.*** [ISSN: 1470-9511] 2001. 4x/yr. USD 430; USD 520 combined subscription for print & online eds. Ed(s): Dr. M A Dorgham. Inderscience

Enterprises Ltd., IEL Editorial Office, PO Box 735, Olney, MK46 5WB, United Kingdom; http://www.inderscience.com. Sample. Refereed. *Indexed:* C&ISA. *Bk. rev.:* Various number and length. *Aud.:* Ac, Sa.

This is a refereed scholarly journal targeting the academician. It addresses all aspects of international automotive technology and management, including product development, research, innovative management, e-commerce, supply chain management, reengineering, efficiency, safety, investment and business, and human resources. Each issue contains referenced articles, charts, graphs, statistics, calls for papers, and a complete index. Some issues contain book reviews. The table of contents, with abstracts, can be accessed at http://www.inderscience.com/ejournal/a/ijatm/ijatmabsindex.html. Appropriate for large academic libraries or special collections

6455. *International Journal of Logistics: research and applications.* [ISSN: 1367-5567] 1998. q. GBP 255 (Individuals, GBP 69). Ed(s): Peter Hines. Carfax Publishing Ltd., 4 Park Sq, Milton Park, Abingdon, OX14 4RN, United Kingdom; enquiry@tandf.co.uk; http://www.tandf.co.uk/. Illus. Sample. Refereed. Vol. ends: Nov. Reprint: PSC. *Indexed:* IBZ. *Bk. rev.:* Various number and length. *Aud.:* Ac, Sa.

This scholarly journal addresses all aspects of the international logistics industry, including intermodal transportation, warehousing, and supply chain management; it is of interest to both the academician and the practitioner. Each issue includes long, researched articles with references, graphs, tables, and charts. There is also a book review section. The journal can be accessed online at http://www.tandf.co.uk/journals/carfax/13675567.html. Appropriate for special collections.

6456. *International Journal of Transport Economics.* [ISSN: 0391-8440] 1974. q. USD 150 print & online eds. (Individuals, EUR 110). Ed(s): Gianrocco Tucci. Istituti Editoriali e Poligrafici Internazionali, Via Giosue' Carducci, 60, Ghezzano La Fontina, 56010, Italy; iepi@iepi.it; http://www.iepi.it. Illus., index, adv. Refereed. Circ: 1000. Vol. ends: Oct. *Indexed:* IBSS, JEL, PAIS. *Bk. rev.:* 7–12, 100–350 words. *Aud.:* Ac, Sa.

This journal, published in Italy but with a worldwide focus, brings together current research in transport economics, marrying theoretical and applied approaches to the subject. Occasional special issues are devoted to a single topic. The editorial board and the authors of the articles come from around the world. The journal is published in English, with some supporting information also included in Italian. In addition to featuring contributed scholarly articles, the journal also features a review article that extends the theoretical discussion to the practical realm. This journal's web site is http://www.libraweb.net/dettagli/INTERNATIONAL%20JOURNAL%20TRANSPORT.htm. Appropriate for special collections.

6457. *International Railway Journal: the first international railway and rapid transit journal.* Former titles (until 1993): *International Railway Journal and Rapid Transit Review;* (until 1979): *International Railway Journal.* 1960. m. USD 72. Ed(s): Mike Knutton. Simmons - Boardman Publishing Corp., 345 Hudson St, 12th floor, New York, NY 10014-4502. Illus., index, adv. Circ: 9101. Vol. ends: Dec. Microform: PQC. Online: Gale Group. Reprint: PQC. *Indexed:* ExcerpMed. *Aud.:* Ac, Sa.

This journal covers the international light-track and heavy-track railroad industries; it is the international version of its sister periodicals for North America, *Railway Age* and *Railway Track and Structures*. Each issue is divided between a section on heavy-rail and a section on light-rail, intra-urban, and interurban rapid transit. These sections include industry news and events, world market reports, feature articles, a list of conferences and seminars, a product showcase, and a list of relevant web sites. Maps of the referenced rail lines are often included in feature articles. The subscription includes an annual supplement, *World Railway Investment*, offering financial data and statistics. The journal can be accessed online at http://www.railjournal.com. Of interest to both the academician and the practitioner, this journal is appropriate for large academic collections and special collections.

6458. *Jane's Airport Review: the global airport business magazine.* [ISSN: 0954-7649] 1989. 10x/yr. GBP 120 United Kingdom; GBP 125 in Europe; USD 190 in the Americas. Jane's Information Group, Sentinel House, 163 Brighton Rd, Coulsdon, CR5 2YH, United Kingdom; info@janes.co.uk; http://www.janes.com. Illus. Vol. ends: Nov/Dec. Online: Gale Group. *Aud.:* Sa.

This journal covers airport business, addressing market intelligence and strategic planning. Its audience is airport management professionals. Coverage is international. Regular features include sections on news, air traffic control, terminal and ground support equipment, and interviews with leading professionals. The journal's online version can be accessed at http://jar.janes.com. Appropriate for special libraries.

6459. *Journal of Advanced Transportation.* Formerly (until vol.12, 1979): *High Speed Ground Transportation Journal.* [ISSN: 0197-6729] 1967. 3x/yr. USD 145. Ed(s): S C Wirasinghe. Institute for Transportation, Inc., #305, 4625 Varsity Dr N W, Ste 68, Calgary, AB T3A 0Z9, Canada. Illus., index. Refereed. Circ: 300 Paid. Vol. ends: Winter. Microform: MIM; PQC. Reprint: PQC. *Indexed:* ApMecR, C&ISA, EngInd, H&SSA, PRA, SUSA. *Bk. rev.:* Occasional. *Aud.:* Ac, Sa.

This scholarly journal, sponsored by the Advanced Transit Association, covers all modes of transportation. The focus is on the engineering and technology behind the analysis, design, economics, operations, and planning of transportation systems. Although the focus of the journal has broadened over the past several years, the editors maintain a special interest in advanced urban rail transit systems. Occasionally, issues focus on a special topic and may include review articles that provide an overall survey of an aspect of the field. The web site features a searchable index of issues back to 1990. The journal's online version can be accessed at http://www.advanced-transport.com. Appropriate for special collections.

6460. *Journal of Air Law and Commerce.* [ISSN: 0021-8642] 1930. q. USD 37 domestic; USD 44 foreign. Ed(s): Zach Garsek. S M U Law Review Association, Southern Methodist University, School of Law, Dallas, TX 75275. Illus., index, adv. Refereed. Circ: 2000. Vol. ends: Fall. Microform: WSH; PMC; PQC. Online: Gale Group; LexisNexis; OCLC Online Computer Library Center, Inc.; West Group; H.W. Wilson. Reprint: PQC; WSH. *Indexed:* CLI, H&SSA, IAA, ILP, LRI, PAIS. *Bk. rev.:* Occasional. *Aud.:* Ac, Sa.

This scholarly publication covers the legal and economic aspects of aviation and space. The journal is managed by a student board of editors in association with the *Southern Methodist University* (SMU) *Law Review.* The issues include comprehensive articles, a review of current-interest topics, coverage of the SMU Air Law Symposium, student comments, case notes, recent decisions, book reviews, and bibliographies of current literature in the industry. Articles are written by lawyers, economists, government officials, and scholars. The journal's online presence can be accessed at http://www.smu.edu/lra/jalc. Appropriate for specialized collections.

6461. *Journal of Air Transport Management.* [ISSN: 0969-6997] 1994. 6x/yr. EUR 511 (Individuals, EUR 126). Ed(s): K Button, S Morrison. Pergamon, The Boulevard, Langford Ln, East Park, Kidlington, OX5 1GB, United Kingdom. Illus., index, adv. Refereed. Vol. ends: No. 4. Microform: PQC. Online: ingenta.com; ScienceDirect. *Bk. rev.:* Occasional. Number and length vary. *Aud.:* Ac, Sa.

Published by Elsevier Science, this journal is of interest to both the academician and the practitioner. It addresses theory and application relative to all aspects of the international air transportation industry, including airlines, infrastructure, airports, traffic control, and management. Each issue consists of lengthy research articles that include graphs, tables, statistics, and detailed references. Some issues offer a book review section. The journal can be accessed online by subscribers at http://www.elsevier.com/locate/jairtraman. Appropriate to special collections.

6462. ***Journal of Air Transportation.*** Formerly: *Journal of Air Transportation World Wide.* [ISSN: 1544-6980] 1996. s-a. USD 68 (Individuals, USD 35). Ed(s): Brent Bowen. University of Nebraska at Omaha, Aviation Institute, Allwie Hall, Rm 422, 600 Dodge St, Omaha, NE 68182-0508. Refereed. Circ: 300. *Indexed:* CIJE. *Bk. rev.:* Occasional. *Aud.:* Ac, Sa.

This scholarly journal addresses all major aspects of air transportation: aviation management and administration, intermodal transportation, airports, air traffic control, aviation, avionics, and space transportation. It is geared to the academician and the specialist. Each issue contains long, researched articles with graphs, tables, charts, and detailed references. This journal's online presence can be accessed at http://www.unomaha.edu/~jatww/index.html. Appropriate for special collections.

6463. ***Journal of Maritime Law and Commerce.*** [ISSN: 0022-2410] 1969. q. USD 245 (Individuals, USD 195). Ed(s): John Paul Jones. Jefferson Law Book Co., 2100 Huntingdon Ave, Baltimore, MD 21211; jefflaw1@juno.com; http://www.jmlc.org. Illus., index, adv. Refereed. Circ: 2500 Paid. Vol. ends: Oct. Reprint: PQC; WSH. *Indexed:* CLI, DSR&OA, ILP, LRI, PAIS, SSCI. *Bk. rev.:* 1-25, 500-2,500 words, signed. *Aud.:* Ac, Sa.

This scholarly journal is dedicated to coverage of all aspects of admiralty and maritime law. It targets the professional and the academician. Its contents concentrate on topics of current interest, but the editorial board will also include historical or theoretical treatments of the field. Special issues on single topics are often published. It is possible to occasionally find case analyses, review articles, and bibliographies. This journal's online presence can be accessed at http://www.jmlc.org. Appropriate for special collections.

6464. ***Journal of Public Transportation.*** [ISSN: 1077-291X] 1997. q. Ed(s): Gary L Brosch. University of South Florida, Center for Urban Transportation Research, College of Engineering, 4202 E Fowler Ave, CUT100, Tampa, FL 33620-5375; http://www.cutr.usf.edu/. *Aud.:* Ac, Sa.

Presenting new case studies and original research, this journal covers public-transportation modes and related policies from all over the world. Although the journal strives to present papers with innovative solutions, approaches can come from any number of disciplines, including engineering, management, and others. The journal is provided free by the Center for Urban Transportation Research at the University of South Florida. The online version can be accessed at http://www.nctr.usf.edu/jpt/journal.htm. Appropriate for special collections

Journal of the Transportation Research Forum. See *Transportation Quarterly.*

6465. ***Journal of Transport Economics and Policy.*** [ISSN: 0022-5258] 1967. 3x/yr. USD 165 (Individuals, USD 55; Students, USD 20). Ed(s): Steven Morrison, Tae Hoon Oum. University of Bath, Claverton Down, Bath, BA2 7AY, United Kingdom; http://www.jtep.org. Illus., index, adv. Refereed. Circ: 1200. Vol. ends: Sep. *Indexed:* ABIn, BAS, BrHumI, EIP, GeogAbPG, IBSS, IBZ, JEL, PAIS, PRA, RRTA, SSCI, SUSA, WAE&RSA. *Bk. rev.:* Occasional, 150–1,500 words, signed. *Aud.:* Ac, Sa.

This scholarly journal focuses on research on economics and policy for intercity and urban transportation. The editorial board, the authors, and the topics they present are international in scope. In addition to the featured articles, there is a section titled "Developments in Transport Policy" that analyzes a particular aspect of current government policies. Occasionally, issues of the journal cover a single topic in depth. The online version can be accessed at http://www.bath.ac.uk/e-journals/jtep. Appropriate for special collections.

6466. ***Journal of Transport Geography.*** [ISSN: 0966-6923] 1993. q. EUR 358. Ed(s): Richard D Knowles. Pergamon, The Boulevard, Langford Ln, East Park, Kidlington, OX5 1GB, United Kingdom. Illus., index. Refereed. Vol. ends: Dec. Microform: PQC. Online: ingenta.com; ScienceDirect; Swets Blackwell. *Indexed:* GeogAbPG, H&SSA, OceAb, PollutAb, RiskAb. *Bk. rev.:* 1–5, 500–1,500 words, signed. *Aud.:* Ac, Sa.

This scholarly publication addresses transport geography and spatial change and land use, including transport policies, infrastructure, operations, and transport networks. Each issue features referenced research articles with bibliographies, charts, graphs, and maps; a viewpoint article; and book reviews. The coverage is international and geared toward the professional and the academician. The journal's online presence can be accessed at http://www.elsevier.nl/inca/publications/store/3/0/4/4/8. Appropriate for special collections.

6467. ***Journal of Transportation and Statistics.*** [ISSN: 1094-8848] 1998. 3x/yr. Free. U.S. Department of Transportation, Bureau of Transportation Statistics, 400 Seventh St SW, 3430, Washington, DC 20590. Illus. Refereed. *Aud.:* Ac, Sa.

This publication, sponsored by the U.S. Department of Transportation, Bureau of Transportation Statistics, features articles on the latest developments in transportation information and data, theory, and analysis. The editors look for articles from all over the world that measure performance and trends in transportation as well as articles that advance the science of acquiring, validating, managing, and disseminating transportation information. Policy studies are not published here. Frequently, issues of the journal center around a specific topic. The web site has the full text of the journal, as well as an index to all volumes, at http://www.bts.gov/jts. Appropriate for large, general collections and special collections.

6468. ***Journal of Transportation Engineering.*** Formerly (until 1983): *American Society of Civil Engineers. Transportation Engineering Journal;* Which was formed by the merger of (1962-1969): *American Society of Civil Engineers. Aero-Space Transport Division. Journal;* Which was formerly (until 1968): *American Society of Civil Engineers. Air Transport Division. Journal;* (1956-1968): *American Society of Civil Engineers. Highway Division. Journal;* (1957-1968): *American Society of Civil Engineers. Pipeline Division. Journal;* All of which superseded in part (1873-1955): *American Society of Civil Engineers. Proceedings.* [ISSN: 0733-947X] 1969. bi-m. Members, USD 72; Non-members, USD 108. Ed(s): Kumares C Sinha. American Society of Civil Engineers, 1801 Alexander Graham Bell Dr, Reston, VA 20191-4400; http://www.pubs.asce.org. Illus., index. Refereed. Circ: 2400. Vol. ends: Nov/Dec. Microform: PQC. Online: EBSCO Publishing; Gale Group; Swets Blackwell. *Indexed:* AS&TI, C&ISA, DSR&OA, EngInd, EnvAb, ExcerpMed, GeoRef, GeogAbPG, H&SSA, PetrolAb, RiskAb, SSCI. *Bk. rev.:* Various number and length. *Aud.:* Ac, Sa.

This scholarly journal is published by the American Society of Civil Engineers and is geared to the academician and the practitioner. It addresses all transportation modalities and covers the construction and maintenance of roads, bridges, airports, and pipelines; traffic management; business management; technology; and transportation economics. Each issue includes lengthy, researched articles with diagrams, charts, tables, and detailed references; a book review section; and a technical report. Current and archived issues can be accessed online at http://www.pubs.asce.org/journals/jrns.html. Appropriate for large academic libraries and special collections.

6469. ***Journal of Transportation Law, Logistics and Policy.*** Former titles (until 1994): *Transportation Practitioners Journal;* (until 1984): *I C C Practitioners' Journal.* [ISSN: 1078-5906] 1933. q. USD 55 domestic; USD 60 Canada; USD 65 elsewhere. Ed(s): James F Bromley. Association for Transportation Law, Logistics and Policy, PMB 250, 3 Church Cir, Annapolis, MD 21401-1933; atllp@aol.com; http://transportlink.com/atllp. Illus., index. Circ: 4000. Vol. ends: Summer. Microform: WSH; PMC. Online: Gale Group. Reprint: WSH. *Indexed:* ABIn, CLI, ILP, LRI. *Bk. rev.:* Occasional, 1,200–2,000 words, signed. *Aud.:* Ac, Sa.

Published by the Association for Transportation Law, Logistics and Policy (ATLLP), this scholarly journal includes articles on transportation law, practice, legislation, regulation, history, theory, logistics, economics, and statistics. Coverage is focused on North America, but occasionally articles on other areas of the world will be included. Every issue includes updates on recent administrative and regulatory developments and recent association news and upcoming activities. Alternate issues contain book reviews and the ATLLP schedule of events. This journal is geared to the professional and the academician. Appropriate for special libraries.

Light Rail and Modern Tramway. See *Tramways & Urban Transit.*

6470. ***Logistics Management.*** Formerly (until Jun., 2002): *Logistics Management & Distribution Report;* Formed by the merger of (1962-1998): *Logistics Management;* Which was formerly (until 1996): *Traffic Management;* (1901-1998): *Distribution;* (until 1992): *Chilton's Distribution;* (until 1986): *Chilton's Distribution for Traffic and Transportation Decision Makers;* (until 1980): *Chilton's Distribution;* (until 1979): *Chilton's Distribution Worldwide;* (until 1977): *Distribution Worldwide;* (until 1972): *Chilton's Distribution Worldwide;* (until 1970): *Distribution Worldwide;* (until 1969): *Distribution Manager.* [ISSN: 1540-3890] 1998. m. Plus annual directory. USD 99 domestic; USD 129.90 Canada; USD 125.90 Mexico. Reed Business Information, 275 Washington St, Newton, MA 02458; http://www.reedbusiness.com. Illus., adv. Circ: 83225. Microform: PQC. Online: Gale Group; ProQuest Information & Learning; H.W. Wilson. *Indexed:* ABIn, B&I, BPI, LogistBibl. *Aud.:* Ac, Sa.

This trade journal provides strong coverage in the areas of transportation operations and policy. Although the focus is on the United States, some coverage is provided on export–import and overseas shipments. Feature articles include company case studies, multipart articles, impacts of government policies and actions, economic analysis, new services, and innovative business practices. The journal includes a large array of monthly columns on various aspects of the industry, e.g., acquisitions, express carriers, railroads, air freight, regulation, etc. Columnists check in regularly with their opinions on a variety of topics. The journal is also full of news summaries, economic indicators, and product and equipment notices; it produces an annual salary survey. Other regular annual features include polls and buyer's guides. This journal's online version can be accessed at http://www.manufacturing.net/lm. Appropriate for special collections.

6471. ***Logistics Today.*** Former titles (until 2003): *Transportation & Distribution;* (until 1987): *Handling and Shipping Management;* (until vol.19, no.10, Oct. 1978): *Handling and Shipping.* [ISSN: 1547-1438] 1960. m. USD 55 domestic; USD 80.25 Canada; USD 95 elsewhere. Ed(s): David Blanchard. Penton Media, Inc., 1300 E 9th St, Cleveland, OH 44114-1503; information@penton.com; http://www.penton.com. Illus., adv. Circ: 71000 Controlled. Vol. ends: Dec. Microform: PQC. Online: bigchalk; The Dialog Corporation; EBSCO Publishing; Florida Center for Library Automation; Gale Group; Northern Light Technology, Inc.; OCLC Online Computer Library Center, Inc.; ProQuest Information & Learning; H.W. Wilson. Reprint: PQC. *Indexed:* ABIn, B&I, BPI, C&ISA, EngInd, ExcerpMed, LogistBibl. *Aud.:* Sa.

As one of the important trade journals on logistics, this publication covers topics related to supply-chain management, covering not only transportation but also other parts of the chain: materials handling, information systems, warehousing, and packaging. While the journal focuses on U.S.-based businesses, it also covers non-U.S. markets and issues. There are several annual features on packaging, integrated warehousing, and distribution. Regular features include columns on hazardous materials, government analysis, event calendars, news, and an industry watch. The journal's web site provides additional news features not included in the print version at http://www.tdmagazine.com. Targeted to industry professionals. Appropriate for special collections.

Marine Log. See Marine Science and Technology section.

Maritime Policy and Management. See Marine Science and Technology section.

6472. ***Mass Transit: better transit through better management.*** [ISSN: 0364-3484] 1974. bi-m. USD 48. Ed(s): Jim Duffy. Cygnus Business Media, Inc., 1233 Janeville Ave, Fort Atkinson, WI 53538-0803; http://www.masstransitmag.com. Illus., adv. Circ: 18000. Vol. ends: Nov/Dec. Online: Florida Center for Library Automation; Gale Group; Northern Light Technology, Inc.; OCLC Online Computer Library Center, Inc. *Indexed:* AIAP, AS&TI, BPI, EIP. *Aud.:* Sa.

This trade publication addresses mass transit for the management practitioner. The journal's focus is on North America, though there is some international coverage. Topics include management, policy, operations, and equipment. Each issue includes feature articles, industry news, legal notes, a forum for transit managers, a calendar of events, and classified ads. The journal's online version can be accessed at http://www.masstransitmag.com. Appropriate for special collections.

6473. ***Metro.*** Former titles (until 1994): *Metro Magazine;* (until 1985): *Metro;* (until 1974): *Metropolitan.* [ISSN: 1098-0083] 1904. 9x/yr. USD 40 domestic; USD 60 Canada; USD 100 elsewhere. Ed(s): Leslie Davis, Cliff Henke. Bobit Publishing Company, 21061 S Western Ave, Torrance, CA 90501. Illus., adv. Circ: 20000 Controlled. Vol. ends: Nov/Dec. *Indexed:* AIAP, FLI. *Aud.:* Sa.

This journal, covering national and international urban and interurban transportation systems, targets the practitioner. It addresses all major urban transportation issues: bus systems, light rail, motor coaches, intelligent transportation systems, high-speed rail, urban transit management, finance, and legislation. Each issue includes industry news and events, feature articles, editorials, product and innovation showcases, a calendar of events, and an industry personnel section. The last issue of the year includes a tear-out calendar highlighting dates of industry interest. There is an annual Top 50 Motorcoach Fleet list. The journal's online version and archived articles can be accessed at http://www.metro-magazine.com/t_home.cfm. Appropriate for special collections.

6474. ***Motor Coach Age.*** [ISSN: 0739-117X] 1948. q. Membership, USD 30. Ed(s): G Mac Sebree. Motor Bus Society, Inc, PO Box 251, Paramus, NJ 07653. Illus., adv. Vol. ends: Dec. *Aud.:* Ga, Sa.

Published by the Motor Bus Society, this journal addresses the history of the bus industry in the United States, for both the enthusiast and the practitioner. It includes feature articles, editorials, old route maps, some statistics, a literature review section, and letters to the editor. Historical photographs, some rare, enhance the text. Each issue emphasizes a city or bus line. Contents of past issues, including cover photographs, can be accessed at http://www.motorbussociety.org/mca. Appropriate for large general collections or special collections.

6475. ***Motor Ship.*** Formerly: *British Motor Ship.* [ISSN: 0027-2000] 1920. m. Free to qualified personnel. Ed(s): Dan Thisdell. Highbury Business Communications, Ann Boleyn House, 9-13 Ewell Rd, Cheam, SM3 8BZ, United Kingdom; http://www.hhc.co.uk/. Illus., index, adv. Circ: 8451. Vol. ends: Dec. Online: Gale Group. *Indexed:* EngInd, ExcerpMed, H&SSA, OceAb. *Aud.:* Sa.

This publication provides news and in-depth coverage of all aspects of the marine industry. The feature articles are often investigative and include coverage of new buildings, in-depth country reviews, descriptions of ships, and exhibition previews. Regular columns cover news on cruise ships, propulsion, and ship repair, as well as equipment, updates on movers and shakers in the industry, and an events calendar. A quarterly supplement covers all aspects of ship repair and usually includes a directory of ship repair yards. Other supplements cover cargo management, port infrastructure, and cruise ships. The web site offers feature articles for current and back issues, as well as other parts of the magazine, at http://www.motorship.com. Appropriate for special collections.

6476. ***National Railway Bulletin.*** [ISSN: 0885-5099] 1935. bi-m. USD 15; USD 19 foreign. Ed(s): Frank G Tatnall. National Railway Historical Society, PO Box 58547, Philadelphia, PA 19102; http://www.nrhs.com. Illus. Circ: 18000. Vol. ends: No. 6. *Bk. rev.:* 5–12, 200–750 words, signed. *Aud.:* Ga, Sa.

Published by the National Railway Historical Society, this journal is targeted at its membership. Rail fans will enjoy the richly illustrated articles on history and current events in the railroad industry. Although many articles focus on passenger transport, there is also historical coverage of freight trains and services. One issue per year is devoted to the activities of the society, with an annual report as well as section-by-section state-of-the-chapter reports. Every issue contains many book reviews, letters to the editor, and a digest of transit news. Appropriate for large general collections and special collections.

6477. ***Overdrive: the magazine for the American trucker.*** Incorporates (1970-2001): *Owner Operator.* [ISSN: 0030-7394] 1961. m. USD 29.97 domestic; USD 60 Canada; USD 4.95 newsstand/cover per issue domestic. Ed(s): Linda Longton. Randall Publishing Company, 3200 Rice Mine Road, N E, Tuscaloosa, AL 35406; tbelk@sandallpub.com; http://www.etrucker.net. Illus., adv. Circ: 21385 Paid. Vol. ends: Dec. Online: EBSCO Publishing. *Indexed:* LRI. *Aud.:* Sa.

This journal addresses the North American trucking industry and targets the truck driver and fleet operator. It covers industry news and events, legislation, safety, technology, product analysis, management, training, and personnel issues. Each issue includes feature articles, a calendar of events, a financial section, an industry-related web site directory, product/equipment reviews, and a job-hunting section. In 2001, this journal took over the publication of content from *Owner Operator*. Recent editions of the journal can be accessed at http://www.etrucker.com/default.asp?magid=1. Appropriate for special collections.

6478. ***P D I.*** Formerly: *Port Development International.* 1985. m. GBP 145 domestic; USD 325 in Europe; USD 403 elsewhere. Ed(s): Chris Orr. Euromoney Institutional Investor plc., Nestor House, Playhouse Yard, London, EC4V 5EX, United Kingdom; http://www.euromoney.com. Illus., adv. Circ: 7900. Vol. ends: Dec. *Indexed:* GeogAbPG. *Aud.:* Sa.

This journal addresses port development throughout the world, covering land usage, terminal design, port-originating intermodal transportation, container handling, bulk handling, port dredging, and general port operations and management. It is geared toward the specialist. Each issue includes industry news and events, feature articles, statistics, a survey of a specific port or region, and technology updates. Detailed diagrams are often used to enhance the text and augment photography. The current issue and archives can be accessed at http://portdev.sksl.com/contents.asp. Appropriate to special collections.

6479. ***Passenger Transport.*** [ISSN: 0364-345X] 1943. w. USD 65 in North America; USD 77 elsewhere. Ed(s): Rhonda Goldberg. American Public Transportation Association, 1666 K St., NW 11th Fl., Washington, DC 20006; sberlin@apta.com. Illus., index, adv. Circ: 4413 Paid. Vol. ends: Dec. *Aud.:* Sa.

This glossy, newspaper-format, weekly publication is targeted to North American transit officials who are likely to be members of the American Public Transportation Association (APTA), the magazine's publisher. There is significant coverage of people involved in the industry, providing interviews and much space to news items about the movement of people in the field. Beyond providing current news on the subject, regular features include industry briefs, international news, classifieds, and regular columns. In conjunction with APTA conferences, special issues are published focusing on city-by-city transit operations. The web site offers excerpts from articles and a year-by-year index back to 1996 at http://www.apta.com/news/pt. Appropriate for special collections.

6480. ***Pipeline & Gas Journal: energy construction, transportation and distribution.*** Incorporates (1928-1990): *Pipeline (Houston);* Which was formerly (until 1974): *Pipe Line News;* Formed by the merger of (19??-1970): *Pipeline Engineer;* Which was formerly (until 1956): *Petroleum Engineer, Oil and Gas Pipelining Edition;* (1859-1970): *American Gas Journal;* Which was formerly (until 1921): *American Gas Engineering Journal;* (until 1917): *American Gas Light Journal.* [ISSN: 0032-0188] 1970. m. USD 33; USD 60 Canada; USD 70 elsewhere. Ed(s): Jeff Share. Oildom Publishing Co. of Texas, Inc., PO Box 941669, Houston, TX 77094-8669; maxine@oildompublishing.com; http://www.oilompublishing.com. Illus., adv. Online: EBSCO Publishing; Factiva; Florida Center for Library Automation; Gale Group; Northern Light Technology, Inc.; OCLC Online Computer Library Center, Inc.; ProQuest Information & Learning; H.W. Wilson. *Indexed:* AS&TI, C&ISA, CEA, EngInd, EnvAb, GeoRef, PetrolAb. *Aud.:* SA.

This journal addresses the international pipeline drilling, maintenance, distribution, and marketing industry, and it is geared to the practitioner. Coverage includes industry news and events, pipeline drilling, pipeline maintenance, the gas and petroleum industries, legislation, safety, technology, equipment, management, distribution, marketing, industry personnel, and the political/economic aspects of the pipeline industry. Each issue includes feature articles, a calendar of events, product reviews, a section on innovative technology, an advertisers index, a section devoted to pipeline projects around the world, and a "Pipeline & Politics" section. There is an extensive annual buyer's guide. The online version of this journal can be accessed at http://www.oildompublishing.com/PGJ/pgj_home.html. Appropriate for special collections.

6481. ***Progressive Railroading.*** [ISSN: 0033-0817] 1958. m. Free to qualified personnel. Ed(s): Pat Foran. Trade Press Publishing Corp., 2100 W Florist Ave, PO Box 694, Milwaukee, WI 53209; http://www.tradepress.com. Illus., adv. Circ: 25000. Vol. ends: Dec. *Indexed:* C&ISA, LogistBibl. *Aud.:* Ac, Sa.

As a major U.S. trade journal in the rail industry, this publication focuses on operations of and equipment used in freight and passenger services as well as on the equipment manufacture and repair aspects of the industry. The feature articles provide profiles of key companies, mechanical items of interest, articles on safety, alliances, and more. Regular features are extensive, including industry and regional news and analysis, statistics, events, regular columnists and commentary, equipment information, and an "Enterprise" column on innovative and excellent business practices. This magazine publishes many annual guides to the industry on the subjects of cars, locomotives and track, finance, and leasing. The web site includes late-breaking news and some of the feature articles from the current issue of the magazine at http://www.progressiverailroading.com. Appropriate for special collections.

6482. ***Public Roads.*** [ISSN: 0033-3735] 1918. q. USD 18. Ed(s): Bob Bryant. U.S. Federal Highway Administration, Office of Highway Information Management, 400 7th St, S W, Washington, DC 20590; bbryant@intergate.dot.gov; http://www.fhwa.dot.gov/. Illus., index. Circ: 5500. Vol. ends: Spring. Microform: CIS; PQC. Online: bigchalk; EBSCO Publishing; Florida Center for Library Automation; Gale Group; Northern Light Technology, Inc.; OCLC Online Computer Library Center, Inc.; ProQuest Information & Learning. Reprint: CIS; PQC. *Indexed:* AS&TI, AgeL, AmStI, C&ISA, ChemAb, EngInd, ExcerpMed, GeoRef, GeogAbPG, IUSGP, PAIS. *Aud.:* Ga, Sa.

This publication covers developments in federal highway policies, programs, research, and development. While the primary audience of the journal is transportation officials, researchers, field technicians, and engineers, the content of the journal could also be used by a general audience that wants to stay informed about transportation issues and progress. Each issue includes features on new research, recent publications, news in the industry, and a calendar of events. Full texts of articles back to 1993 are available on the web site at http://www.tfhrc.gov/pubrds/pubrds.htm. Appropriate for large general collections and special collections.

6483. ***Public Transport International (Edition Francaise).*** Supersedes in part (in 1997): *Public Transport International (Multilingual Edition);* Which was formerly (until 1990): *U I T P Revue; International Union of Tramways, Light Railways and Motor Omnibuses. Review.* [ISSN: 1029-1261] 1952. bi-m. Members, TPE 56; Non-members, EUR 74. Ed(s): Heather Allen. International Union of Public Transport, Av Herrmann Debroux 17, Brussels, 1160, Belgium. Illus., adv. Circ: 3000. Vol. ends: Nov/Dec. *Indexed:* C&ISA. *Aud.:* Sa.

Published by the International Association of Public Transport, this journal addresses the international urban and interurban public-transit industry. It should be of interest to both the academician and the practitioner. Each issue consists of researched articles on the technological, socioeconomic, or political aspects of public transportation. Statistical graphs and tables enhance the text; however, references are not provided for the researched articles. Some references are available upon request. Archived articles can be accessed at http://www.uitp.com. Appropriate for special collections.

6484. *Rail International.* Formerly: *International Railway Congress Association. Monthly Bulletin.* [ISSN: 0020-8442] 1970. m. EUR 80. Ed(s): Antoine Martens. International Railway Congress Association, Rue de France 85, Section 10, Brussels, 1060, Belgium; secretariat@aiccf.org. Illus., index, adv. Circ: 4000. Vol. ends: Dec. *Indexed:* BAS, C&ISA, EngInd, H&SSA. *Bk. rev.:* Occasional, up to 500 words. *Aud.:* Ac, Sa.

This is the official publication of the International Railway Congress Association (IRCA) and the International Union of Railways (UIC). The journal contains original papers dealing with all branches of railway science and management from technical, social, and economic perspectives. Technical papers are also included from IRCA and UIC meetings and conferences. Features of the journal include worldwide industry news, including significant people and policy news, a calendar of events, and a bibliography of resources taken from the UIC Documentation Centre's Railway Database. Contents of the most recent issues of the journal can be accessed at http://www.aiccf.org/E/journal_list.html. Appropriate for special collections.

6485. *Rail Travel News.* [ISSN: 0896-4440] 1970. s-m. USD 26; USD 35 foreign. Ed(s): James Russell. Message Media, PO Box 9007, Berkeley, CA 94709; rtn@trainweb.com; http://trainweb.com/rtn. Illus., adv. Circ: 2000 Paid. Vol. ends: Dec. *Aud.:* Ga.

This is a rail-fan magazine devoted to domestic rail passenger service news. Each issue includes feature articles on rail trips, a "Rail Fantrips" section with suggested rail travel tours and general news on North American rail passenger travel. Selected feature articles and news can be accessed at http://www.railtravelnews.com. Appropriate for large general collections and special collections.

6486. *Railfan & Railroad.* Formerly: *Railfan (Newton);* Incorporates (in 1979): *Railroad Magazine;* Which was formerly: *Railroad Man's Magazine; Railroad Stories.* [ISSN: 0163-7266] 1974. m. USD 27.95 domestic; USD 35.95 Canada; USD 37.95 elsewhere. Ed(s): E Steven Barry. Carstens Publications, Inc., PO Box 700, Newton, NJ 07860-0777; http://www.railfan.com. Illus., adv. Circ: 52000. Vol. ends: Dec. *Bk. rev.:* Number and length vary. *Aud.:* Ga, Sa.

This journal addresses railroading and railway history for the United States, Canada, and occasionally Mexico. It is geared to the enthusiast, although a specialist may be interested in the historical information provided. Contents include railroading news and events; feature articles; book, video, and software reviews; preservation information; sections devoted to railway dining, museums, and tour schedules; and product and hobby reviews. A pull-out index for the previous year is published each spring. Text is enhanced with a large color photography section. The table of contents for the current and forthcoming issues can be accessed at http://www.railfan.com. Appropriate for large general collections and special collections.

6487. *Railroad History.* Formerly (until 1972): *Railway and Locomotive Historical Society. Bulletin.* [ISSN: 0090-7847] 1921. s-a. USD 25. Ed(s): Mark Reutter. Railway & Locomotive Historical Society, c/o Mark Reutter, PO Box 517, Urbana, IL 61803; mreutter@uiuc.edu; http://www.rrhistorical.com/. Illus., index, adv. Refereed. Circ: 4500 Paid. Microform: PQC. Reprint: PQC. *Indexed:* AmH&L. *Bk. rev.:* 20–30, up to 1,500 words, signed. *Aud.:* Ac, Sa.

Published by the Railway & Locomotive Historical Society, this scholarly journal is geared to the academician and advanced student, although the more erudite enthusiast may find it of interest. It addresses the socioeconomic, business, and technological aspects of domestic and international railroad and railway history. It includes feature essays and lengthy researched articles with diagrams, maps, and extensive references. The journal has an impressive book review section and a section on articles recommended for reading. Each issue includes information on preservation, locomotives, a discussion forum, and a photography section. There is a yearly bonus issue devoted to a specific topic. A cumulative index from 1921 forward can be accessed at http://www.rrhistorical-2.com/rlhs. Appropriate for large general collections and special collections.

6488. *Railway Age.* Incorporates (1947-1991, June): *Modern Railroads;* Which was formerly (until 1982): *Modern Railroads - Rail Transit;* (until 1971): *Modern Railroads;* Which incorporated: *Railway Control Systems; Railway Locomotives and Cars.* [ISSN: 0033-8826] 1876. m. USD 56. Ed(s): Luther S Miller, William Vantuono. Simmons - Boardman Publishing Corp., 345 Hudson St, 12th floor, New York, NY 10014-4502. Illus., adv. Circ: 24500. Vol. ends: Dec. Microform: CIS; PQC. Online: EBSCO Publishing; Florida Center for Library Automation; Gale Group; Northern Light Technology, Inc.; OCLC Online Computer Library Center, Inc.; ProQuest Information & Learning; H.W. Wilson. Reprint: PQC. *Indexed:* ABIn, BPI, C&ISA, EngInd, EnvAb, H&SSA, MagInd, PAIS. *Aud.:* Ac, Sa.

As one of the major North American railroad trade journals, *Railway Age* covers all aspects of the railroad industry. The journal includes both freight and passenger service, encompassing commuter, rapid, and light-rail transit, as well as the equipment and supply industry, management, finance, and operational considerations. Annual special issues are published and can include buyer's guides, planner's guides, or year-end outlooks. Regular features include at-a-glance industry indicators and outlooks, people involved, railroader of the year, meeting information, company indexes, professional directories, classifieds, and commentary on a variety of aspects of the industry. The focus is on business rather than technical aspects of the industry. The web site contains late-breaking news as well as selected articles, commentaries, and statistics from the magazine at http://www.railwayage.com. Appropriate for large general collections and special collections.

6489. *Railway Gazette International: a journal of management, engineering and operation.* Formerly: *Railway Gazette.* [ISSN: 0373-5346] 1835. m. GBP 59 domestic; GBP 102 elsewhere; USD 153 elsewhere. Ed(s): Murray Hughes. Reed Business Information Ltd., Quadrant House, The Quadrant, Brighton Rd, Sutton, SM2 5AS, United Kingdom; rbp.subscriptions@rbi.co.uk. Illus., index, adv. Circ: 9616. Vol. ends: Dec. *Indexed:* C&ISA, EngInd. *Bk. rev.:* Occasional. *Aud.:* Sa.

This journal addresses the international rail industry, encompassing heavy and light rail and both freight and passenger services. It is geared to the practitioner and includes industry news and events, technology, legislation, safety, business, finance, management, research, and the socioeconomic and political environments of the rail industry. Each issue contains feature articles, a detailed industry news section, a calendar of events, product reviews, a small book review section, and a section devoted to industry personnel. A different world region is highlighted in each issue. Current and archived issues can be accessed at http://www.railwaygazette.com. Appropriate for a special collection.

6490. *Regional Airline World.* Formerly (until 1999): *Commuter World;* Which incorporates: *Regional Air International.* [ISSN: 1465-6817] 1984. 10x/yr. GBP 80 domestic; USD 130 foreign. Ed(s): Bernie Baldwin. Shephard Press Ltd., 111 High St, Burnham, SL1 7JZ, United Kingdom; publishing@shephard.co.uk. Adv. Circ: 13056. *Aud.:* Sa.

This journal addresses the regional airline industry worldwide and is geared to the practitioner. Coverage includes industry news and events, finances, management and mergers, personnel, technology, and training. Each issue includes a significant international news section, feature articles, the profile of a specific airline, and a calendar of events. The table of contents of the current issue and archived articles can be accessed at http://www.shephard.co.uk/pubs/comwrl. Appropriate for special collections.

6491. *Roads & Bridges.* Former titles (until 1984): *Roads;* (until 1983): *R U R: Rural and Urban Roads; Rural and Urban Roads.* [ISSN: 8750-9229] 1892. m. USD 35. Ed(s): Larry Flynn. Scranton Gillette Communications, Inc., 380 E Northwest Hwy, Ste 200, Des Plaines, IL 60016-2282. Illus., adv. Circ: 70000. Vol. ends: Dec. Microform: PQC. Reprint: PQC. *Indexed:* C&ISA, ExcerpMed. *Aud.:* Sa.

Targeting the practitioner, this journal addresses the domestic transportation construction industry. Coverage includes industry news and events, technology, legislation, safety and regulation, construction materials, construction machinery, products, and equipment. Each issue includes feature articles, a legal section, product and equipment reviews, and sections devoted to technical innovations and construction vehicles. Some issues include information on software and online industry resources. Articles from the current issue and archived issues can be accessed at http://www.roadsbridges.com/rb. Appropriate for special collections.

Seaway Review. See *Great Lakes Seaway Log.*

6492. *Supply Chain Management Review.* [ISSN: 1521-9747] 1997. 6x/yr. USD 209 in US & Canada; USD 241 foreign; USD 59.95 newsstand/cover. Ed(s): Francis J Quinn. Reed Business Information, 275 Washington St, Newton, MA 02458; http://www.reedbusiness.com. Adv. Circ: 10000. Online: EBSCO Publishing; Florida Center for Library Automation; Gale Group; OCLC Online Computer Library Center, Inc. Reprint: PSC. *Indexed:* LogistBibl. *Bk. rev.:* 3–5, 250–750 words. *Aud.:* Ac, Sa.

This journal addresses the international transportation logistics and supply chain management industries; it targets both the academician and the practitioner. Coverage includes logistics, supply chain management, procurement, technology, e-commerce, warehousing, management, training, and information flow. Each issue includes both feature articles and researched articles with references; a resource section for literature, web sites, and networking; a professional-development section listing events, seminars, workshops, and academic programs; and statistics, charts, and graphs. There is at least one subject-specific supplement issued per year. Selected articles, current and archived, along with tables of contents, can be accessed at http://www.manufacturing.net/magazine/scl. Appropriate for large academic collections and special collections.

6493. *T R News.* Former titles: *Transportation Research News; Highway Research News.* [ISSN: 0738-6826] 1963. bi-m. USD 38 in North America; USD 41 elsewhere. Ed(s): Nancy A Ackerman. U.S. National Research Council, Transportation Research Board, 2101 Constitution Ave, N W, Washington, DC 20418. Illus. Circ: 10000. Vol. ends: Nov/Dec. *Indexed:* C&ISA, EngInd. *Bk. rev.:* 4–8, up to 150 words. *Aud.:* Ac, Sa.

This publication covers research and innovations in all modes of transportation. Article contributions come from academics and professionals in the industry. The focus is on U.S.-based initiatives and specifically on Transportation Research Board (TRB) activities. In addition to feature articles, each issue contains profiles of academics and professionals, news briefs and TRB highlights, an events calendar, and a listing of new TRB publications with abstracts. The web site includes the table of contents of each issue as well as full texts of back issues at http://www4.trb.org/trb/onlinepubs.nsf/web/tr_news. Appropriate for special collections.

6494. *Traffic Engineering & Control: the international journal of traffic management and transportation planning.* [ISSN: 0041-0683] 1960. m. GBP 65; USD 120. Ed(s): Keith Lumley. Printerhall Ltd., 29 Newman St, London, W1P 3PE, United Kingdom. Illus., index, adv. Refereed. Circ: 5400. Vol. ends: Dec. Microform: PQC. *Indexed:* BrTechI, C&ISA, EngInd, ErgAb, ExcerpMed, GeogAbPG. *Bk. rev.:* Occasional, up to 750 words. *Aud.:* Ac, Sa.

This British journal primarily covers European countries, with some international coverage. It encompasses industry issues, news, interviews, and current research in traffic engineering. It is targeted at academics, practicing engineers, and students in the field. Regular features also include buyer's guides, classifieds, product news, opinion pieces, and a calendar of events. Annual features include a review of activities of British university transportation research centers. Appropriate for special collections.

6495. *Traffic Technology International.* [ISSN: 1356-9252] 1994. bi-m. Free to qualified personnel. AutoIntermediates Ltd., Abinger House, Church St, 120 South St, Dorking, RH4 1DF, United Kingdom; info@ukintpress.com; http://www.ukintpress.com/. Circ: 18000 Paid. *Aud.:* Sa, Ac.

This bimonthly journal addresses the issues of traffic safety and traffic control. It is global in breadth and targets both the academician and the practitioner. Coverage includes industry news and events, intelligent transportation systems, traffic control devices, traffic safety devices, regulation, legislation, traffic systems operations, research, personnel, management, and training. Each issue includes both feature articles and researched articles with references, a calendar of events, an international news section, a bulletin board that highlights software and innovative technology, statistics, and tables and graphs. The online version of the current issue can be accessed, with password, at http://www.ukintpress.com/recard/tfmcard.html. Appropriate for large academic collections and special collections.

6496. *Traffic World: the logistics news weekly.* [ISSN: 0041-073X] 1907. w. USD 174 in US & Canada; USD 259 elsewhere. Ed(s): William B Cassidy, Clayton Boyce. Journal of Commerce, Inc., 1270 National Press Bldg, Washington, DC 20045; customerservice@cbizmedia.com. Illus., index, adv. Circ: 10500. Vol. ends: No. 13. CD-ROM: The Dialog Corporation. Microform: PQC. Online: bigchalk; The Dialog Corporation; EBSCO Publishing; Factiva; Florida Center for Library Automation; Gale Group; Northern Light Technology, Inc.; OCLC Online Computer Library Center, Inc.; ProQuest Information & Learning; H.W. Wilson. Reprint: PQC. *Indexed:* ABIn, B&I, BPI, LogistBibl. *Aud.:* Sa.

This trade publication provides weekly news and articles on freight transportation and logistics. Coverage is primarily of North America, but articles on Europe and other areas of the world are frequently included. Regular features contain Washington reports; articles about logistics; rail, motor, air, water, and technology; columns on career advancement; commentary; Q&A; e-strategies; classifieds; a calendar of events; and news about people in the industry. The web site offers daily news and a handful of full-text articles and features from each issue at http://www.trafficworld.com. Appropriate for large general collections and special collections.

6497. *Trains.* [ISSN: 0041-0934] 1940. m. USD 39.95; USD 4.95 newsstand/cover per issue. Ed(s): Mark Hemphill. Kalmbach Publishing Co., PO Box 1612, Waukesha, WI 53187-1612; webmaster@kalmbach.com; http://www.trains.com. Illus., index, adv. Circ: 108445. Vol. ends: Dec. Online: bigchalk; EBSCO Publishing; Gale Group; Northern Light Technology, Inc.; ProQuest Information & Learning. *Indexed:* MagInd. *Bk. rev.:* 3–5, 250–750 words, signed. *Aud.:* Ga, Sa.

This journal addresses both the light and heavy rail industries of North America, with some cursory international news. It is geared to the enthusiast; however, the specialist may find the historical and management articles of interest. Coverage includes industry news and events, tours, rail-related hobbies and memorabilia, railroad personnel, preservation, museums, and some management and policy matters. Each issue includes feature articles, book and video reviews, a calendar of events, tour schedules, and a significant photography section that sponsors a readers' photography contest. There is a yearly pull-out recreational-railroading supplement. The journal's web presence can be accessed at http://www.trains.com/maghomepage/maghomepage.asp?idMagazine=1. Appropriate for large public library collections or special collections.

6498. *Tramways & Urban Transit: international light rail magazine.* Former titles (until 1998): *Light Rail and Modern Tramway;* (until 1996): *Modern Tramway and Light Rail Transit;* (until 1980): *Modern Tramway and Rapid Transit;* (until 1977): *Modern Tramway and Light Railway Review.* [ISSN: 1460-8324] 1938. m. Ed(s): Howard Johnston. Ian Allan Publishing Ltd., Riverdene Business Park, Riverdene Industrial Estate, Walton-on-Thames, KT12 4RG, United Kingdom; subs@ianallanpub.co.uk; http://www.ianallan.com/publishing/. Illus., adv. Circ: 7250. Reprint: PQC. *Indexed:* BrTechI. *Bk. rev.:* Number and length vary. *Aud.:* Sa.

Published by the Light Rail Transit Association, this journal has been in continuous publication since 1938. It addresses the global, light-rail, and urban transport industry and is geared to the practitioner. The journal covers industry news and events, technology, funding, legislation, safety, management, and industry personnel. Each issue includes feature articles; an international tram and light-rail news section; reviews of books, databases, and videos; a calendar of events; obituaries; and a product review section. Color and black-and-white photography enhance the text. An archive of selected feature articles can be accessed at http://www.lrta.org/mag.html. Appropriate for special collections.

6499. ***Transport Policy.*** [ISSN: 0967-070X] 1993. q. EUR 375 (Individuals, EUR 96). Ed(s): M Ben-Akiva, Yoshitsugu Hayashi. Pergamon, The Boulevard, Langford Ln, East Park, Kidlington, OX5 1GB, United Kingdom. Illus., index, adv. Refereed. Vol. ends: Oct (No. 8). Microform: PQC. Online: ingenta.com; ScienceDirect; Swets Blackwell. *Indexed:* GeogAbPG, SUSA. *Aud.:* Ac, Sa.

This scholarly publication covers all modes of transportation, addressing theoretical and practical aspects of transportation policy and administration. It targets the practitioner, government official, and academician. Some issues will focus on a single aspect of transport policy. In addition to the scholarly articles, each issue also includes a section on the activities of the Section of the World Conference on Transport Research Society. The online version is available by subscription through Elsevier. Appropriate for special collections.

6500. ***Transport Reviews: a transnational, transdisciplinary journal.*** [ISSN: 0144-1647] 1981. q. GBP 299 (Individuals, USD 77). Ed(s): Juan de Dios Ortuzar, David A Hensher. Taylor & Francis Ltd, 11 New Fetter Ln, London, EC4P 4EE, United Kingdom; info@tandf.co.uk; http://www.tandf.co.uk/journals. Illus., index, adv. Refereed. Vol. ends: Oct/Dec. Online: EBSCO Publishing; Ingenta Select; OCLC Online Computer Library Center, Inc.; RoweCom Information Quest; Swets Blackwell. Reprint: PSC. *Indexed:* C&ISA, ErgAb, GeogAbPG, IBZ, SSCI. *Bk. rev.:* 1–3, 350–750 words, signed. *Aud.:* Ac, Sa.

Like *Transportation*, this scholarly publication covers all modes of transportation in all nations. Topics can touch on social, economic, or technological aspects of the field. The content is aimed at both academic and professional audiences. Occasional issues are organized around a specific topic. Searchable tables of contents are available on the journal's web site at http://www.tandf.co.uk/journals/tf/01441647.html. Appropriate for special collections.

6501. ***Transport Topics: national newspaper of the trucking industry.*** [ISSN: 0041-1558] 1935. w. USD 99 domestic; USD 3.95 newsstand/cover per issue. Ed(s): Howard Abramson. T T Publishing, 2200 Mill Rd, Alexandria, VA 22314-4686; habramso@trucking.org; http://www.TTnews.com. Illus., adv. Circ: 32000 Paid. Microform: PQC. *Indexed:* LogistBibl. *Aud.:* Sa.

This glossy, tabloid-format magazine covers the trucking industry and is published by the American Trucking Association. It is comprised mostly of short articles concerning all aspects of trucking, but especially state and federal regulation, management, policy analysis, finance, operations, equipment, and events. Issues often include special sections on a single topic. Regular features include state news, a weekly business review, fuel prices, products, people news, a calendar of events, job listings, real estate, and equipment. The web site offers late-breaking news and other regular columns at http://www.transporttopics.com. Appropriate for large general collections or special collections

6502. ***Transportation: an international journal devoted to the improvement of transportation planning and practice.*** [ISSN: 0049-4488] 1972. q. EUR 468 print or online ed. Kluwer Academic Publishers, van Godewijckstraat 30, PO Box 17, Dordrecht, 3300 AA, Netherlands; services@wkap.nl; http://www.wkap.nl. Illus., index. Refereed. Vol. ends: No. 4. Microform: PQC. Online: EBSCO Publishing; ingenta.com; Kluwer Online; OCLC Online Computer Library Center, Inc.; Ovid Technologies, Inc.; RoweCom Information Quest; Swets Blackwell. Reprint: SWZ. *Indexed:* AIAP, AS&TI, AgeL, C&ISA, EngInd, EnvAb, ExcerpMed, GeogAbPG, H&SSA, IBSS, RRTA, SCI, SSCI, SUSA, WAE&RSA. *Aud.:* Ac, Sa.

This scholarly publication provides research articles that cover all modes of transportation around the world. The audience is policy makers, transportation planners, and operations managers. Most issues contain four articles, but occasional issues contain many more, focused on a topic. The journal's web site contains tables of contents and a search engine, enabling subject searches of the journal's content. The journal can be accessed, by subscription, at http://www.kluweronline.nl. Appropriate for special collections.

6503. ***Transportation Journal.*** [ISSN: 0041-1612] 1961. q. USD 61.95 domestic; USD 89.95 foreign; USD 17 newsstand/cover per issue. Ed(s): John C Spychalski. American Society of Transportation and Logistics, Inc., 1700 North Moore St., Ste 1900, Arlington, VA 22209-1904; info@astl.org; http://www.astl.org. Illus., index. Refereed. Circ: 3500. Microform: PQC. Online: bigchalk; EBSCO Publishing; Florida Center for Library Automation; Gale Group; Northern Light Technology, Inc.; OCLC Online Computer Library Center, Inc.; ProQuest Information & Learning. Reprint: PQC; WSH. *Indexed:* ABIn, BPI, CLI, EnvAb, ILP, LogistBibl, PAIS, SSCI. *Bk. rev.:* Occasional, 750–1,000 words, signed. *Aud.:* Ac, Sa.

Published by the American Society of Transportation and Logistics, this scholarly journal includes articles on policies, strategies, and techniques relating to the management of transportation and logistics activities. Special theme issues are published regularly. A sample copy of the journal can be accessed at http://www.astl.org/tj.html. Appropriate for special collections.

6504. ***Transportation Law Journal: industry leader in multi-modal law, economics & policy.*** [ISSN: 0049-450X] 1969. 3x/yr. USD 29; USD 39 foreign. Ed(s): Jane Hershey. Transportation Law Journal, University of Denver, College of Law, Denver, CO 80220; tlj@student.law.du.edu; http://du.edu/~transplj/. Illus., index, adv. Refereed. Circ: 2500 Paid. Vol. ends: Spring. Microform: WSH; PMC. Online: Gale Group; LexisNexis; West Group. Reprint: WSH. *Indexed:* CLI, ILP, LRI, PAIS. *Aud.:* Ac, Sa.

Published by the University of Denver College of Law, this journal addresses the international transportation industry and is geared toward the specialist, academician, and transportation law practitioner. It covers transportation law, regulation, and the politico-economic aspects of all transportation modalities. Each issue includes significant researched articles with abundant footnotes. An index to archived articles can be accessed at http://www.law.du.edu/tlj. Appropriate for special collections.

6505. ***Transportation Management & Engineering.*** Formerly: *I T S World.* 1996. 6x/yr. Free. Scranton Gillette Communications, Inc., 380 E Northwest Hwy, Ste 200, Des Plaines, IL 60016-2282. Illus., index, adv. *Indexed:* B&I. *Aud.:* Sa.

This newspaper-formatted journal covers the international intelligent transportation systems (ITS) industry, and it targets the specialist. Coverage includes ITS industry news and events, technology, applications, safety, traffic management, vehicles, and product reviews. Each issue includes a calendar of events, an annotated bibliography of new ITS literature, industry personnel changes, and a product review guide. Current feature articles and an article archive can be accessed online at http://www.tmemag.com. Appropriate for special collections.

6506. ***Transportation Quarterly.*** Formerly (until 1982): *Traffic Quarterly.* [ISSN: 0278-9434] 1947. q. USD 55 domestic; USD 75 foreign. Ed(s): Sandra Selva. Eno Transportation Foundation, 1634 I St, N W Ste 500, Washington, DC 20006-4003. Illus., index, adv. Circ: 1500. Online: EBSCO Publishing; Gale Group; OCLC Online Computer Library Center, Inc.; H.W. Wilson. Reprint: PQC. *Indexed:* AIAP, AS&TI, AgeL, BAS, C&ISA, EngInd, EnvAb, FutSurv, PAIS, SSCI, SUSA. *Bk. rev.:* 1–2, 750–1,500 words, signed. *Aud.:* Ac, Sa.

Beginning in 2000, the *Journal of the Transportation Research Forum* comprises the second half of every issue of *Transportation Quarterly*. While they each maintain their own volume and issue numbering, they share the same ISSN (0278-9434). At the time of this change, *Transportation Quarterly* began publishing both peer- and non–peer-reviewed articles with the aim of covering emerging transportation issues across all modes, particularly focusing on issues that affect policy or have an economic impact. The target audience is transportation officials. The articles contained in the section for the *Journal of the Transportation Research Forum* are all peer-reviewed and cover all modes of transportation that are based on empirical and/or theoretical research of transportation issues. Each issue also contains book reviews and news and activities from the Transportation Research Forum and the Eno Transportation Foundation. Appropriate for special collections.

6507. ***Transportation Research. Parts A-F.*** irreg. Pergamon, The Boulevard, Langford Ln, East Park, Kidlington, OX5 1GB, United Kingdom; nlinfo-f@elsevier.nl; http://www.elsevier.nl. *Bk. rev.:* Occasional, 600–2,500 words. *Aud.:* Ac, Sa.

This six-part set of journals covers the gamut of transportation research occurring around the world. Each part can be purchased separately.

A: Policy & Practice [ISSN: 0965-8564] 10/yr. $1,104. Frank A. Haight. Vol. ends: Dec. Focuses on general-interest articles, particularly on planning and policy and its interaction with political, socioeconomic, and environmental systems.

B: *Methodological* [ISSN: 0191-2615] 10/yr. $1,104. Frank A. Haight. Vol. ends: Apr. Concentrates on the creation, analysis, and performance of models for the movement of freight and people.

C: *Emerging Technologies* [ISSN: 0968-090X] bi-m. $736. Stephen G. Ritchie. Vol. ends: Dec. Discusses implications and applications of new technologies in the field of transportation.

D: *Transport and Environment* [ISSN: 1361-9209] bi-m. $736. Kenneth Button. Covers environmental impacts of transportation, policy issues surrounding that impact, and implications for the design and implementation of transportation systems.

E: *Logistics and Transportation Review* [ISSN: 1366-5545] bi-m. $735. W. K. Talley. Vol. ends: Dec. Features articles on logistics including economics, cost, and production functions; capacity; demand; infrastructure; models; and supply chain topics.

F: *Traffic Psychology and Behaviour* [ISSN: 1369-8478] q. $490. J. A. Rothengatter. Focuses on the behavioral and psychological aspects of traffic and transport.

6508. ***Transportation Research Record.*** Formerly (until 1974): *Highway Research Record.* [ISSN: 0361-1981] 1963. irreg. USD 865 in North America; USD 900 elsewhere. U.S. National Research Council, Transportation Research Board, 2101 Constitution Ave, N W, Washington, DC 20418; http://www.nas.edu/trb/about/pubindex.html. Illus. Refereed. Circ: 3250. *Indexed:* C&ISA, ChemAb, EngInd, GeoRef, S&F, SCI. *Aud.:* Ac, Sa.

Each issue of this publication contains papers on a topic relating to specific transportation modes and subject areas. The papers come from those prepared for presentation at Transportation Research Board (TRB) annual meetings, conferences, and workshops; they cover various aspects of the issue's theme, including technical, social, economic, or operational perspectives. Between 50 and 60 issues are published each year. Authors and topics come from all over the world. The primary emphasis of this journal is on topics relating to the engineering of highways, urban transportation, and traffic safety. Along with other TRB publications, this is an essential series for any transportation collection. An index to this journal's articles can be accessed at http://www.dcdata.com/trb/trb.htm. Appropriate for large academic collections and special collections.

6509. ***Transportation Science.*** [ISSN: 0041-1655] 1967. q. USD 221 print & online eds. (Individuals, USD 155 print & online eds.). Ed(s): Hani Mahmassani. I N F O R M S, 901 Elkridge Landing Rd., Ste. 400, Linthicum, MD 21090-2909; informs@informs.org; http://www.informs.org/pubs/. Illus., index, adv. Refereed. Circ: 1200 Paid and controlled. Vol. ends: Nov. Microform: WWS; NRP. Online: EBSCO Publishing; JSTOR (Web-based Journal Archive); ProQuest Information & Learning. *Indexed:* AS&TI, C&ISA, EngInd, IBSS, SCI, SSCI. *Bk. rev.:* Occasional, 500–1,500 words. *Aud.:* Ac, Sa.

Published by the Institute for Operations Research and Management Sciences (INFORMS), this scholarly journal contains articles on all modes of transportation on operational-management aspects such as planning and the economic and social design, but not the physical design, of transportation-related components. The mission of the journal is to advance the analytical, experimental, and observational tools in the study of transportation. The journal contains research articles, critical-review articles, technical notes, letters to the editor, and book reviews. Annually, dissertation abstracts submitted for the Transportation Science Section Prize are published. Tables of contents can be accessed at http://transci.pubs.informs.org. Appropriate for special collections.

6510. ***Urban Transport International.*** [ISSN: 1268-2241] 1995. bi-m. EUR 45 domestic; EUR 61 in Europe; EUR 73 elsewhere. Ed(s): John Maryon. Urban Transport International, 3 av. Hoche, Paris, 75008, France; urban.transport@free.fr; http://urban.transport.free.fr. Illus., adv. Sample. Circ: 8000. *Aud.:* Sa.

This English-language journal published in France addresses the international urban/public transportation industry. It is geared toward the practitioner and covers industry news and events, legislation, regulation, safety, technology, marketing, economics, management, planning, and intelligent transportation systems. Each issue includes feature articles, relevant web sites, statistics, diagrams, route maps, a highlighted subject section, and a calendar of events. The tables of contents for current and past issues can be accessed at http://lerail.uti.free.fr/uti/index-uti.htm. Appropriate for special collections.

6511. ***Waterways Journal.*** [ISSN: 0043-1524] 1887. w. USD 32. Ed(s): Dan Owen, John Shoulberg. Waterways Journal, Inc., 319 N. Fourth St., 650 Security Bldg., St. Louis, MO 63102. Illus., adv. Circ: 5000 Paid. Vol. ends: No. 52. *Bk. rev.:* Occasional, up to 250 wds. *Aud.:* Ga, Sa.

This U.S.-focused, tabloid-format publication covers all aspects of inland waterways, water transportation, and ports. Written for anyone with an interest in inland water transportation, including enthusiasts, its articles cover news, historical articles, letters, barge data and other statistics, Washington news, and more. Annual features include a yearbook and directory that includes a chronological listing of the year's important news. A weekly news summary and editorial are available on the magazine's web site at http://www.waterwaysjournal.net. Appropriate for special collections.

6512. ***WorkBoat.*** [ISSN: 0043-8014] 1943. m. USD 49; USD 69 in Canada & Mexico; USD 79 elsewhere. Ed(s): Dave Krapf. Diversified Business Communications, PO Box 7438, Portland, ME 04112-7438; http://www.workboat.com. Illus., adv. Circ: 22000. Vol. ends: Dec. Online: Florida Center for Library Automation; Gale Group. *Aud.:* Sa.

A trade magazine for the North American workboat industry, which includes but is not limited to tugs, barges, salvage vessels, crewboats, utility boats, excursion vessels, freighters, tankers, patrol craft, fire boats, and research vessels. It is geared to the practitioner and covers industry news and events, legislation, regulation, safety, technology, vessel construction and maintenance, marine personnel, equipment, and product news. Each issue includes feature articles, a calendar of events, a classified section, a product showcase, and a section highlighting a specific port. The table of contents for the current issue and the full text of archived articles can be accessed at http://www.workboat.com/index.html. Appropriate for special collections.

6513. ***World Highways.*** [ISSN: 0964-4598] 1950. 10x/yr. GBP 100; USD 165. Ed(s): Alan Peterson. Route One Publishing Ltd., Horizon House, Azalea Dr, Swanley, BR8 8JR, United Kingdom; subs@routeonepub.com; http://www.routeonepub.com. Illus., adv. Circ: 18201. *Aud.:* Sa.

This journal addresses the international road and highway construction and maintenance industries and targets the practitioner. It covers industry news and events, materials, signage, lighting, equipment, technology, the environment and weather, traffic, and safety. Each issue includes feature articles, a calendar of events, guides to products and services, relevant web sites, and a highlighted construction site. It includes a whole page devoted to highway construction humor. The current issue's table of contents, news briefs, and full text of feature articles can be accessed at http://www.worldhighways.com/news/index.htm. Appropriate for special collections.

■ TRAVEL AND TOURISM

General/Newsletters/Reference/Research

See also Canada; and City, State, and Regional sections.

Jeff Kosokoff, Head of Reference Services, Lamont Library of the Harvard College Library, Harvard University, Harvard Yard, Cambridge, MA, 02138; kosokoff@fas.harvard.edu

Introduction

The travel industry has been in a gigantic slump with the decline in the world economy after September 11th and rising security concerns. Also, free information on the Internet, from individuals, travel publishers, and travel agents, continues to grow in quantity and quality. The ongoing proliferation of this free information provides a challenge to the publishers of printed travel magazines, and two old favorites are no more (*Travel Holiday* and *Consumer Reports Travel Letter*). Since the last edition, some publications have moved completely online (and out of this chapter), while still others keep publishing pretty much as they have for many years. At least for now, there are still some very useful and valuable publications available to consumers, and libraries can get a lot of bang for their buck. The consumer publications listed here each cover an expansive region or travel theme of wide appeal.

In the academic realm, interest in tourism studies, especially as they relate to economic and development issues, remains strong. Since the 11th edition, many new publications have emerged, and only time will tell if they survive and become important players in library collections. The academic publications listed here continue to be very interdisciplinary in nature, as geography, economics, sociology, environmental studies, and political science come to look at a variety of issues arising out of the growth and spread of tourism. The double-edged sword of tourism as an alternative to more traditional manufacturing or agricultural economies looms large in this realm.

Regarding online resources, counterpart web sites that provide particularly useful or expanded content are noted in the annotation for those publications. "Free-with-print" online access for academic journals is noted in annotations as well. In lieu of providing a separate section of electronic journals, the Yahoo gateway web site URL is listed below. Given the fluidity of many "e-zines" and other web sites, it would be counterproductive to point to specific publications. The Yahoo! listing is an excellent place to look for online publications to begin one's online search for consumer-oriented travel information, especially when the goal is to find more in the way of narratives than is provided by general booking-oriented web sites like Travelocity, Expedia, or Orbitz:

http://dir.yahoo.com/Recreation/Travel/News_and_Media/Magazines/

Basic Periodicals

Ems: *National Geographic Traveler;* Hs: *National Geographic Traveler, Transitions Abroad;* Ga: *Arthur Frommer's Budget Travel, Conde Nast Traveler, National Geographic Traveler, Transitions Abroad, Travel & Leisure;* Ac: *Annals of Tourism Research, Journal of Sustainable Tourism, Journal of Travel Research.*

Basic Abstracts and Indexes

Access; Leisure, Recreation and Tourism Abstracts; Lodging, Restaurant and Travel Abstracts; Magazine Index; Readers' Guide to Periodical Literature.

Pacific Tourism Review. See *Tourism Review International.*

General

6514. ***Adventure Travel.*** [ISSN: 1368-0773] 1995. bi-m. GBP 30; GBP 2.80 newsstand/cover per issue. Ed(s): Alun Davies. Independent & Specialist Travel, PO Box 6254, Alcester, B49 6PF, United Kingdom; alunadtrav@btinternet.com. Circ: 18000 Paid. *Bk. rev.:* 10, 50 words. *Aud.:* Ga.

Readers who want information about resorts, hotels, and restaurants should look elsewhere. This is a down-to-earth magazine for serious globetrotting adventure travelers, written by and for mountain and rock climbers, hikers, and whitewater rafters. It includes feature-length, first-person travel narratives, gear reviews, and general tips and discussion of issues facing the community of travelers on the edge. A U.K. focus means that the prices are in British pounds and the itineraries originate in Britain; however, this publication is packed with useful and detailed information for all adventure travelers. A valuable resource for serious outdoor adventurers, *AT* belongs in larger public libraries and any others that serve this unique clientele.

6515. ***Arthur Frommer's Budget Travel: vacations for real people.*** [ISSN: 1521-5210] 1998. bi-m. USD 11.97 domestic; USD 23.97 Canada; USD 29.97 elsewhere. Ed(s): Arthur Frommer. Arthur Frommer's Budget Travel, 530 Seventh Ave, 2nd Fl, New York, NY 10018. Adv. Circ: 450000. *Aud.:* Ga.

This glossy magazine is geared to the traveler who is willing to do some negotiating and digging to get a better deal. It includes among its features budget tips for families, information on hostels, and a variety of money-saving hints offered in columns and essays. The magazine's audience includes the average traveler who wants to take a relatively affordable vacation. This is a highly readable title suitable for public and academic libraries of all sizes. The free companion web site is provided via MSN as an integrated part of the travel section of the MSNBC travel section (http://www.msnbc.com/news/bt-front_front.asp?).

Backpacker: the magazine of wilderness travel adventure. See Hiking, Climbing, and Outdoor Recreation/General section.

6516. ***Business Traveler (USA Edition).*** 1976. 10x/yr. USD 39.99 domestic; USD 54.99 foreign. Ed(s): Eva Leonard. Perry Publications Inc, 225 Park Ave S, 7th Fl, New York, NY 10003; http://www.btonline.com. Illus., adv. Sample. Circ: 48000 Paid. *Aud.:* Sa.

Business travelers are the audience for this slick magazine, which focuses on destinations, flights, and hotels. There are lots of hotel recommendations along with comparative reviews of airline and other travel services. Most suitable for corporate libraries and other libraries that serve those who travel frequently on business to the world's major cities.

6517. ***Caribbean Travel and Life.*** Formerly (until 1987): *Caribbean Travel and Life Magazine.* [ISSN: 1052-1011] 1986. 9x/yr. USD 23.95 domestic; USD 32.95 Canada; USD 41.95 elsewhere. Ed(s): Bob Friel, Jessica Chapman. World Publications LLC, 460 N Orlando Ave, Ste 200, Winter Park, FL 32789; info@worldpub.net; http://www.worldpub.net. Illus., adv. Circ: 157518 Paid. *Aud.:* Ga.

A wonderful resource for those planning a trip to the Caribbean, which is broadly defined to include Bermuda, the Bahamas, and the Yucatan peninsula. Although the tone can sometimes be more promotional than objective, this magazine offers beautiful photographs and quality articles about travel opportunities throughout the islands. A typical issue has a handful of feature articles on particular islands or styles of travel or accommodations. The two major sections, "Travel" and "Life," give briefer tidbits about particular attractions, accommodations, and events throughout the region. Additional valuable content, also leaning toward the promotional, is available on the magazine's web site (http://www.caribbeantravelmag.com).

6518. ***Conde Nast Traveler: truth in travel.*** Formerly (until 1987): *Signature.* [ISSN: 0893-9683] 1954. m. USD 12 domestic; USD 33.97 Canada; USD 38.97 elsewhere. Ed(s): Thomas J Wallace. Conde Nast Publications Inc., 4 Times Square, 5th Fl, New York, NY 10036. Illus., index, adv. Sample. Circ: 750000. Vol. ends: Dec (No. 12). Microform: PQC. Online: Gale Group. *Indexed:* ASIP, GeoRef, RGPR. *Aud.:* Ga.

The ultimate high-end travel magazine, *Conde Nast Traveler* is targeted at the upscale travel market, but it is of interest to all varieties of travelers. The emphasis is on style, the spectacular, and the extraordinary in travel. Stunning photographs and sumptuous settings make this is a primary component of any public or academic library collection that contains commercial travel and tourism periodicals. The companion web site (http://www.concierge.com/) is a valuable resource for general information and travel planning.

6519. ***Cruise Travel: ships, ports, schedules, prices.*** [ISSN: 0199-5111] 1979. bi-m. USD 29.95 domestic; USD 40 foreign; USD 5.99 newsstand/cover per issue. Ed(s): Robert Meyers. World Publishing Co., 990 Grove St, Evanston, IL 60201; cs@centurysports.net; http://www.cruisetraveling.com. Illus., adv. Sample. Circ: 180400 Paid. Vol. ends: May/Jun. Reprint: PQC. *Aud.:* Ga.

Sister publication of *Travel America* (see below), which features articles about new ships, trends in cruising, and popular and new ports-of-call. Feature articles concentrate on individual ships, activities at various destinations, and tips for making the most of a cruise vacation. A good secondary magazine that is most at home in public libraries.

The Explorers Journal. See Geography section.

Geomundo. See Latin American section.

The Guide: gay travel, entertainment, politics, and sex. See Lesbian, Gay, Bisexual, and Transgender section.

6520. ***National Geographic Adventure.*** [ISSN: 1523-6226] 1999. bi-m. USD 12 domestic; CND 35 Canada; USD 25 elsewhere. Ed(s): John Rasmus. National Geographic Society, 1145 17th St, N W, Washington, DC 20036; adventure@ngs.org; http://www.nationalgeographic.com/adventure. Illus. Circ: 352077 Free. Online: Gale Group. *Bk. rev.:* 3, 500 words. *Aud.:* Ga.

This magazine for adventure travelers is everything you would expect from the folks at National Geographic. Stunning photography accompanies well-written articles about travel on the wilder side. Special attention is paid to ecologically sensitive travel. The feature articles are complemented by shorter pieces on equipment, interviews, and travel tips. Readers that climb, canoe, kayak, or dive while traveling will enjoy finding this magazine in their high school, public, or academic library. Previous articles and valuable information such as gear reviews are preserved on this magazine's web site (http://www.nationalgeographic.com/adventure).

6521. ***National Geographic Traveler.*** [ISSN: 0747-0932] 1984. 8x/yr. USD 17.95 domestic; CND 30.94 Canada; USD 25.50 elsewhere. Ed(s): Keith Bellows. National Geographic Society, 1145 17th St, N W, Washington, DC 20036. Illus., index, adv. Sample. Circ: 715000 Paid. Vol. ends: Nov/Dec. *Indexed:* ASIP, MagInd. *Aud.:* Ga.

An outstanding travel publication from National Geographic. Beautiful photographs complement high-quality and informative articles emphasizing travel to established destinations the world over. Most articles focus on travel to a particular region and its culture, and not all articles include recommendations for lodging or dining. This valuable resource belongs in all public and many academic and school libraries. Web-exclusive content is available on the companion web site (http://www.nationalgeographic.com/traveler).

Our World: international gay & lesbian travel. See Lesbian, Gay, Bisexual, and Transgender section.

6522. ***T & L Golf.*** Formerly (until 2000): *Travel & Leisure Golf.* [ISSN: 1533-3434] 1998. bi-m. USD 27 domestic; USD 23 Canada; USD 30.50 elsewhere. Ed(s): John Atwood. American Express Publishing Corp., 1120 Ave of the Americas, New York, NY 10036; http://www.amexpub.com. Illus., adv. Circ: 305000. *Aud.:* Ga.

If golf is an important part of one's travel experience, then this magazine is a great resource. There are features about famous golfers, celebrity golf enthusiasts, courses, golf destinations, package vacations that include golf, and equipment reviews. Sections on golf homes, golf tips, and the golf lifestyle round out this attractive mass-marketed publication from the *Travel & Leisure* family of publications.

6523. ***Transitions Abroad: the guide to learning, living, and working overseas.*** Formerly (until 1985): *Transitions.* [ISSN: 1061-2343] 1977. bi-m. USD 28 domestic; USD 32 Canada; USD 46 elsewhere. Ed(s): Clayton A Hubbs. Transitions Abroad Publishing, 18 Hulst Rd, Box 1300, Amherst, MA 01004; editor@transitionsabroad.com. Illus., index, adv. Sample. Circ: 20000 Paid. Vol. ends: May/Jun. *Aud.:* Hs, Ga.

A fantastic resource for Americans interested in working or studying outside the United States. This journal's focus is on extended opportunites—how to find out about them, how to apply, and how to adjust to one's new life. *Transitions Abroad* is especially useful for those interested in teaching English overseas. It also includes information for the long-term independent traveler, including travel bargains and volunteer opportunities. Various directory listings of employers and opportunities in each issue are in themselves a valuable resource. Highly recommended for academic, high school, career services, and public libraries. The companion web site (http://www.transitionsabroad.com) is an excellent resource in its own right.

6524. ***Travel 50 & Beyond.*** [ISSN: 1049-6211] 1990. q. USD 11.95; USD 3.95 newsstand/cover per issue. Ed(s): Elizabeth Armstrong. Vacation Publications, Inc., 1502 Augusta Dr, Ste 415, Houston, TX 77057. Illus., adv. Sample. Circ: 150000. Vol. ends: Fall (No. 4). *Aud.:* Ga.

The original travel magazine aimed at the 50-and-older crowd, *Travel 50 and Beyond* stresses destinations in the Americas but increasingly covers destinations in Europe and beyond. Although most of the information is of interest to travelers of all ages, some articles emphasize issues of interest to older people, such as tips for those who have grandchildren or have mobility issues. Suitable for public libraries.

6525. ***Travel & Leisure.*** Formerly: *Travel and Camera.* [ISSN: 0041-2007] 1971. m. USD 26.95 domestic; USD 49 Canada; USD 64 elsewhere. Ed(s): Nancy Novogrod. American Express Publishing Corp., 1120 Ave of the Americas, New York, NY 10036. Illus., index, adv. Sample. Circ: 961000 Paid. Vol. ends: Dec. Microform: PQC. Online: Gale Group. *Indexed:* ASIP, LRI, MagInd. *Aud.:* Ga.

A core publication for the upscale traveler, *T+L* emphasizes stylish travel experiences when only the best will do. It provides high-quality feature articles including destination and trip descriptions, tips and tricks for getting the most out of a visit to a particular location, and restaurant and hotel reviews. This flagship publication of the Travel & Leisure brand is at home in public and academic libraries that serve the stylish business or leisure traveler (or those who wish they were). Supplemental information and articles from previous issues are available at the companion web site (http://www.travelandleisure.com/).

6526. ***Travel & Leisure Family.*** 1998. s-a. Ed(s): Margot Guralnick. American Express Publishing Corp., 1120 Ave of the Americas, New York, NY 10036; http://www.amexpub.com. Illus., adv. Circ: 250000 Paid. *Aud.:* Ga.

For the nuclear family headed off on vacation, *T+L Family* is a family-focused semiannual version of its parent publication *Travel & Leisure* (see above). It identifies and offers suggestions for places that are appropriate for travel with children. It is chock-full of tips and details to help families plan. Strongly focused on the Western Hemisphere, the magazine includes longer feature articles as well as useful sections on health concerns when traveling with children. Appropriate for public libraries. The companion web site provides a nice supplement, including content from recent issues (http://www.tlfamily.com).

6527. ***TravelAmerica.*** Formerly (until 1993): *Tours and Resorts.* [ISSN: 1068-2554] 1985. bi-m. USD 29.95 domestic; USD 40 foreign; USD 5.99 newsstand/cover per issue. Ed(s): Robert Meyers. World Publishing Co., 990 Grove St, Evanston, IL 60201; cs@centurysports.net. Illus., adv. Sample. Circ: 245000 Paid. *Aud.:* Ga.

This basic, general travel magazine includes departments for escorted tours, resort travel, and recreational vehicle enthusiasts. It focuses on destinations within the United States and provides feature articles about individual cities, regions, and states. Well-placed in a public library collection.

6528. ***Wanderlust: travel for the free-spirited.*** [ISSN: 1351-4733] 1993. bi-m. GBP 17.50 domestic; GBP 21 in Europe; GBP 30 rest of world. Ed(s): Lyn Hughes. Wanderlust, PO Box 1832, Windsor, SL4 6YP, United Kingdom; info@wanderlust.co.uk; http://www.wanderlust.co.uk. Illus., adv. Sample. Circ: 35500 Paid. *Bk. rev.:* 8, 250 words. *Aud.:* Ga.

This glossy British publication offers lots of sensible tips and information about exotic travel destinations througout the world. In addition to feature articles, every issue has sections that focus on health and safety, upcoming events, and travel gear. This is a great addition to school, public, and academic libraries that serve adventurous world travelers. Some information, including recent book and CD-ROM reviews, are reproduced on the companion web site (http://www.wanderlust.co.uk/).

Newsletters

6529. ***Artistic Traveler: architecture & travel with art & photography.*** [ISSN: 1060-2569] 1991. bi-m. USD 29. Ed(s): Richard Hovey. S & R Research, PO Box 2038, Vancouver, WA 98668-2038. Illus. Sample. *Aud.:* Ac, Sa.

A wonderful newsletter for travelers who have a special interest in art and architecture. Articles focus on photography, events, and awards. A large portion of each issue is devoted to a national events calendar that lists exhibitions, major renovations, and workshops throughout the United States and major European cities. This is a great resource for anyone interested in the architecture and visual arts scene. Underrepresented in libraries, this publication should be in many more public and arts-oriented academic collections.

6530. ***International Travel News.*** [ISSN: 0191-8761] 1976. m. USD 18 domestic; USD 28 foreign. Ed(s): David Tykol. Martin Publications Inc., 2120 28th St, Sacramento, CA 95818; itn@ns.net; http://www.intltravelnews.com. Illus., adv. Sample. Circ: 50000. *Bk. rev.:* 1, 750 words. *Aud.:* Ga.

Reader-contributors make this massive travel newsletter a wonderful resource for frequent travelers and others who want to hear firsthand accounts of life on the ground at all kinds of destinations worldwide. It announces deals and specials and provides a general forum for travelers. This newsletter is suitable for public libraries of all sizes. The *ITN* web site (http://www.intltravelnews.com) is a nice extension of the print publication.

6531. ***Marco Polo: the magazine for adventure travelers over 50.*** 1997. q. USD 10; USD 2.95 newsstand/cover per issue. Ed(s): James Plouf. Marco Polo Publishing Inc., 1299 Bayshore Blvd Ste B, Dunedin, FL 34698; james@travelroads.com; http://www.marco-polo.net. Adv. Circ: 4000 Paid. *Bk. rev.:* 2, 100-150 words. *Aud.:* Ga.

A casual and fun travel newsletter for the 50-and-over crowd. Freelance writers and newsletter staff contribute feature articles that document travel destinations that are likely to be of interest to older, but still adventurous, travelers. Active independent and escorted travelers will enjoy the tone and scope of this publication. General travel tips and discounts for specific destinations are featured in each issue. At home in public libraries.

6532. ***Travel Smart.*** Incorporates (in 1983): *Joy of Travel;* Which was formerly (1969-1983): *Joyer Travel Report.* [ISSN: 0741-5826] 1976. m. USD 39 domestic; USD 64 foreign. Ed(s): Nancy J Dunnan. Dunnan Communications, Inc., PO Box 397, Dobbs Ferry, NY 10522. Illus., index. Sample. Circ: 18000 Paid. *Aud.:* Ga.

A timely little newsletter with last-minute travel deals and longer feature articles on themes such as immigration, overseas employment, or general safety tips. Each issue also includes the "Insider Report," one or two regional overviews with suggestions for what to see and do, where to stay and eat, and how to get there. Suitable for public libraries.

Reference

Leisure, Recreation and Tourism Abstracts. See Abstracts and Indexes section.

6533. ***O A G Desktop Flight Guide - North American Edition.*** Formerly (until 1991): *Official Airline Guide. North American Edition.* [ISSN: 1057-0918] 1948. s-m. Members, USD 599. O A G Worldwide, 444 N Michigan Ave, Chicago, IL 60611; custsvc@oag.com; http://www.oag.com. Illus., adv. Circ: 30000. *Aud.:* Ga, Sa.

This publication is the complete listing of every airline's scheduled flights in North America, including the United States, Mexico, Canada, and the Caribbean. Each flight's listing includes day(s) of the week, departure/arrival times, airline, flight number, classes of service available, type of aircraft, meals served, and number of intermediate stops. Other editions available include "Worldwide" and regional "pocket guides." Some libraries may want to opt for the online version, which is similar in cost to a print subscription. For reference desks in corporate and larger public and academic libraries.

Research

6534. ***Annals of Tourism Research: a social sciences journal.*** [ISSN: 0160-7383] 1973. q. EUR 529 (Individuals, EUR 142; Students, EUR 61). Ed(s): Jafar Jafari. Pergamon, The Boulevard, Langford Ln, East Park, Kidlington, OX5 1GB, United Kingdom. Illus., index, adv. Sample. Refereed. Circ: 1200. Vol. ends: Oct. Microform: PQC. Online: ingenta.com; ScienceDirect; Swets Blackwell. *Indexed:* ABS&EES, AbAn, AgeL, AnthLit, BPI, CJA, CommAb, ForAb, LR&TI, PAIS, RRTA, RiskAb, S&F, SSCI, SociolAb, SportS, WAE&RSA. *Bk. rev.:* 8, 750 words. *Aud.:* Ac, Sa.

This is one of the top journals in the field. It publishes cross-disciplinary academic research on tourism, with some attention to recreation and hospitality. Articles emphasize theory over practice. Although the articles are in English, abstracts are included in both English and French. Professionals can keep up-to-date with their field through the book reviews, notices of publication, and a conference calendar. Tables of contents and sample issues are free online (www.elsevier.com/locate/atoures). Although a bit overpriced, this journal belongs in every academic tourism collection, and it is also of interest to theory-minded scholars in anthropology, economics, and cultural studies.

6535. ***Current Issues in Tourism.*** [ISSN: 1368-3500] 1998. bi-m. GBP 266 (Individuals, GBP 50). Ed(s): C Hall, Chris Cooper. Channel View Publications, Frankfurt Lodge, Clevedon Hall, Victoria Rd., Clevedon, BS21 7HH, United Kingdom; info@multilingual-matters.com; http://www.channelviewpublications.com. Online: EBSCO Publishing; Ingenta Select; Swets Blackwell. *Indexed:* ForAb, IndVet, PEI, RRTA, S&F, VetBull, WAE&RSA. *Aud.:* Ac.

This scholarly journal addresses contemporary and current issues and perspectives in tourism studies. It explores different and emerging types of tourism worldwide as well as local tourism issues in particular locations. The print subscription includes online access via Ingenta Select (http://www.ingentaselect.com/) at no additional charge. Appropriate for academic libraries with comprehensive collections in tourism studies.

6536. ***Event Management: an international journal.*** Formerly (until 1999): *Festival Management & Event Tourism.* [ISSN: 1525-9951] 1993. q. USD 290 combined subscription domestic print & online eds.; USD 310 combined subscription foreign print & online eds. Ed(s): Dr. Bruce Wicks, Dr. Donald Getz. Cognizant Communication Corporation, 3 Hartsdale Rd, Elmsford, NY 10523-3701; cogcomm@aol.com; http://www.cognizantcommunication.com. Adv. Refereed. *Indexed:* LR&TI. *Bk. rev.:* 1, 750 words. *Aud.:* Ac.

This scholary journal publishes articles concerned with the management of festivals and special events. It attempts to bring coherence to the disparate interests that are involved in the management and execution of conferences, expositions, and other annual or irregular events. A secondary but important publication for geographers, sociologists, economists, and others interested in these issues. Online access is available to subscribers via Ingenta (http://www.ingenta.com/journals/browse/cog/em). Appropriate for large academic collections.

6537. *Information Technology and Tourism: application - methodology - techniques.* [ISSN: 1098-3058] 1998. q. USD 300 combined subscription domestic print & online eds.; USD 325 combined subscription foreign print & online eds. Ed(s): Hannes Werthner. Cognizant Communication Corporation, 3 Hartsdale Rd, Elmsford, NY 10523-3701; cogcomm@aol.com; http://www.cognizantcommunication.com. Refereed. *Indexed:* RRTA, WAE&RSA. *Bk. rev.:* 6, 500 words. *Aud.:* Ac, Sa.

This is composed primarily of practical articles and book reviews at the intersection of digital technology and the tourism industry. The fairly technical articles are aimed at planners and IT managers who are looking to implement and improve the management of tourism through improvements in information technology. This is a publication for academics and practitioners alike. Full text is online for subscribers via Ingenta (http://www.ingenta.com/journals/browse/cog/itt). Appropriate for special and large academic libraries.

6538. *International Journal of Tourism Research.* Formerly (until 1999): *Progress in Tourism and Hospitality Research.* [ISSN: 1099-2340] 1995. bi-m. USD 575. John Wiley & Sons Ltd., The Atrium, Southern Gate, Chichester, PO19 8SQ, United Kingdom; customer@wiley.co.uk; http://www.wiley.co.uk. Adv. Refereed. *Indexed:* ForAb, RRTA, S&F, WAE&RSA. *Bk. rev.:* 5, 1,000 words. *Aud.:* Ac.

This relatively new and somewhat general journal cuts a wide swath across various areas of tourism research. It is international in focus, with an emphasis on new approaches. The most recent special issue (there is one each year) focused on "visitor attractions." For comprehensive, academic tourism collections.

Journal of Hospitality & Leisure Marketing. See Advertising, Marketing, and Public Relations section.

Journal of Hospitality & Tourism Research. See Hospitality/Restaurant section.

6539. *Journal of Sustainable Tourism.* [ISSN: 0966-9582] 1993. bi-m. GBP 240 (Individuals, GBP 50). Ed(s): Bill Bramwell, Bernard Lane. Channel View Publications, Frankfurt Lodge, Clevedon Hall, Victoria Rd., Clevedon, BS21 7HH, United Kingdom; info@multilingual-matters.com; http://www.channelviewpublications.com. Illus., index, adv. Sample. Refereed. Online: EBSCO Publishing; Ingenta Select; Swets Blackwell. *Indexed:* EnvAb, ForAb, GeogAbPG, RRTA, S&F, SociolAb, WAE&RSA. *Bk. rev.:* 3, 1,000 words. *Aud.:* Ac, Sa.

An important journal for scholars looking for ways to reduce the negative ecological and community impacts of tourism. It publishes timely articles that explore projects that strive to balance the needs and expectations of the tourism industry with those of host areas and ecosystems. Online access via Ingenta Select (http://www.ingentaselect.com) is available to subscribers at no additional charge.

6540. *Journal of Travel Research.* Formerly: *Travel Research Bulletin.* [ISSN: 0047-2875] 1962. q. GBP 241 print & online eds. in Europe, Middle East, Africa & Australasia. Ed(s): Charles R Goeldner. Sage Publications, Inc., 2455 Teller Rd, Thousand Oaks, CA 91320; info@sagepub.com; http://www.sagepub.com. Circ: 1600. Online: Florida Center for Library Automation; Gale Group; ingenta.com; Northern Light Technology, Inc.; OCLC Online Computer Library Center, Inc.; ProQuest Information & Learning; RoweCom Information Quest; Swets Blackwell; H.W. Wilson. *Indexed:* ABIn, ABS&EES, BPI, GeogAbPG, LR&TI, RRTA, S&F, SUSA, WAE&RSA. *Bk. rev.:* 2, 750 words. *Aud.:* Ac.

An important journal that emphasizes quantitative research about travel and tourism for scholars interested in tourism marketing. The articles treat topics that range from research on particular destinations to overviews of general issues such as research methodologies, tourist perceptions, and interactions between tourist destinations and local communities. An important resource for scholarly and special collections that serve academics and practitioners interested in the economic and marketing aspects of tourism and leisure studies.

6541. *Journal of Vacation Marketing: an international journal.* [ISSN: 1356-7667] 1995. q. GBP 230 (Individual members, GBP 80 based only at universities or other educational establishments). Ed(s): J S Perry Hobson. Henry Stewart Publications, Russell House, 28-30 Little Russell St, London, WC1A 2HN, United Kingdom; qweny@henrystewart.co.uk; http://www.henrystewart.com/. Adv. Refereed. Circ: 850 Paid. Online: EBSCO Publishing; ingenta.com; OCLC Online Computer Library Center, Inc.; ProQuest Information & Learning. Reprint: PSC. *Indexed:* LR&TI, RRTA, WAE&RSA. *Bk. rev.:* 2, 500 words. *Aud.:* Ac, Sa.

A specialty journal for scholars and practitioners in the travel industry. Peer-reviewed articles appear in the "Academic Papers" section, which is flanked by other articles that tend toward the practical and can vary in quality. This journal is at home in business and business-oriented hospitality and tourism collections. Online access with print subscription via Ingenta (http://www.ingenta.com/journals/browse/hsp/vm?).

6542. *Journeys: the international journal of travel and travel writing.* [ISSN: 1465-2609] 2000. s-a. USD 90 (Individuals, USD 28; USD 15 newsstand/cover per issue). Ed(s): J Eade, G R Marvin. Berghahn Books Inc., 604 W 115th St, New York, NY 10025; journals@berghahnbooks.com; http://www.berghahnbooks.com. Adv. Online: Gale Group. *Indexed:* SociolAb. *Bk. rev.:* 5, 750 words. *Aud.:* Ac.

A niche journal that publishes articles about travel writing. Historians, sociologists, and anthropologists all can find something of interest here. A substantial part of each issue comprises the book reviews, which focus on newly published travel narratives and scholarly books.

6543. *Tourism Analysis.* [ISSN: 1083-5423] 1996. q. USD 295 combined subscription domestic print & online eds.; USD 325 combined subscription foreign print & online eds. Cognizant Communication Corporation, 3 Hartsdale Rd, Elmsford, NY 10523-3701; cogcomm@aol.com; http://www.cognizantcommunication.com. Refereed. *Indexed:* ForAb, RRTA, S&F, WAE&RSA. *Bk. rev.:* 3, 800 words. *Aud.:* Ac.

Aims to provide a forum for the discussion of new and developing models for understanding travel and tourism. This journal has a theoretical and international focus on general issues in the study of tourism, leisure, and hospitality. It belongs only in comprehensive academic travel and tourism collections. Ingenta provides full-text-online for subscribers (http://www.ingenta.com/journals/browse/cog/ta).

6544. *Tourism and Hospitality Research: the Surrey quarterly review.* Formerly (until 1999): *International Journal of Tourism and Hospitality Research.* [ISSN: 1467-3584] 1999. q. GBP 195 (Individuals, GBP 100 full-time academics). Ed(s): Richard Butler, Andrew Lockwood. Henry Stewart Publications, Russell House, 28-30 Little Russell St, London, WC1A 2HN, United Kingdom; qweny@henrystewart.co.uk; http://www.henrystewart.com/. Circ: 1000 Paid. Reprint: PSC. *Indexed:* JEL. *Aud.:* Ac.

A scholarly journal that provides a forum for articles that address theoretical issues in tourism and hospitality. Each issue publishes five or six articles addressing the economics, management, and impact of tourism. A "Practice Papers" section has various short pieces meant to be more practical discussions than formal research. Suitable for strong academic collections.

6545. *Tourism Economics: the business and finance of tourism and recreation.* [ISSN: 1354-8166] 1995. q. USD 303 print & online eds. Ed(s): Stephen Wanhill. I P Publishing Ltd., Coleridge House, 4-5 Coleridge Gardens, London, NW6 3HQ, United Kingdom; JEdmondIP@aol.com; http://www.ippublishing.com. Illus. Sample. Refereed. *Indexed:* ForAb, JEL, RRTA, S&F, WAE&RSA. *Aud.:* Ac.

This international journal presents analysis of current trends in tourism in an economic context. It has a strong quantitative focus and a general emphasis on the treatment of concrete cases as opposed to purely theoretical discussions. *Tourism Economics* is appropriate for academic collections with a strong focus on economics or the tourism industry. Online access is available via Ingenta Select (http://www.ingentaselect.com) at no additional charge.

6546. ***Tourism Review International.*** Formerly (until 2003): *Pacific Tourism Review.* [ISSN: 1544-2721] 1997. q. USD 275 combined subscription domestic print & online eds.; USD 295 combined subscription foreign print & online eds. Cognizant Communication Corporation, 3 Hartsdale Rd, Elmsford, NY 10523-3701; cogcomm@aol.com; http://www.cognizantcommunication.com. Refereed. *Indexed:* BAS, RRTA. *Bk. rev.:* 2, 1,000 words. *Aud.:* Ac.

This journal focuses on tourism patterns and issues within the Pacific and around the Pacific Rim. It applies and develops lessons learned from travel and tourism at specific destinations to inform those interested in the region from geographical, social, economic, and political perspectives. *Pacific Tourism Review* is a second-tier journal that is nonetheless appropriate for academic collections that aim to be strong in Pacific Rim studies, even outside of travel and tourism studies. Online access for print subscribers is via Ingenta (http://www.ingenta.com/journals/browse/cog/ptr).

Electronic Journals

Infiltration. See Zines section.

■ URBAN STUDIES

JoAnn Jacoby, Anthropology and Sociology Subject Specialist, Education and Social Science Library, University of Illinois at Urbana-Champaign, Urbana, IL 61801; E-mail: jacoby@uiuc.edu

Introduction

Urban studies, the design and study of urban and regional areas, is a truly multidisciplinary field with strong ties to city planning, landscape architecture and design, public policy, civil and environmental engineering, and architecture. It also has considerable overlap with other disciplines such as sociology, political science, geography, ecology, anthropology, economics, and history. The field of urban studies encompasses diverse areas of interest including, but not limited to, community and economic development, public health and safety, ecology and environmental management, transportation and public works, housing, land use, sustainable development, cultural heritage and preservation, aesthetics and design, and urban-renewal sprawl and gentrification.

An emerging theme in the academic literature, as well as among practitioners concerned with policy and planning issues, is the interplay between global and local forces that shape urban environments. Globalization is a recurring topic in all but the most narrowly focused titles, perhaps reflecting an increasing interest in this area among scholars and activists across the disciplines. *Environment and Urbanization, International Journal of Urban and Regional Research,* and *Regional Studies* are among the journals that publish extensively in this area, the latter with an emphasis on the impact of the European Union on local and regional development. Not surprisingly, the use of Geographic Information Systems (GIS) technologies is burgeoning within the field, and journals such as *Computer, Environment and Urban Systems* and the *Journal of the Urban and Regional Information Systems Association* highlight the application of GIS to urban studies issues. Ecology and environmental management is another area of growing interest, and a number of journals, including *Environment and Planning A, Journal of Urban Planning and Development,* and *Landscape and Urban Planning: An International Journal of Landscape Ecology, Planning, and Design* publish on environmental and ecological topics.

Most of the serials described in this section are geared toward academics or practitioners and are too theoretical or technical to appeal to a general audience. There are a few notable exceptions, including *American City and Country, National Civic Review, Planning,* and *Urban Land.* Another title that may be appropriate for some public libraries is *New Urban News,* a newsletter devoted to the principles of smart growth that is accessible, timely, and reasonably priced. The scholarly journals included reflect the breadth and depth of the discipline, and most libraries will have to choose carefully among them. The titles designated "Basic Periodicals" can serve loosely as a core list for academic libraries, but they should be supplemented, or in some cases replaced, by other titles selected in accordance with the particular research and curricular needs of the institution.

Basic Periodicals

Ga: *American City & County, Journal of the American Planning Association, Journal of Urban Technology, National Civic Review, Public Management, Planning, Urban Land;* Ac: *Cities, Environment and Urbanization, European Urban and Regional Studies, Growth and Change, International Journal of Urban and Regional Research, Journal of the American Planning Association, Journal of Planning Literature, Journal of Urban Affairs, Planning, Public Administration Review, Urban Affairs Review, Urban History, Urban Studies.*

Basic Abstracts and Indexes

Ekistic Index of Periodicals, Index to Current Urban Documents, PAIS, Sage Urban Studies Abstracts.

6547. ***American City & County: administration, engineering, and operations in relation to local government.*** Formerly: *American City.* [ISSN: 0149-337X] 1909. m. Free to qualified personnel. Ed(s): Beth Wade. Primedia Business Magazines & Media, Inc. (Atlanta), 6151 Powers Ferry Rd, N W, Atlanta, GA 30339-2941; inquiries@primediabusiness.com; http://www.primediabusiness.com/. Illus., index, adv. Circ: 71355. Vol. ends: Dec. Microform: PQC. Online: bigchalk; EBSCO Publishing; Factiva; Florida Center for Library Automation; Gale Group; LexisNexis; Northern Light Technology, Inc.; OCLC Online Computer Library Center, Inc.; ProQuest Information & Learning; H.W. Wilson. Reprint: PQC. *Indexed:* ABIn, AIAP, AS&TI, AgeL, BRI, CBRI, ChemAb, EngInd, ExcerpMed, MagInd, PAIS, RGPR, SSI, WRCInf. *Aud.:* Ga, Ac, Sa.

This glossy trade magazine is geared toward city and county government officials. The focus is on succinct summaries of current news, government trends and programs, policy issues, and projects. Advertisements are also included. This long-standing title (first published in 1909) is widely considered to be essential reading for local government officials and should be included in both public and academic library collections.

6548. ***Axis: the journal of housing, planning and regeneration.*** Formerly (until 1999): *Housing and Planning Review;* which incorporated (in 1998): *Housing Review;* Which was formerly: *Housing Centre Review;* (until 1964): *British Housing and Planning Review.* [ISSN: 1467-9086] bi-m. GBP 42.50 United Kingdom; GBP 47.50 elsewhere. Ed(s): Chris Griffin. ROOM, the National Council for Housing and Planning, 14 Old St, London, EC1V 9BH, United Kingdom. Illus., adv. Circ: 4500. Vol. ends: Nov/Dec. *Indexed:* AIAP, IBZ. *Bk. rev.:* Various number and length. *Aud.:* Ga, Ac, Sa.

Published by the National Council for Housing and Planning (a.k.a. ROOM, an activist organization in the United Kingdom), *Axis* "sets out to bridge the gap between practitioners and academics by reporting research findings in an accessible way." Covers all aspects of housing, planning, policy, and urban renewal in the United Kingdom, with occasional attention to the broader international context. A typical issue includes half a dozen features and reports, editorials or interviews from senior politicians, executives, or regular columnists; a section on innovative products and services; book reviews; and advertisements. Appropriate for both public and academic libraries.

6549. ***Canadian Journal of Urban Research.*** [ISSN: 1188-3774] 1992. s-a. CND 55 (Individuals, CND 40). Ed(s): Dan Chekki. University of Winnipeg, Institute of Urban Studies, 346 Portage Ave, Winnipeg, MB R3C 0C3, Canada; ius@uwinnipeg.ca; http://www.uwinnipeg.ca/~ius. Illus. Sample. Refereed. Circ: 125 Paid. Online: Florida Center for Library Automation; Gale Group; Micromedia ProQuest; ProQuest Information & Learning. *Indexed:* AIAP, CBCARef, EIP, PRA, PSA, SUSA, SWA, SociolAb. *Bk. rev.:* 12-15, 600-1,000 words, signed. *Aud.:* Ac.

Canadian Journal of Urban Research is a scholarly journal covering the field of urban studies from a multidisciplinary perspective. As the title implies, the journal primarily publishes Canadian research, but with considerable space given to studies from Europe. Recent articles include "Ottawa Hull and

Canberra: Implementation of capital city plans" and "The topography of memory in Berlin: The Neue Wache and the Memorial for the Murdered Jews in Berlin." Includes some articles in French, and abstracts in both French and English accompany each article.

6550. ***Cities: the international journal of urban policy and planning.*** [ISSN: 0264-2751] 1983. bi-m. EUR 737 (Individuals, EUR 196). Ed(s): Andrew Kirby. Pergamon, The Boulevard, Langford Ln, East Park, Kidlington, OX5 1GB, United Kingdom. Illus., index, adv. Refereed. Microform: PQC. Online: ingenta.com; ScienceDirect; Swets Blackwell. *Indexed:* AIAP, EIP, EnvAb, IBSS, PAIS, PRA, PSA, SSCI, SUSA, SociolAb. *Aud.:* Ac.

Broadly interdisciplinary and truly international in scope, *Cities* is a core academic journal. Its scholarly articles range in focus from technical ("The statistical modeling of road traffic noise in an urban setting") to theoretical ("The dialectic of development in U.S. urban policies: An alternative theory of poverty"). Each issue also features a profile of a major city, including a brief historical account and a critical assessment of current policy and planning issues. This title is recommended for academic libraries supporting urban studies programs.

6551. ***Community Development Journal.*** Formerly: *Community Development Bulletin.* [ISSN: 0010-3802] 1966. q. GBP 112. Ed(s): Dr. Keith Popple. Oxford University Press, Great Clarendon St, Oxford, OX2 6DP, United Kingdom; jnl.orders@oup.co.uk; http://www3.oup.co.uk/jnls. Illus., index, adv. Sample. Refereed. Circ: 1100. Vol. ends: Oct. Microform: PQC. Online: EBSCO Publishing; HighWire Press; ingenta.com; Oxford University Press Online Journals; RoweCom Information Quest; Swets Blackwell. Reprint: PSC. *Indexed:* ASSIA, BAS, CIJE, ForAb, IBSS, IBZ, IPSA, PAIS, PSA, RRTA, RiskAb, S&F, SSCI, SSI, SUSA, SWA, SWR&A, SociolAb, WAE&RSA. *Bk. rev.:* 5-6, 1,000 words, signed. *Aud.:* Ac.

This journal covers development and planning in communities of all types and sizes across the globe, examining community studies and rural development from political, economic, and sociological perspectives. Recent articles include "Barriers to community participation in development planning: Lessons from the Mutengene (Cameroon) self-help water project" and "The limits to government intervention in fostering an ethnically integrated community: A Singapore case study." Appropriate for college and university libraries.

6552. ***Computers, Environment and Urban Systems.*** Former titles: *Urban Systems; Computers and Urban Society.* [ISSN: 0198-9715] 1975. 6x/yr. EUR 1018. Ed(s): Paul A Longley. Pergamon, The Boulevard, Langford Ln, East Park, Kidlington, OX5 1GB, United Kingdom. Illus., index, adv. Refereed. Circ: 850. Vol. ends: No. 25. Microform: PQC. Online: ingenta.com; ScienceDirect; Swets Blackwell. *Indexed:* AIAP, C&ISA, EngInd, EnvAb, ExcerpMed, GeogAbPG, PsycholAb, SSCI, SUSA, SWRA. *Aud.:* Ac.

Computers, Environment and Urban Systems publishes scholarly and applied research on the use of computer-based technologies in the planning, design, and management of urban areas and the environment. Not surprisingly, GIS and management information systems are a major focus. Articles range from those dealing with rather specific technical issues ("Implementing spatial segregation measures in GIS") to more broadly theoretical studies ("An extensible, modular architecture for simulating urban development, transportation, and environmental impacts"). There are frequent special issues, recent examples of which include a collection of papers presented at the Geocomputation 2000 conference and a special issue on Cadastral systems. Due to its high cost, this title is recommended only for large academic libraries.

6553. ***Ekistics: problems and science of human settlements.*** [ISSN: 0013-2942] 1955. bi-m. Individuals, USD 100; Students, USD 50. Ed(s): Panayotis C Psomopoulos. Athens Technological Organization, Athens Center of Ekistics, 24 Strat Syndesmou, Athens, 106 73, Greece; http://www.energ.polimi.it/development/org/di805.htm. Illus., index. Sample. Refereed. Circ: 1000 Paid. Vol. ends: Nov/Dec. Microform: PQC. Online: OCLC Online Computer Library Center, Inc.; ProQuest Information & Learning. Reprint: PQC. *Indexed:* AIAP, API, BAS, ChemAb, EIP, EnvAb, ExcerpMed, FutSurv, IBSS, PAIS, RRTA, SSCI, SSI, SUSA, WAE&RSA. *Aud.:* Ac.

This scholarly journal from Greece publishes articles dealing with ekistics, defined as the study of human settlements, in both developing and industrialized countries. The authors and the topics addressed are truly international, representing countries and perspectives often overlooked in the rest of the literature. Recent articles include "Applying morphological analysis to a semi-squatter settlement in Turkey" and "Green spaces and the ecological quality of housing: The case of Cypriot settlement," as well as articles on broader issues such as "The quality of growth" and "Global transportation." Publication is running behind schedule, with the 1998 issues appearing in 2001 and 1999 issues in 2002, but lengthy double and triple issues are appearing with a frequency that suggests the editors are making an effort to get back on schedule. One of the few serials in the field published outside the United States or Great Britain, *Ekistics* is a good selection for academic libraries supporting urban studies programs despite the lag in publication time.

6554. ***Environment and Planning A: international journal of urban and regional research.*** Formerly: *Environment and Planning.* [ISSN: 0308-518X] 1969. m. USD 1142; USD 114 newsstand/cover per issue. Ed(s): Nigel Thrift. Pion Ltd., 207 Brondesbury Park, London, NW2 5JN, United Kingdom; sales@pion.co.uk; http://www.pion.co.uk/perception. Illus., index, adv. Sample. Refereed. Vol. ends: Dec. *Indexed:* AIAP, ASG, AgeL, ArtHuCI, ExcerpMed, GeoRef, GeogAbPG, HRA, IBSS, JEL, PRA, PollutAb, RRTA, SSCI, SSI, SUSA, SWA, SWRA, WAE&RSA. *Bk. rev.:* 5-15, 500-1,000 words, signed. *Aud.:* Ac.

This monthly seeks to publish cutting-edge research in urban and regional studies. The flagship journal in a series of titles denoted by different letters and subtitles, *Environment and Planning A (EPA)* has no subtitle, indicating its broad scope. The focus of the others is evident from their names: *EPB: Planning and Design, EPC: Government and Policy,* and *EPD: Society and Space. EPA*'s scope is international and its approach is truly multidisciplinary, with articles dealing with all facets of urban planning, including geography, economics, environmental science, political science, demography, and engineering. Although quite expensive, large academic libraries that support urban studies programs may find it to be worth the price.

6555. ***Environment and Urbanization.*** [ISSN: 0956-2478] 1989. s-a. GBP 60 (Individuals, GBP 26). Ed(s): David Satterthwaite. International Institute for Environment and Development, 3 Endsleigh St, London, WC1H ODD, United Kingdom. Illus., index, adv. Refereed. Circ: 2600. Vol. ends: No. 2. *Indexed:* C&ISA, EIP, EnvAb, IBSS, PAIS, PSA, PollutAb, SSCI, SUSA, SWRA, SociolAb, WAE&RSA, WRCInf. *Bk. rev.:* 25-30, 100-300 words. *Aud.:* Ac.

Environment and Urbanization focuses on development and planning issues in Africa, Asia, and Latin America and strives to include contributions from authors living and working in those regions. Each issue has a special theme selected by subscriber polls and includes 9-14 papers, a guide to the literature, profiles of innovative NGOs working in a related area, and papers on tools and methods. Recent themes include "Globalization and cities" and "Building cities with and for children and youth." Each issue also includes a "Book Notes" section comprised of 20-30 summaries of new books, research reports, and newsletters organized into subject categories such as children, environment and natural resources, governance, health, inequality, land rights and reform, and water and sanitation. The literature reviewed includes works published in English, Spanish, French, and Portuguese, and summaries of every article are given in French and Spanish.

6556. ***European Urban and Regional Studies.*** [ISSN: 0969-7764] 1994. q. GBP 298 in Europe, Middle East, Africa & Australasia. Ed(s): David Sadler, Ray Hudson. Sage Publications Ltd., 6 Bonhill St, London, EC2A 4PU, United Kingdom; info@sagepub.co.uk; http://www.sagepub.co.uk/. Adv. Refereed. Circ: 650. *Indexed:* AgeL, IBSS, IPSA, PRA, PSA, RRTA, SSCI, SUSA, SociolAb, WAE&RSA. *Bk. rev.:* 3-10, 500-1000 words, signed. *Aud.:* Ac.

One of the most highly cited scholarly journals in the field, *European Urban and Regional Studies* publishes substantial research articles on urban policy and planning issues throughout Europe. "Questioning EU cohesion policy in Portugal: A complex systems approach" and "From museum to mass entertainment: The evolution of the role of museums in cities" are typical examples of recent articles. With its focus on European Union policy issues and debates, this title may also be of interest to political scientists. Appropriate for academic libraries.

Geo World. See Geography section.

6557. *Growth and Change: a journal of urban and regional policy.* [ISSN: 0017-4815] 1970. q. USD 183 print & online eds. Blackwell Publishing, Inc., Commerce Place, 350 Main St, Malden, MA 02148; subscrip@blackwellpub.com; http://www.blackwellpublishing.com. Illus., index, adv. Sample. Refereed. Vol. ends: No. 4. Microform: PQC. Online: EBSCO Publishing; Florida Center for Library Automation; Gale Group; ingenta.com; OCLC Online Computer Library Center, Inc.; RoweCom Information Quest; Swets Blackwell. *Indexed:* ABCPolSci, ABIn, AgeL, ArtHuCI, BAS, HRA, IPSA, JEL, PAIS, PRA, PSA, PollutAb, RRTA, S&F, SSCI, SUSA, SWRA, SociolAb, WAE&RSA. *Bk. rev.:* 2-6, 1,000 words, signed. *Aud.:* Ac, Sa.

Growth and Change is a scholarly journal that publishes empirical and theoretical research on urban and regional development, planning, and policy. The approach is multidisciplinary, with an emphasis on economics, public finance, geography, public policy, and agricultural economics. Recent articles include "Knowledge, market structure, and economic coordination: Dynamics of industrial districts" and "Estimating the refugee population from PUMS data: Issues and demographic implications." A good title for both academic libraries and large urban public libraries.

6558. *Habitat International: journal for the study of human settlements.* Formerly (until 1977): *Habitat (Oxford).* [ISSN: 0197-3975] 1976. q. EUR 1062. Ed(s): C L Choguill. Pergamon, The Boulevard, Langford Ln, East Park, Kidlington, OX5 1GB, United Kingdom. Illus., adv. Refereed. Circ: 350. Microform: PQC. Online: ingenta.com; ScienceDirect; Swets Blackwell. *Indexed:* AgeL, BiolAb, DSA, EnvAb, ExcerpMed, FPA, ForAb, GeoRef, IBSS, PRA, PSA, SFSA, SSCI, SUSA, SWA, SociolAb, WAE&RSA. *Bk. rev.:* Variable number and length. *Aud.:* Ac.

Habitat International is a scholarly journal presenting research on urbanization in developing regions and the social, political, and economic linkages between the developing and developed world. It is a substantial and well-respected title, likely to also be of interest to sociologists, anthropologists, and other social scientists. Recent articles include "Learning from the past: International housing policy since 1945—an introduction" and "Impeded self-help: Toleration and the proscription of housing consolidation in Hong Kong's squatter areas." Because of its high price, this title is recommended only for large academic libraries.

6559. *Housing Studies.* [ISSN: 0267-3037] 1986. bi-m. GBP 301 (Individuals, GBP 96). Ed(s): Alan Murie. Carfax Publishing Ltd., 4 Park Sq, Milton Park, Abingdon, OX14 4RN, United Kingdom; enquiry@tandf.co.uk; http://www.tandf.co.uk/. Illus., index, adv. Sample. Refereed. Circ: 800. Online: EBSCO Publishing; Ingenta Select; Northern Light Technology, Inc.; OCLC Online Computer Library Center, Inc.; ProQuest Information & Learning; RoweCom Information Quest; Swets Blackwell. Reprint: PSC. *Indexed:* AgeL, BAS, GeogAbPG, IBZ, JEL, PSA, SSCI, SWA, SociolAb. *Bk. rev.:* 4-7, 500-2,000 words, signed. *Aud.:* Ac, Sa.

Housing Studies is a scholarly journal devoted to the subject of housing from a variety of disciplinary perspectives including urban studies, public administration, sociology, geography, political science, history, and law. The focus is on the United Kingdom, but occasional articles deal with Europe, the United States, and other parts of the world. Recent articles include "Forced relocation vs. voluntary mobility: The effects of dispersal programmes on households" and "Social housing agencies and the governance of anti-social behaviour." Appropriate for undergraduate collections.

6560. *International Journal of Urban and Regional Research.* [ISSN: 0309-1317] 1976. q. GBP 252 print & online eds. Ed(s): Patrick le Gales. Blackwell Publishing Ltd., 9600 Garsington Rd, PO Box 805, Oxford, OX4 2DQ, United Kingdom; customerservices@oxon.blackwellpublishing.com; http://www.blackwellpublishing.com/. Illus., index, adv. Sample. Refereed. Vol. ends: Dec. Online: EBSCO Publishing; Gale Group; ingenta.com; OCLC Online Computer Library Center, Inc.; RoweCom Information Quest; Swets Blackwell. Reprint: SWZ. *Indexed:* ABCPolSci, AIAP, AmH&L, BAS, CJA, IBSS, IPSA, JEL, PAIS, PSA, RRTA, SSCI, SSI, SUSA, SWA, SociolAb, WAE&RSA. *Bk. rev.:* 5-10, length varies, signed. *Aud.:* Ac.

A prestigious scholarly journal with an international scope and a decidedly sociological bent, the *International Journal of Urban and Regional Research* has become one of the core titles in the field. Many of the recent articles focus on the interplay between the global and the local, making this a valuable source for academics from any discipline interested in globalization issues. The September 2002 issue included a substantial section (7 articles) devoted to the theme "Reflections on cities, September 11th and the ~War on Terrorism'—one year on." Highly recommended for academic libraries.

6561. *International Planning Studies.* [ISSN: 1356-3475] 1996. q. GBP 225 (Individuals, GBP 58). Carfax Publishing Ltd., 4 Park Sq, Milton Park, Abingdon, OX14 4RN, United Kingdom; enquiry@tandf.co.uk; http://www.tandf.co.uk/. Illus., index. Refereed. Reprint: PSC. *Indexed:* ABIn, IBZ. *Bk. rev.:* 3-10, signed, variable length. *Aud.:* Ac.

Founded in 1995, this recent addition to the field publishes "transnational and transdisciplinary comparative research in the fields of urban and regional studies." The coverage is truly international—recent issues include articles on Asia, Africa, and Latin America as well as Europe and the United States. The topics addressed span the depth and breadth of urban planning, from "Enhancing collaborative governance for natural area management: Some experiences from Taiwan" to "Romance and tragedy in (post)modern planning: A pragmatist's perspective." A good selection for large academic libraries supporting urban studies programs.

6562. *Journal of Housing and Community Development.* Former titles (until 1995): *Journal of Housing; J O H: Journal of Housing.* [ISSN: 1534-648X] 1944. bi-m. USD 33. Ed(s): Rosana Hemakom. National Association of Housing and Redevelopment Officials, 630 Eye St, N W, Washington, DC 20001-3736; nahro@nahro.org; http://www.nahro.org. Illus., index, adv. Circ: 15000 Paid. Vol. ends: Nov/Dec. Microform: PQC. Online: Gale Group. Reprint: PQC. *Indexed:* ABIn, AIAP, AgeL, EnvAb, PAIS, RiskAb, SSCI, SSI. *Aud.:* Ga, Ac, Sa.

Published by the National Association of Housing and Redevelopment Officials, this glossy magazine is the trade journal for people working in the field of housing and community development. Issues include at least four feature articles on policy issues, best practices, and current developments; several shorter, newsy reports on topics such as federal regulations, technology, data initiatives, and people working in the field; and plenty of advertisements. Appropriate for both large public libraries and academic institutions.

6563. *Journal of Planning Education and Research.* [ISSN: 0739-456X] 1981. q. USD 233 print & online eds. Ed(s): Rene Kane, Michael Hibbard. Sage Publications, Inc., 2455 Teller Rd, Thousand Oaks, CA 91320; info@sagepub.com; http://www.sagepub.com. Adv. Refereed. Circ: 2000. Online: ingenta.com; RoweCom Information Quest; Swets Blackwell. *Indexed:* AIAP, EnvAb, GeogAbPG, PAIS, PSA, SSCI, SUSA. *Bk. rev.:* 2-6 signed, variable length. *Aud.:* Ac.

This scholarly journal published by the Association of Collegiate Schools of Planning covers planning theory, planning pedagogy, and planning practice. Both qualitative and quantitative research are featured, and a typical issue also includes half a dozen lengthy book reviews. Examples of recent articles include "Operationalizing neighborhood accessibility for land use–travel behavior research and regional modeling" and "From racial zoning to community empowerment: The interstate highway system and the African American community in Birmingham, Alabama." Appropriate for academic libraries supporting urban planning programs.

6564. ***Journal of Planning Literature.*** Incorporates (1957-1996): *C P L Bibliographies.* [ISSN: 0885-4122] 1986. q. GBP 470 print & online eds. in Europe, Middle East, Africa & Australasia. Ed(s): Jack Nasar. Sage Publications, Inc., 2455 Teller Rd, Thousand Oaks, CA 91320; info@sagepub.com; http://www.sagepub.com. Adv. Refereed. Circ: 900. Microform: PQC. Online: ingenta.com; OCLC Online Computer Library Center, Inc.; ProQuest Information & Learning; RoweCom Information Quest; Swets Blackwell. *Indexed:* AIAP, GeogAbPG, IBSS, PAIS, SUSA. *Bk. rev.:* Various number and length. *Aud.:* Ac.

An excellent current-awareness source, each issue of the *Journal of Planning Literature* provides reviews and concise abstracts of dozens of books, journal and magazine articles, government reports, city and regional documents and plans, conference papers, and research reports. The abstracts are organized by subject under the broad categories "History/Theory/Administration," "Quantitative/Economic/Methodological" and "Physical/Environmental." In addition, each issue includes several scholarly articles and review essays on topics such as "Visualization tools and methods in community planning: From freehand sketches to virtual reality" and "The effects of impact fees on the price of housing and land: A literature review." Highly recommended for academic libraries.

6565. ***Journal of the American Planning Association.*** Former titles (until 1979): *Planners Journal; American Institute of Planners. Journal.* [ISSN: 0194-4363] 1925. q. Members, USD 33; Non-members, USD 75. Ed(s): Ed Bd. American Planning Association, 122 South Michigan Ave, Ste 1600, Chicago, IL 60603-6107; http://www.planning.org. Illus., adv. Refereed. Circ: 10500. Vol. ends: Oct. Microform: PQC. Online: bigchalk; EBSCO Publishing; Florida Center for Library Automation; Gale Group; OCLC Online Computer Library Center, Inc.; ProQuest Information & Learning; H.W. Wilson. Reprint: PQC; PSC. *Indexed:* ABCPolSci, ABIn, AIAP, API, AgeL, ArtInd, BAS, BHA, EIP, EnvAb, ExcerpMed, GeogAbPG, IBZ, IPSA, MCR, PAIS, SSCI, SSI, SUSA. *Bk. rev.:* 8-10, 500-1,200 words, signed. *Aud.:* Ga, Ac, Sa.

This scholarly journal of the American Planning Association (see also their newsmagazine *Planning*) is a core title in urban studies. Each issue includes six or more substantial articles on all aspects of urban and regional planning. Also included are commentaries on current or previously published articles, the "Planner's Notebook" highlighting best practice tools and techniques, and an extensive review section covering books and multimedia products. The reviews are organized under subject headings such as housing for seniors, economic growth, political economy, radical planning, and sprawl. The articles are academically rigorous but accessible, and this title is recommended for large public libraries as well as academic institutions.

6566. ***Journal of Urban Affairs.*** Formed by the merger of (1979-1982): *Urban Affairs Papers;* (1977-1982): *Urban Interest Journal.* [ISSN: 0735-2166] 1976. q. USD 480 print & online eds. Blackwell Publishing, Inc., Commerce Place, 350 Main St, Malden, MA 02148; subscrip@blackwellpub.com; http://www.blackwellpublishing.com. Illus., adv. Refereed. Circ: 530. Microform: PQC. Online: EBSCO Publishing; Gale Group; ingenta.com; OCLC Online Computer Library Center, Inc.; RoweCom Information Quest; Swets Blackwell; H.W. Wilson. *Indexed:* ABS&EES, AIAP, CJA, IIBP, IPSA, PAIS, PSA, SSCI, SSI, SUSA, SWR&A, SociolAb. *Bk. rev.:* 2-5, 500-1,000 words, signed. *Aud.:* Ga, Ac, Sa.

Sponsored by the Urban Affairs Association (the professional organization for urban studies scholars, researchers, and public service providers), the *Journal of Urban Affairs* is unusually accessible and down-to-earth for a scholarly journal. Recent articles include "Habitat for Humanity: Building social capital through faith-based service" and "Privatization, politics, and urban services: The political behavior of charter schools." An excellent choice for academic libraries as well as some large public libraries.

6567. ***Journal of Urban Design.*** [ISSN: 1357-4809] 1996. 3x/yr. GBP 159 (Individuals, GBP 42). Carfax Publishing Ltd., 4 Park Sq, Milton Park, Abingdon, OX14 4RN, United Kingdom; enquiry@tandf.co.uk; http://www.tandf.co.uk/. Illus., index, adv. Sample. Refereed. Vol. ends: Oct. Online: EBSCO Publishing; Ingenta Select; Northern Light Technology, Inc.; OCLC Online Computer Library Center, Inc.; ProQuest Information & Learning; RoweCom Information Quest; Swets Blackwell. Reprint: PSC. *Indexed:* API, BrHumI, IBZ. *Bk. rev.:* 6-8, 1,000-1,500 words. *Aud.:* Ac, Sa.

This beautifully illustrated scholarly journal focuses on the growing area of design and aesthetics within urban studies, broadly defined to include conservation and preservation as well as historical and sociological perspectives on urban design. A British publication, it also includes numerous American and European contributions. "Stakeholder views on value and urban design," "Transformations and city extensions: Some observations of Copenhagen's city form at a time of global change" and "Brooklyn's vernacular waterfront" are representative examples of recent articles. Appropriate for academic libraries supporting strong programs in urban studies and architecture.

Journal of Urban Economics. See Economics section.

Journal of Urban History. See History section.

6568. ***Journal of Urban Planning and Development.*** Formerly (until 1982): *American Society of Civil Engineers. Urban Planning and Development Division. Journal.* [ISSN: 0733-9488] 1956. q. Members, USD 40; Non-members, USD 60. Ed(s): R Ian Kingham. American Society of Civil Engineers, 1801 Alexander Graham Bell Dr, Reston, VA 20191-4400; http://www.pubs.asce.org. Illus., index. Refereed. Circ: 1575. Microform: PQC. Online: EBSCO Publishing; Gale Group; Swets Blackwell. Reprint: PQC. *Indexed:* AS&TI, C&ISA, DSR&OA, EngInd, EnvAb, GeoRef, GeogAbPG, H&SSA, PAIS, PollutAb, RiskAb, SSCI, SWRA. *Aud.:* Ac, Sa.

A scholarly journal covering the civil engineering aspects of urban planning and development, the *Journal of Urban Planning and Development* covers transportation planning, environmental assessment, and utilities and public works management. Recent issues include editorial pieces and three or four papers on topics such as "Sustainable urban transportation: Performance indicators and some analytical approaches" and "Microanalysis of shopping center location in terms of retail supply quality and environmental impact." Appropriate for academic libraries supporting urban studies and civil engineering programs as well as some large public libraries.

6569. ***Journal of Urban Technology.*** [ISSN: 1063-0732] 1992. 3x/yr. GBP 176 (Individuals, GBP 60). Ed(s): Richard E Hanley. Carfax Publishing Ltd., 4 Park Sq, Milton Park, Abingdon, OX14 4RN, United Kingdom; enquiry@tandf.co.uk; http://www.tandf.co.uk/. Illus., index. Refereed. Circ: 600. Online: EBSCO Publishing; Ingenta Select; OCLC Online Computer Library Center, Inc.; RoweCom Information Quest; Swets Blackwell. Reprint: PSC. *Indexed:* AIAP, CIJE, IBZ, PRA, SSCI, SUSA. *Bk. rev.:* 2-6, variable length. *Aud.:* Ga, Ac, Sa.

Journal of Urban Technology is a scholarly journal that strives to "open a conversation between specialists and nonspecialists" in order to "maximize the positive and minimize the adverse effects of technology on cities." The articles tend to be timely and accessible, with frequent special issues on topics such as "Digital communities" and "Monitoring and reporting the urban environment." Recent articles include "Lead safe yards: A program for improving health in urban neighborhoods," "Environmental data: Finding it, sharing it, and using it," and "When Superman used X-ray vision, did he have a search warrant? Emerging law enforcement technologies and the transformation of urban space." Recommended for both large public libraries and academic institutions.

Landscape and Urban Planning. See Landscape Architecture section.

6570. ***National Civic Review.*** Formerly (until 1959): *National Municipal Review.* [ISSN: 0027-9013] 1911. q. USD 125. Ed(s): Robert Loper. Jossey-Bass Inc., Publishers, 989 Market St, San Francisco, CA 94103-1741; jbsubs@jbp.com; http://www.josseybass.com. Index, adv. Circ: 2100 Paid. Vol. ends: Winter. Microform: WSH; PMC. Online:

EBSCO Publishing; Florida Center for Library Automation; Gale Group; Northern Light Technology, Inc.; OCLC Online Computer Library Center, Inc.; H.W. Wilson. Reprint: PQC; PSC; WSH. *Indexed:* ABCPolSci, BRI, CBRI, CLI, FutSurv, ILP, PAIS, SSI. *Bk. rev.:* Infrequent. *Aud.:* Ga, Ac, Sa.

Published by the National Civic League, this quarterly focuses on civics, government, and citizen involvement. Each issue has a theme, such as the American communties movement or issues in local government structure and performance. Not every theme is directly relevant to urban studies, but the topics covered provide a context for understanding how community action and public policy informs urban development and planning. Appropriate for all academic and many medium-sized to large public libraries.

6571. ***New Urban News.*** [ISSN: 1096-1844] 1996. 8x/yr. USD 79 in North America (Students, USD 45). Ed(s): Robert Steuteville. New Urban Publications, Inc., PO Box 6515, Ithaca, NY 14851-6515; http://www.newurbannews.com. Illus. Sample. Circ: 5000 Paid. *Aud.:* Ga,Ac, Sa.

New Urban News is a bimonthly newsmagazine devoted to promulgating the principles of smart growth within urban and regional planning. Also known as the "new urbanism," smart growth involves limiting sprawl and designing pedestrian-friendly communities with mixed-use development. Topics covered in this magazine include urban design and planning, architecture, construction, finance, public policy, street design, inner-city revitalization, and zoning. This is an accessible, reasonably priced title that would be appropriate for both public and academic libraries.

6572. ***Planning.*** Formerly: *American Society of Planning Officials. A S PO Newsletter;* Which superseded (in 1978): *Practicing Planner;* (in 1971): *Planner's Notebook.* [ISSN: 0001-2610] 1972. m. Non-members, USD 65. Ed(s): Sylvia Lewis. American Planning Association, 122 South Michigan Ave, Ste 1600, Chicago, IL 60603-6107; http://www.planning.org. Illus., index, adv. Circ: 30000 Paid. Vol. ends: Dec. Microform: PQC. Online: EBSCO Publishing; Florida Center for Library Automation; Gale Group; Northern Light Technology, Inc.; OCLC Online Computer Library Center, Inc.; ProQuest Information & Learning. Reprint: PQC. *Indexed:* ABIn, AIAP, BPI, EnvAb, ExcerpMed, GeogAbPG, LRI, PAIS, SUSA. *Bk. rev.:* Variable number and length. *Aud.:* Ga, Ac, Sa.

This glossy magazine from the American Planning Association includes half a dozen or so short feature articles, local and national news briefs, letters, editorials, advertisements, and the "Planner's Library," which provides succinct reviews of significant publications in the field. "Right-sizing urban growth boundaries" and "How the Dutch do housing" are typical examples of recent articles. Timely, insightful, and highly readable, this title is recommended for both public and academic libraries.

6573. ***Planning Perspectives: an international journal of history, planning and the environment.*** [ISSN: 0266-5433] 1986. q. GBP 386 (Individuals, GBP 82). Ed(s): Anthony Sutcliffe. E. & F.N. Spon, 11 New Fetter Ln, London, EC4P 4EE, United Kingdom. Illus. Refereed. Vol. ends: Oct. Online: EBSCO Publishing; Ingenta Select; OCLC Online Computer Library Center, Inc.; RoweCom Information Quest; Swets Blackwell. Reprint: PSC. *Indexed:* AIAP, API, AmH&L, GeogAbPG, IBZ, PRA, SUSA. *Bk. rev.:* 10-15, 500 words. *Aud.:* Ac.

A scholarly journal with an international focus, *Planning Perspectives* publishes articles dealing with urban planning from the perspective of social history. Recent articles include "The origins of town planning in New Zealand, 1900-1926: A divergent path?" and "The industrial suburb is dead, long live the industrial slum: Suburbs and slums in Chicago and Montreal, 1850-1950." Each issue also includes 10 to 15 full-length book reviews as well as a large number of "book notes," mini-reviews of books and journals.

6574. ***Planning Practice and Research.*** [ISSN: 0269-7459] 1986. q. GBP 268 (Individuals, GBP 52). Ed(s): Vincent Nadin. Carfax Publishing Ltd., 4 Park Sq, Milton Park, Abingdon, OX14 4RN, United Kingdom; enquiry@tandf.co.uk; http://www.tandf.co.uk/. Illus. Refereed. Online: EBSCO Publishing; Ingenta Select; OCLC Online Computer Library Center, Inc.; RoweCom Information Quest; Swets Blackwell. Reprint: PSC. *Indexed:* GeogAbPG, IBSS, IBZ, PAIS, RRTA, S&F, WAE&RSA. *Bk. rev.:* 3-6, 500 words. *Aud.:* Ac, Sa.

This scholarly journal includes articles related to city and regional planning in the United Kingsom and around the world, brief but timely research reports, and book reviews. The emphasis is on practice rather than theory, although the articles are substantial and analytical. Perhaps its most notable feature is the "Planning literature information service," a listing of current articles published in core urban studies journals arranged by subject. A good selection for academic libraries.

6575. ***Public Administration.*** [ISSN: 0033-3298] 1923. q. GBP 334 print & online eds. Ed(s): R A W Rhodes. Blackwell Publishing Ltd., 9600 Garsington Rd, PO Box 805, Oxford, OX4 2DQ, United Kingdom; jnlinfo@blackwellpublishers.co.uk; http://www.blackwellpublishing.com/. Illus., index, adv. Refereed. Circ: 4650. Vol. ends: Winter. Microform: PQC. Online: EBSCO Publishing; Gale Group; ingenta.com; OCLC Online Computer Library Center, Inc.; RoweCom Information Quest; Swets Blackwell. Reprint: PSC. *Indexed:* ABCPolSci, BAS, BrHumI, GeogAbPG, HRA, IBSS, IPSA, LRI, PAIS, PRA, PSA, RRTA, SSCI, SSI, SUSA, SWA, SociolAb, WAE&RSA. *Bk. rev.:* 10-15, 500-1,000 words, signed. *Aud.:* Ac.

The focus of this scholarly journal is public policy, administration, and management in the United Kingdom, Europe, and, to a lesser extent, the United States. The editors strive for a comparative perspective on public administration, and every issue includes articles offering an analysis of issues pertaining to the European Union. A typical issue includes ten research articles, and may also include a substantial book review section or a section of shorter articles called "Public management and notes." Appropriate for large academic libraries.

6576. ***Public Administration Review.*** [ISSN: 0033-3352] 1940. bi-m. USD 209 print & online eds. Ed(s): Larry D Terry, Shelly Peffer. Blackwell Publishing, Inc., Commerce Place, 350 Main St, Malden, MA 02148; subscrip@blackwellpub.com; http://www.blackwellpublishing.com. Illus., index, adv. Refereed. Circ: 12000 Paid and controlled. Vol. ends: Nov/Dec. Microform: MIM; PQC. Online: EBSCO Publishing; Florida Center for Library Automation; Gale Group; ingenta.com; Northern Light Technology, Inc.; OCLC Online Computer Library Center, Inc.; ProQuest Information & Learning; RoweCom Information Quest; Swets Blackwell; H.W. Wilson. Reprint: PQC; WSH. *Indexed:* ABCPolSci, ABIn, ABS&EES, AgeL, BPI, BRI, CBRI, CIJE, CJA, CLI, HumInd, IBSS, IPSA, LRI, PAIS, PRA, PSA, SSCI, SSI, SUSA, SWA, SWR&A. *Bk. rev.:* 2, 2,000-3,000 words, signed. *Aud.:* Ga, Ac, Sa.

Published on behalf of the American Society for Public Administration, this journal covers public policy, administration, and management in the United States, with occasional articles dealing with other parts of the world. Geared toward practitioners as well as academics, the articles tend to be timely and fairly accessible. Examples of recent articles include "Organizing for Homeland Security," "The extent and determinants of the utilization of university research in government agencies," and "Devolution and the social welfare of elderly immigrants: Who will bear the burden?" Recommended for most academic libraries and some large public libraries.

Public Management. See Government Periodicals—State and Local section.

6577. ***Regional Studies.*** [ISSN: 0034-3404] 1966. 9x/yr. GBP 530 (Individuals, GBP 156). Ed(s): P McGregor. Carfax Publishing Ltd., 4 Park Sq, Milton Park, Abingdon, OX14 4RN, United Kingdom; enquiry@tandf.co.uk; http://www.tandf.co.uk/. Illus., index, adv. Refereed. Vol. ends: Dec. Microform: PQC. Online: EBSCO Publishing; Florida Center for Library Automation; Gale Group; Ingenta Select; Northern Light Technology, Inc.; OCLC Online Computer Library Center, Inc.; ProQuest Information & Learning; RoweCom Information

Quest; Swets Blackwell. Reprint: PSC; SWZ. *Indexed:* ABIn, AIAP, API, BAS, BrEdI, BrHumI, ExcerpMed, ForAb, GeogAbPG, HRA, IBSS, IBZ, IPSA, JEL, PAIS, PRA, PSA, RRTA, RiskAb, S&F, SSCI, SUSA, SociolAb, WAE&RSA. *Bk. rev.:* 2-10, 500-1,000 words, signed. *Aud.:* Ac.

Regional Studies is an international scholarly journal with a multidisiplinary approach to urban and regional development. The focus is on economic and policy issues, with an emphasis on the European scene. "Technology transfer within multinational firms and its impact on the productivity of Scottish subsidiaries" and "Evaluating policy implementation: The European Union's small and medium sized enterprise policies in Galicia and Sardinia" are typical recent articles. Appropriate for university libraries with large collections.

6578. *Town Planning Review.* [ISSN: 0041-0020] 1910. q. USD 270 (Individuals, USD 155; Students, USD 50). Ed(s): Robin Bloxsidge. Liverpool University Press, 4 Cambridge St, Liverpool, L69 7ZU, United Kingdom; http://www.liverpool-unipress.co.uk/. Illus., index, adv. Refereed. Circ: 1100. Vol. ends: Oct. Reprint: PSC. *Indexed:* AIAP, API, ArtInd, BAS, BrArAb, BrHumI, BrTechI, CJA, EnvAb, ExcerpMed, GeogAbPG, IBSS, NumL, PAIS, PRA, RRTA, SFSA, SSCI, SWA, WAE&RSA. *Bk. rev.:* 10-15, 500-1,000 words, signed. *Aud.:* Ac.

This is a long-standing scholarly journal with broad coverage of city and regional planning research from an interdisciplinary perspective. Most of the contributions reflect the journal's British origins, but some attention is also given to international issues. Each issue includes a brief invited essay, or "Viewpoint," on a current topic, a dozen or so research articles, and six or more book reviews. Selected issues also include a section called "Policy Forum," in which a number of contributors debate issues of planning policy. Appropriate for academic libraries.

6579. *U R I S A Journal.* [ISSN: 1045-8077] 1989. s-a. USD 295. Urban and Regional Information Systems Association, 1460 Renaissance Dr, Ste 305, Park Ridge, IL 60068-1348; info@urisa.org; http://www.urisa.org/index.htm. Refereed. Circ: 3800. *Indexed:* GeogAbPG. *Bk. rev.:* variable number and length. *Aud.:* Ac, Sa.

Published by the Urban and Regional Information Systems Association, a nonprofit international association for information technology professionals, this scholarly journal addresses all aspects of information systems as they relate to urban and regional planning, from techniques for using GIS applications to cognitive studies of how people think about and represent their geographic surroundings. "An object-oriented approach for modeling urban land-use changes" and "Role of multi-scalar GIS-based indicators studies in formulating neighborhood planning policy" are typical examples of recent articles. Appropriate for large academic libraries.

6580. *Urban Affairs Review.* Formerly (until 1995): *Urban Affairs Quarterly.* [ISSN: 1078-0874] 1965. bi-m. GBP 414 print & online eds. in Europe, Middle East, Africa & Australasia. Ed(s): Dennis R Judd. Sage Publications, Inc., 2455 Teller Rd, Thousand Oaks, CA 91320; info@sagepub.com; http://www.sagepub.com. Illus., index, adv. Refereed. Circ: 1900. Vol. ends: Jun. Microform: PQC. Online: Florida Center for Library Automation; Gale Group; ingenta.com; OCLC Online Computer Library Center, Inc.; ProQuest Information & Learning; RoweCom Information Quest; Swets Blackwell. *Indexed:* ABCPolSci, AIAP, ASSIA, ArtHuCI, C&ISA, CIJE, CJA, CommAb, EIP, EnvAb, ExcerpMed, GeogAbPG, HRA, IBSS, IPSA, MagInd, PAIS, PRA, PSA, RI-1, RiskAb, SSCI, SSI, SUSA, SWA, SWR&A, SociolAb. *Bk. rev.:* 2-4, 1,000-2,000 words. *Aud.:* Ac, Sa.

Urban Affairs Review is a respected scholarly journal within the field. The focus is on social and economic dynamics of urban areas in the United States and throughout the world. Recent articles include "Structural change and fiscal flows: A framework for analyzing the effects of urban events" and "The construction of the local and the limits of contemporary community building in the United States." A good choice for academic libraries.

6581. *Urban Geography.* [ISSN: 0272-3638] 1980. 8x/yr. USD 394 in North America; USD 399 elsewhere. V.H. Winston & Son, Inc., c/o Bellwether Publishing, Ltd, 8640 Guilford Rd, Ste 200, Columbia, MD 21046; bellpub@bellpub.com; http://www.bellpub.com. Illus., index. Sample. Refereed. Vol. ends: No. 8. *Indexed:* ABS&EES, ArtHuCI, BAS, CJA, GeogAbPG, IBSS, IPSA, PRA, SSCI, SSI, SUSA, SWA, WAE&RSA. *Bk. rev.:* Various number and length. *Aud.:* Ac.

As the title implies, *Urban Geography* publishes research on urban studies from a geographical perspective. Geography here is broadly defined to include the full range of the social sciences, and the topics covered include race, poverty, and ethnicity; comparative studies of urban areas; historical preservation; housing markets; and economic activity. Appropriate for many academic libraries.

6582. *Urban History.* Formerly: *Urban History Yearbook.* [ISSN: 0963-9268] 1974. 3x/yr. USD 142 (Individuals, USD 54). Ed(s): Rosemary Sweet, Philip J Ethington. Cambridge University Press, The Edinburgh Bldg, Shaftesbury Rd, Cambridge, CB2 2RU, United Kingdom; information@cambridge.org; http://uk.cambridge.org/journals. Adv. Online: EBSCO Publishing; OCLC Online Computer Library Center, Inc.; RoweCom Information Quest. Reprint: SWZ. *Indexed:* AIAP, API, AmH&L, BAS, BHA, BrArAb, GeogAbPG, NumL, PSA, SociolAb. *Bk. rev.:* 15-20 lengthy reviews. *Aud.:* Ac.

This journal focuses on the historiography of towns and cities, publishing scholarly research on the social, economic, political, and cultural aspects of the history of urban areas. Each issues includes 15 or more substantial book reviews and three to five review essays. An annual bibliography featuring as many as 1,000 books and articles is included in the final number of each volume. Recommended for most academic libraries.

6583. *Urban Land.* [ISSN: 0042-0891] 1941. m. 0 membership. Ed(s): Kristina Kessler. Urban Land Institute, 1025 Thomas Jefferson St, N W, Ste 500 W, Washington, DC 20007-5201; kkessler@uli.org; http://www.uli.org/homepage.htm. Illus., index, adv. Circ: 13500. Microform: PQC. Reprint: PQC. *Indexed:* AIAP, API, EnvAb, PAIS, SUSA. *Bk. rev.:* 2-4, 200-300 words, signed. *Aud.:* Ga, Ac, Sa.

Published by the Urban Land Institute (ULI), this glossy magazine focuses on real estate and development. There are advertisements alongside substantial feature articles, opinion pieces, and regular departments, including "Techtrends," "Capital Markets," and the "Solution File." Several supplements to the magazine are included with ULI membership. Recommended for both public and academic libraries.

6584. *Urban Studies: an international journal for research in urban and regional studies.* [ISSN: 0042-0980] 1964. 13x/yr. GBP 638 (Individuals, GBP 164). Carfax Publishing Ltd., 4 Park Sq, Milton Park, Abingdon, OX14 4RN, United Kingdom; enquiry@tandf.co.uk; http://www.tandf.co.uk/. Illus., index, adv. Refereed. Vol. ends: Dec. Online: EBSCO Publishing; Florida Center for Library Automation; Gale Group; Ingenta Select; Northern Light Technology, Inc.; OCLC Online Computer Library Center, Inc.; ProQuest Information & Learning; RoweCom Information Quest; Swets Blackwell. Reprint: PSC. *Indexed:* AIAP, API, AgeL, AmH&L, ArtHuCI, BAS, BHA, BrHumI, CJA, EnvAb, ExcerpMed, GeogAbPG, HRA, IBSS, IBZ, IPSA, JEL, PAIS, PRA, PSA, RRTA, RiskAb, SFSA, SSCI, SSI, SUSA, SWA, SociolAb, WAE&RSA. *Bk. rev.:* 10-15, 300-1,500 words. *Aud.:* Ac.

A scholarly journal with a multidisciplinary approach to urban and regional planning, *Urban Studies* is a well-respected title that publishes research with an economic or sociological focus from top scholars in the field. The scope is truly international, with coverage of both developed and less developed regions. Recent theme issues include "Chinese urban development" and "Social housing policy in the European Union." Recommended for all academic libraries.

Electronic Journals

Public Administration and Management. See Management, Administration, and Human Resources/Electronic Journals section.

■ VETERINARY SCIENCE

C. Trenton Boyd, Director, Veterinary Medical Library, W218 Veterinary Medicine, University of Missouri, Columbia, MO 65211; boydt@missouri.edu; FAX: 573-882-2950

Introduction

The titles in this section have been selected for a library that needs to maintain a very basic core collection of veterinary medical periodicals, such as a medical library in a state with no veterinary library or an academic library that serves a department of veterinary science. The criteria considered in the selection process were journal usage studies, citation analysis studies, and the author's 33 years of experience in the field. The author of this section is the chair of the Serials Committee of the Veterinary Medical Libraries Section of the Medical Library Association, and he would be happy to answer questions about any veterinary-related title.

A collection for a library serving a college of veterinary medicine will carry a much more extensive list of veterinary titles, as well as many nonveterinary titles. (Many useful treatments and techniques can be extrapolated from human medicine and the biological sciences to veterinary medicine.) Examples of basic science titles are *Nature, Science,* and *Scientific American.* Many human medical journals contain comparative and experimental animal studies that are important in the field of veterinary medicine. Some examples of these are *American Journal of Pathology, American Journal of Physiology, Endocrinology, Journal of Bone & Joint Surgery,* and *Comparative Clinical Pathology.*

One should remember there are several refereed animal science titles that serve as a very important adjunct to veterinary medicine. The studies contained therein are frequently valuable to veterinary researchers and practitoner/clinicians. Examples are *Journal of Animal Science, Journal of Dairy Science, Poultry Science,* and *Sheep and Goat Research Journal.* Additionally, one can find many breed-specific titles, such as *Brown Swiss Bulletin, Quarter Horse Journal, Santa Gertrudis Journal,* and *German Shepherd Dog Review,* which will often provide articles on the health, care, and breeding of a particular breed. The majority of the journals selected for this list are for the research scientist and/or practicing veterinarian, and the average reader will probably not find them interesting for leisure reading.

There are several indexing services that offer partial coverage of the veterinary literature (see list of basic abstracts and indexes). However, the only index that attempts to be complete in the coverage of veterinary literature is *Index Veterinarius* and its companion publication, *Veterinary Bulletin.*

The trend of the veterinary specialities to develop their own journals has progressed considerably since the last edition. This is prevalent not only with U.S. associations, but also with the foreign. It has been interesting to watch the publications grow from newsletters to in-house publications to contracting with the major publishers for a professionally edited journal. While the last step is great for the association, it is a killer for the libraries as the subscription rate for institutions suddenly multiplies fivefold. Librarians need to be ever vigilant in promoting SPARC.

Veterinary medicine remains comparatively slow in breaking into electronic publishing as compared to other subject disciplines. However, steady progress has been made since the last edition. Most of the journals that are available in full-text online versions are published by the major scientific publishing houses, such as Blackwell and Elsevier (with its many subsidaries). A few of the association journals are available through BioOne and HighWire. The majority of the smaller publishers have not yet gone electronic. The most widely read veterinary journal in the United States, *Journal of the American Veterinary Medical Association,* only became available online in the past year.

There are approximately five journals that are in electronic format only. Their growth seems to be painfully slow. Even those that are peer reviewed seem to have problems in attracting contributors. It will be interesting to see if these survive and are eventually viewed by the academic world as "acceptable" journals to publish in for promotion and tenure. In addressing this issue, an excellent editorial titled "Present Status and Future of Veterinary Medical Publishing on the Internet" appears in the June 2000 issue of *Veterinary Neurology and Neurosurgery,* which is one of the totally electronic journals. The citation is at http://www.neurovet.org/EditorialText.htm

Basic Periodicals

Ga: *DVM;* Ac: *American Animal Hospital Association. Journal, American Journal of Veterinary Research, American Veterinary Medical Association. Journal, Compendium on Continuing Education for the Practicing Veterinarian, Equine Veterinary Journal, Veterinary Clinics of North America: Equine Practice, Veterinary Clinics of North America: Exotic Animal Practice, Veterinary Clinics of North America: Food Animal Practice, Veterinary Clinics of North America: Small Animal Practice, Veterinary Journal, The Veterinary Record.*

Basic Abstracts and Indexes

Biological Abstracts; Focus On: veterinary science and medicine; Index Medicus; Index Veterinarius; Science Citation Index; Veterinary Bulletin.

6585. ***American Animal Hospital Association. Journal.*** Formerly: *American Animal Hospital Association Bulletin.* [ISSN: 0587-2871] 1965. bi-m. USD 107 in US & Canada. Ed(s): Dr. Walt Ingwersen. American Animal Hospital Association, 12575 W Bayaud Ave, Lakewood, CO 80228. Illus., index, adv. Refereed. Circ: 14100 Paid and controlled. Vol. ends: Nov/Dec. Microform: PQC. Online: ProQuest Information & Learning. Reprint: PQC. *Indexed:* Agr, B&AI, BiolAb, ChemAb, ExcerpMed, FoVS&M, IndMed, IndVet, SCI, VetBull. *Aud.:* Ac, Sa.

This is the official publication of the American Animal Hospital Association, which is an organization of small-animal practitioners; consequently, its articles are limited to dogs and cats. The layout editors do a superb job of intermixing color and black-and-white photographs, tables, and text to make this journal easy to read and pleasing to the eye. The arrangement of the articles is by discipline. Articles include case studies, original research, reviews, and retrospective studies. This is the leading journal in small-animal medicine and is a must for small-animal practitioners, clinicians, and veterinary science collections. Online full text available from 2003 through ProQuest (http://eproxy.lib.hku.hk/login?rl=http://proquest.umi.com/pqdlink?Ver=1&Exp=02-28-2008&REQ=3&Cert=8RkgPFRptdTvV1FKLh3z/cz3/fRY9GCcIdHZawv9OLnkZsgh2BSZKBJxYZqVW6zlO65X6ibpa10-&Pub=49611).

6586. ***American Journal of Veterinary Research.*** [ISSN: 0002-9645] 1940. m. USD 185 domestic; USD 195 foreign. Ed(s): Diane Fagen. American Veterinary Medical Association, c/o AVMA Library, 1931 N Meacham Rd, Ste 100, Schaumburg, IL 60173-4360; afagen@avma.org; http://www.avma.org. Illus., index, adv. Refereed. Circ: 6299 Paid. Vol. ends: Dec. Microform: PMC; PQC. *Indexed:* AbAn, Agr, B&AI, BiolAb, ChemAb, DSA, ExcerpMed, FS&TA, FoVS&M, IndMed, IndVet, S&F, SCI, SSCI, VetBull, WAE&RSA, ZooRec. *Aud.:* Ac, Sa.

A publication of the American Veterinary Medical Association, this journal is devoted to publishing peer-reviewed reports of the highest quality research that has a clear potential to enhance the health, welfare, and performance of animals. The illustrative material is largely black-and-white. An average issue will carry 20 to 30 articles varying in length from 2 to 12 pages. At the front of each issue is a section titled "Veterinary Research News." It reports on the latest happenings in the veterinary research community. This basic research journal is recommended for libraries serving graduate programs in the fields of veterinary medicine, animal science, dairy science, and laboratory animals.

6587. ***American Veterinary Medical Association. Journal.*** Incorporates: *American Veterinary Medical Association. News.* [ISSN: 0003-1488] 1877. s-m. USD 120 domestic; USD 140 foreign. Ed(s): Diane Fagen. American Veterinary Medical Association, c/o AVMA Library, 1931 N Meacham Rd, Ste 100, Schaumburg, IL 60173-4360; afagen@avma.org; http://www.avma.org. Illus., index, adv. Refereed. Circ: 68000 Paid. Vol. ends: Dec. Microform: BHP; PQC. *Indexed:* Agr, B&AI, BiolAb, ChemAb, DSA, ExcerpMed, FS&TA, FoVS&M, IndMed, IndVet, RRTA, S&F, SCI, SSCI, VetBull, WAE&RSA, ZooRec. *Bk. rev.:* 2-3, 200-400 words. *Aud.:* Ac, Sa.

This is the official publication of the American Veterinary Medical Association (AVMA), the largest veterinary association in the United States. Thus, this is the one journal that practically all veterinarians receive. Each issue carries a section on news related to the association and the profession, as well as interpretive summaries of articles, clinical reports, original studies, book reviews, announcements, and job opportunities. Additional features that appear frequently are "Legal Briefs," "What Is Your Diagnosis," and "Special Reports." The announcement section is invaluable for finding information on upcoming national and international meetings, CE offerings, and dates of state board examinations. The signed book reviews are useful to libraries doing book selection in this subject area. The editors certainly fulfill the mission statement of the journal: "to promote the science and art of veterinary medicine and to provide a forum for discussion of ideas important to the profession." This journal must be considered as the first choice for any U.S. veterinary collection.

6588. ***Australian Veterinary Journal.*** [ISSN: 0005-0423] 1925. m. AUD 341. Ed(s): Steve Ireland. Australian Veterinary Association, 134-136 Hampden Rd, Artarmon, NSW 2064, Australia; editor@ava.com.au; http://www.ava.com.au. Illus., index, adv. Refereed. Circ: 4500. Vol. ends: Dec. *Indexed:* Agr, B&AI, BiolAb, ChemAb, DSA, ExcerpMed, FS&TA, FoVS&M, ForAb, HortAb, IndMed, IndVet, RRTA, S&F, SCI, VetBull, WAE&RSA, ZooRec. *Bk. rev.:* 1-3, 300-600 words. *Aud.:* Ac, Sa.

This title is the official journal of the Australian Veterinary Association (AVA). Each issue has six to nine original research articles, one to five short contributions, and occasional case reports, all of which are classified under the general headings of "clinical" and "scientific." Major review articles and signed editorials are frequently included. It also has a news section, classifieds, obituaries, abstracts from other journals and the regular columns "World Watch" and "Viewpoint." Because this publication is designed to serve the practitioner as well as the researcher in Australia, one finds articles on domestic and nondomestic animal species (kangaroos, wallabies, koalas, etc.) native to Australia. Academic libraries serving animal science departments conducting research on sheep and tropical animal production will find this useful. It is also a natural selection for veterinary science collections, as much high-quality, original veterinary research emanates from Australia. Free online access to all, from October 1996 except the most recent six months at: http://www.ava.com.au/content/avj/avj.htm

6589. ***Avian Diseases.*** [ISSN: 0005-2086] 1957. q. USD 160 domestic; USD 170 foreign. Ed(s): Dr. L van der Heide. American Association of Avian Pathologists, Inc., University of Pennsylvania, 382 W. Street Rd., Kennett Sq., PA 19348-1692; AAAP@vet.upenn.edu; http://www.aaap.info/avdis/. Illus., index. Refereed. Circ: 1900. Vol. ends: Oct/Dec. Microform: WSH; PMC; PQC. Online: BioOne. *Indexed:* Agr, BiolAb, ChemAb, FoVS&M, IndMed, IndVet, SCI, VetBull, ZooRec. *Aud.:* Ac, Sa.

This title, the official publication of the American Association of Avian Pathologists, publishes the results of original research conducted in the specialty of avian diseases from throughout the world. While the emphasis is on birds of commercial importance—for example, chickens, turkeys, ducks, and geese—articles also appear on wild birds and pet species, such as budgerigars, parrots, and cockatiels. It is a substantial journal, containing 20 to 40 papers per issue, with each article averaging six to ten pages in length. Illustrations are mostly in black and white. It is highly recommended for poultry science and veterinary science collections. One can view the tables of contents of all issues from 2000 to date at http://www.aaap.info/avdis. Full online text from 2002 through BioOne is available: http://www.bioone.org/bioone/?request=get-journals-list&issn=0005-2086

6590. ***Canadian Journal of Veterinary Research.*** Former titles: *Canadian Journal of Comparative Medicine; Canadian Journal of Comparative Medicine and Veterinary Science.* [ISSN: 0830-9000] 1937. q. CND 110 domestic; USD 125 foreign. Ed(s): Dr. Eva Nagy. Canadian Veterinary Medical Association, 339 Booth St, Ottawa, ON K1R 7K1, Canada; kallen@cvma-acmv.org; http://www.cvma-acmv.org. Illus., index, adv. Refereed. Circ: 2000 Paid. Vol. ends: Dec. *Indexed:* Agr, BiolAb, ChemAb, DSA, ExcerpMed, FS&TA, FoVS&M, IndMed, IndVet, MCR, S&F, SCI, VetBull, WAE&RSA, ZooRec. *Aud.:* Ac, Sa.

This journal, the research journal of the Canadian Veterinary Medical Association, publishes results of original research in veterinary and comparative medicine. It is the Canadian counterpart to the *American Journal of Veterinary Research.* Papers may be full-length (up to eight pages) or short communications (two to three pages). Occasional review articles of general interest are published. All articles are in English, but the abstracts are given in both English and French. All animal species, domestic and nondomestic, are covered. Approximately 98 percent of the illustrations are in black and white. The target audience is scientists in the fields of veterinary science, animal science, and comparative medicine. This is a journal that should be found in all North American veterinary libraries. Although full-text articles are not available online, one can view the tables of contents from 1999 to date at its web site (http://www.canadianveterinarians.net/vetjournals).

6591. ***Canadian Veterinary Journal.*** [ISSN: 0008-5286] 1960. m. CND 140 domestic; USD 150 foreign. Ed(s): Dr. Doug Hare. Canadian Veterinary Medical Association, 339 Booth St, Ottawa, ON K1R 7K1, Canada; http://www.cvma-acmv.org. Illus., index, adv. Refereed. Circ: 5000 Paid. Vol. ends: Dec. Microform: PMC; PQC. *Indexed:* Agr, BiolAb, ChemAb, DSA, ExcerpMed, FoVS&M, IndMed, IndVet, RRTA, S&F, SCI, SSCI, VetBull, WAE&RSA, ZooRec. *Bk. rev.:* 1-6, 300-700 words. *Aud.:* Ac, Sa.

As the official publication of the Canadian Veterinary Medical Association (CVMA), this journal is considered to be the "voice of veterinary medicine in Canada." In addition to carrying scientific articles, review articles, and brief communications, each issue also contains a news section about CVMA activities (in both English and French), notices of upcoming meetings, new-product information, employment opportunities, and short reports on other matters of interest, such as veterinary medical ethics. This journal is recommended for veterinary libraries. The tables of contents, including abstracts, since 1999 are available online at the CVMA web site (http://www.canadianveterinarians.net/vetjournals).

6592. ***Clinical Techniques in Small Animal Practice.*** Formerly (until 1997): *Seminars in Veterinary Medicine and Surgery: Small Animal.* [ISSN: 1096-2867] 1986. q. USD 209 (Individuals, USD 129; Students, USD 64). Ed(s): Dr. Deborah Greco, Dr. James Orsini. W.B. Saunders Co., Independence Sq W, Ste 300, the Curtis Center, Philadelphia, PA 19106-3399; http://www.us.elsevierhealth.com/product.jsp?isbn=1055937x. Illus., index, adv. Refereed. Circ: 1214. Vol. ends: Nov. *Indexed:* Agr, BiolAb, DSA, FoVS&M, IndMed, IndVet, VetBull, WAE&RSA. *Aud.:* Ac, Sa.

This journal fills a unique niche by providing detailed, procedure-oriented information to enhance the practioner's office practice. The journal focuses on techniques in use in the average clinical practice: ophthalmic, dental, reproduction, surgery, and emergency and critical-care techniques. Each issue has a guest editor and focuses on a specific topic. There is an average of six to eight articles per issue. The illustrative photographs are in color and black and white. Recommended for veterinary science collections.

6593. ***Compendium on Continuing Education for the Practicing Veterinarian.*** Formerly: *Compendium on Continuing Education for the Small Animal Practitioner.* [ISSN: 0193-1903] 1979. m. USD 80 (Individuals, USD 58). Ed(s): Lilliane Anstee. Veterinary Learning Systems, 780 Township Line Rd., Yardley, PA 19067-4200; info@vetlearn.com.; http://www.vetlearn.com. Illus., index, adv. Sample. Refereed. Circ: 35000. Vol. ends: Dec. Microform: PQC. *Indexed:* Agr, DSA, FoVS&M, IndVet, VetBull, WAE&RSA. *Aud.:* Ac, Sa.

No other veterinary journal in recent years has exploded on the scene and gained or maintained such a large following as this one. It continues to be the most popular journal among academic veterinary clinicians. As a result, students usually feel this is a must-have journal when they go into practice. All articles are of a didatic nature and are followed by a list of review questions. Continuing-education credit can be received from Auburn University College of Veterinary Medicine by submitting answers to the review questions. The journal is heavily illustrated with color photographs. The articles are categorized under two broad subject headings: small animal/exotics and equine. A *Food Animal*

Medicine and Management supplement is published six times a year. This is a necessary publication for any veterinary practitioner as well as any veterinary science collection.

6594. ***D V M: the newsmagazine of veterinary medicine.*** [ISSN: 0012-7337] 1970. m. USD 39 in North America; USD 85 elsewhere; USD 4 newsstand/cover US & Possessions. Ed(s): Maureen Hrehocik. Advanstar Communications Inc., Healthcare Group, 7500 Old Oak Blvd, Cleveland, OH 44130-3369; info@advanstar.com; http://www.advanstar.com. Illus., adv. Circ: 45320. Vol. ends: Dec. Microform: PQC. Online: OCLC Online Computer Library Center, Inc.; ProQuest Information & Learning; H.W. Wilson. *Indexed:* B&AI. *Aud.:* Ga, Ac, Sa.

As the subtitle indicates, this is the *Newsweek* or *Time* magazine of veterinary medicine. Its size (10.75 × 14.5 inches) makes it stand out from the other magazines in the field. It reports on all relevant news, trends, and developments, and offers practical and authoritative medical information. Regular columnists write on practice management and marketing. Exclusive features include interviews and editorial roundtable discussions with professional leaders, feature reports on hot topics and complete coverage of regulatory and legislative activity. There is a monthly "New Products and Services" section and a quarterly "New Product Review" section in which important new products are introduced. There are occasional educational supplements to provide the clinician with the latest information on selected topics. The two most recent supplements were devoted to parasite control and diagnostic testing and imaging. The journal is interspersed with many color ads. The writing is in a nontechnical jargon so that clients in a veterinary waiting room may find some of its articles interesting. The web site (http://www.dvmnewsmagazine.com) provides the latest breaking news as well as selected feature articles from the magazine's archives.

6595. ***Equine Veterinary Journal.*** [ISSN: 0425-1644] 1968. bi-m. GBP 80 domestic (Students, GBP 40). Ed(s): P D Rossdale. Equine Veterinary Journal Ltd., 351 Exning Rd, Newmarket, CB8 0AU, United Kingdom; evj.editorial@dial.pipex.com; evj.subs@dial.pipex.com. Illus., index, adv. Refereed. Circ: 2000. Vol. ends: Nov. Reprint: PQC. *Indexed:* Agr, BiolAb, DSA, FoVS&M, IndMed, IndVet, RRTA, SCI, VetBull, WAE&RSA. *Aud.:* Ac, Sa.

This is the official publication of the British Equine Veterinary Association. Since its first appearance in 1968, it has become the most respected international scientific equine journal in the world. The average issue carries 10 to 14 full-length articles on original research, plus one to three short communications and case reports of equine medicine on topics such as oncology, exercise, doping, parasitology, physiology, surgery, behavior, reproduction and racing. The illustrations are predominantly in black and white. A must for veterinary libraries, equine practitioners, and libraries serving colleges with equestrian programs or those conducting equine research.

6596. ***Exotic D V M.*** [ISSN: 1521-1363] 1999. bi-m. USD 69 in North America; USD 89 elsewhere. Ed(s): Linda Harrison. Zoological Education Network, PO Box 541749, Lake Worth, FL 33454-1749. Adv. Vol. ends: No. 4. *Bk. rev.:* 1-2, 300-400 words. *Aud.:* Ac,Sa.

This flashy journal has certainly found its niche in the field of exotic animal medicine. It is definitely a practical how-to magazine, and it is somewhat surprising that the idea has not caught on in the other disciplines of veterinary medicine. The major thrust of the magazine is to present a single procedure or tip through a series of step-by-step color images (up to 16). Text is kept to a minimum. Some issues are topic specific, such as dentistry, dermatology, and surgery. In addition, there are regular columns on nutrition, pet care, book reviews, and the exotic marketplace. Each pet care column is devoted to a specific exotic animal providing valuable resource information for the proper care (nutrition, housing, restraint, breeding, sexing) of the animal. Such all-you-need-to-know information on nontraditional companion animals is usually very difficult to locate, and it is exciting to see this as a regular feature. The magazine is essential for any clinic handling exotic animals and veterinary libraries. Zoo libraries would probably find it a useful addition to their collections. Subscribers also have access to an online version, as well as an online forum, at http://www.exoticdvm.com. (CTB)

6597. ***F D A Veterinarian.*** [ISSN: 1057-6223] 1979. bi-m. USD 17. Ed(s): Karan A Kandra. U.S. Food & Drug Administration, Center for Veterinary Medicine, 7500 Standish Pl, Rockville, MD 20855. Circ: 3600. *Indexed:* IndVet. *Aud.:* Ac, Sa.

This federal government title is produced by the Center for Veterinary Medicine, whose purpose is to regulate the manufacture and distribution of food additives and drugs that will be given to animals. This publication is the most reliable source for the latest information regarding changes in veterinary drug regulations, withdrawal times for antibiotics, companies not in compliance with federal regulations, new animal drug approvals, etc. The information is objective and of considerable value for anyone working with animals, from farmers to veterinarians to, for that matter, dedicated pet owners. Issues have short features and articles on such subjects as "Contaminated Animal Feed Supplements Recalled," "Mad Cow Disease," and " Protecting Pets from Mosquito-Borne Diseases." This publication is available both in print and online. The online version, which can be downloaded free, is archived back to the November/December 1995 issue. (CTB)

6598. ***Journal of Avian Medicine and Surgery.*** Former titles (until 1995): *Association of Avian Veterinarians. Journal;* (until 1989): *A A V Today;* (until 1987): *A A V Newsletter.* [ISSN: 1082-6742] 1980. q. USD 130 domestic; USD 135 in Canada & Mexico; USD 145 elsewhere. Ed(s): Dr. James Carpenter. Association of Avian Veterinarians, PO Box 210732, Bedford, TX 76095; aavpubs@aol.com. Illus., index, adv. Sample. Refereed. Circ: 3500. Vol. ends: Dec. *Indexed:* FoVS&M, IndVet, S&F, VetBull, ZooRec. *Bk. rev.:* 1-2, 400-500 words. *Aud.:* Ac, Sa.

This official publication of the Association of Avian Veterinarians (AAV) is an international journal on the medicine and surgery of captive and wild birds. It publishes original research, review articles, case reports, and research briefs. In addition, it has an editorial in each issue plus the sections "What's Your Diagnosis?," "Historical Perspectives," "Selected Abstracts from the Literature," and a calendar of upcoming meetings. The illustrations are chiefly in black and white, with a judicious use of color. An expensive clay-coated paper is used to achieve the highest resolution of photographs. The journal is essential for the avian practitioner and is highly recommended for zoo and veterinary libraries. Online full text is available from 2000 through BioOne: http://www.bioone.org/bioone/?request=get-journals-list&issn=1082-6742

6599. ***Journal of Feline Medicine and Surgery.*** [ISSN: 1098-612X] 1999. bi-m. EUR 290 (Individuals, EUR 139). Ed(s): M Scherk, A H Sparkes. W.B. Saunders Co. Ltd., 32 Jamestown Rd, London, NW1 7BY, United Kingdom; http://www.harcourt-international.com. Illus., adv. Refereed. Circ: 1000. *Indexed:* IndVet, VetBull. *Bk. rev.:* 1, 200-300 words. *Aud.:* Ac, Sa.

The official journal of the European Society of Feline Medicine (ESFM) is international in scope and probably the only scientific, peer-reviewed journal in the world devoted exclusively to feline medicine and surgery. Besides publishing original papers, reviews, and short communications, the editors commission some articles. An international news section provides information about ESFM and other feline veterinary meetings, society news, new developments, and relevant issues from other publications and meetings. This journal is a must for the feline practitioner. Most veterinary libraries will find it to be a necessary journal to have. Online full text is available through ScienceDirect (http://www.sciencedirect.com/science/journal/1098612X).

6600. ***Journal of Small Animal Practice.*** [ISSN: 0022-4510] 1960. m. GBP 152 domestic; GBP 168 elsewhere. Ed(s): Dr. F J Barr. British Veterinary Association, 7 Mansfield St, London, W1G 9NQ, United Kingdom; bvahq@bva.co.uk; http://www.bva.co.uk/. Illus., index, adv. Refereed. Circ: 4500. Vol. ends: Dec. Reprint: ISI. *Indexed:* Agr, BiolAb, ChemAb, DSA, ExcerpMed, FoVS&M, IndMed, IndVet, SCI, VetBull, ZooRec. *Bk. rev.:* 1, 300-375 words. *Aud.:* Ac, Sa.

This is the British counterpart to the *Journal of the American Animal Hospital Association,* representing the British Small Animal Veterinary Association (BSAVA) and the World Small Animal Veterinary Association. It is an international journal publishing original clinical research, review articles, and case histories covering all aspects of medicine and surgery relating to dogs, cats, and other small mammals. Printing on clay-based paper enables the publisher to make excellent use of color layouts that increase eye appeal and readability. Each issue includes a news section providing topical information of interest to companion-animal practitoners. Readership will be limited to small-animal practitioners and clinicians. It is highly recommended for libraries serving veterinary science programs. Tables of contents with abstracts of the current issue can be found at BSAVA web site (http://www.bsava.com/nonmembers.htm), so the reader can get an idea of what the journal is like.

6601. ***Journal of Swine Health and Production.*** Formerly: *Swine Health and Production.* [ISSN: 1537-209X] 1993. bi-m. USD 97.50 in North America; USD 110 elsewhere. Ed(s): Karen Richardson, Cate Dewey. American Association of Swine Veterinarians, 902 1st Ave, Perry, IA 50220-1703; http://www.aasv.org. Refereed. Circ: 1800. Vol. ends: Nov/Dec. *Indexed:* Agr, DSA, FoVS&M, IndVet, VetBull, WAE&RSA. *Aud.:* Ac,Sa.

The American Association of Swine Veterinarians (AASV) publishes the only refereed journal in North America that focuses exclusively on swine. It accepts for publication manuscripts on original research, case reports, literature reviews, brief communications, and practice tips. In addition, it publishes news concering the association as well as other news of interest to its membership. One nice feature is the calendar of upcoming national and international meetings. Most of the articles are illustrated with tables, charts, and graphs, although photographs are used when needed. Color is used judiciously. This journal is a must for the swine practitioner, veterinary libraries, and any institution that is involved with swine research. The journal is available online to subscribers and can be accessed through the AASV web site (http://www.aasv.org).

6602. ***Journal of Veterinary Internal Medicine.*** [ISSN: 0891-6640] 1987. bi-m. USD 100 USD 20 per issue. Ed(s): Stephen P DiBartola, Kenneth W Hinchcliff. American College of Veterinary Internal Medicine, 1997 Wadsworth Blvd, Ste A, Lakewood, CO 80215-3327; acvim@acvim.org ; http://www.acvim.org/. Illus., index, adv. Refereed. Circ: 1000 Paid. Vol. ends: Nov/Dec. *Indexed:* Agr, BiolAb, DSA, FoVS&M, HortAb, IndMed, IndVet, SCI, VetBull. *Aud.:* Ac, Sa.

The last several years have shown a proliferation of specialty journals in the field of veterinary medicine, of which this journal is a good example. It is the official publication of the American College of Veterinary Internal Medicine, one of the largest specialty boards within the American Veterinary Medical Association. The editors particularly seek clinical and research manuscripts in the area of small-animal and large-animal internal medicine, cardiology, neurology, and oncology. In addition, they accept review articles, brief communications, case reports, and clinical vignettes. The use of photographs appears limited, with greater emphasis placed on charts, graphs, and tables. It is a well-edited publication, but readership will be limited to those veterinarians, clinicians, and researchers with an interest in internal medicine. However, it is considered a necessary purchase for veterinary college libraries.

6603. ***Journal of Veterinary Medical Education.*** [ISSN: 0748-321X] 1974. 4x/yr. USD 60 (Individuals, USD 50). Ed(s): Dr. Donald Walsh. Association of American Veterinary Medical Colleges, 1101 Vermont Ave, NW, Ste 710, Washington, DC 20005; journals@utpress.utoronto.edu; http://aavmc.org/. Illus., adv. Refereed. Circ: 3400 Paid. Vol. ends: Dec. Microform: PQC. Reprint: PQC. *Indexed:* CIJE, DSA, FoVS&M, IndVet, SSCI, VetBull, WAE&RSA. *Bk. rev.:* 1-5, 200-350 words. *Aud.:* Ac, Sa.

This is the only journal, in any language, devoted to veterinary medical education. It is the official publication of the Association of American Veterinary Medical Colleges. The journal contains articles on veterinary medical curricula, instructional technology, teaching methodology, and new approaches to the learning paradigm. A unique feature is the peer review of individually created education software. It is a useful journal to monitor for information regarding changes in the profession and how veterinary colleges are reacting to the changes. Readership will mostly be limited to veterinary college administrators, members of curriculum committees, and continuing education personnel.

6604. ***Journal of Wildlife Diseases.*** Former titles: *Wildlife Disease Association. Journal; Wildlife Disease Association. Bulletin.* [ISSN: 0090-3558] 1965. q. USD 250. Ed(s): Elizabeth S Williams. Wildlife Disease Association, Inc., PO Box 1897, Lawrence, KS 66044-8897; orders@allenpress.com; http://www.wildlifedisease.org. Illus., index, adv. Sample. Refereed. Circ: 1350 Paid. Vol. ends: Oct. *Indexed:* Agr, B&AI, BiolAb, BiolDig, ChemAb, DSA, FoVS&M, ForAb, IndMed, IndVet, RRTA, S&F, SCI, VetBull, ZooRec. *Bk. rev.:* 1-5, 500-600 words. *Aud.:* Ac, Sa.

This international journal publishes the results of original research and observations dealing with all aspects of infectious, parasitic, toxic, nutritional, physiologic, developmental, and neoplastic diseases affecting the health and survival of free-living or captive wild animals, including fish. Illustrations are in black and white. As one can surmise from the scope of coverage, each issue carries a diverse array of articles, ranging from chronic wasting disease in deer and elk to spontaneous gallstone formation in deer mice to sarcoptes in common wombats. An average issue has 12 to 17 full-length articles followed by 10 to 18 short communications. The book reviews are exceptionally good. This is a must for academic libraries supporting game biology/wildlife science and veterinary science programs.

6605. ***Journal of Zoo and Wildlife Medicine.*** Formerly: *Journal of Zoo Animal Medicine.* [ISSN: 1042-7260] 1971. q. USD 195 (Individuals, USD 90). Ed(s): Wilbur B Amand. American Association of Zoo Veterinarians, 6 North Pennell Rd, Media, PA 19063; aazv@allnepress.com; http://www.aazv.org. Illus., index, adv. Refereed. Circ: 1200. Vol. ends: Dec. *Indexed:* BiolAb, DSA, EnvAb, FoVS&M, ForAb, IndMed, IndVet, S&F, SCI, VetBull, ZooRec. *Bk. rev.:* 2-3, 300-500 words. *Aud.:* Ac, Sa.

The official publication of the American Association of Zoo Veterinarians emphasizes original-research findings, clinical observations, and case reports in the field of veterinary medicine dealing with captive and free-ranging wild animals. It is generally recognized as the leading journal in this discipline. Abstracts of selected articles appearing elsewhere in the literature are included in each issue. An interesting feature in each issue, "Clinical Challenge," gives insight into how difficult cases were solved and/or resolved. This is a high-quality research journal with black-and-white illustrations. A must for zoo and veterinary libraries and perhaps for libraries supporting marine biology programs. Online version from 2000 available through BioOne (http://www.bioone.org/bioone/?request=get-journals-list&issn=1042-7260).

6606. ***Research in Veterinary Science.*** [ISSN: 0034-5288] 1960. bi-m. EUR 407 (Individuals, EUR 242). Ed(s): G A Hall. W.B. Saunders Co. Ltd., Foots Cray High Street, Sidcup, DA14 5HP, United Kingdom; http://www.harcourt-international.com. Illus., index, adv. Refereed. Circ: 945. Vol. ends: Nov. Microform: PMC; PQC. Online: EBSCO Publishing; OCLC Online Computer Library Center, Inc.; RoweCom Information Quest; ScienceDirect; Swets Blackwell. Reprint: PQC; SWZ. *Indexed:* Agr, BiolAb, ChemAb, DSA, ExcerpMed, FS&TA, FoVS&M, HortAb, IndMed, IndVet, S&F, SCI, SSCI, VetBull, WAE&RSA, ZooRec. *Aud.:* Ac, Sa.

This title, the official publication of the Association of Veterinary Teachers and Research Workers, is perhaps best described as the British Veterinary Association's equivalent of the American Veterinary Medical Association's *American Journal of Veterinary Research.* Original contributions, review articles, and short communications on the health, welfare, and diseases of all animal species as well as comparative medicine are accepted for publication. Color illustrations are used infrequently. Many of the contributors are from outside the United Kingdom, which gives the journal an international flavor. The articles are categorized under specific subject headings. Tables of contents and abstracts since 1999 are available free at its web site (http://www.harcourt-international.com/journals/rvsc), while full text is available through ScienceDirect. Recommended for veterinary libraries.

6607. ***Seminars in Avian and Exotic Pet Medicine.*** [ISSN: 1055-937X] 1992. q. USD 209 (Individuals, USD 112; Students, USD 52). Ed(s): Dr. Alan M Fudge. W.B. Saunders Co., Independence Sq W, Ste 300, the Curtis Center, Philadelphia, PA 19106-3399; elspcs@elsevier.com; http://www.us.elsevierhealth.com/product.jsp?isbn=1055937x. Illus., index, adv. Refereed. Circ: 1530. Vol. ends: Dec. *Indexed:* FoVS&M, ZooRec. *Aud.:* Ac, Sa.

One of the new trends in the field of veterinary medicine has been the development of a specialty dealing with exotic animals and/or pet birds. Although practitioners have been witnessing an increasing number of cases in this area, there has been a lack of scholarly journals devoted to this specialty. Hence, the practitioner has often had difficulty locating reliable information. *Seminars in Avian and Exotic Pet Medicine* is one of three new journals (see also *Journal of Avian Medicine and Surgery* and *Veterinary Clinics of North America: exotic animal practice*) that is successfully filling the void. The format features a subject specialist as a guest editor, and the issue is devoted to the editor's specialty. All papers are invited. The journal is printed on clay-based paper and has an easy-to-read format featuring excellent black-and-white and color photographs. There is an average of six articles, three to ten pages in length, per issue. The concise, topical, and authoritative reviews address problems faced in daily practice. Recent themes have been passerine birds, soft tissue surgery, and endocrinology. This journal is a must for the avian practitioner and for any practitioner handling exotic-animal cases. It is also highly recommended for veterinary and zoo libraries.

6608. ***Veterinary Clinics of North America: Equine Practice.*** [ISSN: 0749-0739] 1985. 3x/yr. USD 211 (Individuals, USD 139; Students, USD 70). Ed(s): A Simon Turner. W.B. Saunders Co., Independence Sq W, Ste 300, the Curtis Center, Philadelphia, PA 19106-3399; http://www.us.elsevierhealth.com/. Illus., index. Refereed. Vol. ends: Dec. *Indexed:* FoVS&M, HortAb, IndMed, IndVet, RRTA, VetBull, WAE&RSA. *Aud.:* Ac, Sa.

As with the other three *Veterinary Clinics of North America* journals, each issue has a guest editor who is responsible for inviting other experts on the featured topic to contribute papers. Recent topics include geriatrics, respiratory disease, pain management and anesthesia, and toxicology. The use of photographs, tables, and charts is kept to a minimum. While this is must reading for equine practitioners and a necessary title for veterinary collections, it is also recommended for animal science and equestrian collections.

6609. ***Veterinary Clinics of North America: Exotic Animal Practice.*** [ISSN: 1094-9194] 1998. 3x/yr. USD 196 (Individuals, USD 125; Students, USD 62). W.B. Saunders Co., Independence Sq W, Ste 300, the Curtis Center, Philadelphia, PA 19106-3399; http://www.us.elsevierhealth.com/. Illus., index. Refereed. Vol. ends: Sep. *Indexed:* IndMed. *Aud.:* Ac, Sa.

The latest entry in the *Veterinary Clinics of North America* series is devoted to exotic-animal practice. The increasing popularity of exotic animals being used as companion animals has created a new specialty in veterinary medicine, which in turn necessitates peer-reviewed scientific literature for the specialist. As with the other titles in this series, each issue is devoted to a single topic. A limited number of photographs and diagrams are used. It is the aim of the publisher to provide detailed information of a special diagnostic and therapeutic nature applicable to exotic species. Essential to wildlife, zoo, and veterinary collections.

6610. ***Veterinary Clinics of North America: Food Animal Practice.*** [ISSN: 0749-0720] 1985. 3x/yr. USD 167 (Individuals, USD 113; Students, USD 57). W.B. Saunders Co., Independence Sq W, Ste 300, the Curtis Center, Philadelphia, PA 19106-3399; http://www.us.elsevierhealth.com/. Illus., index. Refereed. Vol. ends: Nov. *Indexed:* DSA, FoVS&M, IndMed, IndVet, VetBull, WAE&RSA. *Aud.:* Ac, Sa.

As with its companion volumes in the *Veterinary Clinics* series, each issue is under the direction of a guest editor who is an authority in his or her field. Information on new developments in the diagnosis and management of species (cattle, swine, goats, sheep, llamas, deer, and ratites) treated by food animal practitioners is covered. Each issue averages 10 to 15 articles. Recent topics have included mastitis, biosecurity of cattle operations, and immunology. Illustrations are usually in black and white, but occasionally color is used. This title is recommended for veterinary and animal science collections and should be found on every food animal practitioner's bookshelf.

6611. ***Veterinary Clinics of North America: Small Animal Practice.*** Supersedes in part (in 1979): *Veterinary Clinics of North America.* [ISSN: 0195-5616] 1971. bi-m. USD 240 (Individuals, USD 162; Students, USD 81). W.B. Saunders Co., Independence Sq W, Ste 300, the Curtis Center, Philadelphia, PA 19106-3399; http://www.us.elsevierhealth.com/. Illus., index. Refereed. Vol. ends: Nov. Microform: MIM; PQC. Online: ingenta.com. Reprint: ISI; PQC. *Indexed:* BiolAb, DSA, ExcerpMed, FoVS&M, HortAb, IndMed, IndVet, SCI, SSCI, VetBull, WAE&RSA, ZooRec. *Aud.:* Ac, Sa.

Like all of the titles in Saunders's *Veterinary Clinics of North America* series, each hardback volume is devoted to a specific topic, with an expert on the topic serving as a guest editor. The series proved so popular that it split into four sections: small-animal practice, equine practice, food-animal practice, and exotic-animal practice. Recent issues feature medical oncology, topics in feline surgery, critical care, and nutraceuticals. The few illustrations are in black and white. A basic title for a veterinary medicine collection as well as for small-animal practitioners.

6612. ***Veterinary Economics: business solutions for practicing veterinarians.*** [ISSN: 0042-4862] 1960. m. USD 42 domestic (Free to qualified personnel; Students, USD 29.50). Ed(s): Marnette Denell Falley. Thomson Veterinary Healthcare Communications, 8033 Flint, Lenexa, KS 66214; vmpg@vetmed; http://vetmedpub.com. Illus., index, adv. Refereed. Circ: 50000. Vol. ends: Dec. Microform: PQC. Online: Northern Light Technology, Inc. *Indexed:* ATI, FoVS&M, IndVet, VetBull. *Aud.:* Ac, Sa.

This journal has long been recognized for its excellent coverage of all aspects of veterinary practice management, retirement planning, evaluating practices for purchase, partnership arrangement, contracts, client relations, taxes, and other financial matters. Its regular column on hospital designs is very popular. Its special reports on trends, salaries, and economics in the profession are well respected. Among the numerous publishing awards it has received is the 1999 Jesse H. Neal Editorial Achievement Award, which is the Pulitzer Prize of the business press. Recommended for veterinary libraries and practitioners.

6613. ***The Veterinary Journal.*** Former titles (until 1997): *British Veterinary Journal;* (until 1949): *Veterinary Journal;* (until 1900): *Veterinary Journal and Annals of Comparative Pathology.* [ISSN: 1090-0233] 1875. bi-m. EUR 497 (Individuals, EUR 251). Ed(s): A. J. Higgins. W.B. Saunders Co. Ltd., 32 Jamestown Rd, London, NW1 7BY, United Kingdom; http://www.harcourt-international.com. Illus., index, adv. Sample. Refereed. Vol. ends: Dec. Microform: PMC; PQC. Online: EBSCO Publishing; OCLC Online Computer Library Center, Inc.; RoweCom Information Quest; ScienceDirect; Swets Blackwell. Reprint: PQC; SWZ. *Indexed:* Agr, BiolAb, ChemAb, DSA, ExcerpMed, FS&TA, FoVS&M, IndMed, IndVet, S&F, SCI, VetBull, WAE&RSA, ZooRec. *Bk. rev.:* 4-6, 300-500 words. *Aud.:* AC.

This is one of the longest-running English-language veterinary journals, tracing its history back to 1875. It is international in scope and publishes original papers and reviews on all aspects of veterinary science and kindred subjects, with particular emphasis on animal health and preventive medicine. Papers are published under three categories: "Fast Track," "Commissioned Topical Reviews," and "Original Articles." The "Fast Track" section is designed to help authors achieve rapid publication of novel experimental findings or to promote methodologies of unusual and timely significance. The use of photographic materials is minimal, with a greater reliance on charts, tables, and graphs. The signed book reviews are useful to collection development personnel. This is a basic title for veterinary science collections. The table of contents and abstracts are available for free since 1999 at its web site (http://www.harcourt-international.com/journals/rvsc). Full-text coverage is available through ScienceDirect. With the advent of the electronic version, an article is now available within six weeks of acceptance online, before the hard copy is published.

6614. ***Veterinary Medicine.*** Formerly (until 1985): *Veterinary Medicine - Small Animal Clinician.* [ISSN: 8750-7943] 1905. m. USD 59 domestic (Free to qualified personnel; Students, USD 20.95). Ed(s): Margaret Rampey. Thomson Veterinary Healthcare Communications, 8033 Flint, Lenexa, KS 66214; vmpg@vetmed; http://vetmedpub.com. Illus., index, adv. Refereed. Circ: 26020. Vol. ends: Dec. Microform: PQC. Online: Northern Light Technology, Inc.; ProQuest Information & Learning. *Indexed:* Agr, B&AI, BiolAb, DSA, FoVS&M, HortAb, IndMed, IndVet, VetBull, WAE&RSA, ZooRec. *Aud.:* Ac, Sa.

The goal of this journal is to provide solutions to the most common and emerging diagnostic and therapeutic problems seen in clinical practice. Therefore, the emphasis is on articles that give a how-to approach to guide practicing veterinarians in selecting better diagnostic and therapeutic strategies. Hence, the articles are more clinical than research oriented. Because of its practical nature and the fact that the articles are concise, to the point, and well illustrated in color, this journal is popular with practicing veterinarians. Since January 2000, the journal has focused exclusively on dogs, cats, and exotics. A highly recommended title for the small-animal practitioner and all veterinary science collections.

6615. ***Veterinary Pathology.*** Formerly: *Pathologia Veterinaria.* [ISSN: 0300-9858] 1964. bi-m. USD 170 (Individuals, USD 98; Students, USD 55). Ed(s): Donna F. Kusewitt. American College of Veterinary Pathologists, c/o Box 1897, Lawrence, KS 66044-8897; info@acvp.org; http://www.afip.org/. Illus., index, adv. Refereed. Circ: 1200. Vol. ends: Nov. *Indexed:* Agr, BiolAb, ChemAb, DSA, ExcerpMed, FoVS&M, IndMed, IndVet, S&F, SCI, VetBull, ZooRec. *Bk. rev.:* 1-2, 250-350 words. *Aud.:* Ac, Sa.

This is the official publication of the American College of Veterinary Pathologists, but it is international in scope. The journal publishes manuscripts, reviews, brief communications, and case reports dealing with experimental and natural diseases. It also carries advertisements for employment opportunities and new products. The quality of the photographs (color and black-and-white) is exceptional. The scope of coverage includes diseases in domestic animals, laboratory animals, and exotics. This is a recommended title for libraries serving diagnostic laboratories and/or veterinary programs. Online full text is available, through HighWire, from 2000 to the present for all paid subscribers. The journal's web site, giving full subscription information, online accessiblity, instructions to authors, etc., is at http://www.vetpathology.org.

6616. ***Veterinary Record.*** [ISSN: 0042-4900] 1888. w. GBP 145.50 domestic; GBP 157.50 in Africa; GBP 189 elsewhere. Ed(s): Martin Alder. British Veterinary Association, 7 Mansfield St, London, W1G 9NQ, United Kingdom; bvahq@bva.co.uk; http://www.bva.co.uk/. Illus., index, adv. Refereed. Circ: 10000. Vol. ends: Dec. Microform: PQC. Online: ingenta.com. Reprint: PQC. *Indexed:* Agr, B&AI, BiolAb, ChemAb, DSA, ExcerpMed, FS&TA, FoVS&M, HortAb, IndMed, IndVet, RRTA, S&F, SCI, SSCI, VetBull, WAE&RSA, ZooRec. *Bk. rev.:* 1-3, 400-750 words. *Aud.:* Ac, Sa.

Founded in 1888, this publication of the British Veterinary Association is one of the most venerable journals in the field of veterinary medicine. It is a newsy journal carrying information about the association and veterinary matters in the United Kingdom and serves as a forum for British veterinarians to present their viewpoints. However, it is also highly respected for the papers it publishes on original research as well as review articles, clinical case histories, short communications, and letters. All aspects of veterinary medicine and surgery are covered. Illustrations are generally in color. This journal is one of the most cited journals in the veterinary field and is necessary for most veterinary science collections. One can view the table of contents of the current issue at the journal's web site (http://www.vetrecord.co.uk).

6617. ***Veterinary Surgery.*** Incorporates: *Veterinary Anesthesia;* Formerly: *Journal of Veterinary Surgery.* [ISSN: 0161-3499] 1978. bi-m. USD 256 print & online. Blackwell Publishing, Inc., Commerce Place, 350 Main St, Malden, MA 02148; subscrip@blackwellpub.com; http://www.blackwellpublishing.com. Illus., index, adv. Refereed. Circ: 2434. Vol. ends: Nov/Dec. Reprint: PQC. *Indexed:* Agr, BiolAb, DSA, FoVS&M, IndMed, IndVet, SCI, VetBull, WAE&RSA. *Aud.:* Ac, Sa.

Veterinary Surgery is the official publication of the American College of Veterinary Surgeons and the European College of Veterinary Surgeons. It is a journal of continuing education within the broad field of veterinary surgery. Coverage includes, but is not limited to, surgical techniques, management of the surgical patient, diagnostic aids, and the history of veterinary surgery. The periodical covers both large and small animals. The illustrations are high-quality black-and-white photographs. In addition to carrying clinical and research papers, it also publishes scientific abstracts from the annual meetings and a section on job opportunities. A recommended title for veterinary collections. Online full text available since 2000. Further information is available at http://www2.us.elsevierhealth.com/scripts/om.dll/serve?action=searchDB&searchdbfor=home&id=jvet.

Electronic Journals

6618. ***Veterinary Neurology and Neurosurgery.*** [ISSN: 1526-2073] q. Ed(s): T A Holliday. Veterinary Neurology and Neurosurgery, 1507 Alice St, Davis, CA 95616; taholliday@ucdavis.edu; http://www.neurovet.org. Refereed. *Aud.:* Ac, Sa.

Veterinary Neurology and Neurosurgery is a peer-reviewed online journal providing free access to clinical and research information in veterinary neurology and veterinary neurosurgery. The journal considers for publication original clinical or laboratory research, review papers, case reports, and continuing education papers. In addition, it features a "Case of the Month" section, a series of video clips showing various neurological disorders, and a section called "Electrophysiology Notes." As with all of the veterinary journals in an entirely electronic format, the submission of manuscripts has been slow, but encouraging.

■ WEDDINGS

Heidi Gauder, Government Documents and Assistant Collection Management Librarian, Roesch Library, University of Dayton, Dayton, OH 45469; heidi.gauder@notes.udayton.edu

Introduction

Weddings are a big business. It is estimated that over two million weddings take place annually, at an average cost of $19,000. Whether the brides have dreamed about their wedding since they were children or not, a wedding day is often the culmination of months of planning and spending. Bridal magazines help promote many of these wedding fantasies and dreams, most of them following a recognizable pattern in each issue. There is the wedding planning advice, including countdown and budget worksheets, a section on wedding etiquette, as well as ideas for personalizing the wedding ceremony or reception. Sometimes relationship advice is also included. Another part will cover bridal fashion and beauty, from the bride's hair to wedding accessories to bridesmaids' outfits, and always wedding dresses. After the fashion spread there usually follows a section on the bridal registry and then the honeymoon. Many magazines also include stories and pictures of real weddings. Many print titles have online equivalents that contain similar content and also serve as a link to wedding shopping and merchandise. Although there are a fair number of titles within this genre, sadly, most tend to promote the same Judeo-Christian fantasy: white wedding dress, big reception feast, traditional registry, and exotic honeymoon. Very few magazines, however, are written specifically for the ethnic or minority bride. Most titles do report on ethnic traditions, but overall, the models are predominantly Caucasian and wedding fashions do little to encourage dressing in something other than a white dress. This section describes only those wedding magazines that are available nationwide on a serial basis. In doing so, special regional wedding editions and many destination wedding magazines have been excluded, although they are worth a brief mention. There are many regional issues that often serve as vehicles for local vendors to advertise and showcase their talents (especially true for wedding photographers). Nationally distributed magazines including *Weddingbells, Modern Bride,* and *The Knot* all publish local offshoots. In addition to regional magazines, other titles produce special wedding issues. *InStyle,* for example, publishes at least one wedding issue annually in addition to its regular issues, as does *Southern Living, Renaissance Magazine,* and *Better Homes and Gardens.* Lastly, there are destination wedding and honeymoon magazines such as *Pacific Rim Weddings, Bermuda Weddings,* and *Island Weddings and Honeymoons.* The focus of this section, however, is for the most part on those magazines that help fulfill more than one aspect of the wedding day.

Basic Periodicals

Sa: *Bride's, Bridal Guide, Elegant Bride, Martha Stewart Weddings, Modern Bride.*

6619. ***101 Bridal Ideas.*** a. USD 4.99 newsstand/cover per issue; USD 6.95 newsstand/cover per issue Canada. Clapper Communications Companies, 2400 E Devon Ave, Ste 375, Des Plaines, IL 60018-4618; feedback@clapper.com; http://www.craftideas.com. *Aud.:* Sa.

This semi-annual bridal magazine is unlike the others listed because it caters to those brides and interested crafters who want to add a homemade touch to that special day. This magazine contains no couture fashions, wedding planning ideas, relationship advice, registry checklist, or honeymoon travel ideas. Instead, *101 Bridal Ideas* provides craft ideas and instructions for all skill levels using a variety of mediums. An editorial notes, "Whether you stamp your floral ribbon, make clay frames, or arrange your own silk floral bouquet, have a creative, wonderful, memorable day!" This title is also found online and includes selected project ideas, along with many more available for purchase. The web site for *101 Bridal Ideas* is part of set of craft magazines from the publisher's web site. For the bride looking for the handcrafted touch at her wedding, this magazine and its online component offer plenty of ideas.

6620. ***Bridal Guide: the how to for "I do".*** [ISSN: 0882-7451] 1982. bi-m. USD 11.97; USD 4.99 newsstand/cover per issue. Ed(s): Diane Forden. Rosenbloom Family Publishing, 3 E 54th St, 15th Fl, New York, NY 10022-3108; http://www.BridalGuidemag.com. Illus., adv. Sample. Circ: 250000 Paid. Vol. ends: Dec (No. 6). *Aud.:* Sa.

Bridal Guide is a traditional wedding magazine that should appeal to brides planning their ultimate fantasy weddings as well as to brides intending to have more economical affairs. The fashions are particularly telling in this regard: Most couture dresses are displayed in feature articles, while the advertisements promote more moderately priced dresses and utilize more plus-sized models than other magazines. To its credit, however, *Bridal Guide* also includes dresses from inexpensive lines in the fashion articles. The bimonthly magazine has the usual mix of planning advice; gift ideas; beauty, registry, cake, flower, and honeymoon tips; and a real-life wedding story. The online version follows these categories and is mostly text; although there is a link for fashion and beauty, no images of wedding dresses are included. The web site has a number of retail sponsors, but it is not partnered with any single wedding portal like other titles in this genre.

6621. ***Bride's.*** Former titles (until 1995): *Bride's and Your New Home;* (until Nov. 1991): *Bride's; Bride's Magazine.* [ISSN: 1084-1628] 1934. bi-m. USD 21.97 domestic; USD 36 Canada; USD 41 elsewhere. Ed(s): Millie Martini Bratten. Conde Nast Publications Inc., 4 Times Square, 5th Fl, New York, NY 10036; letters@brides.com; http://www.brides.com. Illus., adv. Circ: 500000 Paid. Vol. ends: Nov/Dec. Microform: PQC. Reprint: PQC. *Aud.:* Sa.

Probably the best-known bridal magazine, *Bride's* is certainly the heftiest. One recent issue nearly topped 1,000 pages, much of it advertising. While readers often overlook ads, in this case they may prove useful, especially for brides looking for the perfect wedding dress, invitations, honeymoon destinations, or other items. This magazine seeks to be the only source needed by prospective brides and grooms as they deal with "all aspects of wedding planning and beginning life as a couple. Its articles offer suggestions to meet a variety of styles and budgets." There are sections on fashion, beauty, wedding planning, receptions, registry, and the honeymoon. Numerous Q&A columns answer specific questions on fashion, beauty, reception, etiquette, sex, and travel. Snapshots from real weddings offer plenty of ideas. While magazines in this genre do their best to present the ultimate wedding fantasy, the editors of *Bride's* also realize that many brides are faced with a budget and often include budgeting advice. Produced by the publisher of *Vogue, Glamour,* and *Modern Bride,* this magazine has the familiar look and feel of its sister magazines. The online version follows a similar print format.

6622. ***Elegant Bride.*** Formerly: *Southern Bride.* 1988. q. bi-m. in 2004. USD 15.95 domestic; USD 4.95 newsstand/cover per issue domestic; GBP 3.50 newsstand/cover per issue United Kingdom. Fairchild Publications, Inc., 7 W 34th St, New York, NY 10001-8191; http://www.fairchildpub.com. Illus., adv. Sample. Circ: 142000. Vol. ends: Winter. *Aud.:* Sa.

Elegant Bride is for the woman who can spare no expense for her wedding—or the woman who wishes she could. This quarterly publication is like other bridal magazines except for the high-end couture fashions, accessories, and other wedding details. A recent article titled "Simply the Best" features some of the ultimate wedding and engagement rings, including the pink diamond given to Jennifer Lopez. There are few features here that consider any budgets but the most lavish. Another distinction of this title is its closer resemblance to regular fashion magazines; indeed, the web site notes, "With a nod to the past and clear sense of the present, *Elegant Bride* addresses the needs of fashionable, intelligent women who happen to be getting married." Financial expert Jean Chatzky and relationship expert Dr. Pat Love are regular contributors. One issue profiles lingerie designer Josie Natori and celebrity wedding photographer Dennis Reggie. But it is, after all, a bridal magazine, and there are the usual features: budget worksheet, countdown calendar, registry list, fashion and honeymoon tips, and real-life wedding stories. For all its high-end couture, it is still an accessible and eminently readable title. The online version contains the table of contents of the current issue, selected articles, planning tools, and a link to its retail partner, exclusivelyweddings.com.

6623. ***For the Bride by Demetrios.*** [ISSN: 1064-8089] 1991. q. USD 4.99 per issue. Ed(s): Patricia Canole. D J E Publications, 222 W 37th St, 12th Fl, New York, NY 10018. Adv. Circ: 160000. *Aud.:* Sa.

Billing itself as "the ultimate source for bridal fashion," this quarterly is unique in that its publisher, Demetrios, is also is also a wedding gown designer. Part wedding magazine, part catalog for the moderately priced Demetrios dress lines, it contains elements of a typical bridal magazine including beauty and relationship advice, new home decorating, and honeymoon articles. Advertising and features on bridal fashions, however, display only stock from Demetrios, although there is additional advertising from designers promoting tuxedos and evening wear and bridesmaids' fashions. Also missing from the typical issue are examples of real-life weddings and vendor listings. This magazine is useful for brides seeking that "ultimate source" of ideas and advice, but only if they care to hear from just one voice in a large industry.

6624. ***Grace Ormonde Wedding Style.*** 1999. a. USD 12 per issue domestic. Ed(s): Grace Ormonde. Elegant Publishing, Inc., PO Box 89, Barrington, RI 02806. Adv. *Aud.:* Sa.

Visually stunning, *Grace Ormonde Wedding Style* is an annual publication filled with creative and innovative graphic design. This oversized, award-winning magazine contains the usual fashion and jewelry advertisements, but also many ads for reception venues and photography studios. Clearly aimed at an upscale, sophisticated market, articles cover encore weddings, building a new home (not just furnishing a new home via registry items), and women's health, among other things. Interspersed among these features are numerous real-life "feature weddings" as well. Besides an advertisers' directory, *Wedding Style* also provides its own "Five Star" directory, which is described as "an effort to present the readers with choices among the best wedding professionals in their respective fields." This national magazine has a regional counterpart in the Northeast and a web site that provides access to current and archived articles back to 2000. This title is most useful for the bride who can afford the $8.50 issue price and more.

6625. ***The Knot Weddings Magazine.*** Formerly: *The Knot Wedding Gowns.* 1999. s-a. USD 9.99 newsstand/cover per issue. Ed(s): Carley Roney. The Knot Inc., 462 Broadway, 6th Fl, New York, NY 10013. Adv. Circ: 100000 Paid and controlled. *Aud.:* Sa.

From the creators of the online wedding mega-site, theknot.com, comes a print magazine of the same name. A semi-annual publication, this "one-of-a-kind bridal sourcebook" runs well over 500 pages. The first part of this publication does indeed resemble a typical wedding magazine, with planning and beauty advice, real weddings, and a fashion spread. The back of the magazine contains the usual articles about registries and honeymoons. In between, however, is the real reason for buying it: the directories, most notably the fashion directory. These directories showcase over 800 wedding gowns and bridesmaid fashions, more than 50 honeymoon resorts, and hundreds of wedding accessory and jewelry items. The web site claims to have over two million unique visitors monthly, and to be the leading Internet retailer of wedding favors and supplies. For those who cannot access theknot.com on the web, this magazine is the next best thing.

6626. *Martha Stewart Weddings.* Formerly (until 1999): *Martha Stewart Living Weddings.* [ISSN: 1534-553X] 1990. 4x/yr. USD 16; USD 5.50 newsstand/cover per issue; USD 6.50 newsstand/cover per issue Canada. Martha Stewart Living Omnimedia LLC, 20 W 43rd St, 25th Fl, New York, NY 10036; mstewart@marthastewart.com; http://www.marthastewart.com. Adv. *Aud.:* Sa.

Like the original *Martha Stewart Living* magazine, the *Weddings* magazine follows a similar format. It, too, offers advice on how to create elegant meals, sophisticated flower arrangements, and marvelous cakes as well as clever wedding craft ideas (under the same name, "Good Things"), all showcased in handsome photographs. The cover is distinct; unlike most titles in this genre, it is such wedding accompaniments as flowers and cakes, not the bride, that are the focus of attention. However, there is no mistaking this title for anything but a wedding magazine. In addition to reception meals, flowers, planning calendars, and honeymoon descriptions, it also contains fashion features and it profiles real wedding events, giving attention to unique touches. Various wedding traditions are reviewed and explained in greater detail than in other magazines, with attention paid to ethnic traditions; sex and relationship advice, however, is left to other titles. The web site for *Martha Stewart Weddings* contains articles, but no fashion items, and links to related Marth Stewart products. For the bride who reads *Martha Stewart Living* and enjoys the beautiful creations found there, this magazine is a must-have.

6627. *Modern Bride: a complete guide for the bride-to-be.* [ISSN: 0026-7546] 1949. bi-m. USD 11.97 domestic. Ed(s): Antonia van der Meer. Conde Nast Publications Inc., 4 Times Square, 5th Fl, New York, NY 10036; http://www.condenast.com. Illus., adv. Circ: 377912 Paid. Vol. ends: Nov/Dec. Microform: PQC. Online: The Dialog Corporation; Gale Group. *Indexed:* MagInd. *Aud.:* Sa.

Modern Bride seeks to offer a little something for every bride, whether it's wedding dresses for every shape, bridal accessories in a variety of price ranges, or various reception themes. This effort at mass appeal is also reflected in the advertisements, which include dress designers from across the price spectrum. As the magazine notes to potential advertisers, "The engaged life-stage is among the most compelling sales opportunities for your company," and this title seeks to make the most of those opportunities, with readers of all income levels. Intended as a guide for planning the wedding, honeymoon, and first home, this magazine includes the usual categories of bridal fashion, registry items, relationship advice, and honeymoon ideas. This publication was recently purchased by Conde Nast, which also owns *Bride's* magazine. *Modern Bride* has a somewhat edgier look than its sister publication. Although the print version includes few real-life weddings, the online version shows several, in slide-show format. It also has links to local vendors, and readers can sign up for newsletters or participate in sweepstakes opportunities.

6628. *Wedding Dresses.* s-a. USD 9.98; USD 5.99 newsstand/cover per issue. Ed(s): Severine Ferrari. Gerard Bedouk Publishing, Inc., 575 Madison Ave, 25th Fl, New York, NY 10022. Adv. *Aud.:* Sa.

"Dedicated to women, fashion, and happiness," *Wedding Dresses* magazine seeks to fulfill its masthead promise. Its focus is primarily on preparing the bride's outfit for her wedding day, although additional features presumably attend to the rest of a bride's happiness—wedding planning, cakes, flowers, registry, and honeymoon. Of particular note is the "In the Spotlight" section, which does a good job of showcasing both unknown and leading dress designers. About half of the fashion advertising is found in the "Fashion Album," which promotes a variety of designers and dress price ranges. Although the online version of the magazine offers a brief overview of the current issue, the main purpose of the web site appears to be as a vehicle for attracting subscribers.

6629. *Weddingbells (US General Edition).* [ISSN: 1481-5761] 1999. s-a. USD 4.95 newsstand/cover per issue. Ed(s): Crys Stewart. Weddingbells, 34 King St E, Ste 800, Toronto, ON M5C 2X8, Canada; info@weddingbells.com. *Aud.:* Sa.

A relatively recent newcomer and running well short of 200 pages, the Canadian *Weddingbells* contains a well-balanced mix of ads and features aimed at men and women in their late twenties. Promising to "appeal to the bride's specific interests as well as the needs of the groom, friends and family," this magazine offers the usual fashion, beauty, gift registry, and honeymoon advice as well as a section for the groom, which is actually written by a man. Suggestions for personalizing the ceremony and reception are included, as is the ubiquitous wedding countdown calendar. This magazine also provides coverage for real-life weddings. In addition to the national publication, nine regional editions are published for major metropolitan areas including Boston, Chicago, New York, and San Francisco. The online version of *Weddingbells* has partnered with another wedding web site, the large WeddingChannel.com directory, to provide retailing opportunities and selected content.

6630. *World Class Weddings.* q. USD 4.95 newsstand/cover. World Class Weddings, Inc., 5401 S Kirkman Rd., Ste 310, Orlando, FL 32810; http://www.wcweddings.com. *Aud.:* Sa.

With an emphasis on "world," *World Class Weddings* sometimes reads more like a travel magazine. Offering photos and descriptions of idyllic wedding sites, past issues have covered yacht weddings and castle destinations. This quarterly is shorter than most (one issue was less than 100 pages) in a genre where issues of 500 pages are not uncommon. Because of its size and emphasis on wedding locations, the coverage of wedding fashions is noticeably smaller, both in advertising and in feature spreads. A couple of real-life weddings appear in each issue, along with wedding planning advice, honeymoon recommendations, and interviews with such celebrities as the Duchess of York and the Hawaiian singer, Hoku. The companion web site serves primarily as retailer for wedding-related items.

■ WOMEN

Fashion

Lori A. Goetsch, Director, Public Services, University of Maryland Libraries, 4115 McKeldin Library, College Park, MD 20742; lgoetsch@deans.umd.edu; FAX: 301-405-9191

Monica Fusich, Henry Madden Library, 5200 N. Barton Ave., M/S 34, California State University, Fresno, Fresno, CA 93740-8014 (Fashion subsection)

Introduction

Since the last edition of *Magazines for Libraries*, the power of Oprah Winfrey has pervaded the women's magazine marketplace. Her publication, *O*, continues to be a strong contender and, while Oprah cannot solely be credited with changing an industry, her presence and influence—along with other factors such as the aging of the baby-boom generation and cataclysmic world events—have brought about a subtle shift in both theme and image in women's general interest magazines.

Spirituality, authenticity, simplicity, and self-affirmation—post–millennium and 9/11—themes that are foundational to Oprah's success have crept into magazines that for years have been dominated either by fashion and beauty, sex and relationships, or domesticity and family. Of course, this trend does not mean that these topics have disappeared from the pages by any means. Nevertheless, a growing focus on personal growth and development can be found in most major newsstand titles, with articles on self-improvement beyond the superficiality of clothes and cosmetics. Also, the comforts of home and a desire for a less hectic lifestyle have contributed to more attention to interior decorating and home entertainment. Many magazines have even gone to a cleaner, less cluttered look to communicate this trend toward a simpler life, emulating the look and feel of *O* in the process. Titles on the scene that are devoted to these new-age themes are *Body and Soul* (formerly *New Age Journal*) and *Organic Style*. Also, Meredith Corporation, publisher of *Ladies' Home Journal* and *Better Homes and Gardens* has recently launched *Women's Faith and Spirit* to respond to this area of reader interest.

Oprah is also applauded for advancing images of women that are more likely to fit the reader's image of herself, and again others have followed suit. The recognition that women come in all shapes and sizes is finally beginning to challenge the pencil-thin models that have dominated over the years. Two surprising examples are *Glamour*, which published a recent issue on body acceptance, and *Vogue*, which featured plus-size models and celebrities in a recent "Shape" issue. A new fashion magazine for women size 12 and up, *Grace*, was launched to attract this fast-growing market segment. Perhaps the time will come when there will not be a need for niche magazines to address what is now the mainstream audience, but that transformation is yet to be seen. Some small steps have been taken, however, as the market demands increase.

Women's magazines have continued to be less responsive to reflecting women's racial and ethnic diversity. Minorities are still infrequently shown on covers, with the exception of an occasional celebrity. Halle Berry's appearance on the cover of *Cosmopolitan* in 2002 was only the fifth by an African American woman in nearly 40 years. A *New York Times* study of 471 covers from 31 women's, men's, teen, and entertainment magazines published in 2002 found that one in five depict people of color. While an improvement over a 1998 study, there is still a long way to go in this arena. The growing number of teen magazines and Oprah, yet again, are suggested as catalysts in improving this representation of ethnic and racial minorities.

One area of the women's magazine market that has proven, surprisingly, to be unsuccessful is women's sports magazines. *Women's Sports and Fitness* and *Sports Illustrated Women* have ceased, despite the growing number of girls and women participating in organized sports. *Real Sports* continues to publish, but only collector's editions around key women's sports events. Fitness magazines, however, continue to thrive with several new entries in the market popping up, such as *Oxygen* and *Women's Health and Fitness*.

Since the last edition, we've also said goodbye to some long-standing newsstand and subscription staples, most notably *Mademoiselle* and *Working Woman* as well as the upstart *Rosie*. *Rosie* went down in flames after a very public dispute between its celebrity namesake Rosie O'Donnell and the magazine's publisher. Along with *Grace*, one of the most successful launches has been *Lucky: the magazine about shopping*. *Lucky* is more of a monthly mail-order catalog that is high on graphics and low on content, not unlike *Shuz*, a quarterly publication of, well, shoes! Perhaps it serves to remind us that, despite the search for inner peace and simplicity, the adage "when the going gets tough, the tough go shopping" is, ultimately, still what women's magazines are all about. Even Oprah might agree with that sentiment.

Basic Periodicals

Hs: *Fitness, Glamour, Self, Shape;* Ga: *Allure, Cosmopolitan, Essence, Family Circle, First for Women, Good Housekeeping, Ladies' Home Journal, Marie Claire, O: The Oprah Magazine, Redbook, Woman's Day, Working Mother;* Sa: *Latina, Heart & Soul, Today's Christian Woman.*

Basic Abstracts and Indexes

Access, Health Index, Magazine Index, Readers' Guide to Periodical Literature, Women's Studies Index.

6631. ***Allure.*** [ISSN: 1054-7711] 1991. m. USD 15 domestic; USD 34 Canada; USD 39 elsewhere. Ed(s): Linda Wells. Conde Nast Publications Inc., 4 Times Square, 5th Fl, New York, NY 10036; http://www.condenast.com. Illus., adv. Circ: 865059 Paid. Vol. ends: Feb. Microform: PQC. *Aud.:* Ga.

Allure has become a mainstream women's fashion, health, and beauty magazine. The magazine lacks the nontraditional approach to the definition of "beauty" that it highlighted at its inception, and it now displays the traditional beauty magazine features: fashion, hair, cosmetics, health, and celebrities. Each issue offers clothes, cosmetics and accessory tips, products, and trends through features such as "Beauty Insider," "Beauty 101," and "Fashion Report." Runway news is highlighted in "Fashion Bulletin," and fashion photos, which often feature celebrities in regular features such as "A List," present looks that seem unachievable for the average woman. *Allure* does successfully cover well many of the same topics as competitors such as *Elle*. Also, like its competitors, much of the magazine is photographic, although fashion layouts lack the rough edge of the magazine's earlier days. The magazine's web site highlights the contents of the current issue and provides beauty and fashion tips and product reviews, reader forums and polls, and "Talk to Allure."

Better Homes and Gardens. See Home section.

Body & Soul. See Spirituality and Well-Being section.

6632. ***Bust: for women with something to get off their chest.*** [ISSN: 1089-4713] 1993. q. USD 14.97 domestic; USD 24.97 Canada; USD 34.97 elsewhere. Ed(s): Debbie Stoller. Bust, PO Box 1016, New York, NY 10276; subscription@bust.com; http://www.bust.com. Illus., adv. *Bk. rev.:* 22, 150-300 words. *Aud.:* Hs, Ga.

Subtitled "for women with something to get off their chests," *Bust* provides a newsstand antidote to mainstream women's magazines. While many of the topics are the same, the perspective is decidedly alternative, unconventional, and liberal. For example, the subject matter of the "Broadcast" and "Real Life" sections ranges from political activism, honor killings in Pakistan, and abortion to the history of hair color, instructions for making a charm bracelet, and stereo-buying advice. Each issue has a general theme (e.g., "The Age Issue," "Fight Like a Girl Issue") and includes various takes on that theme through first-person articles, personality profiles, and in-depth, frank celebrity interviews. "The *Bust* Guide" covers a wide range of film, book, and music reviews. A healthy and empowering attitude towards sex is endorsed through sex product advertising, a regular advice column from "sexpert Susie Bright," and "One-Handed Read," a soft-core erotic short story at the end of the issue. The web site is as interesting and varied as the magazine. It offers an online store, subscription and back issue information including sample stories from previous issues, a calendar of events, "News from the Net," chat, message boards, greeting cards, and personals. Also, a directory of web sites of interest to *Bust* readers called "Girl Wide Web" offers links to sites arranged in subject categories such as "Culture Vulture" and "She-Commerce and Services."

6633. ***Chatelaine (English Edition).*** [ISSN: 0009-1995] 1928. m. CND 19.98 domestic; CND 49 United States; CND 54 elsewhere. Ed(s): Rona Maynard. Rogers Media Publishing Ltd, One Mount Pleasant Rd, Toronto, ON M4Y 2Y5, Canada; http://www.rogers.com. Illus., adv. Circ: 750000. Microform: MIM; MML; PQC. Online: bigchalk; EBSCO Publishing; Gale Group; LexisNexis; Micromedia ProQuest; ProQuest Information & Learning. *Indexed:* CBCARef, CPerI, MagInd. *Aud.:* Ga.

This premier Canadian women's service magazine calls itself "Canada's biggest kitchen table." While it offers many of the same features as the well-known U.S. titles, it takes a distinctly national perspective and has been recognized as a Magazine of the Year by the Canadian National Magazine Awards. The magazine features regular columns covering business, health, technology, personal financial management, and parenting. Home life is covered through food columns featuring quick recipes, inexpensive crafts, decorating tips, and make-your-own fashions with mail-order patterns. Articles on health and family, relationships, Canadian celebrities, and personal-interest stories round out *Chatelaine*. There is also a French edition (ISSN: 0317-2635). The magazine offers an electronic version, *Chatelaine Connects*, that has also achieved recognition as the most-used web site by Canadian women. The site offers a number of features and services organized to reflect the magazine's content. There are links to back issues, discussion groups on health, family, work, and money, and to other web sites. A reader poll, promotions, contests, a buyer's guide, a book club, and an e-mail alerting service round out the site. It is well designed and could serve as a model to emulate for other women's service magazines.

6634. ***Cosmopolitan.*** [ISSN: 0010-9541] 1886. m. USD 18 domestic; USD 42 foreign; USD 3.99 newsstand/cover per issue. Hearst Communications, Inc., Cosmopolitan, 1790 Broadway, New York, NY 10019. Illus., adv. Circ: 2486393 Paid. Vol. ends: Dec. Microform: PQC. Online: EBSCO Publishing; Gale Group; Northern Light Technology, Inc.; OCLC Online Computer Library Center, Inc.; ProQuest Information & Learning. *Indexed:* ASIP, BiogInd, LRI, MRD, MagInd, RGPR. *Bk. rev.:* 4-6, brief-500 words. *Aud.:* Ga.

Cosmo continues to adapt to the changing landscape of women's magazine publishing while maintaining its "bad girl" image. The focus is on the "*Cosmo* Girl" and her needs: sex, looks, relationships, success, and more sex as reflected in the advertising as well as the content. Work is less prominently featured, although each issue includes an item or two devoted to careers and personal financial management. Entertainment is featured in "Cosmo Informer," which focuses on trends, films, and celebrity gossip. Much of the magazine is question-and-answer advice columns and regular features like the "Dating Diary" and "Man Manual" that provides male beefcake rivaling *Playgirl* magazine. Feature stories highlight celebrities and sex and relationship articles with a "pop-psych" bent on such topics as extramarital affairs and keeping a man interested. Each issue also includes several reader-contributed features. "Book Club" provides a book adaptation that leans toward soft-core pornography. *Cosmo*'s web site offers various reader advice and survey links, including "Cosmo Quiz," a sex-article archive, "Bedside Astrologer," and a celebrity interview.

6635. *Country Woman.* Former titles (until 1987): *Farm Woman;* (until 1986): *Farm Woman News;* (until 1985): *Farm Wife News.* [ISSN: 0892-8525] 1971. bi-m. USD 21 United States; USD 29.94 Canada; USD 25.98 elsewhere. Ed(s): Ann Kaiser. Reiman Publications, LLC, 5400 S 60th St, Greendale, WI 53129; http://www.reimanpub.com. Illus., adv. Sample. Circ: 1700000 Paid. Vol. ends: Dec. *Aud.:* Hs, Ga.

Country Woman describes itself as a magazine "for farm and country women and those who have moved from the country in body but not in heart." Readers are the writers and contributors that create each issue. Through letters, household hints, farm and garden advice, do-it-yourself information, home photos, craft patterns, personality features about women and their hobbies and interests, travel features, and recipes, this magazine provides a means for rural women as well as those interested in country life to network with one another and share experiences and information. Although geared toward women, it appeals to a broad readership. Frequent contests and surveys are offered and promoted. Pleasure reading is provided through short fiction and readers' poetry. A companion web site provides links to "Country Store," cooking schools, recipes, and tours plus the table of contents and a feature story from the latest issue.

Curve. See Lesbian, Gay, Bisexual, and Transgender section.

6636. *Energy for Women: how to energize your life.* 2001. bi-m. m. until Sep/Oct 2003. USD 19.97 domestic; USD 44.97 foreign. Ed(s): Gretchen Ferraro. Muscle Media, Inc., 555 Corporate Circle, Golden, CO 80401; info@musclemedia.com; http://www.musclemedia.com. Adv. *Aud.:* Sa.

This magazine provides inspiration and motivation for women interested in learning about training, weight loss and diet, health, and nutirition. Much of the information is delivered in quick, easy-to-read question-and-answer columns, brief tips, and news items. Before-and-after success stories including training workouts and nutrition plans. Each issue includes two or three exercise pictorials to work various parts of the body. One or two longer articles cover topics such as metabolism, fad diets, supplements, exercise during pregnancy, and goal-setting. The "FYI" section provides the latest information on health and fitness research, gear and clothing, style, beauty, and a buyer's guide. The audience is women who are serious fitness and body-sculpting buffs who are preparing to enter a competition as well as those who are just interested in working hard to look great in the gym or on the beach. The web site highlights the current issue.

6637. *Essence (New York): the magazine for today's black woman.* [ISSN: 0014-0880] 1970. m. USD 18.96; USD 34.96. Ed(s): Diane Weathers. Essence Communications Inc., 1500 Broadway, New York, NY 10036-4015; info@essence.com; http://www.essence.com. Illus., adv. Circ: 1215000 Paid. Vol. ends: Dec. Microform: PQC. Online: bigchalk; Chadwyck-Healey Incorporated; EBSCO Publishing; Gale Group; LexisNexis; OCLC Online Computer Library Center, Inc.; ProQuest Information & Learning. *Indexed:* BRI, CBRI, IIBP, MRD, MagInd, RGPR, WSI. *Bk. rev.:* 4-5, 75 words; 6, 15 words; unsigned. *Aud.:* Hs, Ac, Sa.

Essence is a well-written, interesting magazine that is marketed to African American women but includes many features of broad interest. Articles are typical of those found in other general-interest women's magazines—male/female relationships, health and fitness, beauty, diet, parenting, financial management, careers, recipes, decorating, fashion, travel—but they are approached from an African American perspective. Several point-of-view and advice columns provide personal perspectives on issues. Each issue contains two or three inspirational articles on prominent African American personalities in the arts, politics, education, and other fields. The magazine also sponsors the annual Essence Awards, highlighting accomplishments of African Americans. There is at least one article in each issue on a social issue relevant to the African American community, such as sexual harassment. Each issue also includes "In the Spirit," a long-standing inspirational message from publication director Susan L. Taylor. *Essence* ranks among the top magazines for readership among African American adults. Its circulation continues to grow, and it appeals to both men and women. A web site provides highlights of the current issue; book, film, and music reviews; celebrity profiles; a calendar of events; "channels" that focus on topics such as "Work & Wealth," and live chat.

6638. *Family Circle.* [ISSN: 0014-7206] 1932. 15x/yr. USD 19.98 domestic; USD 1.95 newsstand/cover per issue domestic; CND 2.69 newsstand/cover per issue Canada. Family Circle, Inc., 375 Lexington Ave, New York, NY 10017-5514; fcfeedback@familycircle.com; http://www.familycircle.com. Illus., adv. Circ: 4600000 Paid. Vol. ends: Dec. Online: Gale Group. *Indexed:* ASIP, AgeL, ConsI, IHTDI, MagInd, WSI. *Aud.:* Ga.

Family Circle continues to wage war at the checkout counter with *Woman's Day.* Each issue's bright, colorful cover promises tips to make women's lives easier or to help them achieve a goal. In addition, departments provide advice from experts on issues of interest to the contemporary working wife, mother, and homemaker on cooking, decorating and crafts, beauty and fashion, medical news, gardening, health and fitness, travel, and even pet care. *Family Circle* recognizes the dual role of a woman as mother and worker, so recipes and decorating tips are quick, practical, and economical. Regular features include "Circle This," which provides consumer news; "Family Answer Book," which features advice on money, marriage, law, family matters, and other topics; and "Buyer's Guide." One or two lengthy features highlight the life of a celebrity or, in the feature "Women Who Make a Difference," offer an inspiring, real-life story that frequently shows a woman's triumph over adversity. The magazine's web site highlights the contents of current and past issues and links to recipes and gardening, decorating, and other advice.

6639. *First for Women.* [ISSN: 1040-9467] 1989. 17x/yr. USD 19.97 domestic; USD 37.97 foreign. Ed(s): Dena Vane. Bauer Publishing Company, L.P., 270 Sylvan Ave, Englewood, NJ 07632-2513; http://www.ffmarket.com. Illus., adv. Circ: 1350000. *Aud.:* Ga.

First for Women has yet to achieve the circulation of its venerable grocery store competitors, *Family Circle* and *Woman's Day.* It has improved in the quality of its advertisers since its inception and looks a little less cluttered in recent years, but it still retains the overcrowded, busy look and feel of supermarket tabloids. Geared toward a young audience, the formula for content is similar to its more successful competitors; casual fashion, beauty, food, health and fitness, diet and nutrition, parenting, crafts and decorating, personalities, money management, and work are major themes. Each issue is heavy on photographs and light on content, which is delivered primarily in the format of tips, lists, and advice columns. Recommended web sites, numerous recipes, a horoscope, cartoons, and a crossword puzzle are included in each issue.

6640. *Fit: strong - smart - sexy.* Formerly (until 1995): *New Body.* [ISSN: 1082-5665] 1982. bi-m. USD 19.97 domestic; USD 25.97 foreign; USD 2.99 newsstand/cover per issue. Ed(s): Lisa Klugman. Goodman Media Group, Inc., 250 W 57th St, Ste 710, New York, NY 10107-0799; http://www.goodmanmediagroup.com. Illus., adv. Circ: 152050. Vol. ends: Jan/Feb (No. 6). *Aud.:* Hs, Ga.

Fit is among several newsstand titles to survive and thrive in the women's health and fitness market. Like *Fitness,* it focuses on news and trends in exercise, sports, diet, nutrition, psychology, health, sexuality, beauty, travel, and fitness gear and equipment. Articles feature training and workout advice and routines, including products. The tone is upbeat, with personal successes and celebrity profiles and trainers providing motivation and inspiration. Diet, food, and nutrition are also a major focus, and an active lifestyle is promoted through features on such activities as hiking, diving, and climbing as well as gym workouts. Recipes are healthful and easy to prepare and are accompanied by a shopping list. There is less emphasis on makeup, hair, and clothes, and models come in all shapes and sizes, emphasizing the magazine's focus on health and body acceptance, not perfection. Two or three lengthy articles in each issue focus on mental and physical health topics, such as contraception and fitness during pregnancy. Regular features include "Fit Scene"—training trends, medical updates, and more—and "Fit Gear," offering information on new products in the fitness marketplace.

6641. *Fitness: mind - body - spirit for women.* Formerly (until 1992): *Family Circle's Fitness Now.* [ISSN: 1060-9237] 1983. m. USD 13.97; USD 29.97 Canada; USD 3.50 newsstand/cover per issue. Gruner + Jahr U.S.A. Publishing, 375 Lexington Ave, New York, NY 10017-5514; corpcomm@gjusa.com; http://www.gjusa.com. Illus. Sample. Circ: 1197638 Paid. Vol. ends: Dec. *Aud.:* Ga.

Along with *Shape, Fitness* is one of the leaders among women's health and fitness magazines that appeal to a young, active female market interested in looking good, particularly at the health club. The focus is exercise, fashion, diet and nutrition, sports, health, medicine, psychology, travel, and beauty. Information lacks depth, and much of the common-sense advice is delivered through news/product information columns, quick tips, and lists. Training features provide step-by-step workout instructions and advice. Inspiration is provided by success stories from celebrities and readers. In addition to equipment and gear evaluations in each issue, there is an annual buyer's guide. Recipes are quick, easy, and nutritional. *Fitness* has placed itself squarely in the competitive and growing health and exercise market. The web site complements the magazine with exercise tips, health and diet news, a recipe finder, reader polls and quizes, a fitness calculator for target heart rate and other health factors, and message boards along with subscription information.

6642. *Flare (Toronto): Canada's fashion magazine.* Formerly: *Miss Chatelaine.* [ISSN: 0708-4927] 1964. m. CND 19.98 domestic; CND 49.50 foreign; CND 3.50 newsstand/cover per issue. Ed(s): Suzanne Boyd. Rogers Media Publishing Ltd, One Mount Pleasant Rd, Toronto, ON M4Y 2Y5, Canada; http://www.rogers.com. Illus., adv. Circ: 201000 Paid. Vol. ends: Dec. Microform: MML. Online: EBSCO Publishing; Gale Group; LexisNexis; Micromedia ProQuest. *Indexed:* CBCARef, CPerI. *Aud.:* Hs, Ga.

Flare is the fashion, beauty, and health magazine for the contemporary Canadian woman. Regular columns and features consist primarily of brief news items and tips on cosmetics, skin and hair care, fitness, health, decorating, and fashion. Although fashion news focuses on both Canadian and international designers, the celebrity and society news reported in the "Flare Was There" column is almost exclusively Canadian. Fashion layouts have become less practical, more youthful—and more expensive—in recent years, suggesting a marketing move towards a younger readership and away from career women seeking more practical and affordable fashion. A buying guide is provided. Relationship advice; information on decorating, health and fitness; and personality features are included in each issue. *Flare Online* provides links to fashion, beauty, and health information and advice and also to fashion resources, fashion/design educational sites, and a salon directory. The site also highlights the current issue of the magazine along with fashion and beauty tips, a horoscope, contests, a store, and a salon directory.

6643. *Glamour.* Incorporates: *Charm.* [ISSN: 0017-0747] 1939. m. USD 16 domestic; USD 34 foreign; USD 3.50 newsstand/cover per issue. Ed(s): Cynthia Leive. Conde Nast Publications Inc., 4 Times Square, 5th Fl, New York, NY 10036; magpr@condenast.com; http://www.glamour.com; http://www.condenast.com; http://www.swoon.com; http://www.phys.com. Illus., adv. Circ: 2100000 Paid. Vol. ends: Dec. Microform: PQC. Online: Gale Group. Reprint: PQC. *Indexed:* ASIP, ConsI, LRI, MRD, MagInd, RGPR, WSI. *Bk. rev.:* 5, 75 words, unsigned. *Aud.:* Hs, Ga, Ac.

Glamour has overcome its tendency to "*Cosmo*-ize," and has re-established its own identity after editorial upheavals. While not the magazine it once was, with a focus on social issues along with health and beauty coverage, *Glamour* has returned to the foundations of health, beauty, relationships beyond sex, work, and money management. It has even responded to the market by featuring women who are not always pencil thin, particularly as part of its annual "body confidence" issue that features women in all shapes and sizes. This is not to say, however, that it is still not a strong competitor with *Cosmo* on the sex front. The magazine regularly features personality profiles, articles on celebrity fashion, and other lifestyle articles and briefs. A number of reader surveys plus advice and self-help columns provide information on sex and personal relationships, including "Jake," "*Glamour* Asks: Men Answer," "Relationtips," and "Sexplanations." The magazine's entertainment coverage highlights books, celebrities, and films. A web site features reader services, polls, and contests, and promotes the recent issue.

6644. *Good Housekeeping.* [ISSN: 0017-209X] 1885. m. USD 10 domestic; USD 32 foreign. Ed(s): Ellen Levine. Hearst Corporation, 250 W 55th St, 5th Fl, New York, NY 10019. Illus., adv. Circ: 4549000 Paid. Vol. ends: Jun/Dec. Microform: NBI; PQC. Online: EBSCO Publishing; Gale Group; Northern Light Technology, Inc.; OCLC Online Computer Library Center, Inc.; ProQuest Information & Learning. Reprint: PQC. *Indexed:* AgeL, CINAHL, ConsI, IHTDI, LRI, MagInd, RGPR. *Aud.:* Ga, Ac.

The *Good Housekeeping* Seal of Approval has stood as the symbol of "unique consumer education and consumer protection" since 1885, and the magazine maintains those ties to consumer information and advice. *Good Housekeeping* is targeted to family-oriented readers who are interested in practical information and a bit of inspiration. Regular departments are written by respected authorities, for example, "Do the Right Thing" by Peggy Post, the "Household Helpline" by Heloise, and "Money Watch" by Jane Bryant Quinn. Consumer information in the way of product recalls, money management, and the environment is provided in each issue. Articles focus on relationships, health, beauty, fitness, and interior decoration as well as celebrity profiles and inspirational personal stories in "Getting Personal." Short stories and novel adaptations are occasional features. And, of course, the extensive recipe section—providing menus, step-by-step guides, and a heavy emphasis on the microwave—has always been a strong selling point. Information from the Good Housekeeping Institute is also provided, featuring consumer information, recalls, and product evaluations. *Good Housekeeping* maintains high editorial standards and strictly reviews all advertising copy before it is accepted for publication. This policy, as well as the magazine's efforts to keep up with a changing society, keeps it one of the premier women's service magazines. The web site complements the magazine with consumer information, a buyer's guide, expert advice, recipes, and the opportunity for reader interaction and advice-sharing.

6645. *Grace Woman Magazine: living life to its fullest.* [ISSN: 1542-9687] 2002. m. Ed(s): Ceslie Armstrong. Grace Magazine, 276 Fifth Ave, Ste 503, New York, NY 10001. *Bk. rev.:* 6 brief, 75 words. *Aud.:* Ga.

Grace Woman celebrated its first anniversary in 2003 and has been declared a success by the media for its response to the need for a fashion and beauty magazine for women size 12 and up. But you really do not have to fit the market to enjoy this publication. While featuring all of the traditional elements of successful women's magazines—sexy fashion layouts, celebrity profiles, health and beauty, fitness, travel, and more—*Grace Woman* uses women of all shapes, sizes, and colors as a means of promoting acceptance and mainstreaming the mainstream, so to speak. The web site is well designed and highlights items from the current issue as well as providing a members-only area, "Graceville," where readers find behind-the-scenes stories, message boards, chat, and reader polls.

6646. *Heart & Soul.* Formerly (until 199?): *Rodale's Heart and Soul.* [ISSN: 1092-1974] 1993. 10x/yr. USD 10 domestic; USD 20 Canada; USD 25 elsewhere. Ed(s): Corynne L. Corbett. Vanguarde Media, Inc, 315 Park Ave S, 11th fl, New York, NY 10010; http://www.vanguarde.com. Illus., adv. Sample. Circ: 200000. *Indexed:* GendWatch, IIBP. *Bk. rev.:* 4-6, 75 words, unsigned. *Aud.:* Sa.

The audience for *Heart & Soul* is young African American women interested in personal development. Originally focused on diet and exercise, the magazine has broadened its appeal by combining health and beauty news and features with information on nutrition, psychology, relationships, sex, decorating, work, and spirituality to present a holistic approach to wellness and success for the African American woman. "You, First!" provides tips, quick facts, news, and reviews on a wide range of topics, from product and book reviews and financial advice to workout tips and self-esteem. Fashion, skin, hair, and makeup advice and product information are also featured. Fitness and health remain a feature of the magazine through the "Body Clinic" section. A celebrity feature and healthful recipes round out each issue. The web site highlights current and past issues. *Heart & Soul* has broad appeal to African American women looking for a balanced, interesting lifestyle magazine.

6647. *InStyle.* [ISSN: 1076-0830] 1994. m. USD 23.88 domestic; USD 34 Canada; USD 3.99 newsstand/cover per issue domestic. Ed(s): Charla Lawhon. Time, Inc, Time & Life Bldg, Rockefeller Center, 1271 Ave of the Americas, New York, NY 10020-1393; letters@instylemag.com. Illus., adv. *Indexed:* RGPR. *Aud.:* Ga.

InStyle combines the celebrity profiles and gossip of magazines like *People* with the fashion, beauty, and home entertaining elements of other women's magazines. The packaging is stylish and clean, appealing to an upscale readership. Fashion features like "The Look" use celebrities to highlight fashion trends, accessories, tips, and Q & A. This approach continues through the beauty coverage, with celebrities providing cosmetics and hair advice, including product recommendations. "Instant Style" and "Runway to Reality" provide advice on how to get that celebrity look for yourself. The magazine also focuses on home entertaining and decorating and includes a few recipes. Celebrity interviews are lengthy and accompanied by photographs taken in the celebrity's home. Information on furniture, interior design, and accessories accompany the article. The web site is available only to magazine subscribers.

6648. *Jane.* [ISSN: 1093-8737] 1997. 10x/yr. USD 10 domestic; USD 33.95 Canada; USD 37.95 elsewhere. Ed(s): Jane Pratt. Fairchild Publications, Inc., 7 W 34th St, New York, NY 10001-8191; http://www.fairchildpub.com. Illus., adv. Circ: 500000. Vol. ends: Dec. *Bk. rev.:* 3-5, brief, unsigned. *Aud.:* Ga.

Launched in 1997 by former *Sassy* editor Pratt, *Jane* has joined the competitive market of women's lifestyle magazines. Its content is similar to that of its competitors: fashion, beauty, personalities, and health, with a heavy dose of gossip, entertainment, and culture through book, film, and music reviews. What made *Jane* unique early on—coverage of "gadgets," automobiles, and other topics usually found in men's magazines as well as articles of political or social interest—has faded into the background, but the tongue-in-cheek style remains. Celebrities have become a prominent focus, but *Jane*'s quirky interviews and profiles are not what you find in other women's magazines. For example, Pamela Anderson of *Baywatch* fame is a regular columnist. Fashion layouts are artsy and edgy, and the high-quality paper stock brings out the best in the photography. The web site is rather irritating, with difficult-to-read color schemes, distracting graphics, and meager content. The current issue's table of contents is offered, and most other links lead to merchandise information. Readers can "Rant" by means of a reader-poll link or explore "Jane's Dates," a personals service.

6649. *Ladies' Home Journal.* Formerly (until 1889): *Ladies Home Journal and Practical Housekeeper.* [ISSN: 0023-7124] 1883. m. USD 16.97 domestic; USD 22.97 foreign. Ed(s): Myrna Blyth. Meredith Corp., 125 Park Ave, 19th Fl, New York, NY 10017; http://www.meredith.com. Illus., adv. Circ: 4100000 Paid. Vol. ends: Dec. Microform: PQC. Online: The Dialog Corporation; Gale Group. *Indexed:* CINAHL, ConsI, LRI, MagInd, RGPR, WSI. *Aud.:* Ga, Ac.

LHJ is a consistently popular women's magazine that works to keep itself in step with the changing role of American women while maintaining a sense of its own history. The magazine was recently redesigned and went to a larger, more readable format. However, tradition is still maintained between the covers through the long-standing feature "Can This Marriage Be Saved?," which is described as "the most popular, most enduring women's magazine feature in the world" and is prominently placed at the beginning of each issue. A more recent addition is "Was This Marriage Saved?," a follow-up on a couple profiled in an earlier issue that tracks their progress. The remainder of the magazine is heavily focused on woman as wife, mother, sister, friend, and worker, with lengthy, often inspirational stories about marriage and family. *LHJ* is one of the few women's magazines where content dominates over image. The balance of each issue is devoted to woman as individual through a number of regular departments on beauty, fashion, health, food, and home decorating. A celebrity is featured on the cover with an accompanying profile. As with other service magazines, *LHJ* offers a large food section with recipes, menu planning, and nutritional information. Although geared to a predominantly white, middle-class audience, efforts have been made to reflect minorities in photographs and advertising. The magazine's web site reprints or supplements articles from recent issues through links on health, beauty, parenting, and food. There is also a shopping guide as well as an opportunity for reader feedback and discussion.

6650. *Latina (New York).* [ISSN: 1099-890X] 1996. m. USD 12. Ed(s): Sylvia A Martinez. Latina Publications LLC, 1500 Broadway, Ste 600, New York, NY 10036; editor@latina.com; http://www.latina.com. Illus., adv. Online: Gale Group. *Aud.:* Sa.

Latina, a bilingual fashion and lifestyle magazine, is the brainchild of Stanford graduate Christy Haubegger, who recognized the need for a publication that addresses the interests of the fastest-growing minority in the United States. The magazine has become a newsstand staple. It emphasizes topics of interest to Latinas and takes subjects covered in established women's magazines and looks at them from a Hispanic perspective. Fashion, beauty, health, fitness, work, travel, parenting, personal finance, food, and relationships are all included, along with celebrity interviews and feature stories. Arts and entertainment features highlight Hispanic musicians, artists, dancers, authors, and actors. Motivational stories about lesser-known but successful Latinas are also included. Social issues such as education, domestic violence, legal rights, health care, and interracial relationships are also covered, although less so in recent issues. A web site promotes the current issue and also provides message boards as well as event and promotional information.

6651. *Lucky: a new magazine about shopping.* [ISSN: 1531-4294] 2000. m. USD 12 domestic; USD 30 Canada; USD 31 newsstand/cover per issue elsewhere. Ed(s): Kim France. Conde Nast Publications Inc., 4 Times Square, 5th Fl, New York, NY 10036; talktous@luckymag.com; http://www.luckymag.com. Adv. *Aud.:* Ga.

Looking for every possible swimsuit style, its cost, and how to buy it? Or comparison shopping for strappy high-heeled sandals? Then *Lucky* is for you. More of a catalog than magazine, *Lucky* targets shopaholics looking for great buys around the country in women's apparel, cosmetics, and home decorating. There is no pretense of providing content comparable to other women's magazines—no relationship stories or sex advice here. Except for an occasional expert tip on topics such as buying jewelry or applying makeup, there is little text in the magazine other than brief descriptions of an item, its cost, and how to order it. It is page after page of products organized into fashion, beauty, and lifestyle sections. "Style Spy" highlights a variety of trendy clothes, shoes, and accessories, and "Beauty Spy" focuses on cosmetics and hair care. Lifestyle coverage is found in sections like "Home Spy" that focuses on decorating, organizing, and do-it-yourself projects. While it hardly matters to the magazine's target readership, it does become difficult to tell where the magazine ends and the advertising begins. Included in each issue is a page of stickers labeled "Yes!" or "Maybe?" for the reader to use to mark items that catch her eye. The magazine's web site features a catch of the day, bargain browser, shopping directory, a locator service for bargains in different areas of the country, reader forums, issue highlights, events, and promotions.

6652. *Marie Claire.* [ISSN: 1081-8626] 1994. m. USD 12 domestic; USD 32 Canada; USD 64 foreign. Hearst Corporation, 250 W 55th St, 5th Fl, New York, NY 10019; marieclaire@hearst.com; http://www.hearstmagsb2b.com. Illus., adv. Circ: 950000 Paid. Online: EBSCO Publishing; Gale Group. *Bk. rev.:* 2-3, 25 words. *Aud.:* Ga.

Marie Claire no longer needs to rely on name recognition from its European counterpart started in France in the 1930s and published in 22 countries. It stands on its own in the marketplace with other fashion, beauty, and lifestyle magazines. Fashion and beauty are major emphases, taking up about half of each issue, with health, fitness, relationships, food, decorating, personal finance, and entertainment rounding out the issue. Layouts are bold, contemporary, and daring, and feature young designers. Cosmetics, accessories, and beauty tips also receive significant coverage. Celebrity news and gossip focus on the young and the hip in fashion and the arts. There is an occasional brief nod to work and career advice. *Marie Claire* leans towards the sensational in its articles, with such topics as shaken-baby syndrome and child abduction in its "First Person" and "Special Report" features. The magazine's web site promotes and supplements the current issue and offers reader services including message boards, chat, and product promotions and freebies.

Martha Stewart Living. See Home section.

6653. ***More (New York).*** [ISSN: 1094-7868] 1997. 10x/yr. USD 20 domestic; USD 30 foreign; USD 2.95 newsstand/cover per issue. Ed(s): Susan Crandell. Meredith Corp., 125 Park Ave, 19th Fl, New York, NY 10017; http://www.meredith.com. Illus., adv. Circ: 850000. *Aud.:* Ga, Sa.

This spinoff of *Ladies Home Journal* is geared to a target audience of women at midlife. Articles focus on the positive aspects of that time of a woman's life, focusing on health, fashion for all sizes and shapes, travel, relationships, and beauty tips. "Notebook" highlights trends, films, books, travel, and the arts, suggesting that the content is geared to women with more leisure time and a fair amount of disposable income on their hands. Interior decorating is also a focus, with work and career de-emphasized. As with *Ladies Home Journal,* a celebrity graces the cover, and other well-known personalities are featured heavily in the magazine. Health-related news and information is a particular strength, through both the "Vital & Vibrant" section and lengthy articles focusing on such topics as breast cancer and osteoporosis. Relationship stories focus on love and sex at middle age and parenting adult children. The web site highlights events and promotions, the current issue, and a reader panel.

Mothering. See Family and Marriage section.

Ms. See Women: Feminist and Special Interest/Feminist and Women's Studies section.

6654. ***Ms. Fitness: fitness lifestyle for today's active woman.*** [ISSN: 1078-0661] 1993. q. USD 15.96 domestic; USD 18 Canada; USD 36 elsewhere. Ed(s): Greta Blackburn. Wally Boyko Productions, Inc., PO Box 2378, Corona, CA 91718-2378; http://www.getbig.com/magazine/msfit/msfit.com. Illus., adv. Sample. Circ: 150000. *Bk. rev.:* 3-5, brief, unsigned. *Aud.:* Sa.

Boyko, publisher of *Ms. Fitness,* is also the mastermind behind the Ms. Fitness USA competitions and a line of Ms. Fitness women's fitness centers, training videos, workout attire, and other products. Clearly, this publication is directed toward the same audience to which these other products are marketed: the serious health and fitness buff interested in tips, techniques, training, inspiration, and, just maybe, competition. The focus is on exercise, nutrition, medicine, diet, physical and emotional health, home equipment, and athletic wear. The magazine takes a strong anti-drug stance and promotes a holistic approach. Famous and not-so-famous fitness personalities are profiled, and before-and-after success stories provide inspiration and advice. All aspects of developing a trim, muscular female physique are covered, including workouts, equipment, various sports, and weight training. Brief product reviews provide information on equipment, videos, and software programs. Ms. Fitness competitions and competitors are highlighted, and a calendar of Ms. Fitness events is included in each issue. The web site highlights the magazine's event and product information and features tables of contents for current and past issues, with ordering information.

6655. ***O: The Oprah Magazine.*** [ISSN: 1531-3247] 2000. m. USD 15 domestic; USD 37 foreign; USD 3.50 newsstand/cover. Ed(s): Amy Gross. Harpo Entertainment Group, 110 N. Carpenter St., Chicago, IL 60607. Illus., adv. Circ: 1900000. Online: Gale Group. *Indexed:* RGPR. *Bk. rev.:* 1 lengthy; 4-5 brief; signed. *Aud.:* Ga.

O is television personality Oprah Winfrey's highly successful foray into publishing. The magazine complements the themes of her popular talk show, emphasizing spirituality, personal development, and celebration. A motivating column from Oprah begins and ends each issue, and the pages in between draw upon many of the same people that have been featured on the television program—Phil McGraw on relationship advice and Suze Orman on personal finance, for example. The magazine combines elements of other popular women's newsstand magazines such as fashion, beauty, health, decorating, family, and celebrities, but adds Oprah's own brand of self-help, inspiration, and faith in the human spirit. As with the audience on television, the magazine's readers play a strong role in the content through reader advice stories and surveys. Another strong feature is inspirational profiles of people overcoming hardships or helping others. "The O List" highlights products for pampering—food, clothes, music, home decor, and the like. Each issue includes an in-depth and intimate interview between Oprah and a well-known personality. The high-quality production and clean, spare cover (with Oprah, of course, featured) set the magazine apart from its competitors and communicate Oprah's sense of style and purpose. A web site highlights the current issue, previews forthcoming issues, and archives back issues. There are links to Oprah's television show web site, chat and message boards, an online photo gallery to which readers can contribute, advice, and recipes.

6656. ***Organic Style: the art of living in the balance.*** [ISSN: 1530-7824] 2001. bi-m. USD 19.96 domestic; CND 24.96 Canada; USD 37 elsewhere. Ed(s): Peggy Northrup. Rodale, 33 E Minor St, Emmaus, PA 18098; info@rodale.com; http://www.rodale.com. Illus., adv. Circ: 750000 Paid. Online: EBSCO Publishing. *Aud.:* Ga.

The subtitle summarizes the focus of this magazine: balancing health and fitness, beauty, home, food, and lifestyle with nature. Continuing in the tradition of other Rodale publications that focus on holistic approaches to health and well-being, *Organic Style* covers eco-trends such as natural fiber clothing, energy-efficient cars and appliances, socially responsible consumerism, wellness, and recycled products. It communicates these themes through content akin to that of traditional women's magazines—fashion, food, travel, decorating, work, and health. Women with "organic style" are profiled, including some celebrities. The web site complements the magazine with events and promotions, contests, the *Organic Style* catalog collection, a book section, reader forums, and an organic product directory.

Parents. See Parenting section.

6657. ***Playgirl: entertainment for women.*** [ISSN: 0273-6918] 1973. m. USD 38 domestic; USD 46 foreign; USD 3.99 newsstand/cover per issue. Ed(s): Tasha Church. Playgirl, Inc., 801 Second Ave, New York, NY 10017-4706; http://www.playgirlmag.com/. Illus., adv. Sample. Circ: 575000 Paid. Vol. ends: May. *Bk. rev.:* 2-3, brief, unsigned. *Aud.:* Ga.

Playgirl is an adult magazine that was the 1970s answer to *Playboy* and has probably surprised many with its longevity. As with its male counterpart, *Playgirl* isn't purchased for the articles. Its numerous photo layouts, including a centerfold, feature men (sometimes with women) in provocative nude poses. Readers vote annually for "Man of the Year" and can even send in photos of their favorite guy to the "Real Men" department. In fact, the men in *Playgirl* have recently been studied as part of research for an article on eating disorders. One of the more amusing and ironic findings, at least for women, is that the images the models portray place stress and expectations on men to reach a difficult-to-achieve physical standard. That bit of trivia aside, the text is dominated by advice columns, reader exchanges, celebrity interviews, and articles with a sexual theme. "Sex Ed" is a cross between "Dear Abby" and "Playboy Advisor," and "Readers' Fantasy Forum" allows readers to share their rich imaginations. Each issue also includes book, music, film, and product reviews and a horoscope. Advertising supports the sexual content of the magazine, promoting 900 telephone numbers, sexual aids and devices, and videos. A web site provides additional nude pictorials. Free access still requires a credit card for identification purposes; a members-only site is accessed with a password.

6658. ***Prima.*** [ISSN: 0951-8622] 1986. m. GBP 22.80 domestic; GBP 41.95 foreign; GBP 2 newsstand/cover per issue. Ed(s): Maire Fahey. Gruner & Jahr (UK), 197 Marsh Wall, London, E14 9SG, United Kingdom; prima@grunerandjahr.co.uk. Illus., adv. *Bk. rev.:* 6-8, brief. *Aud.:* Ga.

Prima, Britain's largest-selling women's monthly, is akin to *Family Circle* and *Woman's Day* in the United States. The magazine takes an affordable, do-it-yourself approach to home and family management in many of its regular features and articles. Topics include health, beauty, family relationships, travel, decorating, gardening, cooking, crafts, and fashion for women on a budget. There are fashion layouts of ready-made, moderately priced clothing as well as patterns for making your own. Consumer and health information is also highlighted. The recipe section is extensive and practical, keeping cost and ease of preparation in mind. The web site promotes the current issue and provides subscription information.

Real Simple. See Home Section.

6659. *Red (London): best things in life.* [ISSN: 1461-1317] 1998. m. GBP 34.80 domestic; GBP 67 foreign; GBP 2.90 newsstand/cover per issue. Ed(s): Sarah Stone, Trish Halpin. Hachette Filipacchi (UK) Ltd., 64 North Row, London, W1K 7LL, United Kingdom; http://www.hachettefilipacchiuk.co.uk/. Illus., adv. *Bk. rev.:* 6, 50-75 words. *Aud.:* Ga.

Red is a popular British women's magazine similar in coverage to lifestyle counterparts such as *Marie Claire* and *Glamour.* Articles focus on celebrities, relationships, style, health and beauty, work, and home and garden. A celebrity interview is included, and entertainment is also covered in the "Talk" section, with brief items on U.S. and U.K. celebrity gossip, music, television, films, and books. "Red Living" focuses on decorating, fashion, food, travel, fitness, and health. *Red* is published in a larger format than U.S. magazines and there is generally more depth to its content, particularly in the first half of each issue. The web site supplements features in the current issue; offers chat, message boards, and contests; and highlights the "Man of the Month."

6660. *Redbook.* [ISSN: 0034-2106] 1903. m. USD 15 domestic; USD 27 foreign; USD 2.95 newsstand/cover. Ed(s): Ellen Kunes. Hearst Corporation, 224 W 57th St 4th Fl, New York, NY 10019; horb@hearst.com; http://www.hearstcorp.com. Illus., adv. Circ: 2800000 Paid. Microform: NBI; PQC. Online: bigchalk; EBSCO Publishing; Gale Group; Northern Light Technology, Inc.; OCLC Online Computer Library Center, Inc.; ProQuest Information & Learning. *Indexed:* ConsI, MagInd, RGPR, RI-1, WSI. *Aud.:* Ac, Ga.

Redbook targets a younger audience than its sister Hearst publication, *Good Housekeeping,* and has spicier, sexier content. It attempts to reach young readers who have married and outgrown *Cosmo* but do not yet place themselves in the readership of more traditional titles such as *Ladies' Home Journal* and *Good Housekeeping.* The magazine begins with a focus on that woman and her health, diet, fitness, beauty, and fashion followed by a heavy dose of information and advice on marriage, parenting, and family life including recipes. Articles focus on sex, relationships, personalities, and personal stories that sometimes border on the sensational, the inspirational, or even the tragic. The web site is similar in content but perhaps a little steamier than the printed magazine, focusing on sex and marriage, reader polls and chats, advice columns, and "Redbook Diaries," serialized stories with accompanying message boards.

6661. *Self.* [ISSN: 0149-0699] 1979. m. USD 12 domestic; USD 27 Canada; USD 30 elsewhere. Ed(s): Lucy Danziger. Conde Nast Publications Inc., 4 Times Square, 5th Fl, New York, NY 10036; magpr@condenast.com; http://www.condenast.com. Illus., adv. Sample. Circ: 1284604 Paid. Vol. ends: Dec. Microform: PQC. Online: Gale Group. Reprint: PQC. *Aud.:* Hs, Ga.

Self is aimed at contemporary women who are looking for an upbeat lifestyle magazine that emphasizes fitness and health along with fashion and beauty coverage. It has evolved over the years from a magazine that included fiction and coverage of political and social issues to one with a strong fitness and health bent. *Self* has now settled into the more broadly focused lifestyle magazine market while returning, at least in some degree, to its roots by covering issues of importance to women such as abortion, body image, and bioengineering in foods. Coverage balances health, beauty, style, and diet while remaining strong in its treatment of fitness with workout routines and other exercise advice offered. The web site highlights current and past issues along with a tip of the day, health calculator, workout slide show, and links to reader surveys and forums.

Seventeen. See Teenagers section.

6662. *Shape.* [ISSN: 0744-5121] 1981. m. USD 14.97 domestic; USD 29.97 foreign; USD 2.99 newsstand/cover per issue. Ed(s): Barbara Harris. Weider Publications, 21100 Erwin St, Woodland Hills, CA 91367; http://www.shapemag.com. Illus., adv. Sample. Circ: 1692690 Paid. Vol. ends: Aug. *Indexed:* MagInd, PEI, SportS. *Aud.:* Hs, Ga, Ac.

Shape is one of a stable of magazines from fitness personality and publisher Joe Weider. It has evolved from a forum for the expression of his philosophy and the promotion of his products to a well-balanced, popular health-and-exercise magazine. Stories focus on exercise and sports; beauty and fashion for the young, active woman; athletic gear and sportswear; health, diet, and nutrition, including recipes; and travel, emphasizing health spas and other locations of interest to *Shape* readers, such as climbing and hiking spots. Mental health and well-being are also emphasized. Departments such as "Shape Your Life," "Get Fit," and "Think Healthy" provide current news, tips, products, and events. "Success Stories" relate personal weight loss or gain or general fitness improvement and are designed to inspire the reader through before-and-after photographs. Much attention is given to training and technique; regular features such as "Do it Right" and "Target Training" teach proper form for various exercises using a "reader model" to illustrate the activity. Product evaluations are useful, and the "Buyer's Guide" advertises a variety of products and services. A companion publication, *Shape Presents Fit Pregnancy,* is published quarterly. The web site promotes the current issue and offers reader surveys, event information, and "Shape Tools" such as fitness calculators, recipes, and expert advice.

Teen. See Teenagers section.

6663. *Today's Black Woman: your guide to love and relationships.* [ISSN: 1099-582X] 1995. 9x/yr. USD 27 domestic. Ed(s): Kate Ferguson. T B W Publishing Group, 210 Rte 4 E, Ste 401, Paramus, NJ 07652. Illus., adv. Circ: 87401. Vol. ends: Dec. *Bk. rev.:* 3- 5, 50 words. *Aud.:* Sa.

Today's Black Woman has much in common with other lifestyle magazines, but it is geared toward an African American female readership. Format and content are familiar: health, fitness, beauty, money, relationships, sex, work and career, celebrities, travel, and fashion. Articles either focus on getting/keeping a man or promoting positive and motivational images of successful women through celebrity features and personal profiles. The magazine places a strong focus on sexuality and intimacy through several articles, Q & A columns, and regular columns such as "Man Talk" and "Men's Room." A book excerpt or short story is included, usually with a romantic theme. A self-test appears in each issue, along with a horoscope. *Today's Black Woman* does not compare in quality to *Essence* but may appeal to a younger readership looking for a magazine that addresses their needs and interests as African American women.

6664. *Today's Christian Woman.* [ISSN: 0163-1799] 1978. bi-m. USD 17.95 domestic; USD 19.95 foreign. Ed(s): Jane Struck. Christianity Today International, 465 Gundersen Dr, Carol Stream, IL 60188. Illus., adv. Sample. Circ: 260000 Paid. Vol. ends: Nov/Dec. Online: EBSCO Publishing; Gale Group. *Indexed:* ChrPI. *Bk. rev.:* 6-8, 60 words. *Aud.:* Ga, Sa.

Today's Christian Woman describes itself as "a practical magazine geared for women in their 20s, 30s, and 40s." Its purpose is to address personal and social issues from a biblical perspective to help women cope with issues that arise in family and marital relationships, work life, and personal development. Letters to the editor and regular columns such as "MomSense," "Your Relationships," and "My Story" offer spiritual and practical guidance for the reader on health, marriage, work, finances, and family. Role models and popular Christian authors and celebrities also provide inspiration through profiles and a cover story. Women of color have become more prominently featured in the magazine in recent years. Articles cover such topics as spiritual development, prayer, relationships, careers, family life, and issues such as addiction and birth control. Advertisements are geared to this special audience and include Christian book, music, and video publishers. Each issue also features book, film, and music reviews. A web site offers information from and about the magazine, chat and interactive Bible study links, a prayer network, advice, and reader polls.

Town & Country. See General Editorial/General section.

Woman Rider. See Automobiles and Motorcycles section.

6665. *Woman's Day.* [ISSN: 0043-7336] 1937. 17x/yr. USD 8.99 domestic; CND 28.99 Canada; USD 28.99 elsewhere. Ed(s): Jane Chesnutt. Hachette Filipacchi Media U.S., Inc., 1633 Broadway, New York, NY 10019; http://www.hfmus.com. Illus., adv. Circ: 4350000 Paid. Vol. ends: Dec. Microform: PQC. Online: America Online, Inc.; Gale Group. *Indexed:* ASIP, ConsI, IHTDI, MagInd. *Aud.:* Ga.

Woman's Day is a perennial checkout counter competitor with *Family Circle* and, in more recent years, *First for Women* and other titles. While it has updated its content and gone to a cleaner cover look, *Woman's Day*'s approach has remained essentially the same: to provide practical information to middle-class wives and mothers who may or may not be working outside the home. Regular features include the editor's column, "All in a Woman's Day," and numerous tips on housekeeping, parenting, and family relationships. Many of the regular departments offer advice on a number of topics of concern to the thrifty woman: health, nutrition and meal planning, home care, money management, crafts, travel, gardening, and decorating. The magazine's strengths are product and consumer information, inexpensive and practical fashions, and recipes. Editorially, the magazine is conservative and patriotic and projects a subtle religious bent through the biblical quote that tops the table of contents and through inspirational articles and personal profiles. A web site reflects the contents of current and past issues and offers reader polls, chat, contests, product information and promotions, and recipes.

6666. *Women & Guns Magazine.* [ISSN: 1045-7704] 1989. bi-m. USD 18. Ed(s): Peggy Tartaro. Second Amendment Foundation, PO Box 488, Buffalo, NY 14209; WAGUNS@aol.com; http://www.womenandguns.com/. Illus., adv. Sample. Circ: 18000 Paid. Vol. ends: No. 6. *Bk. rev.:* 1, 300 words. *Aud.:* Sa.

Recently celebrating its 12th year of publication, *Women & Guns* successfully meets the needs of its specialized audience of women gun owners. Each issue provides current news of interest to gun enthusiasts as well as those interested in the public policy issues related to firearms. Articles cover a variety of topics, such as women's involvement in gun legislation, recreational shooting, self-defense and personal protection, hunting, the public image of women gun owners, and competition. Demands for gun control legislation spark considerable editorial activity in the magazine regarding concealed-weapon laws and gun-manufacturer liability. Detailed product tests of guns and related accessories are also a major focus, as are training tips. Advertising as well as photos that accompany articles prominently feature women using firearms. Video and book reviews appear in some issues. The web site features articles from the current issue, an archive of past articles, products spotlight, resource directory, message board, and links to related sites.

6667. *Working Mother: the smart guide for a whole life.* Incorporates (1986-1988): *Baby; McCall's Working Mother.* [ISSN: 0278-193X] 1978. 10x/yr. USD 9.97 domestic; USD 19 Canada; USD 32 elsewhere. Ed(s): Jill Kirschenbaum. Working Mother Media, 260 Madison Ave, New York, NY 10016; http://www.workingmother.com. Illus., adv. Circ: 75000 Paid. Vol. ends: Dec. Microform: PQC. Online: Gale Group. *Indexed:* MagInd, RGPR, WSI. *Aud.:* Ga.

Working Mother is a valuable and popular resource for working women who are new mothers or who already have older children. The "Work in Progress" department provides helpful and practical information and advice on health, fitness, beauty, food and nutrition, money, and career and workplace concerns, such as child care, maternity leave, technology, and pay equity. "Go Home" focuses on parenting, including games, projects, and other things to do with children. Recipes pay particular attention to nutritional needs and ease of preparation. Each issue closes with "Back Talk," a personal comment piece. Annually, the magazine reports on the best U.S. companies for working mothers and the status of child care in the 50 states, and a report on the "Best Companies for Women of Color" debuted in 2003. The reports are also available on the magazine's web site, along with current issue highlights and articles, a book club, recipes, and events.

WWD. See Business/Trade and Industry section.

YM. See Teenagers section.

Fashion

The major fashion magazines were challenged over the past two years by new launches with a more specific focus, such as *O* and *In Style*. However, magazines such as *Vogue*, *Harper's Bazaar*, *W*, and *Elle* have all remained strong publications as evidenced by their advertisement pages which have all increased, with *Vogue* leading the way with a jump of 19%. The editor shakeups of the past have also settled, with Anna Wintour still at the helm of *Vogue*. Fashion magazines are still manipulating content to reach a larger audience, and *Vogue* has led the way with theme issues focusing on such topics as age, sizes, and couples.

Most of the fashion magazines in this section have a general focus that covers all subjects relating to beauty and fashion. Also included are magazines focusing on a specific niche market, such as bridal or full-sized fashion. Fashion magazines for a specific ethnic market such as *Latina* and *Essence* continue to thrive, emphasizing that fashion and beauty are of interest to all.

Fashion is no longer seen solely in print but has migrated to television and the Internet. Fashion and the Internet are a perfect match. The Internet offers instantaneous access to fashion reporting by using web-streaming to highlight fashion shows and current designer's collections. Internet fashion magazines have proliferated in the past few years, and were first created by individuals disseminating opinions on topics such as punk style, makeup, and designers. The fashion industry quickly saw the value of the Internet as an advertising and information medium and began to develop commercial web sites. Most of these offer the tables of contents of current issues with some special features to lure readers to these sites. The fashion e-zines that are included within the section in the Electronic Journals subsection focus solely on independent sites that are not affiliated with a print publication. The growth of fashion reporting from print to television to the Internet emphasizes the universal interest in fashion.

6668. *B B W: real women - real beauty.* [ISSN: 0192-5938] 1979. bi-m. USD 14.95 domestic; USD 22.95 in Canada & Mexico; USD 46.95 elsewhere. Ed(s): Sally Smith. Aeon Publishing Group, Inc., 88 Sunnyside Blvd, Ste 203, Plainview, NY 11803. Illus., adv. Sample. Circ: 100000. Vol. ends: Dec. *Aud.:* Sa.

Relaunched in June 1999, *BBW* is still a fashion and lifestyle magazine for the full-sized woman. Each issue contains fashion layouts and articles that promote a positive viewpoint of women regardless of size. Fashion articles' coverage runs the gamut from lingerie to wedding to office attire, and many articles are accompanied by a helpful resource guide, which lists catalogues and stores offering this particular kind of attire for the full-sized woman. The models used in the layouts are of the appropriate size to the fashions being displayed and promote a positive view of the full-sized woman. *BBW* also includes profiles and interviews with plus-size individuals and articles on beauty and health. An important part of this magazine is the articles that deal with the discrimination and attitudes full-sized women must deal with on a day-to-day basis. Each issue is rounded out by book reviews, personal ads, and an issue column. *BBW* is not only an excellent resource for the large-sized woman interested in fashion, but also a counterpoint to the fashion magazines featuring the extremely thin model as an ideal that many women are not interested in attaining. The web site has been redesigned and offers excerpts of articles from the current issue as well as book reviews and beauty picks.

6669. *Belle: Black Elegance presents the magazine for full-figured women.* [ISSN: 1082-9679] 1995. q. USD 12.97. Ed(s): Sonia Alleyne. Starlog Group, Inc., 475 Park Ave S, 8th Fl, New York, NY 10016; http://www.starlog.com. Illus., adv. Sample. Circ: 250000 Paid. Vol. ends: Summer (No. 12). *Bk. rev.:* 5-6, length varies. *Aud.:* Sa.

The goal of *Belle* is to encourage self-acceptance among its readership of full-figured African American women. Each issue includes an eye-catching fashion layout featuring full-figured African Americans, but *Belle* is more than a fashion magazine. It includes articles exploring issues facing the full-figured reader such as weight and pregnancy, psychology and weight, and fitness. Interviews with full-figured women and men are also included. All articles are written in a positive and upbeat style that emphasizes *Belle*'s goal of self-acceptance. Each issue includes reviews of current books, vacation getaways, and food. *Belle* does not offer a web version of the magazine.

6670. *Elle.* [ISSN: 0888-0808] 1985. m. USD 12 domestic; USD 32 foreign. Ed(s): Roberta Myers. Hachette Filipacchi Media U.S., Inc., 1633 Broadway, New York, NY 10019; http://www.hfmus.com. Illus., adv. Circ: 9450000 Paid. Vol. ends: Aug. Online: America Online, Inc. *Indexed:* ASIP, DAAI, MRD. *Bk. rev.:* 8-12, brief. *Aud.:* Hs, Ga.

Elle is a well-rounded fashion magazine that includes lifestyle, relationship, health, fitness, and beauty features. A considerable portion of each issue is also devoted to information on culture, politics, and social issues. Articles cover music, literature, and film as well as a celebrity cover story and fiction. Regular columns such as "Ask E. Jean" provide relationship advice. "Elle First" covers fashion news and trends, and "Fashion Notebook" and "Inside Fashion" follow runway news and trends in the industry. Lush, artistic fashion layouts also remain a prominent feature, emphasizing designer wear. Each issue includes a calendar of fashion-related events and museum openings, a retail guide, and numerology and horoscope features. *Elle*'s web site offers online fashion stories, photos from designer collections, an issue preview, events calendar, and "Daily Essentials" highlighting fashion news or products.

6671. *Harper's Bazaar.* [ISSN: 0017-7873] 1867. m. USD 8 domestic; USD 28 foreign. Ed(s): Glenda Bailey, Regan Solmo. Hearst Corporation, 1700 Broadway, Ste 2801, New York, NY 10019; bazaar@hearst.com; http://www.hearstcorp.com. Illus., adv. Circ: 726582. Vol. ends: Dec. Microform: NBI; PMC; PQC. Online: bigchalk; EBSCO Publishing; Gale Group; OCLC Online Computer Library Center, Inc.; ProQuest Information & Learning. Reprint: PQC. *Indexed:* BiogInd, DAAI, MagInd, RGPR, WSI. *Bk. rev.:* Various number and length. *Aud.:* Ga, Ac.

Harper's Bazaar, one of America's oldest fashion magazines, balances lavishly illustrated fashion spreads with substantive feature articles. The magazine is currently divided into five sections: "The Bazaar," "Report," "Image," "Life," and "Features." "The Bazaar" is a thematic shopping guide; "Report" covers fashion news and events; "Image" includes such topics as migraines, beauty and aging, and reviews of new products; and "Life" focuses on the arts, including film and book reviews. The "Features" section includes well-written articles on a variety of issues that relate to some aspect of fashion. *Harper's Bazaar*, a perennial favorite, appeals to women interested in a contemporary interpretation of fashion. The web site provides information on current fashion events, links to advertisers, and excerpts from articles in the current print issue.

6672. *Mode: style beyond size.* [ISSN: 1091-0271] 1997. m. USD 18 domestic; USD 27 foreign; USD 2.95 newsstand/cover per issue. Ed(s): Corynne Corbett. Lewit & LeWinter, Inc., 200 Central Park S., Apt. 26B, New York, NY 10019-1448; editorial@modemag.com. Illus., adv. *Aud.:* Ga, Sa.

The cover of *Mode,* with its subtitle "The New Shape in Fashion," shows in both layout and words that this magazine is created for fashionable women who are not model-sized. *Mode* focuses on women who are sizes 12, 14, 16, and above. The layout is interesting and eye-catching and can be compared to fashion magazines such as *Vogue* or *Elle*. *Mode,* which targets the 25-to-34-year-old market, began in 1997 as a quarterly and is now a monthly. Each issue offers many articles and layouts on fashion, and plus-size models are used. Features include an interview with a plus-size celebrity and articles on romance and health-related topics. Regular features include "Ask Emme" and "Pleasure Zone," among others. The *Mode* web site allows access to either highlights of the current print issue or an online issue that includes access to a chat room and bulletin board.

6673. *shuz: your complete guide to what's underfoot.* q. USD 19.95; USD 9.95 newsstand/cover per issue. Ed(s): Gay Bryant. Magnolia Media Group, 3451 Boston Ave, Fort Worth, TX 76116-6330; info@shuz.com. *Aud.:* Ga, Sa.

First launched in 1998, this is the premier magazine for shoe aficionados. Each issue focuses on all aspects of footwear and includes articles such as "Soles of Serendipity" or "Barbie: the Shoe Diva." Other feature articles include, for example, interviews with shoe designers and artists using shoes in their artwork. Each issue includes a news column covering information relating to the shoe industry, a celebrity section featuring celebrities and their shoes, as well as a listing of new shoe store openings. The guide section lists new shoes arranged by style, such as pumps or sandals, and then by designer. It also includes a photo, the price, and an order form from the "Shuz Concierge." This magazine is beautifully photographed and lavishly illustrated. Its web site does not appear to have been updated since 2000.

6674. *Vogue.* [ISSN: 0042-8000] 1892. m. USD 18 domestic; USD 50 foreign. Ed(s): Anna Wintour. Conde Nast Publications Inc., 4 Times Square, 5th Fl, New York, NY 10036; http://www.condenast.com. Illus., index, adv. Circ: 1100000 Paid. Vol. ends: Dec. Microform: PQC; NRP. Online: Gale Group. Reprint: PQC. *Indexed:* BHA, BiogInd, ConsI, DAAI, MRD, MagInd, RGPR, RI-1. *Bk. rev.:* 3-4, 100-200 words. *Aud.:* Ga, Ac.

Vogue is one of the premier international fashion magazines, offering up-to-date information on current fashion and runway trends. Each issue is divided into four main sections: "Fashion," "Beauty, Health and Fitness" "Features," and "People Are Talking About." The "Fashion" section typically includes articles on haute couture and designers. "Beauty, Health and Fitness" offers information related to fashion such as makeup and hair trends, while the "Features" section includes well-written articles on a variety of topics. "People Are Talking About" covers current events such as museum openings and book and film reviews. The fashion layouts, shot by famous photographers, are always interesting and sometimes controversial. *Vogue* also has Australian, Brazilian, British, French, German, Italian, and Spanish editions. *Vogue* has partnered with *W* to provide a web site called *Style.com*. This site provides videos of fashion shows and slide shows of models and outfits, as well as articles on current trends, people, and parties. *Style.com* also provides a forum for readers to post comments and offers the option to subscribe to a weekly newsletter. This is an essential title for those interested in fashion.

6675. *W.* Incorporates (1987-1988): *Scene (New York)*. [ISSN: 0162-9115] 1971. m. USD 16.95 domestic; USD 65 Canada; USD 97 elsewhere. Fairchild Publications, Inc., 7 W 34th St, New York, NY 10001-8191; customerservice@fairchildpub.com; http://www.fairchildpub.com. Illus., adv. Circ: 416000 Paid. Vol. ends: Dec. Microform: FCM. Online: Gale Group. *Indexed:* ASIP, DAAI. *Aud.:* Ga, Ac.

W is a lavishly illustrated fashion magazine written for and targeted to those in high society or for readers interested in those in high society. It covers all areas of fashion from designers to current collections. It is divided into sections that highlight trends in cosmetics, accessories, beauty, and interior design. The magazine's large size allows for interesting layouts that complement these articles. In addition to fashion coverage, a large part of the magazine is devoted to the doings of various celebrities. Departments such as "Suzy" and "Eye" describe the openings, dinners, and weddings these celebrities are attending. In addition, articles on various actors, directors, and artists add some substance to the magazine. This is the magazine to read to keep up with the lives of newsworthy people while enjoying interesting fashion layouts. *W* has partnered with *Vogue* to create *Style.com*, which highlights features from both magazines while also providing extra features such as fashion shows, beauty trends, and people and parties.

Electronic Journals

6676. *Fashion Net.* 1995. w. Triple International Ltd., http://www.fashionnet.com. Illus. *Aud.:* Ga, Sa.

Fashion Net offers weekly fashion news, videos of runway shows from designers such as Jean Paul Gaultier and Zac Posen, and useful information on the fashion industry for aspiring fashion designers. *Fashion Net* also includes message boards and job listings, and it e-mails news updates.

6677. *FashionClick: the online fashion and style magazine.* 1998. m. Ed(s): Freddy Vicioso-Galan. FashionClick, staff@fashionclick.com; http://www.fashionclick.com. Illus. *Aud.:* Ga, Ac.

Based in Madrid, Spain, and published in both Spanish and English, *FashionClick* covers designers and their collections as well as standard fashion magazine fare. Each issue includes a style article and an overview of international men and women's collections. Since the last review, *FashionClick* has added *FashionClick Premium* and now charges an access fee to interactive/multimedia fashion editorials as well as interviews with models. This site is visually exciting and includes excellent illustrations and graphics.

6678. *Hint.* w. Ed(s): Lee Carter. Hint Magazine, 134 Tenth Ave, Suite 2, New York, NY 10011; leecarter@hintmag.com; http://www.hintmag.com. Adv. *Aud.:* Ga, Ac.

Each issue includes interviews and articles on current and cutting-edge fashion trends and designers. Some of the regular columns include "Chic Happens: Who, What and Wear News Gossip," "Jetsetera, the Art of Parties," and "Model

Mania." *Hint* uses a variety of visuals such as web streaming, photographs, animated gifs, and graphics to add an edgy and au courant feeling to the site. A message board and a chat room are also included.

6679. *Jade Magazine: a fresh perspective for Asian women.* 1999. bi-m. Ed(s): Ellen Hwang. JADE Magazine Inc., Village Station, Box 915, New York, NY 10014; info@jademagazine.com; http://www.jademagazine.com/. Circ: 7000. *Aud.:* Sa.

Started by two ambitious Asian American women, *Jade* is an e-zine designed to create a place to address young English-speaking Asian women's issues and interests, highlight their contributions, and confront the stereotypes surrounding them. Through its clean, uncluttered presentation and well-written content, *Jade* has grown in readership. Many features are common to women's fashion and beauty magazines—clothes, cosmetics, accessories, health, careers, travel, and entertainment—but all are addressed from a unique Asian perspective. In addition to the more typical women's magazine features, *Jade* also provides daily updates of world news relevant to its readership, events of interest in Asia, Canada, and the United States, and "Open Mike," where readers can share their views. The current online issue is available at no charge; articles from past issues are for sale. *Jade* has recently begun publishing a print edition.

6680. *The Look Online.* irreg. USD 108. Look Online, Inc., 529 E 85th St, New York, NY 10028; look@lookonline.com; http://www.lookonline.com/. *Bk. rev.:* 2-4, 150-200 words, signed. *Aud.:* Sa.

The Look Online is an e-zine for both fashion industry professionals and consumers who want "real insider information about New York fashion and how it works." It is available both free and by paid subscription. It offers interviews, editorials, profiles, book reviews, editorial cartoons, and roundtable discussions, as well as original runway photos and special articles written by guest columnists on the New York fashion scene. Subscribers also receive a biweekly newsletter covering New York fashion news and issues; market and trend reports in the beauty, ready-to-wear, resort, and men's wear industries; a New York fashion event schedule; and a directory of sixty fashion public relations firms.

6681. *Skirt! Magazine.* 1994. m. USD 26. Ed(s): Nikki Hardin. Skirt! Magazine, 455 1/2 King St, Charleston, SC 29403; nikki@skirtmag.com; http://www.skirtmag.com. *Aud.:* Ga.

Skirt! began as a print publication in the Charleston area in 1994 but has expanded its focus and readership through its web edition. The magazine is described as "an attitude...spirited, independent, outspoken, serious, playful and irreverent, sometimes controversial, always passionate." The e-zine lives up to its purpose with lively, first-person essays on a wide range of topics—moving back home, living with cancer, even going into the pickle business. Regular departments are entertaining as well. "Short Skirts" offers women's news, "Skirt Salon" highlights entertainment, "Muse Room" provides inspiration, and "Bitch of the Month" invites readers to let off some steam. Recipes, books, and films round out the site. Archives are available, as are reader feedback opportunities through polls and e-mail to the editor.

6682. *Women Today Magazine.* m. Free. Ed(s): Claire Colvin. Women Today Magazine, 20385 64th Ave, Langley, BC V2Y 1N5, Canada; editor@womentodaymagazine.com; http://www.womentodaymagazine.com. *Aud.:* Ga.

Women Today is a Canadian e-zine that covers much of the same ground as newsstand service magazines but with an underlying Christian message that is not readily apparent until the site is explored. Information about fashion, beauty, family, career, relationships, health and wellness, recipes, and parenting is helpful and in-depth. New items are labeled as such, and older items stay on the site for a while, sometimes making the lists under each main topic quite long. Live chat, discussion boards, and polls are available to get readers involved in the site. A feature not found in most service magazines but provided by *Women Today* is first-person news about women from around the world. Here is where a strong evangelical Christian message is delivered, directing readers to information on how they can accept Christ into their lives. There is a companion site, *Christian Women Today,* that has a more overt religious message similar to the print magazine *Today's Christian Woman* and its companion web site.

6683. *WomenOf.com.* 1997. w. Ed(s): S Klann. Prosolutions Inc, 7585 W 66th Ave, Arvada, CO 80003. *Aud.:* Ga.

This e-journal provides comprehensive coverage of a wide-ranging number of issues and topics: business, health, family, travel, law, automobiles, sports, money, cooking, and more. Issued weekly, *WomenOf.com* serves as a national edition or digest of sorts for several community-focused e-journals for women. A pull-down menu to these sites is on the home page, and some of the articles are drawn from these local sites. Articles are, for the most part, well written and authoritative, providing a brief author profile and e-mail address, and there is also a "Woman of the Month" feature. A section called "The Directory" provides a promising listing of services such as health care providers, financial services, lawyers, banks, spas, and more (it is currently light on entries in several categories).

■ WOMEN: FEMINIST AND SPECIAL INTEREST

Feminist and Women's Studies/Literary and Artistic/Special Interest

Lilith R. Kunkel, Library Director, Salem Campus Library, Kent State University Salem Regional Campus, 2491 State Route 45 South, Salem, OH 44460; kunkel@salem.kent.edu; FAX: 330 332-5086

Introduction

Women's studies is an area of study that developed in the context of the women's movement of the 1970s and continues to be shaped by the changing socio-political context of American and world feminism. It deals with the roles, status, and condition of women and, increasingly, with gender relations. From its inception, it has been interdisciplinary and activist in outlook. Programs vary greatly in their blending of theoretical, empirical, and applied studies and in their sexual and other politics. Critics have sometimes challenged the academic credibility of these programs and provided limited financial support compared to more traditional disciplines.

In choosing women's studies and feminist periodicals to meet the needs of library users, selectors need to consider not only these complicated origins but also current trends in publishing. The most notable trends are the growth of web-based publishing and the increased availability of online, full-text databases. The number of resources has proliferated as the web makes cheap, fast publishing possible free from the constraints of mainstream publishing. Many web-based publications prove to be ephemeral, however, and access to their content through major search engines is limited. The growth of databases and full-text services has increased the availability of women's studies and feminist periodicals to some degree. The major vendors appear to attach fairly low priority to the inclusion of women's studies and feminist titles and do not cover smaller, more specialized publications. The online versions of specialized abstracts and indexes such as *Contemporary Women's Issues, Studies on Women,* and *Gender Abstracts* provide better coverage of these, but their price may be beyond the reach of smaller libraries struggling to meet the costs of the big databases.

The titles listed here have been selected to represent the variety and scope of women's studies. The online publications included in the Electronic Journals subsection are free scholarly journals available only online and are feminist news sources. Following the precedent set by earlier editions of *Magazines for Libraries,* this section includes few publications dealing with sexuality. These are covered in the Lesbian, Gay, Bisexual, and Transgender section and the Sexuality section.

Basic Periodicals

FEMINIST AND WOMEN'S STUDIES. Ems: *New Moon*, Hs: *Ms., NWSA Journal, Women in Literature and Life Assembly, Women in Sport & Physical Activity;* Ga: Frontiers, Herizons, Iris, Ms., National NOW Times, Sexing the Political; Ac: *Critical Matrix, Feminist Economics, Feminist Studies, Frontiers, Gender and Education, Gender and History, Gender Issues, Genders, Health Care for Women International, Hypatia, Journal of Women's History, Legacy, Ms., NWSA Journal, Sexing the Political, Signs, Tulsa Studies in Women's Literature, Violence Against Women, WIN News, Woman's Art Journal, Women & Health, Women & Politics, Women in Sport & Physical Activity Journal, Women's Health Issues, Women's Studies Quarterly, Women's Writing.*

LITERARY AND ARTISTIC. Ga: *Bridges, Calyx, Room of One's Own;* Ac: *Calyx, femspec, Kalliope, n.paradoxa.*

SPECIAL INTEREST. Hs: *Melpomene Journal;* Ga: *Conscience, Lilith, Melpomene Journal,* Ac: *Media Report to Women.*

Basic Abstracts and Indexes

Contemporary Women's Issues, Feminist Periodicals, GenderWatch, Studies on Women and Gender Abstracts, Violence & Abuse Abstracts, Women Studies Abstracts, Women's Studies Index, Women's Studies International, , Women's Studies on Disc.

Jenda. See Africa section.

Feminist and Women's Studies

6684. *Abafazi: the Simmons College journal of women of African descent.* 1991. s-a. USD 25 (Individuals, USD 15). Ed(s): Della Scott. Simmons College, 300 The Fenway, Boston, MA 02115; http://www.simmons.edu/. Refereed. *Aud.:* Ac.

Abafazi seeks "to promote feminist scholarship in all fields of study in order to heighten readers' awareness of black women's intellectual traditions, herstories, and socio-political, economic, and cultural issues throughout the African world." It features research articles, essays, and interviews with emerging and established black scholars and activists. It also includes poetry and art work. Published by Simmons College's African American Studies Department, this is an important resource for its focus on black women.

6685. *Affilia: journal of women and social work.* [ISSN: 0886-1099] 1986. q. GBP 273 in Europe, Middle East, Africa & Australasia. Ed(s): Emma Gross. Sage Publications, Inc., 2455 Teller Rd, Thousand Oaks, CA 91320; info@sagepub.com; http://www.sagepub.com. Illus., adv. Refereed. Circ: 1300. Vol. ends: Nov. *Indexed:* ASSIA, AgeL, ArtHuCI, CJA, FemPer, HRA, IMFL, SFSA, SSCI, SWA, SWR&A, SociolAb, WSA, WSI. *Bk. rev.:* 7-14, 350-900 words, signed. *Aud.:* Ac, Sa.

This scholarly journal addresses the concerns of social work and its clients from a feminist perspective. It aims to provide the knowledge and tools needed to improve the delivery of social services through research reports, empirical articles, opinion pieces, and book reviews. Issues also include news updates and literary works. Full text is available through *ingenta* to institutions with print subscriptions.

6686. *Asian Journal of Women's Studies.* [ISSN: 1225-9276] 1995. q. KRW 30000 domestic; USD 70 foreign; KRW 8000 per issue domestic. Ed(s): Philwha Chang. Ewha Womans University Press, Ewha Womans University, Asian Center for Women's Studies, Seoul, 120-750, Korea, Republic of; acwsewha@esha.ac.kr; http://ews.ewha.ac.kr. Adv. Sample. Refereed. Circ: 700 Paid and controlled. *Indexed:* FemPer, GendWatch, SSCI. *Bk. rev.:* 2, 800-1,000 words, signed. *Aud.:* Ac.

This interdisciplinary journal from the Asian Center for Women's Studies provides a feminist perspective on women's issues in Asia and throughout the world. It aims to communicate scholarly ideas and "to develop women's studies in Asia and expand the horizon of western centered women?s studies." It includes scholarly articles, reports, notes on teaching and research, and book reviews

6687. *Atlantis: a women's studies journal - revue d'etudes sur les femmes.* [ISSN: 0702-7818] 1975. s-a. CND 45 (Individuals, CND 25; CND 12 newsstand/cover per issue). Ed(s): Marilyn Porter, Keith Louise Falton. Mount Saint Vincent University, Institute for the Study of Women, Halifax, NS B3M 2J6, Canada; atlantis@msvu.ca. Illus., index, adv. Refereed. Circ: 900. Vol. ends: Spring/Summer. Microform: MML. *Indexed:* AltPI, AmH&L, CBCARef, CPerI, FemPer, MLA-IB, SWA, WSA, WSI. *Bk. rev.:* 8, length varies, signed. *Aud.:* Ac.

This is an established Canadian journal providing critical and creative writing in English and French about women and women's studies. Publication alternates between general, open, and special issues. One recent issue includes a discussion of controversies in Canadian feminism, a conference report, an interview, and articles on family violence and married women teachers in Saskatchewan. Its perspective is international and interdisciplinary. Contributors are academics and feminists.

6688. *Australian Feminist Studies.* [ISSN: 0816-4649] 1986. 3x/yr. GBP 208 (Individuals, GBP 54). Ed(s): Susan Magarey. Carfax Publishing Ltd., 4 Park Sq, Milton Park, Abingdon, OX14 4RN, United Kingdom; enquiry@tandf.co.uk; http://www.tandf.co.uk/. Adv. Refereed. Circ: 600. Online: EBSCO Publishing; Ingenta Select; OCLC Online Computer Library Center, Inc.; RMIT Publishing; RoweCom Information Quest; Swets Blackwell. Reprint: PSC. *Indexed:* AltPI, ArtHuCI, FemPer, PSA, SSCI, SWA, SociolAb. *Bk. rev.:* 6-8, 500 words, essay length, signed. *Aud.:* Ac.

This international journal publishes disciplinary and transdisciplinary scholarship in women's studies and feminist research. It promotes discussion of the interaction between feminist theory and practice. Its contents include scholarly articles, reviews, critiques and correspondence that place it in the academic mainstream. The journal also includes news of government and trade union policies affecting women, conference reports, and discussions of teaching. A free contents alert service (SARA) is available from the publisher.

Bitch. See Zines section.

6689. *Canadian Woman Studies.* Formerly (until vol.3, no.2, 1981): *Canadian Women's Studies.* [ISSN: 0713-3235] 1978. q. CND 42.80 (Individuals, CND 32.10; CND 8 newsstand/cover per issue). Ed(s): Luciana Ricciutelli. Inanna Publications and Education Inc., 212 Founders College, York University, 4700 Keele St, Downsview, ON M3J 1P3, Canada; cwscf@yorku.ca; http://www.yorku.ca/org/cwscf/home.html. Illus., adv. Refereed. Circ: 5000. Vol. ends: Winter (No. 4). Microform: MML. Online: Florida Center for Library Automation; Gale Group; LexisNexis; Micromedia ProQuest; OCLC Online Computer Library Center, Inc.; H.W. Wilson. *Indexed:* ABS&EES, CBCARef, CPI, CPerI, FemPer, HumInd, SWA, WSA, WSI. *Bk. rev.:* 7, 600-1,100, signed. *Aud.:* Ac, Sa.

This bilingual quarterly seeks to make feminist writing and research available to academic and nonacademic women and to provide a middle ground between theory and activism. Issues are theme-based and include scholarly and experiential articles, art, creative writing, and book reviews. Coverage is international. The editors encourage submissions dealing with the diverse lives of "women of color, Aboriginal women, immigrant women, working class women, women with disabilities, lesbians, and other marginalized women."

6690. *Columbia Journal of Gender and the Law.* [ISSN: 1062-6220] 1991. a. USD 45 (Individuals, USD 25). Columbia University School of Law, Jerome Greene Hall, 435 W 116th St, New York, NY 10027; http://law.columbia.edu/. Illus. *Indexed:* FemPer, GendWatch, ILP. *Bk. rev.:* Number varies, essay length, signed. *Aud.:* Ac, Sa.

This law review takes an interdisciplinary approach to the interplay between gender and the law. Articles reflect a broad definition of feminism and feminist jurisprudence and address issues affecting all races, ethnicities, classes, sexual orientations, and cultures. Contributors are judges, law professors, law students, and scholars from other disciplines. Recommended for law libraries and academic collections.

6691. ***Critical Matrix: the Princeton journal of women, gender, and culture.*** [ISSN: 1066-288X] 1985. s-a. USD 30 (Individuals, USD 25; Students, USD 20). Ed(s): Paul Kelleher, Jennifer Waldron. Princeton University, Program in the Study of Women and Gender, 113 Dickinson Hall, Princeton University, Princeton, NJ 08544-1017; matrix@princeton.edu. Illus., index, adv. Refereed. Circ: 500. Vol. ends: No. 2. Online: Gale Group; OCLC Online Computer Library Center, Inc.; SoftLine Information. *Indexed:* CWI, FemPer, GendWatch, MLA-IB, RI-1, WSA. *Aud.:* Ac.

Critical Matrix is a forum for research and creative work in feminism and women's studies by graduate students, faculty, and nonacademics. Recent special issues look at women photographers, the senses, and gendered labor. This award-winning journal from Princeton's Program in Women's Studies and Gender is recommended for women's studies collections.

6692. ***Differences: a journal of feminist cultural studies.*** [ISSN: 1040-7391] 1989. 3x/yr. USD 94 (Individuals, USD 35). Ed(s): Denise Davis, Naomi Schor. Duke University Press, 905 W Main St, Ste 18 B, Durham, NC 27701; dukepress@duke.edu; http://www.dukeupress.edu. Illus., adv. Sample. Circ: 1100. Vol. ends: Fall. Online: bigchalk; Chadwyck-Healey Incorporated; EBSCO Publishing; Florida Center for Library Automation; Gale Group; Ingenta Select; LexisNexis; OCLC Online Computer Library Center, Inc.; Project MUSE; RoweCom Information Quest; SoftLine Information; Swets Blackwell; H.W. Wilson. Reprint: PSC. *Indexed:* AltPI, CWI, FemPer, GendWatch, HumInd, MLA-IB, PSA, SWA, SociolAb, WSA, WSI. *Aud.:* Ac.

This scholarly journal looks at how concepts and categories of "difference" are produced and operate within culture and over time. The main but not exclusive focus is women and gender. Articles are interdisciplinary and cover a broad range of topics. Now published by Duke University Press with full text available online through *ingenta* to institutions with print subscriptions.

6693. ***European Journal of Women's Studies.*** [ISSN: 1350-5068] 1994. q. GBP 298 in Europe, Middle East, Africa & Australasia. Ed(s): Mary Evans, Magda Michielsens. Sage Publications Ltd., 6 Bonhill St, London, EC2A 4PU, United Kingdom; info@sagepub.co.uk; http://www.sagepub.co.uk/. Illus., adv. Refereed. Vol. ends: Nov. *Indexed:* ABS&EES, ASSIA, AgeL, ArtHuCI, BrHumI, CommAb, FemPer, HRA, IBSS, IPSA, PSA, SFSA, SSCI, SWA, SociolAb, WSA. *Bk. rev.:* 2-10, length varies, signed. *Aud.:* Ac.

This multidisciplinary, academic journal publishes theoretical and thematic articles dealing with women and feminism in a varied European context. Issues include open letters, book reviews, and conference reports and provide multiple feminist perspectives. Published with the support of WISE (The European Women's Studies Association).

6694. ***Feminism & Psychology: an international journal.*** [ISSN: 0959-3535] 1991. q. GBP 317 in Europe, Middle East, Africa & Australasia. Ed(s): Sue Wilkinson. Sage Publications Ltd., 6 Bonhill St, London, EC2A 4PU, United Kingdom; info@sagepub.co.uk; http://www.sagepub.co.uk/. Illus., adv. Refereed. Circ: 1000. Vol. ends: Nov. *Indexed:* ASSIA, AgeL, ArtHuCI, FemPer, IBSS, IBZ, PSA, PsycholAb, SFSA, SSCI, SWA, SociolAb, WSA. *Bk. rev.:* 0-10, 600-1,000 words, signed. *Aud.:* Ac, Sa.

This international journal seeks to develop feminist theory and practice and to bridge the divide between academic and applied psychology. It publishes research and scholarly articles, commentaries, and book reviews. A special feature of recent issues has been a critical reappraisal of important earlier feminist scholarship by Diana Scully, Pauline Bart, and others.

6695. ***Feminist Collections: a quarterly of women's studies resources.*** [ISSN: 0742-7441] 1980. 4x/yr. USD 15 Univ. of WI affiliated, Libraries, USD 22.50 (Individuals, USD 8.25 Univ. of WI affiliated). Ed(s): Phyllis Holman Weisbard, JoAnne Lehman. University of Wisconsin System, Women's Studies Librarian, 430 Memorial Library, 728 State St, Madison, WI 53706; wisws1@library.wisc.edu; http://www.library.wisc.edu/libraries/WomensStudies/fcmain.htm. Illus., adv. Circ: 1000. Vol. ends: Summer. Online: Gale Group; LexisNexis; OCLC Online Computer Library Center, Inc.; SoftLine Information. *Indexed:* CWI, FemPer, GendWatch, HEA, LISA, SWA, WSA, WSI. *Bk. rev.:* Number varies, essay length, signed. *Aud.:* Ac, Sa.

Feminist Collections provides information on resources for teaching and research in women's studies. It includes reviews of books, periodicals, and audiovisual and Internet resources as well as news about feminist publishing. Recent articles cover topics such as women in the civil rights movement, domestic violence, women in popular music, and Internet resources on female genital mutilation. Regular features include "New Reference Works in Women's Studies" and "Periodical Notes," which contains information about new and ceased publications. A print subscription includes *Feminist Periodicals*, a current-contents listing service (see Abstracts and Indexes section). An important resource for teaching, research, and collection development.

6696. ***Feminist Economics.*** [ISSN: 1354-5701] 1995. 3x/yr. GBP 129 (Individuals, GBP 46). Ed(s): Diana Strassmann. Routledge, 11 New Fetter Ln, London, EC4P 4EE, United Kingdom. Illus., adv. Sample. Refereed. Vol. ends: No. 3. Online: EBSCO Publishing; Gale Group; Ingenta Select; OCLC Online Computer Library Center, Inc.; RoweCom Information Quest; Swets Blackwell. Reprint: PSC. *Indexed:* AgeL, AltPI, BAS, BrHumI, FemPer, IBSS, IBZ, JEL, PSA, SSCI, SociolAb. *Bk. rev.:* 0-12, length varies, signed. *Aud.:* Ac.

The journal of the International Association for Feminist Economics (IAFFE) applies a feminist perspective to new and diverse areas of economic inquiry in order to develop "more illuminating theories" and to improve living conditions for all. Coverage is interdisciplinary and international. Contents include scholarly articles, book reviews, conference announcements, and explorations of special topics such as teaching feminist economics. A recent special issue is devoted to gender, color, caste, and class.

6697. ***Feminist Media Studies.*** [ISSN: 1468-0777] 2001. 3x/yr. GBP 173 (Individuals, GBP 32). Ed(s): Cynthia Carter, Lisa McLaughlin. Routledge, 11 New Fetter Ln, London, EC4P 4EE, United Kingdom; info@routledge.co.uk; http://www.routledge.co.uk. Reprint: PSC. *Indexed:* SociolAb. *Bk. rev.:* yes. *Aud.:* Ac, Sa.

This transdisciplinary, peer-reviewed journal provides a feminist perspective on media and communication studies. Its goal is to serve as an international forum for discussions between scholarly, professional, and grassroots organizations. Contents include articles, commentary, criticism, and book reviews and reflect a variety of theoretical, analytical, and practical perspectives. A recent special issue focuses on the representation of HIV/AIDs in the media.

6698. ***Feminist Review.*** [ISSN: 0141-7789] 1979. 3x/yr. GBP 198 (Individuals, GBP 35). Palgrave Macmillan Ltd., Houndmills, Basingstoke, RG21 6XS, United Kingdom; journal-info@palgrave.com; http://www.palgrave-journals.com/. Illus., adv. Sample. Refereed. Circ: 3500. Online: EBSCO Publishing; Gale Group; Ingenta Select; ingenta.com; RoweCom Information Quest; Swets Blackwell. *Indexed:* ASSIA, AltPI, ArtHuCI, BrHumI, FemPer, IBSS, IBZ, RI-1, SSCI, SSI, SWA, SociolAb. *Bk. rev.:* 4-17, length varies, signed. *Aud.:* Ga, Ac.

This is a socialist-feminist journal covering a range of feminist academic and political concerns. Articles are grouped around themes such as "drugs" or "fashion and beauty." In addition to scholarly articles, issues include dialogues, review essays, book reviews, and occasional creative writing related to the theme.

6699. ***Feminist Studies.*** [ISSN: 0046-3663] 1972. 3x/yr. USD 120 (Individuals, USD 33). Ed(s): Claire G. Moses. Feminist Studies, Inc., 0103 Taliaferro Hall, University of Maryland, College Park, MD 20742. Illus., index, adv. Refereed. Circ: 5000. Vol. ends: Fall (No. 3).

Microform: PQC. Online: bigchalk; Chadwyck-Healey Incorporated; EBSCO Publishing; Florida Center for Library Automation; Gale Group; Northern Light Technology, Inc.; OCLC Online Computer Library Center, Inc.; ProQuest Information & Learning; SoftLine Information; H.W. Wilson. Reprint: PQC; PSC. *Indexed:* ASSIA, AgeL, AltPI, AmH&L, AnthLit, ArtHuCI, BAS, BHA, FemPer, GendWatch, IBSS, IBZ, IMFL, MLA-IB, PRA, PSA, PhilInd, PsycholAb, RI-1, SFSA, SSCI, SSI, SWA, SociolAb, WSA, WSI. *Bk. rev.:* 0-1, essay length, signed. *Aud.:* Ac.

Feminist Studies seeks to promote discussion among feminist scholars, activists, and writers, to develop an interdisciplinary body of knowledge and theory, and to change women's condition. Contents include scholarly research, essays, book reviews, and creative works. Recent issues include a retrospective of "second wave feminism." Published in association with the University of Maryland's Women's Studies Program.

6700. ***Feminist Teacher: a journal of the practices, theories, and scholarship of feminist teaching.*** [ISSN: 0882-4843] 1984. 3x/yr. USD 45 (Individuals, USD 25). Feminist Teacher Editorial Collective, c/o Theresa D. Kemp, Feminist Teacher Editorial Collective, English Department, PO Box 4004, Eau Claire, WI 54702-4004. Adv. Refereed. Circ: 600. *Indexed:* AltPI, CIJE, CWI, EduInd, FemPer, GendWatch, SWA, WSA, WSI. *Aud.:* Hs, Ga, Ac.

This journal addresses the theory and practice of feminist teaching as well as issues such as sexism, antifeminism, racism, homophobia, and other forms of oppression in the classroom. It is directed toward teachers and administrators at all levels and includes articles, book reviews, review essays, and news and information about resources for teaching.

6701. ***Feminist Theology.*** [ISSN: 0966-7350] 1992. 3x/yr. GBP 75 (Individuals, GBP 35; Students, GBP 26.50). Ed(s): Lisa Isherwood, Janet Wootton. Sheffield Academic Press Ltd, Mansion House, 19 Kingfield Rd, Sheffield, S11 9AS, United Kingdom; jjoyce@continuumbooks.com; http://www.continuumjournals.com/. Online: EBSCO Publishing. *Indexed:* IBZ, R&TA, RI-1, SWA. *Bk. rev.:* 6-8, varies, signed. *Aud.:* Ac, Sa.

Feminist Theology is an academic journal designed "to give a voice to the women . . . in matters of theology and religion" and "to be accessible to a wide range of readers." A recent issue includes a panel response to Argentinian theologian Marcella Althaus-Reid's *Indecent Theology* and a series of articles on violence against women.

6702. ***Feminist Theory: an international interdisciplinary journal.*** [ISSN: 1464-7001] 2000. 3x/yr. GBP 206 in Europe, Middle East, Africa & Australasia. Ed(s): Gabriele Griffin, Rosemary Hennessy. Sage Publications Ltd., 6 Bonhill St, London, EC2A 4PU, United Kingdom; info@sagepub.co.uk; http://www.sagepub.co.uk/. Illus., index, adv. Refereed. Vol. ends: Dec. Online: EBSCO Publishing; ingenta.com; OCLC Online Computer Library Center, Inc.; RoweCom Information Quest; Swets Blackwell. *Indexed:* FemPer, IBZ, PSA, SociolAb. *Bk. rev.:* Various number and length, signed. *Aud.:* Ac.

This international journal focuses on the critical examination and discussion of diverse feminist theoretical and political positions across the humanities and social sciences. Contents include articles, responses, interchanges between theorists, and book reviews.

6703. ***Frontiers (Lincoln): a journal of women studies.*** [ISSN: 0160-9009] 1975. 3x/yr. USD 60 (Individuals, USD 35; USD 27 newsstand/cover per issue). University of Nebraska Press, 233 N 8th St, Lincoln, NE 68588-0255; pressmail@unl.edu; http://www.nebraskapress.unl.edu. Illus., index, adv. Refereed. Microform: PQC. Online: EBSCO Publishing; Florida Center for Library Automation; Gale Group; OCLC Online Computer Library Center, Inc.; Project MUSE; ProQuest Information & Learning; RoweCom Information Quest; Swets Blackwell. Reprint: PQC. *Indexed:* AgeL, AmH&L, AmHI, ArtHuCI, BAS, FemPer, HRA, MLA-IB, PAIS, SSCI, SSI, SWA, WSA, WSI. *Aud.:* Ac.

This multicultural, cross-disciplinary journal features work in women's studies, history, anthropology, sociology, ethnic studies, and American Studies. Its contents are a mix of scholarly work, personal essays, and creative works. Contributions from authors belonging to racial and ethnic minorities are encouraged. Some issues such as the recent "Indigent Women" are theme-based.

6704. ***Gender and Development.*** Formerly: *Focus on Gender.* [ISSN: 1355-2074] 1993. 3x/yr. GBP 107 (Individuals, GBP 43). Ed(s): Caroline Sweetman. Carfax Publishing Ltd., 4 Park Sq, Milton Park, Abingdon, OX14 4RN, United Kingdom; enquiry@tandf.co.uk; http://www.tandf.co.uk/. Circ: 100. Online: EBSCO Publishing; Ingenta Select; Swets Blackwell. Reprint: PSC. *Indexed:* FemPer, HortAb, IBSS, IBZ, PSA, RRTA, SWA, SociolAb, WAE&RSA. *Bk. rev.:* brief-750 words. *Aud.:* Ac, Sa.

This journal is concerned with the relationship between gender and economic development. Issues are thematic and include articles, case studies, conference reports, interviews, resources, and book reviews. Articles are directed toward development practitioners, policy makers, and academics. Recent issues focus on poverty and climate change. Tables of contents and an e-mail contents alert service (SARA) are available on the publisher's web site.

6705. ***Gender and Education.*** [ISSN: 0954-0253] 1989. q. Individuals, GBP 72. Ed(s): Rosemary Preston, Christina Hughes. Carfax Publishing Ltd., 4 Park Sq, Milton Park, Abingdon, OX14 4RN, United Kingdom; enquiry@tandf.co.uk; http://www.tandf.co.uk/. Illus., adv. Sample. Refereed. Vol. ends: Dec (No. 4). Online: EBSCO Publishing; Ingenta Select; OCLC Online Computer Library Center, Inc.; ProQuest Information & Learning; RoweCom Information Quest; Swets Blackwell. Reprint: PSC. *Indexed:* ASSIA, BrEdI, CIJE, CWI, FemPer, IBZ, LT&LA, SSCI, SWA, SociolAb. *Bk. rev.:* 9-15, 500-1,000 words, signed. *Aud.:* Ac.

Gender and Education publishes multidisciplinary research with gender as a main category of analysis. Education is broadly defined as encompassing formal and informal education at all levels and within all contexts. Coverage is international. Tables of contents and an e-mail contents alerting service (SARA)are on available the publisher's web site.

6706. ***Gender and History.*** [ISSN: 0953-5233] 1989. 3x/yr. GBP 252 print & online eds. Ed(s): Keith McClelland. Blackwell Publishing Ltd., 9600 Garsington Rd, PO Box 805, Oxford, OX4 2DQ, United Kingdom; customerservices@oxon.blackwellpublishing.com; http://www.blackwellpublishing.com/. Illus., adv. Sample. Refereed. Vol. ends: Nov. Online: EBSCO Publishing; ingenta.com; OCLC Online Computer Library Center, Inc.; RoweCom Information Quest; Swets Blackwell. Reprint: SWZ. *Indexed:* AmH&L, FemPer, IBSS, PSA, SWA, SociolAb, WSA, WSI. *Bk. rev.:* Number varies, essay length, signed. *Aud.:* Ac.

This journal offers a historical perspective on gender relations, men and masculinity, and women and femininity. It has a broad chronological and geographical scope. It covers both specific episodes in gender history and broader methodological questions in history. It also includes discussions of teaching gender history and extensive book reviews. Special issues focus on themes such as "Dress and Material and Visual Culture" or "Gender, Citizenship, and Subjectivity." Tables of contents of past issues and an online sample issue are available on the publisher's web site.

6707. ***Gender & Society.*** [ISSN: 0891-2432] 1987. bi-m. USD 462. Ed(s): Christine E Bose. Sage Publications, Inc., 2455 Teller Rd, Thousand Oaks, CA 91320; info@sagepub.com; http://www.sagepub.com. Illus., adv. Sample. Refereed. Circ: 2500. Vol. ends: Dec. Reprint: PSC. *Indexed:* ABS&EES, ASSIA, AgeL, ArtHuCI, CJA, CommAb, FemPer, HRA, IBSS, IBZ, IMFL, PsycholAb, RI-1, RiskAb, SFSA, SSCI, SSI, SWA, SociolAb, WSA, WSI. *Bk. rev.:* Number varies, essay length, signed. *Aud.:* Ac.

This official publication of Sociologists for Women in Society presents the latest research and theory on gender and its social and structural implications. Contents include scholarly articles focused around a particular theoretical or policy issue, research reports, and book reviews. An occasional special issue covers a single topic of concern, such as "African American Women: Gender Relations, Work, and the Political Economy in the Twenty-First Century." Articles are available electronically via *ingenta* to members of institutions with print subscriptions. A highly ranked women's studies journal according to the Social Science Citation Index's Journal Citation Reports.

6708. *Gender Issues.* Formerly (until 1998): *Feminist Issues.* [ISSN: 1098-092X] 1980. q. USD 200 (Individuals, USD 68). Ed(s): Rita J Simon. Transaction Publishers, 35 Berrue Circle, Rutgers University, Piscataway, NJ 08854-8042; trans@transactionpub.com; http://www.transactionpub.com. Illus., adv. Refereed. Circ: 500. Vol. ends: Fall. Microform: PQC. Online: bigchalk; EBSCO Publishing; Florida Center for Library Automation; Gale Group; Ingenta Select; Northern Light Technology, Inc.; OCLC Online Computer Library Center, Inc.; ProQuest Information & Learning. Reprint: PQC; PSC. *Indexed:* ABS&EES, AltPI, AnthLit, CJA, FemPer, HRA, IBZ, LRI, PRA, RI-1, SFSA, SSI, SWA, SociolAb, WSA. *Bk. rev.:* 2, essay length, signed. *Aud.:* Ac.

Gender Issues publishes basic and applied research relating to gender, gender roles, and the changing roles and statuses of women throughout the industrial and developing nations of the world. It covers a broad range of topics in gender studies and feminism. Recent issues, for example, include articles on dress norms at work, the sex trade in Thailand, women in prison, how successful women lose their jobs, international adoption, and gender differences in the Canadian economy. It also includes book reviews. Full text is available via *ingenta* to members of institutions with print subscriptions.

Gender, Place and Culture. See Geography section.

6709. *Gender, Technology & Development.* [ISSN: 0971-8524] 1997. 3x/yr. INR 220 (Individuals, INR 125). Ed(s): Cecilia Ng. Sage Publications India Pvt. Ltd., M-32 Market, Greater Kailash-I, PO Box 4215, New Delhi, 110 048, India; http://www.indiasage.com/. Illus., index, adv. Sample. Refereed. Circ: 400. Vol. ends: Nov. *Indexed:* IBSS, PSA, SociolAb. *Bk. rev.:* 4, length varies, signed. *Aud.:* Ac.

This international, refereed journal focuses on gender relations and technological development in non-Western societies and cultures, particularly Asia. Its intended audience is academics and people working in development and natural resource management. In addition to scholarly articles, it includes book reviews, conference reports, and a listing of recent books on development and technology. A "People's Initiative" section profiles efforts to apply gender theory to real-world development problems. One special issue each year focuses on a theme, such as "Women and the Digital Divide" or "Gender Relations in Forest Societies." Table of contents of recent issues are available on the publisher's web site.

6710. *Gender, Work and Organization.* [ISSN: 0968-6673] 1994. bi-m. USD 654 print & online eds. Ed(s): David Knights, Jill Rubery. Blackwell Publishing Ltd., 9600 Garsington Rd, PO Box 805, Oxford, OX4 2DQ, United Kingdom; http://www.blackwellpublishing.com/. Illus., adv. Sample. Refereed. Vol. ends: No. 4. Online: EBSCO Publishing; ingenta.com; OCLC Online Computer Library Center, Inc.; RoweCom Information Quest; Swets Blackwell. *Indexed:* ErgAb, FemPer, IBSS, SWA, SociolAb. *Bk. rev.:* Number and length vary, signed. *Aud.:* Ac.

This interdisciplinary journal publishes theoretical and research articles relating to gender and work. It is concerned with "gender relations at work, the organization of gender and the gendering of organizations." It includes review articles and book reviews of international publications.

6711. *Harvard Women's Law Journal.* [ISSN: 0270-1456] 1978. a. USD 19 domestic; USD 23 Canada; USD 22 elsewhere. Ed(s): Elizabeth Bangs. Harvard University, Law School, Publications Center, Hastings Hall, Cambridge, MA 02138; hlswlj@law.harvard.edu; http://www.harvard.edu/. Adv. Circ: 900. Microform: WSH; PMC. Online: Gale Group; LexisNexis; OCLC Online Computer Library Center, Inc.; West Group; H.W. Wilson. Reprint: WSH. *Indexed:* AltPI, CLI, FemPer, ILP, LRI, PAIS, RI-1, SWA. *Bk. rev.:* Number and length vary. *Aud.:* Ac, Sa.

This law journal addresses a broad range of topics relating to gender and the law and promotes the development of "a feminist jurisprudence." Contents include academic articles analyzing feminist legal issues and essays based on personal experience. A "Recent Developments" section covers new trends while the "Law and Literature" section contains creative and academic pieces dealing with the intersection of law and literature. Issues also include case comments, notes on controversial or current topics, and book reviews.

6712. *Hastings Women's Law Journal.* [ISSN: 1061-0901] 1989. s-a. USD 25 domestic; USD 32 foreign; USD 15 newsstand/cover per issue domestic. University of California at San Francisco, Hastings College of the Law, 200 McAllister St, San Francisco, CA 94102-4978; http://www.uchastings.edu/. Adv. Circ: 600. Microform: WSH. Online: Gale Group; West Group. Reprint: WSH. *Indexed:* CLI, ILP, LRI. *Bk. rev.:* 0-1, length varies, signed. *Aud.:* Ac, Sa.

The focus of this journal is on the intersections of gender with race, class, sexual orientation, and perspectives neglected by other law reviews. It publishes articles, commentaries, essays, personal narratives, and book reviews that take a new and critical view of the issues.

6713. *Health Care for Women International.* Formerly (until 1983): *Issues in Health Care of Women.* [ISSN: 0739-9332] 1979. 10x/yr. USD 560 (Individuals, USD 154). Ed(s): Phyllis Noerager Stern. Taylor & Francis Inc, 325 Chestnut St, Suite 800, Philadelphia, PA 19016; info@taylorandfrancis.com; http://www.taylorandfrancis.com/. Illus., index, adv. Sample. Refereed. Circ: 400. Vol. ends: Nov/Dec (No. 6). Online: EBSCO Publishing; Ingenta Select; OCLC Online Computer Library Center, Inc.; RoweCom Information Quest; Swets Blackwell. Reprint: PQC; PSC. *Indexed:* CINAHL, FemPer, IBSS, PsycholAb, SFSA, SWA, SociolAb, WSI. *Bk. rev.:* 0-1, length varies, signed. *Aud.:* Ac, Sa.

This journal from the International Council on Women's Health Issues provides an interdisciplinary and multicultural perspective on health care and related topics of concern to women. Its intended audience is researchers, scholars, practitioners, and students in nursing and allied health, women's studies, and the social sciences. In addition to scholarly articles, contents include council news and a book review. A current contents alert service and recent tables of contents are available from the publisher's web site.

6714. *Hecate: an interdisciplinary journal of women's liberation.* [ISSN: 0311-4198] 1975. s-a. AUD 154 (Individuals, AUD 35). Ed(s): Carole Ferrier. Hecate Press, c/o School of English, Media Studies & Art History, University of Queensland, St Lucia, QLD 4072, Australia; http://emsah.uq.edu.au/awsr/main.html. Adv. Refereed. Circ: 2000. Online: bigchalk; EBSCO Publishing; Florida Center for Library Automation; Gale Group; Northern Light Technology, Inc.; OCLC Online Computer Library Center, Inc.; ProQuest Information & Learning; RMIT Publishing; SoftLine Information. *Indexed:* AltPI, BEL&L, FemPer, IBZ, SWA, WSA, WSI. *Aud.:* Ga, Ac.

This international journal offers a radical feminist and Marxist perspective on women's experiences in Australia and throughout the world. Contents include research articles, literary analysis, interviews, editorials, creative works, and graphics. The journal also publishes the annual *Hecate's Australian Women's Book Review.*

6715. *Herizons: women's news & feminist views.* Formerly (until 1981): *Manitoba women's newspaper.* [ISSN: 0711-7485] 1979. 4x/yr. CND 30 (Individuals, CND 24.99; CND 5.75 newsstand/cover per issue). Ed(s): Penni Mitchell. Herizons, PO Box 128, Winnipeg, MB R3C 2G1, Canada; herizons@escape.ca; http://www.cmpa.ca/f6.html. Illus., adv. Circ: 4500. Online: EBSCO Publishing; Florida Center for Library Automation; Gale Group; Micromedia ProQuest; Northern Light Technology, Inc.; OCLC Online Computer Library Center, Inc.; SoftLine Information. *Indexed:* AltPI, CBCARef, CPerI, CWI, FemPer, GendWatch, WSI. *Bk. rev.:* 4, 550 words, signed. *Aud.:* Ga, Ac.

This popular Canadian feminist magazine covers topics of interest to women worldwide. A recent issue, for example, includes an interview with Arab feminist Nahla Abdo and a feature article on why lesbians batter. Other sections cover news, opinion, art, and literature. Selected articles from the current and previous issues are posted on the magazine's web site.

6716. *Hypatia: a journal of feminist philosophy.* [ISSN: 0887-5367] 1986. q. USD 102; USD 142.80 combined subscription. Ed(s): Nancy Tuana, Laurie J. Shrage. Indiana University Press, 601 N Morton St, Bloomington, IN 47404; hypatia@cfrvm.cfr.usf.edu; http://www.indiana.edu/~iupress. Illus., adv. Sample. Refereed. Circ: 1700. Vol. ends: Fall. Online: bigchalk; Chadwyck-Healey Incorporated; EBSCO Publishing; Florida Center for Library Automation; Gale Group; LexisNexis; OCLC Online Computer Library Center, Inc.; Project MUSE; ProQuest Information & Learning; RoweCom Information Quest; SoftLine Information; H.W. Wilson. Reprint: PSC. *Indexed:* ABS&EES, AltPI, BHA, CWI, FemPer, GendWatch, HumInd, IBZ, MLA-IB, PSA, PhilInd, RI-1, SWA, SociolAb, WSA, WSI. *Bk. rev.:* 3-5, 1,000-1,500 words, signed. *Aud.:* Ac.

This journal positions itself at "the intersection of philosophy and women's studies" and strives to promote and develop feminist discourse in philosophy. It is also concerned with reclaiming the work of women philosophers. Special issues address themes such as "Feminist Philosophy and the Problem of Evil" and "Feminist Philosophies of Love and Work." Contents also include book reviews.

6717. *Iris: A Journal about Women.* [ISSN: 0896-1301] 1980. s-a. USD 40 (Individuals, USD 9). Ed(s): Eileen Boris. University of Virginia, Women's Center, PO Box 323 HSC, Charlottesville, VA 22908; minerva.acc.virginia.edu/~womenctr/pubs/iris/irishome.html. Illus., adv. Refereed. Circ: 2500 Paid. Vol. ends: Summer/Fall. *Indexed:* CWI, FemPer, GendWatch, WSA. *Bk. rev.:* 2-12, length varies, signed. *Aud.:* Ga, Ac.

Iris is sponsored by the Women's Center and the Studies in Gender and Women program at the University of Virginia. Each issue includes critical essays, news articles, interviews, fiction, poetry, art, and photography representing a variety of feminist perspectives and geared toward "young women who want to make a difference in the world around them." Contributors are writers, artists, and scholars from throughout the world. The editorial staff consists of student interns. Recent theme-based issues feature "Emerging Voices" and "Women in Action."

6718. *Journal of Feminist Family Therapy: an international forum.* [ISSN: 0895-2833] 1989. q. USD 415. Ed(s): Toni Schindler Zimmerman. Haworth Press, Inc., 10 Alice St, Binghamton, NY 13904-1580; getinfo@haworthpressinc.com; http://www.haworthpressinc.com. Illus., adv. Sample. Refereed. Circ: 306 Paid. Vol. ends: No. 4. Microform: PQC. Reprint: HAW. *Indexed:* ASSIA, AltPI, CWI, FemPer, GendWatch, IBZ, IMFL, SFSA, SWA, SWR&A, SociolAb, WSA. *Bk. rev.:* 4-5, 200-1,000 words, signed. *Aud.:* Ac, Sa.

This journal offers a feminist perspective on the theory and practice of family therapy. It publishes theoretical, research, and clinical articles. It also includes book reviews; letters, comments, and discussion; interviews; and historical documents. Tables of contents are available online at the publisher's web site.

6719. *Journal of Feminist Studies in Religion.* [ISSN: 8755-4178] 1985. s-a. USD 50 (Individuals, USD 22). Ed(s): Elizabeth Schussler Fiorenza, Kwok M Pui-Lan. Society of Biblical Literature, P.O. Box 2243, Williston, VT 05495-2243; sblexec@sbl-site.org; http://www.sbl-site.org. Illus., adv. Refereed. Circ: 1000 Paid. *Indexed:* ArtHuCI, FemPer, HumInd, NTA, R&TA, RI-1, SSCI, WSA. *Bk. rev.:* essay length, signed. *Aud.:* Ac, Sa.

This interdisciplinary, feminist journal in religious studies is associated with Harvard Divinity School. Contents include research articles, review articles, reports of feminist projects related to religion, opinion pieces, and roundtable discussions. Special sections or entire issues may be devoted to important theoretical issues or themes. Useful for public and church library collections as well as academic collections in women's studies, philosophy, and religious studies.

6720. *Journal of Gender Studies.* [ISSN: 0958-9236] 1992. 3x/yr. GBP 213 (Individuals, GBP 26). Ed(s): Jenny Hockey, Jenny Wolmark. Carfax Publishing Ltd., 4 Park Sq, Milton Park, Abingdon, OX14 4RN, United Kingdom; enquiry@tandf.co.uk; http://www.tandf.co.uk/. Illus., index, adv. Sample. Refereed. Vol. ends: Nov. Online: bigchalk; EBSCO Publishing; Gale Group; Ingenta Select; LexisNexis; Northern Light Technology, Inc.; OCLC Online Computer Library Center, Inc.; ProQuest Information & Learning; RoweCom Information Quest; Swets Blackwell. Reprint: PSC. *Indexed:* ASSIA, CWI, FemPer, IBSS, PSA, RI-1, SSCI, SSI, SWA, SWR&A, SociolAb. *Bk. rev.:* 8-33, 300-1,500 words, signed. *Aud.:* Ac.

This interdisciplinary, feminist journal uses gender as a framework for analysis in the natural and social sciences, the arts, and popular culture. Articles come from international sources and diverse backgrounds. They provide a variety of perspectives on social and cultural definitions of gender and gender relations. Book reviews are also included. An article alert service and tables of contents are available online from the publisher.

6721. *Journal of Interdisciplinary Gender Studies.* [ISSN: 1325-1848] 1995. s-a. AUD 80 (Individuals, AUD 40). Ed(s): Anne Sullivan, Hilary M Carey. University of Newcastle, Department of Sociology and Anthropology, Faculty of Arts and Social Sciences, Newcastle, NSW 2308, Australia; mgams@cc.newcastle.edu.au; http://www.newcastle.edu.au/department/hi/jigs/. Online: RMIT Publishing. *Bk. rev.:* 800—1200 words, signed. *Aud.:* Ac.

The origins of this refereed journal lie in an annual gender studies conference at the University of Newcastle in New South Wales, Australia. The journal's focus is on the study of gender within and across disciplines. It features contributions from new and established scholars. Articles are concerned with gay and lesbian issues, race, ethnicity, sexuality, and masculinity as well as with women. Contents also include book reviews. Although indexing of this publication is limited, contents information is available online from the journal's web site.

Journal of Lesbian Studies. See Lesbian, Gay, Bisexual, and Transgender section.

Journal of Women and Aging. See Aging section.

6722. *Journal of Women's History.* [ISSN: 1042-7961] 1989. q. USD 90 domestic; USD 97 in Canada & Mexico; USD 103.20 elsewhere. Ed(s): Leila J Rupp. Indiana University Press, 601 N Morton St, Bloomington, IN 47404. Illus., adv. Sample. Refereed. Circ: 1600. Vol. ends: Winter. Microform: PQC. Online: bigchalk; Chadwyck-Healey Incorporated; EBSCO Publishing; Florida Center for Library Automation; Gale Group; LexisNexis; Northern Light Technology, Inc.; OCLC Online Computer Library Center, Inc.; Project MUSE; ProQuest Information & Learning; RoweCom Information Quest; SoftLine Information; Swets Blackwell; H.W. Wilson. Reprint: PSC. *Indexed:* ABS&EES, AltPI, AmH&L, ArtHuCI, CWI, FLI, FemPer, GendWatch, HumInd, IBSS, PSA, SWA, SociolAb, WSA, WSI. *Bk. rev.:* 2-4, essay length; 23-120 brief abstracts. *Aud.:* Ac.

This scholarly journal features theoretical and research articles about women and gender throughout the course of world history. It welcomes a variety of feminist perspectives. Contents also include commentary on historical documents, review essays, book reviews, letters to the editor, and a listing of dissertations in women's history. One recent issue includes an important retrospective analysis of the cult of true womanhood.

6723. *Legacy (Lincoln): a journal of American Women Writers.* [ISSN: 0748-4321] 1984. s-a. USD 55 (Individuals, USD 35; Students, USD 25). Ed(s): Sharon M Harris, Karen Dandurand. University of Nebraska Press, 233 N 8th St, Lincoln, NE 68588-0255; pressmail@unl.edu;

http://www.nebraskapress.unl.edu. Adv. Refereed. Reprint: PQC. *Indexed:* AmH&L, ArtHuCI, BRI, CBRI, FemPer, IBZ, MLA-IB, SSCI, SWA, WSA. *Bk. rev.:* 6, 800 words, signed. *Aud.:* Ac.

The journal of the Society for the Study of American Women Writers examines the work of American women writers and the literary tradition that developed around it. Contents include research articles, profiles of women authors and excerpts from their writings, archival materials, and book reviews. Recommended for academic collections.

6724. *Meridians (Middletown): feminism, race, transnationalism.* 2000. s-a. USD 85 (Individuals, USD 30; USD 20 domestic students). Ed(s): Myriam J A Chancy. Wesleyan University Press, 110 Mt Vernon St, Middletown, CT 06459; http://www.wesleyan.edu/wespress/. Refereed. *Aud.:* Ga, Ac.

Meridians is cosponsored by Smith College and Wesleyan University and offers valuable insight into the interplay of feminism, race, and transnationalism in today's world. It publishes interdisciplinary "scholarship and creative work by and about women of color in the U.S. and international contexts." Contents include articles, essays, multivoiced dialogues, interviews, reports, creative works, and media reviews.

6725. *Michigan Feminist Studies.* Former titles (until 1987): *New Occasional Papers in Women's Studies;* (until 1983): *Michigan Occasional Paper;* Supersedes (in 1978): *University of Michigan Papers in Women's Studies.* [ISSN: 1055-856X] 1974. a. USD 25 (Individuals, USD 10). Ed(s): Cari Carpenter, Karen Miller. University of Michigan, Women's Studies Department, 1122 Lane Hall, 204 S State St, Ann Arbor, MI 48109-1290; mfseditors@umich.edu. Illus., adv. Refereed. Circ: 500. *Indexed:* FemPer, WSA. *Bk. rev.:* 0-4, essay length, signed. *Aud.:* Ac.

This interdisciplinary journal from University of Michigan graduate students explores a variety of theoretical and experiential perspectives on gender. A recent special issue on "deviance" focuses on individuals and behaviors outside traditional moral codes and family structures. Limited indexing.

6726. *Michigan Journal of Gender & Law.* [ISSN: 1095-8835] 1994. s-a. USD 30 domestic; USD 35 foreign. University of Michigan, Law School, 625 South State St, Ann Arbor, MI 48109-1215. Reprint: WSH. *Bk. rev.:* signed. *Aud.:* Ac.

This feminist publication seeks to expand legal discourse by focusing on "how gender and related issues of race, class, sexual orientation, and culture impact the lives of men and women." Topics of recent articles include sexual harassment, domestic violence against household workers, and sexual regulation through welfare law. Contributors include legal scholars, social scientists, practitioners, students, and others.

Mothering. See Family and Marriage section.

6727. *Ms.* [ISSN: 0047-8318] 1972. bi-m. USD 35 domestic; USD 42 Canada; USD 78 elsewhere. Ed(s): Gloria Steinem. Liberty Media for Women, L.L.C., 1600 Wilson Blvd, Ste 801, Arlington, VA 22209; info@msmagazine.com; http://www.msmagazine.com. Illus., adv. Circ: 250000. Vol. ends: Nov/Dec. Microform: PQC. Online: bigchalk; Gale Group; OCLC Online Computer Library Center, Inc.; ProQuest Information & Learning. *Indexed:* ABS&EES, BEL&L, BRD, BRI, CBRI, ConsI, FLI, FemPer, LRI, MRD, MagInd, RGPR, SWA, WSA, WSI. *Bk. rev.:* 8, 124-300 words, signed. *Aud.:* Hs, Ga, Ac.

This well known, widely circulated magazine provides feature articles on feminist issues and concerns. It covers national and international news about women and gender. It publishes news about the arts and original fiction and poetry. It promotes organization and activism on behalf of feminism, peace, environmentalism, workers rights, and a variety of other issues. Recommended for public and academic libraries.

6728. *N W S A Journal.* [ISSN: 1040-0656] 1988. 3x/yr. USD 125 (Individuals, USD 35). Ed(s): Margaret McFadden. Indiana University Press, 601 N Morton St, Bloomington, IN 47404. Illus., adv. Refereed. Circ: 1200. Online: Chadwyck-Healey Incorporated; EBSCO Publishing; Florida Center for Library Automation; Gale Group; LexisNexis; OCLC Online Computer Library Center, Inc.; Project MUSE; ProQuest Information & Learning; RoweCom Information Quest; SoftLine Information; Swets Blackwell; H.W. Wilson. Reprint: PSC. *Indexed:* ASSIA, AbAn, AmH&L, AmHI, BRI, CBRI, CWI, FemPer, GendWatch, PAIS, PSA, SSI, SWA, SociolAb, WSA, WSI. *Bk. rev.:* 9-12, brief and essay length, signed. *Aud.:* Ac.

The journal of the National Women's Studies Association publishes interdisciplinary, multicultural scholarship in women's studies. It seeks to connect feminist scholarship and theory with activism and teaching. In addition to research articles, its contents include articles about the theory and teaching of women's studies and reviews of books, teaching materials, and films. Recent special issues include "25 Years of NWSA" and "Feminist Disability Studies."

6729. *National N O W Times.* Formerly: *Do It N O W.* [ISSN: 0149-4740] 1968. q. Non-members, USD 35. Ed(s): Patricia Ireland. National Organization for Women, 733 15th St NW 2nd FL, Washington, DC 20005-2112; now@now.org; http://www.now.org/nnt/nntindex.html. Illus., adv. Circ: 250000. Vol. ends: Oct (No. 4). *Indexed:* AltPI. *Bk. rev.:* Number varies, 500 words, signed. *Aud.:* Ga, Ac.

The official newsletter of the National Organization of Women provides news about feminist issues and activists' achievements. It offers political commentary, conference reports, and notes on NOW chapter activities. It also includes book reviews, illustrations, and advertising. Full text of current and past issues is available from NOW's web site.

New Moon. See Children section.

6730. *Nin: journal of gender studies in antiquity.* [ISSN: 1567-8474] a. USD 84 print & online eds. (Individuals, EUR 42 print & online eds.). Ed(s): J Asher-Greve, A K Guinan. Brill Academic Publishers, Inc., PO Box 9000, Leiden, 2300 PA, Netherlands; cs@brill.nl; http://www.brill.nl. *Bk. rev.:* Number and length vary. *Aud.:* Ac.

This journal from the Women's Association of Ancient Near Eastern Studies (WANES) examines gender issues in the ancient Near East using the resources of history, literature, and the arts. Research articles address issues such as women and war, mourners' laments in ancient Egypt, and birth incantations in Aeschylus. Issues also include review essays, book reviews, and conference notes. Full text is available online through Ingenta Select.

6731. *Nora: Nordic journal of women's studies.* [ISSN: 0803-8740] 1993. 3x/yr. GBP 53 (Individuals, GBP 33). Ed(s): Susanne V. Knudsen, Bente Meyer. Taylor & Francis A S, Cort Adelersgt. 17, Solli, PO Box 2562, Oslo, 0202, Norway; journals@tandf.no. Illus., adv. Sample. Refereed. Online: EBSCO Publishing; Ingenta Select; OCLC Online Computer Library Center, Inc.; RoweCom Information Quest; Swets Blackwell. Reprint: PSC. *Indexed:* ASSIA, FemPer, IBZ, SWA. *Bk. rev.:* 6, 700 words-essay length, signed. *Aud.:* Ac.

While focusing on women's experiences in Nordic countries both historically and in the present, this journal is also international in outlook and offers discussions of interest to feminist scholars everywhere. A recent issue, for example, features articles offering a gender or feminist perspective on the body and its representations. In addition to research articles, contents include review essays and short communications. An article alert service and table of contents are available through the publisher's web site.

6732. *Off Our Backs: a women's news journal.* [ISSN: 0030-0071] 1970. 6x/yr. USD 40 (Individuals, USD 25; Students, USD 21). Ed(s): Jennie Ruby. Off Our Backs, Inc., 2337B 18th St, N W, Washington, DC 20009-2003; offourbacks@cs.com; http://www.offourbacks.org/. Illus., index, adv. Circ: 15000. Vol. ends: Dec. Microform: PQC. Online: EBSCO Publishing; Florida Center for Library Automation; Gale Group; LexisNexis; Northern Light Technology, Inc.; OCLC Online Computer Library Center, Inc.; ProQuest Information & Learning; SoftLine Information. *Indexed:* AltPI, BRI, CBRI, CWI, FemPer, GendWatch, SWA, WSA, WSI. *Bk. rev.:* 1-5, 1,000-2,000 words. *Aud.:* Ga, Ac.

This long-running feminist newspaper covers news affecting women and the women's movement worldwide. It serves women as a forum for discussion of feminist ideas and theory and as a resource for information on feminist and lesbian culture. It seeks to educate the public about women's issues around the world. Special features include reviews of books, theatre, film, television, and music and a comic strip called "Dykes to Watch Out For." Selected articles from back issues are available at the newspaper's web site.

Psychology of Women Quarterly. See Psychology section.

6733. ***The Public Eye (Somerville).*** [ISSN: 1094-8759] 1977. 3x/yr. USD 39 (Individuals, USD 29; Non-profit organizations, USD 29). Ed(s): Judith Glaubman. Political Research Associates, 1310 Broadway, Ste 201, Somerville, MA 02144-1731; pra@igc.org; http://www.publiceye.org/. Online: ProQuest Information & Learning; SoftLine Information. *Indexed:* AltPI. *Bk. rev.:* 20, brief annotations. *Aud.:* Ga, Ac.

This newsletter from the independent, nonprofit Political Research Associates monitors the political activities of the political right. Each issue contains documented research and analysis about threats to open, democratic, and pluralistic values including, but not limited to, antifeminist policies and activities. The publisher's web site provides full text of the current issue and selected articles from previous issues.

6734. ***Race, Gender & Class: an interdisciplinary journal.*** Formerly (until 1994): *Race, Sex and Class.* [ISSN: 1082-8354] 1993. q. USD 40 (Individuals, USD 24). Ed(s): Jean Ait Belkhir. Southern University at New Orleans, Department of Social Sciences, 6400 Press Dr, New Orleans, LA 70126; jbelkhir@suno.edu; http://www.suno.edu/sunorgc. Circ: 1200. *Indexed:* AltPI, FemPer, GendWatch, HEA. *Bk. rev.:* signed. *Aud.:* Ac.

This interdisciplinary, multicultural journal from Southern University of New Orleans publishes articles and review essays focusing on issues of race, gender, and class in society. It also publishes proceedings of the annual Race, Gender, and Class Conference. The journal aims to publish materials that "have practical implications, direct or indirect, for education" and "that are accessible to undergraduates in introductory and general education classes." Unusual for its focus on race and class. Limited coverage in indexes.

6735. ***Resources for Feminist Research.*** Formerly: *Canadian Newsletter of Research on Women.* [ISSN: 0707-8412] 1972. 2x/yr. CND 82.39 (Individuals, CND 38; CND 15 newsstand/cover per issue). Ed(s): Philinda Masters. University of Toronto, Ontario Institute for Studies in Education, 252 Bloor St W, Toronto, ON M5S 1V6, Canada; rfrdrf@oise.utoronto.ca; http://www.oise.utoronto.ca/rfr. Illus., index, adv. Refereed. Circ: 2000. Vol. ends: Winter. Microform: MML. Online: Florida Center for Library Automation; Gale Group; LexisNexis; Micromedia ProQuest; OCLC Online Computer Library Center, Inc. *Indexed:* AgeL, AmH&L, CBCARef, CEI, CPerI, FemPer, HumInd, SWA, SociolAb, WSA. *Bk. rev.:* 5-20, length varies, signed. *Aud.:* Ac.

This is a bilingual (English/French) journal from the University of Toronto. It publishes articles addressing issues in feminist research and theory in two theme-based double issues a year. These offer new feminist research and explore issues in women's studies. Recent issues focus on "Feminist Cultural Production" and "The Impact of Gender across the Curriculum." Each issue includes research articles and discussion papers or reports as well as book reviews.

Sex Roles. See Sociology and Social Work/General section.

Sexualities. See Sexuality section.

6736. ***Sexualities, Evolution & Gender: an international journal of feminist and evolutionary standpoints.*** Formerly: *Psychology, Evolution and Gender.* [ISSN: 1479-2508] 1999. 3x/yr. GBP 236 (Individuals, GBP 57). Ed(s): Paula Nicolson, David Buss. Routledge, 11 New Fetter Ln, London, EC4P 4EE, United Kingdom; journals@routldege.com; http://journals.routledge.com. Adv. Refereed. Online: EBSCO Publishing; Ingenta Select; OCLC Online Computer Library Center, Inc.; RoweCom Information Quest; Swets Blackwell. Reprint: PSC. *Indexed:* ExcerpMed. *Aud.:* Ac.

This journal publishes empirical and theoretical papers on the psychology of gender and gender relations. Regular features include a "Debate" section presenting diverse views on topical issues such as the glass ceiling and a "Reviews" section featuring review essays. Occasional issues feature a guest editor and a set of papers on a theme such as homosexuality. Full text is available via *ingenta* to members of institutions with print subscriptions.

6737. ***Signs: Journal of Women in Culture and Society.*** [ISSN: 0097-9740] 1975. q. USD 220 print & online eds. (Individuals, USD 44 print & online eds.; Members, USD 34 print & online eds.). Ed(s): Sandra Harding, Kathryn Norberg. University of Chicago Press, Journals Division, PO Box 37005, Chicago, IL 60637; subscriptions@press.uchicago.edu; http://www.journals.uchicago.edu. Illus., adv. Refereed. Circ: 3000 Paid. Vol. ends: Summer. Microform: PMC; PQC. Online: EBSCO Publishing; Florida Center for Library Automation; Gale Group; OCLC Online Computer Library Center, Inc.; ProQuest Information & Learning. Reprint: ISI; PQC; PSC. *Indexed:* ABCPolSci, ABS&EES, ASSIA, AgeL, AmH&L, AmHI, AnthLit, ArtHuCI, BAS, BRI, CBRI, CIJE, CommAb, FemPer, IBSS, IBZ, IMFL, IPSA, MLA-IB, PSA, PsycholAb, RI-1, SSCI, SSI, SWA, SociolAb, WSA, WSI. *Bk. rev.:* 2-12, 1,200-2,000 words, signed. *Aud.:* Ac.

This established journal publishes articles on familiar and emergent areas of women's studies scholarship. Contents reflect the interdisciplinary nature of the field and include research articles, essays, review essays, book reviews, and notes. Some theme issues are published. Tables of contents are available on the publisher's web site.

6738. ***Social Politics: international studies in gender, state, and society.*** [ISSN: 1072-4745] 1994. 3x/yr. GBP 78. Ed(s): Sonya Michel, Ann Orloff. Oxford University Press, Great Clarendon St, Oxford, OX2 6DP, United Kingdom; jnl.orders@oup.co.uk; http://www3.oup.co.uk/jnls. Illus., index, adv. Refereed. Circ: 850. Vol. ends: No. 3. Microform: PQC. Online: HighWire Press; ingenta.com; Project MUSE; Swets Blackwell. Reprint: PSC; SWZ. *Indexed:* AmH&L, FemPer, IBZ, PAIS, PSA, SSCI, SWA, SociolAb. *Bk. rev.:* essay length, signed. *Aud.:* Ac, Sa.

This scholarly journal applies a feminist and gender perspective to the analysis of social policy, the state, and society. It is interdisciplinary and multicultural in scope. Articles in one recent issue deal with themes of gender and globalization, gender and comparative welfare analysis, and gender and discourses about the state. Another issue provides a forum for discussion of gender and welfare. The publisher's web site provides tables of contents, article abstracts, and an e-mail contents alert service.

6739. ***Southern California Review of Law and Women's Studies.*** [ISSN: 1088-3525] 1991. s-a. USD 25. Ed(s): Ann LaClair, Diara Fleming. University of Southern California, Law School, University Park, Los Angeles, CA 90089-0071; http://www.usc.edu/dept/law/rlaws/index.html. Microform: WSH. Reprint: WSH. *Indexed:* ABS&EES, CLI, ILP. *Bk. rev.:* 0-1, length varies, signed. *Aud.:* Ac, Sa.

This journal from the University of Southern California Law School examines the relationship of women and the law from an interdisciplinary and multicultural perspective. Contents include articles, legal notes, and briefs. Tables of contents are available online at the journal's web site. Useful for law libraries and larger academic collections

6740. ***Studies in Gender and Sexuality.*** [ISSN: 1524-0657] 2000. q. USD 165 (Individuals, USD 48.50; USD 15 per issue in US & Canada). Ed(s): Ken Corbett. Analytic Press, Inc., 101 West St, Hillsdale, NJ 07642; TAP@analyticpress.com; http://www.analyticpress.com. Adv. Refereed. *Indexed:* FemPer, SociolAb. *Aud.:* Ac.

Studies in Gender and Sexuality is directed toward clinicians, developmental researchers, and academics in psychology, cultural anthropology, family history, feminism, gender studies, queer studies, social history, sociology, and women's studies. It seeks to provide a variety of perspectives, to promote discussion, and to develop new insights into issues relating to gender and sexuality. Contents include research articles and roundtable discussion papers. Tables of contents are available online at the publisher's web site.

6741. ***Tulsa Studies in Women's Literature.*** [ISSN: 0732-7730] 1982. s-a. USD 14 (Individuals, USD 12; USD 7 newsstand/cover per issue domestic). Ed(s): Holly A Laird. University of Tulsa, 600 S College Ave, Tulsa, OK 74104; linda-frazier@utulsa.edu; http://www.utulsa.edu/tswl/tswlhome.html. Illus., index, adv. Refereed. Circ: 1000. Microform: PQC. Online: Gale Group; JSTOR (Web-based Journal Archive). *Indexed:* AmH&L, ArtHuCI, BRI, CBRI, FemPer, HumInd, MLA-IB, SSCI, SWA, WSA, WSI. *Bk. rev.:* 10, essay length, signed. *Aud.:* Ac.

This journal publishes articles, notes, archival research, and reviews relating to women and writing throughout history. Articles may be literary, historical, or theoretical. The editors welcome work by both new and established scholars. A recent special issue focuses on the theme "Feminism and Time." Contents of the current volume and a 20-year index are available on the journal's web site.

6742. ***Violence Against Women: an international and interdisciplinary journal.*** [ISSN: 1077-8012] 1995. m. GBP 482 print & online eds. in Europe, Middle East, Africa & Australasia. Ed(s): Claire M Renzetti. Sage Publications, Inc., 2455 Teller Rd, Thousand Oaks, CA 91320; info@sagepub.com; http://www.sagepub.com. Illus., adv. Sample. Refereed. Vol. ends: Dec. *Indexed:* ASG, ASSIA, CJA, CJPI, FemPer, H&SSA, HRA, RiskAb, SFSA, SSCI, SSI, SUSA, SWA, SociolAb. *Bk. rev.:* 2, essay length, signed. *Aud.:* Ga, Ac, Sa.

This journal publishes empirical research and cross-cultural and historical analyses of violence against women and girls. It is concerned with both well-known and lesser-known forms of violence including sexual assault, domestic violence, rape, pornography, lesbian battery, sexual harassment, hate crimes, and female circumcision. It seeks to promote dialogue among people of diverse backgrounds working in various fields and disciplines. Some issues are thematic. The journal also includes book reviews. Articles are available electronically via *ingenta* to members of institutions with a print subscription. The publisher also offers a contents alert service.

6743. ***W I N News: all the news that is fit to print by, for, about women.*** [ISSN: 0145-7985] 1975. q. USD 48 (Individuals, USD 35). Ed(s): Fran P Hosken. Women's International Network, 187 Grant St, Lexington, MA 02173-2140; winnews@igc.org; http://feminist.com/win.htm. Illus., index, adv. Circ: 800 Paid. Vol. ends: Autumn (No. 4). Microform: PQC. Online: bigchalk; EBSCO Publishing; Florida Center for Library Automation; Gale Group; OCLC Online Computer Library Center, Inc.; ProQuest Information & Learning; SoftLine Information. *Indexed:* EIP, FemPer, GendWatch, SWA. *Aud.:* Ga, Ac, Sa.

W I N News is an open, participatory newsletter from the Women's International News Network. This organization seeks to foster communication by and about women without the constraints of a male-dominated international press. The quarterly newsletter reports on the status of women and women's rights around the world for a general, international audience. Regular features report on activities at the United Nations, women's health, women and development, violence against women, women and the media, and reports from countries around the world. A recent topic is female genital mutilation. A useful source for activists and others concerned with women in a global context.

Women & Criminal Justice. See Criminology and Law Enforcement section.

6744. ***Women & Environments International Magazine.*** Former titles (until 2001): *W E International Magazine;* (until 1998): *Women and Environments;* (until 1980): *Women and Environments International Newsletter.* [ISSN: 1499-1993] 1976. s-a. CND 35 (Individuals, CND 22). Ed(s): Reggie Modlich. Institute for Women's Studies and Gender Studies, New College, University of Toronto, Toronto, ON M5S 1C6, Canada; we.mag@utoronto.ca; http://www.weimag.com. Illus., adv. Circ: 1000 Paid. Microform: CML. Online: EBSCO Publishing; OCLC Online Computer Library Center, Inc.; ProQuest Information & Learning; SoftLine Information; H.W. Wilson. *Indexed:* AIAP, AltPI, CBCARef, CPerI, FemPer, SFSA, SSI, SWA, WSA, WSI. *Bk. rev.:* 1-4, 175-400 words. *Aud.:* Ga, Ac.

Formerly *W E International Magazine*, this magazine explores women's multiple relationships with their environments from a feminist perspective. It is published by the Institute for Women's Studies, New College, University of Toronto. It also provides a forum for discussions among academics, professionals, and activists. Full text of the current issue and tables of contents for back issues are available on the journal's web site.

6745. ***Women & Health: the multidisciplinary journal of women's health issues.*** [ISSN: 0363-0242] 1976. q. 2 vols./yr. USD 480. Ed(s): Jeanne M Stellman. Haworth Press, Inc., 10 Alice St, Binghamton, NY 13904-1580; getinfo@haworthpressinc.com; http://www.haworthpressinc.com. Illus., adv. Sample. Refereed. Circ: 596 Paid. Vol. ends: No. 4. Microform: PQC. Online: Gale Group. Reprint: HAW; ISI. *Indexed:* AbAn, AgeL, AltPI, BAS, BiolAb, BiolDig, CINAHL, CJA, CWI, DSA, ExcerpMed, FemPer, GSI, GendWatch, H&SSA, HEA, IBZ, IMFL, IndMed, MCR, PAIS, PEI, PsycholAb, RiskAb, SFSA, SSCI, SSI, SWA, SWR&A, SociolAb, WAE&RSA, WSA, WSI. *Bk. rev.:* 8-12, length varies, signed. *Aud.:* Ac, Sa.

Amid ongoing controversies surrounding equitable funding and support for medical research about women and gender equity in health care services, this journal is an important resource for the most current scholarly international information for both health care practitioners and researchers. Some issues are theme-based. Topics include the economics of health care for women, health problems associated with sexual harassment, health services for the disabled, and ethnic, class, and gender factors for specific diseases. In contrast to traditional medicine's reactionary approach to disease, *Women & Health* focuses upon prevention and early diagnosis, which can significantly improve the quality of women's lives. Highly recommended for academic collections and medical libraries.

6746. ***Women & Politics (Binghamton): a quarterly journal of research & policy studies.*** [ISSN: 0195-7732] 1980. q. USD 485. Ed(s): Karen O'Connor, Sarah E. Brewer. Haworth Press, Inc., 10 Alice St, Binghamton, NY 13904-1580; getinfo@haworthpressinc.com; http://www.haworthpressinc.com. Illus., adv. Sample. Refereed. Circ: 566 Paid. Vol. ends: No. 4. Microform: PQC. Online: Gale Group. Reprint: HAW. *Indexed:* ABCPolSci, ABS&EES, AgeL, AltPI, AmH&L, ArtHuCI, CWI, CommAb, ExcerpMed, FemPer, IBZ, IPSA, LRI, PAIS, PSA, SSCI, SSI, SWA, SWR&A, SociolAb, WSA. *Bk. rev.:* 5-14, 600 words–essay length, signed. *Aud.:* Ac, Sa.

This academic journal publishes research and theoretical articles about women's roles in all aspects of politics including political philosophy, international relations, and American and comparative politics. It is also concerned with the impact of politics on women's lives. Book reviews are included. Occasional special issues may be devoted to single themes such as "Mifepristone [RU 486]." Tables of contents and a contents alert service are available from the publisher's web site.

6747. ***Women & Therapy: a feminist quarterly.*** Formerly: *Women - Counseling Therapy and Mental Health Services.* [ISSN: 0270-3149] 1982. q. USD 450. Ed(s): Ellyn Kaschak, Doris Howard. Haworth Press, Inc., 10 Alice St, Binghamton, NY 13904-1580; getinfo@haworthpressinc.com; http://www.haworthpressinc.com. Illus., adv. Sample. Refereed. Circ: 433 Paid. Vol. ends: No. 4. Microform: PQC. Online: Gale Group; LexisNexis; Northern Light Technology, Inc.; ProQuest Information & Learning. Reprint: HAW. *Indexed:* ABS&EES, AgeL, AltPI, BiolAb, CWI, FemPer, GendWatch, HEA, IBZ, IMFL, SFSA, SSCI, SWA, SWR&A, SociolAb, WSA, WSI. *Bk. rev.:* 0-7, 900 words, signed. *Aud.:* Ac, Sa.

The intended audience of this publication is feminist therapists, health practitioners, and other feminist researchers. The journal provides a feminist perspective on women and the experience of therapy. Its concerns include the process of therapy with female clients, problems affecting women more than men, the influence of women's roles on therapy, and the needs of special groups of women. The contents include empirical, clinical, and theoretical articles. Some issues offer several articles on a single theme such as "Violence in the Lives of Black Women." Tables of contents, abstracts, and a contents alert service are available from the publisher's web site.

6748. *Women's Health Issues.* [ISSN: 1049-3867] 1991. bi-m. Individuals, USD 131. Ed(s): Dr. Warren H. Pearse. Elsevier Inc., 360 Park Ave. S, New York, NY 10010-1710; usinfo-f@elsevier.com; http://www.elsevier.com. Illus., adv. Refereed. Circ: 3000 Paid. Vol. ends: Nov (No. 11). Microform: PQC. Online: ingenta.com; ScienceDirect; Swets Blackwell. *Indexed:* AgeL, CINAHL, ExcerpMed, IndMed, SSCI, SWA, SociolAb. *Aud.:* Ac, Sa.

This scholarly journal from the Jacobs Institute of Women's Health publishes research articles, conference reports, and editorials and opinion pieces on issues relating to women's health and wellness. Concerns include gender differences in specific diseases or conditions and the socioeconomic, ethnic, and cultural factors affecting health. For health professionals, policy makers, social scientists, and others.

6749. *Women's History Review.* [ISSN: 0961-2025] 1992. q. GBP 270 (Individuals, GBP 42). Ed(s): June Purvis. Triangle Journals Ltd., Attn: Roger Osborn-King, Publisher, PO Box 65, Wallingford, OX10 0YG, United Kingdom; subscriptions@triangle.co.uk; http://www.triangle.co.uk. Illus., index, adv. Sample. Refereed. Vol. ends: Dec. *Indexed:* AmH&L, ArtHuCI, BrHumI, FemPer, HumInd, IBZ, PSA, SWA, SociolAb, WSI. *Bk. rev.:* 5-8, length varies, signed. *Aud.:* Ac.

This journal provides an interdisciplinary, feminist perspective on women and gender relations in history. Coverage, while heavily British, also includes U.S., European, and world history. Useful features include the "Viewpoints" section featuring experiential and opinion pieces. The journal also includes review essays, and book reviews. Tables of contents and full text of older articles are available on the publisher's web site.

6750. *Women's Policy Journal of Harvard, John F. Kennedy School of Government.* 2001. a. USD 40. Ed(s): Laura Manjarrez, Danielle Levine. Harvard University, John F. Kennedy School of Government, 79 John F. Kennedy St., Cambridge, MA 02138; http://www.ksg.harvard.edu. Adv. *Aud.:* Ga, Ac.

Each issue of this journal from Harvard's John F. Kennedy School of Government is organized around a theme or issue in public policy that affects women. Contributions from academic experts, prominent practitioners, and selected graduate students are presented with a view to promoting discourse and improving decision making.

6751. *The Women's Quarterly: the journal of the Independent Women's Forum.* [ISSN: 1079-6622] 1994. q. USD 30 domestic; USD 36 foreign. Ed(s): Charlotte Hays. Independent Women's Forum, 1726 M Street NW., Ste 1001, Washington, DC 20036; info@jwf.org; http://www.iwf.org. Illus. Sample. *Indexed:* CWI, GendWatch. *Aud.:* Ga, Ac.

This nonacademic magazine from the Independent Women's Forum offers a conservative point of view on public policy and cultural issues affecting women. Its articles, interviews, and opinion pieces promote enterprise and personal responsibility and consistently criticize the liberal feminist agenda (including Title IX). Full text of past issues are available on the publisher's web site. Appropriate for public libraries.

The Women's Review of Books. See Books and Book Reviews section.

6752. *Women's Studies: an interdisciplinary journal.* [ISSN: 0049-7878] 1972. 8x/yr. GBP 413 (Individuals, GBP 100). Ed(s): Wendy Martin. Taylor & Francis Ltd, 11 New Fetter Ln, London, EC4P 4EE, United Kingdom; http://www.tandf.co.uk/journals. Illus., adv. Refereed. Microform: MIM. Online: EBSCO Publishing; Florida Center for Library Automation; Gale Group; Northern Light Technology, Inc.; OCLC Online Computer Library Center, Inc. Reprint: PSC. *Indexed:* ABS&EES, AbAn, AmH&L, AmHI, BHA, BrHumI, CommAb, FLI, FemPer, HumInd, IBSS, IBZ, MLA-IB, SWA, SociolAb, WSA. *Bk. rev.:* Number and length vary. *Aud.:* Ac.

This journal publishes articles, essays, and book reviews focusing largely on women in literature and the arts but is also interdisciplinary in outlook. Its contents include poetry and film and book reviews. Occasional issues focus on special topics. Tables of contents and a contents alerting service are available on the publisher's web site.

Women's Studies in Communication. See Communication section.

6753. *Women's Studies International Forum: a multidisciplinary journal for the rapid publication of research communications and review articles in women's studies.* Former titles (until 1982): *Women's Studies International Quarterly;* (until 1979): *Women's Studies (Oxford).* [ISSN: 0277-5395] 1978. bi-m. EUR 523 (Individuals, EUR 108; Students, EUR 35). Ed(s): Christine Zmroczek, D. Bell. Pergamon, The Boulevard, Langford Ln, East Park, Kidlington, OX5 1GB, United Kingdom; nlinfo-f@elsevier.nl; http://www.elsevier.nl. Illus., index, adv. Sample. Refereed. Circ: 1000. Vol. ends: Nov/Dec (No. 24). Microform: PQC. Online: Gale Group; ingenta.com; ScienceDirect; Swets Blackwell. *Indexed:* ABS&EES, AbAn, AgeL, AltPI, AmH&L, AnthLit, BAS, BrHumI, CJA, CommAb, FemPer, IBSS, IBZ, PSA, PsycholAb, SSCI, SSI, SWA, SociolAb, WSA. *Bk. rev.:* 6-10, length varies, signed. *Aud.:* Ac.

This expensive journal offers truly global coverage of women's studies and feminist research. It publishes research and theoretical articles, review essays, and book reviews. Its "Feminist Forum" offers conference announcements, news about women and women's studies, and notices of new books. One or more theme-based issues a year address special topics such as "Women-Text-Communities," "Understanding Local/Global Identities," and "Women in or from Asia." The publisher's web site offers tables of contents, abstracts, and a contents alerting service.

6754. *Women's Studies Quarterly.* Formerly: *Women's Studies Newsletter.* [ISSN: 0732-1562] 1972. 4x/yr. USD 40 (Individuals, USD 30). Feminist Press, CUNY Graduate Center, 365 5th Ave, New York, NY 10016; mvaux@gc.cuny.edu; http://www.feministpress.org. Illus., adv. Refereed. Circ: 3000 Controlled. Vol. ends: Fall/Winter (No. 3 - No. 4). Reprint: PSC. *Indexed:* ABS&EES, AgeL, AltPI, AmH&L, EduInd, FemPer, PSA, SSI, SWA, SociolAb, WSA. *Bk. rev.:* 0-5, 1,000-1,800 words, signed. *Aud.:* Ga, Ac.

This Feminist Press journal provides an international and cross-cultural perspective on research and teaching in women's studies. Contents include research articles and articles about teaching. Theme-based issues provide diverse viewpoints and in-depth coverage of subjects such as "Gender and Film" and "Women's Studies Then and Now."

Literary and Artistic

6755. *Calyx: a journal of art & literature by women.* [ISSN: 0147-1627] 1976. 2x/yr. USD 25 (Individuals, USD 19.50; USD 9.50 newsstand/ cover per issue). Ed(s): Micki Reaman, Beverly McFarland. Calyx, Inc., PO Box B, Corvallis, OR 97339-0539; calyx@proaxis.com; http://www.proaxis.com/~calyx. Illus., adv. Circ: 4500. Vol. ends: No. 3. *Indexed:* ABS&EES, AmHI, FemPer, HumInd, IAPV, SWA. *Bk. rev.:* 5-12, 500-1,500 words, signed. *Aud.:* Ga, Ac.

Calyx publishes poetry, prose, art, and book reviews by women from many walks of life. This long established literary review is known for publishing high quality work and for nurturing and developing writers. Several past contributors such as Paula Gunn Allen, Julia Alvarez, and Barbara Kingsolver are now well known. The journal has received awards including the 1998 Pushcart Prize and the 1996 Bumbershoot Best Literary Journal Award.

Camera Obscura. See Films section.

6756. ***Femspec.*** [ISSN: 1523-4002] s-a. USD 50 (Individuals, USD 30). Ed(s): Batya Weinbaum, Robin A Reid. Femspec, Department of English, Cleveland State University, Cleveland, OH 44115. Circ: 300. *Indexed:* MLA-IB. *Bk. rev.:* 2, essay length, signed. *Aud.:* Ga, Ac.

Femspec is an interdisciplinary, feminist journal covering areas not well represented in feminist or mainstream literary journals. It is "dedicated to critical and creative works in the realms of science fiction, fantasy, magical realism, surrealism, myth, folklore, and other supernatural agents." Issues feature fiction, poetry, criticism, interviews, and book reviews.

6757. ***Kalliope: a journal of women's literature & art.*** [ISSN: 0735-7885] 1979. 2x/yr. USD 24.95 (Individuals, USD 14.95; USD 7 newsstand/cover per issue). Ed(s): Mary Sue Koeppel. Florida Community College, Kalliope Writers' Collective, 3939 Roosevelt Blvd, Jacksonville, FL 32205; http://www.fccj.org/kalliope. Illus. Refereed. Circ: 1600. Microform: PQC. *Indexed:* AmHI, FemPer, IAPV. *Bk. rev.:* 4, 150-400 words, signed. *Aud.:* Ga, Ac.

This literary journal publishes poetry, short fiction, interviews, reviews, and visual art by women. The editors welcome work from new and established writers. Some issues have themes. Published by a collective actively involved not only in publishing women?s work but in developing women through poetry and fiction workshops.

6758. ***n.paradoxa: international feminist art journal.*** [ISSN: 1461-0434] 1998. s-a. GBP 32 including the UK (Individuals, GBP 18 including the UK; GBP 7.95 newsstand/cover per issue in Europe including the UK). Ed(s): Katy Deepwell. K T Press, 38 Bellot St, East Greenwich, London, SE10 OAQ, United Kingdom. Adv. Refereed. Circ: 1000. *Indexed:* ABM. *Aud.:* Ga, Sa.

This international feminist journal focuses on the visual arts. It publishes in-depth analyses of contemporary women's art and feminist art theory. It also provides information on women's art organizations and exhibitions; chronicles the contemporary women's art movement; and includes reviews of publications about contemporary women artists. It is a valuable resource for students, artists, and academics and is available in online and print editions.

6759. ***Room of One's Own: a feminist journal of literature and criticism.*** [ISSN: 0316-1609] 1975. q. CND 25 (Individuals, CND 22; CND 7 newsstand/cover per issue). Growing Room Collective, PO Box 46160, Vancouver, BC V6J 5G5, Canada; http://www.islandnet.com/room/enter. Adv. Circ: 1000 Paid. Microform: MML; PQC. Reprint: PQC. *Indexed:* AmHI, CBCARef, CPerI, FemPer, MLA-IB, SWA. *Bk. rev.:* 700 words, signed. *Aud.:* Ga, Ac.

For more than 25 years, this Canadian literary magazine has showcased poems, short fiction, essays, reviews, and art by women writers and artists. Many of the works speak to the experiences of Canadian women and their unique environments. Selected content from the current and previous issues is available on the magazine's web site.

6760. ***Salamander: a magazine for poetry, fiction & memoirs.*** [ISSN: 1063-3359] 1992. 2x/yr. USD 22 for 2 yrs.; USD 6 newsstand/cover per issue. Ed(s): Jennifer Barber. Salamander, Inc., 48 Ackers Ave, Brookline, MA 02445-4160. Adv. Circ: 900. *Aud.:* Ga.

Salamander features poetry, fiction, and memoirs. It has received support from the National Endowment for the Arts, the Massachusetts Cultural Council, the Council for Literary Magazines and Presses, the Brookline Council on the Arts and Humanities, and Bradford College. The editors give special attention to the work of established and emerging women writers.

6761. ***Woman's Art Journal.*** [ISSN: 0270-7993] 1980. s-a. USD 38 (Individuals, USD 20). Ed(s): Elsa Honig Fine. Woman's Art, Inc., 1711 Harris Rd., Laverock, PA 19038-7208. Illus., index, adv. Refereed. Circ: 4000. Vol. ends: Fall/Winter (No. 2). Microform: PQC. Online: OCLC Online Computer Library Center, Inc.; H.W. Wilson. *Indexed:* ABM, ABS&EES, AIAP, ArtHuCI, ArtInd, BHA, DAAI, FemPer. *Bk. rev.:* 5-13, 400-3,500 words, signed. *Aud.:* Hs, Ga, Ac, Sa.

This publication covers women and issues relating to women in the visual arts from antiquity to the present. Each 50-page issue includes a "Portraits" section about individual women artists and a "Reviews" section covering exhibitions and publications by and about women writers. Some issues include an "Issues and Insights" section addressing topics relating to women in the visual arts and shorter notes and reviews. Contributors include artists, critics, art professionals, and academics. Issues include high-quality black-and-white illustrations. Of interest for art and women?s studies collections.

6762. ***Women: a cultural review.*** [ISSN: 0957-4042] 1990. 3x/yr. GBP 156 (Individuals, GBP 38). Routledge, 11 New Fetter Ln, London, EC4P 4EE, United Kingdom; info@routledge.co.uk; http://www.routledge.co.uk. Adv. Circ: 450. Online: EBSCO Publishing; Ingenta Select; OCLC Online Computer Library Center, Inc.; RoweCom Information Quest; Swets Blackwell. Reprint: PSC. *Indexed:* AltPI, BrHumI, FLI, FemPer, HumInd, RI-1. *Bk. rev.:* Number and length vary. *Aud.:* Ac.

The focus of this British journal is on "the role and representation of gender and sexuality in the arts and culture." It publishes research articles, essays, review essays, and book reviews about women and gender in literature, the media, history, education, law, philosophy, psychoanalysis, and the fine and performing arts. The publisher's web site provides tables of contents and an article alert service.

6763. ***Women and Music: a journal of gender and culture.*** [ISSN: 1090-7505] 1997. a. USD 55 domestic; USD 61 foreign. Ed(s): Catherine Pickar. University of Nebraska Press, 233 N 8th St, Lincoln, NE 68588-0255; pressmail@unl.edu; http://www.nebraskapress.unl.edu. Adv. Refereed. Online: Florida Center for Library Automation; Gale Group; OCLC Online Computer Library Center, Inc.; SoftLine Information. *Indexed:* IIMP, MusicInd. *Bk. rev.:* 10, essay length, signed. *Aud.:* Ac, Sa.

This refereed journal from the International Alliance for Women in Music takes an interdisciplinary, feminist approach to understanding the relationships among gender, music, and culture. Contents include scholarly articles that examine the role of gender in shaping works of music and women's roles as composers, teachers, performers, and critics. Its coverage is international. The journal also includes review essays and book reviews reflecting the diversity of world music and women's place in it. Recommended for academic collections.

6764. ***Women's Writing.*** [ISSN: 0969-9082] 1994. 3x/yr. GBP 220 includes online access (Individuals, GBP 38). Ed(s): Marie Mulvey-Roberts, Janet Todd. Triangle Journals Ltd., Attn: Roger Osborn-King, Publisher, PO Box 65, Wallingford, OX10 0YG, United Kingdom; subscriptions@triangle.co.uk; http://www.triangle.co.uk. Illus., index. Sample. Refereed. Vol. ends: Dec. *Indexed:* AmH&L, BrHumI, FemPer, IBZ, MLA-IB, SWA, WSI. *Bk. rev.:* 4-6, 1,000 words, signed. *Aud.:* Ac.

This international journal publishes theoretical and historical perspectives and other contributions about gender, culture, race, and class in women's writing before 1900. Special theme issues focus on individual writers such as Harriet Martineau and Mary Shelley or on topics such as "Dissenting Women" and "The Body and Women." It also includes book reviews. Tables of contents, abstracts, and full text are available on the publisher's web site.

Special Interest

Archives of Sexual Behavior. See Psychology section.

6765. ***The Beltane Papers: a journal of women's mysteries.*** Former titles: *T B P's Octava; Beltane Papers.* [ISSN: 1074-3634] 1984. 3x/yr. USD 16 domestic; USD 23 Canada; USD 29 elsewhere. Ed(s): M L Thompson Helland. The Beltane Papers, PO Box 29694, Bellingham, WA 98228-1694; beltane@az.com. Illus., adv. Circ: 5000. *Bk. rev.:* 10, 70-essay length, signed. *Aud.:* Ac, Sa.

This magazine of feminist spirituality and goddess worship provides a forum for women to explore their spirituality, share rituals, and network with others. The content offers an inclusive blend of articles. A recent issue, for example, features stories about Australian, Celtic, and African spirituality and goddess worship. Its review section covers books, music, theater, and divination tools, among other things. Some full-text articles and an e-mail discussion forum are available on the web site.

6766. ***Bridges: a journal for Jewish feminists and our friends.*** [ISSN: 1046-8358] 1990. irreg. USD 18 per issue. Ed(s): Clare Kinberg. Bridges Association, PO Box 24839, Eugene, OR 97402. Illus. Sample. Circ: 3000. *Indexed:* FemPer, IJP. *Bk. rev.:* 2, essay length, signed. *Aud.:* Hs, Ac, Sa.

Bridges is an independent review of Jewish feminist culture and politics founded in 1990. It "celebrates and illustrates Jewish women's identity and social justice activism with articles by and about lesbians, working-class Jews, Jewish women of various ethnic backgrounds, and reports on Israeli women peace workers." Contents include fiction, poetry, art, and reviews. Special issues feature writing and art by Jewish women of color and Israeli women's voices. An audiotape version is available free to print-disabled subscribers through the Jewish Braille Institute.

6767. ***Conscience: a news journal of prochoice Catholic opinion.*** [ISSN: 0740-6835] 1980. q. USD 10; USD 5 newsstand/cover. Ed(s): Patti Miller. Catholics for a Free Choice, 1436 U St, N W, Ste 301, Washington, DC 20009-3997. Index, adv. Sample. Circ: 15000 Paid and controlled. Vol. ends: No. 4. *Indexed:* BRI, CBRI, CWI, GendWatch, IAPV, PAIS, SWA. *Bk. rev.:* 2, 700 words, signed. *Aud.:* Ac, Sa.

This quarterly magazine from Catholics for a Free Choice offers "in-depth coverage of the topics central to CFFC's mission, including women's rights in society and in religions, reproductive rights, sexuality and gender, feminist theology, social justice, church and state issues, and the role of religion in formulating public policy." Contributors include CFFC researchers and staff, clergy, scholars, and activists expressing a range of pro-choice and social justice viewpoints. Recommended for academic and public libraries. Full text of articles from current and past issues are available in English, Spanish, or Portuguese on the web site.

Journal of Gay & Lesbian Psychotherapy. See Lesbian, Gay, Bisexual, and Transgender section.

Journal of Gay & Lesbian Social Services. See Lesbian, Gay, Bisexual, and Transgender section.

6768. ***Lilith: the independent Jewish women's magazine.*** [ISSN: 0146-2334] 1976. q. USD 24 (Individuals, USD 18). Ed(s): Susan Weidman Schneider. Lilith Publications, Inc., 250 W 57th St, Ste 2432, New York, NY 10107-0172; lilithmag@aol.com; http://www.lilithmag.com. Adv. Circ: 10000. Microform: PQC. Online: bigchalk; Factiva; OCLC Online Computer Library Center, Inc.; ProQuest Information & Learning; SoftLine Information. *Indexed:* ABS&EES, ENW, FemPer, GendWatch, IJP, SWA, WSA, WSI. *Bk. rev.:* 5-14, 300 words, signed. *Aud.:* Ga, Sa.

Lilith is still going strong as one of the earliest feminist magazines born in the Second Wave feminist movement of the 1970s. Its nonfiction includes autobiography, interviews, literary criticism, and analyses of wide-ranging topics that impact Jewish women's lives around the world. Reports may focus on local grassroots activism or international events. The "Kol Ishah" section provides alternative news highly relevant to Jewish women that is unlikely to be reported in mainstream media. The "New Ceremonies and Rituals" feature shares ideas for enriching the spiritual observance of key life events. *Lilith* is an inclusive arena where Jewish women can talk and perhaps realize that their values blend with those of feminism. Sample articles are available on its web site.

6769. ***Media Report to Women.*** [ISSN: 0145-9651] 1972. q. USD 55 (Individuals, USD 33). Ed(s): Sheila Gibbons. Communication Research Associates, Inc., 38091 Beach Rd, PO Box 180, Colton's Point, MD 20626-0180; sheilagib@erols.com. Illus., index, adv. Sample. Vol. ends: Fall (No. 4). *Indexed:* FLI, FemPer, WSA, WSI. *Bk. rev.:* 3-5, 50-90 words. *Aud.:* Ga, Ac, Sa.

This quarterly newsletter monitors issues of interest to women and the manner in which all types of media depict women. It also looks at the employment of women by the media. Current and back issue summaries, statistical information, and useful Internet links are available on the newsletter's web site. Useful for journalists and others concerned with the misrepresentation and/or underrepresentation of women in the media.

6770. ***Melpomene Journal: a journal for women's health research.*** Formerly: *Melpomene Report.* [ISSN: 1043-8734] 1981. 3x/yr. USD 75 (Individuals, USD 40). Ed(s): Evelyn Cottle Raedler. Melpomene Institute for Women's Health Research, 1010 University Ave W, Saint Paul, MN 55104-4706; http://www.melpomene.org. Illus. Circ: 2500 Paid. *Indexed:* CWI, SportS. *Aud.:* Ga, Ac.

This journal offers a combination of research and general interest articles on issues relating to women's health and physical activity throughout the life span. A recent special issue focuses on physical education for girls in all types of schools. It is distinctive in coverage and should be useful for public and academic library collections.

Midwifery Today with International Midwife. See Medicine and Health/Family Planning section.

6771. ***SageWoman: celebrating the goddess in every woman.*** [ISSN: 1068-1698] 1983. q. USD 21 domestic; USD 26 foreign; USD 6.95 newsstand/cover per issue domestic. Ed(s): Anne Newkirk Niven. Blessed Bee, Inc., PO Box 641, Point Arena, CA 95468; info@sagewoman.com; http://www.sagewoman.com. Illus., adv. Circ: 21000 Paid. Vol. ends: Winter. Online: OCLC Online Computer Library Center, Inc.; SoftLine Information. *Indexed:* AltPI, FemPer, WSI. *Bk. rev.:* 10, 220-400 words, signed. *Aud.:* Sa.

This quarterly magazine of women's spirituality celebrates "the goddess in every woman" with articles, poetry, columns, photographs, and graphic artwork by women. It invites submissions from "all spiritual paths" but focuses on "material which expresses an Earth-centered spirituality." For a readership that "includes women of a variety of religious faiths, from Roman Catholic to Lesbian Separatist Witch and everywhere in between."

Women in Sport and Physical Activity Journal. See Sports: Physical Education, Coaching, and Sports Sciences section.

Electronic Journals

6772. ***Feminist Majority Foundation Online.*** 1995. d. Membership, USD 15. Feminist Majority Foundation, 1600 Wilson Blvd, Ste 801, Arlington, VA 22209; femmaj@feminist.org; http://www.feminist.org. *Aud.:* Ga, Ac.

The Feminist Majority Foundation, a nonprofit organization headed by Eleanor Smeal, uses "research and action to empower women economically, socially, and politically." Although its Feminist Majority Newsletter has ceased publication, its web site provides an online daily news service covering U.S. and global feminist news. A search engine allows readers to search U.S. news from 1995 to the present and global news from June 2000 to the present. The site includes useful links to in-depth articles from the news wires and the feminist press.

6773. ***Genders (Online Edition).*** s-a. Ed(s): Ann Kibbey, Thomas Foster. University of Colorado, Campus Box 226, Boulder, CO 80309. Refereed. *Bk. rev.:* essay length, signed. *Aud.:* Ac, Ga.

This e-journal from the University of Colorado and Washington State University publishes "essays about gender and sexuality in relation to social, political, artistic, and economic concerns." Contents include discussions of particular works of art, literature, or film and historical and cross-cultural analyses of contemporary gender issues.

6774. ***Intersections: gender, history & culture in the Asian context.*** [ISSN: 1440-9151] 1998. s-a. Ed(s): Anne Marie Medcalf, Carolyn Brewer. Murdoch University, School of Asian Studies, South St, Perth, W.A. 6163, Australia; intrsect@central.murdoch.edu.au; http://wwwsshe.murdoch.edu.au/hum/as/intersections/. Illus., index, adv. Refereed. *Indexed:* MLA-IB. *Bk. rev.:* 2-7, essay length, signed. *Aud.:* Ac.

This refereed electronic journal provides a forum for research and teaching about the multiple historical and cultural gender patterns of Asia. Papers include photos, maps, or artistic reproductions as well as video or sound where they enhance understanding and allow "for new connections to be made." Contents include book and film reviews and "reading notes" as well as research articles. A recent theme-based issue focuses on "Deconstructing Popular and Diasporic Images." Author and geographic indexes are available on the journal web site.

6775. ***Journal of International Women's Studies Online.*** *Bk. rev.:* 0-2, essay length, signed. *Aud.:* Ac.

This journal provides an opportunity for scholars, activists, and students to bridge "the conventional divides of scholarship and activism; 'western' and 'third world' feminisms" by exploring "the relationship between feminist theory and various forms of organizing." Contents include research articles, essays, and film and book reviews. A recent special issue, "Harvesting Our Strengths: Third Wave Feminism and Women's Studies," features papers from a conference on Third Wave feminism at the University of Exeter. Articles are in pdf format.

6776. ***Outskirts: feminisms along the edge.*** Formerly (until 1996): *Outskirts.* [ISSN: 1445-0445] 1981. s-a. USD 6. Ed(s): Delys Bird. University of Western Australia, Centre for Women's Studies, . Refereed. *Bk. rev.:* Number and length vary. *Aud.:* Ac.

This is a refereed, feminist, cultural-studies e-journal issued from the English Department of the University of Western Australia and the Women's Studies program of the University of Adelaide. Articles, fiction, poetry, and reviews of performances and books focus on a broad range of issues in "feminisms along the edge." Full text is available online from 1996 forward.

6777. ***Sexing the Political.*** 2001. m. Free. Ed(s): Krista Jacob. Krista Jacob, sexingthepolitical@aol.com; http://www.sexingthepolitical.com/. *Bk. rev.:* 2-3, 425 words, signed. *Aud.:* Ga, Ac.

Sexing the Political is a monthly online journal covering issues relating to feminist sexuality. It provides "a forum for the creative and radical political expression of third wave feminists from diverse cultural, sexual, and economic perspectives." Contents include articles, columns, and book and music reviews as well as a prominently featured editorial from Krista Jacob and letters to the editor. Topics covered include sexism in the media, parenting, living single, sexuality and popular culture, and queer and other issues. The intended audience is Generation X feminists. Back issues are archived online.

WIN News. See *Women's International Net Magazine.*

6778. ***Women in Literature and Life Assembly.*** 1992. a. USD 15 domestic. National Council of Teachers of English, 1111 W Kenyon Rd, Urbana, IL 61801-1096; suefjohn@grove.iup.edu; http://www.scholar.lib.vt.edu/journals/willa/. Circ: 500. *Aud.:* Hs, Ac.

This journal, originating with the National Council of Teachers of English, addresses gender issues in the teaching of literacy and writing. It is issued in hard-copy form to subscribers; the electronic version appears on a delayed basis. Content includes articles, teaching notes, and the occasional poem. It is appropriate for teachers at all levels.

6779. ***Women's International Net Magazine.*** 1997. m. Ed(s): Judith Colp Rubin. Women's International Net Magazine, 4817 Morgan Dr, Chevy Chase, MD 20815; jrubin@winmagazine.org; http://winmagazine.org. *Aud.:* Ga.

This is the online edition of *WIN News* (see Feminist and Women's Studies subsection).

■ ZINES

Directories Online

See also Alternatives; and Little Magazines sections.

Gail Golderman, Electronic Media Librarian, Union College, Schenectady, NY 12308; goldermg@union.edu; FAX: 518-388-6619

Introduction

It used to be quite easy to define what a zine was—"a nonprofessional, anti-commercial, small-circulation magazine"—and for the most part that definition holds true today. The majority of print zines (and the number is in the thousands) are produced, published, and distributed by those that create them. Zines are sent through the mail or found in small independent bookstores or music stores. Many are still available for free, for the cost of a few stamps, or for trade. Some titles are available only by single issue, and/or only directly through the publisher, while others are available through a subscription, a distributor, "infoshop," or more commercial venue.

The zine world has not remained static. A new category of professional-looking zines has emerged, and it is difficult at times to distinguish them from regular mainstream magazines. Another indication of change has been the impact of the web over the past eight years. The growth of electronic zines, or "e-zines," has been phenomenal. Some are extensions to a counterpart that offer selected material from the current paper issue, similar to traditional print-format periodicals, while others exist solely on the web.

Regardless of the distribution, zines continue to be about the individuals that create them. This form of personal expression is the very essence of how the culture began, and it (and the state of the world) dictates its longevity with the assurance that zines will remain a viable print art form for some time to come.

Whatever appearance these titles currently take, zines have existed for decades. Personal, political, cultural, and philosophical ideologies—and the desire to voice them—define the content. Their popularity has increased, and we continue to see new publishers unified in the quest to keep this medium alive.

The origin of what we call the present zine publication has evolved from the word "fanzine," a term that dates back to the science fiction "fan magazines" of the 1930s and 1940s. The term became popular in the late 1970s and early 1980s as a broad spectrum of people became part of the "DIY"—do-it-yourself culture. Underground and alternative newspapers became popular as fans of punk rock music—and generally those individuals who felt that mainstream media ignored their political, musical, or cultural identification—got involved. According to early editors, there was no representation if you fell outside the conventional spectrum, so many began to create their own media structure. These new publications represented a community of people who exchanged, read, and often reviewed each other's writing, a practice that exists today among zine editors and readers.

The popularity of zines became evident with the success of *Factsheet Five,* a review publication created by Mike Gunderloy, a science fiction fan who began reading other "fanzines," including political, punk, and counterculture newsletters and magazines. He in turn distributed these as lists in a photocopied newsletter to his friends. In 1982, Gunderloy began printing reviews and contact addresses for zines sent to him, and his newsletter grew in size and distribution, becoming crucial for self-publishers, political dissenters, and the growing science fiction and zine culture. What ultimately resulted was a new subculture of zines, and the number of publications increased dramatically. *Factsheet Five* became a focal point and central resource for readers and publishers of zines worldwide, with several editors and over 60 issues before suspending publication in 1998.

Selecting zines for a publication such as *Magazines for Libraries* continues to be a daunting task, and selecting zine publications for library aquisitions raises a multiplicity of concerns as well. A subscription to a zine does not guarantee the regularity of any particular title, and in fact, "published several times a year" might not mean this year at all. Many titles are not available through a subscription and can only be purchased as single issues directly from the publisher or through a distributor.

Irregularity is a common theme and while some zine writers are prolific and diligent, others publish on a schedule that suits their lifestyle, and traditional periodical claiming is not an option for this category of material. Another factor to consider is that editors have great intentions, but many titles fold after one or two issues, and many titles, although still active, haven't released a new issue in several years. However, that being said, the value of adding zines to a library collection is immeasurable for intellectual diversity. Many titles are unique in their cultural or political perspective, are local, national, or international in scope, and contain material that cannot readily be found in mainstream publications, whether it is community news and networking information, first-hand reporting of protests or political actions throughout the world, reviews of independently produced videos or books, or commentary on and conversations with political prisoners.

Those with experience suggest establishing cash accounts to purchase single issues or purchasing through a distributor if subscriptions are not available. Review the lists and anthologies that editors produce when considering what zines to acquire, and see what zine editors read and suggest. As mentioned earlier, editors review other zines and typically publish current lists and distribution/contact information. A zine such as *Xerography Debt* is such a resource. Published by Davida Breier (also known for *Leeking Ink*), it is "a review zine for zine readers by zine writers." Another avenue to explore is *The Zine Yearbook,* published by well-known editor Jen Angel. This is an annual collection of excerpts "from the best zines publishing today," allowing librarians the opportunity to sample new and old titles for content and consistency. Another helpful source for acquiring titles is the *Zine Guide,* which includes a comprehensive subject index "focusing on subjects specific to research, activism, zine/underground culture, music, psychology/therapy, sociology, and travel." Utilizing the available bibliographic tools and directory resources, both online and in print, is essential for successfully procuring zines for your library.

Titles included in this edition have been analyzed with several selection criteria, including longevity (they are still being published from the previous edition, or at least that is the editor's claim), availability (they offer subscriptions, or at least are readily available from a publisher, distributor, or bookstore), and finally, for new titles added, they have published at least one or two issues during the past year. Titles deleted from the previous edition have officially ceased, have not published an issue in several years, or the publisher has announced the demise of the publication. Several titles, however, that have not been published in the past year are included for historical purposes or because of assurance from the publisher that the next issue is "in the works."

For every title included, there are hundreds, if not thousands, not listed here that favorably compare as far as quality, content, and style. As mentioned above, use the sources listed to best choose based on your particular user population.

Basic Periodicals

Hs: *Beer Frame, Bitch, Bust, Cometbus, The Duplex Planet, Maximum Rock'n'roll, Punk Planet, Slug & Lettuce, World War Three Illustrated;* Ga: *Bayou La Rose, Beer Frame, Bitch, Broken Pencil, Bust, Clamor, Cometbus, The Door, The Duplex Planet, Fat!So?, Guinea Pig Zero, Hermenaut, Maximum Rock 'n' roll, Mouth, Nuclear Resister, Progressive Review, Punk Planet, Slug & Lettuce, Stay Free, Ten Page News, World War Three Illustrated;* Ac: *Anarchy, Clamor, Hermenaut, Mouth, Mystery Date, Nuclear Resister, Progressive Review, Race Traitor, Turning the Tide, Umbrella.*

6780. *Ache.* a. USD 2.50 newsstand/cover. Armen Svadjian, Ed. & Pub., 167, Cortleigh Blvd, Toronto, ON M5N 1P6, Canada; achemag@yahoo.com. *Aud.:* Hs, Ga.

A relatively new Toronto-based publication profiling zine and punk culture, *Ache* issues include interviews with musicians, editors, authors, and local artists, as well as a music review column and the editor's own comics, "Freshman Funnies." The latest issue features an interview and cover artwork by Canadian cartoonist Dave Cooper and a look at the Ontario, California--based company responsible for those "fundamental Christian mini-comics," Chick Publications.

6781. *Alabama Grrrl.* irreg. USD 2 newsstand/cover per issue. Alabama Grrrl, PO Box 297, Lawrence, KS 66044; ailecia@tripod.com. *Aud.:* Ga.

Alabama Grrrl is a personal zine, with political content, written by a twenty-something feminist, activist, and novice photographer living in Kansas. Current content includes the history of the co-op she used to live in, coping with debilitating cramps in "I Lost Control Today," girlfriend problems, and an essay about being adopted. Past issues examined have covered a range of topics, such as dealing with roommates, the "Millions for Mumia March" in Pittsburgh, hip-hop web sites, homesickness, political activism, and body image concerns. Issues include lists of zines and reviews, short album reviews, and related web sites.

Alternative Press Review. See Alternatives section.

6782. *Anarchy: a journal of desire armed.* [ISSN: 1044-1387] 1980. s-a. USD 16 for 2 yrs. Ed(s): Jason McQuinn. A A L Press, PO Box 4710, Arlington, VA 22204-4710; jmcquinn@coin.org. Illus. Circ: 6000 Paid. *Indexed:* AltPI. *Bk. rev.:* 6-10, 400-3,600 words. *Aud.:* Ga, Ac.

Anarchy is a long-standing source of alternative media reviews, radical artwork and cartoons, international anarchist news, anarchist web sites, interviews, and essays on such topics as libertarianism, primitivism, and anarchy throughout history. The zine is co-edited by the *Alternative Press Review* founding editor Jason McQuinn and Lawrence Jarach. *Anarchy* offers an "anti-authoritarian point of view; critical of ideology, religion, nationalism, militarism and all political hierarchy." Each issue typically contains 80–100 pages with full-color covers. The current issue begins with a piece titled "No to all wars, not just to some wars!" and includes essays on anarchist collaboration in the Spanish Civil War, perspectives on the war in Iraq, alternative media reviews, news, and extensive letters with editorial comments.

The Baffler. See Alternatives section.

6783. *Bamboo Girl.* 1995. irreg. approx. 2/yr. USD 3 per issue. Ed(s): Sabrina Margarita Alcantara-Tan. Mutya Publishing, PO Box 507, New York, NY 10159-0507. *Aud.:* Ga.

Bamboo Girl regularly features interviews, zine and music reviews (focusing on those with Asian, lesbian, radical, and/or feminist views), excerpts from books of Filipino mythology, photography, and correspondence. Its manifesto is "to challenge the issues of racism/sexism/homophobia from the point of view of smart, loud, non-traditional girls of color, especially from that of the feminist Pinay (Filipina)-mutt perspective." Recent issues include articles on the Filipino/American Coalition for Environmental Solutions (FACES), a personal account of 9/11, women against the war, and the Filipino women behind the 60s/70s rock band Fanny. Issues can be purchased individually at a variety of stands or distributors. Subscriptions are available as well. The web site inlcudes links to Asian American, feminist, government, Hapa-related, Filipino, and queer resources. Archival issues can also be ordered online.

6784. *Bayou La Rose.* 1978. irreg. USD 7.50 for 4 nos. Ed(s): Arthur J Miller, Della Anaya. Bayou La Rose, PO Box 5464, Tacoma, WA 87415-0464; bayou@blarg.net. Illus. *Aud.:* Ga.

More than 20 years in publication, *Bayou La Rose* regularly contains interviews, articles, and contact information on everything from antinuclear organizing to international human rights. Prisoner solidarity, native struggles, and the "new world order" are common themes. A recent "Special Issue on Organization" features a document published by exiled Russian anarchists in 1926, an article titled "A New Union Vision," and views on anarchist revolution in the current world. Local and worldwide resistance events and actions are covered in detail.

6785. *Beer Frame: the journal of inconspicuous consumption.* 1993. irreg. USD 3 newsstand/cover per issue. Ed(s): Paul Lukas. Beer Frame, 671 DeGraw St, Apt 2, Brooklyn, NY 11217; consumer@interport.net; http://www.core77.com/beerframe/. Illus., adv. *Bk. rev.:* Occasional, 200-400 words. *Aud.:* Hs, Ga.

Subtitled "The Journal of Inconspicuous Consumption," Paul Lucas's *Beer Frame* reviews an array of consumer products, from supermarket fare to printed matter. Issues have featured essays on Skee-Balls, multicolored vanilla wafers, those little individualized salt packets (and other single-serving seasonings), and gender-specific tissues such as "Kleenex for Men." The current issue takes a look at "Blastin' Green" ketchup. Music reviews are included.

6786. ***The Big Takeover.*** 1980. 2x/yr. USD 20 domestic for 4 nos.; USD 22 Canada for 4 nos.; USD 24 elsewhere for 4 nos. Ed(s): Jack Rabid. Big Takeover, 249 Eldridge St, 14, New York, NY 10002; jrabid@bigtakeover.com; http://www.bigtakeover.com. Adv. Circ: 11500 Paid. *Aud.:* Hs, Ga.

The Big Takeover supplies interviews and features on major-label and indie artists, with editorial columns, reader letters, comics, and hundreds of music reviews. Past issues have included interviews with Richard Thompson, Idlewild, and Radiohead, to name just a few. Recent article topics include the Bush administration's new tax-cut deal, the expanding Clear Channel monopoly, the American Idol farce, and "Special Report: Sweden Underground Rock Explosion."

6787. ***Bitch: the feminist response to pop culture.*** [ISSN: 1524-5314] 1996. s-a. USD 15 domestic; USD 21 Canada; USD 35 elsewhere. Ed(s): Lisa Jervis. Bitch Publications, 2765 16th St, San Francisco, CA 94103; lisa@bitchmagazine.com; http://www.bitchmagazine.com. Illus., adv. Circ: 15000 Paid. *Indexed:* AltPI, GendWatch. *Bk. rev.:* Number and length vary. *Aud.:* Hs, Ga.

A standard, professional-style zine with thematic issues, *Bitch: Feminist Response to Pop Culture* is "devoted to incisive commentary on our media-driven world." Critiques of television, movies, magazines, and advertising are regular features, as well as in-depth interviews and profiles of women in all areas of pop culture, news blurbs, the "Love It/Shove It" rant column, and "The Bitch List" (favorite things). Reader letters, editorial columns, music and book reviews, and full-length articles round out each issue. Past content includes Afghan women, an interview with "Bend It Like Beckham" director Gurinder Chadha, and writers' obsessions.

6788. ***Broken Pencil: the guide to alternative publications in Canada.*** [ISSN: 1201-8996] 1995. 3x/yr. CND 12 Canada; USD 12 United States; USD 15 elsewhere. Ed(s): Hal Niedzviecki. Broken Pencil, PO Box 203, Toronto, ON M5S 2S7, Canada. Illus., index, adv. Circ: 3000. *Bk. rev.:* 16, 120-300 words. *Aud.:* Ga.

Subtitled "Zine Culture in Canada and the World," *Broken Pencil* is a magazine of over 80 pages that entertains all aspects of alternative culture, including reviews of zines, comics, books, e-zines, and music from across Canada. Reviews are arranged alphabetically, geographically by region, or by issue, and include complete ordering information. Separate sections list international publications (including U.S.-based ones), e-zines (with full-fledged reviews), music, and books. Reprints of the best of the alternative press in Canada are included in each issue, as are original features and fiction, news shorts, zine of the month, product of the issue, and readers' letters. The latest "Almost Famous Issue" includes "Everything you need to know about selling out" and "Ironic Crafting and the Not-Martha Revolution."

Bust. See Women section.

6789. ***Cashiers du Cinemart.*** 1994. irreg. USD 5 per issue. Ed(s): Mike White. Cashiers du Cinemart, PO Box 2401, Riverview, MI 48192; mwhite@impossiblefunky.com; http://www.cashiersducinemart.com. Circ: 6000. *Bk. rev.:* 300-400. *Aud.:* Hs, Ga, Ac.

A well-known film and popular culture zine, *Cashiers du Cinemart* includes interviews with actors and directors, features, letters, and film, zine, and music reviews. A handy feature for film enthusiasts is the detailed coverage and reporting on independent films from the United States and Canada. The current issue includes a look at the 1975 film *Deafula*, a piece on the making of *Takedown*, and reports from the New York Underground Film Festival, the SXSW Film Festival, and the Toronto International Film Festival. Past issues have included "That's a Rap," a look at the short history of rap movies from the mid-1980s to the present, a review of actor Robert Blake in the 1970s film "Electra Glide in Blue," and a piece titled "The 50 Greatest Movies Never Made." Book reviews are included in the "Bibliofinds" column.

6790. ***Clamor: new perspectives on politics, culture, media and life.*** [ISSN: 1534-9489] bi-m. USD 18 domestic; USD 24 foreign; USD 4.50 newsstand/cover domestic. Become the Media, PO Box 1225, Bowling Green, OH 43402; info@clamormagazine.org; http://www.clamormagazine.org. Adv. *Bk. rev.:* Various number and length. *Aud.:* Hs, Ga, Ac.

Edited by Jen Angel of *Fucktooth* fame and Jason Kucsma, this publication centers around politics, people, and culture. It is a professional-format zine, each issue having a particular focus and theme (with a variety of other topics thrown in). Advertising is minimal, and pieces range from the footnoted informative essay to the first-person story to the photo essay. "People," "Media," "Politics," "Gender & Sexuality," "Economics," and "Culture" are regular features. The first issue of *Clamor* was one of the first magazines to contain personal accounts from the front lines of the November 2000 protests against the World Trade Organization (WTO)in Seattle. Past issues have shared perspectives on voting and electoral politics, economic inequality, technotopia, pornography and punk, and prison reform. The current issue, titled the "Food Issue," looks at fair-trade coffee, young women's body image, the WTO, and the latest on San Francisco's Rainbow Cooperative Grocery and the Israeli/Palestinian conflict. Each issue typically includes reader letters and video, zine, music, and book reviews.

6791. ***Cometbus.*** 1991. irreg. USD 2.50. Ed(s): Aaron Cometbus. Cometbus, c/o BBT, PO Box 4279, Berkeley, CA 94704. Illus. *Aud.:* Ga.

Cometbus appears on every "favorite zine" list, and with good reason. It has been around for a long time and continues to include an eclectic mix of interesting material. For many it defines what a zine is—a personal publication about the editor's (Aaron Cometbus) life, travels, and interests. *Cometbus* has also run comics, short stories, and writings by others. Chiefly handwritten (all in caps), it includes interviews, personal stories, and crazy adventures—a quirky diary/novella combination. Past issues have included a teenage punk love story, a series featuring a critical look at the attempt to find a simpler life away from the city titled "Back to the Land," interviews with the collective involved with the Dead End Cafe, an entire issue devoted to the editor's personal stories (23 chapters), a history of 1960s-era letters, short stories, and a veritable novella about living in a houseful of punks. An extensive collection—originally reproduced—of 20 years of *Cometbus* is available in the anthology *Despite Everything: A Cometbus Omnibus* (Last Gasp Press, 2002).

6792. ***The Door Magazine.*** Formerly: *Wittenburg Door.* [ISSN: 1044-7512] 1971. bi-m. USD 29.95 domestic; USD 39.95 foreign. Ed(s): Bob Darden. Trinity Foundation, Inc., PO Box 1444, Waco, TX 76703-1444. Illus., adv. Circ: 10000 Paid. *Indexed:* ChrPI. *Aud.:* Ga.

"The world's pretty much only religious satire magazine," *The Door* successfully manages to provide "a humorous avenue for the expression of the less flattering aspects of the institution, while still embracing the legitimacy of the ideals behind Christianity which are the foundations for faith." Current financial worries have stalled the latest publication, but editors note they have resurrected the next issue and are still in business. *The Door* contains religious satire and humor, includes insightful interviews, a "truth is stranger than fiction" section and the "loser of the month" award. Past issues have included Christian spiritual analogies found within the Harry Potter series, the "Scientology Dictionary of Select Terms," and simple exercise routines from the "Pontius Pilates Fitness Method." *The Door* also regularly features news clippings and cartoons.

6793. ***Doris.*** irreg. USD 1.50 newsstand/cover per issue. Ed(s): Cindy Ovenrack. Cindy Ovenrack, Ed. & Pub., PO Box 1734, Asheville, NC 28802. *Aud.:* Ga.

A long-running publication that is popular among zine readers and editors, *Doris* combines personal stories and comics for an interesting mix. Excerpts of the editor's "D.I.Y. Antidepression Guide" were reprinted in *The Zine Yearbook*, Vol. 5, 2001. Past issues include illustrations and line-drawn comics and the "Doris encyclopedia series" with stories that start with A, B, and C. The latest issue continues with D, E, F, and G, and includes pieces about living in the desert, friendships, abortions, rape, and rediscovering emotions. Zine recommendations and a reader letter are included.

6794. *The Duplex Planet.* [ISSN: 0882-2549] 1979. m. USD 12. Ed(s): David B Greenberger. Duplex Planet, PO Box 1230, Saratoga Springs, NY 12866. Illus. Circ: 800. *Aud.:* Hs, Ga.

One of the longest-running zines in existence, *Duplex Planet* was created when editor David Greenberger began publishing his conversations with residents at the Duplex Nursing Home in Boston. Years later, the publication has inspired a comic book series (*Duplex Planet Illustrated,* Fantagraphics Books), a poetry collection, a five-volume CD set, two documentaries, three plays, a video, and several books. It is a publication about memory and the realities of aging, based on interviews and conversations with nursing home residents and adult center and meal site attendees. Recent questions have included "To what do you attribute your good health?" and "Can you tell me about snakes?" The conversations usually take place with several residents and bounce from topic to topic. Stories about six different residents of the nursing home are available in a new book titled *No More Shaves* (Fantagraphics Books, 2003).

6795. *Dwan.* 1993. irreg. USD 2 newsstand/cover per issue. Ed(s): Donny Smith. Dwan, PO Box 411, Swarthmore, PA 19081; http://www.geocities.com/dwanzine. *Aud.:* Ga, Ac.

Dwan is a bilingual "more or less queer" zine, epitomizing self-expression and community, with no ads and no pretentions toward becoming a "magazine." It combines poetry, excerpts from editor Donny Smith's diaries and correspondence, interviews, and web site listings. The call for submissions is simple: "Queer. Legible. You decide what that means." Issues have recounted conversations about racism, translated poems by Sappho into English (and Emily Dickinson into Spanish), interviewed Mary Harron, the director of "I Shot Andy Warhol," described interesting dreams, and reviewed such micropress publications as *GirlFrenzy* and *Java Turtle.* Occasional poems and prose are translated and reprinted from cited publications.

6796. *Dwelling Portably.* Former titles: *Portable Dwelling; Message Post.* 1980. 3x/yr. USD 2 domestic; USD 3 foreign. Ed(s): Holly Davis. Light Living Library, PO Box 190 UR, Philomath, OR 97370. Illus., adv. Circ: 1300. *Aud.:* Ga.

This small digest will come to the rescue with its array of simple, low-cost, and earth-friendly tips for those "who live in (or out of) tents, buses, vans, and cars." Formerly known as *The Message Post, Dwelling Portably* is a resource zine about ultra-cheap nomadic lifestyles for people seeking the simpler life. If you like living and/or traveling outside the mainstream, *Dwelling Portably* will offer practical tips and commonsense survival skills. Past issues have included essays about cutting twine without a knife, solar cookers, dental care, and building different kinds of tents, shelters, and other furnishings that are low-cost and earth-friendly. Each issue includes want ads, resource listings for other publications, an index to recent issues, and zine reviews.

6797. *East Village Inky.* 1998. irreg. USD 8 for 4 issues. Ed(s): Ayun Halliday. East Village Inky, PO Box 22754, Brooklyn, NY 11202-2754. Illus. *Bk. rev.:* 3, 100-150 words. *Aud.:* Ga.

East Village Inky documents "the ongoing saga of a mother and three-thumbed baby Inky (now in kindergarten) in New York City's East Village" (now transplanted to Brooklyn), with the addition of younger brother, "Milo the fat boy." Hand written and hand drawn, it is an entertaining look at permissive parenting, dwindling naptimes, ethnic dining, and outings with the children. Issues have included "Whence Comest Bitchmother," "Operating Instructions for My Young," "Dismantling the 340 Square Foot Apartment," "Brooklyn Basics," pieces on cleaning tub toys, the World Trade Center collapse, and getting a subscription to the *New York Times.* Earlier issues tell about Inky getting headlice, "The EVI's Guide to Gorilla Marketing," and "Bright New Morning One Year to the Day after the Presidential Election of 2001." Each issue typically includes an "Advice to the Fathers" column, recipes, and zine, comic, film, and kid's book reviews.

6798. *Eat the State!* 1996. w. USD 16 for 20 issues. Ed(s): Maria Tomchick, Troy Skeels. Eat the State!, PO Box 85541, Seattle, WA 98145. Illus., adv. Sample. *Aud.:* Ga.

Eat the State! "is a shamelessly biased political journal. We want an end to poverty, exploitation, imperialism, militarism, racism, sexism, heterosexism, environmental destruction, television, and large ugly buildings, and we want it fucking now." Although the focus is on events and activities in the Seattle, Washington, area, the weekly commentary applies to all and covers national and international concerns. Current issues explore Operation TopOff 2, the terrorism response drills in Chicago and Seattle, the belief that America has designs on Mexico's oil, and North Korea's latest actions. The zine regularly includes the "Nature & Politics" column by Jeffrey St. Clair, comic strips ("This Modern World"), a "Reclaim Our History" timeline, and "Eat These Shorts," a short column of newsworthy items. The publication also includes letters and a calendar of local events. Readers can subscribe to the recycled paper version, check the web site on a weekly basis, get the full contents of the newspaper via e-mail for free, or listen via a local Seattle radio station and on the Internet.

6799. *eXtreme Conformity.* 2000. irreg. USD 6. Larry Nocella, Ed. & Pub., PO Box 122, Royersford, PA 19468-0122. *Aud.:* Hs, Ga, Ac.

Larry Nocella's *eXtreme Conformity,* also known as *XC,* takes readers on a slightly different path from his earlier publication QECE, a political, newsy, thought-provoking zine. *XC* is primarily a pamphlet-style comic-prose zine that plays on conformity and the ordinary with a unique sense of humor. Issues tell mini-stories of icon-type characters.

6800. *Factsheet 5: the definitive guide to the zine revolution.* [ISSN: 0890-6823] 1982. 6x/yr. Individuals, USD 20. Ed(s): Chris Becker. Factsheet 5, PO Box 170099, San Francisco, CA 94117-0099; seth@factsheet5.com; http://www.factsheet5.com. Illus., index, adv. Circ: 15000 Paid. *Bk. rev.:* 55, 125-250 words. *Aud.:* Ga.

Note: Although this is no longer being published, *Factsheet Five* remains an important link to zine history for those involved in the medium both past and present. A complementary web site was still available for viewing, but now it is not. Considered by many to be the world's leading source of zine information and the first zine dedicated solely to the subject of zines, *Factsheet Five* began as a small stapled newsletter sent to friends of Mike Gunderloy, the original editor. It eventually turned into a full-fledged magazine available widely in newsstands and bookstores. Each issue contained more than 1,200 reviews arranged alphabetically within general topical areas (political, personal, queer, science fiction, sex), as well as a half dozen or so longer "Editors' Choice" reviews, address updates, interviews, and articles. Zine publications include the title for legacy purposes and are still waiting for yet another resurrection.

6801. *Fat!So?: for people who don't apologize for their size.* 1994. 4x/yr. USD 12 domestic; USD 20 foreign. Ed(s): Marilyn Wann. Fat! So?, PO Box 423464, San Francisco, CA 94142; marilyn@fatso.com; http://www.fatso.com/. *Aud.:* Ga.

A zine "for people who don't apologize about their size," *Fat!So?* (not to be confused with the 1980s movie) takes on issues concerning America's biggest fear—fat people. It started as a venue to create awareness of the mistreatment of fat people in every aspect of daily life, including work, romance, and medicine. Each issue contains a photo essay showing what real body parts look like, essays, interviews, poetry, and "Aunt Agony," a friendly fat advice column. Past issues have included an interview with the improv comedian Jason Wooten, an article containing statistics on the weight loss culture in the United States ("The Body Mass Index of Fat Culture"), and stories from fat survivors in "Big Fat Truths." Also available, based on content from earlier issues, is *Fat!So? Because You Don't Have to Apologize for Your Size.* (Ten Speed Press, 1999).

6802. *Fish Piss.* [ISSN: 1206-3355] 1997. q. CND 3 newsstand/cover per issue. Ed(s): Louis Rastelli. Spontaneous Productions, Place d'Armes, PO Box 1232, Montreal, PQ H2Y 3K2, Canada; fishpiss@hotmail.com. *Bk. rev.:* Number and length vary. *Aud.:* Ga.

Fish Piss is packed with original prose, poetry, illustrations, cartoons, interviews, music and zine reviews, letters, and even news shorts. Past highlights include Montreal comics, urban ink drawings by Chansigaud, schoolyard fiction by Valerie Joy Kalynchuk, and poetry by Jason Gallagher. Although it is Montreal based, the coverage extends beyond Quebec, with entries in French and English. Current issues include a retrospective look at the bar scene in Montreal during the 1960s, riot stories, a portrait of American aggression across the world, prison life in Guantanamo Bay, Cuba, and a discussion on telemarketing.

6803. ***For the Clerisy: good words for readers.*** 1993. irreg. USD 2 newsstand/cover per issue. Ed(s): Brant Kresovich. For the Clerisy, PO Box 404, Getzville, NY 14068-0404. *Bk. rev.:* Occasional, length varies. *Aud.:* Ga.

This zine, formerly known as *For the Clerisy: About Latvia,* originally studied aspects of Latvian culture "from toilets to bribery" and focused on the editor's travels, teaching job, and language and communication skills. The editor now lives in the United States, and *For the Clerisy* has become a book review zine. The latest issue includes novels by twentieth-century English writers. Past issues have covered comic influences, yippies, true-crime books, and advice for potential English as a Second Language teachers. Additionally, issues typically include essays about films, zine reviews, letters from readers, and "Interview Advice."

6804. ***Giant Robot: Asian pop culture and beyond.*** 1994. q. USD 15. Ed(s): Eric Nakamura, Martin Wong. Giant Robot Publishing, PO Box 2053, Los Angeles, CA 90064; grobot@deltanet.com; http://www.giantrobot.com. Illus., adv. Circ: 40000 Paid. *Aud.:* Hs, Ga.

Giant Robot magazine "covers cool aspects of Asian and Asian-American pop culture." A standard glossy format publication, each issue centers around a topic or theme. There have been reviews of Japanese animated movies and interviews with a variety of personalities such as Michael Lau, the maker of "Crazy Children toys," actress Anita Muia, and Robert Lee, a homeless Korean man in downtown Los Angeles. Past issues have included pieces on Asian junk-food products, haircuts, the tallest Asian-American man, and the Cambodian Landmine Museum. The "Cultural Evolution" issue features an interview with the comedian/actor Stephen Chow, an article on "manpurses" in Japan, and the Beijing punk scene. Regular items include video game, music, and zine reviews, and letters from readers. The web site includes ordering information, links, and excerpts from past issues.

Gray Areas. See Alternatives section.

6805. ***Guide to Lost Wonder: an emanation of the Museum of Lost Wonder.*** 1997. irreg. USD 3 per issue domestic; USD 4 per issue Canada; USD 5 per issue elsewhere. Ed(s): Jeff Hoke. Wonderella Printed, 1204 Neilson St, Berkeley, CA 94706; http://www.onderella.com/pamphlets/lostwonder.htm. Illus. *Aud.:* Ga.

A zine detailed as "an emanation of the Museum of Lost Wonder," this is published by visual artist Jeff Hoke as an activity book for the Museum of Lost Wonder, "a place where people can go to ponder life's big question." Content is philosophical and humorous and often includes cut-and-paste do-it-yourself art objects. One issue ("The Darker Side of Museums") contained a history of the "not so splendid" ways in which collectors, clerics, politicians, and curators have operated, from Ptolemy to the Smithsonian, as well as a piece arguing that P. T. Barnum "put the public in control of their own reasoning machinery." The latest issue ("Revealing the Museum") is the first of a two-part series behind the scenes at the Museum of Lost Wonder. Includes alchemical engravings restored by Hoke.

6806. ***Guinea Pig Zero: a journal for human research subjects.*** [ISSN: 1098-0539] 1996. irreg. Individuals, USD 15 for 4 nos.; USD 5 newsstand/cover per issue domestic. Robert Helms, Ed. & Pub., PO Box 42531, Philadelphia, PA 19101; gpzero@netaxs.com; http://www.geocities.com/hotsprings/villa/2529/. Illus., adv. Refereed. Circ: 4000. *Bk. rev.:* 2-4, 200-400 words. *Aud.:* Ga.

Subtitled "a journal for human research subjects," *Guinea Pig Zero* is an "occupational jobzine for people who volunteer as medical or pharmaceutical research subjects." If you sell yourself to science in any way, this is a must-read. It covers medical experimentation and informed consent from the point of view of an educated "guinea pig." Various sections are devoted to bioethics, the history of medical research subjects, current news and research, evaluations of particular research facilities by volunteers, and true stories of guinea pig adventures. All back issues, 1 through 8, are available, but the publication will resume as a web zine only. The "best of" appears in the new book *Guinea Pig Zero: An Anthology of the Journal for Human Research Subjects* (Garrett County Press, 2002). Past topics have included experimental gene therapy, the serin gas scandal, research unit report cards, the Gulf War experimentation, the CIA's LSD experiments, and the needless deaths of so many research subjects.

6807. ***H2SO4: won't you join us - we're drowning in obscurity but the water is lovely.*** [ISSN: 1083-3897] 1992. s-a. USD 8 domestic; USD 18 foreign; USD 4 newsstand/cover per issue. Ed(s): Jill Stauffer. h2so4, PO Box 423354, San Francisco, CA 94142-3354; h2so4@socrates.berkeley.edu; http://socrates.berkeley.edu/~h2so4. Illus., adv. Circ: 1000. *Bk. rev.:* Number and length varies. *Aud.:* Hs, Ga, Ac.

Subtitled "won't you join us—we're drowning in obscurity but the water is lovely," and "dedicated to provoking thought on politics & philosophy, art & love, without thereby giving up the potential to delight, amuse and entertain." Currently in its seventh year, *h2so4* is a quirky philosophical take on political counterculture with a mixture of essays and commentary on love, art, music, and life. Published twice yearly, it includes a "Dear Philosopher" advice column in which a well-known "thinker" ponders questions from everyday life. Issues regularly feature essays, philosophical letters, poetry, movie, music and book reviews, and illustrations.

6808. ***Hermenaut.*** [ISSN: 1523-8717] 1992. s-a. USD 20 domestic; USD 30 foreign; USD 6 newsstand/cover. Ed(s): Joshua Glenn. Hermenaut, 179 Boylston St, Bldg P, Jamaica Plain, MA 02130-4544; info@hermenaut.com; http://www.hermenaut.com. Illus., adv. Refereed. Circ: 5000 Paid and controlled. *Indexed:* AltPI. *Bk. rev.:* 6, length varies. *Aud.:* Ga, Ac.

Calling itself "the digest of heady philosophy," *Hermenaut* is a full-fledged popular culture journal entertaining contemporary issues surrounding philosophy and culture, with quite a bit of humor thrown in as well. Prominent figures such as Dick Gregory, Walt Whitman, Rosey Grier, The Village People, and David Koresh have been featured. Most issues are theme related, and the current issue is titled "The Stockholm Syndrome," which the editor's define as a psychiatric condition identified in the 1970s that focuses on the emotional dependence a prisoner feels for his or her captor. Back issues have revolved around anorexia/technology, vertigo, camp, and popular culture. Authors regularly include freelance journalists, zine editors, and contributors to numerous publications such as *The New Republic, London Review of Books, Lingua Franca,* and *The Economist.* Book and film reviews are regular features. The current issue presents an essay on the "Origins of Neototalitarianism," an in-depth look at Ti-Grace Atkinson, former president of the New York chapter of the National Organization for Women in the late 1960s, and a personal account of being taken hostage conversationally by a fellow traveler in "Is this Bus Taken?" by Beth Daniels.

6809. ***Hip Mama: the parenting zine.*** [ISSN: 1074-195X] 1994. q. USD 15; USD 22 foreign. Ed(s): Bee Lavender, Ariel Gore. Hip Mama, PO Box 12525, Portland, OR 97212; ariel@hipmama.com. Illus., adv. Circ: 5000. *Indexed:* AltPI. *Bk. rev.:* 4, length varies. *Aud.:* Ga.

"Providing a forum for fresh, authentic writing from the trenches of motherhood," is this zine's mission. *Hip Mama* regularly features practical articles about raising multiracial kids, parenting teenagers, and fighting infringements on public school students' rights. The publication was originally started as a college project to fill the void that traditional parenting and feminist press magazines created when covering single or urban parenting. Glossy print and attractively illustrated with black-and-white photos and drawings, each issue also contains news briefs, short fiction, and poetry. Issues have included first-hand accounts about breast feeding in public, music and book reviews, and suggestions for "kid friendly" restaurants in a variety of locations.

6810. ***Hitch: journal of pop culture absurdity.*** 1994. q. USD 16; USD 4 per issue. Ed(s): Rod M Lott. Hitch Publishing Company, PO Box 23621, Oklahoma City, OK 73123-2621; http://www.hitchmagazine.com. Illus., adv. Circ: 2000. *Bk. rev.:* 2, length varies. *Aud.:* Ga.

Humorous satire aimed at people in the film industry and politics, this publication reports on encounters and interviews with celebrities and offers articles on a variety of topics. A recent issue of *Hitch* features an interview with Gina Gershon('s stand-in), blaxploitation flicks, and 2002's most fascinating people. Each issue also includes film, music, video, book, and zine reviews. Past issues have included articles on trash movie posters, "Hitch Extreme," an entire issue of the early years, karaoke, the Teletubbies, cable TV, and the "Cheap Bastard Christmas Gift Guide."

6811. ***Holy Temple of Mass Consumption.*** 1990. q. Ed(s): Wayne Aiken. Holy Temple of Mass Consumption, PO Box 30904, Raleigh, NC 27622; slack@ncsu.edu. Adv. Circ: 1000. *Aud.:* Ga.

"With strong ties to the finest Subgenius traditions," this zine features scores of reviews, with an emphasis on comics, music, and zines produced by "cranks, weirdos, freaks, net personalities and anyone else who turns us on." The print zine is currently on hold, although the editor claims to have new material in the works. Past issues include clip-art graphics and original artwork. Check out the web site to find atheist-oriented links, freedom/liberty quotes, an animated gif library, and information on how to become a "SubGenius Minister."

6812. ***Holy TitClamps.*** 1989. irreg. USD 3 per issue. Larry-Bob, PO Box 590488, San Francisco, CA 94159-0488; larrybob@io.com; http://www.io.com/~larrybob. Circ: 2000. *Aud.:* Ga.

Published by the editor of the review zine *Queerzine Explosion* (see below), this tabloid-style publication regularly includes articles, fiction, narratives, interviews, artwork, poetry, comics, and zine reviews.

6813. ***Indy Unleashed.*** irreg. USD 1.65 newsstand/cover per issue. Ed(s): Owen Thomas. Indy Unleashed, PO Box 9651, Columbus, OH 43209. *Bk. rev.:* Occasional, 200-300 words. *Aud.:* Ga.

Begun as an all-review supplement to the *Ten Page News* (below in this section), *Indy Unleashed* examines a diverse range of micropress publications. Each issue features substantial and critical reviews of zines, comics, and books. In addition to the reviews, each issue includes review-like articles and commentary. Past topics have focused on the zine industry, and "underground writers."

6814. ***Infiltration.*** irreg. CND 10 for 4 nos.; CND 3 newsstand/cover. Infiltration, PO Box 13, Toronto, ON M6H 4E1, Canada. *Aud.:* Ga.

"The zine about going places you're not supposed to go," *Infiltration* is "devoted to the art of urban exploration" and documenting these escapades with maps, pictures, and diagrams. This Canadian publication features editorials, exploring advice and information, articles on recent expeditions, and interviews, from abandoned building adventures to posh hotel crashing. The current issue, "Twin Cities Spectacular," explores the landscape beneath Minneapolis-St. Paul. Past editions have explored the secret spaces of churches in Toronto, Paris, Lansing, and Bangkok, ferries in British Columbia, abandoned floating restaurants near St. Catharines, tankers in Hamilton harbor, tunnels under Toronto's Degrasi High, and exploring an abandoned missile silo in Roswell, New Mexico. For the curious and mischievous at heart.

6815. ***Leeking Ink.*** 1995. irreg. USD 2. Leeking Inc., c/o Davida Gypsy Breier, PO Box 963, Havre de Grace, MD 21078; http://www.leekinginc.com/. *Aud.:* Hs, Ga.

A personal and quite humorous journal-type zine by the publisher of *Glovebox Chronicles* and *Xerography Debt* (both in this section), the latest issue of *Leeking Ink* at 36 pages includes "The Hardest Year in My Life" and "Memories of Minnesota" as well as the usual on-going journal entries. Past issues have examined shoe love, turning thirty, visits to the doctor, buying an Oliver typewriter at a flea market, vegetarianism, travel essays, and hiking with ticks. Issues typically include hilarious journal excerpts, recipes, letters, and zine reviews.

6816. ***Living Free: a personal journal of self liberation.*** 1979. bi-m. USD 12 domestic; USD 15 overseas; USD 2. Sample. Ed(s): Jim Stumm. Living Free, Box 29, Hiler Branch, Buffalo, NY 14223. Adv. Circ: 200 Paid. *Bk. rev.:* Occasional, 200-600 words. *Aud.:* Ga.

A bimonthly newsletter about "self-reliance, personal freedom, and lifestyle alternatives," *Living Free* is a forum for debate among "freedom-seekers, libertarians, anarchists, and outlaws, since 1979." Topics have included garden seeds and organic gardening, how to make wine, privacy tips, homesteading, survivalists, and fugitives eluding the federal government. Issues include editorial commentary, nonfiction, news items, letters from readers, zine listings, and book reviews.

6817. ***Loving More Magazine: new models for relationships.*** Formerly (until 1991): *P E P Talk - Group Marriage News.* [ISSN: 1523-5858] 1984. q. Members, USD 30; Non-members, USD 24; USD 6 newsstand/cover per issue. Ed(s): Ryam Nearing. P E P Publishing, PO Box 4358, Boulder, CO 80306; ryam@lovemore.com; http://www.lovemore.com. Adv. *Bk. rev.:* Occasional. *Aud.:* Ga, Ac.

Loving More Magazine is "the only magazine in the world dedicated to new models for relationships." This quarterly is dedicated exclusively to topics involving multi-partner relating. It is intended as a resource for people who wish to move beyond traditional monogamy toward what editors call "polyamory (many loves) or Loving More." It regularly includes interviews and narratives related to sexual freedom and polyfidelity, spirituality and sacred sex, alternative communities, and parenting. Past issues have included a bibical perspective on polyamory, how not to enter into a nonmonogamous relationship, and combating jealousy with multiple partners. Each issue contains news briefs, letters from readers, personal ads, and regional resource listings.

6818. ***Lumpen Magazine.*** [ISSN: 1092-3667] 1993. q. m. until 2002. USD 25; USD 35 Canada; USD 45 elsewhere. Lumpen Media Group, 960 W 31st St, Chicago, IL 60608; lumpen@lumpen.com; http://www.lumpen.com. Illus., adv. Circ: 22500 Controlled. *Indexed:* AltPI. *Bk. rev.:* 1-2, length varies. *Aud.:* Ga.

Generally antiauthoritarian, *Lumpen,* loosely translated from German as "a rag," covers progressive politics and underground culture and includes a nice mix of local, national, and interantional items. A recent issue, titled "The Apocalypse Issue," features an interview with Noam Chomsky, diary entries from a member of the Iraq peace team, the latest in an on-going series that details George W. Bush's agenda for world domination, and a listing of the ten worst corporations of 2002. Past issues have covered a Chicago-based activist group, Internet filtering, photos from the G8 summit in Italy, and dispatches from the anti-IMF/World Bank protests in Washington, DC. Occasional fiction is included, and music, book, and zine reviews are regularly featured.

6819. ***Maximum Rock 'n' Roll.*** [ISSN: 0743-3530] 1982. m. USD 18 in US & Canada; USD 24 in Mexico & S. America; USD 33 in Europe. Ed(s): Arwen Curry, Mike Thorn. Maximum Rock'n'Roll, PO Box 460760, San Francisco, CA 94146-0760. Illus., adv. *Bk. rev.:* 5-7, 200-500 words. *Aud.:* Hs, Ga.

An influential punk rock magazine, *Maximum Rock'n'roll* includes a considerable amount of text in each tabloid-style issue—space is not wasted. Issues include band interviews, concert listings, club, zine and book reviews, guest columns, letters, articles, news, and video listings. Substantial political commentary weaves throughout the pages. A recent issue titled "What Happened to Music Zines" features a discussion with five New York City based zine editors, numerous articles on the war in Iraq including a piece by Noam Chomsky, several personal recountings of demonstrations against the ongoing invasion, and commentary on the International Solidarity Movement and a trip to Palestine. Extensive advertising for bands and punk record labels make up a significant portion of each issue.

6820. ***Minimum Security.*** 1999. irreg. USD 2 newsstand/cover per issue. Ed(s): Stephanie McMillan. Minimum Security, PO Box 460673, Ft. Lauderdale, FL 33346; steph@minimumsecurity.net; http://www.minimumsecurity.net. *Aud.:* Ga.

A political cartoon zine that takes on the latest national and word issues with biting humor and satire. Published in one-page strips, the issues have dealt with police brutality, human rights, animal rights, political prisoners, and the WTO. A recent issue deals primarily with the war on terrorism, with views not found in most mainstream news publications. McMillan's work can also be sampled in the anthology *Attitude: The New Subversive Political Cartoonists,* edited by Ted Rall (NBM Publishing, 2002).

6821. *Monozine.* irreg. Ed(s): Todd Lesser. Monozine, PO Box 598, Reisertown, MD 21136. *Aud.:* Ga.

Monozine, originally published after the editor's "bout with mono," covers a nearly universal topic of conversation: doctors, physical ailments, and illness. Touted as an anti-medical magazine, it contains contributors' first-hand accounts of coping with an array of injuries and illnesses, letters from readers, and cartoons. Past content has included a piece on gunshots, "do-it-yourself" surgery, an entire issue ("The Rock Issue") devoted to musicians' sick stories, contacting herpes, vomiting, and doctor's offices. If you're one of those people who can't stand the sight of blood, you probably won't want to read about it either. Slightly delayed with publication. Editors say two new issues are in the works.

6822. *Mouth: voice of the disability nation.* [ISSN: 1071-5657] 1990. bi-m. USD 48 (Individuals, USD 16). Ed(s): Lucy Gwin. Free Hand Press, Inc., 61 Brighton St, Rochester, NY 14607. Illus. Circ: 7500 Paid. *Indexed:* AltPI. *Bk. rev.:* Occasional, length varies. *Aud.:* Ga, Ac.

Mouth, the "voice of the disability nation," is a no-nonsense publication with the intent to increase awareness and understanding of our "Disability Culture." It employs an in-your-face style, confronting such topics as nursing home abuse, wheelchair recalls, accessibility issues, ADA compliancy, assisted suicide, and charitable organizations ("pity peddling, misery merchandising"). The current issue, "Dirty Words," includes a piece by Larry Biondi, an independent-living specialist, and news from a federal district court appeal for the life of Theresa Marie Schiavo, a woman with massive brain damage. Issues include resources, reader letters, disability news briefs, photography, political cartoons, and reviews.

6823. *Musea.* 1992. m. USD 10. Tom Hendricks, Ed. & Pub., 4000 Hawthorne, 5, Dallas, TX 75219-2275; tomhendricks474@cs.com; http://musea.digitalchainsaw.com. Circ: 400 Paid and controlled. *Aud.:* Ga.

Musea, "the zine for ART and the ART REVOLUTION," is a newsletter that comments upon and provides the latest news about the arts industry and media, with special attention to art/media conglomerates such as Paramount/Viacom, AOL Time Warner, Westinghouse, and Disney. With more than 120 issues published, editors construct short newsworthy stories ("Hard News") from a variety of print and AP wire sources. Current issues have reported on animals and art, movie and television scripts, and the current state of radio. Each issue includes prose, poetry, comics, and a monthly write-in contest for readers with questions such as "Who wrote an entire novel without using the letter 'e'?" or "What is the name of the largest mud-brick building in the world?" *Musea* is also well known for its art envelopes made from glossy magazine photos. Each is a one-of-a-kind piece of mailable art. Requests can be sent to the mailing address.

6824. *My Evil Twin Sister.* [ISSN: 1536-7851] 1995. irreg. USD 5. Ed(s): Amber Gayle. Evil Twin Publications, PO Box 351, Williams, OR 97544. Illus. *Aud.:* Hs, Ga.

Originally conceived as a zine project by identical twins Stacy Wakefield and Amber Gayle, *My Evil Twin Sister* has become more novella-like in the past few years. Issues such as "Notta Lotta Love Stories" feature stories by Amber and photos by Stacy about people she's loved and the emotions that accompany the highs and lows of loving and being loved. Past issues available include "Ramble Right," and "Greetings From the Endless Highway." The publications include poetry, prose, and diary entries written by Amber and original design, photography, and illustrations by Stacy.

6825. *Mystery Date.* irreg. Ed(s): Lynn Peril. Mystery Date, PO Box 641592, San Francisco, CA 94164-1592; http://members.tripod.com/~Mystery_Date. *Aud.:* Hs, Ga, Ac.

Subtitled "one gal's guide to good stuff," *Mystery Date* is, according to creator Lynn Peril, "a fanzine devoted to my obsession with used books—particularly old sex and dating manuals, etiquette and self-help books, and health, beauty and fashion guides." Known as the "little pink zine," this publication is regularly used as a text in the University of North Carolina–Chapel Hill Department of Sociology, and it has included such topics as sex education records ("Sex Ed on Vinyl"), Jayne Mansfield, "Marriage Guides for the Perplexed," a survey of advice books from 1878 through 1976, and advice for single living. The most current issue features articles on feminine hygiene products, bra buying, and celebrity advice for teens. Nos. 1-6 are currently out of print, and number 7 is in the works, according to Peril. In edition to the print zine, the web site spotlights a "Find of the Month or So" plus selections from past issues and plans for the upcoming issue. A new book, tentatively titled *Bluestockings and Sex Kittens: A Social History of the College Girl in the 20th Century,* will be published by W.W. Norton in 2004 or 2005, joining *Pink Think: Becoming a Woman in Many Uneasy Lessons,* published by Norton in 2002.

6826. *Nuclear Resister: a chronicle of hope.* Formerly (until 1982): *National No-Nukes Prison Support Collective. Newsletter.* [ISSN: 0883-9875] 1980. 6x/yr. USD 15 domestic; USD 20 Canada; USD 25 elsewhere. Ed(s): Jack Cohen Joppa. National No-Nukes Prison Support Collective, PO Box 43383, Tucson, AZ 85733; nukeresister@igc.org; www.nonviolence.org/nukeresister. Illus. Sample. Circ: 1000. Microform: PQC. *Aud.:* Ga, Ac.

Nuclear Resister provides comprehensive reporting on arrests for antinuclear civil resistance in the United States and Canada, "with an emphasis on providing support for the women and men jailed for these actions." There is also reporting on antiwar arrests and peace-prisoner support. Each issue provides the names and jail addresses of currently imprisoned antinuclear and antiwar activists. Readers are encouraged to provide active support by writing letters and in other ways requested by the prisoners. Each issue includes U.S. and international news about protests, arrests, trials, announcements about publications, events, and future actions. In addition, defendants' statements are occasionally printed, as are letters and essays by prisoners. Current issues include an account of the School of the Americas protest, updates on the three religious sisters imprisoned in Colorado for a Sacred Earth and Space Plowshares action, a memoriam to honor Philip Berrigan, and a day-by-day list of arrests of opponents of the war in Iraq. The last issue of each year includes the "Resistance Reflections" column, which since 1983, has tallied the nuclear resistance arrests with a brief overview of the past year.

6827. *Oblivion.* 1995. q. Oblivion, 120 State Ave, N E, Ste 76, Olympia, WA 98501-8212; oblivion@oblivion.net; http://www.oblivion.net. *Bk. rev.:* Occasional. *Aud.:* Hs, Ga.

Currently on hiatus, *Oblivion* focuses on such "youth rights movement" concerns as curfews, Internet restrictions, and age of consent. Originally started as a zine publication in 1995, it is now a nonprofit youth rights organization, and editors promise that a long overdue issue will be well worth the wait. Each edition contains news briefs about young people, and articles and letters by students struggling against authority. Topics have included WTO stories, post-Columbine hysteria, women and children in Afghanistan, the pledge of allegiance and abstainers, and the latest AOL parental control settings for Internet sites. Each issue includes editorial commentary ("Oblivion Speaks"), reader letters, and reviews of zines that focus on youth issues.

6828. *Oop.* irreg. USD 8 for 4 issues. Ed(s): Joey Harrison. Oop, 4454 Pennfield Rd, Toledo, OH 43612. *Aud.:* Ga.

"Your authoritative source for the oopist perspective," *Oop* is a personal zine that contains the quirky writings of editor Joey Harrison. The latest issue includes a story about a visit to view a taping of Conan O'Brien and ruminations relating to an exchange of letters between the editor and O'Brien before the visit; recollections of Osama bin Laden by various fictional characters; a reprint of a newspaper essay making fun of John Ashcroft; an essay on mnemonics; and more. Issues have examined brushes with celebrities, the bands around broccoli stalks, wierd albums, and killers Harrison has known. Issues include letters from readers, interviews, cartoons, and photos.

6829. *Progressive Review.* Former titles (until 1985): *D.C. Gazette; Capitol East Gazette.* [ISSN: 0889-2202] 1966. bi-m. USD 18 domestic; USD 32 foreign; USD 2.50 newsstand/cover per issue. Ed(s): Sam Smith. Progressive Review, 1312, 18th St, N W, 5th Fl, Washington, DC 20036; news@prorev.com; http://prorev.com. Illus. Circ: 2000. Reprint: PQC. *Indexed:* AltPI. *Aud.:* Ga, Ac.

Progressive Review, billed as the "longest running act on the off-Broadway of Washington journalism," has a long history as an alternative publication. It is the third generation of a magazine started in the '60s as the *Capitol East Gazette,* a community-based newspaper. The paper changed to a more city-wide focus under the name of *DC Gazette,* and then in the mid-'80s to the present title to focus on national politics. Well known for its coverage and support of the antiwar movement, prison reform, and urban planning, *Progressive Review* became an outspoken critic of the "war on drugs" and a voice of the growing Green movement. Current issues regularly report on the "Latest Undernews," "Youth," "Bush News," "Green Politics," "Ecology," and "Peace." A recent issue covers the situation in Iraq, the Israeli-Palestinian peace process, and a "Hillary Watch."

6830. ***Punk Planet.*** [ISSN: 1534-7761] 199?. bi-m. USD 24 domestic; USD 35 Canada; USD 48 in Europe. Ed(s): Daniel Sinker. Punk Planet, 4229 N Honore, Chicago, IL 60613. Adv. *Bk. rev.:* 1-2, 700-800 words. *Aud.:* Hs, Ga.

Consistently ranked among the top twenty zine favorites, *Punk Planet* contains interviews, articles, reviews, letters, and ads with the focus on punk music. It also includes essays and thought-provoking commentary on broader topics such as radio consolidation and the Telecommunications Act, travels in the West Bank, and genetically altered food. A recent issue, titled "Revenge of Print," is a cover-to-cover tribute to those zine makers, authors, and comic artists still churning out their writing and art in print, with interviews and excerpts of their current work. Past issues have included a look at musicians against the war, Clear Channel's monopoly, Chicago politics, and a tribute to Joey Ramone. Each issue includes extensive reader letters; zine, music, and book reviews; and a new, on-going column called "Static," filled with shorter pieces about people, bands, politics, and more.

6831. ***Queer Ramblings: an international publication for queer women and their many admirers.*** Formerly: *Ramblings.* 2000. m. USD 16; USD 3 newsstand/cover. Ed(s): Sandra R Garcia. Queer Ramblings, Inc., 392, 14th St., Ste 1A, Brooklyn, NY 11215; sandy@queerramblings.com; http://www.queerramblings.com. *Aud.:* Ga.

Begun as an outlet for the editor's personal writing, *QueerRamblings*, "an international publication for queer women and their many admirers," regularly publishes original prose, poetry, photography, and beautiful artwork by contributing women as well. Relationships, love, a week of solitude, and facing one's addiction are just a sampling of the well-written content found in each issue.

6832. ***Queerzine Explosion.*** s-a. USD 2 for 4 nos. Ed(s): Laurence Roberts. Queerzine Explosion, PO Box 590488, San Francisco, CA 94159-0488; larrybob@io.com. *Aud.:* Ga.

Laurence Roberts (a.k.a. Larry-Bob) is the expert when it comes to zines by lesbian, gay, bi, and transgender people. *Queerzine Explosion* typically includes short reviews of comic books, newsletters, catalogs, zines, and magazines, as well as information about related books, videos, music, and "non-queer-specific zine resources," with ordering/contact information supplied. Brief excerpts from current and past issues can be found on the *Holy Titclamps* web site. The latest issue was published in 2001, but Larry-Bob maintains that the zine is still alive. He also publishes the zine *Holy Titclamps* (see above).

6833. ***Race Traitor: journal of the new abolitionism.*** 1993. irreg. USD 40 for 4 nos. (Individuals, USD 20 for 4 nos.; USD 5 newsstand/cover per issue). Ed(s): John Garvey, Noel Ignatiev. New Abolitionists, Inc., PO Box 499, Dorchester, MA 02122; http://www.newabolition.org. Adv. Circ: 2000. *Indexed:* AltPI. *Bk. rev.:* 1-9, length varies. *Aud.:* Ga, Ac.

Using the motto "Treason to whiteness is loyalty to humanity," *Race Traitor* confronts head-on the issues of white privilege, race relations, and racism, and continues its dedication to "abolishing the privileges of the white skin." Articles report on a variety of subject matter such as anti-Semitism and white supremacy, magnet schools, the surrealist movement in the United States, sociological examinations of "whiteness," and police-assisted homicide. An anthology of selected essays from the first five issues was published by Routledge (1996). Although not halted, the current issue has been delayed. A recent issue attempts to articulate an abolitionist vision by revealing essential elements in "Abolition and the New Society." A recent special double issue titled "Surrealism in the USA" includes the complete contents of the suppressed surrealist issue of *Socialist Review.* Issues typically include fiction, poetry, reviews, and letters.

6834. ***Ram's Horn: a monthly newsletter of food system analysis.*** [ISSN: 0827-4053] 1980. m. CND 20 domestic; USD 20 United States; USD 26 elsewhere. Ed(s): Cathleen Kneen. Ram's Horn, S-6, C-27, RR#1, Sorrento, BC V0E 2W0, Canada; ramshorn@ramshorn.bc.ca. Illus. *Bk. rev.:* Occasional, 350 words. *Aud.:* Ga, Ac.

Subtitled "a monthly newsletter of food system analysis," *Ram's Horn* presents a critique of the agribusiness status quo and acts as a watchdog on such topics as food aid, food labeling, irradiation, additives, and genetic engineering. The zine also features pieces about agricultural alternatives like farmers' markets and community gardens. Current topics include the U.S. food plan for Iraq, making structural change in the food system, and organic standards and pesticides. There are numerous book reviews, such as "Invisible Giant: Cargill and its Transnational Strategies," which details the strategies and goals of food industry conglomerates. Illustrated with cartoons.

6835. ***Razorcake.*** m. Razorcake Fanzine/Webzine, PO Box 42129, Los Angeles, CA 90042; webzine.editor@razorcake.com. *Aud.:* Ga.

Often reviewed as a "punk genre zine," *Razorcake* is much more than that, with timely articles and interviews as well as the standard comics, plus zine, music, live show, and book reviews. A sampling of recent content includes an in-depth look at anarchy and the Emma Goldman Papers Project in Berkeley, road trips and driving tips, the Hitler and Henry Ford connection, rants about vinyl records vs. CDs, essays on music genre movies, Internet advertising, and mail-order catalogs. As a bonus, each subscription also comes with a free punk rock CD and assorted goodies.

RFD. See Lesbian, Gay, Bisexual, and Transgender section.

6836. ***Rockrgrl: no beauty tips or guilt trips.*** [ISSN: 1086-5985] 1995. bi-m. USD 15 domestic; USD 30 foreign; USD 4.50 newsstand/cover per issue. Ed(s): Carla A Desantis. Rockrgrl, 7683 S E 27th St, Ste 317, Mercer Island, WA 98040-2826; info@rockrgrl.com; http://www.rockrgrl.com. Illus., adv. Circ: 10000. Online: OCLC Online Computer Library Center, Inc.; ProQuest Information & Learning; SoftLine Information. *Indexed:* GendWatch. *Bk. rev.:* Occasional, length varies. *Aud.:* Hs, Ga.

Rockrgrl's cover assertion—"no beauty tips or guilt trips"—holds true. This magazine straightforwardly dispenses "information and inspiration for women in the music business," with columns on legal matters and equipment, interviews, and music reviews. Each issue typically features a different "cover-girl" for the main cover story, although one issue detailed "Rape at Woodstock '99: Still Searching for Answers" and another presented "Rock's 50 Greatest Women of All Time." A recent issue includes an interview with Brody Armstrong of the Australian punk trio The Distillers, a guide to touring in Silverlake, California, more interviews, a sneak peek at the new line of Daisy Rock guitars, and reader letters.

6837. ***Rumpshaker.*** irreg. Ed(s): Eric Weiss. Rumpshaker, 72-38 65th Place, Glendale, NY 11385; rshaker5@aol.com; http://www.rumpshakerzine.com. *Aud.:* Hs, Ga.

Described by the editor as a "hardcore zine," *Rumpshaker* includes a wide variety of material—the primary focus centered around punk bands—with interviews of those involved in the "hardcore" scene and extensive punk band reviews. Each issue contains articles and commentary primarily by the editor. There is also a section titled "Use Your Head," which includes entries by other zine editors. Included in a recent issue is a look at punk rock photography in "The Art of Shooting People—Interviews with Hardcore Photographers," several articles on obsessive-compulsive disorder, an interview with Gene Bauston of Farm Sanctuary, and an interview with Kid Dynamite. Other features include a zine guide and an alphabetical list of punk record labels with addresses. There is a delay in publication of current issue, but those in the know say it is still in print.

6838. *Slingshot.* 1988. q. Free in Bay Area. Slingshot, 3214 Shattuck Ave, Berkeley, CA 94705. Circ: 9000. *Aud.:* Ga.

A long-running anarchist newspaper celebrating its 15th birthday, *Slingshot* covers community struggles in Berkeley and around the San Francisco Bay Area. Although the content generally focuses on East Bay concerns, national and global issues are reported as well. A recent issue reports on the fight against the WTO, the closing of the Lesaffre Yeast (formerly known as Red Star Yeast) factory in West Oakland, antiwar sentiment, and the deaths of the three International Solidarity Movement activists in Palestine. Updates on political prisoners, zine and alternative magazine reviews, and guides to local activities, actions, and events are regular features. Past issues have included articles on "Food Not Bombs," industrialization and pollution in West Oakland, the Yucca Mountain nuclear waste dump, and anti–civil liberty measures. Free in the Bay Area and free to prisoners.

6839. *Slug & Lettuce.* 1986. bi-m. USD 3.30 domestic; USD 1 per issue foreign. Ed(s): Christine Boarts Larson. Slug & Lettuce, PO Box 26632, Richmond, VA 23261-6632. Illus., adv. Circ: 8000. *Aud.:* Hs, Ga.

A jam-packed tabloid for "punk rockers, zine makers, and other do-it-yourselfers," *Slug & Lettuce* heavily emphasizes reviews of zines and music. Each edition also includes classified ads dealing with do-it-yourself projects, distributor information, book reviews, events and gatherings, a "local punks guide to the Bay Area" (and Boston), with listings of restaurants, record stores, book stores, coffee shops, punk friendly bars, and interesting places to go. Also included is an introduction by the editor, short essays, and regular columns (e.g., "ecopunk," "vegan action"), which account for a fair portion of each issue. Recent content covers sex, relationships, love, suicide, anxiety/panic attacks, and gardening.

Small Magazine Review. See *Small Press Review* in the Books and Book Reviews section.

6840. *Snowbound: the frosty zine.* [ISSN: 1097-6043] 1998. a. USD 8 domestic; USD 12 foreign. Keiko Media Inc, Snowbound, PMB 708, 3023 N Clark St, Chicago, IL 60657-5205; http://keikomedia.com/. *Aud.:* Ga.

Snowbound, an annual "zine with ice in its veins," is part literary journal, part ice hockey fanzine, and part Nordic-Baltic music review. Each issue contains a feature section that explores a different topic and serves as an international link to music from Finland. The 2002 "Urban Borealis" issue includes contributor profiles in "Coldsnap," a piece on balancing new technology in Greenland, and a look at the white power movement, with the Scandinavian connection to the neo-fascist variation of black metal. Each issue also includes a cartoon section and "Rekord Reviews," with music from Nordic and Baltic Europe. Additionally, the latest issue contains two reports examining the backstage and behind-the-scenes workings of music festivals; the Nordic Roots Festival in Minneapolis, Minnesota, and the Provinssirock Festival in Seinajoki, Finland. A hiatus is planned for 2003, with new issues in winter 2004/05

6841. *Stay Free!* 1993. 10 every x mos. USD 10 for 3 nos. Ed(s): Carrie McLaren. Stay Free!, PO Box 306, New York, NY 10012; stayfree@sunsite.unc.edu; http://sunsite.unc.edu/stayfree. Adv. Circ: 5000. *Aud.:* Ga.

Stay Free is "focused on issues surrounding commercialism and American culture." Theme-oriented issues typically include interviews and humorous commentary on a variety of advertising concerns. A recent "Copyright Issue" features the "Illegal Art Exhibit," and includes an interview with New York University historian Siva Vaidhyanathan, letters to George W. Bush, and an interview with Public Enemy's Chuck D and Hank Shocklee in "Copyrights and Hip-Hop."

6842. *Steamshovel Press.* [ISSN: 1062-3795] 1988. q. USD 25 domestic; USD 30 foreign. Ed(s): Kenn Thomas. Kenn Thomas, Ed. & Pub., PO Box 210553, St. Louis, MO 63121; kennthomas@umsl.edu; http://www.steamshovelpress.com. Illus., adv. Circ: 700 Paid. *Bk. rev.:* 8, length varies. *Aud.:* Ga, Ac.

Conspiracy theories, mind control projects, flying saucers, extraterrestrials, and the 9/11 attack on America are covered here with a great deal of seriousness in interviews, articles, book reviews, and letters from readers. A recent issue includes author interviews, examines embedded reporters in the invasion of Iraq, and discusses numerous current conspiracies and corruption in the U.S. government. The web site includes selected content, book reviews, and a new conspiracy portal to books, videos, and CDs.

The Sun. See Alternatives section.

6843. *Tablet (Seattle).* 2000. bi-w. Ed(s): De Kwok. Tablet Newspaper, 1122 E. Pike St., PMB #1435, Seattle, WA 98122; editor@tabletnewspaper.com; http://www.tabletnewspaper.com. *Aud.:* Hs, Ga.

Tablet is a biweekly publication dedicated to promoting emerging music, art, and political communities of the Northwest and beyond. Each issue has wide-ranging content organized within "Music," "Politics," "Arts," and "Life" departments. A recent issue contains reports on tactical nuclear weapons, the upcoming presidential election, and rebuilding Iraq, as well as extensive band and film reviews and a segment of the cartoon "Kitties."

6844. *Ten Page News.* irreg. USD 1.32 newsstand/cover per issue. Ed(s): Owen Thomas. Ten Page News, PO Box 9651, Columbus, OH 43209. *Bk. rev.:* Occasional, length varies. *Aud.:* Ga.

At first glance *Ten Page News* appears lacking in organization and design, but it soon becomes clear that what it might lack in appearance it more than makes up for with content. Well known for its incisive and critical reviews of micropress publications, each issue offers a wide range of subject matter. Editor Owen Thomas, who holds a doctorate in mathematics, also publishes the review zine *Indy Unleashed* (above in this section). A recent issue reviews eight comics, including *Guide to Lost Wonder* (above in this section) and the debut of *Eldritch Pulp Adventure,* and reports on the SPACE 2003: Small Press and Alternative Comics Expo that was held in Ohio. Each issue typically reviews seven or eight publications and includes editorial commentary, letters, and zine distribution information, as well as an article or two relating to the academic profession. Past issues have reported on the Underground Publishing Conference, included zine reviews and poetry, described "ten English-language novels I've loved and haven't read in about ten years or more," shared memories of the Monroe County Public Library, and provided a thorough index to the first 15 issues.

6845. *Turning the Tide: journal of anti-racist action, research and education.* [ISSN: 1082-6491] 1988. q. USD 15 in North America; USD 25 elsewhere. Ed(s): Michael Novick. Michael Novick, PO Box 1055, Culver City, CA 90232-1055; part2001@usa.net; http://www.antiracist.org. Illus., adv. Circ: 9000. Vol. ends: Spring/Winter. *Indexed:* AltPI. *Bk. rev.:* 1, 450 words. *Aud.:* Ga, Ac.

Begun as a stapled antiracism newsletter covering police brutality, the neo-Nazi movement, and hate crimes in general, *Turning the Tide* has evolved into a tabloid "journal of antiracist activism, research, and education." Published quarterly by the "People Against Racist Terror (PART)," it contains action alerts and event information, political commentaries, interviews, letters, and occasional book reviews. A recent issue issue includes a critical analysis on lessons learned from war, a piece about the C.R.A.C.K. program, in which people struggling with drug addiction are offered $200 in exchange for becoming sterilized, and contact information for political prisoners in the United States. Past issues include articles on antigay violence, a California high-school anarchist organization, international solidarity, Native American rights, police abuse, political prisoners, and prisoner rights.

6846. *Umbrella.* [ISSN: 0160-0699] 1978. irreg. USD 25 (Individuals, USD 20). Ed(s): Judith A Hoffberg. Umbrella Associates, PO Box 3640, Santa Monica, CA 90408; umbrella@ix.netcom.com; http://colophon.com/journal. Illus., adv. Circ: 500 Paid. *Indexed:* ABM. *Bk. rev.:* 90-100, 100-450 words. *Aud.:* Ac.

Chronicling the small-press culture of artists' books, artist-created zines, mail art, and related disciplines, *Umbrella* is an important source of news and reviews, including a fair sampling of international coverage. It celebrates its

25th anniversary next year as an artist book publication. A typical issue contains information about mail art shows, obituaries, exhibition listings, and short reviews on the latest exhibition catalogs and artists' books published during the year. Issues also include essays, interviews, web sites of interest, memorials to those well known in the art world, and calls for entries of mail art.

6847. ***World War Three Illustrated.*** 1979. irreg. USD 3.50 per issue. World War Three, PO Box 20777, New York, NY 10009. *Aud.:* Hs, Ga.

At first glance, it's hard to comprehend the volume of political content that's packed between the uniquely colorful, illustrated covers of this publication. A regular comic it's not, and in fact, the editors initially had a difficult time getting the publication on the newsstand because it was considered too "heavy" for the comic world and too "comic-like" for the serious political publications. That is no longer the case, as *World War Three Illustrated* is recognized both nationally and internationally as a powerful resource for current events topics, such as religion, gentrification, racism, sexism, homelessness, war, and violence. A recent issue includes the diverse reactions of artists, writers, and cartoonists to September 11th. Highlights of past issues are anthologized in two trade paperbacks as *World War Three Illustrated: 1980-1988* and *World War Three Illustrated: Confrontational Comics* (Four Walls Eight Windows, 1995).

6848. ***Xerography Debt: the review zine with latent per-zine tendencies.*** Formerly (until 2002): *Xerox Debt.* 1999. 3x/yr. USD 9; USD 3 newsstand/cover. Ed(s): Davida Gypsy Breier. Leeking Inc., PO Box 963, Havre de Grace, MD 21078. *Aud.:* Ga.

Formerly known as *Xerox Debt*, *Xerography Debt* is "the review zine with latent per-zine tendencies." A wonderful resource consisting mainly of zine reviews by zine writers, it is publicized by Breier as "a hybrid of review zine and personal zine." What better way to get initiated into the culture than by reading what zine editors have to say about new and old titles? Each issue also includes the latest zine news, announcements and commentary from zine writers, contact information for reviewers, distributor information, art work, and other bits and pieces of valuable information. Some content is available online, as are the beginning stages of a comprehensive index that will eventually include all the zines reviewed in past issues.

6849. ***Zine Guide: the ultimate independent press resource guide.*** [ISSN: 1537-6125] 1997. 2x/yr. USD 12; USD 7.95 newsstand/cover per issue. Ed(s): Brent Ritzel. Tail Spins Magazine, 908 N. Oakley, Ste. 2, Chicago, IL 60622. Adv. Circ: 12000 Paid. *Aud.:* Ga.

Infamous for its favorite and least favorite zine surveys, *Zine Guide* contains contact data and brief annotations for thousands of titles, arranged alphabetically. Survey results of best (and least favorite) zines are included, with compilations based on votes from the general public. Issues include editorials, articles on preserving zines in the library and the zine revolution, "Zine Guide Forum," advertisements, interviews, reader comments, distributor information, and "Dead Letter Office," as well as zines not included in the latest issue, a person index, a record label index, a band/musician index, zine subject and place indexes, and information about zine libraries.

6850. ***Zine World: a reader's guide to the underground press.*** 1996. q. USD 14 domestic; USD 18 in Canada & Mexico; USD 22 elsewhere. Ed(s): Jerianne Thompson. Jerianne Thompson, Ed. & Pub., PO Box 330156, Murfreesboro, TN 37113-0156; jerianne@undergroundpress.org; http://www.undergroundpress.org/. Illus. *Bk. rev.:* 1, 100-200 words. *Aud.:* Ga.

Formerly known (and currently being referred to) as *Zine World*, this is a significant publication devoted to coverage of "small-scale amateur books and periodicals" (generally excluding "anything fancified enough to have a UPC, ISBN, or ISSN"). Although the web site is still "Readers Guide...," the latest issue is titled *Zine World: A Readers Guide to the Underground Press.* Valuable for readers and publishers alike, each issue contains about 300 reviews, with some zines examined by more than one person. Reviewer bios are a helpful addition, as are such details as estimated reading time for each title. Each issue contains news, letters, reviews, address changes, event listings, classifieds for zines and other underground projects (where listings up to 50 words are free for any do-it-yourself project), and a "Word of Mouth" section, where readers send in recommendations on wholesale and retail distributor information and tell whom to avoid buying from and/or what titles to avoid reading. Because of a delay in publishing the current issue, a 12-page supplement will also be released, with more reviews, articles, and current events listings.

Directories Online

Underground Vlorbik: Indy Online. http://members.aol.com/vlorbik/zine.html. Owen Thomas. Created and maintained by the editor of *The Ten Page News* and the reviewzine *Indy Unleashed*, this site includes an extensive alphabetical listing of zines, selected reviews from Thomas's publications, a section on publishers, distributors, and catalogs, and links to online zine reviews and zine resources.

World Wide Punk: Punk Zines. http://www.worldwidepunk.com/zines.html. 1995. Victor Gedris. A directory of "punk/hardcore zines on the net," this site includes a variety of information, such as links to punk web zines, text zines, e-mail addresses for printed zines, and zine reviews. The site contains music reviews, news, an alphabetical listing of punk bands on the web, punk record labels, distributors, and more.

Zines: The Zine & E-Zine Resource Guide. http://www.zinebook.com. Chip Rowe. A mega-site with all kinds of valuable resources including zine directories, distributor information, how and where to buy zines, links and addresses, reviews, new zine listings, zine books, and much more.

*Grrrl Zine Network.*http://www.grrrlzines.net/index.htm. A "resource and transnational network site" for grrrl, lady, queer and transfolk zines. Includes an annotated A-Z list of zines and comics, with ordering information, e-mail and web site links, listing of zine distributors, zine books, d-i-y books, interviews with zine editors and distributors, and more.

Electronic Journals

6851. ***American Newspeak.*** 1996. w. Ed(s): Wayne Grytting. American Newspeak, 2002 S Dearborn, Seattle, WA 98144; wgrytt@blarg.net; http://www.scn.org/news/newspeak/. *Aud.:* Ga.

Humorous commentary on current political and social events. *American Newspeak* also appears in *Z Magazine*, a monthly print periodical. Topics have focused on the Bush administration, Bill Gates, Colin Powell, and the latest feature, "The Orwell Awards" for "cutting edge advances in the mangling of meaning by members of the Empire." Now available in book form, titled *American Newspeak: The Mangling of Meaning for Power and Profit* (New Society Pub., 2002); the web site offers excerpts with table of contents.

6852. ***Conservatively Incorrect.*** Former title: *Conservatively Incorrect (Print Edition).* 1993. m. Ed(s): Rack Jite. Conservatively Incorrect, PO Box 845, Seabrook, TX 77586. *Aud.:* Ga.

With its stated purpose to "clobber conservatives in as many avenues of creative expression as possible, keeping in mind that humor, a little fun and a good wallop are the prerequisites in getting people to listen," *Conservatively Incorrect* is a gold mine of political quotations. Although the print zine is no longer, editor Jite has recently published an e-book titled *Conservatively Incorrect: A Liberal Dose of Political Humor and Opinion* (Hard Response, 2003). Excerpts from each chapter are available online, as well as current commentary, quotes, and articles.

6853. ***Feminista!*** 1997. m. Ed(s): Juliette Cutler Page. Feminista!, 1388 Haight St, PMB 30, San Francisco, CA 94117; editor@feminista.com; http://www.feminista.com/. *Bk. rev.:* Number and length vary. *Aud.:* Hs, Ga, Ac.

"The online journal of feminist construction," *Feminista* includes content revolving around "art, social commentary, philosophy, wit, humor and respect." Issues have included a collection of external links about the state of women in Afghanistan and the Taliban leadership, an article on abortion from the viewpoint of a young Christian woman, and an analogy between cluster bombs and pornography, and a statement on the sexual exploitation of women in "Men Create the Demand; Women Are the Supply." The current issue offers a feminist perspective by Andrea Dworkin titled "The Women Suicide Bombers" and a look at the realities of severe postpartum depression in "When Sadness Follows Childbirth." Issues typically include poetry, announcements, and book reviews.

6854. *Gurl.* 1996. q. Ed(s): Esther Drill. gURL, 1440 Broadway, 21st Fl, New York, NY 10018; jade@gurl.com; http://www.gurl.com. *Aud.:* Hs, Ga.

An e-zine geared to young women, the gURL web site was originally started "as an alternative to traditional girl-directed media." Issues include "news about news," an advice column ("Help me Heather"), comics, games, and a "Dig or Dis" section. Editors have recently published *The Looks Book* (Penguin, 2002), and the first book, *DEAL WITH IT! A Whole New Approach to Your Body, Brain and Life as a gURL!* (Pocket Books, 1999), is still available as well.

6855. *Interracial Voice.* 1995. bi-m. Free. Ed(s): Charles Michael Byrd. Interracial Voice, PO Box 560185, College Point, NY 11356-0185; intvoice@webcom.com; http://www.webcom.com/intvoice/. *Aud.:* Hs, Ga, Ac.

Interracial Voice is an e-zine "serving the mixed-race/interracial community in cyberspace." This publication advocates universal recognition of mixed-race individuals as constituting a separate "racial" entity. The site includes essays, interviews, letters, poetry, speeches, live chat, multiracial resources, and a section devoted to research opportunities and on-going projects.

6856. *Splendid.* Formerly: *Independent Music Reviews.* 1996. w. Ed(s): George Zahora. Splendid WebMedia, 1202 Curtiss St., 2nd Fl., Downers Grove, IL 60515; splendid@splendidezine.com; http://www.splendidezine.com/. *Bk. rev.:* Number and length varies. *Aud.:* Hs, Ga.

Splendid is an online music magazine with a focus on independently released material, although editors claim to review everything they receive, from "DIY" to major labels. Updated daily by writers based in several major U.S. cities, the site includes a massive archive of more than 8,000 music reviews (complete with Real Audio soundclips), interviews, articles, and "Boombox," a repository of full-length streaming audio tracks from staff's favorite new releases. Regular departments feature the "Bookshelf," a small-press book review column, "The Essential Albums," and musical picks in "Ten." Zine and concert reviews and international reports are included. An e-mail edition is also available.

TITLE INDEX

The numbers in this index refer to entry numbers in the text, not page numbers. Titles in boldface indicate those that have been designated basic periodicals in a given subject area.

A

B

D

E

F

G

H

I

J

K

L

M

N

O

P

Q

R

T

U

V

W

X

Y

Z

SUBJECT INDEX

SUBJECT INDEX

D

SUBJECT INDEX

I

J

K

L

SUBJECT INDEX

N

O

Q

R

S

T

U

X

Y

Z